CW00516626

Presented to

Margaret

on this 21st day of July 1998.

with prayers for God's richest
blessings on your future.
Psalm 37. v, 5.

By Norah

Holy Bible

Containing

The Old and New Testaments

The New King James Version

RED LETTER EDITION

with Read-along References™, Read-along Translations™
Topical Index to the Bible
The Christian's Guide to the New Life
Book Introductions and Outlines
Visual Survey of the Bible
Special Study Aids

THOMAS NELSON PUBLISHERS
Nashville

Cover Design: The triquetra (from a Latin word meaning "three-cornered") is an ancient symbol f
comprises three interwoven arcs, distinct yet equal and inseparable, symbolizing that the Father, t
Holy Spirit are three distinct yet equal Persons and indivisibly One God.

Printed in the United States of America

3 4 5 6 7 8 9 10 11 12 13 14 15 16 17 18 19 20—93 92 91 90

Welcome to . . .

THE NEW OPEN BIBLE™ STUDY EDITION

The intent of this study Bible is to make the Scriptures an open and rewarding book for personal Bible study and to give an overview of the whole Bible message. In combining scholarly commentary with the latest revision of the trusted King James Version, the publisher is pleased to present the labors of learned and reverent men who have sought to clarify the meaning of the Scriptures and bring the treasures of God's Holy Word into the possession of the reader. To that end, the following special features are provided.

The text is that of the New King James Version. It has been produced with the conviction that the words of Scripture as originally penned in the Hebrew and Greek were inspired by God. Since they are the eternal Word of God, the Holy Scriptures speak with fresh power to each generation, to give wisdom that leads to salvation, that men and women may serve Christ to the glory of God.

The helps and special features found in this Bible have been prepared by eminent scholars under the supervision of Thomas Nelson Publishers. In this edition Read-along References™ and Read-along Translations™ are used to help you understand the text. The symbol "R" beside a word denotes a Read-along Reference™, which lists at the end of the verse other passages that have similar meanings or further bearing on the word or phrase indicated. This exciting cross-reference method of Bible study ties the magnificent truths of Scripture together.

The symbol "T" beside a word or phrase indicates a Read-along Translation™, an easy-to-understand equivalent, alternate, or literal translation at the end of the verse. When the symbol "*" is used, a textual note is given at the end of the page. When more than one reference or translation follows a verse, a center point "•" is used for division. When space does not allow the symbol letter (R, T, or *) to precede the word or phrase referenced, then the symbol follows immediately at the end of the word or first word of the phrase referenced.

Immediately before each book of the Bible there is an introduction and outline of the book. These introductions are extensive and scholarly, and the outlines are designed to give the reader an overview of the book.

The *Topical Index to the Bible* is one of the major study aids in this edition. A marvel in itself, this distinctive section combines the most useful features of a concordance, reference system, and index, but, in many ways, is better than any of them separately. With the *Topical Index*, the serious Bible student will find the riches of the Word unfolding in logical fashion. The busy pastor or speaker, searching the Scriptures for a message, will find the *Topical Index to the Bible* one of the most helpful tools to the explication of the Scriptures in published form today.

An extremely important study feature is *The Christian's Guide to the New Life*. These twenty-eight outlines cover the major teachings of the Bible and literally help you open the Bible to the point-by-point development of each doctrine. With the study notes at the bottoms of the Bible text pages, you can actually cover the material of an advanced course in systematic theology, but in a much easier and clearer manner.

For convenience in Bible study, the reader is referred to the major classifications of *Bible Study Helps* found in THE NEW OPEN BIBLE™, Study Edition. These helps provide a wealth of information normally found only in a complete library of books.

Among the articles in the *Bible Study Helps* section are *How to Study the Bible*, *Read Your Bible Through in a Year*, *Harmony of the Gospels*, and *Teachings and Illustrations of Christ by Subject*. *The Visual Survey of the Bible*, which appears immediately following the Old Testament, gives you a visual overview of the whole of Scripture. And, for the first time in this new edition of The Open Bible®, we are pleased to introduce **198 additional pages of study material.** Included are 18 charts; 100 illustrated articles on significant people and places of the Bible, as well as subjects of archaeological interest; 30 full-page maps featuring Bible cities and the activities of familiar Bible personalities; and 40 pages of word studies that shed new light on the text. See pages 8 and 9 for an index to these new visual study helps.

The *Biblical Information* section features many items not commonly understood in the Scriptures, plus countless bits of practical information in concise form. Of special interest is the article *The Greatest Archaeological Discoveries*, which includes photographs and scholarly discussion of the most recent archaeological finds.

Messianic Prophecies are indicated in THE NEW OPEN BIBLE™, Study Edition, by stars placed with the references in the appropriate passages. An outline star is used to indicate a prophecy later fulfilled in Jesus Christ. A solid star is used to indicate a prophecy that has been fulfilled in Jesus Christ.

This study edition of the Holy Bible is intended to make it an open Book to the reverent reader. It is hoped that this unique edition will truly make the Scriptures plain enough so all can have an Open Bible.

The Publisher

CONTRIBUTORS
to the Study Aids

KENNETH D. BOA, Ph.D.
Visual Survey of the Bible, Author; Introductions to the Books of the Bible, Co-Author
Director of Publications, Search Ministries
Atlanta, Georgia

†WICK BROOMALL, A.M., Th.M.
Topical Index to the Bible (formerly titled Biblical Cyclopedic Index)
Minister, Presbyterian Church
Augusta, Georgia

W. A. CRISWELL, D.D., Ph.D.
The Scarlet Thread of Redemption
Pastor, First Baptist Church
Dallas, Texas

ARTHUR L. FARSTAD, Th.D.
Consulting Editor
Word Studies, Author
Bible Editor
Dallas, Texas

PAUL R. FINK, Ed.S., Th.D.
The Christian's Guide to the New Life, Contributing Editor
Professor of Pastoral Ministries, Liberty Baptist College
Lynchburg, Virginia

DONALD E. HOKE, D.D.
How to Study the Bible
Pastor, Cedar Springs Presbyterian Church
Knoxville, Tennessee

GEORGE KNIGHT, B.A., B.D., Th.M.
Visual Bible Study Aids, Editor
Nashville, Tennessee

†R. G. LEE, D.D., LL.D., Ph.D.
A Guide to Christian Workers
Pastor-Evangelist
Memphis, Tennessee

†Deceased

MYLES LORENZEN, Th.M.
Visual Survey of the Bible, Contributor
Co-Pastor, Fellowship Bible Church
Roswell, Georgia

JIM BILL McINTEER, B.A.
Harmony of the Gospels
Minister, West End Church of Christ
Nashville, Tennessee

†MERRILL F. UNGER, Th.D., Ph.D.
The Greatest Archaeological Discoveries
Professor Emeritus, Dallas Theological Seminary
Dallas, Texas

C. M. WARD, D.D.
A Guide to Christian Workers
Assemblies of God Radio Evangelist
Santa Cruz, California

WILLIAM WHITE, Ph.D.
The Greatest Archaeological Discoveries
Consulting Editor
Warrington, Pennsylvania

BRUCE H. WILKINSON, Th.M., D.D.
Outlines to the Books of the Bible, Author; Introductions to the Books of the Bible, Co-Author and Executive Editor
Founder and President, Walk Thru the Bible Ministries
Atlanta, Georgia

NEAL D. WILLIAMS, Th.D.
The Christian's Guide to the New Life, Contributing Editor
Assistant Professor of Biblical Studies, Liberty Baptist College
Lynchburg, Virginia

HAROLD L. WILLMINGTON, D.Min.
The Christian's Guide to the New Life, Executive Editor
Vice President, Liberty Baptist College
Lynchburg, Virginia

Books of the Old and New Testaments

CONTENTS
of The New Open Bible™

I. Text

II. Bible Study Helps

III. Biblical Information

Index to Visual Bible Study Aids

Articles

Charts

Maps

Word Studies

FOREWORD

For the past several centuries English-speaking peoples have cherished the King James Version of the Bible. This love does not come from a desire to preserve a tradition for tradition's sake. Rather, the opposite is true: the King James Version has become a tradition because it is loved for its scholarship, literary form, and devotional quality.

During its long history the translation has been revised in accordance with changes in English speech and our growing knowledge of the original text of the Scriptures. Previous major revisions were prepared in 1629, 1638, 1762, and 1769. It is our hope that the present volume, the fifth major revision of the King James Version, will preserve for our own period of history the most revered Bible of the English-speaking world.

The King James Version

In the summer of 1603, when King James was on his way to London to receive the English crown, he was presented with a petition of grievances by clergy holding Puritan convictions, which led the king to call a conference "for hearing and for the determining of things pretended to be amiss in the church." This conference was convened for three days, January 14–16, 1604, and was known as the Hampton Court Conference. During this conference Dr. John Rainolds, the leader of the Puritan party and the president of Corpus Christi College, Oxford, made the motion that a new translation of the Bible be undertaken. Though the majority present were against the motion, it appealed to the king, and he ordered that such a translation be undertaken. Fifty-four of the best biblical scholars in Great Britain were brought together for this great task, divided into six groups—three to work on a translation of the Old Testament and three on the New Testament. Two groups for the Old and New Testaments were to meet at Oxford, two at Cambridge, and two at Westminster.

The result of this action was an English translation which bore the following title: *The Holy Bible, Conteyning the Old Testament, and the New, Newly Translated out of the Originall tongues: & with the former Translations diligently compared and revised: by his Majesties speciall Comandement. Appointed to be read in Churches. Imprinted at London by Robert Barker, Printer to the Kings most excellent Majestie. Anno Dom. 1611.* While this version is called "the Authorized Version," no act of Parliament was ever passed approving it. King James vigorously promoted such an undertaking, but there was no subsequent official act. Nevertheless, the work soon made its own way to a position of leading acceptance among clergy and laity. It was to hold that position for over three centuries.

A New King James Version

In the latter part of the nineteenth century, F. H. A. Scrivener observed that the King James Bible, ". . . so laborious, so generally accurate, so close, so abhorrent of paraphrase, so grave and weighty in word and rhythm, so intimately bound up with the religious convictions of the English people, will never yield its hard earned supremacy, save to some reverential and well-considered revision of which it has been adapted as the basis, that shall be happy enough to retain its characteristic excellence, while amending its venial [trifling] errors and supplying its unavoidable defect."

The versions of 1881, 1901, and 1952 had used a New Testament Greek text that differed considerably from the traditional text and from the great majority of biblical manuscripts. There was growing concern among large segments of the Christian community that there was insufficient reason for many of these differences.

In 1975 Thomas Nelson Publishers, successor to the British firm that had first published the English Revised Version (1885), the American Standard Version (1901), and the Revised Standard Version (1952), determined to evaluate interest in a possible new revision. Such a revision would retain the traditional text while taking account of variant readings in footnotes.

Because any revision of the Scriptures must meet the needs of public worship, Christian education and personal reading and study, leading clergymen and lay Christians were invited to meetings in Chicago, Illinois, and Nashville, Tennessee, in 1975, and in London, England, in 1976, to discuss the need for revision. Almost one hundred church leaders from a broad spectrum of Christian churches gave strong endorsement to a new revision.

Biblical scholars representing a broad cross section of evangelical Christendom were selected to work on this major project. They came from Canada, England, Scotland, New Zealand, Australia, the Netherlands, and Taiwan, as well as from the United States, so that the New King James Version would reflect internationally accepted English usage.

Each translator worked privately and recommended changes in the King James text. In the translator's work he used the *Biblia Hebraica Stuttgartensia* (for the Old Testament) or the Scrivener Greek Text (for the New Testament) and a copy of the 1611 King James Version as revised in 1769 (the edition in general use today). His work was then submitted to the executive editor for the Old or New Testament. An elaborate concordance and word studies of the English, Greek, and Hebrew were prepared especially for this revision by the executive editors and their associates. In addition, using the original texts, the King James Bible, and the guidelines, the executive editor for the Old or New Testament carefully reviewed each scholar's work. Where necessary, they made recommendations for further changes or, in some cases, for restoration of the King James reading.

Each book was then submitted to the English editor to be checked for grammatical accuracy, literary beauty, and the effective communication of the content.

Throughout the entire editing process, the work was regularly reviewed by the clergy and lay advisors who served on the British and North American Overview Committees.

The final exhaustive review process was carried out by a separate Executive Review Committee for each Testament over a period of four years.

All suggested changes were collated by the executive editors. Copies of each book showing all suggested changes were then reviewed in extensive study sessions by the entire Executive Review Committee for each Testament.

The review process was completed in July 1981, at St. Andrews University in northeast Scotland, not far from King James's residence, historic Stirling Castle. During part of this time the North American Committee was joined in its activity by the distinguished members of the British Overview Committee. As in the older version of the King James Bible words added to the English text for purposes of clarity, which were not in the original Hebrew or Greek, were indicated to be shown in italics. This work was carried out by the Old and New Testament executive editors. Subject headings were developed jointly by the executive editors and the English editor.

The New King James Version was thus prepared with profound reverence for the Word of God and with deep appreciation of the wise traditions established by the translators of 1611. It was the prayer of the current revisers that the work in which they labored indeed be, as Dr. Scrivener had said years before, a "reverential and well-considered revision . . . retaining the characteristic excellencies" of the King James Bible.

PREFACE

Purpose

In the Preface to the 1611 edition, the translators of the Authorized Version, known popularly as the King James Bible, state that it was not their purpose "to make a new translation . . . but to make a good one better." Indebted to the earlier work of William Tyndale and others, they saw their best contribution to consist in revising and enhancing the excellence of the English versions which had sprung from the Reformation of the sixteenth century. In harmony with the purpose of the King James scholars, the translators and editors of the present work have not pursued a goal of innovation. They have perceived the Holy Bible, New King James Version, as a continuation of the labors of the earlier translators, thus unlocking for today's readers the spiritual treasures found especially in the Authorized Version of the Holy Scriptures.

A Living Legacy

For nearly four hundred years, and throughout several revisions of its English form, the King James Bible has been deeply revered among the English-speaking peoples of the world. The precision of translation for which it is historically renowned, and its majesty of style, have enabled that monumental version of the Word of God to become the mainspring of the religion, language, and legal foundations of our civilization.

Although the Elizabethan period and our own era share in zeal for technical advance, the former period was more aggressively devoted to classical learning. Along with this awakened concern for the classics came a flourishing companion interest in the Scriptures, an interest that was enlivened by the conviction that the manuscripts were providentially handed down and were a trustworthy record of the inspired Word of God. The King James translators were committed to producing an English Bible that would be a precise translation, and by no means a paraphrase or a broadly approximate rendering. On the one hand, the scholars were almost as familiar with the original languages of the Bible as with their native English. On the other hand, their reverence for the divine Author and His Word assured a translation of the Scriptures in which only a principle of utmost accuracy could be accepted.

In 1786 the Catholic scholar, Alexander Geddes, said of the King James Bible, "If accuracy and strictest attention to the letter of the text be supposed to constitute an excellent version, this is of all versions the most excellent." George Bernard Shaw became a literary legend in our century because of his severe and often humorous criticisms of our most cherished values. Surprisingly, however, Shaw pays the following tribute to the scholars commissioned by King James: "The translation was extraordinarily well done because to the translators what they were translating was not merely a curious collection of ancient books written by different authors in different stages of culture, but the Word of God divinely revealed through His chosen and expressly inspired scribes. In this conviction they carried out their work with boundless reverence and care and achieved a beautifully artistic result." History agrees with these estimates. Therefore, while seeking to unveil the excellent *form* of the traditional English Bible, special care has also been taken in the present edition to preserve the work of *precision* which is the legacy of the 1611 translators.

Complete Equivalence in Translation

Where new translation has been necessary in the New King James Version, the most complete representation of the original has been rendered by considering the history of usage and etymology of words in their contexts. This principle of complete equivalence seeks to preserve *all* of the information in the text, while presenting it in good literary form. Dynamic equivalence, a recent procedure in Bible translation, commonly results in paraphrasing where a more literal rendering is needed to reflect a specific and vital sense. For example, complete equiva lence truly renders the original text in expressions such as "lifted her voice and wept" (Gen. 21:16); "I gave you cleanness of teeth" (Amos 4:6); "Jesus met them, saying, 'Rejoice!'" (Matt. 28:9); and "'Woman, what does your concern have to do with Me?'" (John 2:4). Complete equivalence translates fully, in order to provide an English text that is both accurate and readable.

In keeping with the principle of complete equivalence, it is the policy to translate interjections which are commonly omitted in modern language renderings of the Bible. As an example, the interjection *behold,* in the older King James editions, continues to have a place in English usage, especially in dramatically calling attention to a spectacular scene, or an event of profound importance such as the Immanuel prophecy of Isaiah 7:14. Consequently, *behold* is retained for these occasions in the present edition. However, the Hebrew and Greek originals for this word can be translated variously depending on the circumstances in the passage. Therefore, in addition to *behold,* words such as *indeed, look, see,* and *surely* are also rendered to convey the appropriate sense suggested by the context in each case.

In faithfulness to God and to our readers, it was deemed appropriate that all participating scholars sign a statement affirming their belief in the verbal and plenary inspiration of Scripture, and in the inerrancy of the original autographs.

Devotional Quality

The King James scholars readily appreciated the intrinsic beauty of divine revelation. They accordingly disciplined their talents to render well-chosen English words of their time, as well as a graceful, often musical arrangement of language which has stirred the hearts of Bible readers through the years. The translators, the committees, and the editors of the present edition, while sensitive to the late twentieth-century English idiom, and while adhering faithfully to the Hebrew, Aramaic, and Greek texts, have sought to maintain that lyrical quality which is so highly regarded in the Authorized Version. This devotional quality is especially apparent in the poetic and prophetic books, although even the relatively plain style of the gospels and epistles cannot strictly be likened, as sometimes suggested, to modern newspaper style. The Koine Greek of the New Testament is influenced by the Hebrew background of the writers, for whom even the Gospel narratives were not merely flat utterance, but often song in various degrees of rhythm.

The Style

Students of the Bible applaud the timeless devotional character of our historic Bible. Yet it is also universally understood that our language, like all living languages, has undergone profound change since 1611. Subsequent revisions of the King James Bible have sought to keep abreast of changes in English speech. The present work is a further step toward this objective. Where obsolescence and other reading difficulties exist, present-day vocabulary, punctuation, and grammar have been carefully integrated. Words representing ancient objects, such as *chariot* and *phylactery*, have no modern substitutes and are therefore retained.

A special feature of the New King James Version is its conformity to the thought flow of the 1611 Bible. The reader discovers that the sequence and identity of words, phrases, and clauses of the new edition, while much clearer, are so close to the traditional that there is remarkable ease in listening to the reading of either edition while following with the other.

In the discipline of translating biblical and other ancient languages, a standard method of transliteration, that is, the English spelling of untranslated words, such as names of persons and places, has never been commonly adopted. In keeping with the design of the present work, the King James spelling of untranslated words is retained, although made uniform throughout. For example, instead of the spellings *Isaiah* and *Elijah* now in the Old Testament and *Esaias* and *Elias* in the New Testament, *Isaiah* and *Elijah* now appear in both Testaments.

King James doctrinal and theological terms, for example, *propitiation*, *justification*, and *sanctification*, are generally familiar to English-speaking peoples. Such terms have been retained except where the original language indicates need for a more precise translation.

Readers of the Authorized Version will immediately be struck by the absence of several pronouns: *thee*, *thou*, and *ye* are replaced by the simple *you*, while *your* and *yours* are substituted for *thy* and *thine* as applicable. *Thee*, *thou*, *thy*, and *thine* were once forms of address to express a special relationship to human as well as divine persons. These pronouns are no longer part of our language. However, reverence for God in the present work is preserved by capitalizing pronouns, including *You*, *Your*, and *Yours*, which refer to Him. Additionally, capitalization of these pronouns benefits the reader by clearly distinguishing divine and human persons referred to in a passage. Without such capitalization the distinction is often obscure, because the antecedent of a pronoun is not always clear in the English translation.

In addition to the pronoun usages of the seventeenth century, the *-eth* and *-est* verb endings so familiar in the earlier King James editions are now obsolete. Unless a speaker is schooled in these verb endings, there is common difficulty in selecting the correct form to be used with a given subject of the verb in vocal prayer. That is, should we use *love*, *loveth*, or *lovest*? *do*, *doeth*, *doest*, or *dost*? *have*, *hath*, or *hast*? Because these forms are obsolete, contemporary English usage has been substituted for the previous verb endings.

In older editions of the King James Version, the frequency of the connective *and* far exceeded the limits of present English usage. Also, biblical linguists agree that the Hebrew and Greek original words for this conjunction may commonly be translated otherwise, depending on the immediate context. Therefore, instead of *and*, alternatives such as *also*, *but*, *however*, *now*, *so*, *then*, and *thus* are accordingly rendered in the present edition, when the original language permits.

The real character of the Authorized Version does not reside in its archaic pronouns or verbs or other grammatical forms of the seventeenth century, but rather in the care taken by its scholars to impart the letter and spirit of the original text in a majestic and reverent style.

The Old Testament Text

The Hebrew Bible has come down to us through the scrupulous care of ancient scribes who copied the original text in successive generations. By the sixth century A.D. the scribes were succeeded by a group known as the Masoretes, who continued to preserve the sacred Scriptures for another five hundred years in a form known as the Masoretic Text. Babylonia, Palestine, and Tiberias were the main centers of Masoretic activity; but by the tenth century A.D. the Masoretes of Tiberias, led by the family of ben Asher, gained the ascendancy. Through subsequent editions, the ben Asher text became in the twelfth century the only recognized form of the Hebrew Scriptures.

Daniel Bomberg printed the first Rabbinic Bible in 1516–17; that work was followed in 1524–25 by a second edition prepared by Jacob ben Chayyim and also published by Bomberg. The text of ben Chayyim was adopted in most subsequent Hebrew Bibles, including those used by the King James translators. The ben Chayyim text was also used for the first two editions of Rudolph Kittel's *Biblia Hebraica* of 1906 and 1912. In 1937 Paul Kahle published a third edition of *Biblia Hebraica*. This edition was based on the oldest dated manuscript of the ben Asher text, the Leningrad Manuscript B19a (A.D. 1008), which Kahle regarded as superior to that used by ben Chayyim.

For the New King James Version the text used was the 1967/1977 Stuttgart edition of *Biblica Hebraica*, with frequent comparisons being made with the Bomberg edition of 1524–25. The Septuagint (Greek) Version of the Old Testament and the Latin Vulgate were consulted. In addition to referring to a variety of ancient versions of the Hebrew Scriptures, the New King James Version also draws on the resources of relevant manuscripts from the Dead Sea caves. In the few places where the Hebrew is so obscure that the King James followed one of the versions, but where information is now available to resolve the problems, the New King James Version follows the Hebrew text. Significant variations are recorded in footnotes.

The New Testament Text

There is more manuscript support for the New Testament than for any other body of ancient literature. Over five thousand Greek, eight thousand Latin, and many more manuscripts in other languages attest the integrity of the New Testament. There is only one basic New Testament used by Protestants, Roman Catholics, and Orthodox, by conservatives and liberals. Minor variations in hand copying have appeared through the centuries, before mechanical printing began about A.D. 1450.

Some variations exist in the spelling of Greek words, in word order, and in similar details. These ordinarily do not show up in translation and do not affect the sense of the text in any way.

Other manuscript differences, regarding the omission or inclusion of a word or a clause, as well as two paragraphs in the gospels, should not overshadow the overwhelming degree of *agreement* which exists among the ancient records. Bible readers may be assured that the most important differences in the English New Testament of today are due, not to manuscript divergence, but to the way in which translators view the task of translation: How literally should the text be rendered? How does the translator view the matter of biblical inspiration? Does the translator adopt a paraphrase when a literal rendering would be quite clear and more to the point? The New King James Version follows the historic precedent of the Authorized Version in maintaining a literal approach to translation, except where the idiom of the original language occasionally cannot be translated directly into our tongue.

The King James New Testament was based on the traditional text of the Greek-speaking churches, first published in 1516, and later called the Textus Receptus or Received Text. Although based on relatively few available manuscripts, these were representative of many more which existed at the time but only became known later. In the late nineteenth century, B. Westcott and F. Hort taught that this text had been officially edited by the fourth-century church, but a total lack of historical evidence for this event has forced a revision of the theory. It is now widely held that the Byzantine Text that largely supports the Textus Receptus has as much right to the Alexandrian or any other tradition to be weighed in determining the text of the New Testament. Those readings in the Textus Receptus which have weak support are indicated in the footnotes as being opposed by both critical and majority texts.

Since the 1880s most contemporary translations of the New Testament have relied on a relatively few manuscripts discovered chiefly in the late nineteenth and early twentieth centuries. Such translations depend primarily on two manuscripts, Codex Vaticanus and Codex Sinaiticus, because of their greater age. The Greek text obtained by using these sources and the related papyri (our most ancient manuscripts) is known as the Alexandrian Text. However, some scholars have grounds for doubting the faithfulness of Vaticanus and Sinaiticus, since they often disagree with one another, and Sinaiticus exhibits excessive omission.

A third viewpoint of New Testament scholarship holds that the best text is based on the consensus of the majority of existing Greek manuscripts. This text is called the Majority Text. Most of these manuscripts are in substantial agreement. Even though many are late, and none is earlier than the fifth century, usually their readings are verified by papyri, ancient versions, quotations from the early church fathers, or a combination of these. The Majority Text is similar to the Textus Receptus, but it corrects those readings which have little or no support in the Greek manuscript tradition.

Today, scholars agree that the science of New Testament textual criticism is in a state of flux. Very few scholars still favor the Textus Receptus as such, and then often for its historical prestige as the text of Luther, Calvin, Tyndale, and the King James Version. For about a century most have followed a critical text quite similar to Westcott and Hort, although many have abandoned this for an eclectic text in which individual readings are chosen according to context and other criteria. A small but growing number of scholars prefer the Majority Text, which is close to the traditional text except in the Revelation.

In light of these facts, and also because the New King James Version is the fifth revision of an historic document translated from specific Greek texts, the editors decided to retain the traditional text in the body of the New Testament and to indicate major critical and majority text variant readings in footnotes. Although these variations are duly indicated in the footnotes of the present edition, it is most important to emphasize that fully eighty-five percent of the New Testament text is the same in the Textus Receptus, the Alexandrian Text, and the Majority Text.

Special Abbreviations

Arab.	Arabic
Aram.	Aramaic
Bg.	the 1524–25 edition of the Hebrew Old Testament published by Daniel Bomberg
bu.	bushel, bushels
c.	approximately
cf.	compare
ch., chs.	chapter, chapters
DSS	Dead Sea Scrolls
fem.	feminine
f., ff.	following verse, following verses
ft.	foot, feet
gal.	gallon, gallons
Gr.	Greek
Heb.	Hebrew
i.e.	that is
in.	inch, inches
Kt.	Kethib—the written words of the Hebrew Old Testament preserved by the Masoretes
Lat.	Latin
lb.	pound, pounds
lit.	literally
LXX	Septuagint—an ancient translation of the Old Testament into Greek
M	Majority Text
ms., mss.	manuscript, manuscripts
masc.	masculine
mi.	mile, miles
MT	Masoretic Text—the traditional Hebrew Old Testament
NU	the eclectic Greek text in the twenty-sixth edition of the Nestle-Aland Greek New Testament (N) and in the third edition of the United Bible Societies' Greek New Testament (U)
oz.	ounce, ounces
pl.	plural
pt.	pint, pints
Qr.	Qere—certain words read aloud, differing from the written words, in the Masoretic tradition of the Hebrew Old Testament
qt.	quart, quarts
Sam.	Samaritan Pentateuch—a variant Hebrew edition of the books of Moses
sing.	singular
Syr.	Syriac
Tg.	Targum—an Aramaic paraphrase of the Old Testament
TR	Textus Receptus or Received Text
v., vv.	verse, verses
vss.	versions—ancient translations of the Bible
Vg.	Vulgate—an ancient translation of the Bible into Latin, translated and edited by Jerome

HOW TO USE

ITALIC TYPE in the text indicates words that are not found in the original languages of Hebrew, Aramaic, or Greek, but they are needed for clarity in English.

ALTERNATE TRANSLATIONS are set in italic type and preceded by the word "Or"; these words are different from those in the text, but they are justified by the original languages.

13 So he lodged there that same night, and took what came to his hand as [R]a present for Esau his brother: Gen. 43:11
14 two hundred female goats and twenty male goats, two hundred ewes and twenty rams,
15 thirty milk camels with their colts, forty cows and ten bulls, twenty female donkeys and ten foals.
16 Then he delivered *them* to the hand of his servants, every drove by itself, and said to his servants, "Pass over before me, and put some distance between successive droves."
17 And he commanded the first one, saying, "When Esau my brother meets you and asks you, saying, 'To whom do you belong, and where are you going? Whose *are* these in front of you?'
18 "then you shall say, 'They *are* your servant Jacob's. It *is* a present sent to my lord Esau; and behold, he also *is* behind us.' "
19 So he commanded the second, the third, and all who followed the droves, saying, "In this manner you shall speak to Esau when you find him;
20 "and also say, 'Behold, your servant Jacob *is* behind us.' " For he said, "I will [R]appease him with the present that goes before me, and afterward I will see his face; perhaps he will accept me." [Prov. 21:14]
21 So the present went on over before him, but he himself lodged that night in the camp.
22 And he arose that night and took his two wives, his two maidservants, and his eleven sons, and crossed over the ford of Jabbok.
23 He took them, sent them over the brook, and sent over what he had.
24 Then Jacob was left alone; and a Man wrestled with him until the breaking of day.
25 Now when He saw that He did not prevail against him, He [T]touched the socket of his hip; and the socket of Jacob's hip was out of joint as He wrestled with him. *struck*
26 And [R]He said, "Let Me go, for the day breaks." But he said, [R]"I will not let You go unless You bless me!" Luke 24:28 • Hos. 12:4
27 So He said to him, "What *is* your name?" And he said, "Jacob."
28 And He said, [R]"Your name shall no longer be called Jacob, but [T]Israel; for you have struggled with God and with men, and have prevailed." Gen. 35:10 • Lit. *Prince with God*
29 Then Jacob asked *Him,* saying, "Tell *me* Your name, I pray." And He said, [R]"Why *is* it *that* you ask about My name?" And He [R]blessed him there. Judg. 13:17, 18 • Gen. 35:9
30 And Jacob called the name of the place [T]Peniel: "For I have seen God face to face, and my life is preserved." Lit. *Face of God*
31 Just as he crossed over *Penuel the sun rose on him, and he limped on his hip.
32 Therefore to this day the children of Israel do not eat the muscle that shrank, which *is* on the hip socket, because He [T]touched the socket of Jacob's hip in the muscle that shrank. Or *struck*

CHAPTER 33

Jacob Makes Peace with Esau

NOW Jacob lifted his eyes and looked, and there, [R]Esau was coming, and with him were four hundred men. So he divided the children among Leah, Rachel, and the two maidservants. Gen. 32:6
2 And he put the maidservants and their children in front, Leah and her children behind, and Rachel and Joseph last.
3 Then he crossed over before them and [R]bowed himself to the ground seven times, until he came near to his brother. Gen. 18:2; 42:6
4 [R]But Esau ran to meet him, and embraced him, [R]and fell on his neck and kissed him, and they wept. Gen. 32:28 • Gen. 45:14, 15
5 And he lifted his eyes and saw the women and children, and said, "Who *are* these with you?" And he said, "The children [R]whom God has graciously given your servant." Gen. 48:9
6 Then the maidservants came near, they and their children, and bowed down.
7 And Leah also came near with her children, and they bowed down. Afterward Joseph and Rachel came near, and they bowed down.
8 Then Esau said, "What *do you mean by* [R]all this company which I met?" And he said, "*These are* [R]to find favor in the sight of my lord." Gen. 32:13–16 • Gen. 32:5
9 But Esau said, "I have enough, my brother; keep what you have for yourself."
10 And Jacob said, "No, please, if I have now found favor in your sight, then receive my present from my hand, inasmuch as I [R]have seen your face as though I had seen the face of God, and you were pleased with me. Gen. 43:3
11 "Please, take my blessing that is brought to you, because God has dealt graciously with me, and because I have enough." And he urged him, and he took *it.*
12 Then Esau said, "Let us take our journey; let us go, and I will go before you."
13 But Jacob said to him, "My lord knows that the children *are* weak, and the flocks and herds which are nursing *are* with me. And if the men should drive them hard one day, all the flock will die.
14 "Please let my lord go on ahead before his servant. I will lead on slowly at a pace which the livestock that go before me, and the children, are able to endure, until I come to my lord [R]in Seir." Gen. 32:3; 36:8
15 And Esau said, "Now let me leave with

32:31 Alternate form of *Peniel,* v. 30

CONCEPTUAL REFERENCES are marked with a superior letter "R" to point out verses that will explain the referenced word or phrase in the text. The cross-reference in square brackets refers to a passage similar in concept.

CROSS-REFERENCES, marked with a superior letter "R", point out verses that will explain the referenced word or phrase.

LITERAL TRANSLATION for a particular word or phrase in the text is denoted with a superior letter "T" and the abbreviation "Lit." in the note.

ASTERISKS indicate important textual information. The corresponding notes are found at the foot of the same page. Textual notes point out significant textual variants in both Old and New Testaments.

THE NEW OPEN BIBLE™

An **OUTLINE STAR** and a **SOLID STAR** indicate Messianic references. The outline star indicates a prophecy that at the time of the writing had yet to be fulfilled. The solid star indicates the fulfillment of a prophecy.

RED LETTER type is used in the New Testament to signify words of Jesus Christ.

Jesus Returns to Nazareth—Luke 2:39

19 But when Herod was dead, behold, an
angel of the Lord appeared in a dream to
Joseph in Egypt,
20 [R]saying, "Arise, take the young Child and
His mother, and go to the land of Israel, for
those who [R]sought the young Child's life are
dead." Luke 2:39 • Matt. 2:16
21 Then he arose, took the young Child and
His mother, and came into the land of Israel.
22 But when he heard that Archelaus was
reigning over Judea instead of his father
Herod, he was afraid to go there. And being
warned by God in a [R]dream, he turned aside
into the region of Galilee. Matt. 2:12, 13, 19
23 And he came and dwelt in a city called
[R]Nazareth, that it might be fulfilled [R]which
was spoken by the prophets, "He shall be
called a Nazarene." John 1:45, 46 • Judg. 13:5★

CHAPTER 3

The Person of John the Baptist
Mark 1:2–6; Luke 3:3–6

IN those days John the Baptist came
preaching in the wilderness of Judea,
2 and saying, "Repent, for [R]the kingdom of
heaven is at hand!" Dan. 2:44; Mal. 4:5, 6★
3 For this is he who was spoken of by the
prophet Isaiah, saying:

[R]*"The voice of one crying in the wilderness:* Is. 40:3★
[R]*'Prepare the way of the LORD,*
Make His paths straight.'" Luke 1:76

4 And John himself was clothed in camel's
hair, with a leather belt around his waist; and
his food was locusts and wild honey.
5 Then Jerusalem, all Judea, and all the
region around the Jordan went out to him
6 [R]and were baptized by him in the Jordan,
confessing their sins. Acts 19:4, 18

The Preaching of John the Baptist
Mark 1:7–9; Luke 3:7–9, 16, 17

7 But when he saw many of the Pharisees
and Sadducees coming to his baptism, he said
to them, "Brood of vipers! Who has warned
you to flee from the wrath to come?

8 "Therefore bear fruits worthy of repentance,
9 "and do not think to say to yourselves,
[R]'We have Abraham as *our* father.' For I say
to you that God is able to raise up children to
Abraham from these stones. John 8:33
10 "And even now the ax is laid to the root
of the trees. [R]Therefore every tree which does
not bear good fruit is cut down and thrown
into the fire. Matt. 7:19
11 [R]"I indeed baptize you with water unto
repentance, but He who is coming after me is
mightier than I, whose sandals I am not
worthy to carry. He will baptize you with the
Holy Spirit *and fire. Acts 2:4, 33☆
12 [R]"His winnowing fan *is* in His hand, and
He will thoroughly [T]purge His threshing floor,
and gather His wheat into the barn; but He
will [R]burn up the chaff with unquenchable
fire." Mal. 3:3 • *clean out* • Matt. 13:30

Baptism of Jesus—Mark 1:9–11; Luke 3:21–23

13 Then Jesus came from Galilee to John at
the Jordan to be baptized by him.
14 And John *tried to* prevent Him, saying, "I
have need to be baptized by You, and are
You coming to me?"
15 But Jesus answered and said to him,
"Permit *it to be so* now, for thus it is fitting
for us to fulfill all righteousness." Then he
allowed Him.
16 Then Jesus, when He had been baptized,
came up immediately from the water; and
behold, the heavens were opened to Him, and
He saw the [R]Spirit of God descending like a
dove and alighting upon Him. Is. 11:2; 42:1★
17 [R]And suddenly a voice *came* from
heaven, saying, [R]"This is My beloved Son, in
whom I am well pleased." John 12:28 • Ps. 2:7

CHAPTER 4

First Temptation—Mark 1:12, 13; Luke 4:1–4

THEN Jesus was led up by the Spirit into
the wilderness to be tempted by the devil.
2 And when He had fasted forty days and
forty nights, afterward He was hungry.

3:11 M omits *and fire*

3:17 God the Father of Christ—Every new Christian everntually wonders in what sense God may be called the Father of Christ and Christ the Son of God. The answer to this question is not a simple one. First, one must recognize that the title Son of God does not speak of physical nature, for God is spirit (Page 1241—John 4:24), and Christ was the Son of God before He assumed a human body in Bethlehem (Page 1239—John 3:16; Page 1381—Gal. 4:4). Passages which use terms implying physical origin must be taken in a figurative sense (Page 1450—Heb. 1:5).

Second, the title expresses a unique relationship. Christ distinguished His sonship from that of His disciples (Page 1265—John 20:17). He is begotten of God in a sense that no one else is (Page 1236—John 1:14; 3:16). Some call it "eternal generation," signifying the timelessness of this "God from God" relationship.

(continued on next page)

The superior "T" and italic type in reference indicate an **EQUIVALENT TRANSLATION**, which is similar in meaning; translating the text word helps to clarify meaning.

SUBJECT HEADS and **PARALLEL PASSAGES** have been added to assist the reader in identifying main subjects of the following text and to help locate parallel passages in Scripture.

POETRY and **OBLIQUE TYPE** set certain portions of Bible verse apart for clarification. Poetry is structured as contemporary verse to reflect the poetic form and beauty of the original Hebrew, Aramaic, or Greek language. Oblique type in the New Testament text indicates quotations from the Old Testament.

THE CHRISTIAN'S GUIDE TO THE NEW LIFE is a point-by-point Bible study. The introduction leads you to the page of the first underlined verse. Detailed notes at the bottom of the page discuss the passage. Then they refer you to the next verses for study. You cover the material of an advanced course in systematic theology.

EXPLANATION OF FORMAT

The format of this volume is designed to enhance the vividness and devotional quality of the Holy Scriptures and to assist the reader in personal study. To this end, special features have been incorporated both in the text of the Bible and in special study aids on each page.

Read-along™ Study Aids

*Superior symbols of R, T, or ** usually precede the referenced word or phrase in the text (examples: [R]glory, [T]king of *Israel). When space does not allow the superior symbol to precede the referenced word or phrase, the superior immediately follows the referenced word or the first word of the referenced phrase (examples: [R]glory, [R]king[T] of *Israel).

Superior R's indicate either cross-references or Messianic prophecies. These cross-references point out verses that will explain the referenced word or phrase in the text. A cross-reference in *square brackets* (example: [Deut. 12:5]) refers to a passage similar in theme or a conceptual reference to the passage in the text.

A superior R can also indicate a prophecy of the Messiah. The reference at the end of the verse will be followed by an outline or solid star. The outline star indicates a prophecy that at the time of the writing had yet to be fulfilled. The solid star indicates the fulfillment of a prophecy.

Superior T's indicate either translation notes or monies, weights, or measures. There are four kinds of *translation notes:*

— equivalent translations (in italic type with no introductory words; example: *mercy*), which are roughly similar in meaning to the translation in the text and help to clarify them;

— alternate translations (in italic type, preceded by "Or"; example: Or *mercy*), which are different from those in the text but are justified by the original languages;

— literal translations (in italic type, preceded by "Lit."; example: Lit. *mercy*); and

— notes that explain words or phrases in the text (in roman type; example: Mercy).

Words set in roman type in translation notes are explanatory only and are not translated from the original languages.

The monies, weights, or measures are conversions into modern measures of Bible terms. To further understand these calculations, turn to the article, "Monies, Weights, and Measures."

Asterisks are used to indicate important textual information. The corresponding notes are found at the foot of the same page. *Textual notes* point out significant textual variants in both the Old and New Testaments. The sources of these variant readings are identified by abbreviations listed below.

The notes in the present edition of the New Testament make no evaluation of readings (and so terms such as "better manuscripts" are avoided), but they do clearly indicate the sources of readings that diverge from the traditional text, whether they be from the modern eclectic or "critical" text (NU), which depends heavily upon the Alexandrian type of text, or from the Majority Text (M). (See the Preface, "The New Testament Text," for an explanation of these terms.) Thus a clearly defined statement of the variants, representing all textual persuasions, is provided for the benefit of interested readers.

Subject headings, printed in italic type, indicate the main subjects of the sections of text that follow them. These headings are not found in the original Hebrew, Aramaic, or Greek, but have been added to assist the reader in identifying topics and transitions in the biblical content. Whenever a parallel passage in Scripture exists, reference to that parallel is made with the subject heading.

The Text

Italic type in the text (example: God saw that *it was* good) indicates words that are not found in the original languages, but are needed for clarity in English.

Oblique type in the New Testament text (example: *Behold, a virgin shall be with child*) indicates quotations from the Old Testament. The sources of the quotations are found in cross-references.

Paragraph breaks are indicated by verse numbers in bold-face type (example: **Genesis 1:6**) or, when a new paragraph begins within a verse, by indentation (example: **Genesis 35:22**).

Quotation marks in the text follow modern English usage. For easier reading, only the marks denoting the most recently opened quotations are repeated in a new paragraph.

Personal pronouns and certain nouns are capitalized when they refer to Deity.

Poetry is structured as contemporary verse to reflect the poetic form and beauty of the original language.

The covenant name of God in the Old Testament, represented by the Hebrew consonants, YHWH, is translated "LORD" or "GOD" (using capital letters as shown), as it has been throughout the history of the King James Bible. In this edition, the capitalized form is also used whenever the covenant name is quoted in the New Testament from a passage in the Old Testament.

HOW TO STUDY THE BIBLE

The Bible is the greatest book ever written. In it God Himself speaks to men. It is a book of divine instruction. It offers comfort in sorrow, guidance in perplexity, advice for our problems, rebuke for our sins, and daily inspiration for our every need.

The Bible is not simply one book. It is an entire library of books covering the whole range of literature. It includes history, poetry, drama, biography, prophecy, philosophy, science, and inspirational reading. Little wonder, then, that all or part of the Bible has been translated into more than 1,200 languages, and every year more copies of the Bible are sold than any other single book.

The Bible alone truly answers the greatest questions that men of all ages have asked: **"Where have I come from?" "Where am I going?" "Why am I here?" "How can I know the truth?"** For the Bible reveals the truth about God, explains the origin of man, points out the only way to salvation and eternal life, and explains the age-old problem of sin and suffering.

The great theme of the Bible is the Lord Jesus Christ and His work of redemption for mankind. The person and work of Jesus Christ are promised, prophesied, and pictured in the types and symbols of the Old Testament. In all of His truth and beauty, the Lord Jesus Christ is revealed in the gospels; and the full meanings of His life, His death, and His resurrection are explained in the epistles. His glorious coming again to earth in the future is unmistakably foretold in the book of Revelation. The great purpose of the written Word of God, the Bible, is to reveal the living Word of God, the Lord Jesus Christ (read John 1:1-18).

Dr. Wilbur M. Smith relates seven great things that the study of the Bible will do for us:

1. **The Bible discovers sin and convicts us.**
2. **The Bible helps cleanse us from the pollutions of sin.**
3. **The Bible imparts strength.**
4. **The Bible instructs us in what we are to do.**
5. **The Bible provides us with a sword for victory over sin.**
6. **The Bible makes our lives fruitful.**
7. **The Bible gives us power to pray.**

You do not need a whole library of books to study the Bible. The Bible is its own best commentator and interpreter. With all of the instructive helps that you have in this new Bible, you have a whole lifetime of Bible study.

I. Personal Bible Study

A. *Devotional Bible Study*

The Bible is not an end in itself, but is a means to the end of knowing God and doing His will. The apostle Paul said, "Be diligent to present yourself approved to God, a worker who does not need to be ashamed, rightly dividing the word of truth" (**2 Tim. 2:15**). God has given us the Bible in order that we might know Him and that we might do His will here on earth.

Therefore, devotional Bible study is the most important kind of Bible study. Devotional Bible study means reading and studying the Word of God in order that we may hear God's voice and that we may know how to do His will and to live a better Christian life.

A great scientist and medical doctor, Dr. Howard A. Kelly (Professor of Gynecology at Johns Hopkins University from 1889 through 1940), was also an avid student of the Bible. He once said: "The very best way to study the Bible is simply to read it daily with close attention and with prayer to see the light that shines from its pages, to meditate upon it, and to continue to read it until somehow it works itself, its words, its expressions, its teachings, its habits of thought, and its presentation of God and His Christ into the very warp and woof of one's being."

For your devotional reading and study of the Bible, here are several important, practical suggestions:

1. Begin your Bible reading with prayer (**Ps. 119:18; John 16:13,14,15**).

2. Take brief notes on what you read. Keep a small notebook for your Bible study (see number 4 below).

3. Read slowly through one chapter, or perhaps two or three chapters, or perhaps just one paragraph at a time. After reading, ask yourself what this passage means. Then reread it.

4. It is often very helpful in finding out the true meaning of a chapter or passage to ask yourself the following questions, then write the answers in your notebook:

- **a.** What is the main subject of this passage?
- **b.** Who are the persons revealed in this passage: Who is speaking? About whom is he speaking? Who is acting?
- **c.** What is the key verse of this passage?
- **d.** What does this passage teach me about the Lord Jesus Christ?
- **e.** Does this passage portray any sin for me to confess and forsake?
- **f.** Does this passage contain any command for me to obey?
- **g.** Is there any promise for me to claim?
- **h.** Is there any instruction for me to follow?

Not all of these questions may be answered in every passage.

5. Keep a spiritual diary. Either in your Bible study notebook mentioned above (number 2), or in a separate notebook entitled, "My Spiritual Diary," write down daily what God says to you through the Bible. Write down the sins that you confess or the commands you should obey.

6. Memorize passages of the Word of God. No one is ever too old to memorize the Word of God. Write verses on cards with the reference on one side and the verse on the other. Carry these cards with you and review them while you're waiting for a train, standing in lunch line, etc.

Other persons prefer to memorize whole passages or chapters of the Bible. A small pocket Bible will help you to review these passages when you have spare moments. One of the best ways is to spend a few minutes every night before going to sleep, in order that your subconscious mind may help you fix these passages of God's Word in your mind while you're asleep (**Ps. 119:11**).

To meditate means "to reflect, to ponder, to consider, to dwell in thought." Through meditation the Word of God will become meaningful and real to you, and the Holy Spirit will use this time to apply the Word of God to your own life and its problems.

7. Obey the Word of God. As Paul said to Timothy in Second Timothy 3:16: "All Scripture *is* given by inspiration of God, and *is* profitable for doctrine, for reproof, for correction, for instruction in righteousness." The Bible has been given to us that we may live a holy life, well-pleasing to God. Therefore God says, "But be doers of the word, and not hearers only" (**James 1:22**).

8. The Navigators, a group of men banded together just before World War II to encourage Bible study among Christian servicemen, developed a splendid plan for a personal, devotional study.

- **a.** After prayer, first read the Bible passage slowly and silently; then read it again aloud.
- **b.** In a large notebook divide the paper into columns and head each column as follows: Chapter title, Key verse, Significant truth, Cross-references, Difficulties in this passage (personal or possible), Application to me, and Summary or outline of the passage. In each of these columns, write the information desired.

Do not try to adopt all of these methods at once, but start out slowly, selecting those methods and suggestions which appeal to you. You will find, as millions of others have before you, that the more you read and study the Word of God, the more you'll want to read it. Therefore, the following suggestions of Bible study are made for those who wish to make a more intensive study of the Bible truths.

B. Study for Bible Knowledge

There are many valuable methods of Bible study. One may study the Bible, as if with a telescope, to see the great truths which stand out in every book. Or one may study the Bible as if with a microscope to find all of the marvelous details which are in this mine of spiritual riches. In this section there are several proven methods with which a person may conduct more intensive Bible study. The most important thing is to follow faithfully some systematic method of Bible study.

Bible Study by Chapters. In the Bible there are 1,189 chapters in the Old and New Testaments. In a little over three years, a person could make an intensive study of the whole Bible, taking a chapter a day. It is usually a good practice to start your Bible study in the New Testament.

1. Read through the chapter carefully, seeking to find its main subject or subjects.

2. As you read each chapter, give it a title which suggests its main content. If you are reading the Gospel of John, for example, you might give each chapter titles like this:

ch. 1 "Jesus Christ, the Word of God"
ch. 2 "The Wedding at Cana"
ch. 3 "The New Birth"
ch. 4 "The Woman at the Well"
ch. 5 "The Healing of the Man at the Pool of Bethesda"
ch. 6 "The Feeding of the 5,000"

3. Reread the chapter again and make a simple outline which will include its main thoughts. For example in **John 1**, you might make an outline like this:

"Jesus Christ, the Word of God":

- **a.** Jesus Christ was the eternal Word of God, **1-9.**
- **b.** Jesus Christ came into the world, **10-18.**
- **c.** John witnesses that Christ is to come, **19-28.**
- **d.** John says that Jesus is the Lamb of God, **29-37.**
- **e.** Jesus Christ calls His first disciples, **38-51.**

4. Concerning each chapter, ask and answer the questions suggested in item number 4 of devotional Bible study hints above. Especially take note of any practical or theological problems in this chapter. Then, using your concordance, look up the key words in those verses and find out what other portions of the Bible say about this question or problem. Compare Scripture with Scripture to find its true meaning. Usually, to understand an important Bible chapter, you must study it together with the preceding or following chapters.

Bible Study by Paragraphs. A paragraph is several sentences of thought in writing. When an author changes the subject of emphasis in writing, he usually begins a new paragraph. The beginning of a paragraph in this Bible is indicated by a bold face verse number. Studying the Bible by paragraphs like this is often called analytic Bible study.

1. Read the paragraph carefully for its main thought or subject.

2. In order to find the relation of the important words and sentences in this paragraph, it is often helpful to rewrite the text. For example, if you were going to study the paragraph on prayer in the Sermon on the Mount found in **Matthew 6:5-8,** you could rewrite this text:

"And when you pray, you shall not be like the hypocrites. For they love to pray standing in the synagogues and on the corners of the streets, that they may be seen by men. Assuredly, I say to you, they have their reward.

"But you, when you pray, go into your room, and when you have shut your door, pray to your Father who *is* in the secret *place;* and your Father who sees in secret will reward you openly.

"But when you pray, do not use vain repetitions as the heathen *do.* For they think that they will be heard for their many words.

"Therefore do not be like them. For your Father knows the things you have need of before you ask Him."

3. From the text which you've now rewritten so that you can see the relationship of the various parts of the paragraph, it is easy to make a simple outline. For example, using **Matthew 6:5-15,** your outline of this passage would be something like this:

"Jesus Teaches Us How to Pray"—**Matthew 6:5-15.**

- **a.** How not to pray: **Matthew 6:5, 7, 8.**
  - (1) Hypocritically in public, **6:5.**
  - (2) With useless repetition. **6:7, 8.**
- **b.** How to pray: **Matthew 6:6, 9-13.**
  - (1) In private to your heavenly Father, **6:6.**
  - (2) Following the pattern of Jesus' model prayer, **6:9-13.**

4. It is helpful also to look up in the concordance important words that occur in this paragraph. For example, the words "hypocrites," "heathen," etc. By comparing other passages of the Bible which teach about prayer, you'll be kept from making any mistakes concerning the true nature, conditions, and results of prayer according to the will of God.

Bible Study by Verses. In studying the historical passages of the Bible, such as most of the Old Testament or parts of the gospels, each verse may have only one simple meaning.

But many verses in both the Old and New Testaments are rich with many great Bible truths which will demand more detailed study. There are many ways that you can study a single Bible verse.

1. Study it by the verbs in the verse. For example, if you were studying **John 3:16** you would find the following verbs: "loved . . . gave . . . should not perish . . . have . . ."

You could make a comparative list like this:

God loved Man believes
God gave Man shall not perish
Man has everlasting life.

Or simply take the nouns in this wonderful verse: "God . . . world . . . only begotten Son . . . whoever . . . everlasting life."

2. Study a verse through the personalities revealed. For example, once again taking **John 3:16,** these very simple but significant points are brought to light: "God . . . only begotten Son . . . whoever . . . Him."

3. Study a verse by looking for the great ideas revealed in it. Let us look again at **John 3:16** as our example. We might title this verse, "The greatest verse in the Bible." The following ideas are found in it:

"God"—the greatest person
"so loved"—the greatest devotion
"the world"—the greatest number
"He gave"—the greatest act
"His only begotten Son"—the greatest gift
"that whoever believes"—the greatest condition
"should not perish"—the greatest mercy
"have everlasting life"—the greatest result

4. Sometimes a combination of these various ideas applied to a verse will bring the richest results. For example, take **Romans 5:1:**

"Therefore"—This verse depends on **4:25.** Our justification is based on and is guaranteed by Jesus' resurrection.

"justified"—made righteous.

"by faith"—method of our justification (see also **3:24; 4:9**).

"have"—not future, but present tense—we have this *now.*

"peace with God"—We were enemies, but now there is peace between us and God because of what Christ has done.

"through our Lord Jesus Christ"—the way to peace with God is only through Jesus Christ.

Bible Study by Books. After you have begun to study the Bible by chapters or paragraphs or verses, you will be ready to study the Bible by books.

1. There are several methods of Bible book study.

- **a.** One is called the inductive method. This is a method of studying in detail the contents of a Bible book and then drawing from these details general conclusions or principles concerning the contents and purpose of the book.
- **b.** Another method of book study is called the synthetic method. By this method, one reads the Bible book over several times to receive the general impressions of the main ideas and purpose of the book without attention to the details. (It is sometimes hard to distinguish these two methods.)
- **c.** In some cases the study of a Bible book becomes a historical study, if that book relates the history of a nation or a man in a particular period of time. For example, the book of Exodus tells the history of the children of Israel from the death of Joseph in Egypt until the erection of the tabernacle in the wil-

derness in the time of Moses. This covers approximately 400 years.

The principles of Bible book study, whether inductive or synthetic, are very similar. Such study will require more time than the previous methods mentioned, but it will be amply rewarding.

2. Here are some methods for Bible study by books:

a. Read the book through to get the perspective and the general emphasis of the book.

b. Reread the book many times, each time asking yourself a relevant question and jotting down the answers you find as you read. Here are the most important questions to ask:

First reading: What is the central theme or emphasis of this book? What is the key verse?

Second reading: Remembering the theme of the book, see how it is emphasized and developed. Look for any special problems or applications.

Third reading: What does it tell me about the author and his circumstances when he wrote this book?

Fourth reading: What does the book tell me about the people to whom the book was written and their circumstances, need, or problems?

Fifth reading: What are the main divisions of the book? Is there any outline apparent in the logical organization and development of the book? During this reading, divide the text into the paragraphs as you see them and then give a title to each paragraph. Draw a line down the right side of the outline and on the other side write any problems, questions, words, or ideas that require further study by comparison with other passages in the Bible.

Sixth and successive readings: Look for other facts and/or information that your earlier readings have suggested. By now certain words will stand out in the book. See how often they recur. (For example, as you read the book of Philippians, you will soon find that the word "joy" occurs many times. This is one of the key words of the book, so note its occurrences and the circumstances surrounding it.)

As you read and reread a book, you'll find that you begin to see its structure and its outline very clearly. It is true, however, that there are other outlines for any given book. It depends on the principle of division that you select. For example, as you study the book of Romans, you might adopt the outline that Dr. G. Allen Fleece, president of Columbia Bible College, has written:

The Book of Romans

Subject: "The Gospel," 1:16

I. The Gospel for the lost sinner, 1—5
II. The Gospel for the Christian, 6—8.
III. The Gospel for the whole world, 9—11.
IV. The Gospel applied to daily living, 12—16.

Of course, each of these great sections of this remarkable book can be divided into smaller subjects with great profit.

This method, applied to a book which is mainly historical, will also enable you to find a clear outline. In the case of a historical book, the outline will be largely chronological. The book of Acts lends itself to this kind of study and outline.

The Book of Acts

Subject: "The Gospel Witness in the First Century"

Key verse: 1:8

Outline:

I. Introduction: The apostles receive power, 1:1—2:4
II. The witness in Jerusalem, 2:5—7:60
III. The witness in Judea and Samaria, 8:1—11:18
IV. The beginning of the witness to the end of the earth, 11:19—28:31

Once again more careful study will give the details and further subdivisions of each of these great units of gospel history in this inspired record of the origin of the Christian church.

Bible Study by Words. There are two profitable and helpful ways of studying great words or subjects in the Word of God.

1. Word study by Bible books. Certain words have special significance in certain Bible books. For example, after studying the Gospel of John as a book and by chapters, you'll find it instructive and inspiring to trace the words "believe" and "belief." They occur almost 100 times. By reading the book hurriedly and underlining each passage where the words "believe" and "belief" occur, you'll understand why Bible scholars contend that the purpose of the Gospel of John is expressed by the author in **John 20:31.**

2. General word study. The fine index and concordance in this Bible will be a great help. Through the study of great Bible words, you can soon become familiar with the great doctrines of the Bible and understand the great theological principles which the Bible reveals.

With the concordance you might begin with the study of the word "grace." By tracing the occurrences of this word through the Old Testament and then into the New Testament, you will come to see that God has always dealt with His people in grace, and you will find in a concrete way the great truth of **Ephesians 2:8.**

Bible Study by Topics. Closely related to the method of study by words is the study according to great topics or subjects: Bible prayers, Bible promises, Bible sermons, Bible songs, Bible poems, etc.

Or one might study Bible geography by reading rapidly through and looking for rivers, seas, and mountains highlighted in Scripture. For example, the mountain-top experiences in the life of Abraham are a thrilling study.

Another challenging study is to read rapidly through the Gospels and Epistles looking for the commands of the Lord to us. The list of Bible topics is unlimited.

First, for a topical study on prayer, look up the word "prayer" or "pray" in your concordance. Look up every form of these words and such related words as "ask," "intercession," etc. After you have looked up these verses, study them and bring together all the teaching on prayer that you find. You will find conditions of prayer, words to be used in prayer, results to expect from prayer, when to pray, and where to pray.

Bible Study Through Biography. The Bible is a record of God's revealing Himself to men and through men. The Old Testament as well as the New is rich in such biographical studies. Here are a few:

The life of Noah: Genesis 5:32—10:32
The life of Abraham: Genesis 12—25
The life of Joseph: Genesis 37—50
The life of Deborah: Judges 4, 5

Let us summarize various methods for studying the great Bible biographies:

1. Read the Bible book or passages in which this person's life is prominent, e.g., Abraham in **Genesis 12-25,** plus references to Abraham in **Hebrews 11** and **Romans 4.**

2. Trace character with your concordance.

3. Be careful to note indirect references to the person in other portions of Scripture.

Conclusion. There are many other methods of studying the Bible: the psychological method, the sociological method, the cultural method, the philosophical method, etc. Use all the Bible study methods suggested above. From time to time, change your method so that you'll not become too accustomed to any one method or tired from delving too deeply into one type of study.

The great thrill of Bible study is discovering these eternal truths of God's Word for yourself and embarking on the adventure of obeying them and experiencing the blessing in your personal life.

II. Family Bible Study

Nothing is more important in a Christian home than the family altar. At a convenient time when all members of the family are home, father or mother should lead them in worship of God and in reading His Word. A simple program for family worship includes singing a hymn, an opening prayer by a family member, a brief Bible study, and a concluding period of prayer in which all members take part.

The family altar and Bible study will bind the family together, eliminate juvenile delinquency, foster deeper love, and enable each member to become a stronger, better Christian. Since family Bible study usually includes small children, it is wise to avoid deep, difficult topics and study something of interest and help to all. Such subjects might be Bible biographies as outlined above, stories of miracles and deeds of Jesus as revealed in the Gospels, miracles in the Old Testament, and other narrative portions of the Bible. It is wise to keep the study brief and concentrate on a short passage of Scripture. For example, if the family is going to study the life of Moses, it could be divided into units like this:

First day: The birth of Moses: Exodus 2:1-10
Second day: Moses' great choice and great mistake: Hebrews 11:24-27; Exodus 2:11-15
Third day: Moses' wilderness training: Exodus 2:16-25
Fourth day: Moses' call to serve God: Exodus 3:1-22
Fifth day: Moses' argument with God: Exodus 4:1-17
Sixth day: Moses' return to Egypt: Exodus 4:18-31

Here are several practical hints on how to make your family Bible study interesting and profitable to all:

1. Keep your family Bible study reasonably short: one brief chapter or several paragraphs a day.

2. Have each member read a verse.

3. Appoint one family member to lead in worship each day and select the passage to read. This one may appoint others to help in the family worship.

4. Read through a Bible book, a chapter or several paragraphs each day. As you read, together decide on a name or a title for each chapter and memorize this.

5. After reading the passage, have each member in the family explain one verse or one paragraph.

6. Let the leader (or the father or mother) prepare five or ten questions on the Bible passage and ask various members of the family to answer these questions after the passage has been read.

7. Study the beautiful maps in your Bible together and trace Paul's journeys or the wandering of the children of Israel in Egypt.

8. Study Bible topics together. Assign verses concerning a topic or great word to each member of the family. Let each read a verse and tell what the verse teaches about the topic or word.

9. After the Bible reading, have each member tell what this verse means or how it can be applied to personal life.

10. Make up Bible games by having each member make up questions to try to stump the others.

11. Study a Bible book together, using the hints given above. There are many wonderful ways to make the Bible the heart of your home.

III. Principles of Bible Interpretation

Since the Bible was written by many men over a period covering 1,500 years, and since the last author of the Bible has been dead 1,900 years, there are definite problems in understanding the exact meaning of certain passages of the Bible.

There is a need to interpret clearly certain passages of the Bible because there is a gap between the way we think and the words we use today and the way of thinking and the words that these Bible writers used thousands of years ago. Bible scholars have pointed out that there are language gaps—differences in words that we use; there are cultural gaps—different customs were in vogue then. There are geographical gaps—certain rivers that are spoken of in the Bible have long since dried up. Some places that are spoken of frequently in the Bible are not on our modern maps. And then there are historical gaps—the Bible speaks of kings and empires which existed years ago.

Therefore, there is a need for Bible interpretation. This is a fascinating study in itself, but I want to give you just a few principles of interpretation of the Bible that will keep you from error and help you understand the difficult passages of the Word of God.

1. Always remember that the Bible is God's infallible, inerrantly inspired Word. There are no mistakes in the Bible. God has included everything in the Bible that He wants you to know and is necessary for you to know concerning salvation and your Christian life.

2. The second principle of interpretation is to interpret the Bible in the light of its historical background. There are three aspects of this:

a. Study the personal circumstances of the writer. In studying the book of The Revelation, it is important to understand where John was and what he was doing when God gave him this marvelous revelation. See **Revelation 1:1-10.**

b. The second aspect of this principle is to study the culture and customs of the country at the time that the writing or story was taking place. For example, to understand the book of Ruth, it is important to study the customs concerning widows, redemptions of property, etc., as they are explained in **Leviticus 25** and **Deuteronomy 25.**

c. A third aspect of this principle is to study and interpret the Bible in the light of the actual historical situation and events that were taking place at the time of the story. For example, in studying the Gospels it is important to realize that the entire land of Palestine and all of the Jews were being governed and oppressed by the Roman Empire at that time.

3. Interpret the Bible according to the purpose and plan of each book.

Every Bible book has its specific purpose intended by the Holy Spirit to bring some special message to man. For example, it is important to remember that **First John** (see **1 John 5:13**) was written to Christians. Therefore the promise in **First John 1:9** is specifically applied to Christians.

4. One of the most important principles of interpretation is always to interpret according to the context of a verse.

The "context" includes the verses immediately preceding and immediately following the verse you are studying. If you do not take care to interpret the verse according to the context, you could make the Bible teach atheism. For the Bible itself says, "*There is* no God" (**Ps. 14:1**). But the context makes very clear what this verse means: The immediately preceding sentence says, "The fool has said in his heart, '*There is* no God.'"

Always study the passage immediately preceding and immediately following any verse, word, or topic to make sure that you see this truth in the setting which God intended.

5. Always interpret according to the correct meaning of words. You can find the correct meaning of a word in several ways. First of all, look up the usage of the word in other parts of the Bible to find how it was used in that generation. Another way is to look up its background or its root. You could do this with the use of a dictionary. Still another way is to look up the synonyms—words that are similar in meaning but slightly different: for example, "prayer," "intercession," "supplication."

6. Also interpret the Bible according to all of the parallel passages which deal with the subject and according to the message of the entire Bible.

The more you read the Bible, the more you will understand that in it God is revealing His way of salvation to men from beginning to end. And when you come to a difficult passage, think of it in the light of the overall purpose of the Bible. For example, the animal sacrifices of the Old Testament are meant to be a picture of the perfect sacrifice of Jesus Christ on the cross.

If you will follow these simple rules, you will be kept from error and extremes, and you will be helped to understand correctly the teachings of even the more difficult passages in God's Word.

THE CHRISTIAN'S GUIDE TO THE NEW LIFE

The Christian's Guide to the New Life offers a complete doctrinal overview of the Bible to assist you in a practical, simplified way to study your Bible. The six main areas of study, described below, are further amplified; these systematically cover all the important areas of biblical theology. This unique study feature places before the Bible student an exegesis of Scripture with hundreds of Scriptural references.

For the student just beginning Bible study, *The Christian's Guide to the New Life* covers in a fundamental way how to become a Christian, then steps the believer through the Christian life. The easy-to-use references and cross-references lead the reader toward a comprehensive, practical knowledge of God's Word.

The general organization of *The Christian's Guide to the New Life* includes six main areas of study:

Knowing God's Word
Understanding God's Being
Beginning the New Life
Growing in the New Life
Facing Problems in the New Life
Recognizing God's Institutions

These areas of study are subdivided into twenty-eight individual **Christian's Guides** with appropriate Bible references. All the material is organized in a simple format to assist you in more easily understanding the Bible, the inspired Word of God. Each numbered Christian's Guide has several discussions of Bible texts appearing on the page where the text occurs. For example, within the main area of study **Knowing God's Word** is Christian's Guide (1) **How God's Word Came to Us.** There are three discussions concerning how God's Word came to us: on page 241 is **Revelation of God's Word;** on page 832 is **Inspiration of God's Word;** and on page 719 is **Illumination of God's Word.**

This article, *The Christian's Guide to the New Life*, will serve as a general introduction, index, and guide to the various Christian's Guides. Each time you study one of the discussions in the Bible the last line will tell you where to turn for the next discussion. When you finish a main area of study, such as **Knowing God's Word,** the last line in the last discussion will tell you to turn to this article, *The Christian's Guide to the New Life*. Then, after reading the synopsis of the next main area of study, you will be ready to turn to the first discussion and follow the development of that area of study.

The Christian's Guide to the New Life can be used in three easy ways: for monthly study, daily study, and topical study.

- Monthly study—once a day for twenty-eight days study one of the numbered Christian's Guides. Read each of the discussions and look up the listed references.
- Daily study—once a day for 105 days study a single discussion in the Bible text. Read the complete discussion and look up the listed references.
- Topical study—using this article, *The Christian's Guide to the New Life*, as an index, study individual Christian's Guides and discussions as the need arises.

You are now ready to begin using *The Christian's Guide to the New Life*. For each of the six main areas of study a synopsis and an organization are provided. For each of the Christian's Guides page numbers and Scripture references are provided to help you find the various discussions in the Bible.

Knowing God's Word

Synopsis

Christians should know the Bible for many reasons, but the primary one is because God is its Author. All Bible students know that God is Creator (Gen. 1:1), Redeemer (Is. 60:16), and Judge (Gen. 18:25), but do we think of Him as the Author of the Bible? Human writers feel it vital that we read their books; it is much more important that we read God's book, the Bible.

About fourteen centuries before Christ, our Bible had its beginnings in the Sinai desert. In this arid place God spoke to Moses, who had once been a prince in Egypt and was nearly 120 years old at the time. At the Lord's command, Moses picked up his pen and began writing Scripture's first five books, Genesis through Deuteronomy. More than 1,500 years later, the divine manuscript was completed on a lonely, windswept island in the Mediterranean Sea by a former fisherman, John the apostle. From Genesis through Revelation, the final biblical book, there are sixty-six divinely inspired books. Over the centuries, approximately forty men and women—representing varied backgrounds and writing styles—served as channels for God's Word. Yet, in spite of these variations in time and talent, the completed work displays a marvelous historical, theological, geographical, topical, and biographical unity.

The Bible's practical benefits for us may well be summarized under two headings: knowing and growing. The Bible proclaims the good news of the gospel that we might know God; it explains the will of God that all of us may grow spiritually before Him.

Scripture also reveals our place within God's program and answers crucial questions pertaining to our origin, purpose, and destiny. Because God has revealed His unchanging truths, the Christian faith provides real answers and guidance to every generation. Although we cannot grasp how individual events fit into God's program (Eccl. 11:5), we can understand God's basic plan in order to come to know and serve Him. Few joys can compare with realizing our places in God's program and working to fulfill our destinies.

Organization

Understanding God's Being

Synopsis

The Bible reveals the nature of God as spirit, unity, and trinity. He is a spirit—a personal, infinite being (John 4:24); He is one—one in substance or nature and incapable of being divided into separate parts (Deut. 6:4); and He is three—eternally existing in three coequal persons (Matt. 28:19). While great mystery surrounds God's nature, it is reassuring to know that our God is above us.

God's attributes are merely words we use to describe how God is and how He acts toward us. Among these attributes are love, holiness, constancy, justice, truth, eternality, omniscience (all-knowing), omnipresence (all-present), and omnipotence (all-powerful). The fact that we can grasp and understand this much about God is evidence of God's desire that all peoples may know Him.

The word *Father* is variously applied in the Bible. When God is spoken of as the Father of all men, it is as Creator; as the Father of Christ, it expresses an eternal, unique relationship, as the Father of believers, it denotes a relationship established by grace; and as Father of Israel, it means a bond established by covenant. However Father is used, it is a deliberately chosen word to communicate to men one of the primary ways God wants us to conceive of Him.

The title *Son of God* is one which Jesus never directly applied to Himself, but when others applied it to Him Jesus willingly accepted it as a claim to His own deity (John 10:24–38). Jesus often referred to Himself as "the Son," which was certainly an abbreviation for the Son of God. How significant is this term to the Christian? It is very important, because it helps establish some major truths without which we would be left with little evidence that the words of Jesus Christ were actually true. It can be said that as our relationship with the Son of God determines whether we will become Christians, our relationship with the Spirit of God determines what kind of believers we will be.

Organization

The Ministry of the Son of God
Page 1174—Mark 10:45

8. The Holy Spirit
The Person of the Holy Spirit
Page 1390—Eph. 4:3
The Work of the Holy Spirit in Salvation
Page 1442—Titus 3:5
The Work of the Holy Spirit in Christian Living
Page 1351—1 Cor. 6:19

Beginning the New Life

Synopsis

Mankind is by nature sinful and needs the righteousness of God. We must be separated from sin and set apart to righteousness. If we are to approach God, we must do so on God's terms—we must have new lives in which our sins have been forgiven and obliterated.

It is one thing to be convinced of the need for the new life, but it is an entirely different thing to acquire the new life. When we are "saved" we are said to be new creatures (2 Cor. 5:17); to have passed from death to life (John 5:24); to have been transferred from the rule of darkness to the kingdom of God's Son (Col. 1:13); to have been born again (John 3:3); and to have been adopted by God (Gal. 4:4, 5). These wonderful results of having new life in Christ are offered freely to all who trust in Christ for salvation.

One of the most thrilling benefits of finding new life in Christ is "everlasting [eternal] life." We enter a new, personal relationship with God that gives us a fullness of spiritual vitality, and this new life is a gift which will never die. God can accomplish a life-changing transformation for all who truly believe in Christ.

Organization

9. Need for the New Life
Holiness of God
Page 777—Is. 6:3
Adam's Sin
Page 8—Gen. 3:6, 7
Individual Sin
Page 756—Eccl. 7:20

10. Way to the New Life
New Life: A Free Gift
Page 1331—Rom. 6:23
New Life: Based on Christ's Death
Page 1406—Col. 1:22
New Life: Received by Faith
Page 1295—Acts 16:31

11. Results of the New Life
Everlasting Life
Page 1243—John 5:24
New Nature
Page 1368—2 Cor. 5:17
Christ's Righteousness
Page 834—Is. 61:10
Placed into God's Family
Page 1497—1 John 3:2
Empowered by God
Page 1272—Acts 1:8

12. Assurance of the New Life
Promise of God
Page 1440—Titus 1:2
Witness of the Spirit
Page 1498—1 John 3:24
Changed Life
Page 1349—1 Cor. 6:11

Growing in the New Life

Synopsis

Knowing how to grow in the new life is essential. The old adage is ever true: "Sin will keep you from God's Word, and God's Word will keep you from sin."

No factor in Christian growth is more important than prayer. Prayer may be defined as talking with and listening to God. We talk to Him with our lips and heart, and He talks to us through His will. It involves a two-way conversation. Spiritual maturity is impossible without systematic prayer.

Worship is essential also to spiritual growth. Worship involves honor and respect toward God, the ceremony of private and public worship, and the joyful service of Christians to their Lord. Christians who submit to the lordship of Christ in reverence and service will grow in their spiritual lives.

The Bible describes Christian life as "[walking] in the Spirit" (Gal. 5:16). Walking best represents the step-by-step character of the spiritual life. Living by the Spirit's power is a moment-by-moment yielding to the Spirit's will and control. The evidence that we are walking in the Spirit is simply the display of the fruit of the Spirit (Gal. 5:22, 23). Walking in the Spirit involves confession of sin, yielding to God, and being filled with or controlled by the Spirit.

Organization

13. Bible Study
Reading God's Word
Page 564—Neh. 8:3
Memorizing God's Word
Page 604—Job 22:22
Meditating upon God's Word
Page 252—Josh. 1:8
Obedience to God's Word
Page 242—Deut. 31:12

14. Prayer
Praise
Page 710—Ps. 150:1
Confession

Page 1494—1 John 1:9
Petition
Page 321—1 Sam. 1:17
Thanksgiving
Page 1401—Phil. 4:6
Commitment
Page 728—Prov. 16:3

15. **Stewardship**
Using Spiritual Gifts
Page 1355—1 Cor. 12:1–10
Serving
Page 1382—Gal. 5:13
Giving
Page 1372—2 Cor. 9:6–8

16. **Worship**
The Meaning of Worship
Page 483—1 Chr. 16:29
The Expressions of Worship
Page 1463—Heb. 13:15
The Reasons for Worship
Page 509—2 Chr. 7:3

17. **Participation in the Local Church**
Definition of the Local Church
Page 1341—Rom. 16:5
Reasons for Participation in the Local Church
Page 1458—Heb. 10:25
Benefits of Participation in the Local Church
Page 1274—Acts 2:42–47

18. **Sharing Our Faith**
Sharing Our Faith: Why?
Page 1155—Matt. 28:19
Sharing Our Faith: What?
Page 1359—1 Cor. 15:3, 4
Sharing Our Faith: How?
Page 1413—1 Thess. 1:5
Sharing Our Faith: When?
Page 1436—2 Tim. 4:2

19. **Walking in the Spirit**
Walking in the Spirit: Confession
Page 666—Ps. 73:1
Walking in the Spirit: Yielding
Page 1336—Rom. 12:1
Walking in the Spirit: Filling
Page 1391—Eph. 5:18

Facing Problems in the New Life

Synopsis

Just as we have problems in our physical lives, we also experience problems in our spiritual or new lives. Facing and conquering difficulties cause us to grow and be strengthened, whether those problems are physical or spiritual. As we grow in our new strength, we bring glory to God as He demonstrates His faithfulness and that His grace is sufficient for every need (2 Cor. 12:9). Some of the problems that are common in the new life are sin, temptation, suffering, knowing the will of God, and doubt.

A believer must be especially wary of places, situations, and times in which he or she may be vulnerable to temptation. Certainly the best antidote to temptation is to be a growing Christian. The mind that is occupied with the things of the Lord cannot at the same time be susceptible to temptation.

Of all the possible sins against God, the most serious is that of self-will. This sin led to the fall of Satan (Is. 14:12–14), and it can be said to be the root of Adam's transgression (Gen. 3:1–7). It is, therefore, of utmost importance that the child of God find His will and perform it.

The dismissal of doubt and strengthening of faith are best accomplished by reading and understanding the Word of God (Rom. 10:17). The Holy Spirit will convict the willing heart of its power. Growing in the Word produces growth in faith; reading and understanding the Word are like planting seeds of faith in the heart. They will bear the mature fruit of faith.

Organization

20. **Sin**
What Sin Is
Page 654—Ps. 51:2
What Sin Does
Page 830—Is. 59:2
What Should Be Done About Sin
Page 642—Ps. 32:5

21. **Temptation**
Temptation by the World
Page 1496—1 John 2:15
Temptation by the Flesh
Page 1181—Mark 14:38
Temptation by Satan
Page 487—1 Chr. 21:1

22. **Suffering**
Kinds of Suffering
Page 1481—1 Pet. 3:17
Purposes of Suffering
Page 590—Job 2:7
Response to Suffering
Page 590—Job 1:21
Examples of Suffering
Page 885—Jer. 37:15

23. **Knowing the Will of God**
Knowing the Will of God Through the Scriptures
Page 456—2 Kin. 23:3
Knowing the Will of God Through Prayer and Fasting
Page 988—Dan. 9:3, 4
Knowing the Will of God Through Submission to the Spirit
Page 778—Is. 6:8

Recognizing God's Institutions

Synopsis

God gave humanity four basic institutions: the family, human government, Israel, and the church. It may be observed that each of these institutions demonstrates a characteristic or attribute of God.

- The family illustrates the unity of God (Gen. 2:24; Deut. 6:4).
- Human government illustrates the judgment of God (Rom. 13:1, 2).
- Israel illustrates the election of God (Rom. 9:1–18; 11:1–5).
- The church illustrates the love of God (Eph. 5:22–27).

The family was the first human institution God created. Through the family God illustrates visibly the relationships which exist in the Godhead and the relationship which exists between Christ and His church. Through the family God sought to bring into proper relationship the world with Himself. He created all of the heavens and earth and the things in them that they might prepare the way for and sustain the crown of His creation—humanity.

God's purpose in human government is that it serve as both a custodian and an enforcer of His eternal law. It has been correctly noted that all the thousands of good and practical laws passed by hundreds of legislative bodies and rulers throughout history are in reality only amplifications of the Ten Commandments.

God's selection of Israel as a special nation may puzzle the Bible student, but His choice becomes obvious through study. When God promised Abraham that he would become the father of a great nation, He also promised that He would bless all peoples through that nation (Gen. 12:1–3). Israel was to be a channel of blessing as well as a recipient.

The church, illustrating God's love for us, is the fourth institution through which God works. The universal church—the Body of Christ (Col. 1:18)—comprises all believers since the institution of the church.

Organization

MONIES, WEIGHTS, AND MEASURES

The Hebrews probably first used coins in the Persian period (500–350 B.C.). However, minting began around 700 B.C. in other nations. Prior to this, precious metals were weighed, not counted as money.

Some units appear as both measures of money and measures of weights. This comes from naming the coins after their weight. For example, the shekel was a weight long before it became the name of a coin.

It is helpful to relate biblical monies to current values. But we cannot make exact equivalents. The fluctuating value of money's purchasing power is difficult to determine in our own day. It is even harder to evaluate currencies used two- to three-thousand years ago.

Therefore, it is best to choose a value meaningful over time, such as a common laborer's daily wage. One day's wage corresponds to the ancient Jewish system (a silver shekel is four days' wages) as well as to the Greek and Roman systems (the drachma and the denarius were each coins representing a day's wage).

The monies chart below takes a current day's wage as thirty-two dollars. Though there are differences of economies and standards of living, this measure will help us apply meaningful values to the monetary units in the chart and in the biblical text.

Monies

Unit	*Monetary Value*	*Equivalents*	*Translations*
Jewish Weights			
Talent	gold—$5,760,000[1] silver—$384,000	3,000 shekels; 6,000 bekas	talent
Shekel	gold—$1,920 silver—$128	4 days' wages; 2 bekas; 20 gerahs	shekel
Beka	gold—$960 silver—$64	½ shekel; 10 gerahs	bekah
Gerah	gold—$96 silver—$6.40	1/20 shekel	gerah
Persian Coins			
Daric	gold—$1,280[2] silver—$64	2 days' wages; ½ Jewish silver shekel	drachma
Greek Coins			
Tetradrachma (Stater)	$128	4 drachmas	piece of money
Didrachma	$64	2 drachmas	tribute
Drachma	$32	1 day's wage	piece of silver
Lepton	$.25	½ of a Roman kodrantes	mite
Roman Coins			
Aureus	$800	25 denarii	
Denarius	$32	1 day's wage	denarius
Assarius	$2	1/16 of a denarius	copper coin
Kodrantes	$.50	¼ of an assarius	penny, quadrans

[1]Value of gold is fifteen times the value of silver.
[2]Value of gold is twenty times the value of silver.

Weights

Unit	Weight	Equivalents	Translations
Jewish Weights			
Talent	c. 75 pounds for common talent, c. 150 pounds for royal talent	60 minas; 3,000 shekels	talent
Mina	1.25 pounds	50 shekels	mina
Shekel	c. .4 ounce (11.4 grams) for common shekel c. .8 ounce for royal shekel	2 bekas; 20 gerahs	shekel
Beka	c. .2 ounce (5.7 grams)	½ shekel; 10 gerahs	half a shekel
Gerah	c. .02 ounce (.57 grams)	1/20 shekel	gerah
Roman Weight			
Litra	12 ounces		pound

Measures of Length

Unit	Length	Equivalents	Translations
Day's journey	c. 20 miles		day's journey
Roman mile	4,854 feet	8 stadia	mile
Sabbath day's journey	3,637 feet	6 stadia	Sabbath day's journey
Stadion	606 feet	⅛ Roman mile	furlong
Rod	9 feet (10.5 feet in Ezekiel)	3 paces; 6 cubits	measuring reed, reed
Fathom	6 feet	4 cubits	fathom
Pace	3 feet	⅓ rod; 2 cubits	pace
Cubit	18 inches	½ pace; 2 spans	cubit
Span	9 inches	½ cubit; 3 handbreadths	span
Handbreadth	3 inches	⅓ span; 4 fingers	handbreadth
Finger	.75 inches	¼ handbreadth	finger

Dry Measures

Unit	Measure	Equivalents	Translations
Homer	6.52 bushels	10 ephahs	homer
Kor	6.52 bushels	1 homer; 10 ephahs	kor, measure
Lethech	3.26 bushels	½ kor	half homer
Ephah	.65 bushel, 20.8 quarts	1/10 homer	ephah

Dry Measures—Continued

Unit	Measure	Equivalents	Translations
Modius	7.68 quarts		basket
Seah	7 quarts	1/3 ephah	measure
Omer	2.08 quarts	1/10 ephah; 1 4/5 kab	omer
Kab	1.16 quarts	4 logs	kab
Choenix	1 quart		measure
Xestes	1 1/6 pints		pot
Log	.58 pint	1/4 kab	log

Liquid Measures

Unit	Measure	Equivalents	Translations
Kor	60 gallons	10 baths	kor
Metretes	10.2 gallons		gallons
Bath	6 gallons	6 hins	measure, bath
Hin	1 gallon	2 kabs	hin
Kab	2 quarts	4 logs	kab
Log	1 pint	1/4 kab	log

Topical Index to the Bible

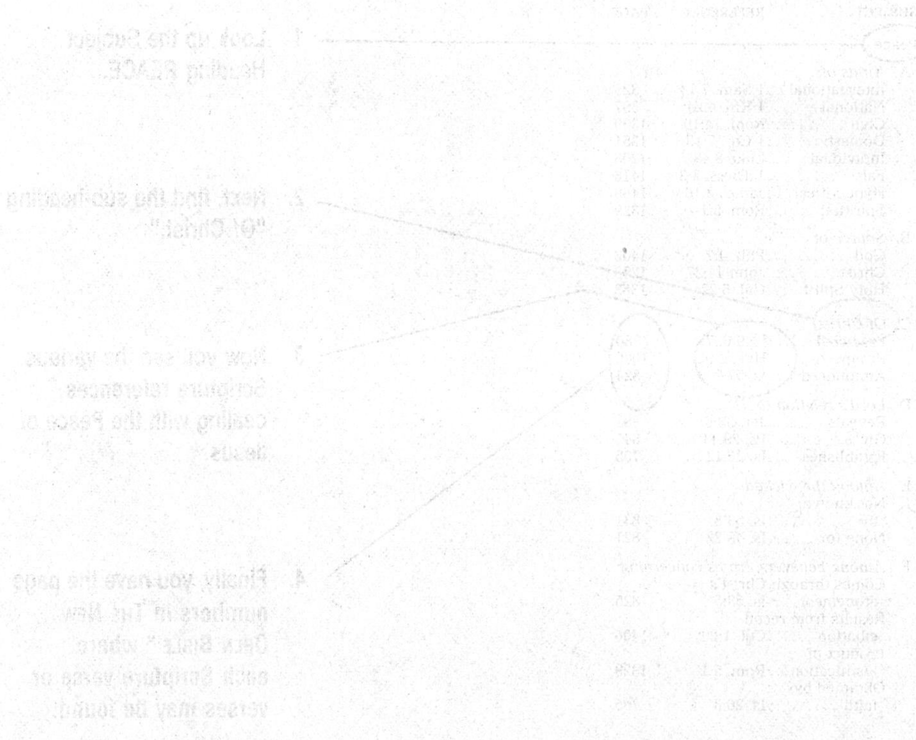

How to Use The Topical Index to the Bible

The Topical Index to the Bible is a special kind of subject index that combines the best features of a concordance, a topical index, the usable study features of a syllabus, and other related study aids into one unique, quick, easy-to-use form. The Index offers advantages for personal Bible study that not even a combination of the above study helps would provide.

With over 8,000 subjects, names, places, things, concepts, events, and doctrines of the Bible, the Topical Index truly "opens" the Bible. It not only includes the Scripture references for the individual subjects (by appropriate sub-headings), it goes one convenient step further: it gives the actual page numbers in THE NEW OPEN BIBLE™ where each Scripture verse or verses may be found.

An example will illustrate. Suppose you need to prepare or study a lesson on "The Peace of Jesus." Follow four easy steps.

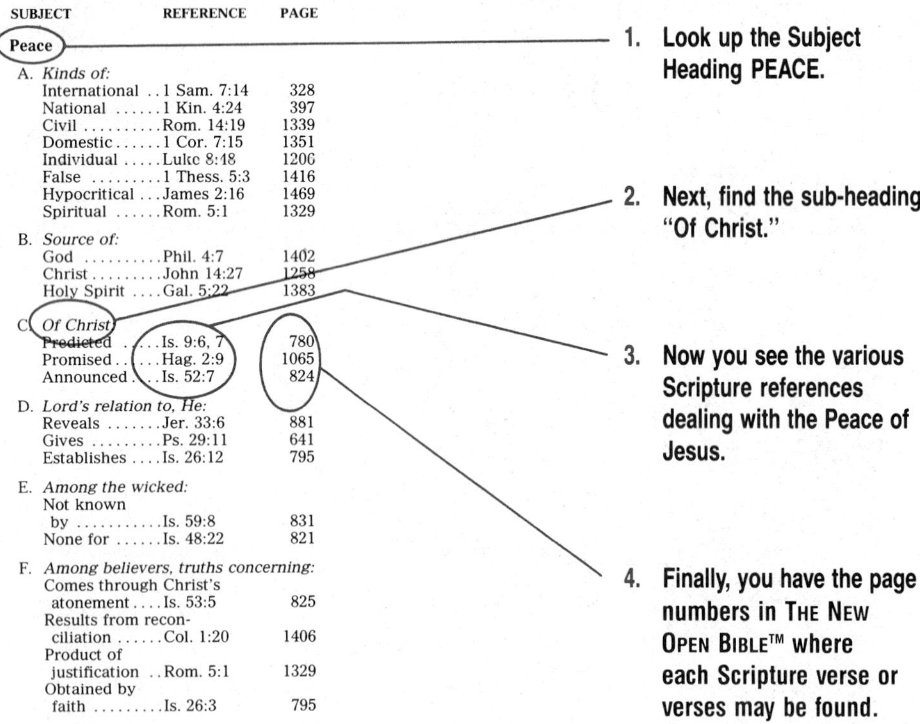

SUBJECT	REFERENCE	PAGE
Peace		
A. *Kinds of:*		
International	1 Sam. 7:14	328
National	1 Kin. 4:24	397
Civil	Rom. 14:19	1339
Domestic	1 Cor. 7:15	1351
Individual	Luke 8:48	1206
False	1 Thess. 5:3	1416
Hypocritical	James 2:16	1469
Spiritual	Rom. 5:1	1329
B. *Source of:*		
God	Phil. 4:7	1402
Christ	John 14:27	1258
Holy Spirit	Gal. 5:22	1383
C. *Of Christ:*		
Predicted	Is. 9:6, 7	780
Promised	Hag. 2:9	1065
Announced	Is. 52:7	824
D. *Lord's relation to, He:*		
Reveals	Jer. 33:6	881
Gives	Ps. 29:11	641
Establishes	Is. 26:12	795
E. *Among the wicked:*		
Not known by	Is. 59:8	831
None for	Is. 48:22	821
F. *Among believers, truths concerning:*		
Comes through Christ's atonement	Is. 53:5	825
Results from reconciliation	Col. 1:20	1406
Product of justification	Rom. 5:1	1329
Obtained by faith	Is. 26:3	795

1. Look up the Subject Heading PEACE.
2. Next, find the sub-heading "Of Christ."
3. Now you see the various Scripture references dealing with the Peace of Jesus.
4. Finally, you have the page numbers in THE NEW OPEN BIBLE™ where each Scripture verse or verses may be found.

The Topical Index has provided two important sources of information for you. First, you have the scriptural material needed to prepare or study your lesson. Second, you have this material in order as it appears in the Bible, so you have a ready-made outline for your personal use.

Topical Index to the Bible

FROM GENESIS TO REVELATION

ARRANGED ALPHABETICALLY GIVING THE BOOK, CHAPTER, VERSE AND PAGE
WHERE EVERY REFERENCE IN THIS INDEX IS FOUND

SUBJECT	REFERENCE	PAGE

A

Aaron—*bright*

A. *Ancestry and family of:*

Descendant of Levi	Ex. 6:16-20	74
Son of Amram and Jochebed	Ex. 6:20	74
Moses' older brother	Ex. 7:1, 7	74
Brother of Miriam	Ex. 15:20	86
Husband of Elisheba	Ex. 6:23	74
Father of Nadab, Abihu, Eleazar, and Ithamar	Ex. 6:23	74

B. *Position of:*

Moses' helper	Ex. 4:13-31	72
Becomes "prophet" to Moses	Ex. 7:1, 2	74
God inspired	Ex. 12:1	80
Commissioned, with Moses to deliver Israelites from Egypt	Ex. 6:13, 26	74
	Josh. 24:5	279
Inferior to that of Melchizedek	Heb. 7:11-19	1455

C. *Special privileges of:*

Appears before Pharaoh	Ex. 5:1-4	73
Performs miracles	Ex. 7:9, 10, 19, 20	74
Supports Moses' hands	Ex. 17:10-12	88
Ascends Mt. Sinai	Ex. 19:24	90
	Ex. 24:1, 9	95
Sees God's glory	Ex. 24:9, 10	95
Judges Israel in Moses' absence	Ex. 24:14	95
Allowed inside the veil	Lev. 16:15	139
Blesses the people	Lev. 9:22	128
Intercedes for Miriam	Num. 12:10-12	175

D. *Sins of:*

Tolerates idolatry	Ex. 32:1-4	105
Permits evil	Ex. 32:21-25	105
Conspires against Moses	Num. 12:1-16	175
With Moses, fails at Meribah	Num. 20:1-13, 24	183

E. *Character of:*

A good speaker	Ex. 4:14	72
Weak in crises	Ex. 32:1-24	105
Subject to jealousy	Num. 12:1, 2	175
Conscious of guilt	Num. 12:11	175
Submissive	Lev. 10:1-7	128
A saint	Ps. 106:16	686

F. *Priesthood of:*

Chosen by God	Ex. 28:1	99
Sons, in office	Lev. 8:1-36	126
Anointed with oil	Ex. 30:25, 30	104
Duties given	Ex. 30:7-10	103
Garments prescribed	Ex. 39:1-31	112
Ordained to teach	Lev. 10:8, 11	130
Set apart to offer sacrifices	Lev. 9:1-24	128
	Heb. 5:1-4	1453
Alone enters within the holy place	Ex. 30:10	103
	Heb. 9:7, 25	1457
Intercedes for others	Num. 16:46-48	181
Confirmed by God	Num. 17:8-10	181
	Heb. 9:4	1457
Hereditary	Num. 20:23-28	184
For lifetime	Heb. 7:23	1456
Inferior to Melchizedek's	Heb. 7:11-19	1455

G. *Death and descendants of:*

Lives 123 years	Num. 33:39	200
Death	Num. 20:23-29	184
Eleazar, son of, successor	Num. 20:25-28	184
	Deut. 10:6	221

Aaronites—*descendants of Aaron*

Fights with David	1 Chr. 12:27	479
Under Zadok	1 Chr. 27:17	493

Ab—*fifth month of the Jewish year*

Aaron died in	Num. 33:38	200

See Jewish calendar

Ab—*father*

A part of many Hebrew names (e.g., Abinadab, Abner, Abijah)	1 Sam. 7:1	328

Abaddon—*a Hebrew word translated "destruction"*

Designates ruin in	Job 31:12	610
Parallel with Sheol in	Job 26:6	607
Refers to death	Job 28:22	608
Personified	Rev. 9:11	1526

Abagtha

A eunuch under King Ahasuerus	Esth. 1:10	577

Abanah—*a river flowing through Damascus*

Spoken of highly by Naaman	2 Kin. 5:12	434

Abandon—*desert*

A. *Required for:*

Safety	Gen. 19:12-26	28
	Acts 27:41-44	1315
Salvation	Phil. 3:7-10	1401
Service	Matt. 10:37-39	1129
Sanctification	2 Cor. 6:14-18	1369
Spiritual success	Heb. 11:24-27	1460

B. *Aspects of:*

Land, commanded	Gen. 12:1-5	18
Idolatry, admonished	Ex. 32:1-10	105
One's ministry, rebuked	1 Kin. 19:3-18	418
Family, regretted	1 Sam. 30:1-6	354
The tabernacle, remembered	Jer. 7:12	853
Jerusalem, lamented	Matt. 23:37, 38	1147

C. *Of men to judgment because of:*

Sin	Gen. 6:5-7	11
Rebellion	1 Sam. 15:16-26	339
Unbelief	Matt. 23:37-39	1147
Rejecting God	Rom. 1:21-32	1324
Sexual immorality	1 Cor. 5:1-5	1348
Apostasy	Heb. 10:26-29	1458

Abarim—*regions beyond*

Moses sees the promised land from	Num. 27:12	192

Abasement—*degradation; humiliation*

A. *As a judgment for:*

Stubbornness	2 Kin. 14:8-14	445
Defaming God	2 Chr. 32:1-22	531
Pride	Is. 14:12-17	786
Hating Jews	Esth. 7:4-10	582
Arrogance	Dan. 4:33, 37	981
	Acts 12:20-23	1289

B. *As a virtue, seen in:*

Nineveh's repentance	Jon. 3:1-10	1032
	Matt. 12:41	1131
A publican's unworthiness	Luke 18:13, 14	1220
Paul's life	1 Cor. 9:19-23	1353
Christ's humiliation	Phil. 2:5-8	1400

C. *Rewards of, seen in:*

Healing	2 Kin. 5:11-14	434
Elevation	Matt. 23:12	1145
Restoration	Luke 15:11-24	1218
Renewed service	1 Cor. 15:9, 10	1359

Abate—*diminish, desist*

Flood waters	Gen. 8:8, 11	12
Moses' natural force not	Deut. 34:7	247

SUBJECT | REFERENCE | PAGE

Abiel—*God is father*

1. The grandfather of Saul and Abner ....1 Sam. 9:1, 2 330
2. David's mighty man ....1 Chr. 11:32 478
   Also called Abi-Albon ....2 Sam. 23:31 385

Abiezer—*the father is help*

1. A descendant of Joseph ....Josh. 17:1, 2 270
   Called Jeezer ....Num. 26:30 191
   Family settles at Ophrah ....Judg. 6:24 290
   Gideon belongs to..........Judg. 6:11, 12 290
   Family rallies to Gideon's call ....Judg. 6:34 291
2. A mighty man and commander in David's army.........2 Sam. 23:27 385

Abiezrite

A member of the family of Abiezer.........Judg. 6:11 290; Judg. 6:24, 34 290

Abigail—*the father is joyful*

1. Nabal's beautiful and wise wife ....1 Sam. 25:3 350
   Appeases David's anger ....1 Sam. 25:14-35 350
   Becomes David's wife.........1 Sam. 25:36-42 351
   Captured and rescued .....1 Sam. 30:5, 18 354
   Mother of Chileab ......2 Sam. 3:3 362
2. A stepsister of David ....1 Chr. 2:16, 17 466

Abihail—*the father is might*

1. A Levite head of the house of Merari ....Num. 3:35 163
2. Abishur's wife ....1 Chr. 2:29 466
3. A Gadite chief in Bashan ....1 Chr. 5:14 468
4. Wife of King Rehoboam ...2 Chr. 11:18 512
5. Father of Queen Esther ....Esth. 2:15 578

Abihu—*he is father*

Second of Aaron's four sons ....Ex. 6:23 74
Ascends Mt. Sinai ....Ex. 24:1, 9 95
Chosen as priest ..Ex. 28:1 99
Offers, with Nadab, strange fire ....Lev. 10:1-7 128
Dies in the presence of the Lord ....Num. 3:4 162
Dies without heirs ....1 Chr. 24:2 490

Abihud—*the father is majesty*

A Benjamite ......1 Chr. 8:3 473

Abijah—*Yahweh is Father*

1. Wife of Hezron.......1 Chr. 2:24 466
2. Son of Becher ....1 Chr. 7:8 472
3. Samuel's second son; follows corrupt ways.........1 Sam. 8:2, 3 330
4. Descendant of Aaron; head of an office of priests.....1 Chr. 24:3, 10 490
   Zechariah belongs to ....Luke 1:5 1190
5. Son of Jeroboam I ...1 Kin. 14:1-18 411
6. Another name for King Abijam.......2 Chr. 11:20 514
7. The mother of Hezekiah ....2 Chr. 29:1 527
   Called Abi ....2 Kin. 18:2 450
8. A priest who signs the document ....Neh. 10:7 569
9. A priest returning from Babylon with Zerubbabel........Neh. 12:1, 4, 17 571

Abijam—another form of *Abijah*

King of Judah ....1 Kin. 14:31 412
Son and successor of King Rehoboam ....1 Kin. 15:1-7 412
Follows in his father's sins ....1 Kin. 15:3, 4 412
Wars against King Jeroboam ....1 Kin. 15:6, 7 412
Also called Abijah ....1 Chr. 3:10 467
Slays 500,000 Israelites ....2 Chr. 13:13-20 515
Fathers 38 children by 14 wives ....2 Chr. 13:21 515

Abilene—*grassy place*

A province or tetrarchy of Syria ....Luke 3:1 1194

Ability—*power to perform*

A. *Descriptive of:*
   Material prosperity ....Deut. 16:17 228
   Emotional strength ......Num. 11:14 173
   Military power.......Num. 13:31 176; 1 Kin. 9:21 406
   Physical strength ......Ex. 18:18, 23 88
   Mental power........Gen. 15:5 21
   Moral power ..1 Cor. 3:2 1346
   Spiritual power........James 3:2 1469
   Divine power........Rom. 4:21 1327

B. *Of God's power to:*
   Deliver.......1 Cor. 10:13 1354
   Humble men ...Dan. 4:37 981
   Create life .....Matt. 3:9 1117
   Destroy ....Matt. 10:28 1129
   Preserve believers ......John 10:28 1252
   Keep His promise ....Rom. 4:21 1327
   Establish us ...Rom. 16:25 1341
   Supply grace ...2 Cor. 9:8 1372
   Exceed our petitions .....Eph. 3:20 1388
   Supply ability........1 Pet. 4:11 1483
   Comfort others.......2 Cor. 1:4 1366
   Keep what we have committed to Him ....2 Tim. 1:12 1433
   Save from death ....Heb. 5:7 1453
   Resurrect men ....Heb. 11:19 1460
   Keep from stumbling .....Jude 24, 25 1512

C. *Of Christ's power to:*
   Heal ....Matt. 9:28, 29 1127
   Subdue all things.........Phil. 3:21 1401
   Help His own ....Heb. 2:18 1452
   Have compassion ..Heb. 4:15, 16 1453
   Save completely ...Heb. 7:25 1456

D. *Of the Christian's power to:*
   Speak for the Lord ....Luke 21:15 1225
   Admonish .....Rom. 15:14 1340
   Survive testings ......1 Cor. 3:13-15 1346
   Withstand Satan ....Eph. 6:11, 13 1393
   Convict opposition ....Titus 1:9 1440
   Bridle the whole body ....James 3:2 1469

Abimael—*God is Father*

A son of Joktan ...Gen. 10:28 16

Abimelech—*the father is king*

1. A Philistine king of Gerar ....Gen. 20:1-18 28
   Makes treaty with Abraham .....Gen. 21:22-34 30
2. A second king of Gerar ....Gen. 26:1-11 34
   Tells Isaac to go home ....Gen. 26:12-16 36
   Makes a treaty with Isaac concerning certain wells.........Gen. 26:17-33 36
3. A son of Gideon by a concubine ....Judg. 8:31 294
   Conspires to become king ....Judg. 9:1-4 294
   Slays his 70 brothers .....Judg. 9:5 294
   Made king of Shechem .....Judg. 9:6 294
   Rebuked by Jotham, lone survivor ......Judg. 9:7-21 295
   Conspired against by Gaal ....Judg. 9:22-29 295
   Captures Shechem and Thebez ....Judg. 9:41-50 296
   Death of ....Judg. 9:51-57 296
4. A son of Abiathar the priest ....1 Chr. 18:16 486
   Also called Ahimelech ...1 Chr. 24:6 491

Abinadab—*the father is generous*

1. A man of Kirjath Jearim whose house tabernacles the ark of the Lord ....1 Sam. 7:1, 2 328
2. The second of Jesse's eight sons ....1 Sam. 16:8 340
   A soldier in Saul's army.........1 Sam. 17:13 342
3. A son of Saul slain at Mt. Gilboa ....1 Sam. 31:1-8 355
   Bones of, buried by men of Jabesh ....1 Chr. 10:1-12 475

Abinoam—*the father is pleasantness*

Father of Barak ...Judg. 4:6 288

Abiram—*the father is exalted*

1. Reubenite who conspired against Moses..........Num. 16:1-50 179
2. The firstborn son of Hiel ......1 Kin. 16:34 414; Josh. 6:26 258

Abishag—*the father wanders*

A Shunammite employed as David's nurse.........1 Kin. 1:1-4, 15 391
Witnessed David's choice of Solomon as successor.........1 Kin. 1:15-31 391
Adonijah slain for desiring to marry her ......1 Kin. 2:13-25 393

Abishai—*father of a gift*

A son of Zeruiah, David's sister ....2 Sam. 2:18 361
Brother of Joab and Asahel ....1 Chr. 2:16 466

SUBJECT | REFERENCE | PAGE

Abishai—continued
- Rebuked by David .... 1 Sam. 26:5-9 351
- Serves under Joab in David's army ... 2 Sam. 2:17, 18 361
- Joins Joab in blood-revenge against Abner ... 2 Sam. 2:18-24 361
- Co-commander of David's army ... 2 Sam. 10:9, 10 369
- Loyal to David during Absalom's uprising .... 2 Sam. 16:9-12 376
- Sternly rebuked by David .... 2 Sam. 19:21-23 379
- Loyal to David during Sheba's rebellion .... 2 Sam. 20:1-6, 10 380
- Slays 300 Philistines .... 2 Sam. 23:18 385
- Slays 18,000 Edomites .... 1 Chr. 18:12, 13 486
- Saves David by killing a giant ... 2 Sam. 21:16, 17 382

Abishalom—*father of peace*
- A variant form of Absalom .... 1 Kin. 15:2, 10 412

Abishua—*the father is salvation*
1. A Benjamite ... 1 Chr. 8:3, 4 473
2. Phinehas' son .... 1 Chr. 6:4, 5, 50 469

Abishur—*the father is a wall*
- A Jerahmeelite .... 1 Chr. 2:28, 29 466

Abital—*the father is dew*
- Wife of David ..... 2 Sam. 3:2, 4 362

Abitub—*the father is goodness*
- A Benjamite ...... 1 Chr. 8:8-11 473

Abiud—Greek form of *Abihud*
- Ancestor of Jesus .... Matt. 1:13 1115

Ablution—*ceremonial washing*
- Of priests .... Ex. 30:18-21 103; Ex. 40:30, 31 116
- Of ceremonially unclean .... Lev. 14:7-9 136; Lev. 15:5-10 138
- Of a house .... Lev. 14:52 137
- By Pharisees ..... Mark 7:1-5 1167

Abner—*the father is a lamp*
- Commands Saul's army ..... 1 Sam. 14:50, 51 337
- Introduces David to Saul .... 1 Sam. 17:55-58 343
- Rebuked by David .... 1 Sam. 26:5, 14-16 351
- Saul's cousin .... 1 Sam. 14:50, 51 337
- Supports Ishbosheth as Saul's successor .... 2 Sam. 2:8-10 361
- Defeated by David's men .... 2 Sam. 2:12-17 361
- Kills Asahel in self-defense ..... 2 Sam. 2:18-23 361
- Pursued by Joab .... 2 Sam. 2:24-32 361
- Slain by Joab ..... 2 Sam. 3:8-27 362
- Death of, condemned by David .... 2 Sam. 3:28-39 362

Abolish—*to do away with*

A. *Of evil things:*
- Idolatry .... Is. 2:18 773
- Man-made ordinances ... Col. 2:20-22 1408
- Death .... 1 Cor. 15:26 1359
- Evil works .... Ezek. 6:6 922
- Enmity .... Eph. 2:15 1388

B. *Of things good for a while:*
- Old covenant .. 2 Cor. 3:13 1367
- Present world .... Heb. 1:10-12 1450
- Temporal rule .... 1 Cor. 15:24 1359
- Partial things .... 1 Cor. 13:10 1356

C. *Of things not to be abolished:*
- God's righteousness .... Is. 51:6 823
- God's Word ... Matt. 5:18 1120

Abominations—*things utterly repulsive*

A. *Descriptive of:*
- Egyptians eating with Hebrews ..... Gen. 43:32 56
- Undesirable social relations ..... Ex. 8:26 76
- Spiritist practices ..... Deut. 18:9-12 229
- Heathen idolatry ...... Deut. 7:25, 26 218
- Child-sacrifice ...... Deut. 12:31 224
- Pagan gods .... 2 Kin. 23:13 457

B. *Applied to perverse sexual relations:*
- Unnatural acts .... Lev. 18:19-29 141
- Wrong clothing ...... Deut. 22:5 232
- Prostitution and sodomy .... Deut. 23:17, 18 233
- Reclaiming a defiled woman .... Deut. 24:4 235
- Racial intermarriage ..... Ezra 9:1-14 551

C. *In ceremonial matters, applied to:*
- Unclean animals ..... Lev. 11:10-23, 41-43 130
- Deformed animals ...... Deut. 17:1 228
- Heathen practices in God's house .... 2 Chr. 36:14 538

D. *Sinfulness of, seen in:*
- Being enticed ...... 1 Kin. 11:5, 7 407
- Delighting in ... Is. 66:3 837
- Rejecting admonitions against .... Jer. 44:4, 5 891
- Polluting God's house .... Jer. 7:30 853
- Being defiled ...... Ezek. 20:7, 30-32 937

E. *Judgments upon, manifested in:*
- Stoning to death .... Deut. 17:2-5 228
- Destroying a city .... Deut. 13:13-17 224
- Diminished by God's vengeance .... Ezek. 5:11-13 922
- Experiencing God's fury .... Ezek. 20:7, 8 937

F. *Things especially classed as:*
- Silver or gold from graven images .... Deut. 7:25 218
- Perverse man .... Prov. 3:32 716
- Seven sins .... Prov. 6:16-19 719
- False balance ...... Prov. 11:1 723
- Lying lips ..... Prov. 12:22 724
- Sacrifices of the wicked .... Prov. 15:8, 9 727
- Proud in heart .... Prov. 16:5 728
- Justifying the wicked .... Prov. 17:15 729
- Scoffer .... Prov. 24:9 737
- Prayer of one who turns away his ear .... Prov. 28:9 742
- False worship ...... Is. 1:13 772
- Scant measures .... Mic. 6:10 1041
- Self-righteousness .... Luke 16:15 1219

Abomination of desolation
- Predicted by Daniel .... Dan. 9:27; 11:31; 12:11 989
- Cited by Christ ... Matt. 24:15 1147

Abortion—*accidental or planned miscarriage*
- Laws concerning ...... Ex. 21:22-25 92
- Pronounced as a judgment .... Hos. 9:14 1002
- Sought to relieve misery .... Job 3:16 591
- Of animals, by thunder .... Ps. 29:9 640
- Figurative of abrupt conversion ...... 1 Cor. 15:8 1359

Abound—*to increase greatly*

A. *Of good things:*
- God's grace ... Rom. 5:15, 20 1329
- Hope .... Rom. 15:13 1340
- God's work .... 1 Cor. 15:58 1360
- Suffering of Christ .... 2 Cor. 1:5 1366
- Joy in suffering ..... 2 Cor. 8:2 1371
- Gracious works .... 2 Cor. 8:7 1371
- Good works ... 2 Cor. 9:8 1372
- Love .... Phil. 1:9 1398
- Fruitfulness ... Phil. 4:17, 18 1402
- Faith .... Col. 2:7 1408
- Pleasing God .... 1 Thess. 4:1 1416
- Christian qualities ..... 2 Pet. 1:5-8 1487
- Blessings ...... Prov. 28:20 742

B. *Source of, in good things:*
- From God ..... 2 Cor. 9:8 1372
- From Christian generosity .... 2 Cor. 8:2, 3 1371
- Faithfulness .. Prov. 28:20 742
- Generosity .... Phil. 4:14-18 1402

C. *Of evil things:*
- Transgressions .... Prov. 29:22 743
- Lawlessness ... Matt. 24:12 1147
- Increasing sins .... Rom. 5:20 1329

Abraham—*the father of a multitude*

A. *Ancestry and family:*
- Descendant of Shem .... 1 Chr. 1:24-27 465
- Son of Terah .. Gen. 11:26 18
- First named Abram .... Gen. 11:27 18
- A native of Ur .... Gen. 11:28, 31 18
- Pagan ancestors .... Josh. 24:2 277
- Weds Sarai .... Gen. 11:29 18

B. *Wanderings of:*
- Goes to Haran .... Gen. 11:31 18
- Receives God's call ... Gen. 12:1-3 18; Acts 7:2-4 1279
- Prompted by faith .... Heb. 11:8 1460
- Enters Canaan ...... Gen. 12:4-6 18
- Canaan promised to, by God .... Gen. 12:1, 7 18
- Pitched his tent near Bethel .... Gen. 12:8 20

SUBJECT REFERENCE PAGE

Abstinence—continued
Hannah .... 1 Sam. 1:15 321
Rechabites .... Jer. 35:1-19 882
Daniel .... Dan. 1:8 976
John the Baptist .... Luke 1:13-15 1190

Abundance—*plentiful supply*

A. *Of material things:*
Spices .... 1 Kin. 10:10 406
Rain .... 1 Kin. 18:41 418
Metals .... 1 Chr. 22:3, 14 489
Trees .... {1 Chr. 22:4 489 / Neh. 9:25 568}
Sacrifices ..... 1 Chr. 29:21 496
Camels .... 2 Chr. 14:15 516
Great numbers ..... 2 Chr. 15:9 516
Flocks and herds .... {2 Chr. 18:2 517 / 2 Chr. 32:29 533}
Money .... 2 Chr. 24:11 523
Weapons ...... 2 Chr. 32:5 531
Riches .... Ps. 52:7 654
Milk .... Is. 7:22 779
Wine .... Is. 56:12 828
Horses .... Ezek. 26:10 948
Labors .... 2 Cor. 11:23 1373

B. *Of God's spiritual blessings:*
Goodness ..... Ex. 34:6 107
Pardon .... Is. 55:7 828
Peace and truth .... Jer. 33:6 881
Answers to our prayers ...... Eph. 3:20 1388
Grace .... 1 Tim. 1:14 1426
Mercy .... 1 Pet. 1:3 1477

C. *Of spiritual things:*
Predicted for Gospel times .... Is. 35:2 806
Realized in the Messiah ...... Ps. 72:7 665
Given to the gentle .... Ps. 37:11 645
Through Christ .... {Rom. 5:17, 18, 20} 1329
By grace ...... Eph. 1:3-6 1387

D. *Of good things for Christians:*
Greater usefulness .... Matt. 13:11-13 1132
Greater reward .... Matt. 25:29 1149
Spiritual life ... John 10:10 1251
Grace .... Rom. 5:17 1329
Christian service .... 1 Cor. 15:10 1359
Joy .... 2 Cor. 8:2 1371
Thanks-giving .... {2 Cor. 4:15 1368 / 2 Cor. 9:12 1372}
Rejoicing ...... Phil. 1:26 1400
Holy Spirit .... Titus 3:5, 6 1442
Entrance in God's kingdom ..... 2 Pet. 1:11 1487

E. *Of undesirable things:*
Witchcraft .... Is. 47:9 819
Idleness .... Ezek. 16:49 932

F. *Characteristics of:*
Given to the obedient ..... Lev. 26:3-13 152
Useful in God's work .... 2 Chr. 24:11 523
Cannot satisfy fully .... Eccl. 5:10-12 753
Not to be trusted .... Ps. 52:7 654
Subject to conditions ... {Mal. 3:10-12 1082 / Matt. 6:32, 33 1123}
Can be taken away .... Luke 12:13-21 1214
Not a sign of real worth .... Luke 12:15 1214

G. *Obtained by:*
Putting away sin .... 2 Chr. 15:8, 9 516
Following God's commands ... 2 Chr. 17:3-5 517

SUBJECT REFERENCE PAGE

Given by God .... Job 36:31 614
Through Christ .... John 10:10 1251

Abuse—*application to a wrong purpose*

A. *Of physical things:*
Sexual per-versions ..... {Gen. 19:5-9, 31-38} 26
Torture .... Judg. 16:21 303

B. *Of spiritual things:*
Misuse of authority .... {Num. 20:10-13 183 / 1 Cor. 9:18 1353}
Using the world wrongly .... 1 Cor. 7:31 1352
Perverting the truth .... 2 Pet. 2:10-22 1489
Corrupting God's ordinances .. {1 Sam. 2:12-17 323 / 1 Cor. 11:17-22 1355}

C. *Manifested by:*
Unbelieving ... Mark 15:29-32 1184

Abyss

Translated:
"bottomless pit" .... {Rev. 9:1, 2, 11 1526 / Rev. 17:8 1533}

Acacia Grove

1. Israel's last camp before crossing the Jordan .... Josh. 3:1 254
Scene of Baalam's attempted curse .... Num. 22–24 186
Sin of Baal of Peor here .... Num. 25:1-18 190
Site of Joshua's commission .. Num. 27:12-23 192
War with Midianites here .... Num. 31:1-54 197
Reuben and Gad receive inheritance here .... Num. 32:1-42 198
Scene of Moses' final address ...... Deut. 1–34 208
Spies sent from .... Josh. 2:1 253
2. Valley blessed by the Lord .... Joel 3:18 1012

Acacia wood

Used in:

Making the ark ... Ex. 25:10, 13 95
Table of showbread ...... Ex. 37:10 110
Altar of incense ... Ex. 30:1 103
Altar of burnt offering .... Ex. 38:1, 6 111
Tabernacle boards .... Ex. 26:15-37 98

Accad—*a city in the land of Shinar*

City in Shinar .... Gen. 10:10 16

Acceptance—*the reception of one's person or service*

A. *Objects of, before God:*
Righteousness and justice .... Prov. 21:3 733
Our words and meditations .. Ps. 19:14 636
Our dedication .... Rom. 12:1, 2 1336
Service .... Rom. 14:18 1339
Giving .... Rom. 15:16, 27 1340
Offerings .... Phil. 4:18 1402
Intercession ... 1 Tim. 2:1-3 1426
Helping parents .... 1 Tim. 5:4 1429
Spiritual sacrifices ..... 1 Pet. 2:5 1479

B. *Qualifications of, seen in:*
Coming at God's time ... {Is. 49:8 821 / 2 Cor. 6:2 1369}

SUBJECT REFERENCE PAGE

Meeting God's require-ments .... Job 42:8, 9 620
Receiving divine sign .... Judg. 6:9-21 290
Noting God's response .... {1 Sam. 7:8-10 328 / John 12:28-30 1256}
Responding to God's renewal ..... {Ezek. 20:40-44} 938
Manifesting spiritual rectitude ..... Mic. 6:6-8 1041

C. *Persons disqualified for, such as:*
Blemished sacrifices .... {Mal. 1:8, 10, 13} 1080
Man's person .... Gal. 2:6 1380
Those who swear deceitfully .... Ps. 24:3-6 638

Access to God

A. *By means of:*
Christ .... John 14:6 1258
Christ's blood .... Eph. 2:13 1388
Holy Spirit .... Eph. 2:18 1388
Faith .... Rom. 5:2 1329
Clean hands ... Ps. 24:3-5 638
God's grace ... Eph. 1:6 1387
Prayer .... Matt. 6:6 1121

B. *Characteristics of:*
On God's choosing ..... Ps. 65:4 661
Sinners com-manded to seek .... {Is. 55:6, 7 828 / James 4:8 1471}
With confidence ... Heb. 4:16 1453
Boldness ...... Eph. 3:12 1388
Results from reconcili-ation .... Col. 1:21, 22 1406
Open to Gentiles ...... Acts 14:27 1293
Experienced in Christ's priesthood ... Heb. 7:19-25 1456
Sought by God's people .... Ps. 27:4 639
Bold in prayer .... Heb. 4:16 1453
A blessing to be chosen .... Ps. 65:4 661

Accident—*event not foreseen*

A. *Caused by:*
An animal .... Num. 22:25 187
A fall .... 2 Sam. 4:4 363

B. *Explanation of:*
Known to God .... {Deut. 29:29 241 / Prov. 16:9, 33 728}
Misunderstood by men .... Luke 13:4, 5 1215
Subject to God's providence ... Rom. 8:28 1333

Acco—*a seaport 8 miles north of Mt. Carmel* (modern Acre)

Assigned to Asher .... Judg. 1:31 284
Called Ptolemais in the New Testament .... Acts 21:7 1305

Accommodation—*adaptation caused by human limitations*

A. *Physically, caused by:*
Age .... Gen. 33:13-15 44
Strength and size .... {1 Sam. 17:38-40} 343
Inability to repay .... Luke 7:41, 42 1204

B. *Spiritually, caused by:*
Man's blindness .... Matt. 13:10-14 1132
Absence of the Spirit .... John 16:12, 13 1259
Carnality ...... 1 Cor. 3:1, 2 1346

SUBJECT REFERENCE PAGE

Spiritual immaturity ... Rom. 14:1-23 1339
Man's present limitations ... 1 Cor. 2:7-16 1346
Degrees of light ... Heb. 9:7-15 1457

Accomplish—*to fulfill*

A. *Of God's Word concerning:*
Judah's captivity ... Dan. 9:2 987
Judah's return ... 2 Chr. 36:22, 23 538
God's sovereign plan ... Is. 55:11 828
Christ's suffering ... Luke 18:31 1221
Christ's death ... John 19:28-30 1264

B. *Of human things:*
Food ... 1 Kin. 5:9 398

Accord—*united agreement*

A. *Descriptive of:*
A spontaneous response ... Acts 12:10 1289
United in spirit ... Acts 12:20 1289
Voluntary action ... 2 Cor. 8:17 1371
Single-mindedness ... Josh. 9:2 260
Spiritual unity ... Acts 1:14 1272

B. *Manifested in:*
Fellowship ... Acts 2:46 1274
Prayer ... Acts 4:24 1277
Opposition ... Acts 7:57 1282
Response ... Acts 8:6 1282
Decisions ... Acts 15:25 1294
Mind ... Phil. 2:2 1400

Accountability—*responsibility for own acts*

A. *Kinds of:*
Universal ... Rom. 14:12 1339
Personal ... 2 Sam. 12:1-15 370
Personal and family ... Josh. 7:1-26 258
Personal and national ... 2 Sam. 24:1-17 387
Delayed but exacted ... 2 Sam. 21:1-14 381
Final ... Rom. 2:1-12 1324

B. *Determined by:*
Federal headship ... Gen. 3:1-24 8; Rom. 5:12-21 1329
Personal responsibility ... Ezek. 18:1-32 934
Faithfulness ... Matt. 25:14-30 1148
Knowledge ... Luke 12:47, 48 1215
Conscience ... Rom. 2:12-16 1324
Greater light ... Rom. 2:17-29 1325
Maturity of judgment ... 1 Cor. 8:1-13 1352

Accursed—*under a curse, doomed*

A. *Caused by:*
Hanging on a tree ... Deut. 21:23 232
Sin among God's people ... Josh. 7:12 258
Possessing a banned thing ... Josh. 6:18 256
Preaching contrary to the Gospel ... Gal. 1:8, 9 1378
Blaspheming Christ ... 1 Cor. 12:3 1355

B. *Objects of being:*
A city ... Josh. 6:17 256
A forbidden thing ... Josh. 22:20 276
An old sinner ... Is. 65:20 837
Christ haters or non-believers ... 1 Cor. 16:22 1361
Paul (for the sake of Israel) ... Rom. 9:3 1333

Accusations—*to charge; speak against*

A. *Kinds of:*
Pagan ... Dan. 3:8 979
Personal ... Dan. 6:24 985
Public ... John 18:29 1263

B. *Sources of, in:*
The devil ... Job 1:6-12 589; Rev. 12:9, 10 1529
Enemies ... Ezra 4:6 546
Man's conscience ... John 8:9 1248
God's Word ... John 5:45 1244
Hypocritical ... John 8:6, 10, 11 1248
The last days ... 2 Tim. 3:1, 3 1434
Apostates ... 2 Pet. 2:10, 11 1489

C. *Forbidden:*
Against servants ... Prov. 30:10 744
Falsely ... Luke 3:14 1195
Among slanderers ... Titus 2:3 1440

D. *False, examples of, against:*
Jacob ... Gen. 31:26-30 42
Joseph ... Gen. 39:10-21 51
Ahimelech ... 1 Sam. 22:11-16 348
David ... 2 Sam. 10:3 369
Job ... Job 2:3-5 590
Jeremiah ... Jer. 26:8-11 872
Amos ... Amos 7:10, 11 1021
Joshua ... Zech. 3:1-5 1069
Christ ... Matt. 26:59-66 1151
Stephen ... Acts 6:11-14 1279
Paul and Silas ... Acts 16:19-21 1295
Paul ... Acts 21:27-29 1305
Christians ... 1 Pet. 2:12 1479

Achaia—*a region of Greece*

Visited by Paul ... Acts 18:1, 12 1299
Gallio proconsul ... Acts 18:12 1299
Apollos preaches in ... Acts 18:24-28 1300
Christians of, very generous ... Rom. 15:26 1340
Saints in all of ... 2 Cor. 1:1 1364
Paul commends Christians of ... 2 Cor. 11:10 1373
Gospel proclaimed throughout ... 1 Thess. 1:7, 8 1413

Achaicus—*belonging to Achaia*

A Corinthian Christian who visited Paul ... 1 Cor. 16:17, 18 1361

Achan, Achar—*trouble*

A son of Carmi ... Josh. 7:1 258
Sin of, caused Israel's defeat ... Josh. 7:1-15 258
Stoned to death ... Josh. 7:16-25 259
Sin of, recalled ... Josh. 22:20 276
Also called Achar ... 1 Chr. 2:7 465

Achbor—*mouse*

1. Father of Edomite king ... Gen. 36:36, 38 48
2. A courtier under Josiah ... 2 Kin. 22:12, 14 456
Called Abdon ... 2 Chr. 34:20 535

Achim—*short form of Jehoiachim*

Ancestor of Jesus ... Matt. 1:14 1115

Achish—*serpent-charmer*

A king of Gath ... 1 Sam. 21:10-15 347
David seeks refuge ... 1 Sam. 27:1-12 352
Forced to expel David by Philistine lords ... 1 Sam. 29:1-11 354
Receives Shimei's servants ... 1 Kin. 2:39, 40 394

Achmetha—*capital of Media* (same as Ecbatana)

Site of Persian archives ... Ezra 6:2 547

Achor, valley of—*trouble*

Site of Achan's stoning ... Josh. 7:24-26 259
On Judah's boundary ... Josh. 15:7 267
Promises concerning ... Is. 65:10 836

Achsah—*anklet*

A daughter of Caleb ... 1 Chr. 2:49 466
Given to Othniel ... Josh. 15:16-19 267
Given springs of water ... Judg. 1:12-15 284

Achshaph—*dedicated*

A royal city of Canaan ... Josh. 11:1 264
Captured by Joshua ... Josh. 12:7, 20 265
Assigned to Asher ... Josh. 19:24, 25 272

Achzib—*a lie*

1. City of Judah ... Josh. 15:44 268
Also called Chezib ... Gen. 38:5 50
2. Town of Asher ... Josh. 19:29 272

Acknowledge—*to recognize*

A. *Evil objects of:*
Sin ... Ps. 32:5 642
Transgressions ... Ps. 51:3 654
Iniquity ... Jer. 3:13 848
Wickedness ... Jer. 14:20 861

B. *Good objects of:*
God ... Prov. 3:6 715
God's might ... Is. 33:13 804
God's people ... Is. 61:9 833
God's mystery ... Col. 2:2 1406
God's truth ... 2 Tim. 2:25 1434
The apostles ... 1 Cor. 14:37 1358
Christian leaders ... 1 Cor. 16:18 1361

Acquaintance—*personal knowledge*

With God, gives peace ... Job 22:21 604
Of God, with man's ways ... Ps. 139:3 704

Acquaintances

Deserted by ... Ps. 31:11 641
Made an abomination ... Ps. 88:8, 18 676
Jesus sought among ... Luke 2:44 1194

SUBJECT REFERENCE PAGE

Acquaintances—continued

Stand afar off from Christ .... Luke 23:49 1230

Acquit—*to declare to be innocent; pardon*

Not possible with the wicked .... Nah. 1:3 1045
Sought by the righteous .... Job 7:21 594
Difficulty of obtaining .... Job 9:28-31 595

Acre—*a land measurement*

Plowing of, by a yoke of oxen .... 1 Sam. 14:14 336
Descriptive of barrenness ...... Is. 5:10 775

Acrostic

A literary device using the Hebrew alphabet; illustrated best in (Hebrew) .... Ps. 119:1-176 694

Acts of the Apostles—*book of New Testament*

Written by Luke .... {Luke 1:1-4 1190; Acts 1:1, 2 1271}
Parts of, written by eyewitness ...... Acts 27:1, 2 1312

Adadah—*holiday*

A city of Judah ... Josh. 15:22 268

Adah—*ornament*

1. One of Lamech's wives .... Gen. 4:19 10
2. One of Esau's wives ...... {Gen. 36:2, 4, 10, 12} 46
Also called Basemath .... Gen. 26:34 36

Adaiah—*Yahweh has adorned*

1. The maternal grandfather of Josiah .... 2 Kin. 22:1 455
2. A Levite ...... 1 Chr. 6:41 470
3. Son of Shimhi .... 1 Chr. 8:21 473
Called Shema .... 1 Chr. 8:13 473
4. Aaronite priest .... 1 Chr. 9:10-12 474
5. The father of Maaseiah ..... 2 Chr. 23:1 522
6. A son of Bani .... Ezra 10:29 553
7. Another of a different family of Bani .... Ezra 10:34, 39 553
8. A descendant of Judah .... Neh. 11:4, 5 570

Adalia

Haman's son ..... Esth. 9:8, 10 583

Adam—*red earth*

A. *Creation of:*
In God's image .... Gen. 1:26, 27 4
By God's breath .... Gen. 2:7 7
A living soul .. 1 Cor. 15:45 1360
From dust ..... Gen. 2:7 7
Before Eve .... 1 Tim. 2:13 1427
Upright .... Eccl. 7:29 756
Intelligent being .... Gen. 2:19, 20 7

B. *Position of, first:*
Worker .... Gen. 2:8, 15 7
To receive God's law .... Gen. 2:16, 17 7
Husband ...... Gen. 2:18-25 7
Man to sin .... Gen. 3:6-12 8
To receive promise of the Messiah .... Gen. 3:15 9
Father .... Gen. 4:1 9
Head of race .. Rom. 5:12-14 1329

C. *Sin of:*
Instigated by Satan .... Gen. 3:1-5 8
Prompted by Eve .... Gen. 3:6 8
Done knowingly .... 1 Tim. 2:14 1427
Resulted in broken fellowship .... Gen. 3:8 8
Brought God's curse .... Gen. 3:14-19 9

D. *Descendants of, are all:*
Sinners .... Rom. 5:12 1329
Subject to death .... Rom. 5:12-14 1329
Scattered over the earth .... Deut. 32:8 244
In need of salvation ..... John 3:16 1239

Adam—*a city near Zaretan*

Site of backing up Jordan's waters to let Israel pass over .... Josh. 3:16 254

Adamah—*red ground*

City of Naphtali ... Josh. 19:35, 36 272

Adami Nekeb—*earthy*

In Naphtali .... Josh. 19:33 272

Adam, Last—*an attribution of Christ*

Prefigured in Adam .... Rom. 5:14 1329
Gift of, abound to many .... Rom. 5:15 1329
A life-giving spirit .... 1 Cor. 15:45 1360
Spiritual and heavenly .... {1 Cor. 15:46-48} 1360

Adam, Second

Expressive of Christ .... {1 Cor. 15:20-24 1359; 1 Cor. 15:45 1360}

Adar—*dark or cloudy*

A town of Judah .... Josh. 15:1, 3 267

Adar—*the twelfth month of the Hebrew year*

Date set by Haman for massacre of Jews .... Esth. 3:7, 13 579
Date adopted for Purim .... {Esth. 9:19, 21, 26-28} 585
Date of completion of Temple .... Ezra 6:15 548

Adbeel—*disciplined of God*

A son of Ishmael .... Gen. 25:13 34

Add—*to increase the sum of*

A. *Of material things:*
Another child .... Gen. 30:24 41
A population .... 2 Sam. 24:3 387
Heavy burdens ..... {1 Kin. 12:11, 14} 409
Years to life ... Prov. 3:2 715
Kingly majesty ...... Dan. 4:36 981
Stature .... Matt. 6:27 1123

B. *Of good things:*
No sorrow .... Prov. 10:22 722
Inspired words .... Jer. 36:32 884
Learning ...... Prov. 16:23 729
Spiritual blessings ..... Matt. 6:33 1123
Converts to Christ .... Acts 2:41, 47 1274
A covenant .... Gal. 3:15 1381
The Law ...... Gal. 3:19 1381

C. *Of evil things:*
Additions to God's Word .... Deut. 4:2 211
National sins .. 1 Sam. 12:19 334
Iniquity .... Ps. 69:27 664
Sin to sin ..... Is. 30:1 800
Grief to sorrow .... Jer. 45:3 893
Personal sin ... Luke 3:19, 20 1195
Afflictions ..... Phil. 1:16 1398

Addan—*strong*

A place in Babylonia whose returnees fail to prove Israelite ancestry .... Ezra 2:59 544

Addar—*wide, open place*

A Benjamite ...... 1 Chr. 8:3 473
Also called Ard ... Num. 26:40 191

Addi—*my witness*

Ancestor of Jesus .... Luke 3:23, 28 1195

Additions to the church

A. *Manner and number of:*
"The Lord added" .... Acts 2:47 1274
"Believers . . . added to the Lord" .... Acts 5:14 1277
"Disciples . . . multiplied" ... Acts 6:1 1278
"A great company of priests" ...... Acts 6:7 1279
"Churches . . . were multiplied" ... Acts 9:31 1286
"A great number believed" ..... Acts 11:21 1288
"Much people added" .... Acts 11:24 1288
"Churches . . . increased in number" ..... Acts 16:5 1294

B. *By means of:*
Word preached ..... Acts 2:14-41 1273
The Spirit's convicting power .... John 16:7-11 1259
The Gospel as God's power .... Rom. 1:16 1324
Responding faith .... Acts 14:1 1292

Addon (see Addan)

Address—*a public message*

A. *In Old Testament:*
Moses' expository .... Deut. 1:1–4:40 208
Moses' second ..... {Deut. 4:44–26:19} 214
Moses' third .... {Deut. 27:1–30:20} 237
Moses' fourth .... Deut. 32:1-43 243
Moses' final ... Deut. 33:1-29 246
Joshua's exhortation ... Josh. 23:2-16 277
Joshua's farewell ...... Josh. 24:1-25 277
Solomon's to God .... 1 Kin. 3:6-9 395

SUBJECT — REFERENCE — PAGE

Ezra's expository ....Neh. 8:1-8 — 564
Jeremiah's Temple sermon ......Jer. 7:1–10:25 — 853

B. *Of Paul:*
First ....Acts 9:20-22 — 1286
Second ....Acts 13:16-41 — 1291
To Peter ......Gal. 2:14-21 — 1380
To women ....Acts 16:13 — 1295
With Silas ....Acts 16:29-32 — 1295
At Athens .....Acts 17:22-31 — 1299
At Troas ......Acts 20:6, 7 — 1302
To elders ......Acts 20:17-35 — 1303
To the crowd ....Acts 22:1-21 — 1306
Before Felix ...Acts 24:10-21 — 1308
Before Agrippa ......Acts 26:1-29 — 1312
On the ship ....Acts 27:21-26 — 1314
Final recorded .....Acts 28:25-28 — 1315

C. *Of Peter:*
In upper room ....Acts 1:13-22 — 1272
Pentecost ......Acts 2:14-40 — 1273
At Temple .....Acts 3:12-26 — 1276
In house of Cornelius ....Acts 10:34-43 — 1287
At Jerusalem council ....Acts 15:7-11 — 1293

D. *Of Others:*
Stephen ....Acts 7:2-60 — 1279
Herod ....Acts 12:21, 22 — 1289
James ....Acts 15:13-21 — 1293
Tertullus .....Acts 24:1-8 — 1308

Adiel—*ornament of God*

1. A Simeonite prince ....1 Chr. 4:24, 36 — 468
2. Aaronite priest ....1 Chr. 9:12, 13 — 474
3. Father of Azmaveth ....1 Chr. 27:25 — 494

Adin—*effeminate*

1. A man whose descendants return with Zerubbabel ...Ezra 2:2, 15 — 542
2. A man whose descendants return with Ezra ....Ezra 8:1, 6 — 549
3. Sealer of the covenant ....Neh. 10:1, 16 — 569

Adina—*delicate*

A Reubenite captain under David ....1 Chr. 11:42 — 479

Adino—*slender*

A mighty man under David ....2 Sam. 23:8 — 385
Compare parallel passage in ....1 Chr. 11:11 — 478

Adithaim—*double ornaments*

A city of Judah ...Josh. 15:21, 36 — 268

Adjuration—*earnest advising; to charge as if under an oath*

Joshua's, to Jericho ....Josh. 6:26 — 258
Saul's, to those breaking a fast ....1 Sam. 14:24-28 — 336
Ahab's, to the prophet Micaiah ....1 Kin. 22:16 — 423
Caiaphas', by God ....Matt. 26:63 — 1151
Demon's, by God ....Mark 5:7 — 1165
Exorcists', by Jesus ....Acts 19:13 — 1300
Paul's charge, by the Lord ....1 Thess. 5:27 — 1418

Adlai—*Yahweh is just*

Father of Shaphat ....1 Chr. 27:29 — 494

Admah—*red earth*

A city near Sodom ....Gen. 10:19 — 16
Joins other cities against Chedorlaomer ...Gen. 14:1-4, 8 — 21
Destroyed with Sodom and Gomorrah ....Gen. 19:24-28 — 28

Admatha—*God-given*

One of Ahasuerus' chamberlains ....Esth. 1:13-15 — 577

Administer—*serve; execute; manage*

Applied to:
Judgment ....1 Kin. 3:28 — 395
Vengeance ....Jer. 21:12 — 867
Justice ....2 Sam. 8:15 — 367

Administration—*the management or disposition of affairs*

Of gifts to Jerusalem saints ....2 Cor. 8:19, 20 — 1371
Of spiritual gifts ....1 Cor. 12:5 — 1355; 2 Cor. 9:12 — 1372

Admiration—*exceptional esteem*

Reserved for saints ....2 Thess. 1:10 — 1421
Flattering, shown by false teachers ....Jude 16 — 1512

Admonition—*wise words spoken against evil acts; warning*

A. *Performed by:*
God ....Heb. 8:5 — 1456
Earthly fathers ....Eph. 6:4 — 1392
Leaders ....1 Thess. 5:12 — 1416
Christians .....Rom. 15:14 — 1340

B. *Directed against:*
A remnant ....Jer. 42:19 — 890
Elders ....Acts 20:28-35 — 1303
Those who will not work ....2 Thess. 3:10, 15 — 1422
Divisive man ..Titus 3:10 — 1442

C. *Sources of in:*
Scriptures .....1 Cor. 10:11 — 1354
Wise words ...Eccl. 12:11, 12 — 759
Spiritual knowledge ...Col. 3:16 — 1408

Adna—*pleasure*

1. Jew who divorced his foreign wife ....Ezra 10:18, 30 — 553
2. Postexilic priest ....Neh. 12:12, 15 — 571

Adnah—*pleasure*

1. Captain of Saul ....1 Chr. 12:20 — 479
2. Chief Captain of Jehoshaphat ..2 Chr. 17:14 — 517

Adonai—*Lord*

The Hebrew title for God (translated "Lord") expressing lordship (found in the following five compound words)

Adoni-Bezek—*lord of Bezek*

A king of Bezek ..Judg. 1:3-7 — 283

Adonijah—*my Lord is Yahweh*

1. David's fourth son ....2 Sam. 3:2, 4 — 362
Attempts to usurp throne ....1 Kin. 1:5-53 — 391
Desires Abishag as wife ....1 Kin. 2:13-18 — 393
Executed by Solomon .....1 Kin. 2:19-25 — 393
2. A teacher .....2 Chr. 17:8, 9 — 517
3. A Jew who signed the document ...Neh. 9:38; 10:16 — 569
Probably the same as Adonikam in ....Ezra 2:13 — 544

Adonikam—*my Lord has risen*

Descendants of, return from exile ....Ezra 2:13 — 544

Adoniram, Adoram—*my Lord is exalted*

A son of Abda ....1 Kin. 4:6 — 395
Official under David, Solomon, and Rehoboam ......2 Sam. 20:24 — 381; 1 Kin. 5:14 — 398; 1 Kin. 12:18 — 409
Stoned by angry Israelites ....1 Kin. 12:18 — 409
Called Hadoram ..2 Chr. 10:18 — 512

Adoni-Zedek—*my Lord is righteous*

An Amorite king of Jerusalem ....Josh. 10:1-5 — 261
Defeated and slain by Joshua ....Josh. 10:6-27 — 261

Adoption—*the legal act of investing with sonship*

A. *Used naturally of:*
Eliezer under Abraham .....Gen. 15:2-4 — 21
Joseph's sons under Jacob ....Gen. 48:5, 14, 16 — 60
Moses under Pharaoh's daughter ....Ex. 2:10 — 69; Acts 7:21 — 1279
Esther under Mordecai .....Esth. 2:7 — 578

B. *Used spiritually of Israel as:*
Elected by God ....Deut. 14:1, 2 — 225; Rom. 11:1-32 — 1335
Blessed by God ....Rom. 9:4 — 1333
Realized in history.......Ex. 4:22, 23 — 72

C. *Used spiritually of the Gentiles as:*
Predicted in the prophets .....Is. 65:1 — 836
Confirmed by faith ....Rom. 10:20 — 1335
Realized in the new covenant .....Eph. 2:12 — 1388; Eph. 3:1-6 — 1388

D. *The time of:*
Past, predestined to ....Rom. 8:29 — 1333
Present, regarded as sons ....John 1:12, 13 — 1236; John 3:1-11 — 1239
Future, glorified as sons ..Rom. 8:19, 23 — 1333; 1 John 3:2 — 1497

E. *The source of:*
By God's grace ....Rom. 4:16, 17 — 1327
By faith ....Gal. 3:7, 26 — 1381
Through Christ ....Gal. 4:4, 5 — 1381

F. *Assurances of, by:*
Spirit's witness ......Rom. 8:16 — 1333
Spirit's leading.......Rom. 8:14 — 1332

SUBJECT REFERENCE PAGE

Adoption—continued

"Abba, Father" ...... Rom. 8:15 1332
Changed life .. 1 John 3:9-17 1497
Father's chastening .. Prov. 3:11, 12 716; Heb. 12:5-11 1462

G. *The blessings of:*
A new nature .... 2 Cor. 5:17 1368
A new name .... Is. 62:2, 12 834; Rev. 3:12 1521
Access to God .... Eph. 2:18 1388
Fatherly love .. 1 John 3:1 1497
Help in prayer .... Matt. 6:5-15 1121
Spiritual unity .... John 17:11, 21 1261; Eph. 2:18-22 1388
A glorious inheritance .. John 14:1-3 1258; Rom. 8:17, 18 1333

Adoraim—*double honor*

A city fortified by Rehoboam .... 2 Chr. 11:5, 9 512

Adoram—*the Lord is exalted*

An official over forced labor .... 2 Sam. 20:24 381; 1 Kin. 12:18 409

See Adoniram

Adoration—*reverential praise*

A. *Rendered falsely to:*
Idols .... Is. 44:15, 17, 19 816
An image ..... Dan. 3:5-7 979
Heavenly hosts .... 2 Kin. 17:16 449
Satan .... Luke 4:6-8 1198
Men .... Acts 10:25, 26 1287
Angels .... Col. 2:18, 23 1408

B. *Rendered properly to God:*
Illustrated ..... Is. 6:1-5 777
Taught .... Ps. 95–100 680
Proclaimed .... Rev. 4:8-11 1523

C. *Rendered properly to Christ as God by:*
Wise men ..... Matt. 2:1, 11 1116
Leper .... Matt. 8:2 1125
Ruler .... Matt. 9:18 1127
Disciples ...... Matt. 14:22, 33 1134
Woman .... Matt. 15:25 1135
Mother .... Matt. 20:20 1140
Blind man ..... John 9:1, 38 1250
Every creature ...... Phil. 2:10, 11 1400

See also Worship

Adornment

A. *Used literally of:*
A harlot .... Rev. 17:3, 4 1533
A woman .... Is. 3:16-24 774; 1 Tim. 2:9 1426
A building .... Luke 21:5 1224
A bride .... Rev. 21:2 1538

B. *Used spiritually of:*
Believer as justified ...... Is. 61:10 834
Believer as sanctified .... Titus 2:10 1442
Israel restored ...... Jer. 31:4 877
Saintly woman .... 1 Tim. 2:9 1426

C. *Guidelines for:*
In modesty .... 1 Tim. 2:9 1426
Not external ... 1 Pet. 3:3-5 1480

Adrammelech—*Adar is king*

1. A god worshiped by the Samarians .... 2 Kin. 17:31 449
2. Killed Sennacherib .... 2 Kin. 19:36, 37 453; Is. 37:38 810

Adramyttium—*a seaport of Mysia in Asia Minor*

Travels of Paul ... Acts 27:2-6 1314

Adriatic Sea

A part or the whole of the Adriatic Sea named after Adria, a city of Italy .... Acts 27:27 1314

Adriel—*my help is God*

Marries Saul's eldest daughter .... 1 Sam. 18:19 344
Sons of, slain to atone Saul's crime .... 2 Sam. 21:8, 9 381

Adullam—*refuge*

A town of Canaan .... Gen. 38:1, 12, 20 50
Conquered by Joshua .... Josh. 12:7, 15 265
Assigned to Judah .... Josh. 15:20, 35 268
Fortified by Rehoboam .... 2 Chr. 11:5-7 512
Symbol of Israel's glory .... Mic. 1:15 1037
Reoccupied .... Neh. 11:25, 30 571
David seeks refuge in caves of .... 1 Sam. 22:1, 2 347
Exploits of mighty men while there .... 2 Sam. 23:13-17 385

Adullamite—*a citizen of Adullam*

Judah's friend ... Gen. 38:1, 12, 20 50

Adulterer—*a man who commits adultery*

Punishment of .... Lev. 20:10 143
Waits for the twilight .... Job 24:15 606
Offspring of ...... Is. 57:3 829
Land is full of .... Jer. 23:10 869
Shall not inherit the kingdom of God .... 1 Cor. 6:9 1349
God will judge .... Heb. 13:4 1463

Adulteress—*a woman guilty of adultery; seductress*

A. *Sin of:*
Punished by death .... Lev. 20:10 143
Ensnares the simple .... Prov. 7:6-23 720
Brings a man to poverty ...... Prov. 6:26 719
Leads to death .... Prov. 2:16-19 715
Increases transgressors ...... Prov. 23:27, 28 736
Defined by Christ .... Matt. 5:32 1120
Forgiven by Christ .... John 8:1-11 1248
Mentioned by Paul .... Rom. 7:3 1331

B. *Examples of:*
Tamar .... Gen. 38:13-24 50
Potiphar's wife (attempted) ... Gen. 39:7-20 51
Midianite women .... Num. 25:6-8 190
Rahab .... Josh. 2:1 253
Bathsheba ..... 2 Sam. 11:4, 5 369
Herodias ...... Matt. 14:3, 4 1134
Unnamed woman .... John 8:1-11 1248

See Harlot

Adultery—*sexual intercourse outside marriage*

A. *Defined:*
In God's Law .... Ex. 20:14 90
By Christ ...... Matt. 5:28, 32 1120
In mental attitude ...... Matt. 5:28 1120
As a work of the flesh .... Gal. 5:19 1383

B. *Sin of:*
Breaks God's Law .... Deut. 5:18 214
Punishable by death .... Lev. 20:10-12 143
Brings death .. Prov. 2:18, 19 715
Makes one poor .... Prov. 29:3 742
Produces moral insensibility .... Prov. 30:20 744; 2 Cor. 12:21 1375
Corrupts a land .... Hos. 4:1-3 998
Justifies divorce ...... Matt. 19:7-9 1139
Excludes from Christian fellowship .... 1 Cor. 5:1-13 1348
Excludes from God's kingdom ..... 1 Cor. 6:9, 10 1349
Merits God's judgments .... Heb. 13:4 1463
Ends in hell (Sheol) .... Prov. 7:27 720; Rev. 21:8 1538

C. *Forgiveness of, by:*
Man .... Judg. 19:1-4 306
Christ .... John 8:10, 11 1248
Repentance ... 2 Sam. 12:7-14 370
Regeneration .... 1 Cor. 6:9-11 1349

D. *Examples of:*
Lot .... Gen. 19:31-38 28
Shechem ...... Gen. 34:2 45
Judah .... Gen. 38:1-24 50
Eli's sons ..... 1 Sam. 2:22 324
David .... 2 Sam. 11:1-5 369
Amnon .... 2 Sam. 13:1-20 371
The Samaritan woman .... John 4:17, 18 1241

Adultery, spiritual

Seen in Israel's idolatry .... Judg. 2:11, 17 285
Described graphically ...... Ezek. 16 931
Symbolized in Hosea's marriage .... Hos. 1:1-3 996
Figurative of friendship with the world .... James 4:4 1471
Figurative of false teaching ... Rev. 2:14, 15, 20-22 1519

Adummim—*red spots*

A hill between Jerusalem and Jericho .... Josh. 15:5, 7, 8 267
The probable site of Good Samaritan parable in .... Luke 10:30-37 1209

Advancement—*progression*

A. *Promotion to a higher office:*
Moses and Aaron, by the Lord .... 1 Sam. 12:6 333
Promised to Balaam ..... Num. 22:16, 17 187
Joseph, by true interpretation .... Gen. 41:38-46 54
Levites, for loyalty .... Ex. 32:26-28 106
Phinehas, by decisive action ...... Num. 25:7-13 190
Haman, by intrigue .... Esth. 3:1, 2 578
Mordecai, by ability .... Esth. 10:2 585
Daniel, by fidelity .... Dan. 2:48 978

SUBJECT | REFERENCE | PAGE

Deacons, by faithfulness . . 1 Tim. 3:10, 13 1427

B. *Conditions of, seen in:*
Humility . . . . . . Matt. 18:4 1138
Faithfulness . . . Matt. 25:14-30 1148
Skilled in work . . . . Prov. 22:29 735
Service to others . . . . Luke 22:24-30 1226

C. *Hindrances to, occasioned by:*
Self-glory . . . Is. 14:12-15 786; 1 Cor. 4:6-9 1348
Pride . . . . Ezek. 28:11-19 951; 1 Pet. 5:5, 6 1483

Advantage—*superior circumstance or ability*

A. *In God's kingdom, none by:*
Birth . . . . Matt. 3:8, 9 1117
Race . . . . Gal. 2:14-16 1380
Position . . . . John 3:1-6 1239
Works . . . . Matt. 5:20 1120
Wealth . . . . Luke 9:25 1207

B. *In God's kingdom, some by:*
Industry . . . . . . 1 Cor. 15:10 1359
Faithfulness . . . Matt. 25:14-30 1148
Kindred spirit . . . . Phil. 2:19-23 1400
Works . . . . 1 Cor. 3:11-15 1346
Dedication . . . . Rev. 14:1-5 1531

Advent of Christ, the First

A. *Announced in the Old Testament by:*
Moses . . . . Deut. 18:18, 19 229
Samuel . . . . Acts 3:24 1276
David . . . . Ps. 40:6-8 648; Heb. 10:5-8 1458
Prophets . . . . . . Luke 24:26, 27 1231

B. *Prophecies fulfilled by His:*
Birth . . . . Is. 7:14 779; Matt. 1:23 1116
Forerunner . . Mal. 3:1, 2 1082; Matt. 3:1-3 1117
Incarnation . . . . Is. 9:6 780
Time of arrival . . . . . . Dan. 9:24, 25 989; Mark 1:15 1159
Rejection . . . . Is. 53:1-4 825; Rom. 10:16-21 1335
Crucifixion . . Ps. 2:1, 2 625; Acts 4:24-28 1277
Atonement . . Is. 53:1-12 825; 1 Pet. 1:18-21 1479
Resurrection . . . . . . Ps. 16:8-11 633; Acts 2:25-31 1273
Priesthood . . . Ps. 110:4, 5 689; Heb. 5:5, 6 1453

C. *His first coming:*
Introduces Gospel age . . . . Acts 3:24 1276
Establishes new covenant . . . Jer. 31:31-34 878; Heb. 8:6-13 1456
Fulfills prophecy . . . . . Luke 24:44, 45 1231
Nullifies the ceremonial system . . . . Heb. 9 1457
Brings Gentiles in . . . . Acts 15:13-18 1293

Advent of Christ, the Second (see Second Coming of Christ)

Advents of Christ, compared

A. *First Advent:*
Prophesied . . . Deut. 18:18, 19 229; Is. 7:14 779
Came as man . . . . Phil. 2:5-8 1400
Announced . . . . Luke 2:10-14 1193
Time predicted . . . . . Dan. 9:25 989
To save the lost . . . . Matt. 18:11 1138
Subject to government . . Matt. 17:24-27 1138

B. *Second Advent:*
Prophesied . . John 14:1-3 1258; 1 Thess. 4:16 1416
Come as God . . . . 1 Thess. 4:16 1416
As a thief . . . . . . 1 Thess. 5:2 1416
At a time unknown . . . . . Matt. 24:36 1148
To judge the lost . . . . Matt. 25:31-33, 41-46 1149
Source of government . . . . Rev. 20:4-6 1536; Rev. 22:3-5 1539

Adversaries—*those who actively oppose*

A. *Descriptive of:*
Satan . . . . 1 Pet. 5:8 1483
Gospel's enemies . . . . . . 1 Cor. 16:9 1361
Israel's enemies . . . . . Josh. 5:13 256
An enemy . . . . . Esth. 7:6 582
A rival . . . . 1 Sam. 1:6 321
God's agent . . 1 Kin. 11:14, 23 407
God's angel . . . Num. 22:22 187

B. *Believer's attitude toward:*
Pray for . . . . Matt. 5:43, 44 1121
Use God's weapons against . . . . Luke 21:15 1225
Not to be terrified by . . . . Phil. 1:28 1400
Not to give opportunity to . . . . 1 Tim. 5:14 1429
Remember God's judgment on . . . . Heb. 10:27 1458

Adversity—*adverse circumstances*

A. *Caused by:*
Man's sin . . . . . Gen. 3:16-19 9
Disobedience to God's Law . . . . Lev. 26:14-20 152

B. *Purposes of, to:*
Punish for sin . . . . 2 Sam. 12:9-12 371
Humble us . . . . 2 Chr. 33:12 533
Lead us to God's Word . . . . Deut. 8:2, 3 218
Chasten and correct . . . . Heb. 12:5-11 1462
Test our faith . . . . 1 Pet. 1:5-8 1477
Give us final rest . . . . Ps. 94:12, 13 679

C. *Reactions to:*
Rebellious . . . Ex. 14:4-8 83; Job 2:9 590
Distrustful . . . . Ex. 6:8, 9 74
Complaining . . Ruth 1:20, 21 313
Questioning . . . . Jer. 20:7-10 866
Fainting . . . . Prov. 24:10 737
Arrogant . . . . . . Ps. 10:6 631
Hopeful . . . . Lam. 3:31-40 912
Submissive . . . . Job 5:17-22 592
Joyful . . . . James 1:2-4 1468

D. *God's relation to, He:*
Troubles nations with . . . . 2 Chr. 15:5, 6 516
Knows the soul in . . . . Ps. 31:7 641
Saves out of . . . 1 Sam. 10:19 332
Redeems out of . . . . 2 Sam. 4:9 363

E. *Helps under:*
By prayer . . . . . . Jon. 2:1-7 1032
By understanding God's purpose . . . . Lam. 3:31-39 912; Rom. 5:3 1329

Advertise—*to make known publicly*

Messiah's advent . . . . Num. 24:14-19 189
A piece of property . . . . Ruth 4:4 315

Advice—*one's judgment or counsel*

A. *Sought by:*
A king . . . . Esth. 1:13-15 577
Another ruler . . . . Acts 25:13-27 1310
A usurper . . . 2 Sam. 16:20-23 376
Five men . . . . . 2 Kin. 22:12-20 456

B. *Sought from:*
The ephod . . . . . . 1 Sam. 23:9-12 348
A prophet . . . . . Jer. 42:1-6 890
A dead prophet . . . . . . 1 Sam. 28:7-20 353
A council . . . . . Acts 15:1-22 1293
A grieving husband . . . . . . Judg. 20:4-7 307

C. *Kinds of:*
Helpful . . . . Ex. 18:12-25 88
Rejected . . . . 1 Kin. 12:6-8 409
Timely . . . . . . 1 Sam. 25:32-34 351
Good . . . . 2 Kin. 5:13, 14 434
God-inspired . . . 2 Sam. 17:6-14 376
Foolish . . . . Job 2:9 590
Humiliating . . . Esth. 6:6-11 582
Fatal . . . . Esth. 5:14 581; Esth. 7:9, 10 582
Ominous . . . . . . Matt. 27:19 1152
Accepted . . . . . . Acts 5:34-41 1278

D. *Sought from:*
Congregation of Israel . . . . Judg. 20:7 307

Advocate, Christ our

A. *His interest in believers, by right of:*
Election . . . . . . John 15:16 1259
Redemption . . . Eph. 1:7 1387
Regeneration . . Col. 1:27 1406
Imputed righteousness . . . . 2 Cor. 5:21 1369; Phil. 3:9 1401

B. *His defense of believers by:*
Prayer . . . . Luke 22:31-34 1226
Protection . . . . . Heb. 13:6 1463
Provision . . . . Ps. 23:1 637; John 10:28 1252
Perseverance . . . . 2 Tim. 4:17, 18 1436

C. *His blessings upon believers:*
Another Helper . . . . John 14:16, 17 1258
New commandment . . . . John 13:34, 35 1257
New nature . . . . 2 Cor. 5:17 1368
New name . . . . Rev. 2:17 1519
New life . . . . John 4:14 1241
New relationship . . John 15:15 1259

D. *Our duties prescribed by Him:*
Our mission—world evangelization . . . . . . Matt. 28:16-20 1155
Our means—the Holy Spirit . . . . Acts 1:8 1272
Our might—the Gospel . . . . . . Rom. 1:16 1324
Our motivation—the love of Christ . . . . 2 Cor. 5:14, 15 1368

Aeneas—*praise*

A paralytic healed by Peter . . . . Acts 9:32-35 1286

Aenon—*springs*

A place near Salim where John the Baptist baptized . . . . John 3:22, 23 1241

SUBJECT — REFERENCE — PAGE

- Spiritual beauty .... Prov. 16:31 — 729
- Fruitfulness ... Ps. 92:12-15 — 679
- Judgment ..... 1 Kin. 12:6-8 — 409
- Strong faith ... Josh. 24:15, 29 — 279

C. *Attitude of others toward:*
- Respect .... Lev. 19:32 — 142
- Disrespect ..... 2 Chr. 36:17 — 538
- Insolence ..... Is. 3:5 — 774

D. *Unusual things connected with:*
- Retaining physical vigor .... Deut. 34:7 — 247
- Becoming a father .... Gen. 18:9-15 — 24; Luke 1:18, 36 — 1190
- Living to see Christ .... Luke 2:25-32 — 1194
- Knowing kind of death in .... John 21:18, 19 — 1267

E. *Attaining unto, by:*
- Honoring parents .... Ex. 20:12 — 90; Eph. 6:2, 3 — 1392
- Keeping God's law .... Prov. 3:1, 2 — 715
- Following wisdom ...... Prov. 3:13, 16 — 716
- The fear of the Lord .... Ps. 128:1, 6 — 701
- Keeping from evil .... Ps. 34:11-14 — 643
- God's promise ...... Gen. 15:15 — 23

F. *Those of Bible times who lived beyond age of 100:*
- Methuselah .... Gen. 5:27 — 11
- Jared .... Gen. 5:20 — 11
- Noah .... Gen. 9:29 — 15
- Adam .... Gen. 5:5 — 10
- Seth .... Gen. 5:8 — 10
- Cainan .... Gen. 5:14 — 10
- Enosh .... Gen. 5:11 — 10
- Mahalaleel .... Gen. 5:17 — 10
- Lamech .... Gen. 5:31 — 11
- Enoch .... Gen. 5:23 — 11
- Terah .... Gen. 11:32 — 18
- Isaac .... Gen. 35:28 — 46
- Abraham .... Gen. 25:7 — 33
- Jacob .... Gen. 47:28 — 60
- Ishmael .... Gen. 25:17 — 34
- Jehoiada ...... 2 Chr. 24:15 — 523
- Sarah .... Gen. 23:1 — 31
- Aaron .... Num. 33:39 — 200
- Moses .... Deut. 34:7 — 247
- Joseph .... Gen. 50:26 — 64
- Joshua .... Josh. 24:29 — 279

Agee—*fugitive*
- Shammah's father .... 2 Sam. 23:11 — 385

Ages—*extended periods of time*
- Descriptive of the times before Christ .... Eph. 3:5 — 1388
- Descriptive of eternity .... Eph. 2:7 — 1387

Agitation—*a disturbance*

A. *Physically of:*
- Mountain ..... Ex. 19:16-18 — 90
- The earth ..... Matt. 27:51-53 — 1154
- The world ..... Ps. 46:2-6 — 651
- End-time events .... Luke 21:25-27 — 1225
- World's end ... 2 Pet. 3:7-12 — 1489

B. *Emotionally of:*
- Extreme grief .... 2 Sam. 19:1-4 — 378
- Remorse ...... Matt. 27:3, 4 — 1152
- Fear .... Matt. 28:1-4 — 1155

C. *Figuratively of:*
- Messiah's advent .... Hag. 2:6, 7 — 1065
- Enraged people .... Acts 4:25-28 — 1277
- The wicked .... Is. 57:20 — 829

- The drunkard ..... Prov. 23:29-35 — 736

Agony—*extreme suffering*

Descriptive of:
- Christ in Gethsemane ...... Luke 22:44 — 1228
- Christ on the cross .... Mark 15:34-37 — 1184
- Paul's sufferings .... 2 Cor. 1:8, 9 — 1366
- The Christians' race .... 1 Cor. 9:24, 25 — 1353

Agree, agreement

A. *Forbidden between:*
- Israel and pagans .... Ex. 34:12-16 — 107
- God and Baal .... 1 Kin. 18:21-40 — 417
- Believers, demons ...... 1 Cor. 10:21 — 1354
- Truth, error ... 1 John 4:1-6 — 1498

B. *Necessary between:*
- Prophecy, fulfillment .... Acts 15:15 — 1293
- Doctrine, life .. James 2:14-21 — 1469
- Words, performance .... 2 Cor. 10:9-11 — 1373
- Believers in prayer .... Matt. 18:19 — 1138
- Adversaries ... Matt. 5:24, 25 — 1120
- Christian workers ...... Gal. 2:7-9 — 1380

C. *Examples of:*
- Laban and Jacob .... Gen. 31:43-53 — 43
- God and Israel .... Ex. 19:3-8 — 89
- David and Jonathan ..... 1 Sam. 18:1-4 — 343
- The wicked and Sheol .... Is. 28:15, 18 — 798
- Employer and employees .... Matt. 20:10-13 — 1140
- Judas and the Sanhedrin .... Matt. 26:14-16 — 1150
- Witnesses ... Mark 14:56, 59 — 1182
- Husband and wife .... Acts 5:9 — 1277
- The Jews and Gamaliel ..... Acts 5:34-40 — 1278
- Conspiring Jews .... Acts 23:20 — 1307
- The people of antichrist .... Rev. 17:17 — 1535

Agriculture—*the cultivation of the soil*

A. *Terms and implements involved:*
- Binding .... Gen. 37:7 — 49
- Cultivating .... Luke 13:6-9 — 1215
- Gleaning ...... Ruth 2:3 — 314
- Grafting ..... Rom. 11:17-19 — 1336
- Harrowing .... Is. 28:24 — 799
- Harvesting .... Matt. 13:30 — 1133
- Mowing .... Amos 7:1 — 1021
- Planting ..... Prov. 31:16 — 745
- Plowing .... Job 1:14 — 589
- Pruning .... Is. 5:6 — 775
- Reaping .... Is. 17:5 — 789
- Removing stones .... Is. 5:2 — 775
- Sowing .... Matt. 13:3 — 1132
- Stacking ...... Ex. 22:6 — 93
- Threshing ..... Judg. 6:11 — 290
- Treading ...... Neh. 13:15 — 572
- Watering ...... 1 Cor. 3:6-8 — 1346
- Weeding ...... Matt. 13:28, 29 — 1133
- Winnowing ..... Ruth 3:2 — 314

B. *Virtues required in:*
- Wisdom ...... Is. 28:24-29 — 799
- Diligence ..... Prov. 27:23-27 — 740
- Labor .... 2 Tim. 2:6 — 1434
- Patience ...... James 5:7 — 1471
- Industry ..... Prov. 28:19 — 742
- Faith .... Hab. 3:17-19 — 1054
- Bountifulness .... 2 Cor. 9:6, 7 — 1372
- Hopefulness ... 1 Cor. 9:10 — 1353

C. *Enemies of:*
- War .... Jer. 50:16 — 900
- Pestilence ..... Joel 1:9-12 — 1008
- Fire .... Joel 1:19 — 1009
- Animals .... Song 2:15 — 763
- Dry seasons ... Jer. 14:1, 4 — 860

D. *Restrictions involving:*
- Coveting another's field .... Deut. 5:21 — 214
- Removing boundaries ... Deut. 19:14 — 230
- Roaming cattle .... Ex. 22:5 — 93
- Spreading fire .... Ex. 22:6 — 93
- Military service ...... Deut. 20:5, 6 — 230
- Working on the Sabbath ..... Ex. 34:21 — 108
- Complete harvest ..... Lev. 19:9, 10 — 142

E. *God's part in:*
- Began in Eden .... Gen. 2:15 — 7
- Sin's penalty .. Gen. 3:17 — 9
- Providence of, impartial ..... Matt. 5:45 — 1121
- Goodness of, recognized .... Acts 14:16, 17 — 1293
- Judgments against, cited .... Hag. 1:10, 11 — 1064

F. *Figurative of:*
- Gospel seed ... Matt. 13:1-9 — 1132
- Gospel dispensation .... Matt. 13:24-30, 36-43 — 1133
- God's workers ...... John 4:36-38 — 1242
- God's Word ... Is. 55:10, 11 — 828
- Spiritual barrenness ... Heb. 6:7, 8 — 1455
- Spiritual bountifulness .... 2 Cor. 9:9, 10 — 1372
- Final harvest .. Mark 4:28, 29 — 1164

Aground—*stranded in shallow water*
- Ship carrying Paul .... Acts 27:41 — 1315

Agur—*collector*
- Writer of proverbs .... Prov. 30:1-33 — 743

Ahab—*father's brother*

1. A wicked king of Israel .... 1 Kin. 16:29 — 414
- Marries Jezebel ...... 1 Kin. 16:31 — 414
- Introduces Baal worship ...... 1 Kin. 16:31-33 — 414
- Denounced by Elijah .... 1 Kin. 17:1 — 414
- Gathers prophets of Baal ..... 1 Kin. 18:17-46 — 417
- Wars against Ben-hadad ... 1 Kin. 20:1-43 — 420
- Covets Naboth's vineyard .... 1 Kin. 21:1-16 — 421
- Death of, predicted .... 1 Kin. 21:17-26 — 422
- Repentance of, delays judgment ..... 1 Kin. 21:27-29 — 422
- Joins Jehoshaphat against Syrians ..... 1 Kin. 22:1-4 — 422
- Rejects Micaiah's warning ...... 1 Kin. 22:5-33 — 423
- Slain in battle ...... 1 Kin. 22:34-37 — 425

SUBJECT **REFERENCE** **PAGE**

Lived with David at Gath ....1 Sam. 27:3 352
Captured by Amalekites at Ziklag ....1 Sam. 30:5 354
Rescued by David ....1 Sam. 30:18 355
Lives with David in Hebron ......2 Sam. 2:1, 2 360
Mother of Amnon ......2 Sam. 3:2 362

Ahio—*brotherly*

1. Abinadab's son ....2 Sam. 6:3 364
2. A Benjamite ...1 Chr. 8:14 473
3. A son of Jehiel ....{1 Chr. 8:31 473; 1 Chr. 9:37 475}

Ahira—*my brother is evil*

A tribal leader ....Num. 1:15 159

Ahisamach—*my brother supports*

A Danite ....Ex. 31:6 104

Ahishahar—*brother of dawn*

A Benjamite ......1 Chr. 7:10 472

Ahishar—*my brother has sung*

A manager of Solomon's household ....1 Kin. 4:6 395

Ahithophel—*brother of folly*

David's counselor.........2 Sam. 15:12 374
Joins Absalom's insurrection .....2 Sam. 15:31 375
Plans of, prepared against by David ....{2 Sam. 15:31-34} 375
Counsels Absalom.........{2 Sam. 16:20-22} 376
Reputed wise ......2 Sam. 16:23 376
Counsel of, rejected by Absalom ....2 Sam. 17:1-22 376
Commits suicide ..2 Sam. 17:23 377

Ahitub—*my brother is goodness*

1. Phinehas' son ....1 Sam. 14:3 336
2. The father of Zadok the priest ....2 Sam. 8:17 367
3. The father of another Zadok ....1 Chr. 6:11, 12 469

Ahlab—*fruitful*

A city of Asher ...Judg. 1:31 284

Ahlai—*O would that!*

1. Father of a warrior of David ....1 Chr. 11:41 479
2. Woman who married an Egyptian servant ....1 Chr. 2:31-35 466

Ahoah—*brotherly*

A son of Bela .....1 Chr. 8:4 473

Ahohite—*a descendant of Ahoah*

Applied to Dodo, Zalmon, and Ilai ....{2 Sam. 23:9, 28 385; 1 Chr. 11:29 478}

Aholiab—*a father's tent*

Son of Ahisamach ......Ex. 31:6 104

Ahumai—*heated by Yahweh*

A descendant of Judah ....1 Chr. 4:2 467

Ahuzzam—*possessor*

A man of Judah ...1 Chr. 4:6 467

Ahuzzath—*possession*

A friend of Abimelech ....Gen. 26:26 36

Ahzai—*Yahweh has grasped*

A postexilic priest ....Neh. 11:13 570
Also called Jahzerah ....1 Chr. 9:12 474

Ai—*ruin*

1. A city east of Bethel in central Palestine .....Josh. 7:2 258
   Abraham camps near ....Gen. 12:8 20
   A royal city of Canaan ......Josh. 10:1 261
   Israel defeated at ....Josh. 7:2-5 258
   Israel destroys completely ...Josh. 8:1-28 259
   Occupied after exile ....Ezra 2:28 544
2. An Ammonite city near Heshbon .....Jer. 49:3 897

Aiah—*falcon*

The father of Rizpah, Saul's concubine ....2 Sam. 3:7 362

Aijalon—*place of gazelles*

1. A town assigned to Dan ....Josh. 19:42 272
   Amorites not driven from ....Judg. 1:35 285
   Miracle there............Josh. 10:12, 13 262
   Assigned to Kohathite Levites ....Josh. 21:24 275
   City of refuge ....1 Chr. 6:66-69 470
   Included in Benjamin's territory ......1 Chr. 8:13 473
   Fortified by Rehoboam ...2 Chr. 11:5, 10 512
   Captured by Philistines .....2 Chr. 28:18 527
2. The burial place of Elon, a judge ....Judg. 12:12 299

Ain—*spring*

1. A town near Riblah ....Num. 34:11 202
2. Town of Judah ....Josh. 15:32 268
   Transferred to Simeon ....Josh. 19:7 271
   Later assigned to the priests ....Josh. 21:16 273
   Called Ashan ....1 Chr. 6:59 470
3. Letter of the Hebrew alphabet ....{Ps. 119:121-128} 698

Air—*the atmosphere around the earth*

Man given dominion over.............Gen. 1:26-30 4
Man names birds of ....Gen. 2:19, 20 7
God destroys birds of ....Gen. 6:7 11
Mystery of eagle in ....Prov. 30:19 744
Satan, prince of ...Eph. 2:2 1387
Believers meet Jesus in ....1 Thess. 4:17 1416
God's wrath poured out in ....Rev. 9:2 1526
Figurative of emptiness ....1 Cor. 9:26 1353

Ajah—*falcon*

A Horite ....Gen. 36:24 48

Akel Dama

Field called "Field of Blood" ....Acts 1:19 1272

Akkub—*cunning*

1. Elioenai's son ....1 Chr. 3:24 467
2. A Levite head of a family of porters ....1 Chr. 9:17 474
3. A family of Nethinim .....Ezra 2:45 544
4. A Levite interpreter ...Neh. 8:7 565

Akrabbim—*scorpions*

An "ascent" on the south of the Dead Sea ....Num. 34:4 202
One border of Judah ....Josh. 15:3 267

Alabaster—*container made of fine textured, usually white and translucent, material*

Used by woman anointing Jesus ....Matt. 26:7 1150

Alameth (see Alemeth)

Alammelech—*oak of a king*

Village of Asher ..Josh. 19:26 272

Alamoth—*virgins*

A musical term probably indicating a women's choir ....1 Chr. 15:20 481

Alarm—*sudden and fearful surprise*

A. *Caused physically by:*
   Sudden attack ....Judg. 7:20-23 292
   Death plague ....Ex. 12:29-33 82
   A mysterious manifestation ....{1 Sam. 28:11-14} 353
   Prodigies of nature ....Matt. 27:50-54 1154

B. *Caused spiritually by:*
   Sin ....{1 Sam. 12:17-19} 333
   Remorse ......Gen. 27:34-40 37
   Conscience ....Acts 24:24, 25 1308
   Hopelessness in hell ....Luke 16:22-31 1219

C. *Shout of jubilee or warning:*
   Instruction to Israel ....Num. 10:9 172
   Causes anguish ......Jer. 4:19 849
   Prophecy of judgment .....Jer. 49:2 897

See Agitation

Alas—*an intense emotional outcry*

A. *Emotional outcry caused by:*
   Israel's defeat ....Josh. 7:7-9 258
   An angel's appearance ....Judg. 6:22 290
   A vow's realization ...{Judg. 11:34, 35} 298
   Army without water ....2 Kin. 3:9, 10 431
   Loss of an ax head ....2 Kin. 6:5 434
   Servant's fear ....2 Kin. 6:14, 15 436

SUBJECT — REFERENCE — PAGE

Alas—continued

B. *Prophetic outcry caused by:*
- Israel's future .... Num. 24:23, 24 — 190
- Israel's punishment .. Amos 5:16-20 — 1020
- Jacob's trouble .... Jer. 30:7-9 — 876
- Babylon's fall .... Rev. 18:10-19 — 1535

Alemeth—*hidden*

1. A Benjamite ... 1 Chr. 7:8 — 472
2. A descendant of Saul .... 1 Chr. 8:36 — 473
3. A Levitical city .... 1 Chr. 6:60 — 470

Aleph

- The first letter in the Hebrew alphabet .... Ps. 119:1-8 — 694

Alert—*watchful*

- In battle .... Judg. 7:15-22 — 292
- In personal safety .... 1 Sam. 19:9, 10 — 345
- In readiness for attack .... Neh. 4:9-23 — 560
- In prayer .... Matt. 26:41 — 1151
- In spiritual combat .... Eph. 6:18 — 1393
- In waiting for Christ's return .... Matt. 24:42-51 — 1148
- Daily living .... 1 Cor. 16:13 — 1361
- Times of testing ... Luke 21:34-36 — 1225
- Against false teachers .... Acts 20:29-31 — 1303

Alexander—*man-defending*

1. A son of Simon of Cyrene ...... Mark 15:21 — 1184
2. A member of the high-priestly family .... Acts 4:6 — 1276
3. A Jew in Ephesus ...... Acts 19:33, 34 — 1302
4. An apostate condemned by Paul .... 1 Tim. 1:19, 20 — 1426

Alexander the Great—*Alexander III of Macedonia* (356–323 B.C.)

A. *Not named in the Bible, but referred to as:*
- The four-headed leopard ...... Dan. 7:6 — 985
- The goat with a great horn .... Dan. 8:5-9, 21 — 986
- A mighty king .... Dan. 11:3 — 991

B. *Rule of, described:*
- His invasion of Palestine ..... Zech. 9:1-8 — 1073
- His kingdom being divided .... Dan. 7:6 — 985

Alexandria—*a city of Egypt founded by Alexander the Great* (332 B.C.)

- Men of, persecute Stephen ...... Acts 6:9 — 1279
- Apollos, native of .... Acts 18:24 — 1300
- Paul sails in ship .... Acts 27:6 — 1314

Algum, almug—*a tree* (probably the red sandalwood)

- Imported from Ophir by Hiram's navy ... 1 Kin. 10:11, 12 — 406
- Used in constructing the temple .... 2 Chr. 9:10, 11 — 511
- Also imported from Lebanon .... 2 Chr. 2:8 — 501

Alienation—*a withdrawing or separation*

Descriptive of
- Israel's apostasy .... Ezek. 23:17, 18, 22, 28 — 942
- Spiritual deadness .... Eph. 4:18 — 1391

Aliens—*citizens of a foreign country; strangers*

A. *Descriptive, naturally, of:*
- Israel in the Egyptian bondage ..... Gen. 15:13 — 23
- Abraham in Canaan ...... Gen. 23:4 — 31
- Moses in Egypt .... Ex. 18:2, 3 — 88
- Israel in Babylon ...... Ps. 137:4 — 704

B. *Descriptive, spiritually, of:*
- Estrangement from friends .... Job 19:15 — 602
- The condition of the Gentiles ...... Eph. 2:12 — 1388

Alive—*the opposite of being dead*

A. *Descriptive of:*
- Natural life .. Gen. 43:7, 27, 28 — 56
- Spiritual life ... Luke 15:24, 32 — 1218
- Restored physical life .... Acts 9:41 — 1286
- Christ's resurrected life .... Acts 1:3 — 1271
- The believer's glorified life .... 1 Cor. 15:22 — 1359
- Korah, Dathan, and Abiram's descent into Sheol .... Num. 16:27, 33 — 180

B. *The power of keeping:*
- Belongs to God .... Deut. 32:39 — 245
- Not in man's power .... Ps. 22:29 — 637
- Promised to the godly .... Ps. 33:18, 19 — 643
- Gratefully acknowledged .... Josh. 14:10 — 267
- Transformed by Christ's return .... 1 Thess. 4:15, 16 — 1416

Allegory—*an extended figure of speech using symbols*

A. *Of natural things:*
- A king's doom .... Judg. 9:8-20 — 295
- Old age .... Eccl. 12:1-7 — 759
- Israel as a transplanted vine .... Ps. 80:8-19 — 672

B. *Of spiritual things:*
- Christian as sheep .... John 10:1-16 — 1251
- Two covenants .... Gal. 4:21-31 — 1382
- Israel and the Gentiles ...... Rom. 11:15-24 — 1336
- Christ and His Church ...... Eph. 5:22-33 — 1392
- The Christian's armor .... Eph. 6:11-17 — 1393

Alleluia—*praise ye the Lord*

- The Greek form of the Hebrew Hallelujah .... Rev. 19:1-6 — 1535

Alliances—*treaties between nations or individuals*

A. *In the time of the patriarchs:*
- Abraham with Canaanite chiefs .... Gen. 14:13 — 21
- Abraham with Abimelech ... Gen. 21:22-34 — 30
- Isaac with Abimelech ... Gen. 26:26-33 — 36
- Jacob with Laban .... Gen. 31:44-54 — 43

B. *In the time of the wilderness:*
- Israel with Moab .... Num. 25:1-3 — 190

C. *In the time of the conquest:*
- Israel with Gibeonites ... Josh. 9:3-27 — 260

D. *In the time of David:*
- David with Achish .... 1 Sam. 27:2-12 — 352

E. *In the time of Solomon:*
- Solomon with Hiram .... 1 Kin. 5:12-18 — 398
- Solomon with Egypt .... 1 Kin. 3:1 — 394

F. *In the time of the divided kingdom:*
- Asa with Ben-Hadad .. 1 Kin. 15:18-20 — 413
- Ahab with Ben-Hadad .. 1 Kin. 20:31-34 — 421
- Israel with Assyria ...... 2 Kin. 16:5-9 — 447
- Hoshea with Egypt .... 2 Kin. 17:1-6 — 448

G. *In the time of Judah's sole kingdom:*
- Hezekiah with Egypt .. 2 Kin. 18:19-24 — 450
- Jehoiakim with Egypt .. 2 Kin. 23:31-35 — 458

Alliance with evil

A. *Forbidden to:*
- Israel .... Ex. 34:11-16 — 107
- Christians ..... Rom. 13:12 — 1339
- Christ .... Matt. 4:1-11 — 1117

B. *Forbidden because:*
- Leads to idolatry ...... Ex. 23:32, 33 — 95
- Deceives .... Num. 25:1-3, 18 — 190
- Enslaves ...... 2 Pet. 2:18, 19 — 1489
- Defiles .... Ezra 9:1, 2 — 551
- Brings God's anger .... Ezra 9:13-15 — 551
- Corrupts ...... 1 Cor. 15:33 — 1360
- Incompatible with Christ .... 2 Cor. 6:14-16 — 1369
- Defiles .... Jude 23 — 1512

C. *The believer should:*
- Avoid .... Prov. 1:10-15 — 714
- Hate .... Ps. 26:4, 5 — 639
- Confess .... Ezra 10:9-11 — 553
- Separate from .... 2 Cor. 6:17 — 1369

D. *Examples of:*
- Solomon ...... 1 Kin. 11:1-11 — 407
- Jeroboam ... 1 Kin. 12:25-33 — 409
- Jehoshaphat . 2 Chr. 20:35-37 — 520
- Judas Iscariot ...... Matt. 26:14-16 — 1150
- Heretics .... Rev. 2:14, 15, 20 — 1519

See Association

All in all—*complete*

Descriptive of:
- God .... 1 Cor. 15:28 — 1359
- Christ .... Eph. 1:23 — 1387

Allon—*oak*

- A Simeonite prince .... 1 Chr. 4:37 — 468

SUBJECT — REFERENCE — PAGE

Allon Bachuth—*oak of weeping*

A tree marking Deborah's grave . . . . Gen. 35:8 — 46

Allowance—*a stipulated amount*

Daily to Jehoiachin . . . . . . 2 Kin. 25:27-30 — 460; Jer. 52:34 — 905

Almighty—*a title of God*

Applied to God . . Gen. 17:1, 2 — 23; 2 Cor. 6:18 — 1369
Applied to Christ . . . . Rev. 1:8 — 1517

Almodad—*the beloved*

Eldest son of Joktan . . . . Gen. 10:26 — 16

Almond—*a small tree bearing fruit*

Sent as a present to Pharaoh . . . . Gen. 43:11 — 56
Used in the tabernacle . . . . Ex. 25:33, 34 — 97
Aaron's rod produces . . . . Num. 17:2, 3, 8 — 181
Used figuratively of old age . . . . Eccl. 12:5 — 759
Used by Jacob . . . . Gen. 30:37 — 41

Almon Diblathaim—*Almon of the double cake of figs*

An Israelite encampment . . . . Num. 33:46, 47 — 200

Alms, almsgiving—*gifts prompted by love to help the needy*

A. *Design of, to:*
Help the poor . . . . Lev. 25:35 — 150
Receive a blessing . . . . . Deut. 15:10, 11 — 227

B. *Manner of bestowing with:*
A willing spirit . . . . Deut. 15:7-11 — 227
Simplicity . . . . . Matt. 6:1-4 — 1121
Cheerfulness . . 2 Cor. 9:7 — 1372
True love . . . . . 1 Cor. 13:3 — 1356
Fairness to all . . . . Acts 4:32-35 — 1277
Regularity . . . . Acts 11:29, 30 — 1289
Law of reciprocity . . . Rom. 15:25-27 — 1340

C. *Cautions concerning:*
Not for man's honor . . . . Matt. 6:1-4 — 1121
Not for lazy . . . 2 Thess. 3:10 — 1422
Needful for the rich . . . . 1 Tim. 6:17, 18 — 1430

D. *Rewarded:*
Now . . . . Deut. 14:28, 29 — 225; 2 Cor. 9:9, 10 — 1372
In heaven . . . . . Matt. 19:21 — 1140

E. *Examples of:*
Zacchaeus . . . . Luke 19:8 — 1222
Dorcas . . . . Acts 9:36 — 1286
Cornelius . . . . . Acts 10:2 — 1286
The early Christians . . . . Acts 4:34-37 — 1277

Aloes—*a perfume-bearing tree*

A. *Used on:*
Beds . . . . Prov. 7:17 — 720
The dead . . . . . . John 19:39 — 1264

B. *Figurative of:*
Israel . . . . Num. 24:5, 6 — 189

Aloth—*ascents, steeps*

A town in Asher . . 1 Kin. 4:16 — 397

Alpha and Omega—*first and last letters of the Greek alphabet* ("A to Z")

Expressive of God and Christ's eternity . . . . Rev. 1:8, 17, 18 — 1517; Rev. 21:6, 7 — 1538

Alphabet—*the letters of a language*

The Hebrew, seen in . . . . Ps. 119 — 694

Alphaeus—*leader, chief*

1. The father of Levi (Matthew) . . . . Mark 2:14 — 1162
2. The father of James . . . . Matt. 10:3 — 1127

Altar—*an elevated structure*

A. *Uses of:*
Sacrifice . . . . Gen. 8:20 — 14
Incense . . . . . Ex. 30:1, 7, 8 — 103; Luke 1:10, 11 — 1190
National unity . . . . Deut. 12:5, 6 — 223
A memorial . . . . Ex. 17:15, 16 — 88
Protection . . . . . Ex. 21:13, 14 — 92

B. *Made of:*
Earth . . . . Ex. 20:24 — 92
Unhewn stone . . . . Ex. 20:25 — 92
Stones . . . . Deut. 27:5, 6 — 237
Natural rock . . Judg. 6:19-21 — 290
Bronze . . . . Ex. 27:1-6 — 98

C. *Built worthily by:*
Noah . . . . Gen. 8:20 — 14
Abraham . . . . . . Gen. 12:7, 8 — 20
Isaac . . . . Gen. 26:25 — 36
Jacob . . . . Gen. 33:18, 20 — 45
Moses . . . . Ex. 17:15 — 88
Joshua . . . . Deut. 27:4-7 — 237
Eastern tribes . . . . Josh. 22:10, 34 — 276
Gideon . . . . Judg. 6:26, 27 — 291
Manoah . . . . . Judg. 13:19, 20 — 299
Israelites . . . . . . Judg. 21:4 — 309
Samuel . . . . 1 Sam. 7:17 — 330
Saul . . . . 1 Sam. 14:35 — 337
David . . . . . . 2 Sam. 24:18-25 — 387
Elijah . . . . 1 Kin. 18:31, 32 — 418

D. *Built unworthily* (for idolatry) *by:*
Gideon's father . . . . Judg. 6:25-32 — 290
King Jeroboam . . . 1 Kin. 12:32, 33 — 410
King Ahab . . . 1 Kin. 16:30-32 — 414
King Ahaz . . . 2 Chr. 28:1, 3, 5 — 526
Israelite people . . . . Is. 65:3 — 836
Athenians . . . . . Acts 17:23 — 1299

E. *Pagan altars destroyed by:*
Gideon . . . . Judg. 6:25-29 — 290
King Asa . . . . 2 Chr. 14:2, 3 — 515
Jehoiada . . . . 2 Kin. 11:17, 18 — 443
King Hezekiah . . . . 2 Kin. 18:22 — 450
King Josiah . . . . 2 Kin. 23:12, 16, 17 — 457

F. *Burnt offering:*

1. *Of the tabernacle, features concerning:*
Specifications . . . . Ex. 27:1-8 — 98
Bezaleel, builder of . . . . Ex. 31:1-6, 9 — 104
Place of, outside tabernacle . . . . Ex. 40:6, 29 — 113
Only priests allowed at . . . . Num. 18:3, 7 — 181
The defective not acceptable on . . . . Lev. 22:22 — 145
The putting on of blood . . . . Ex. 29:12 — 102
2. *Of Solomon's Temple:*
Described . . . . . 1 Kin. 8:63, 64 — 404
Renewed by King Asa . . . . 2 Chr. 15:8 — 516
Cleansed by King Hezekiah . . . . 2 Chr. 29:18-24 — 528
Repaired by King Manasseh . . . 2 Chr. 33:16-18 — 534
Vessels of, carried to Babylon . . . . . 2 Kin. 25:14 — 459
3. *Of the postexilic* (Zerubbabel's) *temple:*
Described . . . . Ezra 3:1-6 — 545
Polluted . . . . Mal. 1:7, 8 — 1080
4. *Of Ezekiel's vision:*
Described . . . . Ezek. 43:13-27 — 967

G. *Incense:*
In the tabernacle, described . . . . Ex. 30:1-10 — 103
Location of . . . . Ex. 30:6 — 103
Anointed with oil . . . . Ex. 30:26, 27 — 104
Annual atonement made at . . . . Ex. 30:10 — 103
In Solomon's Temple . . . . . . 1 Kin. 7:48 — 401
In John's vision . . . . Rev. 8:3 — 1525

H. *New covenant:*
A place of spiritual sacrifices . . . . . Rom. 12:1, 2 — 1336
Christ, our pattern . . . . Heb. 13:10-16 — 1463

Altruism—*living for the good of others*

A. *Manifested in:*
Service . . . . Matt. 20:26-28 — 1141
Doing good . . . . . Acts 10:38 — 1287
Seeking the welfare of others . . . . Gal. 6:1, 2, 10 — 1383
Helping the weak . . . . Acts 20:35 — 1303

B. *Examples of:*
Moses . . . . Ex. 32:30-32 — 106
Samuel . . . . 1 Sam. 12:1-5 — 333
Jonathan . . . . 1 Sam. 18:1-4 — 343
Christ . . . . John 13:4-17 — 1257
Paul . . . . 1 Cor. 9:19-22 — 1353

Alush—*wild place*

An Israelite encampment . . . . . Num. 33:13, 14 — 200

Alvah—*high; tall*

An Edomite chief . . . . Gen. 36:40 — 48
Also called Aliah . . . . 1 Chr. 1:51 — 465

Alvan—*tall*

A son of Shobal the Horite . . . . Gen. 36:23 — 48
Also called Alian . . . . 1 Chr. 1:40 — 465

Always—*continually, forever*

A. *Of God's:*
Care . . . . Deut. 11:12 — 222
Covenant . . . . . . 1 Chr. 16:15 — 482
Striving . . . . Ps. 103:9 — 683

B. *Of Christ's:*
Determination . . . . Ps. 16:8-11 — 633; Acts 2:25-28 — 1273
Rejoicing . . . . . . Prov. 8:30-31 — 721

SUBJECT	REFERENCE	PAGE
Always—continued		
Presence	Matt. 28:20	1155
Obedience	John 8:29	1249
Prayer	John 11:42	1255
C. *Of the believer's:*		
Prayer	Luke 21:36	1225
Peace	2 Thess. 3:16	1422
Obedience	Phil. 2:12	1400
Work	1 Cor. 15:58	1360
Defense	1 Pet. 3:15	1481
Rejoicing	Phil. 4:4	1401
Thanksgiving	1 Thess. 1:2	1413
Victory	2 Cor. 2:14	1367
Conscience	Acts 24:16	1308
Confidence	2 Cor. 5:6	1368
Sufficiency	2 Cor. 9:8	1372
D. *Of the unbeliever's:*		
Probation	Gen. 6:3	11
Turmoil	Mark 5:5	1165
Rebellion	Acts 7:51	1282
Lying	Titus 1:12	1440
Amad—*people of duration*		
A city of Asher	Josh. 19:26	272
Amal—*toil*		
Asher's descendant	1 Chr. 7:35	473
Amalek—*warlike*		
A son of Eliphaz	1 Chr. 1:36	465
Grandson of Esau	Gen. 36:11, 12	48
A chief of Edom	Gen. 36:16	48
First among nations	Num. 24:20	189
Amalekites—*a nation hostile to Israel*		
A. *Defeated by:*		
Chedorlaomer	Gen. 14:5-7	21
Joshua	Ex. 17:8, 13	88
Gideon	Judg. 7:12-25	292
Saul	1 Sam. 14:47, 48	337
David	1 Sam. 27:8, 9	352
Simeonites	1 Chr. 4:42, 43	468
B. *Overcame Israel during:*		
Wilderness	Num. 14:39-45	178
Judges	Judg. 3:13	287
C. *Destruction of:*		
Predicted	Ex. 17:14	88
Reaffirmed	Deut. 25:17-19	236
Fulfilled in part by David	1 Sam. 27:8, 9	352
	2 Sam. 1:1-16	360
Fulfilled by the Simeonites	1 Chr. 4:42, 43	468
Amam—*gathering place*		
A city of Judah	Josh. 15:26	268
Amana—*permanent*		
A summit in the Anti-Lebanon mountain range	Song 4:8	764
Amaranthine—*like the amaranth flower: unfading, perennial*		
This Greek word is used to describe our inheritance and our glory	1 Pet. 1:4	1477
	1 Pet. 5:4	1483
Amariah—*Yahweh said*		
1. The grandfather of Zadok the priest	1 Chr. 6:7, 8, 52	469
2. A priest	1 Chr. 6:11	469
3. Levite in David's time	1 Chr. 23:19	490
4. A high priest	2 Chr. 19:11	519
5. A Levite in Hezekiah's reign	2 Chr. 31:14, 15	530
6. Son of King Hezekiah	Zeph. 1:1	1057
7. One who divorced his foreign wife	Ezra 10:42, 44	554
8. A signer of Nehemiah's document	Neh. 10:3	569
9. A postexilic chief priest	Neh. 12:1, 2, 7	571
Amasa—*burden-bearer*		
1. The son of Jithra; David's nephew	2 Sam. 17:25	377
Commands Absalom's rebels	2 Sam. 17:25	377
Made David's commander	2 Sam. 19:13	379
Treacherously killed by Joab	2 Sam. 20:9-12	380
Death avenged	1 Kin. 2:28-34	394
2. An Ephraimite leader	2 Chr. 28:9-12	527
Amasai—*Yahweh has borne*		
1. A Kohathite Levite	1 Chr. 6:25, 35	469
2. David's officer	1 Chr. 12:18	479
3. A priestly trumpeter in David's time	1 Chr. 15:24	482
4. A Kohathite Levite	2 Chr. 29:12	528
Amashai—*carrying spoil*		
A priest	Neh. 11:13	570
Amasiah—*Yahweh bears*		
One of Jehoshaphat's commanders	2 Chr. 17:16	517
Amazement—*an intense emotional shock*		
A. *Caused by:*		
Christ's miracles	Matt. 12:22, 23	1131
	Luke 5:25, 26	1201
Christ's teaching	Matt. 19:25	1140
God's power	Luke 9:42, 43	1208
Apostolic miracle	Acts 3:7-10	1274
B. *Manifested by:*		
Christ's parents	Luke 2:48	1194
Christ's disciples	Matt. 19:25	1140
The Jews	Mark 9:15	1171
The early Christians	Acts 9:19-21	1286
Amaziah—*Yahweh is strong*		
1. King of Judah	2 Kin. 14:1-4	445
Kills his father's assassinators	2 Kin. 14:5, 6	445
Raises a large army	2 Chr. 25:5	524
Employs troops from Israel	2 Chr. 25:6	524
Rebuked by a man of God	2 Chr. 25:7-10	524
Defeats Edomites	2 Kin. 14:7	445
Worships Edomite gods	2 Chr. 25:14	524
Rebuked by a prophet	2 Chr. 25:15, 16	525
Defeated by Israel	2 Kin. 14:8-14	445
Killed by conspirators	2 Chr. 25:25-28	525
2. A priest of Bethel	Amos 7:10-17	1021
3. A Simeonite	1 Chr. 4:34, 42, 43	468
4. A Merarite Levite	1 Chr. 6:45	470
Ambassador—*an official sent to deal with a foreign government or sovereign*		
A. *Some purposes of, to:*		
Grant safe passage	Num. 20:14-21	184
Settle disputes	Judg. 11:12-28	297
Arrange business	1 Kin. 5:1-12	397
Stir up trouble	1 Kin. 20:1-12	420
Issue an ultimatum	2 Kin. 19:9-14	452
Spy	2 Kin. 20:12-19	454
Learn God's will	Jer. 37:3-10	884
B. *Some examples of:*		
Judah to Egypt	Is. 30:1-4	800
Babylonians to Judah	2 Chr. 32:31	533
Necho to Josiah	2 Chr. 35:20, 21	536
C. *Used figuratively of:*		
Christ's ministers	2 Cor. 5:20	1369
Paul in particular	Eph. 6:19, 20	1393
Amber—*a yellow, fossilized resin*		
Descriptive of the divine glory	Ezek. 1:4, 27	919
Ambidextrous—*equally skilled with either hand*		
True of some of David's warriors	1 Chr. 12:1, 2	479
Ambition, Christian		
A. *Good, if for:*		
The best gifts	1 Cor. 12:31	1356
Spiritual goals	Phil. 3:12-14	1401
The Gospel's extension	Rom. 15:17-20	1340
Acceptance before God	2 Cor. 5:9, 10	1368
Quietness	1 Thess. 4:11	1416
B. *Evil, if it leads to:*		
Strife	Matt. 20:20-28	1140
Sinful superiority	Matt. 18:1-6	1138
A Pharisaical spirit	Mark 12:38-40	1178
Contention about gifts	1 Cor. 3:3-8	1346
Selfish ambition	Phil. 1:14-17	1398
Ambition, worldly		
A. *Inspired by:*		
Satan	Gen. 3:1-6	8
	Luke 4:5-8	1198
Pride	Is. 14:12-15	786
	1 Tim. 3:1, 6	1427
Jealousy	Num. 12:2	175
B. *Leads to:*		
Sin	Acts 8:18-24	1282
Strife	James 4:1, 2	1471
Suicide	2 Sam. 17:23	377
Self-glory	Hab. 2:4, 5	1053

SUBJECT — REFERENCE — PAGE

C. *Examples of:*
- Builders of Babel .... Gen. 11:4 — 16
- Korah's company .... Num. 16:3-35 — 179
- Abimelech .... Judg. 9:1-6 — 294
- Absalom .... 2 Sam. 15:1-13 — 374
- Adonijah .... 1 Kin. 1:5-7 — 391
- Haman .... Esth. 5:9-14 — 581
- Nebuchadnezzar .... Dan. 3:1-7 — 978
- James and John .... Mark 10:35-37 — 1173
- The antichrist .... 2 Thess. 2:3, 4 — 1421
- Diotrephes .... 3 John 9, 10 — 1506

Ambush—*strategic concealment for surprise attack*

- Joshua at Ai .... Josh. 8:1-24 — 259
- Abimelech against Shechem .... Judg. 9:31-40 — 295
- Israel at Gibeah .... Judg. 20:29-48 — 308
- David against the Philistines .... 2 Sam. 5:23-25 — 364
- Jehoshaphat against his enemies .... 2 Chr. 20:22-25 — 520

Amen—*a strong assent to a prayer* (also translated *"assuredly"*)

A. *Used in the Old Testament to:*
- Confirm a statement .... Num. 5:22 — 166
- Close a doxology .... 1 Chr. 16:36 — 483
- Confirm an oath .... Neh. 5:13 — 561
- Give assent to laws .... Deut. 27:15-26 — 237

B. *Used in the New Testament to:*
- Close a doxology .... Rom. 9:5 — 1333
- Close epistle .... Rom. 16:27 — 1341
- Describe God's promises .... 2 Cor. 1:20 — 1366
- Close prayer .... 1 Cor. 14:16 — 1358
- Give assent .... Rev. 1:7 — 1517
- Emphasize a truth (translated "most assuredly") .... John 3:3, 5, 11 — 1239

Amethyst—*a form of quartz purple to blue-violet*

- Worn by the high priest .... Ex. 39:12 — 112; Ex. 28:19 — 100
- In the New Jerusalem .... Rev. 21:20 — 1539

Ami

- Head of a family of Solomon's servants .... Ezra 2:57 — 544
- Called Amon .... Neh. 7:59 — 564

Amittai—*true*

- The father of Jonah the prophet .... Jon. 1:1 — 1030

Ammah—*mother or beginning*

- A hill near Giah .... 2 Sam. 2:24 — 361

Ammiel—*my kinsman is God*

1. A spy representing the tribe of Dan .... Num. 13:12 — 176
2. The father of Machir .... 2 Sam. 9:4, 5 — 367
3. The father of Bathshua (Bathsheba), one of David's wives .... 1 Chr. 3:5 — 467
   - Called Eliam .... 2 Sam. 11:3 — 369
4. A son of Obed-Edom .... 1 Chr. 26:4, 5 — 492

Ammihud—*my kinsman is glorious*

1. An Ephraimite .... Num. 1:10 — 159
2. A Simeonite, father of Shemuel .... Num. 34:20 — 202
3. A Naphtalite .... Num. 34:28 — 202
4. The father of king of Geshur .... 2 Sam. 13:37 — 373
5. A Judahite .... 1 Chr. 9:4 — 474

Amminadab—*my kinsman is noble*

1. Man of Judah .... 1 Chr. 2:10 — 466
   - The father of Nashon .... Num. 1:7 — 159
   - Aaron's father-in-law .... Ex. 6:23 — 74
   - An ancestor of David .... Ruth 4:19, 20 — 317
   - An ancestor of Christ .... Matt. 1:4 — 1115
2. Chief of a Levitical house .... 1 Chr. 15:10, 11 — 481
3. Son of Kohath .... 1 Chr. 6:22 — 469

Ammishaddai—*my kinsman is the Almighty*

- A captain representing the Danites .... Num. 1:12 — 159

Ammizabad—*my kinsman has endowed*

- A son of Benaiah .... 1 Chr. 27:6 — 493

Ammon—*a people*

- A nation fathered by Lot .... Gen. 19:36, 38 — 28

Ammonites—*descendants of Ben-Ammi*

A. *Characterized by:*
- Cruelty .... Amos 1:13 — 1016
- Pride .... Zeph. 2:9, 10 — 1058
- Callousness .... Ezek. 25:3, 6 — 947
- Idolatry .... 1 Kin. 11:7, 33 — 407

B. *Hostility toward Israel, seen in:*
- Not aiding Israel .... Deut. 23:3, 4 — 233
- Helping the Amalekites .... Judg. 3:13 — 287
- Proposing a cruel treaty .... 1 Sam. 11:1-3 — 332
- Abusing David's ambassadors .... 2 Sam. 10:1-4 — 369
- Hiring Syrians against David .... 2 Sam. 10:6 — 369
- Assisting the Chaldeans .... 2 Kin. 24:2 — 458
- Harassing postexilic Jews .... Neh. 4:3, 7, 8 — 560

C. *Defeated by:*
- Jephthah .... Judg. 11:4-33 — 297
- Saul .... 1 Sam. 11:11 — 333
- David .... 2 Sam. 10:7-14 — 369
- Jehoshaphat .... 2 Chr. 20:1-25 — 519
- Jotham .... 2 Chr. 27:5, 6 — 526

D. *Prohibitions concerning:*
- Exclusion from worship .... Deut. 23:3-6 — 233
- No intermarriage with .... Ezra 9:1-3 — 551

E. *Prophecies concerning their:*
- Captivity .... Amos 1:13-15 — 1016
- Subjection .... Jer. 25:9-21 — 871
- Destruction .... Ps. 83:1-18 — 673

Ammonitess—*a female Ammonite*

- Naamah .... 1 Kin. 14:21, 31 — 412
- Shimeath .... 2 Chr. 24:26 — 524

Amnesty—*a pardon granted to political offenders*

- To Shimei .... 2 Sam. 19:16-23 — 379
- To Amasa .... 2 Sam. 17:25 — 377; 2 Sam. 19:13 — 379

Amnon—*faithful*

1. A son of David .... 2 Sam. 3:2 — 362
   - Rapes his half sister .... 2 Sam. 13:1-18 — 371
   - Killed by Absalom .... 2 Sam. 13:19-29 — 372
2. Son of Shimon .... 1 Chr. 4:19-33 — 467

Amok—*deep, inscrutable*

- A chief priest .... Neh. 12:7, 20 — 571

Amon—*master workman*

1. King of Judah .... 2 Kin. 21:18, 19 — 455
   - Follows evil .... 2 Chr. 33:22, 23 — 534
   - Killed by conspiracy .... 2 Kin. 21:23, 24 — 455
2. A governor of Samaria .... 1 Kin. 22:10, 26 — 423

Amorites—*mountain dwellers*

A. *Described as:*
- Descendants of Canaan .... Gen. 10:15, 16 — 16
- Original inhabitants of Palestine .... Ezek. 16:3 — 931
- One of seven nations .... Gen. 15:19-21 — 23
- A confederation .... Josh. 10:1-5 — 261
- Ruled by great kings .... Ps. 136:17-19 — 703
- Of great size .... Amos 2:9 — 1016
- Very wicked .... Gen. 15:16 — 23
- Worshipers of idols .... Judg. 6:10 — 290

B. *Contacts of, with Israel:*
- Their defeat by Joshua .... Josh. 10:1-43 — 261
- Their not being destroyed .... Judg. 1:34-36 — 285
- Peace with .... 1 Sam. 7:14 — 328
- Solomon uses for forced labor .... 1 Kin. 9:20, 21 — 406
- Intermarriage with .... Judg. 3:5, 6 — 287

Amos—*burden-bearer*

1. A prophet of Israel .... Amos 1:1 — 1015
   - Pronounces judgment against nations .... Amos 1:1-3, 15 — 1015
   - Denounces Israel's sins .... Amos 4:1–7:9 — 1017
   - Condemns Amaziah, the priest of Bethel .... Amos 7:10-17 — 1021
   - Predicts Israel's downfall .... Amos 9:1-10 — 1022
   - Foretells great blessings .... Amos 9:11-15 — 1023
2. An ancestor of Christ .... Luke 3:25 — 1195

Amoz—*strong*

- The father of Isaiah the prophet .... Is. 1:1 — 771

Amphipolis—*a city in Macedonia*

- Visited by Paul .... Acts 17:1 — 1297

SUBJECT — REFERENCE — PAGE

Amplias

Christian at Rome .... Rom. 16:8 — 1341

Amram—*a people exalted*

1. Son of Kohath .... Num. 3:17-19 — 162
   The father of Aaron, Moses and Miriam ...... Ex. 6:18-20 — 74; 1 Chr. 6:3 — 469
2. Jew who divorced his foreign wife .... Ezra 10:34 — 553

Amramites—*descendants of Amram*

A subdivision of the Levites .... Num. 3:27 — 162

Amraphel—*powerful people*

A king of Shinar who invaded Canaan during Abraham's time; identified by some as the Hammurabi of the monuments ...... Gen. 14:1, 9 — 21

Amulet—*charm worn to protect against evil*

Condemned ...... Is. 3:18-23 — 774

Amusements—*entertainment*

A. *Found in:*
   - Dancing ..... Ex. 32:18, 19, 25 — 105
   - Music .... 1 Sam. 18:6, 7 — 343
   - Earthly pleasures .... Eccl. 2:1-8 — 749
   - Drunkenness .... Amos 6:1-6 — 1020; 1 Pet. 4:3 — 1481
   - Feasting ...... Mark 6:21, 22 — 1166
   - Games .... Luke 7:32 — 1204
   - Gossip .... Acts 17:21 — 1297

B. *Productive of:*
   - Sorrow .... Prov. 14:13 — 726
   - Poverty .... Prov. 21:17 — 733
   - Vanity .... Eccl. 2:1-11 — 749
   - Immorality .... 1 Cor. 10:6-8 — 1353
   - Spiritual deadness ..... 1 Tim. 5:6 — 1429

C. *Prevalence of:*
   - In the last days .... 2 Tim. 3:1, 4 — 1434
   - In Babylon .... Rev. 18:21-24 — 1535
   - At Christ's return .... Matt. 24:36-39 — 1148

Amzi—*strong one*

1. A Merarite Levite .... 1 Chr. 6:46 — 470
2. A priest .... Neh. 11:12 — 570

Anab—*grapes*

A town of Judah .... Josh. 11:21 — 264

Anah—*answer*

1. Father of Esau's wife .. Gen. 36:2, 14, 18 — 46
2. A Horite chief .... Gen. 36:20, 29 — 48
3. Son of Zibeon .... Gen. 36:24 — 48

Anaharath—*narrow way*

A city in the valley of Jezreel .... Josh. 19:19 — 272

Anaiah—*Yahweh has answered*

1. A Levite assistant ..... Neh. 8:4 — 565
2. One who sealed the new covenant ..... Neh. 10:22 — 569

Anak—*long-necked*

Descendant of Arba .... Josh. 15:13 — 267
Father of three sons .... Num. 13:22 — 176

Anakim—*descendants of Anak; a race of giants*

A. *Described as:*
   - Giants .... Num. 13:28-33 — 176
   - Very strong .. Deut. 2:10, 11, 21 — 209

B. *Defeated by:*
   - Joshua ...... Josh. 10:36-39; 11:21 — 262
   - Caleb .... Josh. 14:6-15 — 266

C. *A remnant left:*
   - Among the Philistines ..... Josh. 11:22 — 264
   - Possibly in Gath .... 1 Sam. 17:4-7 — 340

Anamim—*rockmen*

A tribe or people listed among Mizraim's (Egypt's) descendants ..... Gen. 10:13 — 16

Anammelech—*Anu is king*

A god worshiped at Samaria .... 2 Kin. 17:24, 31 — 449

Anan—*cloud*

A signer of Nehemiah's document .... Neh. 10:26 — 569

Anani—*my cloud*

Son of Elioenai ... 1 Chr. 3:24 — 467

Ananiah—*Yahweh has covered*

1. The father of Maaseiah .... Neh. 3:23 — 560
2. A town inhabited by Benjamite returnees ..... Neh. 11:32 — 571

Ananias—*Yahweh has been gracious*

1. Disciple at Jerusalem slain for lying to God .... Acts 5:1-11 — 1277
2. A Christian disciple at Damascus ... Acts 9:10-19 — 1284; Acts 22:12-16 — 1306
3. A Jewish high priest .... Acts 23:1-5 — 1307

Anarchy—*a reign of lawlessness in society*

A. *Manifested in:*
   - Moral looseness .... Ex. 32:1-8, 25 — 105
   - Idolatry .... Judg. 17:1-13 — 303
   - Religious syncretism .. 2 Kin. 17:27-41 — 449
   - A reign of terror .... Jer. 40:13-16 — 888
   - Perversion of justice .... Hab. 1:1-4 — 1052

B. *Instances of:*
   - At Kadesh .... Num. 14:1-10 — 176
   - During the judges .... Judg. 18:1-31 — 304
   - In the northern kingdom .... 1 Kin. 12:26-33 — 409
   - At the crucifixion .... Matt. 27:15-31 — 1152
   - At Stephen's death .... Acts 7:54, 57, 58 — 1282
   - At Ephesus .... Acts 19:28-34 — 1302
   - In the time of antichrist .... 2 Thess. 2:3-12 — 1421

Anath—*answer*

Father of Shamgar .... Judg. 3:31 — 288

Anathoth—*answers*

1. A Benjamite, son of Becher .... 1 Chr. 7:8 — 472
2. A leader who signed the document .... Neh. 10:19 — 569
3. A Levitical city in Benjamin .... Josh. 21:18 — 273
   - Birthplace of Jeremiah ..... Jer. 1:1 — 844
   - Citizens of, hate Jeremiah ..... Jer. 11:21, 23 — 858
   - Jeremiah bought property there .... Jer. 32:6-15 — 879
   - Home of famous mighty man .... 2 Sam. 23:27 — 385
   - Home of Abiathar, the high priest .... 1 Kin. 2:26 — 394
   - Reoccupied after exile .... Ezra 2:1, 23 — 542
   - To be invaded by Assyria ...... Is. 10:30 — 784
   - Reproved Jeremiah of .... Jer. 29:27 — 875

Anathothite—*a native of Anathoth*

Abiezer thus called .... 2 Sam. 23:27 — 385

Anchor—*a weight used to hold a ship in place*

Literally, of Paul's ship ...... Acts 27:29, 30, 40 — 1314
Figuratively of the believer's hope .... Heb. 6:19 — 1455

Ancient—*that which is old*

Applied to the beginning (eternity) .... Is. 45:21 — 818
Applied to something very old .... Prov. 22:28 — 735
Applied to old men (elders) .... Ps. 119:100 — 697; 1 Sam. 24:13 — 349

Ancient of Days

Title applied to God .... Dan. 7:9, 13, 22 — 985

Andrew—*manly*

A fisherman ...... Matt. 4:18 — 1118
A disciple of John the Baptist .... John 1:40 — 1237
Brought Peter to Christ .... John 1:40-42 — 1237
Called to Christ's discipleship ...... Matt. 4:18, 19 — 1118
Enrolled among the Twelve .... Matt. 10:2 — 1127
Told Jesus about a lad's lunch .... John 6:8, 9 — 1244
Carried a request to Jesus .... John 12:20-22 — 1256
Sought further light on Jesus' words .... Mark 13:3, 4 — 1179
Met in the upper room .... Acts 1:13 — 1272

Andronicus—*conqueror of men*

A notable Christian at Rome .... Rom. 16:7 — 1341

Anem—*double fountain*

Levitical city ..... 1 Chr. 6:73 — 472

SUBJECT REFERENCE PAGE

Anger of man—continued
- Potiphar ...... Gen. 39:1, 19 — 50
- Moses .... Num. 20:10-12 — 183
- Balaam ..... Num. 22:27, 28 — 187
- Saul .... 1 Sam. 20:30 — 346
- Naaman ...... 2 Kin. 5:11, 12 — 434
- Asa .... 2 Chr. 16:10 — 517
- Uzziah .... 2 Chr. 26:19 — 526
- Ahasuerus .... Esth. 1:9, 12 — 577
- Haman .... Esth. 3:5 — 579
- Nebuchadnezzar .... Dan. 3:12, 13 — 979
- Jonah .... Jon. 4:1-11 — 1032
- Herod .... Matt. 2:16 — 1116
- The Jews ...... Luke 4:28 — 1198
- Jewish officialdom ... Acts 5:17 — 1278

D. *The Christian attitude toward:*
- To be slow in .... Prov. 14:17 — 726
- Not to sin in ... Eph. 4:26 — 1391
- To put away ... Eph. 4:31 — 1391

E. *Effects of, seen in:*
- Attempted assassination .... Esth. 2:21 — 578
- Punishment ... Prov. 19:19 — 731
- Mob action .... Acts 19:28, 29 — 1302

F. *Pacified by:*
- Kindly suggestion ... 2 Kin. 5:10-14 — 434
- Righteous execution .... Esth. 7:10 — 582
- Gentle answer .... Prov. 15:1 — 727

Anguish—*extreme pain*

A. *Caused by:*
- Physical hardships .... Ex. 6:9 — 74
- Physical pain .... 2 Sam. 1:9 — 360
- Impending destruction ... Deut. 2:25 — 210
- Conflict of soul .... Job 7:11 — 594
- National distress ...... Is. 8:21, 22 — 780
- Childbirth ..... John 16:21 — 1261
- A spiritual problem ...... 2 Cor. 2:4 — 1366

B. *Reserved for:*
- People who refuse wisdom ...... Prov. 1:20-27 — 714
- The wicked .... Job 15:20, 24 — 599
- Those in Hades .... Luke 16:23, 24 — 1219

Aniam—*lament of the people*
- A Manassite ...... 1 Chr. 7:19 — 472

Anim—*springs*
- A city in south Judah .... Josh. 15:50 — 268

Animals

A. *Described as:*
- Domesticated and wild .... 2 Sam. 12:3 — 370
- Clean and unclean ..... Lev. 11:1-31 — 130; Deut. 14:1-20 — 225
- For sacrifices .... Lev. 16:3, 5 — 139; Ex. 12:3-14 — 80

B. *List of, in the Bible:*
- Antelope ...... Deut. 14:5 — 225
- Ape .... 1 Kin. 10:22 — 407
- Badger .... Ex. 25:5 — 95
- Bat .... Deut. 14:18 — 225
- Bear .... 1 Sam. 17:34 — 342
- Boar .... Ps. 80:13 — 672
- Bull .... Jer. 52:20 — 905
- Calf .... Gen. 18:7 — 24
- Camel .... Gen. 12:16 — 20
- Cattle .... Gen. 1:25 — 4
- Chameleon .... Lev. 11:30 — 132
- Cobra .... Is. 11:8 — 784
- Colt .... Zech. 9:9 — 1073
- Cow .... Gen. 32:15 — 44
- Deer .... Deut. 14:5 — 225
- Dog .... Ex. 22:31 — 94
- Donkey .... Gen. 22:3 — 30
- Elephant ("ivory") ..... 1 Kin. 10:22 — 407
- Ewe lamb ..... Gen. 21:30 — 30
- Fox .... Judg. 15:4 — 302
- Frog .... Ex. 8:2-14 — 75
- Gazelle .... Deut. 14:5 — 225
- Gecko .... Lev. 11:30 — 132
- Goat .... Gen. 27:9 — 36
- Greyhound .... Prov. 30:31 — 744
- Hare .... Deut. 14:7 — 225
- Heifer .... Gen. 15:9 — 23
- Hind .... Hab. 3:19 — 1054
- Horse .... Gen. 47:17 — 60
- Hyena .... Is. 13:22 — 786
- Hyrax .... Lev. 11:5 — 130
- Jackal .... Is. 13:22 — 786
- Lamb .... Ex. 29:39 — 103
- Leopard .... Rev. 13:2 — 1529
- Lion .... 1 Sam. 17:34 — 342
- Lizard .... Lev. 11:29, 30 — 132
- Mole .... Is. 2:20 — 773
- Monkey .... 1 Kin. 10:22 — 407
- Mouse .... Lev. 11:29 — 132
- Mule .... 2 Sam. 13:29 — 372
- Ox .... Ex. 21:28 — 92
- Porcupine .... Is. 14:23 — 787
- Ram .... Gen. 15:9 — 23
- Roe deer ...... Deut. 14:5 — 225
- Scorpion ...... Deut. 8:15 — 220
- Serpent .... Matt. 10:16 — 1129
- Sheep .... Gen. 4:2 — 9
- Spider .... Prov. 30:28 — 744
- Swine .... Is. 65:2-4 — 836
- Whale (great sea creatures) .... Gen. 1:21 — 4
- Wolf .... Is. 11:6 — 784

C. *Used figuratively of:*
- Human traits .... Gen. 49:9-14, 21 — 61
- Universal peace .... Is. 11:6-9 — 784
- Man's innate nature .... Jer. 13:23 — 860
- World empires ...... Dan. 7:2-8 — 985
- Satanic powers .... Rev. 12:4, 9 — 1529
- Christ's sacrifice ...... 1 Pet. 1:18-20 — 1479

Anise—*a plant for seasoning; the dill*
- Tithed by the Jews .... Matt. 23:23 — 1145

Ankle—*joint connecting foot and leg*
- Lame man's healed .... Acts 3:7 — 1274

Anklet—*an ornament worn by women on the ankles*
- Included in Isaiah's denunciation .... Is. 3:16, 18 — 774

Anna—*grace*
- Aged prophetess ...... Luke 2:36-38 — 1194

Annas—*gracious*
- A Jewish high priest .... Luke 3:2 — 1194
- Christ appeared before .... John 18:12-24 — 1262
- Peter and John appeared before .... Acts 4:6 — 1276

Anointing—*pouring oil upon*

A. *Performed upon:*
- The patriarchs ... 1 Chr. 16:15-17, 21, 22 — 482
- Priest .... Ex. 29:1, 7 — 102
- Prophets ...... 1 Kin. 19:16 — 420
- Israel's kings .. 1 Sam. 10:1 — 331
- Foreign kings .... 1 Kin. 19:15 — 420
- The messianic King .... Ps. 2:2 — 625
- Sacred objects .... Ex. 30:26-28 — 104

B. *Ordinary, purposes of, for:*
- Adornment .... Ruth 3:3 — 315
- Invigoration ... 2 Sam. 12:20 — 371
- Hospitality .... Luke 7:38, 46 — 1204
- Battle .... Is. 21:5 — 791
- Burial .... Matt. 26:12 — 1150
- Sanctifying .... Ex. 30:29 — 104

C. *Medicinal, purposes of, for:*
- Wound .... Luke 10:34 — 1209
- Healing ..... Mark 6:13 — 1166; James 5:14 — 1473

D. *Sacred, purposes of, to:*
- Memoralize an event .... Gen. 28:18 — 38
- Confirm a covenant ..... Gen. 35:14 — 46
- Set apart ...... Ex. 30:22-29 — 104
- Institute into office .... 1 Sam. 16:12, 13 — 340

E. *Absence of:*
- Sign of judgment ..... Deut. 28:40 — 239
- Fasting ..... 2 Sam. 12:16, 20 — 371
- Mourning ..... 2 Sam. 14:2 — 373

F. *Of Christ the Messiah "the Anointed One," as:*
- Predicted ..... Ps. 45:7 — 651; Is. 61:1 — 833
- Fulfilled ..... Luke 4:18 — 1198; Heb. 1:9 — 1450
- Interpreted .... Acts 4:27 — 1277
- Symbolized in His name ("the Christ") ..... Matt. 16:16, 20 — 1136; Acts 9:22 — 1286
- Typical of the believer's anointing .... 1 John 2:27 — 1496

G. *Significance of, as indicating:*
- Divine appointment .... 2 Chr. 22:7 — 522
- Special honor .... 1 Sam. 24:6, 10 — 349
- Special privilege ..... Ps. 105:15 — 685
- God's blessing ...... Ps. 23:5 — 638

Anointing of the Holy Spirit

A. *Of Christ:*
- Predicted ..... Is. 61:1 — 833
- Fulfilled .... John 1:32-34 — 1237
- Explained ..... Luke 4:18 — 1198

B. *Of Christians:*
- Predicted ..... Ezek. 47:1-12 — 970
- Foretold by Christ .... John 7:38, 39 — 1248
- Fulfilled at Pentecost .... Acts 2:1-41 — 1273
- Fulfilled at conversion .. 2 Cor. 1:21, 22 — 1366; 1 John 2:20, 27 — 1496

Answer—*a reply*

A. *Good:*
- Soft .... Prov. 15:1 — 727
- Confident ..... Dan. 3:16-18 — 979
- Convicting .... Dan. 5:17-28 — 983
- Astonished .... Luke 2:47 — 1194
- Unanswerable ..... Luke 20:3-8 — 1223

SUBJECT — REFERENCE — PAGE

SUBJECT REFERENCE PAGE

Anxiety—*a disturbed state of mind produced by real or imaginary fears*

A. *Caused by:*
Brother's hatred .... Gen. 32:6-12 43
Son's rebellion .... 2 Sam. 18:24-33 378
King's decree .... Esth. 4:1-17 579
Child's absence ...... Luke 2:48 1194
Son's sickness ...... John 4:46-49 1242
Friend's delay .... 2 Cor. 2:12, 13 1367

B. *Overcome by:*
Trust .... Ps. 37:1-5 645
Reliance upon the Holy Spirit .... Mark 13:11 1179
God's provision ..... Luke 12:22-30 1214
Upward look .. Luke 21:25-28 1225
Assurance of God's sovereignty ... Rom. 8:28 1333
Angel's word .... Acts 27:21-25 1314
Prayer .... Phil. 4:6 1401
God's care .... 1 Pet. 5:6, 7 1483

See Cares, worldly

Ape—*a monkey*

Article of trade ... 1 Kin. 10:22 407

Apelles

A Christian in Rome .... Rom. 16:10 1341

Apharsathchites

Assyrian colonists in Samaria opposing Zerubbabel's work .... Ezra 4:9 546

Aphek—*strength, fortress*

1. A town in Plain of Sharon .... Josh. 12:18 265
Site of Philistine camp ... 1 Sam. 4:1 326; 1 Sam. 29:1 354
2. A city assigned to Asher .... Josh. 19:30 272
3. Border city .... Josh. 13:4 265
4. A city in Jezreel ..... 1 Kin. 20:26-30 421
Syria's defeat prophesied here .... 2 Kin. 13:14-19 444

Aphekah—*fortress*

A city of Judah ... Josh. 15:53 268

Aphiah—*striving*

An ancestor of King Saul .... 1 Sam. 9:1 330

Aphik—*strength, fortress*

Spared by Asher .... Judg. 1:31 284

See Aphek 2

Aphrah—*house of dust*

A Philistine city; symbolic of doom .... Mic. 1:10 1036

Apocalypse—*an unveiling of something unknown*

The Greek word usually translated "revelation" .... Rom. 16:25 1341; Gal. 1:12 1378

Apocrypha—*hidden things*

Writings in Greek written during the period between the Testaments; rejected by Protestants as uninspired

Apollonia—*pertaining to Apollo*

A town between Amphipolis and Thessalonica .... Acts 17:1 1297

Apollos—*a short or pet name for Apollonios*

An Alexandrian Jew mighty in the Scriptures .... Acts 18:24, 25 1300
Receives further instruction .... Acts 18:26 1300
Sent to preach in Achaia .... Acts 18:27, 28 1300
A minister in Corinth .... 1 Cor. 1:12 1345; 1 Cor. 3:4, 22 1346
Cited by Paul ..... 1 Cor. 4:6 1348
Urged to revisit Corinth .... 1 Cor. 16:12 1361
Journey of, noted by Paul .... Titus 3:13 1442

Apollyon—*the destroyer*

Angel of the bottomless pit .... Rev. 9:11 1526

Apostasy—*a falling away from God's truth*

A. *Kinds of:*
National .... 1 Kin. 12:26-33 409
Individual .... 2 Kin. 21:1-9 454; Heb. 3:12 1452
Satanic .... Rev. 12:7-9 1529
Angelic .... 2 Pet. 2:4 1487
General .... 2 Tim. 3:1-5 1434
Imputed .... Acts 21:21 1305
Final .... 2 Thess. 2:3 1421
Irremedial ..... Heb. 6:1-8 1455

B. *Caused by:*
Satan .... Luke 22:31 1226
False teachers ...... Acts 20:29, 30 1303
Perversion of Scripture ..... 2 Tim. 4:3, 4 1436
Persecution ... Matt. 13:21 1132
Unbelief ...... Heb. 4:9-11 1453
Love of world .... 2 Tim. 4:10 1436
Hardened heart .... Acts 7:54, 57 1282
Spiritual blindness .... Acts 28:25-27 1315

C. *Manifested in:*
Resisting truth .... 2 Tim. 3:7, 8 1434
Resorting to deception .... 2 Cor. 11:13-15 1373
Reverting to immorality .. 2 Pet. 2:14, 19-22 1489

D. *Safeguards against, found in:*
God's Word .... Ps. 119:11 694; 2 Tim. 3:13-17 1436
Spiritual growth .... 2 Pet. 1:5-11 1487
Indoctrination ..... Acts 20:29-31 1303
Faithfulness ... Matt. 24:42-51 1148
Spiritual perception .... 1 John 4:1-6 1498
Being grounded in the truth .... Eph. 4:13-16 1390
Using God's armor .... Eph. 6:10-20 1393
Preaching the Word .... 2 Tim. 4:2, 5 1436

E. *Examples of, seen in:*
Israelites ...... Ex. 32:1-35 105
Saul .... 1 Sam. 15:11 339
Solomon ...... 1 Kin. 11:1-10 407
Amaziah .... 2 Chr. 25:14-16 524
Judas .... Matt. 26:14-16 1150
Hymenaeus and Philetus ...... 2 Tim. 2:17, 18 1434
Demas .... 2 Tim. 4:10 1436
Certain men ... Jude 4 1510

Apostles—*men divinely commissioned to represent Christ*

A. *Descriptive of:*
Christ .... Heb. 3:1 1452
The twelve .... Matt. 10:2 1127
Others (Barnabas, James, etc.) .. Acts 14:14 1293; Gal. 1:19 1378
Messengers ... 2 Cor. 8:23 1371
False teachers ...... 2 Cor. 11:13 1373
Simon Peter ... Matt. 10:2 1127
Andrew .... Matt. 10:2 1127
James, son of Zebedee ..... Matt. 10:2 1127
John .... Matt. 10:2 1127
Philip .... Matt. 10:3 1127
Bartholomew (Nathanael) ..... Matt. 10:3 1127; John 1:45 1237
Thomas .... Matt. 10:3 1127
Matthew (Levi) ..... Matt. 10:3 1127; Luke 5:27 1201
James, son of Alphaeus ..... Matt. 10:3 1127
Thaddaeus (Judas) ...... Matt. 10:3 1127; John 14:22 1258
Simon the Zealot .... Luke 6:15 1202
Judas Iscariot ...... Matt. 10:4 1127
Matthias ..... Acts 1:26 1273
Paul .... 2 Cor. 1:1 1364
Barnabas ..... Acts 14:14 1293
James, the Lord's brother .... Gal. 1:19 1378
Silvanus and Timothy ..... 1 Thess. 1:1 1413; 1 Thess. 2:9 1415
Andronicus and Junia .... Rom. 16:7 1341

B. *Mission of, to:*
Perform miracles ..... Matt. 10:1, 8 1127
Preach Gospel .... Matt. 28:19, 20 1155
Witness Christ's resurrection .... Acts 1:22 1272; Acts 10:40-42 1288
Write Scripture ..... Eph. 3:5 1388
Establish the Church ...... Eph. 2:20 1388

C. *Limitations of, before Pentecost:*
Lowly in position ...... Matt. 4:18 1118
Unlearned .... Acts 4:13 1276
Subject to disputes ...... Matt. 20:20-28 1140
Faith often obscure ...... Matt. 16:21-23 1137
Need of instruction ... Matt. 17:4, 9-13 1137

D. *Position of, after Pentecost:*
Interpreted prophecy ..... Acts 2:14-36 1273
Defended truth .... Phil. 1:7, 17 1398
Exposed heretics ...... Gal. 1:6-9 1378
Upheld discipline .... 2 Cor. 13:1-6 1375
Established churches ..... Rom. 15:17-20 1340

Appaim—*nostrils*

A man of Judah ... 1 Chr. 2:30, 31 466

SUBJECT — REFERENCE — PAGE

Apparel—*clothing*

A. *Kinds of:*
- Harlot's ... Gen. 38:14, 15 ... 50
- Virgin's ... 2 Sam. 13:18 ... 372
- Mourner's ... 2 Sam. 12:19, 20 ... 371
- Gorgeous ... Luke 7:25 ... 1204
- Rich ... Ezek. 27:24 ... 950
- Worldly ... 1 Pet. 3:3 ... 1480
- Showy ... Luke 16:19 ... 1219
- Official ... 1 Kin. 10:5 ... 406
- Royal ... Esth. 6:8 ... 582
- Priestly ... Ezra 3:10 ... 545
- Angelic ... Acts 1:10 ... 1272
- Heavenly ... Rev. 19:8 ... 1536

B. *Attitude toward:*
- Not to covet ... Acts 20:33 ... 1303
- Without show ... 1 Pet. 3:3, 4 ... 1480
- Be modest in ... 1 Tim. 2:9, 10 ... 1426

C. *Figurative of:*
- Christ's blood ... Is. 63:1-3 ... 835
- Christ's righteousness ... Zech. 3:1-5 ... 1069
- The Church's purity ... Ps. 45:13, 14 ... 651

Apparition—*appearance of ghost or disembodied spirit*
- Samuel ... 1 Sam. 28:12-14 ... 353
- Christ mistaken for ... Matt. 14:26 ... 1134; Luke 24:37, 39 ... 1231

Appeal—*petition for higher judgment*
- To Christ ... Luke 12:13, 14 ... 1214
- Of Paul, to Caesar ... Acts 25:11, 25-27 ... 1310; Acts 26:32 ... 1312

Appearance, outward

A. *Can conceal:*
- Deception ... James 1:10, 11 ... 1468; Josh. 9:3-16 ... 260
- Hypocrisy ... Matt. 23:25-28 ... 1145
- Rottenness ... Acts 12:21-23 ... 1289
- Rebellion ... 2 Sam. 15:7-13 ... 374
- False apostles ... 2 Cor. 11:13-15 ... 1373
- Inner glory ... Is. 53:1-3 ... 825; Matt. 17:1, 2 ... 1137

B. *Can be:*
- Misunderstood ... Josh. 22:10-31 ... 276
- Mistaken ... 1 Sam. 1:12-18 ... 321
- Misleading ... 2 Cor. 10:7-11 ... 1373
- Misjudged ... John 7:24 ... 1247
- Misinterpreted ... Matt. 11:16-19 ... 1130

Appearances, divine

A. *Of the Lord in the Old Testament:*
- To Abraham ... Gen. 12:7 ... 20
- To Isaac ... Gen. 26:1, 2, 24 ... 34
- To Jacob ... Gen. 35:1, 9 ... 46
- To Moses ... Ex. 3:1, 2, 16 ... 70
- To Israel ... Ex. 16:10 ... 86
- In mercy seat ... Lev. 16:2 ... 139
- In tabernacle ... Num. 14:10 ... 177
- To Gideon ... Judg. 6:11, 12 ... 290
- To Manoah ... Judg. 13:2, 3, 10, 21 ... 299
- To Samuel ... 1 Sam. 3:21 ... 326
- To David ... 2 Chr. 3:1 ... 503
- To Solomon ... 1 Kin. 3:5 ... 395

B. *Of Christ's first advent, in:*
- Nativity ... 2 Tim. 1:10 ... 1433
- Transfiguration ... Luke 9:29-31 ... 1207
- Resurrected form ... Luke 24:34 ... 1231
- Priestly intercession ... Heb. 9:24 ... 1457
- Return ... Col. 3:4 ... 1408

C. *Of Christ resurrected, to, at:*
- Mary Magdalene ... John 20:11-18 ... 1265
- Other women ... Matt. 28:9, 10 ... 1155
- Disciples on road to Emmaus ... Luke 24:13-35 ... 1230
- Ten disciples ... John 20:19-25 ... 1265
- Thomas ... John 20:26-31 ... 1265
- Sea of Galilee ... John 21:1-25 ... 1267
- Give great commission ... Matt. 28:16-20 ... 1155
- Five hundred brethren ... 1 Cor. 15:6 ... 1359
- His ascension ... Acts 1:4-11 ... 1271
- Paul ... Acts 9:3-6 ... 1284
- John ... Rev. 1:10-18 ... 1517

D. *Of Christ's second advent, a time of:*
- Salvation ... Heb. 9:28 ... 1457
- Confidence ... 1 John 2:28 ... 1497
- Judgment ... 2 Tim. 4:1 ... 1436
- Reward ... 2 Tim. 4:8 ... 1436
- Blessedness ... Titus 2:13 ... 1442
- Joy ... 1 Pet. 1:7, 8 ... 1477
- Rulership ... 1 Tim. 6:14, 15 ... 1430

See Theophany

Appeasement—*means used to reconcile two parties*

A. *Kinds of, between:*
- Brothers ... Gen. 32:20 ... 44
- Nations ... 1 Kin. 20:31-34 ... 421
- Tribes ... Josh. 22:10-34 ... 276
- Jews and Gentiles ... Eph. 2:11-17 ... 1388

B. *Means of, by:*
- Gifts ... Gen. 43:11-16 ... 56
- Special pleading ... 1 Sam. 25:17-35 ... 350
- Correcting an abuse ... Acts 6:1-6 ... 1278
- Slowness to anger ... Prov. 15:18 ... 727
- Wisdom ... Prov. 16:14 ... 728

C. *None allowed between:*
- Righteousness, evil ... 2 Cor. 6:14-17 ... 1369
- Truth, error ... Gal. 1:7-9 ... 1378
- Faith, works ... Gal. 5:1-10 ... 1382
- Flesh, Spirit ... Gal. 5:16-26 ... 1383
- Christ, Satan ... Matt. 4:1-11 ... 1117
- Heaven, Sheol ... Is. 28:18 ... 798

D. *Of God's wrath, by:*
- Righteous action ... Num. 16:44-50 ... 181
- Repentance ... 2 Sam. 12:10-14 ... 371
- Atoning for an evil ... 2 Sam. 21:1-14 ... 381
- Christ's death ... Is. 53:1-7 ... 825
- Christ's righteousness ... Zech. 3:1-5 ... 1069; 2 Cor. 5:18-21 ... 1369

Appetite—*desire to fulfill some basic need*

A. *Kinds of:*
- Physical ... 1 Sam. 14:31-33 ... 337
- Sexual ... 1 Cor. 7:1-9 ... 1351
- Lustful ... Matt. 5:28 ... 1120
- Insatiable ... Prov. 27:20 ... 740
- Spiritual ... Ps. 119:20, 131 ... 694

B. *Perversion of, by:*
- Gluttony ... Prov. 23:1, 2 ... 735
- Adultery ... Prov. 6:24-29 ... 719; Ezek. 23:1-49 ... 942
- Impurity ... Rom. 1:24-32 ... 1324

C. *Loss of, by:*
- Age ... 2 Sam. 19:35 ... 380
- Trouble ... 1 Sam. 28:21-23 ... 353
- Visions ... Dan. 10:3-16 ... 989
- Deep concern ... John 4:31-34 ... 1242

D. *Spiritual, characteristics of:*
- Satisfying ... Is. 55:1, 2 ... 827
- Sufficient ... Matt. 5:6 ... 1120
- Spontaneous ... John 7:37-39 ... 1248
- Sanctifying ... 1 Pet. 2:2 ... 1479
- Sublime ... Col. 3:1-3 ... 1408

See Gluttony; Hunger; Temperance

Apphia
- Christian lady of Colossae ... Philem. 2 ... 1445

Appii Forum—*a town about 40 miles south of Rome*
- Paul meets Christians here ... Acts 28:15 ... 1315

Applause—*a visible expression of public approval*
- Men seek after ... Matt. 6:1-5 ... 1121

"Apple of the eye"—*a figurative expression for something very valuable*

A. *Translated as:*
- "The apple of His eye" ... Zech. 2:8 ... 1069

B. *Figurative of:*
- God's care ... Deut. 32:10 ... 244
- God's Law ... Prov. 7:2 ... 720
- The saint's security ... Ps. 17:8 ... 633

Apples of gold—*something of great value*
- A word fitly spoken ... Prov. 25:11 ... 738

Appoint—*to set in an official position or relationship*

A. *Descriptive of ordination, to:*
- Priesthood ... Num. 3:10 ... 162
- Prophetic office ... Heb. 3:2 ... 1452
- Ruler ... 2 Sam. 6:21 ... 365
- Apostleship ... Luke 10:1 ... 1208
- Deacon's office ... Acts 6:3 ... 1278
- Christ as high priest ... Heb. 5:1 ... 1453
- Paul as a preacher ... 1 Tim. 2:7 ... 1426
- Elders ... Titus 1:5 ... 1440
- Royal officer ... Dan. 2:24 ... 978

B. *Descriptive of God's rule, over:*
- Earth ... Ps. 104:19, 20 ... 684
- World history ... Acts 17:26 ... 1299
- Israel's history ... 2 Chr. 33:8 ... 533
- Nations ... Jer. 47:7 ... 895
- Man's life ... Job 14:5 ... 598
- Death ... Heb. 9:27 ... 1457
- Final judgment ... Acts 17:31 ... 1299
- Man's destiny ... Matt. 24:51 ... 1148

C. *Descriptive of the believer's life:*
- Trials ... 1 Thess. 3:3 ... 1415
- Service ... Acts 22:10 ... 1306

See article on Greatest Archaeological Discoveries

SUBJECT — REFERENCE — PAGE

Architect—*one who draws plans for a building*

Plan of, given to Noah — Gen. 6:14-16 — 11
Plan of, shown to Moses — Ex. 25:8, 9, 40 — 95
Bezalel, an inspired — Ex. 35:30-35 — 109
Plan of, given to Solomon — 1 Chr. 28:11-21 — 495
Seen in Ezekiel's vision — Ezek. 40–42 — 963

Archives—*storage place for public and historical documents*

The Book of the Law found in — 2 Kin. 22:8 — 455
Jeremiah's roll placed in — Jer. 36:20, 21 — 884
Record book kept in — Ezra 4:15 — 546
Genealogies kept in — Neh. 7:5, 64 — 563

Ard—*humpbacked*

A son of Benjamin — Gen. 46:21 — 59
Progenitor of the Ardites — Num. 26:40 — 191
Also called Addar — 1 Chr. 8:3 — 473

Ardon—*descendant*

A son of Caleb — 1 Chr. 2:18 — 466

Areli—*valiant, heroic*

A son of Gad — Gen. 46:16 — 59

Areopagite—*a member of the court*

A convert — Acts 17:34 — 1299

Areopagus—*a rocky hill at Athens; also the name of a court*

Paul preached — Acts 17:18-34 — 1297

Aretas—*pleasing*

The title borne by four Nabataean rulers, the last of whom Paul mentions (Aretas IV, Philopatris, 9 B.C.–A.D. 40) — 2 Cor. 11:32, 33 — 1374

Argob—*mound or region of clods*

1. District of Bashan with 60 fortified cities — Deut. 3:4 — 210; 1 Kin. 4:13 — 397
2. Guard killed by Pekah — 2 Kin. 15:25 — 447

Aridai

A son of Haman — Esth. 9:9 — 583

Aridatha

A son of Haman — Esth. 9:8 — 583

Arieh—*lion*

Guard killed by Pekah — 2 Kin. 15:25 — 447

Ariel—*lion of God*

1. Ezra's friend — Ezra 8:15-17 — 550
2. Name applied to Jerusalem — Is. 29:1, 2, 7 — 799

Arimathea—*a height*

Joseph's native city — John 19:38 — 1264

Arioch—*lion-like*

1. King of Ellasar — Gen. 14:1, 9 — 21
2. Captain of Nebuchadnezzar — Dan. 2:14, 15 — 977

Arisai

A son of Haman — Esth. 9:9 — 583

Arise—*to stand up*

A. *Descriptive of:*
Natural events — Eccl. 1:5 — 749
Standing up — 1 Sam. 28:23 — 354
Regeneration — Luke 15:18, 20 — 1218
Resurrection — Matt. 9:24, 25 — 1127
A miracle — Luke 4:38, 39 — 1200

B. *Descriptive of prophetic events:*
World kingdoms — Dan. 2:39 — 978
The Messiah's advent — Is. 60:1-3 — 832
Persecution — Mark 4:16, 17 — 1164
False christs — Matt. 24:24 — 1147

Aristarchus—*the best ruler*

A Macedonian Christian — Acts 19:29 — 1302
Accompanied Paul — Acts 20:1, 4 — 1302
Imprisoned with Paul — Col. 4:10 — 1409

Aristobulus—*the best counselor*

A Christian at Rome — Rom. 16:10 — 1341

Ark of bulrushes—*a basket made of reeds* (papyrus)

Moses placed in — Ex. 2:1-6 — 69
Made by faith — Heb. 11:23 — 1460

Ark of Noah

Construction — Gen. 6:14-16 — 11
Cargo — Gen. 6:19-21 — 11
Ready for the flood — Matt. 24:38, 39 — 1148
Rested on Mt. Ararat — Gen. 8:1-16 — 12
A type of baptism — 1 Pet. 3:20, 21 — 1481

Ark of the Covenant—*a small box containing the tablets of the Law*

A. *Called:*
Ark of the covenant — Num. 10:33 — 173
Ark of the testimony — Ex. 30:6 — 103
Ark of the Lord — Josh. 4:11 — 255
Ark of God — 1 Sam. 3:3 — 324
Ark of God's strength — 2 Chr. 6:41 — 508

B. *Construction of:*
Described — Ex. 25:10-22 — 95
Executed — Ex. 37:1-5 — 110

C. *Contained:*
The Ten Commandments — Deut. 10:4, 5 — 221
Aaron's rod — Num. 17:10 — 181; Heb. 9:4 — 1457
Pot of manna — Ex. 16:33, 34 — 87

D. *Conveyed:*
By Levites — Num. 3:30, 31 — 163
Before Israel — Josh. 3:3-17 — 254
Into battle — 1 Sam. 4:4, 5 — 326
On a cart — 1 Sam. 6:7-15 — 327

E. *Purposes of:*
Symbol of God's Law — Ex. 25:16, 21 — 97
Memorial of God's provision — Ex. 16:33, 34 — 87
Place to know God's will — Ex. 25:22 — 97; Ex. 30:6, 36 — 103
Place of entreaty — Josh. 7:6-15 — 258
Symbol of God's holiness — 1 Sam. 6:19 — 328; 2 Sam. 6:6, 7 — 364
Place of atonement — Lev. 16:2, 14-17 — 139
Symbol of heaven — Rev. 11:19 — 1529

F. *History of:*
Carried across Jordan — Josh. 3:14-17 — 254
Caused Jordan's stoppage — Josh. 4:5-11, 18 — 254
Carried around Jericho — Josh. 6:6-20 — 256
At Mt. Ebal ceremony — Josh. 8:30-33 — 260
Set up at Shiloh — Josh. 18:1 — 270
Moved to house of God — Judg. 20:26, 27 — 308
Returned to Shiloh — 1 Sam. 1:3 — 321
Carried into battle — 1 Sam. 4:3-22 — 326
Captured — 1 Sam. 4:10-22 — 326
Caused Dagon's fall — 1 Sam. 5:1-4 — 327
Brought a plague — 1 Sam. 5:6-12 — 327
Returned to Israel — 1 Sam. 6:1-21 — 327
Set in Abinadab's house — 1 Sam. 7:1, 2 — 328
In Obed-Edom's house — 2 Sam. 6:10-12 — 364
Established in Jerusalem — 2 Sam. 6:12-17 — 365
During Absalom's rebellion — 2 Sam. 15:24-29 — 375
Placed in Temple — 1 Kin. 8:1-11 — 402
Restored by Josiah — 2 Chr. 35:3 — 535
Carried to Babylon — 2 Chr. 36:6, 18 — 538
Prophetic fulfillment — Jer. 3:16, 17 — 848; Acts 15:13-18 — 1293

Arkite—*belonging to Arka*

Canaan's descendants — Gen. 10:17 — 16; 1 Chr. 1:15 — 464

Arm of God

A. *Described as:*
Stretched out — Deut. 4:34 — 212
Everlasting — Deut. 33:27 — 247
Strong, mighty — Ps. 89:10, 13 — 676
Holy — Ps. 98:1 — 681
Glorious — Is. 63:12 — 835

B. *Descriptive of, God's:*
Redeeming — Ex. 6:6 — 73
Saving — Ps. 44:3 — 650
Victorious — Ps. 98:1 — 681
Ruling — Is. 40:10 — 811
Strengthening — Ps. 89:21 — 677
Protecting — Deut. 7:19 — 218
Destroying — Is. 30:30 — 802

Arm of the wicked—*expression for molestation*

Shall be broken — Ps. 10:15 — 631

SUBJECT REFERENCE PAGE

Assembly—continued
The Temple's dedication .... 2 Chr. 5:1-14 506
Josiah's reformation ... 2 Kin. 23:1-3, 21-23 456
Ezra's reading the Law ... Neh. 8:1-18 564
Jesus' trial .... Matt. 27:11-26 1152
Pentecost ..... Acts 2:1-21 1273
The Jerusalem Council ...... Acts 15:5-21 1293

Assent—*agreeing to the truth of a statement or fact*

A. *Concerning good things:*
Accepting God's covenant ..... Ex. 19:7, 8 89
Agreeing to reforms ..... 1 Sam. 7:3, 4 328; Ezra 10:1-12, 19 551
Accepting a scriptural decision ...... Acts 15:13-22 1293
Receiving Christ as Savior .... Rom. 10:9, 10 1335

B. *Concerning evil things:*
Tolerating idolatry ...... Jer. 44:15-19 893
Condemning Christ to death .... Matt. 27:17-25 1152
Putting Stephen to death .... Acts 7:51-60 1282
Refusing to hear the Gospel .... Acts 13:44-51 1292

Asshur—*level plain*

1. One of the sons of Shem; progenitor of the Assyrians ... Gen. 10:22 16; 1 Chr. 1:17 464
2. The chief god of the Assyrians; seen in names like Ashurbanipal (Osnapper) ... Ezra 4:10 546
3. A city in Assyria or the nation of Assyria ..... Num. 24:22, 24 189

Asshurim—*mighty ones*

Descendants of Abraham by Keturah .... Gen. 25:3 33

Assir—*prisoner*

1. A son of Korah .... Ex. 6:24 74; 1 Chr. 6:22 469
2. A son of Ebiasaph ..... 1 Chr. 6:23, 37 469
3. A son of King Jeconiah ..... 1 Chr. 3:17 467

Assistance, divine

A. *Offered, in:*
Battle .... 2 Chr. 20:5-17 519
Trouble .... Ps. 50:15 653
Crises .... Luke 21:14, 15 1225
Prayer .... Rom. 8:16-27 1333
Testimony .... 2 Tim. 4:17 1436
Wisdom .... James 1:5-8 1468

B. *Given:*
Internally ... Phil. 2:13 1400; Heb. 13:21 1464
By God ..... 1 John 4:9, 10 1498; 2 Cor. 8:9 1371
By Christ ...... Phil. 4:13 1402
By the Spirit .. Zech. 4:6 1070
By God's Word .... 1 Thess. 2:13 1415
By grace .... 1 Cor. 15:10 1359
By prayer ..... James 5:15-18 1473
By trusting God .... Ps. 37:3-7 645
By God's providence ... Rom. 8:28 1333

Association—*joining together for mutually beneficial purposes*

A. *Among believers, hindered by:*
Sin .... Acts 5:1-11 1277
Friction .... Acts 6:1-6 1278
Inconsistency .... Gal. 2:11-14 1380
Disagreement .... Acts 15:36-40 1294
Selfishness .... 3 John 9-11 1506
Ambition ...... Matt. 20:20-24 1140
Error .... 2 John 7-11 1502
Partiality ...... James 2:1-5 1469

B. *Among believers, helped by:*
Common faith .... Acts 2:42-47 1274
Mutual helpfulness ... Gal. 6:1-5 1383
United prayer .... Matt. 18:19, 20 1138
Impending dangers ...... Neh. 4:1-23 560
Grateful praise .... Acts 4:23-33 1277

See Alliance with evil; Fellowship

Assos—*a seaport of Mysia in Asia Minor*

Paul walks to, from Troas .... Acts 20:13, 14 1303

Assurance—*the security of knowing that one's name is written in heaven*

A. *Objects of, one's:*
Election .... 1 Thess. 1:4 1413
Adoption ...... Eph. 1:4, 5 1387
Union with Christ .... 1 Cor. 6:15 1349
Possession of eternal life .... John 5:24 1243; 1 John 5:13 1499
Peace .... Rom. 5:1 1329

B. *Steps in:*
Believing God's Word .... 1 Thess. 2:13 1415
Accepting Christ as Savior .... Rom. 10:9, 10 1335
Standing upon the promises ..... John 10:28-30 1252
Desiring spiritual things .... 1 Pet. 2:2 1479
Growing in grace .... 2 Pet. 1:5-11 1487
Knowing life is changed ... 2 Cor. 5:17 1368; 1 John 3:14-22 1497
Having inner peace and joy .... Rom. 15:12, 13 1340; Phil. 4:7 1402
Victorious living .... 1 John 5:4, 5 1499
The Spirit's testimony .... Rom. 8:15, 16 1332
Absolute assurance ... Rom. 8:33-39 1333; 2 Tim. 1:12 1433

C. *Compatible with:*
A nature still subject to sin .... 1 John 1:8-10 1494; 1 John 2:1 1494
Imperfection of life .... Gal. 6:1 1383
Limited knowledge ... 1 Cor. 13:9-12 1356
Fatherly chastisement .... Heb. 12:5-11 1462

Assyria—*the nation ruled from Asshur (first) and Nineveh (later)*

A. *Significant facts regarding:*
Of remote antiquity ..... Gen. 2:14 7
Of Shem's ancestry ..... Gen. 10:22 16
Founded by Nimrod ..... Gen. 10:8-12 16; Mic. 5:6 1039
Nineveh, chief city of .... Gen. 10:11 16
Hiddekel (Tigris) River flows through ...... Gen. 2:14 7
Proud nation .. Is. 10:5-15 782
A cruel military power .... Nah. 3:1-19 1048
Agent of God's purposes .... Is. 7:17-20 779; Is. 10:5, 6 782

B. *Contacts of, with Israel:*
Pul (Tiglath-Pileser III, 745–727 B.C.) captures Damascus .... Is. 8:4 779
Puts Menahem under tribute ...... 2 Kin. 15:19, 20 447
Occasions Isaiah's prophecy ...... Is. 7;8 772
Puts Pekah under tribute .... 2 Kin. 15:29 447
Shalmaneser (727–722 B.C.) besieges Samaria ...... 2 Kin. 17:3-5 448
Sargon II (722–705 B.C.) captures Israel .... 2 Kin. 17:6-41 448

C. *Contacts of, with Judah:*
Sargon's general takes Ashdod (in Philistia) .. Is. 20:1-6 791
Sennacherib (704–681 B.C.) invades Judah .... 2 Kin. 18:13 450
Puts Hezekiah under tribute ...... 2 Kin. 18:14-16 450
Threatens Hezekiah through Rabshakeh .. 2 Kin. 18:17-37 450
Army of, miraculously slain .... 2 Kin. 19:35 453
Assassination of, by his sons .... 2 Kin. 19:37 453

D. *Prophecies concerning:*
Destruction of, anciently foretold ...... Num. 24:22-24 189
Israel captive in land of .... Hos. 10:6 1002; Hos. 11:5 1003
Doom of, mentioned ... Is. 10:12, 19 782; Is. 14:24, 25 787
End eulogized ..... Nah. 3:1-19 1048
Shares, figuratively, in Gospel blessings ..... Is. 19:23-25 790

Astonishment—*an emotion of perplexed amazement*

A. *Caused by:*
God's judgments ... 1 Kin. 9:8, 9 404; Jer. 18:16 865
Racial intermarriage ..... Ezra 9:2-4 551
Urgent message ..... Ezek. 3:14, 15 920
A miracle ..... Dan. 3:24 979
An unexplained vision .... Dan. 8:27 987
Christ's knowledge ... Luke 2:47 1194
Christ's teaching ..... Luke 4:32 1200
Christ's miracles ..... Mark 5:42 1166; Luke 5:9 1200
Gentile conversions .. Acts 10:45 1288
Miracles .... Acts 12:5-7, 13-16 1289; Acts 13:6-12 1291

B. *Applied figuratively to:*
God .... Jer. 14:9 860
Babylon .... Jer. 51:37, 41 903
Jerusalem ..... Ezek. 5:5, 15 921
Priests .... Jer. 4:9 849

Astrologers—*those who search the heavens for supposed revelations*

Cannot save Babylon .... Is. 47:1, 12-15 819

SUBJECT | REFERENCE | PAGE

Cannot interpret dreams .... Dan. 2:2, 10-13 977; Dan. 4:7 980
Cannot decipher handwriting ..... Dan. 5:7, 8 983
Daniel surpasses .... Dan. 1:20 977
Daniel made master of .... Dan. 5:11 983
God does not speak through .... Dan. 2:27, 28 978

Asylum—*protection, refuge*

Afforded by altar .... 1 Kin. 1:50-53 392; 1 Kin. 2:28 394
Cities of refuge .... Ex. 21:12-14 92; Deut. 19:1-13 230

Asyncritus—*incomparable*

A Christian at Rome .... Rom. 16:14 1341

Atad—*thorn*

A mourning site east of Jordan .... Gen. 50:9-13 64

Atarah—*crown*

A wife of Jerahmeel .... 1 Chr. 2:26 466

Ataroth—*crowns*

1. Town of Gad .. Num. 32:3, 34 198
2. A town of Ephraim ..... Josh. 16:7 268
3. A town between Ephraim and Benjamin .... Josh. 16:2 268
   Probably the same as Ataroth Addar .... Josh. 16:5 268; Josh. 18:13 271
4. A village near Bethlehem .... 1 Chr. 2:54 466

Ataroth Addar—*crowns of Addar*

A frontier town of Ephraim .... Josh. 16:5 268

See Ataroth 3

Ater—*crippled one*

1. The ancestor of a family of returnees .... Ezra 2:16 544; Neh. 7:21 563
2. The ancestor of a family of porters .... Ezra 2:42 544; Neh. 7:45 563
3. A signer of Nehemiah's document .... Neh. 10:17 569

Athach—*lodging, inn*

A town in south Judah .... 1 Sam. 30:30 355

Athaiah—*Yahweh is helper*

A Judahite in Nehemiah's time .... Neh. 11:4 570

Athaliah—*Yahweh is exalted*

1. The daughter of Ahab and Jezebel .... 2 Kin. 8:18, 26 438; 2 Chr. 22:2, 3 521
   Destroys all the royal seed except Joash .... 2 Kin. 11:1, 2 442; 2 Chr. 22:10, 11 522
   Usurps throne for six years .... 2 Kin. 11:3 442
   Killed by priestly uprising ..... 2 Kin. 11:4-16 442; 2 Chr. 23:1-21 522
   Called wicked .... 2 Chr. 24:7 523
2. A Benjamite ... 1 Chr. 8:26, 27 473

3. The father of Jeshaiah ..... Ezra 8:7 550

Atharim—*spys*

Israel attacked there .... Num. 21:1 184

Atheism—*the denial of God's existence*

A. *Defined as:*
The fool's philosophy .. Ps. 14:1 632; Ps. 53:1 655
Living without God ..... Rom. 1:20-32 1324; Eph. 2:12 1388

B. *Manifestations of, seen in:*
Defiance of God .... Ex. 5:2 73; 2 Kin. 18:19-35 450
Irreligion ...... Titus 1:16 1440
Corrupt morals ...... Rom. 13:12, 13 1339; 1 Pet. 4:3 1481

C. *Evidences against, seen in:*
Man's inner conscience ... Rom. 2:14, 15 1325
Design in nature ...... Job 38:1-41 615; Job 39:1-30 616
God's works ... Ps. 19:1-6 635
God's providence .. Ps. 104:1-35 683; Acts 14:17 1293
Clear evidence ..... Rom. 1:19, 20 1324
The testimony of pagans .... Dan. 4:24-37 981
Fulfillment of prophecy .... Is. 41:20-23 813; Is. 46:8-11 819

Athens—*a Greek city named after the goddess Athena*

Paul preaches in .... Acts 17:15-34 1297
Paul resides in .... 1 Thess. 3:1 1415

Athlai—*Yahweh is strong*

A Jew who divorced his foreign wife .... Ezra 10:28 553

Athletes

Discipline .... 1 Cor. 9:24-27 1353
Removal of weights .... Heb. 12:1 1462
Prize .... Phil. 3:14 1401

Atonement—*reconciliation of the guilty by divine sacrifice*

A. *Elements involved in, seen in:*
Man's sin .... Ex. 32:30 106; Ps. 51:3, 4 654
The blood sacrificed .... Lev. 16:11, 14-20 139; Heb. 9:13-22 1457
Guilt transferred .. Lev. 1:3, 4 120; 2 Cor. 5:21 1369
Guilt removed .... Lev. 16:21 139; 1 Cor. 6:11 1349
Forgiveness granted .... Lev. 5:10, 11 124; Rom. 4:6, 7 1327
Righteousness given .... Rom. 10:3, 4 1334; Phil. 3:9 1401

B. *Fulfilled by Christ:*
Predicted .... Is. 53:10-12 825; Dan. 9:24-26 989
Symbolized .. Is. 63:1-9 835; Zech. 3:3-9 1069
Realized .... Rom. 3:23-26 1327; 1 Pet. 1:18-21 1479

Atonement, Day of

A. *Features regarding:*
Time specified ..... Lev. 23:26, 27 148
The ritual involved in .... Lev. 16:3, 5-15 139
A time of humiliation ... Lev. 16:29, 31 140
Exclusive ministry of the high priest in ..... Lev. 16:2, 3 139; Heb. 9:7 1457

B. *Benefits of, for:*
The holy place .... Lev. 16:15, 16 139
The people .... Lev. 16:17, 24 139
The high priest .... Lev. 16:11 139; Heb. 9:7 1457

C. *Result of, seen in:*
Atonement for sin .... Rom. 3:24-26 1327
Removal of sin .... Heb. 9:7-28 1457; Heb. 13:10-13 1463

Atonement of Christ

A. *Typified by:*
The paschal lamb .... Ex. 12:5, 11, 14 80; John 1:29 1237; 1 Cor. 5:7 1348
The Day of Atonement .. Lev. 16:30, 34 140; Heb. 9:7-28 1457

B. *What man is:*
A sinner ...... Rom. 5:8 1329
Alienated in mind .... Col. 1:21 1406
Strangers ..... Eph. 2:12 1388

C. *What God does:*
Loves us ...... John 3:16 1239
Demonstrates His love toward us .... Rom. 5:8 1329
Sends Christ to save us .... Gal. 4:4, 5 1381
Spared not His own Son .... Rom. 8:32 1333

D. *What Christ does:*
Becomes a man .... Heb. 2:14 1452
Becomes our ransom ...... Matt. 20:28 1141
Dies in our place .... 1 Pet. 3:18 1481
Dies for our sins .... 1 Pet. 2:24 1480
Dies as a sacrifice ...... Eph. 5:2 1391
Dies willingly ..... John 10:18 1252
Reconciles us to God .... Rom. 5:10 1329
Brings us to God .... 1 Pet. 3:18 1481
Restores our fellowship .... 1 Thess. 5:10 1416

See Blood of Christ

E. *What the believer receives:*
Forgiveness .... Eph. 1:7 1387
Peace .... Rom. 5:1 1329
Reconciliation .... 2 Cor. 5:19 1369
Righteousness .... 2 Cor. 5:21 1369
Justification ... Rom. 3:24-26 1327
Access to God .... Eph. 2:18 1388
Cleansing ..... 1 John 1:7 1494
Liberty .... Gal. 5:1 1382
Freedom from the devil's power .... Heb. 2:14 1452
Christ's intercession .. Heb. 2:17, 18 1452

Atroth Beth Joab

A village near Bethlehem .... 1 Chr. 2:54 466

Atroth Shophan

A city built by the Gadites ..... Num. 32:34, 35 199

SUBJECT — REFERENCE — PAGE

Attai—*timely*
1. A half-Egyptian Judahite ..... 1 Chr. 2:35, 36 — 466
2. A Gadite in David's army .... 1 Chr. 12:11 — 479
3. Rehoboam's son .... 2 Chr. 11:18-20 — 512

Attalia—*a seaport town of Pamphylia named after Attalus II*
Paul sails from, to Antioch .... Acts 14:25, 26 — 1293

Attend
To care for .... Esth. 4:5 — 579

Attendance, church
Taught by example .... Acts 11:25, 26 — 1288; Acts 14:19, 20, 26, 27 — 1293
Not to be neglected .... Heb. 10:25 — 1458

Attitude—*the state of mind toward something*
A. *Of Christians toward Christ, must:*
Confess .... Rom. 10:9, 10 — 1335
Obey .... John 14:15, 23 — 1258
Follow .... Matt. 16:24 — 1137
Imitate .... 1 Pet. 2:21 — 1480
B. *Of Christians toward the world, not to:*
Conform to .... Rom. 12:2 — 1337
Abuse .... 1 Cor. 7:29-31 — 1352
Love .... 1 John 2:15 — 1496
Be friend of ... James 4:4 — 1471
Be entangled with .... 2 Tim. 2:4 — 1434
Be defiled with .... Jude 23 — 1512
C. *Of Christians toward sinners:*
Seek their salvation ..... 1 Cor. 9:22 — 1353
Pray for .... Rom. 9:1-3 — 1333
Plead with .... Acts 17:22-31 — 1299
Rebuke .... Titus 1:10-13 — 1440
Persuade ...... 2 Cor. 5:11 — 1368

Audience—*an assembly of hearers*
Disturbed .... Neh. 13:1-3 — 572
Attentive .... Luke 7:1 — 1203
Hostile .... Luke 4:28-30 — 1198
Receptive .... Acts 2:1-41 — 1273
Menacing .... Acts 7:54-60 — 1282
Rejecting .... Acts 13:44-51 — 1292
Critical .... Acts 17:22-34 — 1299
Sympathetic ...... Acts 20:17-38 — 1303
Vast .... Rev. 5:9 — 1523; Rev. 7:9, 10 — 1525
See Assembly

Auditorium—*a room for assembly*
Hearing .... Acts 25:23 — 1310

Augustus' regiment—*a battalion of Roman soldiers*
Paul placed in custody of .... Acts 27:1 — 1312

Author—*creator; originator; writer*
God of peace ..... 1 Cor. 14:33 — 1358
Christ of salvation .... Heb. 5:9 — 1453
Christ of faith .... Heb. 12:2 — 1462
Solomon of many proverbs and songs .... 1 Kin. 4:32 — 397

Authority—*the lawful right to enforce obedience, power*
A. *As rulers:*
Governor .... Acts 23:24, 26 — 1307; Matt. 10:18 — 1129
B. *Delegated to, man as:*
Created .... Gen. 1:26-31 — 4
A legal state .... Esth. 9:29 — 585; Luke 22:25 — 1226
Agent of the state .... Matt. 8:9 — 1125; Rom. 13:1-6 — 1337
Husband .... 1 Cor. 14:35 — 1358
Agent of religious leaders .... Acts 26:10, 12 — 1312
C. *Christ's, seen in His power:*
Over demons .... Mark 1:27 — 1161
In teaching ... Matt. 7:29 — 1125
To forgive ..... Luke 5:24 — 1201
To judge ...... John 5:22, 27 — 1243
To rule ...... Matt. 2:6 — 1116; 1 Cor. 15:24 — 1359; 1 Pet. 3:22 — 1481
To commission .. Matt. 28:18-20 — 1155
D. *Purpose:*
Protection ...... Heb. 13:17 — 1464
Instruction ..... 1 Pet. 5:2, 3 — 1483
Example of Christ's power .... Matt. 8:5-13 — 1125
Testimony to unbelievers .. 1 Pet. 3:13-15 — 1481; 1 Tim. 6:1 — 1430
E. *Of Christians, given to:*
Apostles ...... 2 Cor. 10:8 — 1373
Ministers ...... Titus 2:15 — 1442
The righteous ..... Prov. 29:2 — 742

Ava—*a region or city in Assyria*
Colonists from, brought to Samaria by Sargon .... 2 Kin. 17:24 — 449
Worshipers of Nibhaz and Tartak .... 2 Kin. 17:31 — 449

Avarice—*covetousness; greed*
A. *Productive of:*
Defeat .... Josh. 7:11, 21 — 258
Death .... 1 Kin. 21:5-16 — 422
Discontent .... James 4:1-4 — 1471
B. *Examples of:*
Balaam .... 2 Pet. 2:15 — 1489
Achan .... Josh. 7:20, 21 — 259
Ahab .... 1 Kin. 21:1-4 — 421
Judas Iscariot ...... Matt. 26:14-16 — 1150
Ananias and Sapphira ..... Acts 5:1-10 — 1277
Rich men .... Luke 12:16-21 — 1214; James 5:1-6 — 1471

Aven—*wickedness*
1. The city of On in Egypt near Cairo; known as Heliopolis ... Gen. 41:45 — 54; Ezek. 30:17 — 953
2. A name contemptuously applied to Bethel ..... Hos. 10:5, 8 — 1002
3. Valley in Syria .... Amos 1:5 — 1015

Avenge—*to retaliate for an evil done*
A. *Kinds of:*
Commanded by God .... Num. 31:1, 2 — 197
Given strength for .... Judg. 16:28-30 — 303
Sought maliciously ... 1 Sam. 18:25 — 344
Possible but not done .... 1 Sam. 24:12 — 349
Attempted but hindered .... 1 Sam. 25:26-33 — 351
Obtained in self-defense .. Esth. 8:12, 13 — 583
B. *Sought because of:*
A murdered neighbor .... Num. 35:12 — 203; Josh. 20:5 — 273
A wife's mistreatment .... Judg. 15:6-8 — 302
Judah's sins ... Jer. 5:9 — 850
Mistreatment .... Acts 7:24, 25 — 1281
Impurity ...... 1 Thess. 4:5-7 — 1416
C. *Performed by:*
God Himself ..... Lev. 26:25 — 153; Luke 18:7, 8 — 1220
Wicked men ... 2 Sam. 4:8-12 — 363
Impetuous general ..... 2 Sam. 18:18, 19, 31 — 378
An anointed king .... 2 Kin. 9:6, 7 — 439
A judge .... Luke 18:3, 5 — 1220
God .... Rev. 19:2 — 1536
D. *Restrictions on:*
Personal, prohibited .... Lev. 19:17, 18 — 142
Christians prohibited .... Rom. 12:19 — 1337

Avenger of blood (literally, "*redeemer of blood*")
An ancient practice .... Gen. 4:14 — 10
Seen in kinsman as "redeemer" of enslaved relative .... Lev. 25:25, 47-49 — 150; Ruth 4:1-10 — 315
Seen also in kinsman as "avenger" of a murdered relative .... Num. 35:11-34 — 203
Avenger alone must kill murderer .... Deut. 19:6, 11-13 — 230
Practice of, set aside by David .... 2 Sam. 14:4-11 — 373
Same word translated "kinsman" and "redeemer" ..... Ruth 4:1 — 315; Job 19:25 — 602
Figurative of a violent person .... Ps. 8:2 — 630

Avim, Avims, Avites—*villagers*
1. A tribe of early Canaanites living near Gaza; absorbed by the Caphtorim (Philistines) .. Deut. 2:23 — 210
2. A city of Benjamin near Bethel ...... Josh. 18:23 — 271
3. Colonists brought from Ava in Assyria .... 2 Kin. 17:24, 31 — 449

Avith—*ruin*
An Edomite city .. Gen. 36:35 — 48

Awakening, spiritual
A. *Produced by:*
Returning to Bethel ...... Gen. 35:1-7 — 46
Discovering God's Word .... 2 Kin. 22:8-13 — 455
Reading God's Word .... Neh. 8:2-18 — 564
Confessing sin .... Ezra 10:1-17 — 551
Receiving the Spirit .... John 7:38, 39 — 1248; Acts 2:1-47 — 1273
B. *Old Testament examples of, under:*
Joshua .... Josh. 24:1-31 — 277
Samuel .... 1 Sam. 7:3-6 — 328
Elijah .... 1 Kin. 18:21-40 — 417
Hezekiah .... 2 Chr. 30:1-27 — 529; 2 Chr. 31:1 — 530
Josiah .... 2 Kin. 23:1-25 — 456
Ezra .... Ezra 10:1-17 — 551

SUBJECT REFERENCE PAGE

C. *New Testament examples of:*
John the Baptist .... Luke 3:2-14 1194
Jesus in Samaria ...... John 4:28-42 1242
Philip in Samaria ...... Acts 8:5-12 1282
Peter at Lydda .... Acts 9:32-35 1286
Peter with Cornelius .... Acts 10:34-48 1287
Paul at Antioch in Pisidia ...... Acts 13:14-52 1291
Paul at Thessalonica ...... Acts 17:11, 12 1297; 1 Thess. 1:1-10 1413
Paul at Corinth ...... 2 Cor. 7:1-16 1369

Awe—*fear mingled with reverence*
Proper attitude toward God .... Ps. 33:8 643
Also toward God's Word .... Ps. 119:161 699

Awl—*a sharp tool for piercing*
Used on the ear as a symbol of perpetual obedience ...... Ex. 21:6 92; Deut. 15:17 227

Ax—*a sharp instrument for cutting wood*
A. *Used in:*
Cutting timber .... Judg. 9:48 296
War .... 1 Chr. 20:3 487
Malicious destruction ... Ps. 74:5-7 667
A miracle; floated in water .... 2 Kin. 6:5, 6 434
B. *As a figure of:*
Judgment ..... Matt. 3:10 1117
God's sovereignty ... Is. 10:15 782

Ayyah
Ephraimite town .... 1 Chr. 7:28 473

Azal, Azel
1. A descendant of Jonathan ..... 1 Chr. 8:37, 38 473
2. A place near Jerusalem .... Zech. 14:5 1076

Azaliah—*Yahweh has set aside*
Father of Shaphan .... 2 Kin. 22:3 455

Azaniah—*Yahweh has heard*
A Levite who signs the document .... Neh. 10:9 569

Azarel, Azareel—*God has helped*
1. A Levite in David's army at Ziklag .... 1 Chr. 12:6 479
2. A musician in David's time .... 1 Chr. 25:18 492
3. A prince of Dan under David .... 1 Chr. 27:22 493
4. A Jew who divorced his foreign wife .... Ezra 10:41 554
5. A postexilic priest .... Neh. 11:13 570
6. A musician in dedication service .... Neh. 12:36 572

Azariah—*Yahweh has helped*
1. Man of Judah .... 1 Chr. 2:8 465
2. A Kohathite Levite .... 1 Chr. 6:36 470
3. A son of Zadok the high priest .... 1 Kin. 4:2 395
4. A son of Ahimaaz ..... 1 Chr. 6:9 469
5. A great-grandson of Ahimaaz ..... 1 Chr. 6:9-10 469
6. Son of Nathan ...... 1 Kin. 4:5 395
7. A son of Jehu, with Egyptian ancestry ..... 1 Chr. 2:34-38 466
8. A prophet who encourages King Asa .... 2 Chr. 15:1-8 516
9. Son of King Jehoshaphat .... 2 Chr. 21:2 521
10. A captain under Jehoiada ..... 2 Chr. 23:1 522
11. Another under Jehoiada ..... 2 Chr. 23:1 522
12. A head of Ephraim ..... 2 Chr. 28:12 527
13. King of Judah .... 2 Kin. 15:1 446
14. A high priest who rebukes King Uzziah ...... 2 Chr. 26:16-20 526
15. Kohathite, father of Joel .... 2 Chr. 29:12 528
16. A reforming Levite .... 2 Chr. 29:12 528
17. Chief priest in time of Hezekiah .... 2 Chr. 31:9, 10 530
18. A high priest, son of Hilkiah ...... 1 Chr. 6:13, 14 469
19. Ancestor of Ezra .... Ezra 7:1-3 548
20. An opponent of Jeremiah ..... Jer. 43:2 890
21. The Hebrew name of Abed-Nego ... Dan. 1:7 976
22. Postexilic Jew .... Neh. 7:6, 7 563
23. A workman under Nehemiah .... Neh. 3:23, 24 560
24. A prince of Judah .... Neh. 12:32, 33 571
25. An expounder of the law .... Neh. 8:7 565
26. A signer of the covenant ..... Neh. 10:1, 2 569
27. A descendant of Hilkiah ...... 1 Chr. 9:11 474

Azaz—*strong*
A Reubenite ...... 1 Chr. 5:8 468

Azaziah—*Yahweh is strong*
1. A musician .... 1 Chr. 15:21 481
2. Father of Hoshea ...... 1 Chr. 27:20 493
3. A temple overseer ..... 2 Chr. 31:13 530

Azbuk—*pardon*
Father of a certain Nehemiah; but not the celebrated one .... Neh. 3:16 559

Azekah—*tilled*
Great stones cast upon .... Josh. 10:11 262
Camp of Goliath .... 1 Sam. 17:1, 4, 17 340
Fortified by Rehoboam .... 2 Chr. 11:5, 9 512
Reoccupied after exile .... Neh. 11:30 571
Besieged by Nebuchadnezzar .... Jer. 34:7 882

Azem, Ezem—*bone*
A town of Judah .... Josh. 15:29 268
Allotted to Simeon .... Josh. 19:3 271
Also called Ezem .... 1 Chr. 4:29 468

Azgad—*fate is hard*
Head of exile family .... Ezra 2:12 542; Ezra 8:12 550
Among document signers .... Neh. 10:15 569

Aziel—*God strengthens*
A Levite musician .... 1 Chr. 15:20 481
Called Jaaziel .... 1 Chr. 15:18 481

Aziza—*strong*
Divorced foreign wife .... Ezra 10:27 553

Azmaveth—*death is strong*
1. One of David's mighty men .... 2 Sam. 23:31 385
2. A Benjamite ... 1 Chr. 12:3 479
3. David's treasurer ..... 1 Chr. 27:25 494
4. A son of Jehoaddah ... 1 Chr. 8:36 473
5. A village near Jerusalem ..... Neh. 12:29 571
Also called Beth Azmaveth .... Neh. 7:28 563

Azmon—*strong*
A place in south Canaan .... Num. 34:4, 5 202

Aznoth Tabor—*peaks of Tabor*
Place in Naphtali .... Josh. 19:34 272

Azor—*helper*
Ancestor of Christ .... Matt. 1:13, 14 1115

Azotus—*fortress*
Philip went there .... Acts 8:40 1284
Same as Ashdod .... 1 Sam. 6:17 328

Azriel—*God is a help*
1. A chief of Manasseh .... 1 Chr. 5:24 469
2. Father of Jerimoth ..... 1 Chr. 27:19 493
3. Father of Seraiah ...... Jer. 36:26 884

Azrikam—*my help has arisen*
1. Son of Neariah ...... 1 Chr. 3:23 467
2. A son of Azel .... 1 Chr. 8:38 473
3. A Merarite Levite .... 1 Chr. 9:14 474
4. Official under King Ahaz .... 2 Chr. 28:7 527

Azubah—*forsaken*
1. Wife of Caleb .... 1 Chr. 2:18, 19 466
2. Mother of Jehoshaphat .... 1 Kin. 22:42 425

Azur, Azzur—*helpful*
1. Father of Hananiah .... Jer. 28:1 874
2. Father of Jaazaniah .... Ezek. 11:1 927
3. A covenant signer .... Neh. 10:17 569

Azzan—*strong*
Father of Paltiel ... Num. 34:26 202

SUBJECT REFERENCE PAGE

B

Baal—*lord, possessor, husband*

A. *The nature of:*
- The male god of the Phoenicians and Canaanites; the counterpart of the female Ashtaroth .... 2 Kin. 23:5 — 457
- Connected with immorality .. Num. 25:1, 3, 5 — 190; Hos. 9:10 — 1002
- Incense burned to .... Jer. 7:9 — 853
- Kissing the image of .... 1 Kin. 19:18 — 420; Hos. 13:1, 2 — 1004
- Dervish rites by priests of .... 1 Kin. 18:26, 28 — 417
- Children burned in fire of .... Jer. 19:5 — 865
- Eating sacrifices .... Ps. 106:28 — 686

B. *History of:*
- Among Moabites in Moses' time .... Num. 22:41 — 188
- Altars built to, during time of judges .... Judg. 2:11-14 — 285; Judg. 6:28-32 — 291
- Jezebel introduces into Israel .... 1 Kin. 16:31, 32 — 414
- Elijah's overthrow of, on Mt. Carmel .... 1 Kin. 18:17-40 — 417
- Athaliah encourages it into Judah ... 2 Kin. 11:14-20 — 443; 2 Chr. 22:2-4 — 521
- Revived again in Israel and Judah ... Hos. 2:8 — 997; Amos 5:26 — 1020
- Manasseh worships .... 2 Kin. 21:3 — 454
- Altars everywhere .. Jer. 11:13 — 858
- Overthrown by Josiah .... 2 Kin. 23:4, 5 — 456
- Denounced by prophets .... Jer. 19:4-6 — 865; Ezek. 16:1, 2, 20, 21 — 931
- Historic retrospect .... Rom. 11:4 — 1335

Baal—*master; possessor*
1. A Benjamite, from Gibeon .... 1 Chr. 8:30 — 473
2. A descendant of Reuben .... 1 Chr. 5:5, 6 — 468
3. A village of Simeon .... 1 Chr. 4:33 — 468
   Also called Baalath Beer .... Josh. 19:8 — 271

Baalah—*mistress*
1. A town also known as Kirjath Jearim .... Josh. 15:9, 10 — 267
2. A hill in Judah .... Josh. 15:11 — 267
3. A town in South Judah .... Josh. 15:29 — 268
   Probably the same as Bilhah .... 1 Chr. 4:29 — 468
   May be the same as Balah .... Josh. 19:3 — 271

Baalath—*mistress*
- A village of Dan .. Josh. 19:44 — 272
- Fortified by Solomon .... 1 Kin. 9:18 — 406

Baalath Beer—*mistress of the well*
- A border town of Simeon .... Josh. 19:8 — 271
- Called Ramah of the South .... Josh. 19:8 — 271
- Also called Baal .. 1 Chr. 4:33 — 468

Baal-Berith—*lord of covenant*
- A god (Baal) of Shechem .... Judg. 8:33 — 294; Judg. 9:4 — 294
- Also called Berith .... Judg. 9:46 — 296

Baale—*Judah*
- A town of Judah .... 2 Sam. 6:2 — 364
- Also called Baalah and Kirjath Jearim .... Josh. 15:9, 10 — 267

Baal Gad—*lord of good fortune*
- A place in the valley of Lebanon .... Josh. 11:17 — 264

Baal Hamon—*lord of a multitude*
- Site of Solomon's vineyard .... Song 8:11 — 767

Baal-Hanan—*lord of grace*
1. Edomite king .... Gen. 36:38 — 48
2. David's gardener .... 1 Chr. 27:28 — 494

Baal Hazor—*lord of a village*
- A place near Ephraim .... 2 Sam. 13:23 — 372

Baal Hermon—*lord of Hermon*
- A mountain east of Jordan .... Judg. 3:3 — 287

Baals—*lords* (plural of Baal)
- Deities of Canaanite polytheism .... Judg. 10:10-14 — 297
- Ensnared Israelites .... Judg. 2:11-14 — 285; Judg. 3:7 — 287
- Rejected in Samuel's time .... 1 Sam. 7:4 — 328
- Historic reminder .... 1 Sam. 12:10 — 333
- Ahaz makes images to .... 2 Chr. 28:1-4 — 526

Baalis
- An Ammonite king .... Jer. 40:14 — 888

Baal Meon—*lord of Meon* (habitation)
- An Amorite city on the Moabite boundary .... Ezek. 25:9 — 947
- Rebuilt by Reubenites .... Num. 32:38 — 199; Josh. 13:15, 17 — 266

Baal Peor, Baal of Peor—*lord of Peor*
- A Moabite god .... Num. 25:1-5 — 190
- Infected Israel; 24,000 died .... Num. 25:1-9 — 190
- Vengeance taken on .... Num. 31:1-18 — 197
- Sin long remembered .... Deut. 4:3, 4 — 211; Josh. 22:17 — 276; Ps. 106:28, 29 — 686
- Historic reminder .... 1 Cor. 10:1-8 — 1353

Baal Perazim—*lord of breaking through*
- Where David defeated the Philistines .... 2 Sam. 5:18-20 — 364
- Same as Perazim .... Is. 28:21 — 798

Baal Shalisha—*lord of Shalisha*
- A place from which Elisha received food .... 2 Kin. 4:42-44 — 433

Baal Tamar—*lord of the palm*
- A place in Benjamin .... Judg. 20:33 — 308

Baal-Zebub—*lord of flies*
- A Philistine god at Ekron .... 2 Kin. 1:2 — 429
- Ahaziah inquired of .... 2 Kin. 1:2, 6, 16 — 429
- Also called Beelzebub .... Matt. 10:25 — 1129; Matt. 12:24 — 1131

Baal Zephon—*lord of darkness*
- Israelite camp site .... Ex. 14:2, 9 — 83; Num. 33:7 — 199

Baana—*affliction*
1. Supply officer .... 1 Kin. 4:12 — 397
2. Zadok's father .... Neh. 3:4 — 559

Baanah—*affliction*
1. A murderer of Ishbosheth ... 2 Sam. 4:1-12 — 363
2. Heled's father .... 1 Chr. 11:30 — 478
3. A returning exile .... Ezra 2:2 — 542; Neh. 7:7 — 563
   Signs document .... Neh. 10:27 — 569
4. Supply officer .... 1 Kin. 4:16 — 397

Baara—*foolish*
- Shaharaim's wife .... 1 Chr. 8:8 — 473

Baaseiah—*work of Yahweh*
- A Levite ancestor of Asaph .... 1 Chr. 6:40 — 470

Baasha—*boldness*
- Gains throne by murder .... 1 Kin. 15:27, 28 — 413
- Kills Jeroboam's household .... 1 Kin. 15:29, 30 — 413
- Wars against Asa .... 1 Kin. 15:16, 32 — 412
- Restricts access to Judah .... 1 Kin. 15:17 — 412
- Contravened by Asa's league with Ben-Hadad .... 1 Kin. 15:18-22 — 413
- Evil reign .... 1 Kin. 15:33, 34 — 413

Babbler—*an inane talker*
- The mumblings of drunkards .... Prov. 23:29-35 — 736
- Like a serpent .... Eccl. 10:11 — 758
- Paul called such .. Acts 17:18 — 1297
- Paul's warnings against .... 1 Tim. 6:20 — 1430; 2 Tim. 2:16 — 1434

Babe, Baby—*an infant child*

A. *Natural:*
- Moses .... Ex. 2:6 — 69
- John Baptist ... Luke 1:41, 44 — 1192
- Christ .... Luke 2:12, 16 — 1193
- Offspring .... Ps. 17:14 — 634

B. *Figurative of:*
- Unenlightened . Rom. 2:20 — 1325
- True believers .... Matt. 11:25 — 1130; Matt. 21:16 — 1141
- New Christians ... 1 Pet. 2:2 — 1479
- Carnal Christians .... 1 Cor. 3:1 — 1346; Heb. 5:13 — 1453

SUBJECT REFERENCE PAGE

Babel—*confusion*

A city built by Nimrod in the plain of Shinar ....Gen. 10:8-10 16

Babel, Tower of

A huge brick structure intended to magnify man and preserve the unity of the race ....Gen. 11:1-4 16
Objectives thwarted by God ....Gen. 11:5-9 16

Babylon, city of

A. *History of:*
Built by Nimrod ......Gen. 10:8-10 16
Tower built there ....Gen. 11:1-9 16
Amraphel's capital ....Gen. 14:1 21
Occupied by Assyrians in Manasseh's time ....2 Chr. 33:11 533
Greatest power under Nebuchadnezzar ....Dan. 4:30 981
A magnificent city .....Is. 13:19 786; Is. 14:4 786
Wide walls of............Jer. 51:44 903
Gates of.......Is. 45:1, 2 817
Bel, god of ....Is. 46:1 818
Jews carried captive to ...2 Kin. 25:1-21 459; 2 Chr. 36:5-21 538

B. *Inhabitants, described as:*
Enslaved by magic........Is. 47:1, 9-13 819
Idolatrous ...Jer. 50:35, 38 901; Dan. 3:18 979
Sacrilegious ...Dan. 5:1-3 983

C. *Prophecies concerning:*
Babylon, God's agent .Jer. 25:9 871; Jer. 27:5-8 873
God fights with ....Jer. 21:1-7 867
Jews, 70 years in .....Jer. 25:12 871; Jer. 29:10 875
First of great empires .....Dan. 2:31-38 978; Dan. 7:2-4 985
Cyrus, God's agent ....Is. 45:1-4 817
Perpetual desolation of..........Is. 13:19-22 786; Jer. 50:13, 39 900
Downfall of..........Is. 13:1-22 785; Jer. 50:1-46 899

Babylon in the New Testament

A. *The city on the Euphrates*
Listed as a point of reference ...Matt. 1:11, 12, 17 1115
As the place of Israel's exile ....Acts 7:43 1281
As the place of Peter's residence ....1 Pet. 5:13 1483

B. *The prophetic city*
Fall predicted .....Rev. 14:8 1531
Wrath taken on ....Rev. 16:19 1533
Called "the Mother of Harlots" .....Rev. 17:1-18 1533
Fall described ....Rev. 18:1-24 1535

Babylonians—*sons of Babel*

Inhabitants of Babylonia ......Ezek. 23:15-23 942

Babylonian garment—*a valuable robe worn in Babylon*

Coveted by Achan ....Josh. 7:21 259

Baca—*weeping*

Figurative of sorrow ....Ps. 84:6 674

Bachelor—*unmarried man*

Described literally ....1 Cor. 7:26-33 1352
Described figuratively .....Is. 56:3-5 828; Matt. 19:12 1139; Rev. 14:1-5 1531
Not for elders ....Titus 1:5, 6 1440

Bachrites

Family of Becher ....Num. 26:35 191

Backbiting—*reviling another in secret; slander*

A fruit of sin .....Rom. 1:28-30 1324
Expressed by the mouth ....Ps. 50:20 653
An offspring of anger ....Prov. 25:23 738
Merits punishment ......Ps. 101:5 682
Keeps from God ..Ps. 15:1, 3 632
To be laid aside ...1 Pet. 2:1 1479
Unworthy of Christians ....2 Cor. 12:20 1374

Backsliding—*to turn away from God after conversion*

A. *Described as:*
Turning from God ....1 Kin. 11:9 407
Turning to evil ....Ps. 125:5 700
Turning to Satan ....1 Tim. 5:15 1429
Turning back to the world ....2 Tim. 4:10 1436
Tempting Christ ....1 Cor. 10:9 1353
Turning from first love ....Rev. 2:4 1519
Turning from the Gospel ......Gal. 1:6, 7 1378; Gal. 3:1-5 1380

B. *Prompted by:*
Haughty spirit.........Prov. 16:18 728
Spiritual blindness ...2 Pet. 1:9 1487; Rev. 3:17 1523
Murmuring ....Ex. 17:3 87
Lusting after evil ....Ps. 106:14 686
Material things ....Mark 4:18, 19 1164; 1 Tim. 6:10 1430
Prosperity .....Deut. 8:11-14 218
Tribulation ....Matt. 13:20, 21 1132

C. *Results:*
Displeases God ....Ps. 78:56-59 671
Punishment ....Num. 14:43-45 178; Jer. 8:5-13 854
Blessings withheld .....Is. 59:2 830
Unworthiness ....Luke 9:62 1208

D. *Examples of Israel's:*
At Meribah ....Ex. 17:1-7 87
At Sinai ....Ex. 32:1-35 105
In wilderness ...Ps. 106:14-33 686
After Joshua's death .....Judg. 2:8-23 285; Ps. 106:34-43 686
In Solomon's life ....1 Kin. 11:4-40 407; Neh. 13:26 573
During Asa's reign.........2 Chr. 15:1-4 516
During Manasseh's reign.........2 Chr. 33:1-10 533

E. *Examples of, among believers:*
Lot ....Gen. 19:1-22 26
David ....2 Sam. 11:1-5 369; Ps. 51:1-19 653
Peter ....Matt. 26:69-75 1151; Luke 22:31, 32 1226
Galatians ....Gal. 1:6 1378; Gal. 4:9-11 1381
Corinthians ...1 Cor. 5:1-13 1348
Churches of Asia ....2 Tim. 1:15 1433; Rev. 2; 3 1517

See Apostasy

Badger

1. *Probably a specie of dolphin or porpoise*
Skins of, used in tabernacle coverings....Ex. 26:14 98; Ex. 35:7 108
Used for sandals ....Ezek. 16:10 931
2. *The Syrian rock hyrax*
Called "rock hyrax" ......Lev. 11:5 130; Deut. 14:7 225
Lives among rocks ....Ps. 104:18 684
Likened to people ....Prov. 30:26 744

Bag—*a purse or pouch*

A. *Used for:*
Money ....2 Kin. 12:10 443
Stones ......1 Sam. 17:40, 49 343
Food ("vessels") ...1 Sam. 9:7 331
Weights .....Deut. 25:13 236; Prov. 16:11 728

B. *Figurative of:*
Forgiveness ...Job 14:17 599
True righteousness ....Prov. 16:11 728
True riches ....Luke 12:33 1214
Insecure riches ....Hag. 1:6 1064

Bahurim—*young men*

A village near Jerusalem ....2 Sam. 3:16 362
Where Shimei cursed David ....2 Sam. 16:5 375
Where two men hid in a well ....2 Sam. 17:17, 18 377

Bakbakkar—*investigator*

A Levite ....1 Chr. 9:15 474

Bakbuk—*a flask*

Head of post-exilic family ....Ezra 2:51 544; Neh. 7:53 564

Bakbukiah—*Yahweh has poured out*

1. A Levite of high position ......Neh. 11:17 570
2. Levite porter ..Neh. 12:25 571

Baker—*one who cooks food* (bread)

A. *Kinds of:*
Household ....Gen. 18:6 24
Public.........Jer. 37:21 885
Royal ....Gen. 40:1, 2 51

B. *Features of:*
Usually a woman's job ....Lev. 26:26 153
Considered menial ....1 Sam. 8:13 330

Balaam—*destroyer of the people*

A. *Information concerning:*
A son of Beor ....Num. 22:5 186

SUBJECT REFERENCE PAGE

Baruch—continued
The Jewish remnant takes him to Egypt ..... Jer. 43:1-7 890
2. Son of Zabbai .... Neh. 3:20 560
Signs document .... Neh. 10:6 569
3. A Shilonite of Judah .... Neh. 11:5 570

Barzillai—*of iron*
1. Helps David with food .... {2 Sam. 17:27-29 377
Age restrains him from following David ...... {2 Sam. 19:31-39 380
2. Father of Adriel .... 2 Sam. 21:8 381
3. A postexilic priest .... Ezra 2:61 544

Basemath—*fragrance*
1. Wife of Esau .. Gen. 26:34 36
Called Adah ... Gen. 36:2, 3 46
2. Wife of Esau .... {Gen. 36:3, 4, 13 46
Called Mahalath .... Gen. 28:9 38
3. A daughter of Solomon ..... 1 Kin. 4:15 397

Bashan—*smooth soil*
A vast highland east of the Sea of Chinnereth (Galilee) .... Num. 21:33-35 186
Ruled by Og ...... Deut. 29:7 240
Conquered by Israel .... Neh. 9:22 568
Assigned to Manasseh .... Deut. 3:13 211
Smitten by Hazael .... {2 Kin. 10:32, 33 442
Fine cattle .... Ezek. 39:18 963
Typical of cruelty .... {Ps. 22:12 637 / Amos 4:1 1017

Bashan Havoth Jair
A district named after Jair .... Deut. 3:14 211

Basin—*cup or bowl for containing liquids*
Moses used .... Ex. 24:6 95
Made for the altar .... {Ex. 38:3 111 / Ex. 27:3 98
Brought for David .... {2 Sam. 17:28, 29 377
Hiram made ...... 1 Kin. 7:40 401

Baskets—*something made to hold objects*
A. *Used for carrying:*
Produce .... Deut. 26:2 236
Food .... Matt. 14:20 1134
Ceremonial offerings ..... Ex. 29:3, 23 102
Paul .... Acts 9:24, 25 1286
Other objects (heads) .... 2 Kin. 10:7 440
B. *Symbolic of:*
Approaching death .... Gen. 40:16-19 52
Israel's judgment ..... Amos 8:1-3 1022
Judah's judgment ..... Jer. 24:1-10 870
Hiding good works .... Matt. 5:15 1120

Bastard—*an illegitimate child*
A. *Penalty attached to* .... Deut. 23:2 233
B. *Examples of:*
Moab and Ammon ...... Gen. 19:36-38 28
Sons of Tamar by Judah .... Gen. 38:12-30 50
Jephthah ...... Judg. 11:1 297
C. *Figurative of:*
A mixed race .... Zech. 9:6 1073
The unregenerate state .... Heb. 12:8 1462

Bat—*a flying mammal*
Listed among unclean birds ... {Lev. 11:19 132 / Deut. 14:18 225
Lives in dark places .... Is. 2:19-21 773

Bath—*a liquid measure* (about 6 gallons)
A tenth of a homer .... {Ezek. 45:10, 11 969
For measuring oil and wine .... {2 Chr. 2:10 501 / Is. 5:10 775

Bathing
A. *For pleasure:*
Pharaoh's daughter ..... Ex. 2:5 69
Bathsheba .... 2 Sam. 11:2, 3 369
B. *For purification:*
Cleansing the feet ...... {Gen. 24:32 32 / John 13:10 1257
Ceremonial cleansing .... {Lev. 14:8 136 / 2 Kin. 5:10-14 434
Jewish rituals .... Mark 7:2 1167
Before performing priestly duties .... {Ex. 30:19-21 104 / Lev. 16:4, 24 139

Bath Rabbim—*daughter of multitudes*
Gate of Heshbon .... Song 7:4 766

Bathsheba—*daughter of an oath*
Wife of Uriah ..... 2 Sam. 11:2, 3 369
Commits adultery with David .... 2 Sam. 11:4, 5 369
Husband's death contrived by David .... 2 Sam. 11:6-25 369
Mourns husband's death .... 2 Sam. 11:26 370
Becomes David's wife .... 2 Sam. 11:27 370
Her first child dies .... {2 Sam. 12:14-19 371
Solomon's mother .... 2 Sam. 12:24 371
Secures throne for Solomon .... 1 Kin. 1:15-31 391
Deceived by Adonijah .... 1 Kin. 2:13-25 393

Bathshua—*daughter of prosperity*
Same as Bathsheba .... 1 Chr. 3:5 467

Batten—*a wooden or metal peg*
Used in a weaver's loom .... {Judg. 16:13, 14 303
See Nail

Battering ram (see Armor)
Used in destroying walls .... {Ezek. 4:2 921 / Ezek. 21:22 940

Battle (see War)

Battle-ax—*an instrument of war*
Applied to Israel .... Jer. 51:19, 20 902

Bavai—*wisher*
Postexilic worker .... Neh. 3:18 560

Bay—*inlet*
Dead Sea's cove at Jordan's mouth .... Josh. 15:5 267

Bazluth—*stripping*
Head of a family .... Ezra 2:52 544
Called Bazlith in .... Neh. 7:54 564

Bdellium—*an oily gum, or a white pearl*
A valuable mineral of Havilah .... Gen. 2:12 7
Manna colored like .... Num. 11:7 173

Beach—*coast; shore*
Place of:
Jesus' preaching .. Matt. 13:2 1132
Fisherman's task .... Matt. 13:48 1133
Jesus' meal with disciples .... John 21:8, 9 1267
A prayer meeting .... Acts 21:5 1303
A notable shipwreck .... Acts 27:39-44 1314
A miracle .... Acts 28:1-6 1315

Bealiah—*Yahweh is Lord*
A warrior .... 1 Chr. 12:5 479

Bealoth—*mistresses*
Village of Judah .. Josh. 15:24 268

Beam
A. *Physical:*
Wood undergirding floors .... 1 Kin. 7:2 400
Part of weaver's frame .... 1 Sam. 17:7 342
B. *Figurative of:*
The cry for vengeance .... Hab. 2:11 1053
God's power ... Ps. 104:3 683

Bean—*a food*
Brought to David by friends ...... {2 Sam. 17:27, 28 377
Mixed with grain for bread .... Ezek. 4:9 921

Bear—*a wild animal*
A. *Natural:*
Killed by David .... {1 Sam. 17:34, 35 342
Two tore up forty-two lads .... 2 Kin. 2:23, 24 431
B. *Figurative of:*
Fierce revenge ...... 2 Sam. 17:8 376
Fool's folly .... Prov. 17:12 729
Wicked rulers .... Prov. 28:15 742
World empire .... Dan. 7:5 985
Final antichrist .... Rev. 13:2 1529
Messianic times .... Is. 11:7 784
A constellation .... Job 9:9 595

Bear—*to carry, yield*
A. *Used literally of:*
Giving birth ... Gen. 17:19 24

SUBJECT	REFERENCE	PAGE
Carrying a load	Josh. 3:13 / Jer. 17:21	254 / 864
Cross	Matt. 27:32	1154
B. *Used figuratively of:*		
Excessive punishment	Gen. 4:13	10
Divine deliverance	Ex. 19:4	89
Responsibility for sin	Lev. 5:17 / Lev. 24:15	124 / 149
Burden of leadership	Deut. 1:9, 12	208
Personal shame	Ezek. 16:54	932
Evangelism	Acts 9:15	1286
Spiritual help	Gal. 6:1, 2	1383
Spiritual productivity	John 15:2, 4, 8	1258

Beard—*hair grown on the face*

SUBJECT	REFERENCE	PAGE
A. *Long, worn by:*		
Aaron	Ps. 133:2	702
David	1 Sam. 21:12, 13	347
B. *In mourning:*		
Plucked	Ezra 9:3	551
Clipped	Jer. 48:37, 38	897
C. *Features regarding:*		
Leper's must be shaven	Lev. 13:29-33	135
Half-shaven, an indignity	2 Sam. 10:4, 5	369
Marring of, forbidden	Lev. 19:27	142
Shaven, by Egyptians	Gen. 41:14	52
Spittle on, sign of lunacy	1 Sam. 21:12, 13	347
Holding to, a token of respect	2 Sam. 20:9	380

Beasts—*four-footed animals; mammals*

SUBJECT	REFERENCE	PAGE
A. *Characteristics of:*		
God-created	Gen. 1:21	4
Of their own order	1 Cor. 15:39	1360
Named by Adam	Gen. 2:20	8
Suffer in man's sin	Rom. 8:20-22	1333
Perish at death	Ps. 49:12-15	652
Follow instincts	Is. 1:3 / Jude 10	771 / 1510
Under God's control	1 Sam. 6:7-14	327
Wild	Mark 1:13	1159
For man's food	Gen. 9:3 / Acts 10:12, 13	14 / 1287
Used in sacrifices	Lev. 27:26-29	154
Spiritual lessons from	1 Kin. 4:30-33 / Job 12:7	397 / 597
Eat people	1 Sam. 17:46 / 1 Cor. 15:32	343 / 1360
B. *Treatment of:*		
No sexual relation with	Lev. 20:15, 16	143
Proper care of, sign of a righteous man	Gen. 33:13, 14 / Prov. 12:10	44 / 724
Abuse of, rebuked	Num. 22:28-32	187
Extra food for, while working	Deut. 25:4 / 1 Tim. 5:18	236 / 1429
C. *Typical of:*		
Man's folly	Ps. 73:22	667
Unregenerate men	Titus 1:12	1440

SUBJECT	REFERENCE	PAGE
False prophets	2 Pet. 2:12	1489
Antichrist	Rev. 13:1-4	1529
See Animals		

Beaten silver—*silver shaped by hammering*

SUBJECT	REFERENCE	PAGE
Overlaid idols	Is. 30:22 / Hab. 2:19	802 / 1054
In trade	Jer. 10:9	856

Beatings—*striking the body with blows; floggings*

SUBJECT	REFERENCE	PAGE
A. *Inflicted on:*		
The wicked	Deut. 25:3	235
The guilty	Lev. 19:20	142
Children	Prov. 22:15	735
The disobedient	Prov. 26:3 / Luke 12:47, 48	739 / 1215
B. *Victims of unjust beatings:*		
A servant	Luke 20:10, 11	1223
Christ	Is. 50:6 / Mark 15:19	823 / 1184
The apostles	Acts 5:40	1278
Paul	Acts 16:18-24	1295

Beatitudes—*pronouncements of blessings*

SUBJECT	REFERENCE	PAGE
Jesus begins His sermon with	Matt. 5:3-12 / Luke 6:20-22	1120 / 1202

Beautiful gate—*gate at east of Temple area*

SUBJECT	REFERENCE	PAGE
Lame man healed there	Acts 3:1-10	1274

Beauty, physical

SUBJECT	REFERENCE	PAGE
A. *Temporal:*		
Seen in nature	Hos. 14:6 / Matt. 6:28, 29	1005 / 1123
Consumed in dissipation	Is. 28:1	796
Contest Abishag, winner of	1 Kin. 1:1-4	391
Esther, winner of	Esth. 2:1-17	577
Destroyed by sin	Ps. 39:11	647
Ends in grave	Ps. 49:14	653
B. *In Women:*		
Vain	Prov. 31:30	745
Without discretion	Prov. 11:22	723
Enticements of	Prov. 6:25	719
Source of temptation	Gen. 6:2 / 2 Sam. 11:2-5	11 / 369
Leads to marriage	Deut. 21:10-13	231
A bride's	Ps. 45:11	651
Sarah's	Gen. 12:11	20
Rebekah's	Gen. 24:15, 16	32
Rachel's	Gen. 29:17	40
Daughters of Job	Job 42:15	620
Abigail's	1 Sam. 25:3	350
Bathsheba's	2 Sam. 11:2, 3	369
Tamar's	2 Sam. 13:1	371
Abishag's	1 Kin. 1:3, 4	391
Vashti's	Esth. 1:11	577
Esther's	Esth. 2:7	578
C. *In Men:*		
Of man	Is. 44:13	816
Of the aged	Prov. 20:29	733
Joseph's	Gen. 39:6	51
David's	1 Sam. 16:12, 13	340
Absalom's	2 Sam. 14:25	374

Beauty, spiritual

SUBJECT	REFERENCE	PAGE
The Messiah	Ps. 110:3 / Is. 52:7	689 / 824
The true Israel	Ps. 45:8-11 / Song 1:8	651 / 763
The meek	Ps. 149:4	709
Spiritual worship	2 Chr. 20:21	520
Christian ministers	Rom. 10:15	1335
Holy garments	Is. 52:1	824
Christ's rejection by Israel	Zech. 11:7-14	1075

Bebai—*fatherly*

SUBJECT	REFERENCE	PAGE
1. Family head	Ezra 2:11	542
2. One who signs document	Neh. 10:15	569

Becher—*young camel*

SUBJECT	REFERENCE	PAGE
1. Benjamin's son	Gen. 46:21	59
2. Son of Ephraim	Num. 26:35	191
Called Bered	1 Chr. 7:20	472

Bechorath—*the first birth*

SUBJECT	REFERENCE	PAGE
Ancestor of Saul	1 Sam. 9:1	330

Bed

SUBJECT	REFERENCE	PAGE
A. *Made of:*		
The ground	Gen. 28:11	38
Iron, 13½ feet long	Deut. 3:11	211
Ivory	Amos 6:4	1020
Gold and silver	Esth. 1:6	577
B. *Used for:*		
Sleep	Luke 11:7	1211
Rest	2 Sam. 4:5-7	363
Sickness	Gen. 49:33	63
Meals	Amos 6:4	1020
Prostitution	Prov. 7:16, 17	720
Evil	Ps. 36:4	645
Marriage	Song 3:1 / Heb. 13:4	764 / 1463
Singing	Ps. 149:5	709
C. *Figurative of:*		
The grave	Job 17:13-16	601
Divine support	Ps. 41:3	649
Worldly security	Is. 57:7	829

Bed—*a garden plot*

SUBJECT	REFERENCE	PAGE
Used literally	Song 6:2	766
Used figuratively	Song 5:13	765

Bedad—*separation*

SUBJECT	REFERENCE	PAGE
Father of Hadad	Gen. 36:35	48

Bedan—*son of judgment*

SUBJECT	REFERENCE	PAGE
1. Judge of Israel	1 Sam. 12:11	333
2. Descendant of Manasseh	1 Chr. 7:17	472

Bedeiah—*servant of Yahweh*

SUBJECT	REFERENCE	PAGE
Son of Bani	Ezra 10:34, 35	553

Bedfellows

SUBJECT	REFERENCE	PAGE
Provide mutual warmth	Eccl. 4:11	753

Bedroom

SUBJECT	REFERENCE	PAGE
A place of sleep	2 Sam. 4:7	363
Elisha's special	2 Kin. 4:8, 10	432
Secrets of	2 Kin. 6:12	436
Joash hidden in	2 Kin. 11:2	442

SUBJECT REFERENCE PAGE

Seeks Daniel's aid ....Dan. 5:13-16 983
Daniel interprets for him ....Dan. 5:17-29 983
Last Chaldean king ....Dan. 5:30, 31 984

Belteshazzar—*Bel protect his life*

Daniel's Babylonian name ....Dan. 1:7 976

Ben—*son*

Levite porter ....1 Chr. 15:18 481

Benaiah—*Yahweh has built*

1. Jehoiada's son ....2 Sam. 23:20 385
A mighty man ....2 Sam. 23:20, 21 385
David's bodyguard ....2 Sam. 8:18 367
Faithful to David ....2 Sam. 15:18 375; 2 Sam. 20:23 381
Escorts Solomon to the throne ....1 Kin. 1:38-40 392
Executes Adonijah, Joab and Shimei ....1 Kin. 2:25, 29-34 394; 1 Kin. 2:46 394
Commander-in-chief ....1 Kin. 2:28-35 394
2. One of David's mighty men ....2 Sam. 23:30 385
Divisional commander ....1 Chr. 27:14 493
3. Levite musician ....1 Chr. 15:18-20 481
4. Priestly trumpeter ....1 Chr. 15:24 482; 1 Chr. 16:6 482
5. Levite of Asaph's family ....2 Chr. 20:14 520
6. Simeonite ....1 Chr. 4:36 468
7. Levite overseer ....2 Chr. 31:13 530
8. Father of leader Pelatiah ....Ezek. 11:1, 13 927
9-12. Four postexilic Jews who divorced their foreign wives ....Ezra 10:25-43 553

Ben-Ammi—*son of my kinsman*

Son of Lot; father of the Ammonites ....Gen. 19:38 28

Bene Berak—*sons of berak* (lightning)

A town of Dan ....Josh. 19:45 272

Ben-Deker—*piercing; mattock*

One of Solomon's officers ....1 Kin. 4:9 397

Benediction—*an act of blessing*

A. *Characteristics of:*
Instituted by God ....Gen. 1:22, 28 4
Divinely approved ....Deut. 10:8 221
Aaronic form ....Num. 6:23-26 168
Apostolic form ....2 Cor. 13:14 1375
Jesus' last words ....Luke 24:50, 51 1231

B. *Pronounced upon:*
Creation ....Gen. 1:22, 28 4
New world ....Gen. 9:1, 2 14
Abraham ....Gen. 14:19, 20 21
Marriage ....Gen. 24:60 33
Son (Jacob) ....Gen. 27:27-29 37
Monarch (Pharaoh) ....Gen. 47:7, 10 59
Sons (Joseph's) ....Gen. 48:15, 16, 20 61
Tribes (Israel's) ....Deut. 33:1-29 246
Foreigner ....Ruth 1:8, 9 313
People ....2 Sam. 6:18 365
Jesus ....Luke 2:34 1194
Song of Zacharias ....Luke 1:68-79 1192
Children's blessing ....Mark 10:16 1173

Benefactor—*one who bestows benefits*

A. *Materially, God as:*
Israel's ....Deut. 7:6-26 217
Unbeliever's ....Acts 14:15-18 1293
Christian's ....Phil. 4:19 1402

B. *Spiritually:*
By God ....Eph. 1:3-6 1387
Through Christ ....Eph. 2:13-22 1388
For enrichment ....Eph. 1:16-19 1387

C. *Attitudes toward:*
Murmuring ....Num. 11:1-10 173
Forgetfulness ....Ps. 106:7-14 686
Rejection ....Acts 13:44-47 1292
Remembrance ....Luke 7:1-5 1203
Gratefulness ....Acts 13:48 1292

Benefice—*an enriching act or gift*

Manifested by a church ....Phil. 4:15-17 1402
Encouraged in a friend ....Philem. 17-22 1445
Justified in works ....James 2:14-17 1469
Remembered in heaven ....1 Tim. 6:17-19 1430

Bene Jaakan—*sons of Jaakan*

A wilderness station ....Num. 33:31 200

Benevolence—*generosity toward others*

A. *Exercised toward:*
The poor ....Gal. 2:10 1380
The needy ....Eph. 4:28 1391
Enemies ....Prov. 25:21 738
God's servant ....Phil. 4:14-17 1402

B. *Measured by:*
Ability ....Acts 11:29 1289
Love ....1 Cor. 13:3 1356
Sacrifice ....Mark 12:41-44 1179
Bountifulness ....2 Cor. 9:6-15 1372

C. *Blessings of:*
Fulfills a grace ....Rom. 12:6, 13 1337
Performs a spiritual sacrifice ....Heb. 13:16 1464
Makes us "more blessed" ....Acts 20:35 1303
Enriches the giver ....Prov. 11:25 724; Is. 58:10, 11 830
Reward ....1 Tim. 6:17-19 1430

Ben-Hadad—*son of the god Hadad*

1. Ben-Hadad I, king of Damascus. Hired by Asa, king of Judah, to attack Baasha, king of Israel ....1 Kin. 15:18-21 413
2. Ben-Hadad II, king of Damascus. Makes war on Ahab, king of Israel ....1 Kin. 20:1-21 420
Defeated by Israel ....1 Kin. 20:26-34 421
Fails in siege against Samaria ....2 Kin. 6:24-33 436; 2 Kin. 7:6-20 437
Killed by Hazael ....2 Kin. 8:7-15 438
3. Ben-Hadad III, king of Damascus. Loses all Israelite conquests made by Hazael, his father ....2 Kin. 13:3-25 444

Ben-Hail—*son of strength*

A teacher ....2 Chr. 17:7 517

Ben-Hanan—*son of the gracious one*

A son of Shimon ....1 Chr. 4:20 467

Beninu—*our son*

A Levite document signer ....Neh. 10:13 569

Benjamin—*son of the right hand*

Jacob's youngest son ....Gen. 35:16-20 46
Jacob's favorite son ....Gen. 42:4 54; Gen. 43:1-14 56
Loved by Joseph ....Gen. 43:29-34 56
Judah intercedes for ....Gen. 44:18-34 57
Joseph's gifts to ....Gen. 45:22 58
Father of five sons ....1 Chr. 8:1, 2 473
Head of a tribe ....Num. 26:38-41 191
Jacob's prophecy concerning ....Gen. 49:27 63

Benjamin (others bearing this name)

1. A son of Bilhan ....1 Chr. 7:10 472
2. Son of Harim ....Ezra 10:18, 31, 32 553
Same as in ....Neh. 3:23 560

Benjamin, tribe of

A. *Background features of:*
Descendants of Jacob's youngest son ....Gen. 35:17, 18, 24 46
Family divisions of ....Num. 26:38-41 191
Strength of ....Num. 1:36, 37 160
Bounds of ....Josh. 18:11-28 271
Prophecies respecting ....Gen. 49:27 63; Deut. 33:12 246

B. *Memorable events of:*
Almost destroyed for protecting men of Gibeah ....Judg. 20:12-48 308
Wives provided for, to preserve the tribe ....Judg. 21:1-23 309
Furnished Israel her first king ....1 Sam. 9:1-17 330
Hailed David's return ....2 Sam. 19:16, 17 379

C. *Celebrities belonging to:*
Ehud, a judge ....Judg. 3:15 287
Saul, Israel's first king ....1 Sam. 9:1 330
Abner, David's general ....1 Sam. 17:55 343
Mordecai ....Esth. 2:5 578
The apostle Paul ....Phil. 3:5 1401

Beno—*his son*

A Merarite Levite ....1 Chr. 24:26, 27 491

Ben-Oni—*son of my sorrow*

Rachel's name for Benjamin ....Gen. 35:16-18 46

Ben-Zoheth—*son of Zoheth*

A man of Judah ....1 Chr. 4:20 467

TOPICAL INDEX

SUBJECT — REFERENCE — PAGE

Beon—*house of On*

A locality east of Jordan ... Num. 32:3 ... 198
Same as Baal Meon ... Num. 32:37, 38 ... 199

Beor—*a burning*

1. Father of Bela ... Gen. 36:32 ... 48
2. Father of Balaam ... Num. 22:5; 2 Pet. 2:15 ... 186, 1489

Bera—*excellent*

A king of Sodom ... Gen. 14:2 ... 21

Berachah—*blessing*

1. David's warrior ... 1 Chr. 12:3 ... 479
2. A valley in Judah near Tekoa ... 2 Chr. 20:26 ... 520

Berachiah—*blessed by Yahweh*

1. Asaph's father ... 1 Chr. 6:39 ... 470
2. Levite door-keepers ... 1 Chr. 15:23, 24 ... 482
3. Head man of Ephraim ... 2 Chr. 28:12 ... 527
4. Son of Zerubbabel ... 1 Chr. 3:20 ... 467
5. Levite ... 1 Chr. 9:16 ... 474
6. Postexilic workman ... Neh. 3:4, 30 ... 559
7. Father of Zechariah ... Zech. 1:1, 7; Matt. 23:35 ... 1068, 1147

Beraiah—*Yahweh has created*

A Benjamite chief ... 1 Chr. 8:21 ... 473

Berea—*watered*

A city of Macedonia visited by Paul ... Acts 17:10-15 ... 1297

Bereavement—*the emotional state after a loved one's death*

A. *General attitudes in:*
Horror ... Ex. 12:29, 30 ... 82
Great emotion ... 2 Sam. 18:33 ... 378
Complaint ... Ruth 1:20, 21 ... 313
Genuine sorrow ... Gen. 37:33-35 ... 49
Submission ... Job 1:18-21 ... 590

B. *Christian attitudes in:*
Unlike world's ... 1 Thess. 4:13-18 ... 1416
Yet sorrow allowed ... John 11:32-35; Acts 9:39 ... 1253, 1286
With hope of reunion ... John 11:20-27 ... 1253

C. *Unusual circumstances of, mourning:*
Forbidden ... Lev. 10:6 ... 130
Of great length ... Gen. 50:1-11 ... 63
Turned to joy ... John 11:41-44 ... 1255

Bered—*hail*

1. A place in the wilderness of Shur ... Gen. 16:7, 14 ... 23
2. An Ephraimite ... 1 Chr. 7:20 ... 472

Beri—*belonging to a well*

An Asherite ... 1 Chr. 7:36 ... 473

Beriah—*evil*

1. Son of Asher ... Gen. 46:17 ... 59
2. Ephraim's son ... 1 Chr. 7:22, 23 ... 472
3. Chief of Benjamin ... 1 Chr. 8:13, 16 ... 473
4. Levite ... 1 Chr. 23:10, 11 ... 490

Beriites

Descendants of Beriah ... Num. 26:44 ... 191

Berites

A people in north Palestine ... 2 Sam. 20:14, 15 ... 381

Berith—*covenant*

Shechem idol ... Judg. 9:46 ... 296
Same as Baal-Berith ... Judg. 8:33; Judg. 9:4 ... 294, 294

Bernice—*victorious*

Sister of Herod Agrippa II ... Acts 25:13, 23 ... 1310
Hears Paul's defense ... Acts 26:1-30 ... 1312

Berodach-Baladan

A king of Babylon ... 2 Kin. 20:12-19 ... 454
Also called Merodach-Baladan ... Is. 39:1 ... 810

Berothah, Berothai—*wells*

City of Syria taken by David ... 2 Sam. 8:8 ... 367
Boundary in the ideal kingdom ... Ezek. 47:16 ... 971

Beryl—*a precious stone*

In breastplate of high priest ... Ex. 28:15-21; Ex. 39:8-14 ... 99, 112
Ornament of a king ... Ezek. 28:12, 13 ... 951
Describes a lover ... Song 5:14 ... 765
Applied to an angel ... Dan. 10:5, 6 ... 989
Wheels like color of ... Ezek. 1:16 ... 919
In New Jerusalem ... Rev. 21:20 ... 1539

Besai

A family head ... Ezra 2:49 ... 544

Besodeiah—*in the counsel of Yahweh*

Father of Meshullam ... Neh. 3:6 ... 559

Besor—*cold*

A brook south of Ziklag ... 1 Sam. 30:9, 10, 21 ... 354

Bestial—*beast like*

Condemned ... Ex. 22:19 ... 93
Punishment of ... Lev. 20:13 ... 143

Best Seats—*seats or places of honor*

Sought by scribes and Pharisees ... Matt. 23:1, 6; Mark 12:38, 39 ... 1145, 1178
Not to be sought ... Luke 14:7-11 ... 1217

Betah—*trust, confidence*

Cities of Hadadezer ... 2 Sam. 8:8 ... 367
Called Tibhath ... 1 Chr. 18:8 ... 486

Beten—*valley*

City of Asher ... Josh. 19:25 ... 272

Beth—*house*

Second letter of the Hebrew alphabet ... Ps. 119:9-16 ... 694

Bethabara—*house of passage*

A place beyond Jordan where John baptized ... John 1:28 ... 1237

Beth Acacia

A town of Judah ... Judg. 7:22 ... 292

Beth Anath—*house of Anath* (the goddess)

A town of Naphtali ... Josh. 19:38, 39 ... 272
Canaanites remain in ... Judg. 1:33 ... 284

Beth Anoth—*house of Anoth* (the goddess)

A town of Judah ... Josh. 15:59 ... 268

Bethany—*house of poverty*

A town on Mt. of Olives ... Luke 19:29 ... 1222
Home of Lazarus ... John 11:1 ... 1253
Home of Simon, the leper ... Matt. 26:6 ... 1149
Jesus visits there ... Mark 11:1, 11, 12 ... 1174
Scene, Ascension ... Luke 24:50, 51 ... 1231

Beth Arabah—*house of desert*

A village of Judah ... Josh. 15:6, 61 ... 267
Assigned to Benjamin ... Josh. 18:21, 22 ... 271

Beth Arbel—*house of God's ambush*

A town destroyed by Shalman ... Hos. 10:14 ... 1003

Beth Aven—*house of nothingness* (vanity)

A town of Benjamin ... Josh. 7:2 ... 258
Israel defeated Philistines there ... 1 Sam. 13:5 ... 334

Beth Baal Meon

City of Reuben ... Josh. 13:17 ... 266

Beth Barah—*house of the ford*

A passage over Jordan ... Judg. 7:24 ... 292

Beth Biri—*house of my creation*

A town of Simeon ... 1 Chr. 4:31 ... 468
Probably same as Beth Lebaoth ... Josh. 19:6 ... 271

Beth Car—*house of a lamb*

Site of Philistines' retreat ... 1 Sam. 7:11 ... 328

SUBJECT	REFERENCE	PAGE
Asa	1 Kin. 15:9-24 2 Chr. 14:1–16:14	412 515
Baasha, Elah, Zimri and Omri	1 Kin. 15:32–16:27	413
J. *Mutual alliance:*		
Ahab and Elijah	1 Kin. 16:28–18:19	414
Contest on Mt. Carmel	1 Kin. 18:20-40	417
Ahab and Ben-Hadad	1 Kin. 20:1-34	420
Murder of Naboth	1 Kin. 21:1-29	421
Revival under Jehoshaphat	1 Kin. 22:41-50 2 Chr. 17:1-19	425 517
Battle of Ramoth Gilead	1 Kin. 22:1-40 2 Chr. 18:1-34	422 517
Wars of Jehoshaphat	2 Chr. 19:1–20:30	519
Translation of Elijah	2 Kin. 2:1-11	430
Jehoshaphat and Jehoram	2 Kin. 3:1-27	431
Ministry of Elisha	2 Kin. 4:1–6:23 2 Kin. 8:1-15	432 437
Siege of Samaria	2 Kin. 6:24–7:20	436
Death of Elisha	2 Kin. 13:14-20	444
K. *Decline of both kingdoms:*		
Accession of Jehu	2 Kin. 9:1–10:31	438
Athaliah and Joash	2 Kin. 11:1–12:21	442
Amaziah and Jeroboam	2 Kin. 14:1-29	445
Captivity of Israel	2 Kin. 15:29 2 Kin. 17:1-6	447 448
Reign of Hezekiah	2 Kin. 18:1–20:21 2 Chr. 29:1–32:33	450 527
Reign of Manasseh	2 Kin. 21:1-18 2 Chr. 33:1-20	454 533
Josiah's reforms	2 Kin. 22:1–23:30 2 Chr. 34:1–35:27	455 534
Captivity of Judah	2 Kin. 24:1–25:30 2 Chr. 36:5-21	458 538
L. *Captivity:*		
Daniel and Nebuchadnezzar	Dan. 1:1–4:37	976
Belshazzar and Darius	Dan. 5:1–6:28	983
Rebuilding the Temple	Ezra 1:1–6:15	542
Rebuilding Jerusalem	Neh. 1:1–6:19	558
Esther and Mordecai	Esth. 2:1–10:3	577
M. *Ministry of Christ:*		
Birth	Matt. 1:18-25 Luke 2:1-20	1116 1193
Childhood	Luke 2:40-52	1194
Baptism	Matt. 3:13-17 Luke 3:21, 22	1117 1195
Temptation	Matt. 4:1-11 Luke 4:1-13	1117 1198
First miracle	John 2:1-11	1237
With Nicodemus	John 3:1-21	1239
The Samaritan woman	John 4:5-42	1241
Healing	Luke 4:31-41	1200
Controversy on the Sabbath	Luke 6:1-11	1201
Apostles chosen	Mark 3:13-19 Luke 6:12-16	1163 1202
Sermon on the Mount	Matt. 5:1–7:29 Luke 6:20-49	1120 1202
Raises dead son	Luke 7:11-17	1203
Anointed	Luke 7:36-50	1204
Accused of blasphemy	Matt. 12:22-37 Mark 3:19-30	1131 1163
Calms the sea	Matt. 8:23-27 Mark 4:35-41	1126 1164
Demoniac healed	Matt. 8:28-34 Mark 5:1-20	1126 1164
Daughter of Jairus healed	Matt. 9:18-26 Luke 8:41-56	1127 1206
Feeds 5,000	Matt. 14:13-21 Mark 6:30-44	1134 1167
Feeds 4,000	Matt. 15:32-39	1136
Peter confesses Jesus is Christ	Matt. 16:5-16 Mark 8:27-29	1136 1170
Foretells death	Matt. 16:21-26 Luke 9:22-25	1137 1207
Transfiguration	Matt. 17:1-13 Luke 9:28-36	1137 1207
Forgiving of adulteress	John 7:53–8:11	1248
Resurrection of Lazarus	John 11:1-44	1253
Blesses the children	Matt. 19:13-15 Mark 10:13-16	1139 1172
Bartimaeus healed	Matt. 20:29-34 Mark 10:46-52	1141 1174
Meets Zacchaeus	Luke 19:1-10	1221
Triumphant entry	Matt. 21:1-9 Luke 19:29-44	1141 1222
Anointed	Matt. 26:6-13 Mark 14:3-9	1149 1180
The Passover	Matt. 26:17-19 Luke 22:7-13	1150 1225
The Lord's Supper	Matt. 26:26-29 Mark 14:22-25	1150 1181
Gethsemane	Luke 22:39-46	1226
Betrayal and arrest	Matt. 26:47-56 John 18:3-12	1151 1262
Before the Sanhedrin	Matt. 26:57-68 Luke 22:54-65	1151 1228
Denied by Peter	John 18:15-27	1262
Before Pilate	Matt. 27:2-14 Luke 23:1-7	1152 1228
Before Herod	Luke 23:6-12	1228
Returns to Pilate	Matt. 27:15-26 Luke 23:13-25	1152 1229
Crucifixion	Matt. 27:35-56 Luke 23:33-49	1154 1229
Burial	Matt. 27:57-66 Luke 23:50-56	1154 1230
Resurrection	Matt. 28:1-15 John 20:1-18	1155 1265
Appearance to disciples	Luke 24:36-43 John 20:19-25	1231 1265
Appearance to Thomas	John 20:26-31	1265
Great commission	Matt. 28:16-20	1155
Ascension	Luke 24:50-53	1231
N. *The early church:*		
Pentecost	Acts 2:1-42	1273
In Jerusalem	Acts 2:3–6:7	1273
Martyrdom of Stephen	Acts 6:8–7:60	1279
In Judea and Samaria	Acts 8:1–12:25	1282
Conversion of Saul	Acts 9:1-18	1284
First missionary journey	Acts 13:1–14:28	1289
Jerusalem conference	Acts 15:1-35	1293
Second missionary journey	Acts 15:36–18:22	1294
Third missionary journey	Acts 18:23–21:16	1300
Captivity of Paul	Acts 21:27–28:31	1305

Bichri—*firstborn*

Father of Sheba	2 Sam. 20:1	380

Bidkar—*servant of Kar*

Captain under Jehu	2 Kin. 9:25	439

Bigamist—*having more than one wife*

First, Lamech	Gen. 4:19	10

Bigamy (see Marriage)

Bigotry—*excessive prejudice; blind fanaticism*

A. *Characteristics of:*		
Name-calling	John 8:48, 49	1250
Spiritual blindness	John 9:39-41	1251
Hatred	Acts 7:54-58	1282
Self-righteousness	Phil. 3:4-6	1401
Ignorance	1 Tim. 1:13	1426
B. *Examples of:*		
Haman	Esth. 3:8-10	579
The Pharisees	John 8:33-48	1249
The Jews	1 Thess. 2:14-16	1415
Saul (Paul)	Acts 9:1, 2	1284
Peter	Acts 10:14, 28	1287

See Intolerance; Persecution

Bigtha—*gift of God*

An officer of Ahasuerus	Esth. 1:10	577

Bigthan, Bigthana—*gift of God*

Conspired against Ahasuerus	Esth. 2:21 Esth. 6:2	578 581

Bigvai—*happy*

1. Zerubbabel's companion	Ezra 2:2 Neh. 7:7, 19	542 563
2. One who signs covenant	Neh. 10:16	569

Bildad—*Bel has loved*

One of Job's friends	Job 2:11	590
Makes three speeches	Job 8:1-22 Job 18:1-21 Job 25:1-6	594 601 606

Bileam—*greed*

A town of Manasseh	1 Chr. 6:70	470

Bilgah—*brightness, cheerfulness*

1. A descendant of Aaron	1 Chr. 24:1, 6, 14	490
2. A chief of the priests	Neh. 12:5, 7, 18	571
Same as Bilgai; signs document	Neh. 10:8	569

Bilhah—*foolish, simple*

1. Rachel's maid	Gen. 29:29	40
The mother of Dan and Naphtali	Gen. 30:1-8	40
Commits incest with Reuben	Gen. 35:22	46
2. Simeonite town	1 Chr. 4:29	468
Same as Baalah	Josh. 15:29	268

SUBJECT REFERENCE PAGE

Bilhan—*foolish, simple*

1. A Horite chief; son of Ezer .... Gen. 36:27 48; 1 Chr. 1:42 465
2. A Benjamite family head .... 1 Chr. 7:10 472

Bilshan—*searcher*

A postexilic leader .... Ezra 2:2 542; Neh. 7:7 563

Bimhal—*with pruning*

An Asherite ...... 1 Chr. 7:33 473

Bin

For food storage .... 1 Kin. 17:12-16 416

Binding—*a restraint; a tying together*

A. *Used literally of:*
- Tying a man ... Gen. 22:9 30
- Imprisonment .... 2 Kin. 17:4 448; Acts 22:4 1306
- Ocean's shores ...... Prov. 30:4 743

B. *Used figuratively of:*
- A fixed agreement .... Num. 30:2 196
- God's Word ... Prov. 3:3 715
- The brokenhearted ...... Is. 61:1 833
- Satan .... Luke 13:16 1216
- The wicked .... Matt. 13:30 1133
- Ceremonialism .... Matt. 23:4 1145
- The keys ...... Matt. 16:19 1136
- A determined plan .... Acts 20:22 1303
- Marriage ...... Rom. 7:2 1331

Binea

A son of Moza .... 1 Chr. 8:37 473

Binnui—*built*

1. Head of postexilic family .... Neh. 7:15 563
   Called Bani .... Ezra 2:10 542
2. Son of Pahath-Moab .... Ezra 10:30 553
3. Son of Bani ... Ezra 10:38 554
4. Postexilic Levite .... Neh. 12:8 571
   Henadad's son .... Neh. 10:9 569
   Family of, builds wall .... Neh. 3:24 560

Bird cage

Used figuratively ...... Jer. 5:27 851

Birds—*vertebrates with feathers and wings*

A. *List of:*
- Buzzard .... Lev. 11:13 132
- Dove .... Gen. 8:8 12
- Eagle .... Job 39:27 617
- Falcon .... Deut. 14:13 225
- Hawk .... Job 39:26 617
- Hen .... Matt. 23:37 1147
- Heron .... Lev. 11:19 132
- Hoopoe .... Lev. 11:19 132
- Jackal .... Job 30:29 609
- Kite .... Deut. 14:13 225
- Ostrich .... Job 30:29 609
- Owls .... Lev. 11:16 132
  - Desert .... Ps. 102:6 682
  - Fisher .... Lev. 11:17 132
  - Screech ...... Lev. 11:17 132
  - Little .... Lev. 11:17 132
- Partridge ...... 1 Sam. 26:20 352
- Pelican .... Ps. 102:6 682
- Pigeon .... Lev. 12:6 133
- Quail .... Num. 11:31, 32 175
- Raven .... Job 38:41 616
- Rooster ..... Matt. 26:34, 74 1150; Mark 14:30 1181; Luke 22:61 1228; John 18:27 1263
- Sparrow ...... Matt. 10:29-31 1129
- Stork .... Ps. 104:17 684
- Swallow ...... Ps. 84:3 674
- Swift .... Jer. 8:7 854
- Turtledove .... Song 2:12 763
- Vulture .... Lev. 11:13 132

B. *Features regarding:*
- Created by God .... Gen. 1:20, 21 4
- Named by Adam .... Gen. 2:19, 20 7
- Clean, unclean ...... Gen. 8:20 14
- Differ from animals ...... 1 Cor. 15:39 1360
- Under man's dominion .... Ps. 8:6-8 630
- For food ...... Gen. 9:2, 3 14
- Belong to God .... Ps. 50:11 653
- God provides for .... Ps. 104:10-12 684; Luke 12:23, 24 1214
- Can be tamed .... James 3:7 1469
- Differ in singing .... Song 2:12 763
- Some migratory .... Jer. 8:7 854
- Solomon writes of .... 1 Kin. 4:33 397
- Clean, used in sacrifices .... Lev. 1:14 120; Luke 2:23, 24 1193
- Worshiped by man .... Rom. 1:23 1324

C. *Figurative of:*
- Escape from evil .... Ps. 124:7 700
- A wanderer ... Prov. 27:8 740
- Snares of death .... Eccl. 9:12 757
- Cruel kings .... Is. 46:11 819
- Hostile nations .... Jer. 12:9 859
- Wicked rich ... Jer. 17:11 863
- Kingdom of heaven .... Matt. 13:32 1133
- Maternal love .... Matt. 23:37 1147

Birsha—*with wickedness*

A king of Gomorrah ...... Gen. 14:2, 8, 10 21

Birth—*the act of coming into life*

A. *Kinds of:*
- Natural .... Eccl. 7:1 754
- Figurative ..... Is. 37:3 808
- Supernatural .... Matt. 1:18-25 1116
- The new ...... John 3:5 1239

See New birth

B. *Natural, features regarding:*
- Pain of, results from sin .... Gen. 3:16 9
- Produces a sinful being .... Ps. 51:5 654
- Makes ceremonially unclean ..... Lev. 12:2, 5 133; Luke 2:22 1193
- Affliction from .... John 9:1 1250
- Twins of, differ .... Gen. 25:21-23 34
- Sometimes brings death .... Gen. 35:16-20 46
- Pain of, forgotten .... John 16:21 1261

Birthday—*date of one's birth*

Job and Jeremiah curse theirs .... Job 3:1-11 591; Jer. 20:14, 15 866

Celebration:
- Pharaoh's .... Gen. 40:20 52
- Herod's .... Mark 6:21 1166

Birthright—*legal rights inherited by birth*

A. *Blessings of:*
- Seniority ...... Gen. 43:33 57
- Double portion .... Deut. 21:15-17 232
- Royal succession ... 2 Chr. 21:3 521

B. *Loss of:*
- Esau's—by sale .... Gen. 25:29-34 34; Heb. 12:16 1462
- Reuben's—as a punishment ..... Gen. 49:3, 4 61; 1 Chr. 5:1, 2 468
- Manasseh's—by Jacob's will .... Gen. 48:15-20 61; 1 Chr. 5:1, 2 468
- David's brother—by divine will .... 1 Sam. 16:2-22 340
- Adonijah's—by the Lord .... 1 Kin. 2:13, 15 393
- Hosah's son's—by his father's will .... 1 Chr. 26:10 492

C. *Transferred to:*
- Jacob .... Gen. 27:6-46 36
- Judah .... Gen. 49:8-10 61
- Solomon ...... 1 Chr. 28:5-7 494

See Firstborn

Births, foretold

A. *Over a short period:*
- Ishmael's ..... Gen. 16:11 23
- Isaac's .... Gen. 18:10 24
- Samson's ..... Judg. 13:3, 24 299
- Samuel's ..... 1 Sam. 1:11, 20 321
- Shunammite's son's .... 2 Kin. 4:16, 17 432
- John the Baptist's ..... Luke 1:13 1190

B. *Over a longer period:*
- Josiah's .... 1 Kin. 13:2 410
- Cyrus' .... Is. 45:1-4 817
- Christ's ...... Gen. 3:15 9; Mic. 5:1-3 1039

Birzaith—*olive well*

An Asherite ...... 1 Chr. 7:31 473

Bishlam—*in peace*

A Persian officer .... Ezra 4:7 546

Bishop—*an overseer; elder*

A. *Qualifications of, given by:*
- Paul .... 1 Tim. 3:1-7 1427
- Peter, called "elder" .... 1 Pet. 5:1-4 1483

B. *Office of:*
- Same as overseer or elder .... Acts 20:17, 28 1303
- Several in a church ...... Acts 20:17, 28 1303; Phil. 1:1 1398
- Follows ordination .... Titus 1:5, 7 1440
- Held by Christ .... 1 Pet. 2:25 1480

C. *Duties of:*
- Oversee the church .... Acts 20:17, 28-31 1303
- Feed God's flock .... 1 Pet. 5:2 1483

SUBJECT REFERENCE PAGE

Watch over men's souls .... Heb. 13:17 1464
Teach .... 1 Tim. 5:17 1429

Bit—*a part of a horse's bridle*

Figurative, of man's stubborn nature .... Ps. 32:9 642; James 3:3 1469

Bithiah—*daughter of Yahweh*

Pharaoh's daughter; wife of Mered .... 1 Chr. 4:18 467

Bithron—*ravine, gorge*

A district east of Jordan .... 2 Sam. 2:29 361

Bithynia—*a province of Asia Minor*

The Spirit keeps Paul from .... Acts 16:7 1295
Peter writes to Christians of .... 1 Pet. 1:1 1477

Bitter

A. *Used of:*
The soul ...... Job 3:20 591
Words .... Ps. 64:3 659
Water .... Num. 5:24 166
Demanding woman .... Eccl. 7:26 756
Sin .... Prov. 5:4 718
Death .... Jer. 31:15 877

B. *Avoidance of:*
Toward a wife .... Col. 3:19 1409
As contrary to the truth .... James 3:14 1471

Bitter herbs

Part of Passover meal .... Ex. 12:8 80; Num. 9:11 171

"Bitter is sweet"

Descriptive of man's hunger .... Prov. 27:7 740

Bittern—*a nocturnal member of heron family*

Sings in desolate windows .... Zeph. 2:14 1058

Bitterness—*extreme enmity; sour temper*

A. *Kinds of:*
The heart ..... Prov. 14:10 726
Death .... 1 Sam. 15:32 339

B. *Causes of:*
Childlessness .. 1 Sam. 1:5, 10 321
A foolish son .... Prov. 17:25 730
Sickness ...... Is. 38:17 810

C. *Avoidance of:*
Toward others .... Eph. 4:31 1391
As a source of defilement .... Heb. 12:15 1462

Bitter waters

Made sweet by a tree .... Ex. 15:23-25 86
Swallowed by suspected wife .... Num. 5:11-31 165

Bizjothjah—*contempt of Yahweh*

A town in south Judah .... Josh. 15:28 268

Biztha—*eunuch*

An officer under Ahasuerus .... Esth. 1:10 577

Blackness—*destitute of light*

A. *Literally of:*
Hair .... Song 5:11 765
Horse .... Zech. 6:2 1071
Sky .... 1 Kin. 18:45 418
Mountain ..... Heb. 12:18 1463
Night .... Prov. 7:9 720

B. *Figuratively of:*
Hell .... Jude 13 1510

C. *Specifically:*
Let blackness of the day .... Job 3:5 591
Clothe heaven with .... Is. 50:3 822

Blamelessness—*freedom from fault; innocency*

A. *Used ritualistically of:*
Priests .... Matt. 12:5 1130
Proper observance .. Luke 1:6 1190
Works, righteousness .... Phil. 3:6 1401

B. *Desirable in:*
Bishops (elders) ..... 1 Tim. 3:2 1427; Titus 1:6, 7 1440
Deacons ...... 1 Tim. 3:10 1427
Widows .... 1 Tim. 5:7 1429

C. *Attainment of:*
Desirable now .... Phil. 2:15 1400
At Christ's return .... 1 Cor. 1:8 1345; 1 Thess. 5:23 1418; 2 Pet. 3:14 1489

Blasphemy—*cursing God*

A. *Arises out of:*
Pride .... Ps. 73:9, 11 666; Ezek. 35:12, 13 959
Hatred .... Ps. 74:18 667
Affliction ..... Is. 8:21 780
Injustice ...... Is. 52:5 824
Defiance ...... Is. 36:15-20 808
Skepticism .. Ezek. 9:8 926; Mal. 3:13, 14 1083
Self-deification ... Dan. 11:36, 37 992; 2 Thess. 2:4 1421
Unworthy conduct ..... 2 Sam. 12:13, 14 371; Rom. 2:24 1325

B. *Instances of:*
Job's wife ..... Job 2:9 590
Shelomith's son .... Lev. 24:11-16, 23 149
Sennacherib .... 2 Kin. 19:4, 10, 22 452
The beast ..... Dan. 7:25 986; Rev. 13:1, 5, 6 1529
The Jews ...... Luke 22:65 1228
Saul of Tarsus .... 1 Tim. 1:13 1426
Gentiles .... Rom. 1:28-32 1324
Hymenaeus .... 1 Tim. 1:20 1426

C. *Those falsely accused of:*
Naboth .... 1 Kin. 21:12, 13 422
Jesus .... Matt. 9:3 1126; Matt. 26:65 1151
Stephen .... Acts 6:11, 13 1279

D. *Guilt of:*
Punishable by death .... Lev. 24:11, 16 149
Christ accused of .... John 10:33, 36 1252

See Revile

Blasphemy against the Holy Spirit

Attributing Christ's miracles to Satan .... Matt. 12:22-32 1131
Never forgivable .... Mark 3:28-30 1163

Blasting—*injure severely*

Shows God's power .... Ex. 15:8 85
Sent as judgment .... Amos 4:9 1018
Figurative of death .... Job 4:9 592

Blastus—*sprout*

Herod's chamberlain ..... Acts 12:20 1289

Blemish—*any deformity or injury*

A. *Those without physical:*
Priests .... Lev. 21:17-24 144
Absalom ...... 2 Sam. 14:25 374
Animals used in sacrifices .... Lev. 22:19-25 145; Mal. 1:8 1080

B. *Those without moral:*
Christ .... Heb. 9:14 1457
The Church ..... Eph. 5:27 1392

C. *Those with:*
Apostates ..... 2 Pet. 2:13 1489

Bless—*to bestow blessings upon*

To give divine blessings .... Gen. 1:22 4; Gen. 9:1-7 14
To adore God for His blessings .... Gen. 24:48 33; Ps. 103:1 683
To invoke blessings upon another .... Gen. 24:60 33; Gen. 27:4, 27 36

Blessed—*the objects of God's favors*

A. *Reasons for, they:*
Are chosen .... Eph. 1:3, 4 1387
Believe .... Gal. 3:9 1381
Are forgiven ... Ps. 32:1, 2 642
Are justified ... Rom. 4:6-9 1327
Are instructed .... Ps. 94:12 679
Keep God's Word .... Rev. 1:3 1517

B. *Time of:*
Eternal past ... Eph. 1:3, 4 1387
Present .... Luke 6:22 1202
Eternal future .... Matt. 25:34 1149

Blessings—*the gift of God's grace*

A. *Physical and temporal:*
Prosperity ..... Mal. 3:10-12 1082
Food, clothing ..... Matt. 6:26, 30-33 1123
Sowing, harvest ...... Acts 14:17 1293
Longevity ..... Ex. 20:12 90
Children ...... Ps. 127:3-5 701

B. *National and Israelitish:*
General .... Gen. 12:1-3 18
Specific .... Rom. 9:4, 5 1333
Fulfilled .... Rom. 11:1-36 1335
Perverted ..... Rom. 2:17-29 1325
Rejected ...... Acts 13:46-52 1292

C. *Spiritual and eternal:*
Salvation .... John 3:16 1239
Election ...... Eph. 1:3-5 1387
Regeneration .... 2 Cor. 5:17 1368
Forgiveness ... Col. 1:14 1406
Adoption ...... Rom. 8:15-17 1332
No condemnation .... Rom. 8:1 1332
Holy Spirit .... Acts 1:8 1272
Justification ... Acts 13:38, 39 1292
New covenant ..... Heb. 8:6-13 1456
Fatherly chastisement . Heb. 12:5-11 1462
Christ's intercession .. Rom. 8:34 1333

SUBJECT REFERENCE PAGE

Book of life—continued

B. *Excludes:*
Renegades ... Ex. 32:33 106; Ps. 69:28 664
Apostates ... Rev. 13:8 1531; Rev. 17:8 1533

C. *Affords, basis of:*
Joy ... Luke 10:20 1209
Hope ... Heb. 12:23 1463
Judgment ... Dan. 7:10 985; Rev. 20:12-15 1538

Booths—*stalls made of branches*

Used for cattle ... Gen. 33:17 45
Required in feast of tabernacle ... Lev. 23:40-43 148; Neh. 8:14-17 565

Booty—*spoils taken in war*

A. *Stipulations concerning:*
No Canaanites ... Deut. 20:14-17 231
No accursed thing ... Josh. 6:17-19 256
Destruction of Amalek ... 1 Sam. 15:2, 3 337
Destruction of Arad ... Num. 21:1-3 184
The Lord's judgment ... Jer. 49:30-32 899

B. *Division of:*
On percentage basis ... Num. 31:26-47 197
Rear troops share in ... 1 Sam. 30:22-25 355

Border—*boundary*

A. *Marked by:*
Natural landmarks ... Josh. 18:16 271
Rivers ... Josh. 18:19 271
Neighbor's landmark ... Deut. 19:14 230

B. *Enlargement of:*
By God's power ... Ex. 34:24 108
A blessing ... 1 Chr. 4:10 467

Born again—*new birth, regeneration*

A. *Necessity of, because of:*
Inability ... John 3:3, 5 1239
The flesh ... John 3:6 1239
Deadness ... Eph. 2:1 1387

B. *Produced by:*
The Holy Spirit ... John 3:5, 8 1239; Titus 3:5 1442
The Word of God ... James 1:18 1468; 1 Pet. 1:23 1479
Faith ... 1 John 5:1 1498

C. *Results of:*
New creature ... 2 Cor. 5:17 1368
Changed life ... Rom. 6:4-11 1329
Holy life ... 1 John 3:9 1497
Righteousness ... 1 John 2:29 1497
Love ... 1 John 3:10 1497
Victory ... 1 John 5:4 1499

Borrow—*to get by loan*

A. *Regulations regarding:*
From other nations, forbidden ... Deut. 15:6 227; Deut. 28:12 238
Obligation to repay ... Ex. 22:14, 15 93
Non-payment, wicked ... Ps. 37:21 646
Involves servitude ... Prov. 22:7 734
Evils of, corrected ... Neh. 5:1-13 561

Christ's words on ... Matt. 5:42 1121

B. *Examples of:*
Jewels ... Ex. 11:2 79
A widow's vessels ... 2 Kin. 4:3 432
A woodsman's ax ... 2 Kin. 6:5 434
Christ's transportation ... Matt. 21:2, 3 1141

Bosom—*the breast as center of affections*

A. *Expressive of:*
Prostitution ... Prov. 6:26, 27 719
Anger ... Eccl. 7:9 754
Protection ... Is. 40:11 811
Iniquity ... Job 31:33 610

B. *Symbolic of:*
Man's impatience ... Ps. 74:11 667
Christ's deity ... John 1:18 1236
Eternal peace ... Luke 16:22, 23 1219

Bottle—*a hollow thing* (vessel)

A. *Used for:*
Milk ... Judg. 4:19 288
Water ... Gen. 21:14 29
Wine ... Hab. 2:15 1053

B. *Made of:*
Clay ... Jer. 19:1, 10, 11 865
Skins ... Matt. 9:17 1126; Mark 2:22 1162

C. *Figurative of:*
God's remembrance ... Ps. 56:8 656
God's judgments ... Jer. 13:12-14 859
Sorrow ... Ps. 119:83 697
Impatience ... Job 32:19 611
Clouds of rain ... Job 38:37 616
Old and new covenants ... Matt. 9:17 1126

Bottomless pit

Apollyon, king of ... Rev. 9:11 1526
Beast comes from ... Rev. 11:7 1528; Rev. 17:8 1533
Devil, cast into ... Rev. 20:1-3 1536
A prison ... Rev. 20:7 1538

Bough—*branch of a tree*

A. *Used:*
To make ceremonial booths ... Lev. 23:39-43 148
In siege of Shechem ... Judg. 9:45-49 296

B. *Figurative of:*
Joseph's offspring ... Gen. 49:22 63
Judgment ... Is. 17:1-11 788
Israel ... Ps. 80:8-11 672

Bow—*an instrument for shooting arrows*

A. *Uses of:*
For hunting ... Gen. 27:3 36
For war ... Is. 7:24 779
As a token of friendship ... 1 Sam. 18:4 343
As a commemorative song ... 2 Sam. 1:18 360

B. *Illustrative of:*
Strength ... Job 29:20 609
The tongue ... Ps. 11:2 631
Defeat ... Hos. 1:5 996
Peace ... Hos. 2:18, 19 998

Bowing, Bowing the knee

A. *Wrong:*
Before idols ... Ex. 20:5 90
In mockery ... Matt. 27:29 1152
Before an angel ... Rev. 22:8, 9 1539

B. *True, in:*
Prayer ... 1 Kin. 8:54 403
Homage ... 2 Kin. 1:13 430
Repentance ... Ezra 9:5, 6 551
Worship ... Ps. 95:6 680
Submission ... Eph. 3:14 1388; Phil. 2:10 1400

Bowl—*a vessel*

Full of incense ... Rev. 5:8 1523
Filled with God's wrath ... Rev. 16:1-17 1532

Box tree—*an evergreen tree*

Descriptive of messianic times ... Is. 41:19, 20 813

Boy—*male child*

Esau and Jacob ... Gen. 25:27 34
Payment for a harlot ... Joel 3:3 1012
Play in streets ... Zech. 8:5 1072

See Children; Young men

Bozez—*shining*

Rock of Michmash ... 1 Sam. 14:4, 5 336

Bozkath—*height*

A town in south Judah ... Josh. 15:39 268
Home of Jedidah ... 2 Kin. 22:1 455

Bozrah—*fortress; sheepfold*

1. City of Edom ... Gen. 36:33 48
Destruction of, foretold ... Amos 1:12 1016
Figurative, of Messiah's victory ... Is. 63:1 835
2. City of Moab ... Jer. 48:24 896

Bracelet—*ornament*

Worn by both sexes ... Ezek. 16:11 931
Given to Rebekah ... Gen. 24:22 32
Worn by King Saul ... 2 Sam. 1:10 360
A sign of worldliness ... Is. 3:19 774

Braided hair

Contrasted to spiritual adornment ... 1 Tim. 2:9, 10 1426

Bramble—*a thorny bush*

Emblem of a tyrant ... Judg. 9:8-15 295
Symbol of destruction ... Is. 34:13 806

Branch—*a limb*

A. *Used naturally of:*
Limbs of tree ... Num. 13:23 176

B. *Used figuratively of:*
Israel ... Rom. 11:16, 21 1336
The Messiah ... Is. 11:1 784
Christians ... John 15:5, 6 1259
Adversity ... Job 15:32 600

SUBJECT REFERENCE PAGE

Nebuchadnezzar's kingdom ..... Dan. 4:10-12 980

Brass—*an alloy of copper and zinc* (tin)

Used of:

Christ's glory .... Rev. 1:15 1519

Bravery, moral

Condemning sin .. 2 Sam. 12:1-14 370
Denouncing hypocrisy .... Matt. 23:1-39 1145
Opposing enemies .... Phil. 1:28 1400
Exposing inconsistency .... Gal. 2:11-15 1380
Uncovering false teachers .... 2 Pet. 2:1-22 1487
Rebuking Christians ...... 1 Cor. 6:1-8 1349; James 4:1-11 1471

Breach—*a break*

Used figuratively of:

Sin .... Is. 30:13 800

Bread—*food*

A. *God's provision for:*
Earned by sweat .... Gen. 3:19 9
Object of prayer .... Matt. 6:11 1121
Without work, condemned .. 2 Thess. 3:8, 12 1422
A gift ...... Ruth 1:6 313; 2 Cor. 9:10 1372

B. *Uses of unleavened, for:*
Heavenly visitors ...... Gen. 19:3 26
The Passover ..... Ex. 12:8 80
Priests .... 2 Kin. 23:9 457
Nazirites ...... Num. 6:13, 15 166
Lord's Supper .... Luke 22:7-19 1225

C. *Special uses of:*
Provided by ravens .... 1 Kin. 17:6 416
Strength ...... 1 Kin. 19:6-8 418
Satan's .... Matt. 4:3 1118
Miracle .... Matt. 14:19-21 1134
Insight .... Luke 24:35 1231

D. *Figurative of:*
Adversity ..... Is. 30:20 802
Christ .... John 6:33-35 1246
Christ's death .... 1 Cor. 11:23-28 1355
Communion with Christ .. Acts 2:46 1274; 1 Cor. 10:17 1354
Extreme poverty ...... Ps. 37:25 646
Heavenly food .... Ps. 78:24 670
Prodigality ..... Ezek. 16:49 932
Wickedness ..... Prov. 4:17 718
Idleness .... Prov. 31:27 745

E. *Bread of life:*
Christ is .... John 6:32-35 1246
Same as manna .... Ex. 16:4, 5 86
Fulfilled in Lord's Supper ...... 1 Cor. 11:23, 24 1355

Breaking of bread—*a meal*

Prayer before ..... Matt. 14:19 1134
Insight through .... Luke 24:35 1231
Fellowship thereby .... Acts 2:42 1274
Strength gained by .... Acts 20:11 1303

See Lord's Supper

Breastplate—*protection*

A. *Worn by:*
High priest ..... Ex. 28:4, 15-20 99
"Locusts" ..... Rev. 9:7, 9 1526

B. *Figurative of:*
Christ's righteousness .... Is. 59:17 831
Faith's righteousness .... Eph. 6:14 1393

Breasts—*the female teats*

A. *Literally of:*
Married love ..... Prov. 5:19 718; Song 1:13 763
An infant's life .... Job 3:12 591; Ps. 22:9 637
Posterity .... Gen. 49:25 63

B. *Figuratively, of:*
Mother Jerusalem .... Is. 66:10, 11 838

Breath

Comes from God .... Gen. 2:7 7
Necessary for all .... Eccl. 3:19 752
Held by God .... Dan. 5:23 983
Taken by God .... Ps. 104:29 684
Figurative, of new life .... Ezek. 37:5-10 960

Breath of God

Cause of:

Life .... Job 33:4 611
Destruction .. 2 Sam. 22:16 382; Is. 11:4 784
Death .... Job 4:9 592

Brevity of human life

A. *Compared to:*
Pilgrimage .... Gen. 47:9 60
A sigh .... Ps. 90:9 678
Sleep .... Ps. 90:5 678
Flower .... Job 14:2 598
Grass .... 1 Pet. 1:24 1479
Vapor .... James 4:14 1471
Shadow .... Eccl. 6:12 754
Moment .... 2 Cor. 4:17 1368
A weaver's shuttle .... Job 7:6 594

B. *Truths arising from:*
Prayer can prolong ...... Is. 38:2-5 810
Incentive to improvement .... Ps. 90:12 678
Some kept from old age .... 1 Sam. 2:32, 33 324
Some know their end .... 2 Pet. 1:13, 14 1487
Hope regarding ..... Phil. 1:21-25 1398
Life's completion ... 2 Tim. 4:6-8 1436

Bribery—*gifts to pervert*

A. *The effects of:*
Makes sinners .... Ps. 26:10 639
Corrupts conscience ... Ex. 23:8 94
Perverts justice .... Is. 1:23 772
Brings chaos .... Amos 5:12 1020
Merits punishment .. Amos 2:6 1016

B. *Examples of:*
Balak .... Num. 22:17, 18, 37 187
Delilah .... Judg. 16:4, 5 302

SUBJECT REFERENCE PAGE

Samuel's sons .... 1 Sam. 8:3 330
Ben-Hadad .... 1 Kin. 15:18, 19 413
Shemaiah ..... Neh. 6:10-13 562
Haman .... Esth. 3:8, 9 579
Judas and priests .... Matt. 27:3-9 1152
Soldiers .... Matt. 28:12-15 1155
Simon .... Acts 8:18 1282
Felix .... Acts 24:25, 26 1308

Brick—*baked clay*

Babel built of ..... Gen. 11:3 16
Israel forced to make .... Ex. 1:14 69
Altars made of ..... Is. 65:3 836
Forts made of ..... Is. 9:10 781

Bridal

Gift:

A burned city ..... 1 Kin. 9:16 406

Veil:

Rebekah wears first .... Gen. 26:64-67 34

Bride—*newly wed woman*

Wears adornments ..... Is. 61:10 834
Receives presents .... Gen. 24:53 33
Has damsels ...... Gen. 24:59, 61 33
Adorned for husband .... Rev. 19:7, 8 1536
Husband rejoices .... Is. 62:5 834
Stands near husband .... Ps. 45:9 651
Receives benediction ...... Ruth 4:11, 12 315
Must forget father's house .... Ruth 1:8-17 313
Must be chaste .... 2 Cor. 11:2 1373
Figurative of Israel .... Ezek. 16:8-14 931
Figurative of Church .... Rev. 21:2, 9 1538

Bridegroom—*newly wed man*

Wears special garments .... Is. 61:10 834
Attended by friends .... John 3:29 1241
Rejoices over bride .... Is. 62:5 834
Returns with bride .... Matt. 25:1-6 1148
Exempted from military service .... Deut. 24:5 235
Figurative of God .... Ezek. 16:8-14 931
Figurative of Christ .... John 3:29 1241

Bridle—*a harness*

A. *Used literally of:*
A donkey ..... Prov. 26:3 739

B. *Used figuratively of:*
God's control .... Is. 30:28 802
Self-control ... James 1:26 1468
Imposed control .... Ps. 32:9 642

Briers—*thorny shrub*

A. *Used literally of:*
Thorns .... Judg. 8:7, 16 292

B. *Used figuratively of:*
Sinful nature .. Mic. 7:4 1041
Change of nature .... Is. 55:13 828
Rejection ...... Is. 5:6 775

SUBJECT — REFERENCE — PAGE

Brimstone—*sulphur*
Falls upon Sodom ..... Gen. 19:24 — 28
Sent as judgment ..... Deut. 29:23 — 241
State of wicked ..... Ps. 11:6 — 631
Condition of hell ..... Rev. 14:10 — 1531

Broiled fish
Eaten by Jesus ..... Luke 24:42, 43 — 1231

Broken-handed
Disqualifies for priesthood ..... Lev. 21:19 — 144

Brokenhearted—*grieving*
Christ's mission to ..... Is. 61:1 — 833

Bronze—*an alloy of copper and tin*
A. *Used for:*
Tabernacle vessels ..... Ex. 38:2-31 — 111
Temple vessels ..... 1 Kin. 7:41-46 — 401
Armor ..... 2 Chr. 12:10 — 514
Mirrors ..... Ex. 38:8 — 111; Is. 45:2 — 817
B. *Workers in:*
Tubal-Cain ..... Gen. 4:22 — 10
Hiram ..... 1 Kin. 7:14 — 400
C. *Figurative of:*
Grecian Empire ..... Dan. 2:39 — 978
Obstinate sinners ..... Is. 48:4 — 820
Endurance ..... Jer. 15:20 — 862
God's decrees ..... Zech. 6:1 — 1071
Christ's glory ..... Dan. 10:6 — 989

Bronze serpent
Occasion of ruin ..... 2 Kin. 18:4 — 450

Brooks—*streams*
A. *Characteristics of:*
Numerous ..... Deut. 8:7 — 218
Produce grass ..... 1 Kin. 18:5 — 416
Abound in fish ..... Is. 19:8 — 790
Afford protection ..... Is. 19:6 — 790
B. *Names of:*
Arnon ..... Num. 21:14, 15 — 186
Besor ..... 1 Sam. 30:9 — 354
Gaash ..... 2 Sam. 23:30 — 385
Cherith ..... 1 Kin. 17:3, 5 — 414
Kidron ..... 2 Sam. 15:23 — 375
Kishon ..... Ps. 83:9 — 674
C. *Figurative of:*
Wisdom ..... Prov. 18:4 — 730
Prosperity ..... Job 20:17 — 603
Deception ..... Job 6:15 — 593
Refreshment ..... Ps. 110:7 — 691

Broth—*thin, watery soup*
Served by Gideon ..... Judg. 6:19, 20 — 290
Figurative of evil ..... Is. 65:4 — 836

Brother, brethren
A. *Used naturally of:*
Sons of same parents ..... Gen. 42:4 — 54
Common ancestry ..... Gen. 14:12-16 — 21
Same race ..... Deut. 23:7 — 233
Same humanity ..... Gen. 9:5 — 14
B. *Used figuratively of:*
An ally ..... Amos 1:9 — 1015
Christian disciples ..... Matt. 23:8 — 1145
A spiritual companion ..... 1 Cor. 1:1 — 1345
C. *Characteristics of Christian brothers:*
One Father ..... Matt. 23:8, 9 — 1145
Believe ..... Luke 8:21 — 1205
Some weak ..... 1 Cor. 8:11-13 — 1352
In need ..... James 2:15 — 1469
Of low degree ..... James 1:9 — 1468
Disorderly ..... 2 Thess. 3:6 — 1422
Evil ..... James 4:11 — 1471
Falsely judge ..... Rom. 14:10-21 — 1339
Need admonishment ..... 2 Thess. 3:15 — 1422

Brotherhood of man
A. *Based on common:*
Creation ..... Gen. 1:27, 28 — 4
Blood ..... Acts 17:26 — 1299
Needs ..... Prov. 22:2 — 734; Mal. 2:10 — 1081
B. *Disrupted by:*
Sin ..... 1 John 3:12 — 1497
Satan ..... John 8:44 — 1250

Brotherly kindness (love)
A. *Toward Christians:*
Taught by God ..... 1 Thess. 4:9 — 1416
Commanded ..... Rom. 12:10 — 1337
Explained ..... 1 John 4:7-21 — 1498
Fulfills the Law ..... Rom. 13:8-10 — 1339
Badge of new birth ..... John 13:34 — 1257
A Christian grace ..... 2 Pet. 1:5-7 — 1487
Must continue ..... Heb. 13:1 — 1463
B. *Toward others:*
Neighbors ..... Matt. 22:39 — 1144
Enemies ..... Matt. 5:44 — 1121

Brothers (brethren) of Christ
Four: James, Joses, Simon, Judas (Jude) ..... Matt. 13:55 — 1134; Mark 6:3 — 1166
Born after Christ ..... Matt. 1:25 — 1116; Luke 2:7 — 1193
Travel with Mary ..... Matt. 12:47-50 — 1132
Disbelieve Christ ..... John 7:4, 5 — 1247
Become believers ..... Acts 1:14 — 1272
Work for Christ ..... 1 Cor. 9:5 — 1353
One (James) becomes prominent ..... Acts 12:17 — 1289
Wrote an epistle ..... James 1:1 — 1468
Another (Jude) wrote an epistle ..... Jude — 1510

Brothers, Twin
Figureheads on Paul's ship to Rome, called Castor and Pollux ..... Acts 28:11 — 1315

Brought up—*reared*
Ephraim's children—by Joseph ..... Gen. 50:23 — 64
Esther—by Mordecai ..... Esth. 2:5-7, 20 — 578
Jesus—at Nazareth ..... Luke 4:16 — 1198
Paul—at Gamaliel's feet ..... Acts 22:3 — 1306

Brow
The forehead ..... Is. 48:4 — 820
Top of hill ..... Luke 4:29 — 1198

Bruised—*injured*
A. *Used literally of:*
Physical injuries ..... Luke 9:39 — 1208
B. *Used figuratively of:*
Evils ..... Is. 1:6 — 772
The Messiah's pains ..... Is. 53:5 — 825
Satan's defeat ..... Gen. 3:15 — 9; Rom. 16:20 — 1341

Bucket—*container for water*
Figurative of blessing ..... Num. 24:7 — 189
Pictures God's magnitude ..... Is. 40:15 — 811

Buffet—*to strike*
Descriptive of Paul ..... 2 Cor. 12:7 — 1374

Build—*construct or erect*
A. *Used literally, of:*
City ..... Gen. 4:17 — 10
Altar ..... Gen. 8:20 — 14
Tower ..... Gen. 11:4 — 16
House ..... Gen. 33:17 — 45
Sheepfolds ..... Num. 32:16 — 198
Fortifications ..... Deut. 20:20 — 231; Ezek. 4:2 — 921
Temple ..... 1 Kin. 6:1, 14 — 398; Ezra 4:1 — 545
High place ..... 1 Kin. 11:7 — 407
Walls ..... Neh. 4:6 — 560
Tombs ..... Matt. 23:29 — 1145; Luke 11:47 — 1212
Synagogue ..... Luke 7:2-5 — 1203
B. *Used figuratively, of:*
Obeying Christ ..... Matt. 7:24-27 — 1125
Church ..... Matt. 16:18 — 1136
Christ's resurrection ..... Matt. 26:61 — 1151; John 2:19-21 — 1239
Return to legalism ..... Gal. 2:16-20 — 1380
Christian unity ..... Eph. 2:19-22 — 1388
Spiritual growth ..... Acts 20:32 — 1303; Col. 2:7 — 1408; 1 Pet. 2:5 — 1479
See Edification

Bukki
1. Danite chief ..... Num. 34:22 — 202
2. A descendant of Aaron ..... 1 Chr. 6:5, 51 — 469

Bukkiah—*proved of Yahweh*
A Levite musician ..... 1 Chr. 25:4, 13 — 491

Bul—*growth*
Eighth Hebrew month ..... 1 Kin. 6:38 — 400

Bull—*male of any bovine animal*
Used in sacrifices ..... Heb. 9:13 — 1457
Blood of, insufficient ..... Heb. 10:4 — 1458

SUBJECT REFERENCE PAGE

Symbol of evil men .... Ps. 22:12 637
Symbol of mighty men .... Ps. 68:30 663
Restrictions on .. Deut. 15:19, 20 227
Sacrifices of, inadequate ...... Ps. 69:30, 31 664
Blood of, unacceptable .... Is. 1:11 772
Figurative of the Lord's sacrifice .... Is. 34:6, 7 805
Figurative of strength .... Deut. 33:17 246

Bullock—*young bull*

Used in sacrifices .... Ex. 29:1, 10-14 102
Figurative of the Lord's sacrifice .... Is. 34:6, 7 805

Bulrush—*a reed*

Used in Moses' ark .... Ex. 2:3 69
Found in river banks .... Job 8:11 595
Figurative of judgment .... Is. 9:14 781
See Papyrus; Rush

Bulwark—*defensive wall*

Around Jerusalem .... Ps. 48:13 652
Used in wars ..... Eccl. 9:14 757

Bunah—*intelligence*

A descendant of Judah .... 1 Chr. 2:25 466

Bunni—*erected*

1. A preexilic Levite .... Neh. 11:15 570
2. A postexilic Levite .... Neh. 9:4 567
3. Signer of document .... Neh. 10:15 569

Burden—*load*

A. *Used physically of:*
Load, cargo ... Neh. 4:17 561

B. *Used figuratively of:*
Care .... Ps. 55:22 656
Prophet's message .... Hab. 1:1 1052
Rules, rites .... Luke 11:46 1212
Sin .... Ps. 38:4 646
Responsibility .... Gal. 6:2, 5 1383
Christ's law ... Matt. 11:30 1130

Burden-bearer

Christ is the believer's .... Ps. 55:22 656

Burial

A. *Features regarding:*
Body washed ...... Acts 9:37 1286
Ointment used .... Matt. 26:12 1150
Embalm sometimes .... Gen. 50:26 64
Body wrapped ..... John 11:44 1255
Placed in coffin .... Gen. 50:26 64
Carried on a bier .... Luke 7:14 1203
Mourners attend .... John 11:19 1253
Graves provided ..... Gen. 23:5-20 31
Tombs erected .... Matt. 23:27-29 1145

B. *Places of:*
Abraham and Sarah .... Gen. 25:7-10 33
Deborah .... Gen. 35:8 46
Rachel .... Gen. 35:19, 20 46
Miriam .... Num. 20:1 183
Moses .... Deut. 34:5, 6 247
Gideon .... Judg. 8:32 294
Samson and Manoah ..... Judg. 16:30, 31 303
Saul and his sons .... 1 Sam. 31:12, 13 356
David .... 1 Kin. 2:10 393
Joab .... 1 Kin. 2:33, 34 394
Solomon .... 1 Kin. 11:43 408
Rehoboam ..... 1 Kin. 14:31 412
Asa .... 1 Kin. 15:24 413
Manasseh ..... 2 Kin. 21:18 455
Amon .... 2 Kin. 21:23-26 455
Josiah .... 2 Chr. 35:23, 24 536
Jesus .... Luke 23:50-53 1230
Lazarus .... John 11:14, 38 1253

Buried alive

Two rebellious families .... Num. 16:27-34 180
Desire of some .... Rev. 6:15, 16 1524

Burning bush

God speaks from .... Ex. 3:2 70

Business—*one's work*

A. *Attitudes toward:*
See God's hand .... James 4:13 1471
Be diligent .... Prov. 22:29 735
Be industrious ... Rom. 12:8, 11 1337
Be honest ..... 2 Cor. 8:20-22 1371
Put God's first .... Matt. 6:33, 34 1123
Keep heaven in mind .... Matt. 6:19-21 1123
Give portion ... Mal. 3:8-12 1082
Avoid anxiety ...... Luke 12:22-30 1214
Remember the fool .... Luke 12:15-21 1214

B. *Those diligent in:*
Joseph .... Gen. 39:11 51
Moses .... Heb. 3:5 1452
Workers in Israel .... 2 Chr. 34:11, 12 534
Daniel .... Dan. 6:4 984
Mordecai ...... Esth. 10:2, 3 585
Paul .... Acts 20:17-35 1303

Busybodies—*meddlers*

Women guilty of .... 1 Tim. 5:13 1429
Some Christians ...... 2 Thess. 3:11, 12 1422
Admonitions against .... 1 Pet. 4:15 1483
See Slander; Whisperer

Butler—*an officer*

Imprisonment of Pharaoh's ...... Gen. 40:1-13 51
Same as "cupbearer" ..... 1 Kin. 10:5 406

Butter—*curdled milk*

Set before visitors .... Gen. 18:8 24
Got by churning .. Prov. 30:33 744
Figurative of smooth words .... Ps. 55:21 656
See Curds

Buz—*contempt*

1. A Gadite ...... 1 Chr. 5:14 468
2. An Aramean tribe descending from Nahor .. Gen. 22:20, 21 31

Buzi—*descendant of Buz*

Father of Ezekiel .... Ezek. 1:3 918

Buzite—*belonging to Buz*

Of the tribe of Buz .... Job 32:2 611

Buzzard

Unclean bird ..... Lev. 11:13 132

Byway—*winding or secluded path*

Used by travelers .... Judg. 5:6 289

Byword—*saying; remark*

Predicted as a taunt .... Deut. 28:37 239
Job describes himself .... Job 17:6 601

C

Cabbon—*surround*

Village of Judah .. Josh. 15:40 268

Cabul—*unproductive*

1. Town of Asher .... Josh. 19:27 272
2. A district of Galilee offered to Hiram .... 1 Kin. 9:12, 13 404
Solomon placed people in .... 2 Chr. 8:2 510

Caesar—*a title of Roman emperors*

A. *Used in reference to:*

1. Augustus Caesar (31 B.C.–A.D. 14)
Decree of brings Joseph and Mary to Bethlehem ... Luke 2:1 1193
2. Tiberius Caesar (A.D. 14–37)
Christ's ministry dated by .... Luke 3:1-23 1194
Tribute paid to .... Matt. 22:17-21 1144
Jews side with .... John 19:12 1263
3. Claudius Caesar (A.D. 41–54)
Famine in time of .... Acts 11:28 1288
Banished Jews from Rome .... Acts 18:2 1299
4. Nero Caesar (A.D. 54–68) Paul appealed to ... Acts 25:8-12 1310
Converts in household of .... Phil. 4:22 1402
Paul before .... 2 Tim. 4:16-18 1436
Called Augustus ..... Acts 25:21 1310

B. *Represented Roman authority:*
Image on coins .... Matt. 22:19-21 1144; Mark 12:15, 16 1178; Luke 20:24 1223
Received tax .... Matt. 22:19, 21 1144; Mark 12:14, 17 1178; Luke 20:25 1224
Jesus called threat to .... Luke 23:2 1228; John 19:12 1263

SUBJECT REFERENCE PAGE

Peace ....1 Cor. 7:15 1351
Glory and virtue ....2 Pet. 1:3 1487
Eternal glory ..2 Thess. 2:14 1421
Eternal life ....1 Tim. 6:12 1430

D. *Attitudes toward:*
Walk worthy of............Eph. 4:1 1390
Make it sure ..2 Pet. 1:10 1487
Of Gentiles ....Eph. 4:17-19 1390

Calneh—*fort of Ana*

1. Nimrod's city ....Gen. 10:9, 10 16
2. A city linked with Hamath and Gath ....Amos 6:2 1020
Same as Calno ....Is. 10:9 782

Calvary—*from the Latin "calvaria"* (skull)

Christ was crucified there ....Luke 23:33 1229
Same as "Golgotha" in Hebrew ....John 19:17 1264

Camel—*humpbacked animal*

A. *Used for:*
Riding ....Gen. 24:61, 64 33
Trade ....Gen. 37:25 49
War ....Judg. 7:12 292
Hair of, for clothing ......Matt. 3:4 1117
Used for garment worn by John the Baptist ...Matt. 3:4 1117
Wealth ....Job 42:12 620

B. *Features of:*
Docile ....Gen. 24:11 32
Unclean ....Lev. 11:4 130
Adorned ....Judg. 8:21, 26 294
Prize for booty ....Job 1:17 589
Treated well ...Gen. 24:31, 32 32
Illustrative of the impossible ...Matt. 19:24 1140

Camon—*elevation*

Jair was buried there ....Judg. 10:5 296

Camp—*to pitch a tent; take residence*

A. *The Lord's guidance of, by:*
An angel ....{Ex. 14:19 85; Ex. 32:34 106}
His presence ..Ex. 33:14 106
A cloud ....Ps. 105:39 685

B. *Israel's:*
On leaving Egypt ....Ex. 13:20 83
At Sinai ....Ex. 18:5 88
Orderly ....Num. 2:2-34 161
Tabernacle in center of...........Num. 2:17 161
Exclusion of:
Unclean ......Deut. 23:10-12 233
Lepers ....Lev. 13:46 135
Dead ....Lev. 10:4, 5 130
Executions outside ....Lev. 24:23 149
Log kept of....Num. 33:1-49 199
In battle .....{Josh. 10:5, 31, 34} 261

C. *Spiritual significance of:*
Christ's crucifixion outside ....Heb. 13:12, 13 1463
God's people ..Rev. 20:9 1538

Cana of Galilee

A village of upper Galilee; home of Nathanael ....John 21:2 1267
Christ's first miracle at ....John 2:1-11 1237
Healing at ....John 4:46-54 1242

Canaan—*low*

1. A son of Ham ....Gen. 10:6 16
Cursed by Noah ....Gen. 9:20-25 15
2. Promised Land.........Gen. 12:5 18

Canaan, Land of

A. *Specifications regarding:*
Boundaries ....Gen. 10:19 16
Fertility ....Ex. 3:8, 17 70
Seven nations.......Deut. 7:1 217
Language .....Is. 19:18 790

B. *God's promises concerning, given to:*
Abraham ....Gen. 12:1-3 18
Isaac ....Gen. 26:2, 3 34
Jacob ....Gen. 28:10-13 38
Israel ....Ex. 3:8 70

C. *Conquest of:*
Announced....Gen. 15:7-21 21
Preceded by spies ....Num. 13:1-33 176
Delayed by unbelief ......Num. 14:1-35 176
Accomplished by the Lord ....Josh. 23:1-16 277
Done only in part ....{Judg. 1:21, 27-36} 284

Canaan, names of

Canaan ....Gen. 11:31 18
Land of Hebrews ....Gen. 40:15 52
Palestina ....Ex. 15:14 86
Land of Israel ....1 Sam. 13:19 334
Immanuel's land ..Is. 8:8 780
Beulah ....Is. 62:4 834
Glorious ....Dan. 8:9 987
The Lord's land ...Hos. 9:3 1001
Holy land ....Zech. 2:12 1069
Land of the Jews ....Acts 10:39 1287
Land of promise ..Heb. 11:9 1460

Canaanites—*original inhabitants of Palestine*

A. *Described as:*
Descendants of Ham ....Gen. 10:5, 6 16
Under a curse ....Gen. 9:25, 26 15
Amorites ....Gen. 15:16 23
Seven nations.......Deut. 7:1 217
Fortified ....Num. 13:28 176
Idolatrous .....Deut. 29:17 241
Defiled ....Lev. 18:24-27 141

B. *Destruction of:*
Commanded by God ......{Ex. 23:23, 28-33} 94
Caused by wickedness ...Deut. 9:4 220
In God's time ....Gen. 15:13-16 23
Done in degrees ......Ex. 23:29, 30 94

C. *Commands prohibiting:*
Common league with ....Deut. 7:1, 2 217
Intermarriage with ....Deut. 7:1, 3 217
Idolatry of .....Ex. 23:24 94
Customs of ....Lev. 18:24-27 141

Canaanites—*of Tyre and Sidon*

Woman from that region ....Matt. 15:22 1135

Candace—*dynastic title of Ethiopian queens*

Conversion of eunuch of...................Acts 8:27-39 1284

Cane—*a tall sedgy grass*

Used in sacrifices ....{Is. 43:24 815; Jer. 6:20 852}
Used in holy oil ...Ex. 30:23 104

Canneh

Trading city ......Ezek. 27:23 950

Cannibalism—*using human flesh as food*

Predicted as a judgment ....Deut. 28:53-57 239
Fulfilled in a siege ....2 Kin. 6:28, 29 436

Capacity—*ability to perform*

Hindered by sin ...Gal. 5:17 1383
Fulfilled in Christ ....Phil. 4:13 1402

Capernaum—*village of Nahum*

A. *Scene of Christ's healing of:*
Centurion's servant ......Matt. 8:5-13 1125
Nobleman's son ....John 4:46-54 1242
Peter's mother-in-law ....Matt. 8:14-17 1125
The demoniac ....Mark 1:21-28 1161
The paralytic .....Matt. 9:1-8 1126
Various diseases ......Matt. 8:16, 17 1125

B. *Other events connected with:*
Jesus' head-quarters ......Matt. 4:13-17 1118
Simon Peter's home ....Mark 1:21, 29 1161
Jesus' sermon on the Bread of Life........John 6:24-71 1246
Other important messages ....Mark 9:33-50 1172
Judgment pronounced upon ....Matt. 11:23, 24 1130

Caph

Eleventh letter of Hebrew alphabet.........Ps. 119:81-88 697

Caphtor—*cup*

The place (probably Crete) from which the Philistines came to Palestine ....Jer. 47:4 895

Caphtorim

Those of Caphtor ....Deut. 2:23 210
Descendants of Mizraim ....Gen. 10:13, 14 16
Conquerors of the Avim ....Deut. 2:23 210

Capital punishment—*the death penalty*

A. *Institution of:*
By God .....{Gen. 9:5, 6 14; Ex. 21:12-17 92}

B. *Crimes punished by:*
Murder ....Gen. 9:5, 6 14
Adultery ......Lev. 20:10 143
Incest ....Lev. 20:11-14 143
Sodomy ....Lev. 20:13 143
Rape ....Deut. 22:25 233
Witchcraft ....Ex. 22:18 93
Disobedience to parents ......Ex. 21:17 92
Blasphemy ..{Lev. 24:11-16, 23} 149
False doctrines .....Deut. 13:1-10 224

SUBJECT REFERENCE PAGE

Capitals—*tops of posts or columns*

Variegated decorations of .... Ex. 36:38 110
Part of temple .... 1 Kin. 7:16, 19, 20 400

Cappadocia—*a province of Asia Minor*

Natives of, at Pentecost .... Acts 2:1, 9 1273
Christians of, addressed by Peter .... 1 Pet. 1:1 1477
Adnah .... 2 Chr. 17:14 517

Capstone

Placed with shouts of "Grace" .... Zech. 4:7 1070

Captain—*a civil or military officer*

A. *Applied literally to:*
Arioch .... Dan. 2:15 977
Potiphar ...... Gen. 37:36 50
David as leader .... 1 Sam. 22:2 347
Jehohanan .... 2 Chr. 17:15 517
Temple police head .... Luke 22:4 1225

B. *Applied spiritually to:*
Angel of the Lord .... Josh. 5:14 256

Captain, chief of the Temple—*priest who kept order*

Conspired with Judas .... Luke 22:3, 4 1225
Arrested Jesus .... Luke 22:52-54 1228
Arrested apostles .... Acts 5:24-26 1278

Captive—*an enslaved person*

A. *Good treatment of:*
Compassion ... Ex. 6:4-8 73
Kindness ...... 2 Chr. 28:15 527
Mercy .... 2 Kin. 6:21-23 436

B. *Bad treatment of:*
Forced labor ... 2 Sam. 12:31 371
Blinded .... Judg. 16:21 303
Maimed .... Judg. 1:6, 7 284
Ravished ...... Lam. 5:11-13 914
Enslaved ...... 2 Kin. 5:2 433
Killed .... 1 Sam. 15:32, 33 339

C. *Applied figuratively to those:*
Under Satan ... 2 Tim. 2:26 1434
Under sin ..... 2 Tim. 3:6 1434
Liberated by Christ .... Luke 4:18 1198

Captivity—*a state of bondage; enslavement*

A. *Foretold regarding:*
Hebrews in Egypt .... Gen. 15:13, 14 23
Israelites ...... Deut. 28:36-41 239
Ten tribes (Israel) .... Amos 7:11 1021
Judah .... Is. 39:6 811

B. *Fulfilled:*
In Egypt .... Ex. 1:11-14 68
In many captivities .... Judg. 2:14-23 285
In Assyria ..... 2 Kin. 17:6-24 448
In Babylon .. 2 Kin. 24:11-16 459
Under Rome ... John 19:15 1264

C. *Causes of:*
Disobedience .... Deut. 28:36-68 239
Idolatry .... Amos 5:26, 27 1020

Caravan—*a group traveling together*

Ishmaelite traders .... Gen. 37:25 49
Jacob's family .... Gen. 46:5, 6 58
Jacob's funeral .... Gen. 50:7-14 64
Queen of Sheba ... 1 Kin. 10:1, 2 406
Returnees from exile .... Ezra 8:31 550

Carcas—*severe*

Eunuch under Ahasuerus .... Esth. 1:10 577

Carcass—*a dead body, corpse*

A. *Used literally of:*
Sacrificial animals ...... Gen. 15:9, 11 23
Unclean beasts .... Lev. 5:2 124
Lion .... Judg. 14:8 300
Men .... Deut. 28:25, 26 238
Idols .... Jer. 16:18 863

B. *Used figuratively of:*
Those in hell .. Is. 66:24 838
Idolatrous kings .... Ezek. 43:7, 9 967
Attraction ..... Matt. 24:28 1147

C. *Laws regarding:*
Dwelling made unclean by .... Num. 19:11-22 183
Contact with, makes unclean ...... Lev. 11:39 132
Food made unclean ...... Lev. 11:40 132

Carchemish

Eastern capital of Hittites on the Euphrates .... 2 Chr. 35:20 536
Conquered by Sargon II .... Is. 10:9 782
Josiah wounded here .... 2 Chr. 35:20-24 536

Care, carefulness—*wise and provident concern*

A. *Natural concern for:*
Children ...... Luke 2:44-49 1194
Duties .... Luke 10:40 1211
Mate .... 1 Cor. 7:32-34 1352
Health .... Is. 38:1-22 810
Life .... Mark 4:38 1164
Possessions ... Gen. 33:12-17 44

B. *Spiritual concern for:*
Duties .... Phil. 2:20 1400
Office .... 1 Tim. 3:1-8 1427
A minister's needs .... Phil. 4:10-12 1402
The flock of God .... John 10:11; 1 Pet. 5:2, 3 1252, 1483
Christians ..... 1 Cor. 12:25 1356
Spiritual things .... Acts 18:12-17 1299

Care, divine—*God's concern for His creatures*

For the world ..... Ps. 104:1-10 683
For animals .... Ps. 104:11-30 684
For pagans .... Jon. 4:11 1033
For Christians .... Matt. 6:25-34 1123
Nineveh .... Zeph. 2:10-15 1058

Careah—*made bold*

Father of Johanan .... 2 Kin. 25:23 460
Same as Kareah .. Jer. 40:8 888

Cares, worldly—*overmuch concern for earthly things, anxiety*

A. *Evils of:*
Chokes the Word .... Matt. 13:7, 22 1132
Gluts the soul .... Luke 21:34 1225
Obstructs the Gospel .... Luke 14:18-20 1217
Hinders Christ's work .... 2 Tim. 2:4 1434
Manifests unbelief ...... Matt. 6:25-32 1123

B. *Antidotes for God's:*
Protection ..... Ps. 37:5-11 645
Provision ..... Matt. 6:25-34 1123
Promises ...... Phil. 4:6, 7 1401

Carelessness—*lack of proper concern*

Babylon .... Is. 47:1, 8-11 819
Ethiopians .... Ezek. 30:9 953
Inhabitants of coastlands .... Ezek. 39:6 962
Nineveh .... Zeph. 2:15 1058
Women of Jerusalem .... Is. 32:9-11 803
Gallio .... Acts 18:12-17 1299

Carmel—*field, park, garden*

1. Rendered as:
"Fruitful field" .... Is. 10:18 782
"Plentiful field" .... Is. 16:10 788
"Bountiful country" ..... Jer. 2:7 845
2. City of Judah .... Josh. 15:55 268
Site of Saul's victory ...... 1 Sam. 15:12 339
Home of David's wife .... 1 Sam. 27:3 352
3. A mountain of Palestine ..... Josh. 19:26 272
Joshua defeated king there .... Josh. 12:22 265
Scene of Elijah's triumph ..... 1 Kin. 18:19-45 417
Elisha visits ... 2 Kin. 2:25 431
Place of beauty .... Song 7:5 766
Figurative of strength ...... Jer. 46:18 894
Barrenness foretold ...... Amos 1:2 1015

Carmelite, Carmelitess

Nabal .... 1 Sam. 30:5; 2 Sam. 2:2 354, 361
Hezrai .... 2 Sam. 23:35 385
Abigail .... 1 Sam. 27:3 352

Carmi—*vinedresser*

1. Son of Reuben ...... Gen. 46:9 59
2. Father of Achan .... Josh. 7:1 258

Carnal—*fleshly, worldly*

Used literally of:

Sexual relations ... Lev. 19:20 142
Paul calls himself .... Rom. 7:14 1332
Paul calls brethren at Corinth .... 1 Cor. 3:1, 3 1346

Carob pod—*seedcase of the carob, or locust tree*

Rendered "pod"; fed to swine .... Luke 15:16 1218

Carpenter—*a skilled woodworker*

David's house built by .... 2 Sam. 5:11 364
Temple repaired by .... 2 Chr. 24:12 523

SUBJECT REFERENCE PAGE

Temple restored by ....Ezra 3:7 545
Joseph works as ..Matt. 13:55 1134

Carpentry tools—*implements for the carpentry trade*

Ax ....Deut. 19:5 230
Hammer ....Jer. 23:29 870
Line ....Zech. 2:1 1069
Nail ....Jer. 10:4 856
Saw ....1 Kin. 7:9 400

Carpus—*fruit*

Paul's friend at Troas ....2 Tim. 4:13 1436

Carriage

A vehicle ....Is. 46:1 818

Carrion vulture

Unclean bird .....Lev. 11:18 132

Carshena—*plowman*

Prince of Persia ...Esth. 1:14 577

Cart—*a wagon*

Used in moving ...Gen. 45:19, 21 58
Made of wood ....1 Sam. 6:14 328
Sometimes covered ....Num. 7:3 168
Drawn by cows ...1 Sam. 6:7 327
Used in threshing ....Is. 28:28 799
Used for hauling ....Amos 2:13 1016
Ark carried by ....2 Sam. 6:3 364
Figurative of sin ..Is. 5:18 777

Carving—*cutting figures in wood or stone; grave*

Used in worship ..Ex. 31:1-7 104
Found in homes ..1 Kin. 6:18 398
Employed by idolators ....Judg. 18:18 306
Used in the Temple ....1 Kin. 6:35 400

Casiphia—*silvery*

Home of exiled Levites ....Ezra 8:17 550

Casluhim

A tribe descended from Mizraim ....Gen. 10:14 16
Descendant of Ham ....1 Chr. 1:8, 12 464

Cassia—*amber*

An ingredient of holy oil ....Ex. 30:24, 25 104
An article of commerce ....Ezek. 27:19 950
Noted for fragrance........Ps. 45:8 651

Castaway—*worthless; reprobated*

The rejected ....{Matt. 25:30 1149 / 2 Pet. 2:4 1487}

Caste—*divisions of society*

Some leaders of low ....Judg. 11:1-11 297
David aware of ....{1 Sam. 18:18, 23} 344
Jews and Samaritans observe ....John 4:9 1241
Abolished ....Acts 10:28-35 1287

Castle—*fortress*

Used figuratively of:

Offended brother..........Prov. 18:19 730

Castor and Pollux—*sons of Jupiter*

Gods in Greek and Roman mythology; figureheads on Paul's ship to Rome ....Acts 28:11 1315

Castration—*removal of male testicles*

Disqualified for congregation ....Deut. 23:1 233
Rights restored in new covenant ....Is. 56:3-5 828
Figurative of absolute devotion.........Matt. 19:12 1139

Caterpillar—*an insect living on vegetation*

Works with locust ....Is. 33:4 804

Cattle—*animals* (collectively)

Created by God ...Gen. 1:24 4
Adam named .....Gen. 2:20 8
Entered the ark ..Gen. 7:13, 14 12
Taken as plunder ....Josh. 8:2, 27 259
Belong to God ....Ps. 50:10 653
Nebuchadnezzar eats like ....Dan. 4:33 981
Pastureless ....Joel 1:18 1009

Caulkers—*sealers*

Used on Tyrian vessels ....Ezek. 27:9, 27 948

Caution—*provident care; alertness*

For safety ......{Acts 23:10, 16-24} 1307
For defense ....Neh. 4:12-23 560
For attack ....1 Sam. 20:1-17 345
A principle ....Prov. 14:15, 16 726
Neglect of ....1 Sam. 26:4-16 351

Cave—*a cavern*

A. *Used for:*
Habitation ....Gen. 19:30 28
Refuge ....1 Kin. 18:4 416
Burial ....John 11:38 1253
Concealment ....1 Sam. 22:1 347
Protection ...{Is. 2:19 773 / Rev. 6:15 1524}

B. *Mentioned in Scripture:*
Machpelah ....Gen. 23:9 31
Makkedah .....Josh. 10:16, 17 262
Adullam ....1 Sam. 22:1 347
En Gedi ....1 Sam. 24:1, 3 349

Cedar—*an evergreen tree*

A. *Used in:*
Ceremonial cleansing ....Lev. 14:4-7 136
Building Temple ......1 Kin. 5:5, 6 397
Building palaces ....2 Sam. 5:11 364
Gifts ....1 Chr. 22:4 489
Making idols ...Is. 44:14, 17 816

B. *Figurative of:*
Israel's glory ..Num. 24:6 189
Christ's glory ......{Ezek. 17:22, 23} 934
Growth of saints ....Ps. 92:12 679
Mighty nations.......Amos 2:9 1016
Arrogant rulers ....Is. 2:13 773

Ceiling—*upper surface of a room*

Temple's ....1 Kin. 6:15 398

Celebrate—*to commemorate; observe; keep*

Feast of Weeks ...Ex. 34:22 108
Feast of Ingathering ......Ex. 34:22 108
The Sabbath ......Lev. 23:32, 41 148
Passover ....2 Kin. 23:21 457
Feast of Unleavened Bread ....2 Chr. 30:13 529
Feast of Tabernacles .....Zech. 14:16 1077

Celestial—*heavenly*

Bodies called .....1 Cor. 15:40 1360

Celibacy—*the unmarried state*

Useful sometimes ....Matt. 19:10, 12 1139
Not for bishops ...1 Tim. 3:2 1427
Requiring, a sign of apostasy ....1 Tim. 4:1-3 1429
Figurative of absolute devotion ....Rev. 14:4 1531

Cemetery—*a burial place*

Bought by Abraham ....Gen. 23:15, 16 31
Pharisees compared to ....Matt. 23:27 1145
Man dwelt in .....Mark 5:2, 3 1165
A resurrection from ....Matt. 27:52 1154

Cenchrea—*millet*

A harbor of Corinth ....Acts 18:18 1300
A church in ......Rom. 16:1 1341

Censer—*firepan*

Used for incense ....{Num. 16:6, 7, 39} 179
Made of bronze ...Num. 16:39 180
Used in idol worship ....Ezek. 8:11 924
Typical of Christ's intercession .....Rev. 8:3, 5 1525

Censoriousness—*a critical spirit*

Rebuked by Jesus ....Matt. 7:1-5 1123
Diotrephes ....3 John 9, 10 1506
Apostates ....Jude 10-16 1510

Census—*counting the population*

At Sinai ....Ex. 38:25, 26 112
Military ....{Num. 1:2, 18, 20} 159
In Moab ....Num. 26:1-64 190
By David ....2 Sam. 24:1-9 387
Provoked by Satan ....1 Chr. 21:1 487
Completed by Solomon ....2 Chr. 2:17 503
Of exiles ....Ezra 2:1-70 542
By Rome ....Luke 2:1, 2 1193

Centurion—*a Roman officer*

Servant of, healed ....Matt. 8:5-13 1125
Watches crucifixion ....Matt. 27:54 1154
Is converted ......Acts 10:1-48 1286
Protects Paul .....Acts 22:25-28 1306
Takes Paul to Rome ....Acts 27:1 1312

Cephas—*stone*

Name of Peter ....John 1:42 1237

SUBJECT	REFERENCE	PAGE
Charitableness—*a generous spirit toward others*		
Bearing burdens	Gal. 6:2-4	1383
Showing forgiveness	2 Cor. 2:1-10	1366
Seeking concord	Phil. 4:1-3	1401
Helping the tempted	Gal. 6:1	1383
Encouraging the weak	Rom. 14:1-15	1339
Not finding fault	Matt. 7:1-3	1123
Descriptive of Dorcas	Acts 9:36	1286
Charmers—*users of magic*		
Falsified by God	Ps. 58:4, 5	657
Chastisement—*fatherly correction*		
A. *Sign of:*		
Sonship	Prov. 3:11, 12	716
God's love	Deut. 8:5	218
B. *Design of, to:*		
Correct	Jer. 24:5, 6	870
Prevent sin	2 Cor. 12:7-9	1374
Bless	Ps. 94:12, 13	679
C. *Response to:*		
Penitence	2 Chr. 6:24-31	508
Submission	2 Cor. 12:7-10	1374
Chastity—*sexual purity*		
A. *Manifested in:*		
Dress	1 Pet. 3:1-6	1480
Looks	Matt. 5:28, 29	1120
Speech	Eph. 5:4	1391
Intentions	Gen. 39:7-12	51
B. *Aids to:*		
Shun the unchaste	1 Cor. 5:11	1349
Consider your sainthood	Eph. 5:3, 4	1391
Dangers of unchastity	Prov. 6:24-35	719
Let marriage suffice	1 Cor. 7:1-7	1351
"Keep yourself pure"	1 Tim. 5:22	1430
C. *Examples of:*		
Job	Job 31:1, 9-12	609
Joseph	Gen. 39:7-20	51
Ruth	Ruth 3:10, 11	315
Boaz	Ruth 3:13, 14	315
Saints	Rev. 14:4	1531
Cheating—*defrauding by deceitful means; depriving*		
The Lord	Mal. 3:8, 9	1082
One's soul	Matt. 16:26	1137
The needy	Amos 8:4, 5	1022
Others	1 Cor. 7:5	1351
See Dishonesty		
Chebar—*joining*		
River in Babylonia	Ezek. 1:3	918
Site of Ezekiel's visions and Jewish captives	Ezek. 10:15, 20	927
Chedorlaomer—*servant of the god Lagamar*		
A king of Elam; invaded Canaan	Gen. 14:1-16	21
Cheek—*side of face*		
Micaiah struck on	1 Kin. 22:24	423
Struck on	Job 16:10	600
Messiah's plucked	Is. 50:6	823
Description of:		
Beauty	Song 5:13	765
Patience	Matt. 5:39	1121
Victory	Ps. 3:7	626
Attack	Mic. 5:1	1039
Cheerfulness—*serene joyfulness*		
A. *Caused by:*		
A merry heart	Prov. 15:13	727
The Lord's goodness	Zech. 9:16, 17	1074
The Lord's presence	Mark 6:54, 55	1167
Victory	John 16:33	1261
Confidence	Acts 24:10	1308
B. *Manifested in:*		
Giving	2 Cor. 9:7	1372
Christian graces	Rom. 12:8	1337
Times of danger	Acts 27:22-36	1314
Cheese—*a dairy product*		
Used for food	1 Sam. 17:18	342
Received by David	2 Sam. 17:29	377
Figurative of trials	Job 10:10	596
Chelal—*completeness; perfection*		
A son of Pahath-Moab	Ezra 10:30	553
Cheluh—*robust*		
A son of Bani	Ezra 10:35	553
Chelub—*basket; bird's cage*		
1. A brother of Shuah	1 Chr. 4:11	467
2. Father of Ezri	1 Chr. 27:26	494
Chelubai		
A son of Hezron	1 Chr. 2:9	465
Chemosh—*fire, hearth*		
The god of the Moabites	Num. 21:29	186
Children sacrificed to	2 Kin. 3:26, 27	432
Solomon builds altars to	1 Kin. 11:7	407
Josiah destroys altars of	2 Kin. 23:13	457
Chenaanah—feminine form of *Canaan*		
1. A Benjamite	1 Chr. 7:10	472
2. Father of Zedekiah	2 Chr. 18:10	518
Chenani—contraction of *Chenaniah*		
A reforming Levite	Neh. 9:4	567
Chenaniah—*Yahweh has established*		
1. A chief Levite in David's reign	1 Chr. 15:22, 27	481
2. A reforming Levite; contracted to Chenani	Neh. 9:4	567
Chephar Haammonai—*village of the Ammonite*		
A village of Benjamin	Josh. 18:24	271
Chephirah—*village*		
A city of the Gibeonites	Josh. 9:17	261
Assigned to Benjamin	Josh. 18:26	271
Residence of exiles	Ezra 2:25	544
Cheran—*lyre*		
A Horite, son of Dishon	1 Chr. 1:41	465
Cherethites—*Cretans in southwest Palestine*		
Tribes in southwest Canaan	1 Sam. 30:14	355
Identified with Philistines	Ezek. 25:16	947
In David's bodyguard	2 Sam. 8:18	367
Serve Solomon	1 Kin. 1:37, 38	392
Cherith—*cut; brook*		
Elijah hid there	1 Kin. 17:3-6	414
Cherub		
A district in Babylonia	Ezra 2:59 Neh. 7:61	544 564
Cherubim (plural of cherub)		
A. *Appearances of:*		
Fully described	Ezek. 1:5-14	919
B. *Functions of:*		
Guard	Gen. 3:22-24	9
Fulfill God's purposes	Ezek. 10:9-16	926
Show God's majesty	2 Sam. 22:11	382
C. *Images of:*		
On the mercy seat	Ex. 25:18-22	97
On the veil	Ex. 26:31	98
On curtains	Ex. 36:8	109
In the Temple	1 Kin. 8:6, 7	402
Chesalon—*trust*		
A town of Judah	Josh. 15:10	267
Chesed		
Fourth son of Nahor	Gen. 22:22	31
Chesil—*a fool*		
A village of Judah	Josh. 15:30	268
Probably same as Bethul and Bethuel	Josh. 19:4 1 Chr. 4:30	271 468
Chest—*case or box*		
For offering	2 Kin. 12:9, 10	443
For levy fixed by Moses	2 Chr. 24:8, 9	523
Used to safeguard valuables	1 Sam. 6:8-15	327
Chestnut tree—*plane tree*		
Used by Jacob	Gen. 30:37	41
In Eden, God's garden	Ezek. 31:8, 9	954
Chesulloth—*loins or slopes*		
A border town of Issachar	Josh. 19:18	272
Chezib—*deceitful*		
Same as Azib; birthplace of Shelah	Gen. 38:5	50

SUBJECT — REFERENCE — PAGE

Chicken—*domestic fowl*

Hen and brood .... Luke 13:34 — 1216
Rooster .... Luke 22:34 — 1226

Chicks—*the young of a hen*

Figurative of Israel .... Matt. 23:37 — 1147

Chiding—*to reprove or rebuke*

A. *Between men:*
Jacob with Laban .... Gen. 31:36 — 43
Israelites with Moses .... Ex. 17:2 — 87
Ephraimites with Gideon ...... Judg. 7:24, 25 — 292; Judg. 8:1 — 292
Paul with Peter .... Gal. 2:11, 14 — 1380

B. *By Christ, because of:*
Unbelief ...... Matt. 11:20-24 — 1130
Spiritual dullness ...... Matt. 16:8-12 — 1136
Censoriousness ..... Mark 10:13-16 — 1172
Sluggishness .. Matt. 26:40 — 1150

Chidon—*a javelin*

Where Uzza was struck dead .... 1 Chr. 13:9, 10 — 480
Called Nachon .... 2 Sam. 6:6 — 364

Childbearing

Agreeable to God's command .... Gen. 1:28 — 7
Result of marriage .... 1 Tim. 5:14 — 1429
Attended with pain .... Gen. 3:16 — 9
Productive of joy .... John 16:21 — 1261
Productive of the Messiah .... Luke 2:7 — 1193
Means of salvation .... 1 Tim. 2:15 — 1427
Expressed in symbols .... Rev. 12:2, 5 — 1529

Childhood, characteristics of

Dependence ...... 1 Thess. 2:7 — 1415
Immaturity .... 1 Cor. 13:11 — 1356
Foolishness ...... Prov. 22:15 — 735
Unstableness ..... Eph. 4:14 — 1390
Humility .... Matt. 18:1-5 — 1138
Need for instruction .... Prov. 22:6 — 734
Influence on adults .... Is. 49:15 — 822

Childishness—*an immature spirit*

Manifested by Saul .... 1 Sam. 18:8, 9 — 343
Seen in Haman ... Esth. 6:6-9 — 582

Childlikeness

Requirement of God's kingdom .... Mark 10:15 — 1173
An element in spiritual growth .... 1 Pet. 2:2 — 1479
A model to be followed .... 1 Cor. 14:20 — 1358

Children, figurative

Disciples of a teacher .... Mark 10:24 — 1173
God's own .... Rom. 8:16, 17 — 1333
Christians .... Eph. 5:8 — 1391
Devil's own .... 1 John 3:10 — 1497
Those who show such trait .... Matt. 11:16-19 — 1130

See Sonship of Believers

Children, illegitimate

No inheritance .... Gal. 4:30 — 1382
No fatherly care ... Heb. 12:8 — 1462
Not in congregation .... Deut. 23:2 — 233
Despised .... Judg. 11:2 — 297

Children, natural

A. *Right estimate of:*
God's gifts .... Gen. 33:5 — 44
God's heritage ...... Ps. 127:3-5 — 701
Crown of old men .... Prov. 17:6 — 729

B. *Characteristics of:*
Imitate parents ...... 1 Kin. 15:11, 26 — 412
Diverse in nature .... Gen. 25:27 — 34
Playful .... Matt. 11:16-19 — 1130

C. *Capacities of:*
Glorify God ... Matt. 21:15, 16 — 1141
Come to Christ .... Mark 10:13-16 — 1172
Understand Scripture ..... 2 Tim. 3:15 — 1436
Receive the promises .... Acts 2:39 — 1274
Believe .... Matt. 18:6 — 1138
Receive training ...... Eph. 6:4 — 1392
Worship in God's house. .. 1 Sam. 1:24, 28 — 323

D. *Parental obligations toward:*
Nourishment .... 1 Sam. 1:22 — 321
Discipline ..... Eph. 6:4 — 1392
Instruction .... Gal. 4:1, 2 — 1381
Employment .. 1 Sam. 17:15 — 342
Inheritance .... Luke 12:13, 14 — 1214

E. *Duties of:*
Obedience ...... Eph. 6:1-3 — 1392
Honor to parents ...... Heb. 12:9 — 1462
Respect for age .... 1 Pet. 5:5 — 1483
Care for parents ...... 1 Tim. 5:4 — 1429
Obedience to God .... Deut. 30:2 — 241
Remembering God .... Eccl. 12:1 — 759

F. *Description of ungrateful:*
Stubborn ...... Deut. 21:18-21 — 232
Scorners ...... Prov. 30:17 — 744
Robbers ...... Prov. 28:24 — 742
Strikers .... Ex. 21:15 — 92
Cursers .... Lev. 20:9 — 143

G. *Examples of good:*
Isaac .... Gen. 22:6-10 — 30
Joseph .... Gen. 45:9, 10 — 58
Jephthah's daughter ..... Judg. 11:34-36 — 298
Samuel .... 1 Sam. 2:26 — 324
David .... 1 Sam. 17:20 — 342
Josiah .... 2 Chr. 34:1-3 — 534
Esther .... Esth. 2:20 — 578
Daniel .... Dan. 1:1-6 — 976
John the Baptist .... Luke 1:80 — 1193
Jesus .... Luke 2:51 — 1194
In the Temple ...... Matt. 21:15, 16 — 1141
Timothy ...... 2 Tim. 3:15 — 1436

H. *Examples of bad:*
Esau .... Gen. 26:34, 35 — 36
Job's haters ... Job 19:18 — 602
Sons of Eli ... 1 Sam. 2:12, 17 — 323
Sons of Samuel ...... 1 Sam. 8:1-3 — 330
Absalom ...... 2 Sam. 15:10 — 374
Adonijah ...... 1 Kin. 1:5, 6 — 391
Elisha's mockers ..... 2 Kin. 2:22, 23 — 431
Adrammelech .... 2 Kin. 19:37 — 453

I. *Acts performed upon:*
Naming ...... Ruth 4:17 — 317
Blessing ..... Luke 1:67, 76-79 — 1192
Circumcision .... Luke 2:21 — 1193

J. *Murder of:*
By Pharaoh ... Ex. 1:15, 16 — 69
By Herod the Great .... Matt. 2:16-18 — 1116
In war .... Num. 31:12-17 — 197

Chileab—*restraint of father*

A son of David .... 2 Sam. 3:3 — 362
Also called Daniel .... 1 Chr. 3:1 — 466

Chilion—*wasting away*

Elimelech's son ... Ruth 1:2 — 313
Orpah's deceased husband .... Ruth 1:4, 5 — 313
Boaz redeems his estate .... Ruth 4:9 — 315

Chilmad

A town or country trading with Tyre .... Ezek. 27:23 — 950

Chimham—*pining*

A son of Barzillai .... 2 Sam. 19:37-40 — 380
Inn bearing his name .... Jer. 41:17 — 890

Chinnereth, Cinneroth—*lyre*

1. A city of Naphtali ..... Deut. 3:17 — 211
2. The region of Chinnereth ... 1 Kin. 15:20 — 413
Same as plain of Gennesaret ... Matt. 14:34 — 1135
3. The Old Testament name for Sea of Galilee .... Num. 34:11 — 202
Also called Lake of Gennesaret and Sea of Galilee .... Luke 5:1 — 1200

Chios—*snow*

An island of the Aegean Sea; on Paul's voyage .... Acts 20:15 — 1303

Chislev

Ninth month of Hebrew year............. Neh. 1:1 — 558

Chislon—*trust, hope*

Father of Elidad .. Num. 34:21 — 202

Chisloth Tabor—*the flanks of Tabor*

A locality near Mt. Tabor .... Josh. 19:12 — 271
Probably same as Chesulloth .... Josh. 19:18 — 272

Chittim, Kittim

The island of Cyprus; inhabited by descendants of Japheth (through Javan) .... Gen. 10:4 — 16
Ships of, in Balaam's prophecy .... Num. 24:24 — 190

Chiun—*detestable thing*

Pagan deity worshiped by Israel .... Amos 5:26 — 1020

SUBJECT REFERENCE PAGE

- Prayer concerning ... Ps. 70:2 ... 664
- Illustrations of ... Acts 19:29 ... 1302

B. *Examples of:*
- Babel ... Gen. 11:9 ... 16
- Philistines ... 1 Sam. 7:10 ... 328
- Egyptians ... Ex. 14:24 ... 85
- City of Shushan ... Esth. 3:15 ... 579
- Jerusalem ... Acts 21:31 ... 1305

Congratulate—*to express happiness to another*

- Tou to David ... 1 Chr. 18:9, 10 ... 486

Congregation—*an assembly of people*

A. *Used of:*
- The political Israel ... Ex. 12:3, 19, 47 ... 80
- A religious assembly ... Acts 13:42, 43 ... 1292

B. *Regulations concerning:*
- Ruled by representatives ... Num. 16:6 ... 179
- Summoned by trumpets ... Num. 10:3, 4, 7 ... 172
- Bound by decisions of representatives ... Josh. 9:15-21 ... 261
- Atonement of sin of ... Lev. 4:13-21 ... 123
- Exclusion of certain ones from ... Deut. 23:1-8 ... 233

Coniah—*Yahweh is creating*

- King of Judah ... Jer. 22:24, 28 ... 868
- Same as Jehoiachin ... 2 Kin. 24:8 ... 458

Connivance at wrong—*tacit approval of evil*

- Involves guilt ... Ps. 50:18-22 ... 653
- Aaron's, at Sinai ... Ex. 32:1, 2, 22 ... 105
- Pilate's, at Jesus' trial ... Matt. 27:17-26 ... 1152
- Saul's (Paul's) at Stephen's death ... Acts 7:57-60 ... 1282; Acts 8:1 ... 1282

Cononiah, Conaniah—*Yahweh has established*

1. A Levite ... 2 Chr. 31:11, 12, 13 ... 530
2. A Levite official ... 2 Chr. 35:9 ... 536

Conscience—*the inner judge of moral issues*

A. *Described as:*
- Good ... Acts 23:1 ... 1307
- Pure ... 1 Tim. 3:9 ... 1427
- Evil ... Heb. 10:22 ... 1458
- Defiled ... 1 Cor. 8:7 ... 1352
- Seared ... 1 Tim. 4:2 ... 1429

B. *Functions of:*
- A witness ... Rom. 2:14, 15 ... 1325
- An accuser ... John 8:9 ... 1248
- An upholder ... 1 Tim. 1:19 ... 1426
- Server of good ... Rom. 13:4, 5 ... 1337
- Source of joy ... 2 Cor. 1:12 ... 1366
- Dead ... Prov. 30:20 ... 744

C. *Limitations of:*
- Needs cleansing ... Heb. 9:14 ... 1457
- Subject to others' ... 1 Cor. 10:28, 29 ... 1354
- Differs ... 1 Cor. 8:7-13 ... 1352
- Fallible ... Prov. 16:25 ... 729

Conscience, clear—*freedom from guilt feelings*

A. *Necessary for:*
- Freedom from dead works ... Heb. 9:13, 14 ... 1457
- Access to God ... Heb. 10:21, 22 ... 1458
- Liberty in witnessing ... 1 Pet. 3:15, 16 ... 1481
- Christian love ... 1 Tim. 1:5 ... 1426
- Confidence in prayer ... 1 John 3:21, 22 ... 1497
- Proud confidence ... 2 Cor. 1:12 ... 1366

B. *Requirements for:*
- Doctrinal purity ... 1 Tim. 1:3-5, 18–2:1 ... 1426; 1 Tim. 4:1, 2 ... 1429
- Proper conduct ... Acts 24:10-13, 16 ... 1308; Rom. 13:4-6 ... 1337
- Faith in Christ's blood ... Heb. 9:14 ... 1457; Heb. 10:19-22 ... 1458
- Knowledge ... 1 Cor. 8:7 ... 1352
- Belief ... Titus 1:15 ... 1440
- Submissive spirit ... 1 Pet. 2:18, 19 ... 1480
- Faith in God's greatness ... 1 John 3:20 ... 1497
- Consideration of others ... 1 Cor. 10:28, 29 ... 1354
- Seeking forgiveness ... Prov. 28:13 ... 742; Matt. 5:23, 24 ... 1120

Conscription—*to enroll for compulsory service*

- Employed by Solomon ... 1 Kin. 7:13, 14 ... 400; 1 Kin. 9:20, 21 ... 406
- To build Temple ... 1 Kin. 5:2, 3, 13 ... 397
- To restore cities ... 1 Kin. 9:15-17 ... 404
- Led to revolt ... 1 Kin. 12:3-16 ... 408

See Levy

Consecration—*dedication to God's service*

A. *Applied to:*
- Israel ... Ex. 19:6 ... 89
- Priests ... Lev. 8:1–13 ... 126
- Levites ... Num. 8:5, 6, 14 ... 170
- Individuals ... 1 Sam. 1:11 ... 321
- Firstborn ... Ex. 13:2, 12 ... 82
- Possessions ... Lev. 27:28, 29 ... 155
- Christ ... Heb. 2:10 ... 1452

B. *The Christian's:*
- By Christ ... John 17:23 ... 1262
- Complete and entire ... Rom. 12:1, 2 ... 1336
- Separation from world ... 2 Cor. 6:14-18 ... 1369
- Devotion to Christ ... Rev. 14:1-7 ... 1531
- Sacred anointing ... 1 John 2:20, 27 ... 1496
- New priesthood ... 1 Pet. 2:5, 9 ... 1479

Conservation—*preserving worthwhile things*

- Material things ... John 6:12, 13 ... 1244
- Spiritual things ... Rev. 3:2, 3 ... 1521
- Good ... Acts 26:22, 23 ... 1312
- Unwise ... Luke 5:36, 37 ... 1201

Consolation—*comfort fortified with encouragement*

- God, source of ... Rom. 15:5 ... 1340
- Simeon waits for ... Luke 2:25 ... 1194
- Source of joy ... Acts 15:30, 31 ... 1294
- To be shared ... 2 Cor. 1:4-11 ... 1366

Conspiracy—*a plot to overthrow lawful authority*

Against:
- Joseph ... Gen. 37:18-20 ... 49
- Moses ... Num. 16:1-35 ... 179
- Samson ... Judg. 16:4-21 ... 302
- Daniel ... Dan. 6:4-17 ... 984
- Jesus ... Matt. 12:14 ... 1131
- Paul ... Acts 23:12-15 ... 1307

Constancy—*firmness of purpose*

- Ruth's, to Naomi ... Ruth 1:16 ... 313
- Jonathan's, to David ... 1 Sam. 20:12-17 ... 346
- Virgins, to Christ ... Rev. 14:4, 5 ... 1531

Constellation—*a group of stars*

- The Great Bear ... Job 9:9 ... 595; Job 38:32 ... 616
- The Serpent ... Job 26:13 ... 607
- Orion ... Job 38:31 ... 616; Amos 5:8 ... 1018
- Pleiades (seven stars) ... Job 9:9 ... 595; Job 38:31 ... 616
- Castor and Pollux ... Acts 28:11 ... 1315
- Judgment on ... Is. 13:10, 11 ... 785
- Incense burned to ... 2 Kin. 23:5 ... 457

Consultation—*seeking advice from others*

- Demonical ... 1 Sam. 28:7-25 ... 353
- Divided ... 1 Kin. 12:6, 8 ... 409
- Determined ... Dan. 6:7 ... 984
- Devilish ... John 12:10, 11 ... 1255; Matt. 26:3, 4 ... 1149

Contempt—*scorn compounded with disrespect*

A. *Forbidden toward:*
- Parents ... Prov. 23:22 ... 736
- Weak Christians ... Matt. 18:10 ... 1138; Rom. 14:3 ... 1339
- Believing masters ... 1 Tim. 6:2 ... 1430
- The poor ... James 2:1-3 ... 1469

B. *Objects of:*
- The righteous ... Ps. 80:6 ... 672
- Spiritual things ... Matt. 22:2-6 ... 1143
- Christ ... John 9:28, 29 ... 1251

C. *Examples of:*
- Nabal ... 1 Sam. 25:10, 11 ... 350
- Michal ... 2 Sam. 6:16 ... 365
- Sanballat ... Neh. 2:19 ... 559
- Jews ... Matt. 26:67, 68 ... 1151
- False teachers ... 2 Cor. 10:10 ... 1373
- The wicked ... Prov. 18:3 ... 730

Contention—*a quarrelsome spirit*

A. *Caused by:*
- Pride ... Prov. 13:10 ... 725
- Disagreement ... Acts 15:36-41 ... 1294
- Divisions ... 1 Cor. 1:11-13 ... 1345
- A quarrelsome spirit ... Gal. 5:15 ... 1383

B. *Antidotes:*
- Avoid the contentious ... Prov. 21:19 ... 733
- Avoid controversies ... Titus 3:9 ... 1442
- Abandon the quarrel ... Prov. 17:14 ... 729
- Follow peace ... Rom. 12:18-21 ... 1337

SUBJECT REFERENCE PAGE

Through conversion ... 1 Pet. 1:18, 23 1479
Perfected in heaven ... 1 Cor. 15:42, 50 1360

Corruption, mount of

Site of pagan altars ... 1 Kin. 11:7 407
Altars of, destroyed ... 2 Kin. 23:13 457

Corruption of body

Results from Adam's sin ... Rom. 8:21 1333
Begins in this life ... 2 Cor. 5:4 1368
Consummated by death ... John 11:39 1253
Freedom from, promised ... Rom. 8:21 1333
Freedom from, accomplished ... 1 Cor. 15:42 1360

Cos

An island between Rhodes and Miletus ... Acts 21:1 1303

Cosam—*a diviner*

Father of Addi ... Luke 3:28 1195

Cosmetics

Used by Jezebel ... 2 Kin. 9:30 440
Futility of ... Jer. 4:30 850

Cosmic conflagration—*to destroy by fire*

Day of judgment ... 2 Pet. 3:7-10 1489

Council—*Jewish Sanhedrin*

A judicial court ... Matt. 5:22 1120
Christ's trial ... Matt. 26:57-59 1151
Powers of, limited ... John 18:31 1263
Apostles before ... Acts 4:5-30 1276
Stephen before ... Acts 6:12-15 1279
Paul before ... Acts 23:1-5 1307

Counsel, God's

A. *Called:*
Immutable ... Heb. 6:17 1455
Faithful ... Is. 25:1 794
Wonderful ... Is. 28:29 799
Great ... Jer. 32:19 879
Sovereign ... Dan. 4:35 981
Eternal ... Eph. 3:11 1388

B. *Events determined by:*
History ... Is. 46:10, 11 819
Christ's death ... Acts 2:23 1273
Salvation ... Rom. 8:28-30 1333
Union in Christ ... Eph. 1:9, 10 1387

C. *Attitudes toward:*
Christians declare ... Acts 20:27 1303
Proper reserve ... Acts 1:7 1272
Wicked despise ... Is. 5:19 777
They reject ... Luke 7:30 1204

Counsel, man's

Jethro's, accepted ... Ex. 18:13-27 88
Hushai's followed ... 2 Sam. 17:14 377
Of a woman, brings peace ... 2 Sam. 20:16-20 381
David's dying ... 1 Kin. 2:1-10 393
Of old men, rejected ... 1 Kin. 12:8, 13 409
Of friends, avenged ... Esth. 5:14 581; Esth. 7:10 582

Counselor—*an advisor*

Christ is ... Is. 9:6 780
Your testimonies are ... Ps. 119:24 694
Safety in many ... Prov. 11:14 723
Brings security ... Prov. 15:22 727
Jonathan, a ... 1 Chr. 27:32 494
Gamaliel ... Acts 5:33-40 1278

Count—*to number*

Things counted:

Stars ... Gen. 15:5 21
Days ... Lev. 15:13 138
Years ... Lev. 25:8 149
Plunder ... Num. 31:26 197
Weeks ... Deut. 16:9 228
Money ... 2 Kin. 22:4 455
People ... 1 Chr. 21:17 488
Bones ... Ps. 22:17 637
Towers ... Ps. 48:12 652
Houses ... Is. 22:10 792

Countenance—*facial expression, visage*

A. *Kinds of:*
Unfriendly ... Gen. 31:1, 2 42
Fierce ... Deut. 28:50 239
Awesome ... Judg. 13:6 299
Sad ... Neh. 2:2, 3 558
Handsome ... 1 Sam. 16:12 340
Cheerful ... Prov. 15:13 727
Angry ... Prov. 25:23 738

B. *Transfigured:*
Moses' ... 2 Cor. 3:7 1367
Christ's ... Matt. 17:1, 2 1137
The believer's ... 2 Cor. 3:18 1367

Counterfeit—*a spurious imitation of the real thing*

A. *Applied to persons:*
Christ ... Matt. 24:4, 5, 24 1147
Apostles ... 2 Cor. 11:13 1373
Ministers ... 2 Cor. 11:14, 15 1373
Christians ... Gal. 2:3, 4 1380
Teachers ... 2 Pet. 2:1 1487
Prophets ... 1 John 4:1 1498
The antichrist ... Rev. 19:20 1536

B. *Applied to things:*
Worship ... Matt. 15:8, 9 1135
Gospel ... Gal. 1:6-12 1378
Miracles ... 2 Thess. 2:7-12 1421
Knowledge ... 1 Tim. 6:20 1430
Commandments ... Titus 1:13, 14 1440
Doctrines ... Heb. 13:9 1463
Religion ... James 1:26 1468
Prayers ... James 4:3 1471

Country—*the land of a nation*

Commanded to leave ... Gen. 12:1-4 18
Love of native ... Gen. 30:25 41
Exiled from ... Ps. 137:1-6 704
A prophet in his own ... Luke 4:24 1198
A heavenly ... Heb. 11:16 1460

Courage—*fearlessness in the face of danger*

A. *Manifested:*
Among enemies ... Ezra 5:1-17 547
In battle ... 1 Sam. 17:46 343
Against great foes ... Judg. 7:7-23 291
Against great odds ... 1 Sam. 17:32, 50 342
When threatened ... Dan. 3:16-18 979
When intimidated ... Dan. 6:7-13 984
When facing death ... Judg. 16:28-30 303
In youth ... 1 Sam. 14:6-45 336
In old age ... Josh. 14:10-12 267
Before a king ... Esth. 4:8, 16 579
In moral crises ... Neh. 13:1-31 572
In preaching Christ ... Acts 3:12-26 1276
In rebuking ... Gal. 2:11-15 1380

B. *Men encouraged to:*
Leaders ... Deut. 31:7 242
Joshua ... Josh. 1:5-7 252
Gideon ... Judg. 7:7-11 291
Philistines ... 1 Sam. 4:9 326
Zerubbabel ... Hag. 2:4 1065
Solomon ... 1 Chr. 28:20 495

Course—*onward movement; advance*

A ship's direction ... Acts 16:11 1295
A prescribed path ... Judg. 5:20 289
The age ... Eph. 2:2 1387
The cycle of life ... James 3:6 1469

Courtesy—*visible signs of respect*

A. *Shown in:*
Manner of address ... Gen. 18:3 24
Gestures of bowing ... Gen. 19:1 26
Rising before superiors ... Lev. 19:32 142
Well-wishing remarks ... Gen. 43:29 56
Expressions of blessing ... Ruth 2:4 314

B. *Among Christians:*
Taught ... Rom. 12:9-21 1337
Illustrated ... 3 John 1-6, 12 1506

Courts—*institution designed for justice*

A. *Kinds of:*
Circuit ... 1 Sam. 7:15-17 330
Superior and inferior ... Ex. 18:21-26 88
Ecclesiastical ... Matt. 18:15-18 1138

B. *Places held:*
At the tabernacle ... Num. 27:1-5 192
Outside the camp ... Lev. 24:13, 14 149
At the city's gates ... Ruth 4:1, 2 315
Under a tree ... Judg. 4:4, 5 288

C. *Features of:*
Witness examined ... Deut. 19:15-21 230
Accused speaks ... Mark 15:1-5 1182
Sentence of, final ... Deut. 17:8-13 228
Contempt of, forbidden ... Acts 23:1-5 1307
Corruption of, deplored ... Matt. 26:59-62 1151

Courtship—*the period leading to marriage*

Isaac and Rebekah ... Gen. 24:1-67 31
Jacob and Rachel ... Gen. 29:9-30 40
Samson ... Judg. 14:1-7 300
Boaz and Ruth ... Ruth 3:4-14 315

SUBJECT REFERENCE PAGE

Creator—*the Supreme Being*

A title of God . . . . Is. 40:28 812
Man's disrespect of . . . . Rom. 1:25 1324
To be remembered . . . . Eccl. 12:1 759

Creditor—*one to whom a debt is payable*

Interest, forbidden . . . . Ex. 22:25 93
Debts remitted . . . . Neh. 5:10-12 561
Some very cruel . . Matt. 18:28-30 1139
Christian principle . . . . Rom. 13:8 1339

Cremation—*burning a body*

Two hundred fifty were consumed . . . . Num. 16:35 180
Zimri's end . . . . 1 Kin. 16:15-19 414

Crescens—*growing*

Paul's assistant . . . 2 Tim. 4:10 1436

Crete—*an island in the Mediterranean Sea*

Some from, at Pentecost . . . . Acts 2:11 1273
Paul visits . . . . Acts 27:7-21 1314
Titus dispatched to . . . . Titus 1:5 1440
Inhabitants of, evil and lazy . . . . Titus 1:12 1440

Crib

Animals feed from . . . . Is. 1:3 771

Criminal—*a lawbreaker*

Paul considered a . . . . Acts 25:16, 27 1310
Christ accused of . . . . John 18:28-30 1263
Christ crucified between . . . . Luke 23:32, 33 1229
One unrepentant; one repentant . . . . Luke 23:39-43 1229

Cripple—*one physically impaired*

Mephibosheth, by a fall . . . . 2 Sam. 4:4 363
Paul's healing of . . . . Acts 14:8-10 1292
Jesus heals . . . . Matt. 15:30, 31 1135

Crisis—*the crest of human endurance*

Bad advice in . . . . Job 2:9, 10 590
God's advice in . . . Luke 21:25-28 1225

Crispus—*curled*

Chief ruler of synagogue at Corinth . . . . Acts 18:8 1299
Baptized by Paul . . . . 1 Cor. 1:14 1345

Crop—*the craw of a bird*

Removed by priest . . . . Lev. 1:16 120

Cross—*a method of execution*

A. *Used literally of:*
Christ's death . . . . Matt. 27:32 1154

B. *Used figuratively of:*
Duty . . . . Matt. 10:38 1129
Christ's sufferings . . . . 1 Cor. 1:17 1345
The Christian faith . . . . 1 Cor. 1:18 1345
Reconciliation . . . . Eph. 2:16 1388

Crown—*an emblem of glory*

A. *Worn by:*
High priest . . . . Lev. 8:9 127
Kings . . . . 2 Sam. 12:30 371
Queens . . . . Esth. 2:17 578
Ministers of state . . . . Esth. 8:15 583

B. *Applied figuratively to:*
A good wife . . . Prov. 12:4 724
Old age . . . . Prov. 16:31 729
Grandchildren . . . . Prov. 17:6 729
Honor . . . . Prov. 27:24 740
Material blessings . . . . Ps. 65:11 661

C. *Applied spiritually to:*
Christ . . . . Ps. 132:18 702
Christ at His return . . . . Rev. 19:12 1536
Christ glorified . . . . Heb. 2:7-9 1450
The church . . . . Is. 62:3 834
The Christian's reward . . . . 2 Tim. 2:5 1434
The minister's reward . . . . Phil. 4:1 1401
Soul winners . . 1 Thess. 2:19 1415
The Christian's incorruptible prize . . . . 1 Cor. 9:25 1353

Crown—*the top of the head*

Figurative of retribution . . . . Ps. 7:16 628

Crown of thorns

Placed on Christ . . . . Matt. 27:29; John 19:2 1152; 1263

Crowns of Christians

Joy . . . . 1 Thess. 2:19 1415
Righteousness . . . . 2 Tim. 4:8 1436
Life . . . . James 1:12 1468
Glory . . . . 1 Pet. 5:4 1483
Imperishable . . . . 1 Cor. 9:25 1353

Crucifixion—*death on a cross*

A. *Jesus' death by:*
Predicted . . . . Matt. 20:19 1140
Demanded . . Mark 15:13, 14 1184
Gentiles . . . . Matt. 20:19 1140
Jews . . . . Acts 2:22, 23, 36 1273
Between thieves . . . . Matt. 27:38 1154
Nature of, unrecognized . . . . 1 Cor. 2:7, 8 1346

B. *Figurative of:*
Utter rejection . . . . Heb. 6:6 1455
Apostasy . . . . Rev. 11:8 1528
Union with Christ . . . . Gal. 2:20 1380
Separation . . . . Gal. 6:14 1383
Sanctification . . . . Rom. 6:6 1329
Dedication . . . . 1 Cor. 2:2 1346

Cruelty—*violence*

Descriptive of the wicked . . . . Ps. 74:20 668
To animals, forbidden . . . . Num. 22:27-35 187

Crumbs—*fragments of bread*

Dogs eat of . . . . Matt. 15:27 1135
Lazarus begs for . . . . Luke 16:20, 21 1219

Crying—*an emotional upheaval*

Accusation . . . . Gen. 4:10 10
Remorse . . . . Heb. 12:17 1463
Pretense . . . . Judg. 14:15-18 300
Sorrow . . . . 2 Sam. 18:33 378
Others' sins . . . . Ps. 119:136 698
Pain . . . . Heb. 5:7, 8 1453
None in heaven . . . Rev. 21:4 1538

Crystal—*rock crystal*

Wisdom surpasses . . . . Job 28:17-20 608
Gates of Zion . . . . Is. 54:12 827
Descriptive of heaven . . . . Rev. 4:6 1523

Cubs—*offspring of beasts*

Figurative of:
Babylonians . . . . Jer. 51:38 903
Assyrians . . . . Nah. 2:11, 12 1048
Princes of Israel . . Ezek. 19:2-9 936

Cucumber—*an edible fruit grown on a vine*

Lusted after . . . . Num. 11:5 173
Grown in gardens . . . . Is. 1:8 772

Cud—*partly digested food*

Animals chew again . . . . Lev. 11:3-8 130

Cummin—*an annual of the parsley family*

Seeds threshed by a rod . . . . Is. 28:25, 27 799
A trifle of tithing . . . . Matt. 23:23 1145

Cup

A. *Literal use of:*
For drinking . . . 2 Sam. 12:3 370

B. *Figurative uses of:*
One's portion . . . . Ps. 11:6 631
Blessings . . . . Ps. 23:5 638
Suffering . . . . Matt. 20:23 1141
New covenant . . . . 1 Cor. 10:16 1354
Hypocrisy . . . Matt. 23:25, 26; Luke 11:39 1145; 1212

Cupbearer—*a high court official*

Many under Solomon . . . . 1 Kin. 10:5 406
Nehemiah, a faithful . . . . Neh. 1:11 558

Curds

Article of diet . . . . 2 Sam. 17:29 377
Fed to infants . . . . Is. 7:15, 22 779
Illustrative of prosperity . . . . Deut. 32:14 244

See Butter

Cure—*to restore to health*

Of the body . . . . Matt. 17:16 1137
Of the mind . . . . Mark 5:15 1165
Of the demonized . . . . Matt. 12:22 1131
With means . . . . Is. 38:21 810
By faith . . . . Num. 21:8, 9 184
By prayer . . . . James 5:14, 15 1473
By God's mercy . . . Phil. 2:27 1400
Hindered . . . . 2 Kin. 8:7-15 438

Curiosity—*seeking to know things forbidden or private*

Into God's secrets, forbidden . . . . John 21:21, 22 1267

D

SUBJECT REFERENCE PAGE

Dead Sea

Called the:

Salt Sea ....Gen. 14:3 21
Sea of the Arabah ....Deut. 3:17 211

Deaf—*unable to hear*

Protection afforded ....Lev. 19:14 142
Healing of ....Matt. 11:5 1129
Figurative of spiritual inability ....Is. 42:18, 19 814
Figurative of patience ....Ps. 38:13 647

Death, eternal

A. *Described as:*
Everlasting punishment ...Matt. 25:46 1149
Resurrection of condemnation ...John 5:29 1243
God's wrath ...1 Thess. 1:10 1413
Destruction ...2 Thess. 1:9 1421; 2 Pet. 2:12 1489
Second death ....Rev. 20:14 1538

B. *Truths regarding:*
A consequence of man's sin ....Gen. 3:17-19 9
The punishment of the wicked ....Matt. 25:41, 46 1149
Separates from God ....2 Thess. 1:9 1421
Christ saves from ....John 3:16 1239
Saints shall escape from ....1 Cor. 15:54-58 1360; Rev. 2:11 1519
Vividly described ...Luke 16:22-26 1219

Death, natural

A. *Features regarding:*
Consequence of sin ....Rom. 5:12 1329
Lot of all ....Heb. 9:27 1457
Ends earthly life ....Eccl. 9:10 757
Christ delivers from fear of ....Heb. 2:14, 15 1452
Some escaped from ....Gen. 5:24 11
Some will escape ....1 Cor. 15:51, 52 1360
All to be raised from ....Acts 24:15 1308
Illustrates regeneration ....Rom. 6:2 1329

B. *Described as:*
Return to dust ....Gen. 3:19 9
Removal of breath ....Gen. 25:8 33; Acts 5:10 1277
Removal from tent ....2 Cor. 5:1 1368
Naked ....2 Cor. 5:3, 4 1368
Sleep ....John 11:11-14 1253
Departure ....Phil. 1:23 1398

C. *Recognition after:*
Departed saints recognized by the living ....Matt. 17:1-8 1137
Greater knowledge in future world ....1 Cor. 13:12 1356
The truth illustrated ...Luke 16:19-24 1219

Death of saints

A. *Described as:*
Sleep in Jesus ....1 Thess. 4:14 1416
Blessed ....Rev. 14:13 1531
A gain ....Phil. 1:21 1398
Peace ....Is. 57:1, 2 829
Crown of righteousness ....2 Tim. 4:8 1436

B. *Exemplified in:*
Abraham ....Gen. 25:8 33
Isaac ....Gen. 35:28, 29 46
Jacob ....Gen. 49:33 63
Elisha ....2 Kin. 13:14, 20 444
The criminal ...Luke 23:39-43 1229

Death of wicked

Result of sin ....Rom. 5:12 1329
Often punishment ....Ex. 23:25-29 94; Is. 65:11, 12 837
Unpleasant for God ....Ezek. 33:11 956
Without hope ....1 Thess. 4:13 1416; Rev. 20:10, 14, 15 1538

Death penalty—*legal execution*

By stoning ....Deut. 13:6-10 224; Deut. 17:5 228

Debate—*discussion, contention*

With a neighbor ...Prov. 25:9 738
Wicked, full of ....Rom. 1:29 1324
Saints must avoid ....2 Cor. 12:20 1374

Debir—*oracle*

1. King of Eglon ....Josh. 10:3-26 261
2. City of Judah ....Josh. 15:15 267
Also called Kirjath Sepher ....Josh. 15:15 267
Captured by Joshua ....Josh. 10:38, 39 262
Recaptured by Othniel ....Josh. 15:15-17 267; Judg. 1:11-13 284
Assigned to priests ....Josh. 21:13, 15 273
3. A place east of the Jordan ....Josh. 13:26 266
4. Town of Judah ....Josh. 15:7 267

Deborah—*a bee*

1. Rebekah's nurse ....Gen. 35:8 46
2. A prophetess and judge ....Judg. 4:4-14 288
Composed song of triumph ....Judg. 5:1-31 288

Debt, debtor

A. *Safeguards regarding:*
No oppression allowed ....Deut. 23:19, 20 233
Collateral protected ....Ex. 22:25-27 93
Time limitation of ....Deut. 15:1-18 227
Non-payment forbidden ....Neh. 5:4, 5 561
Debts to be honored ....Rom. 13:6 1339
Interest (usury) forbidden ....Ezek. 18:8-17 934
Love, the unpayable ....Rom. 13:8 1339
Parable concerning ...Matt. 18:23-35 1139

B. *Evils of:*
Causes complaint ....2 Kin. 4:1-7 432
Produces strife ....Jer. 15:10 862
Makes outlaws ....1 Sam. 22:2 347
Endangers property ....Prov. 6:1-5 718
Brings slavery ....Lev. 25:39, 47, 48 150

C. *Figurative of:*
Sins ....Matt. 6:12 1121
Works ....Rom. 4:4 1327
Moral obligation ....Rom. 1:14 1321
God's mercy ...Ps. 37:26 646

Decalogue (see Ten Commandments)

Decapolis—*league of ten cities*

Multitudes from, follow Jesus ....Matt. 4:25 1118
Healed demon-possessed, preaches in ....Mark 5:20 1165

Deceit, deceivers, deception

A. *The wicked:*
Devise ....Ps. 35:20 644
Speaks ....Jer. 9:8 855
Are full of ....Rom. 1:29 1324
Increase in ....2 Tim. 3:13 1436

B. *Agents of:*
Satan ....2 Cor. 11:13, 14 1373
Sin ....Rom. 7:11 1331
Self ....1 Cor. 3:18 1346; James 1:22 1468
Others ....2 Thess. 2:3 1421; 2 Tim. 3:13 1436

C. *Warnings against:*
Among religious workers ....2 Cor. 11:3-15 1373
As a sign of apostasy ....2 Thess. 2:9, 10 1421
Sign of latter days ....1 Tim. 4:1 1429
As a sign of the antichrist ....1 John 4:1-6 1498

D. *Examples of:*
Eve ....1 Tim. 2:14 1427
Abram ....Gen. 12:11-13 20
Isaac ....Gen. 26:6, 7 34
Jacob ....Gen. 27:18-27 37
Joseph's brothers ....Gen. 37:28-32 49
Pharaoh ....Ex. 8:29 76
David ....1 Sam. 21:12, 13 347
Amnon ....2 Sam. 13:6-14 372
Gehazi ....2 Kin. 5:20-27 434
Elisha ....2 Kin. 6:18-23 436
Herod ....Matt. 2:7, 8 1116
Pharisees ....Matt. 22:15, 16 1144
Peter ....Mark 14:70, 71 1182
Ananias ....Acts 5:1-11 1277
The earth ....Rev. 13:11-14 1531

Deceive—*to delude or mislead*

A. *In Old Testament:*
Eve, by Satan ....Gen. 3:13 9
Israel, by the Midianites ....Num. 25:17, 18 190
Joshua, by the Gibeonites ...Josh. 9:22 261

B. *Of Christians:*
By flattering words ....Rom. 16:18 1341
By false report ....2 Thess. 2:3 1421
By false reasoning ....Col. 2:4 1406
By evil spirits ....1 Tim. 4:1 1429
By false prophets ....Mark 13:22 1179; 2 Tim. 3:13 1436

Decision—*determination to follow a course of action*

A. *Sources of:*
Loyalty ....Ruth 1:16 313
Prayer ....1 Sam. 23:1-13 348
The Lord ....1 Kin. 12:15 409

SUBJECT REFERENCE PAGE

God's truth .... Deut. 32:2 244
The Messiah .. Is. 26:19 796
Man's fickleness .... Hos. 6:4 1000
Peace and harmony ..... Ps. 133:3 702

Dexterity—*skill in using one's hands or body*

Of 700 men .... Judg. 20:16 308
David's .... 1 Sam. 17:40-50 343

Diadem—*a crown*

Reserved for God's people .... Is. 28:5 798
Restored by grace .... Is. 62:3 834

Dial—*an instrument for telling time*

Miraculous movement of .... Is. 38:8 810

Diamond—*crystallized carbon*

Sacred .... Ex. 28:18 100
Precious .... Ezek. 28:13 951

Diblah—*rounded cake*

An unidentified place .... Ezek. 6:14 922

Diblaim—*twin fig cakes*

Hosea's father-in-law .... Hos. 1:3 996

Dibon—*a wasting away*

1. Amorite town .... Num. 21:30 186
Taken by Israel .... Num. 32:2-5 198
Rebuilt by Gadites ...... Num. 32:34 199
Called Dibon Gad .... Num. 33:45, 46 200
Later given to Reubenites .. Josh. 13:9, 15, 17 265
Destruction of, foretold ...... Jer. 48:18, 22 896
2. A village of Judah .... Neh. 11:25 571

Dibri—*loquacious; wordy*

A Danite .... Lev. 24:11-14 149

Dictator—*ruler with absolute authority*

A. *Powers of, to:*
Take life ...... 1 Kin. 2:45, 46 394
Judge .... 1 Kin. 10:9 406
Tax .... 2 Kin. 15:19, 20 447
Levy labor .... 1 Kin. 5:13-15 398
Make war ..... 1 Kin. 20:1 420
Form alliances .... 1 Kin. 15:18, 19 413

B. *Examples, evil:*
Pharaoh ...... Ex. 1:8-22 68
Ahab .... 1 Kin. 16:28-33 414
Herod .... Matt. 2:16 1116

C. *Examples, benevolent:*
Solomon ...... 1 Kin. 8:12-21 402; 1 Kin. 10:23, 24 407
Cyrus .... Ezra 1:1-4 542

Didymus—*twin*

Surname of Thomas .... John 11:16 1253

Diet

Of the Hebrews ... Lev. 11:1-47 130

Differing weights

Prohibited ...... Deut. 25:13, 14 236

Difficulties—*problems hard to solve*

A. *Kinds of:*
Mental .... Ps. 139:6, 14 704
Moral .... Ps. 38:1-22 646
Theological ... John 6:48-60 1246

B. *Examples of:*
Birth of a child in old age .... Gen. 18:9-15 24
Testing of Abraham ..... Gen. 22:1-14 30
Slaughter of Canaanites ... Ex. 23:27-33 94
God's providence ... Ps. 44:1-26 650
Prosperity of wicked .... Ps. 73:1-28 666
Israel's unbelief ...... John 12:39-41 1256

C. *Negative attitudes toward:*
Rebellion against .... Num. 21:4, 5 184
Unbelief under .... Heb. 3:12-19 1452

D. *Positive attitudes toward:*
Submission under .... Num. 14:7-9 177
Prayer concerning ..... Mark 11:23, 24 1175
Admission of .... 2 Pet. 3:15, 16 1489

Diklah—*palm tree*

Son of Joktan .... Gen. 10:27 16

Dilean—*cucumber*

Town of Judah .... Josh. 15:38 268

Dilemma—*unpleasant alternatives*

Given to David .... 1 Chr. 21:9-17 488
Presented to Jews .... Matt. 21:23-27 1143

Diligence—*faithful applications to one's work*

A. *Manifested in:*
A child's education .... Deut. 6:6, 7 215
Dedicated service .... Rom. 12:11 1337
A minister's task .... 2 Tim. 4:1-5 1436

B. *Special objects of:*
The soul ...... Deut. 4:9 211
God's commandments .... Deut. 6:17 217
The heart ...... Prov. 4:23 718
Christian qualities ..... 2 Pet. 1:5-9 1487
One's calling .. 2 Pet. 1:10 1487

C. *Rewards of:*
Prosperity ..... Prov. 10:4 722
Ruling hand ... Prov. 12:24 725
Perseverance .... 2 Pet. 1:10 1487

Dimnah—*dung heap*

City of Zebulun ... Josh. 21:35 275
Same as Rimmon .... 1 Chr. 6:77 472

Dimon—*riverbed*

Place in Moab .... Is. 15:9 788

Dimonah

Town in Judah .... Josh. 15:22 268
Same as Dibon ... Neh. 11:25 571

Dinah—*judgment*

Daughter of Leah .... Gen. 30:20, 21 41
Defiled by Shechem .... Gen. 34:1-24 45
Avenged by brothers .... Gen. 34:25-31 45
Guilt concerning .. Gen. 49:5-7 61

Dinaites

Foreigners who settled in Samaria .... Ezra 4:9 546

Dinhabah—*give judgment*

City of Edom ..... Gen. 36:32 48

Dionysius—*of the* (god) *Dionysos*

Prominent Athenian; converted by Paul .... Acts 17:34 1299

Diotrephes—*nurtured by Zeus*

Unruly church member .... 3 John 9, 10 1506

Diplomacy—*the art of managing affairs of state*

Joseph, an example in .... Gen. 41:33-46 54
Mordecai's advancement in .... Esth. 10:1-3 585
Daniel's ability in .... Dan. 2:48, 49 978
Paul's resort to ... Acts 21:20-25 1305

Disappointment—*the non-fulfillment of one's hopes*

A. *Concerning one's:*
Sons .... 1 Sam. 2:12-17 323
Mate .... 1 Sam. 25:23-31 350
Failure .... 2 Sam. 17:23 377
Wisdom .... Eccl. 1:12-18 749
Acceptance .... Jer. 20:7-9 866
Mission .... Jon. 4:1-9 1032
Hopes .... Luke 24:17-24 1230

B. *Antidotes against:*
Let trust prevail .... Hab. 3:17-19 1054
Put God first .. Hag. 1:2-14 1064
Accept God's plan .... Rom. 8:28 1333
Remember God's promises ..... Heb. 6:10-12 1455

Disarmament—*abolishing weapons of war*

Imposed upon Israel .... 1 Sam. 13:19-22 334
Figurative of peace .... Is. 2:4 773

Discernment, spiritual

Requested by Solomon .... 1 Kin. 3:9-14 395
Prayed for by the psalmist .... Ps. 119:18 694
Sought by Daniel .... Dan. 7:15, 16 986
Denied to the unregenerate .... 1 Cor. 2:14 1346
Necessity of .... 1 John 4:1-6 1498

Disciples—*followers of a teacher*

John the Baptist's .... John 1:35 1237
Jesus' .... John 2:2 1237

SUBJECT REFERENCE PAGE

Joseph ....Gen. 37:5 49
Pharaoh ......Gen. 41:1-13 52
Unnamed person ....Judg. 7:13, 14 292
Solomon ......1 Kin. 3:5-10 395
Job ....Job 7:14 594
Nebuchadnezzar ....Dan. 2:1-13 977
Joseph ....Matt. 1:19, 20 1116
Pilate's wife ...Matt. 27:13, 19 1152

Dregs—*the sediments of liquids; grounds*

Wicked shall drink down ....Ps. 75:8 668
Contains God's fury ....Is. 51:17, 22 824
Figurative of negligence and ease ....Jer. 48:11 896

Drink—*to swallow liquids*

A. *Used literally of:*
Water ....Gen. 24:14 32
Wine ....Gen. 9:21 15

B. *Used figuratively of:*
Famine ....2 Kin. 18:27 452
Misery ....Is. 51:22, 23 824
Married pleasure .....Prov. 5:15-19 718
Unholy alliances ....Jer. 2:18 845
God's blessings .....Zech. 9:15-17 1073
Spiritual communion ..John 6:53, 54 1246
Holy Spirit ....John 7:37-39 1248

Drink offerings

Of wine ....Hos. 9:4 1001
Of water ....1 Sam. 7:6 328

Dromedary—*a specie of camel*

Noted for speed ...Jer. 2:23 845
Figurative of Gospel blessings ....Is. 60:6 832

Dropsy—*an unnatural accumulation of fluid in parts of the body*

Healing of ....Luke 14:2-4 1216

Dross—*impurities separated from metals*

Result of refinement ......Prov. 25:4 738
Figurative of Israel ....Is. 1:22, 25 772

Drought—*an extended dry season*

Unbearable in the day ....Gen. 31:40 43
Seen in the wilderness ....Deut. 8:15 220
Comes in summer ....Ps. 32:4 642
Sent as a judgment ....Hag. 1:11 1064
Only God can stop ....Jer. 14:22 861
Descriptive of spiritual barrenness ......Jer. 14:1-7 860
The wicked dwell in ....Jer. 17:5, 6 863
The righteous endure ....Jer. 17:8 863
Longest ....1 Kin. 18:1; Luke 4:25 416, 1198

Drown

Of the Egyptians ....Ex. 14:27-30 85
Jonah saved from ....Jon. 1:15-17 1030
Of severe judgment ....Matt. 18:6 1138

The woman saved from ....Rev. 12:15, 16 1529
Figurative of lusts ....1 Tim. 6:9 1430

Drowsiness—*the mental state preceding sleep*

Prelude to poverty ....Prov. 23:21 736
Disciples guilty of ....Matt. 26:36-43 1150

Drunkenness—*state of intoxication*

A. *Evils of:*
Debases ......Gen. 9:21, 22 15
Provokes brawling ....Prov. 20:1 732
Poverty ....Prov. 23:21 736
Perverts justice ....Is. 5:22, 23 777
Confuses the mind ....Is. 28:7 798
Licentiousness ....Rom. 13:13 1339
Disorderliness ....Matt. 24:48-51 1148
Hinders watchfulness ....1 Thess. 5:6, 7 1416

B. *Actual instances of the evil of:*
Defeat in battle ....1 Kin. 20:16-21 420
Degradation ...Esth. 1:10, 11 577
Debauchery ....Dan. 5:1-4 983
Weakness .....Amos 4:1 1017
Disorder .....1 Cor. 11:21, 22 1355

C. *Penalties of:*
Death ....Deut. 21:20, 21 232
Exclusion from fellowship ....1 Cor. 5:11 1349
Exclusion from heaven ....1 Cor. 6:9, 10 1349

D. *Figurative of:*
Destruction ...Is. 49:26 822
Roaring waves ....Ps. 107:25-27 687
Giddiness .....Is. 19:14 790
Error ....Is. 28:7 798
Spiritual blindness .....Is. 29:9-11 799
International chaos ....Jer. 25:15-29 871
Persecution ...Rev. 17:6 1533

Drusilla—feminine of *"Drusus"*

Wife of Felix; hears Paul ....Acts 24:24, 25 1308

Dumah—*silence*

1. Descendants (a tribe) of Ishmael ......Gen. 25:14 34
2. Town in Judah ....Josh. 15:52 268

Dumb—*inability to speak*

A. *Used literally of dumbness:*
Imposed ......Ezek. 3:26, 27 921
Demonized ....Mark 9:17, 25 1171

B. *Used figuratively of:*
Inefficient leaders ....Is. 56:10 828
Helplessness ..1 Cor. 12:2 1355

See Mute

Dung—*excrement; refuse*

A. *Used for:*
Fuel ....Ezek. 4:12, 15 921
Food in famine ....2 Kin. 6:25 436

B. *Figurative of:*
Something worthless .....2 Kin. 9:37 440

Dungeon—*an underground prison*

Joseph in ....Gen. 40:8, 15 51
Jeremiah in ....Jer. 37:16 885

Dunghills—*heaps of manure*

Pile of manure ....Luke 14:34, 35 1217

Dura—*circuit, wall*

Site of Nebuchadnezzar's golden image ....Dan. 3:1 978

Dust—*powdery earth*

A. *Used literally of:*
Man's body ....Gen. 2:7 7
Dust of Egypt ....Ex. 8:16, 17 75
Particles of soil ....Num. 5:17 165

B. *Used figuratively of:*
Man's mortality ......Gen. 3:19 9
Descendants ..Gen. 13:16 20
Judgment ......Deut. 28:24 238
Act of cursing ....2 Sam. 16:13 376
Dejection .....Job 2:12 591
Subjection ....Is. 49:23 822
The grave .....Is. 26:19 796
Rejection ......Matt. 10:14 1127

Duty—*an obligation*

A. *Toward men:*
Husband to wife ....Eph. 5:25-33 1392
Wife to husband ......Eph. 5:22-24 1392
Parents to children ....Eph. 6:4 1392
Children to parents ....Eph. 6:1-3 1392
Subjects to rulers ....1 Pet. 2:12-20 1479
Rulers to subjects ....Rom. 13:1-7 1337
Men to men ...1 Pet. 3:8-16 1480
The weak ......1 Cor. 8:1-13 1352

B. *Toward God:*
Love ....Deut. 11:1 222
Obey ....Matt. 12:50 1132
Serve ....1 Thess. 1:9 1413
Worship ....John 4:23 1241

Dwarf—*a diminutive person*

Excluded from priesthood ....Lev. 21:20 144

Dwelling, God

In the tabernacle ....Ex. 29:43-46 103
In the temple ....1 Kin. 6:11-13; 2 Chr. 7:1-3 398, 508
In Zion ....Is. 8:18 780
In Christ ....Col. 2:9 1408
Among men ....John 1:14 1236
In our hearts .....1 John 4:12-16 1498
In the Holy Spirit ....1 Cor. 3:16 1346
In the New Jerusalem ....Rev. 7:15 1525

Dyeing—*coloring*

Leather ....Ex. 25:5 95

Dysentery

Cured by Paul ....Acts 28:8 1315

SUBJECT **REFERENCE** **PAGE**

Anxiety concerning, prohibited .... Matt. 6:24-34 1123

B. *Spiritual significance of:*
Covenant ..... Ex. 24:11 95
Adoption ..... Jer. 52:33, 34 905
Fellowship ..... Luke 22:15-20 1226

C. *Christian attitude toward:*
Tradition rejected ..... Mark 7:1-23 1167
Disorderliness condemned ..... 1 Cor. 11:20-22 1355
Regard for weaker brother ..... Rom. 14:1-23 1339
No work, no eating ..... 2 Thess. 3:7-10 1422

Ebal—*to be bare, stony*

1. Son of Shobal ..... Gen. 36:23 48
Same as Obal ..... Gen. 10:28 16
2. Mountain in Samaria ..... Deut. 27:12, 13 237
Law to be written upon ..... Deut. 27:1-8 237
Fulfilled by Joshua ..... Josh. 8:30-35 260

Ebed—*slave*

1. Gaal's father .. Judg. 9:28, 30 295
2. Son of Jonathan ..... Ezra 8:6 550

Ebed-Melech—*slave of the king*

Ethiopian eunuch; rescues Jeremiah ..... Jer. 38:7-13 886
Promised divine protection ..... Jer. 39:15-18 887

Ebenezer—*stone of help*

Site of Israel's defeat ..... 1 Sam. 4:1-10 326
Ark transferred from ..... 1 Sam. 5:1 327
Site of memorial stone ..... 1 Sam. 7:10, 12 328

Eber—*the region beyond*

1. Great-grandson of Shem . Gen. 10:21-24 16; 1 Chr. 1:25 465
Progenitor of the:
Hebrews ..... Gen. 11:16-26 18
Arabians and Arameans ..... Gen. 10:25-30 16
Ancestor of Christ ..... Luke 3:35 1195
2. Son of Elpaal ..... 1 Chr. 8:12 473
3. Son of Shashak ..... 1 Chr. 8:22, 25 473
4. Postexilic priest ..... Neh. 12:20 571

Ebiasaph—*gatherer*

Forefather of Samuel ..... 1 Chr. 6:23 469
Same as Abiasaph ..... Ex. 6:16, 18, 24 74

Ebony

Black, heavy hardwood; article of trade ..... Ezek. 27:15 950

Ebron—*alliance*

Town of Asher .... Josh. 19:28 272

See Hebron

Ecclesiastes, Book of—from Gr. word "assembly" and Heb. word "one who assembles"

Vanity of earthly things ..... Eccl. 1:2 749
Material goods .... Eccl. 5:10-12 753

Eclipse of the sun

Foretold ..... Amos 8:9 1022

Economy—*living thriftily*

The law of ..... Prov. 11:24 723
The wrong kind ... Hag. 1:6, 9-11 1064
Exemplified by Jesus ..... John 6:11, 12 1244

Eczema

Makes an animal unacceptable ... Lev. 22:22 145

Eden—*delight; pleasantness*

1. First home ..... Gen. 2:8-15 7
Zion becomes like ..... Is. 51:3 823
Called the "garden of God" ..... Ezek. 28:13 951
Terrible contrast ..... Joel 2:3 1009
2. Region in Mesopotamia ..... Is. 37:12 808
3. Gershonite Levite ..... 2 Chr. 29:12 528

Eder—*a flock*

1. Tower ..... Gen. 35:21 46
2. Town in Judah ..... Josh. 15:21 268
3. Benjamite ..... 1 Chr. 8:15 473
4. Levite ..... 1 Chr. 23:23 490

Edification—*building up one's faith*

A. *Objects of:*
The church .... 1 Cor. 14:4-12 1356
The body of Christ ..... Eph. 4:12 1390
One another .... Rom. 14:19 1339

B. *Accomplished by:*
The ministry .. 2 Cor. 12:19 1374
Christian gifts ..... 1 Cor. 14:3-12 1356
Word of God .. Acts 20:32 1303
Love ..... 1 Cor. 8:1 1352
Spiritual things ..... Rom. 14:19 1339
Seeking another's goods ..... Rom. 15:2 1340
God's authority ..... 2 Cor. 10:8 1373

C. *Hindrances of:*
Carnal spirit ... 1 Cor. 3:1-4 1346
Disputes ..... 1 Tim. 1:3, 4 1426
Spiritual lukewarmness .... Rev. 3:14-22 1521
Worldly spirit ..... James 4:1-6 1471

Edom—*red*

1. Name given to Esau ..... Gen. 25:30 34
2. Edomites ..... Num. 20:18-21 184
3. Land of Esau; called Seir ..... Gen. 32:3 43
Called Edom and Idumea ..... Mark 3:8 1163
Mountainous land ..... Jer. 49:16, 17 898
People of, cursed ..... Is. 34:5, 6 805

Edomites—*descendants of Esau*

A. *Character of:*
Warlike ..... Gen. 27:40 37
Idolatrous ..... 2 Chr. 25:14, 20 524
Superstitious ..... Jer. 27:3, 9 873
Proud ..... Jer. 49:16 898
Strong ..... Jer. 49:19 898
Vindictive ..... Ezek. 25:12 947

B. *Relations with Israel:*
Descendants of Esau ..... Gen. 36:9 48
Refused passage to ..... Num. 20:18-20 184
Enemies of .... Ezek. 35:5-7 958
Wars against ..... 1 Sam. 14:47 337
Joined enemies of ..... 2 Chr. 20:10 519
Aided Babylon against ..... Ps. 137:7 704

C. *Prophecies concerning:*
Subjection to Israel ..... Gen. 27:37 37
Punishment for persecuting Israel ..... Is. 34:5-8 805
Utter desolation of ..... Is. 34:9-17 805
Figurative of Gentiles ..... Amos 9:11, 12 1023

Edrei—*mighty*

1. Capital of Bashan ..... Deut. 3:10 211
Site of Og's defeat ..... Num. 21:33-35 186
2. City of Naphtali ..... Josh. 19:37 272

Education—*instruction in knowledge*

A. *Performed by:*
Parents ..... Eph. 6:4 1392
Guardians ..... Gal. 4:1-3 1381
Teachers ..... 2 Chr. 17:7-9 517
Learned men ..... Acts 22:3 1306

B. *Method of:*
Sharing ..... Gal. 6:6 1383
Recalling God's works ..... Ps. 78:1-8 669
Learning from nature ..... Prov. 6:6-11 719
Step by step ... Is. 28:10 798
Asking questions ..... Luke 2:46 1194

C. *Examples of:*
Moses ..... Acts 7:22 1279
Daniel ..... Dan. 1:17 977
Paul ..... Acts 22:3 1306
Timothy ..... 2 Tim. 3:15, 16 1436

Effeminate—*a man with female traits*

Curse on Egypt ... Is. 19:16 790
The weakness of Nineveh ..... Nah. 3:13 1049
Rebuked by Paul ..... 1 Cor. 16:13 1361
Shall not inherit the kingdom of God ..... 1 Cor. 6:9 1349

Effort—*using energy to get something done*

Organized ..... Neh. 4:15-23 561
Diligence in ..... Neh. 6:1-4 562
Inspired to ..... Hag. 1:12-14 1064
Ill-considered ..... Luke 14:28-30 1217
The highest ..... Phil. 3:11-14 1401

Egg

Prohibition concerning that of birds ..... Deut. 22:6 232
Article of food .... Luke 11:12 1211
White of, without taste ..... Job 6:6 593

SUBJECT REFERENCE PAGE

Eglah—*heifer*
Wife of David ....2 Sam. 3:2, 5 362

Eglaim—*two ponds*
Moabite town .....Is. 15:8 788

Eglon—*heifer-like*
1. Moabite king ....Judg. 3:12-15 287
2. City of Judah ....Josh. 15:39 268

Egotism—*a sinful exultation of one's self*
Satan ....Is. 14:13-15 786; Luke 4:5, 6 1198
Goliath ....1 Sam. 17:4-11 340
Haman ....Esth. 6:6-12 582
Simon ....Acts 8:9-11 1282
Herod ....Acts 12:20-23 1289
Diotrephes ....3 John 9, 10 1506
Sign of antichrist ....2 Thess. 2:3, 4 1421
Sign of the last days ....2 Tim. 3:1-5 1434

Egypt—*black*
A. *Israel's contact with:*
Abram visits ..Gen. 12:10 20
Joseph sold into ....Gen. 37:28, 36 49
Joseph becomes leader in............Gen. 39:1-4 50
Hebrews move to...........Gen. 46:5-7 58
Persecution by ....Ex. 1:15-22 69
Israel leaves ...Ex. 12:31-33 82
Army of, perishes ......Ex. 14:26-28 85
B. *Characteristics of:*
Superstitious ....Is. 19:3 790
Unprofitable ...Is. 30:1-7 800
Treacherous ...Is. 36:6 806
Ambitious .....Jer. 46:8, 9 894
C. *Prophecies concerning:*
Israel's sojourn in............Gen. 15:13 23
Destruction of..........Ezek. 30:24, 25 953
Ever a lowly kingdom ......Ezek. 29:14, 15 952
Conversion of............Is. 19:18-25 790
Christ, called out of............Matt. 2:15 1116

Egyptian, the—*an unknown insurrectionist*
Paul mistaken for ....Acts 21:37, 38 1305

Ehi—*brotherly*
Benjamin's son ...Gen. 46:21 59
Same as Ahiram ....Num. 26:38 191

Ehud—*union*
1. Great-grandson of Benjamin ....1 Chr. 7:10 472
2. Son of Gera ...Judg. 3:15 287
Slays Eglon ...Judg. 3:16-26 287

Eker—*offshoot*
Descendant of Judah ....1 Chr. 2:27 466

Ekron—*extermination*
Philistine city .....Josh. 13:3 265
Captured by Judah ....Judg. 1:18 284

Assigned to Dan ..Josh. 19:40, 43 272
Ark sent to ....1 Sam. 5:10 327
Denounced by the prophets ....Jer. 25:9, 20 871

El—*ancient word for God, often used as prefix to Hebrew names*
El Bethel ....Gen. 35:6, 7 46

Eladah—*God has adorned*
A descendant of Ephraim..........1 Chr. 7:20 472

Elah—*an oak*
1. Duke of Edom ....Gen. 36:41 48
2. Son of Caleb ..1 Chr. 4:15 467
3. King of Israel ....1 Kin. 16:6, 8-10 413
4. Benjamite .....1 Chr. 9:8 474
5. Father of Hoshea ......2 Kin. 15:30 447
6. Valley of ....1 Sam. 17:2, 19 340
7. Father of Shimei ....1 Kin. 4:18 397

Elam—*hidden*
1. Son of Shem ..Gen. 10:22 16
2. Benjamite .....1 Chr. 8:24 473
3. Korahite Levite ....1 Chr. 26:1, 3 492
4. Head of postexilic families ......Ezra 2:7 542
5. Another family head ....Ezra 2:31 544
6. One who signs covenant .....Neh. 10:1, 14 569
7. Priest ....Neh. 12:42 572

Elamites—*descendants of Elam*
A Semite (Shem) people ....Gen. 10:22 16
An ancient nation ....Gen. 14:1 21
Connected with Media ....Is. 21:2 791
Destruction of ....Jer. 49:34-39 899
In Persian empire ....Ezra 4:9 546
Jews from, at Pentecost ....Acts 2:9 1273

Elasah—*God has made*
1. Shaphan's son ....Jer. 29:3 874
2. Son of Pashhur ......Ezra 10:22 553

Elath—*a grove*
Seaport on Red Sea ....1 Kin. 9:26 406
Built by Azariah ....2 Kin. 14:21, 22 446
Captured by Syrians ....2 Kin. 16:6 447
Same as Ezion Geber ....2 Chr. 8:17 510

El Bethel—*God of Bethel*
Site of Jacob's altar ....Gen. 35:6, 7 46

Eldaah—*God has called*
Son of Midian ....Gen. 25:4 33

Eldad—*God has loved*
Elder of Moses ....Num. 11:26-29 175

Elderly
A. *Contributions of:*
Counsel .....1 Kin. 12:6-16 409; Job 12:12 597
Spiritual service ....Luke 2:36-38 1194
Fruitfulness ...Ps. 92:13, 14 679
Leadership ...Josh. 24:2, 14, 15, 29 277
B. *Attitude toward:*
Minister to needs ....1 Kin. 1:15 391
Respect ....Ps. 71:18, 19 665
As cared for by God ....Is. 46:4 818
Honor ....Lev. 19:32 142; Prov. 16:31 729

Elders of Israel
A. *Functions of, in Mosaic period:*
Rule the people ....Judg. 2:7 285
Represent the nation ....Ex. 3:16, 18 70
Share in national guilt ....Josh. 7:6 258
Assist in government ..Num. 11:16-25 173
Perform religious acts..........Ex. 12:21, 22 80
B. *Functions of, in later periods:*
Choose a king ....2 Sam. 3:17-21 362
Ratify a covenant .....2 Sam. 5:3 363
Assist at a dedication....1 Kin. 8:1-3 402
Counsel kings........1 Kin. 12:6-8, 13 409
Legislate reforms ......Ezra 10:7-14 553
Try civil cases ....Matt. 26:3-68 1149

Elders in the church
A. *Qualifications of, stated by:*
Paul ....Titus 1:5-14 1440
Peter ....1 Pet. 5:1-4 1483
B. *Duties of:*
Administer relief.........Acts 11:29, 30 1289
Correct error ....Acts 15:4, 6, 23 1293
Hold fast the faithful Word ....Titus 1:5, 9 1440
Rule well ......1 Tim. 5:17 1429
Minister to the sick ....James 5:14, 15 1473
C. *Honors bestowed on:*
Ordination ....Acts 14:21, 23 1293
Obedience ....Heb. 13:7, 17 1463
Due respect ...1 Tim. 5:1, 19 1429
See Bishop

Elead—*God has testified*
Ephraimite ....1 Chr. 7:21 472

Elealeh—*God has ascended*
Moabite town .....Is. 15:1, 4 787
Rebuilt by Reubenites ......Num. 32:37 199

Eleasah—*God has made*
1. Descendant of Judah ....1 Chr. 2:2-39 465
2. Descendant of Saul ....1 Chr. 8:33-37 473

Eleazar—*God has helped*
1. Son of Aaron........Ex. 6:23 74

SUBJECT — REFERENCE — PAGE

Barren .... Luke 1:7, 13 — 1190
Conceives a son .. Luke 1:24, 25 — 1190
Relative of Mary .... Luke 1:36 — 1192
Salutation to Mary .... Luke 1:39-45 — 1192
Mother of John the Baptist .... Luke 1:57-60 — 1192

Elizaphan—*God has concealed*

1. Chief of Kohathites ... Num. 3:30 — 163
Heads family .... 1 Chr. 15:5, 8 — 481
Family consecrated ..... 2 Chr. 29:12-16 — 528
2. Son of Parnach ...... Num. 34:25 — 202

Elizur—*God is a rock*

Reubenite warrior .... Num. 1:5 — 159

Eljehoenai—*toward God are my eyes*

Korahite gatekeeper ...... 1 Chr. 26:1-3 — 492

Elkanah—*God has possessed*

1. Father of Samuel ...... 1 Sam. 1:1-23 — 321
2. Son of Korah .... Ex. 6:24 — 74
Escapes judgment ..... Num. 26:11 — 191
3. Levite .... 1 Chr. 6:23-36 — 469
4. Descendant of Korah .... 1 Chr. 6:22, 23 — 469
5. Levite .... 1 Chr. 9:16 — 474
6. Korahite warrior ...... 1 Chr. 12:1, 6 — 479
7. Officer under Ahaz ...... 2 Chr. 28:7 — 527
8. Doorkeeper of the ark .... 1 Chr. 15:23 — 482

Elkoshite—*an inhabitant of Elkosh*

Descriptive of Nahum .... Nah. 1:1 — 1045

Ellasar

Place in Babylon .... Gen. 14:1, 9 — 21

Elmodam

Ancestor of Christ .... Luke 3:28 — 1195

Elnaam—*God is pleasantness*

Father of two warriors .... 1 Chr. 11:26, 46 — 478

Elnathan—*God has given*

1. Father of Nehushta .... 2 Kin. 24:8 — 458
Goes to Egypt .... Jer. 26:22 — 873
Entreats with king .... Jer. 36:25 — 884
2, 3, 4. Three Levites .... Ezra 8:16 — 550

Eloi (same as Eli)

Jesus' cry .... Mark 15:34 — 1184

Elon—*oak*

1. Hittite .... Gen. 26:34 — 36
2. Son of Zebulun ...... Gen. 46:14 — 59
3. Judge in Israel .... Judg. 12:11, 12 — 299
4. Town of Dan .. Josh. 19:43 — 272

Elon Beth Hanan—*oak of house of grace*

Town of Dan ..... 1 Kin. 4:9 — 397

Elonites—*belonging to Elon*

Descendants of Elon .... Num. 26:26 — 191

Eloquent—*fluent and persuasive in speech*

Moses is not ...... Ex. 4:10 — 72
Paul rejects .... 1 Cor. 2:1, 4, 5 — 1346
Apollos is .... Acts 18:24 — 1300
False prophets boast of .... 2 Pet. 2:18 — 1489

Elpaal—*God has wrought*

Benjamite .... 1 Chr. 8:11-18 — 473

El Paran—*oak of Paran*

Place in Canaan .. Gen. 14:6 — 21

Elpelet—*God of deliverance*

Son of David ..... 1 Chr. 14:3, 5 — 480
Same as Eliphelet .... 1 Chr. 3:6 — 467

Eltekeh—*God is dread*

City of Dan .... Josh. 19:44 — 272
Assigned to Levites .... Josh. 21:23 — 275

Eltekon—*founded by God*

Village in Judah .. Josh. 15:59 — 268

Eltolad—*kindred of God*

Town in Judah .... Josh. 15:21, 30 — 268
Assigned to Simeonites .... Josh. 19:4 — 271
Called Tolad ...... 1 Chr. 4:29 — 468

Elul—*vine*

Sixth month of Hebrew year .... Neh. 6:15 — 562

Eluzai—*God is my defense*

Ambidextrous warrior of David .... 1 Chr. 12:1, 5 — 479

Elymas—*a wise man*

Arabic name of Bar-Jesus, a false prophet .... Acts 13:6-12 — 1291

Elzabad—*God has bestowed*

1. Gadite warrior ...... 1 Chr. 12:8, 12 — 479
2. Korahite Levite .... 1 Chr. 26:7, 8 — 492

Elzaphan (contraction of *Elizaphan*)

Son of Uzziel ..... Ex. 6:22 — 74
Given instructions by Moses .... Lev. 10:4 — 130

Emancipation—*a setting free from slavery*

Of Hebrew nation .... Ex. 12:29-42 — 82
Of Hebrew slaves .... Ex. 21:2 — 92
In the year of jubilee .... Lev. 25:8-41 — 149
Proclaimed by Zedekiah .... Jer. 34:8-11 — 882
By Cyrus .... 2 Chr. 36:23 — 538; Ezra 1:1-4 — 542

Emasculation—*castration*

Penalty of .... Deut. 23:1 — 233

Embalming—*preserving a corpse from decay*

Unknown to Abraham .... Gen. 23:1-4 — 31
Practiced in Egypt .... Gen. 50:2, 3, 26 — 63
Manner of, among Jews .... 2 Chr. 16:14 — 517
Limitation of ..... John 11:39, 44 — 1253

Embroider—*to decorate by needlework*

In tabernacle curtains .... Ex. 26:1, 36 — 97
Bezaleel and Aholiab inspired in .... Ex. 35:30-35 — 109
On Sisera's garments .... Judg. 5:30 — 290

Emek Keziz—*cut off*

City of Benjamin .... Josh. 18:21 — 271

Emerald—*a precious stone of the beryl variety*

In high priests' garments .... Ex. 28:17 — 100
In Tyre's trade .... Ezek. 27:16 — 950
Used for ornamentation ... Ezek. 28:13 — 951
Foundation stone .... Rev. 21:19 — 1539

Emim—*terrors*

Giant race of Anakim east of the Dead Sea .... Gen. 14:5 — 21

Emmaus—*hot spring*

Town near Jerusalem .... Luke 24:13-18 — 1230

Emotion—*a person's response to living situations*

A. *Objects of:*
Self .... Job 3:1-26 — 591
Nation .... Ps. 137:1-6 — 704
Family .... Gen. 49:1-28 — 61
Mate .... 1 Sam. 25:24, 25 — 351
Foreigners .... Ruth 1:16-18 — 313

B. *Kinds of:*
Conviction .... Acts 2:37 — 1274
Contempt ..... 1 Sam. 17:42-44 — 343
Despondency .... 1 Kin. 19:4-10 — 418
Disappointment ...... Luke 18:23 — 1221
Disgust .... Neh. 4:1-3 — 560
Envy .... 1 Sam. 17:28 — 342
Fear .... 1 Kin. 19:1-3 — 418
Flattery ..... 1 Sam. 25:23-31 — 350
Hate .... Acts 7:54, 57 — 1282
Joy .... Luke 15:22-24 — 1218
Love .... Ex. 32:26-29 — 106
Loyalty ..... 2 Sam. 18:32, 33 — 378
Regret .... Luke 16:27-31 — 1219
Revenge ...... Gen. 27:41-45 — 37
Sorrow ...... 2 Sam. 12:13-19 — 371

SUBJECT REFERENCE PAGE

For abundant living ... Rom. 15:13 1340
For edification ... Rom. 15:14 1340
To raise dead ... 1 Cor. 6:14 1349; 2 Cor. 13:4 1375

En Gannim—*fountains of gardens*

1. Village of Judah ... Josh. 15:34 268
2. Border town of Issachar ... Josh. 19:21 272
Assigned to Levites ... Josh. 21:29 275

En Gedi—*fountain of a kid*

May have been originally called Hazazon Tamar ... 2 Chr. 20:2 519
Occupied by the Amorites ... Gen. 14:7 21
Assigned to Judah ... Josh. 15:62, 63 268
David's hiding place ... 1 Sam. 23:29 349
Noted for vineyards ... Song 1:14 763

Engraving—*cutting or carving on some hard substance*

Stone set in priest's breastplate ... Ex. 28:9-11, 21 99
Bezaleel, inspired in ... Ex. 35:30-33 109
Of a signet ... Ex. 28:21 100; Ex. 39:6 112
Of cherubim ... 1 Kin. 6:29 400

En Haddah—*swift fountain*

Frontier village of Issachar ... Josh. 19:17, 21 272

En Hakkore—*fountain of him who called*

Miraculous spring ... Judg. 15:14-19 302

En Hazor—*fountain of a village*

City of Naphtali ... Josh. 19:32, 37 272

Enjoyment—*satisfaction in something*

A. *Of material things:*
Depends upon obedience ... Deut. 7:9-15 217
Withheld for disobedience ... Hag. 1:3-11 1064
Must not trust in ... Luke 12:16-21 1214
Cannot fully satisfy ... Eccl. 2:1-11 749
B. *Of spiritual things:*
Abundant ... 1 Tim. 6:17 1430
Never-ending ... Is. 58:11 830
Satisfying ... Is. 55:1, 2 827
Internal ... John 7:37-39 1248
For God's people only ... Is. 65:22-24 837
Complete in heaven ... Ps. 16:11 633

Enlargement—*extension in quantity or quality*

Japheth's territory ... Gen. 9:27 15
Israel's prosperity ... Ex. 34:24 108
Solomon's kingdom ... 1 Kin. 4:20-25 397
Solomon's wisdom ... 1 Kin. 4:29-34 397
Pharisaical hypocrisy ... Matt. 23:5 1145
Spiritual:
Relationship ... 2 Cor. 6:11, 13 1369
Knowledge ... Eph. 1:15-19 1387
Opportunity ... Is. 54:1-3 825

Enlightenment, spiritual

A. *Source of:*
From God ... Ps. 18:28 635
Through God's Word ... Ps. 19:8 635
By prayer ... Eph. 1:18 1387
By God's ministers ... Acts 26:17, 18 1312
B. *Degrees of:*
Partial now ... 1 Cor. 13:9-12 1356
Hindered by sin ... 1 Cor. 2:14 1346
Complete in heaven ... Is. 60:19 833

Enoch—*dedicated*

1. Son of Cain ... Gen. 4:17 10
2. City built by Cain ... Gen. 4:17 10
3. Father of Methuselah ... Gen. 5:21 11
Walks with God ... Gen. 5:22 11
Taken up to heaven ... Gen. 5:24 11
Prophecy of, cited ... Jude 14, 15 1510

Enos, Enosh—*mortal*

Grandson of Adam ... Gen. 4:25, 26 10
Son of Seth ... Gen. 5:6-11 10
Ancestor of Christ ... Luke 3:38 1195
Genealogy of ... 1 Chr. 1:1 464

En Rimmon—*fount of pomegranates*

Reinhabited after the exile ... Neh. 11:29 571
Same as Rimmon ... Zech. 14:10 1076

En Rogel—*the fuller's fountain*

Fountain outside Jerusalem ... 2 Sam. 17:17 377
On Benjamin's boundary ... Josh. 18:11, 16 271
Seat of Adonijah's plot ... 1 Kin. 1:5-9 391

En Shemesh—*fountain of the sun*

Spring and town near Jericho ... Josh. 15:7 267

En Tappuah—*fountain of the apple tree*

Town of Ephraim ... Josh. 17:7, 8 270

Entertainment—*affording an enjoyable occasion*

A. *Occasions of:*
Child's weaning ... Gen. 21:8 29
Ratifying covenants ... Gen. 31:54 43
King's coronation ... 1 Kin. 1:9, 18, 19 391
National deliverance ... Esth. 9:17-19 585
Marriage ... Matt. 22:2 1143
Return of loved ones ... Luke 15:23-25 1218
B. *Features of:*
Invitations sent ... Luke 14:16 1217
Preparations made ... Matt. 22:4 1144
Helped by servants ... John 2:5 1237
Under a leader ... John 2:8, 9 1237
Often with music ... Luke 15:25 1218
Sometimes out of control ... 1 Sam. 25:36 351
Unusual ... Heb. 13:2 1463

Enthusiasm—*a spirit of intense zeal*

Caleb's ... Num. 13:30-33 176
Phinehas' ... Num. 25:7-13 190
David's ... 2 Sam. 6:12-22 365
Saul's (Paul's) ... Acts 9:1, 2 1284
Paul's ... Phil. 3:7-14 1401

Enticers—*those who allure to evil*

A. *Means of:*
Man ... Ex. 22:16 93
Spirit ... 2 Chr. 18:20 518
Sinners ... Prov. 1:10 714
Lusts ... James 1:14 1468
Human wisdom ... 1 Cor. 2:4 1346
B. *Reasons proposed:*
Turn from God ... Deut. 13:6-8 224
Obtain secrets ... Judg. 16:4, 5 302
Defeat a king ... 2 Chr. 18:4-34 518
Commit a sin ... James 1:14 1468

Entrails—*bowels, intestines*

Used literally:
Amasa's poured out ... 2 Sam. 20:10 380
Jehoram's came out ... 2 Chr. 21:14-19 521
Judas's gushed out ... Acts 1:16-18 1272

Envy—*resentment against another's success, jealousy*

A. *Characterized as:*
Powerful ... Prov. 27:4 740
Dominant in unregenerate nature ... Rom. 1:29 1324
Of the flesh ... Gal. 5:19-21 1383
Source of evil ... 1 Tim. 6:4 1430
B. *The evil of, among Christians:*
Hinders growth ... 1 Pet. 2:1, 2 1479
C. *Examples of:*
Philistines ... Gen. 26:14 36
Joseph's brothers ... Gen. 37:5, 11 49
Aaron and Miriam ... Num. 12:1, 2 175
Korah ... Num. 16:1-3 179
Asaph ... Ps. 73:3, 17-20 666
Haman ... Esth. 5:13 581
Chief priests ... Mark 15:10 1184
The Jews ... Acts 13:45 1292

Epaenetus

Addressed by Paul ... Rom. 16:5 1341

Epaphras

Leader of the Colossian church ... Col. 1:7, 8 1405
Suffers as a prisoner in Rome ... Philem. 23 1445

Epaphroditus—*lovely, charming*

Messenger from Philippi ... Phil. 2:25-27 1400
Brings a gift to Paul ... Phil. 4:18 1402

SUBJECT REFERENCE PAGE

Escape—*to flee from*

A. *Physical things:*
Flood .... Gen. 7:7, 8 12
City of destruction ... Gen. 19:15-30 28
Mob .... Luke 4:28-30 1198
Insane king ... 1 Sam. 19:9-18 345
Wicked queen .... 2 Kin. 11:1-3 442
Assassination .... Esth. 2:21-23 578
Hanging .... {Esth. 5:14 581; Esth. 7:9 582}
Prison .... Acts 5:18-20 1278
Sinking ship ... Acts 27:30-44 1314

B. *Spiritual things:*
Sin .... Gen. 39:10-12 51
Destruction ...... Luke 21:36 1225
Corruption .... 2 Pet. 1:4 1487
God's wrath .... {1 Thess. 1:9, 10} 1413
The great tribulation .... Rev. 7:13-17 1525

Eschatology—*teaching dealing with final destiny*

A. *In Old Testament:*
Judgment ..... Is. 2:12-22 773
Messianic kingdom .... {Jer. 23:4-18 869; Jer. 33:14-17 881}

B. *In New Testament:*
Coming of Christ .... {Matt. 24 1116; Luke 21:5-36 1224}
Resurrection of dead ... {1 Cor. 15:51-58 1360; 1 Thess. 4:13-18 1416}
Destruction of earth .... 2 Pet. 3:10-13 1489
Reign of Christ .... Rev. 20:4, 6 1536

Esek—*strife*

A well in Gerar ... Gen. 26:20 36

Esh-Baal—*man of Baal*

Son of Saul .... 1 Chr. 8:33 473

Eshban—*wise man*

Son of Dishon .... Gen. 36:26 48

Eshcol—*cluster of grapes*

1. Brother of Aner and Mamre .... Gen. 14:13, 24 21
2. Valley near Hebron ..... {Num. 13:22-27 176; Deut. 1:24 208}

Eshean—*support*

City of Judah ..... Josh. 15:52 268

Eshek—*oppression*

Descendant of Saul .... 1 Chr. 8:39 474

Eshtaol—*a way*

Town of Judah .... Josh. 15:20, 33 268
Assigned to Danites .... Josh. 19:40, 41 272
Near Samson's home and burial site .... Judg. 16:31 303

Eshtaolites

Inhabitants of Eshtaol .... 1 Chr. 2:53 466

Eshtemoa, Eshtemoh—*obedience*

Town of Judah .... Josh. 15:20, 50 268
Assigned to Levites .... Josh. 21:14 273

David sends spoils to .... {1 Sam. 30:26, 28} 355

Eshton—*restful*

Man of Judah ..... 1 Chr. 4:1-12 467

Esli—*reserved*

Ancestor of Christ .... Luke 3:25 1195

Establish—*a permanent condition*

A. *Of earthly things:*
Kingdom ...... 2 Chr. 17:5 517
Festival .... Esth. 9:21 585

B. *Of spiritual things:*
Messiah's kingdom ..... 2 Sam. 7:13 366
God's Word .... Ps. 119:38 696
Our:
Hearts .... 1 Thess. 3:13 1415
Faith .... Col. 2:7 1408
Works .... 2 Thess. 2:17 1421
Lives .... 1 Pet. 5:10 1483

C. *Accomplished by:*
God .... 2 Cor. 1:21, 22 1366

Esther—*star*

Daughter of Abihail .... Esth. 2:15 578
Mordecai's cousin .... Esth. 2:7, 15 578
Selected for harem .... Esth. 2:7-16 578
Chosen queen .... Esth. 2:17, 18 578
Seeks to help Mordecai .... Esth. 4:4-6 579
Told of Haman's plot .... Esth. 4:7-9 579
Sends message to Mordecai .... Esth. 4:10-12 579
Told to act ...... Esth. 4:13, 14 581
Seeks Mordecai's aid .... Esth. 4:15-17 581
Appears before Ahasuerus .... Esth. 5:1-5 581
Invites Ahasuerus to banquet .... Esth. 5:4-8 581
Reveals Haman's plot .... Esth. 7:1-7 582
Given Haman's house .... Esth. 8:1, 2 582
Secures change of edict .... Esth. 8:3-6 582
Makes further request .... Esth. 9:12, 13 583
With Mordecai, institutes Purim .... Esth. 9:29-32 585

Estrangement from God

Caused by:
Adam's sin ...... {Gen. 3:8-11, 24} 8
Personal sin ..... Ps. 51:9-12 654
National sin ..... Jer. 2:14-17 845

Etam—*Wild beasts' lair*

1. Village of Simeon ...... 1 Chr. 4:32 468
2. Rock where Samson took refuge .... Judg. 15:8-19 302
3. Town of Judah .... 2 Chr. 11:6 512

Eternal, everlasting—*without end*

A. *Applied to Trinity:*
God .... Ps. 90:2 677
Christ .... Prov. 8:23 721
Holy Spirit .... Heb. 9:14 1457

B. *Applied to God's attributes:*
Home .... Eccl. 12:5 759
Power .... Rom. 1:20 1324
Covenant ..... Is. 55:3 827
Gospel .... Rev. 14:6 1531
Counsels ...... Eph. 3:10, 11 1388
Righteousness .... {Ps. 119:142, 144} 698
Kingdom ...... Ps. 145:13 708
Truth .... Ps. 100:5 682
Love .... Jer. 31:3 877
Father .... Is. 9:6 780

C. *Applied to the believer:*
Comfort .... 2 Thess. 2:16 1421
Life .... John 3:15 1239
Redemption .... Heb. 9:12 1457
Salvation .... Heb. 5:9 1453
Inheritance .... Heb. 9:15 1457
Glory .... 1 Pet. 5:10 1483
Kingdom .... 2 Pet. 1:11 1487
Reward .... John 4:36 1242
Name .... Is. 56:5 828
Glory .... 2 Tim. 2:10 1434
Light .... Is. 60:19, 20 833
Joy .... Is. 51:11 823
Dwellings ..... Luke 16:9 1218
Purpose .... Eph. 3:11 1388

D. *Applied to the wicked:*
Condemnation . Mark 3:29 1163
Judgment ..... Heb. 6:2 1455
Punishment ... Matt. 25:46 1149
Destruction .... 2 Thess. 1:9 1421
Contempt .... Dan. 12:2 993
Bonds .... Jude 6 1510
Fire .... Matt. 25:41 1149
Sin .... Mark 3:29 1163

Eternity—*time without end mentioned once*

God's habitation .. Is. 57:15 829

Etham—*sea bound*

Israel's encampment ..... Ex. 13:20 83

Ethan—*perpetuity*

1. One noted for wisdom .... 1 Kin. 4:31 397
2. Levite .... 1 Chr. 6:44 470
3. Ancestor of Asaph .... 1 Chr. 6:42, 43 470

Ethanim—*incessant rains*

Seventh month in the Hebrew year .... 1 Kin. 8:2 402

Ethbaal—*with Baal*

Father of Jezebel .... 1 Kin. 16:31 414

Ether—*plenty*

Town of Judah .... Josh. 15:42 268

Ethics—*a system setting forth standards of right conduct*

Perversion of ..... Rom. 1:19-32 1324
Law of .... Rom. 2:14-16 1325
Summary of Christian .... Rom. 12:1-21 1336

Ethiopia (Cush)—*burnt face*

Country south of Egypt .... Ezek. 29:10 952
Home of the sons of Ham .... Gen. 10:6 16
Famous for minerals .... Job 28:19 608
Merchandise of ... Is. 45:14 818
Wealth of .... Is. 43:3 815
Militarily strong .. 2 Chr. 12:2, 3 514
Anguished people .... Ezek. 30:4-9 953
Defeated by Asa .. 2 Chr. 14:9-15 515
Subdued .... Dan. 11:43 993

SUBJECT — REFERENCE — PAGE

Ethiopia (Cush)—continued
- Prophecies against ....Is. 20:1-6 — 791
- Hopeful promise ..Ps. 68:31 — 663

Ethiopians—*descendants of Cush*
- Skin of, unchangeable .....Jer. 13:23 — 860
- Moses' marriage to ....Num. 12:1 — 175
- Ebed-Melech saves Jeremiah ....Jer. 38:7 — 886
- Eunuch converted ....Acts 8:26-40 — 1284

Eth Kazin—*time of a judge*
- On border of Zebulun ....Josh. 19:13, 16 — 272

Ethnan—*hire*
- Judahite ....1 Chr. 4:5-7 — 467

Ethni—*liberal*
- Levite ....1 Chr. 6:41 — 470

Eubulus—*prudent*
- Christian at Rome ....2 Tim. 4:21 — 1437

Eucharist (see Lord's Supper)

Eunice—*blessed with victory*
- Mother of Timothy ....2 Tim. 1:5 — 1433

Eunuch—*an officer or official, emasculated*

A. *Rules concerning:*
- Excluded from congregation ....Deut. 23:1 — 233
- Given promise ......Is. 56:3-5 — 828

B. *Duties of:*
- Keeper of harem ....Esth. 2:3, 14 — 578
- Attendant ...Dan. 1:3, 7, 10, 11 — 976
- Treasurer .....Acts 8:27 — 1284
- Seven, serving Ahasuerus ...Esth. 1:10, 15 — 577

Euodias—*good journey*
- Christian woman at Philippi ....Phil. 4:2 — 1401

Euphrates—*that which makes fruitful*
- River of Eden .....Gen. 2:14 — 7
- Assyria bounded by ....2 Kin. 23:29 — 458
- Babylon on ....Jer. 51:13, 36 — 902
- Boundary of God's promise ..Gen. 15:18 — 23; 1 Kin. 4:21, 24 — 397
- Scene of battle ....Jer. 46:2, 6, 10 — 893
- Exiled Jews weep there ....Ps. 137:1 — 704
- Angels bound there ....Rev. 9:14 — 1526

Euroclydon—*east wind*
- Violent wind ......Acts 27:14 — 1314

Eutychus—*fortunate*
- Sleeps during Paul's sermon ....Acts 20:9 — 1302
- Restored to life ...Acts 20:12 — 1303

Evangelism—*declaring Gospel to the unregenerate*

A. *Scope:*
- To all nations ......Matt. 28:19, 20 — 1155; Mark 16:15 — 1185
- House to house ....Acts 5:42 — 1278
- Always ....1 Pet. 3:15 — 1481
- As ambassadors ....2 Cor. 5:18-20 — 1369

B. *Source:*
- Jesus Christ ...Gal. 1:6-12 — 1378
- The Father ....John 6:44, 65 — 1246
- The Spirit .....Acts 1:8 — 1272

Evangelist—*one who proclaims good news*
- Distinct ministry ....Eph. 4:11 — 1390
- Applied to Philip ....Acts 21:8 — 1305
- Timothy works as...............2 Tim. 4:5 — 1436

Eve—*life*
- Made from Adam's rib ....Gen. 2:18-22 — 7
- Named by Adam ....Gen. 3:20 — 9
- Deceived by Satan ....Gen. 3:1-24 — 8
- Leads Adam to sin ....1 Tim. 2:13, 14 — 1427

Evening—*last hours of sunlight*
- Labor ceases .....Judg. 19:16 — 307; Ruth 2:17 — 314
- Workers paid .....Deut. 24:15 — 235
- Ritual impurity ends ....Lev. 11:24-28 — 132; Num. 19:19 — 183
- Meditation ....Gen. 24:63 — 33
- Prayer ....Matt. 14:15, 23 — 1134
- Eating ....Luke 24:29, 30 — 1231
- Sacrifice ....Ex. 29:38-42 — 103; Num. 28:3-8 — 194

Evening sacrifice—*part of Israelite worship*
- Ritual described ..Ex. 29:38-42 — 103
- Part of continual offering ....Num. 28:3-8 — 194

Events, Biblical, classified

A. *Orginating, originating other events:*
- Creation ......Gen. 1 — 4
- Fall of man ....Rom. 5:12 — 1329

B. *Epochal, introducing new period:*
- Flood ....Gen. 6–8 — 11
- The death of Christ ....Matt. 27:50, 51 — 1154; Heb. 9 — 1457

C. *Typical, foreshadowing some New Testament event:*
- The Passover—Christ as Lamb ....Ex. 12 — 80; John 1:35-37 — 1237; 1 Cor. 5:7, 8 — 1348
- Jonah and great fish—Christ's death and resurrection ....Jon. 1; 2 — 1030; Matt. 12:38-41 — 1131

D. *Prophetic, prophesying future events:*
- Return from exile ....2 Chr. 36:22, 23 — 538; Jer. 29:10 — 875
- Destruction of Jerusalem ...Luke 19:41-44 — 1222; Luke 21:20-24 — 1225

E. *Redemptive, connected with man's salvation:*
- Advent of Christ ......Luke 2:11 — 1193; Gal. 4:4, 5 — 1381
- Death of Christ.......Luke 24:44-47 — 1231; 1 Tim. 1:15 — 1426

F. *Unique, those without parallel:*
- Creation ......Gen. 1 — 4
- Virgin birth ....Matt. 1:18-25 — 1116; Luke 1:30-37 — 1192

G. *Miraculous, those produced by supernatural means:*
- Plagues on Egypt ....Ex. 7–12 — 74
- Crossing Red Sea ....Ex. 14–15 — 83
- Fall of Jericho.......Josh. 6 — 252
- Sun's standing still ....Josh. 10:12-14 — 262

H. *Judgmental, those judging people for sins:*
- Flood ....2 Pet. 2:5 — 1487
- Sodom and Gomorrah ...Gen. 19 — 26; 2 Pet. 2:6 — 1487
- Killing of Israelites ....Ex. 32:25-35 — 106; Num. 25:1-9 — 190

I. *Transforming, those producing a change:*
- Christ's transformation ....Matt. 17:1-8 — 1137
- Conversion of Paul ......Acts 9 — 1284; 1 Tim. 1:12-14 — 1426
- Believer's regeneration ....John 3:1-8 — 1239; 2 Cor. 5:17 — 1368

J. *Providential, those manifesting God's providence:*
- Baby's cry ....Ex. 2:5-10 — 69
- Joseph's being sold into Egypt ....Gen. 37:26-28 — 49; Gen. 45:1-9 — 58
- King's sleepless night ....Esth. 6:1-10 — 581

K. *Confirmatory, those confirming some promise:*
- Worship at Sinai ....Ex. 3:12 — 70
- Aaron's rod ...Num. 17:1-11 — 181
- Thunder and rain ....1 Sam. 12:16-18 — 333
- Sun's shadow moved backward ...2 Kin. 20:8-11 — 454; Is. 38:1-8 — 810

L. *Promissory, those fulfilling some promise:*
- Pentecost ....Joel 2:28-32 — 1010; Acts 2 — 1273
- Spirit's coming ......Luke 24:49 — 1231; Acts 1:4, 5, 8 — 1271; Acts 2:1-4 — 1273
- Possession of land ......Gen. 15:18-21 — 23; Josh. 24:3, 11-19 — 279

M. *Eschatological, those connected with Christ's return:*
- Doom of antichrist ....2 Thess. 2:1-12 — 1421
- Resurrection and translation ....1 Cor. 15:35-38, 42 — 1360; 1 Thess. 4:13-18 — 1416
- Resurrection and judgment ....Matt. 25:31-46 — 1149; Acts 17:31 — 1299; Rev. 20:11-15 — 1538
- Destruction of the world ....2 Pet. 3:7-15 — 1489

Evi—*desirous*
- King of Midian ...Num. 31:8 — 197
- Land of, assigned to Reuben ....Josh. 13:15, 21 — 266

SUBJECT — REFERENCE — PAGE

Eye—*the organ of sight*

A. *Affected by:*
- Age ....Gen. 27:1 — 36
- Wine ....Gen. 49:12 — 63
- Sorrow ....Job 17:7 — 601
- Disease ....Lev. 26:16 — 152
- Grief ....Ps. 6:7 — 628
- Light ....Acts 22:11 — 1306

B. *Of God, figurative of:*
- Omniscience ...2 Chr. 16:9 — 517
- Holiness ......Hab. 1:13 — 1053
- Guidance ......Ps. 32:8 — 642
- Protection .....Ps. 33:18 — 643

C. *Of man, figurative of:*
- Revealed knowledge ....Num. 24:3 — 189
- Lawlessness ...Judg. 17:6 — 304
- Jealousy ......1 Sam. 18:9 — 344
- Understanding .....Ps. 19:8 — 635
- Agreement ....Is. 52:8 — 824
- Great sorrow ..Jer. 9:1 — 855
- Retaliation ....Matt. 5:38 — 1121
- The essential nature ....Matt. 6:22, 23 — 1123
- Moral state ....Matt. 7:3-5 — 1123
- Spiritual inability ......Matt. 13:15 — 1132
- Spiritual dullness ......Mark 8:17, 18 — 1170
- Future glory ...1 Cor. 2:9 — 1346
- Illumination ...Eph. 1:18 — 1387
- Unworthy service ....Eph. 6:6 — 1393
- Worldliness ...1 John 2:16 — 1496
- Evil desires ....2 Pet. 2:14 — 1489

D. *Prophecies concerning:*
- Shall see the Redeemer ....Job 19:25-27 — 602
- Gentiles shall see ....Is. 42:6, 7 — 814
- Blind shall see ....Is. 29:18 — 800
- Will see the King ....Is. 33:17 — 805
- Will see Jesus ....Rev. 1:7 — 1517
- Tears of, shall be wiped away ....Rev. 7:17 — 1525

Eyebrows—*the arch of hair over the eyes*
- Of lepers, shaved off ....Lev. 14:2, 9 — 136

Eye salve—*an ointment*
- Christ mentions ...Rev. 3:18 — 1523

Eyeservice—*service performed only when watched by another*
- Highly obnoxious ....Eph. 6:6 — 1393

Eyewitness—*a firsthand observer*
- Consulted by Luke ....Luke 1:1, 2 — 1190
- Of Christ's majesty ....2 Pet. 1:16 — 1487

Ezbai—*shining*
- Naarai's father ....1 Chr. 11:37 — 478

Ezbon—*bright*
1. Son of Gad ....Gen. 46:16 — 59
2. Benjamite .....1 Chr. 7:7 — 472

Ezekiel—*God strengthens*

A. *Life of:*
- Hebrew prophet; son of Buzi ....Ezek. 1:3 — 918
- Carried captive to Babylon ......Ezek. 1:1-3 — 918
- Lived among exiles ....Ezek. 3:15-17 — 920
- His wife died ...Ezek. 24:18 — 946
- Persecuted .....Ezek. 3:25 — 921
- Often consulted ....Ezek. 8:1 — 924
- Prophetic minister ......Ezek. 3:17-21 — 920

B. *Visions of:*
- God's glory ...Ezek. 1:4-28 — 919
- Abominations ....Ezek. 8:5-18 — 924
- Valley of dry bones ....Ezek. 37:1-14 — 960
- Messianic times ....Ezek. 40–48 — 963
- River of life ...Ezek. 47:1-5 — 970

C. *Methods employed by:*
- Threatens dumbness ....Ezek. 3:26 — 921
- Symbolizes siege of Jerusalem ....Ezek. 4:1-3 — 921
- Shaves himself ....Ezek. 5:1-4 — 921
- Removes belongings ....Ezek. 12:3-16 — 928
- Uses boiling pot ....Ezek. 24:1-14 — 946
- Does not mourn for wife ....Ezek. 24:16-27 — 946
- Uses parables .....Ezek. 17:2-10 — 933

Ezekiel, Book of—*a Book of the Old Testament*
- Prophecies against Israel ....Ezek. 1:1–24:27 — 918
- Prophecies against the nations ....Ezek. 25:1–32:32 — 947
- Prophecies of restoration ......Ezek. 33:1–39:29 — 956
- The messianic kingdom ....Ezek. 40:1–48:35 — 963

Ezel—*departure*
- David's hiding place ....1 Sam. 20:19 — 346

Ezem—*bone*
- Village of Judah ..Josh. 15:29 — 268
- Assigned to Simeon ....Josh. 19:3 — 271

Ezer—*help*
1. Horite tribe ....1 Chr. 1:38 — 465
   Son of Seir ....Gen. 36:21 — 48
2. Ephraimite ....1 Chr. 7:21 — 472
3. Judahite ......1 Chr. 4:1, 4 — 467
4. Gadite warrior ......1 Chr. 12:9 — 479
5. Son of Jeshua ....Neh. 3:19 — 560
6. Postexilic priest ....Neh. 12:42 — 572

Ezion Geber—*backbone of a giant*
- Town on the Red Sea ....1 Kin. 9:26 — 406
- Israelite encampment ......Num. 33:35 — 200
- Seaport of Israel's navy ....1 Kin. 22:48 — 425
- See Elath

Eznite—*spear; to be sharp*
- Warrior of David ....2 Sam. 23:8 — 385
- Called Tachmonite ......2 Sam. 23:8 — 385
- Called Hachmonite ......1 Chr. 11:11 — 478

Ezra—*help*
1. Postexilic priest ....Neh. 12:1, 7 — 571
   Called Azariah ....Neh. 10:2 — 569
2. Scribe, priest and reformer of postexilic times ....Ezra 7:1-6 — 548
   - Commissioned by Artaxerxes ....Ezra 7:6-28 — 549
   - Takes exiles with him ....Ezra 8:1-20 — 549
   - Proclaims a fast ....Ezra 8:21-23 — 550
   - Commits treasures to the priests ....Ezra 8:24-30 — 550
   - Comes to Jerusalem ....Ezra 8:31, 32 — 550
   - Institutes reforms ....Ezra 9:1-15 — 551
   - Reads the Law ....Neh. 8:1-18 — 564
   - Helps in dedication .....Neh. 12:27-43 — 571

Ezra, Book of—*a book of the Old Testament*
- Return from exile ....Ezra 1:1–2:70 — 542
- Rebuilding the Temple ....Ezra 3:1–6:22 — 545
- Reformation .....Ezra 9:1–10:44 — 551

Ezrahite—*belonging to Ezrach*
- Family name of Ethan and Heman ....1 Kin. 4:31 — 397

Ezri—*my help*
- David's farm overseer ....1 Chr. 27:26 — 494

F

Fable—*a fictitious story*

A. *Form of allegory:*
- The trees ......Judg. 9:7-15 — 295
- The thistle .....2 Kin. 14:9 — 445

B. *Form of fiction, contrary to:*
- Edification .....1 Tim. 1:4 — 1426
- Godliness ......1 Tim. 4:6, 7 — 1429
- Truth ....2 Tim. 4:4 — 1436
- Facts ....2 Pet. 1:16 — 1487

Face—*front part of head*

A. *Acts performed on:*
- Spitting on ....Deut. 25:9 — 236
- Disfiguring of ....Matt. 6:16 — 1121
- Painting of ....2 Kin. 9:30 — 440
- Hitting ....2 Cor. 11:20 — 1373

B. *Acts indicated by:*
- Falling on—worship ......Gen. 17:3 — 23
- Covering of—mourning .....2 Sam. 19:4 — 379
- Hiding of—disapproval ..Deut. 31:17, 18 — 243
- Turning away of—rejection ......2 Chr. 30:9 — 529
- Setting of—determination ......2 Kin. 12:17 — 444

Face of the Lord

A. *Toward the righteous:*
- Shine on ......Num. 6:25 — 168
- Do not hide ...Ps. 102:2 — 682

SUBJECT REFERENCE PAGE

Feasts, Hebrew—continued
Weeks (Pentecost) ... Ex. 23:16 94
Tabernacle .... Lev. 23:34-44 148

B. *Purposes of:*
Unify the nation .... Deut. 12:5-14 223
Worship God .... Ex. 5:1 73
Illustrate spiritual truths .... John 7:37-39 1248
Foretell the Messiah ..... 1 Cor. 11:23-26 1355

C. *Brief history of:*
Pre-Sinaitic observance ... Ex. 12:1-27 80
Three instituted at Sinai .... Ex. 23:14-17 94
Celebrated in the wilderness .... Num. 9:3-5 171
Again at beginning of conquest ..... Josh. 5:10, 11 256
At dedication of Temple ...... 1 Kin. 8:2, 65 402
"Dedication" introduced by Solomon ..... 2 Chr. 7:9-11 509
Idolatrous counterfeits introduced by Jeroboam ... 1 Kin. 12:27-33 409
Observed in Hezekiah's reign .... 2 Chr. 30:1 529
Perversion of, by Jews .... Is. 1:13, 14 772
Restored in Josiah's reformation .... 2 Kin. 23:22, 23 457
Failure in, cause of exile .... 2 Chr. 36:20, 21 538
Restored after the exile .... Ezra 3:4 545
Purim instituted by Mordecai ..... Esth. 9:17 32 585
Christ attends .... John 2:23 1239
John 13:1 1257
Christ fulfills the Passover .... 1 Cor. 5:7, 8 1348
Christianity begins with Pentecost .... Acts 2:1-41 1273
All fulfilled in Christ .... 2 Cor. 3:3-18 1367

Feasts, social
A. *Worldly, occasions of:*
Idolatry .... Ex. 32:6 105
Drunkenness .... 1 Sam. 25:36 351
Proud display .... Esth. 1:1-8 577
Profane carousals .... Dan. 5:1-16 983
Licentiousness ..... Mark 6:21, 22 1166

B. *Proper, occasions of:*
Refreshment .. Gen. 19:1-3 26
Reconciliation ...... Gen. 31:54, 55 43
Reunion .... Gen. 43:16-34 56
Restoration .... Luke 15:22-24 1218
See Entertainment

Feeble—*powerless*
Moab .... Is. 16:14 788

Feed—*to supply food to*
A. *Used naturally of:*
Food for men .... 2 Sam. 19:33 380
Food for animals ...... Gen. 30:36 41
God's provision ..... Matt. 6:26 1123

B. *Used figuratively of:*
Messiah .... Ezek. 34:23 958
Good deeds ... Matt. 25:37 1149

Supernatural supply .... Rev. 12:6 1529
Elemental teaching ...... 1 Cor. 3:2 1346
Change of nature .... Is. 11:7 784
Corruption ..... Ps. 49:14 653
Vanity .... Hos. 12:1 1003

Feet—*the lower parts of the body*
A. *Acts performed by or on, indicating:*
Subjection ..... Josh. 10:24 262
Conquest .... 2 Sam. 22:39 384
Humiliation ... Judg. 5:27 289
Submission and entreaty ..... 1 Sam. 25:24, 41 351
Great love ..... Luke 7:38, 44-46 1204
Worship .... Rev. 19:10 1536
Learner's position ...... Luke 10:39 1211
Humility ...... John 13:5-14 1257
Changed nature .... Luke 8:35 1206
Rejection ...... Matt. 10:14 1127

B. *Figurative of:*
God's holiness ...... Ex. 3:5 70
God's nature .. Ex. 24:10 95
Clouds .... Nah. 1:3 1045
God's messengers ... Rom. 10:15 1335
Final conquest ..... Rom. 16:20 1341

C. *Unusual features concerning:*
No swelling ... Neh. 9:21 568
Lameness ..... 2 Sam. 9:3, 13 367
Neglected ..... 2 Sam. 19:24 379
Impotent ...... Acts 14:8-10 1292
Binding .... Acts 21:11 1305
See Foot

Feet washing
Performed on guests .... Gen. 18:4 24
Proffered by Abigail .... 1 Sam. 25:40, 41 351
On Jesus, with tears .... Luke 7:44 1204
Performed by Jesus .... John 13:5 1257
Duty of saints .... 1 Tim. 5:10 1429

Felix—*happy*
Governor of Judea .... Acts 23:24, 26 1307
Letter addressed to .... Acts 23:25-30 1307
Paul's defense before .... Acts 24:1-21 1308
Convicted, but unchanged ...... Acts 24:22-25 1308
Subject to bribery .... Acts 24:26, 27 1310

Fellow citizens
With the saints ... Eph. 2:19 1388

Fellow countryman
Shall not hate .... Lev. 19:17 142
Becomes poor .... Lev. 25:25 150
Judge righteously ...... Deut. 1:16 208
Lord gives rest .... Deut. 3:20 211
Save some .... Rom. 11:14 1335

Fellow servant
Who owed a hundred denarii .... Matt. 18:28-33 1139
Evil slave beats ... Matt. 24:48, 49 1148
Were to be killed .... Rev. 6:11 1524
Who hold fast the testimony of Jesus .... Rev. 19:10 1536
Who heed the words .... Rev. 22:9 1539

Fellowship—*sharing together*
A. *Based upon common:*
Purpose .... Ps. 133:1-3 702
Belief .... Acts 2:42 1274
Conviction .... 1 Pet. 3:8 1480
Work .... Neh. 4:1-23 560
Hope .... Heb. 11:39, 40 1462
Faith .... 1 Sam. 20:30-42 346
Suffering ...... Dan. 3:16-30 979
Need .... 2 Cor. 8:1-15 1371

B. *Persons sharing together:*
Father, the Son, and Christians ..... 1 John 1:3 1494
Christ and Christians .... 1 Cor. 1:9 1345
Holy Spirit and Christians .... Phil. 2:1 1400
Apostles ...... Acts 2:42 1274
Believers ...... 1 John 1:7 1494

C. *Things shared together:*
Material things .... 2 Cor. 8:4 1371
Suffering ...... Phil. 3:10 1401
The Gospel ministry ...... Gal. 2:9 1380
Gospel privileges .... Phil. 1:5 1398
Gospel mystery ...... Eph. 3:9 1388

Fellow workers
In the truth ...... 3 John 8 1506
In the kingdom ... Col. 4:11 1409
Prisca and Aquila described as .... Rom. 16:3 1341
Urbanas .... Rom. 16:9 1341
Timothy .... Rom. 16:21 1341
Paul .... 1 Cor. 3:1-9 1346
Titus .... 2 Cor. 8:23 1371
Epaphroditus ..... Phil. 2:25 1400
Philemon .... Philem. 1 1445
Marcus, Aristarchus, Demas, Lucas .... Philem. 24 1445

Ferryboats
David's use of ... 2 Sam. 19:16-18 379

Festus—*feastful, joyful*
Governor of Judaea .... Acts 24:27 1310
Paul's defense made to .... Acts 25:1-22 1310

Fetters—*shackle for binding the feet*
A. *Used literally of:*
Imprisonment .... Ps. 105:18 685

B. *Used figuratively of:*
Trouble .... Job 36:8 614
Subjection .... Ps. 149:8 709

Fetus—*unborn child*
Protected by law .... Ex. 21:22, 23 92
Possesses sin nature .... Ps. 51:5 654
Fashioned by God .... Ps. 139:13-16 705
Called by God ..... Is. 49:1 821
Jer. 1:5 844
Active .... Luke 1:41 1192

Fever—*abnormal body temperature*
Sent as a judgment .... Deut. 28:22 238

SUBJECT | REFERENCE | PAGE

Forethought—*thinking ahead*

- In meeting a danger .... Gen. 32:3-23 — 43
- In anticipating evil .... Prov. 22:3 — 734
- Concerning physical needs .... Phil. 4:10-19 — 1402
- Neglect of, dangerous .... Matt. 25:8-13 — 1148
- Examples of ant, in .... Prov. 6:6-8 — 719
- For eternal riches .... Luke 12:23-34 — 1214

Foretold—*made known beforehand*

- Destruction of Jerusalem .... Mark 13:1, 2 — 1179
- Gospel blessings .... Acts 3:24 — 1276
- Paul's trip to Corinth .... 2 Cor. 13:2 — 1375

Forewarn—*to warn beforehand*

- God's judgment .... Luke 12:5 — 1214
- God's vengeance .... 1 Thess. 4:6 — 1416

Forfeit—*loss incurred by one's failure*

- Leadership .... 1 Sam. 15:16-28 — 339
- Possessions .... Ezra 10:8 — 553
- Salvation .... Matt. 16:26 — 1137

Forfeiting spiritual rights

- Birthright .... Gen. 25:34 — 34
- Headship .... Gen. 49:3, 4 — 61
- Apostleship .... Matt. 26:14-16 — 1150
- Spiritual heritage .... Acts 13:45-48 — 1292

Forger—*a counterfeiter*

- Applied to David's enemies .... Ps. 119:69 — 696

Forget—*be unable to remember*

- God does not .... Is. 49:15 — 822
- Our sinful past .... Phil. 3:13 — 1401

Forgetful—*unable to remember*

- Concerning our hearing .... James 1:25 — 1468

Forgetting of God

A. *Seen in forgetting God's:*

- Covenant .... Deut. 4:23 — 212
- Works .... Ps. 78:7, 11 — 670
- Blessings .... Ps. 103:2 — 683
- Law .... Ps. 119:153, 176 — 699
- Word .... James 1:25 — 1468

B. *Characteristics of:*

- Wicked .... Is. 65:11 — 837
- Form of backsliding .... Jer. 3:21, 22 — 848
- Instigated by false teachers .... Jer. 23:26, 27 — 870

Forgiveness—*an act of pardon*

A. *Synonyms of:*

- "Blots out" .... Is. 43:25 — 816
- "Remission" .... Matt. 26:28 — 1150
- "Pardon" .... Is. 55:7 — 828
- "Remember no more" .... Jer. 31:34 — 879
- "Healed" .... 2 Chr. 30:18-20 — 529

B. *Basis of:*

- God's nature .... Ps. 86:5 — 675
- God's grace .... Luke 7:42 — 1204
- Shedding of blood .... Heb. 9:22 — 1457
- Christ's death .... Col. 1:14 — 1406
- Son's power .... Luke 5:21-24 — 1201
- Man's repentance .... Acts 2:38 — 1274
- Our forgiveness .... Matt. 6:12-14 — 1121
- Faith in Christ .... Acts 10:43 — 1288

C. *Significance of:*

- Shows God's righteousness .... Rom. 3:25, 26 — 1327
- Makes salvation real .... Luke 1:77 — 1193
- Must be preached .... Luke 24:47 — 1231

Forgiving one another

A. *The measure of:*

- Seventy times seven .... Matt. 18:21, 22 — 1139
- Unlimited .... Luke 17:3, 4 — 1219
- As God forgave us .... Eph. 4:32 — 1391

B. *Benefits of:*

- Means of our forgiveness .... Mark 11:25, 26 — 1175
- Restored Christian fellowship .... 2 Cor. 2:7-10 — 1366
- Spiritual cleansing .... James 5:15, 16 — 1473

C. *Examples of:*

- Esau and Jacob .... Gen. 33:4-15 — 44
- Joseph .... Gen. 45:8-15 — 58
- Moses .... Num. 12:1-13 — 175
- David .... 2 Sam. 19:18-23 — 379
- Solomon .... 1 Kin. 1:52, 53 — 393
- Jesus .... Luke 23:34 — 1229
- Stephen .... Acts 7:59, 60 — 1282
- Paul .... 2 Tim. 4:16 — 1436

Fork

- In tabernacle .... Ex. 27:3 — 98; Num. 2:12-14 — 161
- In temple .... 1 Chr. 28:11, 17 — 495; 2 Chr. 4:16 — 506

Form—*the outward appearance*

A. *Of physical things:*

- Earth without .... Gen. 1:2 — 4
- Man in the womb .... Is. 44:24 — 817
- Sexes .... 1 Tim. 2:13 — 1427
- Idols .... Is. 44:10 — 816

B. *Of spiritual realities:*

- Incarnate Christ .... Is. 53:2 — 825; Rom. 9:20 — 1334
- Molder .... Rom. 9:20 — 1334
- Christian truth .... Rom. 6:17 — 1331
- New birth .... Gal. 4:19 — 1382
- World passing away .... 1 Cor. 7:31 — 1352

Formalism—*forms performed mechanically*

A. *Characterized by:*

- Outward forms of religion .... Is. 1:10-15 — 772
- Lifelessness .... Is. 58:1-14 — 829
- Lukewarmness .... Rev. 3:14-18 — 1521

B. *Sign of:*

- Hypocrisy .... Luke 18:10-14 — 1220
- Deadness .... Phil. 3:4-8 — 1401
- Last days .... 2 Tim. 3:1, 5 — 1434

Formula—*a prescribed method*

- Success .... Prov. 22:29 — 735
- Prosperity .... Matt. 6:32, 33 — 1123
- Peace .... Is. 26:3 — 795
- Making friends .... Prov. 18:24 — 731

Fornication—*sex relations among the unmarried*

Evil of:

- Comes from evil heart .... Matt. 15:19 — 1135
- Sins against the body .... 1 Cor. 6:18 — 1349
- Excludes from God's kingdom .... 1 Cor. 6:9 — 1349
- Disrupts Christian fellowship .... 1 Cor. 5:9-11 — 1348
- Spiritual fornication symbolized in final apostasy .... Rev. 17:1-5 — 1533

Forsaken—*left deserted*

- God's house .... Neh. 13:11 — 572
- God's children .... Ps. 37:25 — 646
- Messiah .... Is. 53:3 — 825
- God's Son .... Matt. 27:46 — 1154

Forsaking Christ

- Disciples left .... Matt. 26:56 — 1151
- Cause of separation .... John 6:66-70 — 1247

Forsaking God

A. *Manifested in:*

- Going after idols .... 1 Kin. 11:33 — 408
- Going backward .... Jer. 15:6 — 861
- Following human forms .... Jer. 2:13 — 845

B. *Evil of:*

- Manifests ingratitude .... Jer. 2:5-12 — 845
- Brings confusion .... Jer. 17:13 — 864
- Merits God's wrath .... Ezra 8:22 — 550

C. *Examples of:*

- Israel .... 2 Kin. 17:7-18 — 448
- Judah .... 2 Chr. 12:1, 5 — 514

Fortifications—*walls or towers for protection*

- Cities .... 1 Kin. 9:15 — 404; 2 Chr. 11:5-11 — 512
- City of David .... 2 Sam. 5:7-9 — 364

Fortified cities

- Means of protection .... 2 Sam. 20:6 — 380
- Mighty and strong .... Deut. 9:1 — 220
- Conquerable .... Deut. 3:4, 5 — 210
- Utterly destroyed .... 2 Kin. 3:19, 25 — 431
- No substitute for God .... Hos. 8:14 — 1001

Fortress—*center of military strength*

- Nation's security .... 2 Chr. 26:9 — 525
- Illustrative of God's protection .... Ps. 18:2 — 634
- Typical of Christ .... Is. 33:16, 17 — 805
- Applied to God's prophet .... Jer. 6:27 — 852

Fortunatus—*fortunate*

- Christian at Corinth .... 1 Cor. 16:17 — 1361

SUBJECT — REFERENCE — PAGE

SUBJECT REFERENCE PAGE

Garden—continued
In Egypt ..... Deut. 11:10 222
In Shushan ..... Esth. 1:5 577
In Gethsemane ..... Mark 14:32 1181
A royal ..... 2 Kin. 25:4 459

B. *Used for:*
Festivities ..... Esth. 1:5 577
Idolatry ..... Is. 65:3 836
Meditations ..... Matt. 26:36 1150
Burial ..... John 19:41 1264

C. *Figurative of:*
Desolation ..... Amos 4:9 1018
Fruitfulness ..... Is. 51:3 823
Prosperity ..... Is. 58:11 830
Righteousness ..... Is. 61:11 834

Gardener—*one whose work is gardening*

Adam, the first ..... Gen. 2:15 7
Christ, mistaken for ..... John 20:15, 16 1265

Gareb—*scab*

1. One of David's warriors ..... 2 Sam. 23:38 385
2. Hill near Jerusalem ..... Jer. 31:39 879

Garland—*ceremonial headdress or wreath*

Brought by priests of Jupiter ..... Acts 14:13 1292

Garlic—*an onion-like plant*

Egyptian food ..... Num. 11:5 173

Garments (see Clothing)

Garmite—*bony*

Gentile name applied to Keilah ..... 1 Chr. 4:19 467

Garrison—*a military post*

Smitten by Jonathan ..... 1 Sam. 13:3, 4 334
Attacked by Jonathan ..... 1 Sam. 14:1-15 336

Gatam—*puny*

Esau's grandson; chief of Edomite clan ..... Gen. 36:11-16 48

Gate—*an entrance*

A. *Made of:*
Wood ..... Neh. 2:3, 17 558
Iron ..... Acts 12:10 1289
Bronze ..... Ps. 107:16 687
Stones ..... Rev. 21:12 1538

B. *Opening for:*
Cities ..... Judg. 16:3 302
Citadel ..... Neh. 2:8 558
Sanctuary ..... Ezek. 44:1, 2 967
Tombs ..... Matt. 27:60 1154
Prisons ..... Acts 12:5, 10 1289

C. *Used for:*
Business transactions ..... 1 Kin. 22:10 423
Legal business ..... Ruth 4:1-11 315
Criminal cases ..... Deut. 25:7-9 236
Proclamations ..... Jer. 17:19, 20 864
Festivities ..... Ps. 24:7 638
Protection ..... 2 Sam. 18:24, 33 378

D. *Figurative of:*
Satanic power ..... Matt. 16:18 1136
Death ..... Is. 38:10 810
Righteousness ..... Ps. 118:19, 20 693
Salvation ..... Matt. 7:13 1123
Heaven ..... Rev. 21:25 1539

Gatekeeper

Duty of:
Zechariah ..... 1 Chr. 9:21 474
Shallum ..... 1 Chr. 9:17 474
Akkub ..... 1 Chr. 9:17 474
Talmon ..... 1 Chr. 9:17 474
Ahiman ..... 1 Chr. 9:17 474
Ben ..... 1 Chr. 15:18 481
Jaaziel ..... 1 Chr. 15:18 481
Shemiramoth ..... 1 Chr. 15:18 481
Jehiel ..... 1 Chr. 15:18 481
Unni ..... 1 Chr. 15:18 481
Eliab ..... 1 Chr. 15:18 481
Benaiah ..... 1 Chr. 15:18 481
Maaseiah ..... 1 Chr. 15:18 481
Mattithiah ..... 1 Chr. 15:18 481
Elipheleh ..... 1 Chr. 15:18 481
Mikneiah ..... 1 Chr. 15:18 481
Obed-Edom ..... 1 Chr. 15:18 481
Jeiel ..... 1 Chr. 15:18 481
Heman ..... 1 Chr. 15:17 481
Asaph ..... 1 Chr. 15:17 481
Ethan ..... 1 Chr. 15:17 481
Berechiah ..... 1 Chr. 15:23 482
Elkanah ..... 1 Chr. 15:23 482
Jehiah ..... 1 Chr. 15:24 482
Jeduthun ..... 1 Chr. 16:38 483
Hosah ..... 1 Chr. 16:38 483

Gates of Jerusalem

1. Corner Gate ..... 2 Chr. 26:9 525
2. Refuse Gate ..... Neh. 12:31 571
3. Of Ephraim ..... Neh. 8:16 567
4. Fish Gate ..... Zeph. 1:10 1057
5. Fountain Gate ..... Neh. 12:37 572
6. Horse Gate ..... Jer. 31:40 879
7. Benjamin's Gate ..... Zech. 14:10 1076
8. "Gate of the Prison" ..... Neh. 12:39 572
9. Sheep Gate ..... Neh. 3:1 559
10. Upper Benjamin Gate ..... Jer. 20:2 866
11. Valley Gate ..... Neh. 2:13 559
12. Water Gate ..... Neh. 8:16 567

Gath—*winepress*

1. Philistine city ..... 1 Sam. 6:17 328
Last of Anakim here ..... Josh. 11:22 264
Ark carried to ..... 1 Sam. 5:8 327
Home of Goliath ..... 1 Sam. 17:4 340
David takes refuge in ..... 1 Sam. 21:10-15 347
David's second flight to ..... 1 Sam. 27:3-12 352
Captured by David ..... 1 Chr. 18:1 484
Captured by Hazael ..... 2 Kin. 12:17 444
Rebuilt by Rehoboam ..... 2 Chr. 11:5, 8 512
Uzziah broke down walls of ..... 2 Chr. 26:6 525
Destruction of, prophetic ..... Amos 6:1-3 1020
Name becomes proverbial ..... Mic. 1:10 1036
2. Musical instrument or tune ..... Ps. 8; 81; 84 (titles) 628

Gath Hepher—*winepress of the pit*

Birthplace of Jonah ..... 2 Kin. 14:25 446
Boundary of Zebulun ..... Josh. 19:13 272

Gath Rimmon—*pomegranate press*

1. City of Dan ..... Josh. 19:40-45 272
Assigned to Levites ..... Josh. 21:24 275
2. Town in Manasseh ..... Josh. 21:25 275

Gaza—*strong place*

Philistine city ..... Josh. 13:3 265
Conquered by Joshua ..... Josh. 10:41 264
Refuge of Anakim ..... Josh. 11:22 264
Assigned to Judah ..... Josh. 15:47 268
Gates of, removed by Samson ..... Judg. 16:1-3 302
Samson deceived by Delilah here ..... Judg. 16:1-20 302
Samson blinded here ..... Judg. 16:21 303
Ruled by Solomon ..... 1 Kin. 4:22, 24 397
Sin of, condemned ..... Amos 1:6, 7 1015
Judgment pronounced upon ..... Jer. 25:20 871
Philip journeys to ..... Acts 8:26 1284

Gazelle—*medium-sized antelope; translated "roe"; "roebuck"*

A. *Described as:*
Fit for food ..... Deut. 12:15, 22 223
Swift ..... 1 Chr. 12:8 479
Wild ..... 2 Sam. 2:18 361
Hunted by men ..... Prov. 6:5 719
In Solomon's provisions ..... 1 Kin. 4:23 397

B. *Figurative of:*
Timidity ..... Is. 13:14 786
Swiftness ..... 2 Sam. 2:18 361
Church ..... Song 4:5 764
Christ ..... Song 2:9, 17 763

Gazez—*shearer*

1. Son of Caleb ..... 1 Chr. 2:46 466
2. Grandson of Caleb ..... 1 Chr. 2:46 466

Gazites

Inhabitants of Gaza ..... Judg. 16:2 302

Gazzam—*consuming*

Head of family of Temple servants ..... Ezra 2:48 544

Geba, Gaba—*a hill*

City of Benjamin ..... Josh. 18:24 271
Assigned to Levites ..... Josh. 21:17 273
Rebuilt by Asa ..... 1 Kin. 15:22 413
Idolatrous ..... 2 Kin. 23:8 457
Repossessed after the exile ..... Neh. 11:31 571

Gebal—*mountain*

1. Phoenician maritime town ..... Ezek. 27:9 948
Inhabitants called Gebalites ..... Josh. 13:5 265; 1 Kin. 5:18 398
2. Mountainous region in Edom ..... Ps. 83:7 674

SUBJECT REFERENCE PAGE

Geber—*strong one; hero*
Solomon's purveyors .... 1 Kin. 4:19 397

Gebim—*ditches*
Place north of Jerusalem .... Is. 10:31 784

Gedaliah—*Yahweh has made great*
1. Jeduthun's son .... 1 Chr. 25:3, 9 491
2. Pashur's son .. Jer. 38:1 885
3. Grandfather of Zephaniah ... Zeph. 1:1 1057
4. Ahikam's son .... Jer. 39:14 887
Made governor of Judah ...... 2 Kin. 25:22-26 460
Befriends Jeremiah .... Jer. 40:5, 6 887
Murdered by Ishmael ...... Jer. 41:2, 18 888
Postexilic priest .... Ezra 10:18 553

Geder—*wall*
Town of Judah .... Josh. 12:13 265

Gederah—*sheepfold*
Town in Judah .... Josh. 15:36 268

Gederathite
Native of Gederah .... 1 Chr. 12:4 479

Gederite
Native of Geder ... 1 Chr. 27:28 494

Gederoth—*sheepfolds*
Town of Judah .... Josh. 15:41 268
Captured by Philistines .... 2 Chr. 28:18 527

Gederothaim—*two sheepfolds*
Town of Judah .... Josh. 15:36 268

Gedor—*wall*
1. Town of Judah .... Josh. 15:58 268
2. Simeonite town .... 1 Chr. 4:39 468
3. Town of Benjamin .... 1 Chr. 12:7 479
4. Family in Judah .... 1 Chr. 4:4 467
5. A son of Jeiel and brother of Ner .... 1 Chr. 8:30, 31 473; 1 Chr. 9:35-37 475
6. The son of Jered .... 1 Chr. 4:18 467

Ge Harashim
A craftsman ...... 1 Chr. 4:14 467

Gehazi—*valley of vision*
Elisha's servant ... 2 Kin. 5:25 434
Seeks reward from Naaman .... 2 Kin. 5:20-24 434
Afflicted with leprosy .... 2 Kin. 5:25-27 434
Relates Elisha's deeds to Jehoram .... 2 Kin. 8:4-6 437

Gehenna (see Hell)

Geliloth—*circles*
Probably Gilgal, in the land of Benjamin .... Josh. 18:17 271

Gemalli—*camel driver*
Father of Ammiel .... Num. 13:12 176

Gemariah—*Yahweh has perfected*
1. Hilkiah's son .. Jer. 29:3 874
2. Shaphan's son .... Jer. 36:10-25 883

Gems—*precious stones*
On breastplate .... Ex. 28:15-21 99
Figurative of value .... Prov. 3:15 716; Prov. 31:10 745
In commerce .... Ezek. 27:16 950
In New Jerusalem .... Rev. 21:19-21 1539

Genealogies—*ancestral lineage*
A. *Importance:*
Chronology ... Matt. 1:17 1116
Priesthood claims .... Ezra 2:61, 62 544; Neh. 7:63, 64 564
Messiahship ... Matt. 1:1-17 1115
B. *Lists of:*
Patriarchs' .... Gen. 5:1-32 10
Noah's .... Gen. 10:1-32 15
Shem's .... Gen. 10:21-32 16
Abraham's .... 1 Chr. 1:28-34 465
Jacob's .... Gen. 46:8-27 59
Esau's .... Gen. 36:1-43 46
Israel's .... 1 Chr. 9:1 474
David's .... 1 Chr. 3:1-16 466
Levites' .... 1 Chr. 6:1-81 469

Genealogy of Jesus
Seed of Abraham .... Gal. 3:16 1381
Through Joseph .. Matt. 1:2-17 1115
Through Mary .... Luke 3:23-38 1195

General—*chief military authority*
Commander ...... 1 Chr. 27:34 494; Rev. 6:15 1524
Also rendered "princes" .... Gen. 12:15 20

Generation
Descriptive of:
Period of time .... Gen. 9:12 15
Living people or race .... Matt. 24:34 1148

Genesis, Book of—*first book of the Old Testament*
Creation .... Gen. 1:1–2:25 4
The fall .... Gen. 3:1-24 8
The flood .... Gen. 6:8–7:24 11
Abraham .... Gen. 12:1–25:18 18
Isaac .... Gen. 25:19–26:35 34
Jacob .... Gen. 27:1–36:43 36
Joseph .... Gen. 37:1–50:26 48

Genius—*unusual mental ability*
Applicable to Solomon .... 1 Kin. 4:29-34 397

Gentiles—*non-Jews*
A. *Described as:*
Superstitious .... Deut. 18:14 229
Knowing God .... Rom. 1:21 1324
Without the Law .... Rom. 2:14 1325
Wicked .... Rom. 1:23-32 1324
Idolatrous ..... 1 Cor. 12:2 1355
Uncircumcised .... Eph. 2:11 1388
Without Christ .... Eph. 2:12 1388
Dead in sins ... Eph. 2:1 1387
B. *Blessings promised to:*
Given to Christ .... Ps. 2:8 625
Included in God's covenant .... Gen. 12:3 18; Gal. 3:8 1381
Conversion predicted .... Is. 11:10 784; Rom. 15:9-16 1340
Christ their light .... Is. 49:6 821
Included in "all flesh" .... Joel 2:28-32 1010
Called "other sheep" .... John 10:16 1252
C. *Conversion of:*
Predicted ..... Is. 60:1-14 832
Proclaimed .... Matt. 4:12-17 1118
Anticipated .... John 10:16 1252
Questioned .... Acts 10:9-29 1287
Realized .... Acts 10:34-48 1287
Explained ...... Acts 11:1-18 1288
Hindered .... Acts 13:45-51 1292
Debated .... Acts 15:1-22 1293
Confirmed .... Acts 15:23-31 1294
Vindicated .... Acts 28:25-29 1315
D. *Present position:*
Barrier removed ..... Eph. 2:11-22 1388
Brought near .... Eph. 2:13 1388
Fellow citizens ...... Eph. 2:19 1388
Fellow heirs .... Eph. 3:6 1388
In body .... Eph. 3:6 1388

Gentleness—*mildness combined with tenderness*
A. *Examples of:*
God's .... 2 Sam. 22:36 384
Christ's .... Matt. 11:29 1130
Paul's .... 1 Thess. 2:7 1415
Holy Spirit .... Gal. 5:22, 23 1383
B. *A Christian essential in:*
Living in the world .... Titus 3:1, 2 1442
Instruction .... 2 Tim. 2:24, 25 1434
Restoring a brother .... Gal. 6:1 1383
Calling .... Eph. 4:1, 2 1390
Marriage ...... 1 Pet. 3:1-4 1480
C. *Commandments concerning:*
Follow after ... 1 Tim. 6:11 1430

Genubath—*theft*
Edomite .... 1 Kin. 11:20 408

Geology—*study of the earth*
Allusions to ...... Gen. 1:9, 10 4

Gera—*grain*
1. Son of Bela .... Gen. 46:21 59
2. A descendant of Bela .... 1 Chr. 8:3-8 473
3. Father of Ehud .... Judg. 3:15 287
4. Father of Shimei .... 2 Sam. 16:5 375

Gerah—*smallest coin and weight among the Jews*
Twentieth part of a shekel ..... Ex. 30:13 103; Lev. 27:25 154

Gerar—*region*
Town of Philistia .... Gen. 10:19 16

SUBJECT REFERENCE PAGE

Health ....Phil. 2:25-30 1400
Sleep ....Prov. 3:23-25 716
Rest ....Deut. 12:10 223
All things .....1 Tim. 6:17 1430
All needs ......Phil. 4:19 1402
2. *Spiritual:*
Christ ....John 3:16 1239
Holy Spirit ....Luke 11:13 1211
Grace ....James 4:6 1471
Wisdom ....James 1:5 1468
Repentance ...Acts 11:18 1288
Faith ....Eph. 2:8 1387
New spirit .....Ezek. 11:19 927
Peace ....Phil. 4:7 1402
Rest ....Heb. 4:1, 9 1452
Glory ....1 Pet. 5:10 1483
Eternal life ....John 10:28 1252

B. *Of man:*

1. *Purposes of:*
Confirm covenants ....Gen. 21:27-32 30
Appease anger ....1 Sam. 25:27-35 351
Show respect ....Judg. 6:18-21 290
Manifest friendship ...1 Sam. 30:26-31 355
Reward ......2 Sam. 18:11, 12 378
Memorialize an event ....Esth. 9:20-22 585
Render worship ......Matt. 2:11 1116
Give help .....Phil. 4:10-18 1402
Seal friendship ....1 Sam. 18:3, 4 343
2. *Times given:*
Betrothals .....Gen. 24:50-53 33
Weddings ....Ps. 45:12 651
Departures .....Gen. 45:21-24 58
Returns home ....Luke 15:22, 23 1218
Times of recovery .....Job 42:10, 11 620
Trials, forbidden ....Ex. 23:8 94

C. *Spiritual:*
Listed and explained....Rom. 12:6-8 1337; 1 Cor. 12:4-30 1355
Came from God ....James 1:17 1468
Assigned sovereignty ..1 Cor. 12:11, 28 1355
Cannot be bought ....Acts 8:18-20 1282
Always for edification .....Rom. 1:11 1321
Counterfeited by Satan ....2 Cor. 11:13-15 1373
Spiritually discerned ....1 Cor. 12:2, 3 1355
Love, the supreme .....1 Cor. 13:1-13 1356

Gihon—*bursting forth*

1. River of Eden ....Gen. 2:13 7
2. Spring outside Jerusalem ....1 Kin. 1:33-45 392
3. Source of water supply ....2 Chr. 32:30 533

Gilalai—*weighty*

Levite musician ...Neh. 12:36 572

Gilboa—*bubbling fountain*

Range of limestone hills in Issachar ....1 Sam. 28:4 353
Scene of Saul's death ....1 Sam. 31:1-7 355
Philistines desecrate Saul's body ....1 Sam. 31:8, 9 355
Under David's curse ....2 Sam. 1:17, 21 360

Gilead—*rocky or strong*

1. Grandson of Manasseh ...Num. 26:29, 30 191
2. Father of Jephthah .....Judg. 11:1 297
3. Gadite ....1 Chr. 5:14 468
4. Condemned city ....Hos. 6:8 1000
5. Mountain .....Judg. 7:3 291
6. Tableland east of the Jordan between the Arnon and Jabbok rivers ....Judg. 20:1 307
Possessed by Israel ....Num. 21:21-31 186
Assigned to Reuben, Gad, and Manasseh ....Deut. 3:12-17 211
Rebuked by Deborah ....Judg. 5:17 289
Hebrews flee to ....1 Sam. 13:7 334
Ishbosheth's rule over .....2 Sam. 2:8, 9 361
David takes refuge in ....2 Sam. 17:26, 27 377; 2 Sam. 19:31 380
In David's census ....2 Sam. 24:1, 6 387
Elijah's birthplace ....1 Kin. 17:1 414
Smitten by Hazael ......2 Kin. 10:32, 33 442
Mentioned by Amos ....Amos 1:3, 13 1015

Gilead, Balm of—*an aromatic gum for medicinal purposes*

Figurative of:
National healing ....Jer. 8:22 855; Jer. 51:8 902

Gilgal—*a circle, a wheel*

1. Memorial site between Jordan and Jericho ...Josh. 4:19-24 255
Israel circumcised ..Josh. 5:2-9 255
Passover observed .....Josh. 5:10 256
Site of Gibeonite covenant .....Josh. 9:3-15 260
On Samuel's circuit ....1 Sam. 7:15, 16 330
Saul made king ....1 Sam. 11:15 333
Saul rejected ..1 Sam. 13:4-15 334
Denounced for idolatry ......Hos. 9:15 1002
2. Town near Bethel ....2 Kin. 2:1 430
Home of Elisha ....2 Kin. 4:38 433

Giloh—*exile*

Town of Judah ....Josh. 15:51 268

Gilonite—*Giloh native*

Ahithophel called ....2 Sam. 15:12 374

Gimel

Third letter in Hebrew alphabet ....Ps. 119:17-24 694

Gimzo—*producing sycamores*

Village of Judah ..2 Chr. 28:18 527

Ginath—*protection*

Father of Tibni ..1 Kin. 16:21, 22 414

Ginnethoi—*gardener*

Postexilic priest ...Neh. 12:4 571

Ginnethon—*gardener*

Family head and signer of document ....Neh. 10:6 569
Probably same as Ginnethoi

Gird—*to put on, as a belt*

A. *Purposes of:*
Strengthening ....Prov. 31:17 745

B. *Figurative of:*
Gladness ......Ps. 30:11 641
Truth ....Eph. 6:14 1393
Readiness .....1 Pet. 1:13 1477

C. *Those girding:*
Priests ....Ex. 28:4, 39 99
Warriors ......1 Sam. 18:4 343
Jesus ....John 13:3, 4 1257

Girgashites—*an original tribe of Canaan*

Descendants of Canaan ....Gen. 10:15, 16 16
Land of, given to Abraham's descendants .....Gen. 15:18, 21 23
Delivered to Israel ....Josh. 24:11 279

Girl—*a female child; young woman*

Sold for wine .....Joel 3:3 1012
Prophecy concerning ......Zech. 8:4, 5 1072
Raised by Jesus ...Mark 5:39-42 1166
Demands John's head ....Matt. 14:10, 11 1134
Questions Peter ...John 18:17 1262
Is disbelieved .....Acts 12:13-17 1289
Healed by Paul .....Acts 16:16-18 1295

Girzites—*inhabitants of Gezer*

Raided by David ....1 Sam. 27:8 352

Gishpa—*fondle*

Overseer ....Neh. 11:21 570

Gittaim—*two winepresses*

Village of Benjamin ....Neh. 11:31, 33 571
Refuge of the Beerothites ......2 Sam. 4:2, 3 363

Gittites—*natives of Gath*

600 follow David ....2 Sam. 15:18-23 375

Giving to God

A. *Manner of:*
Without show.........Matt. 6:1-4 1121
According to ability........1 Cor. 16:1, 2 1360
Willingly ......1 Chr. 29:3-9 495
Liberally ......2 Cor. 9:6-15 1372
Cheerfully ....2 Cor. 9:7 1372
Proportionately .....Mal. 3:10 1082

B. *Examples of:*
Israelites ......Ex. 35:21-29 108
Leaders of Israel ....Num. 7:2-28 168
Poor widow ...Luke 21:1-4 1224
Macedonian churches .....2 Cor. 8:1-5 1371

Gizonite

Hashem thus described ....1 Chr. 11:34 478

TOPICAL INDEX

SUBJECT REFERENCE PAGE

Hadassah—*myrtle*
Esther's Jewish name ....Esth. 2:7 578

Hadattah—*new*
Town in south Judah; possibly should be read as Hazor-Hadattah ....Josh. 15:25 268

Hadid—*sharp*
Town of Benjamin........Neh. 11:31, 34 571

Hadlai—*restful*
Ephraimite ....2 Chr. 28:12 527

Hadoram—*Hadar is exalted*
1. Son of Joktan ....Gen. 10:26, 27 16
2. Son of Tou ....1 Chr. 18:9, 10 486
3. Rehoboam's tribute officer ....2 Chr. 10:18 512
Called Adoram ......1 Kin. 12:18 409
Probably same as Adoniram ......1 Kin. 4:6 395

Hadrach—*periodical return*
Place in Syria ....Zech. 9:1 1073

Hagab—*locust*
Head of a family of Temple servants ....Ezra 2:46 544

Hagabah—*locust*
Head of a family of Temple servants ....Neh. 7:46, 48 563; Ezra 2:43, 45 544

Hagar—*flight*
Sarah's Egyptian handmaid ....Gen. 16:1 23
Flees from Sarah ....Gen. 16:5-8 23
Returns; becomes mother of Ishmael ....Gen. 16:3-16 23
Abraham sends her away..............Gen. 21:14 29
Paul's allegory of ....Gal. 4:22-26 1382

Hagerite—*a descendant of Hagar*
Jaziz, keeper of David's flocks ....1 Chr. 27:31 494

Haggai—*festive*
Postexilic prophet ....Ezra 5:1, 2 547
Contemporary of Zechariah ....Ezra 6:14 548
Prophecies of, dated in reign of Darius Hystaspes (520 B.C.) ....Hag. 1:1, 15 1064; Hag. 2:1, 10, 20 1065

Haggai, the Book of—*a book of the Old Testament*
Purpose ....Hag. 1:1-15 1064
The coming glory ....Hag. 2:4-9 1065
On Levitical cleanliness ....Hag. 2:10-14 1065

Hagri—*a Hagerite*
Father of one of David's warriors..........1 Chr. 11:38 478

Called "Bani the Gadite" in ....2 Sam. 23:36 385

Haggi—*festal*
Son of Gad ....Gen. 46:16 59
Head of tribal family ....Num. 26:15 191

Haggiah—*festival of Yahweh*
Merarite Levite ....1 Chr. 6:30 469

Haggith—*festal*
One of David's wives ....2 Sam. 3:4 362
Mother of Adonijah ....1 Kin. 1:5 391

Hagrites
Nomad people east of Gilead ....1 Chr. 5:10-22 468
Called Hagarites........Ps. 83:6 674

Hail—*frozen rain*
Illustrative of God's:
Wonders ....Job 38:22 616
Glory ....Ps. 18:12 634
Chastening ....Is. 28:2, 17 798
Wrath ....Rev. 8:7 1525
Power............Ps. 147:17 709

Hail—*a salutation*
Gabriel to Mary ...Luke 1:26-28 1190
Soldiers to Christ ....Matt. 27:27-29 1152

Hair
A. *Of women:*
Covering ....1 Cor. 11:15 1354
Uses of.........Luke 7:38 1204
Prohibitions concerning ......1 Tim. 2:9 1426; 1 Pet. 3:3 1480

B. *Of men:*
Not to be worn long ....1 Cor. 11:14 1354
Rules for cutting ....Lev. 19:27 142
Long, during Nazirite vow ....Num. 6:5 166
Gray, sign of age ....1 Sam. 12:2 333
Absalom's beautiful ....2 Sam. 14:25, 26 374
Numbered ....Matt. 10:30 1129

C. *Figurative of:*
Minuteness ....Judg. 20:16 308
Complete safety ....1 Sam. 14:45 337
Fear ....Job 4:14, 15 592
Great numbers ....Ps. 40:12 648
Grief..........Ezra 9:3 551
Respect ....Prov. 16:31 729
Attractiveness ......Song 5:2, 11 765
Affliction ....Is. 3:17, 24 774
Entire destruction ....Is. 7:20 779
Decline and fall ....Hos. 7:9 1000

Hakkatan—*the smallest*
Johanan's father ..Ezra 8:12 550

Hakkoz—*the thorn*
Descendant of Aaron ....1 Chr. 24:1, 10 490
Called Koz ....Ezra 2:61, 62 544
Descendants of, kept from priesthood ....Neh. 7:63, 64 564

Hakupha—*crooked*
Ancestor of certain Temple servants ....Ezra 2:42, 43, 51 544

Halah—*a district of Assyria*
Israelite captives carried to ....2 Kin. 17:6 448

Halak—*smooth*
Mountain near Seir ....Josh. 11:17 264

Half-shekel tax—*a temple tax*
Commanded ......Ex. 30:13, 14 103
Christ paid ....Matt. 17:24-27 1138

Half-tribe of Manasseh—*the part of Manasseh east of the Jordan*
Clans of:
Machir ....Josh. 17:1 270

Halhul—*contorted*
A city in Judah ....Josh. 15:20, 21, 58 268

Hali—*necklace*
Town of Asher ....Josh. 19:25 272

Hallohesh—*enchanter*
Repairs walls and signs covenant ....Neh. 3:12 559; Neh. 10:24 569

Ham—*hot*
1. Noah's youngest son ....Gen. 5:32 11
Enters ark.....Gen. 7:7 12
His immoral behavior merits Noah's curse ....Gen. 9:22-25 15
Father of descendants of repopulated earth ...Gen. 10:6-20 16
2. Poetical name of Egypt ....Ps. 105:23, 27 685
3. Hamites at Gedor.........1 Chr. 4:39, 40 468
4. Place where Chedorlaomer defeated the Zuzim ....Gen. 14:5 21

Haman
Plots to destroy Jews ....Esth. 3:3-15 579
Invited to Esther's banquet ....Esth. 5:1-14 581
Forced to honor Mordecai ....Esth. 6:5-14 581
Hanged on his own gallows ....Esth. 7:1-10 582

Hamath—*fortification*
Hittite city north of Damascus ....Josh. 13:5 265
Spies visit ....Num. 13:21 176
Israel's northern limit ....Num. 34:8 202
Solomon's boundary ....1 Kin. 8:65 404
Storage cities built ....2 Chr. 8:3, 4 510
Captured by the Assyrians.......2 Kin. 18:30, 34 452
People of, deported to Samaria ....2 Kin. 17:24, 30 449
Israelites exiled ...Is. 11:11 784
Mentioned by Jeremiah ....Jer. 49:23 898

SUBJECT REFERENCE PAGE

Harem—*group of females associated with one man*

Esther a member of King Ahasuerus' ...... Esth. 2:8-14 578

Hareph—*plucking*

Son of Caleb ..... 1 Chr. 2:50, 51 466

Harhaiah—*Yahweh is protecting*

Father of Uzziel ... Neh. 3:8 559

Harhas—*splendor*

Grandfather of Shallum .... 2 Kin. 22:14 456

Harhur—*fever*

Ancestor of returning Temple servants .... Ezra 2:43, 51 544

Harim—*consecrated to God*

1. Descendant of Aaron .... 1 Chr. 24:1, 6, 8 490
2. Postexilic leader .... Ezra 2:32, 39 544
3. Father of Malchijah .... Neh. 3:11 559
4. Signer of the covenant ..... Neh. 10:1, 5 569
5. Signer of the covenant ..... Neh. 10:1, 27 569
6. Family house of priests .... Neh. 12:12, 15 571
7. Descendants of, divorced foreign wives .... Ezra 10:19, 21 553

Hariph—*autumn rain*

Family of returnees .... Neh. 7:24 563
Signers of covenant .... Neh. 10:19 569
Same as Jorah .... Ezra 2:18 544

Harlot—*a prostitute*

A. *Characteristics of:*
Shameless .... Jer. 3:3 847
Painted ..... Ezek. 23:30, 40 943
Enticing .... Prov. 9:14-18 722
Roaming streets .... Prov. 7:12 720
Expensive ..... Prov. 29:3 742

B. *Evils of:*
Profanes God's name .... Amos 2:7 1016
Connected with idolatry ...... Ex. 34:15, 16 107
Brings spiritual error .... Hos. 4:10-19 998
Cause of divorce ...... Jer. 3:8, 14 847

C. *Prohibitions concerning:*
Forbidden in Israel .... Lev. 19:29 142
Priests not to marry .... Lev. 21:1, 7, 14 143
To be shamed ...... Prov. 5:3-20 718
Punishment ..... Lev. 21:9 144

D. *Examples of:*
Tamar .... Gen. 38:13-20 50
Rahab .... Josh. 2:1-21 253
Jephthah's mother .... Judg. 11:1 297
Samson's ..... Judg. 16:1 302
Hosea's wife ... Hos. 1:2 996
The great ..... Rev. 17:1-18 1533

E. *Figurative of:*
Tyre .... Is. 23:15, 17 793
Israel .... Is. 1:21 772
Spiritual adultery .... Is. 57:7-9 829; Rev. 17:1-18 1533

See Adultery

Harmony—*agreement, cooperation*

Husband and wife .... 1 Cor. 7:3-6 1351; Eph. 5:22-23 1392; Col. 3:18, 19 1409
Christians ..... John 13:34, 35 1257; Rom. 15:5-7 1340
Christians and unbelievers ..... Rom. 12:16-18 1337; Heb. 12:14 1462

Harnepher

Asherite .... 1 Chr. 7:36 473

Harness—*to equip*

Horses .... Jer. 46:4 894

Harod—*fountain of trembling*

Well near Gideon's camp .... Judg. 7:1 291

Harodite

Inhabitant of Harod .... 2 Sam. 23:25 385
Same as Harorite .... 1 Chr. 11:27 478

Haroeh—*the seer*

Judahite .... 1 Chr. 2:50, 52 466
Called Reaiah .... 1 Chr. 4:2 467

Harosheth Hagoyim—*carving of the nations*

Residence of Sisera .... Judg. 4:2, 13, 16 288

Harp—*a stringed musical instrument*

Used by:

The wicked .... Is. 5:11, 12 775
David .... 1 Sam. 16:16, 23 340
Prophets .... 1 Sam. 10:5 331
Temple orchestra .... 1 Chr. 16:5 482
Temple worshipers ...... Ps. 33:2 642
Celebrators ..... 2 Chr. 20:27, 28 520
Jewish captives ... Ps. 137:2 704
Worshipers in heaven .... Rev. 5:8 1523

Harpoon—*a barbed spear for hunting large fish*

Used against Leviathan .... Job 41:7 619

Harsha—*enchanter*

Head of Temple servants .... Ezra 2:43, 52 544; Neh. 7:46, 54 563

Harum—*exalted*

Judahite .... 1 Chr. 4:8 467

Harumaph—*flat-nosed*

Father of Jedaiah .... Neh. 3:10 559

Haruphite

Designation of Shephatiah ...... 1 Chr. 12:5 479
Member of Hariph's family .... Neh. 7:24 563

Haruz—*active*

Father-in-law of King Manasseh .... 2 Kin. 21:19 455

Harvest—*the time when the crops are ripe*

A. *Occasion of:*
Great joy ...... Is. 9:3 780
Bringing the first-fruits .... Lev. 23:10 145
Remembering the poor .... Lev. 19:9, 10 142

B. *Figuratively of:*
Seasons of grace .... Jer. 8:20 855
Judgment ...... Jer. 51:33 903
God's wrath ... Rev. 14:15 1531
Gospel opportunities ...... Matt. 9:37, 38 1127
World's end ... Matt. 13:30, 39 1133
Measure of fruitfulness ... 2 Cor. 9:6 1372

C. *Promises concerning:*
To continue ... Gen. 8:22 14
Rain .... Jer. 5:24 851
Patience ...... James 5:7 1471

D. *Failure caused by:*
Drought .... Amos 4:7 1018
Locusts .... Joel 1:4 1008
Sin .... Is. 17:4-12 789

Hasadiah—*Yahweh has been gracious*

Son of Zerubbabel ...... 1 Chr. 3:20 467

Hashabiah—*Yahweh has imputed*

1. Merarite Levite .... 1 Chr. 6:44, 45 470
Perhaps the same as in .... 1 Chr. 9:14 474
2. Levite musician ..... 1 Chr. 25:3, 19 491
3. Kohathite Levite .... 1 Chr. 26:30 493
4. Levite ruler ... 1 Chr. 27:17 493
5. Chief Levite during Josiah's reign .... 2 Chr. 35:9 536
6. Postexilic Levite .... Ezra 8:19, 24 550
Probably the same in .... Neh. 10:11 569
7. Postexilic ruler .... Neh. 3:17 560
8. Descendant of Asaph .... Neh. 11:22 570
9. Priest in the time of Joiakim ...... Neh. 12:21 571

Hashabnah—*covenant sealer*

Signed covenant .. Neh. 10:25 569

Hashabniah—*Yahweh has regarded me*

1. Father of Hattush ...... Neh. 3:10 559
2. Postexilic Levite .... Neh. 9:5 567

Probably the same as Hashabiah 6.

Hashbadana—*thoughtful judge*

Assistant to Ezra .... Neh. 8:4 565

Hashem—*shining*

Father of David's warriors .... 1 Chr. 11:34 478
Also called Jashen .... 2 Sam. 23:32 385

Hashmonah—*fertility*

Israelite encampment ..... Num. 33:29 200

Hashub, Hasshub—*thoughtful*

1. Postexilic workman .... Neh. 3:11 559

SUBJECT REFERENCE PAGE

Heedfulness—*giving proper attention to something important*

A. *Objects of:*
God's commandments . . . . Josh. 22:5 275
Our ways . . . . Ps. 39:1 647
False teachers . . . . . . Matt. 16:6 1136
God's Word . . . 2 Pet. 1:19 1487

B. *Admonitions to Christians, concerning:*
Deception . . . . . Matt. 24:4 1147
Outward display . . . . Matt. 6:1 1121
Worldliness . . . Luke 21:34 1225
Duty . . . . Acts 20:28-31 1303
Foundation . . . . 1 Cor. 3:10 1346
Liberty . . . . 1 Cor. 8:9 1352
Security . . . . 1 Cor. 10:12 1354
Effectiveness . . . . . . Gal. 5:15 1383
Ministry . . . . . . Col. 4:17 1410
Fables . . . . 1 Tim. 1:4 1426
Unbelief . . . . . . Heb. 3:12 1452

See Caution

Heel—*the back part of the human foot*

Used literally of:
Esau's . . . . Gen. 25:26 34

Used figuratively of:
Seed of the woman . . . . Gen. 3:15 9
Enemy of Dan . . . . Gen. 49:17 63
The wicked . . . . Job 18:5, 9 601
Friend of David . . . Ps. 41:9 649

Hegai—*the sprinkler*

Eunuch under King Ahasuerus . . . . Esth. 2:3, 8, 15 578

Heifer—*a young cow*

A. *Ceremonial uses of:*
In a covenant . . . . . Gen. 15:9 23
In purification . . . Num. 19:1-22 182

B. *Red heifer, ceremony concerning:*
Without spot . . Num. 19:2 182
Never yoked . . Num. 19:2 182
Slaughtered and burned outside the camp . . . . . Num. 19:3-8 182
Ashes kept . . . . Num. 19:9, 10 183
Ashes, with water, used to purify . . . . Num. 19:11-22 183
Significance of . . . . Heb. 9:13, 14 1457

C. *Figurative of:*
Improper advantage . . . . Judg. 14:18 300
Contentment . . . . Jer. 50:11 899

Heirs, natural

A. *Persons and property involved:*
Firstborn . . . . Deut. 21:15-17 232
Sons of concubines . . . Gen. 21:10 29
Daughters . . . . . Num. 27:1-11 192
Widows . . . . Ruth 3:12, 13 315
Order of succession . . . Num. 27:8-11 192

B. *Exceptions:*
Father could make concubines' sons heirs . . . . Gen. 49:1, 12-27 61
Daughters receive marriage portion . . . . Gen. 29:24, 29 40
Daughters sometimes share with sons . . . . Job 42:15 620
Daughters receive, if no sons . . . . Num. 27:8 192

C. *Examples of heirship changes by divine election:*
Ishmael to Isaac . . . . Gen. 21:10, 11 29
Esau to Jacob . . . . Gen. 27:35-37 37; Rom. 9:13 1334
Reuben to Joseph . . . . . . Gen. 49:22-26 63
Adonijah to Solomon . . . . . 1 Kin. 1:11-14 391

See Birthright; Inheritance, earthly

Heirs, spiritual

A. *Of Christ:*
Recognized . . . . Matt. 21:38 1143
Appointed . . . . . Heb. 1:2 1450

B. *Of Christians, means of:*
By promise . . . . Gal. 3:29 1381
Through Christ . . . . Gal. 4:7 1381
Through faith . . . . Rom. 4:13, 14 1327
By grace . . . . . . Gal. 4:21-31 1382

C. *Of Christians, receiving:*
Grace . . . . 1 Pet. 3:7 1480
Promise . . . . Heb. 11:9 1460
Kingdom . . . . . . James 2:5 1469
Salvation . . . . . Heb. 1:14 1450
Righteousness . . . . Heb. 11:7 1460
Eternal life . . . . Titus 3:7 1442

See Inheritance, spiritual

Helah—*ornament*

One of Asher's wives . . . . 1 Chr. 4:5, 7 467

Helam—*fortress*

Place between Damascus and Hamath where David defeated Syrians . . . . 2 Sam. 10:16-19 369

Helbah—*fertility*

City of Asher . . . . . Judg. 1:31 284

Helbon—*fertile*

City north of Damascus . . . . Ezek. 27:18 950

Heldai—*worldly*

1. One of David's captains . . . . 1 Chr. 27:15 493
Probably same as Heled and Heleb . . . . 1 Chr. 11:30 478
2. Exile from Babylon bearing gifts . . . . Zech. 6:10, 11 1071
Called Helem . . . . Zech. 6:14 1071

Helek—*portion*

Son of Gilead . . . . . Num. 26:30 191
Founder of a family . . . . Josh. 17:2 270

Helem—*strength*

1. Asherite . . . . . . 1 Chr. 7:34, 35 473
2. Same as Heldai . . . . Zech. 6:10, 11 1071
Called Hotham . . . . 1 Chr. 7:32 473

Heleph—*strong*

Frontier town of Naphtali . . . . Josh. 19:32, 33 272

Helez—*strong*

1. One of David's captains . . . . . . 2 Sam. 23:26 385
2. Judahite . . . . . . 1 Chr. 2:39 466

Heli—*climbing*

Father of Joseph, husband of Mary . . . . Luke 3:23 1195

Helkai—*portion*

Postexilic priest . . . Neh. 12:15 571

Helkath—*portion, field*

Frontier town of Asher . . . . Josh. 19:24, 25 272
Assigned to Levites . . . . Josh. 21:31 275
Same as Hukok . . . . 1 Chr. 6:75 472

Hell—*the place of eternal torment*

A. *Described as:*
Everlasting fire . . . . Matt. 25:41 1149
Everlasting punishment . . Matt. 25:46 1149
Outer darkness . . . . . Matt. 8:12 1125
Everlasting destruction . . . 2 Thess. 1:9 1421
Lake of fire . . . . Rev. 19:20 1536

B. *Prepared for:*
Devil and his angels . . . . Matt. 25:41 1149
Wicked . . . . Rev. 21:8 1538
Disobedient . . . Rom. 2:8, 9 1324
Fallen angels . . 2 Pet. 2:4 1487
Beast and the false prophet . . . . . . Rev. 19:20 1536
Worshipers of the beast . . . . Rev. 14:11 1531
Rejectors of the Gospel . . . . Matt. 10:15 1129

C. *Punishment of, described as:*
Bodily . . . . Matt. 5:29, 30 1120
In the soul . . . . Matt. 10:28 1129
With degrees . . Matt. 23:14 1145

Hellenists

Greek-speaking Jews . . . . Acts 6:1 1278
Hostile to Paul . . . . Acts 9:29 1286
Gospel preached to . . . . Acts 11:20 1288

Helmet—*armor for the head*

Used figuratively of salvation:
Prepared . . . . Is. 59:17 831
Provided . . . . Eph. 6:17 1393
Promised . . . . 1 Thess. 5:8 1416

Helon—*strong*

Father of Eliab . . . . Num. 1:9 159

Helper—*one who assists another*

A. *Used of:*
God . . . . Heb. 13:6 1463
Christ . . . . Heb. 4:15, 16 1453
Holy Spirit . . . . Rom. 8:26 1333
Angels . . . . Dan. 10:13 989
Woman . . . . Gen. 2:18, 20 7
Christians . . . . . Acts 16:9 1295

B. *As the Holy Spirit:*
Abides with believers . . . . . John 14:16 1258
Teaches . . . . John 14:26 1258
Testifies of Christ . . . . John 15:26 1259
Convicts . . . . . . John 16:7-11 1259
Guides into truth . . . . John 16:13 1259

SUBJECT REFERENCE PAGE

Hope—continued
Joy .... Rom. 12:12 1337
Salvation ..... Rom. 8:23 1333
Assurance .... Heb. 6:18, 19 1455
Stability ...... Col. 1:23 1406

D. *Grounds of:*
God's Word .... Ps. 119:42-81 696; Rom. 15:4 1340
God's promises .... Acts 26:6, 7 1312; Titus 1:2 1440

E. *Objects of:*
God .... Ps. 39:7 647
Christ .... 1 Cor. 15:19 1359
Salvation ..... Rom. 5:1-5 1329
Resurrection .. Acts 23:6 1307
Eternal life .... Titus 1:2 1440
Glory .... Rom. 5:2 1329
Christ's return .... Rom. 8:22-25 1333

Hopelessness—*without hope*
Condition of the wicked .... Eph. 2:12 1388
Their unchangeable condition .... Luke 16:23-31 1219

Hophni—*fighter*
Son of Eli; brother of Phinehas .... 1 Sam. 1:3 321
Called "reprobates" .... 1 Sam. 2:12 323
Guilty of unlawful practices .... 1 Sam. 2:13-17 323
Immoral .... 1 Sam. 2:22 324
Eli's warning rejected by .... 1 Sam. 2:23-25 324
Cursed by a man of God .... 1 Sam. 2:27-36 324
Warned by Samuel .... 1 Sam. 3:11-18 326
Ark taken to battle by .... 1 Sam. 4:1-8 326
Slain in battle .... 1 Sam. 4:11 326
News of, causes Eli's death .... 1 Sam. 4:12-18 326

Hor—*mountain*
1. Mountain of Edom .... Num. 20:23 184
Scene of Aaron's death .... Num. 20:22-29 184; Num. 33:37-39 200
2. Prominent peak of the Lebanon range .... Num. 34:7, 8 202

Horam—*elevated*
King of Gezer .... Josh. 10:33 262

Horeb—*desert*
God appears to Moses .... Ex. 3:1-22 70
Water flows from .... Ex. 17:6 87
Law given here ... Mal. 4:4 1083
Site of Israel's great sin .... Deut. 9:8, 9 220; Ps. 106:19 686
Covenant made ... Deut. 29:1 240
Elijah lodged here 40 days .... 1 Kin. 19:8, 9 418

See Sinai

Horem—*consecrated*
City of Naphtali ... Josh. 19:32, 38 272

Hor Hagidgad—*cavern of Gidgah*
Israelite encampment .... Num. 33:32 200

See Gudgodah

Hori—*cave dweller*
1. Son of Lotan .... Gen. 36:22 48; 1 Chr. 1:39 465
2. Horites .... Gen. 36:21-30 48
3. Father of Shaphat the spy .... Num. 13:5 176

Horites—*cave dwellers*
Inhabitants of Mt. Seir .... Gen. 36:20 48
Defeated by Chedorlaomer ... Gen. 14:5, 6 21
Ruled by chieftains .... Gen. 36:29, 30 48
Driven out by Esau's descendants .... Gen. 36:20-29 48; Deut. 2:12, 22 209

Hormah—*devoted to destruction*
Originally called Zephath .... Judg. 1:17 284
Scene of Israel's defeat .... Num. 14:45 178
Destroyed by Israel .... Num. 21:1-3 184
Assigned to Judah .... Josh. 15:30 268
Transferred to Simeon .... Josh. 19:4 271
David sends spoils to .... 1 Sam. 30:26, 30 355

Horn—*bone-like protrusion from an animal's head*
A. *Descriptive of:*
Ram's .... Gen. 22:13 30
Ox's .... Ex. 21:29 92
Wild ox .... Ps. 92:10 679
Goat's .... Dan. 8:5 986
Altar's .... 1 Kin. 1:50 392

B. *Uses of:*
For trumpets .. Josh. 6:4, 13 256
For vessels .... 1 Sam. 16:1-13 340

C. *Figurative of:*
Christ's power .... Rev. 5:6 1523
Power of the wicked .... Ps. 22:21 637
Power of earthly kingdoms .... Dan. 7:7, 8, 24 985
Power of the antichrist .... Rev. 13:1 1529
Arrogance .... 1 Kin. 22:11 423
Conquests ..... Deut. 33:17 246
Exaltation ..... 1 Sam. 2:1, 10 323
Destruction .... Jer. 48:25 896
Salvation ..... Luke 1:69 1192

D. *As musical instrument:*
Used on occasions .... 1 Chr. 15:28 482
A part of worship ...... 2 Chr. 15:14 516
Used in Babylon ...... Dan. 3:7, 10 979

Hornets—*a large, strong wasp*
God's agents .... Ex. 23:28 94; Deut. 7:20 218
Kings driven out by .... Josh. 24:12 279

Horns of the altar—*the protruding points at the four corners of an altar*
Description .... Ex. 27:2 98
Provides sanctuary .... 1 Kin. 1:50 392

Horonaim—*two caverns*
Moabite city ...... Is. 15:5 788

Horonite
Native of Horonaim .... Neh. 2:10, 19 558

Horoscope—*fortune-telling by astrology*
Forbidden .... Jer. 10:2 856
Unprofitable ...... Deut. 17:2-5 228
Punishment ...... Is. 47:13, 14 819

Horse
A. *Used for:*
Travel .... Deut. 17:16 229
War .... Ex. 14:9 83
Bearing burdens ...... Neh. 7:68 564
Sending messages .... Esth. 8:10 583
Idolatry .... 2 Kin. 23:11 457

B. *Figurative of:*
Human trust ... Hos. 14:3 1005
Obstinacy ... Ps. 32:9 642; James 3:3 1469
Impetuosity in sin .... Jer. 8:6 854
God's protection .... 2 Kin. 2:11 430

Horse Gate—*a gate of Jerusalem*
Restored by Nehemiah .... Neh. 3:28 560

Horse traders
Tyre famous for ... Ezek. 27:2, 14 948

Hosah—*seeking refuge*
1. Village of Asher .... Josh. 19:29 272
2. Temple porter .... 1 Chr. 16:38 483

Hosanna—*save, now, we beseech you*
Triumphal acclaim .... Matt. 21:9, 15 1141; Mark 11:9 1174

Hosea—*salvation*
Son of Beeri, prophet of the northern kingdom .... Hos. 1:1 996
Reproved idolatry .... Hos. 1–2 996
Threatens God's judgment; calls to repentance ...... Hos. 3–6 998
Foretells impending judgment .... Hos. 7–10 1000
Calls an ungrateful people to repentance; promises God's blessings .... Hos. 11–14 1003

Hoshaiah—*Yahweh has saved*
1. Father of Jezaniah and Azariah .... Jer. 42:1 890
2. Participant in a dedication .... Neh. 12:31, 32 571

Hoshama—*Yahweh has heard*
Son of King Jeconiah .... 1 Chr. 3:17, 18 467

Hoshea—*save*
1. Original name of Joshua, the son of Nun .. Deut. 32:44 245; Num. 13:8, 16 176

See Joshua, Jehoshua
2. Ephraimite chieftain ..... 1 Chr. 27:20 493
3. One who signs covenant ..... Neh. 10:1, 23 569
4. Israel's last king; usurps throne .... 2 Kin. 15:30 447
5. Reigns wickedly; Israel taken to Assyria during reign .... 2 Kin. 17:1-23 448

SUBJECT REFERENCE PAGE

Grandfather of Bezalel .... Ex. 31:1, 2 104
Supports Moses' hands .... Ex. 17:10-12 88
Aids Aaron .... Ex. 24:14 95
2. Prince of Midian .... Josh. 13:21 266
3. Father of Rephaiah .... Neh. 3:9 559

Hurai—*free, noble*

One of David's mighty men .... 1 Chr. 11:32 478

Huram—*noble, free*

Son of Bela .... 1 Chr. 8:5 473

Huri—*linen worker*

Gadite .... 1 Chr. 5:14 468

Husband—*married man*

A. *Regulations concerning:*
One flesh ...... Matt. 19:5, 6 1139
Until death .... Rom. 7:2, 3 1331
Rights of ...... 1 Cor. 7:1-5 1351
Sanctified by wife .... 1 Cor. 7:14-16 1351

B. *Duties of, toward wife:*
Love .... Eph. 5:25-33 1392
Live with for life .... Matt. 19:3-9 1139
Be faithful to .. Mal. 2:14, 15 1082
Be satisfied with .... Prov. 5:18, 19 718
Instruct ..... 1 Cor. 14:34, 35 1358
Honor .... 1 Pet. 3:7 1480
Confer with ... Gen. 31:4-16 42
Provide for .... 1 Tim. 5:8 1429
Rule over ..... Gen. 3:16 9

C. *Kinds of:*
Adam, blaming ...... Gen. 3:9-12 8
Isaac, loving .... Gen. 24:67 33
Elkanah, sympathetic .... 1 Sam. 1:8-23 321
Nabal, evil .... 1 Sam. 25:3 350
Ahab, weak ... 1 Kin. 21:5-16 422
David, ridiculed ..... 2 Sam. 6:20 365
Job, strong .... Job 2:7-10 590

Hushah—*haste*

Judahite .... 1 Chr. 4:4 467

Hushai—*hasty*

Archite; David's friend .... 2 Sam. 15:32-37 375
Feigns sympathy with Absalom .. 2 Sam. 16:16-19 376
Defeats Ahithophel's advice .... 2 Sam. 17:5-23 376

Husham—*hastily*

Temanite king of Edom .... Gen. 36:34, 35 48

Hushathite

Inhabitant of Hushah .... 2 Sam. 21:18 382

Hushim—*hasters*

1. Head of a Danite family .... Gen. 46:23 59
Called Shuham ...... Num. 26:42 191
2. Son of Aher ... 1 Chr. 7:12 472
3. Wife of Shaharaim ... 1 Chr. 8:8, 11 473

Huz

Son of Nahor ...... Gen. 22:20, 21 31

Huzzab—*uncertain meaning*

May refer to Assyrian queen or to Nineveh; or may be rendered "it is decreed" .... Nah. 2:7 1048

Hymenaeus—*belonging to Hymen*

False teacher excommunicated by Paul .... 1 Tim. 1:19, 20 1426
Teaches error ..... 2 Tim. 2:17, 18 1434

Hymn—*a spiritual song*

A. *Occasions producing:*
Great deliverance ... Ex. 15:1-19 85
Great victory .. Judg. 5:1-31 288
Prayer answered .... 1 Sam. 2:1-10 323
Mary's "Magnificat" ...... Luke 1:46-55 1192
Father's ecstasy ...... Luke 1:68-79 1192
Angel's delight .... Luke 2:14 1193
Old man's faith .... Luke 2:29-32 1194
Heaven's eternal praise .... Rev. 5:9-14 1523

B. *Purposes of:*
Worship God .... 2 Chr. 23:18 523
Express joy ... Matt. 26:30 1150
Edify .... 1 Cor. 14:15 1358
Testify to others .... Acts 16:25 1295

Hypocrisy, hypocrite—*showy, empty display of religion*

A. *Kinds of:*
Worldly .... Matt. 23:5-7 1145
Legalistic .... Rom. 10:3 1334
Evangelical .... 2 Pet. 2:10-22 1489
Satanic ...... 2 Cor. 11:13-15 1373

B. *Described as:*
Self-righteous . Luke 18:11, 12 1220
"Holier than you" .... Is. 65:5 836
Blind .... Matt. 23:17-26 1145
Covetous .... 2 Pet. 2:3 1487
Showy .... Matt. 6:2, 5, 16 1121
Highly critical .... Matt. 7:3-5 1123
Indignant ..... Luke 13:14-16 1216
Bound by traditions .... Matt. 15:1-9 1135
Neglectful of major duties .... Matt. 23:23, 24 1145
Pretended but unpracticed .... Ezek. 33:31, 32 957
Interested in the externals ...... Luke 20:46, 47 1224
Fond of titles .. Matt. 23:6, 7 1145
Inwardly unregenerate .... Luke 11:39 1212

C. *Examples of:*
Jacob .... Gen. 27:6-35 36
Jacob's sons ... Gen. 37:29-35 49
Delilah .... Judg. 16:4-20 302
Ishmael .... Jer. 41:6, 7 888
Herod .... Matt. 2:7, 8 1116
Pharisees ..... John 8:4-9 1248
Judas .... Matt. 26:25-49 1150
Ananias .... Acts 5:1-10 1277
Peter .... Gal. 2:11-14 1380

Hyssop—*a small plant*

Grows from walls .... 1 Kin. 4:33 397
Used in sprinkling blood .... Ex. 12:22 80
Used to offer Jesus vinegar .... John 19:28, 29 1264
Typical of spiritual cleansing .... Ps. 51:7 654

I

I AM—*a title indicating self-existence*

Revealed to Moses .... Ex. 3:14 70
Said by Christ .... John 8:57, 58 1250

Christ expressing, refers to:

Bread of life .... John 6:35, 41, 48, 51 1246
Light of the world .... John 8:12, John 9:5 1249, 1250
Door of the sheep .... John 10:7, 9 1251
Good shepherd ... John 10:11, 14 1252
Resurrection and the life .... John 11:25 1253
True and living way .... John 14:6 1258
True vine .... John 15:1, 5 1258

Ibleam—*he destroys the people*

City assigned to Manasseh .... Josh. 17:11, 12 270
Canaanites remain in .... Judg. 1:27 284
Called Bileam .... 1 Chr. 6:70 470
Ahaziah slain near .... 2 Kin. 9:27 439

Ibneiah—*Yahweh builds up*

Head of a Benjamite family .... 1 Chr. 9:8 474

Ibnijah—*Yahweh builds up*

Father of Reuel ... 1 Chr. 9:8 474

Ibri—*a Hebrew*

Son of Jaaziah .... 1 Chr. 24:27 491

Ibzan—*active*

Judge of Israel .... Judg. 12:8 299
Father of 60 children .... Judg. 12:8, 9 299

Ice

Figurative of:

By reason of ...... Job 6:16 593

Ichabod—*inglorious*

Son of Phinehas .. 1 Sam. 4:19-22 327

Iconium—*image-like*

City of Asia Minor; visited by Paul .... Acts 13:51 1292
Many converts in .... Acts 14:1-6 1292
Paul visits again .. Acts 14:21 1293
Timothy's ministry .... Acts 16:1, 2 1294
Paul persecuted ... 2 Tim. 3:11 1436

Iconoclast—*a breaker of images*

Moses, an angry .. Ex. 32:19, 20 105
Gideon, an inspired .... Judg. 6:25-32 290
Jehu, a subtle ... 2 Kin. 10:18-31 442
Josiah, a reforming ...... 2 Kin. 23:12-25 457

Idalah—*memorial of God*

Border town of Zebulun .... Josh. 19:15 272

SUBJECT REFERENCE PAGE

Incense—*sweet perfume; frankincense*

A. *Offered:*
By priests .....Lev. 16:12, 13 139
On the altar ...Ex. 30:1-8 103
On day of atonement ....Lev. 16:12, 13 139
According to strict formula ......Ex. 30:34-36 104

B. *Illegal offering of:*
Forbidden .....Ex. 30:37, 38 104
Excluded from certain offerings .....Lev. 5:11 124
Punished severely .....Lev. 10:1, 2 128; 2 Chr. 26:16-21 526
Among idolaters .....Is. 65:3 836

C. *Typical of:*
Worship ......Ps. 141:2 706
Prayer ......Rev. 5:8 1523; Rev. 8:3, 4 1525
Praise.........Mal. 1:11 1080
Approved service ....Eph. 5:2 1391

D. *Purposes of:*
Used in holy oil ....Ex. 30:34-38 104
Used in meal offerings .....Lev. 2:1, 2, 15 120
Excluded from certain offerings .....Lev. 5:11 124
Used in the showbread ...Lev. 24:7 149
Product of Arabia ....Is. 60:6 832
Presented to Jesus ....Matt. 2:11 1116
Figurative of worship ....Ps. 141:2 706

Incentives to good works

Reap kindness ....Hos. 10:12 1003
Remain ....John 15:16 1259
Reap ....Gal. 6:7-10 1383

Incest—*sexual relations between persons related*

A. *Relations prohibited:*
Same family ...Lev. 18:6-12 141
Grandchildren ......Lev. 18:10 141
Aunts and uncles ....Lev. 18:12-14 141
In-laws.........Lev. 18:15, 16 141
Near kin ......Lev. 18:17, 18 141

B. *Punishment for:*
Death ....Lev. 20:11-17 143
Childlessness ......Lev. 20:19-21 143
A curse ....Deut. 27:20-23 237

C. *Examples of:*
Lot—with his daughters .....Gen. 19:30-38 28
Reuben—with his father's concubine .....Gen. 35:22 46

Inconsistency—*the non-agreement of two things*

Between:
Criticism of ourselves and others ....Matt. 7:3 1123
Legalism and human mercy ....John 7:23 1247
Profession and reality ....Luke 22:31-62 1226
Preaching and practice ....Rom. 2:21-23 1325
Private and public convictions ......Gal. 2:11-14 1380
Faith and works ..James 2:14-26 1469
Profession and works ....Titus 1:16 1440

Inconstancy—*inability to stand firm in crisis*

A. *Causes of:*
Little faith .....Matt. 13:19-22 1132
Satan ....Luke 22:31-34 1226
False teachers ......Gal. 1:6-10 1378
Doubt ....James 1:6-8 1468
Immaturity ....2 Pet. 1:5-10 1487

B. *Remedies against:*
Firm foundation ...Matt. 7:24-27 1125
Strong faith ...Hab. 3:16-19 1054
Full armor .....Eph. 6:10-20 1393

Incontinency—*uncontrolled indulgence of the passions*

A. *Expressed in:*
Unbridled sexual morals ....Ex. 32:6, 18, 25 105
Abnormal sexual desires ....2 Sam. 13:1-15 371
Unnatural sexual appetites ....Gen. 19:5-9 26; Rom. 1:26, 27 1324

B. *Sources of:*
Lust ....1 Pet. 4:2, 3 1481
Satan ....1 Cor. 7:5 1351
Apostasy ......2 Tim. 3:3 1434

Incorruptible—*enduring; lasting forever*

Resurrected body ....1 Cor. 15:42, 52, 53 1360
Christian's inheritance ....1 Pet. 1:4 1477
Seed of Christian life..............1 Pet. 1:23 1479

Increase—*to become more abundant*

A. *Used literally of:*
Knowledge ....Dan. 12:4 993

B. *Used spiritually of:*
Messiah's kingdom .....Is. 9:7 781
Wisdom ....Luke 2:52 1194
Faith ....Luke 17:5 1219
Esteem ....John 3:30 1241
Knowledge of God ....Col. 1:10 1406
Love ....1 Thess. 4:9, 10 1416
Ungodliness ...2 Tim. 2:16 1434

Incredulity—*an unwillingness to believe*

Characterized by:

Exaggerated demand for evidence ....John 20:24, 25 1265
Desire for more signs ....Judg. 6:37-40 291
Attempts to nullify plain evidence ....John 9:13-41 1250
Blindness of mind ....Acts 28:22-29 1315

Indecency

Noah guilty of ....Gen. 9:21-23 15
Forbidden, to priests ....Ex. 20:26 92
Michal rebukes David for ....2 Sam. 6:20-23 365
Men committing ..Rom. 1:27 1324

Indecision—*inability to decide between vital issues*

A. *Manifested in, mixing:*
Truth and idolatry ....1 Kin. 18:21 417
Duty and compromise ....John 19:12-16 1263
Holiness and sin ....Gal. 5:1-7 1382
Faith and works ....Gal. 3:1-5 1380

B. *Results in:*
Spiritual unfitness ....Luke 9:59-62 1208
Instability .....James 1:6-8 1468
Sinful compromise ....2 Cor. 6:14-18 1369
Spiritual defeat ....Rom. 6:16-22 1331
Spiritual deadness .....Rev. 3:15-17 1521

C. *Examples of:*
Israel at Kadesh ....Num. 13:26-33 176
Joshua at Ai ...Josh. 7:6-10 258
David at Keilah ....1 Sam. 23:1-5 348
Pilate ....Matt. 27:11-24 1152
Felix ....Acts 24:25, 26 1308

See Inconstancy

Independence—*control of one's affairs apart from outside influences*

A. *Virtues of:*
Freedom of action ....Gen. 14:22-24 21
Responsibility ....John 9:21, 23 1251

B. *Evils of:*
Arbitrary use of authority ....1 Sam. 14:24-45 336
Selfishness ....1 Sam. 25:1-11 350
Mismanagement ....Luke 15:12-16 1218
Arrogance .....3 John 9, 10 1506

India

Eastern limit of Persian Empire ....Esth. 1:1 577

Indictment—*formal accusation for a crime*

A. *For real crimes:*
Korah's company .....Num. 16:1-50 179
Achan ....Josh. 7:1-26 258
Baal worshipers .....1 Kin. 18:19-42 417
David ....2 Sam. 12:1-14 370
Ananias.......Acts 5:1-10 1277

B. *For supposed crimes:*
Certain tribes ....Josh. 22:10-34 276
Naboth ....1 Kin. 21:1-16 421
Three Hebrew men ....Dan. 3:1-28 978
Jews ....Ezra 5:3-17 547; Esth. 3:8, 9 579
Christ..........Matt. 26:61-65 1151
Stephen ....Acts 6:11, 13 1279
Paul ....Acts 16:20, 21 1295; Acts 17:7 1297

Indifference—*not concerned for or against something*

A. *Characteristic of:*
Unbelievers ...Luke 17:26-30 1220
Backsliders....Rev. 3:15, 16 1521

B. *As a good feature concerning, worldly:*
Comforts ......Phil. 4:11-13 1402
Applause ......Gal. 1:10 1378
Traditions .....Col. 2:16-23 1408

C. *As a bad feature:*
Inhumanitarianism .....Luke 10:30-32 1209
In the use of one's talents ....Luke 19:20-26 1222
Moral callousness ...Matt. 27:3, 4 1152

SUBJECT REFERENCE PAGE

Indifference—continued
Religious unconcern .... Acts 18:12-16 1299

Indignation—*boiling wrath against something sinful*

A. *God's:*
Irresistible .... Nah. 1:6 1045
Victorious .... Hab. 3:12 1054
Poured out .... Zeph. 3:8 1059
Toward His enemies ...... Is. 66:14 838
On Israel ...... Deut. 29:28 241
Against Edom forever ...... Mal. 1:4 1080
Angels, instruments of .... Ps. 78:49 671
On believers ... Job 10:17 596
Will hide His own from .... Is. 26:20 796
Entreated, on the wicked .... Ps. 69:24 664
As punishment .. Rom. 2:8 1324

B. *Man's against:*
Others .... Esth. 5:9 581
Jews .... Neh. 4:1 560
Christ .... Luke 13:14 1216
Christians ..... Acts 5:17 1278

Indignities suffered by Christ

A. *Against His body:*
Spit on .... Matt. 26:67 1151
Struck .... John 18:22, 23 1263
Crowned with thorns .... Matt. 27:29 1152
Crucified ...... Matt. 27:31-35 1152

B. *Against His person:*
Called guilty without a trial .... John 18:30, 31 1263
Mocked and derided ..... Matt. 27:29, 31, 39-44 1152
Rejected in favor of a murderer ..... Matt. 27:16-21 1152
Crucified between two men .... John 19:18 1264

Indiscrimination—*showing lack of distinction in*

Devastation ...... Is. 24:1-4 793
Judgment .... Ezek. 18:1-32 934
God's providences ..... Matt. 5:45 1121

Indulge—*to yield to desires*

Fleshly desires .... Eph. 2:3 1387
Corrupt desires .... 2 Pet. 2:10 1489
Gross immorality .... Jude 7 1510

Indulgence—*a kindness often misused*

Parental .... 1 Sam. 3:11-14 326
Kingly .... 2 Sam. 13:21-39 372
Priestly .... Judg. 17:1-13 303

Industry—*diligence in one's work*

A. *Characteristics of:*
Established .... Gen. 2:15 7
Commanded .. 1 Thess. 4:11 1416
Commendable .... Prov. 27:23-27 740
Done willingly ..... Prov. 31:13 745
Mark of wisdom ...... Prov. 10:5 722
Suspended on Sabbath .... Ex. 20:10 90
Neglect of, rebuked ..... 2 Thess. 3:10-12 1422

B. *Necessity of:*
Our needs ..... 1 Thess. 2:9 1415
Needs of others .... Acts 20:35 1303
Faithful witness ...... 1 Tim. 5:8 1429

C. *Blessings of:*
Wealth .... Prov. 10:4, 5 722
Praise .... Prov. 31:28, 31 745
Food sufficient ..... Prov. 12:11 724
Will rule ...... Prov. 12:24 725

Indwelling, of believers

A. *By Christ:*
Through faith .... Eph. 3:14-19 1388
Mystery .... Col. 1:27 1406

B. *Spirit:*
Every believer ...... Rom. 8:9-11 1332
Body, a temple of God .... 1 Cor. 3:16 1346

Infant salvation

Suggested by Scripture .... Matt. 18:3-5, 10 1138; Matt. 19:14 1139

Infants

A. *Acts performed upon:*
Naming .... Ruth 4:17 317
Blessing ..... Luke 1:67, 76-79 1192
Circumcision .. Luke 2:21 1193

B. *Capacity to:*
Believe .... Matt. 18:6 1138
Know the Scriptures .... 2 Tim. 3:15 1436
Receive training ...... Eph. 6:4 1392
Worship in God's house ...... 1 Sam. 1:24, 28 323

C. *Murder of:*
By Pharaoh ... Ex. 1:16 69
By Herod the Great .... Matt. 2:16-18 1116
In war .... Num. 31:17 197

Infidelity—*unbelief in God's revelation*

A. *Causes of:*
Unregenerate heart ...... Rom. 2:5 1324
Hatred of the light .... John 3:19-21 1239
Spiritual blindness .... 1 Cor. 2:8, 14 1346
Self-trust ...... Is. 47:10, 11 819
Unbelief ...... Acts 6:10-15 1279
Inveterate prejudice ..... Acts 7:54, 57 1282
Worldly wisdom ...... 1 Cor. 1:18-22 1345

B. *Manifested in:*
Rejecting God's Word .... 2 Pet. 3:3-5 1489
Scoffing at God's servants ..... 2 Chr. 30:6, 10 529
Hiding under lies .... Is. 28:15 798
Living without God .... Job 22:13-17 604
Using derisive words .... Matt. 12:24 1131
Doubting God's righteousness .... Ps. 10:11, 13 631
Calling religion worthless .... Mal. 3:14 1083

C. *Punishment of:*
Eternal separation from God .... 2 Thess. 1:8, 9 1421
God's wrath .... 1 Thess. 2:14-16 1415
Hell .... Luke 16:23-31 1219
Severe punishment .. Heb. 10:28, 29 1458

D. *Remedies against:*
Remember the end .... Ps. 73:16-28 667
Trust when you can't explain ...... Job 2:9, 10 590
Stand upon the Word .... Matt. 4:3-11 1118
Use God's armor .... Eph. 6:10-19 1393
Grow spiritually .... 2 Pet. 1:4-11 1487

Infinite—*extending immeasurably*

God's understanding ... Ps. 147:5 708

Infirmities—*weaknesses of our human nature*

A. *Kinds of:*
Sickness or disease .... Matt. 8:17 1125
Imperfections of the body .... 2 Cor. 11:30 1374

B. *Our duties with reference to:*
Rejoice in ..... 2 Cor. 12:10 1374
Help those afflicted with .... Gal. 6:1 1383
Not to despise in others .... Gal. 4:13, 14 1382

Influence—*that invisible force in one's personality that causes others to act*

Christians, should be:
As salt .... Matt. 5:13 1120
As light .... Matt. 5:14-16 1120; Phil. 2:15 1400
As examples ...... 1 Thess. 1:7, 8 1413
Beneficial to spouse .... 1 Cor. 7:14, 16 1351; 1 Pet. 3:1, 2 1480
Above criticism .... 1 Cor. 8:10-13 1352
Honorable .... 1 Tim. 6:1 1430
Permanent .... Heb. 11:4 1460
Beneficial to others .... 1 Pet. 2:11, 12 1479
Without reproach .... Phil. 2:15, 16 1400

Ingenuity—*skill shown in unusual contrivances*

Of God .... Job 38:4-41 615; Ps. 139:13-16 705; Gen. 27:7-29 36
Of man .... Ex. 2:1-9 69; Ex. 35:30-33 109

Ingratitude—*unthankfulness for blessings received*

A. *Characteristics of:*
Inconsiderate .... Deut. 32:6, 7 244
Unreasonable .... Jer. 2:5-7 845
Unnatural ...... Is. 1:2, 3 771
Ungrateful .... Jer. 5:7-9, 24 850

B. *Causes of:*
Prosperity ..... Deut. 6:10-12 215
Self-sufficiency ... Deut. 8:12-18 218
Forgetfulness .... Luke 17:12-18 1220
Fear .... 1 Sam. 23:5, 12 348
Greed .... 1 Sam. 25:4-11 350
Pride .... Dan. 5:18-20 983

C. *Attitudes toward:*
Acknowledged .... 1 Sam. 24:17-19 350
Abused .... 2 Chr. 24:22 524
Revealed .... 1 Sam. 23:5-12 348
Forgiven by kindness .... 1 Sam. 25:14-35 350

SUBJECT REFERENCE PAGE

Inner natures, conflict of—continued
Cannot please God .... Rom. 8:8 1332
To be mortified ..... Col. 3:5 1408

B. *New nature:*
By Spirit's indwelling .... 1 Cor. 3:16 1346
Strengthened by Spirit .... Eph. 3:16 1388
Called inward man .... 2 Cor. 4:16 1368
Called new man .... Col. 3:10 1408
Fruits of ...... Gal. 5:22, 23 1383

C. *Conflict:*
Called warfare ..... Rom. 7:19-23 1332; Gal. 5:17 1383

D. *Victory:*
Recognize source .... James 1:14-16 1468
Realize former condition ..... Eph. 2:1-7 1387
Put off former conduct .... Eph. 4:22 1391
Make no provision ..... Rom. 13:14 1339
Complete surrender to God .... Rom. 12:1, 2 1336
Spiritual food .... 1 Pet. 2:1, 2 1479

Innocence—*freedom from guilt or sin*

A. *Loss of, by:*
Disobedience .... Rom. 5:12 1329
Idolatry .... Ps. 106:34-39 686

B. *Kinds of:*
Absolute ...... 2 Cor. 5:21 1369
Legal .... Luke 23:4 1228
Moral .... Josh. 22:10-34 276
Spiritual ...... 2 Pet. 3:14 1489

C. *Of Christ:*
In prophecy ... Is. 53:7-9 825
In type .... 1 Pet. 1:19 1479
In reality ...... 1 Pet. 3:18 1481
By examination .... Luke 23:13-22 1229
By testimony ... Acts 13:28 1291

Innocents, massacre of

Mourning foretold .... Jer. 31:15 877
After Jesus' birth .... Matt. 2:16-18 1116

Inns, Three

Place about 30 miles south of Rome .... Acts 28:15 1315

Innumerable—*uncounted multitude*

Evils .... Ps. 40:12 648
Animal life .... Ps. 104:25 684
Descendants ...... Heb. 11:12 1460
People .... Luke 12:1 1212
Angels .... Heb. 12:22 1463

Inquiry—*a consulting or seeking for counsel*

By Israel .... Ex. 18:15 88
With ephod ..... 1 Sam. 23:9, 11 348
Unlawful method .... 1 Sam. 28:6, 7 353
Through prayer .... 2 Cor. 12:7-9 1374; James 1:5 1468

Insanity—*mental derangement*

A. *Characteristics of:*
Abnormal behavior ..... Dan. 4:32-34 981
Self-destruction ... Matt. 17:14-18 1137
Distinct from demon possession ... Matt. 4:24 1118

B. *Figurative of:*
The result of moral instability ... Jer. 25:15-17 871; Jer. 51:7 902
God's judgment ..... Zech. 12:4 1075

Inscription—*a statement written or engraved*

On Christ's cross .... Luke 23:38 1229; John 19:19-22 1264
On an altar .... Acts 17:23 1299
Roman coin ...... Mark 12:16 1178

Insects of the Bible

A. *Characteristics of:*
Created by God .... Gen. 1:24, 25 4
Some clean ..... Lev. 11:21, 22 132
Some unclean ...... Lev. 11:23, 24 132

B. *List of:*
Ant .... Prov. 6:6 719
Bee .... Judg. 14:8 300
Cricket .... Lev. 11:22 132
Caterpillar .... Ps. 78:46 671
Flea .... 1 Sam. 24:14 349
Fly .... Eccl. 10:1 758
Gnat .... Matt. 23:24 1145
Grasshopper .. Lev. 11:22 132
Hornet .... Deut. 7:20 218
Leech .... Prov. 30:15 744
Locust .... Ex. 10:4 78
Moth .... Is. 50:9 823
Spider .... Prov. 30:28 744
Worms .... Ex. 16:20 87

C. *Illustrative of:*
Design in nature .... Prov. 30:24-28 744
Troubles ...... Ps. 118:12 693
Insignificance .... 1 Sam. 24:14 349
Desolation .... Joel 1:4 1008
Appetite ..... Prov. 30:15 744
Transitoriness .... Is. 51:8 823; Matt. 6:20 1123
Vast numbers ..... Judg. 6:5 290

Insecurity—*a state of anxiety about earthly needs*

A. *Descriptive of:*
Wicked .... Ps. 37:1, 2, 10 645
Riches .... 1 Tim. 6:17 1430
Those trusting in themselves ... Luke 12:16-21 1214

B. *Cure of:*
Steadfast of mind .... Is. 26:3 795
Rely upon God's promises ..... Ps. 37:1-26 645
Remember God's provision ..... Phil. 4:9-19 1402
Put God first .. Matt. 6:25-34 1123

Insensibility—*deadness of spiritual life*

A. *Kinds of:*
Physical ...... Judg. 19:26-29 307
Spiritual ...... Jer. 5:3, 21 850
Judicial .... Acts 28:25-28 1315

B. *Causes of:*
Seared conscience ... 1 Tim. 4:2 1429
Spiritual ignorance .... Eph. 4:18, 19 1391
Wanton pleasure ..... 1 Tim. 5:6 1429

Insincerity—*hypocritical deceitfulness*

A. *Manifested in:*
Mock ceremonies ... Is. 58:3-6 830
Unwilling preaching .... Jon. 4:1-11 1032
Trumped up questions .... Matt. 22:15-22 1144
Boastful pretentions ... Luke 22:33 1226

B. *Those guilty of:*
Hypocrites ..... Luke 11:42-47 1212
False teachers ...... Gal. 6:12, 13 1383
Immature Christians .... 1 Cor. 4:17-21 1348

See Hypocrisy

Insomnia—*inability to sleep*

A. *Causes of:*
Excessive work .... Gen. 31:40 43
Worry .... Esth. 6:1 581
Dreams .... Dan. 2:1 977
Conscience .... Dan. 6:9-18 984

B. *Cure of:*
Trust .... Ps. 3:5, 6 626
Peacefulness .. Ps. 4:8 626
Confidence .... Ps. 127:1, 2 701
Obedience .... Prov. 6:20-22 719

Inspiration of the Scriptures

A. *Expressed by:*
"Thus the LORD said to me" .... Jer. 13:1 859
"The word of the LORD came" .... 1 Kin. 16:1 413
"It is written" ...... Rom. 10:15 1335
"As the Holy Spirit says" .... Heb. 3:7 1452
"According to the Scripture" .... James 2:8 1469
"My words in your mouth" ...... Jer. 1:9, 10 844

B. *Described as:*
Inspired by God .... 2 Tim. 3:16 1436
Moved by the Holy Spirit .... 2 Pet. 1:21 1487
Christ-centered .... Luke 24:27 1231; 2 Cor. 13:3 1375

C. *Modes of:*
Different ...... Heb. 1:1 1450
Inner impulse ..... Judg. 13:25 300; Jer. 20:9 866
A voice .... Rev. 1:10 1517
Dreams .... Dan. 7:1 985
Visions .... Ezek. 11:24, 25 928

D. *Proofs of:*
Fulfilled prophecy .... Jer. 28:15-17 874; Luke 24:27, 44, 45 1231
Miracles attesting .... Ex. 4:1-9 72; 2 Kin. 1:10-14 430
Teachings supporting ... Deut. 4:8 211; Ps. 19:7-11 635

E. *Design of:*
Reveal God's mysteries .... Amos 3:7 1017; 1 Cor. 2:10 1346
Reveal the future ...... Acts 1:16 1272; 1 Pet. 1:10-12 1477
Instruct and edify .... Mic. 3:8 1038; Acts 1:8 1272
Counteract distortion .... 2 Cor. 13:1-3 1375; Gal. 1:6-11 1378

F. *Results of Scriptures:*
Unbreakable .. John 10:34-36 1252
Eternal .... Matt. 24:35 1148
Authoritative .... Matt. 4:4, 7, 10 1118
Trustworthy ... Ps. 119:160 699

SUBJECT REFERENCE PAGE

Verbally accurate ..... Matt. 22:32, 43-46 1144; Gal. 3:16 1381
Sanctifying ..... 2 Tim. 3:16, 17 1436
Effective ..... Jer. 23:29 870; 2 Tim. 3:15 1436

See Word of God

Instability—*lack of firmness of convictions*

A. *Causes of:*
Deception ..... Gal. 3:1 1380; Col. 2:4-8 1406
Immaturity ..... 1 Tim. 3:6 1427
False teaching ..... 2 Cor. 11:3, 4 1373; Gal. 1:6-11 1378
Lack of depth ..... Heb. 5:11-14 1453
Unsettled mind ..... Eph. 4:14 1390; James 1:6-8 1468

B. *Examples of:*
Pharaoh ..... Ex. 10:8-20 79
Israel ..... Judg. 2:17 285
Solomon ..... 1 Kin. 11:1-8 407
Disciples ..... John 6:66 1247
John Mark ..... Acts 15:37, 38 1294
Galatians ..... Gal. 1:6 1378

Instinct—*inbred characteristic of*

Animals ..... Is. 1:3 771
Birds ..... Jer. 8:7 854

Instruction—*imparting knowledge to others*

A. *Given by:*
Parents ..... Deut. 6:6-25 215
Priests ..... Deut. 24:8 235
God ..... Jer. 32:33 880
Pastors ..... Eph. 4:11 1390
Pedagogues ..... Neh. 8:7, 8 565
Paraclete (the Holy Spirit) ..... John 14:26 1258

B. *Means of:*
Nature ..... Prov. 6:6-11 719
Human nature ..... Prov. 24:30-34 737
Law ..... Rom. 2:18 1325
Proverbs ..... Prov. 1:1-30 714
Songs ..... Deut. 32:1-44 243
History ..... 1 Cor. 10:1-11 1353
God's Word ..... 2 Tim. 3:15, 16 1436

See Education; Teaching, teachers

Instrument—*a tool or implement*

For threshing ..... 2 Sam. 24:22 387
For sacrifices ..... Ezek. 40:42 964
Of iron ..... 2 Sam. 12:31 371
Body members, used as ..... Rom. 6:13 1331

Insult—*to treat insolently*

Ignored by King Saul ..... 1 Sam. 10:26, 27 332
Job treated with ..... Job 30:1, 9, 10 609
Children punished because of ..... 2 Kin. 2:23, 24 431
Pharisees treat Jesus with ..... Matt. 12:24, 25 1131
Paul's reaction to ..... Acts 23:1-5 1307
Forbidden ..... 1 Pet. 3:8, 9 1480

Insurrection—*rebellion against constituted authority*

In Jerusalem ..... Ezra 4:19 546
Absalom's miserable ..... 2 Sam. 18:32, 33 378
Attempted by Jews ..... Mark 15:7 1182

Integrity—*moral uprightness*

A. *Manifested in:*
Moral uprightness ..... Gen. 20:3-10 29
Unselfish service ..... Num. 16:15 180
Performing vows ..... Jer. 35:12-19 883
Rejecting bribes ..... Acts 8:18-23 1282
Honest behavior ..... 2 Cor. 7:2 1369

B. *Illustrated in:*
Job's life ..... Job 2:3, 9, 10 590
David's kingship ..... Ps. 7:8 628
Nehemiah's service ..... Neh. 5:14-19 561
Daniel's rule ..... Dan. 6:1-4 984
Paul's ministry ..... 2 Cor. 4:2 1367

Intemperance—*not restraining the appetites*

A. *Manifested in:*
Drunkenness ..... Prov. 23:19-35 736
Gluttony ..... Titus 1:12 1440
Immorality ..... Rom. 1:26, 27 1324

B. *Evils of:*
Puts the flesh first ..... Phil. 3:19 1401
Brings about death ..... 1 Sam. 25:36-38 351

See Drunkenness

Intention—*a fixed determination to do a specified thing*

A. *Good:*
Commended but not allowed ..... 1 Kin. 8:17-19 402
Planned but delayed ..... Rom. 15:24-28 1340

B. *Evil:*
Restrained by God ..... Gen. 31:22-31 42
Turned to good by God ..... Gen. 45:4-8 58
Overruled by God's providence ..... Esth. 9:23-25 585

C. *Of Christ:*
Predicted ..... Ps. 40:6-8 648
Announced ..... Matt. 20:18-28 1140
Misunderstood ..... Matt. 16:21-23 1137
Fulfilled ..... John 19:28-30 1264
Explained ..... Luke 24:25-47 1231

Interbreeding—*crossbreed*

Forbidden:

In animals, vegetables, cloth ..... Lev. 19:19 142

Intercession—*prayer offered in behalf of others*

A. *Purposes of:*
Secure healing ..... James 5:14-16 1473
Avert judgment ..... Num. 14:11-21 177
Insure deliverance ..... 1 Sam. 7:5-9 328
Give blessings ..... Num. 6:23-27 168
Obtain restoration ..... Job 42:8-10 620
Encourage repentance ..... Rom. 10:1-4 1334

B. *Characteristics of:*
Pleading ..... Gen. 18:23-33 26
Specific ..... Gen. 24:12-15 32
Victorious ..... Ex. 17:9-12 88
Very intense ..... Ex. 32:31, 32 106
Quickly answered ..... Num. 27:15-23 194
Confessing ..... 2 Sam. 24:17 387
Personal ..... 1 Chr. 29:19 496
Covenant pleading ..... Neh. 1:4-11 558
Unselfish ..... Acts 7:60 1282

C. *Examples of:*
Moses ..... Ex. 32:11-13 105
Joshua ..... Josh. 7:6-9 258
Jehoshaphat ..... 2 Chr. 20:5-13 519
Isaiah ..... 2 Chr. 32:20 531
Daniel ..... Dan. 9:3-19 988
Christ ..... John 17:1-26 1261
Paul ..... Col. 1:9-12 1405

Intercourse—*copulation*

Kinds of, forbidden:

With neighbor's wife ..... Lev. 18:20 141
With animal ..... Lev. 18:23 141

Interest—*money charged on borrowed money; usury*

From poor man, forbidden ..... Ex. 22:25 93
From a stranger, permitted ..... Deut. 23:19, 20 233
Exaction of, unprofitable ..... Prov. 28:8 742
Condemned as a sin ..... Ezek. 18:8-17 934
Exaction of, rebuked ..... Neh. 5:1-13 561
Reward for non-exaction of ..... Ps. 15:5 632
Used to illustrate ..... Luke 19:23 1222

Intermediate state—*the state of the believer between death and the resurrection*

A. *Described as:*
Like sleep ..... John 11:11-14 1253
"Far better" ..... Phil. 1:21, 23 1398
"Present with the Lord" ..... 2 Cor. 5:6, 8 1368

B. *Characteristics of:*
Persons identifiable ..... Matt. 17:3 1137
Conscious and enjoyable ..... Ps. 17:15 634; Luke 16:25 1219
Unchangeable ..... Luke 16:26 1219
Without the body ..... 2 Cor. 5:1-4 1368; Rev. 6:9 1524
Awaiting the resurrection ..... Phil. 3:20, 21 1401; 1 Thess. 4:13-18 1416

See Immortality

Interpretation—*making the unknown known*

A. *Things in need of:*
Dreams ..... Gen. 41:15-36 52
Languages ..... Gen. 42:23 55
Writings ..... Dan. 5:7-31 983
Scripture ..... Acts 8:30-35 1284
Tongues ..... 1 Cor. 12:10 1355

B. *Agents of:*
Jesus Christ ..... Luke 24:25-47 1231
Holy Spirit ..... 1 Cor. 2:11-16 1346
Angels ..... Luke 1:26-37 1190
Prophets and apostles ..... Eph. 3:2-11 1388

Intestines (see Entrails)

Intimidation—*suggesting possible harm if one acts contrary to another's wishes*

Attitudes toward:

Discovers its deceit ..... Neh. 6:5-13 562

SUBJECT — REFERENCE — PAGE

Ish-Tob—*man of Tob*

Small kingdom of Aram .... 2 Sam. 10:6, 8 369
Jephthah seeks asylum in .... Judg. 11:3, 5 297

Ishuah—*he is equal*

Son of Asher .... Gen. 46:17 59
Called Ishvah .... 1 Chr. 7:30 473

Ishvi—*man of Yahweh*

Son of Asher and chief .... 1 Chr. 7:30 473

Island—*surrounded by water*

List of:

Caphtor (Crete?) .... Jer. 47:4 895
Clauda .... Acts 27:16 1314
Chios .... Acts 20:15 1303
Cos .... Acts 21:1 1303
Crete .... Acts 27:12 1314
Cyprus .... Acts 11:19 1288
Elishah .... Ezek. 27:7 948
Malta .... Acts 28:1, 7, 9 1315
Patmos .... Rev. 1:9 1517
Rhodes .... Acts 21:1 1303
Samos .... Acts 20:15 1303
Samothrace .... Acts 16:11 1295
Syracuse .... Acts 28:12 1315
Tyre .... Is. 23:1, 2 793

Ismachiah—*Yahweh will sustain*

Temple overseer .... 2 Chr. 31:13 530

Ispah—*to lay bear*

Benjamite .... 1 Chr. 8:16 473

Israel—*God strives*

A. *Used literally of:*
Jacob .... Gen. 32:28 44
Descendants of Jacob .... Gen. 49:16, 28 63
Ten northern tribes (in contrast to Judah) .... 1 Sam. 11:8 333
Restored nation after exile .... Ezra 9:1 551

B. *Used spiritually of:*
Messiah .... Is. 49:3 821
God's redeemed ones .... Rom. 9:6-13 1333
True church .... Gal. 6:16 1383

Israelites—*descendants of Israel* (Jacob)

A. *Brief history of:*
Begin as a nation in Egypt .... Ex. 1:12, 20 68
Afflicted in Egypt .... Ex. 1:12-22 68
Moses becomes their leader .... Ex. 3:1-22 70
Saved from plagues .... Ex. 9:4, 6, 26 76
Expelled from Egypt .... Ex. 12:29-36 82
Pass through Red Sea .... Ex. 14:1-31 83
Receive Law at Sinai .... Ex. 19:1-25 89
Sin at Sinai .... Ex. 32:1-35 105
Rebel at Kadesh .... Num. 13:1-33 176
Wander 40 years .... Num. 14:26-39 177
Cross Jordan .... Josh. 4:1-24 254
Conquer Canaan .... Josh. 12:1-24 265
Ruled by judges .... Judg. 2:1-23 285
Samuel becomes leader .... 1 Sam. 7:1-17 328
Seek to have a king .... 1 Sam. 8:1-22 330
Saul chosen king .... 1 Sam. 10:18-27 332
David becomes king .... 2 Sam. 2:1-4 360
Solomon becomes king .... 1 Kin. 1:28-40 392
Kingdom divided .... 1 Kin. 12:1-33 408
Israel (northern kingdom) carried captive .... 2 Kin. 17:5-23 448
Judah (southern kingdom) carried captive .... 2 Kin. 24:1-20 458
70 years in exile .... 2 Chr. 36:20, 21 538
Return after exile .... Ezra 1:1-5 542
Nation rejects Christ .... Matt. 27:20-27 1152
Nation destroyed .... Luke 21:20-24 .... 1225; 1 Thess. 2:14-16 1415

B. *Blessed with:*
Great leaders .... Heb. 11:8-40 1460
Inspired prophets .... 1 Pet. 1:10-12 1477
God's oracles .... Rom. 3:2 1325
Priesthood .... Rom. 9:3-5 1333
The Law .... Gal. 3:16-25 1381
Messianic promises .... Acts 3:18-26 1276
Tabernacle .... Heb. 9:1-10 1457
Messiah .... Dan. 9:24-27 989
God's covenant .... Jer. 31:31-33 878
Regathering .... Is. 27:12 .... 796; Jer. 16:15, 16 863

C. *Sins of:*
Idolatry .... Hos. 13:1-4 1004
Hypocrisy .... Is. 1:11-14 772
Disobedience .... Jer. 7:22-28 853
Externalism .... Matt. 23:1-33 1145
Unbelief .... Rom. 11:1-31 1335
Works—righteousness .... Phil. 3:4-9 1401

D. *Punishments upon:*
Defeat .... Lev. 26:36-38 153
Curses upon .... Deut. 28:15-46 238
Captivity .... Judg. 2:13-23 285
Destruction .... Luke 19:42-44 1223
Dispersion .... Deut. 4:26-28 212
Blindness .... Rom. 11:25 1336
Forfeiture of blessings .... Acts 13:42-49 1292
Replaced by Gentiles .... Rom. 11:11-20 1335

See Jews

Israel, the religion of

A. *History of:*
Call of Abram .... Gen. 12:1-3 18
Canaan promised .... Gen. 15:18-21 23
Covenant at Sinai .... Ex. 20 90
Covenant at Shechem .... Josh. 24:1-28 277
Ark brought to Jerusalem .... 2 Sam. 6 364
Dedication of the Temple .... 1 Kin. 8:1-66 402
Reform movements .... 2 Kin. 23:4-14 .... 456; 2 Chr. 29:3-36 527
Destruction of Jerusalem .... Jer. 6 851
Restoration of the Law .... Neh. 8, 9 564

B. *Beliefs about God:*
Creator .... Gen. 1:1 .... 4; Ps. 104:24 684
Sustainer of creation .... Ps. 104:27-30 684
Active in human affairs .... Deut. 26:5-15 236
Omniscient .... Ps. 139:1-6 704
Omnipresent .... Jer. 23:23, 24 870
Everlasting .... Ps. 90:2 677
Moral .... Ex. 34:6, 7 107

Issachar—*man of hire*

1. Jacob's fifth son .... Gen. 30:17, 18 41
2. Tribe of, descendants of Jacob's fifth son .... Num. 26:23, 24 191
Prophecy concerning .... Gen. 49:14, 15 63
Census at Sinai .... Num. 1:28, 29 160
On Gerizim .... Deut. 27:12 237
Inheritance of .... Josh. 19:17-23 272
Assists Deborah .... Judg. 5:15 289
At David's coronation .... 1 Chr. 12:32 480
Census in David's time .... 1 Chr. 7:1-5 472
Attended Hezekiah's Passover .... 2 Chr. 30:18 529
Prominent person of .... Judg. 10:1 296
3. Doorkeeper .... 1 Chr. 26:1, 5 492

Isshiah, Jisshiah, Jesshiah—*Yahweh exists*

1. Mighty man of David .... 1 Chr. 12:1, 6 479
2. Kohathite Levite .... 1 Chr. 23:20 .... 490; 1 Chr. 24:25 491
3. Levite and family head .... 1 Chr. 24:21 491

Isui (see Ishvi)

Italy—*a peninsula of southern Europe*

Soldiers of, in Caesarea .... Acts 10:1 1286
Jews expelled from .... Acts 18:2 1299
Paul sails for .... Acts 27:1, 6 1312
Christians in .... Acts 28:14 1315

Itching ears—*descriptive of desire for something exciting*

Characteristic of the last days .... 2 Tim. 4:2, 3 1436

Ithai—*with me* (is Yahweh)

Son of Ribai .... 1 Chr. 11:31 478
Also called Ittai .... 2 Sam. 23:29 385

Ithamar—*island of palms*

Youngest son of Aaron .... Ex. 6:23 74
Consecrated as priest .... Ex. 28:1 99
Duty entrusted to .... Ex. 38:21 111
Jurisdiction over Gershonites and Merarites .... Num. 4:21-33 164
Founder of Levitical family .... 1 Chr. 24:4-6 490

Ithiel—*God is with me*

1. Man addressed by Agur .... Prov. 30:1 743
2. Benjamite .... Neh. 11:7 570

Ithmah—*bereavement*

Moabite of David's mighty men .... 1 Chr. 11:46 479

SUBJECT REFERENCE PAGE

Jawbone—*cheekbone*

Weapon used by Samson ....Judg. 15:15-19 302

Jazer—*helpful*

Town east of Jordan near Gilead ....2 Sam. 24:5 387
Amorites driven from ....Num. 21:32 186
Assigned to Gad ..Josh. 13:24, 25 266
Becomes Levitical city ....Josh. 21:34, 39 275
Taken by Moabites ....Is. 16:8, 9 788
Desired by sons of Reuben and Gad ....Num. 32:1-5 198

Jaziz—*shining*

Shepherd over David's flocks ....1 Chr. 27:31 494

Jealous, jealousy

A. *Kinds of:*
Divine ....Ex. 20:5 90
Marital........Num. 5:12-31 165
Motherly ......Gen. 30:1 40
Brotherly .....Gen. 37:4-28 49
Sectional .....2 Sam. 19:41-43 380
National .....Judg. 8:1-3 292

B. *Good causes of:*
Zeal for the Lord ....Num. 25:11 190
Concern over Christians ....2 Cor. 11:2 1373

C. *Evil causes of:*
Favoritism ....Gen. 37:3-11 49
Regard for names ....1 Cor. 3:3-5 1346
Carnality ....Amos 3:12-15 1017; 2 Cor. 12:20 1374

D. *Described as:*
Implacable ....Prov. 6:34, 35 720
Cruel ....Song 8:6 767
Burning ....Deut. 29:20 241
Godly ....2 Cor. 11:2 1373

Jearim—*forests*

Mountain 10 miles west of Jerusalem ....Josh. 15:10 267

Jeatherai—*steadfast*

Descendant of Levi.............1 Chr. 6:21 469
Also called Ethni............1 Chr. 6:41 470

Jeberechiah—*Yahweh blesses*

Father of Zechariah (not the prophet).........Is. 8:2 779

Jebus—*trodden underfoot*

Same as Jerusalem ....1 Chr. 11:4 475
Entry denied to David ....1 Chr. 11:5 478
Levite came near ....Judg. 19:1, 11 306

See Zion; Sion

Jebusites

Descendants of Canaan ....Gen. 10:15, 16 16
Mountain tribe ....Num. 13:29 176
Land of, promised to Israel ....Gen. 15:18-21 23
Adoni-Zedek, their king, raises confederacy .....Josh. 10:1-5 261
Their king killed by Joshua ....Josh. 10:23-26 262
Join fight against Joshua ....Josh. 11:1-5 264
Assigned to Benjamin ....Josh. 18:28 271
Royal city not taken ....Judg. 1:21 284
Taken by David ...2 Sam. 5:6-8 364
Old inhabitants remain ....2 Sam. 24:16-25 387
Become slaves ....1 Kin. 9:20, 21 406

Jecamiah (see Jekamiah)

Jecholiah—*Yahweh is able*

Mother of King Azariah ....2 Kin. 15:2 446; 2 Chr. 26:3 525

Jeconiah—*Yahweh establishes*

Variant form of Jehoiachin ......1 Chr. 3:16, 17 467
Abbreviated to Coniah ....Jer. 22:24, 28 868
Son of Josiah .....Matt. 1:11 1115

See Jehoiachin

Jedaiah—*Yahweh has been kind*

1. Priestly family ......1 Chr. 24:7 491
2. Head of the priests ....Neh. 12:6 571
3. Another head priest ....Neh. 12:7, 21 571
4. Simeonite .....1 Chr. 4:37 468
5. Postexilic worker ....Neh. 3:10 559
6. One who brings gifts for the Temple ......Zech. 6:10, 14 1071

Jediael—*known of God*

1. Son of Benjamin and family head ....1 Chr. 7:6, 10, 11 472
2. Manassite; joins David ....1 Chr. 12:20 479
3. One of David's mighty men ....1 Chr. 11:45 479
4. Korahite porter ....1 Chr. 26:1, 2 492

Jedidah—*beloved*

Mother of King Josiah ....2 Kin. 22:1 455

Jedidiah—*beloved of Yahweh*

Name given to Solomon by Nathan ......2 Sam. 12:24, 25 371

Jeduthun—*praising*

1. Levite musician appointed by David ....1 Chr. 16:41, 42 483
Heads a family of musicians ....2 Chr. 5:12 507
Name appears in Psalm titles ....Ps. 39; 62; 77 647
Family officiates after Exile.........Neh. 11:17 570
Possibly same as Ethan .....1 Chr. 15:17, 19 481
2. Father of Obed-Edom ..1 Chr. 16:38 483

Jegar Sahadutha—*heap of testimony*

Name given by Laban to memorial stones ....Gen. 31:46, 47 43

Jehaleleel, Jehalelel—*God will flash light*

1. Man of Judah and family head ....1 Chr. 4:16 467
2. Merarite Levite ....2 Chr. 29:12 528

Jehdeiah—*Yahweh will make glad*

1. Kohathite Levite ....1 Chr. 24:20 491
2. Meronothite in charge of David's donkeys .....1 Chr. 27:30 494

Jehezekel—*God will strengthen*

Descendant of Aaron ....1 Chr. 24:1, 16 490

Jehiah—*Yahweh lives*

Doorkeeper ......1 Chr. 15:24 482

Jehiel—*God lives*

1. Levite musician ....1 Chr. 15:18, 20 481
2. Gershonite and family head ....1 Chr. 23:8 490
3. Son of Hachmoni ....1 Chr. 27:32 494
4. Son of King Jehoshaphat ....2 Chr. 21:2, 4 521
5. Hemanite Levite ....2 Chr. 29:14 528
6. Overseer in Hezekiah's reign ....2 Chr. 31:13 530
7. Official of the Temple ......2 Chr. 35:8 536
8. Father of Obadiah, a returned exile ....Ezra 8:9 550
9. Father of Shechaniah ..Ezra 10:2 551
10. Postexilic priest ....Ezra 10:21 553
11. Postexilic priest ....Ezra 10:26 553

Jehieli

A Levite family ....1 Chr. 26:21, 22 492

Jehizkiah—*Yahweh strengthens*

Ephraimite chief ..2 Chr. 28:12 527

Jehoaddah—*whom Yahweh adorns*

Descendant of Saul ....1 Chr. 8:36 473
Also called Jarah ....1 Chr. 9:42 475

Jehoaddan—*Yahweh delights*

Mother of Amaziah ....2 Kin. 14:2 445

Jehoahaz—*Yahweh has taken hold of*

1. Son and successor of Jehu, king of Israel ......2 Kin. 10:35 442
Seeks the Lord in defeat ....2 Kin. 13:2-9 444
2. Son and successor of Josiah, king of Judah ....2 Kin. 23:30-34 458
Called Shallum ......1 Chr. 3:15 467
3. Another form of Ahaziah, youngest son of King Joram ....2 Chr. 21:17 521

Jehoash (see Joash)

Jehohanan—*Yahweh is gracious*

1. Korahite Levite ....1 Chr. 26:3 492
2. Captain under Jehoshaphat .2 Chr. 17:10, 15 517
3. Father of Ishmael, Jehoiada's supporter ....2 Chr. 23:1 522

SUBJECT REFERENCE PAGE

Jeshebeab—*may the father tarry* (live)

Descendant of Aaron ....1 Chr. 24:13 491

Jesher—*uprightness*

Caleb's son ....1 Chr. 2:18 466

Jeshimon—*waste*

Wilderness west of the Dead Sea ....1 Sam. 23:19, 24 349

Jeshishai—*aged*

Gadite ....1 Chr. 5:14 468

Jeshohaiah—*humbled by Yahweh*

Leader in Simeon ....1 Chr. 4:36 468

Jeshua—*Yahweh is salvation*

1. Descendant of Aaron........Ezra 2:36 544
2. Levite treasurer ....2 Chr. 31:14, 15 530
3. Postexilic high priest ....Zech. 3:8 1069
   Returns with Zerubbabel ...Ezra 2:2 542
   Aids in Temple rebuilding ....Ezra 3:2-8 545
   Withstands opponents ....Ezra 4:1-3 545
   Figurative act performed on ....Zech. 3:1-10 1069
4. Called Jeshua ......Hag. 1:1 1064
   See Joshua (3)
5. Levite assistant .....Ezra 2:40 544
   Explains the Law ....Neh. 8:7 565
   Leads in worship ......Neh. 9:4, 5 567
   Seals the covenant .....Neh. 10:1, 9 569
6. Repairer of the wall ....Neh. 3:19 560
7. Man of the house of Pahath-Moab ....Ezra 2:6 542
8. Village in south Judah ....Neh. 11:26 571

Jeshurun—*upright one*

Poetic name of endearment for Israel ....Deut. 32:15 244

Jesimiel—*God sets up*

Simeonite leader ....1 Chr. 4:36 468

Jesse—*Yahweh exists*

Grandson of Ruth and Boaz ....Ruth 4:17-22 317
Father of: David ....1 Sam. 16:18, 19 340
Eight sons ......1 Sam. 16:10, 11 340
Two daughters ...1 Chr. 2:15, 16 466
Citizen of Beth-lehem ....1 Sam. 16:1, 18 340
Protected by David ....1 Sam. 22:1-4 347
Of humble origin ....1 Sam. 18:18, 23 344
Mentioned in prophecy ....Is. 11:1, 10 784
Ancestor of Christ ....Matt. 1:5, 6 1115

Jesshiah (see Isshiah)

Jesting—*mocking; joking*

Condemned ......Eph. 5:4 1391
Lot appeared to be ....Gen. 19:14 28
Of godless men ...Ps. 35:16 644

Jesus (see Christ)

Jether—*abundance*

1. Gideon's oldest son ....Judg. 8:20, 21 294
2. Descendant of Judah ....1 Chr. 2:32 466
3. Son of Ezra ...1 Chr. 4:17 467
4. Asherite; probably same as Ithran ....1 Chr. 7:30-38 473
5. Amasa's father ....1 Kin. 2:5, 32 393

Jetheth—*subjection*

Chief of Edom ....Gen. 36:40 48

Jethlah—*an overhanging place*

Danite town ......Josh. 19:42 272

Jethro—*excellent*

Priest of Midian; Moses' father-in-law ....Num. 10:29 172
Also called Reuel ....Num. 10:29 172
Moses marries his daughter Zipporah ....Ex. 2:16-22 69
Moses departs from ....Ex. 4:18-26 72
Visits and counsels Moses ....Ex. 18:1-27 88

Jetur

Son of Ishmael ...Gen. 25:15 34
Conflict with Israel ....1 Chr. 5:18, 19 469
Tribal descendants of; the Itureans ....Luke 3:1 1194

Jeuel—*snatching away*

Son of Zerah .....1 Chr. 9:6 474

Jeush—*may he aid*

1. Son of Esau and Edomite chief ....Gen. 36:5, 18 46
2. Benjamite head ....1 Chr. 7:10 472
3. Gershonite Levite ....1 Chr. 23:10, 11 490
4. Descendant of Jonathan .....1 Chr. 8:39 474
5. Rehoboam's son ....2 Chr. 11:19 514

Jeuz—*counseling*

Benjamite ....1 Chr. 8:8, 10 473

Jewels—*ornaments used on the body*

A. *Used for:*
   Ornaments ....Is. 3:18-24 774
   Evil offering ...Ex. 32:1-5 105
   Good offering ......Ex. 35:22 109
   Spoils of war ....2 Chr. 20:25 520
   Farewell gifts ....Ex. 11:2 79
B. *Significance of:*
   Betrothal present ......Gen. 24:22, 53 32
   Sign of wealth ....James 2:2 1469
   Standard of value ....Prov. 3:15 716
   Tokens of repentance ...Gen. 35:4 46
   Tokens of love ....Ezek. 16:11-13 931
   Indications of worldliness ...1 Tim. 2:9 1426
   Figurative of God's own ....Matt. 13:45, 46 1133

Jewess—*a female Jew*

Woman of the Hebrew race ....Acts 24:24 1308

Jewish alphabet

Given topically ....Ps. 119 694

Jewish calendar

A. *List of months of:*
   Abib, or Nisan (March—April) ....Ex. 13:4 82
   Ziv or Iyar (April—May) ....1 Kin. 6:1, 37 398
   Sivan (May—June) ..Esth. 8:9 583
   Tammuz (June—July) ..Jer. 39:2 887
   Ab (July—August) ......Num. 33:38 200
   Elul (August—September) ...Neh. 6:15 562
   Ethanim or Tishri (September—October) .....1 Kin. 8:2 402
   Bul or Heshvan (October—November) ....1 Kin. 6:38 400
   Chislev (November—December) ...Neh. 1:1 558
   Tebeth (December—January) .....Esth. 2:16 578
   Shebat or Sebat (January—February) ....Zech. 1:7 1068
   Adar (February—March) ....Esth. 3:7 579
B. *Feasts of:*
   Abib (14)—Passover .....Ex. 12:18 80
   Abib (15-21)—Unleavened Bread ....Lev. 23:5, 6 145
   Abib (16)—Firstfruits ....Lev. 23:10, 11 145
   Ziv (14)—Later Passover .....Num. 9:10, 11 171
   Sivan (6)—Pentecost, Feast of Weeks, Harvest .....Lev. 23:15-21 148
   Ethanim (1)—Trumpets ....Lev. 23:24 148
   Ethanim (10)—Day of Atonement ..Lev. 16:29-34 140
   Ethanim (15-21)—Tabernacles ..Lev. 23:34, 35 148
   Ethanim (22)—Holy Convocation ....Lev. 23:36 148
   Chislev (25)—Dedication ...John 10:22 1252

Jewish measures (Metrology)

A. *Long Measures:*
   Finger (¾ inch) ....Jer. 52:21 905
   Handbreadth (3 to 4 inches) ......Ex. 25:25 97
   Span (about 9 inches) ....Ex. 28:16 100
   Cubit of man (about 18 inches) ....Gen. 6:15 11
   Pace (about 3 feet) ....2 Sam. 6:13 365
   Fathom (about 6 feet) ....Acts 27:28 1314
   Rod (about 11 feet) ....Ezek. 40:5 963
   Line ....Ezek. 40:3 963
B. *Land measures:*
   Cubit of God (1¾ feet) ....Josh. 3:4 254

SUBJECT REFERENCE PAGE

Heber separates from Kenites ...... Judg. 4:11 288
Heber's wife (Jael) slays Sisera ...... Judg. 4:17-22 288
Spared by Saul in war with Amalekites ...... 1 Sam. 15:6 339
David shows friendship to ...... 1 Sam. 30:29 355
Recorded among Judahites; ancestors of Rechabites ...... 1 Chr. 2:55 466

Keren-Happuch—*horn of eye paint*

Daughter of Job ..Job 42:14 620

Kerioth—*cities*

1. Town in south Judah ....Josh. 15:25 268
2. City of Moab ..Amos 2:2 1016

Keros—*bent*

Head of a Nethinim family returning from exile ....Ezra 2:44 544

Kettle—*pot*

Large cooking vessel ....1 Sam. 2:14 323
Same word rendered "baskets" ....Ps. 81:6 673

Keturah—*incense*

Abraham's second wife ....Gen. 25:1 33
Sons of:
Listed ....Gen. 25:1, 2 33
Given gifts and sent away ....Gen. 25:6 33

Key—*a small instrument for unlocking doors*

Used literally for:

Doors ....Judg. 3:25 287

Used figuratively of:

Prophetic authority of Christ ....Is. 22:22 792
Present authority of Christ ....Rev. 1:18 1519
Plenary authority of Christ's apostles ....Matt. 16:19 1136
Teachers ....Luke 11:52 1212

Keziah—*cassia*

Daughter of Job ..Job 42:14 620

Kibroth Hattaavah—*graves of lust*

Burial site of Israelites slain by God ....Num. 11:33-35 175

Kibzaim—*double heap*

Ephraimite city assigned to Kohathite
Levites ....Josh. 21:22 275
Called Jokmeam ....1 Chr. 6:68 470
See Jokmeam

Kid—*a young goat*

A. *Used for:*
Food ....Gen. 27:9 36
Payment ......Gen. 38:17-23 50
Sacrifices ......Lev. 4:23 123
Offerings ......{Judg. 13:15, 19} 299
Festive occasions ....Luke 15:29 1218

B. *Figurative of:*
Weakness .....Judg. 14:6 300
Peacefulness ..Is. 11:6 784

See Goat

Kidnappers—*those who seize others by unlawful force*

Condemned by law ....1 Tim. 1:10 1426

Kidnapping

A. *Punishment for:*
Death ....Ex. 21:16 92
Condemned ...1 Tim. 1:10 1426

B. *Examples of:*
Joseph ....Gen. 37:23-28 49
Daughters of Shiloh ....Judg. 21:20-23 310
Joash ....2 Kin. 11:1-12 442
Jeremiah ......Jer. 43:1-8 890

Kidneys

Select internal organs of an animal ....Ex. 29:13, 22 102
Translated "wheat" ....Deut. 32:14 244

Kidron—*dark, turbid*

Valley (dry except for winter torrents) near Jerusalem ....John 18:1 1262
East boundary of Jerusalem ....Jer. 31:40 879
Crossed by David and Christ ....John 18:1 1262
Site of dumping of idols ....2 Chr. 29:16 528

Killing—*causing life to cease*

A. *Reasons for:*
Take another's wife ....Gen. 12:12 20
Take another's property .....1 Kin. 21:19 422
Take revenge ......Gen. 27:42 37
Satisfy anger ....Num. 22:29 187
Hate ....John 5:18 1243
Execute God's wrath ....{Num. 31:2, 16-19} 197
Destroy people ....Ex. 1:16 69
Seize a throne ....2 Kin. 15:25 447
Put down rebellion .....1 Kin. 12:27 409
Fulfill prophecy .....1 Kin. 16:1-11 413
Fear of punishment ..Acts 16:27 1295
Get rid of an unwanted person ......Matt. 21:38 1143

B. *Reasons against:*
God's Law ....Ex. 20:13 90
Regard for:
Life ....Gen. 37:21 49
One's position ....{1 Sam. 11 321; 1 Sam. 24:10 349}

C. *Of Christians:*
In God's hand ....Luke 12:4, 5 1214
Result of persecution ...Matt. 24:9 1147
Time will come ....John 16:2 1259
Under antichrist ....{Rev. 11:7 1528; Rev. 13:15 1531}

Kinah—*lamentation*

Village in south Judah ....Josh. 15:22 268

Kindness—*a friendly attitude toward others*

A. *Kinds of:*
Extra-ordinary ....Acts 28:2 1315
Acquired ....Col. 3:12 1408
Developed .....Prov. 31:26 745
Commended ...2 Cor. 6:6 1369
Divine ....Neh. 9:17 568

B. *Of God, described as:*
Great ....Neh. 9:17 568
Everlasting .....Is. 54:8 827
Shall not depart ....Is. 54:10 827
Manifested ......Ps. 31:21 642
Through Christ ....Eph. 2:7 1387
Cause of man's salvation .....Titus 3:4-7 1442

C. *Manifestation of:*
Rewarded ....1 Sam. 15:6 339
Recalled ......2 Sam. 2:5, 6 361
Rebuffed ....2 Sam. 3:8 362
Remembered ....2 Sam. 9:1-7 367
Refused ....2 Sam. 10:1-6 369

Kindred—*one's family connections*

Manifestation of:

Felt with great emotion ....Esth. 8:6 583
Through faith .....Josh. 6:23 258
By gospel ....{Acts 3:25 1276; Rev. 14:6 1531}

Kine—*archaic for cow, ox, steer*

Used for:

Ox ....Deut. 7:13 218
Cattle ....Deut. 32:14 244
Cow ....{Gen. 32:15 44; 1 Sam. 6:7 327}

King, Christ as

A. *In Old Testament prophecy:*
Judah's tribe ..Gen. 49:10 63
With a scepter ....Num. 24:15-17 189
David's lineage ....2 Sam. 7:1-29 365
Divine origin ..Is. 9:6, 7 780
In righteousness ....Is. 11:1-5 784
At God's appointed time ....Ezek. 21:27 940
Will endure forever ....Dan. 2:44 978
Born in Bethlehem ....Mic. 5:2, 3 1039
As Priest-king ...Zech. 6:9-15 1071
Having salvation .....Zech. 9:9 1073
He is coming ..Mal. 3:1-5 1082

B. *Christ's right to rule, determined by:*
Divine decree ....Ps. 2:6, 7 625
Prophecy .....Ps. 45:6, 7 651
Birth ....Is. 9:6, 7 780
Being seated at God's right hand ...{Ps. 16:8-11 633; Ps. 110:1, 2 689; Acts 2:34-36 1274}
Crowning .....Zech. 6:11-15 1071

C. *Described as:*
Eternal ....Rev. 11:15 1528
Spiritual ......John 18:36, 37 1263
Not for immoral or impure person ....Eph. 5:5 1391
The Son of His love ....Col. 1:13 1406

Kingdom of God

A. *Described as, of:*
God ....Mark 1:15 1159
Heaven ....Matt. 3:2 1117
Christ and God ....Eph. 5:5 1391
Their Father ....Matt. 13:43 1133
My Father's ....Matt. 26:29 1150
His dear Son ...Col. 1:13 1406

SUBJECT REFERENCE PAGE

Kingdom of God—continued

B. *Special features of:*
Gospel of .....Matt. 24:14 1147
Word of ....Matt. 13:19 1132
Mysteries of ...Mark 4:10-13 1164
Key of David ...Rev. 3:7 1521

C. *Entrance into, by:*
New birth .....John 3:1-8 1239
Granted ....Luke 22:29 1226
Divine call ....1 Thess. 2:12 1415
Repentance ....Matt. 3:2 1117

D. *Members of:*
Seek it first ....Matt. 6:33 1123
Suffer tribulation ....Acts 14:22 1293
Preach it ......Acts 8:12 1282
Pray for it .....Matt. 6:10 1121
Work in ....Col. 4:11 1409

E. *Nature of:*
Spiritual ......Rom. 14:17 1339
Eternal ....2 Pet. 1:11 1487

Kings, earthly

A. *Some characteristics of:*
Arose over Egypt ....Ex. 1:8 68
Desired by people ....1 Sam. 8:5, 6 330
Under God's control ......Dan. 4:25, 37 981
Rule by God's permission ...Dan. 2:20, 21 977
Subject to temptations ....2 Sam. 11:1-5 369; Prov. 31:5 744
Good ....2 Kin. 22:1, 2 455
Evil ....2 Kin. 21:1-9 454

B. *Position of before God, by God:*
Chosen ....1 Chr. 28:4-6 494
Anointed ......1 Sam. 16:12 340
Removed and established ...Dan. 2:21 977
Rejected .....1 Sam. 15:10-26 339

C. *Duties of:*
Make covenants ....Gen. 21:22-32 30
Read Scriptures ....Deut. 17:19 229
Make war .....1 Sam. 11:5-11 332
Pardon ....2 Sam. 14:1-11 373; 2 Sam. 19:18-23 379
Judge ....2 Sam. 15:2 374
Govern righteously ...2 Sam. 23:3, 4 384
Keep Law .....1 Kin. 2:3 393
Make decrees ......Dan. 3:1-6, 29 978

King's Garden—*a garden of Jerusalem*
Near a gate ....2 Kin. 25:4 459
By the Pool of Shelah ....Neh. 3:15 559

King's Highway—*an important passageway connecting Damascus and Egypt*
Use of, requested ....Num. 20:17 184

Kings of ancient Israel

A. *Over the United Kingdom:*
Saul ....1 Sam. 11:15–31:13 333
David ....2 Sam. 2:4– 361; 1 Kin. 2:11 393
Solomon .....1 Kin. 1:39–11:43 392

B. *Over Israel* (the northern kingdom):
Jeroboam (22 yrs.) .....1 Kin. 12:20–14:20 409
Nadab (2 yrs.) ....1 Kin. 15:25-27, 31 413
Baasha (24 yrs.) ....1 Kin. 15:28-34 413; 1 Kin. 16:1-7 413
Elah (2 yrs.) ...1 Kin. 16:8-14 413
Zimri (7 days) ....1 Kin. 16:15 414
Omri (12 yrs.) ....1 Kin. 16:23-28 414
Ahab (22 yrs.) ....1 Kin. 16:29–22:40 414
Ahaziah (2 yrs.) ....1 Kin. 22:51-53 425
Jehoram (Joram) (12 yrs.) ....2 Kin. 3:1–9:26 431
Jehu (28 yrs.) .....2 Kin. 9:2–10:36 439
Jehoahaz (17 yrs.) ....2 Kin. 13:1-9 444
Jehoash (Joash) (16 yrs.) ....2 Kin. 13:10-25 444
Jeroboam II (41 yrs.) .....2 Kin. 14:23-29 446
Zechariah (6 mos.) ....2 Kin. 15:8-12 446
Shallum (1 mo.) ....2 Kin. 15:13-15 446
Menahem (10 yrs.) .....2 Kin. 15:16-22 446
Pekahiah (2 yrs.) ....2 Kin. 15:23-26 447
Pekah (20 yrs.) ....2 Kin. 15:27-31 447
Hoshea (9 yrs.) ....2 Kin. 17:1-6 448

C. *Over Judah* (the southern kingdom):
Rehoboam (17 yrs.) .....1 Kin. 12:21-24 409
Abijam (Abijah) (3 yrs.) ....1 Kin. 15:1-8 412
Asa (41 yrs.) ...1 Kin. 15:9-24 412
Jehoshaphat (25 yrs.) .....1 Kin. 22:41-50 425
Jehoram (Joram) (8 yrs.) ....2 Kin. 8:16-24 438
Ahaziah (1 yr.) ....2 Kin. 8:25-29 438
Athaliah (Queen) (usurper) (6 yrs.) ....2 Kin. 11:1-3 442
Joash (Jehoash) (40 yrs.) ....2 Kin. 12:1, 21 443
Amaziah (29 yrs.) ....2 Kin. 14:1-20 445
Azariah (Uzziah) (52 yrs.) ....2 Kin. 15:1, 2 446
Jotham (16 yrs.) ....2 Kin. 15:32-38 447
Ahaz (16 yrs.) ....2 Kin. 16:1-20 447
Hezekiah (29 yrs.) ....2 Kin. 18:1–20:21 450
Manasseh (55 yrs.) ....2 Kin. 21:1-18 454
Amon (2 yrs.) ....2 Kin. 21:19-26 455
Josiah (31 yrs.) ....2 Kin. 22:1–23:30 455
Jehoahaz (Shallum) (3 mos.) ....2 Kin. 23:31-33 458
Jehoiakim (11 yrs.) ....2 Kin. 23:34–24:6 458
Jehoiachin (Jeconiah) (3 mos.) ....2 Kin. 24:8-16 458
Zedekiah (Mattaniah) (11 yrs.) ....2 Kin. 24:17–25:7 459

Kings, the Books of—*books of the Old Testament*

A. *1 Kings*
Solomon ascends to the throne ....1 Kin. 1:1–2:46 391
The kingdom of Solomon ...1 Kin. 3:1–10:29 394
The fall of Solomon .....1 Kin. 11:1-40 407
Rehoboam against Jeroboam .....1 Kin. 12:1-33 408
Ahab and Jezebel ......1 Kin. 16:29-34 414
Ministry of Elijah ....1 Kin. 17:1–19:21 414
Syria against Samaria .....1 Kin. 20:1-34 420
Ahab and Naboth ......1 Kin. 21:1-29 421

B. *2 Kings*
Ministry of Elijah and Elisha ....2 Kin. 1:1–9:11 429
Reign of Jehu ....2 Kin. 9:11–10:36 439
Fall of Israel ...2 Kin. 17:1-41 448
Reign of Hezekiah ....2 Kin. 18:1–20:21 450
Reform of Judah ....2 Kin. 22:1–23:30 455
Fall of Jerusalem .....2 Kin. 25:1-21 459

Kingship of God—*the position of God as sovereign ruler of the universe*
Over Jerusalem ...Matt. 5:35 1121
Over all ....Ps. 103:19 683
Of all kingdoms ...2 Kin. 19:15 452

Kir—*wall*
1. Place mentioned by Amos to which Syrians were taken ....Amos 1:5 1015
Tiglath-Pileser carries people of Damascus here ....2 Kin. 16:9 448
Inhabitants of, against Judah ....Is. 22:6 792
2. Fortified city of Moab ......Is. 15:1 787
Same as Kir Hareseth ....Is. 16:7 788; 2 Kin. 3:25 432

Kirjath—*city*
Town of Benjamin ....Josh. 18:21, 28 271

Kirjathaim—*twin cities*
1. Assigned to Reuben ......Num. 32:37 199
Repossessed by Moabites .....Jer. 48:1-23 895
2. Town in Naphtali .....1 Chr. 6:76 472
Same as Kartan ....Josh. 21:32 275

Kirjath Arba—*city of Arba, or fourfold city*
Ancient name of Hebron ....Gen. 23:2 31
Named after Arba the Anakite ....Josh. 15:54 268
City of refuge .....Josh. 20:7 273
Possessed by Judah ....Judg. 1:10 284

Kirjath Jearim—*city of forests*
Gibeonite town ...Josh. 9:17 261
Assigned to Judah ....Josh. 15:60 268
Reassigned to Benjamin ....Josh. 18:28 271
Ark taken from ....1 Chr. 13:5 480
Home of Urijah ...Jer. 26:20 873
Called:
Baalah ....Josh. 15:9, 10 267
Kirjath ....Josh. 18:28 271
Kirjath Baal .....Josh. 15:60 268
Baale Judah ....2 Sam. 6:2 364
Shortened to Kirjath Arim ....Ezra 2:25 544

SUBJECT — REFERENCE — PAGE

Kirjath Sannah—*city of destruction*
City of Judah; also called Debir .... Josh. 15:49 — 268

Kirjath Sepher—*city of books*
Same as Debir .... Judg. 1:11-13 — 284
Taken by Othniel .... Josh. 15:15-17 — 267

Kish—*bow*
1. Benjamite of Gibeah; father of King Saul .... 1 Sam. 9:1-3 — 330; Acts 13:21 — 1291
2. Benjamite of Jerusalem .... 1 Chr. 8:30 — 473
3. Merarite Levite in David's time .... 1 Chr. 23:21, 22 — 490
4. Another Merarite Levite in Hezekiah's time .... 2 Chr. 29:12 — 528
5. Benjamite and great-grandfather of Mordecai .. Esth. 2:5 — 578

Kishi—*snarer*
One of David's singers .... 1 Chr. 6:31, 44 — 469
Called Kushaiah .. 1 Chr. 15:17 — 481

Kishion—*hardness*
Border town of Issachar .... Josh. 19:17,20 — 272
Called Kishon .... Josh. 21:28 — 275
See Kedesh 2

Kishon—*bending*
River of north Palestine; Sisera's army swept away by .... Judg. 4:7, 13 — 288
Elijah slew Baal prophets here .... 1 Kin. 18:40 — 418

Kiss—*a physical sign of affection*
A. *Times employed, at:*
Departure ..... Gen. 31:28, 55 — 42
Separation .... Acts 20:37 — 1303
Reunions ...... Luke 15:20 — 1218
Great joy ..... Luke 7:38, 45 — 1204
Blessing ...... Gen. 48:10-16 — 61
Anointings .... 1 Sam. 10:1 — 331
Reconciliation ..... Gen. 33:4 — 44
Death .... Gen. 50:1 — 63
B. *Figurative of:*
Complete:
Submission to evil ..... Hos. 13:2 — 1004
Submission to God ..... Ps. 2:12 — 625
Reconciliation ..... Ps. 85:10 — 675
Utmost affection ..... Song 1:2 — 762
C. *Kinds of:*
Deceitful ..... 2 Sam. 20:9, 10 — 380; Luke 22:48 — 1228
Insincere ..... 2 Sam. 15:5 — 374
Fatherly ...... Gen. 27:26, 27 — 37
Friendship .... Ex. 18:7 — 88; 1 Sam. 20:41 — 346
Esteem .... 2 Sam. 19:32, 39 — 380
Sexual love ... Gen. 29:11 — 40; Song 1:2 — 762
Illicit love .... Prov. 7:13 — 720
False religion ..... 1 Kin. 19:18 — 420; Hos. 13:2 — 1004
Holy love ..... Rom. 16:16 — 1341; 1 Cor. 16:20 — 1361

Kite—*a bird of the falcon family*
Ceremonially unclean .... Lev. 11:12-14 — 132

Kithlish—*a man's wall*
Town of Judah .... Josh. 15:1, 40 — 267

Kitron—*shortened, little*
Town in Zebulun .... Judg. 1:30 — 284

Kittim
Sons of Javan .... Gen. 10:4 — 16

Kneading—*mixing elements together*
Part of food process .... Gen. 18:6 — 24
Done by women .... Jer. 7:18 — 853

Kneading bowl—*used for kneading dough*
Overcome by frogs .... Ex. 8:3 — 75
Carried out of Egypt .... Ex. 12:33, 34 — 82

Knee
A. *Place of weakness, due to:*
Terror .... Dan. 5:6 — 983
Fasting ...... Ps. 109:24 — 689
Disease ...... Deut. 28:35 — 239
Lack of faith .. Is. 35:3 — 806
B. *Lying upon:*
Sign of true parentage or adoption .... Gen. 30:3 — 40
Place of fondling ..... Is. 66:12 — 838
Place of sleep .... Judg. 16:19 — 303
C. *Bowing of:*
Act of:
Respect ...... 2 Kin. 1:13 — 430
False worship ..... 1 Kin. 19:18 — 420
True worship ..... Rom. 14:11 — 1339
D. *Bowing of, in prayer:*
Solomon ...... 2 Chr. 6:13, 14 — 507
Daniel .... Dan. 6:10 — 984
Christ .... Luke 22:41 — 1226
Stephen ...... Acts 7:59, 60 — 1282
Peter .... Acts 9:40 — 1286
Paul .... Acts 20:36 — 1303
Christians .... Acts 21:5 — 1303

Knife—*a sharp instrument for cutting*
A. *Used for:*
Slaying animals ..... Gen. 22:6-10 — 30
Circumcision ..... Josh. 5:2, 3 — 255
Dismembering a body ..... Judg. 19:29 — 307
Sharpening pens ..... Jer. 36:23 — 884
B. *Figurative of:*
Inordinate appetite ..... Prov. 23:2 — 735
Cruel oppressors ... Prov. 30:14 — 744

Knob—*an ornament*
Round protrusions on lampstand ..... Ex. 25:31-36 — 97

Knock—*to rap on a door*
Rewarded ...... Luke 11:9, 10 — 1211
Expectant ..... Luke 12:36 — 1214
Disappointed .... Luke 13:25-27 — 1216
Unexpected .... Acts 12:13, 16 — 1289
Invitation .... Rev. 3:20 — 1523

Knowledge
A. *Kinds of:*
Natural ...... Matt. 24:32 — 1148
Deceptive .... Gen. 3:5 — 8
Sinful .... Gen. 3:7 — 8
Personal ..... Josh. 24:31 — 279
Practical .... Ex. 36:1 — 109
Experimental ..... Ex. 14:4, 18 — 83
Friendly ..... Ex. 1:8 — 68
Intuitive .... 1 Sam. 22:22 — 348
Intellectual .... John 7:15, 28 — 1247
Saving .... John 17:3 — 1261
Spiritual .... 1 Cor. 2:14 — 1346
Revealed ..... Luke 10:22 — 1209
B. *Sources of:*
God .... Ps. 94:10 — 679
Nature ...... Ps. 19:1, 2 — 635
Scriptures .... 2 Tim. 3:15 — 1436
Doing God's will ..... John 7:17 — 1247
C. *Believer's attitude toward:*
Not to be puffed up ..... 1 Cor. 8:1 — 1352
Should grow in ..... 2 Pet. 3:18 — 1490
Should add to ..... 2 Pet. 1:5 — 1487
Not to be forgetful of ..... 2 Pet. 3:17 — 1490
Accept our limitations of ..... 1 Cor. 13:8-12 — 1356
Be filled with ..... Phil. 1:9 — 1398
D. *Christ's, of:*
God .... Luke 10:22 — 1209
Man's nature .. John 2:24, 25 — 1239
Man's thoughts ..... Matt. 9:4 — 1126
Believers .... John 10:14, 27 — 1252
Things future ..... 2 Pet. 1:14 — 1487
All things .... Col. 2:3 — 1406
E. *Attitude of sinful men toward:*
Turn from .... Rom. 1:21 — 1324
Ignorant of .... 1 Cor. 1:21 — 1345
Raised up against ..... 2 Cor. 10:5 — 1372
Did not acknowledge God ..... Rom. 1:28 — 1324
Never able to come to ..... 2 Tim. 3:7 — 1434
F. *Value of:*
Superior to gold ..... Prov. 8:10 — 721
Increases strength ..... Prov. 24:5 — 736
Keeps from destruction ... Is. 5:13 — 775
Insures stability ..... Is. 33:6 — 804

Koa
People described as enemies of Jerusalem ..... Ezek. 23:23 — 943

Kohath—*assembly*
Second son of Levi ..... Gen. 46:8, 11 — 59
Goes with Levi to Egypt ..... Gen. 46:11 — 59
Brother of Jochebed, mother of Aaron and Moses ..... Ex. 6:16-20 — 74
Dies at age 133 .... Ex. 6:18 — 74

Kohathites—*descendants of Kohath*
A. *History of:*
Originate in Levi's son (Kohath) ..... Gen. 46:11 — 59
Divided into 4 groups (Amram, Izhar, Hebron, Uzziel) ..... Num. 3:19, 27 — 162

SUBJECT — REFERENCE — PAGE

Kohathites—continued
- Numbering of .... Num. 3:27, 28 — 162
- Duties assigned to .... Num. 4:15-20 — 164
- Cities assigned to .... Josh. 21:4-11 — 273

B. *Privileges of:*
- Aaron and Moses .... Ex. 6:20 — 74
- Special charge of sacred instruments .. Num. 4:15-20 — 164
- Temple music by Heman the Kohathite .... 1 Chr. 6:31-38 — 469
- Under Jehoshaphat, lead in praise .... 2 Chr. 20:19 — 520
- Under Hezekiah, help to cleanse Temple ...... 2 Chr. 29:12, 15 — 528

C. *Sins of:*
- Korah (of Izhar) leads rebellion .... Num. 16:1-35 — 179; Jude 11 — 1510

Kolaiah—*voice of Yahweh*
1. Father of the false prophet Ahab .... Jer. 29:21-23 — 875
2. Postexilic Benjamite family .... Neh. 11:7 — 570

Koph
- Letter of the Hebrew alphabet .... Ps. 119:145-152 — 698

Korah—*baldness*
1. Son of Esau .... Gen. 36:5, 14, 18 — 46
2. Son of Eliphaz and grandson of Esau .... Gen. 36:16 — 48
3. Calebite .... 1 Chr. 2:42, 43 — 466
4. Son of Izhar the Kohathite .... Ex. 6:21, 24 — 74
   - Leads a rebellion against Moses and Aaron .... Num. 16:1-3 — 179
   - Warned by Moses .... Num. 16:4-27 — 179
   - Supernaturally destroyed .... Num. 16:28-35 — 180
   - Sons of, not destroyed .... Num. 26:9-11 — 190
   - Sons of, porters .... 1 Chr. 26:19 — 492

Korahites
- Descendants of Korah .... Ex. 6:24 — 74
- Some become:
  - David's warriors .... 1 Chr. 12:6 — 479
  - Servants .... 1 Chr. 9:19-31 — 474
  - Musicians .... 1 Chr. 6:22-32 — 469
- A contemplation of .... Ps. 42 (Title) — 649

Kore—*a partridge*
1. Korahite Levite .... 1 Chr. 9:19 — 474
2. Porter of the eastern gate .... 2 Chr. 31:14 — 530

Koz—*thorn*
- Father of Anub ... 1 Chr. 4:8 — 467
- See Hakkoz

Kushaiah—*bow of Yahweh* (that is, rainbow)
- Merarite Levite musician .... 1 Chr. 15:17 — 481
- Called Kishi .... 1 Chr. 6:44 — 470

L

Laadah—*festival*
- Judahite .... 1 Chr. 4:21 — 468

Laadan
1. Son of Gershon, the son of Levi .... 1 Chr. 23:7-9 — 490
   - Called Libni ... 1 Chr. 6:17 — 469
2. Ephraimite .... 1 Chr. 7:26 — 473

Laban—*white*
1. Son of Bethuel ...... Gen. 24:24, 29 — 32
   - Brother of Rebekah ...... Gen. 24:15, 29 — 32
   - Father of Leah and Rachel .... Gen. 29:16 — 40
   - Chooses Rebekah for Isaac .... Gen. 24:29-60 — 32
   - Entertains Jacob .... Gen. 29:1-14 — 38
   - Deceives Jacob in marriage arrangement .... Gen. 29:15-30 — 40
   - Agrees to Jacob's business arrangement .... Gen. 30:25-43 — 41
   - Changes attitude toward Jacob .... Gen. 31:1-9 — 42
   - Pursues after fleeing Jacob .... Gen. 31:21-25 — 42
   - Rebukes Jacob .... Gen. 31:26-30 — 42
   - Rebuked by Jacob .... Gen. 31:31-42 — 42
   - Makes covenant with Jacob .... Gen. 31:43-55 — 43
2. City in the wilderness ... Deut. 1:1 — 208

Labor—*physical or mental effort*

A. *Physical:*

Nature of:
- As old as creation ...... Gen. 2:5, 15 — 7
- Ordained by God .... Gen. 3:17-19 — 9
- One of the commandments .... Ex. 20:9 — 90
- From morning until night .... Ps. 104:23 — 684
- With the hands ...... 1 Thess. 4:11 — 1416
- To life's end ... Ps. 90:10 — 678
- Without God, vanity .... Eccl. 2:11 — 751
- Shrinking from, denounced ... 2 Thess. 3:10 — 1422

Benefits of:
- Profit .... Prov. 14:23 — 726
- Happiness ..... Ps. 128:2 — 701
- Proclaim gospel .... 1 Thess. 2:9 — 1415
- Supply of other's needs .... Acts 20:35 — 1303; Eph. 4:28 — 1391
- Restful sleep .. Eccl. 5:12 — 753
- Double honor .... 1 Tim. 5:17 — 1429
- Eternal life .... John 6:27 — 1246
- Not in vain .. 1 Cor. 15:58 — 1360; Phil. 2:16 — 1400

B. *Spiritual:*

Characteristics of:
- Commissioned by Christ .... John 4:38 — 1242
- Accepted by few .... Matt. 9:37, 38 — 1127
- Working with God .... 1 Cor. 3:9 — 1346
- By God's grace .... 1 Cor. 15:10 — 1359
- Result of faith .... 1 Tim. 4:10 — 1429
- Characterized by love .... 1 Thess. 1:3 — 1413
- Done in prayer .... Col. 4:12 — 1409
- Subject to discouragement .... Is. 49:4 — 821; Gal. 4:11 — 1381
- Interrupted by Satan .... 1 Thess. 3:5 — 1415
- See Work, the Christian's

C. *Problems:*
- Inspired by opposition .... Ezra 4:1-6 — 545
- Complaint over wages .... Matt. 20:1-16 — 1140
- Mistreatment of employees .... Matt. 21:33-35 — 1143
- Characteristics of last days .... James 5:1-6 — 1471

Labor, (childbirth)

A. *Of a woman's, described as:*
- Fearful .... Ps. 48:6 — 652
- Painful .... Is. 13:8 — 785
- Hazardous .... Gen. 35:16-19 — 46
- Joyful afterwards ... John 16:21 — 1261

B. *Figurative of:*
- New Israel .... Is. 66:7, 8 — 838
- Messiah's birth .... Mic. 4:9, 10 — 1038
- Redemption ..... Mic. 5:3 — 1039
- New birth ..... Gal. 4:19 — 1382
- Creation's rebirth .... Rom. 8:22 — 1333

Lachish
- Town in south Judah .... Josh. 15:1, 39 — 267
- Joins coalition against Gibeonites .... Josh. 10:3-5 — 261
- Defeated by Joshua .... Josh. 10:6-33 — 261
- Fortified by Rehoboam .... 2 Chr. 11:5, 9 — 512
- City of sin .... Mic. 1:13 — 1037
- Amaziah murdered here ...... 2 Kin. 14:19 — 446; 2 Chr. 25:27 — 525
- Taken by Sennacherib .... 2 Kin. 18:13-17 — 450
- Military headquarters .... Is. 36:1, 2 — 806; Is. 37:8 — 808
- Fights against Nebuchadnezzar .... Jer. 34:1, 7 — 881
- Reoccupied after exile .... Neh. 11:30 — 571

Lack—*something still needed*

A. *How to avoid:*
- Remember God's promises ..... Deut. 2:7 — 209
- Work diligently .... 1 Thess. 4:11, 12 — 1416
- Live chastely ...... Prov. 6:32 — 720
- Share in common ..... Acts 4:34 — 1277
- Obey .... Amos 4:6 — 1018

B. *Things subject to:*
- Food .... 2 Sam. 3:29 — 362
- Physical needs .... 2 Chr. 8:14 — 510; 2 Cor. 11:9 — 1373
- Possessions ... 1 Sam. 30:19 — 355
- Service to others .... Phil. 2:30 — 1401
- Entire commitment .... Luke 18:22 — 1221
- Wisdom .... James 1:5 — 1468
- Graces .... 2 Pet. 1:9 — 1487
- See Want

Lad—*a young boy*
- Heard by God .... Gen. 21:17-20 — 29
- Saved by God .... Gen. 22:12 — 30

SUBJECT REFERENCE PAGE

Loved by his father .... Gen. 44:22-34 57
Slain with Samson .... Judg. 16:26-30 303
Unsuspecting .... 1 Sam. 20:21-41 346
Tattling .... 2 Sam. 17:18 377
Providing .... John 6:9 1244

Ladder

Jacob's .... Gen. 28:10-12 38

Lady

Applied to females of high rank .... Judg. 5:29 290
Among royalty .... Esth. 1:18 577
Elect .... 2 John 1, 5 1502
Figurative of Babylon .... Is. 47:5-7 819

Lael—*belonging to God*

Gershonite Levite .... Num. 3:24 162

Lahad—*oppression*

Judahite .... 1 Chr. 4:2 467

Lahai Roi—*of the Living One who sees me*

Name of a well ... Gen. 16:7, 14 11
Same as Beer Lahai Roi .... Gen. 24:62 33

Lahmam—*place of light*

City of Judah ..... Josh. 15:1, 40 267

Lahmi—*Bethlehemite*

Brother of Goliath slain by Elhanan .... 1 Chr. 20:5 487

Laish—*lion*

1. Benjamite ..... 1 Sam. 25:44 351
2. City in north Palestine at the head of the Jordan .... Judg. 18:7, 14 304
Called Leshem .... Josh. 19:47 272
3. Village in Benjamin between Anathoth and Gallim .... Is. 10:30 784

Lake

Sea of Galilee is called .... Luke 5:1, 2 1200; Luke 8:22-33 1205
Bottomless pit described as .... Rev. 19:20 1536

Lake of fire—*the place of final punishment*

A. *Those consigned to:*
The beast and false prophet ..... Rev. 19:20 1536
The devil ..... Rev. 20:10 1538
Death and hell .... Rev. 20:14 1538
Those whose names are not in book of life ... Rev. 20:15 1538

B. *Described as:*
Burning brimstone ..... Rev. 19:20 1536
Second death .... Rev. 20:14 1538

Lakkum—*obstruction*

Town of Naphtali .... Josh. 19:32, 33 272

Lama—the Aramaic for *why*

Spoken by Christ on the cross .... Matt. 27:46 1154

Lamb—*a young sheep*

A. *Used for:*
Food .... 2 Sam. 12:4 370
Clothing .... Prov. 27:26 740
Trade .... Ezra 7:17 549
Tribute .... 2 Kin. 3:4 431
Covenants .... Gen. 21:28-32 30
Sacrifices ..... Ex. 12:5 80

B. *Figurative of:*
God's people .. Is. 5:17 777
Weak believers ..... Is. 40:11 811
God's ministers ..... Luke 10:3 1208
Messiah's reign .... Is. 11:6 784

Lamb of God, the (Christ)

A. *Descriptive of Christ as:*
Predicted ..... Is. 53:7 825
Presented to Israel .... John 1:29 1237
Preached to world .... Acts 8:32-35 1284
Praised throughout eternity ...... Rev. 5:6, 13 1523

B. *Descriptive of Christ as:*
Sacrifice .... 1 Pet. 1:19 1479; Rev. 7:13, 14 1525
Redeemer ..... Rev. 5:9 1523
King .... Rev. 15:3 1532

Lame, lameness—*inability to walk properly*

A. *Healing of, by:*
Christ .... Matt. 11:5 1129
Peter .... Acts 3:2-7 1274
Philip .... Acts 8:5-7 1282

B. *Figurative of:*
Extreme weakness .... 2 Sam. 5:6, 8 364
Inconsistency ...... Prov. 26:7 739
Weak believers ..... Jer. 31:8 877
Healed .... Is. 35:6 806

C. *Causes of:*
Birth defect .... Acts 3:2 1274
Accident ...... 2 Sam. 4:4 363

D. *Renders unfit for:*
Priesthood .... Lev. 21:17, 18 144
Sacrifice ...... Deut. 15:21 227
Active life .... 2 Sam. 9:13 367; 2 Sam. 19:24-26 379

Lamech—*wild man*

1. Son of Methushael, of Cain's race .... Gen. 4:17, 18 10
Had two wives .... Gen. 4:19 10
2. Son of Methuselah; father of Noah .... Gen. 5:25-31 11
Man of faith ... Gen. 5:29 11
In Christ's ancestry ..... Luke 3:36 1195

Lamed

Letter of the Hebrew alphabet .... Ps. 119:89-96 697

Lamentation—*mournful speeches; elegies; dirges*

A. *Historical of:*
Jeremiah over Josiah .... 2 Chr. 35:25 536
David over Saul .... 2 Sam. 1:17-27 360
David over Abner ...... 2 Sam. 3:33, 34 363
Jeremiah over Jerusalem .... Lam. 1:1 908

B. *Prophetic of:*
Isaiah over Babylon ...... Is. 14:1-32 786
Jeremiah over Jerusalem .... Jer. 7:28-34 853
Ezekiel over Tyre .... Ezek. 27:2-36 948
Christ over Jerusalem .... Luke 19:41-44 1222
Kings over Babylon ..... Rev. 18:1-24 1535

Lamentations, the Book of—*a book of the Old Testament*

The suffering of Zion .... Lam. 1:1–2:22 908
Individual prayer .... Lam. 3:1-66 911
Collective prayer .... Lam. 5:1-22 914

Lamp

A. *Used in:*
Tabernacle .... Ex. 37:23 111
Temple .... 1 Chr. 28:15 495
Processions .... Matt. 25:1-8 1148

B. *Figurative of:*
God .... 2 Sam. 22:29 384
God's Word ...... Ps. 119:105 697; Prov. 6:23 719
God's justice .. Zeph. 1:12 1057
Conscience .... Prov. 20:27 733
Prosperity ..... Job 29:3 608
Industry ...... Prov. 31:18 745
Death .... Job 18:6 601
Churches ...... Rev. 1:20 1519
Christ .... Rev. 1:14 1519

Lampstand, The Golden

A. *Specifications regarding:*
Made of gold .... Ex. 25:31 97
After a divine model .... Ex. 25:31-40 97
Set in holy place .... Heb. 9:2 1457
Continual burning of .... Ex. 27:20, 21 99
Carried by Kohathites ... Num. 4:4, 15 163
Temple's ten branches of .... 1 Kin. 7:48-50 401
Taken to Babylon ...... Jer. 52:19 905

B. *Used figuratively of:*
Christ .... Zech. 4:2, 11 1070
The church .... Rev. 1:13, 20 1519

Lance—*a spear*

Used in war ...... Jer. 50:42 901
Used by Baal's priests .... 1 Kin. 18:28 417

Landmark—*a boundary marker*

Removal of, forbidden .... Deut. 19:14 230

Land of promise (Canaan)

A. *Described as:*
The land of promise ...... Heb. 11:9 1460
The land of Canaan ...... Ezek. 16:3, 29 931
The land of the Jews .... Acts 10:39 1287
The Holy Land .... Zech. 2:12 1069
"Beulah" .... Is. 62:4 834

B. *Conquest of, by:*
Divine command .... Ex. 23:24 94
God's angel .... Ex. 23:20, 23 94
Hornets .... Ex. 23:28 94
Degrees .... Ex. 23:29, 30 94

SUBJECT REFERENCE PAGE

Lions—continued

C. *Figurative of:*
Tribe of Judah ....Gen. 49:9 61
Christ ....Rev. 5:5 1523
Devil ....1 Pet. 5:8 1483
Transformation ....Is. 11:6-8 784
Victory ....Ps. 91:13 678
Boldness ....Prov. 28:1 740
Persecutors ...Ps. 22:13 637
World empire ....Dan. 7:1-4 985
Antichrist .....Rev. 13:2 1529

Lips

A. *Described as:*
Uncircumcised .....Ex. 6:12, 30 74
Unclean ....Is. 6:5, 7 778
Stammering ...Is. 28:11 798
Flattering .....Ps. 12:2, 3 631
Perverse ....Prov. 4:24 718
Righteous .....Prov. 16:13 728
False ....Prov. 17:4 729
Burning ....Prov. 26:23 739

B. *Of the righteous, used for:*
Knowledge ....Job 33:3 611
Prayer ....Ps. 17:1 633
Silent prayer ..1 Sam. 1:13 321
Righteousness ....Ps. 40:9 648
Grace ....Ps. 45:2 651
Praise ....Ps. 51:15 654
Vows ....Ps. 66:13, 14 661
Singing ....Ps. 71:23 665
God's judgments ....Ps. 119:13 694
Feeding many ....Prov. 10:21 722
Spiritual fruitfulness .....Hos. 14:2 1005
Heb. 13:15 1463

C. *Of the wicked, used for:*
Flattery ....Prov. 7:21 720
Mocking ....Ps. 22:7 637
Defiance ....Ps. 12:4 632
Lying ....Is. 59:3 831
Poison ....Ps. 140:3, 9 705
Troublemaking ......Prov. 24:2 736
Evil ....Prov. 16:27, 30 729
Deception .....Prov. 24:28 737

D. *Warnings:*
Put away perverse .....Prov. 4:24 718
Refrain from using ....Prov. 17:28 730
1 Pet. 3:10 1481
Of an adulteress, avoid ....Prov. 5:3-13 718
Hypocrites ....Mark 7:6 1169

Litigation—*a lawsuit*

Christ's warning concerning ......Matt. 5:25, 40 1120
Paul's warning concerning ......1 Cor. 6:1, 2 1349

Litter—*a covered framework for carrying a single passenger*

Of nations ....Is. 66:20 838

Liver—*body organ that secretes bile*

A. *Used literally of:*
Animals:
In sacrifice ...Ex. 29:13, 22 102
For divination ....Ezek. 21:21 940

B. *Used figuratively of:*
Extreme pain or death ....Prov. 7:23 720

Livestock

Struck by God ....Ex. 12:29 82
Firstborn of, belong to God ....Ex. 34:19 107
Can be unclean ...Lev. 5:2 124
East of Jordan good for ....Num. 32:1, 4 198
Given as ransom ....Num. 3:45 163

See Cattle

Living, Christian

Source—Christ ...John 14:19 1258
Length—forever ..John 11:25, 26 1253
Means—faith in Christ ....Rom. 1:17 1324
Kind—resurrected ......2 Cor. 5:15 1368
End—to God ......Rom. 14:7, 8 1339
Purpose—for Christ ....1 Thess. 5:10 1416
Motivation—Christ ....Gal. 2:20 1380
Atmosphere—in the Spirit ....Gal. 5:25 1383
Manner—righteously ......Titus 2:12 1442
Enemies—flesh and sin ....Rom. 8:12, 13 1332
Price—persecution ....2 Tim. 3:12 1436

Living creatures—*a phrase referring to animals or living beings*

Aquatic animals ..Gen. 1:21 4
Land animals .....Gen. 1:24 4
Angelic beings ....Ezek. 1:5 919

Lizard—*a small, swift reptile with legs*

Ceremonially unclean ....Lev. 11:29, 30 132

Lo-Ammi—*not my people*

Symbolic name of Hosea's son ....Hos. 1:8, 9 996

Loan (see Borrow; Lending)

Lock

Doors ....Judg. 3:23, 24 287
Hair ....Judg. 16:13, 19 303
City gates ......Neh. 3:6, 13, 14 559

Locust—*devastating, migratory insects*

A. *Types, or stages, of:*
Eating ....Joel 1:4 1008
Devastating ...Lev. 11:22 132

B. *Used literally of insects:*
Miraculously brought forth ....Ex. 10:12-19 79
Sent as a judgment ....Deut. 28:38 239
1 Kin. 8:37 403
Used for food ....Matt. 3:4 1117

C. *Used figuratively of:*
Weakness .....Ps. 109:23, 24 689
Running men ....Is. 33:4 804
Nineveh's departing glory ....Nah. 3:15, 17 1049
Final plagues ....Rev. 9:3, 7 1526

See Grasshopper

Lod

Benjamite town ...1 Chr. 8:1, 12 473
Mentioned in postexilic books ....Ezra 2:33 544
Aeneas healed here, called Lydda ....Acts 9:32-35 1286

Lo Debar

City in Manasseh (in Gilead) ....2 Sam. 9:4, 5 367
Machir a native of ....2 Sam. 17:27 377

Lodge—*to pass the night*

Travelers—in a house ....Judg. 19:4-20 306
Spies—in a house ....Josh. 2:1 253
Animals—in ruins ....Zeph. 2:14 1058
Righteousness—in a city ....Is. 1:21 772
Thoughts—in Jerusalem ....Jer. 4:14 849

Loft—*a room upstairs*

Dead child taken to ....1 Kin. 17:19-24 416
Young man falls from ....Acts 20:9 1302

Loins

Used figuratively of source of hope ....1 Pet. 1:13 1477

Lois

Timothy's grandmother ....2 Tim. 1:5 1433

Loneliness

Jacob—in prayer ....Gen. 32:23-30 44
Joseph—in weeping ....Gen. 43:30, 31 56
Elijah—in discouragement ....1 Kin. 19:3-14 418
Jeremiah—in witnessing ......Jer. 15:17 862
Nehemiah—in a night vigil ....Neh. 2:12-16 559
Christ—in agony ....Matt. 26:36-45 1150
Paul—in prison ...2 Tim. 4:16 1436

Longevity—*a great span of life*

Allotted years, 70 ....Ps. 90:10 678

See Length of life

Longsuffering—*forbearance*

A. *Manifested in God's:*
Description of His nature ....Ex. 34:6 107
Delay in executing wrath ....Rom. 9:22 1334
Dealing with sinful men ....Rom. 2:4 1324
Desire for man's salvation .....2 Pet. 3:9, 15 1489

B. *As a Christian grace:*
Exemplified by the prophets ("patience") ..James 5:10 1471
Manifested by Old Testament saints ("patience") ..Heb. 6:12 1455
Produced by the Spirit ....Gal. 5:22 1383
Witnessed in Paul's life ....2 Cor. 6:6 1369
Taught as a virtue ....Eph. 4:1 1390
Given power for.............Col. 1:11 1406
Set for imitation .....2 Tim. 3:10 1436
Needed by preachers ....2 Tim. 4:2 1436

SUBJECT REFERENCE PAGE

Maai—*compassionate*

Postexilic trumpeter ....Neh. 12:35, 36 571

Maarath—*barren place*

Town of Judah ....Josh. 15:1, 59 267

Maaseiah—*work of Yahweh*

1. Levite musician during David's reign ... 1 Chr. 15:16, 18 481
2. Levite captain under Jehoiada .....2 Chr. 23:1 522
3. Official during King Uzziah's reign ....2 Chr. 26:11 525
4. Son of Ahaz, slain by Zichri ....2 Chr. 28:7 527
5. Governor of Jerusalem during King Josiah's reign ....2 Chr. 34:1, 8 534
6. Father of the false prophet Zedekiah .....Jer. 29:21 875
7. Father of Zephaniah the priest ....Jer. 21:1 867
8. Temple doorkeeper ...Jer. 35:4 882
9. Judahite postexilic Jew ....Neh. 11:5 570
10. Benjamite ancestor of a postexilic Jew ....Neh. 11:7 570
11, 12, 13. Three priests who divorced their foreign wives .... Ezra 10:18, 21, 22 553
14. Layman who divorced his foreign wife ....Ezra 10:30 553
15. Representative who signs the covenant .....Neh. 10:1, 25 569
16. One who stood by Ezra ....Neh. 8:4 565
17. Levite who explains the Law ....Neh. 8:7 565
18. Priest who takes part in dedication services .....Neh. 12:41 572
19. Another participating priest ....Neh. 12:42 572
20. Father or ancestor of Azariah ......Neh. 3:23 560

Maasai—*work of Yahweh*

Priest of Immer's family ....1 Chr. 9:12 474

Maath—*to be small*

Ancestor of Christ ....Luke 3:26 1195

Maaz—*anger*

Judahite ....1 Chr. 2:27 466

Maaziah—*Yahweh is a refuge*

1. Descendant of Aaron; heads a course of priests ....1 Chr. 24:1-18 490
2. One who signs the covenant .....Neh. 10:1, 8 569

Macedonia—*Greece* (northern)

A. *In Old Testament prophecy:*
Called the kingdom of Greece ....Dan. 11:2 991
Bronze part of Nebuchadnezzar's image ...Dan. 2:32, 39 978
Described as a leopard with four heads ....Dan. 7:6, 17 985
Described as a male goat .. Dan. 8:5, 21 986; Dan. 11:4 991

B. *In New Testament missions:*
Man of, appeals to ....Acts 16:9, 10 1295
Paul preaches in, at Philippi, etc. .... Acts 16:10–17:14 1295

Paul's troubles in ....2 Cor. 7:5 1369
Churches of, very generous .... Rom. 15:26 1340; 2 Cor. 8:1-5 1371

Machbanai—*clad with a cloak*

One of David's mighty men ....1 Chr. 12:13 479

Machbenah—*lump*

Son of Sheva .....1 Chr. 2:49 466

Machi

Father of the Gadite spy ....Num. 13:15 176

Machir—*sold*

1. Manasseh's only son ....Gen. 50:23 64
Founder of the family of Machirites ....Num. 26:29 191
Conqueror of Gilead .... Num. 32:39, 40 199
Name used of Manasseh tribe ....Judg. 5:14 289
2. Son of Ammiel ......2 Sam. 9:4, 5 367
Provides food for David ..... 2 Sam. 17:27-29 377

Machnadebai—*gift of the noble one*

Son of Bani; divorced foreign wife ....Ezra 10:34, 40 553

Machpelah—*double*

Field containing a cave; bought by Abraham ....Gen. 23:9-18 31
Sarah and Abraham buried here .... Gen. 23:19; 25:9, 10 31
Isaac, Rebekah, Leah, and Jacob buried here ......Gen. 49:29-31 63

Madai—*middle*

Third son of Japheth; ancestor of the Medes ....Gen. 10:2 15

Made—*something brought into being*

A. *Why Christ was made for us:*
Sin ....2 Cor. 5:21 1369
In our likeness ......Phil. 2:7 1400
High priest ....Heb. 6:20 1455

B. *What Christians are made by Him:*
Righteous ......2 Cor. 5:21 1369
Heirs ....Titus 3:7 1442

Madmannah—*dunghill*

Town in south Judah ....Josh. 15:20, 31 268
Son of Shaaph ....1 Chr. 2:49 466

Madmen—*dunghill*

Moabite town .....Jer. 48:2 895

Madmenah—*dunghill, or dungheap*

Town near Jerusalem ....Is. 10:31 784

Madness—*emotional or mental derangement*

A. *Kinds of:*
Extreme jealousy ....1 Sam. 18:8-11 343
Extreme rage ....Luke 6:11 1202

B. *Causes of:*
Disobedience to God's Laws ....Deut. 28:28 238
Judgment sent by God .... Dan. 4:31-34 981; Zech. 12:4 1075

C. *Manifestations of:*
Irrational behavior ..... 1 Sam. 21:12-15 347
Uncontrollable emotions .....Mark 5:1-5 1164
Moral decay ...Jer. 50:38 901

See Insanity; Lunatic

Madon—*contention*

Canaanite town ...Josh. 12:19 265
Joins confederacy against Joshua ....Josh. 11:1-12 264

Magbish—*strong*

Town of Judah ....Ezra 2:30 544

Magdala—*tower*

City of Galilee ....Matt. 15:39 1136

Magdalene—*of Magdala*

Descriptive of one of the Marys ....Matt. 27:56 1154

See Mary 3

Magdiel—*God is glory*

Edomite duke .....Gen. 36:43 48

Magi—*a priestly sect in Persia*

Brings gifts to the infant Jesus ....Matt. 2:1, 2 1116

Magic, magician—*the art of doing superhuman things by "supernatural" means*

A. *Special manifestations of:*
At the exodus ....Ex. 7:11 75
During apostolic Christianity ..Acts 8:9, 18-24 1282

B. *Modified power of:*
Acknowledged in history ......Ex. 7:11, 22 75
Recognized in prophecy .... 2 Thess. 2:9-12 1421
Fulfilled in antichrist ......Rev. 13:13-18 1531

C. *Failure of, to:*
Perform miracles .....Ex. 8:18, 19 76
Overcome demons ......Acts 19:13-19 1300

D. *Condemnation of, by:*
Explicit Law ...Lev. 20:27 143
Their inability .....Ex. 8:18 76
Final judgment .....Rev. 21:8 1538

See Divination

Magistrates—*civil rulers*

A. *Descriptive of:*
Ruler ....Judg. 18:7 304
Authorities .....Luke 12:11 1214

B. *Office of:*
Ordained by God ....Rom. 13:1, 2 1337
Due proper respect ....Acts 23:5 1307

C. *Duties of:*
To judge:
Impartially ...Deut. 1:17 208
Righteously ..Deut. 25:1 235

SUBJECT REFERENCE PAGE

Mast—*a vertical support for sails and rigging on a sailing ship*

A. *Used literally of:*
Cedars of Lebanon ..... Ezek. 27:5 948

B. *Used figuratively of:*
Strength of enemies ..... Is. 33:23 805

Master

A. *Descriptive of:*
Owner of slaves .... Ex. 21:4-6 92
King .... 1 Chr. 12:19 479
Prophet .... 2 Kin. 2:3, 5 430

B. *Kinds of:*
Unmerciful ... 1 Sam. 30:13-15 355
Angry .... Luke 14:21 1217
Good .... Gen. 24:9-35 32
Believing ...... 1 Tim. 6:2 1430
Heavenly ..... Col. 4:1 1409

Master builder

Paul describes himself as .... 1 Cor. 3:10 1346

Master workmen—*craftsmen*

Bezaleel .... Ex. 31:1-5 104
Hiram of Tyre .... 1 Kin. 7:13-50 400
Aquila and Priscilla .... Acts 18:2, 3 1299
Demetrius .... Acts 19:24 1302

Mate—*the male or female of a pair*

God provides for .... Is. 34:15, 16 806

Materialistic—*concerned for worldly goods only*

Christ condemns .... Luke 12:16-21 1214
Sadducees described .... Acts 23:8 1307
Christians forbidden to live as .... 1 Cor. 15:30-34 1360

Mathematics, spiritual

A. *General:*

Addition:
God's Word ... Deut. 4:2 211
Knowledge will increase ...... Dan. 12:4 993
Increased riches .... Ps. 62:10 659

Subtraction:
God's commandments .... Deut. 12:32 224

Multiplication:
Human family .... Gen. 1:28 7

B. *Unrighteous:*

Addition:
Wealth .... Ps. 73:12 666
Guilt .... 2 Chr. 28:13 527
Sin .... Is. 30:1 800

Subtraction:
Wealth obtained by fraud .... Prov. 13:11 725
Life shortened ... Ps. 55:23 656; Prov. 10:27 723

Multiplication:
Sorrow by idolatry ...... Ps. 16:4 633
Transgression ...... Prov. 29:16 743

C. *Righteous:*

Addition:
Years .... Prov. 3:1, 2 715; Prov. 4:10 716
Blessing without sorrow .... Prov. 10:22 722
By putting God first .... Matt. 6:33 1123
Graces .... 2 Pet. 1:5-7 1487
In latter years .... Job 42:12 620

Subtraction:
Disease .... Ex. 15:26 86
Taken from evil .... Is. 57:1 829

Multiplication:
Prosperity ... Deut. 8:1, 11-13 218
Length of days .... Deut. 11:18-21 222; Prov. 9:11 722
Mercy, peace, love .... Jude 2 1510
Church .... Acts 9:31 1286

Matred—*expulsion*

Mother-in-law of Hadar (Hadad), an Edomite king .... Gen. 36:39 48

Matri—*rainy*

Saul's Benjamite family .... 1 Sam. 10:21 332

Mattan—*gift*

1. Priest of Baal .... 2 Kin. 11:18 443
Killed by the people ...... 2 Chr. 23:16, 17 523
2. Father of Shephatiah ... Jer. 38:1 885

Mattanah—*gift*

Israelite camp ... Num. 21:18, 19 186

Mattaniah—*gift of Yahweh*

1. King Zedekiah's original name .... 2 Kin. 24:17 459
2. Son of Mica, a Levite and Asaphite ..... 1 Chr. 9:15 474
3. Musician, son of Heman .... 1 Chr. 25:4, 16 491
4. Spirit of the LORD came upon .... 2 Chr. 20:14 520
5. Levite under King Hezekiah .... 2 Chr. 29:13 528
6. Postexilic Levite and singer .... Neh. 11:17 570
7. Levite gatekeeper ... Neh. 12:25 571
8. Postexilic Levite .... Neh. 12:35 571
9. Levite in charge of treasuries .... Neh. 13:13 572
10, 11, 12, 13. Four postexilic Jews who divorced foreign wives .... Ezra 10:26-37 553

Mattathah—*gift* (of God)

Son of Nathan; ancestor of Christ .... Luke 3:31 1195

Mattathias—*Greek form of Mattathiah*

1. Postexilic ancestor of Christ .... Luke 3:25 1195
2. Another postexilic ancestor of Christ .... Luke 3:26 1195

Mattattah—*gift of Yahweh*

Jew who put away his foreign wife .... Ezra 10:33 553

Mattenai—*gift of Yahweh*

1. Priest in the time of Joiakim ...... Neh. 12:19 571
2, 3. Two postexilic Jews who put away their foreign wives .... Ezra 10:33, 37 553

Matter—*something*

A. *Descriptive of:*
Lawsuit .... 1 Cor. 6:1 1349
Sum of something .... Eccl. 12:13 759
Love affair .... Ruth 3:18 315
News .... Mark 1:45 1161

B. *Kinds of:*
Evil .... Ps. 64:5 659
Unknown ..... Dan. 2:5, 10 977

Matthan—*gift*

Ancestor of Joseph .... Matt. 1:15, 16 1115

Matthat—*gift*

1. Ancestor of Christ .... Luke 3:24 1195
2. Another ancestor of Christ .... Luke 3:29 1195

Matthew—*gift of Yahweh*

Tax gatherer ..... Matt. 9:9 1126
Becomes Christ's follower .... Matt. 9:9 1126
Appointed an apostle .... Matt. 10:2, 3 1127
Called Levi, the son of Alphaeus .... Mark 2:14 1162
Entertains Jesus with a great feast .... Mark 2:14, 15 1162
In the upper room .... Acts 1:13 1272
Author of the first Gospel .... Matt. 1:1 (Title) 1115

Matthew, the Gospel of—*a book of the New Testament*

Events of Jesus' birth .... Matt. 1:18–2:23 1116
John the Baptist ... Matt. 3:1-17 1117
The temptation ... Matt. 4:1-11 1117
Jesus begins His ministry .... Matt. 4:12-17 1118
The Great Sermon .... Matt. 5:1–7:29 1120
Christ, about John the Baptist .... Matt. 11:1-19 1129
Conflict with the Pharisees and Sadducees .. Matt. 15:39–16:6 1136
Peter's confession .... Matt. 16:13-20 1136
Prophecy of death and resurrection ..... Matt. 20:17-19 1140
Jerusalem entry ... Matt. 21:1-11 1141
Authority of Jesus .... Matt. 21:23–22:14 1143
Woes to the Pharisees .... Matt. 23:1-36 1145
Garden of Gethsemane ..... Matt. 26:36-56 1150
Crucifixion and burial .... Matt. 27:27-66 1152
Resurrection of Christ .... Matt. 28:1-20 1155

Matthias—*gift of Yahweh*

Chosen by lot to replace Judas .... Acts 1:15-26 1272

Mattithiah—*gift of Yahweh*

1. Korahite Levite .... 1 Chr. 9:31 475

SUBJECT REFERENCE PAGE

2. Levite, son of Jeduthun, and Temple musician .... 1 Chr. 15:18, 21 481
3. Jew who put away his foreign wife ....Ezra 10:43 554
4. Levite attendant to Ezra ....Neh. 8:4 565

Mattock—*an agricultural instrument for digging and hoeing*

Sharpened for battle..........1 Sam. 13:20-22 334

Maturity, spiritual

Do away with childish things ....1 Cor. 13:11 1356
Be mature in your thinking ....1 Cor. 14:20 1358
Solid food is for...Heb. 5:11-14 1453
Overcoming the evil one ....1 John 2:14 1496

Mazzaroth—*the signs of the Zodiac or a constellation*

Descriptive of God's power ....Job 38:32 616

Meah, tower of the

Restored by Eliashib ....Neh. 3:1 559

Meal—*ground grain used for food*

One-tenth of an ephah of ....Num. 5:15 165
Used in offerings ....1 Kin. 4:22 397
"Then bring" .....2 Kin. 4:41 433
Millstones and grind ....Is. 47:2 819
Three measures of ....Matt. 13:33 1133

Meals—*times of eating*

A. *Times of:*
Early morning .....John 21:4-12 1267
At noon (for laborers) .....Ruth 2:14 314
In the evening ......Gen. 19:1-3 26

B. *Extraordinary and festive:*
Guests invited ....Matt. 22:3, 4 1144
Received with a kiss ....Luke 7:45 1204
Feet washed ...Luke 7:44 1204
Anointed with ointment .....Luke 7:38 1204
Proper dress...Matt. 22:11, 12 1144
Seated according to rank ....Matt. 23:6 1145
Special guest honored ......1 Sam. 9:22-24 331
Entertainment provided ......Luke 15:25 1218
Temperate habits taught ....Prov. 23:1-3 735
Intemperance condemned...Amos 6:4-6 1020

See Entertainment; Feasts

Means of grace

A. *Agents of:*
Holy Spirit ....Gal. 5:16-26 1383
God's Word ...1 Thess. 2:13 1415
Prayer ....Rom. 8:15-27 1332
Christian fellowship ....Mal. 3:16-18 1083
Public worship ......1 Thess. 5:6 1416
Christian witnessing ...Acts 8:4 1282

B. *Words expressive of:*
Stir up the gift ....2 Tim. 1:6 1433
Neglect not the spiritual gift ....1 Tim. 4:14 1429
Take heed to the ministry......Col. 4:17 1410
Grow in grace ....2 Pet. 3:18 1490

C. *Use of, brings:*
Assurance ....2 Pet. 1:5-12 1487
Stability ......Eph. 4:11-16 1390

D. *Enemies of:*
Devil ....1 Thess. 3:5 1415
World ....1 John 2:15-17 1496
Coldness ......Rev. 3:14-18 1521

Mearah—*cave*

Unconquered by Joshua ....Josh. 13:1, 4 265

Measure—*a standard of size, quantity or values*

A. *Objectionable:*
Differing (different) ... Deut. 25:14, 15 236
Short ....Mic. 6:10 1041
Using themselves as a gauge ....2 Cor. 10:12 1373

B. *As indicative of:*
Earth's weight ....Is. 40:12 811
Punishment inflicted ....Matt. 7:2 1123

C. *Figurative of:*
Great size .....Hos. 1:10 997
Sin's ripeness ......Matt. 23:32 1145
The Spirit's infilling ......John 3:34 1241
Man's ability ..2 Cor. 10:13 1373
Perfection of faith ....Eph. 4:13, 16 1390

Measuring line—*a cord of specified length for measuring*

Signifies hope ... Jer. 31:38-40 879; Zech. 2:1 1069

Mebunnai—*built*

One of David's mighty men.............2 Sam. 23:27 385
Called Sibbechai ....1 Chr. 11:29 478

Mecherathite—*a dweller in Mecharah*

Descriptive of Hepher, one of David's mighty men.............1 Chr. 11:36 478

Meconah—*foundation*

Town of Judah....Neh. 11:25, 28 571

Medad—*beloved*

One of the seventy elders receiving the Spirit ....Num. 11:26-29 175

Medan—*judgment*

Son of Abraham by Keturah ....Gen. 25:1, 2 33

Meddling—*interfering with the affairs of others*

Brings a king's death..........2 Chr. 35:21-24 536
Christians ....1 Pet. 4:15 1483
Such called "busybodies" ....2 Thess. 3:11 1422

Medeba—*full waters*

Old Moabite town ....Num. 21:29, 30 186
Assigned to Reuben ....Josh. 13:9, 16 265
Syrians defeated here............1 Chr. 19:6, 7 486
Reverts to Moab ..Is. 15:2 787

Medes, Media—*the people and country of the Medes*

A. *Characteristics of:*
Part of Medo-Persian empire ......Esth. 1:19 577
Inflexible laws of......Dan. 6:8, 12, 15 984
Among those at Pentecost ....Acts 2:9 1273

B. *Kings of, mentioned in the Bible:*
Cyrus ....Ezra 1:1 542
Ahasuerus ....Ezra 4:6 546
Artaxerxes I ...Ezra 4:7 546
Darius ....Ezra 6:1 547
Xerxes ....Dan. 11:2 991
Artaxerxes ....Ezra 6:14 548

C. *Place of, in Bible history:*
Israel deported to...........2 Kin. 17:6 448
Babylon falls to............Dan. 5:30, 31 984
"Darius the Mede," new ruler of Babylon......Dan. 5:31 984
Daniel rises high in the kingdom of............Dan. 6:1-28 984
Cyrus, king of Persia, allows Jews to return .... 2 Chr. 36:22, 23 538
Esther and Mordecai live under Ahasuerus, king of...........Esth. 1:3, 19 577

D. *Prophecies concerning:*
Agents in Babylon's fall ....Is. 13:17-19 786
Cyrus, king of, God's servant ....Is. 44:28 817
"Inferior" kingdom .....Dan. 2:39 978
Compared to a bear ....Dan. 7:5 985
Kings of.......Dan. 11:2 991
War with Greece ....Dan. 11:2 991

Mediation—*a friendly intervention designed to render assistance*

A. *Purposes of:*
Save a life ....Gen. 37:21, 22 49
Save a people ....Ex. 32:11-13 105
Obtain a wife ....1 Kin. 2:13-25 393
Obtain justice ....Job 9:33 596

B. *Motives prompting:*
People's fear ..Deut. 5:5 214
Regard for human life ....Jer. 38:7-13 886
Sympathy for a sick man.........2 Kin. 5:6-8 433; Matt. 17:15 1137

C. *Methods used:*
Intense prayer ....Deut. 9:20-29 221
Flattery ..... 1 Sam. 25:23-35 350
Appeal to self-preservation ....Esth. 4:12-17 581

Mediator, Christ our

A. *His qualifications:*
Bears God's image, man's likeness .....Phil. 2:6-8 1400; Heb. 2:14-17 1452

SUBJECT REFERENCE PAGE

Mered—*rebellion*

Judahite ....1 Chr. 4:17 467
Had two wives .....1 Chr. 4:17, 18 467

Meremoth—*elevations*

1. Signer of the covenant .....Neh. 10:5 569
Called Meraioth .....Neh. 12:15 571
2. One who divorced his foreign wife ....Ezra 10:34, 36 553
3. Priest, son of Uriah; weighs silver and gold .....Ezra 8:33 550
Repairs wall of Jerusalem ....Neh. 3:4, 21 559

Meres—*the forgetful one*

Persian prince ....Esth. 1:13, 14 577

Merib-Baal—*Baal contends*

Another name for Mephibosheth ...1 Chr. 8:34 473

Merit—*reward given for something done additionally*

A. *Of man, impossible because:*
None is good ..Rom. 3:12 1325
None is righteous .....Rom. 3:10 1325
We are all sinful ....Is. 6:5 778
Our good comes from God ....1 Cor. 15:9, 10 1359
Our righteousness:
Is unavailing ....Matt. 5:20 1120
Is Christ's ....2 Cor. 5:21 1369
Cannot save ....Rom. 10:1-4 1334
B. *Of Christ:*
Secured by obedience ....Rom. 5:17-21 1329
Secured by His death ....Is. 53:10-12 825
Obtained by faith ....Phil. 3:8, 9 1401

Merodach—*bold*

Supreme deity of the Babylonians .....Jer. 50:2 899
Otherwise called Bel..............Is. 46:1 818

Merodach-Baladan—*Merodach has given a son*

Sends ambassadors to Hezekiah ....Is. 39:1-8 810
Also called Berodach-Baladan ....2 Kin. 20:12 454

Merom—*high place*

Lake on Jordan north of the Sea of Galilee ....Josh. 11:5, 7 264

Meronothite

Citizen of Meronoth ....1 Chr. 27:30 494

Meroz—*refuge*

Town cursed for failing to help the Lord ....Judg. 5:23 289

Merry—*a spirit of gaiety; cheerful*

A. *Good, comes from:*
Heart ....Prov. 15:13, 15 727
Restoration ....Jer. 30:18, 19 876
Christian joy ..James 5:13 1473
B. *Evil, results from:*
Careless unconcern ....Judg. 9:27 295
Drunkenness ..1 Sam. 25:36 351
False optimism .....1 Kin. 21:7 422
Sinful glee ....Rev. 11:10 1528

Mesha—*retreat*

1. Border of Joktan's descendants ....Gen. 10:30 16
2. Benjamite .....1 Chr. 8:8, 9 473
3. Son of Caleb ..1 Chr. 2:42 466
4. King of Moab ....2 Kin. 3:4 431

Meshach—*the shadow of the prince*

Name given to Mishael ....Dan. 1:7 976
Advanced to high position ....Dan. 2:49 978
Remains faithful in testing ....Dan. 3:13-30 979

Meshech—*tall*

1. Son of Japheth ......Gen. 10:2 15
Called Mesech ......Ps. 120:5 699
Famous traders ....Ezek. 27:13 948
Confederates with Gog ....Ezek. 38:2, 3 961
Inhabitants of the nether world ....Ezek. 32:18, 26 955
2. Son of Shem ..1 Chr. 1:17 464
Same as Mash ....Gen. 10:23 16

Meshelemiah—*Yahweh repays*

Father of Zechariah ....1 Chr. 9:21 474
Porter in the Temple..........1 Chr. 26:1 492
Called Shelemiah ....1 Chr. 26:14 492

Meshezabeel—*God delivers*

1. Postexilic wall repairer ......Neh. 3:4 559
2. One who signs covenant ....Neh. 10:21 569
3. Judahite ......Neh. 11:24 571

Meshillemith—*recompense*

Postexilic priest ...1 Chr. 9:10-12 474
Called Meshillemoth ....Neh. 11:13 570

Meshillemoth—*acts of recompense*

Ephraimite leader ....2 Chr. 28:12 527

Meshobab—*restored*

Descendant of Simeon ....1 Chr. 4:34-38 468

Meshullam—*recompensed; rewarded*

1. Benjamite ....1 Chr. 8:17 473
2. Gadite leader........1 Chr. 5:11, 13 468
3. Shaphan's grandfather ..2 Kin. 22:3 455
4. Hilkiah's father ....1 Chr. 9:11 474
5. Son of Zerubbabel ...1 Chr. 3:19 467
6. A priest ....1 Chr. 9:10-12 474
7. Kohathite overseer .....2 Chr. 34:12 534
8. A second Benjamite ....1 Chr. 9:7 474
9. Another Benjamite ....1 Chr. 9:8 474
10. Man commissioned to secure Levites ....Ezra 8:16 550
11. Levite who supports Ezra's reforms ......Ezra 10:15 553
12. One who divorced his foreign wife ....Ezra 10:29 553
13. Postexilic workman ....Neh. 3:4, 30 559
His daughter married Tobiah's son ....Neh. 6:18 562
14. Postexilic workman ....Neh. 3:6 559
15. One of Ezra's attendants....Neh. 8:4 565
16, 17. Two priests who sign covenant .....Neh. 10:7, 20 569
18, 19. Two priests in Joiakim's time ....Neh. 12:13, 16 571
20. Porter..........Neh. 12:25 571
21. Participant in dedication services ......Neh. 12:33 571

Meshullemeth—*feminine form of Meshullam*

Wife of King Manasseh ......2 Kin. 21:18, 19 455

Mesopotamia—*the country between two rivers*

Abraham's native home ....Acts 7:2 1279
Place of Laban's household ......Gen. 24:4, 10, 29 31
Called:
Padan Aram .....Gen. 25:20 34
Syria ....Gen. 31:20, 24 42
Balaam came from ....Deut. 23:4 233
Israel enslaved to ....Judg. 3:8, 10 287
Chariots and horsemen hired from ....1 Chr. 19:6 486
Called Haran; conquered by Sennacherib ....2 Kin. 19:12, 16 452
People from, at Pentecost ....Acts 2:9 1273

Messenger—*one sent on a mission*

A. *Mission of, to:*
Appease wrath ....Gen. 32:3-6 43
Ask for favors........Num. 20:14-17 184
Spy out ....Josh. 6:17, 25 256
Assemble a nation ....Judg. 6:35 291
Secure provisions ....1 Sam. 25:4-14 350
Relay news ....1 Sam. 11:3-9 332
Stir up war ....Judg. 11:12-28 297
Sue for peace ....2 Sam. 3:12, 13 362
Offer sympathy ....1 Chr. 19:2 486
Call for help ...2 Kin. 17:4 448
Issue an ultimatum .....1 Kin. 20:2-9 420
Deliver the LORD's message .....Hag. 1:13 1065
B. *Reception of:*
Rejected ......Deut. 2:26-30 210
Humiliated ....1 Chr. 19:2-4 486
Rebuked ......2 Kin. 1:2-5, 16 429
C. *Significant examples of:*
John the Baptist ....Mal. 3:1 1082
Paul's thorn ....2 Cor. 12:7 1374
Gospel workers .....2 Cor. 8:23 1371; Phil. 2:25 1400

Messiah, the

A. *Described as:*
Seed of woman.......Gen. 3:15 9

SUBJECT REFERENCE PAGE

Moon—continued
Marking time .... Gen. 1:14 4
Designating seasons ...... Ps. 104:19 684
Signaling prophetic events .... Matt. 24:29 1147; Luke 21:25 1225

Morality—*principles of right conduct*

A. *Of the unregenerate:*
Based upon conscience ... Rom. 2:14, 15 1325
Commanded by law .... John 8:3-5 1248
Limited to outward appearance ... Is. 1:14, 15 772
Object of boasting ..... Mark 10:17-20 1173

B. *Of the regenerated:*
Based upon the new birth .... 2 Cor. 5:17 1368
Prompted by the Spirit .... Gal. 5:22, 23 1383
Comes from the heart .... Heb. 8:10 1456
No boasting except in Christ .... 1 Cor. 15:10 1359; Phil. 3:7-10 1401

Morasthite—*a native of Moresheth*

Descriptive of Micah .... Jer. 26:18 873

Mordecai—*dedicated to Mars*

1. Jew exiled in Persia .... Esth. 2:5, 6 578
Brings up Esther .... Esth. 2:7 578
Directs Esther's movements ... Esth. 2:10-20 578
Reveals plot to kill the king .... Esth. 2:22, 23 578
Refuses homage to Haman .... Esth. 3:1-6 578
Gallows made for .... Esth. 5:14 581
Honored by the king .... Esth. 6:1-12 581
Is highly exalted .... Esth. 8:7, 15 583
Becomes famous ...... Esth. 9:4 583
Writes to Jews about Feast of Purim .... Esth. 9:20-31 585
2. Postexilic returnee ..... Ezra 2:2 542

More—*something in addition*

A. *"More than" promises:*
Repentance ... Matt. 18:13 1138
Love .... John 21:15 1267

B. *"Much more" promises:*
Grace .... Rom. 5:9-17 1329
Witnessing .... Phil. 1:14 1398
Obedience .... Phil. 2:12 1400

C. *"No more" promises:*
Christ's death .... Rom. 6:9 1329
Remember sin .... Heb. 8:12 1456

Moreh—*teacher, soothsayer*

1. Place (oak tree or grove) near Shechem ..... Gen. 12:6 20
Probably place of:
Idol-burying .. Gen. 35:4 46
Covenant-stone .... Josh. 24:26 279
2. Hill in the valley of Jezreel .... Judg. 7:1 291

Moresheth Gath—*possession of Gath*

Birthplace of Micah the prophet .... Mic. 1:14 1037

Moriah

God commands Abraham to sacrifice Isaac here ... Gen. 22:1-13 30
Site of Solomon's temple .... 2 Chr. 3:1 503

Morning—*the first part of the day*

A. *Early risers in:*
Do the LORD's will .... Gen. 22:3 30
Worship ...... Ex. 24:4 95
Do the LORD's work .... Josh. 6:12 256
Fight the LORD's battles .... Josh. 8:10 259
Depart on a journey ...... Judg. 19:5, 8 306
Correct an evil .... Dan. 6:19 984
Pray .... Mark 1:35 1161
Visit the tomb .... Mark 16:2 1185
Preach .... Acts 5:21 1278

B. *For the righteous, a time for:*
Joy .... Ps. 30:5 641
God's loving-kindness ..... Ps. 92:2 679
God's mercies ...... Lam. 3:22, 23 911

C. *For the unrighteous, a time of:*
Dread .... Deut. 28:67 240
Destruction ..... Is. 17:14 789

D. *Figurative of:*
Man's unrighteousness .... Hos. 6:4 1000
Judgment ..... Zeph. 3:5 1059
God's light .... Amos 5:8 1018
Christ's return .... Rev. 2:28 1521

Morning sacrifice—*part of Israelite worship*

Ritual described .. Ex. 29:38-42 103
Part of continual offering .... Num. 28:3-8 194
Under Ahaz ...... 2 Kin. 16:15 448

Morning Star

Figurative of Christ:

To church at Thyatira .... Rev. 2:24, 28 1521
Christ, of Himself .... Rev. 22:16 1539
Applied to Christ .... 2 Pet. 1:19 1487

Morsel—*a small piece of food*

Offered to angels .... Gen. 18:5 24
Rejected by a doomed man .... 1 Sam. 28:22 353
Asked of a dying woman .... 1 Kin. 17:11, 12 416
Better than strife .... Prov. 17:1 729
Exchanged for a birthright .... Heb. 12:16 1462

Mortar (I)—*a vessel*

Vessel used for beating grains .... Num. 11:8 173
Used figuratively ...... Prov. 27:22 740

Mortar (II)—*a building material*

Made of:

Clay .... Is. 41:25 813
Asphalt .... Gen. 11:3 16
Plaster .... Lev. 14:42, 45 137

Mortgage—*something given in security for debt*

Postexilic Jews burdened with .... Neh. 5:3 561

Mortification—*a putting to death*

A. *Objects of:*
Law .... Rom. 7:4 1331
Sin .... Rom. 6:6, 11 1329
Flesh .... Rom. 13:14 1339
Members of earthly body .... Col. 3:5 1408

B. *Agents of:*
Holy Spirit .... Rom. 8:13 1332
Our obedience .... Rom. 6:17-19 1331

Moserah (sing.), **Moseroth** (pl.)—*bond*

Place of Aaron's death and burial .... Deut. 10:6 221
Israelite encampment .... Num. 33:30, 31 200

Moses—*drawn out*

A. *Early life of* (first 40 years):
Descendant of Levi .... Ex. 2:1 69
Son of Amram and Jochebed ... Ex. 6:16-20 74
Brother of Aaron and Miriam ...... Ex. 15:20 86
Born under slavery .... Ex. 2:1-10 69
Hid by mother .... Ex. 2:2, 3 69
Educated in Egyptian wisdom ..... Acts 7:22 1279
Refused Egyptian sonship ...... Heb. 11:23-27 1460
Defended his people .... Ex. 2:11-14 69
Rejected, flees to Midian .... Ex. 2:15 69

B. *In Midian* (second 40 years):
Married Zipporah ..... Ex. 2:16-21 69
Father of two sons .... Ex. 2:22 69; Acts 7:29 1281
Became Jethro's shepherd ..... Ex. 3:1 70

C. *Leader of Israel* (last 40 years; to the end of his life):
Heard God's voice .... Ex. 3:2-6 70
God's plan revealed to him .... Ex. 3:7-10 70
Argued with God .... Ex. 4:1-17 72
Met Aaron .... Ex. 4:14-28 72
Assembled elders of Israelites ..... Ex. 4:29-31 72
Rejected by Pharaoh and Israel .... Ex. 5:1-23 73
Conflict with Pharaoh; ten plagues sent .... Ex. 7–12 74
Commanded to institute the Passover .... Ex. 12:1-29 80; Heb. 11:28 1462

D. *From Egypt to Sinai:*
Led people from Egypt .... Ex. 12:30-38 82
Observed the Passover ..... Ex. 12:39-51 82
Healed bitter waters .... Ex. 15:22-27 86

TOPICAL INDEX

SUBJECT REFERENCE PAGE

Mount Gerizim—*rocky*
Place the blessed stood ... Deut. 27:12 237
Jotham spoke to people of Shechem here ... Judg. 9:7 295

Mount Gilboa—*bubbling spring*
Men of Israel slain ... 1 Sam. 31:1 355
Saul and his sons slain here ... 1 Sam. 31:8 355

Mount Gilead—*heap of witness*
Gideon divides the people for battle ... Judg. 7:3 291

Mount Hor—*mountain*
LORD spoke to Moses and Aaron ... Num. 20:23 184
Aaron died there ... Num. 20:25-28 184

Mount Horeb—*desolate*
Sons of Israel stripped of ornaments ... Ex. 33:6 106
The same as Sinai ... Ex. 3:1 70

Mount of Olives
Prophecy concerning ... Zech. 14:4 1076
Jesus sent disciples for donkey ... Matt. 21:1, 2 1141; Mark 11:1, 2 1174
Jesus speaks of the signs of His coming ... Matt. 24:3 1147; Mark 13:3, 4 1179
After the Lord's supper went out to ... Matt. 26:30 1150; Mark 14:26 1181
Called Mount Olivet ... Luke 19:29 1222; Luke 21:37 1225

Mount Seir—*rugged*
Horites defeated by Chedorlaomer ... Gen. 14:5, 6 21

Mount Shepher—*beauty*
Israelites camped at ... Num. 33:23, 24 200

Mount Sinai
Lord descended upon, in fire ... Ex. 19:18 90
Lord called Moses to the top ... Ex. 19:20 90
The glory of the LORD rested on, for six days ... Ex. 24:16 95

Mount Tabor—*broken*
Deborah sent Barak there to defeat Canaanites ... Judg. 4:6-14 288

Mount Zion
Survivors shall go out from ... 2 Kin. 19:31 453

Mountain—*a high elevation of earth*
A. *Mentioned in the Bible:*
Abarim ... Num. 33:47, 48 200
Ararat ... Gen. 8:4 12
Bashan ... Ps. 68:15 662
Carmel ... 1 Kin. 18:19 417
Ebal ... Deut. 27:13 237
Gaash ... Judg. 2:9 285
Gerizim ... Deut. 11:29 223
Gilboa ... 2 Sam. 1:6, 21 360
Hachilah ... 1 Sam. 23:19 349
Hermon ... Josh. 13:11 266
Hor ... Num. 34:7, 8 202
Horeb (same as Sinai) ... Ex. 3:1 70
Lebanon ... Deut. 3:25 211
Moreh ... Judg. 7:1 291
Moriah ... Gen. 22:2 30
Nebo ... Deut. 34:1 247
Olives or Olivet ... Matt. 24:3 1147
Pisgah ... Num. 21:20 186
Sinai ... Ex. 19:2-20 89
Sion or Zion ... 2 Sam. 5:7 364
Tabor ... Judg. 4:6-14 288
B. *In Christ's life, place of:*
Temptation ... Matt. 4:8 1118
Sermon ... Matt. 5:1 1120
Prayer ... Matt. 14:23 1134
Transfiguration ... Matt. 17:1, 2 1137
Prophecy ... Matt. 24:3 1147
Agony ... Matt. 26:30, 31 1150
Ascension ... Luke 24:50 1231
C. *Uses of:*
Boundaries ... Num. 34:7, 8 202
Distant vision ... Deut. 3:27 211
Hunting ... 1 Sam. 26:20 352
Warfare ... 1 Sam. 17:3 340
Protection ... Amos 6:1 1020
Refuge ... Matt. 24:16 1147
Idolatrous worship ... Is. 65:7 836
Assembly sites ... Josh. 8:30-33 260
D. *Significant Old Testament events on:*
Ark rested upon (Ararat) ... Gen. 8:4 12
Abraham's testing (Moriah) ... Gen. 22:1-19 30
Giving of the Law (Sinai) ... Ex. 19:2-25 89
Moses' view of Canaan (Pisgah) ... Deut. 34:1 247
Combat with Baalism (Carmel) ... 1 Kin. 18:19-42 417
David's city (Zion) ... 2 Sam. 5:7 364
E. *Figurative of:*
God's:
Protection ... Is. 31:4 803
Dwelling ... Is. 8:18 780
Judgments ... Jer. 13:16 859
Gospel age ... Is. 27:13 796
Messiah's advent ... Is. 40:9 811
Great joy ... Is. 44:23 817
Great difficulties ... Matt. 21:21 1143
Pride of man ... Luke 3:5 1195
Supposed faith ... 1 Cor. 13:2 1356

Mourning—*expression of sorrow*
A. *Caused by:*
Death ... Gen. 50:10 64
Defection ... 1 Sam. 15:35 339
Disobedience ... Ezra 9:4-7 551
Desolation ... Joel 1:9, 10 1008
Defeat ... Rev. 18:11 1535
Discouragement ... Ps. 42:9 649
Disease ... Job 2:5-8 590
B. *Transformed into:*
Gladness ... Is. 51:11 823
Hope ... John 11:23-28 1253
Everlasting joy ... Is. 35:10 806
C. *Signs of:*
Tearing of clothing ... 2 Sam. 3:31, 32 363
Ashes on head ... 2 Sam. 13:19 372
Sackcloth ... Gen. 37:34 49
Neglect of appearance ... 2 Sam. 19:24 379
Presence of mourners ... John 11:19, 31 1253
Apparel ... 2 Sam. 14:2 373
Shave head ... Jer. 16:6, 7 862

Mouse, mice—*a small quadruped*
Accounted unclean ... Lev. 11:29 132
Eaten by idolatrous Israelites ... Is. 66:17 838

Mouth
A. *Descriptive of:*
Top of a well ... Gen. 29:2, 3, 8 38
Opening of a sack ... Gen. 42:27, 28 55
Man's ... Job 3:1 591
B. *Exhortations concerning:*
Make all acceptable ... Ps. 19:14 636
Keep with a muzzle ... Ps. 39:1 647
Set a guard before ... Ps. 141:3 706
Keep the corrupt from ... Eph. 4:29 1391
Keep filthy language from ... Col. 3:8 1408
C. *Of unregenerate, source of:*
Lying ... 1 Kin. 22:13, 22, 23 423
Idolatry ... 1 Kin. 19:18 420
Unfaithfulness ... Ps. 5:9 626
Cursing ... Ps. 10:7 631
Pride ... Ps. 17:10 633
Evil ... Ps. 50:19 653
Lies ... Ps. 63:11 659
Vanity ... Ps. 144:8, 11 707
Foolishness ... Prov. 15:2, 14 727
D. *Of regenerate, used for:*
Prayer ... 1 Sam. 1:12 321
God's Law ... Josh. 1:8 252
Praise ... Ps. 34:1 643
Wisdom ... Ps. 37:30 646
Testimony ... Eph. 6:9 1393
Confession ... Rom. 10:8-10 1334
Righteousness ... Ps. 71:15 665

Move—*to change the position*
A. *Of God's Spirit in:*
Creation ... Gen. 1:2 4
Man ... Judg. 13:25 300
Prophets ... 2 Pet. 1:21 1487
B. *Of things immovable:*
City of God ... Ps. 46:4, 5 651
Eternal kingdom ... Ps. 96:10 680

Mowing—*to cut grass*
First growth for taxes ... Amos 7:1 1021
Left on the ground ... Ps. 72:6 665

Moza—*a going forth*
1. Descendant of Judah ... 1 Chr. 2:46 466
2. Descendant of Saul ... 1 Chr. 8:36, 37 473

Mozah—*drained*
A Benjamite town ... Josh. 18:21, 26 271

Mulberry tree
Referred to by Jesus ... Luke 17:6 1219

SUBJECT REFERENCE PAGE

Myra—*a city of Lycia*

Paul changes ships here ....Acts 27:5, 6 1314

Myrrh

A. *Dried gum* (Heb., *mor) of a balsam tree, used:*
In anointing oil ....Ex. 30:23 104
As a perfume ....Ps. 45:8 651
For beauty treatment .....Esth. 2:12 578
Brought as gifts ....Matt. 2:11 1116
Given as a sedative ......Mark 15:23 1184
Used for embalming ...John 19:38, 39 1264

B. *Fragrant resin* (Heb., *lot) used:*
In commerce ...Gen. 37:25 49
As presents....Gen. 43:11 56

Myrtle—*a shrub*

Found in mountains; booths made of ....Neh. 8:15 567
Figurative of the Gospel ....Is. 41:19 813
Used symbolically .....Zech. 1:10, 11 1068

Mysia—*a province of Asia Minor*

Paul and Silas pass through ....Acts 16:7, 8 1295

Mystery—*something unknown except by divine revelation*

A. *Concerning God's:*
Secrets........Deut. 29:29 241
Providence ....Rom. 11:33-36 1336
Sovereignty ...Rom. 9:11-23 1334
Prophecies ....1 Pet. 1:10-12 1477
Predestination .....Rom. 8:29, 30 1333

B. *Concerning Christianity:*
Christ's incarnation ...1 Tim. 3:16 1427
Christ's nature ....Col. 2:2 1406
Kingdom of God ....Luke 8:10 1205
Christian faith ....1 Tim. 3:9 1427
Indwelling Christ......Col. 1:26, 27 1406
Union of all believers......Eph. 3:4-9 1388
Israel's blindness ....Rom. 11:25 1336
Lawlessness ...2 Thess. 2:7 1421
Harlot Babylon.....Rev. 17:5, 7 1533
Resurrection of saints ....1 Cor. 15:51 1360
God's completed purpose ......Rev. 10:7 1528

Mythology, referred to

Zeus ....Acts 14:12, 13 1292
Hermes ....Acts 14:12 1292
Pantheon ....Acts 17:16-23 1297
Diana ....Acts 19:24-41 1302
Castor and Pollox (Twin *Brothers)* ....Acts 28:11 1315

Myths—*speculative and philosophical fable or allegory*

Condemned ....1 Tim. 1:4 1426
Fables ....1 Tim. 4:7 1429
False ....2 Tim. 4:4 1436

N

Naam—*pleasantness*

Son of Caleb .....1 Chr. 4:15 467

Naamah—*sweet, pleasant*

1. Daughter of Lamech ......Gen. 4:19-22 10
2. Ammonite wife of Solomon; mother of King Rehoboam ...1 Kin. 14:21, 31 412
3. Town of Judah ....Josh. 15:1, 41 267

Naaman—*pleasant*

1. Son of Benjamin ....Gen. 46:21 59
2. Captain in the Syrian army ....2 Kin. 5:1-17 433
Healed of his leprosy ....2 Kin. 5:14-17 434
Referred to by Christ ....Luke 4:27 1198

Naamathite—*an inhabitant of Naamah*

Applied to Zophar, Job's friend ....Job 2:11 590

Naamites

Descendants of Naaman ....Num. 26:40 191

Naarah—*girl*

1. Wife of Ashur ....1 Chr. 4:5, 6 467
2. Town of Ephraim .....Josh. 16:7 268
Same as Naaran ......1 Chr. 7:28 473

Naarai—*pleasantness of Yahweh*

One of David's mighty men ....1 Chr. 11:37 478

Naashon (see Nahshon)

Nabal—*fool*

Wealthy sheep owner ....1 Sam. 25:2, 3 350
Refuses David's request ....1 Sam. 25:4-12 350
Abigail, wife of, appeases David's wrath against ....1 Sam. 25:13-35 350
Drunk, dies of a stroke ....1 Sam. 25:36-39 351
Widow of, becomes David's wife ....1 Sam. 25:39-42 351

Naboth—*sprout*

Owner of vineyard coveted by King Ahab ....1 Kin. 21:1-4 421
Accused falsely of blasphemy and disloyalty..........1 Kin. 21:5-16 422
Murder of, avenged ....1 Kin. 21:17-25 422

Nachon—*prepared*

Threshing floor, site of Uzzah's death ....2 Sam. 6:6, 7 364

Called:
Perez Uzzah ("breach") ....2 Sam. 6:8 364
Chidon ....1 Chr. 13:9 480

Nadab—*willing, liberal*

1. Eldest of Aaron's four sons ....Ex. 6:23 74
Takes part in affirming covenant .....Ex. 24:1, 9-12 95
Becomes priest ....Ex. 28:1 99
Consumed by fire ....Lev. 10:1-7 128
Dies childless .....Num. 3:4 162
2. Judahite ....1 Chr. 2:28, 30 466
3. Benjamite ......1 Chr. 8:30 473
4. King of Israel ....1 Kin. 14:20 412
Killed by Baasha ....1 Kin. 15:25-31 413

Naggai

Ancestor of Christ ....Luke 3:25 1195

Nahalal, Nahallal, Nahalol—*drinking place for flocks*

Village of Zebulun ....Josh. 19:10, 15 271
Assigned to Merarite Levites ....Josh. 21:35 275
Canaanites not driven from ....Judg. 1:30 284

Nahaliel—*valley of God*

Israelite camp ....Num. 21:19 186

Naham—*consolation*

Father of Keilah ...1 Chr. 4:19 467

Nahamani—*compassionate*

Returned after the exile ....Neh. 7:7 563

Naharai—*snorting*

Armor-bearer of Joab ...2 Sam. 23:37; 1 Chr. 11:39 385, 479

Nahash—*serpent*

1. King of Ammon; makes impossible demands ....1 Sam. 11:1-15 332
2. King of Ammon who treats David kindly..........2 Sam. 10:2 369
Son of, helps David ....2 Sam. 17:27-29 377
3. Father of Abigail and Zeruiah, David's half sisters ....2 Sam. 17:25 377

Nahath—*descent*

1. Edomite chief ....Gen. 36:13 48
2. Kohathite Levite ....1 Chr. 6:26 469
Called Tohu ....1 Sam. 1:1 321
3. Levite in Hezekiah's reign ....2 Chr. 31:13 530

Nahbi—*concealed*

Spy of Naphtali ...Num. 13:14 176

Nahor, Nachor—*snorting*

1. Grandfather of Abraham ....Gen. 11:24-26 18
2. Son of Terah, brother of Abraham .....Gen. 11:27 18
Marries Milcah, fathers eight sons by her and four by concubine ....Gen. 11:29 18
City of Haran.......Gen. 24:10 32
God of ....Gen. 31:53 43

SUBJECT REFERENCE PAGE

Nahshon, Naashon

Judahite leader . . . Num. 1:4, 7 159
Aaron's brother-in-law . . . Ex. 6:23 74
Ancestor of David . . . Ruth 4:20-22 317
Ancestor of Christ . . . Matt. 1:4 1115

Nahum—*full of comfort*

Inspired prophet to Judah concerning Nineveh . . . Nah. 1:1 1045

Nahum, the Book of—*a book of the Old Testament*

The awesomeness of God . . . Nah. 1:1-15 1045
The destruction of Nineveh . . . Nah. 2; 3 1048

Nail

A. *Significant uses of:*
Killing a man . . . Judg. 4:21 288
Fastening Christ to cross . . . John 20:25 1265

B. *Figurative uses of:*
Words fixed in the memory . . . Eccl. 12:11 759
Atonement for man's sin . . . Col. 2:14 1408

Nain—*pleasant*

Village south of Nazareth; Jesus raises widow's son here . . . Luke 7:11-17 1203

Naioth—*habitations*

Prophets' school in Ramah . . . 1 Sam. 19:18, 19, 22, 23 345

Naked, nakedness—*nude, nudity*

A. *Used of man's:*
Original state . . . Gen. 2:25 8
Sinful state . . . Gen. 3:7, 10, 11 8
State of grace . . . Rom. 8:35 1333
Disembodied state . . . 2 Cor. 5:3 1368

B. *Evil of:*
Strictly forbidden . . . Lev. 18:6-20 141
Brings a curse . . . Gen. 9:21-25 15
Judged by God . . . Ezek. 22:10 941

C. *Instances of:*
Noah guilty of . . . Gen. 9:21-23 15
Forbidden, to priests . . . Ex. 20:26 92
Michal rebukes David for . . . 2 Sam. 6:20-23 365

D. *Putting clothing on:*
Indicates a changed life . . . Mark 5:15 1165
Promises a reward . . . Matt. 25:34-40 1149
Takes away shame . . . Rev. 3:18 1523
Sign of true faith . . . James 2:15-17 1469

E. *Figurative of:*
Separation from God . . . Is. 20:3 791
Israel's unworthiness . . . Ezek. 16:7-22 931
Judah's spiritual adultery . . . Ezek. 16:36-38 932
God's judgment . . . Ezek. 16:39 932
Spiritual need . . . Hos. 2:9 997
Wickedness . . . Nah. 3:4, 5 1048
Needy . . . Matt. 25:36, 38 1149
God's knowledge . . . Heb. 4:13 1453
Unpreparedness . . . Rev. 16:15 1533

Name—*a word used to identify a person, animal, or thing*

A. *Determined by:*
Events of the time . . . Gen. 30:8 41
Prophetic position . . . Gen. 25:26 34
Fondness of hope . . . Gen. 29:32-35 40
Change of character . . . John 1:42 1237
Innate character . . . 1 Sam. 25:25 351
Coming events . . . Is. 8:1-4 779
Divine mission . . . Matt. 1:21 1116

B. *Of God, described as:*
Great . . . Josh. 7:9 258
Secret . . . Judg. 13:18 299
Glorious . . . Is. 63:14 835
Everlasting . . . Ps. 135:13 703
Exalted . . . Ps. 148:13 709
Holy . . . Is. 57:15 829

C. *Of God, evil acts against:*
Taken in vain . . . Ex. 20:7 90
Sworn falsely . . . Lev. 19:12 142
Lies spoken in . . . Zech. 13:3 1076
Despised . . . Mal. 1:6 1080

D. *Of God, proper attitude toward:*
Exalt . . . Ps. 34:3 643
Praise . . . Ps. 54:6 655
Love . . . Ps. 69:36 664

E. *Of Christ:*
Given before birth . . . Matt. 1:21, 23 1116
Hated by the world . . . Matt. 10:22 1129
Believers baptized in . . . Acts 2:38 1274
Miracles performed by . . . Acts 3:16 1276
Believers suffer for . . . Acts 5:41 1278
Speaking in . . . Acts 9:27, 29 1286
Gentiles called by . . . Acts 15:14, 17 1293
Final subjection to . . . Phil. 2:9, 10 1400

F. *Of believers:*
Called everlasting . . . Is. 56:5 828
Written in heaven . . . Luke 10:20 1209
Called evil by world . . . Luke 6:22 1202
Known by Christ . . . John 10:3 1251
Confessed by Christ . . . Rev. 3:5 1521
"Called by" . . . Is. 62:2 834; Rev. 3:12 1521

Names of Christ (see Christ, names of)

Naomi—*my delight*

Widow of Elimelech . . . Ruth 1:1-3 313
Returns to Bethlehem with Ruth . . . Ruth 1:14-19 313
Arranges Ruth's marriage to Boaz . . . Ruth 3; 4 314
Considers Ruth's child (Obed) her own . . . Ruth 4:16, 17 317

Naphish—*numerous*

Ishmael's eleventh son . . . Gen. 25:15 34

Naphtali—*my wrestling*

1. Son of Jacob by Bilhah . . . Gen. 30:1, 8 40
Sons of, form tribe . . . Gen. 46:24 59
Receives Jacob's blessing . . . Gen. 49:21, 28 63
2. Tribe of . . . Num. 1:42 160
Stationed last . . . Num. 2:29-31 161
Territory assigned by . . . Josh. 19:32-39 272
Canaanites not driven out by . . . Judg. 1:33 284
Barak becomes famous . . . Judg. 4:6, 14-16 288
Bravery of, praised . . . Judg. 5:18 289
Warriors of, under Gideon . . . Judg. 7:23 292
Warriors of, help David . . . 1 Chr. 12:34 480
Conquered by wars . . . 1 Kin. 15:20 413
Taken captive . . . 2 Kin. 15:29 447
Prophecy of a great light in . . . Is. 9:1-7 780
Fulfilled in Christ's ministry in . . . Matt. 4:12-16 1118

Naphtuhim

Fourth son of Mizraim; probably district around . . . Gen. 10:13 16

Narcissus

Christian in Rome . . . Rom. 16:11 1341

Nathan—*gift*

1. Son of David . . 2 Sam. 5:14 364
Mary's lineage traced through . . . Zech. 12:12 1075
2. Judahite . . . 1 Chr. 2:36 466
3. Prophet under David and Solomon . . . 1 Chr. 29:29 496
Reveals God's plan to David . . . 2 Sam. 7:2-29 365
Rebukes David's sin . . . 2 Sam. 12:1-15 370
Renames Solomon as Jedidiah . . . 2 Sam. 12:24, 25 371
Reveals Adonijah's plot . . . 1 Kin. 1:10-46 391
Sons of, in official positions . . . 1 Kin. 4:1, 2, 5 395
4. Father of Igal . . . 2 Sam. 23:36 385
5. A chief among returnees . . . Ezra 8:16 550
6. One who divorced his foreign wife . . . Ezra 10:34, 39 553

Nathanael—*God has given*

One of Christ's disciples . . . John 1:45-51 1237

Nathan-Melech—*the king has given*

An official in Josiah's reign . . . 2 Kin. 23:11 457

National duties (see Citizen, citizenship)

SUBJECT — REFERENCE — PAGE

Nations—*people under a sovereign government*

A. *Of the world:*
- Descendants of Noah's sons .... Gen. 10:32 — 16
- Originate in a person .... Gen. 19:37, 38 — 28
- Made from one blood .... Acts 17:26 — 1299
- Separated by God .... Deut. 32:8 — 244
- Inherit separate characteristics .... Gen. 25:23 — 34
- Laden with iniquity .... Is. 1:4 — 771
- Destroyed by corruption .... Lev. 18:26-28 — 141
- Exalted by righteousness .... Prov. 14:34 — 727
- Father of many nations .... Gen. 17:4 — 23
- LORD will set you high above all .... Deut. 28:1 — 238
- Subject to repentance .... Jer. 18:7-10 — 864
- Judged by God .... Gen. 15:14 — 23
- Under God's control .... Jer. 25:8-14 — 871
- Future of, revealed .... Dan. 2:27-45 — 978
- Gospel to be preached to all .... Matt. 24:14 — 1147
- Sarah shall be mother of many .... Gen. 17:16 — 24

B. *Of Israel:*
- Descendants of Abraham .... {Gen. 12:2 — 18; John 8:33, 37 — 1249}
- Designated .... Ex. 19:6 — 89
- Given blessings .... {Deut. 4:7, 8 — 211; Rom. 9:4, 5 — 1333}
- Punished by God .... Jer. 25:1-11 — 871
- Scattered among nations .... {Neh. 1:8 — 558; Luke 21:24 — 1225}
- Christ died for .... John 11:51 — 1255

C. *Of the true people of God:*
- Described as righteous .... Is. 26:2 — 795
- Born in a day .... Is. 66:8 — 838
- Accounted fruitful .... Matt. 21:43 — 1143
- Believers are .... 1 Pet. 2:9 — 1479

Nations, table of
- Record .... Gen. 10:1-32 — 15

Natural—*that which is innate and real; not artificial or man-made*

A. *Described as:*
- Physical origin .... James 1:23 — 1468
- Normal .... Rom. 1:26 — 1324
- Unregenerate .... 1 Cor. 2:14 — 1346
- Unnatural .... 2 Pet. 2:12 — 1489
- Temporal .... 1 Cor. 15:46 — 1360

B. *Contrasted with:*
- Acquired .... Rom. 11:21, 24 — 1336
- Perverted .... Rom. 1:26, 27 — 1324
- Spiritual (life) .... 1 Cor. 2:14 — 1346
- Spiritual (body) .... {1 Cor. 15:44-46} — 1360

Naturalization—*becoming a citizen of an adopted country*
- Natural level, rights of .... Acts 22:25-28 — 1306
- Spiritual level, blessings of .... Eph. 2:12-19 — 1388

Natural man
- Does not accept things of God .... 1 Cor. 2:14 — 1346
- Contrasted with spiritual .... {1 Cor. 15:44-46} — 1360

Natural religion

A. *Contents of, God's:*
- Glory .... Ps. 19:1-3 — 635
- Nature .... Rom. 1:19, 20 — 1324
- Sovereignty .... Acts 17:23-31 — 1299
- Goodness .... Acts 14:15-17 — 1293

B. *Characteristics of:*
- Original .... Rom. 1:19, 20 — 1324
- Universal .... Rom. 10:18 — 1335
- Inadequate .... Rom. 2:12-15 — 1324
- Corrupted .... Rom. 1:21-32 — 1324
- Valuable .... Dan. 5:18-23 — 983

Nature—*the essential elements resident in something*

A. *Descriptive of:*
- Right order of things .... Rom. 1:26 — 1324
- Natural sense of right .... Rom. 2:14 — 1325
- Non-existence .... Gal. 4:8 — 1381
- Man's natural depravity .... Eph. 2:3 — 1387
- Divine .... 2 Pet. 1:4 — 1487

B. *Of man's unregenerate, described as:*
- Under wrath .... Eph. 2:3 — 1387
- Source of:
  - Iniquity .... James 3:6 — 1469
  - Corruption .... 2 Pet. 2:12 — 1489

Nature, beauties of
- Reveal God's glory .... Ps. 19:1-6 — 635
- Greater than outward appearance .... Matt. 6:28-30 — 1123
- Descriptive of spiritual blessings .... Is. 35:1, 2 — 806

Navel—*the point at which the umbilical cord is attached*

A. *Used literally of:*
- Lover's appeal .... Song 7:2 — 766

B. *Used figuratively of:*
- Israel's wretched condition .... Ezek. 16:4 — 931

Navy—*ships owned by a country*
- Solomon's .... 1 Kin. 9:26 — 406
- Jehoshaphat's .... 1 Kin. 22:48 — 425

Nazarene—*a native of Nazareth*
- Jesus to be called .... Matt. 2:23 — 1117
- Descriptive of Jesus' followers .... Acts 24:5 — 1308

Nazareth

A. *Town in Galilee:*
- Considered obscure .... John 1:46 — 1237
- City of Jesus' parents .... Matt. 2:23 — 1117
- Early home of Jesus .... Luke 2:39-51 — 1194
- Jesus departs from .... Mark 1:9 — 1159
- Jesus rejected by .... Luke 4:16-30 — 1198

B. *As a title of honor descriptive of Jesus:*
- Anointed by the Spirit .... Acts 10:38 — 1287
- Risen Lord .... Acts 22:8 — 1306

Nazirite—*one especially consecrated to God*

A. *Methods of becoming, by:*
- Birth .... Judg. 13:5, 7 — 299
- Vow .... Num. 6:2 — 166

B. *Requirements of:*
- Separation .... Num. 6:4 — 166
- No:
  - Wine .... Num. 6:3, 4 — 166
  - Shaving .... Num. 6:5 — 166
  - Defilement .... Num. 6:6, 7 — 166
  - Corruption .... Amos 2:11, 12 — 1016
- Holiness .... Num. 6:8 — 166

C. *Examples of:*
- Samson .... Judg. 16:14-17 — 303
- Samuel .... 1 Sam. 1:11-28 — 321
- John the Baptist .... Luke 1:13, 15 — 1190
- Christians .... 2 Cor. 6:17 — 1369

Neah—*the settlement*
- Town in Zebulun .... Josh. 19:13 — 272

Neapolis—*new city*
- Seaport of Philippi .... Acts 16:11 — 1295

Near—*close at hand* (in place or time)

A. *Of dangers, from:*
- Prostitute .... Prov. 7:8 — 720
- Destruction .... Prov. 10:14 — 722
- God's judgment .... Joel 3:14 — 1012

B. *Of the messianic salvation, as:*
- Promised .... Is. 50:8 — 823
- Available .... Is. 51:5 — 823

C. *Of Christ's return, described by:*
- Christ .... Matt. 24:33 — 1148
- Paul .... Rom. 13:11 — 1339

Neariah—*Yahweh drives away*
1. Descendant of David .... 1 Chr. 3:22, 23 — 467
2. Simeonite captain .... 1 Chr. 4:42 — 468

Nearness of God

A. *Old Testament:*
- In sense of time .... {Is. 46:13 — 819; Zeph. 1:14 — 1057}
- In prayer .... Is. 55:6 — 828

B. *New Testament:*
- In sense of time .... {Rev. 1:1-3 — 1517; Rev. 22:10 — 1539}
- In prayer .... Phil. 4:5-9 — 1401

Nebai—*projecting*
- Leader who signs the sealed covenant .... Neh. 10:19 — 569

Nebaioth, Nebajoth
- Descendants of, from Arabian tribe .... Is. 60:7 — 832
- Eldest son of Ishmael .... Gen. 25:13 — 34

Neballat—*hard, firm*
- Postexilic town of Benjamin .... Neh. 11:31, 34 — 571

Nebat—*look*
- Father of Jeroboam .... 1 Kin. 11:26 — 408

Nebo—*height*
1. Babylonian god of literature and science .... Is. 46:1 — 818

SUBJECT REFERENCE PAGE

O

SUBJECT REFERENCE PAGE

Omnipresence—*universal presence of*

God ..... Jer. 23:23, 24 870
Christ ..... Matt. 18:20 1139
Holy Spirit ..... Ps. 139:7-12 704

Omniscience—*infinite knowledge of*

God ..... Is. 40:14 811
Christ ..... Col. 2:2, 3 1406
Holy Spirit ..... 1 Cor. 2:10-13 1346

Omri—*Yahweh apportions*

1. Descendant of Benjamin ..... 1 Chr. 7:8 472
2. Judahite ..... 1 Chr. 9:4 474
3. Chief officer of Issachar ..... 1 Chr. 27:18 493
4. King of Israel; made king by Israel's army ..... 1 Kin. 16:15, 16 414
   Prevails over Zimri and Tibni ..... 1 Kin. 16:17-23 414
   Builds Samaria ..... 1 Kin. 16:24 414
   Reigns wickedly ..... 1 Kin. 16:25-28 414

On—*stone*

1. Reubenite leader; joins Korah's rebellion ..... Num. 16:1 179
2. City of Lower Egypt; center of sun worship .. Gen. 41:45, 50 54
   Called Beth Shemesh ..... Jer. 43:13 891

See Heres

Onam—*vigorous*

1. Horite chief ... Gen. 36:23 48
2. Man of Judah ..... 1 Chr. 2:26, 28 466

Onan—*strong*

Second son of Judah; slain for failure to consummate union ..... Gen. 38:8-10 50

Oneness—*unity*

A. *Of Christ, with:*
The Father ..... John 10:30 1252
Christians ..... Heb. 2:11 1452

B. *Among Christians of:*
Baptized ..... 1 Cor. 12:13 1356
Union ..... Ezek. 37:16-24 961
Headship ..... Ezek. 34:23 958
Faith ..... Eph. 4:4-6 1390
Mind ..... Phil. 2:2 1400
Heart ..... Acts 4:32 1277

See Unity of believers

Onesimus—*useful*

Slave of Philemon converted by Paul in Rome ..... Philem. 10-17 1445
With Tychicus, carries Paul's letters to Colosse and to Philemon ..... Col. 4:7-9 1409

Onesiphorus—*profit-bearing*

Ephesian Christian commended for his service ..... 2 Tim. 1:16-18 1433

Onion—*a bulbous plant used for food*

Lusted after by Israelites ..... Num. 11:5 173

Only begotten

Of Christ's:

Incarnation ..... John 1:14 1236
Godhead ..... John 1:18 1236
Mission ..... John 3:16, 18 1239; 1 John 4:9 1498

Ono—*strong*

Town of Benjamin rebuilt by Shamed ..... 1 Chr. 8:12 473
Reinhabited by returnees ..... Ezra 2:1, 33 542

Onycha—*nail; claw; husk*

Ingredient of holy incense ..... Ex. 30:34 104

Onyx—*fingernail* (Greek)

Translation of a Hebrew word indicating a precious stone ..... Job 28:16 608; Ezek. 28:13 951
Found in Havilah ..... Gen. 2:11, 12 7
Placed in high priest's ephod ..... Ex. 28:9-20 99
Gathered by David ..... 1 Chr. 29:2 495

Open—*to unfasten; to unlock; to expose*

A. *Descriptive of miracles on:*
Earth ..... Num. 16:30, 32 180
Eyes ..... John 9:10-32 1250
Ears ..... Mark 7:34, 35 1169
Mouth ..... Luke 1:64 1192
Prison doors ... Acts 5:19, 23 1278
Death ..... 2 Kin. 4:35 433
Graves ..... Matt. 27:52 1154

B. *Descriptive of spiritual things:*
God's provision ..... Ps. 104:28 684
God's bounty ..... Mal. 3:10 1082
Christ's blood ..... Zech. 13:1 1075
Man's corruption ..... Rom. 3:13 1325
Spiritual eyesight ..... Luke 24:31, 32 1231
Door of faith .. Acts 14:27 1293
Opportunity ... 1 Cor. 16:9 1361

Ophel—*bulge, hill*

South extremity of Jerusalem's eastern hill ..... Neh. 3:15-27 559
Fortified by Jotham and Manasseh ..... 2 Chr. 27:3 526
Residence of Nethinim ..... Neh. 3:26 560

Ophir—*rich*

1. Son of Joktan ..... Gen. 10:26, 29 16
2. Land, probably in southeast Arabia, inhabited by descendants of 1 .... Gen. 10:29, 30 16
   Famous for its gold ..... 1 Chr. 29:4 495

Ophni—*the high place*

Village of Benjamin ..... Josh. 18:24 271

Ophrah—*hind*

1. Judahite ..... 1 Chr. 4:14 467
2. Town in Benjamin near Michmash ..... Josh. 18:21, 23 271
3. Town in Manasseh; home of Gideon ..... Judg. 6:11, 15 290
   Site of Gideon's burial ..... Judg. 8:32 294

Opportunity—*the best time for something*

A. *Kinds of:*
Rejected ..... Matt. 23:37 1147
Spurned ..... Luke 14:16-24 1217
Prepared ..... Acts 8:35-39 1284
Providential ..... 1 Cor. 16:9 1361
Good ..... Gal. 6:10 1383

B. *Loss of, due to:*
Unbelief ..... Num. 14:40-43 178
Neglect ..... Jer. 8:20 855
Unpreparedness ..... Matt. 24:50, 51 1148
Blindness ..... Luke 19:41, 42 1222

Oppression—*subjection to unjust hardships*

A. *Kinds of:*
Personal ..... Is. 38:14 810
National ..... Ex. 3:9 70
Economic ..... Mic. 2:1, 2 1037
Messianic ..... Is. 53:7 825
Spiritual ..... Acts 10:38 1287

B. *Those subject to:*
Widows ..... Zech. 7:10 1071
Hired servant ..... Deut. 24:14 235
Poor ..... Ps. 12:5 632
People ..... Is. 3:5 774
Soul ..... Ps. 54:3 655

C. *Evils of, bring:*
Guilt ..... Is. 59:12, 13 831
Reproach ..... Prov. 14:31 726
Poverty ..... Prov. 22:16 735
Judgment ..... Ezek. 18:12, 13 934

D. *Punishment of:*
God's judgment ..... Is. 49:26 822
Captivity ..... Is. 14:2, 4 786
Destruction of ..... Ps. 72:4 665

E. *Protection against:*
Sought in prayer ..... Deut. 26:7 236
Given by the LORD ..... Ps. 103:6 683
Secured in refuge ..... Ps. 9:9 630

F. *Agents of:*
Nations ..... Judg. 10:12 297
Enemy ..... Ps. 42:9 649; Ps. 106:42 686
Wicked ..... Ps. 55:3 655
Man ..... Ps. 119:134 698
Leaders ..... Prov. 28:16 742
Sword ..... Jer. 46:16 894; Jer. 50:16 900
Devil ..... Acts 10:38 1287
Rich ..... James 2:6 1469

Oracle—*a revelation; a wise saying*

A. *Descriptive of the high priest's ephod:*
Source of truth ..... 1 Sam. 23:9-12 348

B. *Descriptive of God's Word:*
Received by Israel ..... Acts 7:38 1281
Test of truth ... 1 Pet. 4:11 1483

Oration, orator

Character of:

Egotistical ..... Acts 12:21-23 1289
Prejudiced ..... Acts 24:1-9 1308
Inspired ..... Acts 26:1-29 1312

Orchard—*a cultivated garden or park*

Source of fruits ... Song 4:13 765
Source of nuts ... Song 6:11 766

SUBJECT REFERENCE PAGE

Palace—*a royal building*

A. *Descriptive of:*
King's house ... 2 Chr. 9:11 511
Foreign city ... Is. 25:2 794
Dwellings in Zion ... Ps. 48:3 652
Heathen king's residence ... Ezra 6:2 547

B. *Characteristics of:*
Place of luxury ... Luke 7:25 1204
Subject to destruction ... Is. 13:22 786

C. *Figurative of:*
Messiah's temple ... Ps. 45:8, 15 651
Divine workmanship ... Ps. 144:12 707
Eternal city ... Jer. 30:18 876

Palal—*judge*

Postexilic laborer ... Neh. 3:25 560

Pale—*deficient in color*

Figurative of:

Shame ... Is. 29:22 800

Palestine (see Canaan, Land of)

Palliation of sin—*excusing sin*

A. *Manifested by:*
Calling bad men good ... Mal. 2:17 1082
Describing sin as good ... Is. 5:20 777
Justifying the wicked ... Is. 5:23 777
Encouraging the wicked ... Ezek. 13:22 929
Calling the proud blessed ... Mal. 3:13-15 1083
Envying the wicked ... Ps. 73:3-15 666
Supposing God cannot see sin ... Ps. 10:11-13 631
Ignoring reproof ... Job 34:5-36 612
Sinning defiantly ... Is. 5:18, 19 777
Considering God indifferent to evil ... Zeph. 1:12 1057
Misjudging people ... Matt. 11:18, 19 1130
Questioning God's Word ... Ezek. 20:49 938

B. *Caused by:*
Moral darkness ... Matt. 6:23 1123
Man-made concepts ... Matt. 16:3-6 1136
Hypocrisy ... Matt. 23:15-23 1145
Evil heart ... Luke 16:15 1219
False teaching ... 2 Pet. 2:1-19 1487

Pallu—*distinguished*

Son of Reuben; head of tribal family ... Gen. 46:9 59; Ex. 6:14 74; Num. 26:5, 8 190

Palm of the hand

Used literally of:

Priest's hand ... Lev. 14:15, 26 136
Idol's hand ... 1 Sam. 5:4 327
Daniel's hand ... Dan. 10:10 989
Soldier's hand ... Matt. 26:67 1151

Palm tree

A. *Uses of:*
Fruit of, for food ... Joel 1:12 1008
Figures of, carved on Temple ... 1 Kin. 6:29-35 400
Branches of, for booths ... Lev. 23:40-42 148
Places of, at Elim and Jericho ... Ex. 15:27 86
Site of, for judgeship ... Judg. 4:5 288

B. *Figurative of:*
Righteous ... Ps. 92:12 679
Beauty ... Song 7:7 766
Victory ... John 12:13 1255

Palms, city of

Moabites conquer ... Judg. 3:12, 13 287

Palti—*abbreviation of Pelatiah*

1. Benjamite spy ... Num. 13:9 176
2. Man to whom Saul gives Michal, David's wife-to-be, in marriage ... 1 Sam. 25:44 351

Paltiel—*God has delivered*

1. Prince of Issachar ... Num. 34:26 202
2. Same as Palti 2 ... 2 Sam. 3:15 362

Paltite, the

Native of Beth Pelet ... Josh. 15:27 268
Home of one of David's mighty men ... 2 Sam. 23:26 385
Same referred to as the Pelonite ... 1 Chr. 11:27 478

Pamphylia—*coastal region in South Asia Minor*

People from, at Pentecost ... Acts 2:10 1273
Paul visits ... Acts 13:13 1291
John Mark returns home from ... Acts 13:13 1291; Acts 15:38 1294
Paul preaches in cities of ... Acts 14:24, 25 1293
Paul sails past ... Acts 27:5 1314

Pan—*thin plate*

Offering in ... Lev. 2:5 120
Cooking ... Lev. 6:21 125
Pouring ... 2 Sam. 13:9 372

Panic—*fright*

A. *Among Israelites:*
At the Red Sea ... Ex. 14:10-12 83
Before the Philistines ... 1 Sam. 4:10 326
Of Judah before Israel ... 2 Kin. 14:12 445

B. *Among nations:*
Egyptians ... Ex. 14:27 85
Philistines ... 1 Sam. 14:22 336
Syrians ... 2 Kin. 7:6, 7 437
Ammonites and Moabites ... 2 Chr. 20:22-25 520

Paper—*sheet*

Writing material ... 2 John 12 1502

See Papyrus

Paphos—*capital of Cyprus*

Paul blinds Elymas ... Acts 13:6-13 1291

Papyrus—*a tall marsh plant growing in the Nile river region*

Referred to as bulrush in ... Ex. 2:3 69
Cannot grow without marsh ... Job 8:11 595

See Paper

Parables—*an earthly story with a heavenly meaning*

A. *Descriptive of:*
Prophecy ... Num. 23:7-24 188
Discourse ... Job 27:1-23 607
Wise saying ... Prov. 26:7, 9 739
Prophetic message ... Ezek. 17:1-10 933
Illustration (especially true of Christ's) ... Matt. 13:18 1132

B. *Of Christ, characteristics of:*
Numerous ... Mark 4:33, 34 1164
Illustrative ... Luke 12:16-21 1214

Meaning of:
Self-evident ... Mark 12:1-12 1175
Unknown ... Matt. 13:36 1133
Explained ... Luke 8:9-15 1205
Prophetic ... Luke 21:29-36 1225

C. *Design of:*
Bring under conviction ... 2 Sam. 12:1-6 370
Teach a spiritual truth ... Is. 5:1-6 775
Illustrate a point ... Luke 10:25-37 1209
Fulfill prophecy ... Matt. 13:34, 35 1133
Conceal truth from the unbelieving ... Matt. 13:10-16 1132

D. *Of Christ, classification of:*

Concerning God's love in Christ:
Lost sheep ... Luke 15:4-7 1217
Lost money ... Luke 15:8-10 1218
Prodigal son ... Luke 15:11-32 1218
Hidden treasure ... Matt. 13:44 1133
Pearl of great price ... Matt. 13:45, 46 1133

Concerning Israel:
Barren fig tree ... Luke 13:6-9 1215
Two sons ... Matt. 21:28-32 1143
Wicked husbandman ... Matt. 21:33-46 1143

Concerning Christianity (the Gospel) in this age:
New cloth ... Matt. 9:16 1126
New wine ... Matt. 9:17 1126
Sower ... Matt. 13:3-8 1132
Tares ... Matt. 13:24-30 1133
Mustard seed ... Matt. 13:31, 32 1133
Leaven ... Matt. 13:33 1133
Net ... Matt. 13:47-50 1133
Great supper ... Luke 14:16-24 1217
Seed growing secretly ... Mark 4:26-29 1164

Concerning salvation:
House built on the rock ... Matt. 7:24-27 1125
Pharisee and publican ... Luke 18:9-14 1220
Two debtors ... Luke 7:36-50 1204
Marriage of the king's son ... Matt. 22:1-14 1143

Concerning Christian life:
Lamp under a basket ... Matt. 5:15, 16 1120
Unmerciful servant ... Matt. 18:23-35 1139
Friend at midnight ... Luke 11:5-13 1211

SUBJECT REFERENCE PAGE

Partake—continued

C. *Of spiritual things:*
Divine nature ....2 Pet. 1:4 1487
Christ ....Heb. 3:14 1452
Holy Spirit ....Heb. 6:4 1455
Heavenly calling ....Heb. 3:1 1452
Grace ....Phil. 1:7 1398
Gospel ....1 Cor. 9:23 1353
Spiritual blessings .....Rom. 11:17 1336
Future glory ...1 Pet. 5:1 1483
Promise of salvation .....Eph. 3:6 1388
Holiness ......Heb. 12:10 1462
Inheritance ....Col. 1:12 1406

Partakers

A. *Of physical things:*
Sacrifices .....1 Cor. 10:18 1354
Suffering ......2 Cor. 1:7 1366

B. *Of spiritual things:*
Holiness ......Heb. 12:10 1462
Communion .....1 Cor. 10:16, 17 1354
Spiritual things ....Rom. 15:27 1340
Inheritance ....Col. 1:12 1406

Parthians—*inhabitants of Parthia*

Some present at Pentecost ....Acts 2:1, 9 1273

Partiality—*favoritism*

A. *Manifested:*
In marriages Gen. 29:30 40
Among brothers ......Gen. 43:30, 34 56
Between parents and children ......Gen. 25:28 34
In social life ...James 2:1-4 1469

B. *Inconsistent with:*
Household harmony .....Gen. 37:4-35 49
Justice in law ....Lev. 19:15 142

Favoritism in:
Ministry ......1 Tim. 5:21 1429
Restriction of salvation .....Acts 10:28-35 1287

C. *Consistent with:*
Choice of workers ......Acts 15:36-40 1294
Estimate of friends ....Phil. 2:19-22 1400
God's predestination ......Rom. 9:6-24 1333

See Favoritism

Partition—*a dividing wall*

In the sanctuary ..1 Kin. 6:21 398
Between people ...Eph. 2:11-14 1388

Partner—*an associate in*

Crime ....Prov. 29:24 743
Business ....Luke 5:7, 10 1200
Christian work ..2 Cor. 8:23 1371; Philem. 17 1445

Partridge—*a wild bird meaning "the caller"* (in Heb.)

Hunted in mountains ....1 Sam. 26:20 352
Figurative of ill-gotten riches ....Jer. 17:11 863

Paruah—*sprouting*

Father of Jehoshaphat, an officer of Solomon ....1 Kin. 4:17 397

Parvaim

Unidentified place providing gold for Solomon's Temple ....2 Chr. 3:6 503

Parzites

Descendants of Perez ....Num. 26:20 191

Pasach—*divider*

Asherite ....1 Chr. 7:33 473

Pasdammim—*boundary of bloodshed*

Philistines gathered here ....1 Chr. 11:13 478

Paseah—*lame*

1. Judahite ....1 Chr. 4:12 467
2. Head of a family of Nethinim .....Ezra 2:43, 49 544
One of, repairs walls ....Neh. 3:6 559
3. A family of temple servants.......Neh. 7:46, 51 563

Pashur, Pashhur—*free*

1. Official opposing Jeremiah ....Jer. 21:1 867; Jer. 38:1-13 885
Descendants of, returnees ......Neh. 11:12 570
2. Priest who put Jeremiah in jail ....Jer. 20:1-6 866
3. Father of Gedaliah, Jeremiah's opponent ....Jer. 38:1 885
4. Priestly family of returnees ....Ezra 2:38 544
Members of, divorced foreign wives ....Ezra 10:22 553
5. Priest who signs the covenant ....Neh. 10:3 569

Passing away—*ceasing to exist*

A. *Things subject to:*
Our days ......Ps. 90:9 678
Old things .....2 Cor. 5:17 1368
World's fashion ......1 Cor. 7:31 1352
World's lust ...1 John 2:17 1496
Heaven and earth ....2 Pet. 3:10 1489

B. *Things not subject to:*
Christ's words ....Luke 21:33 1225
Christ's dominion ....Dan. 7:14 986

Passion—*suffering*

A. *Descriptive of:*
Christ's sufferings ....Acts 1:3 1271
Lusts ....Rom. 1:26 1324

B. *As applied* (theologically) *to Christ's sufferings:*
Predicted .....Is. 53:1-12 825
Portrayed visibly ....Mark 14:3-8 1180
Preached .....Acts 3:12-18 1276; 1 Pet. 1:10-12 1477

Passover—*a Jewish festival commemorative of the exodus from Egypt*

A. *Features concerning:*
Commemorative of the tenth plague ....Ex. 12:3-28 80
Necessity of blood applied ....Ex. 12:7 80
To be repeated annually ....Ex. 12:24-27 80

B. *Observances of:*
At Sinai ....Num. 9:1-14 171
At the conquest .....Josh. 5:10-12 256
By Christ ......Matt. 26:18, 19 1150

C. *Typical of the Lord's death* (the Lord's Supper):
Lamb without blemish ......1 Pet. 1:19 1479
One of their own ....Ex. 12:5 80; Heb. 2:14, 17 1452
Lamb chosen ....Ex. 12:3 80; 1 Pet. 2:4 1479
Slain at God's appointed time ....Ex. 12:6 80; Acts 2:23 1273
Christ is ....1 Cor. 5:7 1348

See Lamb of God, the

Password—*a secret word used to identify friends*

Used by Gileadites ......Judg. 12:5, 6 298

Pastor—*shepherd*

To perfect the saints ....Eph. 4:11, 12 1390
Appointed by God ....Jer. 3:15 848
Unfaithful ones are punished ....Jer. 22:22 868

See Shepherd

Pasture—*a place for grazing animals*

A. *Used literally of places for:*
Cattle to feed ....Gen. 47:4 59
Wild animals to feed ....Is. 32:14 804
God's material blessings .....Ps. 65:11-13 661

B. *Used figuratively of:*
Restoration and peace ....Ezek. 34:13-15 958
True Israel ....Ps. 95:7 680
Kingdom of God ....Is. 49:9, 10 821
Kingdom of Israel ....Jer. 25:36 872
Gospel ....Is. 30:23 802
Abundant provision for salvation .....Ezek. 45:15 969

C. *Of the true Israel* (the Church), *described as:*
God's people ..Ps. 100:3 681
Provided for ...John 10:9 1251
Purchased .....Ps. 74:1, 2 667
Thankful ......Ps. 79:13 672
Scattered by false shepherds ....Jer. 23:1 868

See Shepherd

Patara—*a port of Lycia in Asia Minor*

Paul changes ships here............Acts 21:1, 2 1303

Path—*a walk; manner of life*

A. *Of the wicked:*
Brought to nothing ......Job 6:18 593
Becomes dark ....Job 24:13 606
Is crooked .....Is. 59:8 831
Leads to death ....Prov. 2:18 715
Filled with wickedness ...Prov. 1:15, 16 714
Is destructive ....Is. 59:7 831
Followed by wicked rulers ....Is. 3:12 774

SUBJECT REFERENCE PAGE

SUBJECT REFERENCE PAGE

Pen

Figurative of tongue ..... Ps. 45:1 650
False ..... Jer. 8:8 854
Not preferred ..... 3 John 13 1506

Penalties—*punishment inflicted for wrongdoing*

A. *For sexual sins:*
Adultery—death ..... Lev. 20:10 143
Incest—death ..... Lev. 20:11-14 143
Sodomy—destruction ..... Gen. 19:13, 17, 24 28

B. *For bodily sins:*
Drunkenness—exclusion ..... 1 Cor. 5:11 1349; 1 Cor. 6:9, 10 1349
Murder—death ..... Ex. 21:12-15 92
Persecution—God's judgment ..... Matt. 23:34-36 1147

C. *For following heathen ways:*
Human sacrifice—death ..... Lev. 20:2-5 142
Witchcraft—death ..... Ex. 22:18 93
Idolatry—death ..... Ex. 22:20 93

D. *For internal sins:*
Ingratitude punished ..... Prov. 17:13 729
Pride—abomination ..... Prov. 16:5 728
Unbelief—exclusion ..... Num. 20:12 183
Lying—curse ..... Jer. 23:10 869; Zech. 5:3 1070
Blasphemy—death ..... Lev. 24:14-16, 23 149

Peninnah—*coral, pearl*

Elkanah's second wife ..... 1 Sam. 1:2, 4 321

Penitence—*state of being sorry for one's sins*

A. *Results of:*
Forgiveness ..... Ps. 32:5, 6 642
Restoration ..... Job 22:23-29 605
Renewed fellowship ..... Ps. 51:12, 13 654

B. *Examples of:*
Job ..... Job 42:1-6 619
David ..... Ps. 51:1-19 653
Josiah ..... 2 Kin. 22:1, 19 455
Tax collector ..... Luke 18:13 1220
Thief on the cross ..... Luke 23:39-42 1229

C. *Elements:*
Acknowledgment of sin ..... Job 33:27, 28 612; Luke 15:18, 21 1218
Plea for mercy ..... Luke 18:13 1220
Broken heart ..... Ps. 34:18 643; Ps. 51:17 654
Confession ..... 1 John 1:9 1494

See Repentance

Pentecost—*fiftieth* (day)

A. *In the Old Testament:*
Called "the Feast of Weeks" ..... Ex. 34:22, 23 108
Marks completion of barley harvest ..... Lev. 23:15, 16 148
Called "Feast of Harvest" ..... Ex. 23:16 94
Work during, prohibited ..... Lev. 23:21 148
Two loaves presented ..... Lev. 23:17, 20 148
Other sacrifices prescribed ..... Lev. 23:18 148
Offerings given by Levites ..... Deut. 16:10-14 228
Time of consecration ..... Deut. 16:12, 13 228
Observed during Solomon's time ..... 2 Chr. 8:12, 13 510

See Feasts, Hebrew

B. *In the New Testament:*
Day of the Spirit's coming; the formation of the Christian Church ..... Acts 2:1-47 1273
Paul desires to attend ..... Acts 20:16 1303
Paul plans to stay in Ephesus until ..... 1 Cor. 16:8 1361

Penuel—*the face of God*

1. Place east of Jordan; site of Jacob's wrestling with angel ..... Gen. 32:24-31 44
Inhabitants of, slain by Gideon ..... Judg. 8:8, 9, 17 292
Later refortified by Jeroboam ..... 1 Kin. 12:25 409
2. Judahite ..... 1 Chr. 4:4 467
3. Benjamite ..... 1 Chr. 8:25 473

Penury—*extreme poverty; destitution*

Widow's gift in, commended ..... Luke 21:1-4 1224

People

Found among Israel ..... Deut. 7:6 217
Not limited to Israel ..... Rom. 2:28, 29 1325
Called the remnant ..... Is. 11:10, 11, 16 784
Gentiles included in ..... Is. 19:25 791; Is. 65:1 836; Rom. 15:10, 11 1340
Became such by covenant ..... Jer. 31:31-34 878
Secured through the Messiah ..... Ezek. 34:22-31 958
Accomplished by Christ's death ..... Matt. 1:21 1116; Luke 1:68, 77 1192
Separated from others ..... 2 Cor. 6:16-18 1369; Rev. 18:4 1535
God's true Church ..... 1 Pet. 2:9, 10 1479
All nations included in ..... Rev. 5:9 1523; Rev. 7:9 1525
God's eternal people ..... Rev. 21:3 1538

People of the land—*the conservative element of the population consisting mainly of landholders*

The influence of ..... 2 Kin. 11:13-15 443
Taxed ..... 2 Kin. 23:35 458

Peor—*opening*

1. Mountain of Moab opposite Jericho ..... Num. 23:28 189
Israel's camp seen from ..... Num. 24:2 189
2. Moabite god called Baal of Peor ..... Num. 25:3, 5, 18 190
Israelites punished for worship of ..... Num. 31:16 197

Perceive, perception—*knowledge derived through one of the senses*

Outward circumstances ..... 2 Sam. 12:19 371; Acts 27:10 1314
Outward intentions ..... John 6:15 1244
Intuition ..... 1 Sam. 3:8 324; John 4:19 1241
Unusual manifestations ..... 1 Sam. 12:17, 18 333; Acts 10:34 1287
Spiritual insight ..... Neh. 6:12 562; Acts 14:9 1292
God's blessings ..... Neh. 6:16 562
Bitter experience ..... Eccl. 1:17 749; Eccl. 3:22 752
Obvious implication ..... Matt. 21:45 1143; Luke 20:19 1223
God's revelation ..... Gal. 2:9 1380; 1 John 3:16 1497
Internal consciousness ..... Luke 8:46 1206; Acts 8:23 1284

Perdition—*the state of the damned; destruction*

Judas Iscariot ..... John 17:12 1261
Lost ..... Phil. 1:28 1400
Antichrist ..... 2 Thess. 2:3 1421; Rev. 17:8, 11 1533

Peres—*to split into pieces*

Sentence of doom ..... Dan. 5:28 984

Peresh—*dung*

Man of Manasseh ..... 1 Chr. 7:16 472

Perez—*a breach*

One of Judah's twin sons by Tamar ..... Gen. 38:24-30 50
Numbered among Judah's sons ..... Gen. 46:12 59
Founder of a tribal family ..... Num. 26:20, 21 191
Descendants of, notable in later times ..... 1 Chr. 27:3 493
Ancestor of David and Christ ..... Ruth 4:12-18 317

Perezites

Descendants of Perez ..... Num. 26:20 191

Perfection—*the extreme degree of excellence; pure; complete; mature*

A. *Applied to natural things:*
Day ..... Prov. 4:18 718
Gold ..... 2 Chr. 4:21 506
Weights ..... Deut. 25:15 236
Beauty ..... Ezek. 28:12 951
Offering ..... Lev. 22:21 145

B. *Applied to spiritual graces:*
Patience ..... James 1:4 1468
Love ..... Col. 3:14 1408
Holiness ..... 2 Cor. 7:1 1369
Praise ..... Matt. 21:16 1141
Faith ..... 1 Thess. 3:10 1415
Good works ..... Heb. 13:21 1464
Unity ..... John 17:23 1262
Strength ..... 2 Cor. 12:9 1374

C. *Means of:*
God ..... 1 Pet. 5:10 1483
Christ ..... Heb. 10:14 1458
Holy Spirit ..... Gal. 3:3 1380
God's Word ..... 2 Tim. 3:16, 17 1436
Ministry ..... Eph. 4:11, 12 1390
Sufferings ..... Heb. 2:10 1452

D. *Stages of:*
Eternally accomplished ..... Heb. 10:14 1458
Objective goal ..... Matt. 5:48 1121
Subjective process ..... 2 Cor. 7:1 1369
Daily activity ..... 2 Cor. 13:9 1375

SUBJECT REFERENCE PAGE

B. *Times of:*
Daily ....Ps. 72:15 666
Continually ...Ps. 71:6 665
Seven times daily ....Ps. 119:164 699
All the day ....Ps. 35:28 645
At midnight ....Ps. 119:62 696; Acts 16:25 1295
While I live ....Ps. 146:2 708

Praise of men

A. *Worthy:*
From another ......Prov. 27:2 739
For:
Faithfulness ....Prov. 31:28 745
Obedience ....Rom. 13:3 1337
Works ....Prov. 31:31 745

B. *Unworthy for:*
Wicked ....Prov. 28:4 740
Disorder ....1 Cor. 11:17, 22 1355
Self-seeking ...John 12:43 1256

Prating—*foolish babbling*

Descriptive of:
Fool ....Prov. 10:8, 10 722
Diotrephes ....3 John 10 1506

Prayer—*a request to God*

A. *Kinds of:*
Secret ....Matt. 6:6 1121
Family ....Acts 10:2, 30 1286
Group ....Matt. 18:20 1139
Public ....1 Cor. 14:14-17 1358

B. *Parts of:*
Adoration .....Dan. 4:34, 35 981
Confession .....1 John 1:9 1494
Supplication ....1 Tim. 2:1-3 1426
Intercession ....James 5:14, 15 1473
Thanksgiving ....Phil. 4:6 1401

C. *Personal requirements of:*
Purity of heart ....Ps. 66:18, 19 662
Believing ....Matt. 21:22 1143
In Christ's name ....John 14:13 1258
According to God's will ....1 John 5:14 1499

D. *General requirements of:*
Forgiving spirit ....Matt. 6:14 1121
Simplicity .....Matt. 6:5, 6 1121
Humility and repentance ...Luke 18:10-14 1220
Unity of believers .....Matt. 18:19, 20 1138
Tenacity ....Luke 18:1-8 1220
Importunity ...Luke 11:5-8 1211
Intensity ....Matt. 7:7-11 1123
Confident expectation ...Mark 11:24 1175
Without many words ....Matt. 6:7 1121
Unceasingly ...1 Thess. 5:17 1416

E. *Answers refused, because of:*
Sin ....Ps. 66:18 662
Selfishness ....James 4:3 1471
Doubt ....James 1:5-7 1468
Disobedience ....Prov. 28:9 742
Inhumanity ....Prov. 21:13 733
Pride ....Luke 18:11, 12, 14 1220

F. *Posture for:*
Standing ....Neh. 9:5 567
Kneeling ....Ezra 9:5 551
Sitting ....1 Chr. 17:16-27 484
Bowing ....Ex. 34:8 107

Hands uplifted ......1 Tim. 2:8 1426

Prayer meetings

In the upper room ....Acts 1:13, 14 1272
In a house ....Acts 12:5-17 1289
By a river ....Acts 16:13 1295
On a beach ....Acts 21:5 1303

Prayers of Christ

A. *Their nature:*
Adoration ......Matt. 11:25-27 1130
Intercession ...John 17:1-26 1261
Thanksgiving ....John 11:41, 42 1255

B. *Their great occasions:*
At His baptism ......Luke 3:21, 22 1195
Before selecting the apostles ......Luke 6:12-16 1202
At His transfiguration ....Luke 9:28, 29 1207
In Gethsemane ....Matt. 26:36-42 1150

C. *Their times and places:*
Early in morning .....Mark 1:35 1161
In secret ....Luke 5:16 1200; Luke 9:18 1207
With others ....Luke 11:1 1211
On mountain ..Matt. 14:23 1134

Preach, preaching—*proclaiming the Gospel*

A. *Of the Gospel:*
Necessity of ...1 Cor. 9:16 1353
Without charge ....1 Cor. 9:18 1353
Extent of, to all ....Col. 1:25 1406
Only one ......Gal. 1:8, 9 1378
Centers in the Cross ....1 Cor. 1:23 1345
Preacher's importance in ....Rom. 10:14, 15 1335

B. *Attitudes toward:*
Accepted ....Luke 11:32 1212
Rejected ....2 Pet. 2:4, 5 1487
Not perfected by ....Heb. 4:2 1452
Perverted .....Gal. 1:6-9 1378
Contentious about ....Phil. 1:15-18 1398
Counted foolishness ...1 Cor. 1:18-21 1345
Ridiculed .....Acts 17:16-18 1297
Not ashamed of ....Rom. 1:15, 16 1321

Preacher—*one who proclaims publically*

Author of Ecclesiastes .....Eccl. 1:1, 2 749
Causes to hear ...Rom. 10:14 1335
Paul, speaking of himself ......1 Tim. 2:7 1426; 2 Tim. 1:11 1433
Noah, of righteousness ....2 Pet. 2:5 1487

Precepts—*specific charges; commandments*

God's:
Commanded ......Heb. 9:19 1457
Corrupted ....Matt. 15:9 1135
Kept ....Ps. 119:56-69 696
Sought ....Ps. 119:40-94 696
Not forgotten .....Ps. 119:93, 141 697
Loved ....Ps. 119:159 699
Source of understanding ....Ps. 119:100, 104 697

See Traditions

Precious—*something extremely valuable*

A. *Applied to spiritual things:*
Wisdom ....Prov. 3:13, 15 716
One's life ....1 Sam. 26:21 352; 2 Kin. 1:13, 14 430
Redemption of a soul ....Ps. 49:8 652
God's thoughts to us ....Ps. 139:17 705
Death of God's people ....Ps. 72:14 666
Christ ....Is. 28:16 798
Christ's blood ....1 Pet. 1:19 1479
Faith ....2 Pet. 1:1 1487
Promises ....2 Pet. 1:4 1487
Trial of faith ...1 Pet. 1:7 1477

B. *Applied figuratively to:*
Knowledge ....Prov. 20:15 732
Sons of Zion ..Lam. 4:2 913
Rewards ....1 Cor. 3:12-14 1346
Final harvest ..James 5:7 1471
Worldly pomp ....Rev. 17:4 1533
Heaven's glory ....Rev. 21:11, 19 1538

Precious promises

A. *To the troubled by:*
Doubts ....Ps. 73:1-28 666
Afflictions ....Ps. 34:1-22 643
Persecution ...Matt. 5:11, 12 1120
Anxiety ....Phil. 4:6 1401
Temptation ....1 Cor. 10:13 1354
Infirmities .....2 Cor. 12:7-10 1374
Discipline .....Heb. 12:3-13 1462

B. *To the sorrowful over:*
Death ....1 Thess. 4:13-18 1416
Sickness .....James 5:13-16 1473
Their sins .....Ps. 32:1-11 642
Disappointment ....Rom. 8:28 1333

C. *To those troubled by:*
World ....1 John 2:15-17 1496
Flesh ....Gal. 5:16-18 1383
Satan ....Luke 22:31, 32 1226
Worry ....Matt. 6:31-34 1123
Sin ....James 1:12-15 1468
Pride ....1 Pet. 5:5-7 1483

D. *To the active Christian in his:*
Giving ....Mal. 3:10 1082
Zeal ....Phil. 4:13 1402
Soul winning ....James 5:20 1473
Fruitfulness ...John 7:38, 39 1248
Graces ....2 Pet. 1:5-11 1487
Prayers ....James 5:16 1473
Perseverance ....Gal. 6:9 1383
Watchfulness ....Eph. 6:10-20 1393
Assurance .....Rom. 8:32-39 1333
Ministry ....Ps. 138:8 704

Predestination—*God's eternal plan*

A. *Described as:*
"Purpose" ......Rom. 8:28 1333
"Prepared beforehand" ..Rom. 9:23 1334
"Foreknowledge" ....Acts 2:23 1273
"Foreknew" ....Rom. 8:29 1333
"Ordained" ...Acts 13:48 1292
"Appointed" ..Acts 22:10 1306
"Determined" ....Luke 22:22 1226
"Foreseeing" ....Gal. 3:8 1381
"Before time began" ....2 Tim. 1:9 1433

B. *Determined by God's:*
Counsel ....Acts 2:23 1273
Foreknowledge ....Acts 2:23 1273

SUBJECT REFERENCE PAGE

Put—continued
2. Warriors (Libyans) allied with Egypt ....Ezek. 27:10 948
Same as Libyans in ....Jer. 46:9 894

Puteoli—*little wells*
Seaport of Italy ...Acts 28:13 1315

Puthites
Descendants of Caleb ....1 Chr. 2:50, 53 466

Putiel—*God enlightens*
Father-in-law of Eleazar ....Ex. 6:25 74

Puvah, Pua, Puah—*utterance*
1. Issachar's second son ....Gen. 46:13 59
Descendants of Punites ......Num. 26:23 191
2. Father of Tola, Israel's judge ....Judg. 10:1 296

Q

Quail—*a small bird*
Sent to satisfy hunger ....Ex. 16:12, 13 87
Sent as a judgment ....Num. 11:31-34 175

Quarantine—*restricted in public contacts*
Required of lepers ....Lev. 13:45, 46 135
Miriam consigned ....Num. 12:14-16 175
Imposed under King Azariah ....2 Kin. 15:1-5 446

Quarrel—*a dispute*
A. *Caused by:*
Flesh ....James 4:1, 2 1471
Hatred ....Mark 6:18, 19 1166
B. *Productive of:*
Friction ....Matt. 20:20-24 1140
Separation ....Acts 15:37-40 1294
C. *Cured by:*
Gentleness ....2 Tim. 2:24-26 1434
Forgiveness ...Col. 3:13 1408
Unity of mind ....Phil. 2:3, 4 1400
See Contention; Strife

Quartus—*fourth*
Christian at Corinth ....Rom. 16:23 1341

Queen—*a king's wife*
A. *Applied to:*
Queen regent ....1 Kin. 10:1-13 406
Heathen deity ....Jer. 44:15-30 893
Mystical Babylon ......Rev. 18:7 1535
B. *Names of:*
Of Sheba ......1 Kin. 10:1 406
Vashti ....Esth. 1:9 577
Esther ....Esth. 5:3 581
Of Heaven ....Jer. 7:18 853
Of the South ..Matt. 12:42 1131

Quench—*to extinguish*
A. *Applied literally to:*
Fire ....Num. 11:2 173
Thirst ....Ps. 104:11 684
B. *Applied figuratively to:*
Love ....Song 8:7 767
God's wrath ...2 Kin. 22:17 456
Spirit ....1 Thess. 5:19 1416
Persecution ...Heb. 11:34 1462

Question—*an inquiry*
Asked by:
Wicked ....Matt. 22:16-40 1144; John 18:33-38 1263
Sincere ....Matt. 18:1-6 1138; Acts 1:6 1272
Jesus ....Matt. 22:41-45 1144

Quietness—*noiselessness*
A. *Descriptive of:*
People ....Judg. 18:7, 27 304
City ....2 Kin. 11:20 443
Nation ....2 Chr. 14:1, 5 515
Earth ....Is. 14:7 786
B. *Realization of:*
Predicted .....Is. 32:17, 18 804
Comes from God ....1 Chr. 22:9 489
Preferred ......Prov. 17:1 729
To be sought ..1 Thess. 4:11 1416
Undeniable ....Acts 19:36 1302
Commanded ..2 Thess. 3:12 1422
Obtainable ....Ps. 131:2 702
Very valuable .....1 Pet. 3:4 1480
Rewarded .....Is. 30:15 802

Quirinius
Roman governor of Syria ....Luke 2:1-4 1193

Quitters, quitting
Unworthy ....Luke 9:62 1208
Believers should not ....Gal. 6:9 1383; 2 Thess. 3:13 1422
Press on ....Phil. 3:12-14 1401
Continue ....2 Tim. 3:14 1436

Quiver—*a case for carrying arrows*
Used by:
Hunters ....Gen. 27:3 36
Soldiers ....Job 39:23 617; Is. 22:6 792
Figurative of:
Children..........Ps. 127:5 701
Messiah ....Is. 49:2 821

Quotations
A. *Introduced by:*
"The Holy Spirit" ....Acts 28:25 1315
"As it is written" ......Rom. 15:9 1340
"The Scripture" ....Gal. 3:8 1381
Old Testament writer ....Rom. 10:5-20 1334
B. *Purposes of:*
Cite fulfillment ....Matt. 1:22, 23 1116
Confirm a truth ....Matt. 4:4 1118
Prove a doctrine ......Rom. 4:5-8 1327
Show the true meaning .....Acts 2:25-36 1273

R

Raamah—*trembling*
Son of Cush ......Gen. 10:6, 7 16
Father of Sheba and Dedan ....Gen. 10:7 16
Noted traders .....Ezek. 27:22 950

Raamiah—*Yahweh has thundered*
Postexilic chief ...Neh. 7:7 563
Same as Reelaiah ....Ezra 2:2 542

Raamses, Rameses—*Ra* (Egyptian sun god) *created him*
Treasure city built by Hebrew slaves ....Ex. 1:11 68

Rabbah, Rabbath—*great*
1. Town of Judah ....Josh. 15:60 268
2. Capital of Ammon ....Amos 1:14 1016
Bedstead of Og here ....Deut. 3:11 211
On Gad's boundary ....Josh. 13:25 266
Besieged by Joab ....2 Sam. 12:26 371
Defeated and enslaved by David ....2 Sam. 12:29-31 371
Destruction of, foretold ......Jer. 49:2, 3 897

Rabbi, Rabboni—*my master*
A. *Applied to:*
John the Baptist ....John 3:26 1241
Jesus Christ ....John 3:2 1239; John 1:38, 49 1237
B. *Significance of:*
Coveted title ...Matt. 23:6, 7 1145
Forbidden by Christ ....Matt. 23:8 1145
Expressive of imperfect faith ....Mark 14:45 1181; John 20:16 1265

Rabbith—*multitude*
Frontier town of Issachar ....Josh. 19:20 272

Rabboni—*Aramaic form of Rabbi*
Mary addresses Christ as ....John 20:16 1265

Rabmag—*head of the Magi*
Title applied to Nergal-Sharezer .Jer. 39:3, 13 887

Rabsaris—*head chamberlain*
Title applied to:
Assyrian officials sent by Sennacherib .....2 Kin. 18:17 450
Babylonian Nebushasban ....Jer. 39:13 887
Babylonian prince ....Jer. 39:3 887

Rabshakeh—*Head of the cupbearers*
Sent ....2 Kin. 18:17 450
King of Assyria sent ....Is. 36:2 806
And told him the words of ....Is. 36:22 808
Hear all the words ....2 Kin. 19:4 452

Raca—*a term of insult*
Use of, forbidden by Christ ....Matt. 5:21, 22 1120

Race, Christian
Requirements of:
Discipline ....1 Cor. 9:24-27 1353
Patience ....Eccl. 9:11 757
Steadfastness .....Gal. 5:7 1382

SUBJECT | REFERENCE | PAGE

SUBJECT REFERENCE PAGE

B. *Used figuratively of:*
Wicked .... Prov. 10:7 722
Foolish wife ... Prov. 12:4 724

Rowing—*to navigate a boat with oars*

Against odds ..... Jon. 1:13 1030
With much labor .... Mark 6:48 1167

Royal—*belonging to a king*

A. *Used literally of:*
King's children ...... 2 Kin. 11:1 442
Robes of royalty .... Esth. 6:8 582
City of a king .... 2 Sam. 12:26 371

B. *Used spiritually of:*
True Israel ..... Is. 62:3 834
True Church ... 1 Pet. 2:9 1479

Ruby—*a valuable gem* (red pearl)

Very valuable .... Prov. 3:15 716
Wisdom more valuable than .... Job 28:18 608
Good wife above price of .... Prov. 31:10 745
Reddish color ..... Lam. 4:7 913

Rudder—*a steering apparatus*

Literally .... Acts 27:40 1315
Figuratively .... James 3:4 1469

Rudeness—*discourtesy*

Shown toward:

Christ .... Matt. 26:67, 68 1151
Paul .... Acts 23:2 1307

Rue—*a pungent perennial shrub*

Tithed by Pharisees .... Luke 11:42 1212

Rufus—*red-haired*

1. Son of Simeon of Cyrene .... Mark 15:21 1184
2. Christian of Rome .... Rom. 16:13 1341
Probably the same as 1.

Rule—*to govern*

A. *Of natural things:*
Sun and moon .... Gen. 1:16, 18 4
Sea .... Ps. 89:9 676

B. *Among men:*
Man over woman .... Gen. 3:16 9
King over people .... Ezra 4:20 546
Diligent over the lazy .... Prov. 12:24 725
Servant over a son .... Prov. 17:2 729
Rich over poor .... Prov. 22:7 734
Servants over a people .... Neh. 5:15 561

C. *Of the Messiah:*
Promised ...... Zech. 6:13 1071
Victorious ..... Ps. 110:2 689
Announced .... Matt. 2:6 1116
Established .... Rev. 12:5 1529
Described ..... Rev. 2:27 1521

Ruler—*one who governs*

A. *Good characteristics of:*
Upholding the good .... Rom. 13:3 1337
Believing ...... Matt. 9:18, 23 1127
Chosen by God .... 2 Sam. 7:8 366

B. *Bad characteristics of:*
Men-pleasers .. John 12:42, 43 1256
Ignorant .... Acts 3:17 1276
Hostile .... Acts 4:26 1277
Loving bribes .... Hos. 4:18 999

C. *Respect toward:*
Commanded .. Ex. 22:28 93
Illustrated ..... Acts 23:5 1307

Ruler of this world

Satan thus called .... John 14:30 1258
To be cast out .... John 12:31 1256
Is judged .... John 16:11 1259
Source of evil ..... Eph. 2:2 1387

Rumah—*high place*

Residence of Pedaiah .... 2 Kin. 23:36 458

Run—*to move swiftly*

A. *Used literally of:*
Man .... Num. 11:27 175
Water .... Ps. 105:41 685
Race .... 1 Cor. 9:24 1353

B. *Used figuratively of:*
Eagerness in:
Evil .... Prov. 1:16 714
Good .... Ps. 119:32 696
Joy of salvation ... Ps. 23:5 638
Christian life .. 1 Cor. 9:26 1353

Rush—*a cylindrical, often hollow marsh plant*

Cut off from Israel; rendered "bulrush" .... Is. 9:14 781
Signifying restoration .... Is. 35:7 806

Rust—*corrosion of metals*

Destruction of earthly treasures .... Matt. 6:19, 20 1123
Of gold and silver .... James 5:3 1471

Ruth—*female companion*

Moabitess .... Ruth 1:4 313
Follows Naomi .... Ruth 1:6-18 313
Marries Boaz ..... Ruth 4:9-13 315
Ancestress of Christ .... Ruth 4:13, 21, 22 317

Ruth, the Book of—*a book of the Old Testament*

Naomi's misfortunes ..... Ruth 1:1-14 313
Ruth's loyalty .... Ruth 1:14-22 313
The favor of Boaz .... Ruth 2:1-23 314
Boaz redeems ..... Ruth 3:8–4:12 315
The generations of Ruth .... Ruth 4:13-22 317

S

Sabachthani—*Why have You forsaken Me?*

Christ's cry on the cross .... Matt. 27:46 1154

Sabaoth—*hosts*

God as Lord of ... Rom. 9:29 1334; James 5:4 1471

Sabbath—*rest*

A. *History of:*
Instituted at creation ...... Gen. 2:2, 3 7
Observed before Sinai .... Ex. 16:22-30 87
Commanded at Sinai .... Ex. 20:8-11 90
Repeated at Canaan's entry .... Deut. 5:12-15 214
References to .... 2 Kin. 4:23 432
Proper observance of, described .... Is. 56:2-7 828
Postexilic Jews encouraged to keep .... Neh. 10:31 569
Perversion of, condemned by Christ .... Luke 13:14-17 1216
Christ teaches on .... Mark 6:2 1166
Paul preached on .... Acts 13:14 1291

B. *Features concerning:*
Commemorative of creation ...... Ex. 20:8-11 90
Seventh day during the Old Testament .... Deut. 5:14 214
Observance of, a perpetual covenant ..... Ex. 31:16, 17 105
Made for man's good .... Mark 2:27 1162
Christ's Lordship over .... Luke 6:5 1201

C. *Regulations concerning:*
Work prohibited on .... Lev. 23:3 145
Cattle must rest on .... Ex. 20:10 90
Business forbidden on .... Jer. 17:21, 22 864
To last from evening until evening ...... Lev. 23:32 148
Worship on ..... Ezek. 46:3 970
Works of mercy on .... Matt. 12:12 1131
Necessities lawful on .... Luke 13:15, 16 1216

See First day of the week

Sabbath day's journey—*about 3,100 feet*

Between Mt. Olivet and Jerusalem .... Acts 1:12 1272

Sabbatical year—*a rest every seventh year*

A. *Purpose of:*
Rest the land .. Ex. 23:10, 11 94
Emancipate slaves .... Ex. 21:2-6 92
Remit debts ... Deut. 15:1-6 227

B. *Allusions to, in history, in:*
Time of the judges .... Ruth 4:1-10 315
Preexilic times .... Jer. 32:6-16 879
Postexilic times .... Neh. 10:31 569

C. *Spiritual significance of:*
Punishment for non-observance ... Lev. 26:33-35 153
Illustrative of spiritual release ...... Is. 61:1-3 833; Luke 4:18-21 1198
Figurative of spiritual rest .... Heb. 4:1-11 1452

See Jubilee, Year of

Sabeans—*descendants of Sheba*

Job's property attacked by .... Job 1:13-15 589
Subject to Israel .. Is. 45:14 818

See Sheba 4, 5, 6

SUBJECT REFERENCE PAGE

Sardites

Descendants of Sered .... Num. 26:26 191

Sardius—*a precious stone*

Used in "breastplate" .... Ex. 28:15-17 99
In the garden of Eden .... Ezek. 28:13 951
Worn by Priest ... Ex. 28:17 100

Sardonyx—*a precious stone*

In John's vision ... Rev. 21:19, 20 1539

Sargon—*the constituted king*

King of Assyria ... Is. 20:1 791

Sarid—*survivor*

Village of Zebulun .... Josh. 19:10, 12 271

Sarsechim

Prince of Nebuchadnezzar .... Jer. 39:3 887

Satan—*adversary*

A. *Names of* (see Devil)

B. *Designs of, to:*
Undo God's work .... Mark 4:15 1164
Make men turn away from God ...... Job 2:4, 5 590
Instigate evil .. John 13:2, 27 1257
Secure men's worship ...... Luke 4:6-8 1198; 2 Thess. 2:3, 4 1421

C. *Character of:*
Deceiver .... Rev. 12:9 1529
Father of lies .. John 8:44 1250
Adversary .... 1 Pet. 5:8 1483

D. *Methods of:*
Disguises himself .... 2 Cor. 11:14 1373
Insinuates doubt .... Gen. 3:1 8
Misuses Scripture ...... Matt. 4:6 1118
Uses schemes ..... 2 Cor. 2:11 1366
Afflicts believers .... Luke 13:16 1216

E. *Judgment upon:*
Bound .... Mark 3:27 1163
Cast out .... John 12:31 1256
Judged .... John 16:11 1259
Bruised .... Rom. 16:20 1341
Assigned to hell .... Matt. 25:41 1149

Satiate(d)—*to be satisfied*

Scorners and fools shall be .... Prov. 1:22, 31 714
The sword shall be .... Jer. 46:10 894
Israel was not .... Ezek. 16:28 931

Satire—*exposing problems to ridicule*

Jesus' devastating use of .... Matt. 23:1-33 1145

Satisfaction—*that which completely fulfills*

A. *Of physical things:*
Sexual pleasures .... Prov. 5:19 718
Bread of heaven .... Ps. 105:40 685
Long life ...... Ps. 91:16 678

B. *Of spiritual things, God's:*
Mercy .... Ps. 90:14 678
Presence .... Ps. 17:15 634

C. *Of things empty of:*
Labor .... Is. 55:2 827
Sinful ways .... Ezek. 16:28, 29 931
Persecution ... Job 19:22 602

Satrap—*protector of the land*

Officials appointed over the kingdom .... Dan. 6:1 984

Saul—*asked* (of God)

1. Son of Kish; first king of Israel .... 1 Sam. 9:1, 2 330
Seeks his father's donkeys ...... 1 Sam. 9:3-14 330
Meets Samuel .... 1 Sam. 9:16-27 331
Anointed as king .... 1 Sam. 10:1-16 331
Victories and family .... 1 Sam. 14:47-52 337
Fights against Philistines; becomes jealous of David ..... 1 Sam. 17:1-58 340; 1 Sam. 18:6-13 343
Promises his daughter to David ..... 1 Sam. 18:14-30 344
Seeks to murder David .... 1 Sam. 19:1-24 344
Pursues David .... 1 Sam. 23:1-28 348
His life spared by David .... 1 Sam. 26:1-25 351
Defeated, commits suicide .... 1 Sam. 31:1-6 355
Burial of .... 1 Sam. 31:7-13 355
David's lament over .... 2 Sam. 1:17-27 360
Sin of, exposed ...... 2 Sam. 21:1-9 381

2. King of Edom .... Gen. 36:37 48

Savior—*one who saves*

Applied to:
God .... Ps. 106:21 686
Christ .... 2 Tim. 1:10 1433

Savior, Jesus as

A. *Characteristics of:*
Only .... Acts 4:10, 12 1276
Complete .... Col. 2:10 1408
Powerful .... Col. 1:12-18 1406
Authoritative .. John 10:18 1252
Universal ..... 1 Tim. 4:10 1429

B. *Announcement of, by:*
Prophets .... Is. 42:6, 7 814
Angels .... Matt. 1:20, 21 1116
John the Baptist .... John 1:29 1237
Christ .... John 12:44-50 1256
Peter .... Acts 5:31 1278
Paul .... 1 Tim. 1:15 1426
John .... 1 John 4:14 1498

C. *Office of, involves His:*
Becoming man .... Heb. 2:14 1452
Perfect righteousness ...... Heb. 5:8, 9 1453
Perfect obedience ...... Rom. 5:19, 20 1329
Dying for us ... 1 Pet. 1:18-20 1479

D. *Saves us from:*
Wrath .... Rom. 5:9 1329
Sin .... John 1:29 1237
Death .... John 11:25, 26 1253

Saw—*a toothed tool for cutting*

Stones .... 1 Kin. 7:9 400
Wood .... Is. 10:15 782
For torture .... 1 Chr. 20:3 487

Scab

Disqualifies an offering .... Lev. 22:21, 22 145
Priest observes ..... Lev. 13:6-8 133
Israel threatened with .... Deut. 28:27 238

Scabbard—*a sheath*

For God's Word ... Jer. 47:6 895

Scandal—*something disgraceful in*

Priesthood .... 1 Sam. 2:22-24 324
Family .... 2 Sam. 13:1-22 371

Scapegoat—*a goat of departure*

Bears sin away ... Lev. 16:8-22 139
Typical of Christ .... Is. 53:6, 11, 12 825

Scarlet—*a brilliant crimson*

A. *Literal uses of, for:*
Tabernacle ... Ex. 26:1, 31, 36 97
Identification .... Gen. 38:28, 30 50

B. *Symbolic uses of:*
Royalty .... Matt. 27:28 1152
Prosperity ...... 2 Sam. 1:24 360
Conquest .... Nah. 2:3 1048
Deep sin ...... Is. 1:18 772

Scatter—*to disperse abroad*

A. *Applied to:*
Nations .... Gen. 11:8, 9 16
Christians ..... Acts 8:1, 4 1282

B. *Caused by:*
Sin .... 1 Kin. 14:15, 16 411
Persecution ...... Acts 11:19 1288

Scepter—*a royal staff*

Sign of authority .... Esth. 4:11 579
Of Judah's tribe ... Gen. 49:10 63
Promise concerning ...... Num. 24:17 189
Fulfilled in Christ .... Heb. 1:8 1450

Sceva

Jewish priest at Ephesus .... Acts 19:14 1300

Schemes of Satan

Known by Christians .... 2 Cor. 2:11 1366
Warnings against .... 2 Cor. 11:3, 13-15 1373
Armor provided against .... Eph. 6:11 1393
World falls before .... Rev. 13:1-18 1529

Schism—*a division within a body*

Prohibition concerning .... 1 Cor. 12:25 1356
Translated "pulls away" .... Matt. 9:16 1126

Scholars—*men reputed for learning*

Numbered by David .... 1 Chr. 25:1, 7, 8 491

SUBJECT — REFERENCE — PAGE

2. "Today you will be with Me in Paradise" .... Luke 23:43 — 1230
3. "Woman, behold your son" .... John 19:26 — 1264
4. "My God, My God" .... Matt. 27:46 — 1154
5. "I thirst" ..... John 19:28 — 1264
6. "It is finished" ..... John 19:30 — 1264
7. "Father, into Your hands" .... Luke 23:46 — 1230

Seventy

Elders appointed .... Ex. 24:1, 9 — 95
Years in Babylon .... Dan. 9:2 — 987
Weeks in prophetic vision .... Dan. 9:24 — 989
In forgiveness .... Matt. 18:22 — 1139
Disciples sent forth .... Luke 10:1 — 1208

Sexes—*male and female*

A. *Creation of:*
By God .... Gen. 1:27 — 4
For:
Union .... Gen. 2:23-25 — 8
Helpfulness .. Gen. 2:18 — 7
Procreation .. Gen. 4:1 — 9
Sexual needs .... Prov. 5:17-19 — 718

B. *Regulations concerning:*
Distinctive clothing for .... Deut. 22:5 — 232
Subordination of .... 1 Cor. 11:3-16 — 1354
Equality in Christ .... Gal. 3:28 — 1381
Different functions of .... 1 Tim. 2:8-15 — 1426
Love between ...... Eph. 5:22-33 — 1392

Sexual love

Good and holy ... Gen. 1:27, 28; Gen. 2:24, 25 — 4, 8
For procreation ... Gen. 4:1 — 9
In marriage only .... Prov. 5:15-20 — 718
Expression of love .... Song 1:12-15; Song 3:1-5 — 763, 764
Mutual responsibility .... 1 Cor. 7:3-5 — 1351

Sexual perversion

A. *Types of:*
Adultery ...... Deut. 22:22-29 — 233
Prostitution ... Deut. 23:17 — 233
Incest .... Lev. 18:6-18 — 141
Homosexuality .... Rom. 1:26, 27 — 1324
Mankind with beasts .... Deut. 27:21 — 237

B. *Judgment upon:*
Defilement ..... Lev. 18:22-28 — 141
Destruction ... 1 Cor. 5:1-5 — 1348
Death .... Lev. 20:13-16 — 143

Shaalbim, Shaalabbin—*jackals*

Amorite city assigned to Danites .... Josh. 19:42 — 272
Subdued by house of Joseph .... Judg. 1:35 — 285

Shaalbonite—*an inhabitant of Shaalbim*

Eliahba called .... 2 Sam. 23:32 — 385

Shaalim—*district of foxes*

Mentioned in Saul's pursuit .... 1 Sam. 9:4 — 330

Shaaph—*friendship*

1. Descendant of Caleb .... 1 Chr. 2:47 — 466
2. Son of Caleb .. 1 Chr. 2:49 — 466

Shaaraim, Sharaim—*double gate*

1. Village in Judah .... Josh. 15:36 — 268
2. City of Simeon ...... 1 Chr. 4:31 — 468

Shaashgaz

Persian eunuch ... Esth. 2:14 — 578

Shabbethai—*Sabbath-born*

Postexilic Levite .. Ezra 10:15 — 553
Interprets the law .... Neh. 8:7, 8 — 565

Shadow

A. *Used literally of:*
Man .... Acts 5:15 — 1278
Mountain ..... Judg. 9:36 — 296
Sundial .... 2 Kin. 20:9-11 — 454

B. *Used figuratively of:*
Protection ..... Ps. 91:1 — 678
Brevity .... Ps. 102:11 — 682
Change .... James 1:17 — 1468
Death .... Matt. 4:16 — 1118
Types .... Col. 2:17 — 1408
Old Testament period .... Heb. 10:1 — 1457

Shadrach

Hananiah's Babylonian name .... Dan. 1:3, 7 — 976
Cast into the fiery furnace .... Dan. 3:1-28 — 978

Shageh—*wandering*

Father of one of David's mighty men .... 1 Chr. 11:34 — 478

Shaharaim—*double dawn*

Benjamite .... 1 Chr. 8:8-11 — 473

Shahazimah—*heights*

Town of Issachar .... Josh. 19:17, 22 — 272

Shake—*to move violently*

A. *Descriptive of:*
Thunder ...... Ps. 77:18 — 669
Earthquakes ... Acts 4:31 — 1277
Fear .... Matt. 28:4 — 1155

B. *Used figuratively of:*
Fear .... Is. 14:16 — 787
Second advent ...... Heb. 12:26, 27 — 1463
Rejection .... Luke 9:5; Acts 18:6 — 1207, 1299

Shalim—*district of foxes*

Mentioned in Saul's pursuit .... 1 Sam. 9:4 — 330

Shalisha—*a third part*

Mentioned in Saul's pursuit .... 1 Sam. 9:4 — 330

Shallecheth—*a casting out*

Gate of Solomon's temple .... 1 Chr. 26:16 — 492

Shallum—*recompense*

1. King of Israel .... 2 Kin. 15:10-15 — 446
2. Husband of Huldah .... 2 Kin. 22:14 — 456
3. Judahite .... 1 Chr. 2:40, 41 — 466
4. Simeonite ..... 1 Chr. 4:25 — 468
5. Father of Hilkiah ...... 1 Chr. 6:12, 13 — 469
6. Naphtali's son .... 1 Chr. 7:13 — 472
7. Family of porters .... Ezra 2:42 — 544
8. Father of Jehizkiah .... 2 Chr. 28:12 — 527
9. One who divorced his foreign wife .... Ezra 10:24 — 553
10. Another who divorced his foreign wife .... Ezra 10:42 — 554
11. Son of Hallohesh .... Neh. 3:12 — 559
12. Jeremiah's uncle .... Jer. 32:7 — 879
13. Father of Maaseiah .... Jer. 35:4 — 882

Shalmai—*Yahweh is recompenser*

Head of a family of Nethinim .... Ezra 2:46 — 544

Shalman

Contraction of Shalmaneser .... Hos. 10:14 — 1003

Shalmaneser—*Shulmanu (a god) is chief*

Assyrian king .... 2 Kin. 17:3 — 448

Shama—*He (God) has heard*

Son of Hotham ... 1 Chr. 11:44 — 479

Shamariah—*Yahweh has kept*

Son of Rehoboam ...... 2 Chr. 11:18, 19 — 512

Shame—*a feeling of guilt*

A. *Caused by:*
Rape .... 2 Sam. 13:13 — 372
Defeat .... 2 Chr. 32:21 — 531
Folly .... Prov. 3:35 — 716
Idleness .... Prov. 10:5 — 722
Pride .... Prov. 11:2 — 723
A wicked wife .... Prov. 12:4 — 724
Lying .... Prov. 13:5 — 725
Stubbornness ..... Prov. 13:18 — 725
Haste in speech .... Prov. 18:13 — 730
Mistreatment of parents ...... Prov. 19:26 — 731
Evil companions .. Prov. 28:7 — 742
Juvenile delinquency .. Prov. 29:15 — 743
Nakedness ..... Is. 47:3 — 819
Idolatry .... Jer. 2:26, 27 — 845
Impropriety .... 1 Cor. 11:6 — 1354
Lust .... Phil. 3:19 — 1401

B. *Of the unregenerate:*
Hardened in ... Jer. 8:12 — 854
Pleasure in ... Rom. 1:26, 27, 32 — 1324
Vessels of ..... Rom. 9:21 — 1334
Glory in ...... Phil. 3:19 — 1401
Like foam ..... Jude 13 — 1510

C. *In the Christian life, of:*
Unregenerate's life .... Rom. 6:21 — 1331
Sinful things .. Eph. 5:12 — 1391
Improper behavior .... 1 Cor. 11:14, 22 — 1354
Christ .... Rom. 1:16 — 1324

Shamer (see Shemer)

SUBJECT REFERENCE PAGE

Shamgar—*cupbearer*

Judge of Israel; struck down 600 Philistines ....Judg. 3:31 288

Shamhuth—*desolation*

Commander in David's army ....1 Chr. 27:8 493

Shamir—*a sharp point*

1. Town in Judah ....Josh. 15:1, 48 267
2. Town in Ephraim .....Judg. 10:1 296
3. Levite ....1 Chr. 24:24 491

Shamma—*astonishment*

Asherite ....1 Chr. 7:36, 37 473

Shammah—*waste*

1. Son of Reuel ..Gen. 36:13, 17 48
2. Son of Jesse ...1 Sam. 16:9 340
   Called Shimea ......1 Chr. 2:13 466
3. One of David's mighty men ....2 Sam. 23:11 385
   Also called Shammoth the Harorite .....1 Chr. 11:27 478

Shammai—*celebrated*

1. Grandson of Jerahmeel ....1 Chr. 2:28, 32 466
2. Descendant of Caleb ....1 Chr. 2:44, 45 466
3. Descendant of Judah ....1 Chr. 4:17 467

Shammoth—*waste*

One of David's mighty men ....1 Chr. 11:27 478

Shammua—*renowned*

1. Reubenite spy ....Num. 13:2-4 176
2. Son of David ....2 Sam. 5:13, 14 364
3. Levite ....Neh. 11:17 570
4. Postexilic priest ....Neh. 12:1, 18 571

Shamsherai—*sun-like*

Son of Jeroham ...1 Chr. 8:26 473

Shapham—*youthful*

Gadite ....1 Chr. 5:12 468

Shaphan—*prudent, shy*

Scribe under Josiah ....2 Kin. 22:3 455
Takes book of the Law to Josiah ....2 Kin. 22:8-10 455
Is sent to Huldah for interpretation ....2 Kin. 22:14 456
Assists in repairs of temple ....2 Chr. 34:8 534
Father of notable son ....Jer. 36:10-12, 25 883

Shaphat—*he has judged*

1. Simeonite spy ....Num. 13:2-5 176
2. Son of Shemaiah ....1 Chr. 3:22 467
3. Gadite chief ...1 Chr. 5:11, 12 468
4. One of David's herdsmen ....1 Chr. 27:29 494
5. Father of the prophet Elisha ....1 Kin. 19:16, 19 420

Shaphir—*glittering*

Town of Judah ....Mic. 1:11 1036

Sharai—*Yahweh is deliverer*

Divorced his foreign wife ....Ezra 10:34, 40 553

Sharar—*firm*

Father of Ahiam ..2 Sam. 23:33 385

Sharers

Of sins ....1 Tim. 5:22 1430

See Partake

Sharezer, Sherezer—*protect the king*

1. Son of Sennacherib ....Is. 37:38 810
2. Sent to Zechariah concerning fasting ....Zech. 7:1-3 1071

Sharon—*plain*

1. Coastal plain between Joppa and Mt. Carmel ...1 Chr. 27:29 494
   Famed for roses.........Song 2:1 763
   Inhabitants turn to the Lord ....Acts 9:35 1286
2. Pasture east of the Jordan ....1 Chr. 5:16 468

Sharonite—*an inhabitant of Sharon*

Shitrai ....1 Chr. 27:29 494

Sharp—*having a keen edge; biting*

A. *Descriptive of:*
   Stone ....Ex. 4:25 72
   Knives ....Josh. 5:2, 3 255
   Share ....1 Sam. 13:20, 21 334
   Rocks ....1 Sam. 14:4 336
   Arrows ....Is. 5:28 777

B. *Used to compare a sword with:*
   Tongue ....Ps. 57:4 656
   Adulteress .....Prov. 5:4 718
   Mouth ....Is. 49:2 821
   God's Word ...Heb. 4:12 1453

C. *Figurative of:*
   Deceitfulness ..Ps. 52:2 654
   Falsehood .....Prov. 25:18 738
   Contention ....Acts 15:39 1294
   Severe rebuke ....2 Cor. 13:10 1375
   Christ's conquest .....Rev. 14:14-18 1531

Sharuhen—*abode of pleasure*

Town of Judah assigned to Simeon ....Josh. 19:1, 6 271
Called Sharaim ...Josh. 15:36 268
Called Shaaraim ..1 Chr. 4:31 468

Shashai—*whitish*

Divorced his foreign wife ....Ezra 10:34, 40 553

Shashak—*assaulter*

Benjamite ....1 Chr. 8:14, 25 473

Shaul—*asked* (of God)

1. Son of Simeon ......Gen. 46:10 59
   Founder of a tribal family ....Num. 26:13 191
2. Kohathite Levite........1 Chr. 6:24 469

Shave—*to cut off the hair*

A. *Used worthily to express:*
   Accommodation ....Gen. 41:14 52
   Cleansing .....Lev. 14:8, 9 136
   Commitment ....Deut. 21:12 231
   Mourning .....Job 1:18-20 590
   Sorrow ....Jer. 41:5 888

B. *Used unworthily to express:*
   Defeat of a Nazirite ......Judg. 16:19 303
   Contempt .....2 Sam. 10:4 369
   Unnaturalness ....1 Cor. 11:5, 6 1354

Shaveh—*plain*

Valley near Salem; Abram meets king of Sodom here.............Gen. 14:17, 18 21

Shaveh Kiriathaim—*plain of Kiriathaim*

Plain near Kiriathaim inhabited by Emim ....Gen. 14:5 21

Shavsha, Shisha—*nobility*

David's secretary ....1 Chr. 18:14, 16 486
Serves under Solomon also ....1 Kin. 4:3 395

Sheal—*asking*

Divorced his foreign wife ....Ezra 10:29 553

Shealtiel—*I have asked God*

Son of King Jeconiah and father of Zerubbabel ......1 Chr. 3:17 467

Sheariah—*Yahweh has esteemed*

Descendant of Saul ....1 Chr. 9:44 475

Shear-Jashub—*a remnant shall return*

Symbolic name given to Isaiah's son ....Is. 7:3 778

Sheba—*seven; an oath*

1. City in territory assigned to Simeon ......Josh. 19:1, 2 271
2. Benjamite insurrectionist .....2 Sam. 20:1-22 380
3. Descendant of Cush through Raamah ....Gen. 10:7 16
4. Descendant of Shem ....Gen. 10:28 16
5. Grandson of Abraham and Keturah ......Gen. 25:3 33
6. Gadite chief ....1 Chr. 5:13 468
7. Land of, occupied by Sabeans, famous traders ....Job 1:15 589; Ps. 72:10 666
   Queen of, visits Solomon; marvels at his wisdom ......1 Kin. 10:1-13 406
   Mentioned by Christ ....Matt. 12:42 1131

Shebah—*seven; an oath*

Name given to a well and town (Beersheba) .....Gen. 26:31-33 36

Shebaniah—*Yahweh has returned me*

1. Levite trumpeter ....1 Chr. 15:24 482
2. Levite; offers prayer and signs covenant .....Neh. 9:4, 5 567
3. Levite who signs covenant .....Neh. 10:12 569

SUBJECT — REFERENCE — PAGE

4. Priest who signs covenant ..... Neh. 10:4 — 569

Shebarim—*breakings*

Place near Ai ..... Josh. 7:5 — 258

Shebat

Eleventh month of the Hebrew year ..... Zech. 1:7 — 1068

Sheber—*breaking*

Son of Caleb ..... 1 Chr. 2:48 — 466

Shebna—*perhaps an abbreviation of Shebaniah*

Treasurer under Hezekiah .... Is. 22:15 — 792
Demoted to position of scribe .... 2 Kin. 19:2 — 452
Man of pride and luxury; replaced by Eliakim ...... Is. 22:19-21 — 792

Shebuel—*God is renown*

1. Son of Gershom ..... 1 Chr. 23:16 — 490
2. Son of Heman .... 1 Chr. 25:4 — 491

Shecaniah, Shechaniah—*Yahweh has dwelt*

1. Descendant of Zerubbabel ... 1 Chr. 3:21, 22 — 467
2. Postexilic returnee ...... Ezra 8:5 — 550
3. Descendant of Aaron .... 1 Chr. 24:11 — 491
4. Priest .... 2 Chr. 31:15 — 530
5. Divorced his foreign wife .... Ezra 10:2, 3 — 551
6. Father of Shemaiah .... Neh. 3:29 — 560
Probably same as number 1
7. Postexilic priest .... Neh. 12:3, 7 — 571
8. Father-in-law of Tobiah .... Neh. 6:18 — 562

Shechem—*shoulder*

1. Son of Hamor; seduces Dinah, Jacob's daughter .... Gen. 34:1-31 — 45
2. Son of Gilead; founder of a tribal family .... Num. 26:31 — 191
3. Son of Shemida ..... 1 Chr. 7:19 — 472
4. Ancient city of Ephraim ..... Gen. 33:18 — 45
Abram camps near .... Gen. 12:6 — 20
Jacob buys ground here .... Gen. 33:18, 19 — 45
Hivites, inhabit .... Gen. 34:2 — 45
Inhabitants of, slaughtered by Simeon and Levi .... Gen. 34:25-29 — 45
Pastures near .... Gen. 37:12, 13 — 49
Becomes city of refuge .... Josh. 20:7 — 273
Joseph buried here .... Josh. 24:32 — 280
Joshua's farewell address here .... Josh. 24:1, 25 — 277
Center of idol worship .. Judg. 9:1, 4-7 — 294
Town destroyed .... Judg. 9:23, 45 — 295
Jeroboam made king here .... 1 Kin. 12:1-19 — 408
Name of, used poetically .... Ps. 108:7 — 688

Shed—*to pour out*

A. *Descriptive of:*
Blood .... Gen. 9:6 — 14
Holy Spirit .... Titus 3:6 — 1442

B. *As applied to blood, indicative of:*
Justifiable execution .... Gen. 9:6 — 14
Unjustifiable murder ...... Gen. 37:22 — 49
Unacceptable sacrifice ...... Lev. 17:1-5 — 140
Attempted vengeance ... 1 Sam. 25:31, 34 — 351
Unpardonable .... 2 Kin. 24:4 — 458
Abomination .... Prov. 6:16, 17 — 719
Heinous crime .... Is. 59:7 — 831
New covenant ..... Matt. 26:28 — 1150

Shedeur—*shedder of light*

Reubenite leader .... Num. 1:5 — 159

Sheep—*a domesticated animal*

A. *Characteristics of:*
Domesticated .... 2 Sam. 12:3 — 370
Gentle .... Jer. 11:19 — 858
Defenseless ...... Mic. 5:8 — 1039
Needful of care .... Ezek. 34:5 — 957

B. *Uses of, for:*
Food .... 1 Sam. 25:18 — 350
Milk .... 1 Cor. 9:7 — 1353
Clothing .... Prov. 31:13 — 745
Presents .... 2 Sam. 17:29 — 377
Tribute .... 2 Kin. 3:4 — 431
Sacrifice ...... Gen. 4:4 — 9

C. *Uses of, in Levitical system as:*
Burnt offering ...... Lev. 1:10 — 120
Sin offering ...... Lev. 4:32 — 123
Trespass offering .... Lev. 5:15 — 124
Peace offering ...... Lev. 22:21 — 145

D. *Needs of, for:*
Protection ..... Job 30:1 — 609
Shepherd ...... John 10:4, 27 — 1251
Fold .... John 10:1 — 1251
Pastures .... Ex. 3:1 — 70
Water .... Gen. 29:8-10 — 40
Rest .... Ps. 23:1, 2 — 637
Shearing ..... 1 Sam. 25:2, 11 — 350

E. *Figurative of:*
Innocent .... 2 Sam. 24:17 — 387
Wicked .... Ps. 49:14 — 653
Jewish people .... Ps. 74:1 — 667
Backsliders ..... Jer. 50:6 — 899
Lost sinners ... Matt. 9:36 — 1127
Christians ..... John 10:1-16 — 1251
Christ .... John 1:29 — 1237
Saved .... Matt. 26:31-34 — 1150
Church .... Acts 20:28 — 1303

See Lamb; Lamb of God

Sheepbreeder

Mesha, king of Moab .... 2 Kin. 3:4 — 431

Sheepfold—*shelter*

Enclosure for flocks .... Num. 32:16 — 198
Entrance to, only by Christ .... John 10:1 — 1251

Sheep Gate—*a gate of the restored Jerusalem*

Repaired .... Neh. 3:32 — 560
Dedicated .... Neh. 12:38, 39 — 572

Sheepshearers

Employed by Judah .... Gen. 38:12 — 50
Many employed by Nabal .... 1 Sam. 25:7, 11 — 350
Used figuratively ...... Is. 53:7 — 825

Sheerah—*blood-relationship*

Daughter of Ephraim; builder of cities .... 1 Chr. 7:24 — 473

Sheets

Large piece of cloth .... Acts 11:5 — 1288

Shehariah—*Yahweh is the dawn*

Benjamite .... 1 Chr. 8:26 — 473

Shekel—*a Jewish measure (approximately .533 oz.)*

A. *As a weight:*
Standard of, defined ...... Ex. 30:13 — 103
Used in weighing ..... Josh. 7:21 — 259
See Weights

B. *As money:*
Used in currency ..... 1 Sam. 9:8 — 331
Fines paid in .... Deut. 22:19, 29 — 232
Revenues of the sanctuary paid in .... Neh. 10:32 — 569

Shekinah—*a word expressing the glory and presence of God*

A. *As indicative of God's presence:*
In nature ...... Ps. 18:7-15 — 634
In the exodus from Egypt .... Ex. 13:21, 22 — 83
At Sinai .... Ex. 24:16-18 — 95
In tabernacle .... Ex. 40:34-38 — 116
Upon the mercy seat .... Ex. 25:22 — 97
In the wilderness ... Num. 9:15-23 — 171; Num. 10:11-36 — 172
In the Temple ...... 2 Chr. 7:1-3 — 508

B. *Illustrated by Christ in His:*
Divine nature .... Col. 2:9 — 1408
Incarnation .... Luke 1:35 — 1192
Nativity .... Luke 2:9 — 1193
Manifestation to Israel ..... Hag. 2:9 — 1065; Zech. 2:5 — 1069
Transfiguration .... 2 Pet. 1:17 — 1487
Ascension ..... Acts 1:9 — 1272
Transforming us by His Spirit .... 2 Cor. 3:18 — 1367; 2 Cor. 4:6 — 1367
Return .... Matt. 24:44 — 1148
Eternal habitation with saints .... Rev. 21:3 — 1538

C. *Accompanied by:*
Angels .... Is. 6:1-4 — 777
Cloud .... Num. 9:15-23 — 171
Fire .... Heb. 12:18-21 — 1463
Earthquake .... Hag. 2:21 — 1065

Shelah—*sprout; request*

1. Son of Arphaxad .... 1 Chr. 1:18 — 465

SUBJECT REFERENCE PAGE

Messiah's advent ....Ps. 72:6 665
Gospel ......Ezek. 34:25, 26 958
Remnant ......Mic. 5:7 1039

Shroud—*to cover or shelter*

Used figuratively ......Ezek. 31:3 954

Shua, Shuah, Shuhah—*prosperity*

1. Son of Abraham by Keturah ......Gen. 25:1, 2 33
2. Father of Judah's wife ....Gen. 38:2, 12 50
3. Descendant of Judah ....1 Chr. 4:1, 11 467
4. Daughter of Heber ....1 Chr. 7:32 473

Shual—*jackal*

1. Asherite ......1 Chr. 7:30, 36 473
2. Region raided by a Philistine company .....1 Sam. 13:17 334

Shubael, Shebuel

1. Levite, son of Amram ......1 Chr. 24:20 491
2. Levite, son of Heman ....1 Chr. 25:4 491

Shuham—*depression*

Son of Dan ....Num. 26:42 191
Called Hushim ....Gen. 46:23 59
Head of the Shuhamites .....Num. 26:42, 43 191

Shuhite—*a descendant of Shua*

Bildad called; a descendant of Abraham by Keturah ....Gen. 25:1-4 33; Job 2:11 590

Shulamite—*a native of Shulam*

Shepherd's sweetheart ......Song 6:13 766

Shumathites

Family of Kirjath Jearim ....1 Chr. 2:53 466

Shunammite—*a native of Shunem*

1. Abishag, David's nurse called ....1 Kin. 1:3, 15 391
2. Woman who cared for Elisha ....2 Kin. 4:8-12 432

Shunem—*uneven*

Border town of Issachar ....Josh. 19:18 272

Shuni—*fortunate*

Son of Gad ....Gen. 46:16 59

Shuppim—*serpent*

Levite porter .....1 Chr. 26:16 492

Shur—*fortification*

Wilderness in south Palestine ....Gen. 16:7 23
Israel went from Red Sea to ....Ex. 15:22 86
On Egypt's border ....1 Sam. 15:7 339
Hagar flees to .....Gen. 16:7 23

Shushan—*a city of Elam*

Residence of Persian monarchs ....Esth. 1:2 577

Located on river Ulai ....Dan. 8:2 986
Court of Ahasuerus here ....Esth. 1:2, 5 577

Shut—*to close securely*

A. *Applied literally to:*
Ark ....Gen. 7:16 12
Door ....Gen. 19:6, 10 26
Animals ....Dan. 6:22 985
Court ....Jer. 33:1 880
Prison ....Acts 26:10 1312

B. *Applied figuratively to:*
God's mercies ....Ps. 77:9 669
Finality of salvation ......Matt. 25:10 1148
Union with Christ ....Song 4:12 765
Spiritual blindness ....Is. 6:10 778
Awe ....Is. 52:15 825
Heaven's glory ....Is. 60:11 832
God's Word ...Jer. 20:9 866
Vision ....Dan. 12:4 993
Secret prayer ....Matt. 6:6 1121
Christ's sovereignty ...Rev. 3:7, 8 1521

Shuthelah

1. Son of Ephraim; head of a family ....Num. 26:35, 36 191
2. Ephraimite ....1 Chr. 7:20, 21 472

Shuttle—*a weaving tool*

Our days swifter than ....Job 7:6 594

Siaha, Sia—*assembly*

Family of returning Nethinim ....Ezra 2:43, 44 544; Neh. 7:47 563

Sibbechai

One of David's mighty men ....1 Chr. 11:29 478
Slays a Philistine giant ....2 Sam. 21:18 382
Commander of a division ....1 Chr. 27:11 493

Sibmah, Shibmah—*balsam*

Town of Reuben ..Num. 32:3, 38 198
Famous for wines ....Is. 16:8, 9 788

Sibraim—*double hope*

Place in north Palestine ....Ezek. 47:16 971

Sick, Sickness—*the state of being unwell*

A. *Caused by:*
Age ....Gen. 48:1, 10 60
Accident ......2 Kin. 1:2 429
Wine ....Hos. 7:5 1000
Sins ....Mic. 6:13 1041
Despondency ..Prov. 13:12 725
Prophetic visions ....Dan. 8:27 987
Love ....Song 2:5 763
God's judgment ....2 Chr. 21:14-19 521
God's sovereignty ...John 11:4 1253

B. *Healing of, by:*
Figs ....2 Kin. 20:7 454
Miracle .....1 Kin. 17:17-23 416
Prayer ....James 5:14, 15 1473
God's mercy ...Phil. 2:25-30 1400

See Diseases; Healing

Sickle—*an instrument for cutting grain*

Literally ....Deut. 16:9 228
Figuratively .....Mark 4:29 1164; Rev. 14:14-19 1531

Siddim, Vale of

Valley of bitumen pits near the Dead Sea ....Gen. 14:3, 8, 10 21

Sidon, Zidon—*fishery*

Canaanite city 20 miles north of Tyre ....Gen. 10:15, 19 16
Israel's northern boundary ....Josh. 19:28 272
Canaanites not expelled from ....Judg. 1:31 284
Israelites oppressed by ....Judg. 10:12 297
Gods of, entice Israelites ....1 Kin. 11:5, 33 407
Judgments pronounced on ....Is. 23:12 793
Israelites sold as slaves by ....Joel 3:4-6 1012
People from, hear Jesus ....Luke 6:17 1202
Visited by Jesus ...Matt. 15:21 1135
Paul visits at .....Acts 27:3 1314

Siege of a city—*a military blockage*

A. *Methods employed in:*
Supplies cut off ....2 Kin. 19:24 453
Ambushes laid ....Judg. 9:34 295
Battering rams used ....Ezek. 4:2 921
Arrows shot ...2 Kin. 19:32 453

B. *Suffering of:*
Famine ....2 Kin. 6:26-29 436
Pestilence .....Jer. 21:6 867

C. *Examples of:*
Jericho ....Josh. 6:2-20 256
Jerusalem ....2 Kin. 24:10, 11 458

See War

Sieve, sift—*screen*

Used figuratively of:
God's judgment ...Amos 9:9 1023
Satan's temptation ....Luke 22:31 1226

Sign—*an outward token having spiritual significance*

A. *Descriptive of:*
Heavenly bodies ....Gen. 1:14 4
Rainbow ....Gen. 9:12-17 15
Circumcision ..Gen. 17:11 24
Bloodshed .....Ex. 12:13 80
God's wonders .....Ps. 65:8 661
Covenant .....Rom. 4:11 1327
Miracles ......Deut. 26:8 236
Memorial ......Num. 16:38 180
Symbolic act ..Is. 8:18 780
Witness ....Is. 19:19, 20 790
Outward display ....John 4:48 1242

B. *Purposes of, to:*
Authenticate a prophecy ..Deut. 13:1 224; 1 Sam. 2:31, 34 324

SUBJECT REFERENCE PAGE

Soul—continued

C. *Abilities of, able to:*
Believe ....Heb. 10:39 1460
Love God .....Luke 10:27 1209
Sin ....Mic. 6:7 1041
Prosper ....3 John 2 1506
Survive death ....Matt. 10:28 1129

D. *Duties of, to:*
Keep itself ....Deut. 4:9 211
Seek the LORD ....Deut. 4:29 212
Love the LORD ....Deut. 6:5 215
Serve the LORD ....Deut. 10:12 221
Store God's Word ....Deut. 11:18 222
Keep God's Law ....Deut. 26:16 237
Obey God ... {Deut. 30:2, 6, 10} 241
Get wisdom ...Prov. 19:8 731

E. *Enemies of, seen in:*
Fleshly lusts ....1 Pet. 2:11 1479
Evil environment ....2 Pet. 2:8 1487
Sin ....Lev. 5:4, 15, 17 124
Adultery ......Prov. 6:32 720
Evil men ......Prov. 22:24, 25 735
Ignorance .....Prov. 8:36 721
Hell ....Prov. 23:14 736

F. *Of the righteous:*
Kept by God ..Ps. 121:7 700
Vexed by sin ..2 Pet. 2:8 1487
Subject to authorities ...Rom. 13:1 1337
Purified by obedience ....1 Pet. 1:22 1479
Not allowed to famish ....Prov. 10:3 722
Restored ......Ps. 23:1, 3 637
Enriched ......Prov. 11:25 724
Satisfied ......Prov. 13:25 725
Reign with Christ ....Rev. 20:4 1536

G. *Of the wicked:*
Desires evil....Prov. 21:10 733
Delights in abominations ....Is. 66:3 837
Has nothing ...Prov. 13:4 725
Required ......Luke 12:19, 20 1214
To be punished .....Rom. 2:9 1324

Soul winning
Importance of ....James 5:20 1473
Christ's command ....Matt. 4:19 1118
Our reward ....Dan. 12:3 993

Sound (see Sober)

Sound doctrine

A. *Manifested in:*
Heart's prayer ....Ps. 119:80 697
Speech ....2 Tim. 1:13 1433
Righteous living ....1 Tim. 1:10 1426

B. *Need of:*
For exhortation ...Titus 1:9 1440
For the faith ...Titus 1:13 1440
Denied by some ....2 Tim. 4:3 1436

Sour grapes—*not yet mature*
Used proverbially .....Jer. 31:29, 30 878

Sowing—*scattering seed*

A. *Restrictions upon, regarding:*
Sabbath year ....Lev. 25:3-22 149
Mingled seed ....Lev. 19:19 142
Weather ......Eccl. 11:4, 6 758

B. *Figurative of evil things:*
Iniquity ....Job 4:8 592
Wind ....Hos. 8:7 1001
Discord ....Prov. 6:14, 19 719
Strife ....Prov. 16:28 729
False teaching .....Matt. 13:25, 39 1133
Sin ....Gal. 6:7, 8 1383

C. *Figurative of good things:*
God's Word ....Is. 55:10 828
Reward ....2 Cor. 9:6, 10 1372
Gospel ...... {Matt. 13:3, 4, 37} 1132
Gospel messengers ...John 4:36, 37 1242
Resurrection ...... {1 Cor. 15:36-44} 1360
Eternal life ...Gal. 6:7-9 1383

Spain—*a country in southwest Europe*
Paul desires to visit ....Rom. 15:24, 28 1340

Sparrow—*a small bird*
Value of ....Matt. 10:29, 31 1129

Spearmen—*infantry men with spears*
One of, pierces Christ's side ....John 19:34 1264
Paul's military escort ....Acts 23:23, 24 1307

Special—*something separated to one's own use*

A. *Applied literally to:*
Israel (God's own) .... {Ex. 19:5 / Deut. 7:6} 89 / 217
Treasure (Solomon's own) ....Eccl. 2:8 751
Translated: "jewels" .....Mal. 3:17 1083

B. *Applied figuratively to:*
True Israel ....Ps. 135:4 703
Christian ......Titus 2:14 1442
True church .....1 Pet. 2:9 1479

Speck—*a small particle*
Used in contrast to a beam ....Matt. 7:3, 5 1123

Speckled
Spotted (of goats) ....Gen. 30:32-39 41
Colored (of birds) ....Jer. 12:9 859

Speech—*the intelligible utterance of the mouth*

A. *Of the wicked, consisting of:*
Lies ....Ps. 58:3 657
Cursing ....Ps. 59:12 658
Enticements ...Prov. 7:21 720
Blasphemies ...Dan. 7:25 986
Earthly things ....John 3:31 1241
Deception .....Rom. 16:18 1341

B. *Of the righteous, consisting of:*
God's righteousness ....Ps. 35:28 645
Wisdom ....1 Cor. 2:6, 7 1346
God's Word ...Ps. 119:172 699
Truth ....Eph. 4:25 1391
Mystery of Christ ....Col. 4:3, 4 1409

Sound doctrine ......Titus 2:1, 8 1440

Speed—*to hasten*
"Let him make" ..Is. 5:19 777
"They shall come with" ....Is. 5:26 777

Spending—*paying out money or service for things*

A. *Wastefully, on:*
Harlots ....Luke 15:30 1218
Physicians ....Mark 5:26 1165

B. *Wisely:*
In Christ's service ....2 Cor. 12:15 1374

Spices—*aromatic vegetable compounds*

A. *Uses of:*
Food ....Song 8:2 767
Incense ....Ex. 30:34-38 104
Fragrance .....Song 4:10 764

B. *Features concerning:*
Used as presents ......Gen. 43:11 56
Objects of commerce ....Gen. 37:25 49
Tokens of royal favor ....1 Kin. 10:2 406
Stored in the temple ....1 Chr. 9:29 474
Sign of wealth ....2 Kin. 20:13 454

Spider

Web of, figurative of:
Insecurity ....Is. 59:5 831
Godless ....Job 8:14 595

Spies—*secret agents of a foreign government*

A. *Purpose of, to:*
Search out Canaan ....Num. 13:1-33 176
Prepare for invasion ....Josh. 2:1-21 253
Search out new land ....Judg. 18:2-17 304
Make false charges ....Luke 20:20 1223

B. *Men accused of, falsely:*
Jacob's sons ...Gen. 42:9-34 55
David's servants ......2 Sam. 10:3 369

Spikenard
Used as a perfume ....Song 1:12 763
Mary uses it in anointing Jesus .... {Mark 14:3 / John 12:3} 1180 / 1255

Spill—*to flow forth*
Water ....2 Sam. 14:14 373
Wine ....Luke 5:37 1201

Spinning—*twisting fibers together to form cloth*
Work done by women ....Ex. 35:25 109
Sign of industry ..Prov. 31:19 745
As an illustration ....Matt. 6:28 1123

Spirit—*an immaterial being*

A. *Descriptive of:*
Holy Spirit ....Gen. 1:2 4
Angels ....Heb. 1:7, 14 1450
Man's immaterial nature ....1 Cor. 2:11 1346

SUBJECT REFERENCE PAGE

State—continued

B. *Duties of Christians to:*
Pray for .... 1 Tim. 2:1, 2 1426
Pay taxes to ... Matt. 22:17-21 1144
Be subject to .. Rom. 13:5, 6 1337
Resist (when evil) .... Acts 4:17-21 1276

Stature—*the natural height of the body*

A. *Used physically of:*
Giants .... Num. 13:32 176
Sabeans .... Is. 45:14 818

B. *Significance of:*
Normal, in human growth .... Luke 2:52 1194
Cannot be changed ..... Matt. 6:27 1123
Not indicative of greatness .... 1 Sam. 16:7 340
In spiritual things .... Eph. 4:13 1390

Statute of limitation

Recognized in the Law .... Deut. 15:1-5, 9 227

Steadfastness—*firm, persistent and determined in one's endeavors*

A. *In human things, following:*
Person .... Ruth 1:18 313
Leader .... Jer. 35:1-19 882
Principle ...... Dan. 1:8 976

B. *In spiritual things:*
Enduring chastisement ...... Heb. 12:7 1462
Bearing persecution .... Rom. 8:35-37 1333
Maintaining perseverance ...... Heb. 3:6, 14 1452
Stability of faith .... Col. 2:5 1406
Persevering in service .... 1 Cor. 15:58 1360
Resisting Satan .... 1 Pet. 5:9 1483
Defending Christian liberty .... Gal. 5:1 1382

C. *Elements of, seen in:*
Having a goal .... Phil. 3:12-14 1401
Discipline ..... 1 Cor. 9:25-27 1353
Run the race .. Heb. 12:1, 2 1462
Never give up .... Rev. 3:10, 21 1521

Stealing—*taking another's property*

Common on earth .... Matt. 6:19 1123
Forbidden in:
Law .... Ex. 20:15 90
Gospel .... Rom. 13:9 1339
Christians not to do .... Eph. 4:28 1391
Excludes from heaven .... 1 Cor. 6:9, 10 1349
None in heaven ... Matt. 6:20 1123

Stephanas—*crowned*

Corinthian Christian .... 1 Cor. 1:16 1345
First convert of Achaia .... 1 Cor. 16:15 1361
Visits Paul .... 1 Cor. 16:17 1361

Stephen—*wreath or crown*

One of the seven deacons .... Acts 6:1-8 1278
Accused falsely by Jews .... Acts 6:9-15 1279
Spoke before the Jewish Sanhedrin .... Acts 7:2-53 1279
Became first Christian martyr .... Acts 7:54-60 1282
Saul (Paul) instigated in death of .... Acts 7:58 1282

Stew—*a thick vegetable soup*

Price of Esau's birthright .... Gen. 25:29-34 34
Eaten by Elisha's disciples .... 2 Kin. 4:38-41 433
Ordinary food .... Hag. 2:12 1065

Steward, stewardship—*a trust granted for profitable use*

A. *Descriptive of:*
One over Joseph's household .... Gen. 43:19 56
Curator or guardian ...... Matt. 20:8 1140
Manager .... Luke 16:2, 3 1218
Management of entrusted duties .... 1 Cor. 9:17 1353

B. *Duties of, to:*
Expend monies .... Rom. 16:23 1341
Serve wisely .. Luke 12:42 1215

C. *Of spiritual things, based on:*
LORD's ownership ... Ps. 24:1, 2 638; Rom. 14:8 1339
Our redemption ... 1 Cor. 6:20 1351
Gifts bestowed upon us ..... Matt. 25:14, 15 1148; 1 Pet. 4:10 1483
Offices given to us .... Eph. 3:2-10 1388; Titus 1:7 1440
Faithful in responsibilities .... Luke 16:1-3 1218

Stewardship, personal financial

Basic principles:
Settling accounts .... Rom. 14:12 1339
God's ownership ...... Ps. 24:1 638; Rom. 14:7, 8 1339
Finances and spirituality inseparable ..... Matt. 19:16-22 1139; Luke 16:10-13 1219; 1 Cor. 6:20 1351; 2 Cor. 8:3-8 1371
Needs will be provided .... Matt. 6:24-34 1123; Phil. 4:19 1402
Content with what God provides .... Ps. 37:25 646; 1 Tim. 6:6-10 1430; Heb. 13:5 1463
Righteousness ...... Prov. 16:8 728; Rom. 12:17 1337; Prov. 22:7 734
Avoid debt .... Rom. 13:8 1339
Do not co-sign ... Prov. 6:1-5 718; Prov. 22:26 735
Inheritance uncertain ...... Prov. 17:2 729; Prov. 20:21 732
Proper priority .... Matt. 6:19-21, 33 1123
Prosperity is from God .... Deut. 29:9 240; Ps. 1:1-3 625; 3 John 2 1506
Saving .... Prov. 21:20 733
Laziness condemned ..... Prov. 24:30, 31 737; Heb. 6:12 1455
Giving is encouraged ...... Prov. 3:9, 10 715; Mal. 3:10-12 1082; 2 Cor. 9:6-8 1372

Sticks—*pieces of wood*

Gathering on Sabbath condemned .... Num. 15:32-35 179
Necessary .... 1 Kin. 17:10-12 416
Miracle producing .... 2 Kin. 6:6 434
Two become one .... Ezek. 37:16-22 961
Viper in bundle of .... Acts 28:3 1315

Stiff-necked—*rebellious; unteachable*

A. *Indicative of Israel's rebelliousness at:*
Sinai .... Ex. 32:9 105
Conquest ...... Deut. 9:6, 13 220
Captivity ...... 2 Chr. 36:13 538
Christ's first advent .... Acts 7:51 1282

B. *Remedies of, seen in:*
Circumcision (regeneration) ...... Deut. 10:16 221
Yield to God .. 2 Chr. 30:8 529

Still

A. *Indicative of:*
God's voice .... 1 Kin. 19:12 420
God's presence ...... Ps. 139:18 705
Fright .... Ex. 15:16 86
Fixed character .... Rev. 22:11 1539
Peace .... Jer. 47:6 895
Quietness ..... Num. 13:30 176

B. *Accomplished by:*
God .... Ps. 107:29 688
Christ .... Mark 4:39 1164
Submission .... Ps. 46:10 651
Communion ... Ps. 4:4 626

Stink, stench—*a foul smell*

A. *Caused by:*
Dead fish ..... Ex. 7:18, 21 75
Corpse .... John 11:39 1253
Wounds .... Ps. 38:5 646

B. *Figurative of:*
Hell .... Is. 34:3, 4 805

Stir up

A. *Of strife, etc., by:*
Wrath .... Prov. 15:18 727
Hatred .... Prov. 10:12 722
Grievous words .... Prov. 15:1 727
Unbelief ...... Acts 13:50 1292
Agitators ...... Acts 6:12 1279
Kings .... Dan. 11:2, 25 991

B. *Of good things:*
Generosity .... Ex. 35:21, 26 108
Repentance ... Is. 64:7 836
Ministry ...... 2 Tim. 1:6 1433
Memory .... 2 Pet. 1:13 1487

C. *Of God's sovereignty in:*
Fulfilling His Word .... 2 Chr. 36:22 538; Ezra 1:1 542
Accomplishing His purpose ...... Is. 13:17 786; Hag. 1:14 1065

Stocks—*blocks of wood*

Instrument of punishment ...... Acts 16:19, 24 1295
Punishment .... Job 33:11 611

Stoics—*pertaining to a colonnade or porch*

Sect of philosophers founded by Zeno around 308 B.C. .... Acts 17:18 1297

Stones—*rocks*

A. *Natural uses of:*
Weighing ..... Lev. 19:36 142
Knives .... Ex. 4:25 72
Weapons ...... 1 Sam. 17:40-50 343
Holding water .... Ex. 17:1-7 87
Covering wells .... Gen. 29:2 38
Covering tombs .... Matt. 27:60 1154

SUBJECT REFERENCE PAGE

Tenderness—*expressing a feeling or sympathy*

Shown toward the young .... Gen. 33:13 44
Expressed toward an enemy .... 1 Sam. 30:11-15 354
Illustrated by a Samaritan ...... Luke 10:33-36 1209
Manifested by a father .... Luke 15:11-24 1218

Tens of the Bible

A. *Descriptive of:*
Brothers ...... Gen. 42:3 54
Cubits .... Ex. 26:16 98
Pillars and sockets ...... Ex. 27:12 99
Command-ments .... Ex. 34:28 108
Shekels .... Num. 7:14 168
Years .... Ruth 1:4 313
Loaves .... 1 Sam. 17:17 342
Tribes .... 1 Kin. 11:31, 35 408
Degrees .... 2 Kin. 20:9-11 454
Virgins .... Matt. 25:1-13 1148
Talents .... Matt. 25:28 1149
Lepers .... Luke 17:11-19 1220
Pieces of money ...... Luke 19:12-27 1222
Horns .... Rev. 12:3 1529

B. *Expressive of:*
Repre-sentation ..... Ruth 4:2 315
Intensity .... Num. 14:22 177
Sufficiency ..... Neh. 4:12 560
Magnitude ...... Dan. 1:20 977
Remnant .... Amos 5:3 1018
Completion .. Dan. 7:7, 20, 24 985
Perfection ..... Luke 19:16-24 1222

Tentmaker

The occupation of:
Aquila and Priscilla .... Acts 18:2, 3 1299
Paul .... Acts 18:2, 3 1299

Tents—*movable habitations*

A. *Used by:*
People .... 1 Chr. 17:5 484
Shepherds .... Is. 38:12 810
Armies .... 1 Sam. 13:2 334
Rechabites ..... Jer. 35:7, 10 883
Women .... Gen. 24:67 33
Maidservants .. Gen. 31:33 42

B. *Features concerning:*
Fastened by cords .... Is. 54:2 825
Door provided ..... Gen. 18:1 24
Used for the ark .... 2 Sam. 7:1-6 365

C. *Figurative of:*
Shortness of life .... Is. 38:12; 2 Cor. 5:1 810; 1368
Heavens ...... Is. 40:22 812
Enlarge .... Is. 54:2 825

Terah—*duration; wandering*

1. Father of Abram .... Gen. 11:26 18
Idolater .... Josh. 24:2 277
Dies in Haran .... Gen. 11:25-32 18
2. Israelite encamp-ment .... Num. 33:1, 27 199

Teraphim—*household idols*

Laban's, stolen by Rachel .... Gen. 31:19-35 42
Used in idolatry ... Hos. 3:4 998

Terebinth tree

A. *Uses of:*
Landmarks .... Judg. 6:11, 19 290
Burial place .... Gen. 35:8 46

B. *Figurative of:*
Judgment ..... Is. 1:29, 30 772

Teresh—*dry*

King's official ..... Esth. 2:21 578

Terrestrial—*belonging to the earth*

Spoken of bodies .... 1 Cor. 15:40 1360

Terror—*extreme fear*

A. *Caused by:*
Lord's presence ..... Heb. 12:21 1463
Fear .... Job 9:34 596
Death .... Job 24:17 606
War .... Ezek. 21:12 940
Fright .... Luke 24:37 1231
Persecutors .... 1 Pet. 3:14 1481

B. *Sent as means of:*
Protection ..... Gen. 35:5 46
Punishment ... Lev. 26:16 152

C. *Safeguards against, found in:*
God's promise ...... Ps. 91:5 678
God's plan .... Luke 21:9 1224

Tertius—*third*

Paul's scribe ...... Rom. 16:22 1341

Tertullus—*diminutive of Tertius*

Orator who accuses Paul .... Acts 24:1-8 1308

Test—*something that manifests a person's real character*

A. *Kinds of:*
Given to Solomon ..... 1 Kin. 10:1-3 406
Physical ...... 1 Sam. 17:38, 39 343
Supernatural .. Ex. 7–11 74
Spiritual ...... Dan. 6:1-28 984
National ...... Ex. 32:1-35 105

B. *Purposes of, to:*
Test obedience ... Gen. 3:1-8; Gen. 22:1-18 8; 30
Learn God's will .... Judg. 6:36-40 291
Accept good diet .... Dan. 1:12-16 976
Refute Satan's claims .... Job 1:6-22 589
Destroy idolatry ..... 1 Kin. 18:22-24 417

C. *Descriptive of:*
Testing physically ... 1 Sam. 17:39; Luke 14:19 343; 1217
Testing morally .... John 6:6 1244
Showing something to be true .... Gen. 42:15, 16 55

D. *Objects of, among Christians:*
Faith .... 2 Cor. 13:5 1375
Abilities .... 1 Tim. 3:10 1427

Testament—*a will or covenant*

Descriptive of a person's will .... Heb. 9:15-17 1457

Testimony—*witness borne in behalf of something*

A. *Necessary elements of, seen in:*
Verbal expression ... 2 Sam. 1:16 360
Witnesses ... Neh. 13:15; John 8:17 572; 1249

B. *Means of:*
Prophets ...... Acts 10:42, 43 1288
Friends .... 3 John 12 1506
Jews .... Acts 22:12 1306
Messengers ... Acts 20:21, 24 1303
Song .... Deut. 31:21 243
Our sins .... Is. 59:12 831

C. *Reaction to:*
Believed ...... 2 Thess. 1:10 1421
Confirmed .... 1 Cor. 1:6 1345

D. *Purpose of, to:*
Establish the Gospel .... Acts 10:42 1288
Prove Jesus was the Christ .... Acts 18:5 1299
Lead to repentance .... Acts 20:21 1303
Qualify for office .... 1 Tim. 3:7 1427

Tests of Faith

By:
Difficult demands .... Gen. 12:1, 2 18
Severe trials ...... Job 1:6-22 589
Prosperity of the wicked .... Ps. 73:1-28 666
Hardships ..... 2 Cor. 11:21-33 1373

Teth

Letter in the Hebrew alphabet .... Ps. 119:65-72 696

Tetrarch—*a ruler over a fourth part of a kingdom*

Applied to Herod Antipas .... Matt. 14:1 1134

Thaddaeus—*breast*

One of the twelve disciples .... Mark 3:18 1163

Thahash—*porpoise, dolphin*

Son of Nahor ..... Gen. 22:24 31

Thankfulness—*gratitude for blessings*

A. *Described as:*
Spiritual sacrifice ...... Ps. 116:17 693
Duty .... 2 Thess. 2:13 1421
Unceasing .... Eph. 1:16 1387
Spontaneous .. Phil. 1:3 1398
In Christ's name .... Eph. 5:20 1392
God's will ..... 1 Thess. 5:18 1416
Heaven's theme .... Rev. 7:12 1525

B. *Expressed for:*
Food .... John 6:11, 23 1244
Wisdom .... Dan. 2:23 977
Converts ...... 1 Thess. 1:2 1413
Prayer answered .... John 11:41 1255
Victory .... 1 Cor. 15:57 1360
Salvation ..... 2 Cor. 9:15 1372
Lord's Supper .... 1 Cor. 11:24 1355
Changed lives .... 1 Thess. 2:13 1415

C. *Expressed by:*
Healed Samaritan .... Luke 17:12-19 1220
Righteous ..... Ps. 140:13 706

Theater—*a place of public assembly*

Paul kept from entering .... Acts 19:29-31 1302

TOPICAL INDEX

SUBJECT	REFERENCE	PAGE
Women of the Bible, named—continued		
Jerioth, wife of Caleb	1 Chr. 2:18	466
Jerusha, daughter of Zadok	2 Kin. 15:33	447
Jezebel, wife of Ahab	1 Kin. 16:30, 31	414
Joanna, wife of Chuza	Luke 8:3	1205
Jochebed, mother of Moses	Ex. 6:20	74
Judith, daughter of Beeri	Gen. 26:34	36
Julia, Christian woman of Rome	Rom. 16:15	1341
Keren-Happuch, Job's daughter	Job 42:14	620
Keturah, second wife of Abraham	Gen. 25:1	33
Keziah, daughter of Job	Job 42:14	620
Leah, wife of Jacob	Gen. 29:21-25	40
Lois, grandmother of Timothy	2 Tim. 1:5	1433
Lo-Ruhamah, daughter of Gomer	Hos. 1:3-6	996
Lydia, first Christian convert in Europe	Acts 16:14	1295
Maachah		
(1) daughter of Nahor	Gen. 22:23, 24	31
(2) daughter of Talmai	2 Sam. 3:3	362
(3) daughter of Abishalom	1 Kin. 15:2	412
(4) mother of Asa	1 Kin. 15:9, 10	412
(5) concubine of Caleb	1 Chr. 2:48	466
(6) wife of Machir	1 Chr. 7:16	472
(7) wife of Jehiel	1 Chr. 8:29	473
Mahalath		
(1) wife of Esau	Gen. 28:9	38
(2) granddaughter of David	2 Chr. 11:18	512
Mahlah, daughter of Zelophehad	Num. 26:33	191
Mara, another name for Naomi	Ruth 1:20	313
Martha, friend of Christ	Luke 10:38-41	1211
Mary		
(1) mother of Jesus	Matt. 1:16	1115
(2) Mary Magdalene	Matt. 27:56-61	1154
(3) Mary, sister of Martha	Luke 10:38, 39	1211
(4) Mary, wife of Clopas	John 19:25	1264
(5) Mary, mother of Mark	Acts 12:12	1289
(6) a Christian at Rome	Rom. 16:6	1341
Matred, mother-in-law of Hadar	Gen. 36:39	48
Mehetabel, daughter of Matred	Gen. 36:39	48
Merab, King Saul's eldest daughter	1 Sam. 14:49	337
Meshullemeth, wife of Manasseh	2 Kin. 21:18, 19	455
Michal, daughter of King Saul	1 Sam. 14:49	337
Milcah		
(1) daughter of Haran	Gen. 11:29	18
(2) daughter of Zelophehad	Num. 26:33	191
Miriam		
(1) sister of Moses	Ex. 15:20	86
(2) disputed daughter of Ezra	1 Chr. 4:17	467
Naamah		
(1) daughter of Lamech	Gen. 4:19-22	10
(2) wife of Solomon	1 Kin. 14:21	412
Naarah, one of the wives of Ashur	1 Chr. 4:5	467
Naomi, wife of Elimelech	Ruth 1:2	313
Nehushta, daughter of Elnathan	2 Kin. 24:8	458
Noadiah, a false prophetess	Neh. 6:14	562
Noah, daughter of Zelophehad	Num. 26:33	191
Oholah	Ezek. 23:4	942
Oholibah	Ezek. 23:4	942
Orpah, sister-in-law of Ruth	Ruth 1:4	313
Peninnah, one of the wives of Elkanah	1 Sam. 1:1, 2	321
Persis, convert of early Church	Rom. 16:12	1341
Phoebe, a deaconess	Rom. 16:1-2	1341
Priscilla, wife of Aquila	Acts 18:2	1299
Puah, a midwife	Ex. 1:15	69
Rachel, wife of Jacob	Gen. 29:28	40
Rahab, aid to Israel's spies	Josh. 2:1-3	253
Reumah, mother of Tebah	Gen. 22:24	31
Rhoda, a girl	Acts 12:13	1289
Rizpah, concubine of Saul	2 Sam. 3:7	362
Ruth, daughter-in-law of Naomi	Ruth 1:3, 4	313
Salome, wife of Zebedee	Matt. 27:56; Mark 15:40	1154; 1184
Sapphira, wife of Ananias	Acts 5:1	1277
Sarah, (Sarai) wife of Abraham (Abram)	Gen. 11:29	18
Serah, daughter of Asher	Gen. 46:17	59
Sheerah, daughter of Beriah	1 Chr. 7:23, 24	472
Shelomith		
(1) daughter of Dibri	Lev. 24:11	149
(2) daughter of Zerubbabel	1 Chr. 3:19	467
Shimeath, mother of Zabad	2 Chr. 24:26	524
Shimrith, mother of Jehozabad	2 Chr. 24:26	524
Shiphrah, a midwife	Ex. 1:15	69
Shua, daughter of Heber	1 Chr. 7:32	473
Susanna, ministered to Jesus	Luke 8:3	1205
Syntyche, convert of Church at Philippi	Phil. 4:2	1401
Tabitha, same as Dorcas	Acts 9:36	1286
Tahpenes, queen of Egypt	1 Kin. 11:19	408
Tamar		
(1) daughter-in-law of Judah	Gen. 38:6	50
(2) a daughter of David	2 Sam. 13:1	371
(3) daughter of Absalom	2 Sam. 14:27	374
Taphath, one of Solomon's daughters	1 Kin. 4:11	397
Timna, concubine of Eliphaz	Gen. 36:12	48
Tirzah, one of daughters of Zelophehad	Num. 26:33	191
Tryphena convert at Rome	Rom. 16:12	1341
Tryphosa, convert at Rome	Rom. 16:12	1341
Vashti, wife of Ahasuerus	Esth. 1:9	577
Zebudah, mother of Jehoiakim	2 Kin. 23:36	458
Zeresh, wife of Haman	Esth. 5:10	581
Zeruah, a widow	1 Kin. 11:26	408
Zeruiah, mother of Joab	2 Sam. 17:25	377
Zibiah, mother of Jehoash	2 Kin. 12:1	443
Zillah, wife of Lamech	Gen. 4:19	10
Zilpah, Leah's handmaid	Gen. 29:24	40
Zipporah, wife of Moses	Ex. 2:21	69
Wonderful—*full of wonder*		
A. *Ascribed to:*		
Human love	2 Sam. 1:26	360
LORD's works	Ps. 78:4	669
Mysterious things	Prov. 30:18	744
Lord's Law	Ps. 119:18	694
Lord's testimonies	Ps. 119:129	698
Lord's knowledge	Ps. 139:6	704
Our being	Ps. 139:14	705
Messiah's name	Is. 9:6	780
B. *Descriptive of the Lord's work, as:*		
Numerous	Ps. 40:5	647
Transmitted	Ps. 78:4	669
Remembered	Ps. 111:4	691
Praised	Is. 25:1	794
Wonders—*miraculous works*		
A. *Performed by:*		
God	Heb. 2:4	1450
Moses and Aaron	Ex. 11:10	80
Christ	Acts 2:22	1273
Apostles	Acts 2:43	1274
Jesus' name	Acts 4:30	1277
Stephen	Acts 6:8	1279
Paul and Barnabas	Acts 14:3	1292
Paul	2 Cor. 12:12	1374
B. *Places of:*		
Egypt	Acts 7:36	1281
Land of Ham	Ps. 105:27	685
Canaan	Josh. 3:5	254
Deep	Ps. 107:24	687
Heaven	Dan. 6:27	985
Among the peoples	Ps. 77:14	669
C. *Described as:*		
Numerous	Ex. 11:9	80
Great	Acts 6:8	1279
Mighty	Dan. 4:3	980
D. *Man's reactions to:*		
Did not remember	Neh. 9:17	568
Forgetful of	Ps. 78:11, 12	670
Not understanding	Ps. 106:7	686
Not believing	Ps. 78:32	670
Inquiring about	Jer. 21:2	867
E. *Believer's attitude toward, to:*		
Remember	1 Chr. 16:9, 12	482
Declare	Ps. 71:17	665
Give thanks for	Ps. 136:1, 4	703
Consider	Job 37:14	615
Wood		
A. *Descriptive of:*		
Part of a tree	Num. 19:6	182
Forest	Josh. 17:15, 18	270

SUBJECT REFERENCE PAGE

SUBJECT REFERENCE PAGE

Works, good—continued

Secure righteousness ... Rom. 9:31, 32 ... 1334
Substitute for grace ... Rom. 11:6 ... 1335

B. *Considered positively:*
Reward for ... 1 Cor. 3:13-15 ... 1346
Created for ... Eph. 2:10 ... 1387
Prepared for ... 2 Tim. 2:21 ... 1434
Equipped for ... 2 Tim. 3:17 ... 1436

Works, Satan's (see Satan)

Works, the unbeliever's

A. *Described as:*
Wicked ... Col. 1:21 ... 1406
Done in darkness ... Is. 29:15 ... 800
Abominable ... Ps. 14:1 ... 632
Deceitful ... Prov. 11:18 ... 723
Evil ... John 7:7 ... 1247
Unfruitful ... Eph. 5:11 ... 1391

B. *God's attitude toward, will:*
Never forget ... Amos 8:7 ... 1022
Reward ... Prov. 24:12 ... 737
Bring to judgment ... Rev. 20:12, 13 ... 1538

C. *Believer's relation to:*
Cast off ... Rom. 13:12 ... 1339
Have no fellowship with ... Eph. 5:11 ... 1391
Be delivered from ... 2 Tim. 4:18 ... 1437

World

A. *God's relation to, as:*
Maker ... Jer. 10:12 ... 857
Possessor ... Ps. 24:1 ... 638
Redeemer ... John 3:16 ... 1239
Judge ... Ps. 96:13 ... 680

B. *Christ's relation to, as:*
Maker ... John 1:10 ... 1236
Sin-bearer ... John 1:29 ... 1237
Savior ... John 12:47 ... 1256
Life ... John 6:33, 51 ... 1246
Light ... John 8:12 ... 1249
Judge ... Acts 17:31 ... 1299
Overcomer ... John 16:33 ... 1261
Reconciler ... 2 Cor. 5:19 ... 1369

C. *Christian's relation to:*
Light of ... Matt. 5:14 ... 1120
Not of ... John 17:14, 16 ... 1262
Chosen out of ... John 15:19 ... 1259
Tribulation in ... John 16:33 ... 1261
Sent into by Christ ... John 17:18 ... 1262
Not conformed to ... Rom. 12:2 ... 1337
Crucified to ... Gal. 6:14 ... 1383
To live soberly ... Titus 2:12 ... 1442
Unspotted from ... James 1:27 ... 1468
Overcomers of ... 1 John 5:4, 5 ... 1499
Denying desires of ... Titus 2:12 ... 1442

D. *Dangers of, arising from:*
Wisdom ... 1 Cor. 3:19 ... 1348
Love of ... 2 Tim. 4:10 ... 1436
Friendship ... James 4:4 ... 1471
Corruptions ... 2 Pet. 1:4 ... 1487
Lusts ... 1 John 2:15-17 ... 1496
False prophets ... 1 John 4:1 ... 1498
Deceivers ... 2 John 7 ... 1502

E. *In the plan of redemption:*
Elect chosen before ... Eph. 1:4 ... 1387
Revelation made before ... Matt. 13:35 ... 1133
Sin's entrance into ... Rom. 5:12 ... 1329
Its guilt before God ... Rom. 3:19 ... 1325
Original revelation to ... Rom. 1:20 ... 1324
God's love for ... John 3:16 ... 1239
Christ's mission to ... John 12:47 ... 1256
Spirit's conviction of ... John 16:8 ... 1259
Gospel preached in ... Matt. 24:14 ... 1147
Reconciliation of ... 2 Cor. 5:19 ... 1369
Destruction of ... 2 Pet. 3:7 ... 1489
Final judgment of ... Acts 17:31 ... 1299
Satan deceives ... Rev. 12:9 ... 1529

Worm—*a soft-bodied, slender, creeping animal*

A. *Ravages of:*
On bread ... Ex. 16:15, 20 ... 87
On plants ... Jon. 4:7 ... 1033
On the body ... Acts 12:23 ... 1289
In the grave ... Job 24:19, 20 ... 606
In hell ... Mark 9:44-48 ... 1172

B. *Figurative of:*
Insignificance ... Job 25:6 ... 606
Messiah ... Ps. 22:6 ... 637

Wormwood—*a bitter-tasting plant*

Figurative of idolatry ... Deut. 29:18 ... 241
Of adultery ... Prov. 5:4 ... 718
Of God's judgments ... Jer. 9:15 ... 855
Symbol of doom ... Rev. 8:11 ... 1526

Worry (see Cares, worldly)

Worship—*an act of reverence*

A. *Of God:*
Defined ... John 4:20-24 ... 1241
Commanded ... 1 Chr. 16:29 ... 483
Corrupted ... Rom. 1:25 ... 1324
Perverted ... 2 Kin. 21:3, 21 ... 454
Debated ... 1 Kin. 18:21-39 ... 417

B. *Of Christ, by:*
Angels ... Heb. 1:6 ... 1450
Magi ... Matt. 2:1-2, 11 ... 1116
Men ... John 9:30-38 ... 1251
Women ... Matt. 15:25 ... 1135
Disciples ... Matt. 28:17 ... 1155
Heavenly choir ... Rev. 4:10, 11 ... 1523

C. *Of wrong objects, such as:*
Heavenly host ... Deut. 17:3 ... 228
Other gods ... Ex. 34:14 ... 107
Demons ... Deut. 32:17 ... 244
Creatures ... Rom. 1:25 ... 1324
Images ... Dan. 3:5-18 ... 979
Man ... Acts 10:25, 26 ... 1287
Antichrist ... Rev. 13:4-13 ... 1529

D. *Of wrong objects, by:*
Israel ... 2 Kin. 21:3, 21 ... 454
Pagans ... Rom. 1:25 ... 1324
Professing Christians ... Col. 2:18 ... 1408
World ... 2 Thess. 2:3-12 ... 1421

Worthiness—*acceptableness for some benefit*

A. *Of Christ:*
For more glory ... Heb. 3:3 ... 1452
To open the book ... Rev. 5:2, 4 ... 1523
To receive worship ... Rev. 5:9-14 ... 1523

B. *Of believers, for:*
Provisions ... Matt. 10:10 ... 1127
Discipleship ... Matt. 10:37 ... 1129
Their calling ... Eph. 4:1 ... 1390
Suffering ... Acts 5:41 ... 1278
Their walk ... Col. 1:10 ... 1406
Honor ... 1 Tim. 6:1 ... 1430
Kingdom ... 2 Thess. 1:5 ... 1421

Worthless—*useless, despicable*

Sacrifice ... Is. 1:13 ... 772
Religion ... James 1:26 ... 1468
Vile things ... 1 Sam. 15:9 ... 339

See Futile

Wound—*to injure*

A. *Of physical injury, by:*
God ... Deut. 32:39 ... 245
Battle ... 1 Sam. 31:3 ... 355
Adultery ... Prov. 6:32, 33 ... 720
Robbers ... Luke 10:30, 34 ... 1209
Evil spirit ... Acts 19:16 ... 1300

B. *Of spiritual injury, by:*
God's punishment ... Jer. 30:14 ... 876
Drunkenness ... Prov. 23:29, 30 ... 736
Adultery ... Prov. 6:32, 33 ... 720
Sin ... Is. 1:6 ... 772

Wrappings—*clothes for the dead*

Lazarus attired in ... John 11:43, 44 ... 1255

Wrath of God

A. *Described as:*
Anger ... Num. 32:10-13 ... 198
Prolonged ... Ps. 90:9 ... 678
Great ... Zech. 7:12 ... 1071
Willing ... Rom. 9:22 ... 1334
Revealed ... Rom. 1:18 ... 1324
Stored up ... Rom. 2:5-8 ... 1324
Abiding ... John 3:36 ... 1241
Accomplished ... Rev. 6:16, 17 ... 1524

B. *Caused by:*
Apostasy ... 2 Chr. 34:24, 25 ... 535
Sympathy with evil ... Lev. 10:1-6 ... 128
Unfaithfulness ... Josh. 22:20 ... 276
Provocations ... 2 Kin. 23:26 ... 458
Fellowship with evil ... 2 Chr. 19:2 ... 519
Mockery ... 2 Chr. 36:16 ... 538
Idolatry ... Ps. 78:58, 59 ... 671
Intermarriage ... Ezra 10:10-14 ... 553
Profaning the Sabbath ... Neh. 13:18 ... 573
Speaking against God ... Ps. 78:19-21 ... 670

C. *Effects of, seen in:*
Egypt's destruction ... Ex. 15:4, 7 ... 85
Great plague ... Num. 11:33 ... 175
Israel's wanderings ... Num. 32:10-13 ... 198
Withholding of rain ... Deut. 11:17 ... 222
Destruction of a people ... 1 Sam. 28:18 ... 353
Trouble ... Ps. 90:7 ... 678
Man's death ... Ps. 90:9 ... 678
Jerusalem's destruction ... Luke 21:23, 24 ... 1225
Punishments of hell ... Rev. 14:10 ... 1531

SUBJECT REFERENCE PAGE

Zererah

Town in the Jordan valley ....Judg. 7:22 292
Same as Zaretan ....1 Kin. 7:46 401

Zeresh—*golden*

Wife of Haman ....Esth. 5:10, 14 581

Zereth—*splendor*

Judahite ....1 Chr. 4:5-7 467

Zereth Shahar—*the splendor of dawn*

City of Reuben ....Josh. 13:19 266

Zeror—*bundle*

Benjamite ....1 Sam. 9:1 330

Zeruah—*smitten; leprous*

Mother of King Jeroboam I ......1 Kin. 11:26 408

Zerubbabel—*seed of Babel*

Descendant of David ....1 Chr. 3:19 467
Leader of Jewish exiles ....Neh. 7:6, 7 563
Restores worship in Jerusalem ....Ezra 3:1-8 545
Rebuilds the Temple ....Zech. 4:1-14 1070
Prophecy concerning ......Hag. 2:23 1065
Ancestor of Christ ....{Matt. 1:12, 13 1115; Luke 3:27 1195}

Zeruiah—*balm*

Mother of Joab ...2 Sam. 17:25 377

Zetham—*olive tree*

Gershonite Levite ....1 Chr. 23:7, 8 490

Zethan—*olive tree*

Benjamite ....1 Chr. 7:6, 10 472

Zethar—*sacrifice*

One of the seven chamberlains of King Ahasuerus ....Esth. 1:10 577

Zia—*the trembler*

Gadite ....1 Chr. 5:11, 13 468

Ziba—*plant*

Saul's servant ....2 Sam. 9:9 367
Befriends David ...2 Sam. 16:1-4 375
Accused of deception by Mephibosheth ....{2 Sam. 19:17-30} 379

Zibeon—*hyena*

Son of Seir and a clan chief ....Gen. 36:20, 21 48

Zibia—*gazelle*

Benjamite and household head ....1 Chr. 8:8, 9 473

Zibiah—*gazelle*

Mother of King Jehoash ....2 Kin. 12:1 443

Zichri—*famous*

1. Kohathite Levite ....Ex. 6:21 74
2, 3, 4. Three Benjamites ..{1 Chr. 8:19, 23, 27} 473
5. Son of Asaph ....1 Chr. 9:15 474
6. Descendant of Moses ....1 Chr. 26:25 493
7. Reubenite .....1 Chr. 27:16 493
8. Judahite ....2 Chr. 17:16 517
9. Mighty man in Pekah's army ....2 Chr. 28:7 527
10. Benjamite ....Neh. 11:9 570
11. Postexilic priest ....Neh. 12:17 571

Ziddim—*sides*

City of Naphtali ..Josh. 19:35 272

Ziha

Head of a Nethinim family ....Ezra 2:43 544

Ziklag—*winding*

City on the border of Judah ....Josh. 15:1, 31 267
Assigned to Simeon ....Josh. 19:1, 5 271
Held by David .....1 Sam. 27:6 352
Overthrown by Amalekites ......1 Sam. 30:1-31 354
Occupied by returnees ....Neh. 11:28 571

Zillah—*shadow*

One of Lamech's wives ....Gen. 4:19-23 10

Zillethai—*shadow of Yahweh*

1. Benjamite ......1 Chr. 8:20 473
2. Manassite captain ....1 Chr. 12:20 479

Zilpah—*a drop*

Leah's maid ......Gen. 29:24 40
Mother of Gad and Asher ....Gen. 30:9-13 41

Zimmah—*counsel*

Gershonite Levite ....{1 Chr. 6:20, 42, 43} 469

Zimran—*antelope*

Son of Abraham and Keturah ....Gen. 25:1, 2 33

Zimri—*pertaining to an antelope*

1. Grandson of Judah ....1 Chr. 2:3-6 465
Called Zabdi ..Josh. 7:1-18 258
2. Simeonite prince slain by Phinehas .....Num. 25:6-14 190
3. Benjamite .....1 Chr. 8:1, 36 473
4. King of Israel for seven days ....1 Kin. 16:8-20 413
5. Place or people otherwise unknown .....Jer. 25:25 871

Zin—*lowland*

Wilderness through which the Israelites passed ....Num. 20:1 183
Border of Judah and Edom ....Josh. 15:1-3 267

Zina—*abundance*

Son of Shimei .....1 Chr. 23:10 490

Zion—*fortress*

A. *Used literally of:*
Jebusite fortress captured by David ....2 Sam. 5:6-9 364
Place from which Solomon brings the ark ....2 Chr. 5:2 506
Area occupied by the Temple ....Is. 8:18 780

B. *Used figuratively of:*
Israel as a people of God ....2 Kin. 19:21 453
God's spiritual kingdom .....Ps. 125:1 700
Eternal city ....Heb. 12:22, 28 1463
Heaven ....Rev. 14:1 1531

Zior—*smallness*

Town of Judah ....Josh. 15:54 268

Ziph—*refining place*

1. Town in south Judah ....Josh. 15:24 268
2. City in the hill country of Judah ....Josh. 15:55 268
David hides from Saul in wilderness here ....{1 Sam. 23:14, 15} 348
3. Son of Jehaleleel .....1 Chr. 4:16 467

Ziphah—*lent*

Son of Jehaleleel ....1 Chr. 4:16 467

Ziphites—*inhabitants of Ziph*

Betray David {1 Sam. 23:19-24} 349

Ziphron—*beautiful top*

Place in north Palestine ....Num. 34:9 202

Zippor—*sparrow*

Father of Balak ....Num. 22:4, 10 186

Zipporah—*bird*

Daughter of Jethro; wife of Moses ....Ex. 18:1, 2 88

Zithri—*my protection*

Grandson of Kohath ....Ex. 6:18, 22 74

Ziv—*splendor, bloom*

Second month of the Jewish year ....1 Kin. 6:1 398

Ziz—*brightness*

Pass leading from Dead Sea to Jerusalem ....2 Chr. 20:16 520

Ziza—*brightness*

1. Simeonite leader ....{1 Chr. 4:24, 37, 38} 468
2. Son of Rehoboam ...{2 Chr. 11:18-20} 512

Zizah

Gershonite Levite ....{1 Chr. 23:7, 10, 11} 490
See Zina

Zoan

City in Lower Egypt ....Num. 13:22 176

SUBJECT	REFERENCE	PAGE
Places of God's miracles	Ps. 78:12, 43	670
Princes resided at	Is. 30:2, 4	800
Object of God's wrath	Ezek. 30:14	953

Zoar—*little*

Ancient city of Canaan originally named Bela	Gen. 14:2, 8	21
Spared destruction at Lot's request	Gen. 19:20-23	28
Seen by Moses from Mt. Pisgah	Deut. 34:1-3	247
Object of prophetic doom	Is. 15:5	788

Zobah

Syrian kingdom; wars against Saul	1 Sam. 14:47	337

Zobebah—*the affable*

Judahite	1 Chr. 4:1, 8	467

Zohar—*gray*

1. Father of Ephron the Hittite	Gen. 23:8	31
2. Son of Simeon	Gen. 46:10	59

Zoheleth—*serpent*

Stone near En Rogel	1 Kin. 1:9	391

Zoheth—*proud*

Descendant of Judah	1 Chr. 4:1, 20	467

Zophah—*pot-bellied jug*

Asherite	1 Chr. 7:30, 35, 36	473

Zophar—*chirper*

Naamathite and friend of Job	Job 2:11	590

Zophim—*watchers*

Field on the top of Mt. Pisgah	Num. 23:14	188

Zorah, Zareah, Zoreah—*hornet*

Town of Judah	Josh. 15:1, 33	267
Inhabited by Danites	Josh. 19:40, 41	272
Place of Samson's birth and burial	Judg. 13:24, 25	300
	Judg. 16:30, 31	303
Inhabited by returnees	Neh. 11:25, 29	571

Zorathite

Native of Zorah	1 Chr. 4:2	467
Descendants of Caleb	1 Chr. 2:50, 53	466

Zorite

Same as Zorathite	1 Chr. 2:54	466

Zuar—*small, little*

Father of Nethanel	Num. 1:8	159

Zuph—*honeycomb*

1. Ancestor of Samuel	1 Chr. 6:33, 35	470
2. Region in Judah	1 Sam. 9:4-6	330

Zur—*rock*

1. A Midianite leader	Num. 25:15, 18	190
2. Son of Jehiel	1 Chr. 8:30	473

Zuriel—*God is a rock*

Merarite Levite	Num. 3:35	163

Zurishaddai—*the Almighty is a rock*

Father of Shelumiel	Num. 7:36, 41	169

Zuzim—*prominent; giant*

Tribe east of the Jordan	Gen. 14:5	21
Probably same as Zamzummims	Deut. 2:20	210

Read Your Bible Through In a Year

A systematic division of the books of the Bible, primarily for reading.

JANUARY

Date	MORNING	EVENING
	MATT.	GEN.
1	1	1, 2, 3
2	2	4, 5, 6
3	3	7, 8, 9
4	4	10, 11, 12
5	5: 1–26	13, 14, 15
6	5:27–48	16, 17
7	6: 1–18	18, 19
8	6:19–34	20, 21, 22
9	7	23, 24
10	8: 1–17	25, 26
11	8:18–34	27, 28
12	9: 1–17	29, 30
13	9:18–38	31, 32
14	10: 1–20	33, 34, 35
15	10:21–42	36, 37, 38
16	11	39, 40
17	12: 1–23	41, 42
18	12:24–50	43, 44, 45
19	13: 1–30	46, 47, 48
20	13:31–58	49, 50
		EX.
21	14: 1–21	1, 2, 3
22	14:22–36	4, 5, 6
23	15: 1–20	7, 8
24	15:21–39	9, 10, 11
25	16	12, 13
26	17	14, 15
27	18: 1–20	16, 17, 18
28	18:21–35	19, 20
29	19	21, 22
30	20: 1–16	23, 24
31	20:17–34	25, 26

FEBRUARY

Date	MORNING	EVENING
	MATT.	EX.
1	21: 1–22	27, 28
2	21:23–46	29, 30
3	22: 1–22	31, 32, 33
4	22:23–46	34, 35
5	23: 1–22	36, 37, 38
6	23:23–39	39, 40
		LEV.
7	24: 1–28	1, 2, 3
8	24:29–51	4, 5
9	25: 1–30	6, 7
10	25:31–46	8, 9, 10
11	26: 1–25	11, 12
12	26:26–50	13
13	26:51–75	14
14	27: 1–26	15, 16
15	27:27–50	17, 18
16	27:51–66	19, 20
17	28	21, 22
	MARK	
18	1: 1–22	23, 24
19	1:23–45	25
20	2	26, 27
		NUM.
21	3: 1–19	1, 2
22	3:20–35	3, 4
23	4: 1–20	5, 6
24	4:21–41	7, 8
25	5: 1–20	9, 10, 11
26	5:21–43	12, 13, 14
27	6: 1–29	15, 16
28	6:30–56	17, 18, 19
29	7: 1–13	20, 21, 22

MARCH

Date	MORNING	EVENING
	MARK	NUM.
1	7:14–37	23, 24, 25
2	8: 1–21	26, 27
3	8:22–38	28, 29, 30
4	9: 1–29	31, 32, 33
5	9:30–50	34, 35, 36
		DEUT.
6	10: 1–31	1, 2
7	10:32–52	3, 4
8	11: 1–18	5, 6, 7
9	11:19–33	8, 9, 10
10	12: 1–27	11, 12, 13
11	12:28–44	14, 15, 16
12	13: 1–20	17, 18, 19
13	13:21–37	20, 21, 22
14	14: 1–26	23, 24, 25
15	14:27–53	26, 27
16	14:54–72	28, 29
17	15: 1–25	30, 31
18	15:26–47	32, 33, 34
		JOSH.
19	16	1, 2, 3
	LUKE	
20	1: 1–20	4, 5, 6
21	1:21–38	7, 8, 9
22	1:39–56	10, 11, 12
23	1:57–80	13, 14, 15
24	2: 1–24	16, 17, 18
25	2:25–52	19, 20, 21
26	3	22, 23, 24
		JUDG.
27	4: 1–30	1, 2, 3
28	4:31–44	4, 5, 6
29	5: 1–16	7, 8
30	5:17–39	9, 10
31	6; 1–26	11, 12

APRIL

Date	MORNING	EVENING
	LUKE	JUDG.
1	6:27–49	13, 14, 15
2	7: 1–30	16, 17, 18
3	7:31–50	19, 20, 21
		RUTH
4	8: 1–25	1, 2, 3, 4
		1 SAM.
5	8:26–56	1, 2, 3
6	9: 1–17	4, 5, 6
7	9:18–36	7, 8, 9
8	9:37–62	10, 11, 12
9	10: 1–24	13, 14
10	10:25–42	15, 16
11	11: 1–28	17, 18
12	11:29–54	19, 20, 21
13	12: 1–31	22, 23, 24
14	12:32–59	25, 26
15	13: 1–22	27, 28, 29
16	13:23–35	30, 31
		2 SAM.
17	14: 1–24	1, 2
18	14:25–35	3, 4, 5
19	15: 1–10	6, 7, 8
20	15:11–32	9, 10, 11
21	16	12, 13
22	17: 1–19	14, 15
23	17:20–37	16, 17, 18
24	18: 1–23	19, 20
25	18:24–43	21, 22
26	19: 1–27	23, 24
		1 KIN.
27	19:28–48	1, 2
28	20: 1–26	3, 4, 5
29	20:27–47	6, 7
30	21: 1–19	8, 9

MAY

Date	MORNING	EVENING
	LUKE	1 KIN.
1	21:20–38	10, 11
2	22: 1–20	12, 13
3	22:21–46	14, 15
4	22:47–71	16, 17, 18
5	23: 1–25	19, 20
6	23:26–56	21, 22
		2 KIN.
7	24: 1–35	1, 2, 3
8	24:36–53	4, 5, 6
	JOHN	
9	1: 1–28	7, 8, 9
10	1:29–51	10, 11, 12
11	2	13, 14
12	3: 1–18	15, 16
13	3:19–38	17, 18
14	4: 1–30	19, 20, 21
15	4:31–54	22, 23
16	5: 1–24	24, 25
		1 CHR.
17	5:25–47	1, 2, 3
18	6: 1–21	4, 5, 6
19	6:22–44	7, 8, 9
20	6:45–71	10, 11, 12
21	7: 1–27	13, 14, 15
22	7:28–53	16, 17, 18
23	8: 1–27	19, 20, 21
24	8:28–59	22, 23, 24
25	9: 1–23	25, 26, 27
26	9:24–41	28, 29
		2 CHR.
27	10: 1–23	1, 2, 3
28	10:24–42	4, 5, 6
29	11: 1–29	7, 8, 9
30	11:30–57	10, 11, 12
31	12: 1–26	13, 14

JUNE

Date	MORNING	EVENING
	JOHN	2 CHR.
1	12:27–50	15, 16
2	13: 1–20	17, 18
3	13:21–38	19, 20
4	14	21, 22
5	15	23, 24
6	16	25, 26, 27
7	17	28, 29
8	18: 1–18	30, 31
9	18:19–40	32, 33
10	19: 1–22	34, 35, 36
		EZRA
11	19:23–42	1, 2
12	20	3, 4, 5
13	21	6, 7, 8
	ACTS	
14	1	9, 10
		NEH.
15	2: 1–21	1, 2, 3
16	2:22–47	4, 5, 6
17	3	7, 8, 9
18	4: 1–22	10, 11
19	4:23–37	12, 13
		ESTH.
20	5: 1–21	1, 2
21	5:22–42	3, 4, 5
22	6	6, 7, 8
23	7: 1–21	9, 10
		JOB
24	7:22–43	1, 2
25	7:44–60	3, 4
26	8: 1–25	5, 6, 7
27	8:26–40	8, 9, 10
28	9: 1–21	11, 12, 13
29	9:22–43	14, 15, 16
30	10: 1–23	17, 18, 19

JULY

Date	MORNING	EVENING
	ACTS	**JOB**
1	10:24–48	20, 21
2	11	22, 23, 24
3	12	25, 26, 27
4	13: 1–25	28, 29
5	13:26–52	30, 31
6	14	32, 33
7	15: 1–21	34, 35
8	15:22–41	36, 37
9	16: 1–21	38, 39, 40
10	16:22–40	41, 42
		PS.
11	17: 1–15	1, 2, 3
12	17:16–34	4, 5, 6
13	18	7, 8, 9
14	19: 1–20	10, 11, 12
15	19:21–41	13, 14, 15
16	20: 1–16	16, 17
17	20:17–38	18, 19
18	21: 1–17	20, 21, 22
19	21:18–40	23, 24, 25
20	22	26, 27, 28
21	23: 1–15	29, 30
22	23:16–35	31, 32
23	24	33, 34
24	25	35, 36
25	26	37, 38, 39
26	27: 1–26	40, 41, 42
27	27:27–44	43, 44, 45
28	28	46, 47, 48
	ROM.	
29	1	49, 50
30	2	51, 52, 53
31	3	54, 55, 56

AUGUST

Date	MORNING	EVENING
	ROM.	**PS.**
1	4	57, 58, 59
2	5	60, 61, 62
3	6	63, 64, 65
4	7	66, 67
5	8: 1–21	68, 69
6	8:22–39	70, 71
7	9: 1–15	72, 73
8	9:16–33	74, 75, 76
9	10	77, 78
10	11: 1–18	79, 80
11	11:19–36	81, 82, 83
12	12	84, 85, 86
13	13	87, 88
14	14	89, 90
15	15: 1–13	91, 92, 93
16	15:14–33	94, 95, 96
17	16	97, 98, 99
	1 COR.	
18	1	100, 101, 102
19	2	103, 104
20	3	105, 106
21	4	107, 108, 109
22	5	110, 111, 112
23	6	113, 114, 115
24	7: 1–19	116, 117, 118
25	7:20–40	119: 1–88
26	8	119: 89–176
27	9	120, 121, 122
28	10: 1–18	123, 124, 125
29	10:19–33	126, 127, 128
30	11: 1–16	129, 130, 131
31	11:17–34	132, 133, 134

SEPTEMBER

Date	MORNING	EVENING
	1 COR.	**PS.**
1	12	135, 136
2	13	137, 138, 139
3	14: 1–20	140, 141, 142
4	14:21–40	143, 144, 145
5	15: 1–28	146, 147
6	15:29–58	148, 149, 150
		PROV.
7	16	1, 2
	2 COR.	
8	1	3, 4, 5
9	2	6, 7
10	3	8, 9
11	4	10, 11, 12
12	5	13, 14, 15
13	6	16, 17, 18
14	7	19, 20, 21
15	8	22, 23, 24
16	9	25, 26
17	10	27, 28, 29
18	11: 1–15	30, 31
		ECCL.
19	11:16–33	1, 2, 3
20	12	4, 5, 6
21	13	7, 8, 9
	GAL.	
22	1	10, 11, 12
		SONG
23	2	1, 2, 3
24	3	4, 5
25	4	6, 7, 8
		IS.
26	5	1, 2
27	6	3, 4
	EPH.	
28	1	5, 6
29	2	7, 8
30	3	9, 10

OCTOBER

Date	MORNING	EVENING
	EPH.	**IS.**
1	4	11, 12, 13
2	5: 1–16	14, 15, 16
3	5:17–33	17, 18, 19
4	6	20, 21, 22
	PHIL.	
5	1	23, 24, 25
6	2	26, 27
7	3	28, 29
8	4	30, 31
	COL.	
9	1	32, 33
10	2	34, 35, 36
11	3	37, 38
12	4	39, 40
	1 THESS.	
13	1	41, 42
14	2	43, 44
15	3	45, 46
16	4	47, 48, 49
17	5	50, 51, 52
	2 THESS.	
18	1	53, 54, 55
19	2	56, 57, 58
20	3	59, 60, 61
	1 TIM.	
21	1	62, 63, 64
22	2	65, 66
		JER.
23	3	1, 2
24	4	3, 4, 5
25	5	6, 7, 8
26	6	9, 10, 11
	2 TIM.	
27	1	12, 13, 14
28	2	15, 16, 17
29	3	18, 19
30	4	20, 21
	TITUS	
31	1	22, 23

NOVEMBER

Date	MORNING	EVENING
	TITUS	**JER.**
1	2	24, 25, 26
2	3	27, 28, 29
3	**PHILEM.**	30, 31
	HEB.	
4	1	32, 33
5	2	34, 35, 36
6	3	37, 38, 39
7	4	40, 41, 42
8	5	43, 44, 45
9	6	46, 47
10	7	48, 49
11	8	50
12	9	51, 52
		LAM.
13	10: 1–18	1, 2
14	10:19–39	3, 4, 5
		EZEK.
15	11: 1–19	1, 2
16	11:20–40	3, 4
17	12	5, 6, 7
18	13	8, 9, 10
	JAMES	
19	1	11, 12, 13
20	2	14, 15
21	3	16, 17
22	4	18, 19
23	5	20, 21
	1 PET.	
24	1	22, 23
25	2	24, 25, 26
26	3	27, 28, 29
27	4	30, 31, 32
28	5	33, 34
	2 PET.	
29	1	35, 36
30	2	37, 38, 39

DECEMBER

Date	MORNING	EVENING
	2 PET.	**EZEK.**
1	3	40, 41
	1 JOHN	
2	1	42, 43, 44
3	2	45, 46
4	3	47, 48
		DAN.
5	4	1, 2
6	5	3, 4
7	**2 JOHN**	5, 6, 7
8	**3 JOHN**	8, 9, 10
9	**JUDE**	11, 12
	REV.	**HOS.**
10	1	1, 2, 3, 4
11	2	5, 6, 7, 8
12	3	9, 10, 11
13	4	12, 13, 14
14	5	**JOEL**
		AMOS
15	6	1, 2, 3
16	7	4, 5, 6
17	8	7, 8, 9
18	9	**OBAD.**
19	10	**JON.**
		MIC.
20	11	1, 2, 3
21	12	4, 5
22	13	6, 7
23	14	**NAH.**
24	15	**HAB.**
25	16	**ZEPH.**
26	17	**HAG.**
		ZECH.
27	18	1, 2, 3, 4
28	19	5, 6, 7, 8
29	20	9, 10, 11, 12
30	21	13, 14
31	22	**MAL.**

The

Old Testament

of

The New King James Version

THE FIRST BOOK OF MOSES CALLED

GENESIS

THE BOOK OF GENESIS

The first part of Genesis focuses on the beginning and spread of sin in the world and culminates in the devastating flood in the days of Noah. The second part of the book focuses on God's dealings with one man, Abraham, through whom God promises to bring salvation and blessing to the world. Abraham and his descendants learn firsthand that it is always safe to trust the Lord in times of famine and feasting, blessing and bondage. From Abraham . . . to Isaac . . . to Jacob . . . to Joseph . . . God's promises begin to come to fruition in a great nation possessing a great land.

Genesis is a Greek word meaning "origin," "source," "generation," or "beginning." The original Hebrew title *Bereshith* means "In the Beginning."

The literary structure of Genesis is clear and is built around eleven separate units, each headed with the word *generations* in the phrase "These are the generations" or "The book of the generations": (1) Introduction to the Generations (1:1—2:3); (2) Heaven and Earth (2:4—4:26); (3) Adam (5:1—6:8); (4) Noah (6:9—9:29); (5) Sons of Noah (10:1—11:9); (6) Shem (11:10-26); (7) Terah (11:27—25:11); (8) Ishmael (25:12-18); (9) Isaac (25:19—35:29); (10) Esau (36:1—37:1); (11) Jacob (37:2—50:26).

THE AUTHOR OF GENESIS

Although Genesis does not directly name its author, and although Genesis ends some three centuries before Moses was born, the whole of Scripture and church history are unified in their adherence to the Mosaic authorship of Genesis.

The Old Testament is replete with both direct and indirect testimonies to the Mosaic authorship of the entire Pentateuch (Ex. 17:14; Lev. 1:1, 2; Num. 33:2; Deut. 1:1; Josh. 1:7; 1 Kin. 2:3; 2 Kin. 14:6; Ezra 6:18; Neh. 13:1; Dan. 9:11-13; Mal. 4:4). The New Testament also contains numerous testimonies (Matt. 8:4; Mark 12:26; Luke 16:29; John 7:19; Acts 26:22; Rom. 10:19; 1 Cor. 9:9; 2 Cor. 3:15).

The Early Church openly held to the Mosaic authorship, as does the first-century Jewish historian Josephus. As would be expected the Jerusalem Talmud supports Moses as author.

It would be difficult to find a man in all the range of Israel's life who was better prepared or qualified to write this history. Trained in the "wisdom of the Egyptians" (Acts 7:22), Moses had been providentially prepared to understand and integrate, under the inspiration of God, all the available records, manuscripts, and oral narratives.

THE TIME OF GENESIS

Genesis divides neatly into three geographical settings: (1) the Fertile Crescent (1—11); (2) Israel (12—36); (3) Egypt (37—50).

The setting of the first eleven chapters changes rapidly as it spans more than two thousand years and fifteen hundred miles, and paints the majestic acts of the Creation, the garden of Eden, the Noahic Flood, and the towering citadel of Babel.

The middle section of Genesis rapidly funnels down from the broad brim of the two millennia spent in the Fertile Crescent to less than two hundred years in the little country of Canaan. Surrounded by the rampant immorality and idolatry of the Canaanites, the godliness of Abraham rapidly degenerates into gross immorality in some of his descendants.

In the last fourteen chapters, God dramatically saves the small Israelite nation from extinction by transferring the "seventy souls" to Egypt so that they may grow and multiply. Egypt is an unexpected womb for the growth of God's chosen nation Israel, to be sure, but one in which they are isolated from the maiming influence of Canaan.

Genesis spans more time than any other book in the Bible; in fact, it covers more than all sixty-five other books of the Bible put together.

Utilizing the same threefold division noted above, the following dates can be assigned:

A. 2,000 or more years, 4000–2090 B.C. (Gen. 1—11)
   1. Creation, 4000 B.C. or earlier (Gen. 1:1)
   2. Death of Terah, 2090 B.C. (Gen. 11:32)

B. 193 years, 2090–1897 B.C. (Gen. 12—36)
   1. Death of Terah, 2090 B.C. (Gen. 11:32)
   2. Joseph to Egypt, c. 1897 B.C. (Gen. 37:2)

C. 93 years, 1897–1804 B.C. (Gen. 37—50)
   1. Joseph to Egypt, c. 1897 B.C. (Gen. 37:2)
   2. Death of Joseph, 1804 B.C. (Gen. 50:26)

THE CHRIST OF GENESIS

Genesis moves from the general to the specific in its messianic predictions: Christ is the seed of the woman (3:15), from the line of Seth (4:25), the son of Shem (9:27), the descendant of Abraham (12:3), of Isaac (21:12), of Jacob (25:23), and of the tribe of Judah (49:10).

Christ is also seen in people and events that serve as types. (A "type" is a historical fact that illustrates a spiritual truth.) Adam is "a type of Him who was to come" (Rom. 5:14). Both entered the world through a special act of God as sinless men. Adam is the head of the old creation; Christ is the Head of the new creation. Abel's acceptable offering of a blood sacrifice points to Christ, and there is a parallel in his murder by Cain. Melchizedek ("righteous king") is "made like the Son of God" (Heb. 7:3). He is the king of Salem ("peace") who brings forth bread and wine and is the priest of the Most High God. Joseph is also a type of Christ. Joseph and Christ are both objects of special love by their fathers, both are hated by their brothers, both are rejected as rulers over their brothers, both are conspired against and sold for silver, both are condemned though innocent, and both are raised from humiliation to glory by the power of God.

KEYS TO GENESIS

Key Word: Beginnings—Genesis gives the beginning of almost everything, including the beginning of the universe, life, man, sabbath, death, marriage, sin, redemption, family, literature, cities, art, language, and sacrifice.

Key Verses: Genesis 3:15; 12:3—"And I will put enmity between you and the woman, and between your seed and her Seed; He shall bruise your head, and you shall bruise His heel" (3:15).

"I will bless those who bless you, and I will curse him who curses you; and in you all the families of the earth shall be blessed" (12:3).

Key Chapter: Genesis 15—Central to all of Scripture is the Abrahamic Covenant, which is given in 12:1–3 and ratified in 15:1–21. Israel receives three specific promises: (1) the promise of a great land—"from the river of Egypt to the great river, the River Euphrates" (15:18); (2) the promise of a great nation—"and I will make your descendants as the dust of the earth" (13:16); and (3) the promise of a great blessing—"I will bless you and make your name great; and you shall be a blessing" (12:2).

SURVEY OF GENESIS

Genesis is not so much a history of man as it is the first chapter in the history of the *redemption* of man. As such, Genesis is a highly selective spiritual interpretation of history. Genesis is divided into four great events (1—11) and four great people (12—50).

The Four Great Events: Chapters 1—11 lay the foundation upon which the whole Bible is built and center on four key events. (1) *Creation:* God is the sovereign Creator of matter, energy, space, and time. Man is the pinnacle of the Creation. (2) *Fall:* Creation is followed by corruption. In the first sin man is separated from God (Adam from God), and in the second sin, man is separated from man (Cain from Abel). In spite of the devastating curse of the Fall, God promises hope of redemption through the seed of the woman (3:15). (3) *Flood:* As man multiplies, sin also multiplies until God is compelled to destroy humanity with the exception of Noah and his family. (4) *Nations:* Genesis teaches the unity of the human race: we are all children of Adam through Noah, but because of rebellion at the Tower of Babel, God fragments the single culture and language of the post-flood world and scatters people over the face of the earth.

The Four Great People: Once the nations are scattered, God focuses on one man and his descendants through whom He will bless all nations (12—50). (1) *Abraham:* The calling of Abraham (12) is the pivotal point of the book. The three covenant promises God makes to Abraham (land, descendants, and blessing) are foundational to His program of bringing salvation upon the earth. (2) *Isaac:* God establishes His covenant with Isaac as the spiritual link with Abraham. (3) *Jacob:* God transforms this man from selfishness to servanthood and changes his name to Israel, the father of the twelve tribes. (4) *Joseph:* Jacob's favorite son suffers at the hands of his brothers

FOCUS	FOUR EVENTS				FOUR PEOPLE			
REFERENCE	1:1—3:1—6:1—10:1—12:1—25:19—27:19—37:1—50:26							
DIVISION	CREATION	FALL	FLOOD	NATIONS	ABRAHAM	ISAAC	JACOB	JOSEPH
TOPIC	HUMAN RACE				HEBREW RACE			
	HISTORICAL				BIOGRAPHICAL			
LOCATION	FERTILE CRESCENT (Eden-Haran)				CANAAN (Haran-Canaan)			EGYPT (Canaan-Egypt)
TIME	c. 2000 YEARS (c. 4004-2090 B.C.)				193 YEARS (2090-1897 B.C.)			93 YEARS (1897-1804 B.C.)

and becomes a slave in Egypt. After his dramatic rise to the rulership of Egypt, Joseph delivers his family from famine and brings them out of Canaan to Goshen.

Genesis ends on a note of impending bondage with the death of Joseph. There is great need for the redemption that is to follow in the Book of Exodus.

OUTLINE OF GENESIS

Part One: Primeval History (1:1—11:9)

I. The Creation .... **1:1—2:25**

A. Creation of the World .... 1:1—2:3
B. Creation of Man 2:4–25

II. The Fall .... **3:1—5:32**

A. The Fall of Man 3:1–24
1. Temptation of Man 3:1–5
2. Fall of Man 3:6, 7
3. Judgment on Man 3:8–24
B. After the Fall: Conflicting Family Lines .... 4:1—5:32
1. The Initial Conflict 4:1–15
2. The Ungodly Line of Cain 4:16–24
3. The Godly Line of Seth .... 4:25—5:32

III. The Judgment of the Flood .... **6:1—9:29**

A. Causes of the Flood 6:1–5
1. The Ungodly Multiply 6:1–4
2. The Ungodly Sin Continually 6:5
B. Judgment of the Flood 6:6–22
1. The Ungodly to Be Destroyed 6:6, 7
2. The Godly to Be Saved 6:8–22
C. The Flood .... 7:1—8:19
1. The Ark Is Entered 7:1–10
2. The Earth Is Flooded 7:11–24
3. The Flood Recedes 8:1–19
D. Results of the Flood .... 8:20—9:17
1. Noah Worships God 8:20–22
2. God's Covenant with Noah 9:1–17
E. After the Flood: The Sin of the Godly Line 9:18–29
1. The Sons of Noah 9:18, 19
2. Ham's Sin 9:20–24
3. The Curse on Canaan 9:25–27
4. Noah's Death 9:28, 29

IV. The Judgment on the Tower of Babel 10:1—11:9

A. Family Lines After the Flood 10:1–32
1. The Family of Japheth 10:1–5
2. The Family of Ham 10:6–14
3. The Family of Canaan 10:15–20
4. The Family of Shem 10:21–32
B. Judgment on All the Family Lines 11:1–9
1. Construction of the Tower 11:1–3
2. Rebellion at the Tower 11:4
3. Judgment on All the Family Lines 11:5–9

Part Two: Patriarchal History (11:10—50:26)

I. The Life of Abraham .... **11:10—25:18**

A. Introduction of Abram 11:10–32
1. Abram's Family Line 11:10–26
2. Abram's Past 11:27–32
B. The Covenant of God with Abram .... 12:1—25:18
1. Initiation of the Covenant 12:1–20
2. Separation to the Covenant ... 13:1—14:24
a. Abram's Separation from Lot 13:1–13
b. God's Promise to Abram 13:14–18
c. Abram Rescues Lot 14:1–16
d. Abram Refuses Reward 14:17–24
3. Ratification of the Covenant .. 15:1—16:16
a. God's Promise of Children 15:1–21
b. A Carnal Plan for Children 16:1–16
4. Institution of the Covenant: Circumcision 17:1–27
5. Testing of the Covenant .... 18:1—20:18
a. Sarah's Faith Is Tested 18:1–15
b. Abraham's Faith Is Tested 18:16–33
c. Destruction of Sodom and Gomorrah 19:1–29
d. The Sin of Lot 19:30–38
e. The Test of Abimelech 20:1–18
6. Consummation of the Covenant .... 21:1—25:18
a. Birth of Isaac 21:1–34
b. Offering of Isaac 22:1–24
c. Death of Sarah 23:1–20
d. Isaac's Marriage 24:1–67
e. Abraham Dies 25:1–18

II. The Life of Isaac .... **25:19—26:35**

A. The Family of Isaac 25:19–34
B. The Failure of Isaac 26:1–33
C. The Failure of Esau 26:34, 35

III. The Life of Jacob .... **27:1—36:43**

A. Jacob Gains Esau's Blessing .... 27:1—28:9
B. Jacob's Life at Haran .... 28:10—32:32
1. Jacob's Dream 28:10–22
2. Jacob's Labors .... 29:1—30:43
3. Jacob's Flight 31:1–55
C. Jacob's Return .... 32:1—33:20
1. Jacob Fights with the Angel 32:1–32
2. Jacob Makes Peace with Esau 33:1–20
D. Jacob's Residence in Canaan .... 34:1—36:43
1. The Defilement of Dinah 34:1–31
2. The Devotion at Bethel 35:1–15
3. The Deaths of Rachel and Isaac 35:16–29
E. The History of Esau 36:1–43

IV. **The Life of Joseph** . . . . 37:1—50:26
- A. The Corruption of Joseph's Family . . . . 37:1—38:30
  - 1. Joseph's Family Sins Against Him 37:1-36
  - 2. Joseph's Family Sins with the Canaanites 38:1-30
- B. The Exaltation of Joseph . . . . 39:1—41:57
  - 1. Joseph's Test with the Egyptian Woman 39:1-23
  - 2. Joseph's Test with the Egyptian Society 40:1-23
  - 3. Joseph's Test with Pharaoh's Dreams. 41:1-36
  - 4. Joseph's Exaltation over Egypt . . . 41:37-57
- C. The Salvation of Jacob's Family 42:1—50:26
  - 1. Joseph's Brothers Visit Egypt 42:1-38
  - 2. Joseph's Brothers' Second Journey to Egypt . . . . 43:1—45:28
  - 3. Jacob's Family Safe in Egypt 46:1—47:26
  - 4. Jacob Blesses the Family in Egypt . . . . 47:27—49:32
  - 5. Jacob Dies in Egypt . . . . 49:33—50:14
  - 6. Joseph Dies in Egypt 50:15-26

CHAPTER 1

Creation of the World

IN the [R]beginning [R]God created the heavens
and the earth. [John 1:1-3] • Acts 17:24
2 The earth was [R]without form, and void;
and darkness *was* on the face of the deep.
[R]And the Spirit of God was hovering over the
face of the waters. Jer. 4:23 • Is. 40:13, 14
3 Then God said, [R]"Let there be [R]light";
and there was light. 2 Cor. 4:6 • [Heb. 11:3]
4 And God saw the light, that *it was* good;
and God divided the light from the darkness.
5 God called the light Day, and the [R]dark-
ness He called Night. So the evening and the
morning were the first day. Ps. 19:2; 33:6
6 Then God said, "Let there be a [T]firma-
ment in the midst of the waters, and let it
divide the waters from the waters." *expanse*
7 Thus God made the firmament, and divided the waters which *were* under the firmament from the waters which *were* above the
firmament; and it was so.
8 And God called the firmament Heaven.
So the evening and the morning were the
second day.
9 Then God said, [R]"Let the waters under
the heavens be gathered together into one
place, and [R]let the dry *land* appear"; and it
was so. Job 26:10 • Ps. 24:1, 2; 33:7; 95:5
10 And God called the dry *land* Earth, and
the gathering together of the waters He
called Seas. And God saw that *it was* good.
11 Then God said, "Let the earth [R]bring
forth grass, the herb *that* yields seed, *and* the
[R]fruit tree *that* yields fruit according to its
kind, whose seed *is* in itself, on the earth";
and it was so. Heb. 6:7 • 2 Sam. 16:1
12 And the earth brought forth grass, the
herb *that* yields seed according to its kind,
and the tree *that* yields fruit, whose seed *is* in
itself according to its kind. And God saw that
it was good.
13 So the evening and the morning were the
third day.
14 Then God said, "Let there be lights in the
firmament of the heavens to divide the day
from the night; and let them be for signs and
seasons, and for days and years;
15 "and let them be for lights in the firmament of the heavens to give light on the
earth"; and it was so.
16 Then God made two great [T]lights: the
[R]greater light to rule the day, and the [R]lesser
light to rule the night. *He made* [R]the stars
also. *luminaries* • Ps. 136:8 • Ps. 8:3 • Job 38:7
17 God set them in the firmament of the
[R]heavens to give light on the earth, Gen. 15:5
18 and to [R]rule over the day and over the
night, and to divide the light from the darkness. And God saw that *it was* good. Jer. 31:35
19 So the evening and the morning were the
fourth day.
20 Then God said, "Let the waters abound
with an abundance of living creatures, and let
birds fly above the earth across the face of
the [T]firmament of the heavens." *expanse*
21 So [R]God created great sea creatures and
every living thing that moves, with which the
waters abounded, according to their kind,
and every winged bird according to its kind.
And God saw that *it was* good. Ps. 104:25-28
22 And God blessed them, saying, "Be fruitful and multiply, and fill the waters in the
seas, and let birds multiply on the earth."
23 So the evening and the morning were the
fifth day.
24 Then God said, "Let the earth bring forth
the living creature according to its kind:
cattle and creeping thing and beast of the
earth, *each* according to its kind"; and it was
so.
25 And God made the beast of the earth
according to its kind, cattle according to its
kind, and everything that creeps on the earth
according to its kind. And God saw that *it*
was good.
26 Then God said, [R]"Let Us make man in
Our image, according to Our likeness; let
them have dominion over the fish of the sea,
over the birds of the air, and over the cattle,
over *all the earth and over every creeping
thing that creeps on the earth." [Eph. 4:24]
27 So God created man [R]in His *own* image;

1:26 Syr. *all the wild animals of*

THE SIX DAYS OF CREATION

"In the beginning God created the heavens and the earth" (Gen. 1:1).

According to the Book of Genesis, God created the world and all that is in it in six days. Then He declared it all to be "very good" (Gen. 1:31). The Creator rested on the seventh day (Gen. 2:1–3).

While there were other "creation stories" among the pagan nations of the ancient world, the biblical account is unique in that God existed before creation and called the physical world into being from nothing (Gen. 1:1, 2; John 1:2, 3). These pagan nations, particularly the Babylonians, believed the material universe was eternal and that it brought their gods into being. But Genesis describes a God who is clearly superior to the physical world.

God began organizing a shapeless and barren earth (Gen. 1:2), providing light (1:3–5), and separating land from water (1:6–10). The creation of plant and animal life followed, including creatures of the sea, air, and land (1:11–25). Man and woman were created on the sixth day (1:26–28), before the Creator's Sabbath rest (2:1–3).

Scholars disagree about the length of the creation "days." Some believe these were actual twenty-four-hour days, while others believe they were periods of undetermined length. Regardless of the length of these days, the biblical writer is declaring that God created the world in orderly fashion as part of a master plan. The world did not just evolve on its own or by accident.

The "gap" theory, advanced to reconcile the biblical account of creation with geology, holds that creation in Genesis 1:1 was followed by catastrophe (1:2), then succeeded by God's re-creation or reshaping of the physical world (1:3–31). But this theory reduces God to a weak being with little control over His own creation. The powerful God who created the world also presides over its destiny.

Man and woman are the crowning achievements of God's creative work (Ps. 8:5). As free moral beings who bear the image of God, they were assigned dominion over the natural world (Gen. 1:27, 28). They alone among the living creatures of the world are equipped for fellowship with their Creator.

THE GARDEN OF EDEN

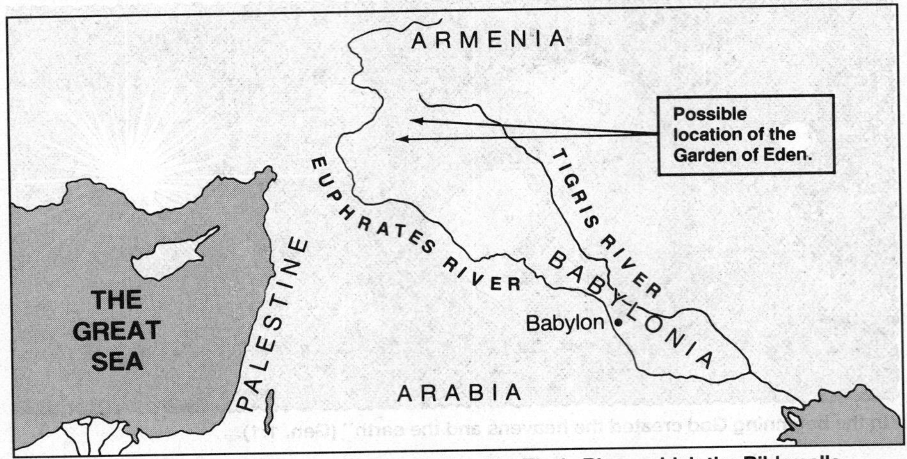

The Garden of Eden may have been located near the Tigris River, which the Bible calls Hiddekel (Gen. 2:14).

The Garden of Eden was the first home of Adam and Eve, the first man and woman (Gen. 2:4—3:24). Eden is a translation of a Hebrew word which means "Delight," suggesting a "Garden of Delight." The garden contained many beautiful and fruitbearing trees, including the "tree of life" and "the tree of the knowledge of good and evil" (Gen. 2:9).

Pinpointing the exact location of the Garden of Eden is difficult, although the best theory places it near the source of the Tigris and Euphrates rivers in the Armenian highlands (see map). A major catastrophe, perhaps the Flood of Noah's time, may have wiped out all traces of the other two rivers mentioned—the Pishon and the Havilah (Gen. 2:11). But modern space photography has produced evidence that two rivers, now dry beds, could have flowed through the area centuries ago.

God commanded Adam and Eve not to eat of the tree of the knowledge of good and evil (Gen. 2:17). They fell from their original state of innocence when Satan approached Eve through the serpent and tempted her to eat of the forbidden fruit (Gen. 3:1–5). She ate the fruit and also gave it to her husband to eat (Gen. 3:6, 7). Their disobedience plunged them and all of the human race into a state of sin and corruption.

Because of their unbelief and rebellion, they were driven from the garden. Other consequences of their sin were loss of their innocence (Gen. 3:7), pain in childbearing and submission of the wife to her husband (Gen. 3:16), the cursing of the ground and the resultant hard labor for man (Gen. 3:17–19), and separation from God (Gen. 3:23, 24).

The apostle Paul thought of Christ as the Second Adam who would save the old sinful Adam through His plan of redemption and salvation. "As in Adam all die, even so in Christ all shall be made alive" (1 Cor. 15:22).

in the image of God He created him; [R]male
and female He created them. Gen. 5:2 • Matt. 19:4
28 Then God blessed them, and God said to
them, "Be fruitful and multiply; fill the earth
and subdue it; have dominion over the fish of
the sea, over the birds of the air, and over
every living thing that moves on the earth."
29 And God said, "See, I have given you
every herb *that* yields seed which *is* on the
face of all the earth, and every tree whose
fruit yields seed; to you it shall be for food.
30 "Also, to [R]every beast of the earth, to
every [R]bird of the air, and to everything that
creeps on the earth, in which *there is* [T]life, *I
have given* every green herb for food"; and it
was so. Ps. 145:15 • Job 38:41 • *a living soul*
31 Then God saw everything that He had
made, and indeed *it was* very good. So the
evening and the morning were the sixth day.

CHAPTER 2

THUS the heavens and the earth, and [R]all
the host of them, were finished. Ps. 33:6
2 [R]And on the seventh day God ended His
work which He had done, and He rested on
the seventh day from all His work which He
had done. Ex. 20:9–11; 31:17
3 Then God blessed the seventh day and
sanctified it, because in it He rested from all
His work which God had created and made.

Creation of Man

4 [R]This *is* the [T]history of the heavens and
the earth when they were created, in the day
that the LORD God made the earth and the
heavens, Gen. 1:1 • Lit. *generations* or *genealogy*
5 before any [R]plant of the field was in the
earth and before any herb of the field had
grown. For the LORD God had not [R]caused it
to rain on the earth, and *there was* no man
[R]to till the ground; Gen. 1:11, 12 • Gen. 7:4 • Gen. 3:23
6 but a mist went up from the earth and
watered the whole face of the ground.
7 And the LORD God formed man *of* the
dust of the ground, and [R]breathed into his
[R]nostrils the breath of life; and [R]man became
a living being. Job 33:4 • Gen. 7:22 • 1 Cor. 15:45
8 The LORD God planted a garden [R]east-
ward in [R]Eden, and there He put the man
whom He had formed. Gen. 3:23, 24 • Gen. 4:16
9 And out of the ground the LORD God
made every tree grow that is pleasant to the
sight and good for food. The tree of life *was*
also in the midst of the garden, and the tree
of the knowledge of good and evil.
10 Now a river went out of Eden to water
the garden, and from there it parted and
became four riverheads.
11 The name of the first *is* Pishon; it *is* the
one which encompasses [R]the whole land of
Havilah, where *there is* gold. Gen. 25:18
12 And the gold of that land *is* good. [R]Bdel-
lium and the onyx stone *are* there. Num. 11:7
13 The name of the second river *is* Gihon; it
is the one which encompasses the whole land
of Cush.
14 The name of the third river *is* *Hiddekel;
it *is* the one which goes toward the east of
Assyria. The fourth river *is* the Euphrates.

15 Then the LORD God took [T]the man and
put him in the garden of Eden to [T]tend and
keep it. Or *Adam* • *cultivate*
16 And the LORD God commanded the man,
saying, "Of every tree of the garden you may
freely eat;
17 "but of the tree of the knowledge of good
and evil you shall not eat, for in the day that
you eat of it you shall surely die."

18 And the LORD God said, "*It is* not good
that man should be alone; [R]I will make him a
helper comparable to him." 1 Cor. 11:8, 9
19 Out of the ground the LORD God formed
every beast of the field and every bird of the
air, and brought *them* to Adam to see what

2:14 Or *Tigris*

2:15–17 The Edenic Covenant—The covenant in Eden is the first of the general or universal covenants. In it, Adam is charged to: (1) populate the earth (Gen. 1:28); (2) subdue the earth (Gen. 1:28); (3) exercise dominion over the animal creation (Gen. 1:28); (4) care for the garden of Eden and enjoy its fruit (Gen. 1:29; 2:15); and (5) refrain from eating the fruit of the tree of the knowledge of good and evil, under penalty of death (Gen. 2:16, 17). The Edenic Covenant was terminated by man's disobedience, when Adam and Eve ate of the fruit of the tree of the knowledge of good and evil, resulting in their spiritual and physical deaths. This failure necessitated the establishment of the covenant with Adam (Page 9—Gen. 3:14–21).

Now turn to Page 9—Gen. 3:14–21: The Adamic Covenant.

2:18–25 How the Family Began—Genesis 2:18–25 fills in the details of the simple statement in Genesis 1:27: "Male and female He created them." This account particularly amplifies the "and female" part of the statement and shows how woman was created. Three observations can be made on the passage that will help us to understand how the family began:

a. The need for woman (vv. 18–20). Woman is absolutely essential in God's plan. It was God who observed, "*It is* not good that man should be alone" (v. 18), and determined to make a "helper" for Adam. Woman's role in the will of God was to be a "helper" who was suitable to man in every particular mental, spiritual, emotional, social, and physical need. God undertook an orientation program to show man the need that He alone had observed. He brought to man the birds and beasts He had created, so that man should exercise his dominion over them (v. 28) and name them (v. 19). However, in verse 20 it is noted that for Adam there was no "helper" similar to himself.

(continued on next page)

he would call them. And whatever Adam
called each living creature, that *was* its name.
20 So Adam gave names to all cattle, to the
birds of the air, and to every beast of the field.
But for Adam there was not found a helper
comparable to him.
21 And the LORD God caused a [R]deep sleep
to fall on Adam, and he slept; and He took
one of his ribs, and closed up the flesh in its
place. 1 Sam. 26:12
22 Then the rib which the LORD God had
taken from man He [T]made into a woman, and
He brought her to the man. Lit. *built*
23 And Adam said:

"This *is* now [R]bone of my bones
And flesh of my flesh;
She shall be called Woman, Gen. 29:14
Because she was taken out of Man."

24 Therefore a man shall leave his father
and mother and [T]be joined to his wife, and
they shall become one flesh. Lit. *cling*
25 And they were both naked, the man and
his wife, and were not [R]ashamed. Is. 47:3

CHAPTER 3

Temptation of Man

NOW the serpent was [R]more cunning than
any beast of the field which the LORD
God had made. And he said to the woman,
"Has God indeed said, 'You shall not eat of
every tree of the garden'?" 2 Cor. 11:3
2 And the woman said to the serpent, "We
may eat the fruit of the trees of the garden;
3 "but of the fruit of the tree which *is* in
the midst of the garden, God has said, 'You
shall not eat it, nor shall you [R]touch it, lest
you die.' " Ex. 19:12, 13
4 [R]And the serpent said to the woman,
"You will not surely die. [2 Cor. 11:3]
5 "For God knows that in the day you eat
of it your eyes will be opened, and you will be
like God, knowing good and evil."

Fall of Man

6 So when the woman saw that the tree
was good for food, that it *was* pleasant to the
eyes, and a tree desirable to make *one* wise,
she took of its fruit and ate. She also gave to
her husband with her, and he ate.
7 Then the eyes of both of them were
opened, [R]and they knew that they *were*
naked; and they sewed fig leaves together
and made themselves coverings. Gen. 2:25

Judgment on Man

8 And they heard the [T]sound of the LORD
God walking in the garden in the [T]cool of the
day, and Adam and his wife hid themselves
from the presence of the LORD God among
the trees of the garden. Or *voice* • *breeze*
9 Then the LORD God called to Adam and
said to him, "Where *are* you?"
10 So he said, "I heard Your voice in the
garden, [R]and I was afraid because I was
naked; and I hid myself." Gen. 2:25
11 And He said, "Who told you that you
were naked? Have you eaten from the tree of
which I commanded you that you should not
eat?"
12 Then the man said, [R]"The woman whom

(continued from previous page)

b. The provision of woman for man (vv. 21–24). God caused Adam to go to sleep, and God removed one of his "ribs." Exactly what God removed is not known, but it was adequate for His purpose. He "made" (lit., *built*) a woman (v. 22) whom Adam recognized as being his equal, "bone of my bones and flesh of my flesh." This resulted in what has become known as the universal law of marriage (v. 24), in which it can be seen that: (1) the responsibility for marriage is on the man's shoulders—he is to "leave his father and mother"; (2) the responsibility for keeping the union together is on the man's shoulders—he is to "be joined to" his wife; and (3) the union is indissoluble—"they shall become one flesh."

c. The state of the first man and woman (v. 25). From the beginning the man and woman were "naked" in each other's presence and "were not ashamed." There is no shame in nudity when it occurs within the right context—the marital union. This passage clearly teaches that (1) sex was God's idea and is not sinful; (2) sex came before the Fall, and if the Fall had never taken place there still would be sexual relations between a man and his wife; and (3) propagation of the species is one, but not the exclusive, purpose for sex. The Bible gives two other reasons for sex: (1) to promote love between the husband and wife (Page 1463—Heb. 13:4), and (2) to prevent fornication—the unlawful satisfaction of the God-given sexual desire (Page 1351—1 Cor. 7:2).

Now turn to Page 215—Deut. 6:4–9: Three Essentials for a Christian Home.

3:6, 7 Adam's Sin—Adam's sin does not seem to be a very great sin from man's perspective. All he did was take a bite of some fruit. Adam's sin is serious in that the fruit was of the tree of the knowledge of good and evil, of which God said that he was not to eat under penalty of death (Page 7—Gen. 2:17). Up to this time Adam was morally innocent. When he sinned, he by nature became a sinner. As such he died. He died spiritually immediately and began to die physically. Adam was the first man ever to live upon the face of the earth. From Adam and Eve come every other human being who ever has lived upon the face of the earth. Thus Adam is the "federal head" from whom every other man came. Like begets like. Apples beget apples. Dogs beget dogs. Human beings beget human beings. Since Adam became a sinner before Eve conceived a child, every human being descended from him is a sinner just like him except Christ. Because of Adam's sin, death entered into the human race (Page 1329—Rom. 5:12–14); every human being needs to have the new life.

Now turn to Page 756—Eccl. 7:20: Individual Sin.

You gave *to be* with me, she gave me of the
tree, and I ate." [Prov. 28:13]
13 And the LORD God said to the woman,
"What *is* this you have done?" And the
woman said, [R]"The serpent deceived me, and
I ate." 2 Cor. 11:3

14 So the LORD God said to the serpent:

"Because you have done this,
You *are* cursed more than all cattle,
And more than every beast of the field;
On your belly you shall go,
And [R]you shall eat dust
All the days of your life. Deut. 28:15–20
15 And I will put enmity
Between you and the woman,
And between your seed and her Seed;
[R]He shall bruise your head, Rom. 16:20☆
And you shall bruise His heel."

16 To the woman He said:

"I will greatly multiply your sorrow and
your conception;
In pain you shall bring forth children;
Your desire *shall be* [T]for your husband,
And he shall rule over you." Lit. *toward*

17 Then to Adam He said, "Because you
have heeded the voice of your wife, and have
eaten from the tree of which I commanded
you, saying, 'You shall not eat of it':

"Cursed *is* the ground for your sake;
[R]In toil you shall eat *of* it
All the days of your life. Eccl. 2:23
18 Both thorns and thistles it shall [T]bring
forth for you, *cause to grow*
And you shall eat the herb of the field.
19 [R]In the sweat of your face you shall eat
bread 2 Thess. 3:10
Till you return to the ground,
For out of it you were taken;
[R]For dust you *are*, Gen. 2:7; 5:5
And [R]to dust you shall return." Job 21:26

20 And Adam called his wife's name Eve,
because she was the mother of all living.
21 Also for Adam and his wife the LORD
God made tunics of skin, and clothed them.

22 Then the LORD God said, "Behold, the
man has become like one of Us, to know good
and evil. And now, lest he put out his hand
and take also of the tree of life, and eat, and
live forever"—
23 therefore the LORD God sent him out of
the garden of Eden [R]to till the ground from
which he was taken. Gen. 4:2; 9:20
24 So He drove out the man; and He placed
cherubim at the east of the garden of Eden,
and a flaming sword which turned every way,
to guard the way to the tree of life.

CHAPTER 4

The Initial Conflict

NOW Adam knew Eve his wife, and she
conceived and bore Cain, and said, "I
have gotten a man from the LORD."
2 Then she bore again, this time his
brother Abel. Now Abel was a keeper of
sheep, but Cain was a tiller of the ground.
3 And in the process of time it came to
pass that Cain brought an offering of the fruit
[R]of the ground to the LORD. Num. 18:12
4 Abel also brought of the firstlings of his
flock and of their fat. And the LORD [R]re-
spected Abel and his offering, Heb. 11:4
5 but He did not respect Cain and his
offering. And Cain was very angry, and his
countenance fell.
6 So the LORD said to Cain, "Why are you

3:14–21 The Adamic Covenant—The covenant with Adam is the second general or universal covenant. It could be called the covenant with mankind, for it sets forth the conditions which will hold sway until the curse of sin is lifted (cf. Page 784—Is. 11:6–10; Page 1333—Rom. 8:18–23). According to the covenant, the conditions which will prevail are:

a. The serpent, the tool used by Satan to effect the fall of man, is cursed. The curse affects not only the instrument, the serpent, but also the indwelling energizer, Satan. Great physical changes took place in the serpent. Apparently it was upright; now it will go on its belly (v. 14). It was the most desirable animal of the animal creation; now it is the most loathsome. The sight or thought of a snake should be an effective reminder of the devastating effects of sin.
b. Satan is judged—he will enjoy limited success ("you shall bruise His heel," v. 15), but ultimately he will be judged ("He shall bruise your head," v. 15).
c. The first prophecy of the coming of Messiah is given (v. 15).
d. There will be a multiplication of conception, necessitated by the introduction of death into the human race (v. 16).
e. There will be pain in childbirth (v. 16).
f. The woman is made subject to her husband (v. 16).
g. The ground is cursed and will bring forth weeds among the food which man must eat for his existence (vv. 17–19).
h. Physical change takes place in man; he will perspire when he works. He will have to work all his life long (v. 19).
i. In sinning, man dies spiritually, and ultimately will die physically. His flesh will decay until it returns to dust from which it was originally taken (v. 19).

Now turn to Page 14—Gen. 9:1–19: The Noahic Covenant.

angry? And why has your countenance fallen?

7 "If you do well, will you not be accepted? And if you do not do well, sin lies at the door. And its desire *is* [T]for you, but you should rule over it." Lit. *toward*

8 Now Cain [T]talked with Abel his *brother; and it came to pass, when they were in the field, that Cain rose against Abel his brother and killed him. Lit. *said to*

9 Then the LORD said to Cain, "Where *is* Abel your brother?" And he said, "I do not know. *Am* I my brother's keeper?"

10 And He said, "What have you done? The voice of your brother's blood [R]cries out to Me from the ground. Heb. 12:24

11 "So now [R]you *are* cursed from the earth, which has opened its mouth to receive your brother's blood from your hand. Gen. 3:14

12 "When you till the ground, it shall no longer yield its strength to you. A fugitive and a vagabond you shall be on the earth."

13 And Cain said to the LORD, "My [T]punishment *is* greater than I can bear! *iniquity*

14 "Surely You have driven me out this day from the face of the ground; [R]I shall be [R]hidden from Your face; I shall be a fugitive and a vagabond on the earth, and it will happen *that* [R]anyone who finds me will kill me." Ps. 51:11 • Is. 1:15 • Num. 35:19, 21, 27

15 And the LORD said to him, *"Therefore, whoever kills Cain, vengeance shall be taken on him [R]sevenfold." And the LORD set a [R]mark on Cain, lest anyone finding him should kill him. Gen. 4:24 • Ezek. 9:4, 6

The Ungodly Line of Cain

16 Then Cain went out from the [R]presence of the LORD and dwelt in the land of [T]Nod on the east of Eden. Jon. 1:3 • Lit. *Wandering*

17 And Cain knew his wife, and she conceived and bore Enoch. And he built a city, [R]and called the name of the city after the name of his son—Enoch. Ps. 49:11

18 To Enoch was born Irad; and Irad begot Mehujael, and Mehujael begot Methushael, and Methushael begot Lamech.

19 Then Lamech took for himself [R]two wives: the name of one *was* Adah, and the name of the second *was* Zillah. Gen. 2:24; 16:3

20 And Adah bore Jabal. He was the father of those who dwell in tents and have livestock.

21 His brother's name *was* Jubal. He was the father of all those who play the harp and [T]flute. *pipe*

22 And as for Zillah, she also bore Tubal-Cain, an instructor of every craftsman in bronze and iron. And the sister of Tubal-Cain *was* Naamah.

23 Then Lamech said to his wives:

"Adah and Zillah, hear my voice;
O wives of Lamech, listen to my speech!
For I have killed a man for wounding
me,
Even a young man for hurting me.
24 If Cain shall be avenged sevenfold,
Then Lamech seventy-sevenfold."

The Godly Line of Seth
1 Chr. 1:1–4; Luke 3:36–38

25 And Adam knew his wife again, and she bore a son and [R]named him [T]Seth, "For God has appointed another seed for me instead of Abel, whom Cain killed." Gen. 5:3 • Lit. *Appointed*

26 And as for Seth, to him also a son was born; and he named him Enosh. Then *men* began to call on the name of the LORD.

CHAPTER 5

THIS is the book of the genealogy of Adam. In the day that God created man, He made him in the likeness of God.

2 He created them male and female, and [R]blessed them and called them Mankind in the day they were created. Gen. 1:28; 9:1

3 And Adam lived one hundred and thirty years, and begot *a son* in his own likeness, after his image, and named him Seth.

4 After he begot Seth, [R]the days of Adam were eight hundred years; [R]and he begot sons and daughters. Luke 3:36–38 • Gen. 1:28; 4:25

5 So all the days that Adam lived were nine hundred and thirty years; and he died.

6 Seth lived one hundred and five years, and begot [R]Enosh. Gen. 4:26

7 After he begot Enosh, Seth lived eight hundred and seven years, and begot sons and daughters.

8 So all the days of Seth were nine hundred and twelve years; and he died.

9 Enosh lived ninety years, and begot [T]Cainan. Heb. *Kenan*

10 After he begot Cainan, Enosh lived eight hundred and fifteen years, and begot sons and daughters.

11 So all the days of Enosh were nine hundred and five years; and he died.

12 Cainan lived seventy years, and begot [T]Mahalaleel. *Mahalalel*, Luke 3:37

13 After he begot Mahalaleel, Cainan lived eight hundred and forty years, and begot sons and daughters.

14 So all the days of Cainan were nine hundred and ten years; and he died.

15 Mahalaleel lived sixty-five years, and begot Jared.

16 After he begot Jared, Mahalaleel lived eight hundred and thirty years, and begot sons and daughters.

17 So all the days of Mahalaleel were eight hundred and ninety-five years; and he died.

4:8 Sam., LXX, Syr., Vg. add *Let us go out to the field*
4:15 LXX, Syr., Vg. *Not so;*

18 Jared lived one hundred and sixty-two years, and begot [R]Enoch. Jude 14, 15

19 After he begot Enoch, Jared lived eight hundred years, and begot sons and daughters.

20 So all the days of Jared were nine hundred and sixty-two years; and he died.

21 Enoch lived sixty-five years, and begot Methuselah.

22 After he begot Methuselah, Enoch [R]walked with God three hundred years, and begot sons and daughters. Gen. 6:9; 17:1; 24:40

23 So all the days of Enoch were three hundred and sixty-five years.

24 And [R]Enoch walked with God; and he *was* not, for God [R]took him. 2 Kin. 2:11 • Heb. 11:5

25 Methuselah lived one hundred and eighty-seven years, and begot Lamech.

26 After he begot Lamech, Methuselah lived seven hundred and eighty-two years, and begot sons and daughters.

27 So all the days of Methuselah were nine hundred and sixty-nine years; and he died.

28 Lamech lived one hundred and eighty-two years, and begot a son.

29 And he called his name [T]Noah, saying, "This *one* will comfort us concerning our work and the toil of our hands, because of the ground which the LORD has cursed." *Rest*

30 After he begot Noah, Lamech lived five hundred and ninety-five years, and begot sons and daughters.

31 So all the days of Lamech were seven hundred and seventy-seven years; and he died.

32 And Noah was five hundred years old, and Noah begot Shem, Ham, and Japheth.

CHAPTER 6

The Ungodly Multiply

NOW it came to pass, [R]when men began to multiply on the face of the earth, and daughters were born to them, Gen. 1:28

2 that the sons of God saw the daughters of men, that they *were* beautiful; and they [R]took wives for themselves of all whom they chose. Deut. 7:3, 4

3 And the LORD said, [R]"My Spirit shall not [R]strive* with man forever, [R]for he *is* indeed flesh; yet his days shall be one hundred and twenty years." [Gal. 5:16, 17] • 2 Thess. 2:7 • Ps. 78:39

4 There were giants on the earth in those days, and also afterward, when the sons of God came in to the daughters of men and they bore *children* to them. Those *were* the mighty men who *were* of old, men of renown.

The Ungodly Sin Continually

5 Then *the LORD saw that the wickedness of man *was* great in the earth, and *that* every [R]intent[T] of the thoughts of his heart *was* only evil [T]continually. Gen. 8:21 • *thought* • *all the day*

The Ungodly to Be Destroyed

6 And [R]the LORD was sorry that He had made man on the earth, and [R]He was grieved in His [R]heart. 1 Sam. 15:11, 29 • Is. 63:10 • Mark 3:5

7 So the LORD said, "I will [R]destroy man whom I have created from the face of the earth, both man and beast, creeping thing and birds of the air, for I am sorry that I have made them." Gen. 7:4, 23

The Godly to Be Saved

8 But Noah [R]found grace in the eyes of the LORD. Gen. 19:19

9 This is the genealogy of Noah. [R]Noah was a just man, [T]perfect in his generations. Noah walked with God. 2 Pet. 2:5 • *blameless*

10 And Noah begot three sons: [R]Shem, Ham, and Japheth. Gen. 5:32; 7:13

11 The earth also was corrupt before God, and the earth was filled with violence.

12 So God looked upon the earth, and indeed it was corrupt; for [R]all flesh had corrupted their way on the earth. Ps. 14:1–3

13 And God said to Noah, "The end of all flesh has come before Me, for the earth is filled with violence through them; and behold, I will destroy them with the earth.

14 "Make yourself an ark of gopherwood; make [T]rooms in the ark, and cover it inside and outside with pitch. Lit. *compartments* or *nests*

15 "And this is how you shall make it: The length of the ark *shall be* [T]three hundred cubits, its width [T]fifty cubits, and its height [T]thirty cubits. 450 ft. • 75 ft. • 45 ft.

16 "You shall make a window for the ark, and you shall finish it to a [T]cubit from above; and set the door of the ark in its side. You shall make it *with* lower, second, and third *decks*. 18 in.

17 [R]"And behold, I Myself am bringing the [R]flood of waters on the earth, to destroy from under heaven all flesh in which *is* the breath of life; *and* everything that *is* on the earth shall [R]die. 2 Pet. 2:5 • 2 Pet. 3:6 • Luke 16:22

18 "But I will establish My [R]covenant with you; and [R]you shall go into the ark—you, your sons, your wife, and your sons' wives with you. Gen. 8:20—9:17; 17:7 • Gen. 7:1, 7, 13

19 "And of every living thing of all flesh you shall bring [R]two of every *sort* into the ark, to keep *them* alive with you; they shall be male and female. Gen. 7:2, 8, 9, 14–16

20 "Of the birds after their kind, of animals after their kind, and of every creeping thing of the earth after its kind, two of every *kind* will come to you to keep *them* alive.

21 "And you shall take for yourself of all food that is eaten, and you shall gather *it* to yourself; and it shall be food for you and for them."

6:3 LXX, Vg. *abide* **6:5** Vg. *God*

22 Thus Noah did; according to all that
[R]God commanded him, so he did. [1 John 5:3]

CHAPTER 7

The Ark Is Entered

THEN the LORD said to Noah, "Come into
the ark, you and all your household,
because I have seen *that* [R]you *are* righteous
before Me in this generation. Gen. 6:9
2 "You shall take with you seven each of
every [R]clean animal, a male and his female;
[R]two each of animals that *are* unclean, a male
and his female; Lev. 11 • Lev. 10:10
3 "also seven each of birds of the air, male
and female, to keep [T]the species alive on the
face of all the earth. Lit. *seed*
4 "For after seven more days I will cause it
to rain on the earth forty days and forty
nights, and I will destroy from the face of the
earth all living things that I have made."
5 [R]And Noah did according to all that the
LORD commanded him. Gen. 6:22
6 Noah *was* six hundred years old when
the flood of waters was on the earth.
7 [R]So Noah, with his sons, his wife, and his
sons' wives, went into the ark because of the
waters of the flood. Matt. 24:38
8 Of clean beasts, of beasts that *are* unclean, of birds, and of everything that creeps
on the earth,
9 two by two they went into the ark to
Noah, male and female, as God had commanded Noah.
10 And it came to pass after seven days that
the waters of the flood were on the earth.

The Earth Is Flooded

11 In the six hundredth year of Noah's life,
in the second month, the seventeenth day of
the month, on that day all the fountains of
the great deep were broken up, and the
[R]windows of heaven were opened. Ps. 78:23
12 [R]And the rain was on the earth forty
days and forty nights. Gen. 7:4, 17
13 On the very same day Noah and Noah's
sons, Shem, Ham, and Japheth, and Noah's
wife and the three wives of his sons with
them, entered the ark—
14 [R]they and every beast after its kind, all
cattle after their kind, every creeping thing
that creeps on the earth after its kind, and
every bird after its kind, every bird of every
[R]sort. Gen. 6:19 • Gen. 1:21
15 And they [R]went into the ark to Noah,
two by two, of all flesh in which *is* the breath
of life. Gen. 6:19, 20; 7:9
16 So those that entered, male and female
of all flesh, went in [R]as God had commanded
him; and the LORD shut him in. Gen. 7:2, 3
17 Now the flood was on the earth forty
days. The waters increased and lifted up the
ark, and it rose high above the earth.
18 The waters prevailed and greatly increased on the earth, [R]and the ark moved
about on the surface of the waters. Ps. 104:26
19 And the waters prevailed exceedingly on
the earth, and all the high hills under the
whole heaven were covered.
20 The waters prevailed fifteen cubits upward, and the mountains were covered.
21 [R]And all flesh died that moved on the
earth: birds and cattle and beasts and every
creeping thing that creeps on the earth, and
every man. Gen. 6:7, 13, 17; 7:4
22 All in [R]whose nostrils *was* the breath *of
the spirit of life, all that *was* on the dry *land*,
died. Gen. 2:7
23 So He destroyed all living things which
were on the face of the ground: both man and
cattle, creeping thing and bird of the air.
They were destroyed from the earth. Only
[R]Noah and those who *were* with him in the
ark remained *alive*. 2 Pet. 2:5
24 [R]And the waters prevailed on the earth
one hundred and fifty days. Gen. 8:3, 4

CHAPTER 8

The Flood Recedes

THEN God [R]remembered Noah, and every
living thing, and all the animals that *were*
with him in the ark. [R]And God made a wind
to pass over the earth, and the waters subsided. Gen. 19:29 • Ex. 14:21; 15:10
2 The fountains of the deep and the windows of heaven were also stopped, and [R]the
rain from heaven was restrained. Job 38:37
3 And the waters receded continually from
the earth. At the end [R]of the hundred and
fifty days the waters decreased. Gen. 7:24
4 Then the ark rested in the seventh
month, the seventeenth day of the month, on
the mountains of Ararat.
5 And the waters decreased continually
until the tenth month. In the tenth *month*, on
the first *day* of the month, the tops of the
mountains were seen.
6 So it came to pass, at the end of forty
days, that Noah opened [R]the window of the
ark which he had made. Gen. 6:16
7 Then he sent out a raven, which kept
going to and fro until the waters had dried up
from the earth.
8 He also sent out from himself a dove, to
see if the waters had abated from the face of
the ground.
9 But the dove found no resting place for
the sole of her foot, and she returned into the
ark to him, for the waters *were* on the face of
the whole earth. So he put out his hand and
took her, and drew her into the ark to himself.
10 And he waited yet another seven days,
and again he sent the dove out from the ark.

7:22 LXX, Vg. omit *of the spirit*

NOAH'S ARK

Artist's conception of Noah's ark.

The ark was a vessel built by Noah to save himself, his family, and animals from the flood sent by God (Gen. 6:14—9:19). The ark was about 450 feet long, 75 feet wide, and 45 feet high, with three decks (see artist's conception of the ark). Scholars have calculated that a vessel of this size would hold more than 43,000 tons.

After almost a year on the water, the ark came to rest on Mount Ararat in what is now Turkey. Numerous attempts across the centuries to find the remains of the vessel have been futile. Shifting glaciers, avalanches, hidden crevices, and sudden storms make mountain climbing in the area extremely dangerous.

The ark reveals both the judgment and mercy of God. His righteous judgment is seen in the destruction of the wicked, but His mercy and care are demonstrated in His preservation of Noah, and, through him, of the human race. The ark is a striking illustration of Christ, who preserves us from the flood of divine judgment through His grace.

From the ancient world there are several other flood stories that are remarkably similar to the biblical account in many details. In the most famous of these, Utnapishti, the Babylonian "Noah," constructed a boat, which was about 180 feet long, 180 feet wide, and 180 feet high—hardly a seaworthy design. In stark contrast to these stories, the Book of Genesis presents a holy and righteous God who sends the flood in judgment against sin and yet mercifully saves Noah and his family because of their righteousness.

In the New Testament, Jesus spoke of the Flood and of Noah and the ark, comparing "the days of Noah" with the time of "the coming of the Son of Man" (Matt. 24:37, 38; Luke 17:26, 27). Other references to the Flood include Hebrews 11:7; 1 Peter 3:20; and 2 Peter 2:5.

11 Then the dove came to him in the evening, and behold, a freshly plucked olive leaf
was in her mouth; and Noah knew that the
waters had abated from the earth.
12 So he waited yet another seven days and
sent out the dove, which did not return again
to him anymore.
13 And it came to pass in the six hundred
and first year, in the first *month*, the first *day*
of the month, that the waters were dried up
from the earth; and Noah removed the covering of the ark and looked, and indeed the
surface of the ground was dry.
14 And in the second month, on the twenty-
seventh day of the month, the earth was
dried.
15 Then God spoke to Noah, saying,
16 "Go out of the ark, you and your wife,
and your sons and your sons' wives with you.
17 "Bring out with you every living thing of
all flesh that *is* with you: birds and cattle and
every creeping thing that creeps on the earth,
so that they may abound on the earth, and be
fruitful and multiply on the earth."
18 So Noah went out, and his sons and his
wife and his sons' wives with him.
19 Every beast, every creeping thing, every
bird, *and* whatever creeps on the earth, according to their families, went out of the ark.

Noah Worships God

20 Then Noah built an [R]altar to the LORD,
and took of [R]every clean animal and of every
clean bird, and offered [R]burnt offerings on the
altar. Gen. 12:7 • Lev. 11 • Ex. 10:25
21 And the LORD smelled a soothing aroma.
Then the LORD said in His heart, "I will never
again curse the ground for man's sake, although the imagination of man's heart *is* evil
from his youth; nor will I again destroy every
living thing as I have done.

22 "While the earth [R]remains,
Seedtime and harvest,
And cold and heat,
And winter and summer,
And [R]day and night
Shall not cease." Is. 54:9 • Jer. 33:20, 25

CHAPTER 9

God's Covenant with Noah

SO God blessed Noah and his sons, and said
to them: [R]"Be fruitful and multiply, and
fill the earth. Gen. 1:28, 29; 8:17; 9:7, 19; 10:32
2 [R]"And the fear of you and the dread of
you shall be on every beast of the earth, on
every bird of the air, on all that move *on* the
earth, and on all the fish of the sea. They are
given into your hand. Ps. 8:6
3 "Every moving thing that lives shall be
food for you. I have given you all things, even
as the [R]green herbs. Rom. 14:14, 20
4 [R]"But you shall not eat flesh with its life,
that is, its blood. 1 Sam. 14:33, 34

5 "Surely for your lifeblood I will demand
a reckoning; from the hand of every beast I
will require it, and [R]from the hand of man.
From the hand of every [R]man's brother I will
require the life of man. Gen. 4:9, 10 • Acts 17:26

6 "Whoever [R]sheds man's blood,
By man his blood shall be shed;

9:1–19 The Noahic Covenant—The covenant with Noah is the third general or universal covenant. Noah has just passed through the universal flood in which all the world's population had been wiped out. Only Noah, his wife, his three sons, and their wives—eight people—constitute the world's population. Noah might have thought that the things provided by the covenant with Adam had now been changed. However, God gives the Noahic Covenant so that Noah and all the human race to follow might know that the provisions made in the Adamic Covenant remain in effect with one notable addition: the principle of human government which includes the responsibility of suppressing the outbreak of sin and violence, so that it will not be necessary to destroy the earth again by a flood. The provisions of the covenant are:

a. The responsibility to populate the earth is reaffirmed (v. 1).
b. The subjection of the animal kingdom to man is reaffirmed (v. 2).
c. Man is permitted to eat the flesh of animals. However, he is to refrain from eating blood (vv. 3, 4).
d. The sacredness of human life is established. Whatever sheds man's blood, whether man or beast, must be put to death (vv. 5, 6).
e. This covenant is confirmed to Noah, all mankind, and every living creature on the face of the earth (vv. 9, 10).
f. The promise is given never to destroy the earth again by a universal flood (v. 11). The next time God destroys the earth, the means will be fire (Page 1489—2 Pet. 3:10).
g. The rainbow is designated as a testimony of the existence of this covenant and the promise never to destroy the earth by flood. As long as we can see the rainbow we will know that the Noahic Covenant is in existence (vv. 12–17).

Now turn to Page 18—Gen. 12:1–3: The Abrahamic Covenant.

9:5 The Origin of Human Government—It has been assumed that human government was officially instituted after the Great Flood in Genesis 9. However, some form of law and order undoubtedly existed prior to this period. This is strongly suggested by both Jesus and Jude. Jesus in Luke 17:26, 27 says that prior to the Flood in Noah's day people conducted their affairs in much the same manner as we do today. Jude gives us the text of a message Enoch preached to sinners prior to the Flood (Page 1510—Jude 14, 15). We learn that one of the main factors which brought about the Flood was man's disobedience to the revealed law of God.

[R]For in the image of God
He made man. Lev. 24:17 • Gen. 1:26, 27
7 And as for you, [R]be fruitful and
multiply;
Bring forth abundantly in the earth
And multiply in it." Gen. 9:1, 19

8 Then God spoke to Noah and to his sons
with him, saying:
9 "And as for Me, [R]behold, I establish [R]My
covenant with you and with your [T]descen-
dants after you, Gen. 6:18 • Is. 54:9 • Lit. *seed*
10 [R]"and with every living creature that *is*
with you: the birds, the cattle, and every
beast of the earth with you, of all that go out
of the ark, every beast of the earth. Ps. 145:9
11 "Thus [R]I establish My covenant with
you: Never again shall all flesh be cut off by
the waters of the flood; never again shall
there be a flood to destroy the earth." Is. 54:9
12 And God said: [R]"This *is* the sign of the
covenant which I make between Me and you,
and every living creature that *is* with you, for
perpetual generations: Gen. 9:13, 17; 17:11
13 "I set [R]My rainbow in the cloud, and it
shall be for the sign of the covenant between
Me and the earth. Ezek. 1:28
14 "It shall be, when I bring a cloud over
the earth, that the rainbow shall be seen in
the cloud;
15 "and [R]I will remember My covenant
which *is* between Me and you and every
living creature of all flesh; the waters shall
never again become a flood to destroy all
flesh. Lev. 26:42, 45
16 "The rainbow shall be in the cloud, and I
will look on it to remember the everlasting
covenant between God and every living creature of all flesh that *is* on the earth."
17 And God said to Noah, "This *is* the sign
of the covenant which I have established
between Me and all flesh that *is* on the
earth."

The Sons of Noah

18 Now the sons of Noah who went out of
the ark were Shem, Ham, and Japheth. [R]And
Ham *was* the father of Canaan. Gen. 9:25–27
19 These three *were* the sons of Noah, and
from these the whole earth was populated.

Ham's Sin

20 And Noah began *to be* [R]a farmer, and he
planted a vineyard. Gen. 3:19, 23; 4:2
21 Then he drank of the wine and was
drunk, and became uncovered in his tent.
22 And Ham, the father of Canaan, saw the
nakedness of his father, and told his two
brothers outside.
23 But Shem and Japheth took a garment,
laid *it* on both their shoulders, and went
backward and covered the nakedness of their
father. Their faces *were* turned away, and
they did not see their father's nakedness.
24 So Noah awoke from his wine, and knew
what his younger son had done to him.

The Curse on Canaan

25 Then he said:

[R]"Cursed *be* Canaan; Deut. 27:16
A [R]servant of servants Josh. 9:23
He shall be to his brethren."

26 And he said:

[R]"Blessed *be* the LORD, Gen. 14:20; 24:27
The God of Shem,
And may Canaan be his servant.
27 May God enlarge Japheth,
And may he dwell in the tents of Shem;
And may Canaan be his servant."

Noah's Death

28 And Noah lived after the flood three
hundred and fifty years.
29 So all the days of Noah were nine hundred and fifty years; and he died.

CHAPTER 10

The Family of Japheth—1 Chr. 1:5–7

NOW this *is* the genealogy of the sons of
Noah: Shem, Ham, and Japheth. And
sons were born to them after the flood.
2 [R]The sons of Japheth *were* Gomer, Magog, Madai, Javan, Tubal, Meshech, and
Tiras. 1 Chr. 1:5–7
3 The sons of Gomer *were* Ashkenaz, *Riphath, and Togarmah.

10:3 *Diphath*, 1 Chr. 1:6

At any rate, there is certainly no doubt concerning the source of human government. God Himself is its divine author. Two individuals give testimony to this fact. Daniel reminds King Nebuchadnezzar that "the Most High rules in the kingdom of men, and gives it to whomever He chooses" (Page 981—Dan. 4:25). The apostle Paul exhorts Christians to be subject to the laws of human government because all earthly powers exist through God's divine permission (Page 1337—Rom. 13).

If one rightly understands the origin of human government, then the conclusion is reached that lawless anarchy is not only rebellion against human authority, but actual blasphemy against the divine Creator Himself.

Now turn to Page 1337—Rom. 13:1-4: The Function of Human Government.

4 The sons of Javan *were* Elishah, Tarshish, Kittim, and *Dodanim.
5 From these the coastland *peoples* of the
Gentiles were separated into their lands,
everyone according to his *own* language,
according to their families, into their nations.

The Family of Ham—1 Chr. 1:8–12

6 [R]The sons of Ham *were* Cush, Mizraim,
[T]Put, and Canaan. 1 Chr. 1:8–16 • Or *Phut*
7 The sons of Cush *were* Seba, Havilah,
Sabtah, Raamah, and Sabtechah; and the
sons of Raamah *were* Sheba and Dedan.
8 Cush begot [R]Nimrod; he began to be a
mighty one on the earth. Mic. 5:6
9 He was a mighty hunter [R]before the
LORD; therefore it is said, "Like Nimrod the
mighty hunter before the LORD." Gen. 21:20
10 [R]And the beginning of his kingdom was
[R]Babel, Erech, Accad, and Calneh, in the land
of Shinar. Mic. 5:6 • Gen. 11:9
11 From that land he went [R]to Assyria and
built Nineveh, Rehoboth Ir, Calah, Mic. 5:6
12 and Resen between Nineveh and Calah
(that *is* the principal city).
13 Mizraim begot Ludim, Anamim, Leha-
bim, Naphtuhim,
14 Pathrusim, and Casluhim (from whom
came the Philistines and Caphtorim).

The Family of Canaan—1 Chr. 1:13–16

15 Canaan begot Sidon his firstborn, and
[R]Heth; Gen. 23:3
16 [R]the Jebusite, the Amorite, and the Gir-
gashite; Gen. 14:7; 15:19–21
17 the Hivite, the Arkite, and the Sinite;
18 the Arvadite, the Zemarite, and the Ha-
mathite. Afterward the families of the Canaanites were dispersed.
19 And the border of the Canaanites was
from Sidon as you go toward Gerar, as far as
Gaza; then as you go toward Sodom, Gomorrah, Admah, and Zeboim, as far as Lasha.
20 These *were* the sons of Ham, according
to their families, according to their languages, in their lands *and* in their nations.

The Family of Shem—1 Chr. 1:17–23

21 And *children* were born also to Shem,
the father of all the children of Eber, the
brother of Japheth the elder.
22 The sons of Shem *were* Elam, Asshur,
[R]Arphaxad, Lud, and Aram. Luke 3:36
23 The sons of Aram *were* Uz, Hul, Gether,
and *Mash.
24 Arphaxad begot [R]Salah, and Salah begot
Eber. Gen. 11:12
25 [R]To Eber were born two sons: the name
of one *was* [T]Peleg, for in his days the earth
was divided; and his brother's name *was*
Joktan. 1 Chr. 1:19 • Lit. *Division*
26 Joktan begot Almodad, Sheleph, Hazarmaveth, Jerah,
27 Hadoram, Uzal, Diklah,
28 [T]Obal, Abimael, Sheba, *Ebal,* 1 Chr. 1:22
29 Ophir, Havilah, and Jobab. All these *were*
the sons of Joktan.
30 And their dwelling place was from Mesha as you go toward Sephar, the mountain
of the east.
31 These *were* the sons of Shem, according
to their families, according to their languages, in their lands, according to their
nations.
32 These *were* the families of the sons of
Noah, according to their generations, in their
nations; and from these the nations were
divided on the earth after the flood.

CHAPTER 11

Construction of the Tower

NOW the whole earth had one language
and one [T]speech. Lit. *lip*
2 And it came to pass, as they journeyed
from the east, that they found a plain in the
land of Shinar, and they dwelt there.
3 Then they said to one another, "Come,
let us make bricks and [T]bake *them* thoroughly." They had brick for stone, and they
had asphalt for mortar. Lit. *burn*

Rebellion at the Tower

4 And they said, "Come, let us build ourselves a city, and a tower whose top *is* in the
heavens; let us make a [R]name for ourselves,
lest we [R]be scattered abroad over the face of
the whole earth." Gen. 6:4 • Deut. 4:27

Judgment on All the Family Lines

5 [R]But the LORD came down to see the city
and the tower which the sons of men had
built. Gen. 18:21
6 And the LORD said, "Indeed [R]the people
are one and they all have [R]one language, and
this is what they begin to do; now nothing
that they [R]propose to do will be withheld
from them. Gen. 9:19 • Gen. 11:1 • Ps. 2:1
7 "Come, [R]let Us go down and there [R]con-
fuse their language, that they may not understand one another's speech." Gen. 1:26 • Ex. 4:11
8 So [R]the LORD scattered them abroad
from there over the face of all the earth, and
they ceased building the city. [Luke 1:51]
9 Therefore its name is called [T]Babel, [R]be-
cause there the LORD confused the language
of all the earth; and from there the LORD
scattered them abroad over the face of all the
earth. Lit. *Confusion,* Babylon • 1 Cor. 14:23

10:4 Sam. *Rodanim* and 1 Chr. 1:7
10:23 LXX *Meshech* and 1 Chr. 1:17

THE TOWER OF BABEL

The Tower of Babel may have been similar to the ziggurats built by the Babylonians as places of worship of their chief god Marduk.

The Tower of Babel was built on the plain of Shinar, a site probably in ancient Babylonia in southern Mesopotamia, some time after the great flood of Noah's time. A symbol of man's sinful pride and rebellion, the structure was built to satisfy the people's vanity: "Let us make a name for ourselves" (Gen. 11:4).

The pyramid-like tower was expected to reach heaven. These people were trying to approach God on their own self-serving terms, but they learned that the gates of heaven cannot be stormed. Men and women must approach the holy God in reverence and humility.

This tower was built of bricks and mortar, since no stones were available on the flat plains of southern Mesopotamia. The Babel Tower appears to be similar to the ziggurats the ancient inhabitants of southern Mesopotamia built as places for the worship of their gods. Both Assyrian and Babylonian kings prided themselves on the height of these pagan temples, boasting of building them as high as heaven.

One such tower, built in Ur, Abraham's ancestral city in southern Mesopotamia, about 2100 B.C., was a pyramid consisting of three terraces of diminishing size (see illustration). The temple was climbed by converging stairways. The uppermost part of the tower was an altar devoted to pagan worship.

God intervened to prevent the builders of Babel from partaking of the power and glory that belongs only to Him. The language of the builders was confused so they could no longer communicate with one another. In their frustration, they abandoned the project. Then the prideful builders were scattered abroad (Gen. 11:7, 8). How small and weak this tower was in comparison to God's power! Humankind's misguided efforts at self-glorification brought on confusion and frustration and their dispersion throughout the world.

Abram's Family Line
1 Chr. 1:24–27; Luke 3:34–36

10 RThis *is* the genealogy of Shem: Shem
was one hundred years old, and begot Arphaxad two years after the flood. Gen. 10:22–25
11 After he begot Arphaxad, Shem lived five
hundred years, and begot sons and daughters.
12 Arphaxad lived thirty-five years, Rand
begot Salah. Luke 3:35
13 After he begot Salah, Arphaxad lived
four hundred and three years, and begot sons
and daughters.
14 Salah lived thirty years, and begot Eber.
15 After he begot Eber, Salah lived four
hundred and three years, and begot sons and
daughters.
16 REber lived thirty-four years, and begot
RPeleg. 1 Chr. 1:19 • Luke 3:35
17 After he begot Peleg, Eber lived four
hundred and thirty years, and begot sons and
daughters.
18 Peleg lived thirty years, and begot Reu.
19 After he begot Reu, Peleg lived two
hundred and nine years, and begot sons and
daughters.
20 Reu lived thirty-two years, and begot
RSerug. Luke 3:35
21 After he begot Serug, Reu lived two
hundred and seven years, and begot sons and
daughters.
22 Serug lived thirty years, and begot Nahor.
23 After he begot Nahor, Serug lived two
hundred years, and begot sons and daughters.
24 Nahor lived twenty-nine years, and begot RTerah. Josh. 24:2
25 After he begot Terah, Nahor lived one
hundred and nineteen years, and begot sons
and daughters.
26 Now Terah lived seventy years, and begot RAbram, Nahor, and Haran. Gen. 17:5

Abram's Past

27 This *is* the genealogy of Terah: Terah
begot RAbram, Nahor, and Haran. Haran
begot Lot. Gen. 11:31; 17:5
28 And Haran died before his father Terah
in his native land, in Ur of the Chaldeans.
29 Then Abram and Nahor took wives: the
name of Abram's wife *was* RSarai, and the
name of Nahor's wife, RMilcah, the daughter
of Haran the father of Milcah and the father
of Iscah. Gen. 17:15; 20:12 • Gen. 22:20, 23; 24:15
30 But Sarai was barren; she had no child.
31 And Terah took his son Abram and his
grandson Lot, the son of Haran, and his
daughter-in-law Sarai, his son Abram's wife,
and they went out with them from Ur of the
Chaldeans to go to the land of Canaan; and
they came to Haran and dwelt there.
32 So the days of Terah were two hundred
and five years, and Terah died in Haran.

CHAPTER 12

Initiation of the Covenant

NOW the RLORD had said to Abram:

"Get Rout of your country,
From your kindred Acts 7:2, 3 • Gen. 13:9
And from your father's house,
To a land that I will show you.
2 RI will make you a great nation; Deut. 26:5
RI will bless you Gen. 22:17; 24:35
And make your name great;
RAnd you shall be a blessing. Gen. 28:4
3 I will bless those who bless you,
And I will curse him who curses you;
And in Ryou all the families of the earth
shall be Rblessed." Gal. 3:8 ☆ • Is. 41:27

4 So Abram departed as the LORD had
spoken to him, and Lot went with him. And
Abram *was* seventy-five years old when he
departed from Haran.
5 Then Abram took Sarai his wife and Lot

12:1–3 The Abrahamic Covenant—The covenant with Abraham is the first of the theocratic covenants (pertaining to the rule of God). It is unconditional, depending solely upon God who obligates Himself in grace, indicated by the unconditional declaration, "I will," to bring to pass the promised blessings. The Abrahamic Covenant is the basis of all the other theocratic covenants and provides for blessings in three areas: (1) national—"I will make you a great nation," (2) personal—"I will bless you and make your name great; and you shall be a blessing," and (3) universal—"in you all families of the earth shall be blessed." This covenant was first given in broad outline and was later confirmed to Abraham in greater detail (cf. Page 20—Gen. 13:14–17; 15:1–7, 18–21; 17:1–8). The Abrahamic Covenant constitutes an important link in all that God began to do, has done throughout history, and will continue to do until the consummation of history. It is the one purpose of God for humans into which all of God's programs and works fit. The personal aspects of the Abrahamic Covenant are fourfold: (1) to be the father of a great nation, (2) to receive personal blessing, (3) to receive personal honor and reputation, and (4) to be the source of blessing to others. The universal aspects of the covenant are threefold: (1) blessings for those people and nations which bless Abraham and the nation which comes from him; (2) cursings upon those people and nations which curse Abraham and Israel; and (3) blessings upon all the families of the earth through the Messiah, who, according to the flesh, is Abraham's son and provides salvation for the entire world.

Now turn to Page 89—Ex. 19:5–8: The Mosaic Covenant.

OLD TESTAMENT JOURNEYS

One of the most famous travelers of the Old Testament was Abraham. He accompanied his family as they moved from Ur in lower Mesopotamia to the city of Haran in upper Mesopotamia (Gen. 11:31, 32). Later he moved his family from Haran to southern Canaan in response to God's call (Gen. 12:1–5). Still later he moved his flocks and herds into Egypt to escape a severe famine throughout Canaan (Gen. 12:10). He eventually returned to southern Canaan, where he spent the rest of his life as a wandering herdsman in the region around Hebron and the central hill country of Shechem. A Moslem mosque in modern Hebron supposedly marks the site of Abraham's tomb in southern Palestine.

Following is a list of some of the journeys made by other Old Testament personalities:

Personality(ies)	Description of Journey	Biblical Reference
Jacob	From Hebron to ancestral Haran to find a wife	Gen. 28; 29
Joseph	From Canaan to Egypt, sold into slavery by his brothers	Gen. 37
Jacob and his family	To Egypt to escape a famine in Canaan	Gen. 42—46
Moses	From Egypt to Midian after killing an Egyptian; back to Egypt to lead his people out of slavery	Ex. 2:14, 15 Ex. 3; 4
Israelites	From Egypt to the Promised Land	Ex. 12 and following
Ruth	From Moab to mother-in-law Naomi's ancestral home in Bethlehem	Ruth 1
Saul	From Gibeah to Ramah to be anointed first king of Israel	1 Sam. 1:1; 9:1—10:1
Samuel	From Ramah to Bethlehem to anoint David as king	1 Sam. 16
David	From Philistia to Hebron to become king of Judah; from Hebron to Jerusalem to capture the city and become king over all Israel	2 Sam. 2:1–4 2 Sam. 5:7–12
Solomon	From Jerusalem to Gibeon to offer sacrifices and ask for wisdom	1 Kin. 3:4–9
Queen of Sheba	From Africa or Arabia to Jerusalem to pay a royal visit to Solomon	1 Kin. 10
Elijah	From Jezreel into the wilderness to escape Jezebel's wrath	1 Kin. 18:46; 19
Naaman	From Syria to Samaria to be healed by Elisha	2 Kin. 5
Captives of Judah	From Jerusalem to captivity in Babylon From captivity in Babylon to freedom in Jerusalem	2 Chr. 36:20 Ezra 1
Ezra	From Babylon to Jerusalem "to teach statutes and ordinances in Israel"	Ezra 7:1–10
Nehemiah	From Babylon to Jerusalem to rebuild the city wall	Neh. 1; 2

his brother's son, and all their possessions
that they had gathered, and the [T]people
whom they had acquired in Haran, and they
departed to go to the land of Canaan. So they
came to the land of Canaan. Lit. *souls*
6 Abram passed through the land to the
place of Shechem, as far as [T]the terebinth
tree of Moreh. [R]And the Canaanites *were*
then in the land. Or *Alon Moreh* • Gen. 10:18, 19
7 Then the LORD appeared to Abram and
said, "To your descendants I will give this
land." And there he built an altar to the
LORD, who had appeared to him.
8 And he moved from there to the mountain east of Bethel, and he pitched his tent
with Bethel on the west and Ai on the east;
there he built an altar to the LORD and [R]called
on the name of the LORD. Gen. 4:26; 13:4; 21:33
9 So Abram journeyed, going on still
toward the [T]South. Heb. *Negev*
10 Now there was a famine in the land, and
Abram went down to Egypt to sojourn there,
for the famine *was* severe in the land.
11 And it came to pass, when he was close
to entering Egypt, that he said to Sarai his
wife, "Indeed I know that you *are* [R]a woman
of beautiful countenance. Gen. 12:14; 26:7; 29:17
12 "Therefore it will happen, when the
Egyptians see you, that they will say, 'This *is*
his wife'; and they [R]will kill me, but they will
let you live. Gen. 20:11; 26:7
13 "Please say you *are* my sister, that it may
be well with me for your sake, and that [T]I
may live because of you." Lit. *my soul*
14 So it was, when Abram came into Egypt,
that the Egyptians saw the woman, that she
was very beautiful.
15 The princes of Pharaoh also saw her and
commended her to Pharaoh. And the woman
was taken to Pharaoh's house.
16 He treated Abram well for her sake. He
had sheep, oxen, male donkeys, male and
female servants, female donkeys, and camels.
17 But the LORD [R]plagued Pharaoh and his
house with great plagues because of Sarai,
Abram's wife. 1 Chr. 16:21
18 And Pharaoh called Abram and said,
"What *is* this you have done to me? Why did
you not tell me that she *was* your wife?
19 "Why did you say, 'She *is* my sister'? I
might have taken her as my wife. Now therefore, here is your wife; take *her* and go your
way."
20 [R]So Pharaoh commanded *his* men concerning him; and they sent him away, with
his wife and all that he had. [Prov. 21:1]

CHAPTER 13

Abram's Separation from Lot

THEN Abram went up from Egypt, he and
his wife and all that he had, and Lot with
him, [R]to the [T]South. Gen. 12:9 • Heb. *Negev*
2 [R]Abram *was* very rich in livestock, in
silver, and in gold. Gen. 24:35; 26:14
3 And he went on his journey [R]from the
South as far as Bethel, to the place where his
tent had been at the beginning, between
Bethel and Ai, Gen. 12:8, 9
4 to the [R]place of the altar which he had
made there at first. And there Abram called
on the name of the LORD. Gen. 12:7, 8; 21:33
5 Lot also, who went with Abram, had
flocks and herds and tents.
6 Now [R]the land was not able to [T]support
them, that they might dwell together, for
their possessions were so great that they
could not dwell together. Gen. 36:7 • Lit. *bear*
7 And there was [R]strife between the herdsmen of Abram's livestock and the herdsmen
of Lot's livestock. The Canaanites and the
Perizzites then dwelt in the land. Gen. 26:20
8 So Abram said to Lot, [R]"Please let there
be no strife between you and me, and between my herdsmen and your herdsmen; for
we *are* brethren. 1 Cor. 6:7
9 "*Is* not the whole land before you? Please
separate from me. If *you take* the left, then I
will go to the right; or, if *you go* to the right,
then I will go to the left."
10 And Lot lifted his eyes and saw all the
plain of Jordan, that it *was* well watered
everywhere (before the LORD [R]destroyed
Sodom and Gomorrah) [R]like the garden of
the LORD, like the land of Egypt as you go
toward [R]Zoar. Gen. 19:24 • Gen. 2:8, 10 • Deut. 34:3
11 Then Lot chose for himself all the plain
of Jordan, and Lot journeyed east. And they
separated from each other.
12 Abram dwelt in the land of Canaan, and
Lot dwelt in the cities of the plain and
pitched *his* tent even as far as Sodom.
13 But the men of Sodom *were* exceedingly
wicked and sinful against the LORD.

God's Promise to Abram

14 And the LORD said to Abram, after Lot
[R]had separated from him: "Lift your eyes now
and look from the place where you are—
[R]northward, southward, eastward, and westward; Gen. 13:11 • Gen. 28:14
15 "for all the land which you see I give to
you and your [T]descendants forever. Lit. *seed*
16 "And I will make your descendants as
the dust of the earth; so that if a man could
number the dust of the earth, *then* your
descendants also could be numbered.
17 "Arise, walk in the land through its
length and its width, for I give it to you."
18 Then Abram moved *his* tent, and went
and [R]dwelt [T]by the terebinth trees of Mamre,
which *are* in Hebron, and built an altar there
to the LORD. Gen. 14:13 • Or *Alon Mamre*

CHAPTER 14

Abram Rescues Lot

AND it came to pass in the days of Amraphel king of Shinar, Arioch king of
Ellasar, Chedorlaomer king of Elam, and
Tidal king of [T]nations, Heb. *Goyim*
2 *that* they made war with Bera king of
Sodom, Birsha king of Gomorrah, Shinab
king of Admah, Shemeber king of Zeboiim,
and the king of Bela (that is, Zoar).
3 All these joined together in the Valley of
Siddim [R](that is, the Salt Sea). Num. 34:12
4 Twelve years they served Chedorlaomer,
and in the thirteenth year they rebelled.
5 In the fourteenth year Chedorlaomer
and the kings that *were* with him came and
attacked the Rephaim in Ashteroth Karnaim,
[R]the Zuzim in Ham, [R]the Emim in Shaveh
Kiriathaim, Deut. 2:20 • Deut. 2:10
6 [R]and the Horites in their mountain of
Seir, as far as El Paran, which *is* by the
wilderness. Deut. 2:12, 22
7 Then they turned back and came to En
Mishpat (that *is*, Kadesh), and attacked all
the country of the Amalekites, and also the
Amorites who dwelt in Hazezon Tamar.
8 And the king of Sodom, the king of
Gomorrah, the king of Admah, the king of
Zeboiim, and the king of Bela (that *is*, Zoar)
went out and joined together in battle in the
Valley of Siddim
9 against Chedorlaomer king of Elam,
Tidal king of [T]nations, Amraphel king of
Shinar, and Arioch king of Ellasar—four
kings against five. Heb. *Goyim*
10 Now the Valley of Siddim *was full of*
[R]asphalt pits; and the kings of Sodom and
Gomorrah fled; *some* fell there, and the remainder fled to the mountains. Gen. 11:3
11 Then they took [R]all the goods of Sodom
and Gomorrah, and all their provisions, and
went their way. Gen. 14:16, 21
12 They also took Lot, Abram's [R]brother's
son [R]who dwelt in Sodom, and his goods, and
departed. Gen. 11:27; 12:5 • Gen. 13:12
13 Then one who had escaped came and
told Abram the Hebrew, for he dwelt by [T]the
terebinth trees of Mamre the Amorite,
brother of Eshcol and brother of Aner; and
they *were* allies with Abram. Or *Alon Mamre*
14 Now when Abram heard that [R]his
brother was taken captive, he armed his
three hundred and eighteen trained *servants*
who were born in his own house, and went in
pursuit as far as Dan. Gen. 13:8; 14:12
15 He divided his forces against them by
night, and he and his servants attacked them
and pursued them as far as Hobah, which *is*
[T]north of Damascus. *to the left of*
16 So he brought back all the goods, and
also brought back his brother Lot and his
goods, as well as the women and the people.

Abram Refuses Reward

17 And the king of Sodom went out to meet
him at the Valley of Shaveh (that *is*, the
[R]King's Valley), [R]after his return from [T]the
defeat of Chedorlaomer and the kings who
were with him. 2 Sam. 18:18 • Heb. 7:1 • Lit. *striking*
18 Then Melchizedek king of Salem
brought out bread and wine; he *was* [R]the
priest of [R]God Most High. Ps. 110:4 • Acts 16:17
19 And he blessed him and said:

"Blessed be Abram of God Most High,
[R]Possessor of heaven and earth; Gen. 14:22
20 And [R]blessed be God Most High,
Who has delivered your enemies into
your hand." Gen. 24:27

And he [R]gave him a tithe of all. Heb. 7:4
21 Now the king of Sodom said to Abram,
"Give me the [T]persons, and take the goods for
yourself." Lit. *souls*
22 But Abram said to the king of Sodom, "I
have lifted my hand to the LORD, God Most
High, the Possessor of heaven and earth,
23 "that [R]I *will take* nothing, from a thread
to a sandal strap, and that I will not take
anything that *is* yours, lest you should say, 'I
have made Abram rich'— 2 Kin. 5:16
24 "except only what the young men have
eaten, and the portion of the men who went
with me: Aner, Eshcol, and Mamre; let them
take their portion."

CHAPTER 15

God's Promise of Children

AFTER these things the word of the LORD
came to Abram [R]in a vision, saying,
"Do not be afraid, Abram. I *am* your shield,
your exceedingly great reward." Dan. 10:1
2 But Abram said, "Lord GOD, what will
You give me, seeing I go childless, and the
heir of my house *is* Eliezer of Damascus?"
3 Then Abram said, "Look, You have given
me no offspring; indeed [T]one born in my
house is my heir!" *a servant*, Gen. 14:14
4 And behold, the word of the LORD *came*
to him, saying, "This one shall not be your
heir, but one who [R]will come from your own
body shall be your heir." 2 Sam. 7:12
5 Then He brought him outside and said,
"Look now toward heaven, and [R]count the
[R]stars if you are able to number them." And
He said to him, [R]"So shall your [R]descendants
be." Ps. 147:4 • Jer. 33:22 • Ex. 32:13 • Gen. 17:19
6 And he believed in the LORD, and He
accounted it to him for righteousness.
7 Then He said to him, "I *am* the LORD,
who brought you out of Ur of the Chaldeans,
to give you this land to inherit it."
8 And he said, "Lord GOD, [R]how shall I
know that I will inherit it?" Luke 1:18

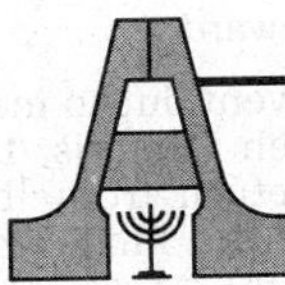

HALLELUJAH! AMEN!

Untold millions—yes, by now billions—of people have used the words *Hallelujah! Amen!* to express aspects of their faith. This word study examines their Old Testament roots.

Hallelujah

Praise Jah—poetic for the LORD or Jehovah—*Hallelujah* is a command (imperative) from the Hebrew verb *hālal, praise.* Sometimes it is used to praise merely human qualities: Sarah's beauty (Gen. 12:14, 15), Absalom's good looks (2 Sam. 14:25), an outstanding wife and mother (Prov. 31:28, 31).

By far the most common use of the verb is to praise the Lord. The *hallelu-* part of the word is not only a command, but the form is plural in Hebrew. This suggests congregational praise. Hence, we are not surprised that the Book of Psalms contains about a third of these uses, because the Psalms constitute the praises of Israel—and now of the church, as well.

The praise of God is very important. It should be a delight to His people, not a chore. All of creation should join in His praise (Ps. 148:1, 2).

Ancient Israel praised the Lord with music, choirs, congregational singing, dance, and even speaking (Jer. 31:7). The modern church does much the same.

Amen

We associate the word *amen* as the last word of a prayer or a choral anthem, an agreement with what someone has said—especially in church. Even unbelievers sometimes use the word to show support for views expressed. All this fits in nicely with the ancient verb *āman* ("confirm," "support," "be established," "believe").

In one form of the Hebrew verb, used in a very important text, we read that Abraham "believed [form of *āman*] in the LORD, and He accounted it to him for righteousness" (Gen. 15:6). Someone has paraphrased this, "Abraham said *amen* to God, and He justified him." While not a literal rendering, it does express the truth of justification by faith. The New Testament uses Abraham as a figure representing salvation by grace through faith. He is the father of the faithful, not only of the Jews who believed God's Word, but also of the Christians.

This also fits in with Hebrews 11, the great faith chapter, where faith is seen basically as a certainty, an established belief.

The popular word *amen* is derived from the verb *āman*. It means "verily," "truly," or "assuredly." Sometimes it is just transliterated from the Hebrew as *amen*. Our Christian usage of *amen* at the end of prayers and hymns has good Old Testament precedent, to say the least. The five books of Psalms all end in *amens,* and the last psalm is itself an "amen" to the whole book.

After David's great psalm in 1 Chronicles 16:8–36 was delivered, "all the people said, 'Amen!' and praised the LORD." A similar response is seen to Ezra's blessing of the Lord in Nehemiah 8:6.

Surprisingly, *amen* is used over twice as often in the New Testament as in the Old. In His letter to the lukewarm Laodiceans, Jesus called Himself "the Amen" (Rev. 3:14). He meant: "You can count on Me to be firm and true!"

A usage of *amen* that is unique to our Lord shows up in the Greek text, the Latin Vulgate, and the old Douay-Rheims Version. Wherever Jesus prefaced His remarks, with *verily* (KJV), *truly* (NASB), or *assuredly* (NKJV), the original reads *amen.* Twenty-five times in John it is a double *amen.* Jesus was saying that His following words were very important. The NKJV translates the double *amen* by "most assuredly," since repeating such a long word ("assuredly, assuredly") would sound odd.

A literal rendering of John 5:24 would read, "*Amen, amen,* I say to you, he who hears My word and believes in Him who sent Me has everlasting life, and shall not come into judgment, but has passed from death into life."

Those who believe this gracious promise can well respond: "Hallelujah! Amen!"

9 So He said to him, "Bring Me a three-year-old heifer, a three-year-old female goat, a three-year-old ram, a turtledove, and a young pigeon."

10 Then he brought all these to Him and [R]cut them in two, down the middle, and placed each piece opposite the other; but he did not cut [R]the birds in two. Jer. 34:18 • Lev. 1:17

11 And when the vultures came down on the carcasses, Abram drove them away.

12 Now when the sun was going down, a deep sleep fell upon Abram; and behold, horror *and* great darkness fell upon him.

13 Then He said to Abram: "Know certainly [R]that your descendants will be strangers in a land *that is* not theirs, and will serve them, and [R]they will afflict them four hundred years. Ex. 1:11 • Ex. 12:40

14 "And also the nation whom they serve [R]I will judge; afterward [R]they shall come out with great possessions. Ex. 6:6 • Ex. 12:36

15 "Now as for you, you shall [T]go to your fathers in peace; you shall be buried at a good old age. Die and join your ancestors

16 "But [R]in the fourth generation they shall return here, for the iniquity [R]of the Amorites *is* not yet complete." Ex. 12:41 • 1 Kin. 21:26

17 And it came to pass, when the sun went down and it was dark, that behold, *there was* a smoking oven and a burning torch that [R]passed between those pieces. Jer. 34:18, 19

18 On the same day the LORD [R]made a covenant with Abram, saying: Gen. 24:7

[R]"To your descendants I have given this land, from the river of Egypt to the great river, the River Euphrates— Gen. 12:7; 17:8

19 "the Kenites, the Kenezzites, and the Kadmonites;

20 "the Hittites, the Perizzites, and the Rephaim;

21 "the Amorites, the Canaanites, the Girgashites, and the Jebusites."

CHAPTER 16

A Carnal Plan for Children

NOW Sarai, Abram's wife, had borne him no *children.* And she had an Egyptian maidservant whose name was Hagar.

2 So Sarai said to Abram, "See now, the LORD has restrained me from bearing *children.* Please, go in to my maid; perhaps I shall [T]obtain children by her." And Abram heeded the voice of Sarai. Lit. *be built up from*

3 Then Sarai, Abram's wife, took Hagar her maid, the Egyptian, and gave her to her husband Abram to be his wife, after Abram had dwelt ten years in the land of Canaan.

4 So he went in to Hagar, and she conceived. And when she saw that she had conceived, her mistress became [R]despised in her eyes. [Prov. 30:21, 23]

5 Then Sarai said to Abram, "My wrong *be* upon you! I gave my maid into your embrace; and when she saw that she had conceived, I became despised in her eyes. The LORD judge between you and me."

6 So Abram said to Sarai, "Indeed your maid *is* in your hand; do to her as you please." And when Sarai dealt harshly with her, [R]she fled from her presence. Ex. 2:15

7 Now the Angel of the LORD found her by a spring of water in the wilderness, by the spring on the way to [R]Shur. Ex. 15:22

8 And He said, "Hagar, Sarai's maid, where have you come from, and where are you going?" And she said, "I am fleeing from the presence of my mistress Sarai."

9 So the Angel of the LORD said to her, "Return to your mistress, and [R]submit yourself under her hand." [Titus 2:9]

10 Then the Angel of the LORD said to her, [R]"I will multiply your descendants exceedingly, so that they shall not be counted for multitude." Gen. 17:20

11 And the Angel of the LORD said to her:

"Behold, you *are* with child,
And you shall bear a son.
You shall call his name [T]Ishmael,
Because the LORD has heard your
affliction. Lit. *God Hears*

12 [R]He shall be a wild man;
His hand *shall be* against every man,
And every man's hand against him.
[R]And he shall dwell in the presence of all
his brethren." Gen. 21:20 • Gen. 25:18

13 Then she called the name of the LORD who spoke to her, You-Are-[T]the-God-Who-Sees; for she said, "Have I also here seen Him [R]who sees me?" Heb. *El Roi* • Gen. 31:42

14 Therefore the well was called [T]Beer Lahai Roi; observe, *it is* between Kadesh and Bered. Lit. *Well of the One Who Lives and Sees Me*

15 So Hagar bore Abram a son; and Abram named his son, whom Hagar bore, Ishmael.

16 Abram *was* eighty-six years old when Hagar bore Ishmael to Abram.

CHAPTER 17

Institution of the Covenant: Circumcision

WHEN Abram was ninety-nine years old, the LORD appeared to Abram and said to him, "I *am* [T]Almighty God; walk before Me and be blameless. Heb. *El Shaddai*

2 "And I will make My [R]covenant between Me and you, and [R]will multiply you exceedingly." Gen. 15:18 • Gen. 12:2; 13:16; 15:5; 18:18

3 Then Abram fell on his face, and God talked with him, saying:

4 "As for Me, behold, My covenant is with you, and you shall be [R]a father of [T]many nations. [Rom. 4:11, 12, 16] • Lit. *multitude of nations*

5 "No longer shall your name be called
Abram, but your name shall be Abraham; for
I have made you a father of many nations.
6 "I will make you exceedingly fruitful;
and I will make [R]nations of you, and [R]kings
shall come from you. Gen. 17:16; 35:11 • Matt. 1:6
7 "And I will [R]establish My covenant between Me and you and your descendants
after you in their generations, for an everlasting covenant, to be God to you and [R]your
descendants after you. [Gal. 3:17] ☆ • Rom. 9:8
8 "Also I give to you and your descendants
after you the land in which you are a stranger, all the land of Canaan, as an everlasting
possession; and I will be their God."
9 And God said to Abraham: "As for you,
[R]you shall keep My covenant, you and your
descendants after you throughout their generations. Ex. 19:5
10 "This *is* My covenant which you shall
keep, between Me and you and your descendants after you: [R]Every male child among you
shall be circumcised; Acts 7:8
11 "and you shall be circumcised in the
flesh of your foreskins, and it shall be a sign
of the covenant between Me and you.
12 "He who is eight days old among you
[R]shall be circumcised, every male child in
your generations, he who is born in your
house or bought with money from any stranger who is not your descendant. Lev. 12:3
13 "He who is born in your house and he
who is bought with your money must be
circumcised, and My covenant shall be in
your flesh for an everlasting covenant.
14 "And the uncircumcised male child, who
is not circumcised in the flesh of his foreskin,
that person [R]shall be cut off from his people;
he has broken My covenant." Ex. 4:24–26
15 Then God said to Abraham, "As for Sarai
your wife, you shall not call her name Sarai,
but [T]Sarah *shall be* her name. Lit. *Princess*
16 "And I will bless her and also give you a
son by her; then I will bless her, and she shall
be *a mother* [R]*of* nations; [R]kings of peoples
shall be from her." Gen. 35:11 • Gen. 17:6; 36:31
17 Then Abraham fell on his face [R]and
laughed, and said in his heart, "Shall *a child*
be born to a man who is one hundred years
old? And shall Sarah, who is ninety years old,
bear *a child*?" Gen. 17:3; 18:12; 21:6
18 And Abraham [R]said to God, "Oh, that
Ishmael might live before You!" Gen. 18:23
19 Then God said: "No, [R]Sarah your wife
shall bear you a son, and you shall call his
name Isaac; I will establish My covenant
with him for an everlasting covenant, *and*
with his descendants after him. [Gal. 4:28] ☆
20 "And as for Ishmael, I have heard you.
Behold, I have blessed him, and will make
him fruitful, and will multiply him exceedingly. He shall beget twelve princes, [R]and I
will make him a great nation. Gen. 21:13, 18
21 "But My covenant I will establish with
Isaac, [R]whom Sarah shall bear to you at this
[R]set time next year." Gen. 21:2 • Gen. 18:14
22 Then He finished talking with him, and
God went up from Abraham.
23 So Abraham took Ishmael his son, all
who were born in his house and all who were
bought with his money, every male among
the men of Abraham's house, and circumcised the flesh of their foreskins that very
same day, as God had said to him.
24 Abraham *was* ninety-nine years old
when he was circumcised in the flesh of his
foreskin.
25 And Ishmael his son *was* thirteen years
old when he was circumcised in the flesh of
his foreskin.
26 That very same day Abraham was circumcised, and his son Ishmael;
27 and [R]all the men of his house, born in the
house or bought with money from a stranger,
were circumcised with him. Gen. 18:19

CHAPTER 18

Sarah's Faith Is Tested

THEN the LORD appeared to him by the
terebinth trees of Mamre, as he was sitting in the tent door in the heat of the day.
2 [R]So he lifted his eyes and looked, and
behold, three men were standing by him;
[R]and when he saw *them*, he ran from the tent
door to meet them, and bowed himself to the
ground, Heb. 13:2 • Gen. 19:1
3 and said, "My Lord, if I have now found
favor in Your sight, do not pass on by Your
servant.
4 "Please let [R]a little water be brought, and
wash your feet, and rest yourselves under the
tree. Gen. 19:2; 24:32; 43:24
5 "And I will bring a morsel of bread, that
[R]you may refresh your hearts. After that you
may pass by, [R]inasmuch as you have come to
your servant." And they said, "Do as you
have said." Judg. 19:5 • Gen. 19:8; 33:10
6 So Abraham hastened into the tent to
Sarah and said, "Quickly, make ready [T]three
measures of fine meal; knead *it* and make
cakes." 6.524 bu.
7 And Abraham ran to the herd, took a
tender and good calf, gave *it* to a young man,
and he hastened to prepare it.
8 So [R]he took butter and milk and the calf
which he had prepared, and set *it* before
them; and he stood by them under the tree as
they ate. Gen. 19:3
9 Then they said to him, "Where *is* Sarah
your wife?" And he said, "Here, in the tent."
10 And He said, "I will certainly return to
you [R]according to the time of life, and behold,
[R]Sarah your wife shall have a son." And
Sarah was listening in the tent door which
was behind him. 2 Kin. 4:16 • Rom. 9:9
11 Now [R]Abraham and Sarah were old, well-

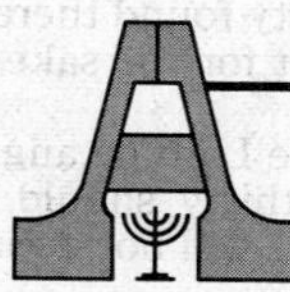

COVENANT

One of the most mysterious and yet theologically significant events is recorded in Genesis 15. In a vision, God told Abram to take a heifer, a goat, a ram, a turtledove, and a young pigeon, and cut all except the birds in half. Then he was told to place each piece opposite the other.

"Now when the sun was going down, a deep sleep fell upon Abram; and behold, horror *and* great darkness fell upon him" (v. 12). Then God predicted the 400-year bondage of Abram's descendants in a foreign land and their return to Canaan at the end of four generations.

"And it came to pass, when the sun went down and it was dark, that behold, *there was* a smoking oven and a burning torch that passed between those pieces. On the same day the LORD made [Heb. *kārat*, lit. *cut*] a covenant [Heb. *berît*] with Abram" (vv. 17, 18). Then followed the prediction of the extent of the land to be given to Abram's descendants.

The Hebrew idiom *cutting a covenant* was based on the custom of cutting up an animal and those who were making the covenant walking between the pieces. In this case, only God (visualized as "a smoking oven and a burning torch") went through. This suggests to many that it was an unconditional covenant on God's part, no matter what Abram did or did not do. (But see below.)

Covenant is a word with many shades of meaning, being used for all sorts of formal agreements between people, or between God and men.

Covenants Between Men

Between friends, such as David and Jonathan, a covenant is an alliance of brotherly love and loyalty (1 Sam. 18:3; 20:8; 23:18). In Proverbs 2:16, 17, the "seductress" who deserts her husband "and forgets the covenant [marriage contract] of her God" is described. A *berît* can also be an agreement or pledge, as between Jehoiada and his captains (2 Kin. 11:4). Between countries it is a treaty or alliance, as between Israel and the Gibeonites (Josh. 9), Solomon and Hiram (1 Kin. 5:2–6), and Judah and Tyre (Amos 1:9). Between a king and his people, as between Saul and Israel, it was not unlike a simpler form of a constitutional monarchy.

Between God and Man

Most important of all, between God and man, a covenant was "cut" with animal sacrifices, an oath and promised blessings for obedience and curses for disobedience.

Meredith Kline maintains that the whole Book of Deuteronomy, plus the Ten Commandments, and passages such as Joshua 24, are all written in the form of an ancient covenant, or treaty, between a monarch and his subjects. In this case the Monarch was God and His subjects were the Israelites.

The five parts that Kline details in his *Treaty of the Great King* are as follows:

1. Preamble, identifying the suzerain, or lord.
2. Prologue, describing previous history of relationships.
3. Stipulations and demands of the suzerain.
4. Ratifications, or swearing allegiance, with benefits for keeping the treaty and curses for breaking it.
5. Witnesses and instructions for implementing the covenant.

The Covenants and Bible Doctrine

All Bible-believing Christians believe in the covenants, but some make them central to their theology and some see them as an important part of a larger framework.

Those who fit the whole Bible into a covenantal framework are known as "covenant theologians." Those who see the covenants as within larger administrations (dispensations) are known as "dispensationalists." Recently, conservative Christians from both groups have found out that they have much more in common than they previously thought. Whether one favors covenants or dispensations, or both, the main program is neither the one nor the other, but the Person of Christ, who is all in all, and in all.

advanced in age; *and* [R]Sarah had passed the age of childbearing. Gen. 17:17 • Gen. 31:35

12 Therefore Sarah laughed within herself, saying, "After I have grown old, shall I have pleasure, my [R]lord being old also?" 1 Pet. 3:6

13 And the LORD said to Abraham, "Why did Sarah laugh, saying, 'Shall I surely bear *a child,* since I am old?'

14 [R]"Is anything too hard for the LORD? [R]At the appointed time I will return to you, according to the time of life, and Sarah shall have a son." Jer. 32:17 • Gen. 17:21; 18:10

15 But Sarah denied *it,* saying, "I did not laugh," for she was afraid. And He said, "No, but you did laugh!"

Abraham's Faith Is Tested

16 Then the men rose from there and looked toward Sodom, and Abraham went with them to send them on the way.

17 And the LORD said, [R]"Shall I hide from Abraham what I am doing, Ps. 25:14

18 "since Abraham shall surely become a great and mighty nation, and all the nations of the earth shall be blessed in him?

19 "For I have known him, in order [R]that he may command his children and his household after him, that they keep the way of the LORD, to do righteousness and justice, that the LORD may bring to Abraham what He has spoken to him." [Deut. 4:9, 10; 6:6, 7]

20 And the LORD said, "Because the outcry against Sodom and Gomorrah is great, and because their sin is very grievous,

21 [R]"I will go down now and see whether they have done altogether according to the outcry against it that has come to Me; and if not, [R]I will know." Gen. 11:5 • Deut. 8:2; 13:3

22 Then the men turned away from there [R]and went toward Sodom, but Abraham still stood before the LORD. Gen. 18:16; 19:1

23 And Abraham [R]came near and said, [R]"Would You also destroy the righteous with the wicked? [Heb. 10:22] • Num. 16:22

24 "Suppose there were fifty righteous within the city; would You also destroy the place and not spare *it* for the fifty righteous that were in it?

25 "Far be it from You to do such a thing as this, to slay the righteous with the wicked, so [R]that the righteous should be as the wicked; far be it from You! [R]Shall not the Judge of all the earth do right?" Is. 3:10, 11 • Deut. 1:16, 17; 32:4

26 And the LORD said, [R]"If I find in Sodom fifty righteous within the city, then I will spare all the place for their sakes." Jer. 5:1

27 Then Abraham answered and said, "Indeed now, I who *am but* dust and ashes have taken it upon myself to speak to the Lord:

28 "Suppose there were five less than the fifty righteous; would You destroy all of the city for *lack of* five?" And He said, "If I find there forty-five, I will not destroy *it.*"

29 Then he spoke to Him yet again and said, "Suppose there should be forty found there?" And He said, "I will not do *it* for the sake of forty."

30 And he said, "Let not the Lord be angry, and I will speak: Suppose thirty should be found there?" And He said, "I will not do *it* if I find thirty there."

31 Then he said, "Indeed now, I have taken it upon myself to speak to the Lord: Suppose twenty should be found there?" And He said, "I will not destroy *it* for the sake of twenty."

32 And he said, [R]"Let not the Lord be angry, and I will speak but once more: Suppose ten should be found there?" And He said, "I will not destroy *it* for the sake of ten." Judg. 6:39

33 So the LORD went His way as soon as He had finished speaking with Abraham; and Abraham returned to his place.

CHAPTER 19

Destruction of Sodom and Gomorrah

NOW the two angels came to Sodom in the evening, and [R]Lot was sitting in the gate of Sodom. When Lot saw *them,* he rose to meet them, and he bowed himself with his face toward the ground. Gen. 18:1–5

2 And he said, "Here now, my lords, please [R]turn in to your servant's house and spend the night, and [R]wash your feet; then you may rise early and go on your way." And they said, "No, but we will spend the night in the open square." [Heb. 13:2] • Gen. 18:4; 24:32

3 But he insisted strongly; so they turned in to him and entered his house. [R]Then he made them a feast, and baked [R]unleavened bread, and they ate. Gen. 18:6–8 • Ex. 12:8

4 Now before they lay down, the men of the city, the men of Sodom, both old and young, all the people from every quarter, surrounded the house.

5 [R]And they called to Lot and said to him, "Where are the men who came to you tonight? [R]Bring them out to us that we [R]may know them *carnally.*" Is. 3:9 • Judg. 19:22 • Gen. 4:1

6 So [R]Lot went out to them through the doorway, shut the door behind him, Judg. 19:23

7 and said, "Please, my brethren, do not do so wickedly!

8 [R]"See now, I have two daughters who have not known a man; please, let me bring them out to you, and you may do to them as you wish; only do nothing to these men, since this is the reason they have come under the shadow of my roof." Judg. 19:24

9 And they said, "Stand back!" Then they said, "This one came in to sojourn, [R]and he keeps acting as a judge; now we will deal worse with you than with them." So they pressed hard against the man Lot, and came near to break down the door. Ex. 2:14

10 But the men reached out their hands and

THE DEAD SEA

The Dead Sea is a lake about 50 miles long and 10 miles wide in southern Palestine. The Jordan River and other smaller streams flow into it, but, because it lies at the lowest point on the earth, no water flows out of it. Because of its rapid water loss through evaporation, salts and other minerals have become highly concentrated in it. This has made the lake unfit for marine life; thus its name "the Dead Sea."

In Abraham's time five cities known as the "cities of the plain" were situated at the south end of the Dead Sea (Gen. 14:2, 8). Because of their great wickedness, four of these cities—Sodom, Gomorrah, Admah, and Zeboiim—were destroyed by earthquake and fire (Gen. 19:28, 29; Deut. 29:23). Many scholars believe the remains of these cities were covered in later years by the Dead Sea as the waters shifted when other earthquakes struck the area.

In addition to the destruction of Sodom and Gomorrah, many other biblical events occurred along the shores of the Dead Sea. The springs of En Gedi provided a refuge for David in his flight from King Saul (1 Sam. 24:1). In the Valley of Salt south of the Dead Sea, David was victorious over the Edomites (2 Sam. 8:13; 1 Chr. 18:12, 13).

The Dead Sea is also famous because of the discovery of ancient biblical manuscripts in the caves on its northwest coast (see photo). Known as the Dead Sea Scrolls, these manuscripts include a complete copy of the Book of Isaiah and portions of several other books of the Bible, as well as many non-biblical manuscripts. They are dated to the period between 250 B.C. and A.D. 135.

These manuscripts, some of the earliest copies of biblical texts yet discovered, helped scholars establish dates for several important biblical events and gave helpful information on the development of the Hebrew language.

Other names for the Dead Sea used in the Bible are the Salt Sea (Josh. 3:16), the Sea of Arabah (Deut. 3:17), and the eastern sea (Joel 2:20).

Photo by Howard Vos

A jar in which some of the Dead Sea Scrolls were stored.

pulled Lot into the house with them, and shut
the door.
11 And they [R]struck the men who *were* at
the doorway of the house with blindness,
both small and great, so that they became
weary *trying* to find the door. Gen. 20:17
12 Then the men said to Lot, "Have you
anyone else here? Son-in-law, your sons, your
daughters, and whomever you have in the
city—take *them* out of this place!
13 "For we will destroy this place, because
the [R]outcry against them has grown great
before the face of the LORD, and [R]the LORD
has sent us to destroy it." Gen. 18:20 • 1 Chr. 21:15
14 So Lot went out and spoke to his sons-in-
law, who had married his daughters, and said,
"Get up, get out of this place; for the LORD
will destroy this city!" [R]But to his sons-in-law
he seemed to be joking. Ex. 9:21
15 When the morning dawned, the angels
urged Lot to hurry, saying, [R]"Arise, take your
wife and your two daughters who are here,
lest you be consumed in the punishment of
the city." Rev. 18:4
16 And while he lingered, the men took hold
of his hand, his wife's hand, and the hands of
his two daughters, the LORD being merciful to
him, [R]and they brought him out and set him
outside the city. Ps. 34:22
17 So it came to pass, when they had
brought them outside, that *he said, "Escape
for your life! Do not look behind you nor stay
anywhere in the plain. Escape [R]to the mountains, lest you be destroyed." Gen. 14:10
18 Then Lot said to them, "Please, [R]no, my
lords! Acts 10:14
19 "Indeed now, your servant has found
favor in your sight, and you have increased
your mercy which you have shown me by
saving my life; but I cannot escape to the
mountains, lest some evil overtake me and I
die.
20 "See now, this city *is* near *enough* to flee
to, and it *is* a little one; please let me escape
there (*is* it not a little one?) and my soul shall
live."
21 And he said to him, "See, [R]I have favored
you concerning this thing also, in that I will
not overthrow this city for which you have
spoken. Job 42:8, 9
22 "Hurry, escape there. For I cannot do
anything until you arrive there." Therefore
the name of the city was called Zoar.
23 The sun had risen upon the earth when
Lot entered Zoar.
24 Then the LORD rained [R]brimstone and
[R]fire on Sodom and Gomorrah, from the LORD
out of the heavens. Deut. 29:23 • Lev. 10:2
25 So He [T]overthrew those cities, all the
plain, all the inhabitants of the cities, and
[R]what grew on the ground. *devastated* • Ps. 107:34
26 But his wife looked back behind him, and
she became [R]a pillar of salt. Luke 17:32
27 And Abraham went early in the morning
to the place where [R]he had stood before the
LORD. Gen. 18:22
28 Then he looked toward Sodom and Gomorrah, and toward all the land of the plain;
and he saw, and behold, [R]the smoke of the
land which went up like the smoke of a
furnace. Rev. 9:2; 18:9
29 And it came to pass, when God destroyed
the cities of the plain, that God [R]remembered
Abraham, and sent Lot out of the midst of the
overthrow, when He overthrew the cities in
which Lot had dwelt. Gen. 8:1; 18:23

The Sin of Lot

30 Then Lot went up out of Zoar and [R]dwelt
in the mountains, and his two daughters were
with him; for he was afraid to dwell in Zoar.
And he and his two daughters dwelt in a
cave. Gen. 19:17, 19
31 Now the firstborn said to the younger,
"Our father *is* old, and *there is* no man on the
earth [R]to come in to us as is the custom of all
the earth. Gen. 16:2, 4; 38:8, 9
32 "Come, let us make our father drink
wine, and we will lie with him, that we may
preserve the [T]lineage of our father." Lit. *seed*
33 So they made their father drink wine
that night. And the firstborn went in and lay
with her father, and he did not know when
she lay down or when she arose.
34 It happened on the next day that the
firstborn said to the younger, "Indeed I lay
with my father last night; let us make him
drink wine tonight also, and you go in *and* lie
with him, that we may preserve the [T]lineage
of our father." Lit. *seed*
35 Then they made their father drink wine
that night also. And the younger arose and
lay with him, and he did not know when she
lay down or when she arose.
36 Thus both the daughters of Lot were
with child by their father.
37 The firstborn bore a son and called his
name Moab; [R]he *is* the father of the Moabites
to this day. Deut. 2:9
38 And the younger, she also bore a son and
called his name Ben-Ammi; [R]he *is* the father
of the people of Ammon to this day. Deut. 2:19

CHAPTER 20

The Test of Abimelech

AND Abraham journeyed from [R]there to
the South, and dwelt between Kadesh
and Shur, and sojourned in Gerar. Gen. 18:1
2 Now Abraham said of Sarah his wife,
"She *is* my sister." And Abimelech king of
Gerar sent and [R]took Sarah. Gen. 12:15

19:17 LXX, Syr., Vg. *they*

3 But God came to Abimelech in a dream
by night, and said to him, "Indeed you *are* a
dead man because of the woman whom you
have taken, for she *is* a man's wife."
4 But Abimelech had not come near her;
and he said, "Lord, [R]will You slay a righteous
nation also? Gen. 18:23–25
5 "Did he not say to me, 'She *is* my sister'?
And she, even she herself said, 'He *is* my
brother.' In the integrity of my heart and
innocence of my hands I have done this."
6 And God said to him in a dream, "Yes, I
know that you did this in the integrity of
your heart. For [R]I also withheld you from
sinning [R]against Me; therefore I did not let
you touch her. 1 Sam. 25:26, 34 • Gen. 39:9
7 "Now therefore, restore the man's wife;
for he *is* a prophet, and he will pray for you
and you shall live. But if you do not restore
her, [R]know that you shall surely die, you [R]and
all who *are* yours." Gen. 2:17 • Num. 16:32, 33
8 So Abimelech rose early in the morning,
called all his servants, and told all these
things in their hearing; and the men were
very afraid.
9 And Abimelech called Abraham and said
to him, "What have you done to us? How
have I [T]offended you, [R]that you have brought
on me and on my kingdom a great sin? You
have done deeds to me [R]that ought not to be
done." *sinned against* • Gen. 26:10; 39:9 • Gen. 34:7
10 Then Abimelech said to Abraham, "What
did you have in view, that you have done this
thing?"
11 And Abraham said, "Because I thought,
surely the fear of God *is* not in this place; and
they will kill me on account of my wife.
12 "But indeed *she is* truly my sister. She *is*
the daughter of my father, but not the daughter of my mother; and she became my wife.
13 "And it came to pass, when God caused
me to wander from my father's house, that I
said to her, 'This *is* your kindness that you
should do for me: in every place, wherever we
go, say of me, "He *is* my brother." ' "
14 Then Abimelech [R]took sheep, oxen, and
male and female servants, and gave *them* to
Abraham; and he restored Sarah his wife to
him. Gen. 12:16
15 And Abimelech said, "See, my land *is*
before you; dwell where it pleases you."
16 Then to Sarah he said, "Behold, I have
given your brother a thousand *pieces* of
silver; indeed this vindicates you [R]before all
who *are* with you and before all *others*."
Thus she was [T]reproved. Gen. 24:65 • Or *justified*
17 So Abraham prayed to God; and God
[R]healed Abimelech, his wife, and his maidservants. Then they bore *children*; Gen. 21:2
18 for the LORD [R]had closed up all the
wombs of the house of Abimelech because of
Sarah, Abraham's wife. Gen. 12:17

CHAPTER 21

Birth of Isaac

AND the LORD [R]visited Sarah as He had
said, and the LORD did for Sarah [R]as He
had spoken. 1 Sam. 2:21 • [Gal. 4:23, 28]
2 For Sarah conceived and bore Abraham
a son in his old age, [R]at the set time of which
God had spoken to him. Gen. 17:21; 18:10, 14
3 And Abraham called the name of his son
who was born to him—whom Sarah bore to
him—[R]Isaac.[T] Gen. 17:19, 21 • Lit. *Laughter*
4 Then Abraham [R]circumcised his son
Isaac when he was eight days old, [R]as God
had commanded him. Acts 7:8 • Gen. 17:10, 12
5 Now Abraham was one hundred years
old when his son Isaac was born to him.
6 And Sarah said, [R]"God has [T]made me
laugh, *so that* all who hear [R]will laugh with
me." Is. 54:1 • Lit. *made laughter for me* • Luke 1:58
7 She also said, "Who would have said to
Abraham that Sarah would nurse children?
For I have borne *him* a son in his old age."
8 So the child grew and was weaned. And
Abraham made a great feast on the same day
that Isaac was weaned.
9 And Sarah saw the son of Hagar [R]the
Egyptian, whom she had borne to Abraham,
[R]scoffing.[T] Gen. 16:1, 4, 15 • [Gal. 4:29] • Lit. *laughing*
10 Therefore she said to Abraham, [R]"Cast
out this bondwoman and her son; for the son
of this bondwoman shall not be heir with my
son, *namely* with Isaac." Gal. 3:18; 4:30
11 And the matter was very [T]displeasing in
Abraham's sight because of his son. *bad*
12 But God said to Abraham, "Do not let it
be displeasing in your sight because of the lad
or because of your bondwoman. Whatever
Sarah has said to you, listen to her voice; for
[R]in Isaac your seed shall be called. [Rom. 9:7, 8] ☆
13 "Yet I will also make a nation of the son
of the bondwoman, because he *is* your seed."
14 So Abraham rose early in the morning,
and took bread and [T]a skin of water; and
putting *it* on her shoulder, he gave *it* and the
boy to Hagar, and [R]sent her away. Then she
departed and wandered in the Wilderness of
Beersheba. A water bottle made of skins • John 8:35
15 And the water in the skin was used up,
and she placed the boy under one of the
shrubs.
16 Then she went and sat down across from
him at a distance of about a bowshot; for she
said to herself, "Let me not see the death of
the boy." So she sat opposite *him*, and lifted
her voice and wept.
17 And [R]God heard the voice of the lad.
Then the [R]angel of God called to Hagar out of
heaven, and said to her, "What ails you,
Hagar? Fear not, for God has heard the voice
of the lad where he *is*. Ex. 3:7 • Gen. 22:11
18 "Arise, lift up the lad and hold him with
your hand, for [R]I will make him a great
nation." Gen. 16:10; 21:13; 25:12–16

19 And God opened her eyes, and she saw a
well of water. Then she went and filled the
skin with water, and gave the lad a drink.
20 So God [R]was with the lad; and he grew
and dwelt in the wilderness, [R]and became an
archer. Gen. 28:15; 39:2, 3, 21 • Gen. 16:12
21 He dwelt in the Wilderness of Paran; and
his mother [R]took a wife for him from the land
of Egypt. Gen. 24:4
22 And it came to pass at that time that
Abimelech and Phichol, the commander of
his army, spoke to Abraham, saying, [R]"God *is*
with you in all that you do. Gen. 26:28
23 "Now therefore, [T]swear to me by God
that you will not deal falsely with me, with
my offspring, or with my posterity; but that
according to the kindness that I have done to
you, you will do to me and to the land in
which you have sojourned." *take an oath*
24 And Abraham said, "I will swear."
25 Then Abraham [T]reproved Abimelech because of a well of water which Abimelech's
servants [R]had seized. *rebuked* • Gen. 26:15, 18, 20–22
26 And Abimelech said, "I do not know who
has done this thing; you did not tell me, nor
had I heard *of it* until today."
27 So Abraham took sheep and oxen and
gave them to Abimelech, and the two of them
[R]made a [T]covenant. Gen. 26:31; 31:44 • *treaty*
28 And Abraham set seven ewe lambs of the
flock by themselves.
29 Then Abimelech asked Abraham, "What
is the meaning of these seven ewe lambs
which you have set by themselves?"
30 And he said, "You will take *these* seven
ewe lambs from my hand, that they may be
my witness that I have dug this well."
31 Therefore he called that place [T]Beer-
sheba, because the two of them swore an
oath there. Lit. *Well of the Oath* or *Well of the Seven*
32 Thus they made a covenant at Beer-
sheba. So Abimelech rose with Phichol, the
commander of his army, and they returned to
the land of the Philistines.
33 Then *Abraham* planted a tamarisk tree
in Beersheba, and there called on the name of
the LORD, the Everlasting God.
34 And Abraham sojourned in the land of
the Philistines many days.

CHAPTER 22

Offering of Isaac

NOW it came to pass after these things
that God tested Abraham, and said to
him, "Abraham!" And he said, "Here I am."
2 And He said, "Take now your son, your
only *son* Isaac, whom you love, and go to the
land of Moriah, and offer him there as a
[R]burnt offering on one of the mountains of
which I shall tell you." Gen. 8:20; 31:54
3 So Abraham rose early in the morning
and saddled his donkey, and took two of his
young men with him, and Isaac his son; and
he split the wood for the burnt offering, and
arose and went to the place of which God had
told him.
4 Then on the third day Abraham lifted his
eyes and saw the place afar off.
5 And Abraham said to his young men,
"Stay here with the donkey; the [T]lad and I
will go yonder and worship, and we will
[R]come back to you." *young man* • [Heb. 11:19]
6 So Abraham took the wood of the burnt
offering and [R]laid *it* on Isaac his son; and he
took the fire in his hand, and a knife, and the
two of them went together. John 19:17
7 But Isaac spoke to Abraham his father
and said, "My father!" And he said, "Here I
am, my son." And he said, "Look, the fire and
the wood, but where *is* the lamb for a burnt
offering?"
8 And Abraham said, "My son, God will
provide for Himself the [R]lamb for a [R]burnt
offering." And the two of them went together. John 1:29, 36 • Ex. 12:3–6
9 Then they came to the place of which
God had told him. And Abraham built an
altar there and placed the wood in order; and
he bound Isaac his son and [R]laid him on the
altar, upon the wood. [Heb. 11:17–19]
10 And Abraham stretched out his hand and
took the knife to slay his son.
11 But the [R]Angel of the LORD called to him
from heaven and said, "Abraham, Abraham!"
And he said, "Here I am." Gen. 16:7-11; 21:17, 18
12 And He said, [R]"Do not lay your hand on
the lad, or do anything to him; for [R]now I
know that you fear God, since you have
not [R]withheld your son, your only *son*, from
Me." 1 Sam. 15:22 • James 2:21, 22 • Gen. 22:2, 16
13 Then Abraham lifted his eyes and
looked, and there behind *him was* a ram
caught in a thicket by its horns. So Abraham
went and took the ram, and offered it up for a
burnt offering instead of his son.
14 And Abraham called the name of the
place, [T]The-LORD-Will-Provide; as it is said *to*
this day, "In the Mount of the LORD it shall
be provided." Heb. *YHWH Yireh*
15 Then the Angel of the LORD called to
Abraham a second time out of heaven,
16 and said: [R]"By Myself I have sworn, says
the LORD, because you have done this thing,
and have not withheld your son, your only
son, Ps. 105:9
17 "in blessing I will bless you, and in
multiplying I will multiply your descendants
as the stars of the heaven and as the sand
which *is* on the seashore; and your descendants shall possess the gate of their enemies.
18 "In your seed [R]all the nations of the
earth shall be blessed, because you have
obeyed My voice." Gal. 3:16☆
19 So Abraham returned to his young men,
and they rose and went together to Beersheba; and Abraham dwelt at Beersheba.

20 Now it came to pass after these things that it was told Abraham, saying, "Indeed [R]Milcah also has borne children to your brother Nahor: Gen. 11:29; 24:15

21 [R]"Huz his firstborn, Buz his brother, Kemuel the father [R]of Aram, Job 1:1 • Job 32:2

22 "Chesed, Hazo, Pildash, Jidlaph, and Bethuel."

23 And [R]Bethuel begot [T]Rebekah. These eight Milcah bore to Nahor, Abraham's brother. Gen. 24:15 • Or *Rebecca*

24 His concubine, whose name was Reumah, also bore Tebah, Gaham, Thahash, and Maachah.

CHAPTER 23

Death of Sarah

SARAH lived one hundred and twenty-seven years; *these were* the years of the life of Sarah.

2 So Sarah died in [R]Kirjath Arba (that *is,* [R]Hebron) in the land of Canaan, and Abraham came to mourn for Sarah and to weep for her. Josh. 14:15; 15:13; 21:11 • Gen. 13:18; 23:19

3 Then Abraham stood up from before his dead, and spoke to the sons of Heth, saying,

4 [R]"I *am* a foreigner and a sojourner among you. [R]Give me property for a burial place among you, that I may bury my dead out of my sight." [Gen. 17:8] • Acts 7:5, 16

5 And the sons of Heth answered Abraham, saying to him,

6 "Hear us, my lord: You *are* a [T]mighty prince among us; bury your dead in the choicest of our burial places. None of us will withhold from you his burial place, that you may bury your dead." Lit. *prince of God*

7 Then Abraham stood up and bowed himself to the people of the land, the sons of Heth.

8 And he spoke with them, saying, "If it is your wish that I bury my dead out of my sight, hear me, and [T]meet with Ephron the son of Zohar for me, *approach*

9 "that he may give me the cave of Machpelah which he has, which *is* at the end of his field. Let him give it to me at the full price, as property for a burial place among you."

10 Now Ephron dwelt among the sons of Heth; and Ephron the Hittite answered Abraham in the presence of the sons of Heth, all who entered at the gate of his city, saying,

11 [R]"No, my lord, hear me: I give you the field and the cave that *is* in it; I give it to you in the presence of the sons of my people. I give it to you. Bury your dead!" 2 Sam. 24:21–24

12 Then Abraham bowed himself down before the people of the land;

13 and he spoke to Ephron in the hearing of the people of the land, saying, "If you *will give it,* please hear me. I will give you money for the field; take *it* from me and I will bury my dead there."

14 And Ephron answered Abraham, saying to him,

15 "My lord, listen to me; the land *is worth* four hundred shekels of silver. What *is* that between you and me? So bury your dead."

16 And Abraham listened to Ephron; and Abraham [R]weighed out the silver for Ephron which he had named in the hearing of the sons of Heth, [T]four hundred shekels of silver, currency of the merchants. Jer. 32:9, 10 • $51,200

17 So [R]the field of Ephron which *was* in Machpelah, which *was* before Mamre, the field and the cave which *was* in it, and all the trees that *were* in the field, which *were* within all the surrounding borders, were deeded Gen. 25:9; 49:29–32; 50:13

18 to Abraham as a possession in the presence of the sons of Heth, before all who went in at the gate of his city.

19 And after this, Abraham buried Sarah his wife in the cave of the field of Machpelah, before Mamre (that *is,* Hebron) in the land of Canaan.

20 So the field and the cave that *is* in it [R]were deeded to Abraham by the sons of Heth as property for a burial place. Jer. 32:10, 11

CHAPTER 24

Isaac's Marriage

NOW Abraham was old, well advanced in age; and the LORD [R]had blessed Abraham in all things. Gen. 12:2; 13:2; 24:35

2 So Abraham said to the oldest servant of his house, who ruled over all that he had, "Please, put your hand under my thigh,

3 "and I will make you [T]swear by the LORD, the God of heaven and the God of the earth, that [R]you will not take a wife for my son from the daughters of the Canaanites, among whom I dwell; *take an oath* • Deut. 7:3

4 [R]"but you shall go [R]to my country and to my kindred, and take a wife for my son Isaac." Gen. 28:2 • Gen. 12:1

5 And the servant said to him, "Perhaps the woman will not be willing to follow me to this land. Must I take your son back to the land from which you came?"

6 But Abraham said to him, "Beware that you do not take my son back there.

7 "The LORD God of heaven, who [R]took me from my father's house and from the land of my kindred, and who spoke to me and swore to me, saying, [R]'To your descendants I give this land,' He will send His angel before you, and you shall take a wife for my son from there. Gen. 12:1; 24:3 • Gen. 12:7; 13:15; 15:18; 17:8

8 "And if the woman is not willing to follow you, then [R]you will be released from this oath; only do not take my son back there." Josh. 2:17–20

9 So the servant put his hand under the thigh of Abraham his master, and swore to him concerning this matter.

10 Then the servant took ten of his master's camels and departed, for all his master's goods *were in* his hand. And he arose and went to Mesopotamia, to the city of Nahor.

11 And he made his camels kneel down outside the city by a well of water at evening time, the time [R]when women go out to draw *water*. Ex. 2:16

12 Then he [R]said, "O LORD God of my master Abraham, please [R]give me success this day, and show kindness to my master Abraham. Ex. 3:6, 15 • Neh. 1:11

13 "Behold, I stand *here* by the well of water, and [R]the daughters of the men of the city are coming out to draw water. Ex. 2:16

14 "Now let it be that the young woman to whom I say, 'Please let down your pitcher that I may drink,' and she says, 'Drink, and I will also give your camels a drink'—*let* her *be the one* whom You have appointed for Your servant Isaac. And by this I will know that You have shown kindness to my master."

15 And it happened, before he had finished speaking, that behold, [T]Rebekah, who was born to Bethuel, son of Milcah, the wife of Nahor, Abraham's brother, came out with her pitcher on her shoulder. Or *Rebecca*

16 Now the young woman [R]*was* very beautiful to behold, a virgin; no man had known her. And she went down to the well, filled her pitcher, and came up. Gen. 12:11; 26:7; 29:17

17 And the servant ran to meet her and said, "Please let me drink a little water from your pitcher."

18 [R]So she said, "Drink, my lord." Then she hastened and let her pitcher down to her hand, and gave him a drink. [1 Pet. 3:8, 9]

19 And when she had finished giving him a drink, she said, "I will draw *water* for your camels also, until they have finished drinking."

20 Then she hastened and emptied her pitcher into the trough, ran back to the well to draw *water*, and drew for all his camels.

21 And the man, wondering at her, remained silent so as to know whether [R]the LORD had made his journey prosperous or not. Gen. 24:12–14, 27, 52

22 So it was, when the camels had finished drinking, that the man took a golden nose ring weighing half a shekel, and two bracelets for her wrists weighing ten *shekels* of gold,

23 and said, "Whose daughter *are* you? Tell me, please, is there room *in* your father's house for us [T]to lodge?" *to spend the night*

24 So she said to him, [R]"I *am* the daughter of Bethuel, Milcah's son, whom she bore to Nahor." Gen. 22:23; 24:15

25 Moreover she said to him, "We have both straw and feed enough, and room to lodge."

26 Then the man [R]bowed down his head and worshiped the LORD. Ex. 4:31

27 And he said, [R]"Blessed *be* the LORD God of my master Abraham, who has not forsaken [R]His mercy and His truth toward my master. As for me, being on the way, the LORD [R]led me to the house of my master's brethren." Ex. 18:10 • Gen. 32:10 • Gen. 24:21, 48

28 So the young woman ran and told *those of* her mother's house these things.

29 Now Rebekah had a brother whose name *was* [R]Laban, and Laban ran out to the man by the well. Gen. 29:5, 13

30 So it came to pass, when he saw the nose ring, and the bracelets on his sister's wrists, and when he heard the words of his sister Rebekah, saying, "Thus the man spoke to me," that he went to the man. And there he stood by the camels at the well.

31 And he said, "Come in, [R]O blessed of the LORD! Why do you stand outside? For I have prepared the house, and a place for the camels." Judg. 17:2

32 Then the man came to the house. And he unloaded the camels, and [R]provided straw and feed for the camels, and water to [R]wash his feet and the feet of the men who *were* with him. Gen. 43:24 • Gen. 19:2

33 And *food* was set before him to eat, but he said, [R]"I will not eat until I have told about my errand." And he said, "Speak on." John 4:34

34 So he said, "I *am* Abraham's servant.

35 "The LORD [R]has blessed my master greatly, and he has become great; and He has given him flocks and herds, silver and gold, male and female servants, and camels and donkeys. Gen. 13:2; 24:1

36 "And Sarah my master's wife bore a son to my master when she was old; and [R]to him he has given all that he has. Gen. 21:10; 25:5

37 "Now my master [R]made me swear, saying, 'You shall not take a wife for my son from the daughters of the Canaanites, in whose land I dwell; Gen. 24:2–4

38 [R]'but you shall go to my father's house and to my kindred, and take a wife for my son.' Gen. 24:4

39 [R]"And I said to my master, 'Perhaps the woman will not follow me.' Gen. 24:5

40 "But he said to me, 'The LORD, before whom I walk, will send His angel with you and [T]prosper your way; and you shall take a wife for my son from my kindred and from my father's house. *make your way successful*

41 [R]'You will be clear from this oath when you arrive among my kindred; for if they will not give *her* to you, then you will be released from my oath.' Gen. 24:8

42 "And this day I came to the well and said, 'O LORD God of my master Abraham, if You will now prosper the way in which I go,

43 [R]'behold, I stand by the well of water; and it shall come to pass that when the virgin comes out to draw *water*, and I say to her,

"Please give me a little water from your
pitcher to drink," Gen. 24:13
44 'and she says to me, "Drink, and I will
draw for your camels also,"—*let* her *be* the
woman whom the LORD has appointed for my
master's son.'
45 "But before I had finished speaking in
my heart, there was Rebekah, coming out
with her pitcher on her shoulder; and she
went down to the well and drew *water*. And I
said to her, 'Please let me drink.'
46 "And she made haste and let her pitcher
down from her *shoulder*, and said, 'Drink, and
I will give your camels a drink also.' So I
drank, and she gave the camels a drink also.
47 "Then I asked her, and said, 'Whose
daughter *are* you?' And she said, 'The daughter of Bethuel, Nahor's son, whom Milcah
bore to him.' So I put the nose ring on her
nose and the bracelets on her wrists.
48 [R]"And I bowed my head and worshiped
the LORD, and blessed the LORD God of my
master Abraham, who had led me in the way
of truth to [R]take the daughter of my master's
brother for his son. Gen. 24:26, 52 • Gen. 22:23; 24:27
49 "Now if you will [R]deal kindly and truly
with my master, tell me. And if not, tell me,
that I may turn to the right hand or to the
left." Josh. 2:14
50 Then Laban and Bethuel answered and
said, "The thing comes from the LORD; we
cannot speak to you either bad or good.
51 [R]"Here *is* Rebekah before you; take *her*
and go, and let her be your master's son's
wife, as the LORD has spoken." Gen. 20:15
52 And it came to pass, when Abraham's
servant heard their words, that he worshiped
the LORD, *bowing himself* to the earth.
53 Then the servant brought out jewelry of
silver, jewelry of gold, and clothing, and gave
them to Rebekah. He also gave precious
things to her brother and to her mother.
54 And he and the men who *were* with him
ate and drank and stayed all night. Then they
arose in the morning, and he said, "Send me
away to my master."
55 But her brother and her mother said,
"Let the young woman stay with us *a few*
days, at least ten; after that she may go."
56 And he said to them, "Do not hinder me,
since the LORD has prospered my way; send
me away so that I may go to my master."
57 So they said, "We will call the young
woman and ask her personally."
58 Then they called Rebekah and said to
her, "Will you go with this man?" And she
said, "I will go."
59 So they sent away Rebekah their sister
[R]and her nurse, and Abraham's servant and
his men. Gen. 35:8
60 And they blessed Rebekah and said to
her:

"Our sister, *may* you *become*
[R]*The mother of* thousands of ten
thousands; Gen. 17:16
And may your descendants possess
The gates of those who hate them."

61 Then Rebekah and her maids arose, and
they rode on the camels and followed the
man. So the servant took Rebekah and departed.
62 Now Isaac came from the way of Beer
Lahai Roi, for he dwelt in the South.
63 And Isaac went out to meditate in the
field in the evening; and he lifted his eyes and
looked, and there, the camels *were* coming.
64 Then Rebekah lifted her eyes, and when
she saw Isaac [R]she dismounted from her
camel; Josh. 15:18
65 for she had said to the servant, "Who *is*
this man walking in the field to meet us?"
And the servant said, "It *is* my master." So
she took a veil and covered herself.
66 And the servant told Isaac all the things
that he had done.
67 Then Isaac brought her into his mother
Sarah's tent; and he took Rebekah and she
became his wife, and he loved her. So Isaac
was comforted after his mother's *death*.

CHAPTER 25

Abraham Dies—1 Chr. 1:28-33

ABRAHAM again took a wife, and her
name *was* [R]Keturah. 1 Chr. 1:32, 33
2 And she bore him Zimran, Jokshan, Medan, Midian, Ishbak, and Shuah.
3 Jokshan begot Sheba and Dedan. And
the sons of Dedan were Asshurim, Letushim,
and Leummim.
4 And the sons of Midian *were* Ephah,
Epher, Hanoch, Abidah, and Eldaah. All these
were the children of Keturah.
5 And [R]Abraham gave all that he had to
Isaac. Gen. 24:35, 36
6 But Abraham gave gifts to the sons of
the concubines which Abraham had; and
while he was still living he [R]sent them eastward, away from Isaac his son, to [R]the country of the east. Gen. 21:14 • Judg. 6:3
7 This *is* the sum of the years of Abraham's
life which he lived: one hundred and seventy-
five years.
8 Then Abraham breathed his last and died
in a good old age, an old man and full *of
years*, and was gathered to his people.
9 And his sons Isaac and Ishmael buried
him in the cave of [R]Machpelah, which *is*
before Mamre, in the field of Ephron the son
of Zohar the Hittite, Gen. 23:9, 17; 49:30
10 the field which Abraham purchased from
the sons of Heth. [R]There Abraham was buried, and Sarah his wife. Gen. 49:31
11 And it came to pass, after the death of

Abraham, that God blessed his son Isaac.
And Isaac dwelt at [R]Beer Lahai Roi. Gen. 16:14
12 Now this *is* the genealogy of Ishmael,
Abraham's son, whom Hagar the Egyptian,
Sarah's maidservant, bore to Abraham.
13 And [R]these *were* the names of the sons of
Ishmael, by their names, according to their
generations: The firstborn of Ishmael, Nebajoth; then Kedar, Adbeel, Mibsam, 1 Chr. 1:29–31
14 Mishma, Dumah, Massa,
15 *Hadar, Tema, Jetur, Naphish, and Kedemah.
16 These *were* the sons of Ishmael and
these *were* their names, by their towns and
their [T]settlements, [R]twelve princes according
to their nations. *camps* • Gen. 17:20
17 These *were* the years of the life of Ishmael: one hundred and thirty-seven years;
and [R]he breathed his last and died, and was
gathered to his people. Gen. 25:8; 49:33
18 (They dwelt from Havilah as far as Shur,
which *is* east of Egypt as you go toward
Assyria.) *And* he [T]died in the presence of all
his brethren. *fell*

The Family of Isaac

19 This *is* the genealogy of Isaac, Abraham's son. [R]Abraham begot Isaac. Matt. 1:2
20 Isaac was forty years old when he took
Rebekah as wife, [R]the daughter of Bethuel
the Syrian of Padan Aram, the sister of Laban
the Syrian. Gen. 22:23; 24:15, 29, 67
21 Now Isaac pleaded with the LORD for his
wife, because she *was* barren; [R]and the LORD
granted his plea, [R]and Rebekah his wife
conceived. 1 Chr. 5:20 • Rom. 9:10–13
22 But the children struggled together
within her; and she said, "If *all is* well, why
am I this *way*?" [R]So she went to inquire of
the LORD. 1 Sam. 1:15; 9:9; 10:22
23 And the LORD said to her:

[R]"Two nations *are* in your womb,
Two peoples shall be separated from
your body; Gen. 17:4–6; 16; 24:60
One people shall be stronger than [R]the
other, 2 Sam. 8:14
And the older shall serve the younger."

24 So when her days were fulfilled *for her* to
give birth, indeed *there were* twins in her
womb.
25 And the first came out red. *He was* [R]like
a hairy garment all over; so they called his
name [T]Esau. Gen. 27:11, 16, 23 • Lit. *Hairy*
26 Afterward his brother came out, and his
hand took hold of Esau's heel; so his name
was called [T]Jacob. Isaac *was* sixty years old
when she bore them. *Supplanter* or *Deceitful*
27 So the boys grew. And Esau was a skillful hunter, a man of the field; but Jacob was a
mild man, dwelling in tents.
28 And Isaac loved Esau because he ate *of*
his game, but Rebekah loved Jacob.
29 Now Jacob cooked a stew; and Esau
came in from the field, and he *was* weary.
30 And Esau said to Jacob, "Please feed me
with that same red *stew*, for I *am* weary."
Therefore his name was called [T]Edom. Lit. *Red*
31 But Jacob said, "Sell me your birthright
as of this day."
32 And Esau said, "Look, I *am* about to die;
so what *profit* shall this birthright be to me?"
33 Then Jacob said, [T]"Swear to me as of this
day." So he swore to him, and [R]sold his
birthright to Jacob. *Take an oath* • Heb. 12:16
34 And Jacob gave Esau bread and stew of
lentils; then [R]he ate and drank, arose, and
went his way. Thus Esau [R]despised *his* birthright. Eccl. 8:15 • Heb. 12:16, 17

CHAPTER 26

The Failure of Isaac

THERE was a famine in the land, besides
the first famine that was in the days of
Abraham. And Isaac went to [R]Abimelech
king of the Philistines, in Gerar. Gen. 20:1, 2
2 Then the LORD appeared to him and said:
"Do not go down to Egypt; dwell in [R]the land
of which I shall tell you. Gen. 12:1
3 [T]"Sojourn in this land, and I will be with
you and bless you; for to you and your
descendants I give all these lands, and I will
perform the oath which I swore to Abraham
your father. Reside temporarily
4 "And [R]I will make your descendants
multiply as the stars of heaven; I will give to
your descendants all these lands; [R]and in your
seed all the nations of the earth shall be
blessed; Gal. 3:8 ☆ • Gen. 12:3; 22:18
5 [R]"because Abraham obeyed My voice
and kept My charge, My commandments, My
statutes, and My laws." Gen. 22:16, 18
6 So Isaac dwelt in Gerar.
7 And the men of the place asked *him*
about his wife. And he said, "She *is* my
sister"; for [R]he was afraid to say, "*She is* my
wife," *because he thought*, "lest the men of
the place should kill me for Rebekah, because
she *is* beautiful to behold." Prov. 29:25
8 Now it came to pass, when he had been
there a long time, that Abimelech king of the
Philistines looked through a window, and
saw, and there was Isaac, [T]showing endearment to Rebekah his wife. *caressing*
9 Then Abimelech called Isaac and said,
"Quite obviously she *is* your wife; so how
could you say, 'She *is* my sister'?" And Isaac
said to him, "Because I said, 'Lest I die on
account of her.'"
10 And Abimelech said, "What *is* this you
have done to us? One of the people might
soon have lain with your wife, and [R]you
would have brought guilt on us." Gen. 20:9

25:15 MT *Hadad*

BIRTHRIGHT IN BIBLE TIMES

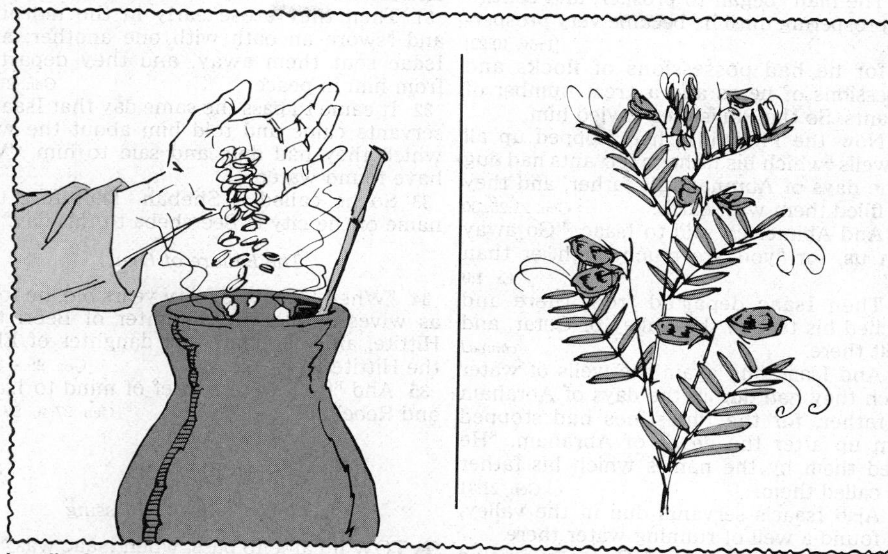

Lentils, from which Jacob made stew, was a common vegetable of Old Testament times. It grew in pods like peas or beans.

The term *birthright* appears several times in the Bible. The word refers to the inheritance rights of the firstborn son in a Hebrew family in Old Testament times. The property of a father was normally divided among his sons at his death. But a larger amount, usually a double portion, went to the oldest son (Deut. 21:17), who assumed the care of his mother and unmarried sisters.

The birthright with its privileges and responsibilities could be forfeited by behavior that was offensive to the father or opposed to God's will. For example, Reuben apparently lost his birthright by committing incest with his father's concubine (Gen. 35:22; 49:3, 4). Esau foolishly squandered his birthright by trading it to his brother Jacob for a bowl of stew made from lentils (Gen. 25:29–34; see illustration).

These ancient accounts about the birthright remind us that we can forfeit God's blessings if we do not live responsibly as the heirs of God.

In New Testament times, inheritance practices were influenced by Greek and Roman regulations, which focused less on the elder son. The Greeks relied on wills to pass on their property. However, if no will existed, property was divided equally among sons in good standing. Under Roman law, the property of a man who died without a will went to his wife and children.

Paul described Jesus as the "firstborn over all creation" (Col. 1:15), and emphasized the spiritual birthright of all Christians as "heirs of God and joint heirs with Christ, if indeed we suffer with *Him*" (Rom. 8:17). A willingness to share in the sufferings of Christ is the condition for the blessings we receive as His spiritual heirs.

11 So Abimelech charged all *his* people,
saying, "He who [R]touches this man or his
wife shall surely be put to death." Ps. 105:15
12 Then Isaac sowed in that land, and
reaped in the same year a hundredfold; and
the LORD [R]blessed him. Gen. 24:1; 25:3, 11; 26:3
13 The man [R]began to prosper, and continued prospering until he became very prosperous; [Prov. 10:22]
14 for he had possessions of flocks and
possessions of herds and a great number of
servants. So the Philistines envied him.
15 Now the Philistines had stopped up all
the wells [R]which his father's servants had dug
in the days of Abraham his father, and they
had filled them with earth. Gen. 21:25, 30
16 And Abimelech said to Isaac, "Go away
from us, for [R]you are much mightier than
we." Ex. 1:9
17 Then Isaac departed from there and
[T]pitched his tent in the Valley of Gerar, and
dwelt there. *camped*
18 And Isaac dug again the wells of water
which they had dug in the days of Abraham
his father, for the Philistines had stopped
them up after the death of Abraham. [R]He
called them by the names which his father
had called them. Gen. 21:31
19 Also Isaac's servants dug in the valley,
and found a well of running water there.
20 But the herdsmen of Gerar quarreled
with Isaac's herdsmen, saying, "The water *is*
ours." So he called the name of the well Esek,
because they quarreled with him.
21 Then they dug another well, and they
quarreled over that *one* also. So he called its
name [T]Sitnah. Lit. *Enmity*
22 And he moved from there and dug another well, and they did not quarrel over it.
So he called its name Rehoboth, because he
said, "For now the LORD has made room for
us, and we shall be fruitful in the land."
23 Then he went up from there to Beersheba.
24 And the LORD appeared to him the same
night and said, "I *am* the God of your father
Abraham; do not fear, for [R]I *am* with you. I
will bless you and multiply your descendants
for My servant Abraham's sake." Gen. 26:3, 4
25 So he built an altar there and called on
the name of the LORD, and he pitched his tent
there; and there Isaac's servants dug a well.
26 Then Abimelech came to him from Gerar
with Ahuzzath, one of his friends, [R]and Phichol the commander of his army. Gen. 21:22
27 And Isaac said to them, "Why have you
come to me, [R]since you hate me and have
[R]sent me away from you?" Judg. 11:7 • Gen. 26:16
28 But they said, "We have certainly seen
that the LORD [R]is with you. So we said, 'Let
there now be an oath between us, between
you and us; and let us make a [T]covenant with
you, Gen. 21:22, 23 • *treaty*
29 'that you will do us no harm, since we
have not touched you, and since we have
done nothing to you but good and have sent
you away in peace. [R]You *are* now the blessed
of the LORD.' " Gen. 24:31
30 [R]So he made them a feast, and they ate
and drank. Gen. 19:3
31 Then they arose early in the morning
and [R]swore an oath with one another; and
Isaac sent them away, and they departed
from him in peace. Gen. 21:31
32 It came to pass the same day that Isaac's
servants came and told him about the well
which they had dug, and said to him, "We
have found water."
33 So he called it Shebah. Therefore the
name of the city *is* Beersheba to this day.

The Failure of Esau

34 [R]When Esau was forty years old, he took
as wives Judith the daughter of Beeri the
Hittite, and Basemath the daughter of Elon
the Hittite. Gen. 28:8; 36:2
35 And [R]they were a grief of mind to Isaac
and Rebekah. Gen. 27:46; 28:1, 8

CHAPTER 27

Jacob Gains Esau's Blessing

NOW it came to pass, when Isaac was [R]old
and [R]his eyes were so dim that he could
not see, that he called Esau his older son and
said to him, "My son." And he answered him,
"Here I am." Gen. 35:28 • Gen. 48:10
2 And he said, "Behold now, I am old. I [R]do
not know the day of my death. [Prov. 27:1]
3 [R]"Now therefore, please take your weapons, your quiver and your bow, and go out to
the field and hunt game for me. Gen. 25:27, 28
4 "And make me savory food, such as I
love, and bring *it* to me that I may eat, that
my soul may bless you before I die."
5 Now Rebekah was listening when Isaac
spoke to Esau his son. And Esau went to the
field to hunt game and to bring *it*.
6 So Rebekah spoke to Jacob her son,
saying, "Indeed I heard your father speak to
Esau your brother, saying,
7 'Bring me game and make savory food
for me, that I may eat it and bless you in the
presence of the LORD before my death.'
8 "Now therefore, my son, obey my voice
according to what I command you.
9 "Go now to the flock and bring me from
there two choice kids of the goats, and I will
make [R]savory food from them for your father,
such as he loves. Gen. 27:4
10 "Then you shall take *it* to your father,
that he may eat *it*, and that he [R]may bless you
before his death." Gen. 27:4; 48:16
11 And Jacob said to Rebekah his mother,
"Look, [R]Esau my brother *is* a hairy man, and
I *am* a smooth-*skinned* man. Gen. 25:25

12 "Perhaps my father will feel me, and I
shall seem to be a deceiver to him; and I shall
bring a curse on myself and not a blessing."
13 But his mother said to him, [R]"*Let* your
curse *be* on me, my son; only obey my voice,
and go, get *them* for me." Gen. 43:9
14 And he went and got *them* and brought
them to his mother, and his mother made
savory food, such as his father loved.
15 Then Rebekah took [R]the choice clothes
of her elder son Esau, which *were* with her in
the house, and put them on Jacob her younger son. Gen. 27:27
16 And she put the skins of the kids of the
goats on his hands and on the smooth part of
his neck.
17 Then she gave the savory food and the
bread, which she had prepared, into the hand
of her son Jacob.
18 So he went to his father and said, "My
father"; and he said, "Here I am. Who *are*
you, my son?"
19 And Jacob said to his father, "I *am* Esau
your firstborn; I have done just as you told
me; please arise, sit and eat of my game, [R]that
your soul may bless me." Gen. 27:4
20 But Isaac said to his son, "How *is it* that
you have found *it* so quickly, my son?" And
he said, "Because the LORD your God brought
it to me."
21 Then Isaac said to Jacob, "Please come
near, that I [R]may feel you, my son, whether
you *are* really my son Esau or not." Gen. 27:12
22 So Jacob went near to Isaac his father,
and he felt him and said, "The voice *is* Jacob's
voice, but the hands *are* the hands of Esau."
23 And he did not recognize him, because
[R]his hands were hairy like his brother Esau's
hands; so he blessed him. Gen. 27:16
24 Then he said, "*Are* you really my son
Esau?" And he said, "I *am*."
25 And he said, "Bring *it* near to me, and I
will eat of my son's game, so [R]that my soul
may bless you." So he brought *it* near to him,
and he ate; and he brought him wine, and he
drank. Gen. 27:4, 10, 19, 31
26 Then his father Isaac said to him, "Come
near now and kiss me, my son."
27 And he came near and [R]kissed him; and
he smelled the smell of his clothing, and
blessed him and said: Gen. 29:13

"Surely, [R]the smell of my son Song 4:11
Is like the smell of a field
Which the LORD has blessed.
28 Therefore may [R]God give you Heb. 11:20
Of [R]the dew of heaven, Deut. 33:13, 28
Of [R]the fatness of the earth, Gen. 45:18
And plenty of grain and wine.
29 [R]Let peoples serve you, Gen. 9:25; 25:23
And nations bow down to you.
Be master over your brethren,
And [R]let your mother's sons bow down
to you. Gen. 37:7, 10; 49:8
Cursed *be* everyone who curses you,
And blessed *be* those who bless you!"

30 Then it happened, as soon as Isaac had
finished blessing Jacob, and Jacob had
scarcely gone out from the presence of Isaac
his father, that Esau his brother came in from
his hunting.
31 He also had made savory food, and
brought it to his father, and said to his father,
"Let my father arise and eat of his son's
game, that your soul may bless me."
32 And his father Isaac said to him, "Who
are you?" And he said, "I *am* your son, your
firstborn, Esau."
33 Then Isaac trembled exceedingly, and
said, "Who? Where *is* the one who hunted
game and brought *it* to me? I ate all *of it*
before you came, and I have blessed him—
[R]*and* indeed he shall be blessed." Gen. 25:23
34 When Esau heard the words of his father, [R]he cried with an exceedingly great and
bitter cry, and said to his father, "Bless me,
even me also, O my father!" [Heb. 12:17]
35 But he said, "Your brother came with
deceit and has taken away your blessing."
36 And Esau said, "Is he not rightly named
[T]Jacob? For he has supplanted me these two
times. He took away my birthright, and now
look, he has taken away my blessing!" And
he said, "Have you not reserved a blessing for
me?" *Supplanter* or *Deceitful*
37 Then Isaac answered and said to Esau,
"Indeed I have made him your master, and all
his brethren I have given to him as servants;
with grain and wine I have sustained him.
What shall I do now for you, my son?"
38 And Esau said to his father, "Have you
only one blessing, my father? Bless me, *even*
me also, O my father!" And Esau lifted up his
voice [R]and wept. Heb. 12:17
39 Then Isaac his father answered and said
to him:

"Behold, [R]your dwelling shall be of the
[T]fatness of the earth, Heb. 11:20 • *fertility*
And of the dew of heaven from above.
40 By your sword you shall live,
And [R]you shall serve your brother;
And [R]it shall come to pass, when you
become restless,
That you shall break his yoke from
your neck." Gen. 25:23; 27:29 • 2 Kin. 8:20–22

41 So Esau hated Jacob because of the
blessing with which his father blessed him,
and Esau said in his heart, [R]"The days of
mourning for my father are at hand; then I
will kill my brother Jacob." Gen. 50:2–4, 10
42 And the words of Esau her older son
were told to Rebekah. So she sent and called
Jacob her younger son, and said to him,
"Surely your brother Esau comforts himself
concerning you *by intending* to kill you.

43 "Now therefore, my son, obey my voice: arise, flee to my brother Laban in Haran.

44 "And stay with him a [R]few days, until your brother's fury turns away, Gen. 31:41

45 "until your brother's anger turns away from you, and he forgets what you have done to him; then I will send and bring you from there. Why should I be bereaved also of you both in one day?"

46 And Rebekah said to Isaac, "I am weary of my life because of the daughters of Heth; if Jacob takes a wife of the daughters of Heth, like these *who are* the daughters of the land, what good will my life be to me?"

CHAPTER 28

THEN Isaac called Jacob and [R]blessed him, and [T]charged him, and said to him: [R]"You shall not take a wife from the daughters of Canaan. Gen. 27:33 · *commanded* · Gen. 24:3

2 "Arise, go to Padan Aram, to the house of [R]Bethuel your mother's father; and take yourself a wife from there of the daughters of Laban your mother's brother. Gen. 22:23

3 "May [R]God Almighty bless you,
And make you [R]fruitful and multiply
you, Gen. 17:16; 35:11; 48:3 · Gen. 26:4, 24
That you may be an assembly of
peoples;
4 And give you the blessing of Abraham,
To you and your descendants with you,
That you may inherit the land
In which you are a stranger,
Which God gave to Abraham."

5 So Isaac sent Jacob away, and he went to Padan Aram, to Laban the son of Bethuel the Syrian, the brother of Rebekah, the mother of Jacob and Esau.

6 Esau saw that Isaac had blessed Jacob and sent him away to Padan Aram to take himself a wife from there, *and that* as he blessed him he gave him a charge, saying, "You shall not take a wife from the daughters of Canaan,"

7 and that Jacob had obeyed his father and his mother and had gone to Padan Aram.

8 Also Esau saw that the daughters of Canaan did not please his father Isaac.

9 So Esau went to Ishmael and took Mahalath the daughter of Ishmael, Abraham's son, [R]the sister of Nebajoth, to be his wife in addition to the wives he had. Gen. 25:13

Jacob's Dream

10 Now Jacob [R]went out from Beersheba and went toward Haran. Hos. 12:12

11 So he came to a certain place and stayed there all night, because the sun had set. And he took one of the stones of that place and put it at his head, and he lay down in that place to sleep.

12 Then he dreamed, and behold, a ladder *was* set up on the earth, and its top reached to heaven; and there [R]the angels of God were ascending and descending on it. John 1:51

13 And behold, the LORD stood above it and said: [R]"I *am* the LORD God of Abraham your father and the God of Isaac; [R]the land on which you lie I will give to you and your descendants. Gen. 26:24 · Gen. 13:15, 17; 26:3; 35:12

14 "Also your descendants shall be as the dust of the earth; you shall spread abroad to the west and the east, to the north and the south; and in you and in your seed all the families of the earth shall be blessed.

15 "Behold, I *am* with you and will keep you wherever you go, and will bring you back to this land; for I will not leave you until I have done what I have spoken to you."

16 Then Jacob awoke from his sleep and said, "Surely the LORD is in [R]this place, and I did not know *it*." Ex. 3:5

17 And he was afraid and said, "How awesome *is* this place! This *is* none other than the house of God, and this *is* the gate of heaven!"

18 Then Jacob rose early in the morning, and took the stone that he had put at his head, [R]set it up as a pillar, [R]and poured oil on top of it. Gen. 31:13, 45 · Lev. 8:10–12

19 And he called the name of [R]that place [T]Bethel; but the name of that city had been Luz previously. Judg. 1:23, 26 · Lit. *House of God*

20 Then Jacob made a vow, saying, "If God will be with me, and keep me in this way that I am going, and give me [R]bread to eat and clothing to put on, 1 Tim. 6:8

21 "so that [R]I come back to my father's house in peace, [R]then the LORD shall be my God. Judg. 11:31 · Deut. 26:17

22 "And this stone which I have set as a pillar [R]shall be God's house, [R]and of all that You give me I will surely give a [T]tenth to You." Gen. 35:7, 14 · Gen. 14:20 · *tithe*

CHAPTER 29

Jacob's Labors

SO Jacob went on his journey and came to the land of the people of the east.

2 And he looked, and saw a [R]well in the field; and behold, there *were* three flocks of sheep lying by it; for out of that well they watered the flocks. A large stone *was* on the well's mouth. Gen. 24:10, 11

3 Now all the flocks would be gathered there; and they would roll the stone from the well's mouth, water the sheep, and put the stone back in its place on the well's mouth.

4 And Jacob said to them, "My brethren, where *are* you from?" And they said, "We *are* from [R]Haran." Gen. 11:31; 28:10

5 Then he said to them, "Do you know [R]Laban the son of Nahor?" And they said, "We know him." Gen. 24:24, 29; 28:2

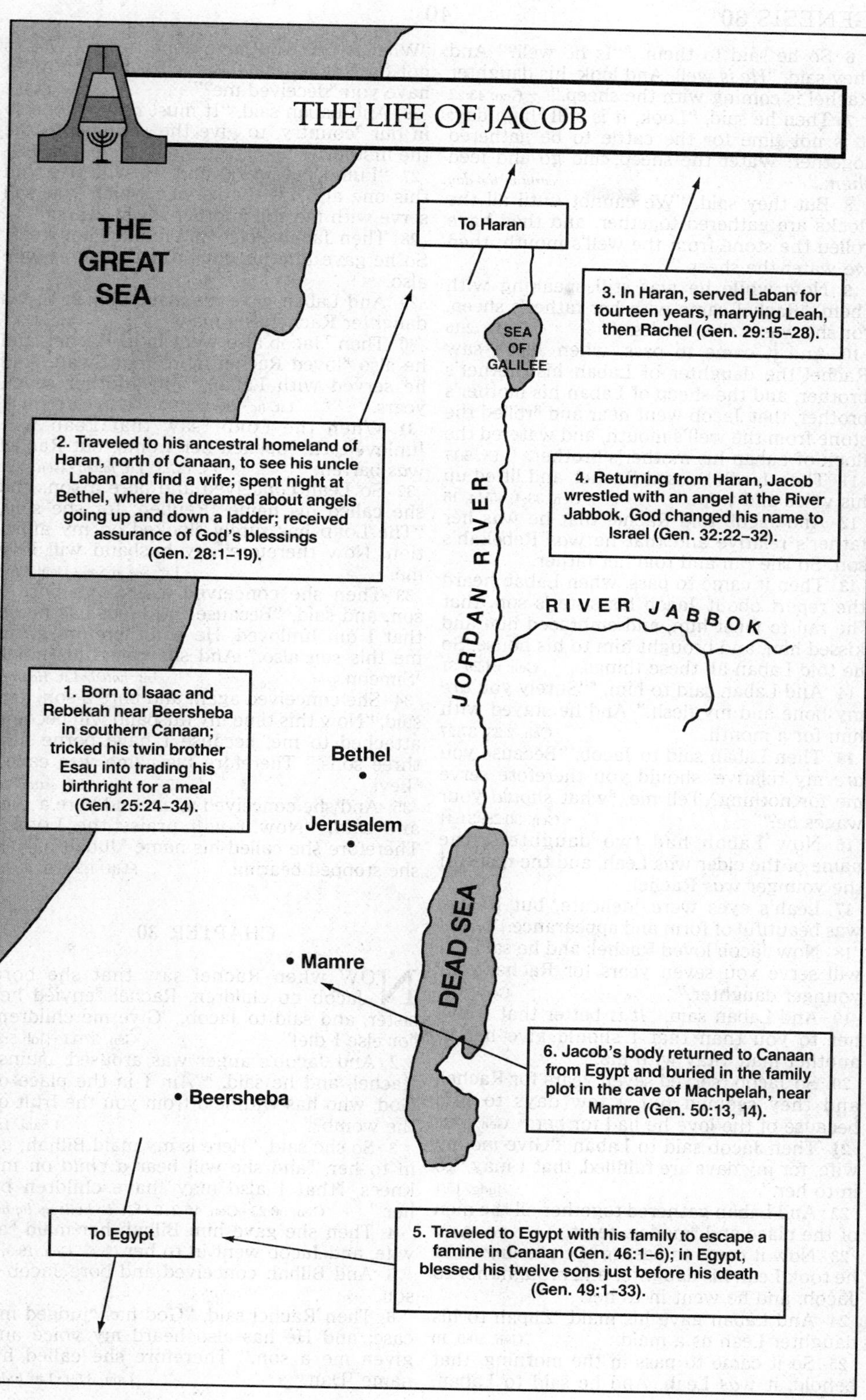

THE LIFE OF JACOB
THE GREAT SEA
To Haran
3. In Haran, served Laban for fourteen years, marrying Leah, then Rachel (Gen. 29:15–28).
SEA OF GALILEE
2. Traveled to his ancestral homeland of Haran, north of Canaan, to see his uncle Laban and find a wife; spent night at Bethel, where he dreamed about angels going up and down a ladder; received assurance of God's blessings (Gen. 28:1–19).
4. Returning from Haran, Jacob wrestled with an angel at the River Jabbok. God changed his name to Israel (Gen. 32:22–32).
JORDAN RIVER
RIVER JABBOK
1. Born to Isaac and Rebekah near Beersheba in southern Canaan; tricked his twin brother Esau into trading his birthright for a meal (Gen. 25:24–34).
Bethel
Jerusalem
DEAD SEA
Mamre
6. Jacob's body returned to Canaan from Egypt and buried in the family plot in the cave of Machpelah, near Mamre (Gen. 50:13, 14).
Beersheba
To Egypt
5. Traveled to Egypt with his family to escape a famine in Canaan (Gen. 46:1–6); in Egypt, blessed his twelve sons just before his death (Gen. 49:1–33).

6 So he said to them, [R]"Is he well?" And
they said, "*He is* well. And look, his daughter
Rachel is coming with the sheep." Gen. 43:27
7 Then he said, "Look, *it is* still [T]high day;
it is not time for the cattle to be gathered
together. Water the sheep, and go and feed
them." *early in the day*
8 But they said, "We cannot until all the
flocks are gathered together, and they have
rolled the stone from the well's mouth; then
we water the sheep."
9 Now while he was still speaking with
them, [R]Rachel came with her father's sheep,
for she was a shepherdess. Ex. 2:16
10 And it came to pass, when Jacob saw
Rachel the daughter of Laban his mother's
brother, and the sheep of Laban his mother's
brother, that Jacob went near and [R]rolled the
stone from the well's mouth, and watered the
flock of Laban his mother's brother. Ex. 2:17
11 Then Jacob [R]kissed Rachel, and lifted up
his voice and wept. Gen. 33:4; 45:14, 15
12 And Jacob told Rachel that he *was* her
father's relative and that he *was* Rebekah's
son. So she ran and told her father.
13 Then it came to pass, when Laban heard
the report about Jacob his sister's son, that
[R]he ran to meet him, and embraced him and
kissed him, and brought him to his house. So
he told Laban all these things. Gen. 24:29–31
14 And Laban said to him, [R]"Surely you *are*
my bone and my flesh." And he stayed with
him for a month. Gen. 2:23; 37:27
15 Then Laban said to Jacob, "Because you
are my relative, should you therefore serve
me for nothing? Tell me, [R]what *should* your
wages *be*?" Gen. 30:28; 31:41
16 Now Laban had two daughters: the
name of the elder *was* Leah, and the name of
the younger *was* Rachel.
17 Leah's eyes *were* [T]delicate, but Rachel
was beautiful of form and appearance. Or *weak*
18 Now Jacob loved Rachel; and he said, [R]"I
will serve you seven years for Rachel your
younger daughter." Gen. 31:41
19 And Laban said, "*It is* better that I give
her to you than that I should give her to
another man. Stay with me."
20 So Jacob [R]served seven years for Rachel,
and they seemed *but* a few days to him
because of the love he had for her. Gen. 30:26
21 Then Jacob said to Laban, "Give *me* my
wife, for my days are fulfilled, that I may [R]go
in to her." Judg. 15:1
22 And Laban gathered together all the men
of the place and [R]made a feast. John 2:1, 2
23 Now it came to pass in the evening, that
he took Leah his daughter and brought her to
Jacob; and he went in to her.
24 And Laban gave his maid [R]Zilpah to his
daughter Leah *as* a maid. Gen. 30:9, 10
25 So it came to pass in the morning, that
behold, it *was* Leah. And he said to Laban,
"What is this you have done to me? Was it
not for Rachel that I served you? Why then
have you [R]deceived me?" 1 Sam. 28:12
26 And Laban said, "It must not be done so
in our [T]country, to give the younger before
the firstborn. Lit. *place*
27 "Fulfill her week, and we will give you
this one also for the service which you will
serve with me still another seven years."
28 Then Jacob did so and fulfilled her week.
So he gave him his daughter Rachel as wife
also.
29 And Laban gave his maid [R]Bilhah to his
daughter Rachel as a maid. Gen. 30:3–5
30 Then [T]Jacob also went in to Rachel, and
he also [R]loved Rachel more than Leah. And
he served with Laban [R]still another seven
years. Lit. *he* • Deut. 21:15–17 • Gen. 30:26; 31:41
31 When the LORD [R]saw that Leah *was*
[T]unloved, He [R]opened her womb; but Rachel
was barren. Ps. 127:3 • Lit. *hated* • Gen. 30:1
32 So Leah conceived and bore a son, and
she called his name [T]Reuben; for she said,
"The LORD has surely [R]looked on my affliction. Now therefore, my husband will love
me." Lit. *See, a Son* • Deut. 26:7
33 Then she conceived again and bore a
son, and said, "Because the LORD has heard
that I *am* [T]unloved, He has therefore given
me this *son* also." And she called his name
[T]Simeon. Lit. *hated* • Lit. *Hearing*
34 She conceived again and bore a son, and
said, "Now this time my husband will become
attached to me, because I have borne him
three sons." Therefore his name was called
[T]Levi. Lit. *Attached*
35 And she conceived again and bore a son,
and said, "Now I will praise the LORD."
Therefore she called his name [R]Judah.[T] Then
she stopped bearing. Matt. 1:2 • Lit. *Praise*

CHAPTER 30

NOW when Rachel saw that she bore
Jacob no children, Rachel [R]envied her
sister, and said to Jacob, "Give me children,
[R]or else I die!" Gen. 37:11 • [Job 5:2]
2 And Jacob's anger was aroused against
Rachel, and he said, [R]"*Am* I in the place of
God, who has withheld from you the fruit of
the womb?" 1 Sam. 1:5
3 So she said, "Here is my maid Bilhah; go
in to her, [R]and she will bear *a child* on my
knees, [R]that I also may [T]have children by
her." Gen. 50:23 • Gen. 16:2, 3 • Lit. *be built up by her*
4 Then she gave him Bilhah her maid [R]as
wife, and Jacob went in to her. Gen. 16:3, 4
5 And Bilhah conceived and bore Jacob a
son.
6 Then Rachel said, "God has [R]judged my
case; and He has also heard my voice and
given me a son." Therefore she called his
name [T]Dan. Lam. 3:59 • Lit. *Judge*

7 And Rachel's maid Bilhah conceived
again and bore Jacob a second son.
8 Then Rachel said, "With [T]great wrestlings I have wrestled with my sister, *and*
indeed I have prevailed." So she called his
name [T]Naphtali. Lit. *wrestlings of God* • *My Wrestling*
9 When Leah saw that she had stopped
bearing, she took Zilpah her maid and [R]gave
her to Jacob as wife. Gen. 30:4
10 And Leah's maid Zilpah bore Jacob a
son.
11 Then Leah said, "A troop comes!" So she
called his name [T]Gad. Lit. *Troop* or *Fortune*
12 And Leah's maid Zilpah bore Jacob a
second son.
13 Then Leah said, "I am happy, for the
daughters [R]will call me blessed." So she called
his name [T]Asher. Luke 1:48 • Lit. *Happy*
14 Now Reuben went in the days of wheat
harvest and found mandrakes in the field,
and brought them to his mother Leah. Then
Rachel said to Leah, [R]"Please give me *some* of
your son's mandrakes." Gen. 25:30
15 But she said to her, "*Is it* a small matter
that you have taken away my husband?
Would you take away my son's mandrakes
also?" And Rachel said, "Therefore he will lie
with you tonight for your son's mandrakes."
16 When Jacob came out of the field in the
evening, Leah went out to meet him and said,
"You must come in to me, for I have surely
hired you with my son's mandrakes." And he
lay with her that night.
17 And God listened to Leah, and she conceived and bore Jacob a fifth son.
18 Leah said, "God has given me my hire,
because I have given my maid to my husband." So she called his name Issachar.
19 Then Leah conceived again and bore
Jacob a sixth son.
20 And Leah said, "God has endowed me
with a good endowment; now my husband
will dwell with me, because I have borne him
six sons." So she called his name Zebulun.
21 Afterward she bore a [R]daughter, and
called her name [T]Dinah. Gen. 34:1 • Lit. *Judgment*
22 Then God remembered Rachel, and God
listened to her and opened her womb.
23 And she conceived and bore a son, and
said, "God has taken away my reproach."
24 So she called his name Joseph, and said,
"The LORD shall add to me another son."
25 And it came to pass, when Rachel had
borne Joseph, that Jacob said to Laban,
"Send me away, that I may go to [R]my own
place and to my country. Gen. 18:33
26 "Give *me* my wives and my children [R]for
whom I have served you, and let me go;
for you know my service which I have done
for you." Gen. 29:18–20, 27, 30
27 And Laban said to him, "Please *stay*, if I
have found favor in your eyes, *for* [R]I have
learned by experience that the LORD has
blessed me for your sake." Gen. 26:24; 39:3
28 Then he said, [R]"Name me your wages,
and I will give *it*." Gen. 29:15; 31:7, 41
29 And [T]Jacob said to him, [R]"You know how
I have served you and how your livestock has
been with me. Lit. *he* • Gen. 31:6, 38–40
30 "For what you had before I *came was*
little, and it is *now* increased to a great
amount; the LORD has blessed you [T]since my
coming. And now, when shall I also [R]provide
for my own house?" Lit. *at my foot* • [1 Tim. 5:8]
31 So he said, "What shall I give you?" And
Jacob said, "You shall not give me anything.
If you will do this thing for me, I will again
feed and keep your flocks:
32 "Let me pass through all your flock
today, removing from there all the speckled
and spotted sheep, and all the brown ones
among the lambs, and the spotted and
speckled among the goats; and [R]*these* shall be
my wages. Gen. 31:8
33 "So my [R]righteousness will answer for
me in time to come, when the subject of my
wages comes before you: every one that *is*
not speckled and spotted among the goats,
and brown among the lambs, will be considered stolen, if *it is* with me." Ps. 37:6
34 And Laban said, "Oh, that it were according to your word!"
35 So he removed that day the male goats
that were [R]speckled and spotted, all the
female goats that were speckled and spotted,
every one that had *some* white in it, and all
the brown ones among the lambs, and gave
them into the hand of his sons. Gen. 31:9–12
36 Then he put [T]three days' journey between himself and Jacob, and Jacob fed the
rest of Laban's flocks. 60 mi.
37 Now Jacob took for himself rods of green
poplar and of the almond and chestnut trees,
peeled white strips in them, and exposed the
white which *was* in the rods.
38 And the rods which he had peeled, he set
before the flocks in the gutters, in the watering troughs where the flocks came to drink,
so that they should conceive when they came
to drink.
39 So the flocks conceived before the rods,
and the flocks brought forth streaked,
speckled, and spotted.
40 Then Jacob separated the lambs, and
made the flocks face toward the streaked and
all the brown in the flock of Laban; but he
put his own flocks by themselves and did not
put them with Laban's flock.
41 And it came to pass, whenever the stronger livestock conceived, that Jacob placed
the rods before the eyes of the livestock in
the gutters, that they might conceive among
the rods.
42 But when the flocks were feeble, he did
not put *them* in; so the feebler were Laban's
and the stronger Jacob's.

43 Thus the man became exceedingly prosperous, and had large flocks, female and male
servants, and camels and donkeys.

CHAPTER 31

Jacob's Flight

NOW Jacob heard the words of Laban's
sons, saying, "Jacob has taken away all
that was our father's, and from what was our
father's he has acquired all this wealth."
2 And Jacob saw the [R]countenance of Laban, and indeed it *was* not [R]*favorable* toward
him as before. Gen. 4:5 • Deut. 28:54
3 Then the LORD said to Jacob, "Return to
the land of your fathers and to your kindred,
and I will [R]be with you." Gen. 46:4
4 So Jacob sent and called Rachel and
Leah to the field, to his flock,
5 and said to them, [R]"I see your father's
[T]countenance, that it *is* not *favorable* toward
me as before; but the God of my father [R]has
been with me. Gen. 31:2, 3 • Lit. *face* • Is. 41:10
6 "And [R]you know that with all my might I
have served your father. Gen. 30:29; 31:38–41
7 "Yet your father has deceived me and
changed my wages [R]ten times, but God [R]did
not allow him to hurt me. Num. 14:22 • Job 1:10
8 "If he said thus: 'The speckled shall be
your wages,' then all the flocks bore speckled.
And if he said thus: 'The streaked shall be
your wages,' then all the flocks bore streaked.
9 "So God has taken away the livestock of
your father and given *them* to me.
10 "And it happened, at the time when the
flocks conceived, that I lifted my eyes and
saw in a dream, and behold, the rams which
leaped upon the flocks *were* streaked,
speckled, and gray-spotted.
11 "Then [R]the Angel of God spoke to me in
a dream, saying, 'Jacob.' And I said, 'Here I
am.' Gen. 16:7–11; 22:11, 15; 31:13; 48:16
12 "And He said, 'Lift your eyes now and
see, all the rams which leap on the flocks *are*
streaked, speckled, and gray-spotted; for I
have seen all that Laban is doing to you.
13 'I *am* the God of Bethel, where you
anointed the pillar *and* where you made a
vow to Me. Now arise, get out of this land,
and return to the land of your kindred.' "
14 Then Rachel and Leah answered and
said to him, "Is there still any portion or
inheritance for us in our father's house?
15 "Are we not considered strangers by
him? For [R]he has sold us, and also completely
consumed our money. Gen. 29:15, 20, 23, 27
16 "For all these riches which God has
taken from our father *are really* ours and our
children's; now then, whatever God has said
to you, do it."
17 Then Jacob rose and set his sons and his
wives on camels.
18 And he carried away all his livestock and
all his possessions which he had gained, his
acquired livestock which he had gained in
Padan Aram, to go to his father Isaac in the
land of [R]Canaan. Gen. 17:8; 33:18; 35:27
19 Now Laban had gone to shear his sheep,
and Rachel had stolen the [R]household[T] idols
that were her father's. Judg. 17:5 • Heb. *teraphim*
20 And Jacob stole away, unknown to La-
ban the Syrian, in that he did not tell him
that he intended to flee.
21 So he fled with all that he had. He arose
and crossed the river, and [T]headed toward the
mountains of Gilead. Lit. *set his face toward*
22 And Laban was told on the third day that
Jacob had fled.
23 Then he took his brethren with him and
pursued him for seven days' journey, and he
overtook him in the mountains of Gilead.
24 But God [R]had come to Laban the Syrian
in a dream by night, and said to him, "Be
careful that you [R]speak to Jacob neither good
nor bad." Gen. 20:3; 31:29; 46:2–4 • Gen. 24:50; 31:7, 29
25 So Laban overtook Jacob. Now Jacob
had pitched his tent in the mountains, and
Laban with his brethren pitched in the mountains of Gilead.
26 And Laban said to Jacob: "What have
you done, that you have stolen away unknown to me, and carried away my daughters like captives *taken* with the sword?
27 "Why did you flee away secretly, and
steal away from me, and not tell me; for I
might have sent you away with joy and
songs, with timbrel and harp?
28 "And you did not allow me [R]to kiss my
sons and my daughters. Now [R]you have done
foolishly in so doing. Gen. 31:55 • 1 Sam. 13:13
29 "It is in my power to do you harm, but
the God of your father spoke to me [R]last
night, saying, 'Be careful that you speak to
Jacob neither good nor bad.' Gen. 31:24
30 "And now you have surely gone because
you greatly long for your father's house, *but*
why did you [R]steal my gods?" Judg. 17:5; 18:24
31 Then Jacob answered and said to Laban,
"Because I was [R]afraid, for I said, 'Perhaps
you would take your daughters from me by
force.' Gen. 26:7; 32:7, 11
32 "With whomever you find your gods, [R]do
not let him live. In the presence of our
brethren, identify what I have of yours and
take *it* with you." For Jacob did not know
that Rachel had stolen them. Gen. 44:9
33 And Laban went into Jacob's tent, into
Leah's tent, and into the two maids' tents,
but he did not find *them*. Then he went out of
Leah's tent and entered Rachel's tent.
34 Now Rachel had taken the [T]household
idols, put them in the camel's saddle, and sat
on them. And Laban [T]searched all about the
tent but did not find *them*. Heb. *teraphim* • Lit. *felt*
35 And she said to her father, "Let it not
displease my lord that I cannot [R]rise before
you, for the manner of women *is* with me."

And he searched but did not find the [T]house-
hold idols. Lev. 19:32 • Heb. *teraphim*
36 Then Jacob was angry and rebuked Laban, and Jacob answered and said to Laban:
"What *is* my [T]trespass? What *is* my sin, that
you have so hotly pursued me? *transgression*
37 "Although you have searched all my
things, what part of your household things
have you found? Set *it* here before my brethren and your brethren, that they may judge
between us both!
38 "These twenty years I *have been* with
you; your ewes and your female goats have
not miscarried their young, and I have not
eaten the rams of your flock.
39 [R]"That which was torn *by beasts* I did
not bring to you; I bore the loss of it. [R]You
required it from my hand, *whether* stolen by
day or stolen by night. Ex. 22:10 • Ex. 22:10–13
40 "*There* I was! In the day the drought
consumed me, and the frost by night, and my
sleep departed from my eyes.
41 "Thus I have been in your house twenty
years; I served you fourteen years for your
two daughters, and six years for your flock,
and you have changed my wages ten times.
42 "Unless the God of my father, the God of
Abraham and the Fear of Isaac, had been
with me, surely now you would have sent me
away empty-handed. [R]God has seen my affliction and the labor of my hands, and [R]rebuked
you last night." Ex. 3:7 • 1 Chr. 12:17
43 And Laban answered and said to Jacob,
"*These* daughters *are* my daughters, and
these children *are* my children, and *this* flock
is my flock; all that you see *is* mine. But what
can I do this day to these my daughters or to
their children whom they have borne?
44 "Now therefore, come, let us make a
[T]covenant, [R]you and I, and let it be a witness
between you and me." *treaty* • Josh. 24:27
45 So Jacob [R]took a stone and set it up *as* a
pillar. Gen. 28:18; 35:14
46 Then Jacob said to his brethren, "Gather
stones." And they took stones and made a
heap, and they ate there on the heap.
47 Laban called it [T]Jegar Sahadutha, but
Jacob called it [T]Galeed. Both mean *Heap of Witness*
48 And Laban said, [R]"This heap *is* a witness
between you and me this day." Therefore its
name was called Galeed, Josh. 24:27
49 also [T]Mizpah, because he said, "May the
LORD watch between you and me when we
are absent one from another. Lit. *Watch*
50 "If you afflict my daughters, or if you
take *other* wives besides my daughters, *although* no man *is* with us—see, God *is* witness between you and me!"
51 Then Laban said to Jacob, "Here is this
heap and here is *this* pillar, which I have
placed between you and me.
52 "This heap *is* a witness, and *this* pillar *is*
a witness, that I will not pass beyond this
heap to you, and you will not pass beyond
this heap and this pillar to me, for harm.
53 "The God of Abraham, the God of Nahor,
and the God of their father judge between
us." And Jacob swore by [R]the [T]Fear of his
father Isaac. Gen. 31:42 • A reference to God
54 Then Jacob offered a sacrifice on the
mountain, and called his brethren to eat
bread. And they ate bread and stayed all
night on the mountain.
55 And early in the morning Laban arose,
and kissed his sons and daughters and
[R]blessed them. Then Laban departed and
[R]returned to his place. Gen. 28:1 • Num. 24:25

CHAPTER 32

Jacob Fights with the Angel

SO Jacob went on his way, and [R]the angels
of God met him. Num. 22:31
2 When Jacob saw them, he said, "This *is*
God's [R]camp." And he called the name of that
place [T]Mahanaim. Josh. 5:14 • Lit. *Double Camp*
3 Then Jacob sent messengers before him
to Esau his brother in the land of Seir, [R]the
[T]country of Edom. Gen. 25:30; 36:6–9 • Lit. *field*
4 And he commanded them, saying,
[R]"Speak thus to my lord Esau, 'Thus your
servant Jacob says: "I have sojourned with
Laban and stayed there until now. Prov. 15:1
5 [R]"I have oxen, donkeys, flocks, and male
and female servants; and I have sent to tell
my lord, that [R]I may find favor in your
sight." ' " Gen. 30:43 • Gen. 33:8, 15
6 Then the messengers returned to Jacob,
saying, "We came to your brother Esau, and
[R]he also is coming to meet you, and four
hundred men *are* with him." Gen. 33:1
7 So Jacob was greatly afraid and [R]dis-
tressed; and he divided the people that *were*
with him, and the flocks and herds and camels, into two companies. Gen. 32:11; 35:3
8 And he said, "If Esau comes to the one
company and [T]attacks it, then the other
company which is left will escape." Lit. *strikes*
9 [R]Then Jacob said, [R]"O God of my father
Abraham and God of my father Isaac, the
LORD [R]who said to me, 'Return to your country and to your kindred, and I will deal well
with you': [Ps. 50:15] • Gen. 28:13; 31:42 • Gen. 31:3, 13
10 "I am not worthy of the least of all the
[R]mercies and of all the truth which You have
shown Your servant; for I crossed over this
Jordan with [R]my staff, and now I have become two companies. Gen. 24:27 • Job 8:7
11 "Deliver me, I pray, from the hand of my
brother, from the hand of Esau; for I fear
him, lest he come and [T]attack me *and* [R]the
mother with the children. Lit. *strike* • Hos. 10:14
12 "For [R]You said, 'I will surely treat you
well, and make your descendants as the [R]sand
of the sea, which cannot be numbered for
multitude.' " Gen. 28:13–15 • Gen. 22:17

13 So he lodged there that same night, and
took what came to his hand as [R]a present for
Esau his brother: Gen. 43:11
14 two hundred female goats and twenty
male goats, two hundred ewes and twenty
rams,
15 thirty milk camels with their colts, forty
cows and ten bulls, twenty female donkeys
and ten foals.
16 Then he delivered *them* to the hand of
his servants, every drove by itself, and said to
his servants, "Pass over before me, and put
some distance between successive droves."
17 And he commanded the first one, saying,
"When Esau my brother meets you and asks
you, saying, 'To whom do you belong, and
where are you going? Whose *are* these in
front of you?'
18 "then you shall say, 'They *are* your servant Jacob's. It *is* a present sent to my lord
Esau; and behold, he also *is* behind us.' "
19 So he commanded the second, the third,
and all who followed the droves, saying, "In
this manner you shall speak to Esau when
you find him;
20 "and also say, 'Behold, your servant
Jacob *is* behind us.' " For he said, "I will
[R]appease him with the present that goes
before me, and afterward I will see his face;
perhaps he will accept me." [Prov. 21:14]
21 So the present went on over before him,
but he himself lodged that night in the camp.
22 And he arose that night and took his two
wives, his two maidservants, and his eleven
sons, and crossed over the ford of Jabbok.
23 He took them, sent them over the brook,
and sent over what he had.
24 Then Jacob was left alone; and a Man
wrestled with him until the breaking of day.
25 Now when He saw that He did not prevail against him, He [T]touched the socket of
his hip; and the socket of Jacob's hip was out
of joint as He wrestled with him. *struck*
26 And [R]He said, "Let Me go, for the day
breaks." But he said, [R]"I will not let You go
unless You bless me!" Luke 24:28 • Hos. 12:4
27 So He said to him, "What *is* your name?"
And he said, "Jacob."
28 And He said, [R]"Your name shall no
longer be called Jacob, but [T]Israel; for you
have struggled with God and with men, and
have prevailed." Gen. 35:10 • Lit. *Prince with God*
29 Then Jacob asked *Him*, saying, "Tell *me*
Your name, I pray." And He said, [R]"Why *is* it
that you ask about My name?" And He
[R]blessed him there. Judg. 13:17, 18 • Gen. 35:9
30 And Jacob called the name of the place
[T]Peniel: "For I have seen God face to face,
and my life is preserved." Lit. *Face of God*
31 Just as he crossed over *Penuel the sun
rose on him, and he limped on his hip.
32 Therefore to this day the children of
Israel do not eat the muscle that shrank,
which *is* on the hip socket, because He
[T]touched the socket of Jacob's hip in the
muscle that shrank. Or *struck*

CHAPTER 33

Jacob Makes Peace with Esau

NOW Jacob lifted his eyes and looked, and
there, [R]Esau was coming, and with him
were four hundred men. So he divided the
children among Leah, Rachel, and the two
maidservants. Gen. 32:6
2 And he put the maidservants and their
children in front, Leah and her children
behind, and Rachel and Joseph last.
3 Then he crossed over before them and
[R]bowed himself to the ground seven times,
until he came near to his brother. Gen. 18:2; 42:6
4 [R]But Esau ran to meet him, and embraced him, [R]and fell on his neck and kissed
him, and they wept. Gen. 32:28 • Gen. 45:14, 15
5 And he lifted his eyes and saw the
women and children, and said, "Who *are*
these with you?" And he said, "The children
[R]whom God has graciously given your servant." Gen. 48:9
6 Then the maidservants came near, they
and their children, and bowed down.
7 And Leah also came near with her children, and they bowed down. Afterward
Joseph and Rachel came near, and they
bowed down.
8 Then Esau said, "What *do* you *mean by*
[R]all this company which I met?" And he said,
"*These are* [R]to find favor in the sight of my
lord." Gen. 32:13–16 • Gen. 32:5
9 But Esau said, "I have enough, my
brother; keep what you have for yourself."
10 And Jacob said, "No, please, if I have
now found favor in your sight, then receive
my present from my hand, inasmuch as I
[R]have seen your face as though I had seen
the face of God, and you were pleased with
me. Gen. 43:3
11 "Please, take my blessing that is brought
to you, because God has dealt graciously with
me, and because I have enough." And he
urged him, and he took *it*.
12 Then Esau said, "Let us take our journey; let us go, and I will go before you."
13 But Jacob said to him, "My lord knows
that the children *are* weak, and the flocks
and herds which are nursing *are* with me.
And if the men should drive them hard one
day, all the flock will die.
14 "Please let my lord go on ahead before
his servant. I will lead on slowly at a pace
which the livestock that go before me, and
the children, are able to endure, until I come
to my lord [R]in Seir." Gen. 32:3; 36:8
15 And Esau said, "Now let me leave with

32:31 Alternate form of *Peniel*, v. 30

you *some* of the people who *are* with me." But he said, "What need is there? [R]Let me find favor in the sight of my lord." Ruth 2:13

16 So Esau returned that day on his way to Seir.

17 And Jacob journeyed to [R]Succoth, built himself a house, and made [T]booths for his livestock. Therefore the name of the place is called [T]Succoth. Josh. 13:27 • *shelters* • Lit. *Booths*

18 Then Jacob came safely to the city of [R]Shechem, which *is* in the land of Canaan, when he came from Padan Aram; and he pitched his tent before the city. Josh. 24:1

19 And [R]he bought the parcel of [T]land, where he had pitched his tent, from the children of Hamor, Shechem's father, for one hundred pieces of money. John 4:5 • Lit. *the field*

20 Then he erected an altar there and called it [T]El Elohe Israel. Lit. *God, the God of Israel*

CHAPTER 34

The Defilement of Dinah

NOW [R]Dinah the daughter of Leah, whom she had borne to Jacob, went out to see the daughters of the land. Gen. 30:21

2 And when Shechem the son of Hamor the Hivite, prince of the country, saw her, he took her and lay with her, and violated her.

3 His soul [T]was strongly attracted to Dinah the daughter of Jacob, and he loved the young woman and spoke [T]kindly to the young woman. Lit. *clung to* • *tenderly*

4 So Shechem [R]spoke to his father Hamor, saying, "Get me this young woman as a wife." Judg. 14:2

5 And Jacob heard that he had defiled Dinah his daughter. Now his sons were with his livestock in the field; so Jacob [R]held[T] his peace until they came. 2 Sam. 13:22 • *kept silent*

6 Then Hamor the father of Shechem went out to Jacob to speak with him.

7 And the sons of Jacob came in from the field when they heard *it*; and the men were grieved and very angry, because he [R]had done a disgraceful thing in Israel by lying with Jacob's daughter, [R]a thing which ought not to be done. Judg. 20:6 • 2 Sam. 13:12

8 But Hamor spoke with them, saying, "The soul of my son Shechem longs for your daughter. Please give her to him as a wife.

9 "And make marriages with us; give your daughters to us, and take our daughters to yourselves.

10 "So you shall dwell with us, and the land shall be before you. Dwell and trade in it, and acquire possessions for yourselves in it."

11 Then Shechem said to her father and her brothers, "Let me find favor in your eyes, and whatever you say to me I will give.

12 "Ask me ever so much dowry and gift, and I will give according to what you say to me; but give me the young woman as a wife."

13 But the sons of Jacob answered Shechem and Hamor his father, and spoke deceitfully, because he had defiled Dinah their sister.

14 And they said to them, "We cannot do this thing, to give our sister to one who is [R]uncircumcised, for [R]that *would be* a reproach to us. Ex. 12:48 • Josh. 5:2–9

15 "But on this *condition* we will consent to you: If you will become as we *are*, if every male of you is circumcised,

16 "then we will give our daughters to you, and we will take your daughters to us; and we will dwell with you, and we will become one people.

17 "But if you will not heed us and be circumcised, then we will take our daughter and be gone."

18 And their words pleased Hamor and Shechem, Hamor's son.

19 So the young man did not delay to do the thing, because he delighted in Jacob's daughter. He *was* [R]more honorable than all the household of his father. 1 Chr. 4:9

20 And Hamor and Shechem his son came to the [R]gate of their city, and spoke with the men of their city, saying: Ruth 4:1, 11

21 "These men *are* at peace with us. Therefore let them dwell in the land and trade in it. For indeed the land *is* large enough for them. Let us take their daughters to us as wives, and let us give them our daughters.

22 "Only on this *condition* will the men consent to dwell with us, to be one people: if every male among us is circumcised as they *are* circumcised.

23 "*Will* not their livestock, their property, and every animal of theirs *be* ours? Only let us consent to them, and they will dwell with us."

24 And all who went out of the gate of his city heeded Hamor and Shechem his son; every male was circumcised, all who [R]went out of the gate of his city. Gen. 23:10, 18

25 Now it came to pass on the third day, when they were in pain, that two of the sons of Jacob, Simeon and Levi, Dinah's brothers, each took his sword and came boldly upon the city and killed all the males.

26 And they killed Hamor and Shechem his son with the edge of the sword, and took Dinah from Shechem's house, and went out.

27 The sons of Jacob came upon the slain, and plundered the city, because their sister had been defiled.

28 They took their sheep, their oxen, and their donkeys, what *was* in the city and what *was* in the field,

29 and all their wealth. All their little ones and their wives they took captive; and they plundered even all that *was* in the houses.

30 Then Jacob said to Simeon and Levi, [R]"You have [R]troubled me [R]by making me obnoxious among the inhabitants of the land,

among the Canaanites and the Perizzites; [R]and since I *am* few in number, they will gather themselves together against me and kill me. I shall be destroyed, my household and I." Gen. 49:6 • Josh. 7:25 • Ex. 5:21 • Deut. 4:27

31 But they said, "Should he treat our sister like a harlot?"

CHAPTER 35

The Devotion at Bethel

THEN God said to Jacob, "Arise, go up to [R]Bethel and dwell there; and make an altar there to God, [R]who appeared to you [R]when you fled from the face of Esau your brother." Gen. 28:19; 31:13 • Gen. 28:13 • Gen. 27:43

2 And Jacob said to his [R]household and to all who *were* with him, "Put away the foreign gods that *are* among you, purify yourselves, and change your garments. Josh. 24:15

3 "Then let us arise and go up to Bethel; and I will make an altar there to God, [R]who answered me in the day of my distress [R]and has been with me in the way which I have gone." Gen. 32:7, 24 • Gen. 28:15, 20; 31:3, 42

4 So they gave Jacob all the foreign [T]gods which *were* in their hands, and *all their* [R]earrings which *were* in their ears; and Jacob hid them under [R]the terebinth tree which *was* by Shechem. *idols* • Hos. 2:13 • Josh. 24:26

5 And they journeyed, and [R]the terror of God was upon the cities that *were* all around them, and they did not pursue the sons of Jacob. Ex. 15:16; 23:27

6 So Jacob came to [R]Luz (that *is*, Bethel), which *is* in the land of Canaan, he and all the people who *were* with him. Gen. 28:19, 22; 48:3

7 And he built an altar there and called the place [T]El Bethel, because there God appeared to him when he fled from the face of his brother. Lit. *God of the House of God*

8 Now [R]Deborah, Rebekah's nurse, died, and she was buried below Bethel under the terebinth tree. So the name of it was called [T]Allon Bachuth. Gen. 24:59 • Lit. *Terebinth of Weeping*

9 Then [R]God appeared to Jacob again, when he came from Padan Aram, and [R]blessed him. Josh. 5:13 • Gen. 32:29

10 And God said to him, "Your name *is* Jacob; [R]your name shall not be called Jacob anymore, [R]but Israel shall be your name." So He called his name Israel. Gen. 17:5 • Gen. 32:28

11 Also God said to him: "I *am* God Almighty. Be fruitful and multiply; a nation and a company of nations shall proceed from you, and kings shall come from your body.

12 "The [R]land which I gave Abraham and Isaac I give to you; and to your descendants after you I give this land." Gen. 12:7; 13:15

13 Then God [T]went up from him in the place where He talked with him. *departed*

14 So Jacob [R]set up a pillar in the place where He talked with him, a pillar of stone; and he poured a drink offering on it, and he poured oil on it. Gen. 28:18, 19; 31:45

15 And Jacob called the name of the place where God spoke with him, [R]Bethel. Gen. 28:19

The Deaths of Rachel and Isaac

16 Then they journeyed from Bethel. And when there was but a [T]little distance to go to Ephrath, Rachel travailed *in childbirth*, and she had hard labor. 5 mi.

17 Now it came to pass, when she was in hard labor, that the midwife said to her, "Do not fear; you will have this son also."

18 And so it was, as her soul was departing (for she died), that she called his name Ben-Oni; but his father called him Benjamin.

19 So Rachel died and was buried on the way to Ephrath (that *is*, Bethlehem).

20 And Jacob set a pillar on her grave, which *is* the pillar of Rachel's grave [R]to this day. 1 Sam. 10:2

21 Then Israel journeyed and pitched his tent beyond [R]the tower of Eder. Mic. 4:8

22 And it happened, when Israel dwelt in that land, that Reuben went and [R]lay with Bilhah his father's concubine; and Israel heard *about it*. Gen. 49:4

Now the sons of Jacob were twelve:

23 the sons of Leah *were* [R]Reuben, Jacob's firstborn, and Simeon, Levi, Judah, Issachar, and Zebulun; Ex. 1:1–4

24 the sons of Rachel *were* Joseph and Benjamin;

25 the sons of Bilhah, Rachel's maidservant, *were* Dan and Naphtali;

26 and the sons of Zilpah, Leah's maidservant, *were* Gad and Asher. These *were* the sons of Jacob who were born to him in Padan Aram.

27 Then Jacob came to his father Isaac at Mamre, or Kirjath Arba (that *is*, Hebron), where Abraham and Isaac had sojourned.

28 Now the days of Isaac were one hundred and eighty years.

29 So Isaac breathed his last and died, and was [T]gathered to his people, *being* old and full of days. And [R]his sons Esau and Jacob buried him. Joined his ancestors • Gen. 25:9; 49:31

CHAPTER 36

The History of Esau—1 Chr. 1:35–42

NOW this *is* the genealogy of Esau, [R]who is Edom. Gen. 25:30

2 Esau took his wives from the daughters of Canaan: Adah the daughter of Elon the [R]Hittite; Aholibamah the daughter of Anah, the daughter of Zibeon the Hivite; 2 Kin. 7:6

3 and [R]Basemath, Ishmael's daughter, sister of Nebajoth. Gen. 28:9

4 Now [R]Adah bore Eliphaz to Esau, and Basemath bore Reuel. 1 Chr. 1:35

5 And Aholibamah bore Jeush, Jaalam,

TRAVELS OF THE PATRIARCHS

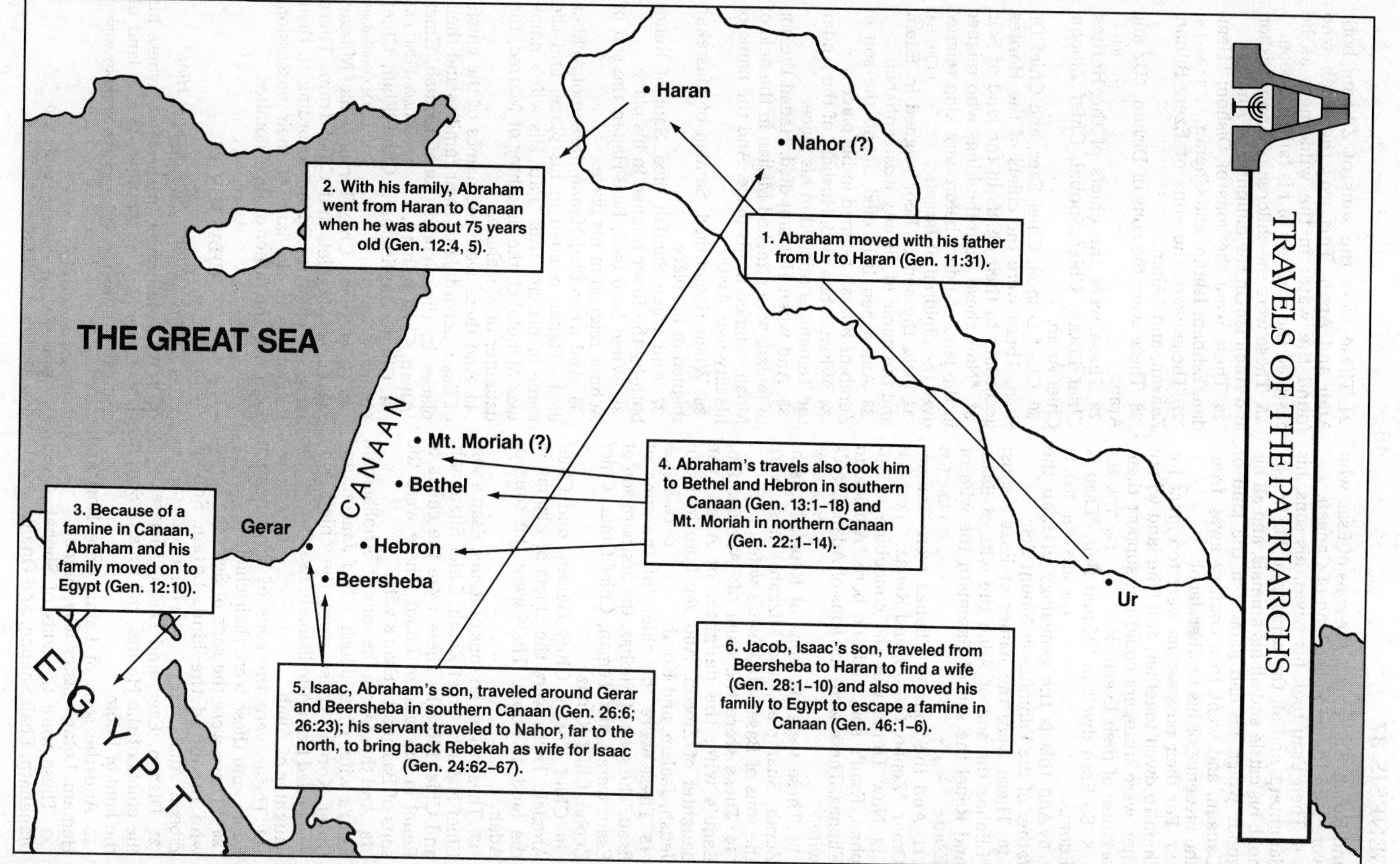

THE GREAT SEA
CANAAN
EGYPT
Haran
Nahor (?)
Ur
Mt. Moriah (?)
Bethel
Hebron
Gerar
Beersheba
1. Abraham moved with his father from Ur to Haran (Gen. 11:31).
2. With his family, Abraham went from Haran to Canaan when he was about 75 years old (Gen. 12:4, 5).
3. Because of a famine in Canaan, Abraham and his family moved on to Egypt (Gen. 12:10).
4. Abraham's travels also took him to Bethel and Hebron in southern Canaan (Gen. 13:1–18) and Mt. Moriah in northern Canaan (Gen. 22:1–14).
5. Isaac, Abraham's son, traveled around Gerar and Beersheba in southern Canaan (Gen. 26:6; 26:23); his servant traveled to Nahor, far to the north, to bring back Rebekah as wife for Isaac (Gen. 24:62–67).
6. Jacob, Isaac's son, traveled from Beersheba to Haran to find a wife (Gen. 28:1–10) and also moved his family to Egypt to escape a famine in Canaan (Gen. 46:1–6).

and Korah. These *were* the sons of Esau who
were born to him in the land of Canaan.
6 Then Esau took his wives, his sons, his
daughters, and all the persons of his household, his cattle and all his animals, and all his
goods which he had gained in the land of
Canaan, and went to a country away from
the presence of his brother Jacob.
7 For their possessions were too great for
them to dwell together, and [R]the land where
they were strangers could not support them
because of their livestock. Gen. 17:8; 28:4
8 So Esau dwelt in [R]Mount Seir. [R]Esau *is*
Edom. Gen. 32:3 • Gen. 36:1, 19
9 And this *is* the genealogy of Esau the
father of the Edomites in Mount Seir.
10 These *were* the names of Esau's sons:
[R]Eliphaz the son of Adah the wife of Esau,
and Reuel the son of Basemath the wife of
Esau. 1 Chr. 1:35
11 And the sons of Eliphaz were Teman,
Omar, [R]Zepho, Gatam, and Kenaz. 1 Chr. 1:36
12 Now Timna was the concubine of Eliphaz, Esau's son, and she bore [R]Amalek to
Eliphaz. These *were* the sons of Adah, Esau's
wife. Num. 24:20
13 These *were* the sons of Reuel: Nahath,
Zerah, Shammah, and Mizzah. These were
the sons of Basemath, Esau's wife.
14 These were the sons of [T]Aholibamah,
Esau's wife, the daughter of Anah, the
daughter of Zibeon. And she bore to Esau:
Jeush, Jaalam, and Korah. Or *Oholibamah*
15 These *were* the chiefs of the sons of
Esau. The sons of Eliphaz, the firstborn *son* of
Esau, were Chief Teman, Chief Omar, Chief
Zepho, Chief Kenaz,
16 Chief Korah, Chief Gatam, *and* Chief
Amalek. These *were* the chiefs of Eliphaz in
the land of Edom. They *were* the sons of
Adah.
17 These *were* the sons of Reuel, Esau's son:
Chief Nahath, Chief Zerah, Chief Shammah,
and Chief Mizzah. These *were* the chiefs of
Reuel in the land of Edom. These *were* the
sons of Basemath, Esau's wife.
18 And these *were* the sons of [T]Aholibamah,
Esau's wife: Chief Jeush, Chief Jaalam, and
Chief Korah. These *were* the chiefs *who*
descended from Aholibamah, Esau's wife, the
daughter of Anah. Or *Oholibamah*
19 These *were* the sons of Esau, who is
Edom, and these *were* their chiefs.
20 [R]These *were* the sons of Seir [R]the Horite
who inhabited the land: Lotan, Shobal,
Zibeon, Anah, 1 Chr. 1:38–42 • Gen. 14:6
21 Dishon, Ezer, and Dishan. These *were*
the chiefs of the Horites, the sons of Seir, in
the land of Edom.
22 And the sons of Lotan were Hori and
Hemam. Lotan's sister *was* Timna.
23 These *were* the sons of Shobal: Alvan,
Manahath, Ebal, Shepho, and Onam.
24 These *were* the sons of Zibeon: both
Ajah and Anah. This *was the* Anah who
found the water in the wilderness as he
pastured the donkeys of his father Zibeon.
25 These *were* the children of Anah: Dishon
and Aholibamah the daughter of Anah.
26 These *were* the sons of Dishon: [R]Hem-
dan, Eshban, Ithran, and Cheran. 1 Chr. 1:41
27 These *were* the sons of Ezer: Bilhan,
Zaavan, and *Akan.
28 These *were* the sons of Dishan: [R]Uz and
Aran. Job 1:1
29 These *were* the chiefs of the Horites:
Chief Lotan, Chief Shobal, Chief Zibeon,
Chief Anah,
30 Chief Dishon, Chief Ezer, and Chief Dishan. These *were* the chiefs of the Horites,
according to their chiefs in the land of Seir.
31 [R]Now these *were* the kings who reigned
in the land of Edom before any king reigned
over the children of Israel: 1 Chr. 1:43
32 Bela the son of Beor reigned in Edom,
and the name of his city *was* Dinhabah.
33 And when Bela died, Jobab the son of
Zerah of Bozrah reigned in his place.
34 When Jobab died, Husham of the land of
the Temanites reigned in his place.
35 And when Husham died, Hadad the son
of Bedad, who attacked Midian in the field of
Moab, reigned in his place. And the name of
his city *was* Avith.
36 When Hadad died, Samlah of Masrekah
reigned in his place.
37 And when Samlah died, Saul of Reho-
both-*by*-the-River reigned in his place.
38 When Saul died, Baal-Hanan the son of
Achbor reigned in his place.
39 And when Baal-Hanan the son of Achbor
died, *Hadar reigned in his place; and the
name of his city *was* *Pau. His wife's name
was Mehetabel, the daughter of Matred, the
daughter of Mezahab.
40 And these *were* the names of the chiefs
of Esau, according to their families and their
places, by their names: Chief Timnah, Chief
[T]Alvah, Chief Jetheth, *Aliah*, 1 Chr. 1:51
41 Chief [T]Aholibamah, Chief Elah, Chief
Pinon, Or *Oholibamah*
42 Chief Kenaz, Chief Teman, Chief Mibzar,
43 Chief Magdiel, and Chief Iram. These
were the chiefs of Edom, according to their
habitations in the land of their possession.
Esau *was* the father of the Edomites.

CHAPTER 37

Joseph's Family Sins Against Him

NOW Jacob dwelt in the land [R]where his
father was a [T]stranger, in the land of
Canaan. Gen. 17:8; 23:4 • *sojourner*, temporary resident

36:27 *Jaakan*, 1 Chr. 1:42
36:39 Sam., Syr. *Hadad* and 1 Chr. 1:50
36:39 *Pai*, 1 Chr. 1:50

2 This *is* the genealogy of Jacob. Joseph,
being seventeen years old, was feeding the
flock with his brothers. And the lad *was* with
the sons of Bilhah and the sons of Zilpah, his
father's wives; and Joseph brought [R]a bad
report of them to his father. 1 Sam. 2:22–24
3 Now Israel loved Joseph more than all
his children, because he *was* [R]the son of his
old age. Also he [R]made him a tunic of *many*
colors. Gen. 44:20 • Gen. 37:23, 32
4 But when his brothers saw that their
father loved him more than all his brothers,
they [R]hated him and could not speak peaceably to him. Gen. 27:41; 49:23
5 Now Joseph dreamed a dream, and he
told *it* to his brothers; and they hated him
even more.
6 So he said to them, "Please hear this
dream which I have dreamed:
7 "There we were, binding sheaves in the
field. Then behold, my sheaf arose and also
stood upright; and indeed your sheaves stood
all around and bowed down to my sheaf."
8 And his brothers said to him, "Shall you
indeed reign over us? Or shall you indeed
have dominion over us?" So they hated him
even more for his dreams and for his words.
9 Then he dreamed still another dream and
told it to his brothers, and said, "Look, I have
dreamed another dream. And this time, [R]the
sun, the moon, and the eleven stars bowed
down to me." Gen. 46:29; 47:25
10 So he told *it* to his father and his brothers; and his father rebuked him and said to
him, "What *is* this dream that you have
dreamed? Shall your mother and I and [R]your
brothers indeed come to bow down to the
earth before you?" Gen. 27:29
11 And his brothers envied him, but his
father [R]kept the matter *in mind.* Dan. 7:28
12 Then his brothers went to feed their
father's flock in [R]Shechem. Gen. 33:18–20
13 And Israel said to Joseph, "Are not your
brothers feeding *the flock* in Shechem?
Come, I will send you to them." So he said to
him, "Here I am."
14 Then he said to him, "Please go and see if
it is well with your brothers and well with the
flocks, and bring back word to me." So he
sent him out of the Valley of [R]Hebron, and he
went to Shechem. Gen. 13:18; 23:2, 19; 35:27
15 Now a certain man found him, and there
he was, wandering in the field. And the man
asked him, saying, "What are you seeking?"
16 So he said, "I am seeking my brothers.
[R]Please tell me where they are feeding *their
flocks.*" Song 1:7
17 And the man said, "They have departed
from here, for I heard them say, 'Let us go to
Dothan.' " So Joseph went after his brothers
and found them in [R]Dothan. 2 Kin. 6:13
18 Now when they saw him afar off, even
before he came near them, [R]they conspired
against him to kill him. Mark 14:1
19 Then they said to one another, "Look,
this [T]dreamer is coming! Lit. *master of dreams*
20 "Come therefore, let us now kill him and
cast him into some pit; and we shall say,
'Some wild beast has devoured him.' We shall
see what will become of his dreams!"
21 But [R]Reuben heard *it*, and he delivered
him out of their hands, and said, "Let us not
kill him." Gen. 42:22
22 And Reuben said to them, "Shed no
blood, *but* cast him into this pit which *is* in
the wilderness, and do not lay a hand on
him"—that he might deliver him out of their
hands, and bring him back to his father.
23 So it came to pass, when Joseph had
come to his brothers, that they [R]stripped
Joseph of *his* tunic, the tunic of *many* colors
that *was* on him. Matt. 27:28
24 Then they took him and cast him into a
pit. And the pit *was* empty; *there was* no
water in it.
25 [R]And they sat down to eat a meal. Then
they lifted their eyes and looked, and there
was a company of Ishmaelites, coming from
Gilead with their camels, bearing spices,
[R]balm, and myrrh, on their way to carry *them*
down to Egypt. Prov. 30:20 • Jer. 8:22
26 So Judah said to his brothers, "What
profit *is there* if we kill our brother and
[R]conceal his blood? Gen. 37:20
27 "Come and let us sell him to the Ishmaelites, and let not our hand be upon him, for he
is [R]our brother *and* [R]our flesh." And his
brothers listened. Gen. 42:21 • Gen. 29:14
28 Then Midianite traders passed by; so *the
brothers* pulled Joseph up and lifted him out
of the pit, [R]and sold him to the Ishmaelites for
[R]twenty[T] *shekels* of silver. And they took
Joseph to Egypt. Ps. 105:17 • Matt. 27:9 • $2,560
29 Then Reuben returned to the pit, and
indeed Joseph *was* not in the pit; and he [R]tore
his clothes. Job 1:20
30 And he returned to his brothers and said,
"The lad [R]*is* no *more*; and I, where shall I
go?" Gen. 42:13, 36
31 So they took [R]Joseph's tunic, killed a kid
of the goats, and dipped the tunic in the
blood. Gen. 37:3, 23
32 Then they sent the tunic of *many* colors,
and they brought *it* to their father and said,
"We have found this. Do you know whether
it *is* your son's tunic or not?"
33 And he recognized it and said, "*It is* my
son's tunic. A wild beast has devoured him.
Without doubt Joseph is torn to pieces."
34 Then Jacob [R]tore his clothes, put sackcloth on his waist, and [R]mourned for his son
many days. 2 Sam. 3:31 • Gen. 50:10
35 And all his sons and all his daughters
[R]arose to comfort him; but he refused to be
comforted, and he said, "For [R]I shall go down
into the grave to my son in mourning." Thus
his father wept for him. 2 Sam. 12:17 • Gen. 25:8

36 Now [R]the Midianites had sold him in
Egypt to Potiphar, an officer of Pharaoh *and*
captain of the guard. Gen. 39:1

CHAPTER 38

Joseph's Family Sins with the Canaanites

IT came to pass at that time that Judah
departed from his brothers, and visited a
certain Adullamite whose name *was* Hirah.
2 And Judah saw there a daughter of a
certain Canaanite whose name *was* Shua,
and he married her and went in to her.
3 So she conceived and bore a son, and he
called his name [R]Er. Gen. 46:12
4 She conceived again and bore a son, and
she called his name [R]Onan. Num. 26:19
5 And she conceived yet again and bore a
son, and called his name [R]Shelah. He was at
Chezib when she bore him. Num. 26:20
6 Then Judah took a wife for Er his firstborn, and her name *was* [R]Tamar. Ruth 4:12
7 But [R]Er, Judah's firstborn, was wicked in
the sight of the LORD, [R]and the LORD killed
him. Gen. 46:12 • 1 Chr. 2:3
8 And Judah said to Onan, "Go in to [R]your
brother's wife and marry her, and raise up an
heir to your brother." Deut. 25:5, 6
9 But Onan knew that the heir would not
be [R]his; and it came to pass, when he went in
to his brother's wife, that he emitted on the
ground, lest he should give an heir to his
brother. Deut. 25:6
10 And the thing which he did displeased
the LORD; therefore He killed him also.
11 Then Judah said to Tamar his daughter-
in-law, [R]"Remain a widow in your father's
house till my son Shelah is grown." For he
said, "Lest he also die as his brothers *did*."
And Tamar went and dwelt [R]in her father's
house. Ruth 1:12, 13 • Lev. 22:13
12 Now in the process of time the daughter
of Shua, Judah's wife, died; and Judah [R]was
comforted, and went up to his sheepshearers
at Timnah, he and his friend Hirah the Adullamite. 2 Sam. 13:39
13 And it was told Tamar, saying, "Look,
your father-in-law is going up [R]to Timnah to
shear his sheep." Josh. 15:10, 57
14 So she took off her widow's garments,
covered *herself* with a veil and wrapped
herself, and [R]sat in an open place which *was*
on the way to Timnah; for she saw [R]that
Shelah was grown, and she was not given to
him as a wife. Prov. 7:12 • Gen. 38:11, 26
15 When Judah saw her, he thought she
was a harlot, because she had covered her
face.
16 Then he turned to her by the way, and
said, "Please let me come in to you"; for he
did not know that she *was* his daughter-in-
law. So she said, "What will you give me, that
you may come in to me?"
17 And he said, "I will send *you* a young
goat from the flock." And she said, "Will you
give *me* a pledge till you send *it*?"
18 Then he said, "What pledge shall I give
you?" So she said, [R]"Your signet and cord,
and your staff that *is* in your hand." Then he
gave *them* to her, and went in to her, and she
conceived by him. Gen. 38:25; 41:42
19 So she arose and went away, and [R]laid
aside her veil and put on the garments of her
widowhood. Gen. 38:14
20 And Judah sent the young goat by the
hand of his friend the Adullamite, to receive
his pledge from the woman's hand, but he did
not find her.
21 Then he asked the men of that place,
saying, "Where is the harlot who *was* openly
by the roadside?" And they said, "There was
no harlot in this *place*."
22 And he returned to Judah and said, "I
cannot find her. Also, the men of the place
said there was no harlot in this *place*."
23 Then Judah said, "Let her take *them* for
herself, lest we be shamed; for I sent this
young goat and you have not found her."
24 And it came to pass, about three months
after, that Judah was told, saying, "Tamar
your daughter-in-law has [R]played the harlot;
furthermore she *is* [T]with child by harlotry."
So Judah said, "Bring her out [R]and let her be
burned!" Judg. 19:2 • *pregnant* • Lev. 20:14; 21:9
25 When she *was* brought out, she sent to
her father-in-law, saying, "By the man to
whom these belong, I *am* with child." And
she said, "Please determine whose these
are—the signet and cord, and staff."
26 So Judah acknowledged *them* and said,
"She has been more righteous than I, because
I did not give her to Shelah my son." And he
[R]never knew her again. Job 34:31, 32
27 Now it came to pass, at the time for
giving birth, that behold, twins *were* in her
womb.
28 And so it was, when she was giving birth,
that *the one* put out *his* hand; and the midwife took a scarlet *thread* and bound it on his
hand, saying, "This one came out first."
29 Then it happened, as he drew back his
hand, that his brother came out unexpectedly; and she said, "How did you break
through? *This* breach *be* upon you!" Therefore his name was called [R]Perez. Gen. 46:12
30 Afterward his brother came out who had
the scarlet *thread* on his hand. And his name
was called [R]Zerah. 1 Chr. 2:4

CHAPTER 39

Joseph's Test with the Egyptian Woman

NOW Joseph had been taken down to
Egypt. And Potiphar, an officer of
Pharaoh, captain of the guard, an Egyptian,

[R]bought him from the Ishmaelites who had
taken him down there. Gen. 37:28; 45:4
2 [R]The LORD was with Joseph, and he was
a successful man; and he was in the house of
his master the Egyptian. Acts 7:9
3 And his master saw that the LORD *was*
with him and that the LORD [R]made all he did
[T]to prosper in his hand. Ps. 1:3 • *to be a success*
4 So Joseph [R]found favor in his sight, and
served him. Then he made him [R]overseer of
his house, and all *that* he had he put in his
hand. Gen. 18:3; 19:19; 39:21 • Gen. 24:2, 10; 39:8, 22
5 So it was, from the time *that* he had
made him overseer of his house and all that
he had, that [R]the LORD blessed the Egyptian's
house for Joseph's sake; and the blessing of
the LORD was on all that he had in the house
and in the field. Gen. 18:26; 30:27
6 So he left all that he had in Joseph's
[T]hand, and he did not know what he had
except for the [T]bread which he ate. And
Joseph [R]was handsome in form and appearance. Care • Food • 1 Sam. 16:12
7 Now it came to pass after these things
that his master's wife cast longing eyes on
Joseph, and she said, "Lie with me."
8 But he refused and said to his master's
wife, "Look, my master does not know what
is with me in the house, and he has committed all that he has to my hand.
9 "*There is* no one greater in this house
than I, nor has he kept back anything from
me but you, because you *are* his wife. [R]How
then can I do this great wickedness, and [R]sin
against God?" Prov. 6:29, 32 • Ps. 51:4
10 So it was, as she spoke to Joseph day by
day, that he [R]did not heed her, to lie with her
or to be with her. Prov. 1:10
11 But it happened about this time, when
Joseph went into the house to do his work,
and none of the men of the house *was* inside,
12 that she caught him by his garment,
saying, "Lie with me." But he left his garment
in her hand, and fled and ran outside.
13 And so it was, when she saw that he had
left his garment in her hand and fled outside,
14 that she called to the men of her house
and spoke to them, saying, "See, he has
brought in to us a [R]Hebrew to [T]mock us. He
came in to me to lie with me, and I cried out
with a loud voice. Gen. 14:13; 41:12 • *laugh at*
15 "And it happened, when he heard that I
lifted my voice and cried out, that he left his
garment with me, and fled and went outside."
16 So she kept his garment with her until
his master came home.
17 Then she spoke to him with words like
these, saying, "The Hebrew servant whom
you brought to us came in to me to mock me;
18 "so it happened, as I lifted my voice and
cried out, that he left his garment with me
and fled outside."
19 So it was, when his master heard the
words which his wife spoke to him, saying,
"Your servant did to me after this manner,"
that his [R]anger was aroused. Prov. 6:34, 35
20 Then Joseph's master took him and [R]put
him into the [R]prison, a place where the king's
prisoners *were* confined. And he was there in
the prison. Ps. 105:18 • Gen. 40:3, 15; 41:14
21 But the LORD was with Joseph and
showed him mercy, and He gave him favor in
the sight of the keeper of the prison.
22 And the keeper of the prison [R]committed
to Joseph's hand all the prisoners who *were*
in the prison; whatever they did there, it was
his doing. Gen. 39:4; 40:3, 4
23 The keeper of the prison did not look
into anything *that was* under Joseph's hand,
because the LORD was with him; and whatever he did, the LORD made *it* prosper.

CHAPTER 40

Joseph's Test with the Egyptian Society

IT came to pass after these things *that* the
butler and the baker of the king of Egypt
offended their lord, the king of Egypt.
2 And Pharaoh was angry with his two
officers, the chief butler and the chief baker.
3 So he put them in custody in the house
of the captain of the guard, in the prison, the
place where Joseph *was* confined.
4 And the captain of the guard charged
Joseph with them, and he served them; so
they were in custody for a while.
5 Then the butler and the baker of the king
of Egypt, who *were* confined in the prison,
[R]dreamed a dream, both of them, each man's
dream in one night *and* each man's dream
with its *own* interpretation. Gen. 37:5; 41:1
6 And Joseph came in to them in the
morning and looked at them, and saw that
they *were* sad.
7 So he asked Pharaoh's officers who *were*
with him in the custody of his lord's house,
saying, "Why do you look so sad today?"
8 And they said to him, [R]"We each have
dreamed a dream, and *there is* no interpreter
of it." And Joseph said to them, [R]"Do not
interpretations belong to God? Tell *them* to
me, please." Gen. 41:15 • [Dan. 2:11, 20–22, 27, 28, 47]
9 Then the chief butler told his dream to
Joseph, and said to him, "Behold, in my
dream a vine *was* before me,
10 "and in the vine *were* three branches; it
was as though it budded, its blossoms shot
forth, and its clusters brought forth ripe
grapes.
11 "Then Pharaoh's cup *was* in my hand;
and I took the grapes and pressed them into
Pharaoh's cup, and placed the cup in Pharaoh's hand."
12 And Joseph said to him, [R]"This *is* the
interpretation of it: The three branches [R]*are*
three days. Dan. 2:36; 4:18, 19 • Gen. 40:18; 42:17
13 "Now within three days Pharaoh will [R]lift

up your head and restore you to your [T]place,
and you will put Pharaoh's cup in his hand
according to the former manner, when you
were his butler. 2 Kin. 25:27 • *position*
14 "But [R]remember me when it is well with
you, and [R]please show kindness to me; make
mention of me to Pharaoh, and get me out of
this house. Luke 23:42 • Josh. 2:12
15 "For indeed I was [R]stolen away from the
land of the Hebrews; [R]and also I have done
nothing here that they should put me into the
dungeon." Gen. 37:26–28 • Gen. 39:20
16 When the chief baker saw that the interpretation was good, he said to Joseph, "I also
was in my dream, and there *I had* three white
baskets on my head.
17 "In the uppermost basket *there were* all
kinds of baked goods for Pharaoh, and the
birds ate them out of the basket on my head."
18 So Joseph answered and said, [R]"This *is*
the interpretation of it: The three baskets *are*
three days. Gen. 40:12
19 "Within three days Pharaoh will lift off
your head from you and hang you on a tree;
and the birds will eat your flesh from you."
20 Now it came to pass on the third day,
which was Pharaoh's birthday, that he made
a feast for all his servants; and he lifted up
the head of the chief butler and of the chief
baker among his servants.
21 Then he [R]restored the chief butler to his
butlership again, and [R]he placed the cup in
Pharaoh's hand. Gen. 40:13 • Neh. 2:1
22 But he [R]hanged the chief baker, as
Joseph had interpreted to them. Gen. 40:19
23 Yet the chief butler did not remember
Joseph, but [R]forgot him. Eccl. 9:15, 16

CHAPTER 41

Joseph's Test with Pharaoh's Dreams

THEN it came to pass, at the end of two
full years, that [R]Pharaoh had a dream;
and behold, he stood by the river. Gen. 40:5
2 Suddenly there came up out of the river
seven cows, fine looking and fat; and they fed
in the meadow.
3 Then behold, seven other cows came up
after them out of the river, ugly and gaunt,
and stood by the *other* cows on the bank of
the river.
4 And the ugly and gaunt cows ate up the
seven fine looking and fat cows. So Pharaoh
awoke.
5 He slept and dreamed a second time; and
suddenly seven heads of grain came up on
one stalk, plump and good.
6 Then behold, seven thin heads, blighted
by the east wind, sprang up after them.
7 And the seven thin heads devoured the
seven plump and full heads. So Pharaoh
awoke, and indeed, *it was* a dream.
8 Now it came to pass in the morning that
his spirit was troubled, and he sent and called
for all the magicians of Egypt and all its [R]wise
men. And Pharaoh told them his dreams, but
there was no one who could interpret them
for Pharaoh. Matt. 2:1
9 Then the chief butler spoke to Pharaoh,
saying: "I remember my faults this day.
10 "When Pharaoh was [R]angry with his
servants, [R]and put me in custody in the house
of the captain of the guard, *both* me and the
chief baker, Gen. 40:2, 3 • Gen. 39:20
11 [R]"we each dreamed a dream in one night,
he and I. Each of us dreamed according to
the interpretation of his *own* dream. Gen. 40:5
12 "Now there *was* a young Hebrew man
with us there, a servant of the captain of the
guard. And we told him, and he [R]interpreted
our dreams for us; to each man he interpreted
according to his *own* dream. Gen. 40:12
13 "And it came to pass just [R]as he interpreted for us; so it happened. He restored me
to my office, and he hanged him." Gen. 40:21, 22
14 Then Pharaoh sent and called Joseph,
and they brought him hastily [R]out of the
dungeon; and he shaved, changed his clothing, and came to Pharaoh. [1 Sam. 2:8]
15 And Pharaoh said to Joseph, "I have
dreamed a dream, and *there is* no one who
can interpret it. [R]But I have heard it said of
you *that* you can understand a dream, to
interpret it." Dan. 5:16
16 So Joseph answered Pharaoh, saying,
[R]"*It is* not in me; [R]God will give Pharaoh an
answer of peace." Dan. 2:30 • Dan. 2:22, 28, 47
17 Then Pharaoh said to Joseph: "Behold, in
my dream I stood on the bank of the river.
18 "Suddenly seven cows came up out of
the river, fine looking and fat; and they fed in
the meadow.
19 "Then behold, seven other cows came up
after them, poor and very ugly and gaunt,
such ugliness as I have never seen in all the
land of Egypt.
20 "And the gaunt and ugly cows ate up the
first seven, the fat cows.
21 "When they had eaten them up, no one
would have known that they had eaten them,
for they *were* just as ugly as at the beginning.
So I awoke.
22 "Also I saw in my dream, and suddenly
seven [T]heads came up on one stalk, full and
good. Heads of grain
23 "Then behold, seven heads, withered,
thin, *and* blighted by the east wind, sprang up
after them.
24 "And the thin heads devoured the seven
good heads. So [R]I told *this* to the magicians,
but *there was* no one who could explain *it* to
me." Is. 8:19
25 Then Joseph said to Pharaoh, "The
dreams of Pharaoh *are* one; [R]God has shown
Pharaoh what He *is* about to do: Dan. 2:28, 29, 45
26 "The seven good cows *are* seven years,

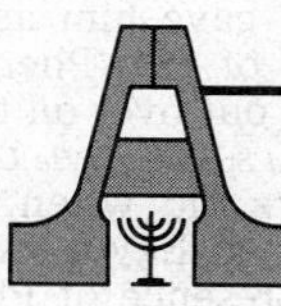

OLD TESTAMENT VISIONS

In Old Testament times, God often used dreams (when a person was asleep) and visions (when a person was awake) to make His will known. The Egyptian Pharaoh's dream could not be interpreted by his magicians. But Joseph told him that it referred to a forthcoming period of famine in the land (Gen. 41).

Does God still speak through dreams and visions today? Interpreters and scholars are divided on this question. Some believe God has no need to speak through dreams, since His Holy Spirit is now available to instruct us in God's will. But others believe just as strongly that dreams are still means of God's revelation.

Joel, one of the minor prophets, foresaw the outpouring of the Spirit of God on believers as a time when "your old men shall dream dreams, your young men shall see visions" (Joel 2:28). This prophecy was fulfilled with the outpouring of God's Spirit at Pentecost (Acts 2:14–21). Other significant dreams and visions in the Old Testament include the following:

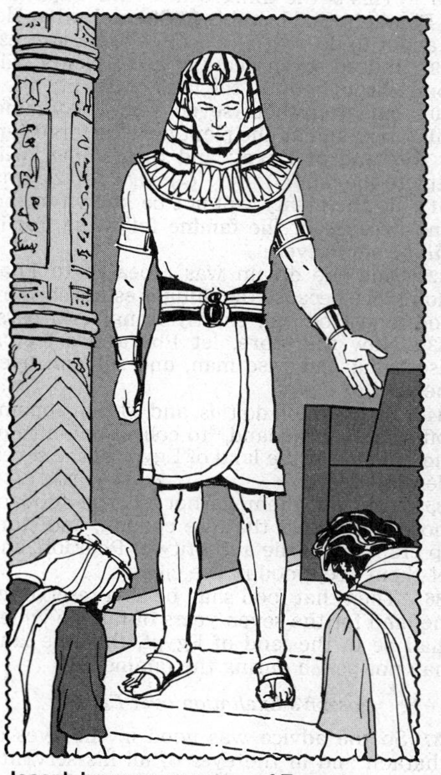

Joseph became governor of Egypt in fulfillment of his dream that he would become prominent over his brothers.

Personality	Message of Dream or Vision	Biblical Reference
	DREAMS	
Jacob	Assurance of God's covenant	Gen. 28:10–15
Joseph	Joseph's future prominence over his brothers	Gen. 37:1–11
Solomon	Assurance of God's wisdom	1 Kin. 3:5–10
	VISIONS	
Jacob	Instructed to go to Egypt	Gen. 46:2–4
Isaiah	A revelation to God's holiness	Is. 6:1–8
Ezekiel	God's promise to restore His people Israel	Ezek. 37
Daniel	The great world powers to come and the glories of Christ	Dan. 7; 8 Dan. 10:5–9

and the seven good [T]heads *are* seven years;
the dreams *are* one. Heads of grain
27 "And the seven thin and ugly cows
which came up after them *are* seven years,
and the seven empty heads blighted by the
east wind are [R]seven years of famine. 2 Kin. 8:1
28 [R]"This *is* the thing which I have spoken
to Pharaoh. God has shown Pharaoh what He
is about to do. [Gen. 41:25, 32]
29 "Indeed seven years of great plenty will
come throughout all the land of Egypt;
30 "but after them seven years of famine
will [R]arise, and all the plenty will be forgotten
in the land of Egypt; and the famine [R]will
deplete the land. Gen. 41:54, 56 • Gen. 47:13
31 "So the plenty will not be known in the
land because of the famine following, for it
will be very severe.
32 "And the dream was repeated to Pharaoh twice because the thing *is* established by
God, and God will shortly bring it to pass.
33 "Now therefore, let Pharaoh select a
discerning and wise man, and set him over
the land of Egypt.
34 "Let Pharaoh do *this*, and let him appoint
[T]officers over the land, [R]to collect one-fifth *of
the produce* of the land of Egypt in the seven
plentiful years. *overseers* • [Prov. 6:6–8]
35 "And let them gather all the food of
those good years that are coming, and store
up grain under the authority of Pharaoh, and
let them keep food in the cities.
36 "Then that food shall be as a reserve for
the land for the seven years of famine which
shall be in the land of Egypt, that the land
may not perish during the famine."

Joseph's Exaltation over Egypt

37 So the advice was good in the eyes of
Pharaoh and in the eyes of all his servants.
38 And Pharaoh said to his servants, "Can
we find *such a one* as this, a man [R]in whom *is*
the Spirit of God?" Num. 27:18
39 Then Pharaoh said to Joseph, "Inasmuch
as God has shown you all this, *there is* no one
as discerning and wise as you.
40 [R]"You shall be [T]over my house, and all
my people shall be ruled according to your
word; only in regard to the throne will I be
greater than you." Ps. 105:21 • In charge of
41 And Pharaoh said to Joseph, "See, I have
[R]set you over all the land of Egypt." Dan. 6:3
42 Then Pharaoh [R]took his signet ring off
his hand and put it on Joseph's hand; and he
clothed him in garments of fine linen and put
a gold chain around his neck. Esth. 3:10
43 And he had him ride in the second
chariot which he had; [R]and they cried out
before him, "Bow the knee!" So he set him
[R]over all the land of Egypt. Esth. 6:9 • Gen. 42:6
44 Pharaoh also said to Joseph, "I *am* Pharaoh, and without your consent no man may
lift his hand or foot in all the land of Egypt."
45 And Pharaoh called Joseph's name
[T]Zaphnath-Paaneah. And he gave him as a
wife Asenath, the daughter of Poti-Pherah
priest of On. So Joseph went out over *all* the
land of Egypt. Probably means *God Speaks and He Lives*
46 Joseph was thirty years old when he
[R]stood before Pharaoh king of Egypt. And
Joseph went out from the presence of Pharaoh, and went throughout all the land of
Egypt. 1 Sam. 16:21
47 Now in the seven plentiful years the
ground brought forth abundantly.
48 So he gathered up all the food of the
seven years which were in the land of Egypt,
and laid up the food in the cities; he laid up in
every city the food of the fields which surrounded them.
49 Joseph gathered very much grain, [R]as the
sand of the sea, until he stopped counting, for
it was without number. Gen. 22:17
50 [R]And to Joseph were born two sons before the years of famine came, whom Asenath, the daughter of Poti-Pherah priest of
On, bore to him. Gen. 46:20; 48:5
51 Joseph called the name of the firstborn
Manasseh: "For God has made me forget all
my toil and all my [R]father's house." Ps. 45:10
52 And the name of the second he called
Ephraim: "For God has caused me to be
fruitful in the land of my affliction."
53 Then the seven years of plenty which
were in the land of Egypt ended,
54 [R]and the seven years of famine began to
come, [R]as Joseph had said. The famine was in
all lands, but in all the land of Egypt there
was bread. Acts 7:11 • Gen. 41:30
55 So when all the land of Egypt was famished, the people cried to Pharaoh for bread.
Then Pharaoh said to all the Egyptians, "Go
to Joseph; whatever he says to you, do."
56 The famine was over all the face of the
earth, and Joseph opened all the storehouses
and [R]sold to the Egyptians. And the famine
became severe in the land of Egypt. Gen. 42:6
57 [R]So all countries came to Joseph in Egypt
to [R]buy *grain*, because the famine was severe
in all lands. Ezek. 29:12 • Gen. 27:28, 37; 42:3

CHAPTER 42

Joseph's Brothers Visit Egypt

WHEN [R]Jacob saw that there was grain
in Egypt, Jacob said to his sons, "Why
do you look at one another?" Acts 7:12
2 And he said, "Indeed I have heard that
there is grain in Egypt; go down to that place
and buy for us there, that we may [R]live and
not die." Gen. 43:8
3 So Joseph's ten brothers went down to
buy grain in Egypt.
4 But Jacob did not send Joseph's brother
Benjamin with his brothers, for he said,
[R]"Lest some calamity befall him." Gen. 42:38

5 And the sons of Israel went to buy *grain*
among those who journeyed, for the famine
was [R]in the land of Canaan. Acts 7:11
6 Now Joseph *was* governor [R]over the
land; and it was he who sold to all the people
of the land. And Joseph's brothers came and
[R]bowed down before him with *their* faces to
the earth. Gen. 41:41, 55 • Gen. 37:7–10; 41:43
7 Joseph saw his brothers and recognized
them, but he acted as a stranger to them and
spoke roughly to them. Then he said to them,
"Where do you come from?" And they said,
"From the land of Canaan to buy food."
8 So Joseph recognized his brothers, but
they did not recognize him.
9 Then Joseph remembered the dreams
which he had dreamed about them, and said
to them, "You *are* spies! You have come to
see the [T]nakedness of the land!" Exposed parts
10 And they said to him, "No, my lord, but
your servants have come to buy food.
11 "We *are* all one man's sons; we *are*
honest *men*; your servants are not spies."
12 But he said to them, "No, but you have
come to see the nakedness of the land."
13 And they said, "Your servants *are* twelve
brothers, the sons of one man in the land of
Canaan; and in fact, the youngest *is* with our
father today, and one [R]*is* no more." Gen. 37:30
14 But Joseph said to them, "It *is* as I spoke
to you, saying, 'You *are* spies!'
15 "In this *manner* you shall be tested: [R]By
the life of Pharaoh, you shall not leave this
place unless your youngest brother comes
here. I Sam. 1:26; 17:55
16 "Send one of you, and let him bring your
brother; and you shall be [T]kept in prison, that
your words may be tested to see whether
there is any truth in you; or else, by the life of
Pharaoh, surely you *are* spies!" Lit. *bound*
17 So he [T]put them all together in prison
[R]three days. Lit. *gathered* • Gen. 40:4, 7, 12
18 Then Joseph said to them the third day,
"Do this and live, [R]*for* I fear God: Lev. 25:43
19 "If you *are* honest *men*, let one of your
brothers be confined to your prison house;
but you, go and carry grain for the famine of
your houses.
20 "And [R]bring your youngest brother to
me; so your words will be verified, and you
shall not die." And they did so. Gen. 44:18–34
21 Then they said to one another, "We *are*
truly guilty concerning our brother, for we
saw the anguish of his soul when he pleaded
with us, and we would not hear; [R]therefore
this distress has come upon us." Prov. 21:13
22 And Reuben answered them, saying,
[R]"Did I not speak to you, saying, 'Do not sin
against the boy'; and you would not listen?
Therefore behold, his blood is now [R]required
of us." Gen. 37:21, 22, 29 • Gen. 9:5, 6
23 But they did not know that Joseph understood *them*, for he spoke to them through
an interpreter.
24 And he turned himself away from them
and wept. Then he returned to them again,
and talked with them. And he took Simeon
from them and bound him before their eyes.
25 Then Joseph [R]gave a command to fill
their sacks with grain, to [R]restore every
man's money to his sack, and to give them
provisions for the journey. [R]Thus he did for
them. Gen. 44:1 • Gen. 43:12 • [Rom. 12:17, 20, 21]
26 So they loaded their donkeys with the
grain and departed from there.
27 But as [R]one *of them* opened his sack to
give his donkey feed at the encampment, he
saw his money; and there it was, in the
mouth of his sack. Gen. 43:21, 22
28 So he said to his brothers, "My money
has been restored, and there it is, in my
sack!" Then their hearts [T]failed *them* and
they were afraid, saying to one another,
"What *is* this *that* God has done to us?" *sank*
29 Then they went to Jacob their father in
the land of Canaan and told him all that had
happened to them, saying:
30 "The man *who is* lord of the land [R]spoke
roughly to us, and took us for spies of the
country. Gen. 42:7
31 "But we said to him, 'We *are* honest
men; we are not spies.
32 'We *are* twelve brothers, sons of our
father; one *is* no *more*, and the youngest *is*
with our father this day in the land of Canaan.'
33 "Then the man, the lord of the country,
said to us, [R]'By this I will know that you *are*
honest *men*: Leave one of your brothers *here*
with me, take *food for* the famine of your
households, and be gone. Gen. 42:15, 19, 20
34 'And bring your [R]youngest brother to
me; so I shall know that you *are* not spies,
but *that* you *are* honest *men*. *And* I will
deliver your brother to you, and you may
[R]trade in the land.'" Gen. 42:20; 43:3, 5 • Gen. 34:10
35 Then it happened as they emptied their
sacks, that surprisingly [R]each man's bundle of
money *was* in his sack; and when *both* they
and their father saw the bundles of money,
they were afraid. Gen. 43:12, 15, 21
36 And Jacob their father said to them,
"You have [R]bereaved me *of my children*:
Joseph is no *more*, Simeon is no *more*, and
you want to take [R]Benjamin *away*. All these
things are against me." Gen. 43:14 • [Rom. 8:28, 31]
37 Then Reuben spoke to his father, saying,
"Kill my two sons if I do not bring him *back*
to you; put him in my hands, and I will bring
him back to you."
38 But he said, "My son shall not go down
with you, for his brother is dead, and he is left
alone. [R]If any calamity should befall him
along the way in which you go, then you
would [R]bring down my gray hair with sorrow
to the grave." Gen. 42:4; 44:29 • Gen. 37:35; 44:31

CHAPTER 43

Joseph's Brothers' Second Journey to Egypt

NOW the famine *was* severe in the land.
2 And it came to pass, when they had
eaten up the grain which they had brought
from Egypt, that their father said to them,
"Go [R]back, buy us a little food." Gen. 42:2; 44:25
3 But Judah spoke to him, saying, "The
man solemnly warned us, saying, 'You shall
not see my face unless your [R]brother *is* with
you.' " Gen. 42:20; 43:5; 44:23
4 "If you send our brother with us, we will
go down and buy you food.
5 "But if you will not send *him*, we will not
go down; for the man said to us, 'You shall
not see my face unless your brother *is* with
you.' "
6 And Israel said, "Why did you deal *so*
wrongfully with me *as* to tell the man
whether you had still *another* brother?"
7 But they said, "The man asked us pointedly about ourselves and our kindred, saying,
'*Is* your father still alive? Have you *another*
brother?' And we told him according to these
words. Could we possibly have known that
he would say, 'Bring your brother down'?"
8 Then Judah said to Israel his father,
"Send the lad with me, and we will arise and
go, that we may [R]live and not die, both we
and you *and* also our little ones. Gen. 42:2; 47:19
9 "I myself will be surety for him; from my
hand you shall require him. [R]If I do not bring
him *back* to you and set him before you, then
let me bear the blame forever. Gen. 42:37; 44:32
10 "For if we had not lingered, surely by
now we would have returned this second
time."
11 And their father Israel said to them, "If *it*
must be so, then do this: Take some of the
best fruits of the land in your vessels and
carry down a present for the man—a little
[R]balm and a little honey, spices and myrrh,
pistachio nuts and almonds. Jer. 8:22
12 "Take double money in your hand, and
take back in your hand the money [R]that was
returned in the mouth of your sacks; perhaps
it was an oversight. Gen. 42:25, 35; 43:21, 22
13 "Take your brother also, and arise, go
back to the man.
14 "And may God Almighty [R]give you
mercy before the man, that he may release
your other brother and Benjamin. [R]If I am
bereaved, I am bereaved!" Ps. 106:46 • Esth. 4:16
15 So the men took that present and Benjamin, and they took double money in their
hand, and arose and went [R]down to Egypt;
and they stood before Joseph. Gen. 39:1; 46:3, 6
16 When Joseph saw Benjamin with them,
he said to the steward of his house, "Take
these men to my home, and slaughter [T]an
animal and make ready; for *these* men will
dine with me at noon." Lit. *a slaughter*
17 Then the man did as Joseph ordered, and
the man brought the men into Joseph's
house.
18 Now the men were afraid because they
were brought into Joseph's house; and they
said, "*It is* because of the money, which was
returned in our sacks the first time, that we
are brought in, so that he may seek [R]an
occasion against us and fall upon us, to take
us as slaves with our donkeys." Judg. 14:4
19 When they drew near to the steward of
Joseph's house, they talked with him at the
door of the house,
20 and said, "O sir, [R]we indeed came down
the first time to buy food; Gen. 42:3, 10
21 "but [R]it happened, when we came to the
encampment, that we opened our sacks, and
there, *each* man's money *was* in the mouth of
his sack, our money in full weight; so we
have brought it back in our hand. Gen. 42:27, 35
22 "And we have brought down other
money in our hands to buy food. We do not
know who put our money in our sacks."
23 But he said, "Peace *be* with you, do not
be afraid. Your God and the God of your
father has given you treasure in your sacks; I
had your money." Then he brought [R]Simeon
out to them. Gen. 42:24
24 So the man brought the men into Joseph's house and [R]gave *them* water, and they
washed their feet; and he gave their donkeys
feed. Gen. 18:4; 19:2; 24:32
25 Then they made the present ready for
Joseph's coming at noon, for they heard that
they would eat bread there.
26 And when Joseph came home, they
brought him the present which *was* in their
hand into the house, and [R]bowed down before
him to the earth. Gen. 37:7, 10; 42:6; 44:14
27 Then he asked them about *their* well-
being, and said, "*Is* your father well, the old
man of whom you spoke? *Is* he still alive?"
28 And they answered, "Your servant our
father *is* in good health; he *is* still alive." [R]And
they bowed their heads down and prostrated
themselves. Gen. 37:7, 10
29 Then he lifted his eyes and saw his
brother Benjamin, his mother's son, and said,
"*Is* this your younger brother [R]of whom you
spoke to me?" And he said, "God be gracious
to you, my son." Gen. 42:13
30 Now [R]his heart yearned for his brother;
so Joseph made haste and sought *somewhere*
to weep. And he went into *his* chamber and
[R]wept there. 1 Kin. 3:26 • Gen. 42:24; 45:2, 14, 15; 46:29
31 Then he washed his face and came out;
and he restrained himself, and said, "Serve
the [R]bread." Gen. 43:25
32 So they set him a place by himself, and
them by themselves, and the Egyptians who
ate with him by themselves; because the
Egyptians could not eat food with the [R]He-
brews, for that *is* [R]an abomination to the
Egyptians. Gen. 41:12 • Gen. 46:34

33 And they sat before him, the firstborn
according to his [R]birthright and the youngest
according to his youth; and the men looked
in astonishment at one another. Gen. 27:36; 42:7
34 Then he took servings to them from
before him, but Benjamin's serving was [R]five
times as much as any of theirs. So they drank
and were merry with him. Gen. 45:22

CHAPTER 44

AND he commanded the steward of his
house, saying, "Fill the men's sacks
with food, as much as they can carry, and put
each man's money in the mouth of his sack.
2 "Also put my cup, the silver cup, in the
mouth of the sack of the youngest, and his
grain money." So he did according to the
word that Joseph had spoken.
3 As soon as the morning dawned, the men
were sent away, they and their donkeys.
4 *And* when they had gone out of the city,
and were not *yet* far off, Joseph said to his
steward, "Get up, follow the men; and when
you overtake them, say to them, 'Why have
you [R]repaid evil for good? 1 Sam. 25:21
5 '*Is* not this *the one* from which my lord
drinks, and with which he indeed practices
divination? You have done evil in so doing.' "
6 So he overtook them, and he spoke to
them these same words.
7 And they said to him, "Why does my lord
say these words? Far be it from us that your
servants should do such a thing.
8 "Look, we brought back to you from the
land of Canaan the money which we found in
the mouth of our sacks. How then could we
steal silver or gold from your lord's house?
9 "With whomever of your servants it is
found, [R]let him die, and we also will be my
lord's slaves." Gen. 31:32
10 And he said, "Now also *let* it *be* according to your words; he with whom it is found
shall be my slave, and you shall be blameless."
11 Then each man speedily let down his
sack to the ground, and each opened his sack.
12 So he searched, *and* he began with the
oldest and [T]left off with the youngest; and the
cup was found in Benjamin's sack. *finished with*
13 Then they [R]tore their clothes, and each
man loaded his donkey and returned to the
city. 2 Sam. 1:11
14 So Judah and his brothers came to Joseph's house, and he *was* still there; and they
[R]fell before him on the ground. Gen. 37:7, 10
15 And Joseph said to them, "What deed *is*
this you have done? Did you not know that
such a man as I can certainly practice divination?"
16 Then Judah said, "What shall we say to
my lord? What shall we speak? Or how shall
we clear ourselves? God has [R]found out the
iniquity of your servants; here [R]we are, my
lord's slaves, both we and *he* also with whom
the cup was found." [Num. 32:23] • Gen. 44:9
17 But he said, "Far be it from me that I
should do so; *but* the man in whose hand the
cup was found, he shall be my slave. And as
for you, go up in peace to your father."
18 Then Judah came near to him and said:
"O my lord, please let your servant speak a
word in my lord's hearing, and [R]do not let
your anger burn against your servant; for
you *are* even like Pharaoh. Ex. 32:22
19 "My lord asked his servants, saying,
'Have you a father or a brother?'
20 "And we said to my lord, 'We have a
father, an old man, and a child of *his* old age,
who is young; his brother is dead, and he
[R]alone is left of his mother's children, and his
[R]father loves him.' Gen. 46:19 • Gen. 42:4
21 "Then you said to your servants, [R]'Bring
him down to me, that I may set my eyes on
him.' Gen. 42:15, 20
22 "And we said to my lord, 'The lad cannot
leave his father, for *if* he should leave his
father, *his father* would die.'
23 "But you said to your servants, [R]'Unless
your youngest brother comes down with you,
you shall see my face no more.' Gen. 43:3, 5
24 "So it was, when we went up to your
servant my father, that we told him the
words of my lord.
25 "And [R]our father said, 'Go back *and* buy
us a little food.' Gen. 43:2
26 "But we said, 'We cannot go down; if our
youngest brother is with us, then we will go
down; for we may not see the man's face
unless our youngest brother *is* with us.'
27 "Then your servant my father said to us,
'You know that my wife bore me two sons;
28 'and the one went out from me, and I
said, [R]"Surely he is torn to pieces"; and I have
not seen him since. Gen. 37:31-35
29 'But if you take this one also from me,
and calamity befalls him, you shall bring
down my gray hair with sorrow to the grave.'
30 "Now therefore, when I come to your
servant my father, and the lad *is* not with us,
since his life is bound up in the lad's life,
31 "it will happen, when he sees that the lad
is not *with us*, that he will die. So your
servants will bring down the gray hair of
your servant our father with sorrow to the
grave.
32 "For your servant became surety for the
lad to my father, saying, [R]'If I do not bring
him *back* to you, then I shall bear the blame
before my father forever.' Gen. 43:9
33 "Now therefore, please let your servant
remain instead of the lad as a slave to my
lord, and let the lad go up with his brothers.
34 "For how shall I go up to my father if the
lad *is* not with me, lest perhaps I see the evil
that would [T]come upon my father?" Lit. *find*

CHAPTER 45

THEN Joseph could not restrain himself
before all those who stood by him, and he
cried out, "Make everyone go out from me!"
So no one stood with him [R]while Joseph made
himself known to his brothers. Acts 7:13
2 And he wept aloud, and the Egyptians
and the house of Pharaoh heard *it*.
3 Then Joseph said to his brothers, [R]"I *am*
Joseph; does my father still live?" But his
brothers could not answer him, for they were
dismayed in his presence. Acts 7:13
4 And Joseph said to his brothers, "Please
come near to me." And they came near. And
he said: "I *am* Joseph your brother, [R]whom
you sold into Egypt. Gen. 37:28; 39:1
5 "But now, do not therefore be grieved or
angry with yourselves because you sold me
here; [R]for God sent me before you to preserve
life. Gen. 45:7, 8; 50:20
6 "For these two years the [R]famine *has
been* in the land, and *there are* still five years
in which *there will be* neither plowing nor
harvesting. Gen. 43:1; 47:4, 13
7 "And God sent me before you to preserve
a posterity for you in the earth, and to save
your lives by a great deliverance.
8 "So now *it was* not you *who* sent me
here, but God; and He has made me a father
to Pharaoh, and lord of all his house, and a
ruler throughout all the land of Egypt.
9 "Hasten and go up to my father, and say
to him, 'Thus says your son Joseph: "God has
made me lord of all Egypt; come down to me,
do not [T]tarry. *delay*
10 "You shall dwell in the land of Goshen,
and you shall be near to me, you and your
children, your children's children, your flocks
and your herds, and all that you have.
11 "There I will [R]provide for you, lest you
and your household, and all that you have,
come to poverty; for *there are* still five years
of famine." ' Gen. 47:12
12 "And behold, your eyes and the eyes of
my brother Benjamin see that *it is* [R]my
mouth that speaks to you. Gen. 42:23
13 "So you shall tell my father of all my
glory in Egypt, and of all that you have seen;
and you shall hasten and [R]bring my father
down here." Acts 7:14
14 Then he fell on his brother Benjamin's
neck and wept, and Benjamin wept on his
neck.
15 Moreover he [R]kissed all his brothers and
wept over them, and after that his brothers
talked with him. Gen. 48:10
16 Now the report of it was heard in Pharaoh's house, saying, "Joseph's brothers have
come." So it pleased Pharaoh and his servants well.
17 And Pharaoh said to Joseph, "Say to
your brothers, 'Do this: Load your beasts and
depart; go to the land of Canaan.
18 'Bring your father and your households
and come to me; I will give you the best of
the land of Egypt, and you will eat [R]the [T]fat of
the land. Gen. 27:28; 47:6 • The choicest produce
19 'Now you are commanded—do this: Take
carts out of the land of Egypt for your little
ones and your wives; bring your father and
come.
20 'Also do not be concerned about your
goods, for the best of all the land of Egypt *is*
yours.' "
21 Then the sons of Israel did so; and
Joseph gave them [R]carts, according to the
command of Pharaoh, and he gave them
provisions for the journey. Gen. 45:19; 46:5
22 He gave to all of them, to each man,
[R]changes of garments; but to Benjamin he
gave three hundred *pieces* of silver and [R]five
changes of garments. 2 Kin. 5:5 • Gen. 43:34
23 And he sent to his father these *things*:
ten donkeys loaded with the good things of
Egypt, and ten female donkeys loaded with
grain, bread, and food for his father for the
journey.
24 So he sent his brothers away, and they
departed; and he said to them, "See that you
do not become troubled along the way."
25 Then they went up out of Egypt, and
came to the land of Canaan to Jacob their
father.
26 And they told him, saying, "Joseph *is* still
alive, and he *is* governor over all the land of
Egypt." [R]And Jacob's heart stood still, because he did not believe them. Job 29:24
27 But when they told him all the words
which Joseph had said to them, and when he
saw the carts which Joseph had sent to carry
him, the spirit of Jacob their father revived.
28 Then Israel said, "*It is* enough. Joseph
my son *is* still alive. I will go and see him
before I die."

CHAPTER 46

Jacob's Family Safe in Egypt

SO Israel took his journey with all that
he had, and came to [R]Beersheba, and
offered sacrifices to the God of his father
Isaac. Gen. 21:31, 33; 26:32, 33; 28:10
2 Then God spoke to Israel [R]in the visions
of the night, and said, "Jacob, Jacob!" And he
said, "Here I am." Gen. 15:1; 22:11; 31:11
3 And He said, "I *am* God, the God of your
father; do not fear to go down to Egypt, for I
will make of you a great nation there.
4 "I will go down with you to Egypt, and I
will also surely bring you up *again*; and
Joseph *will put his hand on your eyes."
5 Then Jacob arose from Beersheba; and
the sons of Israel carried their father Jacob,

46:4 Joseph would close Jacob's eyes in death.

their little ones, and their wives, in the carts which Pharaoh had sent to carry him.

6 So they took their livestock and their goods, which they had acquired in the land of Canaan, and went to Egypt, [R]Jacob and all his descendants with him. Deut. 26:5

7 His sons and his sons' sons, his daughters and his sons' daughters, and all his descendants he brought with him to Egypt.

8 Now these *were* the names of the children of Israel, Jacob and his sons, who went to Egypt: Reuben *was* Jacob's firstborn.

9 The [R]sons of Reuben *were* Hanoch, Pallu, Hezron, and Carmi. Ex. 6:14

10 [R]The sons of Simeon *were* Jemuel, Jamin, Ohad, Jachin, Zohar, and Shaul, the son of a Canaanite woman. Ex. 6:15

11 The sons of [R]Levi *were* Gershon, Kohath, and Merari. 1 Chr. 6:1, 16

12 The sons of Judah *were* Er, Onan, Shelah, Perez, and Zerah (but Er and Onan died in the land of Canaan). [R]The sons of Perez were Hezron and Hamul. Gen. 38:29

13 The sons of Issachar *were* Tola, Puvah, Job, and Shimron.

14 The [R]sons of Zebulun *were* Sered, Elon, and Jahleel. Num. 26:26

15 These *were* the [R]sons of Leah, whom she bore to Jacob in Padan Aram, with his daughter Dinah. All the persons, his sons and his daughters, *were* thirty-three. Gen. 35:23; 49:31

16 The sons of Gad *were* *Ziphion, Haggi, Shuni, *Ezbon, Eri, *Arodi, and Areli.

17 The sons of Asher *were* Jimnah, Ishuah, Isui, Beriah, and Serah, their sister. And the sons of Beriah *were* Heber and Malchiel.

18 These *were* the sons of Zilpah, [R]whom Laban gave to Leah his daughter; and these she bore to Jacob: sixteen persons. Gen. 29:24

19 The [R]sons of Rachel, [R]Jacob's wife, *were* Joseph and Benjamin. Gen. 35:24 • Gen. 44:27

20 [R]And to Joseph in the land of Egypt were born Manasseh and Ephraim, whom Asenath, the daughter of Poti-Pherah priest of On, bore to him. Gen. 41:45, 50–52; 48:1

21 The sons of Benjamin *were* Belah, Becher, Ashbel, Gera, Naaman, Ehi, Rosh, [R]Muppim, Huppim, and Ard. Num. 26:38, 39

22 These *were* the sons of Rachel, who were born to Jacob: fourteen persons in all.

23 The son of Dan *was* Hushim.

24 [R]The sons of Naphtali *were* Jahzeel, Guni, Jezer, and Shillem. Num. 26:48

25 These *were* the sons of Bilhah, whom Laban gave to Rachel his daughter, and she bore these to Jacob: seven persons in all.

26 [R]All the persons who went with Jacob to Egypt, who came from his body, [R]besides Jacob's sons' wives, *were* sixty-six persons in all. Ex. 1:5 • Gen. 35:11

27 And the sons of Joseph who were born to him in Egypt *were* two persons. [R]All the persons of the house of Jacob who went to Egypt were seventy. Deut. 10:22

28 Then he sent Judah before him to Joseph, [R]to point out before him *the way* to Goshen. And they came [R]to the land of Goshen. Gen. 31:21 • Gen. 47:1

29 So Joseph made ready his chariot and went up to Goshen to meet his father Israel; and he presented himself to him, and fell on his neck and wept on his neck a good while.

30 And Israel said to Joseph, [R]"Now let me die, since I have seen your face, because you *are* still alive." Luke 2:29, 30

31 Then Joseph said to his brothers and to his father's household, [R]"I will go up and tell Pharaoh, and say to him, 'My brothers and those of my father's house, who *were* in the land of Canaan, have come to me. Gen. 47:1

32 'And the men *are* [R]shepherds, for their occupation has been to feed livestock; and they have brought their flocks, their herds, and all that they have.' Gen. 47:3

33 "So it shall be, when Pharaoh calls you and says, 'What is your occupation?'

34 "that you shall say, 'Your servants' [R]occupation has been with livestock from our youth even till now, both we *and* also our fathers,' that you may dwell in the land of Goshen; for every shepherd *is* [R]an abomination to the Egyptians." Gen. 47:3 • Gen. 43:32

CHAPTER 47

THEN Joseph went and told Pharaoh, and said, "My father and my brothers, their flocks and their herds and all that they possess, have come from the land of Canaan; and indeed they *are* in the land of Goshen."

2 And he took five men from among his brothers and presented them to Pharaoh.

3 Then Pharaoh said to his brothers, "What *is* your occupation?" And they said to Pharaoh, [R]"Your servants *are* shepherds, both we *and* also our fathers." Gen. 46:32, 34

4 And they said to Pharaoh, [R]"We have come to sojourn in the land, because your servants have no pasture for their flocks, for the famine *is* severe in the land of Canaan. Now therefore, please let your servants dwell in the land of Goshen." Deut. 26:5

5 Then Pharaoh spoke to Joseph, saying, "Your father and your brothers have come to you.

6 "The land of Egypt *is* before you. Have your father and brothers dwell in the best of the land; let them dwell [R]in the land of Goshen. And if you know *any* competent men among them, then make them chief herdsmen over my livestock." Gen. 47:4

7 Then Joseph brought in his father Jacob and set him before Pharaoh; and Jacob [R]blessed Pharaoh. Gen. 47:10; 48:15, 20

46:16 Sam., LXX *Zephon* and Num. 26:15
46:16 *Ozni*, Num. 26:16 **46:16** *Arod*, Num. 26:17

8 Pharaoh said to Jacob, "How old *are*
you?"
9 And Jacob said to Pharaoh, "The days of
the years of my [T]pilgrimage *are* one hundred
and thirty years; [R]few and evil have been the
days of the years of my life, and they have
not attained to the days of the years of the
life of my fathers in the days of their pilgrimage." Lit. *sojourning* • [Job 14:1]
10 So Jacob [R]blessed Pharaoh, and went out
from before Pharaoh. Gen. 47:7
11 And Joseph situated his father and his
brothers, and gave them a possession in the
land of Egypt, in the best of the land, in the
land of [R]Rameses, [R]as Pharaoh had commanded. Ex. 1:11; 12:37 • Gen. 47:6, 27
12 Then Joseph provided [R]his father, his
brothers, and all his father's household with
bread, according to the number in *their*
families. Gen. 45:11; 50:21
13 Now *there was* no bread in all the land;
for the famine *was* very severe, [R]so that the
land of Egypt and *all* the land of Canaan
languished because of the famine. Gen. 41:30
14 [R]And Joseph gathered up all the money
that was found in the land of Egypt and in
the land of Canaan, for the grain which they
bought; and Joseph brought the money into
Pharaoh's house. Gen. 41:56; 42:6
15 So when the money failed in the land of
Egypt and in the land of Canaan, all the
Egyptians came to Joseph and said, "Give us
bread, for [R]why should we die in your presence? For the money has failed." Gen. 47:19
16 Then Joseph said, "Give your livestock,
and I will give you *bread* for your livestock, if
the money is gone."
17 So they brought their livestock to
Joseph, and Joseph gave them bread *in exchange* for the horses, the flocks, the cattle of
the herds, and for the donkeys. Thus he [T]fed
them with bread *in exchange* for all their
livestock that year. *supplied*
18 When that year had ended, they came to
him the next year and said to him, "We will
not hide from my lord that our money is
gone; my lord also has our herds of livestock.
There is nothing left in the sight of my lord
but our bodies and our lands.
19 "Why should we die before your eyes,
both we and our land? Buy us and our land
for bread, and we and our land will be servants of Pharaoh; give *us* seed, that we may
[R]live and not die, that the land may not be
desolate." Gen. 43:8
20 Then Joseph [R]bought all the land of
Egypt for Pharaoh; for every man of the
Egyptians sold his field, because the famine
was severe upon them. So the land became
Pharaoh's. Jer. 32:43
21 And as for the people, he moved them
into the cities, from *one* end of the borders of
Egypt to the *other* end.
22 [R]Only the land of the [R]priests he did not
buy; for the priests had rations *allotted to
them* by Pharaoh, and they ate their rations
which Pharaoh gave them; therefore they did
not sell their lands. Ezra 7:24 • Gen. 41:45
23 Then Joseph said to the people, "Indeed I
have bought you and your land this day for
Pharaoh. Look, *here is* seed for you, and you
shall sow the land.
24 "And it shall come to pass in the harvest
that you shall give one-fifth to Pharaoh.
Four-fifths shall be your own, as seed for the
field and for your food, for those of your
households and as food for your little ones."
25 So they said, "You have saved [R]our lives;
let us find favor in the sight of my lord, and
we will be Pharaoh's servants." Gen. 33:15
26 And Joseph made it a law over the land
of Egypt to this day, *that* Pharaoh should
have one-fifth, except for the land of the
priests only, *which* did not become Pharaoh's.

Jacob Blesses the Family in Egypt

27 So Israel [R]dwelt in the land of Egypt, in
the country of Goshen; and they had possessions there and [R]grew and multiplied exceedingly. Gen. 47:11 • Gen. 17:6; 26:4; 35:11; 46:3
28 And Jacob lived in the land of Egypt
seventeen years. So the length of Jacob's life
was one hundred and forty-seven years.
29 When the time drew near that Israel
must die, he called his son Joseph and said to
him, "Now if I have found favor in your sight,
please put your hand under my thigh, and
[R]deal kindly and truly with me. [R]Please do not
bury me in Egypt, Gen. 24:49 • Gen. 50:25
30 "but [R]let me lie with my fathers; you
shall carry me out of Egypt and [R]bury me in
their burial place." And he said, "I will do as
you have said." 2 Sam. 19:37 • Gen. 49:29; 50:5–13
31 Then he said, "Swear to me." And he
swore to him. So [R]Israel bowed himself on the
head of the bed. 1 Kin. 1:47

CHAPTER 48

NOW it came to pass after these things
that Joseph was told, "Indeed your
father *is* sick"; and he took with him his two
sons, [R]Manasseh and Ephraim. Gen. 41:51, 52
2 And Jacob was told, "Look, your son
Joseph is coming to you"; and Israel
strengthened himself and sat up on the bed.
3 Then Jacob said to Joseph: "God Almighty appeared to me at [R]Luz in the land of
Canaan and blessed me, Gen. 28:13, 19; 35:6, 9
4 "and said to me, 'Behold, I will make you
fruitful and multiply you, and I will make of
you a multitude of people, and [R]give this land
to your descendants after you [R]*as* an everlasting possession.' Ex. 6:8 • Gen. 17:8
5 "And now your [R]two sons, Ephraim and
Manasseh, who were born to you in the land

of Egypt before I came to you in Egypt, *are*
mine; as Reuben and Simeon, they shall be
mine. Josh. 13:7; 14:4
6 "Your offspring whom you beget after
them shall be yours, *and* will be called by the
name of their brothers in their inheritance.
7 "But as for me, when I came from Padan,
[R]Rachel died beside me in the land of Canaan
on the way, when *there was* but a [T]little
distance to go to Ephrath; and I buried her
there on the way to Ephrath (that is, Bethlehem)." Gen. 35:9, 16, 19, 20 • 5 mi.
8 Then Israel saw Joseph's sons, and said,
"Who *are* these?"
9 And Joseph said to his father, "They *are*
my sons, whom God has given me in this
place." And he said, "Please bring them to
me, and [R]I will bless them." Gen. 27:4; 47:15
10 Now the eyes of Israel were dim with
age, *so that* he could not see. Then Joseph
brought them near him, and he [R]kissed them
and embraced them. Gen. 27:27; 45:15; 50:1
11 And Israel said to Joseph, [R]"I had not
thought to see your face; but in fact, God has
also shown me your offspring!" Gen. 45:26
12 So Joseph brought them from beside his
knees, and he bowed down with his face to
the earth.
13 And Joseph took them both, Ephraim
with his right hand toward Israel's left hand,
and Manasseh with his left hand toward
Israel's right hand, and brought *them* near
him.
14 Then Israel stretched out his right hand
and laid *it* on Ephraim's head, who *was* the
younger, and his left hand on Manasseh's
head, [R]guiding his hands knowingly, for Manasseh *was* the [R]firstborn. Gen. 48:19 • Josh. 17:1
15 And [R]he blessed Joseph, and said:

"God, before whom my fathers Abraham
and Isaac walked,
The God who has fed me all my life
long to this day, [Heb. 11:21]
16 The Angel [R]who has redeemed me from
all evil, Gen. 22:11, 15–18; 28:13–15; 31:11
Bless the lads;
Let [R]my name be named upon them,
And the name of my fathers Abraham
and Isaac;
Amos 9:12
And let them [R]grow into a multitude in
the midst of the earth." Num. 26:34, 37

17 Now when Joseph saw that his father
[R]laid his right hand on the head of Ephraim, it
displeased him; so he took hold of his father's
hand to remove it from Ephraim's head to
Manasseh's head. Gen. 48:14
18 And Joseph said to his father, "Not so,
my father, for this *one is* the firstborn; put
your right hand on his head."
19 But his father refused and said, [R]"I know,
my son, I know. He also shall become a
people, and he also shall be great; but truly
[R]his younger brother shall be greater than he,
and his descendants shall become a multitude
of nations." Gen. 48:14 • Num. 1:33, 35
20 So he blessed them that day, saying, [R]"By
you Israel will bless, saying, 'May God make
you as Ephraim and as Manasseh!' " And thus
he set Ephraim before Manasseh. Ruth 4:11, 12
21 Then Israel said to Joseph, "Behold, I am
dying, but God will be with you and bring
you back to the land of your fathers.
22 "Moreover I have given to you one [T]por-
tion above your brothers, which I took from
the hand of the Amorite with my sword and
my bow."
Lit. *shoulder, ridge*

CHAPTER 49

AND Jacob called his sons and said,
"Gather together, that I may tell you
what shall befall you in the last days:

2 "Gather together and hear, you sons of
Jacob,
And listen to Israel your father.

3 "Reuben, you are [R]my firstborn,
My might and the beginning of my
strength,
The excellency of dignity and the
excellency of power. Gen. 29:32
4 Unstable as water, you shall not excel,
Because you [R]went up to your father's
bed;
Then you defiled *it*—
He went up to my couch. Gen. 35:22

5 "Simeon and Levi *are* brothers;
Instruments of [T]cruelty *are in* their
habitation. *violence*
6 [R]Let not my soul enter their council;
Let not my honor be united [R]to their
assembly; Prov. 1:15, 16 • Ps. 26:9
[R]For in their anger they slew a man,
And in their self-will they [T]hamstrung
an ox. Gen. 34:26 • *lamed*
7 Cursed *be* their anger, for *it is* fierce;
And their wrath, for it is cruel!
[R]I will divide them in Jacob
And scatter them in Israel. Josh. 19:1, 9

8 "Judah,[R] you *are he* whom your brothers
shall praise; Deut. 33:7
[R]Your hand *shall be* on the neck of your
enemies; Ps. 18:40
[R]Your father's children shall bow down
before you. 1 Chr. 5:2
9 Judah *is* [R]a lion's whelp; [Rev. 5:5]
From the prey, my son, you have gone
up.
He bows down, he lies down as a lion;
And as a lion, who shall rouse him?

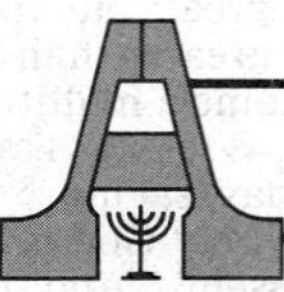

JACOB'S FAREWELL

Jesus, who was called the "Lion of the tribe of Judah," traced His earthly lineage through this tribe.

As the aged Jacob neared death, he summoned his twelve sons to tell them "what shall befall you in the last days" (Gen. 49:1). Some of the sons received predictions of good fortune from their father, while others were told their future looked bleak. These sons became the twelve tribes of Israel, which settled the land of Canaan several centuries later. Jacob's predictions proved to be accurate, as demonstrated by later events in their history.

Jacob's firstborn son Reuben, singled out as "unstable as water" (49:4), was eventually absorbed by the tribe of Gad. Simeon likewise faded into obscurity, and Levi evolved into the priestly tribe that had no separate territory of its own (49:5–7). Benjamin was described as a "ravenous wolf" (49:27), a symbol of greed.

Zebulun's tribe eventually settled on the coast of the Mediterranean Sea and became a "haven for ships" (49:13), in fulfillment of his father's prediction. Two tribes that became particularly prosperous were Asher (49:20) and Joseph (49:22). Naphtali was described as a deer (49:21), perhaps suggesting a spirit of freedom and grace. Gad (49:19), Dan (49:16–18), and Issachar (49:14, 15) were singled out for their physical strength and ability as warriors and military leaders.

But Jacob's most significant words were reserved for Judah, the tribe "whom your brothers shall praise" (49:8) because it would produce a great ruler for the Hebrew people. From this tribe sprang David, the most popular king in the history of Israel, and eventually the Messiah, Jesus Christ, whose earthly father Joseph "was of the house and lineage of David" (Luke 2:4).

Jacob described his son Judah as a "lion's whelp" (or cub), an animal that symbolizes strength and royalty. Because Jesus traced His earthly lineage through this tribe, He was called the "Lion of the tribe of Judah" (Rev. 5:5).

10 [R]The *scepter shall not depart from
Judah, Ps. 60:7; Rev. 5:5 ☆
Nor [R]a lawgiver from between his feet,
[R]Until Shiloh comes; Ps. 60:7 • Is. 11:1
[R]And to Him *shall be* the obedience of
the people. Ps. 2:6–9; 72:8–11
11 Binding his donkey to the vine,
And his donkey's colt to the choice
vine,
He washed his garments in wine,
And his clothes in the blood of grapes.
12 His eyes *are* darker than wine,
And his teeth whiter than milk.

13 "Zebulun[R] shall dwell by the haven of
the sea; Deut. 33:18, 19
He *shall become* a haven for ships,
And his border shall adjoin Sidon.

14 "Issachar[R] is a strong donkey, 1 Chr. 12:32
Lying down between two burdens;
15 He saw that rest *was* good,
And that the land *was* pleasant;
He bowed [R]his shoulder to bear *a*
burden, 1 Sam. 10:9
And became a band of slaves.

16 "Dan[R] shall judge his people
As one of the tribes of Israel. Deut. 33:22
17 [R]Dan shall be a serpent by the way,
A viper by the path, Judg. 18:27
That bites the horse's heels
So that its rider shall fall backward.
18 [R]I have waited for your salvation, O
LORD! Is. 25:9

19 "Gad,[R] a troop shall tramp upon him,
But he shall triumph at last. Deut. 33:20

20 "Bread from Asher *shall be* rich,
And he shall yield royal dainties.

21 "Naphtali[R] *is* a deer let loose; Deut. 33:23
He gives [T]goodly words. Lit. *words of beauty*

22 "Joseph *is* a fruitful bough,
A fruitful bough by a well;
His branches run over the wall.
23 The archers have [R]bitterly grieved him,
Shot *at him* and hated him. Gen. 37:4, 24
24 But his [R]bow remained in strength,
And the arms of his hands were [T]made
strong Job 29:20 • Or *supple*
By the hands of [R]the Mighty *God* of
Jacob Ps. 132:2, 5
(From there [R]*is* the Shepherd, [R]the
Stone of Israel), [Ps. 23:1; 80:1] • Is. 28:16
25 [R]By the God of your father who will help
you, Gen. 28:13; 32:9; 35:3; 43:23; 50:17
[R]And by the Almighty [R]who will bless
you Gen. 17:1; 35:11 • Deut. 33:13
With blessings of heaven above,
Blessings of the deep that lies beneath,
Blessings of the breasts and of the
womb.
26 The blessings of your father
Have excelled the blessings of my
ancestors,
[R]Up to the utmost bound of the
everlasting hills. Deut. 33:15
They shall be on the head of Joseph,
And on the crown of the head of him
who was separate from his brothers.

27 "Benjamin is a [R]ravenous wolf;
In the morning he shall devour the
prey, Judg. 20:21, 25
And at night he shall divide the spoil."

28 All these *are* the twelve tribes of Israel,
and this *is* what their father spoke to them.
And he blessed them; he blessed each one
according to his own blessing.
29 Then he charged them and said to them:
"I am to be gathered to my people; bury me
with my fathers [R]in the cave that *is* in the
field of Ephron the Hittite, Gen. 23:16–20; 50:13
30 "in the cave that *is* in the field of Machpelah, which *is* before Mamre in the land of
Canaan, [R]which Abraham bought with the
field of Ephron the Hittite as a possession for
a burial place. Gen. 23:3–20
31 "There they buried Abraham and Sarah
his wife, there they buried Isaac and Rebekah
his wife, and there I buried Leah.
32 "The field and the cave that *is* there *were*
purchased from the sons of Heth."

Jacob Dies in Egypt

33 And when Jacob had finished commanding his sons, he drew his feet up into the bed
and breathed his last, and was gathered to his
people.

CHAPTER 50

THEN Joseph fell on his father's face, and
wept over him, and kissed him.
2 And Joseph commanded his servants the
physicians to [R]embalm his father. So the
physicians embalmed Israel. Gen. 50:26
3 Forty days were required for him, for
such are the days required for those who are
embalmed; and the Egyptians [R]mourned[T] for
him seventy days. Deut. 34:8 • Lit. *wept*
4 And when the days of his mourning were
past, Joseph spoke to [R]the household of
Pharaoh saying, "If now I have found favor
in your eyes, please speak in the hearing of
Pharaoh, saying, Esth. 4:2
5 [R]'My father made me swear, saying, "Behold, I am dying; in my grave [R]which I dug
for myself in the land of Canaan, there you
shall bury me." Now therefore, please let me

49:10 A symbol of kingship

go up and bury my father, and I will come back.' " Gen. 47:29–31 • Is. 22:16

6 And Pharaoh said, "Go up and bury your father, as he made you swear."

7 So Joseph went up to bury his father; and with him went up all the servants of Pharaoh, the elders of his house, and all the elders of the land of Egypt,

8 as well as all the house of Joseph, his brothers, and his father's house. Only their little ones, their flocks, and their herds they left in the land of Goshen.

9 And there went up with him both chariots and horsemen, and it was a very great gathering.

10 Then they came to the threshing floor of Atad, which *is* beyond the Jordan, and they [R]mourned there with a great and very solemn lamentation. [R]He observed seven days of mourning for his father. Acts 8:2 • 1 Sam. 31:13

11 And when the inhabitants of the land, the Canaanites, saw the mourning at the threshing floor of Atad, they said, "This *is* a grievous mourning of the Egyptians." Therefore its name was called [T]Abel Mizraim, which *is* beyond the Jordan. *Mourning of Egypt*

12 So his sons did for him just as he had commanded them.

13 For his sons carried him to the land of Canaan, and buried him in the cave of the field of Machpelah, before Mamre, which Abraham bought with the field from Ephron the Hittite as property for a burial place.

14 And after he had buried his father, Joseph returned to Egypt, he and his brothers and all who went up with him to bury his father.

Joseph Dies in Egypt

15 When Joseph's brothers saw that their father was dead, they said, "Perhaps Joseph will hate us, and may [T]actually repay us for all the evil which we did to him." *fully*

16 So they sent *messengers* to Joseph, saying, "Before your father died he commanded, saying,

17 'Thus you shall say to Joseph: "I beg you, please forgive the trespass of your brothers and their sin; for they did evil to you." ' Now, please, forgive the trespass of the servants of the God of your father." And Joseph wept when they spoke to him.

18 Then his brothers also went and [R]fell down before his face, and they said, "Behold, we *are* your servants." Gen. 37:7–10; 41:43; 44:14

19 Joseph said to them, "Do not be afraid, [R]for *am* I in the place of God? 2 Kin. 5:7

20 [R]"But as for you, you meant evil against me; *but* [R]God meant it for good, in order to bring it about as *it is* this day, to save many people alive. Ps. 56:5 • [Acts 3:13–15]

21 "Now therefore, do not be afraid; I will provide for you and your little ones." And he comforted them and spoke kindly to them.

22 So Joseph dwelt in Egypt, he and his father's household. And Joseph lived one hundred and ten years.

23 Joseph saw Ephraim's children to the third *generation.* [R]The children of Machir, the son of Manasseh, [R]were also brought up on Joseph's knees. Num. 26:29; 32:39 • Gen. 30:3

24 And Joseph said to his brethren, "I am dying; but [R]God will surely visit you, and bring you out of this land to the land [R]of which He swore to Abraham, to Isaac, and to Jacob." Ex. 3:16, 17 • Gen. 26:3; 35:12; 46:4

25 Then Joseph took an oath from the children of Israel, saying, "God will surely [T]visit you, and [R]you shall carry up my [R]bones from here." *help* • Deut. 1:8; 30:1–8 • Ex. 13:19

26 So Joseph died, *being* one hundred and ten years old; and they embalmed him, and he was put in a coffin in Egypt.

THE SECOND BOOK OF MOSES CALLED

EXODUS

THE BOOK OF EXODUS

Exodus is the record of Israel's birth as a nation. Within the protective "womb" of Egypt, the Jewish family of seventy rapidly multiplies. At the right time, accompanied with severe "birth pains," an infant nation, numbering between two and three million people, is brought into the world where it is divinely protected, fed, and nurtured.

The Hebrew title, *We'elleh Shemoth,* "Now These *Are* the Names," comes from the first phrase in 1:1. Exodus begins with "Now" to show it as a continuation of Genesis. The Greek title is *Exodus,* a word meaning exit, departure, or going out. The Septuagint uses this word to describe the book by its key event (see 19:1, "gone out"). In Luke 9:31 and in Second Peter 1:15, the word *exodus* speaks of physical death (Jesus and Peter). This embodies Exodus's theme of redemption, because redemption is accomplished only through death. The Latin title is *Liber Exodus,* "Book of Departure," taken from the Greek title.

THE AUTHOR OF EXODUS

Critics have challenged the Mosaic authorship of Exodus in favor of a series of oral and written documents that were woven together by editors late in Israel's history. Their arguments are generally weak and far from conclusive, especially in view of the strong external and internal evidence that points to Moses as the author.

External Evidence: Exodus has been attributed to Moses since the time of Joshua (cf. Ex. 20:25 with Josh. 8:30–32). Other biblical writers attribute Exodus to Moses: Malachi (Mal. 4:4), the disciples (John 1:45), and Paul (Rom. 10:5). This is also the testimony of Jesus (Mark 7:10; 12:26; Luke 20:37; John 5:46, 47; 7:19, 22, 23). Jewish and Samaritan traditions consistently hold to the Mosaic authorship of Exodus.

Internal Evidence: Portions of Exodus are directly attributed to Moses (Ex. 15; 17:8–14; 20:1–17; 24:4, 7, 12; 31:18; 34:1–27). Moses' usual procedure was to record events soon after they occurred in the form of historical annals. It is clear from Exodus that the author must have been an eyewitness of the Exodus and an educated man. He was acquainted with details about the customs and climate of Egypt and the plants, animals, and terrain of the wilderness. A consistency of style and development also points to a single author. Its antiquity is supported by the frequent use of ancient literary constructions, words, and expressions.

THE TIME OF EXODUS

If the early date for the Exodus (c. 1445 B.C.) is assumed, this book was composed during the forty-year wilderness journey, between 1445 B.C. and 1405 B.C. Moses probably kept an account of God's work, which he then edited in the plains of Moab shortly before his death. Exodus covers the period from the arrival of Jacob in Egypt (c. 1875 B.C.) to the erection of the tabernacle 431 years later in the wilderness (c. 1445 B.C.).

THE CHRIST OF EXODUS

Exodus contains no direct messianic prophecies, but it is full of types and portraits of Christ. Here are seven: (1) *Moses:* In dozens of ways Moses is a type of Christ (Deut. 18:15). Both Moses and Christ are prophets, priests, and kings (although Moses was never made King, he functioned as the ruler of Israel); both are kinsman-redeemers; both are endangered in infancy; both voluntarily renounce power and wealth; both are deliverers, lawgivers, and mediators. (2) *The Passover:* John 1:29, 36 and First Corinthians 5:7 make it clear that Christ is our slain God and the Passover Lamb. (3) *The seven feasts:* Each of these feasts portrays some aspect of the ministry of Christ. (4) *The Exodus:* Paul relates baptism to the exodus event because baptism symbolizes death to the old and identification with the new (Rom. 6:2, 3; 1 Cor. 10:1, 2). (5) *The manna and water:* The New Testament applies both to Christ (John 6:31–35, 48–63; 1 Cor. 10:3, 4). (6) *The tabernacle:* In its materials, colors, furniture, and arrangement, the tabernacle clearly speaks of the person of Christ and the way of redemption. The development is progressive from suffering, blood, and death, to beauty, holiness, and the glory of God. The tabernacle is theology in a physical form. (7) *The High Priest:* In several ways the high priest foreshadows the ministry of Christ, our great High Priest (Heb. 4:14–16; 9:11, 12, 24–28).

KEYS TO EXODUS

Key Word: Redemption—Central to the Book of Exodus is the concept of redemption. Israel was redeemed *from* bondage in Egypt and *into* a covenant relationship with God. From the redemption of Moses in the Nile to the redeeming presence of God in the Tabernacle, Exodus records God's overwhelming acts of deliverance, by which He demonstrates His right to be Israel's King.

Key Verses: Exodus 6:6; 19:5, 6—"Therefore say to the children of Israel: 'I *am* the LORD; I will bring you out from under the burdens of the Egyptians, I will rescue you from their bondage, and I will redeem you with an outstretched arm and with great judgments' " (6:6).

" 'Now therefore, if you will indeed obey My voice and keep My covenant, then you shall be a special treasure to Me above all people; for all the earth *is* Mine. And you shall be to Me a kingdom of priests and a holy nation' " (19:5, 6).

Key Chapters: Exodus 12—14—The climax of the entire Old Testament is recorded in chapters 12—14: the salvation of Israel through blood (the Passover) and through power (the Red Sea). The exodus is the central event of the Old Testament as the cross is of the New Testament.

SURVEY OF EXODUS

Exodus abounds with God's powerful redemptive acts on behalf of His oppressed people. It begins in pain and ends in liberation; it moves from the groaning of the people to the glory of God. It is the continuation of the story that begins in Genesis with the seventy descendants of Jacob who move from Canaan to Egypt. They have multiplied under adverse conditions to a multitude of over two million people. When the Israelites finally turn to God for deliverance from their bondage, God quickly responds by redeeming them "with an outstretched arm and with great judgments" (6:6). God faithfully fulfills His promise made to Abraham centuries before (Gen. 15:13, 14).

The book falls into two parts: (1) redemption from Egypt (1—18); and (2) revelation from God (19—40).

Redemption from Egypt (1—18): After four centuries of slavery, the people of Israel cry to the God of Abraham, Isaac, and Jacob for deliverance. God has already prepared Moses for this purpose, and has commissioned him at the burning bush to stand before Pharaoh as the advocate for Israel. However, Pharaoh hardens his heart: "Who *is* the LORD, that I should obey His voice to let Israel go?" (5:2).

God soon reveals Himself to Pharaoh through a series of object lessons, the ten plagues. These plagues grow in severity until the tenth brings death to the firstborn of every household of Egypt. Israel is redeemed through this plague by means of the Passover lamb. The Israelites' faith in God at this point becomes the basis for their national redemption. As they leave Egypt, God guides them by a pillar of fire and smoke, and saves them from Egypt's pursuing army through the miraculous crossing of the sea. In the wilderness He protects and sustains them throughout their journeys.

Revelation from God (19—40): Now that the people have experienced God's deliverance, guidance, and protection, they are ready to be taught what God expects of them. The redeemed people must now be set apart to walk with God. This is why the emphasis moves from narration in chapters 1—18 to legislation in chapters 19—40. On Mount Sinai, Moses receives God's moral, civil, and ceremonial laws, as well as the pattern for the tabernacle to be built in the wilderness. After God judges the people for their worship of the golden calf, the tabernacle is constructed and consecrated. It is a building of beauty in a barren land and reveals much about the person of God and the way of redemption.

FOCUS	REDEMPTION FROM EGYPT				REVELATION FROM GOD	
REFERENCE	1:1—	2:1—	5:1—	15:22—	19:1—	32:1—40:38
DIVISION	THE NEED FOR REDEMPTION	THE PREPARATION FOR REDEMPTION	THE REDEMPTION OF ISRAEL	THE PRESERVATION OF ISRAEL	THE REVELATION OF THE COVENANT	THE RESPONSE OF ISRAEL TO THE COVENANT
TOPIC	NARRATION				LEGISLATION	
	SUBJECTION		REDEMPTION		INSTRUCTION	
LOCATION	EGYPT			WILDERNESS	MOUNT SINAI	
TIME	430 YEARS			2 MONTHS	10 MONTHS	

OUTLINE OF EXODUS

Part One: Redemption from Egypt (1:1—18:27)

I. The Need for Redemption from Egypt . . . 1:1–22

A. Israel's Rapid Multiplication. 1:1–7
B. Israel's Severe Affliction 1:8–14
C. Israel's Planned Extinction 1:15–22

II. The Preparation of the Leaders of the Redemption . . . . 2:1—4:31

A. Moses Is Redeemed from Murder 2:1–10
B. Moses Tries to Redeem by Murder . . . 2:11–22
C. Israel Calls upon God 2:23–25
D. God Calls upon Moses . . . . 3:1—4:17
1. God Miraculously Appears. 3:1–6
2. God Calls Moses to Leadership. 3:7–10
3. God Answers Moses' Objections . . . . 3:11—4:17
a. "Who Am I?" 3:11, 12
b. "What Is His Name?" 3:13–22
c. "They Will Not Believe Me" 4:1–9
d. "I Am Slow of Speech" 4:10–17
E. Moses Accepts the Call. 4:18–26
1. Moses Returns to Egypt. 4:18–23
2. Moses Reinstitutes Circumcision. . . 4:24–26
F. Israel Accepts the Call of Moses as Deliverer 4:27–31

III. God's Redemption of Israel from Egypt. . . . . 5:1—15:21

A. Moses Confronts Pharaoh by Word 5:1—6:9
1. Pharaoh Rejects Moses. 5:1–14
2. Israel Rejects Moses 5:15–21
3. Moses Questions God's Plan 5:22, 23
4. God Reassures Moses 6:1–8
5. Moses Reassures Israel 6:9
B. Moses Confronts Pharaoh with Miracles . . . . 6:10—7:13
1. God Recommissions Moses 6:10–27
2. Moses Objects. 6:28–30
3. God Reassures Moses 7:1–7
4. Aaron's Rod Swallows Pharaoh's Rods 7:8–13
C. Moses Confronts Pharaoh Through Plagues. . . . . 7:14—11:10
1. First Plague: Blood. 7:14–25
2. Second Plague: Frogs. 8:1–15
3. Third Plague: Lice 8:16–19
4. Fourth Plague: Flies. 8:20–32
5. Fifth Plague: Disease on Beasts 9:1–7
6. Sixth Plague: Boils on Man and Beast. 9:8–12
7. Seventh Plague: Hail 9:13–35
8. Eighth Plague: Locusts. 10:1–20
9. Ninth Plague: Darkness 10:21–29
10. Tenth Plague: Death Announced 11:1–10
D. Israel Redeemed by Blood Through the Passover. . . . . 12:1—13:16
1. Instructions for the Passover 12:1–20
2. Participation in the Passover 12:21–28
3. Redemption Through the Passover. 12:29–36
4. Freedom Because of the Passover 12:37–51
5. Sanctification as a Result of the Passover 13:1–16
E. Israel Redeemed by Power from Egypt . . . . 13:17—15:21
1. God Leads Israel . . . . 13:17—14:2
2. Pharaoh Follows Israel. 14:3–9
3. Israel Rebels Against God 14:10–12
4. God Opens the Red Sea. 14:13–31
5. Israel Praises God. 15:1–21

IV. The Preservation of Israel in the Wilderness . . . . 15:22—18:27

A. Preserved from Thirst 15:22–27
B. Preserved from Hunger. 16:1–36
C. Preserved from Thirst Again 17:1–7
D. Preserved from Defeat 17:8–16
E. Preserved from Chaos 18:1–27

Part Two: Revelation from God (19:1—40:38)

I. The Revelation of the Old Covenant 19:1—31:18

A. The Preparation of the People. 19:1–25
1. Location of the Giving of the Covenant 19:1, 2
2. Purpose of the Covenant. 19:3–6
3. Israel Accepts the Covenant. 19:7, 8
4. Israelites Sanctify Themselves. 19:9–25
B. The Revelation of the Covenant 20:1–26
1. The Ten Commandments 20:1–17
a. Commandments Relating to God 20:1–11
b. Commandments Relating to Man 20:12–17
2. The Response of Israel. 20:18–21
3. Provision for Approaching God . . . 20:22–26
C. The Judgments. . . . . 21:1—23:33
1. Social Regulations . . . . 21:1—22:15
a. Rights of Persons. 21:1–32
b. Rights of Property . . . . 21:33—22:15
2. Moral Regulations . . . . 22:16—23:9
a. Proper Conduct. 22:16–31
b. Proper Justice 23:1–9
3. Religious Regulations 23:10–33
a. Sabbatical Year 23:10–13
b. Three National Feasts. 23:14–19
4. Conquest Regulations 23:20–33
D. The Formal Ratification of the Covenant. 24:1–11
1. The Covenant Is Ratified Through Blood 24:1–8
2. The God of the Covenant Is Revealed 24:9–11
E. The Tabernacle . . . . 24:12—27:21
1. The Revelation Is Given on Mount Sinai. 24:12–18
2. The Offering for the Tabernacle. 25:1–7
3. The Revelation of the Tabernacle . . . . 25:8—27:21

CHAPTER 1

Israel's Rapid Multiplication

NOW these *are* the names of the children
of Israel who came to Egypt; each man
and his household came with Jacob:
2 Reuben, Simeon, Levi, and Judah;
3 Issachar, Zebulun, and Benjamin;
4 Dan, Naphtali, Gad, and Asher.
5 All those [T]who were descendants of Jacob were *seventy persons (for Joseph was in
Egypt *already*). Lit. *who came from the loins of*
6 And [R]Joseph died, all his brothers, and all
that generation. Gen. 50:26
7 [R]But the children of Israel were fruitful
and increased abundantly, multiplied and
[T]grew exceedingly mighty; and the land was
filled with them. Acts 7:17 • *became very numerous*

Israel's Severe Affliction

8 Now there arose a new king over Egypt,
[R]who did not know Joseph. Acts 7:18, 19
9 And he said to his people, "Look, the
people of the children of Israel *are* more and
[R]mightier than we; Gen. 26:16
10 [R]"come, let us [R]deal [T]wisely with them,
lest they multiply, and it happen, in the event
of war, that they also join our enemies and
fight against us, and *so* go up out of the
land." Ps. 83:3, 4 • Acts 7:19 • *shrewdly toward*
11 Therefore they set taskmasters over
them to afflict them with their burdens. And
they built for Pharaoh [R]supply cities, Pithom
[R]and Raamses. 1 Kin. 9:19 • Gen. 47:11
12 But the more they afflicted them, the

1:5 DSS, LXX *seventy-five*

more they multiplied and grew. And they were in dread of the children of Israel.

13 So the Egyptians made the children of Israel [R]serve with [T]rigor. Gen. 15:13 • *harshness*

14 And they [R]made their lives bitter with hard bondage—[R]in mortar, in brick, and in all manner of service in the field. All their service in which they made them serve *was* with rigor. Num. 20:15 • Ps. 81:6

Israel's Planned Extinction

15 Then the king of Egypt spoke to the [R]Hebrew midwives, of whom the name of one *was* Shiphrah and the name of the other Puah; Ex. 2:6

16 and he said, "When you do the duties of a midwife for the Hebrew women, and see *them* on the birthstools, if it *is* a [R]son, then you shall kill him; but if it *is* a daughter, then she shall live." Acts 7:19

17 But the midwives feared God, and did not do as the king of Egypt commanded them, but saved the male children alive.

18 So the king of Egypt called for the midwives and said to them, "Why have you done this thing, and saved the male children alive?"

19 And the midwives said to Pharaoh, "Because the Hebrew women *are* not like the Egyptian women; for they *are* lively and give birth before the midwives come to them."

20 [R]Therefore God dealt well with the midwives, and the people multiplied and [T]grew very mighty. [Prov. 11:18] • *became very numerous*

21 And so it was, because the midwives feared God, [R]that He [T]provided households for them. 1 Sam. 2:35 • *gave them families*

22 So Pharaoh commanded all his people, saying, [R]"Every son who is *born you shall cast into the river, and every daughter you shall save alive." Acts 7:19

CHAPTER 2

Moses Is Redeemed from Murder

AND a man of the house of Levi went and took *as wife* a daughter of Levi.

2 So the woman conceived and bore a son. And [R]when she saw that he *was* a beautiful *child,* she hid him three months. Acts 7:20

3 But when she could no longer hide him, she took an ark of bulrushes for him, daubed it with asphalt and pitch, put the child in it, and laid *it* in the reeds by the river's bank.

4 [R]And his sister stood afar off, to know what would be done to him. Num. 26:59

5 Then the [R]daughter of Pharaoh came down to wash *herself* at the river. And her maidens walked along the river's side; and when she saw the ark among the reeds, she sent her maid to get it. Acts 7:21

6 And when she had opened *it,* she saw the child, and behold, the baby wept. So she had compassion on him, and said, "This is one of the Hebrews' children."

7 Then his sister said to Pharaoh's daughter, "Shall I go and call a nurse for you from the Hebrew women, that she may nurse the child for you?"

8 And Pharaoh's daughter said to her, "Go." So the maiden went and called the child's mother.

9 Then Pharaoh's daughter said to her, "Take this child away and nurse him for me, and I will give *you* your wages." So the woman took the child and nursed him.

10 And the child grew, and she brought him to Pharaoh's daughter, and he became her son. So she called his name Moses, saying, "Because I drew him out of the water."

Moses Tries to Redeem by Murder

11 Now it came to pass in those days, [R]when Moses was grown, that he went out to his brethren and looked at their burdens. And he saw an Egyptian beating a Hebrew, one of his brethren. Heb. 11:24–26

12 So he looked this way and that way, and when he saw no one, he [R]killed the Egyptian and hid him in the sand. Acts 7:24, 25

13 And when he went out the second day, behold, two Hebrew men [R]were fighting, and he said to the one who did the wrong, "Why are you striking your companion?" Prov. 25:8

14 Then he said, [R]"Who made you a prince and a judge over us? Do you intend to kill me as you killed the Egyptian?" So Moses [R]feared and said, "Surely this thing is known!" Acts 7:27, 28 • Judg. 6:27

15 When Pharaoh heard of this matter, he sought to kill Moses. But Moses fled from the face of Pharaoh and dwelt in the land of [R]Midian; and he sat down by a well. Ex. 3:1

16 Now the priest of Midian had seven daughters. [R]And they came and drew water, and they filled the [R]troughs to water their father's flock. Gen. 24:11, 13, 19; 29:6–10 • Gen. 30:38

17 Then the shepherds came and drove them away; but Moses stood up and helped them, and [R]watered their flock. Gen. 29:3, 10

18 When they came to [R]Reuel[T] their father, [R]he said, "How *is it that* you have come so soon today?" Num. 10:29 • *Jethro,* Ex. 3:1 • Ex. 3:1; 4:18

19 And they said, "An Egyptian delivered us from the hand of the shepherds, and he also drew enough water for us and watered the flock."

20 So he said to his daughters, "And where *is* he? Why *is it that* you have left the man? Call him, that he may eat bread."

21 Then Moses was content to live with the man, and he gave [R]Zipporah his daughter to Moses. Ex. 4:25; 18:2

22 And she bore *him* a son, and he called his

1:22 LXX, Tg. add *to the Hebrews*

name [T]Gershom; for he said, "I have been a
stranger in a foreign land." Lit. *Stranger There*

Israel Calls upon God

23 Now it happened in the process of time
that the king of Egypt died. Then the children
of Israel groaned because of the bondage, and
they cried out; and [R]their cry came up to God
because of the bondage. James 5:4
24 So God [R]heard their groaning, and God
[R]remembered His covenant with Abraham,
with Isaac, and with Jacob. Ex. 6:5 • Gen. 15:13
25 And God looked upon the children of
Israel, and God [R]acknowledged *them.* Ex. 3:7

CHAPTER 3

God Miraculously Appears

NOW Moses kept the flock of Jethro his
father-in-law, the priest of Midian. And
he led the flock to the back of the desert, and
came to Horeb, the mountain of God.
2 And [R]the Angel of the LORD appeared to
him in a flame of fire from the midst of a
bush. So he looked, and behold, the bush
burned with fire, but the bush *was* not consumed. Deut. 33:16
3 Then Moses said, "I will now turn aside
and see this [R]great sight, why the bush does
not burn." Acts 7:31
4 So when the LORD saw that he turned
aside to look, God called [R]to him from the
midst of the bush and said, "Moses, Moses!"
And he said, "Here I am." Deut. 33:16
5 Then He said, "Do not draw near this
place. Take your sandals off your feet, for the
place where you stand *is* holy ground."
6 Moreover He said, [R]"I *am* the God of
your father—the God of Abraham, the God of
Isaac, and the God of Jacob." And Moses
hid his face, for [R]he was afraid to look upon
God. [Matt. 22:32] • 1 Kin. 19:13

God Calls Moses to Leadership

7 And the LORD said: "I have surely seen
the oppression of My people who *are* in
Egypt, and have heard their cry because of
their taskmasters, for I know their sorrows.
8 "So I have come down to deliver them
out of the hand of the Egyptians, and to bring
them up from that land [R]to a good and large
land, to a land flowing with milk and honey,
to the place of the Canaanites and the Hittites and the Amorites and the Perizzites and
the Hivites and the Jebusites. Deut. 1:25
9 "Now therefore, behold, [R]the cry of the
children of Israel has come to Me, and I have
also seen the [R]oppression with which the
Egyptians oppress them. Ex. 2:23 • Ex. 1:11, 13, 14
10 "Come now, therefore, and I will send
you to Pharaoh that you may bring My
people, the children of Israel, out of Egypt."

"Who Am I?"

11 But Moses said to God, "Who *am* I that I
should go to Pharaoh, and that I should bring
the children of Israel out of Egypt?"
12 So He said, [R]"I will certainly be with you.
And this *shall be* a [R]sign to you that I have
sent you: When you have brought the people
out of Egypt, you shall serve God on this
mountain." Gen. 31:3 • Ex. 4:8; 19:3

"What Is His Name?"

13 Then Moses said to God, "Indeed, *when* I
come to the children of Israel and say to
them, 'The God of your fathers has sent me
to you,' and they say to me, 'What *is* His
name?' what shall I say to them?"
14 And God said to Moses, "I AM WHO I
AM." And He said, "Thus you shall say to the
children of Israel, [R]'I AM has sent me to
you.' " [John 8:24, 28, 58]
15 Moreover God said to Moses, "Thus you
shall say to the children of Israel: 'The LORD
God of your fathers, the God of Abraham, the
God of Isaac, and the God of Jacob, has sent
me to you. This *is* My name forever, and this
is My memorial to all generations.'
16 "Go and [R]gather the elders of Israel
together, and say to them, 'The LORD God of
your fathers, the God of Abraham, of Isaac,
and of Jacob, appeared to me, saying, [R]"I
have surely visited you and *seen* what is done
to you in Egypt; Ex. 4:29 • Ex. 2:25; 4:31
17 "and I have said [R]I will bring you up out
of the affliction of Egypt to the land of the
Canaanites and the Hittites and the Amorites
and the Perizzites and the Hivites and the
Jebusites, to a land flowing with milk and
honey." ' Gen. 15:13–21; 46:4; 50:24, 25
18 "Then they will heed your voice; and you
shall come, you and the elders of Israel, to
the king of Egypt; and you shall say to him,
'The LORD God of the Hebrews has met with
us; and now, please, let us go [T]three days'
journey into the wilderness, that we may
sacrifice to the LORD our God.' 60 mi.
19 "But I am sure that the king of Egypt
[R]will not let you go, no, not even by a mighty
hand. Ex. 5:2
20 "So I will [R]stretch out My hand and
strike Egypt with [R]all My wonders which I
will do in its midst; and [R]after that he will let
you go. Ex. 6:6; 9:15 • Deut. 6:22 • Ex. 11:1; 12:31–37
21 "And I will give this people favor in the
sight of the Egyptians; and it shall be, when
you go, that you shall not go empty-handed.
22 [R]"But every woman shall ask of her
neighbor, namely, of her who dwells near her
house, [R]articles of silver, articles of gold, and
clothing; and you shall put *them* on your sons
and on your daughters. So [R]you shall plunder
the Egyptians." Ex. 11:2 • Ex. 33:6 • Job 27:17

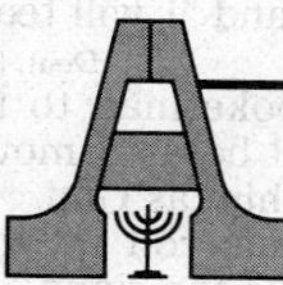

THE NAME OF THE LORD

Exodus 3 records one of the greatest revelations in the Old Testament: the personal name of God. (The words translated *God* in our Bible [*'El, 'Elohim, 'Eloah*] are not names, but the standard vocabulary for the Deity and even for false gods.)

God had told Moses His plan to use Him in delivering the Israelites from Egyptian bondage, and Moses had asked whom He should tell the people had sent him. God answered Moses: "I AM WHO I AM." He told Moses to tell them that "I AM" had sent him, "the LORD God." "I AM" and "LORD" are both probably derived from the Hebrew verb *to be* (*hayah*) because God is the ever-present One, "the Eternal" (Moffatt translation).

Many people are puzzled that in this and many other (over six thousand!) passages some Bibles read *LORD* in all capitals (e.g., KJV, NKJV, NIV), some read "Jehovah" (ASV, Darby), and some read "Yahweh" (Jerusalem Bible). Why such a radical difference? Do the manuscripts vary that much? No, not at all.

Because the name of God is so important—Jews devoutly refer to Him as "the Name" (*ha Shem*)—it is well worth exploring this revelation in some detail. It is merely a question of a Jewish tradition and how various Christian scholars handle that tradition.

In the Ten Commandments, God forbids us to take His name "in vain." That is, we should not bear false witness in oaths and probably should avoid using profanity, as well. In their great fear of violating this command, devout Hebrews went beyond the law, and when they read the Hebrew Scriptures aloud they would read the word *Lord* (*'Adonai*) whenever they saw the four letters (*YHWH*, or traditionally *JHVH* in Latin pronunciation) that spelled out God's revealed covenant name. This was the sacred name by which He had committed Himself to Israel as a nation.

The most ancient copies of the Hebrew text were written in consonants only. As the language became less and less used, scholars (called Masoretes) added little dots and dashes called "vowel points" to indicate how the text was to be pronounced. Oddly enough, they put the vowels that go with the word *'Adonai* together with the sacred four-letter name (called "tetragrammaton") to guide the readers to say *'Adonai* aloud in synagogue services.

Jehovah

This is the origin of the name "Jehovah." It is actually a hybrid name, combining the vowels of *'Adonai* with the consonants of *YHWH* into *JeHoVaH* or *YeHoWaH* (the "a" of *Adonai* is changed for reasons of Hebrew pronunciation). The people who produced this name were medieval Christian Hebrew scholars; the Jews never acknowledged such a name. The defense of this Christian hybrid is the same as the defense of the Jewish avoidance of pronouncing the name—tradition! There are many lovely hymns and paraphrases of the Psalms that use this name, so it would be a loss to eliminate it from our Christian vocabulary. The poetical form of Jehovah is *Jah*.

Yahweh

It is very likely that the name was pronounced very much like "Yahweh." Comparisons with transliterations of the name into other alphabets from very ancient times confirm this. The best argument for the spelling is that it is probably historically accurate. However, the RSV's 1952 introduction explained its reason for rejecting "Yahweh" in the translation. It said that it lacks devotional qualities for English-speaking Christians. It is true that many names beginning with "Y" seem odd to our culture (*all* the names in English Bibles beginning with "J"—including *Jesus* —were pronounced with a *Y* sound, in the original, as in "*hallelu-Yah*").

LORD

Most recent major English Bibles, dissatisfied with both *Jehovah* and *Yahweh*, have retained the KJV's *LORD*. The NASB, which is an updating of the ASV, actually restored *LORD* (the 1901 text read *Jehovah*).

CHAPTER 4

"They Will Not Believe Me"

THEN Moses answered and said, "But
suppose they will not believe me or listen
to my voice; suppose they say, 'The LORD has
not appeared to you.' "
2 So the LORD said to him, "What *is* that in
your hand?" And he said, "A rod."
3 And He said, "Cast it on the ground." So
he cast it on the ground, and it became a
serpent; and Moses fled from it.
4 Then the LORD said to Moses, "Reach out
your hand and take *it* by the tail" (and he
reached out his hand and caught it, and it
became a rod in his hand),
5 "that they may [R]believe that the [R]LORD
God of their fathers, the God of Abraham, the
God of Isaac, and the God of Jacob, has
appeared to you." Ex. 4:31; 19:9 • Ex. 3:6, 15
6 Furthermore the LORD said to him, "Now
put your hand in your bosom." And he put
his hand in his bosom, and when he took it
out, behold, his hand *was* leprous, like snow.
7 And He said, "Put your hand in your
bosom again." So he put his hand in his
bosom again, and drew it out of his bosom,
and behold, [R]it was restored like his *other*
flesh. Deut. 32:39
8 "Then it will be, if they do not believe
you, nor heed the message of the [R]first sign,
that they may believe the message of the
latter sign. Ex. 7:6–13
9 "And it shall be, if they do not believe
even these two signs, or listen to your voice,
that you shall take water from [T]the river and
pour *it* on the dry *land.* And [R]the water which
you take from the river will become blood on
the dry *land.*" The Nile • Ex. 7:19, 20

"I Am Slow of Speech"

10 Then Moses said to the LORD, "O my
Lord, I *am* not eloquent, neither before nor
since You have spoken to Your servant; but I
am slow of speech and slow of tongue."
11 So the LORD said to him, [R]"Who has
made man's mouth? Or who makes the mute,
the deaf, the seeing, or the blind? *Have* not I,
the LORD? Ps. 94:9; 146:8
12 "Now therefore, go, and I will be [R]with
your mouth and teach you what you shall
say." Is. 50:4
13 But he said, "O my Lord, please send by
the hand of whomever *else* You may send."
14 So the anger of the LORD was kindled
against Moses, and He said: "Is not Aaron the
Levite your [R]brother? I know that he can
speak well. And look, [R]he is also coming out
to meet you. When he sees you, he will be
glad in his heart. Num. 26:59 • Ex. 4:27
15 "Now you shall speak to him and put the
words in his mouth. And I will be with your
mouth and with his mouth, and [R]I will teach
you what you shall do. Deut. 5:31
16 "So he shall be your spokesman to the
people. And he himself shall be as a mouth
for you, and you shall be to him as God.
17 "And you shall take this rod in your
hand, with which you shall do the signs."

Moses Returns to Egypt

18 So Moses went and returned to Jethro
his father-in-law, and said to him, "Please let
me go and return to my brethren who *are* in
Egypt, and see whether they are still alive."
And Jethro said to Moses, "Go in peace."
19 And the LORD said to Moses in Midian,
"Go, return to Egypt; for [R]all the men are
dead who sought your life." Ex. 2:15, 23
20 Then Moses [R]took his wife and his sons
and set them on a donkey, and he returned to
the land of Egypt. And Moses took [R]the rod of
God in his hand. Ex. 18:2–5 • Num. 20:8, 9, 11
21 And the LORD said to Moses, "When you
go back to Egypt, see that you do all those
wonders before Pharaoh which I have put in
your hand. But [R]I will harden his heart, so
that he will not let the people go. John 12:40
22 "Then you shall [R]say to Pharaoh, 'Thus
says the LORD: [R]"Israel *is* My son, [R]My firstborn. Ex. 5:1 • Hos. 11:1 • Jer. 31:9
23 "So I say to you, let My son go that he
may serve Me. But if you refuse to let him go,
indeed I will kill your son, your firstborn." ' "

Moses Reinstitutes Circumcision

24 And it came to pass on the way, at the
encampment, that the LORD [R]met him and
sought to [R]kill him. Num. 22:22 • Gen. 17:14
25 Then Zipporah took a sharp stone and
cut off the foreskin of her son and [T]cast *it* at
Moses' feet, and said, "Surely you *are* a
husband of blood to me!" Lit. *made it touch*
26 So He let him go. Then she said, "*You are*
a [T]husband of blood!"—because of the circumcision. *bridegroom*

Israel Accepts the Call of Moses as Deliverer

27 And the LORD said to Aaron, "Go into the
wilderness [R]to meet Moses." So he went and
met him on [R]the mountain of God, and kissed
him. Ex. 4:14 • Ex. 3:1; 18:5; 24:13
28 So Moses told Aaron all the words of the
LORD who had sent him, and all the [R]signs
which He had commanded him. Ex. 4:8, 9
29 Then Moses and Aaron [R]went and gathered together all the elders of the children of
Israel. Ex. 3:16; 12:21
30 [R]And Aaron spoke all the words which
the LORD had spoken to Moses. Then he did
the signs in the sight of the people. Ex. 4:15, 16
31 So the people believed; and when they
heard that the LORD had [R]visited the children
of Israel and that He [R]had looked on their

affliction, then [R]they bowed their heads and
worshiped. Gen. 50:24 • Ex. 2:25; 3:7 • Gen. 24:26

CHAPTER 5

Pharaoh Rejects Moses

AFTERWARD Moses and Aaron went in
and told Pharaoh, "Thus says the LORD
God of Israel: 'Let My people go, that they
may hold a feast to Me in the wilderness.' "
2 And Pharaoh said, [R]"Who *is* the LORD,
that I should obey His voice to let Israel go? I
do not know the LORD, [R]nor will I let Israel
go." 2 Kin. 18:35 • Ex. 3:19; 7:14
3 So they said, "The God of the Hebrews
has met with us. Please, let us go [T]three days'
journey into the desert and sacrifice to the
LORD our God, lest He fall upon us with
[R]pestilence or with the sword." 60 mi. • Ex. 9:15
4 Then the king of Egypt said to them,
"Moses and Aaron, why do you take the
people from their work? Get *back* to your
[R]labor." Ex. 1:11; 2:11; 6:6
5 And Pharaoh said, "Look, the people of
the land *are* [R]many now, and you make them
rest from their labor!" Ex. 1:7, 9
6 So the same day Pharaoh commanded
the [R]taskmasters of the people and their
officers, saying, Ex. 1:11; 3:7; 5:10, 13, 14
7 "You shall no longer give the people
straw to make [R]brick as before. Let them go
and gather straw for themselves. Ex. 1:14
8 "And you shall lay on them the quota of
bricks which they made before. You shall not
diminish it. For they are idle; therefore they
cry out, saying, 'Let us go *and* sacrifice to our
God.'
9 "Let more work be laid on the men, that
they may labor in it, and let them not regard
false words."
10 And the taskmasters of the people and
their officers went out and spoke to the
people, saying, "Thus says Pharaoh: 'I will
not give you straw.
11 'Go, get yourselves straw where you can
find it; yet none of your work will be diminished.' "
12 So the people were scattered abroad
throughout all the land of Egypt to gather
stubble instead of straw.
13 And the taskmasters forced *them* to
hurry, saying, "Fulfill your work, *your* daily
quota, as when there was straw."
14 Also the [R]officers of the children of Israel, whom Pharaoh's taskmasters had set
over them, were [R]beaten *and* were asked,
"Why have you not fulfilled your task in
making brick both yesterday and today, as
before?" Ex. 5:6 • Is. 10:24

Israel Rejects Moses

15 Then the officers of the children of Israel
came and cried out to Pharaoh, saying, "Why
are you dealing thus with your servants?
16 "There is no straw given to your servants, and they say to us, 'Make brick!' And
indeed your servants *are* beaten, but the fault
is in your *own* people."
17 But he said, "You *are* idle! *You are* idle!
Therefore you say, 'Let us go *and* sacrifice to
the LORD.'
18 "Therefore go now *and* work; for no
straw shall be given you, yet you shall deliver
the quota of bricks."
19 And the officers of the children of Israel
saw *that* they *were* in trouble after it was
said, "You shall not diminish *any* bricks from
your daily quota."
20 Then, as they came out from Pharaoh,
they met Moses and Aaron who stood there
to meet them.
21 And they said to them, "Let the LORD
look on you and judge, because you have
made us [T]abhorrent in the sight of Pharaoh
and in the sight of his servants, to put a
sword in their hand to kill us." Lit. *stink*

Moses Questions God's Plan

22 So Moses returned to the LORD and said,
"Lord, why have You brought trouble on this
people? Why *is* it You have sent me?
23 "For since I came to Pharaoh to speak in
Your name, he has done evil to this people;
neither have You delivered Your people at
all."

CHAPTER 6

God Reassures Moses

THEN the LORD said to Moses, "Now you
shall see what I will do to Pharaoh. For
[R]with a strong hand he will let them go, and
with a strong hand [R]he will drive them out of
his land." Ex. 3:19 • Ex. 12:31, 33, 39
2 And God spoke to Moses and said to him:
"I *am* [T]the LORD. Heb. *YHWH*, traditionally *Jehovah*
3 "I appeared to Abraham, to Isaac, and to
Jacob, as God Almighty, but *by* My name
[T]LORD I was not known to them. *YHWH*
4 "I have also established My covenant
with them, to give them the land of Canaan,
the land of their [T]pilgrimage, in which they
were [T]strangers. *sojournings* • Temporary residents
5 "And [R]I have also heard the groaning of
the children of Israel whom the Egyptians
keep in bondage, and I have remembered My
covenant. Ex. 2:24
6 "Therefore say to the children of Israel:
'I *am* the LORD; I will bring you out from
under the burdens of the Egyptians, I will
[R]rescue you from their bondage, and I will
redeem you with [T]an outstretched arm and
with great judgments. Deut. 7:8 • Mighty power
7 'I will take you as My people, and I will
be your God. Then you shall know that I *am*
the LORD your God who brings you out from
under the burdens of the Egyptians.

8 'And I will bring you into the land which
I [T]swore to give to Abraham, Isaac, and
Jacob; and I will give it to you *as* a heritage:
I *am* the LORD.' " *promised,* lit. *lifted up my hand*

Moses Reassures Israel

9 So Moses spoke thus to the children of
Israel; [R]but they would not heed Moses,
because of [R]anguish[T] of spirit and cruel bondage. Ex. 5:21 • Ex. 2:23 • Lit. *shortness*

God Recommissions Moses

10 And the LORD spoke to Moses, saying,
11 "Go in, speak to Pharaoh king of Egypt,
that he must let the children of Israel go out
of his land."
12 And Moses spoke before the LORD, saying, "The children of Israel have not heeded
me. How then shall Pharaoh heed me, for I
am [T]of uncircumcised lips?" A poor speaker
13 Then the LORD spoke to Moses and
Aaron, and gave them a [R]command[T] for the
children of Israel and for Pharaoh king of
Egypt, to bring the children of Israel out of
the land of Egypt. Deut. 31:14 • *charge*
14 These *are* the heads of their fathers'
houses: The sons of Reuben, the firstborn of
Israel, *were* Hanoch, Pallu, Hezron, and
Carmi. These are the families of Reuben.
15 [R]And the sons of Simeon *were* [T]Jemuel,
Jamin, Ohad, Jachin, Zohar, and Shaul the
son of a Canaanite woman. These *are* the
families of Simeon. Gen. 46:10 • *Nemuel,* Num. 26:12
16 These *are* the names of the sons of Levi
according to their generations: Gershon,
Kohath, and Merari. And the years of the life
of Levi *were* one hundred and thirty-seven.
17 [R]The sons of Gershon *were* Libni and
Shimi according to their families. 1 Chr. 6:17
18 And [R]the sons of Kohath *were* Amram,
Izhar, Hebron, and Uzziel. And the years of
the life of Kohath *were* one hundred and
thirty-three. 1 Chr. 6:2, 18
19 [R]The sons of Merari *were* Mahali and
Mushi. These *are* the families of Levi according to their generations. 1 Chr. 6:19; 23:21
20 Now [R]Amram took for himself [R]Joche-
bed, his father's sister, as wife; and she bore
him [R]Aaron and Moses. And the years of the
life of Amram *were* one hundred and thirty-
seven. Ex. 2:1, 2 • Num. 26:59 • Num. 26:59
21 [R]The sons of Izhar *were* Korah, Nepheg,
and Zichri. 1 Chr. 6:37, 38
22 And [R]the sons of Uzziel *were* Mishael,
Elzaphan, and Zithri. Lev. 10:4
23 Aaron took to himself Elisheba, daughter
of [R]Amminadab, sister of Nahshon, as wife;
and she bore him [R]Nadab, Abihu, [R]Eleazar,
and Ithamar. Ruth 4:19, 20 • Lev. 10:1 • Ex. 28:1
24 And [R]the sons of Korah *were* Assir, Elkanah, and Abiasaph. These are the families of
the Korahites. Num. 26:11
25 Eleazar, Aaron's son, took for himself
one of the daughters of Putiel as wife; and
[R]she bore him Phinehas. These *are* the heads
of the fathers of the Levites according to
their families. Num. 25:7, 11
26 These *are the same* Aaron and Moses to
whom the LORD said, "Bring out the children
of Israel from the land of Egypt according to
their [R]armies."[T] Ex. 7:4; 12:17, 51 • *hosts*
27 These *are* the ones who spoke to Pharaoh king of Egypt, [R]to bring out the children
of Israel from Egypt. These *are the same*
Moses and Aaron. Ps. 77:20

Moses Objects

28 And it came to pass, on the day *when* the
LORD spoke to Moses in the land of Egypt,
29 that the LORD spoke to Moses, saying, "I
am the LORD. [R]Speak to Pharaoh king of
Egypt all that I say to you." Ex. 6:11; 7:2
30 But Moses said before the LORD, "Behold,
[R]I *am* [T]of uncircumcised lips, and how shall
Pharaoh heed me?" Ex. 4:10; 6:12 • A poor speaker

CHAPTER 7

God Reassures Moses

SO the LORD said to Moses: "See, I have
made you *as* God to Pharaoh, and Aaron
your brother shall be your prophet.
2 "You [R]shall speak all that I command
you. And Aaron your brother shall speak to
Pharaoh, that he must send the children of
Israel out of his land. Ex. 4:15
3 "And [R]I will harden Pharaoh's heart, and
[R]multiply My [R]signs and My wonders in the
land of Egypt. Ex. 4:21; 9:12 • Ex. 11:9 • Deut. 4:34
4 "But Pharaoh will not heed you, so that I
may lay My hand on Egypt and bring My
armies *and* My people, the children of Israel,
out of the land of Egypt by great judgments.
5 "And the Egyptians shall know that I *am*
the LORD, when I [R]stretch out My hand on
Egypt and [R]bring out the children of Israel
from among them." Ex. 9:15 • Ex. 3:20; 6:6; 12:51
6 Then Moses and Aaron did *so*; just as the
LORD commanded them, so they did.
7 And Moses *was* [R]eighty years old and
[R]Aaron eighty-three years old when they
spoke to Pharaoh. Deut. 29:5; 31:2; 34:7 • Num. 33:39

Aaron's Rod Swallows Pharaoh's Rods

8 Then the LORD spoke to Moses and
Aaron, saying,
9 "When Pharaoh speaks to you, saying,
[R]'Show a miracle for yourselves,' then you
shall say to Aaron, [R]'Take your rod and cast *it*
before Pharaoh, *and* let it become a serpent.' " Is. 7:11 • Ex. 4:2, 3, 17
10 So Moses and Aaron went in to Pharaoh,
and they did so, just [R]as the LORD commanded. And Aaron cast down his rod before

Pharaoh and before his servants, and it [R]be-
came a serpent. Ex. 7:9 • Ex. 4:3
11 But Pharaoh also called the wise men
and [R]the sorcerers; so the magicians of Egypt,
they also [R]did in like manner with their
enchantments. 2 Tim. 3:8 • Ex. 7:22; 8:7, 18
12 For every man threw down his rod, and
they became serpents. But Aaron's rod swallowed up their rods.
13 And Pharaoh's heart grew hard, and he
did not heed them, as the LORD had said.

First Plague: Blood

14 So the LORD said to Moses: [R]"Pharaoh's
heart *is* hard; he refuses to let the people
go. Ex. 8:15; 10:1, 20, 27
15 "Go to Pharaoh in the morning, when he
goes out to the [R]water, and you shall stand by
the river's bank to meet him; and [R]the rod
which was turned to a serpent you shall take
in your hand. Ex. 2:5; 8:20 • Ex. 4:2, 3; 7:10
16 "And you shall say to him, 'The LORD
God of the Hebrews has sent me to you,
saying, "Let My people go, that they may
[T]serve Me in the wilderness"; but indeed,
until now you would not hear! *worship*
17 'Thus says the LORD: "By this you shall
know that I *am* the LORD. Behold, I will strike
the waters which *are* in the river with the rod
that *is* in my hand, and [R]they shall be turned
[R]to blood. Ex. 4:9; 7:20 • Rev. 11:6; 16:4, 6
18 "And the fish that *are* in the river shall
die, the river shall stink, and the Egyptians
will [R]loathe to drink the water of the
river." ' " Ex. 7:24
19 Then the LORD spoke to Moses, "Say to
Aaron, 'Take your rod and stretch out your
hand over the waters of Egypt, over their
streams, over their rivers, over their ponds,
and over all their pools of water, that they
may become blood. And there shall be blood
throughout all the land of Egypt, both in
vessels of wood and *vessels of* stone.' "
20 And Moses and Aaron did so, just as the
LORD commanded. So he lifted up the rod and
struck the waters that *were* in the river, in
the sight of Pharaoh and in the sight of his
servants. And all the [R]waters that *were* in the
river were turned to blood. Ps. 78:44; 105:29, 30
21 The fish that *were* in the river died, the
river stank, and the Egyptians could not
drink the water of the river. So there was
blood throughout all the land of Egypt.
22 Then the magicians of Egypt did [R]so with
their enchantments; and Pharaoh's heart
grew hard, and he did not heed them, [R]as the
LORD had said. Ex. 8:7 • Ex. 3:19; 7:3
23 And Pharaoh turned and went into his
house. Neither was his heart moved by this.
24 So all the Egyptians dug all around the
river for water to drink, because they could
not drink the water of the river.
25 And seven days passed after the LORD
had struck the river.

CHAPTER 8

Second Plague: Frogs

AND the LORD spoke to Moses, "Go to
Pharaoh and say to him, 'Thus says the
LORD: "Let My people go, [R]that they may
serve Me. Ex. 3:12, 18; 4:23; 5:1, 3
2 "But if you [R]refuse to let *them* go, behold, I will smite all your territory with
[R]frogs. Ex. 7:14; 9:2 • Rev. 16:13
3 "So the river shall bring forth frogs
abundantly, which shall go up and come into
your house, into your [R]bedchamber, on your
bed, into the houses of your servants, on your
people, into your ovens, and into your kneading bowls. Ps. 105:30
4 "And the frogs shall come up on you, on
your people, and on all your servants." ' "
5 Then the LORD spoke to Moses, "Say to
Aaron, [R]'Stretch out your hand with your rod
over the streams, over the rivers, and over
the ponds, and cause frogs to come up on the
land of Egypt.' " Ex. 7:19
6 So Aaron stretched out his hand over the
waters of Egypt, and [R]the frogs came up and
covered the land of Egypt. Ps. 78:45; 105:30
7 [R]And the magicians did so with their
[T]enchantments, and brought up frogs on the
land of Egypt. Ex. 7:11, 22 • *secret arts*
8 Then Pharaoh called for Moses and
Aaron, and said, [T]"Entreat the LORD that He
may take away the frogs from me and from
my people; and I will let the people go, that
they may sacrifice to the LORD." *Pray to*
9 And Moses said to Pharaoh, "Accept the
honor of saying when I shall intercede for
you, for your servants, and for your people, to
destroy the frogs from you and your houses,
that they may remain in the river only."
10 So he said, "Tomorrow." And he said,
"*Let it be* according to your word, that you
may know that [R]*there is* no one like the LORD
our God. Ex. 9:14; 15:11
11 "And the frogs shall depart from you,
from your houses, from your servants, and
from your people. They shall remain in the
river only."
12 Then Moses and Aaron went out from
Pharaoh. And Moses [R]cried out to the LORD
concerning the frogs which He had brought
against Pharaoh. Ex. 8:30; 9:33; 10:18; 32:11
13 So the LORD did according to the word of
Moses. And the frogs died out of the houses,
out of the courtyards, and out of the fields.
14 They gathered them together in heaps,
and the land stank.
15 But when Pharaoh saw that there was
[R]relief, he hardened his heart and did not
heed them, as the LORD had said. Eccl. 8:11

Third Plague: Lice

16 So the LORD said to Moses, "Say to
Aaron, 'Stretch out your rod, and strike the

dust of the land, so that it may become [T]lice throughout all the land of Egypt.' " Or *gnats*

17 And they did so. For Aaron stretched out his hand with his rod and struck the dust of the earth, and [R]it became lice on man and beast. All the dust of the land became lice throughout all the land of Egypt. Ps. 105:31

18 Now [R]the magicians so worked with their [T]enchantments to bring forth lice, but they [R]could not. So there were lice on man and beast. Ex. 7:11, 12; 8:7 • *secret arts* • Dan. 5:8

19 Then the magicians said to Pharaoh, "This *is* [T]the finger of God." But Pharaoh's heart grew hard, and he did not heed them, just as the LORD had said. An act of God

Fourth Plague: Flies

20 And the LORD said to Moses, "Rise early in the morning and stand before Pharaoh as he comes out to the water. Then say to him, 'Thus says the LORD: [R]"Let My people go, that they may serve Me. Ex. 3:18; 4:23; 5:1, 3; 8:1

21 "Or else, if you will not let My people go, behold, I will send swarms *of flies* on you and your servants, on your people and into your houses. The houses of the Egyptians shall be full of swarms *of flies,* and also the ground on which they *stand.*

22 "And in that day I will set apart the land of [R]Goshen, in which My people dwell, that no swarms *of flies* shall be there, in order that you may [R]know that I *am* the LORD in the midst of the land. Gen. 50:8 • Ex. 7:5, 17; 10:2

23 "I will [T]make a difference between My people and your people. Tomorrow this [R]sign shall be." ' " Lit. *set a ransom,* Ex. 9:4; 11:7 • Ex. 4:8

24 And the LORD did so. [R]Thick swarms *of flies* came into the house of Pharaoh, *into* his servants' houses, and into all the land of Egypt. The land was corrupted because of the swarms *of flies.* Ps. 78:45; 105:31

25 Then Pharaoh called for Moses and Aaron, and said, "Go, sacrifice to your God in the land."

26 And Moses said, "It is not right to do so, for we would be sacrificing [R]the abomination of the Egyptians to the LORD our God. If we sacrifice the abomination of the Egyptians before their eyes, then will they not [T]stone us? Gen. 43:32; 46:34 • Put us to death by stoning

27 "We will go [R]three days' journey into the wilderness and sacrifice to the LORD our God as [R]He will command us." Ex. 3:18; 5:3 • Ex. 3:12

28 And Pharaoh said, "I will let you go, that you may sacrifice to the LORD your God in the wilderness; only you shall not go very far away. [R]Intercede for me." Ex. 8:8, 15, 29, 32; 9:28

29 Then Moses said, "Indeed I am going out from you, and I will entreat the LORD, that the swarms *of flies* may depart tomorrow from Pharaoh, from his servants, and from his people. But let Pharaoh not [R]deal deceitfully anymore in not letting the people go to sacrifice to the LORD." Ex. 8:8, 15

30 So Moses went out from Pharaoh and [R]entreated the LORD. Ex. 8:12

31 And the LORD did according to the word of Moses; He removed the swarms *of flies* from Pharaoh, from his servants, and from his people. Not one remained.

32 But Pharaoh hardened his heart at this time also; neither would he let the people go.

CHAPTER 9

Fifth Plague: Disease on Beasts

THEN the LORD said to Moses, "Go in to Pharaoh and tell him, 'Thus says the LORD God of the Hebrews: "Let My people go, that they may [R]serve Me. Ex. 7:16

2 "For if you [R]refuse to let *them* go, and still hold them, Ex. 8:2

3 "behold, the [R]hand of the LORD will be on your cattle in the field, on the horses, on the donkeys, on the camels, on the oxen, and on the sheep. *There will be* a very severe pestilence. Ex. 7:4

4 "And the LORD will make a difference between the livestock of Israel and the livestock of Egypt. So nothing shall die of all *that* belongs to the children of Israel." ' "

5 Then the LORD appointed a set time, saying, "Tomorrow the LORD will do this thing in the land."

6 So the LORD did this thing on the next day, and [R]all the livestock of Egypt died; but of the livestock of the children of Israel, not one died. Ps. 78:48, 50

7 Then Pharaoh sent, and indeed, not even one of the livestock of the Israelites was dead. But the heart of Pharaoh became hard, and he did not let the people go.

Sixth Plague: Boils on Man and Beast

8 So the LORD said to Moses and Aaron, "Take for yourselves handfuls of ashes from a furnace, and let Moses scatter it toward the heavens in the sight of Pharaoh.

9 "And it will become fine dust in all the land of Egypt, and it will cause [R]boils that break out in sores on man and beast throughout all the land of Egypt." Rev. 16:2

10 Then they took ashes from the furnace and stood before Pharaoh, and Moses scattered *them* toward heaven. And *they* caused [R]boils that break out in sores on man and beast. Deut. 28:27

11 And the [R]magicians could not stand before Moses because of the [R]boils, for the boils were on the magicians and on all the Egyptians. [Ex. 8:18, 19] • Job 2:7

12 But the LORD hardened the heart of Pharaoh; and he did not heed them, just [R]as the LORD had spoken to Moses. Ex. 4:21

THE TEN PLAGUES OF EGYPT

The overrunning of the land by frogs and swarms of locusts were two of the plagues the Egyptians faced when they refused to free the Israelites.

Pharaoh, the ruler of Egypt, refused to release the Hebrew people from slavery and allow them to leave his country. So the Lord sent ten plagues upon the Egyptians to break Pharaoh's stubborn will and to demonstrate His power and superiority over the pagan gods of the Egyptians.

These plagues occurred within a period of about nine months, in the following order:

1. The water of the Nile River turned into blood (Ex. 7:14–25).
2. Frogs overran the countryside (Ex. 8:1–15).
3. People and animals were infested with lice (Ex. 8:16–19).
4. Swarms of flies covered the land (Ex. 8:20–32).
5. Disease killed the livestock of Egypt (Ex. 9:1–7).
6. Boils and sores infected the Egyptians and their animals (Ex. 9:8–12).
7. Hail destroyed crops and vegetation (Ex. 9:13–35).
8. Swarms of locusts covered the land (Ex. 10:1–20).
9. Thick darkness covered Egypt for three days (Ex. 10:21–29).
10. The Egyptian firstborn, both of the people and their animals, were destroyed by God's death angel (Ex. 11:1—12:30).

In all of these plagues, the Israelites were protected, while the Egyptians and their property were destroyed. The Hebrews were delivered from the final plague when they marked their houses, at God's command, by sprinkling the blood of a lamb on their doorposts. The death angel "passed over" the Hebrew houses.

At this final demonstration of God's power, the Pharaoh gave in and allowed Moses and the Israelites to leave Egypt. This deliverance became one of the most memorable occasions in Hebrew history. The Passover is celebrated annually even today to commemorate God's deliverance of the Hebrew people from slavery. (See the article "Feasts and Festivals," pp. 146, 147.)

Seventh Plague: Hail

13 Then the LORD said to Moses, [R]"Rise
early in the morning and stand before Pharaoh, and say to him, 'Thus says the LORD
God of the Hebrews: "Let My people go, that
they may [R]serve Me, Ex. 8:20 • Ex. 9:1
14 "for at this time I will send all My
plagues to your very heart, and on your
servants and on your people, [R]that you may
know that *there is* none like Me in all the
earth. Ex. 8:10
15 "Now if I had [R]stretched out My hand
and struck you and your people with [R]pesti-
lence, then you would have been cut off from
the earth. Ex. 3:20; 7:5 • Ex. 5:3
16 "But indeed for [R]this *purpose* I have
raised you up, that I may show My power *in*
you, and that My [R]name may be declared in
all the earth. [Rom. 9:17, 18] • 1 Kin. 8:43
17 "As yet you exalt yourself against My
people in that you will not let them go.
18 "Behold, tomorrow about this time I will
cause very heavy hail to rain down, such as
has not been in Egypt since its founding until
now.
19 "Therefore send now *and* gather your
livestock and all that you have in the field,
for the hail shall come down on every man
and every beast which is found in the field
and is not brought home; and they shall
die." ' "
20 He who feared the word of the LORD
among the servants of Pharaoh made his
servants and his livestock flee to the houses.
21 But he who did not regard the word of
the LORD left his servants and his livestock in
the field.
22 Then the LORD said to Moses, "Stretch
out your hand toward heaven, that there may
be [R]hail in all the land of Egypt—on man, on
beast, and on every herb of the field, throughout the land of Egypt." Rev. 16:21
23 And Moses stretched out his rod toward
heaven; and [R]the LORD sent thunder and hail,
and fire darted to the ground. And the LORD
rained hail on the land of Egypt. Josh. 10:11
24 So there was hail, and fire mingled with
the hail, so very heavy that there was none
like it in all the land of Egypt since it became
a nation.
25 And the [R]hail struck throughout the
whole land of Egypt, all that *was* in the field,
both man and beast; and the hail struck
every herb of the field and broke every tree of
the field. Ps. 78:47, 48; 105:32, 33
26 Only in the land of Goshen, where the
children of Israel *were*, there was no hail.
27 And Pharaoh sent and [R]called for Moses
and Aaron, and said to them, "I have sinned
this time. [R]The LORD *is* righteous, and my
people and I *are* wicked. Ex. 8:8 • 2 Chr. 12:6
28 [T]"Entreat the LORD, that there may be no
more [T]mighty thundering and hail, for *it is*
enough. I will let you go, and you shall stay
no longer." *Pray to* • Lit. *sounds of God*
29 And Moses said to him, "As soon as I
have gone out of the city, I will spread out
my hands to the LORD; the thunder will cease,
and there will be no more hail, that you may
know that the [R]earth *is* the LORD's. Ps. 24:1
30 "But as for you and your servants, [R]I
know that you will not yet fear the LORD
God." [Is. 26:10]
31 Now the flax and the barley were struck,
[R]for the barley *was* in the head and the flax
was in bud. Ruth 1:22; 2:23
32 But the wheat and the spelt were not
struck, for they *are* late crops.
33 So Moses went out of the city from
Pharaoh and spread out his hands to the
LORD; then the thunder and the hail ceased,
and the rain was not poured on the earth.
34 And when Pharaoh saw that the rain, the
hail, and the thunder had ceased, he sinned
yet more; and he hardened his heart, he and
his servants.
35 So [R]the heart of Pharaoh was hard; neither would he let the children of Israel go, as
the LORD had spoken by Moses. Ex. 4:21

CHAPTER 10

Eighth Plague: Locusts

NOW the LORD said to Moses, "Go in to
Pharaoh; for I have hardened his heart
and the hearts of his servants, that I may
show these signs of Mine before him,
2 "and that [R]you may tell in the hearing of
your son and your son's son the mighty
things I have done in Egypt, and My signs
which I have done among them, that you
may know that I *am* the LORD." Joel 1:3
3 So Moses and Aaron came in to Pharaoh
and said to him, "Thus says the LORD God of
the Hebrews: 'How long will you refuse to
[R]humble yourself before Me? Let My people
go, that they may serve Me. [1 Kin. 21:29]
4 'Or else, if you refuse to let My people go,
behold, tomorrow I will bring [R]locusts into
your territory. Rev. 9:3
5 'And they shall cover the face of the
earth, so that no one will be able to see the
earth; and [R]they shall eat the residue of what
is left, which remains to you from the hail,
and they shall eat every tree which grows up
for you out of the field. Ex. 9:32
6 'They shall fill your houses, the houses of
all your servants, and the houses of all the
Egyptians—which neither your fathers nor
your fathers' fathers have seen, since the day
that they were on the earth to this day.' "
And he turned and went out from Pharaoh.
7 Then Pharaoh's [R]servants said to him,
"How long shall this man be [R]a snare to us?
Let the men go, that they may serve the LORD

their God. Do you not yet know that Egypt is
destroyed?" Ex. 7:5; 8:19; 9:20; 12:33 • Ex. 23:33
8 So Moses and Aaron were brought again
to Pharaoh, and he said to them, "Go, serve
the LORD your God. *But* who *are* the ones
that are going?"
9 And Moses said, "We will go with our
young and our old; with our sons and our
daughters, with our flocks and our herds we
will go, for [R]we must hold a feast to the
LORD." Ex. 5:1; 7:16
10 Then he said to them, "The LORD had
better be with you when I let you and your
little ones go! Beware, for evil is ahead of you.
11 "Not so! Go now, you *who are* men, and
serve the LORD, for that is what you desired."
And they were driven [R]out from Pharaoh's
presence. Ex. 10:28
12 Then the LORD said to Moses, [R]"Stretch
out your hand over the land of Egypt for the
locusts, that they may come upon the land of
Egypt, and [R]eat every herb of the land—all
that the hail has left." Ex. 7:19 • Ex. 10:5, 15
13 So Moses stretched out his rod over the
land of Egypt, and the LORD brought an east
wind on the land all that day and all *that*
night. *And* when it was morning, the east
wind brought the locusts.
14 And the locusts went up over all the land
of Egypt and rested on all the territory of
Egypt. *They were* very severe; [R]previously
there had been no such locusts as they, nor
shall there be such after them. Joel 2:1–11
15 For they [R]covered the face of the whole
earth, so that the land was darkened; and
they [R]ate every herb of the land and all the
fruit of the trees which the hail had left. So
there remained nothing green on the trees or
on the plants of the field throughout all the
land of Egypt. Ex. 10:5 • Ps. 105:35
16 Then Pharaoh called for Moses and
Aaron in haste, and said, "I have sinned
against the LORD your God and against you.
17 "Now therefore, please forgive my sin
only this once, and [R]entreat[T] the LORD your
God, that He may take away from me this
death only." 1 Kin. 13:6 • *make supplication to*
18 So he [R]went out from Pharaoh and entreated the LORD. Ex. 8:30
19 And the LORD turned a very strong west
wind, which took the locusts away and blew
them [R]*into the* Red Sea. There remained not
one locust in all the territory of Egypt. Joel 2:20
20 But the LORD hardened Pharaoh's heart,
and he did not let the children of Israel go.

Ninth Plague: Darkness

21 Then the LORD said to Moses, [R]"Stretch
out your hand toward heaven, that there may
be darkness over the land of Egypt, darkness
which may even be felt." Ex. 9:22
22 So Moses stretched out his hand toward
heaven, and there was thick darkness in all
the land of Egypt [R]three days. Ex. 3:18
23 They did not see one *another; nor did*
anyone rise from his place for three days.
[R]But all the children of Israel had light in
their dwellings. Ex. 8:22, 23
24 Then Pharaoh called to Moses and [R]said,
"Go, serve the LORD; only let your flocks and
your herds be kept back. Let your [R]little ones
also go with you." Ex. 8:8, 25; 10:8 • Ex. 10:10
25 But Moses said, "You must also give [T]us
sacrifices and burnt offerings, that we may
sacrifice to the LORD our God. Lit. *into our hands*
26 "Our [R]livestock also shall go with us; not
a hoof shall be left behind. For we must take
some of them to serve the LORD our God, and
even we do not know with what we must
serve the LORD until we arrive there." Ex. 10:9
27 But the LORD [R]hardened Pharaoh's heart,
and he would not let them go. Ex. 4:21
28 Then Pharaoh said to him, [R]"Get away
from me! Take heed to yourself and see my
face no more! For in the day you see my face
you shall die!" Ex. 10:11
29 And Moses said, "You have spoken well.
[R]I will never see your face again." Heb. 11:27

CHAPTER 11

Tenth Plague: Death Announced

AND the LORD said to Moses, "I will bring
yet one *more* plague on Pharaoh and on
Egypt. Afterward he will let you go from
here. [R]When he lets *you* go, he will surely
drive you out of here altogether. Ex. 6:1; 12:39
2 "Speak now in the hearing of the people,
and let every man ask from his neighbor and
every woman from her neighbor, [R]articles of
silver and articles of gold." Ex. 3:22; 12:35, 36
3 And the LORD gave the people favor in
the sight of the Egyptians. Moreover the man
[R]Moses *was* very great in the land of Egypt,
in the sight of Pharaoh's servants and in the
sight of the people. Deut. 34:10–12
4 Then Moses said, "Thus says the LORD:
[R]'About midnight I will go out into the midst
of Egypt; Ex. 12:12, 23, 29
5 'and all the firstborn in the land of Egypt
shall die, from the firstborn of Pharaoh who
sits on his throne, even to the firstborn of the
maidservant who *is* behind the handmill, and
all the firstborn of the beasts.
6 'Then there shall be a great cry throughout all the land of Egypt, such as was not like
it *before*, nor shall be like it again.
7 [R]'But against none of the children of
Israel [R]shall a dog [T]move its tongue, against
man or beast, that you may know that the
LORD does make a difference between the
Egyptians and Israel.' Ex. 8:22 • Josh. 10:21 • *sharpen*
8 "And all these your servants shall come
down to me and bow down to me, saying,

'Get out, and all the people who follow you!'
After that I will go out." [R]Then he went out
from Pharaoh in great anger. Heb. 11:27
9 But the LORD said to Moses, "Pharaoh
will not heed you, so that My wonders may
be multiplied in the land of Egypt."
10 So Moses and Aaron did all these wonders before Pharaoh; [R]and the LORD hardened
Pharaoh's heart, and he did not let the children of Israel go out of his land. Rom. 2:5

CHAPTER 12

Instructions for the Passover

NOW the LORD spoke to Moses and Aaron
in the land of Egypt, saying,
2 [R]"This month *shall be* your beginning of
months; it *shall be* the first month of the year
to you. Deut. 16:1
3 "Speak to all the congregation of Israel,
saying: 'On the [R]tenth *day* of this month
every man shall take for himself a lamb,
according to the house of *his* father, a lamb
for a household. Josh. 4:19
4 'And if the household is too small for the
lamb, let him and his neighbor next to his
house take *it* according to the number of the
persons; according to each man's need you
shall make your count for the lamb.
5 'Your lamb shall be [R]without blemish, a
male of the first year. You may take *it* from
the sheep or from the goats. [1 Pet. 1:19]
6 'Now you shall keep it until the [R]four-
teenth day of the same month. Then the
whole assembly of the congregation of Israel
shall kill it at twilight. Lev. 23:5
7 'And they shall take *some* of the blood
and put *it* on the two doorposts and on the
lintel of the houses where they eat it.
8 'Then they shall eat the flesh on that
[R]night; [R]roasted in fire, with [R]unleavened
bread *and* with bitter *herbs* they shall eat
it. Num. 9:12 • Deut. 16:7 • 1 Cor. 5:8
9 'Do not eat it raw, nor boiled at all with
water, but [R]roasted in fire—its head with its
legs and its entrails. Deut. 16:7
10 [R]'You shall let none of it remain until
morning, and what remains of it until morning you shall burn with fire. Ex. 16:19; 23:18; 34:25
11 'And thus you shall eat it: *with* a belt on
your waist, your sandals on your feet, and
your staff in your hand. So you shall eat it in
haste. [R]It *is* the LORD's Passover. Ex. 12:13
12 'For I will pass through the land of Egypt
on that night, and will strike all the firstborn
in the land of Egypt, both man and beast; and
against all the gods of Egypt I will execute
judgment: [R]*I am the* LORD. Ex. 6:2
13 'Now the blood shall be a sign for you on
the houses where you *are.* And when I see
the blood, I will pass over you; and the plague
shall not be on you to destroy *you* when I
strike the land of Egypt.
14 'So this day shall be to you a memorial;
and you shall keep it as a feast to the LORD
throughout your generations. You shall keep
it as a feast by an everlasting ordinance.
15 [R]'Seven days you shall eat unleavened
bread. On the first day you shall remove
leaven from your houses. For whoever eats
leavened bread from the first day until the
seventh day, [R]that [T]person shall be [T]cut off
from Israel. Lev. 23:6 • Gen. 17:14 • *soul* • Put to death
16 'On the first day *there shall be* [R]a holy
convocation, and on the seventh day there
shall be a holy convocation for you. No
manner of work shall be done on them; but
that which everyone must eat—that only
may be prepared by you. Lev. 23:2, 7, 8
17 'So you shall observe *the Feast of* Unleavened Bread, for on this same day I will
have brought your [T]armies [R]out of the land of
Egypt. Therefore you shall observe this day
throughout your generations as an everlasting ordinance. *hosts* • Num. 33:1
18 [R]'In the first *month,* on the fourteenth
day of the month at evening, you shall eat
unleavened bread, until the twenty-first day
of the month at evening. Lev. 23:5–8
19 'For [R]seven days no leaven shall be found
in your houses, since whoever eats what is
leavened, that same person shall be cut off
from the congregation of Israel, whether *he*
is a stranger or a native of the land. Ex. 12:15
20 'You shall eat nothing leavened; in all
your habitations you shall eat unleavened
bread.' "

Participation in the Passover

21 Then [R]Moses called for all the elders of
Israel and said to them, "Pick out and take
lambs for yourselves according to your families, and kill the Passover *lamb.* [Heb. 11:28]
22 [R]"And you shall take a bunch of hyssop,
dip *it* in the blood that *is* in the basin, and
[R]strike the lintel and the two doorposts with
the blood that *is* in the basin. And none of
you shall go out of the door of his house until
morning. Heb. 11:28 • Ex. 12:7
23 "For the LORD will pass through to strike
the Egyptians; and when He sees the blood
on the lintel and on the two doorposts, the
LORD will pass over the door and [R]not allow
[R]the destroyer to come into your houses to
strike *you.* Rev. 7:3; 9:4 • Heb. 11:28
24 "And you shall observe this thing as an
ordinance for you and your sons forever.
25 "It will come to pass when you come to
the land which the LORD will give you, [R]just
as He promised, that you shall keep this
service. Ex. 3:8, 17
26 "And it shall be, when your children say
to you, 'What do you mean by this service?'
27 "that you shall say, [R]'It *is* the Passover
sacrifice of the LORD, who passed over the
houses of the children of Israel in Egypt

ATONEMENT AND REDEMPTION

Atone For, Reconcile (*kāphar*)

Occurring 150 times, *kāphar* has traditionally been thought to be related to an Arabic word for cover. The view that Old Testament sacrifices covered over sins until the Messiah came and actually did away with them is today considered unlikely by some scholars. There is in Genesis 6:14 one usage of a verb meaning "to cover with pitch" (Noah's ark) that is spelled the same but considered to be a different verb.

R. Laird Harris takes the verb to be derived from the noun *kôpher* (see below) and to mean "provide a ransom" (*Theological Wordbook of the Old Testament*, I:453).

Atonement (*kippûr, kippûrîm*)

Atonement (*kippûr, kippûrîm*) is the word in the expression "Day of Atonement." In the Old Testament, the plural form is used, rather than the current *Yôm Kippûr.* The day commemorates redemption by blood and power: the blood of the lamb on the doorposts was a ransom, and it protected the Israelites from destruction. Passing through the Red Sea on dry land illustrates redemption by power.

Atonement, Expiation, Ransom Price (*kōpher*)

The word *kōpher* is used to teach redemption by substitution. The worshiper put his hands on the head of the sacrifice, and as he confessed his sins they were transferred to the innocent animal. Generally the word *kōpher* is used in the sense of removing sin or defilement. It clearly parallels the New Testament doctrine that Christ, the Lamb of God, an innocent—and infinite—sacrifice, bore the sins of those guilty sinners who identify with Him by faith.

Mercy Seat, Place of Propitiation (*kappōret*)

The gold lid to the ark of the covenant where God promised to meet with His people was the mercy seat. Once a year the high priest of Israel sprinkled the blood of atonement on this cover. The New Testament equivalent (from the Septuagint) is *hilastērion*, "place of propitiation." The traditional rendering "mercy seat" is not very literal. For one thing it was not a seat (unless the metaphorical usage, such as "seat of authority," is meant) and the stress is not so much on mercy (*eleos*) as it is on satisfaction (*hilasmos*). (See word study on p. 1451.) Christ Himself is called our mercy seat or propitiation (KJV, NKJV) in Romans 3:25.

Redeem, Make Good a Lapsed Claim (*gā'al*)

Gā'al occurs 118 times in the Old Testament, counting words derived from this verb. The main idea is to redeem one's relatives from difficulty or danger, such as by buying back some family property or purchasing an Israelite out of slavery.

Redeemer, Redeeming Relative (*gō'ēl*)

Gō'ēl is the masculine participle of the above verb. God Himself is presented in the Psalms as Israel's Redeemer, and Job's famous passage "I know *that* my Redeemer lives" (Job. 19:25) is generally taken to refer to Christ and His redemption.

The most famous and most attractive illustration of redemption is the case of Ruth and Boaz. Boaz fulfilled two different functions here. First was *levirate* (from Latin *levir,* "husband's brother") marriage, in that he married the widow Ruth as a near relative ("kinsman redeemer" is the KJV rendering). He also bought back the field that Naomi had sold in her poverty.

The requirements of a *gō'ēl* were fulfilled by Boaz and later on a larger scale by Christ: Boaz was a close relative (Lev. 25:48, 49; cf. Ruth 2:20); Christ was born of a woman, yet was infinite, as God the Son. Boaz was willing to fulfill his duty (Ruth 4:4), and so was Christ (Heb. 10:4–10). As a man of wealth Boaz was able to meet his obligation to Ruth. Likewise, because Christ could "sympathize with our weaknesses" and "was in all *points* tempted as *we are, yet* without sin" (Heb. 4:15), He could fulfill His role as the perfect sacrifice for our sins.

when He struck the Egyptians and delivered
our households.' " So the people [R]bowed their
heads and worshiped. Ex. 12:11 • Ex. 4:31
28 Then the children of Israel went away
and [R]did *so;* just as the LORD had commanded
Moses and Aaron, so they did. [Heb. 11:28]

Redemption Through the Passover

29 And it came to pass at midnight that [R]the
LORD struck all the firstborn in the land of
Egypt, from the firstborn of Pharaoh who sat
on his throne to the firstborn of the captive
who *was* in the dungeon, and all the firstborn
of [R]livestock. Num. 8:17; 33:4 • Ex. 9:6
30 So Pharaoh rose in the night, he, all his
servants, and all the Egyptians; and there
was a great cry in Egypt, for *there was* not a
house where *there was* not one dead.
31 Then he [R]called for Moses and Aaron by
night, and said, "Rise *and* go out from among
my people, [R]both you and the children of
Israel. And go, serve the LORD as you have
[R]said. Ex. 10:28, 29 • Ex. 8:25; 11:1 • Ex. 10:9
32 [R]"Also take your flocks and your herds,
as you have said, and be gone; and bless me
also." Ex. 10:9, 26
33 And the Egyptians urged the people, that
they might send them out of the land in
haste. For they said, "We *shall* all *be* dead."
34 So the people took their dough before it
was leavened, having their kneading bowls
bound up in their clothes on their shoulders.
35 Now the children of Israel had done
according to the word of Moses, and they had
asked from the Egyptians [R]articles of silver,
articles of gold, and clothing. Ex. 3:21, 22; 11:2, 3
36 [R]And the LORD had given the people
favor in the sight of the Egyptians, so that
they granted them *what they requested.*
Thus they plundered the Egyptians. Ex. 3:21

Freedom Because of the Passover

37 Then the children of Israel journeyed
from Rameses to Succoth, about six hundred
thousand men on foot, besides children.
38 A [R]mixed multitude went up with them
also, and flocks and herds—a great deal of
[R]livestock. Num. 11:4 • Deut. 3:19
39 And they baked unleavened cakes of the
dough which they had brought out of Egypt;
for it was not leavened, because they were
driven out of Egypt and could not wait, nor
had they prepared provisions for themselves.
40 Now the [T]sojourn of the children of
Israel who lived in *Egypt *was* [R]four hundred
and thirty years. Length of the stay • Acts 7:6
41 And it came to pass at the end of the four
hundred and thirty years—on that very same
day—it came to pass that all the armies of the
LORD went out from the land of Egypt.
42 It *is* a [T]night of solemn observance to the
LORD for bringing them out of the land of
Egypt. This *is* that night of the LORD, a
solemn observance for all the children of
Israel throughout their generations. *vigil*
43 And the LORD said to Moses and Aaron,
"This *is* [R]the ordinance of the Passover: No
outsider shall eat it. Num. 9:14
44 "But every man's servant who is bought
for money, when you have [R]circumcised him,
then he may eat it. Gen. 17:12, 13
45 [R]"A sojourner and a hired servant shall
not eat it. Lev. 22:10
46 "In one house it shall be eaten; you shall
not carry any of the flesh outside the house,
nor shall you break one of its bones.
47 [R]"All the congregation of Israel shall
keep it. Ex. 12:6
48 "And [R]when a stranger sojourns with
you *and wants* to keep the Passover to the
LORD, let all his males be circumcised, and
then let him come near and keep it; and he
shall be as a native of the land. For no
uncircumcised person shall eat it. Num. 9:14
49 [R]"One law shall be for the native-born
and for the stranger who sojourns among
you." Num. 15:15, 16
50 Thus all the children of Israel did; as the
LORD commanded Moses and Aaron, so they
did.
51 [R]So it came to pass, on that very same
day, that the LORD brought the children of
Israel out of the land of Egypt [R]according to
their armies. Ex. 12:41; 20:2 • Ex. 6:26

CHAPTER 13

Sanctification as a Result of the Passover

THEN the LORD spoke to Moses, saying,
2 [R]"Sanctify to Me all the firstborn,
whatever opens the womb among the children of Israel, *both* of man and animal; it is
Mine." Deut. 15:19; Luke 2:23 ☆
3 And Moses said to the people: "Remember this day in which you went out of Egypt,
out of the house of bondage; for by strength
of hand the LORD brought you out of this
place. No leavened bread shall be eaten.
4 [R]"On this day you are going out, in the
month Abib. Ex. 12:2; 23:15; 34:18
5 "And it shall be, when the LORD brings
you into the [R]land of the Canaanites and the
Hittites and the Amorites and the Hivites and
the Jebusites, which He [R]swore to your fathers to give you, a land flowing with milk
and honey, [R]that you shall keep this service
in this month. Gen. 17:8 • Ex. 6:8 • Ex. 12:25, 26
6 [R]"Seven days you shall eat unleavened
bread, and on the seventh day *there shall be* a
feast to the LORD. Ex. 12:15–20
7 "Unleavened bread shall be eaten seven
days. And [R]no leavened bread shall be seen
among you, nor shall leaven be seen among
you in all your quarters. Ex. 12:19

12:40 Sam., LXX *Egypt and Canaan*

8 "And you shall tell your son in that day, saying, '*This is done* because of what the LORD did for me when I came up from Egypt.'

9 "It shall be as [R]a sign to you on your hand and as a memorial between your eyes, that the LORD's law may be in your mouth; for with a strong hand the LORD has brought you out of Egypt. Deut. 6:8; 11:18

10 "You shall therefore keep this ordinance in its season from year to year.

11 "And it shall be, when the LORD [R]brings you into the land of the [R]Canaanites, as He swore to you and your fathers, and gives it to you, Ex. 13:5 • Num. 21:3

12 [R]"that you shall set apart to the LORD all that open the womb, that is, every firstling that comes from an animal which you have; the males *shall be* the LORD's. Lev. 27:26

13 "But [R]every firstling of a donkey you shall redeem with a lamb; and if you will not redeem *it*, then you shall break its neck. And all the firstborn of man among your sons [R]you shall redeem. Ex. 34:20 • Num. 3:46, 47; 18:15, 16

14 [R]"So it shall be, when your son asks you in time to come, saying, 'What *is* this?' that you shall say to him, [R]'By strength of hand the LORD brought us out of Egypt, out of the house of bondage. Deut. 6:20 • Ex. 13:3, 9

15 'And it came to pass, when Pharaoh was stubborn about letting us go, that [R]the LORD killed all the firstborn in the land of Egypt, both the firstborn of man and the firstborn of animal. Therefore I sacrifice to the LORD all males that open the womb, but all the firstborn of my sons I redeem.' Ex. 12:29

16 "It shall be as [R]a sign on your hand and as frontlets between your eyes, for by strength of hand the LORD brought us out of Egypt." Ex. 13:9

God Leads Israel

17 Then it came to pass, when Pharaoh had let the people go, that God did not lead them *by* way of the land of the Philistines, although that *was* near; for God said, "Lest perhaps the people change their minds when they see war, and return to Egypt."

18 So God [R]led the people around *by* way of the wilderness of the Red Sea. And the children of Israel went up in orderly ranks out of the land of Egypt. Num. 33:6

19 And Moses took the bones of Joseph with him, for he had placed the children of Israel under solemn oath, saying, [R]"God will surely [T]visit you, and you shall carry up my bones from here with you." Ex. 4:31 • *help*

20 So [R]they took their journey from [R]Succoth and camped in Etham at the edge of the wilderness. Num. 33:6–8 • Ex. 12:37

21 And [R]the LORD went before them by day in a pillar of cloud to lead the way, and by night in a pillar of fire to give them light, so as to go by day and night. Deut. 1:33

22 He did not take away the pillar of cloud by day or the pillar of fire by night *from* before the people.

CHAPTER 14

NOW the LORD spoke to Moses, saying:

2 "Speak to the children of Israel, that they turn and camp before Pi Hahiroth, between Migdol and the sea, opposite Baal Zephon; you shall camp before it by the sea.

Pharaoh Follows Israel

3 "For Pharaoh will say of the children of Israel, [R]'They *are* bewildered by the land; the wilderness has closed them in.' Ps. 71:11

4 "Then I will harden Pharaoh's heart, so that he will pursue them; and I [R]will gain honor over Pharaoh and over all his army, [R]that the Egyptians may know that I *am* the LORD." And they did so. Ex. 9:16 • Ex. 7:5; 14:25

5 Now it was told the king of Egypt that the people had fled, and [R]the heart of Pharaoh and his servants was turned against the people; and they said, "Why have we done this, that we have let Israel go from serving us?" Ps. 105:25

6 So he [T]made ready his chariot and took his people with him. *harnessed*

7 Also, he took [R]six hundred choice chariots, and all the chariots of Egypt with captains over every one of them. Ex. 15:4

8 And the LORD [R]hardened the heart of Pharaoh king of Egypt, and he pursued the children of Israel; and [R]the children of Israel went out with boldness. Ex. 14:4 • Num. 33:3

9 So the [R]Egyptians pursued them, all the horses *and* chariots of Pharaoh, his horsemen and his army, and overtook them camping by the sea beside Pi Hahiroth, before Baal Zephon. Josh. 24:6

Israel Rebels Against God

10 And when Pharaoh drew near, the children of Israel lifted their eyes, and behold, the Egyptians marched after them. So they were very afraid, and the children of Israel [R]cried out to the LORD. Neh. 9:9

11 [R]Then they said to Moses, "Because *there were* no graves in Egypt, have you taken us away to die in the wilderness? Why have you so dealt with us, to bring us up out of Egypt? Ps. 106:7, 8

12 [R]"*Is* this not the word that we told you in Egypt, saying, 'Let us alone that we may serve the Egyptians?' For *it would have been* better for us to serve the Egyptians than that we should die in the wilderness." Ex. 5:21; 6:9

God Opens the Red Sea

13 And Moses said to the people, "Do not be afraid. Stand still, and see the salvation of the LORD, which He will accomplish for you

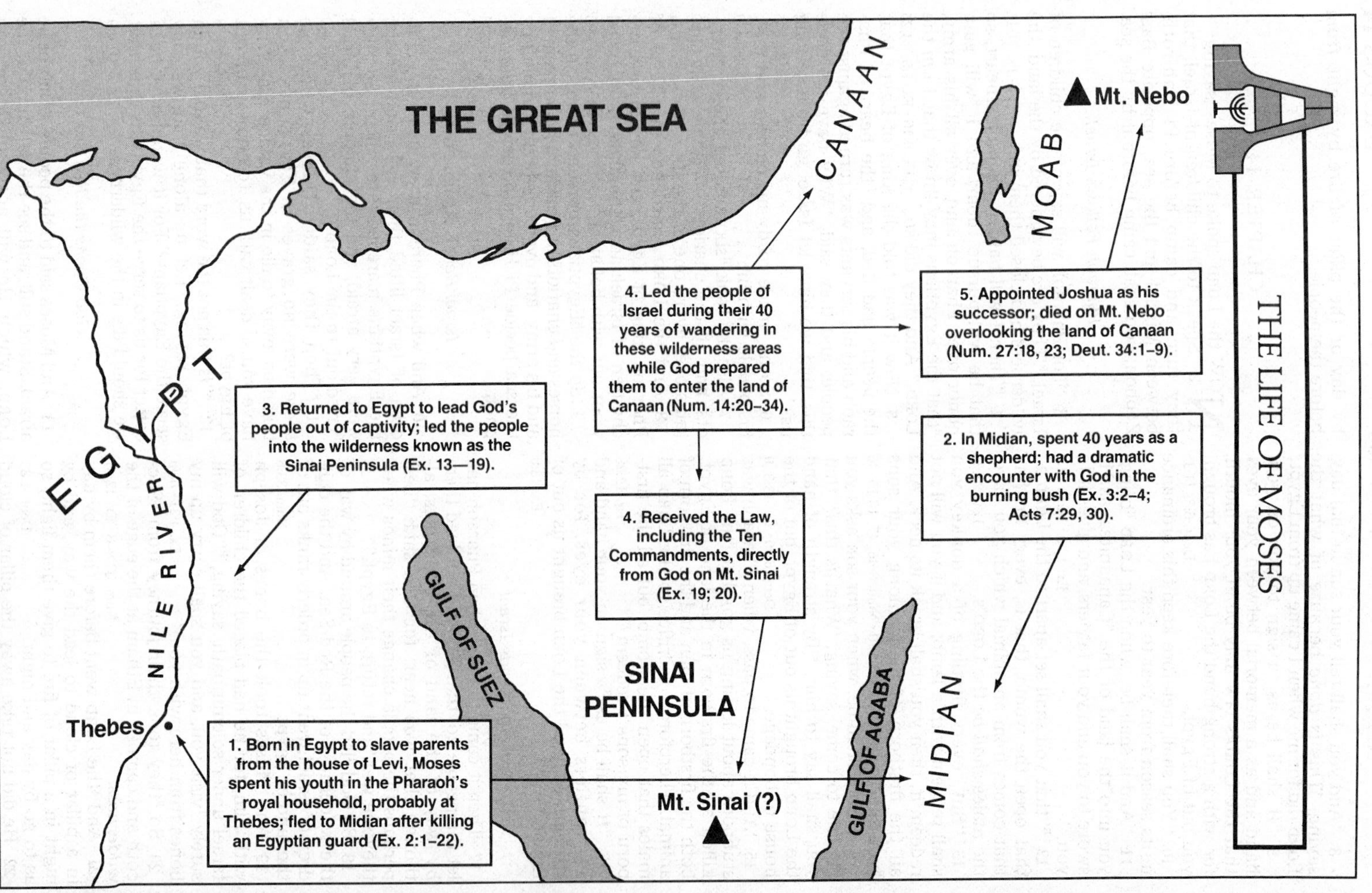
THE LIFE OF MOSES
THE GREAT SEA
CANAAN
MOAB
Mt. Nebo
EGYPT
NILE RIVER
Thebes
GULF OF SUEZ
SINAI PENINSULA
Mt. Sinai (?)
GULF OF AQABA
MIDIAN
1. Born in Egypt to slave parents from the house of Levi, Moses spent his youth in the Pharaoh's royal household, probably at Thebes; fled to Midian after killing an Egyptian guard (Ex. 2:1–22).
2. In Midian, spent 40 years as a shepherd; had a dramatic encounter with God in the burning bush (Ex. 3:2–4; Acts 7:29, 30).
3. Returned to Egypt to lead God's people out of captivity; led the people into the wilderness known as the Sinai Peninsula (Ex. 13—19).
4. Received the Law, including the Ten Commandments, directly from God on Mt. Sinai (Ex. 19; 20).
4. Led the people of Israel during their 40 years of wandering in these wilderness areas while God prepared them to enter the land of Canaan (Num. 14:20–34).
5. Appointed Joshua as his successor; died on Mt. Nebo overlooking the land of Canaan (Num. 27:18, 23; Deut. 34:1–9).

today. For the Egyptians whom you see
today, you shall see again no more forever.
14 "The LORD will fight for you, and you
shall [R]hold[T] your peace." [Is. 30:15] • Lit. *be quiet*
15 And the LORD said to Moses, "Why do
you cry to Me? Tell the children of Israel to
go forward.
16 "But [R]lift up your rod, and stretch out
your hand over the sea and divide it. And the
children of Israel shall go on dry *ground*
through the midst of the sea. Num. 20:8, 9, 11
17 "And I indeed will harden the hearts of
the Egyptians, and they shall follow them. So
I will gain honor over Pharaoh and over all
his army, his chariots, and his horsemen.
18 "Then the Egyptians shall know that I
am the LORD, when I have gained honor for
Myself over Pharaoh, his chariots, and his
horsemen."
19 And the Angel of God, [R]who went before
the camp of Israel, moved and went behind
them; and the pillar of cloud went from
before them and stood behind them. [Is. 63:9]
20 So it came between the camp of the
Egyptians and the camp of Israel. Thus it was
a cloud and darkness *to the one*, and it gave
light by night *to the other*, so that the one did
not come near the other all that night.
21 Then Moses stretched out his hand over
the sea; and the LORD caused the sea to go
back by a strong east wind all that night, and
[R]made the sea into dry *land*, and the waters
were [R]divided. Ps. 66:6; 106:9; 136:13, 14 • Is. 63:12, 13
22 So [R]the children of Israel went into the
midst of the sea on the dry *ground*, and the
waters *were* [R]a wall to them on their right
hand and on their left. Ex. 15:19 • Ex. 14:29; 15:8
23 And the Egyptians pursued and went
after them into the midst of the sea, all
Pharaoh's horses, his chariots, and his horsemen.
24 Now it came to pass, in the morning
[R]watch, that [R]the LORD looked down upon the
army of the Egyptians through the pillar of
fire and cloud, and He [T]troubled the army of
the Egyptians. Judg. 7:19 • Ex. 13:21 • *confused*
25 And He took off their chariot wheels, so
that they drove them with difficulty; and the
Egyptians said, "Let us flee from the face of
Israel, for the LORD [R]fights for them against
the Egyptians." Ex. 7:5; 14:4, 14, 18
26 Then the LORD said to Moses, "Stretch
out your hand over the sea, that the waters
may come back upon the Egyptians, on their
chariots, and on their horsemen."
27 And Moses stretched out his hand over
the sea; and when the morning appeared, the
sea [R]returned to its full depth, while the
Egyptians were fleeing into it. So the LORD
[R]overthrew[T] the Egyptians in the midst of the
sea. Josh. 4:18 • Ex. 15:1, 7 • Lit. *shook off*
28 Then the waters returned and covered
the chariots, the horsemen, *and* all the army
of Pharaoh that came into the sea after them.
Not so much as one of them remained.
29 But [R]the children of Israel had walked on
dry *land* in the midst of the sea, and the
waters *were* a wall to them on their right
hand and on their left. Ps. 66:6; 78:52, 53
30 So the LORD saved Israel that day out of
the hand of the Egyptians, and Israel [R]saw
the Egyptians dead on the seashore. Ps. 59:10
31 Thus Israel saw the great work which
the LORD had done in Egypt; so the people
feared the LORD, and [R]believed the LORD and
His servant Moses. John 2:11; 11:45

CHAPTER 15

Israel Praises God

THEN [R]Moses and the children of Israel
sang this song to the LORD, and spoke,
saying: Ps. 106:12

"I will [R]sing to the LORD, Is. 12:1–6
For He has triumphed gloriously!
The horse and its rider
He has thrown into the sea!
2 The LORD *is* my strength and song,
And He has become my salvation;
He *is* my God, and I will praise Him;
My father's God, and I will exalt Him.
3 The LORD *is* a man of [R]war; Rev. 19:11
The LORD *is* His [R]name. Ps. 24:8; 83:18
4 [R]Pharaoh's chariots and his army He has
cast into the sea; Ex. 14:28
[R]His chosen captains also are drowned in
the Red Sea. Ex. 14:7
5 The depths have covered them;
They sank to the bottom like a stone.

6 "Your [R]right hand, O LORD, has become
glorious in power; Ps. 17:7; 118:15
Your right hand, O LORD, has dashed
the enemy in pieces.
7 And in the greatness of Your
[R]excellence Deut. 33:26
You have overthrown those who rose
against You;
You sent forth Your wrath *which*
consumed them [R]like stubble. Is. 5:24
8 And with the blast of Your nostrils
The waters were gathered together;
[R]The floods stood upright like a heap;
And the depths [T]congealed in the heart
of the sea. Ps. 78:13 • *became firm*
9 [R]The enemy said, 'I will pursue,
I will overtake, Judg. 5:30
I will [R]divide the spoil; Is. 53:12
My desire shall be satisfied on them.
I will draw my sword,
My hand shall destroy them.'
10 You blew with Your wind,
The sea covered them;
They sank like lead in the mighty
waters.

11 "Who[R] *is* like You, O LORD, among the
gods? 1 Kin. 8:23
Who *is* like You, glorious in holiness,
Fearful in praises, doing wonders?
12 You stretched out Your right hand;
The earth swallowed them.
13 You in Your mercy have [R]led forth
The people *whom* You have redeemed;
You have guided *them* in Your strength
To Your holy habitation. [Ps. 77:20]

14 "The people will hear *and* be afraid;
[R]Sorrow will take hold of the inhabitants
of [T]Palestina. Ps. 48:6 · *Philistia*
15 [R]Then [R]the chiefs of Edom will be
dismayed; Gen. 36:15, 40 · Deut. 2:4
[R]The mighty men of Moab, Num. 22:3, 4
Trembling will take hold of them;
[R]All the inhabitants of Canaan will [R]melt
away. Josh. 5:1 · Josh. 2:9–11, 24
16 Fear and dread will fall on them;
By the greatness of Your arm
They will be [R]*as* still as a stone,
Till Your people pass over, O LORD,
Till the people pass over 1 Sam. 25:37
[R]*Whom* You have purchased. Jer. 31:11
17 You will bring them in and [R]plant them
In the [R]mountain of Your inheritance,
In the place, O LORD, *which* You have
made Ps. 44:2; 80:8, 15 · Ps. 2:6; 78:54, 68
For Your own dwelling,
The [R]sanctuary, O LORD, *which* Your
hands have established. Ps. 68:16; 76:2

18 "The LORD shall reign forever and ever."

19 For the horses of Pharaoh went with his
chariots and his horsemen into the sea, and
the LORD brought back the waters of the sea
upon them. But the children of Israel went on
dry *land* in the midst of the sea.
20 Then Miriam the prophetess, the sister of
Aaron, took the timbrel in her hand; and all
the women went out after her [R]with timbrels
and with dances. Judg. 11:34; 21:21
21 And Miriam [R]answered them:

[R]"Sing to the LORD, 1 Sam. 18:7 · Ex. 15:1
For He has triumphed gloriously!
The horse and its rider
He has thrown into the sea!"

Preserved from Thirst

22 So Moses brought Israel from the Red
Sea; then they went out into the Wilderness
of Shur. And they went three days in the
wilderness and found no [R]water. Num. 20:2
23 Now when they came to [R]Marah, they
could not drink the waters of Marah, for they
were bitter. Therefore the name of it was
called [T]Marah. Num. 33:8 · Lit. *Bitter*
24 And the people [R]murmured against Moses, saying, "What shall we drink?" Ex. 14:11
25 So he cried out to the LORD, and the
LORD showed him a tree; *and* when he cast *it*
into the waters, the waters were made sweet.
There He made a statute and an [T]ordinance
for them. And there He tested them, *law*
26 and said, "If you diligently heed the
voice of the LORD your God and do what is
right in His sight, give ear to His commandments and keep all His statutes, I will put
none of the [R]diseases on you which I have
brought on the Egyptians. For I *am* the LORD
[R]who heals you." Deut. 28:27, 58, 60 · Ex. 23:25
27 Then they came to Elim, where there
were twelve wells of water and seventy palm
trees; so they camped there by the waters.

CHAPTER 16

Preserved from Hunger

AND they [R]journeyed from Elim, and all
the congregation of the children of
Israel came to the Wilderness of Sin, which is
between Elim and [R]Sinai, on the fifteenth day
of the second month after they departed from
the land of Egypt. Num. 33:10, 11 · Ex. 12:6, 51; 19:1
2 Then the whole congregation of the
children of Israel [R]murmured against Moses
and Aaron in the wilderness. 1 Cor. 10:10
3 And the children of Israel said to them,
[R]"Oh, that we had died by the hand of the
LORD in the land of Egypt, [R]when we sat by
the pots of meat *and* when we ate bread to
the full! For you have brought us out into this
wilderness to kill this whole assembly with
hunger." Lam. 4:9 · Num. 11:4, 5
4 Then the LORD said to Moses, "Behold, I
will rain bread from heaven for you. And the
people shall go out and gather a certain quota
every day, that I may test them, whether
they will walk in My law or not.
5 "And it shall be on the sixth day that
they shall prepare what they bring in, and it
shall be twice as much as they gather daily."
6 Then Moses and Aaron said to all the
children of Israel, [R]"At evening you shall
know that the LORD has brought you out of
the land of Egypt. Ex. 6:7
7 "And in the morning you shall see the
glory of the LORD; for He hears your murmurings against the LORD. But [R]what *are* we, that
you murmur against us?" Num. 16:11
8 Also Moses said, "*This shall be seen*
when the LORD gives you meat to eat in the
evening, and in the morning bread to the full;
for the LORD hears your [T]murmurings which
you make against Him. And what *are* we?
Your murmurings *are* not against us but
[R]against the LORD." *grumblings* · 1 Sam. 8:7
9 Then Moses spoke to Aaron, "Say to all
the congregation of the children of Israel,
[R]'Come near before the LORD, for He has
heard your murmurings.' " Num. 16:16
10 Now it came to pass, as Aaron spoke to
the whole congregation of the children of

Israel, that they looked toward the wilderness, and behold, the glory of the LORD [R]appeared in the cloud. Num. 16:19

11 And the LORD spoke to Moses, saying,

12 [R]"I have heard the [T]murmurings of the children of Israel. Speak to them, saying, [R]'At twilight you shall eat meat, and [R]in the morning you shall be filled with bread. And you shall know that I *am* the LORD your God.' " Ex. 16:8 • *grumblings* • Ex. 16:6 • Ex. 16:7

13 So it was that quails came up at evening and covered the camp, and in the morning [R]the dew lay all around the camp. Num. 11:9

14 And when the layer of dew lifted, there, on the surface of the wilderness, was a small round [R]substance, *as* fine as [R]frost on the ground. Num. 11:7, 8 • Ps. 147:16

15 So when the children of Israel saw *it,* they said to one another, "What is it?" For they did not know what it *was.* And Moses said to them, [R]"This *is* the bread which the LORD has given you to eat. 1 Cor. 10:3

16 "This is the thing which the LORD has commanded: 'Let every man gather it [R]according to each one's need, one [R]omer[T] for each person, *according to the* number of persons; let every man take for *those* who *are* in his tent.' " Ex. 12:4 • Ex. 16:32, 36 • 2.087 qt.

17 And the children of Israel did so and gathered, some more, some less.

18 So when they measured *it* by omers, he who gathered much had nothing over, and he who gathered little had no lack. Every man had gathered according to each one's need.

19 And Moses said, "Let no one [R]leave any of it till morning." Ex. 12:10; 16:23; 23:18

20 Notwithstanding they did not [T]heed Moses. But some of them left part of it until morning, and it bred worms and stank. And Moses was angry with them. *listen to*

21 So they gathered it every morning, every man according to his need. And when the sun became hot, it melted.

22 And so it was, on the sixth day, *that* they gathered twice as much bread, [T]two omers for each one. And all the rulers of the congregation came and told Moses. 4.174 qt.

23 Then he said to them, "This *is what* the LORD has said: 'Tomorrow *is* [R]a Sabbath rest, a holy Sabbath to the LORD. Bake what you will bake *today,* and boil what you will boil; and lay up for yourselves all that remains, to be kept until morning.' " Gen. 2:3

24 So they laid it up till morning, as Moses commanded; and it did not [R]stink, nor were there any worms in it. Ex. 16:20

25 Then Moses said, "Eat that today, for today *is* a Sabbath to the LORD; today you will not find it in the field.

26 [R]"Six days you shall gather it, but on the seventh day, *which is* the Sabbath, there will be none." Ex. 20:9, 10

27 Now it happened *that some* of the people went out on the seventh day to gather, but they found none.

28 And the LORD said to Moses, "How long [R]do you refuse to keep My commandments and My laws? 2 Kin. 17:14

29 "See! For the LORD has given you the Sabbath; therefore He gives you on the sixth day bread for two days. Let every man remain in his place; let no man go out of his place on the seventh day."

30 So the people rested on the seventh day.

31 And the house of Israel called its name [T]Manna. And [R]it *was* like white coriander seed, and the taste of it *was* like wafers *made* with honey. Lit. *What,* Ex. 16:15 • Num. 11:7-9

32 Then Moses said, "This *is* the thing which the LORD has commanded: 'Fill an [T]omer with it, to be kept for your generations, that they may see the bread with which I fed you in the wilderness, when I brought you out of the land of Egypt.' " 2.087 qt.

33 And Moses said to Aaron, [R]"Take a pot and put an omer of manna in it, and lay it up before the LORD, to be kept for your generations." Heb. 9:4

34 As the LORD commanded Moses, so Aaron laid it up [R]before the Testimony, to be kept. Num. 17:10

35 And the children of Israel ate manna forty years, [R]until they came to an inhabited land; they ate manna until they came to the border of the land of Canaan. Josh. 5:12

36 Now an omer *is* one-tenth of an ephah.

CHAPTER 17

Preserved from Thirst Again

THEN [R]all the congregation of the children of Israel set out on their journey from the Wilderness of [R]Sin, according to the commandment of the LORD, and camped in Rephidim; but *there was* no water for the people to [R]drink. Ex. 16:1 • Num. 33:11-15 • Ex. 15:22

2 [R]Therefore the people contended with Moses, and said, "Give us water, that we may drink." And Moses said to them, "Why do you contend with me? Why do you [R]tempt the LORD?" Num. 20:2, 3, 13 • [Deut. 6:16]

3 And the people thirsted there for water, and the people [R]murmured against Moses, and said, "Why *is* it you have brought us up out of Egypt, to kill us and our children and our [R]livestock with thirst?" Ex. 16:2, 3 • Ex. 12:38

4 So Moses cried out to the LORD, saying, "What shall I do with this people? They are almost ready to [R]stone me!" John 8:59; 10:31

5 And the LORD said to Moses, [R]"Go on before the people, and take with you some of the elders of Israel. Also take in your hand your rod with which [R]you struck the river, and go. Ezek. 2:6 • Num. 20:8

6 [R]"Behold, I will stand before you there on the rock in Horeb; and you shall strike the

rock, and water will come out of it, that the
people may drink." And Moses did so in
the sight of the elders of Israel. Num. 20:10, 11
7 So he called the name of the place [T]Mas-
sah and [T]Meribah, because of the contention
of the children of Israel, and because they
[T]tempted the LORD, saying, "Is the LORD
among us or not?" *Tempted* • *Contention* • *tested*

Preserved from Defeat

8 [R]Now Amalek came and fought with
Israel in Rephidim. Gen. 36:12
9 And Moses said to Joshua, "Choose us
some men and go out, fight with Amalek.
Tomorrow I will stand on the top of the hill
with [R]the rod of God in my hand." Ex. 4:20
10 So Joshua did as Moses said to him, and
fought with Amalek. And Moses, Aaron, and
Hur went up to the top of the hill.
11 And so it was, when Moses [R]held up his
hand, that Israel prevailed; and when he let
down his hand, Amalek prevailed. [James 5:16]
12 But Moses' hands *became* [T]heavy; so
they took a stone and put *it* under him, and
he sat on it. And Aaron and Hur supported
his hands, one on one side, and the other on
the other side; and his hands were steady
until the going down of the sun. *tired*
13 So Joshua defeated Amalek and his people with the edge of the sword.
14 Then the LORD said to Moses, [R]"Write
this *for* a memorial in the book and recount *it*
in the hearing of Joshua, that [R]I will utterly
blot out the remembrance of Amalek from
under heaven." Ex. 24:4; 34:27 • 1 Sam. 15:3
15 And Moses built an altar and called its
name, The-LORD-Is-My-Banner;
16 for he said, "Because the LORD has
[R]sworn: the LORD *will have* war with Amalek
from generation to generation." Gen. 22:14–16

CHAPTER 18

Preserved from Chaos—Deut. 1:12–17

AND [R]Jethro, the priest of Midian, Moses'
father-in-law, heard of all that [R]God had
done for Moses and for Israel His people—
that the LORD had brought Israel out of
Egypt. Ex. 2:16, 18; 3:1 • [Ps. 106:2, 8]
2 Then Jethro, Moses' father-in-law, took
[R]Zipporah, Moses' wife, after he had sent her
back, Ex. 2:21; 4:20–26
3 with her two sons, of whom the [R]name of
one *was* Gershom (for he said, "I have been a
stranger in a foreign land") Ex. 2:22
4 and the name of the other *was* [T]Eliezer
(for *he said*, "The God of my father *was* my
[R]help, and delivered me from the sword of
Pharaoh"); Lit. *My God is Help* • Gen. 49:25
5 and Jethro, Moses' father-in-law, came
with his sons and his wife to Moses in the
wilderness, where he was encamped at [R]the
mountain of God. Ex. 3:1, 12; 4:27; 24:13
6 Now he had said to Moses, "I, your
father-in-law Jethro, am coming to you with
your wife and her two sons with her."
7 So Moses [R]went out to meet his father-
in-law, bowed down, and [R]kissed him. And
they asked each other about *their* well-being,
and they went into the tent. Gen. 18:2 • Ex. 4:27
8 And Moses told his father-in-law all that
the LORD had done to Pharaoh and to the
Egyptians for Israel's sake, all the hardship
that had come upon them on the way, and
how the LORD had [R]delivered them. Ex. 15:6, 16
9 Then Jethro rejoiced for all the [R]good
which the LORD had done for Israel, whom
He had delivered out of the hand of the
Egyptians. [Is. 63:7–14]
10 And Jethro said, [R]"Blessed *be* the LORD,
who has delivered you out of the hand of the
Egyptians and out of the hand of Pharaoh,
and who has delivered the people from under
the hand of the Egyptians. Gen. 14:20
11 "Now I know that the LORD *is* [R]greater
than all the gods; for in the very thing in
which they [T]behaved [R]proudly, *He was* above
them." 2 Chr. 2:5 • *acted presumptuously* • Luke 1:51
12 Then Jethro, Moses' father-in-law, took a
burnt [R]offering and sacrifices to God. And
Aaron came with all the elders of Israel [R]to
eat bread with Moses' father-in-law before
God. Ex. 24:5 • Deut. 12:7
13 And so it was, on the next day, that
Moses [R]sat to judge the people; and the
people stood before Moses from morning
until evening. Matt. 23:2
14 So when Moses' father-in-law saw all
that he did for the people, he said, "What *is*
this thing that you are doing for the people?
Why do you alone [T]sit, and all the people
stand before you from morning until evening?" Sit as judge
15 And Moses said to his father-in-law,
"Because [R]the people come to me to inquire
of God. Lev. 24:12
16 "When they have [R]a [T]difficulty, they
come to me, and I judge between one and
another; and I make known the statutes of
God and His laws." Ex. 24:14 • *dispute*, lit. *matter*
17 So Moses' father-in-law said to him, "The
thing that you do *is* not good.
18 "Both you and these people who *are* with
you will surely wear yourselves out. For this
thing *is* too much for you; [R]you are not able
to perform it by yourself. Num. 11:14, 17
19 "Listen now to my voice; I will give you
counsel, and God will be with you: Stand
before God for the people, so that you may
[R]bring the difficulties to God. Num. 9:8; 27:5
20 "And you shall [R]teach them the statutes
and the laws, and show them the way in
which they must walk and [R]the work they
must do. Deut. 5:1 • Deut. 1:18
21 "Moreover you shall select from all the
people [R]able men, such as [R]fear God, [R]men of

truth, [R]hating covetousness; and place *such*
over them *to be* rulers of thousands, rulers
of hundreds, rulers of fifties, and rulers of
tens. Acts 6:3 • 2 Sam. 23:3 • Ezek. 18:8 • Deut. 16:19
22 "And let them judge the people at all
times. [R]Then it will be *that* every great matter
they shall bring to you, but every small
matter they themselves shall judge. So it will
be easier for you, for [R]they will bear *the*
burden with you. Deut. 1:17 • Num. 11:17
23 "If you do this thing, and God *so* commands you, then you will be able to endure,
and all this people will also go to their [R]place
in peace." Ex. 16:29
24 So Moses heeded the voice of his father-
in-law and did all that he had said.
25 And [R]Moses chose able men out of all
Israel, and made them heads over the people:
rulers of thousands, rulers of hundreds, rulers
of fifties, and rulers of tens. Deut. 1:15
26 So they judged the people at all times;
the hard cases they brought to Moses, but
they judged every small case themselves.
27 Then Moses let his father-in-law depart,
and he went his way to his own land.

CHAPTER 19

Location of the Giving of the Covenant

IN the third month after the children of
Israel had gone out of the land of Egypt,
on the same day, [R]they came *to* the Wilderness of Sinai. Num. 33:15
2 For they had departed from [R]Rephidim,
had come *to* the Desert of Sinai, and camped
in the wilderness. So Israel camped there
before [R]the mountain. Ex. 17:1 • Ex. 3:1, 12; 18:5

Purpose of the Covenant

3 And Moses went up to God, and the
LORD [R]called to him from the mountain,
saying, "Thus you shall say to the house of
Jacob, and tell the children of Israel: Ex. 3:4
4 'You have seen what I did to the Egyptians, and *how* [R]I bore you on eagles' wings
and brought you to Myself. Is. 63:9
5 'Now therefore, if you will indeed obey
My voice and keep My covenant, then you
shall be a special treasure to Me above all
people; for all the earth *is* [R]Mine. Ex. 9:29
6 'And you shall be to Me a [R]kingdom of
priests and a [R]holy nation.' These *are* the
words which you shall speak to the children
of Israel." [1 Pet. 2:5, 9] • Deut. 7:6; 14:21; 26:19

Israel Accepts the Covenant

7 So Moses came and called for the elders
of the people, and [T]laid before them all these
words which the LORD commanded him. *set*
8 Then [R]all the people answered together
and said, "All that the LORD has spoken we
will do." So Moses brought back the words of
the people to the LORD. Deut. 5:27; 26:17

Israelites Sanctify Themselves

9 And the LORD said to Moses, "Behold, I
come to you in the thick cloud, [R]that the
people may hear when I speak with you, and
believe you forever." So Moses told the words
of the people to the LORD. Deut. 4:12
10 Then the LORD said to Moses, "Go to the
people and sanctify them today and tomorrow, and let them wash their clothes.
11 "And let them be ready for the third day.
For on the third day the LORD will come
down upon Mount Sinai in the sight of all the
people.
12 "You shall set bounds for the people all
around, saying, 'Take heed to yourselves *that*
you do *not* go up to the mountain or touch its
base. [R]Whoever touches the mountain shall
surely be put to death. Heb. 12:20
13 'Not a hand shall touch him, but he shall
surely be stoned or shot *with an arrow;*
whether man or beast, he shall not live.'
When the trumpet sounds long, they shall
come near the mountain."

19:5–8 The Mosaic Covenant—The covenant with Moses is the second of the theocratic covenants (pertaining to the rule of God) and is conditional. It is introduced by the conditional formula, "if you will indeed obey My voice . . . then you shall be a special treasure." This covenant was given to the nation Israel so that those who believed God's promise given to Abraham in the Abrahamic Covenant (Page 18—Gen. 12:1–3) would know how they should conduct themselves. The Mosaic Covenant in its entirety governs three areas of their lives: (1) the commandments governed their personal lives particularly as they related to God (Page 90—Ex. 20:1–26); (2) the judgments governed their social lives particularly as they related to one another (Page 92—Ex. 21:1—24:11); and (3) the ordinances governed their religious lives so that the people would know how to approach God on the terms that He dictates (Page 95—Ex. 24:12—31:18). The Mosaic Covenant in no way replaced or set aside the Abrahamic Covenant. Its function is clearly set forth by Paul (Page 1381—Gal. 3:17–19), who points out that the law, the Mosaic Covenant, came 430 years after the Abrahamic Covenant. The Mosaic Covenant was added alongside the Abrahamic Covenant so that the people of Israel would know how to conduct their lives until "the seed," the Christ, comes and makes the complete and perfect sacrifice, toward which the sacrifices of the Mosaic Covenant only point. The Mosaic Covenant was never given so that by keeping it people could be saved, but so that they might realize that they cannot do what God wants them to do even when God writes it down on tablets of stone. The law was given that man might realize that he is helpless and hopeless when left to himself, and realize that his only hope is to receive the righteousness of God by faith in Jesus (Page 1381—Gal. 3:22–24).

Now turn to Page 240—Deut. 29:10–15; 30:11–20: The Palestinian Covenant.

14 Then Moses went down from the mountain to the people and sanctified the people, and they washed their clothes.

15 And he said to the people, "Be ready for the third day; do not come near *your* wives."

16 Then it came to pass on the third day, in the morning, that there were [R]thunderings and lightnings, and a thick cloud on the mountain; and the sound of the trumpet was very loud, so that all the people who *were* in the camp [R]trembled. Heb. 12:18, 19 • Heb. 12:21

17 And [R]Moses brought the people out of the camp to meet with God, and they stood at the foot of the mountain. Deut. 4:10

18 Now [R]Mount Sinai *was* completely in smoke, because the LORD descended upon [R]it in fire. [R]Its smoke ascended like the smoke of a furnace, and *the whole mountain quaked greatly. Deut. 4:11 • Ex. 3:2; 24:17 • Gen. 15:17; 19:28

19 And when the blast of the trumpet sounded long and became louder and louder, [R]Moses spoke, and [R]God answered him by voice. Heb. 12:21 • Ps. 81:7

20 Then the LORD came down upon Mount Sinai, on the top of the mountain. And the LORD called Moses to the top of the mountain, and Moses went up.

21 And the LORD said to Moses, "Go down and warn the people, lest they break through [R]to gaze at the LORD, and many of them perish. 1 Sam. 6:19

22 "Also let the priests who come near the LORD [R]sanctify[T] themselves, lest the LORD break out against them." Lev. 21:6–8 • *consecrate*

23 And Moses said to the LORD, "The people cannot come up to Mount Sinai; for You warned us, saying, [R]'Set bounds around the mountain and [T]sanctify it.'" Ex. 19:12 • *consecrate*

24 Then the LORD said to him, "Away! Get down and then come up, you and Aaron with you. But do not let the priests and the people break through to come up to the LORD, lest He break out against them."

25 So Moses went down to the people and spoke to them.

CHAPTER 20

Commandments Relating to God

AND God spoke all these words, saying:

2 "I *am* the LORD your God, who brought you out of the land of Egypt, out of the house of bondage.

3 "You[R] shall have no other gods before Me. Jer. 25:6; 35:15

4 "You shall not make for yourself any carved image, or any likeness *of anything* that *is* in heaven above, or that *is* in the earth beneath, or that *is* in the water under the earth;
5 you shall not bow down to them nor serve them. For I, the LORD your God, *am* a jealous God, visiting the iniquity of the fathers on the children to the third and fourth *generations* of those who hate Me,
6 but [R]showing mercy to thousands, to those who love Me and keep My commandments. Deut. 7:9

7 "You shall not take the name of the LORD your God in vain, for the LORD [R]will not hold him guiltless who takes His name in vain. Mic. 6:11

8 "Remember[R] the Sabbath day, to keep it holy. Lev. 26:2
9 [R]Six days you shall labor and do all your work, Luke 13:14
10 but the seventh day *is* the Sabbath of the LORD your God. *In it* you shall do no work: you, nor your son, nor your daughter, nor your manservant, nor your maidservant, nor your cattle, [R]nor your stranger who *is* within your gates. Neh. 13:16–19
11 For [R]*in* six days the LORD made the heavens and the earth, the sea, and all that *is* in them, and rested the seventh day. Therefore the LORD blessed the Sabbath day and hallowed it. Ex. 31:17

Commandments Relating to Man

12 "Honor your father and your mother, that your days may be [R]long upon the land which the LORD your God is giving you. Deut. 5:16, 33; 6:2; 11:8, 9

13 "You[R] shall not murder. Rom. 13:9

14 "You shall not commit adultery.

15 "You[R] shall not steal. Lev. 19:11, 13

16 "You[R] shall not bear false witness against your neighbor. Deut. 5:20

17 "You shall not covet your neighbor's house; [R]you shall not covet your neighbor's wife, nor his manservant, nor his maidservant, nor his ox, nor his donkey, nor anything that *is* your neighbor's." [Matt. 5:28]

The Response of Israel

18 Now all the people [R]witnessed the thunderings, the lightning flashes, the sound of the trumpet, and the mountain [R]smoking; and when the people saw *it*, they trembled and stood afar off. Rev. 1:10, 12 • Ex. 19:16, 18

19 Then they said to Moses, "You speak with us, and we will hear; but [R]let not God speak with us, lest we die." Deut. 5:5, 23–27

20 And Moses said to the people, [R]"Do not fear; [R]for God has come to test you, and [R]that His fear may be before you, so that you may not sin." [Is. 41:10, 13] • [Deut. 13:3] • Is. 8:13

19:18 LXX *all the people*

THE TEN COMMANDMENTS

At Mount Sinai Moses received God's commandments to His people.

The Ten Commandments (see Ex. 20:1–17) were laws given by God as guidelines for daily living. Although God gave the commandments to His people through Moses at Mount Sinai (see illustration) more than three thousand years ago, they are still relevant today. These laws are also known as the Decalogue, from the Greek word meaning "ten words."

The Ten Commandments are divided into two sections. The first four commandments govern our relationship to God, while commandments five through ten speak of our relationship to other people. The meaning of the Ten Commandments may be stated briefly as follows:

1. Trust God only (Ex. 20:3, 4).
2. Worship God only (Ex. 20:5, 6).
3. Use God's name in ways that honor Him (Ex. 20:7).
4. Rest on the Sabbath day and think about God (Ex. 20:8–11).
5. Respect and obey your parents (Ex. 20:12).
6. Protect and respect human life (Ex. 20:13).
7. Be true to your husband or wife (Ex. 20:14).
8. Do not take what belongs to others (Ex. 20:15).
9. Do not lie about others (Ex. 20:16).
10. Be satisfied with what you have (Ex. 20:17).

About 1,300 years after God gave these commandments, Jesus upheld them. He actually placed these laws on a higher plane, demanding that the spirit, as well as the legal aspects, of the laws be observed. He placed His stamp of approval on the commandments by declaring, "Do not think that I came to destroy the Law or the Prophets. I did not come to destroy but to fulfill" (Matt. 5:17).

The Code of Hammurabi, an ancient law code named after an early king of Babylonia, bears many similarities to the Ten Commandments. However, the Law given at Mount Sinai reflects a high view of the nature of God and His holiness and His requirements of His people.

21 So the people stood afar off, but Moses
drew near [R]the thick darkness where God
was. Ex. 19:16

Provision for Approaching God

22 Then the LORD said to Moses, "Thus you
shall say to the children of Israel: 'You have
seen that I have talked with you [R]from
heaven. Deut. 4:36; 5:24, 26
23 'You shall not make *anything to be* [R]with
Me—gods of silver or gods of gold you shall
not make for yourselves. Ex. 32:1, 2, 4
24 'An altar of earth you shall make for Me,
and you shall sacrifice on it your burnt offerings and your peace offerings, your sheep and
your oxen. In every place where I [T]record My
name I will come to you, and I will bless
you. *cause my name to be remembered*
25 'And if you make Me an altar of stone,
you shall not build it of hewn stone; for if you
use your tool on it, you have profaned it.
26 'Nor shall you go up by steps to My altar,
that your nakedness may not be exposed
on it.'

CHAPTER 21

Rights of Persons

"NOW these *are* the [T]judgments which
you shall set before them: *ordinances*
2 [R]"If you buy a Hebrew servant, he shall
serve six years; and in the seventh he shall go
out free and pay nothing. Jer. 34:14
3 "If he comes in by himself, he shall go
out by himself; if he *comes in* married, then
his wife shall go out with him.
4 "If his master has given him a wife, and
she has borne him sons or daughters, the wife
and her children shall be her master's, and he
shall go out by himself.
5 [R]"But if the servant plainly says, 'I love
my master, my wife, and my children; I will
not go out free,' Deut. 15:16, 17
6 "then his master shall bring him to the
[R]judges. He shall also bring him to the door,
or to the doorpost, and his master shall pierce
his ear with an awl; and he shall serve him
forever. Ex. 12:12; 22:8, 9
7 "And if a man [R]sells his daughter to be a
maidservant, she shall not go out as the
menservants do. Neh. 5:5
8 "If she [T]does not please her master, who
has betrothed her to himself, then he shall let
her be redeemed. He shall have no right to
sell her to a foreign people, since he has dealt
deceitfully with her. Lit. *is evil in the eyes of*
9 "And if he has betrothed her to his son,
he shall deal with her according to the custom of daughters.
10 "If he takes another *wife*, he shall not
diminish her food, her clothing, [R]and her
marriage rights. [1 Cor. 7:3, 5]
11 "And if he does not do these three for
her, then she shall go out free, without
paying money.
12 [R]"He who strikes a man so that he dies
shall surely be put to death. [Matt. 26:52]
13 "But if he did not lie in wait, but God
delivered *him* into his hand, then I will appoint for you a place where he may flee.
14 "But if a man acts with [R]premeditation
against his neighbor, to kill him with [T]guile,
[R]you shall take him from My altar, that he
may die. Deut. 19:11, 12 • *treachery* • 1 Kin. 2:28–34
15 "And he who strikes his father or his
mother shall surely be put to death.
16 [R]"He who kidnaps a man and [R]sells him,
or if he is [R]found in his hand, shall surely be
put to death. Deut. 24:7 • Gen. 37:28 • Ex. 22:4
17 "And [R]he who curses his father or his
mother shall surely be put to death. Mark 7:10
18 "If men contend with each other, and
one strikes the other with a stone or with *his*
fist, and he does not die but is confined to *his*
bed,
19 "if he rises again and walks about outside with his staff, then he who struck *him*
shall be [T]acquitted. He shall only pay *for* the
loss of his time, and shall provide *for him* to
be thoroughly healed. *exempt from punishment*
20 "And if a man beats his servant or his
maidservant with a rod, so that he dies under
his hand, he shall surely be punished.
21 "Notwithstanding, if he remains alive a
day or two, he shall not be punished; for he *is*
his [R]property. Lev. 25:44–46
22 "If men fight, and hurt a woman with
child, so that [T]she gives birth prematurely,
yet no *lasting* harm follows, he shall surely be
punished accordingly as the woman's husband imposes on him; and he shall pay as the
judges *determine.* Lit. *her children come out*
23 "But if *any lasting* harm follows, then
you shall give life for life,
24 [R]"eye for eye, tooth for tooth, hand for
hand, foot for foot, Lev. 24:20
25 "burn for burn, wound for wound, stripe
for stripe.
26 "And if a man strikes the eye of his
servant, or the eye of his maidservant, and
destroys it, he shall let him go free for the
sake of his eye.
27 "And if he knocks out his servant's
tooth, or his maidservant's tooth, he shall let
him go free for the sake of his tooth.
28 "If an ox gores a man or a woman to
death, then [R]the ox shall surely be stoned,
and its flesh shall not be eaten; but the owner
of the ox *shall be* acquitted. Gen. 9:5
29 "But if the ox [T]tended to thrust with its
horn in times past, and it has been made
known to his owner, and he has not kept it
confined, so that it has killed a man or a
woman, the ox shall be stoned and its owner
also shall be put to death. *was inclined*

30 "If there is imposed on him a sum of money, then he shall pay [R]to redeem his life, whatever is imposed on him. Num. 35:31

31 "Whether it has gored a son or gored a daughter, according to this judgment it shall be done to him.

32 "If the ox gores a manservant or a maidservant, he shall give to their master thirty shekels of silver, and the ox shall be stoned.

Rights of Property

33 "And if a man opens a pit, or if a man digs a pit and does not cover it, and an ox or a donkey falls in it,

34 "the owner of the pit shall make *it* good; he shall give money to their owner, but the dead *beast* shall be his.

35 "And if one man's ox hurts another's, so that it dies, then they shall sell the live ox and divide the money from it; and the dead *ox* they shall also divide.

36 "Or if it was known that the ox tended to thrust in time past, and its owner has not kept it confined, he shall surely pay ox for ox, and the dead beast shall be his own.

CHAPTER 22

"IF a man steals an ox or a sheep, and slaughters it or sells it, he shall [R]restore five oxen for an ox and four sheep for a sheep. 2 Sam. 12:6

2 "If the thief is found [R]breaking in, and he is struck so that he dies, *there shall be* no guilt for his bloodshed. Matt. 6:19; 24:43

3 "If the sun has risen on him, *there shall be* guilt for his bloodshed. He should make full restitution; if he has nothing, then he shall be [R]sold[T] for his theft. Ex. 21:2 • Sold as a slave

4 "If the theft is certainly found alive in his hand, whether it is an ox or donkey or sheep, he shall [R]restore double. Prov. 6:31

5 "If a man causes a field or vineyard to be grazed, and lets loose his animal, and it feeds in another man's field, he shall make restitution from the best of his own field and the best of his own vineyard.

6 "If fire breaks out and catches in thorns, so that stacked grain, standing grain, or the field is consumed, he who kindled the fire shall surely make restitution.

7 "If a man [R]delivers to his neighbor money or articles to keep, and it is stolen out of the man's house, [R]if the thief is found, he shall pay double. Lev. 6:1–7 • Ex. 22:4

8 "If the thief is not found, then the master of the house shall be brought to the [R]judges *to see* whether he has put his hand into his neighbor's goods. Ex. 21:6, 22; 22:28

9 "For any kind of trespass, *whether it concerns* an ox, a donkey, a sheep, or clothing, *or* for any kind of lost thing which *another* claims to be his, the [R]cause of both parties shall come before the judges; *and* whomever the judges condemn shall pay double to his neighbor. Deut. 25:1

10 "If a man delivers to his neighbor a donkey, an ox, a sheep, or any beast to keep, and it dies, is hurt, or driven away, no one seeing *it*,

11 "*then* an [R]oath of the LORD shall be between them both, that he has not put his hand into his neighbor's goods; and the owner of it shall accept *that*, and he shall not make *it* good. Heb. 6:16

12 "But if, in fact, it is stolen from him, he shall make restitution to the owner of it.

13 "If it is [R]torn to pieces *by an animal, then* he shall bring it as evidence, *and* he shall not make good what was torn. Gen. 31:39

14 "And if a man borrows *anything* from his neighbor, and it becomes injured or dies, the owner of it not *being* with it, he shall surely make *it* good.

15 "*But* if its owner *was* with it, he shall not make *it* good; if it *was* hired, it came for its hire.

Proper Conduct

16 "And [R]if a man entices a virgin who is not betrothed, and lies with her, he shall surely pay the bride-price for her *to be* his wife. Deut. 22:28, 29

17 "If her father utterly refuses to give her to him, he shall pay money according to the [R]bride-price of virgins. Gen. 34:12

18 "You shall not permit a sorceress to live.

19 [R]"Whoever lies with a beast shall surely be put to death. Lev. 18:23; 20:15, 16

20 "He who sacrifices to *any* god, except to the LORD only, he shall be utterly destroyed.

21 [R]"You shall neither mistreat a [T]stranger nor oppress him, for you were strangers in the land of Egypt. Deut. 10:19 • *sojourner*

22 [R]"You shall not afflict any widow or fatherless child. [James 1:27]

23 "If you afflict them in any way, *and* they cry at all to Me, I will surely hear their cry;

24 "and My wrath will become hot, and I will kill you with the sword; your wives shall be widows, and your children fatherless.

25 [R]"If you lend money to *any of* My people *who are* poor among you, you shall not be like a moneylender to him; you shall not charge him [R]interest. Lev. 25:35–37 • Ps. 15:5

26 [R]"If you ever take your neighbor's garment as a pledge, you shall return it to him before the sun goes down. Deut. 24:6, 10–13

27 "For that *is* his only covering, it *is* his garment for his skin. What will he sleep in? And it will be that when he cries to Me, I will hear, for I *am* [R]gracious. Ex. 34:6, 7

28 [R]"You shall not revile God, nor curse a [R]ruler of your people. Eccl. 10:20 • Acts 23:5

29 "You shall not delay *to offer* the first of your ripe produce and your juices. The firstborn of your sons you shall give to Me.

30 [R]"Likewise you shall do with your oxen
and your sheep. It shall be with its mother
[R]seven days; on the eighth day you shall give
it to Me. Deut. 15:19 • Lev. 22:27
31 "And you shall be [R]holy men to Me: [R]you
shall not eat *any* meat *which is* torn *by
beasts* in the field; you shall throw it to the
dogs. Lev. 11:44; 19:2 • Ezek. 4:14

CHAPTER 23

Proper Justice

"YOU shall not circulate a false report.
Do not put your hand with the wicked
to be an [R]unrighteous witness. Deut. 19:16–21
2 "You shall not follow a crowd to do evil;
nor shall you testify in a dispute so as to turn
aside after many to pervert *justice.*
3 "You shall not show partiality to a [R]poor
man in his dispute. Deut. 1:17; 16:19
4 [R]"If you meet your enemy's ox or his
donkey going astray, you shall surely bring it
back to him again. [Rom. 12:20]
5 [R]"If you see the donkey of one who hates
you lying under its burden, and you would
refrain from helping it, you shall surely help
him with it. Deut. 22:4
6 [R]"You shall not pervert the judgment of
your poor in his dispute. Eccl. 5:8
7 "Keep yourself far from a false matter;
do not kill the innocent and righteous. For [R]I
will not justify the wicked. Rom. 1:18
8 "And [R]you shall take no bribe, for a bribe
blinds the discerning and perverts the words
of the righteous. Prov. 15:27; 17:8, 23
9 "Also you shall not oppress a stranger,
for you know the heart of a stranger, because
you were strangers in the land of Egypt.

Sabbatical Year

10 [R]"Six years you shall sow your land and
gather in its produce, Lev. 25:1–7
11 "but the seventh *year* you shall let it rest
and lie fallow, that the poor of your people
may eat; and what they leave, the beasts of
the field may eat. In like manner you shall do
with your vineyard *and* your olive grove.
12 [R]"Six days you shall do your work, and
on the seventh day you shall rest, that your
ox and your donkey may rest, and the son of
your maidservant and the stranger may be
refreshed. Luke 13:14
13 "And in all that I have said to you, [R]be
circumspect and [R]make no mention of the
name of other gods, nor let it be heard from
your mouth. 1 Tim. 4:16 • Josh. 23:7

Three National Feasts

14 [R]"Three times you shall keep a feast to
Me in the year: Ex. 23:17; 34:22–24
15 [R]"You shall keep the Feast of Unleavened Bread (you shall eat unleavened bread
seven days, as I commanded you, at the time
appointed in the month of Abib, for in it you
came out of Egypt; [R]none shall appear before
Me empty); Ex. 12:14–20 • Ex. 22:29; 34:20
16 "and the Feast of Harvest, the firstfruits
of your labors which you have sown in the
field; and the Feast of Ingathering, *which is*
at the end of the year, when you have gathered in *the fruit of* your labors from the field.
17 "Three times in the year all your males
shall appear before the Lord [T]GOD. *YHWH*
18 "You shall not offer the blood of My
sacrifice with leavened bread; nor shall the
fat of My sacrifice remain until morning.
19 [R]"The first of the firstfruits of your land
you shall bring into the house of the LORD
your God. [R]You shall not boil a young goat in
its mother's milk. Deut. 26:2, 10 • Deut. 14:21

Conquest Regulations

20 [R]"Behold, I send an Angel before you to
keep you in the way and to bring you into the
place which I have prepared. Ex. 3:2; 13:15; 14:19
21 "Beware of Him and obey His voice; do
not provoke Him, for He will not pardon your
transgressions; for My name *is* in Him.
22 "But if you indeed obey His voice and do
all that I speak, then [R]I will be an enemy to
your enemies and an adversary to your adversaries. Deut. 30:7
23 [R]"For My Angel will go before you and
[R]bring you in to the Amorites and the Hittites
and the Perizzites and the Canaanites and
the Hivites and the Jebusites; and I will [T]cut
them off. Ex. 23:20 • Josh. 24:8, 11 • *annihilate them*
24 "You shall not [R]bow down to their gods,
nor serve them, [R]nor do according to their
works; [R]but you shall utterly overthrow them
and completely break down their *sacred*
pillars. Ex. 20:5; 23:13, 33 • Deut. 12:30, 31 • Num. 33:52
25 "So you shall [R]serve the LORD your God,
and [R]He will bless your bread and your water.
And [R]I will take sickness away from the
midst of you. Deut. 6:13 • Deut. 28:5 • Ex. 15:26
26 [R]"No one shall suffer miscarriage or be
barren in your land; I will [R]fulfill the number
of your days. Deut. 7:14; 28:4 • 1 Chr. 23:1
27 "I will send My fear before you, I will
[R]cause confusion among all the people to
whom you come, and will make all your
enemies turn *their* backs to you. Deut. 7:23
28 "And [R]I will send hornets before you,
which shall drive out the Hivite, the Canaanite, and the Hittite from before you. Josh. 24:12
29 [R]"I will not drive them out from before
you in one year, lest the land become desolate and the beast of the field become too
numerous for you. Deut. 7:22
30 "Little by little I will drive them out from
before you, until you have increased, and you
inherit the land.
31 "And [R]I will set your [T]bounds from the
Red Sea to the Sea of the Philistines, and
from the desert to [T]the River. For I will

[R]deliver the inhabitants of the land into your hand, and you shall drive them out before you. Gen. 15:18 • *boundaries* • The Euphrates • Josh. 21:44

32 [R]"You shall make no [T]covenant with them, nor with their gods. Ex. 34:12, 15 • *treaty*

33 "They shall not dwell in your land, lest they make you sin against Me. For *if* you serve their gods, [R]it will surely be a snare to you." Ps. 106:36

CHAPTER 24

The Covenant Is Ratified Through Blood

NOW He said to Moses, "Come up to the LORD, you and Aaron, [R]Nadab and Abihu, [R]and seventy of the elders of Israel, and worship from afar. Lev. 10:1, 2 • Num. 11:16

2 "And Moses alone shall come near the LORD, but they shall not come near; nor shall the people go up with him."

3 So Moses came and told the people all the words of the LORD and all the [T]judgments. And all the people answered with one voice and said, [R]"All the words which the LORD has said we will do." *ordinances* • Ex. 19:8; 24:7

4 And Moses [R]wrote all the words of the LORD. And he rose early in the morning, and built an altar at the foot of the mountain, and twelve [R]pillars according to the twelve tribes of Israel. Deut. 31:9 • Gen. 28:18

5 Then he sent young men of the children of Israel, who offered [R]burnt offerings and sacrificed peace offerings of oxen to the LORD. Ex. 18:12; 20:24

6 And Moses [R]took half the blood and put *it* in basins, and half the blood he sprinkled on the altar. Heb. 9:18

7 Then he [R]took the Book of the Covenant and read in the hearing of the people. And they said, "All that the LORD has said we will do, and be obedient." Heb. 9:19

8 And Moses took the blood, sprinkled *it* on the people, and said, "Behold, the blood of the covenant which the LORD has made with you according to all these words."

The God of the Covenant Is Revealed

9 Then Moses went up, also Aaron, Nadab, and Abihu, and seventy of the elders of Israel,

10 and they saw the God of Israel. And *there was* under His feet as it were a paved work of sapphire stone, and it was like the [T]very heavens in *its* clarity. Lit. *substance of sky*

11 But on the nobles of the children of Israel He did not [T]lay His hand. So they saw God, and they ate and drank. *stretch out*

The Revelation Is Given on Mount Sinai

12 Then the LORD said to Moses, "Come up to Me on the mountain and be there; and I will give you [R]tablets of stone, and the law and commandments which I have written, that you may teach them." Ex. 31:18; 32:15

13 So Moses arose with [R]his assistant Joshua, and Moses went up to the mountain of God. Ex. 32:17

14 And he said to the elders, "Wait here for us until we come back to you. Indeed, Aaron and [R]Hur *are* with you. If any man has a difficulty, let him go to them." Ex. 17:10, 12

15 Then Moses went up into the mountain, and [R]a cloud covered the mountain. Ex. 19:9

16 Now the glory of the LORD rested on Mount Sinai, and the cloud covered it six days. And on the seventh day He called to Moses out of the midst of the cloud.

17 The sight of the glory of the LORD *was* like a consuming fire on the top of the mountain in the eyes of the children of Israel.

18 So Moses went into the midst of the cloud and went up into the mountain. And [R]Moses was on the mountain forty days and forty nights. Ex. 34:28

CHAPTER 25

The Offering for the Tabernacle

THEN the LORD spoke to Moses, saying:

2 "Speak to the children of Israel, that they bring Me an offering. [R]From everyone who gives it willingly with his heart you shall take My offering. Ex. 35:4–9, 21

3 "And this *is* the offering which you shall take from them: gold, silver, and bronze;

4 "blue and purple and scarlet *yarn*, fine linen *thread*, and goats' *hair*;

5 "rams' skins dyed red, [T]badger skins, and acacia wood; Or *dolphin*

6 "oil for the light, and spices for the anointing oil and for the sweet incense;

7 "onyx stones, and stones to be set in the [R]ephod and in the breastplate. Ex. 28:4, 6–14

The Purpose of the Tabernacle

8 "And let them make Me a sanctuary, that [R]I may dwell among them. [2 Cor. 6:16]

9 "According to all that I show you, *that is*, the pattern of the tabernacle and the pattern of all its furnishings, just so you shall make *it*.

The Ark of the Covenant

10 [R]"And they shall make an ark of acacia wood; [T]two and a half cubits *shall be* its length, a cubit and a half its width, and a cubit and a half its height. Ex. 37:1–9 • 45 in.

11 "And you shall overlay it with pure gold, inside and out you shall overlay it, and shall make on it a molding of gold all around.

12 "You shall cast four rings of gold for it, and put *them* in its four corners; two rings *shall be* on one side, and two rings on the other side.

13 "And you shall make poles *of* acacia wood, and overlay them with gold.

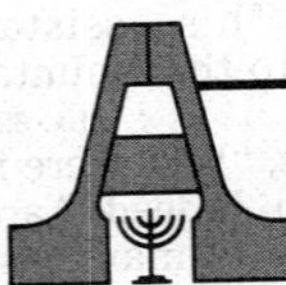

ARK OF THE TESTIMONY

Also known as the ark of the covenant, the ark of the Lord, and the ark of God, the ark of the Testimony was the object most sacred to the Israelites during their time in the Wilderness.

Do we know what the ark of the Testimony looked like? We cannot be positive, but there is a clear and detailed description in the Old Testament (Ex. 25:10–22). Archaeologists have discovered depictions of the ark (for example, a stone carving of the ark was found at the excavation of a synagogue in Capernaum).

From the biblical account, we can determine these facts about its physical appearance: It was a box about 45 inches long, 27 inches wide, and 27 inches high, made from acacia wood. Four poles were inserted into rings on the side of the ark so it could be carried by four men (see illustration).

The lid on the ark, called the mercy seat, was made of gold. The Hebrew word traditionally translated "mercy seat" could be rendered "place of atonement," because this was where the high priest sprinkled blood once each year on the Day of Atonement as the atonement for sin (Lev. 16:15). Mounted on this lid were two winged creatures (cherubim), which faced each other with outstretched wings. Inside the ark were the two stone tablets containing the Ten Commandments, which Moses had received from God at Mount Sinai (Ex. 20). It also contained a golden pot of manna and Aaron's rod that budded (Heb. 9:4), reminders of God's provision for the needs of the Israelites in the Wilderness.

The Israelites believed that God lived among them in the tabernacle between the wings of the cherubim on the mercy seat. God spoke to Moses from this place (Num. 7:89) during their years of wandering in the Wilderness as they were being prepared to enter the Promised Land.

The ark was carried ahead of the Israelites when they left Mount Sinai (Num. 10:33); when they crossed the Jordan River to enter Canaan (Josh. 4:9–11); and when they circled the walls of Jericho before that city fell (Josh. 6:1–20). After many other travels, it was finally placed in Solomon's temple in Jerusalem (1 Kin. 8:1–9), only to disappear after the destruction of Jerusalem by the Babylonians in 586 B.C.

The ark served as a visible reminder of God's presence with the Hebrew people. The mercy seat, covered with gold, symbolized God's throne and His rule in the hearts of those who acknowledge Him as their sovereign Lord.

Artist's conception of the ark of the Testimony.

14 "You shall put the poles into the rings on the sides of the ark, that the ark may be carried by them.

15 [R]"The poles shall be in the rings of the ark; they shall not be taken from it. 1 Kin. 8:8

16 "And you shall put into the ark [R]the Testimony which I will give you. Heb. 9:4

17 [R]"You shall make a mercy seat of pure gold; two and a half cubits *shall be* its length and a cubit and a half its width. Ex. 37:6

18 "And you shall make two cherubim of gold; of hammered work you shall make them at the two ends of the mercy seat.

19 "Make one cherub at one end, and the other cherub at the other end; you shall make the cherubim at the two ends of it *of one piece* with the mercy seat.

20 "And [R]the cherubim shall stretch out *their* wings above, covering the mercy seat with their wings, and they shall face one another; the faces of the cherubim *shall be* toward the mercy seat. 1 Kin. 8:7

21 "You shall put the mercy seat on top of the ark, and [R]in the ark you shall put the Testimony that I will give you. Ex. 25:16

22 "And [R]there I will meet with you, and I will speak with you from above the mercy seat, from [R]between the two cherubim which *are* on the ark of the Testimony, of all *things* which I will give you in commandment to the children of Israel. Ex. 29:42, 43; 30:6, 36 • Num. 7:89

The Table of Showbread

23 "You shall also make a table of acacia wood; two cubits *shall be* its length, a cubit its width, and a cubit and a half its height.

24 "And you shall overlay it with pure gold, and make a molding of gold all around.

25 "You shall make for it a frame of a handbreadth all around, and you shall make a gold molding for the frame all around.

26 "And you shall make for it four rings of gold, and put the rings on the four corners that *are* at its four legs.

27 "The rings shall be close to the frame, as holders for the poles to bear the table.

28 "And you shall make the poles of acacia wood, and overlay them with gold, that the table may be carried with them.

29 "You shall make [R]its dishes, its pans, its pitchers, and its bowls for pouring. You shall make them of pure gold. Ex. 37:16

30 "And you shall set the [R]showbread on the table before Me always. Lev. 24:5–9

The Golden Lampstand

31 [R]"You shall also make a lampstand of pure gold; the lampstand shall be of hammered work. Its shaft, its branches, its bowls, its ornamental knobs, and flowers shall be *of one piece.* Zech. 4:2

32 "And six branches shall come out of its sides: three branches of the lampstand out of one side, and three branches of the lampstand out of the other side.

33 [R]"Three bowls *shall be* made like almond *blossoms* on one branch, *with* an *ornamental* knob and a flower, and three bowls made like almond *blossoms* on the other branch, *with* an *ornamental* knob and a flower—and so for the six branches that come out of the lampstand. Ex. 37:19

34 "On the lampstand itself four bowls *shall be* made like almond *blossoms, each with* its *ornamental* knob and flower.

35 "And *there shall be* a knob under the *first* two branches of the same, a knob under the *second* two branches of the same, and a knob under the *third* two branches of the same, according to the six branches that extend from the lampstand.

36 "Their knobs and their branches *shall be of one piece*; all of it *shall be* one hammered piece of pure gold.

37 "You shall make seven lamps for it, and [R]they shall arrange its lamps so that they [R]give light in front of it. Lev. 24:3, 4 • Num. 8:2

38 "And its wick-trimmers and their trays *shall be* of pure gold.

39 "It shall be made of a [T]talent of pure gold, with all these utensils. $5,760,000

40 "And [R]see to it that you make *them* according to the pattern which was shown you on the mountain. [Heb. 8:5]

CHAPTER 26

The Curtains of Linen

"MOREOVER [R]you shall make the tabernacle *with* ten curtains *woven of* fine linen thread, and blue and purple and scarlet *yarn*; with artistic designs of cherubim you shall weave them. Ex. 36:8–19

2 "The length of each curtain *shall be* twenty-eight cubits, and the width of each curtain four cubits. And every one of the curtains shall have the same measurements.

3 "Five curtains shall be coupled to one another, and *the other* five curtains *shall be* coupled to one another.

4 "And you shall make loops of blue *yarn* on the edge of the curtain on the selvedge of *one* set, and likewise you shall do on the outer edge of *the other* curtain of the second set.

5 "Fifty loops you shall make in the one curtain, and fifty loops you shall make on the edge of the curtain that *is* on the end of the second set, that the loops may be clasped to one another.

6 "And you shall make fifty clasps of gold, and couple the curtains together with the clasps, so that it may be one tabernacle.

7 [R]"You shall also make curtains of goats' *hair*, to be a tent over the tabernacle. You shall make eleven curtains. Ex. 36:14

8 "The length of each curtain *shall be* [T]thirty cubits, and the width of each curtain [T]four cubits; and the eleven curtains shall all have the same measurements. 45 ft. • 6 ft.

9 "And you shall couple five curtains by themselves and six curtains by themselves, and you shall double over the sixth curtain at the forefront of the tent.

10 "You shall make fifty loops on the edge of the curtain that is outermost in *one* set, and fifty loops on the edge of the curtain of the second set.

11 "And you shall make fifty bronze clasps, put the clasps into the loops, and couple the tent together, that it may be one.

12 "The remnant that remains of the curtains of the tent, the half curtain that remains, shall hang over the back of the tabernacle.

13 "And a [T]cubit on one side and a cubit on the other side, of what remains of the length of the curtains of the tent, shall hang over the sides of the tabernacle, on this side and on that side, to cover it. 18 in.

14 "You shall also make a covering of rams' skins dyed red for the tent, and a covering of badger skins above that.

The Boards and Sockets

15 "And for the tabernacle you shall make the boards of acacia wood, standing upright.

16 [T]"Ten cubits *shall be* the length of a board, and a [T]cubit and a half *shall be* the width of each board. 15 ft. • 27 in.

17 "Two [T]tenons *shall be* in each board for binding one to another. Thus you shall make for all the boards of the tabernacle. *tabs*

18 "And you shall make the boards for the tabernacle, twenty boards for the south side.

19 "You shall make forty sockets of silver under the twenty boards: two sockets under one board for its two tenons, and two sockets under another board for its two tenons.

20 "And for the second side of the tabernacle, the north side, *there shall be* twenty boards

21 "and their forty sockets of silver: two sockets under one board, and two sockets under another board.

22 "For the far side of the tabernacle, westward, you shall make six boards.

23 "And you shall also make two boards for the two back corners of the tabernacle.

24 "They shall be coupled together at the bottom and they shall be coupled together at the top by one ring. Thus it shall be for both of them. They shall be for the two corners.

25 "So there shall be eight boards with their sockets of silver—sixteen sockets—two sockets under one board, and two sockets under another board.

26 "And you shall make bars of acacia wood: five for the boards on one side of the tabernacle,

27 "five bars for the boards on the other side of the tabernacle, and five bars for the boards of the side of the tabernacle, for the far side westward.

28 "The [R]middle bar shall pass through the midst of the boards from end to end. Ex. 36:33

29 "You shall overlay the boards with gold, make their rings of gold *as* holders for the bars, and overlay the bars with gold.

30 "And you shall raise up the tabernacle [R]according to its pattern which you were shown on the mountain. Acts 7:44

The Inner Veil

31 [R]"You shall make a veil woven of blue and purple and scarlet *yarn*, and fine linen thread. It shall be woven with an artistic design of cherubim. Matt. 27:51

32 "You shall hang it upon the four pillars of acacia *wood* overlaid with gold. Their hooks *shall be of* gold, upon four sockets of silver.

33 "And you shall hang the veil from the clasps. Then you shall bring the ark of the Testimony in there, behind the veil. The veil shall be a divider for you between [R]the holy *place* and the Most Holy. Heb. 9:2, 3

34 "You shall put the mercy seat upon the ark of the Testimony in the Most Holy.

35 "You shall set the table outside the veil, and the lampstand across from the table on the side of the tabernacle toward the south; and you shall put the table on the north side.

The Outer Veil

36 [R]"You shall make a screen for the door of the tabernacle, *woven of* blue and purple and scarlet *yarn*, and fine linen thread, made by a weaver. Ex. 36:37

37 "And you shall make for the screen five pillars of acacia *wood*, and overlay them with gold; their hooks *shall be of* gold, and you shall cast five sockets of bronze for them.

CHAPTER 27

The Bronze Altar

"YOU shall make [R]an altar of acacia wood, [T]five cubits long and five cubits broad—the altar shall be square—and its height *shall be* three cubits. Ex. 38:1 • 7.5 ft.

2 "You shall make its horns on its four corners; its horns shall be of one piece with it. And you shall overlay it with bronze.

3 "Also you shall make its pans to receive its ashes, and its shovels and its basins and its forks and its firepans; you shall make all its utensils of bronze.

4 "You shall make a grate for it, a network of bronze; and on the network you shall make four bronze rings at its four corners.

5 "You shall put it under the rim of the
altar beneath, that the network may be midway up the altar.
6 "And you shall make poles for the altar,
poles of acacia wood, and overlay them with
bronze.
7 "The poles shall be put in the rings, and
the poles shall be on the two sides of the altar
to bear it.
8 "You shall make it hollow with boards;
[R]as it was shown you on the mountain, so
shall they make *it*. Ex. 25:40; 26:30

The Court of the Tabernacle

9 "You shall also make the court of the
tabernacle. For the south side *there shall be*
hangings for the court *woven of* fine linen
thread, one hundred cubits long for one side.
10 "And its twenty pillars and their twenty
sockets *shall be* of bronze. The hooks of the
pillars and their bands *shall be* of silver.
11 "Likewise along the length of the north
side *there shall be* hangings [T]one hundred
cubits long, with its twenty pillars and their
twenty sockets of bronze, and the hooks of
the pillars and their bands of silver. 150 ft.
12 "And along the width of the court on the
west side *shall be* hangings of fifty cubits,
with their ten pillars and their ten sockets.
13 "The width of the court on the east side
shall be [T]fifty cubits. 75 ft.
14 "The hangings on *one* side *of the gate*
shall be [T]fifteen cubits, *with* their three pillars
and their three sockets. 22.5 ft.
15 "And on the other side *shall be* hangings
of [T]fifteen *cubits, with* their three pillars and
their three sockets. 22.5 ft.
16 "For the gate of the court *there shall be*
a screen [T]twenty cubits long, *woven of* blue
and purple and scarlet *yarn*, and fine linen
thread, made by a weaver. It *shall have* four
pillars and four sockets. 30 ft.
17 "All the pillars around the court shall
have bands of silver; their [R]hooks *shall be* of
silver and their sockets of bronze. Ex. 38:19
18 "The length of the court *shall be* one
hundred cubits, the width fifty throughout,
and the height five cubits, *woven of* fine linen
thread, and its sockets of bronze.
19 "All the utensils of the tabernacle for all
its service, all its pegs, and all the pegs of the
court, *shall be* of bronze.

The Oil for the Lamp

20 "And [R]you shall command the children
of Israel that they bring you pure oil of
pressed olives for the light, to cause the lamp
to [T]burn continually. Lev. 24:1–4 • Lit. *ascend*
21 "In the tabernacle of meeting, outside
the veil which *is* before the Testimony,
[R]Aaron and his sons shall tend it from evening until morning before the LORD. *It shall*
be a statute forever to their generations on
behalf of the children of Israel. Ex. 30:8

CHAPTER 28

The Command to Make the Priests' Clothes

"NOW take Aaron your brother, and his
sons with him, from among the children of Israel, that he may minister to Me as
priest, Aaron *and* Aaron's sons: Nadab,
Abihu, [R]Eleazar, and Ithamar. Ex. 6:23
2 "And you shall make holy garments for
Aaron your brother, for glory and for beauty.
3 "So [R]you shall speak to all *who are* gifted
artisans, [R]whom I have filled with the spirit of
wisdom, that they may make Aaron's garments, to sanctify him, that he may minister
to Me as priest. Ex. 31:6; 36:1 • Ex. 31:3; 35:30, 31
4 "And these *are* the garments which they
shall make: a breastplate, an [T]ephod, a robe, a
skillfully woven tunic, a turban, and a sash.
So they shall make holy garments for Aaron
your brother and his sons, that he may minister to Me as priest. Ornamented vest
5 "They shall take the gold and blue and
purple and scarlet *thread*, and fine linen,

The Ephod

6 [R]"and they shall make the ephod of gold
and blue and purple *and* scarlet *thread*, and
fine linen thread, artistically woven. Ex. 39:2–7
7 "It shall have two shoulder straps joined
at its two edges, and *so* it shall be joined
together.
8 "And the [T]intricately woven band of the
ephod, which *is* on it, shall be of the same
workmanship, *woven of* gold and blue and
purple and scarlet *thread*, and fine linen
thread. *ingenious work of*
9 "Then you shall take two onyx [R]stones
and engrave on them the names of the sons
of Israel: Ex. 35:27
10 "six of their names on one stone, and *the*
remaining six names on the other stone,
according to their [R]birth. Gen. 29:31—30:24
11 "With the work of an [R]engraver in stone,
like the engravings of a signet, you shall
engrave the two stones with the names of the
sons of Israel. You shall set them in settings
of gold. Ex. 35:35
12 "And you shall put the two stones on the
shoulders of the ephod *as* memorial stones
for the sons of Israel. So Aaron shall bear
their names before the LORD on his two
shoulders [R]as a memorial. Josh. 4:7
13 "You shall also make settings of gold,
14 "and you shall make two chains of pure
gold like braided cords, and fasten the
braided chains to the settings.

The Breastplate

15 [R]"You shall make the breastplate of
judgment. Artistically woven according to

the workmanship of the ephod you shall
make it: of gold and blue and purple and
scarlet *thread*, and of fine linen thread, you
shall make it. Ex. 39:8–21
16 "It shall be doubled into a square: a
[T]span *shall be* its length, and a span *shall be*
its width. 9 in.
17 [R]"And you shall put settings of stones in
it, four rows of stones: *The first* row *shall be* a
[T]sardius, a topaz, and an emerald; *this shall
be* the first row; Ex. 39:10 • Or *ruby*
18 "the second row *shall be* a turquoise, a
sapphire, and a diamond;
19 "the third row, a [T]jacinth, an agate, and
an amethyst; Or *amber*
20 "and the fourth row, a [T]beryl, an [T]onyx,
and a jasper. They shall be set in gold settings. Or *yellow jasper* • Or *carnelian*
21 "And the stones shall have the names of
the sons of Israel, twelve according to their
names, *like* the engravings of a signet, each
one with its own name; they shall be according to the twelve tribes.
22 "You shall make chains for the breastplate at the end, like braided cords of pure
gold.
23 "And you shall make two rings of gold
for the breastplate, and put the two rings on
the two ends of the breastplate.
24 "Then you shall put the two braided
chains of gold in the two rings which are on
the ends of the breastplate;
25 "and the *other* two ends of the two
braided chains you shall fasten to the two
settings, and put them on the shoulder straps
of the ephod in the front.
26 "You shall make two rings of gold, and
put them on the two ends of the breastplate,
on the edge of it, which is on the inner side of
the ephod.
27 "And two *other* rings of gold you shall
make, and put them on the two shoulder
straps, underneath the ephod toward its
front, right at the seam above the [T]intricately
woven band of the ephod. *ingenious work of*
28 "They shall bind the breastplate by
means of its rings to the rings of the ephod,
using a blue cord, so that it is above the
intricately woven band of the ephod, and so
that the breastplate does not come loose from
the ephod.
29 "So Aaron shall [R]bear the names of the
sons of Israel on the breastplate of judgment
over his heart, when he goes into the holy
place, as a memorial before the LORD continually. Ex. 28:12

The Urim and Thummim

30 "And you shall put in the breastplate of
judgment the Urim and the Thummim, and
they shall be over Aaron's heart when he
goes in before the LORD. So Aaron shall bear
the judgment of the children of Israel over
his heart before the LORD continually.

The Robe of the Ephod

31 [R]"You shall make the robe of the ephod
all of blue. Ex. 39:22–26
32 "There shall be an opening for his head
in the middle of it; it shall have a woven
binding all around its opening, like the opening in a coat of mail, so that it does not tear.
33 "And upon its hem you shall make pomegranates of blue and purple and scarlet *yarn*,
all around its hem, and bells of gold between
them all around:
34 "a golden bell and a pomegranate, a
golden bell and a pomegranate, upon the hem
of the robe all around.
35 "And it shall be upon Aaron when he
ministers, and its sound will be heard when
he goes into the holy *place* before the LORD
and when he comes out, that he may not die.

The Holy Crown

36 [R]"You shall also make a plate of pure
gold and engrave on it, *like* the engraving of
a signet: Ex. 39:30, 31

HOLINESS TO THE LORD.

37 "And you shall put it on a blue cord, that
it may be on the turban; it shall be on the
front of the turban.
38 "So it shall be on Aaron's forehead, that
Aaron may [R]bear the iniquity of the holy
things which the children of Israel hallow in
all their [T]holy gifts; and it shall always be on
his forehead, that they may be accepted
before the LORD. [1 Pet. 2:24] • *sacred*

The Priest's Coat

39 "You shall [R]skillfully weave the tunic of
fine linen *thread*, you shall make the turban
of fine linen, and you shall make the sash of
woven work. Ex. 35:35; 39:27–29
40 [R]"For Aaron's sons you shall make tunics, and you shall make sashes for them.
And you shall make [T]hats for them, for glory
and beauty. Ezek. 44:17, 18 • *headgear* or *turbans*
41 "So you shall put them on Aaron your
brother and on his sons with him. You shall
[R]anoint them, [R]consecrate them, and [T]sanc-
tify them, that they may minister to Me as
priests. Lev. 10:7 • Lev. 8 • *set them apart*
42 "And you shall make for them linen
trousers to cover their nakedness; they shall
[T]reach from the waist to the thighs. Lit. *be*
43 "They shall be on Aaron and on his sons
when they come into the tabernacle of meeting, or when they come near the altar to
minister in the holy *place*, that they do not
incur iniquity and die. *It shall be* a statute
forever to him and his descendants after him.

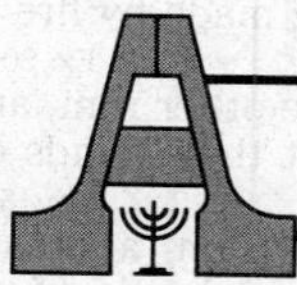

AARON AS HIGH PRIEST

When the priesthood was instituted in the Wilderness, Moses consecrated his brother Aaron as the first high priest of Israel (Ex. 28; 29; Lev. 8; 9). The priesthood was set within the tribe of Levi, from which Aaron was descended, and Aaron's sons inherited the position of high priest from their father.

The high priest's dress (see illustration) represented his function as mediator between God and people. Over his regular priestly garments the high priest wore an ephod, a two-piece apron. He also wore a breastplate of judgment with twelve precious stones. These were engraved with the names of the twelve tribes of Israel (Ex. 28:15–30). In the pocket of the breastplate, directly over the high priest's heart, were the Urim and Thummim (Ex. 28:30), the medium through which God communicated His will to the people.

The high priest was responsible for seeing that the duties of all the priests were carried out (2 Chr. 19:11). His most important responsibility occurred annually on the Day of Atonement. On this day he entered the Holy of Holies, or the Most Holy Place, in the tabernacle and made sacrifice first for his own sins, then for the sins committed by all the people during the year just ended (Ex. 30:10).

The high priest's dress represented his function as mediator between God and people.

David organized twenty-four groups of priests to serve at the tabernacle during his reign as king of Judah. Kings Hezekiah and Josiah assisted the high priest in reform and restoration of the temple. In the New Testament, the high priest was referred to as ruler of the people (Acts 23:4, 5) and was the presider over the Sanhedrin, the highest ruling body of the Jews (Matt. 26:57–59).

The New Testament speaks of Jesus in figurative terms as a "high priest." He was not of the order of Aaron but of Melchizedek, an eternal priesthood (Heb. 5:10). He had no need to offer sacrifice for His own sin, for He had no sin (Heb. 7:27, 28). He offered His own blood, once for all (Heb. 9:12, 26; 10:10, 12). Therefore, we may come boldly into the presence of God through the "one Mediator between God and men, *the* Man Christ Jesus" (1 Tim. 2:5).

CHAPTER 29

The Consecration of the Priests

"AND this is what you shall do to them to hallow them for ministering to Me as priests: [R]Take one young bull and two rams without blemish, [Heb. 7:26–28]

2 "and [R]unleavened bread, unleavened cakes mixed with oil, and unleavened wafers anointed with oil (you shall make them of wheat flour). Lev. 2:4; 6:19–23

3 "You shall put them in one basket and bring them in the basket, with the bull and the two rams.

4 "And Aaron and his sons you shall bring to the door of the tabernacle of meeting, [R]and you shall wash them with water. Ex. 40:12

5 [R]"Then you shall take the garments, put the tunic on Aaron, and the robe of the ephod, the ephod, and the breastplate, and gird him with [R]the intricately woven band of the ephod. Ex. 28:2 • Ex. 28:8

6 [R]"You shall put the turban on his head, and put the holy crown on the turban. Lev. 8:9

7 "And you shall take the anointing oil, pour *it* on his head, and anoint him.

8 "Then [R]you shall bring his sons and put tunics on them. Ex. 28:39, 40

9 "And you shall gird them with sashes, Aaron and his sons, and put the hats on them. [R]The priesthood shall be theirs for a perpetual statute. So you shall [R]consecrate Aaron and his sons. Num. 18:7; 25:13 • Ex. 28:41

10 "You shall also have the bull brought before the tabernacle of meeting, and [R]Aaron and his sons shall put their hands on the head of the bull. Lev. 1:4; 8:14

11 "Then you shall kill the bull before the LORD, *by* the door of the tabernacle of meeting.

12 "You shall take *some* of the blood of the bull and put *it* on [R]the horns of the altar with your finger, and [R]pour all the blood beside the base of the altar. Lev. 8:15 • Ex. 27:2; 30:2

13 "And you shall take all the fat that covers the entrails, the fatty lobe attached to the liver, and the two kidneys and the fat that *is* on them, and burn *them* on the altar.

14 "But [R]the flesh of the bull, with its skin and its offal, you shall burn with fire outside the camp. It *is* a sin offering. Lev. 4:11, 12, 21

15 [R]"You shall also take one ram, and Aaron and his sons shall [R]put their hands on the head of the ram; Lev. 8:18 • Lev. 1:4–9

16 "and you shall kill the ram, and you shall take its blood and [R]sprinkle *it* all around on the altar. Ex. 24:6

17 "Then you shall cut the ram in pieces, wash its entrails and its legs, and put *them* with its pieces and with its head.

18 "And you shall burn the whole ram on the altar. It *is* a [R]burnt offering to the LORD; it *is* a sweet aroma, an offering made by fire to the LORD. Ex. 20:24

19 [R]"You shall also take the other ram, and Aaron and his sons shall put their hands on the head of the ram. Lev. 8:22

20 "Then you shall kill the ram, and take some of its blood and put *it* on the tip of the right ear of Aaron and on the tip of the right ear of his sons, on the thumb of their right hand and on the big toe of their right foot, and sprinkle the blood all around on the altar.

21 "And you shall take some of the blood that is on the altar, and some of [R]the anointing oil, and sprinkle *it* on Aaron and on his garments, on his sons and on the garments of his sons with him; and [R]he and his garments shall be hallowed, and his sons and his sons' garments with him. Ex. 30:25, 31 • [Heb. 9:22]

22 "Also you shall take the fat of the ram, the fat tail, the fat that covers the entrails, the fatty lobe attached to the liver, the two kidneys and the fat on them, the right thigh (for it *is* a ram of consecration),

23 "one loaf of bread, one cake *made with* oil, and one wafer from the basket of the unleavened bread that *is* before the LORD;

24 "and you shall put all these in the hands of Aaron and in the hands of his sons, and you shall [R]wave them *as* a wave offering before the LORD. Lev. 7:30; 10:14

25 "You shall receive them back from their hands and burn *them* on the altar as a burnt offering, as a sweet aroma before the LORD. It *is* an offering made by fire to the LORD.

26 "Then you shall take [R]the breast of the ram of Aaron's consecration and wave it *as* a wave offering before the LORD; and it shall be your portion. Lev. 7:31, 34; 8:29

27 "And from the ram of the consecration you shall sanctify the breast of the wave offering which is waved, and the thigh of the heave offering which is raised, of *that* which *is* for Aaron and of *that* which is for his sons.

28 "It shall be from the children of Israel *for* Aaron and his sons [R]by a statute forever. For it is a heave offering; it shall be a heave offering from the children of Israel from the sacrifices of their peace offerings, *that is*, their heave offering to the LORD. Lev. 10:15

29 "And the holy garments of Aaron shall be his sons' after him, [R]to be anointed in them and to be consecrated in them. Num. 18:8

30 "That son who becomes priest in his place shall put them on for [R]seven days, when he enters the tabernacle of meeting to minister in the [T]holy *place*. Lev. 8:35 • *sanctuary*

31 "And you shall take the ram of the consecration and [R]boil its flesh in the holy place. Lev. 8:31

32 "Then Aaron and his sons shall eat the flesh of the ram, and the [R]bread that *is* in the basket, *by* the door of the tabernacle of meeting. Matt. 12:4

33 "They shall eat those things with which
the atonement was made, to consecrate *and*
to sanctify them; [R]but a stranger shall not eat
them, because they *are* holy. Lev. 22:10
34 "And if any of the flesh of the consecration offerings, or of the bread, remains until
the morning, then [R]you shall burn the remainder with fire. It shall not be eaten,
because it *is* holy. Lev. 7:18; 8:32
35 "Thus you shall do to Aaron and his
sons, according to all that I have commanded
you. Seven days you shall consecrate them.
36 "And you shall offer a bull every day *as* a
sin offering for atonement. You shall cleanse
the altar when you make atonement for it,
and you shall anoint it to sanctify it.
37 "Seven days you shall make atonement
for the altar and sanctify it. And the altar
shall be most holy. [R]Whatever touches the
altar must be holy. Matt. 23:19

The Continual Offerings of the Priests

38 "Now this *is* what you shall offer on the
altar: [R]two lambs of the first year, [R]day by day
continually. Num. 28:3–31; 29:6–38 • Dan. 12:11
39 "One lamb you shall offer [R]in the morning, and the other lamb you shall offer [T]at
twilight. Ezek. 46:13–15 • Lit. *between the two evenings*
40 "With the one lamb shall be [T]one-tenth
of an ephah of flour mixed with [T]one-fourth
of a hin of pressed oil, and one-fourth of a hin
of wine *as* a drink offering. 2.087 qt. • 1 qt.
41 "And the other lamb you shall offer [T]at
twilight; and you shall offer with it the grain
offering and the drink offering, as in the
morning, for a sweet aroma, an offering made
by fire to the LORD. Lit. *between the two evenings*
42 "*This shall be* a continual burnt offering
throughout your generations *at* the door of
the tabernacle of meeting before the LORD,
where I will meet you to speak with you.
43 "And there I will meet with the children
of Israel, and *the tabernacle* [R]shall be sanctified by My glory. 1 Kin. 8:11
44 "So I will sanctify the tabernacle of
meeting and the altar. I will also [R]sanctify
both Aaron and his sons to minister to Me as
priests. Lev. 21:15
45 [R]"I will dwell among the children of
Israel and will be their God. [Rev. 21:3]
46 "And they shall know that I *am* the LORD
their God, who [R]brought them up out of the
land of Egypt, that I may dwell among them.
I *am* the LORD their God. Lev. 11:45

CHAPTER 30

The Altar of Incense

"YOU shall make [R]an altar to burn incense on; you shall make it of acacia
wood. Ex. 37:25–29
2 "A [T]cubit *shall be* its length and a cubit
its width—it shall be square—and [T]two cubits
shall be its height. Its horns *shall be* of one
piece with it. 18 in. • 3 ft.
3 "And you shall overlay its top, its sides
all around, and its horns with pure gold; and
you shall make for it a [T]molding of gold all
around. *border*
4 "Two gold rings you shall make for it,
under the molding on both its sides. You shall
place *them* on its two sides, and they will be
holders for the poles with which to bear it.
5 "You shall make the poles of acacia
wood, and overlay them with gold.
6 "And you shall put it before the veil that
is before the ark of the Testimony, before the
[R]mercy seat that *is* over the Testimony,
where I will meet with you. Ex. 25:21, 22
7 "Aaron shall burn on it [R]sweet incense
every morning; when [R]he tends the lamps, he
shall burn incense on it. 1 Sam. 2:28 • Ex. 27:20, 21
8 "And when Aaron lights the lamps [T]at
twilight, he shall burn incense on it, a perpetual incense before the LORD throughout your
generations. Lit. *between the two evenings*
9 "You shall not offer [R]strange incense on
it, or a burnt offering, or a meal offering; nor
shall you pour a drink offering on it. Lev. 10:1
10 "And [R]Aaron shall make atonement
upon its horns once a year with the blood of
the sin offering of atonement; once a year he
shall make atonement upon it throughout
your generations. It *is* most holy to the
LORD." Lev. 16:3–34

The Ransom Money

11 Then the LORD spoke to Moses, saying:
12 "When you take the census of the children of Israel for their number, then every
man shall give [R]a[T] ransom for himself to the
LORD, when you number them, that there
may be no plague among them when *you*
number them. [1 Pet. 1:18, 19] • the price of a life
13 "This is what everyone among those who
are numbered shall give: half a shekel according to the shekel of the sanctuary (a shekel *is*
twenty gerahs). [R]The [T]half-shekel *shall be* an
offering to the LORD. Ex. 38:26 • $64
14 "Everyone included among those who
are numbered, from twenty years old and
above, shall give an offering to the LORD.
15 "The [R]rich shall not give more and the
poor shall not give less than half a shekel,
when *you* give an offering to the LORD, to
make atonement for yourselves. [Eph. 6:9]
16 "And you shall take the atonement
money of the children of Israel, and [R]shall
[T]appoint it for the service of the tabernacle of
meeting, that it may be a memorial for the
children of Israel before the LORD, to make
atonement for yourselves." Ex. 38:25–31 • *give*

The Laver of Bronze

17 Then the LORD spoke to Moses, saying:
18 [R]"You shall also make a [T]laver of bronze,
with its base also of bronze, for washing. You

shall [R]put it between the tabernacle of meeting and the altar. And you shall put water in
it, Ex. 38:8 • *basin* • Ex. 40:30
19 "for Aaron and his sons shall wash their
hands and their feet in water from it.
20 "When they go into the tabernacle of
meeting, or when they come near the altar to
minister, to burn an offering made by fire to
the LORD, they shall wash with water, lest
they die.
21 "So they shall wash their hands and their
feet, lest they die. And it shall be a [T]statute
forever to them—to him and his descendants
throughout their generations." *requirement*

The Anointing Oil

22 Moreover the LORD spoke to Moses, saying:
23 "Also take for yourself quality spices—
five hundred *shekels* of liquid myrrh, half as
much sweet-smelling cinnamon (two hundred and fifty *shekels*), two hundred and fifty
shekels of sweet-smelling [R]cane, Song 4:14
24 [T]"five hundred *shekels* of [R]cassia, according to the shekel of the sanctuary, and a [R]hin[T]
of olive oil. 12.5 lb • Ps. 45:8 • Ex. 29:40 • 1 gal
25 "And you shall make from these a holy
anointing oil, an ointment compounded according to the art of the perfumer. It shall be
[R]a holy anointing oil. Ex. 37:29; 40:9
26 "With it you shall anoint the tabernacle
of meeting and the ark of the Testimony;
27 "the table and all its utensils, the lampstand and its utensils, and the altar of incense;
28 "the altar of burnt offering with all its
utensils, and the laver and its base.
29 "You shall [T]sanctify them, that they may
be most holy; [R]whatever touches them must
be holy. *consecrate* • Ex. 29:37
30 [R]"And you shall anoint Aaron and his
sons, and sanctify them, that *they* may minister to Me as priests. Lev. 8:12
31 "And you shall speak to the children of
Israel, saying: 'This shall be a holy anointing
oil to Me throughout your generations.
32 'It shall not be poured on man's flesh;
nor shall you make *any other* like it, according to its composition. [R]It *is* holy, *and* it shall
be holy to you. Ex. 30:25, 37
33 'Whoever [T]compounds *any* like it, or
whoever puts *any* of it on an outsider, [R]shall
be cut off from his people.'" *mixes* • Gen. 17:14

The Incense

34 And the LORD said to Moses: "Take
sweet spices, stacte and onycha and galba-
num, and pure frankincense with *these* sweet
spices; there shall be equal amounts of each.
35 "You shall make of these an incense, a
compound [R]according to the art of the perfumer, salted, pure, *and* holy. Ex. 30:25
36 "And you shall beat *some* of it very fine,
and put some of it before the Testimony in
the tabernacle of meeting where I will meet
with you. It shall be most holy to you.
37 "But *as for* the incense which you shall
make, you shall not make any for yourselves,
according to its [T]composition. It shall be to
you holy for the LORD. Lit. *proportion*
38 [R]"Whoever makes *any* like it, to smell it,
he shall be cut off from his people." Ex. 30:33

CHAPTER 31

Instructions for Building the Tabernacle

THEN the LORD spoke to Moses, saying:
2 [R]"See, I have called by name Bezaleel
the [R]son of Uri, the son of Hur, of the tribe
of Judah. Ex. 35:30—36:1 • 1 Chr. 2:20
3 "And I have filled him with the Spirit of
God, in wisdom, in understanding, in knowledge, and in all *manner of* workmanship,
4 "to design artistic works, to work in gold,
in silver, in bronze,
5 "in cutting jewels for setting, in carving
wood, and to work in all *manner of* workmanship.
6 "And I, indeed I, have appointed with
him [R]Aholiab the son of Ahisamach, of the
tribe of Dan; and I have put wisdom in the
hearts of all who are [R]gifted artisans, that
they may make all that I have commanded
you: Ex. 35:34 • Ex. 28:3; 35:10, 35; 36:1
7 "the tabernacle of meeting, the ark of
the Testimony and the mercy seat that *is* on
it, and all the furniture of the tabernacle—
8 [R]"the table and its utensils, [R]the pure
lampstand with all its utensils, the altar of
incense, Ex. 37:10–16 • Ex. 37:17–24
9 "the altar of burnt offering with all its
utensils, and the laver and its base—
10 "the garments of ministry, the holy garments for Aaron the priest and the garments
of his sons, to minister as priests,
11 "and the anointing oil and sweet incense
for the holy *place*. According to all that I
have commanded you they shall do."

Sign of the Covenant: The Sabbath

12 And the LORD spoke to Moses, saying,
13 "Speak also to the children of Israel,
saying: 'Surely My Sabbaths you shall keep,
for it *is* a sign between Me and you throughout your generations, that *you* may know
that I *am* the LORD who sanctifies you.
14 'You shall keep the Sabbath, therefore,
for it *is* holy to you. Everyone who profanes it
shall surely be put to death; for [R]whoever
does *any* work on it, that person shall be cut
off from among his people. Num. 15:32–36
15 'Work shall be done for six days, but the
seventh *is* the Sabbath of rest, holy to the
LORD. Whoever does *any* work on the Sabbath day, he shall surely be put to death.

16 'Therefore the children of Israel shall keep the Sabbath, to observe the Sabbath throughout their generations *as* a perpetual covenant.

17 'It *is* [R]a sign between Me and the children of Israel forever; for [R]*in* six days the LORD made the heavens and the earth, and on the seventh day He rested and was refreshed.' " Ex. 31:13 • Gen. 1:31; 2:2, 3

Two Tablets Are Presented

18 And when He had made an end of speaking with him on Mount Sinai, He gave Moses two tablets of the Testimony, tablets of stone, written with the finger of God.

CHAPTER 32

Israel Willfully Breaks the Covenant

NOW when the people saw that Moses [R]delayed coming down from the mountain, the people [R]gathered together to Aaron, and said to him, [R]"Come, make us gods that shall go before us; for *as for* this Moses, the man who brought us up out of the land of Egypt, we do not know what has become of him." Ex. 24:18; Deut. 9:9–12 • Ex. 17:1–3 • Acts 7:40

2 And Aaron said to them, "Break off the [R]golden earrings which *are* in the ears of your wives, your sons, and your daughters, and bring *them* to me." Ex. 11:2; 35:22

3 So all the people broke off the golden earrings which *were* in their ears, and brought *them* to Aaron.

4 And he received *the gold* from their hand, and he fashioned it with an engraving tool, and made a molded calf. Then they said, "This *is* your god, O Israel, that [R]brought you out of the land of Egypt!" Ex. 29:45, 46

5 So when Aaron saw *it*, he built an altar before it. And Aaron made a proclamation and said, "Tomorrow *is* a feast to the LORD."

6 Then they rose early on the next day, offered burnt offerings, and brought peace offerings; and the people [R]sat down to eat and drink, and rose up to play. Num. 25:2

God to Destroy Israel

7 And the LORD said to Moses, [R]"Go, get down! For your people whom you brought out of the land of Egypt [R]have corrupted *themselves*. Deut. 9:8–21 • Gen. 6:11, 12

8 "They have turned aside quickly out of the way which I commanded them. They have made themselves a molded calf, and worshiped it and sacrificed to it, and said, [R]'This *is* your god, O Israel, that brought you out of the land of Egypt!' " 1 Kin. 12:28

9 And the LORD said to Moses, [R]"I have seen this people, and indeed it *is* a [T]stiff-necked people! [Acts 7:51] • *stubborn*

10 "Now therefore, let Me alone, that [R]My wrath may burn hot against them and I may [T]consume them. And [R]I will make of you a great nation." Ex. 22:24 • *destroy* • Num. 14:12

Moses Intercedes for Israel

11 Then Moses pleaded with the LORD his God, and said: "LORD, why does Your wrath burn hot against Your people whom You have brought out of the land of Egypt with great power and with a mighty hand?

12 [R]"Why should the Egyptians speak, and say, 'He brought them out to harm them, to kill them in the mountains, and to consume them from the face of the earth'? Turn from Your fierce wrath, and [R]relent from this harm to Your people. Num. 14:13–19 • Ex. 32:14

13 "Remember Abraham, Isaac, and Israel, Your servants, to whom You [R]swore by Your own self, and said to them, [R]'I will multiply your descendants as the stars of heaven; and all this land that I have spoken of I give to your descendants, and they shall inherit *it* forever.' " [Heb. 6:13] • Gen. 12:7; 13:15; 15:7, 18

14 So the LORD relented from the harm which He said He would do to His people.

Moses Disciplines Israel

15 And [R]Moses turned and went down from the mountain, and the two tablets of the Testimony *were* in his hand. The tablets *were* written on both sides; on the one *side* and on the other they were written. Deut. 9:15

16 Now the [R]tablets *were* the work of God, and the writing *was* the writing of God engraved on the tablets. Ex. 31:18

17 And when Joshua heard the noise of the people as they shouted, he said to Moses, "*There is* a noise of war in the camp."

18 But he said:

"*It is* not the voice of *those who* shout in
 victory,
Nor *is it* the voice of *those who* cry out
 in defeat,
But the voice of *those who* sing that I
 hear."

19 So it was, as soon as he came near the camp, that [R]he saw the calf *and* the dancing. So Moses' anger became hot, and he cast the tablets out of his hands and broke them at the foot of the mountain. Deut. 9:16, 17

20 [R]Then he took the calf which they had made, burned *it* in the fire, and ground *it* to powder; and he scattered *it* on the water and made the children of Israel drink *it*. Deut. 9:21

21 And Moses said to Aaron, [R]"What did this people do to you that you have brought so great a sin upon them?" Gen. 26:10

22 So Aaron said, "Do not let the anger of my lord become hot. [R]You know the people, that they *are set* on evil. Deut. 9:24

23 "For they said to me, 'Make us gods that
shall go before us; *as for* this Moses, the man
who brought us out of the land of Egypt, we
do not know what has become of him.'
24 "And I said to them, 'Whoever has any
gold, let them break *it* off.' So they gave *it* to
me, and I cast it into the fire, and this calf
came out."
25 Now when Moses saw that the people
were [R]unrestrained (for Aaron [R]had not restrained them, to *their* shame among their
enemies), Ex. 33:4, 5 • 2 Chr. 28:19
26 then Moses stood in the entrance of the
camp, and said, "Whoever *is* on the LORD's
side, *let him come* to me." And all the sons of
Levi gathered themselves together to him.
27 And he said to them, "Thus says the
LORD God of Israel: 'Let every man put his
sword on his side, and go in and out from
entrance to entrance throughout the camp,
and [R]let every man kill his brother, every man
his companion, and every man his neighbor.'" Num. 25:5–13
28 So the sons of Levi did according to the
word of Moses. And about three thousand
men of the people fell that day.
29 [R]Then Moses said, "Consecrate yourselves today to the LORD, that He may bestow
on you a blessing this day, for every man has
opposed his son and his brother." Ex. 28:41

Moses Atones for Israel

30 And it came to pass on the next day that
Moses said to the people, [R]"You have sinned
a great sin. So now I will go up to the LORD;
[R]perhaps I can [R]make atonement for your
sin." 1 Sam. 12:20, 23 • 2 Sam. 16:12 • Num. 25:13
31 Then Moses [R]returned to the LORD and
said, "Oh, these people have sinned a great
sin, and have [R]made for themselves a god of
gold! Deut. 9:18 • Ex. 20:23
32 "Yet now, if You will forgive their sin—
but if not, I pray, [R]blot me [R]out of Your book
which You have written." Ps. 69:28 • Dan. 12:1
33 And the LORD said to Moses, [R]"Whoever
has sinned against Me, I will [R]blot him out of
My book. [Ezek. 18:4; 33:2, 14, 15] • Ex. 17:14

God Sends His Angel

34 "Now therefore, go, lead the people to
the place of which I have [R]spoken to you.
[R]Behold, My Angel shall go before you. Nevertheless, [R]in the day when I [R]visit for punishment, I will visit punishment upon them for
their sin." Ex. 3:17 • Ex. 23:20 • Deut. 32:35 • Ps. 89:32
35 So the LORD plagued the people because
of [R]what they did with the calf which Aaron
made. Neh. 9:18

CHAPTER 33

The Tabernacle Is Moved Outside the Camp

THEN the LORD said to Moses, "Depart
and go up from here, you and the people
whom you have brought out of the land of
Egypt, to the land of which I swore to Abraham, Isaac, and Jacob, saying, [R]'To your
descendants I will give it.' Gen. 12:7
2 [R]"And I will send *My* Angel before you,
[R]and I will drive out the Canaanite and the
Amorite and the Hittite and the Perizzite and
the Hivite and the Jebusite. Ex. 32:34 • Josh. 24:11
3 "*Go up* [R]to a land flowing with milk and
honey; for I will not go up in your midst, lest
I [T]consume you on the way, for you *are* a
[T]stiff-necked people." Ex. 3:8 • *destroy* • *stubborn*
4 And when the people heard these grave
tidings, [R]they mourned, [R]and no one put on
his ornaments. Num. 14:1, 39 • Ezra 9:3
5 For the LORD had said to Moses, "Say to
the children of Israel, 'You *are* a stiff-necked
people. I could come up into your midst in
one moment and consume you. Now therefore, take off your [T]ornaments, that I may
[R]know what to do to you.'" *jewelry* • [Ps. 139:23]
6 So the children of Israel stripped themselves of their ornaments by Mount Horeb.
7 Moses took his tent and pitched it outside the camp, far from the camp, and [R]called
it the tabernacle of meeting. And it came to
pass *that* everyone who [R]sought the LORD
went out to the tabernacle of meeting which
was outside the camp. Ex. 29:42, 43 • Deut. 4:29

Moses Talks to God

8 So it was, whenever Moses went out to
the tabernacle, *that* all the people rose, and
each man stood [R]*at* his tent door and
watched Moses until he had gone into the
tabernacle. Num. 16:27
9 And it came to pass, when Moses entered
the tabernacle, that the pillar of cloud descended and stood *at* the door of the tabernacle, and [T]the LORD talked with Moses. *He*
10 All the people saw the pillar of cloud
standing *at* the tabernacle door, and all the
people rose and [R]worshiped, each man *in* his
tent door. Ex. 4:31
11 So [R]the LORD spoke to Moses face to
face, as a man speaks to his friend. And he
would return to the camp, but [R]his servant
Joshua the son of Nun, a young man, did not
depart from the tabernacle. Num. 12:8 • Ex. 24:13

God Will Show Moses the Way

12 Then Moses said to the LORD, "See, [R]You
say to me, 'Bring up this people.' But You
have not let me know whom You will send
with me. Yet You have said, [R]'I know you by
name, and you have also found grace in My
sight.' Ex. 3:10; 32:34 • Ex. 33:17
13 "Now therefore, I pray, if I have found
grace in Your sight, show me now Your way,
that I may know You and that I may find
grace in Your sight. And consider that this
nation *is* [R]Your people." Deut. 9:26, 29
14 And He said, [R]"My Presence will go *with
you*, and I will give you rest." Is. 63:9

15 Then he said to Him, [R]"If Your Presence does not go *with us*, do not bring us up from here. Ex. 33:3

16 "For how then will it be known that Your people and I have found grace in Your sight, except You go with us? So we shall be separate, Your people and I, from all the people who *are* upon the face of the earth."

17 Then the LORD said to Moses, [R]"I will also do this thing that you have spoken; for you have found grace in My sight, and I know you by name." [James 5:16]

God Shows Moses His Glory

18 And he said, "Please, show me [R]Your glory." [1 Tim. 6:16]

19 Then He said, "I will make all My goodness pass before you, and I will proclaim the name of the LORD before you. [R]I will be gracious to whom I will be [R]gracious, and I will have compassion on whom I will have compassion." [Rom. 9:15, 16, 18] • [Rom. 4:4, 16]

20 But He said, "You cannot see My face; for [R]no man shall see Me, and live." [Gen. 32:30]

21 And the LORD said, "Here is a place by Me, and you shall stand on the rock.

22 "So it shall be, while My glory passes by, that I will put you [R]in the cleft of the rock, and will [R]cover you with My hand while I pass by. Is. 2:21 • Ps. 91:1, 4

23 "Then I will take away My hand, and you shall see My back; but My face shall [R]not be seen." [John 1:18]

CHAPTER 34

Hewing of the Two Tablets

AND the LORD said to Moses, "Cut two tablets of stone like the first *ones*, and I will write on *these* tablets the words that were on the first tablets which you broke.

2 "So be ready in the morning, and come up in the morning to Mount Sinai, and present yourself to Me there [R]on the top of the mountain. Ex. 19:11, 18, 20

3 "And no man shall [R]come up with you, and let no man be seen throughout all the mountain; let neither flocks nor herds feed before that mountain." Ex. 19:12, 13; 24:9–11

4 So he cut two tablets of stone like the first *ones*. Then Moses rose early in the morning and went up Mount Sinai, as the LORD had commanded him; and he took in his hand the two tablets of stone.

The Nature of God Is Revealed

5 Then the LORD descended in the [R]cloud and stood with him there, and [R]proclaimed the name of the LORD. Ex. 19:9 • Ex. 33:19

6 And the LORD passed before him and proclaimed, "The LORD, the LORD God, merciful and gracious, longsuffering, and abounding in goodness and [R]truth, Ps. 108:4

7 [R]"keeping mercy for thousands, [R]forgiving iniquity and transgression and sin, [R]by no means clearing *the guilty*, visiting the iniquity of the fathers upon the children and the children's children to the third and the fourth generation." Ex. 20:6 • Ps. 103:3, 4 • Job 10:14

8 So Moses made haste and [R]bowed his head toward the earth, and worshiped. Ex. 4:31

9 Then he said, "If now I have found grace in Your sight, O Lord, let my Lord, I pray, go among us, even though we *are* a stiff-necked people; and pardon our iniquity and our sin, and take us as Your inheritance."

Renewal of the Covenant

10 And He said: "Behold, I make a covenant. Before all your people I will do marvels such as have not been done in all the earth, nor in any nation; and all the people among whom you *are* shall see the work of the LORD. For it *is* [R]an awesome thing that I will do with you. Ps. 145:6

11 [R]"Observe what I command you this day. Behold, [R]I am driving out from before you the Amorite and the Canaanite and the Hittite and the Perizzite and the Hivite and the Jebusite. Deut. 6:25 • Ex. 23:20–33; 33:2

12 [R]"Take heed to yourself, lest you make a covenant with the inhabitants of the land where you are going, lest it be a snare in your midst. Ex. 23:32, 33

13 "But you shall [R]destroy their altars, break their *sacred* pillars, and [R]cut down their *wooden* images Deut. 12:3 • 2 Kin. 18:4

14 "(for you shall worship [R]no other god, for the LORD, whose [R]name *is* Jealous, *is* a [R]jealous God), [Ex. 20:3–5] • [Is. 9:6; 57:15] • [Deut. 4:24]

15 "lest you make a covenant with the inhabitants of the land, and they play the harlot with their gods and make sacrifice to their gods, and *one of them* invites you and you [R]eat of his sacrifice, 1 Cor. 8:4, 7, 10

16 "and you take of [R]his daughters for your sons, and his daughters [R]play the harlot with their gods and make your sons play the harlot with their gods. Gen. 28:1 • Num. 25:1, 2

17 [R]"You shall make no molded gods for yourselves. Ex. 20:4, 23; 32:8

18 "The Feast of [R]Unleavened Bread you shall keep. Seven days you shall eat unleavened bread, as I commanded you, in the appointed time of the month of Abib; for in the [R]month of Abib you came out from Egypt. Ex. 12:15, 16 • Ex. 12:2; 13:4

19 [R]"All [T]that open the womb *are* Mine, and every male firstling among your livestock, *whether* ox or sheep. Ex. 13:2; 22:29 • *the firstborn*

20 "But [R]the firstling of a donkey you shall redeem with a lamb. And if you will not redeem *him*, then you shall break his neck. All the firstborn of your sons you shall redeem. And none shall appear before Me [R]empty-handed. Ex. 13:13 • Ex. 22:29; 23:15

21 [R]"Six days you shall work, but on the seventh day you shall rest; in plowing time and in harvest you shall rest. Ex. 20:8–11

22 "And you shall observe the Feast of Weeks, of the firstfruits of wheat harvest, and the Feast of Ingathering at the year's end.

23 [R]"Three times in the year all your men shall appear before the Lord, the LORD God of Israel. Ex. 23:14–17

24 "For I will [R]cast out the nations before you and enlarge your borders; neither will any man covet your land when you go up to appear before the LORD your God three times in the year. [Ex. 33:2]

25 "You shall not offer the blood of My sacrifice with leaven, [R]nor shall the sacrifice of the Feast of the Passover be left until morning. Ex. 12:10

26 [R]"The first of the firstfruits of your land you shall bring to the house of the LORD your God. You shall not boil a young goat in its mother's milk." Ex. 23:19

27 Then the LORD said to Moses, "Write [R]these words, for according to the tenor of these words I have made a covenant with you and with Israel." Deut. 31:9

28 [R]So he was there with the LORD forty days and forty nights; he neither ate bread nor drank water. And [R]He wrote on the tablets the words of the covenant, the Ten [T]Commandments. Ex. 24:18 • Ex. 34:1, 4 • Lit. *Words*

Moses Returns from God

29 Now it was so, when Moses came down from Mount Sinai (and the [R]two tablets of the Testimony *were* in Moses' hand when he came down from the mountain), that Moses did not know that [R]the skin of his face shone while he talked with Him. Ex. 32:15 • 2 Cor. 3:7

30 So when Aaron and all the children of Israel saw Moses, behold, the skin of his face shone, and they were afraid to come near him.

31 Then Moses called to them, and Aaron and all the rulers of the congregation returned to him; and Moses talked with them.

32 Afterward all the children of Israel came near, [R]and he gave them as commandments all that the LORD had spoken with him on Mount Sinai. Ex. 24:3

33 And when Moses had finished speaking with them, he put a veil on his face.

34 But [R]whenever Moses went in before the LORD to speak with Him, he would take the veil off until he came out; and he would come out and speak to the children of Israel whatever he had been commanded. [2 Cor. 3:13–16]

35 And whenever the children of Israel saw the face of Moses, that the skin of Moses' face shone, then Moses would put the veil on his face again, until he went in to speak with Him.

CHAPTER 35

Israel Brings Offerings in Abundance

THEN Moses gathered all the congregation of the children of Israel together, and said to them, [R]"These *are* the words which the LORD has commanded *you* to do: Ex. 34:32

2 "Work shall be done for six days, but the seventh day shall be a holy day for you, a Sabbath of rest to the LORD. Whoever does any work on it shall be put to death.

3 "You shall kindle no fire throughout your habitations on the Sabbath day."

4 And Moses spoke to all the congregation of the children of Israel, saying, "This *is* the thing which the LORD commanded, saying:

5 'Take from among you an offering to the LORD. [R]Whoever *is* of a willing heart, let him bring it as an offering to the LORD: [R]gold, silver, and bronze; Ex. 25:2 • Ex. 38:24

6 [R]'blue and purple and scarlet *yarn*, fine linen *thread*, and [R]goats' *hair*; Ex. 36:8 • Ex. 36:14

7 'rams' skins dyed red, badger skins, and acacia wood;

8 'oil for the light, and spices for the anointing oil and for the sweet incense;

9 'onyx stones, and stones to be set in the ephod and in the breastplate.

10 [R]'All who *are* skillful among you shall come and make all that the LORD has commanded: Ex. 31:2–6; 36:1, 2

11 [R]'the tabernacle, its tent, its covering, its clasps, its boards, its bars, its pillars, and its sockets; Ex. 26:1, 2; 36:14

12 [R]'the ark and its poles, *with* the mercy seat, and the veil of the covering; Ex. 25:10–22

13 'the [R]table and its poles, all its utensils, [R]and the showbread; Ex. 25:23 • Ex. 25:30

14 'also the lampstand for the light, its utensils, its lamps, and the oil for the light;

15 'the incense altar, its poles, the anointing oil, the sweet incense, and the screen for the door at the entrance of the tabernacle;

16 [R]'the altar of burnt offering with its bronze grating, its poles, all its utensils, *and* the laver and its base; Ex. 27:1–8

17 [R]'the hangings of the court, its pillars, their sockets, and the screen for the gate of the court; Ex. 27:9–18

18 'the pegs of the tabernacle, the pegs of the court, and their cords;

19 'the [T]garments of ministry, for ministering in the holy *place*—the holy garments for Aaron the priest and the garments of his sons, to minister as priests.' " Or *woven garments*

20 And all the congregation of the children of Israel departed from the presence of Moses.

21 Then everyone came whose heart was stirred, and everyone whose spirit was willing, *and* they brought the LORD's offering for the work of the tabernacle of meeting, for all its service, and for the holy garments.

22 They came, both men and women, as many as had a willing heart, *and* brought earrings and nose rings, rings and necklaces, all jewelry of gold, that is, every man who *offered* an offering of gold to the LORD.

23 And [R]every man, with whom was found blue and purple and scarlet, fine linen, goats' *hair*, red skins of rams, and [T]badger skins, brought *them*. 1 Chr. 29:8 • Or *dolphin*

24 Everyone who offered an offering of silver or bronze brought the LORD's offering. And everyone with whom was found acacia wood for any work of the service, brought *it*.

25 All the women who were [R]gifted artisans spun yarn with their hands, and brought what they had spun, of blue and purple *and* scarlet, and fine linen. Ex. 28:3; 31:6; 36:1

26 And all the women whose hearts stirred with wisdom spun yarn of goats' *hair*.

27 [R]The rulers brought onyx stones, and the stones to be set in the ephod and in the breastplate, Ezra 2:68

28 and spices and oil for the light, for the anointing oil, and for the sweet incense.

29 The children of Israel brought a freewill offering to the LORD, all the men and women whose hearts were willing to bring *material* for all kinds of work which the LORD, by the hand of Moses, had commanded to be done.

30 And Moses said to the children of Israel, "See, [R]the LORD has called by name Bezaleel the son of Uri, the son of Hur, of the tribe of Judah; Ex. 31:1–6

31 "and He has filled him with the Spirit of God, in wisdom and understanding, in knowledge and all manner of workmanship,

32 "to design artistic works, to work in gold and silver and bronze,

33 "in cutting jewels for setting, in carving wood, and to work in all manner of artistic workmanship.

34 "And He has put in his heart the ability to teach, *in* him and [R]Aholiab the son of Ahisamach, of the tribe of Dan. Ex. 31:6

35 "He has [R]filled them with skill to do all manner of work of the engraver and the designer and the tapestry maker, in blue and purple and scarlet and fine linen, and of the weaver—those who do every work and those who design artistic works. 1 Kin. 7:14

CHAPTER 36

"AND Bezaleel and Aholiab, and every gifted artisan in whom the LORD has put wisdom and understanding, to know how to do all manner of work for the service of the [R]sanctuary,[T] shall do according to all that the LORD has commanded." Ex. 25:8 • *holy place*

2 Then Moses called Bezaleel and Aholiab, and every gifted artisan in whose heart the LORD had put wisdom, everyone whose heart was stirred, to come and do the work.

3 And they received from Moses all the [R]offering which the children of Israel had brought for the work of the service of making the sanctuary. So they continued bringing to him freewill offerings every morning. Ex. 35:5

4 Then all the craftsmen who were doing all the work of the sanctuary came, each from the work he was doing,

5 and they spoke to Moses, saying, [R]"The people bring much more than enough for the service of the work which the LORD commanded *us* to do." [2 Cor. 8:2, 3]

6 So Moses gave a commandment, and they caused it to be proclaimed throughout the camp, saying, "Let neither man nor woman do any more work for the offering of the sanctuary." And the people were restrained from bringing,

7 for the material they had was sufficient for all the work to be done—indeed too [R]much. 1 Kin. 8:64

The Curtains

8 Then all the gifted artisans among them who worked on the tabernacle made ten curtains woven of fine linen thread, and blue and purple and scarlet *yarn; with* artistic designs of cherubim they made them.

9 The length of each curtain *was* [T]twenty-eight cubits, and the width of each curtain [T]four cubits; the curtains *were* all the same size. 42 ft. • 6 ft.

10 And he coupled five curtains to one another, and *the other* five curtains he coupled to one another.

11 He made loops of blue yarn on the edge of the curtain on the selvedge of one set; likewise he did on the outer edge of *the other* curtain of the second set.

12 [R]Fifty loops he made on one curtain, and fifty loops he made on the edge of the curtain on the end of the second set; the loops held one *curtain* to another. Ex. 26:5

13 And he made fifty clasps of gold, and coupled the curtains to one another with the clasps, that it might be one tabernacle.

14 [R]He made curtains of goats' *hair* for the tent over the tabernacle; he made eleven curtains. Ex. 26:7

15 The length of each curtain *was* [T]thirty cubits, and the width of each curtain [T]four cubits; the eleven curtains *were* the same size. 45 ft. • 6 ft.

16 He coupled five curtains by themselves and six curtains by themselves.

17 And he made fifty loops on the edge of the curtain that is outermost in one set, and fifty loops he made on the edge of the curtain of the second set.

18 He also made fifty bronze clasps to couple the tent together, that it might be one.

19 [R]Then he made a covering for the tent of rams' skins dyed red, and a covering of [T]badger skins above *that.* Ex. 26:14 • Or *dolphin*

The Boards

20 For the tabernacle [R]he made boards of acacia wood, standing upright. Ex. 26:15–29

21 The length of each board *was* [T]ten cubits, and the width of each board a [T]cubit and a half. 15 ft. • 27 in.

22 Each board had two [T]tenons [R]for binding one to another. Thus he made for all the boards of the tabernacle. *tabs* • Ex. 26:17

23 And he made boards for the tabernacle, twenty boards for the south side.

24 Forty sockets of silver he made to go under the twenty boards: two sockets under one board for its two tenons, and two sockets under another board for its two tenons.

25 And for the other side of the tabernacle, the north side, he made twenty boards

26 and their forty sockets of silver: two sockets under one board and two sockets under another board.

27 For the west side of the tabernacle he made six boards.

28 He also made two boards for the two back corners of the tabernacle.

29 And they were coupled at the bottom and [T]coupled together at the top by one ring. Thus he made both of them for the two corners. Lit. *doubled*

30 So there were eight boards and their sockets—sixteen sockets of silver—two sockets under every board.

31 And he made bars of acacia wood: five for the boards on one side of the tabernacle,

32 five bars for the boards on the other side of the tabernacle, and five bars for the boards of the tabernacle on the far side westward.

33 And he made the middle bar to pass through the boards from one end to the other.

34 He overlaid the boards with gold, made their rings of gold *to be* holders for the bars, and overlaid the bars with gold.

The Veils

35 And he made [R]a veil woven of blue and purple and scarlet *yarn,* and fine linen thread; it was woven *with* an artistic design of cherubim. Ex. 26:31–37

36 He made for it four pillars of acacia *wood,* and overlaid them with gold, with their hooks of gold; and he cast four sockets of silver for them.

37 He also made a [R]screen for the tabernacle door, woven of blue and purple and scarlet *yarn,* and fine linen thread, made by a [T]weaver, Ex. 26:36 • Lit. *variegator,* a weaver in colors

38 and its five pillars with their hooks. And he overlaid their capitals and their rings with gold, but their five sockets *were of* bronze.

CHAPTER 37

The Ark of the Covenant

THEN Bezaleel made [R]the ark of acacia wood; [T]two and a half cubits *was* its length, a cubit and a half its width, and a cubit and a half its height. Ex. 25:10–20 • 45 in.

2 He overlaid it with pure gold inside and outside, and made a molding of gold all around it.

3 And he cast for it four rings of gold *to be set* in its four corners: two rings on one side, and two rings on the other side of it.

4 He made poles of acacia wood, and overlaid them with gold.

5 And he put the poles into the rings at the sides of the ark, to bear the ark.

6 He also made the [R]mercy seat of pure gold; two and a half cubits *was* its length and a cubit and a half its width. Ex. 25:17

7 He made two cherubim of beaten gold; he made them of one piece at the two ends of the mercy seat:

8 one cherub at one end on this side, and the other cherub at the *other* end on that side. He made the cherubim at the two ends *of one piece* with the mercy seat.

9 The cherubim spread out *their* wings above, *and* covered the [R]mercy seat with their wings. They faced one another; the faces of the cherubim were toward the mercy seat. Ex. 25:20

The Table of Showbread

10 He made [R]the table of acacia wood; two cubits *was* its length, a cubit its width, and a [T]cubit and a half its height. Ex. 25:23–29 • 27 in.

11 And he overlaid it with pure gold, and made a molding of gold all around it.

12 Also he made a frame of a [T]handbreadth all around it, and made a molding of gold for the frame all around it. 3 in.

13 And he cast for it four rings of gold, and put the rings on the four corners that *were* at its four legs.

14 The rings were close to the frame, as holders for the poles to bear the table.

15 And he made the poles of acacia wood to bear the table, and overlaid them with gold.

16 He made of pure gold the utensils which were on the table: its [R]dishes, its cups, its bowls, and its pitchers for pouring. Ex. 25:29

The Gold Lampstand

17 He also made the [R]lampstand of pure gold; of hammered work he made the lampstand. Its shaft, its branches, its bowls, its *ornamental* knobs, and its flowers were of the same piece. Ex. 25:31–39

18 And six branches came out of its sides: three branches of the lampstand out of one side, and three branches of the lampstand out of the other side.

19 There were three bowls made like almond *blossoms* on one branch, with an *ornamental* knob and a flower, and three bowls made like almond *blossoms* on the other branch, with an *ornamental* knob and a flower—and so for the six branches coming out of the lampstand.

20 And on the lampstand itself *were* four bowls made like almond *blossoms, each with* its *ornamental* knob and flower.

21 *There was* a knob under the *first* two branches of the same, a knob under the *second* two branches of the same, and a knob under the *third* two branches of the same, according to the six branches extending from it.

22 Their knobs and their branches were of one piece; all of it *was* one hammered piece of pure gold.

23 And he made its seven lamps, its [R]wick-trimmers, and its trays of pure gold. Num. 4:9

24 Of a [T]talent of pure gold he made it, with all its utensils. $5,760,000

The Altar of Incense

25 He made the incense altar of acacia wood. Its length *was* a cubit and its width a cubit—*it was* square—and two cubits *was* its height. Its horns were *of one piece* with it.

26 And he overlaid it with pure gold: its top, its sides all around, and its horns. He also made for it a molding of gold all around it.

27 He made two rings of gold for it under its molding, by its two corners on both sides, as holders for the poles with which to bear it.

28 And he [R]made the poles of acacia wood, and overlaid them with gold. Ex. 30:5

29 He also made [R]the holy anointing oil and the pure incense of sweet spices, according to the work of the perfumer. Ex. 30:23–25

CHAPTER 38

The Altar of Burnt Offerings

HE made the [R]altar of burnt offering of acacia wood; [T]five cubits *was* its length and five cubits its width—*it was* square—and its height *was* three cubits. Ex. 27:1–8 • 7.5 ft.

2 He made its horns on its four corners; the horns were *of one piece* with it. And he overlaid it with bronze.

3 He made all the utensils for the altar: the pans, the shovels, the basins, the forks, and the firepans; all its utensils he made of bronze.

4 And he made a grate of bronze network for the altar, under its rim, midway from the bottom.

5 He cast four rings for the four corners of the bronze grating, *as* holders for the poles.

6 And he made the poles of acacia wood, and overlaid them with bronze.

7 Then he put the poles into the rings on the sides of the altar, with which to bear it. He made the altar hollow with boards.

The Bronze Laver

8 He made [R]the laver of bronze and its base of bronze, from the bronze mirrors of the serving women who assembled at the door of the tabernacle of meeting. Ex. 30:18

The Court

9 Then he made [R]the court on the south side; the hangings of the court *were woven of* fine linen, one hundred cubits long. Ex. 27:9–19

10 There *were* twenty pillars for them, with twenty bronze sockets. The hooks of the pillars and their bands *were of* silver.

11 On the north side *the hangings were* one hundred cubits *long,* with twenty pillars and their twenty bronze sockets. The hooks of the pillars and their bands *were of* silver.

12 And on the west side *there were* hangings of [T]fifty cubits, with ten pillars and their ten sockets. The hooks of the pillars and their bands *were of* silver. 75 ft.

13 For the east side *the hangings were* [T]fifty cubits. 75 ft.

14 The hangings of one side *of the gate were* [T]fifteen cubits *long, with* their three pillars and their three sockets, 22.5 ft.

15 and the same for the other side of the court gate; on this side and that *were* hangings of [T]fifteen cubits, *with* their three pillars and their three sockets. 22.5 ft.

16 All the hangings of the court all around *were woven of* fine linen.

17 The sockets for the pillars *were of* bronze, the hooks of the pillars and their bands *were of* silver, and the overlay of their capitals *was of* silver; and all the pillars of the court had bands of silver.

18 The screen for the gate of the court *was* woven of blue and purple and scarlet *yarn,* and fine linen thread. The length *was* [T]twenty cubits, and the height along its width *was* [T]five cubits, corresponding to the hangings of the court. 30 ft. • 7.5 ft.

19 And *there were* four pillars *with* their four sockets of bronze; their hooks *were* of silver, and the overlay of their capitals and their bands *was of* silver.

20 All the [R]pegs of the tabernacle, and of the court all around, *were of* bronze. Ex. 27:19

The Sum of the Materials

21 This is the inventory of the tabernacle, the tabernacle of the Testimony, which was counted according to the commandment of Moses, for the service of the Levites, by the hand of Ithamar, son of Aaron the priest.

22 [R]Bezaleel the son of Uri, the son of Hur, of the tribe of Judah, made all that the LORD had commanded Moses. Ex. 31:2, 6

23 And with him *was* Aholiab the son of
Ahisamach, of the tribe of Dan, an engraver
and designer, a weaver in blue and purple and
scarlet *yarn*, and fine linen *thread*.
24 All the gold that was used in all the work
of the holy *place*, that is, the gold of the
[R]offering, was twenty-nine talents and seven
hundred and thirty shekels, according to [R]the
shekel of the sanctuary. Ex. 35:5, 22 • Ex. 30:13, 24
25 And the silver from those who were
[R]numbered of the congregation *was* one
hundred talents and one thousand seven
hundred and seventy-five shekels, according
to the shekel of the sanctuary: Ex. 30:11–16
26 [R]a [T]bekah for [T]each man (*that is*, half a
shekel, according to the shekel of the sanctuary), for everyone included in the numbering
from twenty years old and above, for six
hundred and three thousand, five hundred
and fifty *men*. Ex. 30:13, 15 • $64 • Lit. *a head*
27 And from the [T]hundred talents of silver
were cast [R]the sockets of the sanctuary and
the bases of the veil: one hundred sockets
from the hundred talents, one talent for each
socket. $38,400,000 • Ex. 26:19, 21, 25, 32
28 Then from the one thousand seven hundred and seventy-five *shekels* he made hooks
for the pillars, overlaid their capitals, and
[R]made bands for them. Ex. 27:17
29 The offering of bronze *was* seventy talents and two thousand four hundred shekels.
30 And with it he made the sockets for the
door of the tabernacle of meeting, the bronze
altar, the bronze grating for it, and all the
utensils for the altar,
31 the sockets for the court all around, the
bases for the court gate, all the pegs for the
tabernacle, and all the pegs for the court all
around.

CHAPTER 39

The Clothes for the Priests

OF the blue and purple and scarlet *thread*
they made [T]garments of ministry, for
ministering in the holy *place*, and made the
holy garments for Aaron, [R]as the LORD had
commanded Moses. Or *woven garments* • Ex. 28:4
2 [R]He made the [R]ephod of gold and blue
and purple and scarlet *thread*, and of fine
linen thread. Ex. 28:6–14 • Lev. 8:7
3 And they beat the gold into thin sheets
and cut *it into* threads, to work *it* in *with* the
blue and purple and scarlet and fine linen
thread, *into* artistic designs.
4 They made shoulder straps for it to couple *it* together; it was coupled together at its
two edges.
5 And the intricately woven band of his
ephod that *was* on it *was* of the same workmanship, *woven of* gold and blue and purple
and scarlet *thread*, and fine linen thread, as
the LORD had commanded Moses.
6 [R]And they set onyx stones, enclosed in
[T]settings of gold; they were engraved, as
signets are engraved, with the names of the
sons of Israel. Ex. 28:9–11 • *filigrees*
7 He put them on the shoulders of the
ephod, *that they should be* stones for a
[R]memorial for the sons of Israel, as the LORD
had commanded Moses. Ex. 28:12, 29
8 [R]And he made the breastplate, artistically
woven like the workmanship of the ephod, of
gold and blue and purple and scarlet *thread*,
and fine linen thread. Ex. 28:15–30
9 They made the breastplate square by
doubling it; a [T]span *was* its length and a span
its width when doubled. 9 in.
10 [R]And they set in it four rows of stones: a
row with a sardius, a topaz, and an emerald
was the first row; Ex. 28:17
11 the second row, a turquoise, a sapphire,
and a diamond;
12 the third row, a jacinth, an agate, and an
amethyst;
13 the fourth row, a beryl, an onyx, and a
jasper. *They were* enclosed in settings of gold
in their mountings.
14 *There were* [R]twelve stones according to
the names of the sons of Israel: according to
their names, *engraved like* a signet, each one
with its own name according to the twelve
tribes. Rev. 21:12
15 And they made chains for the breastplate
at the ends, like braided cords of pure gold.
16 They also made two settings of gold and
two gold rings, and put the two rings on the
two ends of the breastplate.
17 And they put the two braided chains of
gold in the two rings on the ends of the
breastplate.
18 The two ends of the two braided chains
they fastened in the two settings, and put
them on the shoulder straps of the ephod in
the front.
19 And they made two rings of gold and put
them on the two ends of the breastplate, on
the edge of it, which *was* on the inward side
of the ephod.
20 They made two *other* gold rings and put
them on the two shoulder straps, underneath
the ephod toward its front, right at the seam
above the intricately woven band of the
ephod.
21 And they bound the breastplate by
means of its rings to the rings of the ephod
with a blue cord, so that it would be above
the intricately woven band of the ephod, and
that the breastplate would not come loose
from the ephod, as the LORD had commanded
Moses.
22 [R]He made the [R]robe of the ephod of
woven work, all of blue. Ex. 28:31–35 • Ex. 29:5
23 And *there was* an opening in the middle
of the robe, like the opening in a coat of mail,
with a woven binding all around the opening,
so that it would not tear.

24 They made on the hem of the robe pomegranates of blue and purple and scarlet and fine *linen* thread.

25 And they made [R]bells of pure gold, and put the bells between the pomegranates on the hem of the robe all around between the pomegranates: Ex. 28:33

26 a bell and a pomegranate, a bell and a pomegranate, all around the hem of the robe to [T]minister in, as the LORD had commanded Moses. *serve*

27 [R]They made tunics, artistically woven of fine linen, for Aaron and his sons, Ex. 28:39, 40

28 a turban of fine linen, exquisite hats of fine linen, short trousers of fine linen,

29 [R]and a sash of fine linen and blue and purple and scarlet *thread,* woven as the LORD had commanded Moses. Ex. 28:39

30 Then they made the plate of the holy crown of pure gold, and wrote on it an inscription *like* the engraving of a signet:

HOLINESS TO THE LORD.

31 And they tied to it a blue cord, to fasten *it* above on the turban, as the LORD had commanded Moses.

The Tabernacle Is Inspected by Moses

32 Thus all the work of the tabernacle of the tent of meeting was finished. And the children of Israel did according to all that the LORD had commanded Moses; so they did.

33 And they brought the tabernacle to Moses, the tent and all its furnishings: its clasps, its boards, its bars, its pillars, and its sockets;

34 the covering of rams' skins dyed red, the covering of badger skins, and the veil of the covering;

35 the ark of the Testimony with its poles, and the mercy seat;

36 the table, all its utensils, and the [R]showbread; Ex. 25:23–30

37 the pure lampstand with its lamps (the lamps set in order), all its utensils, and the oil for light;

38 the gold altar, the anointing oil, and the sweet incense; the screen for the tabernacle door;

39 the bronze altar, its grate of bronze, its poles, and all its utensils; the laver with its base;

40 the hangings of the court, its pillars and its sockets, the screen for the court gate, its cords, and its pegs; all the utensils for the service of the tabernacle, for the tent of meeting;

41 and the [T]garments of ministry, to [T]minister in the holy *place*: the holy garments for Aaron the priest, and his sons' garments, to minister as priests. Or *woven garments* • *serve*

42 According to all that the LORD had commanded Moses, so the children of Israel [R]did all the work. Ex. 35:10

43 Then Moses looked over all the work, and indeed they had done it; as the LORD had commanded, just so they had done it. And Moses [R]blessed them. Lev. 9:22, 23

CHAPTER 40

The Tabernacle Is Erected

THEN the LORD spoke to Moses, saying:

2 "On the first day of the [R]first month you shall set up [R]the tabernacle of the tent of meeting. Ex. 12:2; 13:4 • Ex. 26:1, 30; 40:17

3 [R]"You shall put in it the ark of the Testimony, and [T]partition off the ark with the veil. Num. 4:5 • *screen*

4 "You shall bring in the table and [R]arrange the things that are to be set in order on it; [R]and you shall bring in the lampstand and [T]light its lamps. Ex. 25:30; 40:23 • Ex. 40:24, 25 • *set up*

5 [R]"You shall also set the altar of gold for the incense before the ark of the Testimony, and put up the screen for the door of the tabernacle. Ex. 40:26

6 "Then you shall set the [R]altar of the burnt offering before the door of the tabernacle of the tent of meeting. Ex. 39:39

7 "And [R]you shall set the laver between the tabernacle of meeting and the altar, and put water in it. Ex. 30:18; 40:30

8 "You shall set up the court all around, and hang up the screen at the court gate.

9 "And you shall take the anointing oil, and [R]anoint the tabernacle and all that *is* in it; and you shall hallow it and all its utensils, and it shall be holy. Ex. 30:26

10 "You shall anoint the altar of the burnt offering and all its utensils, and sanctify the altar. The altar shall be most holy.

11 "And you shall anoint the laver and its base, and sanctify it.

12 [R]"Then you shall bring Aaron and his sons to the door of the tabernacle of meeting and wash them with water. Lev. 8:1–13

13 "You shall put the holy garments on Aaron, and anoint him and sanctify him, that he may minister to Me as priest.

14 "And you shall bring his sons and clothe them with tunics.

15 "You shall anoint them, as you anointed their father, that they may minister to Me as priests; for their anointing shall surely be [R]an everlasting priesthood throughout their generations." Num. 25:13

16 Thus Moses did; according to all that the LORD had commanded him, so he did.

17 And it came to pass in the first month of the second year, on the first *day* of the month, *that* the tabernacle was raised up.

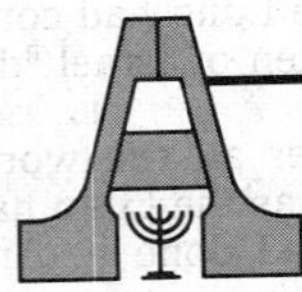

THE TABERNACLE

The tabernacle was a portable tent or sanctuary used by the Israelites as a place for worship during their early history. In the Old Testament, it is frequently called "the tent of meeting," indicating that it was the primary place of encounter between God and His people. The structure was built in accordance with God's instructions to Moses on Mount Sinai during their years of wandering in the Wilderness (Ex. 26; 35). With the people contributing materials and labor, the tabernacle was completed to God's specifications. God blessed their handiwork by covering the tent with a cloud and filling the sanctuary with His glory (Ex. 40:34).

The outer courtyard of the tabernacle was a fenced rectangle about 150 feet long by 75 feet wide (Ex. 27:9–19). The courtyard contained a bronze altar for animal sacrifices (Ex. 27:1–8) and a laver where the priests washed before entering the tent (Ex. 30:17–21).

The tabernacle itself, measuring 15 by 45 feet, had two main sections: the outer room known as the holy place, and the inner room called the Holy of Holies, or Most Holy Place (Ex. 26:33).

The outer room contained an altar where an incense offering was burned (Ex. 30:1–10); the seven-branched gold candlestick (Ex. 25:31–40); and a table for showbread, signifying God's presence (Ex. 25:23–30).

The inner room, or Holy of Holies, was separated from the outer area by a veil, or curtain (Ex. 26:31–37). This sacred part of the tabernacle was entered only once a year by the high priest on the Day of Atonement. In a special ceremony on this day, he made atonement for his own sins and then offered sacrifice to atone for the sins of the people. This most sacred enclosure had only one item of furniture, the ark of the covenant.

The lid of the ark was called the mercy seat. Upon it were two gold cherubim that faced each other. The ark contained the stone tablets with the Ten Commandments (Deut. 10:4, 5), a gold pot filled with manna (Ex. 16:33, 34), and Aaron's rod that budded (Num. 17:10).

During the years when the people of Israel were wandering in the Wilderness, the tabernacle was moved with them from place to place (Ex. 40:36–38). When the Israelites pitched camp in the Wilderness, the tabernacle was to be placed in the center, with the Levites, who were charged with its care (Num. 4), camping next to it (Num. 1:53). Then the tribes were to be arrayed in specific order on the four sides of the tabernacle (Num. 2). This shows what an important role the tabernacle played in the religious life of God's people.

After the conquest of Canaan, the tabernacle was moved to Shiloh, where it remained through the period of the judges (Josh. 18:1). Later the tabernacle was also stationed at Nob (1 Sam. 21:1–6) and Gibeon (1 Kin. 3:4). When the temple was completed, Solomon had the tabernacle moved to Jerusalem (1 Kin. 8:4). Apparently there was no further need for the tabernacle after the completion of the temple, which became the permanent place of worship for the nation and the center of its religious life.

The many references to the tabernacle in the New Testament should be understood in light of the incarnation, when God's Son became a human being. Because the tabernacle was the place where God and His people met, John declared that the Word had become flesh and "tabernacled" among us (John 1:14; the Greek word is translated "dwelt" in the New King James Version). Paul spoke of Christ as the "propitiation" for sin in Romans 3:25. He used the same Greek word that referred to the mercy seat of the ark where the high priest made annual atonement. The laver where priests washed before serving in the tabernacle may be reflected in Titus 3:5.

Revelation 8:3–5 speaks of the golden incense altar. Practically every feature of the tabernacle is found in the epistle to the Hebrews, a book that describes Jesus as the great High Priest and the ultimate and eternal sacrifice for our sins.

Artist's conception of the tabernacle.

18 So Moses raised up the tabernacle, fastened its sockets, set up its boards, put in its bars, and raised up its pillars.
19 And he spread out the tent over the tabernacle and put the covering of the tent on top of it, as the LORD had commanded Moses.
20 He took [R]the Testimony and put *it* into the ark, inserted the poles through the rings of the ark, and put the mercy seat on top of the ark. Ex. 25:16
21 And he brought the ark into the tabernacle, [R]hung up the veil of the covering, and partitioned off the ark of the Testimony, as the LORD had commanded Moses. Ex. 26:33
22 [R]He put the table in the tabernacle of meeting, on the north side of the tabernacle, outside the veil; Ex. 26:35
23 [R]and he set the bread in order upon it before the LORD, as the LORD had commanded Moses. Ex. 40:4
24 [R]He put the lampstand in the tabernacle of meeting, across from the table, on the south side of the tabernacle; Ex. 26:35
25 and [R]he lit the lamps before the LORD, as the LORD had commanded Moses. Ex. 40:4
26 [R]He put the gold altar in the tabernacle of meeting in front of the veil; Ex. 30:1, 6; 40:5
27 [R]and he burned sweet incense on it, as the LORD had commanded Moses. Ex. 30:7
28 [R]He hung up the screen *at* the door of the tabernacle. Ex. 26:36; 40:5
29 [R]And he put the altar of burnt offering *before* the door of the tabernacle of the tent of meeting, and [R]offered upon it the burnt offering and the grain offering, as the LORD had commanded Moses. Ex. 40:6 • Ex. 29:38–42
30 [R]He set the laver between the tabernacle of meeting and the altar, and put water there for washing; Ex. 30:18; 40:7
31 and Moses, Aaron, and his sons washed their hands and their feet *with water* from it.
32 When they went into the tabernacle of meeting, and when they came near the altar, they washed, [R]as the LORD had commanded Moses. Ex. 30:19
33 [R]And he raised up the court all around the tabernacle and the altar, and hung up the screen of the court gate. So Moses [R]finished the work. Ex. 27:9–18; 40:8 • [Heb. 3:2–5]

God Fills the Tabernacle with His Glory

34 Then the [R]cloud covered the tabernacle of meeting, and the [R]glory of the LORD filled the tabernacle. 1 Kin. 8:10, 11 • Lev. 9:6, 23
35 And Moses [R]was not able to enter the tabernacle of meeting, because the cloud rested above it, and the glory of the LORD filled the tabernacle. 1 Kin. 8:11
36 [R]When the cloud was taken up from above the tabernacle, the children of Israel went onward in all their journeys. Num. 9:17
37 But [R]if the cloud was not taken up, then they did not journey till the day that it was taken up. Num. 9:19–22
38 For [R]the cloud of the LORD *was* above the tabernacle by day, and fire was over it by night, in the sight of all the house of Israel, throughout all their journeys. Ex. 13:21

Weights

Unit	*Weight*	*Equivalents*	*Translations*
Jewish Weights			
Talent	c. 75 pounds for common talent, c. 150 pounds for royal talent	60 minas; 3,000 shekels	talent
Mina	1.25 pounds	50 shekels	mina
Shekel	c. .4 ounce (11.4 grams) for common shekel c. .8 ounce for royal shekel	2 bekas; 20 gerahs	shekel
Beka	c. .2 ounce (5.7 grams)	½ shekel; 10 gerahs	half a shekel
Gerah	c. .02 ounce (.57 grams)	1/20 shekel	gerah
Roman Weight			
Litra	12 ounces		pound

THE THIRD BOOK OF MOSES CALLED

LEVITICUS

THE BOOK OF LEVITICUS

Leviticus is God's guidebook for His newly redeemed people, showing them how to worship, serve, and obey a holy God. Fellowship with God through sacrifice and obedience show the awesome holiness of the God of Israel. Indeed, "'you shall be holy, for I the LORD your God *am* holy'" (19:2).

Leviticus focuses on the worship and walk of the nation of God. In Exodus, Israel was redeemed and established as a kingdom of priests and a holy nation. Leviticus shows how God's people are to fulfill their priestly calling.

The Hebrew title is *Wayyiqra,* "And He Called." The Talmud refers to Leviticus as the "Law of the Priests," and the "Law of the Offerings." The Greek title appearing in the Septuagint is *Leuitikon,* "That Which Pertains to the Levites." From this word, the Latin Vulgate derived its name *Leviticus* which was adopted as the English title. This title is slightly misleading because the book does not deal with the Levites as a whole but more with the priests, a segment of the Levites.

THE AUTHOR OF LEVITICUS

The kind of arguments used to confirm the Mosaic authorship of Genesis and Exodus also apply to Leviticus because the Pentateuch is a literary unit. In addition to these arguments, others include the following:

External Evidence: (1) A uniform ancient testimony supports the Mosaic authorship of Leviticus. (2) Ancient parallels to the Levitical system of trespass offerings have been found in the Ras Shamra Tablets dating from about 1400 B.C. and discovered on the coast of northern Syria. (3) Christ ascribes the Pentateuch (which includes Leviticus) to Moses (cf. Matt. 8:2–4 and Lev. 14:1–4; Matt. 12:4 and Lev. 24:9; see also Luke 2:22).

Internal Evidence: (1) Fifty-six times in the twenty-seven chapters of Leviticus it is stated that God imparted these laws to Moses (see 1:1; 4:1; 6:1, 24; 8:1). (2) The Levitical Code fits the time of Moses. Economic, civil, moral, and religious considerations show it to be ancient. Many of the laws are also related to a migratory lifestyle.

THE TIME OF LEVITICUS

No geographical movement takes place in Leviticus: the children of Israel remain camped at the foot of Mount Sinai (25:1, 2; 26:46; 27:34). The new calendar of Israel begins with the first Passover (Ex. 12:2); and, according to Exodus 40:17, the tabernacle is completed exactly one year later.

Leviticus picks up the story at this point and takes place in the first month of the second year. Numbers 1:1 opens at the beginning of the second month. Moses probably wrote much of Leviticus during that first month and may have put it in its final form shortly before his death in Moab, about 1405 B.C.

THE CHRIST OF LEVITICUS

The Book of Leviticus is replete with types and allusions to the person and work of Jesus Christ. Some of the more important include: (1) *The five offerings:* The burnt offering typifies Christ's total offering in submission to His Father's will. The meal offering typifies Christ's sinless service. The peace offering is a type of the fellowship believers have with God through the work of the cross. The sin offering typifies Christ as our guilt-bearer. The trespass offering typifies Christ's payment for the damage of sin. (2) *The high priest:* There are several comparisons and contrasts between Aaron, the first high priest, and Christ, our eternal high priest. (3) *The seven feasts:* Passover speaks of the substitutionary death of the Lamb of God. Christ died on the day of Passover. Unleavened Bread speaks of the holy walk of the believer (1 Cor. 5:6–8). Firstfruits speaks of Christ's resurrection as the firstfruits of the resurrection of all believers (1 Cor. 15:20–23). Christ rose on the day of the Firstfruits. Pentecost speaks of the descent of the Holy Spirit after Christ's ascension. Trumpets, the Day of Atonement, and Tabernacles speak of events associated with the second advent of Christ. This may be why these three are separated by a long gap from the first four in Israel's annual cycle.

KEYS TO LEVITICUS

Key Word: Holiness—Leviticus centers around the concept of the holiness of God, and how an unholy people can acceptably approach Him and then remain in continued fellowship. The way to God is only through blood sacrifice, and the walk with God is only through obedience to His laws.

Key Verses: Leviticus 17:11; 20:7, 8—"'For the life of the flesh *is* in the blood, and I have given it to you upon the altar to make atonement for your souls; for it *is* the blood *that* makes atonement for the soul'" (17:11).

"Sanctify yourselves therefore, and be holy, for I *am* the LORD your God. And you shall keep My statutes, and perform them: I *am* the LORD who sanctifies you" (20:7, 8).

Key Chapter: Leviticus 16—The Day of Atonement *("Yom Kippur")* was the most important single day in the Hebrew calendar as it was the only day the high priest entered into the Holy of Holies to "make atonement for you, to cleanse you, *that* you may be clean from all your sins before the LORD" (16:30).

SURVEY OF LEVITICUS

It has been said that it took God only one night to get Israel out of Egypt, but it took forty years to get Egypt out of Israel. In Exodus, Israel is redeemed and established as a kingdom of priests and a holy nation; and in Leviticus, Israel is taught how to fulfill their priestly call. They have been led out from the land of bondage in Exodus and into the sanctuary of God in Leviticus. They move from redemption to service, from deliverance to dedication. This book serves as a handbook for the Levitical priesthood, giving instructions and regulations for worship. Used to guide a newly redeemed people into worship, service, and obedience to God, Leviticus falls into two major sections: (1) sacrifice (1—17), and (2) sanctification (18—27).

Sacrifice (1—17): This section teaches that God must be approached by the sacrificial offerings (1—7), by the mediation of the priesthood (8—10), by the purification of the nation from uncleanness (11—15), and by the provision for national cleansing and fellowship (16 and 17). The blood sacrifices remind the worshipers that because of sin the holy God requires the costly gift of life (17:11). The blood of the innocent sacrificial animal becomes the substitute for the life of the guilty offerer: "without shedding of blood there is no remission" (Heb. 9:22).

Sanctification (18—27): The Israelites serve a holy God who requires them to be holy as well. To be holy means to be "set apart" or "separated." They are to be separated *from* other nations *unto* God. In Leviticus the idea of holiness appears eighty-seven times, sometimes indicating ceremonial holiness (ritual requirements), and at other times moral holiness (purity of life). This sanctification extends to the people of Israel (18—20), the priesthood (21 and 22), their worship (23 and 24), their life in Canaan (25 and 26), and their special vows (27). It is necessary to remove the defilement that separates the people from God so that they can have a walk of fellowship with their Redeemer.

FOCUS	SACRIFICE				SANCTIFICATION				
REFERENCE	1:1—	8:1—	11:1—	16:1—	18:1—	21:1—	23:1—	25:1—	27:1—27:34
DIVISION	THE LAWS OF				THE LAWS OF SANCTIFICATION				
	THE OFFERINGS	CONSECRATION OF THE PRIESTS	CONSECRATION OF THE PEOPLE	NATIONAL ATONEMENT	FOR THE PEOPLE	FOR THE PRIESTS	IN WORSHIP	IN THE LAND OF CANAAN	THROUGH VOWS
TOPIC	THE WAY TO GOD				THE WALK WITH GOD				
	THE LAWS OF ACCEPTABLE APPROACH TO GOD				THE LAWS OF CONTINUED FELLOWSHIP WITH GOD				
LOCATION	MOUNT SINAI								
TIME	c. 1 MONTH								

OUTLINE OF LEVITICUS

Part One: The Laws of Acceptable Approach to God: Sacrifice (1:1—17:16)

I. The Laws of Acceptable Approach to God . . . . 1:1—7:38

A. Laws of Approach to God When in Fellowship . . . . . . 1:1—3:17
1. The Burnt Offering 1:1–17
2. The Grain Offering 2:1–16
3. The Peace Offering 3:1–17

B. Laws of Approach to God When Out of Fellowship . . . . . . 4:1—6:7
1. The Sin Offering . . . . . . 4:1—5:13
2. The Trespass Offering . . . . . . 5:14—6:7

C. Laws for Administering Offering . . . 6:8—7:38
1. The Burnt Offering 6:8–13
2. The Grain Offering 6:14–23
3. The Sin Offering 6:24–30

Part Two: The Laws of Acceptable Walk with God: Sanctification (18:1—27:34)

2. Conditions and Results
of Obedience 26:3–13
3. Conditions and Results
of Disobedience 26:14–39
4. The Promise of Restoration 26:40–46

**V. The Laws of Sanctification
Through Vows 27:1–34**

A. The Special Consecrating
of Acceptable Things 27:1–25
1. Consecration of Persons 27:1–8
2. Consecration of Animals 27:9–13
3. Consecration of Houses 27:14, 15
4. Consecration of Fields 27:16–25
B. Things Excluded
from Consecration 27:26–34
1. Firstborn Clean Animals 27:26, 27
2. Devoted Things 27:28, 29
3. Tithes 27:30–33
C. The Conclusion of Leviticus 27:34

CHAPTER 1

The Burnt Offering

NOW the LORD [R]called to Moses, and
spoke to him [R]from the tabernacle of
meeting, saying, Ex. 19:3; 25:22 • Ex. 40:34
2 "Speak to the children of Israel, and say
to them: [R]'When any one of you brings an
offering to the LORD, you shall bring your
offering of the livestock—of the herd and of
the flock. Lev. 22:18, 19
3 'If his offering *is* a burnt sacrifice of the
herd, let him offer a male [R]without blemish;
he shall offer it of his own free will at the
door of the tabernacle of meeting before the
LORD. Eph. 5:27
4 'Then he shall put his hand on the head
of the burnt offering, and it will be accepted
on his behalf to make atonement for him.
5 'He shall kill the [R]bull before the LORD;
[R]and the priests, Aaron's sons, shall bring the
blood [R]and sprinkle the blood all around on
the altar that *is by* the door of the tabernacle
of meeting. Mic. 6:6 • 2 Chr. 35:11 • [Heb. 12:24]
6 'And he shall [R]skin the burnt offering and
cut it into its pieces. Lev. 7:8
7 'The sons of Aaron the priest shall put
[R]fire on the altar, and [R]lay the wood in order
on the fire. Mal. 1:10 • Gen. 22:9
8 'Then the priests, Aaron's sons, shall lay
the parts, the head, and the fat in order on
the wood that *is* on the fire upon the altar;
9 'but he shall wash its entrails and its legs
with water. And the priest shall burn all on
the altar as a burnt sacrifice, an offering
made by fire, a sweet aroma to the LORD.
10 'And if his offering *is* of the flocks—of
the sheep or of the goats—as a burnt sacrifice, he shall bring a male without blemish.
11 [R]'He shall kill it on the north side of the
altar before the LORD; and the priests, Aaron's sons, shall sprinkle its blood all around
on the altar. Lev. 1:5
12 'And he shall cut it into its pieces, with
its head and its fat; and the priest shall lay
them in order on the wood that *is* on the fire
upon the altar;
13 'but he shall wash the entrails and the
legs with water. And the priest shall bring *it*
all and burn *it* on the altar; it *is* a burnt
sacrifice, an [R]offering made by fire, a sweet
aroma to the LORD. Num. 15:4–7; 28:12–14
14 'And if the burnt sacrifice of his offering
to the LORD *is* of birds, then he shall bring his
offering of turtledoves or young pigeons.
15 'The priest shall bring it to the altar,
[T]wring off its head, and burn *it* on the altar;
its blood shall be drained out at the side of
the altar. Lit. *nip* or *chop off*
16 'And he shall remove its crop with its
feathers and cast it [R]beside the altar on the
east side, into the place for ashes. Lev. 6:10
17 'Then he shall split it at its wings, *but*
shall not divide *it* completely; and the priest
shall burn it on the altar, on the wood that *is*
on the fire. It *is* a burnt sacrifice, an offering
made by fire, a sweet aroma to the LORD.

CHAPTER 2

The Grain Offering

'WHEN anyone offers [R]a grain offering
to the LORD, his offering shall be *of*
fine flour. And he shall pour oil on it, and put
[R]frankincense on it. Num. 15:4 • Lev. 5:11
2 'He shall bring it to Aaron's sons, the
priests, one of whom shall take from it his
handful of fine flour and oil with all the
frankincense. And the priest shall burn [R]*it as*
a memorial on the altar, an offering made by
fire, a sweet aroma to the LORD. Lev. 2:9
3 [R]'The rest of the grain offering *shall be*
Aaron's and his [R]sons'. [R]*It is* a most holy
offering of the offerings to the LORD made by
fire. Lev. 7:9 • Lev. 6:6; 10:12, 13 • Num. 18:9
4 'And if you bring as an offering a grain
offering baked in the oven, *it shall be* unleavened cakes of fine flour mixed with oil, or
unleavened wafers anointed with oil.
5 'But if your offering *is* a grain offering
baked in a [T]pan, *it shall be of* fine flour,
unleavened, mixed with oil. *flat plate* or *griddle*
6 'You shall break it in pieces and pour oil
on it; it *is* a grain offering.
7 'And if your offering *is* a grain offering
baked in a [R]covered pan, it shall be made *of*
fine flour with oil. Lev. 7:9
8 'You shall bring the grain offering that is
made of these things to the LORD. And when

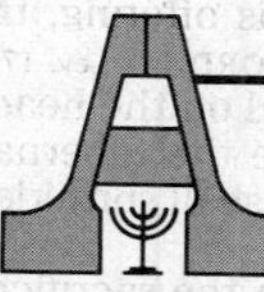

OLD TESTAMENT OFFERINGS

The burnt offering involved a male offering wholly consumed by fire.

The patriarchs of the Old Testament—Abraham, Isaac, and Jacob—built altars and made sacrifices to God wherever they settled (Gen. 12:8; 26:25; 28:18). Cain and Abel made the first offerings recorded in the Bible (Gen. 4:3–5). Noah offered sacrifices of thanksgiving after the great flood (Gen. 8:20). Most of these sacrifices involved the shedding of blood, a method God instituted to prepare His people for the Messiah's ultimate sacrifice for sins.

Several different types of offerings are specified by God throughout the Old Testament. These demonstrate human need and God's merciful provision.

The burnt offering involved a male animal wholly consumed by fire. The animal was killed and the priest collected the blood and sprinkled it about the altar (Num. 28:1–8; see illustration). The burning symbolized the worshiper's desire to be purged of sinful acts. The meal offering, or grain offering, described in Leviticus 2 was similar in purpose to the burnt offering. The grain was brought to the priest, who threw a portion on the fire, accompanied by the burning of incense.

The peace offering was a ritual meal shared with God, the priests, and often other worshipers (Lev. 3). A voluntary animal offering, the sacrifice expressed praise to God and fellowship with others. Jacob and Laban offered this sacrifice when they made a treaty (Gen. 31:43–55). The sin offering, also known as the guilt offering, was offered to make atonement for sins for which restitution was not possible (Lev. 4:5–12). The trespass offering was made for lesser or unintentional offenses for which restitution was possible (Lev. 5:14–19).

The author of the Book of Hebrews identified Jesus as the great High Priest (Heb. 9:11) who replaced the system of animal sacrifices with a once-for-all sacrifice of Himself (Heb. 9:12–28). In the light of Christ's full and final offering for sin, Paul urged Christians to "present your bodies a living sacrifice" (Rom. 12:1).

it is presented to the priest, he shall bring it to
the altar.
9 'Then the priest shall take from the grain
offering [R]a memorial portion, and burn *it* on
the altar. *It is* an [R]offering made by fire, a
sweet aroma to the LORD. Lev. 2:2, 16 • Ex. 29:18
10 'And [R]what is left of the grain offering
shall be Aaron's and his sons'. *It is* a most
holy *offering* of the offerings to the LORD
made by fire. Lev. 2:3; 6:16
11 'No grain offering which you bring to the
LORD shall be made with [R]leaven, for you
shall burn no leaven nor any honey in any
offering to the LORD made by fire. Lev. 6:16, 17
12 'As for the offering of the firstfruits, you
shall offer them to the LORD, but they shall
not be burned on the altar for a sweet aroma.
13 'And every offering of your grain offering
[R]you shall season with salt; you shall not
allow the salt of the covenant of your God to
be lacking from your grain offering. With all
your offerings you shall offer salt. [Col. 4:6]
14 'If you offer a grain offering of your
firstfruits to the LORD, [R]you shall offer for the
grain offering of your firstfruits green heads
of grain roasted on the fire, grain beaten from
[R]full heads. Lev. 23:10, 14 • 2 Kin. 4:42
15 'And you shall put oil on it, and lay
frankincense on it. It *is* a grain offering.
16 'Then the priest shall burn [R]the memorial
portion: *part* of its beaten grain and *part* of
its oil, with all the frankincense, as an offering made by fire to the LORD. Lev. 2:2

CHAPTER 3

The Peace Offering

'WHEN his offering *is* a sacrifice of peace
offering, if he offers *it* of the herd,
whether male or female, he shall offer it
without [T]blemish before the LORD. *defect*
2 'And [R]he shall lay his hand on the head of
his offering, and kill it *at* the door of the
tabernacle of meeting; and Aaron's sons, the
priests, shall [R]sprinkle the blood all around on
the altar. Lev. 1:4, 5; 16:21 • Lev. 1:5
3 'Then he shall offer from the sacrifice of
the peace offering an offering made by fire to
the LORD. The fat that covers the entrails and
all the fat that *is* on the entrails,
4 'the two kidneys and the fat that *is* on
them by the flanks, and the fatty lobe *attached* to the liver above the kidneys, he shall
remove;
5 'and Aaron's sons shall burn it on the
altar upon the burnt sacrifice, which *is* on the
wood that *is* on the fire, *as* an offering made
by fire, a sweet aroma to the LORD.
6 'If his offering as a sacrifice of peace
offering to the LORD *is* of the flock, *whether*
male or female, [R]he shall offer it without
blemish. Lev. 3:1; 22:20–24
7 'If he offers a lamb as his offering, then
he shall offer it [R]before the LORD. Lev. 17:8, 9
8 'And he shall lay his hand on the head of
his offering, and kill it before the tabernacle
of meeting; and Aaron's sons shall sprinkle its
blood all around on the altar.
9 'Then he shall offer from the sacrifice of
the peace offering, as an offering made by fire
to the LORD, its fat *and* the whole fat tail
which he shall remove close to the backbone.
And the fat that covers the entrails and all
the fat that *is* on the entrails,
10 'the two kidneys and the fat that *is* on
them by the flanks, and the fatty lobe *attached* to the liver above the kidneys, he shall
remove;
11 'and the priest shall burn *them* on the
altar *as* [R]food, an offering made by fire to the
LORD. Num. 28:2
12 'And if his offering *is* a goat, then [R]he
shall offer it before the LORD. Lev. 3:1, 7
13 'He shall lay his hand on its head and kill
it before the tabernacle of meeting; and the
sons of Aaron shall sprinkle its blood all
around on the altar.
14 'Then he shall offer from it his offering,
as an offering made by fire to the LORD. The
fat that covers the entrails and all the fat that
is on the entrails,
15 'the two kidneys and the fat that *is* on
them by the flanks, and the fatty lobe attached to the liver above the kidneys, he shall
remove;
16 'and the priest shall burn them on the
altar *as* food, an offering made by fire for a
sweet aroma; all the fat *is* the LORD's.
17 '*This shall be* a perpetual statute
throughout your generations in all your
dwellings: you shall eat neither fat nor
[R]blood.' " Lev. 7:23, 26; 17:10, 14

CHAPTER 4

The Sin Offering

NOW the LORD spoke to Moses, saying,
2 "Speak to the children of Israel, saying: [R]'If a person sins [T]unintentionally against
any of the commandments of the LORD *in
anything* which ought not to be done, and
does any of them, Lev. 5:15–18 • *through error*
3 'if the anointed priest sins, bringing guilt
on the people, then let him offer to the LORD
for his sin which he has sinned a young bull
without blemish as a [R]sin offering. Lev. 9:7
4 'He shall bring the bull [R]to the door of
the tabernacle of meeting before the LORD,
lay his hand on the bull's head, and kill the
bull before the LORD. Lev. 1:3, 4; 4:15
5 'Then the anointed priest [R]shall take
some of the bull's blood and bring it to the
tabernacle of meeting. Lev. 16:14
6 'The priest shall dip his finger in the
blood and sprinkle some of the blood seven

times before the LORD, in front of the [R]veil of the sanctuary. Ex. 40:21, 26

7 'And the priest shall put some of the blood on the horns of the altar of sweet incense before the LORD, which is in the tabernacle of meeting; and he shall pour the remaining blood of the bull at the base of the altar of the burnt offering, which is at the door of the tabernacle of meeting.

8 'He shall take from it all the fat of the bull as the sin offering. The fat that covers the entrails and all the fat which *is* on the entrails,

9 'the two kidneys and the fat that *is* on them by the flanks, and the fatty lobe *attached to* the liver above the kidneys, he shall remove,

10 [R]'as it was taken from the bull of the sacrifice of the peace offering; and the priest shall burn them on the altar of the burnt offering. Lev. 3:3–5

11 'But the bull's hide and all its flesh, with its head and legs, its entrails and offal—

12 'the whole bull he shall carry outside the camp to a clean place, [R]where the ashes are poured out, and [R]burn it on wood with fire; where the ashes are poured out it shall be burned. Lev. 4:21; 6:10, 11; 16:27 • [Heb. 13:11, 12]

13 'Now if the whole congregation of Israel sins unintentionally, [R]and the thing is hidden from the eyes of the assembly, and they have done *something against* any of the commandments of the LORD *in anything* which should not be done, and are guilty; Lev. 5:2–4, 17

14 'when the sin which they have sinned becomes known, then the assembly shall offer a young bull for the sin, and bring it before the tabernacle of meeting.

15 'And the elders of the congregation [R]shall lay their hands on the head of the bull before the LORD. Then the bull shall be killed before the LORD. Lev. 1:3, 4

16 'The anointed priest shall bring some of the bull's blood to the tabernacle of meeting.

17 'Then the priest shall dip his finger in the blood and sprinkle *it* seven times before the LORD, in front of the veil.

18 'And he shall put *some* of the blood on the horns of the altar which *is* before the LORD, which *is* in the tabernacle of meeting; and he shall pour the remaining blood at the base of the altar of burnt offering, which is at the door of the tabernacle of meeting.

19 'He shall take all the fat from it and burn *it* on the altar.

20 'And he shall do with the bull as he did with the bull as a sin offering; thus he shall do with it. So the priest shall make atonement for them, and it shall be forgiven them.

21 'Then he shall carry the bull outside the camp, and burn it as he burned the first bull. It *is* a sin offering for the assembly.

22 'When a ruler has sinned, and done *something* unintentionally *against* any of the commandments of the LORD his God *in anything* which should not be done, and is guilty,

23 'or [R]if his sin which he has sinned [T]comes to his knowledge, he shall bring as his offering a kid of the goats, a male without blemish. Lev. 4:14; 5:4 • *is made known to him*

24 'And [R]he shall lay his hand on the head of the goat, and kill it at the place where they kill the burnt offering before the LORD. It *is* a sin offering. [Is. 53:6]

25 [R]'The priest shall take some of the blood of the sin offering with his finger, put *it* on the horns of the altar of burnt offering, and pour its blood at the base of the altar of burnt offering. Lev. 4:7, 18, 30, 34

26 'And he shall burn all its fat on the altar, like [R]the fat of the sacrifice of peace offering. [R]So the priest shall make atonement for him concerning his sin, and it shall be forgiven him. Lev. 3:3–5 • Lev. 4:20

27 [R]'If [T]anyone of the [T]common people sins unintentionally by doing *something against* any of the commandments of the LORD *in anything* which ought not to be done, and is guilty, Num. 15:27 • Lit. *any soul* • Lit. *people of the land*

28 'or if his sin which he has sinned comes to his knowledge, then he shall bring as his offering a kid of the goats, a female without blemish, for his sin which he has sinned.

29 [R]'And he shall lay his hand on the head of the sin offering, and kill the sin offering in the place of the burnt offering. Lev. 1:4; 4:4, 24

30 'Then the priest shall take *some* of its blood with his finger, put *it* on the horns of the altar of burnt offering, and pour all *the remaining* blood at the base of the altar.

31 'He shall remove all its fat, [R]as fat is removed from the sacrifice of peace offering; and the priest shall burn it on the altar for a [R]sweet aroma to the LORD. [R]So the priest shall make atonement for him, and it shall be forgiven him. Lev. 3:3, 4 • Ex. 29:18 • Lev. 4:26

32 'If he brings a lamb as his sin offering, he shall bring a female without blemish.

33 'Then he shall [R]lay his hand on the head of the sin offering, and slay it as a sin offering at the place where they kill the burnt offering. Num. 8:12

34 'The priest shall take *some* of the blood of the sin offering with his finger, put *it* on the horns of the altar of burnt offering, and pour all *the remaining* blood at the base of the altar.

35 'He shall remove all its fat, as the fat of the lamb is removed from the sacrifice of the peace offering. Then the priest shall burn it on the altar, according to the offerings made by fire to the LORD. [R]So the priest shall make atonement for his sin that he has committed, and it shall be forgiven him. Lev. 4:26, 31

CHAPTER 5

IF a person sins in hearing the utterance of an oath, and *is* a witness, whether he has seen or known *of the matter*—if he does not tell *it*, he bears guilt.

2 'Or [R]if a person touches any unclean thing, whether *it is* the carcass of an unclean beast, or the carcass of unclean livestock, or the carcass of unclean creeping things, and it is hidden from him, he also shall be unclean and [R]guilty. Num. 19:11–16 • Lev. 5:17

3 'Or if he touches [R]human uncleanness, whatever *sort of* uncleanness *it is* with which a man may be defiled, and [T]it is hidden from him—when he realizes *it*, then he shall be guilty. Lev. 5:12, 13, 15 • *he is unaware of it*

4 'Or if a person swears, speaking thoughtlessly with *his* lips to do evil or [R]to do good, whatever *it is* that a man may pronounce by an oath, and it is hidden from him—when he realizes *it*, then he shall be guilty in any of these *matters*. [James 5:12]

5 'And it shall be, when he is guilty in any of these *matters*, that he shall [R]confess that he has sinned in that *thing*; Prov. 28:13

6 'and he shall bring his trespass offering to the LORD for his sin which he has sinned, a female from the flock, a lamb or a kid of the goats as a sin offering. So the priest shall make atonement for him concerning his sin.

7 [R]'If he is not able to bring a lamb, then he shall bring to the LORD, for his trespass which he has committed, two [R]turtledoves or two young pigeons: one as a sin offering and the other as a burnt offering. Lev. 12:6 • Lev. 1:14

8 'And he shall bring them to the priest, who shall offer *that* which *is* for the sin offering first, and wring off its head from its neck, but shall not divide *it* completely.

9 'Then he shall sprinkle *some* of the blood of the sin offering on the side of the altar, and the rest of the blood shall be drained out at the base of the altar. It *is* a sin offering.

10 'And he shall offer the second *as* a burnt offering according to the prescribed manner. So [R]the priest shall make atonement on his behalf for his sin which he has sinned, and it shall be forgiven him. Lev. 4:20, 26; 5:13, 16

11 'But if he is not able to bring two turtledoves or two young pigeons, then he who sinned shall bring for his offering one-tenth of an ephah of fine flour as a sin offering. He shall put no oil on it, nor shall he put *any* frankincense on it, for it *is* a sin offering.

12 'Then he shall bring it to the priest, and the priest shall take his handful of it [R]as a memorial portion, and burn *it* on the altar [R]according to the offerings made by fire to the LORD. It *is* a sin offering. Lev. 2:2 • Lev. 4:35

13 'The priest shall make atonement for him, [T]for his sin that he has sinned in any of these matters; and it shall be forgiven him. [R]*The rest* shall be the priest's as a grain offering.' " *concerning his sin* • Lev. 2:3; 6:17, 26

The Trespass Offering

14 Then the LORD spoke to Moses, saying:

15 "If a person commits a trespass, and sins unintentionally in regard to the holy things of the LORD, then he shall bring to the LORD as his trespass offering a ram without blemish from the flocks, with your valuation in shekels of silver according to the shekel of the sanctuary, as a trespass offering.

16 "And he shall make restitution for the harm that he has done in regard to the holy thing, and shall add one-fifth to it and give it to the priest. So the priest shall make atonement for him with the ram of the trespass offering, and it shall be forgiven him.

17 "If a person sins, and commits any of these things which are forbidden to be done by the commandments of the LORD, though he does not know *it*, yet he is [R]guilty and shall bear his [T]iniquity. Lev. 5:1, 2 • *punishment*

18 [R]"And he shall bring to the priest a ram without blemish from the flock, with your valuation, as a trespass offering. So the priest shall make atonement for him regarding his ignorance in which he erred and did not know *it*, and it shall be forgiven him. Lev. 5:15

19 "It is a trespass offering; [R]he has certainly trespassed against the LORD." Ezra 10:2

CHAPTER 6

AND the LORD spoke to Moses, saying:

2 "If a person sins and commits a trespass against the LORD by lying to his neighbor about what was delivered to him for safekeeping, or about a pledge, or about a robbery, or if he has extorted from his neighbor,

3 "or if he [R]has found what was lost and lies concerning it, and [R]swears falsely—in any one of these things that a man may do in which he sins: Deut. 22:1–4 • Ex. 22:11

4 "then it shall be, because he has sinned and is guilty, that he shall [T]restore [R]what he has stolen, or the thing which he has deceitfully obtained, or what was delivered to him for safekeeping, or the lost thing which he found, *return* • Lev. 24:18, 21

5 "or all that about which he has sworn falsely. He shall restore its full value, add one-fifth more to it, *and* give it to whomever it belongs, on the day of his trespass offering.

6 "And he shall bring his trespass offering to the LORD, [R]a ram without blemish from the flock, with your [T]valuation, as a trespass offering, to the priest. Lev. 1:3; 5:15 • *appraisal*

7 [R]"So the priest shall make atonement for him before the LORD, and he shall be forgiven for any one of these things that he may have done in which he trespasses." Lev. 4:26

The Burnt Offering

8 Then the LORD spoke to Moses, saying,
9 "Command Aaron and his sons, saying,
'This *is* the law of the burnt offering: The
burnt offering *shall be* on the hearth upon
the altar all night until morning, and the fire
of the altar shall be kept burning on it.
10 [R]'And the priest shall put on his linen
garment, and his linen trousers he shall put
on his body, and take up the ashes of the
burnt offering which the fire has consumed
on the altar, and he shall put them [R]beside
the altar. Ex. 28:39–43 • Lev. 1:16
11 'Then he shall take off his garments, put
on other garments, and carry the ashes outside the camp [R]to a clean place. Lev. 4:12
12 'And the fire on the altar shall be kept
burning on it; it shall not be put out. And the
priest shall burn wood on it every morning,
and lay the burnt offering in order on it; and
he shall burn on it [R]the fat of the peace
offerings. Lev. 3:3, 5, 9, 14
13 'A perpetual fire shall burn on the [R]altar;
it shall never go out. Lev. 1:7

The Grain Offering

14 'This *is* the law of the grain offering: The
sons of Aaron shall offer it on the altar before
the LORD.
15 'He shall take from it his handful of the
fine flour of the grain offering, with its oil,
and all the frankincense which *is* on the grain
offering, and shall burn *it* on the altar *for* a
sweet aroma, as a memorial to the LORD.
16 'And the remainder of it Aaron and his
sons shall eat; with unleavened bread it shall
be eaten in a holy place; in the court of the
tabernacle of meeting they shall eat it.
17 'It shall not be baked with leaven. I have
given it *to them as* their [T]portion of My
offerings made by fire; it *is* most holy, like the
sin offering and the trespass offering. *share*
18 'All the males among the children of
Aaron may eat it. *It shall be* a statute forever
in your generations concerning the offerings
made by fire to the LORD. Everyone who
touches them must be holy.' "
19 And the LORD spoke to Moses, saying,
20 [R]"This *is* the offering of Aaron and his
sons, which they shall offer to the LORD,
beginning on the day when he is anointed:
[T]one-tenth of an [R]*ephah* of fine flour as a
daily grain offering, half of it in the morning
and half of it at night. Ex. 29:2 • 2.1 qt. • Ex. 16:36
21 "It shall be made in a [R]pan with oil.
When it is well mixed, you shall bring it in.
And the baked pieces of the grain offering
you shall offer *for* a [T]sweet aroma to the
LORD. Lev. 2:5; 7:9 • *pleasing*
22 "The priest from among his sons, [R]who is
anointed in his place, shall offer it. *It is* a
statute forever to the LORD. [R]It shall be
[T]wholly burned. Lev. 4:3 • Ex. 29:25 • *completely*
23 "For every grain offering for the priest
shall be wholly burned. It shall not be eaten."

The Sin Offering

24 And the LORD spoke to Moses, saying,
25 "Speak to Aaron and to his sons, saying,
'This *is* the law of the sin offering: [R]In the
place where the burnt offering is killed, the
sin offering shall be killed before the LORD. It
is most holy. Lev. 1:1, 3, 5, 11
26 'The priest who offers it for sin shall eat
it. In a holy place it shall be eaten, in the
court of the tabernacle of meeting.
27 'Everyone who touches its flesh [T]must be
holy. And when its blood is sprinkled on any
garment, you shall wash that on which it was
sprinkled, in a holy place. Lit. *shall*
28 'But the earthen vessel in which it is
boiled [R]shall be broken. And if it is boiled in a
bronze pot, it shall be both scoured and
rinsed in water. Lev. 11:33; 15:12
29 'All the males among the priests may eat
it. It *is* most holy.
30 [R]'But no sin offering from which *any* of
the blood is brought into the tabernacle of
meeting, to make atonement in the holy
[R]*place*, shall be eaten. It shall be burned in
the fire. Lev. 4:7, 11, 12, 18, 21; 10:18; 16:27 • Ex. 26:33

CHAPTER 7

The Trespass Offering

'LIKEWISE [R]this *is* the law of the trespass
offering (it *is* most holy): Lev. 5:14—6:7
2 'In the place where they killed the burnt
offering they shall kill the trespass offering.
And its blood he shall sprinkle all around on
the altar.
3 'And he shall offer from it all its fat. The
fat tail and the fat that covers the entrails,
4 'the two kidneys and the fat that *is* on
them by the flanks, and the fatty lobe *attached to* the liver above the kidneys, he shall
remove;
5 'and the priest shall burn them on the
altar *as* an offering made by fire to the LORD.
It *is* a trespass offering.
6 [R]'Every male among the priests may eat
it. It shall be eaten in a holy place. [R]It *is* most
holy. Lev. 6:16–18, 29 • Lev. 2:3
7 [R]'The trespass offering *is* like the sin
offering; *there is* one law for them both: the
priest who makes atonement with it shall
have *it*. Lev. 6:24–30; 14:13
8 'And the priest who offers anyone's
burnt offering, that priest shall have for
himself the skin of the burnt offering which
he has offered.
9 'Also [R]every grain offering that is baked
in the oven and all that is prepared in the
covered pan, or [T]in a pan, shall be the priest's
who offers it. Lev. 2:3, 10 • *on a griddle*

10 'Every grain offering mixed with oil, or dry, shall belong to all the sons of Aaron, to one *as much* as the other.

The Peace Offering

11 'This *is* the law of the sacrifice of peace offerings which he shall offer to the LORD:

12 'If he offers it for a thanksgiving, then he shall offer, with the sacrifice of thanksgiving, unleavened cakes mixed with oil, unleavened wafers [R]anointed with oil, or cakes of *finely* blended flour mixed with oil. Num. 6:15

13 'Besides the cakes, *as* his offering he shall offer [R]leavened bread with the sacrifice of thanksgiving of his peace offering. Amos 4:5

14 'And from it he shall offer one cake from each offering *as* a heave offering to the LORD. [R]It shall belong to the priest who sprinkles the blood of the peace offering. Num. 18:8, 11, 19

15 [R]'The flesh of the sacrifice of his peace offering for thanksgiving shall be eaten the same day it is offered. He shall not leave any of it until morning. Lev. 22:29, 30

16 'But [R]if the sacrifice of his offering *is* a vow or a voluntary offering, it shall be eaten the same day that he offers his sacrifice; but on the next day the remainder of it also may be eaten; Lev. 19:5–8

17 'the remainder of the flesh of the sacrifice on the third day must be burned with fire.

18 'And if *any* of the flesh of the sacrifice of his peace offering is eaten at all on the third day, it shall not be accepted, nor shall it be imputed to him; whoever offers it shall be an [R]abomination, and the person who eats of it shall bear [T]guilt. Lev. 11:10, 11, 41; 19:7 • *his iniquity*

19 'The flesh that touches any unclean thing shall not be eaten. It shall be burned with fire. And as for the *clean* flesh, all who are clean may eat of it.

20 'But the person who eats the flesh of the sacrifice of the peace offering that *belongs* to the [R]LORD, while he is unclean, that person shall be cut off from his people. [Heb. 2:17]

21 'Moreover the person who touches any unclean thing, *such as* human uncleanness, *any* [R]unclean beast, or any [R]abominable unclean thing, and who eats the flesh of the sacrifice of the peace offering that *belongs* to the LORD, that person [R]shall be cut off from his people.'" Lev. 11:24, 28 • Ezek. 4:14 • Lev. 7:20

22 And the LORD spoke to Moses, saying,

23 "Speak to the children of Israel, saying: [R]'You shall not eat any fat, of ox or sheep or goat. Lev. 3:17; 17:10–15

24 'And the fat of a beast that dies *naturally*, and the fat of what is torn by wild animals, may be used in any other way; but you shall by no means eat it.

25 'For whoever eats the fat of the beast of which men offer an offering made by fire to the LORD, the person who eats *it* shall be cut off from his people.

26 [R]'Moreover you shall not eat any blood in any of your dwellings, *whether* of bird or beast. Acts 15:20, 29

27 'Whoever eats any blood, that person shall be cut off from his people.'"

28 Then the LORD spoke to Moses, saying,

29 "Speak to the children of Israel, saying: [R]'He who offers the sacrifice of his peace offering to the LORD shall bring his offering to the LORD from the sacrifice of his peace offering. Lev. 3:1; 22:21

30 'His own hands shall bring the offerings made by fire to the LORD. The fat with the breast he shall bring, that the breast may be waved *as* a wave offering before the LORD.

31 [R]'And the priest shall burn the fat on the altar, but the [R]breast shall be Aaron's and his sons'. Lev. 3:5, 11, 16 • Deut. 18:3

32 [R]'Also the right thigh you shall give to the priest *as* a heave offering from the sacrifices of your peace offerings. Num. 6:20

33 'He among the sons of Aaron, who offers the blood of the peace offering, and the fat, shall have the right thigh for *his* part.

34 'For the breast of the wave offering and the thigh of the heave offering I have taken from the children of Israel, from the sacrifices of their peace offerings, and I have given them to Aaron the priest and to his sons from the children of Israel by a statute forever.'"

35 This *is* the consecrated portion for Aaron and his sons, from the offerings made by fire to the LORD, on the day when Moses presented them to [T]minister to the LORD as priests. *serve as priests to the LORD*

36 The LORD commanded this to be given to them by the children of Israel, [R]on the day that He anointed them, *by* a statute forever throughout their generations. Lev. 8:12, 30

The Summary of the Offerings

37 This *is* the law of the burnt offering, the grain offering, the sin offering, the trespass offering, [R]the consecrations, and the sacrifice of the peace offering, Ex. 29:1

38 which the LORD commanded Moses on Mount Sinai, on the day when He commanded the children of Israel [R]to offer their offerings to the LORD in the Wilderness of Sinai. Lev. 1:1, 2

CHAPTER 8

Consecration Commanded by God

AND the LORD spoke to Moses, saying:

2 "Take Aaron and his sons with him, and the garments, [R]the anointing oil, a [R]bull as the sin offering, two rams, and a basket of unleavened bread; Ex. 30:24, 25 • Ex. 29:10

3 "and gather all the congregation together at the door of the tabernacle of meeting."

4 So Moses did as the LORD commanded him. And the assembly was gathered together at the door of the tabernacle of meeting.
5 And Moses said to the congregation, "This *is* what the LORD commanded to be done."

Cleansing the Priests with Water

6 Then Moses brought Aaron and his sons and [R]washed them with water. Heb. 10:22

Special Garments

7 And he [R]put the tunic on him, girded him with the sash, clothed him with the robe, and put the ephod on him; and he girded him with the intricately woven band of the ephod, and with it tied *the ephod* on him. Ex. 39:1–31
8 Then he put the breastplate on him, and he [R]put the [T]Urim and the Thummim in the breastplate. Ex. 28:30 • Lit. *Lights and the Perfections*
9 [R]And he put the turban on his head. Also on the turban, on its front, he put the golden plate, the holy crown, as the LORD had commanded Moses. Ex. 28:36, 37; 29:6

Anointing with Oil

10 [R]Then Moses took the anointing oil, and anointed the tabernacle and all that *was* in it, and sanctified them. Ex. 30:26–29; 40:10, 11
11 He sprinkled some of it on the altar seven times, anointed the altar and all its utensils, and the laver and its base, to [T]sanctify them. *set them apart* for the LORD
12 And he [R]poured some of the anointing oil on Aaron's head and anointed him, to sanctify him. Ps. 133:2
13 Then Moses brought Aaron's sons and put tunics on them, girded them with sashes, and put [T]hats on them, as the LORD had commanded Moses. *headgear* or *caps*

Consecrating with Blood

14 [R]And he brought the bull for the sin offering. Then Aaron and his sons [R]laid their hands on the head of the bull for the sin offering, Ezek. 43:19 • Lev. 4:4
15 and Moses killed *it*. [R]Then he took the blood, and put *some* on the horns of the altar all around with his finger, and purified the altar; and he poured the blood at the base of the altar, and sanctified it, to make atonement for it. Lev. 4:7
16 [R]Then he took all the fat that *was* on the entrails, the fatty lobe *attached to* the liver, and the two kidneys with their fat, and Moses burned *them* on the altar. Ex. 29:13
17 But the bull, its hide, its flesh, and its offal, he burned with fire outside the camp, as the LORD [R]had commanded Moses. Lev. 4:11, 12
18 [R]Then he brought the ram as the burnt offering. And Aaron and his sons laid their hands on the head of the ram, Ex. 29:15
19 and Moses killed *it*. Then he sprinkled the blood all around on the altar.
20 And he cut the ram into pieces; and Moses [R]burned the head, the pieces, and the fat. Lev. 1:8
21 Then he washed the entrails and the legs in water. And Moses burned the whole ram on the altar. It *was* a burnt sacrifice for a [T]sweet aroma, *and* an offering made by fire to the LORD, [R]as the LORD had commanded Moses. *pleasing* • Ex. 29:18
22 And he brought the second ram, the ram of consecration. Then Aaron and his sons laid their hands on the head of the ram,
23 and Moses killed *it*. And he took *some* of [R]its blood and put it on the tip of Aaron's right ear, on the thumb of his right hand, and on the big toe of his right foot. Lev. 14:14
24 Then he brought Aaron's sons. And Moses put *some* of the [R]blood on the tips of their right ears, on the thumbs of their right hands, and on the big toes of their right feet. And Moses sprinkled the blood all around on the altar. [Heb. 9:13, 14, 18–23]
25 [R]Then he took the fat and the fat tail, all the fat that *was* on the entrails, the fatty lobe *attached to* the liver, the two kidneys and their fat, and the right thigh; Ex. 29:22
26 [R]and from the basket of unleavened bread that was before the LORD he took one unleavened cake, a cake of bread *anointed with* oil, and one wafer, and put *them* on the fat and on the right thigh; Ex. 29:23
27 and he put all *these* [R]in Aaron's hands and in his sons' hands, and waved them *as* a wave offering before the LORD. Ex. 29:24
28 [R]Then Moses took them from their hands and burned *them* on the altar, on the burnt offering. They *were* consecration offerings for a sweet aroma. That *was* an offering made by fire to the LORD. Ex. 29:25
29 And Moses took the breast and waved it *as* a wave offering before the LORD. It was Moses' [R]part of the ram of consecration, as the LORD had commanded Moses. Ex. 29:26
30 Then [R]Moses took some of the anointing oil and some of the blood which *was* on the altar, and sprinkled *it* on Aaron, on his garments, on his sons, and on the garments of his sons with him; and he sanctified Aaron, his garments, his sons, and the garments of his sons with him. Ex. 29:21; 30:30

The Priests Are to Remain in the Tabernacle

31 And Moses said to Aaron and his sons, [R]"Boil the flesh *at* the door of the tabernacle of meeting, and eat it there with the bread that *is* in the basket of consecration offerings, as I commanded, saying, 'Aaron and his sons shall eat it.' Ex. 29:31, 32
32 [R]"What remains of the flesh and of the bread you shall burn with fire. Ex. 29:34

33 "And you shall not go outside the door of
the tabernacle of meeting *for* seven days,
until the days of your consecration are ended.
For seven days he shall consecrate you.
34 [R]"As he has done this day, *so* the LORD
has commanded to do, to make atonement
for you. [Heb. 7:16]
35 "Therefore you shall abide *at* the door of
the tabernacle of meeting day and night for
seven days, and [R]keep the charge of the
LORD, so that you may not die; for so I have
been commanded." Deut. 11:1
36 So Aaron and his sons did all the things
that the LORD had commanded by the hand
of Moses.

CHAPTER 9

Offerings for the Priest

IT came to pass on the [R]eighth day that
Moses called Aaron and his sons and the
elders of Israel. Ezek. 43:27
2 And he said to Aaron, "Take for yourself
a young [R]bull as a sin offering and a ram as a
burnt offering, without blemish, and offer
them before the LORD. Lev. 4:1–12
3 "And to the children of Israel you shall
speak, saying, [R]'Take a kid of the goats as a
sin offering, and a calf and a lamb, *both* of the
first year, without blemish, as a burnt offering, Lev. 4:23, 28
4 'also a bull and a ram as peace offerings,
to sacrifice before the LORD, and [R]a grain
offering mixed with oil; for [R]today the LORD
will appear to you.' " Lev. 2:4 • Ex. 29:43
5 So they brought what Moses commanded before the tabernacle of meeting.
And all the congregation drew near and stood
[T]before the LORD. *in the presence of*
6 Then Moses said, "This *is* the thing
which the LORD commanded you to do, and
the glory of the LORD will appear to you."
7 And Moses said to Aaron, "Go to the
altar, [R]offer your sin offering and your burnt
offering, and make atonement for yourself
and for the people. [R]Offer the offering of the
people, and make atonement for them, as the
LORD commanded." [Heb. 5:3–5; 7:27] • Lev. 4:16, 20
8 Aaron therefore went to the altar and
killed the calf of the sin offering, which *was*
for himself.
9 Then the sons of Aaron brought the
blood to him. And he dipped his finger in the
blood, put *it* on the horns of the altar, and
poured the blood at the base of the altar.
10 [R]But the fat, the kidneys, and the fatty
lobe from the liver of the sin offering he
burned on the altar, as the LORD had commanded Moses. Lev. 8:16
11 [R]The flesh and the hide he burned with
fire outside the camp. Lev. 4:11, 12; 8:17
12 And he killed the burnt offering; and
Aaron's sons presented to him the blood,
which he sprinkled all around on the altar.
13 [R]Then they presented the burnt offering
to him, with its pieces and head, and he
burned *them* on the altar. Lev. 8:20
14 [R]And he washed the entrails and the legs,
and burned *them* with the burnt offering on
the altar. Lev. 8:21

Offerings for the People

15 [R]Then he brought the people's offering,
and took the goat, which *was* the sin offering
for the people, and killed it and offered it for
sin, like the first one. [Is. 53:10]
16 And he brought the burnt offering and
offered it [R]according to the [T]prescribed manner. Lev. 1:1–13 • *ordinance*
17 Then he brought the grain offering, took
a handful of it, and burned *it* on the altar,
besides the burnt sacrifice of the morning.
18 He also killed the bull and the ram *as*
[R]sacrifices of peace offerings, which *were* for
the people. And Aaron's sons presented to
him the blood, which he sprinkled all around
on the altar, Lev. 3:1–11
19 and the fat from the bull and the ram—
the fatty tail, what covers *the entrails* and the
kidneys, and the fatty lobe *attached to* the
liver;
20 and they put the fat on the breasts. Then
he burned the fat on the altar;
21 but the breasts and the right thigh Aaron
waved [R]*as* a wave offering before the LORD,
as Moses had commanded. Lev. 7:30–34

The Lord Accepts the Offerings

22 Then Aaron lifted his hand toward the
people, [R]blessed them, and came down from
offering the sin offering, the burnt offering,
and peace offerings. Luke 24:50
23 And Moses and Aaron went into the
tabernacle of meeting, and came out and
blessed the people. Then the glory of the
LORD appeared to all the people,
24 and fire came out from before the LORD
and consumed the burnt offering and the fat
on the altar. When all the people saw *it*, they
[R]shouted and fell on their faces. Ezra 3:11

CHAPTER 10

The Sin of Nadab and Abihu

THEN [R]Nadab and Abihu, the sons of
Aaron, [R]each took his censer and put fire
in it, put incense on it, and offered [R]profane
fire before the LORD, which He had not commanded them. Num. 3:2–4 • Lev. 16:12 • Ex. 30:9
2 So [R]fire went out from the LORD and
devoured them, and they died before the
LORD. Num. 11:1; 16:35
3 Then Moses said to Aaron, "This is what
the LORD spoke, saying:

THE GLORY OF THE LORD

God showed Himself to Moses in a burning bush in Midian (Ex. 3:1–6).

God has revealed Himself to people in remarkable and unusual ways. Sometimes He has made His will known through dreams (Gen. 37:5–10; Matt. 1:20, 21). He has also shown Himself through nature (Rom. 1:20). But His greatest and most meaningful revelation to the Christian believer is through the second and third persons of the Trinity, Jesus Christ and the Holy Spirit (John 3:16; 14:16).

The Bible speaks often of the "glory of God"—the visible appearance of His moral beauty and perfection. In the Old Testament, He used several different dramatic appearances of His glory to get the attention of His people. He disclosed Himself to Moses in a burning bush in Midian (Ex. 3:1–6; see illustration) and in a cloud on Mount Sinai (Ex. 24:9–17). The cloud of His glory also covered the tabernacle in the Wilderness (Ex. 40:34) and filled the temple in Jerusalem (1 Kin. 8:10, 11).

When Aaron made his first sacrifice in the Wilderness as a priest, God's glory "appeared to all the people" (Lev. 9:23). In these manifestations, He revealed His righteousness, holiness, truth, wisdom, and love. These are all aspects of God's distinctiveness, which may be spoken of as His glory.

Nowhere has God's glory been more fully expressed than through His Son, Jesus Christ (John 1:14). This is a glory in which all believers share (John 17:5, 6, 22). At the end of this age, Christians will be glorified in the heavenly presence of God (Rom. 5:2; Col. 3:4), whose glory will be seen everywhere. The believer's response is one of praise and adoration (Ps. 115:1).

'By those [R]who come near Me
I must be regarded as holy;
And before all the people
I must be glorified.' "

So Aaron held his peace. Ex. 19:22
4 And Moses called Mishael and Elzaphan,
the sons of Uzziel the uncle of Aaron, and
said to them, "Come near, [R]carry your brethren from [T]before the sanctuary out of the
camp." Acts 5:6, 10 • *in front of*
5 So they went near and carried them by
their tunics out of the camp, as Moses had
said.
6 And Moses said to Aaron, and to Eleazar
and Ithamar, his sons, "Do not [T]uncover your
heads nor tear your clothes, lest you die, and
[R]wrath come upon all the people. But let
your brethren, the whole house of Israel,
[T]bewail the burning which the LORD has
kindled. An act of mourning • 2 Sam. 24:1 • *weep bitterly*
7 "You shall not go out from the door of
the tabernacle of meeting, lest you die, for
the anointing oil of the LORD *is* upon you."
And they did according to the word of Moses.
8 Then the LORD spoke to Aaron, saying:
9 [R]"Do not drink wine or intoxicating
drink, you, nor your sons with you, when you
go into the tabernacle of meeting, lest you
die. *It shall be* a statute forever throughout
your generations, Ezek. 44:21
10 "that you may distinguish between holy
and unholy, and between unclean and clean,
11 "and that you may teach the children of
Israel all the statutes which the LORD has
spoken to them by the hand of Moses."

The Sin of Eleazar and Ithamar

12 Then Moses spoke to Aaron, and to
Eleazar and Ithamar, his sons who were left:
[R]"Take the grain offering that remains of the
offerings made by fire to the LORD, and eat it
without leaven beside the altar; [R]for it *is* most
holy. Num. 18:9 • Lev. 21:22
13 "And you shall eat it in a holy place,
because it *is* your [T]due and your sons' due, of
the sacrifices made by fire to the LORD; for so
I have been commanded. *portion*
14 [R]"The breast of the wave offering and the
thigh of the heave offering you shall eat in a
clean place, you, your sons, and your [R]daugh-
ters with you; for *they are* your due and your
sons' [R]due, *which* are given from the sacrifices of peace offerings of the children of
Israel. Num. 18:11 • Lev. 22:13 • Num. 18:10
15 [R]"The thigh of the heave offering and the
breast of the wave offering they shall bring
with the offerings of fat made by fire, to offer
as a wave offering before the LORD. And it
shall be yours and your sons' with you, by a
statute forever, as the LORD has commanded." Lev. 7:29, 30, 34
16 Then Moses diligently made inquiry
about [R]the goat of the sin offering, and there
it was, burned up. And he was angry with
Eleazar and Ithamar, the sons of Aaron *who
were* left, saying, Lev. 9:3, 15
17 [R]"Why have you not eaten the sin offering in a holy place, since it *is* most holy, and
God has given it to you to bear [R]the guilt of
the congregation, to make atonement for
them before the LORD? Lev. 6:24–30 • Ex. 28:38
18 "See! Its blood was not brought inside
the holy *place*; indeed you should have eaten
it in a holy *place*, as I commanded."
19 And Aaron said to Moses, "Look, this
day they have offered their sin offering and
their burnt offering before the LORD, and
such things have befallen me! *If* I had eaten
the sin offering today, would it have been
accepted in the sight of the LORD?"
20 So when Moses heard *that*, he was content.

CHAPTER 11

Animals of the Earth

AND the LORD spoke to Moses and Aaron,
saying to them,
2 "Speak to the children of Israel, saying,
'These *are* the animals which you may eat
among all the beasts that *are* on the earth:
3 'Among the beasts, whatever divides the
hoof, having cloven hooves *and* chewing the
cud—that you may eat.
4 'Nevertheless these you shall [R]not eat
among those that chew the cud or those that
have cloven hooves: the camel, because it
chews the cud but does not have cloven
hooves, is unclean to you; Acts 10:14
5 'the [T]rock hyrax, because it chews the
cud but does not have cloven hooves, *is*
unclean to you; *rock badger*
6 'the hare, because it chews the cud but
does not have cloven hooves, *is* unclean to
you;
7 'and the swine, though it divides the
hoof, having cloven hooves, yet does not
chew the cud, [R]*is* unclean to you. Is. 66:3, 17
8 'Their flesh you shall not eat, and their
carcasses you shall not touch. [R]They *are*
unclean to you. Is. 52:11

Living Things in the Waters

9 [R]'These you may eat of all that *are* in the
water: whatever in the water has fins and
scales, whether in the seas or in the rivers—
that you may eat. Deut. 14:9
10 'But all in the seas or in the rivers that do
not have fins and scales, all that move in the
water or any living thing which *is* in the
water, they *are* an abomination to you.
11 'They shall be an abomination to you;
you shall not eat their flesh, but you shall
regard their carcasses as an abomination.

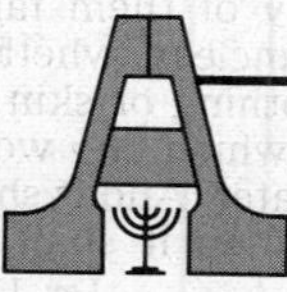

CEREMONIAL LAWS

The hyena was one of the animals considered unclean and forbidden as food to the Hebrews because it ate dead animals.

The concept of ceremonial holiness in Leviticus springs from the truths that God is holy, and only persons ritually clean can approach Him in worship: "For I *am* the LORD your God. You shall therefore sanctify yourselves, and you shall be holy; for I *am* holy" (Lev. 11:44). Chapters 17—26 of Leviticus are known as the "Holiness Code," but the books of Numbers and Deuteronomy also contain many related regulations.

Some actions that were not sinful were considered ceremonially defiling. These included eating unclean foods—such as the vulture or buzzard because of their scavenger habits (see illustration)—and contact with unclean objects or people, such as with a leper or a dead body (Lev. 11:24–47).

Persons guilty of minor offenses could be cleansed simply by ceremonial washing. However, penalties for uncleanness could range from prohibition from the priesthood (Lev. 21:16–24) to expulsion from the camp and social isolation (Lev. 13:44–46).

Priests were especially restricted—in their personal lives, as well as in their conduct at the altar (Lev. 21). Even a descendant of Aaron could not officiate at the altar if he had a physical defect (Lev. 21:17).

Israel was warned that sexual immorality was defiling to them, just as it was to their heathen neighbors (Lev. 18:24). Lust was prohibited, along with all types of unnatural sexual relations, such as incest, homosexuality, and bestiality (Lev. 18; 20).

While this ceremonial system served a valuable purpose for God's people in Old Testament times, the sacrifice of Christ, the great High Priest, has removed the need for ceremonial regulations while stressing the moral law.

12 'Whatever in the water does not have
fins or scales—that *shall be* an abomination
to you.

Birds of the Air

13 [R]'And these you shall regard as an
abomination among the birds; they shall not
be eaten, they *are* an abomination: the eagle,
the vulture, the buzzard, Is. 66:17
14 'the kite, and the falcon after its kind;
15 'every raven after its kind,
16 'the ostrich, the short-eared owl, the
seagull, and the hawk after its kind;
17 'the little owl, the fisher owl, and the
screech owl;
18 'the white owl, the jackdaw, and the
carrion vulture;
19 'the stork, the heron after its kind, the
hoopoe, and the bat.

Winged Insects

20 'All flying insects that creep on *all* fours
shall be an abomination to you.
21 'Yet these you may eat of every flying
insect that creeps on *all* fours: those which
have jointed legs above their feet with which
to leap on the earth.
22 'These you may eat: [R]the locust after its
kind, the destroying locust after its kind, the
cricket after its kind, and the grasshopper
after its kind. Matt. 3:4
23 'But all *other* flying insects which have
four feet *shall be* an abomination to you.

The Carcasses of the Unclean Animals

24 'By these you shall become unclean;
whoever touches the carcass of any of them
shall be unclean until evening;
25 'whoever carries part of the carcass of
any of them [R]shall wash his clothes and be
unclean until evening: Num. 19:10, 21, 22; 31:24
26 '*The carcass* of any beast which divides
the foot, but is not cloven-hoofed or does not
chew the cud, *is* unclean to you. Everyone
who touches it shall be unclean.
27 'And whatever goes on its paws, among
all kinds of animals that go on *all* fours, those
are unclean to you. Whoever touches any
such carcass shall be unclean until evening.
28 'Whoever carries *any such* carcass shall
wash his clothes and be unclean until evening. It *is* unclean to you.

Creeping Things

29 'These also *shall be* unclean to you
among the creeping things that creep on the
earth: the mole, [R]the mouse, and the large
lizard after its kind; Is. 66:17
30 'the gecko, the monitor lizard, the sand
reptile, the sand lizard, and the chameleon.
31 'These *are* unclean to you among all that
creep. Whoever touches them when they are
dead shall be unclean until evening.
32 'Anything on which *any* of them falls,
when they are dead shall be unclean, whether
it is any item of wood or clothing or skin or
sack, whatever item *it is*, in which *any* work
is done, [R]it must be put in water. And it shall
be unclean until evening; then it shall be
clean. Lev. 15:12
33 'Any [R]earthen vessel into which *any* of
them falls [R]you shall break; and whatever *is*
in it shall be unclean: Lev. 6:28 • Lev. 15:12
34 'in such a vessel, any edible food upon
which water falls becomes unclean, and any
drink that may be drunk from it becomes
unclean.
35 'And everything on which *a part* of *any
such* carcass falls shall be unclean; *whether it
is* an oven or cooking stove, it shall be broken
down; *for* they *are* unclean, and shall be
unclean to you.
36 'Nevertheless a spring or a cistern, *in
which there is* plenty of water, shall be clean,
but whatever touches any such carcass becomes unclean.
37 'And if a part of *any such* carcass falls on
any planting seed which is to be sown, it
remains clean.
38 'But if *any* water is put on the seed, and
if *a part* of *any such* carcass falls on it, it
becomes unclean to you.

The Carcasses of the Clean Animals

39 'And if any beast which you may eat
dies, he who touches its carcass shall be
[R]unclean until evening. Hag. 2:11–13
40 'He who eats of its carcass shall wash his
clothes and be unclean until evening. He also
who carries its carcass shall wash his clothes
and be unclean until evening.

The Purpose of Dietary Laws

41 'And every creeping thing that creeps on
the earth *shall be* [T]an abomination. It shall
not be eaten. *detestable*
42 'Whatever crawls on its belly, whatever
goes on *all* fours, or whatever has many feet
among all creeping things that creep on the
earth—these you shall not eat, for they *are*
an abomination.
43 'You shall not make [T]yourselves abominable with any creeping thing that creeps;
nor shall you make yourselves unclean with
them, lest you be defiled by them. Lit. *your souls*
44 'For I *am* the LORD your [R]God. You shall
therefore sanctify yourselves, and [R]you shall
be holy; for I *am* holy. Neither shall you defile
yourselves with any creeping thing that
creeps on the earth. Ex. 6:7 • 1 Pet. 1:15, 16
45 'For I *am* the LORD who brings you up
out of the land of Egypt, to be your God. You
shall therefore be holy, for I *am* holy.
46 'This *is* the law [T]of the beasts and the
birds and every living creature that moves in

the waters, and of every creature that creeps on the earth, *concerning*

47 [R]'to distinguish between the unclean and the clean, and between the animal that may be eaten and the animal that may not be eaten.' " Ezek. 44:23

CHAPTER 12

Laws Concerning Childbirth

THEN the LORD spoke to Moses, saying,

2 "Speak to the children of Israel, saying: 'If a [R]woman has conceived, and borne a male child, then [R]she shall be [T]unclean seven days; as in the days of her customary impurity she shall be unclean. Luke 2:22 • Lev. 18:19 • *impure*

3 'And on the [R]eighth day the flesh of his foreskin shall be circumcised. Gen. 17:12

4 'She shall then continue in the blood of *her* purification thirty-three days. She shall not touch any [T]hallowed thing, nor come into the sanctuary until the days of her purification are fulfilled. *consecrated*

5 'But if she bears a female child, then she shall be unclean two weeks, as in her customary impurity, and she shall continue in the blood of *her* purification sixty-six days.

6 'When the days of her purification are fulfilled, whether for a son or a daughter, she shall bring to the priest a [R]lamb of the first year as a burnt offering, and a young pigeon or a turtledove as a sin offering, to the door of the tabernacle of meeting. [John 1:29]

7 'Then he shall offer it before the LORD, and make atonement for her. And she shall be clean from the flow of her blood. This *is* the law for her who has borne a male or a female.

8 [R]'And if she is not able to bring a lamb, then she may bring two turtledoves or two young pigeons—one as a burnt offering and the other as a sin offering. [R]So the priest shall make atonement for her, and she will be [T]clean.' " Lev. 5:7 • Lev. 4:26 • *pure*

CHAPTER 13

Examination of People

AND the LORD spoke to Moses and Aaron, saying:

2 "When a man has on the skin of his body a swelling, a scab, or a bright spot, and it becomes on the skin of his body *like* a leprous sore, then he shall be brought to Aaron the priest or to one of his sons the priests.

3 "The priest shall look at the sore on the skin of the body; and if the hair on the sore has turned white, and the sore appears *to be* deeper than the skin of his body, it *is* a leprous sore. Then the priest shall look at him, and pronounce him unclean.

4 "But if the bright spot *is* white on the skin of his body, and does not appear *to be* deeper than the skin, and its hair has not turned white, then the priest shall isolate *the one who has* the sore [R]seven days. Lev. 14:8

5 "And the priest shall look at him on the seventh day; and indeed *if* the sore appears to be as it was, *and* the sore has not spread on the skin, then the priest shall isolate him another seven days.

6 "Then the priest shall look at him again on the seventh day; and indeed *if* the sore has darkened, *and* the sore has not spread on the skin, then the priest shall pronounce him clean; it *is only* a scab, and he [R]shall wash his clothes and be clean. Lev. 11:25; 14:8

7 "But if the scab should at all spread over the skin, after he has been seen by the priest for his cleansing, he shall be seen by the priest again.

8 "And *if* the priest sees that the scab has indeed spread on the skin, then the priest shall pronounce him unclean. It *is* leprosy.

9 "When the leprous sore is on a person, then he shall be brought to the priest.

10 [R]"And the priest shall look *at him*; and indeed *if* the swelling on the skin *is* white, and it has turned the hair white, and *there is* a spot of raw flesh in the swelling, Num. 12:10, 12

11 "it *is* an old leprosy on the skin of his body. The priest shall pronounce him unclean, and shall not isolate him, for he *is* unclean.

12 "And if leprosy breaks out all over the skin, and the leprosy covers all the skin of *the one who has* the sore, from his head to his foot, wherever the priest looks,

13 "then the priest shall consider; and indeed *if* the leprosy has covered all his body, he shall pronounce *him* clean *who has* the sore. It has all turned white. He *is* clean.

14 "But when raw flesh appears on him, he shall be unclean.

15 "And the priest shall look at the raw flesh and pronounce him to be unclean; *for* the raw flesh *is* unclean. It *is* leprosy.

16 "Or if the raw flesh changes and turns white again, he shall come to the priest.

17 "And the priest shall look at him; and indeed *if* the sore has turned white, then the priest shall pronounce *him* clean *who has* the sore. He *is* clean.

18 "If the body develops a [R]boil in the skin, and it is healed, Ex. 9:9; 15:26

19 "and in the place of the boil there comes a white swelling or a bright spot, reddish-white, then it shall be shown to the priest;

20 "and *if*, when the priest sees it, it indeed *appears* deeper than the skin, and its hair has turned white, the priest shall pronounce him unclean. It *is* a leprous sore which has broken out of the boil.

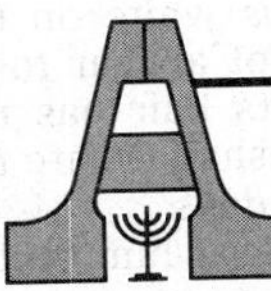

LEPERS AND LEPROSY

One of the lepers healed by Jesus returned to thank Him (Luke 17:15–19).

Leprosy, a disease mentioned often in the Bible, was a dreaded skin affliction in ancient times. Modern medicine has isolated several different types of leprosy, variously characterized by the formation of nodules, ulcers, deformities, and loss of feeling in the skin. In Old Testament times, a symptom used to diagnose the disease was the persistence of shiny white spots under the skin (Lev. 13:3, 4).

Some medical experts believe the ancient disease was a severe type of psoriasis, or scaling of the skin, that is rarely seen today. It was probably more prevalent than Hansen's disease, the term generally used for leprosy today.

The leper, considered to be ceremonially unclean, was isolated and forced to live apart from others. Detailed instructions are given in the Book of Leviticus on how to recognize leprosy and how others were to be protected from those unfortunate enough to contract the dread disease. The leper was cast outside the camp (Lev. 13:46), required to wear mourning clothes, and to cry out "Unclean! Unclean!" to keep others at a safe distance (Lev. 13:45, 46).

Several miraculous cures of leprosy are reported in the Bible. Both Moses (Ex. 4:6, 7) and Miriam (Num. 12:10, 15) were afflicted with leprosy and cured by the Lord. God used the prophet Elisha to heal Naaman, a Syrian military officer, of his leprosy (2 Kin. 5:1–14). In an expression of compassion, Jesus healed ten lepers, then told them to "show yourselves to the priests" (Luke 17:14) for specific instructions on how to reenter society. One of the lepers returned to express his thanks to Jesus (Luke 17:15–19; see illustration).

This miraculous healing of the ten lepers was a clear sign of Jesus' messiahship, since leprosy was curable only by divine intervention.

21 "But if the priest looks at it, and indeed
there are no white hairs in it, and *if* it *is* not
deeper than the skin, but has faded, then the
priest shall isolate him seven days;
22 "and if it should at all spread over the
skin, then the priest shall pronounce him
unclean. It *is* a [T]leprous sore. *infectious*
23 "But if the bright spot stays in one place,
and has not spread, it *is* the scar of the boil;
and the priest shall pronounce him clean.
24 "Or if the body receives a [R]burn on its
skin by fire, and the raw *flesh* of the burn
becomes a bright spot, reddish-white or
white, Is. 3:24
25 "then the priest shall look at it; and
indeed *if* the hair of the bright spot has
turned white, and it appears deeper than the
skin, it *is* leprosy broken out in the burn.
Therefore the priest shall pronounce him
unclean. It *is* a leprous sore.
26 "But if the priest looks at it, and indeed
there are no white hairs in the bright spot,
and it *is* not deeper than the skin, but has
faded, then the priest shall isolate him seven
days.
27 "And the priest shall look at him on the
seventh day. If it has at all spread over the
skin, then the priest shall pronounce him
unclean. It *is* a leprous sore.
28 "But if the bright spot stays in one place,
and has not spread on the skin, but has faded,
it *is* a swelling from the burn. The priest shall
pronounce him clean, for it *is* the scar from
the burn.
29 "If a man or woman has a sore on the
head or the beard,
30 "then the priest shall look at the sore;
and indeed if it appears deeper than the skin,
and there is in it thin yellow hair, then the
priest shall pronounce him unclean. It *is* a
scall, a leprosy of the head or beard.
31 "But if the priest looks at the sore of the
scall, and indeed it does not appear deeper
than the skin, and *there is* no black hair in it,
then the priest shall isolate *the one who has
the sore* of the scall seven days.
32 "And on the seventh day the priest shall
look at the sore; and indeed *if* the scall has
not spread, and there is no yellow hair in it,
and the scall does not appear deeper than the
skin,
33 "he shall shave himself, but the scall he
shall not shave. And the priest shall isolate
the one who has the scall another seven days.
34 "On the seventh day the priest shall look
at the scall; and indeed *if* the scall has not
spread over the skin, and does not appear
deeper than the skin, then the priest shall
pronounce him clean. He shall wash his
clothes and be clean.
35 "But if the scall should at all spread over
the skin after his cleansing,
36 "then the priest shall look at him; and
indeed if the scall has spread over the skin,
the priest need not seek for yellow hair. He *is*
unclean.
37 "But if the scall appears to be at a standstill, and there is black hair grown up in it,
the scall has healed. He *is* clean, and the
priest shall pronounce him clean.
38 "If a man or a woman has bright spots
on the skin of the body, *specifically* white
bright spots,
39 "then the priest shall look; and indeed *if*
the bright spots on the skin of the body *are*
dull white, it *is* a white spot *that* grows on the
skin. He *is* clean.
40 "As for the man whose hair has fallen
from his head, he *is* bald, *but* he *is* clean.
41 "He whose hair has fallen from his forehead, he *is* bald on the forehead, *but* he *is*
clean.
42 "And if there is on the bald head or bald
[R]forehead a reddish-white sore, it *is* leprosy
breaking out on his bald head or his bald
forehead. 2 Chr. 26:19
43 "Then the priest shall look at it; and
indeed *if* the swelling of the sore *is* reddish-
white on his bald head or on his bald forehead, as the appearance of leprosy on the
skin of the body,
44 "he is a leprous man. He *is* unclean. The
priest shall surely pronounce him [T]unclean;
his sore *is* on his [R]head. *altogether defiled* • Is. 1:5
45 "Now the leper on whom the sore *is*, his
clothes shall be torn and his head bare; and
he shall [R]cover his mustache, and cry, [R]'Unclean! Unclean!' Ezek. 24:17, 22 • Lam. 4:15
46 "He shall be unclean. All the days he has
the sore he shall be unclean. He *is* unclean,
and he shall [T]dwell alone; his habitation *shall
be* [R]outside the camp. *live alone* • Num. 5:1–4; 12:14

Examination of Garments

47 "Also, if a garment has a [T]leprous plague
in it, *whether it is* a woolen garment or a
linen garment, Exact identity unclear
48 "whether *it is* in the warp or woof of
linen or wool, whether in leather or in anything made of leather,
49 "and if the plague is greenish or reddish
in the garment or in the leather, whether in
the warp or in the woof, or in anything made
of leather, it *is* a leprous [T]plague and shall be
shown to the priest. *mark*
50 "The priest shall look at the plague and
isolate *that which has* the plague seven days.
51 "And he shall look at the plague on the
seventh day. If the plague has spread in the
garment, either in the warp or in the woof, in
the leather *or* in anything made of leather,
the plague *is* an active leprosy. It *is* unclean.
52 "He shall therefore burn that garment in
which is the plague, whether warp or woof, in
wool or in linen, or anything of leather, for it
is an active leprosy; it shall be burned in the
fire.

53 "But if the priest looks, and indeed the
plague has not spread in the garment, either
in the warp or in the woof, or in anything
made of leather,
54 "then the priest shall command that they
wash *the thing* in which *is* the plague; and he
shall isolate it another seven days.
55 "Then the priest shall look at the plague
after it has been washed; and indeed *if* the
plague has not changed its color, though the
plague has not spread, it *is* unclean, and you
shall burn it in the fire; it continues eating
away, *whether* the damage *is* outside or
inside.
56 "If the priest looks, and indeed the
plague has faded after washing it, then he
shall tear it out of the garment, whether out
of the warp or out of the woof, or out of the
leather.
57 "But if it appears again in the garment,
either in the warp or in the woof, or in
anything made of leather, it *is* a spreading
plague; you shall burn with fire that in which
is the plague.
58 "And if you wash the garment, either
warp or woof, or whatever is made of leather,
if the plague has disappeared from it, then it
shall be washed a second time, and shall be
clean.
59 "This *is* the law of the leprous plague in a
garment of wool or linen, either in the warp
or woof, or in anything made of leather, to
pronounce it clean or to pronounce it unclean."

CHAPTER 14

Cleansing of People

THEN the LORD spoke to Moses, saying,
2 "This shall be the law of the [T]leper for
the day of his cleansing: He [R]shall be brought
to the priest. Medical identity unclear • Matt. 8:2, 4
3 "And the priest shall go out of the camp,
and the priest shall look; and indeed, *if* the
leprosy is healed in the leper,
4 "then the priest shall command to take
for him who is to be cleansed two living *and*
clean birds, [R]cedar wood, [R]scarlet, and [R]hys-
sop. Num. 19:6 • Ex. 25:4 • Ps. 51:7
5 "And the priest shall command that one
of the birds be killed in an earthen vessel over
running water.
6 "As for the living bird, he shall take it,
the cedar wood and the scarlet and the
hyssop, and dip them and the living bird in
the blood of the bird *that was* killed over the
running water.
7 "And he shall sprinkle it seven times on
him who is to be cleansed from the leprosy,
and shall pronounce him clean, and shall let
the living bird loose in the open field.
8 "He who is to be cleansed shall wash his
clothes, shave off all his hair, and [R]wash
himself in water, that he may be clean. After
that he shall come into the camp, and shall
stay outside his tent seven days. [Heb. 10:22]
9 "But on the [R]seventh day he shall shave
all the hair off his head and his beard and his
eyebrows—all his hair he shall shave off. He
shall wash his clothes and wash his body in
water, and he shall be clean. Num. 19:19
10 "And on the eighth day he shall take two
male lambs without blemish, one ewe lamb of
the first year without blemish, three-tenths *of
an ephah* of fine flour mixed with oil as [R]a
grain offering, and one log of oil. Lev. 2:1
11 "Then the priest who makes *him* clean
shall present the man who is to be made
clean, and those things, before the LORD, *at*
the door of the tabernacle of meeting.
12 "And the priest shall take one male lamb
and [R]offer it as a trespass offering, and the log
of oil, and [R]wave them *as* a wave offering
before the LORD. Lev. 5:6, 18 • Ex. 29:22–24, 26
13 "Then he shall kill the lamb in the place
where he kills the sin offering and the burnt
offering, in a holy place; for as the sin offering
is the priest's, so *is* the trespass offering. [R]It *is*
most holy. Lev. 2:3; 7:6; 21:22
14 "The priest shall take *some* of the blood
of the trespass offering, and the priest shall
put *it* on the tip of the right ear of him who is
to be cleansed, on the thumb of his right
hand, and on the big toe of his right foot.
15 "And the priest shall take *some* of the
[T]log of oil, and pour *it* into the palm of his
own left hand. 1 pt.
16 "Then the priest shall dip his right finger
in the oil that *is* in his left hand, and shall
[R]sprinkle some of the oil with his finger seven
times before the LORD. Lev. 4:6
17 "And of the rest of the oil in his hand, the
priest shall put *some* on the tip of the right
ear of him who is to be cleansed, on the
thumb of his right hand, and on the big toe of
his right foot, on the blood of the trespass
offering.
18 "The rest of the oil that *is* in the priest's
hand he shall put on the head of him who is
to be cleansed. So the priest shall make
atonement for him before the LORD.
19 "Then the priest shall offer [R]the sin offering, and make atonement for him who is to
be cleansed from his uncleanness. Afterward
he shall kill the burnt offering. Lev. 5:1, 6; 12:7
20 "And the priest shall offer the burnt
offering and the grain offering on the altar.
So the priest shall make atonement for him,
and he shall be [R]clean. Lev. 14:8, 9
21 "But [R]if he *is* poor and cannot afford it,
then he shall take one male lamb *as* a trespass offering to be waved, to make atonement for him, [T]one-tenth *of an ephah* of fine
flour mixed with oil as a grain offering, a log
of oil, Lev. 5:7, 11; 12:8; 27:8 • 2.087 qt.
22 [R]"and two turtledoves or two young
pigeons, such as he is able to afford: one shall

be a sin offering and the other a burnt offering. Lev. 12:8; 15:14, 15

23 "He shall bring them to the priest on the eighth day for his cleansing, to the door of the tabernacle of meeting, before the LORD.

24 [R]"And the priest shall take the lamb of the trespass offering and the [T]log of oil, and the priest shall wave them *as* a wave offering before the LORD. Lev. 14:12 • 1 pt.

25 "Then he shall kill the lamb of the trespass offering, [R]and the priest shall take *some* of the blood of the trespass offering and put *it* on the tip of the right ear of him who is to be cleansed, on the thumb of his right hand, and on the big toe of his right foot. Lev. 14:14, 17

26 "And the priest shall pour some of the oil into the palm of his own left hand.

27 "Then the priest shall sprinkle with his right finger *some* of the oil that *is* in his left hand seven times before the LORD.

28 "And the priest shall put *some* of the oil that *is* in his hand on the tip of the right ear of him who is to be cleansed, on the thumb of the right hand, and on the big toe of his right foot, on the place of the blood of the trespass offering.

29 "The rest of the oil that *is* in the priest's hand he shall put on the head of him who is to be cleansed, to make atonement for him before the LORD.

30 "And he shall offer one of [R]the turtledoves or young pigeons, such as he can afford— Lev. 14:22; 15:14, 15

31 "such as he is able to afford, the one *as* a sin offering and the other *as* a burnt offering, with the grain offering. So the priest shall make atonement for him who is to be cleansed before the LORD.

32 "This *is* the law *for one* who had a leprous sore, who cannot afford [R]the usual cleansing." Lev. 14:10

Cleansing of Houses

33 And the LORD spoke to Moses and Aaron, saying:

34 "When you have come into the land of Canaan, which I give you as a possession, and [R]I put the leprous plague in a house in the land of your possession, [Prov. 3:33]

35 "and he who owns the house comes and tells the priest, saying, 'It seems to me that *there is* [R]some plague in the house,' [Ps. 91:9, 10]

36 "then the priest shall command that they empty the house, before the priest goes *into it* to look at the plague, that all that *is* in the house may not be made unclean; and afterward the priest shall go in to look at the house.

37 "And he shall look at the plague; and indeed *if* the plague *is* on the walls of the house with ingrained streaks, greenish or reddish, which appear to be deep in the wall,

38 "then the priest shall go out of the house, to the door of the house, and [T]shut up the house seven days. quarantine

39 "And the priest shall come again on the seventh day and look; and indeed *if* the plague has spread on the walls of the house,

40 "then the priest shall command that they take away the stones in which *is* the plague, and they shall cast them into an unclean place outside the city.

41 "And he shall cause the house to be scraped inside, all around, and the dust that they scrape off they shall pour out in an unclean place outside the city.

42 "Then they shall take other stones and put *them* in the place of *those* stones, and he shall take other mortar and plaster the house.

43 "And if the plague comes back and breaks out in the house, after he has taken away the stones, after he has scraped the house, and after it is plastered,

44 "then the priest shall come and look; and indeed *if* the plague has spread in the house, it *is* [R]an active leprosy in the house. It *is* unclean. Lev. 13:51

45 "And he shall break down the house, its stones, its timber, and all the plaster of the house, and he shall carry *them* outside the city to an unclean place.

46 "Moreover he who goes into the house at all while it is shut up shall be unclean [R]until evening. Lev. 11:24; 15:5

47 "And he who lies down in the house shall [R]wash his clothes, and he who eats in the house shall wash his clothes. Lev. 14:8

48 "But if the priest comes in and looks *at it*, and indeed the plague has not spread in the house after the house was plastered, then the priest shall pronounce the house clean, because the plague is healed.

49 "And [R]he shall take, to cleanse the house, two birds, cedar wood, scarlet, and hyssop. Lev. 14:4

50 "Then he shall kill one of the birds in an earthen vessel over running water;

51 "and he shall take the cedar wood, the hyssop, the scarlet, and the living bird, and dip them in the blood of the slain bird and in the running water, and sprinkle the house seven times.

52 "And he shall [T]cleanse the house with the blood of the bird and the running water and the living bird, with the cedar wood, the hyssop, and the scarlet. Ceremonially cleanse

53 "Then he shall let the living bird loose outside the city in the open field, and [R]make atonement for the house, and it shall be clean. Lev. 14:20

The Purpose of the Laws of Leprosy

54 "This *is* the law for any [R]leprous sore and scall, Lev. 13:30; 26:21

55 "for the [R]leprosy of a garment [R]and of a house, Lev. 13:47–52 • Lev. 14:34

56 [R]"for a swelling and a scab and a bright
spot, Lev. 13:2
57 "to teach when *it is* unclean and when *it*
is clean. This *is* the law of leprosy."

CHAPTER 15

Discharges of the Man

AND the LORD spoke to Moses and Aaron,
saying,
2 "Speak to the children of Israel, and say
to them: 'When any man has a discharge
from his body, his discharge *is* unclean.
3 'And this shall be his uncleanness in
regard to his discharge—whether his body
runs with his discharge, or his body is
stopped up by his discharge, it *is* his uncleanness.
4 'Every bed is unclean on which he who
has the discharge lies, and everything on
which he sits shall be unclean.
5 'And whoever touches his bed shall wash
his clothes and [R]bathe in water, and be unclean until evening. Lev. 11:25; 17:15
6 'He who sits on anything on which he
who has the [R]discharge sat shall wash his
clothes and bathe in water, and be unclean
until evening. Deut. 23:10
7 'And he who touches the body of him
who has the discharge shall wash his clothes
and bathe in water, and be unclean until
evening.
8 'If he who has the discharge [R]spits on
him who is clean, then he shall wash his
clothes and bathe in water, and be unclean
until evening. Num. 12:14
9 'Any saddle on which he who has the
discharge rides shall be unclean.
10 'Whoever touches anything that was
under him shall be unclean until evening. He
who carries *any of* those things shall wash
his clothes and bathe in water, and be unclean until evening.
11 'And whomever he who has the discharge touches, and has not rinsed his hands
in water, he shall wash his clothes and bathe
in water, and be unclean until evening.
12 'The vessel of earth that he who has the
discharge touches shall be broken, and every
vessel of wood shall be rinsed in water.
13 'And when he who has a discharge is
cleansed of his discharge, then he shall count
for himself seven days for his cleansing, wash
his clothes, and bathe his body in running
water; then he shall be clean.
14 'On the eighth day he shall take for
himself [R]two turtledoves or two young pigeons, and come before the LORD, to the door
of the tabernacle of meeting, and give them
to the priest. Lev. 14:22, 23, 30, 31
15 'Then the priest shall offer them, [R]the
one *as* a sin offering and the other *as* a burnt
offering. [R]So the priest shall make atonement
for him before the LORD because of his discharge. Lev. 14:30, 31 • Lev. 14:19, 31
16 [R]'If any man has an emission of semen,
then he shall wash all his body in water, and
be unclean until evening. Lev. 22:4
17 'And any garment and any leather on
which there is semen, it shall be washed with
water, and be unclean until evening.
18 'Also, when a woman lies with a man,
and *there is* an emission of semen, they *both*
shall bathe in water, and [R]be unclean until
evening. [1 Sam. 21:4]

Discharges of the Woman

19 [R]'If a woman has a discharge, *and* the
discharge from her body is blood, she shall be
set apart seven days; and whoever touches
her shall be unclean until evening. Lev. 12:2
20 'Everything that she lies on during her
impurity shall be unclean; also everything
that she sits on shall be unclean.
21 'Whoever touches her bed shall wash his
clothes and bathe in water, and be unclean
until evening.
22 'And whoever touches anything that she
sat on shall wash his clothes and bathe in
water, and be unclean until evening.
23 'If *anything* is on *her* bed or on anything
on which she sits, when he touches it, he
shall be unclean until evening.
24 'And [R]if any man lies with her at all, so
that her impurity is on him, he shall be
[T]unclean seven days; and every bed on which
he lies shall be unclean. Lev. 18:19; 20:18 • *defiled*
25 'If [R]a woman has a discharge of blood for
many days, other than at the time of her
customary impurity, or if it runs beyond her
usual time of impurity, all the days of
her unclean discharge shall be as the days of
her *customary* impurity. She *shall be* unclean. Matt. 9:20
26 'Every bed on which she lies all the days
of her discharge shall be to her as the bed of
her impurity; and whatever she sits on shall
be unclean, as the uncleanness of her impurity.
27 'Whoever touches those things shall be
unclean; he shall wash his clothes and bathe
in water, and be unclean until evening.
28 'But [R]if she is cleansed of her discharge,
then she shall count for herself seven days,
and after that she shall be clean. Lev. 15:13–15
29 'And on the eighth day she shall take for
herself two turtledoves or two young pigeons, and bring them to the priest, to the
door of the tabernacle of meeting.
30 'Then the priest shall offer the one *as* a
sin offering and the other *as* a [R]burnt offering, and the priest shall make atonement for
her before the LORD for the discharge of her
uncleanness. Lev. 5:7

The Purpose of the Laws of Discharges

31 'Thus you shall [R]separate the children of Israel from their uncleanness, lest they die in their uncleanness when they defile My tabernacle that *is* among them. Deut. 24:8

32 [R]'This *is* the law for one who has a discharge, [R]and *for him* who emits semen and is unclean thereby, Lev. 15:2 • Lev. 15:16

33 'and for her who is indisposed because of her *customary* impurity, and for one who has a discharge, either man or woman, and for him who lies with her who is unclean.' "

CHAPTER 16

Preparation of the High Priest

NOW the LORD spoke to Moses after [R]the death of the two sons of Aaron, when they offered profane fire before the LORD, and died; Lev. 10:1, 2

2 and the LORD said to Moses: "Tell Aaron your brother not to come at *simply* any time into the Holy *Place* inside the veil, before the mercy seat which *is* on the ark, lest he die; for [R]I will appear in the cloud above the mercy seat. Ex. 25:21, 22; 40:34

3 "Thus Aaron shall come into the Holy *Place:* with *the blood of* a young bull as a sin offering, and *of* a ram as a burnt offering.

4 "He shall put the [R]holy linen tunic and the linen trousers on his body; he shall be girded with a linen sash, and with the linen turban he shall be attired. These *are* holy garments. Therefore he shall wash his body in water, and put them on. Ex. 28:39, 42, 43

5 "And he shall take from [R]the congregation of the children of Israel two kids of the goats as a sin offering, and one ram as a burnt offering. Lev. 4:14

Identification of the Sacrifices

6 "Aaron shall offer the bull as a sin offering, which *is* for himself, and make atonement for himself and for his house.

7 "He shall take the two goats and present them before the LORD *at* the door of the tabernacle of meeting.

8 "Then Aaron shall cast lots for the two goats: one lot for the LORD and the other lot for the scapegoat.

9 "And Aaron shall bring the goat on which the LORD's lot fell, and offer it *as* a sin offering.

10 "But the goat on which the lot fell to be the scapegoat shall be presented alive before the LORD, to make [R]atonement upon it, *and* to let it go as the scapegoat into the wilderness. [1 John 2:2]

Atonement for the Priest

11 "And Aaron shall bring the bull of the sin offering, which is for [R]himself, and make atonement for himself and for his house, and shall kill the bull as the sin offering which *is* for himself. [Heb. 7:27; 9:7]

12 "Then he shall take a censer full of burning coals of fire from the altar before the LORD, with his hands full of sweet incense beaten fine, and bring *it* inside the veil.

13 "And he shall put the incense on the fire before the LORD, that the cloud of incense may cover the [R]mercy seat that *is* on the Testimony, lest he [R]die. Ex. 25:21 • Ex. 28:43

14 "He shall take some of the blood of the bull and sprinkle *it* with his finger on the mercy seat on the east *side*; and before the mercy seat he shall sprinkle some of the blood with his finger seven times.

Atonement for the Tabernacle

15 [R]"Then he shall kill the goat of the sin offering, which *is* for the people, bring its blood [R]inside the veil, do with that blood as he did with the blood of the bull, and sprinkle it on the mercy seat and before the mercy seat. [Heb. 2:17] • [Heb. 6:19; 7:27; 9:3, 7, 12]

16 "So he shall [R]make atonement for the Holy *Place*, because of the uncleanness of the children of Israel, and because of their transgressions, for all their sins; and so he shall do for the tabernacle of meeting which remains among them in the midst of their uncleanness. Ex. 29:36; 30:10

17 "There shall be [R]no man in the tabernacle of meeting when he goes in to make atonement in the Holy *Place*, until he comes out, that he may make atonement for himself, for his household, and for all the congregation of Israel. Luke 1:10

18 "And he shall go out to the altar that *is* before the LORD, and make atonement for [R]it, and shall take some of the blood of the bull and some of the blood of the goat, and put it on the horns of the altar all around. Ex. 29:36

19 "Then he shall sprinkle some of the blood on it with his finger seven times, cleanse it, and [R]sanctify it from the uncleanness of the children of Israel. Ezek. 43:20

Atonement for the People

20 "And when he has made an end of atoning for the Holy *Place*, the tabernacle of meeting, and the altar, he shall bring the live goat;

21 "and Aaron shall lay both his hands on the head of the live goat, [R]confess over it all the iniquities of the children of Israel, and all their transgressions, concerning all their sins, [R]putting them on the head of the goat, and shall send *it* away into the wilderness by the hand of a suitable man. Lev. 5:5; 26:40 • [Is. 53:6]

22 "The goat shall bear on itself all their iniquities to an uninhabited land; and he shall release the goat in the wilderness.

23 "Then Aaron shall come into the tabernacle of meeting, shall take off the linen garments which he put on when he went into the Holy *Place*, and shall leave them there.

24 "And he shall wash his body with water in a holy place, put on his garments, come out and offer his burnt offering and the burnt offering of the people, and make atonement for himself and for the people.

25 [R]"The fat of the sin offering he shall burn on the altar. Lev. 1:8; 4:10

26 "And he who released the goat as the scapegoat shall wash his clothes [R]and bathe his body in water, and afterward he may come into the camp. Lev. 15:5

27 [R]"The bull *for* the sin offering and the goat *for* the sin offering, whose blood was brought in to make atonement in the Holy *Place*, shall be carried outside the camp. And they shall burn in the fire their skins, their flesh, and their offal. Heb. 13:11

28 "Then he who burns them shall wash his clothes and bathe his body in water, and afterward he may come into the camp.

Purpose of the Day of Atonement

29 "*This* shall be a statute forever for you: [R]In the seventh month, on the tenth *day* of the month, you shall [T]afflict your souls, and do no work at all, *whether* a native of your own country or a stranger who sojourns among you. Lev. 23:27–32 • *humble yourselves*

30 "For on that day *the priest* shall make atonement for you, to [R]cleanse you, *that* you may be clean from all your sins before the LORD. Jer. 33:8

31 [R]"It *is* a sabbath of solemn rest for you, and you shall afflict your souls. *It is* a statute forever. Lev. 23:27, 32

32 "And the priest, who is anointed and consecrated to minister as priest in his father's place, shall make atonement, and put on the linen clothes, the holy garments;

33 "then he shall make atonement for [T]the Holy Sanctuary, and he shall make atonement for the tabernacle of meeting and for the altar, and he shall make atonement for the priests and for all the people of the congregation. *The Most Holy Place*

34 "This shall be an everlasting statute for you, to make atonement for the children of Israel, for all their sins, once a year." And he did as the LORD commanded Moses.

CHAPTER 17

Laws Concerning the Location of Sacrifices

AND the LORD spoke to Moses, saying,

2 "Speak to Aaron, to his sons, and to all the children of Israel, and say to them, 'This *is* the thing which the LORD has commanded, saying:

3 "Whatever man of the house of Israel who [R]kills an ox or lamb or goat in the camp, or who kills *it* outside the camp, Deut. 12:5, 15, 21

4 "and does not bring it to the door of the tabernacle of meeting to offer an offering to the LORD before the tabernacle of the LORD, bloodguilt shall be [R]imputed to that man. He has shed blood; and that man shall be cut off from among his people, Rom. 5:13

5 "to the end that the children of Israel may bring their sacrifices [R]which they offer in the open field, that they may bring them to the LORD at the door of the tabernacle of meeting, to the priest, and offer them *as* peace offerings to the LORD. Deut. 12:1–27

6 "And the priest [R]shall sprinkle the blood on the altar of the LORD *at* the door of the tabernacle of meeting, and [R]burn the fat for a sweet aroma to the LORD. Lev. 3:2 • Num. 18:17

7 "They shall no more offer their sacrifices to demons, after whom they have played the harlot. This shall be a statute forever for them throughout their generations." '

8 "And you shall say to them: 'Whatever man of the house of Israel, or of the strangers who sojourn among you, [R]who offers a burnt offering or sacrifice, Lev. 1:2, 3; 18:26

9 'and does not [R]bring it to the door of the tabernacle of meeting, to offer it to the LORD, that man shall be cut off from among his people. Lev. 14:23

Laws Concerning the Use of Blood

10 [R]'And whatever man of the house of Israel, or of the strangers who sojourn among you, who eats any blood, I will set My face against that person who eats blood, and will cut him off from among his people. Gen. 9:4

11 'For the life of the flesh *is* in the blood, and I have given it to you upon the altar to make atonement for your souls; for it *is* the blood *that* makes atonement for the soul.'

12 "Therefore I said to the children of Israel, 'No one among you shall eat blood, nor shall any stranger who sojourns among you eat blood.'

13 "And whatever man of the children of Israel, or of the strangers who sojourn among you, who hunts and catches any animal or bird that may be eaten, he shall pour out its blood and [R]cover it with dust; Ezek. 24:7

14 [R]"for *it is* the life of all flesh. Its blood sustains its life. Therefore I said to the children of Israel, 'You shall not eat the blood of any flesh, for the life of all flesh is its blood. Whoever eats it shall be cut off.' Gen. 9:4

15 "And every person who eats what died *naturally* or what was torn *by beasts*, *whether he is* a native of your own country or a stranger, he shall both wash his clothes and [R]bathe in water, and be unclean until evening. Then he shall be clean. Lev. 15:5

16 "But if he does not wash or bathe his body, then he shall bear his [T]guilt." *iniquity*

CHAPTER 18

Laws of Sexual Sins

THEN the LORD spoke to Moses, saying,

2 "Speak to the children of Israel, and say to them: [R]'I am the LORD your God. Ex. 6:7

3 'According to the doings of the land of Egypt, where you dwelt, you shall not do; and according to the doings of the land of Canaan, where I am bringing you, you shall not do; nor shall you walk in their ordinances.

4 [R]'You shall observe My judgments and keep My ordinances, to walk in them: I *am* the LORD your God. Ezek. 20:19

5 'You shall therefore keep My statutes and My judgments, which if a man does, he shall live by them: I *am* the LORD.

6 'None of you shall approach anyone who is near of kin to him, to uncover his nakedness: I *am* the LORD.

7 'The nakedness of your father or the nakedness of your mother you shall not uncover. She *is* your mother; you shall not uncover her nakedness.

8 'The nakedness of your [R]father's wife you shall not uncover; it *is* your father's nakedness. Gen. 35:22

9 [R]'The nakedness of your sister, the daughter of your father, or the daughter of your mother, *whether* born at home or elsewhere, their nakedness you shall not uncover. Deut. 27:22

10 'The nakedness of your son's daughter or your daughter's daughter, their nakedness you shall not uncover; for theirs *is* your own nakedness.

11 'The nakedness of your father's wife's daughter, begotten by your father—she *is* your sister—you shall not uncover her nakedness.

12 [R]'You shall not uncover the nakedness of your father's sister; she *is* near of kin to your father. Lev. 20:19

13 'You shall not uncover the nakedness of your mother's sister, for she *is* near of kin to your mother.

14 [R]'You shall not uncover the nakedness of your father's brother. You shall not approach his wife; she *is* your aunt. Lev. 20:20

15 'You shall not uncover the nakedness of your daughter-in-law—she *is* your son's wife—you shall not uncover her nakedness.

16 'You shall not uncover the nakedness of your brother's wife; it *is* your brother's nakedness.

17 'You shall not uncover the nakedness of a woman and her daughter, nor shall you take her son's daughter or her daughter's daughter, to uncover her nakedness. They *are* near of kin to her. It *is* wickedness.

18 'Nor shall you take a woman [R]as a rival to her sister, to uncover her nakedness while the other is alive. 1 Sam. 1:6, 8

19 'Also you shall not approach a woman to uncover her nakedness as long as she is in her [R]*customary* impurity. Lev. 15:24; 20:18

20 [R]'Moreover you shall not lie carnally with your [R]neighbor's wife, to defile yourself with her. [Prov. 6:25–33] • Lev. 20:10

21 'And you shall not let any of your descendants pass through [R]*the fire* to [R]Molech, nor shall you profane the name of your God: I *am* the LORD. 2 Kin. 16:3 • 1 Kin. 11:7, 33

22 'You shall not lie with [R]a male as with a woman. It *is* an abomination. Lev. 20:13

23 'Nor shall you mate with any [R]beast, to defile yourself with it. Nor shall any woman stand before a beast to mate with it. It *is* perversion. Ex. 22:19

24 'Do not defile yourselves with any of these things; for by all these the nations are defiled, which I am casting out before you.

25 'For the land is defiled; therefore I visit the punishment of its iniquity upon it, and the land vomits out its inhabitants.

26 [R]'You shall therefore [T]keep My statutes and My judgments, and shall not commit *any* of these abominations, *either* any of your own nation or any stranger who sojourns among you Lev. 18:5, 30 • *obey*

27 '(for all these abominations the men of the land have done, who *were* before you, and thus the land is defiled),

28 'lest [R]the land vomit you out also when you defile it, as it vomited out the nations that *were* before you. Jer. 9:19

29 'For whoever commits any of these abominations, the persons who commit *them* shall be cut off from among their people.

30 'Therefore you shall keep My ordinance, so that *you* do not commit *any* of these abominable customs which were committed before you, and that you do not defile yourselves by them: I *am* the LORD your God.' "

CHAPTER 19

Laws of Social Order

AND the LORD spoke to Moses, saying,

2 "Speak to all the congregation of the children of Israel, and say to them: [R]'You shall be holy, for I the LORD your God *am* holy. Lev. 11:44; 20:7, 26

3 [R]'Every one of you shall revere his mother and his father, and keep My Sabbaths: I *am* the LORD your God. Ex. 20:12

4 [R]'Do not turn to idols, [R]nor make for yourselves [T]molded gods: I *am* the LORD your God. Ex. 20:4 • Ex. 34:17 • Cast metal

5 'And [R]if you offer a sacrifice of peace offering to the LORD, you shall offer it of your own free will. Lev. 7:16

6 'It shall be eaten the same day you offer *it*, and on the next day. And if any remains until the third day, it shall be burned in the fire.

7 'And if it is eaten at all on the third day,
it *is* an abomination. It shall not be accepted.
8 'Therefore *everyone* who eats it shall
bear his iniquity, because he has profaned the
hallowed *offering* of the LORD; and that person shall be cut off from his people.
9 [R]'When you reap the harvest of your
land, you shall not wholly reap the corners of
your field, nor shall you gather the gleanings
of your harvest. Deut. 24:19–22
10 'And you shall not glean your vineyard,
nor shall you gather *every* grape of your
vineyard; you shall leave them for the poor
and the stranger: I *am* the LORD your God.
11 [R]'You shall not steal, nor deal falsely,
[R]nor lie to one another. Ex. 20:15, 16 • Eph. 4:25
12 'And you shall not [R]swear by My name
falsely, [R]nor shall you profane the name of
your God: I *am* the LORD. Deut. 5:11 • Lev. 18:21
13 [R]'You shall not defraud your neighbor,
nor rob *him*. [R]The wages of him who is hired
shall not remain with you all night until
morning. Ex. 22:7–15, 21–27 • Deut. 24:15
14 'You shall not curse the deaf, [R]nor put a
stumblingblock before the blind, but shall
fear your God: I *am* the LORD. Deut. 27:18
15 'You shall do no injustice in judgment.
You shall not be partial to the poor, nor
honor the person of the mighty. *But* in righteousness you shall judge your neighbor.
16 'You shall not go about *as* a [R]talebearer
among your people; nor shall you [R]take a
stand against the life of your neighbor: I *am*
the LORD. Prov. 11:13; 18:8; 20:19 • 1 Kin. 21:7–19
17 'You shall not hate your brother in your
heart. You shall surely rebuke your neighbor,
and not bear sin because of him.
18 [R]'You shall not take vengeance, nor bear
any grudge against the children of your
people, [R]but you shall love your neighbor as
yourself: I *am* the LORD. [Deut. 32:35] • Mark 12:31
19 'You shall keep My statutes. You shall
not let your livestock breed with another
kind. You shall not sow your field with mixed
seed. Nor shall a garment of mixed linen and
wool come upon you.
20 'Whoever lies carnally with a woman
who *is* betrothed as a concubine to *another*
man, and who has not at all been redeemed
nor given her freedom, for this there shall be
[T]scourging; *but* they shall not be put to death,
because she was not free. *punishment*
21 'And he shall bring his trespass offering
to the LORD, to the door of the tabernacle of
meeting, a ram as a trespass offering.
22 'The priest shall make atonement for him
with the ram of the trespass offering before
the LORD for his sin which he has done. And
the sin which he has done shall be forgiven
him.
23 'When you come into the land, and have
planted all kinds of trees for food, then you
shall count their fruit as [T]uncircumcised.
Three years it shall be as uncircumcised to
you. *It* shall not be eaten. *unclean*
24 'But in the fourth year all its fruit shall be
holy, a praise to the LORD.
25 'And in the fifth year you may eat its
fruit, that it may yield to you its increase: I
am the LORD your God.
26 'You shall not eat *anything* with the
blood, nor shall you practice divination or
soothsaying.
27 'You shall not shave around the sides of
your head, nor shall you disfigure the edges
of your beard.
28 'You shall not [R]make any cuttings in
your flesh for the dead, nor tattoo any marks
on you: I *am* the LORD. Jer. 16:6
29 [R]'Do not prostitute your daughter, to
cause her to be a harlot, lest the land fall into
harlotry, and the land become full of wickedness. Deut. 22:21; 23:17, 18
30 'You shall keep My Sabbaths and [R]rever-
ence My sanctuary: I *am* the LORD. Lev. 26:2
31 'Give no regard to mediums and familiar
spirits; do not seek after [R]them, to be defiled
by them: I *am* the LORD your God. Lev. 20:6, 27
32 'You shall [T]rise before the gray headed
and honor the presence of an old man, and
fear your God: I *am* the LORD. *to give honor*
33 'And [R]if a stranger sojourns with you in
your land, you shall not mistreat him. Ex. 22:21
34 [R]'*But* the stranger who dwells among you
shall be to you as [T]one born among you, and
[R]you shall love him as yourself; for you were
strangers in the land of Egypt: I *am* the LORD
your God. Ex. 12:48 • *native among you* • Deut. 10:19
35 'You shall do no injustice in judgment, in
measurement of length, weight, or volume.
36 'You shall have [R]just balances, just
weights, a just [T]ephah, and a just hin: I *am*
the LORD your God, who brought you out of
the land of Egypt. Deut. 25:13–15 • 20.87 qt.
37 [R]'Therefore you shall observe all My
statutes and all My judgments, and perform
them: I *am* the LORD.' " Lev. 18:4, 5

CHAPTER 20

The Penalty for Worshiping Molech

THEN the LORD spoke to Moses, saying,
2 "Again, you shall say to the children of
Israel: 'Whoever of the children of Israel, or
of the strangers who sojourn in Israel, who
gives *any* of his descendants to Molech, he
shall surely be put to death. The people of the
land shall stone him with stones.
3 [R]'I will set My face against that man, and
will [T]cut him off from his people, because he
has given *some* of his descendants to Molech,
to defile My sanctuary and profane My holy
name. Lev. 17:10 • Put him to death
4 'And if the people of the land should in
any way [T]hide their eyes from the man, when

he gives *some* of his descendants to Molech, and they do not kill him, *close*

5 'then I will set My face against that man and against his family; and I will cut him off from his people, and all who prostitute themselves with him to commit harlotry with Molech.

The Penalty for Consulting Spirits

6 'And the person who turns after mediums and familiar spirits, to prostitute himself with them, I will set My face against that person and cut him off from his people.

7 [R]'Sanctify yourselves therefore, and be holy, for I *am* the LORD your God. Lev. 19:2

8 'And you shall keep [R]My statutes, and perform them: [R]I *am* the LORD who [T]sanctifies you. Lev. 19:19, 37 • Ex. 31:13 • *sets you apart*

The Penalty for Cursing Parents

9 'For [R]everyone who curses his father or his mother shall surely be put to death. He has cursed his father or his mother. [R]His blood *shall be* upon him. Ex. 21:17 • 2 Sam. 1:16

The Penalty for Committing Sexual Sins

10 'The man who commits adultery with *another* man's wife, *he* who commits adultery with his neighbor's wife, the adulterer and the adulteress, shall surely be put to death.

11 'The man who lies with his [R]father's wife has uncovered his father's nakedness; both of them shall surely be put to death. Their blood *shall be* upon them. Lev. 18:7, 8

12 'If a man lies with his [R]daughter-in-law, both of them shall surely be put to death. They have committed perversion. Their blood *shall be* upon them. Lev. 18:15

13 'If a man lies with a male as he lies with a woman, both of them have committed an abomination. They shall surely be put to death. Their blood *shall be* upon them.

14 'If a man marries a woman and her [R]mother, it *is* wickedness. They shall be burned with fire, both he and they, that there may be no wickedness among you. Lev. 18:17

15 'If a man mates with a [R]beast, he shall surely be put to death, and you shall kill the beast. Lev. 18:23

16 'If a woman approaches any beast and mates with it, you shall kill the woman and the beast. They shall surely be put to death. Their blood *is* upon them.

17 'If a man takes his [R]sister, his father's daughter or his mother's daughter, and sees her nakedness and she sees his nakedness, it *is* a wicked thing. And they shall be cut off in the sight of their people. He has uncovered his sister's nakedness. He shall bear his [T]guilt. Lev. 18:9 • *iniquity*

18 'If a man lies with a woman during her [T]sickness and uncovers her nakedness, he has discovered her flow, and she has uncovered the flow of her blood. Both of them shall be cut off from their people. Or *customary impurity*

19 'You shall not uncover the nakedness of your [R]mother's sister nor of your [R]father's sister, for that would uncover his near of kin. They shall bear their guilt. Lev. 18:13 • Lev. 18:12

20 'If a man lies with his uncle's wife, he has uncovered his uncle's nakedness. They shall bear their sin; they shall die childless.

21 'If a man takes his brother's wife, it *is* an unclean thing. He has uncovered his brother's nakedness. They shall be childless.

The Purpose of the Laws of Sanctification of the People

22 'You shall therefore keep all My statutes and all My judgments, and perform them, that the land where I am bringing you to dwell [R]may not vomit you out. Lev. 18:25

23 [R]'And you shall not walk in the statutes of the nation which I am casting out before you; for they commit all these things, and [R]therefore I abhor them. Lev. 18:3, 24 • Deut. 9:5

24 'But [R]I have said to you, "You shall inherit their land, and I will give it to you to possess, a land flowing with milk and honey." I *am* the LORD your God, who has separated you from the peoples. Ex. 3:17; 6:8; 13:5; 33:1–3

25 [R]'You shall therefore distinguish between clean beasts and unclean, between unclean birds and clean, [R]and you shall not make yourselves [T]abominable by beast or by bird, or by any kind of living thing that creeps on the ground, which I have separated from you as unclean. Lev. 10:10; 11:1–47 • Lev. 11:43 • *detestable*

26 'And you shall be holy to Me, [R]for I the LORD *am* holy, and have separated you from the peoples, that you should be Mine. Lev. 19:2

27 [R]'A man or a woman who is a medium, or who has familiar spirits, shall surely be put to death; they shall stone them with stones. Their blood *shall be* upon them.' " Lev. 19:31

CHAPTER 21

Laws Concerning Priests

AND the LORD said to Moses, "Speak to the priests, the sons of Aaron, and say to them: [R]'None shall defile himself for the dead among his people, Ezek. 44:25

2 'except for his relatives who are nearest to him: his mother, his father, his son, his daughter, and his brother;

3 'also his virgin sister who is near to him, who has had no husband, for her he may defile himself.

4 '*Otherwise* he shall not defile himself, *being* a [T]chief man among his people, to profane himself. Lit. *master* or *husband*

5 [R]'They shall not make any bald *place* on their heads, nor shall they shave the edges of their beards nor make any cuttings in their flesh. Deut. 14:1

6 'They shall be [R]holy to their God and not
profane the name of their God, for they offer
the offerings of the LORD made by fire, *and*
the [R]bread of their God; [R]therefore they shall
be holy. Ex. 22:31 • Lev. 3:11 • Is. 52:11
7 'They shall not take a wife *who is* a
harlot or a defiled woman, nor shall they take
a woman divorced from her husband; for [T]the
priest is holy to his God. Lit. *he*
8 'Therefore you shall [T]sanctify him, for he
offers the bread of your God. He shall be holy
to you, for [R]I the LORD, who [R]sanctify you,
am holy. *set him apart* • Lev. 11:44, 45 • Lev. 8:12, 30
9 'The daughter of any priest, if she pro-
fanes herself by playing the harlot, she profanes her father. She shall be [R]burned with
fire. Deut. 22:21

Laws Concerning the High Priest

10 'And *he who is* the high priest among his
brethren, on whose head the anointing oil
was poured and who is consecrated to wear
the garments, shall not [R]uncover[T] his head
nor tear his clothes; Lev. 10:6, 7 • In mourning
11 'nor shall he go near any dead body, nor
defile himself for his father or his mother;
12 [R]'nor shall he go out of the sanctuary,
nor profane the sanctuary of his God; for the
[R]consecration of the anointing oil of his God
is upon him: I *am* the LORD. Lev. 10:7 • Ex. 29:6, 7
13 'And he shall take a wife in her virginity.
14 'A widow or a divorced woman or a
defiled woman *or* a harlot—these he shall not
marry; but he shall take a virgin of his own
people as wife.
15 'Nor shall he profane his posterity among
his people, for I the LORD sanctify him.' "

People Prohibited from the Priesthood

16 And the LORD spoke to Moses, saying,
17 "Speak to Aaron, saying: 'No man of
your descendants in *succeeding* generations,
who has *any* defect, may approach to offer
the bread of his God.
18 'For any man who has a defect shall not
approach: a man blind or lame, who has a
marred *face* or any *limb* too long,
19 'a man who has a broken foot or broken
hand,
20 'or is a hunchback or a dwarf, or *a man*
who has a defect in his eye, or eczema or
scab, or is a eunuch.
21 'No man of the descendants of Aaron the
priest, who has a defect, shall come near to
offer the offerings made by fire to the LORD.
He has a defect; he shall not come near to
offer the bread of his God.
22 'He may eat the bread of his God, *both*
the most holy and the holy;
23 'only he shall not go near the [R]veil or
approach the altar, because he has a defect,
lest [R]he profane My sanctuaries; for I the
LORD sanctify them.' " Lev. 16:2 • Lev. 21:12

24 And Moses told *it* to Aaron and his sons,
and to all the children of Israel.

CHAPTER 22

Things Prohibited of the Priesthood

THEN the LORD spoke to Moses, saying,
2 "Speak to Aaron and his sons, that they
separate themselves from the holy things of
the children of Israel, and that they do not
profane My holy name *in those things* which
they sanctify to Me: I *am* the LORD.
3 "Say to them: 'Whoever of all your descendants throughout your generations, who
goes near the holy things which the children
of Israel sanctify to the LORD, while he has
uncleanness upon him, that person shall be
cut off from My presence: I *am* the LORD.
4 'Whatever man of the descendants of
Aaron, who *is* a [R]leper or has a discharge,
shall not eat the holy offerings until he is
clean. And [R]whoever touches anything made
unclean *by* a corpse, or a man who has had
an emission of semen, Num. 5:2 • Num. 19:11
5 'or whoever touches any creeping thing
by which he would be made unclean, or any
person by whom he would become unclean,
whatever his uncleanness may be—
6 'the person who has touched any such
thing shall be unclean until evening, and shall
not eat the holy *offerings* unless he [R]washes
his body with water. Lev. 15:5
7 'And when the sun goes down he shall be
clean; and afterward he may eat the holy
offerings, because [R]it *is* his food. Num. 18:11, 13
8 [R]'Whatever dies *naturally* or is torn *by*
beasts he shall not eat, to defile himself with
it: I *am* the LORD. Lev. 7:24; 11:39, 40; 17:15
9 'They shall therefore keep [R]My [T]ordi-
nance, [R]lest they bear sin for it and die
thereby, if they profane it: I the LORD sanctify them. Lev. 18:30 • *charge* • Ex. 28:43
10 [R]'No outsider shall eat the holy *offering*;
one who sojourns with the priest, or a hired
servant, shall not eat the holy thing. Ex. 29:33
11 'But if the priest [R]buys a person with his
money, he may eat it; and one who is born in
his house may eat his food. Ex. 12:44
12 'If the priest's daughter is married to an
outsider, she may not eat of the holy offerings.
13 'But if the priest's daughter is a widow or
divorced, and has no child, and has returned
to her father's house as in her youth, she may
eat her father's food; but no outsider shall eat
it.
14 'And if a man eats the holy *offering*
unintentionally, then he shall restore a holy
offering to the priest, and add one-fifth to it.
15 'They shall not profane the [R]holy *offer-*
ings of the children of Israel, which they offer
to the LORD, Num. 18:32

16 'or allow them to bear the guilt of trespass when they eat their holy *offerings*; for I the LORD sanctify them.' "

Sacrifices Prohibited of the Priesthood

17 And the LORD spoke to Moses, saying,

18 "Speak to Aaron and his sons, and to all the children of Israel, and say to them: 'Whatever man of the house of Israel, or of the strangers in Israel, who [T]offers his sacrifice for any of his vows or for any of his freewill offerings, which they offer to the LORD as a burnt offering— *brings his offering*

19 [R]'*you shall offer* of your own free will a male without blemish from the cattle, from the sheep, or from the goats. Lev. 1:3

20 [R]'*But* whatever has a defect, you shall not offer, for it shall not be acceptable on your behalf. Deut. 15:21; 17:1

21 'And [R]whoever offers a sacrifice of peace offering to the LORD, [R]to fulfill *his* vow, or a freewill offering from the cattle or the sheep, it must be perfect to be accepted; there shall be no defect in it. Lev. 3:1, 6 • Num. 15:3, 8

22 [R]'Those *that are* blind or broken or maimed, or have an [T]ulcer or eczema or scabs, you shall not offer to the LORD, nor make [R]an offering by fire of them on the altar to the LORD. Mal. 1:8 • *running sore* • Lev. 1:9, 13; 3:3, 5

23 'Either a bull or a lamb that has any limb [R]too long or too short you may offer *as* a freewill offering, but for a vow it shall not be accepted. Lev. 21:18

24 'You shall not offer to the LORD what is bruised or crushed, or torn or cut; nor shall you make *any offering of them* in your land.

25 'Nor from a foreigner's hand shall you offer any of these as [R]the bread of your God, because their [R]corruption *is* in them, *and* defects *are* in them. They shall not be accepted on your behalf.' " Lev. 21:6, 17 • Mal. 1:14

26 And the LORD spoke to Moses, saying:

27 [R]"When a bull or a sheep or a goat is born, it shall be seven days with its mother; and from the eighth day and thereafter it shall be accepted as an offering made by fire to the LORD. Ex. 22:30

28 "*Whether it is* a cow or ewe, do not kill both her and her young on the same day.

29 "And when you [R]offer a sacrifice of thanksgiving to the LORD, offer *it* of your own free will. Lev. 7:12

30 "On the same day it shall be eaten; you shall leave [R]none of it until morning: I *am* the LORD. Lev. 7:15

The Purpose of the Laws of the Priesthood

31 [R]"Therefore you shall keep My commandments, and perform them: I *am* the LORD. Deut. 4:40

32 "You shall not profane My holy name, but I will be hallowed among the children of Israel. I *am* the LORD who sanctifies you,

33 "who brought you out of the land of Egypt, to be your God: I *am* the LORD."

CHAPTER 23

The Weekly Sabbath

AND the LORD spoke to Moses, saying,

2 "Speak to the children of Israel, and say to them: 'The feasts of the LORD, which you shall proclaim *to be* [R]holy convocations, these *are* My feasts. Ex. 12:16

3 [R]'Six days shall work be done, but the seventh day *is* a Sabbath of solemn rest, a holy convocation. You shall do no work *on it*; it *is* the Sabbath of the LORD in all your dwellings. Luke 13:14

Passover

4 [R]'These *are* the feasts of the LORD, holy convocations which you shall proclaim at their appointed times. Ex. 23:14–16

5 'On the fourteenth *day* of the first month at twilight *is* the LORD's Passover.

Unleavened Bread

6 'And on the fifteenth day of the same month *is* the Feast of Unleavened Bread to the LORD; seven days you must eat unleavened bread.

7 [R]'On the first day you shall have a holy convocation; you shall do no [T]customary work on it. Ex. 12:16 • *occupational*

8 'But you shall offer an offering made by fire to the LORD for seven days. The seventh day *shall be* a holy convocation; you shall do no customary work *on it*.' "

Firstfruits

9 And the LORD spoke to Moses, saying,

10 "Speak to the children of Israel, and say to them: 'When you come into the land which I give to you, and reap its harvest, then you shall bring a sheaf of [R]the firstfruits of your harvest to the priest. [Rom. 11:16]

11 'He shall wave the sheaf before the LORD, to be accepted on your behalf; on the day after the Sabbath the priest shall wave it.

12 'And you shall offer on that day, when you wave the [T]sheaf, a male lamb of the first year, without blemish, as a burnt offering to the LORD. 2.087 qt.

13 'Its grain offering *shall be* two-tenths *of an ephah* of fine flour mixed with oil, an offering made by fire to the LORD, for a [T]sweet aroma; and its drink offering *shall be* of wine, [T]one-fourth of a hin. *pleasing* • 1 qt.

14 'You shall eat neither bread nor parched grain nor fresh grain until the same day that you have brought an offering to your God; *it shall be* a statute forever throughout your generations in all your dwellings.

FEASTS AND FESTIVALS

Many religious feasts and festivals were observed by the Jewish people during Old and New Testament times. During these events, the people stopped all manual labor and devoted themselves totally to these celebrations. The accounts of these festivals in the Bible suggest they included a potluck type of meal, with some parts of the meal reserved for the priests and the rest given to those who gathered at the temple or the altar for worship. Observed with thanksgiving, worship, and joyous feasting, these feasts commemorated significant events in Israel's history as God's covenant people.

The three major feasts of Bible times were Passover, Pentecost, and Tabernacles. All males of Israel were required to travel to the temple in Jerusalem to observe these events (Ex. 23:14–19).

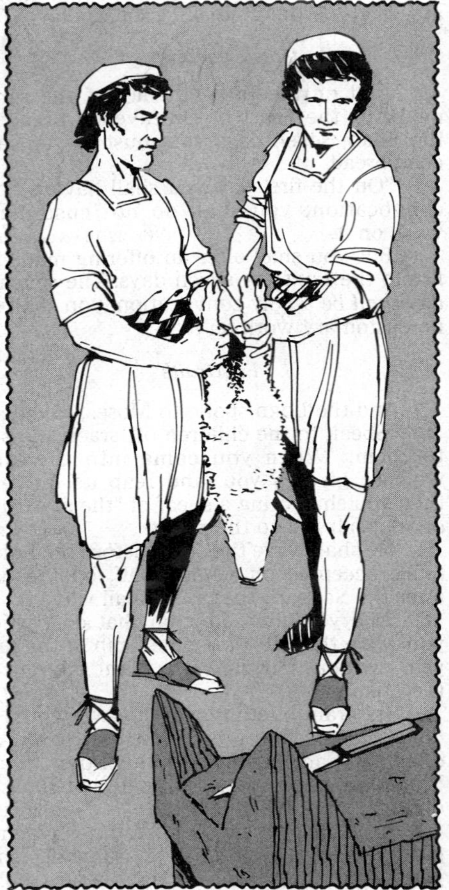

PASSOVER FESTIVAL

This great annual feast recalled the sacrifice of a lamb in Egypt at God's command when the Hebrew people were slaves (Ex. 12:1—13:16). The Hebrews smeared the blood of a lamb on their doorposts as a signal to God that He should "pass over" their houses when He destroyed all the firstborn of Egypt. This miraculous event persuaded the Egyptian Pharaoh to give the Hebrews their freedom. Passover was observed annually from that point on to commemorate this important event in Israel's history.

A custom connected with Passover was the Feast of Unleavened Bread. In this ritual, the people ate bread without leaven to symbolize the haste with which they left Egypt when they were finally released (Ex. 12:15).

In New Testament times, the people gathered in Jerusalem for the annual celebration of Passover. Jesus was crucified in the city during a Passover observance. The blood of the lamb that had saved the Hebrew people from destruction in Egypt had looked forward to this perfect, eternal sacrifice Jesus made for all believers. The words with which John the Baptist greeted Jesus, "Behold! The Lamb of God who takes away the sin of the world!" (John 1:29) portray this sacrificial dimension of His life and ministry.

FEAST OF PENTECOST

This event was a harvest festival, through which the people expressed thanksgiving to God for the grain harvest and other crops (Num. 28:26–31). Other names by which this feast was known were Feast of Weeks and Feast of Firstfruits. The early Christian believers experienced the miraculous outpouring of God's Spirit while gathered in Jerusalem to observe Pentecost (Acts 2:1–4).

FEAST OF TABERNACLES

This great religious celebration commemorated the years of wandering in the Wilderness by the Israelites before they occupied the Promised Land (Deut. 16:13–17). It was also known as the Feast of Ingathering and the Feast of Booths. To observe this festival, the people were commanded to live for seven days in booths, or temporary shelters made of tree branches. Doing so, they relived the experience of the wilderness wandering when no permanent houses were available (Lev. 23:42).

In addition to these three major feasts, other great religious festivals were held at various times during the history of the Israelites to commemorate important events.

FEAST OF PURIM

This feast brought to mind the deliverance of the Hebrew people from a schemer named Haman during the period of their captivity by the Persians. The name comes from the Hebrew word *purim*, meaning "lots," because Haman cast lots to decide when he would carry out his evil plan to destroy the Jewish captives (Esth. 3:6, 7). Esther's quick thinking and brave actions exposed Haman's plot, and he was hanged on the very gallows from which he had planned to hang Esther's uncle Mordecai. Mordecai represented the spirit faithful to God, which Haman detested (Esth. 5:14; 9:18–32). The Feast of Purim, also known as the Feast of Lots, became a national feast after the period of the Exile in Israel's history. It is observed annually by the Jewish people today.

FEAST OF TRUMPETS

This feast was observed by the blowing of trumpets and the offering of animal sacrifices (Lev. 23:24–32; Num. 29:1–40). The exact reason for its observance is not clear. Some scholars believe it originated during Israel's captivity by the Babylonians to counteract the influence of Babylon's new year festival. The Feast of Trumpets is now known as *Rosh Hashanah*.

FEAST OF DEDICATION

Also called the Feast of Lights, or *Hanukkah*, the Feast of Dedication is mentioned only in the apocryphal book of 1 Maccabees. It celebrated the restoration of worship in the temple after its desecration by the pagan ruler Antiochus Epiphanes during the period of the Maccabees about 167 B.C.

DAY OF ATONEMENT

This day was marked by fasting, humiliation, and great reverence (Lev. 16). On this day, the high priest first made atonement for his own sin, then entered the most holy area of the tabernacle to make an appropriate animal sacrifice to atone for the sins of all the people.

Pentecost

15 'And you shall count for yourselves from the day after the Sabbath, from the day that you brought the sheaf of the wave offering: seven Sabbaths shall be completed.

16 'Count [R]fifty days to the day after the seventh Sabbath; then you shall offer [R]a new grain offering to the LORD. Acts 2:1 • Num. 28:26

17 'You shall bring from your habitations two wave *loaves* of two-tenths *of an ephah.* They shall be of fine flour; they shall be baked with leaven. *They are* [R]the firstfruits to the LORD. Num. 15:17–21

18 'And you shall offer with the bread seven lambs of the first year, without blemish, one young bull, and two rams. They shall be *as* a burnt offering to the LORD, with their grain offering and their drink offerings, an offering made by fire for a sweet aroma to the LORD.

19 'Then you shall sacrifice one kid of the goats as a sin offering, and two male lambs of the first year as a sacrifice of peace offering.

20 'The priest shall wave them with the bread of the firstfruits *as* a wave offering before the LORD, with the two lambs. They shall be holy to the LORD for the priest.

21 'And you shall proclaim on the same day *that* it is a holy convocation to you. You shall do no customary work *on it. It shall be* a statute forever in all your dwellings throughout your generations.

22 'When you reap the harvest of your land, you shall not wholly reap the corners of your field when you reap, nor shall you gather any gleaning from your harvest. You shall leave them for the poor and for the stranger: I *am* the LORD your God.' "

Trumpets

23 Then the LORD spoke to Moses, saying,

24 "Speak to the children of Israel, saying: 'In the [R]seventh month, on the first *day* of the month, you shall have a sabbath-*rest,* [R]a memorial of blowing of trumpets, a holy convocation. Num. 29:1 • Lev. 25:9

25 'You shall do no customary work *on it;* and you shall offer an offering made by fire to the LORD.' "

Day of Atonement

26 And the LORD spoke to Moses, saying:

27 [R]"Also the tenth *day* of this seventh month *shall be* the Day of Atonement. It shall be a holy convocation for you; you shall afflict your souls, and offer an offering made by fire to the LORD. Num. 29:7

28 "And you shall do no work on that same day, for it *is* the Day of Atonement, to make atonement for you before the LORD your God.

29 "For any person who is not [R]afflicted *of soul* on that same day, [R]he shall be cut off from his people. Jer. 31:9 • Num. 5:2

30 "And any person who does any work on that same day, [R]that person I will destroy from among his people. Lev. 20:3–6

31 "You shall do no manner of work; *it shall be* a statute forever throughout your generations in all your dwellings.

32 'It *shall be* to you a sabbath of *solemn* rest, and you shall [T]afflict your souls; on the ninth *day* of the month at evening, from evening to evening, you shall [T]celebrate your sabbath." *humble yourselves • observe*

Tabernacles

33 Then the LORD spoke to Moses, saying,

34 "Speak to the children of Israel, saying: [R]'The fifteenth day of this seventh month *shall be* the Feast of Tabernacles *for* seven days to the LORD. Num. 29:12

35 'On the first day *there shall be* a holy convocation. You shall do no customary work *on it.*

36 '*For* seven days you shall offer an offering made by fire to the LORD. On the eighth day you shall have a holy convocation, and you shall offer an offering made by fire to the LORD. It *is* a [R]sacred[T] assembly, *and* you shall do no customary work *on it.* Deut. 16:8 • *solemn*

37 [R]'These *are* the feasts of the LORD which you shall proclaim *to be* holy convocations, to offer an offering made by fire to the LORD, a burnt offering and a grain offering, a sacrifice and drink offerings, everything on its day— Lev. 23:2, 4

38 [R]'besides the Sabbaths of the LORD, besides your gifts, besides all your vows, and besides all your freewill offerings which you give to the LORD. Num. 29:39

39 'Also on the fifteenth day of the seventh month, when you have [R]gathered in the fruit of the land, you shall keep the feast of the LORD *for* seven days; on the first day *there shall be* a sabbath-*rest,* and on the eighth day a sabbath-*rest.* Ex. 23:16

40 'And [R]you shall take for yourselves on the first day the [T]fruit of beautiful trees, branches of palm trees, the boughs of leafy trees, and willows of the brook; [R]and you shall rejoice before the LORD your God for seven days. Neh. 8:15 • Or *foliage* • Deut. 12:7; 16:14, 15

41 'You shall keep it as a feast to the LORD for seven days in the year. *It shall be* a statute forever in your generations. You shall celebrate it in the seventh month.

42 [R]'You shall dwell in [T]booths for seven days. All who are native Israelites shall dwell in booths, [Is. 4:6] • Shelters made of boughs

43 'that your generations may know that I made the children of Israel dwell in booths when [R]I brought them out of the land of Egypt: I *am* the LORD your God.' " Lev. 22:33

44 So Moses [R]declared to the children of Israel the feasts of the LORD. Lev. 23:2

CHAPTER 24

Oil for the Lamps

THEN the LORD spoke to Moses, saying:
2 "Command the children of Israel that
they bring to you pure oil of pressed olives for
the light, to make the lamps burn continually.
3 "Outside the veil of the Testimony, in the
tabernacle of meeting, Aaron shall be in
charge of it from evening until morning
before the LORD continually; *it shall be* a
statute forever in your generations.
4 "He shall [T]be in charge of the lamps on
[R]the pure *gold* lampstand before the LORD
continually. *arrange* or *set in order* • Ex. 25:31; 31:8; 37:17

The Showbread

5 "And you shall take fine flour and bake
twelve [R]cakes with it. Two-tenths *of an
ephah* shall be in each cake. Ex. 25:30; 39:36; 40:23
6 "You shall set them in two rows, six in a
row, on the pure table before the LORD.
7 "And you shall put pure frankincense on
each row, that it may be on the bread for a
[R]memorial, an offering made by fire to the
LORD. Lev. 2:2, 9, 16
8 [R]"Every Sabbath he shall set it in order
before the LORD continually, *being taken*
from the children of Israel by an everlasting
covenant. 1 Chr. 9:32
9 "And it shall be for Aaron and his sons,
and they shall eat it in a holy place; for it *is*
most holy to him from the offerings of the
LORD made by fire, by a perpetual statute."

Law of the Sanctified Name of God

10 Now the son of an Israelite woman,
whose father *was* an Egyptian, went out
among the children of Israel; and this Israelite *woman's* son and a man of Israel fought
each other in the camp.
11 And the Israelite woman's son blasphemed the name *of the LORD* and cursed;
and so they [R]brought him to Moses. (His
mother's name *was* Shelomith the daughter
of Dibri, of the tribe of Dan.) Ex. 18:22, 26
12 Then they [R]put him [T]in custody, [R]that
the mind of the LORD might be shown to
them. Num. 15:34 • *under guard* • Num. 27:5
13 And the LORD spoke to Moses, saying,
14 "Take outside the camp him who has
cursed; then let all who heard *him* [R]lay their
hands on his head, and let all the congregation stone him. Deut. 13:9; 17:7
15 "Then you shall speak to the children of
Israel, saying: 'Whoever curses his God [R]shall
[T]bear his sin. Lev. 20:17 • *be responsible for*
16 'And whoever [R]blasphemes the name of
the LORD shall surely be put to death, *and* all
the congregation shall certainly stone him,
the stranger as well as him who is born in the
land. When he blasphemes the name *of the
LORD*, he shall be put to death. [Mark 3:28, 29]
17 [R]'Whoever kills any man shall surely be
put to death. Ex. 21:12
18 [R]'Whoever kills an animal shall make it
good, animal for animal. Lev. 24:21
19 'If a man causes disfigurement of his
neighbor, as [R]he has done, so shall it be done
to him— Ex. 21:24
20 'fracture for [R]fracture, eye for eye, tooth
for tooth; as he has caused disfigurement of a
man, so shall it be done to him. Ex. 21:23
21 'And whoever kills an animal shall restore it; but whoever kills a man shall be put
to death.
22 'You shall have [R]the same law for the
stranger and for one from your own country;
for I *am* the LORD your God.'" Ex. 12:49
23 Then Moses spoke to the children of
Israel; and they took outside the camp him
who had cursed, and stoned him with stones.
So the children of Israel did as the LORD
commanded Moses.

CHAPTER 25

Law of the Sabbath Year

AND the LORD spoke to Moses on Mount
[R]Sinai, saying, Lev. 26:46
2 "Speak to the children of Israel, and say
to them: 'When you come into the land
which I give you, then the land shall [R]keep a
sabbath to the LORD. Lev. 26:34, 35
3 'Six years you shall sow your field, and
six years you shall prune your vineyard, and
gather in its fruit;
4 'but in the seventh year there shall be a
sabbath of solemn [R]rest for the land, a sabbath to the LORD. You shall neither sow your
field nor prune your vineyard. [Heb. 4:9]
5 [R]'What grows of its own accord of your
harvest you shall not reap, nor gather the
grapes of your untended vine, *for* it is a year
of rest for the land. 2 Kin. 19:29
6 'And the sabbath *produce* of the land
shall be food for you: for you and your
servant, for your maidservant and your hired
servant, for the stranger who sojourns with
you,
7 'for your livestock and the animals that
are in your land—all its produce shall be for
food.

Law of the Year of Jubilee

8 'And you shall count seven sabbaths of
years for yourself, seven times seven years;
and the time of the seven sabbaths of years
shall be to you forty-nine years.
9 'Then you shall cause the trumpet of the
Jubilee to sound on the tenth *day* of the
seventh month; [R]on the Day of Atonement
you shall make the trumpet to sound
throughout all your land. Lev. 23:24, 27
10 'And you shall consecrate the fiftieth
year, and [R]proclaim liberty throughout *all* the

land to all its inhabitants. It shall be a Jubilee
for you; [R]and each of you shall return to his
possession, and each of you shall return to his
family. Jer. 34:8, 15, 17 • Num. 36:4
11 'That fiftieth year shall be a Jubilee to
you; in it [R]you shall neither sow nor reap
what grows of its own accord, nor gather *the
grapes* of your untended vine. Lev. 25:5
12 'For it *is* the Jubilee; it shall be holy to
you; you shall eat its produce from the field.
13 [R]'In this Year of Jubilee, each of you
shall return to his possession. Lev. 25:10; 27:24
14 'And if you sell anything to your neighbor or buy from your neighbor's hand, you
shall not [R]oppress one another. Lev. 19:13
15 [R]'According to the number of years after
the Jubilee you shall buy from your neighbor,
and according to the number of years of
crops he shall sell to you. Lev. 27:18, 23
16 'According to the multitude of years you
shall increase its price, and according to the
fewer number of years you shall diminish its
price; for he sells to you *according* to the
number *of the years* of the crops.
17 'Therefore [R]you shall not [T]oppress one
another, but you shall fear your God; for I *am*
the LORD your God. Lev. 25:14 • *mistreat*
18 'So you shall observe My statutes and
keep My judgments, and perform them; and
you will dwell in the land in safety.
19 'Then the land will yield its fruit, and
[R]you will eat your fill, and dwell there in
safety. Lev. 26:5
20 'And if you say, [R]"What shall we eat in
the seventh year, since [R]we shall not sow nor
gather in our produce?" Matt. 6:25, 31 • Lev. 25:4, 5
21 'Then I will command My blessing on
you in the [R]sixth year, and it will bring forth
produce enough for three years. Ex. 16:29
22 [R]'And you shall sow in the eighth year,
and eat [R]old produce until the ninth year;
until its produce comes in, you shall eat *of*
the old *harvest*. 2 Kin. 19:29 • Josh. 5:11
23 'The land shall not be sold permanently,
for [R]the land *is* Mine; for you *are* [R]strangers
and sojourners with Me. Ex. 19:5 • Ps. 39:12
24 'And in all the land of your possession
you shall grant redemption of the land.
25 'If one of your brethren becomes poor,
and has sold *some* of his possession, and if his
kinsman-redeemer comes to redeem it, then
he may redeem what his brother sold.
26 'Or if the man has no one to redeem it,
but he himself becomes able to redeem it,
27 'then [R]let him count the years since its
sale, and restore the balance to the man to
whom he sold it, that he may return to his
possession. Lev. 25:50–52
28 'But if he is not able to have *it* restored to
himself, then what was sold shall remain in
the hand of him who bought it until the Year
of Jubilee; [R]and in the Jubilee it shall be
released, and he shall return to his possession. Lev. 25:10, 13
29 'And if a man sells a house in a walled
city, then he may redeem it within a whole
year after it is sold; *within* a full year he may
redeem it.
30 'But if it is not redeemed within the
space of a full year, then the house in the
walled city shall belong permanently to him
who bought it, throughout his generations. It
shall not be released in the Jubilee.
31 'However the houses of villages which
have no wall around them shall be counted as
the fields of the country. They may be redeemed, and they shall be released in the
Jubilee.
32 'Nevertheless the cities of the Levites,
and the houses in the cities of their possession, the Levites may redeem at any time.
33 'And if a man purchases a house from
the Levites, then the house that was sold in
the city of his possession shall be released in
the Year of Jubilee; for the houses in the
cities of the Levites *are* their possession
among the children of Israel.
34 'But [R]the field of the common-land of
their cities may not be [R]sold, for it *is* their
perpetual possession. Num. 35:2–5 • Acts 4:36, 37
35 'And if one of your brethren becomes
poor, and falls into poverty among you, then
you shall help him, like a stranger or a
sojourner, that he may live with you.
36 [R]'Take no usury or interest from him; but
[R]fear your God, that your brother may live
with you. Ex. 22:25 • Neh. 5:9
37 'You shall not lend him your money for
usury, nor lend him your food at a profit.
38 'I *am* the LORD your God, who brought
you out of the land of Egypt, to give you the
land of Canaan *and* to be your God.
39 'And if *one of* your brethren *who dwells*
by you becomes poor, and sells himself to
you, you shall not compel him to serve as a
slave.
40 '*But* as a hired servant *and* a sojourner
he shall be with you, *and* shall serve you until
the Year of Jubilee.
41 'And *then* he shall depart from you, *both*
he and his children [R]with him, and shall
return to his own family; he shall return to
the possession of his fathers. Ex. 21:3
42 'For they *are* [R]My servants, whom I
brought out of the land of Egypt; they shall
not be sold as slaves. [Rom. 6:22]
43 'You shall not rule over him with [T]rigor,
but you shall fear your God. *severity*
44 'And as for your male and female slaves
whom you may have—from the nations that
are around you, from them you may buy
male and female slaves.
45 'Moreover you may buy [R]the children of

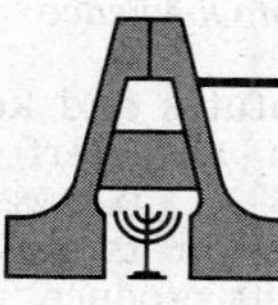

THE JUBILEE YEAR

The Jubilee year was launched with a blast from a ram's horn.

The Jubilee year, also known as the "year of liberty" (Ezek. 46:17), was proclaimed on the fiftieth year after seven cycles of seven years. This fiftieth year was a time when specific instructions about property and slavery outlined in the Jewish law took effect (Lev. 25:8–55).

The word *jubilee* comes from a Hebrew word, meaning "ram's horn," or "trumpet." The Jubilee year was launched with a blast from a ram's horn (see illustration) on the Day of Atonement, signifying a call to celebration, liberation, and the beginning of a year for "doing justice" and "loving mercy."

The fiftieth year was a special year in which to "proclaim liberty throughout *all* the land" (Lev. 25:10). Individuals who had sold themselves as slaves or indentured servants because of indebtedness were released from their debts and set free. If a family's land had been taken away because of indebtedness, this land was returned to the original owners in the Jubilee year.

God apparently established the Jubilee year to prevent the Israelites from oppressing and cheating one another (Lev. 25:17). This law prevented a permanent system of classes from developing; it gave everyone the opportunity to start over, economically and socially.

The Jubilee year reminds us of God's concern for human liberty. God wants people to be free (Luke 4:18, 19). Calling into question any social practice that leads to permanent bondage and loss of economic opportunity, it also stands as a witness to God's desire for justice on earth.

the strangers who sojourn among you, and their families who are with you, which they beget in your land; and they shall become your property. [Is. 56:3, 6, 7]

46 'And [R]you may take them as an inheritance for your children after you, to inherit *them as* a possession; they shall be your permanent slaves. But regarding your brethren, the children of Israel, you shall not rule over one another with rigor. Is. 14:2

47 'Now if a sojourner or stranger close to you becomes rich, and *one of* your brethren *who dwells* by him becomes poor, and sells himself to the stranger *or* sojourner close to you, or to a member of the stranger's family,

48 'after he is sold he may be redeemed again. One of his brothers may redeem him;

49 'or his uncle or his uncle's son may redeem him; or *anyone* who is near of kin to him in his family may redeem him; or if he is able he may redeem himself.

50 'Thus he shall reckon with him who bought him: The price of his release shall be according to the number of years, from the year that he was sold to him until the Year of Jubilee; *it shall be* [R]according to the time of a hired servant for him. Job 7:1

51 'If *there are* still many years *remaining*, according to them he shall repay the price of his redemption from the money with which he was bought.

52 'And if there remain but a few years until the Year of Jubilee, then he shall reckon with him, *and* according to his years he shall repay him the price of his redemption.

53 'He shall be with him as a yearly hired servant, and he shall not rule with rigor over him in your sight.

54 'And if he is not redeemed in these *years*, then he shall be released in the Year of Jubilee, *both* he and his children with him.

55 'For the children of Israel *are* servants to Me; they *are* My servants whom I brought out of the land of Egypt: I *am* the LORD your God.

CHAPTER 26

Basic Requirements of Obedience

'YOU shall [R]not make idols for yourselves; Ex. 20:4, 5
neither a carved image nor a *sacred* pillar
shall you rear up for yourselves;
nor shall you set up an engraved stone in your land, to bow down to it;
for I *am* the LORD your God.
2 [R]You shall [T]keep My Sabbaths and reverence My sanctuary:
I *am* the LORD. Lev. 19:30 • *observe*

Conditions and Results of Obedience

3 [R]'If you walk in My statutes and keep My commandments, and perform them, Deut. 28:1-14
4 [R]then I will give you rain in its season,
[R]the land shall yield its produce, and the trees of the field shall yield their fruit. Is. 30:23 • Ps. 67:6
5 Your threshing shall last till the time of vintage, and the vintage shall last till the time of sowing;
you shall eat your bread to the full, and dwell in your land safely.
6 [R]I will give peace in the land, and [R]you shall lie down, and none will make *you* afraid; Is. 45:7 • Job 11:19
I will rid the land of [R]evil[T] beasts,
and [R]the sword will not go through your land. 2 Kin. 17:25 • *wild* • Ezek. 14:17
7 You will chase your enemies, and they shall fall by the sword before you.
8 [R]Five of you shall chase a hundred, and a hundred of you shall put ten thousand to flight; Deut. 32:30
your enemies shall fall by the sword before you.
9 For I will look on you favorably and make you fruitful, multiply you and confirm My covenant with you.
10 You shall eat the old harvest, and clear out the old because of the new.
11 I will set My tabernacle among you, and My soul shall not abhor you.
12 I will walk among you and be your God, and you shall be My people.
13 I *am* the LORD your God, who brought you out of the land of Egypt, that *you* should not be their slaves;
I have broken the bands of your yoke and made you walk upright.

Conditions and Results of Disobedience

14 'But if you do not obey Me, and do not observe all these commandments,
15 and if you despise My statutes, or if your soul abhors My judgments, so that you do not perform all My commandments, *but* break My covenant,
16 I also will do this to you:
I will even appoint terror over you, [R]wasting disease and fever which shall [R]consume the eyes and cause sorrow of heart. Deut. 28:22 • 1 Sam. 2:33
And you shall sow your seed in vain, for your enemies shall eat it.
17 I will set My face against you, and you shall be defeated by your enemies.
[R]Those who hate you shall reign over you, and you shall [R]flee when no one pursues you. Ps. 106:41 • Prov. 28:1

18 'And after all this, if you do not obey Me,
then I will punish you [R]seven times
more for your sins. 1 Sam. 2:5
19 I will break the pride of your power;
I will make your heavens like iron and
your earth like bronze.
20 And your [R]strength shall be spent in
vain; Ps. 127:1
for your [R]land shall not yield its produce,
nor shall the trees of the land yield
their fruit. Gen. 4:12

21 'Then, if you walk contrary to Me, and
are not willing to obey Me, I will bring
on you seven times more plagues, according to your sins.
22 I will also send wild beasts among you,
which shall rob you of your children,
destroy your livestock, and make you
few in number;
and your highways shall be desolate.

23 'And if [R]by these things you are not
reformed by Me, but walk contrary to
Me, Amos 4:6–12
24 [R]then I also will walk contrary to you, and
I will punish you yet seven times for
your sins. Lev. 26:28, 41
25 And [R]I will bring a sword against you
that will execute the vengeance of *My*
covenant; Ezek. 5:17
when you are gathered together within
your cities [R]I will send pestilence
among you; Deut. 28:21
and you shall be delivered into the hand
of the enemy.
26 [R]When I have cut off your supply of
bread, ten women shall bake your
bread in one oven, and they shall
bring back *to you* your bread by
weight, [R]and you shall eat and not be
satisfied. Ps. 105:16 • Mic. 6:14

27 'And after all this, if you do not obey Me,
but walk contrary to Me,
28 then I also will walk contrary to you in
fury;
and I, even I, will chastise you seven
times for your sins.
29 [T]You shall eat the flesh of your sons, and
you shall eat the flesh of your daughters. In time of famine
30 [R]I will destroy your high places, cut down
your incense altars, and cast your
carcasses on the lifeless forms of your
idols; 2 Chr. 34:3
and My soul shall abhor you.
31 I will lay your cities waste and bring
your sanctuaries to desolation, and I
will not smell the fragrance of your
sweet aromas.
32 [R]I will bring the land to desolation, and
your enemies who dwell in it shall be
astonished at it. Jer. 9:11
33 [R]I will scatter you among the nations and
draw out a sword after you;
your land shall be desolate and your
cities waste. Deut. 4:27
34 [R]Then the land shall enjoy its sabbaths as
long as it lies desolate and you *are* in
your enemies' land;
then the land shall rest and enjoy its
sabbaths. 2 Chr. 36:21
35 As long as *it* lies desolate it shall rest—
for the time it did not rest on your
sabbaths when you dwelt in it.

36 'And as for those of you who are left, I
will send [R]faintness[T] into their hearts
in the lands of their enemies;
the sound of a shaken leaf shall cause
them to flee; Ezek. 21:7, 12, 15 • *fear*
they shall flee as though fleeing from a
sword, and they shall fall when no one
pursues.
37 [R]They shall stumble over one another, as
it were before a sword, when no one
pursues; 1 Sam. 14:15, 16
and [R]you shall have no *power* to stand
before your enemies. Josh. 7:12, 13
38 You shall [R]perish among the nations, and
the land of your enemies shall eat you
up. Deut. 4:26
39 And those of you who are left shall
[T]waste away in their iniquity in your
enemies' lands; *rot*
also in their [R]fathers' iniquities, which
are with them, they shall waste
away. Ex. 34:7

The Promise of Restoration

40 '*But* if they confess their iniquity and the
iniquity of their fathers, with their
unfaithfulness in which they were unfaithful to Me, and that they also have
walked contrary to Me,
41 and *that* I also have walked contrary to
them and have brought them into the
land of their enemies;
if their uncircumcised hearts are humbled, and they accept their guilt—
42 then I will remember My covenant with
Jacob, and My covenant with Isaac
and My covenant with Abraham I will
remember;
I will [R]remember the land. Ps. 136:23
43 [R]The land also shall be left empty by
them, and will enjoy its sabbaths while
it lies desolate without them;
they will accept their guilt, because

they [R]despised My judgments and
because their soul abhorred My
statutes. Lev. 26:34, 35 • Lev. 26:15
44 Yet for all that, when they are in the land
of their enemies, [R]I will not cast them
away, nor shall I abhor them, to utterly destroy them and break My covenant with them;
for I *am* the LORD their God. Deut. 4:31
45 But [R]for their sake I will remember the
covenant of their ancestors, whom I
brought out of the land of Egypt [R]in
the sight of the nations, that I might
be their God:
I *am* the LORD.' " [Rom. 11:28] • Ps. 98:2

46 [R]These *are* the statutes and judgments
and laws which the LORD made between
Himself and the children of Israel [R]on Mount
Sinai by the hand of Moses. [John 1:17] • Lev. 25:1

CHAPTER 27

Consecration of Persons

NOW the LORD spoke to Moses, saying,
2 "Speak to the children of Israel, and
say to them: 'When a man [T]consecrates by a
vow certain persons to the LORD, according
to your valuation, Or *makes a difficult vow*
3 'if your valuation is of a male from
twenty years old up to sixty years old, then
your valuation shall be fifty shekels of silver,
according to the shekel of the sanctuary.
4 'If it *is* a female, then your valuation
shall be [T]thirty shekels; $3,840
5 'and if from five years old up to twenty
years old, then your valuation for a male shall
be [T]twenty shekels, and for a female [T]ten
shekels; $2,560 • $1,280
6 'and if from a month old up to five years
old, then your valuation for a male shall be
five shekels of silver, and for a female your
valuation shall be three shekels of silver;
7 'and if from sixty years old and above, if
it is a male, then your valuation shall be
fifteen shekels, and for a female ten shekels.
8 'But if he is too poor to pay your valuation, then he shall present himself before the
priest, and the priest shall set a value for him;
according to the ability of him who vowed,
the priest shall value him.

Consecration of Animals

9 'And if *it is* a beast such as men may
bring as an offering to the LORD, all such that
any man gives to the LORD shall be holy.
10 'He shall not substitute it or exchange it,
good for bad or bad for good; and if he at all
exchanges beast for beast, then both it and
the one exchanged for it shall be holy.
11 'If *it is* an unclean beast which they do
not offer as a sacrifice to the LORD, then he
shall present the beast before the priest;
12 'and the priest shall set a value for it,
whether it is good or bad; as you, the priest,
value it, so it shall be.
13 'But if he *wants* at all *to* redeem it, then
he must add one-fifth to your valuation.

Consecration of Houses

14 'And when a man [T]sanctifies his house *to
be* holy to the LORD, then the priest shall set a
value for it, whether it is good or bad; as the
priest values it, so it shall stand. *sets apart*
15 'If he who sanctified it *wants to* [T]redeem
his house, then he shall add one-fifth of the
money of your valuation to it, and it shall be
his. *buy back*

Consecration of Fields

16 'And if a man [T]sanctifies to the LORD
some part of a field of his possession, then
your valuation shall be according to the seed
for it. A homer of barley seed *shall be valued*
at [T]fifty shekels of silver. *sets apart* • $6,400
17 'If he sanctifies his field from the Year of
Jubilee, according to your valuation it shall
stand.
18 'But if he sanctifies his field after the
Jubilee, then the priest shall [R]reckon to him
the money due according to the years that
remain till the Year of Jubilee, and it shall be
deducted from your valuation. Lev. 25:15, 16, 28
19 'And if he who sanctifies the field ever
wishes to redeem it, then he must add one-
fifth of the money of your valuation to it, and
it shall belong to him.
20 'But if he does not want to redeem the
field, or if he has sold the field to another
man, it shall not be redeemed anymore;
21 'but the field, [R]when it is released in the
Jubilee, shall be holy to the LORD, as a [R]de-
voted field; it shall be [R]the possession of the
priest. Lev. 25:10, 28, 31 • Lev. 27:28 • Num. 18:14
22 'And if a man sanctifies to the LORD a
field which he has bought, which is not the
field of [R]his possession, Lev. 25:10, 25
23 'then the priest shall reckon to him the
worth of your valuation, up to the Year of
Jubilee, and he shall give your valuation on
that day *as* a holy *offering* to the LORD.
24 'In the Year of Jubilee the field shall
return to him from whom it was bought, to
the one who *owned* the land as a possession.
25 'And all your valuations shall be according to the [T]shekel of the sanctuary: [R]twenty
gerahs to the shekel. $128 • Ex. 30:13

Firstborn Clean Animals

26 'But the [R]firstling[T] of the beasts, which
should be the LORD's firstling, no man shall
sanctify; whether *it is* an ox or sheep, it *is* the
LORD'S. Ex. 13:2, 12; 22:30 • *firstborn among the animals*
27 'And if *it is* an unclean beast, then he
shall redeem *it* according to your valuation,
and [R]shall add one-fifth to it; or if it is not

redeemed, then it shall be sold according to
your valuation. Lev. 27:11, 12

Devoted Things

28 'Nevertheless no devoted *offering* that a
man may devote to the LORD of all that he
has, *both* man and beast, or the field of his
possession, shall be sold or redeemed; every
devoted *offering is* most holy to the LORD.
29 [R]'No person under the ban, who may
become doomed to destruction among men,
shall be redeemed, *but* shall surely be put to
death. Num. 21:2

Tithes

30 'And [R]all the tithe of the land, *whether* of
the seed of the land *or* of the fruit of the tree,
is the LORD's. It *is* holy to the LORD. Gen. 28:22
31 [R]'If a man wants at all to redeem *any* of
his tithes, he shall add one-fifth to it. Lev. 27:13
32 'And concerning the tithe of the herd or
the flock, of whatever passes under the rod,
the tenth one shall be holy to the LORD.
33 'He shall not inquire whether it is good
or bad, [R]nor shall he exchange it; and if he
exchanges it at all, then both it and the one
exchanged for it shall be holy; it shall not be
redeemed.' " Lev. 27:10

The Conclusion of Leviticus

34 These *are* the commandments which the
LORD commanded Moses for the children of
Israel on Mount [R]Sinai. [Heb. 12:18–29]

Liquid Measures

Unit	*Measure*	*Equivalents*	*Translations*
Kor	60 gallons	10 baths	kor
Metretes	10.2 gallons		gallon
Bath	6 gallons	6 hins	measure, bath
Hin	1 gallon	2 kabs	hin
Kab	2 quarts	4 logs	kab
Log	1 pint	¼ kab	log

THE FOURTH BOOK OF MOSES CALLED

NUMBERS

THE BOOK OF NUMBERS

Numbers is the book of wanderings. It takes its name from the two numberings of the Israelites—the first at Mount Sinai and the second on the plains of Moab. Most of the book, however, describes Israel's experiences as they wander in the wilderness. The lesson of Numbers is clear. While it may be necessary to pass through wilderness experiences, one does not have to live there. For Israel, an eleven-day journey became a forty-year agony.

The title of Numbers comes from the first word in the Hebrew text, *Wayyedabber,* "And He Said." Jewish writings, however, usually refer to it by the fifth Hebrew word in 1:1, *Bemidbar,* "In the Wilderness," which more nearly indicates the content of the book. The Greek title in the Septuagint is *Arithmoi,* "Numbers." The Latin Vulgate followed this title and translated it *Liber Numeri,* "Book of Numbers." These titles are based on the two numberings: the generation of Exodus (Num. 1) and the generation that grew up in the wilderness and conquered Canaan (Num. 26). Numbers has also been called the "Book of the Journeyings," the "Book of the Murmurings," and the "Fourth Book of Moses."

THE AUTHOR OF NUMBERS

The evidence that points to Moses as the author of Numbers is similar to that for the previous books of the Pentateuch. These five books form such a literary unit that they rise or fall together on the matter of authorship.

External Evidence: The Jews, the Samaritans, and the early church give testimony to the Mosaic authorship of Numbers. Also a number of New Testament passages cite events from Numbers and associate them with Moses. These include John 3:14; Acts 7 and 13; First Corinthians 10:1–11; Hebrews 3 and 4; and Jude 11.

Internal Evidence: There are more than eighty claims that "the LORD spoke to Moses" (the first is 1:1). In addition, Numbers 33:2 makes this clear statement: "Now Moses wrote down the starting points of their journeys at the command of the LORD." Moses kept detailed records as an eyewitness of the events in this book. As the central character in Exodus through Deuteronomy, he was better qualified than any other man to write these books.

Some scholars have claimed that the third-person references to Moses point to a different author. However, use of the third person was a common practice in the ancient world. Caesar, for example, did the same in his writings.

THE TIME OF NUMBERS

Leviticus covers only one month, but Numbers stretches over almost thirty-nine years (c. 1444–1405 B.C.). It records Israel's movement from the last twenty days at Mount Sinai (1:1; 10:11), the wandering around Kadesh Barnea, and finally the arrival in the plains of Moab in the fortieth year (22:1; 26:3; 33:50; Deut. 1:3). Their tents occupy several square miles whenever they camp since there are probably over two-and-a-half million people (based on the census figures in Numbers 1 and 26). God miraculously feeds and sustains them in the desert—He preserves their clothing and gives them manna, meat, water, leaders, and a promise (14:34).

THE CHRIST OF NUMBERS

Perhaps the clearest portrait of Christ in Numbers is the bronze serpent on the stake, a picture of the Crucifixion (21:4–9): "And as Moses lifted up the serpent in the wilderness, even so must the Son of Man be lifted up" (John 3:14). The rock that quenches the thirst of the multitudes is also a type of Christ: "they drank of that spiritual Rock that followed them, and that Rock was Christ" (1 Cor. 10:4). The daily manna pictures the Bread of Life who later comes down from heaven (John 6:31–33).

Balaam foresees the rulership of Christ: "I see Him, but not now; I behold Him, but not near; a Star shall come out of Jacob; a Scepter shall rise out of Israel" (24:17). The guidance and presence of Christ is seen in the pillar of cloud and fire, and the sinner's refuge in Christ may be seen in the six cities of refuge. The red heifer sacrifice (Num. 19) is also considered a type of Christ.

KEYS TO NUMBERS

Key Word: Wanderings—Numbers records the failure of Israel to believe in the promise of God and the resulting judgment of wandering in the wilderness for forty years.

Key Verses: Numbers 14:22, 23; 20:12—"Because all these men who have seen My glory and the signs which I did in Egypt and in the wilderness, and have put Me to the test now these ten times, and have not heeded My voice, they certainly shall not see the land of which I swore to their fathers, nor shall any of those who rejected Me see it" (14:22, 23).

"Then the LORD spoke to Moses and Aaron, 'Because you did not believe Me, to hallow Me in the eyes of the children of Israel, therefore you shall not bring this congregation into the land which I have given them' " (20:12).

Key Chapter: Numbers 14—The critical turning point of Numbers may be seen in Numbers 14 when Israel rejects God by refusing to go up and conquer the Promised Land. God judges Israel "according to the number of the days in which you spied out the land, forty days, for each day you shall bear your guilt one year, *namely* forty years, and you shall know My rejection" (14:34).

SURVEY OF NUMBERS

Israel as a nation is in its infancy at the outset of this book, only thirteen months after the exodus from Egypt. In Numbers, the book of divine discipline, it becomes necessary for the nation to go through the painful process of testing and maturation. God must teach His people the consequences of irresponsible decisions. The forty years of wilderness experience transforms them from a rabble of ex-slaves into a nation ready to take the Promised Land. Numbers begins with the old generation (1:1—10:10), moves through a tragic transitional period (10:11—25:18), and ends with the new generation (26—36) at the doorway to the land of Canaan.

The Old Generation (1:1—10:10): The generation that witnessed God's miraculous acts of deliverance and preservation receives further direction from God while they are still at the foot of Mount Sinai (1:1—10:10). God's instructions are very explicit, reaching every aspect of their lives. He is the Author of order, not confusion; and this is seen in the way He organizes the people around the tabernacle. Turning from the outward conditions of the camp (1—4) to the inward conditions (5—10), Numbers describes the spiritual preparation of the people.

The Tragic Transition (10:11—25:18): Israel follows God step by step until Canaan is in sight. Then in the crucial moment at Kadesh they draw back in unbelief. Their murmurings had already become incessant, "Now *when* the people complained, it displeased the LORD; for the LORD heard *it*" (11:1). But their unbelief after sending out the twelve spies at Kadesh Barnea is something God will not tolerate. Their rebellion at Kadesh marks the pivotal point of the book. The generation of the Exodus will not be the generation of the conquest.

Unbelief brings discipline and hinders God's blessing. The old generation is doomed to literally kill time for forty years of wilderness wanderings—one year for every day spent by the twelve spies in inspecting the land. They are judged by disinheritance and death as their journey changes from one of anticipation to one of aimlessness. Only Joshua and Caleb, the two spies who believed God, enter Canaan. Almost nothing is recorded about these transitional years.

The New Generation (26—36): When the transition to the new generation is complete, the people move to the plains of Moab, directly east of the Promised Land (22:1). Before they can enter the land they must wait until all is ready. Here they receive new instructions, a new census is taken, Joshua is appointed as Moses' successor, and some of the people settle in the Transjordan.

Numbers records two generations (1—14 and 21—36), two numberings (1 and 26), two journeyings (10—14 and 21—27), and two sets of instructions (5—9 and 28—36). It illustrates both the kindness and severity of God (Rom. 11:22) and teaches that God's people can move forward only as they trust and depend on Him.

FOCUS	THE OLD GENERATION		THE TRAGIC TRANSITION				THE NEW GENERATION		
REFERENCE	1:1	5:1	10:11	13:1	15:1	20:1	26:1	28:1	31:1—36:13
DIVISION	ORGANIZATION OF ISRAEL	SANCTIFICATION OF ISRAEL	TO KADESH	AT KADESH	IN WILDERNESS	TO MOAB	REORGANIZATION OF ISRAEL	REGULATIONS OF OFFERINGS AND VOWS	CONQUEST AND DIVISION OF ISRAEL
TOPIC	ORDER		DISORDER				REORDER		
	PREPARATION		POSTPONEMENT				PREPARATION		
LOCATION	MOUNT SINAI		WILDERNESS				PLAINS OF MOAB		
TIME	20 DAYS		38 YEARS 3 MONTHS AND 10 DAYS				c. 5 MONTHS		

OUTLINE OF NUMBERS

Part One: The Preparation of the Old Generation to Inherit the Promised Land (1:1—10:10)

I. The Organization of Israel . . . . 1:1—4:49

A. Organization of the People . . . . 1:1—2:34
1. The First Census of Israel 1:1–54
2. Arrangement of the Camp. 2:1–34
a. On the East 2:1–9
b. On the South 2:10–16
c. On the Middle 2:17
d. On the West. 2:18–24
e. On the North 2:25–31
f. The Camp Is Arranged. 2:32–34

B. Organization of the Priests . . . . 3:1—4:49
1. The Census of the Levites 3:1–39
a. The Family of Aaron. 3:1–5
b. The Ministry of the Levites 3:6–13
c. The Census Is Commanded 3:14–20
d. The Census of Gershon. 3:21–26
e. The Census of Kohath 3:27–32
f. The Census of Merari 3:33–37
g. The Summary of the Census . . . 3:38, 39
2. The Substitution of the Levites for the Firstborn. 3:40–51
3. The Ministry of the Levites. 4:1–49
a. The Ministry of Kohath 4:1–20
b. The Ministry of Gershon 4:21–28
c. The Ministry of Merari. 4:29–33
d. The Census of the Working Levites 4:34–49

II. Sanctification of Israel. . . . . 5:1—10:10

A. Sanctification Through Separation 5:1–31
1. Separation of Unclean Persons 5:1–4
2. Separation in Restitution for Sin. . . . 5:5–10
3. Separation from Suspected Infidelity 5:11–31

B. Sanctification Through the Nazirite Vow. 6:1–27

C. Sanctification Through Worship . . . . 7:1—9:14
1. Israel Gives Donations 7:1–89
2. The Levites Are Consecrated 8:1–26
3. The Passover Is Celebrated 9:1–14

D. Sanctification Through Divine Guidance . . . . 9:15—10:10
1. Guidance of the Cloud. 9:15–23
2. Guidance of the Silver Trumpets . . 10:1–10

Part Two: The Failure of the Old Generation to Inherit the Promised Land (10:11—25:18)

I. The Failure of Israel En Route to Kadesh . . . . 10:11—12:16

A. Israel Departs Mount Sinai. 10:11–36
B. Failure of the People. 11:1–9
1. Israel Complains About Circumstances. 11:1–3
2. Israel Complains About Food 11:4–9
C. Failure of Moses 11:10–15
1. Moses Complains About the People 11:10–13
2. Moses Complains About His Own Life 11:14, 15
D. God Provides for Moses 11:16–30
E. God Provides for the People. 11:31–35
1. God Provides Quail 11:31, 32
2. God Sends Plagues 11:33–35
F. Failure of Miriam and Aaron 12:1–16
1. Miriam and Aaron Rebel 12:1–3
2. Miriam Is Punished 12:4–10
3. Moses Intercedes 12:11–13
4. Miriam Is Restored. 12:14–16

II. The Climactic Failure of Israel at Kadesh. . . . . 13:1—14:45

A. Investigation of the Promised Land. . . 13:1–33
B. Israel Rebels Against God. 14:1–10
C. Moses Intercedes 14:11–19
D. God Judges Israel. 14:20–38
1. Israel to Wander and Die 14:20–35
2. Spies Die Immediately 14:36–38
E. Israel Rebels Against the Judgment of God. 14:39–45
1. Moses Warns Israel. 14:39–44
2. Amalekites Defeat Israel 14:45

III. The Failure of Israel in the Wilderness . . . . 15:1—19:22

A. Review of the Offerings 15:1–41
1. Offerings to Thank the Lord 15:1–21
2. Offerings for Unintentional Sins . . 15:22–29
3. No Offering for Intentional Sins . . 15:30–36
4. The Tassel on the Garment 15:37–41
B. Rebellion of Korah. 16:1–40
1. Korah Rebels Against Moses and Aaron 16:1–14
2. God Judges Korah. 16:15–40
C. Rebellion of Israel Against Moses and Aaron. 16:41–50
1. Israel Rebels Against Moses and Aaron 16:41
2. God Judges Israel 16:42–50
D. Role of the Priesthood . . . . 17:1—19:22
1. Confirmation of the Divine Call . . . 17:1–13
2. Remuneration of the Priesthood . . . 18:1–32
3. Purification of the Red Heifer. 19:1–22

IV. The Failure of Israel En Route to Moab. . . . . 20:1—25:18

A. Miriam Dies 20:1
B. Moses and Aaron Fail 20:2–13
1. The Sin of Israel. 20:2–6
2. The Command of God. 20:7, 8
3. The Sin of Moses 20:9–13
C. Edom Refuses Passage 20:14–21
D. Aaron Dies 20:22–29
E. Israel's Victory over the Canaanites . . . 21:1–3
F. The Failure of Israel 21:4–9
1. Israel Complains. 21:4, 5
2. God Judges with Serpents 21:6
3. The Bronze Serpent 21:7–9
G. Journey to Moab 21:10–20

Part Three: The Preparation of the New Generation to Inherit the Promised Land (26:1—36:13)

CHAPTER 1

The First Census of Israel

NOW the LORD spoke to Moses in the
Wilderness of Sinai, in the tabernacle of
meeting, on the first *day* of the second
month, in the second year after they had
come out of the land of Egypt, saying:
2 "Take a census of all the congregation of
the children of Israel, by their families, by
their fathers' houses, according to the number of names, every male individually,
3 "from twenty years old and above—all
who *are able to* go to war in Israel. You and
Aaron shall number them by their armies.
4 "And with you there shall be a man from
every tribe, each one the head of his father's
house.
5 "These are the names of the men who
shall stand with you: from Reuben, Elizur the
son of Shedeur;
6 "from Simeon, Shelumiel the son of Zurishaddai;
7 "from Judah, Nahshon the son of Amminadab;
8 "from Issachar, Nethaneel the son of
Zuar;
9 "from Zebulun, Eliab the son of Helon;
10 "from the sons of Joseph: from Ephraim,
Elishama the son of Ammihud; from Manasseh, Gamaliel the son of Pedahzur;
11 "from Benjamin, Abidan the son of Gideoni;
12 "from Dan, Ahiezer the son of Ammishaddai;
13 "from Asher, Pagiel the son of Ocran;
14 "from Gad, Eliasaph the son of Deuel;
15 "from Naphtali, Ahira the son of Enan."
16 These *were* [T]chosen from the congregation, leaders of their fathers' tribes, [R]heads of
the divisions in Israel. *called* • Ex. 18:21, 25
17 Then Moses and Aaron took these men
who had been mentioned [R]by name, Is. 43:1

18 and they assembled all the congregation together on the first *day* of the second month; and they recited their [R]ancestry by families, by their fathers' houses, according to the number of names, from twenty years old and above, each one individually. Ezra 2:59

19 As the LORD commanded Moses, so he numbered them in the Wilderness of Sinai.

20 Now the [R]children of Reuben, Israel's oldest son, their genealogies by their families, by their fathers' house, according to the number of names, every male individually, from twenty years old and above, all who *were able to* go to war: Num. 2:10, 11; 26:5–11

21 those who were numbered of the tribe of Reuben *were* forty-six thousand five hundred.

22 From the children of Simeon, their genealogies by their families, by their fathers' house, of those who were numbered, according to the number of names, every male individually, from twenty years old and above, all who *were able to* go to war:

23 those who were numbered of the tribe of Simeon *were* fifty-nine thousand three hundred.

24 From the [R]children of Gad, their genealogies by their families, by their fathers' house, according to the number of names, from twenty years old and above, all who *were able to* go to war: Num. 26:15–18

25 those who were numbered of the tribe of Gad *were* forty-five thousand six hundred and fifty.

26 From the [R]children of Judah, their genealogies by their families, by their fathers' house, according to the number of names, from twenty years old and above, all who *were able to* go to war: 2 Sam. 24:9

27 those who were numbered of the tribe of Judah *were* [R]seventy-four thousand six hundred. 2 Chr. 17:14

28 From the [R]children of Issachar, their genealogies by their families, by their fathers' house, according to the number of names, from twenty years old and above, all who *were able to* go to war: Num. 2:5, 6

29 those who were numbered of the tribe of Issachar *were* fifty-four thousand four hundred.

30 From the [R]children of Zebulun, their genealogies by their families, by their fathers' house, according to the number of names, from twenty years old and above, all who *were able to* go to war: Num. 2:7, 8; 26:26, 27

31 those who were numbered of the tribe of Zebulun *were* fifty-seven thousand four hundred.

32 From the sons of Joseph, the children of Ephraim, their genealogies by their families, by their fathers' house, according to the number of names, from twenty years old and above, all who *were able to* go to war:

33 those who were numbered of the tribe of Ephraim *were* forty thousand five hundred.

34 From the [R]children of Manasseh, their genealogies by their families, by their fathers' house, according to the number of names, from twenty years old and above, all who *were able to* go to war: Num. 2:20, 21; 26:28–34

35 those who were numbered of the tribe of Manasseh *were* thirty-two thousand two hundred.

36 From the [R]children of Benjamin, their genealogies by their families, by their fathers' house, according to the number of names, from twenty years old and above, all who *were able to* go to war: Num. 26:38–41

37 those who were numbered of the tribe of Benjamin *were* thirty-five thousand four hundred.

38 From the [R]children of Dan, their genealogies by their families, by their fathers' house, according to the number of names, from twenty years old and above, all who *were able to* go to war: Gen. 30:6; 46:23

39 those who were numbered of the tribe of Dan *were* sixty-two thousand seven hundred.

40 From the [R]children of Asher, their genealogies by their families, by their fathers' house, according to the number of names, from twenty years old and above, all who *were able to* go to war: Num. 2:27, 28; 26:44–47

41 those who were numbered of the tribe of Asher *were* forty-one thousand five hundred.

42 From the children of Naphtali, their genealogies by their families, by their fathers' house, according to the number of names, from twenty years old and above, all who *were able to* go to war:

43 those who were numbered of the tribe of Naphtali *were* fifty-three thousand four hundred.

44 [R]These are the ones who were numbered, whom Moses and Aaron numbered, with the leaders of Israel, twelve men, each one representing his father's house. Num. 26:64

45 So all who were numbered of the children of Israel, by their fathers' houses, from twenty years old and above, all who *were able to* go to war in Israel—

46 all who were numbered were [R]six hundred and three thousand five hundred and fifty. Ex. 12:37; 38:26

47 But the Levites were not numbered among them by their fathers' tribe;

48 for the LORD had spoken to Moses, saying:

49 [R]"Only the tribe of Levi you shall not number, nor take a census of them among the children of Israel; Num. 2:33; 26:62

50 "but you shall appoint the Levites over the tabernacle of the Testimony, over all its furnishings, and over all things that belong to it; they shall carry the tabernacle and all its furnishings; they shall attend to it [R]and camp around the tabernacle. Num. 3:23, 29, 35, 38

51 "And when the tabernacle is to go forward, the Levites shall take it down; and when the tabernacle is to be set up, the Levites shall set it [R]up. The outsider who comes near shall be put to death. Num. 10:21

52 "The children of Israel shall pitch their tents, [R]everyone by his own camp, everyone by his own standard, according to their armies; Num. 2:2, 34; 24:2

53 "but the Levites shall camp around the tabernacle of the Testimony, that there may be no wrath on the congregation of the children of Israel; and the Levites shall keep charge of the tabernacle of the Testimony."

54 Thus the children of Israel did; according to all that the LORD commanded Moses, so they did.

CHAPTER 2

On the East

AND the LORD spoke to Moses and Aaron, saying:

2 [R]"Everyone of the children of Israel shall camp by his own [T]standard, beside the emblems of his father's house; they shall camp [R]some distance from the tabernacle of meeting. Num. 1:52; 24:2 • *banner* • Josh. 3:4

3 "On the east side, toward the rising of the sun, those of the standard of the forces with Judah shall camp according to their armies; and Nahshon the son of Amminadab *shall be* the leader of the children of Judah."

4 And his army was numbered at seventy-four thousand six hundred.

5 "Those who camp next to him *shall be* the tribe of Issachar, and Nethanel the son of Zuar *shall be* the leader of the children of Issachar."

6 And his army was numbered at fifty-four thousand four hundred.

7 "Then *shall come* the tribe of Zebulun, and Eliab the son of Helon *shall be* the leader of the children of Zebulun."

8 And his army was numbered at fifty-seven thousand four hundred.

9 "All who were numbered according to their armies of the forces with Judah, one hundred and eighty-six thousand four hundred—these shall [T]break camp first. *set forth*

On the South

10 "On the south side *shall be* the standard of the forces with Reuben according to their armies, and the leader of the children of Reuben *shall be* Elizur the son of Shedeur."

11 And his army was numbered at forty-six thousand five hundred.

12 "Those who camp next to him *shall be* the tribe of Simeon, and the leader of the children of Simeon *shall be* Shelumiel the son of Zurishaddai."

13 And his army was numbered at fifty-nine thousand three hundred.

14 "Then *shall come* the tribe of Gad, and the leader of the children of Gad *shall be* Eliasaph the son of [T]Reuel." *Deuel*, Num. 1:14; 7:42

15 And his army was numbered at forty-five thousand six hundred and fifty.

16 "All who were numbered according to their armies of the forces with Reuben, one hundred and fifty-one thousand four hundred and fifty—[R]they shall [T]be the second to break camp. Num. 10:18 • *set forth second*

On the Middle

17 "Then the tabernacle of meeting shall move out with the [T]camp of the Levites in the middle of the [T]camps; as they camp, so they shall move out, everyone in his place, by their [T]standards. *company* • *whole company* • *banners*

On the West

18 "On the west side *shall be* the standard of the forces with Ephraim according to their armies, and the leader of the children of Ephraim *shall be* Elishama the son of Ammihud."

19 And his army was numbered at forty thousand five hundred.

20 "Next to him *shall be* the tribe of Manasseh, and the leader of the children of Manasseh *shall be* Gamaliel the son of Pedahzur."

21 And his army was numbered at thirty-two thousand two hundred.

22 "Then *shall come* the tribe of Benjamin, and the leader of the children of Benjamin *shall be* Abidan the son of Gideoni."

23 And his army was numbered at thirty-five thousand four hundred.

24 "All who were numbered according to their armies of the forces with Ephraim, one hundred and eight thousand one hundred—they shall be the third to break camp.

On the North

25 "The standard of the forces with Dan *shall be* on the north side according to their armies, and the leader of the children of Dan *shall be* Ahiezer the son of Ammishaddai."

26 And his army was numbered at sixty-two thousand seven hundred.

27 "Those who camp next to him *shall be* the tribe of Asher, and the leader of the children of Asher *shall be* Pagiel the son of Ocran."

28 And his army was numbered at forty-one thousand five hundred.

29 "Then *shall come* the tribe of Naphtali, and the leader of the children of Naphtali *shall be* Ahira the son of Enan."

30 And his army was numbered at fifty-three thousand four hundred.

31 "All who were numbered of the forces with Dan, one hundred and fifty-seven

thousand six hundred—they shall break
camp last, with their [T]standards." *banners*

The Camp Is Arranged

32 These *are* the ones who were numbered
of the children of Israel by their fathers'
houses. All who were numbered according to
their armies of the forces *were* six hundred
and three thousand five hundred and fifty.
33 But [R]the Levites were not numbered
among the children of Israel, just as the LORD
commanded Moses. Num. 1:47; 26:57–62
34 Thus the children of Israel did according
to all that the LORD commanded Moses; so
they camped by their [T]standards and so they
broke camp, each one by his family, according to their fathers' houses. *banners*

CHAPTER 3

The Family of Aaron

NOW these *are* the [R]records[T] of Aaron and
Moses when the LORD spoke with Mo-
ses on Mount Sinai. Ex. 6:16–27 • Lit. *generations*
2 And these *are* the names of the sons of
Aaron: Nadab, the [R]firstborn, and [R]Abihu,
Eleazar, and Ithamar. Ex. 6:23 • Num. 26:60, 61
3 These *are* the names of the sons of
Aaron, [R]the anointed priests, whom he consecrated to minister as priests. Ex. 28:41
4 [R]Nadab and Abihu had died before the
LORD when they offered profane fire before
the LORD in the Wilderness of Sinai; and they
had no children. So Eleazar and Ithamar
ministered as priests under the oversight of
Aaron their father. 1 Chr. 24:2
5 And the LORD spoke to Moses, saying:

The Ministry of the Levites

6 [R]"Bring the tribe of Levi near, and present them before Aaron the priest, that they
may serve him. Num. 8:6–22; 18:1–7
7 "And they shall attend to his needs and
the needs of the whole congregation before
the tabernacle of meeting, to do [R]the work
of the tabernacle. Num. 1:50; 8:11, 15, 24, 26
8 "Also they shall attend to all the furnishings of the tabernacle of meeting, and to the
needs of the children of Israel, to do the work
of the tabernacle.
9 "And you shall give the Levites to Aaron
and his sons; they *are* given entirely to *him
from among the children of Israel.
10 "So you shall appoint Aaron and his
sons, [R]and they shall attend to their priesthood; [R]but the outsider who comes near shall
be put to death." Ex. 29:9 • Num. 1:51; 3:38; 16:40
11 Then the LORD spoke to Moses, saying:
12 "Now behold, I Myself have taken the
Levites from among the children of Israel
instead of every firstborn who opens the
womb among the children of Israel. Therefore the Levites shall be [R]Mine, Num. 3:45
13 "because all the firstborn *are* Mine. [R]On
the day that I struck all the firstborn in the
land of Egypt, I sanctified to Myself all the
firstborn in Israel, both man and beast. They
shall be Mine: I *am* the LORD." Num. 8:17

The Census Is Commanded

14 Then the LORD spoke to Moses in the
Wilderness of Sinai, saying:
15 "Number the children of Levi by their
fathers' houses, by their families; you shall
number [R]every male from a month old and
above." Num. 3:39; 26:62
16 So Moses numbered them according to
the [T]word of the LORD, as he was commanded. Lit. *mouth*
17 These were the sons of Levi by their
names: Gershon, Kohath, and Merari.
18 And these *are* the names of the sons of
Gershon by their families: Libni and Shimei.
19 And the sons of Kohath by their families:
Amram, Izehar, Hebron, and Uzziel.
20 [R]And the sons of Merari by their families:
Mahli and Mushi. These *are* the families of
the Levites by their fathers' houses. Ex. 6:19

The Census of Gershon

21 From Gershon *came* the family of the
Libnites and the family of the Shimites; these
were the families of the Gershonites.
22 Those who were numbered, according to
the number of all the males from a month old
and above—of those who were numbered
there were seven thousand five hundred.
23 The families of the Gershonites were to
camp behind the tabernacle westward.
24 And the leader of the fathers' house of
the Gershonites *was* Eliasaph the son of Lael.
25 The duties of the children of Gershon in
the tabernacle of meeting *included* [R]the tabernacle, [R]the tent with [R]its covering, [R]the
screen for the door of the tabernacle of
meeting, Ex. 25:9 • Ex. 26:1 • Ex. 26:7, 14 • Ex. 26:36
26 the screen for the door of the court, the
hangings of the court which *are* around the
tabernacle and the altar, and their cords,
according to all the work relating to them.

The Census of Kohath

27 [R]From Kohath *came* the family of the
Amramites, the family of the Izharites, the
family of the Hebronites, and the family of
the Uzzielites; these *were* the families of the
Kohathites. 1 Chr. 26:23
28 According to the number of all the
males, from a month old and above, *there
were* eight thousand *six hundred [T]keeping
charge of the sanctuary. *taking care of*
29 [R]The families of the children of Kohath
were to camp on the south side of the tabernacle. Num. 1:53

3:9 Sam., LXX *Me* **3:28** Some LXX mss. *three*

30 And the leader of the fathers' house of the families of the Kohathites *was* Elizaphan the son of [R]Uzziel. Lev. 10:4

31 Their duty *included* the ark, the table, the lampstand, the altars, the utensils of the sanctuary with which they ministered, the screen, and all the work relating to them.

32 And Eleazar the son of Aaron the priest *was to be* chief over the leaders of the Levites, *with* oversight of those who kept charge of the sanctuary.

The Census of Merari

33 From Merari *came* the family of the Mahlites and the family of the Mushites; these *were* the families of Merari.

34 And those who were numbered, according to the number of all the males from a month old and above, *were* six thousand two hundred.

35 The leader of the fathers' house of the families of Merari *was* Zuriel the son of Abihail. [R]These *were* to camp on the north side of the tabernacle. Num. 1:53; 2:25

36 And [R]the appointed duty of the children of Merari *included* the boards of the tabernacle, its bars, its pillars, its sockets, its utensils, all the work relating to them, Num. 4:31, 32

37 and the pillars of the court all around, with their sockets, their pegs, and their cords.

The Summary of the Census

38 Moreover those who were to camp before the tabernacle on the east, before the tabernacle of meeting, *were* Moses, Aaron, and his sons, keeping charge of the sanctuary, [R]to meet the needs of the children of Israel; but [R]the outsider who came near was to be put to death. Num. 3:7, 8 • Num. 3:10

39 [R]All who were numbered of the Levites, whom Moses and Aaron numbered at the commandment of the LORD, by their families, all the males from a month old and above, *were* twenty-two thousand. Num. 3:43; 4:48; 26:62

The Substitution of the Levites for the Firstborn

40 Then the LORD said to Moses: [R]"Number[T] all the firstborn males of the children of Israel from a month old and above, and take the number of their names. Num. 3:15 • *Take a census of*

41 [R]"And you shall take the Levites for Me—I *am* the LORD—instead of all the firstborn among the children of Israel, and the livestock of the Levites instead of all the firstborn among the livestock of the children of Israel." Num. 3:12, 45

42 So Moses numbered all the firstborn among the children of Israel, as the LORD commanded him.

43 And all the firstborn males, according to the number of names from a month old and above, of those who were numbered of them, were twenty-two thousand two hundred and seventy-three.

44 Then the LORD spoke to Moses, saying:

45 [R]"Take the Levites instead of all the firstborn among the children of Israel, and the livestock of the Levites instead of their livestock. The Levites shall be Mine: I *am* the LORD. Num. 3:12, 41

46 "And for [R]the redemption of the two hundred and seventy-three of the firstborn of the children of Israel, [R]who are more than the number of the Levites, Ex. 13:13, 15 • Num. 3:39, 43

47 "you shall take [R]five shekels for each one individually; you shall take *them* in the currency of the shekel of the sanctuary, [R]the shekel of twenty gerahs. Lev. 27:6 • Ex. 30:13

48 "And you shall give the money, with which the excess number of them is redeemed, to Aaron and his sons."

49 So Moses took the redemption money from those who were over and above those who were redeemed by the Levites.

50 From the firstborn of the children of Israel he took the money, [R]one thousand three hundred and sixty-five *shekels*, according to the shekel of the sanctuary. Num. 3:46, 47

51 And Moses [R]gave their redemption money to Aaron and his sons, according to the word of the LORD, as the LORD commanded Moses. Num. 3:48

CHAPTER 4

The Ministry of Kohath

THEN the LORD spoke to Moses and Aaron, saying:

2 "Take a census of the sons of [R]Kohath from among the children of Levi, by their families, by their fathers' house, Num. 3:27–32

3 "from thirty years old and above, even to fifty years old, all who enter the service to do the work in the tabernacle of meeting.

4 [R]"This *is* the service of the sons of Kohath in the tabernacle of meeting, *relating to* [R]the most holy things: Num. 4:15 • Num. 4:19

5 "When the camp prepares to journey, Aaron and his sons shall come, and they shall take down the covering veil and cover the [R]ark of the Testimony with it. Ex. 25:10, 16

6 "Then they shall put on it a covering of badger skins, and spread over *that* a cloth entirely of [R]blue; and they shall insert [R]its poles. Ex. 39:1 • Ex. 25:13

7 "On the table of showbread they shall spread a blue cloth, and put on it the dishes, the pans, the bowls, and the pitchers for pouring; and the showbread shall be on it.

8 "They shall spread over them a scarlet cloth, and cover the same with a covering of badger skins; and they shall insert its poles.

9 "And they shall take a blue cloth and cover the lampstand of the light, with its

lamps, its wick-trimmers, its trays, and all its oil vessels, with which they service it.

10 "Then they shall put it with all its utensils in a covering of badger skins, and put *it* on a carrying beam.

11 "Over the golden altar they shall spread a blue cloth, and cover it with a covering of badger skins; and they shall insert its poles.

12 "Then they shall take all the [R]utensils of service with which they minister in the sanctuary, put *them* in a blue cloth, cover them with a covering of badger skins, and put *them* on a carrying beam. Ex. 25:9

13 "Also they shall take away the ashes from the altar, and spread a purple cloth over it.

14 "They shall put on it all its implements with which they minister there—the firepans, the forks, the shovels, the [T]basins, and all the utensils of the altar—and they shall spread on it a covering of badger skins, and insert its poles. *bowls*

15 "And when Aaron and his sons have finished covering the sanctuary and all the furnishings of the sanctuary, when the camp is set to go, then the sons of Kohath shall come to carry *them*; but they shall not touch any holy thing, lest they die. [R]These *are* the things in the tabernacle of meeting which the sons of Kohath are to carry. Num. 3:31

16 "The appointed duty of Eleazar the son of Aaron the priest *is* the oil for the light, the sweet incense, [R]the daily grain offering, the [R]anointing oil, the oversight of all the tabernacle, of all that *is* in it, with the sanctuary and its furnishings." Ex. 29:38 • Ex. 30:23–25

17 Then the LORD spoke to Moses and Aaron, saying:

18 "Do not cut off the tribe of the families of the Kohathites from among the Levites;

19 "but do this in regard to them, that they may live and not die when they approach [R]the most holy things: Aaron and his sons shall go in and [T]appoint each of them to his service and his task. Num. 4:4 • *assign*

20 [R]"But they shall not go in to watch while the holy things are being covered, lest they die." Ex. 19:21

The Ministry of Gershon

21 Then the LORD spoke to Moses, saying:

22 "Also take a census of the sons of [R]Gershon, by their fathers' house, by their families. Num. 3:22

23 [R]"From thirty years old and above, even to fifty years old, you shall number them, all who enter to perform the service, to do the work in the tabernacle of meeting. Num. 4:3

24 "This *is* the [R]service of the families of the Gershonites, in serving and carrying: Num. 7:7

25 "They shall carry the [R]curtains of the tabernacle and the tabernacle of meeting *with* its covering, the covering of [R]badger skins that *is* on it, the screen for the door of the tabernacle of meeting, Ex. 36:8 • Ex. 26:14

26 "the screen for the door of the gate of the court, the hangings of the court which *are* around the tabernacle and altar, and their cords, all the furnishings for their service and all that is made for these things: so shall they serve.

27 "Aaron and his sons shall assign all the service of the sons of the Gershonites, all their tasks and all their service. And you shall appoint to them all their tasks as their duty.

28 "This *is* the service of the families of the sons of Gershon in the tabernacle of meeting. And their duties *shall be* [R]under the hand of Ithamar the son of Aaron the priest. Num. 4:33

The Ministry of Merari

29 "*As for* the sons of [R]Merari, you shall number them by their families and by their fathers' house. Num. 3:33–37

30 "From thirty years old and above, even to fifty years old, you shall number them, everyone who enters the service to do the work of the tabernacle of meeting.

31 "And this *is* [R]what they must carry as all their service for the tabernacle of meeting: [R]the boards of the tabernacle, its bars, its pillars, its sockets, Num. 7:8 • Ex. 26:15

32 "and the pillars around the court with their sockets, pegs, and cords, with all their furnishings and all their service; and you shall [R]assign *to each man* by name the items he must carry. Ex. 25:9; 38:21

33 "This *is* the service of the families of the sons of Merari, as all their service for the tabernacle of meeting, under the hand of Ithamar the son of Aaron the priest."

The Census of the Working Levites

34 [R]And Moses, Aaron, and the leaders of the congregation numbered the sons of the Kohathites by their families and by their fathers' house, Num. 4:2

35 from thirty years old and above, even to fifty years old, everyone who entered the service for work in the tabernacle of meeting;

36 and those who were numbered by their families were two thousand seven hundred and fifty.

37 These *were* the ones who were numbered of the families of the Kohathites, all who might serve in the tabernacle of meeting, whom Moses and Aaron numbered according to the commandment of the LORD by the hand of Moses.

38 And those who were numbered of the sons of Gershon, by their families and by their fathers' house,

39 from thirty years old and above, even to fifty years old, everyone who entered the

service for work in the tabernacle of meeting—
40 those who were numbered by their families, by their fathers' house, were two thousand six hundred and thirty.
41 These *are* the ones who were numbered
of the families of the sons of Gershon, of all
who might serve in the tabernacle of meeting, whom Moses and Aaron numbered according to the commandment of the LORD.
42 Those of the families of the sons of
Merari who were numbered, by their families,
by their fathers' [T]house, *household*
43 from thirty years old and above, even to
fifty years old, everyone who entered the
service for work in the tabernacle of meeting—
44 those who were numbered by their families were three thousand two hundred.
45 These *are* the ones who were numbered
of the families of the sons of Merari, whom
Moses and Aaron numbered according to the
word of the LORD by the hand of Moses.
46 All who were [R]numbered of the Levites,
whom Moses, Aaron, and the leaders of Israel
numbered, by their families and by their
fathers' houses, 1 Chr. 23:3–23
47 from thirty years old and above, even to
fifty years old, everyone who came to do the
work of service and the work of bearing
burdens in the tabernacle of meeting—
48 those who were numbered were eight
thousand five hundred and eighty.
49 According to the commandment of the
LORD they were numbered by the hand of
Moses, [R]each according to his service and
according to his task; thus were they numbered by him, [R]as the LORD commanded
Moses. Num. 4:15, 24, 31 • Num. 4:1, 21

CHAPTER 5

Separation of Unclean Persons

AND the LORD spoke to Moses, saying:
2 "Command the children of Israel that
they put out of the camp every leper, everyone who has a discharge, and whoever becomes [R]defiled by a *dead* body. Lev. 21:1
3 "You shall put out both male and female;
you shall put them outside the camp, that
they may not defile their camps [R]in the midst
of which I dwell." Lev. 26:11, 12
4 And the children of Israel did so, and put
them outside the camp; as the LORD spoke to
Moses, so the children of Israel did.

Separation in Restitution for Sin

5 Then the LORD spoke to Moses, saying,
6 "Speak to the children of Israel: [R]'When
a man or woman commits any sin that men
commit in unfaithfulness against the LORD,
and that person is guilty, Lev. 5:14—6:7
7 'then he shall confess the sin which he
has done. He shall make restitution for his
trespass in full *value* plus one-fifth of it, and
give *it* to the one he has wronged.
8 'But if the man has no [T]kinsman to
whom restitution may be made for the
wrong, the restitution for the wrong *must* go
to the LORD for the priest, in addition to [R]the
ram of the atonement with which atonement
is made for him. Lit. *redeemer* • Lev. 5:15; 6:6, 7; 7:7
9 'Every [R]offering[T] of all the holy things of
the children of Israel, which they bring to the
priest, shall be his. Ex. 29:28 • *heave offering*
10 'And every man's [T]holy things shall be
his; whatever any man gives the priest shall
be [R]his.'" *consecrated* • Lev. 10:13

Separation from Suspected Infidelity

11 And the LORD spoke to Moses, saying,
12 "Speak to the children of Israel, and say
to them: 'If any man's wife goes astray and
behaves unfaithfully toward him,
13 'and a man [R]lies with her carnally, and it
is hidden from the eyes of her husband, and it
is concealed that she has defiled herself, and
there was no witness against her, nor was she
[R]caught— Lev. 18:20; 20:10 • John 8:4
14 'if the spirit of jealousy comes upon him
and he becomes [R]jealous of his wife, who has
defiled herself; or if the spirit of jealousy
comes upon him and he becomes jealous of
his wife, although she has not defiled herself— Prov. 6:34
15 'then the man shall bring his wife to the
priest. He shall [R]bring the offering required
for her, one-tenth of an ephah of barley meal;
he shall pour no oil on it and put no frankincense on it, because it *is* a grain offering of
jealousy, an offering for remembering, for
bringing iniquity to remembrance. Lev. 5:11
16 'And the priest shall bring her near, and
set her before the LORD.
17 'The priest shall take holy water in an
earthen vessel, and take some of the dust
that is on the floor of the tabernacle and put
it into the water.
18 'Then the priest shall stand the woman
before the [R]LORD, uncover the woman's head,
and put the offering for remembering in her
hands, which *is* the grain offering of jealousy.
And the priest shall have in his hand the
bitter water that brings a curse. Heb. 13:4
19 'And the priest shall put her under oath,
and say to the woman, "If no man has lain
with you, and if you have not gone astray to
uncleanness *while* under your husband's
authority, be free from this bitter water that
brings a curse.
20 "But if you have gone astray *while* under
your husband's *authority*, and if you have
defiled yourself and some man other than
your husband has lain with you"—
21 'then the priest shall [R]put the woman
under the oath of the curse, and he shall say

to the woman—[R]"the LORD make you a curse
and an oath among your people, when the
LORD makes your thigh [T]rot and your belly
swell; Josh. 6:26 • Jer. 29:22 • Lit. *fall away*
22 "and may this water that causes the
curse go into your stomach, and make *your*
belly swell and *your* thigh rot." Then the
woman shall say, "Amen, so be it."
23 'Then the priest shall write these curses
in a book, and he shall scrape *them* off into
the bitter water.
24 'And he shall make the woman drink the
bitter water that brings a curse, and the
water that brings the curse shall enter her *to*
become bitter.
25 [R]'Then the priest shall take the grain
offering of jealousy from the woman's hand,
shall [R]wave the offering before the LORD, and
bring it to the altar; Lev. 8:27 • Lev. 2:2, 9
26 'and the priest shall take a handful of the
offering, [R]as its memorial portion, burn *it* on
the altar, and afterward make the woman
drink the water. Lev. 2:2, 9
27 'When he has made her drink the water,
then it shall be, if she has defiled herself and
behaved unfaithfully toward her husband,
that the water that brings a curse will enter
her *and become* bitter, and her belly will
swell, her thigh will rot, and the woman [R]will
become a curse among her people. Num. 5:21
28 'But if the woman has not defiled herself,
and is clean, then she shall be free and may
conceive children.
29 'This *is* the law of jealousy, when a wife,
while under her husband's *authority*, [R]goes
astray and defiles herself, Num. 5:19
30 'or when the spirit of jealousy comes
upon a man, and he becomes jealous of his
wife; then he shall stand the woman before
the LORD, and the priest shall execute all this
law upon her.
31 'Then the man shall be free from iniquity, but that woman shall bear her guilt.' "

CHAPTER 6

Sanctification Through the Nazirite Vow

THEN the LORD spoke to Moses, saying,
2 "Speak to the children of Israel, and
say to them: 'When either a man or woman
consecrates an offering to take the vow of a
Nazirite, to separate himself to the LORD,
3 'he shall separate himself from wine and
similar drink; he shall drink neither vinegar
made from wine nor vinegar made from
similar drink; neither shall he drink any
grape juice, nor eat fresh grapes or raisins.
4 'All the days of his [T]separation he shall
eat nothing that is produced by the grapevine, from seed to skin. Separation as a Nazirite
5 'All the days of the vow of his separation
no [R]razor shall come upon his head; until the
days are fulfilled for which he separated
himself to the LORD, he shall be holy. *Then* he
shall let the locks of the hair of his head
grow. 1 Sam. 1:11
6 'All the days that he separates himself to
the LORD he shall not go near a dead body.
7 'He shall not make himself unclean even
for his father or his mother, for his brother or
his sister, when they die, because his separation to God *is* on his head.
8 [R]'All the days of his separation he shall
be holy to the LORD. [2 Cor. 6:17, 18]
9 'And if anyone dies very suddenly beside
him, and he defiles his consecrated head, then
he shall [R]shave his head on the day of his
cleansing; on the seventh day he shall shave
it. Lev. 14:8, 9
10 'Then [R]on the eighth day he shall bring
two turtledoves or two young pigeons to the
priest, to the door of the tabernacle of meeting; Lev. 5:7; 14:22; 15:14, 29
11 'and the priest shall offer one as a sin
offering and *the* other as a burnt offering, and
make atonement for him, because he sinned
by reason of the *dead* body; and he shall
sanctify his head that same day.
12 'He shall consecrate to the LORD the days
of his separation, and bring a male lamb in its
first year [R]as a trespass offering; but the
former days shall be [T]lost, because his separation was defiled. Lev. 5:6 • *void*
13 'Now this *is* the law of the Nazirite:
[R]When the days of his separation are fulfilled,
he shall be brought to the door of the tabernacle of meeting. Acts 21:26
14 'And he shall present his offering to the
LORD: one male lamb in its first year without
blemish as a burnt offering, one ewe lamb in
its first year without blemish [R]as a sin offering, one ram without blemish [R]as a peace
offering, Lev. 4:2, 27, 32 • Lev. 3:6
15 'a basket of unleavened bread, cakes of
fine flour mixed with oil, unleavened wafers
anointed with oil, and their grain offering
with their [R]drink offerings. Num. 15:5, 7, 10
16 'Then the priest shall bring *them* before
the LORD and offer his sin offering and his
burnt offering;
17 'and he shall offer the ram as a sacrifice
of peace offering to the LORD, with the basket
of unleavened bread; the priest shall also
offer its grain offering and its drink offering.
18 'Then the Nazirite shall shave his consecrated head *at* the door of the tabernacle of
meeting, and shall take the hair from his
consecrated head and put *it* on the fire which
is under the sacrifice of the peace offering.
19 'And the priest shall take the boiled
shoulder of the ram, one unleavened cake
from the basket, and one unleavened wafer,
and put *them* upon the hands of the Nazirite
after he has shaved his consecrated *hair*,
20 'and the priest shall wave them as a wave
offering before the LORD; [R]they *are* holy for

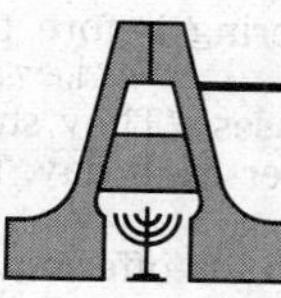

THE NAZIRITE VOW

According to the Jewish historian Josephus, John the Baptist was beheaded at Machaerus.

The Nazirite vow was an oath to abstain from certain worldly influences and to consecrate oneself to God. Among the Jews, the vow was an option for all persons, and it could be taken for a short period or for life. When the specified period was completed, the Nazirite could appear before the priest for the ceremony of release. Nazirites who broke their vows could be restored only by observing specific restoration rites (Num. 6:9–20).

Nazirites expressed their dedication to God by (1) abstaining from all intoxicating drinks and grape products, (2) refusing to cut their hair, (3) avoiding contact with the dead, and (4) refusing to eat food regarded as unclean (Num. 6:3–7).

Persons associated with this Nazirite vow in the Bible include Samson, Samuel, and John the Baptist. Samson's parents were told by the Angel of the Lord that their son would be a Nazirite until his death (Judg. 13:7). Hannah dedicated Samuel to the Nazirite way of life even before his birth (1 Sam. 1:11, 28), although it is not clear from the Bible accounts whether Samuel actually became a Nazirite.

The self-denying life-style of John the Baptist indicates that he may have been a Nazirite (Luke 1:15). John was so outspoken in his condemnation of sin in high places that he was executed by Herod, Roman governor of Palestine (Mark 6:17–28), at Herod's fortress palace in Machaerus (see photo).

The Nazirite vow reminds us that God desires for all Christians to lead holy, separated lives. Such an exemplary witness requires God's grace and strong commitment on the believer's part to avoid corrupting influences. The vow of the Nazirite suggests we need to recover personal Christian discipline.

the priest, together with the breast of the
wave offering and the thigh of the heave
offering. After that the Nazirite may drink
wine.' Ex. 29:27, 28
21 "This is the law of the Nazirite who vows
to the LORD the offering for his separation,
and besides that, whatever else his hand is
able to provide; according to the vow which
he takes, so he must do according to the law
of his separation."
22 And the LORD spoke to Moses, saying:
23 "Speak to Aaron and his sons, saying,
'This is the way you shall bless the children of
Israel. Say to them:

24 "The LORD bless you and keep you;
25 The LORD [R]make His face shine upon
you, Dan. 9:17
And [R]be gracious to you; Mal. 1:9
26 [R]The LORD [T]lift up His countenance upon
you, Ps. 4:6; 89:15 • Look on with favor
And [R]give you peace." ' Lev. 26:6

27 "So they shall put My name on the
children of Israel, and I will bless them."

CHAPTER 7

Israel Gives Donations

NOW it came to pass, when Moses had
finished setting up the tabernacle, that
he anointed it and sanctified it and all its
furnishings, and the altar and all its utensils;
so he anointed them and sanctified them.
2 Then the leaders of Israel, the heads of
their fathers' houses, who *were* the leaders of
the tribes [T]and over those who were numbered, made an offering. Lit. *who stood over*
3 And they brought their offering before
the LORD, six covered carts and twelve oxen,
a cart for *every* two of the leaders, and for
each one an ox; and they presented them
before the tabernacle.
4 Then the LORD spoke to Moses, saying,
5 "Accept *these* from them, that they may
be used in doing the work of the tabernacle
of meeting; and you shall give them to the
Levites, *to* every man according to his service."
6 So Moses took the carts and the oxen,
and gave them to the Levites.
7 Two carts and four oxen he gave to the
sons of Gershon, according to their service;
8 [R]and four carts and eight oxen he gave to
the sons of Merari, according to their service,
under the hand of Ithamar the son of Aaron
the priest. Num. 4:29–33
9 But to the sons of Kohath he gave none,
because theirs *was* [R]the service of the holy
things, [R]*which* they carried on their shoulders. Num. 4:15 • Num. 4:6–14
10 Now the leaders offered [R]the dedication
offering for the altar when it was anointed; so
the leaders offered their offering before the
altar. 2 Chr. 7:5, 9
11 For the LORD said to Moses, "They shall
offer their offering, one leader each day, for
the dedication of the altar."
12 And the one who offered his offering on
the first day *was* [R]Nahshon the son of Amminadab, from the tribe of Judah. Num. 2:3
13 His offering *was* one silver platter, the
weight of which *was* [T]one hundred and thirty
shekels, and one silver bowl of seventy shekels, according to [R]the shekel of the sanctuary,
both of them full of fine flour mixed with oil
as a [R]grain offering; $16,640 • Ex. 30:13 • Lev. 2:1
14 one gold pan of [T]ten *shekels*, full of
[R]incense; $19,200 • Ex. 30:34
15 one young bull, one ram, and one male
lamb in its first year, as a burnt offering;
16 one kid of the goats as a sin offering;
17 and for the sacrifice of peace offerings:
two oxen, five rams, five male goats, and five
male lambs in their first year. This *was* the
offering of Nahshon the son of Amminadab.
18 On the second day Nethaneel the son of
Zuar, leader of Issachar, presented *an offering*.
19 *For* his offering he offered one silver
platter, the weight of which *was* one hundred
and thirty *shekels*, and one silver bowl of
[T]seventy shekels, according to the shekel of
the sanctuary, both of them full of fine flour
mixed with oil as a grain offering; $8,960
20 one gold pan of [T]ten *shekels*, full of
incense; $19,200
21 one young bull, one ram, and one male
lamb in its first year, as a burnt offering;
22 one kid of the goats as a sin offering;
23 and as the sacrifice of peace offerings:
two oxen, five rams, five male goats, and five
male lambs in their first year. This *was* the
offering of Nethaneel the son of Zuar.
24 On the third day Eliab the son of Helon,
leader of the children of Zebulun, *presented
an offering*.
25 His offering *was* one silver platter, the
weight of which *was* one hundred and thirty
shekels, and one silver bowl of seventy shekels, according to the shekel of the sanctuary,
both of them full of fine flour mixed with oil
as a grain offering;
26 one gold pan of ten *shekels*, full of incense;
27 one young bull, one ram, and one male
lamb in its first year, as a burnt offering;
28 one kid of the goats as a sin offering;
29 and for the sacrifice of peace offerings:
two oxen, five rams, five male goats, and five
male lambs in their first year. This *was* the
offering of Eliab the son of Helon.
30 On the fourth day [R]Elizur the son of
Shedeur, leader of the children of Reuben,
presented an offering. Num. 1:5; 2:10

31 His offering *was* one silver platter, the
weight of which *was* [T]one hundred and thirty
shekels, and one silver bowl of [T]seventy
shekels, according to the shekel of the sanctuary, both of them full of fine flour mixed
with oil as a grain offering; $16,640 · $8,960
32 one gold pan of [T]ten *shekels*, full of
incense; $3,640
33 one young bull, one ram, and one male
lamb in its first year, as a burnt offering;
34 one kid of the goats as a sin offering;
35 and as the sacrifice of peace offerings:
two oxen, five rams, five male goats, and five
male lambs in their first year. This *was* the
offering of Elizur the son of Shedeur.
36 On the fifth day [R]Shelumiel the son of
Zurishaddai, leader of the children of Simeon,
presented an offering. Num. 1:6; 2:12; 7:41
37 His offering *was* one silver platter, the
weight of which *was* one hundred and thirty
shekels, and one silver bowl of seventy shekels, according to the shekel of the sanctuary,
both of them full of fine flour mixed with oil
as a grain offering;
38 one gold pan of ten *shekels*, full of incense;
39 one young bull, one ram, and one male
lamb in its first year, as a burnt offering;
40 one kid of the goats as a sin offering;
41 and as the sacrifice of peace offerings:
two oxen, five rams, five male goats, and five
male lambs in their first year. This *was* the
offering of Shelumiel the son of Zurishaddai.
42 On the sixth day [R]Eliasaph the son of
[T]Deuel, leader of the children of Gad, *presented an offering.* Num. 1:14 · *Reuel*, Num. 2:14
43 His offering *was* one silver platter, the
weight of which *was* one hundred and thirty
shekels, and one silver bowl of seventy shekels, according to the shekel of the sanctuary,
both of them full of fine flour mixed with oil
as a grain offering;
44 one gold pan of ten *shekels*, full of incense;
45 one young bull, one ram, and one male
lamb in its first year, as a burnt offering;
46 one kid of the goats as a sin offering;
47 and as the sacrifice of peace offerings:
two oxen, five rams, five male goats, and five
male lambs in their first year. This *was* the
offering of Eliasaph the son of Deuel.
48 On the seventh day [R]Elishama the son of
Ammihud, leader of the children of Ephraim,
presented an offering. Num. 1:10; 2:18
49 His offering *was* one silver platter, the
weight of which *was* one hundred and thirty
shekels, and one silver bowl of seventy shekels, according to the shekel of the sanctuary,
both of them full of fine flour mixed with oil
as a grain offering;
50 one gold pan of ten *shekels*, full of incense;
51 one young bull, one ram, and one male
lamb in its first year, as a burnt offering;
52 one kid of the goats as a sin offering;
53 and as the sacrifice of peace offerings:
two oxen, five rams, five male goats, and five
male lambs in their first year. This *was* the
offering of Elishama the son of Ammihud.
54 On the eighth day [R]Gamaliel the son of
Pedahzur, leader of the children of Manasseh,
presented an offering. Num. 1:10; 2:20
55 His offering *was* one silver platter, the
weight of which *was* one hundred and thirty
shekels, and one silver bowl of seventy shekels, according to the shekel of the sanctuary,
both of them full of fine flour mixed with oil
as a grain offering;
56 one gold pan of ten *shekels*, full of incense;
57 one young bull, one ram, and one male
lamb in its first year, as a burnt offering;
58 one kid of the goats as a sin offering;
59 and as the sacrifice of peace offerings:
two oxen, five rams, five male goats, and five
male lambs in their first year. This *was* the
offering of Gamaliel the son of Pedahzur.
60 On the ninth day [R]Abidan the son of
Gideoni, leader of the children of Benjamin,
presented an offering. Num. 1:11; 2:22
61 His offering *was* one silver platter, the
weight of which *was* [T]one hundred and thirty
shekels, and one silver bowl of [T]seventy
shekels, according to the shekel of the sanctuary, both of them full of fine flour mixed
with oil as a grain offering; $16,640 · $8,960
62 one gold pan of [T]ten *shekels*, full of
incense; $19,200
63 one young bull, one ram, and one male
lamb in its first year, as a burnt offering;
64 one kid of the goats as a sin offering;
65 and as the sacrifice of peace offerings:
two oxen, five rams, five male goats, and five
male lambs in their first year. This *was* the
offering of Abidan the son of Gideoni.
66 On the tenth day [R]Ahiezer the son of
Ammishaddai, leader of the children of Dan,
presented an offering. Num. 1:12; 2:25
67 His offering *was* one silver platter, the
weight of which *was* one hundred and thirty
shekels, and one silver bowl of seventy shekels, according to the shekel of the sanctuary,
both of them full of fine flour mixed with oil
as a grain offering;
68 one gold pan of ten *shekels*, full of incense;
69 one young bull, one ram, and one male
lamb in its first year, as a burnt offering;
70 one kid of the goats as a sin offering;
71 and as the sacrifice of peace offerings:
two oxen, five rams, five male goats, and five
male lambs in their first year. This *was* the
offering of Ahiezer the son of Ammishaddai.
72 On the eleventh day [R]Pagiel the son of
Ocran, leader of the children of Asher, *presented an offering.* Num. 1:13; 2:27
73 His offering *was* one silver platter, the
weight of which *was* one hundred and thirty

shekels, and one silver bowl of seventy shekels, according to the shekel of the sanctuary,
both of them full of fine flour mixed with oil
as a grain offering;
74 one gold pan of ten *shekels*, full of incense;
75 one young bull, one ram, and one male
lamb in its first year, as a burnt offering;
76 one kid of the goats as a sin offering;
77 and as the sacrifice of peace offerings:
two oxen, five rams, five male goats, and five
male lambs in their first year. This *was* the
offering of Pagiel the son of Ocran.
78 On the twelfth day [R]Ahira the son of
Enan, leader of the children of Naphtali,
presented an offering. Num. 1:15; 2:29
79 His offering *was* one silver platter, the
weight of which *was* one hundred and thirty
shekels, and one silver bowl of seventy shekels, according to the shekel of the sanctuary,
both of them full of fine flour mixed with oil
as a grain offering;
80 one gold pan of ten *shekels*, full of incense;
81 one young bull, one ram, and one male
lamb in its first year, as a burnt offering;
82 one kid of the goats as a sin offering;
83 and as the sacrifice of peace offerings:
two oxen, five rams, five male goats, and five
male lambs in their first year. This *was* the
offering of Ahira the son of Enan.
84 This *was* [R]the dedication *offering* for the
altar from the leaders of Israel, when it was
anointed: twelve silver platters, twelve silver
bowls, and twelve gold pans. Num. 7:10
85 Each silver platter *weighed* one hundred
and thirty *shekels* and each bowl seventy
shekels. All the silver of the vessels *weighed*
two thousand four hundred *shekels*, according to the shekel of the sanctuary.
86 The twelve gold pans full of incense
weighed [T]ten *shekels* apiece, according to the
shekel of the sanctuary; all the gold of the
pans *weighed* [T]one hundred and twenty *shekels*. $19,200 • $230,400
87 All the oxen for the burnt offering *were*
twelve young bulls, the rams twelve, the male
lambs in their first year twelve, with their
grain offering, and the kids of the goats as a
sin offering twelve.
88 And all the oxen for the sacrifice of peace
offerings were twenty-four bulls, the rams
sixty, the male goats sixty, and the lambs in
their first year sixty. This *was* the dedication
offering for the altar after it was anointed.
89 Now when Moses went into the tabernacle of meeting [R]to speak with Him, he heard
the voice of One speaking to him from above
the mercy seat that *was* on the ark of the
Testimony, from between the two cherubim;
thus He spoke to him. [Ex. 33:9, 11]

CHAPTER 8

The Levites Are Consecrated

AND the LORD spoke to Moses, saying:
2 "Speak to Aaron, and say to him,
'When you arrange the lamps, the seven
lamps shall give light in front of the lampstand.' "
3 And Aaron did so; he arranged the lamps
to face toward the front of the lampstand, as
the LORD commanded Moses.
4 Now this workmanship of the lampstand
was of hammered gold; from its shaft to its
flowers it *was* hammered work. According to
the pattern which the LORD had shown Moses, so he made the lampstand.
5 Then the LORD spoke to Moses, saying:
6 "Take the Levites from among the children of Israel and cleanse them *ceremonially*.
7 "Thus you shall do to them to cleanse
them: Sprinkle water of purification on them,
and [R]let them [T]shave all their body, and let
them wash their clothes, and *so* make them-
selves clean. Lev. 14:8, 9 • Heb. *cause a razor to pass over*
8 "Then let them take a young bull with
[R]its grain offering of fine flour mixed with oil,
and you shall take another young bull as a sin
offering. Lev. 2:1
9 [R]"And you shall bring the Levites before
the tabernacle of meeting, [R]and you shall
gather together the whole assembly of the
children of Israel. Ex. 29:4; 40:12 • Lev. 8:3
10 "So you shall bring the Levites before
the LORD, and the children of Israel [R]shall lay
their hands on the Levites; Lev. 1:4
11 "and Aaron shall [T]offer the Levites before the LORD, *as though* a [R]wave offering
from the children of Israel, that they may
perform the work of the LORD. *present* • Num. 18:6
12 [R]"Then the Levites shall lay their hands
on the heads of the young bulls, and you shall
offer one as a sin offering and the other as a
burnt offering to the LORD, to make atonement for the Levites. Ex. 29:10
13 "And you shall stand the Levites before
Aaron and his sons, and then offer them *as
though* a wave offering to the LORD.
14 "Thus you shall separate the Levites
from among the children of Israel, and the
Levites shall be [R]Mine. Num. 3:12, 45; 16:9
15 "After that the Levites shall go in to
service the tabernacle of meeting. So you
shall cleanse them and [R]offer them, *as though*
a wave offering. Num. 8:11, 13
16 "For they *are* [R]wholly given to Me from
among the children of Israel; I have taken
them for Myself [R]instead of all who open the
womb, the firstborn of all the children of
Israel. Num. 3:9 • Num. 3:12, 45
17 [R]"For all the firstborn among the children of Israel *are* Mine, *both* man and beast;
on the day that I struck all the firstborn in
the land of Egypt I [T]sanctified them to Myself. Ex. 12:2, 12, 13, 15 • *set them apart*

18 "I have taken the Levites instead of all the firstborn of the children of Israel.

19 "And I have given the Levites as a gift to Aaron and his sons from among the children of Israel, to do the work for the children of Israel in the tabernacle of meeting, and to make atonement for the children of Israel, [R]that there be no plague among the children of Israel when the children of Israel come near the sanctuary." Num. 1:53; 16:46; 18:5

20 Thus Moses and Aaron and all the congregation of the children of Israel did to the Levites; according to all that the LORD commanded Moses concerning the Levites, so the children of Israel did to them.

21 [R]And the Levites purified themselves and washed their clothes; then Aaron presented them, *as though* a wave offering before the LORD, and Aaron made atonement for them to cleanse them. Num. 8:7

22 [R]After that the Levites went in to do their work in the tabernacle of meeting before Aaron and his sons; [R]as the LORD commanded Moses concerning the Levites, so they did to them. Num. 8:15 • Num. 8:5

23 Then the LORD spoke to Moses, saying,

24 "This *is* what *pertains* to the Levites: [R]From twenty-five years old and above one may enter to perform service in the work of the tabernacle of meeting; Num. 4:3

25 "and at the age of fifty years they must cease performing this work, and shall work no more.

26 "They may minister with their brethren in the tabernacle of meeting, [R]to attend to needs, but they *themselves* shall do no work. Thus you shall do to the Levites regarding their duties." Num. 1:53

CHAPTER 9

The Passover Is Celebrated

NOW the LORD spoke to Moses in the Wilderness of Sinai, in the first month of the second year after they had come out of the land of Egypt, saying:

2 "Let the children of Israel keep [R]the Passover at its appointed time. Lev. 23:5

3 "On the fourteenth day of this month, [T]at twilight, you shall keep it at its appointed time. According to all its rites and ceremonies you shall keep it." Lit. *between the evenings*

4 So Moses told the children of Israel that they should keep the Passover.

5 And [R]they kept the Passover on the fourteenth day of the first month, at twilight, in the Wilderness of Sinai; according to all that the LORD commanded Moses, so the children of Israel did. Josh. 5:10

6 Now there were *certain* men who were [R]defiled by *the dead* body of a man, so that they could not keep the Passover on that day; [R]and they came before Moses and Aaron that day. Num. 5:2; 19:11–22 • Num. 27:2

7 And those men said to him, "We *became* defiled by *the dead* body of a man. Why are we kept from presenting the offering of the LORD at its appointed time among the children of Israel?"

8 And Moses said to them, "Stand still, that [R]I may hear what the LORD will command concerning you." Num. 27:5

9 Then the LORD spoke to Moses, saying,

10 "Speak to the children of Israel, saying: 'If anyone of you or your [T]posterity is unclean because of a *dead* body, or *is* far away on a journey, he may still keep the LORD's Passover. *descendants*

11 'On [R]the fourteenth day of the second month, at twilight, they may keep it. They shall [R]eat it with unleavened bread and bitter herbs. 2 Chr. 30:2, 15 • Ex. 12:8

12 [R]'They shall leave none of it until morning, [R]nor break one of its bones. According to all the [T]ordinances of the Passover they shall keep it. Ex. 12:10 • Ex. 12:46; John 19:36 ☆ • *statutes*

13 'But the man who *is* clean and is not on a journey, and ceases to keep the Passover, that same person shall be cut off from among his people, because he did not bring the offering of the LORD at its appointed time; that man shall [R]bear his sin. Num. 5:31

14 'And if a stranger sojourns among you, and would keep the LORD's Passover, he must do so according to the rite of the Passover and according to its ceremony; [R]you shall have one [T]ordinance, both for the stranger and the native of the land.' " Ex. 12:49 • *statute*

Guidance of the Cloud

15 And on the day that the tabernacle was raised up, the cloud covered the tabernacle, the tent of the Testimony; [R]from evening until morning it was above the tabernacle like the appearance of fire. Ex. 13:21, 22; 40:38

16 So it was always: the cloud covered it *by day*, and the appearance of fire by night.

17 Whenever the cloud was [T]taken up from above the tabernacle, after that the children of Israel would journey; and in the place where the cloud settled, there the children of Israel would pitch their tents. *lifted up*

18 At the [T]command of the LORD the children of Israel would journey, and at the command of the LORD they would camp; [R]as long as the cloud stayed above the tabernacle they remained encamped. Lit. *mouth* • 1 Cor. 10:1

19 Even when the cloud continued long, many days above the tabernacle, the children of Israel [R]kept the charge of the LORD and did not journey. Num. 1:53; 3:8

20 So it was, when the cloud was above the tabernacle a few days: according to the command of the LORD they would remain encamped, and according to the command of the LORD they would journey.

21 So it was, when the cloud remained only
from evening until morning: when the cloud
was taken up in the morning, then they
would journey; whether by day or by night,
whenever the cloud was taken up, they
would journey.
22 *Whether it was* two days, a month, or a
year that the cloud remained above the tabernacle, the children of Israel [R]would remain
encamped and not journey; but when it was
taken up, they would journey. Ex. 40:36, 37
23 At the command of the LORD they remained encamped, and at the command of
the LORD they journeyed; they [R]kept the
charge of the LORD, at the command of the
LORD by the hand of Moses. Num. 9:19

CHAPTER 10

Guidance of the Silver Trumpets

AND the LORD spoke to Moses, saying:
2 "Make two silver trumpets for yourself; you shall make them of hammered work;
you shall use them for calling the assembly
and for directing the movement of the camps.
3 "When [R]they blow both of them, all the
assembly shall gather before you at the door
of the tabernacle of meeting. Jer. 4:5
4 "But if they blow *only* one, then the
leaders, the [R]heads of the divisions of Israel,
shall gather to you. Ex. 18:21
5 "When you sound the [R]advance, [R]the
camps that lie on the east side shall then
begin their journey. Joel 2:1 • Num. 2:3
6 "When you sound the advance the second time, then the camps that lie [R]on the
south side shall begin their journey; they
shall sound the call for them to begin their
journeys. Num. 2:10
7 "And when the congregation is to be
gathered together, [R]you shall blow, but not
[R]sound the advance. Num. 10:3 • Joel 2:1
8 [R]"The sons of Aaron, the priests, shall
blow the trumpets; and these shall be to you
as an [T]ordinance forever throughout your
generations. Num. 31:6 • *statute*
9 "When you go to war in your land
against the enemy who [R]oppresses you, then
you shall sound an alarm with the trumpets,
and you will be [R]remembered before the LORD
your God, and you will be saved from your
enemies. Judg. 2:18; 4:3; 6:9; 10:8, 12 • Gen. 8:1
10 "Also [R]in the day of your gladness, in
your appointed feasts, and at the beginning
of your months, you shall blow the trumpets
over your burnt offerings and over the sacrifices of your peace offerings; and they shall
be [R]a memorial for you before your God: I *am*
the LORD your God." Lev. 23:24 • Num. 10:9

Israel Departs Mount Sinai

11 Now it came to pass on the twentieth
day of the second month, in the second year,
that the cloud [R]was taken up from above the
tabernacle of the Testimony. Num. 9:17
12 And the children of Israel set out from
the [R]Wilderness of Sinai on [R]their journeys;
then the cloud settled down in the [R]Wilder-
ness of Paran. Ex. 19:1 • Ex. 40:36 • Gen. 21:21
13 So they started out for the first time
[R]according to the command of the LORD by
the hand of Moses. Num. 10:5, 6
14 The [T]standard of the camp of the children of Judah [R]set out first according to their
armies; over their army was [R]Nahshon the
son of Amminadab. *banner* • Num. 2:3–9 • Num. 1:7
15 Over the army of the tribe of the children
of Issachar *was* Nethaneel the son of Zuar.
16 And over the army of the tribe of the
children of Zebulun *was* Eliab the son of
Helon.
17 Then the tabernacle was taken down;
and the sons of Gershon and the sons of
Merari set out, carrying the tabernacle.
18 And the standard of the camp of Reuben
set out according to their armies; over their
army *was* Elizur the son of Shedeur.
19 Over the army of the tribe of the children
of Simeon *was* Shelumiel the son of Zurishaddai.
20 And over the army of the tribe of the
children of Gad *was* Eliasaph the son of
Deuel.
21 Then the Kohathites set out, carrying
the [R]holy things. (The tabernacle would be
prepared for their arrival.) Num. 4:4–20; 7:9
22 And [R]the standard of the camp of the
children of Ephraim set out according to their
armies; over their army *was* Elishama the son
of Ammihud. Num. 2:18–24
23 Over the army of the tribe of the children
of Manasseh *was* Gamaliel the son of Pedahzur.
24 And over the army of the tribe of the
children of Benjamin *was* Abidan the son of
Gideoni.
25 Then [R]the standard of the camp of the
children of Dan, *which formed* the rear guard
of all the camps, set out according to their
armies; over their army *was* Ahiezer the son
of Ammishaddai. Num. 2:25–31
26 Over the army of the tribe of the children
of Asher *was* Pagiel the son of Ocran.
27 And over the army of the tribe of the
children of Naphtali *was* Ahira the son of
Enan.
28 [R]Thus *was* the order of march of the
children of Israel, according to their armies,
when they began their journey. Num. 2:34
29 Now Moses said to Hobab the son of
*Reuel the Midianite, Moses' father-in-law,
"We are setting out for the place of which the
LORD said, 'I will give it to you.' Come with

10:29 LXX *Raguel*

us, and we will treat you well; for [R]the LORD
has promised good things to Israel." Ex. 3:8
30 And he said to him, "I will not go, but I
will depart to my *own* land and to my kinsmen."
31 So Moses said, "Please do not leave,
inasmuch as you know how we are to camp
in the wilderness, and you can be our eyes.
32 "And it shall be, if you go with us—
indeed it shall be—that [R]whatever good the
LORD will do to us, the same we will do to
you." Judg. 1:16
33 So they departed from [R]the mountain of
the LORD on a journey of three days; and the
ark of the covenant of the LORD [R]went before
them for the three days' journey, to search
out a resting place for them. Ex. 3:1 • Deut. 1:33
34 And [R]the cloud of the LORD *was* above
them by day when they went out from the
camp. Ex. 13:21
35 So it was, whenever the ark set out, that
Moses said:

[R]"Rise up, O LORD!
Let Your enemies be scattered,
And let those who hate You flee before
You." Ps. 68:1, 2; 132:8

36 And when it rested, he said:

"Return, O LORD, *to* the many thousands
of Israel."

CHAPTER 11

Israel Complains About Circumstances

NOW *when* the people complained, it displeased the LORD; for the LORD heard *it*,
and His anger was aroused. So the fire of the
LORD burned among them, and consumed
some in the outskirts of the camp.
2 Then the people [R]cried out to Moses, and
when Moses [R]prayed to the LORD, the fire was
[T]quenched. Num. 12:11, 13 • [James 5:16] • *extinguished*
3 So he called the name of the place [T]Tab-
erah, because the fire of the LORD had burned
among them. Lit. *Burning*

Israel Complains About Food

4 Now the mixed multitude who were
among them yielded to intense craving; so
the children of Israel also wept again and
said: "Who will give us meat to eat?
5 [R]"We remember the fish which we ate
freely in Egypt, the cucumbers, the melons,
the leeks, the onions, and the garlic; Ex. 16:3
6 "but now [R]our whole being *is* dried up;
there is nothing at all except this manna
before our eyes!" Num. 21:5
7 Now the manna *was* like coriander seed,
and its color like the color of bdellium.
8 The people went about and gathered *it*,
ground *it* on millstones or beat *it* in the
mortar, cooked *it* in pans, and made cakes of
it; and [R]its taste was like the taste of pastry
prepared with oil. Ex. 16:31
9 And [R]when the dew fell on the camp in
the night, the manna fell on it. Ex. 16:13, 14

Moses Complains About the People

10 Now Moses heard the people weeping
throughout their families, everyone at the
door of his tent; and [R]the anger of the LORD
was greatly aroused; Moses also was displeased. Ps. 78:21
11 So Moses said to the LORD, "Why have
You afflicted Your servant? And why have I
not found favor in Your sight, that You have
laid the burden of all these people on me?
12 "Did I conceive all these people? Did I
beget them, that You should say to me,
'Carry them in your bosom, as a [R]guardian
carries a nursing child,' to the land which
You [R]swore to their fathers? Is. 49:23 • Gen. 26:3
13 "Where am I to get meat to give to all
these people? For they weep all over me,
saying, 'Give us meat, that we may eat.'

Moses Complains About His Own life

14 [R]"I am not able to bear all these people
alone, because the burden *is* too heavy for
me. Ex. 18:18
15 "If You treat me like this, please kill me
here and now—if I have found favor in Your
sight—and [R]do not let me see my wretched-
ness!" Rev. 3:17

God Provides for Moses

16 So the LORD said to Moses: "Gather to
Me [R]seventy men of the elders of Israel,
whom you know to be the elders of the
people and [R]officers over them; bring them to
the tabernacle of meeting, that they may
stand there with you. Ex. 18:25; 24:1, 9 • Deut. 16:18
17 "Then I will come down and talk with
you there. [R]I will take of the Spirit that *is*
upon you and will put *the same* upon them;
and they shall bear the burden of the people
with you, that you may not bear *it* yourself
alone. 1 Sam. 10:6
18 "Then you shall say to the people,
[T]'Sanctify yourselves for tomorrow, and you
shall eat meat; for you have wept in the
hearing of the LORD, saying, "Who will give
us meat to eat? For *it was* well with us in
Egypt." Therefore the LORD will give you
meat, and you shall eat. *Set yourselves apart*
19 'You shall eat, not one day, nor two days,
nor five days, nor ten days, nor twenty days,
20 [R]'but *for* a whole month, until it comes
out of your nostrils and becomes loathsome
to you, because you have [R]despised the LORD
who is among you, and have wept before
Him, saying, [R]"Why did we ever come up out
of Egypt?" ' " Ps. 106:15 • 1 Sam. 10:19 • Num. 21:5
21 And Moses said, "The people whom I *am*
among *are* six hundred thousand men on

MANNA IN THE WILDERNESS

God supplied manna to the Israelites for forty years.

Manna was the food miraculously supplied by God to the Israelites during their years of wandering in the Wilderness. The Lord told Moses, "I will rain bread from heaven for you" (Ex. 16:4). The spiritual purpose of the daily provision was "that He might humble you and that He might test you, to do you good" (Deut. 8:16).

The manna was to be gathered each day, except the Sabbath, by every household according to need (Ex. 16:16–18; see illustration). Manna gathered in excess of need melted in the sun or became infested with worms (Ex. 16:20, 21). The miracle food, which fell like dew, is described as "a small round substance, *as* fine as frost on the ground" (Ex. 16:14). Although it was sticky when it appeared, the manna soon solidified so that it could be ground and baked into wafers or cakes. It tasted like "wafers *made* with honey" (Ex. 16:31).

The exact nature of this miracle food remains a mystery, although it is compared to "white coriander seed" (Ex. 16:31). Some scholars believe it may have been a substance secreted by plant parasites as they fed on tamarisk trees in the Wilderness. God supplied manna for forty years until the Israelites entered Canaan and the "food of the land" (Josh. 5:12) became available.

During the wilderness years, God provided water for the Israelites when Moses struck a rock with his rod (Ex. 17:6). Quail were also miraculously supplied when the people complained they had no meat to eat with their manna (Ex. 16:13).

Throughout the Bible, references are made to God's provision in the Wilderness to show the Lord's continuing concern for His people. Jesus alluded to the "bread from heaven" given through Moses (John 6:32). But He described Himself as the "bread of life," which permanently satisfies (John 6:35).

foot; yet You have said, 'I will give them
meat, that they may eat *for* a whole month.'
22 [R]"Shall flocks and herds be slaughtered
for them, to provide enough for them? Or
shall all the fish of the sea be gathered
together for them, to provide enough for
them?" 2 Kin. 7:2
23 And the LORD said to Moses, "Has the
LORD's arm been shortened? Now you shall
see whether My word will befall you or not."
24 So Moses went out and told the people
the words of the LORD, and he [R]gathered the
seventy men of the elders of the people and
placed them around the tabernacle. Num. 11:16
25 Then the LORD came down in the cloud,
and spoke to him, and took of the Spirit that
was upon him, and placed *the same* upon the
seventy elders; and it happened, when the
Spirit rested upon them, that they prophesied, *although they never did *so* again.
26 But two men had remained in the camp:
the name of one *was* Eldad, and the name of
the other Medad. And the Spirit rested upon
them. Now they *were* among those listed, but
who [R]had not gone out to the tabernacle; yet
they prophesied in the camp. Jer. 36:5
27 And a young man ran and told Moses,
and said, "Eldad and Medad are prophesying
in the camp."
28 So Joshua the son of Nun, Moses' assistant, *one* of his choice men, answered and
said, "Moses my lord, forbid them!"
29 Then Moses said to him, "Are you [T]zeal-
ous for my sake? Oh, that all the LORD's
people were prophets *and* that the LORD
would put His Spirit upon them!" *jealous*
30 And Moses returned to the camp, *both*
he and the elders of Israel.

God Provides Quail

31 Now a [R]wind went out from the LORD,
and it brought quail from the sea and left
them fluttering near the camp, about a [T]day's
journey on this side and about a day's journey on the other side, all around the camp,
and about [T]two cubits above the surface of
the ground. Ex. 16:13 • 20 mi. • 3 ft.
32 And the people stayed up all that day, all
that night, and all the next day, and gathered
the quail (he who gathered least gathered ten
[R]homers); and they spread *them* out for
themselves all around the camp. Ezek. 45:11

God Sends Plagues

33 But while the [R]meat *was* still between
their teeth, before it was chewed, the wrath
of the LORD was aroused against the people,
and the LORD struck the people with a very
great plague. Ps. 78:29–31; 106:15
34 So he called the name of that place
Kibroth Hattaavah, because there they buried the people who had yielded to craving.
35 From Kibroth Hattaavah the people
moved to Hazeroth, and camped at Hazeroth.

CHAPTER 12

Miriam and Aaron Rebel

THEN Miriam and Aaron [T]spoke against
Moses because of the [T]Ethiopian woman
whom he had married; for [R]he had married an
Ethiopian woman. *criticized* • *Cushite* • Ex. 2:21
2 And they said, "Has the LORD indeed
spoken only through [R]Moses? [R]Has He not
spoken through us also?" And the LORD
[R]heard *it*. Num. 16:3 • Mic. 6:4 • Ezek. 35:12, 13
3 (Now the man Moses *was* very humble,
more than all men who *were* on the face of
the earth.)

Miriam Is Punished

4 [R]Suddenly the LORD said to Moses,
Aaron, and Miriam, "Come out, you three, to
the tabernacle of meeting!" So the three
came out. [Ps. 76:9]
5 [R]Then the LORD came down in the pillar
of cloud and stood *in* the door of the tabernacle, and called Aaron and Miriam. And they
both went forward. Ex. 19:9; 34:5
6 Then He said, "Hear now My words:

If there is a prophet among you,
I, the LORD, make Myself known to him
[R]in a vision,
And I speak to him in a dream. Gen. 46:2
7 Not so with My servant Moses;
He *is* faithful in all My house.
8 I speak with him face to face,
Even plainly, and not in dark sayings;
And he sees the form of the LORD.
Why then were you not afraid
To speak against My servant Moses?"

9 So the anger of the LORD was aroused
against them, and He departed.
10 And when the cloud departed from
above the tabernacle, [R]suddenly Miriam *became* [R]leprous, as *white as* snow. Then Aaron
turned toward Miriam, and there she was, a
leper. Deut. 24:9 • 2 Kin. 5:27; 15:5

Moses Intercedes

11 So Aaron said to Moses, "Oh, my lord!
Please [R]do not lay [T]*this* sin on us, in which we
have done foolishly and in which we have
sinned. 2 Sam. 19:19; 24:10 • *the penalty for this*
12 "Please [R]do not let her be as one dead,
whose flesh is half consumed when he comes
out of his mother's womb!" Ps. 88:4
13 So Moses cried out to the LORD, saying,
"Please [R]heal her, O God, I pray!" Ps. 103:3

Miriam Is Restored

14 Then the LORD said to Moses, "If her
father had but spit in her face, would she not
be shamed seven days? Let her be [R]shut[T] out

11:25 Tg., Vg. *and they did not cease*

of the camp seven days, and after that she
may be received *again*." Lev. 13:46 • *exiled from*
15 [R]So Miriam was shut out of the camp
seven days, and the people did not journey on
till Miriam was brought in *again*. Deut. 24:9
16 And afterward the people moved from
[R]Hazeroth and camped in the Wilderness of
Paran. Num. 11:35; 33:17, 18

CHAPTER 13

Investigation of the Promised Land
Deut. 1:22–40

AND the LORD spoke to Moses, saying,
2 [R]"Send men to spy out the land of
Canaan, which I am giving to the children
of Israel; from each tribe of their fathers
you shall send a man, every one a leader
among them." Deut. 1:22; 9:23
3 So Moses sent them [R]from the Wilderness of Paran according to the command of
the LORD, all of them men who *were* heads of
the children of Israel. Num. 12:16; 32:8
4 Now these *were* their names: from the
tribe of Reuben, Shammua the son of Zaccur;
5 from the tribe of Simeon, Shaphat the
son of Hori;
6 [R]from the tribe of Judah, [R]Caleb the son
of Jephunneh; Num. 34:19 • Josh. 14:6, 7
7 from the tribe of Issachar, Igal the son of
Joseph;
8 from the tribe of Ephraim, *Hoshea the
son of Nun;
9 from the tribe of Benjamin, Palti the son
of Raphu;
10 from the tribe of Zebulun, Gaddiel the
son of Sodi;
11 from the tribe of Joseph, *that is*, from the
tribe of Manasseh, Gaddi the son of Susi;
12 from the tribe of Dan, Ammiel the son of
Gemalli;
13 from the tribe of Asher, Sethur the son of
Michael;
14 from the tribe of Naphtali, Nahbi the son
of Vophsi;
15 from the tribe of Gad, Geuel the son of
Machi.
16 These *are* the names of the men whom
Moses sent to spy out the land. And Moses
called *Hoshea the son of Nun, Joshua.
17 So Moses sent them to spy out the land
of Canaan, and said to them, "Go up this *way*
into the South, and go up to the mountains,
18 "and see what the land is like: whether
the people who dwell in it *are* strong or weak,
few or many;
19 "whether the land they dwell in *is* good
or bad; whether the cities they inhabit *are*
like camps or strongholds;
20 "whether the land *is* [T]rich or poor; and
whether there are forests there or not. [R]Be of
good courage. And bring some of the fruit
of the land." Now the time *was* the season of
the first ripe grapes. *fertile or barren* • Deut. 31:6, 7, 23
21 So they went up and spied out the land
from the Wilderness of Zin as far as Rehob,
near the entrance of [R]Hamath. Josh. 13:5
22 And they went up through the South and
came to [R]Hebron; Ahiman, Sheshai, and Talmai, the descendants of [R]Anak, *were* there.
(Now Hebron was built seven years before
Zoan in Egypt.) Josh. 15:13, 14 • Josh. 11:21, 22
23 [R]Then they came to the [T]Valley of Eshcol, and there cut down a branch with one
cluster of grapes; they carried it between two
of them on a pole. *They* also *brought* some of
the pomegranates and figs. Deut. 1:24, 25 • *Wadi*
24 The place was called the Valley of [T]Esh-
col, because of the cluster which the men of
Israel cut down there. Lit. *Cluster*
25 And they returned from spying out the
land after forty days.
26 So they departed and came back to Moses and Aaron and all the congregation of the
children of Israel in the Wilderness of Paran,
at [R]Kadesh; they brought back word to them
and to all the congregation, and showed them
the fruit of the land. Deut. 1:19
27 Then they told him, and said: "We went
to the land where you sent us. It truly flows
with milk and honey, and this *is* its fruit.
28 "Nevertheless the people who dwell in
the land *are* strong; the cities *are* fortified
and very large; moreover we saw the descendants of [R]Anak there. Josh. 11:21, 22
29 [R]"The Amalekites dwell in the land of the
South; the Hittites, the Jebusites, and the
Amorites dwell in the mountains; and
the Canaanites dwell by the sea and along
the banks of the Jordan." Judg. 6:3
30 Then [R]Caleb quieted the people before
Moses, and said, "Let us go up at once and
take possession, for we are well able to
overcome it." Num. 14:6, 24
31 But the men who had gone up with him
said, "We are not able to go up against the
people, for they *are* stronger than we."
32 And they gave the children of Israel a
bad report of the land which they had spied
out, saying, "The land through which we
have gone as spies *is* a land that devours its
inhabitants, and [R]all the people whom we saw
in it *are* men of *great* stature. Amos 2:9
33 "There we saw the [T]giants (the descendants of Anak came from the giants); and we
were like grasshoppers in our own sight, and
so we were in their sight." Heb. *nephilim*

CHAPTER 14

Israel Rebels Against God

THEN all the congregation lifted up their
voices and cried, and the people [R]wept
that night. Deut. 1:45
2 [R]And all the children of Israel murmured
against Moses and Aaron, and the whole

13:8 LXX, Vg. *Oshea* 13:16 LXX, Vg. *Oshea*

congregation said to them, "If only we had
died in the land of Egypt! Or if only we had
died in this wilderness! Ex. 16:2; 17:3
3 "Why has the LORD brought us to this
land to fall by the sword, that our wives and
children should become victims? Would it not
be better for us to return to Egypt?"
4 So they said to one another, "Let us
select a leader and return to Egypt."
5 Then Moses and Aaron [T]fell on their
faces before all the assembly of the congregation of the children of Israel. *prostrated themselves*
6 And Joshua the son of Nun and Caleb
the son of Jephunneh, *who were* among
those who had spied out the land, tore their
clothes;
7 and they spoke to all the congregation of
the children of Israel, saying: [R]"The land we
passed through to spy out *is* an exceedingly
good land. Num. 13:27
8 "If the LORD delights in us, then He will
bring us into this land and give it to us, 'a
land which flows with milk and honey.'
9 "Only do not rebel against the LORD, nor
fear the people of the land, for [T]they *are* our
bread; their protection has departed from
them, and the LORD *is* with us. Do not fear
them." They shall be as food for our consumption.
10 And all the congregation said to stone
them with stones. Now [R]the glory of the LORD
appeared in the tabernacle of meeting before
all the children of Israel. Ex. 16:10

Moses Intercedes

11 And the LORD said to Moses: "How long
will these people reject Me? And how long
will they not believe Me, with all the signs
which I have performed among them?
12 "I will strike them with the pestilence
and disinherit them, and I will make of you a
nation greater and mightier than they."
13 And Moses said to the LORD: "Then the
Egyptians will hear *it*, for by Your might You
brought these people up from among them,
14 "and they will tell *it* to the inhabitants of
this land. They have [R]heard that You, LORD,
are among these people; that You, LORD, are
seen face to face and *that* Your cloud stands
above them; and You go before them in a
pillar of cloud by day and in a pillar of fire by
night. Deut. 2:25
15 "Now *if* You kill these people as one
man, then the nations which have heard of
Your fame will speak, saying,
16 'Because the LORD was not [R]able to bring
this people to the land which He swore to
give them, therefore He killed them in the
wilderness.' Deut. 9:28
17 "And now, I pray, let the power of my
Lord be great, just as You have spoken,
saying,
18 'The LORD is [R]longsuffering and abundant in mercy, forgiving iniquity and transgression; but He by no means clears *the
guilty*, [R]visiting the iniquity of the fathers on
the children to the third and fourth *generation*.' Ex. 34:6, 7 • Ex. 20:5
19 "Pardon the iniquity of this people, I
pray, according to the greatness of Your
mercy, just [R]as You have forgiven this people, from Egypt even until now." Ps. 78:38

Israel to Wander and Die

20 Then the LORD said: "I have pardoned,
[R]according to your word; Mic. 7:18–20
21 "but truly, as I live, [R]all the earth shall be
filled with the glory of the LORD— Ps. 72:19
22 [R]"because all these men who have seen
My glory and the signs which I did in Egypt
and in the wilderness, and have put Me to the
test now [R]these ten times, and have not
heeded My voice, Deut. 1:35 • Gen. 31:7
23 "they certainly shall not [R]see the land of
which I swore to their fathers, nor shall any
of those who rejected Me see it. Num. 26:65
24 "But My servant Caleb, because he has a
different spirit in him and has followed Me
fully, I will bring into the land where he went,
and his descendants shall inherit it.
25 "Now the Amalekites and the Canaanites dwell in the valley; tomorrow turn and
[R]move out into the wilderness by the Way of
the Red Sea." Deut. 1:40
26 Then the LORD spoke to Moses and
Aaron, saying,
27 "How long *shall I bear with* this evil
congregation who murmur against Me? [R]I
have heard the murmurings which the children of Israel murmur against Me. Ex. 16:12
28 "Say to them, [R]'As I live,' says the LORD,
'just as you have spoken in My hearing, so I
will do to you: Heb. 3:16–19
29 'The carcasses of you who have murmured against Me shall fall in this wilderness,
[R]all of you who were numbered, according to
your entire number, from twenty years old
and above. Num. 1:45, 46; 26:64
30 [R]'Except for Caleb the son of Jephunneh
and Joshua the son of Nun, you shall by no
means enter the land which I swore I would
make you dwell in. Deut. 1:36–38
31 [R]'But your little ones, whom you said
would be victims, I will bring in, and they
shall [T]know the land which [R]you have despised. Deut. 1:39 • *be acquainted with* • Ps. 106:24
32 'But *as for* you, [R]your[T] carcasses shall fall
in this wilderness. Num. 26:64, 65; 32:13 • You shall die
33 'And your sons shall be *shepherds in the
wilderness forty years, and [R]bear the brunt of
your infidelity, until your carcasses are consumed in the wilderness. Ezek. 23:35
34 'According to the number of the days in
which you spied out the land, [R]forty days, for
each day you shall bear your [T]guilt one year,

14:33 Vg. *wanderers*

namely forty years, [R]and you shall know My
[T]rejection. Ezek. 4:6 • *iniquity* • [Heb. 4:1] • *opposition*
35 [R]'I the LORD have spoken this; I will
surely do so to all [R]this evil congregation who
are gathered together against Me. In this
wilderness they shall be consumed, and there
they shall die.' " Num. 23:19 • 1 Cor. 10:5

Spies Die Immediately

36 And the men whom Moses sent to spy
out the land, who returned and made all the
congregation murmur against him by bringing a bad report of the land,
37 those very men who brought the evil
report about the land, [R]died by the plague
before the LORD. [1 Cor. 10:10]
38 [R]But Joshua the son of Nun and Caleb
the son of Jephunneh remained alive, of the
men who went to spy out the land. Josh. 14:6, 10

Moses Warns Israel—Deut. 1:41–44

39 Then Moses told these words to all the
children of Israel, [R]and the people mourned
greatly. Ex. 33:4
40 And they rose early in the morning and
went up to the top of the mountain, saying,
[R]"Here we are, and we will go up to the place
which the LORD has promised, for we have
sinned!" Deut. 1:41–44
41 Then Moses said, "Now why do you
[T]transgress the command of the LORD? For
this will not succeed. *overstep*
42 "Do not go up, lest you be defeated by
your enemies, for the LORD *is* not among you.
43 "For the Amalekites and the Canaanites
are there before you, and you shall fall by the
sword; because you have turned away from
the LORD, the LORD will not be with you."
44 [R]But they presumed to go up to the
mountaintop; nevertheless, neither the ark of
the covenant of the LORD nor Moses departed
from the camp. Deut. 1:43

Amalekites Defeat Israel

45 Then the Amalekites and the Canaanites
who dwelt in that mountain came down and
attacked them, and drove them back as far as
[R]Hormah. Num. 21:3

CHAPTER 15

Offerings to Thank the Lord

AND the LORD spoke to Moses, saying,
2 [R]"Speak to the children of Israel, and
say to them: 'When you have come into the
land you are to inhabit, which I am giving to
you, Lev. 23:10
3 'and you make an offering by fire to the
LORD, a burnt offering or a sacrifice, to fulfill
a vow or as a freewill offering or in your
appointed feasts, to make a sweet aroma to
the LORD, from the herd or the flock,
4 'then he who presents his offering to the
LORD shall bring [R]a grain offering of one-
tenth *of an ephah* of fine flour mixed [R]with
one-fourth of a hin of oil; Ex. 29:40 • Num. 28:5
5 'and one-fourth of a hin of wine as a
drink offering you shall prepare with the
burnt offering or the sacrifice, for each lamb.
6 'Or for a ram you shall prepare as a grain
offering two-tenths *of an ephah* of fine flour
mixed with one-third of a hin of oil;
7 'and as a drink offering you shall offer
[T]one-third of a hin of wine as a sweet aroma
to the LORD. 42.7 oz.
8 'And when you prepare a young bull as a
burnt offering, or as a sacrifice to fulfill a
vow, or as a peace offering to the LORD,
9 'then shall be offered [R]with the young
bull a grain offering of [T]three-tenths *of an
ephah* of fine flour mixed with [T]half a hin of
oil; Num. 28:12, 14 • 6.261 qt. • .5 gal.
10 'and you shall bring as the drink offering
[T]half a hin of wine as an offering made by fire,
a sweet aroma to the LORD. .5 gal.
11 [R]'Thus it shall be done for each young
bull, for each ram, or for each lamb or young
goat. Num. 28
12 'According to the number that you prepare, so you shall do with everyone according
to their number.
13 'All who are native-born shall do these
things in this manner, in presenting an offering made by fire, a sweet aroma to the LORD.
14 'And if a stranger [T]sojourns with you, or
whoever *is* among you throughout your generations, and would present an offering made
by fire, a sweet aroma to the LORD, just as
you do, so shall he do. Resides temporarily
15 'One ordinance *shall be* for you of the
congregation and for the stranger who sojourns *with you*, an ordinance forever
throughout your generations; as you are, so
shall the stranger be before the LORD.
16 [R]'One law and one custom shall be for
you and for the stranger who sojourns with
you.' " Ex. 12:49
17 Again the LORD spoke to Moses, saying,
18 [R]"Speak to the children of Israel, and say
to them: 'When you come into the land to
which I bring you, Deut. 26:1
19 'then it will be, when you eat of [R]the
bread of the land, that you shall offer up a
heave offering to the LORD. Josh. 5:11, 12
20 [R]'You shall offer up a cake of the first of
your ground meal *as* a heave offering; as [R]a
heave offering of the threshing floor, so shall
you offer it up. Lev. 23:10, 14, 17 • Lev. 2:14; 23:10, 16
21 'Of the first of your ground meal you
shall give to the LORD a heave offering
throughout your generations.

Offerings for Unintentional Sins

22 'And [R]if you sin unintentionally, and do
not observe all these commandments which
the LORD has spoken to Moses— Lev. 4:2

23 'all that the LORD has commanded you
by the hand of Moses, from the day the LORD
gave commandment and onward throughout
your generations—
24 'then it will be, if it is unintentionally
committed, [T]without the knowledge of the
congregation, that the whole congregation
shall offer one young bull as a burnt offering,
as a sweet aroma to the LORD, with its grain
offering and its drink offering, according to
the ordinance, and [R]one kid of the goats as a
sin offering. Lit. *away from the eyes* • Lev. 4:23
25 [R]'So the priest shall make atonement for
the whole congregation of the children of
Israel, and it shall be forgiven them, for it was
unintentional; they shall bring their offering,
an offering made by fire to the LORD, and
their sin offering before the LORD, for their
unintended sin. [Heb. 2:17]
26 'It shall be forgiven the whole congregation of the children of Israel and the stranger
who sojourns among them, because all the
people *did it* unintentionally.
27 'And [R]if a person sins unintentionally,
then he shall bring a female goat in its first
year as a sin offering. Lev. 4:27–31
28 [R]'So the priest shall make atonement for
the person who sins unintentionally, when he
sins unintentionally before the LORD, to make
atonement for him; and it shall be forgiven
him. Lev. 4:35
29 'You shall have one law for him who sins
unintentionally, *both for* him who is native-
born among the children of Israel and for the
stranger who sojourns among them.

No Offering for Intentional Sins

30 'But the person who does *anything* [T]pre-
sumptuously, *whether he is* native-born or a
stranger, that one [T]brings reproach on the
LORD, and he shall be cut off from among his
people. *defiantly*, lit. *with a high hand* • *blasphemes*
31 'Because he has [R]despised the word of
the LORD, and has broken His commandment,
that person shall be completely cut off; his
[T]guilt *shall be* upon him.' " Prov. 13:13 • *iniquity*
32 Now while the children of Israel were in
the wilderness, [R]they found a man gathering
sticks on the Sabbath day. Ex. 31:14, 15; 35:2, 3
33 And those who found him gathering
sticks brought him to Moses and Aaron, and
to all the congregation.
34 They put him [R]under guard, because it
had not been explained what should be done
to him. Lev. 24:12
35 Then the LORD said to Moses, [R]"The man
must surely be put to death; all the congregation shall [R]stone him with stones outside the
camp." Ex. 31:14, 15 • Lev. 24:14
36 So, as the LORD commanded Moses, all
the congregation brought him outside the
camp and stoned him with stones, and he
died.

The Tassel on the Garment

37 Again the LORD spoke to Moses, saying,
38 "Speak to the children of Israel: Tell
[R]them to make tassels on the corners of their
garments throughout their generations, and
to put a blue thread in the tassels of the
corners. Matt. 23:5
39 "And you shall have the tassel, that you
may look upon it and [R]remember all the
commandments of the LORD and do them,
and that you [R]*may* not [R]follow the harlotry to
which your own heart and your own eyes are
inclined, Ps. 103:18 • Deut. 29:19 • James 4:4
40 "and that you may remember and do all
My commandments, and be [R]holy for your
God. [Lev. 11:44, 45]
41 "I *am* the LORD your God, who brought
you out of the land of Egypt, to be your God:
I *am* the LORD your God."

CHAPTER 16

Korah Rebels Against Moses and Aaron

NOW Korah the son of Izhar, the son of
Kohath, the son of Levi, with Dathan
and Abiram the sons of Eliab, and On the son
of Peleth, sons of Reuben, took *men*;
2 and they rose up before Moses with some
of the children of Israel, two hundred and
fifty leaders of the congregation, representatives of the congregation, men of renown.
3 They gathered together against Moses
and Aaron, and said to them, "*You* [T]*take* too
much upon yourselves, for [R]all the congregation *is* holy, every one of them, [R]and the LORD
is among them. Why then do you exalt
yourselves above the congregation of the
LORD?" *assume too much for* • Ex. 19:6 • Ex. 29:45
4 So when Moses heard *it*, he [R]fell on his
face; Num. 14:5; 20:6
5 and he spoke to Korah and all his company, saying, "Tomorrow morning the LORD
will show who *is* [R]His and *who is* [T]holy, and
will cause *him* to come near to Him; that one
whom He chooses He will cause to come near
to Him. [2 Tim. 2:19] • *set aside* for His use only
6 "Do this: Take censers, Korah and all
your company;
7 "put fire in them and put incense in them
before the LORD tomorrow, and it shall be
that the man whom the LORD chooses *shall
be* the holy one. *You take* too much upon
yourselves, you sons of Levi!"
8 Then Moses said to Korah, "Hear now,
you sons of Levi:
9 "*Is it* [R]a small thing to you that the God
of Israel has [R]separated you from the congregation of Israel, to bring you near to Himself,
to do the work of the tabernacle of the LORD,
and to stand before the congregation to serve
them; Is. 7:13 • Deut. 10:8
10 "and that He has brought you near *to
Himself*, you and all your brethren, the sons

of Levi, with you? And are you seeking the
priesthood also?
11 "Therefore you and all your company *are*
gathered together against the LORD. [R]And
what *is* Aaron that you murmur against
him?" Ex. 16:7, 8
12 And Moses sent to call Dathan and Abiram the sons of Eliab, but they said, "We will
not come up!
13 "*Is it* a small thing that you have brought
us up out of a land flowing with milk and
honey, to kill us in the wilderness, that you
should keep acting like a prince over us?
14 "Moreover [R]you have not brought us
into [R]a land flowing with milk and honey, nor
given us inheritance of fields and vineyards.
Will you put out the eyes of these men? We
will not come up!" Num. 14:1–4 • Ex. 3:8

God Judges Korah

15 Then Moses was very angry, and said to
the LORD, "Do not [T]respect their offering. I
have not taken one donkey from them, nor
have I hurt one of them." *graciously regard*
16 And Moses said to Korah, "Tomorrow,
you and all your company be present before
the LORD—you and they, as well as Aaron.
17 "Each of you take his censer and put
incense in it, and each of you bring his censer
before the LORD, two hundred and fifty censers; you also, and Aaron, each *of you* with
his censer."
18 So every man took his censer, put fire in
it, laid incense on it, and stood at the door of
the tabernacle of meeting with Moses and
Aaron.
19 And Korah gathered all the congregation
against them at the door of the tabernacle of
meeting. Then [R]the glory of the LORD appeared to all the congregation. Num. 14:10
20 And the LORD spoke to Moses and
Aaron, saying,
21 [R]"Separate yourselves from among this
congregation, that I may [R]consume them in a
moment." Gen. 19:17 • Ex. 32:10; 33:5
22 Then they [R]fell[T] on their faces, and said,
"O God, the God of the spirits of all flesh,
shall one man sin, and You be angry with all
the congregation?" Num. 14:5 • *prostrated themselves*
23 So the LORD spoke to Moses, saying,
24 "Speak to the congregation, saying, 'Get
away from the tents of Korah, Dathan, and
Abiram.' "
25 Then Moses rose and went to Dathan
and Abiram, and the elders of Israel followed
him.
26 And he spoke to the congregation, saying, "Depart now from the tents of these
wicked men! Touch nothing of theirs, lest
you be consumed in all their sins."
27 So they got away from around the tents
of Korah, Dathan, and Abiram; and Dathan
and Abiram came out and stood at the door
of their tents, with their wives, their sons,
and their little [R]children. Num. 26:11
28 Then Moses said: [R]"By this you shall
know that the LORD has sent me to do all
these works, for *I have* not *done them* [R]of my
own will. John 5:36 • John 5:30
29 "If these men die naturally like all men,
or if they are visited by the common fate of
all men, *then* the LORD has not sent me.
30 "But if the LORD creates [R]a new thing,
and the earth opens its mouth and swallows
them up with all that belongs to them, and
they [R]go down alive into the pit, then you will
understand that these men have rejected the
LORD." Job 31:3 • [Ps. 55:15]
31 [R]Then it came to pass, as he finished
speaking all these words, that the ground
split apart under them, Num. 26:10
32 and the earth opened its mouth and
swallowed them up, with their households
and [R]all the men with Korah, with all *their*
goods. Num. 26:11
33 So they and all those with them went
down alive into the pit; the earth closed over
them, and they perished from among the
congregation.
34 Then all Israel who *were* around them
fled at their cry, for they said, "Lest the earth
swallow us up *also*!"
35 And [R]a fire came out from the LORD and
consumed the two hundred and fifty men
who were offering incense. Num. 11:1–3; 26:10
36 Then the LORD spoke to Moses, saying:
37 "Tell Eleazar, the son of Aaron the priest,
to pick up the censers out of the blaze, for
[R]they are holy, and scatter the fire some
distance away. Lev. 27:28
38 "The censers of these men who sinned
against their own souls, let them be made
into hammered plates as a covering for the
altar. Because they presented them before
the LORD, therefore they are holy; and they
shall be a sign to the children of Israel."
39 So Eleazar the priest took the bronze
censers, which those who were burned up
had presented, and they were hammered out
as a covering on the altar,
40 *to be* a memorial to the children of Israel
that no outsider, who *is* not a descendant of
Aaron, should come near to offer incense
before the LORD, that he might not become
like Korah and his companions, just as the
LORD had said to him through Moses.

Israel Rebels Against Moses and Aaron

41 On the next day [R]all the congregation of
the children of Israel murmured against
Moses and Aaron, saying, "You have killed
the people of the LORD." Num. 14:2

God Judges Israel

42 Now it happened, when the congregation
had gathered against Moses and Aaron, that

they turned toward the tabernacle of meeting; and suddenly [R]the cloud covered it, and
the glory of the LORD appeared. Ex. 40:34
43 Then Moses and Aaron came before the
tabernacle of meeting.
44 And the LORD spoke to Moses, saying,
45 "Get away from among this congregation, that I may consume them in a moment."
And they fell on their faces.
46 So Moses said to Aaron, "Take a censer
and put fire in it from the altar, put incense
on it, and take it quickly to the congregation
and make atonement for them; [R]for wrath
has gone out from the LORD. The plague has
begun." Num. 18:5
47 Then Aaron took *it* as Moses commanded, and ran into the midst of the congregation; and already the plague had begun
among the people. So he put in the incense
and made atonement for the people.
48 And he stood between the dead and the
living; so [R]the plague was stopped. Num. 25:8
49 Now those who died in the plague were
fourteen thousand seven hundred, besides
those who died in the Korah incident.
50 So Aaron returned to Moses at the door
of the tabernacle of meeting, for the plague
had stopped.

CHAPTER 17

Confirmation of the Divine Call

AND the LORD spoke to Moses, saying:
2 "Speak to the children of Israel, and
get from them a rod from each father's house,
all their leaders according to their fathers'
houses—twelve rods. Write each man's name
on his rod.
3 "And you shall write Aaron's name on
the rod of Levi. For there shall be one rod for
the head of *each* father's house.
4 "Then you shall place them in the tabernacle of meeting before [R]the Testimony,
[R]where I meet with you. Ex. 25:16 • Ex. 25:22
5 "And it shall be *that* the rod of the man
whom I choose will blossom; thus I will rid
Myself of the murmurings of the children of
Israel, which they murmur against you."
6 So Moses spoke to the children of Israel,
and each of their leaders gave him a rod
apiece, for each leader according to their
fathers' houses, twelve rods; and the rod of
Aaron *was* among their rods.
7 And Moses placed the rods before the
LORD in [R]the tabernacle of witness. Ex. 38:21
8 Now it came to pass on the next day that
Moses went into the tabernacle of witness,
and behold, the rod of Aaron, of the house of
Levi, had sprouted and put forth buds, had
produced blossoms and yielded ripe almonds.
9 Then Moses brought out all the rods
from before the LORD to all the children of
Israel; and they looked, and each man took
his rod.
10 And the LORD said to Moses, "Bring
Aaron's rod back before the Testimony, to be
kept [R]as a sign against the rebels, [R]that you
may put their murmurings away from Me,
lest they die." Deut. 9:7, 24 • Num. 17:5
11 Thus did Moses; just as the LORD had
commanded him, so he did.
12 And the children of Israel spoke to Moses, saying, "Surely we die, we perish, we all
perish!
13 [R]"Whoever even comes near the tabernacle of the LORD must die. Shall we all utterly
die?" Num. 1:51, 53; 18:4, 7

CHAPTER 18

Remuneration of the Priesthood

THEN the LORD said to Aaron: [R]"You and
your sons and your father's house with
you shall [R]bear the [T]iniquity *related to* the
sanctuary, and you and your sons with you
shall bear the iniquity *associated with* your
priesthood. Num. 17:13 • Ex. 28:38 • *guilt*
2 "Also bring with you your brethren of
the tribe of Levi, the tribe of your father, that
they may be joined with you and serve you
while you and your sons *are* with you before
the tabernacle of [T]witness. *testimony*
3 "They shall attend to your [T]needs and all
the needs of the tabernacle; [R]but they shall
not come near the articles of the sanctuary
and the altar, [R]lest they die—they and you
also. *service* • Num. 16:40 • Num. 4:15
4 "They shall be joined with you and attend to the needs of the tabernacle of meeting, for all the work of the tabernacle; [R]but an
outsider shall not come near you. Num. 3:10
5 "And you shall attend to [R]the duties of
the sanctuary and the duties of the altar,
[R]that there *may* be no more wrath on the
children of Israel. Lev. 24:3 • Num. 8:19; 16:46
6 "Behold, I Myself have [R]taken your
brethren the Levites from among the children
of Israel; [R]*they are* a gift to you, given by the
LORD, to do the work of the tabernacle of
meeting. Num. 3:12, 45 • Num. 3:9
7 "Therefore you and your sons with you
shall attend to your priesthood for everything
at the altar and behind the veil; and you shall
serve. I give your priesthood *to you* as a [R]gift
for service, but the outsider who comes near
shall be put to death." 1 Pet. 5:2, 3
8 And the LORD spoke to Aaron: "Here, I
Myself have also given you [T]charge of My
heave offerings, all the holy gifts of the
children of Israel; I have given them [R]as a
portion to you and your sons, as an ordinance
forever. *custody* • Ex. 29:29; 40:13, 15
9 "This shall be yours of the most holy
things *reserved* from the fire: every offering

of theirs, every grain offering and every [R]sin
offering and every [R]trespass offering which
they render to Me, *shall be* most holy for you
and your sons. Lev. 6:25, 26 • Lev. 7:7
10 [R]"In a most holy *place* you shall eat it;
every male shall eat it. It shall be holy to
you. Lev. 6:16, 26
11 "This also *is* yours: the heave offering of
their gift, with all the wave offerings of the
children of Israel; I have given them to you,
and your sons and daughters with you, as an
ordinance forever. [R]Everyone who is [T]clean in
your house may eat it. Lev. 22:1–16 • *purified*
12 [R]"All the [T]best of the oil, all the best of
the new wine and the grain, [R]their firstfruits
which they offer to the LORD, I have given
them to you. Ex. 23:19 • Lit. *fat* • Ex. 22:29
13 "Whatever first ripe fruit is in their land,
[R]which they bring to the LORD, shall be yours.
Everyone who is clean in your house may eat
it. Ex. 22:29; 23:19; 34:26
14 [R]"Every [T]devoted thing in Israel shall be
yours. Lev. 27:1–33 • *consecrated*
15 "Everything that first opens [R]the womb
of all flesh, which they bring to the LORD,
whether man or beast, shall be yours; nevertheless [R]the firstborn of man you shall surely
redeem, and the firstborn of unclean animals
you shall redeem. Ex. 13:2 • Ex. 13:12–15
16 "And those redeemed of the devoted
things you shall redeem when one month old,
according to your valuation, for five shekels
of silver, according to the shekel of the
sanctuary, which *is* [R]twenty gerahs. Ex. 30:13
17 [R]"But the firstborn of a cow, the firstborn
of a sheep, or the firstborn of a goat you shall
not redeem; they *are* holy. [R]You shall sprinkle
their blood on the altar, and burn their fat *as*
an offering made by fire for a sweet aroma to
the LORD. Deut. 15:19 • Lev. 3:2, 5
18 "And their flesh shall be yours, just as
the [R]wave[T] breast and the right thigh are
yours. Ex. 29:26–28 • *breast of the wave offering*
19 "All the heave offerings of the holy
things, which the children of Israel offer to
the LORD, I have given to you and your sons
and daughters with you as an ordinance
forever; [R]it *is* a covenant of salt forever
before the LORD with you and your descendants with you." 2 Chr. 13:5
20 Then the LORD said to Aaron: "You shall
have [R]no inheritance in their land, nor shall
you have any portion among them; [R]I *am*
your portion and your inheritance among the
children of Israel. Josh. 13:14, 33 • Ezek. 44:28
21 "Behold, I have given the children of
Levi all the tithes in Israel as an inheritance
in return for the work which they perform,
the work of the tabernacle of meeting.
22 [R]"Hereafter the children of Israel shall
not come near the tabernacle of meeting,
[R]lest they bear sin and die. Num. 1:51 • Lev. 22:9
23 "But the Levites shall perform the work
of the tabernacle of meeting, and they shall
bear their iniquity; *it shall be* a statute forever, throughout your generations, that
among the children of Israel they shall have
no inheritance.
24 "For the tithes of the children of Israel,
which they offer up *as* a heave offering to the
LORD, I have given to the Levites [T]as an
inheritance; therefore I have said to them,
'Among the children of Israel they shall have
no inheritance.' " *for a possession*
25 Then the LORD spoke to Moses, saying,
26 "Speak thus to the Levites, and say to
them: 'When you take from the children of
Israel the tithes which I have given you from
them as your inheritance, then you shall offer
up a heave offering of it to the LORD, [R]a tenth
of the tithe. Neh. 10:38
27 'And your heave offering shall be reckoned to you as though *it were* the grain of the
[R]threshing floor and as the fullness of the
winepress. Num. 15:20
28 'Thus you shall also offer a heave offering to the LORD from all your tithes which
you receive from the children of Israel, and
you shall give the LORD's heave offering from
it to Aaron the priest.
29 'Of all your gifts you shall offer up every
heave offering due to the LORD, from all the
best of them, the sanctified part of them.'
30 "Therefore you shall say to them: 'When
you have lifted up the best of it, then *the rest*
shall be accounted to the Levites as the
produce of the threshing floor and as the
produce of the winepress.
31 'You may eat it in any place, you and
your households, for it *is* your reward for
your work in the tabernacle of meeting.
32 'And you shall bear no sin because of it,
when you have lifted up the best of it. But
you shall not [R]profane the holy gifts of the
children of Israel, lest you die.' " Lev. 22:2, 15

CHAPTER 19

Purification of the Red Heifer

NOW the LORD spoke to Moses and Aaron,
saying,
2 "This *is* the [T]ordinance of the law which
the LORD has commanded, saying: 'Speak to
the children of Israel, that they bring you a
red heifer without blemish, in which there *is*
no [R]defect [R]*and* on which a yoke has never
come. *statute* • Lev. 22:20–25 • Deut. 21:3
3 'You shall give it to Eleazar the priest,
that he may take it [R]outside the camp, and it
shall be slaughtered before him; Lev. 4:12, 21
4 'and Eleazar the priest shall take some of
its blood with his finger, and [R]sprinkle some
of its blood seven times directly in front of
the tabernacle of meeting. Lev. 4:6
5 'Then the heifer shall be burned in his
sight: [R]its hide, its flesh, its blood, and its offal
shall be burned. Ex. 29:14

6 'And the priest shall take cedar wood and
hyssop and scarlet, and cast *them* into the
midst of the fire burning the heifer.
7 [R]'Then the priest shall wash his clothes,
he shall bathe in water, and afterward he
shall come into the camp; the priest shall be
unclean until evening. Lev. 11:25; 15:5; 16:26, 28
8 'And the one who burns it shall wash his
clothes in water, bathe in water, and shall be
unclean until evening.
9 'Then a man *who is* clean shall gather up
the ashes of the heifer, and store *them* outside the camp in a clean place; and they shall
be kept for the congregation of the children
of Israel for the water of [T]purification; it *is* for
purifying from sin. Lit. *impurity*
10 'And the one who gathers the ashes of
the heifer shall wash his clothes, and be
unclean until evening. It shall be a statute
forever to the children of Israel and to the
stranger who sojourns among them.
11 'He who touches the dead body of anyone shall be unclean seven days.
12 [R]'He shall purify himself with the water
on the third day and on the seventh day; *then*
he will be clean. But if he does not purify
himself on the third day and on the seventh
day, he will not be clean. Num. 19:19; 31:19
13 'Whoever touches the body of anyone
who has died, and does not purify himself,
defiles the tabernacle of the LORD. That
person shall be cut off from Israel. He shall be
unclean, because [R]the water of purification
was not sprinkled on him; [R]his uncleanness *is*
still on him. Num. 8:7; 19:9 • Lev. 7:20; 22:3
14 'This *is* the law when a man dies in a
tent: All who come into the tent and all who
are in the tent shall be unclean seven days;
15 'and every [R]open vessel, which has no
cover fastened on it, *is* unclean. Num. 31:20
16 [R]'Whoever in the open field touches one
who is slain by a sword or who has died, or a
bone of a man, or a grave, shall be unclean
seven days. Num. 19:11; 31:19
17 'And for an unclean *person* they shall
take some of the ashes of the heifer burnt for
purification from sin, and [T]running water
shall be put on them in a vessel. Lit. *living*
18 'A clean person shall take [R]hyssop and
dip *it* in the water, sprinkle *it* on the tent, on
all the vessels, on the persons who were
there, or on the one who touched a bone, the
slain, the dead, or a grave. Ps. 51:7
19 'The clean *person* shall sprinkle the unclean on the third day and on the seventh
day; [R]and on the seventh day he shall purify
himself, wash his clothes, and bathe in water;
and at evening he shall be clean. Lev. 14:9
20 'But the man who is unclean and does
not purify himself, that person shall be cut off
from among the congregation, because he
has [R]defiled the sanctuary of the LORD. The
water of purification has not been sprinkled
on him; he *is* unclean. Num. 19:13
21 'It shall be a perpetual statute for them.
He who sprinkles the water of purification
shall wash his clothes; and he who touches
the water of purification shall be unclean
until evening.
22 'Whatever the unclean *person* touches
shall be unclean; and the person who touches
it shall be unclean until evening.' "

CHAPTER 20

Miriam Dies

THEN the children of Israel, the whole
congregation, came into the Wilderness
of Zin in the first month, and the people
stayed in [R]Kadesh; and [R]Miriam died there
and was buried there. Num. 13:26 • Ex. 15:20

The Sin of Israel

2 [R]Now there was no water for the congregation; [R]so they gathered together against
Moses and Aaron. Ex. 17:1 • Num. 16:19, 42
3 And the people contended with Moses
and spoke, saying: "If only we had died when
our brethren died before the LORD!
4 [R]"Why have you brought up the congregation of the LORD into this wilderness, that
we and our animals should die here? Ex. 17:3
5 "And why have you made us come up
out of Egypt, to bring us to this evil place? It
is not a place of grain or figs or vines or
pomegranates; nor *is* there any water to
drink."
6 So Moses and Aaron went from the presence of the assembly to the door of the
tabernacle of meeting, and they [T]fell on their
faces. And [R]the glory of the LORD appeared to
them. *prostrated themselves* • Num. 14:10

The Command of God

7 Then the LORD spoke to Moses, saying,
8 "Take the rod; you and your brother
Aaron gather the assembly together. Speak
to the rock before their eyes, and it will yield
its water; thus [R]you shall bring water for
them out of the rock, and give drink to the
congregation and their animals." Neh. 9:15

The Sin of Moses

9 So Moses took the rod [R]from before the
LORD as He commanded him. Num. 17:10
10 And Moses and Aaron gathered the congregation together before the rock; and he
said to them, "Hear now, you rebels! Must we
bring water for you out of this rock?"
11 Then Moses lifted his hand and struck
the rock twice with his rod; [R]and water came
out abundantly, and the congregation and
their animals drank. [1 Cor. 10:4]
12 Then the LORD spoke to Moses and
Aaron, "Because [R]you did not believe Me, to

[R]hallow Me in the eyes of the children of
Israel, therefore you shall not bring this
congregation into the land which I have
given them." Deut. 1:37; 3:26, 27; 34:5 • Lev. 10:3
13 This *was* the water of Meribah, because
the children of Israel contended with the
LORD, and He was hallowed among them.

Edom Refuses Passage

14 Now Moses sent messengers from Kadesh to the king of [R]Edom. [R]"Thus says your
brother Israel: 'You know all the hardship
that has befallen us, Gen. 36:31–39 • Deut. 2:4
15 'how our fathers went down to Egypt,
and we dwelt in Egypt a long time, and the
Egyptians afflicted us and our fathers.
16 'When we cried out to the LORD, He
heard our voice and sent the Angel and
brought us up out of Egypt; now here we are
in Kadesh, a city on the edge of your border.
17 'Please let us pass through your country.
We will not pass through fields or vineyards,
nor will we drink water from wells; we will go
along the King's Highway; we will not turn
aside to the right hand or to the left until we
have passed through your territory.' "
18 Then [R]Edom said to him, "You shall not
pass through my *land*, lest I come out against
you with the sword." Num. 24:18
19 So the children of Israel said to him, "We
will go by the Highway, and if I or my
livestock drink any of your water, [R]then I will
pay for it; let me only pass through on foot,
nothing *more*." Deut. 2:6, 28
20 Then he said, "You shall not pass
through." So Edom came out against them
with many men and with a strong hand.
21 Thus Edom [R]refused to give Israel passage through his territory; so Israel [R]turned
away from him. Deut. 2:27, 30 • Judg. 11:18

Aaron Dies

22 Then the children of Israel, the whole
congregation, journeyed from [R]Kadesh [R]and
came to Mount Hor. Num. 33:37 • Num. 21:4
23 And the LORD spoke to Moses and Aaron
in Mount Hor by the border of the land of
Edom, saying:
24 "Aaron shall [T]be [R]gathered to his people,
for he shall not enter the land which I have
given to the children of Israel, because you
rebelled against My word at the water of
Meribah. Die and join his ancestors • Gen. 25:8
25 [R]"Take Aaron and Eleazar his son, and
bring them up to Mount Hor; Num. 33:38
26 "and strip Aaron of his garments and put
them on Eleazar his son; for Aaron shall be
gathered *to his people* and die there."
27 So Moses did just as the LORD commanded, and they went up to Mount Hor in
the sight of all the congregation.
28 [R]Moses stripped Aaron of his garments
and put them on Eleazar his son; and [R]Aaron
died there on the top of the mountain. Then
Moses and Eleazar came down from the
mountain. Ex. 29:29, 30 • Num. 33:38
29 Now when all the congregation saw that
Aaron was dead, all the house of Israel
mourned for Aaron [R]thirty days. Deut. 34:8

CHAPTER 21

Israel's Victory over the Canaanites

WHEN [R]the king of Arad, the Canaanite,
who dwelt in the South, heard that
Israel was coming on the road to Atharim,
then he fought against Israel and took *some*
of them prisoners. Judg. 1:16
2 [R]So Israel made a vow to the LORD, and
said, "If You will indeed deliver this people
into my hand, then [R]I will utterly destroy
their cities." Gen. 28:20 • Deut. 2:34
3 And the LORD listened to the voice of
Israel and delivered up the Canaanites, and
they utterly destroyed them and their cities.
So the name of that place was called [T]Hor-
mah. Lit. *Utter Destruction*

Israel Complains—Deut. 2:1

4 Then they journeyed from Mount Hor by
the Way of the Red Sea, to go around the
land of Edom; and the soul of the people
became very discouraged on the way.
5 And the people spoke against God and
against Moses: "Why have you brought us up
out of Egypt to die in the wilderness? For
there is no food and no water, and our soul
[T]loathes this worthless bread." *detests*

God Judges with Serpents

6 So [R]the LORD sent [R]fiery serpents among
the people, and they bit the people; and many
of the people of Israel died. 1 Cor. 10:9 • Deut. 8:15

The Bronze Serpent

7 [R]Therefore the people came to Moses,
and said, "We have [R]sinned, for we have
spoken against the LORD and against you;
[R]pray to the LORD that He take away the
serpents from us." So Moses prayed for the
people. Num. 11:2 • Lev. 26:40 • Ex. 8:8
8 Then the LORD said to Moses, [R]"Make a
[R]fiery *serpent*, and set it on a pole; and it shall
be that everyone who is bitten, when he
looks at it, shall live." [John 3:14, 15] • Is. 14:29; 30:6
9 So [R]Moses made a bronze serpent, and
put it on a pole; and so it was, if a serpent had
bitten anyone, when he looked at the bronze
serpent, he lived. John 3:14, 15

Journey to Moab

10 Now the children of Israel moved on and
[R]camped in Oboth. Num. 33:43, 44
11 And they journeyed from Oboth and
camped at Ije Abarim, in the wilderness
which *is* east of Moab, toward the sunrise.

HYMNS AND SONGS

The Hebrews were a music-loving people. Several musical instruments, including the tambourine or timbrel (see illustration), are mentioned in the Bible (Ps. 81:2). Merry-making and music were part of their feasts and festivals.

The earliest recorded song in the Bible is referred to as the Song of Moses (see Ex. 15). This hymn was sung by the people to celebrate God's miraculous deliverance of the Hebrews from the Egyptian army at the Red Sea (Ex. 14:3–30). Other significant hymns and songs of the Bible include the following:

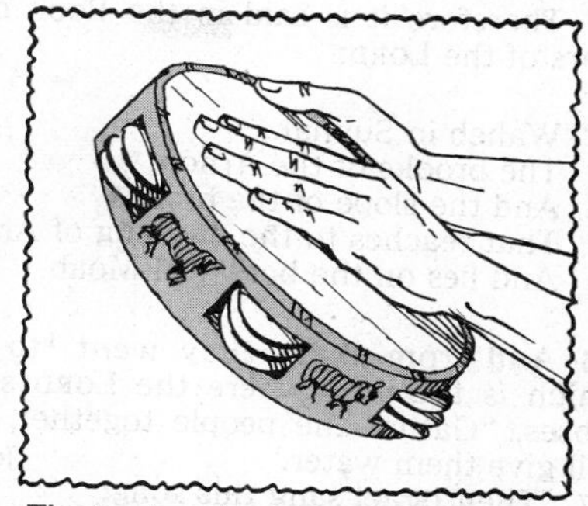

The tambourine, or timbrel, is just one of several musical instruments mentioned in the Bible.

Personality	Description	Biblical Reference
Israelites	Sung by the people as they dug life-saving wells in the Wilderness	Num. 21:14–18
Moses	A song of praise to God by Moses just before his death	Deut. 32:1–44
Deborah and Barak	A victory song after Israel's defeat of the Canaanites	Judg. 5:1–31
Israelite Women	A song to celebrate David's defeat of Goliath	1 Sam. 18:6, 7
Levite Singers	A song of praise at the dedication of the temple in Jerusalem	2 Chr. 5:12–14
Levite Singers	A song of praise, presented as a marching song as the army of Israel prepared for battle	2 Chr. 20:20–23
Levite Singers	A song at the temple restoration ceremony during Hezekiah's reign	2 Chr. 29:25–30
Jesus and Disciples	A song in the Upper Room as they celebrated the Passover together just before the arrest of Jesus	Matt. 26:30
Mary	The Song of Mary, upon learning that she as a virgin would give birth to the Messiah	Luke 1:46–55
Zacharias	A song of joy at the circumcision of his son, who would serve as the Messiah's forerunner	Luke 1:68–79
Paul and Silas	A song of praise to God at midnight from their prison cell in Philippi	Acts 16:25
All Believers	The spiritual songs of thanksgiving and joy, which God wants all believers to sing	Eph. 5:19 Col. 3:16
144,000 Believers	A new song of the redeemed in heaven, sung to glorify God	Rev. 14:1–3

12 [R]From there they moved and camped in
the Valley of Zered. Deut. 2:13
13 From there they moved and camped on
the other side of the Arnon, which *is* in the
wilderness that extends from the border of
the Amorites; for the Arnon *is* the border of
Moab, between Moab and the Amorites.
14 Therefore it is said in the Book of the
Wars of the LORD:

*"Waheb in Suphah,
The brooks of the Arnon,
15 And the slope of the brooks
That reaches to the dwelling of Ar,
And lies on the border of Moab."

16 And from there *they went* [R]to Beer,
which *is* the well where the LORD said to
Moses, "Gather the people together, and I
will give them water." Judg. 9:21
17 [R]Then Israel sang this song: Ex. 15:1

"Spring up, O well!
All of you sing to it—
18 The well the leaders sank,
Dug by the nation's nobles,
By the lawgiver, with their staves."

And from the wilderness *they went* to Mattanah,
19 from Mattanah to Nahaliel, from Nahaliel to Bamoth,
20 and from Bamoth, *in* the valley that *is* in
the country of Moab, to the top of Pisgah
which looks down on the wasteland.

Israel's Victory over Ammon—Deut. 2:26–36

21 Then [R]Israel sent messengers to Sihon
king of the Amorites, saying, Deut. 2:26–37
22 [R]"Let me pass through your land. We will
not turn aside into fields or vineyards; we will
not drink water from wells; *but* we will go by
the King's Highway until we have passed
through your territory." Num. 20:16, 17
23 But Sihon would not allow Israel to pass
through his territory. So Sihon gathered all
his people together and [T]went out against
Israel in the wilderness, and he came to Jahaz
and fought against Israel. *attacked*
24 Then [R]Israel defeated him with the edge
of the sword, and took possession of his land
from the Arnon to the Jabbok, as far as the
people of Ammon; for the border of the
people of Ammon *was* fortified. Amos 2:9
25 So Israel took all these cities, and Israel
[R]dwelt in all the cities of the Amorites, in
Heshbon and in all its villages. Amos 2:10
26 For Heshbon *was* the city of Sihon king
of the Amorites, who had fought against the
former king of Moab, and had taken all his
land from his hand as far as the Arnon.
27 Therefore those who speak in [T]proverbs
say: *parables*

"Come to Heshbon, let it be built;
Let the city of Sihon be repaired.

28 "For fire went out from Heshbon,
A flame from the city of Sihon;
It consumed [R]Ar of Moab, Is. 15:1
The lords of the heights of the Arnon.
29 Woe to you, [R]Moab! Jer. 48:46
You have perished, O people of
[R]Chemosh! Judg. 11:24
He has given his sons as fugitives,
And his [R]daughters into captivity,
To Sihon king of the Amorites. Is. 16:2

30 "But we have shot at them;
Heshbon has perished as far as Dibon.
Then we laid waste as far as Nophah,
Which *reaches* to [R]Medeba." Is. 15:2

31 Thus Israel dwelt in the land of the
Amorites.
32 Then Moses sent to spy out [R]Jazer; and
they took its villages and drove out the
Amorites who *were* there. Jer. 48:32

Israel's Victory over Bashan—Deut. 3:1–4

33 [R]And they turned and went up by the
way to [R]Bashan. So Og king of Bashan went
out against them, he and all his people, to
battle [R]at Edrei. Deut. 29:7 • Deut. 3:1 • Josh. 13:12
34 Then the LORD said to Moses, "Do not
fear him, for I have delivered him into your
hand, with all his people and his land; and
you shall do to him as you did to Sihon king
of the Amorites, who dwelt at Heshbon."
35 So they defeated him, his sons, and all
his people, until there was no survivor left
him; and they took possession of his land.

CHAPTER 22

Balaam Is Sought by Balak

THEN the children of Israel moved, and
camped in the plains of Moab on the side
of the Jordan *across from* Jericho.
2 Now Balak the son of Zippor saw all that
Israel had done to the Amorites.
3 And [R]Moab was exceedingly afraid of the
people because they *were* many, and Moab
was sick with dread because of the children
of Israel. Ex. 15:15
4 So Moab said to the elders of Midian,
"Now this company will [T]lick up all *that is*
around us, as an ox licks up the grass of the
field." And Balak the son of Zippor *was* king
of the Moabites at that time. *consume*
5 Then he sent messengers to Balaam the
son of Beor at [R]Pethor, which *is* near the
River in the land of the sons of his people, to
call him, saying: "Look, a people has come

21:14 Ancient unknown places; Vg. *What he did in the Red Sea* from Egypt. See, they cover the face of the earth, and are settling next to me! Deut. 23:4

6 "Therefore please come at once, [R]curse this people for me, for they *are* too mighty for me. Perhaps I shall be able to defeat them and drive them out of the land, for I know that he whom you bless *is* blessed, and he whom you curse is cursed." Num. 22:12; 24:9

7 So the elders of Moab and the elders of Midian departed with [R]the diviner's fee in their hand, and they came to Balaam and spoke to him the words of Balak. 1 Sam. 9:7, 8

8 And he said to them, [R]"Lodge here tonight, and I will bring back word to you, as the LORD speaks to me." So the princes of Moab stayed with Balaam. Num. 22:19

9 [R]Then God came to Balaam and said, "Who *are* these men with you?" Gen. 20:3

10 And Balaam said to God, "Balak the son of Zippor, king of Moab, has sent to me, *saying*,

11 'Look, a people has come out of Egypt, and they cover the face of the earth. Come now, curse them for me; perhaps I shall be able to overpower them and drive them out.'"

12 And God said to Balaam, "You shall not go with them; you shall not curse the people, for [R]they *are* blessed." [Rom. 11:28]

13 So Balaam rose in the morning and said to the princes of Balak, "Go back to your land, for the LORD has refused to give me permission to go with you."

14 And the princes of Moab rose and went to Balak, and said, "Balaam refuses to come with us."

15 Then Balak again sent princes, more numerous and more honorable than they.

16 And they came to Balaam and said to him, "Thus says Balak the son of Zippor: 'Please let nothing hinder you from coming to me;

17 'for I will certainly honor you greatly, and I will do whatever you say to me. Therefore please come, curse this people for me.'"

18 Then Balaam answered and said to the servants of Balak, "Though Balak were to give me his house full of silver and gold, [R]I could not go beyond the word of the LORD my God, to do less or more. 1 Kin. 22:14

19 "Now therefore, please, you also [R]stay here tonight, that I may know what more the LORD will say to me." Num. 22:8

20 [R]And God came to Balaam at night and said to him, "If the men come to call you, rise *and* go with them; but only the word which I speak to you—that you shall do." Num. 22:9

21 So Balaam rose in the morning, saddled his donkey, and went with the princes of Moab.

22 Then God's anger was aroused because he went, [R]and the Angel of the LORD took His stand in the way as an adversary against him. And he was riding on his donkey, and his two servants *were* with him. Ex. 4:24

23 Now [R]the donkey saw the Angel of the LORD standing in the way with His drawn sword in His hand, and the donkey turned aside out of the way and went into the field. So Balaam struck the donkey to turn her back onto the road. Josh. 5:13

24 Then the Angel of the LORD stood in a narrow path between the vineyards, *with* a wall on this side and a wall on that side.

25 And when the donkey saw the Angel of the LORD, she pushed herself against the wall and crushed Balaam's foot against the wall; so he struck her again.

26 Then the Angel of the LORD went further, and stood in a narrow place where there *was* no way to turn either to the right hand or to the left.

27 And when the donkey saw the Angel of the LORD, she lay down under Balaam; so Balaam's anger was aroused, and he struck the donkey with his staff.

28 Then the LORD [R]opened the mouth of the donkey, and she said to Balaam, "What have I done to you, that you have struck me these three times?" 2 Pet. 2:16

29 And Balaam said to the donkey, "Because you have [T]abused me. I wish there were a sword in my hand, [R]for now I would kill you!" *mocked* • [Prov. 12:10]

30 [R]So the donkey said to Balaam, "*Am* I not your donkey on which you have ridden, ever since *I became* yours, to this day? Was I ever [T]disposed to do this to you?" And he said, "No." 2 Pet. 2:16 • *accustomed*

31 Then the LORD [R]opened Balaam's eyes, and he saw the Angel of the LORD standing in the way with His drawn sword in His hand; and he bowed his head and fell flat on his face. Gen. 21:19

32 And the Angel of the LORD said to him, "Why have you struck your donkey these three times? Behold, I have come out [T]to stand against you, because *your* way is [T]perverse before Me. *as an adversary* • *contrary*

33 "The donkey saw Me and turned aside from Me these three times. If she had not turned aside from Me, surely I would also have killed you by now, and let her live."

34 And Balaam said to the Angel of the LORD, "I have sinned, for I did not know You stood in the way against me. Now therefore, if it displeases You, I will turn back."

35 Then the Angel of the LORD said to Balaam, "Go with the men, [R]but only the word that I speak to you, that you shall speak." So Balaam went with the princes of Balak. Num. 22:20

36 Now when Balak heard that Balaam was coming, he went out to meet him at the city of Moab, which *is* on the border at the Arnon, the boundary of the territory.

37 Then Balak said to Balaam, "Did I not
earnestly send to you, calling for you? Why
did you not come to me? Am I not able [R]to
honor you?" Num. 22:17; 24:11
38 And Balaam said to Balak, "Look, I have
come to you! Now, have I any power at all to
say anything? [R]The word that God puts in my
mouth, that I must speak." 1 Kin. 22:14
39 So Balaam went with Balak, and they
came to Kirjath Huzoth.
40 Then Balak offered oxen and sheep, and
he sent *some* to Balaam and to the princes
who *were* with him.

The First Oracle of Balaam

41 So it was, the next day, that Balak took
Balaam and brought him up to the [R]high
places of Baal, that from there he might
observe the extent of the people. Num. 21:28

CHAPTER 23

THEN Balaam said to Balak, [R]"Build seven
altars for me here, and prepare for me
here seven bulls and seven rams." Num. 23:29
2 And Balak did just as Balaam had spoken, and Balak and Balaam [R]offered a bull
and a ram on *each* altar. Num. 23:14, 30
3 Then Balaam said to Balak, [R]"Stand by
your burnt offering, and I will go; perhaps the
LORD will come [R]to meet me, and whatever
He shows me I will tell you." So he went to a
desolate height. Num. 23:15 • Num. 23:4, 16
4 And God met Balaam, and he said to
Him, "I have prepared the seven altars, and I
have offered on *each* altar a bull and a ram."
5 Then the LORD [R]put a word in Balaam's
mouth, and said, "Return to Balak, and thus
you shall speak." Deut. 18:18
6 So he returned to him, and there he was,
standing by his burnt offering, he and all the
princes of Moab.
7 And he [R]took up his [T]oracle and said:

"Balak the king of Moab has brought me
from Aram, Deut. 23:4 • *prophetic discourse*
From the mountains of the east.
[R]'Come, curse Jacob for me, Num. 22:6, 11, 17
And come, [R]denounce Israel!' 1 Sam. 17:10

8 "How[R] shall I curse whom God has not
cursed? Num. 22:12
And how shall I denounce *whom* the
LORD has not denounced?
9 For from the top of the rocks I see him,
And from the hills I behold him;
There! A people dwelling alone,
Not reckoning itself among the nations.

10 "Who can count the [T]dust of Jacob,
Or number one-fourth of Israel?
Let me die the death of the righteous,
And let my end be like his!" Or *dust cloud*

11 Then Balak said to Balaam, "What have
you done to me? [R]I took you to curse my
enemies, and look, you have blessed *them*
bountifully!" Num. 22:11
12 So he answered and said, [R]"Must I not
take heed to speak what the LORD has put in
my mouth?" Num. 22:38

The Second Oracle of Balaam

13 Then Balak said to him, "Please come
with me to another place from which you
may see them; you shall see only the outer
part of them, and shall not see them all; curse
them for me from there."
14 So he brought him to the field of Zophim,
to the top of Pisgah, and built seven altars,
and offered a bull and a ram on *each* altar.
15 And he said to Balak, "Stand here by
your burnt offering while I meet *the* LORD
over there."
16 Then the LORD met Balaam, and put a
word in his mouth, and said, "Go back to
Balak, and thus you shall speak."
17 So he came to him, and there he was,
standing by his burnt offering, and the
princes of Moab were with him. And Balak
said to him, "What has the LORD spoken?"
18 Then he took up his oracle and said:

[R]"Rise up, Balak, and hear!
Listen to me, son of Zippor! Judg. 3:20

19 "God[R] *is* not a man, that He should lie,
Nor a son of man, that He should
repent. Mal. 3:6
Has He [R]said, and will He not do *it*?
Or has He spoken, and will He not
make it good? 1 Kin. 8:56
20 Behold, I have received *a command* to
bless;
He has blessed, and I cannot reverse it.

21 "He has not observed iniquity in Jacob,
Nor has He seen wickedness in Israel.
The LORD his God *is* with him,
And the shout of a King *is* among them.
22 God brings them out of Egypt;
He has strength like a wild ox.

23 "For *there is* no [T]sorcery against Jacob,
Nor *is there* any [T]divination against
Israel. *enchantment* • *fortune-telling*
It now must be said of Jacob
And of Israel, 'Oh, [R]what God has
done!' Ps. 31:19; 44:1
24 Look, a people rises [R]like a lioness,
And lifts itself up like a lion;
[R]It shall not lie down until it devours the
prey, Gen. 49:9 • Gen. 49:27
And drinks the blood of the slain."

25 Then Balak said to Balaam, "Neither
curse them at all, nor bless them at all!"

26 So Balaam answered and said to Balak,
"Did I not tell you, saying, [R]'All that the LORD
speaks, that I must do'?" Num. 22:38

The Third Oracle of Balaam

27 Then Balak said to Balaam, "Please
come, I will take you to another place; perhaps it will please God that you may curse
them for me from there."
28 So Balak took Balaam to the top of Peor,
that overlooks [T]the wasteland. Or *Jeshimon*
29 Then Balaam said to Balak, "Build for me
here seven altars, and prepare for me here
seven bulls and seven rams."
30 And Balak did as Balaam had said, and
offered a bull and a ram on *every* altar.

CHAPTER 24

NOW when Balaam saw that it pleased the
LORD to bless Israel, he did not go as at
other times, to seek to use sorcery, but he set
his face toward the wilderness.
2 And Balaam raised his eyes, and saw
Israel encamped according to their tribes;
and the Spirit of God came upon him.
3 [R]Then he took up his oracle and said:

"The utterance of Balaam the son of
Beor,
The utterance of the man whose eyes
are opened, Num. 23:7, 18
4 The utterance of him who hears the
words of God,
Who sees the vision of the Almighty,
Who [R]falls down, with eyes opened
wide: Ezek. 1:28

5 "How lovely are your tents, O Jacob!
Your dwellings, O Israel!
6 Like valleys that stretch out,
Like gardens by the riverside,
Like aloes planted by the LORD,
Like cedars beside the waters.
7 He shall pour water from his buckets,
And his seed *shall be* in many waters.

"His king shall be higher than Agag,
And his kingdom shall be exalted.

8 "God[R] brings him out of Egypt;
He has strength like a wild ox;
He shall [R]consume the nations, his
enemies; Num. 23:22 • Num. 14:9; 23:24
He shall [R]break their bones Ps. 2:9
And pierce *them* with his arrows.
9 'He bows down, he lies down as a lion;
And as a lion, who will rouse him?'

"Blessed *is* he who blesses you,
And cursed *is* he who curses you."

10 Then Balak's anger was aroused against
Balaam, and he struck his hands together;
and Balak said to Balaam, "I called you to
curse my enemies, and look, you have bountifully blessed *them* these three times!
11 "Now therefore, flee to your place. I said
I would greatly honor you, but in fact, the
LORD has kept you back from honor."
12 So Balaam said to Balak, "Did I not also
speak to your messengers whom you sent to
me, saying,
13 'Though Balak were to give me his house
full of silver and gold, I could not go beyond
the word of the LORD, to do *either* good or
bad of my own will; *but* what the LORD says,
that I must speak'?

The Fourth Oracle of Balaam

14 "And now, indeed, I am going to my
people. Come, [R]I will advise you what this
people will do to your people in the [R]latter
days." [Mic. 6:5] • Gen. 49:1
15 Then he took up his oracle and said:

"The utterance of Balaam the son of
Beor,
And the utterance of the man whose
eyes are opened;
16 The utterance of him who hears the
words of God,
And knows the knowledge of the Most
High,
Who sees the vision of the Almighty,
Who falls down, with eyes opened wide:

17 "I see Him, but not now;
I behold Him, but not near;
[R]A Star shall come out of Jacob; Matt. 1:2 ☆
A Scepter shall rise out of Israel,
And batter the brow of Moab,
And destroy all the sons of tumult.

18 "And [R]Edom shall be a possession;
Seir also, his enemies, shall be a
possession, 2 Sam. 8:14
While Israel does [T]valiantly. *mightily*
19 Out of Jacob One shall have dominion,
And destroy the remains of the city."

20 Then he looked on Amalek, and he took
up his oracle and said:

"Amalek *was* first among the nations,
But *shall be* last until he perishes."

21 Then he looked on the Kenites, and he
took up his oracle and said:

"Firm is your dwelling place,
And your nest is set in the rock;
22 Nevertheless Kain shall be burned.
How long until Asshur carries you away
captive?"

23 Then he took up his oracle and said:

"Alas! Who shall live when God does
this?
24 But ships *shall come* from the coasts of
[R]Cyprus,[T] Gen. 10:4 • Heb. *Kittim*
And they shall afflict Asshur and afflict
[R]Eber, Gen. 10:21, 25
And so shall [T]Amalek, until he
perishes." Lit. *he* or *that one*

25 Then Balaam rose and departed and [R]returned to his place; Balak also went his way. Num. 21:34; 31:8

CHAPTER 25

Israel Commits Harlotry

THEN Israel remained in [T]Acacia Grove, and the people began to commit harlotry with the women of Moab. Heb. *Shittim*

2 They invited the people to [R]the sacrifices of their gods, and the people ate and [R]bowed down to their gods. Ex. 34:15 • Ex. 20:5

Phinehas Stays the Plague

3 So Israel was joined to Baal of Peor, and [R]the anger of the LORD was aroused against Israel. Ps. 106:28, 29

4 Then the LORD said to Moses, [R]"Take all the leaders of the people and hang the offenders before the LORD, out in the sun, [R]that the fierce anger of the LORD may turn away from Israel." Deut. 4:3 • Num. 25:11

5 So Moses said to [R]the judges of Israel, [R]"Every one of you kill his men who were joined to Baal of Peor." Ex. 18:21 • Deut. 13:6, 9

6 And indeed, one of the children of Israel came and presented to his brethren a Midianite woman in the sight of Moses and in the sight of all the congregation of the children of Israel, [R]who *were* weeping at the door of the tabernacle of meeting. Joel 2:17

7 Now [R]when Phinehas [R]the son of Eleazar, the son of Aaron the priest, saw *it*, he rose from among the congregation and took a javelin in his hand; Ps. 106:30 • Ex. 6:25

8 and he went after the man of Israel into the tent and thrust both of them through, the man of Israel, and the woman through her body. So [R]the plague was [R]stopped among the children of Israel. Ps. 106:30 • Num. 16:46–48

9 And [R]those who died in the plague were twenty-four thousand. Deut. 4:3

10 Then the LORD spoke to Moses, saying:

11 [R]"Phinehas the son of Eleazar, the son of Aaron the priest, has turned back My wrath from the children of Israel, because he was zealous with My zeal among them, so that I did not consume the children of Israel in [R]My zeal. Ps. 106:30 • [Ex. 20:5]

12 "Therefore say, [R]'Behold, I give to him My [R]covenant of peace; [Mal. 2:4, 5; 3:1] • Is. 54:10

13 'and it shall be to him and his descendants after him a covenant of [R]an everlasting priesthood, because he was [R]zealous for his God, and [R]made atonement for the children of Israel.'" Ex. 40:15 • Acts 22:3 • [Heb. 2:17]

14 Now the name of the Israelite who was killed, who was killed with the Midianite woman, *was* Zimri the son of Salu, a leader of a father's house among the Simeonites.

15 And the name of the Midianite woman who was killed *was* Cozbi the daughter of [R]Zur; he *was* head of the people of a father's house in Midian. Num. 31:8

Israel to Destroy Moab

16 Then the LORD spoke to Moses, saying:

17 [R]"Harass the Midianites, and [T]attack them; Num. 31:1–3 • *be hostile toward*

18 "for they harassed you with their [R]schemes[T] by which they seduced you in the matter of Peor and in the matter of Cozbi, the daughter of a leader of Midian, their sister, who was killed in the day of the plague because of Peor." Rev. 2:14 • *tricks*

CHAPTER 26

The Second Census

AND it came to pass, after the [R]plague, that the LORD spoke to Moses and Eleazar the son of Aaron the priest, saying: Num. 25:9

2 "Take a census of all the congregation of the children of Israel from twenty years old and above, by their fathers' houses, all who are able to go to war in Israel."

3 So Moses and Eleazar the priest spoke with them in the plains of Moab by the Jordan, *across from* Jericho, saying:

4 "*Take a census of the people* from twenty years old and above, just as the LORD [R]commanded Moses and the children of Israel who came out of the land of Egypt." Num. 1:1

5 [R]Reuben *was* the firstborn of Israel. The children of Reuben *were: of* Hanoch, the family of the Hanochites; *of* Pallu, the family of the Palluites; Ex. 6:14

6 *of* Hezron, the family of the Hezronites; *of* Carmi, the family of the Carmites.

7 These *are* the families of the Reubenites: those who were numbered of them were forty-three thousand seven hundred and thirty.

8 And the son of Pallu *was* Eliab.

9 The sons of Eliab *were* Nemuel, Dathan, and Abiram. These *are* the Dathan and Abiram, [R]representatives of the congregation, who contended against Moses and Aaron in the company of Korah, when they contended against the LORD; Num. 1:16; 16:1, 2

10 [R]and the earth opened its mouth and swallowed them up together with Korah

when that company died, when the fire devoured two hundred and fifty men; [R]and they
became a sign. Num. 16:32–35 • Num. 16:38–40
11 Nevertheless [R]the children of Korah did
not die. Ex. 6:24
12 The sons of Simeon according to their
families *were: of* Nemuel, the family of the
Nemuelites; *of* [T]Jamin, the family of the
Jaminites; *of* [T]Jachin, the family of the Ja-
chinites; *Jemuel,* Gen. 46:10; Ex. 6:15 • *Jarib,* 1 Chr. 4:24
13 *of* Zerah, the family of the Zarhites; *of*
Shaul, the family of the Shaulites.
14 These *are* the families of the Simeonites:
twenty-two thousand two hundred.
15 The sons of Gad according to their families *were: of* Zephon, the family of the Zeph-
onites; *of* Haggi, the family of the Haggites;
of Shuni, the family of the Shunites;
16 *of* [T]Ozni, the family of the Oznites; *of* Eri,
the family of the Erites; *Ezbon,* Gen. 46:16
17 *of* *Arod, the family of the Arodites; *of*
Areli, the family of the Arelites.
18 These *are* the families of the sons of Gad
according to those who were numbered of
them: forty thousand five hundred.
19 The sons of Judah *were* Er and Onan;
and Er and Onan died in the land of Canaan.
20 And the sons of Judah according to their
families were: *of* Shelah, the family of the
Shelanites; *of* Perez, the family of the Parzites; *of* Zerah, the family of the Zarhites.
21 And the sons of Perez were: *of* Hezron,
the family of the Hezronites; *of* Hamul, the
family of the Hamulites.
22 These *are* the families of Judah according to those who were numbered of them:
seventy-six thousand five hundred.
23 The sons of Issachar according to their
families *were: of* Tola, the family of the
Tolaites; of *Puah, the family of the *Punites;
24 of Jashub, the family of the Jashubites;
of Shimron, the family of the Shimronites.
25 These *are* the families of Issachar according to those who were numbered of
them: sixty-four thousand three hundred.
26 The sons of Zebulun according to their
families *were*: of Sered, the family of the
Sardites; of Elon, the family of the Elonites;
of Jahleel, the family of the Jahleelites.
27 These *are* the families of the Zebulunites
according to those who were numbered of
them: sixty thousand five hundred.
28 The sons of Joseph according to their
families, by Manasseh and Ephraim, *were*:
29 The sons of Manasseh: of Machir, the
family of the Machirites; and Machir begot
Gilead; of Gilead, the family of the Gileadites.
30 These *are* the sons of Gilead: *of* [T]Jeezer,
the family of the Jeezerites; of Helek, the
family of the Helekites; *Abiezer,* Josh. 17:2
31 *of* Asriel, the family of the Asrielites; *of*
Shechem, the family of the Shechemites;
32 *of* Shemida, the family of the Shemida-
ites; *of* Hepher, the family of the Hepherites.
33 Now Zelophehad the son of Hepher had
no sons, but daughters; and the names of the
daughters of Zelophehad *were* Mahlah,
Noah, Hoglah, Milcah, and Tirzah.
34 These *are* the families of Manasseh; and
those who were numbered of them *were* fifty-
two thousand seven hundred.
35 These *are* the sons of Ephraim according
to their families: of Shuthelah, the family of
the Shuthalhites; of [T]Becher, the family of the
Bachrites; of Tahan, the family of the Tahan-
ites. *Bered,* 1 Chr. 7:20
36 And these *are* the sons of Shuthelah: of
Eran, the family of the Eranites.
37 These *are* the families of the sons of
Ephraim according to those who were numbered of them: thirty-two thousand five hundred. These *are* the sons of Joseph according
to their families.
38 The sons of Benjamin according to their
families were: of Bela, the family of the
Belaites; of Ashbel, the family of the Ashbel-
ites; of Ahiram, the family of the Ahiramites;
39 of [R]Shupham,* the family of the Shu-
phamites; of *Hupham, the family of the
Huphamites. 1 Chr. 7:12
40 And the sons of Bela were Ard and Naaman: *of Ard,* the family of the Ardites; of
Naaman, the family of the Naamites.
41 These *are* the sons of Benjamin according to their families; and those who were
numbered of them *were* forty-five thousand
six hundred.
42 These *are* the sons of Dan according to
their families: of [T]Shuham, the family of the
Shuhamites. These *are* the families of Dan
according to their families. *Hushim,* Gen. 46:23
43 All the families of the Shuhamites, according to those who were numbered of
them, *were* sixty-four thousand four hundred.
44 [R]The sons of Asher according to their
families *were*: of Jimna, the family of the
Jimnites; of Jesui, the family of the Jesuites;
of Beriah, the family of the Beriites. Gen. 46:17
45 Of the sons of Beriah: of Heber, the
family of the Heberites; of Malchiel, the
family of the Malchielites.
46 And the name of the daughter of Asher
was Serah.
47 These *are* the families of the sons of
Asher according to those who were numbered of them: fifty-three thousand four
hundred.
48 [R]The sons of Naphtali according to their
families *were*: of Jahzeel, the family of the

26:17 Sam., Syr. *Arodi* and Gen. 46:16
26:23 So with Sam., LXX, Syr., Vg.; Heb. *Puvah,* Gen. 46:13; 1 Chr. 7:1 **26:23** Sam., LXX, Syr., Vg. *Puaites*
26:39 MT *Shephupham; Shephuphan,* 1 Chr. 8:5
26:39 *Huppim,* Gen. 46:21

Jahzeelites; of Guni, the family of the Gun-
ites; 1 Chr. 7:13
49 of Jezer, the family of the Jezerites; of
Shillem, the family of the Shillemites.
50 These *are* the families of Naphtali according to their families; and those who were
numbered of them *were* forty-five thousand
four hundred.
51 These *are* those who were numbered of
the children of Israel: six hundred and one
thousand seven hundred and thirty.

Method for Dividing the Land

52 Then the LORD spoke to Moses, saying:
53 [R]"To these the land shall be [R]divided as
an inheritance, according to the number of
names. Josh. 11:23; 14:1 • Num. 33:54
54 [R]"To a large *tribe* you shall give a larger
inheritance, and to a small *tribe* you shall
give a smaller inheritance. Each shall be
given its inheritance according to those who
were numbered of them. Num. 33:54
55 "But the land shall be [R]divided by lot;
they shall inherit according to the names of
the tribes of their fathers. Num. 33:54; 54:13
56 "According to the lot their inheritance
shall be divided between the larger and the
smaller."

The Levites Have No Inheritance

57 And these *are* those who were numbered
of the Levites according to their families: of
Gershon, the family of the Gershonites;
of Kohath, the family of the Kohathites; of
Merari, the family of the Merarites.
58 These *are* the families of the Levites:
the family of the Libnites, the family of the
Hebronites, the family of the Mahlites,
the family of the Mushites, and the family of
the Korathites. And Kohath begot Amram.
59 The name of Amram's wife *was* Jochebed the daughter of Levi, who was born to
Levi in Egypt; and to Amram she bore Aaron
and Moses and their sister Miriam.
60 [R]To Aaron were born Nadab and Abihu,
Eleazar and Ithamar. Num. 3:2
61 And Nadab and Abihu died when they
offered profane fire before the LORD.
62 Now those who were numbered of them
were twenty-three thousand, every male
from a month old and above; for they were
not numbered among the other children of
Israel, because there was no inheritance
given to them among the children of Israel.

The Old Generation Has No Inheritance

63 These *are* those who were numbered by
Moses and Eleazar the priest, who numbered
the children of Israel [R]in the plains of Moab
by the Jordan, *across from* Jericho. Num. 26:3
64 But among these there was not a man of
those who were numbered by Moses and
Aaron the priest when they numbered the
children of Israel in the Wilderness of Sinai.
65 For the LORD had said of them, "They
shall surely die in the wilderness." So there
was not left a man of them, except Caleb the
son of Jephunneh and Joshua the son of Nun.

CHAPTER 27

The Special Laws of Inheritance

THEN came the daughters of Zelophehad
the son of Hepher, the son of Gilead, the
son of Machir, the son of Manasseh, from the
families of Manasseh the son of Joseph; and
these *were* the names of his daughters: Mahlah, Noah, Hoglah, Milcah, and Tirzah.
2 And they stood before Moses, before
Eleazar the priest, and before the leaders and
all the congregation, *by* the doorway of the
tabernacle of meeting, saying:
3 "Our father died in the wilderness; but he
was not in the company of those who gathered together against the LORD, [R]in company
with Korah, but he died in his own sin; and
he had no sons. Num. 16:1, 2
4 "Why should the name of our father be
removed from among his family because he
had no son? *Therefore* give us a [T]possession
among the brothers of our father." *inheritance*
5 So Moses [R]brought their case before the
LORD. Ex. 18:13–26
6 And the LORD spoke to Moses, saying:
7 "The daughters of Zelophehad speak
what is right; [R]you shall surely give them a
possession of inheritance among their father's brothers, and cause the inheritance of
their father to pass to them. Num. 36:2
8 "And you shall speak to the children of
Israel, saying: 'If a man dies and has no son,
then you shall cause his inheritance to pass
to his daughter.
9 'If he has no daughter, then you shall
give his inheritance to his brothers.
10 'If he has no brothers, then you shall give
his inheritance to his father's brothers.
11 'And if his father has no brothers, then
you shall give his inheritance to the kinsman
nearest him in his family, and he shall possess
it.' " And it shall be to the children of Israel [R]a
statute of judgment, just as the LORD commanded Moses. Num. 35:29

Moses Is Set Aside

12 Now the LORD said to Moses: "Go up into
this Mount Abarim, and see the land which I
have given to the children of Israel.
13 "And when you have seen it, you also
[R]shall be gathered to your people, as Aaron
your brother was gathered. Deut. 10:6; 34:5, 6
14 "For in the Wilderness of Zin, during the
strife of the congregation, you [R]rebelled
against My command to hallow Me at the

CASTING OF LOTS

Several stones, or perhaps precious gems, may have been cast from a clay jug to make important decisions.

The casting of lots was a custom or rite used in ancient times to make important decisions, much as we practice drawing straws or flipping a coin today. Several examples of this practice occur in both the Old and New Testaments.

Lots were cast by the high priest to select the scapegoat on the Day of Atonement (Lev. 16:8–10). This method was also used to divide the land of Canaan after its conquest under Joshua (Num. 26:55, 56; Josh. 14:2). Lots were cast to select warriors to fight against the men of Gibeah (Judg. 20:9, 10) and apparently to choose Saul as the first king of Israel (1 Sam. 10:19–21). Sailors on the ship bound for Tarshish with Jonah on board used lots to determine who had caused the stormy seas (Jon. 1:7).

In the New Testament, Roman soldiers cast lots for Jesus' garments (Matt. 27:35). After prayer, the apostles used lots to choose Matthias as successor to Judas (Acts 1:24–26).

We can only speculate about what materials were used in the casting of lots. Some scholars believe several stones, or perhaps precious gems, were cast from a clay jug (see illustration). Others connect the practice with the Urim and Thummim, precious stones that were on, by, or in the breastplate of the high priest of Israel. The high priest used these stones in making important decisions, but it is not known exactly how this was done (Ex. 28:30).

Proverbs 16:33 demonstrates that casting lots was not considered magic, because the decision was from the Lord. Despite this, there seems to be little justification for this practice today. Since the coming of God's Holy Spirit at Pentecost, we have had this ever-present resource to guide us in our decision making. As enlightened believers, we are urged to bring our needs to the Father in prayer and rely on the direction of the Holy Spirit (John 14:13; 15:16).

waters before their eyes." (These *are* the [R]waters of Meribah, at Kadesh in the Wilderness of Zin.) Ps. 106:32, 33 • Ex. 17:7

Joshua Is Appointed

15 Then Moses spoke to the LORD, saying:
16 "Let the LORD, the God of the spirits of all flesh, set a man over the congregation,
17 [R]"who may go out before them and go in before them, who may lead them out and bring them in, that the congregation of the LORD may not be [R]like sheep which have no shepherd." Deut. 31:2 • Zech. 10:2
18 And the LORD said to Moses: "Take Joshua the son of Nun with you, a man [R]in whom *is* the Spirit, and [R]lay your hand on him; Gen. 41:38 • Deut. 34:9
19 "set him before Eleazar the priest and before all the congregation, and [R]inaugurate[T] him in their sight. Deut. 31:3, 7, 8, 23 • *commission*
20 "And you shall give *some* of your authority to him, that all the congregation of the children of Israel may be obedient.
21 "He shall stand before Eleazar the priest, who shall inquire before the LORD for him by the judgment of the Urim; at his word they shall go out, and at his word they shall come in, *both* he and all the children of Israel with him, all the congregation."
22 So Moses did as the LORD commanded him. He took Joshua and set him before Eleazar the priest and before all the congregation.
23 And he laid his hands on him [R]and [T]inaugurated him, just as the LORD commanded by the hand of Moses. Deut. 3:28; 31:7, 8 • *commissioned*

CHAPTER 28

Daily Offering

NOW the LORD spoke to Moses, saying,
2 "Command the children of Israel, and say to them, 'My offering, [R]My food for My offerings made by fire as a sweet aroma to Me, you shall be careful to offer to Me at their appointed time.' Lev. 3:11; 21:6, 8
3 "And you shall say to them, [R]'This *is* the offering made by fire which you shall offer to the LORD: two male lambs in their first year without blemish, day by day, as a regular burnt offering. Ex. 29:38–42
4 'The one lamb you shall offer in the morning, the other lamb you shall offer in the evening,
5 'and [R]one-tenth[T] of an ephah of fine flour as a [R]grain offering mixed with one-fourth of a hin of pressed oil. Ex. 16:36 • 2.087 qt. • Lev. 2:1
6 '*It is* [R]a regular burnt offering which was ordained at Mount Sinai for a sweet aroma, an offering made by fire to the LORD. Ex. 29:42
7 'And its drink offering *shall be* [T]one-fourth of a hin for each lamb; [R]in a holy *place* you shall pour out the drink to the LORD as an offering. 1 qt. • Ex. 29:42
8 'The other lamb you shall offer in the evening; as the morning grain offering and its drink offering, you shall offer *it* as an offering made by fire, a sweet aroma to the LORD.

Weekly Offering

9 'And on the Sabbath day two lambs in their first year, without blemish, and two-tenths *of an ephah* of fine flour as a grain offering, mixed with oil, with its drink offering—
10 '*this is* [R]the burnt offering for every Sabbath, besides the regular burnt offering with its drink offering. Ezek. 46:4

Monthly Offering

11 [R]'At the beginnings of your months you shall present a burnt offering to the LORD: two young bulls, one ram, and seven lambs in their first year, without blemish; Num. 10:10
12 [R]'three-tenths *of an ephah* of fine flour as a grain offering, mixed with oil, for each bull; two-tenths *of an ephah* of fine flour as a grain offering, mixed with oil, for the one ram; Num. 15:4–12
13 'and [T]one-tenth *of an ephah* of fine flour, mixed with oil, as a grain offering for each lamb, as a burnt offering of sweet aroma, an offering made by fire to the LORD. 2.087 qt.
14 'Their drink offering shall be [T]half a hin of wine for a bull, [T]one-third of a hin for a ram, and one-fourth of a hin for a lamb; this *is* the burnt offering for each month throughout the months of the year. .5 gal • 42.7 oz.
15 'Also [R]one kid of the goats as a sin offering to the LORD shall be offered, besides the regular burnt offering and its drink offering. Num. 15:24; 28:3, 22

Passover

16 [R]'On the fourteenth day of the first month *is* the Passover of the LORD. Lev. 23:5–8

Unleavened Bread

17 [R]'And on the fifteenth day of this month *is* the feast; unleavened bread shall be eaten for seven days. Lev. 23:6
18 'On the [R]first day *you shall have* a holy [T]convocation. You shall do no [T]customary work. Lev. 23:7 • *assembly* or *gathering* • *occupational*
19 'And you shall present an offering made by fire as a burnt offering to the LORD: two young bulls, one ram, and seven lambs in their first year. [R]Be sure they are without blemish. Deut. 15:21
20 'Their grain offering shall be of fine flour mixed with oil: three-tenths *of an ephah* you shall offer for a bull, and two-tenths for a ram;

21 'you shall offer [T]one-tenth *of an ephah* for each of the seven lambs; 2.087 qt.

22 'also [R]one goat *as* a sin offering, to make atonement for you. Num. 28:15

23 'You shall offer these besides the burnt offering of the morning, which *is* for a regular burnt offering.

24 'In this manner you shall offer the food of the offering made by fire daily for seven days, as a sweet aroma to the LORD; it shall be offered besides the regular burnt offering and its drink offering.

25 'And [R]on the seventh day you shall have a holy convocation. You shall do no customary work. Lev. 23:8

Firstfruits

26 'Also [R]on the day of the firstfruits, when you bring a new grain offering to the LORD at your *Feast of* Weeks, you shall have a holy convocation. You shall do no customary work. Deut. 16:9–12

27 'You shall present a burnt offering as a sweet aroma to the LORD: two young bulls, one ram, and seven lambs in their first year,

28 'with their grain offering of fine flour mixed with oil: three-tenths *of an ephah* for each bull, two-tenths for the one ram,

29 'and one-tenth for each of the seven lambs;

30 '*also* one kid of the goats, to make atonement for you.

31 [R]'Be sure they are without [T]blemish. You shall present *them* with their drink offerings, besides the regular burnt offering with its grain offering. Num. 28:3, 19 • *defect*

CHAPTER 29

Trumpets

'AND in the seventh month, on the first *day* of the month, you shall have a holy convocation. You shall do no customary work. For you [R]it is a day of blowing the trumpets. Lev. 23:23–25

2 'You shall offer a burnt offering as a sweet aroma to the LORD: one young bull, one ram, *and* seven lambs in their first year, without blemish.

3 'Their grain offering *shall be* fine flour mixed with oil: [T]three-tenths *of an ephah* for the bull, two-tenths for the ram, 6.261 qt.

4 'and [T]one-tenth for each of the seven lambs; 2.087 qt.

5 'also one kid of the goats *as* a sin offering, to make atonement for you;

6 'besides the burnt offering with its grain offering for the New Moon, the regular burnt offering with its grain offering, and their drink offerings, [R]according to their ordinance, as a sweet aroma, an offering made by fire to the LORD. Num. 15:11, 12

Atonement

7 'On the tenth *day* of this seventh month you shall have a holy convocation. You shall afflict your souls; you shall not do any work.

8 'You shall present a burnt offering to the LORD *as* a sweet aroma: one young bull, one ram, *and* seven lambs in their first year. [R]Be sure they are without blemish. Num. 28:19

9 'Their grain offering *shall be of* fine flour mixed with oil: three-tenths *of an ephah* for the bull, two-tenths for the one ram,

10 'and [T]one-tenth for each of the seven lambs; 2.087 qt.

11 'also one kid of the goats *as* a sin offering, besides [R]the sin offering for atonement, the regular burnt offering with its grain offering, and their drink offerings. Lev. 16:3, 5

Tabernacle

12 'On the fifteenth day of the seventh month you shall have a holy convocation. You shall do no customary work, and you shall keep a feast to the LORD seven days.

13 [R]'You shall present a burnt offering, an offering made by fire as a sweet aroma to the LORD: thirteen young bulls, two rams, *and* fourteen lambs in their first year. They shall be without blemish. Ezra 3:4

14 'Their grain offering *shall be of* fine flour mixed with oil: three-tenths *of an ephah* for each of the thirteen bulls, two-tenths for each of the two rams,

15 'and [T]one-tenth for each of the fourteen lambs; 2.087 qt.

16 'also one kid of the goats *as* a sin offering, besides the regular burnt offering, its grain offering, and its drink offering.

17 'On the [R]second day *present* twelve young bulls, two rams, fourteen lambs in their first year without blemish, Lev. 23:36

18 'and their grain offering and their drink offerings for the bulls, for the rams, and for the lambs, by their number, [R]according to the ordinance; Num. 15:12; 28:7, 14; 29:3, 4, 9, 10

19 'also one kid of the goats *as* a sin offering, besides the regular burnt offering with its grain offering, and their drink offerings.

20 'On the third day *present* eleven bulls, two rams, fourteen lambs in their first year without blemish,

21 'and their grain offering and their drink offerings for the bulls, for the rams, and for the lambs, by their number, [R]according to the ordinance; Num. 29:18

22 'also one goat *as* a sin offering, besides the regular burnt offering, its grain offering, and its drink offering.

23 'On the fourth day *present* ten bulls, two rams, *and* fourteen lambs in their first year, without blemish,

24 'and their grain offering and their drink offerings for the bulls, for the rams, and for

the lambs, by their number, according to the
ordinance;
25 'also one kid of the goats *as* a sin offering, besides the regular burnt offering, its
grain offering, and its drink offering.
26 'On the fifth day *present* nine bulls, two
rams, *and* fourteen lambs in their first year
without blemish,
27 'and their grain offering and their drink
offerings for the bulls, for the rams, and for
the lambs, by their number, according to the
ordinance;
28 'also one goat *as* a sin offering, besides
the regular burnt offering, its grain offering,
and its drink offering.
29 'On the sixth day *present* eight bulls, two
rams, *and* fourteen lambs in their first year
without blemish,
30 'and their grain offering and their drink
offerings for the bulls, for the rams, and for
the lambs, by their number, according to the
ordinance;
31 'also one goat *as* a sin offering, besides
the regular burnt offering, its grain offering,
and its drink offering.
32 'On the seventh day *present* seven bulls,
two rams, *and* fourteen lambs in their first
year without blemish,
33 'and their grain offering and their drink
offerings for the bulls, for the rams, and for
the lambs, by their number, according to the
ordinance;
34 'also one goat *as* a sin offering, besides
the regular burnt offering, its grain offering,
and its drink offering.
35 'On the eighth day you shall have a
[R]sacred[T] assembly. You shall do no customary work. Lev. 23:36 • *solemn*
36 'You shall present a burnt offering, an
offering made by fire as a sweet aroma to the
LORD: one bull, one ram, seven lambs in their
first year without blemish,
37 'and their grain offering and their drink
offerings for the bull, for the ram, and for the
lambs, by their number, according to the
ordinance;
38 'also one goat *as* a sin offering, besides
the regular burnt offering, its grain offering,
and its drink offering.
39 'These *things* you shall present to the
LORD at your [R]appointed feasts (besides your
[R]vowed offerings and your freewill offerings)
as your burnt offerings and your grain offerings, as your drink offerings and your peace
offerings.'" Lev. 23:1–44 • Lev. 7:16; 22:18, 21, 23; 23:38
40 So Moses told the children of Israel
everything, just as the LORD commanded
Moses.

CHAPTER 30

The Regulation of Vows

THEN Moses spoke to [R]the heads of the
tribes concerning the children of Israel,
saying, "This *is* the thing which the LORD has
commanded: Num. 1:4, 16; 7:2
2 [R]"If a man vows a vow to the LORD, or
[R]swears an oath to bind himself by some
agreement, he shall not break his word; he
shall [R]do according to all that proceeds out of
his mouth. Lev. 27:2 • Matt. 14:9 • Job 22:27
3 "Or if a woman vows a vow to the LORD,
and binds *herself* by some agreement while in
her father's house in her youth,
4 "and her father hears her vow and the
agreement by which she has bound herself,
and her father holds his peace, then all her
vows shall stand, and every agreement with
which she has bound herself shall stand.
5 "But if her father overrules her on the
day that he hears, then none of her vows nor
her agreements by which she has bound
herself shall stand; and the LORD will forgive
her, because her father overruled her.
6 "But if indeed she takes a husband, while
bound by her vows or by a rash utterance
from her lips by which she bound herself,
7 "and her husband hears *it*, and makes no
response to her on the day that he hears, then
her vows shall stand, and her agreements by
which she bound herself shall stand.
8 "But if her husband [R]overrules her on the
day that he hears *it*, he shall make void her
vow which she vowed and what she uttered
with her lips, by which she bound herself, and
the LORD will forgive her. [Gen. 3:16]
9 "But any vow of a widow or a divorced
woman, by which she has bound herself, shall
stand against her.
10 "If she vowed in her husband's house, or
bound herself by an agreement with an oath,
11 "and her husband heard *it*, and made no
response to her *and* did not overrule her, then
all her vows shall stand, and every agreement
by which she bound herself shall stand.
12 "But if her husband truly made them
void on the day he heard *them*, then whatever proceeded from her lips concerning her
vows or concerning the agreement binding
her, it shall not stand; her husband has made
them void, and the LORD will forgive her.
13 "Every vow and every binding oath to
afflict her soul, her husband may confirm it,
or her husband may make it void.
14 "But if her husband makes no response
whatever to her from day to day, then he
confirms all her vows or all the agreements
that bind her; he confirms them, because he
made no response to her on the day that he
heard *them*.
15 "But if he does make them void after he
has heard *them*, then he shall bear her guilt."
16 These *are* the statutes which the LORD
commanded Moses, between a man and his
wife, and between a father and his daughter
in her youth in her father's house.

CHAPTER 31

Destruction of the Midianites

AND the LORD spoke to Moses, saying:
2 "Take vengeance for the children of
Israel on the Midianites. Afterward you shall
[R]be gathered to your people." Num. 25:12, 13
3 So Moses spoke to the people, saying,
"Arm some of yourselves for the war, and let
them go against the Midianites to take vengeance for the LORD on [R]Midian. Josh. 13:21
4 "A thousand from each tribe of all the
tribes of Israel you shall send to the war."
5 So there were recruited from the divisions of Israel one thousand from *each* tribe,
twelve thousand armed for war.
6 Then Moses sent them to the war, one
thousand from *each* tribe; he sent them to
the war with Phinehas the son of Eleazar the
priest, with the holy articles and [R]the signal
trumpets in his hand. Num. 10:9
7 And they warred against the Midianites,
just as the LORD commanded Moses, and
[R]they killed all the [R]males. Deut. 20:13 • Gen. 34:25
8 They killed the kings of Midian with *the
rest of* those who were killed, *namely*: Evi,
Rekem, [R]Zur, Hur, and Reba, the five kings of
Midian. [R]Balaam the son of Beor they also
killed with the sword. Num. 25:15 • Josh. 13:22
9 And the children of Israel took *all* the
women of Midian captive, with their little
ones, and took as spoil all their cattle, all
their flocks, and all their goods.
10 They also burned with fire all the cities
where they dwelt, and all their forts.
11 And [R]they took all the spoil and all the
booty, *both* of man and beast. Deut. 20:14
12 Then they brought the captives, the
booty, and the spoil to Moses, to Eleazar the
priest, and to the congregation of the children of Israel, to the camp in the plains of
Moab by the Jordan, *across from* Jericho.
13 And Moses, Eleazar the priest, and all the
leaders of the congregation, went to meet
them outside the camp.
14 But Moses was angry with the officers of
the army, *with* the captains over thousands
and captains over hundreds, who had come
from the battle.
15 And Moses said to them: "Have you kept
[R]all the women alive? Deut. 20:14
16 "Look, these *women* caused the children
of Israel, through the counsel of Balaam, to
trespass against the LORD in the incident of
Peor, and there was a plague among the
congregation of the LORD.
17 "Now therefore, [R]kill every male among
the little ones, and kill every woman who has
known a man intimately. Deut. 7:2; 20:16–18
18 "But keep alive [R]for yourselves all the
young girls who have not known a man
intimately. Deut. 21:10–14

Purification of Israel

19 "And as for you, [R]remain outside the
camp seven days; whoever has killed any
person, and whoever has touched any slain,
purify yourselves and your captives on the
third day and on the seventh day. Num. 5:2
20 "Purify every garment, everything made
of leather, everything woven of goats' *hair*,
and everything made of wood."
21 Then Eleazar the priest said to the men
of war who had gone to the battle, "This *is*
the [T]ordinance of the law which the LORD
commanded Moses: *statute*
22 "Only the gold, the silver, the bronze, the
iron, the tin, and the lead,
23 "everything that can endure fire, you
shall put through the fire, and it shall be
clean; and it shall be purified [R]with the water
of purification. But all that cannot endure fire
you shall put through water. Num. 19:9, 17
24 [R]"And you shall wash your clothes on
the seventh day and be clean, and afterward
you may come into the camp." Lev. 11:25

Distribution of the Spoils

25 And the LORD spoke to Moses, saying:
26 "Count up the plunder that was [T]taken,
both of man and beast, you and Eleazar the
priest and the chief fathers of the congregation; *captured*
27 "and divide the plunder into two parts,
between those who took part in the war, who
went out to battle, and all the congregation.
28 "And levy a [T]tribute for the LORD on the
men of war who went out to battle: [R]one of
every five hundred of the persons, the cattle,
the donkeys, and the sheep; *tax* • Num. 31:30, 47
29 "take *it* from their half, and [R]give *it* to
Eleazar the priest as a heave offering to the
LORD. Deut. 18:1–5
30 "And from the children of Israel's half
you shall take one of every fifty, drawn from
the persons, the cattle, the donkeys, and the
sheep, from all the livestock, and give them
to the Levites who [T]keep charge of the tabernacle of the LORD." *perform the service*
31 So Moses and Eleazar the priest did as
the LORD commanded Moses.
32 And the booty remaining from the plunder, which the men of war had taken, was six
hundred and seventy-five thousand sheep,
33 seventy-two thousand cattle,
34 sixty-one thousand donkeys,
35 and thirty-two thousand persons in all, of
women who had not known a man intimately.
36 And the half, the portion for those who
had gone out to war, was in number three
hundred and thirty-seven thousand five hundred sheep;
37 and the LORD's [T]tribute of the sheep was
six hundred and seventy-five. *tax*

38 The cattle *were* thirty-six thousand, of which the LORD's tribute *was* seventy-two.

39 The donkeys *were* thirty thousand five hundred, of which the LORD's tribute *was* sixty-one.

40 The persons *were* sixteen thousand, of which the LORD's tribute *was* thirty-two persons.

41 So Moses gave the tribute *which was* the LORD's heave offering to Eleazar the priest, [R]as the LORD commanded Moses. Num. 5:9, 10

42 And from the children of Israel's half, which Moses separated from the men who fought—

43 now the half belonging to the congregation was three hundred and thirty-seven thousand five hundred sheep,

44 thirty-six thousand cattle,

45 thirty thousand five hundred donkeys,

46 and sixteen thousand persons—

47 and from the children of Israel's half Moses took one of every fifty, drawn from man and beast, and gave them to the Levites, who kept charge of the tabernacle of the LORD, as the LORD commanded Moses.

48 Then the officers who *were* over thousands of the army, the captains of thousands and captains of hundreds, came near to Moses;

49 and they said to Moses, "Your servants have taken a count of the men of war who *are* under our command, and not a man of us is missing.

50 "Therefore we have brought an offering for the LORD, what every man found of ornaments of gold: armlets and bracelets and signet rings and earrings and necklaces, [R]to make atonement for ourselves before the LORD." Ex. 30:12–16

51 So Moses and Eleazar the priest received the gold from them, all the fashioned ornaments.

52 And all the gold of the offering that they offered to the LORD, from the captains of thousands and captains of hundreds, was [T]sixteen thousand seven hundred and fifty shekels. $32,160,000

53 [R](The men of war had taken spoil, every man for himself.) Deut. 20:14

54 And Moses and Eleazar the priest received the gold from the captains of thousands and of hundreds, and brought it into the tabernacle of meeting as a memorial for the children of Israel before the LORD.

CHAPTER 32

Division of the Land
East of Jordan—Deut. 3:12–19

NOW the children of Reuben and the children of Gad had a very great multitude of livestock; and when they saw the land of Jazer and the land of Gilead, that indeed the region *was* a place for livestock,

2 the children of Gad and the children of Reuben came and spoke to Moses, to Eleazar the priest, and to the leaders of the congregation, saying,

3 "Ataroth, Dibon, Jazer, Nimrah, Heshbon, Elealeh, Shebam, Nebo, and Beon,

4 "the country which the LORD defeated before the congregation of Israel, *is* a land for livestock, and your servants have livestock."

5 Therefore they said, "If we have found favor in your sight, let this land be given to your servants as a possession, *and* do not take us over the Jordan."

6 And Moses said to the children of Gad and to the children of Reuben: "Shall your brethren go to war while you sit here?

7 "Now why will you discourage the heart of the children of Israel from going over into the land which the LORD has given them?

8 "Thus your fathers did [R]when I sent them away from Kadesh Barnea [R]to see the land. Num. 13:3, 26 • Deut. 1:19–25

9 "For [R]when they went up to the Valley of Eshcol and saw the land, they discouraged the heart of the children of Israel, so that they did not go into the land which the LORD had given them. Deut. 1:24, 28

10 "So the LORD's anger was aroused on that day, and He swore an oath, saying,

11 'Surely none of the men who came up from Egypt, from twenty years old and above, shall see the land of which I swore to Abraham, Isaac, and Jacob, because [R]they have not wholly followed Me, Num. 14:24, 30

12 'except Caleb the son of Jephunneh, the Kenizzite, and Joshua the son of Nun, for they have wholly followed the LORD.'

13 "So the LORD's anger was aroused against Israel, and He made them [R]wander in the wilderness forty years, until [R]all the generation that had done evil in the sight of the LORD was gone. Num. 14:33–35 • Num. 26:64, 65

14 "And look! You have risen in your fathers' place, a brood of sinful men, to increase still more the [R]fierce anger of the LORD against Israel. Deut. 1:34

15 "For if you [R]turn away from following Him, He will once again leave them in the wilderness, and you will destroy all these people." Deut. 30:17, 18

16 Then they came near to him and said: "We will build sheepfolds here for our livestock, and cities for our little ones,

17 "but we ourselves will be armed, ready *to* go before the children of Israel until we have brought them to their place; and our little ones will dwell in the fortified cities because of the inhabitants of the land.

18 [R]"We will not return to our homes until every one of the children of Israel has [T]received his inheritance. Josh. 22:1–4 • *possessed*

19 "For we will not inherit with them on the other side of the Jordan and beyond, [R]because our inheritance has fallen to us on this eastern side of the Jordan." Josh. 12:1; 13:8

20 Then [R]Moses said to them: "If you do this thing, if you arm yourselves before the LORD for the war, Deut. 3:18

21 "and all your armed men cross over the Jordan before the LORD until He has driven out His enemies from before Him,

22 "and [R]the land is subdued before the LORD, then afterward [R]you may return and be blameless before the LORD and before Israel; and [R]this land shall be your possession before the LORD. Deut. 3:20 • Josh. 22:4 • Deut. 3:12, 15, 16, 18

23 "But if you do not do so, then take note, you have sinned against the LORD; and be sure [R]your sin will find you out. Is. 59:12

24 "Build cities for your little ones and folds for your sheep, and do [T]what has proceeded out of your mouth." *what you said*

25 And the children of Gad and the children of Reuben spoke to Moses, saying: "Your servants will do as my lord commands.

26 [R]'Our little ones, our wives, our flocks, and all our livestock will be there in the cities of Gilead; Josh. 1:14

27 [R]'but your servants will cross over, every man armed for war, before the LORD to battle, just as my lord says." Josh. 4:12

28 So Moses gave command [R]concerning them to Eleazar the priest, to Joshua the son of Nun, and to the chief fathers of the tribes of the children of Israel. Josh. 1:13

29 And Moses said to them: "If the children of Gad and the children of Reuben cross over the Jordan with you, every man armed for battle before the LORD, and the land is subdued before you, then you shall give them the land of Gilead as a possession.

30 "But if they do not cross over armed with you, they shall have possessions among you in the land of Canaan."

31 Then the children of Gad and the children of Reuben answered, saying: "As the LORD has said to your servants, so we will do.

32 "We will cross over armed before the LORD into the land of Canaan, but the possession of our inheritance *shall remain* with us on this side of the Jordan."

33 So Moses gave to the children of Gad, to the children of Reuben, and to half the tribe of Manasseh the son of Joseph, [R]the kingdom of Sihon king of the Amorites and the kingdom of Og king of Bashan, the land with its cities within the borders, the cities of the surrounding country. Num. 21:24, 33, 35

34 And the children of Gad built [R]Dibon and Ataroth and [R]Aroer, Num. 33:45, 46 • Deut. 2:36

35 Atroth and Shophan and [R]Jazer and Jogbehah, Num. 32:1, 3

36 [R]Beth Nimrah and Beth Haran, [R]fortified cities, and folds for sheep. Num. 32:3 • Num. 32:24

37 And the children of Reuben built [R]Heshbon and Elealeh and Kirjathaim, Num. 21:27

38 Nebo and Baal Meon (*their* names being changed) and Shibmah; and they gave *other* names to the cities which they built.

39 And the children of Machir the son of Manasseh went to Gilead and took it, and dispossessed the Amorites who *were* in it.

40 So Moses [R]gave Gilead to Machir the son of Manasseh, and he dwelt in it. Deut. 3:12, 13, 15

41 Also [R]Jair the son of Manasseh went and took its small towns, and called them [R]Havoth Jair.[T] Deut. 3:14 • Judg. 10:4 • Lit. *Towns of Jair*

42 Then Nobah went and took Kenath and its villages, and he called it Nobah, after his own name.

CHAPTER 33

From Egypt to Sinai

THESE *are* the journeys of the children of Israel, who went out of the land of Egypt by their armies under the [R]hand of Moses and Aaron. Ps. 77:20

2 Now Moses wrote down the starting points of their journeys at the command of the LORD. And these *are* their journeys according to their starting points:

3 They departed from Rameses in the first month, on the fifteenth day of the first month; on the day after the Passover the children of Israel went out [R]with boldness in the sight of all the Egyptians. Ex. 14:8

4 For the Egyptians were burying all *their* firstborn, [R]whom the LORD had killed among them. Also [R]on their gods the LORD had executed judgments. Ex. 12:29 • Is. 19:1

5 [R]Then the children of Israel moved from Rameses and camped at Succoth. Ex. 12:37

6 They departed from [R]Succoth and camped at Etham, which *is* on the edge of the wilderness. Ex. 13:20

7 They moved from Etham and turned back to Pi Hahiroth, which *is* east of Baal Zephon; and they camped near Migdol.

8 They departed *from before Hahiroth and [R]passed through the midst of the sea into the wilderness, went [T]three days' journey in the Wilderness of Etham, and camped at Marah. Ex. 14:22; 15:22, 23 • 60 mi.

9 They moved from Marah and [R]came to Elim. At Elim *were* twelve springs of water and seventy palm trees; so they camped there. Ex. 15:27

10 They moved from Elim and camped by the Red Sea.

11 They moved from the Red Sea and camped in the [R]Wilderness of Sin. Ex. 16:1

12 They journeyed from the Wilderness of Sin and camped at Dophkah.

33:8 Heb. mss., Sam., Syr., Tg., Vg. *from Pi Hahiroth;* cf. Num. 33:7

13 They departed from Dophkah and camped at Alush.

14 They moved from Alush and camped at [R]Rephidim, where there was no water for the people to drink. Ex. 17:1; 19:2

15 They departed from Rephidim and camped in the Wilderness of Sinai.

From Sinai to Kadesh

16 They moved from the Wilderness of Sinai and camped at Kibroth Hattaavah.

17 They departed from Kibroth Hattaavah and [R]camped at Hazeroth. Num. 11:35

The Wilderness Wanderings

18 They departed from Hazeroth and camped at [R]Rithmah. Num. 12:16

19 They departed from Rithmah and camped at Rimmon Perez.

20 They departed from Rimmon Perez and camped at Libnah.

21 They moved from Libnah and camped at Rissah.

22 They journeyed from Rissah and camped at Kehelathah.

23 They went from Kehelathah and camped at Mount Shepher.

24 They moved from Mount Shepher and camped at Haradah.

25 They moved from Haradah and camped at Makheloth.

26 They moved from Makheloth and camped at Tahath.

27 They departed from Tahath and camped at Terah.

28 They moved from Terah and camped at Mithkah.

29 They went from Mithkah and camped at Hashmonah.

30 They departed from Hashmonah and [R]camped at Moseroth. Deut. 10:6

31 They departed from Moseroth and camped at Bene Jaakan.

32 They moved from [R]Bene Jaakan and [R]camped at Hor Hagidgad. Deut. 10:6 • Deut. 10:7

33 They went from Hor Hagidgad and camped at Jotbathah.

34 They moved from Jotbathah and camped at Abronah.

35 They departed from Abronah [R]and camped at Ezion Geber. Deut. 2:8

36 They moved from Ezion Geber and camped in the [R]Wilderness of Zin, which *is* Kadesh. Num. 20:1; 27:14

From Kadesh to Moab

37 They moved from [R]Kadesh and camped at Mount Hor, on the boundary of the land of Edom. Num. 20:22, 23; 21:4

38 Then Aaron the priest went up to Mount Hor at the command of the LORD, and died there in the fortieth year after the children of Israel had come out of the land of Egypt, on the first *day* of the fifth month.

39 Aaron *was* one hundred and twenty-three years old when he died on Mount Hor.

40 Now [R]the king of Arad, the Canaanite, who dwelt in the South in the land of Canaan, heard of the coming of the children of Israel. Num. 21:1

41 So they departed from Mount Hor and camped at Zalmonah.

42 They departed from Zalmonah and camped at Punon.

43 They departed from Punon and [R]camped at Oboth. Num. 21:10

44 They departed from Oboth and camped at Ije Abarim, at the border of Moab.

45 They departed from [T]Ijim and camped at Dibon Gad. Same as *Ije Abarim*, Num. 33:44

46 They moved from Dibon Gad and camped at [R]Almon Diblathaim. Jer. 48:22

47 They moved from Almon Diblathaim [R]and camped in the mountains of Abarim, before Nebo. Deut. 32:49

48 They departed from the mountains of Abarim and [R]camped in the plains of Moab by the Jordan, *across from* Jericho. Num. 22:1

49 They camped by the Jordan, from Beth Jesimoth as far as the [R]Abel Acacia Grove[T] in the plains of Moab. Num. 25:1 • Heb. *Abel Shittim*

Instructions for Conquering Canaan

50 Now the LORD spoke to Moses in the plains of Moab by the Jordan, *across from* Jericho, saying,

51 "Speak to the children of Israel, and say to them: [R]'When you have crossed the Jordan into the land of Canaan, Josh. 3:17

52 [R]'then you shall drive out all the inhabitants of the land from before you, destroy all their engraved stones, destroy all their molded images, and demolish all their [T]high places; Deut. 7:2, 5; 12:3 • Places for pagan worship

53 'you shall dispossess *the inhabitants of* the land and dwell in it, for I have given you the land to [R]possess. Deut. 11:31

54 'And you shall divide the land by lot as an inheritance among your families; to the larger you shall give a larger inheritance, and to the smaller you shall give a smaller inheritance; there everyone's *inheritance* shall be whatever falls to him by lot. You shall inherit according to the tribes of your fathers.

55 'But if you do not drive out the inhabitants of the land from before you, then it shall be that those whom you let remain *shall be* [R]irritants in your eyes and thorns in your sides, and they shall harass you in the land where you dwell. Josh. 23:13

56 'Moreover it shall be *that* I will do to you as I thought to do to them.'"

THE MEDITERRANEAN SEA

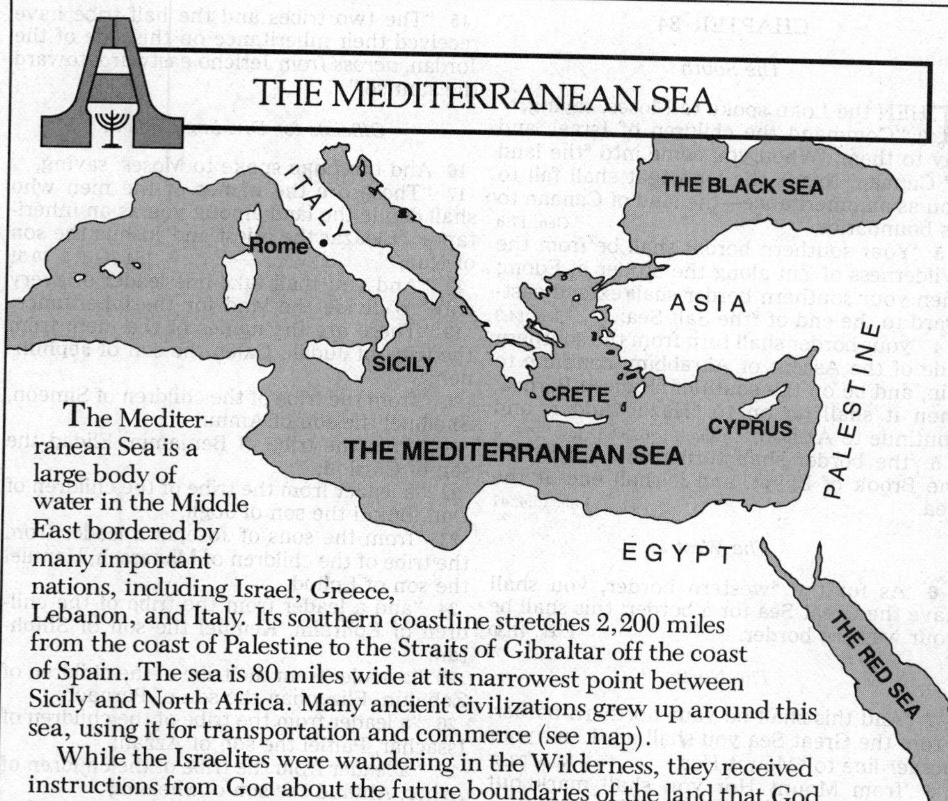

The Mediterranean Sea is a large body of water in the Middle East bordered by many important nations, including Israel, Greece, Lebanon, and Italy. Its southern coastline stretches 2,200 miles from the coast of Palestine to the Straits of Gibraltar off the coast of Spain. The sea is 80 miles wide at its narrowest point between Sicily and North Africa. Many ancient civilizations grew up around this sea, using it for transportation and commerce (see map).

While the Israelites were wandering in the Wilderness, they received instructions from God about the future boundaries of the land that God had promised to Abraham and his descendants. The Mediterranean Sea was established as the western boundary of their territory (Num. 34:6).

In the Bible, the Mediterranean is also referred to as "the Great Sea" (Josh. 1:4), "the Western Sea" (Deut. 11:24), and simply "the sea" (Josh. 16:8). The Romans called it *Mare Nostrum*, or "Our Sea," because of its importance to their empire in trade and commerce. In the time of Jesus and Paul, the Mediterranean was controlled by the Romans, who also used it to transport soldiers to the East to keep order in the provinces.

Perhaps the first people to exploit the trading advantages offered by the Mediterranean Sea were the Phoenicians. Through their fine port cities of Tyre and Sidon, they imported and exported goods from many nations of the ancient world. But the Israelites were never a seafaring people. Even Solomon, with all his wealth, formed an alliance with the Phoenicians under which they conducted import and export services for the Israelites (1 Kin. 9:27).

The Philistines also loved the sea. Some scholars believe they migrated to Palestine from their original home on the island of Crete, or Caphtor, in the Mediterranean. The Mediterranean is called "the Sea of the Philistines" in Exodus 23:31.

The Mediterranean also played a key role in the early expansion of Christianity. Paul crossed the Mediterranean during his missionary journeys and set sail from many of its ports, including Caesarea (Acts 9:30), Seleucia (Acts 13:4), and Cenchrea (Acts 18:18). He was shipwrecked on the Mediterranean while sailing to Rome in late autumn (Acts 27).

CHAPTER 34

The South

THEN the LORD spoke to Moses, saying,

2 "Command the children of Israel, and say to them: 'When you come into [R]the land of Canaan, this *is* the land that shall fall to you as an inheritance—the land of Canaan to its boundaries. Gen. 17:8

3 'Your southern border shall be from the Wilderness of Zin along the border of Edom; then your southern border shall extend eastward to the end of [R]the Salt Sea; Gen. 14:3

4 'your border shall turn from the southern side of the Ascent of Akrabbim, continue to Zin, and be on the south of [R]Kadesh Barnea; then it shall go on to [R]Hazar Addar, and continue to Azmon; Num. 13:26; 32:8 • Josh. 15:3, 4

5 'the border shall turn from Azmon [R]to the Brook of Egypt, and it shall end at the Sea. Josh. 15:4, 47

The West

6 'As for the [R]western border, you shall have the Great Sea for a border; this shall be your western border. Ezek. 47:20

The North

7 'And this shall be your northern border: From the Great Sea you shall mark out your *border* line to [R]Mount Hor; Num. 33:37

8 'from Mount Hor you shall mark out *your border* [R]to the entrance of Hamath; then the direction of the border shall be toward [R]Zedad; Num. 13:21 • Ezek. 47:15

9 'the border shall proceed to Ziphron, and it shall end at [R]Hazar Enan. This shall be your northern border. Ezek. 47:17

The East

10 'You shall mark out your eastern border from Hazar Enan to Shepham;

11 'the border shall go down from Shepham to Riblah on the east side of Ain; the border shall go down and reach to the eastern [T]side of the Sea of Chinnereth; ridge, lit. *shoulder*

12 'the border shall go down along the Jordan, and it shall end at [R]the Salt Sea. This shall be your land with its surrounding boundaries.'" Num. 34:3

13 Then Moses commanded the children of Israel, saying: [R]"This *is* the land which you shall inherit by lot, which the LORD has commanded to give to the nine tribes and to the half-tribe. Josh. 14:1–5

14 [R]"For the tribe of the children of Reuben according to the house of their fathers, and the tribe of the children of Gad according to the house of their fathers, have received *their inheritance*; and the half-tribe of Manasseh has received its inheritance. Num. 32:33

15 "The two tribes and the half-tribe have received their inheritance on this side of the Jordan, *across from* Jericho eastward, toward the sunrise."

Officials for Dividing Canaan

16 And the LORD spoke to Moses, saying,

17 "These *are* the names of the men who shall divide the land among you as an inheritance: [R]Eleazar the priest and Joshua the son of Nun. Josh. 14:1, 2; 19:51

18 "And you shall take one leader of every tribe to divide the land for the inheritance.

19 "These *are* the names of the men: from the tribe of Judah, Caleb the son of Jephunneh;

20 "from the tribe of the children of Simeon, Shemuel the son of Ammihud;

21 "from the tribe of Benjamin, Elidad the son of Chislon;

22 "a leader from the tribe of the children of Dan, Bukki the son of Jogli;

23 "from the sons of Joseph: a leader from the tribe of the children of Manasseh, Hanniel the son of Ephod,

24 "and a leader from the tribe of the children of Ephraim, Kemuel the son of Shiphtan;

25 "a leader from the tribe of the children of Zebulun, Elizaphan the son of Parnach;

26 "a leader from the tribe of the children of Issachar, Paltiel the son of Azzan;

27 "a leader from the tribe of the children of Asher, Ahihud the son of Shelomi;

28 "and a leader from the tribe of the children of Naphtali, Pedahel the son of Ammihud."

29 These *are* the ones the LORD commanded to [T]divide the inheritance among the children of Israel in the land of Canaan. *apportion*

CHAPTER 35

Cities for the Levites

AND the LORD spoke to Moses in [R]the plains of Moab by the Jordan *across from* Jericho, saying: Num. 33:50

2 [R]"Command the children of Israel that they give the Levites cities to dwell in from the inheritance of their possession, and you shall *also* give the Levites [R]common-land around the cities. Josh. 14:3, 4; 21:2, 3 • Lev. 25:22–34

3 "They shall have the cities to dwell in; and their common-land shall be for their cattle, for their herds, and for all their animals.

4 "The common-land of the cities which you shall give the Levites *shall extend* from the wall of the city outward a [T]thousand cubits all around. 1500 ft.

5 "And you shall measure outside the city on the east side [T]two thousand cubits, on the

south side two thousand cubits, on the west
side two thousand cubits, and on the north
side two thousand cubits. The city *shall be* in
the middle. This shall belong to them as
common-land for the cities. 3000 ft.
6 "Now among the cities which you will
give to the Levites *you shall appoint* [R]six
cities of refuge, to which a manslayer may
flee. And to these you shall add forty-two
cities. Josh. 20:2, 7, 8; 21:3, 13
7 "So all the cities you will give to the
Levites *shall be* [R]forty-eight; these *you shall*
give with their common-land. Josh. 21:41
8 "And the cities which you will give *shall*
be [R]from the possession of the children of
Israel; [R]from the larger *tribe* you shall give
many, from the smaller you shall give few;
each shall give some of its cities to the
Levites, in proportion to the inheritance that
each inherits." Josh. 21:3 • Num. 26:54; 33:54

Cities of Refuge

9 Then the LORD spoke to Moses, saying,
10 "Speak to the children of Israel, and say
to them: [R]'When you cross the Jordan into
the land of Canaan, Josh. 20:1–9
11 'then you shall appoint cities to be cities
of refuge for you, that the manslayer who
kills any person accidentally may flee there.
12 [R]'They shall be cities of refuge for you
from the avenger, that the manslayer may
not die until he stands before the congregation in judgment. Deut. 19:6
13 'And of the cities which you give, you
shall have [R]six cities of refuge. Num. 35:6
14 [R]'You shall appoint three cities on this
side of the Jordan, and three cities you shall
appoint in the land of Canaan, *which* will be
cities of refuge. Deut. 4:41
15 'These six cities shall be for refuge for
the children of Israel, [R]for the stranger, and
for the sojourner among them, that anyone
who kills a person accidentally may flee
there. Num. 15:16
16 'But if he strikes him with an iron implement, so that he dies, he *is* a murderer; the
murderer shall surely be put to death.
17 'And if he strikes him with a stone in the
hand, by which one could die, and he does
die, he *is* a murderer; the murderer shall
surely be put to death.
18 'Or *if* he strikes him with a wooden hand
weapon, by which one could die, and he does
die, he *is* a murderer; the murderer shall
surely be put to death.
19 [R]'The avenger of blood himself shall put
the murderer to death; when he meets him,
he shall put him to death. Num. 35:21, 24, 27
20 [R]'If he pushes him out of hatred or,
[R]while lying in wait, hurls something at him
so that he dies, Gen. 4:8 • Ex. 21:14
21 'or in enmity he strikes him with his
hand so that he dies, the one who struck *him*
shall surely be put to death, *for* he *is* a
murderer; the avenger of blood shall put the
murderer to death when he meets him.
22 'But if he pushes him suddenly [R]without
enmity, or throws anything at him without
lying in wait, Ex. 21:13
23 'or uses a stone, by which a man could
die, throwing *it* at him without seeing *him*, so
that he dies, while he was not his enemy or
seeking his harm,
24 'then [R]the congregation shall judge between the manslayer and the avenger of
blood according to these judgments. Josh. 20:6
25 'So the congregation shall deliver the
manslayer from the hand of the avenger of
blood, and the congregation shall return him
to the city of refuge where he had fled, and
[R]he shall remain there until the death of the
high priest [R]who was anointed with the holy
oil. Josh. 20:6 • Ex. 29:7
26 'But if the manslayer at any time goes
outside the limits of the city of refuge where
he fled,
27 'and the avenger of blood finds him outside the limits of his city of refuge, and the
avenger of blood kills the manslayer, he shall
not be guilty of [T]blood, Murder
28 'because he should have remained in his
city of refuge until the death of the high
priest. But after the death of the high priest
the manslayer may return to the land of his
possession.
29 'Now these *things* shall be [R]a statute of
judgment to you throughout your generations in all your dwellings. Num. 27:11
30 'Whoever kills a person, the murderer
shall be put to death on the [R]testimony of
witnesses; but one witness is not *sufficient*
testimony against a person for the death
penalty. Deut. 17:6; 19:15
31 'Moreover you shall take no ransom for
the life of a murderer who *is* guilty of death,
but he shall surely be put to death.
32 'And you shall take no ransom for him
who has fled to his city of refuge, that he may
return to dwell in the land before the death of
the priest.
33 'So you shall not pollute the land where
you *are*; for blood [R]defiles the land, and no
atonement can be made for the land, for the
blood that is shed on it, except [R]by the blood
of him who shed it. Ps. 106:38 • Gen. 9:6
34 'Therefore [R]do not defile the land which
you inhabit, in the midst of which I dwell; for
[R]I the LORD dwell among the children of
Israel.' " Lev. 18:24, 25 • Ex. 29:45, 46

CHAPTER 36

Special Problems of Inheritance in Canaan

NOW the chief fathers of the families of
the children of Gilead the son of Machir, the son of Manasseh, of the families of

the sons of Joseph, came near and [R]spoke
before Moses and before the leaders, the chief
fathers of the children of Israel; Num. 27:1–11
2 and they said: [R]"The LORD commanded
my lord *Moses* to give the land as an inheritance by lot to the children of Israel, and [R]my
lord was commanded by the LORD to give the
inheritance of our brother Zelophehad to his
daughters. Josh. 17:4 • Num. 27:1, 5–7
3 "Now if they are married to any of the
sons of the *other* tribes of the children of
Israel, then their inheritance will be [R]taken
from the inheritance of our fathers, and it will
be added to the inheritance of the tribe into
which they marry; so it will be taken from
the lot of our inheritance. Num. 27:4
4 "And when [R]the Jubilee of the children
of Israel comes, then their inheritance will be
added to the inheritance of the tribe into
which they marry; so their inheritance will be
taken away from the inheritance of the tribe
of our fathers." Lev. 25:10
5 Then Moses commanded the children of
Israel according to the word of the LORD,
saying: [R]"What the tribe of the sons of Joseph
speaks is right. Num. 27:7
6 "This *is* what the LORD commands concerning the daughters of Zelophehad, saying,
'Let them [T]marry whom they think best, [R]but
they may marry only within the family of
their father's tribe.' Lit. *be wives to* • Num. 36:11, 12
7 "So the inheritance of the children of
Israel shall not change hands from tribe to
tribe, for every one of the children of Israel
shall [R]keep the inheritance of the tribe of his
fathers. 1 Kin. 21:3
8 "And [R]every daughter who possesses an
inheritance in any tribe of the children of
Israel shall be the wife of one of the family
of her father's tribe, so that the children of
Israel each may possess the inheritance of his
fathers. 1 Chr. 23:22
9 "Thus no inheritance shall change hands
from *one* tribe to another, but every tribe of
the children of Israel shall keep its own
inheritance."
10 Just as the LORD commanded Moses, so
did the daughters of Zelophehad;
11 for Mahlah, Tirzah, Hoglah, Milcah, and
Noah, the daughters of Zelophehad, were
married to the sons of their father's brothers.
12 They were married into the families of
the children of Manasseh the son of Joseph,
and their inheritance remained in the tribe of
their father's family.
13 These *are* the commandments and the
judgments which the LORD commanded the
children of Israel by the hand of Moses [R]in
the plains of Moab by the Jordan, *across from*
Jericho. Num. 26:3; 33:50

Weights

Unit	*Weight*	*Equivalents*	*Translations*
Jewish Weights			
Talent	c. 75 pounds for common talent, c. 150 pounds for royal talent	60 minas; 3,000 shekels	talent
Mina	1.25 pounds	50 shekels	mina
Shekel	c. .4 ounce (11.4 grams) for common shekel c. .8 ounce for royal shekel	2 bekas; 20 gerahs	shekel
Beka	c. .2 ounce (5.7 grams)	½ shekel; 10 gerahs	half a shekel
Gerah	c. .02 ounce (.57 grams)	1/20 shekel	gerah
Roman Weight			
Litra	12 ounces		pound

THE FIFTH BOOK OF MOSES CALLED

DEUTERONOMY

THE BOOK OF DEUTERONOMY

Deuteronomy, Moses' "Upper Desert Discourse," consists of a series of farewell messages by Israel's 120-year-old leader. It is addressed to the new generation destined to possess the land of promise—those who survived the forty years of wilderness wandering.

Like Leviticus, Deuteronomy contains a vast amount of legal detail, but its emphasis is on the laymen rather than the priests. Moses reminds the new generation of the importance of obedience if they are to learn from the sad example of their parents.

The Hebrew title of Deuteronomy is *Haddebharim,* "The Words," taken from the opening phrase in 1:1, "These *are* the words." The parting words of Moses to the new generation are given in oral and written form so that they will endure to all generations. Deuteronomy has been called "five-fifths of the Law" since it completes the five books of Moses. The Jewish people have also called it *Mishneh Hattorah,* "repetition of the Law," which is translated in the Septuagint as *To Deuteronomion Touto,* "This Second Law." Deuteronomy, however, is not a second law but an adaptation and expansion of much of the original law given on Mount Sinai. The English title comes from the Greek title *Deuteronomion,* "Second Law." Deuteronomy has also been appropriately called the "Book of Remembrance."

THE AUTHOR OF DEUTERONOMY

The Mosaic authorship of Deuteronomy has been vigorously attacked by critics who claim that Moses is only the originator of the tradition on which these laws are based. Some critics grant that part of Deuteronomy may have come from Mosaic times through oral tradition. The usual argument is that it was anonymously written not long before 621 B.C. and used by King Josiah to bring about his reform in that year (2 Kin. 22 and 23). There are several reasons why these arguments are not valid.

External Evidence: (1) The Old Testament attributes Deuteronomy and the rest of the Pentateuch to Moses (see Josh. 1:7; Judg. 3:4; 1 Kin. 2:3; 2 Kin. 14:6; Ezra 3:2; Neh. 1:7; Ps. 103:7; Dan. 9:11; Mal. 4:4). (2) Evidence from Joshua and First Samuel indicates that these laws existed in the form of codified written statutes and exerted an influence on the Israelites in Canaan. (3) Christ quotes it as God's Word in turning back Satan's three temptations (Matt. 4:4, 7, 10) and attributes it directly to Moses (Matt. 19:7–9; Mark 7:10; Luke 20:28; John 5:45–47). (4) Deuteronomy is cited more than eighty times in seventeen of the twenty-seven New Testament books. These citations support the Mosaic authorship (see Acts 3:22; Rom. 10:19). (5) Jewish and Samaritan traditions point to Moses.

Internal Evidence: (1) Deuteronomy includes about forty claims that Moses wrote it. Read Deuteronomy 31: 24–26 (see also 1:1–5; 4:44–46; 29:1; 31:9). (2) Deuteronomy fits the time of Moses, not Josiah: Canaan is viewed from the outside; the Canaanite religion is seen as a future menace; it assumes the hearers remember Egypt and the wilderness; Israel is described as living in tents; and there is no evidence of a divided kingdom. (3) A serious problem of misrepresentation and literary forgery would arise if this book were written in the seventh century B.C. (4) Geographical and historical details indicate a firsthand knowledge. (5) Deuteronomy follows the treaty form used in the fifteenth and fourteenth centuries B.C. (6) Moses' obituary in chapter 34 was probably written by Joshua.

THE TIME OF DEUTERONOMY

Like Leviticus, Deuteronomy does not progress historically. It takes place entirely on the plains of Moab due east of Jericho and the Jordan River (1:1; 29:1; Josh. 1:2). It covers about one month: combine Deuteronomy 1:3 and 34:8 with Joshua 5:6–12. The book was written at the end of the forty-year period in the wilderness (c. 1405 B.C.) when the new generation was on the verge of entering Canaan. Moses wrote it to encourage the people to believe and obey God in order to receive God's blessings.

THE CHRIST OF DEUTERONOMY

The most obvious portrait of Christ is found in 18:15: "The LORD your God will raise up for you a Prophet like me from your midst, from your brethren. Him you shall hear" (see also 18:16–19; Acts 7:37). Moses is a type of Christ in many ways as he is the only biblical figure other than Christ to fill the three offices of prophet (34:10–12), priest (Ex. 32:31–35), and king (although Moses was not king, he functioned as ruler of Israel; 33:4, 5). Both are in danger of death during childhood; both are saviors, intercessors, and believers; and both are rejected by their brethren. Moses is one of the greatest men who ever lived, combining not just one or two memorable virtues but many.

KEYS TO DEUTERONOMY

Key Word: Covenant—The primary theme of the entire Book of Deuteronomy is the renewal of the covenant. Originally established at Mount Sinai, the covenant is enlarged and renewed on the plains of Moab.

Key Verses: Deuteronomy 10:12, 13; 30:19, 20—"And now, Israel, what does the LORD your God require of you, but to fear the LORD your God, to walk in all His ways and to love Him, to serve the LORD your God with all your heart and with all your soul, *and* to keep the commandments of the LORD and His statutes which I command you today for your good?" (10:12, 13).

"I call heaven and earth as witnesses today against you, *that* I have set before you life and death, blessing and cursing; therefore choose life, that both you and your descendants may live; that you may love the LORD your God, that you may obey His voice, and that you may cling to Him, for He *is* your life and the length of your days; and that you may dwell in the land which the LORD swore to your fathers, to Abraham, Isaac, and Jacob, to give them" (30:19, 20).

Key Chapter: Deuteronomy 27—The formal ratification of the covenant occurs in Deuteronomy 27 as Moses, the priests, the Levites, and all of Israel "take heed and listen, O Israel: This day you have become the people of the LORD your God" (27:9).

SURVEY OF DEUTERONOMY

Deuteronomy, in its broadest outline, is the record of the renewal of the Old Covenant given at Mount Sinai. This covenant is reviewed, expanded, enlarged, and finally ratified in the plains of Moab. Moses accomplishes this primarily through three sermons that move from a retrospective, to an introspective, and finally to a prospective look at God's dealings with Israel.

Moses' First Sermon (1:1—4:43): Moses reaches into the past to remind the people of two undeniable facts in their history: (1) the moral judgment of God upon Israel's unbelief, and (2) the deliverance and provision of God during times of obedience. The simple lesson is that obedience brings blessing and disobedience brings punishment.

Moses' Second Sermon (4:44—26:19): This moral and legal section is the longest in the book because Israel's future as a nation in Canaan will depend upon a right relationship with God. These chapters review the three categories of the Law: (1) *The testimonies (5—11).* These are the moral duties—a restatement and expansion of the Ten Commandments plus an exhortation not to forget God's gracious deliverance. (2) *The statutes (12:1—16:17).* These are the ceremonial duties—sacrifices, tithes, and feasts. (3) *The ordinances (16:18—26:19).* These are the civil (16:18—20:20) and social (21—26) duties—the system of justice, criminal laws, laws of warfare, rules of property, personal and family morality, and social justice.

Moses' Third Sermon (27—34): In these chapters Moses writes history in advance. He predicts what will befall Israel in the near future (blessings and cursings) and in the distant future (dispersion among the nations and eventual return). Moses lists the terms of the covenant soon to be ratified by the people. Because Moses will not be allowed to enter the land, he appoints Joshua as his successor and delivers a farewell address to the multitude. God Himself buries Moses in an unknown place, perhaps to prevent idolatry. Moses finally enters the Promised Land when he appears with Christ on the Mount of Transfiguration (Matt. 17:3). The last three verses of the Pentateuch (34:10–12) are an appropriate epitaph for this great man.

FOCUS	FIRST SERMON	SECOND SERMON				THIRD SERMON		
REFERENCE	1:1—4:44—12:1—16:18—21:1—27:1—29:1—31:1—34:12							
DIVISION	REVIEW OF GOD'S ACTS FOR ISRAEL	EXPOSITION OF THE DECALOGUE	CEREMONIAL LAWS	CIVIL LAWS	SOCIAL LAWS	RATIFICATION OF COVENANT	PALESTINIAN COVENANT	TRANSITION OF COVENANT MEDIATOR
TOPIC	WHAT GOD HAS DONE	WHAT GOD EXPECTED OF ISRAEL				WHAT GOD WILL DO		
	HISTORICAL	LEGAL				PROPHETICAL		
LOCATION	PLAINS OF MOAB							
TIME	c. 1 MONTH							

OUTLINE OF DEUTERONOMY

Part One: Moses' First Sermon: "What God Has Done for Israel" (1:1—4:43)

Part Two: Moses' Second Sermon: "What God Expects of Israel" (4:44—26:19)

Part Three: Moses' Third Sermon: "What God Will Do for Israel" (27:1—34:12)

CHAPTER 1

The Preamble of the Covenant

THESE *are* the words which Moses spoke
to all Israel [R]on this side of the Jordan in
the wilderness, in the [T]plain opposite *Suph,
between Paran, Tophel, Laban, Hazeroth, and
Dizahab. Deut. 4:44–46 • Heb. *Arabah*
2 *It is* [T]eleven days' *journey* from Horeb by
way of Mount Seir to Kadesh Barnea. 220 mi.
3 Now it came to pass in the fortieth year,
in the eleventh month, on the first *day* of the
month, *that* Moses spoke to the children of
Israel according to all that the LORD had
given him as commandments to them,
4 [R]after he had killed Sihon king of the
Amorites, who dwelt in Heshbon, and Og
king of Bashan, who dwelt at Ashtaroth [R]in*
Edrei. Num. 21:23, 24, 33–35 • Josh. 13:12
5 On this side of the Jordan in the land of
Moab, Moses began to explain this law, saying,

From Mount Sinai to Kadesh—Ex. 18:18–26

6 "The LORD our God spoke to us [R]in
Horeb, saying: 'You have dwelt long [R]enough
at this mountain. Ex. 3:1, 12 • Ex. 19:1, 2
7 'Turn and take your journey, and go to
the mountains of the Amorites, to all the
neighboring *places* in the [T]plain, in the mountains and in the lowland, in the South and on
the seacoast, to the land of the Canaanites
and to Lebanon, as far as the great river, the
River Euphrates. Heb. *Arabah*
8 'See, I have set the land before you; go in
and possess the land which the LORD [T]swore
to your fathers—to [R]Abraham, Isaac, and
Jacob—to give to them and their descendants
after them.' *promised* • Gen. 12:7; 15:5; 22:17; 26:3; 28:13
9 "And I spoke to you at that time, saying:
'I alone am not able to bear you.
10 'The LORD your God has multiplied you,
[R]and here you *are* today, as the stars of
heaven in multitude. Gen. 15:5; 22:17
11 [R]'May the LORD God of your fathers
make you a thousand times more numerous
than you are, and bless you [R]as He has
promised you! 2 Sam. 24:3 • Gen. 15:5
12 'How can I alone bear your problems and
your burdens and your complaints?
13 'Choose wise, understanding, and knowledgeable men from among your tribes, and I
will make them [T]heads over you.' *rulers*
14 "And you answered me and said, 'The
thing which you have told *us* to do *is* good.'
15 "So I took [R]the heads of your tribes, wise
and knowledgeable men, and [T]made them
heads over you, leaders of thousands, leaders
of hundreds, leaders of fifties, leaders of tens,
and officers for your tribes. Ex. 18:25 • *appointed*
16 "Then I commanded your judges at that
time, saying, 'Hear *the cases* between your
brethren, and [R]judge righteously between a
man and his [R]brother or the stranger who is
with him. Deut. 16:18 • Lev. 24:22
17 'You shall not show partiality in judgment; you shall hear the small as well as the
great; you shall not be afraid in any man's
presence, for [R]the judgment *is* God's. The
case that is too hard for you, [R]bring *it* to me,
and I will hear it.' 2 Chr. 19:6 • Ex. 18:22, 26
18 "And I commanded you at that time all
the things which you should do.

At Kadesh—Num. 13:1—14:45

19 "So we departed from Horeb, [R]and went
through all that great and terrible wilderness
which you saw on the way to the mountains
of the Amorites, as the LORD our God had
commanded us. Then [R]we came to Kadesh
Barnea. Deut. 2:7; 8:15; 32:10 • Num. 13:26
20 "And I said to you, 'You have come to
the mountains of the Amorites, which the
LORD our God is giving us.
21 'Look, the LORD your God has set the
land before you; go up *and* possess *it*, as the
LORD God of your fathers has spoken to you;
[R]do not fear or be discouraged.' Josh. 1:6, 9
22 "And everyone of you came near to me
and said, 'Let us send men before us, and let
them search out the land for us, and bring
back word to us of the way by which we
should go up, and of the cities into which we
shall come.'
23 "And the plan pleased me well; so I took
twelve of your men, one man from *each* tribe.
24 [R]"And they departed and went up into
the mountains, and came to the Valley of
Eshcol, and spied it out. Num. 13:21–25
25 "They also took *some* of the fruit of the
land in their hands and brought *it* down to us;
and they brought back word to us, saying, '*It*
is a [R]good land which the LORD our God is
giving us.' Num. 13:27
26 [R]"Nevertheless you would not go up, but
rebelled against the command of the LORD
your God; Num. 14:1–4
27 "and you [R]murmured in your tents, and
said, 'Because the LORD [R]hates us, He has
brought us out of the land of Egypt to deliver
us into the hand of the Amorites, to destroy
us. Ps. 106:25 • Deut. 9:28
28 'Where can we go up? Our brethren have
[T]discouraged our hearts, saying, [R]"The people
are greater and taller than we; the cities *are*
great and fortified up to heaven; moreover
we have seen the sons of the [R]Anakim
there."' Lit. *melted* • Deut. 9:1, 2 • Num. 13:28
29 "Then I said to you, 'Do not be terrified,
[R]or afraid of them. Num. 14:9

1:1 LXX ms., Tg., Vg. *Red Sea*
1:4 LXX, Syr., Vg. *and;* cf. Josh. 12:4

30 [R]'The LORD your God, who goes before you, He will fight for you, according to all He did for you in Egypt before your eyes, Ex. 14:14

31 'and in the wilderness where you saw how the LORD your God carried you, as a man carries his son, in all the way that you went until you came to this place.'

32 "Yet, for all that, [R]you did not believe the LORD your God, Jude 5

33 "who went in the way before you to search out a place for you to pitch your tents, to show you the way you should go, in the fire by night and in the cloud by day.

34 "And the LORD heard the sound of your words, and was angry, [R]and took an oath, saying, Deut. 2:14, 15

35 [R]'Surely not one of these men of this evil generation shall see that good land of which I swore to give to your fathers, Num. 14:22, 23

36 [R]'except Caleb the son of Jephunneh; he shall see it, and to him and his children I am giving the land on which he walked, because he wholly followed the LORD.' [Josh. 14:9]

37 [R]"The LORD was also angry with me for your sakes, saying, 'Even you shall not go in there; Deut. 3:26; 4:21; 34:4

38 '*but* Joshua the son of Nun, who stands before you, he shall go in there. Encourage him, for he shall cause Israel to inherit it.

39 'Moreover your little ones and your children, who [R]you say will be victims, who today [R]have no knowledge of good and evil, they shall go in there; to them I will give it, and they shall possess it. Num. 14:3 • Is. 7:15, 16

40 [R]'But *as for* you, turn and take your journey into the wilderness by the Way of the Red Sea.' Num. 14:25

41 "Then you answered and said to me, [R]'We have sinned against the LORD; we will go up and fight, just as the LORD our God commanded us.' And when everyone of you had girded on his weapons of war, you were ready to go up into the mountain. Num. 14:40

42 "And the LORD said to me, 'Tell them, [R]"Do not go up nor fight, for I *am* not among you; lest you be defeated before your enemies." ' Num. 14:41–43

43 "So I spoke to you; yet you would not listen, but [R]rebelled against the command of the LORD, and [R]presumptuously[T] went up into the mountain. Num. 14:44 • Deut. 17:12, 13 • *willfully*

44 "And the Amorites who dwelt in that mountain came out against you and chased you [R]as bees do, and drove you back from Seir to Hormah. Ps. 118:12

45 "Then you returned and wept before the LORD, but the LORD would not listen to your voice nor give ear to you.

46 "So you remained in Kadesh many days, according to the days that you spent *there*.

CHAPTER 2

"Do Not Meddle with Edom"—Num. 21:4

"THEN we turned and journeyed into the wilderness of the Way of the Red Sea, as the LORD spoke to me, and we skirted Mount Seir for many days.

2 "And the LORD spoke to me, saying:

3 'You have skirted this mountain [R]long enough; turn northward. Deut. 2:7, 14

4 'And command the people, saying, "You *are about to* pass through the territory of your brethren, the descendants of Esau, who live in Seir; and they will be afraid of you. Therefore watch yourselves carefully.

5 "Do not meddle with them, for I will not give you *any* of their land, no, not so much as one footstep, [R]because I have given Mount Seir to Esau *as* a possession. Gen. 36:8

6 "You shall buy food from them with money, that you may eat; and you shall also buy water from them with money, that you may drink.

7 "For the LORD your God has blessed you in all the work of your hand. He knows your trudging through this great wilderness. These forty years the LORD your God *has been* with you; you have lacked nothing." '

8 "And when we passed beyond our brethren, the descendants of Esau who dwell in Seir, away from the road of the plain, away from Elath and Ezion Geber, we turned and passed by way of the Wilderness of Moab.

"Do Not Harass Moab"

9 "Then the LORD said to me, 'Do not harass Moab, nor contend with them in battle, for I will not give you *any* of their land *as* a possession, because I have given Ar to the descendants of Lot *as* a possession.' "

10 [R](The Emim had dwelt there in times past, a people as great and numerous and tall as [R]the Anakim. Gen. 14:5 • Deut. 9:2

11 They were also regarded as [T]giants, like the Anakim, but the Moabites call them Emim. Heb. *rephaim*

12 [R]The Horites formerly dwelt in Seir, but the descendants of Esau dispossessed them and destroyed them from before them, and dwelt in their [T]place, just as Israel did to the land of their possession which the LORD gave them.) Deut. 2:22 • *stead*

13 " 'Now rise and cross over [R]the [T]Valley of the Zered.' So we crossed over the Valley of the Zered. Num. 21:12 • *Wadi* or *Brook*

14 "And the time we took to come from Kadesh Barnea until we crossed over the Valley of the Zered *was* thirty-eight years, until all the generation of the men of war was consumed from the midst of the camp, just as the LORD had sworn to them.

15 "For indeed the hand of the LORD was
against them, to destroy them from the midst
of the camp until they were consumed.

"Do Not Harass Ammon"

16 "So it was, when all the men of war had
finally perished from among the people,
17 "that the LORD spoke to me, saying:
18 'This day you are to cross over at Ar, the
boundary of Moab.
19 'And *when* you come near the people of
Ammon, do not harass them or meddle with
them, for I will not give you *any* of the land
of the people of Ammon *as* a possession,
because I have given it to [R]the descendants of
Lot *as* a possession.'" Gen. 19:38
20 (That was also regarded as a land of
giants; giants formerly dwelt there. But the
Ammonites call them Zamzummim,
21 [R]a people as great and numerous and tall
as the Anakim. But the LORD destroyed them
before them, and they dispossessed them and
dwelt in their place, Deut. 2:10
22 just as He had done for the descendants
of Esau, [R]who dwelt in Seir, when He destroyed [R]the Horites from before them. They
dispossessed them and dwelt in their place,
even to this day. Gen. 36:8 • Gen. 14:6; 36:20–30
23 And [R]the Avim, who dwelt in villages as
far as Gaza—[R]the Caphtorim, who came from
Caphtor, destroyed them and dwelt in their
place.) Josh. 13:3 • Gen. 10:14

The Conquest of Sihon—Num. 21:21–25

24 " 'Rise, take your journey, and cross over
the River Arnon. Look, I have given into your
hand Sihon the Amorite, king of Heshbon,
and his land. Begin [T]to possess *it*, and engage
him in battle. *to take it over*
25 'This day I will begin to put the dread
and fear of you upon the nations [T]under the
whole heaven, who shall hear the report of
you, and shall tremble and be in anguish
because of you.' *everywhere under the heavens*
26 "And I sent messengers from the Wilderness of Kedemoth to Sihon king of Heshbon,
with words of peace, saying,
27 [R]'Let me pass through your land; I will
keep strictly to the road, and I will turn
neither to the right nor to the left. Judg. 11:19
28 'You shall sell me food for money, that I
may eat, and give me water for money, that I
may drink; only let me pass through on foot,
29 'just as the descendants of Esau who
dwell in Seir and the Moabites who dwell in
Ar did for me, until I cross the Jordan to the
land which the LORD our God is giving us.'
30 "But Sihon king of Heshbon would not
let us pass through, for [R]the LORD your God
[R]hardened his spirit and made his heart obstinate, that He might deliver him into your
hand, as *it is* this day. Josh. 11:20 • Ex. 4:21
31 "And the LORD said to me, 'See, I have
begun to [R]give Sihon and his land over to
you. Begin to possess *it*, that you may inherit
his land.' Deut. 1:3, 8
32 [R]"Then Sihon and all his people came out
against us to fight at Jahaz. Num. 21:23
33 "And [R]the LORD our God delivered him
[T]over to us; so [R]we defeated him, his sons, and
all his people. Deut. 7:2 • Lit. *before us* • Num. 21:24
34 "We took all his cities at that time, and
we [R]utterly destroyed the men, women, and
little ones of every city; we left none remaining. Lev. 27:28
35 "We took only the livestock as plunder
for ourselves, with the spoil of the cities
which we took.
36 "From Aroer, which *is* on the bank of the
River Arnon, and *from* [R]the city that *is* in the
ravine, as far as Gilead, there was not one
city too strong for us; [R]the LORD our God
delivered all to us. Josh. 13:9, 16 • Ps. 44:3
37 "Only you did not go near the land of the
people of Ammon, *or* anywhere along the
River [R]Jabbok, or to the cities of the mountains, or [R]wherever the LORD our God had
forbidden us. Gen. 32:22 • Deut. 2:5, 9, 19

CHAPTER 3

The Conquest of Og—Num. 21:33–35

"THEN we turned and went up the road
to Bashan; and [R]Og king of Bashan
came out against us, he and all his people, to
battle [R]at Edrei. Num. 21:33–35 • Deut. 1:4
2 "And the LORD said to me, 'Do not fear
him, for I have delivered him and all his
people and his land into your hand; you shall
do to him as you did to [R]Sihon king of the
Amorites, who dwelt at Heshbon.' Num. 21:34
3 "So the LORD our God also delivered into
our hands Og king of Bashan, with all his
people, and we [T]attacked him until he had no
survivors remaining. *struck*
4 "And we took all his cities at that time;
there was not a city which we did not take
from them: sixty cities, all the region of
Argob, the kingdom of Og in Bashan.
5 "All these cities *were* fortified with high
walls, gates, and bars, besides a great many
rural towns.
6 "And we utterly destroyed them, as we
did to Sihon king [R]of Heshbon, utterly destroying the men, women, and children of
every city. Deut. 2:24, 34, 35
7 "But all the livestock and the spoil of the
cities we took as booty for ourselves.
8 "And at that time we took the land from
the hand of the two kings of the Amorites
who *were* on this side of the Jordan, from the
River Arnon to Mount [R]Hermon Deut. 4:48
9 "(the Sidonians call [R]Hermon Sirion, and
the Amorites call it Senir), 1 Chr. 5:23

10 [R]"all the cities of the plain, all Gilead, and
all Bashan, as far as Salcah and Edrei, cities
of the kingdom of Og in Bashan. Deut. 4:49
11 "For only Og king of Bashan remained of
the remnant of the [T]giants. Indeed his bedstead *was* an iron bedstead. (*Is* it not in
Rabbah of the people of Ammon?) Nine
cubits *is* its length and four cubits its width,
according to the standard cubit. Heb. *rephaim*

Land Is Granted to Two-and-a-Half Tribes
Num. 32:25–41

12 "And this [R]land, *which* we possessed at
that time, [R]from Aroer, which *is* by the River
Arnon, and half the mountains of Gilead and
[R]its cities, I gave to the Reubenites and the
Gadites. Num. 32:33 • Deut. 2:36 • Num. 34:14
13 "The rest of Gilead, and all Bashan, the
kingdom of Og, I gave to half the tribe of
Manasseh. (All the region of Argob, with all
Bashan, was called the land of the giants.
14 "Jair the son of Manasseh took all the
region of Argob, [R]as far as the border of the
Geshurites and the Maacathites, and [R]called
Bashan after his own name, [T]Havoth Jair, to
this day.) Josh. 13:13 • Num. 32:41 • Lit. *Towns of Jair*
15 "And I gave Gilead to Machir.
16 "And to the Reubenites [R]and the Gadites
I gave from Gilead as far as the River Arnon,
the middle of the river as *the* border, as far as
the River Jabbok, [R]the border of the people of
Ammon; 2 Sam. 24:5 • Num. 21:24
17 "the plain also, with the Jordan as *the*
border, from Chinnereth as far as the east
side of the Sea of the Arabah [R](the Salt Sea),
below the slopes of Pisgah. Gen. 14:3
18 "And I commanded you at that time,
saying: 'The LORD your God has given you
this land to possess. [R]All you men of valor
shall cross over armed before your brethren,
the children of Israel. Num. 32:20
19 'But your wives, your little ones, and
your livestock (I know that you have much
livestock) shall stay in your cities which I
have given you,
20 'until the LORD has given [R]rest to your
brethren as to you, and they also possess the
land which the LORD your God is giving them
beyond the Jordan. Then each of you may
[R]return to his possession which I have given
you.' Deut. 12:9, 10 • Josh. 22:4

Transition of Leadership

21 "And [R]I commanded Joshua at that time,
saying, 'Your eyes have seen all that the
LORD your God has done to these two kings;
so will the LORD do to all the kingdoms
through which you pass. [Num. 27:22, 23]
22 'You must not fear them, for [R]the LORD
your God Himself fights for you.' Ex. 14:14
23 "Then [R]I pleaded with the LORD at that
time, saying: [2 Cor. 12:8, 9]
24 'O Lord GOD, You have begun to show
Your servant Your greatness and Your
[T]mighty hand, for what god *is there* in heaven
or on earth who can do *anything* like Your
works and Your mighty *deeds*? *strong*
25 'I pray, let me cross over and see [R]the
good land beyond the Jordan, those pleasant
mountains, and Lebanon.' Deut. 4:22
26 "But the LORD [R]was angry with me on
your account, and would not listen to me. So
the LORD said to me: 'Enough of that! Speak
no more to Me of this matter. Num. 20:12; 27:14
27 'Go up to the top of Pisgah, and lift your
eyes toward the west, the north, the south,
and the east; behold *it* with your eyes, for you
shall not cross over this Jordan.
28 'But [T]command Joshua, and encourage
him and strengthen him; for he shall go over
before this people, and he shall cause them to
inherit the land which you will see.' *charge*
29 "So we stayed in [R]the valley opposite
Beth Peor. Deut. 4:46; 34:6

CHAPTER 4

Summary of the Covenant

"NOW, O Israel, listen to [R]the statutes
and the judgments which I teach
you to observe, that you may live, and go in
and [T]possess the land which the LORD God of
your fathers is giving you. [Rom. 10:5] • *take over*
2 "You shall not add to the word which I
command you, nor take *anything* from it,
that you may keep the commandments of the
LORD your God which I command you.
3 "Your eyes have seen what the LORD did
at [R]Baal Peor; for the LORD your God has
destroyed from among you all the men who
followed Baal of Peor. Num. 25:1–9
4 "But you who held fast to the LORD your
God *are* alive today, every one of you.
5 "Surely I have taught you statutes and
judgments, just as the LORD my God commanded me, that you should act according *to*
them in the land which you go to possess.
6 "Therefore be careful to observe *them*;
for this *is* [R]your wisdom and your understanding in the sight of the peoples who will
hear all these statutes, and say, 'Surely this
great nation *is* a wise and understanding
people.' [2 Tim. 3:15]
7 "For [R]what great nation *is there* that has
[R]God[T] *so* near to it, as the LORD our God *is* to
us, for whatever *reason* we may call upon
Him? [2 Sam. 7:23] • [Is. 55:6] • Or *a god*
8 "And what great nation *is there* that has
such statutes and righteous judgments as are
in all this law which I set before you this day?
9 "Only take heed to yourself, and diligently keep yourself, lest you [R]forget the
things your eyes have seen, and lest they
depart from your heart all the days of your
life. And [R]teach them to your children and

your grandchildren, Deut. 29:2–8 • Gen. 18:19
10 "*especially concerning* [R]the day you
stood before the LORD your God in Horeb,
when the LORD said to me, 'Gather the people
to Me, and I will let them hear My words,
that they may learn to fear Me all the days
they live on the earth, and *that* they may
teach their children.' Ex. 19:9, 16, 17
11 "Then you came near and stood at the
foot of the mountain, and the mountain
burned with fire to the midst of heaven, with
darkness, cloud, and thick darkness.
12 [R]"And the LORD spoke to you out of the
midst of the fire. You heard the sound of the
words, but saw no [T]form; [R]*you* only *heard* a
voice. Deut. 5:4, 22 • *similitude* • 1 Kin. 19:11–18
13 "So He declared to you His covenant
which He commanded you to perform, *that*
is, the Ten Commandments; and [R]He wrote
them on two tablets of stone. Ex. 24:12
14 "And the LORD commanded me at that
time to teach you statutes and judgments,
that you might [T]observe them in the land
which you cross over to possess. *do* or *perform*
15 "Take careful heed to yourselves, for you
saw no form when the LORD spoke to you at
Horeb out of the midst of the fire,
16 "lest you act corruptly and make for
yourselves a carved image in the form of any
figure: the likeness of male or female,
17 "the likeness of any beast that *is* on the
earth or the likeness of any winged bird that
flies in the air,
18 "the likeness of anything that creeps on
the ground or the likeness of any fish that *is*
in the water beneath the earth.
19 "And *take heed*, lest you [R]lift your eyes
to heaven, and *when* you see the sun, the
moon, and the stars, [R]all the host of heaven,
you feel driven to [R]worship them and serve
them, which the LORD your God has [T]given to
all the peoples under the whole heaven as a
heritage. Deut. 17:3 • 2 Kin. 21:3 • [Rom. 1:25] • *divided*
20 "But the LORD has taken you and
[R]brought you out of the iron furnace, out of
Egypt, to be [R]His people, *His* inheritance, as
you are this day. Jer. 11:4 • Deut. 7:6; 27:9
21 "Furthermore the LORD was angry with
me for your sakes, and swore that I would
not cross over the Jordan, and that I would
not enter the good land which the LORD your
God is giving you as an inheritance.
22 "But I must die in this land, I must not
cross over the Jordan; but you shall cross
over and [T]possess that good land. *take over*
23 "Take heed to yourselves, lest you forget
the covenant of the LORD your God which He
made with you, and make for yourselves a
carved image in the form of anything which
the LORD your God has forbidden you.
24 "For [R]the LORD your God *is* a consuming
fire, [R]a jealous God. Deut. 9:3 • Ex. 20:5; 34:14
25 "When you beget children and grandchildren and have grown old in the land, act
corruptly and make a carved image in the
form of anything, and do evil in the sight of
the LORD your God to provoke Him to anger,
26 [R]"I call heaven and earth to witness
against you this day, that you will soon
utterly perish from the land which you cross
over the Jordan to possess; you will not
[T]prolong *your* days in it, but will be utterly
destroyed. Deut. 30:18, 19 • *live long on it*
27 "And the LORD [R]will scatter you among
the peoples, and you will be left few in
number among the nations where the LORD
will drive you. Deut. 28:62
28 "And there you will serve gods, the work
of men's hands, wood and stone, which neither see nor hear nor eat nor smell.
29 [R]"But from there you will seek the LORD
your God, and you will find *Him* if you seek
Him with all your heart and with all your
soul. [2 Chr. 15:4]
30 "When you are in [T]distress, and all these
things come upon you in the [R]latter days,
when you [R]turn to the LORD your God and
obey His voice *tribulation* • Hos. 3:5 • Joel 2:12
31 "(for the LORD your God *is* a merciful
God), He will not forsake you nor [R]destroy
you, nor forget the covenant of your fathers
which He swore to them. Jer. 30:11
32 "For ask now concerning the days that
are past, which were before you, since the
day that God created man on the earth, and
ask from one end of heaven to the other,
whether *any* great *thing* like this has happened, or *anything* like it has been heard.
33 [R]"Did *any* people *ever* hear the voice of
God speaking out of the midst of the fire, as
you have heard, and live? Deut. 5:24–26
34 "Or did God *ever* try to go *and* take for
Himself a nation from the midst of *another*
nation, by trials, by signs, by wonders, by
war, [R]by a mighty hand and [R]an outstretched
arm, and by great [T]terrors, according to all
that the LORD your God did for you in Egypt
before your eyes? Ex. 13:3 • Ex. 6:6 • *calamities*
35 "To you it was shown, that you might
know that the LORD Himself *is* God; [R]*there is*
none other besides Him. Mark 12:32
36 "Out of heaven He let you hear His
voice, that He might instruct you; on earth
He showed you His great fire, and you heard
His words out of the midst of the fire.
37 "And because He loved your fathers,
therefore He chose their [T]descendants after
them; and He brought you out of Egypt with
His Presence, with His mighty power, *seed*
38 [R]"driving out from before you nations
greater and mightier than you, to bring you
in, to give you their land *as* an inheritance, as
it is this day. Deut. 7:1
39 "Therefore know this day, and consider
it in your heart, that [R]the LORD Himself *is*
God in heaven above and on the earth beneath; *there is* no other. Josh. 2:11

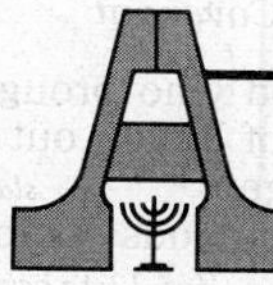

BOOKS OF THE PENTATEUCH

Scrolls were rolls of papyrus, leather, or parchment on which ancient documents were written.

Pentateuch, a Greek word meaning "five volumes," refers to the first five books of the Old Testament—Genesis, Exodus, Leviticus, Numbers, and Deuteronomy. The Jews traditionally refer to this collection as "the Book of the Law" or simply "the Law." Another word for this collection of sacred writings is *Torah*, which means "instruction," "teaching," or "doctrine."

The Pentateuch was also called "the Law of the LORD" (2 Chr. 31:3) and "the Book of the Law of God" (Neh. 8:18). The word *book* should not be understood in the modern sense, however, for many different writing materials were used in Old Testament times, including papyrus and leather scrolls (see illustration) and clay tablets.

The five books of the Pentateuch present a history of humanity from creation to the death of Moses, with particular attention to the development of the Hebrew people. The God revealed in these books is not only the Judge of the earth but also the loving Father of all humankind. In the last book of the Pentateuch, Moses pleaded with the people to observe God's laws and commandments after they settled in their permanent home in the land of Canaan (Deut. 4).

The Pentateuch is generally divided into six major sections: (1) the creation of the world (Gen. 1—11); (2) the period from Abraham to Joseph (Gen. 12—50); (3) Moses and the departure of the Israelites from Egypt (Ex. 1—18); (4) God's revelation at Mount Sinai (Ex. 19—Num. 10); (5) the wilderness wanderings (Num. 11—36); and (6) the addresses of Moses (Book of Deuteronomy).

From the time it was written, the Pentateuch has been accepted as the work of Moses. His specific writing or compiling activity is mentioned in Exodus (17:14; 24:4; 34:27). This tradition was supported by Jesus in New Testament times (Mark 12:26; John 7:23).

40 "You shall therefore keep His statutes and His commandments which I command you today, that it may go well with you and with your children after you, and that you may prolong *your* days in the land which the LORD your God is giving you for all time."

41 Then Moses [R]set apart three cities on this side of the Jordan, toward the rising of the sun, Num. 35:6

42 that the manslayer might flee there, who kills his neighbor unintentionally, without having hated him in time past, and that by fleeing to one of these cities he might live:

43 [R]Bezer in the wilderness on the plateau for the Reubenites, Ramoth in Gilead for the Gadites, and Golan in Bashan for the Manassites. Josh. 20:8

The Introduction to the Law of God

44 And this *is* the law which Moses set before the children of Israel.

45 These *are* the testimonies, the statutes, and the judgments which Moses spoke to the children of Israel after they came out of Egypt,

46 on this side of the Jordan, in the valley opposite Beth Peor, in the land of Sihon king of the Amorites, who dwelt at Heshbon, whom Moses and the children of Israel [T]defeated after they came out of Egypt. *struck*

47 And they took possession of his land and the land of Og king of Bashan, two kings of the Amorites, who *were* on this side of the Jordan, toward the [T]rising of the sun, *east*

48 [R]from Aroer, which *is* on the bank of the River Arnon, even to Mount *Sion (that is, [R]Hermon), Deut. 2:36; 3:12 • Deut. 3:9

49 and all the plain on the east side of the Jordan as far as the Sea of the Arabah, below the [R]slopes of Pisgah. Deut. 3:17

CHAPTER 5

Setting of the Covenant

AND Moses called all Israel, and said to them: "Hear, O Israel, the statutes and judgments which I speak in your hearing today, that you may learn them and be careful to observe them.

2 [R]"The LORD our God made a covenant with us in Horeb. Ex. 19:5

3 "The LORD [R]did not make this covenant with our fathers, but with us, those who *are* here today, all of us who *are* alive. Heb. 8:9

4 "The LORD talked with you face to face on the mountain from the midst of the fire.

5 "I stood between the LORD and you at that time, to declare to you the word of the LORD; for you were afraid because of the fire, and you did not go up the mountain. *He* said:

Commandments of the Covenant

6 'I *am* the LORD your God who brought you out of the land of Egypt, out of the house of [T]bondage. *slaves*

7 [R]'You shall have no other gods [T]before Me. Hos. 13:4 • *besides*

8 'You shall not make for yourself *any* carved image, *or* any likeness *of anything* that *is* in heaven above, or that *is* in the earth beneath, or that *is* in the water under the earth;

9 you shall not bow down to them nor serve them. For I, the LORD your God, *am* a jealous God, visiting the iniquity of the fathers upon the children to the third and fourth *generations* of those who hate Me,

10 [R]but showing mercy to thousands, to those who love Me and [T]keep My commandments. Dan. 9:4 • *observe*

11 'You shall not take the name of the LORD your God in vain, for the LORD will not hold *him* [T]guiltless who takes His name in vain. *innocent*

12 [R]'Observe the Sabbath day, to [T]keep it holy, as the LORD your God commanded you. Ex. 20:8 • *sanctify it*

13 [R]Six days you shall labor and do all your work, Ex. 23:12; 35:2

14 but the seventh day *is* the [R]Sabbath of the LORD your God. *In it* you shall not do any work: you, nor your son, nor your daughter, nor your manservant, nor your maidservant, nor your ox, nor your donkey, nor any of your cattle, nor your stranger who *is* within your gates, that your manservant and your maidservant may rest as well as you. [Heb. 4:4]

15 And remember that you were a slave in the land of Egypt, and *that* the LORD your God brought you out from there [R]by a mighty hand and by an outstretched arm; therefore the LORD your God commanded you to keep the Sabbath day. Deut. 4:34, 37

16 [R]'Honor your father and your mother, as the LORD your God has commanded you, [R]that your days may be long, and that it may be well with [R]you in the land which the LORD your God is giving you. Lev. 19:3 • Deut. 6:2 • Deut. 4:40

17 [R]'You shall not murder. Matt. 5:21

18 [R]'You shall not commit adultery. Ex. 20:14

19 [R]'You shall not steal. [Rom. 13:9]

20 [R]'You shall not bear false witness against your neighbor. Ex. 20:16; 23:1

21 [R]'You shall not covet your neighbor's wife; and you shall not desire your

4:48 Syr. *Sirion*

neighbor's house, his field, his manservant, his maidservant, his ox, his
donkey, or anything that *is* your
neighbor's.' Ex. 20:17

Response of Israel

22 "These words the LORD spoke to all your
assembly, in the mountain from the midst of
the fire, the cloud, and the thick darkness,
with a loud voice; and He added no more.
And [R]He wrote them on two tablets of stone
and gave them to me. Deut. 4:13
23 [R]"So it was, when you heard the voice
from the midst of the darkness, while the
mountain was burning with fire, that you
came near to me, all the heads of your tribes
and your elders. Ex. 20:18, 19
24 "And you said: 'Surely the LORD our God
has shown us His glory and His greatness,
and we have heard His voice from the midst
of the fire. We have seen this day that God
speaks with man; yet he *still* lives.
25 'Now therefore, why should we die? For
this great fire will consume us; [R]if we hear the
voice of the LORD our God anymore, then we
shall die. Deut. 18:16
26 [R]'For who *is there* of all flesh who has
heard the voice of the living God speaking
from the midst of the fire, as we *have*, and
lived? Deut. 4:33
27 'You go near and hear all that the LORD
our God may say, and [R]tell us all that the
LORD our God says to you, and we will hear
and do *it*.' Ex. 20:19

Response of God

28 "Then the LORD heard the voice of your
words when you spoke to me, and the LORD
said to me: 'I have heard the voice of the
words of this people which they have spoken
to you. [R]They are right *in* all that they have
spoken. Deut. 18:17
29 'Oh, that they had such a heart in them
that they would fear Me and always keep all
My commandments, that it might be well
with them and with their children forever!
30 'Go and say to them, "Return to your
tents."
31 'But as for you, stand here by Me, and I
will speak to you all the commandments, the
statutes, and the judgments which you shall
teach them, that they may observe *them* in
the land which I am giving them to possess.'
32 "Therefore you shall [T]be careful to do as
the LORD your God has commanded you;
[R]you shall not turn aside to the right hand or
to the left. *observe* • Deut. 17:20; 28:14
33 "You shall walk in all the ways which
the LORD your God has commanded you, that
you may live [R]and *that it may be* well with
you, and *that* you may prolong *your* days in
the land which you shall possess. Deut. 4:40

CHAPTER 6

The Command to Teach the Law

"NOW this *is* the commandment, *and
these are* the statutes and judgments
which the LORD your God has commanded to
teach you, that you may observe *them* in the
land which you are crossing over to possess,
2 "that you may fear the LORD your God,
to keep all His statutes and His commandments which I command you, you and your
son and your grandson, all the days of your
life, and that your days may be prolonged.
3 "Therefore hear, O Israel, and be careful
to observe *it*, that it may be well with you,
and that you may multiply greatly as the
LORD God of your fathers has promised you—
'a land flowing with milk and honey.'

4 [R]"Hear, O Israel: The LORD our God, the
LORD is one! [1 Cor. 8:4, 6]
5 [R]"You shall love the LORD your God with
all your heart, [R]with all your soul, and with
all your might. Matt. 22:37 • 2 Kin. 23:25
6 "And [R]these words which I command
you today shall be in your heart; Deut. 11:18–20
7 "you shall teach them diligently to your
children, and shall talk of them when you sit
in your house, when you walk by the way,
when you lie down, and when you rise up.
8 [R]"You shall bind them as a sign on your
hand, and they shall be as frontlets between
your eyes. Prov. 3:3; 6:21; 7:3
9 [R]"You shall write them on the doorposts
of your house and on your gates. Deut. 11:20

10 "And it shall be, when the LORD your
God brings you into the land of which He
swore to your fathers, to Abraham, Isaac, and
Jacob, to give you large and beautiful cities
[R]which you did not build, Josh. 24:13

6:4–9 Three Essentials for a Christian Home—A new generation of Israel is gathered on the plains of Moab to hear Moses review the law in preparation for their entrance to the Promised Land. The previous generation had died in unbelief in the wilderness. Moses begins his instruction by telling the people of Israel what a home is all about. He sets forth three components which must be true if the home is rightly related to God:

a. There must be a revelation of God (6:4). God revealed three things about Himself: (1) His eternality (Jehovah; Hebrew *YHWH,* The Eternal); (2) His plurality (*Elohim,* Hebrew plural of God, there are three Persons in the Godhead); and (3) His unity—"one LORD"—the three Persons of the Godhead constitute one God; each is essential.
b. There must be a response to God's revelation (6:5). The response is to be a total response of love with all one's being, heart, soul, and mind. This is the only fitting response to the eternal God who has revealed Himself.

(continued on page 217)

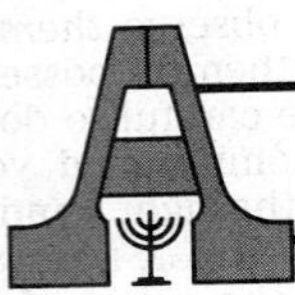

WITH ALL MY HEART

In Deuteronomy 6:5 God tells His people that they must love the Lord their God with all their heart, soul, and strength. Let us look at this word *heart*, and the other physical organs that the Old Testament uses to stand for various emotions and attitudes.

Heart (*lēb* or *lēbāb*)

Our expressions "with all my heart," "my heart wasn't in it," "lionhearted," "heartless," and many more show how similar English and Hebrew are in usage of the word *heart*. The Hebrews used *heart* on a broader scale than we do.

Theologians often divide man's personality into intellect, sensibility (emotion), and will. The Old Testament uses *lēb* to express all three of these, especially, as in English, emotion.

Intellect (mind). Sometimes *heart* is translated *mind* or similarly. Often the context determines when this aspect of heart is emphasized. For example, Proverbs 12:11 tells us that "he who follows frivolity *is* devoid of understanding [*leb*]."

Sensibility (emotion). *Lēb* expresses the whole gamut of emotions, both negative and positive. Second Samuel 17:10 speaks of the "heart of a lion" for bravery. (Compare "Richard the Lionhearted"; also, our word *courage* is from the French for *heart*.) Hannah's heart rejoiced (1 Sam. 2:1). "Jacob's heart stood still" with rapture when he found out that Joseph was still alive (Gen. 45:26). God Himself "was grieved in His heart" because of man's wickedness (Gen. 6:6).

When David says "my heart fails me" (Ps. 40:12), he is not referring to physical "heart failure"; he is oppressed by the innumerable evils opposing him and fearful of his own iniquities overtaking him.

Will. As the seat of being, the heart makes decisions that express a person's will. For example, Moses explained that he was following the Lord's dictates in all his works, and he had "not *done them* of my own will" (lit., "from my heart," Num. 16:28).

Lēb sometimes equals the person as a whole (as does *nephesh*; see study on p. 935). For example, when the Levite's father-in-law asked him to refresh his heart with food, he meant, "Refresh yourself" (Judg. 19:5).

One of the most famous verses in the Bible paints a grim portrait of the natural state of the human heart: "The heart *is* deceitful above all *things*, and desperately wicked; who can know it?" (Jer. 17:9).

Inward Parts (*mēʿîm*)

This word occurs thirty-two times in the Old Testament, always in the plural. The KJV translation "bowels," while acceptable in 1611, is not suitable today. We generally avoid intestines as the seat of emotions, though the informal expression "my gut reaction" is close to the Hebrew.

Besides the literal, physical meaning and references to the reproductive system (Gen. 15:4; Is. 48:19), *mēʿîm* is largely used for emotions, chiefly compassion (Is. 63:15; Jer. 31:20) and anguish (Lam. 1:20).

Paul used this Old Testament expression twice in the New Testament. In both cases the KJV uses "bowels," but even literally the Greek word *splangchna* refers to the heart, lungs, and liver rather than the lower intestine. The NKJV uses "affection" (Phil. 2:1) and "tender mercies" (Col. 3:12) for this concept.

Kidneys (*kelayōt*)

Over half of the thirty-one occurrences of *kelayōt* refer to the organs that filter out impurities. Nine times *kelayōt* refers to one's innermost being. God is seen as "testing the mind [*kelayōt*] and the heart" in Jeremiah 11:20 and elsewhere. Because one's back was vulnerable to arrows in the kidneys, both Job 16:13 (NKJV, "heart") and Lamentations 3:13 (NKJV, "loins") use the idiom for God's severe chastisement.

A main thrust of all three Hebrew metaphors for bodily organs is that our deepest being should be involved in living for God. We should not be passive, but put our whole heart, mind, and soul into our worship and service.

11 "houses full of all good things, which you did not fill, hewn-out wells which you did not dig, vineyards and olive trees which you did not plant—[R]when you have eaten and are full— Deut. 8:10; 11:15; 14:29

12 "*then* beware, lest you forget the [R]LORD who brought you out of the land of Egypt, from the house of bondage. Deut. 8:11–18

13 "You shall fear the LORD your God and serve Him, and shall take oaths in His name.

14 "You shall not go after other gods, the gods of the peoples who *are* all around you

15 "(for [R]the LORD your God *is* a jealous God [R]among you), lest the anger of the LORD your God be aroused against you and destroy you from the face of the earth. Ex. 20:5 • Ex. 33:3

16 "You shall not [T]tempt the LORD your God as you tempted *Him* in Massah. *test*

17 "You shall [R]diligently keep the commandments of the LORD your God, His testimonies, and His statutes which He has commanded you. Deut. 11:22

18 "And you [R]shall do *what is* right and good in the sight of the LORD, that it may be well with you, and that you may go in and possess the good land of which the LORD swore to your fathers, Ex. 15:26

19 [R]"to cast out all your enemies from before you, as the LORD has spoken. Num. 33:52, 53

20 [R]"When your son asks you in time to come, saying, 'What *is the meaning of* the testimonies, the statutes, and the judgments which the LORD our God has commanded you?' Ex. 13:8, 14

21 "then you shall say to your son: 'We were slaves of Pharaoh in Egypt, and the LORD brought us out of Egypt [R]with a mighty hand; Ex. 13:3

22 'and the LORD showed signs and wonders before our eyes, great and severe, against Egypt, Pharaoh, and all his household.

23 'Then He brought us out from there, that He might bring us in, to give us the land of which He swore to our fathers.

24 'And the LORD commanded us to observe all these statutes, to fear the LORD our God, [R]for our good always, that He might preserve us alive, as *it is* this day. Jer. 32:39

25 'Then [R]it will be righteousness for us, if we are careful to observe all these commandments before the LORD our God, as He has commanded us.' [Rom. 10:3, 5]

CHAPTER 7

The Command to Conquer Canaan

"WHEN the LORD your God brings you into the land which you go to possess, and has cast out many nations before you, the Hittites and the Girgashites and the Amorites and the Canaanites and the Perizzites and the Hivites and the Jebusites, seven nations greater and mightier than you,

2 "and when the LORD your God delivers them over to you, you shall conquer them *and* utterly destroy them. You shall make no covenant with them nor show mercy to them.

3 [R]"Nor shall you make marriages with them. You shall not give your daughter to their son, nor take their daughter for your son. 1 Kin. 11:2

4 "For they will turn your sons away from following Me, to serve other gods; [R]so the anger of the LORD will be aroused against you and destroy you suddenly. Deut. 6:15

5 "But thus you shall deal with them: you shall destroy their altars, and break down their *sacred* pillars, and cut down their [T]wooden images, and burn their carved images with fire. Or *Asherim,* Canaanite deities

6 "For you *are* a [T]holy people to the LORD your God; [R]the LORD your God has chosen you to be a people for Himself, a special treasure above all the peoples on the face of the earth. *set apart* • Ex. 19:5, 6

7 "The LORD did not set His [R]love on you nor choose you because you were more in number than any other people, for you were [R]the least of all peoples; Deut. 4:37 • Deut. 10:22

8 "but because the LORD loves you, and because He would keep the oath which He swore to your fathers, the LORD has brought you out with a mighty hand, and redeemed you from the house of [T]bondage, from the hand of Pharaoh king of Egypt. *slaves*

9 "Therefore know that the LORD your God, He *is* God, [R]the faithful God [R]who keeps covenant and mercy for a thousand generations with those who love Him and keep His commandments; 1 Cor. 1:9 • Neh. 1:5

10 "and He repays those who hate Him to their face, to destroy them. He will not [T]be

---

(continued from page 215)

c. There must be a threefold responsibility (6:6–9). This threefold responsibility acts as a check upon the proper response. If the earthly father responds to God with love he will be fulfilling his threefold responsibility. If he fails in any particular, confession of sin is necessary because he does not love God with all his heart, soul, and mind. The threefold responsibility is: (1) to have God's truth govern his heart (6:6)—there must be heart reality, not mere external conformity or ceremony; (2) to have God's truth govern his home—this is evidenced by the fact that the father teaches the truths of God's revelation to his children by both formal (teach diligently) and informal (talk of them) instruction; and (3) to have God's truth govern his habits and conduct personally, privately, and publicly. In short, the home is to be a divine school in which the father is to be the teacher, under Christ.

Now turn to Page 1480—1 Pet. 3:1–6: The Role of the Wife.

[R]slack with him who hates Him; He will repay him to his face. *delay* · [2 Pet. 3:10]

11 "Therefore you shall keep the commandment, the statutes, and the judgments which I command you today, to observe them.

12 "Then it shall come to pass, because you listen to these judgments, and keep and do them, that the LORD your God will keep with you the covenant and the mercy which He swore to your fathers.

13 "And He will love you and bless you and [T]multiply you; He will also bless the fruit of your womb and the fruit of your land, your grain and your new wine and your oil, the increase of your cattle and the offspring of your flock, in the land of which He swore to your fathers to give you. *cause you to increase*

14 "You shall be blessed above all peoples; there shall not be a male or female [R]barren among you or among your livestock. Ex. 23:26

15 "And the LORD will take away from you all sickness, and will afflict you with none of the [R]terrible diseases of Egypt which you have known, but will lay *them* on all those who hate you. Ex. 9:14; 15:26

16 "And you shall [T]destroy all the peoples whom the LORD your God delivers over to you; your eye shall have no pity on them; nor shall you serve their gods, for that *will* [R]*be* a snare to you. *consume* · Judg. 8:27

17 "If you should say in your heart, 'These nations are greater than I; how can I dispossess them?'—

18 "you shall not be afraid of them, *but* you shall [R]remember well what the LORD your God did to Pharaoh and to all Egypt: Ps. 105:5

19 [R]"the great trials which your eyes saw, the signs and the wonders, the mighty hand and the outstretched arm, by which the LORD your God brought you out. So shall the LORD your God do to all the peoples of whom you are afraid. Deut. 4:34; 29:3

20 [R]"Moreover the LORD your God will send the hornet among them until those who are left, who hide themselves from you, are destroyed. Josh. 24:12

21 "You shall not be terrified of them; for the LORD your God, the great and awesome God, *is* among you.

22 "And the LORD your God will drive out those nations before you [R]little by little; you will be unable to [T]destroy them at once, lest the beasts of the field become *too* numerous for you. Ex. 23:29, 30 · *consume*

23 "But the LORD your God will deliver them over to you, and will inflict defeat upon them until they are destroyed.

24 "And [R]He will deliver their kings into your hand, and you will destroy their name from under heaven; [R]no one shall be able to stand [T]against you until you have destroyed them. Josh. 10:24, 42; 12:1–24 · Josh. 23:9 · *before*

25 "You shall burn the carved images of their gods with fire; you shall not covet the silver or gold *that is* on them, nor take *it* for yourselves, lest you be snared by it; for it *is* an abomination to the LORD your God.

26 "Nor shall you bring an abomination into your house, lest you be doomed to destruction like it; *but* you shall utterly detest it and utterly abhor it, for it *is* an accursed thing.

CHAPTER 8

The Command to Remember the Lord

"EVERY commandment which I command you today you must [T]be careful to observe, that you may live and multiply, and go in and possess the land of which the LORD swore to your fathers. *observe to do*

2 "And you shall remember that the LORD your God [R]led you all the way these forty years in the wilderness, to humble you *and* [R]test you, [R]to know what *was* in your heart, whether you would keep His commandments or not. Amos 2:10 · Ex. 16:4 · [John 2:25]

3 "So He humbled you, [R]allowed you to hunger, and [R]fed you with manna which you did not know nor did your fathers know, that He might make you know that man shall [R]not live by bread alone; but man lives by every *word* that proceeds from the mouth of the LORD. Ex. 16:2, 3 · Ex. 16:12, 14, 35 · Matt. 4:4

4 "Your garments did not wear out on you, nor did your foot swell these forty years.

5 [R]"So you should [T]know in your heart that as a man chastens his son, *so* the LORD your God chastens you. 2 Sam. 7:14 · *consider*

6 "Therefore you shall keep the commandments of the LORD your God, [R]to walk in His ways and to fear Him. [Deut. 5:33]

7 "For the LORD your God is bringing you into a good land, [R]a land of brooks of water, of fountains and springs, that flow out of valleys and hills; Deut. 11:9–12

8 "a land of wheat and barley, of vines and fig trees and pomegranates, a land of olive oil and honey;

9 "a land in which you will eat bread without scarcity, in which you will lack nothing; a land whose stones *are* iron and out of whose hills you can dig copper.

10 "When you have eaten and are full, then you shall bless the LORD your God for the good land which He has given you.

11 "Beware that you do not forget the LORD your God by not keeping His commandments, His judgments, and His statutes which I command you today,

12 [R]"lest—*when* you have eaten and are [T]full, and have built beautiful houses and dwell *in them*; Hos. 13:6 · *satisfied*

13 "and *when* your herds and your flocks multiply, and your silver and your gold are [T]multiplied, and all that you have is multiplied; *increased*

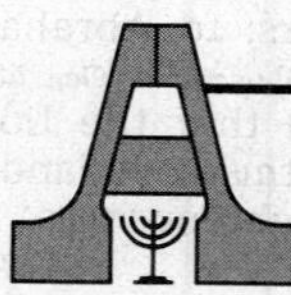

ISRAEL AND THE CANAANITES

The Canaanites, an ancient tribe, highly developed in their culture, occupied Palestine long before the Hebrews arrived to drive them out under the leadership of Joshua about 1405 B.C.

Archaeological evidence indicates the Canaanites must have settled the land of Canaan at least six hundred years before Joshua's time. They had a well-developed system of walled cities, including Jericho, Ai, Lachish, Hebron, Debir, and Hazor. Under God's leadership, Joshua was successful in taking these cities from the Canaanites (Josh. 6—12).

The Canaanites also had their own written language, based upon a unique alphabet, which they apparently developed. Discovery of a number of Canaanite documents at Ras Shamra in northern Palestine has given scholars many insights into Canaanite culture and daily life.

Baal is depicted holding a club, which may symbolize thunder, and a leaf-decorated spear, which may stand for lightning and vegetation.

The religion of the Canaanite people posed a peculiar threat to the new inhabitants of Canaan. The Canaanites worshiped many pagan gods that appealed to their animal instincts. Baal (see illustration), the god who controlled rain and fertility, was their main god.

Baal religion was basically a fertility cult. At temples scattered throughout their land, Canaanite worshipers participated in lewd, immoral acts with sacred prostitutes. Bestiality and child-sacrifice were other evils associated with this depraved form of religion.

The threat of Baal worship explains why Moses issued a stern warning to the people of Israel about the Canaanites several years before they actually occupied the Land of Promise. "You shall conquer them *and* utterly destroy them," Moses commanded. "You shall make no covenant with them nor show mercy to them" (Deut. 7:2).

Canaanite religion continued to exert its influence throughout the land for many years after Joshua's conquest. The Hebrew people had to be called back again and again to worship the one true God, who demanded holy and ethical living from His people.

14 [R]"when your heart [T]is lifted up, and you [R]forget the LORD your God who brought you out of the land of Egypt, from the house of bondage; 1 Cor. 4:7 • *becomes proud* • Ps. 106:21

15 "who led you through that great and terrible wilderness, *in which were* fiery serpents and scorpions and thirsty land where there was no water; who brought water for you out of the rock of flint;

16 "who fed you in the wilderness with manna, which your fathers did not know, that He might humble you and that He might test you, to do you good in the end—

17 "then you say in your heart, 'My power and the might of my hand have gained me this wealth.'

18 "And you shall remember the LORD your God, [R]for *it is* He who gives you power to get wealth, [R]that He may [T]establish His covenant which He swore to your fathers, as *it is* this day. Hos. 2:8 • Deut. 7:8, 12 • *confirm*

19 "Then it shall be, if you by any means forget the LORD your God, and follow other gods, and serve them and worship them, [R]I testify against you this day that you shall surely perish. Deut. 4:26; 30:18

20 "As the nations which the LORD destroys before you, [R]so you shall perish, because you would not be obedient to the voice of the LORD your God. [Dan. 9:11, 12]

CHAPTER 9

Moses Rehearses Israel's Rebellion

"HEAR, O Israel: You *are* to cross over the Jordan today, and go in to dispossess nations greater and mightier than yourself, cities great and fortified up to heaven,

2 "a people great and tall, the descendants of the Anakim, whom you know, and *of whom* you heard *it said*, 'Who can stand before the descendants of Anak?'

3 "Therefore understand today that the LORD your God *is* He who goes over before you *as* a consuming fire. He will destroy them and bring them down before you; so you shall drive them out and destroy them quickly, as the LORD has said to you.

4 [R]"Do not think in your heart, after the LORD your God has cast them out before you, saying, 'Because of my righteousness the LORD has brought me in to possess this land'; but *it is* [R]because of the wickedness of these nations *that* the LORD is driving them out from before you. Deut. 8:17 • Lev. 18:3, 24–30

5 [R]"*It is* not because of your righteousness or the uprightness of your heart *that* you go in to possess their land, but because of the wickedness of these nations *that* the LORD your God drives them out from before you, and that He may [T]fulfill the [R]word which the LORD swore to your fathers, to Abraham, Isaac, and Jacob. [Titus 3:5] • *perform* • Gen. 50:24

6 "Therefore understand that the LORD your God is not giving you this good land to possess because of your righteousness, for you *are* a [T]stiff-necked people. *rebellious*

7 "Remember *and* do not forget how you [R]provoked the LORD your God to wrath in the wilderness; [R]from the day that you departed from the land of Egypt until you came to this place, you have been rebellious against the LORD. Num. 14:22 • Ex. 14:11

8 "Also [R]in Horeb you provoked the LORD to wrath, so that the LORD was angry *enough* with you to have destroyed you. Ex. 32:1–8

9 [R]"When I went up into the mountain to receive the tablets of stone, the tablets of the covenant which the LORD made with you, then I stayed on the mountain forty days and [R]forty nights. I neither ate bread nor drank water. Deut. 5:2–22 • Ex. 24:18

10 "Then the LORD delivered to me two tablets of stone written with the finger of God, and on them *were* all the words which the LORD had spoken to you on the mountain from the midst of the fire [R]in[T] the day of the assembly. Ex. 19:17 • *when you were all gathered together*

11 "And it came to pass, at the end of forty days and forty nights, *that* the LORD gave me the two tablets of stone, the tablets of the covenant.

12 "Then the LORD said to me, 'Arise, go down quickly from here, for your people whom you brought out of Egypt have acted corruptly; they have quickly turned aside from the way which I commanded them; they have made themselves a molded image.'

13 "Furthermore the LORD spoke to me, saying, 'I have seen this people, and indeed they are a [T]stiff-necked people. *rebellious*

14 'Let Me alone, that I may destroy them and [R]blot out their name from under heaven; [R]and I will make of you a nation mightier and greater than they.' Deut. 29:20 • Num. 14:12

15 [R]"So I turned and came down from the mountain, and [R]the mountain burned with fire; and the two tablets of the covenant *were* in my two hands. Ex. 32:15–19 • Ex. 19:18

16 "And [R]I looked, and there, you had sinned against the LORD your God, *and* had made for yourselves a molded calf! You had turned aside quickly from the way which the LORD had commanded you. Ex. 32:19

17 "Then I took the two tablets and threw them out of my two hands and [R]broke them before your eyes. Ex. 32:19

18 "And I [R]fell[T] down before the LORD, as at the first, forty days and forty nights; I neither ate bread nor drank water, because of all your sin which you committed in doing wickedly in the sight of the LORD, to provoke Him to anger. Ex. 34:28 • *prostrated myself*

19 "For I was afraid of the anger and hot displeasure with which the LORD was angry with you, to destroy you. [R]But the LORD listened to me at that time also. Ex. 32:14

20 "And the LORD was very angry with Aaron *and* would have destroyed him; so I prayed for Aaron also at the same time.

21 "Then I took your sin, the calf which you had made, and burned it with fire and crushed it *and* ground *it* very small, until it was as fine as dust; and I threw its dust into the brook that descended from the mountain.

22 "Also at Taberah and Massah and [R]Kibroth Hattaavah you [T]provoked the LORD to wrath. Num. 11:4, 34 • *caused the LORD to be angry*

23 "Likewise, when the LORD sent you from Kadesh Barnea, saying, 'Go up and possess the land which I have given you,' then you rebelled against the commandment of the LORD your God, and [R]you did not believe Him nor obey His voice. Ps. 106:24, 25

24 "You have been rebellious against the LORD from the day that I knew you.

25 [R]"Thus I [T]prostrated myself before the LORD; forty days and forty nights I kept prostrating myself, because the LORD had said He would destroy you. Deut. 9:18 • *fell down*

26 "Therefore I prayed to the LORD, and said: 'O Lord GOD, do not destroy Your people and [R]Your inheritance whom You have redeemed through Your greatness, whom You have brought out of Egypt with a mighty hand. Deut. 32:9

27 'Remember Your servants, Abraham, Isaac, and Jacob; do not look on the stubbornness of this people, or on their wickedness or their sin,

28 'lest the land from which You brought us should say, "Because the LORD was not able to bring them to the land which He promised them, and because He hated them, He has brought them out to kill them in the wilderness."

29 'Yet they *are* Your people and Your inheritance, whom You brought out by Your mighty power and by Your outstretched arm.'

CHAPTER 10

Moses Rehearses God's Mercy

"AT that time the LORD said to me, [T]'Hew for yourself two tablets of stone like the first, and come up to Me on the mountain and make yourself an ark of wood. *Cut out*

2 'And I will write on the tablets the words that were on the first tablets, which you broke; and you shall put them in the ark.'

3 "So I made an ark of acacia wood, hewed two tablets of stone like the first, and went up the mountain, having the two tablets in my hand.

4 "And He wrote on the tablets according to the first writing, the Ten [T]Commandments, [R]which the LORD had spoken to you in the mountain from the midst of the fire in the day of the assembly; and the LORD gave them to me. *Words* • Ex. 20:1; 34:28

5 "Then I turned and came down from the mountain, and put the tablets in the ark which I had made; [R]and there they are, just as the LORD commanded me." 1 Kin. 8:9

6 (Now the children of Israel journeyed from the wells of Bene Jaakan to Moserah. *That was the place* where Aaron died *later*, and where he was buried; and Eleazar his son ministered as priest in his [T]stead. *place*

7 [R]From there they journeyed to Gudgodah, and from Gudgodah to Jotbathah, a land of [T]rivers of water. Num. 33:32–34 • *brooks*

8 At that time the LORD [T]separated the tribe of Levi to bear the ark of the covenant of the LORD, [R]to stand before the LORD to minister to Him and [R]to bless in His name, to this day. *set apart* • Deut. 18:5 • Num. 6:23

9 [R]Therefore Levi has no portion nor inheritance with his brethren; the LORD *is* his inheritance, just as the LORD your God promised him.) Deut. 18:1, 2

10 "As at the first time, I stayed in the mountain forty days and forty nights; [R]the LORD also heard me at that time, *and* the LORD chose not to destroy you. Ex. 32:14

11 [R]"Then the LORD said to me, 'Arise, begin *your* journey before the people, that they may go in and possess the land which I swore to their fathers to give them.' Ex. 33:1

Love God

12 "And now, Israel, what does the LORD your God require of you, but to fear the LORD your God, to walk in all His ways and to [R]love Him, to serve the LORD your God with all your heart and with all your soul, Deut. 6:5

13 "*and* to keep the commandments of the LORD and His statutes which I command you today [R]for your [T]good? Deut. 6:24 • *benefit* or *welfare*

14 "Indeed heaven and the highest heavens belong to the [R]LORD your God, *also* the earth with all that *is* in it. [Neh. 9:6]

15 "The LORD delighted only in your fathers, to love them; and He chose their [T]descendants after them, you above all peoples, as *it is* this day. Lit. *seed*

16 "Therefore circumcise the foreskin of your heart, and be stiff-necked no longer.

17 "For the LORD your God *is* God of gods and [R]Lord of lords, the great God, [R]mighty and awesome, who [R]shows no partiality nor takes a bribe. Rev. 19:16 • Deut. 7:21 • Acts 10:34

18 [R]"He administers justice for the fatherless and the widow, and loves the stranger, giving him food and clothing. Ps. 68:5; 146:9

19 "Therefore love the stranger, for you were strangers in the land of Egypt.

20 [R]"You shall fear the LORD your God; you shall serve Him, and to Him you shall hold fast, and take oaths in His name. Matt. 4:10

21 "He *is* your praise, and He *is* your God, who has done for you these great and awesome things which your eyes have seen.

22 "Your fathers went down to Egypt with seventy persons, and now the LORD your God has made you as the stars of heaven in multitude.

CHAPTER 11

Study and Obey the Commands

"THEREFORE you shall love the LORD your God, and keep His charge, His statutes, His judgments, and His commandments always.

2 "Know today that *I do* not *speak* with your children, who have not known and who have not seen the [T]chastening of the LORD your God, His greatness and His mighty hand and His outstretched arm— *discipline*

3 "His signs and His acts which He did in the midst of Egypt, to Pharaoh king of Egypt, and to all his land;

4 "what He did to the army of Egypt, to their horses and their chariots: [R]how He made the waters of the Red Sea overflow them as they pursued you, and *how* the LORD has destroyed them to this day; Ps. 106:11

5 "what He did for you in the wilderness until you came to this place;

6 "and what He did to Dathan and Abiram the sons of Eliab, the son of Reuben: how the earth opened its mouth and swallowed them up, their households, their tents, and all the substance that *was* [T]in their possession, in the midst of all Israel— *at their feet*

7 "but your eyes have seen every great [T]act of the LORD which He did. *work*

8 "Therefore you shall keep every commandment which I command you today, that you may be strong, and go in and possess the land which you cross over to possess,

9 "and that you may prolong *your* days in the land which the LORD swore to give your fathers, to them and their descendants, [R]'a land flowing with milk and honey.' Ex. 3:8

10 "For the land which you go to possess *is* not like the land of Egypt from which you have come, where you sowed your seed and watered *it* by foot, as a vegetable garden;

11 [R]"but the land which you cross over to possess *is* a land of hills and valleys, which drinks water from the rain of heaven, Deut. 8:7

12 "a land for which the LORD your God cares; [R]the eyes of the LORD your God *are* always on it, from the beginning of the year to the very end of the year. 1 Kin. 9:3

13 'And it shall be that if you diligently [T]obey My commandments which I command you today, to love the LORD your God and serve Him with all your heart and with all your soul, *Lit. listen to*

14 'then [R]I will give *you* the rain for your land in its season, [R]the early rain and the latter rain, that you may gather in your grain, your new wine, and your oil. Deut. 28:12 • Joel 2:23

15 [R]'And I will send grass in your fields for your livestock, that you may [R]eat and be [T]filled.' Ps. 104:14 • Deut. 6:11 • *satisfied*

16 "Take heed to yourselves, lest your heart be deceived, and you turn aside and serve other gods and worship them,

17 "lest the LORD's anger be aroused against you, and He shut up the heavens so that there be no rain, and the land yield no produce, and you perish quickly from the good land which the LORD is giving you.

18 "Therefore [R]you shall [T]lay up these words of mine in your heart and in your [R]soul, and [R]bind them as a sign on your hand, and they shall be as frontlets between your eyes. Deut. 6:6–9 • Lit. *put* • Ps. 119:2, 34 • Deut. 6:8

19 [R]"You shall teach them to your children, speaking of them when you sit in your house, when you walk by the way, when you lie down, and when you rise up. Deut. 4:9, 10; 6:7

20 "And you shall write them on the doorposts of your house and on your gates,

21 "that [R]your days and the days of your children may be multiplied in the land of which the LORD swore to your fathers to give them, like [R]the days of the heavens above the earth. Deut. 4:40 • Ps. 72:5; 89:29

Victory Depends upon Obedience

22 "For if you carefully keep all these commandments which I command you to do—to love the LORD your God, to walk in all His ways, and to hold fast to Him—

23 "then the LORD will [R]drive out all these nations from before you, and you will [R]dispossess greater and mightier nations than yourselves. Deut. 4:38 • Deut. 9:1

24 "Every place on which the sole of your foot treads shall be yours: [R]from the wilderness and Lebanon, from the river, the River Euphrates, even to the [T]Western Sea, shall be your territory. Gen. 15:18 • Mediterranean

25 "No man shall be able to stand against you; the LORD your God will put the dread of you and the fear of you upon all the land where you tread, just as He has said to you.

26 [R]"Behold, I set before you today a blessing and a curse: Deut. 30:1, 15, 19

27 [R]"the blessing, if you obey the commandments of the LORD your God which I command you today; Deut. 28:1–14

28 "and the [R]curse, if you do not obey the commandments of the LORD your God, but turn aside from the way which I command you today, to go after other gods which you have not known. Deut. 28:15–68

29 "And it shall be, when the LORD your God has brought you into the land which you go to possess, that you shall put the [R]blessing on Mount Gerizim and the [R]curse on Mount Ebal. Josh. 8:33 • Deut. 27:13–26

30 "*Are* they not on the other side of the Jordan, toward the setting sun, in the land of the Canaanites who dwell in the plain opposite Gilgal, [R]beside the terebinth trees of Moreh? Gen. 12:6

31 "For you will cross over the Jordan and go in to possess the land which the LORD your God is giving you, and you will possess it and dwell in it.

32 "And you shall be careful to observe all the statutes and judgments which I set before you today.

CHAPTER 12

Law of the Central Sanctuary

"THESE [R]*are* the statutes and judgments which you shall be careful to observe in the land which the LORD God of your fathers is giving you to possess, [T]all the days that you live on the earth. Deut. 6:1 • As long as

2 "You shall utterly destroy all the places where the nations which you shall dispossess served their gods, on the high mountains and on the hills and under every green tree.

3 "And you shall destroy their altars, break their *sacred* pillars, and burn their [T]wooden images with fire; you shall cut down the carved images of their gods and destroy their names from that place. Or *Asherim*

4 "You shall not [R]worship the LORD your God *with* such *things*. Deut. 12:31

5 "But you shall seek the [R]place where the LORD your God chooses, out of all your tribes, to put His name for His [R]habitation;[T] and there you shall go. Ex. 20:24 • Ex. 15:13 • *dwelling*

6 [R]"There you shall take your burnt offerings, your sacrifices, your tithes, the heave offerings of your hand, your vowed offerings, your freewill offerings, and the [R]firstlings of your herds and flocks. Lev. 17:3, 4 • Deut. 14:23

7 "And there you shall eat before the LORD your God, and you shall rejoice in [T]all to which you have put your hand, you and your households, in which the LORD your God has blessed you. *all that you undertake*

8 "You shall not at all do as we are doing here today—[R]every man doing whatever *is* right in his own eyes— Judg. 17:6; 21:25

9 "for as yet you have not come to the [T]rest and the inheritance which the LORD your God is giving you. Or *place of rest*

10 "But *when* you cross over the Jordan and dwell in the land which the LORD your God is giving you to inherit, and *when* He gives you [R]rest from all your enemies round about, so that you dwell in safety, Josh. 11:23

11 "then there will be the place where the LORD your God chooses to make His name abide. There you shall bring all that I command you: your burnt offerings, your sacrifices, your tithes, the heave offerings of your hand, and all your choice offerings which you vow to the LORD.

12 "And [R]you shall rejoice before the LORD your God, you and your sons and your daughters, your menservants and your maidservants, and the [R]Levite who *is* within your gates, since he has no portion nor inheritance with you. Deut. 12:18; 26:11 • Deut. 10:9; 14:29

13 "Take heed to yourself that you do not offer your burnt offerings in every place that you see;

14 "but in the place which the LORD chooses, in one of your tribes, there you shall offer your burnt offerings, and there you shall do all that I command you.

15 "However, you may slaughter and eat meat within all your gates, whatever your heart desires, according to the blessing of the LORD your God which He has given you; the unclean and the clean may eat of it, [R]of the gazelle and the deer alike. Deut. 14:5

16 [R]"Only you shall not eat the blood; you shall pour it on the earth like water. Gen. 9:4

17 "You may not eat within your gates the tithe of your grain or your new wine or your oil, of the firstlings of your herd or your flock, of any of your offerings which you vow, of your freewill offerings, or of the [T]heave offering of your hand. *contribution*

18 "But you must eat them before the LORD your God in the place which the LORD your God chooses, you and your son and your daughter, your manservant and your maidservant, and the Levite who *is* within your gates; and you shall rejoice before the LORD your God in all to which you put your hands.

19 [T]"Take heed to yourself that you do not forsake the Levite as long as you live in your land. *Be careful*

20 "When the LORD your God [R]enlarges your border as He has promised you, and you say, 'Let me eat meat,' because you long to eat meat, you may eat as much meat as your heart desires. Ex. 34:24

21 "If the place where the LORD your God chooses to put His name is too far from [R]you, then you may slaughter from your herd and from your flock which the LORD has given you, just as I have commanded you, and you may eat within your gates as much as your heart desires. Deut. 14:24

22 "Just as the gazelle and the deer are eaten, so you may eat them; the unclean and the clean alike may eat them.

23 "Only be sure that you do not eat the blood, [R]for the blood *is* the life; you may not eat the life with the meat. Gen. 9:4

24 "You shall not eat it; you shall pour it on
the earth like water.
25 "You shall not eat it, that it may go well
with you and your children after you, when
you do *what is* right in the sight of the LORD.
26 "Only the holy things which you have,
and your vowed offerings, you shall take and
go to the place which the LORD chooses.
27 "And [R]you shall offer your burnt offerings, the meat and the blood, on the altar of
the LORD your God; and the blood of your
sacrifices shall be poured out on the altar of
the LORD your God, and you shall eat the
meat. Lev. 1:5, 9, 13, 17
28 "Observe and obey all these words which
I command you, [R]that it may go well with
you and your children after you forever,
when you do *what is* good and right in the
sight of the LORD your God. Deut. 12:25

Law of Idolatry

29 "When [R]the LORD your God cuts off from
before you the nations which you go to
dispossess, and you displace them and dwell
in their land, Ex. 23:23
30 "take heed to yourself that you are not
ensnared to follow them, after they are destroyed from before you, and that you do not
inquire after their gods, saying, 'How did
these nations serve their gods? I also will do
likewise.'
31 "You shall not worship the LORD your
God in that way; for every abomination to
the LORD which He hates they have done to
their gods; for they burn even their sons and
daughters in the fire to their gods.
32 "Whatever I command you, be careful to
observe it; [R]you shall not add to it nor take
away from it. Rev. 22:18, 19

CHAPTER 13

"IF there arises among you a prophet or a
[R]dreamer of dreams, [R]and he gives you
a sign or a wonder, Zech. 10:2 • Matt. 24:24
2 "and [R]the sign or the wonder comes to
pass, of which he spoke to you, saying, 'Let
us go after other gods which you have not
known, and let us serve them,' Deut. 18:22
3 "you shall not listen to the words of that
prophet or that dreamer of dreams, for the
LORD your God [R]is testing you to know
whether you love the LORD your God with all
your heart and with all your soul. Deut. 8:2, 16
4 "You shall [R]walk[T] after the LORD your
God and fear Him, and keep His commandments and obey His voice, and you shall serve
Him and hold fast to Him. 2 Kin. 23:3 • *follow*
5 "But [R]that prophet or that dreamer of
dreams shall be put to death, because he has
spoken in order to turn *you* away from the
LORD your God, who brought you out of the
land of Egypt and redeemed you from
the house of bondage, to entice you from the
way in which the LORD your God commanded you to walk. So you shall [T]put away
the evil from your midst. Jer. 14:15 • *exterminate*
6 [R]"If your brother, the son of your
mother, your son or your daughter, [R]the wife
[T]of your bosom, or your friend who is as your
own soul, secretly entices you, saying, 'Let
us go and serve other gods,' which you
have not known, neither you nor your
fathers, Deut. 17:2 • Gen. 16:5 • Whom you cherish
7 "of the gods of the people which *are* all
around you, near to you or far off from you,
from *one* end of the earth to the *other* end of
the earth,
8 "you shall [R]not [T]consent to him or listen
to him, nor shall your eye pity him, nor shall
you spare him or conceal him; Prov. 1:10 • *yield*
9 "but you shall surely kill him; your hand
shall be first against him to put him to death,
and afterward the hand of all the people.
10 "And you shall stone him with stones
until he dies, because he sought to entice you
away from the LORD your God, who brought
you out of the land of Egypt, from the house
of bondage.
11 "So all Israel shall hear and [R]fear, and
not again do such wickedness as this among
you. Deut. 17:13
12 [R]"If you hear someone in one of your
cities, which the LORD your God gives you to
dwell in, saying, Judg. 20:1–48
13 '*Certain* [T]corrupt men have gone out
from among you and enticed the inhabitants
of their city, saying, "Let us go and serve
other gods," *gods* whom you have not
known,' Lit. *sons of Belial*
14 "then you shall inquire, search out, and
ask diligently. And *if it is* indeed true *and*
certain *that* such an [T]abomination was committed among you, *detestable action*
15 "you shall surely strike the inhabitants
of that city with the edge of the sword—
utterly destroying it, all that is in it and its
livestock, with the edge of the sword.
16 "And you shall gather all its plunder into
the middle of the street, and completely
[R]burn with fire the city and all its plunder, for
the LORD your God; and it shall be a heap
forever. It shall not be built again. Josh. 6:24
17 [R]"So none of the accursed things shall
remain in your hand, that the LORD may
[R]turn from the fierceness of His anger and
show you mercy, have compassion on you
and [T]multiply you, just as He swore to your
fathers, Josh. 6:18 • Josh. 7:26 • *increase*
18 "because you have listened to the voice
of the LORD your God, [R]to keep all His commandments which I command you today, to
do *what is* right in the eyes of the LORD your
God. Deut. 12:25, 28, 32

CHAPTER 14

Law of Food

"YOU *are* the children of the LORD your
God; you shall not cut yourselves nor
shave the front of your head for the dead.
2 [R]"For you *are* a holy people to the LORD
your God, and the LORD has chosen you to be
a people for Himself, a special treasure above
all the peoples who *are* on the face of the
earth. Lev. 20:26
3 "You shall not eat any detestable thing.
4 [R]"These *are* the animals which you may
eat: the ox, the sheep, the goat, Lev. 11:2–45
5 "the deer, the gazelle, the roe deer, the
wild goat, the [T]mountain goat, the antelope,
and the mountain sheep. Or *addax*
6 "And you may eat every animal with
cloven hooves, having the hoof split into two
parts, *and that* chews the cud, among the
animals.
7 "Nevertheless, of those that chew the
cud or have cloven hooves, you shall not eat,
such as these: the camel, the hare, and the
rock hyrax; for they chew the cud but do not
have cloven hooves; they *are* unclean for
you.
8 "Also the swine is unclean for you, because it has cloven hooves, yet *does* not *chew*
the cud; you shall not eat their flesh [R]or touch
their dead carcasses. Lev. 11:26, 27
9 [R]"These you may eat of all that *are* in the
waters: you may eat all that have fins and
scales. Lev. 11:9
10 "And whatever does not have fins and
scales you shall not eat; it *is* unclean for you.
11 "All clean birds you may eat.
12 [R]"But these you shall not eat: the eagle,
the vulture, the buzzard, Lev. 11:13
13 "the red kite, the falcon, and the kite
after their kinds;
14 "every raven after its kind;
15 "the ostrich, the short-eared owl, the
seagull, and the hawk after their kinds;
16 "the little owl, the screech owl, the white
owl,
17 "the jackdaw, the carrion vulture, the
fisher owl,
18 "the stork, the heron after its kind, and
the hoopoe and the bat.
19 "Also every creeping thing that flies is
unclean for you; they shall not be eaten.
20 "You may eat all clean birds.
21 "You shall not eat anything that dies *of
itself*; you may give it to the alien who *is*
within your gates, that he may eat it, or you
may sell it to a foreigner; for you *are* a holy
people to the LORD your God. You shall not
boil a young goat in its mother's milk.

Law of the Tithes

22 [R]"You shall truly tithe all the increase of
your grain that the field produces year by
year. Lev. 27:30
23 "And you shall eat before the LORD your
God, in the place where He chooses to make
His name abide, the tithe of your grain and
your new wine and your oil, of the firstlings
of your herds and your flocks, that you may
learn to fear the LORD your God always.
24 "But if the journey is too long for you, so
that you are not able to carry *the tithe, or* [R]if
the place where the LORD your God chooses
to put His name is too far from you, when the
LORD your God has blessed you, Deut. 12:5, 21
25 "then you shall exchange *it* for money,
take the money in your hand, and go to the
place which the LORD your God chooses.
26 "And you shall spend that money for
whatever your heart desires: for oxen or
sheep, for wine or similar drink, for whatever
your heart desires; you shall eat there before
the LORD your God, and you shall [R]rejoice,
you and your household. Deut. 12:7
27 "You shall not [T]forsake the [R]Levite who
is within your gates, for he has no part nor
inheritance with you. *neglect* • Deut. 12:12
28 "At the end of *every* third year you shall
bring out the tithe of your produce of that
year and store *it* up within your gates.
29 "And the Levite, because he has no
portion nor inheritance with you, and the

14:2 Purpose of Israel—The modern-day student of the Bible may well ask why so much of Scripture is taken up with the history of a single nation. Certainly many Christians wonder why one nation should be called "God's chosen people." The answer to this question is bound up in God's purpose for Israel. When God promised Abraham that he would become the father of a great nation, He also promised that He would bless all peoples through that nation (Page 18—Gen. 12:1–3). Therefore Israel was to be a channel of blessing as well as a recipient. Even their deliverance from Egypt was partially designed to show other nations that Israel's God was the only true God (Page 74—Ex. 7:5; 14:18; Page 253—Josh. 2:9–11). It was further prophesied by Isaiah that the Messiah would bring salvation to the Gentiles (Page 821—Is. 49:6). Also in the Psalms there are many invitations to other nations to come and worship the Lord in Israel (Page 625—Ps. 2:10–12; 117:1). Ruth the Moabitess is an example of a foreigner who believed in Israel's God.

It is clear that God's promise to Abraham to bless the whole world through him is still being fulfilled. The life, ministry, and death of Jesus Christ, and the existence and influence of the church today, all came about through God's choice of Israel. All whom the church wins to Christ, whether Jew or Gentile, enter into those great blessings channeled through Israel.

Now turn to Page 494—1 Chr. 28:4–6: Government of Israel.

WE THE PEOPLE

Gentile, Nation, People, Heathen (*gôy*)

The word *gôy* has several usages and is hard to define. Basically it refers to a defined group of people or a large subdivision of a people.

Genesis 10's "table of nations" uses *gôy* without labeling the mentioned nations as "heathen" or by other pejorative terms.

Unsurprisingly, *gôy* is used for Egypt and Syria, but in view of the tendency to associate the word with Gentiles, it is interesting to note how the Hebrew Old Testament used *gôy* for Israel. God promised to make Abraham "a great nation [*gôy*]" (Gen. 17:20). Moses reminded God to "consider that this nation [*gôy*] *is* Your people [*'am*]" (Ex. 33:13).

While the plural form is used for ethnic groups that would be descendants of Abraham (Gen. 17:16), as time passed, the term more and more came to be used for Gentiles. Even the concept of their being pagan or heathen is evident in some texts. The "uncircumcised" were idolaters, usually wicked, and often enemies of Israel.

Nevertheless, the Old Testament does predict a bright future for the Gentiles when they come to know the Messiah (Is. 11:10; 42:6). The shortest chapter in the Bible, Psalm 117 (perhaps made short to draw attention to a truth that was unpopular in Israel), calls on all the Gentiles (*gôyîm*) and all the peoples to praise the Lord.

People, Nation (*'am*)

The Hebrews, like most nations, had a word they especially liked to call themselves, and *'am* was that term. For example, *'am* was used in Hosea 2:23 to describe God's covenant relationship with Israel: "My people [*'ammî*]." When they apostatized, "not My people [*lo'-'ammî*]" was used. In spite of apostasy, God will always allow a godly remnant that can be called His people: "They will call on My name, and I will answer them. I will say, 'This *is* My people'; and each one will say, 'The LORD *is* my God' " (Zech. 13:9).

The people were a people united by relationships of birth, circumcision, marriage, religion, common language and customs, loyalty to the same leaders, and separation from the *gôyîm*.

The word *'am* also is used in a military sense to mean "troops." First Samuel 11:11 is an example: "So it was, on the next day, that Saul put the people in three companies; and they came into the midst of the camp in the morning watch, and killed Ammonites until the heat of the day." The army of Israel was a citizen army, much as the United States had in the American Revolution or as exists in Israel today. That may well be why they were called "the people."

Nation(s), People(s) (*le'ôm*)

Le'ôm is a poetic word that can be used to parallel either *gôy* or *'am*. The word probably comes from a root meaning "to assemble," and this origin would stress togetherness.

In predicting the future of Rebekah's twins, the Lord told her:

"Two nations [*gôyîm*] are in your womb,
Two peoples [*le'ummîm*] shall be separated from your body;
One people [*le'ôm*] shall be stronger than the other,
And the older shall serve the younger" (Gen. 25:23).

Here the Israelites and the Edomites are called by the same two words, the plurals of both *gôy* and *le'ôm*.

All three words for "people" occur in Psalm 67, where God is petitioned to bless:

"That Your way may be known on earth,
Your salvation among all nations [*gôyim*].
Let the peoples [*'ammîm*] praise You, O God;...
Oh, let the nations [*le'ummîm*] be glad and sing for joy!" (vv. 2–4).

stranger and the fatherless and the widow who *are* within your gates, may come and eat and be satisfied, that the LORD your God may bless you in all the work of your hand which you do.

CHAPTER 15

Law of the Debts

"AT the end of *every* seven years you shall grant a release *of debts.*

2 "And this *is* the form of the release: Every creditor who has lent *anything* to his neighbor shall release *it*; he shall not [T]require *it* of his neighbor or his brother, because it is called the LORD's release. *exact it*

3 "Of a foreigner you may require *it*; but your hand shall release what is owed by your brother,

4 "except when there may be no poor among you; for the LORD will greatly bless you in the land which the LORD your God is giving you to possess *as* an inheritance—

5 "only if you carefully obey the voice of the LORD your God, to observe with care all these commandments which I command you today.

6 "For the LORD your God will bless you just as He promised you; [R]you shall lend to many nations, but you shall not borrow; you shall reign over many nations, but they shall not reign over you. Deut. 28:12, 44

7 "If there is among you a poor man of your brethren, within any of the gates in your land which the LORD your God is giving you, you shall not harden your heart nor shut your hand from your poor brother,

8 "but [R]you shall [T]open your hand wide to him and willingly lend him sufficient for his need, whatever he needs. Matt. 5:42 • *freely open*

9 "Beware lest there be a wicked thought in your heart, saying, 'The seventh year, the year of release, is at hand,' and your eye be evil against your poor brother and you give him nothing, and he cry out to the LORD against you, and it become sin among you.

10 "You shall surely give to him, and your heart should not be grieved when you give to him, because [R]for this thing the LORD your God will bless you in all your works and in all to which you put your hand. Deut. 14:29

11 "For the poor will never cease from the land; therefore I command you, saying, 'You shall open your hand wide to your brother, to your poor and your needy, in your land.'

Law of the Slaves

12 "If your brother, a Hebrew man, or a Hebrew woman, is [R]sold to you and serves you six years, then in the seventh year you shall let him go free from you. Lev. 25:39–46

13 "And when you [T]send him away free from you, you shall not let him go away empty-handed; *set him free*

14 "you shall supply him liberally from your flock, from your threshing floor, and from your winepress. *From what* the LORD has blessed you with, you shall give to him.

15 [R]"You shall remember that you were a slave in the land of Egypt, and the LORD your God redeemed you; therefore I command you this thing today. Deut. 5:15

16 "And [R]if it happens that he says to you, 'I will not go away from you,' because he loves you and your house, since he prospers with you, Ex. 21:5, 6

17 "then you shall take an awl and thrust *it* through his ear to the door, and he shall be your servant forever. Also to your maidservant you shall do likewise.

18 "It shall not seem hard to you when you send him away free from you; for he has been worth [R]a double hired servant in serving you six years. Then the LORD your God will bless you in all that you do. Is. 16:14

Law of Firstborn

19 [R]"All the firstborn males that come from your herd and your flock you shall [T]sanctify to the LORD your God; you shall do no work with the firstborn of your herd, nor shear the firstborn of your flock. Ex. 13:2, 12 • *set apart*

20 [R]"You and your household shall eat *it* before the LORD your God year by year in the place which the LORD chooses. Deut. 12:5; 14:23

21 "But if there is *any* defect in it, *if it is* lame or blind *or has* any serious defect, you shall not sacrifice it to the LORD your God.

22 "You may eat it within your gates; the unclean and the clean *person* alike *may eat it*, as *if it were* a gazelle or a deer.

23 "Only you shall not eat its blood; you shall pour it on the ground like water.

CHAPTER 16

Law of the Feasts

"OBSERVE the month of Abib, and keep the Passover to the LORD your God, for in the month of Abib the LORD your God brought you out of Egypt by night.

2 "Therefore you shall sacrifice the Passover to the LORD your God, from the flock and the herd, in the [R]place where the LORD chooses to put His name. Deut. 12:5, 26; 15:20

3 "You shall eat no leavened bread with it; [R]seven days you shall eat unleavened bread with it, *that is*, the bread of affliction (for you came out of the land of Egypt in haste), that you may [R]remember the day in which you came out of the land of Egypt all the days of your life. Num. 29:12 • Ex. 13:3

4 [R]"And no leaven shall be seen among you in all your territory for seven days, nor shall *any* of the meat which you sacrifice the first day at twilight remain overnight until [R]morning. Ex. 13:7 • Num. 9:12

5 "You may not sacrifice the Passover
within any of your gates which the LORD
your God gives you;
6 "but at the place where the LORD your
God chooses to make His name abide, there
you shall sacrifice the Passover [R]at twilight,
at the going down of the sun, at the time you
came out of Egypt. Ex. 12:7–10
7 "And you shall roast and eat *it* [R]in the
place which the LORD your God chooses, and
in the morning you shall turn and go to your
tents. 2 Kin. 23:23
8 "Six days you shall eat unleavened
bread, and [R]on the seventh day there *shall be*
a sacred assembly to the LORD your God. You
shall do no work *on it*. Lev. 23:8, 36
9 "You shall count seven weeks for yourself; begin to count the seven weeks from *the*
time you begin *to put* the sickle to the grain.
10 "Then you shall keep the [R]Feast of
Weeks to the LORD your God with the tribute
of a freewill offering from your hand, which
you shall give [R]as the LORD your God blesses
you. Ex. 34:22 • 1 Cor. 16:2
11 "You shall rejoice before the LORD your
God, you and your son and your daughter,
your manservant and your maidservant, the
Levite who *is* within your gates, the stranger
and the fatherless and the widow who *are*
among you, at the place where the LORD your
God chooses to make His name abide.
12 [R]"And you shall remember that you were
a slave in Egypt, and you shall be careful to
observe these statutes. Deut. 15:15
13 [R]"You shall observe the Feast of Tabernacles seven days, when you have gathered
from your threshing floor and from your
winepress; Ex. 23:16
14 "and you shall rejoice in your feast, you
and your son and your daughter, your manservant and your maidservant and the Levite,
the stranger and the fatherless and the
widow, who *are* within your [T]gates. *towns*
15 [R]"Seven days you shall keep a sacred
feast to the LORD your God in the place
which the LORD chooses, because the LORD
your God will bless you in all your produce
and in all the work of your hands, so that you
surely rejoice. Lev. 23:39–41
16 "Three times a year all your males shall
appear before the LORD your God in the place
which He chooses: at the Feast of Unleavened Bread, at the Feast of Weeks, and at the
Feast of Tabernacles; and they shall not
appear before the LORD empty-handed.
17 "Every man *shall give* as he is able,
[R]according to the blessing of the LORD your
God which He has given you. Deut. 16:10

Law of the Administration of the Judges

18 "You shall appoint judges and officers in
all your gates, which the LORD your God
gives you, according to your tribes, and they
shall judge the people with just judgment.
19 "You shall not pervert justice; you shall
not show partiality, nor take a bribe, for a
bribe blinds the eyes of the wise and [T]twists
the words of the righteous. *perverts*
20 "You shall follow what is altogether just,
that you may [R]live and inherit the land which
the LORD your God is giving you. Ezek. 18:5–9
21 [R]"You shall not plant for yourself any
tree, as a [T]wooden image, near the altar
which you build for yourself to the LORD your
God. Ex. 34:13 • Or *Asherah*
22 [R]"You shall not set up a sacred pillar,
which the LORD your God hates. Lev. 26:1

CHAPTER 17

"YOU shall not sacrifice to the LORD
your God a bull or sheep which has
any [T]blemish *or* defect, for that *is* an abomination to the LORD your God. Lit. *evil thing*
2 "If there is found among you, within any
of your [T]gates which the LORD your God
gives you, a man or a woman who has been
wicked in the sight of the LORD your God, [R]in
transgressing His covenant, *towns* • Josh. 7:11
3 "who has gone and served other gods
and worshiped them, either [R]the sun or moon
or any of the host of heaven, [R]which I have
not commanded, Deut. 4:19 • Jer. 7:22
4 "and it is told you, and you hear *of it*,
then you shall inquire diligently. And if *it is*
indeed true *and* certain that such an abomination has been committed in Israel,
5 "then you shall bring out to your gates
that man or woman who has committed that
wicked thing, and shall stone [R]to death that
man or woman with stones. Deut. 13:6–18
6 "Whoever is worthy of death shall be put
to death on the testimony of two or three
[R]witnesses, *but* he shall not be put to death
on the testimony of one witness. Num. 35:30
7 "The hands of the witnesses shall be the
first against him to put him to death, and
afterward the hands of all the people. So you
shall put away the evil *person* from among
[R]you. Deut. 13:5; 19:19
8 "If a matter arises which is too hard for
you to judge, between degrees of bloodguiltiness, between one judgment or another, or
between one punishment or another, matters
of controversy within your gates, then you
shall arise and go up to the [R]place which the
LORD your God chooses, Deut. 12:5; 16:2
9 "and you shall come to the priests, the
Levites, and to the judge *there* in those days,
and inquire *of them*; they shall pronounce
upon you the sentence of judgment.
10 "You shall do according to the sentence
which they pronounce upon you in that place
which the LORD chooses. And you shall be

careful to do according to all that they order you.

11 “According to the sentence of the law in which they instruct you, according to the judgment which they tell you, you shall do; you shall not turn aside *to* the right hand or *to* the left from the sentence which they pronounce upon you.

12 “Now the man who acts presumptuously and will not heed the priest who stands to minister there before the LORD your God, or the judge, that man shall die. So you shall put away the evil *person* from Israel.

13 [R]“And all the people shall hear and fear, and no longer act presumptuously. Deut. 13:11

Law of the Administration of the King

14 “When you come to the land which the LORD your God is giving you, and possess it and dwell in it, and say, ‘I will set a king over me like all the nations that *are* around me,’

15 “you shall surely set a king over you whom the LORD your God chooses; *one* [R]from among your brethren you shall set as king over you; you may not set a foreigner over you, who *is* not your brother. Jer. 30:21

16 “But he shall not multiply [R]horses for himself, nor cause the people [R]to return to Egypt to multiply horses, for [R]the LORD has said to you, ‘You shall not return that way again.’ 1 Kin. 4:26; 10:26–29 • Ezek. 17:15 • Ex. 13:17, 18

17 “Neither shall he multiply wives for himself, lest his heart turn away; nor shall he greatly multiply silver and gold for himself.

18 “Also it shall be, when he sits on the throne of his kingdom, that he shall write for himself a copy of this law in a book, from *the one* before the priests, the Levites.

19 “And [R]it shall be with him, and he shall read it all the days of his life, that he may learn to fear the LORD his God and be careful to observe all the words of this law and these statutes, Ps. 119:97, 98

20 [R]“that his heart may not [T]be lifted above his brethren, that he may not turn aside from the commandment *to* the right hand or *to* the left, and that he may prolong *his* days in his kingdom, he and his children in the midst of Israel. John 1:45 ☆ • *become proud*

CHAPTER 18

Law of the Administration of the Priest and Prophet

“THE priests, the Levites, *indeed* all the tribe of Levi, shall have [T]no part nor [R]inheritance with Israel; they shall eat the offerings of the LORD made by fire, and His portion. *no portion* • Deut. 10:9

2 “Therefore they shall have no inheritance among their brethren; the LORD is their inheritance, as He said to them.

3 “And this shall be the priest’s [R]due[T] from the people, from those who offer a sacrifice, whether *it is* bull or sheep: they shall give to the priest the shoulder, the cheeks, and the stomach. Lev. 7:32–34 • *right*

4 “The firstfruits of your grain and your new wine and your oil, and the first of the fleece of your sheep, you shall give him.

5 “For [R]the LORD your God has chosen him out of all your tribes [R]to stand to minister in the name of the LORD, him and his sons forever. Ex. 28:1 • Deut. 10:8

6 “And if a Levite comes from any of your gates, from where he sojourns among all Israel, and comes with all the desire of his mind to the place which the LORD chooses,

7 “then he may serve in the name of the LORD his God as all his brethren the Levites *do,* who stand there before the LORD.

8 “They shall have equal [R]portions to eat, besides what comes from the sale of his inheritance. 2 Chr. 31:4

9 “When you come into the land which the LORD your God is giving you, [R]you shall not learn to follow the [T]abominations of those nations. Deut. 12:29, 30; 20:16–18 • *detestable acts*

10 “There shall not be found among you *anyone* who makes his son or his daughter [T]pass through the fire, *or one* who practices witchcraft, *or* a soothsayer, or one who interprets omens, or a sorcerer, Offering to an idol

11 [R]“or one who conjures spells, or a medium, or a spiritist, or [R]one who calls up the dead. Lev. 20:27 • 1 Sam. 28:7

12 “For all who do these things *are* [T]an abomination to the LORD, and [R]because of these abominations the LORD your God drives them out from before you. *detestable* • Lev. 18:24

13 “You shall be [T]blameless before the LORD your God. Lit. *perfect*

14 “For these nations which you will dispossess listened to soothsayers and diviners; but as for you, the LORD your God has not [T]appointed such for you. *allowed you to do so*

15 [R]“The LORD your God will raise up for you a Prophet like me from your midst, from your brethren. Him you shall hear, Acts 3:22 ☆

16 “according to all you desired of the LORD your God in Horeb in the day of the assembly, saying, [R]‘Let me not hear again the voice of the LORD my God, nor let me see this great fire anymore, lest I die.’ Ex. 20:18, 19

17 “And the LORD said to me: [R]‘What they have spoken is good. Deut. 5:28

18 ‘I will raise up for them a Prophet like you from among their brethren, and will put My words in His mouth, [R]and He shall speak to them all that I command Him. John 4:25 ☆

19 [R]‘And it shall be *that* whoever will not hear My words, which He speaks in My name, I will require *it* of him. Acts 3:23 ☆

20 'But the prophet who presumes to speak a word in My name, which I have not commanded him to speak, or who speaks in the name of other gods, that prophet shall die.'

21 "And if you say in your heart, 'How shall we know the word which the LORD has not spoken?'—

22 [R]"when a prophet speaks in the name of the LORD, [R]if the thing does not happen or come to pass, that *is* the thing which the LORD has not spoken; the prophet has spoken it [R]presumptuously; you shall not be afraid of him. Jer. 28:9 • Deut. 13:2 • Deut. 18:20

CHAPTER 19

Cities of Refuge

"WHEN the LORD your God [R]has cut off the nations whose land the LORD your God is giving you, and you dispossess them and dwell in their cities and in their houses, Deut. 12:29

2 "you shall separate three cities for yourself in the midst of your land which the LORD your God is giving you to possess.

3 "You shall prepare roads for yourself, and divide into three parts the territory of your land which the LORD your God is giving you to inherit, that any manslayer may flee there.

4 "And this *is* the case of the manslayer who flees there, that he may live: Whoever kills his neighbor [T]unintentionally, not having hated him in time past— *ignorantly*

5 "as when *a man* goes to the woods with his neighbor to cut timber, and his hand swings a stroke with the ax to cut down the tree, and the head slips from the handle and strikes his neighbor so that he dies—he shall flee to one of these cities and live;

6 [R]"lest the avenger of blood, while his anger is hot, pursue the manslayer and overtake him, because the way is long, and kill him, though he *was* not worthy of death, since he had not hated the victim in time past. Num. 35:12

7 "Therefore I command you, saying, 'You shall separate three cities for yourself.'

8 "Now if the LORD your God [R]enlarges your territory, as He swore to [R]your fathers, and gives you the land which He promised to give to your fathers, Deut. 12:20 • Gen. 15:18–21

9 "and if you keep all these commandments and do them, which I command you today, to love the LORD your God and to walk always in His ways, then you shall add three more cities for yourself besides these three,

10 [R]"lest innocent blood be shed in the midst of your land which the LORD your God is giving you *as* an inheritance, and *thus* bloodguiltiness be upon you. Deut. 21:1–9

11 "But [R]if anyone hates his neighbor, lies in wait for him, rises against him and strikes him mortally, so that he dies, and he flees to one of these cities, Num. 35:16, 24

12 "then the elders of his city shall send and bring him from there, and deliver him over to the hand of the avenger of blood, that he may die.

13 "Your eye shall not pity him, but you shall put away *the guilt of* innocent blood from Israel, that it may go well with you.

14 [R]"You shall not remove your neighbor's landmark, which the men of old have set, in your inheritance which you will inherit in the land that the LORD your God is giving you to possess. Prov. 22:28

Law of Witnesses

15 "One witness shall not rise against a man concerning any iniquity or any sin that he commits; by the mouth of two or three witnesses the matter shall be established.

16 "If a false witness [R]rises against any man to testify against him of wrongdoing, Ex. 23:1

17 "then both men in the controversy shall stand before the LORD, before the priests and the judges who serve in those days.

18 "And the judges shall make diligent inquiry, and indeed, *if* the witness *is* a false witness, who has testified falsely against his brother,

19 "then you shall do to him as he thought to have done to his brother; so you shall put away the evil *person* from among you.

20 [R]"And those who remain shall hear and fear, and hereafter they shall not again commit such evil among you. Deut. 17:13; 21:21

21 [R]"Your eye shall not pity; *but* [R]life *shall be* for life, eye for eye, tooth for tooth, hand for hand, foot for foot. Deut. 19:13 • Ex. 21:23, 24

CHAPTER 20

Law of Warfare

"WHEN you go out to battle against your enemies, and see horses and chariots *and* people more numerous than you, do not be afraid of them; for the LORD your God *is* [R]with you, who brought you up from the land of Egypt. 2 Chr. 13:12; 32:7, 8

2 "So it shall be, when you are on the verge of battle, that the priest shall approach and speak to the people.

3 "And he shall say to them, 'Hear, O Israel: Today you are on the verge of battle with your enemies; do not let your heart faint, do not be afraid, and do not tremble or be terrified because of them;

4 'for the LORD your God *is* He who goes with you, [R]to fight for you against your enemies, to save you.' Josh. 23:10

5 "Then the officers shall speak to the people, saying: 'What man *is there* who has built a new house and has not dedicated it?

Let him go and return to his house, lest he die in the battle and another man dedicate it.

6 'And what man *is there* who has planted a vineyard and has not *yet* eaten of it? Let him *also* go and return to his house, lest he die in the battle and another man eat of it.

7 [R]'And what man *is there* who is betrothed to a woman and has not *yet* married her? Let him go and return to his house, lest he die in the battle and another man marry her.' Deut. 24:5

8 "Then the officers shall speak further to the people, and say, [R]'What man *is there who is* fearful and fainthearted? Let him go and return to his house, lest the heart of his brethren faint like his heart.' Judg. 7:3

9 "And so it shall be, when the officers have finished speaking to the people, that they shall make captains of the armies to lead the people.

10 "When you go near a city to fight against it, then proclaim an offer of peace to it.

11 "And it shall be that if they accept your offer of peace, and open to you, then all the people *who are* found in it shall be placed under tribute to you, and serve you.

12 "Now if the city will not make peace with you, but would make war against you, then you shall besiege it.

13 "And when the LORD your God delivers it into your hands, [R]you shall strike every male in it with the edge of the sword. Num. 31:7

14 "But the women, the little ones, [R]the livestock, and all that is in the city, all its spoil, you shall plunder for yourself; and [R]you shall eat the enemies' plunder which the LORD your God gives you. Josh. 8:2 • 1 Sam. 14:30

15 "Thus you shall do to all the cities *which are* very far from you, which *are* not of the cities of these nations.

16 "But [R]of the cities of these peoples which the LORD your God gives you *as* an inheritance, you shall let nothing that breathes remain alive, Deut. 7:1–5

17 "but you shall utterly destroy them: the Hittite and the Amorite and the Canaanite and the Perizzite and the Hivite and the Jebusite, just as the LORD your God has commanded you,

18 "lest [R]they teach you to do according to all their [T]abominations which they have done for their gods, and you sin against the LORD your God. Deut. 7:4; 12:30; 18:9 • *detestable things*

19 "When you besiege a city for a long time, while making war against it to take it, you shall not destroy its trees by wielding an ax against them; if you can eat of them, do not cut them down to use in the siege, for the tree of the field *is* man's *food.*

20 "Only the trees which you know *are* not trees for food you may destroy and cut down, to build siegeworks against the city that makes war with you, until it is subdued.

CHAPTER 21

Law of Unknown Murder

"IF *anyone* is found slain, lying in the field in the land which the LORD your God is giving you to possess, *and* it is not known who killed him,

2 "then your elders and your judges shall go out, and they shall measure *the distance* from the slain man to the surrounding cities.

3 "And it shall be *that* the elders of the city nearest to the slain man will take a heifer which has not been worked *and* which has not pulled with a [R]yoke; Num. 19:2

4 "and the elders of that city shall bring the heifer down to a valley with flowing water, which is neither plowed nor sown, and they shall break the heifer's neck there in the valley.

5 "Then the priests, the sons of Levi, shall come near, for [R]the LORD your God has chosen them to minister to Him and to bless in the name of the LORD; [R]by their word every controversy and every [T]assault shall be *settled.* 1 Chr. 23:13 • Deut. 17:8, 9 • Lit. *stroke*

6 "And all the elders of that city nearest to the slain *man* [R]shall wash their hands over the heifer whose neck was broken in the valley. Matt. 27:24

7 "Then they shall answer and say, 'Our hands have not shed this blood, nor have our eyes seen *it.*

8 'Provide atonement, O LORD, for Your people Israel, whom You have redeemed, and do not lay innocent blood to the charge of Your people Israel.' And atonement shall be provided on their behalf for the blood.

9 "So you shall put away the *guilt of* innocent blood from among you when you do *what is* right in the sight of the LORD.

Law of Marriage

10 "When you go out to war against your enemies, and the LORD your God delivers them into your hand, and you take them captive,

11 "and you see among the captives a beautiful woman, and desire her and would take her for your [R]wife, Num. 31:18

12 "then you shall bring her home to your house, and she shall [R]shave her head and trim her nails. Lev. 14:8, 9

13 "She shall put off the clothes of her captivity, remain in your house, and [R]mourn her father and her mother a full month; after that you may go in to her and be her husband, and she shall be your wife. Ps. 45:10

14 "And it shall be, if you have no delight in her, then you shall set her free, but you certainly shall not sell her for money; you shall not treat her brutally, because you have [R]humbled her. Judg. 19:24

15 "If a man has two wives, one loved and the other unloved, and they have borne him children, *both* the loved and the unloved, and *if* the firstborn son is of her who is unloved,

16 "then it shall be, on the day he bequeaths his possessions to his sons, *that* he must not bestow firstborn status on the son of the loved wife in preference to the son of the unloved, *who is truly* the firstborn.

17 "But he shall acknowledge the son of the unloved wife *as* the firstborn [R]by giving him a double portion of all that he has, for he [R]*is* the beginning of his strength; [R]the right of the firstborn *is* his. 2 Kin. 2:9 • Gen. 49:3 • Gen. 25:31, 33

Law of the Rebellious Son

18 "If a man has a stubborn and rebellious son who will not obey the voice of his father or the voice of his mother, and *who,* when they have chastened him, will not heed them,

19 "then his father and his mother shall take hold of him and bring him out to the elders of his city, to the gate of his city.

20 "And they shall say to the elders of his city, 'This son of ours is stubborn and rebellious; he will not obey our voice; he is a glutton and a drunkard.'

21 "Then all the men of his city shall stone him to death with stones; so you shall put away the evil *person* from among you, [R]and all Israel shall hear and fear. Deut. 13:11

22 "If a man has committed a sin [R]worthy of death, and he is put to death, and you hang him on a tree, Acts 23:29

23 [R]"his body shall not remain overnight on the tree, but you shall surely bury him that day, so that [R]you do not defile the land which the LORD your God is giving you *as* an inheritance; for [R]he who is hanged *is* accursed of God. John 19:31 • Lev. 18:25 • Gal. 3:13

CHAPTER 22

Law of the Brother's Property

"YOU [R]shall not see your brother's ox or his sheep going astray, and [T]hide yourself from them; you shall certainly bring them back to your brother. Ex. 23:4 • *ignore them*

2 "And if your brother *is* not near you, or if you do not know him, then you shall bring it to your own house, and it shall remain with you until your brother seeks it; then you shall restore it to him.

3 "You shall do the same with his donkey, and so shall you do with his garment; with any lost thing of your brother's, which he has lost and you have found, you shall do likewise; you must not hide yourself.

4 [R]"You shall not see your brother's donkey or his ox fall down along the road, and hide yourself from them; you shall surely help him lift *them* up again. Ex. 23:5

Law of Separation

5 "A woman shall not wear anything that pertains to a man, nor shall a man put on a woman's garment, for all who do so *are* [T]an abomination to the LORD your God. *detestable*

6 "If a bird's nest happens to be before you along the way, in any tree or on the ground, with young ones or eggs, with the mother sitting on the young or on the eggs, you shall not take the mother with the young;

7 "you shall surely let the mother go, and take the young for yourself, [R]that it may be well with you and *that* you may prolong *your* days. Deut. 4:40

8 "When you build a new house, then you shall make a parapet for your roof, that you may not bring bloodguiltiness on your house if anyone falls from it.

9 [R]"You shall not sow your vineyard with different kinds of seed, lest the yield of the seed which you have sown and the fruit of your vineyard be defiled. Lev. 19:19

10 [R]"You shall not plow with an ox and a donkey together. [2 Cor. 6:14–16]

11 [R]"You shall not wear a garment of different sorts, *such as* wool and linen mixed together. Lev. 19:19

12 "You shall make [R]tassels on the four corners of the clothing with which you cover *yourself.* Num. 15:37–41

Law of Marriage

13 "If any man takes a wife, and goes in to her, and [R]detests her, Deut. 21:15; 24:3

14 "and charges her with shameful conduct, and brings a bad name on her, and says, 'I took this woman, and when I came to her I found she *was* not a virgin,'

15 "then the father and mother of the young woman shall take and bring out *the evidence of* the young woman's virginity to the elders of the city at the gate.

16 "And the young woman's father shall say to the elders, 'I gave my daughter to this man as wife, and he detests her;

17 'now he has charged her with shameful conduct, saying, "I found your daughter *was* not a virgin," and yet these *are the evidences of* my daughter's virginity.' And they shall spread the cloth before the elders of the city.

18 "Then the elders of that city shall take that man and punish him;

19 "and they shall fine him one hundred *shekels* of silver and give *them* to the father of the young woman, because he has brought a bad name on a virgin of Israel. And she shall be his wife; he cannot divorce her all his days.

20 "But if the thing is true, *and evidences of* virginity are not found for the young woman,

21 "then they shall bring out the young woman to the door of her father's house, and

the men of her city shall stone her to death with stones, because she has done a disgraceful thing in Israel, to play the harlot in her father's house; so you shall [T]put away the evil *person* from among you. *purge*

22 [R]"If a man is found lying with a woman married to a husband, then both of them shall die, *both* the man that lay with the woman, and the woman; so you shall put away the evil *person* from Israel. Lev. 20:10

23 "If a young woman *who is* a virgin is [R]betrothed to a husband, and a man finds her in the city and lies with her, Matt. 1:18, 19

24 "then you shall bring them both out to the gate of that city, and you shall stone them to death with stones, the young woman because she did not cry out in the city, and the man because he [R]humbled his neighbor's wife; [R]so you shall put away the evil *person* from among you. Deut. 21:14 • Deut. 22:21, 22

25 "But if a man finds a betrothed young woman in the countryside, and the man forces her and lies with her, then only the man who lay with her shall die.

26 "But you shall do nothing to the young woman; *there is* in the young woman no sin *worthy* of death, for just as when a man rises against his neighbor and kills him, even so *is* this matter;

27 "for he found her in the countryside, *and* the betrothed young woman cried out, but *there was* no one to save her.

28 "If a man finds a young woman *who is* a virgin, who is not betrothed, and he seizes her and lies with her, and they are found out,

29 "then the man who lay with her shall give to the young woman's father fifty *shekels* of silver, and she shall be his wife because he has humbled her; he shall not be permitted to divorce her all his days.

30 "A man shall not take his father's wife, nor [R]uncover his father's bed. Ezek. 16:8

CHAPTER 23

Law of Acceptance into the Congregation

"HE who is emasculated by crushing or mutilation shall [R]not enter the congregation of the LORD. Lev. 21:20; 22:24

2 "One of illegitimate birth shall not enter the congregation of the LORD; even to the tenth generation none of his *descendants* shall enter the congregation of the LORD.

3 [R]"An Ammonite or Moabite shall not enter the congregation of the LORD; even to the tenth generation none of his *descendants* shall enter the congregation of the LORD forever, Neh. 13:1, 2

4 "because they did not meet you with bread and water on the road when you came out of Egypt, and because they hired against you Balaam the son of Beor from Pethor of [T]Mesopotamia, to curse you. *Aram Naharaim*

5 "Nevertheless the LORD your God would not listen to Balaam, but the LORD your God turned the curse into a blessing for you, because the LORD your God loves you.

6 [R]"You shall not seek their peace nor their prosperity all your days forever. Ezra 9:12

7 "You shall not abhor an Edomite, [R]for he *is* your brother. You shall not abhor an Egyptian, because [R]you were an alien in his land. Obad. 10, 12 • Deut. 10:19

8 "The children of the third generation born to them may enter the congregation of the LORD.

9 "When the army goes out against your enemies, then keep yourself from every wicked thing.

10 [R]"If there is any man among you who becomes unclean by some occurrence in the night, then he shall go outside the camp; he shall not come inside the camp. Lev. 15:16

11 "But it shall be, when evening comes, that [R]he shall wash *himself* with water; and when the sun sets, he may come into the camp *again*. Lev. 15:5

12 "Also you shall have a place outside the camp, where you may go out;

13 "and you shall have an implement among your equipment, and when you sit down outside, you shall dig with it and turn and cover your refuse.

14 "For the LORD your God [R]walks in the midst of your camp, to deliver you and give your enemies over to you; therefore your camp shall be holy, that He may see no unclean thing among you, and turn away from you. Lev. 26:12

15 [R]"You shall not give back to his master the slave who has escaped from his master to you. 1 Sam. 30:15

16 "He may dwell with you in your midst, in the place which he chooses within one of your gates, where it [T]seems best to him; [R]you shall not oppress him. *pleases him best* • Ex. 22:21

17 "There shall be no *ritual* harlot [R]of the daughters of Israel, or a [T]perverted one of the sons of Israel. Lev. 19:29 • Male prostitute

18 "You shall not bring the hire of a harlot or the price of a dog to the house of the LORD your God for any vowed offering, for both of these *are* [T]an abomination to the LORD your God. *detestable*

19 [R]"You shall not charge interest to your brother—interest on money *or* food *or* anything that is lent out at interest. Ex. 22:25

20 "To a foreigner you may charge interest, but to your brother you shall not charge interest, that the LORD your God may bless you in all to which you set your hand in the land which you are entering to possess.

21 [R]"When you make a vow to the LORD your God, you shall not delay to pay it; for the LORD your God will surely require it of you, and it would be sin to you. Eccl. 5:4, 5

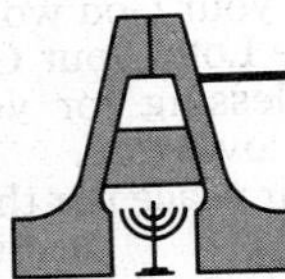

ISRAEL'S TRIBAL RIVALS

The twelve tribes of Israel encountered many tribal enemies, particularly during the Old Testament period before and after the conquest of Canaan. Important tribal rivals mentioned in the Bible are the Amalekites, Ammonites, Amorites, Edomites, Gibeonites, Horites, Hivites, Jebusites, Kenites, Midianites, and Moabites.

These tribal adversaries of Israel were nomadic people, although most of them lived in Canaan at one time or another. The Amorites, Hivites, and Jebusites were among the seven groups God commanded Israel to cast out of Canaan (Deut. 7:1, 2). Several tribes, such as the Kenites, Midianites, and Moabites, were desert wanderers, migrating throughout the desert regions of the Dead Sea or Sinai with their flocks and herds.

Many of these tribal groups were distant relatives of the Israelites. The Midianites traced their ancestry to Midian, the son of Abraham (Gen. 25:2). Three tribes—the Amorites, the Hivites, and Jebusites—were descendants of Canaan, a son of Ham (Gen. 10:6, 15–18). The Moabites and Ammonites were descendants of Lot (Gen. 19:36–38).

Most of these tribes were warlike and often cruel and barbaric, constantly attacking Israel and other nations. Except those retained as slave laborers, they were eventually destroyed or expelled from Canaan. The Gibeonites became woodcutters and water carriers for Israel (Josh. 9:18–21). Solomon used the Hivites and other Canaanites who remained in the land as construction laborers (1 Kin. 9:20, 21).

Israel's tribal rivals were generally idol worshipers. For this reason God commanded His people not to intermarry or make political alliances with these groups (Deut. 7:1–4). The Moabites and Ammonites (see drawing of Ammonite king) were especially rebuked by God because they refused to help the Israelites during their journey from Egypt to the Promised Land (Deut. 23:3, 4).

Ammonites were among the tribal rivals faced by the Israelites.

22 "But if you abstain from vowing, it shall not be sin to you.

23 [R]"That which has gone from your lips you shall keep and perform, for you voluntarily vowed to the LORD your God what you have promised with your mouth. Ps. 66:13, 14

Laws for Harmony in the Nation

24 "When you come into your neighbor's vineyard, you may eat your fill of grapes at your pleasure, but you shall not put *any* in your container.

25 "When you come into your neighbor's standing grain, [R]you may pluck the heads with your hand, but you shall not use a sickle on your neighbor's standing grain. Luke 6:1

CHAPTER 24

"WHEN a man takes a wife and marries her, and it happens that she finds no favor in his eyes because he has found some uncleanness in her, and he writes her a certificate of divorce, puts *it* in her hand, and sends her out of his house,

2 "when she has departed from his house, and goes and becomes another man's *wife*,

3 "*if* the latter husband detests her and writes her a certificate of divorce, puts *it* in her hand, and sends her out of his house, or if the latter husband dies who took her *to be* his wife,

4 "*then* her former husband who divorced her must not take her back to be his wife after she has been defiled; for that *is* an abomination before the LORD, and you shall not bring sin on the land which the LORD your God is giving you *as* an inheritance.

5 [R]"When a man has taken a new wife, he shall not go out to war or be charged with any business; he shall be free at home one year, and [R]bring happiness to his wife whom he has taken. Deut. 20:7 • Prov. 5:18

6 "No man shall take the lower or the upper millstone in pledge, for he takes [T]one's living in pledge. *life*

7 "If a man is found [T]kidnapping any of his brethren of the children of Israel, and mistreats him or sells him, then that kidnapper shall die; and you shall put away the evil *person* from among you. Lit. *stealing*

8 "Take heed in [R]an outbreak of leprosy, that you diligently observe and do according to all that the priests, the Levites, shall teach you; just as I commanded them, *so* you shall be careful to do. Lev. 13:2; 14:2

9 [R]"Remember what the LORD your God did [R]to Miriam on the way when you came out of Egypt. [1 Cor. 10:6] • Num. 12:10

10 "When you [R]lend your brother anything, you shall not go into his house to get his pledge. Matt. 5:42

11 "You shall stand outside, and the man to whom you lend shall bring the pledge out to you.

12 "And if the man *is* poor, you shall not [T]keep his pledge overnight. Lit. *sleep with*

13 "You shall in any case return the pledge to him again when the sun goes down, that he may sleep in his own garment and bless you; and [R]it shall be righteousness to you before the LORD your God. Deut. 6:25

14 "You shall not [R]oppress a hired servant *who is* poor and needy, *whether* one of your brethren or one of the aliens who *is* in your land within your gates. [Mal. 3:5]

15 "Each day [R]you shall give *him* his wages, and not let the sun go down on it, for he *is* poor and has set his heart on it; [R]lest he cry out against you to the LORD, and it be sin to you. Lev. 19:13 • James 5:4

16 [R]"The fathers shall not be put to death for *their* children, nor shall the children be put to death for *their* fathers; a person shall be put to death for his own sin. Ezek. 18:20

17 [R]"You shall not pervert justice due the stranger or the fatherless, [R]nor take a widow's garment as a pledge. Ex. 23:6 • Ex. 22:26

18 "But [R]you shall remember that you were a slave in Egypt, and the LORD your God redeemed you from there; therefore I command you to do this thing. Deut. 24:22

19 [R]"When you reap your harvest in your field, and forget a sheaf in the field, you shall not go back to get it; it shall be for the stranger, the fatherless, and the widow, that the LORD your God may [R]bless you in all the work of your hands. Lev. 19:9, 10 • Ps. 41:1

20 "When you beat your olive trees, you shall not go over the boughs again; it shall be for the stranger, the fatherless, and the widow.

21 "When you gather the grapes of your vineyard, you shall not glean *it* afterward; it shall be for the stranger, the fatherless, and the widow.

22 "And you shall remember that you were a slave in the land of Egypt; therefore I command you to do this thing.

CHAPTER 25

"IF there is a dispute between men, and they come to [T]court, that *the judges* may judge them, and they justify the righteous and condemn the wicked, *the judgment*

2 "then it shall be, if the wicked man [R]deserves to be beaten, that the judge will cause him to lie down [R]and be beaten in his presence, according to his guilt, with a certain number of blows. Prov. 19:29 • Matt. 10:17

3 "Forty blows he may give him *and* no more, lest he should exceed this and beat him with many blows above these, and your brother [R]be humiliated in your sight. Job 18:3

4 [R]"You shall not muzzle an ox while it
[T]treads out *the grain.* [Prov. 12:10] • *threshes*
5 [R]"If brothers dwell together, and one of
them dies and has no son, the widow of the
dead man shall not be *married* to a stranger
outside *the family*; her husband's brother
shall go in to her, take her as his wife, and
perform the duty of a husband's brother to
her. Matt. 22:24
6 "And it shall be *that* the firstborn son
which she bears [R]will succeed to the name of
his dead brother, that [R]his name may not be
blotted out of Israel. Gen. 38:9 • Ruth 4:5, 10
7 "But if the man does not want to take his
brother's wife, then let his brother's wife go
up to the [R]gate to the elders, and say, 'My
husband's brother refuses to raise up a name
to his brother in Israel; he will not perform
the duty of my husband's brother.' Ruth 4:1, 2
8 "Then the elders of his city shall call him
and speak to him; and *if* he stands firm and
says, [R]'I do not want to take her,' Ruth 4:6
9 "then his brother's wife shall come to
him in the presence of the elders, [R]remove his
sandal from his foot, spit in his face, and
answer and say, 'So shall it be done to the
man who will not [R]build up his brother's
house.' Ruth 4:7, 8 • Ruth 4:11
10 "And his name shall be called in Israel,
'The house of him who had his sandal removed.'
11 "If *two* men fight together, and the wife
of one draws near to rescue her husband
from the hand of the one attacking him, and
puts out her hand and seizes him by the
genitals,
12 "then you shall cut off her hand; [R]your
eye shall not pity *her.* Deut. 7:2; 19:13
13 [R]"You shall not have in your bag differing weights, a heavy and a light. Mic. 6:11
14 "You shall not have in your house differing measures, a large and a small.
15 "You shall have a perfect and just
weight, a perfect and just measure, that your
days may be lengthened in the land which
the LORD your God is giving you.
16 "For [R]all who do such things, *and* all who
behave unrighteously, *are* [T]an abomination to
the LORD your God. Prov. 11:1 • *detestable*
17 "Remember what Amalek did to you on
the way as you were coming out of Egypt,
18 "how he met you on the way and attacked your rear ranks, all the stragglers at
your rear, when you *were* tired and weary;
and he [R]did not fear God. Rom. 3:18
19 "Therefore it shall be, [R]when the LORD
your God has given you rest from your enemies all around, in the land which the LORD
your God is giving you to possess *as* an
inheritance, *that* you will [R]blot out the remembrance of Amalek from under heaven.
You shall not forget. 1 Sam. 15:3 • Ex. 17:14

CHAPTER 26

Law of the Tithe

"AND it shall be, when you come into the
land which the LORD your God is
giving you *as* an inheritance, and you possess
it and dwell in it,
2 "that you shall take some of the first of
all the produce of the ground, which you
shall bring from your land that the LORD your
God is giving you, and put *it* in a basket and
[R]go to the place where the LORD your God
chooses to make His name abide. Deut. 12:5
3 "And you shall go to the one who is
priest in those days, and say to him, 'I declare
today to the LORD *your God that I have
come to the country which the LORD swore to
our fathers to give us.'
4 "Then the priest shall take the basket
out of your hand and set it down before the
altar of the LORD your God.
5 "And you shall answer and say before
the LORD your God: 'My father *was* a [T]Syrian,
about to perish, and he went down to Egypt
and sojourned there, [R]few in number; and
there he became a nation, [R]great, mighty, and
populous. Or *Aramean* • Deut. 10:22 • Deut. 1:10
6 'But the Egyptians mistreated us, afflicted us, and laid hard bondage on us.
7 [R]'Then we cried out to the LORD God of
our fathers, and the LORD heard our voice
and looked on our affliction and our labor and
our oppression. Ex. 2:23–25; 3:9; 4:31
8 'So [R]the LORD brought us out of Egypt
with a mighty hand and with an outstretched
arm, [R]with great terror and with signs and
wonders. Deut. 5:15 • Deut. 4:34; 34:11, 12
9 'He has brought us to this place and has
given us this land, [R]"a land flowing with milk
and honey"; Ex. 3:8, 17
10 'and now, behold, I have brought the
firstfruits of the land which you, O LORD,
have given me.' Then you shall set it before
the LORD your God, and worship before the
LORD your God.
11 "So [R]you shall rejoice in every good
thing which the LORD your God has given to
you and your house, you and the Levite and
the stranger who *is* among you. Deut. 12:7; 16:11
12 "When you have finished laying aside all
the [R]tithe of your increase in the third year,
which is [R]the year of tithing, and have given
it to the Levite, the stranger, the fatherless,
and the widow, so that they may eat within
your gates and be filled, Lev. 27:30 • Deut. 14:28, 29
13 "then you shall say before the LORD your
God: 'I have removed the [T]holy *tithe* from *my*
house, and also have given them to the
Levite, the stranger, the fatherless, and the
widow, according to all Your commandments
which You have commanded me; I have not

26:3 LXX *my*

transgressed Your commandments, [R]nor have
I forgotten *them*. *hallowed things* • Ps. 119:141, 153
14 'I have not eaten any of it when in
mourning, nor have I removed *any* of it [T]for
any unclean *use*, nor given *any* of it for the
dead. I have obeyed the voice of the LORD my
God, and have done according to all that You
have commanded me. Or *while unclean*
15 [R]'Look down from Your holy [T]habitation,
from heaven, and bless Your people Israel
and the land which You have given us, just
as You swore to our fathers, [R]"a land flowing
with milk and honey." ' Is. 63:15 • *abode* • Ex. 3:8

Vow of Israel and of God

16 "This day the LORD your God commands
you to observe these statutes and judgments;
therefore you shall be careful to observe
them with all your heart and with all your
soul.
17 "Today you have [R]proclaimed the LORD
to be your God, and that you will walk in His
ways and keep His statutes, His commandments, and His judgments, and that you will
[R]obey His voice. Ex. 20:19 • Deut. 15:5
18 "Also today [R]the LORD has proclaimed
you to be His special people, just as He has
promised you, that *you* should keep all His
commandments, Ex. 6:7; 19:5
19 "and that He will set you [R]high above all
nations which He has made, in praise, in
name, and in honor, and that you may be [R]a
[T]holy people to the LORD your God, just as He
has spoken." Deut. 4:7, 8; 28:1 • [1 Pet. 2:9] • *consecrated*

CHAPTER 27

Erection of the Altar

THEN Moses, with the elders of Israel,
commanded the people, saying: "Keep all
the commandments which I command you
today.
2 "And it shall be, on the day [R]when you
cross over the Jordan to the land which the
LORD your God is giving you, that [R]you shall
set up for yourselves large stones, and whitewash them with lime. Josh. 4:1 • Josh. 8:32
3 "You shall write on them all the words of
this law, when you have crossed over, that
you may enter the land which the LORD your
God is giving you, [R]'a land flowing with milk
and honey,' just as the LORD God of your
fathers has promised you. Ex. 3:8
4 "Therefore it shall be, when you have
crossed over the Jordan, *that* [R]on Mount Ebal
you shall set up these stones, which I command you today, and you shall whitewash
them with lime. Deut. 11:29
5 "And there you shall build an altar to the
LORD your God, an altar of stones; [R]you shall
not use *any* iron *tool* on them. Ex. 20:25
6 "You shall build with [T]whole stones the
altar of the LORD your God, and offer burnt
offerings on it to the LORD your God. *uncut*
7 "You shall offer peace offerings, and
shall eat there, and [R]rejoice before the LORD
your God. Deut. 26:11
8 "And you shall [R]write very plainly on the
stones all the words of this law." Josh. 8:32

Admonition to Obey the Law

9 Then Moses and the priests, the Levites,
spoke to all Israel, saying, "Take heed and
listen, O Israel: [R]This day you have become
the people of the LORD your God. Deut. 26:18
10 "Therefore you shall obey the voice of
the LORD your God, and observe His commandments and His statutes which I command you today."

Proclamation of the Curses

11 And Moses commanded the people on
the same day, saying,
12 "These shall stand [R]on Mount Gerizim to
bless the people, when you have crossed over
the Jordan: Simeon, Levi, Judah, Issachar,
Joseph, and Benjamin; Josh. 8:33
13 "and [R]these shall stand on Mount Ebal to
curse: Reuben, Gad, Asher, Zebulun, Dan,
and Naphtali. Deut. 11:29
14 "And the Levites shall speak with a loud
voice and say to all the men of Israel:
15 'Cursed *is* the one who makes *any*
carved or molded image, an abomination to
the LORD, the work of the hands of the
craftsman, and sets *it* up in secret.' And all
the people shall answer and say, 'Amen!'
16 [R]'Cursed *is* the one who treats his father
or his mother with contempt.' And all the
people shall say, 'Amen!' Ezek. 22:7
17 [R]'Cursed *is* the one who moves his neighbor's landmark.' And all the people shall say,
'Amen!' Deut. 19:14
18 [R]'Cursed *is* the one who makes the blind
to wander off the road.' And all the people
shall say, 'Amen!' Lev. 19:14
19 'Cursed *is* the one who perverts the
justice due the stranger, the fatherless, and
widow.' And all the people shall say, 'Amen!'
20 [R]'Cursed *is* the one who lies with his
father's wife, because he has uncovered his
father's bed.' And all the people shall say,
'Amen!' Deut. 22:30
21 [R]'Cursed *is* the one who lies with any
kind of animal.' And all the people shall say,
'Amen!' Lev. 18:23; 20:15, 16
22 [R]'Cursed *is* the one who lies with his
sister, the daughter of his father or the
daughter of his mother.' And all the people
shall say, 'Amen!' Lev. 18:9
23 [R]'Cursed *is* the one who lies with his
mother-in-law.' And all the people shall say,
'Amen!' Lev. 18:17; 20:14

24 [R]'Cursed *is* the one who attacks his neighbor secretly.' And all the people shall say, 'Amen!' Ex. 20:13; 21:12

25 [R]'Cursed *is* the one who takes a bribe to slay an innocent person.' And all the people shall say, 'Amen!' Ex. 23:7

26 [R]'Cursed *is* the one who does not confirm *all* the words of this law.' And all the people shall say, 'Amen!' Gal. 3:10

CHAPTER 28

Promised Blessings for Obedience

"NOW it shall come to pass, if you diligently obey the voice of the LORD your God, to observe carefully all His commandments which I command you today, that the LORD your God [R]will set you high above all nations of the earth. Deut. 26:19

2 "And all these blessings shall come upon you and [R]overtake you, because you obey the voice of the LORD your God: Deut. 28:15

3 "Blessed *shall* you *be* in the city, and blessed *shall* you *be* in the country.

4 "Blessed *shall be* [R]the [T]fruit of your body, the produce of your ground and the increase of your herds, the increase of your cattle and the offspring of your flocks. Gen. 22:17 • *offspring*

5 "Blessed *shall be* your basket and your kneading bowl.

6 "Blessed *shall* you *be* when you come in, and blessed *shall* you *be* when you go out.

7 "The LORD will cause your enemies who rise against you to be defeated before your face; they shall come out against you one way and flee before you seven ways.

8 "The LORD will [R]command the blessing on you in your storehouses and in all to which you [R]set your hand, and He will bless you in the land which the LORD your God is giving you. Lev. 25:21 • Deut. 15:10

9 "The LORD will establish you as a holy people to Himself, just as He has sworn to you, if you keep the commandments of the LORD your God and walk in His ways.

10 "Then all peoples of the earth shall see that you are called by the name of the LORD, and they shall be [R]afraid of you. Deut. 11:25

11 "And the LORD will grant you plenty of goods, in the fruit of your body, in the increase of your livestock, and in the produce of your ground, in the land of which the LORD swore to your fathers to give you.

12 "The LORD will open to you His good [T]treasure, the heavens, to give the rain to your land in its season, and to bless all the work of your hand. You shall lend to many nations, but you shall not borrow. *storehouse*

13 "And the LORD will make [R]you the head and not the tail; you shall be above only, and not be beneath, if you [T]heed the commandments of the LORD your God, which I command you today, and are careful to observe *them*. [Is. 9:14, 15] • *listen to*

14 [R]"So you shall not turn aside from any of the words which I command you this day, *to* the right *hand* or *to* the left, to go after other gods to serve them. Deut. 5:32

Promised Curses for Disobedience

15 "But it shall come to pass, [R]if you do not obey the voice of the LORD your God, to observe carefully all His commandments and His statutes which I command you today, that all these curses will come upon you and overtake you: Lev. 26:14–39

16 "Cursed *shall* you *be* in the city, and cursed *shall* you *be* in the country.

17 "Cursed *shall be* your basket and your kneading bowl.

18 "Cursed *shall be* the fruit of your body and the produce of your land, the increase of your cattle and the offspring of your flocks.

19 "Cursed *shall* you *be* when you come in, and cursed *shall* you *be* when you go out.

20 "The LORD will send on you [R]cursing, [R]confusion, and [R]rebuke in all that you set your hand to do, until you are destroyed and until you perish quickly, because of the wickedness of your doings in which you have forsaken Me. Mal. 2:2 • Is. 65:14 • Is. 30:17

21 "The LORD will make the [T]plague cling to you until He has consumed you from the land which you are going to possess. *pestilence*

22 "The LORD will strike you with consumption, with fever, with inflammation, with severe burning fever, with the sword, with [R]scorching,[T] and with mildew; they shall pursue you until you perish. Amos 4:9 • *blight*

23 "And [R]your heavens which *are* over your head shall be bronze, and the earth which is under you *shall be* iron. Lev. 26:19

24 "The LORD will change the rain of your land to powder and dust; from the heaven it shall come down on you until you are destroyed.

25 [R]"The LORD will cause you to be defeated before your enemies; you shall go out one way against them and flee seven ways before them; and you shall become [T]troublesome to all the kingdoms of the earth. Deut. 32:30 • *a terror*

26 "Your carcasses shall be food for all the birds of the air and the beasts of the earth, and no one shall frighten *them* away.

27 "The LORD will strike you with [R]the boils of Egypt, with [R]tumors, with the scab, and with the itch, from which you cannot be healed. Ex. 15:26 • 1 Sam. 5:6

28 "The LORD will strike you with madness and blindness and [R]confusion of heart. Jer. 4:9

29 "And you shall [R]grope at noonday, as a blind man gropes in darkness; you shall not prosper in your ways; you shall be only oppressed and plundered continually, and no one shall save *you*. Job 5:14

30 [R]"You shall betroth a wife, but another man shall lie with her; [R]you shall build a house, but you shall not dwell in it; [R]you shall

plant a vineyard, but shall not gather its
grapes. Jer. 8:10 • Amos 5:11 • Deut. 20:6
31 "Your ox *shall be* slaughtered before
your eyes, but you shall not eat of it; your
donkey *shall be* violently taken away from
before you, and shall not be restored to you;
your sheep *shall be* given to your enemies,
and you shall have no one to rescue *them.*
32 "Your sons and your daughters *shall be*
given to another people, and your eyes shall
look and [R]fail *with longing* for them all day
long; and *there shall be* [T]no strength in your
[R]hand. Ps. 119:82 • *nothing you can do* • Neh. 5:5
33 "A nation whom you have not known
shall eat [R]the fruit of your land and the
produce of your labor, and you shall be only
oppressed and crushed continually. Jer. 5:15, 17
34 "So you shall be driven mad because of
the sight which your eyes see.
35 "The LORD will strike you in the knees
and on the legs with severe boils which
cannot be healed, and from the sole of your
foot to the top of your head.
36 "The LORD will [R]bring you and the king
whom you set over you to a nation which
neither you nor your fathers have known,
and [R]there you shall serve other gods—wood
and stone. Jer. 39:1–9 • Deut. 4:28
37 "And you shall become an astonishment,
a proverb, and a byword among all nations
where the LORD will drive you.
38 [R]"You shall carry much seed out to the
field and gather *but* little in, for [R]the locust
shall [T]consume it. Mic. 6:15 • Joel 1:4 • *devour*
39 "You shall plant vineyards and tend
them, but you shall neither drink *of* the [R]wine
nor gather the *grapes*; for the worms shall eat
them. Zeph. 1:13
40 "You shall have olive trees throughout
all your territory, but you shall not anoint
yourself with the oil; for your olives shall
drop off.
41 "You shall beget sons and daughters, but
they shall not be yours; for [R]they shall go into
captivity. Lam. 1:5
42 "Locusts shall [T]consume all your trees
and the produce of your land. *possess*
43 "The alien who *is* among you shall rise
higher and higher above you, and you shall
come down lower and lower.
44 "He shall lend to you, but you shall not
lend to him; he shall be the head, and you
shall be the tail.
45 "Moreover all these curses shall come
upon you and pursue and overtake you, until
you are destroyed, because you [T]did not obey
the voice of the LORD your God, to keep His
commandments and His statutes which He
commanded you. *did not listen to*
46 "And they shall be upon [R]you for a sign
and a wonder, and on your descendants
forever. Is. 8:18
47 "Because you did not serve the LORD
your God with joy and gladness of heart, [R]for
the abundance of all *things,* Deut. 32:15
48 "therefore you shall serve your enemies,
whom the LORD will send against you, in
hunger, in thirst, in nakedness, and in need of
all *things*; and He will put a yoke of iron on
your neck until He has destroyed you.
49 [R]"The LORD will bring a nation against
you from afar, from the end of the earth, *as
swift* as the eagle flies, a nation whose language you will not understand, Jer. 5:15
50 "a nation of fierce countenance, [R]which
does not respect the elderly nor show favor to
the young. 2 Chr. 36:17
51 "And they shall eat the increase of your
livestock and the produce of your land, until
you are destroyed; they shall not leave you
grain or new wine or oil, *or* the increase of
your cattle or the offspring of your flocks,
until they have destroyed you.
52 "They shall [R]besiege you at all your gates
until your high and fortified walls, in which
you trust, come down throughout all your
land; and they shall besiege you at all your
gates throughout all your land which the
LORD your God has given you. 2 Kin. 25:1, 2, 4
53 "You shall eat the [T]fruit of your own
body, the flesh of your sons and your daughters whom the LORD your God has given you,
in the siege and desperate straits in which
your enemy shall distress you. *offspring*
54 "The man among you *who is* [T]sensitive
and very refined [T]will be hostile toward his
brother, toward the wife of his bosom, and
toward the rest of his children whom he
leaves behind, *tender* • Lit. *his eye shall be evil toward*
55 "so that he will not give any of them the
flesh of his children whom he will eat, because he has nothing left in the siege and
desperate straits in which your enemy shall
distress you at all your gates.
56 "The tender and [T]delicate woman among
you, who would not venture to set the sole of
her foot on the ground because of her deli-
cateness and sensitivity, [T]will refuse to the
husband of her bosom, and to her son and her
daughter, *refined* • Lit. *her eye shall be evil toward*
57 "her [T]placenta which comes out [R]from
between her feet, and her children whom she
bears; for she will eat them secretly for lack
of all *things* in the siege and desperate straits
in which your enemy shall distress you at all
your gates. *afterbirth* • Gen. 49:10
58 "If you do not carefully observe all the
words of this law that are written in this
book, that you may fear this glorious and
awesome name, THE LORD YOUR GOD,
59 "then the LORD will bring upon you and
your descendants [R]extraordinary plagues—
great and prolonged plagues—and serious
and prolonged sicknesses. Dan. 9:12
60 "Moreover He will bring back on you all
[R]the diseases of Egypt, of which you were
afraid, and they shall cling to you. Deut. 7:15

61 "Also every sickness and every plague,
which *is* not written in the book of this law,
will the LORD bring upon you until you are
destroyed.
62 "You [R]shall be left few in number,
whereas you were [R]as the stars of heaven in
multitude, because you would not obey the
voice of the LORD your God. Deut. 4:27 • Neh. 9:23
63 "And it shall be, *that* just as the LORD
rejoiced over you to do you good and multiply you, so the LORD will rejoice over you to
destroy you and bring you to nothing; and
you shall be [R]plucked[T] from off the land
which you go to possess. Jer. 12:14; 45:4 • *torn*
64 "Then the LORD [R]will scatter you among
all peoples, from one end of the earth to the
other, and [R]there you shall serve other gods,
which neither you nor your fathers have
known—wood and stone. Jer. 16:13 • Deut. 28:36
65 "And [R]among those nations you shall
find no rest, nor shall the sole of your foot
have a resting place; [R]but there the LORD will
give you a [T]trembling heart, failing eyes, and
anguish of soul. Amos 9:4 • Lev. 26:36 • *anxious*
66 "Your life shall hang in doubt before
you; you shall fear day and night, and have
no assurance of life.
67 "In the morning you shall say, 'Oh, that
it were evening!' And at evening you shall
say, 'Oh, that it were morning!' because of
the fear which terrifies your heart, and because of the sight which your eyes see.
68 "And the LORD [R]will take you back to
Egypt in ships, by the way of which I said to
you, [R]'You shall never see it again.' And there
you shall be offered for sale to your enemies
as male and female slaves, but no one will
buy *you*." Hos. 8:13 • Deut. 17:16

CHAPTER 29

The Covenant Is Based on the Power of God

THESE *are* the words of the covenant
which the LORD commanded Moses to
make with the children of Israel in the land of
Moab, besides the [R]covenant which He made
with them in Horeb. Deut. 5:2, 3
2 Now Moses called all Israel and said to
them: [R]"You have seen all that the LORD did
before your eyes in the land of Egypt, to
Pharaoh and to all his servants and to all his
land— Ex. 19:4
3 "the great trials which your eyes have
seen, the signs, and those great wonders.
4 "Yet [R]the LORD has not given you a heart
to [T]perceive and eyes to see and ears to hear,
to this *very* day. [Acts 28:26, 27] • *understand* or *know*
5 [R]"And I have led you forty years in the
wilderness. [R]Your clothes have not worn out
on you, and your sandals have not worn out
on your feet; Deut. 1:3; 8:2 • Deut. 8:4
6 "you have not eaten bread, nor have you
drunk wine or *similar* drink; that you may
know that I *am* the LORD your God.
7 "And when you came to this place, [R]Si-
hon king of Heshbon and Og king of Bashan
came out against us to battle, and we conquered them. Num. 21:23, 24
8 "We took their land and [R]gave it as an
inheritance to the Reubenites, to the Gadites,
and to half the tribe of Manasseh. Deut. 3:12, 13
9 "Therefore [R]keep the words of this covenant, and do them, that you may [R]prosper in
all that you do. Deut. 4:6 • Josh. 1:7

Parties of the Covenant

10 "All of you stand today before the LORD
your God: your leaders and your tribes and
your elders and your officers, all the men of
Israel,
11 "your little ones and your wives—also
the stranger who *is* in your camp, from [R]the
one who cuts your wood to the one who
draws your water— Josh. 9:21, 23, 27
12 "that you may enter into covenant with
the LORD your God, and into His oath, which
the LORD your God makes with you today,
13 "that He may establish you today as a
people for Himself, and *that* He may be God
to you, just as He has spoken to you, and
[R]just as He has sworn to your fathers, to
Abraham, Isaac, and Jacob. Gen. 17:7, 8
14 "I make this covenant and this oath, [R]not
with you alone, [Jer. 31:31]
15 "but also with *him* who stands here with
us today before the LORD our God, as well as
with *him* who *is* not here with us today

Scattering of Israel

16 (for you know that we dwelt in the land
of Egypt and that we came through the
nations which you passed by,

29:10–15; 30:11–20 The Palestinian Covenant—The covenant concerning Palestine is the third of the theocratic covenants (pertaining to the rule of God). The Palestinian Covenant has two aspects: (1) the legal aspects which are immediate and conditional (Page 237—Deut. 27—29); and (2) the grace aspects which are future and unconditional (Page 241—Deut. 30:1–9). The enjoyment of the immediate blessings are introduced by the conditional formula: "if you diligently obey the voice of the LORD your God . . . the LORD your God will set you high above all nations of the earth" (Page 238—Deut. 28:1). Sadly, Israel did not meet the condition of obedience, and is still experiencing God's curses and punishment for their disobedience (Page 238—Deut. 28:15–68). The unconditional grace aspects of the Palestinian Covenant have yet to be realized. God will regather the scattered people of Israel and establish them in the land He has promised unconditionally to give them. Deuteronomy concludes the Palestinian Covenant with a final warning and challenge for obedience (Page 241—Deut. 30:1–20).

Now turn to Page 365—2 Sam. 7:4–17: The Davidic Covenant.

17 and you saw their [T]abominations and
their idols which *were* among them—wood
and stone and silver and gold); *detestable things*
18 "so that there may not be among you
man or woman or family or tribe, whose
heart turns away today from the LORD our
God, to go *and* serve the gods of these nations, and that there may not be among you a
root bearing bitterness or wormwood;
19 "and so it may not happen, when he
hears the words of this curse, that he blesses
himself in his heart, saying, 'I shall have
peace, even though I walk in the [T]imagina-
tion of my heart'—as though the drunkard
could be included with the sober. *stubbornness*
20 "The LORD would not spare him; for then
the anger of the LORD and [R]His jealousy
would burn against that man, and every
curse that is written in this book would settle
on him, and the LORD [R]would blot out his
name from under heaven. Ps. 79:5 • Deut. 9:14
21 "And the LORD would separate him from
all the tribes of Israel for adversity, according
to all the curses of the covenant that are
written in this Book of the Law,
22 "so that the coming generation of your
children who rise up after you, and the foreigner who comes from a far land, would say,
when they see the plagues of that land and
the sicknesses which the LORD has laid on it:
23 'The whole land *is* brimstone, [R]salt, and
burning; it is not sown, nor does it bear, nor
does any grass grow there, [R]like the overthrow of Sodom and Gomorrah, Admah, and
Zeboim, which the LORD overthrew in His
anger and His wrath.' Zeph. 2:9 • Gen. 19:24, 25
24 "All nations would say, [R]'Why has the
LORD done so to this land? What does the
heat of this great anger mean?' 1 Kin. 9:8
25 "Then *men* would say: 'Because they
have forsaken the covenant of the LORD God
of their fathers, which He made with them
when He brought them out of the land of
Egypt;
26 'for they went and served other gods and
worshiped them, gods that they did not know
and that He had not given to them.
27 'Then the anger of the LORD was aroused
against this land, [R]to bring on it every curse
that is written in this book. Dan. 9:11
28 'And the LORD [R]uprooted them from
their land in anger, in wrath, and in great
indignation, and cast them into another land,
as *it is* this day.' 1 Kin. 14:15

29 "The secret *things belong* to the LORD
our God, but those *things which are* revealed
belong to us and to our children forever, that
we may do all the words of this law.

CHAPTER 30

Restoration of Israel

"NOW it shall come to pass, when all
these things come upon you, the
blessing and the curse which I have set
before you, and you [T]call *them* to mind
among all the nations where the LORD your
God drives you, Lit. *cause them to return to your heart*
2 "and you return to the LORD your God
and obey His voice, according to all that I
command you today, you and your children,
with all your heart and with all your soul,
3 [R]"that the LORD your God will bring you
back from captivity, and have compassion on
you, and [R]gather you again from all the
nations where the LORD your God has scattered you. Jer. 29:14 • Ezek. 34:13
4 [R]"If *any* of you are driven out to the
farthest *parts* under heaven, from there the
LORD your God will gather you, and from
there He will bring you. Neh. 1:9
5 "Then the LORD your God will bring you
to the land which your fathers possessed, and
you shall possess it. He will prosper you and
multiply you more than your fathers.
6 "And the LORD your God will circumcise
your heart and the heart of your descendants,

29:29 Revelation of God's Word—Revelation may be defined as that process by which God imparted to man truths which he otherwise could not know. The details of creation in Genesis 1 and 2 are an example of revelation. As man was not created until the sixth day, we could not have possibly known the events occurring prior to this until God gave the facts to Moses.

We know God spoke to the human authors of our Bible; but just how did He speak? Was it in Hebrew? Greek? Angelic language? He spoke to them in their own language. God's call to young Samuel in the temple (Page 324—1 Sam. 3:1–10) proves this, for the boy at first mistook God's voice for that of the aged priest Eli. Sometimes God spoke through angels: Gabriel was sent from heaven to tell Mary she would give birth to the Messiah (Page 1190—Luke 1:26–37). On other occasions the Lord spoke directly to a man, as He did to Noah concerning the Great Flood (Page 11—Gen. 6:13–21).

One of God's methods of communication in Scripture is to reveal His message through dreams and visions: The wise men (Page 1116—Matt. 2:12) were warned in a dream not to return to Herod, while Peter was later instructed in a vision to minister to Cornelius (Page 1287—Acts 10:10–16). God has communicated in many different ways. He revealed Himself to Moses from a burning bush (Page 70—Ex. 3:4) and to Moses, Aaron, and Miriam out of a cloud (Page 175—Num. 12:4, 5).

One of the most important ways that divine truths were given in the Old Testament was through the Angel of the Lord. Most Bible students perceive this heavenly messenger to be the preincarnate Christ Himself. For example, it is the Angel of the Lord who reassured Joshua on the eve of a battle (Page 256—Josh. 5:13–15).

Now turn to Page 832—Is. 59:21: Inspiration of God's Word.

to love the LORD your God with all your heart
and with all your soul, that you may live.
7 "Also the LORD your God will put all
these curses on your enemies and on those
who hate you, who persecuted you.
8 "And you will [R]again obey the voice of
the LORD and do all His commandments
which I command you today. Zeph. 3:20
9 "The LORD your God will make you
abound in all the work of your hand, in the
fruit of your body, in the increase of your
livestock, and in the produce of your land for
good. For the LORD will again rejoice over
you for good as He rejoiced over your fathers,
10 "if you obey the voice of the LORD your
God, to keep His commandments and His
statutes which are written in this Book of the
Law, *and* if you turn to the LORD your God
with all your heart and with all your soul.

Ratification of the Palestinian Covenant

11 "For this commandment which I command you today, [R]it *is* [T]not *too* mysterious for
you, nor *is* it far off. Is. 45:19 • *not hidden from*
12 "It *is* not in heaven, that you should say,
'Who will ascend into heaven for us and bring
it to us, that we may hear it and do it?'
13 "Nor *is* it beyond the sea, that you
should say, 'Who will go over the sea for us
and bring it to us, that we may hear it and do
it?'
14 "But the word *is* very near you, in your
mouth and in your heart, that you may do it.
15 "See, [R]I have set before you today life
and good, death and evil, Deut. 30:1, 19
16 "in that I command you today to love
the LORD your God, to walk in His ways, and
to keep His commandments, His statutes, and
His judgments, that you may live and multiply; and the LORD your God will bless you in
the land which you go to possess.
17 "But if your heart turns away so that you
do not hear, and are drawn away, and worship other gods and serve them,
18 [R]"I announce to you today that you shall
surely perish; you shall not prolong *your* days
in the land which you cross over the Jordan
to go in and possess. Deut. 4:26; 8:19
19 [R]"I call heaven and earth as witnesses
today against you, *that* [R]I have set before you
life and death, blessing and cursing; therefore
choose life, that both you and your descendants may live; Deut. 4:26 • Deut. 30:15
20 "that you may love the LORD your God,
that you may obey His voice, and that you
may cling to Him, for He *is* your [R]life and the
length of your days; and that you may dwell
in the land which the LORD swore to your
fathers, to Abraham, Isaac, and Jacob, to give
them." [John 11:25; 14:6]

CHAPTER 31

Moses Charges Joshua and Israel

THEN Moses went and spoke these words
to all Israel.
2 And he said to them: "I *am* one hundred
and twenty years old today. I can no longer
go out and come in. Also the LORD has said to
me, 'You shall not cross over this Jordan.'
3 "The LORD your God Himself crosses
over before you; He will destroy these nations
from before you, and you shall dispossess
them. Joshua himself crosses over before you,
just [R]as the LORD has said. Num. 27:21
4 "And the LORD will do to them as He did
to Sihon and Og, the kings of the Amorites
and their land, when He destroyed them.
5 "The LORD will give them over to you,
that you may do to them according to every
commandment which I have commanded
you.
6 "Be strong and of good courage, do not
fear nor be afraid of them; for the LORD your
God, He *is* the One who goes with you. He
will not leave you nor forsake you."
7 Then Moses called Joshua and said to
him in the sight of all Israel, [R]"Be strong and
of good courage, for you must go with this
people to the land which the LORD has sworn
to their fathers to give them, and you shall
cause them to inherit it. Deut. 31:23
8 "And the LORD, [R]He *is* the one who goes
before you. [R]He will be with you, He will not
leave you nor forsake you; do not fear nor be
dismayed." Ex. 13:21 • Josh. 1:5
9 So Moses wrote this law [R]and delivered it
to the priests, the sons of Levi, [R]who bore the
ark of the covenant of the LORD, and to all
the elders of Israel. Deut. 17:18; 31:25, 26 • Josh. 3:3
10 And Moses commanded them, saying:
"At the end of *every* seven years, at the
appointed time in the [R]year of release, [R]at the
Feast of Tabernacles, Deut. 15:1, 2 • Lev. 23:34
11 "when all Israel comes to appear before
the LORD your God in the [R]place which He
chooses, [R]you shall read this law before all
Israel in their hearing. Deut. 12:5 • Josh. 8:34

12 [R]"Gather the people together, men and
women and little ones, and the stranger who
is within your gates, that they may hear and
that they may learn to fear the LORD your
God and carefully observe all the words of
this law, Deut. 4:10

31:12 Obedience to God's Word—Reading, memorizing, and meditating upon the Word of God are of no value without obedience to the Word of God. To obey the Word of God, you do what the Word of God indicates should be done in any situation. Obedience to the Word of God is the only way that the child of God can be pleasing to God in the new life. Obedience to God's Word

13 "and *that* their children, who have not known it, may hear and learn to fear the LORD your God as long as you live in the land which you cross the Jordan to possess."

God Charges Israel

14 Then the LORD said to Moses, [R]"Behold, the days approach when you must die; call Joshua, and present yourselves in the tabernacle of meeting, that [R]I may [T]inaugurate him." So Moses and Joshua went and presented themselves in the tabernacle of meeting. Num. 27:13 • Deut. 3:28 • *commission*

15 Now the LORD appeared at the tabernacle in a pillar of cloud, and the pillar of cloud stood above the door of the tabernacle.

16 And the LORD said to Moses: "Behold, you will [T]rest with your fathers; and this people will rise and play the harlot with the gods of the foreigners of the land, where they go *to be* among them, and they will forsake Me and break My covenant which I have made with them. Die and join your ancestors

17 "Then My anger shall be [R]aroused against them in that day, and [R]I will forsake them, and I will [R]hide My face from them, and they shall be [T]devoured. And many evils and troubles shall befall them, so that they will say in that day, 'Have not these evils come upon us because our God *is* not among us?' Judg. 2:14; 6:13 • 2 Chr. 15:2 • Deut. 32:20 • *consumed*

18 "And I will surely hide My face in that day because of all the evil which they have done, in that they have turned to other gods.

19 "Now therefore, write down this song for yourselves, and teach it to the children of Israel; put it in their mouths, that this song may be [R]a witness for Me against the children of Israel. Deut. 31:22, 26

20 "When I have brought them to the land flowing with milk and honey, of which I swore to their fathers, and they have eaten and filled themselves [R]and grown fat, [R]then they will turn to other gods and serve them; and they will provoke Me and break My covenant. Deut. 32:15–17 • Deut. 31:16

21 "Then it shall be, [R]when many evils and troubles have come upon them, that this song will testify against them as a witness; for it will not be forgotten in the mouths of their descendants, for [R]I know the inclination [R]of their behavior today, even before I have brought them to the land of which I swore *to give them*." Deut. 31:17 • Hos. 5:3 • Amos 5:25, 26

The Book of the Law Is Deposited

22 Therefore Moses wrote this song the same day, and taught it to the children of Israel.

23 [R]Then He inaugurated Joshua the son of Nun, and said, [R]"Be strong and of good courage; for you shall bring the children of Israel into the land of which I swore to them, and I will be with you." Num. 27:23 • Deut. 31:7

24 So it was, when Moses had completed writing the words of this law in a book, when they were finished,

25 that Moses commanded the Levites, who bore the ark of the covenant of the LORD, saying:

26 "Take this Book of the Law, [R]and put it beside the ark of the covenant of the LORD your God, that it may be there [R]as a witness against you; 2 Kin. 22:8 • Deut. 31:19

27 "for I know your rebellion and your stiff neck. *If* today, while I am yet alive with you, you have been rebellious against the LORD, then how much more after my death?

28 "Gather to me all the elders of your tribes, and your officers, that I may speak these words in their hearing [R]and call heaven and earth to witness against them. Deut. 30:19

29 "For I know that after my death you will become utterly corrupt, and turn aside from the way which I have commanded you; and [R]evil will befall you [R]in the latter days, because you will do evil in the sight of the LORD, to provoke Him to anger through the work of your hands." Deut. 28:15 • Gen. 49:1

30 Then Moses spoke in the hearing of all the congregation of Israel the words of this song until they were ended:

CHAPTER 32

The Song of Moses

"GIVE [R]ear, O heavens, and I will speak;
And hear, O [R]earth, the words of my mouth. Deut. 4:26 • Jer. 6:19

---

results in: being treasured by God (Page 89—Ex. 19:5); blessedness (happiness) in life (Page 694—Ps. 119:2); not being ashamed (Page 694—Ps. 119:4–6); understanding (Page 697—Ps. 119:100); avoidance of evil (Page 697—Ps. 119:101); guidance for life (Page 697—Ps. 119:105); safety and freedom from anxiety (Page 715—Prov. 1:33); life (Page 731—Prov. 19:16; Page 934—Ezek. 18:19; Page 1250—John 8:51); God's blessing (Page 772—Is. 1:19); greatness in the kingdom of heaven (Page 1120—Matt. 5:19); bearing fruit for God (Page 1132—Matt. 13:23); manifesting love for God (Page 1258—John 14:23; Page 1494—1 John 2:5); promise of God's presence (Page 1258—John 14:23; Page 1502—2 John 9); abiding in the love of God (Page 1259—John 15:10); evidence of the doctrine that has been taught (Page 1331—Rom. 6:17); assurance of salvation (Page 1494—1 John 2:3); eternal life (Page 1496—1 John 2:17); dwelling in God (Page 1498—1 John 3:24); love of God's children (Page 1498—1 John 5:2); and entrance into heaven (Page 1539—Rev. 22:7).

Now turn to Page 710—Ps. 150:1: Praise.

2 Let my [T]teaching drop as the rain,
My speech distill as the dew, *doctrine*
[R]As raindrops on the tender herb,
And as showers on the grass. Ps. 72:6
3 For I proclaim the [R]name of the LORD:
Ascribe greatness to our God. Deut. 28:58
4 *He is* [R]the Rock, His work *is* perfect;
For all His ways *are* justice, Ps. 18:2
A God of truth and [R]without injustice;
Righteous and upright *is* He. Job 34:10

5 "They[R] have corrupted themselves;
They are not His children, Deut. 4:25; 31:29
Because of their blemish:
A perverse and crooked generation.
6 Do you thus [T]deal with the LORD,
O foolish and unwise people? *repay the*
Is He not [R]your Father, *who* [R]bought
you? Is. 63:16 • Ps. 74:2
Has He not [R]made you and established
you? Deut. 32:15

7 "Remember[R] the days of old, Ps. 44:1
Consider the years of many generations.
Ask your father, and he will show you;
Your elders, and they will tell you:

8 When the Most High [R]divided their
inheritance to the nations, Acts 17:26
When He [R]separated the sons of Adam,
He set the boundaries of the peoples
According to the number of the
*children of Israel. Gen. 11:8
9 For the LORD's portion *is* His people;
Jacob *is* the place of His inheritance.

10 "He found him [R]in a desert land
And in the wasteland, a howling
wilderness; Jer. 2:6
He encircled him, He instructed him,
He kept him as the apple of His eye.
11 [R]As an eagle stirs up its nest, Is. 31:5
Hovers over its young,
Spreading out its wings, taking them
up,
Carrying them on its wings,
12 *So* the LORD alone led him,
And *there was* no foreign god with him.

13 "He[R] made him ride in the heights of the
earth, Is. 58:14
That he might eat the produce of the
fields;
He made him to draw honey from the
rock,
And oil from the flinty rock;
14 Curds from the cattle, and milk of the
flock,
[R]With fat of lambs; Ps. 81:16
And rams of the breed of Bashan, and
goats,
With the choicest wheat;
And you drank wine, the [R]blood of the
grapes. Gen. 49:11

15 "But Jeshurun grew fat and kicked;
[R]You grew fat, you grew thick,
You are covered *with fat*; Deut. 31:20
Then he [R]forsook God *who* [R]made him,
And scornfully esteemed the [R]Rock of
his salvation. Is. 1:4 • Is. 51:13 • Ps. 95:1
16 [R]They provoked Him to jealousy with
foreign *gods*; 1 Cor. 10:22
With [T]abominations they provoked Him
to anger. *detestable acts*
17 [R]They sacrificed to demons, not to God,
To gods they did not know,
To new *gods*, new arrivals
That your fathers did not fear. Rev. 9:20
18 [R]Of the Rock *who* begot you, you are
unmindful, Is. 17:10
And have [R]forgotten the God who
fathered you. Jer. 2:32

32:8 LXX, DSS *angels of God;* Symmachus, Lat. *sons of God*

32:7 God's Work in the Past—The Bible's revelation of God's work in the past provides an informative and exciting panorama of centuries of divine activity toward man.

First, it gives man an *education* in truths unknowable apart from divine revelation. For example, the creation of man described in Genesis 1 and 2 answers man's most basic questions: "Who am I?" and "Where did I come from?" Only God Himself could disclose these facts.

Second, the Bible sets forth a mass of historical *evidence* for the truthfulness of the Christian faith. The most outstanding of these evidences are fulfilled prophecy, the miracles of Christ, and Christ's death and resurrection. The believer's faith is thus grounded in historical events and is far removed from what some have called "a leap into the dark."

Third, the Bible records *examples* to help present-day Christians. Various failures of Israel and the resulting judgments of God are often cited in the New Testament as things to avoid, for example, their idolatry and grumbling in the wilderness (Page 1354—1 Cor. 10:11), and their unbelief at Kadesh (Page 1453—Heb. 4:11). Paul is said to be a living example for believers to follow (Page 1348—1 Cor. 4:16; 11:1), as is Jesus' humility in the midst of suffering (Page 1480—1 Pet. 2:21).

Fourth, the Bible provides *encouragement* for Christians in their life and witness. If God could use an adulterer and murderer like David, then God can certainly use a struggling Christian today if he possesses David's devotion to the Lord. Likewise, if God saved Saul of Tarsus, the chief enemy of the early church (Page 1284—Acts 9:1–31), then surely He can save the people with whom Christians daily share their Faith.

Now turn to Page 705—Ps. 139:14: God's Work in Our Lives.

19 "And[R] when the LORD saw *it*, He spurned
them, Judg. 2:14
Because of the provocation of His sons
and His daughters.
20 And He said: 'I will hide My face from
them,
I will see what their end *will be*,
For they *are* a perverse generation,
[R]Children in whom *is* no faith. Matt. 17:17
21 [R]They have provoked Me to jealousy by
what is not God; Ps. 78:58
They have moved Me to anger by their
[T]foolish idols. *foolishness*, lit. *vanities*
But [R]I will provoke them to jealousy by
those who are not a nation; Rom. 10:19
I will move them to anger by a foolish
nation.
22 For a fire is kindled in My anger,
And shall burn to the [T]lowest hell;
It shall consume the earth with her
increase, *lowest part of Sheol*
And set on fire the foundations of the
mountains.

23 'I will heap disasters upon them;
I will spend My arrows upon them.
24 *They shall be* wasted with hunger,
Devoured by pestilence and bitter
destruction;
I will also send against them the [R]teeth
of beasts, Lev. 26:22
With the poison of serpents of the dust.
25 The sword shall destroy outside;
There shall be terror within
For the young man and virgin,
The nursing child with the man of gray
hairs.
26 [R]I would have said, "I will dash them in
pieces, Ezek. 20:23
I will make the memory of them to
cease from among men,"
27 Had I not feared the wrath of the
enemy,
Lest their adversaries should
misunderstand,
Lest they should say, [R]"Our hand *is*
high; Is. 10:12–15
And it is not the LORD who has done all
this." '

28 "For they *are* a nation void of counsel,
Nor *is there any* understanding in them.
29 [R]Oh, that they were wise, *that* they
understood this, [Luke 19:42]
That they would consider their [R]latter
end! Deut. 31:29
30 How could one chase a thousand,
And two put ten thousand to flight,
Unless their Rock had sold them,
And the LORD had surrendered them?
31 For their rock *is* not like our Rock,
[R]Even our enemies themselves *being*
judges. [1 Sam. 4:7, 8]
32 For [R]their vine *is* of the vine of Sodom
And of the fields of Gomorrah;
Their grapes *are* grapes of gall,
Their clusters *are* bitter. Is. 1:8–10
33 Their wine *is* the poison of serpents,
And the cruel venom of cobras.

34 '*Is* this not laid up in store with Me,
Sealed up among My treasures?
35 [R]Vengeance is Mine, and recompense;
Their foot shall slip in *due* time;
[R]For the day of their calamity *is* at hand,
And the things to come hasten upon
them.' Heb. 10:30 • 2 Pet. 2:3

36 "For[R] the LORD will judge His people
[R]And have compassion on His servants,
When He sees that *their* power is gone,
And [R]*there is* no one *remaining*, bond or
free. Ps. 135:14 • Jer. 31:20 • 2 Kin. 14:26
37 He will say: 'Where *are* their gods,
The rock in which they sought refuge?
38 Who ate the fat of their sacrifices,
And drank the wine of their drink
offering?
Let them rise and help you,
And be your refuge.

39 'Now see that [R]I, *even* I, *am* He,
And [R]*there is* no God besides Me;
[R]I kill and I make alive;
I wound and I heal;
Nor *is there any* who can deliver from
My hand. Is. 41:4; 43:10 • Is. 45:5 • 1 Sam. 2:6
40 For I lift My hand to heaven,
And say, "*As* I live forever,
41 If I [T]whet My glittering sword, *sharpen*
And My hand takes hold on judgment,
I will render vengeance to My enemies,
And repay those who hate Me.
42 I will make My arrows drunk with
blood,
And My sword shall devour flesh,
With the blood of the slain and the
captives,
From the heads of the leaders of the
enemy." '

43 "Rejoice,[R] O Gentiles, *with* His *people;
For He will [R]avenge the blood of His
servants, Rom. 15:10 • Rev. 6:10; 19:2
And render vengeance to His
adversaries;
He [R]will provide atonement for His land
and His people." Ps. 65:3; 79:9; 85:1

44 So Moses came with [T]Joshua the son of
Nun and spoke all the words of this song in
the hearing of the people. Heb. *Hoshea*

32:43 DSS add *And let all the angels worship Him*, see Heb. 1:6

45 Moses finished speaking all these words
to all Israel,
46 and he said to them: R"Set your hearts on
all the words which I testify among you
today, which you shall command your Rchil-
dren to be careful to observe—all the words
of this law. Ezek. 40:4; 44:5 • Deut. 11:19
47 "For it *is* not a Tfutile thing for you,
because it *is* your life, and by this word you
shall prolong *your* days in the land which
you cross over the Jordan to possess." *vain*

Moses Is Ordered to Mount Nebo

48 Then the LORD spoke to Moses that very
same day, saying:
49 R"Go up this mountain of the Abarim,
Mount Nebo, which *is* in the land of Moab,
across from Jericho; view the land of Canaan,
which I give to the children of Israel as a
possession; Num. 27:12–14
50 "and die on the mountain which you
ascend, and be gathered to your people, just
as RAaron your brother died on Mount Hor
and was gathered to his people; Num. 20:25, 28
51 "because you trespassed against Me
among the children of Israel at the waters of
TMeribah Kadesh, in the Wilderness of Zin,
because you did not hallow Me in the midst
of the children of Israel. *Contention at Kadesh*
52 "Yet you shall see the land before *you*,
though you shall not go there, into the land
which I am giving to the children of Israel."

CHAPTER 33

Moses Blesses the Tribes

NOW this *is* the blessing with which Moses Rthe man of God blessed the children of Israel before his death. Ps. 90
2 And he said:

"The LORD came from Sinai,
And dawned on them from RSeir;
He shone forth from RMount Paran,
And He came with Rten thousands of
saints; Deut. 2:1, 4 • Num. 10:12 • Dan. 7:10
From His right hand
Came a fiery law for them.
3 Yes, RHe loves the people; Hos. 11:1
All His saints *are* in Your hand;
They Rsit down at Your feet; [Luke 10:39]
Everyone Rreceives Your words. Prov. 2:1
4 Moses commanded a law for us,
A heritage of the congregation of Jacob.
5 And He was King in Jeshurun,
When the leaders of the people were
gathered,
All the tribes of Israel together.

6 "Let RReuben live, and not die,
Nor let his men be few." Gen. 49:3, 4

7 And this he said of RJudah:

"Hear, LORD, the voice of Judah,
And bring him to his people;
RLet his hands be sufficient for him,
And may You be Ra help against his
enemies." Gen. 49:8-12 • Gen. 49:8 • Ps. 146:5

8 And of RLevi he said: Gen. 49:5

R"*Let* Your Thummim and Your Urim *be*
with Your holy one, Ex. 28:30
RWhom You tested at Massah, Ps. 81:7
And with whom You contended at the
waters of Meribah,
9 Who says of his father and mother,
'I have not Rseen them'; [Gen. 29:32]
RNor did he acknowledge his brothers,
Or know his own children; Ex. 32:26–28
For Rthey have observed Your word
And kept Your covenant. Mal. 2:5, 6
10 RThey shall teach Jacob Your judgments,
And Israel Your law. Lev. 10:11
They shall put incense before You,
RAnd a whole burnt sacrifice on Your
altar. Ps. 51:19
11 Bless his substance, LORD,
And Raccept the work of his hands;
Strike the loins of those who rise
against him, 2 Sam. 24:23
And of those who hate him, that they
rise not again."

12 Of Benjamin he said:

"The beloved of the LORD shall dwell in
safety by Him,
Who shelters him all the day long;
And he shall dwell between His
shoulders."

13 And of Joseph he said:

R"Blessed of the LORD *is* his land,
With the precious things of heaven,
with the Rdew, Gen. 49:22-26 • Gen. 27:28
And the deep lying beneath,
14 With the precious fruits of the sun,
With the precious produce of the
months,
15 With the best things of Rthe ancient
mountains, Gen. 49:26
With the precious things Rof the
everlasting hills, Hab. 3:6
16 With the precious things of the earth
and its fullness,
And the favor of RHim who dwelt in the
bush. Ex. 3:2–4
Let *the blessing* Rcome 'on the head of
Joseph, Gen. 49:26
And on the crown of the head of him
who was separate from his brothers.'
17 His glory *is like* a Rfirstborn bull,
And his horns *are like* the Rhorns of the
wild ox; 1 Chr. 5:1 • Num. 23:22

Together with them
[R]He shall push the peoples Ps. 44:5
To the ends of the earth;
[R]They *are* the ten thousands of Ephraim,
And they *are* the thousands of
Manasseh." Gen. 48:19

18 And of Zebulun he said:

[R]"Rejoice, Zebulun, in your going out,
And Issachar in your tents! Gen. 49:13–15
19 They shall [R]call the peoples *to* the
mountain; Is. 2:3
There [R]they shall offer sacrifices of
righteousness; Ps. 4:5; 51:19
For they shall partake *of* the abundance
of the seas
And *of* treasures hidden in the sand."

20 And of Gad he said:

"Blessed *is* he who [R]enlarges Gad;
He dwells as a lion, 1 Chr. 12:8
And tears the arm and the crown of his
head.
21 [R]He provided the first *part* for himself,
Because a lawgiver's portion was
reserved there. Num. 32:16, 17
He came *with* the heads of the people;
He administered the justice of the LORD,
And His judgments with Israel."

22 And of Dan he said:

"Dan *is* a lion's whelp;
[R]He shall leap from Bashan." Josh. 19:47

23 And of Naphtali he said:

"O Naphtali, satisfied with favor,
And full of the blessing of the LORD,
Possess the west and the south."

24 And of Asher he said:

"Asher *is* most blessed of sons;
Let him be favored by his brothers,
And let him [R]dip his foot in oil. Job 29:6
25 Your sandals *shall be* iron and bronze;
As your days, *so shall* your strength *be*.

26 "*There is* [R]no one like the God of
[R]Jeshurun, Ex. 15:11 • Deut. 32:15
Who rides the heavens to help you,
And in His excellency on the clouds.
27 The eternal God *is your* [R]refuge,
And underneath *are* the everlasting
arms; [Ps. 90:1; 91:2, 9]
[R]He will thrust out the enemy from
before you, Deut. 9:3–5
And will say, 'Destroy!'
28 Then Israel shall dwell in safety,
The fountain of Jacob [R]alone, Num. 23:9
In a land of grain and new wine;
His heavens shall also drop dew.
29 [R]Happy *are* you, O Israel!
[R]Who *is* like you, a people saved by the
LORD, Ps. 144:15 • 2 Sam. 7:23
[R]The shield of your help Ps. 115:9
And the sword of your majesty!
Your enemies shall submit to you,
And [R]you shall tread down their [T]high
places." Num. 33:52 • Places for pagan worship

CHAPTER 34

Moses Views the Promised Land

THEN Moses went up from the plains of
Moab [R]to Mount Nebo, to the top of
Pisgah, which is across from Jericho. And the
LORD showed him all the land of Gilead as far
as Dan, Deut. 32:49
2 all Naphtali and the land of Ephraim and
Manasseh, all the land of Judah as far as the
[T]Western Sea, Mediterranean
3 the South, and the plain of the Valley of
Jericho, the city of palm trees, as far as Zoar.
4 Then the LORD said to him, [R]"This *is* the
land of which I swore to give Abraham,
Isaac, and Jacob, saying, 'I will give it to your
descendants.' [R]I have caused you to see *it*
with your eyes, but you shall not cross over
there." Gen. 12:7 • Deut. 3:27

Moses Dies and Is Mourned

5 [R]So Moses the servant of the LORD died
there in the land of Moab, according to the
word of the LORD. Deut. 32:50
6 And He buried him in a valley in the land
of Moab, opposite Beth Peor; but [R]no one
knows his grave to this day. Jude 9
7 Moses *was* one hundred and twenty
years old when he died. His eyes were not
dim nor his natural vigor [T]abated. *reduced*
8 And the children of Israel wept for Moses in the plains of Moab [R]thirty days. So the
days of weeping *and* mourning for Moses
ended. Gen. 50:3, 10

Moses Is Replaced by Joshua

9 Now Joshua the son of Nun was full of
the [R]spirit of wisdom, for [R]Moses had laid his
hands on him; so the children of Israel
heeded him, and did as the LORD had commanded Moses. Is. 11:2 • Num. 27:18, 23

Moses Is Extolled in Israel

10 But since then there [R]has not arisen in
Israel a prophet like Moses, [R]whom the LORD
knew face to face, Deut. 18:15, 18 • Ex. 33:11
11 in all [R]the signs and wonders which the
LORD sent him to do in the land of Egypt,
before Pharaoh, before all his servants, and in
all his land, Deut. 7:19
12 and by all that mighty power and all the
great terror which Moses performed in the
sight of all Israel.

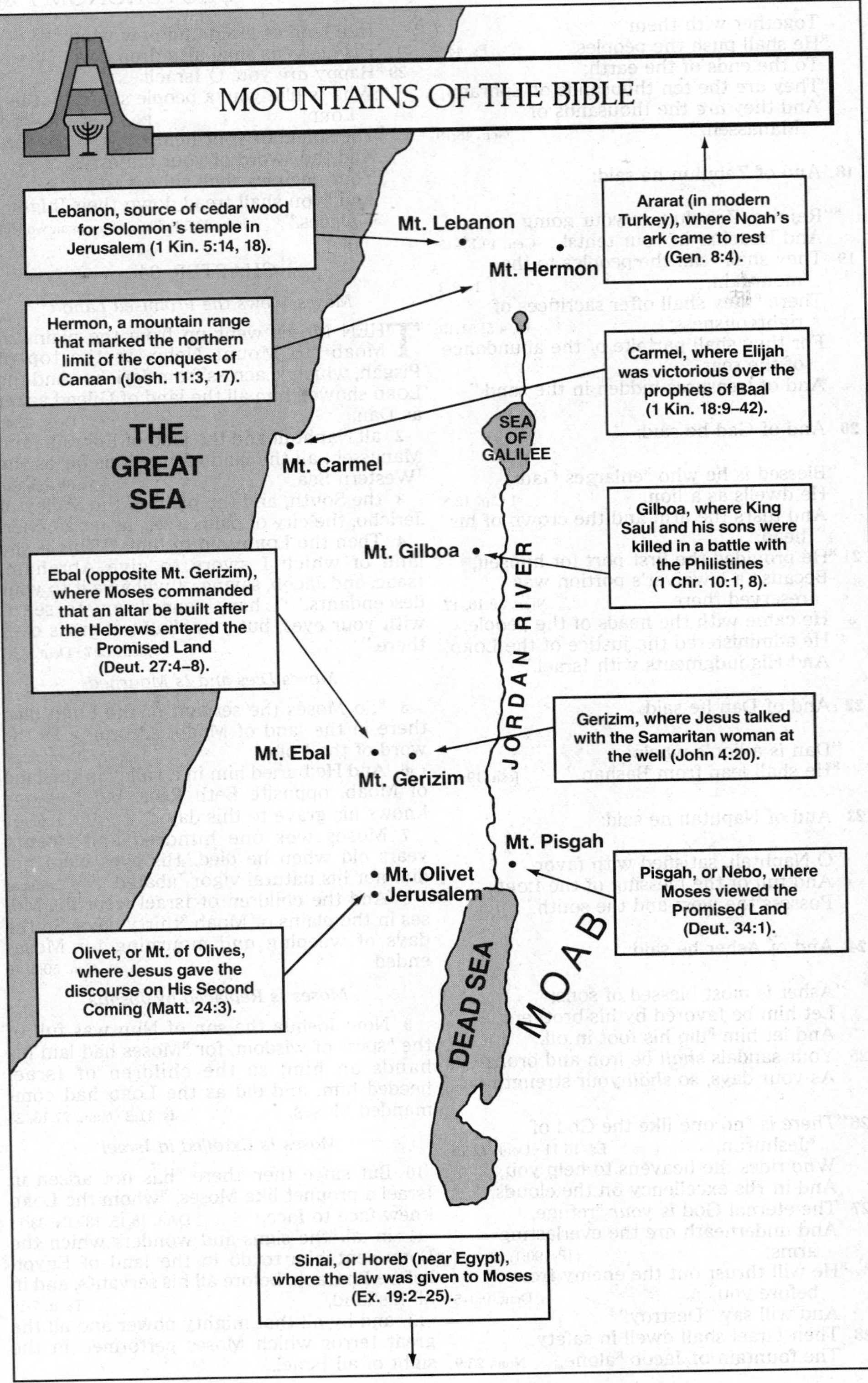

MOUNTAINS OF THE BIBLE
Lebanon, source of cedar wood for Solomon's temple in Jerusalem (1 Kin. 5:14, 18).
Mt. Lebanon
Ararat (in modern Turkey), where Noah's ark came to rest (Gen. 8:4).
Mt. Hermon
Hermon, a mountain range that marked the northern limit of the conquest of Canaan (Josh. 11:3, 17).
Carmel, where Elijah was victorious over the prophets of Baal (1 Kin. 18:9–42).
THE GREAT SEA
SEA OF GALILEE
Mt. Carmel
Gilboa, where King Saul and his sons were killed in a battle with the Philistines (1 Chr. 10:1, 8).
Mt. Gilboa
Ebal (opposite Mt. Gerizim), where Moses commanded that an altar be built after the Hebrews entered the Promised Land (Deut. 27:4–8).
JORDAN RIVER
Gerizim, where Jesus talked with the Samaritan woman at the well (John 4:20).
Mt. Ebal
Mt. Gerizim
Mt. Pisgah
Pisgah, or Nebo, where Moses viewed the Promised Land (Deut. 34:1).
Mt. Olivet
Jerusalem
MOAB
DEAD SEA
Olivet, or Mt. of Olives, where Jesus gave the discourse on His Second Coming (Matt. 24:3).
Sinai, or Horeb (near Egypt), where the law was given to Moses (Ex. 19:2–25).

THE BOOK OF
JOSHUA

THE BOOK OF JOSHUA

Joshua, the first of the twelve historical books (Joshua-Esther), forges a link between the Pentateuch and the remainder of Israel's history. Through three major military campaigns involving more than thirty enemy armies, the people of Israel learn a crucial lesson under Joshua's capable leadership: victory comes through faith in God and obedience to His word, rather than through military might or numerical superiority.

The title of this book is appropriately named after its central figure, Joshua. His original name is *Hoshea,* "Salvation" (Num. 13:8); but Moses evidently changes it to *Yehoshua* (Num. 13:16), "Yahweh Is Salvation." He is also called *Yeshua,* a shortened form of *Yehoshua.* This is the Hebrew equivalent of the Greek name *Iesous* (Jesus). Thus, the Greek title given to the book in the Septuagint is *Iesous Naus,* "Joshua the Son of Nun." The Latin title is *Liber Josue,* the "Book of Joshua."

His name is symbolic of the fact that although he is the leader of the Israelite nation during the conquest, the Lord is the Conqueror.

THE AUTHOR OF JOSHUA

Although it cannot be proven, Jewish tradition seems correct in assigning the authorship of this book to Joshua himself. Joshua 24:26 makes this clear statement: "Then Joshua wrote these words in the Book of the Law of God." This refers at least to Joshua's farewell charge, if not to the book as a whole (see also 18:9). Joshua, as Israel's leader and an eyewitness of most of the events, was the person best qualified to write the book. He even uses the first person in one place (5:6, "us"; "we" appears in some manuscripts of 5:1). The book was written soon after the events occurred: Rahab was still alive (6:25). Other evidences for early authorship are the detailed information about Israel's campaigns and use of the ancient names of Canaanite cities.

The unity of style and organization suggests a single authorship for the majority of the book. Three small portions, however, must have been added after Joshua's death. These are: (1) Othniel's capture of Kirjath Sepher (15:13–19; cf. Judg. 1:9–15), (2) Dan's migration to the north (19:47; cf. Judg. 18:27–29), and (3) Joshua's death and burial (24:29–33). These may have been inserted early in the time of the judges by Eleazer the priest and his son Phinehas (24:33).

Joshua, born a slave in Egypt, becomes a conqueror in Canaan. He serves as personal attendant to Moses, as one of the twelve spies (of whom only he and Caleb believed God), and as Moses' successor. His outstanding qualities are obedient faith, courage, and dedication to God and His Word.

THE TIME OF JOSHUA

Joshua divides neatly into three geographical settings: (1) the Jordan River (1—5); (2) Canaan (6—13:7); and (3) the twelve tribes situated on both sides of the Jordan (13:8—24:33).

The setting of the first five chapters begins east of the Jordan as Joshua replaces Moses, crosses the Jordan on dry land, and finally prepares for war west of the Jordan.

Like a wise general, Joshua utilizes the divide-and-conquer strategy; and his campaign leads him to central Canaan (6—8), southern Canaan (9 and 10), and finally to northern Canaan (11 and 12).

After listing those areas yet to be conquered (13:1–7), Joshua undertakes the long task of dividing the Promised Land to all the tribes. First, he settles those two-and-a-half tribes east of the Jordan (13:8–33) and then the nine-and-a-half tribes west of the Jordan (14:1—19:51). Completing this, he is free to assign the six Cities of Refuge and the forty-eight Cities of Levites, which are scattered among all the tribes.

The Book of Joshua cannot be dated precisely, but utilizing the same threefold division noted above, the following dates can be assigned:

A. One month, March-April, 1405 B.C. (Josh. 1—5)
   1. Death of Moses, March 1405 B.C. (Deut. 34:5–9)
   2. Crossing the Jordan, April 10, 1405 B.C. (Josh. 4:19)

B. Seven years, April 1405–1398 B.C. (Josh. 6:1—13:7)
   1. Caleb forty years old at Kadesh (Josh. 14:7)
   2. Caleb eighty-five years old at that time (Josh. 14:10)
      Note: forty-five years less thirty-eight years of wandering leaves seven years.

C. Eight years, 1398/7–1390 B.C. (Josh. 13:8–24)
   1. Division begun, 1398/7 B.C. (Josh. 14:7–10)
   2. Joshua dies at 110, c. 1390 B.C. (Josh. 24:39)

THE CHRIST OF JOSHUA

Although there are no direct messianic prophecies in the book, Joshua is clearly a type of Christ. His name *Yeshua* ("Yahweh Is

Salvation") is the Hebrew equivalent of the name Jesus. In his role of triumphantly leading his people into their possessions, he foreshadows the One who will bring "many sons to glory" (Heb. 2:10). "Now thanks *be* to God who always leads us in triumph in Christ" (2 Cor. 2:14; see Rom. 8:37). Joshua succeeds Moses and wins the victory unreached by Moses. Christ will succeed the Mosaic law and win the victory unreachable by the Law (John 1:17; Rom. 8:2–4; Gal. 3:23–25; Heb. 7:18, 19).

The "Commander of the army of the LORD" (5:13–15) met by Joshua is evidently a preincarnate appearance of Christ (cf. Josh. 5:15 with Ex. 3:2).

Rahab's scarlet cord portrays safety through the blood (Heb. 9:19–22); and amazingly, this gentile woman is found in Christ's genealogy (Matt. 1:5).

KEYS TO JOSHUA

Key Word: Conquest—The entire Book of Joshua describes the entering, conquering, and occupying of the land of Canaan. The book begins with a statement of the promise of conquest, "Moses My servant is dead. Now therefore, arise, go over this Jordan . . . Every place that the sole of your foot shall tread upon I have given you" (1:2, 3) and ends with the completion of conquest "that not one thing has failed of all the good things which the LORD your God spoke concerning you. All have come to pass for you, *and* not one word of them has failed" (23:14).

Key Verses: Joshua 1:8; 11:23—"This Book of the Law shall not depart from your mouth, but you shall meditate in it day and night, that you may observe to do according to all that is written in it. For then you will make your way prosperous, and then you will have good success" (1:8).

"So Joshua took the whole land, according to all that the LORD had said to Moses; and Joshua gave it as an inheritance to Israel according to their divisions by their tribes. Then the land rested from war" (11:23).

Key Chapter: Joshua 24—Some of the most critical periods in Israel's history are the transitions of leadership: Moses to Joshua; Joshua to the judges; the judges to the kings, and so on. Before his death and in preparation for a major transition of leadership by one man (Joshua) to many (the judges), Joshua reviews for the people God's fulfillment of His promises and then challenges them to review their commitment to the covenant (24:24, 25), which is the foundation for all successful national life.

SURVEY OF JOSHUA

Joshua resumes the narrative where Deuteronomy left off, and takes Israel from the wilderness to the Promised Land. Israel has now reached its climactic point of fulfilling the centuries-old promise in Genesis of a homeland. The first half of Joshua (1:1—13:7) describes the seven-year conquest of the land, and the second half (13:8—24:33) gives the details of the division and settlement of the land.

Conquest (1:1—13:7): The first five chapters record the spiritual, moral, physical, and military preparation of Joshua and the people for the impending conquest of Canaan. Joshua is given a charge by God to complete the task begun by Moses(1:2). After being encouraged by God, Joshua sends out two spies who come back with a favorable report (in contrast to the spies of the previous generation). Obedience and faith are united in the miraculous crossing of the Jordan River (3:1—4:24).

Joshua's campaign in central Canaan (6:1—8:35) places a strategic wedge between the northern and southern cities preventing a massive Canaanite alliance against Israel. This divide-and-conquer strategy proves effective, but God's directions for taking the first city (Jericho) sound like foolishness from a military point of view. The

FOCUS	CONQUEST OF CANAAN		SETTLEMENT IN CANAAN			
REFERENCE	1:1———	6:1———	13:8———	14:1———	20:1———	22:1———24:33
DIVISION	PREPARATION OF ISRAEL	CONQUEST OF CANAAN	SETTLEMENT OF EAST JORDAN	SETTLEMENT OF WEST JORDAN	SETTLEMENT OF RELIGIOUS COMMUNITY	CONDITIONS FOR CONTINUED SETTLEMENT
TOPIC	ENTERING CANAAN	CONQUERING CANAAN	DIVIDING CANAAN			
	PREPARATION	SUBJECTION	POSSESSION			
LOCATION	JORDAN RIVER	CANAAN	TWO AND A HALF TRIBES—EAST JORDAN NINE AND A HALF TRIBES—WEST JORDAN			
TIME	c. 1 MONTH	c. 7 YEARS	c. 8 YEARS			

Lord uses this to test the people and to teach them that Israel's success in battle will always be by His power and not their own might or cleverness. Sin must be dealt with at once because it brings severe consequences and defeat at Ai (7:1–26).

The southern and northern campaigns (9:1—13:7) are also successful, but an unwise oath made to the deceptive Gibeonites forces Israel to protect them and to disobey God's command to eliminate the Canaanites.

Settlement (13:8—24:33): Joshua is growing old, and God tells him to divide the land among the twelve tribes. Much remains to be won, and the tribes are to continue the conquest by faith after Joshua's death. Chapters 13:8—21:45 describe the allocation of the land to the various tribes as well as the inheritances of Caleb (14 and 15) and the Levites (21).

The last chapters (22:1—24:33) record the conditions for continued successful settlement in Canaan. Access to God, as well as His forgiveness, come only through the divinely established sacrificial system; and civil war almost breaks out when the eastern tribes build an altar that is misinterpreted by the western tribes.

Realizing that blessing comes from God only as Israel obeys His covenant, Joshua preaches a moving sermon, climaxed by Israel's renewal of her allegiance to the covenant.

OUTLINE OF JOSHUA

Part One: The Conquest of Canaan (1:1—13:7)

I. Israel Is Prepared for the Conquest. . . . 1:1—5:15
- A. Joshua Replaces Moses . . . 1:1–18
  - 1. Joshua Is Commissioned by God . . . 1:1–9
  - 2. Joshua Commands Israel . . . 1:10–15
    - a. Joshua Commands the Tribes West of the Jordan . . . 1:10, 11
    - b. Joshua Commands the Tribes East of the Jordan . . . 1:12–15
  - 3. Joshua Is Accepted by Israel . . . 1:16–18
- B. Joshua Prepares Israel Militarily . . . 2:1—5:1
  - 1. Joshua Spies Canaan . . . 2:1–24
    - a. The Faith of Rahab . . . 2:1–21
    - b. The Faith of the Spies . . . 2:22–24
  - 2. Joshua Leads Israel into Canaan . . . 3:1—5:1
    - a. The Miraculous Crossing of the Jordan . . . 3:1–17
    - b. The Memorial of the Crossing . . . 4:1–24
    - c. The Canaanites Fear Israel . . . 5:1
- C. Joshua Prepares Israel Spiritually . . . 5:2–12
  - 1. Circumcision Is Practiced . . . 5:2–9
  - 2. Passover Is Celebrated . . . 5:10, 11
  - 3. From Manna to Corn . . . 5:12
- D. The Commander of the Lord Appears . . . 5:13–15

II. The Conquest of Canaan by Israel . . . 6:1—13:7
- A. Conquest of Central Canaan . . . 6:1—8:35
  - 1. Victory at Jericho . . . 6:1–27
  - 2. Defeat at Ai . . . 7:1–26
  - 3. Victory at Ai . . . 8:1–29
  - 4. Result of the Victories . . . 8:30–35
    - a. Israel Worships the Lord . . . 8:30, 31
    - b. Israel Renews the Covenant . . . 8:32–35
- B. Conquest of Southern Canaan . . . 9:1—10:43
  - 1. Failure with the Gibeonites . . . 9:1–27
  - 2. Victory over the Amorites . . . 10:1–43
- C. Conquest of Northern Canaan . . . 11:1–15
- D. Conquest of Canaan Is Summarized . . . 11:16—12:24
  - 1. The Summary of Conquered Territory . . . 11:16–23
  - 2. The Summary of Conquered Kings . . . 12:1–24
    - a. Kings Are Conquered by Moses . . 12:1–6
    - b. Kings Are Conquered by Joshua 12:7–24
- E. Unconquered Parts of Canaan . . . 13:1–7

Part Two: The Settlement in Canaan (13:8—24:33)

I. The Settlement East of the Jordan . . . 13:8–33
- A. Geographical Boundaries . . . 13:8–13
- B. Tribal Boundaries . . . 13:14–23
  - 1. Boundaries of Levi . . . 13:14
  - 2. Boundaries of Reuben . . . 13:15–23
  - 3. Boundaries of Gad . . . 13:24–28
  - 4. Boundaries of the Half-Tribe of Manasseh . . . 13:29–33

II. The Settlement West of the Jordan . . . 14:1—19:51
- A. The First Settlement Done at Gilgal . . . 14:1—17:18
  - 1. Method of Setting Tribal Boundaries 14:1–5
  - 2. Boundaries of Judah . . . 14:6—15:63
    - a. Boundaries of Caleb . . . 14:6–15
    - b. Boundaries of the Remainder of Judah . . . 15:1–63
  - 3. Boundaries of the Tribes of Joseph . . . 16:1—17:18
    - a. Boundaries of Joseph . . . 16:1–4
    - b. Boundaries of Ephraim . . . 16:5–10
    - c. Boundaries of the Half-Tribe of Manasseh . . . 17:1–18
- B. The Second Settlement Done at Shiloh . . . 18:1—19:51
  - 1. The Remaining Tribes Move to Shiloh . . . 18:1

CHAPTER 1

Joshua Is Commissioned by God

AFTER the death of Moses the servant of
the LORD, it came to pass that the LORD
spoke to Joshua the son of Nun, Moses'
[R]assistant, saying: Ex. 24:13
2 [R]"Moses My servant is dead. Now therefore, arise, go over this Jordan, you and all
this people, to the land which I am giving to
them—the children of Israel. Deut. 34:5
3 [R]"Every place that the sole of your foot
will tread upon I have given you, as I said to
Moses. Deut. 11:24
4 [R]"From the wilderness and this Lebanon
as far as the great river, the River Euphrates,
all the land of the Hittites, and to the Great
Sea toward the going down of the sun, shall
be your territory. Gen. 15:18
5 "No man shall *be able to* stand before
you all the days of your life; as I was with
Moses, *so* I will be with you. [R]I will not leave
you nor forsake you. Deut. 31:6, 7
6 [R]"Be strong and of good courage, for to
this people you shall [T]divide as an inheritance
the land which I swore to their fathers to give
them. Deut. 31:7, 23 • *give as a possession*
7 "Only be strong and very courageous,
that you may observe to do according to all
the law which Moses My servant commanded
you; do not turn from it to the right hand or
to the left, that you may [T]prosper wherever
you go. *have success* or *act wisely*

8 "This Book of the Law shall not depart
from your mouth, but you shall [T]meditate in
it day and night, that you may observe to do
according to all that is written in it. For then
you will make your way prosperous, and then
you will have good success. *be constantly in*

9 [R]"Have I not commanded you? Be strong
and of good courage; [R]do not be afraid, nor be
dismayed, for the LORD your God *is* with you
wherever you go." Deut. 31:7 • Ps. 27:1

Joshua Commands the Tribes West of the Jordan

10 Then Joshua commanded the officers of
the people, saying,
11 "Pass through the camp and command
the people, saying, 'Prepare provisions for
yourselves, for [R]within three days you will

1:8 Meditating upon God's Word—Joshua had just succeeded Moses in the leadership of the nation Israel. Moses had led the nation for forty years and had the benefit that all the wisdom and culture of Egypt and the king's household could provide. Moses was a seasoned, multi-talented man who had walked closely with God. Joshua, by contrast, was relatively untried. He was assuming an awesome responsibility in taking command of two-and-a-half million people. If anyone needed a formula for success, Joshua did. Likely there were many well-meaning people with all kinds of advice and formulas to help Joshua in the seemingly impossible task that lay ahead. What comfort and assurance it must have been as the LORD (Yahweh) spoke directly to Joshua, assuring him of His presence with him as He had been with Moses (Josh. 1:5), and giving him the key to success—meditating upon God's Word.

Joshua is to meditate upon the Word of God day and night (i.e., at all times), and is promised (1) prosperity and (2) good success in the God-given task that lies ahead. Reading and memorizing God's Word provide the basis for meditating upon God's Word. You meditate upon the Word of God by rehearsing its thoughts over and over in order to understand its implications for the situations of life. Meditating upon the Word of God will guarantee prosperity and success in the new life.

Now turn to Page 242—Deut. 31:12: Obedience to God's Word.

cross over this Jordan, to go in to possess the land which the LORD your God is giving you to possess.' " Deut. 9:1

Joshua Commands the Tribes East of the Jordan

12 And to the Reubenites, the Gadites, and half the tribe of Manasseh Joshua spoke, saying,

13 "Remember [R]the word which Moses the servant of the LORD commanded you, saying, 'The LORD your God is giving you rest and is giving you this land.' Num. 32:20–28

14 "Your wives, your little ones, and your livestock shall remain in the land which Moses gave you on this side of the Jordan. But you shall [T]pass before your brethren armed, all your mighty men of valor, and help them, *cross over ahead of*

15 "until the LORD has given your brethren rest, as He *has given* you, and they also have taken possession of the land which the LORD your God is giving them. [R]Then you shall return to the land of your possession and enjoy it, which Moses the LORD's servant gave you on this side of the Jordan toward the sunrise." Josh. 22:1–4

Joshua Is Accepted by Israel

16 And they answered Joshua, saying, "All that you command us we will do, and wherever you send us we will go.

17 "Just as we heeded Moses in all things, so we will heed you. Only the LORD your God be with you, as He was with Moses.

18 "Whoever rebels against your command and does not heed your words, in all that you command him, shall be put to death. Only be strong and of good courage."

CHAPTER 2

The Faith of Rahab

NOW Joshua the son of Nun sent out two men [R]from [T]Acacia Grove to spy secretly, saying, "Go, view the land, especially Jericho." So they went, and came to the house of a harlot named [R]Rahab, and [T]lodged there. Num. 25:1 • Heb. *Shittim* • Matt. 1:5 • Lit. *lay down*

2 And [R]it was told the king of Jericho, saying, "Behold, men have come here tonight from the children of Israel to search out the country." Josh. 2:22

3 So the king of Jericho sent to Rahab, saying, "Bring out the men who have come to you, who have entered your house, for they have come to search out all the country."

4 [R]Then the woman took the two men and hid them; and she said, "Yes, the men came to me, but I did not know where they *were* from. 2 Sam. 17:19, 20

5 "And it happened as the gate was being shut, when it was dark, that the men went out. Where the men went I do not know; pursue them quickly, for you may overtake them."

6 (But she had brought them up to the roof and hidden them with the stalks of flax, which she had laid in order on the roof.)

7 Then the men pursued them by the road to the Jordan, to the fords. And as soon as those who pursued them had gone out, they shut the gate.

8 So before they lay down, she came up to them on the roof,

9 and said to the men: [R]"I know that the LORD has given you the land, that [R]the terror of you has fallen on us, and that all the inhabitants of the land [R]are fainthearted because of you. Deut. 1:8 • Deut. 2:25; 11:25 • Josh. 5:1

10 "For we have heard how the LORD dried up the water of the Red Sea for you when you came out of Egypt, and what you did to the two kings of the Amorites who *were* on the other side of the Jordan, Sihon and Og, whom you [R]utterly destroyed. Josh. 6:21

11 "And as soon as we heard *these things*, our hearts melted; neither did there remain any more courage in anyone because of you, for [R]the LORD your God, He *is* God in heaven above and on earth beneath. Deut. 4:39

12 "Now therefore, I beg you, swear to me by the LORD, since I have shown you kindness, that you also will show kindness to my father's house, and give me a true token,

13 "and [R]spare my father, my mother, my brothers, my sisters, and all that they have, and deliver our lives from death." Josh. 6:23–25

14 So the men answered her, "Our lives for yours, if none of you tell this business of ours. And it shall be, when the LORD has given us the land, that [R]we will deal kindly and truly with you." Judg. 1:24

15 Then she [R]let them down by a rope through the window, for her house *was* on the city wall; she dwelt on the wall. Acts 9:25

16 And she said to them, "Get to the mountain, lest the pursuers meet you. Hide there three days, until the pursuers have returned. Afterward you may go your way."

17 Then the men said to her: "We *will be* [T]blameless of this oath of yours which you have made us swear, *free from obligation to*

18 [R]"unless, *when* we come into the land, you bind this line of scarlet cord in the window through which you let us down, [R]and unless you [T]bring your father, your mother, your brothers, and all your father's household to your own home. Josh. 2:12 • Josh. 6:23 • Lit. *gather*

19 "So it shall be *that* whoever goes outside the doors of your house into the street, his blood *shall be* on his own head, and we *will be* guiltless. And whoever is with you in the house, [R]his [T]blood *shall be* on our head if a hand is laid on him. 1 Kin. 2:32 • *guilt of bloodshed*

20 "And if you tell this business of ours,
then we will be [T]free from your oath which
you made us swear." *free from obligation to*
21 Then she said, "According to your words,
so *be* it." And she sent them away, and they
departed. And she bound the scarlet cord in
the window.

The Faith of the Spies

22 Then they departed and went to the
mountain, and stayed there three days until
the pursuers returned. The pursuers sought
them all along the way, but did not find *them*.
23 So the two men returned, descended
from the mountain, and crossed over; and
they came to Joshua the son of Nun, and told
him all that had befallen them.
24 And they said to Joshua, "Truly the LORD
has delivered all the land into our hands, for
indeed all the inhabitants of the country are
fainthearted because of us."

CHAPTER 3

The Miraculous Crossing of the Jordan

THEN Joshua rose early in the morning;
and they set out [R]from [T]Acacia Grove and
came to the Jordan, he and all the children of
Israel, and lodged there before they crossed
over. Josh. 2:1 • Heb. *Shittim*
2 So it was, [R]after three days, that the
officers went through the camp; Josh. 1:10, 11
3 and they commanded the people, saying,
"When you see the ark of the covenant of the
LORD your God, and the priests, the Levites,
[T]bearing it, then you shall set out from your
place and go after it. *carrying*
4 [R]"Yet there shall be a space between you
and it, about two thousand cubits by measure. Do not come near it, that you may
know the way by which you must go, for you
have not passed *this* way before." Ex. 19:12
5 And Joshua said to the people, [R]"Sanctify[T] yourselves, for tomorrow the LORD will
do wonders among you." Josh. 7:13 • *Consecrate*
6 Then Joshua spoke to the priests, saying,
[R]"Take up the ark of the covenant and cross
over before the people." So they took up the
ark of the covenant and went before the
people. Num. 4:15
7 And the LORD said to Joshua, "This day I
will begin to [R]magnify you in the sight of all
Israel, that they may know that, as I was
with Moses, *so* I will be with you. Josh. 4:14
8 "You shall command the priests who
bear the ark of the covenant, saying, 'When
you have come to the edge of the water of
the Jordan, you shall stand in the Jordan.' "
9 So Joshua said to the children of Israel,
"Come here, and hear the words of the LORD
your God."
10 And Joshua said, "By this you shall know
that the living God *is* among you, and *that*
He will without fail [R]drive out from before
you the Canaanites and the Hittites and the
Hivites and the Perizzites and the Girgashites
and the Amorites and the Jebusites: Ex. 33:2
11 "Behold, the ark of the covenant of [R]the
Lord of all the earth is crossing over before
you into the Jordan. Zech. 4:14; 6:5
12 "Now therefore, [R]take for yourselves
twelve men from the tribes of Israel, one man
from every tribe. Josh. 4:2, 4
13 "And it shall come to pass, as soon as the
soles of the feet of the priests who bear the
ark of the LORD, the Lord of all the earth,
shall rest in the waters of the Jordan, *that* the
waters of the Jordan shall be cut off, the
waters that come down from upstream, and
they [R]shall stand as a heap." Ps. 78:13; 114:3
14 So it was, when the people set out from
their camp to cross over the Jordan, with the
priests bearing the [R]ark of the covenant
before the people, Acts 7:44, 45
15 and as those who bore the ark came to
the Jordan, and [R]the feet of the priests who
bore the ark dipped in the edge of the water
(for the Jordan overflows all its banks during
the whole time of harvest), Josh. 3:13
16 that the waters which came down from
upstream stood *still, and* rose in a heap very
far away *at Adam, the city that *is* beside
Zaretan. So the waters that went down into
the Sea of the Arabah, [R]the Salt Sea, failed,
and were cut off; and the people crossed over
opposite Jericho. Gen. 14:3
17 Then the priests who bore the ark of the
covenant of the LORD stood firm on dry
ground in the midst of the Jordan; [R]and all
Israel crossed over on dry ground, until all
the people had crossed completely over the
Jordan. Ex. 3:8; 6:1–8; 14:21, 22, 29; 33:1

CHAPTER 4

The Memorial of the Crossing

AND it came to pass, when all the people
had completely crossed over the Jordan,
that the LORD spoke to Joshua, saying:
2 [R]"Take for yourselves twelve men from
the people, one man from every tribe, Josh. 3:12
3 "and command them, saying, 'Take for
yourselves twelve stones from here, out of
the midst of the Jordan, from the place where
the priests' feet stood firm. You shall carry
them over with you and leave them in the
lodging place where you lodge tonight.' "
4 Then Joshua called the twelve men
whom he had appointed from the children of
Israel, one man from every tribe;
5 and Joshua said to them: "Cross over
before the ark of the LORD your God into the
midst of the Jordan, and each one of you take

3:16 Many mss., vss., and Qr. *from Adam*

up a stone on his shoulder, according to the
number of the tribes of the children of Israel,
6 "that this may be a sign among you
when your children ask in time to come,
saying, 'What do these stones *mean* to you?'
7 "Then you shall answer them that [R]the
waters of the Jordan were cut off before the
ark of the covenant of the LORD; when it
crossed over the Jordan, the waters of the
Jordan were cut off. And these stones shall be
for [R]a memorial to the children of Israel
forever." Josh. 3:13, 16 • Num. 16:40
8 And the children of Israel did so, just as
Joshua commanded, and took up twelve
stones from the midst of the Jordan, as the
LORD had spoken to Joshua, according to the
number of the tribes of the children of Israel,
and carried them over with them to the place
where they lodged, and laid them down there.
9 Then Joshua set up twelve stones in the
midst of the Jordan, in the place where
the feet of the priests who bore the ark of the
covenant stood; and they are there to this
day.
10 So the priests who bore the ark stood in
the midst of the Jordan until everything was
finished that the LORD had commanded
Joshua to speak to the people, according to
all that Moses had commanded Joshua; and
the people [T]hastened and crossed over. *hurried*
11 Then it came to pass, when all the people
had completely crossed over, that the [R]ark of
the LORD and the priests crossed over in the
presence of the people. Josh. 3:11; 6:11
12 And [R]the men of Reuben, the men of
Gad, and half the tribe of Manasseh crossed
over armed before the children of Israel, as
Moses had spoken to them. Num. 32:17, 20, 27, 28
13 About forty thousand [T]prepared for war
crossed over before the LORD for battle, to the
plains of Jericho. *equipped*
14 On that day the LORD [R]magnified[T] Joshua
in the sight of all Israel; and they feared him,
as they had feared Moses, all the days of his
life. Josh. 3:7 • *made Joshua great*
15 Then the LORD spoke to Joshua, saying,
16 "Command the priests who bear [R]the ark
of the Testimony to come up from the Jordan."
Ex. 25:16, 22
17 Joshua therefore commanded the priests,
saying, "Come up from the Jordan."
18 And it came to pass, when the priests
who bore the ark of the covenant of the LORD
had come from the midst of the Jordan, *and*
the soles of the priests' feet touched the dry
land, that the waters of the Jordan returned
to their place [R]and flowed over all its banks as
before. Josh. 3:15
19 Now the people came up from the Jordan
on the tenth *day* of the first month, and they
camped [R]in Gilgal on the east border of
Jericho. Josh. 5:9
20 And [R]those twelve stones which they
took out of the Jordan, Joshua set up in
Gilgal. Josh. 4:3; 5:9, 10
21 Then he spoke to the children of Israel,
saying: [R]"When your children ask their fathers
in time to come, saying, 'What *are* these
stones?' Josh. 4:6
22 "then you shall let your children know,
saying, [R]'Israel crossed over this Jordan on
[R]dry land'; Deut. 26:5–9 • Josh. 3:17
23 "for the LORD your God dried up the
waters of the Jordan before you until you had
crossed over, as the LORD your God did to the
Red Sea, [R]which He dried up before us until
we had crossed over, Ex. 14:21
24 "that all the peoples of the earth may
know the hand of the LORD, that it *is*
[R]mighty, that you may [R]fear the LORD your
God [T]forever." 1 Chr. 29:12 • Jer. 10:7 • Lit. *all days*

CHAPTER 5

The Canaanites Fear Israel

SO it was, when all the kings of the Amorites
who *were* on the west side of the
Jordan, and all the kings of the Canaanites
[R]who *were* by the sea, heard that the LORD
had dried up the waters of the Jordan from
before the children of Israel until *we had
crossed over, that their heart melted; and
there was no spirit in them any longer because
of the children of Israel. Num. 13:29

Circumcision Is Practiced

2 At that time the LORD said to Joshua,
"Make flint knives for yourself, and circumcise
the sons of Israel again the second time."
3 So Joshua made flint knives for himself,
and circumcised the sons of Israel at [T]the hill
of the foreskins. Or *Gibeath Haaraloth*
4 And this *is* the reason why Joshua circumcised
them: [R]All the people who came out
of Egypt *who were* males, all the men of war,
had died in the wilderness on the way, after
they had come out of Egypt. Deut. 2:14–16
5 For all the people who came out had
been circumcised, but all the people *who
were* born in the wilderness on the way as
they came out of Egypt had not been circumcised.
6 For the children of Israel walked forty
years in the wilderness, till all the people *who
were* men of war, who came out of Egypt,
were [T]consumed, because they did not obey
the voice of the LORD—to whom the LORD
swore that He would not show them the land
which the LORD had sworn to their fathers
that He would give us, "a land flowing with
milk and honey." *destroyed*
7 So Joshua circumcised [R]their sons *whom*
He raised up in their place; for they were

5:1 Many mss., vss., and Qr. *their crossing over*

uncircumcised, because they had not been
circumcised on the way. Deut. 1:39
8 So it was, when they had finished cir-
cumcising all the people, that they stayed in
their places in the camp [R]till they were
healed. Gen. 34:25
9 Then the LORD said to Joshua, "This day
I have rolled away the reproach of Egypt
from you." Therefore the name of the place is
called [T]Gilgal to this day. Lit. *rolling*

Passover Is Celebrated

10 So the children of Israel camped in Gilgal, and kept the Passover [R]on the fourteenth
day of the month at twilight on the plains of
Jericho. Ex. 12:6
11 And they ate of the produce of the land
on the day after the Passover, unleavened
bread and [T]parched grain, on the very same
day. *roasted*

From Manna to Corn

12 Now [R]the manna ceased on the day after
they had eaten the produce of the land; and
the children of Israel no longer had manna,
but they ate the food of the land of Canaan
that year. Ex. 16:35

The Commander of the Lord Appears

13 And it came to pass, when Joshua was by
Jericho, that he lifted his eyes and looked,
and behold, [R]a Man stood opposite him [R]with
His sword drawn in His hand. And Joshua
went to Him and said to Him, "*Are* You for us
or for our adversaries?" Gen. 18:1, 2 • Num. 22:23
14 So He said, "No, but *as* Commander of
the army of the LORD I have now come." And
Joshua [R]fell on his face to the earth and
[R]worshiped, and said to Him, "What does my
Lord say to His servant?" Gen. 17:3 • Ex. 34:8
15 Then the Commander of the LORD's
army said to Joshua, [R]"Take your sandal off
your foot, for the place where you stand *is*
holy." And Joshua did so. Ex. 3:5

CHAPTER 6

Victory at Jericho

NOW [R]Jericho was securely shut up because of the children of Israel; none
went out, and none came in. Josh. 2:1
2 And the LORD said to Joshua: "See! I
have given Jericho into your hand, its [R]king,
and the mighty men of valor. Deut. 7:24
3 "You shall march around the city, all *you*
men of war; you shall go all around the city
once. This you shall do six days.
4 "And seven priests shall bear seven
[R]trumpets of rams' horns before the ark. But
the seventh day you shall march around the
city [R]seven times, and [R]the priests shall blow
the trumpets. Lev. 25:9 • 1 Kin. 18:43 • Num. 10:8
5 "Then it shall come to pass, when they
make a long *blast* with the ram's horn, *and*
when you hear the sound of the trumpet, that
all the people shall shout with a great shout;
then the wall of the city will fall down flat.
And the people shall go up every man
straight before him."
6 So Joshua the son of Nun called the
priests and said to them, "Take up the ark of
the covenant, and let seven priests bear seven
trumpets of rams' horns before the ark of the
LORD."
7 And he said to the people, "Proceed, and
march around the city, and let him who is
armed advance before the ark of the LORD."
8 So it was, when Joshua had spoken to
the people, that the seven priests bearing the
seven trumpets of rams' horns before the
LORD advanced and blew the trumpets, and
the ark of the covenant of the LORD followed
them.
9 The armed men went before the priests
who blew the trumpets, [R]and the rear guard
came after the ark, while *the priests* continued blowing the trumpets. Num. 10:25
10 Now Joshua had commanded the people,
saying, "You shall not shout or make any
noise with your voice, nor shall *any* word
proceed out of your mouth, until the day I
say to you, 'Shout!' Then you shall shout."
11 So he had the ark of the LORD circle the
city, going around *it* once. Then they came
into the camp and lodged in the camp.
12 And Joshua rose early in the morning,
and the priests took up the ark of the LORD.
13 Then seven priests bearing seven trumpets of rams' horns before the ark of the
LORD went on continually and blew with the
trumpets. And the armed men went before
them. But the rear guard came after the ark
of the LORD, while *the priests* continued
blowing the trumpets.
14 And the second day they marched
around the city once and returned to the
camp. So they did six days.
15 But it came to pass on the seventh day
that they rose early, about the dawning of
the day, and marched around the city seven
times in the same manner. On that day only
they marched around the city seven times.
16 And the seventh time it was so, when the
priests blew the trumpets, that Joshua said to
the people: "Shout, for the LORD has given
you the city!
17 "Now the city shall be doomed by the
LORD to destruction, it and all who *are* in it.
Only Rahab the harlot shall live, she and all
who *are* with her in the house, because [R]she
hid the messengers that we sent. Josh. 2:4, 6
18 "And you, [R]by all means keep *yourselves*
from the accursed things, lest you become
accursed when you take of the accursed

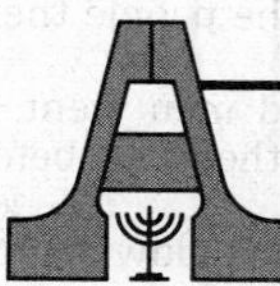

THE CITY OF JERICHO

Located near the Jordan River just north of the Dead Sea, Jericho is the site of one of the oldest continually inhabited cities in the world. Situated seventeen miles northeast of Jerusalem, Jericho has actually been positioned at three different sites within a few miles of one another. Throughout its long history the city has apparently changed location after sieges, earthquakes, and other catastrophes. Present-day Jericho is a small village (er-Riha) on the main highway from Jerusalem to Amman, Jordan.

Known as the "city of palms" (Judg. 3:13) because of the trees that grow in its oasis location, Jericho at 800 feet below sea level sits lower than any other city on earth. Its position at the bottom of a deep gorge contributes to its hot, tropical climate.

Old Testament Jericho was the first city captured by Joshua in his invasion of Canaan during the thirteenth century B.C. Under orders from the Lord, the Israelites marched around the massive walls of the fortified city for six days. On the seventh day the priests blew their trumpets and all the warriors let out a loud shout. The walls came tumbling down, leaving the city exposed to the invaders (Josh. 6).

Excavations of Old Testament Jericho indicate that the site had been occupied for thousands of years before Joshua captured the city. Unfortunately, extensive archaeological excavations there have failed to uncover conclusive evidence of Joshua's conquest, because there are few remains from this period. This lack of evidence is most often attributed to centuries of erosion on the ruin.

New Testament Jericho, located about two miles south of the Old Testament site, is associated with the ministry of Jesus. The rough, hilly road from Jerusalem to Jericho was the setting for Jesus' famous parable of the Good Samaritan (Luke 10:30–37). On visits to Jericho, Jesus healed blind Bartimaeus (Mark 10:46–52) and brought salvation to Zacchaeus (Luke 19:1–10).

Photo by Howard Vos

Mound of Old Testament Jericho with traditional site of the Mount of Temptation in the distance.

things, and make the camp of Israel a curse,
[R]and trouble it. Deut. 7:26 • Josh. 7:1, 12, 25
19 "But all the silver and gold, and vessels
of bronze and iron, *are* [T]consecrated to the
LORD; they [T]shall come into the treasury of
the LORD." *set apart • shall go*
20 So the people shouted when *the priests*
blew the trumpets. And it happened when the
people heard the sound of the trumpet, and
the people shouted with a great shout, that
[R]the wall fell down flat. Then the people went
up into the city, every man straight before
him, and they took the city. Heb. 11:30
21 And they [R]utterly destroyed all that *was*
in the city, both man and woman, young and
old, ox and sheep and donkey, with the edge
of the sword. Deut. 7:2; 20:16, 17
22 But Joshua had said to the two men who
had spied out the country, "Go into the
harlot's house, and from there bring out the
woman and all that she has, [R]as you swore to
her." Josh. 2:12–19
23 And the young men who had been spies
went in and brought out Rahab, [R]her father,
her mother, her brothers, and all that she
had. So they brought out all her relatives and
left them outside the camp of Israel. Josh. 2:13
24 But they burned the city and all that *was*
in it with fire. Only the silver and gold, and
the vessels of bronze and iron, they put into
the treasury of the house of the LORD.
25 And Joshua spared Rahab the harlot, her
father's household, and all that she had. So
[R]she dwells in Israel to this day, because she
hid the messengers whom Joshua sent to spy
out Jericho. [Matt. 1:5]
26 Then Joshua charged *them* at that time,
saying, "Cursed *be* the man before the LORD
who rises up and builds this city Jericho; he
shall lay its foundation with his firstborn, and
with his youngest he shall set up its gates."
27 So the LORD was with Joshua, and his
fame spread throughout all the country.

CHAPTER 7

Defeat at Ai

BUT the children of Israel [T]committed a
trespass regarding the accursed things,
for Achan the son of Carmi, the son of
[T]Zabdi, the son of Zerah, of the tribe of
Judah, took of the accursed things; so the
anger of the LORD burned against the children of Israel. *acted unfaithfully • Zimri,* 1 Chr. 2:6
2 Now Joshua sent men from Jericho to Ai,
which *is* beside Beth Aven, on the east side of
Bethel, and spoke to them, saying, "Go up
and spy out the country." So the men went
up and spied out Ai.
3 And they returned to Joshua and said to
him, "Do not let all the people go up, but let
about two or three thousand men go up and
attack Ai. Do not weary all the people there,
for *the people of Ai are* few."
4 So about three thousand men went up
there from the people, [R]but they fled before
the men of Ai. Lev. 26:17
5 And the men of Ai struck down about
thirty-six men, for they chased them *from*
before the gate as far as Shebarim, and struck
them down on the descent; therefore [R]the[T]
hearts of the people melted and became like
water. Lev. 26:36 • *the people's courage failed*
6 Then Joshua tore his clothes, and fell to
the earth on his face before the ark of the
LORD until evening, *both* he and the elders of
Israel; and they put dust on their heads.
7 And Joshua said, "Alas, Lord [T]GOD, [R]why
have You brought this people over the Jordan at all—to deliver us into the hand of the
Amorites, to destroy us? Oh, that we had
been content, and dwelt on the other side of
the Jordan! Heb. *YHWH, LORD* • Ex. 17:3
8 "O Lord, what shall I say when Israel
turns its [T]back before its enemies? Lit. *neck*
9 "For the Canaanites and all the inhabitants of the land will hear *of it,* and surround
us, and [R]cut off our name from the earth.
Then [R]what will You do for Your great
name?" Deut. 32:26 • Ex. 32:12
10 So the LORD said to Joshua: "Get up!
Why do you lie thus on your face?
11 "Israel has sinned, and they have also
transgressed My covenant which I commanded them. [R]For they have even taken
some of the [T]accursed things, and have both
stolen and deceived; and they have also put *it*
among their own stuff. Josh. 6:17–19 • *devoted*
12 "Therefore the children of Israel could
not stand before their enemies, *but* turned
their backs before their enemies, because
they have become doomed to destruction.
Neither will I be with you anymore, unless
you destroy the accursed from among you.
13 "Get up, [R]sanctify[T] the people, and say,
[R]'Sanctify yourselves for tomorrow, because
thus says the LORD God of Israel: "*There is* an
accursed thing in your midst, O Israel; you
cannot stand before your enemies until you
take away the accursed thing from among
you." Ex. 19:10 • *set apart* • Josh. 3:5
14 'In the morning therefore you shall be
brought according to your tribes. And it shall
be *that* the tribe which [R]the LORD takes shall
come according to families; and the family
which the LORD takes shall come by households; and the household which the LORD
takes shall come man by man. [Prov. 16:33]
15 'Then it shall be *that* he who is taken
with the accursed thing shall be burned with
fire, he and all that he has, because he has
[R]transgressed[T] the covenant of the LORD, and
because he [R]has done a disgraceful thing in
Israel.' " Josh. 7:11 • *overstepped* • Gen. 34:7

16 So Joshua rose early in the morning and brought Israel by their tribes, and the tribe of Judah was taken;

17 and he brought the clan of Judah, and he took the family of the Zarhites; and he brought the family of the Zarhites man by man, and Zabdi was taken.

18 Then he brought his household man by man, and Achan the son of Carmi, the son of Zabdi, the son of Zerah, of the tribe of Judah, [R]was taken. 1 Sam. 14:42

19 So Joshua said to Achan, "My son, I beg you, [R]give glory to the LORD God of Israel, [R]and make confession to Him, and [R]tell me now what you have done; do not hide *it* from me." Jer. 13:16 • Num. 5:6, 7 • 1 Sam. 14:43

20 And Achan answered Joshua and said, "Indeed I have sinned against the LORD God of Israel, and this is what I have done:

21 "When I saw among the spoils a beautiful Babylonian garment, two hundred shekels of silver, and a wedge of gold weighing fifty shekels, I coveted them and took them. And there they are, hidden in the earth in the midst of my tent, with the silver under it."

22 So Joshua sent messengers, and they ran to the tent; and there it was, hidden in his tent, with the silver under it.

23 And they took them from the midst of the tent, brought them to Joshua and to all the children of Israel, and laid them out before the LORD.

24 Then Joshua, and all Israel with him, took Achan the son of Zerah, the silver, the garment, the wedge of gold, his sons, his daughters, his oxen, his donkeys, his sheep, his tent, and all that he had, and they brought them to the Valley of Achor.

25 And Joshua said, [R]"Why have you troubled us? The LORD will trouble you this day." [R]So all Israel stoned him with stones; and they burned them with fire after they had stoned them with stones. Josh. 6:18 • Deut. 17:5

26 Then they raised over him a great heap of stones, still there to this day. So the LORD turned from the fierceness of His anger. Therefore the name of that place has been called the Valley of Achor to this day.

CHAPTER 8

Victory at Ai

THEN the LORD said to Joshua: "Do not be afraid, nor be dismayed; take all the people of war with you, and arise, go up to Ai. See, I have given into your hand the king of Ai, his people, his city, and his land.

2 "And you shall do to Ai and its king as you did to [R]Jericho and its king. Only [R]its spoil and its cattle you shall take as booty for yourselves. Lay an ambush for the city behind it." Josh. 6:21 • Deut. 20:14

3 So Joshua arose, and all the people of war, to go up against Ai; and Joshua chose thirty thousand mighty men of valor and sent them away by night.

4 And he commanded them, saying: "Behold, [R]you shall lie in ambush against the city, behind the city. Do not go very far from the city, but all of you be ready. Judg. 20:29

5 "Then I and all the people who *are* with me will approach the city; and it will come about, when they come out against us as at the first, that we shall flee before them.

6 "For they will come out after us till we have drawn them from the city, for they will say, '*They are* fleeing before us as at the first.' Therefore we will flee before them.

7 "Then you shall rise from the ambush and seize the city, for the LORD your God will deliver it into your hand.

8 "And it will be, when you have taken the city, *that* you shall set the city on fire. According to the commandment of the LORD you shall do. See, I have commanded you."

9 Joshua therefore sent them out; and they went to lie in ambush, and stayed between Bethel and Ai, on the west side of Ai; but Joshua lodged that night among the people.

10 Then Joshua rose up early in the morning and mustered the people, and went up, he and the elders of Israel, before the people to Ai.

11 [R]And all the people of war who *were* with him went up and drew near; and they came before the city and camped on the north side of Ai. Now *there was* a valley between them and Ai. Josh. 8:5

12 So he took about five thousand men and set them in ambush between Bethel and Ai, on the west side of [T]the city. Ai

13 And when they had set the people, all the army that *was* on the north of the city, and its rear guard on the west of the city, Joshua went that night into the midst of the valley.

14 Now it happened, when the king of Ai saw *it*, that the men of the city [T]hastened and rose early and went out against Israel to battle, he and all his people, at an appointed place before the plain. But he [R]did not know that *there was* an ambush against him behind the city. *hurried* • Judg. 20:34

15 And Joshua and all Israel [R]made as if they were beaten before them, and fled by the way of the wilderness. Judg. 20:36

16 So all the people who *were* in Ai were called together to pursue them. And they pursued Joshua and were drawn away from the city.

17 There was not a man left in Ai or Bethel who did not go out after Israel. So they left the city open and pursued Israel.

18 Then the LORD said to Joshua, "Stretch out the spear that *is* in your hand toward Ai, for I will give it into your hand." And Joshua

stretched out the spear that *he had* in his
hand toward the city.
19 So *those in* ambush arose quickly out of
their place; they ran as soon as he had
stretched out his hand, and they entered the
city and took it, and [T]hastened to set the city
on fire. *hurried*
20 And when the men of Ai looked behind
them, they saw, and behold, the smoke of the
city ascended to heaven. So they had no
power to flee this way or that way, and the
people who had fled to the wilderness turned
back on the pursuers.
21 Now when Joshua and all Israel saw that
the ambush had taken the city and that the
smoke of the city ascended, they turned back
and struck down the men of Ai.
22 Then the others came out of the city
against them; so they were *caught* in the
midst of Israel, some on this side and some on
that side. And they struck them down, so
that they let none of them remain or escape.
23 But the king of Ai they took alive, and
brought him to Joshua.
24 And it came to pass when Israel had
made an end of slaying all the inhabitants of
Ai in the field, in the wilderness where they
pursued them, and when they all had fallen
by the edge of the sword until they were
consumed, that all the Israelites returned to
Ai and struck it with the edge of the sword.
25 *So* it was *that* all who fell that day, both
men and women, *were* twelve thousand—all
the people of Ai.
26 For Joshua did not draw back his hand,
with which he stretched out the spear, until
he had [R]utterly destroyed all the inhabitants
of Ai. Josh. 6:21
27 [R]Only the livestock and the spoil of that
city Israel took as booty for themselves,
according to the word of the LORD which He
had [R]commanded Joshua. Num. 31:22, 26 • Josh. 8:2
28 So Joshua burned Ai and made it [R]a heap
forever, a desolation to this day. Deut. 13:16
29 [R]And the king of Ai he hanged on a tree
until evening. [R]And as soon as the sun was
down, Joshua commanded that they should
take his corpse down from the tree, cast it at
the entrance of the gate of the city, and [R]raise
over it a great heap of stones *that remains* to
this day. Josh. 10:26 • Deut. 21:22, 23 • Josh. 7:26; 10:27

Israel Worships the Lord

30 Now Joshua built an altar to the LORD
God of Israel [R]in Mount Ebal, Deut. 27:4–8
31 as Moses the servant of the LORD had
commanded the children of Israel, as it is
written in the [R]Book of the Law of Moses:
"an altar of whole stones over which no man
has wielded *any* [R]iron *tool*." And they offered
on it burnt offerings to the LORD, and sacrificed peace offerings. Ex. 20:25 • Deut. 27:5, 6

Israel Renews the Covenant

32 And there, in the presence of the children of Israel, he wrote on the stones a copy
of the law of Moses, which he had written.
33 Then all Israel, with their elders and
officers and judges, stood on either side of the
ark before the priests, the Levites, who bore
the ark of the covenant of the LORD, the
stranger as well as he who was born among
them. Half of them *were* in front of Mount
Gerizim and half of them in front of Mount
Ebal, [R]as Moses the servant of the LORD had
commanded before, that they should bless
the people of Israel. Deut. 11:29; 27:12
34 And afterward he read all the words of
the law, [R]the blessings and the cursings,
according to all that is written in the [R]Book of
the Law. Deut. 28:2, 15, 45; 29:20, 21; 30:19 • Josh. 1:8
35 There was not a word of all that Moses
had commanded which Joshua did not read
before all the congregation of Israel, with the
women, the little ones, [R]and the strangers
who were living among them. Josh. 8:33

CHAPTER 9

Failure with the Gibeonites

AND it came to pass when [R]all the kings
who *were* on this side of the Jordan, in
the hills and in the lowland and in all the
coasts of [R]the Great Sea toward Lebanon—
[R]the Hittite, the Amorite, the Canaanite, the
Perizzite, the Hivite, and the Jebusite—heard
of it, Josh. 3:10 • Num. 34:6 • Ex. 3:17; 23:23
2 that they gathered together to fight with
Joshua and Israel with one accord.
3 But when the inhabitants of [R]Gibeon
[R]heard what Joshua had done to Jericho and
Ai, Josh. 9:17, 22; 10:2; 21:17 • Josh. 6:27
4 they worked craftily, and went and [T]pre-
tended to be ambassadors. And they took old
sacks on their donkeys, old wineskins torn
and [T]mended, *acted as envoys* • Lit. *tied up*
5 old and patched sandals on their feet,
and old garments on themselves; and all the
bread of their provision was dry *and* moldy.
6 And they went to Joshua, to the camp at
Gilgal, and said to him and to the men of
Israel, "We have come from a far country;
now therefore, make a covenant with us."
7 But the men of Israel said to the Hivites,
"Perhaps you dwell among us; so [R]how can
we make a covenant with you?" Ex. 23:32
8 And they said to Joshua, "We *are* your
servants." And Joshua said to them, "Who
are you, and where do you come from?"
9 So they said to him: [R]"From a very far
country your servants have come, because of
the name of the LORD your God; for we have
[R]heard of His fame, and all that He did in
Egypt, Deut. 20:15 • Josh. 2:9, 10; 5:1

10 "and [R]all that He did to the two kings of
the Amorites who *were* beyond the Jordan—
to Sihon king of Heshbon, and Og king of
Bashan, who was at Ashtaroth. Num. 21:24, 33
11 "Therefore our elders and all the inhabitants of our country spoke to us, saying,
'Take provisions with you for the journey,
and go to meet them, and say to them, "We
are your servants; now therefore, make a
covenant with us." '
12 "This bread of ours we took hot *for* our
provision from our houses on the day we
departed to come to you. But now look, it is
dry and moldy.
13 "And these wineskins which we filled
were new, and see, they are torn; and these
our garments and our sandals have become
old because of the very long journey."
14 Then the men of Israel took some of
their provisions; but they [T]did not ask counsel of the LORD. Lit. *did not inquire at the mouth of*
15 So Joshua [R]made peace with them, and
made a covenant with them to let them live;
and the rulers of the congregation swore to
them. 2 Sam. 21:2
16 And it happened at the end of three days,
after they had made a covenant with them,
that they heard that they *were* their neighbors who dwelt near them.
17 Then the children of Israel journeyed
and came to their cities on the third day. Now
their cities *were* [R]Gibeon, Chephirah, Beeroth, and Kirjath Jearim. Josh. 18:25
18 But the children of Israel did not [T]attack
them, [R]because the rulers of the congregation
had sworn to them by the LORD God of Israel.
And all the congregation murmured against
the rulers. *strike* • Ps. 15:4
19 Then all the rulers said to all the congregation, "We have sworn to them by the LORD
God of Israel; now therefore, we may not
touch them.
20 "This we will do to them: We will let
them live, lest wrath be upon us because of
the oath which we swore to them."
21 And the rulers said to them, "Let them
live, but let them be [R]woodcutters and water
carriers for all the congregation, as the rulers
had [R]promised them." Deut. 29:11 • Josh. 9:15
22 Then Joshua called for them, and he
spoke to them, saying, "Why have you deceived us, saying, 'We *are* very far from you,'
when [R]you dwell near us? Josh. 9:16
23 "Now therefore, you *are* [R]cursed, and
none of you shall be freed from being
slaves—woodcutters and water carriers for
the house of my God." Gen. 9:25
24 So they answered Joshua and said, "Because it was certainly told your servants that
the LORD your God [R]commanded His servant
Moses to give you all the land, and to destroy
all the inhabitants of the land from before
you; therefore [R]we were very much afraid for
our lives because of you, and have done this
thing. Deut. 7:1, 2 • Ex. 15:14
25 "And now, here we *are*, [R]in your hands;
do with us as it seems good and right to do to
us." Gen. 16:6
26 So he did to them, and delivered them
out of the hand of the children of Israel, so
that they did not kill them.
27 And that day Joshua made them [R]wood-
cutters and water carriers for the congregation and for the altar of the LORD, [R]in the
place which He would choose, even to this
day. Josh. 9:21, 23 • Deut. 12:5

CHAPTER 10

Victory over the Amorites

NOW it came to pass when Adoni-Zedek
king of Jerusalem heard how Joshua
had taken Ai and had utterly destroyed it—
[R]as he had done to Jericho and its king, so he
had done to Ai and its king—and how the
inhabitants of Gibeon had made peace with
Israel and were among them, Josh. 6:21
2 that they [R]feared greatly, because Gibeon *was* a great city, like one of the royal
cities, and because it *was* greater than Ai,
and all its men *were* mighty. Ex. 15:14-16
3 Therefore Adoni-Zedek king of Jerusalem sent to Hoham king of Hebron, Piram
king of Jarmuth, Japhia king of Lachish, and
Debir king of Eglon, saying,
4 "Come up to me and help me, that we
may attack Gibeon, for it has made peace
with Joshua and with the children of Israel."
5 Therefore the five kings of the [R]Amo-
rites, the king of Jerusalem, the king of
Hebron, the king of Jarmuth, the king of
Lachish, *and* the king of Eglon, [R]gathered
together and went up, they and all their
armies, and camped before Gibeon and made
war against it. Num. 13:29 • Josh. 9:2
6 And the men of Gibeon sent to Joshua at
the camp [R]at Gilgal, saying, "Do not forsake
your servants; come up to us quickly, save us
and help us, for all the kings of the Amorites
who dwell in the mountains have gathered
together against us." Josh. 5:10; 9:6
7 So Joshua ascended from Gilgal, he and
[R]all the people of war with him, and all the
mighty men of valor. Josh. 8:1
8 And the LORD said to Joshua, [R]"Do not
fear them, for I have delivered them into your
hand; [R]not a man of them shall [R]stand before
you." Josh. 11:6 • Josh. 1:5, 9 • Josh. 21:44
9 Joshua therefore came upon them suddenly, having marched all night from Gilgal.
10 So the LORD routed them before Israel,
killed them with a great slaughter at Gibeon,
chased them along the road that goes [R]to
Beth Horon, and struck them down as far as
[R]Azekah and Makkedah. Josh. 16:3, 5 • Josh. 15:35

11 And it happened, as they fled before
Israel *and* were on the descent of Beth Horon, that the LORD cast down large hailstones
from heaven on them as far as Azekah, and
they died. *There were* more who died from
the hailstones than *those* whom the children
of Israel killed with the sword.
12 Then Joshua spoke to the LORD in the
day when the LORD delivered up the Amorites
before the children of Israel, and he said in
the sight of Israel:

R"Sun, stand still over Gibeon; Hab. 3:11
And Moon, in the Valley of Aijalon."
13 So the sun stood still,
And the moon stopped,
Till the people had revenge
Upon their enemies.

R*Is* this not written in the Book of Jasher? So
the sun stood still in the midst of heaven, and
did not hasten to go *down* for about a whole
day. 2 Sam. 1:18
14 And there has been Rno day like that,
before it or after it, that the LORD heeded the
voice of a man; for Rthe LORD fought for
Israel. Is. 38:7, 8 • Deut. 1:30; 20:4
15 RThen Joshua returned, and all Israel
with him, to the camp at Gilgal. Josh. 10:43
16 But these five kings had fled and hidden
themselves in a cave at Makkedah.
17 And it was told Joshua, saying, "The five
kings have been found hidden in the cave at
Makkedah."
18 So Joshua said, "Roll large stones against
the mouth of the cave, and set men by it to
guard them.
19 "And do not stay *there* yourselves, *but*
pursue your enemies, and attack their rear
ranks; do not allow them to enter their cities,
for the LORD your God has delivered them
into your hand."
20 Then it happened, while Joshua and the
children of Israel made an end of slaying
them with a very great slaughter, till they
had finished, that those who escaped entered
fortified cities.
21 And all the people returned to the camp,
to Joshua at Makkedah, in peace. No one
Tmoved his tongue against any of the children of Israel. *criticized*, lit. *sharpened his tongue*
22 Then Joshua said, "Open the mouth of
the cave, and bring out those five kings to me
from the cave."
23 And they did so, and brought out those
five kings to him from the cave: the king of
Jerusalem, the king of Hebron, the king of
Jarmuth, the king of Lachish, *and* the king
of Eglon.
24 So it was, when they brought out those
kings to Joshua, that Joshua called for all the
men of Israel, and said to the captains of the
men of war who went with him, "Come near,
put your feet on the necks of these kings."
And they drew near and Rput their feet on
their necks. Mal. 4:3
25 Then Joshua said to them, "Do not be
afraid, nor be dismayed; be strong and of
good courage, for thus the LORD will do to all
your enemies against whom you fight."
26 And afterward Joshua struck Tthem and
killed them, and hanged them on five trees;
and they Rwere hanging on the trees until
evening. The kings • Josh. 8:29
27 So it was, at the time of the going down
of the sun *that* Joshua commanded, and they
took them down from the trees, cast them
into the cave where they had been hidden,
and laid large stones against the cave's
mouth, *which remain* until this very day.
28 On that day Joshua took Makkedah, and
struck it and its king with the edge of the
sword. He utterly destroyed *them— all the
people who *were* in it. He let none remain. He
also did to the king of Makkedah Ras he had
done to the king of Jericho. Josh. 6:21
29 Then Joshua passed from Makkedah,
and all Israel with him, to RLibnah; and they
fought against Libnah. Josh. 15:42; 21:13
30 And the LORD also delivered it and its
king into the hand of Israel; he struck it and
all the people who *were* in it with the edge of
the sword. He let none remain in it, but did to
its king as he had done to the king of Jericho.
31 Then Joshua passed from Libnah, and all
Israel with him, to Lachish; and they encamped against it and fought against it.
32 And the LORD delivered Lachish into the
hand of Israel, who took it on the second day,
and struck it and all the people who *were* in it
with the edge of the sword, according to all
that he had done to Libnah.
33 Then Horam king of Gezer came up to
help Lachish; and Joshua struck him and his
people, until he left him none remaining.
34 From Lachish Joshua passed to Eglon,
and all Israel with him; and they encamped
against it and fought against it.
35 They took it on that day and struck it
with the edge of the sword; all the people
who *were* in it he utterly destroyed that day,
according to all that he had done to Lachish.
36 Then Joshua went up from Eglon, and all
Israel with him, to RHebron; and they fought
against it. Josh. 14:13–15; 15:13
37 And they took it and struck it with the
edge of the sword—its king, all its cities, and
all the people who *were* in it; he left none
remaining, according to all that he had done
to Eglon, but utterly destroyed it and all the
people who *were* in it.
38 Then Joshua returned, and all Israel with
him, to Debir; and they fought against it.

10:28 Some ancient authorities read *it*

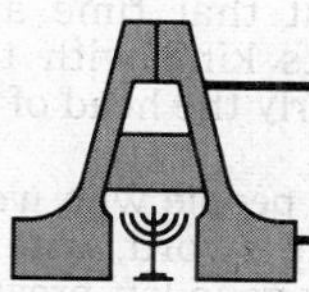

JOSHUA'S VICTORIES

Under Joshua's leadership, the people of Israel entered Canaan about 1405 B.C. to drive out the Canaanites and claim the Land of Promise. A careful study of the military campaigns described in the Book of Joshua shows that Joshua had a carefully planned strategy of conquest. He first established the Israelites in the central part of Canaan, then conducted campaigns into the southern and northern parts of the land to complete the takeover. While these campaigns are described briefly in Joshua 1—11, they probably covered a period of about seven years, from 1405 to 1398. By the time Joshua died (Josh. 24:29), the Israelites had driven most of the Canaanites out of Palestine and divided the land among the twelve tribes of Israel.

Central Campaign

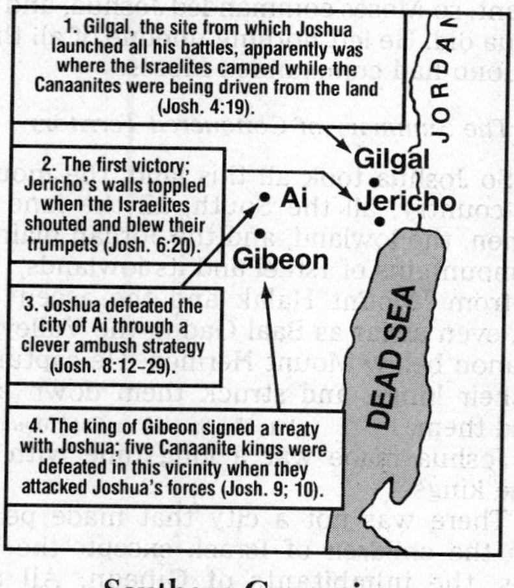

1. Gilgal, the site from which Joshua launched all his battles, apparently was where the Israelites camped while the Canaanites were being driven from the land (Josh. 4:19).

2. The first victory; Jericho's walls toppled when the Israelites shouted and blew their trumpets (Josh. 6:20).

3. Joshua defeated the city of Ai through a clever ambush strategy (Josh. 8:12–29).

4. The king of Gibeon signed a treaty with Joshua; five Canaanite kings were defeated in this vicinity when they attacked Joshua's forces (Josh. 9; 10).

Southern Campaign

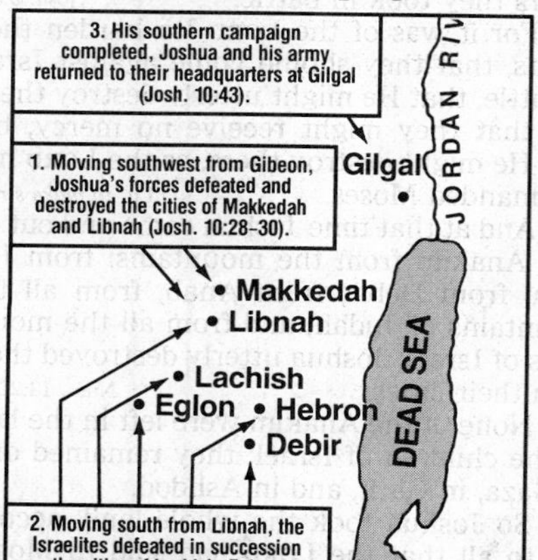

3. His southern campaign completed, Joshua and his army returned to their headquarters at Gilgal (Josh. 10:43).

1. Moving southwest from Gibeon, Joshua's forces defeated and destroyed the cities of Makkedah and Libnah (Josh. 10:28–30).

2. Moving south from Libnah, the Israelites defeated in succession the cities of Lachish, Eglon, Hebron, and Debir (Josh. 10:31–41).

Northern Campaign

Moving his army northward, Joshua met and defeated the combined armies of several Canaanite kings in a fierce battle at the waters of Merom (Josh. 11:1–9).

Joshua sealed his northern victory by destroying the walled city of Hazor, a Canaanite stronghold (Josh. 11:10–12).

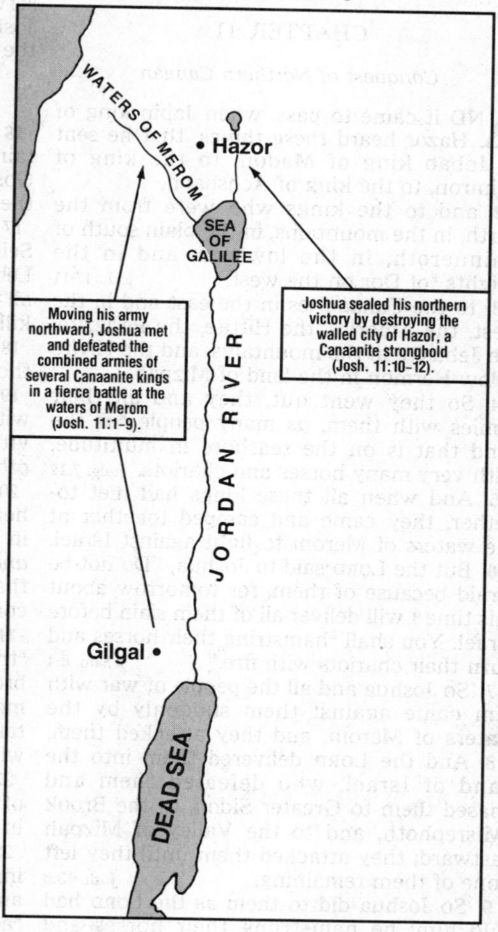

39 And he took it and its king and all its
cities; they struck them with the edge of the
sword and utterly destroyed all the people
who *were* in it. He left none remaining; as he
had done to Hebron, so he did to Debir and its
king, as he had done also to Libnah and its
king.
40 So Joshua conquered all the land: the
mountain country and the [T]South and the
lowland and the wilderness slopes, and all
their kings; he left none remaining, but utterly destroyed all that breathed, as the LORD
God of Israel had commanded. Heb. *Negev*
41 And Joshua conquered them from Kadesh Barnea as far as Gaza, and all the
country of Goshen, even as far as Gibeon.
42 All these kings and their land Joshua
took at one time, [R]because the LORD God of
Israel fought for Israel. Josh. 10:14
43 Then Joshua returned, and all Israel with
him, to the camp at Gilgal.

CHAPTER 11

Conquest of Northern Canaan

AND it came to pass, when Jabin king of
Hazor heard *these things,* that he sent
to Jobab king of Madon, to the king of
Shimron, to the king of Achshaph,
2 and to the kings who *were* from the
north, in the mountains, in the plain south of
Chinneroth, in the lowland, and in the
heights [R]of Dor on the west, Josh. 17:11
3 to the Canaanites in the east and in the
west, the Amorite, the Hittite, the Perizzite,
the Jebusite in the mountains, and the Hivite
below Hermon in the land of Mizpah.
4 So they went out, they and all their
armies with them, *as* many people [R]*as* the
sand that *is* on the seashore in multitude,
with very many horses and chariots. Judg. 7:12
5 And when all these kings had met together, they came and camped together at
the waters of Merom to fight against Israel.
6 But the LORD said to Joshua, "Do not be
afraid because of them, for tomorrow about
this time I will deliver all of them slain before
Israel. You shall [R]hamstring their horses and
burn their chariots with fire." 2 Sam. 8:4
7 So Joshua and all the people of war with
him came against them suddenly by the
waters of Merom, and they attacked them.
8 And the LORD delivered them into the
hand of Israel, who defeated them and
chased them to Greater Sidon, to the Brook
[R]Misrephoth, and to the Valley of Mizpah
eastward; they attacked them until they left
none of them remaining. Josh. 13:6
9 So Joshua did to them as the LORD had
told him: he hamstrung their horses and
burned their chariots with fire.
10 Joshua turned back at that time and
took Hazor, and struck its king with the
sword; for Hazor was formerly the head of all
those kingdoms.
11 And they struck all the people who *were*
in it with the edge of the sword, utterly
destroying *them.* There was none left breathing. Then he burned Hazor with fire.
12 So all the cities of those kings, and all
their kings, Joshua took and struck with the
edge of the sword. He utterly destroyed them,
[R]as Moses the servant of the LORD had commanded. Num. 33:50–56
13 But *as for* the cities that stood on their
[T]mounds, Israel burned none of them, except
Hazor only, *which* Joshua burned. Of ruins
14 And all the spoil of these cities and the
livestock, the children of Israel took as booty
for themselves; but they struck every man
with the edge of the sword until they had
destroyed them, and they left none breathing.
15 As the LORD had commanded Moses his
servant, so Moses commanded Joshua, and so
Joshua did. He left nothing undone of all that
the LORD had commanded Moses.

The Summary of Conquered Territory

16 So Joshua took all this land: the mountain country, all the South, all the land of
Goshen, the lowland, and the Jordan plain—
the mountains of Israel and its lowlands,
17 from [T]Mount Halak and the ascent to
Seir, even as far as Baal Gad in the Valley of
Lebanon below Mount Hermon. He captured
all their kings, and struck them down and
killed them. Lit. *The Smooth* or *Bald Mountain*
18 Joshua made war a long time with all
those kings.
19 There was not a city that made peace
with the children of Israel, except [R]the Hivites, the inhabitants of Gibeon. All *the
others* they took in battle. Josh. 9:3–7
20 For it was of the LORD [T]to harden their
hearts, that they should come against Israel
in battle, that He might utterly destroy them,
and that they might receive no mercy, but
that He might destroy them, as the LORD had
commanded Moses. Lit. *to make strong*
21 And at that time Joshua came and cut off
[R]the Anakim from the mountains: from Hebron, from Debir, from Anab, from all the
mountains of Judah, and from all the mountains of Israel; Joshua utterly destroyed them
with their cities. Num. 13:22, 33
22 None of the Anakim were left in the land
of the children of Israel; they remained only
in Gaza, in Gath, and in Ashdod.
23 So Joshua took the whole land, according to all that the LORD had said to Moses;
and Joshua gave it as an inheritance to Israel
[R]according to their divisions by their tribes.
Then the land rested from war. Num. 26:53

CHAPTER 12

Kings Are Conquered by Moses

THESE *are* the kings of the land whom the children of Israel defeated, and whose land they possessed on the other side of the Jordan toward the rising of the sun, [R]from the River Arnon [R]to Mount Hermon, and all the eastern Jordan plain: Num. 21:24 • Deut. 3:8

2 [R]Sihon king of the Amorites, who dwelt in Heshbon *and* ruled half of Gilead, from Aroer, which is on the bank of the River Arnon, from the middle of that river, even as far as the River Jabbok, *which is* the border of the Ammonites, Deut. 2:24–27

3 and the eastern Jordan plain from the Sea of [T]Chinneroth as far as the [T]Sea of the Arabah (the Salt Sea), the road to Beth Jeshimoth, and [T]southward below the slopes of Pisgah; Galilee • The Dead Sea • Or *Teman*

4 Og king of Bashan and his territory, *who was* of the remnant of the giants, [R]who dwelt at Ashtaroth and at Edrei, Deut. 1:4

5 and reigned over Mount Hermon, [R]over Salcah, over all Bashan, [R]as far as the border of the Geshurites and the Maachathites, and over half of Gilead *as far as* the border of Sihon king of Heshbon. Deut. 3:10 • Deut. 3:14

6 These Moses the servant of the LORD and the children of Israel had conquered; and Moses the servant of the LORD had given it *as* a possession to the Reubenites, the Gadites, and half the tribe of Manasseh.

Kings Are Conquered by Joshua

7 And these *are* the kings of the country [R]which Joshua and the children of Israel conquered on this side of the Jordan, on the west, from Baal Gad in the Valley of Lebanon as far as [T]Mount Halak and the ascent to Seir, which Joshua gave to the tribes of Israel *as* a possession according to their divisions, Josh. 11:17 • Lit. *The Bald Mountain*

8 in the mountain country, in the lowlands, in the *Jordan* plain, in the slopes, in the wilderness, and in the South—[R]the Hittites, the Amorites, the Canaanites, the Perizzites, the Hivites, and the Jebusites: Ex. 3:8; 23:23

9 [R]the king of Jericho, one; [R]the king of Ai, which *is* beside Bethel, one; Josh. 6:2 • Josh. 8:29

10 [R]the king of Jerusalem, one; the king of Hebron, one; Josh. 10:23

11 the king of Jarmuth, one; the king of Lachish, one;

12 the king of Eglon, one; [R]the king of Gezer, one; Josh. 10:33

13 [R]the king of Debir, one; the king of Geder, one; Josh. 10:38, 39

14 the king of Hormah, one; the king of Arad, one;

15 [R]the king of Libnah, one; the king of Adullam, one; Josh. 10:29, 30

16 [R]the king of Makkedah, one; [R]the king of Bethel, one; Josh. 10:28 • Judg. 1:22

17 the king of Tappuah, one; [R]the king of Hepher, one; 1 Kin. 4:10

18 the king of Aphek, one; the king of [T]Lasharon, one; Or *Sharon*

19 the king of Madon, one; [R]the king of Hazor, one; Josh. 11:10

20 the king of [R]Shimron Meron, one; the king of Achshaph, one; Josh. 11:1; 19:15

21 the king of Taanach, one; the king of Megiddo, one;

22 [R]the king of Kedesh, one; the king of Jokneam in Carmel, one; Josh. 19:37; 20:7; 21:32

23 the king of Dor in the heights of Dor, one; the king of the people of Gilgal, one;

24 the king of Tirzah, one—[R]all the kings, thirty-one. Deut. 7:24

CHAPTER 13

Unconquered Parts of Canaan

NOW Joshua [R]was old, advanced in years. And the LORD said to him: "You are old, advanced in years, and there remains very much land yet to be possessed. Josh. 14:10; 23:1, 2

2 [R]"This is the land that yet remains: [R]all the territory of the Philistines and all [R]*that of* the Geshurites, Judg. 3:1–3 • Joel 3:4 • 2 Sam. 3:3

3 [R]"from Sihor, which *is* east of Egypt, as far as the border of Ekron northward (*which* is counted as Canaanite); the [R]five lords of the Philistines—the Gazites, the Ashdodites, the Ashkelonites, the Gittites, and the Ekronites; also [R]the Avites; Jer. 2:18 • Judg. 3:3 • Deut. 2:23

4 "from the south, all the land of the Canaanites, and Mearah that belongs to the Sidonians [R]as far as Aphek, to the border of [R]the Amorites; Josh. 12:18; 19:30 • Judg. 1:34

5 "the land of [R]the [T]Gebalites, and all Lebanon, toward the sunrise, [R]from Baal Gad below Mount Hermon as far as the entrance to Hamath; 1 Kin. 5:18 • Or *Giblites* • Josh. 12:7

6 "all the inhabitants of the mountains from Lebanon as far as the Brook Misrephoth, *and* all the Sidonians—them I will drive out from before the children of Israel; only [T]divide it by lot to Israel as an inheritance, as I have commanded you. *apportion*

7 "Now therefore, divide this land as an inheritance to the nine tribes and half the tribe of Manasseh."

Geographical Boundaries

8 With the other half tribe the Reubenites and the Gadites received their inheritance, [R]which Moses had given them, [R]beyond the Jordan eastward, as Moses the servant of the LORD had given them: Num. 32:33 • Josh. 12:1–6

9 from Aroer which *is* on the bank of the River Arnon, and the town that *is* in the midst of the ravine, [R]and all the plain of Medeba as far as Dibon; Num. 21:30

10 [R]all the cities of Sihon king of the Amorites, who reigned in Heshbon, as far as the
border of the children of Ammon; Num. 21:24, 25
11 [R]Gilead, and the border of the Geshurites
and Maachathites, all Mount Hermon, and all
Bashan as far as Salcah; Josh. 12:5
12 all the kingdom of Og in Bashan, who
reigned in Ashtaroth and Edrei, who remained of the remnant of the giants; for
Moses had defeated and cast out these.
13 Nevertheless the children of Israel [R]did
not drive out the Geshurites or the Maachathites, but the Geshurites and the Maachathites dwell among the Israelites until this
day. Josh. 13:11

Boundaries of Levi

14 Only to the tribe of Levi he had given no
[T]inheritance; the sacrifices of the LORD God
of Israel made by fire *are* their inheritance, as
He said to them. *land as a possession*

Boundaries of Reuben

15 [R]And Moses had given to the tribe of the
children of Reuben *an inheritance* according
to their families. Num. 34:14
16 Their territory was [R]from Aroer, which *is*
on the bank of the River Arnon, [R]and the city
that *is* in the midst of the ravine, [R]and all the
plain by Medeba; Josh. 12:2 • Num. 21:28 • Num. 21:30
17 Heshbon and all its cities that *are* in the
plain: Dibon, Bamoth Baal, Beth Baal Meon,
18 [R]Jahaza, Kedemoth, Mephaath, Num. 21:23
19 Kirjathaim, [R]Sibmah, Zereth Shahar on
the mountain of the valley, Num. 32:38
20 Beth Peor, [R]the slopes of Pisgah, and
Beth Jeshimoth— Deut. 3:17
21 all the cities of the plain and all the
kingdom of Sihon king of the Amorites, who
reigned in Heshbon, whom Moses had struck
with the princes of Midian: Evi, Rekem, Zur,
Hur, and Reba, who *were* princes of Sihon
dwelling in the country.
22 The children of Israel also killed with the
sword Balaam the son of Beor, the soothsayer, among those who were killed by them.
23 And the border of the children of Reuben
was the bank of the Jordan. This *was* the
inheritance of the children of Reuben according to their families, the cities and their
villages.

Boundaries of Gad

24 [R]Moses also had given *an inheritance* to
the tribe of Gad, to the children of Gad
according to their families. Num. 34:14
25 [R]Their territory was Jazer, and all the
cities of Gilead, [R]and half the land of the
Ammonites as far as Aroer, which *is* before
[R]Rabbah, Num. 32:1, 35 • Judg. 11:13, 15 • Deut. 3:11
26 and from Heshbon to Ramath Mizpah
and Betonim, and from Mahanaim to the
border of Debir,
27 and in the valley Beth Haram, Beth Nimrah, Succoth, and Zaphon, the rest of the
kingdom of Sihon king of Heshbon, with
the Jordan as *its* border, as far as the edge [R]of
the [T]Sea of Chinnereth, on the other side of
the Jordan eastward. Num. 34:11 • Sea of Galilee
28 This *is* the inheritance of the children of
Gad according to their families, the cities and
their villages.

Boundaries of the Half-Tribe of Manasseh

29 [R]Moses also gave *an inheritance* to half
the tribe of Manasseh; it was for half the tribe
of the children of Manasseh according to
their families: Num. 34:14
30 Their territory was from Mahanaim, all
Bashan, all the kingdom of Og king of Bashan, and [R]all the towns of Jair which are in
Bashan, sixty cities; Num. 32:41
31 half of Gilead, and Ashtaroth and Edrei,
cities of the kingdom of Og in Bashan, *were*
for the [R]children of Machir the son of Manasseh, for half of the children of Machir according to their families. Num. 32:39, 40
32 These *are the areas* which Moses had
[T]distributed as an inheritance in the plains of
Moab on the other side of the Jordan, by
Jericho eastward. *apportioned*
33 But to the tribe of Levi Moses had given
no inheritance; the LORD God of Israel *was*
their inheritance, as He had said to them.

CHAPTER 14

Method of Setting Tribal Boundaries

THESE *are the areas* which the children of
Israel inherited in the land of Canaan,
[R]which Eleazar the priest, Joshua the son of
Nun, and the heads of the fathers of the
tribes of the children of Israel distributed as
an inheritance to them. Num. 34:16–29
2 Their inheritance *was* by lot, as the LORD
had commanded by the hand of Moses, for
the nine tribes and the half-tribe.
3 For Moses had given the inheritance of
the two tribes and the half-tribe on the other
side of the Jordan; but to the Levites he had
given no inheritance among them.
4 For the children of Joseph were two
tribes: Manasseh and Ephraim. And they
gave no part to the Levites in the land, except
cities to dwell *in*, with their common-lands
for their livestock and their property.
5 [R]As the LORD had commanded Moses, so
the children of Israel did; and they divided
the land. Josh. 21:2

Boundaries of Caleb

6 Then the children of Judah came to
Joshua in Gilgal. And Caleb the son of Jephunneh the Kenizzite said to him: "You
know [R]the word which the LORD said to

Moses the man of God concerning [R]you and
me in Kadesh Barnea. Num. 14:24, 30 • Num. 13:26
7 "I *was* forty years old when Moses the
servant of the LORD sent me from Kadesh
Barnea to spy out the land, and I brought
back word to him as *it was* in my heart.
8 "Nevertheless [R]my brethren who went
up with me made the [T]heart of the people
melt, but I wholly followed the LORD my
God. Num. 13:31, 32 • *courage of the people fail*
9 "So Moses swore on that day, saying,
'Surely the land [R]where your foot has trodden
shall be your inheritance and your children's
forever, because you have wholly followed
the LORD my God.' Deut. 1:36
10 "And now, behold, the LORD has kept me
alive, as He said, these forty-five years, ever
since the LORD spoke this word to Moses
while Israel wandered in the wilderness; and
now, here I am this day, eighty-five years old.
11 "As yet I *am as* strong this day as *I was*
on the day that Moses sent me; just as my
strength *was* then, so now *is* my strength for
war, both for going out and for coming in.
12 "Now therefore, give me this mountain
of which the LORD spoke in that day; for you
heard in that day how the Anakim *were*
there, and *that* the cities *were* great *and*
fortified. [R]It may be that the LORD *will be*
with me, and [R]I shall be able to drive them
out as the LORD said." Rom. 8:31 • Josh. 15:14
13 And Joshua [R]blessed him, [R]and gave
Hebron to Caleb the son of Jephunneh as an
inheritance. Josh. 22:6 • Josh. 10:37; 15:13
14 Hebron therefore became the inheritance
of Caleb the son of Jephunneh the Kenizzite
to this day, because he [R]wholly followed the
LORD God of Israel. Josh. 14:8, 9
15 And [R]the name of Hebron formerly was
Kirjath Arba, *for Arba was* the greatest man
among the Anakim. [R]Then the land had rest
from war. Gen. 23:2 • Josh. 11:23

CHAPTER 15

Boundaries of the Remainder of Judah

'THIS then was the [T]lot of the tribe of the
children of Judah according to their
families: The border of Edom at the [R]Wilder-
ness of Zin southward *was* the extreme
southern boundary. *allotment* • Num. 33:36
2 And their [R]southern border began at the
shore of the Salt Sea, from the bay that faces
southward. Num. 34:3, 4
3 Then it went out to the southern side of
[R]the Ascent of Akrabbim, passed along to
Zin, ascended on the south side of Kadesh
Barnea, passed along to Hezron, went up to
Adar, and went around to Karkaa. Num. 34:4
4 *From there* it passed [R]toward Azmon and
went out to the Brook of Egypt; and the
border ended at the sea. This shall be your
southern border. Num. 34:5
5 The east border *was* the Salt Sea as far
as the mouth of the Jordan. And the border
on the northern quarter *began* at the bay of
the sea at the mouth of the Jordan.
6 The border went up to [R]Beth Hoglah and
passed north of Beth Arabah; and the border
went up [R]to the stone of Bohan the son of
Reuben. Josh. 18:19, 21 • Josh. 18:17
7 Then the border went up toward [R]Debir
from [R]the Valley of Achor, and it turned
northward toward Gilgal, which *is* before the
Ascent of Adummim, which *is* on the south
side of the valley. The border continued
toward the waters of En Shemesh and ended
at [R]En Rogel. Josh. 13:26 • Josh. 7:26 • 2 Sam. 17:17
8 And the border went up by the Valley of
the Son of Hinnom to the southern slope of
the Jebusite *city* (which *is* Jerusalem). The
border went up to the top of the mountain
that *lies* before the Valley of Hinnom westward, which *is* at the end of the Valley [R]of
[T]Rephaim northward. Josh. 18:16 • Lit. *Giants*
9 Then the border went around from the
top of the hill to the fountain of the water of
Nephtoah, and extended to the cities of
Mount Ephron. And the border went around
to Baalah (which *is* Kirjath Jearim).
10 Then the border [T]turned westward from
Baalah to Mount Seir, passed along to the
side of Mount Jearim on the north (which *is*
Chesalon), went down to Beth Shemesh, and
passed on to [R]Timnah. *turned around* • Gen. 38:13
11 And the border went out to the side of
[R]Ekron northward. Then the border went
around to Shicron, passed along to Mount
Baalah, and extended to Jabneel; and the
border ended at the sea. Josh. 19:43
12 The west border *was* [R]the coastline of
the Great Sea. This *is* the boundary of the
children of Judah all around according to
their families. Num. 34:6, 7
13 Now to Caleb the son of Jephunneh he
gave a portion among the children of Judah,
according to the commandment of the LORD
to Joshua, *namely*, Kirjath Arba, which *is*
Hebron (*Arba was* the father of Anak).
14 Caleb drove out [R]the three sons of Anak
from there: [R]Sheshai, Ahiman, and Talmai,
the children of Anak. Judg. 1:10, 20 • Num. 13:22
15 Then [R]he went up from there to the
inhabitants of Debir (formerly the name of
Debir *was* Kirjath Sepher). Judg. 1:11
16 And Caleb said, "He who [T]attacks Kirjath Sepher and takes it, to him I will give
Achsah my daughter as wife." Lit. *strikes*
17 So Othniel the son of Kenaz, the brother
of Caleb, took it; and he gave him [R]Achsah
his daughter as wife. Judg. 1:12
18 Now it was so, when she came *to him*,
that she persuaded him to ask her father for a
field. So she dismounted from *her* donkey,
and Caleb said to her, "What do you wish?"

19 She answered, "Give me a blessing; since
you have given me land in the South, give me
also springs of water." So he gave her the
upper springs and the lower springs.
20 This *was* the inheritance of the tribe of
the children of Judah according to their
families:
21 The cities at the limits of the tribe of the
children of Judah, toward the border of Edom
in the South, were Kabzeel, Eder, Jagur,
22 Kinah, Dimonah, Adadah,
23 Kedesh, Hazor, Ithnan,
24 [R]Ziph, Telem, Bealoth, 1 Sam. 23:14
25 Hazor, Hadattah, Kerioth, Hezron
(which *is* Hazor),
26 Amam, Shema, Moladah,
27 Hazar Gaddah, Heshmon, Beth Pelet,
28 Hazar Shual, Beersheba, Bizjothjah,
29 Baalah, Ijim, Ezem,
30 Eltolad, Chesil, [R]Hormah, Josh. 19:4
31 Ziklag, Madmannah, Sansannah,
32 Lebaoth, Shilhim, Ain, and Rimmon: all
the cities *are* twenty-nine, with their villages.
33 In the lowland: Eshtaol, Zorah, Ashnah,
34 Zanoah, En Gannim, Tappuah, Enam,
35 Jarmuth, Adullam, Socoh, Azekah,
36 Sharaim, Adithaim, Gederah, and Gederothaim: fourteen cities with their villages;
37 Zenan, Hadashah, Migdal Gad,
38 Dilean, Mizpah, [R]Joktheel, 2 Kin. 14:7
39 Lachish, Bozkath, [R]Eglon, Josh. 10:3
40 Cabbon, [T]Lahmas, Kithlish, Or *Lahmam*
41 Gederoth, Beth Dagon, Naamah, and
Makkedah: sixteen cities with their villages;
42 [R]Libnah, Ether, Ashan, Josh. 21:13
43 Jiphtah, Ashnah, Nezib,
44 Keilah, Achzib, and Mareshah: nine
cities with their villages;
45 Ekron, with its towns and villages;
46 from Ekron to the sea, all that *lay* near
[R]Ashdod, with their villages; Josh. 11:22
47 Ashdod with its towns and villages, Gaza
with its towns and villages—as far as [R]the
Brook of Egypt and [R]the Great Sea with *its*
coastline. Josh. 15:4 • Num. 34:6
48 And in the mountain country: Shamir,
Jattir, Sochoh,
49 Dannah, Kirjath Sannah (which *is* Debir),
50 Anab, Eshtemoh, Anim,
51 [R]Goshen, Holon, and Giloh: eleven cities
with their villages; Josh. 10:41; 11:16
52 Arab, Dumah, Eshean,
53 Janum, Beth Tappuah, Aphekah,
54 Humtah, Kirjath Arba (which *is* Hebron), and Zior: nine cities with their villages;
55 Maon, Carmel, Ziph, Juttah,
56 Jezreel, Jokdeam, Zanoah,
57 Kain, Gibeah, and Timnah: ten cities
with their villages;
58 Halhul, Beth Zur, Gedor,
59 Maarath, Beth Anoth, and Eltekon: six
cities with their villages;
60 Kirjath Baal (which *is* Kirjath Jearim)
and Rabbah: two cities with their villages.
61 In the wilderness: Beth Arabah, Middin,
Secacah,
62 Nibshan, the City of Salt, and [R]En Gedi:
six cities with their villages. 1 Sam. 23:29
63 As for the Jebusites, the inhabitants of
Jerusalem, [R]the children of Judah could not
drive them out; [R]but the Jebusites dwell with
the children of Judah at Jerusalem to this
day. 2 Sam. 5:6 • Judg. 1:21

CHAPTER 16

Boundaries of Joseph

THE lot [T]fell to the children of Joseph from
the Jordan, by Jericho, to the waters of
Jericho on the east, to the [R]wilderness that
goes up from Jericho through the mountains
to *Bethel, Lit. *went out* • Josh. 8:15; 18:12
2 then went out *from [R]Bethel to Luz,
passed along to the border of the Archites at
Ataroth, Josh. 18:13
3 and went down westward to the boundary of the Japhletites, as far as the boundary
of Lower Beth Horon to Gezer; and [T]it ended
at the sea. Lit. *the goings out of it were at the sea*
4 So the children of Joseph, Manasseh and
Ephraim, took their inheritance.

Boundaries of Ephraim

5 [R]The border of the children of Ephraim,
according to their families, was *thus*: The
border of their inheritance on the east side
was [R]Ataroth Addar [R]as far as Upper Beth
Horon. Judg. 1:29 • Josh. 18:13 • 2 Chr. 8:5
6 And the border went out toward the sea
on the north side of [R]Michmethath; then the
border went around eastward to Taanath
Shiloh, and passed by it on the east of Janohah. Josh. 17:7
7 Then it went down from Janohah to
Ataroth and Naarah, reached to Jericho, and
came out at the Jordan.
8 The border went out from Tappuah
westward to the Brook Kanah, and [T]it ended
at the sea. This *was* the inheritance of the
tribe of the children of Ephraim according to
their families. Lit. *the goings out of it were at the sea*
9 [R]The separate cities for the children of
Ephraim *were* among the inheritance of the
children of Manasseh, all the cities with their
villages. Josh. 17:9
10 [R]And they did not drive out the Canaanites who dwelt in Gezer; but the Canaanites
dwell among the Ephraimites to this day and
have become forced laborers. Judg. 1:29

16:1 LXX *Bethel Luz*
16:2 LXX *to Bethel* (that is, Luz)

SETTLEMENT OF THE TRIBES

After the conquest of the Promised Land under Joshua, the land formerly occupied by the Canaanites was assigned to the descendants of the sons of Jacob (Josh. 13—21). In a restricted sense, the land stretched from the Jordan River on the east to the Mediterranean Sea on the west. Reuben, Gad, and Manasseh eventually inhabited land east of the Jordan. From north to south, it covered the territory between the Sinai peninsula and the ancient coastal nation of Phoenicia. Land was allotted to the descendants of all Jacob's sons except Levi (Josh. 13:33). Levi's portion went to the two sons of Joseph—Manasseh and Ephraim (Josh. 14:3, 4). The Levites were set apart for priestly service: their portion was to be God Himself (Num. 18:20). However, God provided 48 cities throughout Palestine for use of the Levites (Josh. 21:1–42). This map shows the approximate locations of the tribal settlements, based on the boundaries mentioned in the Book of Joshua.

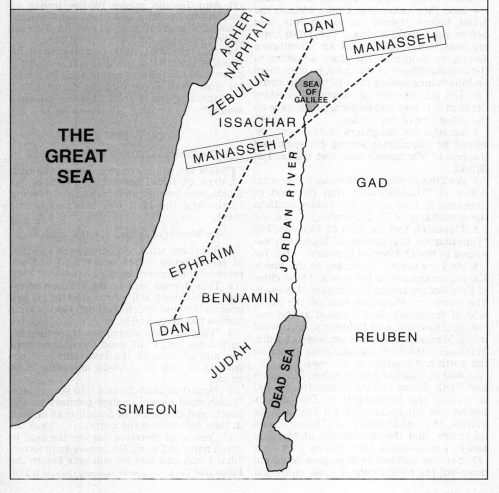

CHAPTER 17

Boundaries of the Half-Tribe of Manasseh

THERE was also a lot for the tribe of Manasseh, for he *was* the firstborn of Joseph: *namely* for [R]Machir the firstborn of Manasseh, the father of Gilead, because he was a man of war; therefore he was given [R]Gilead and Bashan. Gen. 50:23 • Deut. 3:15

2 And there was *a lot* for the rest of the children of Manasseh according to their families: for the children of [T]Abiezer, the children of Helek, the children of Asriel, the children of Shechem, the children of Hepher, and the children of Shemida; these *were* the male children of Manasseh the son of Joseph according to their families. *Jeezer,* Num. 26:30

3 But Zelophehad the son of Hepher, the son of Gilead, the son of Machir, the son of Manasseh, had no sons, but only daughters. And these *are* the names of his daughters: Mahlah, Noah, Hoglah, Milcah, and Tirzah.

4 And they came near before Eleazar the priest, before Joshua the son of Nun, and before the rulers, saying, "The LORD commanded Moses to give us an inheritance among our brothers." Therefore, according to the commandment of the LORD, he gave them an inheritance among their father's brothers.

5 Ten portions fell to [R]Manasseh, besides the land of Gilead and Bashan, which *were* on the other side of the Jordan, Josh. 22:7

6 because the daughters of Manasseh received an inheritance among his sons; and the rest of Manasseh's sons had the land of Gilead.

7 And the territory of Manasseh was from Asher to [R]Michmethath, that *lies* east of Shechem; and the border went along south to the inhabitants of En Tappuah. Josh. 16:6

8 Manasseh had the land of Tappuah, but [R]Tappuah on the border of Manasseh *belonged* to the children of Ephraim. Josh. 16:8

9 And the border descended to the Brook Kanah, southward to the brook. These cities of Ephraim *are* among the cities of Manasseh. The border of Manasseh *was* on the north side of the brook; and it ended at the sea.

10 Southward *it was* Ephraim's, northward *it was* Manasseh's, and the sea was its border. Manasseh's territory was adjoining Asher on the north and Issachar on the east.

11 And in Issachar and in Asher, Manasseh had [R]Beth Shean and its towns, Ibleam and its towns, the inhabitants of Dor and its towns, the inhabitants of En Dor and its towns, the inhabitants of Taanach and its towns, and the inhabitants of Megiddo and its towns—three hilly regions. 1 Kin. 4:12

12 Yet [R]the children of Manasseh could not drive out *the inhabitants of* those cities, but the Canaanites were determined to dwell in that land. Judg. 1:19, 27, 28

13 And it happened, when the children of Israel grew strong, that they put the Canaanites to [R]forced labor, but did not utterly drive them out. Josh. 16:10

14 Then the children of Joseph spoke to Joshua, saying, "Why have you given us *but* one [T]lot and one portion to inherit, since we *are* [R]a great people, inasmuch as the LORD has blessed us until now?" *allotment* • Gen. 48:19

15 So Joshua answered them, "If you *are* a great people, *then* go up to the forest *country* and clear a place for yourself there in the land of the Perizzites and the giants, since the mountains of Ephraim are too confined for you."

16 But the children of Joseph said, "The mountain country is not enough for us; and all the Canaanites who dwell in the land of the valley have chariots of iron, *both those* who *are* of Beth Shean and its towns and *those* who *are* of the Valley of Jezreel."

17 And Joshua spoke to the house of Joseph—to Ephraim and Manasseh—saying, "You *are* a great people and have great power; you shall not have one lot *only,*

18 "but the mountain country shall be yours. Although it *is* wooded, you shall cut it down, and its [T]farthest extent shall be yours; for you shall drive out the Canaanites, [R]though they have iron chariots *and* are strong." Lit. *goings out* • Deut. 20:1

CHAPTER 18

The Remaining Tribes Move to Shiloh

THEN the whole congregation of the children of Israel assembled together [R]at Shiloh, and [R]set up the tabernacle of meeting there. And the land was subdued before them. Jer. 7:12 • Judg. 18:31

New Method of Setting Tribal Boundaries

2 But there remained among the children of Israel seven tribes which had not yet received their inheritance.

3 Then Joshua said to the children of Israel: [R]"How long will you neglect to go and possess the land which the LORD God of your fathers has given you? Judg. 18:9

4 "Pick out from among you three men for *each* tribe, and I will send them; they shall rise and go through the land, survey it according to their inheritance, and come *back* to me.

5 "And they shall divide it into seven parts. [R]Judah shall remain in their territory on the south, and the house of Joseph shall remain in their territory on the north. Josh. 15:1

6 "You shall therefore [T]survey the land in seven parts and bring *the survey* here to me, [R]that I may cast lots for you here before the LORD our God. *describe in writing* • Josh. 14:2; 18:10

7 "But the Levites have no part among
you, for the priesthood of the LORD *is* their
inheritance. And Gad, Reuben, and half the
tribe of Manasseh have received their inheritance beyond the Jordan on the east, which
Moses the servant of the LORD gave them."
8 Then the men arose to go away; and
Joshua charged those who went to [T]survey
the land, saying, "Go, walk [R]through the
land, survey it, and come back to me, that I
may cast lots for you here before the LORD in
Shiloh." *describe in writing* • Gen. 13:17
9 So the men went, passed through the
land, and wrote the survey in a book in seven
parts by cities; and they came to Joshua at
the camp in Shiloh.
10 Then Joshua cast [R]lots for them in Shiloh
before the LORD, and there [R]Joshua divided
the land to the children of Israel according to
their [T]divisions. Acts 13:19 • Num. 34:16–29 • *portions*

Boundaries of Benjamin

11 [R]Now the lot of the tribe of the children
of Benjamin came up according to their
families, and the territory of their lot came
out between the children of Judah and the
children of Joseph. Judg. 1:21
12 [R]Their border on the north side began at
the Jordan, and the border went up to the
side of Jericho on the north, and went up
through the mountains westward; it ended at
the Wilderness of Beth Aven. Josh. 16:1
13 The border went over from there toward
Luz, to the side of Luz (which *is* Bethel)
southward; and the border descended to
Ataroth Addar, near the hill that *lies* on the
south side [R]of Lower Beth Horon. Josh. 16:3
14 Then the border extended *from there*
around the west side to the south, from the
hill that *lies* before Beth Horon southward;
and it ended at [R]Kirjath Baal (which *is* Kirjath Jearim), a city of the children of Judah.
This *was* the west side. Josh. 15:9
15 The south side *began* at the end of Kirjath Jearim, and the border extended on the
west and went out to [R]the spring of the
waters of Nephtoah. Josh. 15:9
16 Then the border came down to the end of
the mountain that *lies* before [R]the Valley
of the Son of Hinnom, which *is* in the Valley
of the [T]Rephaim on the north, descended to
the Valley of Hinnom, to the side of the
Jebusite *city* on the south, and descended to
[R]En Rogel. Josh. 15:8 • Lit. *Giants* • Josh. 15:8
17 And it went around from the north, went
out to En Shemesh, and extended toward
Geliloth, which is before the Ascent of Adummim, and descended to [R]the stone of Bohan
the son of Reuben. Josh. 15:6
18 Then it passed along toward the north
side of Arabah, and went down to Arabah.
19 And the border passed along to the north
side of Beth Hoglah; then [T]the border ended
at the north bay at the Salt Sea, at the south
end of the Jordan. This *was* the southern
boundary. Lit. *the goings out of the border were*
20 The Jordan was its border on the east
side. This *was* the inheritance of the children
of Benjamin, according to its boundaries all
around, according to their families.
21 Now the cities of the tribe of the children
of Benjamin, according to their families, were
Jericho, Beth Hoglah, Emek Keziz,
22 Beth Arabah, Zemaraim, Bethel,
23 Avim, Parah, Ophrah,
24 Chephar Haammoni, Ophni, and Gaba:
twelve cities with their villages;
25 Gibeon, [R]Ramah, Beeroth, Jer. 31:15
26 Mizpah, Chephirah, Mozah,
27 Rekem, Irpeel, Taralah,
28 Zelah, Eleph, [R]Jebus (which *is* Jerusalem), Gibeath, *and* Kirjath: fourteen cities
with their villages. This was the inheritance
of the children of Benjamin according to their
families. Josh. 15:8, 63

CHAPTER 19

Boundaries of Simeon

THE [R]second lot came out for Simeon, for
the tribe of the children of Simeon according to their families. [R]And their inheritance was within the inheritance of the children of Judah. Judg. 1:3 • Josh. 19:9
2 [R]They had in their inheritance Beersheba
(Sheba), Moladah, 1 Chr. 4:28
3 Hazar Shual, Balah, Ezem,
4 Eltolad, Bethul, Hormah,
5 Ziklag, Beth Marcaboth, Hazar Susah,
6 Beth Lebaoth, and Sharuhen: thirteen
cities and their villages;
7 Ain, Rimmon, Ether, and Ashan: four
cities and their villages;
8 and all the villages that *were* all around
these cities as far as Baalath Beer, [R]Ramah of
the South. This *was* the inheritance of the
tribe of the children of Simeon according to
their families. 1 Sam. 30:27
9 The inheritance of the children of Simeon *was included* in the portion of the children of Judah, for the portion of the children
of Judah was too much for them. Therefore
the children of Simeon had *their* inheritance
within the inheritance of that people.

Boundaries of Zebulun

10 The third lot came out for the children of
Zebulun according to their families, and the
border of their inheritance was as far as
Sarid.
11 [R]Their border went toward the west and
to Maralah, went to Dabbasheth, and extended along the brook that is [R]east of Jokneam. Gen. 49:13 • Josh. 12:22
12 Then from Sarid it went eastward toward
the sunrise along the border of Chisloth
Tabor, and went out toward [R]Daberath, bypassing Japhia. 1 Chr. 6:72

13 And from there it passed along on the
east of [R]Gath Hepher, toward Eth Kazin, and
extended to Rimmon, which borders on
Neah. 2 Kin. 14:25
14 Then the border went around it on the
north side of Hannathon, and [T]it ended in the
Valley of Jiphthah El. Lit. *the goings out of it were*
15 Included were Kattath, Nahallal, Shim-
ron, Idalah, and Bethlehem: twelve cities
with their villages.
16 This *was* the inheritance of the children
of Zebulun according to their families, these
cities with their villages.

Boundaries of Issachar

17 The fourth lot came out to Issachar, for
the children of Issachar according to their
families.
18 And their territory went to Jezreel, and
included Chesulloth, Shunem,
19 Haphraim, Shion, Anaharath,
20 Rabbith, Kishion, Abez,
21 Remeth, En Gannim, En Haddah, and
Beth Pazzez.
22 And the border reached to Tabor, Shahazimah, and [R]Beth Shemesh; their border
ended at the Jordan: sixteen cities with their
villages. Josh. 15:10
23 This *was* the inheritance of the tribe of
the children of Issachar according to their
families, the cities and their villages.

Boundaries of Asher

24 [R]The fifth lot came out for the tribe of
the children of Asher according to their
families. Judg. 1:31, 32
25 And their territory included Helkath,
Hali, Beten, Achshaph,
26 Alammelech, Amad, and Mishal; it
reached to [R]Mount Carmel westward, along
the Brook Shihor Libnath. Jer. 46:18
27 It turned toward the sunrise to Beth
Dagon; and it reached to Zebulun and to the
Valley of Jiphthah El, then northward beyond Beth Emek and Neiel, bypassing [R]Cabul
which was on the left, 1 Kin. 9:13
28 including Ebron, Rehob, Hammon, and
Kanah, [R]as far as Greater Sidon. Judg. 1:31
29 And the border turned to Ramah and to
the fortified city of Tyre; then the border
turned to Hosah, and ended at the sea by the
region of [R]Achzib. Judg. 1:31
30 Also Ummah, Aphek, and Rehob *were
included*: twenty-two cities with their villages.
31 This *was* the inheritance of the tribe of
the children of Asher according to their
families, these cities with their villages.

Boundaries of Naphtali

32 [R]The sixth lot came out to the children of
Naphtali, for the children of Naphtali according to their families. Judg. 1:33
33 And their border began at Heleph, en-
closing the territory from the terebinth tree
in Zaanannim, Adami Nekeb, and Jabneel, as
far as Lakkum; it ended at the Jordan.
34 [R]From Heleph the border extended westward to Aznoth Tabor, and went out from
there toward Hukkok; it adjoined Zebulun on
the south side and Asher on the west side,
and ended at Judah by the Jordan toward the
sunrise. Deut. 33:23
35 And the fortified cities *are* Ziddim, Zer,
Hammath, Rakkath, Chinnereth,
36 Adamah, Ramah, Hazor,
37 [R]Kedesh, Edrei, En Hazor, Josh. 20:7
38 Iron, Migdal El, Horem, Beth Anath, and
Beth Shemesh: nineteen cities with their
villages.
39 This *was* the inheritance of the tribe of
the children of Naphtali according to their
families, the cities and their villages.

Boundaries of Dan

40 [R]The seventh lot came out for the tribe of
the children of Dan according to their families. Judg. 1:34–36
41 And the territory of their inheritance
was Zorah, [R]Eshtaol, Ir Shemesh, Josh. 15:33
42 [R]Shaalabbin, Aijalon, Jethlah, Judg. 1:35
43 Elon, Timnah, [R]Ekron, Judg. 1:18
44 Eltekeh, Gibbethon, Baalath,
45 Jehud, Bene Berak, Gath Rimmon,
46 Me Jarkon, and Rakkon, with the region
[T]near [T]Joppa. *over against* • Heb. *Japho*
47 And the [R]border of the children of Dan
went beyond these, because the children of
Dan went up to fight against Leshem and
took it; and they struck it with the edge of
the sword, took possession of it, and dwelt in
it. They called Leshem, [R]Dan, after the name
of Dan their father. Judg. 18 • Judg. 18:29
48 This *is* the inheritance of the tribe of the
children of Dan according to their families,
these cities with their villages.

Boundaries of Joshua

49 When they had made an end of dividing
the land as an inheritance according to their
borders, the children of Israel gave an inheritance among them to Joshua the son of Nun.
50 According to the word of the LORD they
gave him the city which he asked for, Tim-
nath Serah in the mountains of Ephraim; and
he built the city and dwelt in it.
51 These *were* the inheritances which Eleazar the priest, Joshua the son of Nun, and the
heads of the fathers of the tribes of the
children of Israel divided as an inheritance by
lot in Shiloh before the LORD, at the door of
the tabernacle of meeting. So they made an
end of dividing the country.

CHAPTER 20

Six Cities of Refuge

THE LORD also spoke to Joshua, saying,

2 "Speak to the children of Israel, saying: 'Appoint for yourselves cities of refuge, of which I spoke to you through Moses,

3 'that the slayer who kills *any* person accidentally *or* unintentionally may flee there; and they shall be your refuge from the avenger of blood.

4 'And when he flees to one of those cities, and stands at the entrance of the gate of the city, and [T]declares his case in the hearing of the elders of that city, they shall take him into the city as one of them, and give him a place, that he may dwell among them. *states*

5 'Then if the avenger of blood pursues him, they shall not deliver the slayer into his hand, because he struck his neighbor unintentionally, but did not hate him beforehand.

6 'And he shall dwell in that city until he stands before the congregation for judgment, *and* until the death of the one who is high priest in those days. Then the slayer may return and come to his own city and his own house, to the city from which he fled.' "

7 So they appointed Kedesh in Galilee, in the mountains of Naphtali, [R]Shechem in the mountains of Ephraim, and [R]Kirjath Arba (which *is* Hebron) in [R]the mountains of Judah. Josh. 21:21 • Josh. 14:15; 21:11, 13 • Luke 1:39

8 And on the other side of the Jordan, by Jericho eastward, they assigned [R]Bezer in the wilderness on the plain, from the tribe of Reuben, [R]Ramoth in Gilead, from the tribe of Gad, and [R]Golan in Bashan, from the tribe of Manasseh. Deut. 4:43 • Josh. 21:38 • Josh. 21:27

9 [R]These were the cities appointed for all the children of Israel and for the stranger who [T]sojourned among them, that whoever killed *any* person accidentally might flee there, and not die by the hand of the avenger of blood [R]until he stood before the congregation. Num. 35:15 • Resided temporarily • Josh. 20:6

CHAPTER 21

The Families to Be Assigned Cities
1 Chr. 6:54–81

NOW the heads of the fathers of the [R]Levites came near to [R]Eleazar the priest, to Joshua the son of Nun, and to the heads of the fathers of the tribes of the children of Israel. Num. 35:1–8 • Josh. 14:1; 17:4

2 And they spoke to them at [R]Shiloh in the land of Canaan, saying, [R]"The LORD commanded through Moses to give us cities to dwell in, with their common-lands for our livestock." Josh. 18:1 • Num. 35:2

3 So the children of Israel gave to the Levites from their inheritance, at the commandment of the LORD, these cities and their common-lands:

4 Now the lot came out for the families of the Kohathites. And [R]the children of Aaron the priest, *who were* of the Levites, [R]had thirteen cities by lot from the tribe of Judah, from the tribe of Simeon, and from the tribe of Benjamin. Josh. 21:8, 19 • Josh. 19:51

5 [R]The rest of the children of Kohath had ten cities by lot from the families of the tribe of Ephraim, from the tribe of Dan, and from the half-tribe of Manasseh. Josh. 21:20

6 And [R]the children of Gershon had thirteen cities by lot from the families of the tribe of Issachar, from the tribe of Asher, from the tribe of Naphtali, and from the half-tribe of Manasseh in Bashan. Josh. 21:27

7 [R]The children of Merari according to their families had twelve cities from the tribe of Reuben, from the tribe of Gad, and from the tribe of Zebulun. Josh. 21:34

Cities for the Kohathites

8 [R]And the children of Israel gave these cities with their common-lands by lot to the Levites, [R]as the LORD had commanded by the hand of Moses. Josh. 21:3 • Num. 35:2

9 So they gave from the tribe of the children of Judah and from the tribe of the children of Simeon these cities which are [T]mentioned *here* by name, Lit. *called*

10 which were for the children of Aaron, one of the families of the Kohathites, *who were* of the children of Levi; for the lot was theirs first.

11 And they gave them [T]Kirjath Arba (*Arba being* the father of Anak), which *is* Hebron, in the mountains of Judah, with the common-land surrounding it. Lit. *City of Arba*

12 But [R]the fields of the city and its villages they gave to Caleb the son of Jephunneh as his possession. Josh. 14:14

13 Thus to the children of Aaron the priest they gave [R]Hebron with its common-land (a city of refuge for the slayer), [R]Libnah with its common-land, Josh. 15:54; 20:2, 7 • Josh. 15:42

14 [R]Jattir with its common-land, [R]Eshtemoa with its common-land, Josh. 15:48 • Josh. 15:50

15 [R]Holon with its common-land, [R]Debir with its common-land, 1 Chr. 6:58 • Josh. 15:49

16 [R]Ain with its common-land, [R]Juttah with its common-land, and [R]Beth Shemesh with its common-land: nine cities from those two tribes; 1 Chr. 6:59 • Josh. 15:55 • Josh. 15:10

17 and from the tribe of Benjamin, [R]Gibeon with its common-land, [R]Geba with its common-land, Josh. 18:25 • Josh. 18:24

18 Anathoth with its common-land, and Almon with its common-land: four cities.

19 All the cities of the children of Aaron, the priests, *were* thirteen cities with their common-lands.

CITIES OF REFUGE

Six cities of refuge were designated throughout Israel in Old Testament times to provide a haven for people who killed other persons by accident. Protection like this was necessary because of the "avenger of blood," the relative who considered it his duty to slay the killer. Eligibility for refuge was determined by a judge. For convenience, three of the cities were located on either side of the Jordan River.

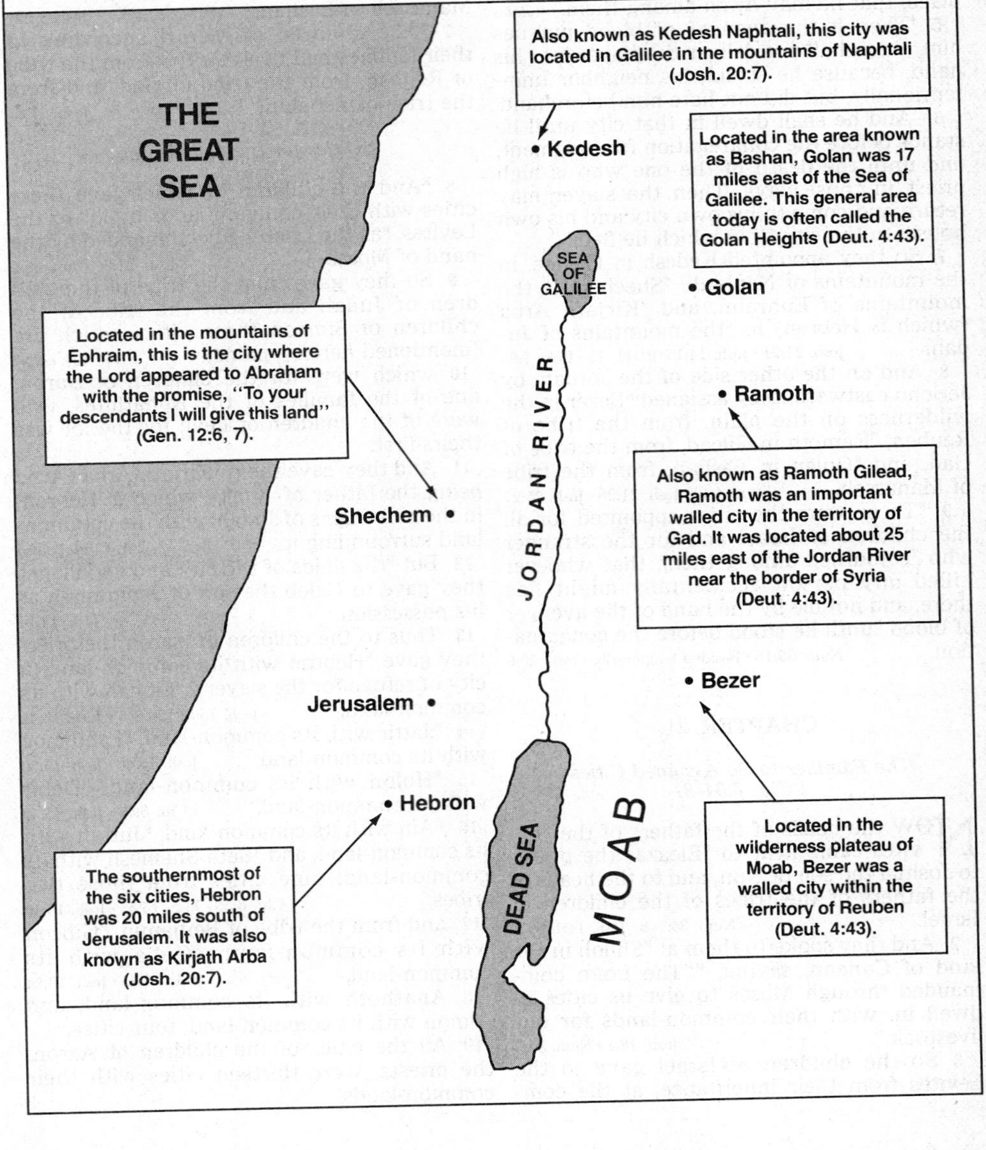

THE GREAT SEA

Also known as Kedesh Naphtali, this city was located in Galilee in the mountains of Naphtali (Josh. 20:7).

• Kedesh

Located in the area known as Bashan, Golan was 17 miles east of the Sea of Galilee. This general area today is often called the Golan Heights (Deut. 4:43).

SEA OF GALILEE

• Golan

Located in the mountains of Ephraim, this is the city where the Lord appeared to Abraham with the promise, "To your descendants I will give this land" (Gen. 12:6, 7).

JORDAN RIVER

• Ramoth

Also known as Ramoth Gilead, Ramoth was an important walled city in the territory of Gad. It was located about 25 miles east of the Jordan River near the border of Syria (Deut. 4:43).

Shechem •

• Bezer

Jerusalem •

• Hebron

MOAB

DEAD SEA

The southernmost of the six cities, Hebron was 20 miles south of Jerusalem. It was also known as Kirjath Arba (Josh. 20:7).

Located in the wilderness plateau of Moab, Bezer was a walled city within the territory of Reuben (Deut. 4:43).

20 [R]And the families of the children of Kohath, the Levites, the rest of the children of Kohath, even they had the cities of their [T]lot from the tribe of Ephraim. 1 Chr. 6:66 • *allotment*
21 For they gave them [R]Shechem with its common-land in the mountains of Ephraim (a city of refuge for the slayer), [R]Gezer with its common-land, Josh. 20:7 • Judg. 1:29
22 Kibzaim with its common-land, and Beth Horon with its common-land: four cities;
23 and from the tribe of Dan, Eltekeh with its common-land, Gibbethon with its common-land,
24 Aijalon with its common-land, *and* Gath Rimmon with its common-land: four cities;
25 and from the half-tribe of Manasseh, Tanach with its common-land and Gath Rimmon with its common-land: two cities.
26 All the ten cities with their common-lands were for the rest of the families of the children of Kohath.

Cities for the Gershonites

27 [R]And to the children of Gershon, of the families of the Levites, from the *other* half-tribe of Manasseh, *they gave* [R]Golan in Bashan with its common-land (a city of refuge for the slayer), and Be Eshterah with its common-land: two cities; 1 Chr. 6:71 • Josh. 20:8
28 and from the tribe of Issachar, Kishion with its common-land, Daberath with its common-land,
29 Jarmuth with its common-land, *and* En Gannim with its common-land: four cities;
30 and from the tribe of Asher, Mishal with its common-land, Abdon with its common-land,
31 Helkath with its common-land, and Rehob with its common-land: four cities;
32 and from the tribe of Naphtali, [R]Kedesh in Galilee with its common-land (a city of refuge for the slayer), Hammoth Dor with its common-land, and Kartan with its common-land: three cities. Josh. 20:7
33 All the cities of the Gershonites according to their families *were* thirteen cities with their common-lands.

Cities for the Merarites

34 [R]And to the families of the children of Merari, the rest of the Levites, from the tribe of Zebulun, Jokneam with its common-land, Kartah with its common-land, 1 Chr. 6:77–81
35 Dimnah with its common-land, *and* Nahalal with its common-land: four cities;
36 and from the tribe of Reuben, [R]Bezer with its common-land, Jahaz with its common-land, Josh. 20:8
37 Kedemoth with its common-land, and Mephaath with its common-land: four cities;
38 and from the tribe of Gad, [R]Ramoth in Gilead with its common-land (a city of refuge for the slayer), Mahanaim with its common-land, Josh. 20:8
39 Heshbon with its common-land, *and* Jazer with its common-land: four cities in all.
40 So all the cities for the children of Merari according to their families, the rest of the families of the Levites, were *by* their lot twelve cities.
41 All the cities of the Levites within the possession of the children of Israel *were* forty-eight cities with their common-lands.
42 Every one of these cities had its common-land surrounding it; thus *were* all these cities.

The Settlement of Israel Is Completed

43 So the LORD gave to Israel [R]all the land of which He had sworn to give to their fathers, and they [R]took possession of it and dwelt in it. Gen. 12:7; 26:3, 4; 28:4, 13, 14 • Num. 33:53
44 The LORD gave them rest all around, according to all that He had sworn to their fathers. And [R]not a man of all their enemies stood against them; the LORD delivered all their enemies into their hand. Deut. 7:24
45 [R]Not a word failed of any good thing which the LORD had spoken to the house of Israel. All came to pass. Josh. 23:14

CHAPTER 22

Joshua Challenges the Eastern Tribes

THEN Joshua called the Reubenites, the Gadites, and half the tribe of Manasseh,
2 and said to them: "You have kept all that Moses the servant of the LORD commanded you, [R]and have obeyed my voice in all that I commanded you. Josh. 1:12–18
3 "You have not [T]left your brethren these many days, up to this day, but have kept the charge of the commandment of the LORD your God. *forsaken*
4 "And now the LORD your God has given rest to your brethren, as He promised them; now therefore, return and go to your tents *and* to the land of your possession, [R]which Moses the servant of the LORD gave you on the other side of the Jordan. Num. 32:33
5 "But [T]take diligent heed to do the commandment and the law which Moses the servant of the LORD commanded you, to love the LORD your God, to walk in all His ways, to keep His commandments, to hold fast to Him, and to serve Him with all your heart and with all your soul." *be very careful to do*
6 So Joshua [R]blessed them and sent them away, and they went to their tents. 2 Sam. 6:18
7 Now to half the tribe of Manasseh Moses had given a possession in Bashan, [R]but to the *other* half of it Joshua gave *a possession* among their brethren on this side of the Jordan, westward. And indeed, when Joshua

sent them away to their tents, he blessed
them, Josh. 17:1-13
8 and spoke to them, saying, "Return with
much riches to your tents, with very much
livestock, with silver, with gold, with bronze,
with iron, and with very much clothing.
[R]Divide the [T]spoil of your enemies with your
brethren." 1 Sam. 30:24 • *plunder*
9 So the children of Reuben, the children
of Gad, and half the tribe of Manasseh returned, and departed from the children of
Israel at Shiloh, which *is* in the land of
Canaan, to go to [R]the country of Gilead, to
the land of their possession, which they
possessed according to the word of the LORD
by the hand of Moses. Num. 32:1, 26, 29

Construction of the Altar

10 And when they came to the region of the
Jordan which *is* in the land of Canaan, the
children of Reuben, the children of Gad, and
half the tribe of Manasseh built an altar there
by the Jordan—a great, impressive altar.

Misunderstanding of the Altar

11 Now the children of Israel [R]heard *some-*
one say, "Behold, the children of Reuben, the
children of Gad, and half the tribe of Manasseh have built an altar on the [T]frontier of the
land of Canaan, in the region of the Jordan,
on the side *occupied by* the children of Israel." Judg. 20:12, 13 • Lit. *front*
12 And when the children of Israel heard *of*
it, [R]the whole congregation of the children of
Israel gathered together at Shiloh to go to
war against them. Josh. 18:1
13 Then the children of Israel [R]sent [R]Phine-
has the son of Eleazar the priest to the
children of Reuben, to the children of Gad,
and to half the tribe of Manasseh, into the
land of Gilead, Deut. 13:14 • Ex. 6:25
14 and with him ten rulers, one ruler each
from the chief house of every tribe of Israel;
and each one *was* the head of the house of
his father among the divisions of Israel.
15 Then they came to the children of Reuben, to the children of Gad, and to half the
tribe of Manasseh, to the land of Gilead, and
they spoke with them, saying,
16 "Thus says the whole congregation of
the LORD: 'What [R]treachery[T] *is* this that you
have committed against the God of Israel, to
turn away this day from following the LORD,
in that you have built for yourselves an altar,
[R]that you might rebel this day against the
LORD? Deut. 12:5-14 • *unfaithful act* • Lev. 17:8, 9
17 '*Is* the iniquity [R]of Peor not enough for
us, from which we are not cleansed until this
day, although there was a plague in the
congregation of the LORD, Num. 25:1-9
18 'but that you must turn away this day
from following the LORD? And it shall be, if
you rebel today against the LORD, that tomorrow [R]He will be angry with the whole congregation of Israel. Num. 16:22
19 'Nevertheless, if the land of your possession *is* unclean, *then* cross over to the land of
the possession of the LORD, [R]where the
LORD's tabernacle stands, and take possession among us; but do not rebel against the
LORD, nor rebel against us, by building yourselves an altar besides the altar of the LORD
our God. Josh. 18:1
20 [R]'Did not Achan the son of Zerah [T]com-
mit a trespass in the [T]accursed thing, and
wrath fell on all the congregation of Israel?
And that man did not perish alone in his
iniquity.' " Josh. 7:1-26 • *act unfaithfully* • *devoted thing*

Explanation of the Altar

21 Then the children of Reuben, the children of Gad, and half the tribe of Manasseh
answered and said to the heads of the [T]divi-
sions of Israel: Lit. *thousands*
22 "The LORD God of gods, the LORD God of
gods, He knows, and let Israel itself know—if
it is in rebellion, or if in treachery against the
LORD, do not save us this day.
23 "If we have built ourselves an altar to
turn from following the LORD, or if to offer on
it burnt offerings or grain offerings, or if to
offer peace offerings on it, let the LORD
Himself [R]require *an account*. 1 Sam. 20:16
24 "But in fact we have done it [T]for fear, for
a reason, saying, 'In time to come your
descendants may speak to our descendants,
saying, "What have you to do with the LORD
God of Israel? Lit. *from fear*
25 "For the LORD has made the Jordan a
border between you and us, *you* children of
Reuben and children of Gad. You have no
part in the LORD." So your descendants
would make our descendants cease fearing
the LORD.'
26 "Therefore we said, 'Let us now prepare
to build ourselves an altar, not for burnt
offering nor for sacrifice,
27 'but *that* it *may be* [R]a [T]witness between
you and us and our generations after us, that
we may [R]perform the service of the LORD
before Him with our burnt offerings, with our
sacrifices, and with our peace offerings; that
your descendants may not say to our descendants in time to come, "You have no part in
the LORD." ' Gen. 31:48 • *testimony* • Deut. 12:5, 14
28 "Therefore we said that it will be, when
they say *this* to us or to our generations in
time to come, that we may say, 'Here is the
replica of the altar of the LORD which our
fathers made, though not for burnt offerings
nor for sacrifices; but it *is* a witness between
you and us.'
29 "Far be it from us that we should rebel
against the LORD, and turn from following
the LORD this day, [R]to build an altar for burnt
offerings, for grain offerings, or for sacrifices,

besides the altar of the LORD our God which
is before His tabernacle." Deut. 12:13, 14

Celebration by the Western Tribes

30 And when Phinehas the priest and the
rulers of the congregation, the heads of the
[T]divisions of Israel who *were* with him, heard
the words that the children of Reuben, the
children of Gad, and the children of Manasseh spoke, it pleased them. Lit. *thousands*
31 Then Phinehas the son of Eleazar the
priest said to the children of Reuben, the
children of Gad, and the children of Manasseh, "This day we perceive that the LORD *is*
[R]among us, because you have not committed
this treachery against the LORD. Now you
have delivered the children of Israel out of
the hand of the LORD." Lev. 26:11, 12
32 And Phinehas the son of Eleazar the
priest, and the rulers, returned from the
children of Reuben and the children of Gad,
from the land of Gilead to the land of Canaan, to the children of Israel, and brought
back word to them.
33 So the thing pleased the children of
Israel, and the children of Israel [R]blessed
God; they spoke no more of going against
them in battle, to destroy the land where the
children of Reuben and Gad dwelt. 1 Chr. 29:20
34 And the children of Reuben and the
children of Gad called the altar, *Witness*,
"For *it is* a witness between us that the LORD
is God."

CHAPTER 23

A Reminder from History

NOW it came to pass, a long time after the
LORD had given rest to Israel from all
their enemies round about, that Joshua [R]was
old, advanced in age. Josh. 13:1; 24:29
2 And Joshua [R]called for all Israel, for their
elders, for their heads, for their judges, and
for their officers, and said to them: "I am old,
advanced in age. Deut. 31:28
3 "You have seen all that the [R]LORD your
God has done to all these nations because of
you, for the [R]LORD your God *is* He who has
fought for you. Ps. 44:3 • Deut. 1:30
4 "See, [R]I have divided to you by lot these
nations that remain, to be an inheritance for
your tribes, from the Jordan, with all the
nations that I have cut off, as far as the Great
Sea westward. Josh. 13:2, 6; 18:10
5 "And the LORD your God will expel them
from before you and drive them out of your
sight. So you shall possess their land, as the
LORD your God has promised you.
6 [R]"Therefore be very courageous to keep
and to do all that is written in the Book of the
Law of Moses, [R]lest you turn aside from it to
the right hand or to the left, Josh. 1:7 • Deut. 5:32
7 "*and* lest you go among these nations,
these who remain among you. You shall not
make mention of the name of their gods, nor
cause *anyone* to swear *by them*; you shall not
serve them nor bow down to them,
8 "but you shall hold fast to the LORD your
God, as you have done to this day.
9 [R]"For the LORD has [T]driven out from
before you great and strong nations; but *as
for* you, no one has been able to stand against
you to this day. Deut. 7:24; 11:23 • *dispossessed*
10 "One man of you shall chase a thousand,
for the LORD your God *is* He who fights for
you, [R]as He has promised you. Ex. 14:14
11 "Therefore take diligent heed to yourselves, that you love the LORD your God.
12 "Or else, if indeed you do [R]go back, and
cling to the remnant of these nations—these
that remain among you—and [R]make marriages with them, and go in to them and they
to you, [2 Pet. 2:20, 21] • Deut. 7:3, 4
13 "know for certain that [R]the LORD your
God will no longer drive out these nations
from before you. [R]But they shall be snares
and traps to you, and scourges on your sides
and thorns in your eyes, until you perish from
this good land which the LORD your God has
given you. Judg. 2:3 • Ex. 23:33; 34:12
14 "Behold, this day [T]I *am* going the way of
all the earth. And you know in all your hearts
and in all your souls that not one thing has
failed of all the good things which the LORD
your God spoke concerning you. All have
come to pass for you, *and* not one word of
them has failed. I am going to die.
15 [R]"Therefore it shall come to pass, that as
all the good things have come upon you
which the LORD your God promised you, so
the LORD will bring upon you [R]all harmful
things, until He has destroyed you from this
good land which the LORD your God has
given you. Deut. 28:63 • Deut. 28:15–68
16 [T]"When you have transgressed the covenant of the LORD your God, which He commanded you, and have gone and served other
gods, and bowed down to them, then the
[R]anger of the LORD will burn against you, and
you shall perish quickly from the good land
which He has given you." Or *If ever* • Deut. 4:24–28

CHAPTER 24

Renewal of the Covenant

THEN Joshua gathered all the tribes of
Israel to Shechem and called for the
elders of Israel, for their heads, for their
judges, and for their officers; and they [R]pre-
sented themselves before God. 1 Sam. 10:19
2 And Joshua said to all the people, "Thus
says the LORD God of Israel: [R]'Your fathers,
including Terah, the father of Abraham and

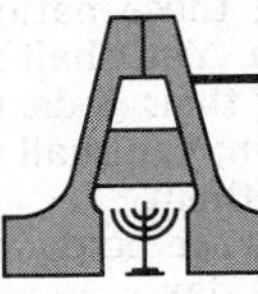

THE CITY OF SHECHEM

City site between Gerizim and Ebal.

Shechem was a fortified city on the edge of a fertile plain in central Palestine where main highways and trade routes converged. Associated particularly with Abraham, Jacob, and Joseph, Shechem was a place where many altars for worship of the one true God were erected.

When Abraham entered Canaan about 2000 B.C., he stopped in Shechem. God appeared to him at Shechem and promised to give the land of Canaan to his descendants (Gen. 12:6, 7). In response, Abraham built an altar to the Lord.

Upon his return to Shechem many years later, Abraham's grandson Jacob also built an altar (Gen. 33:18–20). John 4:12 says he dug a deep well there. Joseph visited his brothers when they were tending their father's herds at Shechem (Gen. 37:12). Joseph's body was taken from Egypt during the Exodus and buried at Shechem (Josh. 24:32).

After Joshua led the Israelites to victory in Canaan, an altar was built at Shechem. Its construction was accompanied by a covenant-renewal ceremony in which offerings were given and the Law was read (Josh. 8:30–35). Shechem's location between barren Mount Ebal and fertile Mount Gerizim gave the ceremony symbolic meaning—the advantages of keeping the covenant were proclaimed from Gerizim, while the curses for breaking it were proclaimed from Ebal.

For a short time after the northern kingdom of Israel was founded, Shechem served as the capital city of this nation before Samaria was built and designated as the capital city (1 Kin. 12:25).

Some scholars identify the New Testament town Sychar (John 4:5) with Shechem. If this is correct, then this is where Jesus spoke with the Samaritan woman at Jacob's well. He promised her living water that would become "a fountain of water springing up into everlasting life" (4:14).

the father of Nahor, dwelt on the other side of [T]the River in old times; and [R]they served other gods. Gen. 11:7–32 • The Euphrates • Josh. 24:14

3 'Then I took your father Abraham from the other side of the River, led him throughout all the land of Canaan, and multiplied his [T]descendants and gave him Isaac. Lit. *seed*

4 'To Isaac I gave [R]Jacob and Esau. To [R]Esau I gave the mountains of Seir to possess, [R]but Jacob and his children went down to Egypt. Gen. 25:24–26 • Deut. 2:5 • Gen. 46:1, 3, 6

5 'Also I sent Moses and Aaron, and I plagued Egypt, according to what I did among them. Afterward I brought you out.

6 'Then I [R]brought your fathers out of Egypt, and you came to the sea; and the Egyptians pursued your fathers with chariots and horsemen to the Red Sea. Ex. 14:2–31

7 'So they cried out to the LORD; and He put [R]darkness between you and the Egyptians, brought the sea upon them, and covered them. And [R]your eyes saw what I did in Egypt. Then you dwelt in the wilderness [R]a long time. Ex. 14:20 • Deut. 4:34 • Josh. 5:6

8 'And I brought you into the land of the Amorites, who dwelt on the other side of the Jordan, [R]and they fought with you. But I gave them into your hand, that you might possess their land, and I destroyed them from before you. Num. 21:21–35

9 'Then [R]Balak the son of Zippor, king of Moab, arose to make war against Israel, and [R]sent and called Balaam the son of Beor to curse you. Judg. 11:25 • Num. 22:2–14

10 [R]'But I would not listen to Balaam; therefore he continued to bless you. So I delivered you out of his hand. Deut. 23:5

11 'Then you went over the Jordan and came to Jericho. And the men of Jericho fought against you—*also* the Amorites, the Perizzites, the Canaanites, the Hittites, the Girgashites, the Hivites, and the Jebusites. But I delivered them into your hand.

12 [R]'I sent the hornet before you which drove them out from before you, *also* the two kings of the Amorites, *but* [R]not with your sword or with your bow. Ex. 23:28 • Ps. 44:3

13 'I have given you a land for which you did not labor, and [R]cities which you did not build, and you dwell in them; you eat of the vineyards and olive groves which you did not plant.' Deut. 6:10, 11

14 "Now therefore, fear the LORD, serve Him in sincerity and in truth, and [R]put away the gods which your fathers served on the other side of [T]the River and [R]in Egypt. Serve the LORD! Ezek. 20:18 • The Euphrates • Ezek. 20:7, 8

15 "And if it seems evil to you to serve the LORD, choose for yourselves this day whom you will serve, whether the gods which your fathers served that *were* on the other side of the River, or the gods of the Amorites, in whose land you dwell. [R]But as for me and my house, we will serve the LORD." Gen. 18:19

16 So the people answered and said: "Far be it from us that we should forsake the LORD to serve other gods;

17 "for the LORD our God *is* He who brought us and our fathers up out of the land of Egypt, from the house of bondage, who did those great signs in our sight, and preserved us in all the way that we went and among all the people through whom we passed.

18 "And the LORD drove out from before us all the people, even the Amorites who dwelt in the land. [R]We also will serve the LORD, for He *is* our God." Ps. 116:16

19 But Joshua said to the people, "You cannot serve the LORD, for He *is* a holy God. He *is* a jealous God; [R]He will not forgive your transgressions nor your sins. Ex. 23:21

20 [R]"If you forsake the LORD and serve foreign gods, [R]then He will turn and do you harm and consume you, after He has done you good." Ezra 8:22 • Deut. 4:24–26

21 And the people said to Joshua, "No, but we will serve the LORD!"

22 So Joshua said to the people, "You *are* witnesses against yourselves that you have chosen the LORD for yourselves, to serve Him." And they said, "*We are* witnesses."

23 "Now therefore," *he said,* [R]"put away the foreign gods which *are* among you, and [R]incline your heart to the LORD God of Israel." Gen. 35:2 • 1 Kin. 8:57, 58

24 And the people [R]said to Joshua, "The LORD our God we will serve, and His voice we will obey." Deut. 5:24–27

25 So Joshua [T]made a covenant with the people that day, and made for them a statute and an ordinance in Shechem. Lit. *cut*

26 Then Joshua wrote these words in the Book of the Law of God. And he took a large stone, and set it up there [R]under the oak that *was* by the sanctuary of the LORD. Gen. 35:4

27 And Joshua said to all the people, "Behold, this stone shall be a witness to us, for it has heard all the words of the LORD which He spoke to us. It shall therefore be a witness to you, lest you deny your God."

28 So [R]Joshua let the people depart, each to his own inheritance. Judg. 2:6, 7

Joshua and Eleazar Die

29 [R]Now it came to pass after these things that Joshua the son of Nun, the servant of the LORD, died, *being* one hundred and ten years old. Judg. 2:8

30 And they buried him within the border of his inheritance at [R]Timnath Serah, which *is* in the mountains of Ephraim, on the north side of Mount Gaash. Josh. 19:50

31 [R]Israel served the LORD all the days of Joshua, and all the days of the elders who

outlived Joshua, who had [R]known all the
works of the LORD which He had done for
Israel. Judg. 2:7 • Deut. 11:2
32 The bones of Joseph, which the children
of Israel had brought up out of Egypt, they
buried at Shechem, in the plot of ground
which Jacob had bought from the sons of
Hamor the father of Shechem for one hundred pieces of silver, and which had become
an inheritance of the children of Joseph.
33 And [R]Eleazar the son of Aaron died; and
they buried him in a hill *that belonged to*
[R]Phinehas his son, which was given to him in
the mountains of Ephraim. Ex. 28:1 • Ex. 6:25

THE BOOK OF

JUDGES

THE BOOK OF JUDGES

The Book of Judges stands in stark contrast to Joshua. In Joshua an obedient people conquered the land through trust in the power of God. In Judges, however, a disobedient and idolatrous people are defeated time and time again because of their rebellion against God.

In seven distinct cycles of sin to salvation, Judges shows how Israel had set aside God's law and in its place substituted *"what was* right in his own eyes" (21:25). The recurring result of abandonment from God's law is corruption from within and oppression from without. During the nearly four centuries spanned by this book, God raises up military champions to throw off the yoke of bondage and to restore the nation to pure worship. But all too soon the "sin cycle" begins again as the nation's spiritual temperature grows steadily colder.

The Hebrew title is *Shophetim,* meaning "judges," "rulers," "deliverers," or "saviors." *Shophet* not only carries the idea of maintaining justice and settling disputes, but it is also used to mean "liberating" and "delivering." First the judges deliver the people; then they rule and administer justice. The Septuagint used the Greek equivalent of this word, *Kritai* ("Judges"). The Latin Vulgate called it *Liber Judicum,* the "Book of Judges." This book could also appropriately be titled "The Book of Failure."

THE AUTHOR OF JUDGES

The author of Judges is anonymous, but Samuel or one of his prophetic students may have written it. Jewish tradition contained in the Talmud attributes Judges to Samuel, and certainly he was the crucial link between the period of the judges and the period of the kings.

It is clear from 18:31 and 20:27 that the book was written after the ark was removed from Shiloh (1 Sam. 4:3–11). The repeated phrase "In those days *there was* no king in Israel" (17:6; 18:1; 19:1; 21:25) shows that Judges was also written after the commencement of Saul's reign but before the divided kingdom. The fact that the Jebusites were dwelling in Jerusalem "to this day" (1:21) means that it was written before 1004 B.C. when David dispossessed the Jebusites (2 Sam. 5:5–9). Thus, the book was written during the time of Samuel; and it is likely that Samuel compiled this book from oral and written source material. His prophetic ministry clearly fits the moral commentary of Judges, and the consistent style and orderly scheme of Judges point to a single compiler.

Judges 18:30 contains a phrase that poses a problem to this early date of composition: "until the day of the captivity of the land." If this refers to the 722 B.C. Assyrian captivity of Israel it could have been inserted by a later editor. It is more likely a reference to the Philistine captivity of the land during the time of the judges. This event is described as "captivity" in Psalm 78:61.

THE TIME OF JUDGES

If Judges was not written by Samuel it was at least written by one of his contemporaries between 1043 B.C. (the beginning of Saul's reign) and 1004 B.C. (David's capture of Jerusalem).

Joshua's seven-year conquest is general in nature; much of the land remains to be possessed (Josh. 13:1). There are still important Canaanite strongholds to be taken by the individual tribes. Some of the nations have been left to "test Israel" (Judg. 3:1, 4). During this time, the Egyptians maintain strong control along the coastal routes, but they are not interested in the hill country where Israel is primarily established.

The events covered in Judges range from about 1380 B.C. to 1045 B.C. (c. 335 years), but the period of the judges extends another thirty years since it includes the life of Samuel (1 Sam. 1:1—25:1). Evidently, the rulerships of some of the judges overlap because not all of them ruled over the entire land. Judges describes the cycles of apostasy, oppression, and deliverance in the southern region (3:7–31), the northern region (4:1—5:31), the central region (6:1—10:5), the eastern region (10:6—12:15), and the western region (13:1—16:31). The spread of apostasy covers the whole land.

THE CHRIST OF JUDGES

Each judge is a savior and a ruler, a spiritual and political deliverer. Thus, the judges portray the role of Christ as the Savior-King of His people. The Book of Judges also illustrates the need for a righteous king.

Including First Samuel, seventeen judges are mentioned altogether. Some are warrior-rulers (e.g., Othniel and Gideon), one is a priest (Eli), and one is a prophet (Samuel). This gives a cumulative picture of the three offices of Christ, who excelled all His predecessors in that He was the ultimate Prophet, Priest, and King.

KEYS TO JUDGES

Key Word: Cycles—The Book of Judges is written primarily on a thematic rather than a chronological basis (chs. 16—21 actually precede chs. 3—15). The author uses the accounts of the various judges to prove the utter failure of living out the closing verse of Judges: "Everyone did *what was* right in his own eyes." To accomplish this, the author uses a five-point cycle to recount the repeated spiral of disobedience, destruction, and defeat. The five parts are: (1) sin, (2) servitude, (3) supplication, (4) salvation, and (5) silence.

Key Verses: Judges 2:20, 21; 21:25—"Then the anger of the LORD was hot against Israel; and He said, 'Because this nation has transgressed My covenant which I commanded their fathers, and has not heeded My voice, I also will no longer drive out before them any of the nations which Joshua left when he died'" (2:20, 21).

"In those days *there was* no king in Israel; everyone did *what was* right in his own eyes" (21:25).

Key Chapter: Judges 2—The second chapter of Judges is a miniature of the whole book as it records the transition of the godly to the ungodly generation, the format of the cycles, and the purpose of God in not destroying the Canaanites.

SURVEY OF JUDGES

Following the death of Joshua, Israel plunges into a 350-year Dark Age. After Joshua and the generation of the conquest pass on, "another generation arose after them who did not know the LORD nor the work which He had done for Israel" (2:10; see also 2:7–10; Josh. 24:31). Judges opens with a description of Israel's deterioration, continues with seven cycles of oppression and deliverance, and concludes with two illustrations of Israel's depravity.

Deterioration (1:1—3:4): Judges begins with short-lived military successes after Joshua's death, but quickly turns to the repeated failure of all the tribes to drive out their enemies. The people feel the lack of a unified central leader, but the primary reasons for their failure are a lack of faith in God and a lack of obedience to Him (2:1–3). Compromise leads to conflict and chaos. Israel does not drive out the inhabitants (1:21, 27, 29, 30); instead of removing the moral cancer spread by the inhabitants of Canaan, they contract the disease. The Canaanite gods literally become a snare to them (2:3). Judges 2:11–23 is a microcosm of the pattern found in chapters 3—16 of Judges.

Deliverances (3:5—16:31): This section describes seven apostasies (fallings away from God), seven servitudes, and seven deliverances. Each of the seven cycles has five steps: sin, servitude, supplication, salvation, and silence. These also can be described by the words *rebellion, retribution, repentance, restoration,* and *rest.* The seven cycles connect together as a descending spiral of sin (2:19). Israel vacillates between obedience and apostasy as the people continually fail to learn from their mistakes. Apostasy grows, but the rebellion is not continual. The times of rest and peace are longer than the times of bondage. The monotony of Israel's sins can be contrasted with the creativity of God's methods of deliverance.

The judges are military and civil leaders during this period of loose confederacy. Thirteen are mentioned in this book, and four more are found in First Samuel (Eli, Samuel, Joel, and Abijah).

Depravity (17:1—21:25): These chapters illustrate (1) religious apostasy (17 and 18) and (2) social and moral depravity (19—21) during the period of the judges. Chapters 19—21 contain one of the worst tales of degradation in the Bible. Judges closes with a key to understanding the period: "everyone did *what was* right in his own eyes" (21:25). The people are not doing what is wrong in their own eyes, but what is "evil in the sight of the LORD."

FOCUS	DETERIORATION		DELIVERANCE						DEPRAVITY		
REFERENCE	1:1	2:1	3:5	4:1	6:1	10:6	12:8	13:1	17:1	19:1	20:1–21:25
DIVISION	ISRAEL FAILS TO COMPLETE THE CONQUEST	GOD JUDGES ISRAEL	SOUTHERN CAMPAIGN	NORTHERN CAMPAIGN (1st)	CENTRAL CAMPAIGN	EASTERN CAMPAIGN	NORTHERN CAMPAIGN (2nd)	WESTERN CAMPAIGN	SIN OF IDOLATRY	SIN OF IMMORALITY	SIN OF CIVIL WAR
TOPIC	CAUSES OF THE CYCLES		CURSE OF THE CYCLES						CONDITIONS DURING THE CYCLES		
	LIVING WITH THE CANAANITES		WAR WITH THE CANAANITES						LIVING LIKE THE CANAANITES		
LOCATION	CANAAN										
TIME	c. 350 YEARS										

OUTLINE OF JUDGES

CHAPTER 1

Failure of Judah

NOW after the death of Joshua it came to
pass that the children of Israel [R]asked
the LORD, saying, "Who shall be first to go up
for us against the [R]Canaanites to fight
against them?" Num. 27:21 • Josh. 17:12, 13
2 And the LORD said, [R]"Judah shall go up.
Indeed I have delivered the land into his
hand." Gen. 49:8, 9
3 So Judah said to [R]Simeon his brother,
"Come up with me to my allotted territory,
that we may fight against the Canaanites;
and [R]I will likewise go with you to your
allotted territory." And Simeon went with
him. Josh. 19:1 • Judg. 1:17
4 Then Judah went up, and the LORD deliv-

ered the Canaanites and the Perizzites into their hand; and they killed ten thousand men at [R]Bezek. 1 Sam. 11:8

5 And they found Adoni-Bezek in Bezek, and fought against him; and they defeated the Canaanites and the Perizzites.

6 Then Adoni-Bezek fled, and they pursued him and caught him and cut off his thumbs and big toes.

7 And Adoni-Bezek said, "Seventy kings with their thumbs and big toes cut off used to gather *their food* under my table; as I have done, so God has repaid me." Then they brought him to Jerusalem, and there he died.

8 Now [R]the children of Judah fought against Jerusalem and took it; they struck it with the edge of the sword and set the city on fire. Josh. 15:63

9 [R]And afterward the children of Judah went down to fight against the Canaanites who dwelt in the mountains, in the [T]South, and in the lowland. Josh. 10:36 • *Negev*

10 Then Judah went against the Canaanites who dwelt in Hebron. (Now the name of Hebron *was* formerly Kirjath Arba.) And they killed Sheshai, Ahiman, and Talmai.

11 [R]From there they went against the inhabitants of Debir. (The name of Debir *was* formerly Kirjath Sepher.) Josh. 15:15

12 [R]Then Caleb said, "He who attacks Kirjath Sepher and takes it, to him I will give my daughter Achsah as wife." Josh. 15:16, 17

13 And Othniel the son of Kenaz, [R]Caleb's younger brother, took it; so he gave him his daughter Achsah as wife. Judg. 3:9

14 Now it was so, when she came *to him*, that *she urged him to ask her father for a field. And she dismounted from *her* donkey, and Caleb said to her, "What do you wish?"

15 So she said to him, [R]"Give me a blessing; since you have given me land in the South, give me also springs of water." Then Caleb gave her the upper springs and the lower springs. Gen. 33:11

16 Now the children of the Kenite, Moses' father-in-law, went up [R]from the city of palms with the children of Judah into the Wilderness of Judah, which *lies* in the South *near* [R]Arad; [R]and they went and dwelt among the people. Deut. 34:3 • Josh. 12:14 • 1 Sam. 15:6

17 And Judah went with his brother Simeon, and they attacked the Canaanites who inhabited Zephath, and utterly destroyed it. So the name of the city was called Hormah.

18 Also Judah took [R]Gaza with its territory, Ashkelon with its territory, and Ekron with its territory. Josh. 11:22

19 So the LORD was with Judah. And they drove out *the inhabitants of* the mountains, but they could not drive out the inhabitants of the lowland, because they had [R]chariots of iron. Josh. 17:16, 18

20 And they gave Hebron to Caleb, as Moses had said. Then he [T]expelled from there the three sons of Anak. *drove out*

Failure of Benjamin

21 But the children of Benjamin did not drive out the Jebusites who inhabited Jerusalem; so the Jebusites dwell with the children of Benjamin in Jerusalem to this day.

Failure of Tribes of Joseph

22 And the house of Joseph also went up against Bethel, and the LORD *was* with them.

23 So the [T]house of Joseph [R]sent men to spy out Bethel. (The name of the city *was* formerly [R]Luz.) *family* • Josh. 2:1; 7:2 • Gen. 28:19

24 And when the spies saw a man coming out of the city, they said to him, "Please show us the entrance to the city, and [R]we will show you mercy." Josh. 2:12, 14

25 So he showed them the entrance to the city, and they struck the city with the edge of the sword; but they let the man and all his family go.

26 And the man went to the land of the Hittites, built a city, and called its name Luz, which *is* its name to this day.

27 [R]However, Manasseh did not drive out *the inhabitants of* Beth Shean and its villages, or [R]Taanach and its villages, or the inhabitants of [R]Dor and its villages, or the inhabitants of Ibleam and its villages, or the inhabitants of Megiddo and its villages; for the Canaanites were determined to dwell in that land. Josh. 17:11–13 • Josh. 21:25 • Josh. 17:11

28 And it came to pass, when Israel was strong, that they put the Canaanites [T]under tribute, but did not completely drive them out. *to forced labor*

29 [R]Nor did Ephraim drive out the Canaanites who dwelt in Gezer; so the Canaanites dwelt in Gezer among them. Josh. 16:10

Failure of Zebulun

30 Nor did Zebulun drive out the inhabitants of Kitron or the inhabitants of Nahalol; so the Canaanites dwelt among them, and [T]were put under tribute. *became forced laborers*

Failure of Asher

31 Nor did Asher drive out the inhabitants of Acco or the inhabitants of Sidon, or of Ahlab, Achzib, Helbah, Aphik, or Rehob.

32 So the Asherites [R]dwelt among the Canaanites, the inhabitants of the land; for they did not drive them out. Ps. 106:34, 35

Failure of Naphtali

33 Nor did Naphtali drive out the inhabitants of Beth Shemesh or the inhabitants of

1:14 LXX, Vg. *he urged her*

Beth Anath; but they dwelt among the Canaanites, the inhabitants of the land. Nevertheless the inhabitants of Beth Shemesh and Beth Anath were put under tribute to them.

Failure of Dan

34 And the Amorites forced the children of Dan into the mountains, for they would not allow them to come down to the valley;

35 and the Amorites were determined to dwell in Mount Heres, [R]in Aijalon, and in Shaalbim; yet when the hand of the house of Joseph became stronger, they [T]were put under tribute. Josh. 19:42 • *became forced laborers*

36 Now the boundary of the Amorites *was* [R]from the Ascent of Akrabbim, from Sela, and upward. Josh. 15:3

CHAPTER 2

Angel Announces Judgment

THEN the Angel of the LORD came up from Gilgal to Bochim, and said: "I led you up from Egypt and brought you to the land of which I swore to your fathers; and I said, 'I will never break My covenant with you.

2 'And you shall make no [T]covenant with the inhabitants of this land; you shall tear down their altars.' But you have not obeyed My voice. Why have you done this? *treaty*

3 "Therefore I also said, 'I will not drive them out before you; but they shall be *thorns* in your side, and [R]their gods shall [T]be a [R]snare to you.' " Judg. 3:6 • *entrap* • Ps. 106:36

4 So it was, when the Angel of the LORD spoke these words to all the children of Israel, that the people lifted up their voice and wept.

5 Then they called the name of that place [T]Bochim; and they sacrificed there to the LORD. Lit. *Weeping*

Godly Generation Dies

6 And when Joshua had dismissed the people, the children of Israel went each to his own inheritance to possess the land.

7 [R]So the people served the LORD all the days of Joshua, and all the days of the elders who outlived Joshua, who had seen all the great works of the LORD which He had done for Israel. Josh. 24:31

8 Now [R]Joshua the son of Nun, the servant of the LORD, died *when he was* one hundred and ten years old. Josh. 24:29

9 [R]And they buried him within the border of his inheritance at [R]Timnath Heres, in the mountains of Ephraim, on the north side of Mount Gaash. Josh. 24:30 • Josh. 19:49, 50

10 When all that generation had been gathered to their fathers, another generation arose after them who did not know the LORD nor the work which He had done for Israel.

Judgment of God Is Described

11 Then the children of Israel did evil in the sight of the LORD, and served the Baals;

12 and they forsook the LORD God of their fathers, who had brought them out of the land of Egypt; and they followed other gods from *among* the gods of the people who *were* all around them, and they bowed down to them; and they provoked the LORD to anger.

13 They forsook the LORD and served Baal and the [T]Ashtoreths. Canaanite goddesses

14 And the anger of the LORD was hot against Israel. So He delivered them into the hands of plunderers who despoiled them; and He sold them into the hands of their enemies all around, so that they [R]could no longer stand before their enemies. Lev. 26:37

15 Wherever they went out, the hand of the LORD was against them for calamity, as the LORD had said, and as the LORD had sworn to them. And they were greatly distressed.

16 Then [R]the LORD raised up judges who delivered them out of the hand of those who plundered them. Ps. 106:43–45

17 Yet they would not listen to their judges, but they [R]played the harlot with other gods, and bowed down to them. They turned quickly from the way in which their fathers walked, in obeying the commandments of the LORD; they did not do so. Ex. 34:15

18 And when the LORD raised up judges for them, [R]the LORD was with the judge and delivered them out of the hand of their enemies all the days of the judge; [R]for the LORD was moved to pity by their groaning because of those who oppressed them and harassed them. Josh. 1:5 • Gen. 6:6

19 And it came to pass, [R]when the judge was dead, that they reverted and behaved more corruptly than their fathers, by following other gods, to serve them and bow down to them. They did not cease from their own doings nor from their stubborn way. Judg. 3:12

Enemy Is Left as a Test

20 Then the anger of the LORD was hot against Israel; and He said, "Because this nation has [R]transgressed My covenant which I commanded their fathers, and has not heeded My voice, [Josh. 23:16]

21 "I also will no longer drive out before them any of the nations which Joshua [R]left when he died, Josh. 23:4, 5, 13

22 "so [R]that through them I may [R]test Israel, whether they will keep the ways of the LORD, to walk in them as their fathers kept *them*, or not." Judg. 3:1, 4 • Deut. 8:2, 16; 13:3

23 Therefore the LORD left those nations, without driving them out immediately; nor did He deliver them into the hand of Joshua.

THE ANGEL OF THE LORD

The Angel of the Lord provided food for the prophet Elijah in the wilderness.

The Angel of the Lord in the Old Testament is a mysterious messenger of God. The Lord used this heavenly emissary to appear to human beings who otherwise would not be able to see Him and live (Ex. 33:20). The Angel of the Lord performed actions associated with God, such as revelation, deliverance, and God's judgment. While similar in nature to other angels, the Angel of the Lord occupies a higher station in heaven than angels in general.

The Angel of the Lord appeared to the following Old Testament personalities and performed the following actions on God's behalf.

Personality	Action	Biblical Reference
Hagar	Instructed Hagar to return to Sarah and told her she would bear many descendants	Gen. 16:7–10
Abraham	Prevented Abraham from sacrificing his son Isaac	Gen. 22:11–13
Jacob	Wrestled with Jacob through the night and blessed him at daybreak	Gen. 32:24–30
Moses	Spoke to Moses from the burning bush, promising to deliver the Israelites from enslavement	Ex. 3:1–8
Israelites	Protected the children of Israel from the pursuing Egyptian army	Ex. 14:19, 20
Israelites	Prepared the children of Israel to enter the Promised Land	Ex. 23:20–23
Balaam	Blocked Balaam's path, then sent him to deliver a message to the prince of Balak	Num. 22:22–35
Joshua	Reassured Joshua in his role as commander of the army of the Lord	Josh. 5:13–15
Israelites	Announced judgment against the Israelites for their sinful alliances with the Canaanites	Judg. 2:1–3
Gideon	Commissioned Gideon to fight against the Midianites	Judg. 6:11–24
Elijah	Provided food for Elijah in the wilderness	1 Kin. 19:4–8
David	Appeared to David on the threshing floor of Ornan, where David built an altar	1 Chr. 21:16–22
Residents of Jerusalem	Delivered the citizens of this city from the Assyrian army	Is. 37:36
Three Hebrew Men	Protected these young Israelites from Nebuchadnezzar's fiery furnace in Babylon	Dan. 3:25

CHAPTER 3

NOW these *are* [R]the nations which the LORD left, that He might test Israel by them, *that is,* all who had not [T]known any of the wars in Canaan Judg. 1:1; 2:21, 22 • *experienced*

2 (*this was* only so that the generations of the children of Israel might be taught to know war, at least those who had not formerly known it),

3 *namely,* [R]five lords of the Philistines, all the Canaanites, the Sidonians, and the Hivites who dwelt in Mount Lebanon, from Mount Baal Hermon to the entrance of Hamath. Josh. 13:3

4 And they were *left, that He might* test Israel by them, to [T]know whether they would obey the commandments of the LORD, which He had commanded their fathers by the hand of Moses. *find out*

The Judge Othniel

5 So the children of Israel dwelt among the Canaanites, the Hittites, the Amorites, the Perizzites, the Hivites, and the Jebusites.

6 And [R]they took their daughters to be their wives, and gave their daughters to their sons; and they served their gods. Ex. 34:15, 16

7 So the children of Israel did evil in the sight of the LORD. They forgot the LORD their God, and served the Baals and [T]Asherahs. Name or symbol for Canaanite goddesses

8 Therefore the anger of the LORD was hot against Israel, and He [R]sold them into the hand of Cushan-Rishathaim king of Mesopotamia; and the children of Israel served Cushan-Rishathaim eight years. Judg. 2:14

9 When the children of Israel [R]cried out to the LORD, the LORD [R]raised up a deliverer for the children of Israel, who delivered them: [R]Othniel the son of Kenaz, Caleb's younger brother. Judg. 3:15 • Judg. 2:16 • Judg. 1:13

10 The Spirit of the LORD came upon him, and he judged Israel. He went out to war, and the LORD delivered Cushan-Rishathaim king of Mesopotamia into his hand; and his hand prevailed over Cushan-Rishathaim.

11 So the land had rest for forty years. Then Othniel the son of Kenaz died.

The Judge Ehud

12 [R]And the children of Israel again did evil in the sight of the LORD. So the LORD strengthened [R]Eglon king of Moab against Israel, because they had done evil in the sight of the LORD. Judg. 2:19 • 1 Sam. 12:9

13 Then he gathered to himself the people of Ammon and [R]Amalek, went and [T]defeated Israel, and took possession of [R]the city of palms. Judg. 5:14 • *struck* • Judg. 1:16

14 So the children of Israel [R]served Eglon king of Moab eighteen years. Deut. 28:48

15 And when the children of Israel [R]cried out to the LORD, the LORD raised up a deliverer for them: Ehud the son of Gera, the Benjamite, a [R]left-handed man. By him the children of Israel sent tribute to Eglon king of Moab. Ps. 78:34 • Judg. 20:16

16 Now Ehud made himself a dagger (it was double-edged and a [T]cubit in length) and fastened it under his clothes on his right thigh. 18 in.

17 So he brought the tribute to Eglon king of Moab. (Now Eglon *was* a very fat man.)

18 And when he had finished presenting the tribute, he sent away the people who had carried the tribute.

19 But he himself turned back [R]from the *stone images that *were* at Gilgal, and said, "I have a secret message for you, O king." He said, "Keep silence!" And all who attended him went out from him. Josh. 4:20

20 And Ehud came to him (now he was sitting upstairs in his cool private chamber). Then Ehud said, "I have a message from God for you." So he arose from *his* seat.

21 Then Ehud reached with his left hand, took the dagger from his right thigh, and thrust it into his belly.

22 Even the [T]hilt went in after the blade, and the fat closed over the blade, for he did not draw the dagger out of his belly; and his entrails came out. *handle*

23 Then Ehud went out through the porch and shut the doors of the upper room behind him and locked them.

24 When he had gone out, [T]Eglon's servants came to look, and *to their* surprise, the doors of the upper room were locked. So they said, "He is probably [T]attending to his needs in the cool chamber." Lit. *his* • Lit. *covering his feet*

25 So they waited till they were [R]embarrassed, and still he had not opened the doors of the upper room. Therefore they took the key and opened *them.* And there was their master, fallen dead on the floor. 2 Kin. 2:17; 8:11

26 But Ehud escaped while they delayed, and passed beyond the *stone images and escaped to Seirah.

27 And it happened, when he arrived, that he blew the trumpet in the [R]mountains of Ephraim, and the children of Israel went down with him from the mountains; and [T]he led them. Josh. 17:15 • Lit. *he went before them*

28 Then he said to them, "Follow *me,* for [R]the LORD has delivered your enemies the Moabites into your hand." So they went down after him, seized the [R]fords of the Jordan leading to Moab, and did not allow anyone to cross over. Judg. 7:9, 15 • Josh. 2:7

29 And at that time they killed about ten thousand men of Moab, all stout men of valor; not a man escaped.

3:19 Tg. *quarries* **3:26** Tg. *quarries*

30 So Moab was subdued that day under the
hand of Israel. And [R]the land had rest for
eighty years. Judg. 3:11

The Judge Shamgar

31 After him was [R]Shamgar the son of
Anath, who killed six hundred men of the
Philistines with an ox goad; [R]and he also
delivered [R]Israel. Judg. 5:6 • Judg. 2:16 • 1 Sam. 4:1

CHAPTER 4

Deborah and Barak Are Called

WHEN Ehud was dead, [R]the children of
Israel again did [R]evil in the sight of the
LORD. Judg. 2:19 • Judg. 2:11
2 So the LORD sold them into the hand of
Jabin king of Canaan, who reigned in Hazor.
The commander of his army *was* Sisera, who
dwelt in [R]Harosheth Hagoyim. Judg. 4:13, 16
3 And the children of Israel cried out to
the LORD; for Jabin had nine hundred chariots of iron, and for twenty years [R]he harshly
oppressed the children of Israel. Ps. 106:42
4 Now Deborah, a prophetess, the wife of
Lapidoth, was judging Israel at that time.
5 [R]And she would sit under the palm tree
of Deborah between Ramah and Bethel in the
mountains of Ephraim. And the children of
Israel came up to her for judgment. Gen. 35:8
6 Then she sent and called for Barak the
son of Abinoam from Kedesh in Naphtali, and
said to him, "Has not the LORD God of Israel
commanded, *saying*, 'Go and [T]deploy *troops*
at Mount [R]Tabor; take with you ten thousand
men of the sons of Naphtali and of the sons of
Zebulun; *march* • Judg. 8:18
7 'and against you I will deploy Sisera, the
commander of Jabin's army, with his chariots
and his multitude at the River Kishon; and I
will [T]deliver him into your hand'?" Lit. *draw*
8 And Barak said to her, "If you will go
with me, then I will go; but if you will not go
with me, I will not go."
9 So she said, "I will surely go with you;
nevertheless there will be no glory for you in
the journey you are taking, for the LORD will
[R]sell Sisera into the hand of a woman." Then
Deborah arose and went with Barak to Kedesh. Judg. 2:14
10 And Barak called Zebulun and Naphtali
to Kedesh; he went up with ten thousand
men [R]under[T] his command, and Deborah
went up with him. 1 Kin. 20:10 • Lit. *at his feet*
11 Now Heber the Kenite, of the children of
Hobab the father-in-law of Moses, had separated himself from the Kenites and pitched
his tent near the terebinth tree at Zaanaim,
[R]which *is* beside Kedesh. Judg. 4:6

Canaanites Are Defeated

12 And they reported to Sisera that Barak
the son of Abinoam had gone up to Mount
Tabor.
13 So Sisera gathered together all his chariots, nine hundred chariots of iron, and all the
people who *were* with him, from Harosheth
Hagoyim to the River Kishon.
14 Then Deborah said to Barak, [T]"Up! For
this *is* the day in which the LORD has delivered Sisera into your hand. [R]Has not the LORD
gone out before you?" So Barak went down
from Mount Tabor with ten thousand men
following him. *Arise!* • Deut. 9:3; 31:3
15 And the LORD routed Sisera and all *his*
chariots and all *his* army with the edge of the
sword before Barak; and Sisera alighted from
his chariot and fled away on foot.
16 But Barak pursued the chariots and the
army as far as Harosheth Hagoyim, and all
the army of Sisera fell by the edge of the
sword; not a man was [R]left. Ex. 14:28
17 However, Sisera had fled away on foot to
the tent of [R]Jael, the wife of Heber the
Kenite; for *there was* peace between Jabin
king of Hazor and the house of Heber the
Kenite. Judg. 5:6
18 And Jael went out to meet Sisera, and
said to him, "Turn aside, my lord, turn aside
to me; do not fear." And when he had turned
aside with her into the tent, she covered him
with a [T]blanket. *rug*
19 Then he said to her, "Please give me a
little water to drink, for I am thirsty." So she
opened [R]a jug of milk, gave him a drink, and
covered him. Judg. 5:24–27
20 And he said to her, "Stand at the door of
the tent, and if any man comes and inquires
of you, and says, 'Is there any man here?' you
shall say, 'No.' "
21 Then Jael, Heber's wife, took a tent peg
and took a hammer in her hand, and went
softly to him and drove the peg into his
temple, and it went down into the ground; for
he was fast asleep and weary. So he died.
22 And then, as Barak pursued Sisera, Jael
came out to meet him, and said to him,
"Come, I will show you the man whom you
seek." And when he went into her *tent*, there
lay Sisera, dead with the peg in his temple.
23 So on that day God subdued Jabin king
of Canaan in the presence of the children of
Israel.
24 And the hand of the children of Israel
grew stronger and stronger against Jabin
king of Canaan, until they had destroyed
Jabin king of Canaan.

CHAPTER 5

Song of Deborah and Barak

THEN Deborah and Barak the son of Abinoam [R]sang on that day, saying: Judg. 4:4

2 "When[T] leaders lead in Israel,
When the people willingly offer
themselves,
Bless the LORD! Or *When locks are loosed*

3 "Hear,[R] O kings! Give ear, O princes!
I, *even* [R]I, will sing to the LORD;
I will sing *praise* to the LORD God of
Israel. Deut. 32:1, 3 • Ps. 27:6

4 "LORD, [R]when You went out from Seir,
When You marched from [R]the field of
Edom, Deut. 33:2 • Ps. 68:8
The earth trembled and the heavens
poured,
The clouds also poured water;
5 [R]The mountains [T]gushed before the
LORD, Ps. 97:5 • *flowed*
[R]This Sinai, before the LORD God of
Israel. Ex. 19:18

6 "In the days of [R]Shamgar, son of Anath,
In the days of [R]Jael, Judg. 3:31 • Judg. 4:17
[R]The highways were deserted, Is. 33:8
And the travelers walked along the
byways.
7 Village life ceased, it ceased in Israel,
Until I, Deborah, arose,
Arose a mother in Israel.
8 They chose [R]new gods; Deut. 32:17
Then *there was* war in the gates;
Not a shield or spear was seen among
forty thousand in Israel.
9 My heart *is* with the rulers of Israel
Who offered themselves willingly with
the people.
Bless the LORD!

10 "Speak, you who ride on white [R]donkeys,
Who sit in judges' attire, Judg. 10:4; 12:14
And who walk along the road.
11 Far from the noise of the archers,
among the watering places,
There they shall recount the righteous
acts of the LORD,
The righteous acts *for* His villagers in
Israel;
Then the people of the LORD shall go
down to the gates.

12 "Awake,[R] awake, Deborah! Ps. 57:8
Awake, awake, sing a song!
Arise, Barak, and lead your captives
away,
O son of Abinoam!

13 "Then the survivors came down, *the
people* against the nobles;
The LORD came down for me against
the mighty.
14 From Ephraim *were* those whose roots
were in [R]Amalek. Judg. 3:13
After you, Benjamin, with your peoples,
From Machir rulers came down,
And from Zebulun those who bear the
recruiter's staff.
15 And the *princes of Issachar *were* with
Deborah;
As Issachar, so *was* Barak
Sent into the valley [T]under his
command; Lit. *at his feet*
Among the divisions of Reuben
There were great resolves of heart.
16 Why did you sit among the sheepfolds,
To hear the pipings for the flocks?
The divisions of Reuben have great
searchings of heart.
17 Gilead stayed beyond the Jordan,
And why did Dan remain on ships?
[R]Asher continued at the seashore,
And stayed by his inlets. Josh. 19:29, 31
18 [R]Zebulun *is* a people *who* jeopardized
their lives to the point of death,
Naphtali also, on the heights of the
battlefield. Judg. 4:6, 10

19 "The kings came *and* fought,
Then the kings of Canaan fought
In [R]Taanach, by the waters of Megiddo;
They took no spoils of silver. Judg. 1:27
20 They fought from the heavens;
The stars from their courses fought
against Sisera.
21 [R]The torrent of Kishon swept them
away, Judg. 4:7
That ancient torrent, the torrent of
Kishon.
O my soul, march on in strength!
22 Then the horses' hooves pounded,
The galloping, galloping of his steeds.
23 'Curse Meroz,' said the [T]angel of the
LORD, Or *Angel*
'Curse its inhabitants bitterly,
Because they did not come to the help
of the LORD,
To the help of the LORD against the
mighty.'

24 "Most blessed among women is Jael,
The wife of Heber the Kenite;
Blessed is she among women in tents.
25 He asked for water, she gave milk;
She brought out cream in a lordly bowl.
26 She stretched her hand to the tent peg,
Her right hand to the workmen's
hammer;
She pounded Sisera, she pierced his
head,
She split and struck through his temple.
27 At her feet he sank, he fell, he lay still;
At her feet he sank, he fell;
Where he sank, there he fell dead.

28 "The mother of Sisera looked through
the window,
And cried out through the lattice,
'Why is his chariot *so* long in coming?
Why tarries the clatter of his chariots?'

5:15 So with vss.; Heb. *And my princes in Issachar*

29 Her wisest [T]ladies answered her,
Yes, she answered herself, *princesses*
30 'Are they not finding and dividing the
spoil:
To every man a girl *or* two;
For Sisera, plunder of dyed garments,
Plunder of garments embroidered and
dyed,
Two pieces of dyed embroidery for the
neck of the looter?'

31 "Thus let all Your enemies [R]perish, O
LORD! Ps. 92:9
But *let* those who love Him *be* [R]like the
[R]sun 2 Sam. 23:4 • Ps. 37:6; 89:36, 37
When it comes out in full strength."

So the land had rest for forty years.

CHAPTER 6

Israel Sins

AND the children of Israel did [R]evil in the
sight of the LORD. So the LORD delivered
them into the hand of [R]Midian for seven
years, Judg. 2:11 • Num. 22:4; 31:1–3
2 and the hand of Midian prevailed against
Israel. Because of the Midianites, the children
of Israel made for themselves the dens, [R]the
caves, and the strongholds which *are* in the
mountains. 1 Sam. 13:6
3 So it was, whenever Israel had sown,
Midianites would come up; also Amalekites
and the [R]people of the East would come up
against them. Judg. 7:12
4 Then they would encamp against them
and [R]destroy the produce of the earth as far
as Gaza, and leave no sustenance for Israel,
neither sheep nor ox nor donkey. Lev. 26:16
5 For they would come up with their livestock and their tents, coming in as numerous
as locusts; both they and their camels were
[T]without number; and they would enter the
land to destroy it. *innumerable*
6 So Israel was greatly impoverished because of the Midianites, and the children of
Israel [R]cried out to the LORD. Hos. 5:15
7 And it came to pass, when the children of
Israel cried out to the LORD because of the
Midianites,
8 that the LORD sent a prophet to the
children of Israel, who said to them, "Thus
says the LORD God of Israel: 'I brought you
up from Egypt and brought you out of the
[R]house of [T]bondage; Josh. 24:17 • *slaves*
9 'and I delivered you out of the hand of
the Egyptians and out of the hand of all who
oppressed you, and [R]drove them out before
you and gave you their land. Ps. 44:2, 3
10 'Also I said to you, "I *am* the LORD your
God; do not fear the gods of the Amorites, in
whose land you dwell. But you have not
obeyed My [R]voice." ' " Judg. 2:1, 2

Gideon Called

11 Now the Angel of the LORD came and sat
under the terebinth tree which *was* in Ophrah, which *belonged* to Joash [R]the Abiezrite,
while his son [R]Gideon threshed wheat in the
winepress, in order to hide *it* from the Midianites. Josh. 17:2 • Heb. 11:32
12 And the [R]Angel of the LORD appeared to
him, and said to him, "The LORD *is* [R]with you,
you mighty man of valor!" Judg. 13:3 • Josh. 1:5
13 And Gideon said to Him, "O [T]my lord, if
the LORD is with us, why then has all this
happened to us? And [R]where *are* all His
miracles [R]which our fathers told us about,
saying, 'Did not the LORD bring us up from
Egypt?' But now the LORD has forsaken us
and delivered us into the hands of the Midianites." Heb. *adoni*, used of man • [Is. 59:1] • Ps. 44:1
14 Then the LORD turned to him and said,
[R]"Go in this might of yours, and you shall
save Israel from the hand of the Midianites.
[R]Have I not sent you?" 1 Sam. 12:11 • Josh. 1:9
15 So he said to Him, "O [T]my Lord, how can
I save Israel? Indeed [R]my clan *is* the weakest
in Manasseh, and I *am* the least in my father's house." Heb. *Adonai*, used of God • 1 Sam. 9:21
16 And the LORD said to him, [R]"Surely I will
be with you, and you shall [T]defeat the Midianites as one man." Ex. 3:12 • Lit. *strike*
17 Then he said to Him, "If now I have
found favor in Your sight, then show me a
sign that it is You who talk with me.
18 [R]"Do not depart from here, I pray, until I
come to You and bring out my offering and
set *it* before You." And He said, "I will wait
until you come back." Gen. 18:3, 5
19 [R]Then Gideon went in and prepared a
young goat, and unleavened bread from an
[T]ephah of flour. The meat he put in a basket,
and he put the broth in a pot; and he brought
them out to Him under the terebinth tree and
presented *them*. Gen. 18:6–8 • 20.87 qt.
20 The Angel of God said to him, "Take the
meat and the unleavened bread and [R]lay
them on this rock, and [R]pour out the broth."
And he did so. Judg. 13:19 • 1 Kin. 18:33, 34
21 Then the Angel of the LORD put out the
end of the staff that *was* in His hand, and
touched the meat and the unleavened bread;
and fire rose out of the rock and consumed
the meat and the unleavened bread. And the
Angel of the LORD departed out of his sight.
22 Now Gideon [R]perceived that He *was* the
Angel of the LORD. So Gideon said, "Alas, O
Lord GOD! [R]For I have seen the Angel of the
LORD face to face." Judg. 13:21, 22 • Gen. 16:13
23 Then the LORD said to him, "Peace *be*
with you; do not fear, you shall not die."
24 So Gideon built an altar there to the
LORD, and called it The-LORD-Shalom. To this
day it *is* still in Ophrah of the Abiezrites.
25 Now it came to pass the same night that
the LORD said to him, "Take your father's

young bull, the second bull of seven years
old, and tear down the altar of Baal that your
father has, and [R]cut down the [T]wooden image
that *is* beside it; Ex. 34:13 • Or *Asherah*
26 "and build an altar to the LORD your God
on top of this [T]rock in the proper arrangement, and take the second bull and offer a
burnt sacrifice with the wood of the image
which you shall cut down." *stronghold*
27 So Gideon took ten men from among his
servants and did as the LORD had said to him.
But because he feared his father's household
and the men of the city too much to do *it* by
day, he did *it* by night.
28 And when the men of the city arose early
in the morning, there was the altar of Baal,
torn down; and the wooden image that *was*
beside it was cut down, and the second bull
was being offered on the altar *which had
been* built.
29 So they said to one another, "Who has
done this thing?" And when they had inquired and asked, they said, "Gideon the son
of Joash has done this thing."
30 Then the men of the city said to Joash,
"Bring out your son, that he may die, because
he has torn down the altar of Baal, and
because he has cut down the wooden image
that *was* beside it."
31 And Joash said to all who stood against
him, "Would you [T]plead for Baal? Would you
save him? Let the one who would plead for
him be put to death by morning! If he *is* a
god, let him plead for himself, because his
altar has been torn down!" *contend*
32 Therefore on that day he called him
Jerubbaal, saying, "Let Baal plead against
him, because he has torn down his altar."
33 Then all [R]the Midianites and Amalekites,
the people of the East, gathered together; and
they crossed over and encamped in [R]the
Valley of Jezreel. Judg. 6:3 • Josh. 17:16
34 But the Spirit of the LORD came upon
Gideon; then he [R]blew the trumpet, and the
Abiezrites gathered behind him. Judg. 3:27
35 And he sent messengers throughout all
Manasseh, who also gathered behind him. He
also sent messengers to [R]Asher, [R]Zebulun,
and Naphtali; and they came up to meet
them. Judg. 5:17; 7:23 • Judg. 4:6, 10; 5:18
36 Then Gideon said to God, "If You will
save Israel by my hand as You have said—
37 [R]"look, I shall put a fleece of wool on the
threshing floor; if there is dew on the fleece
only, and *it is* dry on all the ground, then I
shall know that You will save Israel by my
hand, as You have said." [Ex. 4:3–7]
38 And it was so. When he rose early the
next morning and squeezed the fleece together, he wrung the dew out of the fleece, a
bowl full of water.
39 Then Gideon said to God, "Do not be
angry with me, and let me speak just once
more: Let me test, I pray, just once more with
the fleece; let it now be dry only on the fleece,
but on all the ground let there be dew."
40 And God did so that night. It was dry on
the fleece only, but there was dew on all the
ground.

CHAPTER 7

Midianites Defeated

THEN [R]Jerubbaal (that *is*, Gideon) and all
the people who *were* with him rose early
and encamped beside the well of Harod, so
that the camp of the Midianites was on the
north side of them by the hill of Moreh in the
valley. Judg. 6:32
2 And the LORD said to Gideon, "The people who *are* with you *are* too many for Me to
give the Midianites into their hands, lest
Israel [R]claim glory for itself against Me,
saying, 'My own hand has saved me.' Deut. 8:17
3 "Now therefore, proclaim in the hearing
of the people, saying, [R]'Whoever *is* fearful
and afraid, let him turn and depart at once
from Mount Gilead.' " And twenty-two thousand of the people returned, and ten thousand remained. Deut. 20:8
4 And the LORD said to Gideon, "The people *are* still *too* many; bring them down to the
water, and I will test them for you there.
Then it will be, *that* of whom I say to you,
'This one shall go with you,' the same shall go
with you; and of whomever I say to you,
'This one shall not go with you,' the same
shall not go."
5 So he brought the people down to the
water. And the LORD said to Gideon, "Everyone who laps from the water with his tongue,
as a dog laps, you shall set apart by himself;
likewise everyone who gets down on his
knees to drink."
6 And the number of those who lapped,
putting their hand to their mouth, was three
hundred men; but all the rest of the people
got down on their knees to drink water.
7 Then the LORD said to Gideon, [R]"By the
three hundred men who lapped I will save
you, and deliver the Midianites into your
hand. Let all the *other* people go, every man
to his [T]place." 1 Sam. 14:6 • *home*
8 So the people took provisions and their
trumpets in their hands. And he sent away all
the rest of Israel, every man to his tent, and
retained those three hundred men. Now the
camp of Midian was below him in the valley.
9 And it happened on the same [R]night that
the LORD said to him, "Arise, go down against
the camp, for I have delivered it into your
hand. Judg. 6:25
10 "But if you are afraid to go down, go
down to the camp with Purah your servant,
11 "and you shall hear what they say; and
afterward your hands shall be strengthened

to go down against the camp." Then he went down with Purah his servant to the outpost of the armed men who *were* in the camp.

12 Now the Midianites and Amalekites, all the people of the East, were lying in the valley [R]as numerous as locusts; and their camels *were* [T]without number, as the sand by the seashore in multitude. Judg. 6:5 • *innumerable*

13 And when Gideon had come, there was a man telling a dream to his companion. He said, "I have *just* had a dream: *To my* surprise, a loaf of barley bread tumbled into the camp of Midian; it came to a tent and struck it so that it fell and overturned, and the tent collapsed."

14 Then his companion answered and said, "This *is* nothing else but the sword of Gideon the son of Joash, a man of Israel; *for* into his hand [R]God has delivered Midian and the whole camp." Judg. 6:14, 16

15 And so it was, when Gideon heard the telling of the dream and its interpretation, that he worshiped. He returned to the camp of Israel, and said, "Arise, for the LORD has delivered the camp of Midian into your hand."

16 Then he divided the three hundred men *into* three companies, and he put a trumpet into every man's hand, with empty pitchers, and torches inside the pitchers.

17 And he said to them, "Look at me and do likewise; watch, and when I come to the edge of the camp you shall do *just* as I do:

18 "When I blow the trumpet, I and all who *are* with me, then you also blow the trumpets on every side of the whole camp, and say, '*The sword of* the LORD and of Gideon!' "

19 So Gideon and the hundred men who *were* with him came to the outpost of the camp at the beginning of the middle watch, just as they had posted the watch; and they blew the trumpets and broke the pitchers that *were* in their hands.

20 Then the three companies blew the trumpets and broke the pitchers—they held the torches in their left hands and the trumpets in their right hands for blowing—and they cried, "The sword of the LORD and of Gideon!"

21 And [R]every man stood in his place all around the camp; [R]and the whole army ran and cried out and fled. 2 Chr. 20:17 • 2 Kin. 7:7

22 When the three hundred blew the trumpets, [R]the LORD set every man's sword against his companion throughout the whole camp; and the army fled to [T]Beth Acacia, toward Zererah, as far as the border of Abel Meholah, by Tabbath. Is. 9:4 • Heb. *Beth Shittah*

23 And the men of Israel gathered together from [R]Naphtali, Asher, and all Manasseh, and pursued the Midianites. Judg. 6:35

24 Then Gideon sent messengers throughout all the mountains of Ephraim, saying, "Come down against the Midianites, and seize from them the watering places as far as Beth Barah and the Jordan." Then all the men of Ephraim gathered together and [R]seized the watering places as far as [R]Beth Barah and the Jordan. Judg. 3:28 • John 1:28

25 And they captured two princes of the Midianites, Oreb and Zeeb. They killed Oreb at the rock of Oreb, and Zeeb they killed at the winepress of Zeeb. They pursued Midian and brought the heads of Oreb and Zeeb to Gideon on the other side of the Jordan.

CHAPTER 8

NOW [R]the men of Ephraim said to him, "Why have you done this to us by not calling us when you went to fight with the Midianites?" And they reprimanded him sharply. Judg. 12:1

2 So he said to them, "What have I done now in comparison with you? *Is* not the gleaning *of the grapes* of Ephraim better than [T]the vintage of Abiezer? The whole harvest

3 [R]"God has delivered into your hands the princes of Midian, Oreb and Zeeb. And what was I able to do in comparison with you?" Then their [R]anger toward him [T]abated when he said that. Judg. 7:24, 25 • Prov. 15:1 • *subsided*

4 When Gideon came [R]to the Jordan, he and [R]the three hundred men who *were* with him crossed over, exhausted but still in pursuit. Judg. 7:25 • Judg. 7:6

5 Then he said to the men of [R]Succoth, "Please give loaves of bread to the people who follow me, for they are exhausted, and I am pursuing Zebah and Zalmunna, kings of Midian." Gen. 33:17

6 And the leaders of Succoth said, [R]"*Are*[T] the hands of Zebah and Zalmunna now in your hand, that [R]we should give bread to your army?" Judg. 8:15 • Lit. *Is the palm* • 1 Sam. 25:11

7 So Gideon said, "For this cause, when the LORD has delivered Zebah and Zalmunna into my hand, then I will tear your flesh with the thorns of the wilderness and with briers!"

8 Then he went up from there [R]to Penuel and spoke to them in the same way. And the men of Penuel answered him as the men of Succoth had answered *him*. Gen. 32:30, 31

9 So he also spoke to the men of Penuel, saying, "When I [R]come back in peace, [R]I will tear down this tower!" 1 Kin. 22:27 • Judg. 8:17

10 Now Zebah and Zalmunna *were* at Karkor, and their armies with them, about fifteen thousand *men*, all who were left of [R]all the army of the people of the East; for [R]one hundred and twenty thousand men who drew the sword had fallen. Judg. 7:12 • Judg. 6:5

11 Then Gideon went up by the road of those who dwell in tents on the east of Nobah and Jogbehah; and he [T]attacked the army while the camp felt secure. Lit. *struck*

ISRAEL'S JUDGES
Judges 8—12

After the death of Joshua, the nation of Israel was ruled by judges, or heroic military deliverers, for about 300 years until the united monarchy was established under King Saul. The era of the judges was a time of instability and moral depravity, a dark period when "everyone did what was right in his own eyes" (Judg. 17:6). The judges tried to rally the people against their enemies, but many of the judges were morally weak and the people often turned to idolatry. Along with the well-known judges portrayed on this map, there were several minor judges whose battles are not recorded in the Bible: Abimelech, Tola, Jair, Ibzan, Elon, and Abdon.

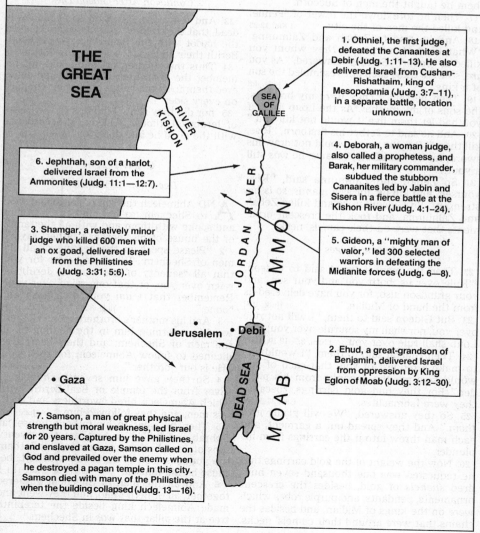

THE GREAT SEA

SEA OF GALILEE

RIVER KISHON

1. Othniel, the first judge, defeated the Canaanites at Debir (Judg. 1:11–13). He also delivered Israel from Cushan-Rishathaim, king of Mesopotamia (Judg. 3:7–11), in a separate battle, location unknown.

6. Jephthah, son of a harlot, delivered Israel from the Ammonites (Judg. 11:1—12:7).

4. Deborah, a woman judge, also called a prophetess, and Barak, her military commander, subdued the stubborn Canaanites led by Jabin and Sisera in a fierce battle at the Kishon River (Judg. 4:1–24).

JORDAN RIVER

AMMON

3. Shamgar, a relatively minor judge who killed 600 men with an ox goad, delivered Israel from the Philistines (Judg. 3:31; 5:6).

5. Gideon, a "mighty man of valor," led 300 selected warriors in defeating the Midianite forces (Judg. 6—8).

Jerusalem

Debir

2. Ehud, a great-grandson of Benjamin, delivered Israel from oppression by King Eglon of Moab (Judg. 3:12–30).

Gaza

DEAD SEA

MOAB

7. Samson, a man of great physical strength but moral weakness, led Israel for 20 years. Captured by the Philistines, and enslaved at Gaza, Samson called on God and prevailed over the enemy when he destroyed a pagan temple in this city. Samson died with many of the Philistines when the building collapsed (Judg. 13—16).

12 When Zebah and Zalmunna fled, he pursued them; and he [R]took the two kings of
Midian, Zebah and Zalmunna, and routed the
whole army. Ps. 83:11
13 Then Gideon the son of Joash returned
from battle, from the Ascent of Heres.
14 And he caught a young man of the men
of Succoth and interrogated him; and he
wrote down for him the leaders of Succoth
and its elders, seventy-seven men.
15 Then he came to the men of Succoth and
said, "Here are Zebah and Zalmunna, about
whom you [R]ridiculed me, saying, 'Are the
hands of Zebah and Zalmunna now in your
hand, that we should give bread to your
weary men?' " Judg. 8:6
16 And he took the elders of the city, and
thorns of the wilderness and briers, and with
them he taught the men of Succoth.
17 Then he tore down the tower of [R]Penuel
and killed the men of the city. 1 Kin. 12:25
18 And he said to Zebah and Zalmunna,
"What kind of men *were they* whom you
killed at [R]Tabor?" So they answered, "As you
are, so *were* they; each one resembled the son
of a king." Judg. 4:6
19 Then he said, "They *were* my brothers,
the sons of my mother. *As* the LORD lives, if
you had let them live, I would not kill you."
20 And he said to Jether his firstborn, "Rise,
kill them!" But the youth would not draw his
sword; for he was afraid, because he *was* still
a youth.
21 So Zebah and Zalmunna said, "Rise
yourself, and kill us; for as a man *is, so is* his
strength." So Gideon arose and killed Zebah
and Zalmunna, and took the crescent ornaments that *were* on their camels' necks.

Gideon Judges

22 Then the men of Israel said to Gideon,
[R]"Rule over us, both you and your son, and
your grandson also; for you have delivered us
from the hand of Midian." [Judg. 9:8]
23 But Gideon said to them, "I will not rule
over you, nor shall my son rule over you; [R]the
LORD shall rule over you." 1 Sam. 8:7; 10:19; 12:12
24 Then Gideon said to them, "I would like
to make a request of you, that each of you
would give me the earrings from his plunder." For they had gold earrings, [R]because
they *were* Ishmaelites. Gen. 37:25, 28
25 So they answered, "We will gladly give
them." And they spread out a garment, and
each man threw into it the earrings from his
plunder.
26 Now the weight of the gold earrings that
he requested was one thousand seven hundred *shekels* of gold, besides the crescent
ornaments, pendants, and purple robes which
were on the kings of Midian, and besides the
chains that *were* around their camels' necks.
27 Then Gideon made it into an ephod and
set it up in his city, Ophrah. And all Israel
[R]played the harlot with it there. It became a
snare to Gideon and to his house. [Ps. 106:39]
28 Thus Midian was subdued before the
children of Israel, so that they lifted their
heads no more. [R]And the country was quiet
for forty years in the days of Gideon. Judg. 5:31
29 Then [R]Jerubbaal the son of Joash went
and dwelt in his own house. Judg. 6:32; 7:1
30 Gideon had seventy sons who were his
own offspring, for he had many wives.
31 [R]And his concubine who *was* in Shechem
also bore him a son, whose name he called
Abimelech. Judg. 9:1
32 Now Gideon the son of Joash died at a
good old age, and was buried in the tomb of
Joash his father, in Ophrah of the Abiezrites.

Confusion After Gideon Dies

33 And it was so, [R]as soon as Gideon was
dead, that the children of Israel again [R]played
the harlot with the Baals, [R]and made Baal-
Berith their god. Judg. 2:19 • Judg. 2:17 • Judg. 9:4, 46
34 Thus the children of Israel [R]did not remember the LORD their God, who had delivered them from the hands of all their enemies
on every side; Deut. 4:9
35 nor did they show kindness to the house
of Jerubbaal (*that is,* Gideon) in accordance
with the good he had done for Israel.

CHAPTER 9

Deception of Abimelech

AND Abimelech the son of Jerubbaal went
to Shechem, to his mother's brothers,
and spoke with them and with all the family
of the house of his mother's father, saying,
2 "Please speak in the hearing of all the
men of Shechem: 'Which is better for you,
that all [R]seventy of the sons of Jerubbaal
reign over you, or that one reign over you?'
Remember that I *am* your own flesh and
[R]bone." Judg. 8:30; 9:5, 18 • Gen. 29:14
3 And his mother's brothers spoke all these
words concerning him in the hearing of all
the men of Shechem; and their heart was
inclined to follow Abimelech, for they said,
"He is our [R]brother." Gen. 29:15
4 So they gave him seventy *shekels* of
silver from the temple of Baal-Berith, with
which Abimelech hired [R]worthless and reckless men; and they followed him. Judg. 11:3
5 Then he went to his father's house [R]at
Ophrah and [R]killed his brothers, the seventy
sons of Jerubbaal, on one stone. But Jotham
the youngest son of Jerubbaal was left, because he hid himself. Judg. 6:24 • 2 Kin. 11:1, 2
6 And all the men of Shechem gathered
together, all of Beth Millo, and they went and
made Abimelech king beside the terebinth
tree at the pillar that *was* in Shechem.

Revelation of Jotham

7 Now when they told *it* to Jotham, he
went and stood on top of [R]Mount Gerizim,
and lifted his voice and cried out, and said to
them: Deut. 11:29; 27:12

"Listen to me, you men of Shechem,
That God may listen to you!

8 "The[R] trees once went forth to anoint a
king over them. 2 Kin. 14:9
And they said to the olive tree,
[R]'Reign over us!' Judg. 8:22, 23
9 But the olive tree said to them,
'Should I cease giving my oil,
[R]With which they honor God and men,
And go to sway over trees?' [John 5:23]

10 "Then the trees said to the fig tree,
'You come *and* reign over us!'
11 But the fig tree said to them,
'Should I cease my sweetness and my
good fruit,
And go to sway over trees?'

12 "Then the trees said to the vine,
'You come *and* reign over us!'
13 But the vine said to them,
'Should I cease my new wine,
[R]Which cheers *both* God and men,
And go to sway over trees?' Ps. 104:15

14 "Then all the trees said to the bramble,
'You come *and* reign over us!'
15 And the bramble said to the trees,
'If in truth you anoint me as king over
you,
Then come *and* take shelter in my
[R]shade; Is. 30:2
But if not, [R]let fire come out of the
bramble Num. 21:28
And devour the cedars of Lebanon!'

16 "Now therefore, if you have acted in
truth and sincerity in making Abimelech
king, and if you have dealt well with Jerubbaal and his house, and have done to him [T]as
he deserves— Lit. *according to the doing of his hands*
17 "for my [R]father fought for you, risked his
life, and [R]delivered you out of the hand of
Midian; Judg. 7 • Judg. 8:22
18 "but you have risen up against my father's house this day, and killed his seventy
sons on one stone, and made Abimelech, the
son of his maidservant, king over the men of
Shechem, because he is your brother—
19 "if then you have acted in truth and
sincerity with Jerubbaal and with his house
this day, *then* [R]rejoice in Abimelech, and let
him also rejoice in you. Is. 8:6
20 "But if not, [R]let fire come from Abimelech and devour the men of Shechem and
Beth Millo; and let fire come from the men of
Shechem and from Beth Millo and devour
Abimelech!" Judg. 9:15, 45, 56, 57
21 And Jotham ran away and fled; and he
went to [R]Beer and dwelt there, for fear of
Abimelech his brother. Num. 21:16

Destruction of Shechem

22 After Abimelech had reigned over Israel
three years,
23 [R]God sent a [R]spirit of ill will between
Abimelech and the men of Shechem; and the
men of Shechem [R]dealt treacherously with
Abimelech, Is. 19:14 • 1 Sam. 16:14; 18:9, 10 • Is. 33:1
24 that the crime *done* to the seventy sons
of Jerubbaal might be settled and their [R]blood
be laid on Abimelech their brother, who killed
them, and on the men of Shechem, who aided
him in the killing of his brothers. Num. 35:33
25 And the men of Shechem set [T]men in
ambush against him on the tops of the mountains, and they robbed all who passed by
them along that way; and it was told Abimelech. Lit. *liers-in-wait for*
26 Now Gaal the son of Ebed came with his
brothers and went over to Shechem; and the
men of Shechem put their confidence in him.
27 So they went out into the fields, and
gathered *grapes* from their vineyards and
trod *them*, and [T]made merry. And they went
into [R]the house of their god, and ate and
drank, and cursed Abimelech. *rejoiced* • Judg. 9:4
28 Then Gaal the son of Ebed said, "Who *is*
Abimelech, and who *is* Shechem, that we
should serve him? *Is he* not the son of Jerubbaal, and *is not* Zebul his officer? Serve the
men of [R]Hamor the father of Shechem; but
why should we serve him? Gen. 34:2, 6
29 [R]"If only this people were under my
hand! Then I would remove Abimelech." So
he said to Abimelech, "Increase your army
and come out!" 2 Sam. 15:4
30 When Zebul, the ruler of the city, heard
the words of Gaal the son of Ebed, his anger
was aroused.
31 And he sent messengers to Abimelech
secretly, saying, "Take note! Gaal the son of
Ebed and his brothers have come to Shechem; and here they are, fortifying the city
against you.
32 "Now therefore, get up by night, you and
the people who *are* with you, and [T]lie in wait
in the field. *set up an ambush*
33 "And it shall be, as soon as the sun is up
in the morning, *that* you shall rise early and
rush upon the city; and *as soon as* he and the
people who are with him come out against
you, you may then do to them [T]as you find
opportunity." Lit. *as your hand can find*
34 So Abimelech and all the people who
were with him rose by night, and laid in wait
against Shechem in four companies.
35 When Gaal the son of Ebed went out
and stood in the entrance to the city gate,

Abimelech and the people who *were* with him
rose [T]from lying in wait. *from the ambush*
36 And when Gaal saw the people, he said
to Zebul, "Look, people are coming down
from the tops of the mountains!" But Zebul
said to him, "You see the shadows of the
mountains as *if they were* men."
37 So Gaal spoke again and said, "See,
people are coming down from the center of
the land, and another company is coming
from the Diviners' Terebinth Tree."
38 Then Zebul said to him, "Where indeed *is*
your mouth now, with which you said, 'Who
is Abimelech, that we should serve him?' *Are*
not these the people whom you despised? Go
out, if you will, and fight with them now."
39 So Gaal went out, leading the men of
Shechem, and fought with Abimelech.
40 And Abimelech chased him, and he fled
from him; and many fell wounded, *even* to
the entrance of the gate.
41 Then Abimelech dwelt at Arumah, and
Zebul [T]drove out Gaal and his brothers, so
that they would not dwell in Shechem. *exiled*
42 And it came about on the next day that
the people went out into the field, and they
told Abimelech.
43 So he took his people, divided them into
three companies, and [T]laid in wait in the field.
And he looked, and there were the people,
coming out of the city; and he rose against
them and attacked them. *made an ambush*
44 Then Abimelech and the company that
was with him rushed forward and stood at
the entrance of the gate of the city; and the
other two companies rushed upon all who
were in the fields and killed them.
45 So Abimelech fought against the city all
that day; he took the city and killed the
people who *were* in it; and he [R]demolished
the city and sowed it with salt. 2 Kin. 3:25
46 Now when all the men of the tower of
Shechem had heard *that*, they entered the
stronghold of the temple of the god Berith.
47 And it was told Abimelech that all the
men of the tower of Shechem were gathered
together.
48 Then Abimelech went up to Mount [R]Zal-
mon, he and all the people who *were* with
him. And Abimelech took an ax in his hand
and cut down a bough from the trees, and
took it and laid *it* on his shoulder; then he
said to the people who were with him, "What
you have seen me do, make haste *and* do as I
have done." Ps. 68:14
49 So each of the people likewise cut down
his own bough and followed Abimelech, put
them against the [T]stronghold, and set the
stronghold on fire above them, so that all the
people of the tower of Shechem died, about a
thousand men and women. *fortified room*

Death of Abimelech

50 Then Abimelech went to Thebez, and he
[T]encamped against Thebez and took it. *besieged*
51 But there was a strong tower in the city,
and all the men and women—all the people of
the city—fled there and shut themselves in;
then they went up to the top of the tower.
52 So Abimelech came as far as the tower
and fought against it; and he drew near the
door of the tower to burn it with fire.
53 But a certain woman [R]dropped an upper
millstone on Abimelech's head and crushed
his skull. 2 Sam. 11:21
54 Then [R]he called quickly to the young
man, his armorbearer, and said to him, "Draw
your sword and kill me, lest men say of me,
'A woman killed him.' " So his young man
thrust him through, and he died. 1 Sam. 31:4
55 And when the men of Israel saw that
Abimelech was dead, they departed, every
man to his *own* [T]place. *home*
56 [R]Thus God repaid the wickedness of
Abimelech, which he had done to his father
by killing his seventy brothers. Job 31:3
57 And all the evil of the men of Shechem
God returned on their own heads, and on
them came [R]the curse of Jotham the son of
Jerubbaal. Judg. 9:20

CHAPTER 10

The Judge Tola

AFTER Abimelech there [R]arose to save
Israel Tola the son of Puah, the son of
Dodo, a man of Issachar; and he dwelt in
Shamir in the mountains of Ephraim. Judg. 2:16
2 He judged Israel twenty-three years; and
he died and was buried in Shamir.

The Judge Jair

3 After him arose Jair, a Gileadite; and he
judged Israel twenty-two years.
4 Now he had thirty sons who rode on
thirty donkeys; they also had thirty towns,
[R]which are called "Havoth Jair" to this day,
which *are* in the land of Gilead. Deut. 3:14
5 And Jair died and was buried in Camon.

Israel Sins

6 Then the children of Israel again did evil
in the sight of the LORD, and served the Baals
and the Ashtoreths, [R]the gods of Syria, the
gods of [R]Sidon, the gods of Moab, the gods of
the people of Ammon, and the gods of the
Philistines; and they forsook the LORD and
did not serve Him. Judg. 2:12 • 1 Kin. 11:33
7 So the anger of the LORD was hot against
Israel; and He sold them into the hands of the
[R]Philistines and into the hands of the people
of [R]Ammon. Judg. 13:1 • Judg. 3:13

8 From that year they [T]harassed and oppressed the children of Israel for eighteen years—all the children of Israel who *were* on the other side of the Jordan in the [R]land of the Amorites, in Gilead. Lit. *shattered* • Num. 32:33

9 Moreover the people of Ammon crossed over the Jordan to fight against Judah also, against Benjamin, and against the house of Ephraim, so that Israel was severely distressed.

10 [R]And the children of Israel cried out to the LORD, saying, "We have [R]sinned against You, because we have both forsaken our God and served the Baals!" 1 Sam. 12:10 • Deut. 1:41

11 So the LORD said to the children of Israel, "*Did I* not *deliver you* from the Egyptians and from the Amorites and from the people of Ammon and from the Philistines?

12 "Also [R]the Sidonians [R]and Amalekites and *Maonites [R]oppressed you; and you cried out to Me, and I delivered you from their hand. Judg. 1:31; 5:19 • Judg. 6:3; 7:12 • Ps. 106:42, 43

13 [R]"Yet you have forsaken Me and served other gods. Therefore I will deliver you no more. [Jer. 2:13]

14 "Go and [R]cry out to the gods which you have chosen; let them deliver you in your time of distress." Deut. 32:37, 38

15 Then the children of Israel said to the LORD, "We have sinned! [R]Do to us whatever seems best to You; only deliver us this day, we pray." 1 Sam. 3:18

16 [R]So they put away the foreign gods from among them and served the LORD. And [R]His soul could no longer endure the misery of Israel. Jer. 18:7, 8 • Is. 63:9

17 Then the people of Ammon gathered together and encamped in Gilead. And the children of Israel assembled together and encamped in [R]Mizpah. Judg. 11:11, 29

18 And the people, the leaders of Gilead, said to one another, "Who *is* the man who will begin the fight against the people of Ammon? He shall [R]be head over all the inhabitants of Gilead." Judg. 11:8, 11

CHAPTER 11

Jephthah Is Called

NOW Jephthah the Gileadite was a mighty man of valor, but he *was* the son of a harlot; and Gilead begot Jephthah.

2 Gilead's wife bore sons; and when his wife's sons grew up, they drove Jephthah out, and said to him, "You shall have [R]no inheritance in our father's house, for you *are* the son of another woman." Gen. 21:10

3 Then Jephthah fled from his brothers and dwelt in the land of Tob; and [R]worthless men banded together with Jephthah and went out *raiding* with him. 1 Sam. 22:2

4 Now it came to pass after a time that the people of Ammon made war against Israel.

5 And so it was, when the people of Ammon made war against Israel, that the elders of Gilead went to get Jephthah from the land of Tob.

6 Then they said to Jephthah, "Come and be our commander, that we may fight against the people of Ammon."

7 So Jephthah said to the elders of Gilead, "Did you not hate me, and expel me from my father's house? Why have you come to me now when you are in [T]distress?" *trouble*

8 And the elders of Gilead said to Jephthah, "That is why we have turned again to you now, that you may go with us and fight against the people of Ammon, and be our head over all the inhabitants of Gilead."

9 So Jephthah said to the elders of Gilead, "If you take me back home to fight against the people of Ammon, and the LORD delivers them to me, shall I be your head?"

10 And the elders of Gilead said to Jephthah, "The LORD will be a witness between us, if we do not do according to your words."

11 Then Jephthah went with the elders of Gilead, and the people made him head and commander over them; and Jephthah spoke all his words before the LORD in Mizpah.

Jephthah Judges

12 Now Jephthah sent messengers to the king of the people of Ammon, saying, [R]"What do you have against me, that you have come to fight against me in my land?" 2 Sam. 16:10

13 And the king of the people of Ammon answered the messengers of Jephthah, "Because Israel took away my land when they came up out of Egypt, from the Arnon as far as the Jabbok, and to the Jordan. Now therefore, restore those *lands* peaceably."

14 So Jephthah again sent messengers to the king of the people of Ammon,

15 and said to him, "Thus says Jephthah: 'Israel did not take away the land of Moab, nor the land of the people of Ammon;

16 'for when Israel came up from Egypt, they walked through the wilderness as far as the Red Sea and came to Kadesh.

17 'Then Israel sent messengers to the king of Edom, saying, "Please let me pass through your land." But the king of Edom would not heed. And in like manner they sent to the king of Moab, but he would not *consent*. So Israel [R]remained in Kadesh. Num. 20:1

18 'And they [R]went along through the wilderness and [R]bypassed the land of Edom and the land of Moab, came to the east side of the land of Moab, and encamped on the other side of the Arnon. But they did not enter the border of Moab, for the Arnon *was* the border of Moab. Deut. 2:9, 18, 19 • Num. 21:4

10:12 LXX mss. *Midianites*

19 'Then Israel sent messengers to Sihon king of the Amorites, king of Heshbon; and Israel said to him, "Please [R]let us pass through your land into our place." Deut. 2:27

20 [R]'But Sihon did not trust Israel to pass through his territory. So Sihon gathered all his people together, encamped in Jahaz, and fought against Israel. Deut. 2:27

21 'And the LORD God of Israel delivered Sihon and all his people into the hand of Israel, and they [T]defeated them. Thus Israel gained possession of all the land of the Amorites, who inhabited that country. Lit. *struck*

22 'They took possession of [R]all the territory of the Amorites, from the Arnon to the Jabbok and from the wilderness to the Jordan. Deut. 2:36, 37

23 'So now the LORD God of Israel has dispossessed the Amorites from before His people Israel; should you then possess it?

24 'Will you not possess whatever Chemosh your god gives you to possess? So whatever [R]the LORD our God takes possession of before us, we will possess. [Deut. 9:4, 5]

25 'And now, *are* you any better than [R]Balak the son of Zippor, king of Moab? Did he ever strive against Israel? Did he ever fight against them? Num. 22:2

26 'While Israel dwelt in [R]Heshbon and its villages, in [R]Aroer and its villages, and in all the cities along the banks of the Arnon, for three hundred years, why did you not recover *them* within that time? Num. 21:25, 26 • Deut. 2:36

27 'Therefore I have not sinned against you, but you wronged me by fighting against me. May the LORD, the Judge, [R]render judgment this day between the children of Israel and the people of Ammon.' " Gen. 16:5; 31:53

28 However, the king of the people of Ammon did not heed the words which Jephthah sent him.

Jephthah Vows

29 Then the Spirit of the LORD came upon Jephthah, and he passed through Gilead and Manasseh, and passed through Mizpah of Gilead; and from Mizpah of Gilead he advanced *toward* the people of Ammon.

30 And Jephthah [R]made a vow to the LORD, and said, "If You will indeed deliver the people of Ammon into my hands, Gen. 28:20

31 "then it will be that whatever comes out of the doors of my house to meet me, when I return in peace from the people of Ammon, [R]shall surely be the LORD's, [R]and I will offer it up as a burnt offering." Lev. 27:2, 3, 28 • Ps. 66:13

32 So Jephthah advanced toward the people of Ammon to fight against them, and the LORD delivered them into his hands.

33 And he defeated them from Aroer as far as Minnith—twenty cities—and to [T]Abel Keramim, with a very great slaughter. Thus the people of Ammon were subdued before the children of Israel. Lit. *Plain of Vineyards*

34 When Jephthah came to his house at Mizpah, there was [R]his daughter, coming out to meet him with timbrels and dancing; and she *was his* only child. Besides her he had neither son nor daughter. Ex. 15:20

35 And it came to pass, when he saw her, that he tore his clothes, and said, "Alas, my daughter! You have brought me very low! You are among those who trouble me! For I have [T]given my word to the LORD, and I cannot go back on it." Lit. *opened my mouth*

36 So she said to him, "My father, *if* you have given your word to the LORD, do to me according to what has gone out of your mouth, because the LORD has avenged you of your enemies, the people of Ammon."

37 Then she said to her father, "Let this thing be done for me: let me alone for two months, that I may go and wander on the mountains and [T]bewail my virginity, my [T]friends and I." *lament* • *companions*

38 So he said, "Go." And he sent her away *for* two months; and she went with her friends, and bewailed her virginity on the mountains.

39 And it was so at the end of two months that she returned to her father, and he [R]carried out his vow with her which he had vowed. She [T]knew no man. And it became a custom in Israel Judg. 11:31 • Remained a virgin

40 *that* the daughters of Israel went four days each year to [T]lament the daughter of Jephthah the Gileadite. *commemorate*

CHAPTER 12

Ephraim Is Conquered

THEN the men of Ephraim gathered together, crossed over toward Zaphon, and said to Jephthah, "Why did you cross over to fight against the people of Ammon, and did not call us to go with you? We will burn your house down on you with fire!"

2 And Jephthah said to them, "My people and I were in a great struggle with the people of Ammon; and when I called you, you did not deliver me out of their hands.

3 "So when I saw that you would not deliver *me*, I [R]took my life in my hands and crossed over against the people of Ammon; and the LORD delivered them into my hand. Why then have you come up to me this day to fight against me?" 1 Sam. 19:5; 28:21

4 Now Jephthah gathered together all the men of Gilead and fought against Ephraim. And the men of Gilead defeated Ephraim, because they said, "You Gileadites [R]*are* fugitives of Ephraim among the Ephraimites *and* among the Manassites." 1 Sam. 25:10

5 The Gileadites seized the [R]fords of the Jordan before the Ephraimites *arrived*. And

when *any* Ephraimite who escaped said, "Let me cross over," the men of Gilead would say to him, "*Are* you an Ephraimite?" If he said, "No," Josh. 22:11

6 then they would say to him, "Then say, 'Shibboleth'!" And he would say, "Sibboleth," for he could not [T]pronounce *it* right. Then they would take him and kill him at the fords of the Jordan. There fell at that time forty-two thousand Ephraimites. Lit. *speak so*

7 And Jephthah judged Israel six years. Then Jephthah the Gileadite died and was buried in *one of* the cities of Gilead.

The Judge Ibzan

8 After him, Ibzan of Bethlehem judged Israel.

9 He had thirty sons. And he gave away thirty daughters in marriage, and brought in thirty daughters from elsewhere for his sons. He judged Israel seven years.

10 Then Ibzan died and was buried at Bethlehem.

The Judge Elon

11 After him, Elon the Zebulunite judged Israel. He judged Israel ten years.

12 And Elon the Zebulunite died and was buried at Aijalon in the country of Zebulun.

The Judge Abdon

13 After him, Abdon the son of Hillel the Pirathonite judged Israel.

14 He had forty sons and thirty grandsons, who [R]rode on seventy young donkeys. He judged Israel eight years. Judg. 5:10; 10:4

15 Then Abdon the son of Hillel the Pirathonite died and was buried in Pirathon in the land of Ephraim, [R]in the mountains of the Amalekites. Judg. 3:13, 27; 5:14

CHAPTER 13

Miraculous Birth of Samson

AGAIN the children of Israel [R]did evil in the sight of the LORD, and the LORD delivered them [R]into the hand of the Philistines for forty years. Judg. 2:11 · 1 Sam. 12:9

2 Now there was a certain man from [R]Zorah, of the family of the Danites, whose name *was* Manoah; and his wife *was* barren and had no children. Josh. 19:41

3 And the [R]Angel of the LORD appeared to the woman and said to her, "Indeed now, you are barren and have borne no children, but you shall conceive and bear a son. Judg. 6:12

4 "Now therefore, please be careful [R]not to drink wine or *similar* drink, and not to eat any unclean *thing*. Num. 6:2, 3, 20

5 "For behold, you shall conceive and bear a son. And no razor shall come upon his head, for the child shall be a Nazirite to God from the womb; and he shall begin to deliver Israel out of the hand of the Philistines."

6 So the woman came and told her husband, saying, "A Man of God came to me, and His [T]countenance *was* like the countenance of the Angel of God, very awesome; but I did not ask Him where He *was* from, and He did not tell me His name. *appearance*

7 "And He said to me, 'Behold, you shall conceive and bear a son. Now drink no wine or *similar* drink, nor eat anything unclean, for the child shall be a Nazirite to God from the womb to the day of his death.' "

8 Then Manoah prayed to the LORD, and said, "O my Lord, please let the Man of God whom You sent come to us again and teach us what we shall do for the child who will be born."

9 And God listened to the voice of Manoah, and the Angel of God came to the woman again as she was sitting in the field; but Manoah her husband *was* not with her.

10 Then the woman ran in haste and told her husband, and said to him, "Look, the Man has just now appeared to me, *the One* who came to me the *other* day!"

11 So Manoah arose and followed his wife. When he came to the Man, he said to Him, "Are You the Man who spoke to this woman?" And He said, "I *am*."

12 And Manoah said, "Now let Your words come *to pass*! What will be the boy's rule of life, and his work?"

13 So the Angel of the LORD said to Manoah, "Of all that I said to the woman let her be careful.

14 "She may not eat anything that comes from the vine, nor may she drink wine or *similar* drink, nor eat anything unclean. All that I commanded her let her observe."

15 Then Manoah said to the Angel of the LORD, "Please [R]let us detain You, and we will prepare a young goat for You." Gen. 18:5

16 And the Angel of the LORD said to Manoah, "Though you detain Me, I will not eat your food. But if you offer a burnt offering, you must offer it to the LORD." (For Manoah did not know He *was* the Angel of the LORD.)

17 Then Manoah said to the Angel of the LORD, "What *is* Your name, that when Your words come *to pass* we may honor You?"

18 And the Angel of the LORD said to him, [R]"Why do you ask My name, seeing it *is* wonderful?" Gen. 32:29

19 So Manoah took the young goat with the grain offering, and offered it upon the rock to the LORD. And He did a wondrous thing while Manoah and his wife looked on:

20 as the flame went up toward heaven from the altar, it happened that the Angel of the LORD ascended in the flame of the altar. When Manoah and his wife saw *this*, they [R]fell on their faces to the ground. Ezek. 1:28

21 When the Angel of the LORD appeared no
more to Manoah and his wife, then Manoah
knew that He *was* the Angel of the LORD.
22 And Manoah said to his wife, "We shall
surely die, because we have seen God!"
23 Then his wife said to him, "If the LORD
had desired to kill us, He would not have
accepted a burnt offering and a grain offering
from our hands, nor would He have shown us
all these *things*, nor would He have told us
such things as these at this time."
24 So the woman bore a son and called his
name [R]Samson; and [R]the child grew, and the
LORD blessed him. Heb. 11:32 • 1 Sam. 3:19
25 And the Spirit of the LORD began to
move upon him at [T]Mahaneh Dan between
Zorah and [R]Eshtaol. Lit. *Camp of Dan* • Judg. 16:31

CHAPTER 14

Sinful Marriage of Samson

NOW Samson went down [R]to Timnah, and
[R]saw a woman in Timnah of the daugh-
ters of the Philistines. Josh. 15:10, 57 • Gen. 34:2
2 So he went up and told his father and
mother, saying, "I have seen a woman in
Timnah of the daughters of the Philistines;
now therefore, get her for me as a wife."
3 Then his father and mother said to him,
"*Is there* no woman among the daughters of
your brethren, or among all my people, that
you must go and get a wife from the [R]uncir-
cumcised Philistines?" And Samson said to
his father, "Get her for me, for [T]she pleases
me well." Gen. 34:14 • Lit. *she is right in my eyes*
4 But his father and mother did not know
that it was [R]of the LORD—that He was seeking an occasion to move against the Philistines. For at that time [R]the Philistines had
dominion over Israel. Josh. 11:20 • Deut. 28:48
5 So Samson went down to Timnah with
his father and mother, and came to the
vineyards of Timnah.
Now *to his* surprise, a young lion *came*
roaring against him.
6 And [R]the Spirit of the LORD came mightily upon him, and he tore the lion apart as
one would have torn apart a young goat,
though *he had* nothing in his hand. But he
did not tell his father or his mother what he
had done. Judg. 3:10
7 Then he went down and talked with the
woman; and she pleased Samson well.
8 After some time, when he returned to get
her, he turned aside to see the carcass of the
lion. And behold, a swarm of bees and honey
were in the carcass of the lion.
9 He took some of it in his hands and went
along, eating. When he came to his father
and mother, he gave *some* to them, and they
also ate. But he did not tell them that he had
taken the honey out of the [R]carcass of the
lion. Lev. 11:27
10 So his father went down to the woman.
And Samson gave a feast there, for young
men used to do so.
11 And it was so, when they saw him, that
they brought thirty companions to be with
him.
12 Then Samson said to them, "Let me
[R]pose a riddle to you. If you can correctly
solve and explain it to me [R]within the seven
days of the feast, then I will give you thirty
linen garments and thirty [R]changes of clothing. Ezek. 17:2 • Gen. 29:27 • 2 Kin. 5:22
13 "But if you cannot explain *it* to me, then
you shall give me thirty linen garments and
thirty changes of clothing." And they said to
him, "Pose your riddle, that we may hear it."
14 So he said to them:

"Out of the eater came something to eat,
And out of the strong came something
sweet."

Now for three days they could not explain
the riddle.
15 So it came to pass on the seventh day
that they said to Samson's wife, "Entice your
husband, that he may explain the riddle to us,
or else we will burn you and your father's
house with fire. Have you invited us in order
to take what is ours? *Is that* not *so*?"
16 Then Samson's wife wept on him, and
said, [R]"You only hate me! You do not love
me! You have posed a riddle to the sons of
my people, but you have not explained *it* to
me." And he said to her, "Look, I have not
explained *it* to my father or my mother; so
should I explain *it* to you?" Judg. 16:15
17 Now she had wept on him the seven days
while their feast lasted. And it happened on
the seventh day that he told her, because she
pressed him so much. Then she explained the
riddle to the sons of her people.
18 So the men of the city said to him on the
seventh day before the sun went down:

"What *is* sweeter than honey?
And what *is* stronger than a lion?"

And he said to them:

"If you had not plowed with my heifer,
You would not have solved my riddle!"

19 Then [R]the Spirit of the LORD came upon
him mightily, and he went down to Ashkelon
and killed thirty of their men, took their
apparel, and gave the changes *of clothing* to
those who had explained the riddle. So his
anger was aroused, and he went back up to
his father's house. Judg. 3:10; 13:25
20 And Samson's wife was *given* to his
companion, who had been his best man.

ISRAEL AND THE PHILISTINES

The Philistines were a fierce tribal people who lived in southwest Palestine. Also referred to as the "sea people," the Philistines probably migrated to central Palestine from the island of Crete, or Caphtor, in the Mediterranean Sea (Gen. 10:14; Amos 9:7). Their presence in their new home was so prominent in Bible times that the entire land of Palestine was named for the coastal territory, Philistia, which they occupied along the Mediterranean.

The Philistines are mentioned prominently in the Bible during two distinct periods of biblical history—in Abraham's time about 1900 B.C. and during the period of the judges and Kings Saul and David from about 1200 to 1000 B.C.

The Philistines of Abraham's time were peaceful, in contrast to those who are mentioned later. The earlier Philistines were governed in a single city-state by one king, Abimelech (Gen. 26:1, 8). But the later Philistines were ruled by five lords, who united the Philistines into a confederation of five city-states—Ashkelon, Ashdod, Ekron, Gath, and Gaza (Josh. 13:3; Judg. 3:3).

Archaeologists have discovered weapons of iron used by the Philistines against the Israelites. So strong was their threat that the tribe of Dan retreated to the north away from their territory. In Samuel's time, the Philistines destroyed the city of Shiloh, which served as the center of worship for the Israelites.

The threat of the Philistines was one factor that led the Israelites to ask for a king and a united kingdom. The first Hebrew ruler, King Saul, and his sons were killed in a battle with the Philistines (1 Sam. 31:1–4). But Saul's successor David was able to defeat the Philistines and break their power (1 Chr. 18:1).

Photo by Gustav Jeeninga

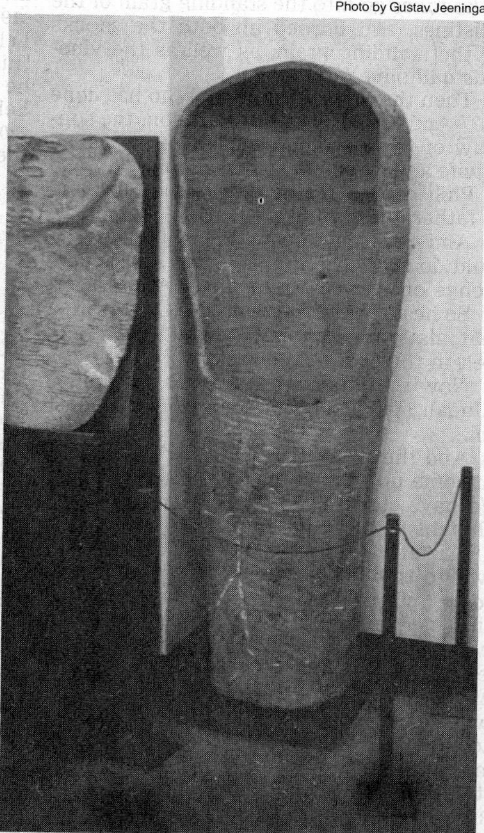

The Philistines were buried in unusual stone coffins. After the body was placed inside, the opening was sealed with a lid engraved with human features.

CHAPTER 15

Judgeship of Samson

AND after a while, in the time of wheat
harvest, it happened that Samson visited his wife with a young goat. And he said,
"Let me go in to my wife, into *her* room." But
her father would not permit him to go in.
2 Her father said, "I really thought that
you thoroughly [R]hated her; therefore I gave
her to your companion. *Is* not her younger
sister better than she? Please, take her instead." Judg. 14:20
3 And Samson said to them, "This time I
shall be blameless regarding the Philistines if
I harm them!"
4 Then Samson went and caught three
hundred foxes; and he took torches, turned
the foxes tail to tail, and put a torch between
each pair of tails.
5 When he had set the torches on fire, he
let *the foxes* go into the standing grain of the
Philistines, and burned up both the shocks
and the standing grain, as well as the vineyards *and* olive groves.
6 Then the Philistines said, "Who has done
this?" And they answered, "Samson, the son-
in-law of the Timnite, because he has taken
his wife and given her to his companion." [R]So
the Philistines came up and burned her and
her father with fire. Judg. 14:15
7 And Samson said to them, "Since you
would do a thing like this, I will surely take
revenge on you, and after that I will cease."
8 So he attacked them hip and thigh with a
great slaughter; then he went down and
dwelt in the cleft of the rock of Etam.
9 Now the Philistines went up, encamped
in Judah, and deployed themselves [R]against
Lehi. Judg. 15:19
10 And the men of Judah said, "Why have
you come up against us?" So they answered,
"We have come up to [T]arrest Samson, to do
to him as he has done to us." Lit. *bind*
11 Then three thousand men of Judah went
down to the cleft of the rock of Etam, and
said to Samson, "Do you not know that the
Philistines rule over us? What *is* this you
have done to us?" And he said to them, "As
they did to me, so I have done to them."
12 And they said to him, "We have come
down to arrest you, that we may deliver you
into the hand of the Philistines." Then Samson said to them, "Swear to me that you will
not kill me yourselves."
13 So they spoke to him, saying, "No, but
we will tie you securely and deliver you into
their hand; but we will surely not kill you."
And they bound him with two new ropes and
brought him up from the rock.
14 When he came to Lehi, the Philistines
came shouting against him. Then the Spirit of
the LORD came mightily upon him; and the
ropes that *were* on his arms became like flax
that is burned with fire, and his bonds [T]broke
loose from his hands. Lit. *melted*
15 He found a fresh jawbone of a donkey,
reached out his hand and took it, and [R]killed
a thousand men with it. Lev. 26:8
16 Then Samson said:

"With the jawbone of a donkey,
Heaps upon heaps,
With the jawbone of a donkey
I have slain a thousand men!"

17 And so it was, when he had finished
speaking, that he threw the jawbone from his
hand, and called that place Ramath Lehi.
18 Then he became very thirsty; so he cried
out to the LORD and said, [R]"You have given
this great deliverance by the hand of Your
servant; and now shall I die of thirst and fall
into the hand of the uncircumcised?" Ps. 3:7
19 So God split the hollow place that *is* in
Lehi, and water came out, and he drank; and
[R]his spirit returned, and he revived. Therefore
he called its name [T]En Hakkore, which is in
Lehi to this day. Is. 40:29 • *Spring of the Caller*
20 And he judged Israel twenty years [R]in
the days of the Philistines. Judg. 13:1

CHAPTER 16

Failure of Samson

THEN Samson went to [R]Gaza and saw a
harlot there, and went in to her. Josh. 15:47
2 *When* the Gazites *were told*, "Samson
has come here!" they [R]surrounded *the place*
and lay in wait for him all night at the gate of
the city. They were quiet all night, saying,
"In the morning, when it is daylight, we will
kill him." 1 Sam. 23:26
3 And Samson lay *low* till midnight; then
he arose at midnight, took hold of the doors
of the gate of the city and the two gateposts,
pulled them up, bar and all, put *them* on his
shoulders, and carried them to the top of the
hill that faces Hebron.
4 Now afterward it happened that he loved
a woman in the Valley of Sorek, whose name
was Delilah.
5 And the [R]lords of the Philistines came up
to her and said to her, [R]"Entice him, and find
out where his great strength *lies*, and by
what *means* we may overpower him, that we
may bind him to afflict him; and every one of
us will give you [T]eleven hundred *pieces* of
silver." Josh. 13:3 • Judg. 14:15 • $8000
6 So Delilah said to Samson, "Please tell
me where your great strength *lies*, and with
what you may be bound to afflict you."
7 And Samson said to her, "If they bind me
with seven fresh bowstrings, not yet dried,

then I shall become weak, and be like any
other man."
8 So the lords of the Philistines brought up
to her seven fresh bowstrings, not yet dried,
and she bound him with them.
9 Now *there were men* lying in wait, staying with her in the room. And she said to him,
"The Philistines *are* upon you, Samson!" But
he broke the bowstrings as a strand of yarn
breaks when it touches fire. So the secret of
his strength was not known.
10 Then Delilah said to Samson, "Look, you
have mocked me and told me lies. Now,
please tell me what you may be bound with."
11 So he said to her, "If they bind me
securely with [R]new ropes that have never
been used, then I shall become weak, and be
like any *other* man." Judg. 15:13
12 Therefore Delilah took new ropes and
bound him with them, and said to him, "The
Philistines *are* upon you, Samson!" And *there
were men* lying in wait, staying in the room.
But he broke them off his arms like a thread.
13 Then Delilah said to Samson, "Until now
you have mocked me and told me lies. Tell
me what you may be bound with." And he
said to her, "If you weave the seven locks of
my head into the web of the loom"—
14 So she wove *it* tightly with the batten of
the loom, and said to him, "The Philistines
are upon you, Samson!" But he awoke from
his sleep, and pulled out the batten and the
web from the loom.
15 Then she said to him, [R]"How can you
say, 'I love you,' when your heart *is* not with
me? You have mocked me these three times,
and have not told me where your great
strength *lies*." Judg. 14:16
16 And it came to pass, when she pestered
him daily with her words and pressed him, *so*
that his soul was vexed to death,
17 that he [R]told her all his heart, and said to
her, "No razor has ever come upon my head,
for I *have been* a Nazirite to God from my
mother's womb. If I am shaven, then my
strength will leave me, and I shall become
weak, and be like any *other* man." [Mic. 7:5]
18 When Delilah saw that he had told her
all his heart, she sent and called for the lords
of the Philistines, saying, "Come up once
more, for he has told me all his heart." So the
lords of the Philistines came up to her and
brought the money in their hand.
19 [R]Then she lulled him to sleep on her
knees, and called for a man and had him
shave off the seven locks of his head. Then
she began to torment him, and his strength
left him. Prov. 7:26, 27
20 And she said, "The Philistines *are* upon
you, Samson!" So he awoke from his sleep,
and said, "I will go out as before, at other
times, and shake myself free!" But he did not
know that the LORD had departed from him.
21 Then the Philistines took him and [T]put
out his eyes, and brought him down to Gaza.
They bound him with bronze fetters, and he
became a grinder in the prison. Lit. *bored out*
22 However, the hair of his head began to
grow again after it had been shaven.
23 Now the lords of the Philistines gathered
together to offer a great sacrifice to [R]Dagon
their god, and to rejoice. And they said:

"Our god has delivered into our hands
Samson our enemy!" 1 Sam. 5:2

24 When the people saw him, they [R]praised
their god; for they said: Dan. 5:4

"Our god has delivered into our hands
our enemy,
The destroyer of our land,
And the one who multiplied our dead."

25 So it happened, when their hearts were
[R]merry, that they said, "Call for Samson, that
he may perform for us." So they called for
Samson from the prison, and he performed
for them. And they stationed him between
the pillars. Judg. 9:27
26 Then Samson said to the lad who held
him by the hand, "Let me feel the pillars
which support the temple, so that I can lean
on them."
27 Now the temple was full of men and
women; all the lords of the Philistines *were*
there. *In fact, there were* about three thousand men and women on the [R]roof who
watched while Samson performed. Deut. 22:8
28 Then Samson called to the LORD, saying,
"O Lord GOD, [R]remember me, I pray!
Strengthen me, I pray, just this once, O God,
that I may with one *blow* take vengeance on
the Philistines for my two eyes!" Jer. 15:15
29 And Samson took hold of the two middle
pillars which supported the temple, and he
braced himself against them, one on his right
and the other on his left.
30 Then Samson said, "Let me die with the
Philistines!" And he pushed with *all his*
might, and the temple fell on the lords and all
the people who *were* in it. So the dead that he
killed at his death were more than he had
killed in his life.
31 And his brothers and all his father's
household came down and took him, and
brought *him* up and buried him between
Zorah and Eshtaol in the tomb of his father
Manoah. He had judged Israel twenty years.

CHAPTER 17

Example of Personal Idolatry

NOW there was a man from the mountains of Ephraim, whose name *was*
[R]Micah. Judg. 18:2

2 And he said to his mother, "The eleven
hundred *shekels* of silver that were taken
from you, and on which you put a curse, even
saying it in my ears—here *is* the silver with
me; I took it." And his mother said, "*May you
be* blessed by the LORD, my son!"
3 So when he had returned the eleven
hundred *shekels* of silver to his mother, his
mother said, "I had wholly dedicated the
silver from my hand to the LORD for my son,
to make a carved image and a molded image;
now therefore, I will return it to you."
4 Thus he returned the silver to his
mother. Then his mother [R]took two hundred
shekels of silver and gave them to the silversmith, and he made it into a carved image
and a molded image; and they were in the
house of Micah. Is. 46:6
5 The man Micah had a shrine, and made
an [R]ephod and [R]household[T] idols; and he
consecrated one of his sons, who became his
priest. Judg. 8:27; 18:14 • Gen. 31:19, 30 • Heb. *teraphim*
6 [R]In those days *there was* no king in
Israel; [R]everyone did *what was* right in his
own eyes. Judg. 18:1; 19:1 • Deut. 12:8
7 Now there was a young man from Bethlehem in Judah, of the family of Judah; he
was a Levite, and was sojourning there.
8 The man departed from the city of Bethlehem in Judah to [T]sojourn wherever he
could find *a place*. Then he came to the
mountains of Ephraim, to the house of Micah, as he journeyed. Reside temporarily
9 And Micah said to him, "Where do you
come from?" So he said to him, "I *am* a
Levite from Bethlehem in Judah, and I am on
my way to find *a place* to sojourn."
10 Micah said to him, "Dwell with me, [R]and
be a [R]father and a priest to me, and I will give
you ten *shekels* of silver per year, a suit of
clothes, and your sustenance." So the Levite
went in. Judg. 18:19 • Gen. 45:8
11 Then the Levite was content to dwell
with the man; and the young man became
like one of his sons to him.
12 So Micah [T]consecrated the Levite, and
the young man became his priest, and lived in
the house of Micah. Lit. *filled the hand of*
13 Then Micah said, "Now I know that the
LORD will be good to me, since I have a Levite
as [R]priest!" Judg. 18:4

CHAPTER 18

Example of Tribal Idolatry

IN [R]those days *there was* no king in Israel.
And in those days [R]the tribe of the Danites was seeking an inheritance for itself to
dwell in; for until that day *their whole* inheritance among the tribes of Israel had not *yet*
fallen to them. Judg. 17:6; 19:1; 21:25 • Josh. 19:40–48
2 So the children of Dan sent five men of
their family from their territory, men of valor
from [R]Zorah and Eshtaol, [R]to spy out the land
and search it. They said to them, "Go, search
the land." So they went to the mountains of
Ephraim, to the [R]house of Micah, and lodged
there. Judg. 13:25 • Num. 13:17 • Judg. 17:1
3 While they *were* at the house of Micah,
they recognized the voice of the young Levite. They turned aside and said to him, "Who
brought you here? What are you doing in this
place? What do you have here?"
4 He said to them, "Thus and so Micah did
for me. He has [R]hired me, and I have become
his priest." Judg. 17:10, 12
5 So they said to him, "Please inquire of
God, that we may know whether the journey
on which we go will be prosperous."
6 And the priest said to them, [R]"Go in
peace. *May* the presence of the LORD *be* with
you on your way." 1 Kin. 22:6
7 So the five men departed and went to
Laish. They saw the people who *were* there,
how they dwelt safely, in the manner of the
Sidonians, quiet and secure. *There were* no
rulers in the land who might put *them* to
shame for anything. They *were* far from the
Sidonians, and they had no ties with anyone.
8 Then [T]the spies came back to their brethren at Zorah and Eshtaol, and their brethren
said to them, "What *is* your *report*?" *they*
9 So they said, [R]"Arise, let us go up against
them. For we have seen the land, and indeed
it *is* very good. *Would* you [R]*do* nothing? Do
not hesitate to go, *that you may* enter to
possess the land. Num. 13:30 • 1 Kin. 22:3
10 "When you go, you will come to a secure
people and a large land. For God has given it
into your hands, a place where *there is* no
lack of anything that *is* on the earth."
11 And six hundred men of the family of the
Danites went from there, from Zorah and
Eshtaol, armed with weapons of war.
12 Then they went up and encamped in
Kirjath Jearim in Judah. (Therefore they call
that place [T]Mahaneh Dan to this day. There *it
is*, west of Kirjath Jearim.) *Camp of*
13 And they passed from there to the mountains of Ephraim, and came to [R]the house of
Micah. Judg. 18:2
14 Then the five men who had gone to spy
out the country of Laish answered and said to
their brethren, "Do you know that there are
in these houses an ephod, household idols, a
carved image, and a molded image? Now
therefore, consider what you should do."
15 So they turned aside there, and came to
the house of the young Levite man, *that is*, to
the house of Micah, and greeted him.
16 The six hundred men armed with their
weapons of war, who *were* of the children of
Dan, stood by the entrance of the gate.
17 Then [R]the five men who had gone to spy
out the land went up, *and* entering there,
they took [R]the carved image, the ephod, the

THE CITY OF SHILOH

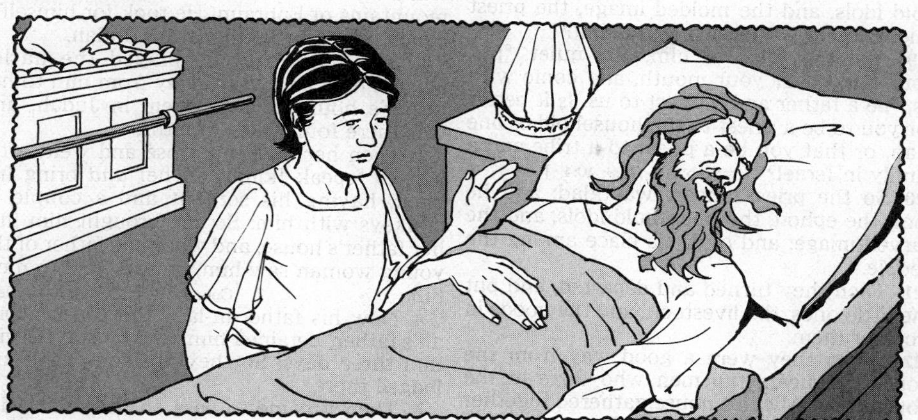

When the Lord called to Samuel, the boy mistook His call for that of his master Eli, whom he awakened.

Shiloh was a small Old Testament village about twenty miles north of Jerusalem. It was important because it served as the religious center for the Hebrew people during the period of the judges before the kingdom was united under the leadership of David.

Numerous references are made to Shiloh during this period as the city where the "house of God" was located (Judg. 18:31). These references are probably to the tabernacle with its ark of the Testimony—or perhaps a permanent building that housed the tabernacle—because the temple was not constructed until about 960 B.C. during Solomon's time.

Hannah prayed for a son at Shiloh. God granted this request by sending Samuel. During his boyhood, Samuel worked with the high priest Eli at Shiloh. One of the most beautiful stories of the Old Testament is about Samuel's response to the voice of the Lord. Thinking his master Eli was calling him, he awakened the high priest to find out what the high priest wanted (see illustration). Finally, it dawned on both that God was calling Samuel in a unique revelation of His will for the boy. Samuel's response to God's next call was, "Speak, LORD, for Your servant hears" (1 Sam. 3:1–10).

Samuel eventually succeeded Eli. The tabernacle was located in Shiloh during Samuel's early years as priest (1 Sam. 1:9; 4:3, 4). However, during a battle with the Philistines, the ark of the Testimony was captured by Israel's enemies because God had forsaken Shiloh as the center of worship (Ps. 78:60). When the ark was returned to Israel by the Philistines, it was not placed at Shiloh (2 Sam. 6:2–17). It was lodged instead at Kirjath Jearim (1 Chr. 13:3–14).

After the ark was moved to another city, Shiloh gradually lost its importance. This loss was made complete when Jerusalem was established as capital of the kingdom in David's time. In the days of the prophet Jeremiah, Shiloh was in ruin (Jer. 7:12, 14). It became an inhabited town again in the days of the Greeks and Romans several centuries later.

household idols, and the molded image. The priest stood at the entrance of the gate with the six hundred men *who were* armed with weapons of war. Judg. 18:2, 14 • Judg. 17:4, 5

18 When these went into Micah's house and took the graven image, the ephod, the household idols, and the molded image, the priest said to them, "What are you doing?"

19 And they said to him, "Be quiet, [R]put your hand over your mouth, and come with us; [R]be a father and a priest to us. *Is it* better for you to be a priest to the household of one man, or that you be a priest to a tribe and a family in Israel?" Job 21:5; 29:9; 40:4 • Judg. 17:10

20 So the priest's heart was glad; and he took the ephod, the household idols, and the carved image, and took his place among the people.

21 Then they turned and departed, and put the little ones, the livestock, and the goods in front of them.

22 When they were a good way from the house of Micah, the men who *were* in the houses near Micah's house gathered together and overtook the children of Dan.

23 And they called out to the children of Dan. So they turned around and said to Micah, [R]"What ails you, that you have gathered such a company?" 2 Kin. 6:28

24 So he said, "You have taken away my gods which I made, and the priest, and you have gone away. Now what more do I have? How can you say to me, 'What ails you?'"

25 And the children of Dan said to him, "Do not let your voice be heard among us, lest angry men fall upon you, and you lose your life, with the lives of your household!"

26 Then the children of Dan went their way. And when Micah saw that they *were* too strong for him, he turned and went back to his house.

27 So they took *the things* Micah had made, and the priest who had belonged to him, and went to Laish, to a people *who were* quiet and secure; [R]and they struck them with the edge of the sword and burned the city with fire. Josh. 19:47

28 *There was* no deliverer, because it *was* [R]far from Sidon, and they had no ties with anyone. It was in the valley that belongs [R]to Beth Rehob. So they rebuilt the city and dwelt there. Judg. 18:7 • 2 Sam. 10:6

29 And [R]they called the name of the city [R]Dan, after the name of Dan their father, who was born to Israel. However, the name of the city formerly *was* Laish. Josh. 19:47 • Judg. 20:1

30 Then the children of Dan set up for themselves the carved image; and Jonathan the son of Gershom, the son of Manasseh, and his sons were priests to the tribe of Dan until the day of the captivity of the land.

31 So they set up for themselves Micah's carved image which he made, all the time that the house of God was in Shiloh.

CHAPTER 19

Example of Personal Immorality

AND it came to pass in those days, when *there was* no king in Israel, that there was a certain Levite sojourning in the remote mountains of Ephraim. He took for himself a concubine from Bethlehem in Judah.

2 But his concubine played the harlot against him, and went away from him to her father's house at Bethlehem in Judah, and was there four whole months.

3 Then her husband arose and went after her, to [R]speak [T]kindly to her *and* bring her back, having his servant and a couple of donkeys with him. So she brought him into her father's house; and when the father of the young woman saw him, he was glad to meet him. Gen. 34:3; 50:21 • Lit. *to her heart*

4 Now his father-in-law, the young woman's father, detained him; and he stayed with him three days. So they ate and drank and lodged there.

5 Then it came to pass on the fourth day that they arose early in the morning, and he stood to depart; but the young woman's father said to his son-in-law, [R]"Refresh your heart with a morsel of bread, and afterward go your way." Gen. 18:5

6 So they sat down, and the two of them ate and drank together. Then the young woman's father said to the man, "Please be content to stay all night, and let your heart be merry."

7 And when the man stood to depart, his father-in-law urged him; so he lodged there again.

8 Then he arose early in the morning on the fifth day to depart, but the young woman's father said, "Please refresh your heart." So they delayed until afternoon; and both of them ate.

9 And when the man stood to depart—he and his concubine and his servant—his father-in-law, the young woman's father, said to him, "Look, the day is now drawing toward evening; please spend the night. See, the day is coming to an end; lodge here, that your heart may be merry. Tomorrow go your way early, so that you may get home."

10 But the man was not willing to spend that night; so he rose and departed, and came to *a place* opposite Jebus (that *is*, Jerusalem). With him were the two saddled donkeys; his concubine *was* also with him.

Example of Tribal Immorality

11 They *were* near Jebus, and the day was far spent; and the servant said to his master, "Come, please, and let us turn aside into this city of the Jebusites and lodge in it."

12 But his master said to him, "We will not turn aside here into a city of foreigners, who

are not of the children of Israel; we will go on [R]to Gibeah." Josh. 18:28

13 So he said to his servant, "Come, let us draw near to one of these places, and spend the night in Gibeah or in [R]Ramah." Josh. 18:25

14 And they passed by and went their way; and the sun went down on them near Gibeah, which belongs to Benjamin.

15 They turned aside there to go in to lodge in Gibeah. And when he went in, he sat down in the open square of the city, for no one would [R]take them into *his* house to spend the night. Matt. 25:43

16 Just then an old man came in from [R]his work in the field at evening, who also *was* from the mountains of Ephraim; he was sojourning in Gibeah, whereas the men of the place *were* Benjamites. Ps. 104:23

17 And when he raised his eyes, he saw the traveler in the open square of the city; and the old man said, "Where are you going, and where do you come from?"

18 So he said to him, "We *are* passing from Bethlehem in Judah toward the remote mountains of Ephraim; I *am* from there. I went to Bethlehem in Judah, *and now* I am going to the house of the LORD. But there *is* no one who will take me into his house,

19 "although we have both straw and fodder for our donkeys, and bread and wine for myself, for your maidservant, and for the young man *who is* with your servant; *there is* no lack of anything."

20 And the old man said, [R]"Peace *be* with you! However, *let* all your needs *be* my responsibility; [R]only do not spend the night in the open square." Gen. 43:23 • Gen. 19:2

21 So he brought him into his house, and gave fodder to the donkeys. And they washed their feet, and ate and drank.

22 *Now* as they were enjoying themselves, suddenly certain men of the city, [T]perverted men, surrounded the house *and* beat on the door. They spoke to the master of the house, the old man, saying, [R]"Bring out the man who came to your house, that we may know him *carnally*!" Lit. *sons of Belial* • [Rom. 1:26, 27]

23 But [R]the man, the master of the house, went out to them and said to them, "No, my brethren! I beg you, do not act *so* wickedly! Seeing this man has come into my house, [R]do not commit this outrage. Gen. 19:6, 7 • 2 Sam. 13:12

24 [R]"Look, *here is* my virgin daughter and [T]the man's concubine; let me bring them out now. [R]Humble them, and do with them as you please; but to this man do not do such a vile thing!" Gen. 19:8 • Lit. *his* • Gen. 34:2

25 But the men would not heed him. So the man took his concubine and brought *her* out to them. And they [R]knew her and abused her all night until morning; and when the day began to break, they let her go. Gen. 4:1

26 Then the woman came as the day was dawning, and fell down at the door of the man's house where her master *was*, till it was light.

27 When her master arose in the morning, and opened the doors of the house and went out to go his way, there was his concubine, fallen *at* the door of the house with her hands on the threshold.

28 And he said to her, "Get up and let us be going." But [R]there was no answer. So the man lifted her onto the donkey; and the man got up and went to his place. Judg. 20:5

29 When he entered his house he took a knife, laid hold of his concubine, and [R]dismembered her into twelve pieces, [T]limb by limb, and sent her throughout all the territory of Israel. 1 Sam. 11:7 • Lit. *with her bones*

30 And so it was that all who saw it said, "No such deed has been done or seen from the day that the children of Israel came up from the land of Egypt until this day. Consider it, take counsel, and speak up!"

CHAPTER 20

War Between Israel and Benjamin

THEN [R]all the children of Israel came out, from Dan to [R]Beersheba, as well as from the land of Gilead, and the congregation gathered together as one man before the LORD [R]at Mizpah. Josh. 22:12 • Josh. 19:2 • 1 Sam. 7:5

2 And the leaders of all the people, all the tribes of Israel, presented themselves in the assembly of the people of God, four hundred thousand foot soldiers who drew the sword.

3 (Now the children of Benjamin heard that the children of Israel had gone up to Mizpah.) Then the children of Israel said, "Tell *us*, how did this wicked deed happen?"

4 So the Levite, the husband of the woman who was murdered, answered and said, "My concubine and I went into Gibeah, which belongs to Benjamin, to spend the night.

5 [R]"And the men of Gibeah rose against me, and surrounded the house at night because of me. They intended to kill me, [R]but instead they ravished my concubine so that she died. Judg. 19:22 • Judg. 19:25, 26

6 "So [R]I took hold of my concubine, cut her in pieces, and sent her throughout all the territory of the inheritance of Israel, because they [R]committed lewdness and outrage in Israel. Judg. 19:29 • Josh. 7:15

7 "Look! All of you *are* children of Israel; give your advice and counsel here and now!"

8 Then all the people arose as one man, saying, "None *of us* will go to his tent, nor will any *of us* turn back to his house;

9 "but now this *is* the thing which we will do to Gibeah: *We will go up* against it by lot.

10 "We will take ten men out of *every* hundred throughout all the tribes of Israel, a

hundred out of *every* thousand, and a thousand out of *every* ten thousand, to make
provisions for the people, that when they
come to Gibeah in Benjamin, they may repay
all the vileness that they have done in Israel."
11 So all the men of Israel were gathered
against the city, united together as one man.
12 [R]Then the tribes of Israel sent men
through all the tribe of Benjamin, saying,
"What *is* this wickedness that has occurred
among you? Deut. 13:14
13 "Now therefore, deliver up the men, the
[T]perverted men who *are* in Gibeah, that we
may put them to death and remove the evil
from Israel!" But the children of Benjamin
would not listen to the voice of their brethren, the children of Israel. Lit. *sons of Belial*
14 Instead, the children of Benjamin gathered together from their cities to Gibeah, to
go to battle against the children of Israel.
15 And from their cities at that time [R]the
children of Benjamin numbered twenty-six
thousand men who drew the sword, besides
the inhabitants of Gibeah, who numbered
seven hundred select men. Num. 1:36, 37
16 Among all this people *there were* seven
hundred select men *who were* [R]left-handed;
every one could sling a stone at a hair's
breadth and not miss. 1 Chr. 12:2
17 Now besides Benjamin, the men of Israel
numbered four hundred thousand men who
drew the sword; all of these *were* men of war.
18 And the children of Israel arose and went
up to [T]the house of God [R]to ask counsel of
God. They said, "Which of us shall go up first
to battle against the children of Benjamin?"
And the LORD said, [R]"Judah *shall go up*
first." Or *Bethel* • Num. 27:21 • Judg. 1:1, 2
19 So the children of Israel rose in the
morning and encamped against Gibeah.
20 And the men of Israel went out to battle
against Benjamin, and the men of Israel put
themselves in battle array to fight against
them at Gibeah.
21 Then [R]the children of Benjamin came out
of Gibeah, and on that day cut down to the
ground twenty-two thousand men of the
Israelites. [Gen. 49:27]
22 And the people, that is, the men of Israel,
encouraged themselves and again formed the
battle line at the place where they had put
themselves in array on the first day.
23 [R]Then the children of Israel went up and
wept before the LORD until evening, and
asked counsel of the LORD, saying, "Shall I
again draw near for battle against the children of my brother Benjamin?" And the LORD
said, "Go up against him." Judg. 20:26, 27
24 So the children of Israel approached the
children of Benjamin on the second day.
25 And [R]Benjamin went out against them
from Gibeah on the second day, and cut
down to the ground eighteen thousand more
of the children of Israel; all these drew the
sword. Judg. 20:21
26 Then all the children of Israel, that is, all
the people, [R]went up and came to [T]the house
of God and wept. They sat there before the
LORD and fasted that day until evening; and
they offered burnt offerings and peace offerings before the LORD. Judg. 20:18, 23; 21:2 • Or *Bethel*
27 So the children of Israel inquired of the
LORD ([R]the ark of the covenant of God *was*
there in those days, Josh. 18:1
28 [R]and Phinehas the son of Eleazar, the son
of Aaron, [R]stood before it in those days),
saying, "Shall I yet again go out to battle
against the children of my brother Benjamin,
or shall I cease?" And the LORD said, "Go up,
for tomorrow I will deliver them into your
hand." Josh. 24:33 • Deut. 10:8; 18:5
29 Then Israel [R]set men in ambush all
around Gibeah. Josh. 8:4
30 And the children of Israel went up
against the children of Benjamin on the third
day, and put themselves in battle array
against Gibeah as at the other times.
31 So the children of Benjamin went out
against the people, *and* were drawn away
from the city. They began to strike down *and*
kill some of the people, as at the other times,
in the highways [R](one of which goes up to
Bethel and the other to Gibeah) and in the
field, about thirty men of Israel. Judg. 21:19
32 And the children of Benjamin said,
"They *are* struck down before us, as at first."
But the children of Israel said, "Let us flee
and draw them away from the city to the
highways."
33 So all the men of Israel rose from their
place and put themselves in battle array at
Baal Tamar. Then Israel's men in ambush
burst forth from their position in the plain of
Geba.
34 And ten thousand select men from all
Israel came against Gibeah, and the battle
was fierce. [T]But the Benjamites did not know
that disaster *was* upon them. Lit. *they*
35 The LORD [T]defeated Benjamin before
Israel. And the children of Israel destroyed
that day twenty-five thousand one hundred
Benjamites; all these drew the sword. *struck*
36 So the children of Benjamin saw that
they were defeated. [R]The men of Israel had
given ground to the Benjamites, because they
relied on the men in ambush whom they had
set against Gibeah. Josh. 8:15
37 [R]And the men in ambush quickly rushed
upon Gibeah; the men in ambush spread out
and struck the whole city with the edge of
the sword. Josh. 8:19
38 Now the appointed signal between the
men of Israel and the men in ambush was
that they would make a great cloud of
[R]smoke rise up from the city, Josh. 8:20

39 whereupon the men of Israel would turn in battle. Now Benjamin had begun [T]to strike *and* kill about thirty of the men of Israel. For they said, "Surely they are defeated before us, as *in* the first battle." Lit. *to strike the slain ones*

40 But when the cloud began to rise from the city in a column of smoke, the Benjamites looked behind them, and there was the whole city going up *in smoke* to heaven.

41 And when the men of Israel turned back, the men of Benjamin panicked, for they saw that disaster had come upon them.

42 Therefore they [T]turned *their backs* before the men of Israel in the direction of the wilderness; but the battle overtook them, and whoever *had come* out of the cities they destroyed in their midst. *fled*

43 They surrounded the Benjamites *and* chased them, *and* easily trampled them down as far as the front of Gibeah toward the east.

44 And eighteen thousand men of Benjamin fell; all these *were* men of valor.

45 Then *they turned and fled toward the wilderness to the rock of [R]Rimmon; and they cut down five thousand of them on the highways. Then they pursued them relentlessly up to Gidom, and killed two thousand of them. Josh. 15:32

46 So all who fell of Benjamin that day were twenty-five thousand men who drew the sword; all these *were* [T]men of valor. *warriors*

47 [R]But six hundred men turned and fled toward the wilderness to the rock of Rimmon, and they stayed at the rock of Rimmon for four months. Judg. 21:13

48 And the men of Israel turned back against the children of Benjamin, and struck them down with the edge of the sword—from *every* city, men and beasts, all who were found. They also set fire to all the cities they came to.

CHAPTER 21

Israel's Foolish Vow

NOW [R]the men of Israel had sworn an oath at Mizpah, saying, "None of us shall give his daughter to Benjamin as a wife." Judg. 20:1

2 Then the people came [R]to [T]the house of God, and remained there before God till evening. They lifted up their voices and wept bitterly, Judg. 20:18, 26 • Or *Bethel*

3 and said, "O LORD God of Israel, why has this come to pass in Israel, that today there should be one tribe *missing* in Israel?"

4 So it was, on the next morning, that the people rose early and [R]built an altar there, and offered burnt offerings and peace offerings. 2 Sam. 24:25

5 The children of Israel said, "Who *is there* among all the tribes of Israel who did not come up with the assembly to the LORD?" [R]For they had made a great oath concerning anyone who had not come up to the LORD at Mizpah, saying, "He shall surely be put to death." Judg. 20:1–3

6 And the children of Israel grieved for Benjamin their brother, and said, "One tribe is cut off from Israel today.

7 "What shall we do for wives for those who remain, seeing we have sworn by the LORD that we will not give them our daughters as wives?"

Men at Jabesh Gilead Murdered

8 And they said, "What one *is there* from the tribes of Israel who did not come up to Mizpah to the LORD?" And, in fact, no one had come to the camp from [R]Jabesh Gilead to the assembly. 1 Sam. 11:1; 31:11

9 For when the people were counted, indeed, not one of the inhabitants of Jabesh Gilead *was* there.

10 So the congregation sent out there twelve thousand of their most valiant men, and commanded them, saying, [R]"Go and strike the inhabitants of Jabesh Gilead with the edge of the sword, including the women and children. Num. 31:17

11 "And this *is* the thing that you shall do: [R]You shall utterly destroy every male, and every woman who has known a man intimately." Num. 31:17

12 So they found among the inhabitants of Jabesh Gilead four hundred young virgins who had not known a man intimately; and they brought them to the camp at [R]Shiloh, which is in the land of Canaan. Josh. 18:1

13 Then the whole congregation sent *word* to the children of Benjamin [R]who *were* at the rock of Rimmon, and announced peace to them. Judg. 20:47

14 So Benjamin came back at that time, and they gave them the women whom they had saved alive of the women of Jabesh Gilead; and yet they had not found enough for them.

15 And the people [R]grieved for Benjamin, because the LORD had made a void in the tribes of Israel. Judg. 21:6

Women of Shiloh Kidnapped

16 Then the elders of the congregation said, "What shall we do for wives for those who remain, since the women of Benjamin have been destroyed?"

17 And they said, "*There must be* an inheritance for the survivors of Benjamin, that a tribe may not be destroyed from Israel.

18 "However, we cannot give them wives from our daughters, for the children of Israel have sworn an oath, saying, 'Cursed *be* the one who gives a wife to Benjamin.' "

20:45 LXX *the rest*

19 Then they said, "In fact, *there is* a yearly
feast of the LORD in [R]Shiloh, which *is* north of
Bethel, on the east side of the [R]highway that
goes up from Bethel to Shechem, and south
of Lebonah." 1 Sam. 1:3 • Judg. 20:31
20 Therefore they instructed the children of
Benjamin, saying, "Go, lie in wait in the
vineyards,
21 "and watch; and just when the daughters of Shiloh come out [R]to perform their
dances, then come out from the vineyards,
and every man catch a wife for himself from
the daughters of Shiloh; then go to the land
of Benjamin. Judg. 11:34
22 "Then it shall be, when their fathers or
their brothers come to us to complain, that
we will say to them, 'Be kind to them for our
sakes, because we did not take a wife for any
of them in the war; for *it is* not *as though* you
have given the *young women* to them at this
time, making yourselves guilty of your
oath.'"
23 And the children of Benjamin did so;
they took *themselves* enough wives for their
number from those who danced, whom they
caught. Then they went and returned to their
inheritance, and they [R]rebuilt the cities and
dwelt in them. Judg. 20:48
24 So the children of Israel departed from
there at that time, every man to his tribe and
family; they went out from there, every man
to his inheritance.
25 [R]In those days *there was* no king in
Israel; [R]everyone did *what was* right in his
own eyes. Judg. 17:6; 18:1; 19:1 • Judg. 17:6

THE BOOK OF

RUTH

THE BOOK OF RUTH

Ruth is a cameo story of love, devotion, and redemption set in the black context of the days of the judges. It is the story of a Moabite woman who forsakes her pagan heritage in order to cling to the people of Israel and to the God of Israel. Because of her *faithfulness* in a time of national *faithlessness*, God rewards her by giving her a new husband (Boaz), a son (Obed), and a privileged position in the lineage of David and Christ (she is the great-grandmother of David).

Ruth is the Hebrew title of this book. This name may be a Moabite modification of the Hebrew word *reuit*, meaning friendship or association. The Septuagint entitles the book *Routh*, the Greek equivalent of the Hebrew name. The Latin title is *Ruth*, a transliteration of *Routh*.

THE AUTHOR OF RUTH

The author of Ruth is not given anywhere in the book, nor is he known from any other biblical passage. Talmudic tradition attributes it to Samuel but this is unlikely since David appears in Ruth 4:17, 22, and Samuel died before David's coronation (1 Sam. 25:1). Ruth was probably written during David's reign since Solomon's name is not included in the genealogy. The anonymity of the book, however, should not detract from its spiritual value or literary beauty.

THE TIME OF RUTH

Ruth divides neatly into four distinct settings: (1) the country of Moab (1:1–18); (2) a field in Bethlehem (1:19—2:23); (3) a threshing floor in Bethlehem (3:1–18); and (4) the city of Bethlehem (4:1–22).

The setting of the first eighteen verses is Moab, a region northeast of the Dead Sea. The Moabites, descendants of Lot, worshiped Chemosh and other pagan gods. Scripture records two times when they fight against Israel (Judg. 3:12–30 and 1 Sam. 14:47). Ruth takes place about two centuries after the first war and about eighty years before the second.

Ruth 1:1 gives the setting of the remainder of the book: "Now it came to pass, in the days when the judges ruled." This is a time of apostasy, warfare, decline, violence, moral decay, and anarchy. Ruth provides a cameo of the other side of the story—the godly remnant who remain true to the laws of God.

Because Ruth is written more to tell a beautiful story than to give all the historical facts of that period, the assignment of time is somewhat difficult. Utilizing the same fourfold division noted above, the following can be assigned:

A. Ruth 1:1–18 (note 1:4): The country of Moab (c. ten years)
B. Ruth 1:19—2:23 (note 1:22; 2:23): A field in Bethlehem (months)
C. Ruth 3:1–18 (note 3:2, 8, 14, 18): A threshing floor in Bethlehem (one day)
D. Ruth 4:1–22 (note 4:13–16): The city of Bethlehem (c. one year)

THE CHRIST OF RUTH

The concept of the kinsman-redeemer or *goel* (3:9, "close relative") is an important portrayal of the work of Christ. The *goel* must (1) be related by blood to those he redeems (Deut. 25:5, 7–10; John 1:14; Rom. 1:3; Phil. 2:5–8; Heb. 2:14, 15); (2) be able to pay the price of redemption (2:1; 1 Pet. 1:18, 19); (3) be willing to redeem (3:11; Matt. 20:28; John 10:15, 18; Heb. 10:7); (4) be free himself (Christ was free from the curse of sin). The word *goel*, used thirteen times in this short book, presents a clear picture of the mediating work of Christ.

KEYS TO RUTH

Key Word: Kinsman-Redeemer—The Hebrew word for kinsman *(goel)* appears thirteen times in Ruth and basically means "one who redeems." By buying back the land of Naomi, as well as marrying Ruth and fathering a son to keep the family line alive, Boaz acts as a redeemer.

Key Verses: Ruth 1:16; 3:11—"But Ruth said: 'Entreat me not to leave you, *or to* turn back from following after you; for wherever you go, I will go; and wherever you lodge, I will lodge; your people *shall be* my people, and your God my God' " (1:16).

"And now, my daughter, do not fear. I will do for you all that you request, for all the people of my town know that you *are* a virtuous woman" (3:11).

Key Chapter: Ruth 4—In twenty-two short verses, Ruth moves from widowhood and poverty to marriage and wealth (2:1). In exercising the law regulating the redemption of property (Lev. 25:25–34) and the law concerning a brother's duty to raise up seed (children) in the name of the deceased (Deut. 25:5–10), Boaz brings a Moabite woman into the family line of David and eventually of Jesus Christ.

SURVEY OF RUTH

Ruth is the story of a virtuous woman who lives above the norm of her day. Although it was probably written during the time of David, the events take place during the time of the judges. This period in Israel's history was generally a desert of rebellion and immorality, but the story of Ruth stands in contrast as an oasis of integrity and righteousness.

Ruth is "a virtuous woman" (3:11) who shows loyal love to her mother-in-law Naomi and her near-kinsman Boaz. In both relationships, goodness and love are clearly manifested. Her love is demonstrated in chapters 1 and 2 and rewarded in chapters 3 and 4.

Ruth's Love Is Demonstrated (1 and 2): The story begins with a famine in Israel, a sign of disobedience and apostasy (Deut. 28—30). An Israelite named Elimelech ("My God Is King") in a desperate act moves from Bethlehem ("House of Bread"—note the irony) to Moab. Although he seeks life in that land, he and his two sons Mahlon ("Sick") and Chilion ("Pining") find only death. The deceased sons leave two Moabite widows, Orpah ("Stubbornness") and Ruth ("Friendship"). Elimelech's widow, Naomi, hears that the famine in Israel is over and decides to return, no longer as Naomi ("Pleasant") but as Mara ("Bitter"). She tells her daughters-in-law to remain in Moab and remarry since there was no security for an unmarried woman in those days. Orpah chooses to leave Naomi and is never mentioned again. Ruth, on the other hand, resolves to cling to Naomi and follow Yahweh, the God of Israel. She therefore gives up her culture, people, and language because of her love.

Naomi's misfortune leads her to think that God is her enemy, but He has plans she does not yet realize. In her plight, she must let Ruth glean at the edge of a field. This is a humiliating and dangerous task because of the character of many of the reapers. However, God's providential care brings her to the field of Boaz, Naomi's kinsman. Boaz ("In Him Is Strength") begins to love, protect, and provide for her.

Ruth's Love Is Rewarded (3 and 4): Boaz takes no further steps toward marriage, so Naomi follows the accepted customs of the day and requests that Boaz exercise his right as kinsman-redeemer. In 3:10–13, Boaz reveals why he has taken no action: he is older than Ruth (perhaps twenty years her senior), and he is not the nearest kinsman. Nevertheless, God rewards Ruth's devotion by giving her Boaz as a husband and by providing her with a son, Obed, the grandfather of David.

FOCUS	RUTH'S LOVE DEMONSTRATED		RUTH'S LOVE REWARDED	
REFERENCE	1:1—	1:19—	3:1—	4:1—4:22
DIVISION	RUTH'S DECISION TO STAY WITH NAOMI	RUTH'S DEVOTION TO CARE FOR NAOMI	RUTH'S REQUEST FOR REDEMPTION BY BOAZ	RUTH'S REWARD OF REDEMPTION BY BOAZ
TOPIC	RUTH AND NAOMI		RUTH AND BOAZ	
	DEATH OF FAMILY	RUTH CARES FOR NAOMI	BOAZ CARES FOR RUTH	BIRTH OF FAMILY
LOCATION	MOAB	FIELDS OF BETHLEHEM	THRESHING FLOOR OF BETHLEHEM	BETHLEHEM
TIME	c. 12 YEARS			

OUTLINE OF RUTH

Part One: Ruth's Love Is Demonstrated (1:1—2:23)

Part Two: Ruth's Love Is Rewarded (3:1—4:22)

I. Ruth's Request for Redemption by Boaz . . . 3:1–18
A. Naomi Seeks Redemption for Ruth 3:1–5
B. Ruth Obeys Naomi 3:6–9
C. Boaz Desires to Redeem Ruth 3:10–18

II. Ruth's Reward of Redemption by Boaz 4:1–22
A. Boaz Marries Ruth 4:1–12
B. Ruth Bears a Son, Obed 4:13–15
C. Naomi Receives a New Family 4:16
D. Ruth Is the Great-Grandmother of David 4:17–22

CHAPTER 1

Ruth's Need to Remain with Naomi

NOW it came to pass, in the days when the
judges [T]ruled, that there was a famine
in the land. And a certain man of Bethlehem,
Judah, went to [T]sojourn in the country of
[R]Moab, he and his wife and his two
sons. Lit. *judged* • Reside temporarily • Gen. 19:37
2 The name of the man *was* Elimelech, the
name of his wife *was* Naomi, and the names
of his two sons *were* Mahlon and Chilion—
[R]Ephrathites of Bethlehem, Judah. And they
went [R]to the country of Moab and remained
there. Gen. 35:19 • Judg. 3:30
3 Then Elimelech, Naomi's husband, died;
and she was left, and her two sons.
4 Now they took wives of the women of
Moab: the name of the one *was* Orpah, and
the name of the other Ruth. And they dwelt
there about ten years.
5 Then both Mahlon and Chilion also died;
so the woman survived her two sons and her
husband.

Ruth's Opportunity to Leave Naomi

6 Then she arose with her daughters-in-
law that she might return from the country
of Moab, for she had heard in the country of
Moab that the LORD had [T]visited His people in
[R]giving them bread. *aided* • Matt. 6:11
7 Therefore she went out from the place
where she was, and her two daughters-in-law
with her; and they went on the way to return
to the land of Judah.
8 And Naomi said to her two daughters-in-
law, [R]"Go, return each to her mother's house.
The LORD deal kindly with you, as you have
dealt with the dead and with me. Josh. 24:15
9 "The LORD grant that you may find [R]rest,
each in the house of her husband." Then she
kissed them, and they lifted up their voices
and wept. Ruth 3:1
10 And they said to her, "Surely we will
return with you to your people."
11 But Naomi said, "Turn back, my daughters; why will you go with me? *Are* there still
sons in my womb, [R]that they may be your
husbands? Deut. 25:5
12 "Turn back, my daughters, go *your way*;
for I am too old to have a husband. If I
should say I have hope, *even if* I should have
a husband tonight and should also bear sons,
13 "would you wait for them till they were
grown? Would you restrain yourselves from
having husbands? No, my daughters; for it
grieves me very much for your sakes that
[R]the hand of the LORD has gone out against
me!" Judg. 2:15
14 Then they lifted up their voices and wept
again; and Orpah kissed her mother-in-law,
but Ruth [R]clung to her. [Prov. 17:17]
15 And she said, "Look, your sister-in-law
has gone back to [R]her people and to her gods;
return after your sister-in-law." Judg. 11:24

Ruth's Choice to Remain with Naomi

16 But Ruth said:

[R]"Entreat[T] me not to leave you,
Or to turn back from following after
you; 2 Kin. 2:2, 4, 6 • *Urge*
For wherever you go, I will go;
And wherever you lodge, I will lodge;
[R]Your people *shall be* my people,
And your God, my God. Ruth. 2:11, 12
17 Where you die, I will die,
And there will I be buried.
[R]The LORD do so to me, and more also,
If *anything but* death parts you and
me." 1 Sam. 3:17

18 When she saw that she was determined
to go with her, she stopped speaking to her.

Ruth and Naomi Return to Bethlehem

19 Now the two of them went until they
came to Bethlehem. And it happened, when
they had come to Bethlehem, that [R]all the
city was excited because of them; and the
women said, "*Is* this Naomi?" Matt. 21:10
20 So she said to them, "Do not call me
[T]Naomi; call me [T]Mara, for the Almighty has
dealt very bitterly with me. *Pleasant* • *Bitter*
21 "I went out full, [R]and the LORD has
brought me home again empty. Why do you
call me Naomi, since the LORD has testified
against me, and [T]the Almighty has afflicted
me?" Job 1:21 • Heb. *Shaddai*
22 So Naomi returned, and Ruth the Moabitess her daughter-in-law with her, who

returned from the country of Moab. Now
they came to Bethlehem [R]at the beginning
of barley harvest. 2 Sam. 21:9

CHAPTER 2

Boaz Meets Ruth

AND Naomi had a kinsman of her husband's, a man of great wealth, of the
family of Elimelech; his name *was* Boaz.
2 So Ruth the Moabitess said to Naomi,
"Please let me go to the [R]field, and glean
heads of grain after *him* in whose sight I may
find favor." And she said to her, "Go, my
daughter." Lev. 19:9, 10; 23:22
3 Then she left, and went and gleaned in
the field after the reapers. And she happened
to come to the part of the field *belonging* to
Boaz, who *was* of the family of Elimelech.
4 Now behold, Boaz came from [R]Bethle-
hem, and said to the reapers, [R]"The LORD *be*
with you!" And they answered him, "The
LORD bless you!" Ruth 1:1 • Ps. 129:7, 8
5 Then Boaz said to his servant who was in
charge of the reapers, "Whose young woman
is this?"
6 So the servant who was in charge of the
reapers answered and said, "It *is* the young
Moabite woman [R]who came back with Naomi
from the country of Moab. Ruth 1:22
7 "And she said, 'Please let me glean and
gather after the reapers among the sheaves.'
So she came and has continued from morning
until now, though she rested a little in the
house."

Boaz Protects Ruth

8 Then Boaz said to Ruth, "You will listen,
my daughter, will you not? Do not go to
glean in another field, nor go from here, but
stay close by my young women.
9 "*Let* your eyes *be* on the field which they
reap, and go after them. Have I not commanded the young men not to touch you?
And when you are thirsty, go to the vessels
and drink from what the young men have
drawn."
10 Then she fell on her face, bowed down to
the ground, and said to him, "Why have I
found favor in your eyes, that you should
take notice of me, since I *am* a foreigner?"
11 And Boaz answered and said to her, "It
has been fully reported to me, [R]all that you
have done for your mother-in-law since the
death of your husband, and *how* you have
left your father and your mother and the land
of your birth, and have come to a people
whom you did not know before. Ruth 1:14–18
12 [R]"The LORD repay your work, and a full
reward be given you by the LORD God of
Israel, [R]under whose wings you have come
for refuge." 1 Sam. 24:19 • Ruth 1:16
13 Then she said, "Let me find favor in your
sight, my lord; for you have comforted me,
and have spoken [T]kindly to your maidservant, [R]though I am not like one of your
maidservants." Lit. *to the heart of* • 1 Sam. 25:41
14 Now Boaz said to her at mealtime,
"Come here, and eat of the bread, and dip
your piece of bread in the vinegar." So she sat
beside the reapers, and he passed parched
grain to her; and she ate and [R]was satisfied,
and kept some back. Ruth 2:18
15 And when she rose up to [T]glean, Boaz
commanded his young men, saying, "Let her
glean even among the sheaves, and do not
[T]reproach her. Gather after the reapers • *rebuke*
16 "Also let *some grain* from the bundles
fall purposely for her; leave *it* that she may
glean, and do not rebuke her."

Boaz Provides for Ruth

17 So she gleaned in the field until evening,
and beat out what she had gleaned, and it
was about an [T]ephah of [R]barley. .65 bu. • Ruth 1:22
18 Then she took *it* up and went into the
city, and her mother-in-law saw what she had
gleaned. So she brought out and gave to her
[R]what she had kept back after she had been
satisfied. Ruth 2:14
19 And her mother-in-law said to her,
"Where have you gleaned today? And where
did you work? Blessed be the one who [R]took
notice of you." So she told her mother-in-law
with whom she had worked, and said, "The
man's name with whom I worked today *is*
Boaz." [Ps. 41:1]
20 Then Naomi said to her daughter-in-law,
"Blessed *be* he of the LORD, who has not
forsaken His kindness to the living and the
dead!" And Naomi said to her, "The man *is* a
relative of ours, one of our near kinsmen."
21 Then Ruth the Moabitess said, "He also
said to me, 'You shall stay close by my young
men until they have finished all my harvest.' "
22 And Naomi said to Ruth her daughter-in-
law, "*It is* good, my daughter, that you go out
with his young women, and that people do
not [T]meet you in any other field." *encounter*
23 So she stayed close by the young women
of Boaz, to glean until the end of barley
harvest and wheat harvest; and she dwelt
with her mother-in-law.

CHAPTER 3

Naomi Seeks Redemption for Ruth

THEN Naomi her mother-in-law said to
her, "My daughter, [R]shall I not seek
[R]security[T] for you, that it may be well with
you? 1 Tim. 5:8 • Ruth 1:9 • *rest*
2 "Now Boaz, [R]whose young women you
were with, *is he* not our kinsman? In fact, he

is winnowing barley tonight at the threshing floor. Ruth 2:3, 8

3 "Therefore wash yourself and [R]anoint yourself, put on your *best* garment and go down to the threshing floor; *but* do not make yourself known to the man until he has finished eating and drinking. 2 Sam. 14:2

4 "Then it shall be, when he lies down, that you shall notice the place where he lies; and you shall go in, uncover his feet, and lie down; and he will tell you what you should do."

5 And she said to her, "All that you say to me I will do."

Ruth Obeys Naomi

6 So she went down to the threshing floor and did according to all that her mother-in-law instructed her.

7 And after Boaz had eaten and drunk, and his heart was cheerful, he went to lie down at the end of the heap of grain; and she came softly, uncovered his feet, and lay down.

8 Now it happened at midnight that the man was startled, and turned himself; and there, a woman was lying at his feet.

9 And he said, "Who *are* you?" So she answered, "I *am* Ruth, your maidservant. Take your maidservant under your wing, for you are a [T]near kinsman." *redeemer*

Boaz Desires to Redeem Ruth

10 Then he said, [R]"Blessed *are* you of the LORD, my daughter! For you have shown more kindness at the end than [R]at the beginning, in that you did not go after young men, whether poor or rich. Ruth 2:20 • Ruth 1:8

11 "And now, my daughter, do not fear. I will do for you all that you request, for all the people of my town know that you *are* [R]a virtuous woman. Prov. 12:4; 31:10–31

12 "Now it is true that I *am your* [R]near kinsman; however, [R]there is a kinsman nearer than I. Ruth 3:9 • Ruth 4:1

13 "Stay this night, and in the morning it shall be *that* if he will perform the duty of a near kinsman for you—good; let him do it. But if he does not want to perform the duty for you, then I will perform the duty for you, *as* the LORD lives! Lie down until morning."

14 So she lay at his feet until morning, and she arose before one could recognize another. Then he said, "Do not let it be known that the woman came to the threshing floor."

15 Also he said, "Bring the [T]shawl that *is* on you and hold it." And when she held it, he measured six *ephahs* of barley, and laid *it* on her. Then *she went into the city. *cloak*

16 So when she came to her mother-in-law, she said, "*Is* that you, my daughter?" Then she told her all that the man had done for her.

17 And she said, "These six *ephahs* of barley he gave me; for he said to me, 'Do not go empty-handed to your mother-in-law.' "

18 Then she said, [R]"Sit still, my daughter, until you know how the matter will turn out; for the man will not rest until he has concluded the matter this day." [Ps. 37:3, 5]

CHAPTER 4

Boaz Marries Ruth

NOW Boaz went up to the gate and sat down there; and behold, the near kinsman of whom Boaz had spoken came by. So Boaz said, "Come aside, friend, sit down here." So he came aside and sat down.

2 And he took ten men of [R]the elders of the city, and said, "Sit down here." So they sat down. 1 Kin. 21:8

3 Then he said to the near kinsman, "Naomi, who has come back from the country of Moab, sold the piece of land [R]which *belonged* to our brother Elimelech. Lev. 25:25

4 "And I thought to [T]inform you, saying, 'Buy *it* back [R]in the presence of the inhabitants and the elders of my people. If you will redeem *it*, redeem *it*; but if you will not redeem *it, then* tell me, that I may know; [R]for *there is* no one but you to redeem *it*, and I *am* next after you.' " And he said, "I will redeem *it*." Lit. *uncover your ear* • Gen. 23:18 • Lev. 25:25

5 Then Boaz said, "On the day you buy the field from the hand of Naomi, you must also buy *it* from Ruth the Moabitess, the wife of the dead, [R]to raise up the name of the dead on his inheritance." Matt. 22:24

6 And the near kinsman said, "I cannot redeem *it* for myself, lest I ruin my own inheritance. You redeem my right of redemption for yourself, for I cannot redeem *it*."

7 Now this *was the custom* in former times in Israel concerning redeeming and exchanging, to confirm anything: one man took off his sandal and gave *it* to the other, and this *was* an attestation in Israel.

8 Therefore the near kinsman said to Boaz, "Buy *it* for yourself." So he took off his sandal.

9 And Boaz said to the elders and *to* all the people, "You *are* witnesses this day that I have bought all that was Elimelech's, and all that *was* Chilion's and Mahlon's, from the hand of Naomi.

10 "Moreover, Ruth the Moabitess, the wife of Mahlon, I have acquired as my wife, to raise up the name of the dead on his inheritance, [R]that the name of the dead may not be cut off from among his brethren and from the gate of his place. You *are* witnesses this day." Deut. 25:6

11 And all the people who *were* at the gate, and the elders, said, "*We are* witnesses. The LORD make the woman who is coming to your house like Rachel and Leah, the two

3:15 MT *he;* some Heb. mss., Syr., Vg. *she*

LEVIRATIC MARRIAGE

The fields of Boaz, near the city of Bethlehem. Photo by Howard Vos

Leviratic marriage, a family and inheritance custom among the Jewish people, is clearly demonstrated in the Book of Ruth. A near kinsman of the widowed Ruth gave up his right to buy the family property and marry Ruth, making it possible for Boaz to take her as his wife (Ruth 4).

The custom of leviratic marriage specified that when an Israelite died without leaving a male heir, his nearest relative should marry the widow in order to continue the family name of the deceased brother. The term *levirate* means "husband's brother."

If brothers on the father's side of the same family lived in the same area and one of them died childless, the widow was not to marry a stranger; rather, the surviving brother was to take her as his wife. The firstborn son by her took the name of the deceased brother, continuing his name in the family register.

Such marriages were not strictly required under Jewish law but were considered an act of love. If a brother-in-law did not wish to marry the widow, he was not forced to do so. Apparently, the next male relative in such cases then had the right to do so. This was the situation that led to the marriage of Boaz and Ruth in the Book of Ruth.

The first mention of the concept of leviratic marriage occurs in Genesis, when Onan was called upon to marry his brother Er's widow (Gen. 38:8). However, Onan refused to "give an heir to his brother" (Gen. 38:9).

Leviratic marriage was the basis for the question asked of Jesus by the Sadducees (Matt. 22:23–28). The rabbis taught that in the next world a widow who had been taken by her brother-in-law reverted to her first husband at the resurrection. Jesus answered that "in the resurrection they neither marry nor are given in marriage" (Matt. 22:30). In other words, the resurrected life will be a different type of life, one that cannot be judged in earthly terms.

who [R]built the house of Israel; and may you
prosper in [R]Ephrathah and be famous in
[R]Bethlehem. Gen. 29:25–30 • Gen. 35:16–18 • Mic. 5:2
12 "May your house be like the house of
Perez, whom Tamar bore to Judah, because
of [R]the offspring which the LORD will give you
from this young woman." 1 Sam. 2:20

Ruth Bears a Son, Obed

13 So Boaz took Ruth and she became his
wife; and when he went in to her, the LORD
gave her conception, and she bore a son.
14 Then [R]the women said to Naomi,
"Blessed *be* the LORD, who has not left you
this day without a [T]near kinsman; and may
his name be famous in Israel! Luke 1:58 • *redeemer*
15 "And may he be to you a restorer of life
and a nourisher of your old age; for your
daughter-in-law, who loves you, who is better
to you than seven sons, has borne him."

Naomi Receives a New Family

16 Then Naomi took the child and laid him
on her bosom, and became a nurse to him.

Ruth Is the Great-Grandmother of David
Matt. 1:3–6

17 Also the neighbor women gave him a
name, saying, "There is a son born to Naomi." And they called his name Obed. He *is*
the father of Jesse, the father of David.
18 [R]Now this *is* the genealogy of Perez:
[R]Perez begot Hezron; 1 Chr. 2:4, 5 • Num. 26:20, 21
19 Hezron begot Ram, and Ram begot Amminadab;
20 Amminadab begot Nahshon, and Nah-
shon begot [R]Salmon;[T] Matt. 1:4 • Heb. *Salmah*
21 Salmon begot Boaz, and Boaz begot
Obed;
22 Obed begot Jesse, and Jesse begot [R]Da-
vid. Matt. 1:6

The Jewish Calendar

The Jews used two kinds of calendars:
Civil Calendar—official calendar of kings, childbirth, and contracts.
Sacred Calendar—from which festivals were computed.

NAMES OF MONTHS	CORRESPONDS WITH	NO. OF DAYS	MONTH OF CIVIL YEAR	MONTH OF SACRED YEAR
TISHRI	Sept.–Oct.	30 days	1st	7th
HESHVAN	Oct.–Nov.	29 or 30	2nd	8th
CHISLEV	Nov.–Dec.	29 or 30	3rd	9th
TEBETH	Dec.–Jan.	29	4th	10th
SHEBAT	Jan.–Feb.	30	5th	11th
ADAR	Feb.–Mar.	29 or 30	6th	12th
NISAN	Mar.–Apr.	30	7th	1st
IYAR	Apr.–May	29	8th	2nd
SIVAN	May–June	30	9th	3rd
TAMMUZ	June–July	29	10th	4th
AB	July–Aug.	30	11th	5th
*ELUL	Aug.–Sept.	29	12th	6th

The Jewish day was from sunset to sunset, in 8 equal parts:

FIRST WATCH . . . .SUNSET TO 9 P.M.
SECOND WATCH .9 P.M. TO MIDNIGHT
THIRD WATCH . . . .MIDNIGHT TO 3 A.M.
FOURTH WATCH . .3 A.M. TO SUNRISE

FIRST HOUR . . . . .SUNRISE TO 9 A.M.
THIRD HOUR . . . . .9 A.M. TO NOON
SIXTH HOUR . . . . .NOON TO 3 P.M.
NINTH HOUR . . . . .3 P.M. TO SUNSET

*Hebrew months were alternately 30 and 29 days long. Their year, shorter than ours, had 354 days. Therefore, about every 3 years (7 times in 19 years) an extra 29-day-month, VEADAR, was added between ADAR and NISAN.

THE FIRST BOOK OF

SAMUEL

THE BOOK OF FIRST SAMUEL

The Book of First Samuel describes the transition of leadership in Israel from judges to kings. Three characters are prominent in the book: Samuel, the last judge and first prophet; Saul, the first king of Israel; and David, the king-elect, anointed but not yet recognized as Saul's successor.

The books of First and Second Samuel were originally one book in the Hebrew Bible, known as the "Book of Samuel" or simply "Samuel." This name has been variously translated "The Name of God," "His Name Is God," "Heard of God," and "Asked of God." The Septuagint divides Samuel into two books even though it is one continuous account. This division artificially breaks up the history of David. The Greek (Septuagint) title is *Bibloi Basileion,* "Books of Kingdoms," referring to the later kingdoms of Israel and Judah. First Samuel is called *Basileion Alpha,* "First Kingdoms." Second Samuel and First and Second Kings are called "Second, Third, and Fourth Kingdoms." The Latin Vulgate originally called the books of Samuel and Kings *Libri Regum,* "Books of the Kings." Later the Latin Bible combined the Hebrew and Greek titles for the first of these books, calling it *Liber I Samuelis,* the "First Book of Samuel," or simply "First Samuel."

THE AUTHOR OF FIRST SAMUEL

The author of First and Second Samuel is anonymous, but Jewish talmudic tradition says that it was written by Samuel. Samuel may have written the first portion of the book, but his death recorded in First Samuel 25:1 makes it clear that he did not write all of First and Second Samuel. Samuel did write a book (10:25), and written records were available. As the head of a company of prophets (10:5; 19:20), Samuel would be a logical candidate for biblical authorship.

First Chronicles 29:29 refers to "the book of Samuel the Seer," "the book of Nathan the Prophet," and "the book of Gad the Seer." All three men evidently contributed to these two books; and it is very possible that a single compiler, perhaps a member of the prophetic school, used these chronicles to put together the Book of Samuel. This is also suggested by the unity of plan and purpose and by the smooth transitions between sections.

THE TIME OF FIRST SAMUEL

If Samuel wrote the material in the first twenty-four chapters, he did so soon before his death (c. 1015 B.C.). He was born around 1105 B.C., and ministered as a judge and prophet in Israel between about 1067 and 1015 B.C. The books of Samuel end in the last days of David; so they must have been compiled after 971 B.C. The reference in First Samuel 27:6 to the divided monarchy in which Judah is separate from Israel indicates a compilation date after Solomon's death in 931 B.C. However, the silence regarding the Assyrian captivity of Israel in 722 B.C. probably means that First Samuel was written before this key event.

First Samuel covers the ninety-four-year period from the birth of Samuel to the death of Saul (c. 1105–1011 B.C.) The Philistines strongly oppress Israel from 1087 B.C. until the battle of Ebenezer in 1047 B.C. (7:10–14). However, even after this time the Philistines exercise military and economic control. They live in the coastal plains; and the hill country in which the Israelites dwell protects them from total conquest by the Philistines.

THE CHRIST OF FIRST SAMUEL

Samuel is a type of Christ in that he is a prophet, priest, and judge. Highly revered by the people, he brings in a new age.

David is one of the primary Old Testament portrayals of the person of Christ. He is born in Bethlehem, works as a shepherd, and rules as king of Israel. He is the anointed king who becomes the forerunner of the messianic King. His typical messianic psalms are born of his years of rejection and danger (see Ps. 22). God enables David, a man "after His own heart" (13:14), to become Israel's greatest king. The New Testament specifically calls Christ the "seed of David according to the flesh" (Rom. 1:3) and "the Root and the Offspring of David" (Rev. 22:16).

KEYS TO FIRST SAMUEL

Key Word: Transition—First Samuel records the critical transition in Israel from the rule of God through the judges to His rule through the kings.

This transition goes through three stages: Eli to Samuel, Samuel to Saul, and Saul to David.

Key Verses: First Samuel 13:14; 15:22—"But now your kingdom shall not continue. The LORD has sought for Himself a man after His own heart, and the LORD has commanded him *to be* commander over His people, because you have not kept what the LORD commanded you" (13:14).

"Then Samuel said, 'Has the LORD *as great* delight in burnt offerings and sacrifices, as in obeying the voice of the LORD? Behold, to obey is better than sacrifice, and to heed than the fat of rams' " (15:22).

Key Chapter: First Samuel 15—First Samuel 15 records the tragic transition of kingship from Saul to David. As in all three changes recorded in First Samuel, God removes His blessing from one and gives it to another because of sin. "Because you have rejected the word of the LORD, He also has rejected you from *being* king" (15:23).

SURVEY OF FIRST SAMUEL

First Samuel records the crucial transition from the theocracy under the judges to the monarchy under the kings. The book is built around three key men: Samuel (1—7), Saul (8—31), and David (16—31).

Samuel (1—7): Samuel's story begins late in the turbulent time of the judges when Eli is the judge-priest of Israel. The birth of Samuel and his early call by Yahweh are found in chapters 1—3. Because of his responsiveness to God (3:19), he is confirmed as a prophet (3:20, 21) at a time when the "word of the LORD was rare . . . *there was* no widespread revelation" (3:1).

Corruption at Shiloh by Eli's notoriously wicked sons leads to Israel's defeat in the crucial battle with the Philistines (4:1–11). The ark of the covenant, God's "throne" among the people, is lost to the Philistines; the priesthood is disrupted by the deaths of Eli and his sons; and the glory of God departs from the tabernacle (Ichabod, "No Glory," 4:21). Samuel begins to function as the last of the judges and the first in the order of the prophets (Acts 3:24). His prophetic ministry (7:3–17) leads to a revival in Israel, the return of the ark, and the defeat of the Philistines. When Samuel is old and his sons prove to be unjust judges, the people wrongly cry out for a king. They want a visible military and judicial ruler so they can be "like all the nations" (8:5–20).

Saul (8—15): In their impatient demand for a king, Israel chooses less than God's best. Their motive (8:5) and criteria (9:2) are wrong. Saul begins well (9—11), but his good characteristics soon degenerate. In spite of Samuel's solemn prophetic warning (12), Saul and the people begin to act wickedly. Saul presumptuously assumes the role of a priest (cf. 2 Chr. 26:18) and offers up sacrifices (13). He makes a foolish vow (14) and disobeys God's command to destroy the Amalekites (15). Samuel's powerful words in 15:22, 23 evoke a pathetic response in 15:24–31.

Saul and David (16—31): When God rejects Saul, He commissions Samuel to anoint David as Israel's next king. God's king-elect serves in Saul's court (16:14—23:29) and defeats the Philistine Goliath (17). Jonathan's devotion to David leads him to sacrifice the throne (20:30, 31) in acknowledgment of David's divine right to it (18). David becomes a growing threat to the insanely jealous Saul; but he is protected from Saul's wrath by Jonathan, Michal, and Samuel (19).

Saul's open rebellion against God is manifested in his refusal to give up what God has said cannot be his. David is protected again by Jonathan from Saul's murderous intent (20), but Saul becomes more active in his pursuit of David. The future king flees to a Philistine city where he feigns insanity (21), and flees again to Adullam where a band of men forms around him (22).

David continues to escape from the hand of Saul, and on two occasions spares Saul's life when he has the opportunity to take it (24—26). David again seeks refuge among the Philistines, but is not allowed to fight on their side against Israel. Saul, afraid of impending battle against the Philistines, foolishly consults a medium at En Dor to hear the deceased Samuel's advice (28). The Lord rebukes Saul and pronounces his doom; he and his sons are killed by the Philistines on Mount Gilboa (31).

FOCUS	SAMUEL		SAUL		
REFERENCE	1:1 — 4:1 —	— 8:1	— 13:1	— 15:10	— 31:13
DIVISION	FIRST TRANSITION OF LEADERSHIP: ELI—SAMUEL	JUDGESHIP OF SAMUEL	SECOND TRANSITION OF LEADERSHIP: SAMUEL—SAUL	REIGN OF SAUL	THIRD TRANSITION OF LEADERSHIP: SAUL—DAVID
TOPIC	DECLINE OF JUDGES		RISE OF KINGS		
	ELI	SAMUEL	SAUL		DAVID
LOCATION	CANAAN				
TIME	c. 94 YEARS				

OUTLINE OF FIRST SAMUEL

Part One: Samuel, the Last Judge (1:1—7:17)

I. The First Transition of National Leadership: Eli–Samuel .... 1:1—3:21

A. The Birth of the New Leader ...... 1:1—2:11
1. Hannah's Barrenness 1:1–18
2. Samuel's Birth 1:19–28
3. Hannah's Prophetic Prayer 2:1–11

B. The Need of the New Leader ..... 2:12—3:36
1. Sinfulness of Eli's Son 2:12–21
2. Compromise of Eli as Father 2:22–36

C. The Transition from Eli to Samuel 3:1–18
1. The Word of the Lord Does Not Come to Eli 3:1
2. The Word of the Lord Comes to Samuel 3:2–18

D. Samuel Is Recognized as the New Leader of Israel 3:19–21

II. The Judgeship of Samuel .... 4:1—7:17

A. The Need for Samuel's Leadership .... 4:1—6:21
1. Conquest of Israel by Philistia 4:1–10
2. Eli and His Sons Die 4:11–22
3. The Sin with the Ark .... 5:1—7:2
a. The Philistines' Sin with the Ark .... 5:1—6:9
b. The Israelites' Sin with the Ark 6:10–21

B. The Victories Under Samuel's Leadership 7:1–17
1. The Acceptable Return of the Ark... 7:1, 2
2. Israel Returns to the Lord 7:3–6
3. Israel's Victory over Philistia 7:7–17

Part Two: Saul, the First King (8:1—31:13)

I. The Second Transition of National Leadership: Samuel–Saul .... 8:1—12:25

A. The Causes of the Transition 8:1–9
1. Israel Rejects Samuel's Sons as Leaders 8:1–5
2. Israel Rejects God as King 8:6–9

B. The Transition from Samuel to Saul .... 8:10—12:25
1. Samuel Warns Israel 8:10–22
2. God Chooses Saul .... 9:1—10:16
3. Samuel Anoints Saul 10:17–27
4. Israel Makes Saul King 11:1–15
5. Samuel Confirms Saul 12:1–25

II. The Reign of King Saul .... 13:1—15:9

A. The Early Success of King Saul 13:1–4
B. The Failures of King Saul .... 13:5—15:9
1. Saul's Sinful Sacrifices 13:5–23
2. Saul's Selfish Curse 14:1–52
3. Saul's Incomplete Obedience 15:1–9

III. The Third Transition of National Leadership: Saul–David .... 15:10—31:13

A. The Transition of Kingship from Saul to David .... 15:10—16:13
1. God Rejects Saul as King 15:10–35
2. God Anoints David as King 16:1–13
3. God Takes His Spirit from Saul 16:14–23
4. God Confirms David over Saul .... 17:1—18:9
a. David Defeats Goliath 17:1–58
b. Jonathan Loves David 18:1–4
c. Israel Elevates David over Saul 18:5–9

B. The Attempts of Saul to Slay David .... 18:10—20:42
1. By Throwing a Spear at David 18:10–16
2. By Tricking David to Fight the Philistines 18:17–30
3. By Commanding His Servants to Kill David 19:1–7
4. By Throwing a Spear at David Again 19:8–10
5. By Sending His Messengers to Kill David 19:11–17
6. By Coming to Kill David at Samuel's House 19:18–24
7. By Commanding Jonathan to Bring David to Be Killed 20:1–42

C. The Rise of David in Exile .... 21:1—28:2
1. David Is Protected by the Priest 21:1–9
2. David Pretends to Be Mad 21:10–15
3. David Builds an Army in the Wilderness .... 22:1—26:25
a. David Flees to Adullam 22:1–5
b. Saul Slays the Priests of God ... 22:6–23
c. David Smites the Philistines 23:1–12
d. Saul Chases David 23:13–29
e. David Saves Saul's Life 24:1–22
f. Samuel the Judge Dies 25:1
g. David Marries Abigail 25:2–44
h. David Saves Saul's Life Again .. 26:1–20
i. Saul Admits His Guilt 26:21–25
4. David Joins with the Philistines .... 27:1—28:2

D. The Final Decline of Saul .... 28:3—31:13
1. God Does Not Answer Saul 28:3–6
2. Saul Visits the Medium 28:7–25
3. David Is Spared from Fighting Saul 29:1–11
4. God Answers David 30:1–8
5. David Kills the Enemy 30:9–31
6. The Enemy Kills Saul 31:1–13

CHAPTER 1

Hannah's Barrenness

NOW there was a certain man of Ramathaim Zophim, of the mountains of Ephraim, and his name *was* Elkanah the son of Jeroham, the son of Elihu, the son of Tohu, the son of Zuph, an Ephraimite.

2 And he had [R]two wives: the name of one *was* Hannah, and the name of the other Peninnah. Peninnah had children, but Hannah had no children. Deut. 21:15–17

3 This man went up from his city [R]yearly [R]to worship and sacrifice to the LORD of hosts in [R]Shiloh. Also the two sons of Eli, Hophni and Phinehas, the priests of the LORD, *were* there. Luke 2:41 • Deut. 12:5–7; 16:16 • Josh 18:1

4 And whenever the time came for Elkanah to make an [R]offering, he would give portions to Peninnah his wife and to all her sons and daughters. Deut. 12:17, 18

5 But to Hannah he would give a double portion, for he loved Hannah, [R]although the LORD had closed her womb. Gen. 16:1; 30:1, 2

6 And her rival also [R]provoked her severely, to make her miserable, because the LORD had closed her womb. Job 24:21

7 So it was, year by year, when she went up to the house of the LORD, that she provoked her; therefore she wept and did not eat.

8 Then Elkanah her husband said to her, "Hannah, why do you weep? Why do you not eat? And why is your heart grieved? *Am* I not [R]better to you than ten sons?" Ruth 4:15

9 So Hannah arose after they had finished eating and drinking in Shiloh. Now Eli the priest was sitting on the seat by the doorpost of [R]the tabernacle of the LORD. 1 Sam. 3:3

10 And she *was* in bitterness of soul, and prayed to the LORD and wept in anguish.

11 Then she made a vow and said, "O LORD of hosts, if You will indeed look on the affliction of your maidservant and remember me, and not forget your maidservant, but will give your maidservant a male child, then I will give him to the LORD all the days of his life, and no razor shall come upon his head."

12 And it happened, as she continued praying before the LORD, that Eli watched her mouth.

13 Now Hannah spoke in her heart; only her lips moved, but her voice was not heard. Therefore Eli thought she was drunk.

14 So Eli said to her, "How long will you be drunk? Put your wine away from you!"

15 And Hannah answered and said, "No, my lord, I *am* a woman of sorrowful spirit. I have drunk neither wine nor intoxicating drink, but have [R]poured out my soul before the LORD. Ps. 42:4; 62:8

16 "Do not consider your maidservant a [R]wicked[T] woman, for out of the abundance of my complaint and grief I have spoken until now." Deut. 13:13 • Lit. *daughter of Belial*

17 Then Eli answered and said, "Go in peace, and the God of Israel grant your petition which you have asked of Him."

18 And she said, [R]"Let your maidservant find favor in your sight." So the woman [R]went her way and ate, and her face was no longer *sad*. Ruth 2:13 • Rom. 15:13

Samuel's Birth

19 Then they rose early in the morning and worshiped before the LORD, and returned and came to their house at Ramah. And Elkanah [R]knew Hannah his wife, and the LORD [R]remembered her. Gen. 4:1 • Gen. 21:1; 30:22

20 So it came to pass in the process of time that Hannah conceived and bore a son, and called his name Samuel, *saying*, "Because I have asked for him from the LORD."

21 And the man Elkanah and all his house [R]went up to offer to the LORD the yearly sacrifice and his vow. 1 Sam. 1:3

22 But Hannah did not go up, for she said to her husband, "*I will not go up* until the child is weaned; then I will [R]take him, that he may appear before the LORD and [R]remain there [R]forever." Luke 2:22 • 1 Sam. 1:11, 28 • Ex. 21:6

1:17 Petition—One great difference between Christianity and all other religions is that the believer has a prayer-hearing and prayer-answering God. In the Old Testament during a contest with Elijah, the priests of Baal make desperate efforts to speak with their god by crying out and cutting themselves, but to no avail. "But *there was* no voice; no one answered" (Page 417—1 Kin. 18:26). How different from these words are those of the Psalmist: "*But* certainly God has heard *me;* He has attended to the voice of my prayer" (Page 662—Ps. 66:19).

a. The nature of our petitions. First of all, God has commanded us to pray (Page 1123—Matt. 7:7, 8; Page 1426—1 Tim. 2:8). When we pray, our petitions should be made by faith (Page 1468—James 1:6) in the name of Jesus (Page 1258—John 14:13). If these simple rules are followed, we can rest assured our prayers are being heard (Page 1498—1 John 3:22; 5:14, 15).

b. The objects of our prayers. For whom or what should we pray? First of all, we need to pray for ourselves, because unless we are in God's will, He cannot hear our petitions about other things. Thus we should begin by asking for cleansing (Page 1494—1 John 1:9) and wisdom (Page 1468—James 1:5). Other areas of our petitions concern spiritual leaders (Page 1409—Col. 4:3), sick believers (Page 1473—James 5:14, 15), rulers (Page 1426—1 Tim. 2:1–3), and even for our enemies (Page 1121—Matt. 5:44).

Now turn to Page 1401—Phil 4:6: Thanksgiving.

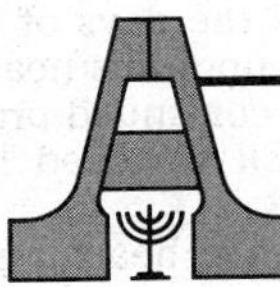

OLD TESTAMENT WOMEN

One of the outstanding women of the Old Testament was Hannah, who prayed for a son and then dedicated him to the Lord even before he was born. Hannah's faithfulness was rewarded in the person of Samuel, who served his nation as prophet, priest, and judge during a crucial time in its history (1 Sam. 1—7).

Other outstanding women of the Old Testament include the following:

Hannah prays for a child.

Name	Description	Biblical Reference
Bathsheba	Wife of David; mother of Solomon	2 Sam. 11:3, 27
Deborah	A judge who defeated the Canaanites under Sisera	Judg. 4:4
Delilah	Philistine woman who tricked Samson	Judg. 16:4, 5
Dinah	Only daughter of Jacob	Gen. 30:21
Esther	Jewish captive in Persia; saved her people from destruction by the schemer Haman	Esth. 2:16, 17
Eve	First woman	Gen. 3:20
Gomer	The prophet Hosea's unfaithful wife	Hos. 1:2, 3
Hagar	Sarah's maid; mother of Ishmael	Gen. 16:3–16
Jezebel	Wicked wife of King Ahab of the Northern Kingdom	1 Kin. 16:30, 31
Jochebed	Mother of Moses	Ex. 6:20
Miriam	Sister of Moses; a prophetess	Ex. 15:20
Naomi	Ruth's mother-in-law	Ruth 1:2, 4
Orpah	Ruth's sister-in-law	Ruth 1:4
Rachel	Wife of Jacob	Gen. 29:28
Rahab	Harlot who harbored Israel's spies; ancestor of Jesus	Josh. 2:1–3; Matt. 1:5
Ruth	Wife of Boaz and mother of Obed; ancestor of Jesus	Ruth 4:13, 17; Matt. 1:5
Sarah	Wife of Abraham; mother of Isaac	Gen. 11:29; 21:2, 3
Tamar	A daughter of David	2 Sam. 13:1
Zipporah	Wife of Moses	Ex. 2:21

23 And Elkanah her husband said to her,
"Do what seems best to you; wait until you
have weaned him. Only let the LORD establish
His word." So the woman stayed and nursed
her son until she had weaned him.
24 Now when she had weaned him, she
took him up with her, with *three bulls, one
ephah of flour, and a skin of wine, and
brought him to [R]the house of the LORD in
Shiloh. And the child *was* young. Josh. 18:1
25 Then they slaughtered a bull, and
[R]brought the child to Eli. Luke 2:22
26 And she said, "O my lord! [R]As your soul
lives, my lord, I *am* the woman who stood by
you here, praying to the LORD. 2 Kin. 2:2, 4, 6
27 [R]"For this child I prayed, and the LORD
has granted me my petition which I asked of
Him. [Matt. 7:7]
28 "Therefore I also have lent him to the
LORD; as long as he lives he shall be [T]lent to
the LORD." So they [R]worshiped the LORD
there. *granted* • Gen. 24:26, 52

CHAPTER 2

Hannah's Prophetic Prayer

AND Hannah [R]prayed and said: Phil. 4:6

"My heart rejoices in the LORD;
My [T]horn is exalted in the LORD.
I smile at my enemies, Strength
Because I rejoice in Your salvation.

2 "*There is* none holy like the LORD,
For *there is* none besides You,
Nor *is there* any rock like our God.

3 "Talk no more so very proudly;
[R]Let no arrogance come from your
mouth, Ps. 94:4
For the LORD *is* the God of knowledge;
And by Him actions are weighed.

4 "The[R] bows of the mighty men *are*
broken, Ps. 37:15; 46:9
And those who stumbled are girded
with strength.
5 *Those who were* full have hired
themselves out for bread,
And *those who were* hungry have
ceased *to hunger.*
Even [R]the barren has borne seven,
And [R]she who has many children has
become feeble. Ps. 113:9 • Is. 54:1

6 "The[R] LORD kills and makes alive;
He brings down to the grave and brings
up. Deut. 32:39
7 The LORD makes poor and makes rich;
[R]He brings low and lifts up. Ps. 75:7
8 [R]He raises the poor from the dust
And lifts the beggar from the ash heap,
[R]To set *them* among princes
And make them inherit the throne of
glory. Luke 1:52 • Job 36:7

[R]"For the pillars of the earth *are* the
LORD'S,
And He has set the world upon
them. Job 38:4–6
9 [R]He will guard the feet of His saints,
But the [R]wicked shall be silent in
darkness. [1 Pet. 1:5] • Rom. 3:19

"For by strength no man shall prevail.
10 The adversaries of the LORD shall be
[R]broken in pieces; Ps. 2:9
[R]From heaven He will thunder against
them. Ps. 18:13, 14
[R]The LORD will judge the ends of the
earth. Ps. 96:13; 98:9

"He will give strength to His king,
And exalt the horn of His anointed."

11 Then Elkanah went to his house at Ramah. But the child [T]ministered to the LORD
before Eli the priest. *served*

Sinfulness of Eli's Son

12 Now the sons of Eli *were* [T]corrupt; they
did not know the LORD. Lit. *sons of Belial*
13 And the priests' custom with the people
was that when any man offered a sacrifice,
the priest's servant would come with a three-
pronged fleshhook in his hand while the meat
was boiling.
14 Then he would thrust *it* into the pan, or
kettle, or caldron, or pot; and the priest
would take for himself all that the fleshhook
brought up. So they did in [R]Shiloh to all the
Israelites who came there. 1 Sam. 1:3
15 Also, before they [R]burned the fat, the
priest's servant would come and say to the
man who sacrificed, "Give meat for roasting
to the priest, for he will not take boiled meat
from you, but raw." Lev. 3:3–5, 16
16 And *if* the man said to him, "They should
really burn the fat first; *then* you may take *as
much* as your heart desires," he would then
answer him, "*No*, but you must give *it to me*
now; and if not, I will take *it* by force."
17 Therefore the sin of the young men was
very great before the LORD, for men [T]ab-
horred the offering of the LORD. *despised*
18 But Samuel ministered before the LORD,
even as a child, wearing a linen ephod.
19 Moreover his mother used to make him a
little robe, and bring *it* to him year by year
when she [R]came up with her husband to offer
the yearly sacrifice. 1 Sam. 1:3, 21

1:24 DSS, LXX, Syr., *a three-year-old bull*

20 And Eli would bless Elkanah and his
wife, and say, "The LORD give you descendants from this woman for the [T]loan that was
[R]lent[T] to the LORD." Then they would go to
their own home. *gift* • 1 Sam. 1:11, 27, 28 • *granted*
21 And the LORD [R]visited[T] Hannah, so that
she conceived and bore three sons and two
daughters. Meanwhile the child Samuel grew
before the LORD. Gen. 21:1 • *aided*

Compromise of Eli as Father

22 Now Eli was very old; and he heard
everything his sons did to all Israel, and how
they lay with [R]the women who assembled at
the door of the tabernacle of meeting. Ex. 38:8
23 So he said to them, "Why do you do such
things? For I hear of your evil dealings from
all the people.
24 "No, my sons! For *it is* not a good report
that I hear. You make the LORD's people
transgress.
25 "If one man sins against another, [R]God*
will judge him. But if a man [R]sins against the
LORD, who will intercede for him?" Nevertheless they did not heed the voice of their
father, [R]because the LORD desired to kill
them. Deut. 1:17; 25:1, 2 • Num. 15:30 • Josh. 11:20
26 And the child Samuel grew in stature,
and in favor both with the LORD and men.
27 Then a [R]man of God came to Eli and said
to him, "Thus says the LORD: [R]'Did I not
clearly reveal Myself to the house of your
father when they were in Egypt in Pharaoh's
house? 1 Kin. 13:1 • Ex. 4:14–16; 12:1
28 'Did I not choose him out of all the tribes
of Israel *to be* My priest, to offer upon My
altar, to burn incense, and to wear an ephod
before Me? And [R]did I not give to the house
of your father all the offerings of the children
of Israel made by fire? Num. 5:9
29 'Why do you kick at My sacrifice and My
offering which I have commanded *in My*
habitation, and honor your sons more than
Me, to make yourselves fat with the best of
all the offerings of Israel My people?'
30 "Therefore the LORD God of Israel says:
[R]'I said indeed *that* your house and the house
of your father would walk before Me forever';
but now the LORD says: [R]'Far be it from Me;
for those who honor Me I will honor, and
[R]those who despise Me shall be lightly esteemed. Ex. 29:9 • Jer. 18:9, 10 • Mal. 2:9–12
31 'Behold, [R]the days are coming that I will
cut off your [T]arm and the arm of your father's
house, so that there will not be an old man in
your house. 1 Kin. 2:27, 35 • *strength*
32 'And you will see an enemy *in My* habitation, *despite* all the good which God does for
Israel. And there shall not be [R]an old man in
your house forever. Zech. 8:4
33 'But any of your men *whom* I do not cut
off from My altar shall consume your eyes
and grieve your heart. And all the descendants of your house shall die in the flower of
their age.
34 'Now this *shall be* [R]a sign to you that will
come upon your two sons, on Hophni and
Phinehas: [R]in one day they shall die, both of
them. 1 Kin. 13:3 • 1 Sam. 4:11, 17
35 'Then [R]I will raise up for Myself a faithful
priest *who* shall do according to what *is* in
My heart and in My mind. [R]I will build him a
sure house, and he shall walk before [R]My
anointed forever. 1 Kin. 2:35 • 1 Kin. 11:38 • Ps. 18:50
36 [R]'And it shall come to pass that everyone
who is left in your house will come *and* bow
down to him for a [T]piece of silver and a
morsel of bread, and say, "Please, [T]put me in
one of the priestly positions, that I may eat a
piece of bread." ' " 1 Kin. 2:27 • $7.28 • *assign*

CHAPTER 3

The Word of the Lord Does Not Come to Eli

THEN [R]the boy Samuel ministered to the
LORD before Eli. And [R]the word of the
LORD was rare in those days; *there was* no
widespread revelation. 1 Sam. 2:11, 18 • Ps. 74:9

The Word of the Lord Comes to Samuel

2 And it came to pass at that time, while
Eli *was* lying down in his place, and when his
eyes had begun to grow [R]so dim that he could
not see, 1 Sam. 4:15
3 and before [R]the lamp of God went out in
the [T]tabernacle of the LORD where the ark of
God *was*, and while Samuel was lying down
to sleep, Ex. 27:20, 21 • Heb. *heykal, palace* or *temple*
4 that the LORD called Samuel. And he
answered, "Here I am!"
5 So he ran to Eli and said, "Here I am, for
you called me." And he said, "I did not call;
lie down again." And he went and lay down.
6 And the LORD called yet again, "Samuel!" So Samuel arose and went to Eli, and
said, "Here I am, for you called me." And he
answered, "I did not call, my son; lie down
again."
7 (Now Samuel [R]did not yet know the
LORD, nor was the word of the LORD yet
revealed to him.) 1 Sam. 2:12
8 And the LORD called Samuel again the
third time. Then he arose and went to Eli, and
said, "Here I am, for you did call me." Then
Eli perceived that the LORD had called the
boy.
9 Therefore Eli said to Samuel, "Go, lie
down; and it shall be, if He calls you, that you
must say, [R]'Speak, LORD, for Your servant
hears.' " So Samuel went and lay down in his
place. 1 Kin. 2:17
10 Then the LORD came and stood and
called as at other times, "Samuel! Samuel!"
And Samuel answered, "Speak, for Your
servant hears."

2:25 Tg. *the Judge*

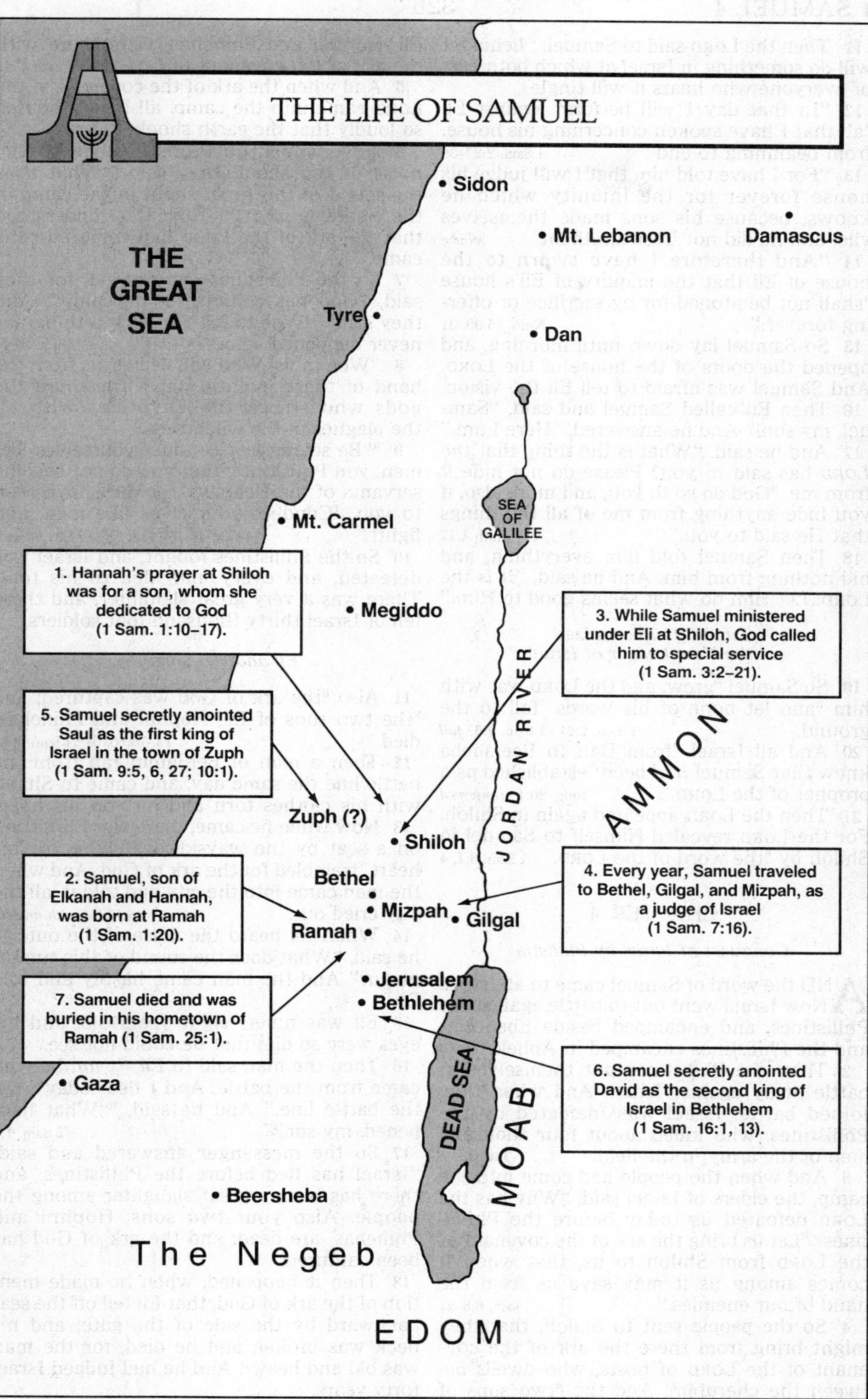

THE LIFE OF SAMUEL
THE GREAT SEA
Sidon
Mt. Lebanon
Damascus
Tyre
Dan
SEA OF GALILEE
Mt. Carmel
Megiddo
1. Hannah's prayer at Shiloh was for a son, whom she dedicated to God (1 Sam. 1:10–17).
3. While Samuel ministered under Eli at Shiloh, God called him to special service (1 Sam. 3:2–21).
JORDAN RIVER
AMMON
5. Samuel secretly anointed Saul as the first king of Israel in the town of Zuph (1 Sam. 9:5, 6, 27; 10:1).
Zuph (?)
Shiloh
Bethel
Mizpah
Gilgal
Ramah
2. Samuel, son of Elkanah and Hannah, was born at Ramah (1 Sam. 1:20).
4. Every year, Samuel traveled to Bethel, Gilgal, and Mizpah, as a judge of Israel (1 Sam. 7:16).
Jerusalem
Bethlehem
7. Samuel died and was buried in his hometown of Ramah (1 Sam. 25:1).
6. Samuel secretly anointed David as the second king of Israel in Bethlehem (1 Sam. 16:1, 13).
Gaza
DEAD SEA
MOAB
Beersheba
The Negeb
EDOM

11 Then the LORD said to Samuel: "Behold, I
will do something in Israel at which both ears
of everyone who hears it will tingle.
12 "In that day I will perform against Eli
[R]all that I have spoken concerning his house,
from beginning to end. 1 Sam. 2:27–36
13 "For I have told him that I will judge his
house forever for the iniquity which he
knows, because his sons made themselves
vile, and he did not [T]restrain them. *rebuke*
14 "And therefore I have sworn to the
house of Eli that the iniquity of Eli's house
[R]shall not be atoned for by sacrifice or offering forever." Num. 15:30, 31
15 So Samuel lay down until morning, and
opened the doors of the house of the LORD.
And Samuel was afraid to tell Eli the vision.
16 Then Eli called Samuel and said, "Samuel, my son!" And he answered, "Here I am."
17 And he said, "What *is* the thing that *the*
LORD has said to you? Please do not hide *it*
from me. [R]God do so to you, and more also, if
you hide anything from me of all the things
that He said to you." Ruth 1:17
18 Then Samuel told him everything, and
hid nothing from him. And he said, "It *is* the
LORD. Let Him do what seems good to Him."

Samuel Is Recognized as the New Leader of Israel

19 So Samuel [R]grew, and the LORD was with
him [R]and let none of his words [T]fall to the
ground. 1 Sam. 2:21 • 1 Sam. 9:6 • *fail*
20 And all Israel [R]from Dan to Beersheba
knew that Samuel *had been* [T]established as a
prophet of the LORD. Judg. 20:1 • *confirmed*
21 Then the LORD appeared again in Shiloh.
For the LORD revealed Himself to Samuel in
Shiloh by [R]the word of the LORD. 1 Sam. 3:1, 4

CHAPTER 4

Conquest of Israel by Philistia

AND the word of Samuel came to all Israel.
Now Israel went out to battle against the
Philistines, and encamped beside Ebenezer;
and the Philistines encamped in Aphek.
2 Then the Philistines put themselves in
battle array against Israel. And when they
joined battle, Israel was [T]defeated by the
Philistines, who killed about four thousand
men of the army in the field. Lit. *struck*
3 And when the people had come into the
camp, the elders of Israel said, "Why has the
LORD defeated us today before the Philistines? [R]Let us bring the ark of the covenant of
the LORD from Shiloh to us, that when it
comes among us it may save us from the
hand of our enemies." Josh. 6:6–21
4 So the people sent to Shiloh, that they
might bring from there the ark of the covenant of the LORD of hosts, who dwells *be-*
tween the cherubim. And the [R]two sons of
Eli, Hophni and Phinehas, *were* there with
the ark of the covenant of God. 1 Sam. 2:12
5 And when the ark of the covenant of the
LORD came into the camp, all Israel shouted
so loudly that the earth shook.
6 Now when the Philistines heard the
noise of the shout, they said, "What *does*
the sound of this great shout in the camp of
the Hebrews *mean*?" Then they understood
that the ark of the LORD had come into the
camp.
7 So the Philistines were afraid, for they
said, "God has come into the camp!" And
they said, [R]"Woe to us! For such a thing has
never happened before. Ex. 15:14
8 "Woe to us! Who will deliver us from the
hand of these mighty gods? These *are* the
gods who struck the Egyptians with all
the plagues in the wilderness.
9 [R]"Be strong and conduct yourselves like
men, you Philistines, that you do not become
servants of the Hebrews, [R]as they have been
to you. [T]Conduct yourselves like men, and
fight!" 1 Cor. 16:13 • Judg. 13:1 • Lit. *Be men*
10 So the Philistines fought, and Israel was
defeated, and every man fled to his tent.
There was a very great slaughter, and there
fell of Israel thirty thousand foot soldiers.

Eli and His Sons Die

11 Also [R]the ark of God was captured; and
[R]the two sons of Eli, Hophni and Phinehas,
died. Ps. 78:60, 61 • 1 Sam. 2:34
12 Then a man of Benjamin ran from the
battle line the same day, and came to Shiloh
with his clothes torn and dirt on his head.
13 Now when he came, there was Eli, sitting
on a seat by the wayside watching, for his
heart [T]trembled for the ark of God. And when
the man came into the city and told *it*, all the
city cried out. *trembled with anxiety*
14 When Eli heard the noise of the outcry,
he said, "What *does* the sound of this tumult
mean?" And the man came hastily and told
Eli.
15 Eli was ninety-eight years old, and his
eyes were so dim that he could not see.
16 Then the man said to Eli, "I *am* he who
came from the battle. And I fled today from
the battle line." And he said, [R]"What happened, my son?" 2 Sam. 1:4
17 So the messenger answered and said,
"Israel has fled before the Philistines, and
there has been a great slaughter among the
people. Also your two sons, Hophni and
Phinehas, are dead; and the ark of God has
been captured."
18 Then it happened, when he made mention of the ark of God, that Eli fell off the seat
backward by the side of the gate; and his
neck was broken and he died, for the man
was old and heavy. And he had judged Israel
forty years.

19 Now his daughter-in-law, Phinehas' wife,
was with child, *due* to be delivered; and when
she heard the news that the ark of God was
captured, and that her father-in-law and her
husband were dead, she bowed herself and
gave birth, for her labor pains came upon her.
20 And about the time of her death the
women who stood by her said to her, "Do not
fear, for you have borne a son." But she did
not answer, nor did she regard *it*.
21 Then she named the child [T]Ichabod,
saying, [R]"The glory has departed from Israel!" because the ark of God had been
captured and because of her father-in-law
and her husband. Lit. *Inglorious* • Ps. 26:8; 78:61
22 And she said, "The glory has departed
from Israel, for the ark of God has been
captured."

CHAPTER 5

The Philistines' Sin with the Ark

THEN the Philistines took the ark of God
and brought it from Ebenezer to Ashdod.
2 When the Philistines took the ark of
God, they brought it into the house of [T]Da-
gon and set it by Dagon. A Philistine idol
3 And when the people of Ashdod arose
early in the morning, there was Dagon,
[R]fallen on its face to the earth before the ark
of the LORD. So they took Dagon and [R]set it
in its place again. Is. 19:1; 46:1, 2 • Is. 46:7
4 And when they arose early the next
morning, there was Dagon, fallen on its face
to the ground before the ark of the LORD.
[R]The head of Dagon and both the palms of its
hands *were* broken off on the threshold; only
the torso of Dagon was left of it. Mic. 1:7
5 Therefore neither the priests of Dagon
nor any who come into Dagon's house [R]tread
on the threshold of Dagon in Ashdod to this
day. Zeph. 1:9
6 But the hand of the LORD was heavy on
the people of Ashdod, and He ravaged them
and struck them with [R]tumors,[T] *both* Ashdod
and its territory. Deut. 28:27 • Probably bubonic plague
7 And when the men of Ashdod saw how *it*
was, they said, "The ark of the God of Israel
must not remain with us, for His hand is
harsh toward us and Dagon our god."
8 Therefore they sent and gathered to
themselves all the [R]lords of the Philistines,
and said, "What shall we do with the ark of
the God of Israel?" And they answered, "Let
the ark of the God of Israel be carried away
to [R]Gath." So they carried the ark of the God
of Israel away. 1 Sam. 6:4 • Josh. 11:22
9 And *so* it was, after they had carried it
away, that the hand of the LORD was against
the city with a very great destruction; and He
struck the men of the city, both small and
great, *and tumors broke out on them.
10 Therefore they sent the ark of God to
Ekron. So it was, as the ark of God came to
Ekron, that the Ekronites cried out, saying,
"They have brought the ark of the God of
Israel to us, to kill us and our people!"
11 So they sent and gathered together all
the lords of the Philistines, and said, "Send
away the ark of the God of Israel, and let it
go back to its own place, so that it does not
kill us and our people." For there was a
deadly destruction throughout all the city;
the hand of God was very heavy there.
12 And the men who did not die were
stricken with the tumors, and the [R]cry of the
city went up to heaven. Jer. 14:2

CHAPTER 6

NOW the ark of the LORD was in the
country of the Philistines seven
months.
2 And the Philistines [R]called for the priests
and the diviners, saying, "What shall we do
with the ark of the LORD? Tell us how we
should send it to its place." Gen. 41:8
3 So they said, "If you send away the ark
of the God of Israel, do not send it [R]empty;
but by all means return *it* to Him *with* [R]a
trespass offering. Then you will be healed,
and it will be known to you why His hand is
not removed from you." Deut. 16:16 • Lev. 5:15, 16
4 Then they said, "What *is* the trespass
offering which we shall return to Him?" They
answered, "Five golden tumors and five
golden rats, *according to* the number of the
lords of the Philistines. For the same plague
was on all of you and on your lords.
5 "Therefore you shall make images of
your tumors and images of your rats that
ravage the land, and you shall [R]give glory to
the God of Israel; perhaps He will [R]lighten[T]
His hand from you, from your gods, and from
your land. Josh. 7:19 • 1 Sam. 5:6, 11 • *ease*
6 "Why then do you harden your hearts
[R]as the Egyptians and Pharaoh hardened
their hearts? When He did mighty things
among them, [R]did they not let the people go,
that they might depart? Ex. 9:34; 14:17 • Ex. 12:31
7 "Now therefore, make a new cart, take
two milk cows which have never been yoked,
and hitch the cows to the cart; and take their
calves home, away from them.
8 "Then take the ark of the LORD and set it
on the cart; and put [R]the articles of gold
which you are returning to Him *as* a trespass
offering in a chest by its side. Then send it
away, and let it go. 1 Sam. 6:4, 5
9 "And watch: if it goes up the road to its
own territory, to Beth Shemesh, *then* He has
done us this great evil. But if not, then we
shall know that *it is* not His hand *that* struck
us; it *was* by chance *that* it happened to us."

5:9 Vg. *and they had tumors in their secret parts*

The Israelites' Sin with the Ark

10 Then the men did so; they took two milk
cows and hitched them to the cart, and shut
up their calves at home.
11 And they set the ark of the LORD on the
cart, and the chest with the gold rats and the
images of their tumors.
12 Then the cows headed straight for the
road to Beth Shemesh, *and* went along the
[R]highway, lowing as they went, and did not
turn aside to the right hand or the left. And
the lords of the Philistines went after them to
the border of Beth Shemesh. Num. 20:19
13 Now *the people of* Beth Shemesh *were*
reaping their [R]wheat harvest in the valley;
and they lifted their eyes and saw the ark,
and rejoiced to see *it*. 1 Sam. 12:17
14 Then the cart came into the field of
Joshua of Beth Shemesh, and stood there; a
large stone *was* there. So they split the wood
of the cart and offered the cows as a burnt
offering to the LORD.
15 The Levites took down the ark of the
LORD and the chest that *was* with it, in which
were the articles of gold, and put *them* on the
large stone. Then the men of Beth Shemesh
offered burnt offerings and made sacrifices
the same day to the LORD.
16 So when [R]the five lords of the Philistines
had seen *it*, they returned to Ekron the same
day. Josh. 13:3
17 [R]Now these *are* the gold tumors which
the Philistines returned *as* a trespass offering
to the LORD: one for Ashdod, one for Gaza,
one for Ashkelon, one for [R]Gath, one for
Ekron; 1 Sam. 6:4 • 1 Sam. 5:8
18 and the gold rats, *according to* the number of all the cities of the Philistines *belonging* to the five lords, *both* fortified cities and
country villages, even as far as the large
stone of Abel on which they set the ark of the
LORD, *which stone remains* to this day in the
field of Joshua of Beth Shemesh.
19 Then He struck the men of Beth Shemesh, because they had looked into the ark
of the LORD. He [R]struck fifty thousand and
seventy men of the people, and the people
lamented because the LORD had struck the
people with a great slaughter. 2 Sam. 6:7
20 And the men of Beth Shemesh said,
"Who is able to stand before this holy LORD
God? And to whom shall it go up from us?"
21 So they sent messengers to the inhabitants of Kirjath Jearim, saying, "The Philistines have brought back the ark of the LORD;
come down *and* take it up with you."

CHAPTER 7

The Acceptable Return of the Ark

THEN the men of Kirjath Jearim came and
took the ark of the LORD, and brought it
into the house of [R]Abinadab on the hill, and
[R]consecrated Eleazar his son to keep the ark
of the LORD. 2 Sam. 6:3, 4 • Lev. 21:8
2 So it was that the ark remained in Kirjath Jearim a long time; it was there twenty
years. And all the house of Israel lamented
after the LORD.

Israel Returns to the Lord

3 Then Samuel spoke to all the house of
Israel, saying, "If you return to the LORD
with all your hearts, *then* put away the
foreign gods and the Ashtoreths from among
you, and prepare your hearts for the LORD,
and serve Him only; and He will deliver you
from the hand of the Philistines."
4 So the children of Israel put away the
[R]Baals and the [T]Ashtoreths, and served the
LORD only. Judg. 2:11 • Images of Canaanite goddesses
5 And Samuel said, "Gather all Israel to
Mizpah, and I will pray to the LORD for you."
6 So they gathered together at Mizpah,
[R]drew water, and poured *it* out before the
LORD. And they [R]fasted that day, and said
there, [R]"We have sinned against the LORD."
And Samuel judged the children of Israel at
Mizpah. 2 Sam. 14:14 • Neh. 9:1, 2 • 1 Sam. 12:10

Israel's Victory over Philistia

7 Now when the Philistines heard that the
children of Israel had gathered together at
Mizpah, the lords of the Philistines went up
against Israel. And when the children of
Israel heard *of it*, they were afraid of the
Philistines.
8 So the children of Israel said to Samuel,
[R]"Do not cease to cry out to the LORD our
God for us, that He may save us from the
hand of the Philistines." Is. 37:4
9 And Samuel took a suckling lamb and
offered *it as* a whole burnt offering to the
LORD. Then Samuel cried out to the LORD for
Israel, and the LORD answered him.
10 Now as Samuel was offering up the
burnt offering, the Philistines drew near to
battle against Israel. But the LORD thundered
with a loud thunder upon the Philistines that
day, and so confused them that they were
overcome before Israel.
11 And the men of Israel went out of Mizpah and pursued the Philistines, and drove
them back as far as below Beth Car.
12 Then Samuel [R]took a stone and set *it* up
between Mizpah and Shen, and called its
name [T]Ebenezer, saying, "Thus far the LORD
has helped us." Josh. 4:9; 24:26 • Lit. *Stone of Help*
13 So the Philistines were subdued, and
they did not come anymore into the territory
of Israel. And the hand of the LORD was
against the Philistines all the days of Samuel.
14 Then the cities which the Philistines had
taken from Israel were restored to Israel,
from Ekron to Gath; and Israel recovered its
territory from the hands of the Philistines.

CAPTURE OF THE ARK

1 Samuel 4—7

The ark of the covenant, a sacred portable chest, was the most sacred object in the tabernacle and the temple. It symbolized God's presence and His covenant with Israel. Believing the ark would protect them in battle, the army of Israel carried the sacred chest into conflict with the Philistines. The Philistines captured the ark but were eager to return it when they were visited by a series of plagues.

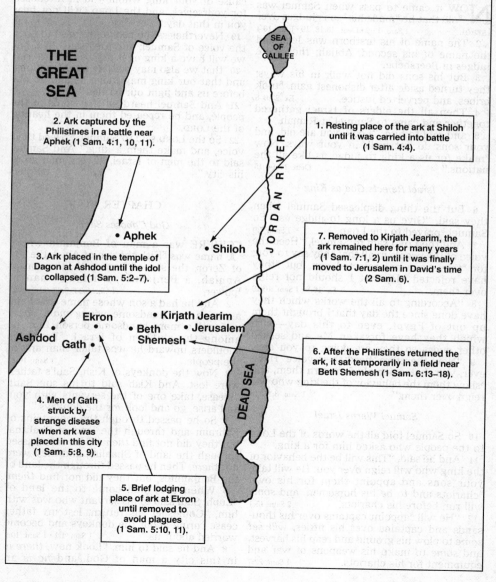

SEA OF GALILEE

THE GREAT SEA

JORDAN RIVER

DEAD SEA

Aphek

Shiloh

Kirjath Jearim

Jerusalem

Ekron

Beth Shemesh

Ashdod

Gath

1. Resting place of the ark at Shiloh until it was carried into battle (1 Sam. 4:4).

2. Ark captured by the Philistines in a battle near Aphek (1 Sam. 4:1, 10, 11).

3. Ark placed in the temple of Dagon at Ashdod until the idol collapsed (1 Sam. 5:2–7).

4. Men of Gath struck by strange disease when ark was placed in this city (1 Sam. 5:8, 9).

5. Brief lodging place of ark at Ekron until removed to avoid plagues (1 Sam. 5:10, 11).

6. After the Philistines returned the ark, it sat temporarily in a field near Beth Shemesh (1 Sam. 6:13–18).

7. Removed to Kirjath Jearim, the ark remained here for many years (1 Sam. 7:1, 2) until it was finally moved to Jerusalem in David's time (2 Sam. 6).

Also there was peace between Israel and the Amorites.

15 So Samuel [R]judged Israel all the days of his life. 1 Sam. 12:11

16 He went from year to year on a circuit to Bethel, Gilgal, and Mizpah, and judged Israel in all those places.

17 But he always returned to Ramah, for his home *was* there. There he judged Israel, and there he built an altar to the LORD.

CHAPTER 8

Israel Rejects Samuel's Sons as Leaders

NOW it came to pass when Samuel was [R]old that he [R]made his [R]sons judges over Israel. 1 Sam. 12:2 • Deut. 16:18, 19 • Judg. 10:4

2 The name of his firstborn was Joel, and the name of his second, Abijah; *they were* judges in Beersheba.

3 But his sons did not walk in his ways; they turned aside after dishonest gain, [R]took bribes, and perverted justice. Ex. 23:6–8

4 Then all the elders of Israel gathered together and came to Samuel at Ramah,

5 and said to him, "Look, you are old, and your sons do not walk in your ways. Now [R]make *for* us a king to judge us like all the nations." Deut. 17:14, 15

Israel Rejects God as King

6 But the thing displeased Samuel when they said, "Give us a king to judge us." So Samuel [R]prayed to the LORD. 1 Sam. 7:9

7 And the LORD said to Samuel, "Heed the voice of the people in all that they say to you; for [R]they have not rejected you, but [R]they have rejected Me, that I should not reign over them. Ex. 16:8 • 1 Sam. 10:19

8 "According to all the works which they have done since the day that I brought them up out of Egypt, even to this day—with which they have forsaken Me and served other gods—so they are doing to you also.

9 "Now therefore, heed their voice. However, you shall solemnly forewarn them, and [R]show them the behavior of the king who will reign over them." 1 Sam. 8:11–18

Samuel Warns Israel

10 So Samuel told all the words of the LORD to the people who asked him for a king.

11 And he said, "This will be the behavior of the king who will reign over you: He will take your sons and appoint *them* for his own [R]chariots and *to be* his horsemen, and *some* will run before his chariots. 2 Sam. 15:1

12 "He will [R]appoint captains over his thousands and captains over his fifties, *will set some* to plow his ground and reap his harvest, and *some* to make his weapons of war and equipment for his chariots. 1 Sam. 22:7

13 "He will take your daughters *to be* perfumers, cooks, and bakers.

14 "And [R]he will take the best of your fields, your vineyards, and your olive groves, and give *them* to his servants. 1 Kin. 21:7

15 "He will take a tenth of your grain and your vintage, and give it to his officers and servants.

16 "And he will take your menservants and your maidservants and your finest young men and your donkeys, and put *them* to his work.

17 "He will take a tenth of your sheep. And you will be his servants.

18 "And you will cry out in that day because of your king whom you have chosen for yourselves, and the LORD [R]will not hear you in that day." Is. 1:15

19 Nevertheless the people [R]refused to obey the voice of Samuel; and they said, "No, but we will have a king over us, Jer. 44:16

20 that we also may be [R]like all the nations, and that our king may judge us and go out before us and fight our battles." 1 Sam. 8:5

21 And Samuel heard all the words of the people, and he repeated them in the hearing of the LORD.

22 So the LORD said to Samuel, [R]"Heed their voice, and make them a king." And Samuel said to the men of Israel, "Every man go to his city." Hos. 13:11

CHAPTER 9

God Chooses Saul

THERE was a man of Benjamin whose name *was* [R]Kish the son of Abiel, the son of Zeror, the son of Bechorath, the son of Aphiah, a Benjamite, a mighty man of [T]power. 1 Chr. 8:33; 9:36–39 • *wealth*

2 And he had a son whose name *was* Saul, a choice and handsome *young man. There was* not a more handsome person than he among the children of Israel. [R]From his shoulders upward *he was* taller than any of the people. 1 Sam. 10:23

3 Now the donkeys of Kish, Saul's father, were lost. And Kish said to his son Saul, "Please, take one of the servants with you, and arise, go and look for the donkeys."

4 So he passed through the mountains of Ephraim and through the land of Shalisha, but they did not find *them*. Then they passed through the land of Shaalim, and *they were* not *there*. Then he passed through the land of the Benjamites, but they did not find *them*.

5 When they had come to the land of [R]Zuph, Saul said to his servant who *was* with him, "Come, let [R]us return, lest my father cease *caring* about the donkeys and become worried about us." 1 Sam. 1:1 • 1 Sam. 10:2

6 And he said to him, "Look now, *there is* in this city a man of God, and *he is* an

honorable man; all that he says surely comes
to pass. So let us go there; perhaps he can
show us the way that we should go."
7 Then Saul said to his servant, "But look,
if we go, [R]what shall we bring the man? For
the bread in our vessels is all gone, and *there*
is no present to bring to the man of God.
What do we have?" Judg. 6:18; 13:17
8 And the servant answered Saul again
and said, "Look, I have here at hand [T]one
fourth of a shekel of silver. I will give *that* to
the man of God, to tell us our way." $1.82
9 (Formerly in Israel, when a man went to
[T]inquire of God, he spoke thus: "Come, let us
go to the seer"; for *he who is* now *called* a
prophet was formerly called a seer.) *seek*
10 Then Saul said to his servant, "Well said;
come, let us go." So they went to the city
where the man of God *was*.
11 As they went up the hill to the city, they
met some young women going out to draw
water, and said to them, "Is the seer here?"
12 And they answered them and said, "Yes,
there he is, just ahead of you. Hurry now; for
today he came to this city, because [R]there is a
sacrifice of the people today [R]on the high
place. Gen. 31:54 • 1 Kin. 3:2
13 "As soon as you come into the city, you
will surely find him before he goes up to the
high place to eat. For the people will not eat
until he comes, because he must bless the
sacrifice; afterward those who are invited will
eat. Now therefore, go up, for about this time
you will find him."
14 So they went up to the city. *And* as they
were coming into the city, there was Samuel,
coming out toward them on his way up to the
high place.
15 Now the LORD had told Samuel in his ear
the day before Saul came, saying,
16 "Tomorrow about this time I will send
you a man from the land of Benjamin, [R]and
you shall anoint him [T]commander over My
people Israel, that he may save My people
from the hand of the Philistines; for I have
looked upon My people, because their cry has
come to me." 1 Sam. 10:1 • *prince* or *ruler*
17 And when Samuel saw Saul, the LORD
said to him, [R]"There he is, the man of whom I
spoke to you. This one shall reign over My
people." 1 Sam. 16:12
18 Then Saul drew near to Samuel in the
gate, and said, "Please tell me, where *is* the
seer's house?"
19 And Samuel answered Saul and said, "I
am the seer. Go up before me to the high
place, for you shall eat with me today; and
tomorrow I will let you go and will tell you all
that *is* in your heart.
20 "But as for your donkeys that were lost
three days ago, do not be anxious about
them, for they have been found. And [T]on
whom *is* all the desire of Israel? *Is it* not on
you and on all your father's house?" *for*
21 And Saul answered and said, "*Am* I not a
Benjamite, of the smallest of the tribes of
Israel, and [R]my family the least of all the
families of the tribe of Benjamin? Why then
do you speak like this to me?" Judg. 6:15
22 Then Samuel took Saul and his servant
and brought them into the hall, and had them
sit in the place of honor among those who
were invited; there *were* about thirty persons.
23 And Samuel said to the cook, "Bring the
portion which I gave you, of which I said to
you, 'Set it apart.'"
24 So the cook took up [R]the thigh with its
upper part and set *it* before Saul. And Samuel
said, "Here it is, what was kept back. *It* was
set apart for you. Eat; for until this time it has
been kept for you, since I said I invited the
people." So Saul ate with Samuel that
day. Lev. 7:32, 33
25 When they had come down from the
high place into the city, *Samuel* spoke with
Saul on [R]the top of the house. Deut. 22:8
26 They arose early; and it was about the
dawning of the day that Samuel called to
Saul on the top of the house, saying, "Get up,
that I may send you on your way." And Saul
arose, and both of them went outside, he and
Samuel.
27 *Now* as they were going down to the
outskirts of the city, Samuel said to Saul,
"Tell the servant to go on ahead of us." And
he went on. "But you stand here [T]awhile, that
I may announce to you the word of God." *now*

CHAPTER 10

THEN [R]Samuel took a flask of oil and
poured *it* on his head, [R]and kissed him
and said: "*Is it* not because [R]the LORD has
anointed you commander over [R]His inheritance? 2 Kin. 9:3, 6 • Ps. 2:12 • Acts 13:21 • Deut. 32:9
2 "When you have departed from me to-
day, you will find two men by Rachel's tomb
in the territory of Benjamin [R]at Zelzah; and
they will say to you, 'The donkeys which you
went to look for have been found. And now
your father has ceased caring about the
donkeys and is worrying about you, saying,
"What shall I do about my son?"' Josh. 18:28
3 "Then you shall go on forward from
there and come to the terebinth tree of
Tabor. There three men going up to God at
Bethel will meet you, one carrying three
young goats, another carrying three loaves of
bread, and another carrying a skin of wine.
4 "And they will [T]greet you and give you
two *loaves* of bread, which you shall receive
from their hands. *ask you about your welfare*
5 "After that you shall come to the hill of
God where the Philistine garrison *is*. And it
will happen, when you have come there to

the city, that you will meet a group of prophets coming down [R]from the high place with a
stringed instrument, a tambourine, a flute,
and a harp before them; [R]and they will be
prophesying. 1 Sam. 19:12, 20 • 2 Kin. 3:15
6 "Then the Spirit of the LORD will come
upon you, and [R]you will prophesy with them
and be turned into another man. 1 Sam. 10:10
7 "And let it be, when these [R]signs come to
you, *that* you do as the occasion demands;
for [R]God *is* with you. Ex. 4:8 • Judg. 6:12
8 "You shall go down before me [R]to Gilgal;
and surely I will come down to you to offer
burnt offerings *and* make sacrifices of peace
offerings. [R]Seven days you shall wait, till I
come to you and show you what you should
do." 1 Sam. 11:14, 15; 13:8 • 1 Sam. 13:8–10
9 And *so* it was, when he had turned his
back to go from Samuel, that God [T]gave him
another heart; and all those signs came to
pass that day. *changed his heart*
10 [R]When they came there to the hill, there
was [R]a group of prophets to meet him; then
the Spirit of God came upon him, and he
prophesied among them. 1 Sam. 10:5 • 1 Sam. 19:20
11 And it happened, when all who knew
him formerly saw that he indeed prophesied
among the prophets, that the people said to
one another, "What *is* this *that* has come
upon the son of Kish? [R]*Is* Saul also among the
prophets?" Matt. 13:54–57
12 Then a man from there answered and
said, "But [R]who *is* their father?" Therefore it
became a proverb: "*Is* Saul also among the
prophets?" John 5:30, 36
13 And when he had finished prophesying,
he went to the high place.
14 Then Saul's [R]uncle said to him and his
servant, "Where did you go?" And he said,
"To look for the donkeys. When we saw that
they were nowhere *to be found*, we went to
Samuel." 1 Sam. 14:50
15 And Saul's uncle said, "Tell me, please,
what Samuel said to you."
16 So Saul said to his uncle, "He told us
plainly that the donkeys had been [R]found."
But about the matter of the kingdom, he did
not tell him what Samuel had said. 1 Sam. 9:20

Samuel Anoints Saul

17 Then Samuel called the people together
[R]to the LORD [R]at Mizpah, Judg. 20:1 • 1 Sam. 7:5, 6
18 and said to the children of Israel, [R]"Thus
says the LORD God of Israel: 'I brought up
Israel out of Egypt, and delivered you from
the hand of the Egyptians *and* from the hand
of all kingdoms and from those who oppressed you.' Judg. 6:8, 9
19 "But you have today rejected your God,
who Himself saved you out of all your adversities and your tribulations; and you have
said to Him, '*No*, but set a king over us!' Now
therefore, present yourselves before the LORD
by your tribes and by your [T]clans." *thousands*
20 And when Samuel had [R]caused all the
tribes of Israel to come near, the tribe of
Benjamin was chosen. Acts 1:24, 26
21 When he had caused the tribe of Benjamin to come near by their families, the family
of Matri was chosen. And Saul the son of
Kish was chosen. But when they sought him,
he could not be found.
22 Therefore they [R]inquired of the LORD
further, "Has the man come here yet?" And
the LORD answered, "There he is, hidden
among the equipment." 1 Sam. 23:2, 4, 10, 11
23 So they ran and brought him from there;
and when he stood among the people, [R]he
was taller than any of the people from his
shoulders upward. 1 Sam. 9:2
24 And Samuel said to all the people, "Do
you see him whom the LORD has chosen, that
there is no one like him among all the people?" So all the people shouted and said,
[T]"Long live the king!" Lit. *May the king live*
25 Then Samuel explained to the people
[R]the behavior of royalty, and wrote *it* in a
book and laid *it* up before the LORD. And
Samuel sent all the people away, every man
to his house. 1 Sam. 8:11–18
26 And Saul also went home [R]to Gibeah;
and valiant *men* went with him, whose hearts
God had touched. Judg. 20:14
27 But some [R]rebels said, "How can this
man save us?" So they despised him, [R]and
brought him no presents. But he [T]held his
peace. Deut. 13:13 • 1 Kin. 4:21; 10:25 • *kept silent*

CHAPTER 11

Israel Makes Saul King

THEN [R]Nahash the Ammonite came up
and [T]encamped against [R]Jabesh Gilead;
and all the men of Jabesh said to Nahash,
[R]"Make a covenant with us, and we will serve
you." 1 Sam. 12:12 • *besieged* • Judg. 21:8 • Gen. 26:28
2 And Nahash the Ammonite answered
them, "On this *condition* I will make *a covenant* with you, that I may put out all your
right eyes, and bring reproach on all Israel."
3 Then the elders of Jabesh said to him,
"Hold off for seven days, that we may send
messengers to all the territory of Israel. And
then, if *there is* no one to [T]save us, we will
come out to you." *deliver*
4 So the messengers came to Gibeah of
Saul and told the news in the hearing of the
people. And [R]all the people lifted up their
voices and wept. Judg. 2:4; 20:23, 26; 21:2
5 Now there was Saul, coming behind the
herd from the field; and Saul said, "What
troubles the people, that they weep?" And
they told him the words of the men of Jabesh.
6 [R]Then the Spirit of God came upon Saul
when he heard this news, and his anger was
greatly aroused. Judg. 3:10; 6:34; 11:29; 13:25; 14:6

7 So he took a yoke of oxen and [R]cut them in pieces, and sent *them* throughout all the territory of Israel by the hands of messengers, saying, [R]"Whoever does not go out with Saul and Samuel to battle, so it shall be done to his oxen." And the fear of the LORD fell on the people, and they came out [T]with one consent. Judg. 19:29 • Judg. 21:5, 8, 10 • Lit. *as one man*

8 When he numbered them in Bezek, the children of Israel were three hundred thousand, and the men of Judah thirty thousand.

9 And they said to the messengers who came, "Thus you shall say to the men of Jabesh Gilead: 'Tomorrow, by *the time* the sun is hot, you shall have help.' " Then the messengers came and reported *it* to the men of Jabesh, and they were glad.

10 Therefore the men of Jabesh said, "Tomorrow we will come out to you, and you may do with us whatever seems good to you."

11 So it was, on the next day, that Saul put the people in three companies; and they came into the midst of the camp in the morning watch, and killed Ammonites until the heat of the day. And it happened that those who survived were scattered, so that no two of them were left together.

12 Then the people said to Samuel, [R]"Who *is* he who said, 'Shall Saul reign over us?' [R]Bring the men, that we may put them to death." 1 Sam. 10:27 • Luke 19:27

13 But Saul said, "Not a man shall be put to death this day, for today [R]the LORD has accomplished salvation in Israel." Ex. 14:13, 30

14 Then Samuel said to the people, "Come, let us go [R]to Gilgal and renew the kingdom there." 1 Sam. 7:16; 10:8

15 So all the people went to Gilgal, and there they made Saul king [R]before the LORD in Gilgal. [R]There they made sacrifices of peace offerings before the LORD, and there Saul and all the men of Israel rejoiced greatly. 1 Sam. 10:17 • 1 Sam. 10:8

CHAPTER 12

Samuel Confirms Saul

NOW Samuel said to all Israel: "Indeed I have heeded your voice in all that you said to me, and have made a king over you.

2 "And now here is the king, [R]walking before you; [R]and I am old and gray headed, and look, my sons *are* with you. I have walked before you from my childhood to this day. Num. 27:17 • 1 Sam. 8:1, 5

3 "Here I am. Witness against me before the LORD and before His anointed: Whose ox have I taken, or whose donkey have I taken, or whom have I defrauded? Whom have I oppressed, or from whose hand have I received *any* bribe with which to [R]blind my eyes? I will restore *it* to you." Deut. 16:19

4 And they said, [R]"You have not defrauded us or oppressed us, nor have you taken anything from any man's hand." Lev. 19:13

5 Then he said to them, "The LORD *is* witness against you, and His anointed *is* witness this day, [R]that you have not found anything [R]in my hand." And they answered, "*He is* witness." Acts 23:9; 24:20 • Ex. 22:4

6 And Samuel said to the people, [R]"*It is* the LORD who raised up Moses and Aaron, and who brought your fathers up from the land of Egypt. Mic. 6:4

7 "Now therefore, stand still, that I may [R]reason with you before the LORD concerning all the [R]righteous acts of the LORD which He did to you and your fathers: Is. 1:18 • Judg. 5:11

8 "When Jacob had gone into Egypt, and your fathers [R]cried out to the LORD, then the LORD [R]sent Moses and Aaron, who brought your fathers out of Egypt and made them dwell in this place. Ex. 2:23–25 • Ex. 3:10; 4:14–16

9 "And when they forgot the LORD their God, He sold them into the hand of [R]Sisera, commander of the army of Hazor, into the hand of the [R]Philistines, and into the hand of the king of [R]Moab; and they fought against them. Judg. 4:2 • Judg. 3:31; 10:7; 13:1 • Judg. 3:12–30

10 "Then they cried out to the LORD, and said, 'We have sinned, because we have forsaken the LORD and served the Baals and Ashtoreths; but now deliver us from the hand of our enemies, and we will serve You.'

11 "And the LORD sent [T]Jerubbaal, *Bedan, Jephthah, and Samuel, and delivered you out of the hand of your enemies on every side; and you dwelt in safety. *Gideon*, Judg. 6:32

12 "And when you saw that Nahash king of the Ammonites came against you, you said to me, 'No, but a king shall reign over us,' when the LORD your God *was* your king.

13 "Now therefore, here is the king [R]whom you have chosen *and* whom you have desired. And take note, [R]the LORD has set a king over you. 1 Sam. 8:5; 12:17, 19 • Hos. 13:11

14 "If you fear the LORD and serve Him and obey His voice, and do not rebel against the commandment of the LORD, then both you and the king who reigns over you will continue following the LORD your God.

15 "However, if you do [R]not obey the voice of the LORD, but [R]rebel against the commandment of the LORD, then the hand of the LORD will be against you, as *it was* against your fathers. Deut. 28:15 • Is. 1:20

16 "Now therefore, [R]stand and see this great thing which the LORD will do before your eyes: Ex. 14:13, 31

17 "*Is* today not the wheat harvest? [R]I will call to the LORD, and He will send thunder and [R]rain, that you may perceive and see that your wickedness *is* great, which you have

12:11 LXX, Syr. *Barak*

done in the sight of the LORD, in asking a
king for yourselves." [James 5:16–18] • Ezra 10:9
18 So Samuel called to the LORD, and the
LORD sent thunder and rain that day; and [R]all
the people greatly feared the LORD and Samuel. Ex. 14:31
19 And all the people said to Samuel, "Pray
for your servants to the LORD your God, that
we may not die; for we have added to all our
sins the evil of asking a king for ourselves."
20 Then Samuel said to the people, "Do not
fear. You have done all this wickedness; yet
do not turn aside from following the LORD,
but serve the LORD with all your heart.
21 "And do not turn aside; for *then you
would go* after empty things which cannot
profit or deliver, for they *are* nothing.
22 "For the LORD will not forsake His people, for His great name's sake, because it has
pleased the LORD to make you His people.
23 "Moreover, as for me, far be it from me
that I should sin against the LORD in ceasing
to pray for you; but [R]I will teach you the
[R]good and the right way. Ps. 34:11 • 1 Kin. 8:36
24 "Only fear the LORD, and serve Him in
truth with all your heart; for [R]consider what
[R]great things He has done for you. Is. 5:12
25 "But if you still do wickedly, you shall be
swept away, both you and your king."

CHAPTER 13

The Early Success of King Saul

SAUL* reigned one year; and when he had
reigned two years over Israel,
2 Saul chose for himself three thousand
men of Israel. Two thousand were with Saul
in Michmash and in the mountains of Bethel,
and a thousand were with Jonathan in Gibeah of Benjamin. The rest of the people he
sent away, every man to his tent.
3 And Jonathan attacked [R]the garrison of
the Philistines that *was* in [R]Geba, and the
Philistines heard *of it*. Then Saul blew the
trumpet throughout all the land, saying, "Let
the Hebrews hear!" 1 Sam. 10:5 • 2 Sam. 5:25
4 Now all Israel heard it said *that* Saul had
attacked a garrison of the Philistines, and
that Israel had also become [T]an abomination
to the Philistines. And the people were called
together to Saul at Gilgal. *odious*

Saul's Sinful Sacrifices

5 Then the Philistines gathered together to
fight with Israel, thirty thousand chariots and
six thousand horsemen, and people as the
sand which *is* on the seashore in multitude.
And they came up and encamped in Michmash, to the east of [R]Beth Aven. Josh. 7:2
6 When the men of Israel saw that they
were in danger (for the people were distressed), then the people hid in caves, in
thickets, in rocks, in holes, and in pits.
7 And *some of* the Hebrews crossed over
the Jordan to the [R]land of Gad and Gilead. As
for Saul, he *was* still in Gilgal, and all the
people followed him trembling. Num. 32:1–42
8 [R]Then he waited seven days, according
to the time set by Samuel. But Samuel did not
come to Gilgal; and the people were scattered
from him. 1 Sam. 10:8
9 So Saul said, "Bring a burnt offering and
peace offerings here to me." And he offered
the burnt offering.
10 Now it happened, as soon as he had
finished offering the burnt offering, that
Samuel came; and Saul went out to meet
him, that he might [T]greet him. Lit. *bless him*
11 And Samuel said, "What have you
done?" And Saul said, "When I saw that the
people were scattered from me, and *that* you
did not come within the days appointed, and
that the Philistines gathered together at
Michmash,
12 "then I said, 'The Philistines will now
come down on me at Gilgal, and I have not
made supplication to the LORD.' Therefore I
felt compelled, and offered a burnt offering."
13 And Samuel said to Saul, [R]"You have
done foolishly. [R]You have not kept the commandment of the LORD your God, which He
commanded you. For now the LORD would
have established your kingdom over Israel
forever. 2 Chr. 16:9 • 1 Sam. 5:11, 22, 28
14 "But now your kingdom shall not continue. The LORD has sought for Himself a
man [R]after His own heart, and the LORD has
commanded him *to be* commander over His
people, because you have not kept what the
LORD commanded you." Acts 7:46; 13:22
15 Then Samuel arose and went up from
Gilgal to Gibeah of Benjamin. And Saul
numbered the people *who were* present with
him, [R]about six hundred men. 1 Sam. 13:2, 6, 7
16 Saul, Jonathan his son, and the people
who were present with them remained in
[T]Gibeah of Benjamin. But the Philistines
encamped in Michmash. Heb. *Geba*
17 Then raiders came out of the camp of the
Philistines in three companies. One company
turned to the road *that leads* to [R]Ophrah, to
the land of Shual, Josh. 18:23
18 another company turned to the road *to*
Beth Horon, and another company turned *to*
the road of the border that overlooks the
Valley of Zeboim toward the wilderness.
19 Now [R]there was no blacksmith to be
found throughout all the land of Israel, for
the Philistines said, "Lest the Hebrews make
swords or spears." Judg. 5:8
20 But all the Israelites would go down to
the Philistines to sharpen each man's plow-
share, his mattock, his ax, and his sickle;

13:1 Heb. is difficult; cf. 2 Sam. 5:4; 1 Kin. 14:2 see also 2 Sam. 2:10; Acts 13:21

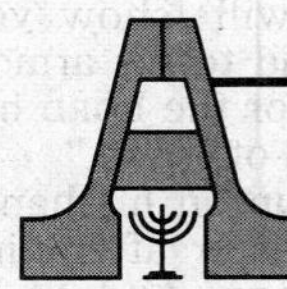

SAUL'S MILITARY CAMPAIGNS

As the first king of the united kingdom of Israel, Saul's major task was to subdue the nation's enemies. At first, he won several decisive battles. But his campaigns bogged down when he turned his attention to David, attempting to wipe out what he perceived as a threat to his power. Saul and his sons were eventually killed by the Philistines.

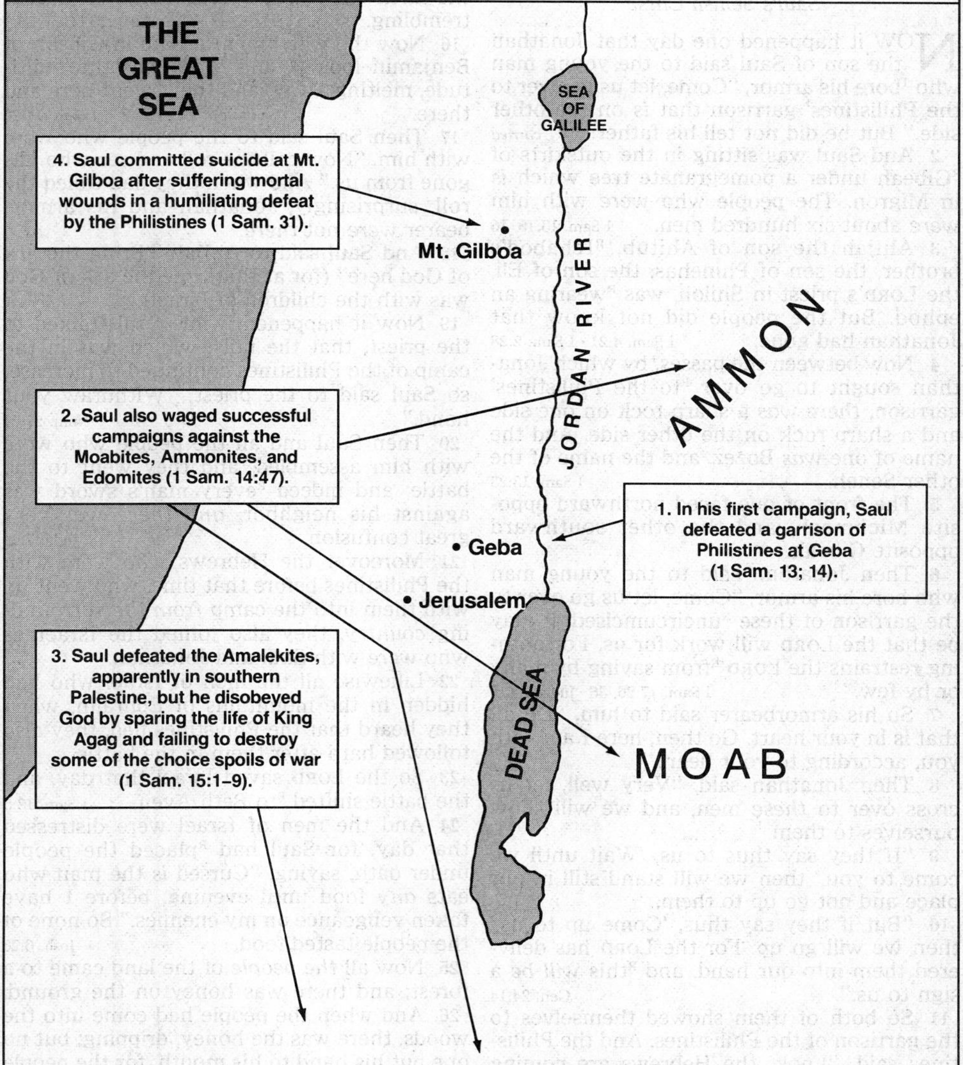

THE GREAT SEA

SEA OF GALILEE

JORDAN RIVER

DEAD SEA

AMMON

MOAB

EDOM

Mt. Gilboa

Geba

Jerusalem

1. In his first campaign, Saul defeated a garrison of Philistines at Geba (1 Sam. 13; 14).

2. Saul also waged successful campaigns against the Moabites, Ammonites, and Edomites (1 Sam. 14:47).

3. Saul defeated the Amalekites, apparently in southern Palestine, but he disobeyed God by sparing the life of King Agag and failing to destroy some of the choice spoils of war (1 Sam. 15:1–9).

4. Saul committed suicide at Mt. Gilboa after suffering mortal wounds in a humiliating defeat by the Philistines (1 Sam. 31).

21 and the charge for a sharpening was a
[T]pim for the plowshares, the mattocks, the
forks, and the axes, and to set the points of
the goads. About two-thirds shekel weight
22 So it came about, on the day of battle,
that there was neither sword nor spear found
in the hand of any of the people who *were*
with Saul and Jonathan. But they were found
with Saul and Jonathan his son.
23 [R]And the garrison of the Philistines went
out to the pass of Michmash. 1 Sam. 14:1, 4

CHAPTER 14

Saul's Selfish Curse

NOW it happened one day that Jonathan
the son of Saul said to the young man
who [T]bore his armor, "Come, let us go over to
the Philistines' garrison that *is* on the other
side." But he did not tell his father. *carried*
2 And Saul was sitting in the outskirts of
[R]Gibeah under a pomegranate tree which *is*
in Migron. The people who *were* with him
were about six hundred men. 1 Sam. 13:15, 16
3 Ahijah the son of Ahitub, [R]Ichabod's
brother, the son of Phinehas, the son of Eli,
the LORD's priest in Shiloh, was [R]wearing an
ephod. But the people did not know that
Jonathan had gone. 1 Sam. 4:21 • 1 Sam. 2:28
4 Now between the passes, by which Jonathan sought to go over [R]to the Philistines'
garrison, *there was* a sharp rock on one side
and a sharp rock on the other side. And the
name of one *was* Bozez, and the name of the
other Seneh. 1 Sam. 13:23
5 The front of one faced northward opposite Michmash, and the other southward
opposite Gibeah.
6 Then Jonathan said to the young man
who bore his armor, "Come, let us go over to
the garrison of these [R]uncircumcised; it may
be that the LORD will work for us. For nothing restrains the LORD [R]from saving by many
or by few." 1 Sam. 17:26, 36 • Judg. 7:4, 7
7 So his armorbearer said to him, "Do all
that is in your heart. Go then; here I am with
you, according to your heart."
8 Then Jonathan said, "Very well, let us
cross over to *these* men, and we will show
ourselves to them.
9 "If they say thus to us, 'Wait until we
come to you,' then we will stand still in our
place and not go up to them.
10 "But if they say thus, 'Come up to us,'
then we will go up. For the LORD has delivered them into our hand, and [R]this *will be* a
sign to us." Gen. 24:14
11 So both of them showed themselves to
the garrison of the Philistines. And the Philistines said, "Look, the Hebrews are coming
out of the holes where they have hidden."
12 Then the men of the garrison called to
Jonathan and his armorbearer, and said,
"Come up to us, and we will [T]show you
something." So Jonathan said to his armorbearer, "Come up after me, for the LORD has
delivered them into the hand of Israel." *teach*
13 And Jonathan climbed up on his hands
and knees with his armorbearer after him;
and they fell before Jonathan. And as he
came after him, his armorbearer killed them.
14 That first slaughter which Jonathan and
his armorbearer made was about twenty men
within about half an acre of land.
15 And [R]there was [T]trembling in the camp,
in the field, and among all the people. The
garrison and [R]the raiders also trembled; and
the earth quaked, so that it was [R]a very great
trembling. Job 18:11 • *terror* • 1 Sam. 13:17 • Gen. 35:5
16 Now the watchmen of Saul in Gibeah of
Benjamin looked, and *there* was the multitude, melting away; and they [R]went here and
there. 1 Sam. 14:20
17 Then Saul said to the people who *were*
with him, "Now call the roll and see who has
gone from us." And when they had called the
roll, surprisingly, Jonathan and his armorbearer *were* not *there*.
18 And Saul said to Ahijah, "Bring the ark
of God here" (for at that time the ark of God
was with the children of Israel).
19 Now it happened, while Saul [R]talked to
the priest, that the noise which *was* in the
camp of the Philistines continued to increase;
so Saul said to the priest, "Withdraw your
hand." Num. 27:21
20 Then Saul and all the people who *were*
with him assembled, and they went to the
battle; and indeed [R]every man's sword was
against his neighbor, *and there was* very
great confusion. Judg. 7:22
21 Moreover the Hebrews *who* were with
the Philistines before that time, who went up
with them into the camp *from the* surrounding *country*, they also joined the Israelites
who *were* with Saul and Jonathan.
22 Likewise all the men of Israel who had
hidden in the mountains of Ephraim, *when*
they heard that the Philistines fled, they also
followed hard after them in the battle.
23 So the LORD saved Israel that day, and
the battle shifted [R]to Beth Aven. 1 Sam. 13:5
24 And the men of Israel were distressed
that day, for Saul had [R]placed the people
under oath, saying, "Cursed *is* the man who
eats *any* food until evening, before I have
taken vengeance on my enemies." So none of
the people tasted food. Josh. 6:26
25 Now all *the people* of the land came to a
forest; and there was honey on the ground.
26 And when the people had come into the
woods, there was the honey, dripping; but no
one put his hand to his mouth, for the people
feared the oath.
27 But Jonathan had not heard his father
charge the people with the oath; therefore he

stretched out the end of the rod that *was* in his hand and dipped it in a honeycomb, and put his hand to his mouth; and his [T]countenance brightened. Lit. *eyes*

28 Then one of the people said, "Your father strictly charged the people with an oath, saying, 'Cursed *is* the man who eats food this day.' " And the people were faint.

29 But Jonathan said, "My father has troubled the land. Look now, how my countenance has brightened because I tasted a little of this honey.

30 "How much better if the people had eaten freely today of the spoil of their enemies which they found! For now would there not have been a much greater slaughter among the Philistines?"

31 Now they had [T]driven back the Philistines that day from Michmash to Aijalon. So the people were very faint. Lit. *struck*

32 And the people rushed on the [T]spoil, and took sheep, oxen, and calves, and slaughtered *them* on the ground; and the people ate *them* [R]with the blood. *plunder* • Deut. 12:16, 23, 24

33 Then they told Saul, saying, "Look, the people are sinning against the LORD by eating with the blood!" And he said, "You have dealt treacherously; roll a large stone to me this day."

34 And Saul said, "Disperse yourselves among the people, and say to them, 'Bring me here every man's ox and every man's sheep, slaughter *them* here, and eat; and do not sin against the LORD by eating with the blood.' " So every one of the people brought his ox with him that night, and slaughtered *it* there.

35 Then Saul [R]built an altar to the LORD. This was the first altar that he built to the LORD. 1 Sam. 7:12, 17

36 And Saul said, "Let us go down after the Philistines by night, and plunder them until the morning light; and let us not leave a man of them." And they said, "Do whatever seems good to you." Then the priest said, "Let us draw near to God here."

37 So Saul asked counsel of God, "Shall I go down after the Philistines? Will You deliver them into the hand of Israel?" But [R]He did not answer him that day. 1 Sam. 28:6

38 And Saul said, [R]"Come over here, all you chiefs of the people, and know and see what this sin was today. Josh. 7:14

39 "For [R]*as* the LORD lives, who saves Israel, though it be in Jonathan my son, he shall surely die." But not a man among all the people answered him. 2 Sam. 12:5

40 Then he said to all Israel, "You be on one side, and my son Jonathan and I will be on the other side." And the people said to Saul, "Do what seems good to you."

41 Therefore Saul said to the LORD God of Israel, "Give a perfect *lot.*" So Saul and Jonathan were taken, but the people escaped.

42 And Saul said, "Cast *lots* between my son Jonathan and me." So Jonathan was taken.

43 Then Saul said to Jonathan, [R]"Tell me what you have done." And Jonathan told him, and said, [R]"I only tasted a little honey with the end of the rod that *was* in my hand. So now I must die!" Josh. 7:19 • 1 Sam. 14:27

44 And Saul answered, [R]"God do so and more also; [R]for you shall surely die, Jonathan." Ruth 1:17 • 1 Sam. 14:39

45 But the people said to Saul, "Shall Jonathan die, who has accomplished this great salvation in Israel? Certainly not! [R]*As* the LORD lives, not one hair of his head shall fall to the ground, for he has worked [R]with God this day." So the people rescued Jonathan, and he did not die. 1 Kin. 1:52 • [2 Cor. 6:1]

46 Then Saul returned from pursuing the Philistines, and the Philistines went to their own place.

47 So Saul established his sovereignty over Israel, and fought against all his enemies on every side, against Moab, against the people of Ammon, against Edom, against the kings of [R]Zobah, and against the Philistines. Wherever he turned, he harassed *them.* 2 Sam. 10:6

48 And he gathered an army and [T]attacked the Amalekites, and delivered Israel from the hands of those who plundered them. *struck*

49 Now the sons of Saul were Jonathan and [T]Jishui and Malchishua. And the names of his two daughters *were these*: the name of the firstborn Merab, and the name of the younger Michal. *Abinadab,* 1 Chr. 8:33; 9:39

50 The name of Saul's wife *was* Ahinoam the daughter of Ahimaaz. And the name of the commander of his army *was* Abner the son of Ner, Saul's [R]uncle. 1 Sam. 10:14

51 Kish *was* the father of Saul, and Ner the father of Abner *was* the son of Abiel.

52 Now there was fierce war with the Philistines all the days of Saul. And when Saul saw any strong man or any valiant man, [R]he took him for himself. 1 Sam. 8:11

CHAPTER 15

Saul's Incomplete Obedience

SAMUEL also said to Saul, [R]"The LORD sent me to anoint you king over His people, over Israel. Now therefore, heed the voice of the words of the LORD. 1 Sam. 9:16; 10:1

2 "Thus says the LORD of hosts: 'I will punish Amalek *for* what he did to Israel, [R]how he laid *wait* for him on the way when he came up from Egypt. Deut. 25:17–19

3 'Now go and [R]attack[T] Amalek, and [R]utterly destroy all that they have, and do not spare them. But kill both man and woman, infant and nursing child, ox and sheep, camel and donkey.' " Deut. 25:19 • Lit. *strike* • Num. 24:20

LORD OF HOSTS

The LORD *of Hosts* is an important title of God, judging from its frequency in the Old Testament.

Although they were writing in Greek, both Paul and James nevertheless used the Hebrew word for "hosts" (*tsebā'ôt*) in the transliterated form of *Sabaoth*. Paul quotes Isaiah, which along with 1 Samuel, is the book in the Greek version of the Old Testament that includes this transliterated (rather than translated) form. The quotation occurs in Romans 9—11 where the great apostle to the Gentiles nevertheless expressed his love for his own nation, as well as his faith that God still has a bright future for Israel. He wrote: "And as Isaiah said before: 'Unless the LORD of Sabaoth had left us a seed, we would have become like Sodom, and we would have been made like Gomorrah'" (Rom. 9:29).

Even though *Sabaoth* looks like *Sabbath* in English letters, the two words are totally unrelated. *Sabbath* comes from the word meaning "to cease" or "rest," and *Sabaoth* is from the Hebrew plural form meaning "host" or "army."

James also used the term: "Indeed the wages of the laborers who mowed your fields, which you kept back by fraud, cry out; and the cries of the reapers have reached the ears of the Lord of Sabaoth" (James 5:4).

Why did James use this name of God out of the many he could have chosen from the Old Testament? How did this fit in with his warning to the selfish rich people? To find out we must look back at some of the Old Testament usages of the name.

LORD of Hosts (*YHWH Tsebāôt*)

The personal name of God is used (LORD in all capitals equals "Jehovah" or "Yahweh"; see word study on p. 71). It is not *Adōnay*—"Lord" or "Master"—even though the Jews read it aloud that way for fear of taking the Lord's name in vain. "God of hosts" (*'Elōhîm tsebāôt*) also occurs, the two expressions together being used almost three hundred times.

The "hosts" part of this divine name is the plural of the noun *tsābā'*. In itself this word can refer to the host of heaven (singular) or hosts of soldiers, that is, armies.

As we have noted, the Greek Old Testament (LXX) sometimes transliterated the word as *sabaōth*, apparently taking it as a technical term. This is probably the source of Paul's and James's transliteration.

Another LXX rendering of the word *hosts* is *Pantokratōr*, or "All-Powerful." This translation has the disadvantage of obscuring the military motif that lies right on the surface of the original name. (The NIV paraphrases much the same with "Sovereign LORD.") To the reader who knows no Hebrew it tends to confuse the name with another title, *God Almighty*. Another LXX translation that does bring out the genitive plural ("of Hosts") of the original is *Kyrios* (*ho*) *Theos tōn dynameōn*, literally, "Lord (the) God of the powers."

This name does not occur in the Pentateuch, Joshua, or Judges. It first appears in 1 Samuel 1:3: Elkanah "went up from his city yearly to worship and sacrifice to the LORD of hosts in Shiloh." Now that Israel had become a nation it became necessary to stress that the head of their forces was the Lord (1 Sam. 17:45). However, He was not merely the head of Israel's armies, but of all hosts, celestial and terrestrial—angelic and human. God could and did rule all the armies of the whole world. Also, perhaps as a warning against joining the heathen in worshiping the host of heaven—sun, moon, and stars—God stresses that He controls all the heavenly host.

One of the most familiar passages using this regal title is Psalm 24: "Who is this King of glory? The LORD of hosts, He *is* the King of glory" (v. 10).

The title is not always military: "Even the sparrow has found a home, and the swallow a nest for herself, where she may lay her young—*even* Your altars, O LORD of hosts" (Ps. 84:3).

Jeremiah loves the title and uses it seventy-three times, and Isaiah, sixty-two. Considering the much smaller size of their books, Zechariah's fondness for the name is great (fifty-three usages in fourteen chapters) and Malachi, twenty-four in just four chapters.

4 So Saul gathered the people together and
numbered them in Telaim, two hundred
thousand foot soldiers and ten thousand men
of Judah.
5 And Saul came to a city of Amalek, and
lay in wait in the valley.
6 Then Saul said to [R]the Kenites, [R]"Go,
depart, get down from among the Amalekites, lest I destroy you with them. For [R]you
showed kindness to all the children of Israel
when they came up out of Egypt." So the
Kenites departed from among the Amalek-
ites. Num. 24:21 • Gen. 18:25; 19:12, 14 • Ex. 18:10, 19
7 [R]And Saul attacked the Amalekites, from
[R]Havilah all the way to [R]Shur, which is east of
Egypt. 1 Sam. 14:48 • Gen. 2:11; 25:17, 18 • Gen. 16:7
8 He also took Agag king of the Amalek-
ites alive, and utterly destroyed all the people
with the edge of the sword.
9 But Saul and the people [R]spared Agag
and the best of the sheep, the oxen, the
fatlings, the lambs, and all *that was* good, and
were unwilling to utterly destroy them. But
everything despised and worthless, that they
utterly destroyed. 1 Sam. 15:3, 15, 19

God Rejects Saul as King

10 Now the word of the LORD came to
Samuel, saying,
11 "I greatly regret that I have set up Saul
as king, for he has [R]turned back from following Me, and has not performed My commandments." And it grieved Samuel, and he cried
out to the LORD all night. 1 Kin. 9:6
12 So when Samuel rose early in the morning to meet Saul, it was told Samuel, saying,
"Saul went to Carmel, and indeed, he set up a
monument for himself; and he has gone on
around, passed by, and gone down to Gilgal."
13 Then Samuel went to Saul, and Saul said
to him, "Blessed *are* you of the LORD! I have
performed the commandment of the LORD."
14 But Samuel said, "What then *is* this
bleating of the sheep in my ears, and the
lowing of the oxen which I hear?"
15 And Saul said, "They have brought them
from the Amalekites; [R]for the people spared
the best of the sheep and the oxen, to sacrifice to the LORD your God; and the rest we
have utterly destroyed." Gen. 3:12, 13
16 Then Samuel said to Saul, "Be quiet! And
I will tell you what the LORD said to me last
night." And he said to him, "Speak on."
17 So Samuel said, [R]"When you *were* little
in your own eyes, *were* you not head of the
tribes of Israel? And did not the LORD anoint
you king over Israel? 1 Sam. 9:21; 10:22
18 "Now the LORD sent you on a mission,
and said, 'Go, and utterly destroy the sinners,
the Amalekites, and fight against them until
they are [T]consumed.' *exterminated*
19 "Why then did you not obey the voice of
the LORD? Why did you swoop down on the
spoil, and do evil in the sight of the LORD?"
20 And Saul said to Samuel, [R]"But I have
obeyed the voice of the LORD, and gone on
the mission on which the LORD sent me, and
brought back Agag king of Amalek; I have
utterly destroyed the Amalekites. 1 Sam. 15:13
21 "But the people took of the plunder,
sheep and oxen, the best of the things which
should have been utterly destroyed, to sacrifice to the LORD your God in Gilgal."
22 Then Samuel said:

[R]"Has the LORD *as great* delight in burnt
offerings and sacrifices, [Is. 1:11–17]
As in obeying the voice of the LORD?
Behold, to obey is better than sacrifice,
And to heed than the fat of rams.
23 For rebellion *is as* the sin of [T]witchcraft,
And stubbornness *is as* iniquity and
idolatry. *divination*
Because you have rejected the word of
the LORD,
[R]He also has rejected you from *being*
king." 1 Sam. 13:14; 16:1

24 Then Saul said to Samuel, "I have
sinned, for I have transgressed the commandment of the LORD and your words, because I
feared the people and obeyed their voice.
25 "Now therefore, please pardon my sin,
and return with me, that I may worship the
LORD."
26 But Samuel said to Saul, "I will not
return with you, [R]for you have rejected the
word of the LORD, and the LORD has rejected
you from being king over Israel." 1 Sam. 2:30
27 And as Samuel turned around to go
away, [R]*Saul* seized the edge of his robe, and it
tore. 1 Kin. 11:30, 31
28 So Samuel said to him, [R]"The LORD has
torn the kingdom of Israel from you today,
and has given it to a neighbor of yours, *who
is* better than you. 1 Kin. 11:31
29 "And also the Strength of Israel [R]will not
lie nor relent. For He *is* not a man, that He
should relent." Num. 23:19
30 Then he said, "I have sinned; *yet* honor
me now, please, before the elders of my
people and before Israel, and return with me,
that I may worship the LORD your God."
31 So Samuel turned back after Saul, and
Saul worshiped the LORD.
32 Then Samuel said, "Bring Agag king of
the Amalekites here to me." So Agag came to
him cautiously. And Agag said, "Surely the
bitterness of death is past."
33 But Samuel said, [R]"As your sword has
made women childless, so shall your mother
be childless among women." And Samuel
hacked Agag in pieces before the LORD in
Gilgal. [Gen. 9:6]
34 Then Samuel went to Ramah, and Saul
went up to his house at Gibeah of Saul.
35 And [R]Samuel went no more to see Saul
until the day of his death. Nevertheless

Samuel mourned for Saul, and the LORD regretted that He had made Saul king over
Israel. 1 Sam. 19:24

CHAPTER 16

God Anoints David as King

THEN the LORD said to Samuel, "How long
will you mourn for Saul, seeing I have
rejected him from reigning over Israel? Fill
your horn with oil, and go; I am sending you
to Jesse the Bethlehemite. For I have provided Myself a king among his sons."
2 And Samuel said, "How can I go? If Saul
hears *it*, he will kill me." And the LORD said,
"Take a heifer with you, and say, [R]'I have
come to sacrifice to the LORD.' 1 Sam. 9:12
3 "Then invite Jesse to the sacrifice, and I
will show you what you shall do; you shall
anoint for Me the one I name to you."
4 So Samuel did what the LORD said, and
went to Bethlehem. And the elders of the
town [R]trembled at his coming, and said, [R]"Do
you come peaceably?" 1 Sam. 21:1 • 1 Kin. 2:13
5 And he said, "Peaceably; I have come to
sacrifice to the LORD. [R]Sanctify[T] yourselves,
and come with me to the sacrifice." Then he
sanctified Jesse and his sons, and invited
them to the sacrifice. Ex. 19:10 • *Consecrate*
6 So it was, when they came, that he
looked at Eliab and [R]said, "Surely the LORD's
anointed *is* before Him." 1 Kin. 12:26
7 But the LORD said to Samuel, "Do not
look at his appearance or at the height of his
stature, because I have [T]refused him. For *the
LORD does* not *see* as man sees; for man looks
at the outward appearance, but the LORD
looks at the [R]heart." *rejected* • 1 Kin. 8:39
8 So Jesse called Abinadab, and made him
pass before Samuel. And he said, "Neither
has the LORD chosen this one."
9 Then Jesse made Shammah pass by. And
he said, "Neither has the LORD chosen this
one."
10 Thus Jesse made seven of his sons pass
before Samuel. And Samuel said to Jesse,
"The LORD has not chosen these."
11 And Samuel said to Jesse, "Are all the
young men here?" Then he said, "There
remains yet the youngest, and there he is,
keeping the [R]sheep." And Samuel said to
Jesse, "Send and bring him. For we will not
sit down till he comes here." 2 Sam. 7:8
12 So he sent and brought him in. Now he
was ruddy, [R]with [T]bright eyes, and good-
looking. And the LORD said, "Arise, anoint
him; for this *is* the one!" Gen. 39:6 • Lit. *beautiful*
13 Then Samuel took the horn of oil and
anointed him in the midst of his brothers; and
[R]the Spirit of the LORD came upon David
from that day forward. So Samuel arose and
went to Ramah. Num. 27:18

God Takes His Spirit from Saul

14 [R]But the Spirit of the LORD departed from
Saul, and [R]a distressing spirit from the LORD
troubled him. Judg. 16:20 • Judg. 9:23
15 And Saul's servants said to him, "Surely,
a distressing spirit from God is troubling you.
16 "Let our master now command your
servants, *who are* before you, to seek out a
man *who is* a skillful player on the harp; and
it shall be that he will play it with his hand
when the [T]distressing spirit from God is upon
you, and you shall be well." Lit. *evil*
17 So Saul said to his servants, [T]"Provide
me now a man who can play well, and bring
him to me." Lit. *Look now for a man for me*
18 Then one of the servants answered and
said, "Look, I have seen a son of Jesse the
Bethlehemite, *who is* skillful in playing, a
mighty man of valor, a man of war, prudent
in speech, and a handsome person; and [R]the
LORD *is* with him." 1 Sam. 3:19; 18:12, 14
19 Therefore Saul sent messengers to Jesse,
and said, "Send me your son David, who *is*
with the sheep."
20 And Jesse took a donkey *loaded with*
bread, a skin of wine, and a young goat, and
sent *them* by his son David to Saul.
21 So David came to Saul and [R]stood before
him. And he loved him greatly, and he became his armorbearer. Gen. 41:46
22 Then Saul sent to Jesse, saying, "Please
let David stand before me, for he has found
favor in my sight."
23 And so it was, whenever the spirit from
God was upon Saul, that David would take a
harp and play *it* with his hand. Then Saul
would become refreshed and well, and the
distressing spirit would depart from him.

CHAPTER 17

David Defeats Goliath

NOW the Philistines gathered their armies
together to battle, and were gathered
together at [R]Sochoh, which *belongs* to Judah;
they encamped between Sochoh and Azekah,
in Ephes Dammim. Josh. 15:35
2 And Saul and the men of Israel were
gathered together, and they encamped in the
Valley of Elah, and drew up in battle array
against the Philistines.
3 The Philistines stood on a mountain on
one side, and Israel stood on a mountain on
the other side, with a valley between them.
4 And a champion went out from the camp
of the Philistines, named [R]Goliath, from
[R]Gath, whose height *was* [T]six cubits and a
span. 2 Sam. 21:19 • Josh. 11:21, 22 • 9.75 ft
5 *He had* a bronze helmet on his head, and
he *was* [T]armed with a coat of mail, and the
weight of the coat *was* [T]five thousand shekels
of bronze. *clothed with scaled body armor* • 125 lb.

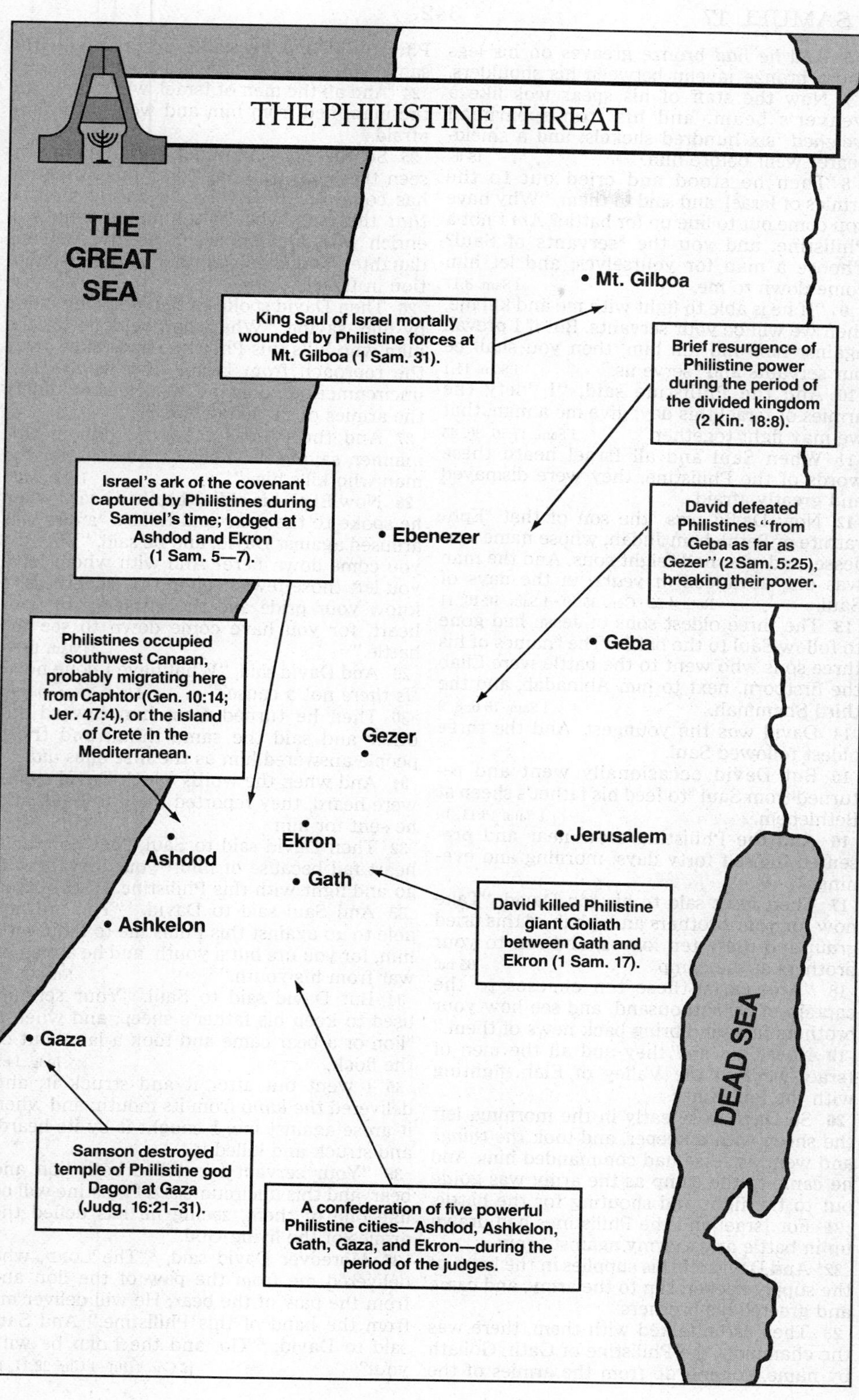
THE PHILISTINE THREAT
THE GREAT SEA
Mt. Gilboa
King Saul of Israel mortally wounded by Philistine forces at Mt. Gilboa (1 Sam. 31).
Brief resurgence of Philistine power during the period of the divided kingdom (2 Kin. 18:8).
Israel's ark of the covenant captured by Philistines during Samuel's time; lodged at Ashdod and Ekron (1 Sam. 5—7).
Ebenezer
David defeated Philistines "from Geba as far as Gezer" (2 Sam. 5:25), breaking their power.
Geba
Philistines occupied southwest Canaan, probably migrating here from Caphtor (Gen. 10:14; Jer. 47:4), or the island of Crete in the Mediterranean.
Gezer
Jerusalem
Ekron
Ashdod
Gath
David killed Philistine giant Goliath between Gath and Ekron (1 Sam. 17).
Ashkelon
Gaza
DEAD SEA
Samson destroyed temple of Philistine god Dagon at Gaza (Judg. 16:21–31).
A confederation of five powerful Philistine cities—Ashdod, Ashkelon, Gath, Gaza, and Ekron—during the period of the judges.

6 And *he had* bronze greaves on his legs
and a bronze javelin between his shoulders.
7 Now the staff of his spear *was* like a
weaver's beam, and his iron spearhead
weighed [T]six hundred shekels; and a shield-
bearer went before him. 15 lb.
8 Then he stood and cried out to the
armies of Israel, and said to them, "Why have
you come out to line up for battle? *Am* I not a
Philistine, and you the [R]servants of Saul?
Choose a man for yourselves, and let him
come down to me. 1 Sam. 8:17
9 "If he is able to fight with me and kill me,
then we will be your servants. But if I prevail
against him and kill him, then you shall be
our servants and [R]serve us." 1 Sam. 11:1
10 And the Philistine said, "I [R]defy the
armies of Israel this day; give me a man, that
we may fight together." 1 Sam. 17:26, 36, 45
11 When Saul and all Israel heard these
words of the Philistine, they were dismayed
and greatly afraid.
12 Now David *was* [R]the son of that [R]Eph-
rathite of Bethlehem Judah, whose name *was*
Jesse, and who had [R]eight sons. And the man
was old, advanced *in years*, in the days of
Saul. Ruth 4:22 • Gen. 35:19 • 1 Sam. 16:10, 11
13 The three oldest sons of Jesse had gone
to follow Saul to the battle. The [R]names of his
three sons who went to the battle *were* Eliab
the firstborn, next to him Abinadab, and the
third Shammah. 1 Sam. 16:6, 8, 9
14 David *was* the youngest. And the three
oldest followed Saul.
15 But David occasionally went and returned from Saul [R]to feed his father's sheep at
Bethlehem. 1 Sam. 16:11, 19
16 And the Philistine drew near and presented himself forty days, morning and evening.
17 Then Jesse said to his son David, "Take
now for your brothers an [T]ephah of this dried
grain and these ten loaves, and run to your
brothers at the camp. .65 bu.
18 "And carry these ten cheeses to the
captain of *their* thousand, and see how your
brothers fare, and bring back news of them."
19 Now Saul and they and all the men of
Israel *were* in the Valley of Elah, fighting
with the Philistines.
20 So David rose early in the morning, left
the sheep with a keeper, and took *the things*
and went as Jesse had commanded him. And
he came to the camp as the army was going
out to the fight and shouting for the battle.
21 For Israel and the Philistines had drawn
up in battle array, army against army.
22 And David left his supplies in the hand of
the supply keeper, ran to the army, and came
and greeted his brothers.
23 Then as he talked with them, there was
the champion, the Philistine of Gath, Goliath
by name, coming up from the armies of the
Philistines; and he spoke according to the
same words. So David heard *them*.
24 And all the men of Israel, when they saw
the man, fled from him and were dreadfully
afraid.
25 So the men of Israel said, "Have you
seen this man who has come up? Surely he
has come up to defy Israel; and it shall be
that the man who kills him the king will
enrich with great riches, [R]will give him his
daughter, and give his father's house exemp-
tion in Israel." Josh. 15:16
26 Then David spoke to the men who stood
by him, saying, "What shall be done for the
man who kills this Philistine and takes away
the reproach from Israel? For who *is* this
uncircumcised Philistine, that he should defy
the armies of the living God?"
27 And the people answered him in this
manner, saying, [R]"So shall it be done for the
man who kills him." 1 Sam. 17:25
28 Now Eliab his oldest brother heard when
he spoke to the men; and Eliab's [R]anger was
aroused against David, and he said, "Why did
you come down here? And with whom have
you left those few sheep in the wilderness? I
know your pride and the insolence of your
heart, for you have come down to see the
battle." [Matt. 10:36]
29 And David said, "What have I done now?
[T]*Is there* not a cause?" Lit. *Is it not a matter*
30 Then he turned from him toward an-
other and said the same thing; and these
people answered him as the first ones *did*.
31 And when the words which David spoke
were heard, they reported *them* to Saul; and
he sent for him.
32 Then David said to Saul, "Let no man's
heart fail because of him; [R]your servant will
go and fight with this Philistine." 1 Sam. 16:18
33 And Saul said to David, [R]"You are not
able to go against this Philistine to fight with
him; for you *are but* a youth, and he a man of
war from his youth." Num. 13:31
34 But David said to Saul, "Your servant
used to keep his father's sheep, and when a
[R]lion or a bear came and took a lamb out of
the flock, Judg. 14:5
35 I went out after it and struck it, and
delivered *the lamb* from its mouth; and when
it arose against me, I caught *it* by its beard,
and struck and killed it.
36 "Your servant has killed both lion and
bear; and this uncircumcised Philistine will be
like one of them, seeing he has defied the
armies of the living God."
37 Moreover David said, [R]"The LORD, who
delivered me from the paw of the lion and
from the paw of the bear, He will deliver me
from the hand of this Philistine." And Saul
said to David, [R]"Go, and the LORD be with
you!" [2 Cor. 1:10] • 1 Chr. 22:11, 16

38 So Saul clothed David with his [T]armor, and he put a bronze helmet on his head; he also clothed him with a coat of mail. Lit. *clothes*

39 And David fastened his sword to his armor, and he tried to walk, for he had not tested *them*. And David said to Saul, "I cannot walk with these, for I have not tested *them*." So David took them off.

40 Then he took his staff in his hand; and he chose for himself five smooth stones from the brook, and put them in a shepherd's bag, in a pouch which he had, and his sling was in his hand. And he drew near to the Philistine.

41 So the Philistine came, and began drawing near to David, and the man who bore the shield *went* before him.

42 And when the Philistine looked about and saw David, he disdained him; for he was *but* a youth, ruddy and good-looking.

43 So the Philistine said to David, "*Am* I a dog, that you come to me with sticks?" And the Philistine cursed David by his gods.

44 And the Philistine said to David, "Come to me, and I will give your flesh to the birds of the air and the beasts of the field!"

45 Then David said to the Philistine, "You come to me with a sword, with a spear, and with a javelin. But I come to you in the name of the LORD of hosts, the God of the armies of Israel, whom you have defied.

46 "This day the LORD will deliver you into my hand, and I will strike you and take your head from you. And this day I will give [R]the carcasses of the camp of the Philistines to the birds of the air and the wild beasts of the earth, [R]that all the earth may know that there is a God in Israel. Deut. 28:26 • Josh. 4:24

47 "Then all this assembly shall know that the LORD does not save with sword and spear; for [R]the battle *is* the LORD's, and He will give you into our hands." 2 Chr. 20:15

48 And it was so, when the Philistine arose and came and drew near to meet David, that David hastened and [R]ran toward the army to meet the Philistine. Ps. 27:3

49 Then David put his hand in his bag and took out a stone; and he slung *it* and struck the Philistine in his forehead, so that the stone sank into his forehead, and he fell on his face to the earth.

50 So David prevailed over the Philistine with a [R]sling and a stone, and struck the Philistine and killed him. But *there was* no sword in the hand of David. Judg. 20:16

51 Therefore David ran and stood over the Philistine, took his sword and drew it out of its sheath and killed him, and cut off his head with it. And when the Philistines saw that their champion was dead, they fled.

52 Now the men of Israel and Judah arose and shouted, and pursued the Philistines as far as the entrance of the valley and to the gates of Ekron. And the wounded of the Philistines fell along the road to [R]Shaaraim, even as far as Gath and Ekron. Josh. 15:36

53 Then the children of Israel returned from chasing the Philistines, and they plundered their tents.

54 And David took the head of the Philistine and brought it to Jerusalem, but he put his armor in his tent.

55 Now when Saul saw David going out against the Philistine, he said to Abner, the commander of the army, "Abner, [R]whose son *is* this youth?" And Abner said, "As your soul lives, O king, I do not know." 1 Sam. 16:21, 22

56 And the king said, "Inquire whose son this young man *is*."

57 Then, as David returned from the slaughter of the Philistine, Abner took him and brought him before Saul [R]with the head of the Philistine in his hand. 1 Sam. 17:54

58 And Saul said to him, "Whose son *are* you, young man?" And David answered, [R]"I *am* the son of your servant Jesse the Bethlehemite." 1 Sam. 17:12

CHAPTER 18

Jonathan Loves David

AND it was so, when he had finished speaking to Saul, that the soul of Jonathan was knit to the soul of David, and Jonathan loved him as his own soul.

2 Saul took him that day, [R]and would not let him go home to his father's house anymore. 1 Sam. 17:15

3 Then Jonathan and David made a covenant, because he loved him as his own soul.

4 And Jonathan took off the robe that *was* on him and gave it to David, with his armor, even to his sword and his bow and his belt.

Israel Elevates David over Saul

5 So David went out wherever Saul sent him, *and* [T]behaved wisely. And Saul set him over the men of war, and he was accepted in the sight of all the people and also in the sight of Saul's servants. Or *prospered*

6 Now it had happened as they were coming *home*, when David was returning from the slaughter of the [T]Philistine, that [R]the women had come out of all the cities of Israel, singing and dancing, to meet King Saul, with tambourines, with joy, and with musical instruments. *Philistines* • Ex. 15:20, 21

7 So the women [R]sang as they danced, and said: Ex. 15:21

"Saul has slain his thousands,
And David his ten thousands."

8 Then Saul was very angry, and the saying displeased him; and he said, "They have ascribed to David ten thousands, and to me

they have ascribed *but* thousands. Now *what* more can he have but the kingdom?"

9 So Saul [T]eyed David from that day forward. Viewed with suspicion

The Attempts of Saul to Slay David: By Throwing a Spear at David

10 And it happened on the next day that the distressing spirit from God came upon Saul, [R]and he prophesied inside the house. So David [R]played *music* with his hand, as at other times; [R]but *there was* a spear in Saul's hand. 1 Sam. 19:24 • 1 Sam. 16:23 • 1 Sam. 19:9, 10

11 And Saul [R]cast the spear, for he said, "I will pin David to the wall *with it.*" But David escaped his presence twice. 1 Sam. 19:10; 20:33

12 Now Saul was afraid of David, because [R]the LORD was with him, but had [R]departed from Saul. 1 Sam. 16:13, 18 • 1 Sam. 16:14; 28:15

13 Therefore Saul removed him from [T]his presence, and made him his captain over a thousand; and [R]he went out and came in before the people. Lit. *himself* • Num. 27:17

14 And David behaved wisely in all his ways, and [R]the LORD *was* with him. Josh. 6:27

15 Therefore, when Saul saw that he behaved very wisely, he was afraid of him.

16 But [R]all Israel and Judah loved David, because he went out and came in before them. 1 Sam. 18:5

By Tricking David to Fight the Philistines

17 Then Saul said to David, "Here is my older daughter Merab; I will give her to you as a wife. Only be valiant for me, and fight the LORD's battles." For Saul thought, "Let my hand not be against him, but let the hand of the Philistines be against him."

18 So David said to Saul, "Who *am* I, and what *is* my life *or* my father's family in Israel, that I should be son-in-law to the king?"

19 But it happened at the time when Merab, Saul's daughter, should have been given to David, that she was given to [R]Adriel the [R]Meholathite as a wife. 2 Sam. 21:8 • Judg. 7:22

20 [R]Now Michal, Saul's daughter, loved David. And they told Saul, and the thing pleased him. 1 Sam. 18:28

21 So Saul said, "I will give her to him, that she may be a snare to him, and that the hand of the Philistines may be against him." Therefore Saul said to David a second time, "You shall be my son-in-law today."

22 And Saul commanded his servants, "Communicate with David secretly, and say, 'Look, the king has delight in you, and all his servants love you. Now therefore, become the king's son-in-law.' "

23 So Saul's servants spoke those words in the hearing of David. And David said, "Does it seem to you *a* light *thing* to be a king's son-in-law, seeing I *am* a poor and lightly esteemed man?"

24 And the servants of Saul told him, saying, "In this manner David spoke."

25 Then Saul said, "Thus you shall say to David: 'The king does not desire any [R]dowry but one hundred foreskins of the Philistines, to take vengeance on the king's enemies.' " But Saul [R]thought to make David fall by the hand of the Philistines. Ex. 22:17 • 1 Sam. 18:17

26 So when his servants told David these words, it pleased David well to become the king's son-in-law. Now [R]the days had not expired; 1 Sam. 18:21

27 therefore David arose and went, he and [R]his men, and killed two hundred men of the Philistines. And [R]David brought their foreskins, and they gave them in full count to the king, that he might become the king's son-in-law. Then Saul gave him Michal his daughter as a wife. 1 Sam. 18:13 • 2 Sam. 3:14

28 Thus Saul saw and knew that the LORD *was* with David, and *that* Michal, Saul's daughter, loved him;

29 and Saul was still more afraid of David. So Saul became David's enemy continually.

30 Then the princes of the Philistines [R]went out *to war.* And so it was, whenever they went out, *that* David [R]behaved more wisely than all the servants of Saul, so that his name became highly esteemed. 2 Sam. 11:1 • 1 Sam. 18:5

CHAPTER 19

By Commanding His Servants to Kill David

NOW Saul spoke to Jonathan his son and to all his servants, that they should kill [R]David; but Jonathan, Saul's son, [R]delighted much in David. 1 Sam. 8:8, 9 • 1 Sam. 18:1

2 So Jonathan told David, saying, "My father Saul seeks to kill you. Therefore please be on your guard until morning, and stay in a secret *place* and hide.

3 "And I will go out and stand beside my father in the field where you *are,* and I will speak with my father about you. Then what I observe, I will tell [R]you." 1 Sam. 20:8–13

4 Now Jonathan [R]spoke well of David to Saul his father, and said to him, "Let not the king [R]sin against his servant, against David, because he has not sinned against you, and because his works *have been* very good toward you. [Prov. 31:8, 9] • [Prov. 17:13]

5 "For he took his life in his hands and killed the Philistine, and [R]the LORD brought about a great salvation for all Israel. You saw *it* and rejoiced. Why then will you [R]sin against innocent blood, to kill David without a cause?" 1 Sam. 11:13 • [Deut. 19:10–13]

6 So Saul heeded the voice of Jonathan, and Saul swore, "*As* the LORD lives, he shall not be killed."

7 Then Jonathan called David, and Jonathan told him all these things. So Jonathan

brought David to Saul, and he was in his
presence [R]as in times past. 1 Sam. 16:21

By Throwing a Spear at David Again

8 And there was war again; and David
went out and fought with the Philistines,
[R]and struck them with a mighty blow, and
they fled from him. 1 Sam. 18:27; 23:5
9 Now [R]the distressing spirit from the
LORD came upon Saul as he sat in his house
with his spear in his hand. And David was
playing *music* with *his* hand. 1 Sam. 16:14
10 Then Saul sought to pin David to the
wall with the spear, but he slipped away from
Saul's presence; and he drove the spear into
the wall. So David fled and escaped that
night.

By Sending His Messengers to Kill David

11 [R]Saul also sent messengers to David's
house to watch him and to kill him in the
morning. And Michal, David's wife, told him,
saying, "If you do not save your life tonight,
tomorrow you will be killed." Ps. 59:title
12 So Michal let David down through a
window. And he went and fled and escaped.
13 And Michal took [T]an image and laid *it* in
the bed, put a cover of goats' *hair* for his
head, and covered *it* with clothes. *idols*
14 So when Saul sent messengers to take
David, she said, "He *is* sick."
15 Then Saul sent the messengers *back* to
see David, saying, "Bring him up to me in the
bed, that I may kill him."
16 And when the messengers had come in,
there was the image in the bed, with a cover
of goats' *hair* for his head.
17 Then Saul said to Michal, "Why have
you deceived me like this, and sent my enemy
away, so that he has escaped?" And Michal
answered Saul, "He said to me, 'Let me go!
[R]Why should I kill you?' " 2 Sam. 2:22

By Coming to Kill David at Samuel's House

18 So David fled and escaped, and went to
Samuel at [R]Ramah, and told him all that Saul
had done to him. And he and Samuel went
and stayed in Naioth. 1 Sam. 7:17
19 Now it was told Saul, saying, "Take note,
David *is* at Naioth in Ramah!"
20 Then [R]Saul sent messengers to take David. [R]And when they saw the group of prophets prophesying, and Samuel standing *as*
leader over them, the Spirit of God came
upon the messengers of Saul, and they also
[R]prophesied. John 7:32 • 1 Sam. 10:5, 6, 10 • Joel 2:28
21 And when Saul was told, he sent other
messengers, and they prophesied likewise.
Then Saul sent messengers again the third
time, and they prophesied also.
22 Then he also went to Ramah, and came
to the great well that *is* at Sechu. So he
asked, and said, "Where *are* Samuel and
David?" And *someone* said, "Indeed *they are*
at Naioth in Ramah."
23 So he went there to Naioth in Ramah.
Then [R]the Spirit of God was upon him also,
and he went on and prophesied until he came
to Naioth in Ramah. 1 Sam. 10:10
24 And he also stripped off his clothes and
prophesied before Samuel in like manner, and
lay down [R]naked all that day and all that
night. Therefore they say, [R]"*Is* Saul also
among the prophets?" Mic. 1:8 • 1 Sam. 10:10–12

CHAPTER 20

By Commanding Jonathan to Bring David to Be Killed

THEN David fled from Naioth in Ramah,
and went and said to Jonathan, "What
have I done? What *is* my iniquity, and what *is*
my sin before your father, that he seeks my
life?"
2 So Jonathan said to him, "By no means!
You shall not die! Indeed, my father will do
nothing either great or small without first
telling me. And why should my father hide
this thing from me? It *is* not *so*!"
3 Then David took an oath again, and said,
"Your father certainly knows that I have
found favor in your eyes, and he has said, 'Do
not let Jonathan know this, lest he be
grieved.' But [R]truly, *as* the LORD lives and *as*
your soul lives, *there is* but a step between
me and death." 1 Sam. 27:1
4 So Jonathan said to David, "Whatever
you yourself desire, I will do *it* for you."
5 And David said to Jonathan, "Indeed
tomorrow *is* the [R]New Moon, and I should
not fail to sit with the king to eat. But let me
go, that I may [R]hide in the field until the third
day at evening. Num. 10:10; 28:11–15 • 1 Sam. 19:2, 3
6 "If your father misses me at all, then say,
'David earnestly asked *permission* of me that
he might run over [R]to Bethlehem, his city, for
there is a yearly sacrifice there for all the
family.' 1 Sam. 16:4; 17:12
7 "If he says thus: '*It is* well,' your servant
will be safe. But if he is very angry, *then* be
sure that evil is determined by him.
8 "Therefore you shall [R]deal kindly with
your servant, for you have brought your
servant into a covenant of the LORD with
you. Nevertheless, [R]if there is iniquity in me,
kill me yourself, for why should you bring me
to your father?" Josh. 2:14 • 2 Sam. 14:32
9 And Jonathan said, "Far be it from you!
For if I knew certainly that evil was determined by my father to come upon you, then
would I not tell you?"
10 Then David said to Jonathan, "Who will
tell me, or what *if* your father answers you
roughly?"

11 And Jonathan said to David, "Come, and
let us go out into the field." So both of them
went out into the field.
12 Then Jonathan said to David: "The LORD
God of Israel *is witness*! When I have
[T]sounded out my father sometime tomorrow,
or the third *day*, and indeed *there is* good
toward David, and I do not send to you and
tell you, *searched out*
13 "may [R]the LORD do so and much more to
Jonathan. But if it pleases my father *to do*
you evil, then I will report it to you and send
you away, that you may go in safety. And
[R]the LORD be with you as He has [R]been with
my father. Ruth 1:17 • Josh. 1:5 • 1 Sam. 10:7
14 "And you shall not only show me the
kindness of the LORD while I still live, that I
may not die;
15 "but you shall not cut off your kindness
from my [T]house forever, no, not when the
LORD has cut off every one of the enemies of
David from the face of the earth." *family*
16 So Jonathan made *a covenant* with the
house of David, *saying*, "Let the LORD require
it at the hand of David's enemies."
17 And Jonathan again caused David to
vow, because he loved him; [R]for he loved him
as he loved his own soul. 1 Sam. 18:1
18 Then Jonathan said to David, [R]"Tomorrow *is* the New Moon; and you will be missed,
because your seat will be empty. 1 Sam. 20:5, 24
19 "And *when* you have stayed three days,
go down quickly and come to [R]the place
where you hid on the day of the deed; and
remain by the stone Ezel. 1 Sam. 19:2
20 "Then I will shoot three arrows to the
side *of it*, as though I shot at a target;
21 "and there I will send a lad, *saying*, 'Go,
find the arrows.' If I expressly say to the lad,
'Look, the arrows *are* on this side of you; get
them and come'—then, [R]as the LORD lives,
there is safety for you and no harm. Jer. 4:2
22 "But if I say thus to the young man,
'Look, the arrows *are* beyond you'—go your
way, for the LORD has sent you away.
23 "And as for [R]the matter which you and I
have spoken of, indeed the LORD *be* between
you and me forever." 1 Sam. 20:14, 15
24 So David hid in the field. And when the
New Moon had come, the king sat down to
eat the feast.
25 Now the king sat on his seat, as at other
times, on a seat by the wall. And Jonathan
arose, and Abner sat by Saul's side, but
David's place was empty.
26 Nevertheless Saul did not say anything
that day, for he thought, "Something has
happened to him; he *is* unclean, surely he *is*
[R]unclean." Lev. 7:20, 21; 15:5
27 And it happened the next day, the second *day* of the month, that David's place was
empty. And Saul said to Jonathan his son,
"Why has the son of Jesse not come to eat,
either yesterday or today?"
28 So Jonathan [R]answered Saul, "David
earnestly asked *permission* of me *to go* to
Bethlehem. 1 Sam. 20:6
29 "And he said, 'Please let me go, for our
family has a sacrifice in the city, and my
brother has commanded me *to be there*. And
now, if I have found favor in your eyes,
please let me get away and see my brothers.'
Therefore he has not come to the king's
table."
30 Then Saul's anger was aroused against
Jonathan, and he said to him, "You son of a
perverse, rebellious *woman*! Do I not know
that you have chosen the son of Jesse to your
own shame and to the shame of your mother's nakedness?
31 "For as long as the son of Jesse lives on
the earth, you shall not be established, nor
your kingdom. Now therefore, send and bring
him to me, for he shall surely die."
32 And Jonathan answered Saul his father,
and said to him, [R]"Why should he be killed?
What has he done?" Gen. 31:36
33 Then Saul cast a spear at him to kill him,
by which Jonathan knew that it was determined by his father to kill David.
34 So Jonathan arose from the table in
fierce anger, and ate no food the second day
of the month, for he was grieved for David,
because his father had treated him shamefully.
35 And so it was, in the morning, that
Jonathan went out into the field at the time
appointed with David, and a little lad *was*
with him.
36 Then he said to his lad, "Now run, find
the arrows which I shoot." As the lad ran, he
shot an arrow beyond him.
37 When the lad had come to the place
where the arrow was which Jonathan had
shot, Jonathan cried out after the lad and
said, "*Is* not the arrow beyond you?"
38 And Jonathan cried out after the lad,
"Make haste, hurry, do not delay!" So Jonathan's lad gathered up the arrows and came
back to his master.
39 But the lad did not know anything. Only
Jonathan and David knew of the matter.
40 Then Jonathan gave his [T]weapons to his
lad, and said to him, "Go, carry *them* to the
city." *equipment*
41 Now as soon as the lad had gone, David
arose from *a place* toward the south, fell on
his face to the ground, and bowed down three
times. And they kissed one another; and they
wept together, but David more so.
42 Then Jonathan said to David, [R]"Go in
peace, since we have both sworn in the name

of the LORD, saying, 'May the LORD be between you and me, and between your descendants and my descendants, forever.' " So he
arose and departed, and Jonathan went into
the city. 1 Sam. 1:17

CHAPTER 21

David Is Protected by the Priest

NOW David came to Nob, to Ahimelech
the priest. And Ahimelech was afraid
when he met David, and said to him, "Why
are you alone, and no one is with you?"
2 So David said to Ahimelech the priest,
"The king has ordered me on some business,
and said to me, 'Do not let anyone know
anything about the business on which I send
you, or what I have commanded you.' And I
have directed *my* young men to such and
such a place.
3 "Now therefore, what have you on hand?
Give *me* five *loaves of* bread in my hand, or
whatever can be found."
4 And the priest answered David and said,
"*There is* no common bread on hand; but
there is holy bread, if the young men have at
least kept themselves from women."
5 Then David answered the priest, and said
to him, "Truly, women *have been* kept from
us about three days since I came out. And the
vessels of the young men are holy, and *the
bread is* in effect common, even though it
was sanctified in the vessel this day."
6 So the priest gave him holy *bread;* for
there was no bread there but the showbread
[R]which had been taken from before the LORD,
in order to put hot bread *in its place* on the
day when it was taken away. Lev. 24:8, 9
7 Now a certain man of the servants of
Saul *was* there that day, detained before the
LORD. And his name *was* [R]Doeg, an Edomite,
the chief of the herdsmen who *belonged* to
Saul. 1 Sam. 14:47; 22:9
8 And David said to Ahimelech, "Is there
not here on hand a spear or a sword? For I
have brought neither my sword nor my
weapons with me, because the king's business required haste."
9 So the priest said, "The sword of Goliath
the Philistine, whom you killed in [R]the Valley
of Elah, [R]there it is, wrapped in a cloth behind
the ephod. If you will take that, take *it.* For
there is no other except that one here." And
David said, "*There is* none like it; give it to
me." 1 Sam. 17:2, 50 • 1 Sam. 31:10

David Pretends to Be Mad

10 Then David arose and fled that day from
before Saul, and went to Achish the king of
Gath.
11 And [R]the servants of Achish said to him,
[R]"*Is* this not David the king of the land? Did
they not sing of him to one another in
dances, saying: Ps. 56:title • 1 Sam. 18:6–8; 29:5

'Saul has slain his thousands,
And David his ten thousands'?"

12 Now David [R]took these words [T]to heart,
and was very much afraid of Achish the king
of Gath. Luke 2:19 • Lit. *in his heart*
13 So he changed his behavior before them,
feigned madness in their hands, [T]scratched on
the doors of the gate, and let his saliva fall
down on his beard. *scribbled*
14 Then Achish said to his servants, "Look,
you see the man is insane. Why have you
brought him to me?
15 "Have I need of madmen, that you have
brought this *fellow* to play the madman in
my presence? Shall this *fellow* come into my
house?"

CHAPTER 22

David Flees to Adullam—1 Chr. 12:16–18

DAVID therefore departed from there and
escaped to the cave of Adullam. And
when his brothers and all his father's house
heard *it,* they went down there to him.
2 And everyone *who was* in distress,
everyone who *was* in debt, and everyone *who
was* discontented gathered to him. So he
became captain over them. And there were
about four hundred men with him.
3 Then David went from there to Mizpah
of [R]Moab; and he said to the king of Moab,
"Please let my father and mother come here
with you, till I know what God will do for
me." 2 Sam. 8:2
4 So he brought them before the king of
Moab, and they dwelt with him all the time
that David was in the stronghold.
5 Then the prophet [R]Gad said to David,
"Do not stay in the stronghold; depart, and
go to the land of Judah." So David departed
and went into the forest of Hereth. 2 Sam. 24:11

Saul Slays the Priests of God

6 When Saul heard that David and the
men who *were* with him had been discovered—now Saul was staying in [R]Gibeah under
a tamarisk tree in Ramah, with his spear in
his hand, and all his servants standing about
him— 1 Sam. 15:34
7 then Saul said to his servants who stood
about him, "Hear now, you Benjamites! Will
the son of Jesse give every one of you fields
and vineyards, *and* make you all captains of
thousands and captains of hundreds?
8 "All of you have conspired against me,
and *there is* no one who reveals to me that
[R]my son has made a covenant with the son of
Jesse; and *there is* not one of you who is

sorry for me or reveals to me that my son has stirred up my servant against me, to lie in wait, as *it is* this day." 1 Sam. 18:3; 20:16, 30

9 Then answered Doeg the Edomite, who was set over the servants of Saul, and said, "I saw the son of Jesse going to Nob, to [R]Ahimelech the son of [R]Ahitub. 1 Sam. 21:1 • 1 Sam. 14:3

10 "And he inquired of the LORD for him, [R]gave him provisions, and gave him the sword of Goliath the Philistine." 1 Sam. 21:6, 9

11 Then the king sent to call Ahimelech the priest, the son of Ahitub, and all his father's house, the priests who *were* in Nob. And they all came to the king.

12 And Saul said, "Hear now, son of Ahitub!" And he answered, "Here I am, my lord."

13 Then Saul said to him, "Why have you conspired against me, you and the son of Jesse, in that you have given him bread and a sword, and have inquired of God for him, that he should rise against me, to lie in wait, as it is this day?"

14 So Ahimelech answered the king and said, "And who among all your servants *is so* [R]faithful as David, who is the king's son-in-law, who goes at your bidding, and is honorable in your house? 1 Sam. 19:4, 5; 20:32; 24:11

15 "Did I then begin to inquire of God for him? Far be it from me! Let not the king impute anything to his servant, *or* to any in the house of my father. For your servant knew nothing of all this, little or much."

16 And the king said, "You shall surely die, Ahimelech, you and all your father's house!"

17 Then the king said to the guards who stood about him, "Turn and kill the priests of the LORD, because their hand also *is* with David, and because they knew when he fled and did not tell it to me." But the servants of the king [R]would not lift their hands to strike the priests of the LORD. Ex. 1:17

18 And the king said to Doeg, "You turn and kill the priests!" So Doeg the Edomite turned and [T]struck the priests, and [R]killed on that day eighty-five men who wore a linen ephod. *attacked* • 1 Sam. 2:31

19 [R]Also Nob, the city of the priests, he struck with the edge of the sword, both men and women, children and nursing infants, oxen and donkeys and sheep—with the edge of the sword. 1 Sam. 22:9, 11

20 [R]Now one of the sons of Ahimelech the son of Ahitub, named Abiathar, [R]escaped and fled after David. 1 Sam. 23:6, 9; 30:7 • 1 Sam. 2:33

21 And Abiathar told David that Saul had killed the LORD's priests.

22 So David said to Abiathar, "I knew that day, when Doeg the Edomite *was* there, that he would surely tell Saul. I have caused *the death* of all the persons of your father's [T]house. *family*

23 "Stay with me; do not fear. [R]For he who seeks my life seeks your life, but with me you *shall be* safe." 1 Kin. 2:26

CHAPTER 23

David Smites the Philistines

THEN they told David, saying, "Look, the Philistines are fighting against Keilah, and they are robbing the threshing floors."

2 Therefore David inquired of the LORD, saying, "Shall I go and attack these Philistines?" And the LORD said to David, "Go and attack the Philistines, and save Keilah."

3 And David's men said to him, "Look, we are afraid here in Judah. How much more then if we go to Keilah against the armies of the Philistines?"

4 Then David inquired of the LORD once again. And the LORD answered him and said, "Arise, go down to Keilah. For I will deliver the Philistines into your hand."

5 And David and his men went to Keilah and [R]fought with the Philistines, struck them with a mighty blow, and took away their livestock. So David saved the inhabitants of Keilah. 1 Sam. 19:8

6 Now it happened, when Abiathar the son of Ahimelech fled to David at Keilah, *that* he went down *with* an ephod in his hand.

7 And Saul was told that David had gone to Keilah. So Saul said, "God has delivered him into my hand, for he has shut himself in by entering a town that has gates and bars."

8 Then Saul called all the people together for war, to go down to Keilah to besiege David and his men.

9 When David knew that Saul plotted evil against him, [R]he said to Abiathar the priest, "Bring the ephod here." 1 Sam. 23:6; 30:7

10 Then David said, "O LORD God of Israel, Your servant has certainly heard that Saul seeks to come to Keilah [R]to destroy the city for my sake. 1 Sam. 22:19

11 "Will the men of Keilah deliver me into his hand? Will Saul come down, as Your servant has heard? O LORD God of Israel, I pray, tell Your servant." And the LORD said, "He will come down."

12 Then David said, "Will the men of Keilah [T]deliver me and my men into the hand of Saul?" And the LORD said, "They will deliver *you*." Lit. *shut up*

Saul Chases David

13 So David and his men, about six hundred, arose and departed from Keilah and went wherever they could go. Then it was told Saul that David had escaped from Keilah; so he halted the expedition.

14 And David stayed in strongholds in the wilderness, and remained in [R]the mountains in the Wilderness of [R]Ziph. Saul [R]sought him every day, but God did not deliver him into his hand. Ps. 11:1 • Josh. 15:55 • Ps. 32:7; 54:3, 4

15 So David saw that Saul had come out to seek his life. And David *was* in the Wilderness of Ziph [T]in a forest. Or *in Horesh*

16 Then Jonathan, Saul's son, arose and
went to David in the woods and
[T]strengthened his hand in God. *encouraged him*
17 And he said to him, [R]"Do not fear, for the
hand of Saul my father shall not find you.
You shall be king over Israel, and I shall be
next to you. [R]Even my father Saul knows
that." [Heb. 13:6] • 1 Sam. 20:31; 24:20
18 So the two of them made a covenant
before the LORD. And David stayed in the
woods, and Jonathan went to his own house.
19 Then the Ziphites came up to Saul at
Gibeah, saying, "Is David not hiding with us
in strongholds in the woods, in the hill of
Hachilah, which *is* on the south of Jeshimon?
20 "Now therefore, O king, come down
according to all the desire of your soul to
come down; and [R]our part *shall be* to deliver
him into the king's hand." Ps. 54:3
21 And Saul said, "Blessed *are* you of the
LORD, for you have compassion on me.
22 "Please go and find out for sure, and see
the place where his hideout is, *and* who has
seen him there. For I am told *that* he is very
crafty.
23 "See therefore, and take knowledge of all
the lurking places where he hides; and come
back to me with certainty, and I will go with
you. And it shall be, if he is in the land, that I
will search for him throughout all the [T]clans
of Judah." Or *thousands*
24 So they arose and went to Ziph before
Saul. But David and his men *were* in the
Wilderness [R]of Maon, in the plain on the
south of Jeshimon. 1 Sam. 25:2
25 When Saul and his men went to seek
him, they told David. Therefore he went
down to the rock, and stayed in the Wilderness of Maon. And when Saul heard *that*, he
pursued David in the Wilderness of Maon.
26 Then Saul went on one side of the mountain, and David and his men on the other side
of the mountain. [R]So David made haste to
get away from Saul, for Saul and his men
[R]were encircling David and his men to take
them. Ps. 31:22 • Ps. 17:9
27 [R]But a messenger came to Saul, saying,
"Hasten and come, for the Philistines have
invaded the land!" 2 Kin. 19:9
28 Therefore Saul returned from pursuing
David, and went against the Philistines; so
they called that place the Rock of Escaping.
29 Then David went up from there and
dwelt in strongholds at [R]En Gedi. 2 Chr. 20:2

CHAPTER 24

David Saves Saul's Life

NOW it happened, when Saul had returned from following the Philistines,
that it was told him, saying, "Take note!
David *is* in the Wilderness of En Gedi."
2 Then Saul took three thousand chosen
men from all Israel, and went to seek David
and his men on the Rocks of the Wild Goats.
3 So he came to the sheepfolds by the
road, where there *was* a cave; and Saul went
in to attend to his needs. (David and his men
were staying in the recesses of the cave.)
4 Then the men of David said to him, "This
is the day of which the LORD said to you,
'Behold, I will deliver your enemy into your
hand, that you may do to him as it seems
good to you.' " And David arose and secretly
cut off a corner of Saul's robe.
5 Now it happened afterward that [R]David's
heart troubled him because he had cut Saul's
robe. 2 Sam. 24:10
6 And he said to his men, [R]"The LORD
forbid that I should do this thing to my
master, the LORD's anointed, to stretch out
my hand against him, seeing he *is* the
anointed of the LORD." 1 Sam. 26:11
7 So David [R]restrained his servants with
these words, and did not allow them to rise
against Saul. And Saul got up from the cave
and went on *his* way. [Matt. 5:44]
8 David also arose afterward, went out of
the cave, and called out to Saul, saying, "My
lord the king!" And when Saul looked behind
him, David stooped with his face to the earth,
and bowed down.
9 And David said to Saul: [R]"Why do you
listen to the words of men who say, 'Indeed
David seeks your harm'? Ps. 141:6
10 "Look, this day your eyes have seen that
the LORD delivered you today into my hand in
the cave, and *someone* urged *me* to kill you.
But *my eye* spared you, and I said, 'I will not
stretch out my hand against my lord, for he *is*
the LORD's anointed.'
11 "Moreover, my father, see! Yes, see the
corner of your robe in my hand! For in that I
cut off the corner of your robe, and did not
kill you, know and see that *there is* [R]neither
evil nor rebellion in my hand, and I have not
sinned against you. Yet you [R]hunt my life to
take it. Ps. 7:3; 35:7 • 1 Sam. 26:20
12 "Let the LORD judge between you and
me, and let the LORD avenge me on you. But
my hand shall not be against you.
13 "As the proverb of the ancients says,
'Wickedness proceeds from the wicked.' But
my hand shall not be against you.
14 "After whom has the king of Israel come
out? Whom do you pursue? [R]A dead dog? [R]A
flea? 2 Sam. 9:8 • 1 Sam. 26:20
15 "Therefore let the LORD be judge, and
judge between you and me, and [R]see and
[R]plead my case, and deliver me out of your
hand." 2 Chr. 24:22 • Ps. 35:1; 43:1; 119:154
16 So it was, when David had finished
speaking these words to Saul, that Saul said,
[R]"*Is* this your voice, my son David?" And Saul
lifted up his voice and wept. 1 Sam. 26:17

17 [R]Then he said to David: "You *are* [R]more
righteous than I; for [R]you have rewarded me
with good, whereas I have rewarded you with
evil. 1 Sam. 26:21 • Gen. 38:26 • [Matt. 5:44]
18 "And you have shown this day how you
have dealt well with me; for when [R]the LORD
delivered me into your hand, you did not kill
me. 1 Sam. 26:23
19 "For if a man finds his enemy, will he let
him get away safely? Therefore may the
LORD reward you with good for what you
have done to me this day.
20 "And now [R]I know indeed that you shall
surely be king, and that the kingdom of Israel
shall be established in your hand. 1 Sam. 23:17
21 "Therefore swear now to me by the LORD
that you will not cut off my descendants after
me, and that you will not destroy my name
from my father's house."
22 So David swore to Saul. And Saul went
home, but David and his men went up to [R]the
stronghold. 1 Sam. 23:29

CHAPTER 25

Samuel the Judge Dies

THEN [R]Samuel died; and the Israelites
gathered together and [R]lamented for him,
and buried him at his home in Ramah. And
David arose and went down [R]to the Wilderness of *Paran. 1 Sam. 28:3 • Deut. 34:8 • Gen. 21:21

David Marries Abigail

2 Now *there was* a man [R]in Maon whose
business *was* in [R]Carmel, and the man *was*
very rich. He had three thousand sheep and a
thousand goats. And he was shearing his
sheep in Carmel. 1 Sam. 23:24 • Josh. 15:55
3 The name of the man *was* Nabal, and the
name of his wife Abigail. And *she was* a
woman of good understanding and beautiful
appearance; but the man *was* harsh and evil
in *his* doings. And he *was of the house of*
[R]Caleb. Josh. 15:13
4 When David heard in the wilderness that
Nabal was [R]shearing his sheep, Gen. 38:13
5 David sent ten young men; and David
said to the young men, "Go up to Carmel, go
to Nabal, and greet him in my name.
6 "And thus you shall say to him who lives
in prosperity: 'Peace *be* to you, peace to your
house, and peace to all that you have!
7 'Now I have heard that you have shearers. Your shepherds were with us, and we did
not hurt them, [R]nor was there anything
missing from them all the while they were in
Carmel. 1 Sam. 25:15, 21
8 'Ask your young men, and they will tell
you. Therefore let *my* young men find favor
in your eyes, for we come on a feast day.
Please give whatever comes to your hand to
your servants and to your son David.' "
9 So when David's young men came, they
spoke to Nabal according to all these words
in the name of David, and waited.
10 Then Nabal answered David's servants,
and said, "Who *is* David, and who *is* the son
of Jesse? There are many servants nowadays
who break away each one from his master.
11 "Shall I then take my bread and my
water and my [T]meat that I have killed for my
shearers, and give *it* to men when I do not
know where they *are* from?" Lit. *slaughter*
12 So David's young men turned on their
heels and went back; and they came and told
him all these words.
13 Then David said to his men, "Every man
gird on his sword." So every man girded on
his sword, and David also girded on his
sword. And about four hundred men went
with David, and two hundred [R]stayed with
the supplies. 1 Sam. 30:24
14 Now one of the young men told Abigail,
Nabal's wife, saying, "Look, David sent messengers from the wilderness to greet our
master; and he [T]reviled them. *scolded* or *scorned at*
15 "But the men *were* very good to us, and
[R]we were not hurt, nor did we miss anything
as long as we accompanied them, when we
were in the fields. 1 Sam. 25:7, 21
16 "They were [R]a wall to us both by night
and day, all the time we were with them
keeping the sheep. Ex. 14:22
17 "Now therefore, know and consider
what you will do, for harm is determined
against our master and against all his household. For he *is such* a [T]scoundrel that *one*
cannot speak to him." Lit. *son of Belial*
18 Then Abigail made haste and [R]took two
hundred *loaves* of bread, two skins of wine,
five sheep already dressed, [T]five seahs of
roasted *grain*, one hundred clusters of raisins,
and two hundred cakes of figs, and loaded
them on donkeys. Gen. 32:13 • 10.873 bu.
19 And she said to her servants, "Go on
before me; see, I am coming after you." But
she did not tell her husband Nabal.
20 So it was, *as* she rode on the donkey,
that she went down under cover of the hill;
and there were David and his men, coming
down toward her, and she met them.
21 Now David had said, "Surely in vain I
have protected all that this *fellow* has in the
wilderness, so that nothing was missed of all
that *belongs* to him. And he has [R]repaid me
evil for good. Ps. 109:5
22 "May God do so, and more also, to the
enemies of David, if I leave one male of all
who *belong* to him by morning light."
23 Now when Abigail saw David, she hastened [R]to dismount from the donkey, fell on
her face before David, and bowed down to
the ground. Judg. 1:14

25:1 LXX *Maon*

24 So she fell at his feet and said: "On me,
my lord, *on* me *let* this iniquity *be*! And please
let your maidservant [T]speak in your ears, and
hear the words of your maidservant. *speak to you*
25 "Please, let not my lord regard this
scoundrel Nabal. For as his name *is*, so *is* he:
[T]Nabal *is* his name, and folly *is* with him. But
I, your maidservant, did not see the young
men of my lord whom you sent. Lit. *Fool*
26 "Now therefore, my lord, *as* the LORD
lives and *as* your soul lives, since the LORD
has held you back from coming to bloodshed
and from avenging yourself with your own
hand, now then, let your enemies and those
who seek harm for my lord be as Nabal.
27 "And now this present which your maidservant has brought to my lord, let it be given
to the young men who follow my lord.
28 "Please forgive the trespass of your
maidservant. For [R]the LORD will certainly
make for my lord an enduring house, because
my lord [R]fights the battles of the LORD, [R]and
evil is not found in you throughout your
days. 2 Sam. 7:11–16, 27 • 1 Sam. 18:17 • 1 Sam. 24:11
29 "Yet a man has risen to pursue you and
seek your life, but the life of my lord shall be
[R]bound in the bundle of the living with the
LORD your God; and the lives of your enemies
He shall [R]sling out, *as from* the pocket of a
sling. [Col. 3:3] • Jer. 10:18
30 "And it shall come to pass, when the
LORD has done for my lord according to all
the good that He has spoken concerning you,
and has appointed you ruler over Israel,
31 "that this will be no grief to you, nor
offense of heart to my lord, either that you
have shed blood without cause, or that my
lord has avenged himself. But when the LORD
has dealt well with my lord, then remember
your maidservant."
32 Then David said to Abigail: [R]"Blessed *be*
the LORD God of Israel, who sent you this day
to meet me! Luke 1:68
33 "And blessed *is* your advice and blessed
are you, because you have [R]kept me this day
from coming to bloodshed and from avenging
myself with my own hand. 1 Sam. 25:26
34 "For indeed, *as* the LORD God of Israel
lives, who has kept me back from hurting
you, unless you had hastened and come to
meet me, surely [R]by morning light no males
would have been left to Nabal." 1 Sam. 25:22
35 So David received from her hand what
she had brought him, and said to her, "Go up
in peace to your house. See, I have heeded
your voice and respected your person."
36 Then Abigail went to Nabal, and there he
was, [R]holding a feast in his house, like the
feast of a king. And Nabal's heart *was* merry
within him, for he *was* very drunk; therefore
she told him nothing, little or much, until
morning light. 2 Sam. 13:28
37 So it was, in the morning, when the wine
had gone from Nabal, and his wife had told
him these things, that his heart died within
him, and he became *like* a stone.
38 Then it happened, *after* about ten days,
that the LORD struck Nabal, and he died.
39 So when David heard that Nabal was
dead, he said, "Blessed *be* the LORD, who has
pleaded the cause of my reproach from the
hand of Nabal, and has [R]kept His servant
from evil! For the LORD has [R]returned the
wickedness of Nabal on his own head." And
David sent and proposed to Abigail, to take
her as his wife. 1 Sam. 25:26, 34 • 1 Kin. 2:44
40 And when the servants of David had
come to Abigail at Carmel, they spoke to her
saying, "David sent us to you, to ask you to
become his wife."
41 Then she arose, bowed her face to the
earth, and said, "Here is your maidservant, a
servant to [R]wash the feet of the servants of
my lord." Luke 7:38, 44
42 So Abigail rose in haste and rode on a
donkey, [T]attended by five of her maidens; and
she followed the messengers of David, and
became his wife. Lit. *with five of her maidens at her feet*
43 David also took Ahinoam of Jezreel, and
so both of them were his wives.
44 But Saul had given Michal his daughter,
David's wife, to [T]Palti the son of Laish, who
was from [R]Gallim. *Paltiel,* 2 Sam. 3:15 • Is. 10:30

CHAPTER 26

David Saves Saul's Life Again

NOW the Ziphites came to Saul at Gibeah,
saying, "Is David not hiding in the hill
of Hachilah, *which is* opposite Jeshimon?"
2 Then Saul arose and went down to the
Wilderness of Ziph, having [R]three thousand
chosen men of Israel with him, to seek David
in the Wilderness of Ziph. 1 Sam. 13:2; 24:2
3 And Saul encamped in the hill of Hachilah, which *is* opposite Jeshimon, by the road.
But David stayed in the wilderness, and he
saw that Saul came after him into the wilderness.
4 David therefore sent out spies, and understood that Saul had indeed come.
5 So David arose and came to the place
where Saul had encamped. And David saw
the place where Saul lay, and [R]Abner the son
of Ner, the commander of his army. Now Saul
lay within the camp, with the people encamped all around him. 1 Sam. 14:50, 51; 17:55
6 Then David answered, and said to
Ahimelech the Hittite and to Abishai the son
of Zeruiah, brother of Joab, saying, "Who will
go down with me to Saul in the camp?" And
Abishai said, "I will go down with you."
7 So David and Abishai came to the people
by night; and there Saul lay sleeping within

the camp, with his spear stuck in the ground
by his head. And Abner and the people lay all
around him.
8 Then Abishai said to David, [R]"God has
delivered your enemy into your hand this
day. Now therefore, please, let me strike him
[T]at once with the spear, right to the earth;
and I will not *have to strike* him a second
time!" 1 Sam. 24:4 • Or *one time*
9 And David said to Abishai, "Do not destroy him; [R]for who can stretch out his hand
against the LORD's anointed, and be guiltless?" 1 Sam. 24:6, 7
10 David said furthermore, "*As* the LORD
lives, [R]the LORD shall strike him, or [R]his day
shall come to die, or he shall [R]go out to battle
and perish. 1 Sam. 25:26, 38 • [Job 7:1; 14:5] • 1 Sam. 31:6
11 "The LORD forbid that I should stretch
out my hand against the LORD's anointed.
But please, take now the spear and the jug of
water that *are* by his head, and let us go."
12 So David took the spear and the jug of
water *by* Saul's head, and they got away; and
no man saw *it* or knew *it* or awoke. For they
were all asleep, because [R]a deep sleep from
the LORD had fallen on them. Gen. 2:21; 15:12
13 Then David went over to the other side,
and stood on the top of a hill afar off, a great
distance *being* between them.
14 And David called out to the people and
to Abner the son of Ner, saying, "Do you not
answer, Abner?" Then Abner answered and
said, "Who *are* you, calling out to the king?"
15 So David said to Abner, "*Are* you not a
man? And who *is* like you in Israel? Why
then have you not guarded your lord the
king? For one of the people came in to destroy your lord the king.
16 "This thing that you have done *is* not
good. *As* the LORD lives, you *are* worthy to
die, because you have not guarded your
master, the LORD's anointed. And now see
where the king's spear *is*, and the jug of
water that *was* by his head."
17 Then Saul knew David's voice, and said,
"*Is* that your voice, my son David?" And
David said, "*It is* my voice, my lord, O king."
18 And he said, [R]"Why does my lord thus
pursue his servant? For what have I done, or
what evil *is* in my hand? 1 Sam. 24:9, 11–14
19 "Now therefore, please, let my lord the
king hear the words of his servant: If the
LORD has stirred you up against me, let Him
accept an offering. But if *it is* the children of
men, *may* they *be* cursed before the LORD,
[R]for they have driven me out this day from
abiding in the inheritance of the LORD, saying, 'Go, serve other gods.' Deut. 4:27, 28
20 "Now therefore, do not let my blood fall
to the earth before the face of the LORD. For
the king of Israel has come out to seek [R]a
flea, as when one hunts a partridge in the
mountains." 1 Sam. 24:14

Saul Admits His Guilt

21 Then Saul said, [R]"I have sinned. Return,
my son David. For I will harm you no more,
because my life was precious in your eyes
this day. Indeed I have played the fool and
erred exceedingly." 1 Sam. 15:24, 30; 24:17
22 And David answered and said, "Here is
the king's spear. Let one of the young men
come over and get it.
23 [R]"May the LORD [R]repay every man *for* his
righteousness and his faithfulness; for the
LORD delivered you into *my* hand today, but I
would not stretch out my hand against the
LORD's anointed. Ps. 7:8; 18:20; 62:12 • 2 Sam. 22:21
24 "And indeed, as your life was valued
much this day in my eyes, so let my life be
valued much in the eyes of the LORD, and let
Him deliver me out of all tribulation."
25 Then Saul said to David, "*May* you *be*
blessed, my son David! You shall both do
great things and also still [R]prevail." So David
went on his way, and Saul returned to his
place. Gen. 32:28

CHAPTER 27

David Joins with the Philistines

AND David said in his heart, "Now I shall
perish someday by the hand of Saul.
There is nothing better for me than that I
should speedily escape to the land of the
Philistines; and Saul will despair of [T]me, to
seek me anymore in any part of Israel. So I
shall escape out of his hand." Searching for me
2 Then David arose and went over with
the six hundred men who *were* with him to
Achish the son of Maoch, king of Gath.
3 So David dwelt with Achish at Gath, he
and his men, each man with his household,
and David [R]with his two wives, Ahinoam the
Jezreelitess, and Abigail the Carmelitess,
Nabal's widow. 1 Sam. 25:42, 43
4 And it was told Saul that David had fled
to Gath; so he sought him no more.
5 Then David said to Achish, "If I have
now found favor in your eyes, let them give
me a place in some town in the country, that
I may dwell there. For why should your
servant dwell in the royal city with you?"
6 So Achish gave him Ziklag that day.
Therefore [R]Ziklag has belonged to the kings
of Judah to this day. Josh. 15:31; 19:5
7 Now [T]the time that David [R]dwelt in the
country of the Philistines was one full year
and four months. Lit. *the number of days* • 1 Sam. 29:3
8 And David and his men went up and
raided the Geshurites, the Girzites, and the
Amalekites. For those nations were the inhabitants of the land from of old, as you go to
Shur, even as far as the land of Egypt.
9 Whenever David [T]attacked the land, he
left neither man nor woman alive, but took

away the sheep, the oxen, the donkeys, the
camels, and the apparel, and returned and
came to Achish. Lit. *struck*
10 Then Achish would say, "Where have
you made a raid today?" And David would
say, "Against the southern area of Judah, or
against the southern area of [R]the Jerahmeelites, or against the southern area of [R]the
Kenites." 1 Chr. 2:9, 25 • Judg. 1:16
11 David would save neither man nor
woman alive, to bring *news* to Gath, saying,
"Lest they should inform on us, saying, 'Thus
David did.' " And so *was* his behavior all the
time he dwelt in the country of the Philistines.
12 So Achish believed David, saying, "He
has made his people Israel utterly abhor him;
therefore he will be my servant forever."

CHAPTER 28

NOW [R]it happened in those days that the
Philistines gathered their armies together for war, to fight with Israel. And
Achish said to David, "You assuredly know
that you will go out with me to battle, you
and your men." 1 Sam. 29:1, 2
2 And David said to Achish, "Surely you
know what your servant can do." And Achish
said to David, "Therefore I will make you one
of my chief guardians forever."

God Does Not Answer Saul

3 Now Samuel had died, and all Israel had
lamented for him and buried him in Ramah,
in his own city. And Saul had put the mediums and the spiritists out of the land.
4 Then the Philistines gathered together,
and came and encamped at [R]Shunem. So Saul
gathered all Israel together, and they encamped at [R]Gilboa. Josh. 19:18 • 1 Sam. 31:1
5 When Saul saw the army of the Philistines, he was [R]afraid, and his heart trembled
greatly. Job 18:11
6 And when Saul inquired of the LORD, the
LORD did not answer him, either by dreams or
by Urim or by the prophets.

Saul Visits the Medium

7 Then Saul said to his servants, "Find me
a woman who is a medium, [R]that I may go to
her and inquire of her." And his servants said
to him, "In fact, *there is* a woman who is a
medium at En Dor." 1 Chr. 10:13
8 So Saul disguised himself and put on
other clothes, and he went, and two men with
him; and they came to the woman by night.
And [R]he said, "Please conduct a séance for
me, and bring up for me the one I shall name
to you." Deut. 18:10, 11
9 Then the woman said to him, "Look, you
know what Saul has done, how he has [R]cut
off the mediums and the spiritists from the
land. Why then do you lay a snare for my life,
to cause me to die?" 1 Sam. 28:3
10 And Saul swore to her by the LORD,
saying, "*As* the LORD lives, no punishment
shall come upon you for this thing."
11 Then the woman said, "Whom shall I
bring up for you?" And he said, "Bring up
Samuel for me."
12 When the woman saw Samuel, she cried
out with a loud voice. And the woman spoke
to Saul, saying, "Why have you deceived me?
For you *are* Saul!"
13 And the king said to her, "Do not be
afraid. What did you see?" And the woman
said to Saul, "I saw [R]a[T] spirit ascending out of
the earth." Ex. 22:28 • Heb. *elohim*
14 So he said to her, "What *is* his form?"
And she said, "An old man is coming up, and
he *is* covered with a mantle." And Saul
perceived that it *was* Samuel, and he stooped
with *his* face to the ground and bowed down.
15 Now Samuel said to Saul, "Why have
you disturbed me by bringing me up?" And
Saul answered, "I am deeply distressed; for
the Philistines make war against me, and God
has departed from me and does not answer
me anymore, neither by prophets nor by
dreams. Therefore I have called you, that you
may reveal to me what I should do."
16 Then Samuel said: "Why then do you ask
me, seeing the LORD has departed from you
and has become your enemy?
17 "And the LORD has done for [T]Himself as
He spoke by me. For the LORD has torn the
kingdom out of your hand and given it to
your neighbor, *namely,* David. Or *him,* David
18 [R]"Because you did not obey the voice of
the LORD nor execute His fierce wrath upon
[R]Amalek, therefore the LORD has done this
thing to you this day. 1 Chr. 10:13 • 1 Sam. 15:3–9
19 "Moreover the LORD will also deliver
Israel with you into the hand of the Philistines. And tomorrow you and your sons *will
be* with [R]me. The LORD will also deliver the
army of Israel into the hand of the Philistines." Job 3:17–19
20 Then immediately Saul fell full length on
the ground, and was dreadfully afraid because of the words of Samuel. And there was
no strength in him, for he had eaten no food
all day or all night.
21 And the woman came to Saul and saw
that he was severely troubled, and said to
him, "Look, your maidservant has obeyed
your voice, and I have [R]put my life in my
hands and heeded the words which you
spoke to me. Job 13:14
22 "Now therefore, please, heed also the
voice of your maidservant, and let me set a
piece of bread before you; and eat, that you
may have strength when you go on *your*
way."

23 But he refused and said, "I will not eat."
But his servants, together with the woman,
urged him; and he heeded their voice. So he
arose from the ground and sat on the bed.
24 Now the woman had a fatted calf in the
house, and she hastened to kill it. And she
took flour and kneaded *it*, and baked unleavened bread from it.
25 So she brought *it* before Saul and his
servants, and they ate. Then they rose and
went away that night.

CHAPTER 29

David Is Spared from Fighting Saul

THEN the Philistines gathered together all
their armies at Aphek, and the Israelites
encamped by a fountain which *is* in Jezreel.
2 And the lords of the Philistines [T]passed in
review by hundreds and by thousands, but
David and his men passed in review at the
rear with Achish. *passed on in the rear*
3 Then the princes of the Philistines said,
"What *are* these Hebrews *doing here*?" And
Achish said to the princes of the Philistines,
"*Is* this not David, the servant of Saul king of
Israel, who has been with me these days, or
these years? And to this day I have found no
fault in him since he defected *to me*."
4 But the princes of the Philistines were
angry with him; so the princes of the Philistines said to him, "Make this fellow return,
that he may go back to the place which you
have appointed for him, and do not let him go
down with us to battle, lest in the battle he
become our adversary. For with what could
he reconcile himself to his master, if not with
the heads of these [R]men? 1 Chr. 12:19, 20
5 "*Is* this not David, [R]of whom they sang to
one another in dances, saying: 1 Sam. 21:11

[R]'Saul has slain his thousands, 1 Sam. 18:7
And David his ten thousands'?"

6 Then Achish called David and said to
him, "Surely, *as* the LORD lives, you have
been upright, and your going out and your
coming in with me in the army *is* good in my
sight. For to this day I have not found evil in
you since the day of your coming to me.
Nevertheless the lords do not favor you.
7 "Therefore return now, and go in peace,
that you may not displease the lords of the
Philistines."
8 Then David said to Achish, "But what
have I done? And to this day what have you
found in your servant as long as I have been
with you, that I may not go and fight against
the enemies of my lord the king?"
9 But Achish answered and said to David,
"I know that you *are* as good in my sight as
an angel of God; nevertheless [R]the princes of
the Philistines have said, 'He shall not go up
with us to the battle.' 1 Sam. 29:4
10 "Now therefore, rise early in the morning
with your master's servants who have come
with you. And as soon as you are up early in
the morning and have light, depart."
11 So David and his men rose early to
depart in the morning, to return to the land
of the Philistines. [R]And the Philistines went
up to Jezreel. 2 Sam. 4:4

CHAPTER 30

God Answers David

NOW it happened, when David and his
men came to [R]Ziklag, on the third day,
that the [R]Amalekites had invaded the South
and Ziklag, attacked Ziklag and burned it
with fire, 1 Sam. 27:6 • 1 Sam. 15:7; 27:8
2 and had taken captive the [R]women and
those who *were* there, from small to great;
they did not kill anyone, but carried *them*
away and went their way. 1 Sam. 27:2, 3
3 So David and his men came to the city,
and there it was, burned with fire; and their
wives, their sons, and their daughters had
been taken captive.
4 Then David and the people who *were*
with him lifted up their voices and wept, until
they had no more power to weep.
5 And David's two wives, Ahinoam the
Jezreelitess, and Abigail the widow of Nabal
the Carmelite, had been taken captive.
6 Then David was greatly distressed, for
the people spoke of stoning him, because the
soul of all the people was grieved, every man
for his sons and his daughters. But David
strengthened himself in the LORD his God.
7 [R]Then David said to Abiathar the priest,
Ahimelech's son, "Please bring the ephod
here to me." And [R]Abiathar brought the
ephod to David. 1 Sam. 23:2–9 • 1 Sam. 23:6
8 [R]So David inquired of the LORD, saying,
"Shall I pursue this troop? Shall I overtake
them?" And He answered him, "Pursue, for
you shall surely overtake *them* and without
fail recover *all*." 1 Sam. 23:2, 4

David Kills the Enemy

9 So David went, he and the six hundred
men who *were* with him, and came to the
Brook Besor, where those stayed who were
left behind.
10 But David pursued, he and four hundred
men; [R]for two hundred stayed *behind*, who
were so weary that they could not cross the
Brook Besor. 1 Sam. 30:9, 21
11 Then they found an Egyptian in the field,
and brought him to David; and they gave him
bread and he ate, and they let him drink
water.
12 And they gave him a piece of a cake of
figs and two clusters of raisins. So [R]when he

had eaten, his strength came back to him; for
he had eaten no bread nor drunk *any* water
for three days and three nights. Judg. 15:19
13 Then David said to him, "To whom do
you *belong,* and where *are* you from?" And
he said, "I *am* a young man from Egypt,
servant of an Amalekite; and my master left
me behind, because three days ago I fell sick.
14 "We made an invasion of the southern
area of [R]the Cherethites, in the *territory*
which *belongs* to Judah, and of the southern
area [R]of Caleb; and we burned Ziklag with
fire." 2 Sam. 8:18 • Josh. 14:13; 15:13
15 And David said to him, "Can you take
me down to this troop?" And he said, "Swear
to me by God that you will neither kill me nor
deliver me into the hands of my [R]master, and
I will take you down to this troop." Deut. 23:15
16 So when he had brought him down,
there they were, spread out over all the land,
[R]eating and drinking and dancing, because of
all the great spoil which they had taken from
the land of the Philistines and from the land
of Judah. 1 Thess. 5:3
17 And David attacked them from twilight
until the evening of the next day. Not a man
of them escaped, except four hundred young
men who rode on camels and fled.
18 So David recovered all that the Amalekites had carried away, and David rescued his
two wives.
19 And nothing of theirs was lacking, either
small or great, sons or daughters, spoil or
anything which they had taken from them;
[R]David recovered all. 1 Sam. 30:8
20 Then David took all the flocks and herds
which they had driven before those *other*
livestock, and said, "This *is* David's spoil."
21 Now David came to the [R]two hundred
men who had been so weary that they could
not follow David, whom they also had made
to stay at the Brook Besor. So they went out
to meet David and to meet the people who
were with him. And when David came near
the people, he greeted them. 1 Sam. 30:10
22 Then all the wicked and [R]worthless[T] men
of those who went with David answered and
said, "Because they did not go with us, we
will not give them *any* of the spoil that we
have recovered, except for every man's wife
and children, that they may lead *them* away
and depart." Deut. 13:13 • Lit. *men of Belial*
23 But David said, "My brethren, you shall
not do so with what the LORD has given us,
who has preserved us and delivered into our
hand the troop that came against us.
24 "For who will heed you in this matter?
But [R]as his part *is* who goes down to the
battle, so *shall* his part *be* who stays by the
supplies; they shall share alike." Josh. 22:8
25 And *so* it was, from that day forward; he
made it a statute and an ordinance for Israel
to this day.
26 Now when David came to Ziklag, he sent
some of the spoil to the elders of Judah, to his
friends, saying, "Here is a present for you
from the spoil of the enemies of the LORD"—
27 to *those* who *were* in Bethel, *those* who
were in [R]Ramoth of the South, *those* who
were in [R]Jattir, Josh. 19:8 • Josh. 15:48; 21:14
28 *those* who *were* in [R]Aroer, *those* who
were in [R]Siphmoth, *those* who *were* in [R]Esh-
temoa, Josh. 13:16 • 1 Chr. 27:27 • Josh. 15:50
29 *those* who *were* in Rachal, *those* who
were in the cities of the Jerahmeelites, *those*
who *were* in the cities of the Kenites,
30 *those* who *were* in [R]Hormah, *those* who
were in [T]Chorashan, *those* who *were* in
Athach, Judg. 1:17 • Or *Borashan*
31 *those* who *were* in Hebron, and to all the
places where David himself and his men were
accustomed to [R]rove. 1 Sam. 23:22

CHAPTER 31

The Enemy Kills Saul—1 Chr. 10:1–14

SO [R]the Philistines fought against Israel;
and the men of Israel fled from before
the Philistines, and fell slain on Mount [R]Gil-
boa. 1 Chr. 10:1–12 • 1 Sam. 28:4
2 Then the Philistines followed hard after
Saul and his sons. And the Philistines killed
[R]Jonathan, Abinadab, and Malchishua, Saul's
sons. 1 Sam. 14:49
3 Now the battle became intense against
Saul; and the archers [T]hit him, and he was
severely wounded by the archers. Lit. *found*
4 [R]Then Saul said to his armorbearer,
"Draw your sword, and thrust me through
with it, lest [R]these uncircumcised men come
and thrust me through and [T]abuse me." But
his armorbearer would not, for he was greatly
afraid. Therefore Saul took a sword and fell
on it. Judg. 9:54 • 1 Sam. 14:6; 17:26, 36 • *torture*
5 And when his armorbearer saw that Saul
was dead, he also fell on his sword, and died
with him.
6 So Saul, his three sons, his armorbearer,
and all his men died together that same day.
7 And when the men of Israel who *were* on
the other side of the valley, and *those* who
were on the other side of the Jordan, saw that
the men of Israel had fled and that Saul and
his sons were dead, they forsook the cities
and fled; and the Philistines came and dwelt
in them.
8 So it came to pass the next day, when
the Philistines came to strip the slain, that
they found Saul and his three sons fallen on
Mount Gilboa.
9 And they cut off his head and stripped off
his armor, and sent *word* throughout the land
of the Philistines, to proclaim *it in* the temple
of their idols and among the people.

10 Then they put his armor in the temple of
the Ashtoreths, and they fastened his body to
the wall of [R]Beth Shan. Judg. 1:27
11 [R]And when the inhabitants of Jabesh
Gilead heard what the Philistines had done to
Saul, 1 Sam. 11:1–13
12 [R]all the valiant men arose and traveled
all night, and took the body of Saul and the
bodies of his sons from the wall of Beth Shan;
and they came to Jabesh and [R]burned them
there. 2 Sam. 2:4–7 • 2 Chr. 16:14
13 Then they took their bones and [R]buried
them under the tamarisk tree at Jabesh, [R]and
fasted seven days. 2 Sam. 2:4, 5; 21:12–14 • Gen. 50:10

Weights

Unit	*Weight*	*Equivalents*	*Translations*
Jewish Weights			
Talent	c. 75 pounds for common talent, c. 150 pounds for royal talent	60 minas; 3,000 shekels	talent
Mina	1.25 pounds	50 shekels	mina
Shekel	c. .4 ounce (11.4 grams) for common shekel c. .8 ounce for royal shekel	2 bekas; 20 gerahs	shekel
Beka	c. .2 ounce (5.7 grams)	½ shekel; 10 gerahs	half a shekel
Gerah	c. .02 ounce (.57 grams)	1/20 shekel	gerah
Roman Weight			
Litra	12 ounces		pound

Liquid Measures

Unit	*Measure*	*Equivalents*	*Translations*
Kor	60 gallons	10 baths	kor
Metretes	10.2 gallons		gallon
Bath	6 gallons	6 hins	measure, bath
Hin	1 gallon	2 kabs	hin
Kab	2 quarts	4 logs	kab
Log	1 pint	¼ kab	log

THE SECOND BOOK OF

SAMUEL

THE BOOK OF SECOND SAMUEL

The Book of Second Samuel records the highlights of David's reign, first over the territory of Judah, and finally over the entire nation of Israel. It traces the ascension of David to the throne, his climactic sins of adultery and murder, and the shattering consequences of those sins upon his family and the nation.

See First Samuel for details on the titles of the books of Samuel. The Hebrew title for both books (originally one) is Samuel. The Greek title for Second Samuel is *Basileion Beta*, "Second Kingdoms." The Latin title is *Liber II Samuelis*, the "Second Book of Samuel," or simply "Second Samuel."

THE AUTHOR OF SECOND SAMUEL

Second Samuel was probably compiled by one man who combined the written chronicles of Nathan the prophet and Gad the seer (1 Chr. 29:29). In addition to these written sources, the compiler evidently used another source called "the Book of Jasher" (1:18). See comments under First Samuel.

THE TIME OF SECOND SAMUEL

The date of the composition for First and Second Samuel was sometime after the death of Solomon (931 B.C.) but before the Assyrian captivity of the northern kingdom (722 B.C.). It is likely that Samuel was composed early in the divided kingdom, perhaps around 900 B.C.

The story of David begins in First Samuel 16 and ends in First Kings 2. Second Samuel records the major events of David's forty-year rule. His reign in Hebron begins in 1011 B.C. and ends in 1004 B.C. (5:5). His thirty-three-year reign over the united Judah and Israel lasts from 1004 B.C. to 971 B.C.

THE CHRIST OF SECOND SAMUEL

As seen in the introduction to First Samuel, David is one of the most important types of Christ in the Old Testament. In spite of his sins, he remains a man after God's own heart because of his responsive and faithful attitude toward God. He sometimes fails in his personal life, but he never flags in his relationship to the Lord. Unlike most of the kings who succeed him, he never allows idolatry to become a problem during his reign. He is a true servant of Yahweh, obedient to His law, and an ideal king. His rule is usually characterized by justice, wisdom, integrity, courage, and compassion. Having conquered Jerusalem, he sits upon the throne of Melchizedek, the "righteous king" (Gen. 14:18). David is the standard by which all subsequent kings are measured.

Of course, David's life as recorded in chapters 1—10 is a far better portrayal of the future Messiah than is his life as it is seen in 11—24. Sin mars potential. The closest way in which he foreshadows the coming King can be seen in the important covenant God makes with him (7:4–17). David wants to build a house for God; but instead, God makes a house for David. The same three promises of an eternal kingdom, throne, and seed are later given to Christ (Luke 1:32, 33). There are nine different dynasties in the northern kingdom of Israel, but there is only one dynasty in Judah. The promise of a permanent dynasty is fulfilled in Christ, the "Son of David" (Matt. 21:9; 22:45), who will sit upon the throne of David (Is. 9:7; Luke 1:32).

KEYS TO SECOND SAMUEL

Key Word: David—The central character of Second Samuel is David, around whom the entire book is written. The key truth illustrated is the same as the theme of Deuteronomy: obedience brings blessing and disobedience brings judgment.

Key Verses: Second Samuel 7:12, 13; 22:21—"When your days are fulfilled and you rest with your fathers, I will set up your seed after you, who will come from your body, and I will establish his kingdom. He shall build a house for My name, and I will establish the throne of his kingdom forever" (7:12, 13).

"The LORD rewarded me according to my righteousness; according to the cleanness of my hands He has recompensed me" (22:21).

Key Chapter: Second Samuel 11—The eleventh chapter of Second Samuel is pivotal for the entire book. This chapter records the tragic sins of David regarding Bathsheba and her husband Uriah. All of the widespread blessings on David's family and his kingdom are quickly removed as God chastises His anointed one.

SURVEY OF SECOND SAMUEL

Second Samuel continues the account of the life of David at the point where First Samuel concludes. Soon after the death of Saul, the king-elect becomes the king enthroned, first over Judah when he reigns in Hebron for seven-and-a-half years and finally over all Israel when he reigns in Jerusalem for thirty-three years. This book reviews the key events in the forty-year reign of the man who is the halfway point between Abraham and Christ. It can be surveyed in the three divisions: the triumphs of David (1—10), the transgressions of David (11), and the troubles of David (12—24).

The Triumphs of David (1—10): Chapters 1—4 record the seven-year reign of David over the territory of Judah. Even though Saul is David's murderous pursuer, David does not rejoice in his death because he recognizes that Saul has been divinely anointed as king. Saul's son Ishbosheth is installed by Abner as a puppet king over the northern tribes of Israel. David's allies led by Joab defeat Abner and Israel (2:17; 3:1). Abner defects and arranges to unite Israel and Judah under David, but Joab kills Abner in revenge. The powerless Ishbosheth is murdered by his own men, and David is made king of Israel (5:3). David soon captures and fortifies Jerusalem and makes it the civil and religious center of the now united kingdom. Under David's rule the nation prospers politically, spiritually, and militarily. David brings the ark to Jerusalem and seeks to build a house for God (7). His obedience in placing the Lord at the center of his rule leads to great national blessing (8—10). "And the LORD preserved David wherever he went" (8:14).

The Transgressions of David (11): David's crimes of adultery and murder mark the pivotal point of the book. Because of these transgressions, David's victories and successes are changed to the personal, family, and national troubles which are recorded throughout the rest of Second Samuel.

The Troubles of David (12—24): The disobedience of the king produces chastisement and confusion at every level. David's glory and fame fade, never to be the same again. Nevertheless, David confesses his guilt when confronted by Nathan the prophet and is restored by God. A sword remains in David's house as a consequence of the sin: the baby born to David and Bathsheba dies, his son Amnon commits incest, and his son Absalom murders Amnon.

The consequences continue with Absalom's rebellion against his father. He shrewdly "stole the hearts of the men of Israel" (15:6). David is forced to flee from Jerusalem, and Absalom sets himself up as king. David would have been ruined, but God keeps Absalom from pursuing him until David has time to regroup his forces. Absalom's army is defeated by David's, and Joab kills Absalom in disobedience of David's orders to have him spared.

David seeks to amalgamate the kingdom, but conflict breaks out between the ten northern tribes of Israel and the two southern tribes of Judah and Benjamin. Israel decides to follow a man named Sheba in a revolt against David, but Judah remains faithful to him. This leads to war, and Joab defeats the rebels.

The closing chapters are actually an appendix to the book because they summarize David's words and deeds. They show how intimately the affairs of the people as a whole are tied to the spiritual and moral condition of the king. The nation enjoys God's blessing when David is obedient to the Lord, and suffers hardship when David disobeys God.

FOCUS	DAVID'S TRIUMPHS			DAVID'S TRANSGRESSIONS	DAVID'S TROUBLES	
REFERENCE	1:1 — 6:1	— 8:1	— 11:1	— 12:1	— 13:37	— 24:25
DIVISION	POLITICAL TRIUMPHS	SPIRITUAL TRIUMPHS	MILITARY TRIUMPHS	SINS OF ADULTERY AND MURDER	TROUBLES IN DAVID'S HOUSE	TROUBLES IN THE KINGDOM
TOPIC	SUCCESS			SIN	FAILURE	
	OBEDIENCE			DISOBEDIENCE	JUDGMENT	
LOCATION	DAVID IN HEBRON	DAVID IN JERUSALEM				
TIME	7½ YEARS	33 YEARS				

OUTLINE OF SECOND SAMUEL

Part One: The Triumphs of David (1:1—10:19)

I. The Political Triumphs of David ...... 1:1—5:25

A. The Reign of David in Hebron over Judah ...... 1:1—4:12
1. King Saul Dies 1:1–27
2. David Is Anointed as King over Judah 2:1–7
3. Ishbosheth Is Made King over Israel 2:8–11
4. David and Ishbosheth Fight ...... 2:12—4:12
a. David's Victory over Ishbosheth 2:12–32
b. David's Growth over Ishbosheth 3:1–5
c. Abner's Murder 3:6–39
d. Ishbosheth's Murder 4:1–8
e. Judgment on the Murder of Ishbosheth 4:9–12

B. The Reign of David in Jerusalem 5:1–25
1. David Is Anointed to Reign over Israel 5:1–5
2. Conquest of Jerusalem 5:6–10
3. Alliance with Tyre 5:11, 12
4. David's Family 5:13–16
5. Conquest of Philistia 5:17–25

II. The Spiritual Triumphs of David ...... 6:1—7:29

A. The Transportation of the Ark 6:1–23
1. Incorrect Transportation of the Ark 6:1–11
2. Correct Transportation of the Ark 6:12
3. David Rejoices over the Ark 6:13–15
4. Michal Despises David 6:16–23

B. The Institution of the Davidic Covenant 7:1–29
1. David Is Forbidden to Build God a House 7:1–3
2. God Promises David an Eternal House 7:4–17
3. David Praises God 7:18–29

III. The Military Triumphs of David ...... 8:1—10:19

A. The Triumphs of David over His Enemies 8:1–12
1. David Defeats Philistia 8:1
2. David Defeats Moab 8:2
3. David Defeats Zobah and Syria 8:3–8
4. David Receives Spoil from His Enemies 8:9–12

B. The Righteous Rule of David ...... 8:13—9:13
1. David's Righteous Rule over Israel 8:13–18
2. David's Righteous Rule over Mephibosheth 9:1–13

C. The Triumphs of David over Ammon and Syria 10:1–19
1. Insult of Ammon 10:1–5
2. Ammon Is Defeated 10:6–14
3. Syria Is Defeated 10:15–19

Part Two: The Transgressions of David (11:1–27)

I. The Sin of Adultery 11:1–5

II. The Sin of Murder 11:6–27

A. Uriah Does Not Sleep with Bathsheba 11:6–13
B. David Commands Uriah's Murder 11:14–25
C. David and Bathsheba Marry 11:26, 27

Part Three: The Troubles of David (12:1—24:25)

I. The Troubles in David's House ...... 12:1—13:36

A. Prophecy by Nathan 12:1–14
1. Prophecy of the Sword 12:1–12
2. David Repents for His Sin 12:13, 14

B. David's Son Dies 12:15–25
1. God Takes Away the Son of Adultery 12:15–23
2. God Gives Another Son 12:24, 25

C. Joab's Loyalty to David 12:26–31
D. Incest in David's House 13:1–20
E. Amnon Is Murdered 13:21–36

II. The Troubles in David's Kingdom 13:37—24:25

A. Rebellion of Absalom ...... 13:37—17:29
1. Flight of Absalom 13:37–39
2. Return of Absalom 14:1–24
3. Deceit of Absalom ...... 14:25—15:6
4. Rebellion of Absalom 15:7–12
5. Flight of David ...... 15:13—16:14
6. Reign of Absalom ...... 16:15—17:29

B. Absalom's Murder 18:1–33

C. David Is Restored as King ...... 19:1—20:26
1. Reproof of Joab 19:1–7
2. Restoration of David ...... 19:8—20:26

D. The Commentary on the Reign of David ...... 21:1—24:25
1. Famine 21:1–14
2. War with Philistia 21:15–22
3. Psalms of Thanksgiving ...... 22:1—23:7
4. Deeds of David's Mighty Men 23:8–39
5. The Census and the Plague 24:1–25

CHAPTER 1

King Saul Dies

NOW it came to pass after the [R]death of
Saul, when David had returned from
the slaughter of the Amalekites, and David
had stayed two days in Ziklag, 1 Sam. 31:6
2 on the third day, behold, it happened
that a man came from Saul's camp with his
clothes [T]torn and dust on his head. So it was,
when he came to David, that he fell to the
ground and prostrated himself. To show grief
3 And David said to him, "Where have you
come from?" So he said to him, "I have
escaped from the camp of Israel."
4 Then David said to him, [R]"How did the
matter go? Please tell me." And he answered,
"The people have fled from the battle,
many of the people are fallen and dead,
and Saul and [R]Jonathan his son are dead
also." 1 Sam. 4:16; 31:3 • 1 Sam. 31:2
5 So David said to the young man who told
him, "How do you know that Saul and Jonathan his son are dead?"
6 And the young man who told him said,
"As I happened by chance *to be* on [R]Mount
Gilboa, there was [R]Saul, leaning on his spear;
and indeed the chariots and horsemen followed hard after him. 1 Sam. 31:1 • 1 Sam. 31:2–4
7 "Now when he looked behind him, he
saw me and called to me. And I answered,
'Here I am.'
8 "And he said to me, 'Who *are* you?' So I
answered him, 'I *am* an Amalekite.'
9 "He said to me again, 'Please stand over
me and kill me, for [T]anguish has come upon
me, but my life still *remains* in me.' agony
10 "So I stood over him and [R]killed him,
because I was sure that he could not live
after he had fallen. And I took the crown that
was on his head and the bracelet that *was* on
his arm, and have brought them here to my
lord." Judg. 9:54
11 Then David took hold of his own clothes
and [R]tore them, and *so did* all the men who
were with him. 2 Sam. 3:31; 13:31
12 And they [R]mourned and wept and [R]fasted
until evening for Saul and for Jonathan his
son, for the [R]people of the LORD and for the
house of Israel, because they had fallen by
the sword. 2 Sam. 3:31 • 1 Sam. 31:13 • 2 Sam. 6:21
13 Then David said to the young man who
told him, "Where *are* you from?" And he
answered, "I *am* the son of an alien, an
Amalekite."
14 And David said to him, "How [R]was it you
were not afraid to put forth your hand to
destroy the LORD's anointed?" Num. 12:8
15 Then [R]David called one of the young
men and said, "Go near, *and* execute him!"
And he struck him so that he died. 2 Sam. 4:10, 12
16 So David said to him, [R]"Your blood *is* on
your own head, for [R]your own mouth has
testified against you, saying, 'I have killed the
LORD's anointed.'" 1 Kin. 2:32–37 • Luke 19:22
17 Then David lamented with this lamentation over Saul and over Jonathan his son,
18 and he told *them* to teach the children of
Judah *the Song of* the Bow; indeed *it is*
written in the Book of [T]Jasher: Lit. *Upright*

19 "The beauty of Israel is slain on your
high places!
How the mighty have fallen!
20 [R]Tell *it* not in Gath, Mic. 1:10
Proclaim *it* not in the streets of
[R]Ashkelon— Jer. 25:20
Lest [R]the daughters of the Philistines
rejoice, Ex. 15:20
Lest the daughters of [R]the
uncircumcised triumph. 1 Sam. 31:4

21 "O [R]mountains of Gilboa, 1 Sam. 31:1
[R]*Let there be* no dew, nor *let there be*
rain upon you, Ezek. 31:15
Nor fields of offerings.
For the shield of the mighty is [T]cast
away there! Lit. *defiled*
The shield of Saul, not [R]anointed with
oil. 1 Sam. 10:1
22 From the blood of the slain,
From the fat of the mighty,
[R]The bow of Jonathan did not turn back,
And the sword of Saul did not return
empty. 1 Sam. 18:4

23 "Saul and Jonathan *were* beloved and
pleasant in their lives,
And in their [R]death they were not
divided; 1 Sam. 31:2–4
They were swifter than eagles,
They were [R]stronger than lions. Judg. 14:18

24 "O daughters of Israel, weep over Saul,
Who clothed you in scarlet, with
luxury;
Who put ornaments of gold on your
apparel.

25 "How the mighty have fallen in the
midst of the battle!
Jonathan *was* slain in your high places.
26 I am distressed for you, my brother
Jonathan;
You have been very pleasant to me;
Your love to me was wonderful,
Surpassing the love of women.

27 "How the mighty have fallen,
And the weapons of war perished!"

CHAPTER 2

David Is Anointed as King over Judah

IT happened after this that David [R]inquired
of the LORD, saying, "Shall I go up to any
of the cities of Judah?" And the LORD said to

him, "Go up." David said, "Where shall I go
up?" And He said, "To Hebron." Judg. 1:1
2 So David went up there, and his two
wives also, Ahinoam the Jezreelitess, and
Abigail the widow of Nabal the Carmelite.
3 And David brought up the men who
were with him, every man with his household. So they dwelt in the cities of Hebron.
4 Then the men of Judah came, and there
they [R]anointed David king over the house of
Judah. And they told David, saying, [R]"The
men of Jabesh Gilead *were the ones* who
buried Saul." 1 Sam. 16:13 • 1 Sam. 31:11–13
5 So David sent messengers to the men of
Jabesh Gilead, and said to them, [R]"You *are*
blessed of the LORD, for you have shown this
kindness to your lord, to Saul, and have
buried him. Ruth 2:20; 3:10
6 "And now may the LORD show kindness
and truth to you. I also will repay you this
kindness, because you have done this thing.
7 "Now therefore, let your hands be
strengthened, and be valiant; for your master
Saul is dead, and also the house of Judah has
anointed me king over them."

Ishbosheth Is Made King over Israel

8 But Abner the son of Ner, commander of
Saul's army, took Ishbosheth the son of Saul
and brought him over to Mahanaim;
9 and he made him king over [R]Gilead, over
the Ashurites, over Jezreel, over Ephraim,
over Benjamin, and over all Israel. Josh. 22:9
10 Ishbosheth, Saul's son, *was* forty years
old when he began to reign over Israel, and
he reigned two years. Only the house of
Judah followed David.
11 And the [T]time that David was king in
Hebron over the house of Judah was seven
years and six months. Lit. *number of days*

David's Victory over Ishbosheth

12 Now Abner the son of Ner, and the
servants of Ishbosheth the son of Saul, went
out from Mahanaim to [R]Gibeon. Josh. 10:2–12
13 And [R]Joab the son of Zeruiah, and the
servants of David, went out and met them by
[R]the pool of Gibeon. So they sat down, one on
one side of the pool and the other on the
other side of the pool. 1 Chr. 2:16; 11:6 • Jer. 41:12
14 Then Abner said to Joab, "Let the young
men now arise and compete before us." And
Joab said, "Let them arise."
15 So they arose and went over by number,
twelve from Benjamin, *followers* of Ishbosheth the son of Saul, and twelve from the
servants of David.
16 And each one grasped his opponent by
the head and *thrust* his sword in his opponent's side; so they fell down together. Therefore that place was called the Field of Sharp
Swords, which *is* in Gibeon.
17 So there was a very fierce battle that
day, and Abner and the men of Israel were
beaten before the servants of David.
18 Now the [R]three sons of Zeruiah were
there: Joab and Abishai and Asahel. And
Asahel *was* [R]*as* fleet of foot [R]as a wild
gazelle. 1 Chr. 2:16 • 1 Chr. 12:8 • Ps. 18:33
19 So Asahel pursued Abner, and in going
he did not turn to the right hand or to the left
from following Abner.
20 Then Abner looked behind him and said,
"*Are* you Asahel?" And he answered, "I *am*."
21 And Abner said to him, "Turn aside to
your right hand or to your left, and lay hold
on one of the young men and take his armor
for yourself." But Asahel would not turn
aside from following him.
22 So Abner said again to Asahel, "Turn
aside from following me. Why should I strike
you to the ground? How then could I face
your brother Joab?"
23 However, he refused to turn aside.
Therefore Abner struck him in the stomach
with the blunt end of the spear, so that the
spear came out of his back; and he fell down
there and died on the spot. So it was *that* as
many as came to the place where Asahel fell
down and died, stood [R]still. 2 Sam. 20:12
24 Joab and Abishai also pursued Abner.
And the sun was going down when they
came to the hill of Ammah, which *is* before
Giah by the road to the Wilderness of Gibeon.
25 Now the children of Benjamin gathered
together behind Abner and became a unit,
and took their stand on top of a hill.
26 Then Abner called to Joab and said,
"Shall the sword devour forever? Do you not
know that it will be bitter in the latter end?
How long will it be then until you tell the
people to return from pursuing their brethren?"
27 And Joab said, "*As* God lives, [T]unless
[R]you had spoken, surely then by morning all
the people would have given up pursuing
their brethren." *if you had not spoken* • 2 Sam. 2:14
28 So Joab blew a trumpet; and all the
people stood still and did not pursue Israel
anymore, nor did they fight anymore.
29 Then Abner and his men went on all that
night through the plain, crossed over the
Jordan, and went through all Bithron; and
they came to Mahanaim.
30 So Joab returned from pursuing Abner.
And when he had gathered all the people
together, there were missing of David's servants nineteen men and Asahel.
31 But the servants of David had struck
down, of Benjamin and Abner's men, three
hundred and sixty men who died.
32 Then they took up Asahel and buried
him in his father's tomb, which *was in* Bethlehem. And Joab and his men went all night,
and they came to Hebron at daybreak.

CHAPTER 3

David's Growth over Ishbosheth

NOW there was a long war between the
house of Saul and the house of David.
But David grew stronger and stronger, and
the house of Saul grew weaker and weaker.
2 Sons were born [R]to David in Hebron: His
firstborn was Amnon [R]by Ahinoam the Jezreelitess; 1 Chr. 3:1–4 • 1 Sam. 25:42, 43
3 his second, [T]Chileab, by Abigail the
widow of Nabal the Carmelite; the third,
Absalom the son of Maacah, the daughter of
Talmai, king of Geshur; *Daniel,* 1 Chr. 3:1
4 the fourth, Adonijah the son of Haggith;
the fifth, Shephatiah the son of Abital;
5 and the sixth, Ithream, by David's wife
Eglah. These were born to David in Hebron.

Abner's Murder

6 Now it was so, while there was war
between the house of Saul and the house of
David, that Abner was strengthening *his hold*
on the house of Saul.
7 And Saul had a concubine, whose name
was Rizpah, the daughter of Aiah. So *Ishbosheth* said to Abner, "Why have you [R]gone in
to my father's concubine?" 2 Sam. 16:21
8 Then Abner became very angry at the
words of Ishbosheth, and said, "*Am* I [R]a dog's
head that belongs to Judah? Today I show
loyalty to the house of Saul your father, to
his brothers, and to his friends, and have not
delivered you into the hand of David; and you
charge me today with a fault concerning this
woman? 1 Sam. 24:14
9 [R]"May God do so to Abner, and more
also, if I do not do for David [R]as the LORD has
sworn to him— 1 Kin. 19:2 • 1 Chr. 12:23
10 "to transfer the kingdom from the
[T]house of Saul, and set up the throne of
David over Israel and over Judah, [R]from Dan
to Beersheba." *family* • 1 Sam. 3:20
11 And he could not answer Abner another
word, because he feared him.
12 Then Abner sent messengers on his behalf to David, saying, "Whose *is* the land?"
saying *also,* "Make your covenant with me,
and indeed my hand *shall be* with you to
bring all Israel to you."
13 And [T]David said, "Good, I will make a
covenant with you. But one thing I require of
you: [R]you shall not see my face unless you
first bring Michal, Saul's daughter, when you
come to see my face." Lit. *he* • Gen. 43:3
14 So David sent messengers to Ishbosheth,
Saul's son, saying, "Give *me* my wife Michal,
whom I betrothed to myself for a hundred
foreskins of the Philistines."
15 And Ishbosheth sent and took her from
her husband, from Paltiel the son of Laish.
16 Then her husband went along with her
to Bahurim, weeping behind her. So Abner
said to him, "Go, return!" And he returned.
17 Now Abner had communicated with the
elders of Israel, saying, "In time past you
were seeking for David *to be* king over you.
18 "Now then, do *it!* [R]For the LORD has
spoken of David, saying, 'By the hand of My
servant David, *I will save My people Israel
from the hand of the Philistines and the hand
of all their enemies.' " 2 Sam. 3:9
19 And Abner also spoke in the hearing of
[R]Benjamin. Then Abner also went to speak in
the hearing of David in Hebron all that
seemed good to Israel and the whole house of
Benjamin. 1 Chr. 12:29
20 So Abner and twenty men with him
came to David at Hebron. And David made a
feast for Abner and the men who *were* with
him.
21 Then Abner said to David, "I will arise
and go, and gather all Israel to my lord the
king, that they may make a covenant with
you, and that you may [R]reign over all that
your heart desires." So David sent Abner
away, and he went in peace. 1 Kin. 11:37
22 At that moment the servants of David
and Joab came from a raid and brought much
[T]spoil with them. But Abner *was* not with
David in Hebron, for he had sent him away,
and he had gone in peace. *booty*
23 When Joab and all the troops that *were*
with him had come, they told Joab, saying,
"Abner the son of Ner came to the king, and
he sent him away, and he has gone in peace."
24 Then Joab came to the king and said,
"What have you done? Look, Abner came to
you; why *is* it *that* you sent him away, and he
has already gone?
25 "Surely you realize that Abner the son of
Ner came to deceive you, to know [R]your
going out and your coming in, and to know
all that you are doing." 1 Sam. 29:6
26 And when Joab had gone from David's
presence, he sent messengers after Abner,
who brought him back from the well of Sirah.
But David did not know *it.*
27 Now when Abner had returned to Hebron, Joab took him aside in the gate to
speak with him privately, and there [T]stabbed
him in the stomach, so that he died for the
blood of Asahel his brother. Lit. *struck*
28 And afterward, when David heard *it,* he
said, "My kingdom and I *are* [T]guiltless before
the LORD forever of the blood of Abner the
son of Ner. *innocent*
29 "Let it rest on the head of Joab and on all
his father's house; and let there never fail to
be in the house of Joab one who has a
discharge or is a leper, who leans on a staff or
falls by the sword, or who lacks bread."

3:18 MT *he;* vss. and many Heb. mss. *I*

30 So Joab and Abishai his brother killed
Abner, because he had killed their brother
[R]Asahel at Gibeon in the battle. 2 Sam. 2:23
31 Then David said to Joab and to all the
people who were with him, [R]"Tear your
clothes, [R]gird yourselves with sackcloth, and
mourn for Abner." And King David followed
the coffin. Josh. 7:6 • Gen. 37:34
32 So they buried Abner in Hebron; and the
king lifted up his voice and wept at the grave
of Abner, and all the people wept.
33 And the king sang *a lament* over Abner
and said:

"Should Abner die as a fool dies?
34 Your hands were not bound
Nor your feet put into fetters;
As a man falls before wicked men, *so*
you fell."

Then all the people wept over him again.
35 And when all the people came to persuade David to eat food while it was still day,
David took an oath, saying, [R]"God do so to
me, and more also, if I taste bread or anything else till the sun goes down!" Ruth 1:17
36 Now all the people took note *of it*, and it
pleased them, since whatever the king did
pleased all the people.
37 For all the people and all Israel understood that day that it had not been the king's
intent to kill Abner the son of Ner.
38 Then the king said to his servants, "Do
you not know that a prince and a great man
has fallen this day in Israel?
39 "And I *am* weak today, though anointed
king; and these men, the sons of Zeruiah, *are*
too harsh for me. The LORD shall repay the
evildoer according to his wickedness."

CHAPTER 4

Ishbosheth's Murder

AND when Saul's son heard that Abner
had died in Hebron, he [T]lost heart, and
all Israel was troubled. Lit. *his hands dropped*
2 Now Saul's son *had* two men *who were*
captains of troops. The name of one *was*
Baanah and the name of the other Rechab,
the sons of Rimmon the Beerothite, of the
children of Benjamin. (For [R]Beeroth also was
[T]*part* of Benjamin, Josh. 18:25 • *considered part of*
3 because the Beerothites fled to [R]Gittaim
and have been sojourners there until this
day.) Neh. 11:33
4 [R]Jonathan, Saul's son, had a son *who
was* lame in *his* feet. He was five years old
when the news about Saul and Jonathan
came from Jezreel; and his nurse took him up
and fled. And it happened, as she made haste
to flee, that he fell and became lame. So his
name *was* Mephibosheth. 2 Sam. 9:3

5 Then the sons of Rimmon the Beerothite,
Rechab and Baanah, set out and came at
about the heat of the day to the [R]house of
Ishbosheth, who was lying on his bed at
noon. 2 Sam. 2:8, 9
6 And they came there, all the way into
the house, *as though* to get wheat, and they
[T]stabbed him in the stomach. Then Rechab
and Baanah his brother escaped. Lit. *struck*
7 For when they came into the house, he
was lying on his bed in his bedroom; then
they struck him and killed him, beheaded him
and took his head, and were all night escaping through the plain.
8 And they brought the head of Ishbosheth to David at Hebron, and said to the
king, "Here is the head of Ishbosheth, the son
of Saul your enemy, who sought your life;
and the LORD has avenged my lord the king
this day of Saul and his descendants."

Judgment on the Murder of Ishbosheth

9 Then David answered Rechab and Baanah his brother, the sons of Rimmon the
Beerothite, and said to them, "*As* the LORD
lives, [R]who has redeemed my life from all
adversity, Gen. 48:16
10 "when [R]someone told me, saying, 'Look,
Saul is dead,' thinking to have brought good
news, I arrested him and had him executed in
Ziklag—the one who *thought* I would give
him a reward for *his* news. 2 Sam. 1:2–16
11 "How much more, when wicked men
have killed a righteous person in his own
house on his bed? Therefore, shall I not now
[R]require his blood at your hand and [T]remove
you from the earth?" [Gen. 9:5, 6] • Lit. *consume you*
12 So David [R]commanded his young men,
and they executed them, cut off their hands
and feet, and hanged *them* by the pool in
Hebron. But they took the head of Ishbosheth and buried *it* in the [R]tomb of Abner in
Hebron. 2 Sam. 1:15 • 2 Sam. 3:32

CHAPTER 5

David Is Anointed to Reign over Israel
1 Chr. 11:1–3

THEN all the tribes of Israel came to David
at Hebron and spoke, saying, "Indeed we
are your bone and your flesh.
2 "Also, in time past, when Saul was king
over us, you were the one who led Israel out
and brought them in; and the LORD said to
you, [R]'You shall shepherd My people Israel,
and be ruler over Israel.' " 1 Sam. 16:1
3 [R]So all the elders of Israel came to the
king at Hebron, [R]and King David made a
covenant with them at Hebron [R]before the
LORD. And they anointed David king over
Israel. 2 Sam. 3:17 • 2 Kin. 11:17 • 1 Sam. 23:18
4 David *was* thirty years old when he
began to reign, *and* he reigned forty years.

5 In Hebron he reigned over Judah [R]seven
years and six months, and in Jerusalem he
reigned thirty-three years over all Israel and
Judah. 2 Sam. 2:11

Conquest of Jerusalem—1 Chr. 11:4–9

6 [R]And the king and his men went to
Jerusalem against [R]the Jebusites, the inhabitants of the land, who spoke to David, saying,
"You shall not come in here; but the blind
and the lame will repel you," thinking, "David cannot come in here." Judg. 1:21 • Josh. 15:63
7 Nevertheless David took the stronghold
of Zion (that *is,* the City of David).
8 Now David said on that day, "Whoever
climbs up by way of the water shaft and
defeats the Jebusites (the lame and the blind,
who are hated by David's soul), [R]*he shall be
chief and captain.*" Therefore they say, "The
blind and the lame shall not come into the
house." 1 Chr. 11:6
9 So David dwelt in the stronghold, and
called it the City of David. Then David built
all around from the Millo and inward.
10 So David went on and became great, and
the LORD God of hosts *was* with him.

Alliance with Tyre—1 Chr. 14:1, 2

11 Then Hiram king of Tyre sent messengers to David, and cedar trees, and carpenters
and masons. And they built David a house.
12 So David knew that the LORD had established him as king over Israel, and that He
had [R]exalted His kingdom for His people
Israel's [R]sake. Num. 24:7 • Is. 45:4

David's Family

13 And [R]David took more concubines and
wives from Jerusalem, after he had come
from Hebron. Also more sons and daughters
were born to David. [Deut. 17:17]
14 Now these *are* the names of those who
were born to him in Jerusalem: [T]Shammua,
Shobab, Nathan, Solomon, *Shimea,* 1 Chr. 3:5
15 Ibhar, Elishua, Nepheg, Japhia,
16 Elishama, Eliada, and Eliphelet.

Conquest of Philistia—1 Chr. 14:9–17

17 [R]Now when the Philistines heard that
they had anointed David king over Israel, all
the Philistines went up to search for David.
And David heard *of it* [R]and went down to the
stronghold. 1 Chr. 11:16 • 2 Sam. 23:14
18 The Philistines also went and deployed
themselves in the Valley of Rephaim.
19 And David inquired of the LORD, saying,
"Shall I go up against the Philistines? Will
You deliver them into my hand?" And the
LORD said to David, "Go up, for I will doubtless deliver the Philistines into your hand."
20 So David went to [R]Baal Perazim, and
David defeated them there; and he said, "The
LORD has broken through my enemies before
me, like a breakthrough of water." Therefore
he called the name of that place [T]Baal Perazim. Is. 28:21 • Lit. *Master of Breakthroughs*
21 And they left their images there, and
David and his men carried them away.
22 [R]Then the Philistines went up once again
and deployed themselves in the Valley of
Rephaim. 1 Chr. 14:13
23 And when [R]David inquired of the LORD,
He said, "You shall not go up; circle around
behind them, and come upon them in front of
the mulberry trees. 2 Sam. 5:19
24 "So it shall be, when you [R]hear the sound
of marching in the tops of the mulberry trees,
then you shall advance quickly. For then [R]the
LORD will go out before you to strike the
camp of the Philistines." 1 Chr. 14:15 • Judg. 4:14
25 And David did so, as the LORD commanded him; and he drove back the Philistines from Geba as far as [R]Gezer. Josh. 16:10

CHAPTER 6

Incorrect Transportation of the Ark
1 Chr. 13:1–14

AGAIN David gathered all *the* choice *men*
of Israel, thirty thousand.
2 And David arose and went with all the
people who *were* with him from Baale Judah
to bring up from there the ark of God, whose
name is called by the Name, the LORD of
Hosts, who dwells *between* the cherubim.
3 So they set the ark of God on a new cart,
and brought it out of the house of Abinadab,
which *was* on the hill; and Uzzah and Ahio,
the sons of Abinadab, drove the new cart.
4 And they brought it out of [R]the house of
Abinadab, which *was* on the hill, accompanying the ark of God; and Ahio went before the
ark. 1 Sam. 7:1
5 Then David and all the house of Israel
[R]played *music* before the LORD on all kinds of
instruments made of fir wood, on harps, on
stringed instruments, on tambourines, on
sistrums, and on cymbals. 1 Sam. 18:6, 7
6 And when they came to [R]Nachon's
threshing floor, Uzzah put out *his* [R]*hand* to
the ark of God and [T]took hold of it, for the
oxen stumbled. 1 Chr. 13:9 • Num. 4:15, 19, 20 • *held it*
7 Then the anger of the LORD was aroused
against Uzzah, and God struck him there for
his [T]error; and he died there by the ark of
God. Or *irreverence*
8 And David became angry because of the
LORD's outbreak against Uzzah; and he called
the name of the place [T]Perez Uzzah to this
day. Lit. *Outburst Against Uzzah*
9 [R]David was afraid of the LORD that day;
and he said, "How can the ark of the LORD
come to me?" Ps. 119:120
10 So David would not move the ark of the
LORD with him into the [R]City of David; but
David took it aside into the house of Obed-
Edom the [R]Gittite. 2 Sam. 5:7 • 1 Chr. 13:13; 26:4–8

11 [R]The ark of the LORD remained in the house of Obed-Edom the Gittite three months. And the LORD [R]blessed Obed-Edom and all his household. 1 Chr. 13:14 • Gen. 30:27; 39:5

Correct Transportation of the Ark
1 Chr. 15:25

12 And it was told King David, saying, "The LORD has blessed the house of Obed-Edom and all that *belongs* to him, because of the ark of God." So David went and brought up the ark of God from the house of Obed-Edom to the City of David with gladness.

David Rejoices over the Ark—1 Chr. 15:26–28

13 And *so* it was, when those bearing the ark of the LORD had gone six paces, that he sacrificed [R]oxen and fatted sheep. 1 Kin. 8:5
14 Then David [R]danced[T] before the LORD with all *his* might; and David *was* wearing a linen ephod. Ps. 30:11; 149:3 • *whirled about*
15 [R]So David and all the house of Israel brought up the ark of the LORD with shouting and with the sound of the trumpet. 1 Chr. 15:28

Michal Despises David—1 Chr. 15:29—16:3

16 And as the ark of the LORD came into the City of David, [R]Michal, Saul's daughter, looked through a window and saw King David leaping and whirling before the LORD; and she despised him in her heart. 2 Sam. 3:14
17 So they brought the ark of the LORD, and set it in [R]its place in the midst of the tabernacle that David had erected for it. Then David offered burnt offerings and peace offerings before the LORD. 1 Chr. 15:1
18 And when David had finished offering burnt offerings and peace offerings, [R]he blessed the people in the name of the LORD of hosts. 1 Kin. 8:14, 15, 55
19 [R]Then he distributed among all the people, among the whole multitude of Israel, both the women and the men, to everyone a loaf of bread, a piece *of meat*, and a cake of raisins. So all the people departed, everyone to his house. 1 Chr. 16:3
20 Then David returned to bless his household. And Michal the daughter of Saul came out to meet David, and said, "How glorious was the king of Israel today, uncovering himself today in the eyes of the maids of his servants, as one of the [R]base fellows [T]shamelessly uncovers himself!" Judg. 9:4 • *openly*
21 So David said to Michal, "*It was* before the LORD, who chose me instead of your father and all his house, to appoint me ruler over the people of the LORD, over Israel. Therefore I will play *music* before the LORD.
22 "And I will be even more undignified than this, and will be humble in my own sight. But as for the maidservants of whom you have spoken, by them I will be held in honor."
23 Therefore Michal the daughter of Saul had no children to the day of her death.

CHAPTER 7

David Is Forbidden to Build God a House
1 Chr. 17:1, 2

NOW it came to pass [R]when the king was dwelling in his house, and the LORD had given him rest from all his enemies all around, 1 Chr. 17:1–27
2 that the king said to Nathan the prophet, "See now, I dwell in a house of cedar, but the ark of God dwells inside tent curtains."
3 Then Nathan said to the king, "Go, do all that *is* in your [R]heart, for the LORD *is* with you." 1 Kin. 8:17, 18

God Promises David an Eternal House
1 Chr. 17:3–15

4 But it happened that night that the word of the LORD came to Nathan, saying,
5 "Go and tell My servant David, 'Thus says the LORD: [R]"Would you build a house for Me to dwell in? 1 Kin. 5:3, 4; 8:19
6 "For I have not dwelt in a house since the time that I brought the children of Israel up from Egypt, even to this day, but have moved about in a tent and in a tabernacle.

7:4–17 The Davidic Covenant—The covenant with David is the fourth of the theocratic covenants (pertaining to the rule of God). In this covenant David is promised three things: (1) a land forever (v. 10); (2) an unending dynasty (vv. 11, 16); and (3) an everlasting kingdom (vv. 13, 16). The birth of Solomon, David's son who is to succeed him, is predicted (v. 12). His particular role is to establish the throne of the Davidic Kingdom forever (v. 13). His throne continues, though his seed is cursed in the person of Jeconiah (Coniah), who was the king under whom the nation was carried captive to Babylon. Jeremiah prophesies that no one whose genealogical descent could be traced back to David through Jeconiah and Solomon would ever sit on David's throne (Page 868—Jer. 22:24–30). Joseph, the legal, but not physical, father of Jesus traces his lineage to David through Jeconiah (Page 1115—Matt. 1:1–17). David, however, had another son, Nathan. His line was not cursed. Mary, the physical mother of Jesus, traces her lineage back to David through Nathan (Page 1195—Luke 3:23–38). Notice the care and the extent to which God goes to keep His word and to preserve its truthfulness. The virgin birth was absolutely essential not only to assure the sinless character of Jesus but also to fulfill the Davidic Covenant. Jesus receives His "blood right" to David's throne through His earthly mother, Mary, and His "legal right" to David's throne through His adoptive earthly father, Joseph. The virgin birth guarantees that one of David's line will sit on David's throne and rule forever, while at the same time preserving intact the curse and restriction on the line of descent through Jeconiah.

Now turn to Page 878—Jer. 31:31–34: The New Covenant.

7 "In all *the places* where I have [R]walked with all the children of Israel, have I ever spoken a word to anyone from the tribes of Israel, whom I commanded [R]to shepherd My people Israel, saying, 'Why have you not built Me a house of cedar?' " ' Lev. 26:11, 12 • 2 Sam. 5:2

8 "Now therefore, thus shall you say to My servant David, 'Thus says the LORD of hosts: [R]"I took you from the sheepfold, from following the sheep, to be ruler over My people, over Israel. 1 Sam. 16:11, 12

9 "And I have been with you wherever you have gone, [R]and have [T]cut off all your enemies from before you, and have made you a great name, like the name of the great *men* who *are* on the earth. 1 Sam. 31:6 • *destroyed*

10 "Moreover I will appoint a place for My people Israel, and will plant them, that they may dwell in a place of their own and move no more; nor shall the sons of wickedness oppress them anymore, as previously,

11 [R]"since the time that I commanded judges *to be* over My people Israel, and have caused you to rest from all your enemies. Also the LORD [T]tells you [R]that He will make you a house. Judg. 2:14–16 • *declares to you* • 2 Sam. 7:27

12 "When your days are fulfilled and you rest with your fathers, I will set up your seed after you, who will come from your body, and I will establish his kingdom.

13 [R]"He shall build a house for My name, and I will [R]establish the throne of his kingdom forever. 1 Kin. 5:5; 8:19 • [Is. 9:7; 49:8]

14 [R]"I will be his Father, and he shall be My son. If he commits iniquity, I will chasten him with the rod of men and with the [T]blows of the sons of men. [Heb. 1:5] • *strokes*

15 "But My mercy shall not depart from him, [R]as I took *it* from Saul, whom I removed from before you. 1 Sam. 15:23, 28; 16:14

16 "And your house and your kingdom shall be established forever before *you. Your throne shall be established forever." ' "

17 According to all these words and according to all this vision, so Nathan spoke to David.

David Praises God—1 Chr. 17:16–27

18 Then King David went in and sat before the LORD; and he said: [R]"Who *am* I, O Lord GOD? And what is my house, that You have brought me this far? Ex. 3:11

19 "And yet this was a small thing in Your sight, O Lord GOD; and You have also spoken of Your servant's house for a great while to come. [R]Is this the manner of man, O Lord GOD? [Is. 55:8, 9]

20 "Now what more can David say to You? For You, Lord GOD, know Your servant.

21 "For Your word's sake, and according to Your own heart, You have done all these great things, to make Your servant know *them.*

22 "Therefore You are great, *O Lord GOD. For [R]*there is* none like You, nor *is there any* God besides You, according to all that we have heard with our [R]ears. Ex. 15:11 • Ex. 10:2

23 "And who *is* like Your people, like Israel, [R]the one nation on the earth whom God went to redeem for Himself as a people, to make for Himself a name— and to do for You great and awesome deeds for Your land—before [R]Your people whom You redeemed for Yourself from Egypt, *from* the nations and their gods? Ps. 147:20 • Deut. 9:26; 33:29

24 "For [R]You have made Your people Israel Your very own people forever; and You, LORD, have become their God. [Deut. 26:18]

25 [R]"And now, O LORD God, the word which You have spoken concerning Your servant and concerning his house, establish *it* forever and do as You have said. Matt. 19:28 ☆

26 "So let Your name be magnified forever, saying, 'The LORD of hosts *is* the God over Israel.' [R]And let the house of Your servant David be established before You. Matt. 25:31 ☆

27 "For You, O LORD of hosts, God of Israel, have revealed *this* to Your servant, saying, 'I will build you a house.' Therefore Your servant found it in his heart to pray this prayer to You.

28 "And now, O Lord GOD, You *are* God, and Your words are true, and You have promised this goodness to Your servant.

29 "Now therefore, let it please You to bless the house of Your servant, that it may continue forever before You; for You, O Lord GOD, have spoken *it*, and with Your blessing let the house of Your servant be blessed [R]forever." 2 Sam. 22:51

CHAPTER 8

David Defeats Philistia—1 Chr. 18:1

AFTER this it came to pass that David [T]attacked the Philistines and subdued them. And David took Metheg Ammah from the hand of the Philistines. Lit. *struck*

David Defeats Moab—1 Chr. 18:2

2 Then [R]he defeated Moab. Forcing them down to the ground, he measured them off with a line. With two lines he measured off those to be put to death, and with one full line those to be kept alive. So the Moabites became David's [R]servants, *and* [R]brought tribute. Num. 24:17 • 2 Sam. 12:31 • 1 Kin. 4:21

David Defeats Zobah and Syria—1 Chr. 18:3–8

3 David also defeated Hadadezer the son of Rehob, king of Zobah, as he went to recover his territory at the River Euphrates.

7:16 LXX *Me* **7:22** Tg., Syr. *O LORD God*

4 David took from him one thousand *chariots*, [T]seven hundred horsemen, and twenty thousand foot soldiers. Also David [R]hamstrung all the chariot horses, except that he spared *enough* of them for one hundred chariots. *seven thousand,* 1 Chr. 18:4 • Josh. 11:6, 9

5 When the Syrians of Damascus came to help Hadadezer king of Zobah, David killed twenty-two thousand of the Syrians.

6 Then David put garrisons in Syria of Damascus; and the Syrians became David's servants, *and* brought tribute. The LORD preserved David wherever he went.

7 And David took [R]the shields of gold that had belonged to the servants of Hadadezer, and brought them to Jerusalem. 1 Kin. 10:16

8 Also from [T]Betah and from [R]Berothai, cities of Hadadezer, King David took a large amount of bronze. *Tibhath,* 1 Chr. 18:8 • Ezek 47:16

David Receives Spoil from His Enemies
1 Chr. 18:9–12

9 When [T]Toi king of [R]Hamath heard that David had defeated all the army of Hadadezer, *Tou,* 1 Chr. 18:9 • 1 Kin. 8:65

10 then Toi sent Joram his son to King David, to greet him and bless him, because he had fought against Hadadezer and defeated him; for Hadadezer had wars with Toi. And *Joram* brought with him articles of silver, articles of gold, and articles of bronze.

11 King David [R]dedicated these to the LORD, along with the silver and gold that he had dedicated from all the nations which he had subdued— 1 Kin. 7:51

12 from *Syria, from Moab, from the people of Ammon, from the [R]Philistines, from Amalek, and from the spoil of Hadadezer the son of Rehob, king of Zobah. 2 Sam. 5:17–25

David's Righteous Rule over Israel
1 Chr. 18:13–17

13 And David made *himself* a name when he returned from killing eighteen thousand *Syrians in [R]the Valley of Salt. 1 Chr. 18:12

14 He also put garrisons in Edom; throughout all Edom he put garrisons, and all the Edomites became David's servants. And the LORD preserved David wherever he went.

15 So David reigned over all Israel; and David administered judgment and justice to all his people.

16 [R]Joab the son of Zeruiah *was* over the army; [R]Jehoshaphat the son of Ahilud *was* recorder; 2 Sam. 19:13; 20:23 • 1 Kin. 4:3

17 Zadok the son of Ahitub and Ahimelech the son of Abiathar *were* the priests; [T]Seraiah *was* the [T]scribe; *Shavsha,* 1 Chr. 18:16 • *secretary*

18 Benaiah the son of Jehoiada *was over* both the Cherethites and the Pelethites; and David's sons were [T]chief ministers. Lit. *priests*

CHAPTER 9

David's Righteous Rule over Mephibosheth

NOW David said, "Is there still anyone who is left of the house of Saul, that I may [R]show him [T]kindness for Jonathan's sake?" 1 Sam. 18:3; 20:14–16 • *covenant faithfulness*

2 And *there was* a servant of the house of Saul whose name *was* [R]Ziba. So when they had called him to David, the king said to him, "*Are* you Ziba?" And he said, "At your service!" 2 Sam. 16:1–4; 19:17, 29

3 Then the king said, "*Is* there not still someone of the house of Saul, to whom I may show [R]the kindness of God?" And Ziba said to the king, "There is still a son of Jonathan *who is* [R]lame in *his* feet." 1 Sam. 20:14 • 2 Sam. 4:4

4 So the king said to him, "Where *is* he?" And Ziba said to the king, "Indeed he *is* in the house of [R]Machir the son of Ammiel, in Lo Debar." 2 Sam. 17:27–29

5 Then King David sent and brought him out of the house of Machir the son of Ammiel, from Lo Debar.

6 Now when Mephibosheth the son of Jonathan, the son of Saul, had come to David, he fell on his face and prostrated himself. Then David said, "Mephibosheth?" And he answered, "Here is your servant!"

7 So David said to him, "Do not fear, for I will surely show you kindness for Jonathan your father's sake, and will restore to you all the land of Saul your grandfather; and you shall eat bread at my table continually."

8 Then he bowed himself, and said, "What *is* your servant, that you should look upon such [R]a dead dog as I?" 2 Sam. 16:9

9 And the king called to Ziba, Saul's servant, and said to him, [R]"I have given to your master's son all that belonged to Saul and to all his house. 2 Sam. 16:4; 19:29

10 "You therefore, and your sons and your servants, shall work the land for him, and you shall bring in *the harvest*, that your master's son may have food to eat. But Mephibosheth your master's son [R]shall eat bread at my table always." Now Ziba had [R]fifteen sons and twenty servants. 2 Sam. 9:7, 11, 13 • 2 Sam. 19:17

11 Then Ziba said to the king, "According to all that my lord the king has commanded his servant, so will your servant do." "As for Mephibosheth," *said the king*, "he shall eat at my table like one of the king's sons."

12 Mephibosheth had a young son [R]whose name *was* Micha. And all who dwelt in the house of Ziba *were* servants of Mephibosheth. 1 Chr. 8:34

13 So Mephibosheth dwelt in Jerusalem, for he ate continually at the king's table. And he was lame in both his feet.

8:12 LXX, Syr., Heb. mss. *Edom*
8:13 LXX, Syr., Heb. mss. *Edomites* and 1 Chr. 18:12

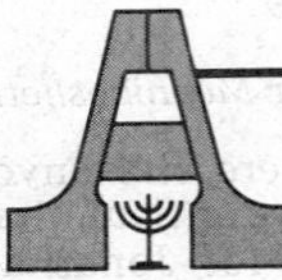

ISRAEL AND THE HITTITES

The Hittites were a people of the ancient world who flourished in Asia Minor and surrounding regions between about 1900 B.C. and 1200 B.C. While the Hittites are mentioned prominently in the Bible, some scholars questioned the existence of these people for many years because there was little physical evidence of their empire. But recent discoveries of Hittite culture by archaeologists have confirmed the accuracy of the biblical accounts.

The Hittite nation, with Hattusa as capital (see photo), eventually spread into northern Syria, then into the land of Canaan. Hittites are mentioned in the Bible during the earliest time of Israel's history.

When Sarah died, Abraham bought a burial cave from Ephron the Hittite (Gen. 23:10–20). Isaac's son Esau took two Hittite women as wives (Gen. 26:34). Several centuries later, the Hittites were included among the groups that would have to be driven out of Canaan before Israel could possess the land (Ex. 3:8; Deut. 7:1).

In David's time, Ahimelech the Hittite was a trusted companion of David during his flight from Saul (1 Sam. 26:6). Uriah the Hittite, Bathsheba's husband, was sent to his death by David to cover up his adultery with Bathsheba (2 Sam. 11:14, 15). Since Uriah was a brave soldier in David's army, this shows that at least some of the Hittites had been assimilated into Israelite culture by this time in their history.

In Solomon's time, Solomon disobeyed God's instructions and married a Hittite woman to seal an alliance with these ancient people (1 Kin. 11:1, 2). This shows how objectionable the Hittite religious system was in God's eyes. The Hittites worshiped many different pagan gods, including several adopted from the Egyptians and the Babylonians. Solomon's marriages became a corrupting influence that pulled the nation of Israel away from worship of the one true God (1 Kin. 11:9–13).

Photo by Howard Vos

Remains of the King Gate in the city wall of Hattusa, ancient capital of the Hittite Empire.

CHAPTER 10

Insult of Ammon—1 Chr. 19:1–5

AND it happened after this that the [R]king of the people of Ammon died, and Hanun his son reigned in his place. 1 Chr. 19:1

2 Then David said, "I will show kindness to Hanun the son of Nahash, as his father showed kindness to me." So David sent by the hand of his servants to comfort him concerning his father. And David's servants came into the land of the people of Ammon.

3 Then the princes of the people of Ammon said to Hanun their lord, "Do you think that David really honors your father because he has sent comforters to you? Has David not *rather* sent his servants to you to search the city, to spy it out, and to overthrow it?"

4 Therefore Hanun took David's servants, shaved off half of their beards, cut off their garments in the middle, [R]at their buttocks, and sent them away. Is. 20:4; 47:2

5 When they told David, he sent to meet them, because the men were greatly [T]ashamed. And the king said, "Wait at Jericho until your beards have grown, and *then* return." *humiliated*

Ammon Is Defeated—1 Chr. 19:6–15

6 So when the people of Ammon saw that they had made themselves repulsive to David, the people of Ammon sent and hired the Syrians of Beth Rehob and the Syrians of Zoba, twenty thousand foot soldiers; and from King Maacah one thousand men, and from Ish-Tob twelve thousand men.

7 Now when David heard *of it,* he sent Joab and all the army of the mighty men.

8 Then the people of Ammon came out and put themselves in battle array at the entrance of the gate. And [R]the Syrians of Zoba, Rehob, Ish-Tob, and Maacah *were* by themselves in the field. 2 Sam. 10:6

9 When Joab saw that the battle line was against him before and behind, he chose some of the choice *men* of Israel and put *them* in battle array against the Syrians.

10 And the rest of the people he put under the command of [R]Abishai his brother, that he might put *them* in battle array against the people of Ammon. 2 Sam. 3:30

11 Then he said, "If the Syrians are too strong for me, then you shall help me. But if the people of Ammon are too strong for you, then I will come and help you.

12 [R]"Be of good courage, and let us [R]be strong for our people and for the cities of our God. And may [R]the LORD do what seems good to Him." Deut. 31:6 • 1 Cor. 16:13 • 1 Sam. 3:18

13 So Joab and the people who *were* with him drew near for the battle against the Syrians, and they fled before him.

14 And when the people of Ammon saw that the Syrians were fleeing, they *also* fled before Abishai, and entered the city. So Joab returned from the people of Ammon and went to [R]Jerusalem. 2 Sam. 11:1

Syria Is Defeated—1 Chr. 19:16–19

15 Now when the Syrians saw that they had been defeated before Israel, they gathered together.

16 Then Hadadezer sent and brought out the Syrians who *were* beyond [T]the River, and they came to Helam. And [T]Shobach the commander of Hadadezer's army *went* before them. The Euphrates • *Shophach,* 1 Chr. 19:16

17 When it was told David, he gathered all Israel, crossed over the Jordan, and came to Helam. And the Syrians set themselves in battle array against David and fought with him.

18 Then the Syrians fled before Israel; and David killed seven hundred charioteers and forty thousand [R]horsemen of the Syrians, and struck Shobach the commander of their army, who died there. 1 Chr. 19:18

19 And when all the kings *who were* servants to Hadadezer saw that they were defeated by Israel, they made peace with Israel and served them. So the Syrians were afraid to help the people of Ammon anymore.

CHAPTER 11

The Sin of Adultery

NOW it came to pass in the spring of the year, at the time when kings go out *to battle,* that [R]David sent Joab and his servants with him, and all Israel; and they destroyed the people of Ammon and besieged Rabbah. But David remained at Jerusalem. 1 Chr. 20:1

2 Then it happened one evening that David arose from his bed and walked on the roof of the king's house. And from the roof he [R]saw a woman bathing, and the woman *was* very beautiful to behold. Gen. 34:2

3 So David sent and inquired about the woman. And *someone* said, "*Is* this not [T]Bathsheba, the daughter of Eliam, the wife of Uriah the Hittite?" *Bathshua,* 1 Chr. 3:5

4 Then David sent messengers, and took her; and she came to him, and [R]he lay with her, for she was cleansed from her impurity; and she returned to her house. [James 1:14, 15]

5 And the woman conceived; so she sent and told David, and said, "I *am* with child."

Uriah Does Not Sleep with Bathsheba

6 Then David sent to Joab, *saying,* "Send me Uriah the Hittite." And Joab sent Uriah to David.

7 When Uriah had come to him, David asked how Joab was doing, and how the

people were doing, and how the war prospered.
8 And David said to Uriah, "Go down to
your house and [R]wash your feet." So Uriah
departed from the king's house, and a gift *of*
food from the king followed him. Gen. 18:4; 19:2
9 But Uriah slept at the [R]door of the king's
house with all the servants of his lord, and
did not go down to his house. 1 Kin. 14:27, 28
10 So when they told David, saying, "Uriah
did not go down to his house," David said to
Uriah, "Did you not come from a journey?
Why did you not go down to your house?"
11 And Uriah said to David, "The ark and
Israel and Judah are dwelling in tents, and
[R]my lord Joab and the servants of my lord are
encamped in the open fields. Shall I then go
to my house to eat and drink, and to lie with
my wife? *As* you live, and *as* your soul lives, I
will not do this thing." 2 Sam. 20:6–22
12 Then David said to Uriah, "Wait here
today also, and tomorrow I will let you
depart." So Uriah remained in Jerusalem that
day and the next.
13 Now when David called him, he ate and
drank before him; and he made him [R]drunk.
And at evening he went out to lie on his bed
[R]with the servants of his lord, but he did not
go down to his house. Gen. 19:33, 35 • 2 Sam. 11:9

David Commands Uriah's Murder

14 Then in the morning it was so that David
[R]wrote a letter to Joab and sent *it* by the hand
of Uriah. 1 Kin. 21:8, 9
15 And he wrote in the letter, saying, "Set
Uriah in the forefront of the [T]hottest battle,
and retreat from him, that he may [R]be struck
down and die." *fiercest* • 2 Sam. 12:9
16 So it happened, while Joab besieged the
city, that he assigned Uriah to a place where
he knew there *were* valiant men.
17 Then the men of the city came out and
fought with Joab. And *some* of the people of
the servants of David fell; and Uriah the
Hittite died also.
18 Then Joab sent and told David all the
things concerning the war,
19 and charged the messenger, saying,
"When you have finished telling the matters
of the war to the king,
20 if it happens that the king's wrath rises,
and he says to you: 'Why did you approach so
near to the city when you fought? Did you
not know that they would shoot from the
wall?
21 'Who struck Abimelech the son of [T]Jer-
ubbesheth? Was it not a woman who cast a
piece of a millstone on him from the wall, so
that he died in Thebez? Why did you go near
the wall?'—then you shall say, 'Your servant
Uriah the Hittite is dead also.' " *Gideon*
22 So the messenger went, and came and
told David all that Joab had sent by him.
23 And the messenger said to David,
"Surely the men prevailed against us and
came out to us in the field; then we drove
them back as far as the entrance of the gate.
24 "The archers shot from the wall at your
servants; and *some* of the king's servants are
dead, and your servant Uriah the Hittite is
dead also."
25 Then David said to the messenger, "Thus
you shall say to Joab: 'Do not let this thing
[T]displease you, for the sword devours one as
well as another. Strengthen your attack
against the city, and overthrow it.' So encourage him." Lit. *be evil in your sight*

David and Bathsheba Marry

26 When the wife of Uriah heard that Uriah
her husband was dead, she mourned for her
husband.
27 And when her mourning was over, David
sent and brought her to his house, and she
[R]became his wife and bore him a son. But the
thing that David had done [R]displeased[T] the
LORD. 2 Sam. 12:9 • 1 Chr. 21:7 • Lit. *was evil in the eyes of*

CHAPTER 12

Prophecy of the Sword

THEN the LORD sent Nathan to David. And
[R]he came to him, and [R]said to him: "There
were two men in one city, one rich and the
other poor. Ps. 51:title • 1 Kin. 20:35–41
2 "The rich *man* had exceedingly many
flocks and herds.
3 "But the poor *man* had nothing, except
one little ewe lamb which he had bought and
nourished; and it grew up together with him
and with his children. It ate of his own food
and drank from his own cup and lay in his
bosom; and it was like a daughter to him.
4 "And a traveler came to the rich man,
who refused to take from his own flock and
from his own herd to prepare one for the
wayfaring man who had come to him; but he
took the poor man's lamb and prepared it for
the man who had come to him."
5 Then David's anger was greatly aroused
against the man, and he said to Nathan, "*As*
the LORD lives, the man who has done this
[T]shall surely die! *deserves to die,* lit. *is a son of death*
6 "And he shall restore [R]fourfold for the
lamb, because he did this thing and because
he had no pity." [Ex. 22:1]
7 Then Nathan said to David, "You *are* the
man! Thus says the LORD God of Israel: 'I
[R]anointed you king over Israel, and I delivered you from the hand of Saul. 1 Sam. 16:13
8 'I gave you your master's house and your
master's wives into your keeping, and gave
you the house of Israel and Judah. And if
that had been too little, I also would have
given you much more!

9 'Why have you despised the commandment of the LORD, to do evil in His sight? [R]You have killed Uriah the Hittite with the sword; you have taken his wife *to be* your wife, and have killed him with the sword of the people of Ammon. 2 Sam. 11:14–17, 27

10 'Now therefore, [R]the sword shall never depart from your house, because you have despised Me, and have taken the wife of Uriah the Hittite to be your wife.' [Amos 7:9]

11 "Thus says the LORD: 'Behold, I will raise up adversity against you from your own house; and I will [R]take your wives before your eyes and give *them* to your neighbor, and he shall lie with your wives in the sight of this sun. 2 Sam. 16:21, 22

12 'For you did *it* secretly, but I will do this thing before all Israel, before the sun.' "

David Repents for His Sin

13 Then David said to Nathan, [R]"I have sinned against the LORD." And Nathan said to David, "The LORD also has [R]put away your sin; you shall not die. 2 Sam. 24:10 • [Mic. 7:18]

14 "However, because by this deed you have given great occasion to the enemies of the LORD [R]to blaspheme, the child also *who is* born to you shall surely die." Is. 52:5

God Takes Away the Son of Adultery

15 Then Nathan departed to his house.
And the [R]LORD struck the child that Uriah's wife bore to David, and it became *very* ill. 1 Sam. 25:38

16 David therefore pleaded with God for the child, and David fasted and went in and [R]lay all night on the ground. 2 Sam. 13:31

17 So the elders of his house arose *and went* to him, to raise him up from the ground. But he would not, nor did he eat food with them.

18 Then on the seventh day it came to pass that the child died. And the servants of David were afraid to tell him that the child was dead. For they said, "Indeed, while the child was *still* alive, we spoke to him, and he would not heed our voice. How can we tell him that the child is dead? He may do some harm!"

19 When David saw that his servants were whispering, David perceived that the child was dead. Therefore David said to his servants, "Is the child dead?" And they said, "He is dead."

20 So David arose from the ground, washed and [R]anointed himself, and changed his clothes; and he went into the house of the LORD and [R]worshiped. Then he went to his own house; and when he requested, they set food before him, and he ate. Ruth 3:3 • Job 1:20

21 Then his servants said to him, "What *is* this that you have done? You fasted and wept for the child *while he was* alive, but when the child died, you arose and ate food."

22 So he said, "While the child was *still* alive, I fasted and wept; [R]for I said, 'Who can tell *whether* *the LORD will be gracious to me, that the child may live?' Jon. 3:9

23 "But now he is dead; why should I fast? Can I bring him back again? I shall go to him, but he shall not return to me."

God Gives Another Son

24 Then David comforted Bathsheba his wife, and went in to her and lay with her. So [R]she bore a son, and he called his name Solomon. And the LORD loved him. Matt. 1:6

25 And He sent *word* by the hand of Nathan the prophet; so *he called his name *Jedidiah, because of the LORD.

Joab's Loyalty to David—1 Chr. 20:1–3

26 Now [R]Joab fought against [R]Rabbah of the people of Ammon, and took the royal city. 1 Chr. 20:1 • Deut. 3:11

27 And Joab sent messengers to David, and said, "I have fought against Rabbah, and I have taken the city's water *supply*.

28 "Now therefore, gather the rest of the people together and encamp against the city and take it, lest I take the city and it be called after my name."

29 So David gathered all the people together and went to Rabbah, fought against it, and took it.

30 Then he took their king's crown from his head. Its weight *was* a [T]talent of gold, with precious stones. And it was *set* on David's head. Also he brought out the spoil of the city in great abundance. 91 lb. or $5,760,000

31 And he brought out the people who *were* in it, and put *them to work* with saws and iron picks and iron axes, and made them cross over to the brick works. So he did with all the cities of the people of Ammon. Then David and all the people returned to Jerusalem.

CHAPTER 13

Incest in David's House

NOW after this it was so that Absalom the son of David had a lovely sister, whose name *was* [R]Tamar; and [R]Amnon the son of David loved her. 1 Chr. 3:9 • 2 Sam. 3:2

2 Amnon was so distressed over his sister Tamar that he became sick; for she *was* a virgin. And it was improper for Amnon to do anything to her.

3 But Amnon had a friend whose name *was* Jonadab the son of Shimeah, David's brother. Now Jonadab *was* a very crafty man.

12:22 Heb. mss., Syr. *God*
12:25 Qr., Syr., Tg., Heb. mss. *she*
12:25 Lit. *Beloved of the LORD*

4 And he said to him, "Why *are* you, the
king's son, becoming thinner day after day?
Will you not tell me?" And Amnon said to
him, "I love Tamar, my brother Absalom's
sister."
5 So Jonadab said to him, "Lie down on
your bed and pretend to be ill. And when
your father comes to see you, say to him,
'Please let my sister Tamar come and give me
food, and prepare the food in my sight, that I
may see *it* and eat it from her hand.' "
6 Then Amnon lay down and pretended to
be ill; and when the king came to see him,
Amnon said to the king, "Please let Tamar
my sister come and [R]make a couple of cakes
for me in my sight, that I may eat from her
hand." Gen. 18:6
7 And David sent home to Tamar, saying,
"Now go to your brother Amnon's house, and
prepare food for him."
8 So Tamar went to her brother Amnon's
house; and he was lying down. Then she took
flour and kneaded *it*, made cakes in his sight,
and baked the cakes.
9 And she took the pan and placed *them*
out before him, but he refused to eat. Then
Amnon said, "Have everyone go out from
me." And they all went out from him.
10 Then Amnon said to Tamar, "Bring the
food into the bedroom, that I may eat from
your hand." And Tamar took the cakes which
she had made, and brought *them* to Amnon
her brother in the bedroom.
11 Now when she had brought *them* to him
to eat, [R]he took hold of her and said to her,
"Come, lie with me, my sister." Gen. 39:12
12 And she answered him, "No, my brother,
do not [T]force me, for [R]no such thing should be
done in Israel. Do not do this disgraceful
thing! Lit. *humble me* • [Lev. 18:9–11; 20:17]
13 "And I, where could I take my shame?
And as for you, you would be like one of the
fools in Israel. Now therefore, please speak to
the king; [R]for he will not withhold me from
you." Gen. 20:12
14 However, he would not heed her voice;
and being stronger than she, he [R]forced her
and lay with her. 2 Sam. 12:11
15 Then Amnon hated her [T]exceedingly, so
that the hatred with which he hated her *was*
greater than the love with which he had
loved her. And Amnon said to her, "Arise, be
gone!" *with a very great hatred*
16 And she said to him, "No, indeed! This
evil of sending me away *is* worse than the
other that you did to me." But he would not
listen to her.
17 Then he called his servant who attended
him, and said, "Here! Put this *woman* out,
away from me, and bolt the door behind her."
18 Now she had on [R]a robe of many colors,
for the king's virgin daughters wore such
apparel. And his servant put her out and
bolted the door behind her. Gen. 37:3
19 Then Tamar put [R]ashes on her head, and
tore her robe of many colors that *was* on her,
and [R]laid her hand on her head and went
away crying bitterly. Josh. 7:6 • Jer. 2:37
20 And Absalom her brother said to her,
"Has Amnon your brother been with you?
But now hold your peace, my sister. He *is*
your brother; do not take this thing to heart."
So Tamar remained desolate in her brother
Absalom's house.

Amnon Is Murdered

21 But when King David heard of all these
things, he was very angry.
22 And Absalom spoke to his brother Amnon [R]neither good nor bad. For Absalom
[R]hated Amnon, because he had forced his
sister Tamar. Gen. 24:50; 31:24 • [Lev. 19:17, 18]
23 And it came to pass, after two full years,
that Absalom [R]had sheepshearers in Baal
Hazor, which *is* near Ephraim; so Absalom
invited all the king's sons. 1 Sam. 25:4
24 Then Absalom came to the king and said,
"Kindly note, your servant has sheepshearers; please, let the king and his servants go
with your servant."
25 But the king said to Absalom, "No, my
son, let us not all go now, lest we be a burden
to you." Then he urged him, but he would not
go; and he blessed him.
26 Then Absalom said, "If not, please let my
brother Amnon go with us." And the king
said to him, "Why should he go with you?"
27 But Absalom urged him; so he let Amnon
and all the king's sons go with him.
28 Now Absalom had commanded his servants, saying, "Watch now, when Amnon's
heart is merry with wine, and when I say to
you, 'Strike Amnon!' then kill him. Do not be
afraid. Have I not commanded you? Be courageous and [T]valiant." Lit. *sons of valor*
29 So the servants of Absalom [R]did to Amnon as Absalom had commanded. Then all
the king's sons arose, and each one got on
[R]his mule and fled. 2 Sam. 12:10 • 2 Sam. 18:9
30 And it came to pass, while they were on
the way, that news came to David, saying,
"Absalom has killed all the king's sons, and
not one of them is left!"
31 So the king arose and tore his garments
and [R]lay on the ground, and all his servants
stood by with their clothes torn. 2 Sam. 12:16
32 Then [R]Jonadab the son of Shimeah, David's brother, answered and said, "Let not my
lord suppose *that* they have killed all the
young men, the king's sons, for only Amnon
is dead. For by the command of Absalom this
has been determined from the day that he
forced his sister Tamar. 2 Sam. 13:3–5
33 "Now therefore, [R]let not my lord the king
take the thing to his heart, to think that all

the king's sons are dead. For only Amnon is
dead." 2 Sam. 19:19
34 Then Absalom fled. And the young man
who was keeping watch lifted his eyes and
looked, and there, many people were coming
from the road on the hillside behind him.
35 And Jonadab said to the king, "Look, the
king's sons are coming; as your servant said,
so it is."
36 So it was, as soon as he had finished
speaking, that the king's sons indeed came,
and they lifted up their voice and wept. Also
the king and all his servants wept very bitterly.

Flight of Absalom

37 But Absalom fled and went to Talmai the
son of Ammihud, king of Geshur. And *David*
mourned for his son every day.
38 So Absalom fled and went to [R]Geshur,
and was there three years. 2 Sam. 14:23, 32; 15:8
39 And King David longed to go to Absalom. For he had been [R]comforted concerning
Amnon, because he was dead. 2 Sam. 12:19, 23

CHAPTER 14

Return of Absalom

SO Joab the son of Zeruiah perceived that
the king's heart *was* concerned [R]about
Absalom. 2 Sam. 13:39
2 And Joab sent to Tekoa and brought
from there a wise woman, and said to her,
"Please pretend to be a mourner, [R]and put on
mourning apparel; do not anoint yourself
with oil, but act like a woman who has been
mourning a long time for the dead. Ruth 3:3
3 "Go to the king and speak to him in this
manner." So Joab [R]put the words in her
mouth. 2 Sam. 14:19
4 And when the woman of Tekoa *spoke
to the king, she [R]fell on her face to the
ground and prostrated herself, and said,
[R]"Help, O king!" 1 Sam. 20:41; 25:23 • 2 Kin. 6:26, 28
5 Then the king said to her, "What trou-
bles you?" And she answered, [R]"Indeed I *am*
a widow, my husband is dead. [Zech. 7:10]
6 "Now your maidservant had two sons;
and the two fought with each other in the
field, and *there was* no one to part them, but
the one struck the other and killed him.
7 "And now the whole family has risen up
against your maidservant, and they said,
'Deliver him who struck his brother, that we
may execute him [R]for the life of his brother
whom he killed; and we will destroy the heir
also.' So they would extinguish my ember
that is left, and leave to my husband *neither*
name nor remnant on the earth." Deut. 19:12, 13
8 Then the king said to the woman, "Go to
your house, and I will give orders concerning
you."
9 And the woman of Tekoa said to the
king, "My lord, O king, *let* the [T]iniquity *be* on
me and on my father's house, and the king
and his throne *be* guiltless." *guilt*
10 So the king said, "Whoever says *anything* to you, bring him to me, and he shall
not touch you anymore."
11 Then she said, "Please let the king remember the LORD your God, and do not
permit the avenger of blood to destroy anymore, lest they destroy my son." And he said,
[R]"*As* the LORD lives, not one hair of your son
shall fall to the ground." 1 Sam. 14:45
12 Then the woman said, "Please, let your
maidservant speak *another* word to my lord
the king." And he said, "Say on."
13 And the woman said: "Why then have
you schemed such a thing against [R]the people
of God? For the king speaks this thing as one
who is guilty, *in that* the king does not bring
his banished one home again. Judg. 20:2
14 "For we [R]will surely die and *become* like
water spilled on the ground, which cannot be
gathered up again. Yet God does not [R]take
away a life; but He [R]devises means, so that
His banished ones are not [T]expelled from
Him. [Heb. 9:27] • Job 34:19 • Num. 35:15 • *cast out*
15 "Now therefore, I have come to speak of
this thing to my lord the king because the
people have made me afraid. And your maidservant said, 'I will now speak to the king; it
may be that the king will perform the request
of his maidservant.
16 'For the king will hear and deliver his
maidservant from the hand of the man *who
would* destroy me and my son together from
the [R]inheritance of God.' Deut. 32:9
17 "Your maidservant said, 'The word of my
lord the king will now be comforting; for [R]as
the angel of God, so *is* my lord the king in
[R]discerning good and evil. And may the LORD
your God be with you.' " 2 Sam. 19:27 • 1 Kin. 3:9
18 Then the king answered and said to the
woman, "Please do not hide from me anything that I ask you." And the woman said,
"Please, let my lord the king speak."
19 And the king said, "*Is* the hand of Joab
with you in all this?" And the woman answered and said, "*As* you live, my lord the
king, no one can turn to the right hand or to
the left from anything that my lord the king
has spoken. For your servant Joab commanded me, and [R]he put all these words in
the mouth of your maidservant. 2 Sam. 14:3
20 "To bring about this change of affairs
your servant Joab has done this thing; but
my lord *is* wise, [R]according to the wisdom of
the angel of God, to know all *things* that *are*
in the earth." 2 Sam. 14:17; 19:27
21 And the king said to Joab, "All right, I
have granted this thing. Go therefore, bring
back the young man Absalom."

14:4 LXX, Syr., Vg., Heb. mss. *came*

22 Then Joab fell to the ground on his face
and bowed himself, and [T]thanked the king.
And Joab said, "Today your servant knows
that I have found favor in your sight, my
lord, O king, in that the king has fulfilled the
request of his servant." Lit. *blessed*
23 So Joab arose [R]and went to Geshur, and
brought Absalom to Jerusalem. 2 Sam. 13:37, 38
24 And the king said, "Let him return to his
own house, but [R]do not let him see my face."
So Absalom returned to his own house, but
did not see the king's face. 2 Sam. 3:13

Deceit of Absalom

25 Now in all Israel there was no one who
was praised as much as Absalom for his good
looks. [R]From the sole of his foot to the crown
of his head there was no blemish in him. Is. 1:6
26 And when he cut the hair of his head—at
the end of every year he cut *it* because it was
heavy on him—when he cut it, he weighed
the hair of his head at [T]two hundred shekels
according to the king's standard. 5 lb.
27 To Absalom were born three sons, and
one daughter whose name *was* Tamar. She
was a woman of beautiful appearance.
28 And Absalom dwelt two full years in
Jerusalem, but did not see the king's face.
29 Therefore Absalom sent for Joab, to send
him to the king, but he would not come to
him. And when he sent again the second
time, he would not come.
30 So he said to his servants, "See, Joab's
field is near mine, and he has barley there; go
and set it on fire." And Absalom's servants
set the field on fire.
31 Then Joab arose and came to Absalom's
house, and said to him, "Why have your
servants set my field on fire?"
32 And Absalom answered Joab, "Look, I
sent to you, saying, 'Come here, so that I may
send you to the king, to say, "Why have I
come from Geshur? *It would be* better for me
to be there still."' Now therefore, let me see
the king's face; but [R]if there is *any* iniquity in
me, let him execute me." 1 Sam. 20:8
33 So Joab went to the king and told him.
And when he had called for Absalom, he
came to the king and bowed himself on his
face to the ground before the king. Then the
king [R]kissed Absalom. Luke 15:20

CHAPTER 15

AFTER this it happened that Absalom
provided himself with chariots and
horses, and fifty men to run before him.
2 Now Absalom would rise early and stand
beside the way to the gate. *So* it was, whenever anyone who had a lawsuit[T] came to the
king for a decision, that Absalom would call
to him and say, "What city *are* you from?"
And he would say, "Your servant *is* from
such and such a tribe of Israel." *controversy*
3 Then Absalom would say to him, "Look,
your case *is* good and right; but *there is* no
[T]deputy of the king to hear you." Lit. *listener*
4 Moreover Absalom would say, [R]"Oh, that
I were made judge in the land, and everyone
who has any suit or cause would come to me;
then I would give him justice." Judg. 9:29
5 And *so* it was, whenever anyone came
near *him* to bow down to him, that he would
put out his hand and take him and kiss him.
6 In this manner Absalom acted toward all
Israel who came to the king for judgment.
[R]So Absalom stole the hearts of the men of
Israel. [Rom. 16:18]

Rebellion of Absalom

7 And it came to pass [R]after *forty years
that Absalom said to the king, "Please, let me
go to [R]Hebron and pay the vow which I
vowed to the LORD. [Deut. 23:21] • 2 Sam. 3:2, 3
8 "For your servant vowed a vow [R]while I
dwelt at Geshur in Syria, saying, 'If the LORD
indeed brings me back to Jerusalem, then I
will serve the LORD.'" 2 Sam. 13:38
9 And the king said to him, "Go in peace."
So he arose and went to Hebron.
10 Then Absalom sent spies throughout all
the tribes of Israel, saying, "As soon as you
hear the sound of the trumpet, then you shall
say, 'Absalom [R]reigns in Hebron!'" 1 Kin. 1:34
11 And with Absalom went two hundred
men from Jerusalem *who were* [R]invited, and
they [R]went along innocently and did not
know anything. 1 Sam. 16:3, 5 • Gen. 20:5
12 Then Absalom sent for Ahithophel the
Gilonite, [R]David's counselor, from his city,
namely from [R]Giloh, while he offered sacrifices. And the conspiracy grew strong, for the
people with Absalom [R]continually increased
in number. 1 Chr. 27:33 • Josh. 15:51 • Ps. 3:1

Flight of David

13 And a messenger came to David, saying,
[R]"The hearts of the men of Israel are [T]with
Absalom." Judg. 9:3 • Lit. *after*
14 So David said to all his servants who
were with him at Jerusalem, "Arise, and let
us [R]flee; or *else* we shall not escape from
Absalom. Make haste to depart, lest he overtake us suddenly and bring disaster upon us,
and strike the city with the edge of the
sword." Ps. 3:title
15 And the king's servants said to the king,
"We *are* your servants, *ready to do* whatever
my lord the king commands."
16 Then the king went out with all his
household after him. But the king left ten
women, concubines, to keep the house.

15:7 LXX mss., Syr., Josephus *four*

17 And the king went out with all the people after him, and stopped at the outskirts.
18 Then all his servants passed [T]before him;
and all the Cherethites, all the Pelethites, and
all the Gittites, [R]six hundred men who had
followed him from Gath, passed before the
king. Lit. *by his hand* • 1 Sam. 23:13; 25:13; 30:1, 9
19 And the king said to [R]Ittai the Gittite,
"Why are you also going with us? Return
and remain with the king. For you *are* a
foreigner and also an exile from your own
place. 2 Sam. 18:2
20 "In fact, you came *only* yesterday.
Should I make you wander up and down with
us today, since I go [R]I know not where?
Return, and take your brethren back. Mercy
and truth *be* with you." 1 Sam. 23:13
21 And Ittai answered the king and said,
[R]"*As* the LORD lives, and *as* my lord the king
lives, surely in whatever place my lord the
king shall be, whether in death or life, even
there also your servant will be." Ruth 1:16, 17
22 So David said to Ittai, "Go, and cross
over." Then Ittai the Gittite and all his men
and all the little ones who *were* with him
crossed over.
23 And all the country wept with a loud
voice, and all the people crossed over. The
king himself also crossed over the Brook
Kidron, and all the people crossed over
toward the way of the wilderness.
24 There was [R]Zadok also, and all the Levites with him, bearing the [R]ark of the covenant of God. And they set down the ark of
God, and [R]Abiathar went up until all the
people had finished crossing over from the
city. 2 Sam. 8:17 • Num. 4:15 • 1 Sam. 22:20
25 Then the king said to Zadok, "Carry the
ark of God back into the city. If I find favor
in the eyes of the LORD, He [R]will bring me
back and show me *both* it and [R]His habitation. [Ps. 43:3] • Ex. 15:13
26 "But if He says thus: 'I have no [R]delight
in you,' here I am, [R]let Him do to me as seems
good to Him." Num. 14:8 • 1 Sam. 3:18
27 The king also said to Zadok the priest,
"*Are* you *not* a seer? Return to the city in
peace, and your two sons with you, Ahimaaz
your son, and Jonathan the son of Abiathar.
28 "See, [R]I will wait in the plains of the
wilderness until word comes from you to
inform me." 2 Sam. 17:16
29 Therefore Zadok and Abiathar carried
the ark of God back to Jerusalem. And they
remained there.
30 So David went up by the ascent of the
Mount of Olives, and wept as he went up; and
he had his head covered and went [R]barefoot.
And all the people who *were* with him [R]cov-
ered their heads and went up, [R]weeping as
they went up. Is. 20:2–4 • Jer. 14:3, 4 • [Ps. 126:6]
31 Then *someone* told David, saying,
[R]"Ahithophel *is* among the conspirators with
Absalom." And David said, "O LORD, I pray,
[R]turn the counsel of Ahithophel into foolishness!" Ps. 3:1, 2; 55:12 • 2 Sam. 16:23; 17:14, 23
32 Now it happened when David had come
to the top *of the mountain*, where he worshiped God, that there was Hushai the [R]Arch-
ite, coming to meet him [R]with his robe torn
and dust on his head. Josh. 16:2 • 2 Sam. 1:2
33 David said to him, "If you go on with me,
then you will become a burden to me.
34 "But if you return to the city, and say to
Absalom, [R]'I will be your servant, O king; *just*
as I *have been* your father's servant previously, so I *will* now also *be* your servant,'
then you may defeat the counsel of Ahithophel for me. 2 Sam. 16:19
35 "And *do* you not *have* Zadok and Abiathar the priests with you there? Therefore it
will be *that* whatever you hear from the
king's house, you shall tell to [R]Zadok and
Abiathar the priests. 2 Sam. 17:15, 16
36 "Indeed *they have* there with them their
two sons, Ahimaaz, Zadok's *son*, and Jonathan, Abiathar's *son*; and by them you shall
send me everything you hear."
37 So Hushai, David's friend, went into the
city. And Absalom came into Jerusalem.

CHAPTER 16

WHEN David was a little past the top *of*
the mountain, there was [R]Ziba the servant of Mephibosheth, who met him with a
couple of saddled donkeys, and on them two
hundred *loaves* of bread, one hundred clusters of raisins, one hundred summer fruits,
and a skin of wine. 2 Sam. 9:2; 19:17, 29
2 And the king said to Ziba, "What do you
mean to do with these?" So Ziba said, "The
donkeys *are* for the king's household to ride
on, the bread and summer fruit for the young
men to eat, and the wine for those who are
faint in the wilderness to drink."
3 Then the king said, "And where *is* your
master's son?" And Ziba said to the king,
"Indeed he is staying in Jerusalem, for he
said, 'Today the house of Israel will restore
the kingdom of my father to me.'"
4 So the king said to Ziba, "Here, all that
belongs to Mephibosheth *is* yours." And Ziba
said, "I humbly bow before you, *that* I may
find favor in your sight, my lord, O king!"
5 Now when King David came to Bahurim,
there was a man from the family of the house
of Saul, whose name *was* Shimei the son of
Gera, coming from there. He came out, cursing continuously as he came.
6 And he threw stones at David and at all
the servants of King David. And all the
people and all the mighty men *were* on his
right hand and on his left.

7 Also Shimei said thus when he cursed: "Come out! Come out! You bloodthirsty man, [R]you [T]rogue! Deut. 13:13 • *worthless man*

8 "The LORD has [R]brought upon you all the blood of the house of Saul, in whose place you have reigned; and the LORD has delivered the kingdom into the hand of Absalom your son. So now you *are caught* in your own evil, because you are a [T]bloodthirsty man!" Judg. 9:24, 56, 57 • Lit. *man of bloodshed*

9 Then Abishai the son of Zeruiah said to the king, "Why should this [R]dead dog [R]curse my lord the king? Please, let me go over and take off his head!" 2 Sam. 9:8 • Ex. 22:28

10 And the king said, "What have I to do with you, you sons of Zeruiah? So let him curse, because [R]the LORD has said to him, 'Curse David.' [R]Who then shall say, 'Why have you done so?' " [Lam. 3:38] • [Rom. 9:20]

11 And David said to Abishai and all his servants, "See how [R]my son who [R]came from my own body seeks my life. How much more now *may this* Benjamite? Let him alone, and let him curse; for so the LORD has ordered him. 2 Sam. 12:11 • Gen. 15:4

12 "It may be that the LORD will look on my *affliction, and that the LORD will repay me with good for his cursing this day."

13 And as David and his men went along the road, Shimei went along the hillside opposite him and cursed as he went, threw stones at him and kicked up dust.

14 Now the king and all the people who *were* with him became weary; so they refreshed themselves there.

Reign of Absalom

15 Meanwhile [R]Absalom and all the people, the men of Israel, came to Jerusalem; and Ahithophel *was* with him. 2 Sam. 15:12, 37

16 And so it was, when Hushai the Archite, [R]David's friend, came to Absalom, that [R]Hushai said to Absalom, "*Long* live the king! *Long* live the king!" 2 Sam. 15:37 • 2 Sam. 15:34

17 So Absalom said to Hushai, "*Is* this your loyalty to your friend? [R]Why did you not go with your friend?" 2 Sam. 19:25

18 And Hushai said to Absalom, "No, but whom the LORD and this people and all the men of Israel choose, his I will be, and with him I will remain.

19 "Furthermore, [R]whom should I serve? *Should I* not *serve* in the presence of his son? As I have served in your father's presence, so will I be in your presence." 2 Sam. 15:34

20 Then Absalom said to [R]Ahithophel, "Give counsel as to what we should do." 2 Sam. 15:12

21 And Ahithophel said to Absalom, "Go in to your father's [R]concubines, whom he has left to keep the house; and all Israel will hear that you [R]are abhorred by your father. Then [R]the hands of all who are with you will be strong." 2 Sam. 15:16; 20:3 • Gen. 34:30 • 2 Sam. 2:7

22 So they pitched a tent for Absalom on the top of the house, and Absalom went in to his father's concubines [R]in the sight of all Israel. 2 Sam. 12:11, 12

23 And the counsel of Ahithophel, which he gave in those days, *was* as if one had inquired at the oracle of God. So *was* all the counsel of Ahithophel [R]both with David and with Absalom. 2 Sam. 15:12

CHAPTER 17

MOREOVER Ahithophel said to Absalom, "Now let me choose twelve thousand men, and I will arise and pursue David tonight.

2 "I will come upon him while he *is* weary and weak, and make him [T]afraid. And all the people who *are* with him will flee, and I will [R]strike only the king. *tremble with fear* • Zech. 13:7

3 "Then I will bring back all the people to you. When all return except the man whom you seek, *then* all the people will be at peace."

4 And the saying pleased Absalom and all the [R]elders of Israel. 2 Sam. 5:3; 19:11

5 Then Absalom said, "Now call Hushai the Archite also, and let us hear what he [R]says too." 2 Sam. 15:32–34

6 And when Hushai came to Absalom, Absalom spoke to him, saying, "Ahithophel has spoken in this manner. Shall we do as he says? If not, speak up."

7 So Hushai said to Absalom: "The counsel that Ahithophel has given *is* not good at this time."

8 "For," said Hushai, "you know your father and his men, that they *are* mighty men, and they *are* enraged in their minds, like [R]a bear robbed of her cubs in the field; and your father *is* a man of war, and will not camp with the people. Hos. 13:8

9 "Surely by now he is hidden in some pit, or in some *other* place. And it will be, when some of them are overthrown at the first, that whoever hears *it* will say, 'There is a slaughter among the people who follow Absalom.'

10 "And even he *who is* valiant, whose heart *is* like the heart of a lion, will [R]melt completely. For all Israel knows that your father *is* a mighty man, and *those* who *are* with him *are* valiant men. Josh. 2:11

11 "Therefore I counsel that all Israel be fully gathered to you, [R]from Dan to Beersheba, [R]like the sand that *is* by the sea for multitude, and that you go to battle in person. 2 Sam. 3:10 • Gen. 22:17

12 "So we will come upon him in some place where he may be found, and we will fall on him as the dew falls on the ground. And of

16:12 MT *iniquity*

him and all the men who *are* with him there
shall not be left so much as one.
13 "Moreover, if he has withdrawn into a
city, then all Israel shall bring ropes to that
city; and we will pull it into the river, until
there is not one small stone found there."
14 So Absalom and all the men of Israel
said, "The counsel of Hushai the Archite *is*
better than the counsel of Ahithophel." For
the LORD had purposed to defeat the good
counsel of Ahithophel, to the intent that the
LORD might bring disaster on Absalom.
15 Then Hushai said to Zadok and Abiathar
the priests, "Thus and so Ahithophel counseled Absalom and the elders of Israel, and
thus and so I have counseled.
16 "Now therefore, send quickly and tell
David, saying, 'Do not spend this night in the
plains of the wilderness, but speedily cross
over, lest the king and all the people who *are*
with him be swallowed up.'"
17 Now Jonathan and Ahimaaz [R]stayed at
[R]En Rogel, for they dared not be seen coming
into the city; so a maidservant would come
and tell them, and they would go and tell
King David. Josh. 2:4–6 • Josh. 15:7; 18:16
18 Nevertheless a lad saw them, and told
Absalom. But both of them went away
quickly and came to a man's house [R]in Bahurim, who had a well in his court; and they
went down into it. 2 Sam. 3:16; 16:5
19 [R]Then the woman took and spread a
covering over the well's mouth, and spread
ground grain on it; and the thing was not
known. Josh. 2:4–6
20 And when Absalom's servants came to
the woman at the house, they said, "Where
are Ahimaaz and Jonathan?" So [R]the woman
said to them, "They have gone over the water
brook." And when they had searched and
could not find *them*, they returned to Jerusalem. Josh. 2:3–5
21 Now it came to pass, after they had
departed, that they came up out of the well
and went and told King David, and said to
David, [R]"Arise and cross over the water
quickly. For thus has Ahithophel counseled
against you." 2 Sam. 17:15, 16
22 So David and all the people who *were*
with him arose and crossed over the Jordan.
By morning light not one of them was left
who had not gone over the Jordan.
23 Now when Ahithophel saw that his
counsel was not followed, he saddled
his donkey, and arose and went home to his
house, to his city. Then he put his household
in order, and hanged himself, and died; and
he was buried in his father's tomb.
24 Then David went to [R]Mahanaim. And
Absalom crossed over the Jordan, he and all
the men of Israel with him. 2 Sam. 2:8; 19:32
25 And Absalom made [R]Amasa captain of
the army instead of Joab. This Amasa *was*
the son of a man whose name *was* [T]Jithra, an
Israelite, who had gone in to [R]Abigail the
daughter of Nahash, sister of Zeruiah, Joab's
mother. 1 Kin. 2:5, 32 • *Jether,* 1 Chr. 2:17 • 1 Chr. 2:16
26 So Israel and Absalom encamped in the
land of Gilead.
27 Now it happened, when David had come
to Mahanaim, that Shobi the son of Nahash
from Rabbah of the people of Ammon, Machir the son of Ammiel from Lo Debar, and
Barzillai the Gileadite from Rogelim,
28 brought beds and basins, earthen vessels
and wheat, barley and flour, parched *grain*
and beans, lentils and parched *seeds,*
29 honey and curds, sheep and cheese of the
herd, for David and the people who *were* with
him to eat. For they said, "The people are
hungry and weary and thirsty [R]in the wilderness." 2 Sam. 16:2, 14

CHAPTER 18

Absalom's Murder

AND David [T]numbered the people who
were with him, and [R]set captains of
thousands and captains of hundreds over
them. Lit. *attended to* • Ex. 18:25
2 Then David sent out one third of the
people under the hand of Joab, [R]one third
under the hand of Abishai the son of Zeruiah,
Joab's brother, and one third under the hand
of [R]Ittai the Gittite. And the king said to the
people, "I also will surely go out with you
myself." Judg. 7:16 • 2 Sam. 15:19–22
3 [R]But the people answered, "You shall not
go out. For if we flee away, they will not care
about us; nor if half of us die, will they care
about us. But *you are* worth ten thousand of
us now. For you are now more help to us in
the city." 2 Sam. 21:17
4 So the king said to them, "Whatever
seems best to you I will do." So the king
stood beside the gate, and all the people went
out by hundreds and by thousands.
5 Now the king had commanded Joab,
Abishai, and Ittai, saying, "*Deal* gently for
my sake with the young man Absalom." And
all the people heard when the king gave all
the captains orders concerning Absalom.
6 So the people went out into the field of
battle against Israel. And the battle was in
the [R]woods of Ephraim. Josh. 17:15, 18
7 The people of Israel were overthrown
there before the servants of David, and a
great slaughter of twenty thousand *men* took
place there that day.
8 For the battle there was scattered over
the face of the whole countryside, and the
woods devoured more people that day than
the sword devoured.
9 Then Absalom met the servants of David. Absalom rode on a mule. The mule went

under the thick boughs of a great terebinth
tree, and [R]his head caught in the terebinth; so
he was left hanging between heaven and
earth. And the mule which *was* under him
went on. 2 Sam. 14:26
10 Now a certain man saw *it* and told Joab,
and said, "I just saw Absalom hanging in a
terebinth tree!"
11 So Joab said to the man who told him,
"You just saw *him*! And why did you not
strike him there to the ground? I would have
given you ten *shekels* of silver and a belt."
12 But the man said to Joab, "Though I
were to receive a thousand *shekels* of silver
in my hand, I would not raise my hand
against the king's son. [R]For in our hearing the
king commanded you and Abishai and Ittai,
saying, *'Beware lest anyone *touch* the
young man Absalom!' 2 Sam. 18:5
13 "Otherwise I would have dealt falsely
against my own life. For there is nothing
hidden from the king, and you yourself would
have set yourself against *me*."
14 Then Joab said, "I cannot linger with
you." And he took three spears in his hand
and thrust them through Absalom's heart,
while he was *still* alive in the midst of the
terebinth tree.
15 And ten young men who bore Joab's
armor surrounded Absalom, and struck and
killed him.
16 Then Joab blew the trumpet, and the
people returned from pursuing Israel. For
Joab held back the people.
17 And they took Absalom and cast him
into a large pit in the woods, and laid a very
large heap of stones over him. Then all Israel
[R]fled, everyone to his tent. 2 Sam. 19:8; 20:1, 22
18 Now Absalom in his lifetime had taken
and set up a pillar for himself, which *is* in the
King's Valley. For he said, "I have no son to
keep my name in remembrance." He called
the pillar after his own name. And to this day
it is called Absalom's Monument.
19 Then [R]Ahimaaz the son of Zadok said,
"Let me run now and take the news to the
king, how the LORD has [T]avenged him of his
enemies." 2 Sam. 15:36; 17:17 • *vindicated*
20 And Joab said to him, "You shall not
take the news this day, for you shall take the
news another day. But today you shall take
no news, because the king's son is dead."
21 Then Joab said to the Cushite, "Go, tell
the king what you have seen." So the Cushite
bowed himself to Joab and ran.
22 And Ahimaaz the son of Zadok said
again to Joab, "But [T]whatever happens,
please let me also run after the Cushite." And
Joab said, "Why will you run, my son, since
you have no news ready?" Lit. *be what may*
23 "But whatever happens," *he said*, "let me
run." So he said to him, "Run." Then Ahimaaz ran by way of the plain, and outran the
Cushite.
24 Now David was sitting between the two
gates. And the watchman went up to the roof
over the gate, to the wall, lifted his eyes and
looked, and there was a man, running alone.
25 Then the watchman cried out and told
the king. And the king said, "If he *is* alone,
there is news in his mouth." And he came
rapidly and drew near.
26 Then the watchman saw *another* man
running, and the watchman called to the
gatekeeper and said, "There is *another* man,
running alone!" And the king said, "He also
brings news."
27 So the watchman said, [T]"I think the
running of the first is like the running of
Ahimaaz the son of Zadok." And the king
said, "He *is* a good man, and comes with
[R]good news." Lit. *I see the running* • 1 Kin. 1:42
28 And Ahimaaz called out and said to the
king, [T]"All is well!" Then he bowed down
with his face to the earth before the king, and
said, "Blessed *be* the LORD your God, who has
delivered up the men who raised their hand
against my lord the king!" *Peace to you*
29 The king said, "Is the young man Absalom safe?" And Ahimaaz answered, "When
Joab sent the king's servant and *me* your
servant, I saw a great tumult, but I did not
know what *it was about*."
30 And the king said, "Turn aside *and* stand
here." So he turned aside and stood still.
31 Just then the Cushite came, and the
Cushite said, "There is good news, my lord
the king! For the LORD has avenged you this
day of all those who rose against you."
32 And the king said to the Cushite, "Is the
young man Absalom safe?" And the Cushite
answered, "May the enemies of my lord the
king, and all who rise against you to do *you*
harm, be as *that* young man *is*!"
33 Then the king was deeply moved, and
went up to the chamber over the gate, and
wept. And as he went, he said thus: [R]"O my
son Absalom—my son, my son Absalom—if
only I had died in your place! O Absalom my
son, [R]my son!" 2 Sam. 12:10 • 2 Sam. 19:4

CHAPTER 19

Reproof of Joab

AND Joab was told, "Behold, the king is
weeping and mourning for Absalom."
2 So the victory that day was *turned* into
[R]mourning for all the people. For the people
heard it said that day, "The king is grieved
for his son." Esth. 4:3
3 And the people [T]stole back into the city
that day, as people who are ashamed steal
away when they flee in battle. *went by stealth*

18:12 Vss. *'Protect the young man Absalom for me!'*

4 But the king covered his face, and the
king cried out with a loud voice, "O my son
Absalom! O Absalom, my son, my son!"
5 Then [R]Joab came into the house to the
king, and said, "Today you have disgraced all
your servants who today have saved your
life, the lives of your sons and daughters, the
lives of your wives and the lives of your
concubines, 2 Sam. 18:14
6 "in that you love your enemies and hate
your friends. For you have declared today
that you [T]regard neither princes nor servants;
for today I perceive that if Absalom had lived
and all of us had died today, then it would
have pleased you well. *have no respect for*
7 "Now therefore, arise, go out and speak
[T]comfort to your servants. For I swear by the
LORD, if you do not go out, not one will stay
with you this night. And that will be worse
for you than all the evil that has befallen you
from your youth until now." Lit. *to the heart of*

Restoration of David

8 Then the king arose and sat in the gate.
And they told all the people, saying, "There is
the king, sitting in the gate." So all the people
came before the king. For everyone of Israel
had [R]fled to his tent. 2 Sam. 18:17
9 Now all the people were in a dispute
throughout all the tribes of Israel, saying,
"The king saved us from the hand of our
enemies, he delivered us from the hand of the
Philistines, and now he has [R]fled from the
land because of Absalom. 2 Sam. 15:14
10 "But Absalom, whom we anointed over
us, has died in battle. Now therefore, why do
you say nothing about bringing back the
king?"
11 Then King David sent to [R]Zadok and
Abiathar the priests, saying, "Speak to the
elders of Judah, saying, 'Why are you the last
to bring the king back to his house, since the
words of all Israel have come to the king,
even to his house? 2 Sam. 15:24
12 'You *are* my brethren, you *are* [R]my bone
and my flesh. Why then are you the last to
bring back the king?' 2 Sam. 5:1
13 [R]"And say to Amasa, '*Are* you not my
bone and my flesh? [R]God do so to me, and
more also, if you are not commander of the
army before me [T]continually in place of
Joab.' " 2 Sam. 17:25 • Ruth 1:17 • *permanently*
14 So he swayed the hearts of all the men of
Judah, [R]just as *the heart of* one man, so that
they sent *this word* to the king: "Return, you
and all your servants!" Judg. 20:1
15 Then the king returned and came to the
Jordan. And Judah came to [R]Gilgal, to go to
meet the king, to escort the king [R]across the
Jordan. Josh. 5:9 • 2 Sam. 17:22
16 And [R]Shimei the son of Gera, a Benjamite, who *was* from Bahurim, hastened and
came down with the men of Judah to meet
King David. 2 Sam. 16:5
17 *There were* a thousand men of [R]Benja-
min with him, and Ziba the servant of the
house of Saul, and his fifteen sons and his
twenty servants with him; and they went
over the Jordan before the king. 1 Kin. 12:21
18 Then a ferryboat went across to carry
over the king's household, and to do what he
thought good.
Now Shimei the son of Gera fell down
before the king when he had crossed the
Jordan.
19 Then he said to the king, "Do not let my
lord [T]impute iniquity to me, or remember
what wrong your servant did on the day that
my lord the king left Jerusalem, that the king
should take *it* to heart. *charge me with iniquity*
20 "For I, your servant, know that I have
sinned. Therefore here I am, the first to come
today of all [R]the house of Joseph to go down
to meet my lord the king." Judg. 1:22
21 But Abishai the son of Zeruiah answered
and said, "Shall not Shimei be put to death
for this, [R]because he [R]cursed the LORD's
anointed?" [Ex. 22:28] • [1 Sam. 26:9]
22 And David said, [R]"What have I to do
with you, you sons of Zeruiah, that you
should be adversaries to me today? [R]Shall
any man be put to death today in Israel? For
do I not know that today I *am* king over
Israel?" 2 Sam. 3:39; 16:10 • 1 Sam. 11:13
23 Therefore the king said to Shimei, "You
shall not die." And the king swore to him.
24 Now Mephibosheth the son of Saul came
down to meet the king. And he had not cared
for his feet, nor trimmed his mustache, nor
washed his clothes, from the day the king
departed until the day he came *back* in peace.
25 So it was, when he had come to Jerusalem to meet the king, that the king said to
him, [R]"Why did you not go with me, Mephibosheth?" 2 Sam. 16:7
26 And he answered, "My lord, O king, my
servant deceived me. For your servant said, 'I
will saddle a donkey for myself, that I may
ride on it and go to the king,' because your
servant *is* lame.
27 "And [R]he has slandered your servant to
my lord the king, [R]but my lord the king *is* like
the angel of God. Therefore do *what is* good
in your eyes. 2 Sam. 16:3, 4 • 2 Sam. 14:17, 20
28 "For all *of* my father's house were but
dead men before my lord the king. Yet you
set your servant among those who eat at
your own table. Therefore what right have I
still to cry out anymore to the king?"
29 So the king said to him, "Why do you
speak anymore of your matters? I have said,
'You and Ziba divide the land.' "
30 Then Mephibosheth said to the king,
"Rather, let him take it all, inasmuch as my

lord the king has come back in peace to his
own house."
31 And [R]Barzillai the Gileadite came down
from Rogelim and went across the Jordan
with the king, to escort him across the Jordan. 1 Kin. 2:7
32 Now Barzillai was a very aged man,
eighty years old. And he had provided the
king with supplies while he stayed at Mahanaim, for he *was* a very rich man.
33 And the king said to Barzillai, "Come
across with me, and I will provide for you
while you are with me in Jerusalem."
34 But Barzillai said to the king, "How long
have I to live, that I should go up with the
king to Jerusalem?
35 "I *am* today [R]eighty years old. Can I
discern between the good and bad? Can your
servant taste what I eat or what I drink? Can
I hear any longer the voice of singing men
and singing women? Why then should your
servant be a further burden to my lord the
king? Ps. 90:10
36 "Your servant will go a little way across
the Jordan with the king. And why should
the king repay me *with* such a reward?
37 "Please let your servant turn back again,
that I may die in my own city, *and be buried*
by the grave of my father and mother. But
here is your servant [R]Chimham; let him cross
over with my lord the king, and do for him
what seems good to you." Jer. 41:17
38 And the king answered, "Chimham shall
cross over with me, and I will do for him
what seems good to you. Now whatever you
request of me, I will do for you."
39 Then all the people went over the Jordan. And when the king had crossed over, the
king [R]kissed Barzillai and blessed him, and he
returned to his own place. Gen. 31:55
40 Now the king went on to Gilgal, and
*Chimham went on with him. And all the
people of Judah escorted the king, and also
half the people of Israel.
41 Just then all the men of Israel came to
the king, and said to the king, "Why have our
brethren, the men of Judah, stolen you away
and brought the king, his household, and all
David's men with him across the Jordan?"
42 So all the men of Judah answered the
men of Israel, "Because the king *is* a close
relative of ours. Why then are you angry over
this matter? Have we ever eaten at the king's
expense? Or has he given us any gift?"
43 And the men of Israel answered the men
of Judah, and said, "We have [R]ten shares in
the king; therefore we also have more *right*
to David than you. Why then do you despise
us—were we not the first to advise bringing
back our king?" Yet [R]the words of the men of
Judah were [T]fiercer than the words of the
men of Israel. 1 Kin. 11:30, 31 • Judg. 8:1; 12:1 • *harsher*

CHAPTER 20

AND there happened to be there a [T]rebel,
whose name *was* Sheba the son of
Bichri, a Benjamite. And he blew a trumpet,
and said: Lit. *man of Belial*

"We have no [T]part in David, *portion*
Nor do we have inheritance in the son
of Jesse;
Every man to his tents, O Israel!"

2 So every man of Israel deserted David,
and followed Sheba the son of Bichri. But the
men of Judah, from the Jordan as far as
Jerusalem, remained loyal to their king.
3 Now David came to his house at Jerusalem. And the king took the ten women, [R]his
concubines whom he had left to keep the
house, and put them in seclusion and supported them, but did not go in to them. So
they were shut up to the day of their death,
living in widowhood. 2 Sam. 15:16; 16:21, 22
4 Then the king said to Amasa, [R]"Assemble
the men of Judah for me within three days,
and be present here yourself." 2 Sam. 17:25; 19:13
5 So Amasa went to assemble *the men of*
Judah. But he delayed longer than the set
time which David had appointed him.
6 And David said to [R]Abishai, "Now Sheba
the son of Bichri will do us more harm than
Absalom. Take [R]your lord's servants and
pursue him, lest he find for himself fortified
cities, and escape us." 2 Sam. 21:17 • 2 Sam. 11:11
7 So Joab's men, with the Cherethites, the
Pelethites, and [R]all the mighty men, went out
after him. And they went out of Jerusalem to
pursue Sheba the son of Bichri. 2 Sam. 15:18
8 When they *were* at the large stone which
is in Gibeon, Amasa came before them. Now
Joab was dressed in battle armor; on it was a
belt *with* a sword fastened in its sheath at his
hips; and as he was going forward, it fell out.
9 Then Joab said to Amasa, "*Are* you in
health, my brother?" And Joab took Amasa
by the beard with his right hand to kiss him.
10 But Amasa did not notice the sword that
was in Joab's hand. And he struck him with it
in the stomach, and his entrails poured out
on the ground; and he did not *strike* him
again. Thus he died. Then Joab and Abishai
his brother pursued Sheba the son of Bichri.
11 Meanwhile one of Joab's men stood near
Amasa, and said, "Whoever favors Joab and
whoever *is* for David, *let him* follow Joab!"
12 But Amasa wallowed in *his* blood in the
middle of the highway. And when the man
saw that all the people stood still, he moved
Amasa from the highway to the field and
threw a garment over him, when he saw that
everyone who came upon him halted.

19:40 MT *Chimhan*

13 When he was removed from the highway, all the people went on after Joab to
pursue Sheba the son of Bichri.
14 And he went through all the tribes of
Israel to [R]Abel and Beth Maachah and all the
Berites. So they were gathered together and
also went after *Sheba*. 2 Kin. 15:29
15 Then they came and besieged him in
Abel of Beth Maachah; and they cast up a
siege mound against the city, and it stood by
the rampart. And all the people who *were*
with Joab battered the wall to throw it down.
16 Then a wise woman cried out from the
city, "Hear, Hear! Please say to Joab, 'Come
nearby, that I may speak with you.' "
17 When he had come near to her, the
woman said, "*Are* you Joab?" He answered,
"I *am.*" Then she said to him, "Hear the
words of your maidservant." And he answered, "I am listening."
18 Then she spoke, saying, "They used to
talk in former times, saying, 'They shall
surely ask *counsel* at Abel,' and so they
would end *disputes*.
19 "I *am among the* peaceable *and* faithful
in Israel. You seek to destroy a city and a
mother in Israel. Why would you swallow up
[R]the inheritance of the LORD?" 1 Sam. 26:19
20 And Joab answered and said, "Far be it,
far be it from me, that I should swallow up or
destroy!
21 "That *is* not so. But a man from the
mountains of Ephraim, Sheba the son of
Bichri by name, has raised his hand against
the king, against David. Deliver him only,
and I will depart from the city." And the
woman said to Joab, "Watch, his head will be
thrown to you over the wall."
22 Then the woman [R]in her wisdom went to
all the people. And they cut off the head of
Sheba the son of Bichri, and threw *it* out to
Joab. Then he blew a trumpet, and they
withdrew from the city, every man to his
tent. So Joab returned to the king at Jerusalem. [Eccl. 9:13–16]
23 And Joab *was* over all the army of Israel;
Benaiah the son of Jehoiada *was* over the
Cherethites and the Pelethites;
24 Adoram *was* in charge of revenue; Jehoshaphat the son of Ahilud *was* recorder;
25 Sheva *was* scribe; [R]Zadok and Abiathar
were the priests; 1 Kin. 4:4
26 [R]and Ira the Jairite was [T]a chief minister
under David. 2 Sam. 8:18 • Or *David's priest*

CHAPTER 21

Famine

NOW there was a famine in the days of
David for three years, year after year;
and David [R]inquired of the LORD. And the
LORD answered, "*It is* because of Saul and *his*
[T]bloodthirsty house, because he killed the
Gibeonites." Num. 27:21 • Lit. *house of bloodshed*
2 So the king called the Gibeonites and
spoke to them. Now the Gibeonites *were* not
of the children of Israel, but of the remnant
of the Amorites; the children of Israel had
sworn protection to them, but Saul had
sought to kill them [R]in his zeal for the children of Israel and Judah. [Ex. 34:11–16]
3 Therefore David said to the Gibeonites,
"What shall I do for you? And with what
shall I make atonement, that you may bless
[R]the inheritance of the LORD?" 2 Sam. 20:19
4 And the Gibeonites said to him, "We will
have no silver or gold from Saul or from his
house, nor shall you kill any man in Israel for
us." And he said, "Whatever you say, *that*
will I do for you."
5 So they answered the king, "As for the
man who consumed us and plotted against
us, *that* we should be destroyed from remaining in any of the territories of Israel,
6 "let seven men of his descendants be
delivered [R]to us, and we will hang them
before the LORD [R]in Gibeah of Saul, [R]*whom*
the LORD chose." And the king said, "I will
give *them*." Num. 25:4 • 1 Sam. 10:26 • 1 Sam. 10:24
7 But the king spared Mephibosheth the
son of Jonathan, the son of Saul, because of
the LORD's oath that *was* between them,
between David and Jonathan the son of Saul.
8 So the king took Armoni and Mephibosheth, the two sons of Rizpah the
daughter of Aiah, whom she bore to Saul, and
the five sons of Michal the daughter of Saul,
whom she [T]brought up for Adriel the son of
Barzillai the Meholathite; Lit. *bore to Adriel*
9 and he delivered them into the hands of
the Gibeonites, and they hanged them on the
hill [R]before the LORD. So they fell, *all* seven
together, and were put to death in the days of
harvest, in the first *days*, in the beginning of
barley harvest. 2 Sam. 6:17
10 Now [R]Rizpah the daughter of Aiah took
sackcloth and spread it for herself on the
rock, [R]from the beginning of harvest until the
late rains poured on them from heaven. And
she did not allow the birds of the air to rest
on them by day nor the beasts of the field by
night. 2 Sam. 3:7; 21:8 • Deut. 21:23
11 And David was told what Rizpah the
daughter of Aiah, the concubine of Saul, had
done.
12 Then David went and took the bones of
Saul, and the bones of Jonathan his son, from
the men of Jabesh Gilead who had stolen
them from the street of Beth Shan, where the
Philistines had hung them up, after the Philistines had struck down Saul in Gilboa.
13 So he brought up the bones of Saul and
the bones of Jonathan his son from there; and
they gathered the bones of those who had
been hanged.

14 They buried the bones of Saul and Jonathan his son in the country of Benjamin in
[R]Zelah, in the tomb of Kish his father. So they
performed all that the king commanded. And
after that [R]God heeded the prayer for the
land. Josh. 18:28 • 2 Sam. 24:25

War with Philistia—1 Chr. 20:4–8

15 When the Philistines were at war again
with Israel, David and his servants with him
went down and fought against the Philistines; and David grew faint.
16 Then Ishbi-Benob, who *was* one of the
sons of [T]the [R]giant, the weight of whose
bronze spear *was* three hundred *shekels*, who
was bearing a new *sword*, thought he could
kill David. Or *Rapha* • 2 Sam. 21:18–22
17 But Abishai the son of Zeruiah came to
his aid, and struck the Philistine and killed
him. Then the men of David swore to him,
saying, "You shall go out no more with us to
battle, lest you quench the lamp of Israel."
18 Now it happened afterward that there
was again a battle with the Philistines at Gob.
Then Sibbechai the Hushathite killed Saph,
who *was* one of the sons of the giant.
19 Again there was a battle in Gob with the
Philistines, where [R]Elhanan the son of Jaare-
Oregim the Bethlehemite killed *the brother of*
Goliath the Gittite, the shaft of whose spear
was like a weaver's beam. 1 Chr. 20:5
20 Yet again [R]there was a battle in Gath,
where there was a man of *great* stature, who
had six fingers on each hand and six toes on
each foot, twenty-four in number; and he also
was born to [T]the giant. 1 Chr. 20:6 • Or *Rapha*
21 So when he [R]defied Israel, Jonathan the
son of [T]Shimeah, the brother of David, killed
him. 1 Sam. 17:10 • *Shammah*, 1 Sam. 16:9 and elsewhere
22 [R]These four were born to [T]the giant in
Gath, and fell by the hand of David and by
the hand of his servants. 1 Chr. 20:8 • Or *Rapha*

CHAPTER 22

Psalms of Thanksgiving

THEN David spoke to the LORD the words
of this song, on the day when the LORD
had delivered him from the hand of all his
enemies, and from the hand of Saul.
2 And he [R]said: Ps. 18

[R]"The LORD *is* my rock, my [R]fortress and
my deliverer; Deut. 32:4 • Ps. 91:2
3 The God of my strength, [R]in Him I will
trust, Heb. 2:13
My [R]shield and the [R]horn[T] of my
salvation, Gen. 15:1 • Luke 1:69 • Strength
My stronghold and my refuge;
My Savior, You save me from violence.
4 I will call upon the LORD, *who is* worthy
to be praised;
So shall I be saved from my enemies.

5 "When the waves of death encompassed
me,
The floods of ungodliness [T]made me
afraid; Or *overwhelmed*
6 The sorrows of Sheol surrounded me,
The snares of death confronted me.
7 In my distress [R]I called upon the LORD,
And cried to my God. Ps. 116:4; 120:1
He [R]heard my voice from His temple,
And my cry *entered* His ears. Ex. 3:7

8 "Then [R]the earth shook and trembled;
[R]The foundations of heaven moved and
shook, Judg. 5:4 • Job 26:11
Because He was angry.
9 Smoke went up from His nostrils,
And devouring [R]fire from His mouth;
Coals were kindled by it. Heb. 12:29
10 He [R]bowed the heavens also, and came
down Is. 64:1
With [R]darkness under His feet. Ex. 20:21
11 He rode upon a cherub, and flew;
And He was seen [R]upon the wings of
the wind. Ps. 104:3
12 He made [R]darkness canopies around
Him, Job 36:29
Dark waters *and* thick clouds of the
skies.
13 From the brightness before Him
Coals of fire were kindled.

14 "The LORD thundered from heaven,
And the Most High uttered His voice.
15 He sent out [R]arrows and scattered
them; Deut. 32:23
Lightning bolts, and He vanquished
them.
16 Then the channels of the sea [R]were
seen, Nah. 1:4
The foundations of the world were
uncovered,
At the [R]rebuke of the LORD, Ex. 15:8
At the blast of the breath of His
nostrils.

17 "He sent from above, He took me,
He drew me out of many waters.
18 He delivered me from my strong enemy,
From those who hated me;
For they were too strong for me.
19 They confronted me in the day of my
calamity,
But the LORD was my [R]support. Is. 10:20
20 [R]He also brought me out into a broad
place; Ps. 31:8; 118:5
He delivered me, because He [R]delighted
in me. 2 Sam. 15:26

21 "The[R] LORD rewarded me according to
my righteousness; 1 Sam. 26:23
According to the [R]cleanness of my
hands Ps. 24:4
He has recompensed me.

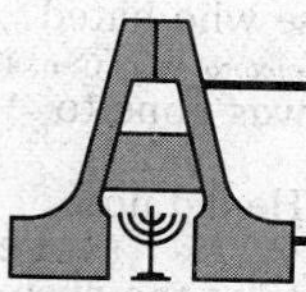

SHEOL AND GEHENNA

Everyone who reads the Old Testament is agreed that *She'ôl* has to do with a place or state to which one (or one's body) goes after death. Because of differing theological views, there is agreement on little else regarding this word, however.

Sheol (*She'ôl*)

The Hebrew word is apparently related to *shā'al*, "to ask," but exactly how is unknown. It occurs sixty-four times in the Old Testament. The KJV translates about half of them by "grave," nearly half by "hell," and three by "pit." Most modern versions, such as NKJV, also sometimes transliterate the Hebrew word, and frequently do so in footnotes.

She'ôl as the Grave. Jacob uses the term four times in Genesis in reference to his being brought down in sorrow "to the grave" (e.g., Gen. 42:38). This meaning is undoubted. It frequently occurs in a parallel construction with *qeber*, "grave."

Job's descriptions of *She'ôl* as a place of darkness, dust, worms, and decay certainly describe the physical grave (Job 17:13–16; 21:13; 24:19, 20).

Peter quoted Psalm 16:10 in Acts 2:27 to prove that Christ arose from the grave, and Paul quoted Hosea 13:14 in 1 Corinthians 15:55 to teach the resurrection of Christians from the grave.

She'ôl as Hell. When the context suggests a negative, fearful future, the translation "hell" is called for. For example, using "grave" or "Sheol" rather than "hell" in Psalm 9:17 would weaken that text considerably: "The wicked shall be turned into hell, *and* all the nations that forget God." Righteous people also go to the grave and the unseen world, so punishment for disobedience must inspire a more fearful response. Proverbs 7:27 describes the harlot's temptations as "the way to hell." "Grave" could be used here, but would not provide as forceful a warning to a young man.

She'ôl is paired with *'abaddôn* ("destruction") in both Proverbs 15:11 and 27:20. This is capitalized as "Hell and Destruction" in the NKJV to indicate personification. Since even the wise go to the grave, it is likely that avoiding eternal punishment in hell is meant here: "The way of life *winds* upward for the wise, that he may turn away from hell below" (Prov. 15:24).

Several of the occurrences of *She'ôl* translated "hell" in the KJV probably refer to the grave. Unfortunately, when these are changed, some people insist that the translators do not believe in the doctrine of hell. This is certainly not true for the translators of the NASB, NIV, and NKJV, all of whose translators held orthodox views on eternal punishment (however unpopular that doctrine may be to modern man).

She'ôl as Pit. In Numbers 16:30, 33, Korah and his fellow rebels went "down alive into the pit." KJV and NKJV translators believed this should be taken in quite a physical sense, as the ground opened up to swallow the rebels.

The KJV's third occurrence of *She'ôl* as "pit" (Job 17:16) in the NKJV is transliterated to allow other interpretations, since the second line of the parallelism uses "dust," which would suggest "grave" to many Bible readers.

Gehenna (a Greek representation of *Gay' Hinnōm* by way of Aramaic)

The Valley of Hinnōm south of Jerusalem became notorious as a place of child sacrifice to Molech (2 Chr. 28:3; 33:6). King Josiah wiped out this dreadful practice (2 Kin. 23:10), and the place later became a garbage dump with its continually burning fires.

The place name was already beginning to take on the New Testament meaning of the place of judgment for sinners in Jeremiah 7:32 and 19:6. Three terms are combined in both verses: "The Valley of the Son of Hinnom," "Tophet," and "the Valley of Slaughter."

In the New Testament James uses *Gehenna* once for "hell" (3:6), and Christ Himself uses it eleven times in the Synoptic Gospels with the same meaning.

Since hell is a fearful place, it is a comfort to know that the One who talked the most about it also made a way to escape its torments (see word study on *faith* on p. 1461).

22 For I have [R]kept the ways of the LORD,
And have not wickedly departed from
my God. Ps. 119:3
23 For all His [R]judgments *were* before me;
And *as for* His statutes, I did not depart
from them. [Deut. 6:6–9; 7:12]
24 I was also blameless before Him,
And I kept myself from my iniquity.
25 Therefore the LORD has recompensed
me according to my righteousness,
According to my cleanness in His eyes.

26 "With [R]the merciful You will show
Yourself merciful; [Matt. 5:7]
With a blameless man You will show
Yourself blameless;
27 With the pure You will show Yourself
pure;
And [R]with the devious You will show
Yourself shrewd. [Lev. 26:23, 24]
28 You will save the humble people;
But Your eyes *are* on the haughty, *that*
You may bring *them* down.

29 "For You *are* my lamp, O LORD;
The LORD shall enlighten my darkness.
30 For by You I can run against a troop;
By my God I can leap over a wall.
31 *As for* God, [R]His way *is* perfect; [Matt. 5:48]
[R]The word of the LORD *is* proven; Ps. 12:6
He *is* a shield to all who trust in Him.

32 "For who *is* God, except the LORD?
And who *is* a rock, except our God?
33 God *is* my [R]strength *and* power, Ps. 27:1
And He makes my way perfect.
34 He makes my feet like the *feet* of deer,
And sets me on my high places.
35 He teaches my hands [T]to make war,
So that my arms can bend a bow of
bronze. Lit. *for the war*

36 "You have also given me the shield of
Your salvation,
And Your gentleness has made me
great.
37 You [R]enlarged my path under me;
So my feet did not slip. Prov. 4:12

38 "I have pursued my enemies and
destroyed them;
Neither did I turn back again till they
were destroyed.
39 And I have destroyed them and
wounded them,
So that they could not rise;
They have fallen [R]under my feet. Mal. 4:3
40 For You have armed me with strength
for the battle;
You have [T]subdued under me those
who rose against me. *caused to bow down*
41 You have also [T]given me the [R]necks of
my enemies,
So that I destroyed those who hated
me. *given me victory over* • Gen. 49:8
42 They looked, but *there was* none to
save;
Even [R]to the LORD, but He did not
answer them. 1 Sam. 28:6
43 Then I beat them as fine [R]as the dust of
the earth; Ps. 18:42
I trod them like dirt in the streets,
And I [T]spread them out. *scattered*

44 "You have also delivered me from the
[T]strivings of my people; *contentions*
You have kept me as the [R]head of the
nations. Deut. 28:13
[R]A people *whom* I have not known shall
serve me. [Is. 55:5]
45 The foreigners submit to me;
As soon as they hear, they obey me.
46 The foreigners fade away,
And come frightened [R]from their
hideouts. [Mic. 7:17]

47 "The LORD lives!
Blessed *be* my Rock!
Let God be exalted,
The [R]Rock of my salvation! Ps. 89:26
48 It *is* God who avenges me,
Who subdues the people under me,
49 Who delivers me from my enemies.
You also lift me above those who rise
against me;
You have delivered me from the
[R]violent man. Ps. 140:1, 4, 11
50 Therefore I will give thanks to You, O
LORD, among the Gentiles,
And sing praises to Your name.
51 *He is* the tower of salvation to His king,
And shows mercy to His [R]anointed,
To David and [R]his descendants
forevermore." Ps. 89:20 • 2 Sam. 7:12–16

CHAPTER 23

NOW these *are* the last words of David.
Thus says David the son of Jesse;
Thus says the man raised up on high,
The anointed of the God of Jacob,
And the sweet psalmist of Israel:

2 "The Spirit of the LORD spoke by me,
And His word *was* on my tongue.
3 The God of Israel said,
[R]The Rock of Israel spoke to me:
'He who rules over men *must be* just,
Ruling in the fear of God. [Deut. 32:4]
4 And [R]*he shall be* like the light of the
morning *when* the sun rises,
A morning without clouds,
Like the tender grass *springing* out of
the earth,
By clear shining after rain.' Ps. 89:36

5 "Although my house *is* not so with God,
[R]Yet He has made with me an
everlasting covenant, Ps. 89:29
Ordered in all *things* and secure.
For *this is* all my salvation and all *my*
desire;
Will He not make *it* increase?
6 But *the sons* of rebellion *shall* all *be* as
thorns thrust away,
Because they cannot be taken with
hands.
7 But the man *who* touches them
Must be [T]armed with iron and the shaft
of a spear, Lit. *filled*
And they shall be utterly burned with
fire in *their* place."

Deeds of David's Mighty Men—1 Chr. 11:10–41

8 These *are* the names of the mighty men
whom David had: Josheb-Basshebeth the
Tachmonite, chief among the captains. He
was called Adino the Eznite, because he had
killed eight hundred men at one time.
9 And after him *was* Eleazar the son of
Dodo, the Ahohite, *one* of the three mighty
men with David when they defied the Philistines *who* were gathered there for battle, and
the men of Israel had retreated.
10 He arose and attacked the Philistines
until his hand was weary, and his hand stuck
to the sword. The LORD brought about a great
victory that day; and the people returned
after him only to plunder.
11 And after him *was* [R]Shammah the son of
Agee the Hararite. The Philistines had gathered together into a troop where there was a
piece of ground full of lentils. Then the people
fled from the Philistines. 1 Chr. 11:27
12 But he stationed himself in the middle of
the field, defended it, and killed the Philistines. And the LORD brought about a great
victory.
13 Then three of the thirty chief men went
down at harvest time and came to David at
the cave of Adullam. And the troop of Philistines encamped in the Valley of Rephaim.
14 David *was* then in [R]the stronghold, and
the garrison of the Philistines *was* then *in*
Bethlehem. 1 Sam. 22:4, 5
15 And David said with longing, "Oh, that
someone would give me a drink of the water
from the well of Bethlehem, which *is* by the
gate!"
16 So the three mighty men broke through
the camp of the Philistines, drew water from
the well of Bethlehem that *was* by the gate,
and took it and brought *it* to David. Nevertheless he would not drink it, but poured it
out to the LORD.
17 And he said, "Far be it from me, O LORD,
that I should do this! *Is this not* the blood of
the men who went in *jeopardy* of their lives?"
Therefore he would not drink it. These things
were done by the three mighty men.
18 Now [R]Abishai the brother of Joab, the
son of Zeruiah, was chief of *another* three. He
lifted his spear against three hundred *men*
and killed *them*, and won a name among
these three. 1 Chr. 11:20
19 Was he not the most honored of three?
Therefore he became their captain. However,
he did not attain to the *first* three.
20 Benaiah *was* the son of Jehoiada, the son
of a valiant man from [R]Kabzeel, [T]who had
done many deeds. [R]He had killed two lion-like
heroes of Moab. He also went down and
killed a lion in the midst of a pit on a snowy
day. Josh. 15:21 • Lit. *great of acts* • Ex. 15:15
21 And he killed an Egyptian, a spectacular
man. The Egyptian *had* a spear in his hand;
so he went down to him with a staff, wrested
the spear out of the Egyptian's hand, and
killed him with his own spear.
22 These *things* Benaiah the son of Jehoiada
did, and won a name among three mighty
men.
23 He was more honored than the thirty,
but he did not attain to the *first* three. And
David appointed him over his guard.
24 [R]Asahel the brother of Joab *was* one of
the thirty; Elhanan the son of Dodo of Bethlehem, 2 Sam. 2:18
25 [R]Shammah the Harodite, Elika the Harodite, 1 Chr. 11:27
26 Helez the Paltite, Ira the son of Ikkesh
the Tekoite,
27 Abiezer the Anathothite, Mebunnai the
Hushathite,
28 Zalmon the Ahohite, Maharai the Netophathite,
29 Heleb the son of Baanah (the Netophathite), Ittai the son of Ribai from Gibeah of
the children of Benjamin,
30 Benaiah a Pirathonite, Hiddai from the
brooks of [R]Gaash, Judg. 2:9
31 Abi-Albon the Arbathite, Azmaveth the
Barhumite,
32 Eliahba the Shaalbonite (of the sons of
Jashen), Jonathan,
33 [R]Shammah the [T]Hararite, Ahiam the son
of Sharar the Hararite, 2 Sam. 23:11 • Or *Ararite*
34 Eliphelet the son of Ahasbai, the son of
the Maacathite, Eliam the son of [R]Ahithophel
the Gilonite, 2 Sam. 15:12
35 Hezrai the Carmelite, Paarai the Arbite,
36 Igal the son of Nathan of [R]Zobah, Bani
the Gadite, 2 Sam. 8:3
37 Zelek the Ammonite, Naharai the Beerothite (armorbearer of Joab the son of
Zeruiah),
38 Ira the Ithrite, Gareb the Ithrite,
39 *and* Uriah the Hittite: thirty-seven in all.

ALTARS IN THE BIBLE

Stone altar on which burnt offerings were placed.

An altar was a platform or elevated place on which a priest placed a sacrifice as an offering to God. The Hebrew word for altar means "a place of slaughter or sacrifice," but the altars of the Old Testament were not limited to sacrificial purposes. Sometimes an altar was built as a testimony of one's faith for future generations (Josh. 22:26–29).

The first altar in the Bible was built by Noah after the Flood (Gen. 8:20). The next several mentioned were built by Abraham (Gen. 12:7, 8; 13:18). These altars were probably little more than piles of stones on which burnt offerings were placed (see illustration).

As the first king of Israel, Saul built an altar during his conquest of the Philistines (1 Sam. 14:35). King David of Judah erected an altar on a threshing floor (2 Sam. 24:15–25). This site became the central place of sacrifice in the temple after it was constructed by Solomon. After building the temple in Jerusalem, Solomon constructed an altar larger than the one David had built, probably adapting it to the size of the temple (2 Chr. 4:1).

The Bible speaks frequently of pagan altars, particularly those associated with the false worship of the Canaanites. God gave specific instructions that pagan altars should be destroyed before altars dedicated to His worship were built (Deut. 12:2, 3). The New Testament also refers to a pagan altar in Athens, erected to an unknown god (Acts 17:23).

Worship in the early Christian church did not include an altar for sacrifices. The statement "We have an altar" (Heb. 13:10) refers to the sacrifice of Christ. Christians have no need for an altar of burnt offerings because atonement for our sins is complete through the sacrificial death of Christ on the cross. We remember our personal acceptance of His sacrifice through participation in the Lord's Supper (also known as Communion, the Lord's Table, and the Eucharist).

CHAPTER 24

The Census and the Plague—1 Chr. 29:26–30

AGAIN the anger of the LORD was aroused against Israel, and He moved David against them to say, [R]"Go, [T]number Israel and Judah." 1 Chr. 27:23, 24 • *take a census of*

2 So the king said to Joab the commander of the army who *was* with him, "Now go throughout all the tribes of Israel, from Dan to Beersheba, and count the people, that I may know the number of the people."

3 And Joab said to the king, "Now may the LORD your God [R]add to the people a hundredfold more than there are, and may the eyes of my lord the king see *it*. But why does my lord the king desire this thing?" Deut. 1:11

4 Nevertheless the king's word [T]prevailed against Joab and against the captains of the army. So Joab and the captains of the army went out from the presence of the king to count the people of Israel. *overruled*

5 And they crossed over the Jordan and camped in [R]Aroer, on the right side of the town which *is* in the midst of the ravine of Gad, and toward [R]Jazer. Deut. 2:36 • Num. 32:1, 3

6 Then they came to Gilead and to the land of Tahtim Hodshi; they came to [R]Dan Jaan and around to [R]Sidon; Judg. 18:29 • Josh. 19:28

7 and they came to the stronghold of [R]Tyre and to all the cities of the [R]Hivites and the Canaanites. Then they went out to South Judah *as far as* Beersheba. Josh. 19:29 • Josh. 11:3

8 So when they had gone through all the land, they came to Jerusalem at the end of nine months and twenty days.

9 Then Joab gave the sum of the number of the people to the king. [R]And there were in Israel eight hundred thousand valiant men who drew the sword, and the men of Judah were five hundred thousand men. 1 Chr. 21:5

10 And David's heart condemned him after he had numbered the people. So David said to the LORD, [R]"I have sinned greatly in what I have done; but now, I pray, O LORD, take away the iniquity of Your servant, for I have [R]done very foolishly." 2 Sam. 12:13 • 1 Sam. 13:13

11 Now when David arose in the morning, the word of the LORD came to the prophet [R]Gad, David's [R]seer, saying, 1 Sam. 22:5 • 1 Sam. 9:9

12 "Go and tell David, 'Thus says the LORD: "I offer you three *things*; choose one of them for yourself, that I may do *it* to you." ' "

13 So Gad came to David and told him; and he said to him, "Shall [R]seven[T] years of famine come to you in your land? Or shall you flee three months before your enemies, while they pursue you? Or shall there be three days' plague in your land? Now consider and see what answer I should take back to Him who sent me." 1 Chr. 21:12 • *three,* 1 Chr. 21:12

14 And David said to Gad, "I am in great distress. Please let us fall into the hand of the LORD, for His mercies *are* great; but [R]do not let me fall into the hand of man." [Is. 47:6]

15 So [R]the LORD sent a plague upon Israel from the morning till the appointed time. From Dan to Beersheba seventy thousand men of the people died. 1 Chr. 21:14

16 [R]And when the angel stretched out his hand over Jerusalem to destroy it, [R]the LORD relented from the destruction, and said to the angel who was destroying the people, "It is enough; now restrain your hand." And the angel of the LORD was by the threshing floor of Araunah the Jebusite. Ex. 12:23 • Gen. 6:6

17 Then David spoke to the LORD when he saw the angel who was striking the people, and said, "Surely [R]I have sinned, and I have done wickedly; but these sheep, what have they done? Let Your hand, I pray, be against me and against my father's house." Ps. 74:1

18 And Gad came that day to David and said to him, [R]"Go up, erect an altar to the LORD on the threshing floor of Araunah the Jebusite." 1 Chr. 21:18

19 So David, according to the word of Gad, went up as the LORD commanded.

20 Now Araunah looked, and saw the king and his servants coming toward him. So Araunah went out and bowed before the king with his face to the ground.

21 Then Araunah said, "Why has my lord the king come to his servant?" And David said, "To buy the threshing floor from you, to build an altar to the LORD, that the plague may be withdrawn from the people."

22 Now Araunah said to David, "Let my lord the king take and offer up whatever *seems* good to him. [R]Look, *here are* oxen for burnt sacrifice, and threshing implements and the yokes of the oxen for wood. 1 Kin. 19:21

23 "All these, O king, Araunah has given to the king." And Araunah said to the king, "May the LORD your God accept you."

24 Then the king said to Araunah, "No, but I will surely buy *it* from you for a price; nor will I offer burnt offerings to the LORD my God with that which costs me nothing." So [R]David bought the threshing floor and the oxen for fifty shekels of silver. 1 Chr. 21:24, 25

25 And David built there an altar to the LORD, and offered burnt offerings and peace offerings. [R]So the LORD heeded the prayers for the land, and [R]the plague was withdrawn from Israel. 2 Sam. 21:14 • 2 Sam. 24:21

THE FIRST BOOK OF THE

KINGS

THE BOOK OF FIRST KINGS

The first half of First Kings traces the life of Solomon. Under his leadership Israel rises to the peak of her size and glory. Solomon's great accomplishments, including the unsurpassed splendor of the temple which he constructs in Jerusalem, bring him worldwide fame and respect. However, Solomon's zeal for God diminishes in his later years, as pagan wives turn his heart away from worship in the temple of God. As a result, the king with the divided heart leaves behind a divided kingdom. For the next century, the Book of First Kings traces the twin histories of two sets of kings and two nations of disobedient people who are growing indifferent to God's prophets and precepts.

Like the two books of Samuel, the two books of Kings were originally one in the Hebrew Bible. The original title was *Melechim*, "Kings," taken from the first word in 1:1, *Vehamelech*, "Now King." The Septuagint artificially divided the book of Kings in the middle of the story of Ahaziah into two books. It called the books of Samuel "First and Second Kingdoms" and the books of Kings "Third and Fourth Kingdoms." The Septuagint may have divided Samuel, Kings, and Chronicles into two books each because the Greek required a greater amount of scroll space than did the Hebrew. The Latin title for these books is *Liber Regum Tertius et Quartus*, "Third and Fourth Book of Kings."

THE AUTHOR OF FIRST KINGS

The author of First and Second Kings is unknown, but evidence supports the talmudic tradition that Kings was written by the prophet Jeremiah. The author was clearly a prophet/historian as seen in the prophetic exposé of apostasy. Both First and Second Kings emphasize God's righteous judgment on idolatry and immorality. The style of these books is also similar to that found in Jeremiah. The phrase "to this day" in First Kings 8:8 and 12:19 indicates a time of authorship prior to the Babylonian captivity (586 B.C.). However, the last two chapters of Second Kings were written after the captivity, probably by a Jewish captive in Babylon.

Evidently, the majority of First and Second Kings was written before 586 B.C. by a compiler who had access to several historical documents. Some of these are mentioned: "the book of the acts of Solomon" (11:41), "the book of the chronicles of the kings of Israel" (14:19), and "the book of the chronicles of the kings of Judah" (14:29; 15:7). These books may have been a part of the official court records (see 2 Kin. 18:18). In addition, Isaiah 36—39 was probably used as a source (cf. 2 Kin. 18—20).

THE TIME OF FIRST KINGS

The Book of Kings was written to the remaining kingdom of Judah before and after its Babylonian exile. The majority was compiled by a contemporary of Jeremiah, if not by Jeremiah himself (c. 646-570 B.C.). It is a record of disobedience, idolatry, and ungodliness which serves as an explanation for the Assyrian captivity of Israel (722 B.C.) and the Babylonian captivity of Judah (586 B.C.). First Kings covers the 120 years from the beginning of Solomon's reign in 971 B.C. through Ahaziah's reign ending in 851 B.C. The key date is 931 B.C., the year the kingdom was divided into the northern nation of Israel and the southern nation of Judah.

THE CHRIST OF FIRST KINGS

Solomon typifies Christ in a number of ways. His fabled wisdom points ahead to "Christ Jesus, who became for us wisdom from God" (1 Cor. 1:30). Solomon's fame, glory, wealth, and honor foreshadow Christ in His kingdom. Solomon's rulership brings knowledge, peace, and worship. However, despite Solomon's splendor, the Son of Man later says of His coming, "indeed a greater than Solomon *is* here" (Matt. 12:42).

The prophet Elijah is more typical of John the Baptist than of Christ, but his prophetic ministry and miraculous works illustrate aspects of the life of Christ.

KEYS TO FIRST KINGS

Key Word: Division of the Kingdom— The theme of First Kings centers around the fact that the welfare of Israel and Judah depends upon the faithfulness of the people and their king to the covenant. Historically, it was written to give an account of the reigns of the kings from Solomon to Jehoshaphat (Judah) and Ahaziah (Israel). The two books of Kings as a whole trace the monarchy from the point of its greatest prosperity under Solomon to its demise and destruction in the Assyrian and Babylonian captivities.

Theologically, First Kings provides a prophetically oriented evaluation of the spiritual and moral causes that led to the political and economic demise of the two kingdoms. The material is too selective to be considered a biography of the kings. For example, Omri was one of Israel's most important rulers from a political point of view, but because of his moral corruption, his achievements are dismissed in a mere eight verses. The lives of these kings are used to teach that observance of God's law produces blessing, but apostasy is rewarded by judgment.

Key Verses: First Kings 9:4, 5; 11:11—"Now if you walk before Me as your father David walked, in integrity of heart and in uprightness, to do according to all that I have commanded you, *and* if you keep My statutes and My judgments, then I will establish the throne of your kingdom over Israel forever, as I promised David your father, saying, 'You shall not fail to have a man on the throne of Israel' " (9:4, 5).

"Therefore the LORD said to Solomon, 'Because you have done this, and have not kept My covenant and My statutes, which I have commanded you, I will surely tear the kingdom away from you and give it to your servant' " (11:11).

Key Chapter: First Kings 12—The critical turning point in First Kings occurs in chapter 12 when the united kingdom becomes the divided kingdom. Solomon dies, and his son Rehoboam becomes king and unwisely leads the nation into a civil war which tragically rips the nation into two separate, and at times conflicting, nations. Instead of unity, First Kings records the history of the two kings, two capitals, and two religions.

SURVEY OF FIRST KINGS

The first half of First Kings concerns the life of one of the most amazing men who ever lived. More than any man before or since, he knew how to amass and creatively use great wealth. With the sole exception of Jesus Christ, Solomon is the wisest man in human history. He brings Israel to the peak of its size and glory, and yet, the kingdom is disrupted soon after his death, torn in two by civil strife. This book divides clearly into two sections: the united kingdom (1—11) and the divided kingdom (12—22).

United Kingdom (1—11): These chapters give an account of Solomon's attainment of the throne, wisdom, architectural achievements, fame, wealth, and tragic unfaithfulness. Solomon's half-brother Adonijah attempts to take the throne as David's death is nearing, but Nathan the prophet alerts David who quickly directs the coronation of Solomon as coregent (ch. 1). Solomon still has to consolidate his power and deal with those who oppose his rule. Only when this is done is the kingdom "established in the hand of Solomon" (2:46). Solomon's ungodly marriages (cf. 3:1) eventually turn his heart from the Lord, but he begins well with a genuine love for Yahweh and a desire for wisdom. This wisdom leads to the expansion of Israel to the zenith of her power. Solomon's empire stretches from the border of Egypt to the border of Babylonia, and peace prevails.

From a theocratic perspective, Solomon's greatest achievement is the building of the temple. The ark is placed in this exquisite building, which is filled with the glory of God. Solomon offers a magnificent prayer of dedication and binds the people with an oath to remain faithful to Yahweh.

Because the Lord is with him Solomon continues to grow in fame, power, and wealth. However, his wealth later becomes a source of trouble when he begins to purchase forbidden items. He acquires many foreign wives who lead him into idolatry. It is an irony of history that this wisest of men acts as a fool in his old age. God pronounces judgment and foretells that Solomon's son will rule only a fraction of the kingdom (Judah).

Divided Kingdom (12—22): Upon Solomon's death, God's words come to pass. Solomon's son Rehoboam chooses the foolish course of promising more severe taxation. Jeroboam, an officer in Solomon's army, leads the ten northern tribes in revolt. They make him their king, leaving only Judah and Benjamin in the south under Rehoboam. This is the beginning of a chaotic period with two nations and two sets of kings. Continual enmity and strife exists between the northern and

FOCUS	UNITED KINGDOM			DIVIDED KINGDOM		
REFERENCE	1:1—	3:1—	9:1—	12:1—	15:1—	16:29—22:53
DIVISION	ESTABLISHMENT OF SOLOMON	RISE OF SOLOMON	DECLINE OF SOLOMON	DIVISION OF THE KINGDOM	REIGNS OF VARIOUS KINGS	REIGN OF AHAB WITH ELIJAH
TOPIC	SOLOMON			MANY KINGS		
	KINGDOM IN TRANQUILLITY			KINGDOMS IN TURMOIL		
LOCATION	JERUSALEM: CAPITAL OF UNITED KINGDOM			SAMARIA: CAPITAL OF ISRAEL JERUSALEM: CAPITAL OF JUDAH		
TIME	c. 40 YEARS			c. 90 YEARS		

southern kingdoms. The north is plagued by apostasy (Jeroboam sets up a false system of worship) and the south by idolatry. Of all the northern and southern kings listed in this book, only Asa (15:9–24) and Jehoshaphat (22:41–50) do "*what was* right in the eyes of the LORD" (15:11; 22:43). All of the others are idolaters, usurpers, and murderers.

Ahab brings a measure of cooperation between the northern and southern kingdoms, but he reaches new depths of wickedness as a king. He is the man who introduces Jezebel's Baal worship to Israel. The prophet Elijah ministers during this low period in Israel's history, providing a ray of light and witness of the word and power of God. But Ahab's encounter with Elijah never brings him to turn from his false gods to God. Ahab's treachery in the matter of Naboth's vineyard causes a prophetic rebuke from Elijah (21). Ahab repents (21:27–29) but later dies in battle because of his refusal to heed the words of Micaiah, another prophet of God.

OUTLINE OF FIRST KINGS

Part One: The United Kingdom (1:1—11:43)

I. The Establishment of Solomon as King 1:1—2:46

- A. Appointment of Solomon as King 1:1–53
  - 1. Decline of David 1:1–4
  - 2. Plot of Adonijah to Be King 1:5–9
  - 3. Anointing of Solomon 1:10–40
  - 4. Submission of Adonijah 1:41–53
- B. Solidification of Solomon as King 2:1–46
  - 1. David's Charge to Solomon 2:1–9
  - 2. David Dies 2:10, 11
  - 3. Solomon Is Established as King 2:12
  - 4. The Kingdom Is Purged 2:13–46
    - a. Adonijah Is Executed 2:13–25
    - b. Abiathar Is Removed 2:26, 27
    - c. Joab Is Executed 2:28–35
    - d. Shimei Is Executed 2:36–46

II. The Rise of Solomon as King ..... 3:1—8:66

- A. Solomon's Request for Wisdom 3:1–28
  - 1. Unwise Marriage of Solomon 3:1, 2
  - 2. Request for Wisdom 3:3–15
  - 3. Display of Solomon's Wisdom 3:16–27
  - 4. National Recognition of Solomon's Wisdom 3:28
- B. Solomon's Administration of Israel 4:1–34
  - 1. Eleven Princes 4:1–6
  - 2. Twelve Governors 4:7–19
  - 3. Solomon Reigns in Wisdom 4:20–34
- C. The Temple and Solomon's House Are Constructed ..... 5:1—8:66
  - 1. Construction of the Temple 5:1–6:38
    - a. Temple Materials 5:1–12
    - b. Temple Laborers 5:13–18
    - c. The Temple Is Completed 6:1–38
  - 2. Construction of Solomon's House 7:1–12
  - 3. Furnishings of the Temple 7:13–51
  - 4. Dedication of the Temple 8:1–66
    - a. The Ark Returns 8:1–9
    - b. The Shechinah Returns 8:10, 11
    - c. Solomon's Sermon 8:12–21
    - d. Solomon's Prayer 8:22–61
    - e. Israel Rejoices 8:62–66

III. The Decline of Solomon as King ..... 9:1—11:43

- A. Reiteration of the Davidic Covenant 9:1–9
- B. Disobedience of Solomon to the Covenant ..... 9:10—11:8
  - 1. Sale of Cities in Israel 9:10–14
  - 2. Enslavement of the Canaanites 9:15–28
  - 3. Multiplication of Wealth 10:1–25
  - 4. Multiplication of Horses 10:26–29
  - 5. Intermarriage with Foreign Women 11:1–3
  - 6. Worship of Idols 11:4–8
- C. Chastening of Solomon for Breaking the Covenant 11:9–40
  - 1. The Rebuke of God 11:9–13
  - 2. The Chastisement of God 11:14–40
- D. Death of Solomon 11:41–43

Part Two: The Divided Kingdom (12:1—22:53)

I. The Division of the Kingdom ..... 12:1—14:31

- A. Cause of the Division 12:1–24
  - 1. Request of Israel to Rehoboam 12:1–5
  - 2. Foolish Response of Rehoboam 12:6–15
  - 3. Revolt of the Northern Tribes 12:16–24
- B. Reign of Jeroboam in Israel ..... 12:25—14:20
  - 1. Sin of Jeroboam 12:25–33
  - 2. Warning of the Prophet 13:1–6
  - 3. Sin of the Prophet 13:7–19
  - 4. Judgment on the Prophet 13:20–32
  - 5. Continued Sin of Jeroboam 13:33, 34
  - 6. Judgment on Jeroboam 14:1–20
- C. Reign of Rehoboam in Judah 14:21–31
  - 1. Sin of Rehoboam 14:21–24
  - 2. Judgment on Rehoboam 14:25–31

II. The Reigns of Two Kings in Judah 15:1–24

- A. Reign of Abijam in Judah 15:1–8
- B. Reign of Asa in Judah 15:9–24
  - 1. Obedience of Asa 15:9–15
  - 2. Disobedience of Asa 15:16–22
  - 3. Death of Asa 15:23, 24

III. The Reigns of Five Kings in Israel 15:25—16:28

- A. Reign of Nadab in Israel 15:25–31
- B. Reign of Baasha in Israel ..... 15:32—16:7

CHAPTER 1

Decline of David

NOW King David was [R]old, [T]advanced in
years; and they put covers on him, but
he could not get warm. 1 Chr. 23:1 • 70 years
2 Therefore his servants said to him, "Let a
young woman, a virgin, be sought for our
lord the king, and let her [T]stand before the
king, and let her care for him; and let her lie
in your bosom, that our lord the king may be
warm." Or *serve*
3 So they sought for a lovely young
woman throughout all the territory of Israel,
and found [R]Abishag the [R]Shunammite, and
brought her to the king. 1 Kin. 2:17 • Josh. 19:18
4 And the young woman *was* very lovely;
and she cared for the king, and served him;
but the king did not know her.

Plot of Adonijah to Be King

5 Now Adonijah the son of Haggith exalted himself, saying, "I will be king"; and he
prepared for himself chariots and horsemen,
and fifty men to run before him.
6 (And his father had not rebuked him at
any time by saying, "Why have you done
so?" He *was* also a very good-looking *man.*
His mother had borne him after Absalom.)
7 Then he conferred with Joab the son of
Zeruiah and with Abiathar the priest, and
they followed and helped Adonijah.
8 But Zadok the priest, Benaiah the son of
Jehoiada, Nathan the prophet, [R]Shimei, Rei,
and the mighty men who *belonged* to David
were not with Adonijah. 1 Kin. 4:18
9 And Adonijah sacrificed sheep and oxen
and fattened cattle by the stone of [T]Zoheleth,
which *is* by En Rogel; he also invited all his
brothers, the king's sons, and all the men of
Judah, the king's servants. Lit. *Serpent*

Anointing of Solomon

10 But he did not invite Nathan the prophet,
Benaiah, the mighty men, or [R]Solomon his
brother. 2 Sam. 12:24
11 So Nathan spoke to Bathsheba the
mother of Solomon, saying, "Have you not
heard that Adonijah the son of [R]Haggith has
become king, and David our lord does not
know *it*? 2 Sam. 3:4
12 "Come, please, let me now give you
counsel, that you may save your own life and
the life of your son Solomon.
13 "Go immediately to King David and say
to him, 'Did you not, my lord, O king, swear
to your maidservant, saying, [R]"Assuredly
your son Solomon shall reign after me, and
he shall sit on my throne"? Why then has
Adonijah become king?' 1 Chr. 22:9–13
14 "Then, while you are still talking there
with the king, I also will come in after you
and confirm your words."
15 So Bathsheba went into the chamber to
the king. (Now the king was very old, and
Abishag the Shunammite was serving the
king.)
16 And Bathsheba bowed and did homage
to the king. Then the king said, "What is your
wish?"
17 Then she said to him, "My lord, [R]you
swore by the LORD your God to your maidservant, *saying,* 'Assuredly Solomon your son
shall reign after me, and he shall sit on my
throne.' 1 Kin. 1:13, 30
18 "So now, look! Adonijah has become
king; and now, my lord the king, you do not
know about *it.*
19 "He has sacrificed oxen and fattened
cattle and sheep in abundance, and has invited all the sons of the king, Abiathar the
priest, and Joab the commander of the army;
but Solomon your servant he has not invited.

20 "And as for you, my lord, O king, the
eyes of all Israel *are* on you, that you should
tell them who will sit on the throne of my
lord the king after him.
21 "Otherwise it will happen, when my lord
the king rests with his fathers, that I and my
son Solomon will be counted as offenders."
22 And just then, while she was still talking
with the king, Nathan the prophet also came
in.
23 So they told the king, saying, "Here is
Nathan the prophet." And when he came in
before the king, he bowed down before the
king with his face to the ground.
24 And Nathan said, "My lord, O king, have
you said, 'Adonijah shall reign after me, and
he shall sit on my throne'?
25 "For he has gone down today, and has
sacrificed oxen and fattened cattle and sheep
in abundance, and has invited all the king's
sons, and the commanders of the army, and
Abiathar the priest; and look! They are eating
and drinking before him; and they say, [R]'*Long*
live King Adonijah!' 1 Sam. 10:24
26 "But he has not invited me, *even* me
your servant, nor Zadok the priest, nor Benaiah the son of Jehoiada, nor your servant
Solomon.
27 "Has this thing been done by my lord the
king, and you have not told your servant who
should sit on the throne of my lord the king
after him?"
28 Then King David answered and said,
"Call Bathsheba to me." So she came into the
king's presence and stood before the king.
29 And the king took an oath and said, [R]"*As*
the LORD lives, who has redeemed my life
from every distress, 2 Sam. 4:9; 12:5
30 [R]"just as I swore to you by the LORD God
of Israel, saying, 'Assuredly Solomon your
son shall be king after me, and he shall sit on
my throne in my place,' so I certainly will do
this day." 1 Kin. 1:13, 17
31 Then Bathsheba bowed with *her* face to
the earth, and did homage to the king, and
said, "Let my lord King David live forever!"
32 And King David said, "Call to me Zadok
the priest, Nathan the prophet, and Benaiah
the son of Jehoiada." So they came before the
king.
33 The king also said to them, "Take with
you the servants of your lord, and have
Solomon my son ride on my own mule, and
take him down to [T]Gihon. Spring east of Jerusalem
34 "There let Zadok the priest and Nathan
the prophet anoint him king over Israel; and
[R]blow the horn, and say, [T]'*Long* live King
Solomon!' 2 Sam. 15:10 • Lit. *Let King Solomon live*
35 "Then you shall come up after him, and
he shall come and sit on my throne, and he
shall be king in my place. For I have appointed him to be ruler over Israel and Judah."
36 And Benaiah the son of Jehoiada answered the king and said, "Amen! May the
LORD God of my lord the king say so *too.*
37 [R]"As the LORD has been with my lord the
king, even so may He be with Solomon, and
[R]make his throne greater than the throne of
my lord King David." 1 Sam. 20:13 • 1 Kin. 1:47
38 So Zadok the priest, Nathan the prophet,
[R]Benaiah the son of Jehoiada, the [R]Chereth-
ites, and the Pelethites went down and had
Solomon ride on King David's mule, and took
him to Gihon. 2 Sam. 8:18; 23:20–23 • 2 Sam. 20:7
39 Then Zadok the priest took a horn of [R]oil
from the tabernacle and anointed Solomon.
And they blew the horn, and all the people
said, "Long live King Solomon!" Ps. 89:20
40 And all the people went up after him;
and the people played the flutes and rejoiced
with great joy, so that the earth *seemed to*
split with their sound.

Submission of Adonijah

41 So Adonijah and all the guests who *were*
with him heard *it* as they finished eating. And
when Joab heard the sound of the horn, he
said, "Why *is* the city in such a noisy uproar?"
42 While he was still speaking, there came
[R]Jonathan, the son of Abiathar the priest.
And Adonijah said to him, "Come in, for [R]you
are a prominent man, and bring good tidings." 2 Sam. 17:17, 20 • 2 Sam. 18:27
43 Then Jonathan answered and said to
Adonijah, "No! Our lord King David has
made Solomon king.
44 "The king has sent with him Zadok the
priest, Nathan the prophet, Benaiah the son
of Jehoiada, the Cherethites, and the Pelethites; and they have made him ride on the
king's mule.
45 "So Zadok the priest and Nathan the
prophet have anointed him king at Gihon;
and they have gone up from there rejoicing,
so that the city is in an uproar. This *is* the
noise that you have heard.
46 "Also Solomon [R]sits on the throne of the
kingdom. 1 Chr. 29:23
47 "And moreover the king's servants have
gone to bless our lord King David, saying,
'May God make the name of Solomon better
than your name, and may He make his
throne greater than your throne.' [R]Then the
king bowed himself on the bed. Gen. 47:31
48 "Also the king said thus, 'Blessed *be* the
LORD God of Israel, who has [R]given *one* to sit
on my throne this day, while my eyes see
[R]*it!*'" 1 Kin. 3:6 • 2 Sam. 7:12
49 Then all the guests who were with Adonijah were afraid, and arose, and each one
went his way.
50 Now Adonijah was afraid of Solomon; so
he arose, and went and [R]took hold of the
horns of the altar. 1 Kin. 2:28

51 And it was told Solomon, saying, "Indeed Adonijah is afraid of King Solomon; for look, he has taken hold of the horns of the altar, saying, 'Let King Solomon swear to me today that he will not put his servant to death with the sword.'"
52 Then Solomon said, "If he proves himself a worthy man, [R]not one hair of him shall fall to the earth; but if wickedness is found in him, he shall die." 1 Sam. 14:45
53 So King Solomon sent them to bring him down from the altar. And he came and fell down before King Solomon; and Solomon said to him, "Go to your house."

CHAPTER 2

David's Charge to Solomon

THEN [R]the days of David drew near that he should die, and he [T]charged Solomon his son, saying: Gen. 47:29 · *commanded*
2 "I go the way of all the earth; be strong, therefore, and prove yourself a man.
3 "And keep the charge of the LORD your God: to walk in His ways, to keep His statutes, His commandments, His judgments, and His testimonies, as it is written in the Law of Moses, that you may [R]prosper in all that you do and wherever you turn; [Deut. 29:9]
4 "that the LORD may fulfill His word which He spoke concerning me, saying, 'If your sons take heed to their way, to walk before Me in truth with all their heart and with all their soul,' He said, 'you shall not lack a man on the throne of Israel.'
5 "Moreover you know also what Joab the son of Zeruiah did to me, *and* what he did to the two commanders of the armies of Israel, to Abner the son of Ner and Amasa the son of Jether, whom he killed. And he shed the blood of war in peacetime, and put the blood of war on his belt that *was* around his waist, and on his sandals that *were* on his feet.
6 "Therefore do [R]according to your wisdom, and do not let his gray hair go down to the grave in peace. 1 Kin. 2:9
7 "But show kindness to the sons of Barzillai the Gileadite, and let them be among those who [R]eat at your table, for so [R]they came to me when I fled from Absalom your brother. 2 Sam. 9:7, 10; 19:28 · 2 Sam. 17:17–29
8 "And see, *you have* with you Shimei the son of Gera, a Benjamite from Bahurim, who cursed me with a malicious curse in the day when I went to Mahanaim. But he came down to meet me at the Jordan, and [R]I swore to him by the LORD, saying, 'I will not put you to death with the sword.' 2 Sam. 19:23
9 "Now therefore, [R]do not hold him guiltless, for you *are* a wise man and know what you ought to do to him; but bring his gray hair down to the grave with blood." Ex. 20:7

David Dies—1 Chr. 3:4; 29:26–28

10 So David rested with his fathers, and was buried in [R]the City of David. 2 Sam. 5:7
11 The period that David [R]reigned over Israel *was* forty years; seven years he reigned in Hebron, and in Jerusalem he reigned thirty-three years. 2 Sam. 5:4, 5

Solomon Is Established as King—1 Chr. 29:23

12 [R]Then Solomon sat on the throne of his father David; and his kingdom was [R]firmly established. 1 Chr. 29:23 · 2 Chr. 1:1

Adonijah Is Executed

13 Now Adonijah the son of Haggith came to Bathsheba the mother of Solomon. And she said, [R]"Do you come peaceably?" And he said, "Peaceably." 1 Sam. 16:4, 5
14 Moreover he said, "I have something *to say* to you." And she said, "Say it."
15 Then he said, "You know that the kingdom was [R]mine, and all Israel had set their expectations on me, that I should reign. However, the kingdom has been turned over, and has become my brother's; for [R]it was his from the LORD. 1 Kin. 1:11, 18 · [Dan. 2:21]
16 "Now I ask one petition of you; do not deny me." And she said to him, "Say it."
17 Then he said, "Please speak to King Solomon, for he will not refuse you, that he may give me [R]Abishag the Shunammite as wife." 1 Kin. 1:3, 4
18 So Bathsheba said, "Very well, I will speak for you to the king."
19 Bathsheba therefore went to King Solomon, to speak to him for Adonijah. And the king rose up to meet her and [R]bowed down to her, and sat down on his throne and had a throne set for the king's mother; [R]so she sat at his right hand. [Ex. 20:12] · Ps. 45:9
20 Then she said, "I desire one small petition of you; do not [T]refuse me." And the king said to her, "Ask it, my mother, for I will not refuse you." Lit. *turn away the face*
21 So she said, "Let Abishag the Shunammite be given to Adonijah your brother as wife."
22 And King Solomon answered and said to his mother, "Now why do you ask Abishag the Shunammite for Adonijah? Ask for him the kingdom also—for he *is* my older brother—for him, and for Abiathar the priest, and for Joab the son of Zeruiah."
23 Then King Solomon swore by the LORD, saying, [R]"May God do so to me, and more also, if Adonijah has not spoken this word against his own life! Ruth 1:17
24 "Now therefore, *as* the LORD lives, who has established me and set me on the throne of David my father, and who has made me a house, as He [R]promised, Adonijah shall be put to death today!" 2 Sam. 7:11, 13

25 So King Solomon sent by the hand of [R]Benaiah the son of Jehoiada; and he struck him down, and he died. 2 Sam. 8:18

Abiathar Is Removed

26 And to Abiathar the priest the king said, "Go to Anathoth, to your own fields, for you *are* worthy of death; but I will not put you to death at this time, because you carried the ark of the Lord GOD before my father David, and because you were afflicted every time my father was afflicted."

27 So Solomon removed Abiathar from being priest to the LORD, that he might fulfill the word of the LORD which He spoke concerning the house of Eli at Shiloh.

Joab Is Executed

28 Then news came to Joab, for Joab [R]had defected to Adonijah, though he had not defected to Absalom. So Joab fled to the tabernacle of the LORD, and [R]took hold of the horns of the altar. 1 Kin. 1:7 • 1 Kin. 1:50

29 And King Solomon was told, "Joab has fled to the tabernacle of the LORD; there *he is*, by the altar." Then Solomon sent Benaiah the son of Jehoiada, saying, "Go, [R]strike him down." 1 Kin. 2:5, 6

30 So Benaiah went to the tabernacle of the LORD, and said to him, "Thus says the king, [R]'Come out!' " And he said, "No, but I will die here." And Benaiah brought back word to the king, saying, "Thus said Joab, and thus he answered me." [Ex. 21:14]

31 And the king said to him, [R]"Do as he has said, and strike him down and bury him, [R]that you may take away from me and from the house of my father the innocent blood which Joab shed. [Ex. 21:14] • [Num. 35:33]

32 "So the LORD will return his [T]blood on his head, because he struck down two men more righteous and better than he, and killed them with the sword—Abner the son of Ner, the commander of the army of Israel, and Amasa the son of Jether, the commander of the army of Judah—though my father David did not know *it*. Or *bloodshed*

33 "Their blood shall therefore return upon the head of Joab and upon the head of his descendants forever. But upon David and his descendants, upon his house and his throne, there shall be peace forever from the LORD."

34 So Benaiah the son of Jehoiada went up and struck and killed him; and he was buried in his own house in the wilderness.

35 The king put Benaiah the son of Jehoiada in his place over the army, and the king put [R]Zadok the priest in the place of [R]Abiathar. 1 Sam. 2:35 • 1 Kin. 2:27

Shimei Is Executed

36 Then the king sent and called for [R]Shimei, and said to him, "Build yourself a house in Jerusalem and dwell there, and do not go out from there anywhere. 1 Kin. 2:8

37 "For it shall be, on the day you go out and cross the Brook Kidron, know for certain you shall surely die; [R]your [T]blood shall be on your own head." Josh. 2:19 • Or *bloodshed*

38 And Shimei said to the king, "The saying *is* good. As my lord the king has said, so your servant will do." So Shimei dwelt in Jerusalem many days.

39 Now it happened at the end of three years, that two slaves of Shimei ran away to [R]Achish the son of Maachah, king of Gath. And they told Shimei, saying, "Look, your slaves *are* in Gath!" 1 Sam. 27:2

40 So Shimei arose, saddled his donkey, and went to Achish at Gath to seek his slaves. And Shimei went and brought his slaves from Gath.

41 And Solomon was told that Shimei had gone from Jerusalem to Gath and had come back.

42 Then the king sent and called for Shimei, and said to him, "Did I not make you swear by the LORD, and warn you, saying, 'Know for certain that on the day you go out and travel anywhere, you shall surely die'? And you said to me, 'The word I have heard *is* good.'

43 "Why then have you not kept the oath of the LORD and the commandment that I gave you?"

44 The king said moreover to Shimei, "You know, as your heart acknowledges, all the wickedness that you did to my father David; therefore the LORD will [R]return your wickedness on your own head. 1 Sam. 25:39

45 "But King Solomon *shall be* blessed, and [R]the throne of David shall be established before the LORD forever." [Prov. 25:5]

46 So the king commanded Benaiah the son of Jehoiada; and he went out and struck him down, and he died. Thus the [R]kingdom was established in the hand of Solomon. 2 Chr. 1:1

CHAPTER 3

Unwise Marriage of Solomon

NOW Solomon made a treaty with Pharaoh king of Egypt, and married Pharaoh's daughter; then he brought her to the City of David until he had finished building his own house, and [R]the house of the LORD, and the wall all around Jerusalem. 1 Kin. 6

2 Meanwhile the people sacrificed at the high places, because there was no house built for the name of the LORD until those days.

Request for Wisdom—2 Chr. 1:2–13

3 And Solomon [R]loved the LORD, [R]walking in the statutes of his father David, except that he sacrificed and burned incense at the high places. [Rom. 8:28] • [1 Kin. 3:6, 14]

4 Now [R]the king went to Gibeon to sacrifice there, [R]for that *was* the great high place:

Solomon offered a thousand burnt offerings
on that altar. 2 Chr. 1:3 • 1 Chr. 16:39; 21:29
5 At Gibeon the LORD appeared to Solomon [R]in a dream by night; and God said,
"Ask! What shall I give you?" Num. 12:6
6 And Solomon said: "You have shown
great mercy to your servant David my father,
because he walked before You in truth, in
righteousness, and in uprightness of heart
with You; You have continued this great
kindness for him, and You have given him a
son to sit on his throne, as *it is* this day.
7 "Now, O LORD my God, You have made
Your servant king instead of my father David, but I *am* a [R]little child; I do not know
how [R]to go out or come in. Jer. 1:6, 7 • Num. 27:17
8 "And Your servant *is* in the midst of
Your people whom You [R]have chosen, a great
people, [R]too numerous to be numbered or
counted. [Deut. 7:6] • Gen. 13:6; 15:5; 22:17
9 "Therefore give to Your servant an [T]un-
derstanding heart [R]to judge Your people, that
I may [R]discern between good and evil. For
who is able to judge this great people of
Yours?" Lit. *hearing* • Ps. 72:1, 2 • [Heb. 5:14]
10 And the speech pleased the LORD, that
Solomon had asked this thing.
11 Then God said to him: "Because you
have asked this thing, and have [R]not asked
long life for yourself, nor have asked riches
for yourself, nor have asked the life of your
enemies, but have asked for yourself understanding to discern justice, [James 4:3]
12 [R]"behold, I have done according to your
words; see, I have given you a wise and
understanding heart, so that there has not
been anyone like you before you, nor shall
any like you arise after you. [1 John 5:14, 15]
13 "And I have also [R]given you what you
have not asked: both riches and honor, so
that there shall not be anyone like you
among the kings all your days. [Matt. 6:33]
14 "So [R]if you walk in My ways, to keep My
statutes and My commandments, as your
father David walked, then I will [R]lengthen[T]
your days." [1 Kin. 6:12] • Ps. 91:16 • *prolong*
15 Then Solomon [R]awoke; and indeed it had
been a dream. And he came to Jerusalem and
stood before the ark of the covenant of the
LORD, offered up burnt offerings, offered
peace offerings, and [R]made a feast for all his
servants. Gen. 41:7 • 1 Kin. 8:65

Display of Solomon's Wisdom

16 Then two women *who were* harlots came
to the king, and [R]stood before him. Num. 27:2
17 And one woman said, "O my lord, this
woman and I dwell in the same house; and I
gave birth while she *was* in the house.
18 "Then it happened, the third day after I
had given birth, that this woman also gave
birth. And we *were* together; *there was* [T]no
one with us in the house, except the two of us
in the house. Lit. *no stranger*
19 "And this woman's son died in the night,
because she lay on him.
20 "So she arose in the middle of the night
and took my son from my side, while your
maidservant slept, and laid him in her bosom,
and laid her dead child in my bosom.
21 "And when I rose in the morning to
nurse my son, there he was, dead. But when I
had examined him in the morning, indeed, he
was not my son whom I had borne."
22 Then the other woman said, "No! But the
living one *is* my son, and the dead one *is* your
son." And the first woman said, "No! But the
dead one *is* your son, and the living one *is* my
son." Thus they spoke before the king.
23 And the king said, "The one says, 'This *is*
my son, who lives, and your son *is* the dead
one'; and the other says, 'No! But your son *is*
the dead one, and my son *is* the living one.' "
24 Then the king said, "Bring me a sword."
So they brought a sword before the king.
25 And the king said, "Divide the living
child in two, and give half to one, and half to
the other."
26 Then the woman whose son *was* living
spoke to the king, for she yearned with
compassion for her son; and she said, "O my
lord, give her the living child, and by no
means kill him!" But the other said, "Let him
be neither mine nor yours, *but* divide *him*."
27 So the king answered and said, "Give the
first woman the living child, and by no means
kill him; she *is* his mother."

National Recognition of Solomon's Wisdom

28 And all Israel heard of the judgment
which the king had rendered; and they feared
the king, for they saw that the wisdom of
God *was* in him to administer justice.

CHAPTER 4

Eleven Princes

SO King Solomon was king over all Israel.
2 And these *were* his officials: Azariah
the son of Zadok, the priest;
3 Elihoreph and Ahijah, the sons of Shisha,
[T]scribes; [R]Jehoshaphat the son of Ahilud, the
recorder; *secretaries* • 2 Sam. 8:16; 20:24
4 Benaiah the son of Jehoiada, over the
army; Zadok and Abiathar, the priests;
5 Azariah the son of Nathan, over the
officers; Zabud the son of Nathan, a priest
and [R]the king's friend; 2 Sam. 15:37; 16:16
6 Ahishar, over the household; and Adoniram the son of Abda, over the labor force.

Twelve Governors

7 And Solomon had twelve governors over
all Israel, who provided food for the king and
his household; each one made provision for
one month of the year.

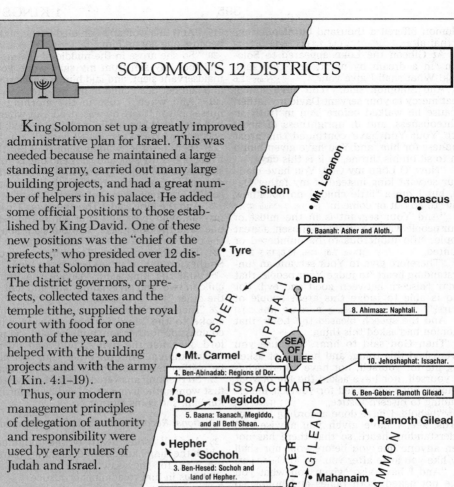

SOLOMON'S 12 DISTRICTS

King Solomon set up a greatly improved administrative plan for Israel. This was needed because he maintained a large standing army, carried out many large building projects, and had a great number of helpers in his palace. He added some official positions to those established by King David. One of these new positions was the "chief of the prefects," who presided over 12 districts that Solomon had created. The district governors, or prefects, collected taxes and the temple tithe, supplied the royal court with food for one month of the year, and helped with the building projects and with the army (1 Kin. 4:1–19).

Thus, our modern management principles of delegation of authority and responsibility were used by early rulers of Judah and Israel.

8 These *are* their names: [T]Ben-Hur, in the
mountains of Ephraim; Lit. *Son of Hur*
9 [T]Ben-Deker, in Makaz, Shaalbim, Beth
Shemesh, and Elon Beth Hanan; Lit. *Son of Deker*
10 Ben-Hesed, in Arubboth; to him *belonged*
Sochoh and all the land of Hepher;
11 [T]Ben-Abinadab, *in* all the regions of Dor;
he had Taphath the daughter of Solomon as
wife; Lit. *Son of Abinadab*
12 Baana the son of Ahilud, *in* Taanach,
Megiddo, and all Beth Shean, which *is* beside
Zaretan below Jezreel, from Beth Shean to
Abel Meholah, as far as the other side of
Jokneam;
13 [T]Ben-Geber, in Ramoth Gilead; to him
belonged the towns of Jair the son of Manasseh, in Gilead; to him *also belonged* the
region of Argob in Bashan—sixty large cities
with walls and bronze gate-bars; *Son of Geber*
14 Ahinadab the son of Iddo, *in* Mahanaim;
15 Ahimaaz, in Naphtali; he also took Basemath the daughter of Solomon as wife;
16 Baanah the son of [R]Hushai, in Asher and
Aloth; 1 Chr. 27:33
17 Jehoshaphat the son of Paruah, in Issachar;
18 Shimei the son of Elah, in Benjamin;
19 Geber the son of Uri, in the land of
Gilead, *in* the country of Sihon king of the
Amorites and of Og king of Bashan; and *he*
was the only governor who *was* in the land.

Solomon Reigns in Wisdom

20 Judah and Israel *were* as numerous [R]as
the sand by the sea in multitude, [R]eating and
drinking and rejoicing. Gen. 22:17; 32:12 • Mic. 4:4
21 So [R]Solomon reigned over all kingdoms
from [R]the[T] River *to* the land of the Philistines,
as far as the border of Egypt. [R]*They* brought
tribute and served Solomon all the days of his
life. Ps. 72:8 • Gen. 15:18 • The Euphrates • Ps. 68:29
22 [R]Now Solomon's [T]provision for one day
was [T]thirty kors of fine flour, sixty kors of
meal, Neh. 5:18 • Lit. *bread* • 195.72 bu.
23 ten fatted oxen, twenty oxen from the
pastures, and one hundred sheep, besides
deer, gazelles, roebucks, and fatted fowl.
24 For he had dominion over all *the region*
on this side of [T]the River from Tiphsah even
to Gaza, namely over [R]all the kings on this
side of the River; and he had peace on every
side all around him. The Euphrates • Ps. 72:11
25 And Judah and Israel [R]dwelt[T] safely,
[R]each man under his vine and his fig tree,
from Dan as far as Beersheba, all the days of
Solomon. [Jer. 23:6] • *lived in safety* • [Mic. 4:4]
26 [R]Solomon had forty thousand stalls of
[R]horses for his chariots, and twelve thousand
horsemen. 1 Kin. 10:26 • [Deut. 17:16]
27 And [R]these governors, each man in his
month, provided food for King Solomon and
for all who came to King Solomon's table.
There was no lack in their supply. 1 Kin. 4:7
28 They also brought barley and straw to
the proper place, for the horses and steeds,
each man according to his charge.
29 And God gave Solomon wisdom and
exceedingly great understanding, and large-
ness of heart like the sand on the seashore.
30 Thus Solomon's wisdom excelled the
wisdom of all the men [R]of the East and all
[R]the wisdom of Egypt. Gen. 25:6 • Is. 19:11, 12
31 For he was wiser than all men—than
Ethan the Ezrahite, [R]and Heman, Chalcol,
and Darda, the sons of Mahol; and his fame
was in all the surrounding nations. 1 Chr. 2:6
32 He spoke three thousand proverbs, and
his songs were one thousand and five.
33 Also he spoke of trees, from the cedar
tree of Lebanon even to the hyssop that
springs out of the wall; he spoke also of
animals, of birds, of creeping things, and of
fish.
34 And men of all nations, from all the kings
of the earth who had heard of his wisdom,
came to hear the wisdom of Solomon.

CHAPTER 5

Temple Materials—2 Chr. 2:3–12

NOW [R]Hiram king of Tyre sent his servants to Solomon, because he heard
that they had anointed him king in place of
his father, [R]for Hiram had always loved David. 2 Chr. 2:3 • 2 Sam. 5:11
2 Then Solomon sent to Hiram, saying:
3 "You know how my father David could
not build a house for the name of the LORD
his God because of the wars which were
fought against him on every side, until the
LORD put his foes under the soles of his feet.
4 "But now the LORD my God has given me
[T]rest on every side, *so that there is* neither
adversary nor evil occurrence. *peace*
5 "And behold, I propose to build a house
for the name of the LORD my God, as the
LORD spoke to my father David, saying, 'Your
son, whom I will set on your throne in your
place, he shall build the house for My name.'
6 "Now therefore, command that they cut
down [R]cedars for me from Lebanon; and my
servants will be with your servants, and I will
pay you wages for your servants according to
whatever you say. For you know *there is*
none among us who has skill to cut timber
like the Sidonians." 2 Chr. 2:8, 10
7 So it was, when Hiram heard the words
of Solomon, that he rejoiced greatly and said,
"Blessed *be* the LORD this day, for He has
given David a wise son over this great people!"
8 Then Hiram sent to Solomon, saying: "I
have considered *the message* which you sent
me, *and* I will do all you desire concerning
the cedar and cypress logs.

9 "My servants shall bring *them* down
from Lebanon to the sea; I will float them in
rafts by sea to the place you indicate to me,
and will have them broken apart there; then
you can take *them* away. And you shall fulfill
my desire by giving food for my household."
10 So Hiram gave Solomon cedar and cypress logs *according to* all his desire.
11 And Solomon gave Hiram twenty thousand kors of wheat *as* food for his household,
and twenty kors of pressed oil. Thus Solomon
gave to Hiram year by year.
12 So the LORD gave Solomon wisdom, [R]as
He had promised him; and there was peace
between Hiram and Solomon, and the two of
them made a treaty together. 1 Kin. 3:12

Temple Laborers

13 Then King Solomon raised up a labor
force out of all Israel; and the labor force was
thirty thousand men.
14 And he sent them to Lebanon, ten thousand a month in shifts: they were one month
in Lebanon *and* two months at home; Adoniram *was* in charge of the labor force.
15 [R]Solomon had seventy thousand who
carried burdens, and eighty thousand who
quarried *stone* in the mountains, 2 Chr. 2:17, 18
16 besides three thousand three hundred
from the [R]chiefs of Solomon's deputies, who
supervised the people who labored in the
work. 1 Kin. 9:23
17 And the king commanded them to
quarry large stones, costly stones, *and* hewn
stones, to lay the foundation of the temple.
18 So Solomon's builders, Hiram's builders,
and the Gebalites quarried *them*; and they
prepared timber and stones to build the
[T]temple. Lit. *house*

CHAPTER 6

The Temple Is Completed—2 Chr. 3:1–14

AND it came to pass in the four hundred
and eightieth year after the children of
Israel had come out of the land of Egypt, in
the fourth year of Solomon's reign over
Israel, in the month of [T]Ziv, which *is* the
second month, that he began to build the
house of the LORD. Or *Ayyar*, April or May
2 Now the house which King Solomon
built for the LORD, its length *was* sixty cubits,
its width twenty, and its height thirty cubits.
3 The vestibule in front of the [R]sanctuary
of the house *was* [T]twenty cubits long across
the breadth of the house, *and* its width *ex-*
tended [T]ten cubits from the front of the
house. Ex. 26:33; Ezek. 41:1 • 30 ft. • 15 ft.
4 And he made for the house [R]windows
with beveled frames. Ezek. 40:16; 41:16
5 Against the wall of the [T]temple he built
[R]chambers all around, *against* the walls of the
temple, all around *both* the sanctuary and the
inner sanctuary. Thus he made side chambers
all around it. Lit. *house* • Ezek. 41:6
6 The lowest chamber *was* five cubits
wide, the middle *was* six cubits wide, and the
third *was* seven cubits wide; for he made
narrow ledges around the outside of the
temple, so that *the support beams* would not
be fastened into the walls of the temple.
7 And the temple, when it was being built,
was built with stone finished at the quarry, so
that no hammer or chisel *or* any iron tool was
heard in the temple while it was being built.
8 The doorway for the middle story *was* on
the right side of the temple. They went up by
stairs to the middle *story*, and from the
middle to the third.
9 [R]So he built the [T]temple and finished it,
and he paneled the temple with beams and
boards of cedar. 1 Kin. 6:14, 38 • Lit. *house*
10 And he built side chambers against the
entire temple, each [T]five cubits high; they
were attached to the temple with cedar
beams. 7.5 ft.
11 Then the word of the LORD came to
Solomon, saying:
12 "*Concerning* this [T]temple which you are
building, if you walk in My statutes, execute
My judgments, keep all My commandments,
and walk in them, then I will perform My
[T]word with you, [R]which I spoke to your
father David. Lit. *house* • *promise* • [2 Sam. 7:13]
13 "And [R]I will dwell among the children of
Israel, and will not [R]forsake My people Israel." Ex. 25:8 • [Deut. 31:6]
14 So Solomon built the temple and finished
it.
15 And he built the inside walls of the
temple with cedar boards; from the floor of
the temple to the ceiling he paneled *them* on
the inside with wood; and he covered the
floor of the temple with planks of cypress.
16 Then he built the twenty-cubit room at
the rear of the temple, from floor to ceiling,
with cedar boards; he built *it* inside as the
inner sanctuary, as the Most Holy *Place*.
17 And in front of it the temple sanctuary
was [T]forty cubits *long*. 60 ft.
18 The inside of the temple was cedar,
carved with ornamental buds and open flowers. All *was* cedar; there was no stone *to be*
seen.
19 And he prepared the [T]inner sanctuary
inside the temple, to set the ark of the covenant of the LORD there. The Most Holy Place
20 The inner sanctuary *was* [T]twenty cubits
long, twenty cubits wide, and twenty cubits
high. He overlaid it with pure gold, and
overlaid the altar of cedar. 30 ft.
21 So Solomon overlaid the inside of the
temple with pure gold. He stretched gold
chains across the front of the inner sanctuary; and he overlaid it with gold.
22 The whole temple he overlaid with gold,
until he had finished all the temple; also he

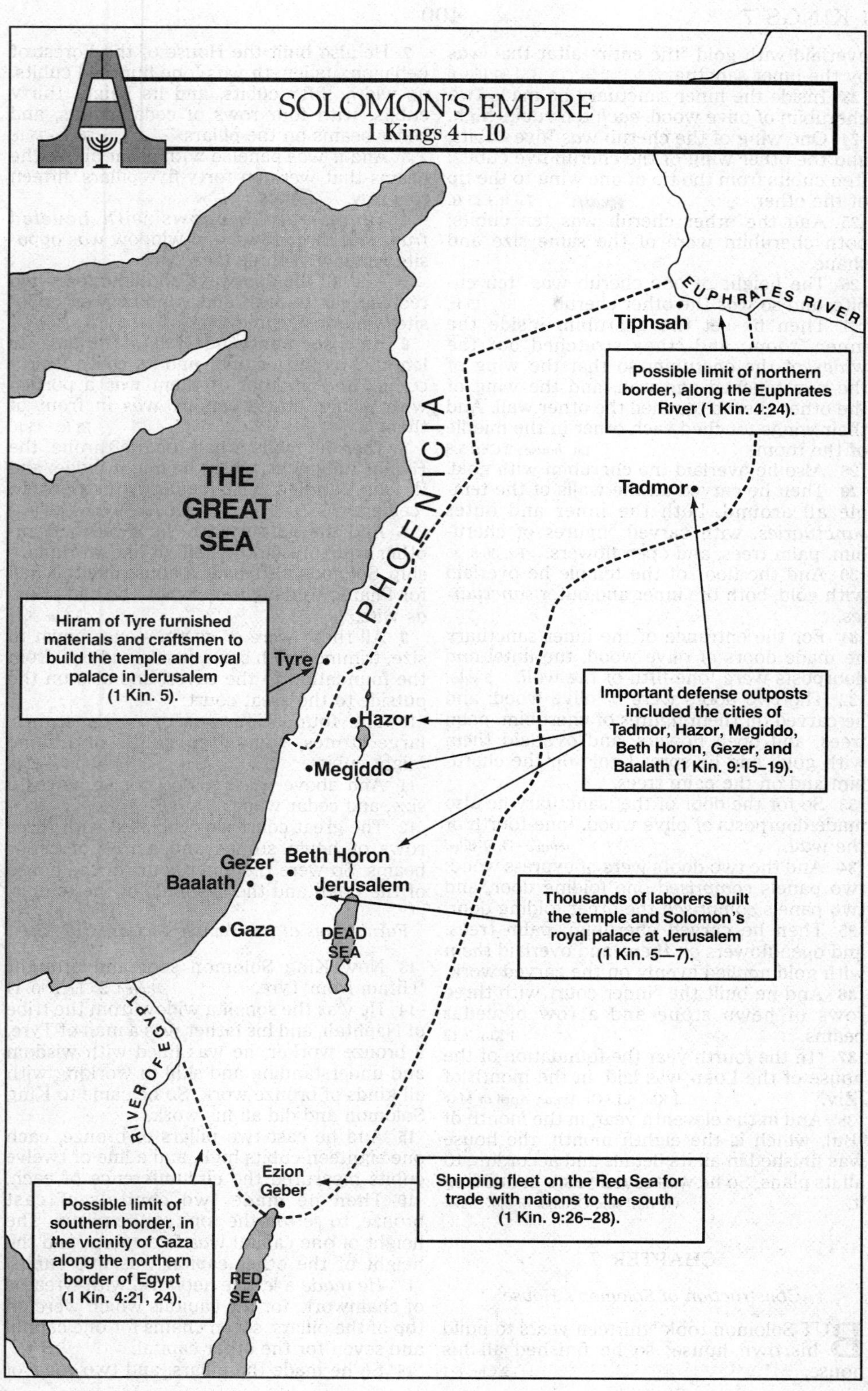
SOLOMON'S EMPIRE
1 Kings 4—10
THE GREAT SEA
PHOENICIA
EUPHRATES RIVER
Tiphsah
Possible limit of northern border, along the Euphrates River (1 Kin. 4:24).
Tadmor
Hiram of Tyre furnished materials and craftsmen to build the temple and royal palace in Jerusalem (1 Kin. 5).
Tyre
Hazor
Megiddo
Important defense outposts included the cities of Tadmor, Hazor, Megiddo, Beth Horon, Gezer, and Baalath (1 Kin. 9:15–19).
Gezer
Beth Horon
Baalath
Jerusalem
Thousands of laborers built the temple and Solomon's royal palace at Jerusalem (1 Kin. 5—7).
Gaza
DEAD SEA
RIVER OF EGYPT
Ezion Geber
Shipping fleet on the Red Sea for trade with nations to the south (1 Kin. 9:26–28).
Possible limit of southern border, in the vicinity of Gaza along the northern border of Egypt (1 Kin. 4:21, 24).
RED SEA

overlaid with gold [R]the entire altar that *was*
by the inner sanctuary. Ex. 30:1, 3, 6
23 Inside the inner sanctuary he made two
cherubim *of* olive wood, *each* ten cubits high.
24 One wing of the cherub *was* [T]five cubits,
and the other wing of the cherub five cubits:
[T]ten cubits from the tip of one wing to the tip
of the other. 7.5 ft. • 15 ft.
25 And the other cherub *was* ten cubits;
both cherubim *were* of the same size and
shape.
26 The height of one cherub *was* [T]ten cubits, and so *was* the other cherub. 15 ft.
27 Then he set the cherubim inside the
inner [T]room; and [R]they stretched out the
wings of the cherubim so that the wing of
the one touched *one* wall, and the wing of
the other cherub touched the other wall. And
their wings touched each other in the middle
of the room. Lit. *house* • 2 Chr. 5:8
28 Also he overlaid the cherubim with gold.
29 Then he carved all the walls of the temple all around, both the inner and outer
sanctuaries, with carved [R]figures of cherubim, palm trees, and open flowers. Ex. 36:8, 35
30 And the floor of the temple he overlaid
with gold, both the inner and outer *sanctuaries*.
31 For the entrance of the inner sanctuary
he made doors *of* olive wood; the lintel *and*
doorposts *were* [T]one-fifth *of the wall*. *5-sided*
32 The two doors *were of* olive wood; and
he carved on them figures of cherubim, palm
trees, and open flowers, and overlaid *them*
with gold; and he spread gold on the cherubim and on the palm trees.
33 So for the door of the [T]sanctuary he also
made doorposts *of* olive wood, [T]one-fourth *of
the wall*. *temple* • Or *4-sided*
34 And the two doors *were of* cypress wood;
two panels *comprised* one folding door, and
two panels *comprised* the other folding door.
35 Then he carved cherubim, palm trees,
and open flowers *on them*, and overlaid *them*
with gold applied evenly on the carved work.
36 And he built the [R]inner court with three
rows of hewn stone and a row of cedar
beams. 1 Kin. 7:12
37 [R]In the fourth year the foundation of the
house of the LORD was laid, in the month of
[T]Ziv. 1 Kin. 6:1 • Or *Ayyar*, April or May
38 And in the eleventh year, in the month of
[T]Bul, which is the eighth month, the house
was finished in all its details and according to
all its plans. So he was seven years in building
it. Or *Heshvan*, October or November

CHAPTER 7

Construction of Solomon's House

BUT Solomon took [R]thirteen years to build
his own house; so he finished all his
house. 2 Chr. 8:1
2 He also built the House of the Forest of
Lebanon; its length *was* [T]one hundred cubits,
its width [T]fifty cubits, and its height thirty
cubits, with four rows of cedar pillars, and
cedar beams on the pillars. 150 ft. • 75 ft.
3 And *it was* paneled with cedar above the
beams that *were* on forty-five pillars, fifteen
to a row.
4 *There were* windows *with beveled
frames in* three rows, and window *was* opposite window *in* three tiers.
5 And all the doorways and doorposts *had*
rectangular frames; and window *was* opposite window *in* three tiers.
6 He also made the Hall of Pillars: its
length *was* [T]fifty cubits, and its width [T]thirty
cubits; and in front of them *was* a portico
with pillars, and a canopy *was* in front of
them. 75 ft. • 45 ft.
7 Then he made a hall for the throne, the
Hall of Judgment, where he might judge; and
it was paneled with cedar from floor to
[T]ceiling. Lit. *floor* of the upper level
8 And the house where he dwelt *had* another court inside the hall, of like workmanship. Solomon also made a house like this hall
for Pharaoh's daughter, [R]whom he had taken
as wife. 2 Chr. 8:11
9 All these *were of* costly stones hewn to
size, trimmed with saws, inside and out, from
the foundation to the eaves, and also on the
outside to the great court.
10 The foundation *was of* costly stones,
large stones, some [T]ten cubits and some
[T]eight cubits. 15 ft. • 12 ft.
11 And above *were* costly stones, hewn to
size, and cedar wood.
12 The great court *was* enclosed with three
rows of hewn stones and a row of cedar
beams. So were the inner court of the house
of the LORD and the vestibule of the temple.

Furnishings of the Temple—2 Chr. 3:15—5:1

13 Now King Solomon sent and brought
[T]Hiram from Tyre. *Huram*, 2 Chr. 2:13, 14
14 He *was* the son of a widow from the tribe
of Naphtali, and his father *was* a man of Tyre,
a bronze worker; he was filled with wisdom
and understanding and skill in working with
all kinds of bronze work. So he came to King
Solomon and did all his work.
15 And he cast two pillars of bronze, each
one eighteen cubits high, and a line of twelve
cubits measured the circumference of each.
16 Then he made two capitals *of* cast
bronze, to set on the tops of the pillars. The
height of one capital *was* five cubits, and the
height of the other capital *was* five cubits.
17 *He made* a lattice network, with wreaths
of chainwork, for the capitals which *were* on
top of the pillars: seven chains for one capital
and seven for the other capital.
18 So he made the pillars, and two rows of

pomegranates above the network all around to cover the capitals that *were* on top; and thus he did for the other capital.

19 And the capitals which *were* on top of the pillars in the hall *were* in the shape of lilies, [T]four cubits. 6 ft.

20 The capitals on the two pillars also *had pomegranates* above, by the convex surface which *was* next to the network; and there *were* two hundred such pomegranates in rows on each of the capitals all around.

21 Then he set up the pillars by the vestibule of the temple; he set up the pillar on the right and called its name [T]Jachin, and he set up the pillar on the left and called its name [T]Boaz. Lit. *He Shall Establish* • Lit. *In It Is Strength*

22 The tops of the pillars were in the shape of lilies. So the work of the pillars was finished.

23 Then he made [R]the Sea of cast bronze, [T]ten cubits from one brim to the other; *it was* completely round. Its height *was* [T]five cubits, and a line of [T]thirty cubits measured its circumference. 2 Chr. 4:2 • 15 ft. • 7.5 ft. • 45 ft.

24 And below its brim *were* ornamental buds encircling it all around, ten to a cubit, all the way around the Sea. The ornamental buds *were* cast in two rows when it was cast.

25 It stood on [R]twelve oxen: three looking toward the north, three looking toward the west, three looking toward the south, and three looking toward the east; the Sea *was set* upon them, and all their back parts *pointed* inward. Jer. 52:20

26 It *was* a handbreadth thick; and its brim was shaped like the brim of a cup, *like* a lily blossom. It contained two thousand baths.

27 He also made ten [T]carts of bronze; four cubits *was* the length of each cart, four cubits its width, and three cubits its height. Or *stands*

28 And this *was* the design of the carts: They had panels, and the panels *were* between frames;

29 on the panels that *were* between the frames *were* lions, oxen, and cherubim. And on the frames *was* a pedestal on top. Below the lions and oxen *were* wreaths of plaited work.

30 Every cart had four bronze wheels and axles of bronze, and its four feet had supports. Under the laver *were* supports of cast *bronze* beside each wreath.

31 Its opening inside the crown at the top *was* [T]one cubit in diameter; and the opening *was* round, shaped *like* a pedestal, [T]one and a half cubits in outside diameter; and also on the opening *were* engravings, but the panels were square, not round. 18 in. • 27 in.

32 Under the panels *were* the four wheels, and the axles of the wheels *were joined* to the cart. The height of a wheel *was* [T]one and a half cubits. 27 in.

33 The workmanship of the wheels *was* like the workmanship of a chariot wheel; their axle pins, their rims, their spokes, and their hubs *were* all of cast *bronze*.

34 And *there were* four supports at the four corners of each cart, *and* its supports *were* part of the cart itself.

35 On the top of the cart, at the height of [T]half a cubit, *it was* perfectly round. And on the top of the cart, its flanges and its panels *were* of the same casting. 9 in.

36 On the plates of its flanges and on its panels he engraved cherubim, lions, and palm trees, wherever there was a clear space on each, with wreaths all around.

37 After this *manner* he made the ten carts. All of them were of [T]the same mold, one measure, *and* one shape. *one*

38 Then [R]he made ten lavers of bronze; each laver contained [T]forty baths, *and* each laver *was* [T]four cubits. On each of the ten carts *was* a laver. 2 Chr. 4:6 • 240 gal. • 6 ft.

39 And he put five carts on the right side of the house, and five on the left side of the house. He set the Sea on the right side of the house toward the southeast.

40 [R]Hiram made the lavers and the shovels and the bowls. So Hiram finished doing all the work that he was to do for King Solomon *on* the house of the LORD: 2 Chr. 4:11—5:1

41 the two pillars, the *two* bowl-shaped capitals that *were* on top of the two pillars, and the two [R]networks covering the two bowl-shaped capitals which *were* on top of the pillars; 1 Kin. 7:17, 18

42 four hundred pomegranates for the two networks (two rows of pomegranates for each network, to cover the two bowl-shaped capitals that *were* on top of the pillars);

43 the ten carts, and ten lavers on the carts;

44 one Sea, and twelve oxen under the Sea;

45 [R]the pots, the shovels, and the bowls. All these articles which Hiram made for King Solomon *for* the house of the LORD *were of* burnished bronze. Ex. 27:3

46 [R]In the plain of Jordan the king had them cast in clay molds, between [R]Succoth and [R]Zaretan. 2 Chr. 4:17 • Gen. 33:17 • Josh. 3:16

47 And Solomon did not weigh all the articles, because *there were* so many; the weight of the bronze was not determined.

48 Solomon had all the furnishings made for the house of the LORD: [R]the altar of gold, and [R]the table of gold on which *was* [R]the showbread; Ex. 37:25, 26 • Ex. 37:10, 11 • Lev. 24:5–8

49 the lampstands of pure gold, five on the right *side* and five on the left in front of the inner sanctuary, with the flowers and the lamps and the wick-trimmers *of* gold;

50 the basins, the trimmers, the bowls, the ladles, and the [T]censers *of* pure gold; and the hinges *of* gold, *both* for the doors of the inner room (the Most Holy *Place*) *and* for the doors of the main hall of the temple. *fire pans*

51 Thus all the work that King Solomon

had done *for* the house of the LORD was
finished; and Solomon brought in the things
[R]which his father David had dedicated: the
silver and the gold and the furnishings. *And*
he put them in the treasuries of the house of
the LORD. 2 Sam. 8:11

CHAPTER 8

The Ark Returns—2 Chr. 5:2-12

NOW Solomon assembled the elders of
Israel and all the heads of the tribes, the
chief fathers of the children of Israel, to King
Solomon in Jerusalem, that they might bring
up the ark of the covenant of the LORD from
the City of David, which *is* Zion.
2 And all the men of Israel assembled to
King Solomon at the feast in the month of
Ethanim, which *is* the seventh month.
3 Then all the elders of Israel came, [R]and
the priests took up the ark. Num. 4:15; 7:9
4 And they brought up the ark of the
LORD, the tabernacle of meeting, and all the
holy furnishings that *were* in the tabernacle.
The priests and the Levites brought them up.
5 Also King Solomon, and all the congregation of Israel who were assembled to him,
were with him before the ark, [R]sacrificing
sheep and oxen that could not be counted or
numbered for multitude. 2 Sam. 6:13
6 Then the priests [R]brought in the ark of
the covenant of the LORD to [R]its place, into
the inner sanctuary of the temple, to the
Most Holy *Place*, [R]under the wings of the
cherubim. 2 Sam. 6:17 • 1 Kin. 6:19 • 1 Kin. 6:27
7 For the cherubim spread *their* two wings
over the place of the ark, and the cherubim
overshadowed the ark and its poles.
8 And the poles [R]extended so that the
[T]ends of the poles could be seen from the holy
place, in front of the inner sanctuary; but
they could not be seen from outside. So they
are there to this day. Ex. 25:13–15; 37:4, 5 • *heads*
9 *There was* nothing in the ark except the
two tablets of stone which Moses put there at
Horeb, when the LORD made *a covenant* with
the children of Israel, when they came out of
the land of Egypt.

The Shechinah Returns—2 Chr. 5:13, 14

10 And it came to pass, when the priests
came out of the holy *place*, that the cloud
[R]filled the house of the LORD, Ex. 40:34, 35
11 so that the priests could not continue
ministering because of the cloud; for the
[R]glory of the LORD filled the house of the
LORD. 2 Chr. 7:1, 2

Solomon's Sermon—2 Chr. 6:1-11

12 [R]Then Solomon spoke: 2 Chr. 6:1

"The LORD said He would dwell [R]in the
dark cloud. Ps. 18:11; 97:2
13 [R]I have surely built You an exalted
house, 2 Sam. 7:13
[R]And a place for You to dwell in
forever." Ps. 132:14

14 And the king turned around and blessed
the whole congregation of Israel, while all
the congregation of Israel was standing.
15 Then he said: [R]"Blessed *be* the LORD God
of Israel, who [R]spoke with His mouth to my
father David, and with His hand has fulfilled
it, saying, Luke 1:68 • 2 Sam. 7:2, 12, 13, 25
16 'Since the day that I brought My people
Israel out of Egypt, I have chosen no city
from any tribe of Israel *in which* to build a
house, that My name might be there; but I
chose David to be over My people Israel.'
17 "Now [R]it was in the heart of my father
David to build a house for the name of the
LORD God of Israel. 2 Sam. 7:2, 3
18 [R]"But the LORD said to my father David,
'Whereas it was in your heart to build a
house for My name, you did well that it was
in your heart. 2 Chr. 6:8, 9
19 'Nevertheless [R]you shall not build the
house, but your son, who shall come from
your loins, he shall build the house for My
name.' 2 Sam. 7:5, 12, 13
20 "So the LORD has fulfilled His word
which He spoke; and I have [T]filled the position of my father David, and sit on the throne
of Israel, [R]as the LORD promised; and I have
built a house for the name of the LORD God of
Israel. *risen in the place of* • 1 Chr. 28:5, 6
21 "And there I have made a place for the
ark, in which *is* the covenant of the LORD
which He made with our fathers, when He
brought them out of the land of Egypt."

Solomon's Prayer—2 Chr. 6:12-39

22 Then Solomon stood before [R]the altar of
the LORD in the presence of all the congregation of Israel, and [R]spread out his hands
toward heaven; 2 Chr. 6:12 • Ezra 9:5
23 and he said: "LORD God of Israel, *there is*
no God in heaven above or on earth below
like You, [R]who keep Your covenant and
mercy with Your servants who [R]walk before
You with all their heart. [Neh. 1:5] • [Gen. 17:1]
24 "You have kept what You promised
Your servant David my father; You have
both spoken with Your mouth and fulfilled *it*
with Your hand, as *it is* this day.
25 "Therefore, LORD God of Israel, now
keep what You promised Your servant David
my father, saying, [R]'You shall not fail to have
a man sit before Me on the throne of Israel,
only if your sons take heed to their way, that
they walk before Me as you have walked
before Me.' 1 Kin. 2:4; 9:5
26 "And now I pray, O God of Israel, let
Your word come true, which You have spoken to Your servant David my father.

27 "But [R]will God indeed dwell on the earth?
Behold, heaven and the heaven of heavens
cannot contain You. How much less this
temple which I have built! [Acts 7:49; 17:24]
28 "Yet regard the prayer of Your servant
and his supplication, O LORD my God, and
listen to the cry and the prayer which Your
servant is praying before You today:
29 "that Your eyes may be open toward this
[T]temple night and day, toward the place of
which You said, 'My name shall be there,'
that You may hear the prayer which Your
servant makes toward this place. Lit. *house*
30 [R]"And may You hear the supplication of
Your servant and of Your people Israel.
When they pray toward this place, then hear
in heaven Your dwelling place; and when
You hear, forgive. Neh. 1:6
31 "When anyone sins against his neighbor,
and is forced to take [R]an oath, and comes *and*
takes an oath before Your altar in this temple, Ex. 22:8–11
32 "then hear in heaven, and act and judge
Your servants, [R]condemning the wicked,
bringing his way on his head, and justifying
the righteous by giving him according to his
righteousness. Deut. 25:1
33 "When Your people Israel are defeated
before an enemy because they have sinned
against You, and when they turn back to You
and confess Your name, and pray and make
supplication to You in this temple,
34 "then hear in heaven, and forgive the sin
of Your people Israel, and bring them back to
the land which You gave to their fathers.
35 [R]"When the heavens are shut up and
there is no rain because they have sinned
against You, when they pray toward this
place and confess Your name, and turn from
their sin because You afflict them, Deut. 28:23
36 "then hear in heaven, and forgive the sin
of Your servants, Your people Israel, that
You may teach them [R]the good way in which
they should walk; and give rain on Your land
which You have given to Your people as an
inheritance. 1 Sam. 12:23
37 "When there is famine in the land, *or*
pestilence, blight *or* mildew, locusts *or* grasshoppers; when their enemy besieges them in
the land of their [T]cities; whatever plague or
whatever sickness *there is*; Lit. *gates*
38 "whatever prayer, whatever supplication
is *made* by anyone, *or* by all Your people
Israel, when each one knows the plague of
his own heart, and spreads out his hands
toward this temple:
39 "then hear in heaven Your dwelling
place, and forgive, and act, and give to everyone according to all his ways, whose heart
You know (for You, only You, [R]know the
hearts of all the sons of men), [1 Sam. 16:7]
40 [R]"that they may fear You all the days
that they live in the land which You gave to
our fathers. [Ps. 130:4]

41 "Moreover, concerning a foreigner, who
is not of Your people Israel, but has come
from a far country for Your name's sake
42 "(for they will hear of Your great name
and Your [R]strong hand and Your outstretched arm), when he comes and prays
toward this temple, Deut. 3:24
43 "hear in heaven Your dwelling place, and
do according to all for which the foreigner
calls to You, [R]that all peoples of the earth
may know Your name and [R]fear You, as *do*
Your people Israel, and that they may know
that this temple which I have built is called
by Your name. [1 Sam. 17:46] • Ps. 102:15
44 "When Your people go out to battle
against their enemy, wherever You send
them, and when they pray to the LORD
toward the city which You have chosen and
toward the temple which I have built for
Your name,
45 "then hear in heaven their prayer and
their supplication, and maintain their cause.
46 "When they sin against You (for *there is*
no one who does not sin), and You become
angry with them and deliver them to the
enemy, and they take them captive [R]to the
land of the enemy, far or near; Lev. 26:34, 44
47 [R]"*yet* when they come to themselves in
the land where they were carried captive, and
repent, and make supplication to You in the
land of those who took them captive, [R]saying,
'We have sinned and done wrong, we have
committed wickedness'; [Lev. 26:40–42] • Dan. 9:5
48 "and *when* they [R]return to You with all
their heart and with all their soul in the land
of their enemies who led them away captive,
and [R]pray to You toward their land which
You gave to their fathers, the city which You
have chosen and the temple which I have
built for Your name: Jer. 29:12–14 • Dan. 6:10
49 "then hear in heaven Your dwelling
place their prayer and their supplication, and
maintain their [T]cause, *justice*
50 "and forgive Your people who have
sinned against You, and all their transgressions which they have transgressed against
You; and [R]grant them compassion before
those who took them captive, that they may
have compassion on them Ps. 106:46
51 "(for [R]they *are* Your people and Your
inheritance, whom You brought out of Egypt,
[R]out of the iron furnace), Deut. 9:26–29 • Jer. 11:4
52 [R]"that Your eyes may be open to the
supplication of Your servant and the supplication of Your people Israel, to listen to them
whenever they call to You. 1 Kin. 8:29
53 "For You separated them from among all
the peoples of the earth *to be* Your inheritance, [R]as You spoke by the hand of Your
servant Moses, when You brought our fathers out of Egypt, O Lord GOD." Ex. 19:5, 6
54 [R]And so it was, when Solomon had finished praying all this prayer and supplication
to the LORD, that he arose from before the

altar of the LORD, from kneeling on his knees
with his hands spread up to heaven. 2 Chr. 7:1
55 Then he stood and blessed all the congregation of Israel with a loud voice, saying:
56 "Blessed *be* the LORD, who has given
[T]rest to His people Israel, according to all that
He promised. There has not failed one word
of all His good promise, which He promised
through His servant Moses. *peace*
57 "May the LORD our God be with us, as
He was with our fathers. [R]May He not leave
us nor forsake us, Deut. 31:6
58 "that He may [R]incline our hearts to
Himself, to walk in all His ways, and to keep
His commandments and His statutes and His
judgments, which He commanded our fathers. Ps. 119:36
59 "And may these words of mine, with
which I have made supplication before the
LORD, be near the LORD our God day and
night, that He may maintain the cause of His
servant and the cause of His people Israel, as
each day may require,
60 [R]"that all the peoples of the earth may
know that [R]the LORD *is* God; *there is* no
other. 1 Sam. 17:46 • Deut. 4:35, 39
61 "Let your heart therefore be loyal to the
LORD our God, to walk in His statutes and
keep His commandments, as at this day."

Israel Rejoices—2 Chr. 7:4-10

62 Then [R]the king and all Israel with him
offered sacrifices before the LORD. 2 Chr. 7:4-10
63 And Solomon offered a sacrifice of peace
offerings, which he offered to the LORD,
twenty-two thousand bulls and one hundred
and twenty thousand sheep. So the king and
all the children of Israel dedicated the house
of the LORD.
64 On the same day the king consecrated
the middle of the court that *was* in front of
the house of the LORD; for there he offered
burnt offerings, grain offerings, and the fat of
the peace offerings, because the bronze altar
that *was* before the LORD *was* too small to
receive the burnt offerings, the grain offerings, and the fat of the peace offerings.
65 At that time Solomon held a feast, and
all Israel with him, a great congregation from
the entrance of Hamath to the Brook of
Egypt, before the LORD our God, seven days
and seven *more* days—fourteen days.
66 On the eighth day he sent the people
away; and they blessed the king, and went to
their tents joyful and glad of heart for all the
goodness that the LORD had done for His
servant David, and for Israel His people.

CHAPTER 9

Reiteration of the Davidic Covenant
2 Chr. 7:11-22

AND it came to pass, when Solomon had
finished building the house of the LORD
and the king's house, and [R]all Solomon's
desire which he wanted to do, 2 Chr. 8:6
2 that the LORD appeared to Solomon the
second time, [R]as He had appeared to him at
Gibeon. 1 Kin. 3:5; 11:9
3 And the LORD said to him: "I have heard
your prayer and your supplication that you
have made before Me; I have sanctified this
house which you have built [R]to put My name
there forever, [R]and My eyes and My heart will
be there perpetually. 1 Kin. 8:29 • Deut. 11:12
4 "Now if you walk before Me as your
father David walked, in integrity of heart and
in uprightness, to do according to all that I
have commanded you, *and* if you [R]keep My
statutes and My judgments, 1 Kin. 8:61
5 "then I will establish the throne of your
kingdom over Israel forever, as I promised
David your father, saying, 'You shall not fail
to have a man on the throne of Israel.'
6 [R]"*But* if you or your sons at all [T]turn
from following Me, and do not keep My
commandments *and* My statutes which I
have set before you, but go and serve other
gods and worship them, 2 Sam. 7:14-16 • *turn back*
7 "then I will [T]cut off Israel from the land
which I have given them; and this house
which I have sanctified for My name I will
cast out of My sight. Israel will be a proverb
and a byword among all peoples. *destroy*
8 "And this house will be exalted; yet
everyone who passes by it will be astonished
and will hiss, and say, 'Why has the LORD
done thus to this land and to this house?'
9 "Then they will answer, 'Because they
forsook the LORD their God, who brought
their fathers out of the land of Egypt, and
have embraced other gods, and worshiped
them and served them; therefore the LORD
has brought all this calamity on them.' "

Sale of Cities in Israel—2 Chr. 8:1, 2

10 Now [R]it happened at the end of twenty
years, when Solomon had built the two
houses, the house of the LORD and the king's
house 2 Chr. 8:1
11 [R](Hiram the king of Tyre had supplied
Solomon with cedar and cypress and gold, as
much as he desired), *that* King Solomon then
gave Hiram twenty cities in the land of
Galilee. 1 Kin. 5:1
12 Then Hiram went from Tyre to see the
cities which Solomon had given him, but they
did not please him.
13 So he said, "What *kind of* cities *are* these
which you have given me, my brother?" And
he called them the land of [T]Cabul, as they are
to this day. Lit. *Good for Nothing*
14 Then Hiram sent the king [T]one hundred
and twenty talents of gold. $691,200,000

Enslavement of the Canaanites
2 Chr. 8:4-18

15 And this *is* the reason for the labor force

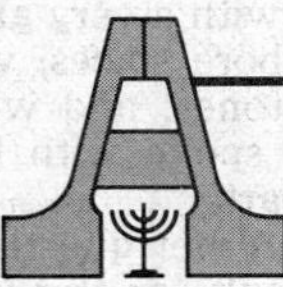

ISRAEL AND THE PHOENICIANS

The Phoenicians lived on a narrow strip of land northwest of Palestine on the eastern shore of the Mediterranean Sea in the area now known as Lebanon and coastal Syria. A people who once occupied the land of Canaan, the Phoenicians were driven out by Israel around 1380 B.C. and crowded onto this narrow strip of coastline.

Hemmed in by the ocean and the Lebanon mountains, the Phoenicians took to the sea to expand their empire. This led them to become distinguished seafaring merchants who founded many colonies along the Mediterranean. The nation was at the pinnacle of its power and prosperity from 1050 to 850 B.C.

With excellent ports such as Tyre and Sidon and a good supply of timber (cypress, pine, and cedar), the Phoenicians became noted shipbuilders (see illustration) and sea merchants (Ezek. 27:8, 9). Since the Israelites disliked the sea, the Phoenicians generally enjoyed good working relations with Israel. Hiram of Tyre, a friend of David and Solomon, helped Israel equip its merchant fleet (1 Kin. 9:26–28).

Phoenician religion was largely a carryover from the Canaanite worship system, which included child sacrifice. The gods were mainly male and female nature deities with Baal as the primary god. The marriage of King Ahab to Jezebel, a Phoenician woman, was a corrupting influence on Israel. Ahab allowed Jezebel to place the prophets of Baal in influential positions (1 Kin. 18:19). King Solomon lapsed into idolatry by worshiping Ashtoreth, the supreme goddess of the Sidonians (1 Kin. 11:5).

The Phoenician cities of Tyre and Sidon are mentioned often in the New Testament. Jesus healed a demon-possessed girl in this area (Matt. 15:21–28). Early Christian believers witnessed in Phoenicia after leaving Jerusalem (Acts 11:19). Paul often traveled through the area (Acts 15:3).

The Phoenicians were noted as shipbuilders and sea merchants.

which King Solomon raised: to build the
house of the LORD, his own house, the [R]Millo,
the wall of Jerusalem, [R]Hazor, [R]Megiddo, and
Gezer. 2 Sam. 5:9 • Josh. 11:1; 19:36 • Josh. 17:11
16 (Pharaoh king of Egypt had gone up and
taken Gezer and burned it with fire, [R]had
killed the Canaanites who dwelt in the city,
and had given it *as* a dowry to his daughter,
Solomon's wife.) Josh. 16:10
17 And Solomon built Gezer, Lower [R]Beth
Horon, 2 Chr. 8:5
18 [R]Baalath, and Tadmor in the wilderness,
in the land *of Judah,* Josh. 19:44
19 all the storage cities that Solomon had,
cities for his chariots and cities for his [R]cav-
alry, and whatever Solomon [R]desired to build
in Jerusalem, in Lebanon, and in all the land
of his dominion. 1 Kin. 4:26 • 1 Kin. 9:1
20 [R]All the people *who were* left of the
Amorites, Hittites, Perizzites, Hivites, and
Jebusites, who *were* not of the children of
Israel— 2 Chr. 8:7
21 that is, their descendants who were left
in the land after them, whom the children of
Israel had not been able to destroy completely—from these Solomon raised [R]forced
labor, as it is to this day. Ezra 2:55, 58
22 But of the children of Israel Solomon
[R]made no forced laborers, because they *were*
men of war and his servants: his officers, his
captains, commanders of his chariots, and his
cavalry. [Lev. 25:39]
23 Others *were* chiefs of the officials who
were over Solomon's work: [R]five hundred and
fifty, who ruled over the people who did the
work. 2 Chr. 8:10
24 But [R]Pharaoh's daughter came up from
the City of David to [R]her house which *Solomon* had built for her. [R]Then he built the
Millo. 2 Chr. 8:11 • 1 Kin. 7:8 • 2 Sam. 5:9
25 [R]Now three times a year Solomon offered
burnt offerings and peace offerings on the
altar which he had built for the LORD, and he
burned incense with them *on the altar* that
was before the LORD. So he finished the
temple. Ex. 23:14-17
26 King Solomon also built a fleet of ships
at Ezion Geber, which *is* near Elath on the
shore of the Red Sea, in the land of Edom.
27 [R]Then Hiram sent his servants with the
fleet, seamen who knew the sea, to work with
the servants of Solomon. 1 Kin. 5:6, 9; 10:11
28 And they went to Ophir, and acquired
four hundred and twenty talents of gold from
there, and brought *it* to King Solomon.

CHAPTER 10

Multiplication of Wealth—2 Chr. 9:1-24

NOW when the [R]queen of Sheba heard of
the fame of Solomon concerning the
name of the LORD, she came [R]to test him with
hard questions. Matt. 12:42 • Judg. 14:12
2 She came to Jerusalem with a very great
[T]retinue, with camels that bore spices, very
much gold, and precious stones; and when
she came to Solomon, she spoke with him
about all that was in her heart. *company*
3 So Solomon answered all her questions;
there was nothing [T]so difficult for the king
that he could not explain it to her. *too*
4 And when the queen of Sheba had seen
all the wisdom of Solomon, the house that he
had built,
5 the food on his table, the seating of his
servants, the service of his waiters and their
apparel, his cupbearers, [R]and his entryway by
which he went up to the house of the LORD,
there was no more spirit in her. 1 Chr. 26:16
6 Then she said to the king: "It was a true
report which I heard in my own land about
your words and your wisdom.
7 "However I did not believe the words
until I came and saw *it* with my own eyes;
and indeed the half was not told me. Your
wisdom and prosperity exceed the fame of
which I heard.
8 [R]"Happy *are* your men and happy *are*
these your servants, who stand continually
before you *and* hear your wisdom! Prov. 8:34
9 [R]"Blessed be the LORD your God, who
delighted in you, setting you on the throne of
Israel! Because the LORD has loved Israel
forever, therefore He made you king, [R]to do
justice and righteousness." 1 Kin. 5:7 • Ps. 72:2
10 Then she gave the king one hundred and
twenty talents of gold, spices in great *abundance,* and precious stones. There never
again came such abundance of spices as the
queen of Sheba gave to King Solomon.
11 Also, the ships of Hiram, which brought
gold from Ophir, brought great *quantities* of
almug wood and precious stones from Ophir.
12 [R]And the king made [T]steps of the almug
wood for the house of the LORD and for the
king's house, also harps and stringed instruments for singers. There never again came
such [R]almug wood, nor has the like been seen
to this day. 2 Chr. 9:11 • Or *supports* • 2 Chr. 9:10
13 And King Solomon gave the queen of
Sheba all she desired, whatever she asked,
besides what Solomon had given her according to the royal bounty. So she turned and
went to her own country, she and her servants.
14 The weight of gold that came to Solomon yearly was [T]six hundred and sixty-six
talents of gold, $3,836,160,000
15 besides *that* from the [R]traveling merchants, from the income of traders, [R]from all
the kings of Arabia, and from the governors
of the country. 2 Chr. 1:16 • Ps. 72:10
16 And King Solomon made two hundred
large shields *of* hammered gold; six hundred
shekels of gold went into each shield.
17 He also *made* three hundred shields *of*
hammered gold; three minas of gold went

into each shield. And the king put them in the House of the Forest of Lebanon.

18 Moreover the king made a great throne of ivory, and overlaid it with pure gold.

19 The throne had six steps, and the top of the throne *was* round at the back; *there were* armrests on either side of the place of the seat, and two lions stood beside the armrests.

20 Twelve lions stood there, one on each side of the six steps; nothing like *this* had been made for any other kingdom.

21 [R]All King Solomon's drinking vessels *were of* gold, and all the vessels of the House of the Forest of Lebanon *were of* pure gold; not *one was of* silver, for this was accounted as nothing in the days of Solomon. 2 Chr. 9:20

22 For the king had merchant ships at sea with the fleet of Hiram. Once every three years the merchant ships came bringing gold, silver, ivory, apes, and monkeys.

23 So King Solomon surpassed all the kings of the earth in riches and wisdom.

24 And all the earth sought the presence of Solomon to hear his wisdom, which God had put in his heart.

25 Each man brought his present: articles of silver and gold, garments, armor, spices, horses, and mules, at a set rate year by year.

Multiplication of Horses
2 Chr. 1:14–17; 9:25–28

26 And Solomon [R]gathered chariots and horsemen; he had one thousand four hundred chariots and twelve thousand horsemen, whom he stationed in the chariot cities and with the king in Jerusalem. 1 Kin. 9:19

27 [R]The king made silver *as common* in Jerusalem as stones, and he made cedars as abundant as the sycamores which are in the lowland. 2 Chr. 1:15–17

28 And Solomon had horses imported from Egypt and Keveh; the king's merchants bought them in Keveh at the *current* price.

29 Now a chariot that was imported from Egypt cost six hundred *shekels* of silver, and a horse one hundred and fifty; [R]and [T]thus, through their agents, they exported *them* to all the kings of the Hittites and the kings of Syria. 2 Kin. 7:6, 7 • Lit. *by their hands*

CHAPTER 11

Intermarriage with Foreign Women

BUT King Solomon loved many foreign women, as well as the daughter of Pharaoh: women of the Moabites, Ammonites, Edomites, Sidonians, *and* Hittites—

2 from the nations of whom the LORD had said to the children of Israel, [R]"You shall not intermarry with them, nor they with you. *For* surely they will turn away your hearts after their gods." Solomon clung to these in love. [Deut. 7:3, 4]

3 And he had seven hundred wives, princesses, and three hundred concubines; and his wives turned away his heart.

Worship of Idols

4 For it was so, when Solomon was old, [R]that his wives turned his heart after other gods; and his heart was not [T]loyal to the LORD his God, [R]as *was* the heart of his father David. [Deut. 17:17] • Lit. *at peace with* • 1 Kin. 9:4

5 For Solomon went after Ashtoreth the goddess of the Sidonians, and after Milcom the abomination of the Ammonites.

6 Solomon did evil in the sight of the LORD, and did not fully follow the LORD, as *did* his father David.

7 Then Solomon built a high place for Chemosh the abomination of Moab, on the hill that *is* east of Jerusalem, and for Molech the abomination of the people of Ammon.

8 And he did likewise for all his foreign wives, who burned incense and sacrificed to their gods.

The Rebuke of God

9 So the LORD became angry with Solomon, because his heart had turned from the LORD God of Israel, [R]who had appeared to him twice, 1 Kin. 3:5; 9:2

10 and [R]had commanded him concerning this thing, that he should not go after other gods; but he did not keep what the LORD had commanded. 1 Kin. 6:12; 9:6, 7

11 Therefore the LORD said to Solomon, "Because you have done this, and have not kept My covenant and My statutes, which I have commanded you, [R]I will surely tear the kingdom away from you and give it to your [R]servant. 1 Kin. 11:31; 12:15, 16 • 1 Kin. 11:31, 37

12 "Nevertheless I will not do it in your days, for the sake of your father David; *but* I will tear it out of the hand of your son.

13 "However I will not tear away the whole kingdom, *but* I will give [R]one tribe to your son [R]for the sake of my servant David, and for the sake of Jerusalem [R]which I have chosen." 1 Kin. 12:20 • 2 Sam. 7:15, 16 • Deut. 12:11

The Chastisement of God

14 Now the LORD [R]raised up an adversary against Solomon, Hadad the Edomite; he *was* a descendant of the king in Edom. 1 Chr. 5:26

15 For it happened, when David was in Edom, and Joab the commander of the army had gone up to bury the slain, [R]after he had killed every male in Edom Num. 24:18, 19

16 (because for six months Joab remained there with all Israel, until he had cut down every male in Edom),

17 that Hadad fled to go to Egypt, he and certain Edomites of his father's servants with him. Hadad *was* still a little child.

18 Then they arose from Midian and came to Paran; and they took men with them from

Paran and came to Egypt, to Pharaoh king of
Egypt, who gave him a house, apportioned
food for him, and gave him land.
19 And Hadad found great favor in the sight
of Pharaoh, so that he gave him as wife the
sister of his own wife, that is, the sister of
Queen Tahpenes.
20 Then the sister of Tahpenes bore him
Genubath his son, whom Tahpenes weaned
in Pharaoh's house. And Genubath was in
Pharaoh's household among the sons of
Pharaoh.
21 Now when Hadad heard in Egypt that
David rested with his fathers, and that Joab
the commander of the army was dead, Hadad
said to Pharaoh, [T]"Let me depart, that I may
go to my own country." Lit. *Send me away*
22 Then Pharaoh said to him, "But what
have you lacked with me, that suddenly you
seek to go to your own country?" So he
answered, "Nothing, but do let me go anyway."
23 And God raised up *another* adversary
against him, Rezon the son of Eliadah, who
had fled from his lord, [R]Hadadezer king of
Zobah. 2 Sam. 8:3; 10:16
24 So he gathered men to him and became
captain over a band *of raiders*, [R]when David
killed those *of Zobah*. And they went to
Damascus and dwelt there, and reigned in
Damascus. 2 Sam. 8:3; 10:8, 18
25 He was an adversary of Israel all the
days of Solomon (besides the trouble that
Hadad *caused*); and he abhorred Israel, and
reigned over Syria.
26 Then Solomon's servant, Jeroboam the
son of Nebat, an Ephraimite from Zereda,
whose mother's name *was* Zeruah, a widow,
also [R]rebelled against the king. 2 Sam. 20:21
27 And this *is* what caused him to rebel
against the king: Solomon had built the Millo
and [T]repaired the damages to the City of
David his father. Lit. *closed up the breaches*
28 The man Jeroboam *was* a mighty man of
valor; and Solomon, seeing that the young
man was [R]industrious, made him the officer
over all the labor force of the house of
Joseph. [Prov. 22:29]
29 Now it happened at that time, when
Jeroboam went out of Jerusalem, that the
prophet Ahijah the Shilonite met him on the
way; and he had clothed himself with a new
garment, and the two *were* alone in the field.
30 Then Ahijah took hold of the new garment that *was* on him, and [R]tore it *into*
twelve pieces. 1 Sam. 15:27, 28; 24:5
31 And he said to Jeroboam, "Take for
yourself ten pieces, for [R]thus says the LORD,
the God of Israel: 'Behold, I will tear the
kingdom out of the hand of Solomon and will
give ten tribes to you 1 Kin. 11:11, 13
32 '(but he shall have one tribe for the sake
of My servant David, and for the sake of
Jerusalem, the city which I have chosen out
of all the tribes of Israel),
33 'because they have forsaken Me, and
worshiped Ashtoreth the goddess of the Sidonians, Chemosh the god of the Moabites, and
Milcom the god of the people of Ammon, and
have not walked in My ways to do *what is*
right in My eyes and *keep* My statutes and
My judgments, as *did* his father David.
34 'However I will not take the whole kingdom out of his hand, because I have made
him ruler all the days of his life for the sake of
My servant David, whom I chose because he
kept My commandments and My statutes.
35 'But I will take the kingdom out of his
son's hand and give it to you—ten tribes.
36 'And to his son I will give one tribe, that
My servant David may always have a lamp
before Me in Jerusalem, the city which I have
chosen for Myself, to put My name there.
37 'So I will take you, and you shall reign
over all your heart desires, and you shall be
king over Israel.
38 'Then it shall be, if you heed all that I
command you, walk in My ways, and do
what is right in My sight, to keep My statutes
and My commandments, as My servant David did, then I will be with you and [R]build for
you an enduring house, as I built for David,
and will give Israel to you. 2 Sam. 7:11, 27
39 'And I will afflict the descendants of
David because of this, but not forever.' "
40 Solomon therefore sought to kill Jeroboam. But Jeroboam arose and fled to Egypt,
to [R]Shishak king of Egypt, and was in Egypt
until the death of Solomon. 2 Chr. 12:2–9

Death of Solomon—2 Chr. 9:29–31

41 Now the rest of the acts of Solomon, all
that he did, and his wisdom, *are* they not
written in the book of the acts of Solomon?
42 And the period that Solomon reigned in
Jerusalem over all Israel *was* forty years.
43 Then Solomon [T]rested with his fathers,
and was buried in the City of David his
father. And Rehoboam his son reigned in his
[R]place. Died and joined his ancestors • 2 Chr. 10:1

CHAPTER 12

Request of Israel to Rehoboam—2 Chr. 10:1–5

NOW [R]Rehoboam went to [R]Shechem, for
all Israel had gone to Shechem to make
him king. 2 Chr. 10:1 • Judg. 9:6
2 So it was, when Jeroboam the son of
Nebat heard *it* (he was still in [R]Egypt, for he
had fled from the presence of King Solomon
and had been dwelling in Egypt), 1 Kin. 11:40
3 that they sent and called him. Then
Jeroboam and the whole congregation of
Israel came and spoke to Rehoboam, saying,
4 "Your father made our yoke [T]heavy; now
therefore, lighten the burdensome service of

your father, and his heavy yoke which he put on us, and we will serve you." *hard*

5 So he said to them, "Depart *for* three days, then come back to me." And the people departed.

Foolish Response of Rehoboam—2 Chr. 10:6–15

6 Then King Rehoboam consulted the elders who stood before his father Solomon while he still lived, and he said, "How do you advise *me* to answer these people?"

7 And they spoke to him, saying, [R]"If you will be a servant to these people today, and serve them, and answer them, and speak good words to them, then they will be your servants forever." 2 Chr. 10:7

8 But he rejected the counsel which the elders gave him, and consulted the young men who had grown up with him, who stood before him.

9 And he said to them, "What counsel do you give? How should we answer this people who have spoken to me, saying, 'Lighten the yoke which your father put on us'?"

10 Then the young men who had grown up with him spoke to him, saying, "Thus you should speak to this people who have spoken to you, saying, 'Your father made our yoke heavy, but you make *it* lighter on us'—thus you shall say to them: 'My little *finger* shall be thicker than my father's waist!

11 'And now, whereas my father laid a heavy yoke on you, I will add to your yoke; my father chastised you with whips, but I will chastise you with scourges!' "

12 So Jeroboam and all the people came to Rehoboam the third day, as the king directed, saying, "Come back to me the third day."

13 Then the king answered the people [T]roughly, and rejected the [T]counsel which the elders had given him; *harshly • advice*

14 and he spoke to them according to the counsel of the young men, saying, "My father made your yoke heavy, but I will add to your yoke; my father chastised you with whips, but I will chastise you with scourges!"

15 So the king did not listen to the people; for the turn *of affairs* was from the LORD, that He might fulfill His word, which the LORD had [R]spoken by Ahijah the Shilonite to Jeroboam the son of Nebat. 1 Kin. 11:11, 29, 31

Revolt of the Northern Tribes
2 Chr. 10:16–19; 11:1–4

16 Now when all Israel saw that the king did not listen to them, the people answered the king, saying:

[R]"What portion have we in David?
We have no inheritance in the son of
Jesse. 2 Sam. 20:1
To your tents, O Israel!
Now, see to your own house, O David!"

So Israel departed to their tents.

17 But Rehoboam reigned over [R]the children of Israel who dwelt in the cities of Judah. 1 Kin. 11:13, 36

18 Then King Rehoboam sent Adoram, who *was* in charge of the revenue; but all Israel stoned him with stones, and he died. Therefore King Rehoboam mounted his chariot in haste to flee to Jerusalem.

19 So [R]Israel has been in rebellion against the house of David to this day. 2 Kin. 17:21

20 Now it came to pass when all Israel heard that Jeroboam had come back, they sent for him and called him to the congregation, and made him king over all Israel. There was none who followed the house of David, but the tribe of Judah only.

21 And when [R]Rehoboam came to Jerusalem, he assembled all the house of Judah with the tribe of [R]Benjamin, one hundred and eighty thousand chosen men who were warriors, to fight against the house of Israel, that he might restore the kingdom to Rehoboam the son of Solomon. 2 Chr. 11:1–4 • 2 Sam. 19:17

22 But [R]the word of God came to Shemaiah the man of God, saying, 2 Chr. 11:2; 12:5–7

23 "Speak to Rehoboam the son of Solomon, king of Judah, to all the house of Judah and Benjamin, and to the rest of the people, saying,

24 'Thus says the LORD: "You shall not go up nor fight against your brethren the children of Israel. Let every man return to his house, [R]for this thing is from Me." ' " Therefore they obeyed the word of the LORD, and turned back, according to the word of the LORD. 1 Kin. 12:15

Sin of Jeroboam

25 Then Jeroboam built Shechem in the mountains of Ephraim, and dwelt there. Also he went out from there and built Penuel.

26 And Jeroboam said in his heart, "Now the kingdom may return to the house of David:

27 "If these people [R]go up to offer sacrifices in the house of the LORD at Jerusalem, then the heart of this people will turn back to their lord, Rehoboam king of Judah, and they will kill me and go back to Rehoboam king of Judah." [Deut. 12:5–7, 14]

28 Therefore the king took counsel and [R]made two calves *of* gold, and said to the people, "It is too much for you to go up to Jerusalem. [R]Here are your gods, O Israel, which brought you up from the land of Egypt!" 2 Kin. 10:29; 17:16 • Ex. 32:4, 8

29 And he set up one in [R]Bethel, and the other he put in [R]Dan. Gen. 28:19 • Judg. 18:26–31

30 Now this thing became [R]a sin, for the people went *to worship* before the one as far as Dan. 1 Kin. 13:34

31 He made [T]shrines on the high places, and
made priests from every class of people, who
were not of the sons of Levi. Lit. *houses*
32 Jeroboam [T]ordained a feast on the fifteenth day of the eighth month, like the feast
that *was* in Judah, and offered sacrifices on
the altar. So he did at Bethel, sacrificing to
the calves that he had made. And at Bethel
he installed the priests of the high places
which he had made. *instituted*
33 So he made offerings on the altar which
he had made at Bethel on the fifteenth day of
the eighth month, in the month which he had
devised in his own heart. And he ordained a
feast for the children of Israel, and offered
sacrifices on the altar and burned incense.

CHAPTER 13

Warning of the Prophet

AND behold, [R]a man of God went from
Judah to Bethel [T]by the word of the
LORD, and Jeroboam stood by the altar to
burn incense. 2 Kin. 23:17 • *at the LORD's command*
2 Then he cried out against the altar [T]by
the word of the LORD, and said, "O altar,
altar! Thus says the LORD: 'Behold, a child,
Josiah by name, shall be born to the house of
David; and on you he shall sacrifice the
priests of the high places who burn incense
on you, and men's bones shall be [R]burned on
you.' " *at the LORD's command* • [Lev. 26:30]
3 And he gave a sign the same day, saying,
"This *is* the sign which the LORD has spoken:
Surely the altar shall split apart, and the
ashes on it shall be poured out."
4 So it came to pass when King Jeroboam
heard the saying of the man of God, who
cried out against the altar in Bethel, that he
stretched out his hand from the altar, saying,
"Arrest him!" Then his hand, which he
stretched out toward him, withered, so that
he could not pull it back to himself.
5 The altar also was split apart, and the
ashes poured out from the altar, according to
the sign which the man of God had given by
the word of the LORD.
6 Then the king answered and said to the
man of God, "Please [R]entreat the favor of the
LORD your God, and pray for me, that my
hand may be restored to me." So the man of
God entreated the LORD, and the king's hand
was restored to him, and became as *it was*
before. James 5:16

Sin of the Prophet

7 Then the king said to the man of God,
"Come home with me and refresh yourself,
and [R]I will give you a reward." 1 Sam. 9:7
8 But the man of God said to the king, [R]"If
you were to give me half your house, I would
not go in with you; nor would I eat bread nor
drink water in this place. Num. 22:18; 24:13
9 "For so it was commanded me by the
word of the LORD, saying, [R]'You shall not eat
bread, nor drink water, nor return by the
same way you came.' " [1 Cor. 5:11]
10 So he went another way and did not
return by the way he came to Bethel.
11 Now an old prophet dwelt in Bethel, and
his [T]sons came and told him all the works
that the man of God had done that day in
Bethel; they also told their father the words
which he had spoken to the king. Lit. *son*
12 And their father said to them, "Which
way did he go?" For his sons had seen which
way the man of God went who came from
Judah.
13 Then he said to his sons, "Saddle the
donkey for me." So they saddled the donkey
for him; and he rode on it,
14 and went after the man of God, and
found him sitting under an oak. Then he said
to him, "*Are* you the man of God who came
from Judah?" And he said, "I *am*."
15 Then he said to him, "Come home with
me and eat bread."
16 And he said, "I cannot return with you
nor go in with you; neither can I eat bread
nor drink water with you in this place.
17 "For [T]I have been told [R]by the word of
the LORD, 'You shall not eat bread nor drink
water there, nor return by going the way you
came.' " Lit. *a command came to me by* • 1 Kin. 20:35
18 He said to him, "I too *am* a prophet as
you *are*, and an angel spoke to me by the
word of the LORD, saying, 'Bring him back
with you to your house, that he may eat
bread and drink water.' " *But* he lied to him.
19 So he went back with him, and ate bread
in his house, and drank water.

Judgment on the Prophet

20 Now it happened, as they sat at the table,
that the word of the LORD came to the
prophet who had brought him back;
21 and he cried out to the man of God who
came from Judah, saying, "Thus says the
LORD: 'Because you have disobeyed the word
of the LORD, and have not kept the commandment which the LORD your God commanded you,
22 'but you came back, ate bread, and drank
water in the [R]place of which *the LORD* said to
you, "Eat no bread and drink no water," your
corpse shall not come to the tomb of your
fathers.' " 1 Kin. 13:9
23 So it was, after he had eaten bread and
after he had drunk, that he saddled the
donkey for him, the prophet whom he had
brought back.
24 So when he was gone, [R]a lion met him on
the road and killed him. And his corpse was
thrown on the road, and the donkey stood by
it; the lion also stood by the corpse. 1 Kin. 20:36
25 And there, men passed by and saw the

corpse thrown on the road, and the lion standing by the corpse. Then they went and told *it* in the city where the old prophet dwelt.

26 So when the prophet who had brought him back from the way heard *it*, he said, "It *is* the man of God who was disobedient to the word of the LORD. Therefore the LORD has delivered him to the lion, which has torn him and killed him, according to the word of the LORD which He spoke to him."

27 And he spoke to his sons, saying, "Saddle the donkey for me." And they saddled *it*.

28 Then he went and found his corpse thrown on the road, and the donkey and the lion standing by the corpse. The lion had not eaten the corpse nor torn the donkey.

29 And the prophet took up the corpse of the man of God, laid it on the donkey, and brought it back. So the old prophet came to the city to mourn, and to bury him.

30 Then he laid the corpse in his own tomb; and they mourned over him, *saying*, [R]"Alas, my brother!" Jer. 22:18

31 So it was, after he had buried him, that he spoke to his sons, saying, "When I am dead, then bury me in the tomb where the man of God *is* buried; [R]lay my bones beside his bones. 2 Kin. 23:17, 18

32 "For the saying which he cried out by the word of the LORD against the altar in Bethel, and against all the [T]shrines on the high places which *are* in the cities of Samaria, will surely come to pass." Lit. *houses*

Continued Sin of Jeroboam

33 After this event Jeroboam did not turn from his evil way, but again he made priests from every class of people for the high places; whoever wished, he consecrated him, and he became *one* of the priests of the high places.

34 [R]And this thing was the sin of the house of Jeroboam, so as to exterminate and destroy *it* from the face of the earth. 1 Kin. 12:30

CHAPTER 14

Judgment on Jeroboam

AT that time Abijah the son of Jeroboam became sick.

2 And Jeroboam said to his wife, "Please arise, and disguise yourself, that they may not recognize you as the wife of Jeroboam, and go to Shiloh. Indeed, Ahijah the prophet *is* there, who told me that [R]*I would be* king over this people. 1 Kin. 11:29–31

3 "Also take with you ten loaves, *some* cakes, and a jar of honey, and go to him; he will tell you what will become of the child."

4 And Jeroboam's wife did so; she arose and went to Shiloh, and came to the house of Ahijah. But Ahijah could not see, for his eyes were [T]glazed by reason of his age. *set*

5 Now the LORD had said to Ahijah, "Here is the wife of Jeroboam, coming to ask you something about her son, for he *is* sick. Thus and thus you shall say to her; for it will be, when she comes in, that she will pretend *to be* another *woman*."

6 And so it was, when Ahijah heard the sound of her footsteps as she came through the door, he said, "Come in, wife of Jeroboam. Why do you pretend *to be* another *person*? For I *have been* sent to you *with* bad *news*.

7 "Go, tell Jeroboam, 'Thus says the LORD God of Israel: [R]"Because I exalted you from among the people, and made you ruler over My people Israel, 1 Kin. 16:2

8 "and tore the kingdom away from the house of David, and gave it to you; and *yet* you have not been as My servant David, [R]who kept My commandments and who followed Me with all his heart, to do only *what was* right in My eyes; 1 Kin. 11:33, 38; 15:5

9 "but you have done more evil than all who were before you, [R]for you have gone and made for yourself other gods and molded images to provoke Me to anger, and [R]have cast Me behind your back— 1 Kin. 12:28 • Ps. 50:17

10 "therefore behold! I will bring disaster on the house of Jeroboam, and will cut off from Jeroboam every male in Israel, [R]bond and free; *and* I will take away the remnant of the house of Jeroboam, as one takes away refuse until it is all gone. Deut. 32:36

11 "The dogs shall eat [R]whoever belongs to Jeroboam and dies in the city, and the birds of the air shall eat whoever dies in the field; for the LORD has spoken *it*!"' 1 Kin. 16:4; 21:24

12 "Arise therefore, go to your own house. [R]When your feet enter the city, the child shall die. 1 Kin. 14:17

13 "And all Israel shall mourn for him and bury him, for he is the only one of Jeroboam who shall come to the grave, because in him there is found something good toward the LORD God of Israel in the house of Jeroboam.

14 "Moreover the LORD will raise up for Himself a king over Israel who shall cut off the house of Jeroboam; [T]this is the day. What? Even now! Or *this day and from now on*

15 "For the LORD will strike Israel, as a reed is shaken in the water. He will uproot Israel from this good land which He gave to their fathers, and will scatter them beyond [T]the River, [R]because they have made their [T]wooden images, provoking the LORD to anger. The Euphrates • [Ex. 34:13, 14] • Or *Asherim*

16 "And He will give Israel up because of the sins of Jeroboam, [R]who sinned and who made Israel sin." 1 Kin. 12:30; 13:34; 15:30, 34; 16:2

17 Then Jeroboam's wife arose and departed, and came to [R]Tirzah. [R]When she came to the threshold of the house, the child died. Song 6:4 • 1 Kin. 14:12

18 And they buried him; and all Israel mourned for him, [R]according to the word of the LORD which He spoke through His servant Ahijah the prophet. 1 Kin. 14:13

19 Now the rest of the acts of Jeroboam, how he [R]made war and how he reigned, indeed they *are* written in the book of the chronicles of the kings of Israel. 2 Chr. 13:2–20

20 The period that Jeroboam reigned *was* twenty-two years. So he rested with his fathers. Then [R]Nadab his son reigned in his place. 1 Kin. 15:25

Sin of Rehoboam

21 And Rehoboam the son of Solomon reigned in Judah. Rehoboam *was* forty-one years old when he became king. He reigned seventeen years in Jerusalem, the city which the LORD had chosen out of all the tribes of Israel, to put His name there. His mother's name *was* Naamah, an Ammonitess.

22 Now Judah did evil in the sight of the LORD, and they provoked Him to jealousy with their sins which they committed, more than all that their fathers had done.

23 For they also built for themselves [T]high places, [R]*sacred* pillars, and wooden images on every high hill and under every green tree. Places for pagan worship • [Deut. 16:22]

24 And there were also perverted persons in the land. They did according to all the abominations of the nations which the LORD had cast out before the children of Israel.

Judgment on Rehoboam—2 Chr. 12:2–16

25 [R]Now it happened, in the fifth year of King Rehoboam, *that* Shishak king of Egypt came up against Jerusalem. 1 Kin. 11:40

26 [R]And he took away the treasures of the house of the LORD and the treasures of the king's house; he took away everything. He also took away all the gold shields [R]which Solomon had made. 2 Chr. 12:9–11 • 1 Kin. 10:17

27 Then King Rehoboam made bronze shields in their place, and [T]committed *them* to the hands of the captains of the [T]guards, who guarded the doorway of the king's house. *entrusted* • Lit. *runners*

28 And so it was, whenever the king went into the house of the LORD, *that* the guards carried them, then brought them back into the guard chamber.

29 Now the rest of the acts of Rehoboam, and all that he did, *are* they not written in the book of the chronicles of the kings of Judah?

30 And there was [R]war between Rehoboam and Jeroboam all *their* days. 1 Kin. 12:21–24; 15:6

31 So Rehoboam rested with his fathers, and was buried with his fathers in the City of David. His mother's name *was* Naamah, an Ammonitess. Then [T]Abijam his son reigned in his place. *Abijah,* 2 Chr. 12:16

CHAPTER 15

Reign of Abijam in Judah—2 Chr. 13:1, 2; 14:1

NOW [R]in the eighteenth year of King Jeroboam the son of Nebat, Abijam became king over Judah. 2 Chr. 13:1

2 He reigned three years in Jerusalem. His mother's name *was* Maachah the granddaughter of [R]Abishalom. 2 Chr. 11:21

3 And he walked in all the sins of his father, which he had done before him; [R]his heart was not loyal to the LORD his God, as was the heart of his father David. Ps. 119:80

4 Nevertheless [R]for David's sake the LORD his God gave him a lamp in Jerusalem, by setting up his son after him and by establishing Jerusalem; 2 Sam. 21:17

5 because David did *what was* right in the eyes of the LORD, and had not turned aside from anything that He commanded him all the days of his life, [R]except in the matter of Uriah the Hittite. 2 Sam. 11:3, 15–17; 12:9, 10

6 And there was war between Rehoboam and Jeroboam all the days of his life.

7 [R]Now the rest of the acts of Abijam, and all that he did, *are* they not written in the book of the chronicles of the kings of Judah? And there was war between Abijam and Jeroboam. 2 Chr. 13:2–22

8 [R]So Abijam rested with his fathers, and they buried him in the City of David. Then Asa his son reigned in his place. 2 Chr. 14:1

Obedience of Asa—2 Chr. 14:2; 15:16–18

9 In the twentieth year of Jeroboam king of Israel, Asa became king over Judah.

10 And he reigned forty-one years in Jerusalem. His grandmother's name *was* Maachah the granddaughter of Abishalom.

11 [R]Asa did *what was* right in the eyes of the LORD, as *did* his father David. 2 Chr. 14:2

12 [R]And he banished the perverted persons from the land, and removed all the idols that his fathers had made. 1 Kin. 14:24; 22:46

13 Also he removed Maachah his grandmother from *being* queen mother, because she had made an obscene image of Asherah. And Asa cut down her obscene image and [R]burned *it* by the Brook Kidron. Ex. 32:20

14 But the [T]high places were not removed. Nevertheless Asa's heart was loyal to the LORD all his days. Places for pagan worship

15 He also brought into the house of the LORD the things which his father had dedicated, and the things which he himself had dedicated: silver and gold and utensils.

Disobedience of Asa—2 Chr. 16:1–6

16 Now there was war between Asa and Baasha king of Israel all their days.

17 And [R]Baasha king of Israel came up against Judah, and built [R]Ramah, [R]that he

might let none go out or come in to Asa king
of Judah. 2 Chr. 16:1–6 • Josh. 18:25 • 1 Kin. 12:26–29
18 Then Asa took all the silver and gold *that*
was left in the treasuries of the house of the
LORD and the treasuries of the king's house,
and delivered them into the hand of his
servants. And King Asa sent them to [R]Ben-
Hadad the son of Tabrimmon, the son of
Hezion, king of Syria, who dwelt in [R]Damas-
cus, saying, 2 Chr. 16:2 • 1 Kin. 11:23, 24
19 "*Let there be* a treaty between you and
me, as there was between my father and your
father. See, I have sent you a present of silver
and gold. Come and break your treaty with
Baasha king of Israel, so that he will withdraw from me."
20 So Ben-Hadad heeded King Asa, and sent
the captains of his armies against the cities of
Israel. He attacked Ijon, Dan, [R]Abel Beth
Maachah, and all Chinneroth, with all the
land of Naphtali. 2 Sam. 20:14, 15
21 Now it happened, when Baasha heard *it*,
that he stopped building Ramah, and remained in [R]Tirzah. 1 Kin. 14:17; 16:15–18
22 Then King Asa made a proclamation
throughout all Judah; none *was* exempted.
And they took away the stones and timber of
Ramah, which Baasha had used for building;
and with them King Asa built [R]Geba of Benjamin, and [R]Mizpah. Josh. 21:17 • Josh. 18:26

Death of Asa—2 Chr. 16:12—17:1

23 The rest of all the acts of Asa, all his
might, all that he did, and the cities which he
built, *are* they not written in the book of the
chronicles of the kings of Judah? But in the
time of his old age he was diseased in his feet.
24 So Asa rested with his fathers, and was
buried with his fathers in the City of David
his father. [R]Then [R]Jehoshaphat his son
reigned in his place. 2 Chr. 17:1 • Matt. 1:8

Reign of Nadab in Israel

25 Now [R]Nadab the son of Jeroboam became king over Israel in the second year of
Asa king of Judah, and he reigned over Israel
two years. 1 Kin. 14:20
26 And he did evil in the sight of the LORD,
and walked in the way of his father, and in
his sin by which he had made Israel sin.
27 [R]Then Baasha the son of Ahijah, of the
house of Issachar, conspired against him.
And Baasha killed him at Gibbethon, which
belonged to the Philistines, while Nadab and
all Israel laid siege to Gibbethon. 1 Kin. 14:14
28 Baasha killed him in the third year of Asa
king of Judah, and reigned in his place.
29 And it was so, when he became king,
that he killed all the house of Jeroboam. He
did not leave to Jeroboam anyone that
breathed, until he had destroyed him, according to the word of the LORD which He had
spoken by His servant Ahijah the Shilonite,
30 [R]because of the sins of Jeroboam, which
he had sinned and by which he had made
Israel sin, because of his provocation with
which he had provoked the LORD God of
Israel to anger. 1 Kin. 14:9, 16
31 Now the rest of the acts of Nadab, and all
that he did, *are* they not written in the book
of the chronicles of the kings of Israel?

Reign of Baasha in Israel

32 [R]And there was war between Asa and
Baasha king of Israel all their days. 1 Kin. 15:16
33 In the third year of Asa king of Judah,
Baasha the son of Ahijah became king over
all Israel in Tirzah, and *reigned* twenty-four
years.
34 He did evil in the sight of the LORD, and
walked in the way of Jeroboam, and in his sin
by which he had made Israel sin.

CHAPTER 16

THEN the word of the LORD came to [R]Jehu
the son of [R]Hanani, against [R]Baasha,
saying: 2 Chr. 19:2; 20:34 • 2 Chr. 16:7–10 • 1 Kin. 15:27
2 "Inasmuch as I lifted you out of the dust
and made you ruler over My people Israel,
and you have walked in the way of Jeroboam, and have made My people Israel sin, to
provoke Me to anger with their sins,
3 "surely I will [T]take away the posterity of
Baasha and the posterity of his house, and I
will make your house like the house of Jeroboam the son of Nebat. *consume*
4 "The dogs shall eat whoever belongs to
Baasha and dies in the city, and the birds of
the air shall eat whoever dies in the fields."
5 Now the rest of the acts of Baasha, what
he did, and his might, [R]*are* they not written in
the book of the chronicles of the kings of
Israel? 2 Chr. 16:11
6 So Baasha [T]rested with his fathers and
was buried in Tirzah. Then Elah his son
reigned in his place. Died and joined his ancestors
7 And also the word of the LORD came by
the prophet Jehu the son of Hanani against
Baasha and his house, because of all the evil
that he did in the sight of the LORD in provoking Him to anger with the work of his hands,
in being like the house of Jeroboam, and
because [R]he killed them. 1 Kin. 15:27, 29

Reign of Elah in Israel

8 In the twenty-sixth year of Asa king of
Judah, Elah the son of Baasha became king
over Israel, *and reigned* two years in Tirzah.
9 Now his servant Zimri, commander of
half *his* chariots, conspired against him as he
was in Tirzah drinking himself drunk in the
house of Arza, [R]steward[T] of *his* house in
Tirzah; 1 Kin. 18:3 • Lit. *who was over the house*
10 and Zimri went in and struck him and

killed him in the twenty-seventh year of Asa
king of Judah, and reigned in his place.
11 Then it came to pass, when he began to
reign, as soon as he was seated on his throne,
that he killed all the household of Baasha; he
[R]did not leave him one male, neither of his
kinsmen nor of his friends. 1 Sam. 25:22
12 Thus Zimri destroyed all the household
of Baasha, [R]according to the word of the
LORD, which He spoke against Baasha by
Jehu the prophet, 1 Kin. 16:3
13 for all the sins of Baasha and the sins of
Elah his son, by which they had sinned and
by which they had made Israel sin, in provoking the LORD God of Israel to anger [R]with
their [T]idols. Deut. 32:21 • Lit. *vanities*
14 Now the rest of the acts of Elah, and all
that he did, *are* they not written in the book
of the chronicles of the kings of Israel?

Reign of Zimri in Israel

15 In the twenty-seventh year of Asa king
of Judah, Zimri had reigned in Tirzah seven
days. And the people *were* encamped [R]against
Gibbethon, which *belonged* to the Philistines. 1 Kin. 15:27
16 Now the people *who were* encamped
heard it said, "Zimri has conspired and also
has killed the king." So all Israel made Omri,
the commander of the army, king over Israel
that day in the camp.
17 Then Omri and all Israel with him went
up from Gibbethon, and they besieged Tirzah.
18 And it happened, when Zimri saw that
the city was [T]taken, that he went into the
citadel of the king's house and burned the
king's house [T]down upon himself with fire,
and died, *captured* • Lit. *over him*
19 because of the sins which he had sinned
in doing evil in the sight of the LORD, [R]in
walking in the [R]way of Jeroboam, and in his
sin which he had committed to make Israel
sin. 1 Kin. 15:26, 34 • 1 Kin. 12:25–33
20 Now the rest of the acts of Zimri, and the
treason he committed, *are* they not written in
the book of the chronicles of the kings of
Israel?

Reign of Omri in Israel

21 Then the people of Israel were divided
into two parts: half of the people followed
Tibni the son of Ginath, to make him king,
and half followed Omri.
22 But the people who followed Omri prevailed over the people who followed Tibni the
son of Ginath. So Tibni died and Omri
reigned.
23 In the thirty-first year of Asa king of
Judah, Omri became king over Israel, *and
reigned* twelve years. Six years he reigned in
[R]Tirzah. 1 Kin. 15:21
24 And he bought the hill of Samaria from
Shemer for two talents of silver; then he built
on the hill, and called the name of the city
which he built, [T]Samaria, after the name of
Shemer, owner of the hill. Heb. *Shomeron*
25 Omri did evil in the eyes of the LORD, and
did worse than all who *were* before him.
26 For he walked in all the ways of Jeroboam the son of Nebat, and in his sin by
which he had made Israel sin, provoking the
LORD God of Israel to anger with their idols.
27 Now the rest of the acts of Omri which
he did, and the might that he showed, *are*
they not written in the book of the chronicles
of the kings of Israel?
28 So Omri rested with his fathers and was
buried in Samaria. Then Ahab his son reigned
in his place.

Sin of Ahab

29 In the thirty-eighth year of Asa king of
Judah, Ahab the son of Omri became king
over Israel; and Ahab the son of Omri reigned
over Israel in Samaria twenty-two years.
30 Now Ahab the son of Omri did evil in the
sight of the LORD, more than all who *were*
before him.
31 And it came to pass, as though it had
been a trivial thing for him to walk in the sins
of Jeroboam the son of Nebat, that he took as
wife Jezebel the daughter of Ethbaal, king of
the Sidonians; [R]and he went and served Baal
and worshiped him. 1 Kin. 21:25, 26
32 Then he set up an altar for Baal in [R]the
temple of Baal, which he had built in Samaria. 2 Kin. 10:21, 26, 27
33 [R]And Ahab made a [T]wooden image. Ahab
did more to provoke the LORD God of Israel
to anger than all the kings of Israel who were
before him. 2 Kin. 13:6 • Or *Asherah*
34 In his days Hiel of Bethel built Jericho.
He laid its foundation [T]with Abiram his firstborn, and with his youngest *son* Segub he set
up its gates, [R]according to the word of the
LORD, which He had spoken through Joshua
the son of Nun. At the cost of the life of • Josh. 6:26

CHAPTER 17

Prophecy of the Drought

AND Elijah the Tishbite, of the inhabitants
of Gilead, said to Ahab, "*As* the LORD
God of Israel lives, before whom I stand,
[R]there shall not be dew nor rain [R]these years,
except at my word." James 5:17 • Luke 4:25

Miracle of Food

2 Then the word of the LORD came to him,
saying,
3 "Get away from here and turn eastward,
and hide by the Brook Cherith, which flows
into the Jordan.
4 "And it will be *that* you shall drink from
the brook, and I have commanded the [R]ra-
vens to feed you there." Job 38:41

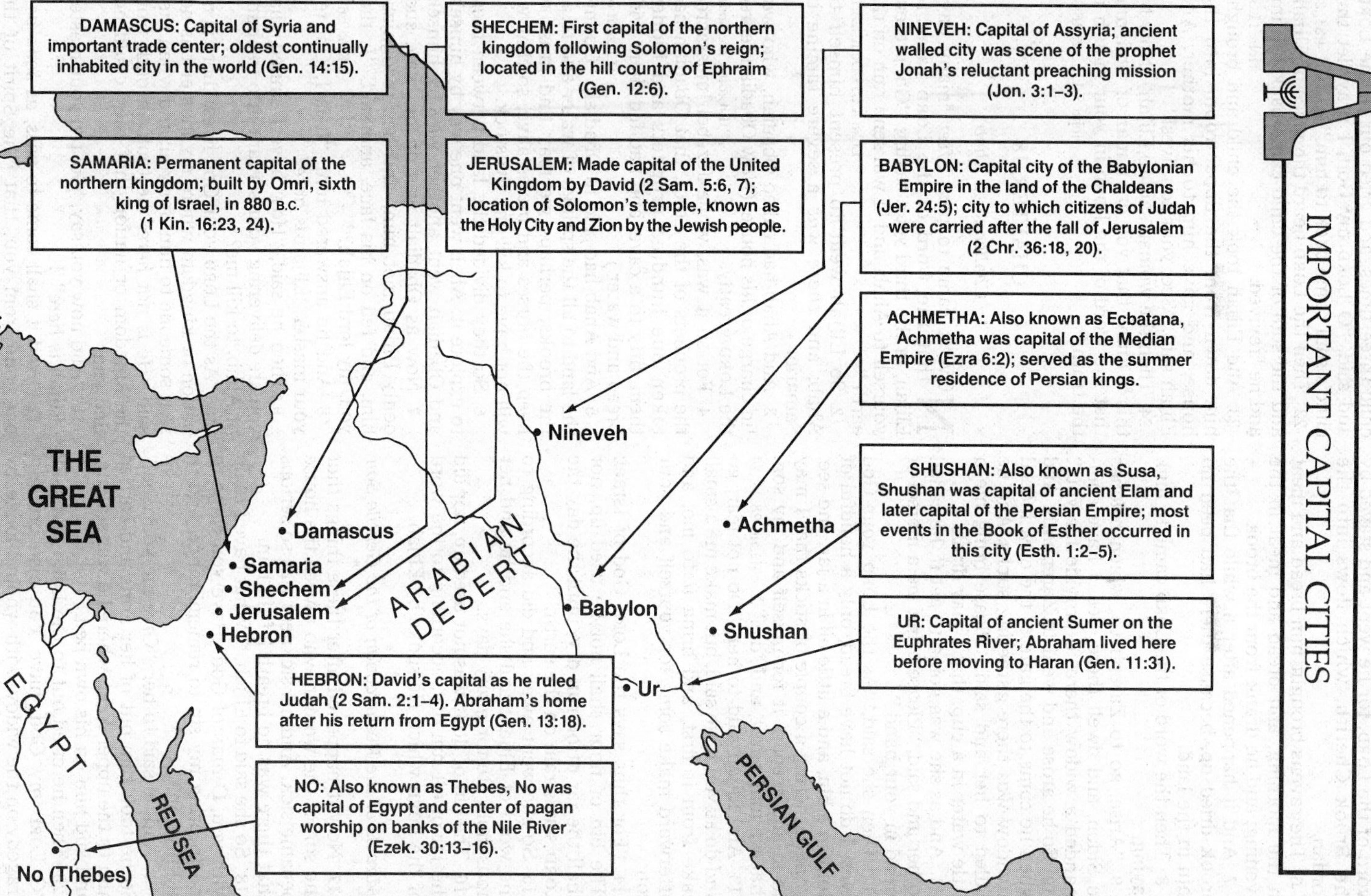
IMPORTANT CAPITAL CITIES
DAMASCUS: Capital of Syria and important trade center; oldest continually inhabited city in the world (Gen. 14:15).
SAMARIA: Permanent capital of the northern kingdom; built by Omri, sixth king of Israel, in 880 B.C. (1 Kin. 16:23, 24).
SHECHEM: First capital of the northern kingdom following Solomon's reign; located in the hill country of Ephraim (Gen. 12:6).
JERUSALEM: Made capital of the United Kingdom by David (2 Sam. 5:6, 7); location of Solomon's temple, known as the Holy City and Zion by the Jewish people.
NINEVEH: Capital of Assyria; ancient walled city was scene of the prophet Jonah's reluctant preaching mission (Jon. 3:1–3).
BABYLON: Capital city of the Babylonian Empire in the land of the Chaldeans (Jer. 24:5); city to which citizens of Judah were carried after the fall of Jerusalem (2 Chr. 36:18, 20).
ACHMETHA: Also known as Ecbatana, Achmetha was capital of the Median Empire (Ezra 6:2); served as the summer residence of Persian kings.
SHUSHAN: Also known as Susa, Shushan was capital of ancient Elam and later capital of the Persian Empire; most events in the Book of Esther occurred in this city (Esth. 1:2–5).
UR: Capital of ancient Sumer on the Euphrates River; Abraham lived here before moving to Haran (Gen. 11:31).
HEBRON: David's capital as he ruled Judah (2 Sam. 2:1–4). Abraham's home after his return from Egypt (Gen. 13:18).
NO: Also known as Thebes, No was capital of Egypt and center of pagan worship on banks of the Nile River (Ezek. 30:13–16).
THE GREAT SEA
Damascus
Samaria
Shechem
Jerusalem
Hebron
Nineveh
ARABIAN DESERT
Babylon
Achmetha
Shushan
Ur
PERSIAN GULF
EGYPT
RED SEA
No (Thebes)

5 So he went and did according to the
word of the LORD, for he went and stayed by
the Brook Cherith, which flows into the
Jordan.
6 The ravens brought him bread and meat
in the morning, and bread and meat in the
evening; and he drank from the brook.
7 And it happened after a while that the
brook dried up, because there had been no
rain in the land.
8 Then the word of the LORD came to him,
saying,
9 "Arise, go to Zarephath, which *belongs*
to Sidon, and dwell there. See, I have commanded a widow there to provide for you."
10 So he arose and went to Zarephath. And
when he came to the gate of the city, indeed
a widow *was* there gathering sticks. And he
called to her and said, "Please bring me a
little water in a cup, that I may drink."
11 And as she was going to get *it*, he called
to her and said, "Please bring me a morsel of
bread in your hand."
12 Then she said, "As the LORD your God
lives, I do not have bread, only a handful of
flour in a bin, and a little oil in a jar; and see,
I *am* gathering a couple of sticks that I may
go in and prepare it for myself and my son,
that we may eat it, and [R]die." Deut. 28:23, 24
13 And Elijah said to her, "Do not fear; go
and do as you have said, but make me a small
cake from it first, and bring *it* to me; and
afterward make *some* for yourself and your
son.
14 "For thus says the LORD God of Israel:
'The bin of flour shall not be used up, nor
shall the jar of oil run dry, until the day the
LORD sends rain on the earth.' "
15 So she went away and did according to
the word of Elijah; and she and he and her
household ate for *many* days.
16 The bin of flour was not used up, nor did
the jar of oil run dry, according to the word
of the LORD which He spoke by Elijah.

Miracle of the Resurrection of the Gentile Son

17 Now it happened after these things *that*
the son of the woman who owned the house
became sick. And his sickness was so serious
that there was no breath left in him.
18 So she said to Elijah, [R]"What have I to do
with you, O man of God? Have you come to
me to bring my sin to remembrance, and to
kill my son?" Luke 5:8
19 And he said to her, "Give me your son."
So he took him out of her arms and carried
him to the upper room where he was staying,
and laid him on his own bed.
20 Then he cried out to the LORD and said,
"O LORD my God, have You also brought
tragedy on the widow with whom I lodge, by
killing her son?"
21 [R]And he stretched himself out on the
child three times, and cried out to the LORD
and said, "O LORD my God, I pray, let this
child's soul come back to him." 2 Kin. 4:34, 35
22 Then the LORD heard the voice of Elijah;
and the soul of the child came back to him,
and he [R]revived. Heb. 11:35
23 And Elijah took the child and brought
him down from the upper room into the
house, and gave him to his mother. And
Elijah said, "See, your son lives!"
24 Then the woman said to Elijah, "Now by
this [R]I know that you *are* a man of God, *and*
that the word of the LORD in your mouth *is*
the truth." John 2:11; 3:2; 16:30

CHAPTER 18

Challenge to Ahab

NOW it came to pass *after* [R]many days
that the word of the LORD came to
Elijah, in the third year, saying, "Go, present
yourself to Ahab, and [R]I will send rain on the
earth." Luke 4:25 • Deut. 28:12
2 So Elijah went to present himself to
Ahab; and *there was* a severe famine in
Samaria.
3 And Ahab had called Obadiah, who *was*
[T]in charge of *his* house. (Now Obadiah feared
the LORD greatly. Lit. *over the house*
4 For so it was, while Jezebel [T]massacred
the prophets of the LORD, that Obadiah had
taken one hundred prophets and hidden
them, fifty to a cave, and had fed them with
bread and water.) Lit. *cut off*
5 And Ahab had said to Obadiah, "Go into
the land to all the springs of water and to all
the brooks; perhaps we may find grass to
keep the horses and mules alive, so that we
will not have to kill any livestock.
6 So they divided the land between them
to explore it; Ahab went one way by himself,
and Obadiah went another way by himself.
7 Now as Obadiah was on his way, suddenly Elijah met him; and he [R]recognized
him, and fell on his face, and said, "*Is* that
you, my lord Elijah?" 2 Kin. 1:6–8
8 And he answered him, "*It is* I. Go, tell
your master, 'Elijah *is here*.' "
9 Then he said, "How have I sinned, that
you are delivering your servant into the hand
of Ahab, to kill me?
10 "*As* the LORD your God lives, there is no
nation or kingdom where my master has not
sent someone to hunt for you; and when they
said, '*He is* not *here*,' he took an oath from
the kingdom or nation that they could not
find you.
11 "And now you say, 'Go, tell your master,
"Elijah *is here*" '!
12 "And it shall come to pass, *as soon as* I
am gone from you, that [R]the Spirit of the
LORD will carry you to a place I do not know;

so when I go and tell Ahab, an[illegible]annot
find you, he will kill me. But I [illegible]rvant
have feared the LORD from my yo[illegible]. Acts 8:39
13 "Was it not reported to my [illegible]what I
did when Jezebel killed the pro[illegible]of the
LORD, how I hid one hundred [illegible]of the
LORD's prophets, fifty to a cave, a[illegible]d them
with bread and water?
14 "And now you say, 'Go, tell [illegible] master,
"Elijah *is here!*" ' and he will kill [illegible]."
15 Then Elijah said, "*As* the L[illegible] of hosts
lives, before whom I stand, I [illegible]l surely
present myself to him today."
16 So Obadiah went to meet Aha[illegible] and told
him; and Ahab went to meet Elija[illegible].
17 Then it happened, when Aha[illegible] saw Elijah, that Ahab said to him, [R]"*Is t*[illegible]*t* you, O
[R]trouble of Israel?" 1 Kin. 21:20 · Josh. 7:25
18 And he answered, "I have not troubled
Israel, but you and your father's house *have,*
[R]in that you have forsaken the commandments of the LORD, and you have followed
the Baals. [2 Chr. 15:2]
19 "Now therefore, send *and* gather all
Israel to me on Mount [R]Carmel, the four
hundred and fifty prophets of Baal, and the
four hundred prophets of [T]Asherah, who eat
at Jezebel's table." Josh. 19:26 · A Canaanite goddess

Victory on Mount Carmel

20 So Ahab sent for all the children of
Israel, and [R]gathered the prophets together
on Mount Carmel. 1 Kin. 22:6

21 And Elijah came to all the people, and
said, [R]"How long will you falter between two
opinions? If the LORD *is* God, follow Him; but
if Baal, [R]*then* follow him." But the people
answered him not a word. [Matt. 6:24] · Josh. 24:15
22 Then Elijah said to the people, "I alone
am left a prophet of the LORD; but Baal's
prophets *are* four hundred and fifty men.
23 "Therefore let them give us two bulls;
and let them choose one bull for themselves,
cut it in pieces, and lay *it* on the wood, but
put no fire *under it;* and I will prepare the
other bull, and lay *it* on the wood, but put no
fire *under it.*
24 "Then you call on the name of your gods,
and I will call on the name of the LORD; and
the God who [R]answers by fire, He is God." So
all the people answered and said, [T]"It is well
spoken." 1 Chr. 21:26 · Lit. *The word is good*
25 Now Elijah said to the prophets of Baal,
"Choose one bull for yourselves and prepare
it first, for you *are* many; and call on the
name of your god, but put no fire *under it.*"
26 So they took the bull which was given
them, and they prepared *it,* and called on the
name of Baal from morning even till noon,
saying, "O Baal, hear us!" But *there was* no
voice; no one answered. And they leaped
about the altar which they had made.
27 And so it was, at noon, that Elijah
mocked them and said, "Cry [T]aloud, for he *is*
a god; either he is meditating, or he is busy,
or he is on a journey, *or* perhaps he is sleeping and must be awakened." *with a loud voice*
28 So they cried aloud, and cut themselves,
as was their custom, with [T]knives and lances,
until the blood gushed out on them. *swords*
29 And it was so, when midday was past,
[R]that they prophesied until the *time* of the
offering of the *evening* sacrifice. But *there
was* [R]no voice; no one answered, no one paid
attention. Ex. 29:39, 41 · 1 Kin. 18:26
30 Then Elijah said to all the people, "Come
near to me." So all the people came near to

18:21 Cure for Doubt—The cure for doubt depends to some extent on the thing doubted. However, the real problem is not in the object doubted but in the subject who doubts. Therefore, the following steps should be taken by the doubting Christian:

a. Confess the doubt to God as sin. Doubt is basically unbelief in God and His Word and is therefore sin (Page 1339—Rom. 14:23; Page 1460—Heb. 11:6). God has promised to hear our confession of even the darkest unbelief.

b. Study the evidence for the Christian faith. Christians have nothing to fear by looking into the facts from any source of knowledge. The greatest evidence for the validity of Christianity, the resurrection of Christ, is attested by many proofs. Among these are the empty tomb, post-resurrection appearances, and transformed disciples. Since the Resurrection is true, it verifies everything the Bible says.

c. Make certain of your salvation. Paul exhorts Christians to examine themselves to make sure they are Christians (Page 1375—2 Cor. 13:5). So did the author of Hebrews (Page 1455—Heb. 6:1–9). Salvation from sin is by simple trust in Jesus Christ. Until you are assured of your salvation you will be troubled by enormous doubts.

d. Faithfully study the Word of God. "Faith *comes* by hearing, and hearing by the word of God" (Page 1335—Rom. 10:17). Through study and application of the Bible, our faith is strengthened and matured. Most especially, we must master the doctrines or basic teachings of the Bible if we are to be stable, mature Christians (Page 1429—1 Tim. 4:13, 16; Page 1436—2 Tim. 3:16; Page 1440—Titus 2:1, 10).

e. Pray. The surest way to face doubts when they come is to have an extensive past history of answered prayer. The more a Christian prays with faith, the more that Christian sees God answer prayer; the more a person sees God answer prayer, the stronger that person's faith becomes while the doubt becomes less.

Now turn to Page 29—THE CHRISTIAN'S GUIDE: Recognizing God's Institutions.

him. [R]And he repaired the altar of the LORD
that was broken down. 2 Chr. 33:16
31 And Elijah took twelve stones, according
to the number of the tribes of the sons of
Jacob, to whom the word of the LORD had
come, saying, "Israel shall be your name."
32 Then with the stones he built an altar [R]in
the name of the LORD; and he made a trench
around the altar large enough to hold [T]two
seahs of seed. [Col. 3:17] • 4.349 bu.
33 And he [R]put the wood in order, cut the
bull in pieces, and laid *it* on the wood, and
said, "Fill four waterpots with water, and
[R]pour *it* on the burnt sacrifice and on the
wood." Lev. 1:6–8 • Judg. 6:20
34 Then he said, "Do *it* a second time," and
they did *it* a second time; and he said, "Do *it*
a third time," and they did *it* a third time.
35 So the water ran all around the altar; and
he also filled the trench with water.
36 And it came to pass, at *the time of* the
offering of the *evening* sacrifice, that Elijah
the prophet came near and said, "LORD God
of Abraham, Isaac, and Israel, let it be known
this day that You *are* God in Israel, and *that*
I *am* Your servant, and *that* I have done all
these things at Your word.
37 "Hear me, O LORD, hear me, that this
people may know that You *are* the LORD
God, and *that* You have turned their hearts
back *to You* again."
38 Then [R]the fire of the LORD fell and consumed the burnt sacrifice, and the wood and
the stones and the dust, and it licked up the
water that *was* in the trench. 1 Chr. 21:26
39 Now when all the people saw *it*, they fell
on their faces; and they said, [R]"The LORD, He
is God! The LORD, He *is* God!" 1 Kin. 18:21, 24
40 And Elijah said to them, "Seize the
prophets of Baal! Do not let one of them
escape!" So they seized them; and Elijah
brought them down to the Brook Kishon and
[R]executed them there. [Deut. 13:5; 18:20]

Miracle of the Rain

41 Then Elijah said to Ahab, "Go up, eat
and drink; for *there is* the sound of abundance of rain."
42 So Ahab went up to eat and drink. And
Elijah went up to the top of Carmel; [R]then he
bowed down on the ground, and put his face
between his knees, James 5:17, 18
43 and said to his servant, "Go up now, look
toward the sea." So he went up and looked,
and said, "*There is* nothing." And seven times
he said, "Go again."
44 Then it came to pass the seventh *time*,
that he said, "There is a cloud, as small as a
man's hand, rising out of the sea!" So he said,
"Go up, say to Ahab, [T]'Prepare *your chariot*,
and go down before the rain stops
you.'" Lit. *Bind* or *Harness*
45 And it happened in the meantime that
the sky became black with clouds and wind,
and there was a heavy rain. So Ahab rode
away and went to Jezreel.
46 Then the hand of the LORD came upon
Elijah; and he girded up his loins and ran
ahead of Ahab to the entrance of Jezreel.

CHAPTER 19

Elijah Flees from Jezebel

AND Ahab told Jezebel all that Elijah had
done, also how he had [R]executed all the
prophets with the sword. 1 Kin. 18:40
2 Then Jezebel sent a messenger to Elijah,
saying, "So let the gods do *to me*, and more
also, if I do not make your life as the life of
one of them by tomorrow about this time."
3 And when he saw *that*, he arose and ran
for his life, and went to Beersheba, which
belongs to Judah, and left his servant there.

Elijah Desires to Die

4 But he himself went a day's journey into
the wilderness, and came and sat down under
a broom tree. And he prayed that he might
die, and said, "It is enough! Now, LORD, take
my life, for I *am* no better than my fathers!"
5 Then as he lay and slept under a broom
tree, suddenly an [T]angel touched him, and
said to him, "Arise *and* eat." Or *Angel*
6 Then he looked, and *there* by his head
was a cake baked on [T]coals, and a jar of
water. So he ate and drank, and lay down
again. *hot stones*
7 And the [T]angel of the LORD came back
the second time, and touched him, and said,
"Arise *and* eat, because the journey *is* too
great for you." Or *Angel*
8 So he arose, and ate and drank; and he
went in the strength of that food forty days
and [R]forty nights as far as [R]Horeb, the mountain of God. Matt. 4:2 • Ex. 3:1; 4:27

Elijah Has Self-Pity

9 And there he went into a cave, and spent
the night in that place; and behold, the word
of the LORD *came* to him, and He said to him,
"What are you doing here, Elijah?"
10 So he said, "I have been very zealous for
the LORD God of hosts; for the children of
Israel have forsaken Your covenant, torn
down Your altars, and [R]killed Your prophets
with the sword. [R]I alone am left; and they
seek to take my life." 1 Kin. 18:4 • 1 Kin. 18:22
11 Then He said, "Go out, and stand on the
mountain before the LORD." And behold, the
LORD [R]passed by, and [R]a great and strong
wind tore into the mountains and broke the
rocks in pieces before the LORD, *but* the LORD
was not in the wind; and after the wind an
earthquake, *but* the LORD *was* not in the
earthquake; Ex. 33:21, 22 • Ezek. 1:4; 37:7

12 and after the earthquake a fire, *but* the
LORD *was* not in the fire; and after the fire [T]a
still small voice. *a delicate, whispering voice*
13 So it was, when Elijah heard *it*, that [R]he
wrapped his face in his mantle and went out
and stood in the entrance of the cave. And
suddenly a voice *came* to him, and said,
"What are you doing here, Elijah?" Ex. 3:6
14 [R]So he said, "I have been very zealous for
the LORD God of hosts; because the children
of Israel have forsaken Your covenant, torn
down Your altars, and killed Your prophets
with the sword. I alone am left; and they seek
to take my life." 1 Kin. 19:10
15 Then the LORD said to him: "Go, return
on your way to the Wilderness of Damascus;
[R]and when you arrive, anoint Hazael *as* king
over Syria. 2 Kin. 8:8–15
16 "Also you shall anoint Jehu the son of
Nimshi *as* king over Israel. And [R]Elisha the
son of Shaphat of Abel Meholah you shall
anoint *as* prophet in your place. 2 Kin. 2:9–15
17 [R]"It shall be *that* whoever escapes the
sword of Hazael, Jehu will [R]kill; and whoever
escapes from the sword of Jehu, [R]Elisha will
kill. 2 Kin. 8:12; 13:3, 22 • 2 Kin. 9:14—10:28 • [Hos. 6:5]
18 [R]"Yet I have reserved seven thousand in
Israel, all whose knees have not bowed to
Baal, [R]and every mouth that has not kissed
him." Rom. 11:4 • Hos. 13:2

Call of Elisha

19 So he departed from there, and found
Elisha the son of Shaphat, who *was* plowing
with twelve yoke *of oxen* before him, and he
was with the twelfth. Then Elijah passed by
him and threw his mantle on him.
20 And he left the oxen and ran after Elijah,
and said, [R]"Please let me kiss my father and
my mother, and *then* I will follow you." And
he said to him, "Go back again, for what have
I done to you?" [Matt. 8:21, 22]
21 So [T]Elisha turned back from him, and
took a yoke of oxen and slaughtered them
and [R]boiled their flesh, using the oxen's
equipment, and gave it to the people, and
they ate. Then he arose and followed Elijah,
and served him. Lit. *he* • 2 Sam. 24:22

CHAPTER 20

First Victory over Syria

NOW Ben-Hadad the king of Syria gathered all his forces together; *there were*
thirty-two kings with him, with horses and
chariots. And he went up and besieged Samaria, and made war against it.
2 Then he sent messengers into the city to
Ahab king of Israel, and said to him, "Thus
says Ben-Hadad:
3 'Your silver and your gold *are* mine; your
loveliest wives and children are mine.' "
4 And the king of Israel answered and said,
"My lord, O king, just as you say, I and all
that I have *are* yours."
5 Then the messengers came back and
said, "Thus speaks Ben-Hadad, saying, 'Indeed I have sent to you, saying, "You shall
deliver to me your silver and your gold, your
wives and your children";
6 'but I will send my servants to you tomorrow about this time, and they shall
search your house and the houses of your
servants. And it shall be, *that* whatever is
[T]pleasant in your eyes, they shall put in their
hands and take *it*.' " *pleasing*
7 Then the king of Israel called all the
elders of the land, and said, "Notice, please,
and see how this *man* seeks trouble, for he
sent to me for my wives, my children, my
silver, and my gold; and I did not deny him."
8 And all the elders and all the people said
to him, "Do not listen or consent."
9 Therefore he said to the messengers of
Ben-Hadad, "Tell my lord the king, 'All that
you sent for to your servant the first time I
will do, but this thing I cannot do.' " And the
messengers departed and brought back word
to him.
10 Then Ben-Hadad sent to him and said,
"The gods do so to me, and more also, if
enough dust is left of Samaria for a handful
for each of the people who follow me."
11 So the king of Israel answered and said,
"Tell *him*, 'Let not the one who puts on *his*
armor boast like the one who takes *it off*.' "
12 And it happened when *Ben-Hadad* heard
this message, as he and the kings *were* drinking at the [T]command post, that he said to his
servants, "Get ready." And they got ready to
attack the city. Lit. *booths* or *shelters*
13 Suddenly a prophet approached Ahab
king of Israel, saying, "Thus says the LORD:
'Have you seen all this great multitude?
Behold, I will deliver it into your hand today,
and you shall know that I *am* the LORD.' "
14 So Ahab said, "By whom?" And he said,
"Thus says the LORD: 'By the young leaders
of the provinces.' " Then he said, "Who will
set the battle in order?" And he answered,
"You."
15 Then he mustered the young leaders of
the provinces, and there were two hundred
and thirty-two; and after them he mustered
all the people, all the children of Israel—
seven thousand.
16 So they went out at noon. Meanwhile
Ben-Hadad and the thirty-two kings helping
him were [R]getting drunk at the command
post. 1 Kin. 16:9; 20:12
17 The young leaders of the provinces went
out first. And Ben-Hadad sent out *a patrol*,
and they told him, saying, "Men are coming
out of Samaria!"
18 So he said, "If they have come out for

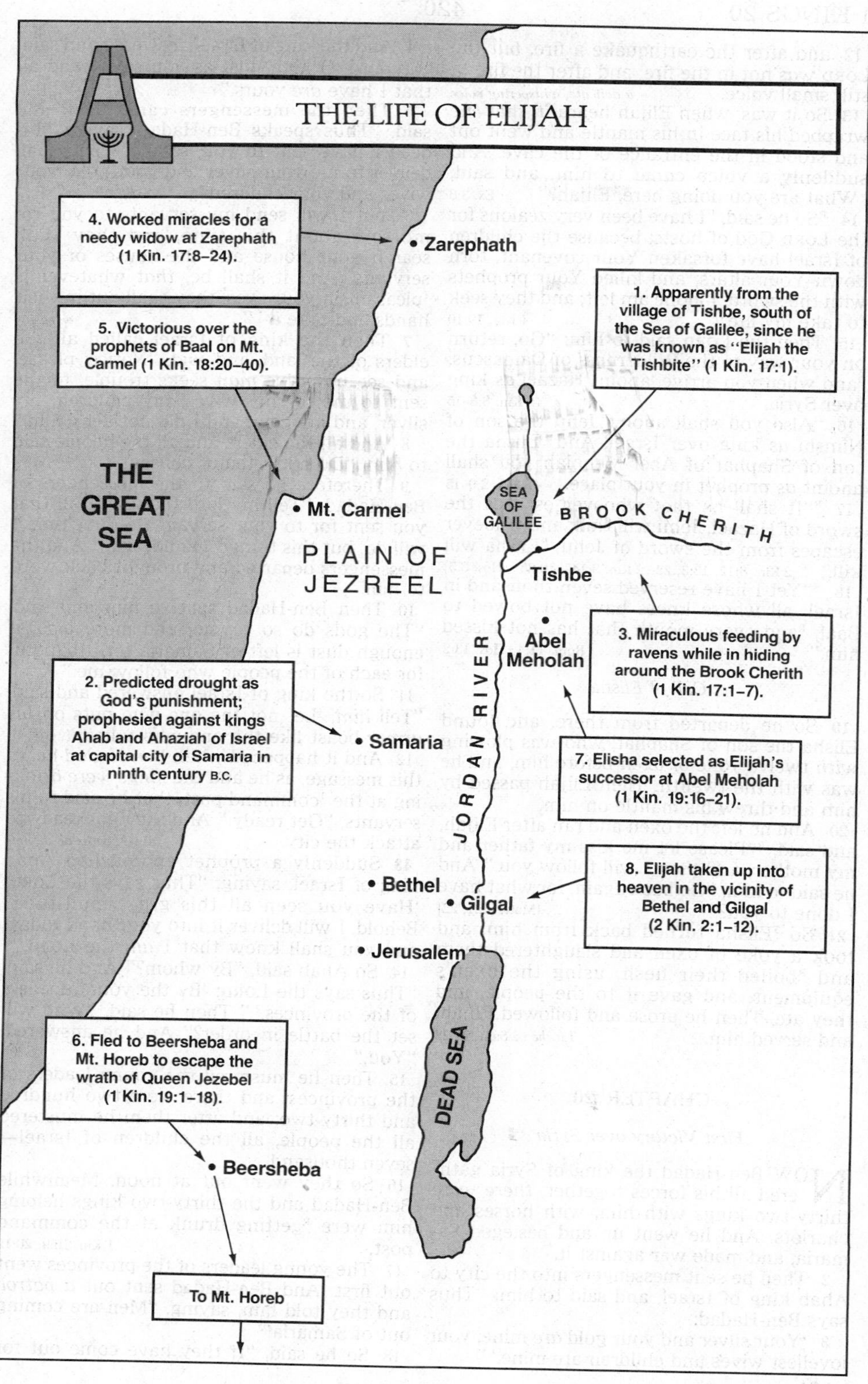

THE LIFE OF ELIJAH
4. Worked miracles for a needy widow at Zarephath (1 Kin. 17:8–24).
Zarephath
5. Victorious over the prophets of Baal on Mt. Carmel (1 Kin. 18:20–40).
1. Apparently from the village of Tishbe, south of the Sea of Galilee, since he was known as "Elijah the Tishbite" (1 Kin. 17:1).
THE GREAT SEA
SEA OF GALILEE
BROOK CHERITH
Mt. Carmel
PLAIN OF JEZREEL
Tishbe
Abel Meholah
JORDAN RIVER
3. Miraculous feeding by ravens while in hiding around the Brook Cherith (1 Kin. 17:1–7).
2. Predicted drought as God's punishment; prophesied against kings Ahab and Ahaziah of Israel at capital city of Samaria in ninth century B.C.
Samaria
7. Elisha selected as Elijah's successor at Abel Meholah (1 Kin. 19:16–21).
8. Elijah taken up into heaven in the vicinity of Bethel and Gilgal (2 Kin. 2:1–12).
Bethel
Gilgal
Jerusalem
6. Fled to Beersheba and Mt. Horeb to escape the wrath of Queen Jezebel (1 Kin. 19:1–18).
DEAD SEA
Beersheba
To Mt. Horeb

peace, take them alive; and if they have come
out for war, take them alive."
19 Then these young leaders of the provinces went out of the city with the army
which followed them.
20 And each one killed his man; so the
Syrians fled, and Israel pursued them; and
Ben-Hadad the king of Syria escaped on a
horse with the cavalry.
21 Then the king of Israel went out and
attacked the horses and chariots, and killed
the Syrians with a great slaughter.

Second Victory over Syria

22 And the prophet came to the king of
Israel and said to him, "Go, strengthen yourself; take note, and see what you should do,
[R]for in the spring of the year the king of Syria
will come up against you." 2 Sam. 11:1
23 Then the servants of the king of Syria
said to him, "Their gods *are* gods of the hills.
Therefore they were stronger than we; but if
we fight against them in the plain, *then*
surely we will be stronger than they.
24 "So do this thing: Dismiss the kings,
each from his position, and put captains in
their [T]places; *positions*
25 "and you shall muster an army like the
army [T]that you have lost, horse for horse and
chariot for chariot. Then we will fight against
them in the plain; surely we will be stronger
than they." And he listened to their voice and
did so. Lit. *that fell from you*
26 So it was, in the spring of the year, that
Ben-Hadad mustered the Syrians and went
up to [R]Aphek to fight against Israel. Josh. 13:4
27 And the children of Israel were mustered
and given provisions, and they went against
them. Now the children of Israel encamped
before them like two little flocks of goats,
while the Syrians filled the countryside.
28 Then a man of God came and spoke to
the king of Israel, and said, "Thus says the
LORD: 'Because the Syrians have said, "The
LORD *is* God of the hills, but He *is* not God of
the valleys," therefore [R]I will deliver all this
great multitude into your hand, and you shall
know that I *am* the LORD.' " 1 Kin. 20:13
29 And they encamped opposite each other
for seven days. So it was that on the seventh
day the battle was joined; and the children of
Israel killed one hundred thousand foot soldiers *of* the Syrians in one day.
30 But the rest fled to Aphek, into the city;
then a wall fell on twenty-seven thousand of
the men *who were* left. And Ben-Hadad fled
and went into the city, into an inner chamber.
31 And his servants said to him, "Look now,
we have heard that the kings of the house of
Israel *are* merciful kings. Please, let us put
sackcloth around our waists and ropes
around our heads, and go out to the king of
Israel; perhaps he will spare your life."
32 So they wore sackcloth around their
waists and *put* ropes around their heads, and
came to the king of Israel and said, "Your
servant Ben-Hadad says, 'Please let me live.' "
And he said, "*Is* he still alive? He *is* my
brother."
33 Now the men were diligently watching
to see whether *any sign of mercy would come*
from him; and they quickly grasped *at this*
word and said, "Your brother Ben-Hadad." So
he said, "Go, bring him." Then Ben-Hadad
came out to him; and he had him come up
into the chariot.
34 Then *Ben-Hadad* said to him, [R]"The cities
which my father took from your father I will
restore; and you may set up marketplaces for
yourself in Damascus, as my father did in
Samaria." Then *Ahab said,* "I will send you
away with this treaty." So he made a treaty
with him and sent him away. 1 Kin. 15:20
35 Now a certain man of the sons of the
prophets said to his neighbor [R]by the word of
the LORD, "Strike me, please." And the man
refused to strike him. 1 Kin. 13:17, 18
36 Then he said to him, "Because you have
not obeyed the voice of the LORD, surely, as
soon as you depart from me, a lion shall kill
you." And as soon as he left him, [R]a lion
found him and killed him. 1 Kin. 13:24
37 And he found another man, and said,
"Strike me, please." So the man struck him,
inflicting a wound.
38 Then the prophet departed and waited
for the king by the road, and disguised himself with a bandage over his eyes.
39 Now as the king passed by, he cried out
to the king and said, "Your servant went out
into the midst of the battle; and there, a man
came over and brought a man to me, and
said, 'Guard this man; if by any means he is
missing, your life shall be for his life, or else
you shall [T]pay a talent of silver.' Lit. *weigh*
40 "And while your servant was busy here
and there, he was gone." And the king of
Israel said to him, "So *shall* your judgment
be; you yourself have decided *it.*"
41 Then he hastened to take the bandage
away from his eyes; and the king of Israel
recognized him as one of the prophets.
42 And he said to him, "Thus says the LORD:
[R]'Because you have let slip out of *your* hand a
man whom I appointed to utter destruction,
therefore your life shall go for his life, and
your people for his people.' " 1 Kin. 22:31–37
43 So the king of Israel went to his house
sullen and displeased, and came to Samaria.

CHAPTER 21

Murder of Naboth

AND it came to pass after these things *that*
Naboth the Jezreelite had a vineyard

which *was* in [R]Jezreel, next to the palace of
Ahab king of Samaria. 1 Kin. 18:45, 46
2 So Ahab spoke to Naboth, saying, "Give
me your vineyard, that I may have it for a
vegetable garden, because it *is* near, next to
my house; and for it I will give you a vineyard better than it. *Or,* if it seems good to
you, I will give you its worth in money."
3 And Naboth said to Ahab, "The LORD
forbid [R]that I should give the inheritance of
my fathers to you!" [Num. 36:7]
4 So Ahab went into his house sullen and
displeased because of the word which Naboth
the Jezreelite had spoken to him; for he had
said, "I will not give you the inheritance of
my fathers." And he lay down on his bed, and
turned away his face, and would eat no food.
5 But [R]Jezebel his wife came to him, and
said to him, "Why is your spirit so sullen that
you eat no food?" 1 Kin. 19:1, 2
6 So he said to her, "Because I spoke to
Naboth the Jezreelite, and said to him, 'Give
me your vineyard for money; or else, if it
pleases you, I will give you *another* vineyard
for it.' And he answered, 'I will not give you
my vineyard.' "
7 Then Jezebel his wife said to him, "You
now exercise authority over Israel! Arise *and*
eat food, and let your heart be cheerful; I will
give you the vineyard of Naboth the Jezreelite."
8 So she wrote letters in Ahab's name,
sealed *them* with his seal, and sent the letters
to the elders and the nobles who *were* dwelling in the city with Naboth.
9 And she wrote in the letters, saying,
"Proclaim a fast, and seat Naboth [T]with high
honor among the people; Lit. *at the head*
10 "and seat two men, scoundrels, before
him to bear witness against him, saying, 'You
have [R]blasphemed God and the king.' *Then*
take him out, and [R]stone him, that he may
die." [Ex. 22:28] • [Lev. 24:14]
11 So the men of his city, the elders and
nobles who were inhabitants of his city, did
as Jezebel had sent to them, as it *was* written
in the letters which she had sent to them.
12 They proclaimed a fast, and seated Naboth with high honor among the people.
13 And two men, scoundrels, came in and
sat before him; and the scoundrels [R]witnessed
against him, against Naboth, in the presence
of the people, saying, "Naboth has blasphemed God and the king!" Then they took
him outside the city and stoned him with
stones, so that he died. [Ex. 20:16; 23:1, 7]
14 Then they sent to Jezebel, saying, "Naboth has been stoned and is dead."
15 And it came to pass, when Jezebel heard
that Naboth had been stoned and was dead,
that Jezebel said to Ahab, "Arise, take possession of the vineyard of Naboth the Jezreelite, which he refused to give you for money;
for Naboth is not alive, but dead."
16 So it was, when Ahab heard that Naboth
was dead, that Ahab got up and went down
to take possession of the vineyard of Naboth
the Jezreelite.

Prediction of Ahab's Death

17 [R]Then the word of the LORD came to
[R]Elijah the Tishbite, saying, [Ps. 9:12] • 1 Kin. 19:1
18 "Arise, go down to meet Ahab king of
Israel, [R]who *lives* in Samaria. There *he is,* in
the vineyard of Naboth, where he has gone
down to take possession of it. 2 Chr. 22:9
19 "You shall speak to him, saying, 'Thus
says the LORD: "Have you murdered and also
taken possession?" ' And you shall speak to
him, saying, 'Thus says the LORD: "In the
place where dogs licked the blood of Naboth,
dogs shall lick your blood, even yours." ' "
20 Then Ahab said to Elijah, "Have you
found me, O my enemy?" And he answered,
"I have found *you,* because you have sold
yourself to do evil in the sight of the LORD:
21 'Behold, I will bring calamity on you. I
will take away your posterity, and will cut off
from Ahab [R]every male in Israel, both [R]bond
and free. 1 Sam. 25:22 • 1 Kin. 14:10
22 'I will make your house like the house of
Jeroboam the son of Nebat, and like the
house of Baasha the son of Ahijah, because of
the provocation with which you have provoked *Me* to anger, and made Israel sin.'
23 "And [R]concerning Jezebel the LORD also
spoke, saying, 'The dogs shall eat Jezebel by
the wall of Jezreel.' 2 Kin. 9:10, 30–37
24 "The dogs shall eat whoever belongs to
Ahab and dies in the city, and the birds of the
air shall eat whoever dies in the field."
25 But [R]there was no one like Ahab who
sold himself to do wickedness in the sight of
the LORD, [R]because Jezebel his wife [T]stirred
him up. 1 Kin. 16:30–33; 21:20 • 1 Kin. 16:31 • *incited him*
26 And he behaved very abominably in
following idols, according to all [R]*that* the
Amorites had done, whom the LORD had cast
out before the children of Israel. 2 Kin. 21:11
27 So it was, when Ahab heard those words,
that he tore his clothes and [R]put sackcloth on
his body, and fasted and lay in sackcloth, and
went about mourning. Gen. 37:34
28 And the word of the LORD came to Elijah
the Tishbite, saying,
29 "See how Ahab has humbled himself
before Me? Because he [R]has humbled himself
before Me, I will not bring the calamity in his
days; *but* in the days of his son I will bring
the calamity on his house." [2 Kin. 22:19]

CHAPTER 22

Promise of Victory by the False Prophets
2 Chr. 18:2–11

NOW three years passed without war
between Syria and Israel.

2 Then it came to pass, in the third year,
that [R]Jehoshaphat the king of Judah went
down to *visit* the king of Israel. 2 Chr. 18:2
3 And the king of Israel said to his servants, "Do you know that [R]Ramoth in Gilead
is ours, but we hesitate to take it out of the
hand of the king of Syria?" Deut. 4:43
4 So he said to Jehoshaphat, "Will you go
with me to fight at Ramoth Gilead?" And
Jehoshaphat said to the king of Israel, [R]"I *am*
as you *are*, my people as your people, my
horses as your horses." 2 Kin. 3:7
5 And Jehoshaphat said to the king of
Israel, [R]"Please inquire for the word of the
LORD today." 2 Kin. 3:11
6 Then the king of Israel gathered [T]the
prophets together, about four hundred men,
and said to them, "Shall I go against Ramoth
Gilead to fight, or shall I refrain?" So they
said, "Go up, for the Lord will deliver *it* into
the hand of the king." The false prophets
7 And [R]Jehoshaphat said, "*Is there* not still
a prophet of the LORD here, that we may
inquire of [T]Him?" 2 Kin. 3:11 • Or *him*
8 So the king of Israel said to Jehoshaphat,
"*There is* still one man, Micaiah the son of
Imlah, by whom we may inquire of the LORD;
but I hate him, because he does not prophesy
good concerning me, but evil." And Jehoshaphat said, "Let not the king say such things!"
9 Then the king of Israel called an officer
and said, "Bring Micaiah the son of Imlah
quickly!"
10 The king of Israel and Jehoshaphat the
king of Judah, having put on *their* robes, sat
each on his throne, at a threshing floor at the
entrance of the gate of Samaria; and all the
prophets prophesied before them.
11 Now Zedekiah the son of Chenaanah
had made [R]horns of iron for himself; and he
said, "Thus says the LORD: 'With these you
shall [R]gore the Syrians until they are destroyed.'" Zech. 1:18–21 • Deut. 33:17
12 And all the prophets prophesied so, saying, "Go up to Ramoth Gilead and prosper,
for the LORD will deliver *it* into the king's
hand."

Promise of Defeat by Micaiah—2 Chr. 18:12–27

13 Then the messenger who had gone to
call Micaiah spoke to him, saying, "Now
listen, the words of the prophets with one
accord *encourage* the king. Please, let your
word be like *the word of* one of them, and
speak encouragement."
14 And Micaiah said, "*As* the LORD lives,
[R]whatever the LORD says to me, that I will
speak." Num. 22:38; 24:13
15 Then he came to the king; and the king
said to him, "Micaiah, shall we go to war
against Ramoth Gilead, or shall we refrain?"
And he answered him, "Go and prosper, for
the LORD will deliver *it* into the hand of the
king!"
16 So the king said to him, "How many
times shall I make you swear that you tell me
nothing but the truth in the name of the
LORD?"
17 Then he said, "I saw all Israel [R]scattered
on the mountains, as sheep that have no
shepherd. And the LORD said, 'These have no
master. Let each return to his house in
peace.'" Matt. 9:36
18 And the king of Israel said to Jehoshaphat, "Did I not tell you that he would not
prophesy good concerning me, but evil?"
19 Then Micaiah said, "Therefore hear the
word of the LORD: I saw the LORD sitting on
His throne, and all the host of heaven standing by, on His right hand and on His left.
20 "And the LORD said, 'Who will persuade
Ahab to go up, that he may fall at Ramoth
Gilead?' So one spoke in this manner, and
another spoke in that manner.
21 "Then a spirit came forward and stood
before the LORD, and said, 'I will persuade
him.'
22 "The LORD said to him, 'In what way?' So
he said, 'I will go out and be a lying spirit in
the mouth of all his prophets.' And He said,
[R]'You shall persuade *him*, and also prevail. Go
out and do so.' Judg. 9:23
23 [R]"Now therefore, look! The LORD has put
a lying spirit in the mouth of all these prophets of yours, and the LORD has declared
disaster against you." [Ezek. 14:9]
24 Then Zedekiah the son of Chenaanah
went near and struck Micaiah on the cheek,
and said, "Which way did the spirit from the
LORD go from me to speak to you?"
25 And Micaiah said, "Indeed, you shall see
on that day when you go into an [R]inner
chamber to hide!" 1 Kin. 20:30
26 Then the king of Israel said, "Take Micaiah, and return him to Amon the governor of
the city and to Joash the king's son;
27 "and say, 'Thus says the king: "Put this
fellow in [R]prison, and feed him with bread of
affliction and water of affliction, until I come
in peace."'" 2 Chr. 16:10; 18:25–27
28 Then Micaiah said, "If you ever return in
peace, the LORD has not spoken by me." And
he said, "Take heed, all you people!"

Defeat of Israel—2 Chr. 18:18–34

29 So the king of Israel and Jehoshaphat
the king of Judah went up to Ramoth Gilead.
30 And the king of Israel said to Jehoshaphat, "I will disguise myself and go into
battle; but you put on your robes." So the
king of Israel [R]disguised himself and went
into battle. 2 Chr. 35:22
31 Now the king of Syria had commanded
the thirty-two [R]captains of his chariots, saying, "Fight with no one small or great, but
only with the king of Israel." 1 Kin. 20:24

AHAB'S IVORY HOUSE AT SAMARIA

During Old Testament times, ivory was a rare and expensive item found only in the palaces of kings and the homes of the very wealthy. Ornate ivory carvings were inlaid in furniture and the wooden paneling used in elegant homes. A mark of the wealth of King Solomon (reigned 971–931 B.C.) was his royal throne made of ivory (2 Chr. 9:17).

After Solomon's reign and the division of his kingdom into two separate nations, the upper classes of the northern kingdom continued the lavish display of their wealth by using ivory in their homes and palaces. The prophet Amos condemned these people for these excesses and for exploiting the poor, predicting that those who rested upon "beds of ivory" would be judged by God (Amos 6:4).

King Ahab of Israel (reigned 874–853 B.C.) was an avid builder who loved to display his wealth with ornate buildings and elegant furnishings. He completed and adorned the capital city of Samaria, which his father Omri (reigned 880–874 B.C.) had begun several years before. Excavations of the royal palace in Samaria have yielded evidence of the extravagant practices Amos condemned. The outside of Ahab's "ivory house" (1 Kin. 22:39; Amos 3:15) was faced with white stone, which gave it the appearance of ivory. It was also decorated throughout with numerous ivory carvings and inlaid ivory panels, like the one shown here.

The two-story palace was constructed on a high hill, surrounded by numerous courtyards. One of these courtyards featured a large pool. Excavators believe this may have been the pool where the blood of Ahab was washed from his chariot after he was killed in battle (1 Kin. 22:38). Discovered nearby was a large storeroom, which contained five hundred pieces of ivory, ready to be inlaid in walls and furniture throughout the royal palace.

Ivory carvings and inlaid ivory panels decorated Ahab's palace.

Ahab's ivory palace is a symbol of the fleeting nature of power and riches. He is remembered as a cruel and idolatrous king whose wealth passed to others after his violent and inglorious death.

32 So it was, when the captains of the
chariots saw Jehoshaphat, that they said,
"Surely it *is* the king of Israel!" Therefore
they turned aside to fight against him, and
Jehoshaphat [R]cried out. 2 Chr. 18:31
33 And it happened, when the captains of
the chariots saw that it *was* not the king of
Israel, that they turned back from pursuing
him.
34 Now a *certain* man drew a bow at ran-
dom, and struck the king of Israel between
the joints of his armor. So he said to the
driver of his chariot, "Turn around and take
me out of the battle, for I am wounded."
35 The battle increased that day; and the
king was propped up in his chariot, facing the
Syrians, and died at evening. The blood ran
out from the wound onto the floor of the
chariot.
36 Then, as the sun was going down, a
shout went throughout the army, saying,
"Every man to his city, and every man to his
own country!"

Death of Ahab

37 So the king died, and was brought to
Samaria. And they buried the king in Samaria.
38 Then *someone* washed the chariot at a
pool in Samaria, and the dogs licked up his
blood while *the harlots bathed, according to
the word of the LORD which He had spoken.
39 Now the rest of the acts of Ahab and all
that he did, [R]the ivory house which he built
and all the cities that he built, *are* they not
written in the book of the chronicles of the
kings of Israel? Amos 3:15
40 So Ahab rested with his fathers. Then
Ahaziah his son reigned in his place.

The Reign of Jehoshaphat in Judah
2 Chr. 20:31—21:1

41 Now [R]Jehoshaphat the son of Asa had
become king over Judah in the fourth year of
Ahab king of Israel. 2 Chr. 20:31
42 Jehoshaphat *was* thirty-five years old
when he became king, and he reigned
twenty-five years in Jerusalem. His mother's
name *was* Azubah the daughter of Shilhi.
43 And he walked in all the ways of his
father Asa. He did not turn aside from them,
doing *what was* right in the eyes of the LORD.
Nevertheless [R]the high places were not taken
away, *for* the people offered sacrifices and
burned incense on the high places. 2 Kin. 12:3
44 Also [R]Jehoshaphat made [R]peace with the
king of Israel. 2 Chr. 19:2 • 2 Chr. 18:1
45 Now the rest of the acts of Jehoshaphat,
the might that he showed, and how he made
war, *are* they not written [R]in the book of the
chronicles of the kings of Judah? 2 Chr. 20:34
46 [R]And the rest of the perverted persons,
who remained in the days of his father Asa,
he banished from the land. 1 Kin. 14:24; 15:12
47 [R]*There was* then no king in Edom, only a
deputy of the king. 2 Sam. 8:14
48 Jehoshaphat made merchant ships to go
to Ophir for gold; but they never sailed, for
the ships were wrecked at Ezion Geber.
49 Then Ahaziah the son of Ahab said to
Jehoshaphat, "Let my servants go with your
servants in the ships." But Jehoshaphat
would not.
50 And [R]Jehoshaphat rested with his fathers, and was buried with his fathers in the
City of David his father. Then Jehoram his
son reigned in his place. 2 Chr. 21:1

The Reign of Ahaziah in Israel

51 [R]Ahaziah the son of Ahab became king
over Israel in Samaria in the seventeenth
year of Jehoshaphat king of Judah, and
reigned two years over Israel. 1 Kin. 22:40
52 He did evil in the sight of the LORD, and
[R]walked in the way of his father and in the
way of his mother and in the way of Jeroboam the son of Nebat, who had made Israel
sin; 1 Kin. 15:26; 21:25
53 for [R]he served Baal and worshiped him,
and provoked the LORD God of Israel to
anger, [R]according[T] to all that his father had
done. Judg. 2:11 • 1 Kin. 16:30–32 • In the same way that

22:38 Tg., Syr. *they washed his armor*

THE SECOND BOOK OF THE
KINGS

THE BOOK OF SECOND KINGS

The Book of Second Kings continues the drama begun in First Kings—the tragic history of two nations on a collision course with captivity. The author systematically traces the reigning monarchs of Israel and Judah, first by carrying one nation's history forward, then retracing the same period for the other nation.

Nineteen consecutive evil kings rule in Israel, leading to the captivity by Assyria. The picture is somewhat brighter in Judah, where godly kings occasionally emerge to reform the evils of their predecessors. In the end, however, sin outweighs righteousness and Judah is marched off to Babylon. See "The Book of First Kings" for more detail concerning the title.

THE AUTHOR OF SECOND KINGS

See "The Author of First Kings" for a discussion of authorship. If this now divided book was not written by Jeremiah, it probably was written by a prophetic contemporary of his. The majority of Second Kings was written before the Babylonian captivity (see "to this day" in 17:34, 41).

The literary style of Second Kings is similar to that of the Book of Jeremiah, and it has been observed that the omission of Jeremiah's ministry in the account of King Josiah and his successors may indicate that Jeremiah himself was the recorder of the events. However, the last two chapters were evidently added to the book after the Babylonian captivity and written by someone other than Jeremiah. The prophet Jeremiah was forced to flee to Egypt (Jer. 43:1–8), not to Babylon. It is interesting that Second Kings 24:18—25:30 is almost the same as Jeremiah 52.

THE TIME OF SECOND KINGS

The last recorded event in Second Kings is the release of Jehoiachin (25:27–30), which takes place in 560 B.C. Most of First and Second Kings probably was written just prior to 586 B.C., but chapters 24 and 25 were written after Jehoiachin's release, perhaps about 550 B.C.

Chapters 1—17 cover the 131 years from 853 B.C. (King Ahaziah of Israel) to 722 B.C. (the Assyrian captivity of Israel). Chapters 18—25 cover the 155 years from the beginning of Hezekiah's reign in 715 B.C. to the release of Jehoiachin in Babylon in 560 B.C. The united kingdom lasts for 112 years (1043–931 B.C.), the northern kingdom of Israel exists for another 209 years (931–722 B.C.), and the southern kingdom of Judah continues for an additional 136 years (722–586 B.C.). During this 457-year kingdom period, there are great shifts of world power. Egyptian and Assyrian control over Palestine fluctuates; Assyria rises to preeminence, declines, and is finally conquered by Babylon.

The books of Kings show that judgment comes to the kingdoms of Israel and Judah because of their idolatry, immorality, and disunity. Judah lasts 136 years longer than Israel because of the relative goodness of eight of its twenty kings. Israel never breaks away from Jeroboam's idolatrous calf worship, but Judah experiences some periods of revival in the worship of Yahweh. During these years, God sends many of His prophets. Elijah, Elisha, Amos, and Hosea are in the northern kingdom, while in the southern kingdom Obadiah, Joel, Isaiah, Micah, Nahum, Zephaniah, Jeremiah, and Habakkuk are prophesying.

THE CHRIST OF SECOND KINGS

Unlike the nine different dynasties in the northern kingdom, the kings of Judah reign as one continuous dynasty. In spite of Queen Athaliah's attempt to destroy the house of David, God remains faithful to His covenant with David (2 Sam. 7) by preserving his lineage. Jesus the Messiah is his direct descendant.

While Elijah is a type of John the Baptist (Matt. 11:14; 17:10–12; Luke 1:17), Elisha reminds us of Christ. Elijah generally lives apart from the people and stresses law, judgment, and repentance. Elisha lives among the people and emphasizes grace, life, and hope.

KEYS TO SECOND KINGS

Key Word: Captivities of the Kingdom—Second Kings records both the destruction and captivity of Israel by the Assyrians (2 Kin. 17), as well as the destruction and captivity of Judah by the Babylonians (2 Kin. 25).

The book was written selectively, not exhaustively, from a prophetic viewpoint to teach that the decline and collapse of the two kingdoms occurred because of failure on the part of the rulers and people to heed the warnings of God's messengers. The spiritual climate of the nation determined its political and economic conditions.

The prophets of Jehovah play a prominent role in First and Second Kings as God uses them to remind the kings of their covenant responsibilities as His theocratic administrators. When the king keeps the covenant, he and the nation are richly blessed. But judgment consistently falls upon those who refuse to obey God's law. God is seen in Kings as the controller of history who reveals His plan and purpose to His people. Unhappily, the people are concerned more with their own plans, and their rejection of God's rule leads to exile at the hands of the Assyrians and Babylonians.

Key Verses: Second Kings 17:22, 23; 23:27—"For the children of Israel walked in all the sins of Jeroboam which he did; they did not depart from them, until the LORD removed Israel out of His sight, as He had said by all His servants the prophets. So Israel was carried away from their own land to Assyria, *as it is* to this day" (17:22, 23).

"And the LORD said, 'I will also remove Judah from My sight, as I have removed Israel, and will cast off this city Jerusalem which I have chosen, and the house of which I said, "My name shall be there"'" (23:27).

Key Chapter: Second Kings 25—The last chapter of Second Kings records the utter destruction of the city of Jerusalem and its glorious temple. Only the poor of Israel are left, and even some of them flee for their lives to Egypt. Hope is still alive, however, with the remnant in the Babylonian captivity as Evil-Merodach frees Jehoiachin from prison and treats him kindly.

SURVEY OF SECOND KINGS

Without interruption Second Kings continues the narrative of First Kings. The twin kingdoms of Israel and Judah pursue a collision course with captivity as the glory of the once united kingdom becomes increasingly diminished. Division has led to decline and now ends in double deportation with Israel captured by Assyria and Judah by Babylon. This book traces the history of the divided kingdom in chapters 1—17 and the history of the surviving kingdom in chapters 18—25.

Divided Kingdom (1—17): These chapters record the story of Israel's corruption in a relentless succession of bad kings from Ahaziah to Hoshea. The situation in Judah during this time (Jehoram to Ahaz) is somewhat better, but far from ideal. This dark period in the northern kingdom of Israel is interrupted only by the ministries of such godly prophets as Elijah and Elisha. At the end of Elijah's miraculous ministry, Elisha is installed and authenticated as his successor. He is a force for righteousness in a nation that never served the true God or worshiped at the temple in Jerusalem. Elisha's ministry is characterized by miraculous provisions of sustenance and life. Through him God demonstrates His gracious care for the nation and His concern for any person who desires to come to Him. However, like his forerunner Elijah, Elisha is basically rejected by Israel's leadership.

Elisha instructs one of his prophetic assistants to anoint Jehu king over Israel. Jehu fulfills the prophecies concerning Ahab's descendants by putting them to death. He kills Ahab's wife Jezebel, his sons, and also the priests of Baal. But he does not depart from the calf worship originally set up by Jeroboam. The loss of the house of Ahab means the alienation of Israel and Judah and the weakening of both. Israel's enemies begin to get the upper hand. Meanwhile, in Judah, Jezebel's daughter Athaliah kills all the descendants of David, except for Joash, and usurps the throne. However, Jehoiada the priest eventually removes her from the throne and places Joash in power. Joash restores the temple and serves God.

Syria gains virtual control over Israel, but there is no response to God's chastisement: the kings and people refuse to repent. Nevertheless, there is a period of restoration under Jeroboam II, but the continuing series of wicked kings in Israel leads to its overthrow by Assyria.

Surviving Kingdom (18—25): Of Israel's nineteen kings, not one is righteous in God's sight. All but one of its nine dynasties are created by murdering the previous king. In Judah, where there is only one dynasty, eight of its twenty

FOCUS	DIVIDED KINGDOM			SURVIVING KINGDOM		
REFERENCE	1:1—— 9:1	——17:1	——18:1	——22:1	——25:1	——25:30
DIVISION	MINISTRY OF ELISHA UNDER AHAZIAH AND JEHORAM	REIGNS OF TEN KINGS OF ISRAEL AND EIGHT KINGS OF JUDAH	FALL OF ISRAEL	REIGNS OF HEZEKIAH AND TWO EVIL KINGS	REIGNS OF JOSIAH AND FOUR EVIL KINGS	FALL OF JUDAH
TOPIC	ISRAEL AND JUDAH			JUDAH		
	AHAZIAH TO HOSHEA			HEZEKIAH TO ZEDEKIAH		
LOCATION	ISRAEL DEPORTED TO ASSYRIA			JUDAH DEPORTED TO BABYLONIA		
TIME	131 YEARS (853 – 722 B.C.)			155 YEARS (715 – 560 B.C.)		

rulers do what is right before God. Nevertheless, Judah's collapse finally comes, resulting in the Babylonian exile. Chapters 18—25 read more easily than chapters 1—17 because alternating the histories of the northern and southern kingdoms is no longer necessary. Only Judah remains.

Six years before the overthrow of Israel's capital of Samaria, Hezekiah becomes king of Judah. Because of his exemplary faith and reforms, God spares Jerusalem from Assyria and brings a measure of prosperity to Judah. However, Hezekiah's son Manasseh is so idolatrous that his long reign leads to the downfall of Judah. Even Josiah's later reforms cannot stem the tide of evil, and the four kings who succeed him are exceedingly wicked. Judgment comes with three deportations to Babylon. The third occurs in 586 B.C. when Nebuchadnezzar destroys Jerusalem and the temple. Still, the book ends on a note of hope with God preserving a remnant for Himself.

OUTLINE OF SECOND KINGS

Part One: The Divided Kingdom (1:1—17:41)

I. The Reign of Ahaziah in Israel . . . . 1 Kin. 22:51—2 Kin. 1:18

A. Spiritual Evaluation of Ahaziah . . . . 1 Kin. 22:51–53
B. Political Situation Under Ahaziah. 1:1
C. Death of Ahaziah 1:2–18

II. The Reign of Jehoram in Israel . . . . 2:1—8:15

A. Transition from Elijah to Elisha 2:1–25
 1. Chariot of Fire Takes Elijah. 2:1–11
 2. Authority of Elijah Is Taken by Elisha 2:12–25
B. Spiritual Evaluation of Jehoram 3:1–3
C. Political Situation Under Jehoram . . 3:4–27
D. Ministry of Elisha . . . . 4:1—8:15
 1. Miracle of the Increase of the Widow's Oil 4:1–7
 2. Miracle of the Shunammite's Son 4:8–37
 3. Miracle of the Deadly Stew . . . 4:38–41
 4. Miracle of the Multiplication of the Loaves 4:42–44
 5. Miracle of the Healing of Naaman 5:1–27
 6. Miracle of the Floating Ax Head 6:1–7
 7. Miracles During the First Syrian Attack 6:8–23
  a. Syria's War Plan. 6:8–12
  b. God's Chariots and Horses 6:13–17
  c. Syria's Army Is Blinded. . . . 6:18–23
 8. Miracles of Elisha During the Second Syrian Attack . . . . 6:24—7:20
  a. Siege of Samaria Causes Famine 6:24–29
  b. Elisha's Prophecies . . . . . 6:30—7:20
 9. Elisha's Ministry with the Shunammite Woman. 8:1–6
 10. Elisha's Ministry with the King of Syria. 8:7–15

III. The Reign of Jehoram in Judah. 8:16–24

IV. The Reign of Ahaziah in Judah . . . 8:25—9:29

A. Spiritual Evaluation of Ahaziah . . . 8:25–27
B. Political Situation Under Ahaziah . . . . 8:28—9:26
 1. Battle Against Syria 8:28, 29
 2. Anointing of Jehu King over Israel 9:1–13
 3. Execution of Joram 9:14–26
C. Death of Ahaziah 9:27–29

V. The Reign of Jehu in Israel. . . . . . 9:30—10:36

A. Fulfillment of Elisha's Prophecy . . . . 9:30—10:28
B. Spiritual Evaluation of Jehu 10:29–31
C. Political Situation Under Jehu . . . 10:32, 33
D. Death of Jehu 10:34–36

VI. The Reign of Queen Athaliah in Judah 11:1–16

A. Salvation of Joash. 11:1–3
B. Overthrow of Athaliah by Jehoiada 11:4–12
C. Death of Athaliah. 11:13–16

VII. The Reign of Joash in Judah. . . . 11:17—12:21

A. Renewal of the Covenant 11:17–21
B. Spiritual Evaluation of Joash. 12:1–3
C. Spiritual Situation Under Joash. . . . 12:4–16
D. Political Situation Under Joash . . . 12:17, 18
E. Death of Joash 12:19–21

VIII. The Reign of Jehoahaz in Israel. 13:1–9

IX. The Reign of Jehoash in Israel. 13:10–25

A. Rule of Jehoash. 13:10–13
B. Last Prophecies and Death of Elisha 13:14–25
 1. Prophecy of Israel's Victory . . . 13:14–19
 2. Death of Elisha 13:20
 3. Miracle of Resurrection at Elisha's Tomb 13:21
 4. Israel's Victory over Syria. 13:22–25

X. The Reign of Amaziah in Judah 14:1–22

A. Spiritual Evaluation of Amaziah. . . . 14:1–6
B. Political Situation Under Amaziah 14:7–14
C. Death of Jehoash 14:15, 16
D. Death of Amaziah 14:17–22

XI. The Reign of Jeroboam II in Israel 14:23–29

XII. The Reign of Azariah in Judah 15:1–7

XIII. The Reign of Zechariah in Israel. 15:8–12

XIV. The Reign of Shallum in Israel 15:13–15

XV. The Reign of Menahem in Israel. . . . 15:16–22

XVI. The Reign of Pekahiah in Israel. 15:23–26

CHAPTER 1

Political Situation Under Ahaziah—2 Kin. 3:5

MOAB [R]rebelled against Israel [R]after the death of Ahab. 2 Sam. 8:2 · 2 Kin. 3:5

Death of Ahaziah

2 Now Ahaziah fell through the lattice of
his upper room in Samaria, and was injured;
so he sent messengers and said to them, "Go,
inquire of Baal-Zebub, the god of Ekron,
whether I shall recover from this injury."
3 But the [T]angel of the LORD said to Elijah
the Tishbite, "Arise, go up to meet the messengers of the king of Samaria, and say to
them, *'Is it* because *there is* no God in Israel
that you are going to inquire of Baal-Zebub,
the god of Ekron?' Or *Angel*
4 "Now therefore, thus says the LORD:
'You shall not come down from the bed to
which you have gone up, but you shall surely
die.' " So Elijah departed.
5 And when the messengers returned to
[T]him, he said to them, "Why have you come
back?" Ahaziah
6 So they said to him, "A man came up to
meet us, and said to us, 'Go, return to the
king who sent you, and say to him, "Thus
says the LORD: *'Is it* because *there is* no God
in Israel *that* you are sending to inquire of
Baal-Zebub, the god of Ekron? Therefore you
shall not come down from the bed to which
you have gone up, but you shall surely
die.' " ' "
7 Then he said to them, "What kind of
man *was it* who came up to meet you and
told you these words?"
8 So they answered him, *"He was* [R]a hairy
man, and wore a leather belt around his
waist." And he said, [R]"It *is* Elijah the Tishbite." Zech. 13:4 · 1 Kin. 18:7
9 Then the king sent to him a captain of
fifty with his fifty men. So he went up to him;
and there he was, sitting on the top of a hill.
And he spoke to him: "Man of God, the king
has said, 'Come down!' "

10 So Elijah answered and said to the captain of fifty, "If I *am* a man of God, then let fire come down from heaven and consume you and your fifty men." And fire came down from heaven and consumed him and his fifty.

11 Then he sent to him another captain of fifty with his fifty men. And he answered and said to him: "Man of God, thus has the king said, 'Come down quickly!' "

12 So Elijah answered and said to them, "If I *am* a man of God, let fire come down from heaven and consume you and your fifty men." And the fire of God came down from heaven and consumed him and his fifty.

13 Again, he sent a third captain of fifty with his fifty men. And the third captain of fifty went up, and came and [T]fell on his knees before Elijah, and pleaded with him, and said to him: "Man of God, please let my life and the life of these fifty servants of yours be precious in your sight. Lit. *bowed down*

14 "Look, fire has come down from heaven and burned up the first two captains of fifties with their fifties. But let my life now be precious in your sight."

15 And the [T]angel of the LORD said to Elijah, "Go down with him; do not be afraid of him." So he arose and went down with him to the king. Or *Angel*

16 Then he said to him, "Thus says the LORD: 'Because you have sent messengers to inquire of Baal-Zebub, the god of Ekron, *is it* because *there is* no God in Israel to inquire of His word? Therefore you shall not come down from the bed to which you have gone up, but you shall surely die.' "

17 So [T]Ahaziah died according to the word of the LORD which Elijah had spoken. Because he had no son, Jehoram became king in his place, in the second year of Jehoram the son of Jehoshaphat, king of Judah. *he*

18 Now the rest of the acts of Ahaziah which he did, *are* they not written in the book of the chronicles of the kings of Israel?

CHAPTER 2

Chariot of Fire Takes Elijah

AND it came to pass, when the LORD was about to [R]take up Elijah into heaven by a whirlwind, that Elijah went with [R]Elisha from Gilgal. Gen. 5:24 • 1 Kin. 19:16–21

2 Then Elijah said to Elisha, "Stay here, please, for the LORD has sent me on to Bethel." And Elisha said, "*As* the LORD lives, and [R]*as* your soul lives, I will not leave you!" So they went down to Bethel. 1 Sam. 1:26

3 And the sons of the prophets who *were* at Bethel came out to Elisha, and said to him, "Do you know that the LORD will take away your master from [T]over you today?" And he said, "Yes, I know; keep silent!" Lit. *your head*

4 Then Elijah said to him, "Elisha, stay here, please, for the LORD has sent me on to Jericho." And he said, "*As* the LORD lives, and *as* your soul lives, I will not leave you!" So they came to Jericho.

5 And the sons of the prophets who *were* at Jericho came to Elisha and said to him, "Do you know that the LORD will take away your master from over you today?" So he answered, "Yes, I know; keep silent!"

6 Then Elijah said to him, "Stay here, please, for the LORD has sent me on to the Jordan." And he said, "*As* the LORD lives, and *as* your soul lives, I will not leave you!" So the two of them went on.

7 And fifty men of the sons of the prophets went and stood facing *them* at a distance, while the two of them stood by the Jordan.

8 Now Elijah took his mantle, rolled *it* up, and struck the water; and [R]it was divided this way and that, so that the two of them crossed over on dry [R]ground. Ex. 14:21, 22 • Josh. 3:17

9 And so it was, when they had crossed over, that Elijah said to Elisha, "Ask! What may I do for you, before I am taken away from you?" And Elisha said, "Please let a double portion of your spirit be upon me."

10 So he said, "You have asked a hard thing. *Nevertheless*, if you see me *when I am* taken from you, it shall be so for you; but if not, it shall not be *so*."

11 Then it happened, as they continued on and talked, that suddenly [R]a chariot of fire *appeared* with horses of fire, and separated the two of them; and Elijah [R]went up by a whirlwind into heaven. 2 Kin. 6:17 • Heb. 11:5

Authority of Elijah Is Taken by Elisha

12 Now Elisha saw *it*, and he cried out, [R]"My father, my father, the chariot of Israel and its horsemen!" So he saw him no more. And he took hold of his own clothes and tore them into two pieces. 2 Kin. 13:14

13 He also took up the mantle of Elijah that had fallen from him, and went back and stood by the bank of the Jordan.

14 Then he took the mantle of Elijah that had fallen from him, and struck the water, and said, "Where *is* the LORD God of Elijah?" And when he also had struck the water, [R]it was divided this way and that; and Elisha crossed over. 2 Kin. 2:8

15 Now when the sons of the prophets who *were* [R]from[T] Jericho saw him, they said, "The spirit of Elijah rests on Elisha." And they came to meet him, and bowed to the ground before him. 2 Kin. 2:7 • Or *at Jericho opposite him saw*

16 Then they said to him, "Look now, there are fifty strong men with your servants. Please let them go and search for your master, [R]lest perhaps the Spirit of the LORD has taken him up and cast him upon some mountain or into some valley." And he said, "You shall not send anyone." 1 Kin. 18:12

17 But when they urged him till he was
[R]ashamed, he said, "Send *them out.*" Therefore they sent fifty men, and they searched
for three days but did not find him. 2 Kin. 8:11
18 And when they came back to him, for he
had stayed in Jericho, he said to them, "Did I
not say to you, 'Do not go'?"
19 Then the men of the city said to Elisha,
"Please notice, the situation of this city *is*
pleasant, as my lord sees; but the water *is*
bad, and the ground barren."
20 And he said, "Bring me a new bowl, and
put salt in it." So they brought *it* to him.
21 Then he went out to the source of the
water, and [R]cast in the salt there, and said,
"Thus says the LORD: 'I have [T]healed this
water; from it there shall be no more death or
barrenness.' " Ex. 15:25, 26 · *purified*
22 So the water remains [R]healed to this day,
according to the saying of Elisha which he
spoke. Ezek. 47:8, 9
23 And he went up from there to Bethel;
and as he was going up the road, some
youths came from the city and mocked him,
and said to him, "Go up, you baldhead! Go
up, you baldhead!"
24 So he turned around and looked at them,
and [R]pronounced a curse on them in the
name of the LORD. And two female bears
came out of the woods and mauled forty-two
of the youths. Deut. 27:13–26
25 Then he went from there to [R]Mount
Carmel, and from there he returned to Samaria. 2 Kin. 4:25

CHAPTER 3

Spiritual Evaluation of Jehoram

NOW [R]Jehoram the son of Ahab became
king over Israel at Samaria in the eighteenth year of Jehoshaphat king of Judah,
and reigned twelve years. 2 Kin. 1:17
2 And he did evil in the sight of the LORD,
but not like his father and mother; for he put
away the *sacred* pillar of Baal [R]that his father
had made. 1 Kin. 16:31, 32
3 Nevertheless he persisted in the sins of
Jeroboam the son of Nebat, who had made
Israel sin; he did not depart from them.

Political Situation Under Jehoram

4 Now Mesha king of Moab was a sheepbreeder, and he regularly paid the king of
Israel one hundred thousand lambs and the
wool of one hundred thousand rams.
5 But it happened, when [R]Ahab died, that
the king of Moab rebelled against the king of
Israel. 2 Kin. 1:1
6 So King Jehoram went out of Samaria at
that time and mustered all Israel.
7 Then he went and sent to Jehoshaphat
king of Judah, saying, "The king of Moab has
rebelled against me. Will you go with me to
fight against Moab?" And he said, "I will go
up; [R]I *am* as you *are,* my people as your
people, my horses as your horses." 1 Kin. 22:4
8 And he said, "Which way shall we go
up?" And he answered, "By way of the Wilderness of Edom."
9 So the king of Israel went with the king
of Judah and the king of Edom, and they
marched on that roundabout route seven
days; and there was no water for the army,
nor for the animals that followed them.
10 And the king of Israel said, "Alas! For
the LORD has called these three kings together to deliver them into the hand of
Moab."
11 But Jehoshaphat said, "*Is there* no
prophet of the LORD here, that we may inquire of the LORD by him?" And one of the
servants of the king of Israel answered and
said, "Elisha the son of Shaphat *is* here, who
poured water on the hands of Elijah."
12 And Jehoshaphat said, "The word of the
LORD is with him." So the king of Israel and
Jehoshaphat and the king of Edom [R]went
down to him. 2 Kin. 2:25
13 Then Elisha said to the king of Israel,
[R]"What have I to do with you? [R]Go to [R]the
prophets of your father and the prophets of
your mother." And the king of Israel said to
him, "No, for the LORD has called these three
kings *together* to deliver them into the hand
of Moab." [Ezek. 14:3] · Judg. 10:14 · 1 Kin. 22:6–11
14 And Elisha said, [R]"*As* the LORD of hosts
lives, before whom I stand, surely were it not
that I regard the presence of Jehoshaphat
king of Judah, I would not look at you, nor
see you. 1 Kin. 17:1
15 "But now bring me a musician." And it
happened, when the musician played, that
the hand of the LORD came upon him.
16 And he said, "Thus says the LORD: 'Make
this valley full of [T]ditches.' *canals*
17 "For thus says the LORD: 'You shall not
see wind, nor shall you see rain; yet that
valley shall be filled with water, so that you,
your cattle, and your animals may drink.'
18 "And this is *but* a trivial thing in the
sight of the LORD; He will also deliver the
Moabites into your hand.
19 "Also you shall attack every fortified city
and every choice city, and shall cut down
every good tree, and stop up every spring of
water, and ruin every good piece of land with
stones."
20 Now it happened in the morning, when
[R]the grain offering was offered, that suddenly
water came by way of Edom, and the land
was filled with water. Ex. 29:39, 40
21 And when all the Moabites heard that
the kings had come up to fight against them,
all who were able to bear arms and older
were gathered; and they stood at the border.
22 Then they rose up early in the morning,

and the sun was shining on the water; and
the Moabites saw the water on the other side
as red as blood.
23 And they said, "This is blood; the kings
have surely struck swords and have killed
one another; now therefore, Moab, to the
spoil!"
24 So when they came to the camp of Israel,
Israel rose up and attacked the Moabites, so
that they fled before them; and they entered
their land, killing the Moabites.
25 Then they destroyed the cities, and each
man threw a stone on every good piece of
land and filled it; and they stopped up all the
springs of water and cut down all the good
trees, except that they left *intact* the stones
of [R]Kir Haraseth. However the slingers surrounded and attacked it. Is. 16:7, 11
26 And when the king of Moab saw that the
battle was too intense for him, he took with
him seven hundred men who drew swords, to
break through to the king of Edom, but they
could not.
27 Then [R]he took his eldest son who would
have reigned in his place, and offered him *as*
a burnt offering upon the wall; and there was
great [T]indignation against Israel. [R]So they
departed from him and returned to *their own*
land. [Amos 2:1] • *wrath* • 2 Kin. 8:20

CHAPTER 4

Miracle of the Increase of the Widow's Oil

A CERTAIN woman of the wives of the
sons of the prophets cried out to Elisha,
saying, "Your servant my husband is dead,
and you know that your servant feared the
LORD. And the creditor is coming [R]to take my
two sons to be his slaves." [Lev. 25:39–41, 48]
2 So Elisha said to her, "What shall I do for
you? Tell me, what do you have in the
house?" And she said, "Your maidservant has
nothing in the house but a jar of oil."
3 Then he said, "Go, borrow vessels from
everywhere, from all your neighbors—empty
vessels; [R]do not gather just a few. 2 Kin. 3:16
4 "And when you have come in, you shall
shut the door behind you and your sons; then
pour it into all those vessels, and set aside the
full ones."
5 So she went from him and shut the door
behind her and her sons, who brought *the
vessels* to her; and she poured *it* out.
6 Now it came to pass, when the vessels
were full, that she said to her son, "Bring me
another vessel." And he said to her, "*There is*
not another vessel." So the oil ceased.
7 Then she came and told the man of God.
And he said, "*Go, sell the oil* and pay your
debt; and you *and* your sons live on the rest."

Miracle of the Shunammite's Son

8 Now it happened one day that Elisha
went to Shunem, where there *was* a notable
woman, and she constrained him to eat some
food. So it was, as often as he passed by, *that*
he turned in there to eat some food.
9 And she said to her husband, "Look now,
I know that this *is* a holy man of God, who
passes by us regularly.
10 "Please, let us make [T]a small upper room
on the wall; and let us put a bed for him
there, and a table and a chair and a lampstand; so it will be, whenever he comes to us,
he can turn in there." *a small walled upper chamber*
11 And it happened one day that he came
there, and he turned in to the upper room and
lay down there.
12 Then he said to Gehazi his servant, "Call
this Shunammite woman." When he had
called her, she stood before him.
13 And he said to him, "Say now to her,
'Look, you have been concerned for us with
all this care. What *can I* do for you? Do you
want me to speak on your behalf to the king
or to the commander of the army?' " And she
answered, "I dwell among my own people."
14 So he said, "What then *is* to be done for
her?" And Gehazi answered, "Actually, she
has no son, and her husband is old."
15 And he said, "Call her." When he had
called her, she stood in the doorway.
16 Then he said, [T]"About this time next year
you shall embrace a son." And she said, "No,
my lord. Man of God, do not lie to your
maidservant!" Lit. *About this season, as the time of life*
17 And the woman conceived, and bore a
son when the appointed time had come, of
which Elisha had told her.
18 So the child grew. Now it happened one
day that he went out to his father, to the
reapers.
19 And he said to his father, "My head, my
head!" So he said to a servant, "Carry him to
his mother."
20 When he had taken him and brought him
to his mother, he sat on her knees till noon,
and *then* died.
21 And she went up and laid him on the bed
of the man of God, shut *the door* upon him,
and went out.
22 Then she called to her husband, and said,
"Please send me one of the young men and
one of the donkeys, that I may run to the
man of God and come back."
23 So he said, "Why are you going to him
today? *It is* neither the New Moon nor the
Sabbath." And she said, "*It is* well."
24 Then she saddled a donkey, and said to
her servant, "Drive, and go forward; do not
slacken the pace for me unless I tell you."
25 So she departed, and went to the man of
God [R]at Mount Carmel. 2 Kin. 2:25
And so it was, when the man of God saw
her afar off, that he said to his servant Gehazi, "Look, *there is* the Shunammite
woman.

26 "Please run now to meet her, and say to
her, '*Is it* well with you? *Is it* well with your
husband? *Is it* well with the child?' " And she
answered, "*It is* well."
27 Now when she came to the man of God
at the hill, she caught him by the feet, but
Gehazi came near to push her away. But the
man of God said, "Let her alone; for her soul
is in deep distress, and the LORD has hidden *it*
from me, and has not told me."
28 And she said, "Did I ask a son of my
lord? Did I not say, 'Do not deceive me'?"
29 Then he said to Gehazi, [T]"Get yourself
ready, and take my staff in your hand, and be
on your way. If you meet anyone, do not
greet him; and if anyone greets you, do not
answer him; but [R]lay my staff on the face of
the child." Lit. *Gird up your loins* • Ex. 7:19; 14:16
30 And the mother of the child said, [R]"*As*
the LORD lives, and *as* your soul lives, I will
not [R]leave you." So he arose and followed
her. 2 Kin. 2:2 • 2 Kin. 2:4
31 Now Gehazi went on ahead of them, and
laid the staff on the face of the child; but
there was neither voice nor hearing. Therefore he went back to meet him, and told him,
saying, "The child has not awakened."
32 And when Elisha came into the house,
there was the child, lying dead on his bed.
33 He [R]went in therefore, shut the door
behind the two of them, [R]and prayed to the
LORD. [Matt. 6:6] • 1 Kin. 17:20
34 And he went up and lay on the child, and
put his mouth on his mouth, his eyes on his
eyes, and his hands on his hands; and [R]he
stretched himself out on the child, and the
flesh of the child became warm. 1 Kin. 17:21–23
35 He returned and walked back and forth
in the house, and again went up [R]and
stretched himself out on him; then [R]the child
sneezed seven times, and the child opened his
eyes. 1 Kin. 17:21 • 2 Kin. 8:1, 5
36 And he called Gehazi and said, "Call this
Shunammite woman." So he called her. And
when she came in to him, he said, "Pick up
your son."
37 So she went in, fell at his feet, and bowed
to the ground; then she [R]picked up her son
and went out. [Heb. 11:35]

Miracle of the Deadly Stew

38 And Elisha returned to Gilgal, and *there*
was a famine in the land. Now the sons of the
prophets *were* sitting before him; and he said
to his servant, "Put on the large pot, and boil
stew for the sons of the prophets."
39 So one went out into the field to gather
herbs, and found a wild vine, and gathered
from it a lap full of wild gourds, and came and
sliced *them* into the pot of stew, though they
did not know *what they were*.
40 Then they served it to the men to eat.
Now it happened, as they were eating the
stew, that they cried out and said, "O man of
God, *there is* [R]death in the pot!" And they
could not eat *it*. Ex. 10:17
41 So he said, "Then bring some flour." And
[R]he put *it* into the pot, and said, "Serve *it* to
the people, that they may eat." And there
was nothing harmful in the pot. Ex. 15:25

Miracle of the Multiplication of the Loaves

42 Then a man came from [R]Baal Shalisha,
[R]and brought the man of God bread of the
firstfruits, twenty loaves of barley bread, and
newly ripened grain in his knapsack. And he
said, "Give *it* to the people, that they may
eat." 1 Sam. 9:4 • [1 Cor. 9:11]
43 And his servant said, [R]"What? Shall I set
this before one hundred men?" He said again,
"Give it to the people, that they may eat; for
thus says the LORD: [R]'They shall eat and have
some left over.' " John 6:9 • Luke 9:17
44 So he set *it* before them; and they ate
[R]and had *some* left over, according to the
word of the LORD. John 6:13

CHAPTER 5

Miracle of the Healing of Naaman

NOW [R]Naaman, commander of the army
of the king of Syria, was [R]a great and
honorable man in the eyes of his master,
because by him the LORD had given victory to
Syria. He was also a mighty man of valor, *but*
he was a leper. Luke 4:27 • Ex. 11:3
2 And the Syrians had gone out [T]on raids,
and had brought back captive a young girl
from the land of Israel. She [T]waited on Naaman's wife. Or in bands • Served, lit. *was before*
3 Then she said to her mistress, "If only
my master *were* with the prophet who *is* in
Samaria! For he would heal him of his leprosy."
4 And [T]Naaman went in and told his master, saying, "Thus and thus said the girl who
is from the land of Israel." Lit. *he*
5 So the king of Syria said, "Go now, and I
will send a letter to the king of Israel." So he
departed and [R]took with him [T]ten talents of
silver, six thousand *shekels* of gold, and ten
changes of clothing. 1 Sam. 9:8 • $3,840,000
6 Then he brought the letter to the king of
Israel, which said,

> Now be advised, when this letter comes
> to you, that I have sent Naaman my
> servant to you, that you may heal him
> of his leprosy.

7 And it happened, when the king of Israel
read the letter, that he tore his clothes and
said, "*Am* I [R]God, to kill and make alive, that
this man sends a man to me to heal him of his
leprosy? Therefore please consider, and see
how he seeks a quarrel with me." [Gen. 30:2]

8 So it was, when Elisha the man of God heard that the king of Israel had torn his clothes, that he sent to the king, saying, "Why have you torn your clothes? Please let him come to me, and he shall know that there is a prophet in Israel."

9 Then Naaman went with his horses and chariot, and he stood at the door of the house of Elisha.

10 And Elisha sent a messenger to him, saying, "Go and [R]wash in the Jordan seven times, and your flesh shall be restored to you, and *you shall* be clean." John 9:7

11 But Naaman became furious, and went away and said, "Indeed, I said to myself, 'He will surely come out to me, and stand and call on the name of the LORD his God, and wave his hand over the place, and heal the leprosy.'

12 "*Are* not the *Abanah and the Pharpar, the rivers of Damascus, better than all the waters of Israel? Could I not wash in them and be clean?" So he turned and went away in a rage.

13 And his servants came near and spoke to him, and said, "My father, *if* the prophet had told you *to do* something great, would you not have done *it*? How much more then, when he says to you, 'Wash, and be clean'?"

14 So he went down and dipped seven times in the Jordan, according to the saying of the man of God; and his flesh was restored like the flesh of a little child, and he was clean.

15 Then he returned to the man of God, he and all his aides, and came and stood before him; and he said, "Indeed, now I know that *there is* [R]no God in all the earth, except in Israel; now therefore, please take [R]a gift from your servant." Dan. 2:47; 3:29; 6:26, 27 • Gen. 33:11

16 But he said, "*As* the LORD lives, before whom I stand, I will receive nothing." And he urged him to take *it*, but he refused.

17 So Naaman said, "Then, if not, please let your servant be given two mule-loads of earth; for your servant will no longer offer either burnt offering or sacrifice to other gods, but to the LORD.

18 "Yet in this thing may the LORD pardon your servant: when my master goes into the temple of Rimmon to worship there, and [R]he leans on my hand, and I bow down in the temple of Rimmon—when I bow down in the temple of Rimmon, may the LORD please pardon your servant in this thing." 2 Kin. 7:2, 17

19 Then he said to him, "Go in peace." So he departed from him a [T]short distance. 5 mi.

20 But [R]Gehazi, the servant of Elisha the man of God, said, "Look, my master has spared Naaman this Syrian, while not receiving from his hands what he brought; but *as* the LORD lives, I will run after him and take something from him." 2 Kin. 4:12; 8:4, 5

21 So Gehazi pursued Naaman. When Naaman saw *him* running after him, he got down from the chariot to meet him, and said, "*Is* all well?"

22 And he said, "All *is* [R]well. My master has sent me, saying, 'Indeed, just now two young men of the sons of the prophets have come to me from the mountains of Ephraim. Please give them a [T]talent of silver and two changes of garments.' " 2 Kin. 4:26 • $384,000

23 So Naaman said, "Please, take two talents." And he urged him, and bound two talents of silver in two bags, with two changes of garments, and handed *them* to two of his servants; and they carried *them* on ahead of him.

24 When he came to [T]the citadel, he took *them* from their hand, and stored *them* away in the house; then he let the men go, and they departed. Lit. *the hill*

25 Now he went in and stood before his master. And Elisha said to him, "Where *did you go*, Gehazi?" And he said, "Your servant did not go anywhere."

26 Then he said to him, "Did not my heart go *with you* when the man turned back from his chariot to meet you? *Is it* [R]time to receive money and to receive clothing, olive groves and vineyards, sheep and oxen, male and female servants? [Eccl. 3:1, 6]

27 "Therefore the leprosy of Naaman [R]shall cling to you and your descendants forever." And he went out from his presence [R]leprous, *as white* as snow. [1 Tim. 6:10] • Ex. 4:6

CHAPTER 6

Miracle of the Floating Ax Head

AND [R]the sons of the prophets said to Elisha, "See now, the place where we dwell with you is too small for us. 2 Kin. 4:38

2 "Please, let us go to the Jordan, and let every man take a beam from there, and let us make there a place where we may dwell." And he answered, "Go."

3 Then one said, [R]"Please consent to go with your servants." And he answered, "I will go." 2 Kin. 5:23

4 So he went with them. And when they came to the Jordan, they cut down trees.

5 But as one was cutting down a tree, the iron *ax head* fell into the water; and he cried out and said, "Alas, master! For it was [R]borrowed." [Ex. 22:14]

6 And the man of God said, "Where did it fall?" And he showed him the place. So [R]he cut off a stick, and threw *it* in there; and he made the iron float. 2 Kin. 2:21; 4:41

7 Therefore he said, "Pick *it* up for yourself." So he reached out his hand and took it.

Syria's War Plan

8 Now the [R]king of Syria was making war against Israel; and he took counsel with his

5:12 Many mss., Qr., Tg., Syr. *Amanah*

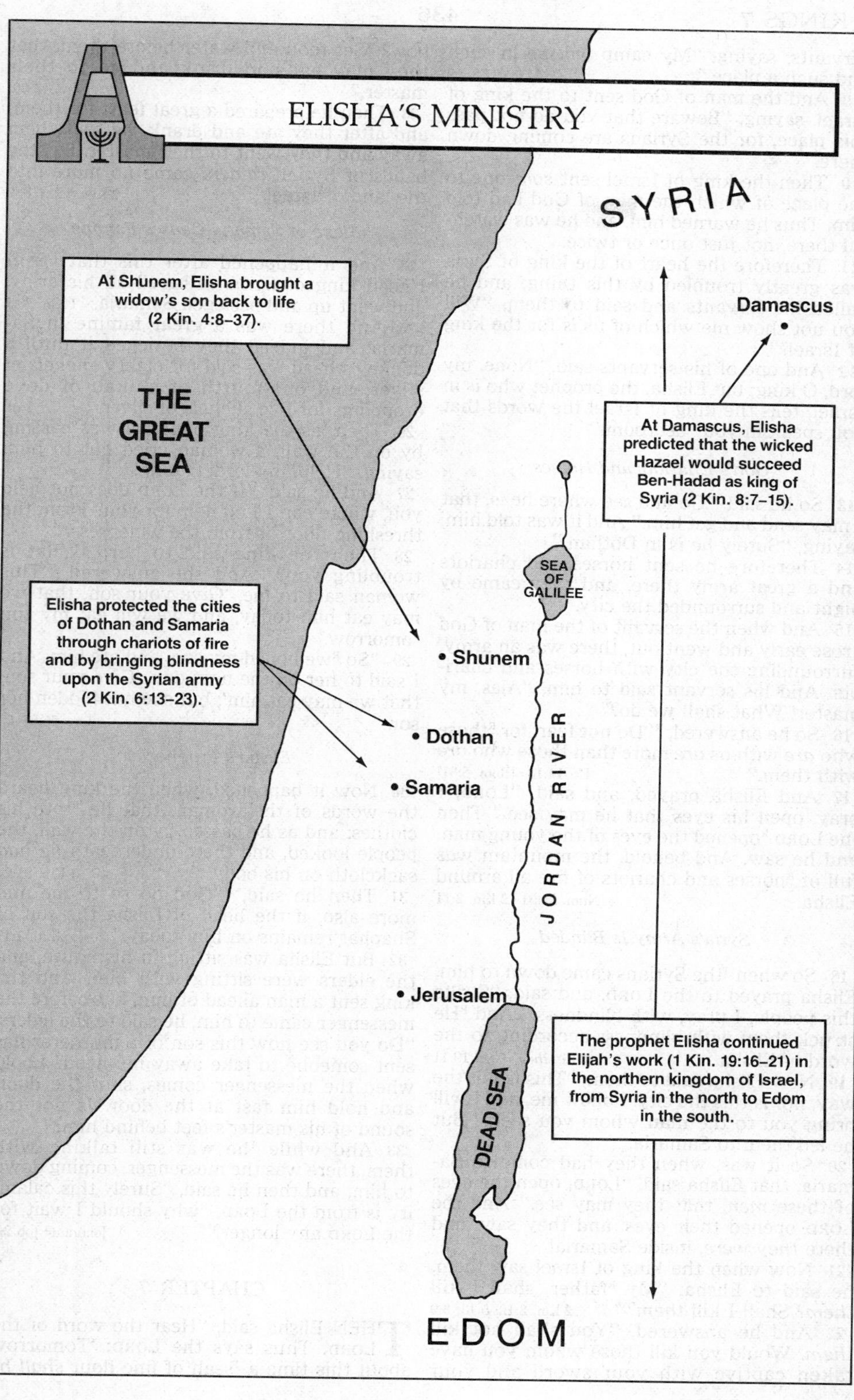
ELISHA'S MINISTRY
SYRIA
At Shunem, Elisha brought a widow's son back to life (2 Kin. 4:8–37).
Damascus
THE GREAT SEA
At Damascus, Elisha predicted that the wicked Hazael would succeed Ben-Hadad as king of Syria (2 Kin. 8:7–15).
SEA OF GALILEE
Elisha protected the cities of Dothan and Samaria through chariots of fire and by bringing blindness upon the Syrian army (2 Kin. 6:13–23).
Shunem
Dothan
Samaria
JORDAN RIVER
Jerusalem
DEAD SEA
The prophet Elisha continued Elijah's work (1 Kin. 19:16–21) in the northern kingdom of Israel, from Syria in the north to Edom in the south.
EDOM

servants, saying, "My camp *will be* in such
and such a place." 2 Kin. 8:28, 29
9 And the man of God sent to the king of
Israel, saying, "Beware that you do not pass
this place, for the Syrians are coming down
there."
10 Then the king of Israel sent *someone* to
the place of which the man of God had told
him. Thus he warned him, and he was watchful there, not just once or twice.
11 Therefore the heart of the king of Syria
was greatly troubled by this thing; and he
called his servants and said to them, "Will
you not show me which of us *is* for the king
of Israel?"
12 And one of his servants said, "None, my
lord, O king; but Elisha, the prophet who *is* in
Israel, tells the king of Israel the words that
you speak in your bedroom."

God's Chariots and Horses

13 So he said, "Go and see where he *is*, that
I may send and get him." And it was told him,
saying, "Surely *he is* in Dothan."
14 Therefore he sent horses and chariots
and a great army there, and they came by
night and surrounded the city.
15 And when the servant of the man of God
arose early and went out, there was an army,
surrounding the city with horses and chariots. And his servant said to him, "Alas, my
master! What shall we do?"
16 So he answered, [R]"Do not fear, for [R]those
who *are* with us *are* more than those who *are*
with them." Ex. 14:13 • [Rom. 8:31]
17 And Elisha prayed, and said, "LORD, I
pray, open his eyes that he may see." Then
the LORD [R]opened the eyes of the young man,
and he saw. And behold, the mountain *was*
full of [R]horses and chariots of fire all around
Elisha. Num. 22:31 • 2 Kin. 2:11

Syria's Army Is Blinded

18 So when [T]the Syrians came down to him,
Elisha prayed to the LORD, and said, "Strike
this people, I pray, with blindness." And [R]He
struck them with blindness according to the
word of Elisha. Lit. *they* • Gen. 19:11
19 Now Elisha said to them, "This *is* not the
way, nor *is* this the city. Follow me, and I will
bring you to the man whom you seek." But
he led them to Samaria.
20 So it was, when they had come to Samaria, that Elisha said, "LORD, open the eyes
of these *men*, that they may see." And the
LORD opened their eyes, and they saw; and
there *they were*, inside Samaria!
21 Now when the king of Israel saw them,
he said to Elisha, "My [R]father, shall I kill
them? Shall I kill *them*?" 2 Kin. 2:12; 5:13; 8:9
22 And he answered, "You shall not kill
them. Would you kill those whom you have
taken captive with your sword and your
bow? [R]Set food and water before them, that
they may eat and drink and go to their
master." [Rom. 12:20]
23 Then he prepared a great feast for them;
and after they ate and drank, he sent them
away and they went to their master. So [R]the
bands of Syrian *raiders* came no more into
the land of Israel. 2 Kin. 5:2; 6:8, 9

Siege of Samaria Causes Famine

24 And it happened after this that [R]Ben-
Hadad king of Syria gathered all his army,
and went up and besieged Samaria. 1 Kin. 20:1
25 And there was a great famine in Samaria; and indeed they besieged it until a
donkey's head was *sold* for eighty *shekels* of
silver, and one-fourth of a [T]kab of dove
droppings for five *shekels* of silver. 1 pt.
26 Then, as the king of Israel was passing
by on the wall, a woman cried out to him,
saying, "Help, my lord, O king!"
27 And he said, "If the LORD does not help
you, where can I find help for you? From the
threshing floor or from the winepress?"
28 Then the king said to her, "What is
troubling you?" And she answered, "This
woman said to me, 'Give your son, that we
may eat him today, and we will eat my son
tomorrow.'
29 "So [R]we boiled my son, and ate him. And
I said to her on the next day, 'Give your son,
that we may eat him'; but she has hidden her
son." Lev. 26:27–29

Elisha's Prophecies

30 Now it happened, when the king heard
the words of the woman, that he [R]tore his
clothes; and as he passed by on the wall, the
people looked, and there underneath *he had*
sackcloth on his body. 1 Kin. 21:27
31 Then he said, [R]"God do so to me and
more also, if the head of Elisha the son of
Shaphat remains on him today." Ruth 1:17
32 But Elisha was sitting in his house, and
the elders were sitting with him. And the
king sent a man ahead of him, but before the
messenger came to him, he said to the elders,
"Do you see how this son of a murderer has
sent someone to take away my head? Look,
when the messenger comes, shut the door,
and hold him fast at the door. *Is* not the
sound of his master's feet behind him?"
33 And while [T]he was still talking with
them, there was the messenger, coming down
to him; and then he said, "Surely this calamity *is* from the LORD; [R]why should I wait for
the LORD any longer?" Jehoram • Job 2:9

CHAPTER 7

THEN Elisha said, "Hear the word of the
LORD. Thus says the LORD: 'Tomorrow
about this time a [T]seah of fine flour *shall be*

sold for a shekel, and two seahs of barley for
a shekel, at the gate of Samaria.' " 8 gal.
2 So an officer on whose hand the king
leaned answered the man of God and said,
"Look, [R]*if* the LORD would make windows in
heaven, could this thing be?" And he said, "In
fact, you shall see *it* with your eyes, but you
shall not eat of it." Mal. 3:10
3 Now there were four leprous men [R]at the
entrance of the gate; and they said to one
another, "Why are we sitting here until we
die? [Num. 5:2–4; 12:10–14]
4 "If we say, 'We will enter the city,' the
famine *is* in the city, and we shall die there.
And if we sit here, we die also. Now therefore,
come, let us surrender to the army of the
Syrians. If they keep us alive, we shall live;
and if they kill us, we shall but die."
5 And they rose at twilight to go to the
camp of the Syrians; and when they had
come to the outskirts of the Syrian camp, to
their surprise no one *was* there.
6 For the LORD had caused the army of the
Syrians [R]to hear the noise of chariots and the
noise of horses—the noise of a great army; so
they said to one another, "Look, the king of
Israel has hired against us [R]the kings of the
Hittites and the kings of the Egyptians to
attack us!" 2 Sam. 5:24 • 1 Kin. 10:29
7 Therefore they [R]arose and fled at twilight, and left the camp intact—their tents,
their horses, and their donkeys—and they
fled for their lives. Ps. 48:4–6
8 And when these lepers came to the outskirts of the camp, they went into one tent
and ate and drank, and carried from it silver
and gold and clothing, and went and hid
them; then they came back and entered
another tent, and carried *some* from there
also, and went and hid *it*.
9 Then they said to one another, "We are
not doing what is right. This day *is* a day of
good news, and we remain silent. If we wait
until morning light, some [T]punishment will
come upon us. Now therefore, come, let us go
and tell the king's household." Calamity
10 So they went and called to the gatekeepers of the city, and told them, saying, "We
went to the Syrian camp, and surprisingly no
one *was* there, not a human sound—only
horses and donkeys tied, and the tents intact."
11 And the gatekeepers called out, and they
told *it* to the king's household inside.
12 Then the king arose in the night and said
to his servants, "Let me now tell you what
the Syrians have done to us. They know that
we *are* [R]hungry; therefore they have gone out
of the camp to [T]hide themselves in the field,
saying, 'When they come out of the city, we
shall catch them alive, and get into the
city.' " 2 Kin. 6:24–29 • Hide themselves in ambush
13 And one of his servants answered and
said, "Please, let several *men* take five of the
remaining horses which are left in the city.
Look, they *may either become* like all the
multitude of Israel that are left in it; or
indeed, *I say*, they *may become* like all the
multitude of Israel left from those who are
consumed; so let us send them and see."
14 Therefore they took two chariots with
horses; and the king sent them in the direction of the Syrian army, saying, "Go and see."
15 And they went after them to the Jordan;
and indeed all the road *was* full of garments
and weapons which the Syrians had thrown
away in their haste. So the messengers returned and told the king.
16 Then the people went out and plundered
the tents of the Syrians. So a seah of fine
flour was *sold* for a [T]shekel, and two seahs of
barley for a shekel, [R]according to the word of
the LORD. $128. • 2 Kin. 7:1
17 Now the king had appointed the officer
on whose hand he leaned to have charge of
the gate. But the people trampled him in the
gate, and he died, just [R]as the man of God
had said, who spoke when the king came
down to him. 2 Kin. 6:32; 7:2
18 So it happened just as the man of God
had spoken to the king, saying, [R]"Two seahs
of barley for a shekel, and a seah of fine flour
for a shekel, shall be *sold* tomorrow about
this time in the gate of Samaria." 2 Kin. 7:1
19 Then that officer had answered the man
of God, and said, "Now look, *if* the LORD
would make windows in heaven, could such a
thing be?" And he had said, "In fact, you
shall see it with your eyes, but you shall not
eat of it."
20 And so it happened to him, for the people
trampled him in the gate, and he died.

CHAPTER 8

Elisha's Ministry with the Shunammite Woman

THEN Elisha spoke to the woman whose
son he had restored to life, saying, "Arise
and go, you and your household, and [T]so-
journ wherever you can sojourn; for the
LORD [R]has called for a [R]famine, and furthermore, it will come upon the land for seven
years." Reside temporarily • Hag. 1:11 • 2 Sam. 21:1
2 So the woman arose and did according to
the saying of the man of God, and she went
with her household and sojourned in the land
of the Philistines seven years.
3 It came to pass, at the end of seven
years, that the woman returned from the land
of the Philistines; and she went to make an
appeal to the king for her house and for her
land.
4 Then the king talked with Gehazi, the
servant of the man of God, saying, "Tell me,
please, all the great things Elisha has done."

5 Now it happened, as he was telling the
king how he had restored the dead to life,
that there was the woman whose son he had
restored to life, appealing to the king for her
house and for her land. And Gehazi said, "My
lord, O king, this *is* the woman, and this *is* her
son whom Elisha restored to life."
6 And when the king asked the woman,
she told him. So the king appointed a certain
officer for her, saying, "Restore all that *was*
hers, and all the proceeds of the field from the
day that she left the land until now."

Elisha's Ministry with the King of Syria

7 Then Elisha went to Damascus, and
[R]Ben-Hadad king of Syria was sick; and it
was told him, saying, "The man of God has
come here." 2 Kin. 6:24
8 And the king said to Hazael, "Take a
present in your hand, and go to meet the man
of God, and inquire of the LORD by him,
saying, 'Shall I recover from this disease?' "
9 So Hazael went to meet him and took a
present with him, of every good thing of
Damascus, forty camel-loads; and he came
and stood before him, and said, "Your son
Ben-Hadad king of Syria has sent me to you,
saying, 'Shall I recover from this disease?' "
10 And Elisha said to him, "Go, say to him,
'You shall certainly recover.' However the
LORD has shown me that he will really die."
11 Then he [T]set his countenance in a stare
until he was ashamed; and the man of God
[R]wept. *fixed his gaze* • Luke 19:41
12 And Hazael said, "Why is my lord weeping?" And he answered, "Because I know the
evil that you will do to the children of Israel:
Their strongholds you will set on fire, and
their young men you will kill with the sword;
and you [R]will dash their children, and rip
open their women with child." Hos. 13:16
13 So Hazael said, "But what [R]*is* your servant—a dog, that he should do this gross
thing?" And Elisha answered, [R]"The LORD has
shown me that you *will become* king over
Syria." 1 Sam. 17:43 • 1 Kin. 19:15
14 Then he departed from Elisha, and came
to his master, who said to him, "What did
Elisha say to you?" And he answered, "He
told me *that* you would surely recover."
15 But it happened on the next day that he
took a thick cloth and dipped *it* in water, and
spread *it* over his face so that he died; and
Hazael reigned in his place.

The Reign of Jehoram in Judah
2 Chr. 21:5–10, 20

16 Now [R]in the fifth year of Joram the son
of Ahab, king of Israel, Jehoshaphat *having
been* king of Judah, [R]Jehoram the son of
Jehoshaphat began to reign as [T]king of Ju-
dah. 2 Kin. 1:17; 3:1 • 2 Chr. 21:3 • Co-regent with his father
17 He was [R]thirty-two years old when he
became king, and he reigned eight years in
Jerusalem. 2 Chr. 21:5–10
18 And he walked in the way of the kings of
Israel, just as the house of Ahab had done,
for the daughter of Ahab was his wife; and he
did evil in the sight of the LORD.
19 Yet the LORD would not destroy Judah,
for the sake of his servant David, [R]as He
promised him to give a lamp to him *and* his
sons forever. 2 Sam. 7:13
20 In his days [R]Edom revolted against Judah's authority, [R]and made a king over themselves. Gen. 27:40 • 1 Kin. 22:47
21 So Joram went to Zair, and all his chariots with him. And he rose by night and
attacked the Edomites who had surrounded
him and the captains of the chariots, but *his*
people fled to their tents.
22 Thus Edom has been in revolt against
Judah's authority to this day. [R]And Libnah
revolted at that time. Josh. 21:13
23 Now the rest of the acts of Joram, and all
that he did, *are* they not written in the book
of the chronicles of the kings of Judah?
24 So Joram rested with his fathers, and
was buried with his fathers in the City of
David. Then [R]Ahaziah[T] his son reigned in his
place. 2 Chr. 22:1, 7 • Or *Azariah* or *Jehoahaz*

Spiritual Evaluation of Ahaziah
2 Kin. 9:29; 2 Chr. 22:1–4

25 In the twelfth year of Joram the son of
Ahab, king of Israel, Ahaziah the son of
Jehoram, king of Judah, began to reign.
26 Ahaziah *was* [R]twenty-two years old
when he became king, and he reigned one
year in Jerusalem. His mother's name *was*
Athaliah the granddaughter of Omri, king of
Israel. 2 Chr. 22:2
27 And he walked in the way of the house
of Ahab, and did evil in the sight of the LORD,
as the house of Ahab *had done*, for he *was*
the son-in-law of the house of Ahab.

Battle Against Syria
2 Kin. 9:15, 16; 2 Chr. 22:5, 6

28 Now he went [R]with Joram the son of
Ahab to war against Hazael king of Syria at
[R]Ramoth Gilead; and the Syrians wounded
Joram. 2 Chr. 22:5 • 1 Kin. 22:3, 29
29 Then King Joram went back to Jezreel to
recover from the wounds which the Syrians
had inflicted on him at [T]Ramah, when he
fought against Hazael king of Syria. And
Ahaziah the son of Jehoram, king of Judah,
went down to see Joram the son of Ahab in
Jezreel, because he was sick. *Ramoth*, v. 28

CHAPTER 9

Anointing of Jehu King over Israel

AND Elisha the prophet called one of the
sons of the prophets, and said to him,

"Get yourself ready, take this flask of oil in
your hand, and go to Ramoth Gilead.
2 "Now when you arrive at that place, look
there for Jehu the son of Jehoshaphat, the
son of Nimshi, and go in and make him rise
up from among [R]his associates, and take him
to an inner room. 2 Kin. 9:5, 11
3 "Then take the flask of oil, and pour *it* on
his head, and say, 'Thus says the LORD: "I
have anointed you king over Israel." ' Then
open the door and flee, and do not delay."
4 So the young man, the servant of the
prophet, went to Ramoth Gilead.
5 And when he arrived, there *were* the
captains of the army sitting; and he said, "I
have a message for you, O commander." And
Jehu said, "For which *one* of us?" And he
said, "For you, commander."
6 Then he arose and went into the house.
And he poured the oil on his head, and said to
him, [R]"Thus says the LORD God of Israel: 'I
have anointed you king over the people of
the LORD, over Israel. 2 Chr. 22:7
7 'You shall strike down the house of Ahab
your master, that I may [R]avenge the blood of
My servants the prophets, and the blood of all
the servants of the LORD, [R]at the hand of
Jezebel. [Deut. 32:35, 41] • 1 Kin. 18:4; 21:15
8 'For the whole house of Ahab shall perish; and I will cut off from Ahab all the males
in Israel, both bond and free.
9 'So I will make the house of Ahab like
the house of Jeroboam the son of Nebat, and
like the house of Baasha the son of Ahijah.
10 'The dogs shall eat Jezebel in the vicinity
of Jezreel, and *there shall be* none to bury
her.' " And he opened the door and fled.
11 Then Jehu came out to the servants of
his master, and *one* said to him, "*Is* all well?
Why did [R]this madman come to you?" And he
said to them, "You know the man and his
babble." Jer. 29:26
12 And they said, "A lie! Tell us now." So he
said, "Thus and thus he spoke to me, saying,
'Thus says the LORD: "I have anointed you
king over Israel." ' "
13 Then each man hastened [R]to take his
garment and put *it* [T]under him on the top of
the steps; and they blew trumpets, saying,
"Jehu is king!" Matt. 21:7, 8 • Lit. *under his feet*

Execution of Joram

14 So Jehu the son of Jehoshaphat, the son
of Nimshi, conspired against Joram. (Now
Joram had been defending Ramoth Gilead, he
and all Israel, against Hazael king of Syria.
15 But King Joram had returned to Jezreel
to recover from the wounds which the Syrians had inflicted on him when he fought
with Hazael king of Syria.) And Jehu said, "If
you are so minded, let no one leave *or* escape
from the city to go and tell *it* in Jezreel."
16 So Jehu rode in a chariot and went to
Jezreel, for Joram was laid up there; [R]and
Ahaziah king of Judah had come down to see
Joram. 2 Kin. 8:29
17 Now a watchman stood on the tower in
Jezreel, and he saw the company of Jehu as
he came, and said, "I see a company of men."
And Joram said, "Get a horseman and send
him to meet them, and let him say, [T]'*Is it*
peace?' " *Are you peaceful?*
18 So the horseman went to meet him, and
said, "Thus says the king: '*Is it* peace?' " And
Jehu said, "What have you to do with peace?
Turn around and follow me." And the watchman reported, saying, "The messenger went
to them, but is not coming back."
19 Then he sent out a second horseman
who came to them, and said, "Thus says the
king: '*Is it* peace?' " And Jehu answered,
"What have you to do with peace? Turn
around and follow me."
20 And the watchman reported, saying, "He
went up to them and is not coming back; and
the driving *is* like the driving of Jehu the son
of Nimshi, for he drives furiously!"
21 So Joram said, [T]"Make ready." And his
chariot was made ready. Then Joram king of
Israel and Ahaziah king of Judah went out,
each in his chariot; and they went out to
meet Jehu, and [T]met him on the property of
Naboth the Jezreelite. *Harness up* • Lit. *found*
22 Now it happened, when Joram saw Jehu,
that he said, "*Is it* peace, Jehu?" So he
answered, "What peace, as long as the harlotries of your mother Jezebel and her witchcraft *are so* many?"
23 Then Joram turned around and fled, and
said to Ahaziah, "Treachery, Ahaziah!"
24 Now Jehu [T]drew his bow with full
strength and shot Jehoram between his arms;
and the arrow came out at his heart, and he
sank down in his chariot. Lit. *filled his hand*
25 Then *Jehu* said to Bidkar his captain,
"Pick *him* up, *and* throw him into the tract of
the field of Naboth the Jezreelite; for remember, when you and I were riding together
behind Ahab his father, that [R]the LORD laid
this [R]burden upon him: 1 Kin. 21:19, 24–29 • Is. 13:1
26 'Surely I saw yesterday the blood of
Naboth and the blood of his sons,' says the
LORD, [R]'and I will repay you [T]in this plot,' says
the LORD. Now therefore, take *and* throw him
on the plot *of ground,* according to the word
of the LORD." 1 Kin. 21:13, 19 • *on this property*

Death of Ahaziah—2 Kin. 8:25; 2 Chr. 22:9

27 But when Ahaziah king of Judah saw
this, he fled by the road to [T]Beth Haggan. So
Jehu pursued him, and said, "Shoot him also
in the chariot." *And they did so* at the ascent
to Gur, which is by Ibleam. Then he fled to
Megiddo, and died there. Lit. *The Garden House*
28 And his servants carried him in the
chariot to Jerusalem, and buried him in his
tomb with his fathers in the City of David.

29 In the eleventh year of Joram the son of Ahab, Ahaziah had become king over Judah.

Fulfillment of Elisha's Prophecy

30 And when Jehu had come to Jezreel, Jezebel heard *of it*; [R]and she put paint on her eyes and adorned her head, and looked through a window. Ezek. 23:40

31 Then, as Jehu entered at the gate, she said, [R]"*Is it* peace, Zimri, murderer of your master?" 1 Kin. 16:9–20

32 And he looked up at the window, and said, "Who *is* on my side? Who?" And two *or* three eunuchs looked out at him.

33 Then he said, "Throw her down." So they threw her down, and *some* of her blood spattered on the wall and on the horses; and he trampled her underfoot.

34 And when he had gone in, he ate and drank. Then he said, "Go now, see to this accursed *woman*, and bury her, for [R]she was a king's daughter." 1 Kin. 16:31

35 So they went to bury her, but they found no more of her than the skull and the feet and the palms of *her* hands.

36 Therefore they came back and told him. And he said, "This *is* the word of the LORD, which He spoke by His servant Elijah the Tishbite, saying, 'On the plot *of ground* at Jezreel dogs shall eat the flesh of Jezebel;

37 'and the corpse of Jezebel shall be [R]as refuse on the surface of the field, in the plot at Jezreel, so that they shall not say, "Here *lies* Jezebel." ' " Ps. 83:10

CHAPTER 10

NOW Ahab had seventy sons in Samaria. And Jehu wrote letters and sent *them* to Samaria, to the rulers of Jezreel, to the elders, and to [T]those who reared Ahab's *sons*, saying: *the guardians of*

> 2 Now as soon as this letter comes to you, since your master's sons *are* with you, and you have chariots and horses, a fortified city also, and weapons,
>
> 3 choose the [T]best qualified of your master's sons, set *him* on his father's throne, and fight for your master's house. *most upright*

4 But they were exceedingly afraid, and said, "Look, two kings could not [T]stand up to him; how then can we stand?" Lit. *stand before*

5 And he who *was* in charge of the house, and he who *was* in charge of the city, the elders also, and those who reared *the sons*, sent to Jehu, saying, "We *are* your servants, we will do all you tell us; but we will not make anyone king. Do *what is* good in your sight."

6 Then he wrote a second letter to them, saying:

> If you *are* for me, and *if* you will obey my voice, take the heads of the men, your master's sons, and come to me at Jezreel by this time tomorrow.

Now the king's sons, seventy persons, *were* with the great men of the city, *who* were rearing them.

7 So it was, when the letter came to them, that they took the king's sons and slaughtered seventy persons, put their heads in baskets and sent *them* to him at Jezreel.

8 Then a messenger came and told him, saying, "They have brought the heads of the king's sons." And he said, "Lay them in two heaps at the entrance of the gate until morning."

9 So it was, in the morning, that he went out and stood, and said to all the people, "You *are* righteous. Indeed [R]I conspired against my master and killed him; but who killed all these? 2 Kin. 9:14–24

10 "Know now that nothing shall [R]fall to the earth of the word of the LORD which the LORD spoke concerning the house of Ahab; for the LORD has done what He spoke [R]by His servant Elijah." 1 Sam. 3:19 • 1 Kin. 21:17–24, 29

11 So Jehu killed all who remained of the house of Ahab in Jezreel, and all his great men and his close acquaintances and his priests, until he left him none remaining.

12 And he arose and departed and went to Samaria. On the way, at [T]Beth Eked of the Shepherds, Lit. *The Shearing House*

13 [R]Jehu met with the brothers of Ahaziah king of Judah, and said, "Who *are* you?" And they answered, "We *are* the brothers of Ahaziah; we have come down to greet the sons of the king and the sons of the queen mother." 2 Chr. 22:8

14 And he said, "Take them alive!" So they took them alive, and [R]killed them at the well of [T]Beth Eked, forty-two men; and he left none of them. 2 Chr. 22:8 • Lit. *The Shearing House*

15 Now when he departed from there, he [T]met Jehonadab the son of Rechab, *coming* to meet him; and he greeted him and said to him, "Is your heart right, as my heart *is* toward your heart?" And Jehonadab answered, "It is." *Jehu said*, "If it is, give *me* your hand." So he gave *him* his hand, and he took him up to him into the chariot. *found*

16 Then he said, "Come with me, and see my [R]zeal for the LORD." So they had him ride in his chariot. 1 Kin. 19:10

17 And when he came to Samaria, [R]he killed all who remained to Ahab in Samaria, till he had destroyed them, according to the word of the LORD which He spoke to Elijah. 2 Kin. 9:8

KING JEHU'S BLACK OBELISK

During the period of Old Testament history from about 900 to 700 B.C., the Assyrians were the dominant world power. One of the powerful Assyrian kings, Shalmaneser III (reigned 859–824 B.C.), erected a large stone monument on which he recorded his military victories. This impressive archaeological find, known as the Black Obelisk, contains a relief sculpture depicting the visit of King Jehu of Israel (reigned 841–814 B.C.) to pay tribute to Shalmaneser.

Placed outside the royal palace at Nimrud in Assyria, the monument is more than six feet high. Chiseled carefully in stone is a series of detailed drawings, with accompanying inscriptions that commemorate Shalmaneser's numerous military campaigns. The obelisk shows an event not mentioned in the Bible—Jehu bowing before Shalmaneser, with numerous Israelite servants and aids standing by with gifts for the Assyrian king.

Tribute, or compulsory payments to protect a weaker nation against a more powerful foe, was often levied by aggressor nations such as the Assyrians during Old Testament times.

After being anointed king of Israel by the prophet Elisha, Jehu eliminated all threats to his rule by killing all members of the family of Ahab, whom he succeeded (2 Kin. 9; 10). As a ruler, Jehu was a weak king who failed to eliminate Baal worship from the land.

The Black Obelisk is a valuable archaeological find, because it helps establish a date for Jehu's rule, as well as an overall chronology for this period of Israel's history. It also shows us what an Israelite king from this period must have looked like. This is the only image or drawing of an Israelite king that has been discovered by archaeologists.

Photo by Gustav Jeeninga

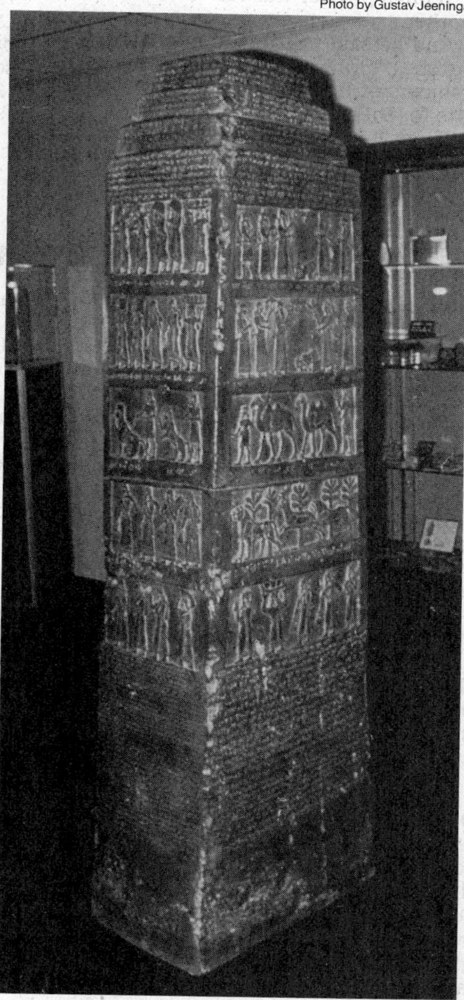

On this large stone monument, Shalmaneser III recorded his military victories.

18 Then Jehu gathered all the people together, and said to them, "Ahab served Baal a
little, *but* Jehu will serve him much.
19 "Now therefore, call to me all the
[R]prophets of Baal, all his servants, and all his
priests. Let no one be missing, for I have a
great sacrifice *to make* to Baal. Whoever is
missing shall not live." But Jehu acted decep-
tively, with the intent of destroying the
worshipers of Baal. 1 Kin. 18:19; 22:6
20 And Jehu said, "Proclaim a solemn assembly for Baal." So they proclaimed *it*.
21 Then Jehu sent throughout all Israel;
and all the worshipers of Baal came, so that
there was not a man left who did not come.
So they came into the [T]temple of Baal, and
the [R]temple of Baal was full from one end to
the other. Lit. *house* • 1 Kin. 16:32
22 And he said to the one in charge of the
wardrobe, "Bring out vestments for all the
worshipers of Baal." So he brought out vestments for them.
23 Then Jehu and Jehonadab the son of
Rechab went into the temple of Baal, and said
to the worshipers of Baal, "Search and see
that no servants of the LORD are here with
you, but only the worshipers of Baal."
24 So they went in to offer sacrifices and
burnt offerings. Now Jehu had appointed for
himself eighty men on the outside, and had
said, "*If* any of the men whom I have brought
into your hands escapes, *whoever lets him
escape, it shall be* [R]his life for the life of the
other." 1 Kin. 20:39
25 Now it was so, as soon as he had made
an end of offering the burnt offering, that
Jehu said to the guard and to the captains,
"Go in *and* kill them; let no one come out!"
And they killed them with the edge of the
sword; then the guards and the officers threw
them out, and went into the [T]inner room of
the temple of Baal. Lit. *city*
26 And they brought the *sacred* pillars out
of the temple of Baal and burned them.
27 Then they broke down the *sacred* pillar
of Baal, and tore down the temple of Baal and
made it a refuse dump to this day.
28 Thus Jehu destroyed Baal from Israel.

Spiritual Evaluation of Jehu

29 However Jehu did not turn away from
the sins of Jeroboam the son of Nebat, who
had made Israel sin, *that is*, from the golden
calves that *were* at Bethel and Dan.
30 And the LORD said to Jehu, "Because you
have done well in doing *what is* right in My
sight, *and* have done to the house of Ahab all
that *was* in My heart, [R]your sons shall sit on
the throne of Israel to the fourth
generation." 2 Kin. 13:1, 10; 14:23; 15:8, 12
31 But Jehu took no heed to walk in the law
of the LORD God of Israel with all his heart;
for he did not depart from the sins of Jeroboam, who had made Israel sin.

Political Situation Under Jehu

32 In those days the LORD began to cut off
parts of Israel; and [R]Hazael conquered them
in all the territory of Israel 2 Kin. 8:12; 13:22
33 from the Jordan eastward: all the land of
Gilead—Gad, Reuben, and Manasseh—from
[R]Aroer, which *is* by the River Arnon, including [R]Gilead and Bashan. Deut. 2:36 • Amos 1:3–5

Death of Jehu

34 Now the rest of the acts of Jehu, all that
he did, and all his might, *are* they not written
in the book of the chronicles of the kings of
Israel?
35 So Jehu rested with his fathers, and they
buried him in Samaria. Then [R]Jehoahaz his
son reigned in his place. 2 Kin. 13:1
36 And the period that Jehu reigned over
Israel in Samaria *was* twenty-eight years.

CHAPTER 11

Salvation of Joash—2 Chr. 22:10–12

WHEN Athaliah the mother of Ahaziah
saw that her son was [R]dead, she arose
and destroyed all the royal heirs. 2 Kin. 9:27
2 But [T]Jehosheba, the daughter of King
Joram, sister of Ahaziah, took [T]Joash the son
of Ahaziah, and stole him away from among
the king's sons *who were* being murdered;
and they hid him and his nurse in the bedroom, from Athaliah, so that he was not
killed. *Jehoshabeath*, 2 Chr. 22:11 • Or *Jehoash*
3 So he was hidden with her in the house
of the LORD for six years, while Athaliah
reigned over the land.

Overthrow of Athaliah by Jehoiada
2 Chr. 23:1–11

4 In [R]the seventh year Jehoiada sent and
brought the captains of hundreds, of the
bodyguards and the [T]escorts, and brought
them into the house of the LORD to him. And
he made a covenant with them and took an
oath from them in the house of the LORD, and
showed them the king's son. 2 Chr. 23:1 • *guards*
5 Then he commanded them, saying, "This
is what you shall do: One-third of you who
come on duty on the Sabbath shall be keeping watch over the king's house,
6 "one-third *shall be* at the gate of Sur,
and one-third at the gate behind the escorts.
You shall keep the watch of the house, lest it
be broken down.
7 "The two [T]contingents of you who go off
duty on the Sabbath shall keep the watch of
the house of the LORD for the king. *companies*
8 "But you shall surround the king on all
sides, every man with his weapons in his

hand; and whoever comes within range, let
him be put to death. You are to be with the
king as he goes out and as he comes in."
9 So the captains of the hundreds did
according to all that Jehoiada the priest
commanded. Each of them took his men who
were to be on duty on the Sabbath, with
those who were going off duty on the Sabbath, and came to Jehoiada the priest.
10 And the priest gave the captains of hundreds the spears and shields which *had belonged* to King David, [R]that were in the
temple of the LORD. 2 Sam. 8:7
11 Then the escorts stood, every man with
his weapons in his hand, all around the king,
from the right [T]side of the temple to the left
side of the temple, by the altar and the
temple. Lit. *shoulder*
12 And he brought out the king's son, put
the crown on him, and *gave him* the [T]Testi-
mony; they made him king and anointed him,
and they clapped their hands and said, "Long
live the king!" Law, Ex. 25:16, 21

Death of Athaliah—2 Chr. 23:12–15

13 [R]Now when Athaliah heard the noise of
the escorts *and* the people, she came to the
people, into the temple of the LORD. 2 Chr. 23:12
14 When she looked, there was the king,
standing by [R]a pillar according to custom;
and the leaders and the trumpeters were by
the king. All the people of the land were
rejoicing and blowing trumpets. And Athaliah tore her clothes and cried out, "Treason!
Treason!" 2 Chr. 34:31
15 Then Jehoiada the priest commanded the
captains of the hundreds, the officers of the
army, and said to them, "Take her outside
[T]under guard, and slay with the sword whoever follows her." For the priest had said, "Do
not let her be killed in the house of the
LORD." Lit. *between ranks*
16 So they seized her; and she went by way
of the horses' entrance to the king's house,
and there she was killed.

Renewal of the Covenant—2 Chr. 23:16–24:1

17 Then Jehoiada made a covenant between
the LORD, the king, and the people, that they
should be the LORD's people, and *also* between the king and the people.
18 And all the people of the land went to the
temple of Baal, and tore it down. They thoroughly broke in pieces its altars and [T]images,
and killed Mattan the priest of Baal before
the altars. And the priest appointed officers
over the house of the LORD. Idols
19 Then he took the captains of hundreds,
the bodyguards, the escorts, and all the
people of the land; and they brought the king
down from the house of the LORD, and went
by way of the gate of the escorts to the king's
house; and he sat on the throne of the kings.
20 So all the people of the land rejoiced; and
the city was quiet, for they had slain Athaliah
with the sword *in* the king's house.
21 Jehoash *was* [R]seven years old when he
became king. 2 Chr. 24:1–14

CHAPTER 12

Spiritual Evaluation of Joash—2 Chr. 24:1, 2

IN the seventh year of Jehu, [R]Jehoash[T]
became king, and he reigned forty years
in Jerusalem. His mother's name *was* Zibiah
of Beersheba. 2 Chr. 24:1 • *Joash,* 2 Kin. 11:2ff.
2 Jehoash did *what was* right in the sight
of the LORD all the days in which [R]Jehoiada
the priest instructed him. 2 Kin. 11:4
3 But the [T]high places were not taken
away; the people still sacrificed and burned
incense on the high places. For pagan worship

Spiritual Situation Under Joash
2 Chr. 24:5–14

4 And Jehoash said to the priests, "All the
money of the dedicated gifts that are brought
into the house of the LORD—each man's
census money, each man's assessment
money—*and* all the money that [T]a man purposes in his heart to bring into the house of
the LORD, *any man's heart prompts him to bring*
5 "let the priests take *it* themselves, each
from his constituency; and let them repair
the [T]damages of the temple, wherever any
dilapidation is found." Lit. *breaches*
6 Now it was so, by the twenty-third year
of King Jehoash, [R]*that* the priests had not
repaired the damages of the temple. 2 Chr. 24:5
7 [R]So King Jehoash called Jehoiada the
priest and the *other* priests, and said to them,
"Why have you not repaired the damages of
the temple? Now therefore, do not take *any
more* money from your constituency, but
deliver it for repairing the damages of the
temple." 2 Chr. 24:6
8 And the priests agreed that they would
neither receive any *more* money from the
people, nor repair the damages of the temple.
9 Then Jehoiada the priest took a chest,
bored a hole in its lid, and set it beside the
altar, on the right side as one comes into the
house of the LORD; and the priests who kept
the door put [R]there all the money *that was*
brought into the house of the LORD. Mark 12:41
10 So it was, whenever they saw that *there
was* much money in the chest, that the king's
[T]scribe and the high priest came up and put it
in bags, and counted the money that was
found in the house of the LORD. *secretary*
11 Then they gave the money, which had
been apportioned, into the hands of those
who did the work, who had the oversight of
the house of the LORD; and they [T]paid it out
to the carpenters and builders who worked
on the house of the LORD, Lit. *weighed*

12 and to masons and stonecutters, and for
buying timber and hewn stone, to repair the
damage of the house of the LORD, and for all
that was paid out to repair the temple.
13 However there were not made for the
house of the LORD basins of silver, trimmers,
sprinkling-bowls, trumpets, any articles of
gold, or articles of silver, from the money
that was brought into the house of the LORD.
14 But they gave that to the workmen, and
they repaired the house of the LORD with it.
15 Moreover [R]they did not require an account from the men into whose hand they
delivered the money to be paid to workmen,
for they dealt faithfully. 2 Kin. 22:7
16 [R]The money from the trespass offerings
and the money from the sin offerings was not
brought into the house of the LORD. [R]It
belonged to the priests. [Lev. 5:15, 18] • [Num. 18:9]

Political Situation Under Joash

17 Now Hazael king of Syria went up and
fought against Gath, and took it; so Hazael
set his face to go up to Jerusalem.
18 And Jehoash king of Judah [R]took all the
sacred things that his fathers, Jehoshaphat
and Jehoram and Ahaziah, kings of Judah,
had dedicated, and his own sacred things, and
all the gold found in the treasuries of the
house of the LORD and in the king's house,
and sent *them* to Hazael king of Syria. Then
he went away from Jerusalem. 1 Kin. 15:18

Death of Joash—2 Chr. 24:25–27

19 Now the rest of the acts of Joash, and all
that he did, *are* they not written in the book
of the chronicles of the kings of Judah?
20 And [R]his servants arose and made a
conspiracy, and killed Joash in the house of
the Millo, which goes down to Silla. 2 Kin. 14:5
21 For Jozachar the son of Shimeath and
Jehozabad the son of Shomer, his servants,
struck him. So he died, and they buried him
with his fathers in the City of David. Then
Amaziah his son reigned in his place.

CHAPTER 13

The Reign of Jehoahaz in Israel

IN the twenty-third year of [T]Joash the son
of Ahaziah, king of Judah, Jehoahaz the
son of Jehu became king over Israel in Samaria, *and reigned* seventeen years. *Jehoash*
2 And he did evil in the sight of the LORD,
and followed the [R]sins of Jeroboam the son of
Nebat, who had made Israel sin. He did not
[T]depart from them. 1 Kin. 12:26–33 • Lit. *turn*
3 Then [R]the anger of the LORD was aroused
against Israel, and He delivered them into the
hand of [R]Hazael king of Syria, and into the
hand of [R]Ben-Hadad the son of Hazael, all
their days. Judg. 2:14 • 2 Kin. 8:12 • Amos 1:4
4 So Jehoahaz [R]pleaded with the LORD, and
the LORD listened to him; for [R]He saw the
oppression of Israel, because the king of
Syria oppressed them. [Ps. 78:34] • [Ex. 3:7, 9]
5 [R]Then the LORD gave Israel a deliverer,
so that they escaped from under the hand of
the Syrians; and the children of Israel dwelt
in their tents as before. 2 Kin. 13:25; 14:25, 27
6 Nevertheless they did not depart from
the sins of the house of Jeroboam, who had
made Israel sin, *but* walked in them; and the
wooden images also remained in Samaria.
7 For He left of the army of Jehoahaz only
fifty horsemen, ten chariots, and ten thousand foot soldiers; for the king of Syria had
destroyed them [R]and made them [R]like the
dust at threshing. 2 Kin. 10:32 • [Amos 1:3]
8 Now the rest of the acts of Jehoahaz, all
that he did, and his might, *are* they not
written in the book of the chronicles of the
kings of Israel?
9 So Jehoahaz rested with his fathers, and
they buried him in Samaria. Then [T]Joash his
son reigned in his place. Or *Jehoash*

Rule of Jehoash—2 Kin. 14:15, 16

10 In the thirty-seventh year of Joash king
of Judah, [T]Jehoash the son of Jehoahaz became king over Israel in Samaria, *and*
reigned sixteen years. *Joash,* v. 9
11 And he did evil in the sight of the LORD;
he did not depart from all the sins of Jeroboam the son of Nebat, who had made Israel
sin; *but* he walked in them.
12 Now the rest of the acts of Joash, all that
he did, and [R]his might with which he fought
against Amaziah king of Judah, *are* they not
written in the book of the chronicles of the
kings of Israel? 2 Kin. 14:9
13 So Joash rested with his fathers. Then
Jeroboam sat on his throne. And Joash was
buried in Samaria with the kings of Israel.

Prophecy of Israel's Victory

14 Elisha had become sick with the illness
of which he would die. Then Joash the king
of Israel came down to him, and wept over
his face, and said, "O my father, my father,
the chariots of Israel and their horsemen!"
15 And Elisha said to him, "Take a bow and
some arrows." So he took himself a bow and
some arrows.
16 Then he said to the king of Israel, "Put
your hand on the bow." So he put his hand *on*
it, and Elisha put his hands on the king's
hands.
17 And he said, "Open the east window";
and he opened *it.* Then Elisha said, "Shoot";
and he shot. And he said, "The arrow of the
LORD's deliverance and the arrow of deliverance from Syria; for you must strike the
Syrians at [R]Aphek till you have destroyed
them." 1 Kin. 20:26

18 Then he said, "Take the arrows"; so he
took *them.* And he said to the king of Israel,
"Strike the ground"; so he struck three times,
and stopped.
19 And the man of God was angry with him,
and said, "You should have struck five or six
times; then you would have struck Syria till
you had destroyed *it.* [R]But now you will strike
Syria *only* three times." 2 Kin. 13:25

Death of Elisha

20 Then Elisha died, and they buried him.
And the [R]*raiding* bands from Moab invaded
the land in the spring of the year. 2 Kin. 3:5

Miracle of Resurrection at Elisha's Tomb

21 So it was, as they were burying a man,
that suddenly they spied a band *of raiders;*
and they put the man in the tomb of Elisha;
and when the man was let down and touched
the bones of Elisha, he revived and stood on
his feet.

Israel's Victory over Syria

22 And [R]Hazael king of Syria oppressed
Israel all the days of Jehoahaz. 2 Kin. 8:12, 13
23 But the LORD was gracious to them, had
compassion on them, and regarded them,
because of His covenant with Abraham,
Isaac, and Jacob, and would not yet destroy
them or cast them from His presence.
24 Now Hazael king of Syria died. Then
Ben-Hadad his son reigned in his place.
25 And [T]Jehoash the son of Jehoahaz recaptured from the hand of Ben-Hadad, the son of
Hazael, the cities which he had taken out of
the hand of Jehoahaz his father by war.
Three times Joash defeated him and recaptured the cities of Israel. *Joash,* vv. 12–14

CHAPTER 14

Spiritual Evaluation of Amaziah—2 Chr. 25:1–4

IN the second year of Joash the son of
Jehoahaz, king of Israel, Amaziah the son
of Joash, king of Judah, became king.
2 He was twenty-five years old when he
became king, and he reigned twenty-nine
years in Jerusalem. His mother's name was
Jehoaddan of Jerusalem.
3 And he did *what was* right in the sight of
the LORD, yet not like his father David; he did
everything as his father Joash had done.
4 However the high places were not taken
away, and the people still sacrificed and
burned incense on the high places.
5 Now it happened, as soon as the kingdom was established in his hand, that he
executed his servants [R]who had murdered his
father the king. 2 Kin. 12:20
6 But the children of the murderers he did
not execute, according to what is written in
the Book of the Law of Moses, in which the
LORD commanded, saying, [R]"The fathers shall
not be put to death for the children, nor shall
the children be put to death for the fathers;
but a person shall be put to death for his own
sin." [Ezek. 18:4, 20]

Political Situation Under Amaziah
2 Chr. 25:11, 17–24

7 He killed ten thousand Edomites in the
Valley of Salt, and took [T]Sela by war, and
called its name Joktheel to this day. Petra
8 Then Amaziah sent messengers to [T]Jeho-
ash the son of Jehoahaz, the son of Jehu,
king of Israel, saying, "Come, let us face one
another *in battle.*" *Joash,* 2 Kin. 13:9, 12–14, 25
9 And Jehoash king of Israel sent to Amaziah king of Judah, saying, "The thistle that
was in Lebanon sent to the cedar that *was* in
Lebanon, saying, 'Give your daughter to my
son as wife'; and a wild beast that *was* in
Lebanon passed by and trampled the thistle.
10 "You have indeed defeated Edom, and
your heart has [T]lifted you up. Glory *in your
success,* and stay at home; for why should
you meddle with trouble so that you fall—
you and Judah with you?" Made you proud
11 But Amaziah would not heed. Therefore
Jehoash king of Israel went out; so he and
Amaziah king of Judah faced one another at
Beth Shemesh, which *belongs* to Judah.
12 And Judah was defeated by Israel, and
every man fled to his tent.
13 Then Jehoash king of Israel captured
Amaziah king of Judah, the son of Jehoash,
the son of Ahaziah, at Beth Shemesh; and he
went to Jerusalem, and broke down the wall
of Jerusalem from the Gate of Ephraim to
the Corner Gate—four hundred cubits.
14 And he took all [R]the gold and silver, all
the articles that were found in the house of
the LORD and in the treasuries of the king's
house, and hostages, and returned to Samaria. 1 Kin. 7:51

Death of Jehoash—2 Kin. 13:12, 13

15 [R]Now the rest of the acts of Jehoash
which he did—his might, and how he fought
with Amaziah king of Judah—*are* they not
written in the book of the chronicles of the
kings of Israel? 2 Kin. 13:12, 13
16 So Jehoash [T]rested with his fathers, and
was buried in Samaria with the kings of
Israel. Then Jeroboam his son reigned in his
place. Died and joined his ancestors

Death of Amaziah—2 Chr. 25:25–26:2

17 Amaziah the son of Joash, king of Judah,
lived fifteen years after the death of Jehoash
the son of Jehoahaz, king of Israel.
18 Now the rest of the acts of Amaziah, *are*
they not written in the book of the chronicles
of the kings of Judah?

19 And [R]they made a conspiracy against
him in Jerusalem, and he fled to [R]Lachish; but
they sent after him to Lachish and killed him
there. 2 Chr. 25:27 • Josh. 10:31
20 Then they brought him on horses, and he
was buried at Jerusalem with his fathers in
the City of David.
21 And all the people of Judah took Azariah, who *was* sixteen years old, and made
him king instead of his father Amaziah.
22 He built Elath and restored it to Judah,
after the king rested with his fathers.

The Reign of Jeroboam II in Israel

23 In the fifteenth year of Amaziah the son
of Joash, king of Judah, Jeroboam the son of
Joash, king of Israel, became king in Samaria,
and reigned forty-one years.
24 And he did evil in the sight of the LORD;
he did not depart from all the sins of Jeroboam the son of Nebat, who had made Israel
sin.
25 He restored the territory of Israel from
the entrance of Hamath to the Sea of the
Arabah, according to the word of the LORD
God of Israel, which He had spoken through
His servant Jonah the son of Amittai, the
prophet who *was* from Gath Hepher.
26 For the LORD saw *that* the affliction of
Israel *was* very bitter; and whether bond or
free, there was no helper for Israel.
27 [R]And the LORD did not say that He would
blot out the name of Israel from under
heaven; but He saved them by the hand of
Jeroboam the son of Joash. [2 Kin. 13:5, 23]
28 Now the rest of the acts of Jeroboam,
and all that he did—his might, how he made
war, and how he recaptured for Israel, from
Damascus and Hamath, *what had belonged*
to Judah—*are* they not written in the book of
the chronicles of the kings of Israel?
29 So Jeroboam [T]rested with his fathers, the
kings of Israel. Then Zechariah his son
reigned in his place. Died and joined his ancestors

CHAPTER 15

The Reign of Azariah in Judah
2 Chr. 26:3–23

IN the twenty-seventh year of Jeroboam
king of Israel, Azariah the son of Amaziah, king of Judah, became king.
2 He was sixteen years old when he became king, and he reigned fifty-two years in
Jerusalem. His mother's name *was* Jecholiah
of Jerusalem.
3 And he did *what was* right in the sight of
the LORD, according to all that his father
Amaziah had done,
4 [R]except that the high places were not
removed; the people still sacrificed and
burned incense on the high places. 2 Kin. 12:3
5 Then the LORD struck the king, so that
he was a leper until the day of his death; so
he [R]dwelt in an isolated house. And Jotham
the king's son *was* over the *royal* house,
judging the people of the land. [Lev. 13:46]
6 Now the rest of the acts of Azariah, and
all that he did, *are* they not written in the
book of the chronicles of the kings of Judah?
7 So Azariah [T]rested with his fathers, and
[R]they buried him with his fathers in the City
of David. Then Jotham his son reigned in his
place. Died and joined his ancestors • 2 Chr. 26:23

The Reign of Zechariah in Israel

8 In the thirty-eighth year of Azariah king
of Judah, Zechariah the son of Jeroboam
reigned over Israel in Samaria six months.
9 And he did evil in the sight of the LORD,
[R]as his fathers had done; he did not depart
from the sins of Jeroboam the son of Nebat,
who had made Israel sin. 2 Kin. 14:24
10 Then Shallum the son of Jabesh conspired against him, and [R]struck and killed him
in front of the people; and he reigned in his
place. Amos 7:9
11 Now the rest of the acts of Zechariah,
indeed they *are* written in the book of the
chronicles of the kings of Israel.
12 This *was* the [R]word of the LORD which
He spoke to Jehu, saying, "Your sons shall sit
on the throne of Israel to the fourth *generation*." And so it was. 2 Kin. 10:30

The Reign of Shallum in Israel

13 Shallum the son of Jabesh became king
in the thirty-ninth year of [T]Uzziah king of
Judah; and he reigned a full month in Samaria. *Azariah*, 2 Kin. 14:21ff.; 15:1ff.
14 For Menahem the son of Gadi went up
from Tirzah, came to Samaria, and struck
Shallum the son of Jabesh in Samaria and
killed him; and he reigned in his place.
15 Now the rest of the acts of Shallum, and
the conspiracy which he [T]led, indeed they *are*
written in the book of the chronicles of the
kings of Israel. Lit. *conspired*

The Reign of Menahem in Israel

16 Then from Tirzah, Menahem attacked
Tiphsah, all who *were* there, and its territory;
because they did not open *it to him*, therefore
he attacked *it*. *And* all the women there who
were with child he ripped open.
17 In the thirty-ninth year of Azariah king
of Judah, Menahem the son of Gadi became
king over Israel, *and reigned* ten years in
Samaria.
18 And he did evil in the sight of the LORD;
he did not depart all his days from the sins of
Jeroboam the son of Nebat, who had made
Israel sin.

19 Pul king of Assyria came against the land; and Menahem gave Pul a thousand talents of silver, that his hand might be with him to strengthen the kingdom in his hand.

20 And Menahem [R]exacted[T] the money from Israel, from all the very wealthy, from each man [T]fifty shekels of silver, to give to the king of Assyria. So the king of Assyria turned back, and did not stay there in the land. 2 Kin. 23:35 • *took* • $6,400

21 Now the rest of the acts of Menahem, and all that he did, *are* they not written in the book of the chronicles of the kings of Israel?

22 So Menahem rested with his fathers. Then Pekahiah his son reigned in his place.

The Reign of Pekahiah in Israel

23 In the fiftieth year of Azariah king of Judah, Pekahiah the son of Menahem became king over Israel in Samaria, *and reigned* two years.

24 And he did evil in the sight of the LORD; he did not depart from the sins of Jeroboam the son of Nebat, who had made Israel sin.

25 Then Pekah the son of Remaliah, an officer of his, conspired against him and [T]killed him in Samaria, in the citadel of the king's house, along with Argob and Arieh; and with him were fifty men of Gilead. He killed him and reigned in his place. *struck*

26 Now the rest of the acts of Pekahiah, and all that he did, indeed they *are* written in the book of the chronicles of the kings of Israel.

The Reign of Pekah in Israel

27 In the fifty-second year of Azariah king of Judah, [R]Pekah the son of Remaliah became king over Israel in Samaria, *and reigned* twenty years. Is. 7:1

28 And he did evil in the sight of the LORD; he did not depart from the sins of Jeroboam the son of Nebat, who had made Israel sin.

29 In the days of Pekah king of Israel, [T]Tiglath-Pileser king of Assyria came and took Ijon, Abel Beth Maachah, Janoah, Kedesh, Hazor, Gilead, and Galilee, all the land of Naphtali; and he [R]carried them captive to Assyria. A later name of *Pul*, v. 19 • 2 Kin. 17:6

30 Then Hoshea the son of Elah led a conspiracy against Pekah the son of Remaliah, and struck and killed him; so he [R]reigned in his place in the twentieth year of Jotham the son of Uzziah. [Hos. 10:3, 7, 15]

31 Now the rest of the acts of Pekah, and all that he did, indeed they *are* written in the book of the chronicles of the kings of Israel.

The Reign of Jotham in Judah—2 Chr. 27:1–9

32 In the second year of Pekah the son of Remaliah, king of Israel, Jotham the son of Uzziah, king of Judah, began to reign.

33 He was twenty-five years old when he became king, and he reigned sixteen years in Jerusalem. His mother's name *was* [T]Jerusha the daughter of Zadok. *Jerushah*, 2 Chr. 27:1

34 And he did *what was* right in the sight of the LORD; he did [R]according to all that his father Uzziah had done. 2 Kin. 15:3, 4

35 However the high places were not removed; the people still sacrificed and burned incense on the high places. He built the Upper Gate of the house of the LORD.

36 Now the rest of the acts of Jotham, and all that he did, *are* they not written in the book of the chronicles of the kings of Judah?

37 In those days the LORD began to send Rezin king of Syria and [R]Pekah the son of Remaliah against Judah. 2 Kin. 15:26, 27

38 So Jotham [T]rested with his fathers, and was buried with his fathers in the City of David his father. Then Ahaz his son reigned in his place. Died and joined his ancestors

CHAPTER 16

Spiritual Evaluation of Ahaz—2 Chr. 28:1–4

IN the seventeenth year of Pekah the son of Remaliah, Ahaz the son of Jotham, king of Judah, began to reign.

2 Ahaz *was* twenty years old when he became king, and he reigned sixteen years in Jerusalem; and he did not do *what was* right in the sight of the LORD his God, as his father David *had done.*

3 But he walked in the way of the kings of Israel; indeed he made his son pass through the fire, according to the [R]abominations of the nations whom the LORD had cast out from before the children of Israel. [Lev. 18:21]

4 And he sacrificed and burned incense on the [R]high places, [R]on the hills, and under every green tree. 2 Kin. 15:34, 35 • [Deut. 12:2]

Political Situation Under Ahaz
2 Chr. 28:5, 16, 21; Is. 7:1

5 [R]Then Rezin king of Syria and Pekah the son of Remaliah, king of Israel, came up to Jerusalem to *make* war; and they besieged Ahaz but could not overcome *him.* Is. 7:1, 4

6 At that time Rezin king of Syria captured Elath for Syria, and drove the men of Judah from Elath. Then the *Edomites went to Elath, and dwell there to this day.

7 So Ahaz sent messengers to [T]Tiglath-Pileser king of Assyria, saying, "I *am* your servant and your son. Come up and save me from the hand of the king of Syria and from the hand of the king of Israel, who rise up against me." A later name of *Pul*, 2 Kin. 15:19

8 And Ahaz took the silver and gold that was found in the house of the LORD, and in the treasuries of the king's house, and sent *it as* a present to the king of Assyria.

16:6 A few ancient mss. *Syrians*

9 So the king of Assyria heeded him; for
the king of Assyria went up against Damascus and [R]took it, carried *its people* captive to
[R]Kir, and killed Rezin. Amos 1:5 • Amos 9:7
10 Now King Ahaz went to Damascus to
meet Tiglath-Pileser king of Assyria, and saw
an altar that *was* at Damascus; and King
Ahaz sent to Urijah the priest the design of
the altar and its pattern, according to all its
workmanship.
11 Then Urijah the priest built an altar
according to all that King Ahaz had sent
from Damascus. So Urijah the priest made *it*
before King Ahaz came from Damascus.
12 And when the king came from Damascus, the king saw the altar; and [R]the king
approached the altar and made offerings on
it. 2 Chr. 26:16, 19
13 So he burned his burnt offering and his
grain offering; and he poured his drink offering and sprinkled the blood of his peace
offerings on the altar.
14 He also brought [R]the bronze altar which
was before the LORD, from the front of the
[T]temple—from between the *new* altar and the
house of the LORD—and put it on the north
side of the *new* altar. 2 Chr. 4:1 • Lit. *house*
15 Then King Ahaz commanded Urijah the
priest, saying, "On the great *new* altar burn
[R]the morning burnt offering, the evening
grain offering, the king's burnt sacrifice, and
his grain offering, with the burnt offering of
all the people of the land, their grain offering,
and their drink offerings; and sprinkle on it
all the blood of the burnt offering and all the
blood of the sacrifice. And the bronze altar
shall be for me to inquire *by*." Ex. 29:39–41
16 Thus did Urijah the priest, according to
all that King Ahaz commanded.
17 And King Ahaz cut off [R]the panels of the
carts, and removed the lavers from them; and
he took down [R]the Sea from the bronze oxen
that *were* under it, and put it on a pavement
of stones. 1 Kin. 7:27–29 • 1 Kin. 7:23–25
18 Also he removed the Sabbath pavilion
which they had built in the temple, and he
removed the king's outer entrance from the
house of the LORD, on account of the king of
Assyria.

Death of Ahaz—2 Chr. 28:26, 27

19 Now the rest of the acts of Ahaz which
he did, *are* they not written in the book of the
chronicles of the kings of Judah?
20 So Ahaz rested with his fathers, and
[R]was buried with his fathers in the City of
David. Then Hezekiah his son reigned in his
place. 2 Chr. 28:27

CHAPTER 17

Spiritual Evaluation of Hoshea

IN the twelfth year of Ahaz king of Judah,
Hoshea the son of Elah became king of
Israel in Samaria, *and he reigned* nine years.
2 And he did evil in the sight of the LORD,
but not as the kings of Israel who were
before him.

Imprisonment of Hoshea

3 Shalmaneser king of Assyria came up
against him; and Hoshea [R]became his vassal,
and paid him tribute money. 2 Kin. 24:1
4 And the king of Assyria uncovered a
conspiracy by Hoshea; for he had sent messengers to So, king of Egypt, and brought no
tribute to the king of Assyria, as *he had done*
year by year. Therefore the king of Assyria
shut him up, and bound him in prison.

Captivity of Samaria—2 Kin. 18:9–12

5 Now [R]the king of Assyria went throughout all the land, and went up to Samaria and
besieged it for three years. Hos. 13:16
6 In the ninth year of Hoshea, the king of
Assyria took Samaria and [R]carried Israel
away to Assyria, and placed them in Halah
and by the Habor, the River of Gozan, and in
the cities of the Medes. [Deut. 28:36, 64; 29:27, 28]

Causes of the Captivity

7 For so it was that the children of Israel
had sinned against the LORD their God, who
had brought them up out of the land of
Egypt, from under the hand of Pharaoh king
of Egypt; and they had feared other gods,
8 and [R]had walked in the statutes of the
nations whom the LORD had cast out from
before the children of Israel, and of the kings
of Israel, which they had made. [Lev. 18:3]
9 Also the children of Israel secretly did
against the LORD their God things that *were*
not right, and they built for themselves [T]high
places in all their cities, [R]from watchtower to
fortified city. Places for pagan worship • 2 Kin. 18:8
10 They set up for themselves *sacred* pillars
and [T]wooden images on every high hill and
under every green tree; Or *Asherim*
11 and there they burned incense on all the
high places, as the nations *had done* whom
the LORD had carried away before them; and
they did wicked things to provoke the LORD
to anger,
12 for they served idols, [R]of which the LORD
had said to them, [R]"You shall not do this
thing." [Ex. 20:3–5] • [Deut. 4:19]
13 Yet the LORD testified against Israel and
against Judah, by all of His prophets, *namely*
[R]every seer, saying, "Turn from your evil
ways, and keep My commandments *and* My
statutes, according to all the law which I
commanded your fathers, and which I sent to
you by My servants the prophets." 1 Sam. 9:9
14 Nevertheless they would not hear, but
[R]stiffened their necks, like the necks of their

fathers, who [R]did not believe in the LORD their God. [Acts 7:51] • Deut. 9:23

15 And they rejected His statutes and His covenant that He had made with their fathers, and His testimonies which He had testified against them; they followed idols, [R]became idolaters, and *went* after the nations who *were* all around them, *concerning* whom the LORD had charged them that they should [R]not do like them. [Rom. 1:21–23] • [Deut. 12:30, 31]

16 So they left all the commandments of the LORD their God, made for themselves a molded image *and* two calves, made a wooden image and worshiped all the [R]host of heaven, and served Baal. [Deut. 4:19]

17 And they caused their sons and daughters to pass through the fire, [R]practiced witchcraft and soothsaying, and sold themselves to do evil in the sight of the LORD, to provoke Him to anger. [Deut. 18:10–12]

18 Therefore the LORD was very angry with Israel, and removed them from His sight; there was none left [R]but the tribe of Judah alone. 1 Kin. 11:13, 32

19 Also [R]Judah did not keep the commandments of the LORD their God, but walked in the statutes of Israel which they made. Jer. 3:8

20 And the LORD rejected all the descendants of Israel, afflicted them, and delivered them into the hand of plunderers, until He had cast them from His [R]sight. 2 Kin. 24:20

21 For [R]He tore Israel from the house of David, and [R]they made Jeroboam the son of Nebat king. Then Jeroboam drove Israel from following the LORD, and made them commit a great sin. 1 Kin. 11:11, 31 • 1 Kin. 12:20, 28

22 For the children of Israel walked in all the sins of Jeroboam which he did; they did not depart from them,

23 until the LORD removed Israel out of His sight, as He had said by all His servants the prophets. So Israel was carried away from their own land to Assyria, *as it is* to this day.

Sins of the Foreigners

24 [R]Then the king of Assyria brought *people* from Babylon, Cuthah, [R]Ava, Hamath, and from Sepharvaim, and placed *them* in the cities of Samaria instead of the children of Israel; and they took possession of Samaria and dwelt in its cities. Ezra 4:2, 10 • 2 Kin. 18:34

25 And it was so, at the beginning of their dwelling there, *that* they did not fear the LORD; therefore the LORD sent lions among them, which killed *some* of them.

26 So they spoke to the king of Assyria, saying, "The nations whom you have removed and placed in the cities of Samaria do not know the rituals of the God of the land; therefore He has sent lions among them, and indeed, they are killing them because they do not know the rituals of the God of the land."

27 Then the king of Assyria commanded, saying, "Send there one of the priests whom you brought from there; let him go and dwell there, and let him teach them the rituals of the God of the land."

28 Then one of the priests whom they had carried away from Samaria came and dwelt in Bethel, and taught them how they should fear the LORD.

29 However every nation continued to make gods of its own, and put *them* [R]in the houses of the high places which the Samaritans had made, *every* nation in the cities where they dwelt. 1 Kin. 12:31; 13:32

30 The men of [R]Babylon made Succoth Benoth, the men of Cuth made Nergal, the men of Hamath made Ashima, 2 Kin. 17:24

31 and the Avites made Nibhaz and Tartak; and the Sepharvites [R]burned their children in fire to Adrammelech and Anammelech, the gods of Sepharvaim. [Deut. 12:31]

32 So they feared the LORD, and from every class they appointed for themselves priests of the high places, who sacrificed for them in the shrines of the high places.

33 [R]They feared the LORD, yet served their own gods—according to the rituals of the nations from among whom they were carried away. Zeph. 1:5

34 To this day they continue practicing the former rituals; they do not fear the LORD, nor do they follow their statutes or their ordinances, or the law and commandment which the LORD had commanded the children of Jacob, [R]whom He named Israel, Gen. 32:28; 35:10

35 with whom the LORD had made a covenant and charged them, saying: "You shall not fear other gods, nor bow down to them nor serve them nor sacrifice to them;

36 "but the LORD, who brought you up from the land of Egypt with great power and [R]an outstretched arm, [R]Him you shall fear, Him you shall worship, and to Him you shall offer sacrifice. Ex. 6:6; 9:15 • [Deut. 10:20]

37 "And the statutes, the ordinances, the law, and the commandment which He wrote for you, you shall be careful to observe forever; you shall not fear other gods.

38 "And the covenant that I have made with you, [R]you shall not forget, nor shall you fear other gods. Deut. 4:23; 6:12

39 "But the LORD your God you shall fear; and He will deliver you from the hand of all your enemies."

40 However they did not obey, but they followed their former rituals.

41 [R]So these nations feared the LORD, yet served their carved images; also their children and their children's children have continued doing as their fathers did, even to this day. 2 Kin. 17:32, 33

CHAPTER 18

Spiritual Evaluation of Hezekiah
2 Chr. 29:1, 2; 31:1

NOW it came to pass in the third year of
Hoshea the son of Elah, king of Israel,
that [R]Hezekiah the son of Ahaz, king of
Judah, began to reign. 2 Chr. 28:27; 29:1
2 He was twenty-five years old when he
became king, and he reigned twenty-nine
years in Jerusalem. His mother's name *was*
[R]Abi the daughter of Zechariah. 2 Chr. 29:1, 2
3 And he did *what was* right in the sight of
the LORD, according to all that his father
David had done.
4 He removed the high places and broke
the *sacred* pillars, cut down the wooden
images and broke in pieces the bronze serpent that Moses had made; for until those
days the children of Israel burned incense to
it, and called it [T]Nehushtan. Lit. *Bronze Thing*
5 He [R]trusted in the LORD God of Israel, [R]so
that after him was none like him among all
the kings of Judah, nor *any* who were before
him. 2 Kin. 19:10 • 2 Kin. 23:25
6 For he [R]held fast to the LORD; he did not
depart from following Him, but kept His
commandments, which the LORD had commanded Moses. Deut. 10:20
7 The LORD was with him; he prospered
wherever he went. And he rebelled against
the king of Assyria and did not serve him.
8 [R]He [T]subdued the Philistines, as far as
Gaza and its territory, [R]from watchtower to
fortified city. Is. 14:29 • Lit. *struck* • 2 Kin. 17:9

Invasion of Israel by Assyria
2 Kin. 17:5–7

9 Now [R]it came to pass in the fourth year
of King Hezekiah, which *was* the seventh
year of Hoshea the son of Elah, king of Israel,
that Shalmaneser king of Assyria came up
against Samaria and besieged it. 2 Kin. 17:3
10 And at the end of three years they took
it. In the sixth year of Hezekiah, that *is,* [R]the
ninth year of Hoshea king of Israel, Samaria
was taken. 2 Kin. 17:6
11 Then the king of Assyria carried Israel
away captive to Assyria, and put them [R]in
Halah and by the Habor, the River of Gozan,
and in the cities of the Medes, 1 Chr. 5:26
12 because they [R]did not obey the voice of
the LORD their God, but transgressed His
covenant *and* all that Moses the servant of
the LORD had commanded; and they would
neither hear nor do *them.* 2 Kin. 17:7–18

First Invasion of Judah by Assyria
Is. 36:1

13 And [R]in the fourteenth year of King
Hezekiah, Sennacherib king of Assyria came
up against all the fortified cities of Judah and
took them. 2 Chr. 32:1
14 Then Hezekiah king of Judah sent to the
king of Assyria at Lachish, saying, "I have
done wrong; turn away from me; whatever
you impose on me I will pay." And the king
of Assyria assessed Hezekiah king of Judah
[T]three hundred talents of silver and [T]thirty
talents of gold. $115,200,000 • $172,800,000
15 So Hezekiah gave *him* all the silver that
was found in the house of the LORD and in
the treasuries of the king's house.
16 At that time Hezekiah stripped *the gold*
from the doors of the temple of the LORD, and
from the pillars which Hezekiah king of
Judah had overlaid, and gave [T]it to the king
of Assyria. Lit. *them*

Second Invasion of Judah by Assyria
2 Chr. 32:9–21; Is. 36:2—37:38

17 Then the king of Assyria sent the Tartan,
the Rabsaris, and the Rabshakeh from Lachish, with a great army against Jerusalem,
to King Hezekiah. And they went up and
came to Jerusalem. When they had come up,
they came and stood by the [R]aqueduct from
the upper pool, which *was* on the highway to
the Fuller's Field. 2 Kin. 20:20
18 And when they had called to the king,
[R]Eliakim the son of Hilkiah, who *was* over
the household, Shebna the [T]scribe, and Joah
the son of Asaph, the recorder, came out to
them. Is. 22:20 • *secretary*
19 Then the Rabshakeh said to them, "Say
now to Hezekiah, 'Thus says the great king,
the king of Assyria: [R]"What confidence *is* this
in which you trust? 2 Chr. 32:10
20 "You speak of *having* counsel and
strength for war; but *they are* [T]vain words.
And in whom do you trust, that you rebel
against me? Lit. *a word of the lips*
21 [R]"Now look! You are trusting in the staff
of this broken reed, Egypt, on which if a man
leans, it will go into his hand and pierce it. So
is Pharaoh king of Egypt to all who trust in
him. Ezek. 29:6, 7
22 "But if you say to me, 'We trust in the
LORD our God,' *is* it not He [R]whose [T]high
places and whose altars Hezekiah has taken
away, and said to Judah and Jerusalem, 'You
shall worship before this altar in Jerusalem'?" ' 2 Kin. 18:4 • Places for pagan worship
23 "Now therefore, I urge you, give a pledge
to my master the king of Assyria, and I will
give you two thousand horses—if you are
able on your part to put riders on them!
24 "How then will you repel one captain of
the least of my master's servants, and put
your trust in Egypt for chariots and horsemen?
25 "Have I now come up without the LORD
against this place to destroy it? The LORD said
to me, 'Go up against this land, and destroy
it.' "

SENNACHERIB'S PRISM

The monument known as Sennacherib's Prism is a fascinating artifact from Assyria's past. It gives a different account than the Bible about an important event in Israel's history—a siege against Jerusalem conducted by King Sennacherib of Assyria (ruled 705–681 B.C.) about 690 B.C. (Is. 36; 37).

The fifteen-inch high clay prism contains well-preserved Assyrian script that verifies the attack on Jerusalem and King Hezekiah of Judah by Assyrian forces. "As to Hezekiah, the Jew, he did not submit to my yoke," the prism reads. "I laid siege to 46 of his strong cities, walled forts and to countless small cities in their vicinity, and conquered them. . . . [Hezekiah] I made a prisoner in Jerusalem, his royal residence, like a bird in a cage."

While Sennacherib's siege against Jerusalem is a verified historical fact, it is interesting that Sennacherib's account does not mention how the siege ended. This leads to suspicion among historians that the siege failed, since the Assyrians never mentioned their defeats in their official records—only their victories.

The biblical account indicates that Sennacherib suffered a crushing defeat in his siege of Jerusalem because of divine intervention. During the night, thousands of soldiers in the Assyrian army died through the action of the angel of the Lord (2 Kin. 19:35). Some scholars believe God used a deadly plague as an instrument of judgment against the enemies of His people.

Rulers of the ancient world used monuments such as this prism on which to record their exploits. These documents of stone and clay have survived for centuries in the rubble and ruin of ancient cities. They provide valuable insight into life in Bible times, confirming and, in many cases, adding valuable information about biblical events.

Photo by Howard Vos

Sennacherib's prism records the Assyrian account of Sennacherib's attack on Jerusalem.

26 Then Eliakim the son of Hilkiah, Shebna,
and Joah said to the Rabshakeh, "Please
speak to your servants in the Aramaic language, for we understand *it*; and do not speak
to us in [T]Hebrew in the hearing of the people
who *are* on the wall." Lit. *Judean*
27 But the Rabshakeh said to them, "Has
my master sent me to your master and to you
to speak these words, and not to the men
who sit on the wall, who will eat and drink
their own waste with you?"
28 Then the Rabshakeh stood and called
out with a loud voice in [T]Hebrew, and spoke,
saying, "Hear the word of the great king, the
king of Assyria! Lit. *Judean*
29 "Thus says the king: [R]'Do not let Hezekiah deceive you, for he shall not be able to
deliver you from his hand; 2 Chr. 32:15
30 'nor let Hezekiah make you trust in the
LORD, saying, "The LORD will surely deliver
us; this city shall not be given into the hand
of the king of Assyria." '
31 "Do not listen to Hezekiah; for thus says
the king of Assyria: 'Make *peace* with me by
a [T]present and come out to me; and every one
of you eat from his own vine and every one
from his own fig tree, and every one of you
drink the waters of his own cistern; Tribute
32 'until I come and take you away to a
land like your own land, [R]a land of grain and
new wine, a land of bread and vineyards, a
land of olive groves and honey, that you may
live and not die. But do not listen to Hezekiah, lest he persuade you, saying, "The
LORD will deliver us." ' Deut. 8:7–9; 11:12
33 [R]'Has any of the gods of the nations at all
delivered its land from the hand of the king of
Assyria? 2 Kin. 19:12
34 'Where *are* the gods of Hamath and
Arpad? Where *are* the gods of Sepharvaim
and Hena and [R]Ivah? Indeed, have they
delivered Samaria from my hand? 2 Kin. 17:24
35 'Who among all the gods of the lands
have delivered their countries from my hand,
[R]that the LORD should deliver Jerusalem from
my hand?' " Dan. 3:15
36 But the people held their peace and
answered him not a word; for the king's
commandment was, "Do not answer him."
37 Then Eliakim the son of Hilkiah, who
was over the household, Shebna the scribe,
and Joah the son of Asaph, the recorder,
came to Hezekiah with *their* clothes torn, and
told him the words of the Rabshakeh.

CHAPTER 19

AND [R]so *it was, when King Hezekiah*
heard *it*, that he tore his clothes, covered himself with [R]sackcloth, and went into
the house of the LORD. Is. 37:1 • Ps. 69:11
2 Then he sent Eliakim, who *was* over the
household, Shebna the scribe, and the elders
of the priests, covered with sackcloth, to
Isaiah the prophet, the son of Amoz.
3 And they said to him, "Thus says Hezekiah: 'This day *is* a day of trouble, and
rebuke, and blasphemy; for the children have
come to birth, but *there is* no strength to
[T]bring them forth. *give birth*
4 'It may be that the LORD your God will
hear all the words of the Rabshakeh, whom
his master the king of Assyria has sent to
[R]reproach the living God, and will [R]reprove
the words which the LORD your God has
heard. Therefore lift up *your* prayer for the
remnant that is left.' " 2 Kin. 18:35 • Ps. 50:21
5 So the servants of King Hezekiah came
to Isaiah.
6 And Isaiah said to them, "Thus you shall
say to your master, 'Thus says the LORD: "Do
not be afraid of the words which you have
heard, with which the servants of the king of
Assyria have blasphemed Me.
7 "Surely I will send [R]a spirit upon him,
and he shall hear a rumor and return to his
own land; and I will cause him to fall by the
sword in his own land." ' " 2 Kin. 19:35–37
8 So the Rabshakeh returned and found
the king of Assyria warring against Libnah,
for he heard that he had departed [R]from
Lachish. 2 Kin. 18:14, 17
9 And [R]the king heard concerning Tirhakah king of Ethiopia, "Look, he has come out
to make war with you." So he again sent
messengers to Hezekiah, saying, 1 Sam. 23:27
10 "Thus you shall speak to Hezekiah king
of Judah, saying: 'Do not let your God [R]in
whom you trust deceive you, saying, "Jerusalem shall not be given into the hand of the
king of Assyria." 2 Kin. 18:5
11 'Look! You have heard what the kings of
Assyria have done to all lands by utterly
destroying them; and shall you be delivered?
12 'Have the gods of the nations delivered
those whom my fathers have destroyed, Gozan and Haran and Rezeph, and the people of
[R]Eden who *were* in Telassar? Ezek. 27:23
13 [R]'Where *is* the king of Hamath, the king
of Arpad, and the king of the city of Sepharvaim, Hena, and Ivah?' " 2 Kin. 18:34
14 [R]And Hezekiah received the letter from
the hand of the messengers, and read it; and
Hezekiah went up to the house of the LORD,
and spread it before the LORD. Is. 37:14
15 Then Hezekiah prayed before the LORD,
and said: "O LORD God of Israel, *the One* who
dwells *between* the cherubim, You are God,
You alone, of all the kingdoms of the earth.
You have made heaven and earth.
16 [R]"Incline Your ear, O LORD, and hear;
open Your eyes, O LORD, and see; and hear
the words of Sennacherib, [R]which he has sent
to reproach the living God. Ps. 31:2 • 2 Kin. 19:4
17 "Truly, LORD, the kings of Assyria have
laid waste the nations and their lands,

18 “and have cast their gods into the fire;
for they *were* not gods, but [R]the work of
men’s hands—wood and stone. Therefore
they have destroyed them. [Acts 17:29]
19 “Now therefore, O LORD our God, I pray,
save us from his hand, [R]that all the kingdoms
of the earth may [R]know that You *are* the
LORD God, You alone.” Ps. 83:18 • 1 Kin. 8:42, 43
20 Then Isaiah the son of Amoz sent to
Hezekiah, saying, “Thus says the LORD God
of Israel: [R]‘*That* which you have prayed to Me
against Sennacherib king of Assyria [R]I have
heard.’ Is. 37:21 • 2 Kin. 20:5
21 “This *is* the word which the LORD has
spoken concerning him:

‘The virgin, [R]the daughter of Zion,
Has despised you, laughed you to scorn;
The daughter of Jerusalem Lam. 2:13
Has shaken *her* head behind your back!

22 ‘Whom have you reproached and
blasphemed?
Against whom have you raised *your*
voice,
And lifted up your eyes on high?
Against the Holy *One* of Israel.
23 [R]By your messengers you have
reproached the Lord, 2 Kin. 18:17
And said: [R]“By the multitude of my
chariots Ps. 20:7
I have come up to the height of the
mountains,
To the limits of Lebanon;
I will cut down its tall cedars
And its choice cypress trees;
I will enter the extremity of its borders,
To its fruitful forest.
24 I have dug and drunk strange water,
And with the soles of my feet I have
[R]dried up Is. 19:6
All the brooks of defense.”

25 ‘Did you not hear long ago
How [R]I made it, [Is. 45:7]
From ancient times that I formed it?
Now I have brought it to pass,
That [R]you should be Is. 10:5, 6
For crushing fortified cities *into* heaps
of ruins.
26 Therefore their inhabitants had little
power;
They were dismayed and confounded;
They were *as* the grass of the field
And the green herb,
As the grass on the housetops
And *grain* blighted before it is grown.

27 ‘But [R]I know your dwelling place,
Your going out and your coming in,
And your rage against Me. Ps. 139:1–3
28 Because your rage against Me and your
tumult
Have come up to My ears,
Therefore [R]I will put My hook in your
nose Ezek. 29:4; 38:4
And My bridle in your lips,
And I will turn you back
By the way which you came.

29 ‘This *shall be* a [R]sign to you:

You shall eat this year such as grows
[T]of itself,
And in the second year what springs
from the same;
Also in the third year sow and reap,
Plant vineyards and eat the fruit of
them. 2 Kin. 20:8, 9 • Without cultivation
30 [R]And the remnant who have escaped of
the house of Judah
Shall again take root downward,
And bear fruit upward. 2 Chr. 32:22, 23
31 For out of Jerusalem shall go a
remnant,
And those who escape from Mount
Zion.
[R]The zeal of the LORD *of hosts* shall do
this.’ Is. 9:7

32 “Therefore thus says the LORD concerning the king of Assyria:

‘He shall [R]not come into this city,
Nor shoot an arrow there, Is. 8:7–10
Nor come before it with shield,
Nor build a siege mound against it.
33 By the way that he came,
By the same shall he return;
And he shall not come into this city,’
Says the LORD.
34 ‘For I will [R]defend this city, to save it
For My own sake and [R]for My servant
David’s sake.’ ” Is. 31:5 • 1 Kin. 11:12, 13

35 And it came to pass on a certain night
that the [T]angel of the LORD went out, and
killed in the camp of the Assyrians one
hundred and eighty-five thousand; and when
[T]people arose early in the morning, there
were the corpses—all dead. Or *Angel* • Lit. *they*
36 So Sennacherib king of Assyria departed
and went away, returned *home*, and remained at [R]Nineveh. Gen. 10:11
37 Now it came to pass, as he was worshiping in the temple of Nisroch his god, that his
sons Adrammelech and Sharezer struck him
down with the sword; and they escaped into
the land of Ararat. Then [R]Esarhaddon his son
reigned in his place. Ezra 4:2

CHAPTER 20

Miraculous Recovery of Hezekiah
2 Chr. 32:24; Is. 38:1–8

IN [R]those days Hezekiah was sick and near
death. And Isaiah the prophet, the son of

Amoz, went to him and said to him, "Thus
says the LORD: 'Set your house in order, for
you shall die, and not live.' " Is. 38:1-22
2 Then he turned his face toward the wall,
and prayed to the LORD, saying,
3 "Remember now, O LORD, I pray, how I
have walked before You in truth and with a
loyal heart, and have done *what was* good in
Your sight." And Hezekiah wept bitterly.
4 Then it happened, before Isaiah had gone
out into the middle court, that the word of
the LORD came to him, saying,
5 "Return and tell Hezekiah the leader of
My people, 'Thus says the LORD, the God of
David your father: [R]"I have heard your
prayer, I have seen [R]your tears; surely I will
heal you. On the third day you shall go up to
the house of the LORD. Ps. 65:2 • Ps. 39:12; 56:8
6 "And I will add to your days fifteen
years. I will deliver you and this city from the
hand of the king of Assyria; and [R]I will
defend this city for My own sake, and for the
sake of My servant David." ' " 2 Kin. 19:34
7 Then [R]Isaiah said, "Take a lump of figs."
So they took and laid *it* on the boil, and he
recovered. Is. 38:21
8 And Hezekiah said to Isaiah, [R]"What *is*
the sign that the LORD will heal me, and that
I shall go up to the house of the LORD the
third day?" Judg. 6:17, 37, 39
9 Then Isaiah said, [R]"This is the sign to
you from the LORD, that the LORD will do the
thing which He has spoken: *shall* the shadow
go forward ten degrees or go backward ten
degrees?" Is. 38:7, 8
10 And Hezekiah answered, "It is an easy
thing for the shadow to go down ten [T]de-
grees; no, but let the shadow go backward
ten degrees." Lit. *steps*
11 So Isaiah the prophet cried out to the
LORD, and [R]He brought the shadow ten [T]de-
grees backward, by which it had gone down
on the sundial of Ahaz. Is. 38:8 • Lit. *steps*

Judah's Wealth Is Exposed to Babylon
Is. 39:1, 2

12 [R]At that time Berodach-Baladan the son
of Baladan, king of Babylon, sent letters and
a present to Hezekiah, for he heard that
Hezekiah had been sick. Is. 39:1-8
13 And Hezekiah was attentive to them,
and showed them all the house of his treasures—the silver and gold, the spices and
precious ointment, and *all* his armory—all
that was found among his treasures. There
was nothing in his house or in all his dominion that Hezekiah did not show them.

Babylonian Exile Is Prophesied
Is. 39:3-8

14 Then Isaiah the prophet went to King
Hezekiah, and said to him, "What did these
men say, and from where did they come to
you?" And Hezekiah said, "They came from a
far country, from Babylon."
15 And he said, "What have they seen in
your house?" So Hezekiah answered, [R]"They
have seen all that *is* in my house; there is
nothing among my treasures that I have not
shown them." 2 Kin. 20:13
16 Then Isaiah said to Hezekiah, "Hear the
word of the LORD:
17 'Behold, the days are coming when all
that *is* in your house, and what your fathers
have accumulated until this day, [R]shall be
carried to Babylon; nothing shall be left,' says
the LORD. Jer. 27:21, 22; 52:17
18 'And they shall take away some of your
sons who will [T]descend from you, whom you
will beget; and they shall be eunuchs in the
palace of the king of Babylon.' " *be born from*
19 Then Hezekiah said to Isaiah, [R]"The
word of the LORD which you have spoken *is*
good!" For he said, "Will there not be peace
and truth at least in my days?" 1 Sam. 3:18

Death of Hezekiah—2 Chr. 32:32, 33

20 Now the rest of the acts of Hezekiah—all
his might, and how he made a pool and a
[T]tunnel and [R]brought water into the city—*are*
they not written in the book of the chronicles
of the kings of Judah? *aqueduct* • 2 Chr. 32:3, 30
21 So Hezekiah rested with his fathers.
Then Manasseh his son reigned in his place.

CHAPTER 21

Spiritual Evaluation of Manasseh
2 Chr. 32:1-9

MANASSEH [R]*was* twelve years old when
he became king, and he reigned fifty-
five years in Jerusalem. His mother's name
was Hephzibah. 2 Chr. 33:1-9
2 And he did evil in the sight of the LORD,
[R]according to the abominations of the nations
whom the LORD had cast out before the
children of Israel. 2 Kin. 16:3
3 For he rebuilt the high places which
Hezekiah his father had destroyed; he raised
up altars for Baal, and made a wooden image,
as Ahab king of Israel had done; and he
[R]worshiped all [T]the host of heaven and served
them. [Deut. 4:19; 17:2-5] • The Assyrian gods
4 He also built altars in the house of the
LORD, of which the LORD had said, [R]"In
Jerusalem I will put My name." 1 Kin. 11:13
5 And he built altars for all the host of
heaven in the [R]two courts of the house of the
LORD. 1 Kin. 6:36; 7:12
6 [R]Also he made his son pass through the
fire, practiced [R]soothsaying, used witchcraft,
and consulted spiritists and mediums. He did
much evil in the sight of the LORD, to provoke
Him to anger. [Lev. 18:21; 20:2] • [Deut. 18:10-14]

7 He even set a carved image of Asherah that he had made, in the [T]house of which the LORD had said to David and to Solomon his son, "In this house and in Jerusalem, which I have chosen out of all the tribes of Israel, I will put My name forever; Temple

8 [R]"and I will not make the feet of Israel wander anymore from the land which I gave their fathers—only if they are careful to do according to all that I have commanded them, and according to all the law that My servant Moses commanded them." 2 Sam. 7:10

9 But they paid no attention, and Manasseh [R]seduced them to do more evil than the nations whom the LORD had destroyed before the children of Israel. [Prov. 29:12]

10 And the LORD spoke [R]by His servants the prophets, saying, 2 Kin. 17:13

11 "Because Manasseh king of Judah has done these abominations ([R]he has acted more wickedly than all the [R]Amorites who *were* before him, and [R]has also made Judah sin with his idols), 1 Kin. 21:26 • Gen. 15:16 • 2 Kin. 21:9

12 "therefore thus says the LORD God of Israel: 'Behold, *I* am bringing *such* calamity upon Jerusalem and Judah, that whoever hears of it, both [R]his ears will tingle. Jer. 19:3

13 'And I will stretch over Jerusalem [R]the measuring line of Samaria and the plummet of the house of Ahab; [R]I will wipe Jerusalem as *one* wipes a dish, wiping *it* and turning *it* upside down. Amos 7:7, 8 • 2 Kin. 22:16–19; 25:4–11

14 'So I will forsake the [R]remnant of My inheritance and deliver them into the hand of their enemies; and they shall become victims of plunder to all their enemies, Jer. 6:9

15 'because they have done evil in My sight, and have provoked Me to anger since the day their fathers came out of Egypt, even to this day.' "

Political Situation Under Manasseh

16 [R]Moreover Manasseh shed very much innocent blood, till he had filled Jerusalem from one end to another, besides his sin with which he made Judah sin, in doing evil in the sight of the LORD. 2 Kin. 24:4

Death of Manasseh

17 Now the rest of the acts of Manasseh—all that he did, and the sin that he committed—*are* they not written in the book of the chronicles of the kings of Judah?

18 So [R]Manasseh rested with his fathers, and was buried in the garden of his own house, in the garden of Uzza. Then his son Amon reigned in his place. 2 Chr. 33:20

The Reign of Amon in Judah—2 Chr. 33:21–25

19 Amon *was* twenty-two years old when he became king, and he reigned two years in Jerusalem. His mother's name *was* Meshullemeth the daughter of Haruz of Jotbah.

20 And he did evil in the sight of the LORD, as his father Manasseh had done.

21 So he walked in all the ways that his father had walked; and he served the idols that his father had served, and worshiped them.

22 He forsook the LORD God of his fathers, and did not walk in the way of the LORD.

23 [R]Then the servants of Amon [R]conspired against him, and killed the king in his own house. 2 Chr. 33:24, 25 • 2 Kin. 12:20; 14:19

24 But the people of the land [R]executed all those who had conspired against King Amon. Then the people of the land made his son Josiah king in his place. 2 Kin. 14:5

25 Now the rest of the acts of Amon which he did, *are* they not written in the book of the chronicles of the kings of Judah?

26 And he was buried in his tomb in the garden of Uzza. Then Josiah his son reigned in his place.

CHAPTER 22

Spiritual Evaluation of Josiah—2 Chr. 34:1, 2

JOSIAH *was* eight years old when he became king, and he reigned thirty-one years in Jerusalem. His mother's name *was* Jedidah the daughter of Adaiah of Bozkath.

2 And he did *what was* right in the sight of the LORD, and walked in all the ways of his father David; he [R]did not turn aside to the right hand or to the left. Deut. 5:32

The Temple Is Repaired—2 Chr. 34:8–13

3 Now it came to pass, in the eighteenth year of King Josiah, *that* the king sent Shaphan the scribe, the son of Azaliah, the son of Meshullam, to the house of the LORD, saying:

4 "Go up to Hilkiah the high priest, that he may count the money which has been [R]brought into the house of the LORD, which [R]the doorkeepers have gathered from the people. 2 Kin. 12:4 • 2 Kin. 12:9, 10

5 "And let them [R]deliver it into the hand of those doing the work, who are the overseers in the house of the LORD; let them give it to those who *are* in the house of the LORD doing the work, to repair the damages of the house— 2 Kin. 12:11–14

6 "to carpenters and builders and masons—and to buy timber and hewn stone to repair the house.

7 "However there need be no accounting made with them of the money delivered into their hand, because they deal faithfully."

The Book of the Law Is Discovered 2 Chr. 34:15–18

8 Then Hilkiah the high priest said to Shaphan the scribe, [R]"I have found the Book

of the Law in the house of the LORD." And
Hilkiah gave the book to Shaphan, and he
read it. Deut. 31:24-26
9 So Shaphan the scribe went to the king,
bringing the king word, saying, "Your servants have [T]gathered the money that was
found in the house, and have delivered it into
the hand of those who do the work, who
oversee the house of the LORD." Lit. *poured out*
10 Then Shaphan the scribe showed the
king, saying, "Hilkiah the priest has given me
a book." And Shaphan read it before the
king.

Repentance of Josiah—2 Chr. 34:19–22

11 Now it happened, when the king heard
the words of the Book of the Law, that he
tore his clothes.
12 Then the king commanded Hilkiah the
priest, [R]Ahikam the son of Shaphan, Achbor
the son of Michaiah, Shaphan the scribe, and
Asaiah a servant of the king, saying, Jer. 26:24
13 "Go, inquire of the LORD for me, for the
people and for all Judah, concerning the
words of this book that has been found; for
great *is* [R]the wrath of the LORD that is
aroused against us, because our fathers have
not obeyed the words of this book, to do
according to all that is written concerning
us." [Deut. 29:23-28; 31:17, 18]
14 So Hilkiah the priest, Ahikam, Achbor,
Shaphan, and Asaiah went to Huldah the
prophetess, the wife of Shallum the son of
Tikvah, the son of Harhas, keeper of the
wardrobe. (She dwelt in Jerusalem in the
Second Quarter.) And they spoke with her.

Prophecy of Blessing—2 Chr. 34:23–28

15 Then she said to them, "Thus says the
LORD God of Israel, 'Tell the man who sent
you to me,
16 "Thus says the LORD: 'Behold, [R]I will
bring calamity on this place and on its inhabitants—all the words of the book which the
king of Judah has read— Deut. 29:27
17 [R]'because they have forsaken Me and
burned incense to other gods, that they might
provoke Me to anger with all the works of
their hands. Therefore My wrath shall be
aroused against this place and shall not be
quenched.' "' Deut. 29:25-27
18 "But to [R]the king of Judah, who sent you
to inquire of the LORD, in this manner you
shall speak to him, 'Thus says the LORD God
of Israel: "*Concerning* the words which you
have heard— 2 Chr. 34:26
19 "because your heart was tender, and you
humbled yourself before the LORD when you
heard what I spoke against this place and
against its inhabitants, that they would become a desolation and [R]a curse, and you tore
your clothes and wept before Me, I also have
heard *you*," says the LORD. Jer. 26:6; 44:22
20 "Surely, therefore, I will gather you to
your fathers, and you shall be gathered to
your grave in peace; and your eyes shall not
see all the calamity which I will bring on this
place."'" So they brought word to the king.

CHAPTER 23

Institution of the Covenant—2 Chr. 34:29–32

THEN the king sent them to gather all the
elders of Judah and Jerusalem to him.
2 And the king went up to the house of the
LORD with all the men of Judah, and with him
all the inhabitants of Jerusalem—the priests
and the prophets and all the people, both
small and great; and he [R]read in their hearing
all the words of the Book of the Covenant
[R]which had been found in the house of the
LORD. Deut. 31:10-13 • 2 Kin. 22:8

3 Then the king [R]stood by a pillar and
made a [R]covenant before the LORD, to follow
the LORD and to keep His commandments
and His testimonies and His statutes, with all
his heart and all *his* soul, to perform the
words of this covenant that were written in
this book. And all the people took their stand
for the covenant. 2 Kin. 11:14 • 2 Kin. 11:17

Reforms Because of the Covenant
2 Chr. 34:33—35:19

4 And the king commanded Hilkiah the
high priest, the priests of the second order,

23:3 Knowing the Will of God Through the Scriptures—The best way to study a subject often begins with a definition of that subject. What do we mean by the will of God? It is that holy and stated purpose of the Father to make His dear children as much like Christ as possible.

Without doubt the most important factor in finding God's will is the Bible itself. God speaks to us not in some loud voice, but through the Scriptures. *First,* the Scriptures declare He does have a definite will for my life. "The steps of a *good* man are ordered by the LORD" (Page 646—Ps. 37:23). "I will instruct you *and teach you in the way you should go*" (Page 642—Ps. 32:8). See also Ephesians 2:10; Hebrews 12:1. *Second,* God desires us to know this will for our lives. "Therefore do not be unwise, but understand what the will of the Lord *is*" (Page 1391—Eph. 5:17). *Third,* this will is continuous. It does not begin when I am thirty years of age. God has a will for children, young people, adults, and senior citizens. See Isaiah 58:11. *Fourth,* God's will is specific. "Your ears shall hear a word behind you, saying, 'This *is* the way, walk in it'" (Page 802—Is. 30:21). "But the way of the upright *is* a highway" (Page 727—Prov. 15:19). *Fifth,* God's will is profitable (Page 252—Josh. 1:8; Page 625—Ps. 1:1–3).

and the doorkeepers, to bring out of the temple of the LORD all the articles that were made for Baal, for Asherah, and for all [T]the host of heaven; and he burned them outside Jerusalem in the fields of Kidron, and carried their ashes to Bethel. The gods of the Assyrians

5 Then he removed the idolatrous priests whom the kings of Judah had ordained to burn incense on the high places in the cities of Judah and in the places all around Jerusalem, and those who burned incense to Baal, to the sun, to the moon, to the [T]constellations, and to all the host of heaven. Zodiac

6 And he brought out the [T]wooden image from the house of the LORD, to the Brook Kidron outside Jerusalem, burned it at the Brook Kidron and ground *it* to ashes, and threw its ashes on [R]the graves of the common people. Or *Asherah*, a Canaanite goddess • 2 Chr. 34:4

7 Then he tore down the *ritual* [T]booths of the perverted persons that *were* in the house of the LORD, where the [R]women wove hangings for the wooden image. Lit. *houses* • Ex. 38:8

8 And he brought all the priests from the cities of Judah, and defiled the high places where the priests had burned incense, from [R]Geba to Beersheba; also he broke down the high places at the gates which *were* at the entrance of the Gate of Joshua the governor of the city, which *were* to the left of the city gate. Josh. 21:17

9 [R]Nevertheless the priests of the high places did not come up to the altar of the LORD in Jerusalem, but they ate unleavened bread among their brethren. [Ezek. 44:10–14]

10 And he defiled [R]Topheth, which *is* in the Valley of the [T]Son of Hinnom, that no man might make his son or his daughter pass through the fire to Molech. Is. 30:33 • Kt. *Sons*

11 Then he removed the horses that the kings of Judah had [T]dedicated to the sun, at the entrance to the house of the LORD, by the chamber of Nathan-Melech, the officer who *was* in the court; and he burned the chariots of the sun with fire. *given*

12 The altars that *were* [R]on the roof, the upper chamber of Ahaz, which the kings of Judah had made, and the altars which [R]Manasseh had made in the two courts of the house of the LORD, the king broke down and pulverized there, and threw their dust into the Brook Kidron. Jer. 19:13 • 2 Kin. 21:5

13 Then the king defiled the high places that *were* east of Jerusalem, which *were* on the [T]south of the [T]Mount of Corruption, which Solomon king of Israel had built for Ashtoreth the abomination of the Sidonians, for Chemosh the abomination of the Moabites, and for Milcom the abomination of the people of Ammon. Lit. *right of* • *Mount of Olives*

14 And he [R]broke in pieces the *sacred* pillars and cut down the wooden images, and filled their places with the bones of men. [Ex. 23:24]

15 Moreover the altar that *was* at Bethel, *and* the [T]high place [R]which Jeroboam the son of Nebat, who made Israel sin, had made, both that altar and the high place he broke down; and he burned the high place *and* crushed *it* to powder, and burned the wooden image. A place for pagan worship • 1 Kin. 12:28–33

16 As Josiah turned, he saw the tombs that *were* there on the mountain. And he sent and took the bones out of the tombs and burned *them* on the altar, and defiled it according to the word of the LORD which the man of God proclaimed, who proclaimed these words.

17 Then he said, "What gravestone *is* this that I see?"And the men of the city told him, "*It is* [R]the tomb of the man of God who came from Judah and proclaimed these things which you have done against the altar of Bethel." 1 Kin. 13:1, 30, 31

18 And he said, "Let him alone; let no one move his bones." So they let his bones alone, with the bones of [R]the prophet who came from Samaria. 1 Kin. 13:11, 31

19 Then Josiah also took away all the [T]shrines of the high places that *were* [R]in the cities of Samaria, which the kings of Israel had made to provoke *the LORD* to anger; and he did to them according to all the deeds he had done in Bethel. Lit. *houses* • 2 Chr. 34:6, 7

20 He executed all the priests of the [T]high places who *were* there, on the altars, and burned men's bones on them; and he returned to Jerusalem. Places for pagan worship

21 Then the king commanded all the people, saying, [R]"Keep the Passover to the LORD your God, [R]as *it is* written in this Book of the Covenant." 2 Chr. 35:1 • Deut. 16:2–8

22 Surely [R]such a Passover had never been held since the days of the judges who judged Israel, nor in all the days of the kings of Israel and the kings of Judah. 2 Chr. 35:18, 19

What is the will of God for us? As we have already noted, it differs from believer to believer. But here are four aspects in the will of God which apply to every Christian:

a. It is His will that we learn more about God (Page 1405—Col. 1:9).
b. It is His will that we grow in grace (Page 1416—1 Thess. 4:3).
c. It is His will that we study His Word (Page 1436—2 Tim. 3:14–17).
d. It is His will that we share our faith (Page 1272—Acts 1:8; Page 1426—1 Tim. 2:4; Page 1489—2 Pet. 3:9).

Now turn to Page 988—Dan. 9:3, 4: Knowing the Will of God Through Prayer and Fasting.

23 But in the eighteenth year of King Josiah this Passover was held before the LORD in Jerusalem.

24 Moreover Josiah put away those who consulted mediums and spiritists, the household gods and idols, all the abominations that were seen in the land of Judah and in Jerusalem, that he might perform the words of [R]the law which were written in the book [R]that Hilkiah the priest found in the house of the LORD. [Lev. 19:31; 20:27] • 2 Kin. 22:8

25 [R]Now before him there was no king like him, who turned to the LORD with all his heart, with all his soul, and with all his might, according to all the Law of Moses; nor after him did *any* arise like him. 2 Kin. 18:5

26 Nevertheless the LORD did not turn from the fierceness of His great wrath, with which His anger was aroused against Judah, [R]because of all the provocations with which Manasseh had provoked Him. Jer. 15:4

27 And the LORD said, "I will also remove Judah from My sight, as I have removed Israel, and will cast off this city Jerusalem which I have chosen, and the house of which I said, 'My name shall be there.' "

Political Situation Under Josiah
2 Chr. 35:20–23

28 Now the rest of the acts of Josiah, and all that he did, *are* they not written in the book of the chronicles of the kings of Judah?

29 In his days Pharaoh Necho king of Egypt went to the aid of the king of Assyria, to the River Euphrates; and King Josiah went against him. And Pharaoh Necho killed him at Megiddo when he confronted him.

Death of Josiah—2 Chr. 35:24—36:1

30 [R]Then his servants moved his body in a chariot from Megiddo, brought him to Jerusalem, and buried him in his own tomb. And [R]the people of the land took Jehoahaz the son of Josiah, anointed him, and made him king in his father's place. 2 Chr. 35:24 • 2 Chr. 36:1–4

The Reign of Jehoahaz in Judah
2 Chr. 36:2–4

31 [R]Jehoahaz *was* twenty-three years old when he became king, and he reigned three months in Jerusalem. His mother's name *was* [R]Hamutal the daughter of Jeremiah of Libnah. Jer. 22:11 • 2 Kin. 24:18

32 And he did evil in the sight of the LORD, according to all that his fathers had done.

33 Now Pharaoh Necho put him in prison [R]at Riblah in the land of Hamath, that he might not reign in Jerusalem; and he imposed on the land a tribute of one hundred talents of silver and a talent of gold. 2 Kin. 25:6

34 Then Pharaoh Necho made Eliakim the son of Josiah king in place of his father Josiah, and changed his name to Jehoiakim. And [T]Pharaoh took Jehoahaz and went to Egypt, and [T]he died there. Lit. *he* • *Jehoahaz*

The Reign of Jehoiakim in Judah
2 Chr. 36:5–8

35 So Jehoiakim gave [R]the silver and gold to Pharaoh; but he taxed the land to give money according to the commandment of Pharaoh; he exacted the silver and gold from the people of the land, from every one according to his assessment, to give *it* to Pharaoh Necho. 2 Kin. 23:33

36 Jehoiakim *was* twenty-five years old when he became king, and he reigned eleven years in Jerusalem. His mother's name *was* Zebudah the daughter of Pedaiah of Rumah.

37 And he did evil in the sight of the LORD, according to all that his fathers had done.

CHAPTER 24

IN [R]his days Nebuchadnezzar king of [R]Babylon came up, and Jehoiakim became his vassal *for* three years. Then he turned and rebelled against him. Dan. 1:1 • 2 Kin. 20:14

2 And the LORD sent against him *raiding* [T]bands of Chaldeans, bands of Syrians, bands of Moabites, and bands of the people of Ammon; He sent them against Judah to destroy it, [R]according to the word of the LORD which He had spoken by His servants the prophets. *troops* • 2 Kin. 20:17; 21:12–14; 23:27

3 Surely at the commandment of the LORD *this* came upon Judah, to remove *them* from His sight because of the sins of Manasseh, according to all that he had done,

4 [R]and also because of the innocent blood that he had shed; for he had filled Jerusalem with innocent blood, which the LORD would not pardon. 2 Kin. 21:16

5 Now the rest of the acts of Jehoiakim, and all that he did, *are* they not written in the book of the chronicles of the kings of Judah?

6 So Jehoiakim rested with his fathers. Then Jehoiachin his son reigned in his place.

7 And [R]the king of Egypt did not come out of his land anymore, for [R]the king of Babylon had taken all that belonged to the king of Egypt from the Brook of Egypt to the River Euphrates. Jer. 37:57 • Jer. 46:2

The Reign of Jehoiachin in Judah
2 Chr. 36:9, 10

8 [T]Jehoiachin *was* eighteen years old when he became king, and he reigned in Jerusalem three months. His mother's name *was* Nehushta the daughter of Elnathan of Jerusalem. *Jeconiah*, Jer. 24:1; or *Coniah*, Jer. 22:24, 28

9 And he did evil in the sight of the LORD, according to all that his father had done.

10 [R]At that time the servants of Nebuchadnezzar king of Babylon came up against Jerusalem, and the city was besieged. Dan. 1:1

11 And Nebuchadnezzar king of Babylon
came against the city, as his servants were
besieging it.
12 Then Jehoiachin king of Judah, his
mother, his servants, his princes, and his
officers went out to the king of Babylon; and
the king of Babylon, [R]in the eighth year of his
reign, took him prisoner. 2 Chr. 36:10
13 And he carried out from there all the
treasures of the house of the LORD and the
treasures of the king's house, and he cut in
pieces all the articles of gold which Solomon
king of Israel had made in the temple of the
LORD, [R]as the LORD had said. Jer. 20:5
14 Also he carried into captivity all Jerusalem: all the captains and all the mighty men
of valor, ten thousand captives, and all the
craftsmen and smiths. None remained except
[R]the poorest people of the land. 2 Kin. 25:12
15 And [R]he carried Jehoiachin captive to
Babylon. The king's mother, the king's wives,
his officers, and the mighty of the land he
carried into captivity from Jerusalem to
Babylon. Jer. 22:24–28
16 All the valiant men, seven thousand, and
craftsmen and smiths, one thousand, all *who
were* strong *and* fit for war, these the king of
Babylon brought captive to Babylon.

Spiritual Evaluation of Zedekiah
2 Chr. 36:10–16; Jer. 52:1, 2

17 Then the king of Babylon made Mattaniah, [T]Jehoiachin's uncle, king in his place,
and changed his name to Zedekiah. Lit. *his*
18 [R]Zedekiah *was* twenty-one years old
when he became king, and he reigned eleven
years in Jerusalem. His mother's name *was*
[R]Hamutal the daughter of Jeremiah of Libnah. Jer. 52:1 • 2 Kin. 23:31
19 He also did evil in the sight of the LORD,
according to all that Jehoiakim had done.

Political Situation Under Zedekiah
2 Chr. 36:17–20; Jer. 52:3–27

20 For because of the anger of the LORD *this*
happened in Jerusalem and Judah, that He
finally cast them out from His presence.
[R]Then Zedekiah rebelled against the king of
Babylon. Ezek. 17:15

CHAPTER 25

NOW it came to pass [R]in the ninth year of
his reign, in the tenth month, on the
tenth *day* of the month, *that* Nebuchadnezzar king of Babylon and all his army came
against Jerusalem and encamped against it;
and they built a siege wall against it all
around. Jer. 6:6; 34:2
2 So the city was besieged until the eleventh year of King Zedekiah.
3 By the ninth *day* of the [R]*fourth* month
the famine had become so severe in the city
that there was no food for the people of the
land. Lam. 4:9, 10
4 Then the city wall was broken through,
and all the men of war *fled* at night by way of
the gate between two walls, which was by
the king's garden, even though the Chaldeans *were* still encamped all around against
the city. And [R]*the king* went by way of the
[T]plain. Ezek. 12:12 • Or *Arabah,* The Jordan Valley
5 But the army of the Chaldeans pursued
the king, and they overtook him in the plains
of Jericho. All his army was scattered from
him.
6 So they took the king and brought him
up to the king of Babylon [R]at Riblah, and
they pronounced judgment on him. Jer. 52:9
7 Then they killed the sons of Zedekiah
before his eyes, [R]put[T] out the eyes of Zedekiah, bound him with bronze fetters, and
took him to Babylon. Jer. 39:7 • *blinded*
8 Now in the fifth month, [R]on the seventh
day of the month (which *was* [R]the nineteenth
year of King Nebuchadnezzar king of Babylon), [R]Nebuzaradan the captain of the
guard, a servant of the king of Babylon, came
to Jerusalem. Jer. 52:12 • 2 Kin. 24:12 • Jer. 39:9
9 [R]He burned the house of the LORD [R]and
the king's house; all the houses of Jerusalem,
that is, all the houses of the great *men,* [R]he
burned with fire. 2 Chr. 36:19 • Jer. 39:8 • Jer. 17:27
10 And all the army of the Chaldeans who
were with the captain of the guard broke
down the walls of Jerusalem all around.
11 Then Nebuzaradan the captain of the
guard carried away captive the rest of the
people *who* remained in the city and
the defectors who had deserted to the king of
Babylon, with the rest of the multitude.
12 But the captain of the guard [R]left *some* of
the poor of the land as vinedressers and
farmers. Jer. 39:10; 40:7; 52:16
13 The bronze pillars that *were* in the house
of the LORD, and the carts and [R]the bronze
Sea that *were* in the house of the
LORD, the Chaldeans broke in pieces, and
carried their bronze to Babylon. 1 Kin. 7:23
14 They also took away [R]the pots, the shovels, the trimmers, the spoons, and all the
bronze utensils with which the priests ministered. Ex. 27:3
15 The firepans and the basins, the things
made of solid gold and solid silver, the captain of the guard took away.
16 The two pillars, one Sea, and the carts,
which Solomon had made for the house of
the LORD, [R]the bronze of all these articles was
beyond measure. 1 Kin. 7:47
17 The height of one pillar *was* eighteen
cubits, and the capital on it *was* of bronze.
The height of the capital was three cubits,

and the network and pomegranates all
around the capital were all of bronze. The
second pillar was the same, with a network.
18 And the captain of the guard took Seraiah the chief priest, Zephaniah the second
priest, and the three doorkeepers.
19 He also took out of the city an officer
who had charge of the men of war, [R]five men
of the king's close associates who were found
in the city, the principal scribe of the army
who mustered the people of the land, and
sixty men of the people of the land *who were*
found in the city. Jer. 52:25
20 So Nebuzaradan, captain of the guard,
took these and brought them to the king of
Babylon at Riblah.
21 Then the king of Babylon struck them
and put them to death at Riblah in the land of
Hamath. [R]Thus Judah was carried away captive from its own land. Deut. 28:36, 64

The Governorship of Gedaliah
Jer. 40:5—41:18

22 Then he made Gedaliah the son of [R]Ahi-
kam, the son of Shaphan, governor over [R]the
people who remained in the land of Judah,
whom Nebuchadnezzar king of Babylon had
left. 2 Kin. 22:12 • Is. 1:9; Jer. 40:5
23 Now when all the [R]captains of the
armies, they and *their* men, heard that the
king of Babylon had made Gedaliah governor, they came to Gedaliah at Mizpah—
Ishmael the son of Nethaniah, Johanan the
son of Careah, Seraiah the son of Tanhumeth
the Netophathite, and Jaazaniah the son of a
Maachathite, they and their men. Jer. 40:7–9
24 And Gedaliah took an oath before them
and their men, and said to them, "Do not be
afraid of the servants of the Chaldeans. Dwell
in the land and serve the king of Babylon,
and it shall be well with you."
25 Now [R]it happened in the seventh month
that Ishmael the son of Nethaniah, the son of
Elishama, of the royal family, came with ten
men and struck and killed Gedaliah, the
Jews, and the Chaldeans who were with him
at Mizpah. Jer. 41:1–3
26 And all the people, small and great, and
the captains of the armies, arose and went to
Egypt; for they were afraid of the Chaldeans.

The Release of Jehoiachin in Babylon
Jer. 52:31–34

27 Now it came to pass in the thirty-seventh
year of the captivity of Jehoiachin king of
Judah, in the twelfth month, on the twenty-
seventh *day* of the month, *that* [T]Evil-
Merodach king of Babylon, in the year that
he began to reign, released Jehoiachin king of
Judah from prison. Lit. *The Man of Marduk*
28 He spoke kindly to him, and gave him a
more prominent seat than those of the kings
who *were* with him in Babylon.
29 So Jehoiachin changed from his prison
garments, and he [R]ate [T]bread regularly before
the king all the days of his life. 2 Sam. 9:7 • Food
30 And as for his provisions, *there was* a
regular ration given him by the king, a portion for each day, all the days of his life.

THE FIRST BOOK OF THE

CHRONICLES

THE BOOK OF FIRST CHRONICLES

The books of First and Second Chronicles cover the same period of Jewish history described in Second Samuel through Second Kings, but the perspective is different. These books are no mere repetition of the same material, but rather form a divine editorial on the history of God's people. While Second Samuel and First and Second Kings give a political history of Israel and Judah, First and Second Chronicles present a religious history of the Davidic dynasty of Judah. The former are written from a prophetic and moral viewpoint, and the latter from a priestly and spiritual perspective. The Book of First Chronicles begins with the royal line of David and then traces the spiritual significance of David's righteous reign.

The books of First and Second Chronicles were originally one continuous work in the Hebrew. The title was *Dibere Hayyamim,* meaning "The Words [accounts, events] of the Days." The equivalent meaning today would be "The Events of the Times." Chronicles was divided into two parts in the third-century B.C. Greek translation of the Hebrew Bible (the Septuagint). At that time it was given the name *Paraleipomenon,* "Of Things Omitted," referring to the things omitted from Samuel and Kings. Some copies add the phrase, *Basileon Iouda,* "Concerning the Kings of Judah." The first book of Chronicles was called *Paraleipomenon Primus,* "The First Book of Things Omitted." The name "Chronicles" comes from Jerome in his Latin Vulgate Bible (A.D. 385–405): *Chronicorum Liber.* He meant his title in the sense of "The Chronicles of the Whole of Sacred History."

THE AUTHOR OF FIRST CHRONICLES

Although the text does not identify the author, several facts seem to support the tradition in the Jewish Talmud that Ezra the priest was the author. The content points to a priestly authorship because of the emphasis on the temple, the priesthood, and the theocratic line of David in the southern kingdom of Judah. The narrative also indicates that Chronicles was at least written by a contemporary of Ezra. Chronicles is quite similar in style to the Book of Ezra, and both share a priestly perspective: genealogies, temple worship, ministry of the priesthood, and obedience to the law of God. In addition, the closing verses of Second Chronicles (36:22, 23) are repeated with minor changes as the opening verses of Ezra (1:1–3). Thus, Chronicles and Ezra may have been one consecutive history as were Luke and Acts.

Ezra was an educated scribe (Ezra 7:6), and according to the apocryphal book of Second Maccabees 2:13–15, Nehemiah collected an extensive library which was available to Ezra for his use in compiling Chronicles. Many of these documents and sources are listed in the book (see "The Author of Second Chronicles"). Scholars of Israel accumulated and compared historical material, and the author of Chronicles was actually a compiler who drew from many sources under the guidance and inspiration of the Holy Spirit.

THE TIME OF FIRST CHRONICLES

The genealogies in chapters 1—9 cover the time from Adam to David, and chapters 10—29 focus on the thirty-three years of David's rule over the united kingdoms of Israel and Judah (1004–971 B.C.). However, the genealogies extend to about 500 B.C., as seen in the mention of Zerubbabel, grandson of King Jeconiah, who leads the first return of the Jews from exile in 538 B.C., and also Zerubbabel's two grandsons Pelatiah and Jeshaiah (3:21).

Ezra probably completed Chronicles between 450 and 430 B.C. and addressed it to the returned remnant. Ezra leads some of the exiles to Jerusalem in 457 B.C. and ministers to the people as their spiritual leader. During Ezra's time, Nehemiah is the political leader and Malachi is the moral leader. Chronicles spends a disproportionate time on the reigns of David and Solomon because they bring the nation to its pinnacle. The book is written to the people of Israel's "Second Commonwealth" to encourage them and to remind them that they must remain the covenant people of God. This reminds the Jews of their spiritual heritage and identity during the difficult times they are facing.

THE CHRIST OF FIRST CHRONICLES

See the introductions to First and Second Samuel for descriptions of David as a type of Christ. The Davidic Covenant of Second Samuel 7 is found again in First Chronicles 7:11–14. Solomon fulfilled part, but the promise of the eternality of David's throne can only point to the coming of the Messiah.

The tribe of Judah is placed first in the national genealogy in First Chronicles because the monarchy, temple, and Messiah (Gen. 49:10) will come from this tribe. Since the books of Chronicles are the last books of the Hebrew Bible, the genealogies in chapters 1—9 are a preamble to the genealogy of Christ in the first book of the New Testament.

KEYS TO FIRST CHRONICLES

Key Verses: First Chronicles 17:11–14; 29:11—"And it shall be, when your days are fulfilled, when you must go *to be* with your fathers, that I will set up your seed after you, who will be of your sons; and I will establish his kingdom. He shall build Me a house, and I will establish his throne forever. I will be his Father, and he shall be My son; and I will not take My mercy away from him, as I took *it* from *him* who was before you. And I will establish him in My house and in My kingdom forever; and his throne shall be established forever" (17:11–14).

"Yours, O LORD, *is* the greatness, the power and the glory, the victory and the majesty; for all *that is* in heaven and in earth *is Yours;* Yours *is* the kingdom, O LORD, and You are exalted as head over all" (29:11).

Key Chapter: First Chronicles 17—Pivotal for the Book of First Chronicles as well as for the rest of the Scriptures is the Davidic Covenant recorded in Second Samuel 7 and First Chronicles 17. God promises David that He will "establish him [David's ultimate offspring, Jesus Christ] in My house and in My kingdom forever; and his throne shall be established forever" (1 Chr. 17:14).

SURVEY OF FIRST CHRONICLES

Chronicles retraces the whole story of Israel's history up to the return from captivity in order to give the returned remnant a divine perspective on the developments of their past. The whole Book of First Chronicles, like Second Samuel, is dedicated to the life of David. It begins with the royal line of David (1—9) before surveying key events of the reign of David (10—29).

Royal Line of David (1—9): These nine chapters are the most comprehensive genealogical tables in the Bible. They trace the family tree of David and Israel as a whole, but in a highly selective manner. The genealogies place a disproportionate emphasis on the tribes of Judah and Benjamin because Chronicles is not concerned with the northern kingdom but with the southern kingdom and the Davidic dynasty. They show God at work in selecting and preserving a people for Himself from the beginning of human history to the period after the Babylonian exile. The genealogies move from the patriarchal period (Adam to Jacob; 1:1—2:2) to the national period (Judah, Levi, and the other tribes of Israel; 2:3—9:44). They demonstrate God's keeping of His covenant promises in maintaining the Davidic line through the centuries. The priestly perspective of Chronicles is evident in the special attention given to the tribe of Levi.

Reign of David (10—29): Compared with Second Samuel, David's life in First Chronicles is seen in an entirely different light. This is clear from both the omissions and the additions. Chronicles completely omits David's struggles with Saul, his seven-year reign in Hebron, his various wives, and Absalom's rebellion. It also omits the event in Second Samuel that hurt the rest of his life—his sin with Bathsheba. Chronicles is written from a more positive perspective, emphasizing God's grace and forgiveness, in order to encourage the Jews who have just returned from captivity. Chronicles adds events not found in Second Samuel, such as David's preparations for the temple and its worship services.

Only one chapter is given to Saul's reign (10), because his heart was not right with God. David's story begins with his coronation over all Israel after he has already reigned for seven years as king over Judah. Chronicles stresses his deep

FOCUS	ROYAL LINE OF DAVID	REIGN OF DAVID				
REFERENCE	1:1—	10:1—	13:1—	18:1—	21:1—	28:1—29:30
DIVISION	GENEALOGIES OF DAVID AND ISRAEL	ACCESSION OF DAVID AS KING	ACQUISITION OF THE ARK	VICTORIES OF DAVID	PREPARATION FOR THE TEMPLE	LAST DAYS OF DAVID
TOPIC	GENEALOGY	HISTORY				
	ANCESTRY	ACTIVITY				
LOCATION	ISRAEL					
TIME	THOUSANDS OF YEARS	c. 33 YEARS				

spiritual commitment, courage, and integrity. It emphasizes his concern for the things of the Lord, including his return of the ark and his desire to build a temple for God. God establishes His crucial covenant with David (17), and the kingdom is strengthened and expanded under his reign (18—20). His sin in numbering the people is recorded to teach the consequences of disobeying God's law. Most of the rest of the book (22—29) is concerned with David's preparations for the building of the temple and the worship associated with it. The priestly perspective of Chronicles can be seen in the disproportionate space given to the temple and the priests. David is not allowed to build the temple (28:3), but he designs the plans, gathers the materials, prepares the site, and arranges for the Levites, priests, choirs, porters, soldiers, and stewards. The book closes with his beautiful public prayer of praise and the accession of Solomon.

OUTLINE OF FIRST CHRONICLES

Part One: The Royal Line of David (1:1—9:44)

I. The Genealogy from Adam to Abraham 1:1–27

A. The Genealogy from Adam to Noah ... 1:1–4
B. The Genealogy from Noah to Abraham 1:5–27
1. Sons of Japheth ... 1:5–7
2. Sons of Ham ... 1:8–16
3. Sons of Shem ... 1:17–27

II. The Genealogy from Abraham to Jacob 1:28–54

A. The Genealogy from Abraham to Isaac ... 1:28–34
B. The Genealogy from Isaac to Jacob 1:35–54
1. Sons of Esau ... 1:35–42
2. Kings of Edom ... 1:43–50
3. Chiefs of Edom ... 1:51–54

III. The Genealogy from Jacob to David ... 2:1–55

A. The Genealogy of the Sons of Jacob ... 2:1, 2
B. The Genealogy of the Sons of Judah 2:3–55

IV. The Genealogy from David to the Captivity ... 3:1–24

A. The Genealogy of the Sons of David ... 3:1–9
B. The Genealogy of the Sons of Solomon ... 3:10–24

V. The Genealogies of the Twelve Tribes 4:1—8:40

A. The Genealogy of Judah ... 4:1–23
B. The Genealogy of Simeon ... 4:24–43
C. The Genealogy of Reuben ... 5:1–10
D. The Genealogy of Gad ... 5:11–22
E. The Genealogy of Manasseh ... 5:23–26
F. The Genealogy of Levi ... 6:1–81
1. The High Priestly Line ... 6:1–15
2. The Levitical Line ... 6:16–30
3. The Musicians' Guild ... 6:31–48
4. The Generations of Aaron ... 6:49–53
5. Cities of the Priests and Levites .. 6:54–81
G. The Genealogy of Issachar ... 7:1–5
H. The Genealogy of Benjamin ... 7:6–12
I. The Genealogy of Naphtali ... 7:13
J. The Genealogy of Manasseh ... 7:14–19
K. The Genealogy of Ephraim ... 7:20–29
L. The Genealogy of Asher ... 7:30–40
M. The Genealogy of Benjamin ... 8:1–40

VI. The Genealogy of the Remnant ... 9:1–34

A. The Genealogy of the Twelve Tribes Who Returned ... 9:1–9
B. The Genealogy of the Priests Who Returned ... 9:10–13
C. The Genealogy of the Levites Who Returned ... 9:14–34

VII. The Genealogy of Saul ... 9:35–44

Part Two: The Reign of David (10:1—29:30)

I. The Accession of David ... 10:1—12:40

A. Death of Saul ... 10:1–14
1. The House of Saul Dies in Battle 10:1–7
2. The Philistines Defile Saul ... 10:8–12
3. The Cause of Saul's Death ... 10:13, 14
B. Anointing of David as King ... 11:1–3
C. Conquest of Jerusalem ... 11:4–9
D. Account of David's Mighty Men 11:10—12:40
1. The Chiefs ... 11:10–14
2. The Thirty Chief Men ... 11:15–25
3. The Mighty Warriors ... 11:26–47
4. The Mighty Men at Ziklag ... 12:1–22
5. The Mighty Men at Hebron ... 12:23–40

II. The Acquisition of the Ark of the Covenant ... 13:1—17:27

A. Improper Transportation of the Ark 13:1–14
1. Preparation to Move the Ark ... 13:1–5
2. Uzza Dies for Touching the Ark 13:6–14
B. Prosperity of David's Reign ... 14:1–17
1. David's House Is Constructed ... 14:1, 2
2. David's Children in Jerusalem ... 14:3–7
3. David's Victory over the Philistines ... 14:8–17
C. Proper Transportation of the Ark ... 15:1–29
1. Spiritual Preparation to Move the Ark ... 15:1–24
2. Joyful Transportation of the Ark 15:25–29
D. Celebration at the Ark in Jerusalem 16:1–43
1. Offering of Sacrifices ... 16:1–3
2. Appointing Musicians ... 16:4–6
3. Praise Psalm of David ... 16:7–36
4. Constant Ministry at the Ark ... 16:37–43
E. Institution of the Davidic Covenant 17:1–27

CHAPTER 1

The Genealogy from Adam to Noah
Gen. 5:1–32; Luke 3:36–38

ADAM, [R]Seth, Enosh, Gen. 4:25, 26; 5:3–9
2 [T]Cainan, Mahalaleel, Jared, Heb. *Qenan*
3 Enoch, Methuselah, Lamech,
4 Noah, Shem, Ham, and Japheth.

Sons of Japheth—Gen. 10:2–5

5 [R]The sons of Japheth *were* Gomer, Magog, Madai, Javan, Tubal, Meshech, and
Tiras. Gen. 10:2–4
6 The sons of Gomer *were* Ashkenaz, [T]Di-
phath, and Togarmah. *Riphath*, Gen. 10:3
7 The sons of Javan *were* Elishah, Tar-
shishah, Kittim, and [R]Rodanim. Gen. 10:4

Sons of Ham—Gen. 10:6–18

8 [R]The sons of Ham *were* Cush, Mizraim,
Put, and Canaan. Gen. 10:6
9 The sons of Cush *were* Seba, Havilah,
Sabta, [R]Raama, and Sabtecha. The sons of
Raama *were* Sheba and Dedan. Gen. 10:7
10 Cush [R]begot Nimrod; he began to be a
mighty one on the earth. Gen. 10:8–10, 13
11 Mizraim begot Ludim, Anamim, Leha-
bim, Naphtuhim,
12 Pathrusim, Casluhim (from whom came
the Philistines and the [R]Caphtorim). Deut. 2:23
13 [R]Canaan begot Sidon, his firstborn, and
Heth; Gen. 9:18, 25–27; 10:15
14 the Jebusite, the Amorite, and the Girga-
shite;
15 the Hivite, the Arkite, and the Sinite;
16 the Arvadite, the Zemarite, and the Ha-
mathite.

Sons of Shem
Gen. 10:21–29; 11:10–26; Luke 3:34–36

17 The sons of Shem *were* Elam, Asshur,
[R]Arphaxad, Lud, Aram, Uz, Hul, Gether, and
[T]Meshech. Luke 3:36 • *Mash*, Gen. 10:23

18 Arphaxad begot Shelah, and Shelah begot Eber.

19 To Eber were born two sons: the name of one *was* Peleg, for in his days the earth was divided; and his brother's name *was* Joktan.

20 [R]Joktan begot Almodad, Sheleph, Hazarmaveth, Jerah, Gen. 10:26

21 Hadoram, Uzal, Diklah,

22 [T]Ebal, Abimael, Sheba, *Obal*, Gen. 10:28

23 Ophir, Havilah, and Jobab. All these *were* the sons of Joktan.

24 [R]Shem, Arphaxad, Shelah, Luke 3:34–36

25 [R]Eber, Peleg, Reu, Gen. 11:15

26 Serug, Nahor, Terah,

27 and [R]Abram, who *is* Abraham. Gen. 17:5

The Genealogy from Abraham to Isaac
Gen. 25:1–4, 12–16

28 [R]The sons of Abraham *were* [R]Isaac and [R]Ishmael. Gen. 21:2, 3 • Gen. 21:2 • Gen. 16:11, 15

29 These *are* their genealogies: The [R]firstborn of Ishmael *was* Nebajoth; then Kedar, Adbeel, Mibsam, Gen. 25:13–16

30 Mishma, Dumah, Massa, Hadad, Tema,

31 Jetur, Naphish, and Kedemah. These *were* the sons of Ishmael.

32 Now [R]the sons born to Keturah, Abraham's concubine, *were* Zimran, Jokshan, Medan, Midian, Ishbak, and Shuah. The sons of Jokshan *were* Sheba and Dedan. Gen. 25:1–4

33 The sons of Midian *were* Ephah, Epher, Hanoch, Abida, and Eldaah. All these were the children of Keturah.

34 And [R]Abraham begot Isaac. The sons of Isaac *were* Esau and Israel. Gen. 21:2

Sons of Esau—Gen. 36:1–30

35 The sons of [R]Esau *were* Eliphaz, Reuel, Jeush, Jaalam, and Korah. Gen. 36:10–19

36 And the sons of Eliphaz *were* Teman, Omar, [T]Zephi, Gatam, *and* Kenaz; and *by* [R]Timna, Amalek. *Zepho*, Gen. 36:11 • Gen. 36:12

37 The sons of Reuel *were* Nahath, Zerah, Shammah, and Mizzah.

38 The sons of Seir *were* Lotan, Shobal, Zibeon, Anah, Dishon, Ezer, and Dishan.

39 And the sons of Lotan *were* Hori and Homam; Lotan's sister *was* Timna.

40 The sons of Shobal *were* [T]Alian, Manahath, Ebal, Shephi, and Onam. The sons of Zibeon *were* Ajah and Anah. *Alvan*, Gen. 36:23

41 The son of Anah *was* [R]Dishon. The sons of Dishon *were* [T]Hamran, Eshban, Ithran, and Cheran. Gen. 36:25 • *Hemdan*, Gen. 36:26

42 The sons of Ezer *were* Bilhan, Zaavan, *and* [T]Jaakan. The sons of Dishan *were* Uz and Aran. *Akan*, Gen. 36:27

Kings of Edom

43 Now these *were* the kings who reigned in the land of Edom before *any* king reigned over the children of Israel: Bela the son of Beor, and the name of his city was Dinhabah.

44 And when Bela died, Jobab the son of Zerah of Bozrah reigned in his place.

45 When Jobab died, Husham of the land of the Temanites reigned in his place.

46 And when Husham died, Hadad the son of Bedad, who [T]attacked Midian in the field of Moab, reigned in his place. The name of his city *was* Avith. Lit. *struck*

47 When Hadad died, Samlah of Masrekah reigned in his place.

48 And when Samlah died, Saul of Rehoboth-by-the-River reigned in his place.

49 When Saul died, Baal-Hanan the son of Achbor reigned in his place.

50 And when Baal-Hanan died, [T]Hadad reigned in his place; and the name of his city was [T]Pai. His wife's name was Mehetabel the daughter of Matred, the daughter of Mezahab. *Hadar*, Gen. 36:39 • *Pau*, Gen. 36:39

Chiefs of Edom

51 Hadad died also. And the chiefs of Edom were Chief Timnah, Chief [T]Aliah, Chief Jetheth, *Alvah*, Gen. 36:40

52 Chief Aholibamah, Chief Elah, Chief Pinon,

53 Chief Kenaz, Chief Teman, Chief Mibzar,

54 Chief Magdiel, and Chief Iram. These *were* the chiefs of Edom.

CHAPTER 2

The Genealogy of the Sons of Jacob
Gen. 29:31—30:24; 35:16–18

THESE *were* the sons of Israel: Reuben, Simeon, Levi, Judah, Issachar, Zebulun,

2 Dan, Joseph, Benjamin, Naphtali, Gad, and Asher.

The Genealogy of the Sons of Judah
Gen. 46:12; Ruth 4:18–22; Matt. 1:3–6; Luke 3:31–33

3 The sons of Judah *were* Er, Onan, and Shelah. *These* three were born to him by the daughter of Shua, the Canaanitess. [R]Er, the firstborn of Judah, was wicked in the sight of the LORD; and He killed him. Gen. 38:7

4 And [R]Tamar, his daughter-in-law, [R]bore him Perez and Zerah. All the sons of Judah *were* five. Gen. 38:6 • Matt. 1:3

5 The sons of [R]Perez *were* Hezron and Hamul. Ruth 4:18

6 The sons of Zerah *were* [T]Zimri, [R]Ethan, Heman, Calcol, and [T]Dara—five of them in all. *Zabdi*, Josh. 7:1 • 1 Kin. 4:31 • *Darda*, 1 Kin. 4:31

7 The son of Carmi *was* [T]Achar, the troubler of Israel, who transgressed in the [T]accursed thing. *Achan*, Josh. 7:1 • *banned* or *devoted*

8 The son of Ethan *was* Azariah.

9 Also the sons of Hezron who were born to him *were* Jerahmeel, Ram, and Chelubai.

10 Ram [R]begot Amminadab, and Amminadab begot Nahshon, [R]leader of the children of Judah; Matt. 1:4 • Num. 1:7; 2:3

11 Nahshon begot [T]Salma, and Salma begot Boaz; *Salmon*, Ruth 4:21; Luke 3:32

12 Boaz begot Obed, and Obed begot Jesse;

13 [R]Jesse begot Eliab his firstborn, Abinadab the second, Shimea the third, 1 Sam. 16:6

14 Nethanel the fourth, Raddai the fifth,

15 Ozem the sixth, *and* David the seventh.

16 Now their sisters *were* Zeruiah and Abigail. [R]And the sons of Zeruiah *were* Abishai, Joab, and Asahel—three. 2 Sam. 2:18

17 Abigail bore Amasa; and the father of Amasa *was* Jether the Ishmaelite.

18 Caleb the son of Hezron begot *children* by Azubah, *his* wife, and by Jerioth. Now these were her sons: Jesher, Shobab, and Ardon.

19 When Azubah died, Caleb took Ephrath as his wife, who bore him Hur.

20 And Hur begot Uri, and Uri begot [R]Bezaleel. Ex. 31:2; 38:22

21 Now afterward Hezron went in to the daughter of [R]Machir the father of Gilead, whom he married when he *was* sixty years old; and she bore him Segub. Num. 27:1

22 Segub begot [R]Jair, who had twenty-three cities in the land of Gilead. Judg. 10:3

23 [R](Geshur and Syria took from them the towns of Jair, with Kenath and its towns—sixty towns.) All these *belonged to* the sons of Machir the father of Gilead. Deut. 3:14

24 After Hezron died in Caleb Ephrathah, Hezron's wife Abijah bore him [R]Ashhur the father of Tekoa. 1 Chr. 4:5

25 The sons of Jerahmeel, the firstborn of Hezron, *were* Ram, the firstborn, and Bunah, Oren, Ozem, *and* Ahijah.

26 Jerahmeel had another wife, whose name was Atarah; she was the mother of Onam.

27 The sons of Ram, the firstborn of Jerahmeel, were Maaz, Jamin, and Eker.

28 The sons of Onam were Shammai and Jada. The sons of Shammai *were* Nadab and Abishur.

29 And the name of the wife of Abishur *was* Abihail, and she bore him Ahban and Molid.

30 The sons of Nadab *were* Seled and Appaim; Seled died without children.

31 The son of Appaim *was* Ishi, the son of Ishi *was* Sheshan, and [R]Sheshan's child *was* Ahlai. 1 Chr. 2:34, 35

32 The sons of Jada, the brother of Shammai, *were* Jether and Jonathan; Jether died without children.

33 The sons of Jonathan *were* Peleth and Zaza. These were the sons of Jerahmeel.

34 Now Sheshan had no sons, only daughters. And Sheshan had an Egyptian servant whose name *was* Jarha.

35 Sheshan gave his daughter to Jarha his servant as wife, and she bore him Attai.

36 Attai begot Nathan, and Nathan begot [R]Zabad; 1 Chr. 11:41

37 Zabad begot Ephlal, and Ephlal begot [R]Obed; 2 Chr. 23:1

38 Obed begot Jehu, and Jehu begot Azariah;

39 Azariah begot Helez, and Helez begot Eleasah;

40 Eleasah begot Sismai, and Sismai begot Shallum;

41 Shallum begot Jekamiah, and Jekamiah begot Elishama.

42 The descendants of Caleb the brother of Jerahmeel *were* Mesha, his firstborn, who was the father of Ziph, and the sons of Mareshah the father of Hebron.

43 The sons of Hebron *were* Korah, Tappuah, Rekem, and Shema.

44 Shema begot Raham the father of Jorkoam, and Rekem begot Shammai.

45 And the son of Shammai *was* Maon, and Maon *was* the father of Beth Zur.

46 Ephah, Caleb's concubine, bore Haran, Moza, and Gazez; and Haran begot Gazez.

47 And the sons of Jahdai *were* Regem, Jotham, Geshan, Pelet, Ephah, and Shaaph.

48 Maachah, Caleb's concubine, bore Sheber and Tirhanah.

49 She also bore Shaaph the father of Madmannah, Sheva the father of Machbenah and the father of Gibea; and the daughter of Caleb *was* [R]Achsah.[T] Josh. 15:17 • Or *Achsa*

50 These were the descendants of Caleb: The sons of Hur, the firstborn of Ephrathah, *were* Shobal the father of Kirjath Jearim,

51 Salma the father of Bethlehem, *and* Hareph the father of Beth Gader.

52 And Shobal the father of Kirjath Jearim had descendants: Haroeh, *and* half of the [T]families of Manuhoth. Same as *Manahethites*, v. 54

53 The families of Kirjath Jearim *were* the Ithrites, the Puthites, the Shumathites, and the Mishraites. From these came the Zorathites and the Eshtaolites.

54 The sons of Salma *were* Bethlehem, the Netophathites, Atroth Beth Joab, half of the Manahethites, and the Zorites.

55 And the families of the scribes who dwelt at Jabez *were* the Tirathites, the Shimeathites, *and* the Suchathites. These *were* the [R]Kenites who came from Hammath, the father of the house of [R]Rechab. Judg. 1:16 • Jer. 35:2

CHAPTER 3

The Genealogy of the Sons of David

NOW these were the sons of David who were born to him in Hebron: The firstborn *was* Amnon, by Ahinoam the Jezreel-

itess; the second, [T]Daniel, by [R]Abigail the
Carmelitess; *Chileab,* 2 Sam. 3:3 • 1 Sam. 25:39–42
2 the third, Absalom the son of Maacah,
the daughter of Talmai, king of Geshur; the
fourth, Adonijah the son of Haggith;
3 the fifth, Shephatiah, by Abital; the sixth,
Ithream, by his wife [R]Eglah. 2 Sam. 3:5
4 *These* six were born to him in Hebron.
[R]There he reigned seven years and six
months, and [R]in Jerusalem he reigned thirty-
three years. 2 Sam. 2:11 • 2 Sam. 5:5
5 And these were born to him in Jerusalem: [T]Shimea, Shobab, Nathan, and Solomon—four by Bathshua the daughter of
[T]Ammiel. *Shammua,* 1 Chr. 14:4 • *Eliam,* 2 Sam. 11:3
6 Also *there* were Ibhar, [T]Elishama, [T]Eliph-
elet, *Elishua,* 1 Chr. 14:5; 2 Sam. 5:15 • *Elpelet,* 1 Chr. 14:5
7 Nogah, Nepheg, Japhia,
8 Elishama, [T]Eliada, and Eliphelet—[R]nine
in all. *Beeliada,* 1 Chr. 14:7 • 2 Sam. 5:14–16
9 *These were* all the sons of David, besides
the sons of the concubines, and [R]Tamar their
sister. 2 Sam. 13:1

The Genealogy of the Sons of Solomon
Matt. 1:7–12

10 Solomon's son *was* [R]Rehoboam; [T]Abijah
was his son, Asa his son, Jehoshaphat his
son, 1 Kin. 11:43 • *Abijam,* 1 Kin. 15:1
11 [T]Joram his son, Ahaziah his son, [T]Joash
his son, *Jehoram,* 2 Kin. 1:17; 8:16 • *Jehoash,* 2 Kin. 12:1
12 Amaziah his son, [T]Azariah his son, Jo-
tham his son, *Uzziah,* Is. 6:1
13 Ahaz his son, Hezekiah his son, Manasseh his son,
14 Amon his son, *and* Josiah his son.
15 The sons of Josiah *were* Johanan the
firstborn, the second Jehoiakim, the third
Zedekiah, and the fourth Shallum.
16 The sons of Jehoiakim *were* Jeconiah his
son *and* [T]Zedekiah his son. *Mattaniah,* 2 Kin. 24:17
17 And the sons of Jeconiah [T]*were* Assir,
Shealtiel his son, Or *the captive were*
18 *and* Malchiram, Pedaiah, Shenazzar, Jecamiah, Hoshama, and Nedabiah.
19 The sons of Pedaiah *were* Zerubbabel
and Shimei. The sons of Zerubbabel *were*
Meshullam, Hananiah, Shelomith their sister,
20 and Hashubah, Ohel, Berechiah, Hasadiah, and Jushab-Hesed—five *in all.*
21 The sons of Hananiah *were* Pelatiah and
Jeshaiah, the sons of Rephaiah, the sons of
Arnan, the sons of Obadiah, and the sons of
Shechaniah.
22 The son of Shechaniah was Shemaiah.
The sons of Shemaiah *were* Hattush, Igal,
Bariah, Neariah, and Shaphat—six *in all.*
23 The sons of Neariah *were* Elioenai, Hezekiah, and Azrikam—three *in all.*
24 The sons of Elioenai *were* Hodaviah,
Eliashib, Pelaiah, Akkub, Johanan, Delaiah,
and Anani—seven *in all.*

CHAPTER 4

The Genealogy of Judah

THE sons of Judah *were* [R]Perez, Hezron,
Carmi, Hur, and Shobal. Gen. 38:29; 46:12
2 And Reaiah the son of Shobal begot
Jahath, and Jahath begot Ahumai and Lahad.
These *were* the families of the Zorathites.
3 These *were* the sons *of the father* of
Etam: Jezreel, Ishma, and Idbash; and the
name of their sister *was* Hazelelponi;
4 and Penuel *was* the father of Gedor, and
Ezer *was the* father of Hushah. These *were*
the sons of [R]Hur, the firstborn of Ephrathah
the father of Bethlehem. 1 Chr. 2:50
5 And [R]Ashhur the father of Tekoa had
two wives, Helah and Naarah. 1 Chr. 2:24
6 Naarah bore him Ahuzzam, Hepher,
Temeni, and Haahashtari. These *were* the
sons of Naarah.
7 The sons of Helah *were* Zereth, Zohar,
and Ethnan;
8 and Koz begot Anub, Zobebah, and the
families of Aharhel the son of Harum.
9 Now Jabez was more honorable than his
brothers, and his mother called his name
Jabez, saying, "Because I bore *him* in pain."
10 And Jabez called on the God of Israel
saying, "Oh, that You would bless me indeed,
and enlarge my [T]territory, that Your hand
would be with me, and that You would keep
me from evil, that I may not cause pain!" So
God granted him what he requested. *border*
11 Chelub the brother of Shuhah begot
Mehir, who *was* the father of Eshton.
12 And Eshton begot Beth-Rapha, Paseah,
and Tehinnah the father of [T]Ir-Nahash. These
were the men of Rechah. *City of Nahash*
13 The sons of Kenaz *were* Othniel and
Seraiah. The sons of Othniel *were* Hathath,
14 and Meonothai who begot Ophrah. Seraiah begot Joab the father of [T]Ge Harashim,
for they were craftsmen. Lit. *Valley of Craftsmen*
15 The sons of [R]Caleb the son of Jephunneh
were Iru, Elah, and Naam. The son of Elah
was [T]Kenaz. 1 Chr. 6:56 • Or *Uknaz*
16 The sons of Jahaleleel *were* Ziph,
Ziphah, Tiria, and Asarel.
17 The sons of Ezrah *were* Jether, Mered,
Epher, and Jalon. And [T]Mered's wife *bore*
Miriam, Shammai, and Ishbah the father of
Eshtemoa. Lit. *she*
18 ([T]His wife Jehudijah bore Jered the father of Gedor, Heber the father of Sochoh,
and Jekuthiel the father of Zanoah.) And
these were the sons of Bithiah the daughter
of Pharaoh, whom Mered took. Or *His Judean wife*
19 The sons of Hodiah's wife, the sister of
Naham, *were* the fathers of Keilah the Garmite and of Eshtemoa the Maachathite.
20 And the sons of Shimon *were* Amnon,

Rinnah, Ben-Hanan, and Tilon. And the sons
of Ishi *were* Zoheth and Ben-Zoheth.
21 The sons of [R]Shelah [R]the son of Judah
were Er the father of Lecah, Laadah the
father of Mareshah, and the families of the
house of the linen workers of the house of
Ashbea; Gen. 38:11, 14 • Gen. 38:1–5; 46:12
22 also Jokim, the men of Chozeba, and
Joash; Saraph, who ruled in Moab, and
Jashubi-Lehem. Now the records are ancient.
23 These *were* the potters and those who
dwell at Netaim and [T]Gederah; there they
dwelt with the king for his work. Lit. *Hedges*

The Genealogy of Simeon—Gen. 46:10

24 The [R]sons of Simeon *were* Nemuel, Jamin, Jarib, Zerah, *and* Shaul, Num. 26:12–14
25 Shallum his son, Mibsam his son, and
Mishma his son.
26 And the sons of Mishma *were* Hamuel
his son, Zacchur his son, and Shimei his son.
27 Shimei had sixteen sons and six daughters; but his brothers did not have many
children, [R]nor did any of their families multiply as much as the children of Judah. Num. 2:9
28 They dwelt at Beersheba, Moladah,
Hazar Shual,
29 [T]Bilhah, Ezem, Tolad, *Balah,* Josh. 19:3
30 Bethuel, Hormah, Ziklag,
31 Beth Marcaboth, [T]Hazar Susim, Beth
Biri, and at Shaaraim. These *were* their cities
until the reign of David. *Hazar Susah,* Josh. 19:5
32 And their villages *were* Etam, Ain, Rimmon, Tochen, and Ashan—five cities—
33 and all the villages that *were* around
these cities as far as [T]Baal. These *were* their
[T]habitations, and they maintained their genealogy: *Baalath Beer,* Josh. 19:8 • *dwelling places*
34 Meshobab, Jamlech, and Joshah the son
of Amaziah;
35 Joel, and Jehu the son of Joshibiah, the
son of Seraiah, the son of Asiel;
36 Elioenai, Jaakobah, Jeshohaiah, Asaiah,
Adiel, Jesimiel, and Benaiah;
37 Ziza the son of Shiphi, the son of Allon,
the son of Jedaiah, the son of Shimri, the son
of Shemaiah—
38 these mentioned by name *were* leaders in
their families, and their father's house increased greatly.
39 So they went to the entrance of Gedor,
as far as the east side of the valley, to seek
pasture for their flocks.
40 And they found rich, good pasture, and
the land *was* broad, quiet, and peaceful; for
some Hamites formerly lived there.
41 These recorded by name came in the
days of Hezekiah king of Judah; and they
[T]attacked their tents and the Meunites who
were found there, and [R]utterly destroyed
them, as it is to this day. So they dwelt in
their place, because *there was* pasture for
their flocks there. Lit. *struck* • 2 Kin. 19:11
42 Now *some* of them, five hundred men of
the sons of Simeon, went to Mount Seir,
having as their captains Pelatiah, Neariah,
Rephaiah, and Uzziel, the sons of Ishi.
43 And they [T]defeated [R]the rest of the Amalekites who had escaped. They have dwelt
there to this day. Lit. *struck* • 1 Sam. 15:8; 30:17

CHAPTER 5

The Genealogy of Reuben—Gen. 46:8, 9

NOW the sons of Reuben the firstborn of
Israel—he *was* indeed the firstborn, but
because he [R]defiled his father's bed, his birthright was given to the sons of Joseph, the son
of Israel, so that the genealogy is not listed
according to the birthright; Gen. 35:22
2 yet Judah prevailed over his brothers,
and from him *came* a ruler, although [T]the
birthright was Joseph's— *the right of the firstborn*
3 the sons of [R]Reuben the firstborn of
Israel were Hanoch, Pallu, Hezron, and
Carmi. Ex. 6:14
4 The sons of Joel *were* Shemaiah his son,
Gog his son, Shimei his son,
5 Micah his son, Reaiah his son, Baal his
son,
6 and Beerah his son, whom Tiglath-
Pileser king of Assyria [R]carried into captivity.
He *was* leader of the Reubenites. 2 Kin. 18:11
7 And his brethren by their families, [R]when
the genealogy of their generations was registered: the chief, Jeiel, and Zechariah, 1 Chr. 5:17
8 and Bela the son of Azaz, the son of
Shema, the son of Joel, who dwelt in [R]Aroer,
as far as Nebo and Baal Meon. Josh. 12:2
9 Eastward they settled as far as the [T]en-
trance of the wilderness this side of the River
Euphrates, because their cattle had [T]multi-
plied in the land of Gilead. *beginning* • *increased*
10 Now in the days of Saul they made war
[R]with the Hagrites, who fell by their hand;
and they dwelt in their tents throughout the
entire *area* east of Gilead. Gen. 25:12

The Genealogy of Gad

11 And the children of Gad dwelt next to
them in the land of Bashan as far as Salcah:
12 Joel *was* the chief, Shapham the next,
then Jaanai and Shaphat in Bashan,
13 and their brethren of their father's
house: Michael, Meshullam, Sheba, Jorai,
Jachan, Zia, and Heber—seven *in all.*
14 These *were* the children of Abihail the
son of Huri, the son of Jaroah, the son of
Gilead, the son of Michael, the son of Jeshishai, the son of Jahdo, the son of Buz;
15 Ahi the son of Abdiel, the son of Guni,
was chief of their father's house.
16 And [T]the Gadites dwelt in Gilead, in
Bashan and in its villages, and in all the

[T]common-lands of [R]Sharon within their borders. Lit. *they* · *open lands* · 1 Chr. 27:29
17 All these were registered by genealogies
in the days of Jotham king of Judah, and in
the days of Jeroboam king of Israel.
18 The sons of Reuben, the Gadites, and
half the tribe of Manasseh *had* forty-four
thousand seven hundred and sixty valiant
men, men able to bear shield and sword, to
shoot with the bow, and skillful in war, who
went to war.
19 They made war with the Hagrites, [R]Jetur,
Naphish, and Nodab. Gen. 25:15
20 And they were helped against them, and
the Hagrites were delivered into their hand,
and all who *were* with them, for they cried
out to God in the battle. He heeded their
prayer, because they put their trust in Him.
21 Then they took away their livestock—
fifty thousand of their camels, two hundred
and fifty thousand of their sheep, and two
thousand of their donkeys—also one hundred
thousand of their men;
22 for many fell dead, because the war [R]*was*
God's. And they dwelt in their place until [R]the
captivity. [Josh. 23:10] · 2 Kin. 15:29; 17:6

The Genealogy of Manasseh

23 So the children of the half-tribe of Manasseh dwelt in the land. Their *numbers*
increased from Bashan to Baal Hermon, that
is, to [R]Senir, or Mount Hermon. Deut. 3:9
24 These *were* the heads of their fathers'
houses: Epher, Ishi, Eliel, Azriel, Jeremiah,
Hodaviah, and Jahdiel. They were mighty
men of valor, famous men, *and* heads of their
fathers' houses.
25 And they were unfaithful to the God of
their fathers, and [R]played the harlot after the
gods of the peoples of the land, whom God
had destroyed before them. 2 Kin. 17:7
26 So the God of Israel stirred up the spirit
of Pul king of Assyria, that is, Tiglath-Pileser
king of Assyria. He carried the Reubenites,
the Gadites, and the half-tribe of Manasseh
into captivity. He took them to Halah, Habor,
Hara, and the river of Gozan to this day.

CHAPTER 6

The High Priestly Line
Gen. 46:11; 1 Chr. 6:50–53

THE sons of Levi *were* [R]Gershon,[T] Kohath,
and Merari. Ex. 6:16 · Or *Gershom*, v. 16
2 The sons of Kohath *were* Amram, [R]Izhar,
Hebron, and Uzziel. 1 Chr. 6:18, 22
3 The children of Amram *were* Aaron,
Moses, and Miriam. And the sons of Aaron
were Nadab, Abihu, Eleazar, and Ithamar.
4 Eleazar begot Phinehas, *and* Phinehas
begot Abishua;
5 Abishua begot Bukki, and Bukki begot
Uzzi;
6 Uzzi begot Zerahiah, and Zerahiah begot
Meraioth;
7 Meraioth begot Amariah, and Amariah
begot Ahitub;
8 [R]Ahitub begot [R]Zadok, and Zadok begot
Ahimaaz; 2 Sam. 8:17 · 2 Sam. 15:27
9 Ahimaaz begot Azariah, and Azariah
begot Johanan;
10 Johanan begot Azariah (it was he who
ministered as priest in the [T]temple that Solomon built in Jerusalem); Lit. *house*
11 [R]Azariah begot [R]Amariah, and Amariah
begot Ahitub; Ezra 7:3 · 2 Chr. 19:11
12 Ahitub begot Zadok, and Zadok begot
[T]Shallum; *Meshullam*, 1 Chr. 9:11
13 Shallum begot Hilkiah, and Hilkiah begot Azariah;
14 Azariah begot [R]Seraiah, and Seraiah begot Jehozadak. Neh. 11:11
15 Jehozadak went *into captivity* when the
LORD carried Judah and Jerusalem into captivity by the hand of Nebuchadnezzar.

The Levitical Line

16 The sons of Levi *were* [R]Gershon,[T] Kohath, and Merari. Ex. 6:16 · Heb. *Gershom*
17 These are the names of the sons of Gershon: Libni and Shimei.
18 The sons of Kohath *were* Amram, Izhar,
Hebron, and Uzziel.
19 The sons of Merari *were* Mahli and Mushi. Now these *are* the families of the Levites
according to their fathers:
20 Of Gershon *were* Libni his son, Jahath
his son, [R]Zimmah his son, 1 Chr. 6:42
21 Joah his son, Iddo his son, Zerah his son,
and Jeatherai his son.
22 The sons of Kohath *were* Amminadab his
son, Korah his son, Assir his son,
23 Elkanah his son, Ebiasaph his son, Assir
his son,
24 Tahath his son, Uriel his son, Uzziah his
son, and Shaul his son.
25 The sons of Elkanah *were* [R]Amasai and
Ahimoth. 1 Chr. 6:35, 36
26 *As for* Elkanah, the sons of Elkanah *were*
Zophai his son, [T]Nahath his son, *Toah*, v. 34
27 [T]Eliab his son, Jeroham his son, *and*
Elkanah his son. *Eliel*, v. 34
28 The sons of Samuel *were* **Joel* the firstborn, and Abijah [T]the second. Heb. *Vasheni*
29 The sons of Merari *were* Mahli, Libni his
son, Shimei his son, Uzzah his son,
30 Shimea his son, Haggiah his son, *and*
Asaiah his son.

The Musicians' Guild

31 Now these are [R]the men whom David
appointed over the service of song in the

6:28 So with LXX, Syr., Arab.; cf. v. 33 and 1 Sam. 8:2

house of the LORD, after the [R]ark came to
rest. 1 Chr. 15:16–22, 27; 16:4–6 • 1 Chr. 15:25—16:1
32 They were ministering with music before
the dwelling place of the tabernacle of meeting, until Solomon had built the house of the
LORD in Jerusalem, and they served in their
office according to their order.
33 And these *are* the ones who [T]ministered
with their sons: Of the sons of the [R]Kohath-
ites *were* Heman the singer, the son of Joel,
the son of Samuel, Lit. *stood with* • Num. 26:57
34 the son of Elkanah, the son of Jeroham,
the son of Eliel, the son of [R]Toah, 1 Sam. 1:1
35 the son of Zuph, the son of Elkanah, the
son of Mahath, the son of Amasai,
36 the son of Elkanah, the son of Joel, the
son of Azariah, the son of Zephaniah,
37 the son of Tahath, the son of Assir, the
son of [R]Ebiasaph, the son of Korah, Ex. 6:24
38 the son of Izhar, the son of Kohath, the
son of Levi, the son of Israel.
39 And his brother [R]Asaph, who stood at his
right hand, *was* Asaph the son of Berachiah,
the son of Shimea, 2 Chr. 5:12
40 the son of Michael, the son of Baaseiah,
the son of Malchijah,
41 the son of [R]Ethni, the son of Zerah, the
son of Adaiah, 1 Chr. 6:21
42 the son of Ethan, the son of Zimmah, the
son of Shimei,
43 the son of Jahath, the son of Gershon,
the son of Levi.
44 And their brethren, the sons of Merari,
on the left hand, *were* Ethan the son of Kishi,
the son of Abdi, the son of Malluch,
45 the son of Hashabiah, the son of Amaziah, the son of Hilkiah,
46 the son of Amzi, the son of Bani, the son
of Shamer,
47 the son of Mahli, the son of Mushi, the
son of Merari, the son of Levi.
48 And their brethren, the Levites, *were*
appointed to every [R]kind of service of the
tabernacle of the house of God. 1 Chr. 9:14–34

The Generations of Aaron—1 Chr. 6:3–8

49 [R]But Aaron and his sons offered sacrifices on the altar of burnt offering and on the
altar of incense, for all the work of the Most
Holy *Place*, and to make atonement for Israel, according to all that Moses the servant
of God had commanded. [Num. 18:1–8]
50 Now these *are* the [R]sons of Aaron: Eleazar his son, Phinehas his son, Abishua his
son, 1 Chr. 6:4–8
51 Bukki his son, Uzzi his son, Zerahiah his
son,
52 Meraioth his son, Amariah his son, Ahitub his son,
53 Zadok his son, *and* Ahimaaz his son.

Cities of the Priests and Levites
Josh. 21:1–42

54 Now these *are* their dwelling places
throughout their settlements in their territory, for they were *assigned* by lot to the sons
of Aaron, of the family of the Kohathites:
55 They gave them Hebron in the land of
Judah, with its surrounding common-lands.
56 But the fields of the city and its villages
they gave to Caleb the son of Jephunneh.
57 And [R]to the sons of Aaron they gave *one*
of the cities of refuge, Hebron; also Libnah
with its common-lands, Jattir, Eshtemoa with
its common-lands, Josh. 21:13, 19
58 [T]Hilen with its common-lands, Debir
with its common-lands, *Holon*, Josh. 21:15
59 [T]Ashan with its common-lands, and Beth
Shemesh with its common-lands. *Ain*, Josh. 21:16
60 And from the tribe of Benjamin: Geba
with its common-lands, [T]Alemeth with its
common-lands, and Anathoth with its
common-lands. All their cities among their
families *were* thirteen. *Almon*, Josh. 21:18
61 To the rest of the family of the tribe of
the Kohathites *they gave* [R]by lot ten cities
from half the tribe of Manasseh. Josh. 21:5
62 And to the sons of Gershon, throughout
their families, *they gave* thirteen cities from
the tribe of Issachar, from the tribe of Asher,
from the tribe of Naphtali, and from the tribe
of Manasseh in Bashan.
63 To the sons of Merari, throughout their
families, *they gave* [R]twelve cities from the
tribe of Reuben, from the tribe of Gad, and
from the tribe of Zebulun. Josh. 21:7, 34–40
64 So the children of Israel gave *these* cities
with their common-lands to the Levites.
65 And they gave by lot from the tribe of
the children of Judah, from the tribe of the
children of Simeon, and from the tribe of the
children of Benjamin these cities which are
called by *their* names.
66 Now [R]some of the families of the sons of
Kohath *were given* cities as their territory
from the tribe of Ephraim. 1 Chr. 6:61
67 [R]And they gave them *one of* the cities of
refuge, Shechem with its common-lands, in
the mountains of Ephraim, also Gezer with
its common-lands, Josh. 21:21
68 [R]Jokmeam with its common-lands, Beth
Horon with its common-lands, Josh. 21:22
69 Aijalon with its common-lands, and Gath
Rimmon with its common-lands.
70 And from the half-tribe of Manasseh:
Aner with its common-lands and Bileam with
its common-lands, for the rest of the family of
the sons of Kohath.
71 From the family of the half-tribe of Manasseh the sons of Gershon *were given* Golan
in Bashan with its common-lands and [R]Ashta-
roth with its common-lands. Josh. 21:27

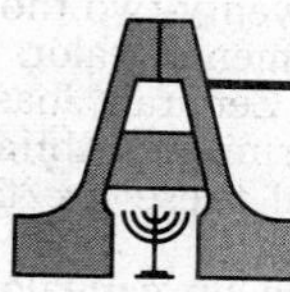

GENEALOGICAL TABLES

Even as many families do today, the Jewish people of Bible times kept detailed family histories. These were important records that helped determine inheritances and provided identification and continuity with the past. These lists of descendants also helped identify the people who were qualified to serve as priests—descendants of Levi and the house of Aaron.

During the Hebrews' years of wilderness wandering, the military organization of the tribes was established by these family records, or genealogies (Num. 1:2–4). These lists were also used to allocate taxes and offerings for the sanctuary (Num. 7:11–89). The first genealogies of the Hebrews were probably memorized and passed down by word of mouth to succeeding generations, as well as being written down.

The Book of Genesis contains several important genealogical tables, including the descendants of Adam (ch. 5), Noah (ch. 10), and Jacob (46:8–25) and the ancestors of Abraham (11:10–32; see illustration of Abraham's tomb).

In the New Testament, both Matthew (1:2–17) and Luke (3:23–38) listed the earthly ancestors of Jesus to show that Jesus the Messiah was descended from the line of David.

Scholars who have studied these genealogical tables in the Bible have noted that not all the ancestors or descendants are included. Apparently, the purpose of the biblical writers who compiled genealogies was to establish the broad line of descent without including all the details.

The apostle Paul cautioned his young minister colleague Timothy to avoid "fables and endless genealogies, which cause disputes rather than godly edification" (1 Tim. 1:4). This should serve as a warning to all persons not to place undue emphasis on their family history. What really matters is not our line of descent but our commitment as individuals to Jesus Christ and His will for our lives.

Abraham's tomb.

72 And from the tribe of Issachar: [T]Kedesh
with its common-lands, Daberath with its
common-lands, *Kishon,* Josh. 21:28
73 Ramoth with its common-lands, and
Anem with its common-lands.
74 And from the tribe of Asher: Mashal with
its common-lands, Abdon with its common-
lands,
75 Hukok with its common-lands, and Rehob with its common-lands.
76 And from the tribe of Naphtali: Kedesh
in Galilee with its common-lands, Hammon
with its common-lands, and Kirjathaim with
its common-lands.
77 From the tribe of Zebulun the rest of the
children of Merari *were given* [T]Rimmon with
its common-lands and Tabor with its
common-lands. Heb. *Rimmono,* 1 Chr. 4:32
78 And on the other side of the Jordan,
across from Jericho, on the east side of the
Jordan, *they were given* from the tribe of
Reuben: Bezer in the wilderness with its
common-lands, Jahzah with its common-
lands,
79 Kedemoth with its common-lands, and
Mephaath with its common-lands.
80 And from the tribe of Gad: Ramoth in
Gilead with its common-lands, Mahanaim
with its common-lands,
81 Heshbon with its common-lands, and
Jazer with its common-lands.

CHAPTER 7

The Genealogy of Issachar—Gen. 46:13

THE sons of Issachar *were* Tola, Puah,
[T]Jashub, and Shimron—four *in all.* *Job*
2 The sons of Tola *were* Uzzi, Rephaiah,
Jeriel, Jahmai, Jibsam, and Shemuel, heads of
their father's house. *The sons* of Tola *were*
mighty men of valor in their generations;
their number in the days of David *was*
twenty-two thousand six hundred.
3 The son of Uzzi *was* Izrahiah, and the
sons of Izrahiah *were* Michael, Obadiah, Joel,
and Ishiah. All five of them *were* chief men.
4 And with them, by their generations,
according to their fathers' houses, *were*
thirty-six thousand *troops* of the army ready
for war; for they had many wives and sons.
5 Now their brethren among all the families of Issachar *were* mighty men of valor,
listed by their genealogies, eighty-seven
thousand in all.

The Genealogy of Benjamin—Gen. 46:21

6 *The sons* of [R]Benjamin *were* Bela, Becher, and Jediael—three *in all.* Gen. 46:21
7 The sons of Bela were Ezbon, Uzzi, Uzziel, Jerimoth, and Iri—five *in all.* They *were*
heads of *their* fathers' houses, and they were
listed by their genealogies, twenty-two thousand and thirty-four mighty men of valor.
8 The sons of Becher *were* Zemirah, Joash,
Eliezer, Elioenai, Omri, Jerimoth, Abijah,
Anathoth, and Alemeth. All these *are* the
sons of Becher.
9 And they were recorded by genealogy
according to their generations, heads of their
fathers' houses, twenty thousand two hundred mighty men of valor.
10 The son of Jediael *was* Bilhan, and the
sons of Bilhan *were* Jeush, Benjamin, Ehud,
Chenaanah, Zethan, Tharshish, and Ahishahar.
11 All these sons of Jediael *were* heads of
their fathers' houses; *there were* seventeen
thousand two hundred mighty men of valor
fit to go out for war *and* battle.
12 Shuppim and Huppim *were* the sons of
Ir, *and* Hushim *was* the son of Aher.

The Genealogy of Naphtali—Gen. 46:24

13 The sons of Naphtali *were* Jahziel, Guni,
Jezer, and Shallum, the sons of Bilhah.

The Genealogy of Manasseh

14 The [R]descendants of Manasseh: his Syrian concubine bore him Machir the father of
Gilead, the father of Asriel. Num. 26:29–34
15 Machir took as his wife *the sister* of
[T]Huppim and [T]Shuppim, whose name *was*
Maachah. The name of *Gilead's* [T]grandson
was Zelophehad, but Zelophehad begot only
daughters. *Hupham,* v. 12 • *Shupham,* v. 12 • Lit. *the second*
16 (Maachah the wife of Machir bore a son,
and she called his name Peresh. The name of
his brother *was* Sheresh, and his sons *were*
Ulam and Rakem.
17 The son of Ulam *was* [R]Bedan.) These
were the descendants of Gilead the son of
Machir, the son of Manasseh. 1 Sam. 12:11
18 His sister Hammoleketh bore Ishhod,
[T]Abiezer, and Mahlah. *Jeezer,* Num. 26:30
19 And the sons of Shemida were Ahian,
Shechem, Likhi, and Aniam.

The Genealogy of Ephraim

20 [R]The sons of Ephraim *were* Shuthelah,
Bered his son, Tahath his son, Eladah his son,
Tahath his son, Num. 26:35–37
21 Zabad his son, Shuthelah his son, and
Ezer and Elead. The men of Gath who were
born in *that* land killed *them* because they
came down to take away their cattle.
22 Then Ephraim their father mourned
many days, and his brethren came to comfort
him.
23 And when he went in to his wife, she
conceived and bore a son; and he called his
name [T]Beriah, because tragedy had come
upon his house. Lit. *In Tragedy*

24 Now his daughter *was* Sheerah, who
built Lower and Upper [R]Beth Horon and
Uzzen Sheerah; Josh. 16:3, 5
25 and Rephah *was* his son, *as well* as
Resheph, and Telah his son, Tahan his son,
26 Laadan his son, Ammihud his son, [R]Elish-
ama his son, Num. 10:22
27 Nun his son, and Joshua his son.
28 Now their [R]possessions and habitations
were Bethel and its towns: to the east [T]Naa-
ran, to the west Gezer and its towns, and
Shechem and its towns, as far as *Ayyah and
its towns; Josh. 16:1–10 • *Naarath,* Josh. 16:7
29 and by the borders of the children of
Manasseh *were* Beth Shean and its towns,
Taanach and its towns, Megiddo and its
towns, Dor and its towns. In these dwelt the
children of Joseph, the son of Israel.

The Genealogy of Asher—Gen. 46:17

30 The sons of Asher *were* Imnah, Ishvah,
Ishvi, Beriah, and their sister Serah.
31 The sons of Beriah *were* Heber and Malchiel, who was the father of Birzaith.
32 And Heber begot Japhlet, Shomer, [T]Ho-
tham, and their sister Shua. *Helem,* 1 Chr. 7:35
33 The sons of Japhlet *were* Pasach, Bimhal,
and Ashvath. These *were* the children of
Japhlet.
34 The sons of [R]Shemer *were* Ahi, Rohgah,
Jehubbah, and Aram. 1 Chr. 7:32
35 And the sons of his brother Helem *were*
Zophah, Imna, Shelesh, and Amal.
36 The sons of Zophah *were* Suah, Harnepher, Shual, Beri, Imrah,
37 Bezer, Hod, Shamma, Shilshah, [T]Jithran,
and Beera. *Jether,* v. 38
38 The sons of Jether *were* Jephunneh,
Pispah, and Ara.
39 The sons of Ulla *were* Arah, Haniel, and
Rizia.
40 All these *were* the children of Asher,
heads of *their* fathers' houses, choice men,
mighty men of valor, chief leaders. And they
were recorded by genealogies among the
army fit for battle; their number *was* twenty-
six thousand.

CHAPTER 8

The Genealogy of Benjamin—Gen. 46:21

NOW Benjamin begot Bela his firstborn,
Ashbel the second, Aharah the third,
2 Nohah the fourth, and Rapha the fifth.
3 The sons of Bela *were* [T]Addar, Gera,
Abihud, *Ard,* Num. 26:40
4 Abishua, Naaman, Ahoah,
5 Gera, Shephuphan, and Huram.
6 And these *are* the sons of Ehud, who
were the heads of the fathers' *houses* of the
inhabitants of [R]Geba, and who forced them to
move to [R]Manahath: 1 Chr. 6:60 • 1 Chr. 2:52
7 Naaman, Ahijah, and Gera who forced
them to move. He begot Uzza and Ahihud.
8 And Shaharaim begot *children* in the
country of Moab, after he had sent away
Hushim and Baara his wives.
9 By Hodesh his wife he begot Jobab,
Zibia, Mesha, Malcam,
10 Jeuz, Sachiah, and Mirmah. These *were*
his sons, heads of their fathers' *houses.*
11 And by Hushim he begot Abitub and
Elpaal.
12 The sons of Elpaal *were* Eber, Misham,
and Shemed, who built Ono and Lod with its
towns;
13 and Beriah and [R]Shema, who *were* heads
of their fathers' *houses* of the inhabitants of
Aijalon, who drove out the inhabitants of
Gath. 1 Chr. 8:21
14 Ahio, Shashak, Jeremoth,
15 Zebadiah, Arad, Eder,
16 Michael, Ispah, and Joha *were* the sons
of Beriah.
17 Zebadiah, Meshullam, Hizki, Heber,
18 Ishmerai, Jizliah, and Jobab *were* the
sons of Elpaal.
19 Jakim, Zichri, Zabdi,
20 Elienai, Zillethai, Eliel,
21 Adaiah, Beraiah, and Shimrath *were* the
sons of [T]Shimei. *Shema,* 1 Chr. 7:13
22 Ishpan, Eber, Eliel,
23 Abdon, Zichri, Hanan,
24 Hananiah, Elam, Antothijah,
25 Iphdeiah, and Penuel *were* the sons of
Shashak.
26 Shamsherai, Shehariah, Athaliah,
27 Jaareshiah, Elijah, and Zichri *were* the
sons of Jeroham.
28 These *were* heads of the fathers' *houses*
by their generations, chief men. These dwelt
in Jerusalem.
29 Now the father of Gibeon, whose wife's
name *was* Maacah, dwelt at Gibeon.
30 And his firstborn son *was* Abdon, then
Zur, Kish, Baal, Nadab,
31 Gedor, Ahio, [T]Zecher, *Zechariah,* 1 Chr. 9:37
32 and Mikloth, *who* begot Shimeah. They
also dwelt [T]alongside their [T]relatives in Jerusalem, with their brethren. Lit. *opposite* • *brethren*
33 [R]Ner begot Kish, Kish begot Saul, and
Saul begot Jonathan, Malchishua, Abinadab,
and [T]Esh-Baal. 1 Sam. 14:51 • *Ishbosheth,* 2 Sam. 2:8
34 The son of Jonathan *was* Merib-Baal,
and Merib-Baal begot [R]Micah. 2 Sam. 9:12
35 The sons of Micah *were* Pithon, Melech,
[T]Tarea, and Ahaz. *Tahrea,* 1 Chr. 9:41
36 And Ahaz begot [T]Jehoaddah; Jehoaddah
begot Alemeth, Azmaveth, and Zimri; and
Zimri begot Moza. *Jarah,* 1 Chr. 9:42
37 Moza begot Binea, [R]Raphah his son,
Eleasah his son, *and* Azel his son. 1 Chr. 9:43
38 Azel had six sons whose names *were*

7:28 Many mss., Bomberg, LXX, Tg., Vg., *Gazza*

these: Azrikam, Bocheru, Ishmael, Sheariah,
Obadiah, and Hanan. All these *were* the sons
of Azel.
39 And the sons of Eshek his brother *were*
Ulam his firstborn, Jeush the second, and
Eliphelet the third.
40 The sons of Ulam were mighty men of
valor—archers. *They* had many sons and
grandsons, one hundred and fifty *in all*. These
were all sons of Benjamin.

CHAPTER 9

The Genealogy of the Twelve Tribes Who Returned

SO [R]all Israel was [T]recorded by genealogies,
and indeed, they *were* inscribed in the
book of the kings of Israel. But Judah was
carried away captive to Babylon because of
their unfaithfulness. Ezra 2:59 • *enrolled*
2 And the first inhabitants who *dwelt* in
their possessions in their cities *were* Israelites, priests, Levites, and the Nethinim.
3 Now in [R]Jerusalem the children of Judah
dwelt, and some of the children of Benjamin,
and of the children of Ephraim and Manasseh: Neh. 11:1, 2
4 Uthai the son of Ammihud, the son of
Omri, the son of Imri, the son of Bani, of the
descendants of Perez, the son of Judah.
5 Of the Shilonites: Asaiah the firstborn
and his sons.
6 Of the sons of Zerah: Jeuel, and their
brethren—six hundred and ninety.
7 Of the sons of Benjamin: Sallu the son of
Meshullam, the son of Hodaviah, the son of
Hassenuah;
8 Ibneiah the son of Jeroham; Elah the son
of Uzzi, the son of Michri; Meshullam the son
of Shephatiah, the son of Reuel, the son of
Ibnijah;
9 and their brethren, according to their
generations—nine hundred and fifty-six. All
these men *were* heads of a father's *house* in
their fathers' houses.

The Genealogy of the Priests Who Returned

10 [R]Of the priests: Jedaiah, Jehoiarib, and
Jachin; Neh. 11:10–14
11 [T]Azariah the son of Hilkiah, the son of
Meshullam, the son of Zadok, the son of
Meraioth, the son of Ahitub, the [R]officer over
the house of God; *Seraiah*, Neh. 11:11 • Jer. 20:1
12 Adaiah the son of Jeroham, the son of
Pashur, the son of Malchijah; Maasai the son
of Adiel, the son of Jahzerah, the son of
Meshullam, the son of Meshillemith, the son
of Immer;
13 and their brethren, heads of their fathers'
houses—one thousand seven hundred and
sixty. *They were* very able men for the work
of the service of the house of God.

The Genealogy of the Levites Who Returned

14 Of the Levites: Shemaiah the son of
Hasshub, the son of Azrikam, the son of
Hashabiah, of the sons of Merari;
15 Bakbakkar, Heresh, Galal, and Mattaniah the son of Micah, the son of [R]Zichri, the
son of Asaph; Neh. 11:17
16 Obadiah the son of Shemaiah, the son of
Galal, the son of Jeduthun; and Berechiah the
son of Asa, the son of Elkanah, who lived in
the villages of the Netophathites.
17 And the gatekeepers *were* Shallum, Akkub, Talmon, Ahiman, and their brethren.
Shallum *was* the chief.
18 Until then *they had been* gatekeepers for
the camps of the children of Levi at the
King's Gate on the east.
19 Shallum the son of Kore, the son of
Ebiasaph, the son of Korah, and his brethren,
from his father's house, the Korahites, *were*
in charge of the work of the service, [T]gate-
keepers of the tabernacle. Their fathers had
been keepers of the entrance to the camp of
the LORD. Lit. *thresholds*
20 And [R]Phinehas the son of Eleazar had
been the officer over them in time past; the
LORD *was* with him. Num. 25:6–13; 31:6
21 [R]Zechariah the son of Meshelemiah *was*
[T]keeper of the door of the tabernacle of
meeting. 1 Chr. 26:2, 14 • *gatekeeper*
22 All those chosen as gatekeepers *were*
two hundred and twelve. They were recorded
by their genealogy, in their villages. David
and Samuel [R]the seer had appointed them to
their trusted office. 1 Sam. 9:9
23 So they and their children *were* in charge
of the gates of the house of the LORD, the
house of the tabernacle, by assignment.
24 The gatekeepers were assigned to the
four directions: the east, west, north, and
south.
25 And their brethren in their villages *had*
to come with them from time to time [R]for
seven days. 2 Kin. 11:4–7
26 For in this trusted office *were* four chief
gatekeepers; they were Levites. And they had
charge over the chambers and treasuries of
the house of God.
27 And they lodged *all* around the house of
God because [T]they *had* the responsibility, and
they *were* in charge of opening *it* every
morning. *the watch was committed to them*
28 Now *some* of them were in charge of the
serving vessels, for they brought them in and
took them out by count.
29 *Some* of them *were* appointed over the
furnishings and over all the implements of
the sanctuary, and over the [R]fine flour and
the wine and the oil and the incense and the
spices. 1 Chr. 23:29
30 And *some* of the sons of the priests made
[R]the ointment of the spices. Ex. 30:22–25

31 Mattithiah of the Levites, the firstborn of
Shallum the Korahite, had the trusted office
over the things that were baked in the pans.
32 And some of their brethren of the sons of
the Kohathites [R]*were* in charge of preparing
the showbread for every Sabbath. Lev. 24:5–8
33 These are [R]the singers, heads of the
fathers' *houses* of the Levites, *who lodged* in
the chambers, *and were* free *from other
duties*; for they were employed in *that* work
day and night. 1 Chr. 6:31; 25:1
34 These heads of the fathers' *houses* of the
Levites *were* heads throughout their generations. They dwelt at Jerusalem.

The Genealogy of Saul

35 Jeiel the father of Gibeon, whose wife's
name *was* Maacah, dwelt at Gibeon.
36 His firstborn son *was* Abdon, then Zur,
Kish, Baal, Ner, Nadab,
37 Gedor, Ahio, Zechariah, and Mikloth.
38 And Mikloth begot [T]Shimeam. They also
dwelt alongside their relatives in Jerusalem,
with their brethren. *Shimeah*, 1 Chr. 8:32
39 [R]Ner begot Kish, Kish begot Saul, and
Saul begot Jonathan, Malchishua, Abinadab,
and Esh-Baal. 1 Chr. 8:33–38
40 The son of Jonathan *was* Merib-Baal,
and Merib-Baal begot Micah.
41 The sons of Micah *were* Pithon, Melech,
[T]Tahrea, [R]*and Ahaz*. *Tarea*, 1 Chr. 8:35 • 1 Chr. 8:35
42 And Ahaz begot [T]Jarah; Jarah begot
Alemeth, Azmaveth, and Zimri; and Zimri
begot Moza; *Jehoaddah*, 1 Chr. 8:36
43 Moza begot Binea, [R]Rephaiah his son,
Eleasah his son, and Azel his son. 1 Chr. 8:37
44 And Azel had six sons whose names
were these: Azrikam, Bocheru, Ishmael, Sheariah, Obadiah, and Hanan; these *were* the
sons of Azel.

CHAPTER 10

The House of Saul Dies in Battle
1 Sam. 31:1–7

NOW [R]the Philistines fought against Israel; and the men of Israel fled from
before the Philistines, and fell slain on Mount
Gilboa. 1 Sam. 31:1, 2
2 Then the Philistines followed hard after
Saul and his sons. And the Philistines killed
Jonathan, [T]Abinadab, and Malchishua, Saul's
sons. *Jishui*, 1 Sam. 14:49
3 The battle became intense against Saul;
and the archers hit him, and he was wounded
by the archers.
4 Then Saul said to his armorbearer,
"Draw your sword, and thrust me through
with it, lest these uncircumcised *men* come
and abuse me." But his armorbearer would
not, for he was greatly afraid. Therefore Saul
took a sword and fell on it.
5 And when his armorbearer saw that Saul
was dead, he also fell on his sword and died.
6 So Saul and his three sons died, and all
his house died together.
7 And when all the men of Israel who *were*
in the valley saw that they had fled and that
Saul and his sons were dead, they forsook
their cities and fled; then the Philistines came
and dwelt in them.

The Philistines Defile Saul—1 Sam. 31:8–13

8 So it happened the next day, when the
Philistines came to [T]strip the slain, that they
found Saul and his sons fallen on Mount
Gilboa. *plunder*
9 And they stripped him and took his head
and his armor, and sent word *throughout* the
land of the Philistines to proclaim the news *in
the temple* of their idols and among the
people.
10 [R]Then they put his armor in the [T]temple
of their gods, and fastened his head in the
temple of Dagon. 1 Sam. 31:10 • Lit. *house*
11 And when all Jabesh Gilead heard all
that the Philistines had done to Saul,
12 all the valiant men arose and took the
body of Saul and the bodies of his sons; and
they brought them to [R]Jabesh, and buried
their bones under the tamarisk tree at Jabesh, and fasted seven days. 2 Sam. 21:12

The Cause of Saul's Death

13 So Saul died for his unfaithfulness which
he had [T]committed against the LORD, because
he did not keep the word of the LORD, and
also because [R]he consulted a medium for
guidance. Lit. *transgressed* • 1 Sam. 28:7
14 But *he* did not inquire of the LORD;
therefore He killed him, and turned the kingdom over to David the son of Jesse.

CHAPTER 11

Anointing of David as King—2 Sam. 5:1–3

THEN [R]all Israel came together to David at
Hebron, saying, "Indeed we *are* your
bone and your flesh. 2 Sam. 5:1
2 "Also, in time past, even when Saul was
king, you *were* the one who led Israel out and
brought them in; and the LORD your God said
to you, 'You shall shepherd My people Israel,
and be ruler over My people Israel.' "
3 Therefore all the elders of Israel came to
the king at Hebron, and David made a covenant with them at Hebron before the LORD.
Then they anointed David king over Israel,
according to the word of the LORD [T]by [R]Sam-
uel. Lit. *by the hand of Samuel* • 1 Sam. 16:1, 4, 12, 13

Conquest of Jerusalem—2 Sam. 5:6–10

4 And David and all Israel [R]went to Jerusalem, which is Jebus, where the Jebusites
were, the inhabitants of the land. 2 Sam. 5:6

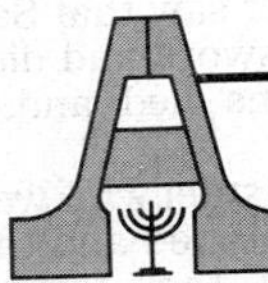

THE CITY OF JERUSALEM

When David became king of Judah, one of his first acts was to capture Jerusalem from the Jebusites and make the city the capital of his kingdom (2 Sam. 5:6–10; 1 Chr. 11:4–9). The city served from that point on as the religious and political capital of the Jewish nation.

Jerusalem was a good choice as a capital city site. Easy to defend because of its hilltop location, it was also centrally located between the northern and southern tribes of the nation. David's first task as king was to unite these tribes under his leadership. This is probably why he selected Jerusalem as his capital.

Jerusalem grew into a magnificent city under Solomon, David's son and successor. Solomon built the temple as the place of worship for the Israelites (1 Kin. 6; 7; 2 Chr. 3; 4). He also planted many vineyards, orchards, and gardens to beautify the city.

Several centuries after Solomon's time, in 586 B.C., the Babylonians destroyed Jerusalem and carried its inhabitants into captivity. Although the temple and the city and its surrounding walls were rebuilt by the returning Jewish exiles some time later, Jerusalem was not restored to its previous splendor. This task, ironically, fell to Herod the Great, Roman ruler of Palestine about the time of Jesus. He restored the temple to its previous state in an attempt to appease the Jewish people and also built several other beautiful buildings in Jerusalem. This building program continued throughout the period of Jesus' public ministry.

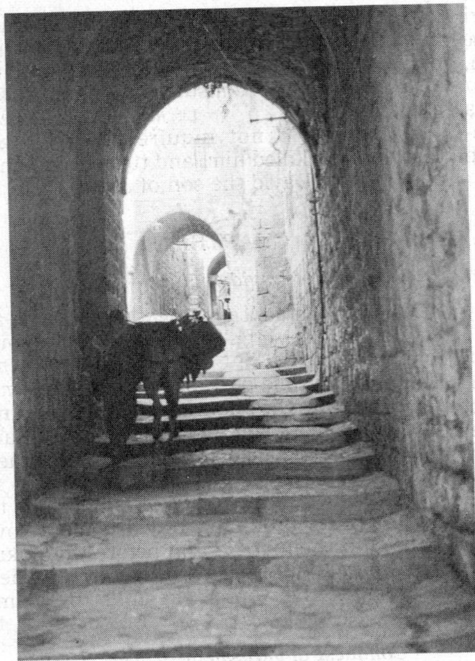

Narrow street through old city section of Jerusalem.

The Holy City played a significant role in the life and ministry of Jesus. At the age of twelve, He went to Jerusalem, where He amazed the temple leaders with His wisdom and knowledge (Luke 2:47). At the close of His public ministry, He was crucified, buried, and resurrected at Jerusalem.

As Jesus had predicted (Matt. 23:37–39), the city of Jerusalem was destroyed in A.D. 70 when the Jewish people rebelled against Roman authority. Rome eventually built a city on the site, but it was considered off-limits for the Jews. This situation changed in 1919, when Israel regained its status as a Jewish nation and Jerusalem was reestablished as its capital city.

Golgotha, a skull-shaped rock outside Jerusalem.

After the reinstatement of Israel, many Jews from throughout the world moved back to their homeland. Most of these Jews settled in a new city west of the old city of Jerusalem. Following the Arab-Israeli War of 1948–49, the new city was allotted to the Jews, while the old city remained in Moslem hands. But Israel reunited Jerusalem during the Six-Day War of 1967, when it took control of the Moslem section of the city.

The modern visitor to the city is impressed with the stark contrast between the old city section, with its crooked, narrow streets (see illustration), and the modern architecture of the new city section of Jerusalem.

One of the most popular tourist sites in Jerusalem is known as "Gordon's Calvary," a rocky knoll just outside the walls of the old city (see illustration), identified by Charles Gordon in 1885 as the site of Jesus' crucifixion. This rock formation does seem to resemble a skull. The Hebrew word for Calvary is *Golgotha,* which means "Place of a Skull" (Mark 15:22). However, another possible location of the crucifixion site is found at the Church of the Sepulcher inside the walls of the old city.

Jerusalem is revered as a holy city by three world religions: Christianity, Judaism, and Islam.

5 Then the inhabitants of Jebus said to David, "You shall not come in here." Nevertheless David took the stronghold of Zion (that is, the City of David).

6 Now David said, "Whoever attacks the Jebusites first shall be [T]chief and captain." And Joab the son of Zeruiah went up first, and became chief. Lit. *head*

7 Then David dwelt in the stronghold; therefore they called it the City of David.

8 And he built the city around it, from the Millo to the surrounding area. Joab [T]repaired the rest of the city. Lit. *revived*

9 Then David went on and became great, and the LORD of hosts *was* with him.

The Chiefs—2 Sam. 23:8–12

10 Now these *were* the heads of the mighty men whom David had, who strengthened themselves with him in his kingdom, with all Israel, to make him king, according to the word of the LORD concerning Israel.

11 And this *is* the number of the mighty men whom David had: [R]Jashobeam the son of a Hachmonite, [R]chief of the captains; he had lifted up his spear against three hundred, killed *by him* at one time. 1 Chr. 27:2 • 1 Chr. 12:18

12 After him *was* Eleazar the son of [R]Dodo, the Ahohite, who *was one* of the three mighty men. 1 Chr. 27:4

13 He was with David at Pasdammim. Now there the Philistines were gathered for battle, and there was a piece of ground full of barley. And the people fled from the Philistines.

14 But they [T]stationed themselves in the midst of *that* field, defended it, and killed the Philistines. And the LORD saved *them* by a great deliverance. Lit. *took their stand*

The Thirty Chief Men
2 Sam. 23:13–23

15 Now three of the thirty chief men went down to the rock to David, into the cave of Adullam; and the army of the Philistines encamped in the Valley of [T]Rephaim. *Giants*

16 David *was* then in the stronghold, and the garrison of the Philistines *was* then in Bethlehem.

17 And David said with longing, "Oh, that someone would give me a drink of water from the well of Bethlehem, which is by the gate!"

18 So the three broke through the camp of the Philistines, drew water from the well of Bethlehem that *was* by the gate, and took *it* and brought *it* to David. Nevertheless David would not drink it, but poured it out to the LORD.

19 And he said, "Far be it from me, O my God, that I should do this! Shall I drink the blood of these men who have put their lives in jeopardy? For at the risk of their lives they brought it." Therefore he would not drink it. These things were done by the three mighty men.

20 Now Abishai the brother of Joab was chief of *another* three. He had lifted up his spear against three hundred men and killed *them*, and won a name among *these* three.

21 [R]Of the three he was more honored than the other two men. Therefore he became their captain. However he did not attain to the *first* three. 2 Sam. 23:19

22 Benaiah was the son of Jehoiada, the son of a valiant man from Kabzeel, who [T]had done many deeds. [R]He had killed two lion-like heroes of Moab. He also had gone down and killed a lion in the midst of a pit on a snowy day. *was great in deeds* • 2 Sam. 23:20

23 And he killed an Egyptian, a man of *great* height, [T]five cubits tall. In the Egyptian's hand *there had been* a spear like a weaver's beam; and he went down to him with a staff, wrested the spear out of the Egyptian's hand, and killed him with his own spear. 7.5 ft.

24 These *things* Benaiah the son of Jehoiada had done, and won a name among three mighty men.

25 Indeed he was more honored than the thirty, but he did not attain to the *first* three. And David appointed him over his guard.

The Mighty Warriors
2 Sam. 23:24–39

26 Also the mighty warriors *were* [R]Asahel the brother of Joab, Elhanan the son of Dodo of Bethlehem, 2 Sam. 23:24

27 [T]Shammoth the Harorite, Helez the Pelonite, *Shammah the Harodite,* 2 Sam. 23:25

28 [R]Ira the son of Ikkesh the Tekoite, [R]Abiezer the Anathothite, 1 Chr. 27:9 • 1 Chr. 27:12

29 [T]Sibbechai the Hushathite, [T]Ilai the Ahohite, *Mebunnai,* 2 Sam. 23:27 • *Zalmon,* 2 Sam. 23:28

30 [R]Maharai the Netophathite, Heled the son of Baanah the Netophathite, 1 Chr. 27:13

31 [T]Ithai the son of Ribai of Gibeah, of the children of Benjamin, [R]Benaiah the Pirathonite, *Ittai,* 2 Sam. 23:29 • 1 Chr. 27:14

32 [T]Hurai of the brooks of Gaash, [T]Abiel the Arbathite, *Hiddai,* 2 Sam. 23:30 • *Abi-Albon,* 2 Sam. 23:31

33 Azmaveth the [T]Baharumite, Eliahba the Shaalbonite, *Barhumite,* 2 Sam. 23:31

34 the sons of Hashem the Gizonite, Jonathan the son of Shageh the Hararite,

35 Ahiam the son of Sacar the Hararite, [R]Eliphal the son of Ur, *Eliphelet,* 2 Sam. 23:34

36 Hepher the Mecherathite, Ahijah the Pelonite,

37 [T]Hezro the Carmelite, [T]Naarai the son of Ezbai, *Hezrai,* 2 Sam. 23:35 • *Paarai the Arbite,* 2 Sam. 23:35

38 Joel the brother of Nathan, Mibhar the son of Hagri,

39 Zelek the Ammonite, Naharai the [T]Be-
rothite (the armorbearer of Joab the son of
Zeruiah), *Beerothite,* 2 Sam. 23:37
40 Ira the Ithrite, Gareb the Ithrite,
41 Uriah the Hittite, [T]Zabad the son of
Ahlai, The last sixteen are not in 2 Sam. 23.
42 Adina the son of Shiza the Reubenite (a
chief of the Reubenites) and thirty with him,
43 Hanan the son of Maachah, Joshaphat
the Mithnite,
44 Uzzia the Ashterathite, Shama and Jeiel
the sons of Hotham the Aroerite,
45 Jediael the son of Shimri, and Joha his
brother, the Tizite,
46 Eliel the Mahavite, Jeribai and Joshaviah
the sons of Elnaam, Ithmah the Moabite,
47 Eliel, Obed, and Jaasiel the Mezobaite.

CHAPTER 12

The Mighty Men at Ziklag

NOW [R]these *were* the men who came to
David at [R]Ziklag while he was still a
fugitive from Saul the son of Kish; and they
were among the mighty men, helpers in the
war, 1 Sam. 27:2 • 1 Sam. 27:6
2 armed with bows, using both the right
hand and [R]the left in *hurling* stones and
shooting arrows with the bow. *They were* of
Benjamin, Saul's brethren. Judg. 3:15; 20:16
3 The chief *was* Ahiezer, then Joash, the
sons of [T]Shemaah the Gibeathite; Jeziel and
Pelet the sons of Azmaveth; Berachah, and
Jehu the Anathothite; Or *Hasmaah*
4 Ishmaiah the Gibeonite, a mighty man
among the thirty, and over the thirty; Jeremiah, Jahaziel, Johanan, and Jozabad the
Gederathite;
5 Eluzai, Jerimoth, Bealiah, Shemariah,
and Shephatiah the Haruphite;
6 Elkanah, Jisshiah, Azareel, Joezer, and
Jashobeam, the Korahites;
7 and Joelah and Zebadiah the sons of
Jeroham of Gedor.
8 *Some* Gadites joined David at the stronghold in the wilderness, mighty men of valor,
men trained for battle, who could handle
shield and spear, whose faces *were like* the
faces of lions, and *were* [R]as swift as gazelles
on the mountains: 2 Sam. 2:18
9 Ezer the first, Obadiah the second, Eliab
the third,
10 Mishmannah the fourth, Jeremiah the
fifth,
11 Attai the sixth, Eliel the seventh,
12 Johanan the eighth, Elzabad the ninth,
13 Jeremiah the tenth, and Machbanai the
eleventh.
14 These *were* from the sons of Gad, captains of the army; the least was over a hundred, and the greatest was over a thousand.
15 These *are* the ones who crossed the
Jordan in the first month, when it had overflowed all its [R]banks; and they put to flight all
those in the valleys, to the east and to the
west. Josh. 3:15; 4:18, 19
16 Then some of the children of Benjamin
and Judah came to David at the stronghold.
17 And David went out [T]to meet them, and
answered and said to them, "If you have
come peaceably to me to help me, my heart
will be united with you; but if to betray me to
my enemies, since *there is* no [T]wrong in my
hands, may the God of our fathers look and
bring judgment." Lit. *before them* • Lit. *violence*
18 Then the Spirit [T]came upon [R]Amasai,
chief of the captains, *and he said:*

"*We are* yours, O David;
We *are* on your side, O son of Jesse!
Peace, peace to you,
And peace to your helpers!
For your God helps you."

So David received them, and made them
captains of the troop. Lit. *clothed* • 2 Sam. 17:25
19 And *some* from Manasseh defected to
David [R]when he was going with the Philistines to battle against Saul; but they did not
help them, for the lords of the Philistines sent
him away by counsel, saying, [R]"He may
defect to his master Saul *and endanger* our
heads." 1 Sam. 29:2 • 1 Sam. 29:4
20 When he went to Ziklag, those of Manasseh who defected to him were Adnah, Jozabad, Jediael, Michael, Jozabad, Elihu, and
Zillethai, captains of the thousands who *were*
from Manasseh.
21 And they helped David against [R]the
bands *of raiders*, for they *were* all mighty
men of valor, and they were captains in the
army. 1 Sam. 30:1, 9, 10
22 For at *that* time they came to David day
by day to help him, until *it was* a great army,
[R]like the army of God. Josh. 5:13–15

The Mighty Men at Hebron

23 Now these *were* the numbers of the
[T]divisions *that were* equipped for the war,
and came to David at Hebron to turn *over* the
kingdom of Saul to him, [R]according to the
word of the LORD: Lit. *heads of those* • 1 Sam. 16:1–4
24 of the children of Judah bearing shield
and spear, six thousand eight hundred
[T]armed for war; *equipped*
25 of the children of Simeon, mighty men of
valor fit for war, seven thousand one hundred;
26 of the children of Levi four thousand six
hundred;
27 Jehoiada, the leader of the Aaronites,
and with him three thousand seven hundred;

28 [R]Zadok, a young man, a valiant warrior,
and from his father's house twenty-two captains; 2 Sam. 8:17
29 of the children of Benjamin, kinsmen of
Saul, three thousand (until then [R]the greatest
part of them had remained loyal to the house
of Saul); 2 Sam. 2:8, 9
30 of the children of Ephraim twenty thousand eight hundred, mighty men of valor,
[T]famous men throughout their father's
house; Lit. *men of names*
31 of the half-tribe of Manasseh eighteen
thousand, who were designated by name to
come and make David king;
32 of the children of Issachar [R]who had
understanding of the times, to know what
Israel ought to do, their chiefs were two
hundred; and all their brethren were at their
command; Esth. 1:13
33 of Zebulun there were fifty thousand
who went out to battle, expert in war with all
weapons of war, [R]stouthearted men who
could keep ranks; Ps. 12:2
34 of Naphtali one thousand captains, and
with them thirty-seven thousand with shield
and spear;
35 of the Danites who could keep battle
formation, twenty-eight thousand six hundred;
36 of Asher, those who could go out to war,
able to keep battle formation, forty thousand;
37 of the Reubenites and the Gadites and
the half-tribe of Manasseh, from the other
side of the Jordan, one hundred and twenty
thousand armed for battle with every *kind* of
weapon of war.
38 All these men of war, who could keep
ranks, came to Hebron with a loyal heart, to
make David king over all Israel; and all the
rest of Israel *were* of [R]one mind to make
David king. 2 Chr. 30:12
39 And they were there with David three
days, eating and drinking, for their brethren
had prepared for them.
40 Moreover those who were near to them,
from as far away as Issachar and Zebulun
and Naphtali, were bringing food on donkeys
and camels, on mules and oxen—provisions
of flour and cakes of figs and cakes of raisins,
wine and oil and oxen and sheep abundantly,
for *there was* joy in Israel.

CHAPTER 13

Preparation to Move the Ark

THEN David consulted with the [R]captains
of thousands and hundreds, *and* with
every leader. 1 Chr. 11:15; 12:34
2 And David said to all the congregation of
Israel, "If *it seems* good to you, and if it is of
the LORD our God, let us send out to our
brethren everywhere *who are* [R]left in all the
land of Israel, and with them to the priests
and Levites *who are* in their cities *and* their
common-lands, that they may gather together to us; Is. 37:4
3 "and let us bring the ark of our God back
to us, [R]for we have not inquired at it since the
days of Saul." 1 Sam. 7:1, 2
4 Then all the congregation said that they
would do so, for the thing was right in the
eyes of all the people.
5 So [R]David gathered all Israel together,
from [R]Shihor in Egypt to as far as the entrance of Hamath, to bring the ark of God
from Kirjath Jearim. 1 Sam. 7:5 • Josh. 13:3

Uzza Dies for Touching the Ark
2 Sam. 6:1–11

6 And David and all Israel went up to
Baalah, to Kirjath Jearim, which belonged to
Judah, to bring up from there the ark of God
the LORD, who dwells *between* the cherubim,
where *His* name is proclaimed.
7 So they carried the ark of God on a new
cart [R]from the house of Abinadab, and Uzza
and Ahio drove the cart. 1 Sam. 7:1
8 Then David and all Israel played *music*
before God with all *their* might, with singing,
on harps, on stringed instruments, on tambourines, on cymbals, and with trumpets.
9 And when they came to [T]Chidon's
threshing floor, Uzza put out his hand to hold
the ark, for the oxen stumbled. *Nachon*, 2 Sam. 6:6
10 Then the anger of the LORD was aroused
against Uzza, and He struck him [R]because he
put his hand to the ark; and he [R]died there
before God. [Num. 4:15] • Lev. 10:2
11 And David became angry because of the
LORD's outbreak against Uzza; therefore that
place is called Perez Uzza to this day.
12 David was afraid of God that day, saying,
"How can I bring the ark of God to me?"
13 And David would not move the ark with
him into the City of David, but took it aside
into the house of Obed-Edom the Gittite.
14 The ark of God remained with the family
of Obed-Edom in his house three months.
And the LORD blessed [R]the house of Obed-
Edom and all that he had. 1 Chr. 26:4–8

CHAPTER 14

David's House Is Constructed—2 Sam. 5:11, 12

NOW Hiram king of Tyre sent messengers
to David, and cedar trees, with masons
and carpenters, to build him a house.
2 And David perceived that the LORD had
established him as king over Israel, for his
kingdom was [R]highly exalted because of His
people Israel. Num. 24:7

David's Children in Jerusalem

3 Then David took more wives in Jerusalem, and David begot more sons and daughters.

4 And these are the names of his children whom he had in Jerusalem: [T]Shammua, Shobab, Nathan, Solomon, *Shimea,* 1 Chr. 3:5

5 Ibhar, Elishua, [T]Elpelet, *Eliphelet,* 1 Chr. 3:6

6 Nogah, Nepheg, Japhia,

7 Elishama, Beeliada, and Eliphelet.

David's Victory over the Philistines
2 Sam. 5:17–25

8 Now when the Philistines heard that [R]David had been anointed king over all Israel, all the Philistines went up to search for David. And David heard *of it* and went out against them. 2 Sam. 5:17–21

9 Then the Philistines went and made a raid on the Valley of [T]Rephaim. Lit. *Giants*

10 And David [R]inquired of God, saying, "Shall I go up against the Philistines? Will You deliver them into my hand?" And the LORD said to him, "Go up, for I will deliver them into your hand." 1 Sam. 23:2, 4; 30:8

11 So they went up to Baal Perazim, and David defeated them there. Then David said, "God has broken through my enemies by my hand like a breakthrough of water." Therefore they called the name of that place [T]Baal Perazim. Lit. *Master of Breakthroughs*

12 And when they left their gods there, David gave a commandment, and they were burned with fire.

13 [R]Then the Philistines once again made a raid on the valley. 2 Sam. 5:22–25

14 Therefore David inquired again of God, and God said to him, "You shall not go up after them; circle around them, and come upon them in front of the mulberry trees.

15 "And it shall be, when you hear a sound of marching in the tops of the mulberry trees, then you shall go out to battle, for God has gone out before you to strike the camp of the Philistines."

16 So David did as God commanded him, and they drove back the army of the Philistines from Gibeon as far as Gezer.

17 Then [R]the fame of David went out into all lands, and the LORD [R]brought the fear of him upon all nations. Josh. 6:27 • [Deut. 2:25; 11:25]

CHAPTER 15

Spiritual Preparation to Move the Ark

DAVID built houses for himself in the City of David; and he prepared a place for the ark of God, and pitched a tent for it.

2 Then David said, "No one may carry the [R]ark of God but the Levites, for the LORD has chosen them to carry the ark of God and to minister before Him forever." [Num. 4:15]

3 And David gathered all Israel together at Jerusalem, to bring up the ark of the LORD to its place, which he had prepared for it.

4 Then David assembled the children of Aaron and the Levites:

5 of the sons of Kohath, Uriel the chief, and one hundred and twenty of his brethren;

6 of the sons of Merari, Asaiah the chief, and two hundred and twenty of his brethren;

7 of the sons of Gershom, Joel the chief, and one hundred and thirty of his brethren;

8 of the sons of [R]Elizaphan, Shemaiah the chief, and two hundred of his brethren; Ex. 6:22

9 of the sons of [R]Hebron, Eliel the chief, and eighty of his brethren; Ex. 6:18

10 of the sons of Uzziel, Amminadab the chief, and one hundred and twelve of his brethren.

11 And David called for [R]Zadok and [R]Abiathar the priests, and for the Levites: for Uriel, Asaiah, Joel, Shemaiah, Eliel, and Amminadab. 1 Chr. 12:28 • 1 Kin. 2:22, 26, 27

12 *Then* he said to them, "You *are* the heads of the fathers' *houses* of the Levites; [T]sanctify yourselves, you and your brethren, that you may bring up the ark of the LORD God of Israel to *the place* I have prepared for it. *consecrate*

13 "For because you *did* not *do it* the first *time,* the LORD our God broke out against us, because we did not consult Him [T]about the proper order." *regarding the ordinance*

14 So the priests and the Levites [T]sanctified themselves to bring up the ark of the LORD God of Israel. *consecrated*

15 And the children of the Levites bore the ark of God on their shoulders, by its poles, as [R]Moses had commanded according to the word of the LORD. Ex. 25:14

16 Then David spoke to the leaders of the Levites to appoint their brethren *to be* the singers accompanied by instruments of music, stringed instruments, harps, and cymbals, by raising the voice with resounding joy.

17 So the Levites appointed Heman the son of Joel; and of his brethren, Asaph the son of Berechiah; and of their brethren, the sons of Merari, Ethan the son of Kushaiah;

18 and with them their brethren of the second *rank*: Zechariah, Ben, Jaaziel, Shemiramoth, Jehiel, Unni, Eliab, Benaiah, Maaseiah, Mattithiah, Elipheleh, Mikneiah, Obed-Edom, and Jeiel, the gatekeepers;

19 the singers, Heman, Asaph, and Ethan, *were* to sound the cymbals of bronze;

20 Zechariah, [T]Aziel, Shemiramoth, Jehiel, Unni, Eliab, Maaseiah, and Benaiah, with strings according to Alamoth; *Jaaziel,* v. 18

21 Mattithiah, Elipheleh, Mikneiah, Obed-Edom, Jeiel, and Azaziah, to direct with harps on the [R]Sheminith; Ps. 6:title

22 Chenaniah, leader of the Levites, was instructor *in charge of* the music, because he *was* skillful;

23 Berechiah and Elkanah *were* doorkeepers for the ark;
24 Shebaniah, Joshaphat, Nethaneel, Amasai, Zechariah, Benaiah, and Eliezer, the
priests, [R]were to blow the trumpets before the
ark of God; and Obed-Edom and Jehiah,
doorkeepers for the ark. [Num. 10:8]

Joyful Transportation of the Ark
2 Sam. 6:12–16

25 So [R]David, the elders of Israel, and the
captains over thousands went to bring up
the ark of the covenant of the LORD from the
house of Obed-Edom with joy. 1 Kin. 8:1
26 And so it was, when God helped the
Levites who bore the ark of the covenant of
the LORD, that they offered seven bulls and
seven rams.
27 David was clothed with a robe of fine
[R]linen, as were all the Levites who bore the
ark, the singers, and Chenaniah the music
master *with* the singers. David also wore a
linen ephod. 1 Sam. 2:18, 28
28 [R]Thus all Israel brought up the ark of the
covenant of the LORD with shouting and with
the sound of the horn, with trumpets and
with cymbals, making music with stringed
instruments and harps. 1 Chr. 13:8
29 And it happened, [R]*as* the ark of the
covenant of the LORD came to the City of
David, that Michal the daughter of Saul,
looking through a window, saw King David
whirling and playing music; and she despised
him in her heart. 2 Sam. 3:13, 14; 6:16, 20–23

CHAPTER 16

Offering of Sacrifices—2 Sam. 6:17–19

SO they brought the ark of God, and set it
in the midst of the tabernacle that David
had erected for it. Then they offered burnt
offerings and peace offerings before God.
2 And when David had finished offering
the burnt offerings and the peace offerings,
[R]he blessed the people in the name of the
LORD. 1 Kin. 8:14
3 Then he distributed to everyone of Israel,
both man and woman, to everyone a loaf of
bread, a piece *of meat*, and a cake of raisins.

Appointing Musicians

4 And he appointed some of the Levites to
minister before the ark of the LORD, to [R]com-
memorate, to thank, and to praise the LORD
God of Israel: Ps. 38:title; 70:title
5 Asaph the chief, and next to him Zechariah, *then* [R]Jeiel, Shemiramoth, Jehiel, Mattithiah, Eliab, Benaiah, and Obed-Edom: Jeiel
with stringed instruments and harps, but
Asaph made music with cymbals; 1 Chr. 15:18
6 Benaiah and Jahaziel the priests regularly *blew* the trumpets before the ark of the
covenant of God.

Praise Psalm of David

7 And on that day David [R]first delivered
this psalm into the hand of Asaph and his
brethren, to thank the LORD: Ps. 105:1–15

8 Oh, [R]give thanks to the LORD!
Call upon His name; 1 Chr. 17:19, 20
Make known His deeds among the
peoples!
9 Sing to Him, sing psalms to Him;
Talk of all His wondrous works!
10 Glory in His holy name;
Let the hearts of those rejoice who seek
the LORD!
11 Seek the LORD and His strength;
Seek His face evermore!
12 Remember His marvelous works which
He has done,
His wonders and the judgments of His
mouth,
13 O seed of Israel His servant,
You children of Jacob, His chosen ones!

14 He *is* the LORD our God;
His judgments *are* in all the earth.
15 Remember His covenant always,
The word which He commanded, for a
thousand generations,
16 *The* [R]*covenant* which He made with
Abraham, Gen. 17:2; 26:3, 28:13; 35:11
And His oath to Isaac,
17 And [R]confirmed it to [R]Jacob for a
statute, Gen. 35:11, 12 • Gen. 28:10–15
To Israel *for* an everlasting covenant,
18 Saying, "To you I will give the land of
Canaan
As the allotment of your inheritance,"
19 When you were but few in number,
Indeed very few, and strangers in it.

20 *When* they went from one nation to
another,
And from *one* kingdom to another
people,
21 He permitted no man to do them
wrong;
Yes, He reproved kings for their sakes,
22 *Saying*, [R]"Do not touch My anointed
ones, Ps. 105:1–15
And do My prophets no harm."

23 [R]Sing to the LORD, all the earth; Ps. 96:1–13
Proclaim the good news of His salvation
from day to day.
24 Declare His glory among the nations,
His wonders among all peoples.

25 For the LORD *is* great and greatly to be
praised;
He *is* also to be feared above all gods.

26 For all the gods [R]of the peoples *are*
[T]idols, Lev. 19:4 • *worthless things*
But the LORD made the heavens.
27 Honor and majesty *are* before Him;
Strength and gladness are in His place.

28 Give to the LORD, O kindreds of the
peoples,
Give to the LORD glory and strength.

29 Give to the LORD the glory *due* His
name;
Bring an offering, and come before Him.
Oh, worship the LORD in the beauty of
holiness!

30 Tremble before Him, all the earth.
The world also is firmly established,
It shall not be moved.

31 Let the heavens rejoice, and let the
earth be glad;
And let them say among the nations,
"The LORD reigns."
32 Let the sea roar, and all its fullness;
Let the field rejoice, and all that *is* in it.
33 Then the [R]trees of the woods shall
rejoice before the LORD, Is. 55:12, 13
For He is coming to judge the earth.

34 [R]Oh, give thanks to the LORD, for *He is*
good! Ps. 106:1; 107:1; 118:1; 136:1
For His mercy *endures* forever.
35 [R]And say, "Save us, O God of our
salvation; Ps. 106:47, 48
Gather us together, and deliver us from
the Gentiles,
To give thanks to Your holy name,
To triumph in Your praise."

36 [R]Blessed *be* the LORD God of Israel
From everlasting to everlasting!

And all [R]the people said, "Amen!" and
praised the LORD. 1 Kin. 8:15, 56 • Deut. 27:15

Constant Ministry at the Ark

37 So he left [R]Asaph and his brothers there
before the ark of the covenant of the LORD to
minister before the ark regularly, as every
day's work [R]required; 1 Chr. 16:4, 5 • Ezra 3:4
38 and Obed-Edom with his sixty-eight
brethren, including Obed-Edom the son of
Jeduthun, and Hosah, *to be* gatekeepers;
39 and Zadok the priest and his brethren
the priests, before the tabernacle of the LORD
at the high place that *was* at Gibeon,
40 to offer burnt offerings to the LORD on
the altar of burnt offering regularly [R]morning
and evening, and *to do* according to all that is
written in the Law of the LORD which He
commanded Israel; [Ex. 29:38–42]
41 and with them Heman and Jeduthun and
the rest who were chosen, who were designated by name, to give thanks to the LORD,
because His mercy *endures* forever;
42 and with them Heman and Jeduthun, to
sound aloud with trumpets and cymbals and
the musical instruments of God. Now the
sons of Jeduthun *were* gatekeepers.
43 [R]Then all the people departed, every man
to his house; and David returned to bless his
house. 2 Sam. 6:18–20

CHAPTER 17

Desire of David to Build God's House
2 Sam. 7:1–3

AND [R]it came to pass, when David was
dwelling in his house, that David said to

16:29 The Meaning of Worship—Worship refers to the supreme honor or veneration given either in thought or deed to a person or thing. The Bible teaches that God alone is worthy of worship (Page 640—Ps. 29:2), but it also sadly records accounts of those who worshiped other objects. Among those were people (Page 978—Dan. 2:46), false gods (Page 442—2 Kin. 10:19), images and idols (Page 773—Is. 2:8; Page 979—Dan. 3:5), heavenly bodies (Page 454—2 Kin. 21:3), Satan (Page 1529—Rev. 13:4), and demons (Page 1526—Rev. 9:20). It is indeed tragic that many worshiped gods they could carry and not the God who could carry them. God Almighty alone is worthy of worship (Page 1523—Rev. 4:11).

True worship involves at least three important elements:

a. Worship requires reverence. This includes the honor and respect directed toward the Lord in thought and feeling. It is one thing to obey a superior unwillingly; it is quite another to commit one's thoughts and emotions in that obedience. Jesus said that those who worship God must do so "in spirit and in truth" (Page 1241—John 4:24). The term *spirit* speaks of the personal nature of worship: It is from my person to God's person and involves the intellect, emotions, and will. The word *truth* speaks of the content of worship: God is pleased when we worship Him, understanding His true character.
b. Worship includes public expression. This was particularly prevalent in the Old Testament because of the sacrificial system. For example, when a believer received a particular blessing for which he wanted to thank God, it was not sufficient to say it privately; he expressed his thanks publicly with a thank-offering (Page 126—Lev. 7:12).
c. Worship means service. These two concepts are often linked together in Scripture (Page 220—Deut. 8:19). Furthermore, the words for worship in both Testaments originally referred to the labor of slaves for the master. Worship especially includes the joyful service which Christians render to Christ their Master. The concept of worship must not be restricted to church attendance, but should embrace an entire life of obedience to God.

Now turn to Page 1463—Heb. 13:15: The Expressions of Worship.

Nathan the prophet, "See now, I dwell in a
house of cedar, but the ark of the covenant of
the LORD *is* under tent curtains." 2 Sam. 7:1
2 Then Nathan said to David, "Do all that
is in your heart, for God *is* with you."

Covenant of God to Build David's House
2 Sam. 7:4–17

3 But it happened that night that the word
of God came to Nathan, saying,
4 "Go and tell My servant David, 'Thus
says the LORD: "You shall [R]not build Me a
house to dwell in. [1 Chr. 28:2, 3]
5 "For I have not dwelt in a house since
the time that I brought up Israel, even to this
day, but have gone from tent to tent, and
from *one* tabernacle *to another.*
6 "Wherever I have moved about with all
Israel, have I ever spoken a word to any of
the judges of Israel, whom I commanded to
shepherd My people, saying, 'Why have you
not built Me a house of cedar?' " '
7 "Now therefore, thus shall you say to My
servant David, 'Thus says the LORD of hosts:
"I took you [R]from the sheepfold, from following the sheep, that you should be [T]ruler over
My people Israel. 1 Sam. 16:11–13 • *leader*
8 "And I have been with you wherever you
have gone, and have cut off all your enemies
from before you, and have [T]made you a name
like the name of the great men who *are* on
the earth. *given you prestige*
9 "Moreover I will appoint a place for My
people Israel, and will [R]plant them, that they
may dwell in a place of their own and move
no more; nor shall the sons of wickedness
oppress them anymore, as previously, Amos 9:14
10 "since the time that I commanded judges
to be over My people Israel. Also I will
subdue all your enemies. Furthermore I tell
you that the LORD will build you a house.
11 "And it shall be, when your days are
[R]fulfilled, when you must go *to be* with your
fathers, that I will [R]set up your seed after
you, who will be of your sons; and I will
establish his kingdom. 1 Kin. 2:10 • Matt. 1:6☆
12 "He shall build Me a house, and I will
establish his throne [R]forever. [Luke 1:33]☆
13 [R]"I will be his Father, and he shall be My
son; and I will not take My mercy away from
him, [R]as I took *it* from *him* who was before
you. Heb. 1:5 • 1 Chr. 10:14☆
14 "And I will establish him in My house
and in My kingdom forever; and his [R]throne
shall be established forever." ' " Acts 2:30☆
15 According to all these words and according to all this vision, so did Nathan speak to
David.

Praise Prayer of David—2 Sam. 7:18–29

16 [R]Then King David went in and sat before
the LORD; and he said: "Who *am* I, O LORD
God? And what is my house, that You have
brought me this far? 2 Sam. 7:18
17 "And *yet* this was a small thing in Your
sight, O God; and You have *also* spoken of
Your servant's house for a great while to
come, and have regarded me according to the
estate of a man of high degree, O LORD God.
18 "What more can David *say* to You for
the honor of Your servant? For You know
Your servant.
19 "O LORD, for Your servant's sake, and
according to Your own heart, You have done
all this greatness, in making known all *these*
great things.
20 "O LORD, *there is* none like You, nor *is*
there any God besides You, according to all
that we have heard with our ears.
21 [R]"And who *is* like Your people Israel, the
one nation on the earth whom God went to
redeem for Himself *as* a people—to make for
Yourself a name by great and awesome
deeds, by driving out nations from before
Your people whom You redeemed from
Egypt? Ps. 147:20
22 "For You have made Your people Israel
Your very own people forever; and You,
LORD, have become their God.
23 "And now, O LORD, the word which You
have spoken concerning Your servant and
concerning his house, *let it* be established
forever, and do as You have said.
24 "So let it be established, that Your name
may be magnified forever, saying, 'The LORD
of hosts, the God of Israel, is Israel's God; and
let the house of Your servant David *be* established before You.'
25 "For You, O my God, have [T]told Your
servant that You will build him a house.
Therefore Your servant has found it *in his*
heart to pray before You. Lit. *uncovered the ear of*
26 "And now, LORD, You are God, and have
promised this goodness to Your servant.
27 "Now You have been pleased to bless the
house of Your servant, that it may continue
before You forever; for You have blessed it, O
LORD, and *it shall be* blessed forever."

CHAPTER 18

Victory over Philistia—2 Sam. 8:1

AFTER this [R]it came to pass that David
[T]attacked the Philistines, subdued them,
and took Gath and its towns from the hand of
the Philistines. 2 Sam. 8:1–18 • Lit. *struck*

Victory over Moab—2 Sam. 8:2

2 Then he [T]defeated [R]Moab, and the Moabites became David's [R]servants, *and* brought
tribute. Lit. *struck* • 2 Sam. 8:2 • Ps. 60:8

Victory over Zobah—2 Sam. 8:3, 4

3 And David defeated Hadadezer king of

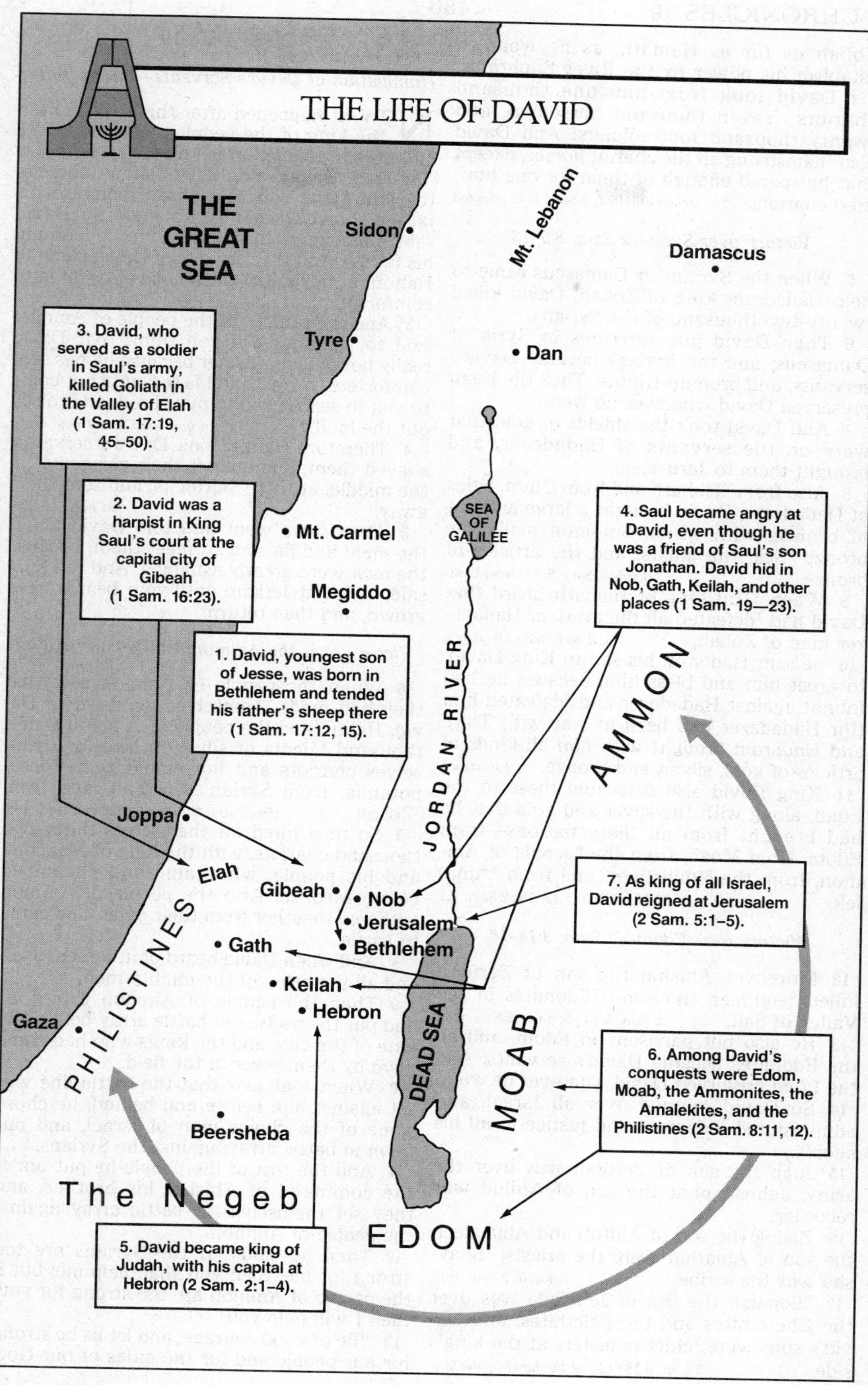

THE LIFE OF DAVID
THE GREAT SEA
Sidon
Mt. Lebanon
Damascus
Tyre
Dan
3. David, who served as a soldier in Saul's army, killed Goliath in the Valley of Elah (1 Sam. 17:19, 45–50).
2. David was a harpist in King Saul's court at the capital city of Gibeah (1 Sam. 16:23).
SEA OF GALILEE
4. Saul became angry at David, even though he was a friend of Saul's son Jonathan. David hid in Nob, Gath, Keilah, and other places (1 Sam. 19—23).
Mt. Carmel
Megiddo
1. David, youngest son of Jesse, was born in Bethlehem and tended his father's sheep there (1 Sam. 17:12, 15).
JORDAN RIVER
AMMON
Joppa
Elah
Gibeah
Nob
Jerusalem
7. As king of all Israel, David reigned at Jerusalem (2 Sam. 5:1–5).
Gath
Bethlehem
Keilah
Hebron
Gaza
PHILISTINES
DEAD SEA
MOAB
6. Among David's conquests were Edom, Moab, the Ammonites, the Amalekites, and the Philistines (2 Sam. 8:11, 12).
Beersheba
The Negeb
EDOM
5. David became king of Judah, with his capital at Hebron (2 Sam. 2:1–4).

Zobah *as far as* Hamath, as he went to
establish his power by the River Euphrates.
4 David took from him one thousand
chariots, [T]seven thousand horsemen, and
twenty thousand foot soldiers. And David
also [T]hamstrung all the chariot *horses*, except
that he spared enough of them for one hundred chariots. *seven hundred,* 2 Sam. 8:4 • *crippled*

Victory over Syria—2 Sam. 8:5–13

5 When the Syrians of Damascus came to
help Hadadezer king of Zobah, David killed
twenty-two thousand of the Syrians.
6 Then David put *garrisons* in Syria of
Damascus; and the Syrians became David's
servants, *and* brought tribute. Thus the LORD
preserved David wherever he went.
7 And David took the shields of gold that
were on the servants of Hadadezer, and
brought them to Jerusalem.
8 Also from [T]Tibhath and from Chun, cities
of Hadadezer, David brought a large amount
of bronze, with which Solomon made the
bronze [T]Sea, the pillars, and the articles of
bronze. *Betah,* 2 Sam. 8:8 • Great basin
9 When [T]Tou king of Hamath heard that
David had [T]defeated all the army of Hadadezer king of Zobah, *Toi,* 2 Sam. 8:9 • Lit. *struck*
10 he sent Hadoram his son to King David,
to greet him and bless him, because he had
fought against Hadadezer and [T]defeated him
(for Hadadezer had been at war with Tou);
and *Hadoram brought with him* all kinds of
articles of gold, silver, and bronze. Lit. *struck*
11 King David also dedicated these to the
LORD, along with the silver and gold that he
had brought from all *these* nations—from
Edom, from Moab, from the [R]people of Ammon, from the [R]Philistines, and from [R]Ama-
lek. 2 Sam. 10:12 • 2 Sam. 5:17–25 • 2 Sam. 1:1

Victory over Edom—2 Sam. 8:14–18

12 Moreover Abishai the son of Zeruiah
killed [R]eighteen thousand [T]Edomites in the
Valley of Salt. 2 Sam. 8:13 • *Syrians,* 2 Sam. 8:13
13 He also put garrisons in Edom, and all
the Edomites became David's servants. And
the LORD preserved David wherever he went.
14 So David reigned over all Israel, and
administered judgment and justice to all his
people.
15 Joab the son of Zeruiah *was* over the
army; Jehoshaphat the son of Ahilud *was*
recorder;
16 Zadok the son of Ahitub and Abimelech
the son of Abiathar *were* the priests; [T]Shav-
sha *was* the scribe; *Seraiah,* 2 Sam. 8:17
17 [R]Benaiah the son of Jehoiada *was* over
the Cherethites and the Pelethites; and David's sons *were* [T]chief ministers at the king's
side. 2 Sam. 8:18 • Lit. *at the hand of the king*

CHAPTER 19

Humiliation of David's Servants—2 Sam. 10:1–5

NOW [R]it happened after this that Nahash
the king of the people of Ammon died,
and his son reigned in his place. 2 Sam. 10:1–19
2 Then David said, "I will show kindness
to Hanun the son of Nahash, because his
father showed kindness to me." So David
sent messengers to comfort him concerning
his father. And the servants of David came to
Hanun in the land of the people of Ammon to
comfort him.
3 And the princes of the people of Ammon
said to Hanun, [T]"Do you think that David
really honors your father because he has sent
comforters to you? Did his servants not come
to you to search and to overthrow and to spy
out the land?" Lit. *In your eyes does David honor*
4 Therefore Hanun took David's servants,
shaved them, and cut off their garments [T]in
the middle, at their [R]buttocks, and sent them
away. *in half* • Is. 20:4
5 Then *some* went and told David about
the men; and he sent to meet them, because
the men were greatly ashamed. And the king
said, "Wait at Jericho until your beards have
grown, and *then* return."

Victory over the Ammonites—2 Sam. 10:6–14

6 When the people of Ammon saw that
they had made themselves repulsive to David, Hanun and the people of Ammon sent a
thousand talents of silver to hire for themselves chariots and horsemen from [T]Meso-
potamia, from Syrian Maachah, and from
[T]Zobah. Heb. *Aram Naharaim* • *Zoba,* 2 Sam. 10:6
7 So they hired for themselves thirty-two
thousand chariots, with the king of Maachah
and his people, who came and encamped
before Medeba. Also the people of Ammon
gathered together from their cities, and came
to battle.
8 And when David heard *of it,* he sent Joab
and all the army of the mighty men.
9 Then the people of Ammon came out
and put themselves in battle array before the
gate of the city, and the kings who had come
were by themselves in the field.
10 When Joab saw that the battle line was
set against him before and behind, he chose
some of the choice men of Israel, and put
them in battle array against the Syrians.
11 And the rest of the people he put under
the command of Abishai his brother, and
they set *themselves* in battle array against
the people of Ammon.
12 Then he said, "If the Syrians are too
strong for me, then you shall help me; but if
the people of Ammon are too strong for you,
then I will help you.
13 "Be of good courage, and let us be strong
for our people and for the cities of our God.

And may the LORD do *what is* good in His
sight."
14 So Joab and the people who *were* with
him drew near for the battle against the
Syrians, and they fled before him.
15 When the people of Ammon saw that the
Syrians were fleeing, they also fled before
Abishai his brother, and entered the city. So
Joab went to Jerusalem.

Victory over the Syrians—2 Sam. 10:15–19

16 Now when the Syrians saw that they had
been defeated by Israel, they sent messengers
and brought the Syrians who were beyond
the River, and Shophach the commander of
Hadadezer's army *went* before them.
17 When it was told David, he gathered all
Israel, crossed over the Jordan and came
upon them, and set up in battle array against
them. So when David had set up in *battle*
array against the Syrians, they fought with
him.
18 Then the Syrians fled before Israel; and
David killed seven [T]thousand charioteers and
forty thousand [T]foot soldiers of the Syrians,
and killed Shophach the commander of the
army. *hundred,* 2 Sam. 10:18 • *horsemen,* 2 Sam. 10:18
19 And when the servants of Hadadezer
saw that they were defeated by Israel, they
made peace with David and became his servants. So the Syrians were not willing to help
the people of Ammon anymore.

CHAPTER 20

Victory over the Ammonites
2 Sam. 11:1; 12:26–31

AND it happened, [T]in the spring of the
year, at the time kings go out *to battle,*
that Joab led out the armed forces and ravaged the country of the people of Ammon,
and came and besieged Rabbah. But David
stayed at Jerusalem. And Joab defeated Rabbah and overthrew it. Lit. *at the return*
2 Then David [R]took their king's crown
from his head, and found it to weigh a [T]talent
of gold, and *there were* precious stones in it.
And it was set on David's head. Also he
brought out the [T]spoil of the city in great
abundance. 2 Sam. 12:30, 31 • $5,760,000 • *plunder*
3 And he brought out the people who *were*
in it, and *put *them* to work with saws, with
iron picks, and with axes. So David did to all
the cities of the people of Ammon. Then
David and all the people returned *to* Jerusalem.

Victory over the Philistine Giants
2 Sam. 21:18–22

4 Now it happened afterward that war
broke out at Gezer with the Philistines, at
which time Sibbechai the Hushathite killed
Sippai, *who was one* of the sons of [T]the giant.
And they were subdued. Or *Raphah*
5 Again there was war with the Philistines,
and Elhanan the son of Jair killed Lahmi the
brother of Goliath the Gittite, the shaft of
whose spear *was* like a weaver's beam.
6 Yet again [R]there was war at Gath, where
there was a man of *great* stature, with
twenty-four fingers and toes, six *on each
hand* and six *on each foot;* and he also was
born to [T]the giant. 2 Sam. 21:20 • Or *Raphah*
7 So when he defied Israel, Jonathan the
son of Shimea, David's brother, killed him.
8 These were born to the giant in Gath,
and they fell by the hand of David and by the
hand of his servants.

CHAPTER 21

Temptation of David by Satan

NOW Satan stood up against Israel, and
moved David to number Israel.
2 So David said to Joab and to the leaders
of the people, "Go, number Israel from Beer-

20:3 LXX *cut them with*

21:1 Temptation by Satan—The role of Satan against the Christian is well summed up by the meaning of the name Satan—"adversary." He is also called "the devil," meaning "accuser." He can appear as a hideous dragon (Page 1529—Rev. 12:3, 4, 9) or as a beautifully deceptive "angel of light" (Page 1373—2 Cor. 11:14). He stands hatefully opposed to all the work of God and resourcefully promotes defiance among men (Page 1164—Mark 4:15; Page 590—Job 2:4, 5).

When Satan sinned he was expelled from heaven (Page 1209—Luke 10:18), although apparently he still had some access to God (Page 589—Job 1:6). A multitude of angels cast in their lot with him in his fall and subsequently became the demons mentioned often in the Bible (Page 1131—Matt. 12:24; Page 1529—Rev. 12:7). Although Satan's doom was secured by Jesus' death on the cross (Page 1259—John 16:11), he will continue to hinder God's program until he and his angels are cast into the lake of fire (Page 1149—Matt. 25:41; Page 1538—Rev. 20:10).

The terrifying work of Satan in the unbeliever is described in Scripture as follows: he blinds their minds (Page 1367—2 Cor. 4:4); he takes the Word of God from their hearts (Page 1205—Luke 8:12); and he controls them (Page 1291—Acts 13:8). In regard to Christians, Satan may accuse them (Page 1529—Rev. 12:10), devour their testimony for Christ (Page 1483—1 Pet. 5:8), deceive them (Page 1373—2 Cor. 11:14), hinder their work (Page 1415—1 Thess. 2:18), tempt them to immorality (Page 1351—1 Cor. 7:5), and even be used by God to discipline Christians (Page 1348—1 Cor. 5:5; Page 1374—2 Cor. 12:7).

(continued on next page)

sheba to Dan, [R]and bring the number of them
to me that I may know *it*." 1 Chr. 27:23, 24
3 And Joab answered, "May the LORD
make His people a hundred times more than
they are. But, my lord the king, *are* they not
all my lord's servants? Why then does my
lord require this thing? Why should he be a
cause of guilt in Israel?"
4 Nevertheless the king's word prevailed
against Joab. Therefore Joab departed and
went throughout all Israel and came to Jerusalem.

Enumeration of Israel

5 Then Joab gave the sum of the number
of the people to David. All Israel *had* one
million one hundred thousand men who drew
the sword, and Judah *had* four hundred and
seventy thousand men who drew the sword.
6 [R]But he did not count Levi and Benjamin
among them, for the king's [T]word was abominable to Joab. 1 Chr. 27:24 • *command*

Prayer of David

7 And God was displeased with this thing;
therefore He struck Israel.
8 So David said to God, "I have sinned
greatly, because I have done this thing; but
now, I pray, take away the iniquity of Your
servant, for I have done very foolishly."

Three Choices of David

9 And the LORD spoke to Gad, David's
[R]seer, saying, 1 Sam. 9:9
10 "Go and tell David, [R]saying, 'Thus says
the LORD: "I offer you three *things*; choose
one of them for yourself, that I may do *it* to
you." ' " 2 Sam. 24:12–14
11 So Gad came to David and said to him,
"Thus says the LORD: 'Choose for yourself,
12 'either three years of famine, or three
months to be defeated by your foes with the
sword of your enemies overtaking *you*, or
else for three days the sword of the LORD—
the plague in the land, with the angel of the
LORD destroying throughout all the territory
of Israel.' Now consider what answer I should
take back to Him who sent me."
13 And David said to Gad, "I am in great
distress. Please let me fall into the hand of the
LORD, for His mercies *are* very great; but do
not let me fall into the hand of man."

Judgment of Pestilence

14 So the LORD sent a plague upon Israel,
and seventy thousand men of Israel fell.
15 And God sent [T]an angel to Jerusalem to
destroy it. As he was destroying, the LORD
looked and relented of the disaster, and said
to the angel who was destroying, "It is
enough; now restrain your hand." And the
angel of the LORD stood by the threshing
floor of Ornan the Jebusite. Or *the Angel*
16 Then David lifted his eyes and [R]saw the
angel of the LORD standing between earth
and heaven, having in his hand a drawn
sword stretched out over Jerusalem. So David and the elders, clothed in sackcloth, fell
on their faces. 2 Chr. 3:1
17 And David said to God, "Was it not I
who commanded the people to be numbered?
I am the one who has sinned and done evil
indeed; but these [R]sheep, what have they
done? Let Your hand, I pray, O LORD my God,
be against me and my father's house, but not
against Your people that they should be
plagued." 2 Sam. 7:8

Withholding of Judgment by Sacrifices

18 Then the [R]angel of the LORD commanded
Gad to say to David that David should go and
erect an altar to the LORD on the threshing
floor of Ornan the Jebusite. 2 Chr. 3:1
19 So David went up at the word of Gad,
which he had spoken in the name of the
LORD.
20 Now Ornan turned and saw the angel;
and his four sons *who were* with him hid
themselves, but Ornan continued threshing
wheat.
21 Then David came to Ornan, and Ornan
looked and saw David. And he went out from
the threshing floor, and bowed *down* to David with *his* face to the ground.
22 Then David said to Ornan, [T]"Grant me
the place of *this* threshing floor, that I may
build an altar on it to the LORD. You shall
grant it to me at the full price, that the plague
may be withdrawn from the people." Lit. *Give*
23 And Ornan said to David, "Take *it* to
yourself, and let my lord the king do *what is*
good in his eyes. Look, I *also* give *you* the
oxen for burnt offerings, the threshing imple-

(continued from previous page)

The Christian's response to Satan is to recognize his power and deception (Page 1366—2 Cor. 2:11; Page 1393—Eph. 6:11), to adhere steadfastly to the faith (Page 1483—1 Pet. 5:9), to resist him openly (Page 1471—James 4:7), and not to give him opportunities (Page 1391—Eph. 4:27). In practice, the best way to oppose him is to be a growing Christian. Also, in the light of his tremendous power to blind men to the gospel, Christians must always be aggressively and compassionately witnessing to the lost in order to snatch them from Satan's control (Page 1312—Acts 26:18). Believers can respond to temptation by Satan with confidence. We know that nothing can separate us from the love of God (Page 1333—Rom. 8:28–39).

Now turn to Page 1481—1 Pet. 3:17: Kinds of Suffering.

ments for wood, and the wheat for the grain
offering; I give *it* all."
24 Then King David said to Ornan, "No, but
I will surely buy *it* for the full price, for I will
not take what is yours for the LORD, nor offer
burnt offerings with *that which* costs *me*
nothing."
25 So [R]David gave Ornan six hundred shekels of gold by weight for the place. 2 Sam. 24:24
26 And David built there an altar to the
LORD, and offered burnt offerings and peace
offerings, and called on the LORD; and [R]He
answered him from heaven by fire on the
altar of burnt offering. Lev. 9:24
27 Then the LORD commanded the angel,
and he returned his sword to its sheath.
28 At that time, when David saw that the
LORD had answered him on the threshing
floor of Ornan the Jebusite, he sacrificed
there.
29 [R]For the tabernacle of the LORD and the
altar of the burnt offering, which Moses had
made in the wilderness, *were* at that time at
the high place in [R]Gibeon. 1 Kin. 3:4 • 1 Chr. 16:39
30 But David could not go before it to
inquire of God, for he was afraid of the sword
of the angel of the LORD.

CHAPTER 22

Material Provisions for the Temple's Construction

THEN David said, [R]"This *is* the house of
the LORD God, and this *is* the altar of
burnt offering for Israel." Deut. 12:5
2 So David commanded to gather the
aliens who *were* in the land of Israel; and he
appointed masons to [R]cut hewn stones to
build the house of God. 1 Kin. 5:17, 18
3 And David prepared iron in abundance
for the nails of the doors of the gates and for
the joints, and bronze in abundance [R]beyond
measure, 1 Kin. 7:47
4 and cedar trees in abundance; for the
[R]Sidonians and those from Tyre brought
much cedar wood to David. 1 Kin. 5:6–10
5 Now David said, [R]"Solomon my son *is*
young and inexperienced, and the house *that*
is to be built for the LORD *must be* exceedingly magnificent, famous and glorious
throughout all countries. I will now make
preparation for it." So David made abundant
preparations before his death. 1 Chr. 29:1, 2

David's Charge to Solomon

6 Then he called for his son Solomon, and
[T]charged him to build a house for the LORD
God of Israel. *commanded*
7 And David said to Solomon: "My son, as
for me, it was in my mind to build a house to
the name of the LORD my God;
8 "but the word of the LORD came to me,
saying, 'You have shed much blood and have
made great wars; you shall not build a house
for My name, because you have shed much
blood on the earth in My sight.
9 'Behold, a son shall be born to you, who
shall be a man of rest; and I will give him rest
from all his enemies all around. His name
shall be [T]Solomon, for I will give peace and
quietness to Israel in his days. *Peaceful*
10 'He shall build a house for My name, and
[R]he shall be My son, and I *will be* his Father;
and I will establish the throne of his kingdom
over Israel forever.' Matt. 1:6 ☆
11 "Now, my son, may [R]the LORD be with
you; and may you prosper, and build the
house of the LORD your God, as He has said
to you. 1 Chr. 22:16
12 "Only may the LORD [R]give you wisdom
and understanding, and give you charge
concerning Israel, that you may keep the law
of the LORD your God. 1 Kin. 3:9–12
13 "Then you will prosper, if you take care
to fulfill the statutes and judgments with
which the LORD [T]charged Moses concerning
Israel. Be strong and of good courage; do not
fear nor be dismayed. *commanded*
14 "Indeed I have taken much trouble to
prepare for the house of the LORD [T]one hundred thousand talents of gold and [T]one million talents of silver, and bronze and iron
[R]beyond measure, for it is so abundant. I have
prepared timber and stone also, and you may
add to them. $576 billion • $384 billion • 1 Chr. 22:3
15 "Moreover *there are* workmen with you
in abundance: [T]hewers and workers of stone
and timber, and all types of skillful men for
every kind of work. *stonecutters, masons, carpenters*
16 "Of gold and silver and bronze and iron
there is no limit. Arise and begin working,
and [R]the LORD be with you." 1 Chr. 22:11

David's Charge to the Leaders

17 David also commanded all the leaders of
Israel to help Solomon his son, *saying*,
18 "*Is* not the LORD your God with you?
[R]And has He *not* given you rest on every side?
For He has given the inhabitants of the land
into my hand, and the land is subdued before
the LORD and before His people. Josh. 22:4
19 "Now set your heart and your soul to
seek the LORD your God. Therefore arise and
build the sanctuary of the LORD God, to bring
the ark of the covenant of the LORD and the
holy articles of God into the house that is to
be built for the name of the LORD."

CHAPTER 23

Enumeration of the Levites

SO when David was old and full of days, he
made his son Solomon king over Israel.

2 And he gathered together all the leaders of Israel, with the priests and the Levites.

3 Now the Levites were numbered from the age of [R]thirty years and above; and the number of individual males was thirty-eight thousand. Num. 4:1-3

4 Of these, twenty-four thousand *were* to look after the work of the house of the LORD, six thousand *were* officers and judges,

5 four thousand *were* gatekeepers, and four thousand [R]praised the LORD with *musical* instruments, [R]"which I made," *said David,* "for giving praise." 1 Chr. 15:16 • 2 Chr. 29:25–27

6 And [R]David divided them into [T]divisions among the sons of Levi: Gershon, Kohath, and Merari. Ex. 6:16 • *groups*

Organization of the Gershonites

7 Of the [R]Gershonites: [T]Laadan and Shimei. 1 Chr. 26:21 • *Libni,* Ex. 6:17

8 The sons of Laadan: the first Jehiel, then Zetham and Joel—three *in all.*

9 The sons of Shimei: Shelomith, Haziel, and Haran—three *in all.* These were the heads of the fathers' *houses* of Laadan.

10 And the sons of Shimei: Jahath, *Zina, Jeush, and Beriah. These *were* the four sons of Shimei.

11 Jahath was the first and Zizah the second. But Jeush and Beriah did not have many sons; therefore they were assigned as one father's house.

Organization of the Kohathites

12 [R]The sons of Kohath: Amram, Izhar, Hebron, and Uzziel—four *in all.* Ex. 6:18

13 The sons of Amram: Aaron and Moses; and Aaron was set apart, he and his sons forever, that he should [T]sanctify the most holy things, to burn incense before the LORD, [R]to minister to Him, and to give the blessing in His name forever. *consecrate* • [Deut. 21:5]

14 Now the sons of Moses the man of God were reckoned to the tribe of Levi.

15 [R]The sons of Moses *were* [T]Gershon and Eliezer. Ex. 18:3, 4 • Heb. *Gershom,* 1 Chr. 6:16

16 Of the sons of Gershon, [R]Shebuel[T] *was* the first. 1 Chr. 26:24 • *Shubael,* 1 Chr. 24:20

17 Of the descendants of Eliezer, Rehabiah was the first. And Eliezer had no other sons, but the sons of Rehabiah were very many.

18 Of the sons of Izhar, [R]Shelomith *was* the first. 1 Chr. 24:22

19 [R]Of the sons of Hebron, Jeriah *was* the first, Amariah the second, Jahaziel the third, and Jekameam the fourth. 1 Chr. 24:23

20 Of the sons of Uzziel, Michah *was* the first and Jesshiah the second.

Organization of the Merarites

21 [R]The sons of Merari *were* Mahli and Mushi. The sons of Mahli *were* Eleazar and [R]Kish. 1 Chr. 24:26 • 1 Chr. 24:29

22 And Eleazar died, and had no sons, but only daughters; and their [T]brethren, the sons of Kish, took them *as wives.* *kinsmen*

23 [R]The sons of Mushi *were* Mahli, Eder, and Jeremoth—three *in all.* 1 Chr. 24:30

Duties of the Levites

24 These *were* the sons of Levi by their fathers' houses—the heads of the fathers' *houses* as they were counted individually by the number of their names, who did the work for the service of the house of the LORD, from the age of [R]twenty years and above. Ezra 3:8

25 For David said, "The LORD God of Israel [R]has given rest to His people, that they may dwell in Jerusalem forever"; 1 Chr. 22:18

26 and also to the Levites, "They shall no longer [R]carry the tabernacle, or any of the articles for its service." Num. 4:5, 15; 7:9

27 For by the [R]last words of David the Levites *were* numbered from twenty years old and above; 2 Sam. 23:1

28 because their duty *was* to help the sons of Aaron in the service of the house of the LORD, in the courts and in the chambers, in the purifying of all holy things and the work of the service of the house of God,

29 both with the showbread and the fine flour for the grain offering, with the unleavened cakes and [R]*what is baked in* the pan, with what is mixed and with all kinds of [R]measures and sizes; Lev. 2:5, 7 • Lev. 19:35

30 to stand every morning to thank and praise the LORD, and likewise at evening;

31 and at every presentation of a burnt offering to the LORD on the Sabbaths and on the New Moons and on the set feasts, by number according to the ordinance governing them, regularly before the LORD;

32 and that they should attend to the [R]needs of the tabernacle of meeting, the needs of the holy *place,* and the needs of the sons of Aaron their brethren in the work of the house of the LORD. [Num. 1:53]

CHAPTER 24

Divisions of the Sons of Aaron

NOW *these are* the divisions of the sons of Aaron. [R]The sons of Aaron *were* Nadab, Abihu, Eleazar, and Ithamar. Lev. 10:1-6

2 And Nadab and Abihu died before their father, and had no children; therefore Eleazar and Ithamar ministered as priests.

3 Then David with Zadok of the sons of Eleazar, and [R]Ahimelech of the sons of Ithamar, divided them according to the schedule of their service. 1 Chr. 18:16

4 Now there were more leaders found of the sons of Eleazar than of the sons of Ithamar, and *thus* they were divided. Among the

23:10 LXX, Vg. *Zizah* and v. 11

sons of Eleazar *there were* sixteen heads of
their fathers' houses, and eight heads of their
fathers' houses among the sons of Ithamar.
5 Thus they were divided by lot, one group
as another, for there were officials of the
sanctuary and officials *of the house* of God,
from the sons of Eleazar and from the sons of
Ithamar.
6 And the scribe, Shemaiah the son of
Nethaneel, *one of* the Levites, wrote them
down before the king, the leaders, Zadok the
priest, Ahimelech the son of Abiathar, and
the heads of the fathers' *houses* of the priests
and Levites, one father's house taken for
Eleazar and *one* for Ithamar.
7 Now the first lot fell to Jehoiarib, the
second to Jedaiah,
8 the third to Harim, the fourth to Seorim,
9 the fifth to Malchijah, the sixth to Mijamin,
10 the seventh to Hakkoz, the eighth to
[R]Abijah, Luke 1:5
11 the ninth to Jeshua, the tenth to Shecaniah,
12 the eleventh to Eliashib, the twelfth to
Jakim,
13 the thirteenth to Huppah, the fourteenth
to Jeshebeab,
14 the fifteenth to Bilgah, the sixteenth to
Immer,
15 the seventeenth to Hezir, the eighteenth
to *Happizzez,
16 the nineteenth to Pethahiah, the twentieth to *Jehezekel,
17 the twenty-first to Jachin, the twenty-
second to Gamul,
18 the twenty-third to Delaiah, the twenty-
fourth to Maaziah.
19 This *was* the schedule of their service
[R]for coming into the house of the LORD
according to their ordinance by the hand of
Aaron their father, as the LORD God of Israel
had commanded him. 1 Chr. 9:25

Organizaiton of the Kohathites

20 Now the rest of the sons of Levi: of the
sons of Amram, [T]Shubael; of the sons of
Shubael, Jehdeiah. *Shebuel,* 1 Chr. 23:16
21 Concerning [R]Rehabiah, of the sons of
Rehabiah, the first *was* Isshiah. 1 Chr. 23:17
22 Of the Izharites, [T]Shelomoth; of the sons
of Shelomoth, Jahath. *Shelomith,* 1 Chr. 23:18
23 Of the sons *of* [R]*Hebron*, Jeriah *was the*
first, Amariah the second, Jahaziel the third,
and Jekameam the fourth. 1 Chr. 23:19; 26:31
24 *Of* the sons of Uzziel, Michah; of the
sons of Michah, Shamir.
25 The brother of Michah, Isshiah; of the
sons of Isshiah, Zechariah.

Organization of the Merarites

26 [R]The sons of Merari *were* Mahli and
Mushi; the son of Jaaziah, Beno. Ex. 6:19
27 The sons of Merari by Jaaziah *were*
Beno, Shoham, Zaccur, and Ibri.
28 Of Mahli: Eleazar, who had no sons.
29 Of Kish: the son of Kish, Jerahmeel.
30 Also the sons of Mushi *were* Mahli, Eder,
and Jerimoth. These *were* the sons of the
Levites according to their fathers' houses.
31 These also cast lots just as their brothers
the sons of Aaron did, in the presence of King
David, Zadok, Ahimelech, and the heads of
the fathers' *houses* of the priests and Levites.
The chief fathers *did* just as their younger
brethren.

CHAPTER 25

Organization of the Orders of the Musicians

MOREOVER David and the captains of
the army separated for the service
some of the sons of [R]Asaph, of Heman, and of
Jeduthun, who *should* prophesy with harps,
stringed instruments, and cymbals. And the
number of the workmen according to their
service was: 1 Chr. 6:30, 33, 39, 44
2 Of the sons of Asaph: Zaccur, Joseph,
Nethaniah, and [T]Asharelah; the sons of
Asaph *were* [T]under the direction of Asaph,
who prophesied according to the order of the
king. *Jesharelah,* v. 14 • Lit. *at the hands of*
3 Of Jeduthun, the sons of Jeduthun:
Gedaliah, [T]Zeri, Jeshaiah, **Shimei*, Hashabiah, and Mattithiah, [T]six, under the direction of their father Jeduthun, who prophesied
with a harp to give thanks and to praise the
LORD. *Jizri,* v. 11 • Shimei is the sixth, v. 17
4 Of Heman, the sons of Heman: Bukkiah,
Mattaniah, [T]Uzziel, [T]Shebuel, Jerimoth,
Hananiah, Hanani, Eliathah, Giddalti, Romamti-Ezer, Joshbekashah, Mallothi, Hothir,
and Mahazioth. *Azarel,* v. 18 • *Shubael,* v. 20
5 All these *were* the sons of Heman the
king's seer in the words of God, to [T]exalt his
horn. For God gave Heman fourteen sons and
three daughters. Increase his power or influence
6 All these *were* under the direction of
their father for the music *in* the house of the
LORD, with cymbals, stringed instruments,
and [R]harps, for the service of the house of
God. Asaph, Jeduthun, and Heman *were*
under the authority of the king. 1 Chr. 15:16
7 So the [R]number of them, with their
brethren who were instructed in the songs of
the LORD, all who were skillful, *was* two
hundred and eighty-eight. 1 Chr. 23:5
8 And they cast lots for their duty, the
small as well as the great, [R]the teacher with
the student. 2 Chr. 23:13
9 Now the first lot for Asaph came out for
Joseph; the second for Gedaliah, him with his
brethren and sons, twelve;

24:15 LXX, Vg. *Aphses* **24:16** MT *Jehezkel*
25:3 So with a Heb. ms., LXX mss.

10 the third for Zaccur, his sons and his
brethren, twelve;
11 the fourth for [T]Jizri, his sons and his
brethren, twelve; *Zeri*, v. 3
12 the fifth for Nethaniah, his sons and his
brethren, twelve;
13 the sixth for Bukkiah, his sons and his
brethren, twelve;
14 the seventh for [T]Jesharelah, his sons and
his brethren, twelve; *Asharelah*, v. 2
15 the eighth for Jeshaiah, his sons and his
brethren, twelve;
16 the ninth for Mattaniah, his sons and his
brethren, twelve;
17 the tenth for Shimei, his sons and his
brethren, twelve;
18 the eleventh for [T]Azarel, his sons and his
brethren, twelve; *Uzziel*, v. 4
19 the twelfth for Hashabiah, his sons and
his brethren, twelve;
20 the thirteenth for [T]Shubael, his sons and
his brethren, twelve; *Shebuel*, v. 4
21 the fourteenth for Mattithiah, his sons
and his brethren, twelve;
22 the fifteenth for [T]Jeremoth, his sons and
his brethren, twelve; *Jerimoth*, v. 4
23 the sixteenth for Hananiah, his sons and
his brethren, twelve;
24 the seventeenth for Joshbekashah, his
sons and his brethren, twelve;
25 the eighteenth for Hanani, his sons and
his brethren, twelve;
26 the nineteenth for Mallothi, his sons and
his brethren, twelve;
27 the twentieth for Eliathah, his sons and
his brethren, twelve;
28 the twenty-first for Hothir, his sons and
his brethren, twelve;
29 the twenty-second for Giddalti, his sons
and his brethren, twelve;
30 the twenty-third for Mahazioth, his sons
and his brethren, twelve;
31 the twenty-fourth for Romamti-Ezer, his
sons and his brethren, twelve.

CHAPTER 26

Organization of the Gatekeepers

CONCERNING the divisions of the gatekeepers: of the Korahites, Meshelemiah
the son of Kore, of the sons of Asaph.
2 And the sons of Meshelemiah *were*
Zechariah the firstborn, Jediael the second,
Zebadiah the third, Jathniel the fourth,
3 Elam the fifth, Jehohanan the sixth,
Eljehoenai the seventh.
4 Moreover the sons of [R]Obed-Edom *were*
Shemaiah the firstborn, Jehozabad the second, Joah the third, Sacar the fourth, Nethanel the fifth, 1 Chr. 15:18, 21
5 Ammiel the sixth, Issachar the seventh,
Peulthai the eighth; for God blessed him.
6 Also to Shemaiah his son were sons born
who governed their fathers' houses, because
they *were* men of great ability.
7 The sons of Shemaiah *were* Othni, Re-
phael, Obed, and Elzabad, whose brothers
Elihu and Semachiah *were* able men.
8 All these *were* of the sons of Obed-Edom,
they and their sons and their brethren, [R]able
men with strength for the work: sixty-two of
Obed-Edom. 1 Chr. 9:13
9 And Meshelemiah had sons and brethren, eighteen able men.
10 Also Hosah, of the children of Merari,
had sons: Shimri the first (for *though* he was
not the firstborn, his father made him the
first),
11 Hilkiah the second, Tebaliah the third,
Zechariah the fourth; all the sons and brethren of Hosah *were* thirteen.
12 Among these *were* the divisions of the
gatekeepers, among the chief men, *having*
duties just like their brethren, to serve in the
house of the LORD.
13 And they [R]cast lots for each gate, the
small as well as the great, according to their
father's house. 1 Chr. 24:5, 31; 25:8
14 The lot for the East *Gate* fell to [T]Shele-
miah. Then they cast lots *for* his son Zechariah, a wise counselor, and his lot came out
for the North Gate; *Meshelemiah*, v. 1
15 to Obed-Edom the South Gate, and to his
sons the [T]storehouse. Heb. *asuppim*
16 To Shuppim and Hosah *the lot came out*
for the West Gate, with the Shallecheth Gate
on the [R]ascending highway—watchman opposite watchman. 1 Kin. 10:5
17 On the east were *six* Levites, on the
north four each day, on the south four each
day, and for the storehouse two by two.
18 As for the [T]Parbar on the west, *there*
were four on the highway *and* two at the
Parbar. Probably a court extending west of the temple
19 These were the divisions of the gatekeepers among the sons of Korah and among the
sons of Merari.

Organization of the Treasuries of the Temple

20 Of the Levites, Ahijah *was* over the
treasuries of the house of God and over the
treasuries of the [T]dedicated things. *holy*
21 The sons of [T]Laadan, the descendants of
the Gershonites of Laadan, heads of their
fathers' *houses*, of Laadan the Gershonite:
[T]Jehieli. *Libni*, 1 Chr. 6:17 • *Jehiel*, 1 Chr. 23:8; 29:8
22 The sons of Jehieli, Zetham and Joel his
brother, *were* over the treasuries of the house
of the LORD.
23 Of the [R]Amramites, the Izharites, the
Hebronites, and the Uzzielites: Ex. 6:18
24 Shebuel the son of Gershom, the son of
Moses, *was* overseer of the treasuries.

25 And his brethren by Eliezer *were* Rehabiah his son, Jeshaiah his son, Joram his son, Zichri his son, and Shelomith his son.

26 This Shelomith and his brethren *were* over all the treasuries of the dedicated things [R]which King David and the heads of fathers' *houses*, the captains over thousands and hundreds, and the captains of the army, had dedicated. 2 Sam. 8:11

27 Some of the spoils won in battles they dedicated to maintain the house of the LORD.

28 And all that Samuel [R]the seer, Saul the son of Kish, Abner the son of Ner, and Joab the son of Zeruiah had dedicated, every dedicated *thing*, was under the hand of Shelomith and his brethren. 1 Sam. 9:9

Organization of the Officers Outside of the Temple

29 Of the Izharites, Chenaniah and his sons *performed* duties as [R]officials and judges over Israel outside Jerusalem. 1 Chr. 23:4

30 Of the Hebronites, Hashabiah and his brethren, one thousand seven hundred able men, had the oversight of Israel on the west side of the Jordan for all the business of the LORD, and in the service of the king.

31 Among the Hebronites, [R]Jerijah *was* head of the Hebronites according to his genealogy of the fathers. In the fortieth year of the reign of David they were sought, and there were found among them capable men [R]at Jazer of Gilead. 1 Chr. 23:19 • Josh. 21:39

32 And his brethren *were* two thousand seven hundred able men, heads of fathers' *houses*, whom King David made officials over the Reubenites, the Gadites, and the half-tribe of Manasseh, for every matter pertaining to God and the affairs of the king.

CHAPTER 27

The Twelve Captains of Israel

AND the children of Israel, according to their number, the heads of fathers' *houses*, the captains of thousands and hundreds and their officers, served the king in every matter of the *military* divisions. *These divisions* came in and went out month by month throughout all the months of the year, each division *having* twenty-four thousand.

2 Over the first division for the first month *was* Jashobeam the son of Zabdiel, and in his division *were* twenty-four thousand;

3 *he was* of the children of Perez, and the chief of all the captains of the army for the first month.

4 Over the division of the second month *was* [T]Dodai an Ahohite, and of his division Mikloth also *was* the leader; in his division *were* twenty-four thousand. Usually spelled *Dodo*

5 The third captain of the army for the third month *was* Benaiah, the son of Jehoiada the priest, who was chief; in his division *were* twenty-four thousand.

6 This was the Benaiah *who was* mighty *among* the thirty, and was over the thirty; in his division *was* Ammizabad his son.

7 The fourth *captain* for the fourth month *was* [R]Asahel the brother of Joab, and Zebadiah his son after him; in his division *were* twenty-four thousand. 1 Chr. 11:26

8 The fifth *captain* for the fifth month *was* [T]Shamhuth the Izrahite; in his division were twenty-four thousand. *Shammah*, 2 Sam. 23:11

9 The sixth *captain* for the sixth month *was* Ira the son of Ikkesh the Tekoite; in his division *were* twenty-four thousand.

10 The seventh *captain* for the seventh month *was* [R]Helez the Pelonite, of the children of Ephraim; in his division *were* twenty-four thousand. 1 Chr. 11:27

11 The eighth *captain* for the eighth month *was* [R]Sibbechai the Hushathite, of the Zarhites; in his division *were* twenty-four thousand. 2 Sam. 21:18

12 The ninth *captain* for the ninth month *was* [R]Abiezer the Anathothite, of the Benjamites; in his division *were* twenty-four thousand. 1 Chr. 11:28

13 The tenth *captain* for the tenth month *was* [R]Maharai the Netophathite, of the Zarhites; in his division *were* twenty-four thousand. 1 Chr. 11:30

14 The eleventh *captain* for the eleventh month *was* [R]Benaiah the Pirathonite, of the children of Ephraim; in his division *were* twenty-four thousand. 1 Chr. 11:31

15 The twelfth *captain* for the twelfth month *was* [T]Heldai the Netophathite, of Othniel; in his division *were* twenty-four thousand. *Heleb*, 2 Sam. 23:29, or *Heled*, 1 Chr. 11:30

The Leaders of the Twelve Tribes

16 Furthermore, over the tribes of Israel: the officer over the Reubenites *was* Eliezer the son of Zichri; over the Simeonites, Shephatiah the son of Maachah;

17 *over* the Levites, [R]Hashabiah the son of Kemuel; over the Aaronites, Zadok; 1 Chr. 26:30

18 *over* Judah, Elihu, *one* of David's brothers; *over* Issachar, Omri the son of Michael;

19 *over* Zebulun, Ishmaiah the son of Obadiah; *over* Naphtali, Jerimoth the son of Azriel;

20 *over* the children of Ephraim, Hoshea the son of Azaziah; *over* the half-tribe of Manasseh, Joel the son of Pedaiah;

21 *over* the half-*tribe* of Manasseh in Gilead, Iddo the son of Zechariah; *over* Benjamin, Jaasiel the son of Abner;

22 *over* Dan, Azarel the son of Jeroham. These *were* the leaders of the tribes of Israel.

23 But David did not take the number of
those twenty years old and under, because
[R]the LORD had said He would multiply Israel
like the stars of the heavens. [Deut. 6:3]
24 Joab the son of Zeruiah began a census,
but he did not finish, for [R]wrath came upon
Israel because of this census; nor was the
number recorded in the account of the chronicles of King David. 1 Chr. 7, 8; 21:7

The Royal Officers of David

25 And Azmaveth the son of Adiel *was* over
the king's treasuries; and Jehonathan the son
of Uzziah was over the storehouses in the
field, in the cities, in the villages, and in the
fortresses.
26 Ezri the son of Chelub was over those
who did the work of the field for tilling the
ground.
27 And Shimei the Ramathite *was* over the
vineyards, and Zabdi the Shiphmite was over
the produce of the vineyards for the supply of
wine.
28 Baal-Hanan the Gederite was over the
olive trees and the sycamore trees that *were*
in the lowlands, and Joash *was* over the store
of oil.
29 And Shitrai the Sharonite *was* over the
herds that fed in Sharon, and Shaphat the
son of Adlai was over the herds *that were* in
the valleys.
30 Obil the Ishmaelite *was* over the camels,
Jehdeiah the Meronothite *was* over the donkeys,
31 and Jaziz the [R]Hagerite *was* over the
flocks. All these *were* the officials over King
David's property. 1 Chr. 5:10

The Counselors of David

32 Also Jehonathan, David's uncle, *was* a
counselor, a wise man, and a [T]scribe; and
Jehiel the [T]son of Hachmoni *was* with the
king's sons. *secretary* • Or *Hachmonite*
33 [R]Ahithophel *was* the king's counselor,
and [R]Hushai the Archite *was* the king's companion. 2 Sam. 15:12 • 2 Sam. 15:32–37
34 After Ahithophel *was* Jehoiada the son
of Benaiah, then Abiathar. And the general of
the king's army *was* [R]Joab. 1 Chr. 11:6

CHAPTER 28

Charge to Israel

NOW David assembled at Jerusalem all
the leaders of Israel: the officers of the
tribes and the captains of the divisions who
served the king, the captains over thousands
and captains over hundreds, and [R]the stewards over all the substance and [T]possessions
of the king and of his sons, with the officials,
the valiant men, and all [R]the mighty men of
valor. 1 Chr. 27:25 • Or *livestock* • 1 Chr. 11:10–47
2 Then King David rose to his feet and
said, "Hear me, my brethren and my people:
[R]I *had* it in my heart to build a house of rest
for the ark of the covenant of the LORD, and
for [R]the footstool of our God, and had made
preparations to build it. 2 Sam. 7:2 • Ps. 99:5; 132:7
3 "But God said to me, 'You shall not build
a house for My name, because you *have been*
a man of war and have shed blood.'
4 "However the LORD God of Israel chose
me above all the house of my father to be
king over Israel forever, for He has chosen
Judah *to be* the ruler; and of the house of
Judah, [R]the house of my father, and among
the sons of my father, He was pleased with
me to make *me* king over all Israel. 1 Sam. 16:1
5 "And of all my sons (for the LORD has
given me many sons) [R]He has chosen my son
Solomon to sit on the throne of the kingdom
of the LORD over Israel. 1 Chr. 22:9; 29:1
6 "Now He said to me, 'It is [R]your son
Solomon *who* shall build My house and My
courts; for I have chosen him *to be* My son,
and I will be his Father. 2 Sam. 7:13, 14

28:4–6 Government of Israel—The government of Israel may be considered under two important headings: the laws, and the leaders.

The laws:

a. The "commandments," especially the Ten Commandments, revealed God's holiness and set up a divine standard of righteousness for the people to follow (Page 90—Ex. 20:1–17).
b. The judgments governed the social life of the people and concerned masters and servants (Page 92—Ex. 21:1–11), physical injuries (Page 92—Ex. 21:12–36), protection of property rights (Page 93—Ex. 22:1–15), etc.
c. The ordinances included the sacrifices that showed that blood must be shed for sinners to be forgiven (Page 120—Lev. 1—17).

The leaders: At first Moses was the sole leader; then he was replaced by Joshua. After Joshua's death the nation was governed for many years by judges, who were usually raised up by God to oppose a specific enemy. Finally, at the people's request, God granted them a king, thus establishing the monarchy (Page 330—1 Sam. 8:5, 22). Under the monarchy there were four key leaders:

a. The *king* was the Lord's representative who ruled the people, but only as the Lord's servant. He led in war (Page 330—1 Sam. 8:20) and made judicial decisions (Page 374—2 Sam. 15:2); but he could not make law, since he himself was under the law (Page 229—Deut. 17:19). His relationship was so close to the Lord that he was adopted by the Lord (Page 366—2 Sam. 7:14; Page 625—Ps. 2:7).

7 'Moreover [R]I will establish his kingdom forever, [R]if he is steadfast to observe My commandments and My judgments, as it is this day.' Matt. 1:6☆ • 1 Chr. 22:13
8 "Now therefore, in the sight of all Israel, the congregation of the LORD, and in the hearing of our God, be careful to seek out all the commandments of the LORD your God, that you may possess this good land, and leave *it* as an inheritance for your children after you forever.

Charge to Solomon

9 "As for you, my son Solomon, [R]know the God of your father, and serve Him with a loyal heart and with a willing mind; for the LORD searches all hearts and understands all the intent of the thoughts. If you seek Him, He will be found by you; but if you forsake Him, He will cast you off forever. [John 17:3]
10 "Consider now, [R]for the LORD has chosen you to build a house for the sanctuary; be strong, and do it." 1 Chr. 22:13; 28:6

Pattern for the Temple

11 Then David gave his son Solomon [R]the plans for the vestibule, its houses, its treasuries, its upper chambers, its inner chambers, and the place of the mercy seat; 1 Chr. 28:19
12 and the plans for all that he had by the Spirit, of the courts of the house of the LORD, of all the chambers all around, [R]of the treasuries of the house of God, and of the treasuries for the dedicated things; 1 Chr. 26:20, 28
13 also for the division of the priests and the [R]Levites, for all the work of the service of the house of the LORD, and for all the articles of service in the house of the LORD. 1 Chr. 23:6
14 *He gave* gold by weight for *things* of gold, for all articles used in every kind of service; also *silver* for all articles of silver by weight, for all articles used in every kind of service;
15 the weight for the [R]lampstands of gold, and their lamps of gold, by weight for each lampstand and its lamps; for the lampstands of silver by weight, for the lampstand and its lamps, according to the use of each lampstand. Ex. 25:31-39
16 And by weight *he gave* gold for the tables of the showbread, for each [R]table, and silver for the tables of silver; 1 Kin. 7:48
17 also pure gold for the forks, the basins, the pitchers of pure gold, and the golden bowls—*he gave gold* by weight for every bowl; and for the silver bowls, *silver* by weight for every bowl;
18 and refined gold by weight for the altar of incense, and for the construction of the chariot, that is, the gold [R]cherubim that spread *their wings* and overshadowed the ark of the covenant of the LORD. Ex. 25:18-22
19 "All *this*," *said David*, "the LORD made me understand in writing, by *His* hand upon me, all the [T]works of these plans." *details*
20 And David said to his son Solomon, [R]"Be strong and of good courage, and do *it*; do not fear nor be dismayed, for the LORD God—my God—*will be* with you. [R]He will not leave you nor forsake you, until you have finished all the work for the service of the house of the LORD. 1 Chr. 22:13 • Josh. 1:5
21 "*Here are* [R]the divisions of the priests and the Levites for all the service of the house of God; and [R]every willing craftsman *will be* with you for all manner of workmanship, for every kind of service; also the leaders and all the people *will be* completely at your command." 1 Chr. 24—26 • Ex. 35:25-35; 36:1, 2

CHAPTER 29

Provisions of David for the Temple

FURTHERMORE King David said to all the congregation: "My son Solomon, whom alone God has [R]chosen, *is* [R]young and inexperienced; and the work *is* great, because the [T]temple *is* not for man but for the LORD God. 1 Chr. 28:5 • 1 Kin. 3:7 • Lit. *palace*
2 "Now for the house of my God I have prepared with all my might: gold for *things to be made of* gold, silver for *things of* silver, bronze for *things of* bronze, iron for *things of* iron, wood for *things of* wood, [R]onyx stones, *stones* to be set, glistening stones of various colors, all kinds of precious stones, and marble slabs in abundance. Is. 54:11, 12
3 "Moreover, because I have set my affection on the house of my God, I have given to the house of my God, over and above all that I have prepared for the holy house, my own special treasure of gold and silver:
4 [T]"three thousand talents of gold, of the gold of [R]Ophir, and [T]seven thousand talents

---

b. The *priest* taught the Lord's laws and officiated at the offering of the sacrifices (Page 120—Lev. 1:5; Page 865—Jer. 18:18).
c. The *prophet* was the man of God who spoke for God and gave divine pronouncements for the present (forthtelling) or for the future (foretelling).
d. The *wise man* produced literary works stressing practical wisdom (Page 714—Prov. 1:1), taught discipline of character to the young (Page 735—Prov. 22:17), and gave counsel to the king (Page 376—2 Sam. 16:20). The choice of these men indicates an important biblical principle: God uses people to reach other people, a principle that is also evident in the Great Commission given to Christians (Page 1155—Matt. 28:19, 20).

Now turn to Page 640—Ps. 29:2: Worship by Israel.

of refined silver, to overlay the walls of the
houses; $17,280,000,000 • 1 Kin. 9:28 • $2,688,000,000
5 "the gold for *things of* gold and the silver
for *things of* silver, and for all kinds of work
to be done by the hands of craftsmen. Who
then is [R]willing to [T]consecrate himself this
day to the LORD?" [2 Cor. 8:5, 12] • Lit. *fill his hand*

Provisions of Israel for the Temple

6 Then the leaders of the fathers' *houses*,
leaders of the tribes of Israel, the captains of
thousands and of hundreds, with the officers
over the king's work, offered willingly.
7 They gave for the work of the house of
God five thousand talents and ten thousand
darics of gold, [T]ten thousand talents of silver,
eighteen thousand talents of bronze, and one
hundred thousand talents of iron. $3,840 billion
8 And whoever had *precious* stones gave
them to the treasury of the house of the
LORD, into the hand of [R]Jehiel[T] the Gershon-
ite. 1 Chr. 23:8 • Possibly the same as *Jehieli*, 1 Chr. 26:21, 22
9 Then the people rejoiced, for they had
offered willingly, because with a loyal heart
they had [R]offered willingly to the LORD; and
King David also rejoiced greatly. 2 Cor. 9:7

David's Final Prayer of Thanksgiving

10 Therefore David blessed the LORD before
all the congregation; and David said:

"Blessed are You, LORD God of Israel,
our Father, forever and ever.
11 [R]Yours, O LORD, *is* the greatness,
The power and the glory, 1 Tim. 1:17
The victory and the majesty;
For all *that is* in heaven and in earth *is*
Yours;
Yours *is* the kingdom, O LORD,
And You are exalted as head over all.
12 [R]Both riches and honor *come* from You,
And You reign over all. Rom. 11:36
In Your hand *is* power and might;
In Your hand *it is* to make great
And to give strength to all.

13 "Now therefore, our God,
We thank You
And praise Your glorious name.
14 But who *am* I, and who *are* my people,
That we should be able to offer so
willingly as this?
For all things *come* from You,
And of Your own we have given You.
15 For [R]we *are* [T]aliens and [T]pilgrims before
You, Heb. 11:13, 14 • *sojourners* • *transients*
As *were* all our fathers;
[R]Our days on earth *are* as a shadow,
And without hope. Job 14:2

16 "O LORD our God, all this abundance that
we have prepared to build You a house for
Your holy name is from Your hand, and *is* all
Your own.
17 "I know also, my God, that You test the
heart and have pleasure in uprightness. As
for me, in the uprightness of my heart I have
willingly offered all these *things*; and now
with joy I have seen Your people, who are
present here to offer willingly to You.
18 "O LORD God of Abraham, Isaac, and
Israel, our fathers, keep this forever in the
intent of the thoughts of the heart of Your
people, and fix their heart toward You.
19 "And [R]give my son Solomon a loyal heart
to keep Your commandments and Your testimonies and Your statutes, to do all *these*
things, and to build the [T]temple for which I
have made provision." [1 Chr. 28:9] • Lit. *palace*

Coronation of Solomon—1 Kin. 1:38–40; 2:12

20 Then David said to all the congregation,
"Now bless the LORD your God." So all the
congregation blessed the LORD God of their
fathers, and bowed their heads and prostrated themselves before the LORD and the
king.
21 And they made sacrifices to the LORD
and offered burnt offerings to the LORD on
the next day: a thousand bulls, a thousand
rams, a thousand lambs, with their drink
offerings, and [R]sacrifices in abundance for all
Israel. 1 Kin. 8:62, 63
22 So they ate and drank before the LORD
with great gladness on that day. And they
made Solomon the son of David king the
second time, and anointed *him* before the
LORD *to be* the leader, and Zadok *to be* priest.
23 Then Solomon sat on the throne of the
LORD as king instead of David his father, and
prospered; and all Israel obeyed him.
24 All the leaders and the mighty men, and
also all the sons of King David, [T]submitted
themselves to King Solomon. Lit. *gave the hand*
25 So the LORD exalted Solomon exceedingly in the sight of all Israel, and [R]bestowed
on him *such* royal majesty as had not been
on any king before him in Israel. 1 Kin. 3:13

Death of King David

26 Thus David the son of Jesse reigned over
all Israel.
27 [R]And the period that he reigned over
Israel *was* forty years; [R]seven years he
reigned in Hebron, and thirty-three *years* he
reigned in Jerusalem. 1 Kin. 2:11 • 2 Sam. 5:5
28 So he [R]died in a good old age, [R]full of
days and riches and honor; and Solomon his
son reigned in his place. Gen. 25:8 • 1 Chr. 23:1
29 Now the acts of King David, first and
last, indeed they *are* written in the book of
Samuel the seer, in the book of Nathan the
prophet, and in the book of Gad the seer,
30 with all his reign and his might, [R]and the
events that happened to him, to Israel, and to
all the kingdoms of the lands. Dan. 2:21; 4:23, 25

THE SECOND BOOK OF THE
CHRONICLES

THE BOOK OF SECOND CHRONICLES

The Book of Second Chronicles parallels First and Second Kings but virtually ignores the northern kingdom of Israel because of its false worship and refusal to acknowledge the temple in Jerusalem. Chronicles focuses on those kings who pattern their lives and reigns after the life and reign of godly King David. It gives extended treatment to such zealous reformers as Asa, Jehoshaphat, Joash, Hezekiah, and Josiah.

The temple and temple worship, central throughout the book, befit a nation whose worship of God is central to its very survival. The book begins with Solomon's glorious temple and concludes with Cyrus's edict to rebuild the temple more than four hundred years later.

See "The Book of First Chronicles" for more detail on the title.

THE AUTHOR OF SECOND CHRONICLES

For a discussion of the author of First and Second Chronicles, see "The Author of First Chronicles." The sources of First and Second Chronicles include official and prophetic records: (1) The Book of the Kings of Israel and Judah (or Judah and Israel) (1 Chr. 9:1; 2 Chr. 16:11; 20:34; 25:26; 27:7; 28:26; 32:32; 35:27; 36:8), (2) A Commentary on the Book of the Kings (2 Chr. 24:27), (3) Chronicles of Samuel the Seer (1 Chr. 29:29), (4) Chronicles of Nathan the Prophet (1 Chr. 29:29; 2 Chr. 9:29), (5) Chronicles of Gad the Seer (1 Chr. 29:29), (6) The Prophecy of Ahijah the Shilonite (2 Chr. 9:29), (7) The Visions of Iddo the Seer (2 Chr. 9:29; 12:15; 13:22), (8) Records of Shemaiah the Prophet (2 Chr. 12:15), (9) Records of Iddo the Prophet on Genealogies (2 Chr. 12:15), (10) Treatise of the Prophet Iddo (2 Chr. 13:22), (11) The Annals of Jehu the Son of Hanani (2 Chr. 20:34), (12) The Acts of Uzziah by Isaiah the Prophet (2 Chr. 26:22), (13) The Vision of Isaiah the Prophet (2 Chr. 32:32), (14) The Records of the Hozai (2 Chr. 33:19), (15) The Account of the Chronicles of King David (1 Chr. 27:24), (16) The Writing of David and His Son Solomon (2 Chr. 35:4). In addition to these, the author-compiler had access to genealogical lists and documents, such as the message and letters of Sennacherib (2 Chr. 32:10–17).

THE TIME OF SECOND CHRONICLES

See "The Time of First Chronicles" for the background of First and Second Chronicles. Chapters 1—9 cover the forty years from 971 B.C. to 931 B.C., and chapters 10—36 cover the 393 years from 931 B.C. to 538 B.C. Jeremiah's prediction of a seventy-year captivity in Babylon (36:21; Jer. 29:10) is fulfilled in two ways: (1) a political captivity in which Jerusalem is overcome from 605 B.C. to 536 B.C., and (2) a religious captivity involving the destruction of the temple in 586 B.C. and the completion of the new temple in 516 or 515 B.C.

THE CHRIST OF SECOND CHRONICLES

The throne of David has been destroyed, but the line of David remains. Murders, treachery, battles, and captivity all threaten the messianic line; but it remains clear and unbroken from Adam to Zerubbabel. The fulfillment in Christ can be seen in the genealogies of Matthew 1 and Luke 3.

The temple also prefigures Christ. Jesus says, "in this place there is *One* greater than the temple" (Matt. 12:6). He also likens His body to the temple: "Destroy this temple, and in three days I will raise it up" (John 2:19). In Revelation 21:22 He replaces the temple: "But I saw no temple in it, for the Lord God Almighty and the Lamb are its temple."

KEYS TO SECOND CHRONICLES

Key Word: Priestly View of Judah—The Book of Second Chronicles provides topical histories of the end of the united kingdom (Solomon) and the kingdom of Judah. More than historical annals, Chronicles is a divine editorial on the spiritual characteristics of the Davidic dynasty. This is why it focuses on the southern rather than the northern kingdom. Most of the kings fail to realize that apart from the true mission as a covenant nation called to bring others to Yahweh, Judah has no calling, no destiny, and no hope of becoming great on her own. Only what is done in accordance with God's will has any lasting value. Chronicles concentrates on the kings who are concerned with maintaining the proper service of God and the times of spiritual reform. However, growing apostasy inevitably leads to judgment.

The temple in Jerusalem is the major unifying theme of First and Second Chronicles. Much of the material found in Second Samuel to Second Kings is omitted from Chronicles because it does not develop this theme. In First Chronicles 11—29, the central message is David's preparation for the construction and service of the temple. Most of Second Chronicles 1—9 is devoted to the building and consecration of the temple. Chapters 10—36 omit the kings of Israel in the north because they have no ties with the temple. Prominence is given to the reigns of Judah's temple restorers (Asa, Jehoshaphat, Joash, Hezekiah, and Josiah). The temple symbolizes God's presence among His people and reminds them of their high calling. It provides the spiritual link between their past and future. Thus, Ezra wrote this book to encourage the people to accept the new temple raised on the site of the old and to remind them of their true calling and God's faithfulness despite their low circumstances. The Davidic line, temple, and priesthood are still theirs.

Key Verses: Second Chronicles 7:14; 16:9—"If My people who are called by My name will humble themselves, and pray and seek My face, and turn from their wicked ways, then I will hear from heaven, and will forgive their sin and heal their land" (7:14).

"For the eyes of the LORD run to and fro throughout the whole earth, to show Himself strong on behalf of *those* whose heart *is* loyal to Him. In this you have done foolishly; therefore from now on you shall have wars" (16:9).

Key Chapter: Second Chronicles 34—Second Chronicles records the reforms and revivals under such kings as Asa, Jehoshaphat, Joash, Hezekiah, and Josiah. Chapter 34 traces the dramatic revival that takes place under Josiah when the "Book of the Law" is found, read, and obeyed.

SURVEY OF SECOND CHRONICLES

This book repeatedly teaches that whenever God's people forsake Him, He withdraws His blessings, but trust in and obedience to the Lord bring victory. Since everything in Chronicles is related to the temple, it is not surprising that this concludes with Cyrus's edict to rebuild it. Solomon's glory is seen in chapters 1—9, and Judah's decline and deportation in chapters 10—36.

Solomon's Reign (1—9): The reign of Solomon brings in Israel's golden age of peace, prosperity, and temple worship. The kingdom is united and its boundaries extend to their greatest point. Solomon's wealth, wisdom, palace, and temple become legendary. His mighty spiritual, political, and architectural feats raise Israel to her zenith. However, it is in keeping with the purpose of Chronicles that six of these nine chapters concern the construction and dedication of the temple.

The Reign of Judah's Kings (10—36): Unfortunately, Israel's glory is short-lived. Soon after Solomon's death the nation is divided, and both kingdoms begin a downward spiral that can only be delayed by the religious reforms. The nation generally forsakes the temple and the worship of Yahweh, and is soon torn by warfare and unrest. The reformation efforts on the part of some of Judah's kings are valiant, but never last beyond one generation. Nevertheless, about seventy percent of chapters 10—36 deals with the eight good kings, leaving only thirty percent to cover the twelve evil rulers. Each king is seen with respect to his relationship to the temple as the center of worship and spiritual strength. When the king serves Yahweh, Judah is blessed with political and economic prosperity.

Here is a brief survey of Judah's twenty rulers: (1) *Rehoboam*—Although he is not righteous, he humbles himself before God and averts His wrath (12:12). (2) *Abijah*—He enjoys a short and evil reign, but he conquers Israel because "the children of Judah . . . relied on the LORD God" (13:18). (3) *Asa*—Although he destroys foreign altars and idols, conquers Ethiopia against great odds through his trust in God, and restores the altar of the Lord, yet he fails to trust God when threatened by Israel. (4) *Jehoshaphat*—He brings

FOCUS	REIGN OF SOLOMON			REIGNS OF THE KINGS OF JUDAH		
REFERENCE	1:1———	2:1———	8:1———	10:1———	14:1———	36:1—36:23
DIVISION	INAUGURATION OF SOLOMON	COMPLETION OF THE TEMPLE	THE GLORY OF SOLOMON'S REIGN	THE DIVISION OF THE KINGDOM	THE REFORMS UNDER ASA, JEHOSHAPHAT, JOASH, HEZEKIAH, AND JOSIAH	THE FALL OF JUDAH
TOPIC	THE TEMPLE IS CONSTRUCTED			THE TEMPLE IS DESTROYED		
	SPLENDOR			DISASTER		
LOCATION	JUDAH					
TIME	c. 40 YEARS			c. 393 YEARS		

in a great revival; "his heart took delight in the ways of the LORD" (17:6). Jehoshaphat overthrows idols, teaches God's Word to the people, and trusts in God before battle. (5) *Jehoram*—A wicked king, he follows the ways of Ahab and marries his daughter. He leads Judah into idolatry and when he dies in pain, departs "to no one's sorrow" (21:20). (6 and 7) *Ahaziah* and *Athaliah*—Ahaziah is as wicked as his father, as is his mother Athaliah. Both are murdered. (8) *Joash*—Although he repairs the temple and restores the worship of God, when Jehoiada the priest dies, Joash allows the people to abandon the temple and return to idolatry. (9) *Amaziah*—Mixed in his relationship to God, he later forsakes the Lord for the gods of Edom. He is defeated by Israel and later murdered. (10) *Uzziah*—He begins well with the Lord and is blessed with military victories. However, when he becomes strong, he proudly and presumptuously plays the role of a priest by offering incense in the temple and therefore is struck with leprosy. (11) *Jotham*—Because he rebuilds the gate of the temple and reveres God, the Lord blesses him with prosperity and victory. (12) *Ahaz*—A wicked king and an idolater, he is oppressed by his enemies and forced to give tribute to the Assyrians from the temple treasures. (13) *Hezekiah*—He repairs and reopens the temple and puts away the altars and idols set up by his father, Ahaz. Judah is spared destruction by Assyria because of his righteousness. His reforms are given only a few verses in Kings but three chapters in Chronicles. (14 and 15) *Manasseh* and *Amon*—Manasseh is Judah's most wicked king. He sets up idols and altars all over the land. However, he repents when he is carried away by Assyria. God brings him back to Judah and he makes a halfway reform, but it comes too late. Amon follows in his father's wickedness. Both kings are murdered. (16) *Josiah*—A leader in reforms and spiritual revival, he centers worship around the temple, finds the law and obeys it, and reinstitutes the Passover. (17, 18, and 19) *Jehoahaz, Jehoiakim, Jehoiachin*—Their relentless evil finally brings the downfall of Judah. The temple is ravaged in each of their reigns. (20) *Zedekiah*—Judah's last king is also wicked. Jerusalem and the temple are destroyed, and the captivity begins. Second Chronicles nevertheless ends on a note of hope at the end of the captivity, when Cyrus issues the decree for the restoration of Judah: "Who *is there* among you of all His people? May the LORD his God *be* with him, and let him go up" (36:23).

OUTLINE OF SECOND CHRONICLES

Part One: The Reign of Solomon (1:1—9:31)

I. The Inauguration of Solomon as King 1:1–17

A. The Worship of Solomon.......... 1:1–6
B. The Petition for Wisdom.......... 1:7–10
C. The Provision of Wisdom.......... 1:11, 12
D. The Wealth of Solomon.......... 1:13–17

II. The Completion of the Temple..... 2:1—7:22

A. Preparation to Build the Temple ... 2:1–18
  1. Selection of the Temple Builders 2:1, 2
  2. Selection of the Temple Materials.......... 2:3–18
B. Construction of the Temple...... 3:1—5:1
C. Dedication of the Temple ...... 5:2—7:22
  1. The Installation of the Ark...... 5:2–12
  2. The Glory of the Lord Fills the Temple 5:13, 14
  3. The Sermon of Solomon........ 6:1–11
  4. The Prayer of Solomon........ 6:12–42
  5. The Fire of the Lord Consumes the Sacrifices 7:1–3
  6. The Nation Offers Sacrifices...... 7:4–7
  7. The Nation Celebrates the Feasts of Tabernacles.......... 7:8–11
  8. The Lord Confirms the Covenant 7:12–22

III. The Glory of the Reign of Solomon 8:1—9:28

A. Enlargement of Solomon's Territory 8:1–6
B. Subjugation of the Enemies of Solomon 8:7–10
C. Religious Practices of Solomon.... 8:11–16
D. Economic Operations of Solomon 8:17, 18
E. The Queen of Sheba Visits 9:1–12
F. Solomon's Wealth.......... 9:13–28

IV. The Death of Solomon 9:29–31

Part Two: The Reigns of the Kings of Judah (10:1—36:23)

I. The Reign of Rehoboam .... 10:1—12:16

A. Division of the Kingdom......... 10:1–19
B. Kingdom of Judah Is Strengthened 11:1–23
C. Kingdom of Judah Is Weakened... 12:1–12
D. Death of Rehoboam.......... 12:13–16

II. The Reign of Abijah 13:1–22

A. War of Abijah and Jeroboam 13:1–20
B. Death of Abijah 13:21, 22

III. The Reign of Asa .... 14:1—16:14

A. Evaluation of Asa.......... 14:1–8
B. Victory over the Ethiopians 14:9–15
C. Exhortation of Azariah.......... 15:1–7
D. Reforms of Asa.......... 15:8–19
E. Victory over the Syrians 16:1–6

CHAPTER 1

The Worship of Solomon—1 Kin. 3:4

NOW [R]Solomon the son of David was
strengthened in his kingdom, and [R]the
LORD his God *was* with him and [R]exalted him
exceedingly. 1 Kin. 2:46 • Gen. 39:2 • 1 Chr. 29:25
2 And Solomon spoke to all Israel, to [R]the
captains of thousands and of hundreds, to
the judges, and to every leader in all Israel,
the heads of the fathers' *houses*. 1 Chr. 27:1–34
3 Then Solomon, and all the congregation
with him, went to the high place that *was* at
Gibeon; for the tabernacle of meeting with
God was there, which Moses the servant of
the LORD had made in the wilderness.
4 [R]But David had brought up the ark of
God from Kirjath Jearim to *the place* David
had prepared for it, for he had pitched a tent
for it at Jerusalem. 2 Sam. 6:2–17
5 Now the bronze altar that Bezaleel the
son of Uri, the son of Hur, had made, *he put
before the tabernacle of the LORD; Solomon
and the congregation sought Him *there*.
6 And Solomon went up there to the
bronze altar before the LORD, which *was* at

1:5 Some authorities *it was there*

the tabernacle of meeting, and [R]offered a
thousand burnt offerings on it. 1 Kin. 3:4

The Petition for Wisdom—1 Kin. 3:5–9

7 [R]On that night God appeared to Solomon, and said to him, "Ask! What shall I give
you?" 1 Kin. 3:5–14; 9:2
8 And Solomon said to God: "You have
shown great mercy to David my father, and
have made me [R]king in his place. 1 Chr. 28:5
9 "Now, O LORD God, let Your promise to
David my father be established, for You have
made me king over a people like the [R]dust of
the earth in multitude. Gen. 13:16
10 [R]"Now give me wisdom and knowledge,
that I may [R]go out and come in before this
people; for who can judge this great people of
Yours?" 1 Kin. 3:9 • Deut. 31:2

The Provision of Wisdom—1 Kin. 3:10–14

11 [R]And God said to Solomon: "Because this
was in your heart, and you have not asked
riches or wealth or honor or the life of your
enemies, nor have you asked long life—but
have asked wisdom and knowledge for yourself, that you may judge My people over
whom I have made you king— 1 Kin. 3:11–13
12 "wisdom and knowledge *are* granted to
you; and I will give you riches and wealth
and honor, such as [R]none of the kings have
had who *have been* before you, nor shall any
after you have the like." 2 Chr. 9:22

The Wealth of Solomon
1 Kin. 10:26–29; 2 Chr. 9:25–28

13 So Solomon came to Jerusalem from [T]the
high place that *was* at Gibeon, from before
the tabernacle of meeting, and reigned over
Israel. Place for worship
14 [R]And Solomon gathered chariots and
horsemen; he had one thousand four hundred
chariots and twelve thousand horsemen,
whom he stationed in the chariot cities and
with the king in Jerusalem. 1 Kin. 10:26
15 [R]Also the king made silver and gold as
common in Jerusalem as stones, and he made
cedars as abundant as the sycamores which
are in the lowland. 2 Chr. 9:27
16 And Solomon had horses imported from
Egypt and Keveh; the king's merchants
bought them in Keveh at the *current* price.
17 They also acquired and imported from
Egypt a chariot for six hundred *shekels* of
silver, and a horse for one hundred and fifty;
thus, [T]through their agents, they exported
them to all the kings of the Hittites and the
kings of Syria. Lit. *by their hands*

CHAPTER 2

Selection of the Temple Builders
1 Kin. 5:15, 16

THEN Solomon [R]determined to build a
temple for the name of the LORD, and a
royal house for himself. 1 Kin. 5:5
2 Solomon selected seventy thousand men
to bear burdens, eighty thousand to quarry
stone in the mountains, and three thousand
six hundred to oversee them.

Selection of the Temple Materials

3 Then Solomon sent to [T]Hiram king of
Tyre, saying: Heb. *Huram*

[R]As you have dealt with David my
father, and sent him cedars to build
himself a house to dwell in, *so deal with*
me. 1 Chr. 14:1
4 Behold, I am building a temple for the
name of the LORD my God, to dedicate
it to Him, to burn before Him [T]sweet
incense, for the continual showbread,
for the burnt offerings morning and
evening, on the Sabbaths, on the New
Moons, and on the [T]set feasts of the
LORD our God. This *is an ordinance*
forever to Israel. *incense of spices • appointed*
5 And the temple which I build *will be*
great, for [R]our God is greater than all
gods. Ps. 135:5
6 But who is able to build Him a temple,
since heaven and the heaven of heavens
cannot contain Him? Who *am* I then,
that I should build Him a temple,
except to burn sacrifice before Him?
7 Therefore send me at once a man
skillful to work in gold and silver, in
bronze and iron, in purple and crimson
and blue, who has skill to engrave with
the skillful men who are with me in
Judah and Jerusalem, [R]whom David my
father provided. 1 Chr. 22:15
8 Also send me cedar and cypress and
algum logs from Lebanon, for I know
that your servants have skill to cut
timber in Lebanon; and indeed my
servants *will be* with your servants,
9 to prepare timber *for* me in abundance,
for the [T]temple which I am about to
build *shall be* great and wonderful. *house*
10 [R]And indeed I will give to your 1 Kin. 5:11
servants, the hewers who cut timber,
[T]twenty thousand kors of ground
wheat, twenty thousand kors of barley,
twenty thousand baths of wine, and
twenty thousand baths of oil. 13,480 bu.

11 Then Hiram king of Tyre answered in
writing, which he sent to Solomon:

[R]Because the LORD loves His people, He
has made you king over them. 2 Chr. 9:8

12 Hiram also said:

[R]Blessed *be* the LORD God of Israel,

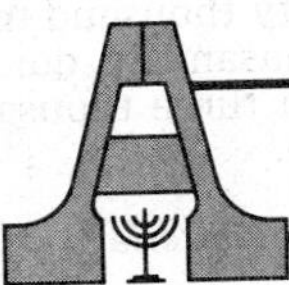

THE CITY OF JOPPA

The modern city of Jaffa, a suburb of Tel Aviv, Israel, is located on the coast of the Mediterranean Sea, about midway between the northern and southern borders of the country. In Bible times, the city was called Joppa, a name that means "Beautiful."

This city is first mentioned in the Bible as a portion of the land allotted to the tribe of Dan (Josh. 19:46). In later years, the prophet Jonah tried to escape his call to preach to the city of Nineveh by going to Joppa to catch a ship bound for Tarshish (Jon. 1:3).

Joppa was the only natural harbor on the Mediterranean Sea between Egypt and Accho (or Ptolemais), north of Mount Carmel. It served as a maritime shipping center for the inland city of Jerusalem in both Old and New Testament times. Solomon's temple at Jerusalem was built in part with cedar logs from Phoenicia. These were floated on rafts from the forests of Lebanon to Joppa, where they were hauled by land to the temple site (2 Chr. 2:16).

Two New Testament personalities are connected with Joppa. The city was the home of Tabitha, or Dorcas (Acts 9:36–43). After Tabitha was restored to life by Simon Peter, many people believed on the Lord.

Simon the tanner also lived at Joppa (Acts 10:32). While praying on the roof of Simon's house, Simon Peter received his famous vision of a sheet descending from heaven (Acts 10:9–22). This vision led Peter to the conviction that "God shows no partiality. But in every nation whoever fears Him and works righteousness is accepted by Him" (Acts 10:34, 35). From that point on, Peter preached the gospel of Christ to Gentiles, as well as to his own Jewish countrymen.

The view from a housetop in Jaffa (Joppa) across the bay to Tel Aviv. Photo by Howard Vos

[R]who made heaven and earth, for He
has given King David a wise son,
endowed with prudence and
understanding, who will build a temple
for the LORD and a royal house for
himself! 1 Kin. 5:7 • Rev. 10:6

13 And now I have sent a skillful man,
endowed with understanding, [T]Huram
my [T]master *craftsman* *Hiram* • Lit. *father*

14 [R](the son of a woman of the daughters
of Dan, and his father was a man of
Tyre), skilled to work in gold and silver,
bronze and iron, stone and wood, purple
and blue, fine linen and crimson, and to
make any engraving and to accomplish
any plan which may be given to him,
with your skillful men and with the
skillful men of my lord David your
father. 1 Kin. 7:13, 14

15 Now therefore, the wheat, the barley,
the oil, and the wine which [R]my lord
has spoken of, let him send to his
servants. 2 Chr. 2:10

16 And we will cut wood from Lebanon, as
much as you need; we will bring it to
you in rafts by sea to [T]Joppa, and you
will carry it up to Jerusalem. Heb. *Japho*

17 [R]Then Solomon numbered all the aliens who *were* in the land of Israel, after the census in which [R]David his father had numbered them; and there were found to be one hundred and fifty-three thousand six hundred. 1 Kin. 5:13 • 1 Chr. 22:2

18 And he made [R]seventy thousand of them bearers of burdens, eighty thousand hewers of *stone* in the mountain, and three thousand six hundred overseers to make the people work. 2 Chr. 2:2

CHAPTER 3

Construction of the Temple—1 Kin. 6:1–7:51

NOW Solomon began to build the house of the LORD at Jerusalem on Mount Moriah, where *the LORD had* appeared to his father David, at the place that David had prepared on the threshing floor of [R]Ornan[T] the Jebusite. 1 Chr. 21:18; 22:1 • *Araunah,* 2 Sam. 24:16

2 And he began to build on the second *day* of the second month in the fourth year of his reign.

3 This is the foundation which Solomon laid for building the house of God: The length *was* sixty cubits (by cubits according to the former measure) and the width twenty cubits.

4 And the vestibule that *was* in front *of* [T]*the sanctuary* was twenty cubits long across the width of the house, and the height *was* one hundred and twenty. He overlaid the inside with pure gold. The main room of the temple

5 The larger room he paneled with cypress which he overlaid with fine gold, and he carved palm trees and chainwork on it.

6 And he decorated the house with precious stones for beauty, and the gold *was* gold from Parvaim.

7 He also overlaid the house—the beams and doorposts, its walls and doors—with gold; and he carved cherubim on the walls.

8 And he made the [R]Most Holy Place. Its length was according to the width of the house, [T]twenty cubits, and its width twenty cubits. He overlaid it with [T]six hundred talents of fine gold. Ex. 26:33 • 30 ft. • $3,456,000,000

9 The weight of the nails *was* [T]fifty shekels of gold; and he overlaid the upper [R]area with gold. $96,000 • 1 Chr. 28:11

10 [R]In the Most Holy Place he made two cherubim, fashioned by carving, and overlaid them with gold. 1 Kin. 6:23–28

11 The wings of the cherubim *were* twenty cubits in *overall* length: one wing *of the one cherub was* five cubits, touching the wall of the room, and the other wing *was* five cubits, touching the wing of the other cherub;

12 *one* wing of the other cherub *was* [T]five cubits, touching the wall of the room, and the other wing *also was* five cubits, touching the wing of the other cherub. 7.5 ft.

13 The wings of these cherubim spanned [T]twenty cubits overall. They stood on their feet, and they faced inward. 30 ft.

14 And he made the [R]veil of blue and purple and crimson and fine linen, and wove cherubim into it. Ex. 26:31

15 Also he made in front of the [T]temple [R]two pillars thirty-five cubits [T]high, and the capital that *was* on the top of each of *them* was five cubits. Lit. *house* • 1 Kin. 7:15–20 • Lit. *long*

16 He made wreaths of chainwork, as in the inner sanctuary, and put *them* on top of the pillars; and he made [R]one hundred pomegranates, and put *them* on the wreaths of chainwork. 1 Kin. 7:20

17 Then he [R]set up the pillars before the temple, one on the right hand and the other on the left; he called the name of the one on the right hand Jachin, and the name of the one on the left Boaz. 1 Kin. 7:21

CHAPTER 4

MOREOVER he made a bronze altar: twenty cubits was its length, twenty cubits its width, and ten cubits its height.

2 [R]Then he made the [T]Sea of cast *bronze,* ten cubits from one brim to the other; it was completely round. Its height *was* five cubits, and a line of thirty cubits measured its circumference. 1 Kin. 7:23–26 • Great laver or basin

3 [R]And under it *was* the likeness of oxen

THE TEMPLE

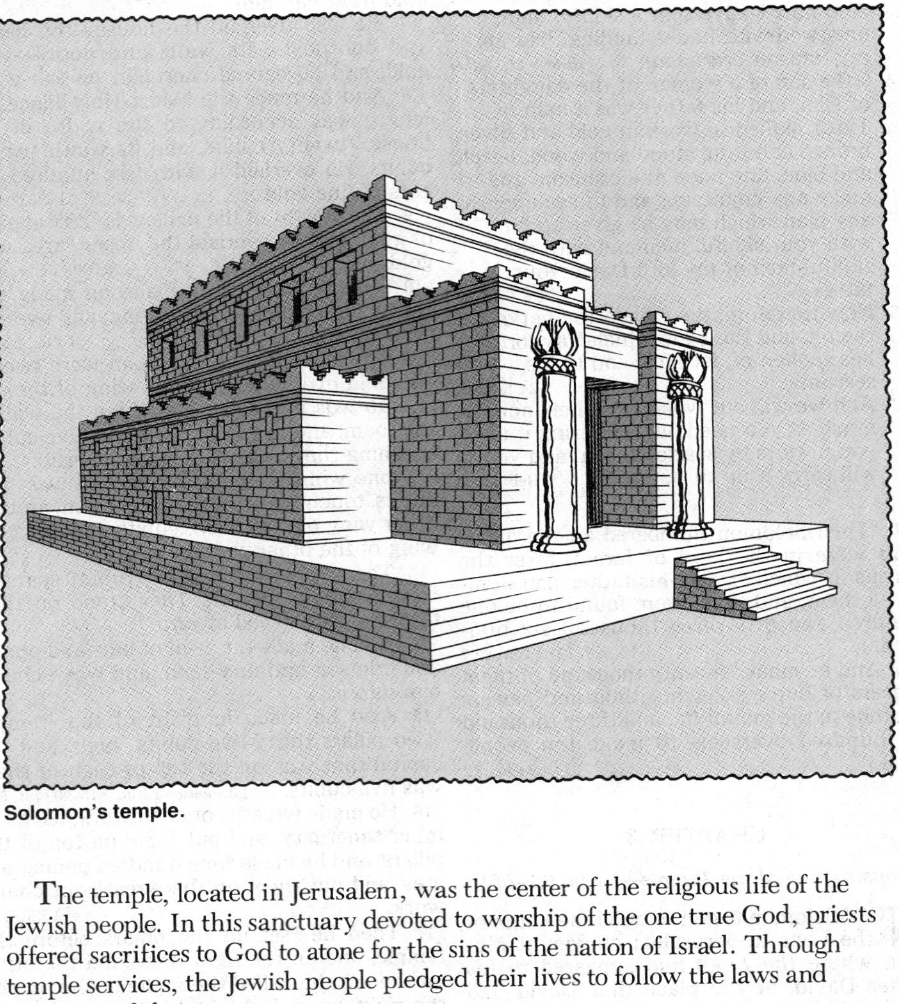

Solomon's temple.

The temple, located in Jerusalem, was the center of the religious life of the Jewish people. In this sanctuary devoted to worship of the one true God, priests offered sacrifices to God to atone for the sins of the nation of Israel. Through temple services, the Jewish people pledged their lives to follow the laws and teachings of their creator.

Before the temple was built, the tabernacle was used as a place of worship by the Hebrew people. During much of their history, the tabernacle was moved from place to place to accompany the nation of Israel in their wanderings (Ex. 40). But after they settled in their permanent home in the Land of Promise, God commanded through His servant David that the temple be constructed. This more ornate structure, devoted to worship, would be a permanent fixture in their capital city (1 Chr. 28).

Three separate temples were actually built in Jerusalem across a period of about a thousand years in Jewish history. All three were built on the same site—on a hill known as Mount Moriah in the eastern section of the Holy City (2 Chr. 3:1).

The first temple, built by King Solomon about 960 B.C., stood on a platform about ten feet high with ten steps leading to an entrance flanked by two stone pillars (see illustration). Thousands of common laborers and skilled craftsmen were involved in its construction (1 Kin. 6; 7; 2 Chr. 3; 4). This building was destroyed by the Babylonians when they captured Jerusalem in 586 B.C. But Cyrus, king of Persia, authorized reconstruction of this building on the same site when he allowed the Jewish people to return to Jerusalem (Ezra 1). This structure, known as Zerubbabel's temple, was completed about 515 B.C. at the urging of the prophets Haggai and Zechariah (Ezra 6:13–15).

Several centuries later, Herod the Great, Roman ruler of Palestine, ordered construction of the third temple—an ornate, cream-colored building of stone and gold—to appease the Jewish people. This temple was the structure to which Jesus referred in speaking of His resurrection (John 2:19, 20). As He predicted, this temple was destroyed by the Romans about 40 years after His resurrection and ascension—in A.D. 70.

The accounts of Solomon's temple in the Old Testament suggest it had an inner courtyard, as well as an outer courtyard. The three main objects in the inner courtyard were (1) the bronze altar used for burnt offerings (1 Kin. 8:22, 64; 9:25); (2) the Sea of cast bronze, which held water for ritual washings by the priests (1 Kin. 7:23–26); and (3) twelve oxen, apparently also cast bronze, which held the Sea of bronze on their backs (1 Kin. 7:25).

In the inner courtyard was an area known as the holy place, which contained the golden incense altar, the table with showbread, five pairs of lampstands, and utensils used for offering sacrifices (1 Kin. 7:48–50). Beyond this area was a room known as the Most Holy Place, or the Holy of Holies, a restricted place which only the high priest could enter. Even he could go into this area only once a year—on the Day of Atonement when he went inside to make atonement for his own sins and then for the sins of the people (Lev. 16). In this room was the ark of the covenant, containing the stone tablets on which the Ten Commandments were written. God's presence was manifested in the Most Holy Place as a cloud (1 Kin. 8:5–11).

Jesus related to the temple in several ways. He showed respect for the temple and referred to it as "My Father's house" (John 2:16). His zeal led Him to purge the temple of merchants who were selling sacrificial animals, thus defiling the "house of prayer" (Mark 11:15–17). But as much as He respected the house of God, Jesus also taught that He was greater than the temple (Matt. 12:6).

His superiority to the temple was clearly shown when the veil of the temple was split from top to bottom at His death (Matt. 27:51). The veil hung before the most sacred place in the temple to keep out all persons except the Jewish high priest. The tearing of the veil symbolized that every believer has unhindered access to God through His Son Jesus Christ because of His sacrificial death on our behalf.

encircling it all around, ten to a [T]cubit, all the way around the Sea. The oxen *were* cast in two rows, when it was cast. 1 Kin. 7:24–26 • 18 in.

4 It stood on twelve [R]oxen: three looking toward the north, three looking toward the west, three looking toward the south, and three looking toward the east; the Sea *was set* upon them, and all their back parts pointed inward. 1 Kin. 7:25

5 It *was* a handbreadth thick; and its brim was shaped like the brim of a cup, *like* a lily blossom. It contained three thousand baths.

6 He also made ten lavers, and put five on the right side and five on the left, to wash in them; such things as they offered for the burnt offering they would wash in them, but the Sea *was* for the priests to wash in.

7 [R]And he made ten lampstands of gold [R]according to their design, and set *them* in the temple, five on the right side and five on the left. 1 Kin. 7:49 • Ex. 25:31

8 [R]He also made ten tables, and placed *them* in the temple, five on the right side and five on the left. And he made one hundred [R]bowls of gold. 1 Kin. 7:48 • 1 Chr. 28:17

9 Furthermore [R]he made the court of the priests, and the [R]great court and doors for the court; and he overlaid these doors with bronze. 1 Kin. 6:36 • 2 Kin. 21:5

10 [R]He set the Sea on the right side, to the southeast. 1 Kin. 7:39

11 Then [R]Huram made the pots and the shovels and the bowls. So Huram finished doing the work that he was to do for King Solomon for the house of God: 1 Kin. 7:40–51

12 the two pillars and [R]the bowl-shaped capitals *that were* on top of the two pillars; the two networks covering the two bowl-shaped capitals which *were* on top of the pillars; 1 Kin. 7:41

13 [R]four hundred pomegranates for the two networks (two rows of pomegranates for each network, to cover the two bowl-shaped capitals that *were* on the pillars); 1 Kin. 7:20

14 he also made [R]carts and the lavers on the carts; 1 Kin. 7:27, 43

15 one Sea and twelve oxen under it;

16 also the pots, the shovels, the forks—and all their articles Huram his [T]master *craftsman* made of burnished bronze for King Solomon for the house of the LORD. *father*

17 In the plain of Jordan the king had them cast in clay molds, between Succoth and [T]Zeredah. *Zaretan*, 1 Kin. 7:46

18 And Solomon had all these articles made in such great abundance that the weight of the bronze was not determined.

19 Thus Solomon had all the furnishings made for the house of God: the altar of gold and the tables on which *was* the showbread;

20 the lampstands with their lamps of pure gold, to burn [R]in the prescribed manner in front of the inner sanctuary, Ex. 27:20, 21

21 with [R]the flowers and the lamps and the wick-trimmers of gold, of purest gold; Ex. 25:31

22 the trimmers, the bowls, the ladles, and the censers of pure gold. As for the entry of the [T]sanctuary, its inner doors to the Most Holy *Place*, and the doors of the main hall of the temple, *were of* gold. Lit. *house*

CHAPTER 5

SO all the work that Solomon had done for the house of the LORD was finished; and Solomon brought in *all* the things which his father David had dedicated: the silver and the gold and all the furnishings. And he put *them* in the treasuries of the house of God.

The Installation of the Ark—1 Kin. 8:1–9

2 [R]Now Solomon assembled the elders of Israel and all the heads of the tribes, the chief fathers of the children of Israel, in Jerusalem, that they might bring the ark of the covenant of the LORD up [R]from the City of David, which *is* Zion. 1 Kin. 8:1–9 • 2 Sam. 6:12

3 [R]Therefore all the men of Israel assembled together with the king at the feast, which *was* in the seventh month. 1 Kin. 8:2

4 So all the elders of Israel came, and the [R]Levites took up the ark. 1 Chr. 15:2, 15

5 Then they brought up the ark, the tabernacle of meeting, and all the holy furnishings that *were* in the tabernacle. The priests and the Levites brought them up.

6 Also King Solomon, and all the congregation of Israel who were assembled with him before the ark, were sacrificing sheep and oxen that could not be counted or numbered for multitude.

7 Then the priests brought in the ark of the covenant of the LORD to its place, into the inner sanctuary of the temple, to the Most Holy *Place*, under the wings of the cherubim.

8 For the cherubim spread *their* wings over the place of the ark, and the cherubim overshadowed the ark and its poles.

9 And the poles extended so that the ends of the poles of the ark could be seen from *the holy place*, in front of the inner sanctuary; but they could not be seen from outside. And [T]they are there to this day. Lit. *it is*

10 *There was* nothing in the ark except the two tablets which Moses [R]put *there* at Horeb, [T]when the LORD made *a covenant* with the children of Israel, when they had come out of Egypt. Deut. 10:2, 5 • Or *where*

11 And it came to pass when the priests came out of the *Most* Holy *Place* (for all the priests who *were* present had [T]sanctified themselves, without keeping to their [R]divisions), *consecrated* • 1 Chr. 24:1–5

12 and the Levites *who were* the singers, all those of Asaph and Heman and Jeduthun, with their sons and their brethren, stood at the east end of the altar, clothed in white linen, having cymbals, stringed instruments and harps, and with them one hundred and twenty priests sounding with trumpets—

The Glory of the Lord Fills the Temple
1 Kin. 8:10, 11

13 indeed it came to pass, when the trumpeters and singers *were* as one, to make one sound to be heard in praising and thanking the LORD, and when they lifted up their voice with the trumpets and cymbals and instruments of music, and praised the LORD, *saying*:

[R]"*For He is* good,
For His mercy *endures* forever,"

that the house, the house of the LORD, was filled with a cloud, 1 Chr. 16:34, 41

14 so that the priests could not continue ministering because of the cloud; for the glory of the LORD filled the house of God.

CHAPTER 6

The Sermon of Solomon—1 Kin. 8:12–21

THEN Solomon said:

"The LORD said
He would dwell in the dark cloud.
2 But I have built You an exalted house,
And [R]a place for You to dwell in
forever." 2 Chr. 7:12

3 Then the king turned around and blessed the whole congregation of Israel, while all the congregation of Israel stood.

4 And he said: "Blessed *be* the LORD God of Israel, who has fulfilled with His hands *what* He spoke with His mouth to my father David, [R]saying, 1 Chr. 17:5

5 'Since the day that I brought My people out of the land of Egypt, I have chosen no city from any tribe of Israel *in which* to build a house, that My name might be there, nor did I choose any man to be a ruler over My people Israel;

6 'but I have chosen Jerusalem, that My name may be there; and I have chosen David to be over My people Israel.'

7 "Now [R]it was in the heart of my father David to build a temple for the name of the LORD God of Israel. 2 Sam. 7:2

8 "But the LORD said to my father David, 'Whereas it was in your heart to build a temple for My name, you did well in that it was in your heart.

9 'Nevertheless you shall not build the house, but your son who will come forth from your own loins, he shall build the temple for My [R]name.' 1 Chr. 28:3–6

10 "So the LORD has fulfilled His word which He spoke, and I have filled the position of my father David, and [R]sit on the throne of Israel, as the LORD promised; and I have built the temple for the name of the LORD God of Israel. 1 Kin. 2:12; 10:9

11 "And there I have put the ark, [R]in which *is* the covenant of the LORD which He made with the children of Israel." 2 Chr. 5:7–10

The Prayer of Solomon—1 Kin. 8:22–53

12 Then [T]*Solomon* stood before the altar of the LORD in the presence of all the congregation of Israel, and spread out his hands *he*

13 (for Solomon had made a bronze platform [T]five cubits long, five cubits broad, and [T]three cubits high, and had set it in the midst of the court; and he stood on it, knelt down on his knees before all the congregation of Israel, and spread out his hands toward heaven), 7.5 ft. • 4.5 ft.

14 and said: "LORD God of Israel, [R]*there is* no God in heaven or on earth like You, who keep *Your* [R]covenant and mercy with Your servants who walk before You with all their hearts. [Ex. 15:11] • [Deut. 7:9]

15 [R]"You have kept what You promised Your servant David my father; You have both spoken with Your mouth and fulfilled *it* with Your hand, as *it is* this day. 1 Chr. 22:9, 10

16 "Therefore, LORD God of Israel, now keep what You promised Your servant David my father, saying, [R]'You shall not fail to have a man sit before Me on the throne of Israel, [R]only if your sons take heed to their way, to walk in My law as you have walked before Me.' 2 Chr. 7:18 • Ps. 132:12

17 "Now then, O LORD God of Israel, let Your word come true, which You have spoken to Your servant David.

18 "But will God indeed dwell with men on the earth? Behold, heaven and the heaven of heavens cannot contain You; how much less this [T]temple which I have built! *house*

19 "Yet regard the prayer of Your servant and his supplication, O LORD my God, and listen to the cry and to the prayer which Your servant is praying before You:

20 "that Your eyes may be open toward this temple day and night, toward the place where *You* said *You would* put Your name, that You may hear the prayer which Your servant prays [R]toward this place. Dan. 6:10

21 "And may You hear the supplications of Your servant and of Your people Israel, when they pray toward this place; hear from Your dwelling place, in heaven; and when You hear, [R]forgive. [Mic. 7:18]

22 "If anyone sins against his neighbor, and is forced to take an [R]oath, and comes *and* takes an oath before Your altar in this temple, Ex. 22:8–11
23 "then hear from heaven, and act, and judge Your servants, bringing retribution on the wicked by bringing his way on his own head, and justifying the righteous by giving him according to his [R]righteousness. [Job 34:11]
24 "Or if Your people Israel are defeated before an [R]enemy because they have sinned against You, and return and confess Your name, and pray and make supplication before You in this temple, 2 Kin. 21:14, 15
25 "then hear from heaven and forgive the sin of Your people Israel, and bring them back to the land which You gave to them and their fathers.
26 "When [R]heaven is shut up and there is no rain because they have sinned against You, when they pray toward this place and confess Your name, and turn from their sin because You afflict them, 1 Kin. 17:1
27 "then hear *in* heaven, and forgive the sin of Your servants, Your people Israel, that You may teach them the good way in which they should walk; and send rain on Your land which You have given to Your people as an inheritance.
28 "When there is famine in the land, pestilence or blight or mildew, locusts or grasshoppers; when their enemies besiege them in the land of their cities; whatever plague or whatever sickness *there is*;
29 "whatever prayer, whatever supplication is made by anyone, or by all Your people Israel, when each one knows his own burden and his own grief, and spreads out his hands to this house:
30 "then hear from heaven Your dwelling place, and forgive, and give to everyone according to all his ways, whose heart You know (for You alone [R]know the [R]hearts of the sons of men), [1 Chr. 28:9] • [1 Sam. 16:7]
31 "that they may fear You, to walk in Your ways as long as they live in the land which You gave to our fathers.
32 "Moreover, concerning a foreigner, [R]who is not of Your people Israel, but who comes from a far country for the sake of Your great name and Your mighty hand and Your outstretched arm, when they come and pray in this temple; John 12:20
33 "then hear from heaven Your dwelling place, and do according to all for which the foreigner calls to You, that all people of the earth may know Your name and fear You, as *do* Your people Israel, and that they may know that this temple which I have built is called by Your name.
34 "When Your people go out to battle against their enemies, wherever You send them, and when they pray to You toward this city which You have chosen and toward the temple which I have built for Your name,
35 "then hear from heaven their prayer and their supplication, and maintain their cause.
36 "When they sin against You (for *there is* [R]no one who does not sin), and You become angry with them and deliver them to the enemy, and they take them [R]captive to a land far or near, [Rom. 3:9, 19; 5:12] • Deut. 28:63–68
37 "yet when they [T]come to themselves in the land where they were carried captive, and repent, and make supplication to You in the land of their captivity, saying, 'We have sinned, we have done wrong, and have acted wickedly'; Lit. *bring back to their hearts*
38 "and when they return to You with all their heart and with all their soul in the land of their captivity, where they have been carried captive, and pray toward their land which You gave to their fathers, *toward* the city which You have chosen, and toward the temple which I have built for Your name:
39 "then hear from heaven Your dwelling place their prayer and their supplications, and maintain their cause, and forgive Your people who have sinned against You.
40 "Now, my God, I pray, let Your eyes be [R]open and *let* Your ears *be* attentive to the prayer *made* in this place. 2 Chr. 6:20

41 "Now [R]therefore, Ps. 132:8–10, 16
Arise, O LORD God, to Your [R]resting
place, 1 Chr. 28:2
You and the ark of Your strength.
Let Your priests, O LORD God, be
clothed with salvation,
And let Your saints [R]rejoice in
goodness. Neh. 9:25
42 "O LORD God, do not turn away the face
of Your anointed;
[R]Remember the mercies of Your servant
David." Ps. 89:49; 132:1, 8–10

CHAPTER 7

The Fire of the Lord Consumes the Sacrifices

NOW when Solomon had finished praying, [R]fire came down from heaven and consumed the burnt offering and the sacrifices; and [R]the glory of the LORD filled the [T]temple. Lev. 9:24 • 1 Kin. 8:10, 11 • Lit. *house*
2 [R]And the priests could not enter the house of the LORD, because the glory of the LORD had filled the LORD's house. 2 Chr. 5:14

3 *When all the children of Israel saw how the fire came down, and the glory of the LORD on the temple, they bowed their faces to the ground on the pavement, and worshiped and praised the LORD, [R]*saying*: Ps. 106:1; 136:1

7:3 See Reader's Guide note on page 434.

"For *He is* good,
For His mercy *endures* forever."

The Nation Offers Sacrifices—1 Kin. 8:62-64

4 [R]Then the king and all the people offered
sacrifices before the LORD. 1 Kin. 8:62, 63
5 King Solomon offered a sacrifice of
twenty-two thousand bulls and one hundred
and twenty thousand sheep. So the king and
all the people dedicated the house of God.
6 [R]And the priests attended to their services; the Levites also with instruments of
the music of the LORD, which King David had
made to praise the LORD, saying, "For His
mercy *endures* forever," whenever David
offered praise by their [T]ministry. [R]The priests
sounded trumpets opposite them, while all
Israel stood. 1 Chr. 15:16 • Lit. *hand* • 2 Chr. 5:12
7 Furthermore Solomon consecrated the
middle of the court that *was* in front of the
house of the LORD; for there he offered burnt
offerings and the fat of the peace offerings,
because the bronze altar which Solomon had
made was not able to receive the burnt
offerings, the grain offerings, and the fat.

The Nation Celebrates the Feasts of Tabernacles 1 Kin. 8:65—9:1

8 At that time Solomon kept the feast
seven days, and all Israel with him, a very
great congregation from the entrance of
Hamath to [T]the Brook of Egypt. The Shihor
9 And on the eighth day they held a [R]sa-
cred assembly, for they observed the dedication of the altar seven days, and the feast
seven days. Lev. 23:36
10 [R]On the twenty-third day of the seventh
month he sent the people away to their tents,
joyful and glad of heart for the goodness that
the LORD had done for David, for Solomon,
and for His people Israel. 1 Kin. 8:66
11 Thus [R]Solomon finished the house of the
LORD and the king's house; and Solomon
successfully accomplished all that came into
his heart to make in the house of the LORD
and in his own house. 1 Kin. 9:1

The Lord Confirms the Covenant 1 Kin. 9:2-9

12 Then the LORD appeared to Solomon by
night, and said to him: "I have heard your
prayer, and have chosen this [R]place for Myself as a house of sacrifice. 2 Chr. 6:20
13 "When I shut up heaven and there is no
rain, or command the locusts to devour the
land, or send pestilence among My people,
14 "if My people who are [R]called by My
name will humble themselves, and pray and
seek My face, and turn from their wicked
ways, then I will hear from heaven, and will
forgive their sin and heal their land. [Is. 43:7]
15 "Now My eyes will be open and My ears
attentive to prayer *made* in this place.
16 "For now I have chosen and [T]sanctified
this house, that My name may be there
forever; and [T]My eyes and [T]My heart will be
there perpetually. *set apart* • *My attention* • *My concern*
17 [R]"As for you, if you walk before Me as
your father David walked, and do according
to all that I have commanded you, and if you
keep My statutes and My judgments, 1 Kin. 9:4
18 "then I will establish the throne of your
kingdom, as I covenanted with David your
father, saying, [R]'You shall never fail *to have* a
man as ruler in Israel.' 2 Chr. 6:16
19 [R]"But if you turn away and forsake My
statutes and My commandments which I
have set before you, and go and serve other
gods, and worship them, Lev. 26:14, 33
20 "then I will uproot them from My land
which I have given them; and this house
which I have sanctified for My name I will
cast out of My sight, and will make it *to be* a
proverb and a byword among all nations.
21 "And *as for* this house, which is exalted,
everyone who passes by it will be astonished

7:3 The Reasons for Worship—The first reason for worship is simply that God commands it (Page 483—1 Chr. 16:29; Page 1118—Matt. 4:10). The first four of the Ten Commandments, which are also the longest, clearly charge men to worship the one true God and Him alone (Page 90—Ex. 20:3–10). To allow any person or thing to usurp the position of lordship over us constitutes gross disobedience to the will of God and incurs His terrible wrath (Page 90—Ex. 20:5; Page 237—Deut. 27:15). All people are destined to pay homage to God anyway, even if unwillingly (Page 1400—Phil. 2:10).

An equally important reason for worship is that God deserves our worship. He alone possesses the attributes that merit our worship and service. Among these are goodness (Page 682—Ps. 100:4, 5), mercy (Page 72—Ex. 4:31), holiness (Page 681—Ps. 99:5, 9), and creative power (Page 1523—Rev. 4:11). When men of biblical times clearly saw the unveiled glory of God, they could not help but fall prostrate in worship. Examples of this response can be seen in the actions of Moses (Page 107—Ex. 34:5–8), Paul (Page 1284—Acts 9:3–6), and John (Page 1517—Rev. 1:9–17).

A final reason for worship is that men need to give it. People cannot find personal fulfillment apart from the glad submission of themselves in worshipful obedience to God. He is the Creator and they are the creatures (Page 1523—Rev. 4:11). People who adopt as their master anything less than God are building their lives on quicksand. They will be no stronger than the object they worship (Page 692—Ps. 115:4–8). One who worships God, however, not only participates in the occupation of heaven (Page 1525—Rev. 7:9–12), but finds joyful satisfaction for the present (Page 1337—Rom. 12:2; Page 1409—Col. 3:24).

Now turn to Page 1341—Rom. 16:5: Definition of the Local Church.

and say, 'Why has the LORD done thus to this land and this house?'

22 "Then they will answer, 'Because they forsook the LORD God of their fathers, who brought them out of the land of Egypt, and embraced other gods, and worshiped them and served them; therefore He has brought all this calamity on them.'"

CHAPTER 8

Enlargement of Solomon's Territory
1 Kin. 9:10–19

IT came to pass at the end of twenty years, in which Solomon had built the house of the LORD and his own house,

2 that the cities which [T]Hiram had given to Solomon, Solomon built them; and he settled the children of Israel there. Heb. *Huram*, 2 Chr. 2:3

3 And Solomon went to Hamath Zobah and seized it.

4 [R]He also built Tadmor in the wilderness, and all the storage cities which he built in [R]Hamath. 1 Kin. 9:17, 18 • 1 Chr. 18:3, 9

5 He built Upper Beth Horon and [R]Lower Beth Horon, fortified cities *with* walls, gates, and bars, 1 Chr. 7:24

6 also Baalath and all the storage cities that Solomon had, and all the chariot cities and the cities of the cavalry, and all that Solomon [R]desired to build in Jerusalem, in Lebanon, and throughout all the land of his dominion. 2 Chr. 7:11

Subjugation of the Enemies of Solomon
1 Kin. 9:20–23

7 [R]All the people *who were* left of the Hittites, Amorites, Perizzites, Hivites, and Jebusites, who *were* not of Israel 1 Kin. 9:20

8 (that is, their descendants who were left in the land after them, whom the children of Israel did not destroy), from these Solomon raised forced labor, as it is to this day.

9 But Solomon did not make the children of Israel [T]servants for his work. Some *were* men of war, captains of his officers, captains of his chariots, and his cavalry. Or *slaves*

10 And others *were* chiefs of the officials of King Solomon: [R]two hundred and fifty, who ruled over the people. 1 Kin. 9:23

Religious Practices of Solomon
1 Kin. 9:24, 25

11 Now Solomon brought the daughter of Pharaoh up from the City of David to the house he had built for her, for he said, "My wife shall not dwell in the house of David king of Israel, because *the places* to which the ark of the LORD has come are holy."

12 Then Solomon offered burnt offerings to the LORD on the altar of the LORD which he had built before the vestibule,

13 according to the daily rate, offering according to the commandment of Moses, for the Sabbaths, the New Moons, and the [R]three appointed yearly feasts—the Feast of Unleavened Bread, the Feast of Weeks, and the Feast of Tabernacles. Ex. 23:14–17; 34:22, 23

14 And, according to the [T]order of David his father, he appointed the divisions of the priests for their service, [R]the Levites for their duties (to praise and serve before the priests) as the duty of each day required, and the [R]gatekeepers by their divisions at each gate; for so David the man of God had commanded. *ordinance* • 1 Chr. 25:1 • 1 Chr. 9:17; 26:1

15 They did not depart from the command of the king to the priests and Levites concerning any matter or concerning the [R]treasuries. 1 Chr. 26:20–28

16 Now all the work of Solomon was well-ordered from the day of the foundation of the house of the LORD until it was finished. So the house of the LORD was completed.

Economic Operations of Solomon
1 Kin. 9:26–28

17 Then Solomon went to Ezion Geber and Elath on the seacoast, in the land of Edom.

18 [R]And Hiram sent him ships by the hand of his servants, and servants who knew the sea. They went with the servants of Solomon to [R]Ophir, and acquired four hundred and fifty talents of gold from there, and brought it to King Solomon. 2 Chr. 9:10, 13 • 1 Chr. 29:4

CHAPTER 9

The Queen of Sheba Visits—1 Kin. 10:1–13

NOW [R]when the queen of Sheba heard of the fame of Solomon, she came to Jerusalem to test Solomon with hard questions, *having* a very great retinue, camels that bore spices, gold in abundance, and precious stones; and when she came to Solomon, she spoke with him about all that was in her heart. [Matt. 12:42]

2 So Solomon answered all her questions; there was nothing so difficult for Solomon that he could not explain it to her.

3 And when the queen of Sheba had seen the wisdom of Solomon, the house that he had built,

4 the food on his table, the seating of his servants, the service of his waiters and their apparel, his [R]cupbearers and their apparel, and his entryway by which he went up to the house of the LORD, there was no more spirit in her. Neh. 1:11

5 Then she said to the king: "*It was* a true report which I heard in my own land about your words and your wisdom.

6 "However I did not believe their words until I came and saw with my own eyes; and

indeed, the half of the greatness of your
wisdom was not told me. You exceed the
fame of which I heard.
7 "Happy *are* your men and happy *are*
these your servants, who stand continually
before you and hear your wisdom!
8 "Blessed be the LORD your God, who
delighted in you, setting you on His throne *to*
be king for the LORD your God! Because your
God has loved Israel, to establish them forever, therefore He made you king over them,
to do justice and righteousness."
9 Then she gave the king [T]one hundred
and twenty talents of gold, spices in great
abundance, and precious stones; there never
were any spices such as those the queen of
Sheba gave to King Solomon. $691,200,000
10 Also, the servants of Hiram and the
servants of Solomon, [R]who brought gold from
Ophir, brought [T]algum wood and precious
stones. 2 Chr. 8:18 • *almug,* 1 Kin. 10:11, 12
11 And the king made walkways *of* the
[T]algum wood for the house of the LORD and
for the king's house, also harps and stringed
instruments for singers; and there were none
such *as these* seen before in the land of
Judah. *almug,* 1 Kin. 10:11, 12
12 Now King Solomon gave to the queen of
Sheba all she desired, whatever she asked,
much more than she had brought to the king.
So she turned and went to her own country,
she and her servants.

Solomon's Wealth
1 Kin. 10:14–29; 2 Chr. 1:14–17

13 [R]The weight of gold that came to Solomon yearly was [T]six hundred and sixty-six
talents of gold, 1 Kin. 10:14–29 • $3,836,160,000
14 besides *what* the traveling merchants
and traders brought. And all the kings of
Arabia and governors of the country brought
gold and silver to Solomon.
15 And King Solomon made two hundred
large shields of hammered gold; six hundred
shekels of hammered gold went into each
shield.
16 *He* also *made* three hundred shields of
hammered gold; three hundred *shekels* of
gold went into each shield. The king put
them in the House of the Forest of Lebanon.
17 Moreover the king made a great throne
of ivory, and overlaid it with pure gold.
18 The throne *had* six steps, with a footstool
of gold, *which were* fastened to the throne;
there were [T]armrests on either side of the
place of the seat, and two lions stood beside
the armrests. Lit. *hands*
19 Twelve lions stood there, one on each
side of the six steps; nothing like *this* had
been made for any *other* kingdom.
20 All King Solomon's drinking vessels *were*
of gold, and all the vessels of the House of the
Forest of Lebanon *were of* pure gold. Not one
was of silver, for this was accounted as
nothing in the days of Solomon.
21 For the king's ships went to Tarshish
with the servants of Huram. Once every three
years the merchant ships came, bringing
gold, silver, ivory, apes, and monkeys.
22 So King Solomon surpassed all the kings
of the earth in riches and wisdom.
23 And all the kings of the earth sought the
presence of Solomon to hear his wisdom,
which God had put in his heart.
24 Each man brought his present: articles of
silver and gold, garments, armor, spices,
horses, and mules, at a set rate year by year.
25 Solomon had four thousand stalls for
horses and chariots, and twelve thousand
horsemen whom he stationed in the chariot
cities and with the king at Jerusalem.
26 So he reigned over all the kings from
[T]the River to the land of the Philistines, as far
as the border of Egypt. The Euphrates
27 [R]The king made silver *as common* in
Jerusalem as stones, and he made cedar trees
[R]as abundant as the sycamores which *are* in
the lowland. 1 Kin. 10:27 • 2 Chr. 1:15–17
28 [R]And they brought horses to Solomon
from Egypt and from all lands. 2 Chr. 1:16

The Death of Solomon—1 Kin. 11:41–43

29 [R]Now the rest of the acts of Solomon,
first and last, *are* they not written in the book
of Nathan the prophet, in the prophecy of
[R]Ahijah the Shilonite, and in the visions of
[R]Iddo the seer concerning Jeroboam the son
of Nebat? 1 Kin. 11:41 • 1 Kin. 11:29 • 2 Chr. 12:15; 13:22
30 [R]Solomon reigned in Jerusalem over all
Israel forty years. 1 Kin. 4:21; 11:42, 43
31 Then Solomon [T]rested with his fathers,
and was buried in the City of David his
father. And Rehoboam his son reigned in his
place. Died and joined his ancestors

CHAPTER 10

Division of the Kingdom—1 Kin. 12:1–19

AND [R]Rehoboam went to Shechem, for all
Israel had gone to Shechem to make
him king. 1 Kin. 12:1–20
2 So it happened when Jeroboam the son
of Nebat heard *it* (he was in Egypt, where he
had fled from the presence of Solomon the
king), that Jeroboam returned from Egypt.
3 Then they sent for him and called him.
And Jeroboam and all Israel came and spoke
to Rehoboam, saying,
4 "Your father made our yoke heavy; now
therefore, lighten the burdensome service of
your father and his heavy yoke which he put
on us, and we will serve you."
5 So he said to them, "Come back to me
after three days." And the people departed.

6 Then King Rehoboam consulted the elders who stood before his father Solomon
while he still lived, saying, "How do you
advise *me* to answer these people?"
7 And they spoke to him, saying, "If you
are kind to these people, and please them,
and speak good words to them, they will be
your servants forever."
8 [R]But he rejected the counsel which the
elders had given him, and consulted the
young men who had grown up with him, who
stood before him. 1 Kin. 12:8–11
9 And he said to them, "What advice do
you give? How should we answer this people
who have spoken to me, saying, 'Lighten the
yoke which your father put on us'?"
10 Then the young men who had grown up
with him spoke to him, saying, "Thus you
should speak to the people who have spoken
to you, saying, 'Your father made our yoke
heavy, but you make *it* lighter on us'—thus
you shall say to them: 'My little *finger* shall
be thicker than my father's waist!
11 'And now, whereas my father put a
heavy yoke on you, I will add to your yoke;
my father chastised you with whips, but I *will*
chastise you with scourges!' "
12 So [R]Jeroboam and all the people came to
Rehoboam on the third day, as the king had
appointed, saying, "Come back to me the
third day." 1 Kin. 12:12–14
13 Then the king answered them roughly.
King Rehoboam rejected the counsel of the
elders,
14 and he spoke to them according to the
counsel of the young men, saying, "My father
made your yoke heavy, but I will add to it;
my father chastised you with whips, but I *will*
chastise you with [T]scourges!" Lit. *scorpions*
15 So the king did not listen to the people;
for the turn *of affairs* was from God, that the
LORD might fulfill His [R]word, which He had
spoken by the hand of Ahijah the Shilonite to
Jeroboam the son of Nebat. 1 Kin. 11:29–39
16 Now when all Israel *saw* that the king
did not listen to them, the people answered
the king, saying:

"What portion *have we* in David?
We have no inheritance in the son of
Jesse.
Every man to your tents, O Israel!
Now see to your own house, O David!"

So all Israel departed to their tents.
17 But Rehoboam reigned over the children
of Israel who dwelt in the cities of Judah.
18 Then King Rehoboam sent Hadoram,
who *was* in charge of revenue; but the children of Israel stoned him with stones, and he
died. Therefore King Rehoboam mounted *his*
chariot in haste to flee to Jerusalem.
19 [R]So Israel has been in rebellion against
the house of David to this day. 1 Kin. 12:19

CHAPTER 11

Kingdom of Judah Is Strengthened
1 Kin. 12:21–24

NOW [R]when Rehoboam came to Jerusalem, he assembled from the house of
Judah and Benjamin one hundred and eighty
thousand chosen *men* who were warriors, to
fight against Israel, that he might restore the
kingdom to Rehoboam. 1 Kin. 12:21–24
2 But the word of the LORD came [R]to
Shemaiah the man of God, saying, 1 Chr. 12:5
3 "Speak to Rehoboam the son of Solomon, king of Judah, and to all Israel in Judah
and Benjamin, saying,
4 'Thus says the LORD: "You shall not go
up or fight against your brethren! Let every
man return to his house, for this thing is from
Me." ' " Therefore they obeyed the words of
the LORD, and turned back from attacking
Jeroboam.
5 So Rehoboam dwelt in Jerusalem, and
built cities for defense in Judah.
6 And he built Bethlehem, Etam, Tekoa,
7 Beth Zur, Sochoh, Adullam,
8 Gath, Mareshah, Ziph,
9 Adoraim, Lachish, Azekah,
10 Zorah, Aijalon, and Hebron, which are in
Judah and Benjamin, fortified cities.
11 And he fortified the strongholds, and put
captains in them, and stores of food, oil, and
wine.
12 Also in every city *he put* shields and
spears, and made them very strong, having
Judah and Benjamin on his side.
13 And from all their territories the priests
and the Levites who *were* in all Israel took
their stand with him.
14 For the Levites left [R]their common-lands
and their possessions and came to Judah and
Jerusalem, for [R]Jeroboam and his sons had
rejected them from serving as priests to the
LORD. Num. 35:2–5 • 2 Chr. 13:9
15 Then he appointed for himself priests for
the [T]high places, for the demons, and the calf
idols which he had made. Center of worship
16 And after [T]the Levites *left*, those from all
the tribes of Israel, such as set their heart to
seek the LORD God of Israel, [R]came to Jerusalem to sacrifice to the LORD God of their
fathers. Lit. *they* • 2 Chr. 15:9, 10; 30:11, 18
17 So they [R]strengthened the kingdom of
Judah, and made Rehoboam the son of Solomon strong for three years, because they
walked in the way of David and Solomon for
three years. 2 Chr. 12:1, 13
18 Then Rehoboam took for himself as wife
Mahalath the daughter of Jerimoth the son of

THE HISTORICAL BOOKS

The books from Joshua through Esther in the Old Testament are known as the historical books. They cover about seven hundred years in the history of God's chosen people, the nation of Israel.

Major events covered by these books include (1) the settlement of the people in the Promised Land after their escape from Egypt and their years of wandering in the Wilderness; (2) the transition from rule by judges to rule by kings; (3) David's anointing as king of the united kingdom (see illustration); (4) the division of the nation into northern and southern factions; (5) the destruction of he northern kingdom; and (6) the captivity and return of the southern kingdom.

Here are brief summaries of the themes of the twelve books in this significant n of the Old Testament:

Joshua: The capture and settlement of the Promised Land.

he nation of Israel is rescued by a series of judges, or military leaders. e best-known deliverers were Deborah, Gideon, and Samson.

Samuel anoints David as king.

Ruth: A beautiful story of God's love and care.

1 and 2 Samuel: The early history of Israel, including the reigns of Saul and David.

1 and 2 Kings: A political history of Israel, focusing on the reigns of selected kings from the time of Solomon to the captivity of the Jewish people by the Babylonians.

1 and 2 Chronicles: A religious history of Israel, covering the same period as 2 Samuel and 1 and 2 Kings.

Ezra: The return of the Jewish people from captivity in Babylon to Jerusalem.

Nehemiah: The rebuilding of the walls of Jerusalem after the Jewish exiles returned from Babylon.

Esther: God's care for His people under Gentile rule.

David, *and of* Abihail the daughter of [R]Eliah
the son of Jesse. 1 Sam. 16:6
19 And she bore him children: Jeush, Shamariah, and Zaham.
20 After her he took [R]Maachah the granddaughter of Absalom; and she bore him Abijah, Attai, Ziza, and Shelomith. 2 Chr. 13:2
21 Now Rehoboam loved Maachah the granddaughter of Absalom more than all his wives and his concubines; for he took eighteen wives and sixty concubines, and begot twenty-eight sons and sixty daughters.
22 And Rehoboam [R]appointed [R]Abijah the son of Maachah as chief, *to be* leader among his brothers; for he *intended* to make him king. Deut. 21:15–17 • 2 Chr. 13:1
23 He dealt wisely, and dispersed some of his sons throughout all the territories of Judah and Benjamin, to every fortified city; and he gave them provisions in abundance. He also sought many wives *for them.*

CHAPTER 12

Kingdom of Judah Is Weakened
1 Kin. 14:25–28

NOW [R]it came to pass, when Rehoboam had established the kingdom and had strengthened himself, that [R]he forsook the law of the LORD, and all Israel along with him. 2 Chr. 11:17 • 1 Kin. 14:22–24
2 [R]And it happened, in the fifth year of King Rehoboam, that Shishak king of Egypt came up against Jerusalem, because they had transgressed against the LORD, 1 Kin. 11:40; 14:25
3 with twelve hundred chariots, sixty thousand horsemen, and people without number who came with him out of Egypt—[R]the Lubim and the Sukkiim and the Ethiopians. 2 Chr. 16:8
4 And he took the fortified cities of Judah and came to Jerusalem.
5 Then Shemaiah the prophet came to Rehoboam and the leaders of Judah, who were gathered together in Jerusalem because of Shishak, and said to them, "Thus says the LORD: 'You have forsaken Me, and therefore I also have left you in the hand of Shishak.'"
6 So the leaders of Israel and the king [R]humbled themselves; and they said, [R]"The LORD *is* righteous." [James 4:10] • Ex. 9:27
7 Now when the LORD saw that they humbled themselves, [R]the word of the LORD came to Shemaiah, saying, "They have humbled themselves; *therefore* I will not destroy them, *but I will grant them some deliverance. My* wrath shall not be poured out on Jerusalem by the hand of Shishak. 1 Kin. 21:28, 29
8 "Nevertheless they will be his servants, that they may distinguish My service from the service of the kingdoms of the nations."
9 So Shishak king of Egypt came up against Jerusalem, and took away the treasures of the house of the LORD and the treasures of the king's house; he took everything. He also carried away the gold shields which Solomon had [R]made. 2 Chr. 9:15, 16
10 In their place King Rehoboam made bronze shields and committed *them* to the hands of the captains of the guard, who guarded the entrance of the king's house.
11 And whenever the king entered the house of the LORD, the guard *would go and* bring them out; *then* they would take them back into the guardroom.
12 When he humbled himself, the wrath of the LORD turned from him, so as not to destroy *him* completely; and things also we
well in Judah.

Death of Rehoboam—1 Kin. 14:21, 22, 2

13 So King Rehoboam strengthen
in Jerusalem and reigned. Now
was forty-one years old wh
king; and he reigned se
Jerusalem, the city whic
chosen out of all the tribes
His name there. His mot
Naamah, an [R]Ammonitess.
14 And he did evil, bec
prepare his heart to seek t
15 The acts of Rehoboa
they not written in the b
prophet, and of Iddo
genealogies? And *ther*
Rehoboam and Jerobo
16 So Rehoboam rested w
and was buried in the City of
[T]Abijah his son reigned in his place.

CHAPTER 13

War of Abijah and Jeroboam—1 Kin. 15:1, 2, 7

IN the eighteenth year of King Jeroboam, Abijah became king over Judah.
2 He reigned three years in Jerusalem. His mother's name *was* [R]Michaiah the daughter of Uriel of Gibeah. And there was war between Abijah and Jeroboam. 2 Chr. 11:20
3 Abijah set the battle in order with an army of valiant warriors, four hundred thousand choice men. Jeroboam also drew up in battle formation against him with eight hundred thousand choice men, mighty men of valor.
4 Then Abijah stood on Mount Zemaraim, which *is* in the mountains of Ephraim, and said, "Hear me, Jeroboam and all Israel:
5 "Should you not know that the LORD God of Israel [R]gave the dominion over Israel to David forever, to him and his sons, [R]by a covenant of salt? 2 Sam. 7:8–16 • Num. 18:19

6 "Yet Jeroboam the son of Nebat, the servant of Solomon the son of David, rose up and [R]rebelled against his lord. 1 Kin. 11:28; 12:20

7 "Then [R]worthless rogues gathered to him, and strengthened themselves against Rehoboam the son of Solomon, when Rehoboam was [R]young and inexperienced and could not withstand them. Judg. 9:4 • 2 Chr. 12:13

8 "And now you think to withstand the kingdom of the LORD, which is in the hand of the sons of David; and you *are* a great multitude, and with you are the gold calves which Jeroboam made for you as gods.

9 "Have you not cast out the priests of the LORD, the sons of Aaron, and the Levites, and made for yourselves priests, like the peoples of *other* lands, [R]so that whoever comes to consecrate himself with a young bull and seven rams may be a priest of [R]*things that are* not gods? Ex. 29:29–33 • Jer. 2:11; 5:7

10 "But as for us, the LORD *is* our God, and we have not forsaken Him; and the priests who minister to the LORD *are* the sons of Aaron, and the Levites *attend* to *their* duties.

11 [R]"And they burn to the LORD every morning and every evening burnt sacrifices and sweet incense; *they* also *set* the [R]showbread *in order on* the pure table, and the lampstand of gold with its lamps [R]to burn every evening; for we keep the command of the LORD our God, but you have forsaken Him. 2 Chr. 2:4 • Lev. 24:5–9 • Ex. 27:20, 21

12 "Now look, God Himself is with us as *our* [R]head, [R]and His priests with sounding trumpets to sound the alarm against you. O children of Israel, do not fight against the LORD God of your fathers, for you shall not prosper!" [Heb. 2:10] • [Num. 10:8–10]

13 But Jeroboam caused an ambush to go around behind them; so they were in front of Judah, and the ambush *was* behind them.

14 And when Judah looked around, to their surprise the battle line *was* at both front and rear; and they [R]cried out to the LORD, and the priests sounded the trumpets. 2 Chr. 6:34, 35

15 Then the men of Judah gave a shout; and as the men of Judah shouted, it happened that God [R]struck Jeroboam and all Israel before Abijah and Judah. 2 Chr. 14:12

16 And the children of Israel fled before Judah, and God delivered them into their hand.

17 Then Abijah and his people struck them with a great slaughter; so five hundred thousand choice men of Israel fell slain.

18 Thus the children of Israel were subdued at that time; and the children of Judah prevailed, [R]because they relied on the LORD God of their fathers. 2 Chr. 14:11

19 And Abijah pursued Jeroboam and took cities from him: Bethel with its villages, Jeshanah with its villages, and [R]Ephrain[T] with its villages. Josh. 15:9 • Or *Ephron*

20 So Jeroboam did not recover strength again in the days of Abijah; and the LORD struck him, and [R]he died. 1 Kin. 14:20

Death of Abijah

21 But Abijah grew mighty, married fourteen wives, and begot twenty-two sons and sixteen daughters.

22 Now the rest of the acts of Abijah, his ways, and his sayings *are* written in the [T]annals of the prophet Iddo. Or *commentary*

CHAPTER 14

Evaluation of Asa—1 Kin. 15:8–12

SO Abijah rested with his fathers, and they buried him in the City of David. Then [R]Asa his son reigned in his place. In his days the land was quiet for ten years. 1 Kin. 15:8

2 Asa did *what was* good and right in the eyes of the LORD his God,

3 for he removed the altars of the foreign *gods* and the [T]high places, and [R]broke down the *sacred* pillars and cut down the wooden images. Places for pagan worship • [Ex. 34:13]

4 He commanded Judah to [R]seek the LORD God of their fathers, and to observe the law and the commandment. [2 Chr. 7:14]

5 He also removed the high places and the incense altars from all the cities of Judah, and the kingdom was quiet under him.

6 And he built fortified cities in Judah, for the land had rest; he had no war in those years, because the LORD had given him rest.

7 Therefore he said to Judah, "Let us build these cities and make walls around *them*, and towers, gates, and bars, *while* the land *is* yet before us, because we have sought the LORD our God; we have sought *Him*, and He has given us rest on every side." So they built and prospered.

8 And Asa had an army of three hundred thousand *men* from Judah who carried [T]shields and spears, and from Benjamin two hundred and eighty thousand men who carried shields and drew bows; all these *were* mighty men of [R]valor. *large shields* • 2 Chr. 13:3

Victory over the Ethiopians

9 [R]Then Zerah the Ethiopian came out against them with an army of a million men and three hundred chariots, and he came to [R]Mareshah. 2 Chr. 12:2, 3; 16:8 • Josh. 15:44

10 So Asa went out against him, and they set the troops in battle array in the Valley of Zephathah at Mareshah.

11 And Asa cried out to the LORD his God, and said, "LORD, *it is* nothing for You to help, whether with many or with those who have no power; help us, O LORD our God, for we rest on You, and in Your name we go against this multitude. O LORD, You *are* our God; do not let man prevail against You!"

12 So the LORD struck the Ethiopians before
Asa and Judah, and the Ethiopians fled.
13 And Asa and the people who *were* with
him pursued them to [R]Gerar. So the Ethiopians were overthrown, and they could not
recover, for they were broken before the
LORD and His army. And they carried away
very much [T]spoil. Gen. 10:19; 20:1 • *plunder*
14 Then they defeated all the cities around
Gerar, for the fear of the LORD came upon
them; and they plundered all the cities, for
there was exceedingly much spoil in them.
15 They also [T]attacked the livestock enclo-
sures, and carried off sheep and camels in
abundance, and returned to Jerusalem. *struck*

CHAPTER 15

Exhortation of Azariah

NOW [R]the Spirit of God came upon Azariah the son of Oded. 2 Chr. 20:14; 24:20
2 And he went out to meet Asa, and said to
him: "Hear me, Asa, and all Judah and Benjamin. [R]The LORD *is* with you while you are
with Him. [R]If you seek Him, He will be found
by you; but if you forsake Him, He will
forsake you. [James 4:8] • [1 Chr. 28:9]
3 [R]"For a long time Israel *has been* without the true God, without a [R]teaching priest,
and without [R]law; Hos. 3:4 • 2 Kin. 12:2 • Lev. 10:11
4 "but [R]when in their trouble they turned
to the LORD God of Israel, and sought Him,
He was found by them. [Deut. 4:29]
5 "And in those times *there was* no peace
to the one who went out, nor to the one who
came in, but great turmoil *was* on all the
inhabitants of the lands.
6 [R]"So nation was [T]destroyed by nation,
and city by city, for God troubled them with
every adversity. Matt. 24:7 • Lit. *beaten in pieces*
7 "But you, be strong and do not let your
hands be weak, for your work shall be rewarded!"

Reforms of Asa—1 Kin. 15:13–15

8 And when Asa heard these words and
the prophecy of Oded the prophet, he took
courage, and removed the abominable idols
from all the land of Judah and Benjamin and
from the cities [R]which he had taken in the
mountains of Ephraim; and he restored the
altar of the LORD that *was* before the vestibule of the LORD. 2 Chr. 13:19
9 Then he gathered all Judah and Benjamin, and [R]those who sojourned with them
from Ephraim, Manasseh, and Simeon, for
they came over to him in great numbers from
Israel when they saw that the LORD his God
was with him. 2 Chr. 11:16
10 So they gathered together at Jerusalem
in the third month, in the fifteenth year of the
reign of Asa.
11 [R]And they offered to the LORD [T]at that
time seven hundred bulls and seven thousand
sheep from the [T]spoil *which* they had
brought. 2 Chr. 14:13–15 • Lit. *in that day* • *plunder*
12 Then they [R]entered into a covenant to
seek the LORD God of their fathers with all
their heart and with all their soul; 2 Kin. 23:3
13 [R]and whoever would not seek the LORD
God of Israel [R]was to be put to death,
whether small or great, whether man or
woman. Ex. 22:20 • Deut. 13:5–15
14 Then they took an oath before the LORD
with a loud voice, with shouting and trumpets and rams' horns.
15 And all Judah rejoiced at the oath, for
they had sworn with all their heart and
[R]sought Him with all their soul; and He was
found by them, and the LORD gave them [R]rest
all around. 2 Chr. 15:2 • 2 Chr. 14:7
16 Also he removed Maachah, the [T]mother
of Asa the king, from *being* queen mother,
because she had made an obscene image of
[T]Asherah; and Asa cut down her obscene
image, crushed *it*, and burned *it* by the Brook
Kidron. Or *grandmother* • A Canaanite goddess
17 But the [T]high places were not removed
from Israel. Nevertheless the heart of Asa
was loyal all his days. Places for pagan worship
18 He also brought into the house of God
the things that his father had dedicated and
that he himself had dedicated: silver and gold
and utensils.
19 And there was no *more* war until the
thirty-fifth year of the reign of Asa.

CHAPTER 16

Victory over the Syrians—1 Kin. 15:16–22

IN the thirty-sixth year of the reign of Asa,
Baasha king of Israel came up against
Judah and built Ramah, that he might let
none go out or come in to Asa king of Judah.
2 Then Asa brought silver and gold from
the treasuries of the house of the LORD and of
the king's house, and sent to Ben-Hadad king
of Syria, who dwelt in Damascus, saying,
3 "*Let there be* a treaty between you and
me, as there was between my father and your
father. Here, I have sent you silver and gold;
come, break your treaty with Baasha king of
Israel, so that he will withdraw from me."
4 So Ben-Hadad heeded King Asa, and sent
the captains of his armies against the cities of
Israel. They attacked Ijon, Dan, Abel Maim,
and all the storage cities of Naphtali.
5 Now it happened, when Baasha heard *it*,
that he stopped building Ramah and ceased
his work.
6 Then King Asa took all Judah, and they
carried away the stones and timber of Ramah, which Baasha had used for building;
and with them he built Geba and Mizpah.

Rebuke of Hanani

7 And at that time [R]Hanani the seer came to Asa king of Judah, and said to him: [R]"Because you have relied on the king of Syria, and have not relied on the LORD your God, therefore the army of the king of Syria has escaped from your hand. 2 Chr. 19:2 · [Jer. 17:5]

8 "Were the Ethiopians and the Lubim not a huge army with very many chariots and horsemen? Yet, because you relied on the LORD, He delivered them into your hand.

9 "For the eyes of the LORD run to and fro throughout the whole earth, to show Himself strong on behalf of *those* whose heart *is* loyal to Him. In this you have done foolishly; therefore from now on you shall have wars."

10 Then Asa was angry with the seer, and [R]put him in prison, for *he was* enraged at him because of this. And Asa oppressed *some* of the people at that time. Jer. 20:2

Death of Asa—1 Kin. 15:23, 24

11 [R]Note that the acts of Asa, first and last, are indeed written in the book of the kings of Judah and Israel. 1 Kin. 15:23, 24

12 And in the thirty-ninth year of his reign, Asa became diseased in his feet, and his malady was *very* severe; yet in his disease he did not seek the LORD, but the physicians.

13 [R]So Asa rested with his fathers; he died in the forty-first year of his reign. 1 Kin. 15:24

14 They buried him in his own tomb, which he had [T]made for himself in the City of David; and they laid him in the bed which was filled with spices and various ingredients prepared in a mixture of ointments. They made a very great burning for him. Lit. *dug*

CHAPTER 17

Evaluation of Jehoshaphat

THEN [R]Jehoshaphat his son reigned in his place, and strengthened himself against Israel. 1 Kin. 15:24

2 And he placed troops in all the fortified cities of Judah, and set garrisons in the land of [R]Judah and in the cities of Ephraim [R]which Asa his father had taken. 2 Chr. 11:5 · 2 Chr. 15:8

3 Now the LORD was with Jehoshaphat, because he walked in the former ways of his father David; he did not seek the Baals,

4 but sought *the God of his father, and walked in His commandments and not according to [R]the acts of Israel. 1 Kin. 12:28

5 Therefore the LORD established the kingdom in his hand; and all Judah [R]gave presents to Jehoshaphat, [R]and he had riches and honor in abundance. 1 Kin. 10:25 · 2 Chr. 18:1

6 And his heart took delight in the ways of the LORD; moreover he removed the high places and wooden images from Judah.

Instruction by the Priests and Levites

7 Also in the third year of his reign he sent his leaders, Ben-Hail, Obadiah, Zechariah, Nethaneel, and Michaiah, [R]to teach in the cities of Judah. 2 Chr. 15:3; 35:3

8 And with them *he sent* Levites: Shemaiah, Nethaniah, Zebadiah, Asahel, Shemiramoth, Jehonathan, Adonijah, Tobijah, and Tobadonijah—the Levites; and with them Elishama and Jehoram, the priests.

9 [R]So they taught in Judah, and *had* the Book of the Law of the LORD with them; they went throughout all the cities of Judah and taught the people. Neh. 8:3, 7

Expansion of the Kingdom

10 And [R]the fear of the LORD fell on all the kingdoms of the lands that *were* around Judah, so that they did not make war against Jehoshaphat. 2 Chr. 14:14

11 Also *some* of the Philistines brought Jehoshaphat presents and silver as tribute; and the Arabians brought him flocks, seven thousand seven hundred rams and seven thousand seven hundred male goats.

12 So Jehoshaphat became increasingly powerful, and he built fortresses and storage cities in Judah.

13 He had much property in the cities of Judah; and the men of war, mighty men of valor, *were* in Jerusalem.

14 These *are* their numbers, according to their fathers' houses. Of Judah, the captains of thousands: Adnah the captain, and with him three hundred thousand mighty men of valor;

15 and next to him *was* Jehohanan the captain, and with him two hundred and eighty thousand;

16 and next to him *was* Amasiah the son of Zichri, [R]who willingly offered himself to the LORD, and with him two hundred thousand mighty men of valor. Judg. 5:2, 9

17 Of Benjamin: Eliada a mighty man of valor, and with him two hundred thousand men armed with bow and shield;

18 and next to him *was* Jehozabad, and with him one hundred and eighty thousand prepared for war.

19 These served the king, besides [R]*those* whom the king put in the fortified cities throughout all Judah. 2 Chr. 17:2

CHAPTER 18

Alliance with Ahab—1 Kin. 22:2–35

JEHOSHAPHAT had riches and honor in abundance; and by marriage he [R]allied himself with [R]Ahab. 2 Kin. 8:18 · 1 Kin. 22:40

2 [R]After some years he went down to *visit* Ahab in Samaria; and Ahab killed sheep and

17:4 LXX *the* LORD *God*

oxen in abundance for him and the people
who were with him, and persuaded him to go
up *with him* to Ramoth Gilead. 1 Kin. 22:2
3 So Ahab king of Israel said to Jehoshaphat king of Judah, "Will you go with me
against Ramoth Gilead?" And he answered
him, "I *am* as you *are*, and my people as your
people; *we will be* with you in the war."
4 And Jehoshaphat said to the king of
Israel, [R]"Please inquire for the word of the
LORD today." 2 Sam. 2:1
5 Then the king of Israel gathered the
prophets together, four hundred men, and
said to them, "Shall we go to war against
Ramoth Gilead, or shall I refrain?" And they
said, "Go up, for God will deliver it into the
king's hand."
6 But Jehoshaphat said, "*Is there* not still a
prophet of the LORD here, that we may inquire of [R]Him?"[T] 2 Kin. 3:11 • Or *him*
7 So the king of Israel said to Jehoshaphat,
"*There is* still one man by whom we may
inquire of the LORD; but I hate him, because
he never prophesies good concerning me, but
always evil. He *is* Micaiah the son of Imla."
And Jehoshaphat said, "Let not the king say
such things!"
8 Then the king of Israel called one *of his*
officers and said, "Bring Micaiah the son of
Imla quickly!"
9 And the king of Israel and Jehoshaphat
king of Judah, clothed in *their* robes, sat each
on his throne; and they sat at a threshing
floor at the entrance of the gate of Samaria;
and all the prophets prophesied before them.
10 Now Zedekiah the son of Chenaanah
had made [R]horns of iron for himself; and he
said, "Thus says the LORD: 'With these you
shall gore the Syrians until they are destroyed.'" Zech. 1:18–21
11 And all the prophets prophesied so, saying, "Go up to Ramoth Gilead and prosper,
for the LORD will deliver *it* into the king's
hand."
12 Then the messenger who had gone to
call Micaiah spoke to him, saying, "Now
listen, the words of the prophets with one
accord encourage the king. Therefore please
let your word be like *the word of* one of them,
and speak encouragement."
13 And Micaiah said, "*As* the LORD lives,
whatever my God says, that I will speak."
14 Then he came to the king; and the king
said to him, "Micaiah, shall we go to war
against Ramoth Gilead, or shall I refrain?"
And he said, "Go and prosper, and they shall
be delivered into your hand!"
15 So the king said to him, "How many
times shall I make you swear that you tell me
nothing but the truth in the name of the
LORD?"
16 Then he said, "I saw all Israel [R]scattered
on the mountains, as sheep that have no
[R]shepherd. And the LORD said, 'These have no
master. Let each return to his house in
peace.'" [Jer. 23:1–8; 31:10] • Matt. 9:36
17 And the king of Israel said to Jehoshaphat, "Did I not tell you *that* he would not
prophesy good concerning me, but evil?"
18 Then [T]Micaiah said, "Therefore hear the
word of the LORD: I saw the LORD sitting on
His throne, and all the host of heaven standing on His right hand and *on* His left. *he*
19 "And the LORD said, 'Who will persuade
Ahab king of Israel to go up, that he may fall
at Ramoth Gilead?' And one spoke in this
manner, and another spoke in that manner.
20 "Then a spirit came forward and stood
before the LORD, and said, 'I will persuade
him.' The LORD said to him, 'In what way?'
21 "So he said, 'I will go out and be a lying
spirit in the mouth of all his prophets.' And
the LORD said, 'You shall persuade *him* and
also prevail; go out and do so.'
22 "Now therefore, look! [R]The LORD has put
a lying spirit in the mouth of these prophets
of yours, and the LORD has declared disaster
against you." Ezek. 14:9
23 Then Zedekiah the son of Chenaanah
went near and [R]struck Micaiah on the cheek,
and said, "Which way did the spirit from the
LORD go from me to speak to you?" Jer. 20:2
24 And Micaiah said, "Indeed you shall see
on that day when you go into an inner
chamber to hide!"
25 Then the king of Israel said, "Take Micaiah, and return him to Amon the governor of
the city and to Joash the king's son;
26 "and say, 'Thus says the king: [R]"Put this
fellow in prison, and feed him with bread of
affliction and water of affliction until I return
in peace."'" 2 Chr. 16:10
27 Then Micaiah said, "If you ever return in
peace, the LORD has not spoken by me." And
he said, "Take heed, all you people!"
28 So the king of Israel and Jehoshaphat
the king of Judah went up to Ramoth Gilead.
29 And the king of Israel said to Jehoshaphat, "I will [R]disguise myself and go into
battle; but you put on your robes." So the
king of Israel disguised himself, and they
went into battle. 2 Chr. 35:22
30 Now the king of Syria had commanded
the captains of the chariots who *were* with
him, saying, "Fight with no one small or
great, but only with the king of Israel."
31 So it was, when the captains of the
chariots saw Jehoshaphat, that they said, "It
is the king of Israel!" Therefore they surrounded him to attack; but Jehoshaphat cried
out, and the LORD helped him, and God
moved them *to turn away* from him.
32 For so it was, when the captains of the
chariots saw that it was not the king of

Israel, that they turned back from pursuing
him.
33 Now a certain man drew a bow at ran-
dom, and struck the king of Israel between
the joints of his armor. So he said to the
driver of his chariot, "Turn around and take
me out of the battle, for I am wounded."
34 The battle increased that day, and the
king of Israel propped *himself* up in *his*
chariot facing the Syrians until evening; and
about the time of sunset he died.

CHAPTER 19

THEN Jehoshaphat the king of Judah returned safely to his house in Jerusalem.
2 And Jehu the son of Hanani the seer
went out to meet him, and said to King
Jehoshaphat, "Should you help the wicked
and love those who hate the LORD? Therefore
the wrath of the LORD *is* upon you.
3 "Nevertheless good things are found in
you, in that you have removed the [T]wooden
images from the land, and have prepared
your heart to seek God." Heb. *Asheroth*
4 So Jehoshaphat dwelt at Jerusalem; and
he went out again among the people from
Beersheba to the mountains of Ephraim, and
brought them back to the LORD God of their
[R]fathers. 2 Chr. 15:8–13

Organization of the Kingdom

5 Then he set [R]judges in the land throughout all the fortified cities of Judah, city by
city, [Deut. 16:18–20]
6 and said to the judges, "Take heed to
what you are doing, for you do not judge for
man but for the LORD, who *is* with you [T]in the
judgment. Lit. *in the matter of the judgment*
7 "Now therefore, let the fear of the LORD
be upon you; take care and do *it,* for *there is*
no iniquity with the LORD our God, no [R]par-
tiality, nor taking of bribes." [Deut. 10:17, 18]
8 Moreover in Jerusalem, for the judgment
of the LORD and for controversies, Jehoshaphat appointed some of the Levites and
priests, and some of the chief fathers of
Israel, when they returned to Jerusalem.
9 And he commanded them, saying, "Thus
you shall act [R]in the fear of the LORD, faithfully and with a loyal heart: [2 Sam. 23:3]
10 [R]"Whatever case comes to you from your
brethren who dwell in their cities, whether of
bloodshed or offenses against law or commandment, against statutes or ordinances,
you shall warn them, lest they trespass
against the LORD and [R]wrath come upon [R]you
and your brethren. Do this, and you will not
be guilty. Deut. 17:8 • Num. 16:46 • [Ezek. 3:18]
11 "And take notice: Amariah the chief
priest *is* over you [R]in all matters of the LORD;
and Zebadiah the son of Ishmael, the ruler of
the house of Judah, for all the king's matters;
also the Levites *will be* officials before you.
Behave courageously, and the LORD will be
[R]with the good." 1 Chr. 26:30 • [2 Chr. 15:2; 20:17]

CHAPTER 20

Victory over Moab and Ammon

IT happened after this *that* the people of
Moab with the people of Ammon, and
others with them besides the Ammonites,
came to battle against Jehoshaphat.
2 Then some came and told Jehoshaphat,
saying, "A great multitude is coming against
you from beyond the sea, from Syria; and
they are [R]in Hazazon Tamar" (which *is* [R]En
Gedi). Gen. 14:7 • Josh. 15:62
3 And Jehoshaphat feared, and set [T]himself
to seek the LORD, and [R]proclaimed a fast
throughout all Judah. Lit. *his face* • Ezra 8:21
4 So Judah gathered together to ask [R]*help*
from the LORD; and from all the cities of
Judah they came to seek the LORD. 2 Chr. 14:11
5 Then Jehoshaphat stood in the congregation of Judah and Jerusalem, in the house
of the LORD, before the new court,
6 and said: "O LORD God of our fathers, *are*
You not God in heaven, and do You *not* rule
over all the kingdoms of the nations, and in
Your hand *is there not* power and might, so
that no one is able to withstand You?
7 "*Are* You not our God, *who* drove out
the inhabitants of this land before Your
people Israel, and gave it to the descendants
of Abraham [R]Your friend forever? Is. 41:8
8 "And they dwell in it, and have built You
a sanctuary in it for Your name, saying,
9 [R]'If disaster comes upon us, *such as* the
sword, judgment, pestilence, or famine, we
will stand before this temple and in Your
presence (for Your [R]name *is* in this temple),
and cry out to You in our affliction, and You
will hear and save.' 2 Chr. 6:28–30 • 2 Chr. 6:20
10 "And now, here are the people of Ammon, Moab, and Mount Seir—whom You
would not let Israel invade when they came
out of the land of Egypt, but they turned
from them and did not destroy them—
11 "here they are, rewarding us [R]by coming
to throw us out of Your possession which
You have given us to inherit. Ps. 83:1–18
12 "O our God, will You not [R]judge them?
For we have no power against this great
multitude that is coming against us; nor do
we know what to do, but [R]our eyes *are* upon
You." Judg. 11:27 • Ps. 25:15; 121:1, 2; 123:1, 2; 141:8
13 Now all Judah, with their little ones,
their wives, and their children, stood before
the LORD.

14 Then [R]the Spirit of the LORD came upon
Jahaziel the son of Zechariah, the son of
Benaiah, the son of Jeiel, the son of Mattaniah, a Levite of the sons of Asaph, in the
midst of the congregation; 2 Chr. 15:1; 24:20
15 and he said, "Listen, all you of Judah and
you inhabitants of Jerusalem, and you, King
Jehoshaphat! Thus says the LORD to you:
[R]'Do not be afraid nor dismayed because of
this great multitude, for the battle *is* not
yours, but God's. [Deut. 1:29, 30; 31:6, 8]
16 'Tomorrow go down against them. They
will surely come up by the ascent of Ziz, and
you will find them at the end of the [T]brook
before the Wilderness of Jeruel. *ravine* or *wadi*
17 'You will not *need* to fight in this *battle*.
Position yourselves, stand still and see the
salvation of the LORD, who is with you, O
Judah and Jerusalem!' Do not fear or be
dismayed; tomorrow go out against them,
[R]for the LORD *is* with you." Num. 14:9
18 And Jehoshaphat [R]bowed his head with
his face to the ground, and all Judah and the
inhabitants of Jerusalem bowed before the
LORD, worshiping the LORD. Ex. 4:31
19 Then the Levites of the children of the
Kohathites and of the children of the Korahites stood up to praise the LORD God of Israel
with voices loud and high.
20 And they rose early in the morning and
went out into the Wilderness of Tekoa; and
as they went out, Jehoshaphat stood and
said, "Hear me, O Judah and you inhabitants
of Jerusalem: [R]Believe in the LORD your God,
and you shall be established; believe His
prophets, and you shall prosper." Is. 7:9
21 And when he had consulted with the
people, he appointed those who should sing
to the LORD, [R]and who should praise the
beauty of holiness, as they went out before
the army and were saying: 1 Chr. 16:29

> [R]"Praise the LORD, Ps. 106:1; 136:1
> For His mercy *endures* forever."

22 Now when they began to sing and to
praise, [R]the LORD set ambushes against the
people of Ammon, Moab, and Mount Seir,
who had come against Judah; and they were
defeated. Judg. 7:22
23 For the people of Ammon and Moab
stood up against the inhabitants of Mount
Seir to utterly kill and destroy *them*. And
when they [T]had made an end of the inhabitants of Seir, [R]they helped to destroy one
another. *had finished* • 1 Sam. 14:20
24 So when Judah came to a place overlooking the wilderness, they looked toward
the multitude; and there *were* their dead
bodies, fallen on the earth. No one had escaped.
25 When Jehoshaphat and his people came
to take away their spoil, they found among
them an abundance of valuables on the *dead
bodies, and precious jewelry, which they
stripped off for themselves, more than they
could carry away; and they were three days
gathering the spoil because there was so
much.
26 And on the fourth day they assembled in
the Valley of [T]Berachah, for there they
blessed the LORD; therefore the name of that
place was called The Valley of Berachah until
this day. Lit. *Blessing*
27 Then they returned, every man of Judah
and Jerusalem, with Jehoshaphat in front of
them, to go back to Jerusalem with joy, for
the LORD had [R]made them rejoice over their
enemies. Neh. 12:43
28 So they came to Jerusalem, with stringed
instruments and harps and trumpets, to the
house of the LORD.
29 And [R]the fear of God was on all the
kingdoms of *those* countries when they heard
that the LORD had fought against the enemies
of Israel. 2 Chr. 14:14; 17:10
30 Then the realm of Jehoshaphat was
quiet, for his God gave him rest all around.

Summary of the Reign of Jehoshaphat
1 Kin. 22:41–45

31 [R]So Jehoshaphat was king over Judah.
He was thirty-five years old when he became
king, and he reigned twenty-five years in
Jerusalem. His mother's name *was* Azubah
the daughter of Shilhi. [1 Kin. 22:41–43]
32 And he walked in the way of his father
Asa, and did not turn aside from it, doing
what was right in the sight of the LORD.
33 Nevertheless the [T]high places were not
taken away, for as yet the people had not
[R]directed their hearts to the God of their
fathers. Places for pagan worship • 2 Chr. 12:14; 19:3
34 Now the rest of the acts of Jehoshaphat,
first and last, indeed they *are* written in the
book of Jehu the son of Hanani, which *is*
mentioned in the book of the kings of Israel.

The Sin and Death of Jehoshaphat
1 Kin. 22:48

35 After this Jehoshaphat king of Judah
allied himself with Ahaziah king of Israel,
who acted very [R]wickedly. [2 Chr. 19:2]
36 And he allied himself with him [R]to make
ships to go to Tarshish, and they made the
ships in Ezion Geber. 1 Kin. 9:26; 10:22
37 But Eliezer the son of Dodavah of Mareshah prophesied against Jehoshaphat, saying,
"Because you have allied yourself with Ahaziah, the LORD has destroyed your works."
Then the ships were wrecked, so that they
were not able to go [R]to Tarshish. 2 Chr. 9:21

20:25 A few mss., Lat., Vg. *garments;* LXX *armor*

CHAPTER 21

Evaluation of Jehoram
1 Kin. 22:50; 2 Kin. 8:17–19

AND [R]Jehoshaphat [T]rested with his fathers, and was buried with his fathers in the City of David. Then Jehoram his son reigned in his place. 1 Kin. 22:50 • Died and joined his ancestors

2 He had brothers, the sons of Jehoshaphat: Azariah, Jehiel, Zechariah, Azaryahu, Michael, and Shephatiah; all these *were* the sons of Jehoshaphat king of Israel.

3 Their father gave them great gifts of silver and gold and precious things, with fortified cities in Judah; but he gave the kingdom to Jehoram, because he *was* the firstborn.

4 Now when Jehoram [T]was established over the kingdom of his father, he strengthened himself and killed all his brothers with the sword, and also *others* of the princes of Israel. Lit. *arose*

5 [R]Jehoram *was* thirty-two years old when he became king, and he reigned eight years in Jerusalem. 2 Kin. 8:17–22

6 And he walked in the way of the kings of Israel, just as the house of Ahab had done, for he had the daughter of Ahab as a wife; and he did evil in the sight of the LORD.

7 Yet the LORD would not destroy the house of David, because of the [R]covenant that He had made with David, and since He had promised to give a lamp to him and to his [R]sons forever. 2 Sam. 7:8–17 • 1 Kin. 11:36

Revolt by Edom and Libnah—2 Kin. 8:20–22

8 [R]In his days the Edomites revolted against Judah's authority, and made a king over themselves. 2 Kin. 8:20; 14:7, 10

9 So Jehoram went out with his officers, and all his chariots with him. And he rose by night and attacked the Edomites who had surrounded him and the captains of the chariots.

10 Thus the Edomites have been in revolt against Judah's authority to this day. At that time Libnah revolted against his rule, because he had forsaken the LORD God of his fathers.

11 Moreover he made [T]high places in the mountains of Judah, and caused the inhabitants of Jerusalem to [R]commit harlotry, and led Judah astray. Places for pagan worship • [Lev. 20:5]

Warning of Elijah

12 And a letter came to him from Elijah the prophet, saying,

Thus says the LORD God of your father David:
Because you have not walked in the ways of Jehoshaphat your father, or in the ways of Asa king of Judah,
13 but have walked in the way of the kings of Israel, and have made Judah and the inhabitants of Jerusalem to [R]play the harlot like the [R]harlotry of the house of Ahab, and also have [R]killed your brothers, those of your father's household, *who were* better than yourself, Deut. 31:16 • 2 Kin. 9:22 • 2 Chr. 21:4
14 behold, the LORD will strike your people with a serious affliction—your children, your wives, and all your possessions;
15 and you *will become* very sick with a [R]disease of your intestines, until your intestines come out by reason of the sickness, day by day. 2 Chr. 21:18, 19

Invasion by Philistia and Arabia

16 Moreover the LORD stirred up against Jehoram the spirit of the Philistines and the Arabians who *were* near the Ethiopians.

17 And they came up into Judah and invaded it, and carried away all the possessions that were found in the king's house, and also his sons and his wives, so that there was not a son left to him except [T]Jehoahaz, the youngest of his sons. *Ahaziah,* 2 Chr. 22:1

Death of Jehoram

18 After all this the LORD struck him in his intestines with an incurable disease.

19 Then it happened in the course of time, after the end of two years, that his intestines came out because of his sickness; so he died in severe pain. And his people made no [T]burning for him, like [R]the burning for his fathers. Burning of spices • 2 Chr. 16:14

20 He was thirty-two years old when he became king. He reigned in Jerusalem eight years and, to no one's sorrow, departed. However they buried him in the City of David, but not in the tombs of the kings.

CHAPTER 22

The Reign of Ahaziah
2 Kin. 8:27–29; 9:15, 16, 27, 28; 10:12–14

THEN the inhabitants of Jerusalem made Ahaziah his youngest son king in his place, for the raiders who came with the [R]Arabians into the camp had killed all the [R]older *sons*. So Ahaziah the son of Jehoram, king of Judah, reigned. 2 Chr. 21:16 • 2 Chr. 21:17

2 Ahaziah *was* forty-two years old when he became king, and he reigned one year in Jerusalem. His mother's name *was* Athaliah the [T]granddaughter of Omri. Lit. *daughter*

3 He also walked in the ways of the house of Ahab, for his mother counseled him to do wickedly.

4 Therefore he did evil in the sight of the LORD, like the house of Ahab; for they were his counselors after the death of his father, to his destruction.

5 He also walked in their counsel, and went with [T]Jehoram the son of Ahab king of Israel to *make* war against Hazael king of Syria at Ramoth Gilead; and the Syrians wounded Joram. *Joram,* vv. 5, 7; 2 Kin. 8:28

6 Then he returned to Jezreel to recover from the wounds which he had received at Ramah, when he fought against Hazael king of Syria. And *Azariah the son of Jehoram, king of Judah, went down to see Jehoram the son of Ahab in Jezreel, because he was sick.

7 His going to Joram was God's occasion for Ahaziah's [T]downfall; for when he arrived, he went out with Jehoram against Jehu the son of Nimshi, whom the LORD had anointed to cut off the house of Ahab. *crushing*

8 And it happened, when Jehu was [R]executing judgment on the house of Ahab, and [R]found the princes of Judah and the sons of Ahaziah's brothers who served Ahaziah, that he killed them. 2 Kin. 9:22–24 • 2 Kin. 10:10–14

9 [R]Then he searched for Ahaziah; and they caught him (he was hiding in Samaria), and brought him to Jehu. When they had killed him, they buried him, "because," they said, "he is the son of [R]Jehoshaphat, who sought the LORD with all his heart." So the house of Ahaziah had no one to assume power over the kingdom. [2 Kin. 9:27] • 1 Kin. 15:24

The Reign of Athaliah—2 Kin. 11:1–16

10 [R]Now when Athaliah the mother of Ahaziah saw that her son was dead, she arose and destroyed all the royal heirs of the house of Judah. 2 Kin. 11:1–3

11 But [T]Jehoshabeath, the daughter of the king, took [R]Joash the son of Ahaziah, and stole him away from among the king's sons who were being murdered, and put him and his nurse in a bedroom. So Jehoshabeath, the daughter of King Jehoram, the wife of Jehoiada the priest (for she was the sister of Ahaziah), hid him from Athaliah so that she did not kill him. *Jehosheba,* 2 Kin. 11:2 • 2 Kin. 12:18

12 And he was hidden with them in the house of God for six years, while Athaliah reigned over the land.

CHAPTER 23

IN [R]the seventh year [R]Jehoiada strengthened himself, *and made a* covenant with the captains of hundreds: Azariah the son of Jeroham, Ishmael the son of Jehohanan, Azariah the son of [R]Obed, Maaseiah the son of Adaiah, and Elishaphat the son of Zichri. 2 Kin. 11:4 • 2 Kin. 12:2 • 1 Chr. 2:37, 38

2 And they went throughout Judah and gathered the Levites from all the cities of Judah, and the [R]chief fathers of Israel, and they came to Jerusalem. Ezra 1:5

3 Then all the congregation made a covenant with the king in the house of God. And he said to them, "Behold, the king's son shall reign, as the LORD has [R]said of the sons of David. 2 Sam. 7:12

4 "This *is* what you shall do: One-third of you [R]entering on the Sabbath, of the priests and the Levites, *shall be* keeping watch over the doors; 1 Chr. 9:25

5 "one-third *shall be* at the king's house; and one-third at the Gate of the Foundation. All the people *shall be* in the courts of the house of the LORD.

6 "But let no one come into the house of the LORD except the priests and [R]those of the Levites who serve. They may go in, for they *are* holy; but all the people shall keep the watch of the LORD. 1 Chr. 23:28–32

7 "And the Levites shall surround the king on all sides, every man with his weapons in his hand; and whoever comes into the house, let him be put to death. You are to be with the king when he comes in and when he goes out."

8 So the Levites and all Judah did according to all that Jehoiada the priest commanded. And each man took his men who were to be on duty on the Sabbath, with those who were going *off duty* on the Sabbath; for Jehoiada the priest had not dismissed [R]the divisions. 1 Chr. 24:1–31

9 And Jehoiada the priest gave to the captains of hundreds the spears and the large and small shields which *had been* King David's, that *were* in the temple of God.

10 Then he set all the people, every man with his weapon in his hand, from the right side of the temple to the left side of the temple, along by the altar and by the temple, all around the king.

11 And they brought out the king's son, put the crown on him, [R]*gave him* the [T]Testimony, and made him king. Then Jehoiada and his sons anointed him, and said, "*Long* live the king!" Deut. 17:18 • Law, Ex. 25:16, 21

12 Now when Athaliah heard the noise of the people running and praising the king, she came to the people in the temple of the LORD.

13 And *when* she looked, there was the king standing by his pillar at the entrance; and the leaders and the trumpeters *were* by the king. All the people of the land were rejoicing and blowing trumpets, also the singers with instruments of music, and [R]those who led in praise. So Athaliah tore her clothes and said, [R]"Treason! Treason!" 1 Chr. 25:8 • 2 Kin. 9:23

14 Then Jehoiada the priest brought out the captains of hundreds who were set over the army, and said to them, "Take her outside under guard, and slay with the sword whoever follows her." For the priest said, "Do not kill her in the house of the LORD."

22:6 Heb. mss., LXX, Syr., Vg. *Ahaziah* and 2 Kin. 8:29

15 So they seized her; and she went by way
of the entrance of the Horse Gate into the
king's house, and they killed her there.

Revival of Jehoiada—2 Kin. 11:17–20

16 Then Jehoiada made a [R]covenant between himself, the people, and the king, that
they should be the LORD's people. Josh. 24:24, 25
17 And all the people went to the [T]temple of
Baal, and tore it down. They broke in pieces
its altars and images, and killed Mattan the
priest of Baal before the altars. Lit. *house*
18 Also Jehoiada appointed the oversight of
the house of the LORD to the hand of the
priests, the Levites, whom David had assigned in the house of the LORD, to offer the
burnt offerings of the LORD, as *it is* written in
the Law of Moses, with rejoicing and with
singing, *as it was established* by David.
19 And he set the gatekeepers at the gates
of the house of the LORD, so that no one *who*
was in any way unclean should enter.
20 [R]Then he took the captains of hundreds,
the nobles, the governors of the people, and
all the people of the land, and brought the
king down from the house of the LORD; and
they went through the Upper Gate to the
king's house, and set the king on the throne
of the kingdom. 2 Kin. 11:19
21 So all the people of the land rejoiced; and
the city was quiet, for they had slain Athaliah
with the sword.

CHAPTER 24

Evaluation of Joash—2 Kin. 11:21—12:2

JOASH [R]*was* seven years old when he became king, and he reigned forty years in
Jerusalem. His mother's name *was* Zibiah of
Beersheba. 2 Kin. 11:21; 12:1–15
2 Joash did *what was* right in the sight of
the LORD all the days of Jehoiada the priest.
3 And Jehoiada took for him two wives,
and he had sons and daughters.

Repair of the Temple—2 Kin. 12:4–16

4 Now it happened after this *that* Joash set
his heart on repairing the house of the LORD.
5 Then he gathered the priests and the
Levites, and said to them, "Go out to the
cities of Judah, and gather from all Israel
money to repair the house of your God from
year to year, and see that you do it quickly."
However the Levites did not do it quickly.
6 So the king called Jehoiada the chief
priest, and said to him, "Why have you not
required the Levites to bring in from Judah
and from Jerusalem the collection, *according*
to the commandment of Moses the servant of
the LORD and of the congregation of Israel,
for the [R]tabernacle of witness?" Num. 1:50

7 For the sons of Athaliah, that wicked
woman, had broken into the house of God,
and had also presented all the dedicated
things of the house of the LORD to the Baals.
8 Then at the king's commandment [R]they
made a chest, and set it outside at the gate of
the house of the LORD. 2 Kin. 12:9
9 And they made a proclamation throughout Judah and Jerusalem to bring to the LORD
the collection *that* Moses the servant of God
had imposed on Israel in the wilderness.
10 Then all the leaders and all the people
rejoiced, brought their contributions, and put
them into the chest until all had given.
11 So it was, at that time, when the chest
was brought to the king's official by the hand
of the Levites, and [R]when they saw that *there*
was much money, that the king's scribe and
the high priest's officer came and emptied the
chest, and took it and returned it to its place.
Thus they did day by day, and gathered
money in abundance. 2 Kin. 12:10
12 Then the king and Jehoiada gave it to
those who did the work of the service of the
house of the LORD; and they hired masons
and carpenters to repair the house of the
LORD, and also those who worked in iron and
bronze to restore the house of the LORD.
13 So the workmen labored, and the work
was completed by them; they restored the
house of God to its original condition and
reinforced it.
14 When they had finished, they brought
the rest of the money before the king and
Jehoiada; [R]they made from it articles for the
house of the LORD, articles for serving and
offering, spoons and vessels of gold and
silver. And they offered burnt offerings in the
house of the LORD continually all the days of
Jehoiada. 2 Kin. 12:13

Death of Jehoiada

15 But Jehoiada grew old and was full of
days, and he died; *he was* one hundred and
thirty years old when he died.
16 And they buried him in the City of David
among the kings, because he had done good
in Israel, both toward God and His house.

Murder of Jehoiada's Son

17 Now after the death of Jehoiada the
leaders of Judah came and bowed down to
the king. And the king listened to them.
18 Therefore they left the house of the LORD
God of their fathers, and served [R]wooden
images and idols; and [R]wrath came upon
Judah and Jerusalem because of their trespass. 1 Kin. 14:23 • [Ex. 34:12–14]
19 Yet He sent prophets to them, to bring
them back to the LORD; and they testified
against them, but they would not listen.

20 Then the Spirit of God [T]came upon Zechariah the son of Jehoiada the priest, who stood above the people, and said to them, "Thus says God: [R]'Why do you transgress the commandments of the LORD, so that you cannot prosper? [R]Because you have forsaken the LORD, He also has forsaken you.' " Lit. *clothed* • Num. 14:41 • [2 Chr. 15:2]

21 So they conspired against him, and at the commandment of the king they [R]stoned him with stones in the court of the house of the LORD. [Neh. 9:26]

22 Thus Joash the king did not remember the kindness which Jehoiada his [T]father had done to him, but killed his son; and as he died, he said, "The LORD look on *it*, and [R]repay!" Foster father • [Gen. 9:5]

Destruction of Judah by Syria

23 So it happened in the spring of the year *that* [R]the army of Syria came up against him; and they came to Judah and Jerusalem, and destroyed all the leaders of the people from among the people, and sent all their [T]spoil to the king of Damascus. 2 Kin. 12:17 • *plunder*

24 For the army of the Syrians [R]came with a small company of men; but the LORD [R]delivered a very great army into their hand, because they had forsaken the LORD God of their fathers. So they [R]executed judgment against Joash. Lev. 26:8 • Lev. 26:25 • 2 Chr. 22:8

Death of Joash—2 Kin. 12:20, 21

25 And when they had withdrawn from him (for they left him severely wounded), [R]his own servants conspired against him because of the blood of the *sons of Jehoiada the priest, and killed him on his bed. So he died. And they buried him in the City of David, but they did not bury him in the tombs of the kings. 2 Kin. 12:20, 21

26 These are the ones who conspired against him: [T]Zabad the son of Shimeath the Ammonitess, and Jehozabad the son of Shimrith the Moabitess. *Jozachar,* 2 Kin. 12:21

27 Now *concerning* his sons, and the many oracles about him, and the repairing of the house of God, indeed they *are* written in the annals of the book of the kings. Then Amaziah his son reigned in his place.

CHAPTER 25

Evaluation of Amaziah—2 Kin. 14:1–6

AMAZIAH *was* twenty-five years old *when* he became king, and he reigned twenty-nine years in Jerusalem. His mother's name *was* Jehoaddan of Jerusalem.

2 And he did *what was* right in the sight of the LORD, but not with a loyal heart.

3 Now it was so, when the kingdom was established for him, that he executed his servants who had murdered his father the king.

4 However he did not execute their children, but *did* as *it is* written in the Law in the Book of Moses, where the LORD commanded, saying, [R]"The fathers shall not be put to death for their children, nor shall the children be put to death for their fathers; but a person shall die for his own sin." Deut. 24:16

Victory over Edom

5 Moreover Amaziah gathered Judah together and set over them captains of thousands and captains of hundreds, according to *their* fathers' houses, throughout all Judah and Benjamin; and he numbered them [R]from twenty years old and above, and found them to be three hundred thousand choice *men, able* to go to war, who could handle spear and shield. Num. 1:3

6 He also hired one hundred thousand mighty men of valor from Israel for [T]one hundred talents of silver. $38,400,000

7 But a [R]man of God came to him, saying, "O king, do not let the army of Israel go with you, for the LORD *is* not with Israel—*not with* any of the children of Ephraim. 2 Chr. 11:2

8 "But if you go, be gone! Be strong in battle! *Even so,* God shall make you fall before the enemy; for God has [R]power to help and to overthrow." 2 Chr. 14:11; 20:6

9 Then Amaziah said to the man of God, "But what *shall we* do about the [T]hundred talents which I have given to the troops of Israel?" And the man of God answered, [R]"The LORD is able to give you much more than this." $38,400,000 • [Deut. 8:18]

10 So Amaziah discharged the troops that had come to him from Ephraim, to go back home. Therefore their anger was greatly aroused against Judah, and they returned home in great anger.

11 Then Amaziah strengthened himself, and leading his people, he went to [R]the Valley of Salt and killed ten thousand of the people of Seir. 2 Kin. 14:7

12 And the children of Judah took captive *another* ten thousand alive, brought them to the top of the rock, and cast them down from the top of the rock, so that they all were dashed in pieces.

13 But as for the soldiers of the army which Amaziah had discharged, so that they would not go with him to battle, they raided the cities of Judah from Samaria to Beth Horon, killed three thousand in them, and took much [T]spoil. *plunder*

Idolatry of Amaziah

14 Now it was so, after Amaziah came from the slaughter of the Edomites, that he

24:25 LXX, Vg. *son* and vv. 20–22

brought the gods of the people of Seir, set them up *to be* his gods, and bowed down before them and burned incense to them.
15 Therefore the anger of the LORD was aroused against Amaziah, and He sent him a prophet who said to him, "Why have you sought [R]the gods of the people, which [R]could not rescue their own people from your hand?" [Ps. 96:5] • 2 Chr. 25:11
16 So it was, as he talked with him, that *the king* said to him, "Have we made you the king's counsel? Cease! Why should you be killed?" Then the prophet ceased, and said, "I know that God has [R]determined to destroy you, because you have done this and have not heeded my counsel." [1 Sam. 2:25]

Defeat of Judah by Israel—2 Kin. 14:8–14

17 Then Amaziah king of Judah took counsel and sent to Joash the son of Jehoahaz, the son of Jehu, king of Israel, saying, "Come, let us face one another in battle."
18 And Joash king of Israel sent to Amaziah king of Judah, saying, "The thistle that *was* in Lebanon sent to the cedar that was in Lebanon, saying, 'Give your daughter to my son as wife'; and a wild beast that *was* in Lebanon passed by and trampled the thistle.
19 "Indeed you say that you have defeated the Edomites, and your heart is lifted up to [R]boast. Stay at home now; why should you meddle with trouble, that you should fall—you and Judah with you?" 2 Chr. 26:16; 32:25
20 But Amaziah would not heed, for it *came* from God, that He might give them into the hand *of their enemies*, because they [R]sought the gods of Edom. 2 Chr. 25:14
21 So Joash king of Israel went out; and he and Amaziah king of Judah faced one another at [R]Beth Shemesh, which *belongs* to Judah. Josh. 19:38
22 And Judah was defeated by Israel, and every man fled to his tent.
23 Then Joash the king of Israel captured Amaziah king of Judah, the son of Joash, the son of [R]Jehoahaz, at Beth Shemesh; and he brought him to Jerusalem, and broke down the wall of Jerusalem from the Gate of Ephraim to the Corner Gate—[T]four hundred cubits. 2 Chr. 21:17; 22:1, 6 • 600 ft.
24 And *he took* all the gold and silver, all the articles that were found in the house of God with [R]Obed-Edom, the treasures of the king's house, and hostages, and returned to Samaria. 1 Chr. 26:15

Death of Amaziah—2 Kin. 14:17–20

25 Amaziah the son of Joash, king of Judah, lived fifteen years after the death of Joash the son of Jehoahaz, king of Israel.
26 Now the rest of the acts of Amaziah, from first to last, indeed *are* they not written in the book of the kings of Judah and Israel?
27 After the time that Amaziah turned away from following the LORD, they made a conspiracy against him in Jerusalem, and he fled to Lachish; but they sent after him to Lachish and killed him there.
28 Then they brought him on horses and buried him with his fathers in [T]the City of Judah. *The City of David*

CHAPTER 26

Evaluation of Uzziah
2 Kin. 14:21, 22; 15:1–3

NOW all the people of Judah took Uzziah, who *was* sixteen years old, and made him king instead of his father Amaziah.
2 He built [T]Elath and restored it to Judah, after the king rested with his fathers. *Eloth*
3 Uzziah *was* sixteen years old when he became king, and he reigned fifty-two years in Jerusalem. His mother's name was Jecholiah of Jerusalem.
4 And he did *what was* [R]right in the sight of the LORD, according to all that his father Amaziah had done. 2 Chr. 24:2
5 He sought God in the days of Zechariah, who had understanding in the *visions of God; and as long as he sought the LORD, God made him [R]prosper. [2 Chr. 15:2; 20:20; 31:21]

Victories of Uzziah

6 Now he went out and [R]made war against the Philistines, and broke down the wall of Gath, the wall of Jabneh, and the wall of Ashdod; and he built cities *around* Ashdod and among the Philistines. Is. 14:29
7 God helped him against [R]the Philistines, against the Arabians who lived in Gur Baal, and against the Meunites. 2 Chr. 21:16
8 Also the Ammonites [R]brought tribute to Uzziah. His fame spread as far as the entrance of Egypt, for he strengthened *himself* exceedingly. 2 Chr. 17:11
9 And Uzziah built towers in Jerusalem at the [R]Corner Gate, at the Valley Gate, and at the corner buttress of the wall; then he fortified them. Neh. 3:13, 19, 32
10 Also he built towers in the desert. He dug many wells, for he had much livestock, both in the lowlands and in the plains; *he also had* farmers and vinedressers in the mountains and in Carmel, for he loved the soil.
11 Moreover Uzziah had an army of fighting men who went out to war by companies, according to the number on their roll as prepared by Jeiel the scribe and Maaseiah the officer, under the hand of Hananiah, *one* of the king's captains.
12 The total number of [T]chief officers of the mighty men of valor *was* two thousand six hundred. Lit. *chief fathers*

26:5 Heb. mss., LXX, Syr., Tg., Arab. *fear*

13 And under their hand *was* an army of three hundred and seven thousand five hundred, that made war with mighty power, to help the king against the enemy.

14 Then Uzziah prepared for them, for the entire army, shields, spears, helmets, body armor, bows, and slings *to cast* stones.

15 And he made devices in Jerusalem, invented by [R]skillful men, to be on the towers and the corners, to shoot arrows and large stones. So his fame spread far and wide, for he was marvelously helped till he *became* strong. Ex. 39:3, 8

Sinful Offering of Uzziah

16 But [R]when he was strong his heart was [R]lifted up, to *his* destruction, for he transgressed against the LORD his God by entering the temple of the LORD to burn incense on the altar of incense. [Deut. 32:15] • 2 Chr. 25:19

17 So [R]Azariah the priest went in after him, and with him were eighty priests of the LORD, *who were* valiant men. 1 Chr. 6:10

18 And they withstood King Uzziah, and said to him, "*It* [R]*is* not for you, Uzziah, to burn incense to the LORD, but for the priests, the sons of Aaron, who are consecrated to burn incense. Get out of the sanctuary, for you have trespassed! You *shall have* no honor from the LORD God." [Num. 3:10]

19 Then Uzziah became furious; and he *had* a censer in his hand to burn incense. And while he was angry with the priests, [R]leprosy broke out on his forehead, before the priests in the house of the LORD, beside the incense altar. 2 Kin. 5:25–27

20 And Azariah the chief priest and all the priests looked at him, and there, on his forehead, he *was* leprous; so they thrust him out of that place. Indeed he also hurried to get out, because the LORD had struck him.

21 [R]King Uzziah was a leper until the day of his death. He dwelt in an [R]isolated house, because he was a leper; for he was cut off from the house of the LORD. Then Jotham his son *was* over the king's house, judging the people of the land. 2 Kin. 15:5 • [Lev. 13:46]

Death of Uzziah—2 Kin. 15:7

22 Now the rest of the acts of Uzziah, from first to last, the prophet [R]Isaiah the son of Amoz wrote. Is. 1:1

23 So Uzziah [T]rested with his fathers, and they buried him with his fathers in the field of burial which *belonged* to the kings, for they said, "He is a leper." Then Jotham his son reigned in his place. Died and joined his ancestors

CHAPTER 27

The Reign of Jotham—2 Kin. 15:33–38

JOTHAM *was* twenty-five years old when he became king, and he reigned sixteen years in Jerusalem. His mother's name *was* [R]Jerushah the daughter of Zadok. 2 Kin. 15:33

2 And he did *what was* right in the sight of the LORD, according to all that his father Uzziah had done (although he did not enter the temple of the LORD). But still [R]the people acted corruptly. 2 Kin. 15:35

3 He built the Upper Gate of the house of the LORD, and he built extensively on the wall of [R]Ophel. 2 Chr. 33:14

4 Moreover he built cities in the mountains of Judah, and in the forests he built fortresses and towers.

5 He also fought with the king of the [R]Ammonites and defeated them. And the people of Ammon gave him in that year one hundred talents of silver, ten thousand kors of wheat, and ten thousand of barley. The people of Ammon paid him this *amount* in the second and third years also. 2 Chr. 26:8

6 So Jotham became mighty, because he prepared his ways before the LORD his God.

7 Now the rest of the acts of Jotham, and all his wars and his ways, indeed they *are* written in the book of the kings of Israel and Judah.

8 He was twenty-five years old when he became king, and he reigned sixteen years in Jerusalem.

9 [R]So Jotham rested with his fathers, and they buried him in the City of David. Then Ahaz his son reigned in his place. 2 Kin. 15:38

CHAPTER 28

Evaluation of Ahaz—2 Kin. 16:1–4

AHAZ [R]*was* twenty years old when he became king, and he reigned sixteen years in Jerusalem; and he did not do *what was* right in the sight of the LORD, as his father David *had done.* 2 Kin. 16:2–4

2 For he walked in the ways of the kings of Israel, and made [R]molded images for [R]the Baals. Ex. 34:17 • Judg. 2:11

3 He burned incense in the Valley of the Son of Hinnom, and burned his children in the fire, according to the abominations of the nations whom the LORD had [R]cast out before the children of Israel. [Lev. 18:24–30]

4 And he sacrificed and burned incense on the [T]high places, on the hills, and under every green tree. Places for pagan worship

Defeat of Judah—2 Kin. 16:5–8; Is. 7:1

5 Therefore [R]the LORD his God delivered him into the hand of the king of Syria. They defeated him, and carried away a great multitude of them as captives, and brought *them* to Damascus. Then he was also delivered into the hand of the king of Israel, who defeated him with a great slaughter. [Is. 10:5]

6 For Pekah the son of Remaliah killed one hundred and twenty thousand in Judah in one day, all valiant men, because they had forsaken the LORD God of their fathers.

7 Zichri, a mighty man of Ephraim, killed Maaseiah the king's son, Azrikam the officer over the house, and Elkanah *who was* second to the king.

8 And the children of Israel carried away captive of their brethren two hundred thousand women, sons, and daughters; and they also took away much [T]spoil from them, and brought the spoil to Samaria. *plunder*

9 But a [R]prophet of the LORD was there, whose name *was* Oded; and he went out before the army that came to Samaria, and said to them: "Look, [R]because the LORD God of your fathers was angry with Judah, He has delivered them into your hand; but you have killed them in a rage *that* [R]reaches up to heaven. 2 Chr. 25:15 • [Is. 10:5; 47:6] • Rev. 18:5

10 "And now you propose to force the children of Judah and Jerusalem to be your [R]male and female slaves; *but are* you not also guilty before the LORD your God? [Lev. 25:39, 42, 43, 46]

11 "Now hear me, therefore, and return the captives, whom you have taken captive from your brethren, [R]for the fierce wrath of the LORD *is* upon you." James 2:13

12 Then some of the heads of the children of Ephraim, Azariah the son of Johanan, Berechiah the son of Meshillemoth, Jehizkiah the son of Shallum, and Amasa the son of Hadlai, stood up against those who came from the war,

13 and said to them, "You shall not bring the captives here, for we *already* have offended the LORD. You intend to add to our sins and to our guilt; for our guilt is great, and *there is* fierce wrath against Israel."

14 So the armed men left the captives and the [T]spoil before the leaders and all the congregation. *plunder*

15 Then the men who were designated by name rose up and took the captives, and from the spoil they clothed all who were naked among them, dressed them and gave them sandals, gave them food and drink, and anointed them; and they let all the feeble ones ride on donkeys. So they brought them to their brethren at Jericho, the city of palm trees. Then they returned to Samaria.

16 [R]At the same time King Ahaz sent to the kings of Assyria to help him. 2 Kin. 16:7

17 For again the Edomites had come, attacked Judah, and carried away captives.

18 [R]The Philistines also had invaded the cities of the lowland and of the South of Judah, and had taken Beth Shemesh, Aijalon, Gederoth, Sochoh with its villages, Timnah with its villages, and Gimzo with its villages; and they dwelt there. Ezek. 16:27, 57

19 For the LORD brought Judah low because of Ahaz king of Israel, for he had [R]encouraged moral decline in Judah and had been continually unfaithful to the LORD. Ex. 32:25

20 Also [R]Tiglath-Pileser[T] king of Assyria came to him and distressed him, and did not assist him. 1 Chr. 5:26 • Heb. *Tilgath-Pilneser*

21 For Ahaz took part *of the treasures* from the house of the LORD, from the house of the king, and from the leaders, and he gave *it* to the king of Assyria; but he did not help him.

Idolatry of Ahaz—2 Kin. 16:12

22 Now in the time of his distress King Ahaz became increasingly unfaithful to the LORD. This *is that* King Ahaz.

23 For [R]he sacrificed to the gods of Damascus which had defeated him, saying, "Because the gods of the kings of Syria help them, I will sacrifice to them [R]that they may help me." But they were the ruin of him and of all Israel. 2 Chr. 25:14 • Jer. 44:17, 18

24 So Ahaz gathered the articles of the house of God, cut in pieces the articles of the house of God, [R]shut up the doors of the house of the LORD, and made for himself altars in every corner of Jerusalem. 2 Chr. 29:3, 7

25 And in every single city of Judah he made [T]high places to burn incense to other gods, and provoked to anger the LORD God of his fathers. Places for pagan worship

Death of Ahaz—2 Kin. 16:20

26 Now the rest of his acts and all his ways, from first to last, indeed they *are* written in the book of the kings of Judah and Israel.

27 So Ahaz [T]rested with his fathers, and they buried him in the city, in Jerusalem; but they did not bring him into the tombs of the kings of Israel. Then Hezekiah his son reigned in his place. Died and joined his ancestors

CHAPTER 29

Evaluation of Hezekiah—2 Kin. 18:2, 3

HEZEKIAH [R]became king *when he was* twenty-five years old, and he reigned twenty-nine years in Jerusalem. His mother's name *was* [T]Abijah the daughter [R]of Zechariah. 2 Kin. 18:1 • *Abi,* 2 Kin. 18:2 • 2 Chr. 26:5

2 And he did *what was* right in the sight of the LORD, according to all that his father David had done.

Purification of the Temple

3 In the first year of his reign, in the first month, he [R]opened the doors of the house of the LORD and repaired them. 2 Chr. 28:24; 29:7

4 Then he brought in the priests and the Levites, and gathered them in the East Square,

5 and said to them: "Hear me, Levites!
Now sanctify yourselves, sanctify the house
of the LORD God of your fathers, and carry
out the rubbish from the holy *place*.
6 "For our fathers have trespassed and
done evil in the eyes of the LORD our God;
they have forsaken Him, have turned their
faces away from the [T]habitation of the LORD,
and turned *their* backs *on Him*. Temple
7 [R]"They have also shut up the doors of
the vestibule, put out the lamps, and have not
burned incense or offered burnt offerings in
the holy *place* to the God of Israel. 2 Chr. 28:24
8 "Therefore the wrath of the LORD fell
upon Judah and Jerusalem, and He has given
them up to trouble, to astonishment, and to
jeering, as you see with your eyes.
9 "For indeed, because of this our fathers
have fallen by the sword; and our sons, our
daughters, and our wives *are* in captivity.
10 "Now *it is* in my heart to make a covenant with the LORD God of Israel, that His
fierce wrath may turn away from us.
11 "My sons, do not be negligent now, for
the LORD has [R]chosen you to stand before
Him, to serve Him, and that you should
minister to Him and burn incense." Num. 3:6
12 Then these Levites arose: Mahath the
son of Amasai and Joel the son of Azariah, of
the sons of the Kohathites; of the sons of
Merari, Kish the son of Abdi and Azariah the
son of Jehalelel; of the Gershonites, Joah the
son of Zimmah and Eden the son of Joah;
13 of the sons of Elizaphan, Shimri and
Jeiel; of the sons of Asaph, Zechariah and
Mattaniah;
14 of the sons of Heman, Jehiel and Shimei;
and of the sons of Jeduthun, Shemaiah and
Uzziel.
15 And they gathered their brethren, sanctified themselves, and went according to the
commandment of the king, at the words of
the LORD, to cleanse the house of the LORD.
16 Then the priests went into the inner part
of the house of the LORD to cleanse *it*, and
brought out all the debris that they found in
the temple of the LORD to the court of the
house of the LORD. And the Levites took *it*
out and carried *it* to the Brook Kidron.
17 Now they began to [T]sanctify on the first
day of the first month, and on the eighth day
of the month they came to the vestibule of
the LORD. Then they sanctified the house of
the LORD in eight days, and on the sixteenth
day of the first month they finished. *consecrate*
18 Then they went in to King Hezekiah and
said, "We have cleansed all the house of the
LORD, the altar of burnt offerings with all its
articles, and the table of the showbread with
all its articles.
19 "Moreover all the articles which King
Ahaz in his reign had [R]cast aside in his
transgression we have prepared and [T]sancti-
fied; and there they *are*, before the altar of
the LORD." 2 Chr. 28:24 • *consecrated*

Restoration of Temple Worship

20 Then King Hezekiah rose early, gathered
the rulers of the city, and went up to the
house of the LORD.
21 And they brought seven bulls, seven
rams, seven lambs, and seven male goats for
a [R]sin offering for the kingdom, for the sanctuary, and for Judah. Then he commanded
the priests, the sons of Aaron, to offer *them*
on the altar of the LORD. Lev. 4:3–14
22 So they killed the bulls, and the priests
received the blood and [R]sprinkled *it* on the
altar. Likewise they killed the rams and
sprinkled the blood on the altar. They also
killed the lambs and sprinkled the blood on
the altar. Lev. 8:14, 15, 19, 24
23 Then they brought out the male goats
for the sin offering before the king and the
congregation, and they laid their [R]hands on
them. Lev. 4:15, 24; 8:14
24 And the priests killed them; and they
presented their blood on the altar as a sin
offering to make an atonement for all Israel,
for the king commanded *that* the burnt offering and the sin offering *be made* for all Israel.
25 Then he stationed the Levites in the
house of the LORD with cymbals, with
stringed instruments, and with harps, according to the commandment of David, of Gad
the king's seer, and of Nathan the prophet;
[R]for thus *was* the commandment of the LORD
by his prophets. 2 Chr. 30:12
26 The Levites stood with the instruments
of David, and the priests with the trumpets.
27 Then Hezekiah commanded *them* to offer the burnt offering on the altar. And when
the burnt offering began, the song of the
LORD *also* began, with the trumpets and with
the instruments of David king of Israel.
28 So all the congregation worshiped, the
singers sang, and the trumpeters sounded; all
this continued until the burnt offering was
finished.
29 And when they had finished offering,
[R]the king and all who were present with him
bowed and worshiped. 2 Chr. 20:18
30 Moreover King Hezekiah and the leaders
commanded the Levites to sing praise to the
LORD with the words of David and of Asaph
the seer. So they sang praises with gladness,
and they bowed their heads and worshiped.
31 Then Hezekiah answered and said, "Now
that you have consecrated yourselves to the
LORD, come near, and bring sacrifices and
thank offerings into the house of the LORD."
So the congregation brought in sacrifices and
thank offerings, and as many as were of a
willing heart *brought* burnt offerings.

32 And the number of the burnt offerings which the congregation brought was seventy bulls, one hundred rams, *and* two hundred lambs; all these *were* for a burnt offering to the LORD.

33 The consecrated things *were* six hundred bulls and three thousand sheep.

34 But the priests were too few, so that they could not skin all the burnt offerings; therefore their brethren the Levites helped them until the work was ended and until the *other* priests had [T]sanctified themselves, for the Levites were more diligent in sanctifying themselves than the priests. *consecrated*

35 Also the burnt offerings *were* in abundance, with [R]the fat of the peace offerings and *with* [R]the drink offerings for *every* burnt offering. So the service of the house of the LORD was set in order. Lev. 3:16 • Num. 15:5–10

36 Then Hezekiah and all the people rejoiced that God had prepared the people, since the events took place so suddenly.

CHAPTER 30

Celebration of the Passover

AND Hezekiah sent to all Israel and Judah, and also wrote letters to Ephraim and Manasseh, that they should come to the house of the LORD at Jerusalem, to keep the Passover to the LORD God of Israel.

2 For the king and his leaders and all the congregation in Jerusalem had agreed to keep the Passover in the second month.

3 For they could not keep it at that time, because a sufficient number of priests had not sanctified themselves, nor had the people gathered together at Jerusalem.

4 And the matter pleased the king and all the congregation.

5 So they [T]resolved to make a proclamation throughout all Israel, from Beersheba to Dan, that they should come to keep the Passover to the LORD God of Israel at Jerusalem, since they had not done *it* for a long *time* in the *prescribed* manner. *established a decree to*

6 Then the runners went throughout all Israel and Judah with the letters from the king and his leaders, and spoke according to the commandment of the king: "Children of Israel, [R]return to the LORD God of Abraham, Isaac, and Israel; then He will return to the remnant of you who have escaped from the hand of the kings of Assyria. [Jer. 4:1]

7 "And do not be like your fathers and your brethren, who trespassed against the LORD God of their fathers, so that He gave them up to astonishment, as you see.

8 "Now do not be [T]stiff-necked, as your fathers *were, but* yield yourselves to the LORD; and enter His sanctuary, which He has sanctified forever, and serve the LORD your God, [R]that the fierceness of His wrath may turn away from you. Rebellious • 2 Chr. 29:10

9 "For if you return to the LORD, your brethren and your children *will be treated* with compassion by those who lead them captive, so that they may come back to this land; for the LORD your God *is* [R]gracious and merciful, and will not turn *His* face from you if you [R]return to Him." [Ex. 34:6] • [Is. 55:7]

10 So the runners passed from city to city through the country of Ephraim and Manasseh, as far as Zebulun; but [R]they laughed them to scorn and mocked them. 2 Chr. 36:16

11 Nevertheless [R]some from Asher, Manasseh, and Zebulun humbled themselves and came to Jerusalem. 2 Chr. 11:16; 30:18, 21

12 Also [R]the hand of God was on Judah to give them singleness of heart to do the commandment of the king and the leaders, [R]at the word of the LORD. [Phil. 2:13] • 2 Chr. 29:25

13 Now many people, a very great congregation, assembled at Jerusalem to keep the Feast of [R]Unleavened Bread in the second month. Lev. 23:6

14 They arose and took away the [R]altars that *were* in Jerusalem, and they took away all the incense altars and cast *them* into the Brook [R]Kidron. 2 Chr. 28:24 • 2 Chr. 29:16

15 Then they slaughtered the Passover *lambs* on the fourteenth *day* of the second month. The priests and the Levites [T]were ashamed, and [T]sanctified themselves, and brought the burnt offerings to the house of the LORD. *humbled themselves • set themselves apart*

16 They stood in their [R]place [T]according to their custom, according to the Law of Moses the man of God; the priests sprinkled the blood *which they received* from the hand of the Levites. 2 Chr. 35:10, 15 • Or *in their proper order*

17 For *there were* many in the congregation who had not sanctified themselves; therefore the Levites had charge of the slaughter of the Passover *lambs* for everyone *who was* not clean, to sanctify *them* to the LORD.

18 For a multitude of the people, [R]many from Ephraim, Manasseh, Issachar, and Zebulun, had not cleansed themselves, [R]yet they ate the Passover contrary to what was written. But Hezekiah prayed for them, saying, "May the good LORD provide atonement for everyone 2 Chr. 30:1, 11, 25 • [Num. 9:10]

19 "*who* [R]prepares his heart to seek God, the LORD God of his fathers, though *he is* not *cleansed* according to the purification of the sanctuary." 2 Chr. 19:3

20 And the LORD listened to Hezekiah and healed the people.

21 So the children of Israel who were present at Jerusalem kept [R]the Feast of Unleavened Bread seven days with great gladness;

and the Levites and the priests praised the
LORD day by day, *singing* to the LORD, accompanied by loud instruments. Ex. 12:15; 13:6
22 And Hezekiah gave encouragement to all
the Levites [R]who taught the good knowledge
of the LORD; and they ate throughout the
feast seven days, offering peace offerings and
[R]making confession to the LORD God of their
fathers. 2 Chr. 17:9; 35:3 • Ezra 10:11

Extra Feast Days

23 Then the whole assembly agreed to keep
the feast [R]another seven days, and they kept
it *another* seven days with gladness. 1 Kin. 8:65
24 For Hezekiah king of Judah gave to the
congregation a thousand bulls and seven
thousand sheep, and the leaders gave to the
congregation a thousand bulls and ten thousand sheep; and a great number of priests
[R]sanctified[T] themselves. 2 Chr. 29:34 • *consecrated*
25 The whole congregation of Judah re-
joiced, also the priests and Levites, all the
congregation that came from Israel, the
sojourners [R]who came from the land of Israel,
and those who dwelt in Judah. 2 Chr. 30:11, 18
26 So there was great joy in Jerusalem, for
since the time of [R]Solomon the son of David,
king of Israel, *there had* been nothing like
this in Jerusalem. 2 Chr. 7:8–10
27 Then the priests, the Levites, arose and
[R]blessed the people, and their voice was
heard; and their prayer came *up* to [R]His holy
dwelling place, to heaven. Num. 6:23 • Deut. 26:15

CHAPTER 31

Destruction of the Idols—2 Kin. 18:4

NOW when all this was finished, all Israel
who were present went out to the cities
of Judah and [R]broke the sacred pillars in
pieces, cut down the wooden images, and
threw down the [T]high places and the altars—
from all Judah, Benjamin, Ephraim, and Manasseh—until they had utterly destroyed
them all. Then all the children of Israel
returned to their own cities, every man to his
possession. 2 Kin. 18:4 • Places for pagan worship

Contribution for the Priests and Levites

2 And Hezekiah appointed [R]the divisions of
the priests and the Levites according to their
divisions, each man according to his service,
the priests and Levites [R]for burnt offerings
and peace offerings, to serve, to give thanks,
and to praise in the gates of the [T]camp of the
LORD. 1 Chr. 23:6; 24:1 • 1 Chr. 23:30, 31 • Temple
3 The king also *appointed* a [T]portion of his
[T]possessions for the burnt offerings: for the
morning and evening burnt offerings, the
burnt offerings for the Sabbaths and the New
Moons and the set feasts, as *it is* written in
the Law of the LORD. *share* • *property*
4 Moreover he commanded the people who
dwelt in Jerusalem to contribute [R]support[T]
for the priests and the Levites, that they
might devote themselves to [R]the Law of the
LORD. Num. 18:8 • *the portion due* • Mal. 2:7
5 As soon as the commandment was circulated, the children of Israel brought in abundance [R]the firstfruits of grain and wine, oil
and honey, and of all the produce of the field;
and they brought in abundantly the [R]tithe of
everything. Ex. 22:29 • [Lev. 27:30]
6 And the children of Israel and Judah,
who dwelt in the cities of Judah, brought the
tithe of oxen and sheep; also the [R]tithe of
holy things which were consecrated to the
LORD their God they laid in heaps. Deut. 14:28
7 In the third month they began laying
them in heaps, and they finished in the seventh month.
8 And when Hezekiah and the leaders
came and saw the heaps, they blessed the
LORD and His people Israel.
9 Then Hezekiah questioned the priests
and the Levites concerning the heaps.
10 And Azariah the chief priest, from the
house of Zadok, answered him and said,
[R]"Since *the people* began to bring the offerings into the house of the LORD, we have had
enough to eat and have plenty left, for the
LORD has blessed His people; and what is left
is this great [R]abundance." [Mal. 3:10] • Ex. 36:5

Reorganization of the Priests and Levites

11 Now Hezekiah commanded *them* to prepare [R]rooms[T] in the house of the LORD, and
they prepared them. 1 Kin. 6:5–8 • *storerooms*
12 Then they faithfully brought in the offerings, the tithes, and the dedicated things;
Cononiah the Levite *was* ruler over them,
and Shimei his brother *was* the next.
13 Jehiel, Azaziah, Nahath, Asahel, Jerimoth, Jozabad, Eliel, Ismachiah, Mahath, and
Benaiah *were* overseers under the hand of
Cononiah and Shimei his brother, at the
commandment of Hezekiah the king and
Azariah the ruler of the house of God.
14 Kore the son of Imnah the Levite, the
keeper of the East Gate, *was* over the freewill
offerings to God, to distribute the offerings of
the LORD and the most holy things.
15 And under him *were* [R]Eden, Miniamin,
Jeshua, Shemaiah, Amariah, and Shecaniah,
his faithful assistants in [R]the cities of the
priests, to distribute [R]allotments to their
brethren by divisions, to the great as well as
the small. 2 Chr. 29:12 • Josh. 21:1–3, 9 • 1 Chr. 9:26
16 Besides those males from three years old
and up who were written in the genealogy,
they distributed to everyone who entered the
house of the LORD his daily portion for the
work of his service, by his division,

17 and to the priests who were written in the genealogy according to their father's house, and to the Levites [R]from twenty years old and up according to their work, by their divisions, 1 Chr. 23:24, 27

18 and to all who were written in the genealogy—their little ones and their wives, their sons and daughters, the whole company of them—for in their faithfulness they [T]sanctified themselves in holiness. *consecrated*

19 Also for the sons of Aaron the priests, *who were* in the fields of the common-lands of their cities, in every single city, *there were* men who were [R]designated by name to distribute portions to all the males among the priests and to all who were listed by genealogies among the Levites. 2 Chr. 31:12–15

20 Thus Hezekiah did throughout all Judah, and he [R]did what *was* good and right and true before the LORD his God. 2 Kin. 20:3; 22:2

21 And in every work that he began in the service of the house of God, in the law and in the commandment, to seek his God, he did *it* with all his heart. So he [R]prospered. Ps. 1:3

CHAPTER 32

Invasion by Assyria
2 Kin. 18:17—19:37; Is. 36:2—37:38

AFTER [R]these deeds of faithfulness, Sennacherib king of Assyria came and entered Judah; he encamped against the fortified cities, thinking to win them over to himself. 2 Kin. 18:13—19:37

2 And when Hezekiah saw that Sennacherib had come, and that his purpose was to make war against Jerusalem,

3 he took counsel with his leaders and [T]commanders to stop the water from the springs which *were* outside the city; and they helped him. Lit. *mighty men*

4 Thus many people gathered together who stopped all the [R]springs and the brook that ran through the land, saying, "Why should the kings of Assyria come and find much water?" 2 Kin. 20:20

5 And he strengthened himself, [R]built up all the wall that was broken, raised *it* up to the towers, and *built* another wall outside; also he repaired the [R]Millo *in* the City of David, and made [T]weapons and shields in abundance. 2 Chr. 25:23 • 2 Sam. 5:9 • *javelins*

6 Then he set military captains over the people, gathered them together to him in the open square of the city gate, and [R]gave them encouragement, saying, 2 Chr. 30:22

7 [R]"Be strong and courageous; [R]do not be afraid nor dismayed before the king of Assyria, nor before all the multitude that *is* with him; for [R]*there are* more with us than with him. [Deut. 31:6] • 2 Chr. 20:15 • 2 Kin. 6:16

8 "With him *is* an [R]arm of flesh; but [R]with us *is* the LORD our God, to help us and to fight our battles." And the people were strengthened by the words of Hezekiah king of Judah. [Jer. 17:5] • [Rom. 8:31]

9 [R]After this Sennacherib king of Assyria sent his servants to Jerusalem (but he *himself*, and all the forces with him, *laid siege* against Lachish), to Hezekiah king of Judah, and to all Judah who *were* in Jerusalem, saying, 2 Kin. 18:17

10 [R]"Thus says Sennacherib king of Assyria: 'In what do you trust, that you remain under siege in Jerusalem? 2 Kin. 18:19

11 'Does not Hezekiah persuade you to give yourselves over to die by famine and by thirst, saying, [R]"The LORD our God will deliver us from the hand of the king of Assyria"? 2 Kin. 18:30

12 'Has not the same Hezekiah taken away His high places and His altars, and commanded Judah and Jerusalem, saying, "You shall worship before one altar and burn incense on [R]it"? 2 Chr. 31:1, 2

13 'Do you not know what I and my fathers have done to all the peoples of *other* lands? [R]Were the gods of the nations of those lands in any way able to deliver their lands out of my hand? 2 Kin. 18:33–35

14 'Who *was there* among all the gods of those nations that my fathers utterly destroyed that could deliver his people from my hand, that your God should be able to deliver you from my [R]hand? [Is. 10:5–12]

15 'Now therefore, [R]do not let Hezekiah deceive you or persuade you like this, and do not believe him; for no god of any nation or kingdom was able to deliver his people from my hand or the hand of my fathers. How much less will your God deliver you from my hand?' " 2 Kin. 18:29

16 And his servants spoke even *more* against the LORD God and against His servant Hezekiah.

17 He also wrote letters to revile the LORD God of Israel, and to speak against Him, saying, "As the gods of the nations of *other* lands have not delivered their people from my hand, so the God of Hezekiah will not deliver His people from my hand."

18 Then they called out with a loud voice in Hebrew to the people of Jerusalem who *were* on the wall, to frighten them and trouble them, that they might take the city.

19 And they spoke against the God of Jerusalem, as against the gods of the people of the earth—[R]the work of men's hands. [Ps. 96:5]

20 [R]Now for this *cause* King Hezekiah and [R]the prophet Isaiah, the son of Amoz, prayed and cried out to heaven. 2 Kin. 19:15 • 2 Kin. 19:2

21 [R]Then the LORD sent an angel who cut down every mighty man of valor, leader, and

HEZEKIAH'S WATER TUNNEL

The long underground shaft known as Hezekiah's water tunnel or the Siloam tunnel was dug through solid rock under the city wall of Jerusalem by King Hezekiah of Judah in the eighth century B.C. (2 Kin. 20:20). The tunnel linking the Gihon Spring outside the city walls to the water reservoir known as the Pool of Siloam inside the city walls was dug to provide water to the city in case of a prolonged siege by Assyrian forces.

Built about 700 B.C., the crooked shaft is 1,750 feet long, often running 60 feet below the surface of the earth. It was discovered in 1838, but little scientific exploration and excavation work was done on the channel until 1866. Not until 1910 was it cleared of debris left by the destruction of Jerusalem in 586 B.C. A walk through Hezekiah's tunnel is a popular activity for modern tourists while visiting Jerusalem.

An inscription in Hebrew found in the tunnel near the Pool of Siloam describes the construction project. Two separate crews worked from opposite ends and eventually met in the middle of the shaft. Digging far below the earth's surface in bedrock, they labored for months in semidarkness with crude hand tools under difficult breathing conditions. But their hard work was rewarded when the Pool of Siloam began to fill with precious water that would spell the difference between life and death for Jerusalem if the Assyrians should attack the city.

A tactic used by besieging armies against walled cities was to cut off food and water supplies to the people inside (2 Kin. 6:26–29). Hezekiah's tunnel and pool was more than a marvel of ancient engineering; it was a brilliant survival strategy.

Hezekiah's tunnel may not have been the first water shaft dug at Jerusalem. Some scholars believe David captured the city from the Jebusites about three hundred years before Hezekiah's time by gaining entrance to the walled city through a water shaft (2 Sam. 5:6–8).

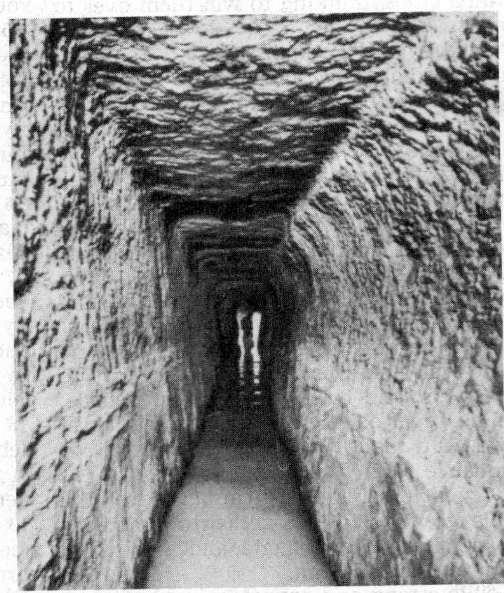

Hezekiah's tunnel was dug to provide water to Jerusalem in case of a prolonged siege by Assyrian forces.

captain in the camp of the king of Assyria. So
he returned [R]shamefaced to his own land.
And when he had gone into the temple of his
god, some of his own offspring struck him
down with the sword there. Zech. 14:3 • Ps. 44:7
22 Thus the LORD saved Hezekiah and the
inhabitants of Jerusalem from the hand of
Sennacherib the king of Assyria, and from
the hand of all *others*, and guided them on
every side.

Restoration of Hezekiah
2 Kin. 20:1–11; Is. 38:1–8

23 And many brought gifts to the LORD at
Jerusalem, and [T]presents to Hezekiah king of
Judah, so that he was exalted in the sight of
all nations thereafter. Lit. *precious things*
24 [R]In those days Hezekiah was sick and
near death, and he prayed to the LORD; and
He spoke to him and gave him a sign. Is. 38:1–8
25 But Hezekiah did not repay according to
the favor *shown* him, for [R]his heart was lifted
up; therefore wrath was looming over him
and over Judah and Jerusalem. [Hab. 2:4]
26 [R]Then Hezekiah humbled himself for the
pride of his heart, he and the inhabitants of
Jerusalem, so that the wrath of the LORD did
not come upon them [R]in the days of Hezekiah. Jer. 26:18, 19 • 2 Kin. 20:19

Wealth of Hezekiah

27 Hezekiah had very great riches and
honor. And he made himself treasuries for
silver, for gold, for precious stones, for spices,
for shields, and for all kinds of desirable
items;
28 storehouses for the harvest of grain,
wine, and oil; and stalls for all kinds of
livestock, and folds for flocks.
29 Moreover he provided cities for himself,
and possessions of flocks and herds in abundance; for [R]God had given him very much
property. 1 Chr. 29:12
30 This same Hezekiah also stopped the
water outlet of Upper Gihon, and [T]brought
the water by tunnel to the west side of the
City of David. Hezekiah prospered in all his
works. Lit. *brought it straight to,* 2 Kin. 20:20

Sin of Hezekiah—2 Kin. 20:12–19; Is. 39:1–8

31 However, *regarding* the ambassadors of
the princes of Babylon, whom they [R]sent to
him to inquire about the wonder that was
done in the land, God withdrew from him, in
order to [R]test him, that He might know all
that was in his heart. Is. 39:1 • [Deut. 8:2, 16]

Death of Hezekiah—2 Kin. 20:20, 21

32 Now the rest of the acts of Hezekiah, and
his goodness, indeed they *are* written in [R]the
vision of Isaiah the prophet, the son of Amoz,
and in the [R]book of the kings of Judah and
Israel. Is. 36—39 • 2 Kin. 18—20
33 So Hezekiah [T]rested with his fathers, and
they buried him in the upper tombs of the
sons of David; and all Judah and the inhabitants of Jerusalem [R]honored him at his death.
Then Manasseh his son reigned in his
place. Died and joined his ancestors • Prov. 10:7

CHAPTER 33

The Reign of Manasseh—2 Kin. 21:1–9, 17, 18

MANASSEH [R]*was* twelve years old when
he became king, and he reigned fifty-
five years in Jerusalem. 2 Kin. 21:1–9
2 But he did evil in the sight of the LORD,
according to the [R]abominations of the nations
whom the LORD had cast out before the
children of Israel. 2 Chr. 28:3
3 For he rebuilt the high places which
Hezekiah his father had broken down; he
raised up altars for the Baals, and made
wooden images; and he worshiped all [T]the
host of heaven and served them. *Assyrian gods*
4 He also built altars in the house of the
LORD, of which the LORD had said, "In Jerusalem shall My name be forever."
5 And he built altars for all the host of
heaven [R]in the two courts of the house of the
LORD. 2 Chr. 4:9
6 [R]Also he caused his sons to pass through
the fire in the Valley of the Son of Hinnom;
he practiced soothsaying, used witchcraft
and sorcery, and consulted mediums and
spiritists. He did much evil in the sight of the
LORD, to provoke Him *to anger*. [Lev. 18:21]
7 He even set a carved image, the idol
which he had made, in the [T]house of God, of
which God had said to David and to Solomon
his son, "In this house and in Jerusalem,
which I have chosen out of all the tribes of
Israel, I will put My name forever; Temple
8 [R]"and I will not again remove the foot of
Israel from the land which I have appointed
for your fathers—only if they are careful to
do all that I have commanded them, according to the whole law and the statutes and the
ordinances by the hand of Moses." 2 Sam. 7:10
9 So Manasseh seduced Judah and the
inhabitants of Jerusalem to do more evil than
the nations whom the LORD had destroyed
before the children of Israel.
10 And the LORD spoke to Manasseh and his
people, but they would not [T]listen. *obey*
11 Therefore the LORD brought upon them
the captains of the army of the king of
Assyria, who took Manasseh with [T]hooks,
bound him with [T]bronze *fetters*, and carried
him off to Babylon. Nose hooks, 2 Kin. 19:28 • *chains*
12 Now when he was in affliction, he implored the LORD his God, and humbled himself greatly before the God of his fathers,

13 and prayed to Him; and He [R]received his
entreaty, heard his supplication, and brought
him back to Jerusalem into his kingdom.
Then Manasseh [R]knew that the LORD *was*
God. Ezra 8:23 • Dan. 4:25
14 After this he built a wall outside the City
of David on the west side of Gihon, in the
valley, as far as the entrance of the Fish Gate;
and *it* enclosed Ophel, and he raised it to a
very great height. Then he put military captains in all the fortified cities of Judah.
15 He took away [R]the foreign gods and the
idol from the house of the LORD, and all the
altars that he had built in the mount of
the house of the LORD and in Jerusalem; and
he cast *them* out of the city. 2 Chr. 33:3, 5, 7
16 He also repaired the altar of the LORD,
sacrificed peace offerings and [R]thank offerings on it, and commanded Judah to serve
the LORD God of Israel. Lev. 7:12
17 [R]Nevertheless the people still sacrificed
on the [T]high places, *but* only to the LORD
their God. 2 Chr. 32:12 • Places for pagan worship
18 Now the rest of the acts of Manasseh, his
prayer to his God, and the words of [R]the seers
who spoke to him in the name of the LORD
God of Israel, indeed they *are written* in the
[T]book of the kings of Israel. 1 Sam. 9:9 • Lit. *words*
19 Also his prayer and *how God* received his
entreaty, and all his sin and trespass, and the
sites where he built [T]high places and set up
wooden images and carved images, before he
was humbled, indeed they *are* written among
the sayings of *Hozai. Places for pagan worship
20 [R]So Manasseh rested with his fathers,
and they buried him in his own house. Then
his son Amon reigned in his place. 2 Kin. 21:18

The Reign of Amon—2 Kin. 21:19–26

21 [R]Amon *was* twenty-two years old when
he became king, and he reigned two years in
Jerusalem. 2 Kin. 21:19–24
22 But he did evil in the sight of the LORD,
as his father Manasseh had done; for Amon
sacrificed to all the carved images which his
father Manasseh had made, and served them.
23 And he did not humble himself before
the LORD, as his father Manasseh had humbled himself; but Amon trespassed more and
more.
24 Then his servants conspired against him,
and killed him in his own house.
25 But the people of the land executed all
those who had conspired against King Amon.
Then the people of the land made his son
Josiah king in his place.

CHAPTER 34

Evaluation of Josiah—2 Kin. 22:1, 2

JOSIAH [R]*was* eight years old when he
became king, and he reigned thirty-one
years in Jerusalem. 2 Kin. 22:1, 2
2 And he did *what was* right in the sight of
the LORD, and walked in the ways of his
father David; *he* did *not* turn aside to the
right hand or to the left.

Early Reforms of Josiah

3 For in the eighth year of his reign, while
he was still young, he began to seek the God
of his father David; and in the twelfth year he
began to purge Judah and Jerusalem of the
high places, the wooden images, the carved
images, and the molded images.
4 They broke down the altars of the Baals
in his presence, and the incense altars which
were above them he cut down; and the
wooden images, the carved images, and the
molded images he broke in pieces, and made
dust of them and scattered *it* on the graves of
those who had sacrificed to them.
5 He also [R]burned the bones of the priests
on their [R]altars, and cleansed Judah and
Jerusalem. 1 Kin. 13:2 • 2 Kin. 23:20
6 And *so he did* in the cities of Manasseh,
Ephraim, and Simeon, as far as Naphtali and
all around, with [T]axes. Lit. *swords*
7 When he had broken down the altars and
the wooden images, had [R]beaten the carved
images into powder, and cut down all the
incense altars throughout all the land of
Israel, he returned to Jerusalem. Deut. 9:21

Repair of the Temple—2 Kin. 22:3–7

8 Now in the eighteenth year of his reign,
when he had purged the land and the [T]tem-
ple, he sent Shaphan the son of Azaliah,
Maaseiah the governor of the city, and Joah
the son of Joahaz the recorder, to repair the
house of the LORD his God. Lit. *house*
9 When they came to Hilkiah the high
priest, they delivered the money that was
brought into the house of God, which the
Levites who kept the doors had gathered
from the hand of Manasseh and Ephraim,
from all the [R]remnant of Israel, from all
Judah and Benjamin, and *which* they had
brought back to Jerusalem. 2 Chr. 30:6
10 Then they put *it* in the hand of the
workmen who had the oversight of the house
of the LORD; and they gave it to the workmen
who worked in the house of the LORD, to
repair and restore the house.
11 They gave *it* to the craftsmen and builders to buy hewn stone and timber for beams,
and to floor the houses which the kings of
Judah had destroyed.
12 And the men did the work faithfully.
Their overseers *were* Jahath and Obadiah the
Levites, of the sons of Merari, and Zechariah
and Meshullam, of the sons of the Kohathites, to supervise. *Others of* the Levites, all of

33:19 LXX *the seers*

whom were skillful with instruments of music,
13 *were* [R]over the burden bearers and *were*
overseers of all who did work in any kind of
service. And *some* of the Levites *were* scribes,
officers, and gatekeepers. 2 Chr. 8:10

Discovery of the Law—2 Kin. 22:8—23:20

14 Now when they brought out the money
that was brought into the house of the LORD,
Hilkiah the priest [R]found the Book of the Law
of the LORD *given* by Moses. 2 Kin. 22:8
15 Then Hilkiah answered and said to Shaphan the scribe, "I have found the Book of
the Law in the house of the LORD." And
Hilkiah gave the book to Shaphan.
16 So Shaphan carried the book to the king,
bringing the king word, saying, "All that was
committed to your servants they are doing.
17 "And they have [T]gathered the money
that was found in the house of the LORD, and
have delivered it into the hand of the overseers and the workmen." Lit. *poured out*
18 Then Shaphan the scribe told the king,
saying, "Hilkiah the priest has given me a
book." And Shaphan read it before the king.
19 Now it happened, when the king heard
the words of the Law, that he tore his clothes.
20 Then the king commanded Hilkiah, Ahikam the son of Shaphan, [T]Abdon the son of
Micah, Shaphan the scribe, and Asaiah a
servant of the king, saying, *Achbor*, 2 Kin. 22:12
21 "Go, inquire of the LORD for me, and for
those who are left in Israel and Judah, concerning the words of the book that is found;
for great *is* the wrath of the LORD that is
poured out on us, because our fathers have
not kept the word of the LORD, to do according to all that is written in this book."
22 So Hilkiah and *those* whom the king *had*
appointed went to Huldah the prophetess, the
wife of Shallum the son of Tokhath, the son
of Hasrah, keeper of the wardrobe. (She
dwelt in Jerusalem in the Second Quarter.)
And they spoke to her to that *effect.*
23 Then she answered them, "Thus says the
LORD God of Israel, 'Tell the man who sent
you to Me,
24 "Thus says the LORD: 'Behold, I will
[R]bring calamity on this place and on its
inhabitants, all the curses that are written in
the [R]book which they have read before the
king of Judah, 2 Chr. 36:14–20 • Deut. 28:15–68
25 'because they have forsaken Me and
burned incense to other gods, that they might
provoke Me to anger with all the works of
their hands. Therefore My wrath will be
poured out on this place, and not be
quenched.' " '
26 "And as for the king of Judah, who sent
you to inquire of the LORD, in this manner
you shall speak to him, 'Thus says the LORD
God of Israel: "*Concerning* the words which
you have heard—
27 "because your heart was tender, and you
humbled yourself before God when you heard
His words against this place and against its
inhabitants, and you humbled yourself before
Me, and you tore your clothes and wept
before Me, I also have heard *you*," says the
[R]LORD. 2 Chr. 12:7; 30:6; 33:12, 13
28 "Surely I will gather you to your fathers,
and you shall be gathered to your grave in
peace; and your eyes shall not see all the
calamity which I will bring on this place and
its inhabitants." ' " So they brought back
word to the king.
29 [R]Then the king sent and gathered all the
elders of Judah and Jerusalem. 2 Kin. 23:1–3
30 And the king went up to the house of the
LORD, with all the men of Judah and the
inhabitants of Jerusalem: the priests and
the Levites, and all the people, great and
small; and he [R]read in their hearing all the
words of the book of the covenant which had
been found in the house of the LORD. Neh. 8:1–3
31 Then the king stood in [R]his place and
made a [R]covenant before the LORD, to follow
the LORD, and to keep His commandments
and His testimonies and His statutes with all
his heart and all his soul, to perform the
words of the covenant that were written in
this book. 2 Kin. 11:14; 23:3 • 2 Chr. 23:16; 29:10
32 And he made all who were present in
Jerusalem and Benjamin take their stand *for*
it. So the inhabitants of Jerusalem did according to the covenant of God, the God of
their fathers.
33 Thus Josiah removed all the abominations from all the country that *belonged* to
the children of Israel, and made all who were
present in Israel diligently serve the LORD
their God. All his days they did not depart
from following the LORD God of their fathers.

CHAPTER 35

Celebration of the Passover—2 Kin. 23:21–23

NOW [R]Josiah kept a Passover to the LORD
in Jerusalem, and they slaughtered the
Passover *lambs* on the [R]fourteenth *day* of the
first month. 2 Kin. 23:21, 22 • Ex. 12:6
2 And he set the priests in their [R]duties and
[R]encouraged them for the service of the
house of the LORD. 2 Chr. 23:18 • 2 Chr. 29:5–15
3 Then he said to the Levites who taught
all Israel, who were holy to the LORD: [R]"Put
the holy ark [R]in the house which Solomon
the son of David, king of Israel, built. [R]*It shall*
no longer *be* a burden on *your* shoulders.
Now serve the LORD your God and His people
Israel. 2 Chr. 34:14 • 2 Chr. 5:7 • 1 Chr. 23:26
4 "Prepare *yourselves* according to your
fathers' [T]houses, according to your divisions,

following the written instruction of David
king of Israel and the [R]written instruction of
Solomon his son. *households* • 2 Chr. 8:14
5 "And stand in the holy *place* according
to the divisions of the fathers' houses of your
brethren the *lay* people, and *according to* the
division of the father's house of the Levites.
6 "So slaughter the Passover *offerings*,
sanctify yourselves, and prepare *them* for
your brethren, that *they* may do according to
the word of the LORD by the hand of Moses."
7 Then Josiah [R]gave the *lay* people lambs
and young goats from the flock, all for Passover *offerings* for all who were present, to the
number of thirty thousand, as well as three
thousand cattle; these *were* from the king's
[R]possessions. 2 Chr. 30:24 • 2 Chr. 31:3
8 And his leaders gave willingly to the
people, to the priests, and to the Levites.
Hilkiah, Zechariah, and Jehiel, rulers of the
house of God, gave to the priests for the
Passover *offerings* two thousand six hundred
from the flock, and three hundred cattle;
9 also Conaniah, his brothers Shemaiah
and Nethaneel, and Hashabiah and Jeiel and
Jozabad, chief of the Levites, gave to the
Levites for Passover *offerings* five thousand
from the flock and five hundred cattle.
10 So the service was prepared, and the
priests stood in their places, and the [R]Levites
in their divisions, according to the king's
command. 2 Chr. 5:12; 7:6; 8:14, 15; 13:10; 29:25–34
11 And they slaughtered the Passover *offerings*; and the priests [R]sprinkled *the blood* with
their hands, while the Levites [R]skinned *the
animals*. 2 Chr. 29:22 • 2 Chr. 29:34
12 Then they removed the burnt offerings
that *they* might give them to the divisions of
the fathers' houses of the *lay* people, to offer
to the LORD, as *it is* written in the Book of
Moses. And so *they did* with the cattle.
13 Also they [R]roasted the Passover *offerings*
with fire according to the ordinance; but the
other holy *offerings* they boiled in pots, in
caldrons, and in pans, and divided *them*
quickly among all the *lay* people. Ex. 12:8, 9
14 Then afterward they prepared portions
for themselves and for the priests, because
the priests, the sons of Aaron, *were busy* in
offering burnt offerings and fat until night;
therefore the Levites prepared portions for
themselves and for the priests, the sons of
Aaron.
15 And the singers, the sons of Asaph, *were*
in their places, according to the command of
David, Asaph, Heman, and Jeduthun the
king's seer. Also the gatekeepers [R]were at
each gate; they did not have to leave their
position, because their brethren the Levites
prepared portions for them. 1 Chr. 9:17, 18
16 So all the service of the LORD was prepared the same day, to keep the Passover and
to offer burnt offerings on the altar of the
LORD, according to the command of King
Josiah.
17 And the children of Israel who were
present kept the Passover at that time, and
the Feast of [R]Unleavened Bread for seven
days. Ex. 12:15; 13:6
18 [R]There had been no Passover kept in
Israel like that since the days of Samuel the
prophet; and none of the kings of Israel had
kept such a Passover as Josiah kept, with the
priests and the Levites, all Judah and Israel
who were present, and the inhabitants of
Jerusalem. 2 Kin. 23:22, 23
19 In the eighteenth year of the reign of
Josiah this Passover was kept.

Death of Josiah—2 Kin. 23:28–30

20 After all this, when Josiah had prepared
the temple, Necho king of Egypt came up to
fight against [R]Carchemish by the Euphrates;
and Josiah went out against him. Jer. 46:2
21 But he sent messengers to him, saying,
"What have I to do with you, king of Judah?
I have not *come* against you this day, but
against the house with which I have war; for
God commanded me to make haste. Refrain
from meddling with God, who *is* with me, lest
He destroy you."
22 Nevertheless Josiah would not turn his
face from him, but disguised himself so that
he might fight with him, and did not heed the
words of Necho from the mouth of God. So
he came to fight in the Valley of Megiddo.
23 And the archers shot King Josiah; and
the king said to his servants, "Take me away,
for I am severely wounded."
24 His servants therefore took him out of
that chariot and put him in the second
chariot that he had, and they brought him to
Jerusalem. So he died, and was buried in *one
of* the tombs of his fathers. And all Judah and
Jerusalem mourned for Josiah.
25 Jeremiah also lamented for Josiah. And
to this day all the singing men and the
singing women speak of Josiah in their lamentations. They made it a custom in Israel;
and indeed they *are* written in the Laments.
26 Now the rest of the acts of Josiah and his
goodness, according to *what was* written in
the Law of the LORD,
27 and his deeds from first to last, indeed
they *are* written in the book of the kings of
Israel and Judah.

CHAPTER 36

The Reign of Jehoahaz—2 Kin. 23:30–33

THEN [R]the people of the land took Jehoahaz the son of Josiah, and made him king
in his father's place in Jerusalem. 2 Kin. 23:30–34

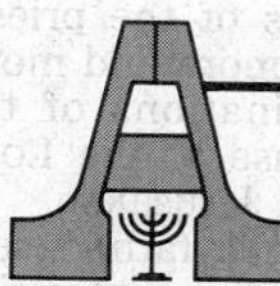

ISRAEL AND THE PERSIANS

The Persians apparently sprang from a people from the hills of Russia who began to settle in upper Mesopotamia and along the Black Sea as early as 2000 B.C. Ancient Media was located in what is now northwestern Iran, west of the Caspian Sea. Cyrus the Great, first ruler of the Persian Empire, united the Medes and Persians to conquer Babylonia and Assyria, thus becoming the dominant power of the ancient world.

After his conquest of Babylonia about 539 B.C., Cyrus authorized the rebuilding of the temple at Jerusalem and the resettlement of the Jewish community in their homeland (2 Chr. 36:22, 23). Many of the Israelites had been carried to Babylonia as captives after the fall of Jerusalem about 586 B.C. (2 Chr. 36:17–21).

Of all the ancient peoples who lived in the upper reaches of the Tigris and Euphrates Rivers, the Medes and Persians probably had the greatest influence on the Israelites. The prophet Isaiah wrote that Cyrus, although he did not know God, was anointed by God for the special mission of returning God's people to Jerusalem (Is. 45:1, 4).

Daniel 6:8, 9 refers to "the law of the Medes and Persians." Once a Persian law was handed down by the king, it could not be changed or revoked. While he was a captive in the royal court of the Babylonians, Daniel predicted that Babylonia would fall to the Medes and Persians (Dan. 5).

The Book of Esther records events that occurred during the reign of King Ahasuerus, or Xerxes, of Persia in the fifth century B.C. By faithfully recording the manners and customs of the Persian Empire, the book serves as a reliable historical record of the period.

Among the nations of the ancient world, Persia is noted for its beautiful cities. Persepolis, the nation's ceremonial capital, was a showplace of Persian culture (see photo). Ecbatana, capital of the Median Empire, became a resort city for the Persians. Susa, called Shushan in the Book of Esther, was the capital of the Elamites before it became the administrative capital of the Persian Empire.

Photo by Howard Vos

Ruins of palace at Persepolis, Persia's ceremonial capital.

2 *Jehoahaz *was* twenty-three years old
when he became king, and he reigned three
months in Jerusalem.
3 Now the king of Egypt deposed him at
Jerusalem; and he imposed on the land a
tribute of [T]one hundred talents of silver and a
[T]talent of gold. $38,400,000 • $5,760,000

The Reign of Jehoiakim—2 Kin. 23:24—24:6

4 Then the king of Egypt made his brother
Eliakim king over Judah and Jerusalem, and
changed his name to Jehoiakim. And Necho
took *Jehoahaz his brother and carried him
off to Egypt.
5 Jehoiakim *was* twenty-five years old
when he became king, and he reigned eleven
years in Jerusalem. And he did [R]evil in the
sight of the LORD his God. [Jer. 22:13–19]
6 Nebuchadnezzar king of Babylon came
up against him, and bound him in [T]bronze
fetters to carry him off to Babylon. *chains*
7 [R]Nebuchadnezzar also carried off *some*
of the articles from the house of the LORD to
Babylon, and put them in his temple at Babylon. Dan. 1:1, 2
8 Now the rest of the acts of Jehoiakim,
the abominations which he did, and what was
found against him, indeed they *are* written in
the book of the kings of Israel and Judah.
Then Jehoiachin his son reigned in his place.

The Reign of Jehoiachin
2 Kin. 24:8–17; Jer. 37:1

9 [R]Jehoiachin *was* *eight years old when
he became king, and he reigned in Jerusalem
three months and ten days. And he did evil in
the sight of the LORD. 2 Kin. 24:8–17
10 At the turn of the year [R]King Nebuchadnezzar summoned *him* and took him to Babylon, [R]with the costly articles from the house
of the LORD, and made [R]Zedekiah,[T] Jehoiakim's brother, king over Judah and Jerusa-
lem. 2 Kin. 24:10–17 • Dan. 1:1, 2 • Jer. 37:1 • Or *Mattaniah*

Evaluation of Zedekiah
2 Kin. 24:18, 19; Jer. 52:1, 2

11 [R]Zedekiah *was* twenty-one years old
when he became king, and he reigned eleven
years in Jerusalem. Jer. 52:1
12 He *also* did evil in the sight of the LORD
his God, *and* [R]did not humble himself before
Jeremiah the prophet, *who spoke* from the
mouth of the LORD. Jer. 21:3–7; 44:10

Destruction of Jerusalem
2 Kin. 24:20—25:21; Jer. 52:3–27

13 And he also [R]rebelled against King Nebuchadnezzar, who had made him swear *an
oath* by God; but he [R]stiffened his neck and
hardened his heart against turning to the
LORD God of Israel. Ezek. 17:15 • 2 Kin. 17:14
14 Moreover all the leaders of the priests
and the people transgressed more and more,
according to all the abominations of the
nations, and defiled the house of the LORD
which He had consecrated in Jerusalem.
15 [R]And the LORD God of their fathers sent
warnings to them by His messengers, rising
up early and sending *them*, because He had
compassion on His people and on His dwelling place. Jer. 7:13; 25:3, 4
16 But they mocked the messengers of God,
despised His words, and scoffed at His prophets, until the wrath of the LORD arose against
His people, till *there was* no remedy.
17 Therefore He brought against them the
king of the Chaldeans, who killed their young
men with the sword in the house of their
sanctuary, and had no compassion on young
man or virgin, on the aged or the weak; He
gave *them* all into his hand.
18 [R]And all the articles from the house of
God, great and small, the treasures of the
house of the LORD, and the treasures of the
king and of his leaders, all *these* he took to
Babylon. 2 Kin. 25:13–15
19 [R]Then they burned the house of God,
broke down the wall of Jerusalem, burned all
its palaces with fire, and destroyed all its
precious possessions. 2 Kin. 25:9
20 And those who escaped from the sword
he carried away to Babylon, [R]where they
became servants to him and his sons until the
reign of the kingdom of Persia, Jer. 17:4; 27:7
21 to fulfill the word of the LORD by the
mouth of Jeremiah, until the land [R]had enjoyed her Sabbaths. As long as she lay desolate [R]she kept Sabbath, to fulfill seventy
years. Lev. 26:34–43 • Lev. 25:4, 5

The Proclamation by Cyrus
to Return to Jerusalem—Ezra 1:1–3

22 [R]Now in the first year of Cyrus king of
Persia, that the word of the LORD *spoken* by
the mouth of [R]Jeremiah might be fulfilled, the
LORD stirred up the spirit of [R]Cyrus king of
Persia, so that he made a proclamation
throughout all his kingdom, and also *put it* in
writing, saying, Ezra 1:1–3 • Jer. 29:10 • Is. 44:28; 45:1

23 [R]Thus says Cyrus king of Persia: All the
kingdoms of the earth the LORD God of
heaven has given me. And He has
commanded me to build Him a [T]house
at Jerusalem which is in Judah. Who *is
there* among you of all His people? May
the LORD his God *be* with him, and let
him go up! Ezra 1:2, 3 • Temple

36:2 MT *Joahaz* **36:4** MT *Joahaz*
36:9 Heb. mss., LXX, Syr. *eighteen* and 2 Kin. 24:8

THE BOOK OF

EZRA

THE BOOK OF EZRA

Ezra continues the Old Testament narrative of Second Chronicles by showing how God fulfills His promise to return His people to the land of promise after seventy years of exile. Israel's "second exodus," this one from Babylon, is less impressive than the return from Egypt because only a remnant chooses to leave Babylon.

Ezra relates the story of two returns from Babylon—the first led by Zerubbabel to rebuild the temple (1—6), and the second under the leadership of Ezra to rebuild the spiritual condition of the people (7—10). Sandwiched between these two accounts is a gap of nearly six decades, during which Esther lives and rules as queen in Persia.

Ezra is the Aramaic form of the Hebrew word *ezer*, "help," and perhaps means "Yahweh helps." Ezra and Nehemiah were originally bound together as one book because Chronicles, Ezra, and Nehemiah were viewed as one continuous history. The Septuagint, a Greek-language version of the Old Testament translated in the third century B.C., calls Ezra-Nehemiah, *Esdras Deuteron*, "Second Esdras." First Esdras is the name of the apocryphal book of Esdras. The Latin title is *Liber Primus Esdrae*, "First Book of Ezra." In the Latin Bible, Ezra is called First Ezra and Nehemiah is called Second Ezra.

THE AUTHOR OF EZRA

Although Ezra is not specifically mentioned as the author, he is certainly the best candidate. Jewish tradition (the Talmud) attributes the Book to Ezra, and portions of the book (7:28—9:15) are written in the first person, from Ezra's point of view. The vividness of the details and descriptions favors an author who was an eyewitness of the later events of the book. As in Chronicles, there is a strong priestly emphasis, and Ezra was a direct priestly descendant of Aaron through Eleazar, Phineas, and Zadok (7:1-5). He studied, practiced, and taught the law of the Lord as an educated scribe (7:1-12). Also according to Second Maccabees 2:13-15, he had access to the library of written documents gathered by Nehemiah. Ezra no doubt used this material in writing Ezra 1—6 as he did in writing Chronicles. Some think that Ezra composed Nehemiah as well by making use of Nehemiah's personal diary.

Ezra was a godly man marked by strong trust in the Lord, moral integrity, and grief over sin. He was a contemporary of Nehemiah (Neh. 8:1-9; 12:36) who arrived in Jerusalem in 444 B.C. Tradition holds that Ezra was the founder of the Great Synagogue where the canon of Old Testament Scripture was settled. Another tradition says that he collected the biblical books into a unit and that he originated the synagogue form of worship.

Ezra wrote this book probably between 457 B.C. (the events of Ezra 7—10) and 444 B.C. (Nehemiah's arrival in Jerusalem). During the period covered by the Book of Ezra, Gautama Buddha (c. 560-480 B.C.) is in India, Confucius (551-479 B.C.) is in China, and Socrates (470-399 B.C.) is in Greece.

THE TIME OF EZRA

The following table shows the chronological relationship of the books of Ezra, Nehemiah, and Esther:

538-515 B.C.	483-473 B.C.
Zerubbabel	Esther
Ezra 1—6	Book of Esther
First Return	–

457 B.C.	444-c. 425 B.C.
Ezra	Nehemiah
Ezra 7—10	Book of Nehemiah
Second Return	Third Return

These books fit against the background of these Persian kings:

Cyrus	(559-530 B.C.)
Cambyses	(530-522 B.C.)
Smerdis	(522 B.C.)
Darius I	(521-486 B.C.)
Ahasuerus	(486-464 B.C.)
Artaxerxes I	(464-423 B.C.)
Darius II	(423-404 B.C.)

Cyrus the Persian overthrows Babylon in October 539 B.C. and issues his decree allowing the Jews to return in 538 B.C. The temple is begun in 536 B.C. The exile lasts only fifty years after 586 B.C., but the seventy-year figure for the captivity is taken from a beginning date of 606 B.C. when the first deportation to Babylon takes place. The rebuilding of the temple is discontinued in 534 B.C., resumed in 520 B.C., and completed in 515 B.C. It is begun under Cyrus and finished under Darius I. The two intervening kings, Cambyses and Smerdis, are not mentioned in any of these books. The prophets Haggai and Zechariah minister during Zerubbabel's time, about 520 B.C. and following years. Esther's story fits entirely in the reign of Xerxes, and Ezra ministers during the reign of Artaxerxes I, as does Nehemiah. There were three waves of deportation to Babylon (606, 597, and 586 B.C.) and three returns from Babylon: 538 B.C. (Zerubbabel), 457 B.C. (Ezra), and 444 B.C. (Nehemiah).

THE CHRIST OF EZRA

Ezra reveals God's continued fulfillment of His promise to keep David's descendants alive. Zerubbabel himself is part of the messianic line as the grandson of Jeconiah (Jehoiachin, 1 Chr. 3:17–19; see Matt. 1:12, 13). There is a positive note of hope in Ezra and Nehemiah because the remnant has returned to the land of promise. In this land the messianic promises will be fulfilled, because they are connected with such places as Bethlehem, Jerusalem, and Zion. Christ will be born in Bethlehem (Mic. 5:2), not in Babylon.

The Book of Ezra as a whole also typifies Christ's work of forgiveness and restoration.

KEYS TO EZRA

Key Word: Temple—The basic theme of Ezra is the restoration of the temple and the spiritual, moral, and social restoration of the returned remnant in Jerusalem under the leadership of Zerubbabel and Ezra. Israel's worship is revitalized and the people are purified. God's faithfulness is seen in the way He sovereignly protects His people through a powerful empire while they are in captivity. They prosper in their exile, and God raises up pagan kings who are sympathetic to their cause and encourage them to rebuild their homeland. God also provides zealous and capable spiritual leaders who direct the return and the rebuilding. He keeps His promise: "I will be found by you, says the LORD, and I will bring you back from your captivity; I will gather you from all the nations and from all the places where I have driven you, says the LORD, and I will bring you to the place from which I cause you to be carried away captive" (Jer. 29:14).

Key Verses: Ezra 1:3; 7:10—"Who *is there* among you of all His people? May his God be with him! Now let him go up to Jerusalem, which *is* in Judah, and build the house of the LORD God of Israel (He *is* God), which *is* in Jerusalem" (1:3).

"For Ezra had prepared his heart to seek the Law of the LORD, and to do *it,* and to teach statutes and ordinances in Israel" (7:10).

Key Chapter: Ezra 6—Ezra 6 records the completion and dedication of the temple which stimulates the obedience of the remnant to keep the Passover and separate themselves from the "filth of the nations of the land" (6:21).

SURVEY OF EZRA

Ezra continues the story exactly where Second Chronicles ends and shows how God's promise to bring His people back to their land is fulfilled (Jer. 29:10–14). God is with these people; and although their days of glory seem over, their spiritual heritage still remains and God's rich promises will be fulfilled. Ezra relates the story of the first two returns from Babylon, the first led by Zerubbabel and the second led decades later by Ezra. Its two divisions are the restoration of the temple (1—6) and the reformation of the people (7—10), and they are separated by a fifty-eight-year gap during which the story of Esther takes place.

The Restoration of the Temple (1—6): King Cyrus of Persia overthrows Babylon in 539 B.C. and issues a decree in 538 B.C. that allows the exiled Jews to return to their homeland. Isaiah prophesied two centuries before that the temple would be rebuilt and actually named Cyrus as the one who would bring it about (Is. 44:28—45:4). Cyrus may have read and responded to this passage.

FOCUS	RESTORATION OF THE TEMPLE		REFORMATION OF THE PEOPLE	
REFERENCE	1:1——3:1	——7:1	——9:1	——10:44
DIVISION	FIRST RETURN TO JERUSALEM	CONSTRUCTION OF THE TEMPLE	SECOND RETURN TO JERUSALEM	RESTORATION OF THE PEOPLE
TOPIC	ZERUBBABEL		EZRA	
	FIRST RETURN OF 49,897		SECOND RETURN OF 1,754	
LOCATION	PERSIA TO JERUSALEM		PERSIA TO JERUSALEM	
TIME	22 YEARS (538 – 516 B.C.)		1 YEAR (458 – 457 B.C.)	

Out of a total Jewish population of perhaps 2 or 3 million, only 49,897 choose to take advantage of this offer. Only the most committed are willing to leave a life of relative comfort in Babylon, endure a trek of nine hundred miles, and face further hardship by rebuilding a destroyed temple and city. Zerubbabel, a "prince" of Judah (a direct descendant of King David), leads the faithful remnant back to Jerusalem. Those who return are from the tribes of Judah, Benjamin, and Levi; but it is evident that representatives from the other ten tribes eventually return as well. The ten "lost tribes" are not entirely lost.

Zerubbabel's priorities are in the right place: he first restores the altar and the religious feasts before beginning work on the temple itself. The foundation of the temple is laid in 536 B.C., but opposition arises and the work ceases from 534 to 520 B.C. While Ezra 4:1–5, 24 concerns Zerubbabel, 4:6–23 concerns opposition to the building of the wall of Jerusalem some time between 464 and 444 B.C. These verses may have been placed here to illustrate the antagonism to the work of rebuilding. The prophets Haggai and Zechariah exhort the people to get back to building the temple (5:1, 2), and the work begins again under Zerubbabel and Joshua the high priest. Tattenai, a Persian governor, protests to King Darius I about the temple building and challenges their authority to continue. King Darius finds the decree of Cyrus and confirms it, even forcing Tattenai to provide whatever is needed to complete the work. It is finished in 515 B.C.

The Reformation of the People (7—10): A smaller return under Ezra takes place in 457 B.C., eighty-one years after the first return under Zerubbabel. Ezra the priest is given authority by King Artaxerxes I to bring people and contributions for the temple in Jerusalem. God protects this band of less than two thousand men and they safely reach Jerusalem with their valuable gifts from Persia. Many priests but few Levites return with Zerubbabel and Ezra (2:36–42; 8:15–19). God uses Ezra to rebuild the people spiritually and morally. When Ezra discovers that the people and the priests have intermarried with foreign women, he identifies with the sin of his people and offers a great intercessory prayer on their behalf. During the gap of fifty-eight years between Ezra 6 and 7, the people fall into a confused spiritual state and Ezra is alarmed. They quickly respond to Ezra's confession and weeping by making a covenant to put away their foreign wives and to live in accordance with God's law. This confession and response to the Word of God brings about a great revival and changes lives.

OUTLINE OF EZRA

Part One: The Restoration of the Temple of God (1:1—6:22)

I. The First Return to Jerusalem Under Zerubbabel .... **1:1—2:70**

A. Decree of Cyrus 1:1–4
B. Gifts from Israel and Cyrus 1:5–11
C. Census of the Returning People 2:1–63
1. The People of Known Descent 2:1–58
a. The Leaders 2:1, 2
b. The People 2:3–35
c. The Priests 2:36–39
d. The Levites 2:40–42
e. The Servants 2:43–58
2. The People of Unknown Descent 2:59–63
a. The People 2:59, 60
b. The Priests 2:61–63
D. The Return Completed 2:64–70
1. The People Who Returned 2:64–67
2. The Gifts the People Gave 2:68–70

II. The Construction of the Temple .... **3:1—6:22**

A. Construction of the Temple Foundation 3:1–13
1. Spiritual Preparation of the People 3:1–6
2. Completion of the Temple Foundation 3:7–13
B. Interruption of the Temple Construction 4:1–24
1. Present Opposition Under Darius 4:1–5
2. Later Opposition Under Ahasuerus 4:6
3. Later Opposition Under Artaxerxes 4:7–23
4. Present Interruption of Construction Under Darius 4:24
C. Completion of the Temple .... 5:1—6:18
1. Resumption of the Temple Construction 5:1, 2
2. Opposition to the Construction 5:3–17
a. Opposition by Tattenai 5:3–5
b. The Letter to Darius 5:6–17
3. Confirmation of the Temple Construction 6:1–12
4. Completion of the Temple 6:13–15
5. Dedication of the Temple 6:16–18
D. Celebration of the Passover 6:19–22

Part Two: The Reformation of the People of God (7:1—10:44)

I. The Second Return to Jerusalem Under Ezra .... **7:1—8:36**

A. The Decree of Artaxerxes 7:1–28
1. Ezra's Qualifications 7:1–10
2. Artaxerxes' Letter 7:11–26
3. Ezra's Response 7:27, 28
B. Census of the Returning Israelites 8:1–14
C. Spiritual Preparation for the Return 8:15–23

1. Acquisition of Temple Leadership . . 8:15–20
2. Proclamation of a Fast. 8:21–23

D. The Return Is Completed. 8:24–36

II. The Restoration of the People . . . . 9:1—10:44

A. Israel Intermarries. 9:1, 2
B. Ezra Intercedes with God 9:3–15
1. Lamentation of Ezra 9:3, 4
2. Confession of Ezra. 9:5–15
a. God's Faithfulness. 9:5–9
b. Israel's Unfaithfulness. 9:10–15

C. Reformation of Israel 10:1–44
1. Israel Laments 10:1, 2
2. The Covenant Is Instituted. 10:3–5
3. Solution for Intermarriage. 10:6–44
a. Separation Is Accepted. 10:6–17
b. Separation of Priests 10:18–22
c. Separation of Levites 10:23, 24
d. Separation of People. 10:25–44

CHAPTER 1

Decree of Cyrus—2 Chr. 36:22, 23

NOW in the first year of Cyrus king of
Persia, that the word of the LORD *spo-*
ken by the mouth of Jeremiah might be
fulfilled, the LORD stirred up the spirit of
Cyrus king of Persia, so that he made a
proclamation throughout all his kingdom,
and also *put it* in writing, saying,

2 Thus says Cyrus king of Persia: All the
kingdoms of the earth the LORD God of
heaven has given me. And He has
commanded me to build Him a [T]house
at Jerusalem which *is* in Judah. Temple
3 Who *is there* among you of all His
people? May his God be with him! Now
let him go up to Jerusalem, which *is* in
Judah, and build the house of the LORD
God of Israel [R](He *is* God), which *is* in
Jerusalem. Dan. 6:26
4 And whoever remains in any place
where he sojourns, let the men of his
place help him with silver and gold,
with goods and livestock, besides the
freewill offerings for the house of God
which *is* in Jerusalem.

Gifts from Israel and Cyrus

5 Then the heads of the fathers' *houses* of
Judah and Benjamin, and the priests and the
Levites, with all *those* whose spirits God had
moved, arose to go up and build the house of
the LORD which *is* in Jerusalem.
6 And all those who *were* around them
[T]encouraged them with articles of silver and
gold, with goods and livestock, and with
precious things, besides all *that* was [R]will-
ingly offered. Lit. *strengthened their hands* • Ezra 2:68
7 King Cyrus also brought out the articles
of the house of the LORD, [R]which Nebuchadnezzar had taken from Jerusalem and put in
the [T]temple of his gods; 2 Kin. 24:13 • Lit. *house*
8 and Cyrus king of Persia brought them
out by the hand of Mithredath the treasurer,
and counted them out to [R]Sheshbazzar the
prince of Judah. Ezra 5:14, 16
9 This *is* the number of them: thirty gold
platters, one thousand silver platters, twenty-
nine knives,
10 thirty gold basins, four hundred and ten
silver basins of a similar *kind, and* one thousand other articles.
11 All the articles of gold and silver *were*
five thousand four hundred. All *these* Sheshbazzar took with the captives who were
brought from Babylon to Jerusalem.

CHAPTER 2

The Leaders

NOW [R]these *are* the people of the province
who came back from the captivity, of
those who had been carried away, [R]whom
Nebuchadnezzar the king of Babylon had
carried away to Babylon, and who returned
to Jerusalem and Judah, everyone to his *own*
city. Neh. 7:6–73 • 2 Kin. 24:14–16; 25:11
2 *Those* who came with Zerubbabel *were*
Jeshua, Nehemiah, Seraiah, Reelaiah, Mordecai, Bilshan, [T]Mispar, Bigvai, [T]Rehum, *and*
Baanah. The number of the men of the people
of Israel: *Mispereth,* Neh. 7:7 • *Nehum,* Neh. 7:7

The People

3 the people of Parosh, two thousand one
hundred and seventy-two;
4 the people of Shephatiah, three hundred
and seventy-two;
5 the people of Arah, [R]seven hundred and
seventy-five; Neh. 7:10
6 the people of [R]Pahath-Moab, of the people of Jeshua *and* Joab, two thousand eight
hundred and twelve; Neh. 7:11
7 the people of Elam, one thousand two
hundred and fifty-four;
8 the people of Zattu, nine hundred and
forty-five;
9 the people of Zaccai, seven hundred and
sixty;
10 the people of Bani, six hundred and
forty-two;
11 the people of Bebai, six hundred and
twenty-three;
12 the people of Azgad, one thousand two
hundred and twenty-two;

OLD TESTAMENT EVENTS

CREATION*	Before recorded history	Gen. 1
ABRAHAM IN CANAAN	2000 B.C.	Gen. 12—25
DEATH OF ABRAHAM	1980 B.C.	Gen. 25
JOSEPH IN EGYPT	1975 B.C.	Gen. 37—45
JACOB'S FAMILY MOVES TO EGYPT	1960 B.C.	Gen. 46
DEATH OF JOSEPH	1925 B.C.	Gen. 49
EGYPTIAN ENSLAVEMENT BEGINS	1900 B.C.	Ex. 1:8—12:42
BIRTH OF MOSES	1525 B.C.	Ex. 2:1–4
EXODUS FROM EGYPT	1445 B.C.	Ex. 12—15
PERIOD OF WILDERNESS WANDERING	1445–1405 B.C.	Deut. 34
DEATH OF MOSES	1405 B.C.	Deut. 34:1–7
CONQUEST OF CANAAN	1405–1398 B.C.	Josh. 6—12
DEATH OF JOSHUA	1390 B.C.	Josh. 24
PERIOD OF THE JUDGES	1374–1107 B.C.	Judg. 3—16
BIRTH OF SAMUEL	1105 B.C.	1 Sam. 1:19, 20
SAUL ANOINTED FIRST KING	1043 B.C.	1 Sam. 10
DAVID ANOINTED KING	1025 B.C.	1 Sam. 16
DAVID'S REIGN OVER ALL ISRAEL	1011–971 B.C.	2 Sam. 5; 1 Kin. 2:11
SOLOMON'S REIGN	971–931 B.C.	1 Kin. 1—12
KINGDOM DIVIDES	931 B.C.	1 Kin. 12
FALL OF NORTHERN KINGDOM	722 B.C.	2 Kin. 17
FALL OF JERUSALEM TO BABYLONIANS	586 B.C.	2 Kin. 25
PERIOD OF EXILE IN BABYLON	586–538 B.C.	Ezra 1
RETURN FROM EXILE	536 B.C.	Ezra 1—6
TEMPLE REBUILT IN JERUSALEM	516 B.C.	Ezra 6:15
JERUSALEM'S WALLS REBUILT	444 B.C.	Neh. 6:15

***Pinning down exact dates for some of the events listed in this chart is difficult. Therefore, the dates given should be considered to be approximate.**

13 the people of Adonikam, six hundred and sixty-six;
14 the people of Bigvai, two thousand and fifty-six;
15 the people of Adin, four hundred and fifty-four;
16 the people of Ater of Hezekiah, ninety-eight;
17 the people of Bezai, three hundred and twenty-three;
18 the people of [T]Jorah, one hundred and twelve; *Hariph,* Neh. 7:24
19 the people of Hashum, two hundred and twenty-three;
20 the people of Gibbar, ninety-five;
21 the people of Bethlehem, one hundred and twenty-three;
22 the men of Netophah, fifty-six;
23 the men of Anathoth, one hundred and twenty-eight;
24 the people of Azmaveth, forty-two;
25 the people of Kirjath Arim, Chephirah, and Beeroth, seven hundred and forty-three;
26 the people of Ramah and Geba, six hundred and twenty-one;
27 the men of Michmas, one hundred and twenty-two;
28 the men of Bethel and Ai, two hundred and twenty-three;
29 the people of Nebo, fifty-two;
30 the people of Magbish, one hundred and fifty-six;
31 the people of the other [R]Elam, one thousand two hundred and fifty-four; Ezra 2:7
32 the people of Harim, three hundred and twenty;
33 the people of Lod, Hadid, and Ono, seven hundred and twenty-five;
34 the people of Jericho, three hundred and forty-five;
35 the people of Senaah, three thousand six hundred and thirty.

The Priests

36 The priests: the sons of [R]Jedaiah, of the house of Jeshua, nine hundred and seventy-three; 1 Chr. 24:7–18
37 the sons of [R]Immer, one thousand and fifty-two; 1 Chr. 24:14
38 the sons of [R]Pashhur, one thousand two hundred and forty-seven; 1 Chr. 9:12
39 the sons of [R]Harim, one thousand and seventeen. 1 Chr. 24:8

The Levites

40 The Levites: the sons of Jeshua and Kadmiel, of the sons of [T]Hodaviah, seventy-four. *Judah,* Ezra 3:9, or *Hodevah,* Neh. 7:43
41 The singers: the sons of Asaph, one hundred and twenty-eight.
42 The sons of the gatekeepers: the sons of Shallum, the sons of Ater, the sons of Talmon, the sons of Akkub, the sons of Hatita, and the sons of Shobai, one hundred and thirty-nine *in* all.

The Servants

43 [R]The Nethinim: the sons of Ziha, the sons of Hasupha, the sons of Tabbaoth, 1 Chr. 9:2
44 the sons of Keros, the sons of [T]Siaha, the sons of Padon, *Sia,* Neh. 7:47
45 the sons of Lebanah, the sons of Hagabah, the sons of Akkub,
46 the sons of Hagab, the sons of Shalmai, the sons of Hanan,
47 the sons of Giddel, the sons of Gahar, the sons of Reaiah,
48 the sons of Rezin, the sons of Nekoda, the sons of Gazzam,
49 the sons of Uzza, the sons of Paseah, the sons of Besai,
50 the sons of Asnah, the sons of Meunim, the sons of [T]Nephusim, *Nephishesim,* Neh. 7:52
51 the sons of Bakbuk, the sons of Hakupha, the sons of Harhur,
52 the sons of [T]Bazluth, the sons of Mehida, the sons of Harsha, *Bazlith,* Neh. 7:54
53 the sons of Barkos, the sons of Sisera, the sons of Tamah,
54 the sons of Neziah, and the sons of Hatipha.
55 The sons of Solomon's servants: the sons of Sotai, the sons of [R]Sophereth, the sons of [T]Peruda, Neh. 7:57–60 • *Perida,* Neh. 7:57
56 the sons of Jaala, the sons of Darkon, the sons of Giddel,
57 the sons of Shephatiah, the sons of Hattil, the sons of Pochereth of Zebaim, and the sons of [T]Ami. *Amon,* Neh. 7:59
58 All the [R]Nethinim and the children of [R]Solomon's servants were three hundred and ninety-two. 1 Chr. 9:2 • 1 Kin. 9:21

The People

59 And these *were* the ones who came up from Tel Melah, Tel Harsha, Cherub, Addan, and Immer; but they could not [T]identify their father's house or their [T]genealogy, whether they *were* of Israel: Lit. *tell* • Lit. *seed*
60 the sons of Delaiah, the sons of Tobiah, and the sons of Nekoda, six hundred and fifty-two;

The Priests

61 and of the sons of the priests: the sons of [R]Habaiah, the sons of [T]Koz, and the sons of [R]Barzillai, who took a wife of the daughters of Barzillai the Gileadite, and was called by their name. Neh. 7:63 • Or *Hakkoz* • 2 Sam. 17:27
62 These sought their listing *among* those who were registered by genealogy, but they were not found; therefore they *were excluded* from the priesthood as defiled.

63 And the [T]governor said to them that they
should not eat of the most holy things till a
priest could consult with the [R]Urim and
Thummim. Or *Tirshatha* • Ex. 28:30

The People Who Returned

64 The whole congregation together *was*
forty-two thousand three hundred *and* sixty,
65 besides their male and female servants,
of whom *there were* seven thousand three
hundred and thirty-seven; and they had two
hundred men and women singers.
66 Their horses *were* seven hundred and
thirty-six, their mules two hundred and forty-five,
67 their camels four hundred and thirty-five, and *their* donkeys six thousand seven
hundred and twenty.

The Gifts the People Gave

68 *Some* of the heads of the fathers' *houses,*
when they came to the house of the LORD
which *is* in Jerusalem, offered freely for the
house of God, to erect it in its place:
69 According to their ability, they gave to
the treasury for the work sixty-one thousand
gold drachmas, five thousand minas of silver,
and one hundred priestly garments.
70 [R]So the priests and the Levites, *some* of
the people, the singers, the gatekeepers, and
the Nethinim, dwelt in their cities, and all
Israel in their cities. Neh. 7:73

CHAPTER 3

Spiritual Preparation of the People

AND when the [R]seventh month had come,
and the children of Israel *were* in the
cities, the people gathered together as one
man to Jerusalem. Neh. 7:73; 8:1, 2
2 Then [T]Jeshua the son of Jozadak and his
brethren the priests, and Zerubbabel the son
of Shealtiel and his brethren, arose and built
the altar of the God of Israel, to offer burnt
offerings on it, as *it is* written in the Law of
Moses the man of God. Or *Joshua*
3 Though fear *had come* upon them because of the people of those countries, they
set the altar on its bases; and they offered
[R]burnt offerings on it to the LORD, *both* the
morning and evening burnt offerings. Num. 28:3
4 They also kept the Feast of Tabernacles,
[R]as *it is* written, and [R]*offered* the daily burnt
offerings in the number required by ordinance for each day; Ex. 23:16 • Num. 29:12, 13
5 and afterward *they offered* the [R]regular
burnt offering, and *those* for New Moons and
for all the appointed feasts of the LORD that
were consecrated, and *those* of everyone who
willingly offered a freewill offering to the
LORD. Ex. 29:38
6 From the first day of the seventh month
they began to offer burnt offerings to the
LORD. But the foundation of the temple of the
LORD had not *yet* been laid.

Completion of the Temple Foundation

7 They also gave money to the masons and
the carpenters, and food, drink, and oil to the
people of Sidon and Tyre to bring cedar logs
from Lebanon to the sea at Joppa, [R]according
to the permission which they had from Cyrus
king of Persia. Ezra 1:2; 6:3
8 Now in the second month of the second
year of their coming to the house of God at
Jerusalem, Zerubbabel the son of Shealtiel,
Jeshua the son of Jozadak, and the rest of
their brethren the priests and the Levites, and
all those who had come out of the captivity
to Jerusalem, began *work* and appointed the
Levites from twenty years old and above to
oversee the work of the house of the LORD.
9 Then [R]Jeshua *with* his sons and brothers,
Kadmiel *with* his sons, and the sons of [T]Judah, arose as one to oversee those working
on the house of God: the sons of Henadad
with their sons and their brethren the Levites. Ezra 2:40 • *Hodaviah,* Ezra 2:40
10 When the builders laid the foundation of
the temple of the LORD, the priests stood in
their apparel with trumpets, and the Levites,
the sons of Asaph, with cymbals, to praise the
LORD, according to the [R]ordinance[T] of David
king of Israel. 1 Chr. 6:31; 16:4; 25:1 • Lit. *hands*
11 [R]And they sang responsively, praising
and giving thanks to the LORD: Neh. 12:24

[R]"For *He is* good, Ps. 136:1
[R]For His mercy *endures* forever toward
Israel." Jer. 33:11

Then all the people shouted with a great
shout, when they praised the LORD, because
the foundation of the house of the LORD was
laid.
12 But many of the priests and Levites and
[R]heads of the fathers' *houses, who were* old
men, who had seen the first temple, wept
with a loud voice when the foundation of this
temple was laid before their eyes; yet many
shouted aloud for joy, Ezra 2:68
13 so that the people could not discern the
noise of the shout of joy from the noise of the
weeping of the people, for the people shouted
with a loud shout, and the sound was heard
afar off.

CHAPTER 4

Present Opposition Under Darius

NOW when [R]the [T]adversaries of Judah and
Benjamin heard that the descendants of
the captivity were building the temple of the
LORD God of Israel, Ezra 4:7–9 • *enemies*

2 they came to Zerubbabel and the heads
of the fathers' *houses*, and said to them, "Let
us build with you, for we seek your God as
you *do*; and we have sacrificed to Him [R]since
the days of Esarhaddon king of Assyria, who
brought us here." 2 Kin. 17:24; 19:37
3 But Zerubbabel and Jeshua and the rest
of the heads of the fathers' *houses* of Israel
said to them, "You may do nothing with us to
build a house for our God; but we alone will
build to the LORD God of Israel, as King
Cyrus the king of Persia has commanded us."
4 Then [R]the people of the land tried to
discourage the people of Judah. They troubled them in building, Ezra 3:3
5 and hired counselors against them to
frustrate their purpose all the days of Cyrus
king of Persia, even until the reign of [R]Darius
king of Persia. Ezra 5:5; 6:1

Later Opposition Under Ahasuerus

6 Now in the reign of Ahasuerus, in the
beginning of his reign, they wrote an accusation against the inhabitants of Judah and
Jerusalem.

Later Opposition Under Artaxerxes

7 In the days of [R]Artaxerxes also, [T]Bishlam,
Mithredath, Tabeel, and the rest of their
companions wrote to Artaxerxes king of
Persia; and the letter *was* written in [R]Aramaic
script, and translated into the Aramaic language. Ezra 7:1, 7, 21 • Or *in peace* • 2 Kin. 18:26
8 *Rehum the commander and Shimshai
the scribe wrote a letter against Jerusalem to
King Artaxerxes in this fashion:

9 [T]From Rehum the commander,
Shimshai the scribe, and the rest of
their companions—*representatives* of
the Dinaites, the Apharsathchites, the
Tarpelites, the people of Persia and
Erech and Babylon and [T]Shushan, the
Dehavites, the Elamites, Lit. *Then* • Or *Susa*
10 and the rest of the nations whom the
great and noble Osnapper took captive
and settled in the cities of Samaria and
the rest *of the region* beyond the
River—[T]and so forth. Lit. *and now*

11 This *is* a copy of the letter that they sent
him—

To King Artaxerxes from your servants
the men *of the region* beyond the River,
[T]and so forth: Lit. *and now*
12 Let it be known to the king that the
Jews who came up from you have come
to us at Jerusalem, and are building the
[R]rebellious and evil city, and are
finishing *its* [R]walls and repairing the
foundations. 2 Chr. 36:13 • Ezra 5:3, 9
13 Let it now be known to the king that, if
this city is built and the walls
completed, they will not pay [R]tax,
tribute, or custom, and the king's
treasury will be diminished. Ezra 4:20; 7:24
14 Now because we receive support from
the palace, it was not proper for us to
see the king's dishonor; therefore we
have sent and informed the king,
15 that search may be made in the book of
the records of your fathers. And you
will find in the book of the records and
know that this city *is* a rebellious city,
harmful to kings and provinces, and
that they have incited sedition within
the city in former times, for which
cause this city was destroyed.
16 We inform the king that if this city is
rebuilt and its walls are completed, the
result will be that you will have no
dominion *over the region* beyond the
River.

17 *Then* the king sent an answer:

To Rehum the commander, *to* Shimshai
the scribe, *to* the rest of their
companions who dwell in Samaria,
and *to* the rest *in the region* beyond
the River:
Peace, [T]and so forth. Lit. *and now*
18 The letter which you sent to us has
been clearly read before me.
19 And [T]I gave the command, and a search
has been made, and it was found that
this city in former times has made
insurrection against kings, and *that*
rebellion and sedition have been
fostered in it. Lit. *by me a decree was put forth*
20 There have also been mighty kings over
Jerusalem, who have ruled over all *the
provinces* beyond the River; and tax,
tribute, and custom were paid to them.
21 Now give the command to make these
men cease, that this city may not be
built until the command is given by me.
22 Take heed now that you do not fail to
do this. Why should damage increase to
the hurt of the kings?

23 Now when the copy of King Artaxerxes'
letter *was* read before Rehum, Shimshai the
scribe, and their companions, they went up in
haste to Jerusalem against the Jews, and by
force of arms made them cease.

*Present Interruption
of Construction Under Darius*

24 Thus the work of the house of God
which *is* at Jerusalem ceased, and it was

4:8 The original language of Ezra 4:8 through 6:18 is Aramaic

discontinued until the second year of the
reign of Darius king of Persia.

CHAPTER 5

Resumption of the Temple Construction
Hag. 1:1; Zech. 1:1

THEN the prophet [R]Haggai and [R]Zechariah
the son of Iddo, prophets, prophesied to
the Jews who *were* in Judah and Jerusalem,
in the name of the God of Israel, *who was*
over them. Hag. 1:1 • Zech. 1:1
2 So Zerubbabel the son of Shealtiel and
Jeshua the son of [T]Jozadak rose up and began
to build the house of God which *is* in Jerusalem; and the prophets of God *were* with
them, helping them. *Jehozadak*, 1 Chr. 6:14

Opposition by Tattenai

3 At the same time Tattenai the governor
of *the region* beyond [T]the River and Shethar-
Boznai and their companions came to them
and spoke thus to them: [R]"Who has commanded you to build this [T]temple and finish
this wall?" The Euphrates • Ezra 1:3; 5:9 • Lit. *house*
4 [R]Then, accordingly, we told them the
names of the men who were constructing this
building. Ezra 5:10
5 But [R]the eye of their God was upon the
elders of the Jews, so that they could not
make them cease till a report could go to
Darius. Then a [R]written answer was returned
concerning this *matter.* Ps. 33:18 • Ezra 6:6

The Letter to Darius

6 This is a copy of the letter that Tattenai
sent:

The governor of *the region* beyond the
River, and Shethar-Boznai, [R]and his
companions, the Persians who *were in*
the region beyond the River, to Darius
the king. Ezra 4:7–10

7 They sent a letter to him, in which was
written thus—

To Darius the king:
All peace.
8 Let it be known to the king that we
went into the province of Judea, to the
[T]temple of the great God, which is being
built with [T]heavy stones, and timber is
being laid in the walls; and this work
goes on diligently and prospers in their
hands. Lit. *house* • Lit. *stones of rolling*
9 Then we asked those elders, *and* spoke
thus to them: [R]"Who commanded you
to build this temple and to finish these
walls?" Ezra 5:3, 4
10 We also asked them their names to
inform you, that we might write the
names of the men who *were* chief
among them.
11 And thus they returned us an answer,
saying: "We are the servants of the God
of heaven and earth, and we are
rebuilding the [T]temple that was built
many years ago, which a great king of
Israel built and completed. Lit. *house*
12 "But because our fathers provoked the
God of heaven to wrath, He gave them
into the hand of Nebuchadnezzar king
of Babylon, the Chaldean, *who*
destroyed this temple and [R]carried the
people away to Babylon. Jer. 13:19
13 "However, in the first year of Cyrus
king of Babylon, King Cyrus issued a
decree to build this house of God.
14 "Also, the gold and silver articles of the
house of God, which Nebuchadnezzar
had taken from the temple that *was* in
Jerusalem and carried into the temple
of Babylon—those King Cyrus took
from the temple of Babylon, and they
were given to one named Sheshbazzar,
whom he had made governor.
15 "And he said to him, 'Take these
articles; go, carry them to the temple
site that *is* in Jerusalem, and let the
house of God be rebuilt on its former
site.'
16 "Then the same Sheshbazzar came *and*
[R]laid the foundation of the house of
God which *is* in Jerusalem; and from
that time even until now it has been
under construction, and [R]it is not *yet*
finished." Ezra 3:8–10 • Ezra 6:15
17 Now therefore, if *it seems* good to the
king, [R]let a search be made in the king's
treasure house, which *is* there in
Babylon, whether it is *so* that a decree
was issued by King Cyrus to build this
house of God at Jerusalem, and let the
king send us his pleasure concerning
this *matter.* Ezra 6:1, 2

CHAPTER 6

Confirmation of the Temple Construction

THEN King Darius issued a decree, [R]and a
search was made in the archives, where
the treasures were stored in Babylon. Ezra 5:17
2 And at Achmetha, in the palace that *is* in
the province of [R]Media, a scroll was found,
and in it a record *was* written thus: 2 Kin. 17:6

3 In the first year of King Cyrus, King
Cyrus issued a [R]decree *concerning* the
house of God at Jerusalem: "Let the
house be rebuilt, the place where they
offered sacrifices; and let the
foundations of it be firmly laid, its

height ^T^sixty cubits *and* its width sixty cubits, Ezra 1:1; 5:13 • 90 ft.
4 ^R^*with* three rows of heavy stones and one row of new timber. Let the ^R^expenses be paid from the king's treasury. 1 Kin. 6:36 • Ezra 3:7
5 Also let ^R^the gold and silver articles of the house of God, which Nebuchadnezzar took from the temple which *is* in Jerusalem and brought to Babylon, be restored and taken back to the temple which *is* in Jerusalem, *each* to its place; and deposit *them* in the house of God"— Ezra 1:7, 8; 5:14
6 ^R^Now *therefore,* Tattenai, governor of *the region* beyond the River, and Shethar-Boznai, and your companions the Persians who *are* beyond the River, keep yourselves far from there. Ezra 5:3, 6
7 Let the work of this ^T^house of God alone; let the governor of the Jews and the elders of the Jews build this house of God on its site. Temple
8 Moreover I issue a decree *as to* what you shall do for the elders of these Jews, for the building of this ^T^house of God: Let the cost be paid at the king's expense from taxes *on the region* beyond the River; this is to be given immediately to these men, so that they are not hindered. Temple
9 And whatever they need—young bulls, rams, and lambs for the burnt offerings of the God of heaven, wheat, salt, wine, and oil, according to the request of the priests who *are* in Jerusalem—let it be given them day by day without fail,
10 that they may offer sacrifices of sweet aroma to the God of heaven, and pray for the life of the king and his sons.
11 Also I issue a decree that whoever alters this edict, let a timber be pulled from his house and erected, and let him be hanged on it; and let his house be made a refuse heap because of this.
12 And may the God who causes His name to dwell there destroy any king or people who put their hand to alter it, or to destroy this ^T^house of God which is in Jerusalem. I Darius issue *the* decree; let it be done diligently. Temple

Completion of the Temple

13 Then Tattenai, governor of *the region*
beyond the River, Shethar-Boznai, and their
companions diligently did according to what
King Darius had sent.
14 So the elders of the Jews built, and they
prospered through the prophesying of Haggai
the prophet and Zechariah the son of Iddo.
And they built and finished *it,* according to
the commandment of the God of Israel, and
according to the ^T^command of Cyrus, Darius,
and Artaxerxes king of Persia. *decree*
15 Now the temple was finished on the third
day of the month of Adar, which was in the
sixth year of the reign of King Darius.

Dedication of the Temple

16 Then the children of Israel, the priests
and the Levites and the rest of the descendants of the captivity, celebrated the dedication of this ^T^house of God with joy. Temple
17 And they ^R^offered sacrifices at the dedication of this house of God, one hundred
bulls, two hundred rams, four hundred lambs,
and as a sin offering for all Israel twelve male
goats, according to the number of the tribes
of Israel. Ezra 8:35
18 They assigned the priests to their divisions and the Levites to their divisions, over
the service of God in Jerusalem, ^R^as it is
written in the Book of Moses. Num. 3:6; 8:9

Celebration of the Passover

19 *And the descendants of the captivity
kept the Passover ^R^on the fourteenth *day* of
the first month. Ex. 12:6
20 For the priests and the Levites had ^R^puri-
fied themselves; all of them *were ritually*
clean. And they ^R^slaughtered the Passover
lambs for all the descendants of the captivity,
for their brethren the priests, and for themselves. 2 Chr. 29:34; 30:15 • 2 Chr. 35:11
21 Then the children of Israel who had
returned from the captivity ate together with
all who had separated themselves from the
^T^filth of the nations of the land in order to
seek the LORD God of Israel. *uncleanness*
22 And they kept the Feast of Unleavened
Bread seven days with joy; for the LORD
made them joyful, and ^R^turned the heart of
the king of Assyria toward them, to
strengthen their hands in the work of the
house of God, the God of Israel. [Prov. 21:1]

CHAPTER 7

Ezra's Qualifications

NOW after these things, in the reign of
Artaxerxes king of Persia, Ezra the ^R^son
of Seraiah, ^R^the son of Azariah, the son of
^R^Hilkiah, 1 Chr. 6:14 • Jer. 52:24 • 2 Chr. 35:8
2 the son of Shallum, the son of Zadok, the
son of Ahitub,
3 the son of Amariah, the son of Azariah,
the son of Meraioth,
4 the son of Zerahiah, the son of Uzzi, the
son of Bukki,
5 the son of Abishua, the son of Phinehas,
the son of Eleazar, the son of Aaron the chief
priest—

6:19 The Hebrew language resumes in Ezra 6:19 and continues through 7:11

6 this Ezra came up from Babylon; and he
was a skilled scribe in the Law of Moses,
which the LORD God of Israel had given. The
king granted him all his request, according to
the hand of the LORD his God upon him.
7 *Some* of the children of Israel, the
priests, the Levites, the singers, the gatekeepers, and the Nethinim came up to Jerusalem
in the seventh year of King Artaxerxes.
8 And Ezra came to Jerusalem in the fifth
month, which *was* in the seventh year of the
king.
9 On the first *day* of the first month he
began *his* journey from Babylon, and on the
first *day* of the fifth month he came to Jerusalem, [R]according to the good hand of his
God upon him. Neh. 2:8, 18
10 For Ezra had prepared his heart to seek
the Law of the LORD, and to do *it*, and to
teach statutes and ordinances in Israel.

Artaxerxes' Letter

11 Now this *is* the copy of the letter that
King Artaxerxes gave Ezra the priest, the
scribe, expert in the words of the commandments of the LORD, and of His statutes to
Israel:

12 *Artaxerxes, [R]king of kings, Dan. 2:37
To Ezra the priest, a scribe of the Law
of the God of heaven:
Perfect *peace*, [R]and so forth. Ezra 4:10
13 I issue a decree that all those of the
people of Israel and the priests and
Levites in my realm, who volunteer to
go up to Jerusalem, may go with you.
14 And whereas you are being sent by the
king and his seven counselors to inquire
concerning Judah and Jerusalem, with
regard to the Law of your God which *is*
in your hand;
15 and *whereas you are* to carry the silver
and gold which the king and his
counselors have freely offered to the
God of Israel, [R]whose dwelling *is* in
Jerusalem; Ezra 6:12
16 and *whereas* all the silver and gold that
you may find in all the province of
Babylon, along with the freewill offering
of the people and the priests, *are to be*
[R]freely offered for the [T]house of their
God in Jerusalem— 1 Chr. 29:6, 9 • Temple
17 now therefore, be careful to buy with
this money bulls, rams, and lambs, with
their grain offerings and their drink
offerings, and offer them on the altar of
the house of your God in Jerusalem.
18 And whatever seems good to you and
your brethren to do with the rest of the
silver and the gold, do it according to
the will of your God.
19 Also the articles that are given to you
for the service of the house of your
God, deliver in full before the God of
Jerusalem.
20 And whatever more may be needed for
the house of your God, which you may
have occasion to provide, pay *for it*
from the king's treasury.
21 And I, *even* I, Artaxerxes the king, do
issue a decree to all the treasurers who
are in the region beyond the River, that
whatever Ezra the priest, the scribe of
the Law of the God of heaven, may
require of you, let it be done diligently,
22 up to one hundred talents of silver, one
hundred kors of wheat, [T]one hundred
baths of wine, one hundred baths of oil,
and salt without prescribed limit. 600 gal.
23 Whatever is commanded by the God of
heaven, let it diligently be done for the
[T]house of the God of heaven. For why
should there be wrath against the realm
of the king and his sons? Temple
24 Also we inform you that it shall not be
lawful to impose tax, tribute, or custom
on any of the priests, Levites, singers,
gatekeepers, Nethinim, or servants of
this house of God.
25 And you, Ezra, according to your God-
given wisdom, [R]set magistrates and
judges who may judge all the people
who *are in the region* beyond the River,
all such as know the laws of your God;
and [R]teach those who do not know
them. Ex. 18:21, 22 • [Mal. 2:7]
26 Whoever will not observe the law of
your God and the law of the king, let
judgment be executed speedily on him,
whether *it be* death, or banishment, or
confiscation of goods, or imprisonment.

Ezra's Response

27 [R]Blessed* *be* the LORD God of our fathers, [R]who has put *such a thing* as this in the
king's heart, to beautify the house of the
LORD which *is* in Jerusalem, 1 Chr. 29:10 • Ezra 6:22
28 and [R]has extended mercy to me before
the king and his counselors, and before all
the king's mighty princes. Ezra 9:9
So I was encouraged, as the hand of the
LORD my God *was* upon me; and I gathered
chief men of Israel to go up with me.

CHAPTER 8

Census of the Returning Israelites

THESE *are* the heads of their fathers'
houses, and *this is* the genealogy of those
who went up with me from Babylon, in the
reign of King Artaxerxes:

7:12 The original language of Ezra 7:12 through 7:26 is Aramaic. **7:27** The Hebrew language resumes in Ezra 7:27.

2 of the sons of Phinehas, Gershom; of the
sons of Ithamar, Daniel; of the sons of David,
[R]Hattush; 1 Chr. 3:22
3 of the sons of Shecaniah, of the sons of
[R]Parosh, Zechariah; and registered with him
were one hundred and fifty males; Ezra 2:3
4 of the sons of [R]Pahath-Moab, Elihoenai
the son of Zerahiah, and with him two hundred males; Ezra 10:30
5 of the sons of Shechaniah, Ben-Jahaziel,
and with him three hundred males;
6 of the sons of Adin, Ebed the son of
Jonathan, and with him fifty males;
7 of the sons of Elam, Jeshaiah the son of
Athaliah, and with him seventy males;
8 of the sons of Shephatiah, Zebadiah the
son of Michael, and with him eighty males;
9 of the sons of Joab, Obadiah the son of
Jehiel, and with him two hundred and eighteen males;
10 of the sons of Shelomith, Ben-Josiphiah,
and with him one hundred and sixty males;
11 of the sons of Bebai, Zechariah the son of
Bebai, and with him twenty-eight males;
12 of the sons of Azgad, Johanan [T]the son of
Hakkatan, and with him one hundred and ten
males; Or *the youngest son,*
13 of the last sons of Adonikam, whose
names *are* these—Eliphelet, Jeiel, and
Shemaiah—and with them sixty males;
14 also of the sons of Bigvai, Uthai and
Zabbud, and with them seventy males.

Acquisition of Temple Leadership

15 Now I gathered them by the river that
flows to Ahava, and we camped there three
days. And I looked among the people and the
priests, and found none of the [R]sons of Levi
there. Ezra 7:7; 8:2
16 Then I sent for Eliezer, Ariel, Shemaiah,
Elnathan, Jarib, Elnathan, Nathan, Zechariah, and [R]Meshullam, leaders; also for Joiarib
and Elnathan, men of understanding. Ezra 10:15
17 And I gave them a command for Iddo
the chief man at the place Casiphia, and I
told them what they should say to Iddo *and*
his brethren the Nethinim at the place Casiphia—that they should bring us servants for
the house of our God.
18 Then, by the good hand of our God upon
us, they [R]brought us a man of understanding,
of the sons of Mahli the son of Levi, the son
of Israel, namely Sherebiah, with his sons and
brothers, eighteen men; Neh. 8:7
19 and [R]Hashabiah, and with him Jeshaiah
of the sons of Merari, his brothers and their
sons, twenty men; Neh. 12:24
20 also of the Nethinim, whom David and
the leaders had appointed for the service of
the Levites, two hundred and twenty Nethinim. All of them were designated by name.

Proclamation of a Fast

21 Then I [R]proclaimed a fast there at the
river of Ahava, that we might [R]humble ourselves before our God, to seek from Him the
[R]right way for us and our little ones and all
our possessions. 1 Sam. 7:6 • Is. 58:3, 5 • Ps. 5:8
22 For [R]I was ashamed to request of the
king an escort of soldiers and horsemen to
help us against the enemy on the road, because we had spoken to the king, saying,
"The hand of our God *is* upon all those for
[R]good who seek Him, but His power and His
wrath *are* [R]against all those who [R]forsake
Him." 1 Cor. 9:15 • [Rom. 8:28] • [Ps. 34:16] • [2 Chr. 15:2]
23 So we fasted and entreated our God for
this, and He [R]answered our prayer. 2 Chr. 33:13

The Return Is Completed

24 Then I separated twelve of the leaders of
the priests—Sherebiah, Hashabiah, and ten of
their brethren with them—
25 and weighed out to them [R]the silver, the
gold, and the articles, the offering for the
house of our God which the king and his
counselors and his princes, and all Israel *who*
were present, had offered. Ezra 7:15, 16
26 I even weighed into their hand [T]six hundred and fifty talents of silver, silver articles
weighing one hundred talents, [T]one hundred
talents of gold, $249,600,000 • $576,000,000
27 twenty gold basins *worth* a [T]thousand
drachmas, and two vessels of fine polished
bronze, precious as gold. $1,424,176
28 And I said to them, "You *are* [T]holy to the
LORD; the articles *are* holy also; and the silver
and the gold *are* a freewill offering to the
LORD God of your fathers. *consecrated*
29 "Watch and keep *them* until you weigh
them before the leaders of the priests and the
Levites and [R]heads of the fathers' *houses* of
Israel in Jerusalem, *in* the chambers of the
house of the LORD." Ezra 4:3
30 So the priests and the Levites received
the silver and the gold and the articles by
weight, to bring *them* to Jerusalem to the
house of our God.
31 Then we departed from the river of
Ahava on the twelfth *day* of the first month,
to go to Jerusalem. And [R]the hand of our God
was upon us, and He delivered us from the
hand of the enemy and from ambush along
the road. Ezra 7:6, 9, 28
32 So we [R]came to Jerusalem, and stayed
there three days. Neh. 2:11
33 Now on the fourth day the silver and the
gold and the articles were weighed in the
house of our God by the hand of Meremoth
the son of Uriah the priest, and with him *was*
Eleazar the son of Phinehas; with them *were*
the Levites, [R]Jozabad the son of Jeshua and
Noadiah the son of Binnui, Neh. 11:16

34 with the number *and* weight of everything. All the weight was written down at that time.

35 The children of those who had been carried away captive, who had come from the captivity, [R]offered burnt offerings to the God of Israel: twelve bulls for all Israel, ninety-six rams, seventy-seven lambs, and twelve male goats *as* a sin offering. All *this was* a burnt offering to the LORD. Ezra 6:17

36 And they delivered the king's orders to the king's satraps and the governors *in the region* beyond the River. So they gave support to the people and the house of God.

CHAPTER 9

Israel Intermarries

WHEN these things were done, the leaders came to me, saying, "The people of Israel and the priests and the Levites have not separated themselves from the peoples of the lands, with respect to the abominations of the Canaanites, the Hittites, the Perizzites, the Jebusites, the Ammonites, the Moabites, the Egyptians, and the Amorites.

2 "For they have taken some of their daughters *as wives* for themselves and their sons, so that the holy seed is intermingled with the peoples of *those* lands. Indeed, the hand of the leaders and rulers has been foremost in this [T]trespass." *unfaithfulness*

Lamentation of Ezra

3 So when I heard this thing, [R]I tore my garment and my robe, and plucked out some of the hair of my head and beard, and sat down [R]astonished. Job 1:20 • Ps. 143:4

4 Then everyone who trembled at the words of the God of Israel assembled to me, because of the transgression of those who had been carried away captive, and I sat astonished until the evening sacrifice.

God's Faithfulness

5 At the evening sacrifice I arose from my fasting; and having torn my garment and my robe, I fell on my knees and [R]spread out my hands to the LORD my God, Ex. 9:29

6 and said, "O my God: I am too [R]ashamed and humiliated to lift up my face to You, my God; for [R]our iniquities have risen higher than *our* heads, and our guilt has [R]grown up to the heavens. Dan. 9:7, 8 • Ps. 38:4 • Rev. 18:5

7 "Since the days of our fathers to this day we *have been* very guilty, and for our iniquities we, our kings, *and* our priests have been delivered into the hand of the kings of the lands, to the sword, to captivity, to plunder, and to humiliation, as *it is* this day.

8 "And now for a little while grace has been *shown* from the LORD our God, to leave us a remnant to escape, and to give us a peg in His holy place, that our God may [R]enlighten our eyes and give us a measure of revival in our bondage. Ps. 34:5

9 "For we *were* slaves. Yet our God did not forsake us in our bondage; but [R]He extended mercy to us in the sight of the kings of Persia, to revive us, to repair the house of our God, to rebuild its ruins, and to give us [R]a wall in Judah and Jerusalem. Ezra 7:28 • Is. 5:2

Israel's Unfaithfulness

10 "And now, O our God, what shall we say after this? For we have forsaken Your commandments,

11 "which You have commanded by Your servants the prophets, saying, 'The land which you are entering to possess is an unclean land, with the [R]uncleanness of the peoples of the lands, with their abominations which have filled it from one end to another with their impurity. Ezra 6:21

12 'Now therefore, do not give your daughters as wives for their sons, nor take their daughters to your sons; and never seek their peace or prosperity, that you may be strong and eat the good of the land, and leave *it* as an inheritance to your children forever.'

13 "And after all that has come upon us for our evil deeds and for our great guilt, since You our God [R]have punished us less than our iniquities *deserve,* and have given us *such* deliverance as this, [Ps. 103:10]

14 "should we [R]again break Your commandments, and join in marriage with the people of these abominations? Would You not be [R]angry with us until You had [T]consumed *us,* so that *there would be* no remnant or survivor? [John 5:14] • Deut. 9:8 • *destroyed*

15 "O LORD God of Israel, [R]You *are* righteous, for we are left as a remnant, as *it is* this day. [R]Here we *are* before You, [R]in our guilt, though no one can stand before You because of this!" Dan. 9:14 • [Rom. 3:19] • 1 Cor. 15:17

CHAPTER 10

Israel Laments

NOW while Ezra was praying, and while he was confessing, weeping, and bowing down before the house of God, a very large congregation of men, women, and children assembled to him from Israel; for the people wept very [R]bitterly. Neh. 8:1–9

2 And Shechaniah the son of Jehiel, *one* of the sons of Elam, spoke up and said to Ezra, "We have [R]trespassed[T] against our God, and have taken pagan wives from the peoples of the land; yet now there is hope in Israel in spite of this. Neh. 13:23–27 • *been unfaithful to*

SHALOM!

Most people, whether they know any Hebrew words other than *amen, hallelujah,* and *cherubim* or not, have heard the word *shālôm*. This noun comes from the root word *shālēm*, "to be complete" or "whole." The basic idea of the root is one of wholeness, unity, fulfillment, and good relationships. *Shālôm* occurs about 250 times in the Old Testament and is a doctrinally significant word.

Shālôm as a Greeting

While not the most common usage, *shālôm* as a greeting is probably the best known today, occurring about twenty-five times in the Old Testament. Second Kings 4:26 is a good example: "*Is it* well with you? *Is it* well with your husband? *Is it* well with the child?" (In each case, "well" is *shālôm*.) The idea is: "Are you in a safe and sound condition?" When young David went to the battlefield in 1 Samuel 17:22, we read that he "greeted [lit. "asked regarding the peace of"] his brothers" (NKJV). The old man in Judges 19:20 greeted the strangers in town, "Peace *be* with you!" This famous expression has come to the West in its Latin form *pax tecum* (singular) or *pax vobiscum* (plural).

Modern Israelis use *shālôm* almost like the Hawaiian *aloha*, both as "hello" and "good-bye." Our idiom "How are you?" in today's Hebrew becomes literally, "What is your *shālôm* ["welfare," "peace," "prosperity"]?" The related Arabic greeting is *salaam*.

Shālôm as Good Relationships

We tend to think of peace as the absence of war or hostilities. The Hebrew word is more positive, suggesting the presence of unity and amicable relationships. This most common usage in the Old Testament occurs between fifty and sixty times.

Regarding King Solomon (Heb. *Shelōmōh*), whose very name is related to this concept, we read that "he had peace on every side all around him" (1 Kin. 4:24). Because David had been a warrior and a man of blood, God rather chose his son Solomon, who was a man of peace, to build the temple.

Peace with God

"Peace with God" is theologically the most important usage, and also the most common (about two-thirds of the Old Testament occurrences of *shālôm*). This peace is a gift from God, and cannot be earned. It often occurs in context of a covenant of peace (see the word study on *covenant* on p. 25). God made such a covenant with Abram in Genesis 15:15.

One of the best-known and best-loved passages in the Old Testament has God's representatives, the Levites, giving a blessing of peace. It is called the Aaronic benediction: "The LORD bless you and keep you; the LORD make His face shine upon you, and be gracious to you; the LORD lift up His countenance upon you, and give you peace" (Num. 6:24–26).

Prince of Peace (*Sar Shālôm*)

"Prince of Peace" (*Sar Shālôm*) is one of Isaiah's several titles of the Messiah (9:6). The enmity and hostility of men against the Lord and against His Messiah are clearly drawn in Psalm 2 and several other texts.

Peace in the New Testament

One of the benefits of the Greek version of the Old Testament (LXX) is that it brought into a world language much of the truth of the Old Testament revelation. Then, building on the Hebrew original, the New Testament picks up these rich concepts and pours them into the Greek word *eirēnē*.

In Ephesians 2:14, Paul writes that "[Jesus] Himself is our peace." Good relationships are restored between God and those who accept Christ as their Savior. Christ also initiates good relationships between those Jews and Gentiles accepting the Messiah, who pulls down the barriers between us and creates in Himself "one new man" (2:15).

Because we have been "justified by faith, we have peace with God through our Lord Jesus Christ" (Rom. 5:1). His Spirit at work in our lives grants us this peace (Gal. 5:22).

The Covenant Is Instituted

3 "Now therefore, let us make a covenant with our God to put away all these wives and those who have been born to them, according to the counsel of my master and of those who tremble at the commandment of our God; and let it be done according to the law.

4 "Arise, for *this* matter *is* your *responsibility*. We also *will be* with you. [R]Be of good courage, and do *it*." 1 Chr. 28:10

5 Then Ezra arose, and made the leaders of the priests, the Levites, and all Israel [R]swear an oath that they would do according to this word. So they swore an oath. Neh. 5:12; 13:25

Separation Is Accepted

6 Then Ezra rose up from before the house of God, and went into the chamber of Jehohanan the son of Eliashib; and *when* he came there, he [R]ate no bread and drank no water, for he mourned because of the guilt of those from the captivity. Deut. 9:18

7 And they issued a proclamation throughout Judah and Jerusalem to all the descendants of the captivity, that they must gather at Jerusalem,

8 and that whoever would not come within three days, according to the counsel of the leaders and elders, all his property would be confiscated, and he himself would be separated from the congregation of those from the captivity.

9 So all the men of Judah and Benjamin gathered at Jerusalem within three days. It *was* the ninth month, on the twentieth *day* of the month; and [R]all the people sat in the open square of the house of God, trembling because of *this* matter and because of heavy rain. 1 Sam. 12:18

10 Then Ezra the priest stood up and said to them, "You have [T]transgressed and have [T]taken pagan wives, adding to the guilt of Israel. *acted unfaithfully* • Heb. *brought back*

11 "Now therefore, make confession to the LORD God of your fathers, and do His will; [R]separate yourselves from the peoples of the land, and from the pagan wives." Ezra 10:3

12 Then all the congregation answered and said with a loud voice, "Yes! As you have said, so we must do.

13 "But *there are* many people; *it is* the season for heavy rain, and we are not able to stand outside. Nor *is this* the work of one or two days, for *there are* many of us who have transgressed in this matter.

14 "Please, let the leaders of our entire congregation stand; and let all those in our cities who have taken pagan wives come at appointed times, together with the elders and judges of their cities, until [R]the fierce wrath of our God is turned away from us in this matter." 2 Chr. 28:11–13; 29:10; 30:8

15 Only Jonathan the son of Asahel and Jahaziah the son of Tikvah opposed this, and [R]Meshullam and Shabbethai the Levite gave them support. Neh. 3:4

16 Then the descendants of the captivity did so. And Ezra the priest, *with* certain heads of the fathers' *households*, were set apart by the fathers' *households*, each of them by name; and they sat down on the first day of the tenth month to examine the matter.

17 By the first day of the first month they finished *questioning* all the men who had taken pagan wives.

Separation of Priests

18 And among the sons of the priests who had taken pagan wives *the following* were found of the sons of [R]Jeshua the son of [T]Jozadak, and his brothers: Maaseiah, Eliezer, Jarib, and Gedaliah. Ezra 5:2 • *Jehozadak*, 1 Chr. 6:14

19 And they gave their promise that they would put away their wives; and *being* [R]guilty, *they presented* a ram of the flock as their [R]trespass offering. Lev. 6:4, 6 • Lev. 5:6, 15

20 Also of the sons of Immer: Hanani and Zebadiah;

21 of the sons of Harim: Maaseiah, Elijah, Shemaiah, Jehiel, and Uzziah;

22 of the sons of Pashhur: Elioenai, Maaseiah, Ishmael, Nethaneel, Jozabad, and Elasah.

Separation of Levites

23 Also of the Levites: Jozabad, Shimei, Kelaiah (the same *is* Kelita), Pethahiah, Judah, and Eliezer.

24 Also of the singers: Eliashib; and of the gatekeepers: Shallum, Telem, and Uri.

Separation of People

25 And others of Israel: of the [R]sons of Parosh: Ramiah, Jeziah, Malchiah, Mijamin, Eleazar, Malchijah, and Benaiah; Ezra 2:3; 8:3

26 of the sons of Elam: Mattaniah, Zechariah, Jehiel, Abdi, Jeremoth, and Eliah;

27 of the sons of Zattu: Elioenai, Eliashib, Mattaniah, Jeremoth, Zabad, and Aziza;

28 of the [R]sons of Bebai: Jehohanan, Hananiah, Zabbai, *and* Athlai; Ezra 8:11

29 of the sons of Bani: Meshullam, Malluch, Adaiah, Jashub, Sheal, *and* Ramoth;

30 of the [R]sons of Pahath-Moab: Adna, Chelal, Benaiah, Maaseiah, Mattaniah, Bezaleel, Binnui, and Manasseh; Ezra 8:4

31 *of* the sons of Harim: Eliezer, Ishijah, Malchijah, Shemaiah, Shimeon,

32 Benjamin, Malluch, *and* Shemariah;

33 of the sons of Hashum: Mattenai, Mattattah, Zabad, Eliphelet, Jeremai, Manasseh, *and* Shimei;

34 of the sons of Bani: Maadai, Amram, Uel,

35 Benaiah, Bedeiah, [T]Cheluh, Or *Cheluhi*

36 Vaniah, Meremoth, Eliashib,
37 Mattaniah, Mattenai, [T]Jaasai, Or *Jaasu*
38 Bani, Binnui, Shimei,
39 Shelemiah, Nathan, Adaiah,
40 Machnadebai, Shashai, Sharai,
41 Azareel, Shelemiah, Shemariah,
42 Shallum, Amariah, *and* Joseph;
43 of the sons of Nebo: Jeiel, Mattithiah,
Zabad, Zebina, Jaddai, Joel, *and* Benaiah.
44 All these had taken pagan wives, and
some of them had wives *by whom* they had
children.

Weights

Unit	*Weight*	*Equivalents*	*Translations*
Jewish Weights			
Talent	c. 75 pounds for common talent, c. 150 pounds for royal talent	60 minas; 3,000 shekels	talent
Mina	1.25 pounds	50 shekels	mina
Shekel	c. .4 ounce (11.4 grams) for common shekel c. .8 ounce for royal shekel	2 bekas; 20 gerahs	shekel
Beka	c. .2 ounce (5.7 grams)	½ shekel; 10 gerahs	half a shekel
Gerah	c. .02 ounce (.57 grams)	1/20 shekel	gerah
Roman Weight			
Litra	12 ounces		pound

Measures of Length

Unit	*Length*	*Equivalents*	*Translations*
Day's journey	c. 20 miles		day's journey
Roman mile	4,854 feet	8 stadia	mile
Sabbath day's journey	3,637 feet	6 stadia	Sabbath day's journey
Stadion	606 feet	⅛ Roman mile	furlong
Rod	9 feet (10.5 feet in Ezekiel)	3 paces; 6 cubits	measuring reed, reed
Fathom	6 feet	4 cubits	fathom
Pace	3 feet	⅓ rod; 2 cubits	pace
Cubit	18 inches	½ pace; 2 spans	cubit
Span	9 inches	½ cubit; 3 handbreadths	span
Handbreadth	3 inches	⅓ span; 4 fingers	handbreadth
Finger	.75 inches	¼ handbreadth	finger

THE BOOK OF

NEHEMIAH

THE BOOK OF NEHEMIAH

Nehemiah, contemporary of Ezra and cupbearer to the king in the Persian palace, leads the third and last return to Jerusalem after the Babylonian exile. His concern for the welfare of Jerusalem and its inhabitants prompts him to take bold action. Granted permission to return to his homeland, Nehemiah challenges his countrymen to arise and rebuild the shattered wall of Jerusalem. In spite of opposition from without and abuse from within, the task is completed in only fifty-two days, a feat even the enemies of Israel must attribute to God's enabling. By contrast, the task of reviving and reforming the people of God within the rebuilt wall demands years of Nehemiah's godly life and leadership.

The Hebrew for Nehemiah is *Nehemyah,* "Comfort of Yahweh." The book is named after its chief character, whose name appears in the opening verse. The combined book of Ezra-Nehemiah is given the Greek title *Esdras Deuteron,* "Second Esdras" (see "The Book of Ezra") in the Septuagint, a third-century B.C. Greek-language translation of the Hebrew Old Testament. The Latin title of Nehemiah is *Liber Secundus Esdrae,* "Second Book of Ezra" (Ezra was the first). At this point, it is considered a separate book from Ezra, and is later called *Liber Nehemiae,* "Book of Nehemiah."

THE AUTHOR OF NEHEMIAH

Clearly, much of this book came from Nehemiah's personal memoirs. The reporting is remarkably candid and vivid. Certainly 1:1—7:5; 12:27–43; and 13:4–31 are the "words of Nehemiah" (1:1). Some scholars think that Nehemiah composed those portions and compiled the rest. Others think that Ezra wrote 7:6—12:26 and 12:44—13:3, and that he compiled the rest making use of Nehemiah's diary. A third view that neither wrote it seems least likely from the evidence. Nehemiah 7:5–73 is almost the same as Ezra 2:1–70, and both lists may have been taken from another record of the same period.

As cupbearer to Artaxerxes I, Nehemiah holds a position of great responsibility. His role of tasting the king's wine to prevent him from being poisoned places Nehemiah in a position of trust and confidence as one of the king's advisers. As governor of Jerusalem from 444 to 432 B.C. (5:14; 8:9; 10:1; 13:6), Nehemiah demonstrates courage, compassion for the oppressed, integrity, godliness, and selflessness. He is willing to give up the luxury and ease of the palace to help his people. He is a dedicated layman who has the right priorities and is concerned for God's work, who is able to encourage and rebuke at the right times, who is strong in prayer, and who gives all glory and credit to God.

THE TIME OF NEHEMIAH

See "The Time of Ezra," because both Ezra and Nehemiah share the same historical background. The Book of Nehemiah fits within the reign of Artaxerxes I of Persia (464–423 B.C.). Esther is Artaxerxes' stepmother, and it is possible that she is instrumental in Nehemiah's appointment as the king's cupbearer. Nehemiah leaves Persia in the twentieth year of Artaxerxes (2:1), returns to Persia in the thirty-second year of Artaxerxes (13:6), and leaves again for Jerusalem "after certain days" (13:6), perhaps about 425 B.C. This book could not have been completed until after his second visit to Jerusalem.

The historical reliability of this book is supported by the Elephantine papyri. These ancient documents mention Sanballat (2:19) and Jehohanan (6:18; 12:23) and indicate that Bigvai replaces Nehemiah as governor of Judah by 410 B.C.

Malachi lives and ministers during Nehemiah's time, and a comparison of the books shows that many of the evils encountered by Nehemiah are specifically denounced by Malachi. The cold-hearted indifference toward God described in both books remains a problem in Israel during the four hundred years before Christ, during which there is no revelation from God.

THE CHRIST OF NEHEMIAH

Like Ezra, Nehemiah portrays Christ in His ministry of restoration. Nehemiah illustrates Christ in that he gives up a high position in order to identify with the plight of his people; he comes with a specific mission and fulfills it; and his life is characterized by prayerful dependence upon God.

In this book, everything is restored except the king. The temple is rebuilt, Jerusalem is reconstructed, the covenant is renewed, and the people are reformed. The messianic line is intact, but the King is yet to come. The decree of Artaxerxes in his twentieth year (2:2) marks the beginning point of Daniel's prophecy of the seventy weeks (see Dan. 9:25–27). "Know therefore and understand, *that* from the going forth of the command to restore and build Jerusalem until Messiah the Prince, *there shall be* seven weeks and sixty-two weeks; the street shall be built again, and the wall, even in troublesome times" (Dan. 9:25). The Messiah will come at the end of the sixty-nine weeks, and this is exactly fulfilled in A.D. 33 (see "The Christ of Daniel").

KEYS TO NEHEMIAH

Key Word: Jerusalem Walls—While Ezra deals with the religious restoration of Judah, Nehemiah is primarily concerned with Judah's political and geographical restoration. The first seven chapters are devoted to the rebuilding of Jerusalem's walls, because Jerusalem was the spiritual and political center of Judah. Without walls, Jerusalem could hardly be considered a city at all. As governor, Nehemiah also establishes firm civil authority. Ezra and Nehemiah work together to build the people spiritually and morally so that the restoration will be complete.

Key Verses: Nehemiah 6:15, 16; 8:8—"So the wall was finished on the twenty-fifth *day* of *the month* of Elul, in fifty-two days. And it happened, when all our enemies heard *of it,* and all the nations around us saw *these things,* that they were very disheartened in their own eyes; for they perceived that this work was done by our God" (6:15, 16).

"So they read distinctly from the book, in the Law of God; and they gave the sense, and helped *them* to understand the reading" (8:8).

Key Chapter: Nehemiah 9—The key to the Old Testament is the covenant, which is its theme and unifying factor. Israel's history can be divided according to the nation's obedience or disobedience to God's conditional covenant: blessings from obedience and destruction from disobedience. Nehemiah 9 records that upon completion of the Jerusalem wall the nation reaffirmed its loyalty to the covenant.

SURVEY OF NEHEMIAH

Nehemiah is closely associated with the ministry of his contemporary, Ezra. Ezra is a priest who brings spiritual revival; Nehemiah is a governor who brings physical and political reconstruction and leads the people in moral reform. They combine to make an effective team in rebuilding the postexilic remnant. Malachi, the last Old Testament prophet, also ministers during this time to provide additional moral and spiritual direction. The Book of Nehemiah takes us to the end of the historical account in the Old Testament, about four hundred years before the birth of the promised Messiah. Its two divisions are: the reconstruction of the wall (1—7), and the restoration of the people (8—13).

The Reconstruction of the Wall (1—7): Nehemiah's great concern for his people and the welfare of Jerusalem leads him to take bold action. The walls of Jerusalem, destroyed by Nebuchadnezzar in 586 B.C., evidently have been almost rebuilt after 464 B.C. when Artaxerxes I took the throne of Persia (see Ezra 4:6–23). When he hears that opposition led to their second destruction, Nehemiah prays on behalf of his people and then secures Artaxerxes' permission, provision, and protection for the massive project of rebuilding the walls.

The return under Nehemiah in 444 B.C. takes place thirteen years after the return led by Ezra, and ninety-four years after the return led by Zerubbabel. Nehemiah inspects the walls and challenges the people to "rise up and build" (2:18). Work begins immediately on the wall and its gates, with people building portions corresponding to where they are living.

However, opposition quickly arises, first in the form of mockery, then in the form of conspiracy when the work is progressing at an alarming rate. Nehemiah overcomes threats of force by setting half of the people on military watch and half on construction. While the external opposition continues to mount, internal opposition also surfaces. The wealthier Jews are abusing and oppressing the people, forcing them to mortgage their property and sell their children into slavery. Nehemiah

FOCUS	RECONSTRUCTION OF THE WALL		RESTORATION OF THE PEOPLE	
REFERENCE	1:1	3:1	8:1	11:1 — 13:31
DIVISION	PREPARATION TO RECONSTRUCT THE WALL	RECONSTRUCTION OF THE WALL	RENEWAL OF THE COVENANT	OBEDIENCE TO THE COVENANT
TOPIC	POLITICAL		SPIRITUAL	
	CONSTRUCTION		INSTRUCTION	
LOCATION	JERUSALEM			
TIME	19 YEARS (444 – 425 B.C.)			

again deals with the problem by the twin means of prayer and action. He also leads by example when he sacrifices his governor's salary. In spite of deceit, slander, and treachery, Nehemiah continues to trust in God and to press on with singleness of mind until the work is completed. The task is accomplished in an incredible fifty-two days, and even the enemies recognize that it can only have been accomplished with the help of God (6:16).

The Restoration of the People (8—13): The construction of the walls is followed by consecration and consolidation of the people. Ezra the priest is the leader of the spiritual revival (8—10), reminiscent of the reforms he led thirteen years earlier (Ezra 9 and 10). Ezra stands on a special wooden podium after the completion of the walls and gives the people a marathon reading of the law, translating from the Hebrew into Aramaic so they can understand. They respond with weeping, confession, obedience, and rejoicing. The Levites and priests lead them in a great prayer that surveys God's past work of deliverance and loyalty on behalf of His people, and magnifies God's attributes of holiness, justice, mercy, and love. The covenant is then renewed with God as the people commit themselves to separate from the Gentiles in marriage and to obey God's commandments.

Lots are drawn to determine who will remain in Jerusalem and who will return to the cities of their inheritance. One-tenth are required to stay in Jerusalem, and the rest of the land is resettled by the people and priests. The walls of Jerusalem are dedicated to the Lord in a joyful ceremony accompanied by instrumental and vocal music.

Unfortunately, Ezra's revival is short-lived; and Nehemiah, who returned to Persia in 432 B.C. (13:6), makes a second trip to Jerusalem about 425 B.C. to reform the people. He cleanses the temple, enforces the Sabbath, and requires the people to put away all foreign wives.

OUTLINE OF NEHEMIAH

Part One: The Reconstruction of the Wall (1:1—7:73)

I. The Preparation to Reconstruct the Wall . . . 1:1—2:20

- A. Discovery of the Broken Wall . . . 1:1–3
- B. Intercession of Nehemiah . . . 1:4—2:8
  - 1. Nehemiah Intercedes with God . . . 1:4–11
  - 2. Nehemiah Intercedes with Artaxerxes 2:1–8
- C. Arrival of Nehemiah in Jerusalem . . . 2:9–11
- D. Preparation to Reconstruct the Wall . . . 2:12–20
  - 1. Nehemiah Inspects the Broken Walls . . . 2:12–16
  - 2. Nehemiah Exhorts the People . . . 2:17, 18
  - 3. Nehemiah Answers the Enemies . . . 2:19, 20

II. The Reconstruction of the Wall . . . 3:1—7:73

- A. Record of the Builders . . . 3:1–32
- B. Opposition to the Reconstruction . . . 4:1—6:14
  - 1. Opposition Through Ridicule . . . 4:1–6
  - 2. Opposition Through Threat of Attack 4:7–9
  - 3. Opposition Through Discouragement . . . 4:10–23
  - 4. Opposition Through Extortion . . . 5:1–13
  - 5. Nehemiah's Unselfish Example . . . 5:14–19
  - 6. Opposition Through Compromise . . . 6:1–4
  - 7. Opposition Through Slander . . . 6:5–9
  - 8. Opposition Through Treachery . . . 6:10–14
- C. Completion of the Reconstruction . . . 6:15–19
- D. Organization of Jerusalem . . . 7:1–4
- E. Registration of Jerusalem . . . 7:5–73
  - 1. The Plan . . . 7:5, 6
  - 2. The Remnant of Known Descent . . . 7:7–60
    - a. The Leaders . . . 7:7
    - b. The Men of Israel . . . 7:8–38
    - c. The Priests . . . 7:39–42
    - d. The Levites . . . 7:43–45
    - e. The Servants . . . 7:46–60
  - 3. The Remnant of Unknown Descent 7:61–65
    - a. The Men of Israel . . . 7:61, 62
    - b. The Priests . . . 7:63–65
  - 4. The Total of the Remnant . . . 7:66–69
  - 5. The Gifts of the Remnant for the Temple . . . 7:70–73

Part Two: The Restoration of the People (8:1—13:31)

I. The Renewal of the Covenant . . . 8:1—10:39

- A. Interpretation of the Law . . . 8:1–18
  - 1. Reading of the Law . . . 8:1–8
  - 2. Response to the Reading . . . 8:9–18
    - a. Israel Celebrates Her Understanding of the Law . . . 8:9–12
    - b. Israel Obeys the Law . . . 8:13–18
- B. Reaffirmation of the Covenant . . . 9:1—10:39
  - 1. Spiritual Preparation of Israel . . . 9:1–3
  - 2. Reiteration of the Acts of Parties of the Covenant . . . 9:4–31
    - a. The Great Deliverances of God . . . 9:4–15
    - b. The Great Sins of Israel . . . 9:16–31
  - 3. Renewal of the Covenant . . . 9:32–38
  - 4. Ratifiers of the Covenant . . . 10:1–27
  - 5. Stipulations of the Covenant . . . 10:28–39

II. The Obedience to the Covenant . . . 11:1—13:31

- A. Resettlement of the People . . . 11:1–36
  - 1. Plan for the Resettlement . . . 11:1, 2
  - 2. Resettlement Within Jerusalem . . . 11:3–24
  - 3. Resettlement Outside of Jerusalem 11:25–36

CHAPTER 1

Discovery of the Broken Wall

THE words of [R]Nehemiah the son of Ha-
chaliah. Neh. 10:1
It came to pass in the month of Chislev,
in the twentieth year, as I was in [R]Shushan[T]
the [T]citadel, Esth. 1:1, 2, 5 • Or *Susa* • Or *fortified palace*
2 that [R]Hanani one of my brethren came
with men from Judah; and I asked them
concerning the Jews who had escaped, who
had survived the captivity, and concerning
Jerusalem. Neh. 7:2
3 And they said to me, "The survivors who
are left from the captivity in the [R]province
are there in great distress and reproach. The
wall of Jerusalem *is* also broken down, and its
gates *are* burned with fire." Neh. 7:6

Nehemiah Intercedes with God

4 So it was, when I heard these words, that
I sat down and wept, and mourned *for many*
days; I was fasting and praying before the
God of heaven.
5 And I said: "I pray, LORD God of heaven,
O great and awesome God, [R]*You* who keep
Your covenant and mercy with those who
love [T]You and observe [T]Your commandments, [Ex. 20:6; 34:6, 7] • Lit. *Him* • Lit. *His*
6 "please let Your ear be attentive and
[R]Your eyes open, that You may hear the
prayer of Your servant which I pray before
You now, day and night, for the children of
Israel Your servants, and [R]confess the sins of
the children of Israel which we have sinned
against You. Both my father's house and I
have sinned. 2 Chr. 6:40 • Dan. 9:20
7 "We have acted very corruptly against
You, and have [R]not kept the commandments,
the statutes, nor the ordinances which You
commanded Your servant Moses. Deut. 28:15
8 "Remember, I pray, the word that You
commanded Your servant Moses, saying, [R]'*If*
you [T]are unfaithful, I will scatter you among
the nations, Lev. 26:33 • *act treacherously*
9 'but *if* you return to Me, and keep My
commandments and do them, though some
of you were cast out to the farthest part of
the heavens, *yet* I will gather them from
there, and bring them to the place which I
have chosen as a dwelling for My name.'
10 "Now these *are* Your servants and Your
people, whom You have redeemed by Your
great power, and by Your strong hand.
11 "O Lord, I pray, please [R]let Your ear be
attentive to the prayer of Your servant, and
to the prayer of Your servants who [R]desire to
fear Your name; and let Your servant prosper
this day, I pray, and grant him mercy in the
sight of this man." For I was the king's
[R]cupbearer. Neh. 1:6 • Is. 26:8 • Neh. 2:1

CHAPTER 2

Nehemiah Intercedes with Artaxerxes

AND it came to pass in the month of Nisan,
in the twentieth year of King Artaxerxes, *when* wine *was* before him, that I took
the wine and gave it to the king. Now I had
never been sad in his presence before.
2 Therefore the king said to me, "Why *is*
your face sad, since you *are* not sick? This *is*
nothing but [R]sorrow of heart." Then I became
[T]dreadfully afraid, Prov. 15:13 • Lit. *very much*
3 and said to the king, "May the king live
forever! Why should my face not be sad,
when [R]the city, the place of my fathers'
tombs, *lies* waste, and its gates are burned
with [R]fire?" 2 Chr. 36:19 • Neh. 1:3
4 Then the king said to me, "What do you
request?" So I prayed to the God of heaven.
5 And I said to the king, "If it pleases the
king, and if your servant has found favor in
your sight, I ask that you send me to Judah,
to the city of my fathers' tombs, that I may
rebuild it."
6 So the king said to me (the queen also
sitting beside him), "How long will your
journey be? And when will you return?" So it
pleased the king to send me; and I set him [R]a
time. Neh. 5:14; 13:6
7 Furthermore I said to the king, "If it
pleases the king, let letters be given to me for
the governors *of the region* beyond [T]the
River, that they must permit me to pass
through till I come to Judah, The Euphrates
8 "and a letter to Asaph the keeper of the
king's forest, that he must give me timber to
make beams for the gates of the citadel
which *pertains* to the temple, for the city
wall, and for the house that I will occupy."
And the king granted *them* to me according
to the good hand of my God upon me.

Arrival of Nehemiah in Jerusalem

9 Then I went to the governors *in the*
region beyond the River, and gave them the
king's letters. Now the king had sent captains
of the army and horsemen with me.
10 When [R]Sanballat the Horonite and Tobiah the Ammonite [T]official heard *of it*, they

were deeply disturbed that a man had come to seek the well-being of the children of Israel. Neh. 2:19; 4:1 • Lit. *servant*

11 So I [R]came to Jerusalem and was there three days. Ezra 8:32

Nehemiah Inspects the Broken Walls

12 Then I arose in the night, I and a few men with me; I told no one what my God had put in my heart to do at Jerusalem; nor was there any animal with me, except the one on which I rode.

13 And I went out by night through the Valley Gate to the Serpent Well and the [T]Refuse Gate, and [T]viewed the walls of Jerusalem which were broken down and its gates which were burned with fire. *Dung* • *examined*

14 Then I went on to the [R]Fountain Gate and to the [R]King's Pool, but *there was* no room for the animal *that was* under me to pass. Neh. 3:15 • 2 Kin. 20:20

15 So I went up in the night by the valley, and viewed the wall; then I turned back and entered by the Valley Gate, and so returned.

16 And the officials did not know where I had gone or what I had done; I had not yet told the Jews, the priests, the nobles, the officials, or the others who did the work.

Nehemiah Exhorts the People

17 Then I said to them, "You see the distress that we *are* in, how Jerusalem *lies* waste, and its gates are burned with fire. Come and let us build the wall of Jerusalem, that we may no longer be a reproach."

18 And I told them of the hand of my God which had been good upon me, and also of the king's words that he had spoken to me. So they said, "Let us rise up and build." Then they set their hands to *do this* good *work*.

Nehemiah Answers the Enemies

19 But when Sanballat the Horonite, Tobiah the Ammonite official, and Geshem the Arab heard *of it*, they laughed us to scorn and despised us, and said, "What *is* this thing that you are doing? [R]Will you rebel against the king?" Neh. 6:6

20 So I answered them, and said to them, "The God of heaven Himself will prosper us; therefore we His servants will arise and build, [R]but you have no heritage or right or memorial in Jerusalem." Ezra 4:3

CHAPTER 3

Record of the Builders

THEN Eliashib the high priest rose up with his brethren the priests and built the Sheep Gate; they consecrated it and hung its doors. They built as far as the Tower of [T]the Hundred, *and* consecrated it, then as far as the Tower of Hananeel. Heb. *Hammeah*

2 Next to [T]Eliashib [R]the men of Jericho built. And next to them Zaccur the son of Imri built. Lit. *him* • Neh. 7:36

3 Also the sons of Hassenaah built the Fish Gate; they laid its beams and [R]hung its doors with its bolts and bars. Neh. 6:1; 7:1

4 And next to them [R]Meremoth the son of Urijah, the son of [T]Koz, made repairs. Next to them [R]Meshullam the son of Berechiah, the son of Meshezabeel, made repairs. Next to them Zadok the son of Baana made repairs. Ezra 8:33 • Or *Hakkoz* • Ezra 10:15

5 Next to them the Tekoites made repairs; but their nobles did not put their [T]shoulders to [R]the work of their Lord. Lit. *necks* • [Judg. 5:23]

6 Moreover Jehoiada the son of Paseah and Meshullam the son of Besodeiah repaired [R]the Old Gate; they laid its beams and hung its doors, with its bolts and bars. Neh. 12:39

7 And next to them Melatiah the Gibeonite, Jadon the Meronothite, the men of Gibeon and Mizpah, repaired the [R]residence[T] of the governor *of the region* [T]beyond the River. Neh. 2:7–9 • Lit. *throne* • West of the Euphrates

8 Next to him Uzziel the son of Harhaiah, one of the goldsmiths, made repairs. Also next to him Hananiah, [T]one of the perfumers, made repairs; and they [T]fortified Jerusalem as far as the Broad Wall. Lit. *the son* • *restored*

9 And next to them Rephaiah the son of Hur, leader of half the district of Jerusalem, made repairs.

10 Next to them Jedaiah the son of Harumaph made repairs in front of his house. And next to him Hattush the son of Hashabniah made repairs.

11 Malchijah the son of Harim and Hashub the son of Pahath-Moab repaired another section, as well as the Tower of the Ovens.

12 And next to him was Shallum the son of Hallohesh, leader of half the district of Jerusalem; he and his daughters made repairs.

13 Hanun and the inhabitants of Zanoah repaired [R]the Valley Gate. They built it, hung its doors with its bolts and bars, and *repaired* a [T]thousand cubits of the wall as far as [R]the Refuse Gate. Neh. 2:13, 15 • 1500 ft. • Neh. 2:13

14 Malchijah the son of Rechab, leader of the district of [R]Beth Haccerem, repaired the Refuse Gate; he built it and hung its doors with its bolts and bars. Jer. 6:1

15 Shallun the son of Col-Hozeh, leader of the district of Mizpah, repaired the Fountain Gate; he built it, covered it, hung its doors with its bolts and bars, and repaired the wall of the Pool of [R]Shelah[T] by the [R]King's Garden, as far as the stairs that go down from the City of David. Is. 8:6 • Or *Shiloah* • 2 Kin. 25:4

16 After him Nehemiah the son of Azbuk, leader of half the district of Beth Zur, made repairs as far as *the place* in front of the

tombs of David, to the [R]man-made pool, and as far as the House of the Mighty. 2 Kin. 20:20

17 After him the Levites, *under* Rehum the son of Bani, made repairs. Next to him Hashabiah, leader of half the district of Keilah, made repairs for his district.

18 After him their brethren, *under* Bavai the son of Henadad, leader of the *other* half of the district of Keilah, made repairs.

19 And next to him Ezer the son of Jeshua, the leader of Mizpah, repaired another section in front of the Ascent to the Armory at the [R]buttress.[T] 2 Chr. 26:9 • Lit. *turning*

20 After him Baruch the son of *Zabbai diligently repaired the other section, from the [T]buttress to the door of the house of Eliashib the high priest. Lit. *turning*

21 After him Meremoth the son of Urijah, the son of [T]Koz, repaired another section, from the door of the house of Eliashib to the end of the house of Eliashib. Or *Hakkoz*

22 And after him the priests, the men of the plain, made repairs.

23 After him Benjamin and Hasshub made repairs opposite their house. After them Azariah the son of Maaseiah, the son of Ananiah, made repairs by his house.

24 After him [R]Binnui the son of Henadad repaired another section, from the house of Azariah to [R]the [T]buttress, even as far as the corner. Ezra 8:33 • Neh. 3:19 • Lit. *turning*

25 Palal the son of Uzai *made repairs* opposite the buttress, and on the tower which projects from the king's upper house that *was* by the court of the prison. After him Pedaiah the son of Parosh *made repairs*.

26 Moreover [R]the Nethinim who dwelt in [R]Ophel *made repairs* as far as *the place* in front of the Water Gate toward the east, and on the projecting tower. Neh. 11:21 • 2 Chr. 27:3

27 After them the Tekoites repaired another section, next to the great projecting tower, and as far as the wall of Ophel.

28 Beyond the Horse Gate the priests made repairs, each in front of his *own* house.

29 After them Zadok the son of Immer made repairs in front of his *own* house. After him Shemaiah the son of Shechaniah, the keeper of the East Gate, made repairs.

30 After him Hananiah the son of Shelemiah, and Hanun, the sixth son of Zalaph, repaired another section. After him Meshullam the son of Berechiah made repairs in front of his [T]dwelling. Lit. *room*

31 After him Malchijah, one of the goldsmiths, made repairs as far as the house of the Nethinim and of the merchants, in front of the [T]Miphkad Gate, and as far as the upper room at the corner. Lit. *Inspection* or *Recruiting*

32 And between the upper room at the corner, as far as the Sheep Gate, the goldsmiths and the merchants made repairs.

CHAPTER 4

Opposition Through Ridicule

BUT it so happened, [R]when Sanballat heard that we were rebuilding the wall, that he was furious and very indignant, and mocked the Jews. Neh. 2:10, 19

2 And he spoke before his brethren and the army of Samaria, and said, "What are these feeble Jews doing? Will they fortify themselves? Will they offer sacrifices? Will they complete it in a day? Will they revive the stones from the heaps of rubbish—*stones* that are burned?"

3 Now [R]Tobiah the Ammonite *was* beside him, and he said, "Whatever they build, if even a fox goes up *on it*, he will break down their stone wall." Neh. 2:10, 19

4 Hear, O our God, for we are despised; turn their reproach on their own heads, and give them as plunder to a land of captivity!

5 [R]Do not cover their iniquity, and do not let their sin be blotted out from before You; for they have provoked *You* to anger before the builders. Jer. 18:23

6 So we built the wall, and the entire wall was joined together up to half its *height*, for the people had a mind to work.

Opposition Through Threat of Attack

7 Now it happened, [R]when Sanballat, Tobiah, [R]the Arabs, the Ammonites, and the Ashdodites heard that the walls of Jerusalem were being restored and the [T]gaps were beginning to be closed, that they became very angry, Neh. 4:1 • Neh. 2:19 • Lit. *breaks*

8 and all of them [R]conspired together to come *and* attack Jerusalem and create confusion. Ps. 83:3–5

9 Nevertheless [R]we made our prayer to our God, and because of them we set a watch against them day and night. [Ps. 50:15]

Opposition Through Discouragement

10 Then Judah said, "The strength of the laborers is failing, and *there is* so much rubbish that we are not able to build the wall."

11 And our adversaries said, "They will neither know nor see anything, till we come into their midst and kill them and cause the work to cease."

12 So it was, when the Jews who dwelt near them came, that they told us ten times, "From whatever place you turn, *they will be* upon us."

13 Therefore I positioned *men* behind the lower parts of the wall, at the openings; and I set the people according to their families, with their swords, their spears, and their bows.

3:20 A few Heb. mss., Syr., Vg. *Zaccai*

14 And I looked, and arose and said to the
nobles, to the leaders, and to the rest of the
people, "Do not be afraid of them. Remember
the Lord, [R]great and awesome, and fight for
your brethren, your sons, your daughters,
your wives, and your houses." [Deut. 10:17]
15 And it happened, when our enemies
heard that it was known to us, and [R]*that* God
had brought their counsel to nothing, that all
of us returned to the wall, everyone to his
work. Job 5:12
16 So it was, from that time on, *that* half of
my servants worked at construction, while
the other half held the spears, the shields, the
bows, and *wore* armor; and the leaders [T]*were*
behind all the house of Judah. Supported
17 Those who built on the wall, and those
who carried burdens, loaded themselves so
that with one hand they worked at construction, and with the other held a weapon.
18 Every one of the builders had his sword
girded at his side as he built. And the one
who sounded the trumpet *was* beside me.
19 Then I said to the nobles, the rulers, and
the rest of the people, "The work *is* great and
extensive, and we are separated far from one
another on the wall.
20 "*Therefore*, wherever you hear the sound
of the trumpet, rally to us there. [R]Our God
will fight for us." Ex. 14:14, 25
21 So we labored in the work, and half of
[T]the men held the spears from daybreak until
the stars appeared. Lit. *them*
22 At the same time I also said to the
people, "Let each man and his servant stay at
night in Jerusalem, that they may be our
guard by night and a working party by day."
23 So neither I, my brethren, my servants,
nor the men of the guard who followed me
took off our clothes, *except* that everyone
took them off for washing.

CHAPTER 5

Opposition Through Extortion

AND there was a great [R]outcry of the
people and their wives against their
[R]Jewish brethren. Neh. 5:7, 8 • Deut. 15:7
2 For there were those who said, "We, our
sons, and our daughters *are* many; therefore
let us get grain *for them*, that we may eat and
live."
3 There were also *some* who said, "We
have mortgaged our lands and vineyards and
houses, that we might buy grain because of
the famine."
4 There were also those who said, "We
have borrowed money for the king's tax *on*
our lands and vineyards.
5 "Yet now our flesh *is* as the flesh of our
brethren, our children as their children; and
indeed we are forcing our sons and our
daughters to be slaves, and *some* of our
daughters are brought into slavery *already. It
is* not in our power *to redeem them*, for other
men have our lands and vineyards."
6 And I became very angry when I heard
their outcry and these words.
7 After serious thought, I rebuked the
nobles and rulers, and said to them, "Each of
you is exacting usury from his brother." So I
called a great assembly against them.
8 And I said to them, "According to our
ability we have [R]redeemed our Jewish brethren who were sold to the nations. Now indeed, will you even sell your brethren? Or
should they be sold to us?" Then they were
silenced and found nothing *to say*. Lev. 25:48
9 Then I said, "What you are doing *is* not
good. Should you not walk [R]in the fear of our
God [R]because of the reproach of the nations,
our enemies?" Lev. 25:36 • 2 Sam. 12:14
10 "I also, *with* my brethren and my servants, am lending them money and grain.
Please, let us stop this [T]usury! *interest*
11 "Restore now to them, even this day,
their lands, their vineyards, their olive groves,
and their houses, also the hundredth *part* of
the money and the grain, the new wine and
the oil, that you have charged them."
12 So they said, "We will restore *it*, and will
require nothing from them; we will do as you
say." Then I called the priests, [R]and required
an oath from them that they would do according to this promise. Ezra 10:5
13 Then I shook out [T]the fold of my garment and said, "So may God shake out each
man from his house, and from his property,
who does not perform this promise. Even
thus may he be shaken out and emptied."
And all the congregation said, "Amen!" and
praised the LORD. [R]Then the people did according to this promise. Lit. *my lap* • 2 Kin. 23:3

Nehemiah's Unselfish Example

14 Moreover, from the time that I was
appointed to be their governor in the land of
Judah, from the twentieth year until the
thirty-second year of King Artaxerxes,
twelve years, neither I nor my brothers [R]ate
the governor's provisions. [1 Cor. 9:4–15]
15 But the former governors who *had been*
before me laid burdens on the people, and
took from them bread and wine, besides forty
shekels of silver; yes, even their servants bore
rule over the people, but I did not do so,
because of the [R]fear of God. Neh. 5:9
16 Indeed, I also continued the work on this
wall, and we did not buy any land. All my
servants *were* gathered there for the work.
17 Moreover *there were* [R]at my table one
hundred and fifty Jews and rulers, besides
those who came to us from the nations
around us. 1 Kin. 18:19
18 Now *that* which was prepared *for me*
daily *was* one ox *and* six choice sheep; also

fowl were prepared for me, and once every
ten days an abundance of all kinds of wine;
yet in spite of this [R]I did not demand the
governor's provisions, because the bondage
was heavy on this people. Neh. 5:14, 15
19 Remember me, my God, for good, *according to* all that I have done for this people.

CHAPTER 6

Opposition Through Compromise

NOW it happened when Sanballat, Tobiah,
[T]Geshem the Arab, and the rest of our
enemies heard that I had rebuilt the wall, and
that there were no breaks left in it [R](though
at that time I had not hung the doors in the
gates), Or *Gashmu* • Neh. 3:1, 3
2 that Sanballat and Geshem sent to me,
saying, "Come, let us meet together in [T]*one of*
the villages in the plain of Ono." But they
thought to do me harm. Or *Kephirim*
3 So I sent messengers to them, saying, "I
am doing a great work, so that I cannot come
down. Why should the work cease while I
leave it and go down to you?"
4 But they sent me this message four
times, and I answered them in the same
manner.

Opposition Through Slander

5 Then Sanballat sent his servant to me as
before, the fifth time, with an open letter in
his hand.
6 In it *was* written:

> It is reported among the nations, and
> Geshem says, *that* you and the Jews
> plan to rebel; therefore, according to
> these rumors, you are rebuilding the
> wall, that you may be their king.
> 7 And you have also appointed prophets
> to proclaim concerning you at
> Jerusalem, saying, "*There is* a king in
> Judah!" Now these matters will be
> reported to the king. So come,
> therefore, and let us take counsel
> together.

8 Then I sent to him, saying, "No such
things as you say are being done, but you
invent them in your own heart."
9 For they all *were trying to* make us
afraid, saying, "Their hands will be weakened
in the work, and it will not be done."
Now therefore, *O God,* strengthen my
hands.

Opposition Through Treachery

10 Afterward I came to the house of Shemaiah the son of Delaiah, the son of Mehetabeel,
who *was* a secret informer; and he said, "Let
us meet together in the house of God, within
the temple, and let us close the doors of the
temple, for they are coming to kill you;
indeed, at night they will come to kill you."
11 And I said, "Should such a man as I flee?
And who *is there* such as I who would go into
the temple to save his life? I will not go in!"
12 Then I perceived that God had not sent
him at all, but that [R]he pronounced *this*
prophecy against me because Tobiah and
Sanballat had hired him. Ezek. 13:22
13 For this reason he *was* hired, that I
should be afraid and act that way and sin, so
that they might have *occasion* for an evil
report, that they might reproach me.
14 My God, remember Tobiah and Sanballat, according to these their works, and the
prophetess Noadiah and the rest of the
prophets who would have made me afraid.

Completion of the Reconstruction

15 So the wall was finished on the twenty-
fifth *day of the month* of Elul, in fifty-two
days.
16 And it happened, when all our enemies
heard *of it,* and all the nations around us saw
these things, that they were very disheartened in their own eyes; for they perceived
that this work was done by our God.
17 Moreover in those days the nobles of
Judah sent many letters to Tobiah, and *the
letters of* Tobiah came to them.
18 For many in Judah were pledged to him,
because he was the [R]son-in-law of Shechaniah the son of Arah, and his son Jehohanan
had married the daughter of [R]Meshullam the
son of Berechiah. Neh. 13:4, 28 • Ezra 10:15
19 Also they reported his good deeds before
me, and reported my [T]words to him. *And*
Tobiah sent letters to frighten me. Or *affairs*

CHAPTER 7

Organization of Jerusalem

THEN it was, when the wall was built and I
had [R]hung the doors, when the gatekeepers, the singers, and the Levites had been
appointed, Neh. 6:1, 15
2 that I gave the charge of Jerusalem to
my brother Hanani, and Hananiah the leader
of the [T]citadel, for he *was* a faithful man and
[R]feared God more than many. *palace* • Ex. 18:21
3 And I said to them, "Do not let the gates
of Jerusalem be opened until the sun is hot;
and while they stand *guard,* let them shut the
doors and bar *them;* and appoint guards from
among the inhabitants of Jerusalem, one at
his watch station and another in front of his
own house."
4 Now the city *was* large and spacious, but
the people in it *were* [R]few, and the houses
were not rebuilt. Deut. 4:27

The Plan

5 Then my God put it into my heart to
gather the nobles, the rulers, and the people,
that they might be registered by genealogy.
And I found a register of the genealogy of
those who had come up in the first *return*,
and found written in it:

6 [R]These *are* the people of the province
who came back from the captivity, of
those who had been carried away,
whom Nebuchadnezzar the king of
Babylon had carried away *captive*, and
who returned to Jerusalem and Judah,
everyone to his *own* city. Ezra 2:1–70

The Leaders

7 Those who came with Zerubbabel *were*
Jeshua, Nehemiah, [T]Azariah, Raamiah,
Nahamani, Mordecai, Bilshan,
[T]Mispereth, Bigvai, Nehum, and Baanah.
The number of the men of the people
of Israel: *Seraiah*, Ezra 2:2 • *Mispar*, Ezra 2:2

The Men of Israel

8 the children of Parosh, two thousand
one hundred and seventy-two;
9 the children of Shephatiah, three
hundred and seventy-two;
10 the children of Arah, six hundred and
fifty-two;
11 the children of Pahath-Moab, of the
children of Jeshua and Joab, two
thousand eight hundred and eighteen;
12 the children of Elam, one thousand two
hundred and fifty-four;
13 the children of Zattu, eight hundred
and forty-five;
14 the children of Zaccai, seven hundred
and sixty;
15 the children of [T]Binnui, six hundred and
forty-eight; *Bani*, Ezra 2:10
16 the children of Bebai, six hundred and
twenty-eight;
17 the children of Azgad, two thousand
three hundred and twenty-two;
18 the children of Adonikam, six hundred
and sixty-seven;
19 the children of Bigvai, two thousand
and sixty-seven;
20 the children of Adin, six hundred and
fifty-five;
21 the children of Ater of Hezekiah,
ninety-eight;
22 the children of Hashum, three hundred
and twenty-eight;
23 the children of Bezai, three hundred and
twenty-four;
24 the children of [T]Hariph, one hundred
and twelve; *Jorah*, Ezra 2:18
25 the children of Gibeon, ninety-five;
26 the men of Bethlehem and Netophah,
one hundred and eighty-eight;
27 the men of Anathoth, one hundred and
twenty-eight;
28 the men of Beth Azmaveth, forty-two;
29 the men of [T]Kirjath Jearim, Chephirah,
and Beeroth, seven hundred and forty-
three; *Kirjath Arim*, Ezra 2:25
30 the men of Ramah and Geba, six
hundred and twenty-one;
31 the men of Michmas, one hundred and
twenty-two;
32 the men of Bethel and Ai, one hundred
and twenty-three;
33 the men of the other Nebo, fifty-two;
34 the children of the other Elam, one
thousand two hundred and fifty-four;
35 the children of Harim, three hundred
and twenty;
36 the children of Jericho, three hundred
and forty-five;
37 the children of Lod, Hadid, and Ono,
seven hundred and twenty-one;
38 the children of Senaah, three thousand
nine hundred and thirty.

The Priests

39 The priests: the children of [R]Jedaiah, of
the house of Jeshua, nine hundred and
seventy-three; 1 Chr. 24:7
40 the children of [R]Immer, one thousand
and fifty-two; 1 Chr. 9:12
41 the children of Pashhur, one thousand
two hundred and forty-seven;
42 the children of [R]Harim, one thousand
and seventeen. 1 Chr. 24:8

The Levites

43 The Levites: the children of Jeshua, of
Kadmiel, *and* of the children of
[T]Hodevah, seventy-four. *Hodaviah*, Ezra 2:40
44 The singers: the children of Asaph, one
hundred and forty-eight.
45 The gatekeepers: the children of
Shallum, the children of Ater, the
children of Talmon, the children of
Akkub, the children of Hatita, the
children of Shobai, one hundred and
thirty-eight.

The Servants

46 The Nethinim: the children of Ziha, the
children of Hasupha, the children of
Tabbaoth,
47 the children of Keros, the children of
[T]Sia, the children of Padon, *Siaha*, Ezra 2:44
48 the children of *Lebana, the children of
*Hagaba, the children of Salmai,
49 the children of Hanan, the children of
Giddel, the children of Gahar,
50 the children of Reaiah, the children of
Rezin, the children of Nekoda,

7:48 MT *Lebanah* 7:48 MT *Hogabah*

51 the children of Gazzam, the children of Uzza, the children of Paseah,
52 the children of Besai, the children of Meunim, the children of Nephishesim,
53 the children of Bakbuk, the children of Hakupha, the children of Harhur,
54 the children of Bazlith, the children of Mehida, the children of Harsha,
55 the children of Barkos, the children of Sisera, the children of Tamah,
56 the children of Neziah, and the children of Hatipha.
57 The children of Solomon's servants: the children of Sotai, the children of Sophereth, the children of Perida,
58 the children of Jaala, the children of Darkon, the children of Giddel,
59 the children of Shephatiah, the children of Hattil, the children of Pochereth of Zebaim, and the children of Amon.
60 All the Nethinim, and the children of Solomon's servants, *were* three hundred and ninety-two.

The Men of Israel

61 And these *were* the ones who came up from Tel Melah, Tel Harsha, Cherub, Addon, and Immer, but they could not identify their father's house nor their lineage, whether they *were* of Israel:
62 the children of Delaiah, the children of Tobiah, the children of Nekoda, six hundred and forty-two;

The Priests

63 and of the priests: the children of Habaiah, the children of [T]Koz, the children of Barzillai, who took a wife of the daughters of Barzillai the Gileadite, and was called by their name. Or *Hakkoz*
64 These sought their listing *among* those who were registered by genealogy, but it was not found; therefore they were excluded from the priesthood as defiled.
65 And the [T]governor said to them that they should not eat of the most holy things till a priest could consult with the Urim and Thummim. Or *Tirshatha*

The Total of the Remnant

66 Altogether the whole congregation *was* forty-two thousand three hundred and sixty,
67 besides their male and female servants, of whom *there were* seven thousand three hundred and thirty-seven; and they had two hundred and forty-five men and women singers.
68 Their horses were seven hundred and thirty-six, their mules two hundred and forty-five,
69 *their* camels four hundred and thirty-five, *and* donkeys six thousand seven hundred and twenty.

The Gifts of the Remnant for the Temple

70 And some of the heads of the fathers' houses gave to the work. [R]The [T]governor gave to the treasury [T]one thousand gold drachmas, fifty basins, and five hundred and thirty priestly garments. Neh. 8:9 • Or *Tirshatha* • $1,424,176
71 Some of the heads of the fathers' *houses* gave to the treasury of the work twenty thousand gold drachmas, and two thousand two hundred silver minas.
72 And *that* which the rest of the people gave *was* twenty thousand gold drachmas, two thousand silver minas, and sixty-seven priestly garments.

73 So the priests, the Levites, the gatekeepers, the singers, *some* of the people, the
Nethinim, and all Israel dwelt in their cities.
[R]When the seventh month came, the
children of Israel *were* in their cities. Ezra 3:1

CHAPTER 8

Reading of the Law

NOW all [R]the people gathered together as one man in the open square that *was* [R]in front of the Water Gate; and they told Ezra the [R]scribe to bring the Book of the Law of Moses, which the LORD had commanded Israel. Ezra 3:1 • Neh. 3:26 • Ezra 7:6
2 So Ezra the priest brought the Law be-
fore the congregation, of men and women
and all who *could* hear with understanding,
on the first day of the seventh month.

3 Then he [R]read from it in the open square
that *was* in front of the Water Gate [T]from
morning until midday, before the men and
women and those who could understand; and
the ears of all the people *were attentive* to
the Book of the Law. 2 Kin. 23:2 • Lit. *from the light*

8:3 Reading God's Word—The person who can read well has a much better opportunity of knowing and understanding God's Word than the person who has to rely upon what others tell him about the Word of God. Reading the Word of God is a very important part of communicating God's Word to God's people. Public Scripture reading was a regular part of the worship services in Israel and in the early church. Today we are blessed above all people in history, for not only does nearly everyone know how to read, but there also are enough copies of the Bible available so that everyone may have a personal copy. Here are some suggestions to aid you in receiving the greatest benefit from reading the Bible:

a. Read the Bible prayerfully. Ask the Spirit of God to meet your heart's need as you read (Page 694—Ps. 119:18).

4 So Ezra the scribe stood on a platform of
wood which they had made for the purpose;
and beside him, at his right hand, stood
Mattithiah, Shema, Anaiah, Urijah, Hilkiah,
and Maaseiah; and at his left hand Pedaiah,
Mishael, Malchijah, Hashum, Hashbadana,
Zechariah, *and* Meshullam.
5 And Ezra opened the book in the sight of
all the people, for he was *standing* above all
the people; and when he opened it, all the
people [R]stood up. Judg. 3:20
6 And Ezra blessed the LORD, the great
God. Then all the people answered, "Amen,
Amen!" while lifting up their hands. And they
bowed their heads and worshiped the LORD
with *their* faces to the ground.
7 Also Jeshua, Bani, Sherebiah, Jamin,
Akkub, Shabbethai, Hodijah, Maaseiah, Kelita, Azariah, Jozabad, Hanan, Pelaiah, and
the Levites, helped the people to understand
the Law; and the people *stood* in their place.
8 So they read distinctly from the book, in
the Law of God; and they gave the sense, and
helped *them* to understand the reading.

Israel Celebrates Her Understanding of the Law

9 And Nehemiah, who *was* the governor,
Ezra the priest *and* scribe, and the Levites
who taught the people said to all the people,
"This day *is* holy to the LORD your God; do
not mourn nor weep." For all the people
wept, when they heard the words of the Law.
10 Then he said to them, "Go your way, eat
the fat, drink the sweet, and send portions to
those for whom nothing is prepared; for *this*
day *is* holy to our LORD. Do not sorrow, for
the joy of the LORD is your strength."
11 So the Levites quieted all the people,
saying, "Be still, for the day *is* holy; do not be
grieved."
12 And all the people went their way to eat
and drink, to [R]send portions and rejoice
greatly, because they [R]understood the words
that were declared to them. Neh. 8:10 • Neh. 8:7, 8

Israel Obeys the Law

13 Now on the second day the heads of the
fathers' *houses* of all the people, with the
priests and Levites, were gathered to Ezra
the scribe, in order to understand the words
of the Law.
14 And they found written in the Law,
which the LORD had commanded by Moses,
that the children of Israel should dwell in
[R]booths[T] during the feast of the seventh
month, Lev. 23:34, 40, 42 • Temporary shelters

---

b. Read the Bible thoughtfully. Think about the meaning and implications of what you are reading.
c. Read the Bible carefully. Take careful note not only of the words that are used but also of how they relate to one another.
d. Read the Bible repeatedly. It may be of great help to read the same portion over daily for a month's time. This is a good way for its words to take root in your heart. If you are reading a short book, read it every day. Divide longer books into manageable portions of two or three chapters and read that portion through every day.
e. Read the Bible extensively. Sometimes it is of great help to read large portions of the Word of God through at one sitting. If you do this, do it at a time when you are alert and not likely to be disturbed during your reading.
f. Read the Bible regularly. It is good to have a particular time every day when you habitually give yourself to the reading of the Word of God.
g. Read the Bible faithfully. Inevitably there will be days when you will fail to read the Bible. Do not let your momentary lapse discourage you. Faithfully resume your practice of reading God's Word.
h. Read the Bible obediently. Because the Bible is God's Word written to you, it is essential to obey it (Page 95—Ex. 24:3).

Now turn to Page 604—Job 22:22: Memorizing God's Word.

8:9 God's Word Convicts—One of the great proofs that the Bible is really God's inspired Word is its unique ability to convict men and women of their sins. Let us consider but a few Old and New Testament examples which demonstrate the lifesaving power of the Scriptures.

Old Testament examples:

a. Josiah, a young and godly Judean king who ruled the Lord's people more than six centuries before Christ, succeeds a wicked ruler who hated righteousness. At the beginning of Josiah's rule a copy of God's Word is found in the temple. When it is read to the king, both he and his people are convicted of their sins in not keeping God's law. A great revival takes place (Page 535—2 Chr. 34:18–21).
b. Nehemiah returns to help the returning Jews rebuild the gates in the Jerusalem wall. This great wall builder thinks the Word of God to be so important that he assembles the people and has the Scriptures read to them for three hours per day. This soon causes them to confess their sins (Page 567—Neh. 9:3).

New Testament examples: Before Jesus left this earth He promised that the Holy Spirit would soon come upon the apostles. "And when He has come, He will convict the world of sin, and of righteousness, and of judgment" (Page 1259—John 16:8). There are many instances in the New Testament where we see the Holy Spirit using God's Word to convict people of their sin. At Pentecost Peter uses the Scriptures to rebuke Israel for crucifying its Messiah. This sermon results in three thousand souls being convicted and accepting Christ (Page 1274—Acts 2:37, 41).

Now turn to Page 633—Ps. 17:4: God's Word Corrects.

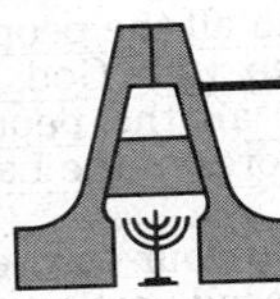

THE EXILES RETURN

After the city of Jerusalem was destroyed by the Babylonians about 586 B.C., the leading citizens of Judah were carried away as captives and resettled in the pagan city of Babylon. When the Babylonians were overthrown by the Persians about seventy years later, the stage was set for God's people to return to their beloved homeland.

There were actually three separate groups of Jewish citizens who made the return from Babylon and Persia to Jerusalem. Each of these groups had a specific task to accomplish.

1. The first group under Zerubbabel returned about 525 B.C. to rebuild the temple. Completed about 515 B.C., the temple was dedicated with great celebration and rejoicing by the Jewish people (Ezra 6:15–22).
2. The second group of Jewish exiles, under the leadership of Ezra the priest, returned to Jerusalem about 458 B.C. Ezra's task was to reestablish the Law as the basis of Jewish life. In a special assembly in the city of Jerusalem, Ezra read from the Law and challenged the people to follow the Lord's teachings (Neh. 8:1–12; see illustration).
3. The third group under Nehemiah returned about 444 B.C. Nehemiah led the people to rebuild the wall around Jerusalem. In spite of opposition from their enemies, Nehemiah rallied and encouraged the people so effectively that the entire project was completed in fifty-two days (Neh. 6:15).

Three prophets of the Old Testament—Haggai, Zechariah, and Malachi—lived and ministered in Jerusalem during this time known as the postexilic period. Haggai and Zechariah encouraged the people to complete the task of building the temple, while Malachi rebuked the returned captives for their sin, idolatry, and shallow worship practices.

Ezra reads from the Law.

15 and that they should announce and proclaim in all their cities and in Jerusalem, saying, "Go out to the mountain, and bring olive branches, branches of oil trees, myrtle branches, palm branches, and branches of leafy trees, to make booths, as *it is* written."
16 Then the people went out and brought *them* and made themselves booths, each one on the roof of his house, or in their courtyards or the courts of the house of God, and in the open square of the Water Gate and in the open square of the Gate of Ephraim.
17 So the whole congregation of those who had returned from the captivity made [T]booths and sat under the booths; for since the days of Joshua the son of Nun until that day the children of Israel had not done so. And there was very great gladness. Temporary shelters
18 Also [R]day by day, from the first day until the last day, he read from the Book of the Law of God. And they kept the feast [R]seven days; and on the [R]eighth day *there was* a sacred assembly, according to the *prescribed* manner. Deut. 31:11 • Lev. 23:36 • Num. 29:35

CHAPTER 9

Spiritual Preparation of Israel

NOW on the twenty-fourth day of [R]this month the children of Israel were assembled with fasting, in sackcloth, and with [T]dust on their heads. Neh. 8:2 • Lit. *earth on them*
2 Then [R]those of Israelite lineage separated themselves from all foreigners; and they stood and [R]confessed their sins and the iniquities of their fathers. Neh. 13:3, 30 • Neh. 1:6
3 And they stood up in their place and [R]read from the Book of the Law of the LORD their God *for one*-fourth of the day; and *for another* fourth they confessed and worshiped the LORD their God. Neh. 8:7, 8

The Great Deliverances of God

4 Then Jeshua, Bani, Kadmiel, Shebaniah, Bunni, Sherebiah, Bani, *and* Chenani stood on the stairs of the Levites and cried out with a loud voice to the LORD their God.
5 Then the Levites, Jeshua, Kadmiel, Bani, Hashabniah, Sherebiah, Hodijah, Shebaniah, *and* Pethahiah, said:

"Stand up *and* bless the LORD your God
Forever and ever!

"Blessed be [R]Your glorious name,
Which is exalted above all blessing and praise! 1 Chr. 29:13
6 [R]You alone *are* the LORD; 2 Kin. 19:15, 19
[R]You have made heaven, Rev. 14:7
[R]The heaven of heavens, with [R]all their host, [Deut. 10:14] • Gen. 2:1
The earth and all *things* on it,
The seas and all that is in them,
And You [R]preserve them all. [Ps. 36:6]
The host of heaven worships You.

7 "You *are* the LORD God,
Who chose [R]Abram, Gen. 11:31
And brought him out of Ur of the Chaldees,
And gave him the name Abraham;
8 You found his heart [R]faithful before You, Gen. 15:6; 22:1–3
And made a covenant with him
To give the land of the Canaanites,
The Hittites, the Amorites,
The Perizzites, the Jebusites,
And the Girgashites—
To give *it* to his descendants.
You [R]have performed Your words,
For You *are* righteous. Josh. 23:14

9 "You[R] saw the affliction of our fathers in Egypt, Ex. 2:25; 3:7
And heard their cry by the Red Sea.
10 You [R]showed signs and wonders against Pharaoh, Ex. 7—14
Against all his servants,
And against all the people of his land.
For You knew that they acted [T]proudly against them. *presumptuously* or *insolently*
So You [R]made a name for Yourself, as *it is* this day. Jer. 32:20
11 [R]And You divided the sea before them,
So that they went through the midst of the sea on the dry land; Ex. 14:20–28
And their persecutors You threw into the deep,
As a stone into the mighty waters.
12 Moreover You [R]led them by day with a cloudy pillar, Ex. 13:21, 22
And by night with a pillar of fire,
To give them light on the road
Which they should travel.

13 "You[R] came down also on Mount Sinai,
And spoke with them from heaven,
And gave them [R]just ordinances and true laws, Ex. 20:1–18 • [Rom. 7:12]
Good statutes and commandments.
14 You made known to them Your [R]holy Sabbath, Gen. 2:3
And commanded them precepts, statutes and laws,
By the hand of Moses Your servant.
15 You [R]gave them bread from heaven for their hunger, Ex. 16:14–17
And [R]brought them water out of the rock for their thirst, Ex. 17:6
And told them to [R]go in to possess the land Deut. 1:8
Which You had sworn to give them.

The Great Sins of Israel

16 "But they and our fathers acted [T]proudly, *presumptuously*

[T]Hardened their necks, Became stubborn
And did not heed Your commandments.
17 They refused to obey,
And [R]they were not mindful of Your wonders Ps. 78:11, 42–45
That You did among them.
But they hardened their necks,
And in their rebellion
They appointed [R]a leader Num. 14:4
To return to their bondage.
But You *are* God,
Ready to pardon,
[R]Gracious and merciful, Joel 2:13
Slow to anger,
Abundant in kindness,
And did not forsake them.

18 "Even [R]when they made a molded calf for themselves, Ex. 32:4–8, 31
And said, 'This *is* your god
That brought you up out of Egypt,'
And worked great provocations,
19 Yet in Your [R]manifold mercies
You did not forsake them in the wilderness. Ps. 106:45
The [R]pillar of the cloud did not depart from them by day, 1 Cor. 10:1
To lead them on the road;
Nor the pillar of fire by night,
To show them light,
And the way they should go.
20 You also gave Your [R]good Spirit to instruct them, Num. 11:17
And did not withhold Your [R]manna from their mouth, Ex. 16:14–16
And gave them water for their thirst.
21 [R]Forty years You sustained them in the wilderness, Deut. 2:7
So that they lacked nothing;
Their [R]clothes did not wear out Deut. 29:5
And their feet did not swell.

22 "Moreover You gave them kingdoms and nations,
And divided them into [T]districts.
So they took possession of the land of [R]Sihon, Lit. *corners* • Num. 21:21–35
The land of the king of Heshbon,
And the land of Og king of Bashan.
23 You also multiplied [R]their children as the stars of heaven, Gen. 15:5; 22:17
And brought them into the land
Which You had told their fathers
To go in and possess.
24 So [R]the [T]people went in Josh. 1:2–4
And possessed the land; Lit. *sons*
[R]You subdued before them the inhabitants of the land, [Ps. 44:2, 3]
The Canaanites,
And gave them into their hands,
With their kings
And the people of the land,
That they might do with them as they would.
25 And they took strong cities and a [R]rich land, Num. 13:27
And possessed [R]houses full of all goods,
Cisterns *already* dug, vineyards, olive groves, Deut. 6:11
And [T]fruit trees in abundance.
So they ate and were filled and [R]grew fat, Lit. *trees for eating* • [Deut. 32:15]
And delighted themselves in Your great [R]goodness. Hos. 3:5

26 "Nevertheless they [R]were disobedient
And rebelled against You, Judg. 2:11
Cast Your law behind their backs
And killed Your prophets, who [T]testified against them *warned them*
To turn them to Yourself;
And they worked great provocations.
27 [R]Therefore You delivered them into the hand of their enemies, Judg. 2:14
Who oppressed them;
And in the time of their trouble,
When they cried to You,
You [R]heard from heaven; Ps. 106:44
And according to Your abundant mercies
[R]You gave them deliverers who saved them Judg. 2:18
From the hand of their enemies.

28 "But after they had rest,
[R]They again did evil before You.
Therefore You left them in the hand of their enemies, Judg. 3:12
So that they had dominion over them;
Yet when they returned and cried out to You,
You heard from heaven;
And [R]many times You delivered them according to Your mercies, Ps. 106:43
29 And [T]testified against them,
That You might bring them back to Your law. *admonished them*
Yet they acted [T]proudly, *presumptuously*
And did not heed Your commandments,
But sinned against Your judgments,
[R]'Which if a man does, he shall live by them.' Lev. 18:5
And they shrugged their shoulders,
[T]Stiffened their necks, Became stubborn
And would not hear.
30 Yet for many years You had patience with them,
And testified against them by Your Spirit [R]in Your prophets. [Acts 7:51]
Yet they would not listen;
[R]Therefore You gave them into the hand of the peoples of the lands. Is. 5:5
31 Nevertheless in Your great mercy
[R]You did not utterly consume them nor forsake them; Jer. 4:27
For You *are* God, gracious and merciful.

Renewal of the Covenant

32 "Now therefore, our God,
The great, the [R]mighty, and awesome God, [Ex. 34:6, 7]
Who keeps covenant and mercy:
Do not let all the [T]trouble seem small before You *hardship*
That has come upon us,
Our kings and our princes,
Our priests and our prophets,
Our fathers and on all Your people,
[R]From the days of the kings of Assyria until this day. 2 Kin. 15:19; 17:3–6
33 However [R]You *are* just in all that has befallen us; [Dan. 9:14]
For You have dealt faithfully,
But we have done wickedly.
34 Neither our kings nor our princes,
Our priests nor our fathers,
Have kept Your law,
Nor heeded Your commandments and Your testimonies,
With which You testified against them.
35 For they have [R]not served You in their kingdom, Deut. 28:47
Or in the many good *things* that You gave them,
Or in the large and rich land which You set before them;
Nor did they turn from their wicked works.

36 "Here [R]we *are*, servants today!
And the land that You gave to our fathers, Deut. 28:48
To eat its fruit and its good *things*,
Here we *are*, servants in it!
37 And [R]it yields much increase to the kings Deut. 28:33, 51
You have set over us,
Because of our sins;
Also they have [R]dominion over our bodies and our cattle Deut. 28:48
At their pleasure;
And we *are* in great distress.

38 "And because of all this,
We [R]make a sure *covenant*, and write *it*;
And our leaders *and* our Levites *and* our priests [R]seal *it*." 2 Kin. 23:3 • Neh. 10:1

CHAPTER 10

Ratifiers of the Covenant

NOW those who placed *their* seal on *the document were*:
Nehemiah the [T]governor, [R]the son of
Hacaliah, and Zedekiah, Or *Tirshatha* • Neh. 1:1
2 [R]Seraiah, Azariah, Jeremiah, Neh. 12:1–21
3 Pashhur, Amariah, Malchijah,
4 Hattush, Shebaniah, Malluch,
5 Harim, Meremoth, Obadiah,
6 Daniel, Ginnethon, Baruch,
7 Meshullam, Abijah, Mijamin,
8 Maaziah, Bilgai, *and* Shemaiah. These
were the priests.
9 The Levites: Jeshua the son of Azaniah,
Binnui of the sons of Henadad, *and* Kadmiel.
10 Their brethren: Shebaniah, Hodijah, Kelita, Pelaiah, Hanan,
11 Micha, Rehob, Hashabiah,
12 Zaccur, Sherebiah, Shebaniah,
13 Hodijah, Bani, *and* Beninu.
14 The leaders of the people: [R]Parosh, Pahath-Moab, Elam, Zattu, Bani, Ezra 2:3
15 Bunni, Azgad, Bebai,
16 Adonijah, Bigvai, Adin,
17 Ater, Hezekiah, Azzur,
18 Hodijah, Hashum, Bezai,
19 Hariph, Anathoth, Nebai,
20 Magpiash, Meshullam, Hezir,
21 Meshezabeel, Zadok, Jaddua,
22 Pelatiah, Hanan, Anaiah,
23 Hoshea, Hananiah, Hasshub,
24 Hallohesh, Pilha, Shobek,
25 Rehum, Hashabnah, Maaseiah,
26 Ahijah, Hanan, Anan,
27 Malluch, Harim, *and* Baanah.

Stipulations of the Covenant

28 [R]Now the rest of the people (the priests,
the Levites, the gatekeepers, the singers, the
Nethinim, [R]and all those who had separated
themselves from the peoples of the lands to
the Law of God, their wives, their sons, and
their daughters, everyone who had knowledge and understanding), Ezra 2:36–43 • Neh. 13:3
29 they joined with their brethren, their
nobles, and entered into a curse and an oath
to walk in God's Law, which was given by
Moses the servant of God, and to observe and
do all the commandments of the LORD our
Lord, and His ordinances and His statutes—
30 that we would not give [R]our daughters as
wives to the peoples of the land, nor take
their daughters for our sons; Ex. 34:16
31 *that if* the peoples of the land bring
[T]wares or any grain to sell on the Sabbath
day, we would not buy it from them on the
Sabbath, or on a holy day; and *that* we would
forego the seventh year's *produce* and the
[T]exaction of every debt. *merchandise • collection*
32 Also we made ordinances for ourselves,
to exact from ourselves yearly [R]one-third[T] of
a shekel for the service of the house of our
God: Matt. 17:24 • $45
33 for [R]the showbread, for the regular grain
offering, for the [R]regular burnt offering of the
Sabbaths, the New Moons, and the set feasts;
for the holy things, for the sin offerings to
make atonement for Israel, and all the work
of the house of our God. Lev. 24:5 • Num. 28; 29
34 We cast lots among the priests, the Levites, and the people, for *bringing* the wood

offering into the house of our God, according
to our fathers' houses, at the appointed times
year by year, to burn on the altar of the LORD
our God as *it is* written in the Law.
35 And *we made ordinances* [R]to bring the
firstfruits of our ground and the firstfruits of
all fruit of all trees, year by year, to the house
of the LORD; Ex. 23:19; 34:26
36 to bring the [R]firstborn of our sons and
our cattle, as *it is* written in the Law, and the
firstlings of our herds and our flocks, to the
house of our God, to the priests who minister
in the house of our God; Ex. 13:2, 12, 13
37 to bring the firstfruits of our dough, our
offerings, the fruit from all kinds of trees, *the*
new wine and oil, to the priests, to the storerooms of the [T]house of our God; and to bring
[R]the tithes of our land to the Levites, for the
Levites should receive the tithes in all our
farming communities. Temple • Lev. 27:30
38 And the priest, the descendant of Aaron,
shall be with the Levites when the Levites
receive tithes; and the Levites shall bring up a
tenth of the tithes to the house of our God, to
[R]the rooms of the storehouse. 1 Chr. 9:26
39 For the children of Israel and the children of Levi shall bring the offering of the
grain, of the new wine and the oil, to the
storerooms where the articles of the sanctuary *are, where* the priests who minister and
the gatekeepers and the singers *are*; and we
will not neglect the house of our God.

CHAPTER 11

Plan for the Resettlement

NOW the leaders of the people dwelt at
Jerusalem; the rest of the people cast
lots to bring one out of ten to dwell in
Jerusalem, [R]the holy city, and nine-tenths
were to dwell in *other* cities. Matt. 4:5; 5:35; 27:53
2 And the people blessed all the men who
[R]willingly offered themselves to dwell at
Jerusalem. Judg. 5:9

Resettlement Within Jerusalem

3 [R]Now these *are* the heads of the province
who dwelt in Jerusalem. (But in the cities of
Judah everyone dwelt in his own possession
in their cities—Israelites, priests, Levites,
[R]Nethinim, and [R]descendants of Solomon's
servants.) 1 Chr. 9:2, 3 • Ezra 2:43 • Ezra 2:55
4 Also [R]in Jerusalem dwelt *certain* of the
children of Judah and of the children of
Benjamin. 1 Chr. 9:3
The children of Judah: Athaiah the son
of Uzziah, the son of Zechariah, the son of
Amariah, the son of Shephatiah, the son of
Mahalaleel, of the children of Perez;
5 and Maaseiah the son of Baruch, the son
of Col-Hozeh, the son of Hazaiah, the son of
Adaiah, the son of Joiarib, the son of Zechariah, the son of Shiloni.
6 All the sons of Perez who dwelt at Jerusalem *were* four hundred and sixty-eight
valiant men.
7 And these are the sons of Benjamin:
Sallu the son of Meshullam, the son of Joed,
the son of Pedaiah, the son of Kolaiah, the
son of Maaseiah, the son of Ithiel, the son of
Jeshaiah;
8 and after him Gabbai *and* Sallai, nine
hundred and twenty-eight.
9 Joel the son of Zichri *was* their overseer,
and Judah the son of [T]Senuah *was* second
over the city. Or *Hassenuah*
10 [R]Of the priests: Jedaiah the son of Joiarib, and Jachin; 1 Chr. 9:10
11 Seraiah the son of Hilkiah, the son of
Meshullam, the son of Zadok, the son of
Meraioth, the son of Ahitub, *was* the leader
of the house of God.
12 Their brethren who did the work of the
house *were* eight hundred and twenty-two;
and Adaiah the son of Jeroham, the son of
Pelaliah, the son of Amzi, the son of Zechariah, the son of Pashhur, the son of Malchijah,
13 and his brethren, heads of the fathers'
houses, were two hundred and forty-two; and
Amashai the son of Azareel, the son of Ahzai,
the son of Meshillemoth, the son of Immer,
14 and their brethren, mighty men of valor,
were one hundred and twenty-eight. Their
overseer *was* Zabdiel [T]the son of *one of* the
great men. Or *the son of Haggedolim*
15 Also of the Levites: Shemaiah the son of
Hasshub, the son of Azrikam, the son of
Hashabiah, the son of Bunni;
16 Shabbethai and Jozabad, of the heads of
the Levites, *had* the oversight of the business
outside of the house of God;
17 and Mattaniah the son of [T]Micha, the son
of Zabdi, the son of Asaph, *who was* the
leader *who* began the thanksgiving with
prayer, and Bakbukiah the second among his
brethren, and Abda the son of Shammua, the
son of Galal, the son of Jeduthun. Or *Michah*
18 All the Levites in [R]the holy city *were* two
hundred and eighty-four. Neh. 11:1
19 Moreover the gatekeepers, Akkub, Talmon, and their brethren who kept the gates,
were one hundred and seventy-two.
20 And the rest of Israel, of the priests *and*
Levites, *were* in all the cities of Judah, everyone in his *own* inheritance.
21 But the Nethinim dwelt in Ophel. And
Ziha and Gishpa *were* over the Nethinim.
22 Also the overseer of the Levites at Jerusalem *was* Uzzi the son of Bani, the son of
Hashabiah, the son of Mattaniah, the son of
Micha, of the sons of Asaph, the singers in
charge of the service of the house of God.
23 For *it was* the king's command concerning them that a [T]certain portion should be for
the singers, a quota day by day. *fixed share*

24 Pethahiah the son of Meshezabeel, of the children of Zerah the son of Judah, *was* [R]the[T] king's deputy in all matters concerning the people. 1 Chr. 18:17 • Lit. *at the king's hand*

Resettlement Outside of Jerusalem

25 And as for the villages with their fields, *some* of the children of Judah dwelt in [R]Kirjath Arba and its villages, Dibon and its villages, Jekabzeel and its villages; Josh. 14:15
26 in Jeshua, Moladah, Beth Pelet,
27 Hazar Shual, and Beersheba and its villages;
28 in Ziklag and Meconah and its villages;
29 in En Rimmon, Zorah, Jarmuth,
30 Zanoah, Adullam, and their villages; in Lachish and its fields; in Azekah and its villages. They dwelt from Beersheba to the Valley of Hinnom.
31 Also the children of Benjamin from Geba *dwelt* in Michmash, Aija, and Bethel, and their villages;
32 in Anathoth, Nob, Ananiah;
33 in Hazor, Ramah, Gittaim;
34 in Hadid, Zeboim, Neballat;
35 in Lod, Ono, *and* [R]the Valley of Craftsmen. 1 Chr. 4:14
36 Some of the Judean divisions of Levites *were* in Benjamin.

CHAPTER 12

Register of the Priests and the Levites

NOW these *are* the [R]priests and the Levites who came up with [R]Zerubbabel the son of Shealtiel, and Jeshua: [R]Seraiah, Jeremiah, Ezra, Ezra 2:1, 2; 7:7 • Neh. 7:7 • Neh. 10:2–8
2 Amariah, [T]Malluch, Hattush, *Melichu*, v. 14
3 Shechaniah, Rehum, Meremoth,
4 Iddo, [T]Ginnethoi, Abijah, *Ginnethon*, v. 16
5 Mijamin, [T]Maadiah, Bilgah, *Moadiah*, v. 17
6 Shemaiah, Joiarib, Jedaiah,
7 Sallu, Amok, Hilkiah, *and* Jedaiah.

These *were* the heads of the priests and their brethren in the days of [R]Jeshua. Zech. 3:1
8 Moreover the Levites *were* Jeshua, Binnui, Kadmiel, Sherebiah, Judah, *and* Mattaniah [R]*who led* the thanksgiving *psalms*, he and his brethren. Neh. 11:17
9 Also Bakbukiah and Unni, their brethren, *stood* across from them in *their* duties.
10 Jeshua begot Joiakim, Joiakim begot Eliashib, Eliashib begot Joiada,
11 Joiada begot Jonathan, and Jonathan begot Jaddua.
12 Now in the days of Joiakim, the priests, the heads of the fathers' *houses were*: of Seraiah, Meraiah; of Jeremiah, Hananiah;
13 of Ezra, Meshullam; of Amariah, Jehohanan;
14 of [T]Melichu, Jonathan; of [T]Shebaniah, Joseph; *Malluch*, v. 2 • *Shechaniah*, v. 3
15 of Harim, Adna; of Meraioth, Helkai;
16 of Iddo, Zechariah; of Ginnethon, Meshullam;
17 of Abijah, Zichri; *the son* of [T]Minjamin; of [T]Moadiah, Piltai; *Mijamin*, v. 5 • *Maadiah*, v. 5
18 of Bilgah, Shammua; of Shemaiah, Jehonathan;
19 of Joiarib, Mattenai; of Jedaiah, Uzzi;
20 of [T]Sallai, Kallai; of Amok, Eber; *Sallu*, v. 7
21 of Hilkiah, Hashabiah; *and* of Jedaiah, Nethaneal.
22 During the reign of Darius the Persian, a record *was also kept* of the Levites and priests *who had been* [R]heads of their fathers' *houses* in the days of Eliashib, Joiada, Johanan, and Jaddua. 1 Chr. 24:6
23 The sons of Levi, the heads of the fathers' *houses* until the days of Johanan the son of Eliashib, *were* written in the book of the [R]chronicles. 1 Chr. 9:14–22
24 And the heads of the Levites *were* Hashabiah, Sherebiah, and Jeshua the son of Kadmiel, with their brothers across from them, to praise *and* give thanks, group alternating with group, according to the command of David the man of God.
25 Mattaniah, Bakbukiah, Obadiah, Meshullam, Talmon, and Akkub *were* gatekeepers keeping the watch at the storerooms of the gates.
26 These *lived* in the days of Joiakim the son of Jeshua, the son of [T]Jozadak, and in the days of Nehemiah the governor, and of Ezra the priest, the scribe. *Jehozadak*, 1 Chr. 6:14

Dedication of the Jerusalem Wall

27 Now at the dedication of the wall of Jerusalem they sought out the Levites in all their places, to bring them to Jerusalem to celebrate the dedication with gladness, both with thanksgivings and singing, *with* cymbals and stringed instruments and harps.
28 And the sons of the singers gathered together from the countryside around Jerusalem, from the villages of the Netophathites,
29 from the house of Gilgal, and from the fields of Geba and Azmaveth; for the singers had built themselves villages all around Jerusalem.
30 Then the priests and Levites [R]purified themselves, and purified the people, the gates, and the wall. Neh. 13:22, 30
31 So I brought the leaders of Judah up on the wall, and appointed two large thanksgiving choirs, *one of which* went to the right hand on the wall toward the Refuse Gate;
32 after them went Hoshaiah and half of the leaders of Judah,
33 and Azariah, Ezra, Meshullam,
34 Judah, Benjamin, Shemaiah, Jeremiah,
35 and *certain* of the priests' sons [R]with trumpets, *namely*, Zechariah the son of Jonathan, the son of Shemaiah, the son of Matta-

niah, the son of Michaiah, the son of Zaccur,
the son of Asaph, Num. 10:2, 8
36 and his brethren, Shemaiah, Azarel, Mi-
lalai, Gilalai, Maai, Nethaneal, Judah, *and*
Hanani, with [R]the musical [R]instruments of
David the man of God; and Ezra the scribe
went before them. 1 Chr. 23:5 • 2 Chr. 29:26, 27
37 By the Fountain Gate, in front of them,
they went up the stairs of the City of David,
on the stairway of the wall, beyond the house
of David, as far as the Water Gate eastward.
38 [R]The other thanksgiving choir went the
opposite *way,* and I *was* behind them with
half of the people on the wall, going past the
[R]Tower of the Ovens as far as [R]the Broad
Wall, Neh. 12:31 • Neh. 3:11 • Neh. 3:8
39 and above the Gate of Ephraim, above
the Old Gate, above [R]the Fish Gate, the
Tower of Hananeel, the Tower of the Hundred, as far as the Sheep Gate; and they
stopped by the Gate of the Prison. Neh. 3:3
40 So the two thanksgiving choirs stood in
the house of God, likewise I and the half of
the rulers with me;
41 and the priests, Eliakim, Maaseiah, [T]Min-
jamin, Michaiah, Elioenai, Zechariah, *and*
Hananiah, with trumpets; Or *Mijamin,* v. 5
42 also Maaseiah, Shemaiah, Eleazar, Uzzi,
Jehohanan, Malchijah, Elam, and Ezer. The
singers [T]sang loudly with Jezrahiah *as their*
director. Lit. *made their voice to be heard*
43 Also that day they offered great sacrifices, and rejoiced, for God had made them
rejoice with great joy; the women and the
children also rejoiced, so that the joy of
Jerusalem was heard [R]afar off. Ezra 3:13
44 And at the same time some were appointed over the rooms of the storehouse for
the offerings, the firstfruits, and the tithes, to
gather into them from the fields of the cities
the portions specified by the Law for the
priests and Levites; for Judah rejoiced over
the priests and Levites who ministered.
45 Both the singers and the gatekeepers
kept the charge of their God and the charge
of the purification, according to the command of David *and* Solomon his son.
46 For in the days of David and Asaph of
old *there were* chiefs of the singers, and
songs of praise and thanksgiving to God.
47 In the days of Zerubbabel and in the
days of Nehemiah all Israel gave the portions
for the singers and the gatekeepers, a portion
for each day. They also consecrated *holy
things* for the Levites, and the Levites consecrated *them* for the children of Aaron.

CHAPTER 13

Separation from the Heathen

ON that day [R]they read from the Book of
Moses in the hearing of the people, and
in it was found written [R]that no Ammonite or
Moabite should ever come into the congregation of God, Neh. 8:3, 8; 9:3 • Deut. 23:3, 4
2 because they had not met the children of
Israel with bread and water, but hired Balaam against them to curse them. However,
our God turned the curse into a blessing.
3 So it was, when they had heard the Law,
[R]that they separated all the mixed multitude
from Israel. Neh. 9:2; 10:28
4 Now before this, Eliashib the priest,
having authority over the storerooms of the
house of our God, *was* allied with Tobiah.
5 And he had prepared for him a large
room, [R]where previously they had stored the
grain offerings, the frankincense, the articles,
the tithes of grain, the new wine and oil,
[R]which were commanded *to be given* to the
Levites and singers and gatekeepers, and the
offerings for the priests. Neh. 12:44 • Num. 18:21, 24
6 But during all this I was not in Jerusalem, [R]for in the thirty-second year of Artaxerxes king of Babylon I had returned to the
king. Then after certain days I obtained leave
from the king, Neh. 5:14–16
7 and I came to Jerusalem and discovered
the evil that Eliashib had done for Tobiah, in
[R]preparing a room for him in the courts of the
[T]house of God. Neh. 13:1, 5 • Temple
8 And it grieved me bitterly; therefore I
threw all the household goods of Tobiah out
of the room.
9 Then I commanded them to [R]cleanse the
rooms; and I brought back into them the
articles of the house of God, with the grain
offering and the frankincense. 2 Chr. 29:5, 15, 16

Restoration of Levitical Support

10 I also realized that the portions for the
Levites had [R]not been given *them;* for each of
the Levites and the singers who did the work
had gone back to [R]his field. Neh. 10:37 • Num. 35:2
11 So [R]I contended with the rulers, and said,
[R]"Why is the house of God forsaken?" And I
gathered them together and set them in their
place. Neh. 13:17, 25 • Neh. 10:39
12 [R]Then all Judah brought the tithe of the
grain and the new wine and the oil to the
storehouse. Neh. 10:38; 12:44
13 [R]And I appointed as treasurers over the
storehouse Shelemiah the priest and Zadok
the scribe, and of the Levites, Pedaiah; and
next to them *was* Hanan the son of Zaccur,
the son of Mattaniah; for they were considered [R]faithful, and their task *was* to distribute
to their brethren. 2 Chr. 31:12 • 1 Cor. 4:2
14 [R]Remember me, O my God, concerning
this, and do not wipe out my good deeds that
I have done for the house of my God, and for
its services! Neh. 5:19; 13:22, 31

Restoration of the Sabbath

15 In those days I saw in Judah *some people*
treading wine presses [R]on the Sabbath, and

bringing in sheaves, and loading donkeys
with wine, grapes, figs, and all *kinds of*
burdens, [R]which they brought into Jerusalem
on the Sabbath day. And I warned *them*
about the day on which they were selling
provisions. [Ex. 20:10] • [Jer. 17:21]
16 Men of Tyre dwelt there also, who
brought in fish and all kinds of goods, and
sold *them* on the Sabbath to the children of
Judah, and in Jerusalem.
17 Then I contended with the nobles of
Judah, and said to them, "What evil thing *is*
this that you do, by which you profane the
Sabbath day?
18 [R]"Did not your fathers do thus, and did
not our God bring all this disaster on us and
on this city? Yet you bring added wrath on
Israel by profaning the Sabbath." [Jer. 17:21]
19 So it was, at the gates of Jerusalem, as it
began to be dark before the Sabbath, that I
commanded the gates to be shut, and
charged that they must not be opened till
after the Sabbath. Then I posted *some* of my
servants at the gates, *so that* no burdens
would be brought in on the Sabbath day.
20 Now the merchants and sellers of all
kinds of [T]wares [T]lodged outside Jerusalem
once or twice. *merchandise* • *spent the night*
21 So I warned them, and said to them,
"Why do you spend the night [T]around the
wall? If you do *so* again, I will lay hands on
you!" From that time on they came no *more*
on the Sabbath. Lit. *before*
22 And I commanded the Levites that [R]they
should cleanse themselves, and that they
should go and guard the gates, to sanctify the
Sabbath day.

Remember me, O my God, *concerning*
this also, and spare me according to the
greatness of Your mercy! Neh. 12:30

Restoration from Mixed Marriages

23 In those days I also saw Jews *who* [R]had
married women of [R]Ashdod, Ammon, *and*
Moab. Ezra 9:2 • Neh. 4:7
24 And half of their children spoke the
language of Ashdod, and could not speak the
language of Judah, but spoke according to
the language of one or the other people.
25 So I [R]contended with them and cursed
them, struck some of them and pulled out
their hair, and made them swear by God,
saying, "You shall not give your daughters as
wives to their sons, nor take their daughters
for your sons or yourselves. Prov. 28:4
26 [R]"Did not Solomon king of Israel sin by
these things? Yet among many nations there
was no king like him, who was beloved of his
God; and God made him king over all Israel.
[R]Nevertheless pagan women caused even him
to sin. 1 Kin. 11:1, 2 • 1 Kin. 11:4–8
27 "Should we then hear of your doing all
this great evil, [R]transgressing against our God
by marrying pagan women?" [Ezra 10:2]
28 And *one* of the sons [R]of Joiada, the son of
Eliashib the high priest, *was* a son-in-law of
[R]Sanballat the Horonite; therefore I drove
him from me. Neh. 12:10, 12 • Neh. 4:1, 7; 6:1, 2
29 Remember them, O my God, because
they have defiled the priesthood and the
covenant of the priesthood and the Levites.

Restoration in Summary

30 Thus I cleansed them of everything pagan. I also assigned duties to the priests and
the Levites, each to his service,
31 and *to bringing* [R]the wood offering and
the firstfruits at appointed times. Neh. 10:34

Remember me, O my God, for good!

THE BOOK OF
ESTHER

THE BOOK OF ESTHER

God's hand of providence and protection on behalf of His people is evident throughout the Book of Esther, though His name does not appear once. Haman's plot brings grave danger to the Jews and is countered by the courage of beautiful Esther and the counsel of her wise cousin Mordecai, resulting in a great deliverance. The Feast of Purim becomes an annual reminder of God's faithfulness on behalf of His people.

Esther's Hebrew name was *Hadassah,* "Myrtle" (2:7), but her Persian name *Ester* was derived from the Persian word for "Star" *(stara).* The Greek title for this book is *Esther,* and the Latin title is *Hester.*

THE AUTHOR OF ESTHER

While the author's identity is not indicated in the text, the evident knowledge of Persian etiquette and customs, the palace in Susa, and details of the events in the reign of Ahasuerus indicate that the author lived in Persia during this period. The obvious Jewish nationalism and knowledge of Jewish customs further suggest that the author was Jewish. If this Persian Jew was not an eyewitness, he probably knew people who were. The book must have been written soon after the death of King Ahasuerus (464 B.C.), because 10:2, 3 speaks of his reign in the past tense. Some writers suggest that Mordecai himself wrote the book; this seems unlikely, for although Mordecai did keep records (9:20), 10:2, 3 imply that his career was already over. Nevertheless, the author certainly made use of Mordecai's records and may have had access to the Book of the Chronicles of the Kings of Media and Persia (2:23; 10:2). Ezra and Nehemiah have also been suggested for authorship, but the vocabulary and style of Esther is dissimilar to that found in their books. It seems likely that a younger contemporary of Mordecai composed the book.

THE TIME OF ESTHER

Ahasuerus is the Hebrew name and Xerxes the Greek name of Khshayarsh, king of Persia in 486–464 B.C. According to 1:3, the feast of Xerxes took place in his third year, or 483 B.C. The historian Herodotus refers to this banquet as the occasion of Xerxes' planning for a military campaign against Greece. But in 479 B.C. he was defeated by the Greeks at Salamis, and Herodotus tells us that he sought consolation in his harem. This corresponds to the time when he held a "contest" and crowned Esther queen of Persia (2:16, 17). Since the events of the rest of the book took place in 473 B.C. (3:7–12), the chronological span is ten years (483–473 B.C.). The probable time of authorship was between 464 B.C. (the end of Xerxes' reign; see 10:2, 3) and about 435 B.C. (the palace at Susa was destroyed by fire during that period, and such an event would probably have been mentioned). The historical and linguistic features of Esther do not support a date later than 400 B.C., as there is no trace of Greek influence.

Xerxes was a boisterous man of emotional extremes, whose actions were often strange and contradictory. This fact sheds light on his ability to sign a decree for the annihilation of the Jews, and two months later to sign a second decree allowing them to overthrow their enemies.

Esther was addressed to the many Jews who did not return to their homeland. Not all the godly people left—some did not return for legitimate reasons. Most were disobedient in staying in Persia. Nevertheless, God continued to care for His people in voluntary exile.

THE CHRIST OF ESTHER

Esther, like Christ, puts herself in the place of death for her people but receives the approval of the king. She also portrays Christ's work as Advocate on our behalf. This book reveals another satanic threat to destroy the Jewish people and thus, the messianic line. God continues to preserve His people in spite of opposition and danger, and nothing can prevent the coming of the Messiah.

KEYS TO ESTHER

Key Word: Providence—The Book of Esther was written to show how the Jewish people were protected and preserved by the gracious hand of God from the threat of annihilation. Although God disciplines His covenant people, He never abandons them. The God of Israel is the sovereign controller of history, and His providential care can be seen throughout this book: He raises a Jewish girl out of obscurity to become the queen of the most powerful empire in the world; He ensures that Mordecai's loyal deed is recorded in the palace records; He guides Esther's admission to the king's court; He superintends the timing of Esther's two feasts; He is involved in Ahasuerus' insomnia and the cure he uses for it; He sees that Haman's gallows will be utilized in an unexpected way; He gives Esther great favor in the sight of the king; and He brings about the new decree and the eventual victory of the Jews.

Key Verses: Esther 4:14; 8:17—"For if you remain completely silent at this time, relief and deliverance will arise for the Jews from another place, but you and your father's house will perish. Yet who knows whether you have come to the kingdom for *such* a time as this?" (4:14).

"And in every province and city, wherever the king's command and decree came, the Jews had joy and gladness, a feast and a holiday. Then many of the people of the land became Jews, because fear of the Jews fell upon them" (8:17).

Key Chapter: Esther 8—According to the Book of Esther, the salvation of the Jews is accomplished through the second decree of King Ahasuerus, allowing the Jews to defend themselves against their enemies. Chapter 8 records this pivotal event with the accompanying result that "many of the people of the land became Jews" (8:17).

SURVEY OF ESTHER

The story of Esther fits between chapters 6 and 7 of Ezra, between the first return led by Zerubbabel and the second return led by Ezra. It provides the only biblical portrait of the vast majority of Jews who choose to remain in Persia rather than return to Palestine. God's guiding and protective hand on behalf of His people is evident throughout this book, even though His name does not appear in it. The clearly emerging message is that God uses ordinary men and women to overcome impossible circumstances to accomplish His gracious purposes. Chapters 1—4 describe the threat to the Jews, and chapters 5—10 describe the triumph of the Jews.

The Threat to the Jews (1—4): The story begins in Ahasuerus's winter palace at Susa. The king provides a lavish banquet and display of royal glory for the people of Susa, and proudly seeks to make Queen Vashti's beauty a part of the program. When she refuses to appear, the king is counseled to depose her and seek another queen, because it is feared that the other women will become insolent if Vashti goes unpunished. Esther later finds favor in the eyes of Ahasuerus and wins the royal "beauty pageant." At her cousin Mordecai's instruction, she does not reveal that she is Jewish. With her help, Mordecai is able to warn the king of an assassination plot, and his deed is recorded in the palace records. Meanwhile, Haman becomes captain of the princes, but Mordecai refuses to bow to him. When he learns that Mordecai is Jewish, Haman plots for a year to eliminate all Jews, as his rage and hatred grow. He casts lots (purim) daily during this period until he determines the best day to have them massacred. Through bribery and lies he convinces Ahasuerus to issue an edict that all Jews in the empire will be slain eleven months hence in a single day. Haman conceives his plot in envy and a vengeful spirit, and he executes it with malicious craft. The decree creates a state of confusion, and Mordecai asks Esther to appeal to the king to spare the Jews. At the peril of her life, Esther decides to see the king and reveal her nationality in a desperate attempt to dissuade Ahasuerus. Mordecai convinces her that she has been called to her high position for this purpose.

The Triumph of the Jews (5—10): After fasting, Esther appears before the king and wisely invites him to a banquet along with Haman. At the banquet she requests that they attend a second banquet, as she seeks the right moment to divulge her request. Haman is flattered but later enraged when he sees Mordecai. He takes his wife's suggestion to build a large gallows for Mordecai (he cannot wait the eleven months for Mordecai to be slain). That night Ahasuerus decides to treat his insomnia by reading the palace records. Reading about Mordecai's deed,

FOCUS	THREAT TO THE JEWS		TRIUMPH OF THE JEWS	
REFERENCE	1:1 — 2:21	—	5:1 — 8:4	— 10:3
DIVISION	SELECTION OF ESTHER AS QUEEN	FORMULATION OF THE PLOT BY HAMAN	TRIUMPH OF MORDECAI OVER HAMAN	TRIUMPH OF ISRAEL OVER HER ENEMIES
TOPIC	FEASTS OF AHASUERUS		FEASTS OF ESTHER AND PURIM	
	GRAVE DANGER		GREAT DELIVERANCE	
LOCATION	PERSIA			
TIME	10 YEARS (483–473 B.C.)			

he wants him to be honored. Haman, mistakenly thinking the king wants to honor him, tells the king how the honor should be bestowed, only to find out that the reward is for Mordecai. He is humbled and infuriated by being forced to honor the man he loathes. At Esther's second banquet Ahasuerus offers her as much as half of his kingdom for the third time. She then makes her plea for her people and accuses Haman of his treachery. The infuriated king has Haman hanged on the gallows that Haman intended for Mordecai. The gallows, seventy-five feet high, was designed to make Mordecai's downfall a city-wide spectacle, but it ironically provides Haman with unexpected public attention—posthumously.

Persian law sealed with the king's ring (3:12) cannot be revoked, but at Esther's request the king issues a new decree to all the provinces that the Jews may assemble and defend themselves on the day when they are attacked by their enemies. This decree changes the outcome intended by the first order and produces great joy. Mordecai is also elevated and set over the house of Haman. When the fateful day of the two decrees arrives, the Jews defeat their enemies in their cities throughout the Persian provinces, but do not take the plunder. The next day becomes a day of celebration and an annual Jewish holiday called the Feast of Purim. The word is derived from the Assyrian *puru,* meaning "lot," referring to the lots cast by Haman to determine the day decreed for the Jewish annihilation. The narrative closes with the advancement of Mordecai to a position second only to the king.

OUTLINE OF ESTHER

Part One: The Threat to the Jews (1:1—4:17)

I. The Selection of Esther as Queen . . . . . . 1:1—2:20

- A. The Divorce of Vashti 1:1–22
  - 1. The Feasts of Ahasuerus 1:1–8
  - 2. Refusal of Queen Vashti 1:9–12
  - 3. Removal of Vashti 1:13–22
    - a. Counsel to King Ahasuerus 1:13–18
    - b. Commandment of King Ahasuerus. 1:19–22
- B. The Marriage to Esther 2:1–20
  - 1. Decree to Search for Vashti's Replacement 2:1–4
  - 2. Preparation of Esther. 2:5–14
  - 3. Selection of Queen Esther. 2:15–20

II. The Formulation of the Plot by Haman . . . . 2:21—4:17

- A. Mordecai Reveals the Plot to Murder the King 2:21–23
- B. Haman Plots to Murder the Jews. . . . 3:1—4:17
  - 1. Haman Is Promoted. 3:1
  - 2. The Reason for Haman's Plot 3:2–6
  - 3. Ahasuerus's Decree to Destroy the Jews . . . . 3:7—4:17
    - a. Presentation of the Plot 3:7–9
    - b. Publication of the Decree. 3:10–15
    - c. Response of the Jews 4:1–17
      - (1) The Lamentation of the Jews . . 4:1–3
      - (2) The Plan of Mordecai 4:4–14
      - (3) The Promise of Queen Esther. 4:15–17

Part Two: The Triumph of the Jews (5:1—10:3)

I. The Triumph of Mordecai over Haman 5:1—8:3

- A. Setting for the Triumph . . . . 5:1—6:3
  - 1. Esther's First Feast 5:1–8
  - 2. Haman Plots to Kill Mordecai. 5:9–14
  - 3. King Ahasuerus's Plan to Honor Mordecai 6:1–3
- B. Mordecai Is Honored 6:4–14
  - 1. Haman's Plan to Honor Himself. 6:4–9
  - 2. Haman Is Forced to Honor Mordecai. 6:10–14
- C. Haman Dies on Gallows Prepared for Mordecai 7:1–10
  - 1. Esther's Second Feast 7:1–4
  - 2. Haman Is Indicted. 7:5–8
  - 3. Haman Is Hanged 7:9, 10
- D. Mordecai Is Given Haman's House. 8:1–3

II. The Triumph of Israel over Her Enemies . . . . 8:4—10:3

- A. Preparation for the Victory of Israel. . . . 8:4–17
  - 1. Esther's Petition to King Ahasuerus. . . 8:4–6
  - 2. King Ahasuerus's Counter-Decree . . . 8:7–14
  - 3. Many Gentiles Are Converted 8:15–17
- B. Israel's Victory over Her Enemies. 9:1–16
  - 1. Victories on the First Day. 9:1–11
  - 2. Victories on the Second Day. 9:12–16
- C. Israel's Celebration. . . . . 9:17—10:3
  - 1. The Feast of Purim 9:17–32
  - 2. The Fame of Mordecai 10:1–3

CHAPTER 1

The Feasts of Ahasuerus

NOW it came to pass in the days of Ahasuerus (this *was* the Ahasuerus who
reigned from India to Ethiopia, *over* one
hundred and twenty-seven provinces),
2 in those days when King Ahasuerus sat
on the throne of his kingdom, which *was* in
[T]Shushan the [T]citadel, Or *Susa* • Or *fortified palace*
3 *that* in the third year of his reign he
[R]made a feast for all his officials and servants—the powers of Persia and Media, the
nobles, and the princes of the provinces *being*
before him— Gen. 40:20
4 when he showed the riches of his glorious kingdom and the splendor of his excellent
majesty for many days, one hundred and
eighty days *in all.*
5 And when these days were completed,
the king made a feast lasting seven days for
all the people who were present in Shushan
the [T]citadel, from great to small, in the court
of the garden of the king's palace. *palace*
6 *There were* white and blue linen *curtains*
fastened with cords of fine linen and purple
on silver rods and marble pillars; *and the*
[R]couches *were* of gold and silver on a *mosaic*
pavement of alabaster, turquoise, and white
and black marble. Amos 2:8; 6:4
7 And they served drinks in golden vessels,
each vessel being different from the other,
with royal wine in abundance, [R]according to
the [T]generosity of the king. Esth. 2:18 • Lit. *hand*
8 In accordance with the law, the drinking
was not compulsory; for so the king had
ordered all the officers of his household, that
they should do according to each man's
pleasure.

Refusal of Queen Vashti

9 Queen Vashti also made a feast for the
women *in* the royal palace which *belonged* to
King Ahasuerus.
10 On the seventh day, when the heart of
the king was merry with wine, he commanded Mehuman, Biztha, [R]Harbona, Bigtha,
Abagtha, Zethar, and Carcas, seven eunuchs
who served in the presence of King Ahasuerus, Esth. 7:9
11 to bring Queen Vashti before the king,
wearing her royal crown, in order to show
her beauty to the people and the officials, for
she *was* beautiful to behold.
12 But Queen Vashti refused to come at the
king's command *brought* by *his* eunuchs;
therefore the king was furious, and his anger
burned within him.

Counsel to King Ahasuerus

13 Then the king said to the [R]wise men
[R]who understood the times (for this *was* the
king's manner toward all who knew law and
justice, Dan. 2:12 • 1 Chr. 12:32
14 those closest to him *being* Carshena,
Shethar, Admatha, Tarshish, Meres, Marsena,
and Memucan, the [R]seven princes of Persia
and Media, [R]who had access to the king's
presence, *and* who [T]ranked highest in the
kingdom): Ezra 7:14 • 2 Kin. 25:19 • Lit. *sat in first place*
15 "What *shall we* do to Queen Vashti,
according to law, because she did not obey
the command of King Ahasuerus *brought to
her* by the eunuchs?"
16 And Memucan answered before the king
and the princes: "Queen Vashti has not only
wronged the king, but also all the princes,
and all the people who *are* in all the provinces
of King Ahasuerus.
17 "For the queen's behavior will become
known to all women, so that they will [R]de-
spise their husbands in their eyes, when they
report, 'King Ahasuerus commanded Queen
Vashti to be brought in before him, but she
did not come.' [Eph. 5:33]
18 "This very day the *noble* ladies of Persia
and Media will say to all the king's officials
that they have heard of the behavior of the
queen. Thus *there will be* excessive contempt
and wrath.

Commandment of King Ahasuerus

19 "If it pleases the king, let a royal [T]decree
go out from him, and let it be recorded in the
laws of the Persians and the Medes, so that it
will [R]not [T]be altered, that Vashti shall come
no more before King Ahasuerus; and let the
king give her royal position to another who is
better than she. Lit. *word* • Esth. 8:8 • *pass away*
20 "When the king's decree which he will
make is proclaimed throughout all his empire
(for it is great), all wives will [R]honor their
husbands, both great and small." [Col. 3:18]
21 And the reply pleased the king and the
princes, and the king did according to the
word of Memucan.
22 Then he sent letters to all the king's
provinces, [R]to each province in its own script,
and to every people in their own language,
that each man should [R]be master in his own
house, and speak in the language of his own
people. Esth. 3:12; 8:9 • [Eph. 5:22–24]

CHAPTER 2

Decree to Search for Vashti's Replacement

AFTER these things, when the wrath of
King Ahasuerus subsided, he remembered Vashti, [R]what she had done, and what
had been decreed against her. Esth. 1:19, 20
2 Then the king's servants who attended
him said: "Let beautiful young virgins be
sought for the king;

3 "and let the king appoint officers in all the provinces of his kingdom, that they may gather all the beautiful young virgins to Shushan the citadel, into the women's quarters, under the custody of Hegai the king's eunuch, custodian of the women. And let beauty preparations be given *them*.

4 "Then let the young woman who pleases the king be queen instead of Vashti." This thing pleased the king, and he did so.

Preparation of Esther

5 *Now* in [T]Shushan the [T]citadel there was a certain Jew whose name *was* Mordecai the son of Jair, the son of Shimei, the son of [R]Kish, a Benjamite. Or *Susa* • *palace* • 1 Sam. 9:1

6 [T]Kish had been carried away from Jerusalem with the captives who had been captured with [T]Jeconiah king of Judah, whom Nebuchadnezzar the king of Babylon had carried away. Lit. *Who* • *Jehoiachin*, 2 Kin. 24:6

7 And [T]Mordecai had brought up Hadassah, that *is*, Esther, [R]his uncle's daughter, for she had neither father nor mother. The young woman *was* lovely and beautiful. When her father and mother died, Mordecai took her as his own daughter. Lit. *he* • Esth. 2:15

8 So it was, when the king's command and decree were heard, and when many young women were gathered at Shushan the citadel, *under* the custody of Hegai, that Esther also was taken to the king's palace, into the care of Hegai the custodian of the women.

9 Now the young woman pleased him, and she obtained his favor; so he readily gave beauty preparations to her, besides her allowance. Then seven choice maidservants were provided for her from the king's palace, and he moved her and her maidservants to the best *place* in the house of the women.

10 [R]Esther had not [T]revealed her people or kindred, for Mordecai had charged her not to reveal *it*. Esth. 2:20 • Revealed the identity of

11 And every day Mordecai paced in front of the court of the women's quarters, to learn of Esther's welfare and what was happening to her.

12 Each young woman's turn came to go in to King Ahasuerus after she had completed twelve months' preparation, according to the regulations for the women, for thus were the days of their preparation apportioned: six months with oil of myrrh, and six months with perfumes and preparations for beautifying women.

13 Thus *prepared, each* young woman went to the king, and she was given whatever she desired to take with her from the women's quarters to the king's palace.

14 In the evening she went, and in the morning she returned to the second house of the women, to the custody of Shaashgaz, the king's eunuch who kept the concubines. She would not go in to the king again unless the king delighted in her and called for her by name.

Selection of Queen Esther

15 Now when the turn came for Esther the daughter of Abihail the uncle of Mordecai, who had taken her as his daughter, to go in to the king, she requested nothing but what Hegai the king's eunuch, the custodian of the women, advised. And Esther [R]obtained favor in the sight of all who saw her. Esth. 5:2, 8

16 So Esther was taken to King Ahasuerus, into his royal palace, in the tenth month, which *is* the month of Tebeth, in the seventh year of his reign.

17 The king loved Esther more than all the *other* women, and she obtained grace and favor in his sight more than all the virgins; so he set the royal [R]crown upon her head and made her queen instead of Vashti. Esth. 1:11

18 Then the king [R]made a great feast, the Feast of Esther, for all his officials and servants; and he proclaimed a holiday in the provinces and gave gifts according to the [T]generosity of a king. Esth. 1:3 • Lit. *hand*

19 When virgins were gathered together a second time, Mordecai sat within the king's gate.

20 [R]*Now* Esther had not *yet* revealed her kindred and her people, just as Mordecai had charged her, for Esther obeyed the command of Mordecai as when she was brought up by him. Esth. 2:10

Mordecai Reveals the Plot to Murder the King

21 In those days, while Mordecai sat within the king's gate, two of the king's eunuchs, [T]Bigthan and Teresh, doorkeepers, became furious and sought to lay hands on King Ahasuerus. *Bigthana*, Esth. 6:2

22 So the matter became known to Mordecai, who told Queen Esther, and Esther informed the king in Mordecai's name.

23 And when an inquiry was made into the matter, it was confirmed, and both were hanged on a gallows; and it was written in [R]the book of the chronicles in the presence of the king. Esth. 6:1

CHAPTER 3

Haman Is Promoted

AFTER these things King Ahasuerus promoted Haman, the son of Hammedatha the Agagite, and advanced him and set his seat above all the princes who *were* with him.

The Reason for Haman's Plot

2 And all the king's servants who *were* within the king's gate bowed and paid

homage to Haman, for so the king had commanded concerning him. But Mordecai [R]would not bow or pay homage. Ps. 15:4

3 Then the king's servants who *were* within the king's gate said to Mordecai, "Why do you transgress the [R]king's command?" Esth. 3:2

4 Now it happened, when they spoke to him daily and he would not listen to them, that they told *it* to Haman, to see whether Mordecai's words would stand; for [T]Mordecai had told them that he *was* a Jew. Lit. *he*

5 When Haman saw that Mordecai [R]did not bow or pay him homage, Haman was [R]filled with wrath. Esth. 3:2; 5:9 • Dan. 3:19

6 But he disdained to lay hands on Mordecai alone, for they had told him of the people of Mordecai. Instead, Haman [R]sought to destroy all the Jews who *were* throughout the whole kingdom of Ahasuerus—the people of Mordecai. Ps. 83:4

Presentation of the Plot

7 In the first month, which is the month of Nisan, in the twelfth year of King Ahasuerus, they cast Pur (that *is*, the lot), before Haman [T]to determine the day and the month, until *it fell on the* twelfth *month*, which *is* the month of Adar. Lit. *from day to day and month to month*

8 Then Haman said to King Ahasuerus, "There is a certain people scattered and dispersed among the people in all the provinces of your kingdom; their laws *are* different from all *other* people's, and they do not keep the king's laws. Therefore it *is* not fitting for the king to let them remain.

9 "If it pleases the king, let *a decree* be written that they be destroyed, and I will pay [T]ten thousand talents of silver into the hands of those who do the work, to bring *it* into the king's treasuries." $3,840,000,000

Publication of the Decree

10 So the king [R]took [R]his signet ring from his hand and gave it to Haman, the son of Hammedatha the Agagite, the [R]enemy of the Jews. Gen. 41:42 • Esth. 8:2, 8 • Esth. 7:6

11 And the king said to Haman, "The money and the people *are* given to you, to do with them as seems good to you."

12 [R]Then the king's scribes were called on the thirteenth day of the first month, and *a decree* was written according to all that Haman commanded—to the king's satraps, to the governors who *were* over each province, to the officials of all people, to every province [R]according to its script, and to every people in their language. [R]In the name of King Ahasuerus it was written, and sealed with the king's signet ring. Esth. 8:9 • Esth. 1:22 • Esth. 8:8–10

13 And the letters were sent by couriers into all the king's provinces, to destroy, to kill, and to annihilate all the Jews, both young and old, little children and women, in one day, on the thirteenth *day* of the twelfth *month*, which *is* the month of Adar, and [R]to plunder their possessions. Esth. 8:11; 9:10

14 [R]A copy of the document was to be issued as law in every province, being published for all people, that they should be ready for that day. Esth. 8:13, 14

15 The couriers went out, hastened by the king's command; and the decree was proclaimed in Shushan the [T]citadel. So the king and Haman sat down to drink, but the city of Shushan was [T]perplexed. *palace* • *in confusion*

CHAPTER 4

The Lamentation of the Jews

WHEN Mordecai learned all that had happened, [T]he tore his clothes and put on sackcloth and ashes, and went out into the midst of the city. He [R]cried out with a loud and bitter cry. Lit. *Mordecai* • Gen. 27:34

2 He went as far as *the square* in front of the king's gate, for no one *might* enter the king's gate clothed with sackcloth.

3 And in every province where the king's command and decree arrived, *there was* great mourning among the Jews, with fasting, weeping, and wailing; and many lay in sackcloth and ashes.

The Plan of Mordecai

4 So Esther's maids and eunuchs came and told her, and the queen was deeply distressed. Then she sent garments to clothe Mordecai and take his sackcloth away from him, but he would not accept *them*.

5 Then Esther called Hathach, *one* of the king's eunuchs whom he had appointed to attend her, and she gave him a command concerning Mordecai, to learn what and why this *was*.

6 So Hathach went out to Mordecai in the city square that *was* in front of the king's gate.

7 And Mordecai told him all that had happened to him, and [R]the sum of money that Haman had promised to pay into the king's treasuries to destroy the Jews. Esth. 3:9

8 He also gave him [R]a copy of the written decree for their destruction, which was given at [T]Shushan, that he might show it to Esther and explain it to her, and that he might command her to go in to the king to make supplication to him and plead before him for her people. Esth. 3:14, 15 • Or *Susa*

9 So Hathach returned and told Esther the words of Mordecai.

10 Then Esther spoke to Hathach, and gave him a command for Mordecai:

11 "All the king's servants and the people of the king's provinces know that any man or

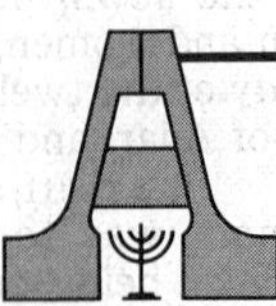

PERSIAN CUSTOMS IN THE BOOK OF ESTHER

The Book of Esther records events during the reign of King Ahasuerus (Xerxes) in the fifth century B.C. at Shushan (Susa), administrative capital of the Persian Empire. After the death of Darius I (the Persian king who had allowed any Jews who desired to return to their homeland to do so), his son Ahasuerus became king. Ahasuerus was the king who became dissatisfied with his queen Vashti and banished her, marrying Esther.

Royal Persian feasts were noted for their splendor and opulence. Esther describes the Persian custom of eating while reclining on beds or couches. All eating utensils were made of gold, "each vessel being different from the other" (Esth. 1:7).

Special laws protected the Persian king. Esther 1:14 refers to the seven princes who "had access to the king's presence." These were the chief nobles who were his advisors. Only a person summoned by the king could visit him, a custom which signified his royalty, as well as protected him from would-be assassins. Esther feared going to Ahasuerus without being called, because the punishment for such a visit was death (Esth. 4:11).

The Persian Empire boasted a well-organized postal system (Esth. 3:13). The king's ring (Esth. 8:8) was the signet ring with which official documents were signed. In ancient Persia documents were sealed in two ways: with a signet ring if they were written on papyrus, or with a cylinder seal if written on clay tablets. Among the objects excavated at the royal city of Persepolis (see photo) was a cylinder seal, which belonged to King Xerxes.

The Book of Esther also refers to "the laws of the Persians and the Medes" (1:19). This phrase describes the ironclad nature of the laws that governed the Persian Empire. Once a law was issued, it could not be changed or revoked—not even by the king himself.

Ruins of the palace of King Darius I at Persepolis. Photo by Howard Vos

woman who goes into the inner court to the
king, who has not been called, *he has* but one
law: put *all* to death, except the one to whom
the king holds out the golden scepter, that he
may live. Yet I myself have not been called to
go in to the king these thirty days."
12 So they told Mordecai Esther's words.
13 Then Mordecai told *them* to answer Esther: "Do not think in your heart that you
will escape in the king's palace any more
than all the other Jews.
14 "For if you remain completely silent at
this time, relief and deliverance will arise for
the Jews from another place, but you and
your father's house will perish. Yet who
knows whether you have come to the kingdom for *such* a time as this?"

The Promise of Queen Esther

15 Then Esther told *them* to return *this*
answer to Mordecai:
16 "Go, gather all the Jews who are present
in [T]Shushan, and fast for me; neither eat nor
drink for [R]three days, night or day. My maids
and I will fast likewise. And so I will go to the
king, which *is* against the law; [R]and if I
perish, I perish!" Or *Susa* • Esth. 5:1 • Gen. 43:14
17 Then Mordecai went his way and did
according to all that Esther commanded him.

CHAPTER 5

Esther's First Feast

NOW it happened [R]on the third day that
Esther put on *her* royal *robes* and stood
in [R]the inner court of the king's palace, across
from the king's house, while the king sat on
his royal throne in the royal house, facing the
entrance of the house. Esth. 4:16 • Esth. 4:11; 6:4
2 So it was, when the king saw Queen
Esther standing in the court, *that* [R]she found
favor in his sight, and [R]the king held out to
Esther the golden scepter that *was* in his
hand. Then Esther went near and touched
the top of the scepter. [Prov. 21:1] • Esth. 4:11; 8:4
3 And the king said to her, "What do you
wish, Queen Esther? What *is* your request?
[R]It shall be given to you—up to half *my*
kingdom!" Mark 6:23
4 So Esther answered, "If it pleases the
king, let the king and Haman come today to
the banquet that I have prepared for him."
5 Then the king said, "Bring Haman
quickly, that he may do as Esther has said."
So the king and Haman went to the banquet
that Esther had prepared.
6 At the banquet of wine the king said to
Esther, [R]"What *is* your petition? It shall be
granted you. What *is* your request, up to half
my kingdom? It shall be done!" Esth. 9:12
7 Then Esther answered and said, "My
petition and request *is this*:
8 "If I have found favor in the sight of the
king, and if it pleases the king to grant my
petition and [T]fulfill my request, then let the
king and Haman come to the [R]banquet which
I will prepare for them, and tomorrow I will
do as the king has said." Lit. *to do* • Esth. 6:14

Haman Plots to Kill Mordecai

9 So Haman went out that day [R]joyful and
with a glad heart; but when Haman saw
Mordecai in the king's gate, and that he did
not stand or tremble before him, he was filled
with indignation against Mordecai. [Job 20:5]
10 Nevertheless Haman [R]restrained himself
and went home, and he sent and called for his
friends and his wife Zeresh. 2 Sam. 13:22
11 Then Haman told them of his great
riches, the multitude of his children, all *the*
ways in which the king had promoted him,
and how he had [R]advanced him above the
officials and servants of the king. Esth. 3:1
12 Moreover Haman said, "Besides, Queen
Esther invited no one but me to come in with
the king to the banquet that she prepared;
and tomorrow I am again invited by her,
along with the king.
13 "Yet all this avails me nothing, so long as
I see Mordecai the Jew sitting at the king's
gate."
14 Then his wife Zeresh and all his friends
said to him, "Let a gallows[T] be made, fifty
cubits high, and in the morning [R]suggest to
the king that Mordecai be hanged on it; then
go merrily with the king to the banquet."
And the thing pleased Haman; so he had [R]the
gallows made. Lit. *tree* or *wood* • Esth. 6:4 • Esth. 7:10

CHAPTER 6

King Ahasuerus's Plan to Honor Mordecai

THAT night [T]the king could not sleep. So
one was commanded to bring the book of
the records of the chronicles; and they were
read before the king. *the king's sleep fled*
2 And it was found written that Mordecai
had told of Bigthana and Teresh, two of the
king's eunuchs, the doorkeepers who had
sought to lay hands on King Ahasuerus.
3 Then the king said, "What honor or
dignity has been bestowed on Mordecai for
this?" And the king's servants who attended
him said, "Nothing has been done for him."

Haman's Plan to Honor Himself

4 And the king said, "Who *is* in the court?"
Now Haman had *just* entered [R]the outer
court of the king's palace [R]to suggest that the
king hang Mordecai on the gallows that he
had prepared for him. Esth. 5:1 • Esth. 5:14
5 The king's servants said to him, "Haman
is there, standing in the court." And the king
said, "Let him come in."

6 So Haman came in, and the king asked
him, "What shall be done for the man whom
the king delights to honor?" Now Haman
thought in his heart, "Whom would the king
delight to honor more than [R]me?" [Prov. 16:18]
7 And Haman answered the king, "*For* the
man whom the king delights to honor,
8 "let a royal robe be brought which the
king has worn, and [R]a horse on which the
king has ridden, which has a royal [T]crest
placed on its head. 1 Kin. 1:33 • *crown*
9 "Then let this robe and horse be delivered to the hand of one of the king's most
noble princes, that he may array the man
whom the king delights to honor. Then [T]pa-
rade him on horseback through the city
square, [R]and proclaim before him: 'Thus shall
it be done to the man whom the king delights
to honor!' " Lit. *cause him to ride* • Gen. 41:43

Haman Is Forced to Honor Mordecai

10 Then the king said to Haman, "Hasten,
take the robe and the horse, as you have
suggested, and do so for Mordecai the Jew
who sits within the king's gate. Leave nothing undone of all that you have spoken."
11 So Haman took the robe and the horse,
arrayed Mordecai and led him on horseback
through the city square, and proclaimed
before him, "Thus shall it be done to the man
the king delights to honor."
12 Afterward Mordecai went back to the
king's gate. But Haman hastened to his
house, mourning and with his head covered.
13 When Haman told his wife Zeresh and all
his friends everything that had happened to
him, his wise men and his wife Zeresh said to
him, "If Mordecai, before whom you have
begun to fall, is of Jewish descent, you will
not prevail against [R]him but will surely fall
before him." Zech. 2:8
14 While they *were* still talking with him,
the king's eunuchs came, and hastened to
bring Haman to [R]the banquet which Esther
had prepared. Esth. 5:8

CHAPTER 7

Esther's Second Feast

SO the king and Haman went to dine with
Queen Esther.
2 And on the second day, [R]at the banquet
of wine, the king again said to Esther, "What
is your petition, Queen Esther? It shall be
granted you. And what *is* your request, up to
half *my* kingdom? It shall be done!" Esth. 5:6
3 Then Queen Esther answered and said,
"If I have found favor in your sight, O king,
and if it pleases the king, let my life be given
me at my petition, and my people at my
request.
4 "For we have been [R]sold, my people and
I, to be destroyed, to be killed, and to be
annihilated. Had we been sold as [R]male and
female slaves, I would have held my tongue,
although the enemy could never compensate
for the king's loss." Esth. 3:9; 4:7 • Deut. 28:68

Haman Is Indicted

5 Then King Ahasuerus answered and said
to Queen Esther, "Who is he, and where is he,
who would dare presume in his heart to do
such a thing?"
6 And Esther said, "The adversary and
enemy *is* this wicked Haman!" So Haman
was terrified before the king and queen.
7 Then the king arose in his wrath from
the banquet of wine *and went* into the palace
garden; but Haman stood before Queen Esther, pleading for his life, for he saw that evil
was determined against him by the king.
8 When the king returned from the palace
garden to the place of the banquet of wine,
Haman had fallen across [R]the couch where
Esther *was*. Then the king said, "Will he also
assault the queen while I *am* in the house?"
As the word left the king's mouth, they
[R]covered Haman's face. Esth. 1:6 • Job 9:24

Haman Is Hanged

9 Now Harbonah, one of the eunuchs, said
to the king, "Look! The [T]gallows, fifty cubits
high, which Haman made for Mordecai, who
spoke good on the king's behalf, is standing
at the house of Haman." Then the king said,
"Hang him on it!" Lit. *tree* or *wood*
10 So [R]they [R]hanged Haman on the gallows
that he had prepared for Mordecai. Then the
king's wrath subsided. [Ps. 7:16; 94:23] • Dan. 6:24

CHAPTER 8

Mordecai Is Given Haman's House

ON that day King Ahasuerus gave Queen
Esther the house of Haman, the [R]enemy
of the Jews. And Mordecai came before the
king, for Esther had told [R]how he *was related*
to her. Esth. 7:6 • Esth. 2:7, 15
2 So the king took off [R]his signet ring,
which he had taken from Haman, and gave it
to Mordecai; and Esther appointed Mordecai
over the house of Haman. Esth. 3:10
3 Now Esther spoke again to the king, fell
down at his feet, and implored him with tears
to counteract the evil *plot* of Haman the
Agagite, and the scheme which he had devised against the Jews.

Esther's Petition to King Ahasuerus

4 And [R]the king held out the golden scepter toward Esther. So Esther arose and stood
before the king, Esth. 4:11; 5:2
5 and said, "If it pleases the king, and if I
have found favor in his sight and the thing
seems right to the king and I am pleasing in

his eyes, let it be written to revoke the
[R]letters devised by Haman, the son of Hammedatha the Agagite, which he wrote to
annihilate the Jews who *are* in all the king's
provinces. Esth. 3:13
6 "For how can I endure to see the evil
that will come to my people? Or how can I
endure to see the destruction of my kindred?"

King Ahasuerus's Counter-Decree

7 Then King Ahasuerus said to Queen
Esther and Mordecai the Jew, "Indeed, I have
given Esther the house of Haman, and they
have hanged him on the gallows because he
tried to lay his hand on the Jews.
8 "You yourselves write *a decree* for the
Jews, [T]as you please, in the king's name, and
seal *it* with the king's signet ring; for a letter
which is written in the king's name and
sealed with the king's signet ring [R]no one can
revoke." Lit. *as is good in your eyes* • Dan. 6:8, 12, 15
9 [R]So the king's scribes were called at that
time, in the third month, which *is* the month
of Sivan, on the twenty-third *day*; and it was
written, according to all that Mordecai commanded, to the Jews, the satraps, the governors, and the princes of the provinces [R]from
India to Ethiopia, one hundred and twenty-
seven provinces *in all*, to every province [R]in
its own script, to every people in their own
language, and to the Jews in their own script
and language. Esth. 3:12 • Esth. 1:1 • Esth. 1:22; 3:12
10 [R]And he wrote in the name of King
Ahasuerus, sealed *it* with the king's signet
ring, and sent letters by couriers on horseback, riding on royal horses [T]bred from swift
steeds. 1 Kin. 21:8 • Lit. *sons of the swift horses*
11 By these letters the king permitted the
Jews who *were* in every city to [R]gather
together and protect their lives—to [R]destroy,
kill, and annihilate all the forces of any
people or province that would assault them,
both little children and women, and to plunder their possessions, Esth. 9:2 • Esth. 9:10, 15, 16
12 on one day in all the provinces of King
Ahasuerus, on the thirteenth *day* of the
twelfth month, which *is* the month of Adar.
13 [R]A copy of the document was to be
issued as a decree in every province and
published to all people, so that the Jews
would be ready on that day to avenge themselves on their enemies. Esth. 3:14, 15
14 *Then* the couriers who rode on royal
horses went out, hastened and pressed on by
the king's command. And the decree was
issued in [T]Shushan the [T]citadel. Or *Susa* • *palace*

Many Gentiles Are Converted

15 Now Mordecai went out from the presence of the king in royal apparel of blue and
white, with a great crown of gold and a
garment of fine linen and purple; and the city
of Shushan rejoiced and was glad.
16 The Jews had [R]light and gladness, joy
and honor. Ps. 97:11; 112:4
17 And in every province and city, wherever
the king's command and decree came, the
Jews had joy and gladness, a feast [R]and a
holiday. Then many of the people of the land
[R]became Jews, because [R]fear of the Jews fell
upon them. Esth. 9:19 • Ps. 18:43 • Gen. 35:5

CHAPTER 9

Victories on the First Day

NOW [R]in the twelfth month, that *is*, the
month of Adar, on the thirteenth day,
[R]*the time* came for the king's command and
his decree to be executed. On the day that the
enemies of the Jews had hoped to overpower
them, the opposite occurred, in that the Jews
themselves [R]overpowered those who hated
them. Esth. 8:12 • Esth. 3:13 • 2 Sam. 22:41
2 The Jews [R]gathered together in their
cities throughout all the provinces of King
Ahasuerus to lay hands on those who [R]sought
their harm. And no one could withstand
them, [R]because fear of them fell upon all
people. Esth. 8:11; 9:15–18 • Ps. 71:13, 14 • Esth. 8:17
3 And all the officials of the provinces, the
satraps, the governors, and all those doing
the king's work, helped the Jews, because the
fear of Mordecai fell upon them.
4 For Mordecai *was* great in the king's
palace, and his fame spread throughout all
the provinces; for this man Mordecai [R]be-
came increasingly prominent. 2 Sam. 3:1
5 Thus the Jews defeated all their enemies
with the stroke of the sword, with slaughter
and destruction, and did what they pleased
with those who hated them.
6 And in Shushan the citadel the Jews
killed and destroyed five hundred men.
7 Also Parshandatha, Dalphon, Aspatha,
8 Poratha, Adalia, Aridatha,
9 Parmashta, Arisai, Aridai, and Vajez-
atha—
10 the ten sons of Haman the son of Hammedatha, the enemy of the Jews—they killed;
but they did not lay a hand on the plunder.
11 On that day the number of those who
were killed in [T]Shushan the [T]citadel [T]was
brought to the king. Or *Susa* • *palace* • Lit. *came*

Victories on the Second Day

12 And the king said to Queen Esther, "The
Jews have killed and destroyed five hundred
men in Shushan the citadel, and the ten sons
of Haman. What have they done in the rest of
the king's provinces? Now what *is* your
petition? It shall be granted to you. Or what
is your further request? It shall be done."
13 Then Esther said, "If it pleases the king,
let it be granted to the Jews who *are* in
Shushan to do again tomorrow according to

MIRACULOUS DELIVERANCES

With his large army and instruments of siege warfare, the Assyrian king Sennacherib was certain he could prevail over the weaker Judean forces led by King Hezekiah.

One of the clearest messages of the Old Testament is that God is a compassionate deliverer who will use His power to help His people. Sennacherib, king of Assyria, discovered this truth about 701 B.C. when he attacked the city of Jerusalem. With his large army and instruments of siege warfare (see illustration), he felt certain he could prevail over the weaker Judean forces under King Hezekiah. But the Lord intervened on behalf of His people: "The angel of the LORD went out, and killed in the camp of the Assyrians one hundred and eighty-five thousand; and when people arose early in the morning, there *were* the corpses—all dead" (2 Kin. 19:35).

God has the power to deliver, even today, if we will give Him control and let Him work His will in our lives. Here are several other specific cases of God's miraculous deliverance of His people in Old Testament times:

Name	God's Action	Biblical Reference
Noah and his family	Delivered from the flood by the ark	Gen. 6—8
Lot and his family	Saved from the fiery destruction of Sodom and Gomorrah	Gen. 19:29
Nation of Israel	Delivered from Egyptian slavery through the Exodus; preserved by miraculous feedings in the Wilderness	Ex. 12—17
Israelites	Saved from fiery serpents by looking at a bronze serpent on a pole	Num. 21:6–9
David and his army	Saved from capture by Saul's army on numerous occasions	1 Sam. 23
Elijah	Fed by the ravens in the wilderness	1 Kin. 17:2–6
Three young Hebrew men	Delivered from Nebuchadnezzar's fiery furnace	Dan. 3:19–30
Daniel	Preserved, unharmed, among the lions	Dan. 6:1–24

today's decree, and let Haman's ten sons [R]be
hanged on the gallows." 2 Sam. 21:6, 9
14 So the king commanded this to be done;
the decree was issued in Shushan, and they
hanged Haman's ten sons.
15 And the Jews who *were* in [T]Shushan
gathered together again on the fourteenth
day of the month of Adar and killed three
hundred men at Shushan; [R]but they did not
lay a hand on the plunder. Or *Susa* • Esth. 9:10
16 The remainder of the Jews in the king's
provinces gathered together and protected
their lives, had rest from their enemies, and
killed seventy-five thousand of their enemies;
but they did not lay a hand on the plunder.

The Feast of Purim

17 *This was* on the thirteenth day of the
month of Adar. And on the fourteenth day of
[T]the month they rested and made it a day of
feasting and gladness. Lit. *it*
18 But the Jews who *were* at Shushan assembled together on the thirteenth *day*, as
well as on the fourteenth *day*; and on the
fifteenth *day* of the month they rested, and
made it a day of feasting and gladness.
19 Therefore the Jews of the villages who
dwelt in the unwalled towns celebrated the
fourteenth day of the month of Adar *as a day
of* gladness and feasting, as a holiday, and for
sending presents to one another.
20 And Mordecai wrote these things and
sent letters to all the Jews who *were* in all the
provinces of King Ahasuerus, *both* near and
far,
21 to establish among them that they
should celebrate yearly the fourteenth and
fifteenth days of the month of Adar,
22 as the days on which the Jews had rest
from their enemies, as the month which was
turned from sorrow to joy for them, and from
mourning to a holiday; that they should
make them days of feasting and joy, of [R]send-
ing presents to one another and gifts to the
[R]poor. Neh. 8:10 • [Deut. 15:7–11]
23 So the Jews accepted the custom which
they had begun, as Mordecai had written to
them,
24 because Haman, the son of Hammedatha
the Agagite, the enemy of all the Jews, [R]had
plotted against the Jews to annihilate them,
and had cast Pur (that *is*, the lot), to consume
them and destroy them; Esth. 3:6, 7; 9:26
25 but when [T]Esther came before the king,
he commanded by letter that this wicked plot
which [T]Haman had devised against the Jews
should [R]return on his own head, and that he
and his sons should be hanged on the gallows. Lit. *she* or *it* • Lit. *he* • Esth. 7:10
26 So they called these days Purim, after
the name [T]Pur. Therefore, because of all the
words of [R]this letter, what they had seen
concerning this matter, and what had happened to them, Lit. *Lot* • Esth. 9:20
27 the Jews established and imposed it upon
themselves and their descendants and all who
should [R]join them, that without fail they
should celebrate these two days every year,
according to the written *instructions* and
according to the *prescribed* time, Esth. 8:17
28 *that* these days *should be* remembered
and kept throughout every generation, every
family, every province, and every city, that
these days of Purim should not fail *to be
observed* among the Jews, and *that* the memory of them should not perish among their
descendants.
29 Then Queen Esther, [R]the daughter of
Abihail, with Mordecai the Jew, wrote with
full authority to confirm this [R]second letter
about Purim. Esth. 2:15 • Esth. 8:10; 9:20, 21
30 And [T]Mordecai sent letters to all the
Jews, to [R]the one hundred and twenty-seven
provinces of the kingdom of Ahasuerus, *with*
words of peace and truth, Lit. *he* • Esth. 1:1
31 to confirm these days of Purim at their
appointed time, as Mordecai the Jew and
Queen Esther had prescribed for them, and as
they had decreed for themselves and their
descendants concerning matters of their
[R]fasting and lamenting. Esth. 4:3, 16
32 So the decree of Esther confirmed these
matters of Purim, and it was written in the
book.

CHAPTER 10

The Fame of Mordecai

AND King Ahasuerus imposed tribute on
the land and *on* the islands of the sea.
2 Now all the acts of his power and his
might, and the account of the greatness of
Mordecai, to which the king advanced him,
are they not written in the book of the
chronicles of the kings of Media and Persia?
3 For Mordecai the Jew *was* second to
King Ahasuerus, and was great among the
Jews and well received by the multitude of
his brethren, seeking the good of his people
and speaking peace to all his [T]kindred. *seed*

THE BOOK OF
JOB

THE BOOK OF JOB

Job is perhaps the earliest book of the Bible. Set in the period of the patriarchs (Abraham, Isaac, Jacob, and Joseph), it tells the story of a man who loses everything—his wealth, his family, his health—and wrestles with the question, Why?

The book begins with a heavenly debate between God and Satan, moves through three cycles of earthly debates between Job and his friends, and concludes with a dramatic "divine diagnosis" of Job's problem. In the end, Job acknowledges the sovereignty of God in his life and receives back more than he had before his trials.

Iyyōb is the Hebrew title for this book, and the name has two possible meanings. If derived from the Hebrew word for persecution, it means "Persecuted One." It is more likely that it comes from the Arabic word meaning "To Come Back" or "Repent." If so, it may be defined "Repentant One." Both meanings apply to the book. The Greek title is *Iob*, and the Latin title is *Iob*.

THE AUTHOR OF JOB

The author of Job is unknown, and there are no textual hints as to his identity. Commentators, however, have been generous with suggestions: Job, Elihu, Moses, Solomon, Isaiah, Hezekiah, Jeremiah, Baruch, and Ezra have all been nominated. The non-Hebraic cultural background of this book may point to gentile authorship. The rabbinic traditions are inconsistent, but one talmudic tradition suggests that Moses wrote the book. The land of Uz (1:1) is adjacent to Midian, where Moses lived for forty years, and it is conceivable that Moses obtained a record of the dialogue left by Job or Elihu.

THE TIME OF JOB

Lamentations 4:21 locates Uz in the area of Edom, southeast of the Dead Sea. This is also in the region of northern Arabia, and Job's friends come from nearby countries.

It is important to distinguish the date of the events in Job from the date of its writing. Accurate dating of the events is difficult because there are no references to contemporary historical occurrences. However, a number of facts indicate a patriarchal date for Job, perhaps between Genesis 11 and 12 or not long after the time of Abraham: (1) Job lived 140 years *after* the events in the book (42:16); his lifespan must have been close to 200 years. This fits the patriarchal period (Abraham lived 175 years, Gen. 25:7). (2) Job's wealth is measured in terms of livestock (1:3; 42:12) rather than gold and silver. (3) Like Abraham, Isaac, and Jacob, Job is the priest of his family and offers sacrifices. (4) There are no references to Israel, the Exodus, the Mosaic law, or the tabernacle. (5) Fitting Abraham's time, the social unit in Job is the patriarchal family-clan. (6) The Chaldeans who murder Job's servants (1:17) are nomads and have not yet become city-dwellers. (7) Job uses the characteristic patriarchal name for God, *Shaddai* ("the Almighty"), thirty-one times. This early term is found only seventeen times in the rest of the Old Testament. The rare use of Yahweh "the LORD" also suggests a pre-Mosaic date. Ezekiel 14:14, 20 and James 5:11 show that Job was a historical person.

Several theories have been advanced for the date of writing: (1) It was written shortly after the events occurred, perhaps by Job or Elihu. (2) It was written by Moses in Midian (1485–1445 B.C.). (3) It was written in the time of Solomon (c. 950 B.C.). (Job is similar to other wisdom literature of this time; compare the praises of wisdom in Job 28 and Proverbs 8. The problem here is the great time lag of about a thousand years.) (4) It was written during or after the Babylonian captivity.

THE CHRIST OF JOB

Job acknowledges a redeemer (see 19:25–27) and cries out for a mediator (9:33; 25:4; 33:23). The book raises problems and questions which are answered perfectly in Christ who identifies with our sufferings (Heb. 4:15). Christ is the believer's Life, Redeemer, Mediator, and Advocate.

KEYS TO JOB

Key Word: Sovereignty—The basic question of the book is, "Why do the righteous suffer if God is loving and all-powerful?" Suffering itself is not the central theme; rather, the focus is on what Job *learns* from his suffering—the sovereignty of God over all creation. The debate in chapters 3—37 regards whether God would allow this suffering to happen to a person who is innocent. The oversimplified solutions offered by Job's three friends are simply inadequate. Elihu's claim that God can use suffering to purify the righteous is closer to the mark. The conclusion at the whirlwind is that God is sovereign and worthy of worship in *whatever* He chooses to do. Job must learn to trust in the goodness and power of God in adversity by enlarging his concept of God. Even this "blameless" man (1:1) needs to repent when he becomes proud and self-righteous. He has to come to the end of his own resources, humble himself, and acknowledge the greatness and majesty of the

Lord. Job teaches that God is Lord "of those in heaven, and of those on earth, and of those under the earth" (Phil. 2:10). He is omniscient, omnipotent, and good. As such, His ways are sometimes incomprehensible to men and women, but He can always be trusted. Without the divine perspective in chapters 1 and 2 and in 38—42, chapters 3—37 are a mystery. Job does not have access to chapters 1 and 2, but he is responsible to trust God when all appearances are contrary. Suffering is not always associated with sin; God often sovereignly uses it to test and teach.

Key Verses: Job 13:15; 37:23, 24—"Though He slay me, yet will I trust Him. Even so, I will defend my own ways before Him" (13:15).

"*As for* the Almighty, we cannot find Him; *He is* excellent in power, *in* judgment and abundant justice; He does not oppress. Therefore men fear Him; He shows no partiality to any *who are* wise of heart" (37:23, 24).

Key Chapter: Job 42—The last chapter of the book records the climax of the long and difficult struggle Job has with himself, his wife, his friends, and even his God. Upon Job's full recognition of the utter majesty and sovereignty of the Lord, he repents and no longer demands an answer as to the "why" of his plight.

SURVEY OF JOB

The Book of Job concerns the transforming crisis in the life of a great man who lived perhaps four thousand years ago. Job's trust in God (1 and 2) changes to complaining and growing self-righteousness (3—31; see 32:1 and 40:8), but his repentance (42:1–6) leads to his restoration (42:7–17). The trials bring about an important transformation: The man after the process is different from the man before the process. The Book of Job divides into three parts: the dilemma of Job (1 and 2), the debates of Job (3—37), and the deliverance of Job (38—42).

The Dilemma of Job (1 and 2): Job is not a logical candidate for disaster (see 1:1, 8). His moral integrity and his selfless service to God heighten the dilemma. Behind the scene, Satan ("Accuser") charges that no one loves God from pure motives, but only for material blessings (1:10). To refute Satan's accusations, God allows him to strike Job with two series of assaults. In his sorrow Job laments the day of his birth but does not deny God (1:21; 2:10).

The Debates of Job (3—37): Although Job's "comforters" reach wrong conclusions, they are his friends: of all who know Job, they are the only ones who come; they mourn with him in seven days of silent sympathy; they confront Job without talking behind his back. However, after Job breaks the silence, a three-round debate follows in which his friends say Job must be suffering because of his sin. Job's responses to their simplistic assumptions make the debate cycles increase in emotional fervor. He first accuses his friends of judging him, and later appeals to the Lord as his judge and refuge.

Job makes three basic complaints: (1) God does not hear me (13:3, 24; 19:7; 23:3-5; 30:20); (2) God is punishing me (6:4; 7:20; 9:17); and (3) God allows the wicked to prosper (21:7). His defenses are much longer than his friends' accusations; in the process of defending his innocence, he becomes guilty of self-righteousness.

After Job's five-chapter closing monologue (27—31), Elihu freshens the air with a more perceptive and accurate view than those offered by Eliphaz, Bildad, or Zophar (32—37). He tells Job that he needs to humble himself before God and submit to God's process of purifying his life through trials.

The Deliverance of Job (38—42): After Elihu's preparatory discourse, God Himself ends the debate by speaking to Job from the whirlwind. In

FOCUS	DILEMMA OF JOB	DEBATES OF JOB					DELIVERANCE OF JOB
REFERENCE	1:1	3:1	15:1	22:1	27:1	32:1	38:1—42:17
DIVISION	CONTROVERSY OF GOD AND SATAN	FIRST CYCLE OF DEBATE	SECOND CYCLE OF DEBATE	THIRD CYCLE OF DEBATE	FINAL DEFENSE OF JOB	SOLUTION OF ELIHU	CONTROVERSY OF GOD WITH JOB
TOPIC	CONFLICT	DEBATE					REPENTANCE
	PROSE	POETRY					PROSE
LOCATION	LAND OF UZ (NORTH ARABIA)						
TIME	PATRIARCHAL PERIOD (c. 2000 B.C.)						

His first speech God reveals His power and wisdom as Creator and Preserver of the physical and animal world. Job responds by acknowledging his own ignorance and insignificance; he can offer no rebuttal (40:3–5). In His second speech God reveals His sovereign authority and challenges Job with two illustrations of His power to control the uncontrollable. This time Job responds by acknowledging his error with a repentant heart (42:1–6). If Job cannot understand God's ways in the realm of nature, how then can he understand God's ways in the spiritual realm? God makes no reference to Job's personal sufferings and hardly touches on the real issue of the debate. However, Job catches a glimpse of the divine perspective; and when he acknowledges God's sovereignty over his life, his worldly goods are restored twofold. Job prays for his three friends who have cut him so deeply, but Elihu's speech is never rebuked. Thus, Satan's challenge becomes God's opportunity to build up Job's life. "Indeed we count them blessed who endure. You have heard of the perseverance of Job and seen the end *intended by* the Lord—that the Lord is very compassionate and merciful" (James 5:11; see James 1:12).

OUTLINE OF JOB

Part One: The Dilemma of Job (1:1—2:13)

I. The Circumstances of Job **1:1–5**
II. The First Assault of Satan **1:6–22**
III. The Second Assault of Satan **2:1–10**
IV. The Arrival of Job's Friends **2:11–13**

Part Two: The Debates of Job (3:1—37:24)

I. The First Cycle of Debate .... **3:1—14:22**

A. Job's First Speech 3:1–26
B. Eliphaz's First Speech .... 4:1—5:27
1. Eliphaz Believes the Innocent Do Not Suffer 4:1–21
2. Eliphaz Calls Job Foolish.......... 5:1–7
3. Eliphaz Encourages Job to Appeal to God 5:8–16
4. Eliphaz Encourages Job to Not Despise God's Discipline 5:17–27
C. Job's Reply to Eliphaz .... 6:1—7:21
1. Job's Deep Anguish 6:1–13
2. Job Seeks His Friends' Sympathy 6:14–30
3. Job Questions God's Continuing Trials 7:1–21
D. Bildad's First Speech.............. 8:1–22
E. Job's Response to Bildad .... 9:1—10:22
1. Job Argues His Case............. 9:1–35
2. Job Questions His Oppression..... 10:1–22
F. Zophar's First Speech 11:1–20
G. Job's Response to Zophar .... 12:1—14:22
1. Job Tells His Friends Only God Knows 12:1–25
2. Job Begs God to Speak to Him.... 13:1–28
3. Job Mourns That Man Has Only One Life.................. 14:1–22

II. The Second Cycle of Debate .... **15:1—21:34**

A. Eliphaz's Second Speech............ 15:1–35
1. Job's Mouth Condemns Him...... 15:1–13
2. The Wicked Suffer 15:14–35
B. Job's Response to Eliphaz .... 16:1—17:16
1. Job Calls His Friends Miserable Comforters............. 16:1–5
2. Job Laments His Situation........ 16:6–14
3. Job Defends His Innocence...... 16:15–22
4. God Makes Job a Byword 17:1–16
C. Bildad's Second Speech............ 18:1–21
D. Job's Response to Bildad............ 19:1–29
E. Zophar's Second Speech 20:1–29
F. Job's Response to Zophar 21:1–34

III. The Third Cycle of Debate......... **22:1—26:14**

A. Eliphaz's Third Speech.............. 22:1–30
B. Job's Response to Eliphaz .... 23:1—24:25
1. Job Will Come Forth as Gold 23:1–17
2. God Seems Indifferent to the Wicked 24:1–25
C. Bildad's Third Speech............... 25:1–6
D. Job's Response to Bildad............ 26:1–14

IV. The Final Defense of Job .... **27:1—31:40**

A. Job's First Monologue .... 27:1—28:28
1. Job Affirms His Righteousness..... 27:1–23
2. Job Observes That Man Cannot Discover Wisdom 28:1–28
B. Job's Second Monologue .... 29:1—31:40
1. Job Remembers His Happy Past... 29:1–25
2. Job Describes His Present Humiliation 30:1–31
3. Job Defends His Innocency........ 31:1–34
a. Innocent of Sensual Sins....... 31:1–12
b. Innocent of Abusing His Power.................. 31:13–23
c. Innocent of Trusting in His Wealth............... 31:24–28
d. Innocent of Not Caring for His Enemies............ 31:29–34
4. Job Pleads to Meet God and Defend Himself........... 31:35–40

V. The Solution of Elihu .... **32:1—37:24**

A. Elihu Intervenes in the Debate 32:1–22
B. Elihu's First Rebuttal 33:1–33

Part Three: The Deliverance of Job (38:1—42:17)

CHAPTER 1

The Circumstances of Job

THERE was a man in the land of Uz,
whose name *was* Job; and that man was
blameless and upright, and one who feared
God and [T]shunned evil. Lit. *turned away from*
2 And seven sons and three daughters
were born to him.
3 Also, his possessions were seven thousand sheep, three thousand camels, five hundred yoke of oxen, five hundred female
donkeys, and a very large household, so that
this man was the greatest of all the [T]people of
the East. Lit. *sons*
4 Now his sons would go and feast *in their*
houses, each on his appointed day, and would
send and invite their three sisters to eat and
drink with them.
5 So it was, when the days of feasting had
run their course, that Job would send and
[T]sanctify them, and he would rise early in the
morning and offer burnt offerings *according*
to the number of them all. For Job said, "It
may be that my sons have sinned and
[T]cursed God in their hearts." Thus Job did
regularly. *consecrate* • Lit. *blessed*, but in an evil sense

The First Assault of Satan

6 Now there was a day when the sons of
God came to present themselves before the
LORD, and Satan also came among them.
7 And the LORD said to [T]Satan, "From
where do you come?" So Satan answered the
LORD and said, "From [R]going to and fro on
the earth, and from walking back and forth
on it." Lit. *the Adversary* • [1 Pet. 5:8]
8 Then the LORD said to Satan, "Have you
[T]considered My servant Job, that *there is*
none like him on the earth, a blameless and
upright man, one who fears God and [T]shuns
evil?" Lit. *set your heart on* • Lit. *turns away from*
9 So Satan answered the LORD and said,
"Does Job fear God for nothing?
10 "Have You not [T]made a hedge around
him, around his household, and around all
that he has on every side? You have blessed
the work of his hands, and his possessions
have increased in the land. Protected him
11 [R]"But now, stretch out Your hand and
touch all that he has, and he will surely
[R]curse You to Your face!" Job 2:5; 19:21 • Is. 8:21
12 So the LORD said to Satan, "Behold, all
that he has *is* in your [T]power; only do not lay
a hand on his *person*." Then Satan went out
from the presence of the LORD. Lit. *hand*
13 Now there was a day [R]when his sons and
daughters *were* eating and drinking wine in
their oldest brother's house; [Eccl. 9:12]
14 and a messenger came to Job and said,
"The oxen were plowing and the donkeys
feeding beside them,
15 "when the Sabeans [T]raided *them* and
took them away—indeed they have killed the
servants with the edge of the sword; and I
alone have escaped to tell you!" Lit. *fell upon*
16 While he *was* still speaking, another also
came and said, "The fire of God fell from
heaven and burned up the sheep and the
servants, and [T]consumed them; and I alone
have escaped to tell you!" *destroyed*
17 While he *was* still speaking, another also
came and said, "The Chaldeans formed three

bands, raided the camels and took them
away, yes, and killed the servants with the
edge of the sword; and I alone have escaped
to tell you!"
18 While he *was* still speaking, another also
came and said, [R]"Your sons and daughters
were eating and drinking wine in their oldest
brother's house, Job 1:4, 13
19 "and suddenly a great wind came from
*across the wilderness and struck the four
corners of the house, and it fell on the young
men, and they are dead; and I alone have
escaped to tell you!"
20 Then Job arose [R]and tore his robe and
shaved his head, and he [R]fell to the ground
and worshiped. Gen. 37:29, 34 • [1 Pet. 5:6]

21 And he said:

"Naked I came from my mother's womb,
And naked shall I return there.
The LORD [R]gave, and the LORD has
[R]taken away; [James 1:17] • Gen. 31:16
Blessed be the name of the LORD."

22 [R]In all this Job did not sin nor charge
God with wrong. Job 2:10

CHAPTER 2

The Second Assault of Satan

AGAIN [R]there was a day when the sons of
God came to present themselves before
the LORD, and Satan came also among them
to present himself before the LORD. Job 1:6–8
2 And the LORD said to Satan, "From
where do you come?" So [R]Satan answered
the LORD and said, "From going to and fro on
the earth, and from walking back and forth
on it." Job 1:7
3 Then the LORD said to Satan, "Have you
considered My servant Job, that *there is* none
like him on the earth, a blameless and upright
man, one who fears God and shuns evil? And
still he holds fast to his integrity, although
you incited Me against him, [R]to [T]destroy him
without cause." Job 9:17 • Lit. *consume*
4 So Satan answered the LORD and said,
"Skin for skin! Yes, all that a man has he will
give for his life.
5 "But stretch out Your hand now, and
touch his [R]bone and his flesh, and he will
surely curse You to Your face!" Job 19:20
6 [R]So the LORD said to Satan, "Behold, he
is in your hand, but spare his life." Job 1:12

7 Then Satan went out from the presence
of the LORD, and struck Job with painful boils
[R]from the sole of his foot to the crown of his
head. Is. 1:6

8 And he took for himself a potsherd with
which to scrape himself [R]while he sat in the
midst of the ashes. Ezek. 27:30
9 Then his wife said to him, "Do you still
hold to your integrity? Curse God and die!"
10 But he said to her, "You speak as one of
the foolish women speaks. [R]Shall we indeed
accept good from God, and shall we not
accept adversity?" [R]In all this Job did not [R]sin
with his lips. Job 1:21, 22 • Job 1:22 • Ps. 39:1

The Arrival of Job's Friends

11 Now when Job's three friends heard of
all this adversity that had come upon him,

1:19 LXX omits *across*

1:21 Response to Suffering—In the hour of suffering the Christian should attempt to determine first of all just why he may be suffering. One can suffer because of his position or his disposition. Peter brings this truth out in his first epistle: "Servants, *be* submissive to *your* masters with all fear, not only to the good and gentle, but also to the harsh. For this *is* commendable, if because of conscience toward God one endures grief, suffering wrongfully" (Page 1480—1 Pet. 2:18, 19).

Suffering is often a two-sided coin. On the one side suffering may be viewed as coming from God to bring out the best in us. See Genesis 22:1, 2, 15–18; Hebrews 11:17. On the other side Satan attempts to use the same temptation and suffering to bring out the worst in us (Page 1468—James 1:13, 14). Finally, the believer can react to suffering in three different ways:

a. Despise it, that is, treat it too lightly, as did Esau his birthright (Page 1462—Heb. 12:5, 16).
b. Faint under it, that is, treat it too seriously (Page 1462—Heb. 12:5).
c. Be exercised by it, that is, receive instruction from it. This is the reaction desired by God (Page 1462—Heb. 12:11–13).

During this time both Peter and Paul advise us to commit our pain and suffering to God, realizing He is faithful to work out all things for our good and God's glory (Page 1333—Rom. 8:28; Page 1483—1 Pet. 4:19). James tells us to count it all joy when we experience these dark hours (Page 1468—James 1:2).

Now turn to Page 885—Jer. 37:15: Examples of Suffering.

2:7 Purposes of Suffering—Perhaps the most painful question confronting the believer is the problem of suffering. Why does a loving and wise God permit His children to suffer? The Scriptures offer a number of reasons for this.

a. To produce fruit. If we allow suffering to accomplish its purpose, it can bring forth patience (Page 1460—Heb. 10:36; Page 1468—James 1:3), joy (Page 641—Ps. 30:5; 126:6), knowledge (Page 679—Ps. 94:12), and maturity (Page 1483—1 Pet. 5:10).
b. To silence the devil. Satan once accused Job of merely serving God for the material blessings involved. But the Lord allowed the devil to torment Job to demonstrate that His servant loved God because of who He was, and not for what he could get from Him (Page 589—Job 1:9–12; 2:3–7).

each one came from his own place—Eliphaz
the Temanite, Bildad the Shuhite, and Zophar
the Naamathite. For they had made an appointment together to come [R]and mourn with
him, and to comfort him. Rom. 12:15
12 And when they raised their eyes from
afar, and did not recognize him, they lifted
their voices and wept; and each one tore his
robe and [R]sprinkled dust on his head toward
heaven. Neh. 9:1
13 So they sat down with him on the
ground [R]seven days and seven nights, and no
one spoke a word to him, for they saw that
his grief was very great. Gen. 50:10

CHAPTER 3

Job's First Speech

AFTER this Job opened his mouth and cursed the day of his *birth*.
2 And Job [T]spoke, and said: Lit. *answered*

3 "May[R] the day perish on which I was born, Jer. 20:14-18
And the night *in which* it was said,
'A male child is conceived.'
4 May that day be darkness;
May God above not seek it,
Nor the light shine upon it.
5 May darkness and [R]the shadow of death claim it; Jer. 13:16
May a cloud settle on it;
May the blackness of the day terrify it.
6 *As for* that night, may darkness seize it;
May it not be included among the days of the year,
May it not come into the number of the months.
7 Oh, may that night be barren!
May no joyful shout come into it!
8 May those curse it who curse the day,
Those [R]who are ready to arouse Leviathan. Jer. 9:17
9 May the stars of its morning be dark;
May it look for light, but *have* none,
And not see the dawning of the day;
10 Because it did not shut up the doors of my *mother's* womb,
Nor hide sorrow from my eyes.

11 "Why[R] did I not die at birth?
Why did I *not* [T]perish when I came from the womb? Job 10:18, 19 • *expire*
12 [R]Why did the knees receive me? Gen. 30:3
Or why the breasts, that I should nurse?
13 For now I would have lain still and been quiet,
I would have been asleep;
Then I would have been at rest
14 With kings and counselors of the earth,
Who [R]built ruins for themselves, Job 15:28
15 Or with princes who had gold,
Who filled their houses *with* silver;
16 Or *why* was I not hidden [R]like a stillborn child, Ps. 58:8
Like infants who never saw light?
17 There the wicked cease *from* troubling,
And there the weary are at rest.
18 *There* the prisoners [T]rest together;
[R]They do not hear the voice of the oppressor. *are at ease* • Job 39:7
19 The small and great are there,
And the servant *is* free from his master.

20 "Why[R] is light given to him who is in misery, Jer. 20:18
And life to the [R]bitter of soul, 2 Kin. 4:27
21 Who [R]long[T] for death, but it does not *come*,
And search for it more than [R]hidden treasures; Rev. 9:6 • Lit. *wait* • Prov. 2:4
22 Who rejoice exceedingly,
And are glad when they can find the [R]grave? Job 7:15, 16
23 *Why is light given* to a man whose way is hidden,
[R]And whom God has hedged in? Job 19:8
24 For my sighing comes before I eat,
And my groanings pour out like water.
25 For the thing I greatly [R]feared has come upon me,
And what I dreaded has happened to me. [Job 9:28; 30:15]
26 I am not at ease, nor am I quiet;
I have no rest, for trouble comes."

CHAPTER 4

Eliphaz Believes the Innocent Do Not Suffer

THEN Eliphaz the Temanite answered and said:

---

c. To glorify God (Page 1250—John 9:1–3; 11:1–4).
d. To make us like Jesus. "That I may know Him and the power of His resurrection, and the fellowship of His sufferings, being conformed to His death" (Page 1401—Phil. 3:10).
e. To teach us dependence. This is brought out by both Christ (Page 1258—John 15:1–5) and the apostle Paul (Page 1374—2 Cor. 12:1–10).
f. To refine our lives (Page 661—Ps. 66:10–12; Page 729—Prov. 17:3; Page 1477—1 Pet. 1:6, 7).
g. To rebuke our sin (Page 1480—1 Pet. 2:20; 3:17; 4:15). As a faithful earthly father must in love punish his erring child, so does our heavenly Father (Page 1462—Heb. 12:5–9).
h. To enlarge our ministry toward others (Page 1366—2 Cor. 1:3–7). It has been observed that he who has suffered much speaks many languages (understands others).
Now turn to Page 590—Job 1:21: Response to Suffering.

2 "If one attempts a word with you, will
you become weary?
But who can withhold himself from
speaking?
3 Surely you have instructed many,
And you [R]have strengthened weak
hands. Is. 35:3
4 Your words have upheld him who was
stumbling,
And you [R]have strengthened the [T]feeble
knees; Is. 35:3 • Lit. *bending*
5 But now it comes upon you, and you
are weary;
It touches you, and you are troubled.
6 *Is* not [R]your reverence [R]your
confidence?
And the integrity of your ways your
hope? Job 1:1 • Prov. 3:26

7 "Remember now, [R]who *ever* perished
being innocent? [Ps. 37:25]
Or where were the upright *ever* cut off?
8 Even as I have seen,
[R]Those who plow iniquity [Prov. 22:8]
And sow trouble reap the same.
9 By the blast of God they perish,
And by the breath of His anger they are
consumed.
10 The roaring of the lion,
The voice of the fierce lion,
And [R]the teeth of the young lions are
broken. Ps. 58:6
11 [R]The old lion perishes for lack of prey,
And the cubs of the lioness are
scattered. Ps. 34:10

12 "Now a word was secretly brought to
me,
And my ear received a whisper of it.
13 [R]In disquieting thoughts from the visions
of the night, Job 33:15
When deep sleep falls on men,
14 Fear came upon me, and trembling,
Which made all my bones shake.
15 Then a spirit passed before my face;
The hair on my body stood up.
16 It stood still,
But I could not discern its appearance.
A form *was* before my eyes;
There was silence;
Then I heard a voice *saying:*
17 'Can a mortal be more righteous than
God?
Can a man be more pure than his
Maker?
18 If He puts no trust in His servants,
If He charges His angels with error,
19 How much more those who dwell in
houses of clay,
Whose foundation is in the dust,
Who are crushed before a moth?
20 [R]They are broken in pieces from morning
till evening;
They perish forever, with no one
regarding. Ps. 90:5, 6
21 Does not their own excellence go away?
They die, even without wisdom.'

CHAPTER 5

Eliphaz Calls Job Foolish

"CALL out now;
Is there anyone who will answer
you?
And to which of the holy ones will you
turn?
2 For wrath kills a foolish man,
And envy slays a simple one.
3 I have seen the foolish taking root,
But suddenly I cursed his habitation.
4 His sons are [R]far from safety, Ps. 119:155
They are crushed in the gate,
And [R]*there is* no deliverer. Ps. 109:12
5 Because the hungry eat up his harvest,
Taking it even from the thorns,
And a snare snatches their substance.
6 For affliction does not come from the
dust,
Nor does trouble spring from the
ground;
7 Yet man is [R]born to [T]trouble,
As the sparks fly upward. Job 14:1 • *labor*

Eliphaz Encourages Job to Appeal to God

8 "But as for me, I would seek God,
And to God I would commit my
cause—
9 Who does great things, and
unsearchable,
Marvelous things without number.
10 He gives rain on the earth,
And sends waters on the fields.
11 [R]He sets on high those who are lowly,
And those who mourn are lifted to
safety. Ps. 113:7
12 [R]He frustrates the devices of the crafty,
So that their hands cannot carry out
their plans. Neh. 4:15
13 He catches the [R]wise in their own
craftiness,
And the counsel of the cunning comes
quickly upon them. [1 Cor. 3:19]
14 They meet with darkness in the
daytime,
And grope at noontime as in the night.
15 But [R]He saves the needy from the
sword,
From the mouth of the mighty,
And from their hand. Ps. 35:10
16 [R]So the poor have hope, 1 Sam. 2:8
And injustice shuts her mouth.

Eliphaz Encourages Job to Not Despise God's Discipline

17 "Behold,[R] happy *is* the man whom God
corrects; Ps. 94:12

Therefore do not despise the chastening
of the Almighty.
18 For He bruises, but He binds up;
He wounds, but His hands make whole.
19 He shall deliver you in six troubles,
Yes, in seven no evil shall touch you.
20 [R]In famine He shall redeem you from
death, Ps. 33:19, 20; 37:19
And in war from the [T]power of the
sword. Lit. *hand*
21 [R]You shall be hidden from the scourge of
the tongue,
And you shall not be afraid of
destruction when it comes. Ps. 31:20
22 You shall laugh at destruction and
famine,
And [R]you shall not be afraid of the
[R]beasts of the earth. Ezek. 34:25 • Hos. 2:18
23 [R]For you shall have a covenant with the
stones of the field,
And the beasts of the field shall be at
peace with you. Ps. 91:12
24 You shall know that your tent *is* in
peace;
You shall visit your habitation and find
nothing amiss.
25 You shall also know that [R]your
descendants *shall be* many,
And your offspring [R]like the grass of the
earth. Ps. 112:2 • Ps. 72:16
26 [R]You shall come to the grave at a full
age, [Prov. 9:11; 10:27]
As a sheaf of grain ripens in its season.
27 Behold, this we have [R]searched out;
It *is* true.
Hear it, and know for yourself." Ps. 111:2

CHAPTER 6

Job's Deep Anguish

THEN Job answered and said:

2 "Oh, that my grief were fully weighed,
And my calamity laid with it in the
balances!
3 For then it would be heavier than the
sand of the sea—
therefore my words have been rash.
4 [R]For the arrows of the Almighty *are*
within me;
My spirit drinks in their poison;
[R]The terrors of God are arrayed [R]against
me. Ps. 38:2 • Ps. 88:15, 16 • Job 30:15
5 Does the [R]wild donkey bray when it has
grass, Job 39:5–8
Or does the ox low over its fodder?
6 Can flavorless food be eaten without
salt?
Or is there *any* taste in the white of an
egg?
7 My soul refuses to touch them;
They *are* as loathsome food to me.

8 "Oh, that I might have my request,
That God would grant *me* the thing
that I long for!
9 That it would please God to crush me,
That He would loose His hand and [R]cut
me off! Job 7:16; 9:21; 10:1
10 Then I would still have comfort;
Though in anguish, I would exult.
Let Him not spare,
For [R]I have not concealed the words of
[R]the Holy One. Acts 20:20 • [Is. 57:15]

11 "What strength do I have, that I should
hope?
And what *is* my end, that I should
prolong my life?
12 *Is* my strength the strength of stones?
Or is my flesh bronze?
13 *Is* my help not within me?
And is success driven from me?

Job Seeks His Friends' Sympathy

14 "To[R] him who is [T]afflicted, kindness
should be shown by his friend,
Even though he forsakes the fear of the
Almighty. [Prov. 17:17] • Or *despairing*
15 [R]My brothers have dealt deceitfully like a
brook,
[R]Like the streams of the brooks that pass
away, Ps. 38:11 • Jer. 15:18
16 Which are dark because of the ice,
And into which the snow vanishes.
17 When it is warm, they cease to flow;
When it is hot, they vanish from their
place.
18 The paths of their way turn aside,
They go nowhere and perish.
19 The caravans of [R]Tema look, Gen. 25:15
The travelers of Sheba hope for them.
20 They are [R]disappointed[T] because they
were confident; Jer. 14:3 • Lit. *ashamed*
They come there and are confused.
21 For now [R]you are nothing, Job 13:4
You see terror and [R]are afraid. Ps. 38:11
22 Did I ever say, 'Bring *something* to me'?
Or, 'Offer a bribe for me from your
wealth'?
23 Or, 'Deliver me from the enemy's hand'?
Or, 'Redeem me from the hand of
oppressors'?

24 "Teach me, and I will hold my tongue;
Cause me to understand wherein I have
erred.
25 How forceful are right words!
But what does your arguing prove?
26 Do you intend to reprove *my* words,
And the speeches of a desperate one,
which are as wind?
27 Yes, you overwhelm the fatherless,
And you [R]undermine your friend. Ps. 57:6

28 Now therefore, be pleased to look at
me;
For I would never lie to your face.
29 [R]Turn now, let there be no injustice;
Yes, turn again, my [R]righteousness [T]still
stands. Job 17:10 • Job 27:5, 6; 34:5 • Lit. *is in it*
30 Is there injustice on my tongue?
Cannot my taste discern the unsavory?

CHAPTER 7

Job Questions God's Continuing Trials

"IS *there* not [R]a time of hard service for
man on earth?
Are not his days also like the days of a
hired man? [Job 14:5, 13, 14]
2 Like a servant who [T]earnestly desires
the shade,
And like a hired man who eagerly looks
for his wages, Lit. *pants for*
3 So I have been allotted [R]months of
futility,
And wearisome nights have been
appointed to me. [Job 15:31]
4 [R]When I lie down, I say, 'When shall I
arise,
And the night be ended?'
For I have had my fill of tossing till
dawn. Deut. 28:67
5 My flesh is [R]caked with worms and
dust,
My skin is cracked and breaks out
afresh. Is. 14:11

6 "My[R] days are swifter than a weaver's
shuttle, Job 9:25; 16:22; 17:11
And are spent without hope.
7 Oh, remember that my life *is* a breath!
My eye will never again see good.
8 [R]The eye of him who sees me will see me
no *more*;
While your *eyes are* upon me, I shall no
longer *be*. Job 8:18; 20:9
9 *As* the cloud disappears and vanishes
away,
So [R]he who goes down to the grave
does not come up. 2 Sam. 12:23
10 He shall never return to his house,
Nor shall his place know him anymore.

11 "Therefore I will [R]not restrain my mouth;
I will speak in the anguish of my spirit;
I will [R]complain in the bitterness of my
soul. Ps. 39:1, 9 • 1 Sam. 1:10
12 *Am* I a sea, or a sea serpent,
That You set a guard over me?
13 When I say, 'My bed will comfort me,
My couch will ease my complaint,'
14 Then You scare me with dreams
And terrify me with visions,
15 So that my soul chooses strangling
And death rather than my body.
16 [R]I loathe *my life*; Job 10:1
I would not live forever.
[R]Let me alone, Job 14:6
For my days *are but* a breath.

17 "What[R] *is* man, that You should magnify
him, Ps. 8:4; 144:3
That You should set Your heart on him,
18 That You should [T]visit him every
morning,
And test him every moment? *attend to*
19 How long?
Will You not look away from me,
And let me alone till I swallow my
saliva?
20 Have I sinned?
What have I done to You, [R]O watcher
of men? Ps. 36:6
Why have You set me as Your target,
So that I am a burden *to myself?
21 Why then do You not pardon my
transgression,
And take away my iniquity?
For now I will lie down in the dust,
And You will seek me diligently,
But I *will* no longer *be*."

CHAPTER 8

Bildad's First Speech

THEN Bildad the Shuhite answered and
said:

2 "How long will you speak these *things*,
And the words of your mouth *be like* a
strong wind?
3 [R]Does God subvert judgment? [Deut. 32:4]
Or does the Almighty pervert justice?
4 If your sons have sinned against Him,
He has cast them away [T]for their
transgression. Lit. *into the hand of*
5 [R]If you would earnestly seek God
And make your supplication to the
Almighty, [Job 5:17–27; 11:13]
6 If you *were* pure and upright,
Surely now He would awake for you,
And prosper your rightful habitation.
7 Though your beginning was small,
Yet your latter end would [R]increase
abundantly. Job 42:12

8 "For [R] inquire, please, of the former age,
And consider the things discovered by
their fathers; Deut. 4:32; 32:7
9 For [R]we *are but of* yesterday, and know
[T]nothing,
Because our days on earth *are* a
shadow. Gen. 47:9 • Lit. *not*
10 Will they not teach you and tell you,
And utter words from their heart?

7:20 LXX *to you*

11 "Can the papyrus grow up without a
marsh?
Can the reeds flourish without water?
12 While it *is* yet green *and* not cut down,
It withers before any *other* plant.
13 So *are* the paths of all who [R]forget God;
And the hope of the [R]hypocrite shall
perish, Ps. 9:17 • Job 11:20; 18:14; 27:8
14 Whose confidence shall be cut off,
And whose trust *is* a spider's [T]web. *house*
15 [R]He leans on his house, but it does not
stand. Job 8:22; 27:18
He holds it fast, but it does not endure.
16 He grows green in the sun,
And his branches spread out in his
garden.
17 His roots wrap around the rock heap,
And look for a place in the stones.
18 [R]If he is destroyed from his place,
Then *it* will deny him, *saying,* 'I have
not seen you.' Job 7:10

19 "Behold, this is the joy of His way,
And out of the earth others will grow.
20 Behold, [R]God will not [T]cast away the
blameless, Job 4:7 • *reject*
Nor will He uphold the evildoers.
21 He will yet fill your mouth with
laughing,
And your lips with [T]rejoicing. *shouts of joy*
22 Those who hate you will be [R]clothed
with shame, Ps. 35:26; 109:29
And the dwelling place of the wicked
[T]will come to nothing." Lit. *will not be*

CHAPTER 9

Job Argues His Case

THEN Job answered and said:

2 "Truly I know *it is* so,
But how can a [R]man be [R]righteous
before God? [Job 4:17; 15:14–16] • [Hab. 2:4]
3 If one wished to [T]contend with Him,
He could not answer Him one time out
of a thousand. *argue*
4 [R]God[T] *is* wise in heart and mighty in
strength.
Who has hardened *himself* against Him
and prospered? Job 36:5 • Lit. *He*
5 He removes the mountains, and they do
not know
When He overturns them in His anger;
6 He shakes the earth out of its place,
And its [R]pillars tremble; Job 26:11
7 He commands the sun, and it does not
rise;
He seals off the stars;
8 He alone spreads out the heavens,
And treads on the waves of the sea;
9 [R]He made [T]the Bear, Orion, and the
Pleiades, Amos 5:8 • Heb. *Ash, Kesil,* and *Kimah*
And the chambers of the south;
10 [R]He does great things past finding out,
Yes, wonders without number. Job 5:9
11 [R]If He goes by me, I do not see *Him;*
If He moves past, I do not perceive
Him; [Job 23:8, 9; 35:14]
12 [R]If He takes away, [T]who can hinder
Him?
Who can say to Him, 'What are You
doing?' [Is. 45:9] • Lit. *who can turn him back?*
13 God will not withdraw His anger,
[R]The allies of [T]the proud lie prostrate
beneath Him. Job 26:12 • Heb. *rahab*

14 "How then can I answer Him,
And choose my words *to reason* with
Him?
15 [R]For though I were righteous, I could
not answer Him; Job 10:15; 23:1–7
I would beg mercy of my Judge.
16 If I called and He answered me,
I would not believe that He was
listening to my voice.
17 For He crushes me with a tempest,
And multiplies my wounds [R]without
cause. Job 2:3
18 He will not allow me to catch my
breath,
But fills me with bitterness.
19 If *it is a matter* of strength, indeed *He*
is strong;
And if of justice, who will appoint my
day *in court?*
20 Though I were righteous, my own
mouth would condemn me;
Though I *were* blameless, it would
prove me perverse.

21 "I am blameless, yet I do not know
myself;
I despise my life.
22 It *is* all one *thing;*
Therefore I say, [R]'He destroys the
blameless and the wicked.' Ezek. 21:3
23 If the scourge slays suddenly,
He laughs at the plight of the innocent.
24 The earth is given into the hand of the
wicked.
He covers the faces of its judges.
If it is not *He,* who else could it be?

25 "Now [R]my days are swifter than a
runner; Job 7:6, 7
They flee away, they see no good.
26 They pass by like swift ships,
Like an eagle swooping on its prey.
27 [R]If I say, 'I will forget my complaint,
I will put off my sad face and wear a
smile,' Job 7:13
28 [R]I am afraid of all my sufferings;
I know that You [R]will not hold me
innocent. Ps. 119:120 • Ex. 20:7
29 *If* I am condemned,
Why then do I labor in vain?

30 If I wash myself with snow water,
And cleanse my hands with [T]soap, *lye*
31 Yet You will plunge me into the pit,
And my own clothes will abhor me.

32 "For [R]*He is* not a man, as I *am*,
That I may answer Him,
And that we should go to court
together. [Is. 45:9]
33 Nor is there any mediator between us,
Who may lay his hand on us both.
34 Let Him take His rod away from me,
And do not let dread of Him terrify me.
35 *Then* I would speak and not fear Him,
But it is not so with me.

CHAPTER 10

Job Questions His Oppression

"MY [R]soul loathes my life;
I will give free course to my
complaint, Job 7:16
I will speak in the bitterness of my soul.
2 I will say to God, 'Do not condemn me;
Show me why You contend with me.
3 *Does it* seem good to You that You
should oppress,
That You should despise the work of
Your hands,
And [T]shine on the counsel of the
wicked? *Look favorably*
4 Do You have eyes of flesh?
Or [R]do You see as man sees? [1 Sam. 16:7]
5 *Are* Your days like the days of a mortal
man?
Are Your years like the days of a
mighty man,
6 That You should seek for my iniquity
And search out my sin,
7 Although You know that I am not
wicked,
And *there is* no one who can deliver
from Your hand?

8 'Your [R] hands have made me and
fashioned me, Ps. 119:73
An intricate unity;
Yet You would [R]destroy me. [Job 9:22]
9 Remember, I pray, [R]that You have
made me like clay. Gen. 2:7
And will You turn me into dust again?
10 [R]Did You not pour me out like milk,
And curdle me like cheese, [Ps. 139:14–16]
11 Clothe me with skin and flesh,
And knit me together with bones and
sinews?
12 You have granted me life and favor,
And Your care has preserved my spirit.

13 'And these *things* You have hidden in
Your heart;
I know that this *was* with You:
14 If I sin, then [R]You mark me, Ps. 139:1
And will not acquit me of my iniquity.
15 If I am wicked, [R]woe to me; Is. 3:11
[R]Even *if* I am righteous, I [T]cannot lift up
my head. [Job 9:12, 15] • Lit. *will not*
I am full of disgrace;
[R]See my misery! Ps. 25:18
16 If [T]my head is exalted,
[R]You hunt me like a fierce lion,
And again You show Yourself awesome
against me. Lit. *it* • Is. 38:13
17 You renew Your witnesses against me,
And increase Your indignation toward
me;
Changes and war are *ever* with me.

18 'Why[R] then have You brought me out of
the womb?
Oh, that I had perished and no eye had
seen me! Job 3:11-13
19 I would have been as though I had not
been.
I would have been carried from the
womb to the grave.
20 [R]Are not my days few? Ps. 39:5
Cease! [R]Leave me alone, that I may
take a little comfort, Job 7:16, 19
21 Before I go *to the place from which* I
shall not return,
[R]To the land of darkness [R]and the
shadow of death, Ps. 88:12 • Ps. 23:4
22 A land as dark as darkness *itself*,
As the shadow of death, without any
order,
Where even the light *is* like darkness.' "

CHAPTER 11

Zophar's First Speech

THEN Zophar the Naamathite answered
and said:

2 "Should not the multitude of words be
answered?
And should [T]a man full of talk be
vindicated? Lit. *a man of lips*
3 Should your empty talk make men
[T]hold their peace?
And when you mock, should no one
rebuke you? *be silent*
4 For you have said,
[R]'My doctrine *is* pure,
And I am clean in your eyes.' Job 6:30
5 But oh, that God would speak,
And open His lips against you,
6 That He would show you the secrets of
wisdom!
For *they would* double *your* prudence.
Know therefore that God [T]exacts from
you Lit. *forgets some of your iniquity for you*
Less than your iniquity *deserves*.

7 "Can[R] you search out the deep things of
God?
Can you find out the limits of the
Almighty? [Eccl. 3:11]
8 *They are* higher than heaven—what can
you do?
Deeper than [T]Sheol—what can you
know? The abode of the dead
9 Their measure *is* longer than the earth
And broader than the sea.

10 "If [R] He passes by, imprisons, and gathers
to judgment, [Rev. 3:7]
Then who can [T]hinder Him? *restrain*
11 For [R]He knows deceitful men;
He sees wickedness also.
Will He not then consider *it?* [Ps. 10:14]
12 For an [R]empty-headed man will be wise,
When a wild donkey's colt is born a
man. Rom. 1:22

13 "If you would [R]prepare your heart,
And [R]stretch out your hands toward
Him; [1 Sam. 7:3] • Ps. 88:9
14 If iniquity *were* in your hand, *and you*
put it far away,
And [R]would not let wickedness dwell in
your tents; Ps. 101:3
15 [R]Then surely you could lift up your face
without spot;
Yes, you could be steadfast, and not
fear; Ps. 119:6
16 Because you would [R]forget *your* misery,
And remember *it* as waters *that have*
passed away, Is. 65:16
17 And *your* life [R]would be brighter than
noonday.
Though you were dark, you would be
like the morning. Is. 58:8, 10
18 And you would be secure, because there
is hope;
Yes, you would dig *about you, and*
[R]take your rest in safety. Lev. 26:5, 6
19 You would also lie down, and no one
would make *you* afraid;
Yes, many would court your favor.
20 But [R]the eyes of the wicked will fail,
And they shall not escape, Deut. 28:65
And [R]their hope—loss of life!" [Prov. 11:7]

CHAPTER 12

Job Tells His Friends Only God Knows

THEN Job answered and said:

2 "No doubt you *are* the people,
And wisdom will die with you!
3 But I have [T]understanding as well as
you;
I *am* not [R]inferior to you.
Indeed, who does not *know* such things
as these? Lit. *a heart* • Job 13:2

4 "I[R] am one mocked by his friends,
Who [R]called on God, and He answered
him,
The just and blameless *who is* laughed
to scorn. Job 21:3 • Ps. 91:15
5 A [T]lamp is despised in the thought of
one who is at ease;
It is made ready for [R]those whose feet
slip. Or *disaster* • Prov. 14:2
6 [R]The tents of robbers prosper,
And those who provoke God are
secure— [Job 9:24; 21:6–16]
In what God provides by His hand.

7 "But now ask the beasts, and they will
teach you;
And the birds of the air, and they will
tell you;
8 Or speak to the earth, and it will teach
you;
And the fish of the sea will explain to
you.
9 Who among all these does not know
That the hand of the LORD has done
this,
10 [R]In whose hand *is* the [T]life of every
living thing, [Acts 17:28] • *soul*
And the breath of all mankind?
11 Does not the ear test words
And the [T]mouth taste its food? *palate*
12 Wisdom *is* with aged men,
And with [T]length of days,
understanding. *Long life*

13 "With Him *are* wisdom and strength,
He has counsel and understanding.
14 If [R]He breaks *a thing* down, it cannot
be rebuilt;
If He imprisons a man, there can be no
release. Job 11:10
15 If He [R]withholds the waters, they dry
up;
If He [R]sends them out, they overwhelm
the earth. [1 Kin. 8:35, 36] • Gen. 7:11–24
16 With Him *are* strength and prudence.
The deceived and the deceiver *are* His.
17 He leads counselors away plundered,
And makes fools of the judges.
18 He loosens the bonds of kings,
And binds their waist with a belt.
19 He leads [T]princes away plundered,
And overthrows the mighty. Lit. *priests*
20 [R]He deprives the trusted ones of speech,
And takes away the discernment of the
elders. Job 32:9
21 [R]He pours contempt on princes, Ps. 107:40
And [T]disarms the mighty. *loosens the belt of*
22 He [R]uncovers deep things out of
darkness,
And brings the shadow of death to
light. [1 Cor. 4:5]

23 [R]He makes nations great, and destroys
them; Is. 9:3; 26:15
He enlarges nations, and guides them.
24 He takes away the [T]understanding of
the chiefs of the people of the earth,
And [R]makes them wander in a pathless
wilderness. Lit. *heart* • Ps. 107:4
25 They grope in the dark without light,
And He makes them [R]stagger like a
drunken *man*. Ps. 107:27

CHAPTER 13

Job Begs God to Speak to Him

"BEHOLD, my eye has seen all *this*,
My ear has heard and understood it.
2 [R]What you know, I also know;
I *am* not inferior to you. Job 12:3
3 But I would speak to the Almighty,
And I desire to reason with God.
4 But you forgers of lies,
[R]You *are* all worthless physicians. Job 6:21
5 Oh, that you would be silent,
And it would be your wisdom!
6 Now hear my reasoning,
And heed the pleadings of my lips.
7 Will you speak [T]wickedly for God,
And talk deceitfully for Him? *unrighteously*
8 Will you show partiality for Him?
Will you contend for God?
9 Will it be well when He searches you
out?
Or can you mock Him as one mocks a
man?
10 He will surely reprove you
If you secretly show partiality.
11 Will not His [T]excellence make you
afraid, Lit. *exaltation*
And the dread of Him fall upon you?
12 Your platitudes *are* proverbs of ashes,
Your defenses are defenses of clay.

13 "Hold[T] your peace with me, and let me
speak,
Then let come on me what *may!* *Be silent*
14 Why [R]do I take my flesh in my teeth,
And put my life in my hands? Job 18:4
15 [R]Though He slay me, yet will I trust
Him.
[R]Even so, I will defend my own ways
before Him. Ps. 23:4 • Job 27:5
16 He also *shall* be my salvation,
For a [R]hypocrite could not come before
Him. Job 8:13
17 Listen diligently to my speech,
And to my declaration with your ears.
18 See now, I have prepared *my* case,
I know that I shall be vindicated.
19 Who *is* he *who* will contend with me?
If now I hold my tongue, I perish.

20 "Only two *things* do not do to me,
Then I will not hide myself from You:
21 [R]Withdraw Your hand far from me,
And let not the dread of You make me
afraid. Ps. 39:10
22 Then call, and I will [R]answer;
Or let me speak, then You respond to
me. Job 9:16; 14:15
23 How many *are* my iniquities and sins?
Make me know my transgression and
my sin.
24 [R]Why do You hide Your face, [Deut. 32:30]
And [R]regard me as Your enemy? Lam. 2:5
25 [R]Will You frighten a leaf driven to and
fro?
And will You pursue dry stubble? Is. 42:3
26 For You write bitter things against me,
And [R]make me inherit the iniquities of
my youth. Job 20:11
27 You put my feet in the stocks,
And watch closely all my paths.
You [T]set a limit for the [T]soles of my
feet. Lit. *inscribe a print* • *roots*

28 "Man[T] decays like a rotten thing, Lit. *He*
Like a garment that is moth-eaten.

CHAPTER 14

Job Mourns That Man Has Only One Life

"MAN *who is* born of woman
Is of few days and full of trouble.
2 [R]He comes forth like a flower and fades
away;
He flees like a shadow and does not
continue. Job 8:9
3 And [R]do You open Your eyes on such a
one,
And [R]bring *me to judgment with
Yourself? Ps. 8:4; 144:3 • [Ps. 143:2]
4 Who [R]can bring a clean *thing* out of an
unclean?
No one! [Ps. 51:2, 5, 10]
5 [R]Since his days *are* determined,
The number of his months *is* with You;
You have appointed his limits, so that
he cannot pass. Job 7:1; 21:21
6 [R]Look away from him that he may [T]rest,
Till [R]like a hired man he finishes his
day. Ps. 39:13 • Lit. *cease* • Job 7:1

7 "For there is hope for a tree,
If it is cut down, that it will sprout
again,
And that its tender shoots will not
cease.
8 Though its root may grow old in the
earth,
And its stump may die in the ground,
9 *Yet* at the scent of water it will bud
And bring forth branches like a plant.

14:3 LXX, Syr., Vg. *him*

10 But man dies and [T]is laid away;
Indeed he [T]breathes his last
And where *is* he? *lies prostrate • expires*
11 *As* water disappears from the sea,
And a river becomes parched and dries
up,
12 So man lies down and does not rise.
[R]Till the heavens *are* no more,
They will not awake [Is. 51:6; 65:17; 66:22]
Nor be roused from their sleep.

13 "Oh, that You would hide me in the
grave,
That You would conceal me until Your
wrath is past,
That You would appoint me a set time,
and remember me!
14 If a man dies, shall he live *again?*
All the days of my hard service [R]I will
wait,
Till my change comes. Job 13:15
15 [R]You shall call, and I will answer You;
You shall desire the work of Your
hands. Job 13:22
16 For now [R]You number my steps,
But do not watch over my sin. Prov. 5:21
17 My transgression *is* sealed up in a bag,
And You cover my iniquity.

18 "But *as* a mountain falls *and* crumbles
away,
And *as* a rock is moved from its place;
19 *As* water wears away stones,
And as torrents wash away the soil of
the earth;
So You destroy the hope of man.
20 You prevail forever against him, and he
passes on;
You change his countenance and send
him away.
21 His sons come to honor, and [R]he does
not know *it;*
They are brought low, and he does not
perceive *it.* Eccl. 9:5
22 But his flesh will be in pain over it,
And his soul will mourn over it."

CHAPTER 15

Job's Mouth Condemns Him

THEN [R]Eliphaz the Temanite answered
and said: Job 4:1

2 "Should a wise man answer with empty
knowledge,
And fill himself with the east wind?
3 Should he reason with unprofitable talk,
Or by speeches with which he can do
no good?
4 Yes, you cast off fear,
And restrain prayer before God.
5 For your iniquity teaches your mouth,
And you choose the tongue of the
crafty.
6 [R]Your own mouth condemns you, and
not I; [Luke 19:22]
Yes, your own lips testify against you.

7 "*Are* you the first man *who* was born?
Or were you made before the hills?
8 Have you heard the counsel of God?
Do you limit wisdom to yourself?
9 [R]What do you know that we do not
know?
What do you understand that *is* not in
us? Job 12:3; 13:2
10 [R]Both the gray haired and the aged *are*
among us, Job 8:8–10; 12:12; 32:6, 7
Much older than your father.
11 *Are* the consolations of God too small
for you,
And the word *spoken* *gently with you?
12 Why does your heart carry you away,
And what do your eyes wink at,
13 That you turn your spirit against God,
And let *such* words go out of your
mouth?

The Wicked Suffer

14 "What[R] *is* man, that he could be pure?
And *he who is* born of a woman, that
he could be righteous? Prov. 20:9
15 [R]If [T]God puts no trust in His saints,
And the heavens are not pure in His
sight, Job 4:18; 25:5 • Lit. *He*
16 [R]How much less man, *who is* abominable
and filthy, Ps. 14:3; 53:3
[R]Who drinks iniquity like water! Prov. 19:28

17 "I will tell you, hear me;
What I have seen I will declare,
18 What wise men have told,
Not hiding *anything received* [R]from
their fathers, Job 8:8; 20:4
19 To whom alone the [T]land was given,
And no alien passed among them: *earth*
20 The wicked man writhes with pain all
his days,
[R]And the number of years is hidden from
the oppressor. Ps. 90:12
21 [T]Dreadful sounds *are* in his ears;
[R]In prosperity the destroyer comes upon
him. *Terrifying* • 1 Thess. 5:3
22 He does not believe that he will [R]return
from darkness, Job 14:10–12
And he watches for the sword.
23 He [R]wanders about for bread, *saying,*
'Where *is it?*' Ps. 59:15; 109:10
He knows [R]that a day of darkness is
ready at his hand. Job 18:12

15:11 LXX *a secret thing*

24 Trouble and anguish make him afraid;
They overpower him, like a king ready
for [T]battle. *attack*
25 For he stretches out his hand against
God,
And acts defiantly against the Almighty,
26 Running stubbornly against Him
With his strong, embossed shield.

27 "Though[R] he has covered his face with
his fatness, Ps. 17:10; 73:7; 119:70
And made *his* waist heavy with fat,
28 He dwells in desolate cities,
In houses which no one inhabits,
Which are destined to become ruins.
29 He will not be rich,
Nor will his wealth [R]continue,
Nor will his possessions overspread the
earth. Job 20:28; 27:16, 17
30 He will not depart from darkness;
The flame will dry out his branches,
And [R]by the breath of His mouth he will
go away. Job 4:9
31 Let him not [R]trust in futile *things*,
deceiving himself,
For futility will be his reward. Is. 59:4
32 It will be accomplished before his time,
And his branch will not be green.
33 He will shake off his unripe grape like a
vine,
And cast off his blossom like an olive
tree.
34 For the company of hypocrites *will be*
barren,
And fire will consume the tents of
bribery.
35 [R]They conceive trouble and bring forth
futility;
Their womb prepares deceit." Is. 59:4

CHAPTER 16

Job Calls His Friends Miserable Comforters

THEN Job answered and said:

2 "I have heard many such things;
Miserable comforters *are* you all!
3 Shall words of wind have an end?
Or what provokes you that you answer?
4 I also could speak as you *do*,
If your soul were in my soul's place.
I could heap up words against you,
And shake my head at you;
5 *But* I would strengthen you with my
mouth,
And the comfort of my lips would
relieve *your grief*.

Job Laments His Situation

6 "Though I speak, my grief is not
relieved;
And *though* I remain silent, how am I
eased?
7 But now He has [R]worn me out;
You [R]have made desolate all my
company. Job 7:3 • Job 16:20; 19:13–15
8 You have shriveled me up,
And it is a [R]witness *against me*;
My leanness rises up against me
And bears witness to my face. Job 10:17
9 He tears *me* in His wrath, and hates me;
He gnashes at me with His teeth;
My adversary sharpens His gaze on me.
10 They [R]gape at me with their mouth,
They [R]strike me reproachfully on the
cheek, Ps. 22:13; 35:21 • Lam. 3:30
They gather together against me.
11 God [R]has delivered me to the ungodly,
And turned me over to the hands of the
wicked. Job 1:15, 17
12 I was at ease, but He has [R]shattered me;
He also has taken *me* by my neck, and
shaken me to pieces; Job 9:17
He has set me up for His target,
13 His archers surround me.
He pierces my heart and does not pity;
He pours out my gall on the ground.
14 He breaks me with wound upon wound;
He runs at me like a *warrior.

Job Defends His Innocence

15 "I have sewn sackcloth over my skin,
And laid my [T]head in the dust. Lit. *horn*
16 My face is [T]flushed from weeping,
And on my eyelids *is* the shadow of
death; Lit. *red*
17 Although no violence *is* in my hands,
And my prayer *is* pure.

18 "O earth, do not cover my blood,
And let my cry have no *resting* place!
19 Surely even now [R]my witness *is* in
heaven,
And my evidence *is* on high. Rom. 1:9
20 My friends scorn me;
My eyes pour out *tears* to God.
21 [R]Oh, that one might plead for a man
with God, Job 31:35
As a man *pleads* for his [T]neighbor! *friend*
22 For when a few years are finished,
I shall go the way of no return.

CHAPTER 17

God Makes Job A Byword

"MY spirit is broken,
My days are extinguished,
[R]The grave *is ready* for me. Ps. 88:3, 4
2 *Are* not mockers with me?
And does not my eye [T]dwell on their
provocation? Lit. *lodge*

16:14 Vg. *giant*

3 "Now put down a pledge for me with
Yourself.
Who *is* he *who* [R]will shake hands with
me? Prov. 6:1; 17:18; 22:26
4 For You have hidden their heart from
[R]understanding; Job 12:20; 32:9
Therefore You will not exalt *them.*
5 He who speaks flattery to *his* friends,
Even the eyes of his children will fail.

6 "But He has made me [R]a byword of the
people, Job 30:9
And I have become one in whose face
men spit.
7 [R]My eye has also grown dim because of
sorrow, Ps. 6:7; 31:9
And all my members *are* like shadows.
8 Upright *men* are astonished at this,
And the innocent stirs himself up
against the hypocrite.
9 Yet the righteous will hold to his [R]way,
And he who has [R]clean hands will be
stronger and stronger. Prov. 4:18 • Ps. 24:4

10 "But please, [R]come back again, all of
you, Job 6:29
For I shall not find *one* wise *man*
among you.
11 [R]My days are past, Job 7:6
My purposes are broken off,
Even the [T]thoughts of my heart. *desires*
12 They change the night into day;
'The light *is* near,' *they say,* in the face
of darkness.
13 If I wait *for* the grave *as* my house,
If I make my bed in the darkness,
14 If I say to corruption, 'You *are* my
father,'
And to the worm, 'You *are* my mother
and my sister,'
15 Where then *is* my [R]hope? Job 7:6; 13:15
As for my hope, who can see it?
16 *Will* they go down [R]to the gates of
[T]Sheol? Jon. 2:6 • The abode of the dead
Shall *we have* [R]rest together in the
dust?" Job 3:17–19; 21:33

CHAPTER 18

Bildad's Second Speech

THEN [R]Bildad the Shuhite answered and
said: Job 8:1

2 "How long *till* you put an end to words?
Gain understanding, and afterward we
will speak.
3 Why are we counted [R]as beasts, Ps. 73:22
And regarded as stupid in your sight?
4 [R]You[T] who tear yourself in anger,
Shall the earth be forsaken for you?
Or shall the rock be removed from its
place? Job 13:14 • Lit. *one who tears his soul*

5 "The[R] light of the wicked indeed goes
out, Prov. 13:9; 20:20; 24:20
And the flame of his fire does not shine.
6 The light is dark in his tent,
And his lamp beside him is put out.
7 The steps of his strength are shortened,
And his own counsel casts him down.
8 For [R]he is cast into a net by his own
feet,
And he walks into a snare. Job 22:10
9 The net takes *him* by the heel,
And [R]a snare lays hold of him. Job 5:5
10 A noose *is* hidden for him on the
ground,
And a trap for him in the road.
11 [R]Terrors frighten him on every side,
And drive him to his feet. Jer. 6:25
12 His strength is starved,
And destruction *is* ready at his side.
13 It devours patches of his skin;
The firstborn of death devours his
[T]limbs. *parts*
14 He is uprooted from [R]the shelter of his
tent,
And they parade him before the king of
terrors. Job 11:20
15 They dwell in his tent *who are* none of
his;
Brimstone is scattered on his habitation.
16 [R]His roots are dried out below,
And his branch withers above. Job 29:19
17 [R]The memory of him perishes from the
earth, [Ps. 34:16]
And he has no name [T]among the
renowned. Lit. *before the outside*
18 He is driven from light into darkness,
And chased out of the world.
19 [R]He has neither son nor posterity among
his people, Is. 14:22
Nor any remaining in his dwellings.
20 Those [T]in the west are astonished [R]at
his day, Lit. *who came after* • Ps. 37:13
As those in the east are frightened.
21 Surely such *are* the dwellings of the
wicked,
And this *is* the place *of him who* [R]does
not know God." Jer. 9:3

CHAPTER 19

Job's Response to Bildad

THEN Job answered and said:

2 "How long will you torment my soul,
And break me in pieces with words?
3 These ten times you have [T]reproached
me; *shamed* or *disgraced*
You are not ashamed *that* you *have
wronged me.

19:3 A Jewish tradition reads *make yourselves strange to me*

4 And if indeed I have erred,
My error remains with me.
5 If indeed you [R]magnify *yourselves*
against me, Ps. 35:26; 38:16; 55:12, 13
And plead my disgrace against me,
6 Know then that God has wronged me,
And has surrounded me with His net.

7 "If I cry out concerning [T]wrong, I am
not heard.
If I cry aloud, *there is* no justice. *violence*
8 [R]He has [T]fenced up my way, so that I
cannot pass; Job 3:23 · *walled off my way*
And He has set darkness in my paths.
9 [R]He has stripped me of my glory, Ps. 89:44
And taken the crown *from* my head.
10 He breaks me down on every side,
And I am gone;
My hope He has uprooted like a tree.
11 He has also kindled His wrath against
me,
And [R]He counts me as *one of* His
enemies. Job 13:24; 33:10
12 His troops come together
And build up their road against me;
They encamp all around my tent.

13 "He[R] has removed my brothers far from
me, Ps. 31:11; 38:11; 69:8; 88:8, 18
And my acquaintances are completely
estranged from me.
14 My relatives have failed,
And my close friends have forgotten
me.
15 Those who dwell in my house, and my
maidservants,
Count me as a stranger;
I am an alien in their sight.
16 I call my servant, but he gives no
answer;
I beg him with my mouth.
17 My breath is offensive to my wife,
And I am [T]repulsive to the children of
my own body. Lit. *strange*
18 Even young children despise me;
I arise, and they speak against me.
19 [R]All my close friends abhor me,
And those whom I love have turned
against me. Ps. 38:11; 55:12, 13
20 [R]My bone clings to my skin and to my
flesh, Ps. 102:5
And I have escaped by the skin of my
teeth.

21 "Have pity on me, have pity on me, O
you my friends,
For the hand of God has struck me!
22 Why do you persecute me as God *does*,
And are not satisfied with my flesh?

23 "Oh, that my words were written!
Oh, that they were inscribed in a book!
24 That they were engraved on a rock
With an iron pen and lead, forever!
25 For I know *that* my Redeemer lives,
And He shall stand at last on the earth;
26 And after my skin is [T]destroyed, this *I*
know, Lit. *struck off*
That in my flesh I shall see God,
27 Whom I shall see for myself,
And my eyes shall behold, and not
another.
How my [T]heart yearns within me! *kidneys*
28 If you should say, 'How shall we
persecute him?'—
Since the root of the matter is found in
me,
29 Be afraid of the sword for yourselves;
For wrath *brings* the punishment of the
sword,
That you may know *there is* a
judgment."

CHAPTER 20

Zophar's Second Speech

THEN [R]Zophar the Naamathite answered
and said: Job 11:1

2 "Therefore my anxious thoughts make
me answer,
Because of the turmoil within me.
3 I have heard the reproof [T]that
reproaches me, Lit. *of my insulting correction*
And the spirit of my understanding
causes me to answer.

4 "Do you *not* know this of old,
Since man was placed on earth,
5 [R]That the triumphing of the wicked is
short, Ps. 37:35, 36
And the joy of the hypocrite is *but* for a
[R]moment? [Job 8:13; 13:16; 15:34; 27:8]
6 [R]Though his haughtiness mounts up to
the heavens, Is. 14:13, 14
And his head reaches to the clouds,
7 *Yet* he will perish forever like his own
refuse;
Those who have seen him will say,
'Where is he?'
8 He will fly away [R]like a dream, and not
be found; Ps. 73:20; 90:5
Yes, he [R]will be chased away like a
vision of the night. Job 18:18; 27:21–23
9 The eye *that* saw him will *see him* no
more,
Nor will his place behold him anymore.
10 His children will seek the favor of the
poor,
And his hands will restore his wealth.
11 His bones are full of [R]his youthful vigor,
[R]But it will lie down with him in the
dust. Job 13:26 · Job 21:26

12 "Though evil is sweet in his mouth,
And he hides it under his tongue,

13 *Though* he spares it and does not
forsake it,
But still keeps it in his [T]mouth, Lit. *palate*
14 *Yet* his food in his stomach turns sour;
It becomes cobra venom within him.
15 He swallows down riches
And vomits them up again;
God casts them out of his belly.
16 He will suck the poison of cobras;
The viper's tongue will slay him.
17 He will not see [R]the streams,
The rivers flowing with honey and
cream. Jer. 17:8
18 He will restore that for which he
labored,
And will not swallow *it* down;
From the proceeds of *his* business
He will get no enjoyment.
19 For he has [T]oppressed *and* forsaken the
poor,
He has violently seized a house which
he did not build. *crushed*

20 "Because[R] he knows no quietness in his
[T]heart, Eccl. 5:13–15 • Lit. *belly*
He will not save anything he desires.
21 Nothing is left for him to eat;
Therefore his well-being will not last.
22 In his self-sufficiency he will be in
distress;
Every hand of [T]misery will come against
him. Or *the wretched* or *sufferer*
23 *When* he is about to fill his stomach,
God will cast on him the fury of His
wrath,
And will rain *it* on him while he is
eating.
24 He will flee from the iron weapon;
A bronze bow will pierce him through.
25 It is drawn, and comes out of the body;
Yes, [R]the glittering *point comes* out of
his [T]gall. Job 16:13 • Gall bladder
[R]Terrors *come* upon him; Job 18:11, 14
26 Total darkness *is* reserved for his
treasures.
[R]An unfanned fire will consume him;
It shall go ill with him who is left in his
tent. Ps. 21:9
27 The heavens will reveal his iniquity,
And the earth will rise up against him.
28 The increase of his house will depart,
And his goods will flow away in the day
of His [R]wrath. Job 20:15; 21:30
29 [R]This *is* the portion from God for a
wicked man, Job 27:13; 31:2, 3
The heritage appointed to him by God."

CHAPTER 21

Job's Response to Zophar

THEN Job answered and said:

2 "Listen carefully to my speech,
And let this be your [T]consolation. *comfort*
3 Bear with me that I may speak,
And after I have spoken, keep
[R]mocking. Job 16:10

4 "As for me, *is* my complaint against
man?
And if *it were*, why should I not be
impatient?
5 Look at me and be astonished;
Put *your* hand over *your* mouth.
6 Even when I remember I am terrified,
And trembling takes hold of my flesh.
7 [R]Why do the wicked live *and* become
old,
Yes, become mighty in power? [Jer. 12:1]
8 Their descendants are established with
them in their sight,
And their offspring before their eyes.
9 Their houses *are* safe from fear,
Neither *is* the rod of God upon them.
10 Their bull breeds without failure;
Their cow calves without miscarriage.
11 They send forth their little ones like a
flock,
And their children dance.
12 They sing to the tambourine and harp,
And rejoice to the sound of the flute.
13 They spend their days in wealth,
And [T]in a moment go down to the
[T]grave. Without lingering • Or *Sheol*
14 [R]Yet they say to God, 'Depart from us,
For we do not desire the knowledge of
Your ways. Job 22:17
15 [R]Who *is* the Almighty, that we should
serve Him?
And [R]what profit do we have if we pray
to Him?' Ex. 5:2 • Mal. 3:14
16 Indeed [T]their prosperity *is* not in their
hand; Lit. *their goal*
[R]The counsel of the wicked is far from
me. Prov. 1:10

17 "How often is the lamp of the wicked
put out?
How often does their destruction come
upon them,
The sorrows *God* [R]distributes in His
anger? [Luke 12:46]
18 [R]They are like straw before the wind,
And like chaff that a storm [T]carries
away. Ps. 1:4; 35:5 • *steals away*
19 *They say*, 'God [T]lays up [T]one's iniquity
[R]for his children';
Let Him recompense him, that he may
know *it*. *stores up* • Lit. *his* • [Ex. 20:5]
20 Let his eyes see his destruction,
And [R]let him drink of the wrath of the
Almighty. Is. 51:17
21 For what does he care about his
household after him,
When the number of his months is cut
in half?

22 "Can *anyone* teach God knowledge,
Since He judges those *who are* on high?
23 One dies in his full strength,
Being wholly at ease and secure;
24 His pails are full of milk,
And the marrow of his bones is moist.
25 Another man dies in the bitterness of his soul,
Never having eaten with pleasure.
26 They [R]lie down alike in the dust,
And worms cover them. Eccl. 9:2

27 "Look, I know your thoughts,
And the schemes *with which* you would wrong me.
28 For you say,
'Where *is* the house of the prince?
And where *is* *the tent,
The dwelling place of the wicked?'
29 Have you not asked those who travel the road?
And do you not know their signs?
30 [R]For the wicked are reserved for the day of doom;
They shall be brought out on the day of wrath. [Prov. 16:4]
31 Who condemns his way to his face?
And who repays him *for what* he has done?
32 Yet he shall be brought to the grave,
And a vigil kept over the tomb.
33 The clods of the valley shall be sweet to him;
[R]Everyone shall follow him, Heb. 9:27
As countless *have gone* before him.
34 How then can you comfort me with empty words,
Since [T]falsehood remains in your answers?" *faithlessness*

CHAPTER 22

Eliphaz's Third Speech

THEN [R]Eliphaz the Temanite answered and said: Job 4:1; 15:1; 42:9

2 "Can[R] a man be profitable to God,
Though he who is wise may be profitable to himself? [Luke 17:10]
3 *Is it* any pleasure to the Almighty that you are righteous?
Or *is it* gain *to Him* that you make your ways blameless?

4 "Is it because of your fear of Him that He reproves you,
And enters into judgment with you?
5 *Is* not your wickedness great,
And your iniquity without end?
6 For you have [R]taken pledges from your brother for no reason,
And stripped the naked of their clothing. [Ex. 22:26, 27]
7 You have not given the weary water to drink,
And you [R]have withheld bread from the hungry. Deut. 15:7
8 But the [T]mighty man possessed the land, Lit. *men of arm*
And the honorable man dwelt in it.
9 You have sent widows away empty,
And the [T]strength of the fatherless was crushed. Lit. *arms*
10 Therefore snares *are* all around you,
And sudden fear troubles you,
11 Or darkness *so that* you cannot see;
And an abundance of [R]water covers you. Ps. 69:1, 2; 124:5

12 "Is not God in the height of heaven?
And see the highest stars, how lofty they are!
13 And you say, [R]'What does God know?
Can He judge through the deep darkness? Ps. 73:11
14 [R]Thick clouds cover Him, so that He cannot see,
And He walks above the circle of heaven.' Ps. 139:11, 12
15 Will you keep to the old way
Which wicked men have trod,
16 Who [R]were cut down before their time,
Whose foundations were swept away by a flood? Job 14:19; 15:32
17 They said to God, 'Depart from us!
What can the Almighty do to *them?'
18 Yet He filled their houses with good *things;*
But the counsel of the wicked is far from me.

19 "The righteous see *it* and are glad,
And the innocent laugh them to scorn:
20 'Surely our *adversaries are cut down,
And the fire consumes their remnant.'

21 "Now acquaint yourself with Him, and [R]be at peace; Is. 27:5
Thereby good will come to you.

22 Receive, please, [R]instruction from His mouth, Prov. 2:6
And lay up His words in your heart.

21:28 Vg. omits *the tent* **22:17** LXX, Syr. *us*
22:20 LXX *substance is*

22:22 Memorizing God's Word—You are not always able to study the Bible by reading it. If you have memorized a portion of the Word of God, you are able to gain insights into its meaning at times when a Bible is not readily available. The Bible recognizes the importance of Scripture memorization. The following benefits can be cited:

23 If you return to the Almighty, you will
be built up;
You will remove iniquity far from your
tents.
24 Then you will [R]lay your gold in the
dust,
And the *gold* of Ophir among the stones
of the brooks. 2 Chr. 1:15
25 Yes, the Almighty will be your *gold
And your precious silver;
26 For then you will have your [R]delight in
the Almighty,
And lift up your face to God. Job 27:10
27 [R]You will make your prayer to Him,
He will hear you,
And you will pay your vows. [Is. 58:9–11]
28 You will also declare a thing,
And it will be established for you;
So light will shine on your ways.
29 When they cast *you* down, and you say,
'Exaltation *will come!*'
Then He will save the humble *person.*
30 He will *even* deliver one who is not
innocent;
Yes, he will be delivered by the purity
of your hands."

CHAPTER 23

Job Will Come Forth as Gold

THEN Job answered and said:
2 "Even today my [R]complaint is bitter;
My hand is listless because of my
groaning. Job 7:11
3 [R]Oh, that I knew where I might find
Him, Job 13:3, 18; 16:21; 31:35
That I might come to His seat!
4 I would present *my* case before Him,
And fill my mouth with arguments.
5 I would know the words *which* He
would answer me,
And understand what He would say to
me.
6 [R]Would He contend with me in His great
power? Is. 57:16
No! But He would take *note* of me.
7 There the upright could reason with
Him,
And I would be delivered forever from
my Judge.

8 "Look,[R] I go forward, but He is not
there,
And backward, but I cannot perceive
Him; Job 9:11; 35:14
9 When He works on the left hand, I
cannot behold *Him;*
When He turns to the right hand, I
cannot see *Him.*
10 But [R]He knows the way that I take;
When [R]He has tested me, I shall come
forth as gold. [Ps. 1:6; 139:1–3] • [James 1:12]
11 [R]My foot has held fast to His steps;
I have kept His way and not turned
aside. Ps. 17:5
12 I have not departed from the
[R]commandment of His lips;
[R]I have treasured the words of His
mouth Job 6:10; 22:22 • Ps. 44:18
More than my necessary *food.*

13 "But He *is* unique, and who can make
Him change?
And *whatever* [R]His soul desires, *that* He
does. [Ps. 115:3]
14 For He performs *what is* [R]appointed for
me, [1 Thess. 3:2–4]
And many such *things are* with Him.
15 Therefore I am terrified at His presence;
When I consider *this,* I am afraid of
Him.
16 For God [R]made my heart weak,
And the Almighty terrifies me; Ps. 22:14
17 Because I was not [R]cut off [T]from the
presence of darkness,
And He did *not* hide deep darkness from
my face. Job 10:18, 19 • Or *by* or *before*

CHAPTER 24

God Seems Indifferent to the Wicked

"SINCE [R]times are not hidden from the
Almighty,
Why do those who know Him see not
His [R]days? [Acts 1:7] • [Is. 2:12]

2 "*Some* remove [R]landmarks;
They seize flocks violently and feed *on*
them; [Deut. 19:14; 27:17]
3 They drive away the donkey of the
fatherless;
They take the widow's ox as a pledge.
4 They push the needy off the road,
So that the [R]poor of the land are forced
to hide. Prov. 28:28

22:25 Ancient vss. suggest *defense;* MT *gold,* as in v. 24

---

a. It keeps the child of God from sinning (Page 694—Ps. 119:11).
b. It provides comfort in times of trouble (Page 696—Ps. 119:52, 92).
c. It stays your mind upon God (Page 649—Ps. 43:3).
d. It provides daily sustenance for the spiritual life (Page 218—Deut. 8:3).
e. It provides continual and ready guidance in all the situations of life (Page 719—Prov. 6:20–23).
f. It provides the basis for formal and informal instruction of your children (Page 215—Deut. 6:6, 7).

Now turn to Page 252—Josh. 1:8: Meditating upon God's Word.

5 Indeed, *like* wild donkeys in the desert,
They go out to their work, seeking diligently for food.
The wilderness *yields* food for them *and* for *their* children.
6 They gather their fodder in the field
And glean in the vineyard of the wicked.
7 They [R]spend the night naked, without clothing, Ex. 22:26, 27
And have no covering in the cold.
8 They are wet with the showers of the mountains,
And [R]huddle around the rock for want of shelter. Lam. 4:5

9 "*Some* snatch the fatherless from the breast,
And take a pledge from the poor.
10 They cause *the poor* to go naked, without [R]clothing;
And they take away the sheaves from the hungry. Job 31:19
11 They press out oil within their walls,
And tread winepresses, yet suffer thirst.
12 The dying groan in the city,
And the souls of the wounded cry out;
Yet God does not charge *them* with wrong.

13 "There are those who rebel against the light;
They do not know its ways
Nor abide in its paths.
14 The murderer rises with the light;
He kills the poor and needy;
And in the night he is like a thief.
15 [R]The eye of the adulterer waits for the twilight, Prov. 7:7–10
[R]Saying, 'No eye will see me'; Ps. 10:11
And he disguises *his* face.
16 In the dark they break into houses
Which they marked for themselves in the daytime;
[R]They do not know the light. [John 3:20]
17 For the morning is the same to them as the shadow of death;
If *someone* recognizes *them*,
They are in the terrors of the shadow of death.

18 "They *should be* swift on the face of the waters,
Their portion *should be* cursed in the earth,
So that no *one would* turn into the way of their vineyards.
19 As drought and heat [T]consume the snow waters,
So should the [T]grave *those who* have sinned. Lit. *seize* • Or *Sheol*
20 The womb should forget him,
The worm *should* feed sweetly on him;
[R]He should be remembered no more,
And wickedness should be broken like a tree. Prov. 10:7
21 For he [T]preys on the barren *who* do not bear, Lit. *feeds on*
And does no good for the widow.

22 "But [T]God draws the mighty away with His power; Lit. *He*
He rises up, but no *man* is sure of life.
23 He gives them security, and they rely *on it*;
Yet His eyes *are* on their ways.
24 They are exalted for a little while,
Then they are gone.
They are brought low;
They are taken out of the way like all *others*;
They dry out like the heads of grain.

25 "Now if *it is* not *so*, who will prove me a liar,
And make my speech worth nothing?"

CHAPTER 25

Bildad's Third Speech

THEN [R]Bildad the Shuhite answered and said: Job 8:1; 18:1

2 "Dominion and fear *belong* to Him;
He makes peace in His high places.
3 Is there any number to His armies?
Upon whom does His light not rise?
4 [R]How then can man be righteous before God? Job 4:17; 15:14
Or how can he be [R]pure *who is* born of a woman? [Job 14:4]
5 If even the moon does not shine,
And the stars are not pure in His sight,
6 How much less man, *who is* a maggot,
And a son of man, *who is* a worm?"

CHAPTER 26

Job's Response to Bildad

BUT Job answered and said:

2 "How have you helped *him who is* without power?
How have you saved the arm *that has* no strength?
3 How have you counseled *one who has* no wisdom?
And *how* have you declared sound advice to many?
4 To whom have you uttered words?
And whose spirit came from you?

5 "The dead tremble,
Those under the waters and those inhabiting them.
6 Sheol *is* naked before Him,
And Destruction has no covering.
7 [R]He stretches out the north over empty space; Job 9:8
He hangs the earth on nothing.
8 [R]He binds up the water in His thick clouds, Prov. 30:4
Yet the clouds are not broken under it.
9 He covers the face of *His* throne,
And spreads His cloud over it.
10 [R]He drew a circular horizon on the face of the waters, Prov. 8:29
At the boundary of light and darkness.
11 The pillars of heaven tremble,
And are astonished at His reproof.
12 [R]He stirs up the sea with His power,
And by His understanding He breaks up [T]the storm. Is. 51:15 • Lit. *rahab*
13 By His Spirit He adorned the heavens;
His hand pierced the fleeing serpent.
14 Indeed these *are* the mere edges of His ways,
And how small a whisper we hear of Him!
But the thunder of His power who can understand?"

CHAPTER 27

Job Affirms His Righteousness

MOREOVER Job continued his discourse, and said:

2 "*As* God lives, [R]*who* has taken away my justice, Job 34:5
And the Almighty, *who* has made my soul bitter,
3 As long as my breath *is* in me,
And the breath of God in my nostrils,
4 My lips will not speak wickedness,
Nor my tongue utter deceit.
5 Far be it from me
That I should say you are right;
Till I die [R]I will not put away my integrity from me. Job 2:9; 13:15
6 My righteousness I [R]hold fast, and will not let it go; Job 2:3; 33:9
[R]My heart shall not [T]reproach *me* as long as I live. Acts 24:16 • *reprove*

7 "May my enemy be like the wicked,
And he who rises up against me like the unrighteous.
8 [R]For what is the hope of the hypocrite,
Though he may gain *much*, Matt. 16:26
If God takes away his life?
9 [R]Will God hear his cry Jer. 14:12
When trouble comes upon him?
10 [R]Will he delight himself in the Almighty?
Will he always call on God? Job 22:26, 27

11 "I will teach you [T]about the hand of God; *by*
What *is* with the Almighty I will not conceal.
12 Surely all of you have seen *it*;
Why then do you behave with complete nonsense?

13 "This[R] is the portion of a wicked man with God, Job 20:29
And the heritage of oppressors, received from the Almighty:
14 [R]If his children are multiplied, *it is* for the sword; Deut. 28:41
And his offspring shall not be satisfied with bread.
15 Those who survive him shall be buried in death,
And [T]their widows shall not weep, Lit. *his*
16 Though he heaps up silver like dust,
And piles up clothing like clay—
17 He may pile *it* up, but [R]the just will wear *it*, Prov. 28:8
And the innocent will divide the silver.
18 He builds his house like a moth,
[R]Like a [T]booth *which* a watchman makes. Is. 1:8 • Temporary shelter
19 The rich man will lie down,
But not be gathered *up*;
He opens his eyes,
And he *is* [R]no more. Job 7:8, 21; 20:7
20 Terrors overtake him like a flood;
A tempest steals him away in the night.
21 The east wind carries him away, and he is gone;
It sweeps him out of his place.
22 It hurls against him and does not [R]spare; Jer. 13:14
He flees desperately from its power.
23 *Men* shall clap their hands at him,
And shall hiss him out of his place.

CHAPTER 28

Job Observes That Man Cannot Discover Wisdom

"SURELY there is a mine for silver,
And a place *where* gold is refined.
2 Iron is taken from the [T]earth,
And copper *is* smelted *from* ore. Lit. *dust*
3 *Man* puts an end to darkness,
And searches every recess
For ore in the darkness and the shadow of death.
4 He breaks open a shaft away from people;
In places forgotten by feet
They hang far away from men;
They swing to and fro.
5 *As for* the earth, from it comes bread,
But underneath it is turned up as by fire;

6 Its stones *are* the source of sapphires,
And it contains gold dust.
7 *That* path no bird knows,
Nor has the falcon's eye seen it.
8 The proud lions have not trodden it,
Nor has the fierce lion passed over it.
9 He puts his hand on the flint;
He overturns the mountains [T]at the roots. At the base
10 He cuts out channels in the rocks,
And his eye sees every precious thing.
11 He dams up the streams from trickling;
What is hidden he brings forth to light.

12 "But[R] where can wisdom be found?
And where *is* the place of understanding? Eccl. 7:24
13 Man does not know its [R]value, Prov. 3:15
Nor is it found in the land of the living.
14 [R]The deep says, *'It is* not in me'; Job 28:22
And the sea says, *'It is* not with me.'
15 It cannot be purchased for gold,
Nor can silver be weighed *for* its price.
16 It cannot be valued in the gold of Ophir,
In precious onyx or sapphire.
17 Neither [R]gold nor crystal can equal it,
Nor can it be exchanged for [T]jewelry of fine gold. Prov. 8:10; 16:16 • *vessels*
18 No mention shall be made of [T]coral or quartz,
For the price of wisdom *is* above [R]rubies. Heb. *ramoth* • Prov. 3:15; 8:11
19 The topaz of Ethiopia cannot equal it,
Nor can it be valued in pure gold.

20 "From[R] where then does wisdom come?
And where *is* the place of understanding? Job 28:12
21 It is hidden from the eyes of all living,
And concealed from the birds of the [T]air. *heaven*
22 [R]Destruction[T] and Death say,
'We have heard a report about it with our ears.' Job 28:14 • Heb. *Abaddon*
23 God understands its way,
And He knows its place.
24 For He looks to the ends of the earth,
And sees under the whole heavens,
25 To establish a weight for the wind,
And mete out the waters by measure.
26 When He made a law for the rain,
And a path for the thunderbolt,
27 Then He saw [T]wisdom and declared it;
He prepared it, indeed, He searched it out. Lit. *it*
28 And to man He said,
'Behold, [R]the fear of the Lord, that *is* wisdom,
And to depart from evil *is* understanding.' " [Prov. 1:7; 9:10]

CHAPTER 29

Job Remembers His Happy Past

JOB further continued his discourse, and said:

2 "Oh, that I were as *in* months [R]past,
As *in* the days *when* God [R]watched over me; Job 1:1–5 • Job 1:10
3 [R]When His lamp shone upon my head,
And when by His light I walked *through* darkness; Job 18:6
4 Just as I was in the days of my prime,
When [R]the friendly counsel of God *was* over my tent; [Ps. 25:14]
5 When the Almighty *was* yet with me,
When my children *were* around me;
6 When [R]my steps were bathed with *cream,
And [R]the rock poured out rivers of oil for me! Deut. 32:14 • Ps. 81:16

7 "When I went out to the gate by the city,
When I took my seat in the open square,
8 The young men saw me and hid,
And the aged arose *and* stood;
9 The princes refrained from talking,
And put *their* hand on their mouth;
10 The voice of nobles was hushed,
And their [R]tongue stuck to the roof of their mouth. Ps. 137:6
11 When the ear heard, then it blessed me,
And when the eye saw, then it approved me;
12 Because [R]I delivered the poor who cried out,
And the fatherless and *he who had* no helper. [Ps. 72:12]
13 The blessing of a perishing *man* came upon me,
And I caused the widow's heart to sing for joy.
14 [R]I put on righteousness, and it clothed me;
My justice *was* like a robe and a turban. [Is. 59:17; 61:10]
15 I *was* [R]eyes to the blind,
And I *was* feet to the lame. Num. 10:31
16 I *was* a father to the poor,
And [R]I searched out the case *that* I did not know. Prov. 29:7
17 I broke the fangs of the wicked,
And plucked the victim from his teeth.

18 "Then I said, 'I shall die in my nest,
And multiply *my* days as the sand.
19 [R]My root *is* spread out [R]to the waters,
And the dew lies all night on my branch. Job 18:16 • Ps. 1:3

29:6 MT *wrath;* Ancient vss. and a few Heb. mss. *cream* and Job 20:17

20 My glory *is* fresh within me,
And my bow is renewed in my hand.'

21 "*Men* listened to me and waited,
And kept silence for my counsel.
22 After my words they did not speak
again,
And my speech settled on them *as dew*.
23 They waited for me *as* for the rain,
And they opened their mouth wide *as*
for [R]the spring rain. [Zech. 10:1]
24 *If* I mocked at them, they did not
believe *it*,
And the light of my countenance they
did not cast down.
25 I chose the way for them, and sat as
chief;
So I dwelt as a king in the army,
As one *who* comforts mourners.

CHAPTER 30

Job Describes His Present Humiliation

"BUT now they mock at me, *men*
[T]younger than I,
Whose fathers I disdained to put with
the dogs of my flock. Lit. *of fewer days*
2 Indeed, what *profit* is the strength of
their hands to me?
Their vigor has perished.
3 *They are* gaunt from want and famine,
Fleeing late to the wilderness, desolate
and waste,
4 Who pluck mallow by the bushes,
And broom tree roots *for* their food.
5 They were driven out from among *men*,
They shouted at them as *at* a thief.
6 *They had* to live in the clefts of the
[T]valleys, *wadis*
In caves of the earth and the rocks.
7 Among the bushes they brayed,
Under the nettles they nestled.
8 *They were* sons of fools,
Yes, sons of vile men;
They were scourged from the land.

9 "And[R] now I am their taunt-song;
Yes, I am their byword. Job 17:6
10 They abhor me, they keep far from me;
They do not hesitate to spit in my face.
11 Because [R]He has loosed *my bowstring
and afflicted me, Job 12:18
They have cast off restraint before me.
12 At *my* right *hand* the rabble arises;
They push away my feet,
And [R]they raise against me their ways
of destruction. Job 19:12
13 They break up my path,
They promote my calamity;
They have no helper.
14 They come as broad breakers;
Under the ruinous storm they roll
along.

15 Terrors are turned upon me;
They pursue my honor as the wind,
And my prosperity has passed like a
cloud.

16 "And[R] now my soul is [R]poured out
because of my *plight*; Ps. 42:4 • Ps. 22:14
The days of affliction take hold of me.
17 My bones are pierced in me at night,
And my gnawing pains take no rest.
18 By great force my garment is disfigured;
It binds me about as the collar of my
coat.
19 He has cast me into the mire,
And I have become like dust and ashes.

20 "I [R]cry out to You, but You do not
answer me;
I stand up, and You regard me. Job 19:7
21 *But* You have become cruel to me;
With the strength of Your hand You
[R]oppose me. Job 10:3; 16:9, 14; 19:6, 22
22 You lift me up to the wind and cause
me to ride *on it*;
You spoil my success.
23 For I know *that* You will bring me *to*
death,
And *to* the house [R]appointed for all
living. [Heb. 9:27]

24 "Surely He would not stretch out *His*
hand against a heap of ruins,
If they cry out when He destroys *it*.
25 [R]Have I not wept for him who was in
trouble? Ps. 35:13, 14
Has *not* my soul grieved for the poor?
26 [R]But when I looked for good, evil came
to me;
And when I waited for light, then came
darkness. Jer. 8:15
27 My heart is in turmoil and cannot rest;
Days of affliction confront me.
28 [R]I go about mourning, but not in the
sun;
I stand up in the congregation *and* cry
out for help. Ps. 38:6; 42:9; 43:2
29 [R]I am a brother of jackals,
And a companion of ostriches. Mic. 1:8
30 My skin grows black and falls from me;
[R]My bones burn with fever. Ps. 102:3
31 My harp is *turned* to mourning,
And my flute to the voice of those who
weep.

CHAPTER 31

Innocent of Sensual Sins

"I HAVE made a covenant with my eyes;
Why then should I [T]look upon a
young woman? *look intently* or *gaze*

30:11 Kt., LXX *His bowstring*

2 For what *is* the [R]allotment of God from
above,
And the inheritance of the Almighty
from on high? Job 20:29
3 *Is* it not destruction for the wicked,
And disaster for the workers of
iniquity?
4 [R]Does He not see my ways,
And count all my steps? [2 Chr. 16:9]

5 "If I have walked with falsehood,
Or if my foot has hastened to deceit,
6 Let me be weighed in a just balance,
That God may know my integrity.
7 If my step has turned from the way,
Or my heart walked after my eyes,
Or if any spot adheres to my hands,
8 *Then* let me sow, and another eat;
Yes, let my harvest be rooted out.

9 "If my heart has been enticed by a
woman,
Or *if* I have lurked at my neighbor's
door,
10 *Then* let my wife grind for another,
And let others bow down over her.
11 For that *would be* wickedness;
Yes, [R]it *would be* iniquity *worthy of*
judgment. Gen. 38:24
12 For that *would be* a fire *that* consumes
to destruction,
And would root out all my increase.

Innocent of Abusing His Power

13 "If I have despised the cause of my
manservant or my maidservant
When they complained against me,
14 What then shall I do when [R]God rises
up?
When He punishes, how shall I answer
Him? [Ps. 44:21]
15 [R]Did not He who made me in the womb
make them?
Did not the same One fashion us in the
womb? Job 34:19

16 "If I have kept the poor from *their*
desire,
Or caused the eyes of the widow to
[R]fail, Job 29:12
17 Or eaten my morsel by myself,
So that the fatherless may not eat of it
18 (But from my youth I reared him as a
father,
And from my mother's womb I guided
[T]the widow); Lit. *her*
19 If I have seen anyone perish for lack of
clothing,
Or any poor *man* without covering;
20 If his [T]heart has not [R]blessed me,
And *if* he was *not* warmed with the
fleece of my sheep; Lit. *loins* • [Deut. 24:13]
21 If I have raised my hand [R]against the
fatherless, Job 22:9
When I saw I had help in the gate;
22 *Then* let my arm fall from my shoulder,
Let my arm be torn from the socket.
23 For [R]destruction *from* God *is* a terror to
me,
And because of His magnificence I
could not endure. Is. 13:6

Innocent of Trusting in His Wealth

24 "If [R] I have made gold my hope,
Or said to fine gold, '*You are* my
confidence'; [Mark 10:23–25]
25 [R]If I have rejoiced because my wealth
was great,
And because my hand had gained
much; Ps. 62:10
26 [R]If I have observed the [T]sun when it
shines, Ezek. 8:16 • Lit. *light*
Or the moon moving *in* brightness,
27 So that my heart has been secretly
enticed,
And my mouth has kissed my hand;
28 This also *would be* an iniquity *worthy
of* judgment,
For I would have denied God *who is*
above.

Innocent of Not Caring for His Enemies

29 "If [R] I have rejoiced at the destruction of
him who hated me, [Prov. 17:5; 24:17]
Or lifted myself up when evil found him
30 [R](Indeed I have not allowed my mouth
to sin [Matt. 5:44]
By asking for a curse on his soul);
31 If the men of my tent have not said,
'Who is there that has not been satisfied
with his meat?'
32 [R](*But* no sojourner had to lodge in the
street,
For I have opened my doors to the
traveler); Gen. 19:2, 3
33 If I have covered my transgressions [R]as[T]
Adam, [Prov. 28:13] • Or *as men do*
By hiding my iniquity in my bosom,
34 Because I feared the great [R]multitude,
And dreaded the contempt of families,
So that I kept silence
And did not go out of the door— Ex. 23:2

Job Pleads to Meet God and Defend Himself

35 [R]Oh, that I had one to hear me!
Here is my mark. Job 19:7; 30:20, 24, 28
Oh, [R]*that* the Almighty would answer
me, Job 13:22, 24; 33:10
That my [T]Prosecutor had written a
book! Lit. *Accuser*
36 Surely I would carry it on my shoulder,
And bind it on me *like* a crown;
37 I would declare to Him the number of
my steps;
Like a prince I would approach Him.

38 "If my land cries out against me,
And its furrows weep together;
39 If [R]I have eaten its [T]fruit without
money, Job 24:6, 10–12 • Lit. *strength*
Or caused its owners to lose their lives;
40 *Then* let [R]thistles grow instead of
wheat,
And weeds instead of barley." Gen. 3:18

The words of Job are ended.

CHAPTER 32

Elihu Intervenes in the Debate

SO these three men ceased answering Job,
because he *was* [R]righteous in his own
eyes. Job 6:29; 31:6; 33:9
2 Then the wrath of Elihu, the son of
Barachel the [R]Buzite, of the family of Ram,
was aroused against Job; his wrath was
aroused because he [R]justified himself rather
than God. Gen. 22:21 • Job 27:5, 6
3 Also against his three friends his wrath
was aroused, because they had found no
answer, and *yet* had condemned Job.
4 Now because they *were* years older than
he, Elihu had waited *to speak to Job.
5 When Elihu saw that *there was* no answer in the mouth of these three men, his
wrath was aroused.
6 So Elihu, the son of Barachel the Buzite,
answered and said:

"I *am* [R]young in years, and you *are* very
old;
Therefore I was afraid,
And dared not declare my opinion to
you. Lev. 19:32
7 I said, [T]'Age should speak,
And multitude of years should teach
wisdom.' Lit. *Days,* years
8 But *there is* a spirit in man,
And [R]the breath of the Almighty gives
him understanding. [Prov. 2:6]
9 [R]Great[T] men are not *always* wise,
Nor do the aged *always* understand
justice. [1 Cor. 1:26] • Or *Men of many years*

10 "Therefore I say, 'Listen to me,
I also will declare my opinion.'
11 Indeed I waited for your words,
I listened to your reasonings, while you
searched out what to say.
12 I paid close attention to you;
And surely not one of you convinced
Job,
Or answered his words—
13 [R]Lest you say, [Jer. 9:23]
'We have found wisdom';
God will vanquish him, not man.
14 Now he has not [T]directed *his* words
against me;
So I will not answer him with your
words. *ordered*

15 "They are dismayed and answer no
more;
Words escape them.
16 And I have waited, because they did
not speak,
Because they stood still *and* answered
no more.
17 I also will answer my part,
I too will declare my opinion.
18 For I am full of words;
The spirit within me compels me.
19 Indeed my [T]belly *is* like wine *that* has
no [T]vent; *bosom* • *opening*
It is ready to burst like new wineskins.
20 I will speak, that I may find relief;
I must open my lips and answer.
21 Let me not, I pray, show partiality to
anyone;
Nor let me flatter any man.
22 For I do not know how to flatter,
Else my Maker would soon take me
[R]away. Job 27:8

CHAPTER 33

Elihu Challenges Job to Debate

"BUT please, Job, hear my speech,
And listen to all my words.
2 Now, I open my mouth;
My tongue speaks in my mouth.
3 My words *come* from my upright heart;
My lips utter pure knowledge.
4 [R]The Spirit of God has made me,
And the breath of the Almighty gives
me life. [Gen. 2:7]
5 If you can answer me,
Set *your words* in order before me;
Take your stand.
6 [R]Truly I *am* [T]as your spokesman before
God; Job 4:19 • Lit. *as your mouth*
I also have been formed out of clay.
7 Surely no fear of me will terrify you,
Nor will my hand be heavy on you.

Elihu Quotes Job's Complaints

8 "Surely you have spoken in my[T] hearing,
And I have heard the sound of *your*
words, *saying,* Lit. *ears*
9 'I[R] *am* pure, without transgression;
I *am* innocent, and *there is* no iniquity
in me. Job 10:7
10 Yet He finds occasions against me,
[R]He counts me as His enemy; Job 13:24; 16:9
11 [R]He puts my feet in the stocks,
He watches all my paths.' Job 13:27; 19:8

Elihu Answers Job's Complaints

12 "Look, *in* this you are not righteous.
I will answer you,
For God is greater than man.

32:4 Vg. *till Job had spoken*

13 Why do you [R]contend with Him?
For He does not give an accounting of
any of His words. [Is. 45:9]
14 [R]For God may speak in one way, or in
another,
Yet man does not perceive it. Ps. 62:11
15 In a dream, in a vision of the night,
When deep sleep falls upon men,
While slumbering on their beds,
16 [R]Then He opens the ears of men,
And seals their instruction. [Job 36:10, 15]
17 In order to turn man *from his* deed,
And conceal pride from man,
18 He keeps back his soul from the Pit,
And his life from [T]perishing by the
sword. Lit. *passing*

19 "Man[T] is also chastened with pain on his
[R]bed, Lit. *He* • Job 30:17
And with strong *pain* in many of his
bones,
20 [R]So that his life abhors bread, Ps. 107:18
And his soul [T]succulent food. *desirable*
21 His flesh wastes away from sight,
And his bones stick out *which once*
were not seen.
22 Yes, his soul draws near the Pit,
And his life to the executioners.

23 "If there is a messenger for him,
A mediator, one among a thousand,
To show man His uprightness,
24 Then He is gracious to him, and says,
'Deliver him from going down to the Pit;
I have found [T]a ransom'; *an atonement*
25 His flesh shall be young like a child's,
He shall return to the days of his youth.
26 He shall pray to God, and He will
delight in him,
He shall see His face with joy,
For He restores to man His
righteousness.
27 And he looks at men and [R]says,
'I have sinned, and perverted *what was*
right, [Luke 15:21]
And it [R]did not profit me.' [Rom. 6:21]
28 He will [R]redeem his soul from going
down to the Pit, Is. 38:17
And *his life shall see the light.

29 "Behold, God works all these *things*,
Twice, *in fact*, three *times* with a man,
30 [R]To bring back his soul from the Pit,
That he may be enlightened with the
light of life. Ps. 56:13

31 "Give ear, Job, listen to me;
Hold your peace, and I will speak.
32 If you have anything to say, answer
me;
Speak, for I desire to justify you.
33 If not, [R]listen to me;
[T]Hold your peace, and I will teach you
wisdom." Ps. 34:11 • *Keep silent*

CHAPTER 34

Elihu Challenges Job to Debate Again

ELIHU further answered and said:
2 "Hear my words, you wise *men*;
Give ear to me, you who have
knowledge.
3 [R]For the ear tests words
As the palate tastes food. Job 6:30; 12:11
4 Let us choose justice for ourselves;
Let us know among ourselves what *is*
good.

Elihu Quotes Job's Complaints

5 "For Job has said, 'I am righteous,
But God has taken away my justice;
6 Should I lie concerning my right?
My [T]wound *is* incurable, *though I am*
without transgression.' Lit. *arrow*
7 What man *is* like Job,
Who drinks [T]scorn like water, *derision*
8 Who goes in company with the workers
of iniquity,
And walks with wicked men?
9 For [R]he has said, 'It profits a man
nothing Mal. 3:14
That he should delight in God.'

Elihu Answers Job's Complaints

10 "Therefore listen to me, you men of
[T]understanding: Lit. *heart*
[R]Far be it from God *to do* wickedness,
And *from* the Almighty *to commit*
iniquity. Job 8:3; 36:23
11 [R]For He repays man *according to* his
work,
And makes man to find a reward
according to *his* way. Ps. 62:12
12 Surely God will never do wickedly,
Nor will the Almighty pervert justice.
13 Who gave Him charge over the earth?
Or who appointed *Him over* the whole
world?
14 If He should set His heart on it,
If He should [R]gather to Himself His
Spirit and His breath, Ps. 104:29
15 All flesh would perish together,
And man would return to dust.

16 "If *you have* understanding, hear this;
Listen to the sound of my words:
17 [R]Should one who hates justice govern?
Will you [R]condemn *Him who is* most
just? 2 Sam. 23:3 • Job 40:8
18 [R]*Is it fitting* to say to a king, '*You are*
worthless,' Ex. 22:28
And to nobles, '*You are* wicked'?
19 Yet He [R]is not partial to princes,
Nor does He regard the rich more than
the poor; [Deut. 10:17]
For they *are* all the work of His hands.

33:28 Kt. *my*

20 In a moment they die, [R]in the middle of
the night;
The people are shaken and pass away;
The mighty are taken away without a
hand. Ex. 12:29

21 "For[R] His eyes *are* on the ways of man,
And He sees all his steps. Job 31:4
22 [R]There is no darkness nor shadow of
death
Where the workers of iniquity may hide
themselves. [Amos 9:2, 3]
23 For He need not further consider a
man,
That he should go before God in
judgment.
24 [R]He breaks in pieces mighty men
without inquiry,
And sets others in their place. [Dan. 2:21]
25 Therefore He knows their works;
He overthrows *them* in the night,
And they are crushed.
26 He strikes them as wicked *men*
In the open sight of others,
27 Because they [R]turned back from Him,
And [R]would not consider any of His
ways, 1 Sam. 15:11 • Is. 5:12
28 So that they [R]caused the cry of the poor
to come to Him; Job 35:9
For He hears the cry of the afflicted.
29 When He gives quietness, who then can
make trouble?
And when He hides *His* face, who then
can see Him,
Whether *it is* against a nation or a man
alone?—
30 That the hypocrite should not reign,
Lest the people be ensnared.

31 "For has *anyone* said to God,
'I have borne *chastening*;
I will offend no more;
32 Teach me *what* I do not see;
If I have done iniquity, I will do no
more'?
33 Should He repay *it* according to your
terms,
Just because you disavow it?
You must choose, and not I;
Therefore speak what you know.

34 "Men of understanding say to me,
Wise men who listen to me:
35 'Job speaks without knowledge,
His words *are* without wisdom.'
36 Oh, that Job were tried to the utmost,
Because *his* answers *are like* those of
wicked men!
37 For he adds rebellion to his sin;
He claps *his hands* among us,
And multiplies his words against God."

CHAPTER 35

Elihu's Third Rebuttal

MOREOVER Elihu answered and said:

2 "Do you think this is right?
Do you say,
'My righteousness is more than God's'?
3 For [R]you say, Job 21:15; 34:9
'What advantage will it be to You?
What profit shall I have, more than *if* I
had sinned?'

4 "I will answer you,
And your companions with you.
5 [R]Look to the heavens, and see;
And behold the clouds *which* are higher
than you. [Job 22:12]
6 If you sin, what do you accomplish
[R]against Him?
Or, *if* your transgressions are multiplied,
what do you do to Him? [Jer. 7:19]
7 [R]If you are righteous, what do you give
Him?
Or what does He receive from your
hand? Prov. 9:12
8 Your wickedness affects a man such as
you,
And your righteousness a son of man.

9 "Because[R] of the multitude of
oppressions they cry out;
They cry out for help because of the
arm of the mighty. Job 34:28
10 But no one says, [R]'Where *is* God my
Maker,
[R]Who gives songs in the night, Is. 51:13 • Acts 16:25
11 Who [R]teaches us more than the beasts
of the earth,
And makes us wiser than the birds of
heaven?' Ps. 94:12
12 [R]There they cry out, but He does not
answer, Prov. 1:28
Because of the pride of evil men.
13 [R]Surely God will not listen to empty *talk*,
Nor will the Almighty regard it. [Is. 1:15]
14 [R]Although you say you do not see Him,
Yet justice *is* before Him, and [R]you
must wait for Him. Job 9:11 • [Ps. 37:5, 6]
15 And now, because He has not [R]punished
in His anger,
Nor taken much notice of folly, Ps. 89:32
16 [R]Therefore Job opens his mouth in vain;
He multiplies words without
knowledge." Job 34:35; 38:2

CHAPTER 36

Elihu Believes That God Is Disciplining Job

ELIHU also proceeded and said:

2 "Bear with me a little, and I will show
you

That *there are* yet words to speak on
God's behalf.
3 I will fetch my knowledge from afar;
I will ascribe righteousness to my
Maker.
4 For truly my words *are* not false;
One who is perfect in knowledge *is* with
you.

5 "Behold, God *is* mighty, but despises *no*
one;
[R]*He is* mighty in strength [T]of
understanding. Job 12:13, 16; 37:23 • *of heart*
6 He does not preserve the life of the
wicked,
But gives justice to the oppressed.
7 [R]He does not withdraw His eyes from the
righteous; [Ps. 33:18; 34:15]
But [R]*they are* on the throne with kings,
For He has seated them forever,
And they are exalted. Ps. 113:8
8 And if *they are* bound in [T]fetters,
Held in the cords of affliction, *chains*
9 Then He tells them their work and their
transgressions—
That they have acted [T]defiantly. *proudly*
10 [R]He also opens their ear to [T]instruction,
And commands that they turn from
iniquity. Job 33:16; 36:15 • *discipline*
11 If they obey and serve *Him*,
They shall [R]spend their days in
prosperity,
And their years in pleasures. [Is. 1:19, 20]
12 But if they do not obey,
They shall perish by the sword,
And they shall die *without knowledge.

13 "But the hypocrites in heart [R]store up
wrath; [Rom. 2:5]
They do not cry for help when He binds
them.
14 [T]They die in youth,
And their life *ends* among the perverted
persons. Lit. *Their soul dies*
15 He delivers the poor in their affliction,
And opens their ears in oppression.

16 "Indeed He would have brought you out
of dire distress,
[R]*Into* a broad place where *there is* no
restraint; Ps. 18:19; 31:8; 118:5
And [R]what is set on your table *would be*
full of [R]richness. Ps. 23:5 • Ps. 36:8
17 But you are filled with the judgment
due the [R]wicked; Job 22:5, 10, 11
Judgment and justice take hold *of you*.
18 Because *there is* wrath, *beware* lest He
take you away with *one* blow;
For [R]a large ransom would not help you
avoid *it*. Ps. 49:7
19 [R]Will your riches,
Or all the mighty forces,
Keep you from distress? [Prov. 11:4]

20 Do not desire the night,
When people are cut off in their place.
21 Take heed, [R]do not turn to iniquity,
For [R]you have chosen this rather than
affliction. [Ps. 31:6; 66:18] • [Heb. 11:25]

Elihu Reminds Job of the Greatness of God

22 "Behold, God is exalted by His power;
Who teaches like Him?
23 [R]Who has assigned Him His way,
Or who has said, 'You have done
[R]wrong'? Job 34:13 • Job 8:3
24 "Remember to [R]magnify His work,
Of which men have sung. [Rev. 15:3]
25 Everyone has seen it;
Man looks on *it* from afar.

26 "Behold, God *is* great, and we [R]do not
know *Him*;
[R]Nor can the number of His years *be*
discovered. [1 Cor. 13:12] • Heb. 1:12
27 For He draws up drops of water,
Which distill as rain from the mist,
28 [R]Which the clouds drop down
And pour abundantly on man. [Prov. 3:20]
29 Indeed, can *anyone* understand the
spreading of clouds,
The thunder from His canopy?
30 Look, He [R]scatters His light upon it,
And covers the depths of the sea. Job 37:3
31 For [R]by these He judges the peoples;
He gives food in abundance. [Acts 14:17]
32 He covers *His* hands with lightning,
And commands it to [T]strike. *strike the mark*
33 [R]His thunder declares it,
The cattle also, concerning [T]the rising
storm. 1 Kin. 18:41 • Lit. *what is rising*

CHAPTER 37

"AT this also my heart trembles,
And leaps from its place.
2 Hear attentively the thunder of His
voice,
And the rumbling *that* comes from His
mouth.
3 He sends it forth under the whole
heaven,
His lightning to the ends of the earth.
4 After it [R]a voice roars;
He thunders with His majestic voice,
And He does not restrain them when
His voice is heard. Ps. 29:3
5 God thunders marvelously with His
voice;
[R]He does great things which we cannot
comprehend. Job 5:9; 9:10; 36:26
6 For [R]He says to the snow, 'Be *on* the
earth'; Ps. 147:16, 17
Likewise to the [T]gentle rain and the
heavy rain of His strength. *shower of rain*

36:12 MT *as one without knowledge*

7 He seals the hand of every man,
That all men may know His work.
8 The animals [R]enter dens,
And remain in their lairs. Ps. 104:21, 22
9 From the chamber *of the south* comes
the whirlwind,
And cold from the scattering winds *of*
the north.
10 By the breath of God ice is given,
And the broad waters are frozen.
11 Also with moisture He saturates the
thick clouds;
He scatters His bright clouds.
12 And they swirl about, being turned by
His guidance,
That they may [R]do whatever He
commands them Job 36:32
On the face of the whole earth.
13 [R]He causes it to come, Ex. 9:18, 23
Whether for [T]correction, Lit. *a rod*
Or [R]for His land, Job 38:26, 27
Or [R]for mercy. 1 Kin. 18:41–46

14 "Listen to this, O Job;
Stand still and [R]consider the wondrous
works of God. Ps. 111:2
15 Do you know when God [T]dispatches
them,
And causes the light of His cloud to
shine? *places them*
16 [R]Do you know the balance of clouds,
Those wondrous works of [R]Him who is
perfect in knowledge? Job 36:29 • Job 36:4
17 Why *are* your garments hot,
When He quiets the earth by the south
wind?
18 With Him, have you [R]spread out the
[R]skies, [Is. 44:24] • Ps. 104:2
Strong as a cast metal mirror?

19 "Teach us what we should say to Him,
For we can prepare nothing because of
the darkness.
20 Should He be told that I *wish to* speak?
If a man were to speak, surely he would
be swallowed up.
21 Even now *men* cannot look at the light
when it is bright in the skies,
When the wind has passed and cleared
them.
22 He comes from the north *as* golden
splendor;
With God *is* awesome majesty.
23 *As for* the Almighty, [R]we cannot find
Him; [1 Tim. 6:16]
[R]*He is* excellent in power,
In judgment and abundant justice;
He does not oppress. [Job 9:4; 36:5]
24 Therefore men [R]fear Him;
He shows no partiality to any *who are*
[R]wise of heart." [Matt. 10:28] • [Matt. 11:25]

CHAPTER 38

God Questions Job from the Realm of Creation

THEN the LORD answered Job [R]out of the
whirlwind, and said: Ex. 19:16

2 "Who *is* this who darkens counsel
By [R]words without knowledge? 1 Tim. 1:7
3 [R]Now [T]prepare yourself like a man;
I will question you, and you shall
answer Me. Job 40:7 • *gird up your loins*

4 "Where[R] were you when I laid the
foundations of the earth? Ps. 104:5
Tell *Me,* if you have understanding.
5 Who determined its measurements?
Surely you know!
Or who stretched the line upon it?
6 To what were its foundations fastened?
Or who laid its cornerstone,
7 When the morning stars sang together,
And all [R]the sons of God shouted for
joy? Job 1:6

8 "Or[R] *who* shut in the sea with doors,
When it burst forth *and* issued from the
womb; Gen. 1:9
9 When I made the clouds its garment,
And thick darkness its swaddling band;
10 When [R]I fixed My limit for it,
And set bars and doors; Job 26:10
11 When I said,
'This far you may come, but no farther,
And here your proud waves must stop!'

12 "Have you [R]commanded the morning
since your days *began,* [Ps. 74:6; 148:5]
And caused the dawn to know its place,
13 That it might take hold of the ends of
the earth,
And the wicked be shaken out of it?
14 It takes on form like clay *under* a seal,
And stands out like a garment.
15 From the wicked their [R]light is
withheld, Job 18:5
And the [T]upraised arm is broken. *high*

16 "Have you [R]entered the springs of the
sea?
Or have you walked in search of the
depths? [Ps. 77:19]
17 Have [R]the gates of death been [T]revealed
to you?
Or have you seen the doors of the
shadow of death? Ps. 9:13 • Lit. *opened*
18 Have you comprehended the breadth of
the earth?
Tell *Me,* if you know all this.

19 "Where *is* the way *to* the dwelling of
light?
And darkness, where *is* its place,

20 That you may take it to its territory,
That you may know the paths *to* its home?
21 Do you know *it*, because you were born then,
Or *because* the number of your days *is* great?

22 "Have you entered [R]the treasury of snow, Ps. 135:7
Or have you seen the treasury of hail,
23 [R]Which I have reserved for the time of trouble,
For the day of battle and war? Is. 30:30
24 By what way is light [T]diffused,
Or the east wind scattered over the earth? Lit. *divided*

25 "Who [R]has divided a channel for the overflowing *water*,
Or a path for the thunderbolt, Job 28:26
26 To cause it to rain on a land *where there is* no one,
A wilderness in which *there is* no man;
27 [R]To satisfy the desolate waste,
And cause to spring forth the growth of tender grass? Ps. 104:13, 14; 107:35
28 [R]Has the rain a father? Job 36:27, 28
Or who has begotten the drops of dew?
29 From whose womb comes the ice?
And the [R]frost of heaven, who gives it birth? Ps. 147:16, 17
30 The waters harden like stone,
And the surface of the deep is frozen.

31 "Can you bind the cluster of the [R]Pleiades,[T] Amos 5:8 • *the Seven Stars*
Or loose the belt of Orion?
32 Can you bring out [T]Mazzaroth in its season?
Or can you guide [T]the Great Bear with its cubs? Lit. *Constellations* • Or *Arcturus*
33 Do you know [R]the ordinances of the heavens?
Can you set their dominion over the earth? Jer. 31:35, 36

34 "Can you lift up your voice to the clouds,
That an abundance of water may cover you?
35 Can you send out lightnings, that they may go,
And say to you, 'Here we *are!*'?
36 [R]Who has put wisdom in [T]the mind?
Or who has given understanding to the heart? [Ps. 51:6] • Lit. *the inward parts*
37 Who can number the clouds by wisdom?
Or who can pour out the bottles of heaven,
38 When the dust hardens in clumps,
And the clods cling together?

God Questions Job from the Realm of Animals

39 "Can[R] you hunt the prey for the lion,
Or satisfy the appetite of the young lions, Ps. 104:21
40 When they crouch in *their* dens,
Or lurk in their lairs to lie in wait?
41 Who provides food for the raven,
When its young ones cry to God,
And wander about for lack of food?

CHAPTER 39

"DO you know the time when the wild [R]mountain goats bear young?
Or can you mark when [R]the deer gives birth? Ps. 104:18 • Ps. 29:9
2 Can you number the months *that* they fulfill?
Or do you know the time when they bear young?
3 They bow down,
They bring forth their young,
They deliver their [T]offspring. Lit. *pangs*
4 Their young ones are healthy,
They grow strong with grain;
They depart and do not return to them.

5 "Who set the wild donkey free?
Who loosed the bonds of the onager,
6 [R]Whose home I have made the wilderness, Jer. 2:24
And the barren land his dwelling?
7 He scorns the tumult of the city;
He does not heed the shouts of the driver.
8 The range of the mountains *is* his pasture,
And he searches after [R]every green thing. Gen. 1:29

9 "Will the [R]wild ox be willing to serve you?
Will he bed by your manger? Num. 23:22
10 Can you bind the wild ox in the furrow with ropes?
Or will he plow the valleys behind you?
11 Will you trust him because his strength *is* great?
Or will you leave your labor to him?
12 Will you trust him to bring home your [T]grain, Lit. *seed*
And gather it to your threshing floor?

13 "The wings of the ostrich wave proudly,
But are her wings and pinions *like the* kindly stork's?
14 For she leaves her eggs on the ground,
And warms them in the dust;
15 She forgets that a foot may crush them,
Or that a wild beast may break them.

16 She treats her young harshly, as though
they were not hers;
Her labor is in vain, without concern,
17 Because God deprived her of wisdom,
And did not [R]endow her with
understanding. Job 35:11
18 When she lifts herself on high,
She scorns the horse and its rider.

19 "Have you given the horse strength?
Have you clothed his neck with
[T]thunder? Or *a mane*
20 Can you frighten him like a locust?
His majestic snorting strikes terror.
21 He paws in the valley, and rejoices in
his strength;
[R]He gallops into the clash of arms. Jer. 8:6
22 He mocks at fear, and is not frightened;
Nor does he turn back from the sword.
23 The quiver rattles against him,
The glittering spear and javelin.
24 He devours the distance with fierceness
and rage;
Nor does he stand firm, because the
trumpet *has* sounded.
25 At the *blast of* the trumpet he says,
'Aha!'
He smells the battle from afar,
The thunder of captains and shouting.

26 "Does the hawk fly by your wisdom,
And spread its wings toward the south?
27 Does the [R]eagle mount up at your
command, Prov. 30:18, 19
And [R]make its nest on high? Jer. 49:16
28 It dwells on the rock, and resides
On the crag of the rock and the
stronghold.
29 From there it spies out the prey;
Its eyes observe from afar.
30 Its young ones suck up blood;
And where the slain *are*, there it *is*."

CHAPTER 40

God Demands an Answer to His Questions

MOREOVER the LORD [R]answered Job,
and said: Job 38:1

2 "Shall [R]the one who contends with the
Almighty correct *Him?* Job 9:3; 10:2
He who rebukes God, let him answer
it."

Job's First Answer to God

3 Then Job answered the LORD and said:

4 "Behold,[R] I am vile; Ezra 9:6
What shall I answer You?
[R]I lay my hand over my mouth. Job 29:9
5 Once I have spoken, but I will not
answer;
Yes, twice, but I will proceed no
further."

God Tells Job to Save Himself

6 [R]Then the LORD answered Job out of the
whirlwind, and said: Job 38:1

7 "Now [T]prepare yourself like a man;
[R]I will question you, and you shall
answer Me: Lit. *gird up your loins* • Job 42:4

8 "Would[R] you indeed [T]annul My
judgment?
Would you condemn Me that you may
be justified? [Rom. 3:4] • *nullify*
9 Have you an arm like God?
Or can you thunder with [R]a voice like
His? [Ps. 29:3, 4]
10 [R]Then adorn yourself *with* majesty and
splendor,
And array yourself with glory and
beauty. Ps. 93:1; 104:1
11 Disperse the rage of your wrath;
Look on everyone *who is* proud, and
humble him.
12 Look on everyone *who is* [R]proud, *and*
bring him low; Dan. 4:37
Tread down the wicked in their place.
13 Hide them in the dust together,
Bind their faces in hidden *darkness*.
14 Then I will also confess to you
That your own right hand can save you.

God Compares the Power of Job with That of the Behemoth

15 "Look now at the [T]behemoth, which I
made *along* with you;
He eats grass like an ox. Identity unknown
16 See now, his strength *is* in his hips,
And his power *is* in his stomach
muscles.
17 He moves his tail like a cedar;
The sinews of his thighs are tightly
knit.
18 His bones *are like* beams of bronze,
His ribs like bars of iron.
19 He *is* the first of the [R]ways of God;
Only He who made him can bring near
His sword. Job 26:14
20 Surely the mountains [R]yield food for
him,
And all the beasts of the field play
there. Ps. 104:14
21 He lies under the lotus trees,
In a covert of reeds and marsh.
22 The lotus trees cover him *with* their
shade;
The willows by the brook surround him.
23 Indeed the river may rage,
Yet he is not disturbed;
He is confident, though the Jordan
gushes into his mouth,
24 *Though* he takes it in his eyes,
Or one pierces *his* nose with a snare.

LEVIATHAN AND BEHEMOTH

When European explorers first brought back reports from Africa of a spotted animal with legs like stilts and a neck so tall that it reached to the treetops, many people scoffed and said no such creature existed or could exist. Today every major zoo has at least a giraffe or two.

There are creatures described in the Old Testament, likewise, that many rationalistic scholars classify as myths. Others believe the descriptions are poetically exaggerated for dramatic effect and that these are well-known creatures found in our zoos. Still others believe they represent large animals that existed in Old Testament times but are now either extinct or only found in very remote areas or in very deep seas. Here we examine two of these.

Leviathan (*liwyātān*)

Leviathan (*liwyātān*) occurs only six times in the Old Testament but the term has stirred up great interest and controversy. *Leviathan* has become a word for anything of enormous size and power. The word is thought to be derived from a verb meaning "to twist." Job 41 is devoted to a detailed description of Leviathan, with God challenging Job to master him.

Some scholars believe that in Job the word poetically describes the Nile crocodile with his scaly hide, terrible teeth, and fast swimming. They feel that this fits in with the overthrow of Egypt in the Red Sea, since "Leviathan" is used for Egyptian troops in Psalm 74:13, 14. But in Psalm 104:25, 26, some envision a dolphin or a whale. However, the description in Job 41:33, 34 seems too majestic for a crocodile or dolphin, or even for a whale: "On earth there is nothing like him, which is made without fear. He beholds every high *thing;* he *is* king over all the children of pride." Since we really do not know for certain what a Leviathan was (or is!), the NKJV note to 41:1 is well stated: "A large sea creature, identity unknown."

Behemoth (*Behēmôt*)

Behemoth (*Behēmôt*) is the plural of the common Hebrew word for cattle or animal (*behēmah*, 137 times). *Behēmôt*, however, occurs only once, in Job 40:15. The ASV of 1901 and the French Louis Segond Version translate the word "hippopotamus." The NASB, an updating of the ASV, changes the text to "Behemoth," probably because there are a number of details in the passage's description of the beast that do not fit a hippopotamus. For example, a hippo's tail is what children at the zoo would call "cute," not impressive "like a cedar" (v. 17). Second, verse 19's observation that the behemoth "*is* the first of the ways of God" is a bit too grandiose for a hippopotamus, no matter how "poetic" one may become.

It has been suggested that perhaps the Hebrew word for "tail" (*zānāb*) really means a "trunk," which is somewhat tail-like in shape. This would suggest an elephant or mammoth, a much more majestic creature than a hippopotamus.

Those who believe that the Bible contains mythology have no problem with these creatures; to them, they simply never existed. Aside from putting the Bible on a purely human level, it also destroys the whole argument of the passage. God is contending with Job and using Behemoth as a proof of His own creativity. How can Job consider a nonexistent species to be proof of God's majesty?

Some creationists are convinced that God is describing His most impressive of all land animals, a dinosaur, such as the brontosaurus or brachiosaurus, which dragged behind them enormous tails the size of cedar trees. Of course, most people believe that dinosaurs were long extinct when Job lived and they rule this out. But there are extrabiblical records of sightings of creatures that sound just like Job 40:15–24.

The "tail like a cedar" (v. 17) fits perfectly. Some dinosaurs ate "grass like an ox" (v. 15) and were at home in marshy reeds and overflowing rivers (vv. 21–23). Other dinosaur-like traits mentioned in the passage are strong hips and powerful stomach muscles (v. 16), tightly knit sinews (v. 17), bones like bronze beams and ribs like iron bars (v. 18).

Again, the NKJV note in verse 15 is relevant: "Identity unknown."

CHAPTER 41

God Compares the Power of Job with That of the Leviathan

"CAN you draw out [T]Leviathan with a hook, A large creature, identity unknown
Or *snare* his tongue with a line *which* you lower?
2 Can you put a reed through his nose,
Or pierce his jaw with a [T]hook? thorn
3 Will he make many supplications to you?
Will he speak softly to you?
4 Will he make a covenant with you?
Will you take him as a servant forever?
5 Will you play with him as *with* a bird,
Or will you leash him for your maidens?
6 Will *your* companions [T]make a banquet of him?
Will they apportion him among the merchants? Or *bargain over him*
7 Can you fill his skin with harpoons,
Or his head with fishing spears?
8 Lay your hand on him;
Remember the battle—
Never do it again!
9 Indeed, *any* hope of *overcoming* him is [T]vain;
Shall *one not* be overwhelmed at the sight of him? Lit. *false*
10 No one *is so* fierce that he would dare stir him up.
Who then is able to stand against Me?
11 [R]Who has preceded Me, that I should pay *him*? [Rom. 11:35]
Everything under heaven is Mine.

12 "I will not [T]conceal his limbs,
His mighty power, or his graceful proportions. Lit. *keep silent about*
13 Who can [T]remove his outer coat?
Who can approach *him* with a double bridle? Lit. *take off the face of his garment*
14 Who can open the doors of his face,
With his terrible teeth all around?
15 *His* rows of [T]scales are *his* pride,
Shut up tightly *as with* a seal; Lit. *shields*
16 One is so near another
That no air can come between them;
17 They are joined one to another,
They stick together and cannot be parted.
18 His sneezings flash forth light,
And his eyes *are* like the eyelids of the morning.
19 Out of his mouth go burning lights;
Sparks of fire shoot out.
20 Smoke goes out of his nostrils,
As *from* a boiling pot and burning rushes.
21 His breath kindles coals,
And a flame goes out of his mouth.
22 Strength dwells in his neck,
And [T]sorrow dances before him. despair
23 The folds of his flesh are joined together;
They are firm on him and cannot be moved.
24 His heart is as hard as stone,
Even as hard as the lower *millstone*.
25 When he raises himself up, the mighty are afraid;
Because of his crashings they [T]are beside themselves. Or *purify themselves*
26 *Though* the sword reaches him, it cannot avail;
Nor does spear, dart, or javelin.
27 He regards iron as straw,
And bronze as rotten wood.
28 The arrow cannot make him flee;
Slingstones become like stubble to him.
29 Darts are regarded as straw;
He laughs at the threat of javelins.
30 His undersides *are* like sharp potsherds;
He spreads pointed *marks* in the mire.
31 He makes the deep boil like a pot;
He makes the sea like a pot of ointment.
32 He leaves a shining wake behind him;
One would think the deep had white hair.
33 On earth there is nothing like him,
Which is made without fear.
34 He beholds every high *thing*;
He *is* king over all the children of pride."

CHAPTER 42

Job Confesses Lack of Understanding

THEN Job answered the LORD and said:

2 "I know that You [R]can do everything,
And that no purpose *of Yours* can be withheld from You. [Matt. 19:26]
3 *You asked*, [R]'Who *is* this who hides counsel without knowledge?' Job 38:2
Therefore I have uttered what I did not understand,
[R]Things too wonderful for me, which I did not know. Ps. 40:5; 131:1; 139:6

Job Repents of His Rebellion

4 Listen, please, and let me speak;
You said, [R]'I will question you, and you shall answer Me.' Job 38:3; 40:7

5 "I have [R]heard of You by the hearing of the ear,
But now my eye sees You. Job 26:14
6 Therefore I [R]abhor *myself*,
And repent in dust and ashes." Ezra 9:6

The Deliverance of Job and His Friends

7 And so it was, after the LORD had spoken
these words to Job, that the LORD said to
Eliphaz the Temanite, "My wrath is aroused

against you and your two friends, for you
have not spoken of Me *what is* right, as My
servant Job *has*.
8 "Now therefore, take for yourselves
seven bulls and seven rams, go to My servant
Job, and offer up for yourselves a burnt
offering; and My servant Job shall pray for
you. For I will accept [T]him, lest I deal with
you *according to your* folly; because you
have not spoken of Me *what is* right, as My
servant Job *has*." Lit. *his face*
9 So Eliphaz the Temanite and Bildad the
Shuhite *and* Zophar the Naamathite went
and did as the LORD commanded them; for
the LORD had [T]accepted Job. Lit. *Job's face*
10 And the LORD [T]restored Job's losses
when he prayed for his friends. Indeed the
LORD gave Job [R]twice as much as he had
before. Lit. *turned the captivity of Job* • Is. 40:2
11 Then [R]all his brothers, all his sisters, and
all those who had been his acquaintances
before, came to him and ate food with him in
his house; and they consoled him and comforted him for all the adversity that the LORD
had brought upon him. Each one gave him a
piece of silver and each a ring of gold. Job 19:13
12 Now the LORD blessed [R]the latter *days* of
Job more than his beginning; for he had
[R]fourteen thousand sheep, six thousand camels, one thousand yoke of oxen, and one
thousand female donkeys. James 5:11 • Job 1:3
13 [R]He also had seven sons and three
daughters. Job 1:2
14 And he called the name of the first Jemi-
mah, the name of the second Keziah, and the
name of the third Keren-Happuch.
15 In all the land were found no women so
beautiful as the daughters of Job; and their
father gave them an inheritance among their
brothers.
16 After this Job [R]lived one hundred and
forty years, and saw his children and grandchildren *for* four generations. Job 5:26
17 So Job died, old and full of days.

THE BOOK OF

PSALMS

THE BOOK OF PSALMS

The Book of Psalms is the largest and perhaps most widely used book in the Bible. It explores the full range of human experience in a very personal and practical way. Its 150 "songs" run from the Creation through the patriarchal, theocratic, monarchical, exilic, and postexilic periods. The tremendous breadth of subject matter in the Psalms includes diverse topics, such as jubilation, war, peace, worship, judgment, messianic prophecy, praise, and lament. The Psalms were set to the accompaniment of stringed instruments and served as the temple hymnbook and devotional guide for the Jewish people.

The Book of Psalms was gradually collected and originally unnamed, perhaps due to the great variety of material. It came to be known as *Sepher Tehillim*—"Book of Praises"—because almost every psalm contains some note of praise to God. The Septuagint uses the Greek word *Psalmoi* as its title for this book, meaning poems sung to the accompaniment of musical instruments. It also calls it the *Psalterium* ("a collection of songs"), and this word is the basis for the term *Psalter*. The Latin title is *Liber Psalmorum*, "Book of Psalms."

THE AUTHOR OF PSALMS

Although critics have challenged the historical accuracy of the superscriptions regarding authorship, the evidence is strongly in their favor. Almost half (seventy-three) of the psalms are designated as Davidic: 3—9; 11—32; 34—41; 51—65; 68—70; 86; 101; 103; 108—110; 122; 124; 131; 133; and 138—145. David's wide experience as shepherd, musician, warrior, and king (1011-971 B.C.) is reflected in these psalms. The New Testament reveals that the anonymous psalms 2 and 95 were also written by this king whose name means "Beloved of Yahweh" (Acts 4:25; Heb. 4:7). In addition to the seventy-five by David, twelve were by Asaph, "Collector," a priest who headed the service of music (50; 73—83; Ezra 2:41); ten were by the sons of Korah, "Bald," a guild of singers and composers (42; 44—49; 84; 85; 87; Num. 26:9-11); two were by Solomon, "Peaceful," Israel's most powerful king (72; 127); one was by Moses, "Son of the Water," a prince, herdsman, and deliverer (90); one was by Heman, "Faithful," a wise man (88; 1 Kin. 4:31; 1 Chr. 15:19); and one was by Ethan, "Enduring," a wise man (89; 1 Kin. 4:31; 1 Chr. 15:19). The remaining fifty psalms are anonymous: 1; 2; 10; 33; 43; 66; 67; 71; 91—100; 102; 104—107; 111—121; 123; 125; 126; 128—130; 132; 134—137; and 146—150. Some of the anonymous psalms are traditionally attributed to Ezra.

THE TIME OF PSALMS

The psalms cover a wide time span from Moses (c. 1410 B.C.) to the postexilic community under Ezra and Nehemiah (c. 430 B.C.). Because of their broad chronological and thematic range, the psalms were written to different audiences under many conditions. They therefore reflect a multitude of moods and as such are relevant to every reader.

The five books were compiled over several centuries. As individual psalms were written, some were used in Israel's worship. A number of small collections were independently made, like the pilgrimage songs and groups of Davidic psalms (1—41, 51—70, 138—145). These smaller anthologies were gradually collected into the five books. The last stage was the uniting and editing of the five books themselves. David (1 Chr. 15:16), Hezekiah (2 Chr. 29:30; Prov. 25:1), and Ezra (Neh. 8) were involved in various stages of collecting the psalms. David was the originator of the temple liturgy of which his psalms were a part. The superscriptions of thirteen psalms specify key events in his life: First Samuel 19:11 (Ps. 59); 21:11 (Ps. 56); 21:13 (Ps. 34); 22:1 (Ps. 142); 22:9 (Ps. 52); 23:19 (Ps. 54); 24:3 (Ps. 57); Second Samuel 8:13 (Ps. 60); 12:13 (Ps. 51); 15:16 (Ps. 3); 15:23 (Ps. 63); 16:5 (Ps. 7); 22:2-51 (Ps. 18).

Here are four things to remember when interpreting the psalms: (1) When the superscription gives the historical event, the psalm should be interpreted in that light. When it is not given, there is little hope in reconstructing the historical occasion. Assuming occasions will probably hurt more than help the interpretive process. (2) Some of the psalms are associated with definite aspects of Israel's worship (e.g., 5:7; 66:13; 68:24, 25), and this can help in understanding those psalms. (3) Many of the psalms use definite structure and motifs. (4) Many psalms anticipate Israel's Messiah and are fulfilled in Christ. However, care must be taken not to allegorize them and forget the grammatical-historical method of interpretation.

THE CHRIST OF PSALMS

Many of the psalms specifically anticipated the life and ministry of Jesus Christ, the One who came centuries later as the promised Messiah ("Anointed One").

There are five different kinds of messianic

psalms: (1) *Typical Messianic.* The subject of the psalm is in some respects a type of Christ (see 34:20; 69:4, 9). (2) *Typical Prophetic.* The psalmist uses language to describe his present experience, which points beyond his own life and becomes historically true only in Christ (see 22). (3) *Indirectly Messianic.* At the time of composition the psalm refers to a king or the house of David in general, but awaits final fulfillment in Christ (see 2; 45; 72). (4) *Purely Prophetic.* Refers solely to Christ without reference to any other son of David (see 110). (5) *Enthronement.* Anticipates the coming of Yahweh and the consummation of His kingdom, which will be fulfilled in the person of Christ (see 96—99).

Some of the specific messianic prophecies in the Book of Psalms include:

	Prophecy	*Fulfillment*
2:7	God will declare Him to be His Son.	Matthew 3:17
8:6	All things will be put under His feet.	Hebrews 2:8
16:10	He will be resurrected from the dead.	Mark 16:6, 7
22:1	God will forsake Him in His hour of need.	Matthew 27:46
22:7, 8	He will be scorned and mocked.	Luke 23:35
22:16	His hands and feet will be pierced.	John 20:25, 27
22:18	Others will gamble for His clothes.	Matthew 27:35, 36
34:20	Not one of His bones will be broken.	John 19:32, 33, 36
35:11	He will be accused by false witnesses.	Mark 14:57
35:19	He will be hated without a cause.	John 15:25
40:7, 8	He will come to do God's will.	Hebrews 10:7
41:9	He will be betrayed by a friend.	Luke 22:47
45:6	His throne will be forever.	Hebrews 1:8
68:18	He will ascend to God's right hand.	Mark 16:19
69:9	Zeal for God's house will consume Him.	John 2:17
69:21	He will be given vinegar and gall to drink.	Matthew 27:34
109:4	He will pray for His enemies.	Luke 23:34
109:8	His betrayer's office will be fulfilled by another.	Acts 1:20
110:1	His enemies will be made subject to Him.	Matthew 22:44
110:4	He will be a priest like Melchizedek.	Hebrews 5:6
118:22	He will be the chief cornerstone.	Matthew 21:42
118:26	He will come in the name of the Lord.	Matthew 21:9

KEYS TO PSALMS

Key Word: Worship—The central theme of the Book of Psalms is worship—God is worthy of all praise because of who He is, what He has done, and what He will do. His goodness extends through all time and eternity. The psalms present personal responses to God as they reflect on His program for His people. There is a keen desire to see His program fulfilled and His name extolled. Many of the psalms survey the Word of God and the attributes of God, especially during difficult times. This kind of faith produces confidence in His power in spite of circumstances.

The psalms were used in the two temples and some were part of the liturgical service. They also served as an individual and communal devotional guide.

Key Verses: Psalm 19:14; 145:21—"Let the words of my mouth and the meditation of my heart be acceptable in Your sight, O LORD, my strength and my redeemer" (19:14).

"My mouth shall speak the praise of the LORD, and all flesh shall bless His holy name forever and ever" (145:21).

Key Chapter: Psalm 100—So many of the favorite chapters of the Bible are contained in the Book of Psalms that it is difficult to select the key chapter among such psalms as Psalms 1; 22; 23; 24; 37; 72; 100; 101; 119; 121; and 150. The two central themes of worship and praise are beautifully wed in Psalm 100.

SURVEY OF PSALMS

The Psalter is really five books in one, and each book ends with a doxology (see chart). The last psalm is the closing doxology for Book 5 and for the Psalter as a whole. After the psalms were written, editorial superscriptions or instructions were added to 116 of them. These superscriptions are historically accurate and are even numbered as the first verses in the Hebrew text. They designate fifty-seven psalms as *mizmor*, "psalm"—a song accompanied by a stringed instrument. Another twenty-nine are called *shir*, "song," and thirteen are called *maschil*, "contemplative poem." Six are called *miktam*, perhaps meaning "epigram" or "inscription poem." Five are termed *tepillah*, "prayer" (see Hab. 3), and only one is called *tehillah*, "praise" (145). In addition to these technical terms, the psalms can be classified according to certain themes: Creation psalms (8; 19), Exodus psalm (78), penitence psalm (6), pilgrimage psalms (120—134), and messianic psalms (see Christ in Psalms). There are even nine acrostic psalms in which the first verse or line begins with the first letter of the Hebrew alphabet, the next begins with the second, and so on (9; 10; 25; 34; 37; 111; 112; 119; 145).

First Chronicles 16:4 supports another approach to classification: "to invoke, to thank, and to praise the LORD, the God of Israel" (RSV). This leads to three basic types—lament, thanksgiving, and praise psalms. The following classification further divides the psalms into ten types: (1) *Individual Lament Psalms:* Directly addressed to God, these psalms petition Him to rescue and defend an individual. They have these elements: (a) an introduction (usually a cry to God), (b) the lament, (c) a confession of trust in God, (d) the petition, (e) a declaration or vow of praise. Most psalms are of this type (e.g., 3—7; 12; 13; 22; 25—28; 35; 38—40; 42; 43; 51; 54—57; 59; 61; 63; 64; 69—71; 86; 88; 102; 109; 120; 130; 140—143). (2) *Communal Lament Psalms:* The only difference is that the nation rather than an individual makes the lament (e.g., 44; 60; 74; 79; 80; 83; 85; 90; and 123). (3) *Individual Thanksgiving Psalms:* The psalmist publicly acknowledges God's activity on his behalf. These psalms thank God for something He has already done or express confidence in what He will yet do. They have these elements: (a) a proclamation to praise God, (b) a summary statement, (c) a report of deliverance, and (d) a renewed vow of praise (e.g., 18; 30; 32; 34; 40; 41; 66; 106; 116; and 138). (4) *Communal Thanksgiving Psalms:* In these psalms the acknowledgement is made by the nation rather than by an individual (see 124 and 129). (5) *General Praise Psalms:* These psalms are more general than the thanksgiving psalms. The psalmist attempts to magnify the name of God and boast about His greatness (see 8; 19; 29; 103; 104; 139; 148; 150). The joyous exclamation "hallelujah" ("praise the LORD!") is found in several of these psalms. (6) *Descriptive Praise Psalms:* These psalms praise God for His attributes and acts (e.g., 33; 36; 105; 111; 113; 117; 135; 136; 146; 147). (7) *Enthronement Psalms:* These psalms describe Yahweh's sovereign reign over all (see 47; 93; 96—99). Some anticipate the kingdom rule of Christ. (8) *Pilgrimage Songs:* Also known as Songs of Zion, these psalms were sung by pilgrims traveling up to Jerusalem for the three annual religious feasts of Passover, Pentecost, and Tabernacles (see 43; 46; 48; 76; 84; 87; 120—134). (9) *Royal Psalms:* The reigns of the earthly King and the heavenly King are portrayed in most of these psalms (e.g., 2; 18; 20; 21; 45; 72; 89; 101; 110; 132; and 144). (10) *Wisdom and Didactic Psalms:* The reader is exhorted and instructed in the way of righteousness (see 1; 37; 119).

There is a problem with the so-called imprecatory ("to call down a curse") psalms. These psalms invoke divine judgment on one's enemies (see 7; 35; 40; 55; 58; 59; 69; 79; 109; 137; 139; and 144). Although some of them seem unreasonably harsh, a few things should be kept in mind: (1) they call for divine justice rather than human vengeance; (2) they ask for God to punish the wicked and thus vindicate His righteousness; (3) they condemn sin (in Hebrew thinking no sharp distinction exists between a sinner and his sin); and (4) even Jesus calls down a curse on several cities and tells His disciples to curse cities that do not receive the gospel (Matt. 10:14, 15).

A number of special musical terms (some obscure) are used in the superscriptions of the psalms. "To the Chief Musician" appears in fifty-five psalms indicating that there is a collection of psalms used by the conductor of music in the temple, perhaps for special occasions. "Selah" is used seventy-one times in the psalms and three times in Habakkuk 3. This word may mark a pause, a musical interlude, or a crescendo.

BOOK	BOOK I (1-41)	BOOK II (42-72)	BOOK III (73-89)	BOOK IV (90-106)	BOOK V (107-150)
CHIEF AUTHOR	DAVID	DAVID AND KORAH	ASAPH	ANONYMOUS	DAVID AND ANONYMOUS
NUMBER OF PSALMS	41	31	17	17	44
BASIC CONTENT	SONGS OF WORSHIP	HYMNS OF NATIONAL INTEREST		ANTHEMS OF PRAISE	
TOPICAL LIKENESS TO PENTATEUCH	GENESIS: MAN AND CREATION	EXODUS: DELIVERANCE AND REDEMPTION	LEVITICUS: WORSHIP AND SANCTUARY	NUMBERS: WILDERNESS AND WANDERING	DEUTERONOMY: SCRIPTURE AND PRAISE
CLOSING DOXOLOGY	41:13	72:18, 19	89:52	106:48	150:1-6
POSSIBLE COMPILER	DAVID	HEZEKIAH OR JOSIAH		EZRA OR NEHEMIAH	
POSSIBLE DATES OF COMPILATION	c. 1020-970 B.C.	c. 970-610 B.C.		UNTIL c. 430 B.C.	
SPAN OF AUTHORSHIP	ABOUT 1,000 YEARS (c. 1410-430 B.C.)				

OUTLINE OF PSALMS

Book One: Psalms 1—41

1. Two Ways of Life Contrasted
2. Coronation of the Lord's Anointed
3. Victory in the Face of Defeat
4. Evening Prayer for Deliverance
5. Morning Prayer for Guidance
6. Prayer for God's Mercy
7. Wickedness Justly Rewarded
8. God's Glory and Man's Dominion
9. Praise for Victory over Enemies
10. Petition for God's Judgment
11. God Tests the Sons of Men
12. The Pure Words of the Lord
13. The Prayer for God's Answer—Now
14. The Characteristics of the Godless
15. The Characteristics of the Godly
16. Eternal Life for One Who Trusts
17. "Hide Me Under the Shadow of Your Wings"
18. Thanksgiving for Deliverance by God
19. The Works and Words of God
20. Trust Not in Chariots and Horses but in God
21. Triumph of the King
22. Psalm of the Cross
23. Psalm of the Divine Shepherd
24. Psalm of the King of Glory
25. Acrostic Prayer for Instruction
26. "Examine Me, O LORD, and Prove Me"
27. Trust in the Lord and Be Not Afraid
28. Rejoice Because of Answered Prayer
29. The Powerful Voice of God
30. Praise for Dramatic Deliverance
31. "Be of Good Courage"
32. The Blessedness of Forgiveness
33. God Considers All Man's Works
34. Seek the Lord
35. Petition for God's Intervention
36. The Excellent Lovingkindness of God
37. "Rest in the LORD"
38. The Heavy Burden of Sin
39. Know the Measure of Man's Days
40. Delight to Do God's Will
41. The Blessedness of Helping the Poor

Book Two: Psalms 42—72

42. Seek After the Lord
43. "Hope in God"
44. Prayer for Deliverance by God
45. The Psalm of the Great King
46. "God Is Our Refuge and Strength"
47. The Lord Shall Subdue All Nations
48. The Praise of Mount Zion
49. Riches Cannot Redeem
50. The Lord Shall Judge All People
51. Confession and Forgiveness of Sin
52. The Lord Shall Judge the Deceitful
53. A Portrait of the Godless
54. The Lord Is Our Helper
55. "Cast Your Burden on the LORD"
56. Fears in the Midst of Trials
57. Prayers in the Midst of Perils
58. Wicked Judges Will Be Judged
59. Petition for Deliverance from Violent Men
60. A Prayer for Deliverance of the Nation
61. A Prayer When Overwhelmed
62. Wait for God
63. Thirst for God
64. A Prayer for God's Protection
65. God's Provision Through Nature
66. Remember What God Has Done
67. God Shall Govern the Earth
68. God Is the Father of the Fatherless
69. Petition for God to Draw Near
70. Prayer for the Poor and Needy
71. Prayer for the Aged
72. The Reign of the Messiah

Book Three: Psalms 73—89

73. The Perspective of Eternity
74. Request for God to Remember His Covenant
75. "God Is the Judge"
76. The Glorious Might of God
77. When Overwhelmed, Remember God's Greatness
78. God's Continued Guidance in Spite of Unbelief
79. Avenge the Defilement of Jerusalem
80. Israel's Plea for God's Mercy
81. God's Plea for Israel's Obedience
82. Rebuke of Israel's Unjust Judges
83. Plea for God to Destroy Israel's Enemies
84. The Joy of Dwelling with God
85. Prayer for Revival
86. "Teach Me Your Way, O LORD"
87. Glorious Zion, City of God
88. Crying from Deepest Affliction
89. Claiming God's Promises in Affliction

Book Four: Psalms 90—106

90. "Teach Us to Number Our Days"
91. Abiding in "the Shadow of the Almighty"
92. It Is Good to Praise the Lord
93. The Majesty of God
94. Vengeance Belongs Only to God
95. Call to Worship the Lord
96. Declare the Glory of God
97. Rejoice! The Lord Reigns!
98. Sing a New Song to the Lord
99. "Exalt the LORD Our God"
100. "Serve the LORD with Gladness"
101. Commitments of a Holy Life
102. Prayer of an Overwhelmed Saint
103. Bless the Lord, All You People!
104. Psalm Rehearsing Creation
105. Remember, God Keeps His Promises
106. "We Have Sinned"

Book Five: Psalms 107—150

107. God Satisfies the Longing Soul
108. Awake Early and Praise the Lord
109. Song of the Slandered
110. The Coming of the Priest-King-Judge
111. Praise for God's Tender Care
112. The Blessings of Those Who Fear God
113. The Condescending Grace of God
114. In Praise for the Exodus
115. To God Alone Be the Glory
116. Love the Lord for What He Has Done

117. The Praise of All Peoples
118. Better to Trust God than Man
119. An Acrostic in Praise of the Scriptures
120. A Cry in Distress
121. God Is Our Keeper
122. "Pray for the Peace of Jerusalem"
123. Plea for the Mercy of God
124. God Is on Our Side
125. Trust in the Lord and Abide Forever
126. "Sow in Tears . . . Reap in Joy"
127. Children Are God's Heritage
128. Blessing on the House of the God-Fearing
129. Plea of the Persecuted
130. "My Soul Waits for the Lord"
131. A Childlike Faith
132. Trust in the God of David
133. Beauty of the Unity of the Brethren
134. Praise the Lord in the Evening
135. God Has Done Great Things!
136. God's Mercy Endures Forever
137. Tears in Exile
138. God Answered My Prayer
139. "Search Me, O God"
140. Preserve Me from Violence
141. "Set a Guard, O LORD, over My Mouth"
142. "No One Cares for My Soul"
143. "Teach Me to Do Your Will"
144. "What Is Man?"
145. Testify to God's Great Acts
146. "Do Not Put Your Trust in Princes"
147. God Heals the Brokenhearted
148. All Creation Praises the Lord
149. "The LORD Takes Pleasure in His People"
150. "Praise the LORD"

BOOK ONE
Psalms 1–41

PSALM 1

Two Ways of Life Contrasted

BLESSED [R]*is* the man
Who walks not in the counsel of the
[T]ungodly, Prov. 4:14 • *wicked*
Nor stands in the path of sinners,
Nor sits in the seat of the scornful;
2 But [R]his delight *is* in the law of the
LORD, Ps. 119:14, 16, 35
And in His law he [T]meditates day and
night. *ponders* by talking to himself
3 He shall be like a tree
[R]Planted by the [T]rivers of water,
That brings forth its fruit in its
season, Jer. 17:8 • *channels*
Whose leaf also shall not wither;
And whatever he does shall prosper.

4 The ungodly *are* not so,
But *are* [R]like the chaff which the wind
drives away. Job 21:18
5 Therefore the ungodly shall not stand in
the judgment,
Nor sinners in the congregation of the
righteous.

6 For [R]the LORD knows the way of the
righteous, Ps. 37:18
But the way of the ungodly shall perish.

PSALM 2

Coronation of the Lord's Anointed

WHY [R]do the nations rage, [Acts 4:25–28] ☆
And the people plot a vain thing?
2 The kings of the earth set themselves,
And the rulers take counsel together,
[R]Against the LORD and against His
[T]Anointed, *saying*, [John 1:41] ☆ • Christ
3 "Let us break Their bonds in pieces
And cast away Their cords from us."

4 He who sits in the heavens shall laugh;
The LORD shall hold them in derision.
5 Then He shall speak to them in His
wrath,
And distress them in His deep
displeasure:
6 "Yet I have [T]set My King Lit. *installed*
On My holy hill of Zion."

7 "I will declare the decree:
The LORD has said to Me,
[R]'You *are* My Son, [Luke 1:35] ☆
Today I have begotten You.
8 Ask of Me, and I will give *You*
The nations *for* Your inheritance,
And the ends of the earth *for* Your
possession.
9 [R]You shall break them with a rod of
iron;
You shall dash them in pieces like a
potter's vessel.' " Ps. 89:23; 110:5, 6 ☆

10 Now therefore, be wise, O kings;
Be instructed, you judges of the earth.
11 Serve the LORD with fear,
And rejoice with trembling.
12 [T]Kiss the Son, lest He be angry,
And you perish *in* the way,
When His wrath is kindled but a little.
Blessed *are* all those who put their trust
in Him. An act of homage and submission

PSALM 3

Victory in the Face of Defeat

A Psalm of David when he fled
from Absalom his son.

LORD, how they have increased who
trouble me!

Many *are* they who rise up against me.
2 Many *are* they who say of me,
"*There is* no help for him in God."
Selah

3 But You, O LORD, *are* [R]a shield [T]for me,
My glory and [R]the One who lifts up my head. Ps. 5:12; 28:7 • Lit. *around* • Ps. 9:13; 27:6
4 I cried to the LORD with my voice,
And [R]He heard me from His [R]holy hill.
Selah Ps. 4:3; 34:4 • Ps. 2:6; 15:1; 43:3

5 [R]I lay down and slept; Lev. 26:6
I awoke, for the LORD sustained me.
6 [R]I will not be afraid of ten thousands of people
Who have set *themselves* against me all around. Ps. 23:4; 27:3

7 Arise, O LORD;
Save me, O my God!
[R]For You have struck all my enemies on the cheekbone;
You have broken the teeth of the ungodly. Job 16:10
8 [R]Salvation *belongs* to the LORD.
Your blessing *is* upon Your people.
Selah [Is. 43:11]

PSALM 4

Evening Prayer for Deliverance

To the Chief Musician. With stringed instruments. A Psalm of David.

HEAR me when I call, O God of my righteousness!
You have relieved me *when I was* in distress;
Have mercy on me, and hear my prayer.

2 How long, O you sons of men,
Will you turn my glory to shame?
How long will you love worthlessness
And seek falsehood? Selah
3 But know that the LORD has set apart for Himself him who is godly;
The LORD will hear when I call to Him.

4 [R]Be angry, and do not sin. [Eph. 4:26]
[R]Meditate within your heart on your bed, and be still. Selah Ps. 77:6
5 Offer the sacrifices of righteousness,
And put your trust in the LORD.

6 *There are* many who say,
"Who will show us *any* good?"
[R]LORD, lift up the light of Your countenance upon us. Num. 6:26
7 You have put [R]gladness in my heart,
More than in the season that their grain and wine increased. Is. 9:3
8 [R]I will both lie down in peace, and sleep;
[R]For You alone, O LORD, make me dwell in safety. Ps. 3:5 • [Lev. 25:18]

PSALM 5

Morning Prayer for Guidance

To the Chief Musician. With *flutes. A Psalm of David.

GIVE [R]ear to my words, O LORD, Ps. 4:1
Consider my [T]meditation. Lit. *groaning*
2 Give heed to the voice of my cry,
My King and my God,
For to You I will pray.
3 My voice You shall hear in the morning, O LORD;
[R]In the morning I will direct *it* to You,
And I will look up. Ps. 55:17; 88:13

4 For You *are* not a God who takes pleasure in wickedness,
Nor shall evil [T]dwell with You. Lit. *sojourn*
5 The [R]boastful shall not [R]stand in Your sight; [Hab. 1:13] • Ps. 1:5
You hate all workers of iniquity.
6 You shall destroy those who speak falsehood;
The LORD abhors the [R]bloodthirsty and deceitful man. Ps. 55:23

7 But as for me, I will come into Your house in the multitude of Your mercy;
In fear of You I will worship toward Your holy temple.
8 [R]Lead me, O LORD, in Your righteousness because of my enemies;
Make Your way straight before my face. Ps. 25:4, 5; 27:11; 31:3

9 For *there is* no [T]faithfulness in their mouth; *uprightness*
Their inward part *is* destruction;
[R]Their throat *is* an open tomb; Rom. 3:13
They flatter with their tongue.
10 Pronounce them guilty, O God!
Let them fall by their own counsels;
Cast them out in the multitude of their transgressions,
For they have rebelled against You.

11 But let all those rejoice who put their trust in You;
Let them ever shout for joy, because You [T]defend them;
Let those also who love Your name
Be joyful in You. *protect*, lit. *cover*
12 For You, O LORD, will bless the righteous;
With favor You will surround him as *with* a shield.

5:title, Heb. *nehiloth*

TYPES OF PSALMS

The Book of Psalms is a collection of prayers, poems, and hymns that focus the worshiper's thoughts on God in praise and adoration. Parts of the book were used as a hymnal in the worship services of ancient Israel. The book contains 150 individual psalms, which may be grouped into the following types or categories.

1. **Individual and communal lament psalms,** or prayers for God's deliverance. Psalms of this type are 3—7; 12; 13; 22; 25—28; 35; 38—40; 42—44; 51; 54—57; 59—61; 63; 64; 69—71; 74; 79; 80; 83; 85; 86; 88; 90; 102; 109; 120; 123; 130; and 140—143. These psalms speak to believers in moments of desperation and despair, when our need is for God's deliverance.

2. **Thanksgiving psalms,** consisting of praise to God for His gracious acts. This theme occurs in Psalms 8; 18; 19; 29; 30; 32—34; 36; 40; 41; 66; 103—106; 111; 113; 116; 117; 124; 129; 135; 136; 138; 139; 146—148; and 150. Every prayer we utter should include the element of thanksgiving. These psalms make us aware of God's blessings and lead us to express our thanks with feeling and conviction.

3. **Enthronement psalms,** which describe God's sovereign rule. Psalms of this type are 47; 93; and 96—99. Through these psalms we acknowledge God as powerful Creator and sovereign Lord over all His creation.

4. **Pilgrimage psalms,** which were sung by worshipers as they traveled to Jerusalem to celebrate the Jewish festivals. Pilgrimage psalms are 43; 46; 48; 76; 84; 87; and 120—134. These psalms can help us establish a mood of reverent worship.

5. **Royal psalms,** which portray the reign of the earthly king, as well as of the heavenly King of Israel. This theme is evident in Psalms 2; 18; 20; 21; 45; 72; 89; 101; 110; 132; and 144. These psalms can make us aware of our daily need to make Christ the sovereign ruler of our lives.

6. **Wisdom psalms,** which instruct the worshiper in the way of wisdom and righteousness. Individual wisdom psalms are 1; 37; and 119. These psalms are especially appropriate in times of decision when we are searching for God's will and direction in our lives.

7. **Imprecatory psalms,** in which the worshiper invokes God's wrath and judgment against his enemies. This theme occurs in Psalms 7; 35; 40; 55; 58; 59; 69; 79; 109; 137; 139; and 144. These psalms can help us be honest about our feelings toward people who have done us wrong and work our way through these feelings to a point of forgiveness.

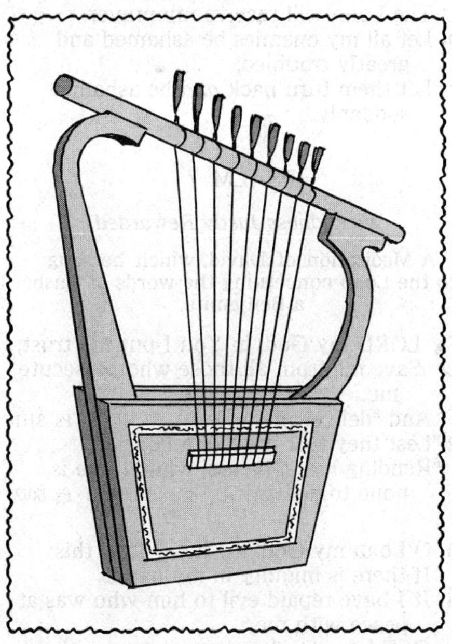

The lyre was one of the musical instruments used to accompany psalms that were sung.

PSALM 6

Prayer for God's Mercy

To the Chief Musician. With stringed instruments. On an *eight-stringed harp. A Psalm of David.

O LORD, [R]do not rebuke me in Your
anger, Ps. 38:1; 118:18
Nor chasten me in Your hot displeasure.
2 Have mercy on me, O LORD, for I *am*
weak;
O LORD, [R]heal me, for my bones are
troubled. [Hos. 6:1]
3 My soul also is greatly [R]troubled;
But You, O LORD—how long? Ps. 88:3

4 Return, O LORD, deliver me!
Oh, save me for Your mercies' sake!
5 [R]For in death *there is* no remembrance
of You; [Eccl. 9:10]
In the grave who will give You thanks?

6 I am weary with my groaning;
[T]All night I make my bed swim; Or *Every*
I drench my couch with my tears.
7 My eye wastes away because of grief;
It grows old because of all my enemies.

8 [R]Depart from me, all you workers of
iniquity;
For the LORD has [R]heard the voice of
my weeping. [Matt. 25:41] • Ps. 3:4; 28:6
9 The LORD has heard my supplication;
The LORD will receive my prayer.
10 Let all my enemies be ashamed and
greatly troubled;
Let them turn back *and* be ashamed
suddenly.

PSALM 7

Wickedness Justly Rewarded

A Meditation of David, which he sang to the LORD concerning the words of Cush, a Benjamite.

O LORD my God, in You I put my trust;
Save me from all those who persecute
me;
And [R]deliver me, Ps. 31:15
2 [R]Lest they tear me like a lion,
[R]Rending *me* in pieces, while *there is*
none to deliver. Is. 38:13 • Ps. 50:22

3 O LORD my God, if I have done this:
If there is iniquity in my hands,
4 If I have repaid evil to him who was at
peace with me,
Or [R]have plundered my enemy without
cause, 1 Sam. 24:7; 26:9
5 Let the enemy pursue me and overtake
me;
Yes, let him trample my life to the
earth,
And lay my honor in the dust. Selah

6 Arise, O LORD, in Your anger;
[R]Lift Yourself up because of the rage of
my enemies, Ps. 94:2
And [R]awake for me *to* the judgment
You have commanded! Ps. 35:23; 44:23
7 So the congregation of the peoples shall
surround You;
For their sakes, therefore, return on
high.
8 The LORD shall judge the peoples;
[R]Judge me, O LORD, [R]according to my
righteousness,
And according to my integrity within
me. Ps. 26:1; 35:24; 43:1 • Ps. 18:20; 35:24

9 Oh, let the wickedness of the wicked
come to an end,
But establish the just;
For the righteous God tests the hearts
and [T]minds. Lit. *kidneys*, secret part of man
10 [T]My defense *is* of God, Lit. *My shield is God*
Who saves the upright in heart.

11 God *is* a just judge,
And God is angry *with the wicked*
every day.
12 If he does not turn back,
He will [R]sharpen His sword; Deut. 32:41
He bends His bow and makes it ready.
13 He also prepares for Himself
instruments of death;
He makes His arrows into fiery shafts.

14 [R]Behold, *the wicked* travails with
iniquity,
Conceives trouble and brings forth
falsehood. Is. 59:4
15 He made a pit and dug it out,
[R]And has fallen into the ditch *which* he
made. [Job 4:8]
16 [R]His trouble shall return upon his own
head, Esth. 9:25
And his violent dealing shall come
down on [T]his own crown. *of his own head*

17 I will praise the LORD according to His
righteousness,
And will sing praise to the name of the
LORD Most High.

PSALM 8

God's Glory and Man's Dominion

To the Chief Musician. *On the instrument of Gath. A Psalm of David.

O LORD, our Lord,
How [R]excellent *is* Your name in all the
earth,

6:title, Heb. *sheminith* **8:title,** Heb. *Al Gittith*

WHAT IS MAN?

At least part of the controversy regarding so-called "sexist" language springs from the fact that English uses the word *man* with two entirely different meanings: "human being" and "adult male." A "chairman" actually indicates a "chairperson," not a "chairmale." Latin (*homo* and *vir*) and Greek (*anthrōpos* and *anēr*) generally differentiate these two concepts. While English has the richest vocabulary of any language (100,000 roots and 500,000 words) in popular usage it has not kept these two concepts separate. When the KJV says "If any man..." it translates the Greek word *tis,* meaning "anyone" (NKJV).

Following are some of the Hebrew words to describe humanity in its various aspects:

'Ādām

'Ādām is the term used in the first three chapters of Genesis for "man" (both male and female) as the pinnacle of God's creation, and as having been created in God's image and likeness. The word is also the personal name of the first man, Adam. Adam was this in both senses of our English word: first human and first male. The root word is believed to suggest ruddiness, and is related to the word for "ground" (*'adāmah*), from which man was formed. Genesis 1:27 is very important here: "So God created man in His *own* image; in the image of God He created him; male and female He created them."

'Ādām is in the image of God in the sense that he is a reasoning, moral being with emotions and a spiritual nature. It is the moral and spiritual nature that is lacking in the rest of the creatures on earth. Animals do not build churches.

'Îsh and 'Ishshah ("man" and "woman")

When husband and wife relationships are in view, *'îsh* and *'ishshah* are common forms (there are separate words for male and female in the sense of gender). Though the two forms may not be from the same root, at the very least Adam makes a pun when he says: "She shall be called Woman [*'ishshah*], because she was taken out of Man [*'îsh*]" (Gen. 2:23).

'Îsh is also commonly used for any male individual and can even simply mean "each" or "whoever."

Both *'ādām* and *'îsh* stress the value of humankind. Since man is created in God's image, it is an attack on that image to destroy a fellow man or woman.

'Enôsh

'Enôsh is the word for mankind that often stresses its mortality and frailty. Psalm 8:4, for example, reads, "What is man [*'enôsh*] that You are mindful of him, and the son of man that You visit him?" The word is also more likely to appear in poetry, as in Psalm 8. If *'enôsh* is derived from *'ānash,* "to be weak or sick," this would fit the common Hebrew usage. Some scholars prefer to derive the word from a similar root not proven to exist in Hebrew but definitely found in the related Semitic tongues, Arabic and Ugaritic. This root stresses sociability and companionship. Humans certainly are social creatures. If this origin is correct, the "frailty" motif would come more from the context and the Old Testament's stress on God's majesty and man's lowly position.

Geber and Gibbôr

Geber and *gibbôr* both come from the root *gābar,* to "prevail," "be strong or great." Both of these words are the opposite of the common understanding of *'enôsh.* If *'enôsh* is man in his frailty, these words stress man in his strength.

Geber occurs sixty-six times and describes a man at the height of his masculine strength. It is somewhat similar to the Hispanic term *macho,* which has become so popular in everyday English, as well.

Gibbôr is usually a military term for warriors and heroes, "mighty men of valor." It is used for Nimrod, the "mighty hunter before the LORD" (Gen. 10:9), for the Philistine "champion," Goliath (1 Sam. 17:51), and for David's mighty men (2 Sam. 23:8).

You who [R]set Your glory above the
heavens! Ps. 148:13 • Ps. 113:4

2 [R]Out of the mouth of babes and infants
You have ordained strength,
Because of Your enemies, Matt. 21:15, 16☆
That You may silence [R]the enemy and
the avenger. Ps. 44:16

3 When I [R]consider Your heavens, the
work of Your fingers,
The moon and the stars, which You
have ordained, Ps. 111:2
4 [R]What is man that You are mindful of
him, Job 7:17, 18
And the son of man that You [R]visit[T]
him? [Job 10:12] • *give attention to* or *care for*
5 For You have made him a little lower
than *the angels,
And You have crowned him with glory
and honor.

6 You have made him to have dominion
over the works of Your hands;
You have put all *things* under his feet,
7 All sheep and oxen—
Even the beasts of the field,
8 The birds of the air,
And the fish of the sea
That pass through the paths of the seas.

9 [R]O LORD, our Lord,
How excellent *is* Your name in all the
earth! Ps. 8:1

PSALM 9

Praise for Victory over Enemies

To the Chief Musician. To *the tune of* *"Death of the Son." A Psalm of David.

I WILL praise *You*, O LORD, with my
whole heart;
I will tell of all Your marvelous works.
2 I will be glad and [R]rejoice in You;
I will sing praise to Your name, [R]O
Most High. Ps. 5:11; 104:34 • [Ps. 83:18; 92:1]

3 When my enemies turn back,
They shall fall and perish at Your
presence.
4 For You have maintained my right and
my cause;
You sat on the throne judging in
righteousness.
5 You have rebuked the [T]nations,
You have destroyed the wicked;
You have [R]blotted out their name
forever and ever. *Gentiles* • Prov. 10:7

6 O enemy, destructions are finished
forever!
And you have destroyed cities;
Even their memory has perished.
7 [R]But the LORD shall endure forever;
He has prepared His throne for
judgment. Heb. 1:11
8 [R]He shall judge the world in
righteousness, [Ps. 96:13; 98:9]
And He shall administer judgment for
the peoples in uprightness.

9 The LORD also will be a [R]refuge[T] for the
oppressed, Ps. 32:7; 46:1 • Lit. *secure height*
A refuge in times of trouble.
10 And those who [R]know Your name will
put their trust in You;
For You, LORD, have not forsaken those
who seek You. Ps. 91:14

11 Sing praises to the LORD, who dwells in
Zion!
Declare His deeds among the people.
12 [R]When He avenges blood, He remembers
them;
He does not forget the cry of the
[T]humble. [Ps. 72:14] • *afflicted*

13 Have mercy on me, O LORD!
Consider my trouble from those who
hate me,
You who lift me up from the gates of
death,
14 That I may tell of all Your praise
In the gates of the daughter of [T]Zion.
I will rejoice in Your salvation. Jerusalem

15 [R]The [T]nations have sunk down in the pit
which they made;
In the net which they hid, their own
foot is caught. Ps. 7:15, 16 • *Gentiles*
16 The LORD is [R]known *by* the judgment
He executes;
The wicked is snared in the work of his
own hands.
*Meditation. Selah Ex. 7:5

17 The wicked shall be turned into hell,
And all the nations that forget God.
18 [R]For the needy shall not always be
forgotten;
[R]The expectation of the poor shall *not*
perish forever. Ps. 9:12; 12:5 • Prov. 23:18

19 Arise, O LORD,
Do not let man prevail;
Let the nations be judged in Your sight.
20 Put them in fear, O LORD,
That the [T]nations may know themselves
to be but men. Selah *Gentiles*

8:5 Heb. *Elohim, God;* LXX, Syr., Tg., Jewish tradition *angels* **9:title**, Heb. *Muth Labben*
9:16 Heb. *Higgaion*

PSALM 10

Petition for God's Judgment

WHY do You stand afar off, O LORD?
Why do You hide *Yourself* in times of
trouble?
2 The wicked in *his* pride [T]persecutes the
poor; *hotly pursues*
[R]Let them be caught in the plots which
they have devised. Ps. 7:16; 9:16

3 For the wicked [R]boasts of his heart's
desire;
He [R]blesses the greedy *and* renounces
the LORD. Ps. 49:6; 94:3, 4 • Prov. 28:4
4 The wicked in his proud countenance
does not seek *God;*
God *is* in none of his [R]thoughts. Ps. 36:1

5 His ways [T]are always prospering;
Your judgments *are* far above, out of
his sight;
As for all his enemies, he sneers at
them. Lit. *are strong*
6 [R]He has said in his heart, [Eccl. 8:11]
"I shall not be moved;
[R]I shall never be in adversity." Rev. 18:7
7 [R]His mouth is full of cursing and deceit
and oppression;
Under his tongue *is* trouble and
iniquity. [Rom. 3:14]

8 He sits in the lurking places of the
villages;
In the secret places he murders the
innocent;
His eyes are secretly fixed on the
helpless.
9 He lies in wait secretly, as a lion in his
den;
He lies in wait to catch the poor;
He catches the poor when he draws him
into his net.
10 So he [T]crouches, he lies low,
That the helpless may fall by his
[T]strength. Or *is crushed* • Or *mighty ones*
11 He has said in his heart,
"God has forgotten;
He hides His face;
He will never see *it.*"

12 Arise, O LORD! O God, [R]lift up Your
hand! Mic. 5:9
Do not forget the [R]humble. Ps. 9:12
13 Why do the wicked renounce God?
He has said in his heart,
"You will not require *an account.*"

14 But You have [R]seen *it,* for You observe
trouble and grief, [Ps. 11:4]
To repay *it* by Your hand.
The helpless commits himself to You;
You are the helper of the fatherless.
15 Break the arm of the wicked and the
evil *man;*
Seek out his wickedness *until* You find
none.

16 [R]The LORD *is* King forever and ever;
The nations have perished out of His
land. Ps. 29:10
17 LORD, You have heard the desire of the
humble;
You will prepare their heart;
You will cause Your ear to hear,
18 To [T]do justice to the fatherless and the
oppressed,
That the man of the earth may [T]oppress
no more. *vindicate* • *terrify*

PSALM 11

God Tests the Sons of Men

To the Chief Musician. A Psalm of David.

IN [R]the LORD I put my trust; Ps. 56:11
How can you say to my soul,
"Flee *as* a bird to your mountain"?
2 For look! [R]The wicked bend *their* bow,
They make ready their arrow on the
string,
That they may shoot [T]secretly at the
upright in heart. Ps. 64:3, 4 • Lit. *in darkness*
3 [R]If the foundations are destroyed,
What can the righteous do? Ps. 82:5

4 The LORD *is* in His holy temple,
The LORD's [R]throne *is* in heaven;
[R]His eyes behold, [Is. 66:1] • [Ps. 33:18]
His eyelids test the sons of men.
5 The LORD [R]tests the righteous,
But the wicked and the one who loves
violence His soul hates. Gen. 22:1
6 Upon the wicked He will rain coals,
Fire and brimstone and a burning wind;
This shall be the portion of their cup.

7 For the LORD *is* righteous,
He [R]loves righteousness; Ps. 33:5; 45:7
His countenance beholds the upright.

PSALM 12

The Pure Words of the Lord

To the Chief Musician. On an *eight-stringed
harp. A Psalm of David.

HELP,[T] LORD, for the godly man [R]ceases!
For the faithful disappear from among
the sons of men. *Save* • [Is. 57:1]
2 [R]They speak idly everyone with his
neighbor; Ps. 10:7; 41:6
With flattering lips *and* [T]a double heart
they speak. An inconsistent mind

12:title, Heb. *sheminith*

3 May the LORD [T]cut off all flattering lips,
And the tongue that speaks [T]proud things, *destroy • great*
4 Who have said,
"With our tongue we will prevail;
Our lips *are* our own;
Who *is* lord over us?"

5 "For the oppression of the poor, for the sighing of the needy,
Now I will arise," says the LORD;
"I will set *him* in the safety for which he yearns."

6 The words of the LORD *are* [R]pure words,
Like silver tried in a furnace of earth,
Purified seven times. 2 Sam. 22:31
7 You shall keep them, O LORD,
You shall preserve them from this generation forever.

8 The wicked prowl on every side,
When vileness is exalted among the sons of men.

PSALM 13

The Prayer for God's Answer—Now

To the Chief Musician. A Psalm of David.

HOW long, O LORD? Will You forget me forever?
[R]How long will You hide Your face from me? Job 13:24
2 How long shall I take counsel in my soul,
Having sorrow in my heart daily?
How long will my enemy be exalted over me?

3 Consider *and* hear me, O LORD my God;
[R]Enlighten my eyes, Ezra 9:8
[R]Lest I sleep the *sleep of* death; Jer. 51:39
4 Lest my enemy say,
"I have prevailed against him";
Lest those who trouble me rejoice when I am moved.

5 But I have trusted in Your mercy;
My heart shall rejoice in Your salvation.
6 I will sing to the LORD,
Because He has dealt bountifully with me.

PSALM 14

The Characteristics of the Godless

To the Chief Musician. A Psalm of David.

THE [R]fool has said in his heart,
"*There is* no God." Ps. 10:4; 53:1
They are corrupt,
They have done abominable works,
There is none who does good.

2 [R]The LORD looks down from heaven upon the children of men,
To see if there are any who understand, who seek God. Ps. 33:13, 14; 102:19
3 [R]They have all turned aside,
They have together become corrupt;
There is none who does good,
No, not one. Rom. 3:12

4 Have all the workers of iniquity no knowledge,
Who eat up my people *as* they eat bread,
And [R]do not call on the LORD? Is. 64:7
5 There they are in great fear,
For God *is* with the generation of the righteous.
6 You shame the counsel of the poor,
But the LORD *is* his [R]refuge. Ps. 9:9; 40:17

7 [R]Oh, that the salvation of Israel *would come* out of Zion! Ps. 53:6
[R]When the LORD brings back the captivity of His people, Job 42:10
Let Jacob rejoice *and* Israel be glad.

PSALM 15

The Characteristics of the Godly

A Psalm of David.

LORD, [R]who may [T]abide in Your tabernacle? Ps. 24:3–5 • *sojurn*
Who may dwell in Your holy hill?

2 He who walks uprightly,
And works righteousness,
And speaks the truth in his heart;
3 He *who* [R]does not backbite with his tongue, [Lev. 19:16–18]
Nor does evil to his neighbor,
[R]Nor does he [T]take up a reproach against his friend; Ex. 23:1 • *receive*
4 [R]In whose eyes a vile person is despised,
But he honors those who fear the LORD;
He *who* [R]swears to his own hurt and does not change; Esth. 3:2 • Lev. 5:4
5 He *who* does not put out his money at usury,
Nor does he take a bribe against the innocent.

He who does these *things* [R]shall never be moved. 2 Pet. 1:10

PSALM 16

Eternal Life for One Who Trusts

A Michtam of David.

PRESERVE me, O God, for in You I put my trust.

2 O *my soul,* you have said to the LORD,
"You *are* my Lord,
[R]My goodness is nothing apart from
You"— Job 35:7
3 *And* to the saints who *are* on the earth,
"They are the excellent ones, in [R]whom
is all my delight." Ps. 119:63

4 Their sorrows shall be multiplied who
hasten *after* another *god;*
Their drink offerings of [R]blood I will not
offer, Ps. 106:37, 38
Nor take up their names on my lips.

5 *You,* O LORD, *are* the portion of my
inheritance and my cup;
You [T]maintain my lot. Lit. *uphold*
6 The lines have fallen to me in pleasant
places;
Yes, I have a good inheritance.

7 I will bless the LORD who has given me
counsel;
My [T]heart also instructs me in the night
seasons. Mind, lit. *kidneys*
8 [R]I have set the LORD always before me;
Because *He is* at my right hand I shall
not be moved. [Acts 2:25–28]

9 Therefore my heart is glad, and my
glory rejoices;
My flesh also will rest in hope.
10 [R]For You will not leave my soul in Sheol,
Nor will You allow Your Holy One to
see corruption. [Ps. 49:15; Acts 2:31, 32] ☆
11 You will show me the [R]path of life;
In Your presence *is* fullness of joy;
At Your right hand *are* pleasures
forevermore. [Matt. 7:14]

PSALM 17

"Hide Me Under the Shadow of Your Wings"

A Prayer of David.

HEAR a just cause, O LORD,
Attend to my cry;
Give ear to my prayer *that is* not from
deceitful lips.
2 Let my vindication come from Your
presence;
Let Your eyes look on the things that
are upright.

3 You have tested my heart;
You have visited *me* in the night;
[R]You have [T]tried me and have found
[T]nothing; Job. 23:10 • examined • Nothing evil
I have purposed that my mouth shall
not [R]transgress. Ps. 39:1

4 Concerning the works of men,
By the word of Your lips,
I have kept *myself* from the paths of
the destroyer.

5 [R]Uphold my steps in Your paths, Ps. 44:18
That my footsteps may not slip.

6 [R]I have called upon You, for You will
hear me, O God;
Incline Your ear to me, *and* hear my
speech. Ps. 86:7; 116:2
7 Show Your marvelous lovingkindness
by Your right hand,
O You who save those who trust *in You*
From those who rise up *against them.*
8 Keep me as the [T]apple of Your eye;
Hide me under the shadow of Your
wings, *pupil*
9 From the wicked who oppress me,
From my deadly enemies who surround
me.

10 They have closed up their fat *hearts;*
With their mouths they speak proudly.
11 They have now surrounded us in our
steps;
They have set their eyes, crouching
down to the earth,
12 Like a lion *that* is eager to tear his prey,
And as a young lion lurking in secret
places.

17:4 God's Word Corrects—There are many symbols for God's Word that can be found in the Bible itself. It can be thought of as a mirror (Page 1468—James 1:23–25), a seed (Page 1479—1 Pet. 1:23), a lamp (Page 697—Ps. 119:105), a sword (Page 1393—Eph. 6:17), and even as food (Page 1453—Heb. 5:12–14). But the Bible also serves as a measuring rod or ruler. Many teachers have used wooden rulers in their classes not only to give the right measurement but, on occasion, to correct a misbehaving pupil. God's Word likewise can do both of these things. It should be used as a standard against which to measure our beliefs. What about certain religious groups which claim Christ was not God, or that the Bible is filled with silly tales? Immediately we can reject such claims by using our divine written ruler to discover that such arguments simply do not measure up.

Sometimes our heavenly teacher uses His written ruler to correct us when we are in the wrong. Israel's great king David once experienced this. "You have dealt well with Your sevant, O LORD, according to Your word. . . . Before I was afflicted I went astray, but now I keep Your word" (Page 696—Ps. 119:65, 67).

There are times when God's Word can correct believers when they are in honest and unintentional error. Aquila and Priscilla, a godly Christian couple, use the Scriptures to help a powerful young preacher named Apollos (Page 1300—Acts 18:24–26). Paul does the same thing for some former disciples of John the Baptist he meets in the city of Ephesus (Page 1300—Acts 19:1–7).

Now turn to Page 694—Ps. 119:9: God's Word Cleanses.

13 Arise, O LORD,
Confront him, cast him down;
Deliver my life from the wicked with
Your sword,
14 With Your hand from men, O LORD,
From men of the world *who have* their
portion in *this* life,
And whose belly You fill with Your
hidden treasure.
They are satisfied with children,
And leave the rest of their *substance*
for their babes.

15 As for me, [R]I will see Your face in
righteousness; [1 John 3:2]
[R]I shall be satisfied when I [R]awake in
Your likeness. Ps. 4:6, 7; 16:11 • [Is. 26:19]

PSALM 18

Thanksgiving for Deliverance by God

To the Chief Musician. A Psalm of David the servant of the LORD, who spoke to the LORD the words of this song on the day that the LORD delivered him from the hand of all his enemies and from the hand of Saul. And he said:

I WILL love You, O LORD, my strength.
2 The LORD is my rock and my fortress
and my deliverer;
My God, [T]my strength, [R]in whom I will
trust; Lit. *rock* • Heb. 2:13
My shield and the [T]horn of my
salvation, my stronghold. Strength
3 I will call upon the LORD, [R]*who is*
worthy to be praised; Rev. 5:12
So shall I be saved from my enemies.

4 [R]The pangs of death encompassed me,
And the floods of [T]ungodliness made me
afraid. Ps. 116:3 • Lit. *Belial*
5 The sorrows of Sheol surrounded me;
The snares of death confronted me.
6 In my distress I called upon the LORD,
And cried out to my God;
He heard my voice from His temple,
And my cry came before Him, *even* to
His ears.

7 [R]Then the earth shook and trembled;
The foundations of the hills also quaked
and were shaken,
Because He was angry. Acts 4:31
8 Smoke went up from His nostrils,
And devouring fire from His mouth;
Coals were kindled by it.
9 [R]He bowed the heavens also, and came
down
With darkness under His feet. Ps. 144:5
10 And He rode upon a cherub, and flew;
He flew upon the wings of the wind.
11 He made darkness His secret place;
[R]His canopy around Him *was* dark
waters
And thick clouds of the skies. Ps. 97:2
12 [R]From the brightness before Him,
His thick clouds passed with hailstones
and coals of fire. Ps. 97:3; 140:10

13 The LORD also thundered in the
heavens,
And the Most High uttered His voice,
Hailstones and coals of fire.
14 [R]He sent out His arrows and scattered
the foe,
Lightnings in abundance, and He
vanquished them. Ps. 144:6
15 Then the channels of waters were seen,
And the foundations of the world were
uncovered
At Your rebuke, O LORD,
At the blast of the breath of Your
nostrils.

16 He sent from above, He took me;
He drew me out of many waters.
17 He delivered me from my strong enemy,
From those who hated me,
For they were too strong for me.
18 They confronted me in the day of my
calamity,
But the LORD was my support.
19 [R]He also brought me out into a broad
place;
He delivered me because He delighted
in me. Ps. 4:1; 31:8; 118:5

20 [R]The LORD rewarded me according to my
righteousness;
According to the cleanness of my hands
He has recompensed me. 1 Sam. 24:19
21 For I have kept the ways of the LORD,
And have not wickedly departed from
my God.
22 For all His judgments *were* before me,
And I did not put away His statutes
from me.
23 I was also blameless [T]before Him, *with*
And I kept myself from my iniquity.
24 [R]Therefore the LORD has recompensed
me according to my righteousness,
According to the cleanness of my hands
in His sight. 1 Sam. 26:23

25 [R]With the merciful You will show
Yourself merciful;
With a blameless man You will show
Yourself blameless; [1 Kin. 8:32]
26 With the pure You will show Yourself
pure;
And [R]with the devious You will show
Yourself shrewd. [Lev. 26:23–28]
27 For You will save the humble people,
But will bring down haughty looks.

28 [R]For You will light my lamp;
The LORD my God will enlighten my
darkness. Job 18:6
29 For by You I can run against a troop,
And by my God I can leap over a wall.
30 *As for* God, His way *is* perfect;
The word of the LORD is proven;
He *is* a shield to all who trust in Him.

31 For who *is* God, except the LORD?
And who *is* a rock, except our God?
32 *It is* God who [R]arms me with strength,
And makes my way perfect. [Ps. 91:2]
33 He makes my feet like the *feet of* deer,
And sets me on my high places.
34 [R]He teaches my hands to make war,
So that my arms can bend a bow of
bronze. Ps. 144:1

35 You have also given me the shield of
Your salvation;
Your right hand has held me up,
Your gentleness has made me great.
36 You enlarged my path under me;
[R]So that my feet did not slip. Prov. 4:12

37 I have pursued my enemies and
overtaken them;
Neither did I turn back again till they
were destroyed.
38 I have wounded them,
So that they were not able to rise;
They have fallen under my feet.
39 For You have armed me with strength
for the battle;
You have subdued under me those who
rose up against me.
40 You have also given me
the necks of my enemies,
So that I destroyed those who hated
me.
41 They cried out, but *there was* none to
save *them,*
[R]*Even* to the LORD, but He did not
answer them. Job 27:9
42 Then I beat them as fine as the dust
before the wind;
I cast them out like dirt in the streets.

43 You have delivered me from the
strivings of the people;
[R]You have made me the head of the
[T]nations;
[R]A people I have not known shall serve
me. 2 Sam. 8 • *Gentiles* • Is. 52:15
44 As soon as they hear of me they obey
me;
The foreigners submit to me.
45 [R]The foreigners fade away,
And come frightened from their
hideouts. Mic. 7:17

46 The LORD lives!
Blessed *be* my Rock!
Let the God of my salvation be exalted.
47 *It is* God who avenges me,
And subdues the peoples under me;
48 He delivers me from my enemies.
[R]You also lift me up above those who
rise against me;
You have delivered me from the violent
man. Ps. 27:6; 59:1
49 Therefore I will give thanks to You,
O LORD, among the [T]Gentiles, *nations*
And sing praises to Your name.

50 [R]Great deliverance He gives to His king,
And shows mercy to His anointed,
To David and his [T]descendants
forevermore. Ps. 21:1; 144:10 • Lit. *seed*

PSALM 19

The Works and Words of God

To the Chief Musician. A Psalm of David.

THE [T]heavens declare the glory of God;
And the [T]firmament shows His
handiwork. *expanse* • *the work of His hands*
2 Day unto day utters speech,
And night unto night reveals
knowledge.
3 *There is* no speech nor language
Where their voice is not heard.
4 [R]Their [T]line has gone out through all the
earth, Rom. 10:18 • *measuring line*
And their words to the end of the
world.

In them He has set a [T]tabernacle for the
sun, *tent*
5 Which *is* like a bridegroom coming out
of his chamber,
[R]*And* rejoices like a strong man to run
its race. Eccl. 1:5
6 Its rising *is* from one end of heaven,
And its circuit to the other end;
And there is nothing hidden from its
heat.

7 [R]The law of the LORD *is* perfect,
[T]converting the soul; Ps. 111:7 • *restoring*
The testimony of the LORD *is* sure,
making [R]wise the simple; Ps. 119:130
8 The statutes of the LORD *are* right,
rejoicing the heart;
The commandment of the LORD *is* pure,
enlightening the eyes;
9 The fear of the LORD *is* clean, enduring
forever;
The judgments of the LORD *are* true
and righteous altogether.
10 More to be desired *are they* than [R]gold,
Yea, than much fine gold; Ps. 119:72, 127

Sweeter also than honey and the
ᵀhoneycomb. *honey in the combs*
11 Moreover by them Your servant is
warned,
And in keeping them *there is* great
reward.

12 Who can understand *his* errors?
ᴿCleanse me from secret *faults.* [Ps. 51:1, 2]
13 Keep back Your servant also from
ᴿpresumptuous *sins;* Num. 15:30
Let them not have ᴿdominion over me.
Then I shall be blameless,
And I shall be innocent of ᵀgreat
transgression. Ps. 119:133 • Or *much*

14 ᴿLet the words of my mouth and the
meditation of my heart
Be acceptable in Your sight,
O LORD, my ᵀstrength and my
ᴿredeemer. Ps. 51:15 • Lit. *rock* • Is. 47:4

PSALM 20

Trust Not in Chariots and Horses but in God

To the Chief Musician. A Psalm of David.

MAY the LORD answer you in the day of
trouble;
May the name of the God of Jacob
ᵀdefend you; Lit. *set you on high*
2 May He send you help from the
sanctuary,
And strengthen you out of Zion;
3 May He remember all your offerings,
And accept your burnt sacrifice. Selah

4 May He grant you according to your
heart's *desire,*
And fulfill all your ᵀpurpose. *counsel*
5 We will rejoice in your salvation,
And in the name of our God we will set
up *our* banners!
May the LORD fulfill all your petitions.

6 Now I know that the LORD saves His
ᵀanointed;
He will answer him from His holy
heaven
With the saving strength of His right
hand. Commissioned one, Heb. *messiah*

7 Some *trust* in chariots, and some in
ᴿhorses;
But we will remember the name of the
LORD our God. Ps. 33:16, 17
8 They have bowed down and fallen;
But we have risen and stand upright.

9 Save, LORD!
May the King answer us when we call.

PSALM 21

Triumph of the King

To the Chief Musician. A Psalm of David.

THE king shall have joy in Your strength,
O LORD;
And in Your salvation how greatly shall
he rejoice!
2 You have given him his heart's desire,
And have not withheld the ᴿrequest of
his lips. Selah 2 Sam. 7:26–29

3 For You meet him with the blessings of
goodness;
You set a crown of pure gold upon his
head.
4 ᴿHe asked life from You, *and* You gave
it to him— Ps. 61:5, 6; 133:3
Length of days forever and ever.
5 His glory *is* great in Your salvation;
Honor and majesty You have placed
upon him.
6 For You have made him most blessed
forever;
You have made him exceedingly glad
with Your presence.
7 For the king trusts in the LORD,
And through the mercy of the Most
High he shall not be ᵀmoved. *shaken*

8 Your hand will find all Your enemies;
Your right hand will find those who
hate You.
9 You shall make them as a fiery oven in
the time of Your anger;
The LORD shall swallow them up in His
wrath,
And the fire shall devour them.
10 Their offspring You shall destroy from
the earth,
And their ᵀdescendants from among the
sons of men. Lit. *seed*
11 For they intended evil against You;
They devised a plot *which* they are not
able *to* ᴿ*perform.* Ps. 2:1–4
12 Therefore You will make them turn
their back;
You will make ready *Your arrows* on
Your string toward their faces.

13 Be exalted, O LORD, in Your own
strength!
We will sing and praise Your power.

PSALM 22

Psalm of the Cross

To the Chief Musician. Set to *"The Deer
of the Dawn." A Psalm of David.

MY ᴿGod, My God, [Mark 15:34] ☆
why have You forsaken Me?

22:title, Heb. *Aijeleth Hashahar*

Why are You so far from helping Me,
And from the words of My groaning?
2 O My God, I cry in the daytime, but
You do not hear;
And in the night season, and am not
silent.

3 But You *are* holy,
Who inhabit the praises of Israel.
4 Our fathers trusted in You;
They trusted, and You delivered them.
5 They cried to You, and were delivered;
[R]They trusted in You, and were not
ashamed. Is. 49:23

6 But I [R]*am* a worm, and no man;
[R]A reproach of men, and despised of the
people. Is. 41:14 • [Is. 53:3]
7 [R]All those who see Me laugh Me to
scorn; Matt. 27:39☆
[T]They shoot out the lip, they shake the
head, *saying,* Show contempt with their mouth
8 "He[T] trusted in the LORD, let Him rescue
Him; Lit. *He rolled himself on the LORD*
[R]Let Him deliver Him, since He delights
in Him!" Ps. 91:14; Matt. 27:43☆

9 [R]But You *are* He who took Me out of the
womb;
You made Me trust *when I was* on My
mother's breasts. [Ps. 71:5, 6]
10 I was cast upon You from birth.
From My mother's womb
[R]You *have been* My God. [Is. 46:3; 49:1]
11 Be not far from Me,
For trouble *is* near;
For *there is* none to help.

12 [R]Many bulls have surrounded Me;
Strong *bulls* of [R]Bashan have encircled
Me. Ps. 22:21; 68:30 • Deut. 32:14
13 [R]They gape at Me *with* their mouths,
As a raging and roaring lion. Job 16:10

14 I am poured out like water,
[R]And all My bones are out of joint;
My heart is like wax;
It has melted within Me. Dan. 5:6
15 [R]My strength is dried up like a potsherd,
And [R]My tongue clings to My jaws;
You have brought Me to the dust of
death. Prov. 17:22 • John 19:28

16 For dogs have surrounded Me;
The assembly of the wicked has
enclosed Me.
They pierced My hands and My feet;
17 I can count all My bones.
[R]They look *and* stare at Me. John 19:37☆

18 They divide My garments among them,
And for My clothing they cast lots.

19 But You, O LORD, do not be far from
Me;
O My Strength, hasten to help Me!
20 Deliver Me from the sword,
[R]My[T] precious *life* from the power of the
dog. Ps. 35:17 • Lit. *My only one*
21 [R]Save Me from the lion's mouth
And from the horns of the wild oxen!

[R]You have answered Me. 2 Tim. 4:17 • Is. 34:7

22 [R]I will declare Your name to My
brethren;
In the midst of the congregation I will
praise You. Mark 1:21, 39; Heb. 2:12☆
23 [R]You who fear the LORD, praise Him!
All you [T]descendants of Jacob, glorify
Him,
And fear Him, all you offspring of
Israel! Ps. 135:19, 20 • Lit. *seed*
24 For He has not despised nor abhorred
the affliction of the afflicted;
Nor has He hidden His face from Him;
But when He cried to Him, He heard.

25 [R]My praise *shall be* of You in the great
congregation;
[R]I will pay My vows before those who
fear Him. Ps. 35:18; 40:9, 10 • Eccl. 5:4
26 The poor shall eat and be satisfied;
Those who seek Him will praise the
LORD.
Let your heart live forever!

27 All the ends of the world
Shall remember and turn to the LORD,
And all the families of the [T]nations
Shall worship before You. *Gentiles*
28 [R]For the kingdom *is* the LORD's,
And He rules over the nations. Matt. 6:13

29 [R]All the prosperous of the earth
Shall eat and worship; Ps. 17:10; 45:12
[R]All those who go down to [T]the dust
Shall bow before Him, [Is. 26:19] • Death
Even he who cannot keep himself alive.

30 A posterity shall serve Him.
It will be recounted of the Lord to the
next generation,
31 They will come and declare His
righteousness to a people who will be
born,
That He has done *this.*

PSALM 23

Psalm of the Divine Shepherd

A Psalm of David.

THE LORD *is* [R]my shepherd;
[R]I shall not [T]want. [Is. 40:11] • [Phil. 4:19] • *lack*

2 He makes me to lie down in [T]green
pastures; Lit. *pastures of tender grass*
He leads me beside the still waters.
3 He restores my soul;
[R]He leads me in the paths of
righteousness
For His name's sake. Ps. 5:8; 31:3

4 Yea, though I walk through the valley
of the shadow of death,
[R]I will fear no evil;
[R]For You *are* with me;
Your rod and Your staff, they comfort
me. [Ps. 3:6; 27:1] • [Is. 43:2]

5 You [R]prepare a table before me in the
presence of my enemies;
You [R]anoint my head with oil;
My cup runs over. Ps. 104:15 • Ps. 92:10
6 Surely goodness and mercy shall follow
me
All the days of my life;
And I will dwell in the house of the
LORD
[T]Forever. Lit. *For length of days*

PSALM 24

Psalm of the King of Glory

A Psalm of David.

THE [R]earth *is* the LORD's, and all its
fullness, 1 Cor. 10:26, 28
The world and those who dwell therein.
2 For He has founded it upon the seas,
And established it upon the waters.

3 [R]Who may ascend into the hill of the
LORD? Ps. 15:1–5
Or who may stand in His holy place?
4 He who has [R]clean hands and [R]a pure
heart, [Job 17:9] • [Matt. 5:8]
Who has not lifted up his soul to an
idol,
Nor [R]sworn deceitfully. Ps. 15:4
5 He shall receive blessing from the LORD,
And righteousness from the God of his
salvation.
6 This *is* Jacob, the generation of those
who [R]seek Him,
Who seek Your face. Selah Ps. 27:4, 8

7 Lift up your heads, O you gates!
And be lifted up, you everlasting doors!
And the King of glory shall come in.
8 Who *is* this King of glory?
The LORD strong and mighty,
The LORD mighty in [R]battle. Rev. 19:13–16
9 Lift up your heads, O you gates!
And lift *them* up, you everlasting doors!
And the King of glory shall come in.
10 Who is this King of glory?
The LORD of hosts,
He *is* the King of glory. Selah

PSALM 25

Acrostic Prayer for Instruction

A Psalm of David.

TO You, O LORD, I lift up my soul.
2 O my God, I [R]trust in You; Ps. 34:8
Let me not be ashamed;
Let not my enemies triumph over me.
3 Indeed, let no one [T]who waits on You
be ashamed; Waits for You in faith
Let those be ashamed who deal
treacherously without cause.

4 [R]Show me Your ways, O LORD;
Teach me Your paths. Ex. 33:13
5 Lead me in Your truth and teach me,
For You *are* the God of my salvation;
On You I wait all the day.

6 Remember, O LORD, Your tender
mercies and Your lovingkindnesses,
For they *have been* from of old.
7 Do not remember the sins of my youth,
nor my transgressions;
According to Your mercy remember me,
For Your goodness' sake, O LORD.

8 Good and upright *is* the LORD;
Therefore He teaches sinners in the
way.
9 The humble He guides in justice,
And the humble He teaches His way.
10 All the paths of the LORD *are* mercy and
truth,
To such as keep His covenant and His
testimonies.
11 [R]For Your name's sake, O LORD, Ps. 79:9
Pardon my iniquity, for it *is* great.

12 Who *is* the man that fears the LORD?
[R]Him shall [T]He teach in the way [T]He
chooses. [Ps. 25:8; 37:23] • Or *he*
13 [R]He himself shall dwell in [T]prosperity,
And [R]his descendants shall inherit the
earth. [Prov. 19:23] • Lit. *goodness* • Matt. 5:5
14 [R]The secret of the LORD *is* with those
who fear Him, [John 7:17]
And He will show them His covenant.
15 [R]My eyes *are* ever toward the LORD,
For He shall [T]pluck my feet out of the
net. [Ps. 123:2; 141:8] • Lit. *bring out*

16 [R]Turn Yourself to me, and have mercy
on me, Ps. 69:16
For I *am* [T]desolate and afflicted. *lonely*
17 The troubles of my heart have enlarged;
Oh, bring me out of my distresses!

18 [R]Look on my affliction and my pain,
And forgive all my sins. 2 Sam. 16:12
19 Consider my enemies, for they are many;
And they hate me with cruel hatred.
20 Oh, keep my soul, and deliver me;
Let me not be ashamed, for I put my trust in You.
21 Let integrity and uprightness preserve me,
For I wait for You.

22 [R]Redeem Israel, O God,
Out of all their troubles! [Ps. 130:8]

PSALM 26

"Examine Me, O LORD, and Prove Me"

A Psalm of David.

VINDICATE [R]me, O LORD, Ps. 7:8
For I have [R]walked in my integrity.
[R]I have also trusted in the LORD;
I shall not slip. 2 Kin. 20:3 • [Ps. 13:5; 28:7]
2 Examine me, O LORD, and [T]prove me;
Try my mind and my heart. *try*
3 For Your lovingkindness *is* before my eyes,
And I have walked in Your truth.
4 I have not [R]sat with idolatrous mortals,
Nor will I go in with hypocrites. Ps. 1:1
5 I have [R]hated the congregation of evildoers, Ps. 31:6; 139:21
And will not sit with the wicked.

6 I will wash my hands in innocence;
So I will go about Your altar, O LORD,
7 That I may proclaim with the voice of thanksgiving,
And tell of all Your wondrous works.
8 LORD, [R]I have loved the habitation of Your house, Ps. 27:4; 84:1–4, 10
And the place where Your glory dwells.

9 [R]Do[T] not gather my soul *together* with sinners, Ps. 28:3 • *Do not take away*
Nor my life with bloodthirsty men,
10 In whose hands *is* a sinister scheme,
And whose right hand is full of bribes.

11 But as for me, I will walk in my integrity;
Redeem me and be merciful to me.
12 [R]My foot stands in an even place;
In the congregations I will bless the LORD. Ps. 40:2

PSALM 27

Trust in the Lord and Be Not Afraid

A Psalm of David.

THE LORD *is* my [R]light and my salvation;
Whom shall I fear? [Mic. 7:8]
The [R]LORD *is* the strength of my life;
Of whom shall I be afraid? Ps. 62:7; 118:14
2 When the wicked came against me
To [R]eat[T] up my flesh, Ps. 14:4 • *devour*
My enemies and foes,
They [R]stumbled and fell. John 18:6 ☆
3 [R]Though an army should encamp against me,
My heart shall not fear;
Though war should rise against me,
In this I *will be* confident. Ps. 3:6

4 [R]One *thing* I have desired of the LORD,
That will I seek: Ps. 26:8; 65:4
That I may [R]dwell in the house of the LORD
All the days of my life, Luke 2:37
To behold the [T]beauty of the LORD,
And to inquire in His temple. *delightfulness*
5 For [R]in the time of trouble
He shall hide me in His pavilion;
In the secret place of His tabernacle
He shall hide me; Ps. 31:20; 91:1
He shall set me high upon a rock.

6 And now [R]my head shall be [T]lifted up above my enemies all around me;
Therefore I will offer sacrifices of [T]joy in His tabernacle;
I will sing, yes, I will sing praises to the LORD. Ps. 3:3 • Lifted up in honor • *joyous shouts*

7 Hear, O LORD, *when* I cry with my voice!
Have mercy also upon me, and answer me.
8 *When You said,* "Seek My face,"
My heart said to You, "Your face, LORD, I will seek."
9 [R]Do not hide Your face from me;
Do not turn Your servant away in anger;
You have been my help;
Do not leave me nor forsake me,
O God of my salvation. Ps. 69:17; 143:7
10 [R]When my father and my mother forsake me, Is. 49:15
Then the LORD will take care of me.

11 [R]Teach me Your way, O LORD,
And lead me in a smooth path, because of my enemies. Ps. 25:4; 86:11; 119:33
12 Do not deliver me to the will of my adversaries;
For [R]false witnesses have risen against me, Ps. 35:11; Matt. 26:60, 61 ☆
And such as breathe out violence.
13 *I would have lost heart,* unless I had believed
That I would see the goodness of the LORD
[R]In the land of the living. Ezek. 26:20

14 [R]Wait[T] on the LORD; Is. 25:9 • Wait in faith
Be of good courage,
And He shall strengthen your heart;
Wait, I say, on the LORD!

PSALM 28

Rejoice Because of Answered Prayer

A Psalm of David.

TO You I will cry, O LORD my Rock:
[R]Do not be silent to me,
[R]Lest, if You *are* silent to me,
I become like those who go down to the pit. Ps. 35:22; 39:12; 83:1 • Ps. 88:4; 143:7
2 Hear the voice of my supplications
When I cry to You,
[R]When I lift up my hands [R]toward Your holy sanctuary. Ps. 5:7 • Ps. 138:2

3 Do not [T]take me away with the wicked
And with the workers of iniquity,
[R]Who speak peace to their neighbors,
But evil *is* in their hearts. *drag* • Ps. 12:2
4 [R]Give to them according to their deeds,
And according to the wickedness of their endeavors; [Rev. 18:6; 22:12]
Give to them according to the work of their hands;
Render to them what they deserve.
5 Because [R]they do not regard the works of the LORD,
Nor the operation of His hands,
He shall destroy them
And not build them up. Is. 5:12

6 Blessed *be* the LORD,
Because He has heard the voice of my supplications!
7 The LORD *is* [R]my strength and my shield; Ps. 18:2; 59:17
My heart [R]trusted in Him, and I am helped; Ps. 13:5; 112:7
Therefore my heart greatly rejoices,
And with my song I will praise Him.
8 The LORD *is* their strength,
And He *is* the saving refuge of His [T]anointed. Commissioned one, Heb. *messiah*
9 Save Your people,
And bless [R]Your inheritance;
Shepherd them also, [Deut. 9:29; 32:9]
[R]And bear them up forever. Deut. 1:31

PSALM 29

The Powerful Voice of God

A Psalm of David.

GIVE[T] [R]unto the LORD, O you mighty ones, *Ascribe* • 1 Chr. 16:28, 29
Give unto the LORD glory and strength.

2 [T]Give unto the LORD the glory due to His name; Lit. *of His name*
Worship the LORD in [R]the [T]beauty of holiness. 2 Chr. 20:21 • *majesty*

3 The voice of the LORD *is* over the waters;
[R]The God of glory thunders; [Job 37:4, 5]
The LORD *is* over many waters.
4 The voice of the LORD *is* powerful;
The voice of the LORD *is* full of majesty.

5 The voice of the LORD breaks [R]the cedars,
Yes, the LORD splinters the cedars of Lebanon. Is. 2:13; 14:8
6 [R]He makes them also skip like a calf,
Lebanon and [R]Sirion like a young wild ox. Ps. 114:4 • Deut. 3:9
7 The voice of the LORD [T]divides the flames of fire. *stirs up*, lit. *hews out*

8 The voice of the LORD shakes the wilderness;
The LORD shakes the Wilderness of [R]Kadesh. Num. 13:26
9 The voice of the LORD makes the [R]deer give birth,
And strips the forests bare;

29:2 Worship by Israel—The central aspect of Israel's worship was the object of their worship, the Lord. While other nations paid homage to many gods (Page 241—Deut. 29:18), only Israel worshiped the one true God (Page 90—Ex. 20:3). This worship could be private (Page 107—Ex. 34:8), as a family (Page 30—Gen. 22:5), or corporate (Page 496—1 Chr. 29:20), as a congregation.

Since so much of the Bible is devoted to Israel's public worship, it deserves special notice. It included offering sacrifices (Page 321—1 Sam. 1:3), adopting a reverent posture (Page 509—2 Chr. 7:6), verbal praise—either spoken (Page 483—1 Chr. 16:36) or sung (Page 657—Ps. 57:7), instrumental praise (Page 710—Ps. 150:3–5), prayer (Page 507—2 Chr. 6:14–42), and the great feasts (Page 145—Lev. 23; 25). One need only read the Psalms to see the excellent form and spirit in which the godly of Israel worshiped.

The first place of worship for the people of Israel was the tabernacle constructed by Moses (Page 95—Ex. 25—27; 30; 31; 35—40) and later the magnificent temple constructed by Solomon (Page 489—1 Chr. 22:5). These structures served to localize the worship of the entire nation. This geographic limitation stands in bold contrast to the privilege of immediate and direct access to God now available to the New Testament believer who himself is the temple of God (Page 1453—Heb. 4:16; Page 1351—1 Cor. 6:19).

Now turn to Page 1281—Acts 7:38: The Meaning of the Church.

And in His temple everyone says,
"Glory!" Job 39:1

10 The LORD sat *enthroned* at the Flood,
And the LORD sits as King forever.
11 RThe LORD will give strength to His
people;
The LORD will bless His people with
peace. Ps. 28:8; 68:35

PSALM 30

Praise for Dramatic Deliverance

A Psalm. A Song at the dedication
of the house of David.

I WILL extol You, O LORD, for You have
Rlifted me up,
And have not let my foes Rrejoice over
me. Ps. 28:9 • Ps. 25:2
2 O LORD my God, I cried out to You,
And You have Rhealed me. Ps. 6:2; 103:3
3 O LORD, RYou have brought my soul up
from the grave;
You have kept me alive, that I should
not go down to the pit. Ps. 86:13

4 RSing praise to the LORD, you saints of
His,
And give thanks at the remembrance of
His Tholy name. Ps. 97:12 • Or *His holiness*
5 For RHis anger *is but for* a moment,
RHis favor *is for* life; Ps. 103:9 • Ps. 63:3
Weeping may endure for a night,
But joy *comes* in the morning.

6 Now in my prosperity I said,
"I shall never be Tmoved." *shaken*
7 LORD, by Your favor You have made
my mountain stand strong;
You hid Your face, *and* I was troubled.

8 I cried out to You, O LORD;
And to the LORD I made supplication:
9 "What profit *is there* in my blood,
When I go down to the pit?
RWill the dust praise You?
Will it declare Your truth? [Ps. 6:5]
10 Hear, O LORD, and have mercy on me;
LORD, be my helper!"

11 RYou have turned for me my mourning
into dancing; Jer. 31:4
You have put off my sackcloth and
clothed me with gladness,
12 To the end that *my* Tglory may sing
praise to You and not be silent.
O LORD my God, I will give thanks to
You forever. *soul*

PSALM 31

"Be of Good Courage"

To the Chief Musician. A Psalm of David.

IN You, O LORD, TI put my trust;
Let me never be ashamed; *have taken refuge*
Deliver me in Your righteousness.
2 Bow down Your ear to me,
Deliver me speedily;
Be my rock of Trefuge, *strength*
A fortress of defense to save me.

3 RFor You *are* my rock and my fortress;
Therefore, for Your name's sake,
Lead me and guide me. [Ps. 18:2]
4 Pull me out of the net which they have
secretly laid for me,
For You *are* my strength.
5 RInto Your hand I commit my spirit;
You have redeemed me, O LORD God of
Rtruth. Luke 23:46 • [Deut. 32:4]

6 I have hated those Rwho regard vain
idols;
But I trust in the LORD. Jon. 2:8
7 I will be glad and rejoice in Your
mercy,
For You have considered my trouble;
You have Rknown my soul in
Tadversities, [John 10:27] • *troubles*
8 And have not Tshut me up into the
hand of the enemy; *given me over*
You have set my feet in a wide place.

9 Have mercy on me, O LORD, for I am in
trouble;
RMy eye wastes away with grief, Ps. 6:7
Yes, my soul and my Tbody! Lit. *belly*
10 For my life is spent with grief,
And my years with sighing;
My strength fails because of my
iniquity,
And my bones waste away.
11 I am a reproach among all my enemies,
But especially among my neighbors,
And *am* repulsive to my acquaintances;
Those who see me outside flee from me.
12 RI am forgotten like a dead man, out of
mind; Ps. 88:4, 5
I am like Ta broken vessel. Lit. *perishing*
13 RFor I hear the slander of many;
RFear *is* on every side;
While they Rtake counsel together
against me, Jer. 20:10 • Lam. 2:22 • Matt. 27:1
They scheme to take away my life.

14 But as for me, I trust in You, O LORD;
I say, "You *are* my God."
15 My times *are* in Your Rhand;
Deliver me from the hand of my
enemies, [Job 14:5; 24:1]
And from those who persecute me.
16 RMake Your face shine upon Your
servant; Ps. 4:6; 80:3
Save me for Your mercies' sake.
17 RDo not let me be ashamed, O LORD, for
I have called upon You; Ps. 25:2, 20
Let the wicked be ashamed;
Let them be silent in the grave.

18 [R]Let the lying lips be put to silence,
Which [R]speak insolent things proudly
and contemptuously against the
righteous. Ps. 109:2; 120:2 • Ps. 94:4

19 [R]Oh, how great *is* Your goodness,
Which You have laid up for those who
fear You, [Rom. 2:4; 11:22]
Which You have prepared for those
who trust in You
In the presence of the sons of men!
20 [R]You shall hide them in the secret place
of Your presence [Ps. 27:5; 32:7]
From the plots of man;
[R]You shall keep them secretly in [T]a
pavilion Job 5:21 • *shelter*
From the strife of tongues.

21 Blessed *be* the LORD,
For He has shown me His marvelous
kindness in a [T]strong city! *fortified*
22 For I said in my haste,
"I am cut off from before Your eyes";
Nevertheless You heard the voice of my
supplications
When I cried out to You.

23 Oh, love the LORD, all you His saints!
For the LORD preserves the faithful,
And fully repays the proud person.
24 [R]Be of good courage,
And He shall strengthen your heart,
All you who hope in the LORD. [Ps. 27:14]

PSALM 32

The Blessedness of Forgiveness

A Psalm of David. *A Contemplation.

BLESSED *is he whose* [R]transgression *is*
forgiven,
Whose sin *is* covered. [Ps. 85:2; 103:3]
2 Blessed *is* the man to whom the LORD
does not [T]impute iniquity, *charge*
And in whose spirit *there is* no guile.

3 When I kept silent, my bones grew old
Through my groaning all the day long.
4 For day and night Your [R]hand was
heavy upon me;
My vitality was turned into the drought
of summer. Selah 1 Sam. 5:6

5 I acknowledged my sin to You,
And my iniquity I have not hidden.
[R]I said, "I will confess my transgressions
to the LORD,"
And You forgave the iniquity of my sin.
Selah [Prov. 28:13]

6 [R]For this cause everyone who is godly
shall [R]pray to You [1 Tim. 1:16] • Is. 55:6
In a time when You may be found;
Surely in a flood of great waters
They shall not come near him.
7 [R]You *are* my hiding place;
You shall preserve me from trouble;
You shall surround me with [R]songs of
deliverance. Selah Ps. 9:9 • Ex. 15:1

8 I will instruct you and teach you in the
way you should go;
I will guide you with My eye.
9 Do not be like the [R]horse *or* like the
mule, Prov. 26:3
Which have no understanding,
Which must be harnessed with bit and
bridle,
Else they will not come near you.

10 [R]Many sorrows *shall be* to the wicked;
But [R]he who trusts in the LORD, mercy
shall surround him. [Rom. 2:9] • Prov. 16:20
11 [R]Be glad in the LORD and rejoice, you
righteous;
And shout for joy, all *you* upright in
heart! Ps. 64:10; 68:3; 97:12

PSALM 33

God Considers All Man's Works

REJOICE in the LORD, O you righteous!
For praise from the upright is beautiful.
2 Praise the LORD with the harp;
[T]Make melody to Him with an
instrument of ten strings. Lit. *Sing to Him*
3 Sing to Him a new song;
Play skillfully with a shout of joy.

32:title, Heb. *Maschil*

32:5 What Should Be Done About Sin—The believer should never condone or attempt to excuse his sin. There are only two things that should be done about sin: confess it and forsake it. The Old and New Testaments are agreed on this. David confessed his sin and experienced the Lord's forgiveness. John agrees as he points out: "If we confess our sins, He is faithful and just to forgive us *our* sins and to cleanse us from all unrighteousness" (Page 1494—1 John 1:9). To "confess" means *to acknowledge* or *to say the same thing as*. The believer is instructed that he is to say the same thing as God says about his sin, "It is sin." When the believer confesses his sin he has the assurance that God "is faithful" (He can be counted upon to keep His word) and "just" (He is just in dealing with our sins because He paid the price for them) "to forgive us *our* sins and to cleanse us from all unrighteousness." There is no sin too great and no sin too small—God is able to cleanse us completely from anything that is inconsistent with His own moral character. Having received forgiveness and cleansing, the believer is to forsake his sin and yield himself completely to God. In doing this the believer is restored to full fellowship with God.

Now turn to Page 1496—1 John 2:15: Temptation by the World.

4 For the word of the LORD *is* right,
And all His work *is done* in truth.
5 He loves righteousness and justice;
The earth is full of the goodness of the
LORD.

6 [R]By the word of the LORD the heavens
were made, [Heb. 11:3]
And all the [R]host of them [R]by the
breath of His mouth. Gen. 2:1 • [Job 26:13]
7 [R]He gathers the waters of the sea
together as a heap; Job 26:10, 38:8
He lays up the deep in storehouses.

8 Let all the earth fear the LORD;
Let all the inhabitants of the world
stand in awe of Him.
9 For [R]He spoke, and it was *done;*
He commanded, and it stood fast. Gen. 1:3

10 [R]The LORD brings the counsel of the
nations to nothing;
He makes the plans of the peoples of no
effect. Is. 8:10; 19:3
11 [R]The counsel of the LORD stands forever,
The plans of His heart to all
generations. [Job 23:13]
12 Blessed *is* the nation whose God *is* the
LORD,
And the people *whom* He has [R]chosen
as His own inheritance. [Ex. 19:5]

13 [R]The LORD looks from heaven;
He sees all the sons of men. Job 28:24
14 From the place of His habitation He
looks
On all the inhabitants of the earth;
15 He fashions their hearts individually;
He [T]considers all their works. *understands*

16 [R]No king *is* saved by the multitude of an
army;
A mighty man is not delivered by great
strength. Ps. 44:6; 60:11
17 [R]A horse *is* a [T]vain hope for safety;
Neither shall it deliver *any* by its great
strength. [Prov. 21:31] • *false*

18 [R]Behold, the eye of the LORD *is* on those
who fear Him, [Job 36:7]
On those who hope in His mercy,
19 To deliver their soul from death,
And to keep them alive in famine.

20 Our soul waits for the LORD;
He *is* our help and our shield.
21 For our heart shall rejoice in Him,
Because we have trusted in His holy
name.
22 Let Your mercy, O LORD, be upon us,
Just as we hope in You.

PSALM 34

Seek the Lord

A Psalm of David when he pretended madness
before Abimelech, who drove him away,
and he departed.

I WILL [R]bless the LORD at all times;
His praise *shall* continually *be* in my
mouth. [Eph. 5:20]
2 My soul shall make its boast in the
LORD;
The humble shall hear *of it* and be glad.
3 Oh, magnify the LORD with me,
And let us exalt His name together.

4 I sought the LORD, and He heard me,
And delivered me from all my fears.
5 They looked to Him and were radiant,
And their faces were not ashamed.
6 This poor man cried out, and the LORD
heard *him,*
And saved him out of all his troubles.
7 The [T]angel of the LORD [R]encamps all
around those who fear Him,
And delivers them. Or *Angel* • 2 Kin. 6:17

8 Oh, [R]taste and see that the LORD *is*
good; 1 Pet. 2:3
Blessed *is* the man *who* trusts in Him!
9 Oh, fear the LORD, you His saints!
There is no [T]want to those who fear
Him. *lack*
10 The young lions lack and suffer hunger;
[R]But those who seek the LORD shall not
lack any good *thing.* [Ps. 84:11]

11 Come, you children, listen to me;
I will teach you the fear of the LORD.
12 [R]Who *is* the man *who* desires life,
And loves *many* days, that he may see
good? [1 Pet. 3:10–12]
13 Keep your tongue from evil,
And your lips from speaking guile.
14 [R]Depart from evil, and do good; Ps. 37:27
[R]Seek peace, and pursue it. [Rom. 14:19]

15 [R]The eyes of the LORD *are* on the
righteous, Job 36:7
And His ears *are open* to their cry.
16 [R]The face of the LORD *is* against those
who do evil, Lev. 17:10
[R]To [T]cut off the remembrance of them
from the earth. [Prov. 10:7] • *destroy*

17 *The righteous* cry out, and [R]the LORD
hears,
And delivers them out of all their
troubles. Ps. 34:6; 145:19
18 [R]The LORD *is* near [R]to those who have a
broken heart, [Ps. 145:18] • [Is. 57:15]
And saves such as [T]have a contrite
spirit. *are crushed in spirit*

19 [R]Many *are* the afflictions of the
righteous,
[R]But the LORD delivers him out of them
all. Prov. 24:16 • Ps. 34:4, 6, 17
20 He guards all his bones;
[R]Not one of them is broken. John 19:33, 36☆
21 [R]Evil shall slay the wicked,
And those who hate the righteous shall
be [T]condemned. Ps. 94:23; 140:11 • *held guilty*
22 The LORD [R]redeems the soul of His
servants,
And none of those who trust in Him
shall be condemned. 1 Kin. 1:29

PSALM 35

Petition for God's Intervention

A Psalm of David.

PLEAD[T] *my cause,* O LORD, with those
who strive with me;
Fight against those who fight against
me. *Contend for me*
2 Take hold of shield and [T]buckler,
And stand up for my help. A small shield
3 Also draw out the spear,
And stop those who pursue me.
Say to my soul,
"I *am* your salvation."

4 [R]Let those be put to shame and brought
to dishonor Ps. 40:14, 15; 70:2, 3
Who seek after my life;
Let those be [R]turned back and brought
to confusion
Who plot my hurt. Ps. 129:5
5 [R]Let them be like chaff before the wind,
And let the [T]angel of the LORD chase
them. Job 21:18 • Or *Angel*
6 Let their way be [R]dark and slippery,
And let the angel of the LORD pursue
them. Ps. 73:18
7 For without cause they have [R]hidden
their net for me *in* a pit,
Which they have dug without cause for
my life. Ps. 9:15
8 Let [R]destruction come upon him
unexpectedly, [1 Thess. 5:3]
And let his net that he has hidden catch
himself;
Into that very destruction let him fall.

9 And my soul shall be joyful in the
LORD;
It shall rejoice in His salvation.
10 [R]All my bones shall say,
"LORD, [R]who *is* like You,
Delivering the poor from him who is
too strong for him,
Yes, the poor and the needy from him
who plunders him?" Ps. 51:8 • [Ex. 15:11]

11 [R]Fierce witnesses rise up; Mark 14:57, 58☆
They ask me *things* that I do not know.
12 [R]They reward me evil for good,
To the sorrow of my soul. John 10:32
13 But as for me, [R]when they were sick,
My clothing *was* sackcloth;
I humbled myself with fasting;
And my prayer would return to my own
[T]heart. Job 30:25 • Lit. *bosom*
14 I paced about as though *he were* my
friend *or* brother;
I bowed down [T]heavily, as one who
mourns *for his* mother. *in mourning*

15 But in my [T]adversity they rejoiced
And gathered together; *limping, stumbling*
Attackers gathered against me,
And I did not know *it;*
They tore *at me* and did not cease;
16 With ungodly mockers at feasts
They gnashed at me with their teeth.

17 Lord, how long will You [R]look on?
Rescue me from their destructions,
My precious *life* from the lions. [Hab. 1:13]
18 I will give You thanks in the great
congregation;
I will praise You among many people.

19 [R]Let them not rejoice over me who are
wrongfully my enemies; Ps. 69:4; 109:3
Nor let them wink with the eye who
[R]hate me without a cause. John 15:24, 25☆
20 For they do not speak peace,
But they devise deceitful matters
Against *those who are* quiet in the land.
21 They also opened their mouth wide
against me,
And said, "Aha, aha!
Our eyes have seen *it.*"

22 *This* You have seen, O LORD;
Do not keep silence.
O Lord, do not be far from me.
23 Stir up Yourself, and awake to my
vindication,
To my cause, my God and my Lord.
24 Vindicate me, O LORD my God,
according to Your righteousness;
And let them not rejoice over me.
25 Let them not say in their hearts, "Ah,
so we would have it!"
Let them not say, "We have swallowed
him up."

26 Let them be ashamed and brought to
mutual confusion
Who rejoice at my hurt;
Let them be [R]clothed with shame and
dishonor Ps. 109:29
Who magnify themselves against me.

27 [R]Let them shout for joy and be glad,

Who favor my righteous cause;
And let them say continually,
"Let the LORD be magnified,
Who has pleasure in the prosperity of
His servant." Rom. 12:15
28 And my tongue shall speak of Your
righteousness
And of Your praise all the day long.

PSALM 36

The Excellent Lovingkindness of God

To the Chief Musician. A Psalm of David
the servant of the LORD.

AN oracle within my heart concerning the
transgression of the wicked:
There is no fear of God before his eyes.
2 For he flatters himself in his own eyes,
When he finds out his iniquity *and*
when he hates.
3 The words of his mouth *are* wickedness
and deceit;
[R]He has ceased to be wise *and* to do
good. Jer. 4:22
4 [R]He devises wickedness on his bed;
He sets himself [R]in a way *that is* not
good; Prov. 4:16 • Is. 65:2
He does not [T]abhor evil. *reject, loathe*

5 Your mercy, O LORD, *is* in the heavens,
And Your faithfulness *reaches* to the
clouds.
6 Your righteousness *is* like the [T]great
mountains; Lit. *mountains of God*
Your judgments *are* a great deep;
O LORD, You preserve man and beast.

7 How precious *is* Your lovingkindness, O
God!
Therefore the children of men [R]put their
trust under the shadow of Your
wings. Ps. 17:8; 57:1; 91:4
8 [R]They are abundantly satisfied with the
fullness of Your house, Ps. 63:5; 65:4
And You give them drink from [R]the
river of Your pleasures. Rev. 22:1
9 For with You *is* the fountain of life;
[R]In Your light we see light. [1 Pet. 2:9]

10 Oh, continue Your lovingkindness to
those who know You,
And Your righteousness to the upright
in heart.
11 Let not the foot of pride come against
me,
And let not the hand of the wicked
drive me away.
12 There the workers of iniquity have
fallen;
They have been cast down and are not
able to rise.

PSALM 37

"Rest in the LORD"

A Psalm of David.

DO[R] not fret because of evildoers,
Nor be envious of the workers of
iniquity. Ps. 73:3
2 For they shall soon be cut down [R]like
the grass, Ps. 90:5, 6; 92:7
And wither as the green herb.

3 Trust in the LORD, and do good;
Dwell in the land, and feed on His
faithfulness.
4 [R]Delight yourself also in the LORD,
And He shall give you the desires of
your [R]heart. Is. 58:14 • Ps. 21:2; 145:19

5 [R]Commit [T]your way to the LORD,
Trust also in Him, [Ps. 55:22] • Lit. *Roll off onto*
And He shall bring *it* to pass.
6 [R]He shall bring forth your righteousness
as the light, Job 11:17
And your justice as the noonday.

7 Rest in the LORD, [R]and wait patiently
for Him;
Do not fret because of him who
[R]prospers in his way,
Because of the man who brings wicked
schemes to pass. [Lam. 3:26] • [Ps. 73:3–12]
8 Cease from anger, and forsake wrath;
Do not fret—*it* only *causes* harm.

9 For evildoers shall be [T]cut off;
But those who wait on the LORD,
They shall inherit the earth. *destroyed*
10 For [R]yet a little while and the wicked
shall be no *more;* [Heb. 10:36]
Indeed, [R]you will look diligently for his
place,
But it *shall be* no *more.* Job 7:10
11 [R]But the meek shall inherit the earth,
And shall delight themselves in the
abundance of peace. [Matt. 5:5]

12 The wicked plots against the just,
And gnashes at him with his teeth.
13 [R]The Lord laughs at him, Ps. 2:4; 59:8
For He sees that his day is coming.
14 The wicked have drawn the sword
And have bent their bow,
To cast down the poor and needy,
To slay those who are of upright
conduct.
15 Their sword shall enter their own heart,
And their bows shall be broken.

16 [R]A little that a righteous man has
Is better than the riches of many
wicked. Prov. 15:16; 16:8

17 For the arms of the wicked shall be
broken,
But the LORD upholds the righteous.

18 The LORD knows the days of the
upright,
And their inheritance shall be forever.
19 They shall not be ashamed in the evil
time,
And in the days of famine they shall be
satisfied.
20 But the wicked shall perish;
And the enemies of the LORD,
Like the splendor of the meadows, shall
vanish.
Into smoke they shall vanish away.

21 The wicked borrows and does not
repay,
But [R]the righteous shows mercy and
gives. Ps. 112:5, 9
22 [R]For *those who are* blessed by Him shall
inherit the earth,
But *those who are* cursed by Him shall
be [T]cut off. [Prov. 3:33] • *destroyed*

23 [R]The steps of a *good* man are [T]ordered by
the LORD, [1 Sam. 2:9] • *established*
And He delights in his way.
24 [R]Though he fall, he shall not be utterly
cast down;
For the LORD upholds *him with* His
hand. Prov. 24:16

25 I have been young, and *now* am old;
Yet I have not seen the righteous
forsaken,
Nor his descendants begging bread.
26 *He is* [T]ever merciful, and lends; *all the day*
And his descendants *are* blessed.

27 Depart from evil, and do good;
And dwell forevermore.
28 For the LORD loves justice,
And does not forsake His saints;
They are preserved forever,
But the descendants of the wicked shall
be cut off.
29 [R]The righteous shall inherit the land,
And dwell in it forever. Prov. 2:21

30 [R]The mouth of the righteous speaks
wisdom, [Matt. 12:35]
And his tongue talks of justice.
31 The law of his God *is* in his heart;
None of his steps shall [T]slide. *slip*

32 The wicked [R]watches the righteous,
And seeks to slay him. Ps. 10:8; 17:11
33 The LORD [R]will not leave him in his
hand, [2 Pet. 2:9]
Nor condemn him when he is judged.

34 [R]Wait on the LORD,
And keep His way,
And He shall exalt you to inherit the
land;
When the wicked are cut off, you shall
see *it*. Ps. 27:14; 37:9
35 I have seen the wicked in great power,
And spreading himself like a native
green tree.
36 Yet he passed away, and behold, he *was*
no *more;*
Indeed I sought him, but he could not
be found.

37 Mark the blameless *man*, and observe
the upright;
For the future of *that* man *is* peace.
38 [R]But the transgressors shall be destroyed
together;
The future of the wicked shall be cut
off. [Ps. 1:4–6; 37:20, 28]

39 But the salvation of the righteous *is*
from the LORD;
He is their strength [R]in the time of
trouble. Ps. 9:9; 37:19
40 And [R]the LORD shall help them and
deliver them; Is. 31:5
He shall deliver them from the wicked,
And save them,
[R]Because they trust in Him. 1 Chr. 5:20

PSALM 38

The Heavy Burden of Sin

A Psalm of David. To bring to remembrance.

O LORD, do not [R]rebuke me in Your
wrath,
Nor chasten me in Your hot
displeasure! Ps. 6:1
2 For Your arrows pierce me deeply,
And Your hand presses me down.

3 *There is* no soundness in my flesh
Because of Your anger,
Nor *is there any* health in my bones
Because of my sin.
4 For my iniquities have gone over my
head;
Like a heavy burden they are too heavy
for me.
5 My wounds are foul *and* festering
Because of my foolishness.

6 I am [T]troubled, I am bowed down
greatly; Lit. *bent down*
I go mourning all the day long.
7 For my loins are full of inflammation,
And *there is* no soundness in my flesh.
8 I am feeble and severely broken;
I groan because of the turmoil of my
heart.

9 Lord, all my desire *is* before You;
And my sighing is not hidden from You.
10 My heart pants, my strength fails me;
As for the light of my eyes, it also has
gone from me.

11 My loved ones and my friends stand
aloof from my plague,
And [T]my kinsmen stand afar off. *neighbors*
12 Those also who seek my life lay snares
for me;
Those who seek my hurt speak of
destruction,
And plan deception all the day long.

13 But I, like a deaf *man,* do not hear;
And *I am* like a [R]mute *who* does not
open his mouth. Matt. 27:12–14☆
14 Thus I am like a man who does not
hear,
And in whose mouth *is* no response.

15 For in You, O LORD, [R]I hope; [Ps. 39:7]
You will [T]hear, O Lord my God. *answer*
16 For I said, "*Hear me,* lest they rejoice
over me,
Lest, when my foot slips, they magnify
themselves against me."

17 [R]For I *am* ready to fall,
And my sorrow *is* continually before
me. Ps. 51:3
18 For I will [R]declare my iniquity; Ps. 32:5
I will be in anguish over my sin.
19 But my enemies *are* vigorous, *and* they
are strong;
And those who hate me wrongfully
have multiplied.
20 Those also [R]who render evil for good,
They are my adversaries, because I
follow *what is* good. Ps. 35:12

21 Do not forsake me, O LORD;
O my God, be not far from me!
22 Make haste to help me,
O Lord, my salvation!

PSALM 39

Know the Measure of Man's Days

To the Chief Musician. To Jeduthun. A Psalm of David.

I SAID, "I will guard my ways,
Lest I sin with my [R]tongue; [James 3:5–12]
I will restrain my mouth with a muzzle,
While the wicked are before me."
2 [R]I was mute with silence,
I held my peace *even* from good;
And my sorrow was stirred up. Ps. 38:13
3 My heart was hot within me;
While I was [T]musing, the fire burned.
Then I spoke with my tongue: *meditating*

4 "LORD, make me to know my end,
And what *is* the measure of my days,
That I may know how frail I *am.*
5 Indeed, You have made my days *as*
handbreadths,
And my age *is* as nothing before You;
Certainly every man at his best state *is*
but [R]vapor. Selah Ps. 62:9
6 Surely every man walks about like a
shadow;
Surely they [T]busy themselves in vain;
He heaps up *riches,*
And does not know who will gather
them. *make an uproar for nothing*

7 "And now, Lord, what do I wait for?
My [R]hope *is* in You. Ps. 38:15
8 Deliver me from all my transgressions;
Do not make me [R]the reproach of the
foolish. Ps. 44:13; 79:4; 119:22
9 I was mute, I did not open my mouth,
Because it was [R]You who did *it.* Job 2:10
10 [R]Remove Your plague from me;
I am consumed by the blow of Your
hand. Job 9:34; 13:21
11 When with rebukes You correct man
for iniquity,
You make his beauty [R]melt away like a
moth; Job 13:28
Surely every man *is* vapor. Selah

12 "Hear my prayer, O LORD,
And give ear to my cry;
Do not be silent at my tears;
For I *am* a stranger with You,
A sojourner, as all my fathers *were.*
13 [R]Remove Your gaze from me, that I may
regain strength, Job 7:19; 10:20, 21; 14:6
Before I go away and am no more."

PSALM 40

Delight to Do God's Will

To the Chief Musician. A Psalm of David.

I [R]WAITED patiently for the LORD;
And He inclined to me,
And heard my cry. Ps. 25:5; 27:14; 37:7
2 He also brought me up out of a horrible
pit,
Out of [R]the miry clay, Ps. 69:2, 14
And [R]set my feet upon a rock, Ps. 27:5
And established my steps.
3 [R]He has put a new song in my mouth—
Praise to our God;
Many will see *it* and fear,
And will trust in the LORD. Ps. 32:7; 33:3

4 [R]Blessed *is* that man who makes the
LORD his trust,
And does not respect the proud, nor
such as turn aside to lies. Ps. 34:8; 84:12
5 [R]Many, O LORD my God, *are* Your
wonderful works Job 9:10

Which You have done;
[R]And Your thoughts *which are* toward
us [Is. 55:8]
Cannot be recounted to You in order;
If I would declare and speak *of them,*
They are more than can be numbered.

6 [R]Sacrifice and offering You did not
desire;
My ears You have opened;
Burnt offering and sin offering You did
not require. [Heb. 10:5–9]
7 Then I said, "Behold, I come;
In the scroll of the Book *it is* written of
me.

8 I delight to do Your will, O my God,
And Your law *is* within my heart."

9 [R]I have proclaimed the good news of
righteousness Ps. 22:22, 25
In the great congregation;
Indeed, [R]I do not restrain my lips,
O LORD, You Yourself know. Ps. 119:13
10 [R]I have not hidden Your righteousness
within my heart; Acts 20:20, 27
I have declared Your faithfulness and
Your salvation;
I have not concealed Your
lovingkindness and Your truth
From the great congregation.

11 Do not withhold Your tender mercies
from me, O LORD;
[R]Let Your lovingkindness and Your truth
continually preserve me. Ps. 61:7
12 For innumerable evils have surrounded
me;
[R]My iniquities have overtaken me, so
that I am not able to look up;
They are more than the hairs of my
head;
Therefore my heart fails me. Ps. 38:4; 65:3

13 [R]Be pleased, O LORD, to deliver me;
O LORD, make haste to help me! Ps. 70:1
14 [R]Let them be ashamed and brought to
mutual confusion Ps. 35:4, 26; 70:2
Who seek to destroy my [T]life; Or *soul*
Let them be driven backward and
brought to dishonor
Who wish me evil.
15 Let them be [R]appalled because of their
shame,
Who say to me, "Aha, aha!" Ps. 73:19

16 [R]Let all those who seek You rejoice and
be glad in You;
Let such as love Your salvation [R]say
continually,
"The LORD be magnified!" Ps. 70:4 • Ps. 35:27
17 [R]But I *am* poor and needy; Ps. 70:5; 86:1
Yet the LORD thinks upon me.
You *are* my help and my deliverer;
[R]Do not delay, O my God. 1 Pet. 5:7

PSALM 41

The Blessedness of Helping the Poor

To the Chief Musician. A Psalm of David.

BLESSED *is* he who considers the [T]poor;
The LORD will deliver him in time of
trouble. *helpless* or *powerless*
2 The LORD will preserve him and keep
him alive,
And he will be blessed on the earth;
[R]You will not deliver him to the will of
his enemies. Ps. 27:12

40:8 We Know God's Will Through His Word—Knowing the will of God must not be thought of merely as finding a certain vocation in life. That aspect represents only a small part of God's will. Rather, the will of God is for everyone to live in conformity to His revealed will in His Word.

a. First of all, and most important, the will of God means believing Christ (Page 1246—John 6:40). If we do not take this first step in doing God's will, we will not be saved from judgment (Page 1125—Matt. 7:21; 12:50); if we do, we will live forever (Page 1496—1 John 2:17).
b. Second, there are clear statements of Scripture which teach that God's will for every Christian includes sanctification (Page 1416—1 Thess. 4:13), giving thanks to God (Page 1416—1 Thess. 5:18), doing good (Page 1480—1 Pet. 2:15), and suffering for doing the right thing (Page 1481—1 Pet. 3:17).
c. Third, the Bible is God's will and must be applied to our lives (Page 241—Deut. 29:29). This fact involves commands to be obeyed, principles to be followed, prohibitions of things to be avoided, and living examples to be imitated or shunned. An attitude of delightful desire should fill all attempts to do God's will (Ps. 40:8). God takes great joy in those who cheerfully do His will.

Although the Bible is a complete revelation of God's will, there are always decisions we must make that are not covered by specific statements of Scripture. In order to know God's will in such instances we must be in fellowship with the Lord (Page 1494—1 John 1:6, 7), seek principles from the Word (Page 1353—1 Cor. 10:6), obtain advice from godly counselors (Page 723—Prov. 11:14; 15:22; 24:6), use common sense, and remember that God works through our own minds and desires to do His will (Page 1400—Phil. 2:13). When none of these principles seem to work, we must simply make the best possible decision, realizing that God will shut the door if it is not His will. Paul, for example, planned to go and see the Roman Christians, although not knowing if God would actually permit it in His will (Page 1340—Rom. 15:22–32). In most cases, however, the believer who thoroughly searches the Word will find the basis for an intelligent decision.

Now turn to Page 244—Deut. 32:7: God's Work in the Past.

3 The LORD will strengthen him on his
bed of illness;
You will sustain him on his sickbed.

4 I said, "LORD, be merciful to me;
[R]Heal my soul, for I have sinned against
You." Ps. 6:2; 103:3; 147:3
5 My enemies speak evil of me:
"When will he die, and his name perish?"
6 And if he comes to see *me,* he speaks
[T]vain *words;*
His heart gathers iniquity to itself;
When he goes out, he tells *it.* *empty*

7 All who hate me whisper together
against me;
Against me they [T]devise my hurt. *plot*
8 "An[T] evil disease," *they say,* "clings to
him.
And *now* that he lies down, he will rise
up no more." Lit. *A thing of Belial*
9 [R]Even my own familiar friend in whom I
trusted, 2 Sam. 15:12
[R]Who ate my bread, John 13:18, 21–30☆
Has lifted up *his* heel against me.

10 But You, O LORD, be merciful to me,
and raise me up,
That I may repay them.
11 By this I know that You are well
pleased with me,
Because my enemy does not triumph
over me.
12 As for me, You uphold me in my
integrity,
And set me before Your face forever.

13 [R]Blessed *be* the LORD God of Israel
From everlasting to everlasting!
Amen and Amen. Ps. 72:18, 19; 89:52; 106:48

BOOK TWO
Psalms 42–72

PSALM 42

Seek After the Lord

To the Chief Musician. *A Contemplation
of the sons of Korah.

AS the deer pants for the water brooks,
So pants my soul for You, O God.
2 [R]My soul thirsts for God, for the [R]living
God.
When shall I come and appear before
God? Ps. 63:1; 84:2; 143:6 • 1 Thess. 1:9
3 [R]My tears have been my food day and
night, Ps. 80:5; 102:9
While they continually say to me,
[R]"Where *is* your God?" Ps. 79:10; 115:2

4 When I remember these *things,*
[R]I pour out my soul within me.
For I used to go with the multitude;
[R]I went with them to the house of God,
With the voice of joy and praise,
With a multitude that kept a pilgrim
feast. Job 30:16 • Is. 30:29

5 Why are you cast down, O my soul?
And *why* are you disquieted within me?
Hope in God, for I shall yet praise Him
For the help of His countenance.

6 O my God, my soul is cast down within
me;
Therefore I will remember You from
the land of the Jordan,
And from the heights of Hermon,
From [T]the Hill Mizar. Or *Mount*
7 Deep calls unto deep at the noise of
Your waterfalls;
[R]All Your waves and billows have gone
over me. Ps. 69:1, 2; 88:7
8 The LORD will [R]command His
lovingkindness in the daytime,
And [R]in the night His song *shall be* with
me— Deut. 28:8 • Job 35:10
A prayer to the God of my life.

9 I will say to God my Rock,
[R]"Why have You forgotten me?
Why do I go mourning because of the
oppression of the enemy?" Ps. 38:6
10 *As* with a [T]breaking of my bones,
My enemies [T]reproach me,
While they say to me all day long,
"Where *is* your God?" Lit. *shattering* • *revile*

11 [R]Why are you cast down, O my soul?
And why are you disquieted within me?
Hope in God;
For I shall yet praise Him,
The [T]help of my countenance and my
God. Ps. 43:5 • Lit. *salvation*

PSALM 43

"Hope in God"

VINDICATE [R]me, O God,
And [R]plead my cause against an
ungodly nation;
Oh, deliver me from the deceitful and
unjust man! [Ps. 26:1; 35:24] • Ps. 35:1
2 For You *are* the God of my strength;
Why do You cast me off?
[R]Why do I go mourning because of the
oppression of the enemy? Ps. 42:9

3 [R]Oh, send out Your light and Your truth!
Let them lead me;

42:title, Heb. *Maschil*

Let them bring me to [R]Your holy hill
And to Your tabernacle. [Ps. 40:11] • Ps. 3:4
4 Then I will go to the altar of God,
To God my exceeding joy;
And on the harp I will praise You,
O God, my God.

5 [R]Why are you cast down, O my soul?
And why are you disquieted within me?
Hope in God;
For I shall yet praise Him,
The [T]help of my countenance and my
God. Ps. 42:5, 11 • Lit. *salvation*

PSALM 44

Prayer for Deliverance by God

To the Chief Musician. *A Contemplation of the sons of Korah.

WE have heard with our ears, O God,
[R]Our fathers have told us,
What deeds You did in their days,
In days of old: [Ex. 12:26, 27]
2 *How* [R]You drove out the [T]nations with
Your hand,
But them You planted;
How You afflicted the peoples, and cast
them out. Ex. 15:17 • *Gentiles, heathen*
3 For [R]they did not gain possession of the
land by their own sword, [Deut. 8:17, 18]
Nor did their own arm save them;
But it was Your right hand, Your arm,
and the light of Your countenance,
Because You favored them.

4 [R]You are my King, O God;
Command victories for Jacob. [Ps. 74:12]
5 Through You [R]we will push down our
enemies;
Through Your name we will trample
those who rise up against us. [Dan. 8:4]
6 For [R]I will not trust in my bow,
Nor shall my sword save me. Ps. 33:16
7 But You have saved us from our
enemies,
And have put to shame those who
hated us.
8 [R]In God we boast all day long, Ps. 34:2
And praise Your name forever. Selah

9 But [R]You have cast *us* off and put us
to shame, Ps. 60:1
And You do not go out with our armies.
10 You make us [R]turn back from the
enemy,
And those who hate us have taken
[T]spoil for themselves. Lev. 26:17 • *plunder*
11 [R]You have given us up like sheep
intended for food,
And have [R]scattered us among the
nations. Rom. 8:36 • Deut. 4:27; 28:64
12 You sell Your people for naught,
And are not enriched by their price.
13 [R]You make us a reproach to our
neighbors,
A scorn and a derision to those all
around us. Deut. 28:37
14 [R]You make us a byword among the
nations,
[R]A shaking of the head among the
peoples. Jer. 24:9 • Job 16:4
15 My dishonor *is* continually before me,
And the shame of my face has covered
me,
16 Because of the voice of him who
reproaches and reviles,
Because of the enemy and the avenger.

17 [R]All this has come upon us;
But we have not forgotten You,
Nor have we dealt falsely with Your
covenant. Dan. 9:13
18 Our heart has not turned back,
[R]Nor have our steps departed from Your
way; Job 23:11
19 But You have severely broken us in
[R]the place of jackals,
And covered us [R]with the shadow of
death. Is. 34:13 • [Ps. 23:4]

20 If we had forgotten the name of our
God,
Or [R]stretched[T] out our hands to a
foreign god, [Deut. 6:14] • Worshiped
21 Would not God search this out?
For He knows the secrets of the heart.
22 [R]Yet for Your sake we are killed all day
long;
We are accounted as sheep for the
slaughter. Rom. 8:36

23 [R]Awake! Why do You sleep, O Lord?
Arise! Do not cast *us* off forever. Ps. 7:6
24 [R]Why do You hide Your face,
And forget our affliction and our
oppression? Job 13:24
25 For [R]our soul is bowed down [T]to the
dust; Ps. 119:25 • Ground, in humiliation
Our body clings to the ground.
26 Arise for our help,
And redeem us for Your mercies' sake.

PSALM 45

The Psalm of the Great King

To the Chief Musician. Set to *"The Lilies." *A Contemplation of the sons of Korah. A Song of Love.

MY heart is overflowing with a good
theme;
I recite my composition concerning the
King;

44:title, Heb. *Maschil* **45:title,** Heb. *Shoshannim*
45:title, Heb. *Maschil*

My tongue *is* the pen of a ready writer.

2 You are fairer than the sons of men;
Grace is poured upon Your lips;
Therefore God has blessed You forever.
3 [T]Gird Your [R]sword upon *Your* thigh,
[R]O Mighty One, *Belt on* • [Heb. 4:12] • [Is. 9:6]
With Your glory and Your majesty.
4 [R]And in Your majesty ride prosperously
because of truth, humility, *and* righteousness;
And Your right hand shall teach You
awesome things. Rev. 6:2
5 Your arrows *are* sharp in the heart of
the King's enemies;
The peoples fall under You.

6 [R]Your throne, O God, *is* forever and
ever; Heb. 1:8☆
A [R]scepter of righteousness *is* the
scepter of Your kingdom. [Num. 24:17]
7 You love righteousness and hate
wickedness;
Therefore God, Your God, has [R]anointed
You
With the oil of [R]gladness more than
Your companions. Ps. 2:2 • Ps. 21:6
8 All Your garments are [R]scented with
myrrh and aloes *and* cassia,
Out of the ivory palaces, by which they
have made You glad. Song 1:12, 13
9 [R]Kings' daughters *are* among Your
honorable women;
[R]At Your right hand stands the queen in
gold from Ophir. Song 6:8 • 1 Kin. 2:19

10 Listen, O daughter,
Consider and incline your ear;
[R]Forget your own people also, and your
father's house; Deut. 21:13
11 So the King will greatly desire your
beauty;
Because He *is* your Lord, worship Him.
12 And the daughter of Tyre *will be there*
with a gift;
[R]The rich among the people will seek
your favor. Is. 49:23

13 The royal daughter *is* all glorious within
the palace;
Her clothing *is* woven with gold.
14 [R]She shall be brought to the King in
robes of many colors;
The virgins, her companions who follow
her, shall be brought to You. Song 1:4
15 With gladness and rejoicing they shall
be brought;
They shall enter the King's palace.

16 Instead of Your fathers shall be Your
sons,
[R]Whom You shall make princes in all the
earth. [1 Pet. 2:9]
17 [R]I will make Your name to be
remembered in all generations;
Therefore the people shall praise You
forever and ever. Mal. 1:11

PSALM 46

"God Is Our Refuge and Strength"

To the Chief Musician. A Psalm of the sons of Korah. A Song for Alamoth.

GOD *is* our [R]refuge and strength, Ps. 62:7, 8
A very present help in trouble.
2 Therefore we will not fear,
Though the earth be removed,
And though the mountains be carried
into the [T]midst of the sea; Lit. *heart*
3 [R]*Though* its waters roar *and* be troubled,
Though the mountains shake with its
swelling. Selah [Ps. 93:3, 4]

4 *There is* a [R]river whose streams shall
make glad the city of God,
The holy *place* of the [T]tabernacle of the
Most High. [Ezek. 47:1–12] • *dwelling places*
5 God *is* [R]in the midst of her, she shall
not be [T]moved; [Zeph. 3:15] • *shaken*
God shall help her, just [T]at the break of
dawn. Lit. *at the turning of the morning*
6 [R]The nations raged, the kingdoms were
moved; Ps. 2:1, 2
He uttered His voice, the earth melted.

7 The [R]LORD of hosts *is* with us; Num. 14:9
The God of Jacob *is* our refuge. Selah

8 Come, behold the works of the LORD,
Who has made desolations in the earth.
9 [R]He makes wars cease to the end of the
earth; Is. 2:4
[R]He breaks the bow and cuts the spear
in two; Ps. 76:3
[R]He burns the chariot in the fire. Ezek. 39:9

10 Be still, and know that I *am* God;
[R]I will be exalted among the nations,
I will be exalted in the earth! [Is. 2:11, 17]

11 The LORD of hosts *is* with us;
The God of Jacob *is* our refuge. Selah

PSALM 47

The Lord Shall Subdue All Nations

To the Chief Musician.
A Psalm of the sons of Korah.

OH, clap your hands, all you peoples!
Shout to God with the voice of
triumph!
2 For the LORD Most High *is* awesome;
He is a great King over all the earth.
3 [R]He will subdue the peoples under us,
And the nations under our feet. Ps. 18:47

4 He will choose our [R]inheritance for us,
The excellence of Jacob whom He loves.
Selah [1 Pet. 1:4]

5 God has gone up with a shout,
The LORD with the sound of a trumpet.
6 Sing praises to God, sing praises!
Sing praises to our King, sing praises!
7 For God *is* the King of all the earth;
Sing praises with understanding.

8 [R]God reigns over the nations; 1 Chr. 16:31
God sits on His [R]holy throne. Ps. 48:1
9 The princes of the people have gathered
together,
[R]The people of the God of Abraham.
[R]For the shields of the earth *belong* to
God; [Rom. 4:11, 12] • [Ps. 89:18]
He is greatly exalted.

PSALM 48

The Praise of Mount Zion

A Song. A Psalm of the sons of Korah.

GREAT *is* the LORD, and greatly to be
praised
In the [R]city of our God,
In His holy mountain. Ps. 46:4; 87:3
2 [R]Beautiful in [T]elevation,
The joy of the whole earth,
Is Mount Zion *on* the sides of the north,
The city of the great King. Ps. 50:2 • *height*
3 God *is* in her palaces;
He is known as her refuge.

4 For behold, [R]the kings assembled,
They passed by together. 2 Sam. 10:6, 14
5 They saw *it, and* so they marveled;
They were troubled, they hastened
away.
6 Fear [R]took hold of them there, Ex. 15:15
And pain, as of a woman in travail,
7 *As when* You break the [R]ships of
Tarshish
With an east wind. Ezek. 27:25

8 As we have heard,
So we have seen
In the city of the LORD of hosts,
In the city of our God:
God will establish it forever. Selah

9 We have thought, O God, on [R]Your
lovingkindness,
In the midst of Your temple. Ps. 26:3
10 According to [R]Your name, O God,
So *is* Your praise to the ends of the
earth; Mal. 1:11
Your right hand is full of righteousness.
11 Let Mount Zion rejoice,
Let the daughters of Judah be glad,
Because of Your judgments.

12 Walk about Zion,
And go all around her.
Count her towers;
13 Mark well her bulwarks;
Consider her palaces;
That you may [R]tell *it* to the generation
following. [Ps. 78:5–7]
14 For this *is* God,
Our God forever and ever;
[R]He will be our guide
Even to death. Is. 58:11

PSALM 49

Riches Cannot Redeem

To the Chief Musician.
A Psalm of the sons of Korah.

HEAR this, all *you* peoples;
Give ear, all *you* inhabitants of the
world,
2 Both low and high,
Rich and poor together.
3 My mouth shall speak wisdom,
And the meditation of my heart *shall*
bring understanding.
4 I will incline my ear to a proverb;
I will disclose my [T]dark saying on the
harp. *riddle*

5 Why should I fear in the days of evil,
When the iniquity at my heels
surrounds me?
6 Those who [R]trust in their wealth
And boast in the multitude of their
riches, [Mark 10:24]
7 None *of them* can by any means
redeem *his* brother,
Nor give to God a ransom for him—
8 For [R]the redemption of their souls *is*
costly,
And it shall cease forever— [Matt. 16:26]
9 That he should continue to live
eternally,
And not [T]see the Pit. *experience corruption*

10 For he sees *that* wise men die;
Likewise the fool and the senseless
person perish,
And leave their wealth to others.
11 Their inner thought *is that* their houses
will continue forever,
And their dwelling places to all
generations;
They [R]call *their* lands after their own
names. Gen. 4:17
12 Nevertheless man, *though* in honor,
does not [T]remain;
He is like the beasts *that* perish. *endure*

13 This is the way of those who *are*
[R]foolish,
And of their posterity who approve
their sayings. Selah [Luke 12:20]

14 Like sheep they are laid in the grave;
Death shall feed on them;
[R]The upright shall have dominion over
them in the morning; [Dan. 7:18]
And their beauty shall be consumed in
the grave, far from their dwelling.
15 But God [R]will redeem my soul from the
power of the grave, Acts 2:31, 32 ☆
For He shall receive me. Selah

16 Do not be afraid when one becomes
rich,
When the glory of his house is
increased;
17 For when he dies he shall carry nothing
away;
His glory shall not descend after him.
18 Though while he lives [R]he blesses
himself
(For *men* will praise you when you do
well for yourself), Deut. 29:19
19 He shall go to the generation of his
fathers;
They shall never see [T]light. The light of life
20 Man *who is* in honor, yet does not
understand,
[R]Is like the beasts *that* perish. Eccl. 3:19

PSALM 50

The Lord Shall Judge All People

A Psalm of Asaph.

THE [R]Mighty One, God the LORD,
Has spoken and called the earth
From the rising of the sun to its going
down. Is. 9:6
2 Out of Zion, the perfection of beauty,
[R]God will shine forth. Ps. 80:1
3 Our God shall come, and shall not keep
silent;
[R]A fire shall devour before Him,
And it shall be very tempestuous all
around Him. [Ps. 97:3]

4 [R]He shall call to the heavens from above,
And to the earth, that He may judge
His people: Is. 1:2
5 "Gather My saints together to Me,
[R]Those who have [T]made a covenant with
Me by sacrifice." Ex. 24:7 • Lit. *cut*
6 Let the [R]heavens declare His
righteousness, [Ps. 97:6]
For God Himself *is* Judge. Selah

7 "Hear, O My people, and I will speak,
O Israel, and I will testify against you;
[R]I *am* God, your God! Ex. 20:2
8 [R]I will not [T]reprove you [R]for your
sacrifices Jer. 7:22 • *rebuke* • [Hos. 6:6]
Or your burnt offerings,
Which are continually before Me.
9 [R]I will not take a bull from your house,
Nor goats out of your folds. Ps. 69:31
10 For every beast of the forest *is* Mine,
And the cattle on a thousand hills.
11 I know all the birds of the mountains,
And the wild beasts of the field *are*
Mine.

12 "If I were hungry, I would not tell you;
[R]For the world *is* Mine, and all its
fullness. Ex. 19:5
13 [R]Will I eat the flesh of bulls,
Or drink the blood of goats? [Ps. 51:15–17]
14 [R]Offer to God thanksgiving, Heb. 13:15
And pay your vows to the Most High.
15 [R]Call upon Me in the day of trouble;
I will deliver you, and you shall glorify
Me." [Zech. 13:9]

16 But to the wicked God says:
"What *right* have you to declare My
statutes,
Or take My covenant in your mouth,
17 [R]Seeing you hate instruction Rom. 2:21
And cast My words behind you?
18 When you saw a thief, you [R]consented
with him,
And have been a [R]partaker with
adulterers. [Rom. 1:32] • 1 Tim. 5:22
19 You give your mouth to evil,
And [R]your tongue frames deceit. Ps. 52:2
20 You sit *and* speak against your brother;
You slander your own mother's son.
21 These *things* you have done, and I kept
silent;
[R]You thought that I was altogether like
you;
But I will reprove you,
And [R]set *them* in order before your
eyes. [Rom. 2:4] • [Ps. 90:8]

22 "Now consider this, you who [R]forget
God,
Lest I tear *you* in pieces,
And *there be* none to deliver: [Job 8:13]
23 Whoever offers praise glorifies Me;
And [R]to him who orders *his* conduct
aright Gal. 6:16
I will show the salvation of God."

PSALM 51

Confession and Forgiveness of Sin

To the Chief Musician. A Psalm of David when Nathan the prophet went to him, after he had gone in to Bathsheba.

HAVE mercy upon me, O God,
According to Your lovingkindness;
According to the multitude of Your
tender mercies,
[R]Blot out my transgressions. [Is. 43:25; 44:22]

2 [R]Wash me thoroughly from my iniquity,
And cleanse me from my sin. [Heb. 9:14]

3 For I acknowledge my transgressions,
And my sin *is* ever before me.
4 [R]Against You, You only, have I sinned,
And done *this* evil [R]in Your sight—
[R]That You may be found just when You speak, 2 Sam. 12:13 • [Luke 5:21] • Rom. 3:4
And blameless when You judge.

5 Behold, I was brought forth in iniquity,
And in sin my mother conceived me.
6 Behold, You desire truth in the inward parts,
And in the hidden *part* You will make me to know wisdom.

7 [R]Purge me with hyssop, and I shall be clean;
Wash me, and I shall be [R]whiter than snow. Heb. 9:19 • [Is. 1:18]
8 Make me to hear joy and gladness,
That the bones *which* You have broken [R]may rejoice. [Matt. 5:4]
9 Hide Your face from my sins,
And blot out all my iniquities.

10 Create in me a clean heart, O God,
And renew a steadfast spirit within me.
11 Do not cast me away from Your presence,
And do not take Your [R]Holy Spirit from me. [Luke 11:13]

12 Restore to me the joy of Your salvation,
And uphold me *with Your* [R]generous Spirit. [2 Cor. 3:17]
13 *Then* I will teach transgressors Your ways,
And sinners shall be converted to You.

14 Deliver me from bloodguiltiness, O God,
The God of my salvation,
And my tongue shall sing aloud of Your righteousness.
15 O Lord, open my lips,
And my mouth shall show forth Your praise.
16 For [R]You do not desire sacrifice, or else I would give *it;* [1 Sam. 15:22]
You do not delight in burnt offering.
17 [R]The sacrifices of God *are* a broken spirit, Ps. 34:18
A broken and a contrite heart—
These, O God, You will not despise.

18 Do good in Your good pleasure to Zion;
Build the walls of Jerusalem.
19 Then You shall be pleased with [R]the sacrifices of righteousness,
With burnt offering and whole burnt offering;
Then they shall offer bulls on Your altar. Ps. 4:5

PSALM 52

The Lord Shall Judge the Deceitful

To the Chief Musician. *A Contemplation of David when Doeg the Edomite went and told Saul, and said to him, "David has gone to the house of Ahimelech."

WHY do you boast in evil, O mighty man?
The goodness of God *endures* continually.
2 Your tongue devises destruction,
Like a sharp razor, working deceitfully.
3 You love evil more than good,
And lying rather than speaking righteousness. Selah
4 You love all devouring words,
You deceitful tongue.

5 God shall likewise destroy you forever;
He shall take you away, and pluck you out of *your* dwelling place,
And uproot you from the land of the living. Selah
6 The righteous also shall see and fear,
And shall laugh at him, *saying,*
7 "Here is the man *who* did not make God his strength,
But trusted in the abundance of his riches,
And strengthened himself in his [T]wickedness." Lit. *desire,* in evil sense

8 But I *am* [R]like a green olive tree in the house of God;
I trust in the mercy of God forever and ever. Jer. 11:16

52:title, Heb. *Maschil*

51:2 What Sin Is—In dealing with sin it is important to know what sin is. If asked to define sin, people will come up with many different definitions as to what sin is—usually the things that the individual does not like. One of the most common definitions of sin is *missing the mark*—a failure to live up to an expected standard. The problem with this definition is that it fails to take into account that when the mark is missed, something is hit. Another definition of sin is found in First John 3:4, "sin is lawlessness." Put simply according to this verse, sin is anything that is contrary to what the Word of God commands or forbids. This definition, however, does not take into account those things about which the Word of God is silent. The best definition for sin is found in First John 5:17, "All unrighteousness is sin."

Now turn to Page 830—Is. 59:2: What Sin Does.

9 I will praise You forever,
Because You have done *it;*
And in the presence of Your saints
I will wait on Your name, for *it is* good.

PSALM 53

A Portrait of the Godless

To the Chief Musician. Set to "Mahalath." *A Contemplation of David.

THE [R]fool has said in his heart,
[R]"*There is* no God." Ps. 10:4 • Rom. 3:10–12
They are corrupt,
and have done abominable iniquity;
There is none who does good.

2 God looks down from heaven upon the children of men,
To see if there are *any* who understand,
who [R]seek God. [2 Chr. 15:2]
3 Every one of them has turned aside;
They have together become corrupt;
There is none who does good,
No, not one.

4 Have the workers of iniquity [R]no knowledge,
Who eat up my people *as* they eat bread,
And do not call upon God? Jer. 4:22
5 [R]There they are in great fear Prov. 28:1
Where no fear was,
For God has scattered the bones of him who encamps against you;
You have put *them* to shame,
Because God has despised them.

6 [R]Oh, that the salvation of Israel would come out of Zion! Ps. 14:7
When God brings back [T]the captivity of His people, Or *His captive people*
Let Jacob rejoice *and* Israel be glad.

PSALM 54

The Lord Is Our Helper

To the Chief Musician. With *stringed instruments. *A Contemplation of David when the Ziphites went and said to Saul, "Is David not hiding with us?"

SAVE me, O God, by Your name,
And vindicate me by Your strength.
2 Hear my prayer, O God;
Give ear to the words of my mouth.
3 For strangers have risen up against me,
And oppressors have sought after my life;
They have not set God before them.
Selah
4 Behold, God *is* my helper;
The Lord *is* with those who [T]uphold my life. *sustain my soul*

5 He will repay my enemies for their evil.
Cut them off in Your [T]truth. Or *faithfulness*
6 I will freely sacrifice to You;
I will praise Your name, O LORD, for *it is* good.
7 For He has delivered me out of all trouble;
[R]And my eye has seen *its desire* upon my enemies. Ps. 59:10

PSALM 55

"Cast Your Burden on the LORD"

To the Chief Musician. With stringed instruments. A Contemplation of David.

GIVE ear to my prayer, O God,
And do not hide Yourself from my supplication.
2 Attend to me, and hear me;
I [R]am[T] restless in my complaint, and moan noisily, Is. 38:14; 59:11 • *wander*
3 Because of the voice of the enemy,
Because of the oppression of the wicked;
[R]For they bring down trouble upon me,
And in wrath they hate me. 2 Sam. 16:7, 8
4 [R]My heart is severely pained within me,
And the terrors of death have fallen upon me. Ps. 116:3
5 Fearfulness and trembling have come upon me,
And horror has overwhelmed me.
6 And I said, "Oh, that I had wings like a dove!
For then I would fly away and be at rest.
7 Indeed, I would wander far off,
And remain in the wilderness. Selah
8 I would hasten my escape
From the windy storm *and* tempest."

9 Destroy, O Lord, *and* divide their [T]tongues,
For I have seen [R]violence and strife in the city. *speech,* counsel • Jer. 6:7
10 Day and night they go around it on its walls;
Iniquity and trouble *are* also in the midst of it.
11 Destruction *is* in its midst;
Deceit and guile do not depart from its streets.

12 [R]For *it is* not an enemy *who* reproaches me; Ps. 41:9
Then I could bear *it.*
Nor *is it* one *who* hates me who has magnified *himself* against me;
Then I could hide from him.

53:title, Heb. *Maschil* 54:title, Heb. *neginoth*
54:title, Heb. *Maschil*

13 But *it was* you, a man my equal,
My companion and my acquaintance.
14 We took sweet counsel together,
And [R]walked to the house of God in the
throng. Ps. 42:4

15 Let death seize them;
Let them [R]go down alive into [T]hell,
For wickedness *is* in their dwellings *and*
among them. Num. 16:30, 33 • Or *Sheol*

16 As for me, I will call upon God,
And the LORD shall save me.
17 [R]Evening and morning and at noon
I will pray, and cry aloud,
And He shall hear my voice. Dan. 6:10
18 He has redeemed my soul in peace from
the battle *which was* against me,
For there were many against me.
19 God will hear, and afflict them,
[R]Even He who abides from of old. Selah
Because they do not change, [Deut. 33:27]
Therefore they do not fear God.

20 He has put forth his hands against
those who [R]were at peace with him;
He has broken his [T]covenant. Ps. 7:4 • *treaty*
21 [R]*The words* of his mouth were smoother
than butter, Ps. 28:3; 57:4
But war *was* in his heart;
His words were softer than oil,
Yet they *were* drawn swords.

22 [R]Cast your burden on the LORD,
And [R]He shall sustain you;
He shall never permit the righteous to
be [T]moved. [Ps. 37:5] • Ps. 37:24 • *shaken*

23 But You, O God, shall bring them down
to the pit of destruction;
[R]Bloodthirsty and deceitful men [R]shall
not live out half their days;
But I will trust in You. Ps. 5:6 • Prov. 10:27

PSALM 56

Fears in the Midst of Trials

To the Chief Musician. Set to *"The Silent Dove in Distant Lands." A Michtam of David when the Philistines captured him in Gath.

BE [R]merciful to me, O God, for man
would swallow me up; Ps. 57:1
Fighting all day he oppresses me.
2 My enemies would [R]hound *me* all day,
For *there are* many who fight against
me, O Most High. Ps. 57:3

3 Whenever I am afraid,
I will trust in You.
4 In God (I will praise His word),
In God I have put my trust;
[R]I will not fear.
What can flesh do to me? Ps. 118:6

5 All day they twist my words;
All their thoughts *are* against me for
evil.
6 They gather together,
They hide, they mark my steps,
When they lie in wait for my life.
7 Shall they escape by iniquity?
In anger cast down the peoples, O God!

8 You number my wanderings;
Put my tears into Your bottle;
[R]*Are they* not in Your book? [Mal. 3:16]
9 When I cry out *to You*,
Then my enemies will turn back;
This I know, because God *is* for me.
10 In God (I will praise *His* word),
In the LORD (I will praise *His* word),
11 In God I have put my trust;
I will not be afraid.
What can man do to me?

12 Vows *made* to You *are binding* upon
me, O God;
I will render praises to You,
13 [R]For You have delivered my soul from
death. Ps. 116:8, 9
Have You not *delivered* my feet from
falling,
That I may walk before God
In the [R]light of the living? Job 33:30

PSALM 57

Prayers in the Midst of Perils

To the Chief Musician. Set to *"Do Not Destroy." A Michtam of David when he fled from Saul into the cave.

BE merciful to me, O God, be merciful to
me!
For my soul trusts in You;
[R]And in the shadow of Your wings I will
make my refuge, Ps. 17:8, 63:7
Until *these* calamities have passed by.

2 I will cry out to God Most High,
To God [R]who performs *all things* for
me. [Ps. 138:8]
3 He shall send from heaven and save me;
He reproaches the one who would
[T]swallow me up. Selah
God shall send forth His mercy and His
truth. *snaps at* or *hounds me*, or *crushes me*

4 My soul *is* among lions;
I lie *among* the sons of men
Who are set on fire,
Whose teeth *are* spears and arrows,
And their tongue a sharp sword.
5 Be exalted, O God, above the heavens;
Let Your glory *be* above all the earth.

56:title, Heb. *Jonath Elem Rechokim*
57:title, Heb. *Al Tashcheth*

6 [R]They have prepared a net for my steps;
My soul is bowed down;
They have dug a pit before me;
Into the midst of it they *themselves*
have fallen. Selah Ps. 9:15

7 [R]My heart is steadfast, O God, my heart
is steadfast;
I will sing and give praise. Ps. 108:1–5
8 Awake, [R]my glory!
Awake, lute and harp!
I will awaken the dawn. Ps. 16:9

9 [R]I will praise You, O Lord, among the
peoples; Ps. 108:3
I will sing to You among the nations.
10 [R]For Your mercy reaches unto the
heavens, Ps. 103:11
And Your truth unto the clouds.

11 Be exalted, O God, above the heavens;
Let Your glory *be* above all the earth.

PSALM 58

Wicked Judges Will Be Judged

To the Chief Musician. Set to *"Do Not Destroy." A Michtam of David.

DO you indeed speak righteousness, you
silent ones?
Do you judge uprightly, you sons of
men?
2 No, in heart you work wickedness;
You weigh out the violence of your
hands in the earth.

3 [R]The wicked are estranged from the
womb;
They go astray as soon as they are
born, speaking lies. [Is. 48:8]
4 [R]Their poison *is* like the poison of a
serpent;
They are like the deaf cobra *that* stops
its ear, Eccl. 10:11
5 Which will not [R]heed the voice of
charmers,
Charming ever so skillfully. Jer. 8:17

6 [R]Break their teeth in their mouth, O
God!
[T]Break out the fangs of the young lions,
O LORD! Job 4:10 • *Break away*
7 [R]Let them flow away as waters *which*
run continually; Josh. 2:11; 7:5
When he bends *his bow,*
Let his arrows be as if cut in pieces.
8 *Let them be* like a snail which melts
away as it goes,
[R]*Like* a stillborn child of a woman, that
they may not see the sun. Job 3:16

9 Before your [R]pots can feel *the burning*
thorns,
He shall take them away [R]as with a
whirlwind, Eccl. 7:6 • Prov. 10:25
As in His living and burning wrath.
10 The righteous shall rejoice when he
sees the [R]vengeance;
[R]He shall wash his feet in the blood of
the wicked, Jer. 11:20 • Ps. 68:23
11 [R]So that men will say,
"Surely *there is* a reward for the
righteous;
Surely He is God who [R]judges in the
earth." Ps. 92:15 • Ps. 50:6; 75:7

PSALM 59

Petition for Deliverance from Violent Men

To the Chief Musician. Set to *"Do Not Destroy." A Michtam of David when Saul sent men, and they watched the house in order to kill him.

DELIVER me from my enemies, O my
God;
[T]Defend me from those who rise up
against me. Lit. *Set me on high*
2 Deliver me from the workers of
iniquity,
And save me from bloodthirsty men.

3 For look, they lie in wait for my life;
[R]The mighty gather against me,
Not *for* my transgression nor *for* my
sin, O LORD. Ps. 56:6
4 They run and prepare themselves
through no fault of *mine.*

[R]Awake to help me, and behold! Ps. 35:23
5 You therefore, O LORD God of hosts,
the God of Israel,
Awake to punish all the [T]nations;
Do not be merciful to any wicked
transgressors. Selah *Gentiles*

6 [R]At evening they return,
They growl like a dog,
And go all around the city. Ps. 59:14
7 Indeed, they belch out with their
mouth;
[R]Swords *are* in their lips; Prov. 12:18
For *they say,* [R]"Who hears?" Ps. 10:11

8 But [R]You, O LORD, shall laugh at them;
You shall have all the [T]nations in
derision. Prov. 1:26 • *Gentiles*
9 *O You* his Strength, I will wait for You.

For God *is* my [T]defense; Lit. *fortress*
10 My merciful God shall [R]come to meet
me;
God shall let [R]me see *my desire* on my
enemies. Ps. 21:3 • Ps. 54:7

58:title, Heb. *Al Tashcheth*
59:title, Heb. *Al Tashcheth*

11 Do not slay them, lest my people forget;
Scatter them by Your power,
And bring them down,
O Lord our shield.
12 [R]*For* the sin of their mouth *and* the words of their lips,
Let them even be taken in their pride,
And for the cursing and lying *which* they speak. Prov. 12:13
13 [R]Consume *them* in wrath, consume *them*,
That they *may* not *be;*
And [R]let them know that God rules in Jacob Ps. 104:35 • Ps. 83:18
To the ends of the earth. Selah

14 And [R]at evening they return,
They growl like a dog,
And go all around the city. Ps. 59:6
15 They wander up and down for food,
And howl if they are not satisfied.

16 But I will sing of Your power;
Yes, I will sing aloud of Your mercy in the morning;
For You have been my defense
And refuge in the day of my trouble.
17 To You, [R]O my Strength, I will sing praises;
For God *is* my defense,
The God of my mercy. Ps. 18:1

PSALM 60

A Prayer for Deliverance of the Nation

To the Chief Musician. Set to *"Lily of the Testimony." A Michtam of David. For teaching. When he fought against Mesopotamia and Syria of Zobah, and Joab returned and killed twelve thousand Edomites in the Valley of Salt.

O GOD, [R]You have cast us off;
You have broken us down;
You have been displeased;
Oh, restore us again! Ps. 44:9
2 You have made the earth tremble;
You have broken it;
Heal its breaches, for it is shaking.
3 [R]You have shown Your people hard things;
[R]You have made us drink the wine of [T]confusion. Ps. 71:20 • Jer. 25:15 • *staggering*

4 [R]You have given a banner to those who fear You,
That it may be displayed because of the truth. Selah Ps. 20:5
5 [R]That Your beloved may be delivered,
Save *with* Your right hand, and hear me. Ps. 108:6–13

6 God has [R]spoken in His holiness:
"I will rejoice; Ps. 89:35
I will [R]divide [R]Shechem
And measure out [R]the Valley of Succoth. Josh. 1:6 • Gen. 12:6 • Josh. 13:27
7 Gilead *is* Mine, and Manasseh *is* Mine;
Ephraim also *is* the [T]helmet for My head;
Judah *is* My lawgiver. Lit. *protection*
8 [R]Moab *is* My washpot;
[R]Over Edom I will cast My shoe;
[R]Philistia, shout in triumph because of Me." 2 Sam. 8:2 • 2 Sam. 8:14 • 2 Sam. 8:1

9 Who will bring me *into* the strong city?
Who will lead me to Edom?
10 *Is it* not You, O God, [R]*who* cast us off?
And *You*, O God, *who* did [R]not go out with our armies? Ps. 108:11 • Josh. 7:12
11 Give us help from trouble,
[R]For vain *is* the help of man. Ps. 118:8; 146:3
12 Through God [R]we will do valiantly,
For *it is* He *who* shall tread down our enemies. Num. 24:18

PSALM 61

A Prayer When Overwhelmed

To the Chief Musician. On *a stringed instrument. A Psalm of David.

HEAR my cry, O God;
Attend to my prayer.
2 From the end of the earth I will cry to You,
When my heart is overwhelmed;
Lead me to the rock that is higher than I.

3 For You have been a shelter for me,
And a strong tower from the enemy.
4 I will abide in Your [T]tabernacle forever;
[R]I will trust in the shelter of Your wings. Selah *tent* • Ps. 91:4

5 For You, O God, have heard my vows;
You have given *me* the heritage of those who fear Your name.
6 You will prolong the king's life,
His years as many generations.
7 He shall abide before God forever.
Oh, prepare mercy and truth, *which* may [T]preserve him! Lit. *guard* or *keep*

8 So I will sing praise to Your name forever,
That I may daily perform my vows.

PSALM 62

Wait for God

To the Chief Musician. To Jeduthun. A Psalm of David.

TRULY [R]my soul silently *waits* for God;
From Him *comes* my salvation. Ps. 33:20

60:title, Heb. *Shushan Eduth* **61:title,** Heb. *neginah*

2 He only *is* my rock and my salvation;
He is my [T]defense; *strong tower*
I shall not be greatly [T]moved. *shaken*

3 How long will you attack a man?
You shall be slain, all of you,
[R]Like a leaning wall and a tottering
fence. Is. 30:13
4 They only consult to cast *him* down
from his high position;
They [R]delight in lies;
They bless with their mouth,
But they curse inwardly. Selah Ps. 28:3

5 My soul, wait silently for God alone,
For my [T]expectation *is* from Him. *hope*
6 He only *is* my rock and my salvation;
He is my defense;
I shall not be [T]moved. *shaken*
7 [R]In God *is* my salvation and my glory;
The rock of my strength,
And my refuge, *is* in God. [Jer. 3:23]

8 Trust in Him at all times, you people;
[R]Pour out your heart before Him;
God *is* a refuge for us. Selah 1 Sam. 1:15

9 Surely men of low degree *are* [T]a vapor,
Men of high degree *are* a lie; *vanity*
If they are weighed in the balances,
They *are* altogether *lighter* than vapor.
10 Do not trust in oppression,
Nor vainly hope in robbery;
[R]If riches increase, [Luke 12:15]
Do not set *your* heart *on them.*

11 God has spoken once,
Twice I have heard this:
That power *belongs* to God.
12 Also to You, O Lord, *belongs* mercy;
For [R]You [T]render to each one according
to his work. [Matt. 16:27] • *reward*

PSALM 63

Thirst for God

A Psalm of David when he was
in the wilderness of Judah.

O GOD, You *are* my God;
Early will I seek You;
[R]My soul thirsts for You;
My flesh longs for You
In a dry and thirsty land
Where there is no water. Ps. 42:2
2 So I have looked for You in the
sanctuary,
To see Your power and Your glory.

3 [R]Because Your lovingkindness *is* better
than life,
My lips shall praise You. Ps. 138:2
4 Thus I will bless You while I live;
I will lift up my hands in Your name.
5 My soul shall be satisfied as with
[T]marrow and [T]fatness,
And my mouth shall praise You with
joyful lips. Lit. *fat* • Abundance

6 When I remember You on my bed,
I meditate on You in the *night* watches.
7 Because You have been my help,
Therefore in the shadow of Your wings
I will rejoice.
8 My soul follows close behind You;
Your right hand upholds me.

9 But those *who* seek my life, to destroy
it,
Shall go into the lower parts of the
earth.
10 They shall fall by the sword;
They shall be [T]a portion for jackals. Prey

11 But the king shall rejoice in God;
[R]Everyone who swears by Him shall
glory;
But the mouth of those who speak lies
shall be stopped. Deut. 6:13

PSALM 64

A Prayer for God's Protection

To the Chief Musician. A Psalm of David.

HEAR my voice, O God, in my
[T]meditation;
Preserve my life from fear of the
enemy. *complaint*
2 Hide me from the secret counsel of the
wicked,
From the [T]insurrection of the workers
of iniquity, *tumult*
3 Who sharpen their tongue like a sword,
[R]And bend *their bows to shoot* their
arrows—bitter words, Ps. 58:7
4 That they may shoot in secret at the
blameless;
Suddenly they shoot at him and do not
fear.

5 They encourage themselves *in* an evil
matter;
They talk of laying snares secretly;
They say, "Who will see them?"
6 They devise iniquities:
"We have perfected a shrewd scheme."
Both the inward thought and the heart
of man are deep.

7 But God shall shoot at them *with* an
arrow;
Suddenly they shall be wounded.
8 So He will make them stumble over
their own tongue;

LOVINGKINDNESS

Lovingkindness or Loyal Love (*hesed*)

The traditional understanding of *hesed* is that it means "lovingkindness" (KJV, NKJV), "mercy," "love," and for those who are not averse to using a typically New Testament word to translate *hesed*—even "grace." The ancient versions would seem to bear out this understanding. The Septuagint (LXX) translates *hesed* chiefly by "mercy" (*eleos*) and so does the Vulgate (*misericordia*).

Starting with Nelson Glueck's study on this word, it became popular to connect *hesed* with covenant obligations. In other words, people, as well as God, acted in a kind way out of loyalty to a covenant obligation. Such translations as "loyalty," "loyal love," and so forth usually go with this view.

R. Laird Harris maintains that *hesed* is deeper than a covenant relationship. For example, while David did make a covenant with Jonathan and was kind to Mephibosheth after his death, behind the covenant lay a gracious love that was even deeper than a solemn contract. Dr. Harris says that the old KJV rendering "lovingkindness" is "not far from the fulness of meaning of the word" (*Theological Wordbook of the Old Testament*, I:307). In the light of this viewpoint, the quite recent NKJV (1982) retained this KJ rendering. This word study agrees with this viewpoint.

The *Hesed* of People

All scholars seem to agree that the traditional idea is correct in Esther 2:9, 17. The LXX even uses the word *charis* ("grace") in 2:9 (see Gal. 1 for this word study), and the NKJV uses "grace" in 2:17: "The king loved Esther more than all the *other* women, and she obtained grace [*hēn*] and favor [*hesed*] in his sight more than all the virgins." The king certainly had no covenant obligations to this Jewish girl, no matter how lovely she was.

After Saul's death in battle, the men of Jabesh Gilead marched all night to provide him and his sons a decent burial (2 Sam. 2:5). They acted out of kindness because he had saved them from each one having an eye gouged out.

Boaz commended Ruth as follows: "You have shown more kindness [*hesed*] at the end than at the beginning" (Ruth 3:10).

The Lord compared Israel's former attitude to that of a bride: "I remember you, the kindness [*hesed*] of your youth, the love of your betrothal" (Jer. 2:2). Of course, a bride does make a marriage covenant, but lying behind that covenant is love.

The *Hesed* of the Lord

In the Ten Commandments (Ex. 20 and Deut. 5), the Lord describes Himself as "a jealous God, visiting the iniquity of the fathers on the children to the third and fourth *generations* of those who hate Me, but showing mercy [*hesed*] to thousands, to those who love Me and keep My commandments" (Ex. 20:5, 6).

Even more gracious is the Lord's self-description spoken after the apostasy of the golden calf, when the Israelites had shown how disloyal they were to God's covenant. "The LORD God, merciful and gracious, longsuffering, and abounding in goodness and truth, keeping mercy [*hesed*] for thousands, forgiving iniquity..." (Ex. 34:67).

Jonah, like many religious but harsh people, was displeased with the Lord's graciousness. Saying, "I told You so," the sulky prophet says, "I know that You *are* a gracious and merciful God, slow to anger and abundant in lovingkindness [*hesed*]" (Jon. 4:2).

Fifteen times in the Old Testament, *hesed* is paired with a word for mercy as a close synonym. For example: "Remember, O LORD, Your tender mercies and Your lovingkindnesses, for they have been from of old" (Ps. 25:6). A concordance check under "lovingkindness" (KJV or NKJV) will show how full of grace the Psalms really are.

Saints (*hasidîm*)

A related noun referring to holy or godly people may mean that they receive grace or practice it—probably both. Only those who have experienced God's grace can show it to others—especially to unlovely people.

[R]All who see them shall flee away. Ps. 31:11
9 All men shall fear,
And shall declare the work of God;
For they shall wisely consider His doing.

10 [R]The righteous shall be glad in the LORD,
and trust in Him. Ps. 32:11
And all the upright in heart shall glory.

PSALM 65

God's Provision Through Nature

To the Chief Musician.
A Psalm of David. A Song.

PRAISE is awaiting You, O God, in Zion;
And to You the [T]vow shall be
performed. Promised deed
2 O You who hear prayer,
[R]To You all flesh will come. [Is. 66:23]
3 Iniquities prevail against me;
As for our transgressions,
You will provide atonement for them.

4 [R]Blessed *is the man whom* You [R]choose,
And cause to approach *You,*
That he may dwell in Your courts.
[R]We shall be satisfied with the goodness
of Your house, Ps. 33:12 • Ps. 4:3 • Ps. 36:8
Of Your holy temple.

5 *By* awesome deeds in righteousness You
will answer us,
O God of our salvation,
You who are the confidence of all the
ends of the earth,
And of the far-off seas;
6 Who established the mountains by His
strength,
[R]*Being* clothed with power; Ps. 93:1
7 [R]You who still the noise of the seas,
The noise of their waves, Matt. 8:26
[R]And the tumult of the peoples. Is. 17:12, 13
8 They also who dwell in the farthest
parts are afraid of Your signs;
You make the outgoings of the morning
and evening [T]rejoice. *shout for joy*

9 You [T]visit the earth and water it,
You greatly enrich it; *give attention to*
[R]The river of God is full of water;
You provide their grain, Ps. 46:4; 104:13
For so You have prepared it.
10 You water its ridges abundantly,
You settle its furrows;
You make it soft with showers,
You bless its growth.

11 You crown the year with Your
goodness,
And Your paths drip *with* abundance.
12 They drop *on* the pastures of the
wilderness,
And the little hills rejoice on every side.
13 The pastures are clothed with flocks;
The valleys also are covered with grain;
They shout for joy, they also sing.

PSALM 66

Remember What God Has Done

To the Chief Musician. A Song. A Psalm.

MAKE [R]a joyful shout to God, all the
earth! Ps. 100:1
2 Sing out the honor of His name;
Make His praise glorious.
3 Say to God,
"How [R]awesome are Your works!
[R]Through the greatness of Your power
Your enemies shall submit themselves
to You. Ps. 65:5 • Ps. 18:44
4 [R]All the earth shall worship You
And sing praises to You;
They shall sing praises *to* Your name."
Selah Ps. 117:1

5 Come and see the works of God;
He is awesome *in His* doing toward the
sons of men.
6 [R]He turned the sea into dry *land;*
They went through the river on foot.
There we will rejoice in Him. Ex. 14:21
7 He rules by His power forever;
His eyes observe the nations;
Do not let the rebellious exalt
themselves. Selah

8 Oh, bless our God, you peoples!
And make the voice of His praise to be
heard,
9 Who keeps our soul among the living,
And does not allow our feet to [T]be
moved. *slip*
10 For You, O God, have proved us;
You have refined us as silver is refined.
11 [R]You brought us into the net;
You laid affliction on our backs. Lam. 1:13
12 [R]You have caused men to ride over our
heads;
[R]We went through fire and through
water;
But You brought us out to [T]rich
fulfillment. Is. 51:23 • Is. 43:2 • *abundance*

13 [R]I will go into Your house with burnt
offerings; Ps. 100:4; 116:14, 17–19
I will pay You my [T]vows, Promises
14 Which my lips have uttered
And my mouth has spoken when I was
in trouble.
15 I will offer You burnt sacrifices of fat
animals,
With the sweet aroma of rams;
I will offer bulls with goats. Selah

16 Come *and* hear, all you who fear God,
And I will declare what He has done for
my soul.
17 I cried to Him with my mouth,
And He was extolled with my tongue.
18 [R]If I regard iniquity in my heart,
The Lord will not hear. Is. 1:15
19 *But* certainly God [R]has heard *me;*
He has attended to the voice of my
prayer. Ps. 116:1, 2

20 Blessed *be* God,
Who has not turned away my prayer,
Nor His mercy from me!

PSALM 67

God Shall Govern the Earth

To the Chief Musician. On *stringed
instruments. A Psalm. A Song.

GOD be merciful to us and bless us,
And [R]cause His face to shine upon us.
Selah Num. 6:25
2 That [R]Your way may be known on
earth, Acts 18:25
Your salvation among all nations.

3 Let the peoples praise You, O God;
Let all the peoples praise You.
4 Oh, let the nations be glad and sing for
joy!
For [R]You shall judge the people
righteously,
And govern the nations on earth.
Selah [Ps. 96:10, 13; 98:9]

5 Let the peoples praise You, O God;
Let all the peoples praise You.
6 *Then* the earth shall yield her increase;
God, our own God, shall bless us.
7 God shall bless us,
And all the ends of the earth shall fear
Him.

PSALM 68

God Is the Father of the Fatherless

To the Chief Musician.
A Psalm of David. A Song.

LET [R]God arise,
Let His enemies be scattered;
Let those also who hate Him flee before
Him. Num. 10:35
2 [R]As smoke is driven away,
So drive *them* away;
[R]As wax melts before the fire,
So let the wicked perish at the presence
of God. [Is. 9:18] • Mic. 1:4
3 But [R]let the righteous be glad;
Let them rejoice before God; Ps. 32:11
Yes, let them rejoice exceedingly.

4 Sing to God, sing praises to His name;
[T]Extol Him who rides on the *clouds,
[R]By His name YAH, *Praise* • [Ex. 6:3]
And rejoice before Him.

5 [R]A father of the fatherless, a defender of
widows, [Ps. 10:14, 18; 146:9]
Is God in His holy habitation.
6 [R]God sets the solitary in families;
[R]He brings out those who are bound into
prosperity; Ps. 107:4–7 • Acts 12:6
But the rebellious dwell in a dry *land.*

7 O God, [R]when You went out before
Your people,
When You marched through the
wilderness, Selah Ex. 13:21
8 The earth shook;
The heavens also dropped *rain* at the
presence of God;
Sinai itself *was moved* at the presence
of God, the God of Israel.
9 [R]You, O God, sent a plentiful rain,
Whereby You confirmed Your
inheritance,
When it was weary. Deut. 11:11
10 Your congregation dwelt in it;
[R]You, O God, provided from Your
goodness for the poor. Deut. 26:5

11 The Lord gave the word;
Great *was* the [T]company of those who
proclaimed *it:* *host*
12 "Kings[R] of armies flee, they flee,
And she who remains at home divides
the [T]spoil. Josh. 10:16 • *plunder*
13 [R]Though you lie down among the
[T]sheepfolds, Ps. 81:6 • Or *saddlebags*
[R]*Yet you will be* like the wings of a dove
covered with silver, Ps. 105:37
And her feathers with yellow gold."
14 [R]When the Almighty scattered kings in
it, Josh. 10:10
It was *white* as snow in Zalmon.

15 A mountain of God *is* the mountain of
Bashan;
A mountain *of many* peaks *is* the
mountain of Bashan.
16 Why do you [T]fume with envy, you
mountains of *many* peaks? Lit. *stare*
[R]*This is* the mountain *which* God desires
to dwell in; [Deut. 12:5]
Yes, the LORD will dwell *in it* forever.

17 [R]The chariots of God *are* twenty
thousand,
Even thousands of thousands;
The Lord is among them *as in* Sinai, in
the Holy *Place.* Deut. 33:2
18 [R]You have ascended on high, Eph. 4:8

67:title, Heb. *neginoth*
68:4 MT *deserts;* Tg. *heavens,* cf. v. 34 and Is. 19:1

[R]You have led captivity captive; Judg. 5:12
You have received gifts among men,
Even *among* [R]the rebellious, 1 Tim. 1:13
That the LORD God might dwell *there.*

19 Blessed *be* the Lord,
Who daily loads us *with benefits,*
The God of our salvation! Selah
20 Our God *is* the God of salvation;
And [R]to GOD the Lord *belong* escapes
from death. [Deut. 32:39]

21 But [R]God will wound the head of His
enemies, Hab. 3:13
[R]The hairy scalp of the one who still
goes on in his trespasses. Ps. 55:23
22 The Lord said, "I will bring [R]back from
Bashan,
I will bring *them* back [R]from the depths
of the sea, Num. 21:33 • Ex. 14:22
23 [R]That your foot may crush *them* in
blood, Ps. 58:10
And the tongues of your dogs *may have*
their portion from *your* enemies."

24 They have seen Your [T]procession, O
God,
The procession of my God, my King,
into the sanctuary. Lit. *goings*
25 [R]The singers went before, the players on
instruments *followed* after;
Among *them were* the maidens playing
timbrels. 1 Chr. 13:8
26 Bless God in the congregations,
The Lord, from the fountain of Israel.
27 [R]There *is* little Benjamin, their leader,
The princes of Judah *and* their
[T]company,
The princes of Zebulun *and* the princes
of Naphtali. 1 Sam. 9:21 • *throng*

28 Your God has [R]commanded your
strength;
Strengthen, O God, what You have
done for us. Is. 26:12
29 Because of Your temple at Jerusalem,
Kings will bring presents to You.
30 Rebuke the beasts of the reeds,
[R]The herd of bulls with the calves of the
peoples, Ps. 22:12
Till everyone [R]submits himself with
pieces of silver. 2 Sam. 8:2
Scatter the peoples *who* delight in war.
31 Envoys will come out of Egypt;
[R]Ethiopia will quickly [R]stretch out her
hands to God. Is. 45:14 • Ps. 44:20

32 Sing to God, you [R]kingdoms of the
earth; [Ps. 67:3, 4]
Oh, sing praises to the Lord, Selah
33 To Him [R]who rides on the heaven of
heavens, *which were* of old!
Indeed, He sends out His voice, a
[R]mighty voice. Ps. 18:10 • Ps. 46:6
34 [R]Ascribe strength to God;
His excellence *is* over Israel, Ps. 29:1
And His strength *is* in the clouds.
35 O God, [R]*You are* more awesome than
Your holy places. Ps. 76:12
The God of Israel *is* He who gives
strength and power to *His* people.

Blessed *be* God!

PSALM 69

Petition for God to Draw Near

To the Chief Musician.
Set to *"The Lilies." A Psalm of David.

SAVE me, O God!
For [R]the waters have come up to *my*
[T]neck. Jon. 2:5 • Lit. *soul*
2 [R]I sink in deep mire,
Where *there is* no standing;
I have come into deep waters,
Where the floods overflow me. Ps. 40:2
3 [R]I am weary with my crying;
My throat is dry; Ps. 6:6
My eyes fail while I wait for my God.

4 Those who [R]hate me without a cause
Are more than the hairs of my head;
They are mighty who would destroy
me,
Being my enemies wrongfully;
Though I have stolen nothing,
I *still* must restore *it.* John 15:25 ☆

5 O God, You know my foolishness;
And my sins are not hidden from You.
6 Let not those who [T]wait for You, O
Lord GOD of hosts, be [T]ashamed
because of me;
Let not those who seek You be
confounded because of me, O God of
Israel. Wait in faith • *dishonored*
7 Because [R]for Your sake I have borne
reproach; Rom. 15:3 ☆
Shame has covered my face.
8 [R]I have become a stranger to my
brothers, Is. 53:3; Mark 3:21 ☆
And an alien to my mother's children;
9 [R]Because zeal for Your house has eaten
me up, John 2:17
And the reproaches of those who
reproach You have fallen on me.
10 When I wept *and chastened* my soul
with fasting,
That became my reproach.
11 I also made [T]sackcloth my garment;
I became a byword to them. Symbol of grief
12 Those who [T]sit in the gate speak
against me, Sit as judges

69:title, Heb. *Shoshannim*

And I *am* the song of the drunkards.

13 But as for me, my prayer *is* to You,
O LORD, *in* the acceptable time;
O God, in the multitude of Your mercy,
Hear me in the truth of Your salvation.
14 Deliver me out of the mire,
And let me not sink;
Let me be delivered from those who hate me,
And out of the deep waters.
15 Let not the floodwater overflow me,
Nor let the deep swallow me up;
And let not the pit shut its mouth on me.

16 Hear me, O LORD, for Your lovingkindness *is* good;
Turn to me according to the multitude of Your tender mercies.
17 And do not hide Your face from Your servant,
For I am in trouble;
Hear me speedily.
18 Draw near to my soul, *and* redeem it;
Deliver me because of my enemies.

19 You know [R]my reproach, my shame, and my dishonor; Ps. 22:6, 7
My adversaries *are* all before You.
20 [R]Reproach has broken my heart,
And I am full of heaviness; Rom. 15:3☆
[R]I looked *for someone* to take pity, but *there was* none; Is. 63:5
And for comforters, but I found none.
21 They also gave me gall for my food,
[R]And for my thirst they gave me vinegar to drink. Matt. 27:34, 48☆

22 [R]Let their table become a snare before them,
And their well-being a trap. Rom. 11:9, 10
23 [R]Let their eyes be darkened, so that they do not see; Is. 6:9, 10
And make their loins shake continually.
24 [R]Pour out Your indignation upon them,
And let Your wrathful anger take hold of them. [1 Thess. 2:16]
25 [R]Let their habitation be desolate;
Let no one dwell in their tents. Matt. 23:38
26 For they persecute [R]*him* whom You have struck,
And talk of the grief of those You have wounded. [Is. 53:4]
27 [R]Add iniquity to their iniquity,
[R]And let them not come into Your righteousness. [Rom. 1:28] • [Is. 26:10]
28 Let them [R]be blotted out of the book of the living, [Ex. 32:32]
And not be written with the righteous.

29 But I *am* poor and sorrowful;
Let Your salvation, O God, set me up on high.
30 [R]I will praise the name of God with a song,
And will magnify Him with thanksgiving. [Ps. 28:7]
31 [R]*This* also shall please the LORD better than an ox *or* bull, Ps. 50:13, 14, 23; 51:16
Which has horns and hooves.
32 [R]The humble shall see *this and* be glad;
And you who seek God, [R]your hearts shall live. Ps. 34:2 • Ps. 22:26
33 For the LORD hears the poor,
And does not despise His prisoners.

34 [R]Let heaven and earth praise Him,
The seas [R]and everything that moves in them. Ps. 96:11 • Is. 55:12
35 [R]For God will save Zion
And build the cities of Judah,
That they may dwell there and possess it. Is. 44:26
36 Also, [R]the [T]descendants of His servants shall inherit it,
And those who love His name shall dwell in it. Ps. 102:28 • Lit. *seed*

PSALM 70

Prayer for the Poor and Needy

To the Chief Musician. *A Psalm* of David. To bring to remembrance.

MAKE *haste,* O God, to deliver me!
Make haste to help me, O LORD!

2 [R]Let them be ashamed and confounded
Who seek my life;
Let them be turned back and confused
Who desire my hurt. Ps. 35:4, 26
3 [R]Let them be turned back because of their shame, Ps. 40:15
Who say, [T]"Aha, aha!" An expression of scorn

4 Let all those who seek You rejoice and be glad in You;
And let those who love Your salvation say continually,
"Let God be magnified!"

5 [R]But I *am* poor and needy; Ps. 72:12, 13
[R]Make haste to me, O God! Ps. 141:1
You *are* my help and my deliverer;
O LORD, do not delay.

PSALM 71

Prayer for the Aged

IN [R]You, O LORD, I put my trust;
Let me never be put to shame. Ps. 25:2, 3
2 [R]Deliver me in Your righteousness, and cause me to escape; Ps. 31:1
Incline Your ear to me, and save me.

3 Be my [T]strong habitation,
To which I may resort continually;
You have given the commandment to
save me, Lit. *rock of habitation* or *refuge*
For You *are* my rock and my fortress.

4 [R]Deliver me, O my God, out of the hand
of the wicked,
Out of the hand of the unrighteous and
cruel man. Ps. 140:1, 3
5 For You are my hope, O Lord GOD;
You are my trust from my youth.
6 [R]By You I have been [T]upheld from *my*
birth; Ps. 22:9, 10 • *sustained from the womb*
You are He who took me out of my
mother's womb.
My praise *shall be* continually of You.

7 [R]I have become as a wonder to many,
But You *are* my strong refuge. Is. 8:18
8 Let [R]my mouth be filled *with* Your
praise Ps. 35:28
And with Your glory all the day.

9 Do not cast me off in the time of old
age;
Do not forsake me when my strength
fails.
10 For my enemies speak against me;
And those who lie in wait for my life
[R]take counsel together, 2 Sam. 17:1
11 Saying, "God has forsaken him;
Pursue and take him, for *there is* none
to deliver *him.*"

12 [R]O God, do not be far from me; Ps. 35:22
O my God, make haste to help me!
13 Let them be [T]confounded *and* consumed
Who are adversaries of my life;
Let them be covered *with* reproach and
dishonor
Who seek my hurt. *ashamed*

14 But I will hope continually,
And will praise You yet more and more.
15 My mouth shall tell of Your
righteousness
And Your salvation all the day,
For I do not know *their* limits.
16 I will go in the strength of the Lord
GOD;
I will make mention of Your
righteousness, of Yours only.

17 O God, You have taught me from my
[R]youth;
And to this *day* I declare Your
wondrous works. Deut. 4:5; 6:7
18 Now also [R]when *I am* old and gray
headed,
O God, do not forsake me,
Until I declare Your strength to *this*
generation,
Your power to everyone *who* is to
come. [Is. 46:4]

Also Your righteousness, O God, *is* very
[T]high, *great,* lit. *to the height of heaven*
You who have done great things;
O God, who *is* like You?
20 [R]*You,* who have shown me great and
severe troubles,
[R]Shall revive me again,
And bring me up again from the depths
of the earth. Ps. 60:3 • Hos. 6:1, 2
21 You shall increase my greatness,
And comfort me on every side.

22 Also [R]with the lute I will praise you—
And Your faithfulness, O my God!
To You I will sing with the harp,
O [R]Holy One of Israel. Ps. 92:1–3 • 2 Kin. 19:22
23 My lips shall greatly rejoice when I sing
to You,
And [R]my soul, which You have
redeemed. Ps. 103:4
24 My tongue also shall talk of Your
righteousness all the day long;
For they are confounded,
For they are brought to shame
Who seek my hurt.

PSALM 72

The Reign of the Messiah

A Psalm of Solomon.

GIVE the king Your judgments, O God,
And Your righteousness to the king's
Son.
2 [R]He will judge Your people with
righteousness, [Is. 9:7; 11:2–5; 32:1] ☆
And Your poor with justice.
3 [R]The mountains will bring peace to the
people, Ps. 85:10
And the little hills, by righteousness.
4 [R]He will bring justice to the poor of the
people; Is. 11:4 ☆
He will save the children of the needy,
And will break in pieces the oppressor.

5 They shall fear You
[R]As long as the sun and moon endure,
Throughout all generations. [Ps. 89:36] ☆
6 [R]He shall come down like rain upon the
mown grass, Hos. 6:3
Like showers *that* water the earth.
7 In His days the righteous shall flourish,
[R]And abundance of peace,
Until the moon is no more. Is. 2:4 ☆

8 [R]He shall have dominion also from sea to
sea,
And from the River to the ends of the
earth. Ex. 23:31
9 Those who dwell in the wilderness will
[R]bow before Him, Is. 49:23 ☆

And His enemies will lick the dust.
10 [R]The kings of Tarshish and of the isles
Will bring presents;
The kings of Sheba and Seba
Will offer gifts. 2 Chr. 9:21
11 [R]Yes, all kings shall fall down before
Him;
All nations shall serve Him. Is. 49:23☆

12 For He [R]will deliver the needy when he
cries, Job. 29:12
The [R]poor also, and *him* who has no
helper. [Ps. 72:4]☆
13 He will spare the poor and needy,
And will save the souls of the needy.
14 He will redeem their life from
oppression and violence;
And [R]precious shall be their blood in His
sight. [Ps. 116:15]☆

15 And He shall live;
And the gold of [R]Sheba will be given to
Him;
Prayer also will be made for Him
continually,
And daily He shall be praised. Is. 60:6☆

16 There will be an abundance of grain in
the earth,
On the top of the mountains;
Its fruit shall wave like Lebanon;
[R]And *those* of the city shall flourish like
grass of the earth. 1 Kin. 4:20

17 [R]His name shall endure forever;
His name shall continue as long as the
sun. [Ps. 89:36]☆
And *men* shall be blessed in Him;
All nations shall call Him blessed.

18 [R]Blessed *be* the LORD God, the God of
Israel, 1 Chr. 29:10
Who only does wondrous things!
19 And [R]blessed *be* His glorious name
forever!
[R]And let the whole earth be filled *with*
His glory. [Neh. 9:5] • Num. 14:21
Amen and Amen.

20 The prayers of David the son of Jesse
are ended.

BOOK THREE

Psalms 73–89

PSALM 73

The Perspective of Eternity

A Psalm of Asaph.

TRULY God *is* good to Israel,
To such as are pure in heart.

2 But as for me, my feet had almost
stumbled;
My steps had nearly [R]slipped. Job 12:5
3 [R]For I *was* envious of the boastful,
When I saw the prosperity of the
[R]wicked. Ps. 37:1, 7 • Job 21:5–16

4 For *there are* no [T]pangs in their death,
But their strength *is* firm. *pains*
5 They *are* not in trouble *as other* men,
Nor are they plagued like *other* men.
6 Therefore pride serves as their necklace;
Violence covers them *like* a garment.
7 Their eyes bulge with abundance;
They have more than heart could wish.
8 [R]They scoff and speak wickedly Ps. 53:1
concerning oppression;
They [R]speak [T]loftily. 2 Pet. 2:18 • Proudly
9 They set their mouth [R]against the
heavens,
And their tongue walks through the
earth. Rev. 13:6

10 Therefore his people return here,
[R]And waters of a full *cup* are drained by
them. [Ps. 75:8]
11 And they say, [R]"How does God know?
And is there knowledge in the Most
High?" Job 22:13
12 Behold, these *are* the ungodly,
Who are always at ease;
They increase *in* riches.

73:1 Walking in the Spirit: Confession—An important prerequisite to walking in the Spirit is the confession of sin. Sin must be confessed in order to restore fellowship and to continue receiving God's power (Page 1494—1 John 1:5–10). Confession means that we agree with God about our sin. This involves much more than simply acknowledging the sin. Confession requires an attitude of sorrow for the sin and a willingness to turn from it. It does not mean that we will never commit the same sin again, but it does mean that the attitude of repentance is present.

Confession should be made at the moment the Christian becomes aware of sin. Apart from this rule, moreover, the Scriptures mention two specific times for confession: before the close of the day (Page 1391—Eph. 4:26) and before the Lord's Supper is observed (Page 1355—1 Cor. 11:27–32). Failure to do the latter is a special cause for discipline from the Lord.

Confession of sin should normally involve only those who have knowledge of the sin. This means that private sins should be confessed privately (Page 1494—1 John 1:9); sins between individuals confessed between those involved (Page 1120—Matt. 5:23, 24); and public sins confessed publicly (Page 1138—Matt. 18:17). Public confession normally is made for the edification of the church (Page 1358—1 Cor. 14:26).

Now turn to Page 1336—Rom. 12:1, 2: Walking in the Spirit: Yielding.

13 Surely I have [T]cleansed my heart [R]*in*
vain, *kept my heart pure in vain* • Job 21:15; 35:3
And washed my hands in innocence.
14 For all day long I have been plagued,
And chastened every morning.

15 If I had said, "I will speak thus,"
Behold, I would have been untrue to
the generation of Your children.
16 When I thought *how* to understand
this,
It *was* too [T]painful for me— *troublesome*
17 Until I went into the sanctuary of God;
Then I understood their [R]end. [Ps. 37:38]

18 Surely You set them in slippery places;
You cast them down to destruction.
19 Oh, how they are *brought* to desolation,
as in a moment!
They are utterly consumed with terrors.
20 As a dream when *one* awakes,
So, Lord, when You awake,
You shall despise their image.

21 Thus my heart was grieved,
And I was vexed in my mind.
22 [R]I *was* so foolish and ignorant;
I was *like* a beast before You. Ps. 92:6
23 Nevertheless I *am* continually with
You;
You hold *me* by my right hand.
24 You will guide me with Your counsel,
And afterward receive me *to* glory.

25 [R]Whom have I in heaven *but You?*
And *there is* none upon earth *that* I
desire besides You. [Phil. 3:8]
26 [R]My flesh and my heart fail; Ps. 84:2
But God *is* the [T]strength of my heart
and my [R]portion forever. Lit. *rock* • Ps. 16:5

27 For indeed, [R]those who are far from
You shall perish; [Ps. 119:155]
You have destroyed all those who
desert You for harlotry.
28 But *it is* good for me to [R]draw near to
God; [Heb. 10:22]
I have put my trust in the Lord GOD,
That I may declare all Your works.

PSALM 74

Request for God to Remember His Covenant

*A Contemplation of Asaph.

O GOD, why have You cast *us* off
forever?
Why does Your anger smoke against
the sheep of Your pasture?
2 Remember Your congregation, *which*
You have purchased of old,
The tribe of Your inheritance, *which*
You have redeemed—
This Mount Zion where You have
dwelt.
3 Lift up Your feet to the perpetual
desolations.
The enemy has damaged everything in
the sanctuary.
4 [R]Your enemies roar in the midst of Your
meeting place; Lam. 2:7
They set up their banners *for* signs.
5 They seem like men who lift up
Axes among the thick trees.
6 And now they break down its carved
work, all at once,
With axes and hammers.
7 They have set fire to Your sanctuary;
They have defiled the dwelling place of
Your name to the ground.
8 [R]They said in their hearts,
"Let us [T]destroy them altogether."
They have burned up all the meeting
places of God in the land. Ps. 83:4 • *oppress*

9 We do not see our signs;
[R]*There is* no longer any prophet;
Nor *is there* any among us who knows
how long. Amos 8:11
10 O God, how long will the adversary
[T]reproach?
Will the enemy blaspheme Your name
forever? *revile*
11 [R]Why do You withdraw Your hand, even
Your right hand?
Take it out of Your bosom and destroy
them. Lam. 2:3
12 For [R]God *is* my King from of old,
Working salvation in the midst of the
earth. Ps. 44:4
13 You divided the sea by Your strength;
You broke the heads of the [T]sea
serpents in the waters. *sea monsters*
14 You broke the heads of [T]Leviathan in
pieces, A large sea creature of unknown identity
And gave him *as* food to the people
inhabiting the wilderness.
15 [R]You broke open the fountain and the
flood; Ex. 17:5, 6
[R]You dried up mighty rivers. Josh. 2:10; 3:13
16 The day *is* Yours, the night also *is*
[R]Yours;
[R]You have prepared the light and the
sun. Job 38:12 • Gen. 1:14–18
17 You have [R]set all the borders of the
earth; Acts 17:26
You have made summer and winter.

18 Remember this, *that* the enemy has
reproached, O LORD,
And *that* a foolish people has
blasphemed Your name.
19 Oh, do not deliver the life of Your
turtledove to the wild beast!

74:title, Heb. *Maschil*

Do not forget the life of Your poor
forever.
20 Have respect to the covenant;
For the dark places of the earth are full
of the habitations of cruelty.
21 Oh, do not let the oppressed return
ashamed!
Let the poor and needy praise Your
name.

22 Arise, O God, plead Your own cause;
Remember how the foolish man
[T]reproaches You daily. *reviles* or *taunts*
23 Do not forget the voice of Your
enemies;
The tumult of those who rise up against
You increases continually.

PSALM 75

"God Is the Judge"

To the Chief Musician. Set to *"Do Not Destroy." A Psalm of Asaph. A Song.

WE give thanks to You, O God, we give
thanks!
For Your wondrous works declare *that*
Your name is near.

2 "When I choose the [T]proper time,
I will judge uprightly. *appointed*
3 The earth and all its inhabitants are
dissolved;
I set up its pillars firmly. Selah

4 "I said to the boastful, 'Do not deal
boastfully,'
And to the wicked, 'Do not [T]lift up the
horn. Raise the head proudly like a horned animal
5 Do not lift up your horn on high;
Do *not* speak with [T]a stiff neck.' " Pride

6 For exaltation *comes* neither from the
east
Nor from the west nor from the south.
7 But [R]God *is* the Judge:
[R]He puts down one,
And exalts another. Ps. 50:6 • 1 Sam. 2:7
8 For [R]in the hand of the LORD *there is* a
cup,
And the wine is red;
It is fully mixed, and He pours it out;
Surely its dregs shall all the wicked of
the earth
Drain *and* drink down. Jer. 25:15

9 But I will declare forever,
I will sing praises to the God of Jacob.

10 "All[R] the [T]horns of the wicked I will also
cut off, Jer. 48:25 • Strength
But [R]the horns of the righteous shall be
[R]exalted." Ps. 89:17; 148:14 • 1 Sam. 2:1

PSALM 76

The Glorious Might of God

To the Chief Musician. On *stringed instruments. A Psalm of Asaph. A Song.

IN [R]Judah God *is* known;
His name *is* great in Israel. Ps. 48:1, 3
2 In [T]Salem also is His tabernacle,
And His dwelling place in Zion. Jerusalem
3 There He broke the arrows of the bow,
The shield and sword of battle. Selah

4 You *are* more glorious and excellent
[R]*Than* the mountains of prey. Ezek. 38:12
5 The stouthearted were plundered;
[R]They have sunk into their sleep;
And none of the mighty men have
found the use of their hands. Ps. 13:3
6 [R]At Your rebuke, O God of Jacob,
Both the chariot and horse were cast
into a dead sleep. Ex. 15:1–21

7 You, Yourself, *are* to be feared;
And [R]who may stand in Your presence
When once You are angry? [Nah. 1:6]
8 [R]You caused judgment to be heard from
heaven; Ex. 19:9
[R]The earth feared and was still, 2 Chr. 20:29
9 When God [R]arose to judgment,
To deliver all the oppressed of the
earth. Selah [Ps. 9:7–9]

10 [R]Surely the wrath of man shall praise
You;
With the remainder of wrath You shall
gird Yourself. Rom. 9:17

11 [R]Make vows to the LORD your God, and
pay *them;*
[R]Let all who are around Him bring
presents to Him who ought to be
feared. [Eccl. 5:4–6] • 2 Chr. 32:22, 23
12 He shall cut off the spirit of princes;
[R]*He is* awesome to the kings of the
earth. Ps. 68:35

PSALM 77

When Overwhelmed, Remember God's Greatness

To the Chief Musician. To Jeduthun. A Psalm of Asaph.

I CRIED out to God with my voice—
To God with my voice;
And He gave ear to me.
2 In the day of my trouble I sought the
Lord;
My hand was stretched out in the night
without ceasing;
My soul refused to be comforted.

75:title, Heb. *Al Tashcheth* 76:title, Heb. *neginoth*

3 I remembered God, and was troubled;
I complained, and my spirit was
overwhelmed. Selah
4 You hold my eyelids *open;*
I am so troubled that I cannot speak.
5 I have considered the days of old,
The years of ancient times.
6 I call to remembrance my song in the
night;
I meditate within my heart,
And my spirit makes diligent search.

7 Will the Lord cast off forever?
And will He be favorable no more?
8 Has His mercy ceased forever?
Has *His* promise failed forevermore?
9 Has God forgotten to be gracious?
Has He in anger shut up His tender
mercies? Selah

10 And I said, "This *is* my [T]anguish;
But I will remember the years of the
right hand of the Most High." *infirmity*
11 I will remember the works of the LORD;
Surely I will remember Your wonders of
old.
12 I will also meditate on all Your work,
And talk of Your deeds.
13 Your way, O God, *is* in the sanctuary;
Who *is* so great a God as *our* God?
14 You *are* the God who does wonders;
You have declared Your strength
among the peoples.
15 You have with *Your* arm redeemed
Your people,
The sons of Jacob and Joseph. Selah

16 The waters saw You, O God;
The waters saw You, they were [R]afraid;
The depths also trembled. Ex. 14:21
17 The clouds poured out water;
The skies sent out a sound;
Your arrows also flashed about.
18 The voice of Your thunder *was* in the
whirlwind;
The lightnings lit up the world;
The earth trembled and shook.
19 Your way *was* in the sea,
Your path in the great waters,
And Your footsteps were not known.
20 You led Your people like a flock
By the hand of Moses and Aaron.

PSALM 78

God's Continued Guidance in Spite of Unbelief

*A Contemplation of Asaph.

GIVE ear, O my people, *to* my law;
Incline your ears to the words of my
mouth.
2 I will open my mouth in a parable;
I will utter [T]dark sayings of old, *riddles*
3 Which we have heard and known,
And our fathers have told us.

4 [R]We will not hide *them* from their
children, Deut. 4:9; 6:7
[R]Telling to the generation to come the
praises of the LORD, Ex. 13:8, 14
And His strength and His wonderful
works that He has done.

5 For [R]He established a testimony in
Jacob,
And appointed a law in Israel,
Which He commanded our fathers,
That [R]they should make them known to
their children; Ps. 147:19 • Deut. 4:9; 11:19

78:title, Heb. *Maschil*

78:4 History of Israel—The biblical history of Israel covers 1,800 years and represents a marvelous panorama of God's gracious working through promise, miracle, blessing, and judgment. Israel begins as only a promise to Abraham (Page 18—Gen. 12:2). For over four hundred years the people of Israel rely on that promise, especially during the period of bondage to Egypt. Finally, in God's perfect timing, He brings the nation out of Egypt with the greatest series of miracles known in the entire Old Testament (Page 74—Ex. 7—15). This event is called the Exodus, meaning *a going out*. Since it constitutes the miraculous birth of the nation, it is to this great act of redemption that the nation always looks back as the foremost example of God's care for His people (Ps. 77:14-20; 78:12-55; Page 1003—Hos. 11:1).

Once God has redeemed Israel He establishes His covenant with them at Mount Sinai (Page 89—Ex.19:5-8). From that point forward the nation is truly the Lord's possession, and He is their God. The covenant foretells gracious blessings for obedience and severe judgments for disobedience. The rest of Israel's history demonstrates the certainty of that prophecy. Through the periods of conquest, judges, monarchy, exile, restoration, and gentile domination, Israel is blessed when she obeys and judged when she disobeys. The nation is finally destroyed in A.D. 70, although this event is not described in the New Testament. Many prophecies, however, promise a future redemption for Israel (Page 1336—Rom. 11:26).

The practical value of studying Israel's history is threefold:

a. It sets forth examples to be followed or avoided (Page 1353—1 Cor. 10:6).
b. It shows God's control of all historical events, in that He was able to deal with Israel as He chose (Ps. 78).
c. It serves as a model for all ages of God's kindness and mercy toward His people (Page 683—Ps. 103:14).

Now turn to page 225—Deut. 14:2: Purpose of Israel.

6 [R]That the generation to come might
know *them,*
The children *who* would be born,
That they may arise and declare *them*
to their children, Ps. 102:18
7 That they may set their hope in God,
And not forget the works of God,
But keep His commandments;
8 And may not be like their fathers,
A stubborn and rebellious generation,
A generation [R]*that* did not [T]set its heart
aright, Ps. 78:37 • Lit. *prepare its heart*
And whose spirit was not faithful to
God.

9 The children of Ephraim, *being* armed
and [T]carrying bows, Lit. *bow shooters*
Turned back in the day of battle.
10 They did not keep the covenant of God;
They refused to walk in His law,
11 And [R]forgot His works
And His wonders that He had shown
them. Ps. 106:13

12 [R]Marvelous things He did in the sight of
their fathers,
In the land of Egypt, [R]*in* the field of
Zoan. Ex. 7—12 • Num. 13:22
13 [R]He divided the sea and caused them to
pass through;
And [R]He made the waters stand up like
a heap. Ex. 14:21 • Ex. 15:8
14 [R]In the daytime also He led them with
the cloud, Ex. 13:21
And all the night with a light of fire.
15 [R]He split the rocks in the wilderness,
And gave *them* drink in abundance like
the depths. Num. 20:11
16 He also brought [R]streams out of the
rock,
And caused waters to run down like
rivers. Num. 20:8, 10, 11

17 But they sinned even more against Him
By [R]rebelling against the Most High in
the wilderness. Heb. 3:16
18 And they tested God in their heart
By asking for the food of their fancy.
19 [R]Yes, they spoke against God:
They said, "Can God prepare a table in
the wilderness? Num. 11:4; 20:3; 21:5
20 [R]Behold, He struck the rock,
So that the waters gushed out,
And the streams overflowed.
Can He give bread also? Num. 20:11
Can He provide meat for His people?"

21 Therefore the LORD heard *this* and [R]was
furious; Num. 11:1
So a fire was kindled against Jacob,
And anger also came up against Israel,
22 Because they did not believe in God,
And did not trust in His salvation.
23 Yet He had commanded the clouds
above,
And opened the doors of heaven,
24 [R]Had rained down manna on them to
eat,
And given them of the [T]bread of
[R]heaven. Ex. 16:4 • Lit. *grain* • John 6:31
25 Men ate angels' food;
He sent them food to the [T]full. *satiation*

26 [R]He caused an east wind to blow in the
heavens;
And by His power He brought in the
south wind. Num. 11:31
27 He also rained meat on them like the
dust,
Feathered fowl like the sand of the
seas;
28 And He let *them* fall in the midst of
their camp,
All around their [T]habitations. *dwellings*
29 So they ate and were well filled,
For He gave them their own desire.
30 They were not [T]deprived of their
craving; Lit. *separated from*
But [R]while their food *was* still in their
mouths, Num. 11:33
31 The wrath of God came against them,
And slew the stoutest of them,
And struck down the choice *men* of
Israel.

32 In spite of this [R]they still sinned,
And [R]did not believe in His wondrous
works. Num. 14:16, 17 • Num. 14:11
33 [R]Therefore their days He consumed in
futility,
And their years in fear. Num. 14:29, 35

34 [R]When He slew them, then they sought
Him;
And they returned and sought diligently
for God. [Hos. 5:15]
35 Then they remembered that [R]God *was*
their rock, [Deut. 32:4, 15]
And the Most High God [R]their
redeemer. Is. 41:14; 44:6; 63:9
36 Nevertheless they [R]flattered Him with
their mouth, Ezek. 33:31
And they lied to Him with their tongue;
37 For their heart was not steadfast with
Him,
Nor were they faithful in His covenant.
38 [R]But He, *being* full of compassion,
forgave *their* iniquity, [Num. 14:18–20]
And did not destroy *them.*
Yes, many a time [R]He turned His anger
away, [Is. 48:9]
And did not stir up all His wrath;
39 For [R]He remembered [R]that they *were*
but flesh,
[R]A breath that passes away and does not
come again. Job 10:9 • John 3:6 • [Job 7:7, 16]

40 How often they [R]provoked[T] Him in the
wilderness, Heb. 3:16 • *rebelled against Him*
And grieved Him in the desert!
41 Yes, [R]again and again they tempted
God, Num. 14:22
And limited the Holy One of Israel.
42 They did not remember His [T]power:
The day when He redeemed them from
the enemy, Lit. *hand*
43 When He worked His signs in Egypt,
And His wonders in the field of Zoan;
44 [R]Turned their rivers into blood,
And their streams, that they could not
drink. Ex. 7:20
45 [R]He sent swarms of flies among them,
which devoured them, Ex. 8:24
And frogs, which destroyed them.
46 He also gave their crops to the
caterpillar,
And their labor to the [R]locust. Ex. 10:14
47 He destroyed their vines with hail,
And their sycamore trees with frost.
48 He also gave up their cattle to the hail,
And their flocks to fiery lightning.
49 He cast on them the fierceness of His
anger,
Wrath, indignation, and trouble,
By sending angels of destruction *among*
them.
50 He made a path for His anger;
He did not spare their soul from death,
But gave their life over to the plague,
51 And destroyed all the [R]firstborn in
Egypt,
The first of *their* strength in the tents of
Ham. Ex. 12:29, 30
52 But He [R]made His own people go forth
like sheep,
And guided them in the wilderness like
a flock; Ps. 77:20
53 And He [R]led them on safely, so that
they did not fear;
But the sea [R]overwhelmed their
enemies. Ex. 14:19, 20 • Ex. 14:27, 28
54 And He brought them to His [R]holy
border,
This mountain [R]*which* His right hand
had acquired. Ex. 15:17 • Ps. 44:3
55 [R]He also drove out the nations before
them, Ps. 44:2
[R]Allotted them an inheritance by
[T]survey,
And made the tribes of Israel dwell in
their tents. Josh. 13:7 • Lit. *measuring cord*

56 [R]Yet they tested and provoked the Most
High God, Judg. 2:11–13
And did not keep His testimonies,
57 But [R]turned back and acted unfaithfully
like their fathers;
They were turned aside [R]like a deceitful
bow. Ezek. 20:27, 28 • Hos. 7:16
58 [R]For they provoked Him to anger with
their [R]high places,
And moved Him to jealousy with their
carved images. Judg. 2:12 • Deut. 12:2
59 When God heard *this,* He was furious,
And greatly abhorred Israel,
60 [R]So that He forsook the tabernacle of
Shiloh,
The tent *which* He had placed among
men, 1 Sam. 4:11
61 [R]And delivered His strength into
captivity, Judg. 18:30
And His glory into the enemy's hand.
62 [R]He also gave His people over to the
sword, 1 Sam. 4:10
And was furious with His inheritance.
63 The fire consumed their young men,
And [R]their maidens were not given in
marriage. Jer. 7:34; 16:9; 25:10
64 [R]Their priests fell by the sword,
And [R]their widows made no
lamentation. 1 Sam. 4:17; 22:18 • Job 27:15

65 Then the Lord awoke as *one out of*
sleep,
And [R]like a mighty man who shouts
because of wine. Is. 42:13
66 And [R]He beat back His enemies; 1 Sam. 5:6
He put them to a perpetual reproach.

67 Moreover He rejected the tent of
Joseph,
And did not choose the tribe of
Ephraim,
68 But chose the tribe of Judah,
Mount Zion [R]which He loved. [Ps. 87:2]
69 And He built His [R]sanctuary like the
heights,
Like the earth which He has established
forever. 1 Kin. 6:1–38
70 He also chose David His servant,
And took him from the sheepfolds;
71 From following [R]the ewes that had
young He brought him, [Is. 40:11]
[R]To shepherd Jacob His people,
And Israel His inheritance. 2 Sam. 5:2
72 So he shepherded them according to the
[R]integrity of his heart,
And guided them by the skillfulness of
his hands. 1 Kin. 9:4

PSALM 79

Avenge the Defilement of Jerusalem

A Psalm of Asaph.

O GOD, the nations have come into
[R]Your inheritance; Ps. 74:2
Your holy temple they have defiled;
They have laid Jerusalem in [T]heaps. *ruins*
2 [R]The dead bodies of Your servants
They have given *as* food for the birds of
the heavens,

The flesh of Your saints to the beasts of
the earth. Jer. 7:33; 19:7; 34:20
3 Their blood they have shed like water
all around Jerusalem,
And *there was* no one to bury *them.*
4 We have become a reproach to our
[R]neighbors,
A scorn and derision to those who are
around us. Ps. 44:13

5 [R]How long, LORD? Ps. 74:1, 9
Will You be angry forever?
Will Your jealousy burn like fire?
6 [R]Pour out Your wrath on the nations
that do not know You, Jer. 10:25
And on the kingdoms that [R]do not call
on Your name. Ps. 53:4
7 For they have devoured Jacob,
And laid waste his dwelling place.

8 Oh, do not remember [T]former iniquities
against us! Or *iniquities of those before us*
Let Your tender mercies come speedily
to meet us,
For we have been brought very low.
9 Help us, O God of our salvation,
For the glory of Your name;
And deliver us, and provide atonement
for our sins,
[R]For Your name's sake! Jer. 14:7, 21
10 [R]Why should the nations say, Ps. 42:10
"Where *is* their God?"
Let there be known among the [T]nations
in our sight *Gentiles*
The avenging of the blood of Your
servants *which has been* shed.

11 Let [R]the groaning of the prisoner come
before You;
According to the greatness of Your
[T]power
Preserve those who are appointed to
die; Ps. 102:20 • Lit. *arm*
12 And return to our neighbors [R]sevenfold
into their bosom Gen. 4:15
[R]Their reproach with which they have
reproached You, O Lord. Ps. 74:10, 18, 22

13 So [R]we, Your people and sheep of Your
pasture,
Will give You thanks forever;
[R]We will show forth Your praise to all
generations. Ps. 74:1; 95:7 • Is. 43:21

PSALM 80

Israel's Plea for God's Mercy

To the Chief Musician. Set to *"The Lilies."
*A Testimony of Asaph. A Psalm.

GIVE ear, O Shepherd of Israel,
[R]You who lead Joseph like a flock;
You who dwell *between* the cherubim,
[R]shine forth! [Ex. 25:20–22] • Deut. 33:2
2 Before [R]Ephraim, Benjamin, and
Manasseh,
Stir up Your strength,
And come *and* save us! Ps. 78:9, 67

3 [R]Restore us, O God;
[R]Cause Your face to shine,
And we shall be saved! Lam. 5:21 • Num. 6:25

4 O LORD God of hosts,
[R]How long will You be angry Ps. 79:5
Against the prayer of Your people?
5 [R]You have fed them with the bread of
tears,
And given them tears to drink in great
measure. Is. 30:20
6 You have made us a strife to our
neighbors,
And our enemies laugh among
themselves.

7 Restore us, O God of hosts;
Cause Your face to shine,
And we shall be saved!

8 You have brought [R]a vine out of Egypt;
[R]You have cast out the [T]nations, and
planted it. [Is. 5:1, 7] • Ps. 44:2 • *Gentiles*
9 You prepared *room* for it,
And caused it to take deep root,
And it filled the land.
10 The hills were covered with its shadow,
And the [T]mighty cedars with its
[R]boughs. Lit. *cedars of God* • Lev. 23:40
11 She sent out her boughs to the Sea,
And her branches to the River.

12 Why have You [R]broken down her
[T]hedges,
So that all who pass by the way pluck
her *fruit?* Is. 5:5 • *walls* or *fences*
13 The boar out of the woods uproots it,
And the wild beast of the field devours
it.

14 Return, we beseech You, O God of
hosts;
[R]Look down from heaven and see,
And visit this vine Is. 63:15
15 And the vineyard which Your right
hand has planted,
And the branch *that* You made strong
[R]for Yourself. [Is. 49:5]
16 *It is* burned with fire, *it is* cut down;
[R]They perish at the rebuke of Your
countenance. [Ps. 39:11]
17 [R]Let Your hand be upon the man of
Your right hand,
Upon the son of man *whom* You made
strong for Yourself. Ps. 89:21
18 Then we will not turn back from You;

80:title, Heb. *Shoshannim* **80:title**, Heb. *Eduth*

Revive us, and we will call upon Your
name.

19 Restore us, O LORD God of hosts;
Cause Your face to shine,
And we shall be saved!

PSALM 81

God's Plea for Israel's Obedience

To the Chief Musician. *On an instrument of Gath. A Psalm of Asaph.

SING aloud to God our strength;
Make a joyful shout to the God of
Jacob.
2 Raise a song and strike the timbrel,
The pleasant harp with the lute.

3 Blow the trumpet at the time of the
New Moon,
At the full moon, on our solemn feast
day.
4 For [R]this *is* a statute for Israel,
And a law of the God of Jacob. Num. 10:10
5 This He established in Joseph *for* a
testimony,
When He went throughout the land of
Egypt,
[R]*Where* I heard a language *that* I did not
understand. Ps. 114:1

6 "I removed his shoulder from the
burden;
His hands were freed from the baskets.
7 [R]You called in trouble, and I delivered
you; Ex. 2:23; 14:10
[R]I answered you in the secret place of
thunder; Ex. 19:19; 20:18
I [R]proved you at the waters of
Meribah. Selah Ex. 17:6, 7

8 "Hear,[R] O My people, and I will
admonish you! [Ps. 50:7]
O Israel, if you will listen to Me!
9 There shall be no [R]foreign god among
you; [Is. 43:12]
Nor shall you worship any foreign god.
10 [R]I *am* the LORD your God, Ex. 20:2
Who brought you out of the land of
Egypt;
Open your mouth wide, and I will fill it.

11 "But My people would not heed My
voice,
And Israel would *have* none of Me.
12 [R]So I gave them over to their own
stubborn heart,
To walk in their own counsels. [Acts 7:42]

13 "Oh, that My people would listen to Me,
That Israel would walk in My ways!
14 I would soon subdue their enemies,
And turn My hand against their
adversaries.
15 [R]The haters of the LORD would pretend
submission to Him, Rom. 1:30
But their fate would endure forever.
16 He would have fed them also with [T]the
finest of wheat; Lit. *fat of wheat*
And with honey [R]from the rock I would
have satisfied you." Job 29:6

PSALM 82

Rebuke of Israel's Unjust Judges

A Psalm of Asaph.

GOD [R]stands in the congregation of the
[T]mighty; [2 Chr. 19:6] • Heb. *El,* lit. *God*
He judges among the gods.
2 How long will you judge unjustly,
And [R]show partiality to the wicked?
Selah [Deut. 1:17]
3 [T]Defend the poor and fatherless; *Vindicate*
Do justice to the afflicted and needy.
4 Deliver the poor and needy;
Free *them* from the hand of the wicked.

5 They do not know, nor do they
understand;
They walk about in darkness;
All the [R]foundations of the earth are
[T]unstable. Ps. 11:3 • *moved*

6 I said, "You *are* [T]gods, *judges,* Heb. *elohim*
And all of you *are* children of the Most
High.
7 But you shall die like men,
And fall like one of the princes."

8 Arise, O God, judge the earth;
For You shall inherit all nations.

PSALM 83

Plea for God to Destroy Israel's Enemies

A Song. A Psalm of Asaph.

DO[R] not keep silent, O God!
Do not hold Your peace,
And do not be still, O God! Ps. 28:1
2 For behold, [R]Your enemies make a
[T]tumult; Ps. 81:15 • *uproar*
And those who hate You have [T]lifted up
their head. Exalted themselves
3 They have taken crafty counsel against
Your people,
And consulted together [R]against Your
sheltered ones. [Ps. 27:5]
4 They have said, "Come, and [R]let us cut
them off from *being* a nation,
That the name of Israel may be
remembered no more." Jer. 11:19; 31:36

81:title, Heb. *Al Gittith*

5 For they have consulted together with
one [T]consent; Lit. *heart*
They form a confederacy against You:
6 [R]The tents of Edom and the Ishmaelites;
Moab and the Hagarites; 2 Chr. 20:1, 10, 11
7 Gebal, Ammon, and Amalek;
Philistia with the inhabitants of Tyre;
8 Assyria also has joined with them;
They have helped the children of Lot.
Selah

9 Deal with them as *with* Midian,
As *with* [R]Sisera, Judg. 4:15–24; 5:20, 21
As *with* Jabin at the Brook Kishon,
10 Who perished at En Dor,
Who became *as* refuse on the earth.
11 Make their nobles like Oreb and like
[R]Zeeb, Judg. 7:25
Yes, all their princes like [R]Zebah and
Zalmunna, Judg. 8:12–21
12 Who said, "Let us take for ourselves
The pastures of God for a possession."

13 [R]O my God, make them like the whirling
dust, Is. 17:13
[R]Like the chaff before the wind! Ps. 35:5
14 As the fire burns the woods,
And as the flame [R]sets the mountains
on fire, Deut. 32:22
15 So pursue them with Your tempest,
And frighten them with Your storm.
16 Fill their faces with shame,
That they may seek Your name, O
LORD.
17 Let them be [T]confounded and dismayed
forever;
Yes, let them be put to shame and
perish, *ashamed*
18 [R]That *men* may know that You, whose
name alone *is* the LORD, Ps. 59:13
Are the Most High over all the earth.

PSALM 84

The Joy of Dwelling with God

To the Chief Musician. *On an instrument
of Gath. A Psalm of the sons of Korah.

HOW lovely [T]*is* Your tabernacle,
O LORD of hosts! *are your dwellings*
2 [R]My soul longs, yes, even faints
For the courts of the LORD;
My heart and my flesh cry out for the
living God. Ps. 42:1, 2

3 Even the sparrow has found a home,
And the swallow a nest for herself,
Where she may lay her young—
Even Your altars, O LORD of hosts,
My King and my God.
4 Blessed *are* those who dwell in Your
[R]house; [Ps. 65:4]
They will still be praising You. Selah

5 Blessed *is* the man whose strength *is* in
You,
Whose heart *is* set on pilgrimage.
6 *As they* pass through the Valley [R]of
[T]Baca, 2 Sam. 5:22–25 • Lit. *Weeping*
They make it a spring;
The rain also covers it with pools.
7 They go [R]from strength to strength;
Every one of them [R]appears before God
in Zion. Prov. 4:18 • Deut. 16:16

8 O LORD God of hosts, hear my prayer;
Give ear, O God of Jacob! Selah
9 [R]O God, behold our shield, Gen. 15:1
And look upon the face of Your
[T]anointed. Commissioned one, Heb. *messiah*

10 For a day in Your courts *is* better than
a thousand.
I would rather [T]be a doorkeeper in the
house of my God *stand at the threshold*
Than dwell in the tents of wickedness.
11 For the LORD God *is* a sun and shield;
The LORD will give grace and glory;
No good *thing* will He withhold
From those who walk uprightly.

12 O LORD of hosts,
Blessed *is* the man who trusts in You!

PSALM 85

Prayer for Revival

To the Chief Musician.
A Psalm of the sons of Korah.

LORD, You have been favorable to Your
land;
You have [R]brought back the captivity
of Jacob. Joel 3:1
2 You have forgiven the iniquity of Your
people;
You have covered all their sin. Selah
3 You have taken away all Your wrath;
You have turned from the fierceness of
Your anger.

4 [R]Restore us, O God of our salvation,
And cause Your anger toward us to
cease. Ps. 80:3, 7
5 [R]Will You be angry with us forever?
Will You prolong Your anger to all
generations? Ps. 79:5
6 Will You not [R]revive us again, Hab. 3:2
That Your people may rejoice in You?
7 Show us Your mercy, O LORD,
And grant us Your salvation.

8 I will hear what God the LORD will
speak,
For He will speak peace

84:title, Heb. *Al Gittith*

To His people and to His saints;
But let them not turn back to folly.
9 Surely [R]His salvation *is* near to those
who fear Him, Is. 46:13
That glory may dwell in our land.

10 Mercy and truth have met together;
[R]Righteousness and peace have kissed
each other. Ps. 72:3
11 Truth shall spring out of the earth,
And righteousness shall look down from
heaven.
12 Yes, the LORD will give *what is* good;
And our land will yield its increase.
13 Righteousness will go before Him,
And shall make His footsteps *our*
pathway.

PSALM 86

"Teach Me Your Way, O LORD"

A Prayer of David.

BOW down Your ear, O LORD, hear me;
For I *am* poor and needy.
2 Preserve my [T]life, for I *am* holy;
You are my God; Lit. *soul*
Save Your servant who trusts in You!
3 Be merciful to me, O Lord,
For I cry to You all day long.
4 Rejoice the soul of Your servant,
For to You, O Lord, I lift up my soul.
5 For [R]You, Lord, *are* good, and ready to
forgive,
And abundant in mercy to all those
who call upon You. [Joel 2:13]

6 Give ear, O LORD, to my prayer;
And attend to the voice of my
supplications.
7 In the day of my trouble I will call upon
You,
For You will answer me.

8 [R]Among the gods *there is* none like You,
O Lord;
Nor *are there any works* like Your
works. [Ex. 15:11]
9 All nations whom You have made
Shall come and worship before You,
O Lord,
And shall glorify Your name.
10 For You *are* great, and [R]do wondrous
things;
[R]You alone *are* God. [Ex. 15:11] • Deut. 6:4

11 [R]Teach me Your way, O LORD;
I will walk in Your truth; Ps. 27:11; 143:8
Unite my heart to fear Your name.
12 I will praise You, O Lord my God, with
all my heart,
And I will glorify Your name
forevermore.

13 For great *is* Your mercy toward me,
And You have delivered my soul from
the [T]depths of Sheol. The abode of the dead

14 O God, the proud have risen against me,
And a mob of violent *men* have sought
my life,
And have not set You before them.
15 But [R]You, O Lord, *are* a God full of
compassion, and gracious,
Longsuffering and abundant in mercy
and truth. Ex. 34:6

16 Oh, turn to me, and have mercy on me!
Give Your strength to Your servant,
And save the son of Your maidservant.
17 Show me a sign for good,
That those who hate me may see *it* and
be ashamed,
Because You, LORD, have helped me
and comforted me.

PSALM 87

Glorious Zion, City of God

A Psalm of the sons of Korah. A Song.

HIS foundation *is* in the holy mountains.
2 The LORD loves the gates of Zion
More than all the dwellings of Jacob.
3 [R]Glorious things are spoken of you,
O city of God! Selah Is. 60:1

4 "I will make mention of [T]Rahab and
Babylon to those who know Me;
Behold, O Philistia and Tyre, with
Ethiopia:
'This *one* was born there.' " Egypt

5 And of Zion it will be said,
"This *one* and that *one* were born in her;
And the Most High Himself shall
establish her."
6 The LORD will record,
When He [R]registers the peoples:
"This *one* was born there." Selah Is. 4:3

7 Both the singers and the players on
instruments *say,*
"All my springs *are* in you."

PSALM 88

Crying from Deepest Affliction

A Song. A Psalm of the sons of Korah. To the
Chief Musician. Set to "Mahalath Leannoth."
*A Contemplation of Heman the Ezrahite.

O LORD, [R]God of my salvation,
I have cried out day and night before
You. Ps. 27:9
2 Let my prayer come before You;
[T]Incline Your ear to my cry. Listen to

88:title, Heb. *Maschil*

3 For my soul is full of troubles,
And my life draws near to the grave.
4 I am counted with those who [R]go[T]
down to the pit; [Ps. 28:1] • Die
I am like a man *who has* no strength,
5 [T]Adrift among the dead, Lit. *Free*
Like the slain who lie in the grave,
Whom You remember no more,
And who are cut off from Your hand.

6 You have laid me in the lowest pit,
In darkness, in the depths.
7 Your wrath lies heavy upon me,
And You have afflicted *me* with all
[R]Your waves. Selah Ps. 42:7
8 [R]You have [T]put away my acquaintances
far from me;
You have made me an abomination to
them; Job 19:13, 19 • *taken away my friends*
I am shut up, and I cannot get out;
9 My eye wastes away because of
affliction.

LORD, I have called daily upon You;
I have stretched out my hands to You.
10 Will You work wonders for the dead?
Shall [T]the dead arise *and* praise You?
Selah *shades, ghosts*
11 Shall Your lovingkindness be declared
in the grave?
Or Your faithfulness in the place of
destruction?
12 Shall Your wonders be known in the
dark?
And Your righteousness in the land of
forgetfulness?

13 But to You I have cried out, O LORD,
And in the morning my prayer comes
before You.
14 LORD, why do You cast off my soul?
Why do You hide Your face from me?
15 I *have been* afflicted and ready to die
from *my* youth *up;*
I suffer Your terrors;
I am distraught.
16 Your fierce wrath has gone over me;
Your terrors have [T]cut me off. *destroyed me*
17 They came around me all day long like
water;
They engulfed me altogether.
18 [R]Loved one and friend You have put far
from me, Ps. 31:11; 38:11
And my acquaintances into darkness.

PSALM 89

Claiming God's Promises in Affliction

*A Contemplation of Ethan the Ezrahite.

I WILL sing of the mercies of the LORD
forever;
With my mouth will I make known
Your faithfulness to all generations.
2 For I have said, "Mercy shall be built
up forever;
[R]Your faithfulness You shall establish in
the very heavens." [Ps. 119:89, 90]

3 "I[R] have made a covenant with My
chosen, 1 Kin. 8:16
I have sworn to My servant David:
4 'Your seed I will establish forever,
And build up your throne [R]to all
generations.' " Selah [Luke 1:33]

5 And [R]the heavens will praise Your
wonders, O LORD;
Your faithfulness also in the
congregation of the saints. [Ps. 19:1]
6 [R]For who in the heavens can be
compared to the LORD?
Who among the sons of the mighty can
be likened to the LORD? Ps. 86:8; 113:5
7 [R]God is greatly to be feared in the
assembly of the saints,
And to be held in reverence by all *those*
around Him. Ps. 76:7, 11
8 O LORD God of hosts,
Who *is* mighty like You, O LORD?
Your faithfulness also surrounds You.
9 You rule the raging of the sea;
When its waves rise, You still them.
10 [R]You have broken [T]Rahab in pieces, as
one who is slain;
You have scattered Your enemies with
Your mighty arm. Ps. 87:4 • Egypt

11 [R]The heavens *are* Yours, the earth also *is*
Yours;
The world and all its fullness, You have
founded them. [Gen. 1:1]
12 The north and the south, You have
created them;
[R]Tabor and [R]Hermon rejoice in Your
name. Josh. 19:22 • Josh. 11:17; 12:1
13 You have a mighty arm;
Strong is Your hand, *and* high is Your
right hand.
14 Righteousness and justice *are* the
foundation of Your throne;
Mercy and truth go before Your face.
15 Blessed *are* the people who know the
[R]joyful sound!
They walk, O LORD, in the light of Your
countenance. Ps. 98:6
16 In Your name they rejoice all day long,
And in Your righteousness they are
exalted.
17 For You *are* the glory of their strength,
And in Your favor our horn is exalted.
18 For our shield *belongs* to the LORD,
And our king to the Holy One of Israel.

89:title, Heb. *Maschil*

19 Then You spoke in a vision to Your
holy *one,
And said: "I have given help to *one who*
is mighty;
I have exalted one [R]chosen from the
people. 1 Kin. 11:34
20 I have found My servant David;
With My holy oil I have anointed him,
21 [R]With whom My hand shall be
established; Ps. 80:17
Also My arm shall strengthen him.
22 The enemy shall not outwit him,
Nor the son of wickedness afflict him.
23 I will beat down his foes before his face,
And plague those who hate him.

24 "But My faithfulness and My mercy *shall*
be with him,
And in My name his horn shall be
exalted.
25 Also I will set his hand over the sea,
And his right hand over the rivers.
26 He shall cry to Me, 'You *are* my Father,
My God, and the rock of my salvation.'
27 Also I will make him *My* firstborn,
The highest of the kings of the earth.
28 [R]My mercy I will keep for him forever,
And My covenant shall stand firm with
him. Is. 55:3
29 His seed also I will make *to endure*
forever,
And his throne as the days of heaven.

30 "If[R] his sons forsake My law [2 Sam. 7:14]
And do not walk in My judgments,
31 If they [T]break My statutes *profane*
And do not keep My commandments,
32 Then I will [T]visit their transgression
with the rod,
And their iniquity with stripes. *attend to*
33 Nevertheless My lovingkindness I will
not [T]utterly take from him, Lit. *break off*
Nor allow My faithfulness to fail.
34 My covenant I will not break,
Nor [R]alter the word that has gone out
of My lips. Jer. 33:20–22
35 Once I have sworn [R]by My holiness;
I will not lie to David: Amos 4:2
36 [R]His seed shall endure forever, [Luke 1:33]
And his throne as the sun before Me;
37 It shall be established forever like the
moon,
Even *like* the faithful witness in the
sky." Selah

38 But You have cast off and [T]abhorred,
You have been furious with Your
[T]anointed. *rejected* • Commissioned one
39 You have renounced the covenant of
Your servant;
[R]You have [T]profaned his crown *by*
casting it to the ground. Lam. 5:16 • *defiled*
40 You have broken down all his hedges;
You have brought his [T]strongholds to
ruin. *fortresses*
41 All who pass by the way plunder him;
He is a reproach to his neighbors.
42 You have exalted the right hand of his
adversaries;
You have made all his enemies rejoice.
43 You have also turned back the edge of
his sword,
And have not sustained him in the
battle.
44 You have made his [T]glory cease,
And cast his throne down to the
ground. *splendor* or *brightness*
45 The days of his youth You have
shortened;
You have covered him with shame.
Selah

46 How long, LORD?
Will You hide Yourself forever?
Will Your wrath burn like fire?
47 Remember how short my time [R]is;
For what [R]futility have You created all
the children of men? Ps. 90:9 • Ps. 62:9
48 What man can live and not [T]see death?
Can he deliver his life from the power
of [T]the grave? Selah *experience* • *Sheol*

49 Lord, where *are* Your former
lovingkindnesses,
Which You [R]swore to David [R]in Your
truth? [2 Sam. 7:15] • Ps. 54:5
50 Remember, Lord, the reproach of Your
servants—
[R]*How* I bear in my bosom *the reproach*
of all the many peoples, Ps. 69:9, 19
51 [R]With which Your enemies have
reproached, O LORD, Ps. 74:10, 18, 22
With which they have reproached the
footsteps of Your [T]anointed. Heb. *messiah*

52 [R]Blessed *be* the LORD forevermore!
Amen and Amen. Ps. 41:13

BOOK FOUR
Psalms 90–106

PSALM 90

"Teach Us to Number Our Days"

A Prayer of Moses the man of God.

LORD, [R]You have been our dwelling place
in all generations. [Ezek. 11:16]
2 [R]Before the mountains were brought
forth, [Prov. 8:25, 26]
Or ever You [T]had formed the earth and
the world, Lit. *gave birth to*

89:19 MT, LXX, Vg. *ones;* many Heb. mss. *one*

Even from everlasting to everlasting,
You *are* God.

3 You turn man to destruction,
And say, "Return, O children of men."
4 [R]For a thousand years in Your sight
Are like yesterday when it is past,
And *like* a watch in the night. 2 Pet. 3:8
5 You carry them away *like* a flood;
[R]*They are* like a sleep.
In the morning [R]they are like grass
which grows up: Ps. 73:20 • Is. 40:6
6 In the morning it flourishes and grows
up;
In the evening it is cut down and
withers.

7 For we have been consumed by Your
anger,
And by Your wrath we are terrified.
8 [R]You have set our iniquities before You,
Our [R]secret *sins* in the light of Your
countenance. Ps. 50:21 • Ps. 19:12
9 For all our days have passed away in
Your wrath;
We finish our years like a sigh.
10 The days of our lives *are* seventy years;
And if by reason of strength *they are*
eighty years,
Yet their boast *is* only labor and
sorrow;
For it is soon cut off, and we fly away.
11 Who knows the power of Your anger?
For as the fear of You, *so is* Your
wrath.
12 So teach *us* to number our days,
That we may gain a heart of wisdom.

13 Return, O LORD!
How long?
And [R]have compassion on Your
servants. Deut. 32:36
14 Oh, satisfy us early with Your mercy,
[R]That we may rejoice and be glad all our
days! Ps. 85:6
15 Make us glad according to the days *in
which* You have afflicted us,
And the years *in which* we have seen
evil.
16 Let [R]Your work appear to Your
servants,
And Your glory to their children. Hab. 3:2
17 [R]And let the beauty of the LORD our God
be upon us,
And [R]establish the work of our hands
for us; Ps. 27:4 • Is. 26:12
Yes, establish the work of our hands.

PSALM 91

Abiding in "the Shadow of the Almighty"

HE [R]who dwells in the secret place of the
Most High
Shall abide [R]under the shadow of the
Almighty. Ps. 27:5; 31:20; 32:7 • Ps. 17:8
2 [R]I will say of the LORD, "*He is* my refuge
and my fortress;
My God, in Him I will trust." Ps. 142:5

3 Surely He shall deliver you from the
snare of the [T]fowler *trapper of birds*
And from the perilous pestilence.
4 [R]He shall cover you with His feathers,
And under His wings you shall take
refuge;
His truth *shall be your* shield and
[T]buckler. Ps. 17:8 • A small shield
5 [R]You shall not be afraid of the terror by
night, [Job 5:19]
Nor of the arrow *that* flies by day,
6 *Nor* of the pestilence *that* walks in
darkness,
Nor of the destruction *that* lays waste
at noonday.

7 A thousand may fall at your side,
And ten thousand at your right hand;
But it shall not come near you.
8 Only with your eyes shall you look,
And see the reward of the wicked.

9 Because you have made the LORD, *who
is* [R]my refuge, Ps. 91:2
Even the Most High, your habitation,
10 [R]No evil shall befall you,
Nor shall any plague come near your
dwelling; [Prov. 12:21]
11 [R]For He shall give His angels charge over
you,
To keep you in all your ways. [Heb. 1:14]
12 They shall bear you up in *their* hands,
Lest you dash your foot against a stone.
13 You shall tread upon the lion and the
cobra,
The young lion and the serpent you
shall trample underfoot.

14 Because he has set his love upon Me,
therefore I will deliver him;
I will [T]set him on high, because he has
[R]known My name. *exalt him* • [Ps. 9:10]
15 He shall [R]call upon Me, and I will
answer him; Ps. 50:15
I *will be* with him in trouble;
I will deliver him and honor him.
16 With [T]long life I will satisfy him,
And show him My salvation. *length of days*

PSALM 92

It Is Good to Praise the Lord

A Psalm. A Song for the Sabbath day.

IT *is* [R]good to give thanks to the LORD,
And to sing praises to Your name, O
Most High; Ps. 147:1

2 To [R]declare Your lovingkindness in the
morning, Ps. 89:1
And Your faithfulness every night,
3 [R]On an instrument of ten strings,
On the lute, 1 Chr. 23:5
And on the harp,
With [T]harmonious sound. *melodic*
4 For You, LORD, have made me glad
through Your work;
I will triumph in the works of Your
hands.

5 O LORD, how great are Your works!
[R]Your thoughts are very deep. [Is. 28:29]
6 [R]A senseless man does not know,
Nor does a fool understand this. Ps. 73:22
7 When [R]the wicked [T]spring up like grass,
And when all the workers of iniquity
flourish, Job 12:6 • *sprout*
It is that they may be destroyed forever.

8 [R]But You, LORD, *are* on high
forevermore. [Ps. 83:18]
9 For behold, Your enemies, O LORD,
For behold, Your enemies shall perish;
All the workers of iniquity shall [R]be
scattered. Ps. 68:1

10 But [R]my [T]horn You have exalted like a
wild ox; Ps. 89:17 • Strength
I have been anointed with fresh oil.
11 [R]My eye also has seen *my desire* on my
enemies;
My ears hear *my desire* on the wicked
Who rise up against me. Ps. 54:7

12 [R]The righteous shall flourish like a palm
tree, Ps. 52:8
He shall grow like a cedar in Lebanon.
13 Those who are planted in the house of
the LORD
Shall flourish in the courts of our God.
14 They shall still bear fruit in old age;
They shall be fresh and flourishing,
15 To declare that the LORD is upright;
He is my rock, and [R]*there is* no
unrighteousness in Him. [Rom. 9:14]

PSALM 93

The Majesty of God

THE [R]LORD reigns, He is clothed with
majesty; Ps. 96:10
The LORD is clothed,
[R]He has girded Himself with strength.
Surely the world is established, so that
it cannot be [T]moved. Ps. 65:6 • *shaken*
2 [R]Your throne *is* established from of old;
You *are* from everlasting. Ps. 45:6

3 The floods have [T]lifted up, O LORD,
The floods have lifted up their voice;
The floods lift up their waves. *raised up*
4 [R]The LORD on high *is* mightier Ps. 65:7
Than the noise of many waters,
Than the mighty waves of the sea.

5 Your testimonies are very sure;
Holiness adorns Your house,
O LORD, [T]forever. Lit. *for length of days*

PSALM 94

Vengeance Belongs Only to God

O LORD God, [R]to whom vengeance
belongs—
O God, to whom vengeance belongs,
shine forth! [Nah. 1:2]
2 Rise up, O [R]Judge of the earth; [Gen. 18:25]
Render punishment to the proud.
3 LORD, how long will the wicked,
How long will the wicked triumph?

4 They [R]utter speech, *and* speak insolent
things;
All the workers of iniquity boast in
themselves. Ps. 31:18
5 They break in pieces Your people, O
LORD,
And afflict Your heritage.
6 They slay the widow and the stranger,
And murder the fatherless.
7 [R]Yet they say, "The LORD does not see,
Nor does the God of Jacob
[T]understand." Ps. 10:11 • *pay attention*

8 Understand, you senseless among the
people;
And *you* fools, when will you be wise?
9 [R]He who planted the ear, shall He not
hear?
He who formed the eye, shall He not
see? [Ex. 4:11]
10 He who [T]instructs the [T]nations, shall He
not correct, *disciplines* • *Gentiles*
He who teaches man knowledge?
11 The LORD [R]knows the thoughts of man,
That they *are* futile. 1 Cor. 3:20

12 Blessed *is* the man whom You [R]instruct,
O LORD,
And teach out of Your law, [Heb. 12:5, 6]
13 That You may give him [T]rest from the
days of adversity,
Until the pit is dug for the wicked. *relief*
14 For the LORD will not [T]cast off His
people, *abandon*
Nor will He forsake His inheritance.
15 But judgment will return to
righteousness,
And all the upright in heart will follow
it.

16 Who will rise up for me against the
evildoers?

Who will stand up for me against the
workers of iniquity?
17 Unless the LORD *had been* my help,
My soul would soon have settled in
silence.
18 If I say, "My foot slips,"
Your mercy, O LORD, will hold me up.
19 In the multitude of my anxieties within
me,
Your comforts delight my soul.

20 Shall [R]the throne of iniquity, which
devises evil by law,
Have fellowship with You? Amos 6:3
21 They gather together against the life of
the righteous,
And condemn [R]innocent blood. [Ex. 23:7]
22 But the LORD has been my defense,
And my God the rock of my refuge.
23 He has brought on them their own
iniquity,
And shall cut them off in their own
wickedness;
The LORD our God shall cut them off.

PSALM 95

Call to Worship the Lord

OH come, let us sing to the LORD!
Let us shout joyfully to the Rock of
our salvation.
2 Let us come before His presence with
thanksgiving;
Let us shout joyfully to Him with
[R]psalms. James 5:13
3 For [R]the LORD *is* the great God, [Ps. 96:4]
And the great King above all gods.
4 [T]In His hand *are* the deep places of the
earth; *In His possession*
The heights of the hills *are* His also.
5 [R]The sea *is* His, for He made it; Gen. 1:9, 10
And His hands formed the dry *land.*

6 Oh come, let us worship and bow down;
Let [R]us kneel before the LORD our
Maker. [Phil. 2:10]
7 For He *is* our God,
And we *are* the people of His pasture,
And the sheep [T]of His hand. Under His care

Today, if you will hear His voice:
8 "Do not harden your hearts, as in the
[T]rebellion, Heb. *Meribah*
And [R]as *in* the day of [T]trial in the
wilderness, Ex. 17:2–7 • Heb. *Massah,* lit. *testing*
9 When [R]your fathers tested Me;
They proved Me, though they [R]saw My
work. Ps. 78:18 • Num. 14:22
10 For [R]forty years I was [T]grieved with
that generation, Heb. 3:10, 17 • *disgusted*
And said, 'It *is* a people who go astray
in their hearts,
And they do not know My ways.'
11 So [R]I swore in My wrath,
'They shall not enter My rest.' " Heb. 4:3, 5

PSALM 96

Declare the Glory of God

OH, sing to the LORD a new song!
Sing to the LORD, all the earth.
2 Sing to the LORD, bless His name;
Proclaim the good news of His salvation
from day to day.
3 Declare His glory among the [T]nations,
His wonders among all peoples. *Gentiles*

4 For [R]the LORD *is* great and [R]greatly to
be praised; Ps. 145:3 • Ps. 18:3
[R]He *is* to be feared above all gods. Ps. 95:3
5 For [R]*all* the gods of the peoples *are*
idols, [Jer. 10:11]
[R]But the LORD made the heavens. Is. 42:5
6 Honor and majesty *are* before Him;
Strength and [R]beauty *are* in His
sanctuary. Ps. 29:2

7 [R]Give[T] to the LORD, O kindreds of the
peoples, Ps. 29:1, 2 • *Ascribe*
Give to the LORD glory and strength.
8 [T]Give to the LORD the glory *due* His
name;
Bring an offering, and come into His
courts. *Ascribe*
9 Oh, worship the LORD [R]in the beauty of
holiness!
Tremble before Him, all the earth. Ps. 29:2

10 Say among the [T]nations, [R]"The LORD
reigns; *Gentiles* • Ps. 93:1; 97:1
The world also is firmly established,
It shall not be [T]moved; *shaken*
He shall judge the peoples righteously."

11 [R]Let the heavens rejoice, and let the
earth be glad; Ps. 69:34
Let the sea roar, and all its fullness;
12 Let the field be joyful, and all that *is* in
it.
Then all the trees of the woods will
rejoice before the LORD.
13 For He is coming, for He is coming to
judge the earth.
[R]He shall judge the world with
righteousness, [Rev. 19:11]
And the peoples with His truth.

PSALM 97

Rejoice! The Lord Reigns!

THE LORD [R]reigns; [Ps. 96:10]
Let the earth rejoice;
Let the multitude of isles be glad!

2 Clouds and darkness surround Him;

[R]Righteousness and justice *are* the
foundation of His throne. [Ps. 89:14]
3 [R]A fire goes before Him, Ps. 18:8
And burns up His enemies round about.
4 [R]His lightnings light the world;
The earth sees and trembles. Ex. 19:18
5 [R]The mountains melt like wax at the
presence of the LORD,
At the presence of the Lord of the
whole earth. Mic. 1:4
6 [R]The heavens declare His righteousness,
And all the peoples see His glory. Ps. 19:1

7 [R]Let all be put to shame who serve
carved images, [Ex. 20:4]
Who boast of idols.
[R]Worship Him, all *you* gods. [Heb. 1:6]
8 Zion hears and is glad,
And the daughters of Judah rejoice
Because of Your judgments, O LORD.
9 For You, LORD, [R]*are* most high above all
the earth; Ps. 83:18
You are exalted far above all gods.

10 You who love the LORD, [R]hate evil!
[R]He preserves the souls of His saints;
[R]He delivers them out of the hand of the
wicked. [Ps. 34:14] • Prov. 2:8 • Ps. 37:40
11 [R]Light is sown for the righteous, Job 22:28
And gladness for the upright in heart.
12 Rejoice in the LORD, you righteous,
[R]And give thanks at the remembrance of
[T]His holy name. Ps. 30:4 • Or *His holiness*

PSALM 98

Sing a New Song to the Lord

A Psalm.

OH, [R]sing to the LORD a new song!
For He has [R]done marvelous things;
His right hand and His holy arm have
gained Him the victory. Is. 42:10 • Ex. 15:11
2 [R]The LORD has made known His
salvation; Is. 52:10
His righteousness He has openly shown
in the sight of the [T]nations. *Gentiles*
3 He has remembered His mercy and His
faithfulness to the house of Israel;
[R]All the ends of the earth have seen the
salvation of our God. Luke 3:6

4 Shout joyfully to the LORD, all the
earth;
Break forth in song, rejoice, and sing
praises.
5 Sing to the LORD with the harp,
With the harp and the sound of a
psalm,
6 With trumpets and the sound of a horn;
Shout joyfully before the LORD, the
King.

7 Let the sea roar, and all its fullness,
The world and those who dwell in it;
8 Let the rivers clap *their* hands;
Let the hills be joyful together before
the LORD,
9 For He is coming to [R]judge the earth.
With righteousness He shall judge the
world, [Ps. 96:10, 13]
And the peoples with [T]equity. *uprightness*

PSALM 99

"Exalt the LORD Our God"

THE LORD reigns;
Let the peoples tremble!
[R]He dwells *between* the cherubim;
Let the earth be [T]moved! Ex. 25:22 • *shaken*
2 The LORD *is* great in Zion,
And He *is* high above all the peoples.
3 Let them praise Your great and
awesome name—
[T]He *is* holy. Or *It*

4 The King's strength also loves justice;
You have established equity;
You have executed justice and
righteousness in Jacob.
5 Exalt the LORD our God,
And worship at His footstool;
For He *is* holy.

6 Moses and Aaron were among His
priests,
And Samuel was among those who
[R]called upon His name;
They called upon the LORD, and He
answered them. 1 Sam. 7:9; 12:18
7 He spoke to them in the cloudy pillar;
They kept His testimonies and the
[T]ordinance *that* He gave them. *statute*

8 You answered them, O LORD our God;
You were to them God-Who-Forgives,
Though You took vengeance on their
deeds.
9 Exalt the LORD our God,
And worship at His holy hill;
For the LORD our God *is* holy.

PSALM 100

"Serve the LORD with Gladness"

A Psalm of Thanksgiving.

MAKE [R]a joyful shout to the LORD, [T]all
you lands! Ps. 95:1 • Lit. *all the earth*
2 Serve the LORD with gladness;
Come before His presence with singing.
3 Know that the LORD, He *is* God;
[R]*It is* He *who* has made us, *and not we
ourselves;

100:3 Some mss. *and His we are*

[R]*We are* His people and the sheep of His
pasture. [Eph. 2:10] • Ezek. 34:30, 31

4 Enter into His gates with thanksgiving,
And into His courts with praise.
Be thankful to Him, *and* bless His name.
5 For the LORD *is* good;
[R]His mercy *is* everlasting,
And His truth *endures* to all
generations. Ps. 136:1

PSALM 101

Commitments of a Holy Life

A Psalm of David.

I WILL sing of mercy and justice;
To You, O LORD, I will sing praises.

2 I will behave wisely in a [T]perfect way.
Oh, when will You come to me?
I will [R]walk within my house with a
perfect heart. *blameless* • 1 Kin. 11:4

3 I will set nothing [T]wicked before my
eyes; *worthless*
[R]I hate the work of those [R]who fall
away; Ps. 97:10 • Josh. 23:6
It shall not cling to me.
4 A perverse heart shall depart from me;
I will not [R]know wickedness. [Ps. 119:115]

5 Whoever secretly slanders his neighbor,
Him I will destroy;
[R]The one who has a haughty look and a
proud heart,
Him I will not endure. Prov. 6:17

6 My eyes *shall be* on the faithful of the
land,
That they may dwell with me;
He who walks in a [T]perfect way,
He shall serve me. *blameless*
7 He who works deceit shall not dwell
within my house;
He who tells lies [T]shall not continue in
my presence. Lit. *be established*
8 [R]Early I will destroy all the wicked of the
land, Jer. 21:12
That I may cut off all the evildoers
[R]from the city of the LORD. Ps. 48:2, 8

PSALM 102

Prayer of an Overwhelmed Saint

A Prayer of the afflicted, when he is
overwhelmed and pours out his complaint
before the LORD.

HEAR my prayer, O LORD,
And let my cry come to You.
2 [R]Do not hide Your face from me in the
day of my trouble;
Incline Your ear to me;
In the day that I call, answer me
speedily. Ps. 27:9; 69:17

3 For my days [T]are [R]consumed like
smoke, Lit. *end in* • James 4:14
And my bones are burned like a hearth.
4 My heart is stricken and withered like
grass,
So that I forget to eat my bread.
5 Because of the sound of my groaning
My bones cling to my [T]skin. *flesh*
6 I am like a pelican of the wilderness;
I am like an owl of the desert.
7 I lie awake,
And am like a sparrow alone on the
housetop.

8 My enemies reproach me all day long,
And those who deride me swear an oath
against me.
9 For I have eaten ashes like bread,
And mingled my drink with weeping,
10 Because of Your indignation and Your
wrath;
For You have lifted me up and cast me
away.
11 My days *are* like a shadow that
lengthens,
And I wither away like grass.

12 But You, O LORD, shall endure forever,
And the remembrance of Your name to
all generations.
13 You will arise *and* have mercy on Zion;
For the time to favor her,
Yes, the set time, has come.
14 For Your servants take pleasure in her
stones,
And show favor to her dust.
15 So the [T]nations shall [R]fear the name of
the LORD,
And all the kings of the earth Your
glory. *Gentiles* • 1 Kin. 8:43
16 For the LORD shall build up Zion;
[R]He shall appear in His glory. [Is. 60:1, 2]
17 [R]He shall regard the prayer of the
destitute, Neh. 1:6
And shall not despise their prayer.

18 This will be [R]written for the generation
to come,
That [R]a people yet to be created may
praise the LORD. [Rom. 15:4] • Ps. 22:31
19 For He [R]looked down from the height of
His sanctuary;
From heaven the LORD viewed the
earth, Deut. 26:15
20 To hear the groaning of the prisoner,
To loose those appointed to death,
21 To [R]declare the name of the LORD in
Zion,
And His praise in Jerusalem, Ps. 22:22

22 [R]When the peoples are gathered
together, [Is. 2:2, 3; 49:22, 23; 60:3]
And the kingdoms, to serve the LORD.

23 He weakened my strength in the way;
He [R]shortened my days. Job 21:21
24 [R]I said, "O my God,
Do not take me away in the midst of
my days;
[R]Your years *are* throughout all
generations. Is. 38:10 • [Ps. 90:2]
25 [R]Of old You laid the foundation of the
earth,
And the heavens *are* the work of Your
hands. [Heb. 1:10–12]
26 [R]They will perish, but You will [T]endure;
Yes, all of them will grow old like a
garment; Is. 34:4; 51:6 • *continue*
Like a cloak You will change them,
And they will be changed.
27 But [R]You *are* the same, [Mal. 3:6]
And Your years will have no end.
28 [R]The children of Your servants will
continue,
And their descendants will be
established before You." Ps. 69:36

PSALM 103

Bless the Lord, All You People!

A Psalm of David.

BLESS [R]the LORD, O my soul;
And all that is within me, *bless* His
holy name! Ps. 104:1, 35
2 Bless the LORD, O my soul,
And forget not all His benefits:
3 Who forgives all your iniquities,
Who [R]heals all your diseases, [Ex. 15:26]
4 Who redeems your life from
destruction,
[R]Who crowns you with lovingkindness
and tender mercies, [Ps. 5:12]
5 Who satisfies your mouth with good
things,
So that [R]your youth is renewed like the
eagle's. [Is. 40:31]

6 The LORD executes righteousness
And justice for all who are oppressed.
7 He made known His ways to Moses,
His acts to the children of Israel.
8 The LORD *is* merciful and gracious,
Slow to anger, and abounding in mercy.
9 He will not always strive *with us*,
Nor will He keep *His anger* forever.
10 [R]He has not dealt with us according to
our sins,
Nor punished us according to our
iniquities. [Ezra 9:13]

11 For as the heavens are high above the
earth,
So great is His mercy toward those who
fear Him;
12 As far as the east is from the west,
So far has He [R]removed our
transgressions from us. [Is. 38:17; 43:25]
13 [R]As a father pities *his* children, Mal. 3:17
So the LORD pities those who fear Him.
14 For He [T]knows our frame; Understands
He remembers that we *are* dust.

15 *As for* man, his days *are* like grass;
As a flower of the field, so he flourishes.
16 [R]For the wind passes over it, and it is
[T]gone, [Is. 40:7] • *not*
And its place remembers it no more.
17 But the mercy of the LORD *is* from
everlasting to everlasting
On those who fear Him,
And His righteousness to children's
children,
18 [R]To such as keep His covenant,
And to those who remember His
commandments to do them. [Deut. 7:9]

19 The LORD has established His throne in
heaven,
And His kingdom rules over all.

20 [R]Bless the LORD, you His angels,
Who excel in strength, who [R]do His
word, Ps. 148:2 • [Matt. 6:10]
Heeding the voice of His word.
21 Bless the LORD, all *you* His hosts,
[R]*You* [T]ministers of His, who do His
pleasure. [Heb. 1:14] • *servants*
22 Bless the LORD, all His works,
In all places of His dominion.

Bless the LORD, O my soul!

PSALM 104

Psalm Rehearsing Creation

BLESS [R]the LORD, O my soul!

O LORD my God, You are very great:
You are clothed with honor and
majesty, Ps. 103:1
2 Who cover *Yourself* with light as *with* a
garment,
Who stretch out the heavens like a
curtain.

3 [R]He lays the beams of His upper
chambers in the waters, [Amos 9:6]
Who makes the clouds His chariot,
Who walks on the wings of the wind,
4 Who makes His angels spirits,
His [T]ministers a flame of fire. *servants*

5 *You who* [T]laid the foundations of the
earth, Lit. *founded the earth upon her bases*

So *that* it should not be moved forever,
6 You [R]covered it with the deep as *with* a
garment; Gen. 1:6
The waters stood above the mountains.
7 At Your rebuke they fled;
At the voice of Your thunder they
hastened away.
8 [T]They went up over the mountains;
They went down into the valleys,
To the place which You founded for
them. Or *The mountains rose; The valleys sank*
9 You have [R]set a boundary that they
may not pass over,
[R]That they may not return to cover the
earth. [Jer. 5:22] • Gen. 9:11–15

10 He sends the springs into the valleys,
Which flow among the hills.
11 They give drink to every beast of the
field;
The wild donkeys quench their thirst.
12 By them the birds of the heavens have
their habitation;
They sing among the branches.
13 [R]He waters the hills from His upper
chambers;
The earth is satisfied with [R]the fruit of
Your works. Ps. 147:8 • Jer. 10:13

14 [R]He causes the grass to grow for the
cattle,
And vegetation for the service of man,
That he may bring forth [R]food from the
earth, Gen. 1:29 • Job 28:5
15 And [R]wine *that* makes glad the heart of
man,
Oil to make *his* face shine,
And bread *which* strengthens man's
heart. Judg. 9:13
16 The trees of the LORD are full *of sap*,
The cedars of Lebanon which He
planted,
17 Where the birds make their nests;
The stork has her home in the fir trees.
18 The high hills *are* for the wild goats;
The cliffs are a refuge for the [R]rock[T]
badgers. Lev. 11:5 • *rock hyraxes*

19 He appointed the moon for seasons;
The [R]sun knows its going down. Ps. 19:6
20 [R]You make darkness, and it is night,
In which all the beasts of the forest
creep about. [Is. 45:7]
21 [R]The young lions roar after their prey,
And seek their food from God. Job 38:39
22 *When* the sun arises, they gather
together
And lie down in their dens.
23 Man goes out to [R]his work Gen. 3:19
And to his labor until the evening.

24 O LORD, how manifold are Your works!
In wisdom You have made them all.
The earth is full of Your possessions—
25 This great and wide sea,
In which *are* innumerable teeming
things,
Living things both small and great.
26 There the ships sail about;
And there is that [R]Leviathan Job 41:1
Which You have made to play there.

27 [R]These all wait for You,
That You may give *them* their food in
due season. Ps. 136:25
28 *What* You give them they gather in;
You open Your hand, they are filled
with good.
29 You hide Your face, they are troubled;
[R]You take away their breath, they die
and return to their dust. Job 34:15
30 [R]You send forth Your Spirit, they are
created; Is. 32:15
And You renew the face of the earth.

31 May the glory of the LORD endure
forever;
May the LORD rejoice in His works.
32 He looks on the earth, and it trembles;
He touches the hills, and they smoke.

33 [R]I will sing to the LORD as long as I live;
I will sing praise to my God while I
have my being. Ps. 63:4
34 May my [R]meditation be sweet to Him;
I will be glad in the LORD. Ps. 19:14
35 May [R]sinners be consumed from the
earth,
And the wicked be no more.

Bless the LORD, O my soul!
[T]Praise the LORD! Ps. 37:38 • Heb. *Hallelujah*

PSALM 105

Remember, God Keeps His Promises

OH, [R]give thanks to the LORD!
Call upon His name;
[R]Make known His deeds among the
peoples. Is. 12:4 • Ps. 145:12
2 Sing to Him, sing psalms to Him;
[R]Talk of all His wondrous works. Ps. 119:27
3 Glory in His holy name;
Let the hearts of those rejoice who seek
the LORD.
4 Seek the LORD and His strength;
[R]Seek His face evermore. Ps. 27:8
5 [R]Remember His marvelous works which
He has done,
His wonders, and the judgments of His
mouth, Ps. 77:11
6 O seed of Abraham His servant,
You children of Jacob, His chosen ones!

7 He *is* the LORD our God;
His judgments *are* in all the earth.

8 He has [R]remembered His covenant
forever,
The word *which* He commanded, for a
thousand generations, Luke 1:72
9 [R]*The covenant* which He made with
Abraham,
And His oath to Isaac, Gen. 17:2
10 And confirmed it to Jacob for a statute,
To Israel *for* an everlasting covenant,
11 Saying, [R]"To you I will give the land of
Canaan Gen. 13:15; 15:18
As the allotment of your inheritance,"
12 When they were *but* few in number,
Indeed very few, and strangers in it.

13 When they went from one nation to
another,
From *one* kingdom to another people,
14 He permitted no one to do them wrong;
Yes, He reproved kings for their sakes,
15 *Saying*, "Do not touch My anointed
ones,
And do My prophets no harm."

16 Moreover [R]He called for a famine in the
land; Gen. 41:54
He destroyed all the provision of bread.
17 [R]He sent a man before them— [Gen. 45:5]
Joseph—*who* was sold as a slave.
18 [R]They hurt his feet with fetters, Gen. 40:15
[T]He was laid in irons. *His soul came into iron*
19 Until the time that his word came to
pass,
The word of the LORD tested him.
20 The king sent and released him,
The ruler of the people let him go free.
21 He made him lord of his house,
And ruler of all his possessions,
22 To [T]bind his princes at his pleasure,
And teach his elders wisdom. As prisoners

23 [R]Israel also came into Egypt, Gen. 46:6
And Jacob sojourned in the land of
Ham.
24 And [R]He increased His people greatly,
And made them stronger than their
enemies. Ex. 1:7, 9
25 [R]He turned their heart to hate His
people, Ex. 1:8–10; 4:21
To deal craftily with His servants.

26 [R]He sent Moses His servant, Ex. 3:10; 4:12–15
And Aaron whom He had chosen.
27 They [R]performed His signs among them,
And wonders in the land of Ham. Ps. 78:43
28 He sent darkness, and made *it* dark;
And they did not rebel against His
word.
29 [R]He turned their waters into blood,
And killed their fish. Ex. 7:20, 21
30 [R]Their land abounded with frogs, Ex. 8:6
Even in the chambers of their kings.
31 [R]He spoke, and there came swarms of
flies,
And lice in all their territory. Ex. 8:16, 17
32 [R]He gave them hail for rain,
And flaming fire in their land. Ex. 9:23–25
33 [R]He struck their vines also, and their fig
trees,
And splintered the trees of their
territory. Ps. 78:47
34 [R]He spoke, and locusts came,
Young locusts without number, Ex. 10:4
35 And ate up all the vegetation in their
land,
And devoured the fruit of their ground.
36 [R]He also [T]destroyed all the firstborn in
their land, Ex. 12:29; 13:15 • Lit. *struck down*
[R]The first of all their strength. Gen. 49:3

37 [R]He also brought them out with silver
and gold,
And *there was* none feeble among His
tribes. Ex. 12:35, 36
38 [R]Egypt was glad when they departed,
For the fear of them had fallen upon
them. Ex. 12:33
39 He spread a cloud for a covering,
And fire to give light in the night.
40 [R]*The people* asked, and He brought quail,
And [R]satisfied them with the bread of
heaven. Ex. 16:12 • Ps. 78:24
41 [R]He opened the rock, and water gushed
out; Ex. 17:6
It ran in the dry places *like* a river.

42 For He remembered [R]His holy promise,
And Abraham His servant. Gen. 15:13, 14
43 He brought out His people with joy,
His chosen ones with [T]gladness. *glad shout*
44 [R]He gave them the lands of the [T]Gentiles,
And they inherited the labor of the
nations, Josh. 11:16–23; 13:7 • *nations*
45 [R]That they might observe His statutes
And keep His laws.

[T]Praise the LORD! [Deut. 4:1, 40] • Heb. *Hallelujah*

PSALM 106

"We Have Sinned"

PRAISE[T] the LORD!

Oh, [R]give thanks to the LORD, for *He is*
good! Heb. *Hallelujah* • 1 Chr. 16:34, 41
For His mercy *endures* forever.

2 Who can [T]utter the mighty acts of the
LORD?
Or can declare all His praise? *express*
3 Blessed *are* those who keep justice,
And he who [R]does righteousness at [R]all
times! Ps. 15:2 • [Gal. 6:9]

4 Remember me, O LORD, with the favor
You have toward Your people;
Oh, visit me with Your salvation,
5 That I may see the benefit of Your
chosen ones,
That I may rejoice in the gladness of
Your nation,
That I may glory with [T]Your
inheritance. The people of Your inheritance

6 [R]We have sinned with our fathers,
We have committed iniquity,
We have done wickedly. [Dan. 9:5]
7 Our fathers in Egypt did not understand
Your wonders;
They did not remember the multitude of
Your mercies,
But rebelled by the sea—the Red Sea.

8 Nevertheless He saved them for His
name's sake,
[R]That He might make His mighty power
known. Ex. 9:16
9 [R]He rebuked the Red Sea also, and it
dried up; Ex. 14:21
So [R]He led them through the depths,
As through the wilderness. Is. 63:11–13
10 He [R]saved them from the hand of him
who hated *them,*
And redeemed them from the hand of
the enemy. Ex. 14:30
11 The waters covered their enemies;
There was not one of them left.
12 [R]Then they believed His words;
They sang His praise. Ex. 15:1–21

13 [R]They soon forgot His works; Ex. 17:1–7
They did not wait for His counsel,
14 [R]But lusted exceedingly in the
wilderness,
And tested God in the desert. 1 Cor. 10:6
15 And He gave them their request,
But sent leanness into their soul.

16 When they envied Moses in the camp,
And Aaron the saint of the LORD,
17 [R]The earth opened up and swallowed
Dathan, Deut. 11:6
And covered the faction of Abiram.
18 A fire was kindled in their company;
The flame burned up the wicked.

19 [R]They made a calf in Horeb, Ex. 32:1–4
And worshiped the molded image.
20 Thus [R]they changed their glory Rom. 1:23
Into the image of an ox that eats grass.
21 They forgot God their Savior,
Who had done great things in Egypt,
22 Wondrous works in the land of Ham,
Awesome things by the Red Sea.
23 [R]Therefore He said that He would
destroy them,
Had not Moses His chosen one [R]stood
before Him in the breach,
To turn away His wrath, lest He destroy
them. Ex. 32:10 • Ezek. 22:30

24 Then they despised [R]the pleasant land;
They did not believe His word, Deut. 8:7
25 [R]But murmured in their tents, Num. 14:2, 27
And did not heed the voice of the LORD.
26 [R]Therefore He lifted up His hand *in an
oath* against them, Ezek. 20:15, 16
To overthrow them in the wilderness,
27 To [T]overthrow their descendants among
the nations, *make their descendants fall also*
And to scatter them in the lands.

28 [R]They joined themselves also to Baal of
Peor, Hos. 9:10
And ate sacrifices made to the dead.
29 Thus they provoked *Him* to anger with
their deeds,
And the plague broke out among them.
30 Then Phinehas stood up and intervened,
And *so* the plague was stopped.
31 And that was accounted to him [R]for
righteousness Num. 25:11–13
To all generations forevermore.

32 [R]They angered *Him* also at the waters of
[T]strife, Num. 20:3–13 • Heb. *Meribah*
[R]So that it went ill with Moses on
account of them; Deut. 1:37; 3:26
33 Because they rebelled against His Spirit,
So that he spoke rashly with his lips.

34 [R]They did not destroy the peoples,
[R]Concerning whom the LORD had
commanded them, Judg. 1:21 • [Deut. 7:2, 16]
35 [R]But they mingled with the Gentiles
And learned their works; Judg. 3:5, 6
36 [R]They served their idols, Judg. 2:12
[R]Which became a snare to them. Deut. 7:16
37 They even sacrificed their sons
And their daughters to demons,
38 And shed innocent blood,
Even the blood of their sons and
daughters,
Whom they sacrificed to the idols of
Canaan;
And the land was polluted with blood.
39 Thus they [T]were [R]defiled by their own
works, *became unclean* • Ezek. 20:18
And [R]played the [T]harlot by their own
deeds. [Lev. 17:7] • Were unfaithful

40 Therefore [R]the wrath of the LORD was
kindled against His people,
So that He abhorred [R]His own
inheritance. Judg. 2:14 • [Deut. 9:29; 32:9]
41 And [R]He gave them into the hand of the
Gentiles,
And those who hated them ruled over
them. Judg. 2:14
42 Their enemies also oppressed them,
And they were brought into subjection
under their hand.

43 [R]Many times He delivered them;
But they rebelled *against Him* by their
counsel, Judg. 2:16
And were brought low for their iniquity.

44 Nevertheless He regarded their
affliction,
When [R]He heard their cry; Judg. 3:9
45 [R]And for their sake He remembered His
covenant, [Lev. 26:41, 42]
And relented [R]according to the
multitude of His mercies. Ps. 69:16
46 [R]He also made them to be pitied
By all those who carried them away
captive. Ezra 9:9

47 [R]Save us, O LORD our God, 1 Chr. 16:35, 36
And gather us from among the Gentiles,
To give thanks to Your holy name,
And to triumph in Your praise.

48 [R]Blessed *be* the LORD God of Israel
From everlasting to everlasting!
And let all the people say, "Amen!"

[T]Praise the LORD! Ps. 41:13 • Heb. *Hallelujah*

BOOK FIVE
Psalms 107–150

PSALM 107

God Satisfies the Longing Soul

OH, [R]give thanks to the LORD, for *He is*
good! Ps. 106:1
For His mercy *endures* forever.
2 Let the redeemed of the LORD say *so,*
Whom He has redeemed from the hand
of the enemy,
3 And [R]gathered out of the lands, Is. 43:5, 6
From the east and from the west,
From the north and from the south.

4 They wandered in [R]the wilderness in a
desolate way; [Deut. 2:7; 32:10]
They found no city to dwell in.
5 Hungry and thirsty,
Their soul fainted in them.
6 [R]Then they cried out to the LORD in their
trouble,
And He delivered them out of their
distresses. Ps. 50:15
7 And He led them forth by the [R]right
way,
That they might go to a city for
habitation. Ezra 8:21
8 [R]Oh, that *men* would give thanks to the
LORD *for* His goodness,
And *for* His wonderful works to the
children of men! Ps. 107:15, 21
9 For He satisfies the longing soul,
And fills the hungry soul with goodness.

10 Those who [R]sat in darkness and in the
shadow of death, [Luke 1:79]
[T]Bound in affliction and irons— *Prisoners*
11 Because they [R]rebelled against the
words of God,
And [T]despised [R]the counsel of the Most
High, Lam. 3:42 • *scorned* • [Ps. 73:24]
12 Therefore He brought down their heart
with labor;
They fell down, and *there was* [R]none to
help. Ps. 22:11
13 Then they cried out to the LORD in their
trouble,
And He saved them out of their
distresses.
14 [R]He brought them out of darkness and
the shadow of death,
And broke their chains in pieces. Ps. 68:6
15 Oh, that *men* would give thanks to the
LORD *for* His goodness,
And *for* His wonderful works to the
children of men!
16 For He has [R]broken the gates of bronze,
And cut the bars of iron in two. Is. 45:1, 2

17 Fools, [R]because of their transgression,
And because of their iniquities, were
afflicted. Lam. 3:39
18 [R]Their soul abhorred all manner of food,
And they [R]drew near to the gates of
death. Job 33:20 • Job 33:22
19 Then they cried out to the LORD in their
trouble,
And He saved them out of their
distresses.
20 [R]He sent His word and [R]healed them,
And [R]delivered *them* from their
destructions. Matt. 8:8 • Ps. 30:2 • Job 33:28, 30
21 Oh, that *men* would give thanks to the
LORD *for* His goodness,
And *for* His wonderful works to the
children of men!
22 [R]Let them sacrifice the sacrifices of
thanksgiving, Lev. 7:12
And declare His works with rejoicing.

23 Those who go down to the sea in ships,
Who do business on great waters,
24 They see the works of the LORD,
And His wonders in the deep.
25 For He commands and [R]raises the
stormy wind, Jon. 1:4
Which lifts up the waves of the sea.
26 They mount up to the heavens,
They go down again to the depths;
Their soul melts because of trouble.
27 They reel to and fro, and stagger like a
drunken man,
And are at their wits' end.

28 Then they cry out to the LORD in their
trouble,
And He brings them out of their
distresses.
29 [R]He calms the storm,
So that its waves are still. Ps. 89:9
30 Then they are glad because they are
quiet;
So He guides them to their desired
haven.
31 [R]Oh, that *men* would give thanks to the
LORD *for* His goodness,
And *for* His wonderful works to the
children of men! Ps. 107:8, 15, 21
32 Let them exalt Him also [R]in the
congregation of the people,
And praise Him in the assembly of the
elders. Ps. 22:22, 25

33 He turns rivers into a wilderness,
And the watersprings into dry ground;
34 A [R]fruitful land into [T]barrenness,
For the wickedness of those who dwell
in it. Gen. 13:10 • Lit. *a salty waste*
35 [R]He turns a wilderness into pools of
water,
And dry land into watersprings. Ps. 114:8
36 There He makes the hungry dwell,
That they may establish a city for
habitation,
37 And sow fields and plant vineyards,
That they may yield a fruitful harvest.
38 [R]He also blesses them, and they multiply
greatly;
And He does not let their cattle
[R]decrease. Gen. 12:2; 17:16, 20 • [Deut. 7:14]

39 When they are [R]diminished and brought
low
Through oppression, affliction and
sorrow, 2 Kin. 10:32
40 He pours contempt on princes,
And causes them to wander in the
wilderness *where there is* no way;
41 [R]Yet He sets the poor on high, far from
affliction, 1 Sam. 2:8
And makes *their* families like a flock.
42 The righteous see *it* and rejoice,
And all iniquity stops its mouth.

43 [R]Whoever *is* wise will observe these
things,
And they will understand the
lovingkindness of the LORD. Jer. 9:12

PSALM 108

Awake Early and Praise the Lord

A Song. A Psalm of David.

O [R]GOD, my heart is steadfast;
I will sing and give praise, even with
my glory. Ps. 57:7–11
2 [R]Awake, lute and harp!
I will awaken the dawn. Ps. 57:8–11
3 I will praise You, O LORD, among the
peoples,
And I will sing praises to You among
the nations.
4 For Your mercy *is* great above the
[T]heavens, *skies*
And Your truth *reaches* to the clouds.

5 Be exalted, O God, above the heavens,
And Your glory above all the earth;
6 [R]That Your beloved may be delivered,
Save *with* Your right hand, and [T]hear
me. Ps. 60:5–12 • Lit. *answer*

7 God has spoken in His holiness:
"I will rejoice;
I will divide Shechem
And measure out the Valley of Succoth.
8 Gilead *is* Mine;
Manasseh *is* Mine;
Ephraim also *is* the [T]helmet for My
head;
Judah *is* My lawgiver. Lit. *protection*
9 Moab *is* My washpot;
Over Edom I will cast My shoe;
Over Philistia I will triumph."

10 [R]Who will bring me into the strong city?
Who will lead me to Edom? Ps. 60:9
11 *Is it* not You, O God, *who* cast us off?
And You, O God, *who* did not go out
with our armies?
12 Give us help from trouble,
For vain *is* the help of man.
13 [R]Through God we will do valiantly,
For *it is* He *who* shall tread down our
enemies. Ps. 60:12

PSALM 109

Song of the Slandered

To the Chief Musician. A Psalm of David.

DO[R] not keep silent,
O God of my praise! Ps. 83:1
2 For the mouth of the wicked and the
mouth of the deceitful
Have opened against me;
They have spoken against me with a
[R]lying tongue. Ps. 27:12
3 They have also surrounded me with
words of hatred,
And fought against me [R]without a
cause. John 15:23–25☆
4 In return for my love they are my
accusers,
But I *give myself to* prayer.
5 Thus [R]they have rewarded me evil for
good,
And hatred for my love. Ps. 35:7, 12; 38:20

6 Set a wicked man over him,
And let [R]an [T]accuser stand at his right
hand. Zech. 3:1 • Heb. *Satan*
7 When he is judged, let him be found
guilty,
And [R]let his prayer become sin. [Prov. 28:9]
8 Let his days be [R]few, [Ps. 55:23]
And [R]let another take his office. Acts 1:20 ☆
9 [R]Let his children be fatherless,
And his wife a widow. Ex. 22:24
10 Let his children [T]continually be
vagabonds, and beg;
Let them seek *their bread* also from
their desolate places. *wander continuously*
11 Let the creditor seize all that he has,
And let strangers plunder his labor.
12 Let there be none to extend mercy to
him,
Nor let there be any to favor his
fatherless children.
13 Let his posterity be [T]cut off, *destroyed*
And in the generation following let
their [R]name be blotted out. Prov. 10:7

14 [R]Let the iniquity of his fathers be
remembered before the LORD,
And let not the sin of his mother [R]be
blotted out. [Ex. 20:5] • Neh. 4:5
15 Let them be continually before the
LORD,
That He may [R]cut off the memory of
them from the earth; Job 18:17
16 Because he did not remember to show
mercy,
But persecuted the poor and needy
man,
That he might even slay the [R]broken in
heart. [Ps. 34:18]
17 [R]As he loved cursing, so let it come to
him;
As he did not delight in blessing, so let
it be far from him. Prov. 14:14
18 As he clothed himself with cursing as
with his garment,
So let it [R]enter his body like water,
And like oil into his bones. Num. 5:22
19 Let it be to him like the garment which
covers him,
And for a belt with which he girds
himself continually.
20 *Let* this *be* the LORD's reward to my
accusers,
And to those who speak evil against my
person.

21 But You, O GOD the Lord,
Deal with me for Your name's sake;
Because Your mercy *is* good, deliver
me.
22 For I *am* poor and needy,
And my heart is wounded within me.
23 I am gone [R]like a shadow when it
lengthens;
I am shaken off like a locust. Ps. 102:11
24 My [R]knees are weak through fasting,
And my flesh is feeble from lack of
fatness. Heb. 12:12
25 I also have become [R]a reproach to
them;
When they look at me, [R]they shake
their heads. Ps. 22:7 • Matt. 27:39

26 Help me, O LORD my God!
Oh, save me according to Your mercy,
27 [R]That they may know that this *is* Your
hand—
That You, LORD, have done it! Job 37:7
28 Let them curse, but You bless;
When they arise, let them be ashamed,
But let [R]Your servant rejoice. Is. 65:14
29 Let my accusers be clothed with shame,
And let them cover themselves with
their own disgrace as with a mantle.

30 I will greatly praise the LORD with my
mouth;
Yes, [R]I will praise Him among the
multitude. Ps. 35:18; 111:1
31 For [R]He shall stand at the right hand of
the poor,
To save *him* from those [T]who condemn
him. [Ps. 16:8] • Lit. *judging his soul*

PSALM 110

The Coming of the Priest-King-Judge

A Psalm of David.

THE [R]LORD said to my Lord,
"Sit at My right hand,
Till I make Your enemies Your
[R]footstool." Matt. 22:44 ☆ • [1 Cor. 15:25]
2 The LORD shall send the rod of Your
strength [R]out of Zion. [Rom. 11:26, 27]
Rule in the midst of Your enemies!

3 [R]Your people *shall be* volunteers
In the day of Your power;
[R]In the beauties of holiness, from the
womb of the morning, Judg. 5:2 • Ps. 96:9
You have the dew of Your youth.
4 The LORD has sworn
And [R]will not relent, [Num. 23:19]
"You *are* a [R]priest forever [Zech. 6:13]
According to the order of
[R]Melchizedek." [Heb. 5:6,10; 6:20] ☆

5 The Lord *is* [R]at Your right hand;
He shall [T]execute kings in the day of
His wrath. [Ps. 16:8] • Lit. *break kings in pieces*
6 He shall judge among the nations,
He shall fill *the places* with dead bodies,
[R]He shall [T]execute the heads of many
countries. Ps. 68:21 • Lit. *break in pieces*

LORD, Lord, lord

Having trounced the critical scribes and Pharisees by successfully answering their hard questions, Jesus posed some Bible questions of His own. He asked, "What do you think about the Christ? Whose Son is He?" That was an easy one.

When they correctly answered, "*The Son* of David," He asked a second, much harder question: "How then does David in the Spirit call Him *'Lord,'* saying: 'The LORD said to my Lord, "Sit at my right hand, till I make Your enemies Your footstools" '? If David then calls Him 'Lord,' how is He his Son?" (Matt. 22:42–45). They were stumped, as we would be, if we didn't have the New Testament to enlighten us.

This one short passage illustrates nicely the three meanings of lordship indicated by the three varieties of capitalization of the words in the title to this word study. The KJV tradition (followed by many modern Bibles) is to use all capitals in the Old Testament when "LORD" represents the personal name of the one true God, Jehovah or Yahweh. The NKJV goes a step further and also does this in the New Testament (as in v. 44), but only where it is a direct quotation from the Old Testament and the original Hebrew reads the sacred name of *YHWH*.

The *Lord* to whom Jehovah was speaking is capitalized to indicate dignity and deity. Whoever is meant, He is David's Lord and Master, yet He is seen as separate from YHWH in some way. Also, David himself is a lord, and, as king, is so called in several passages. For example, the woman of Tekoa addressed him as "my lord, O king" in 2 Samuel 14:9. These variations in the English text are not arbitrary, but represent differences in the Hebrew original.

LORD (*YHWH*)

For a fuller treatment of this name, the sacred tetragrammaton, see the word study on page 71.

Lord (*'Adôn*)

In many passages, especially in the Psalms, *'Adôn* means "Master" or "Lord" when applied to Deity.

For example, if you look closely at Psalm 8, you will notice the capitalization. "O LORD, our Lord" means "O Jehovah [Yahweh] our Lord [Master]." In Psalm 136:3, we are told to "give thanks to the Lord of lords [*'adōnê hā 'adōnîm*]." As so often when *Lord* refers to God, the plural form is used (even the *'adōnê* part is plural, which refers to one Person, God).

When the personal suffix for "my" in Hebrew is put on *'adōn*, it is generally *'adōnî* (singular) for men and *'Adōnai* (plural) for God. However, in Psalm 110:1, the singular form is used. Perhaps this is to stress the dual nature of our Lord: He is both God and Man. As God He is David's Lord, but as Man He is David's Son. Also, if the ancient text had used a plural for "my Lord," it might have seemed to be a copyist's error, since it would have Deity speaking to Deity before the revelation of the three Persons of the Trinity had been clearly made to humankind. However, there are Old Testament verses that certainly demand plurality of Persons in the Godhead (e.g., Gen. 1:26; 11:7; Prov. 30:4; Zech. 12:10).

lord (*'adōn*)

We use lowercase letters in the English Bible when the word *lord* refers to a mortal man. We have already noticed that David was called "lord." Other rulers so designated in the Old Testament include the Pharaoh (Gen. 40:1) and Saul (1 Sam. 16:16). Other important leaders called *'adōn* include Joseph (Gen. 42:10), Eli the priest (1 Sam. 1:15), David's commander Joab (2 Sam. 11:9), and the prophet Elijah (1 Kin. 18:7).

The concept of human "lords" is easier for Britons than for Americans to relate to, since Britain still has lords and the House of Lords. Even ordinary people were called by this title of respect, however: Abraham by Sarah (Gen. 18:12) and by his servant Eliezer (Gen. 24, many times). Ruth also called Boaz "my lord" (*'adōnî*) in Ruth 2:13.

7 He shall drink of the brook by the
wayside;
Therefore He shall lift up the head.

PSALM 111

Praise for God's Tender Care

PRAISE[T] the LORD!

I will [R]praise the LORD with *my* whole
heart,
In the assembly of the upright and *in*
the congregation. Heb. *Hallelujah* • Ps. 35:18

2 [R]The works of the LORD *are* great,
[R]Studied by all who have pleasure in
them. Ps. 92:5 • Ps. 143:5
3 His work *is* honorable and glorious,
And His righteousness endures forever.
4 He has made His wonderful works to be
remembered;
[R]The LORD *is* gracious and full of
compassion. [Ps. 86:5]
5 He has given food to those who fear
Him;
He will ever be mindful of His covenant.
6 He has declared to His people the power
of His works,
In giving them the [T]heritage of the
nations. *inheritance*

7 The works of His hands *are* [R]verity[T] and
justice;
All His precepts *are* sure. [Rev. 15:3] • *truth*
8 They stand fast forever and ever,
And are done in truth and uprightness.
9 [R]He has sent redemption to His people;
He has commanded His covenant
forever: Luke 1:68
[R]Holy and awesome *is* His name. Luke 1:49

10 [R]The fear of the LORD *is* the beginning of
wisdom;
A good understanding have all those
who do *His commandments.*
His praise endures forever. Eccl. 12:13

PSALM 112

The Blessings of Those Who Fear God

PRAISE[T] the LORD!

Blessed *is* the man *who* fears the LORD,
Who [R]delights greatly in His
commandments. Heb. *Hallelujah* • Ps. 128:1

2 [R]His descendants will be mighty on
earth;
The generation of the upright will be
blessed. [Ps. 102:28]
3 Wealth and riches *will be* in his house,
And his righteousness endures forever.
4 [R]Unto the upright there arises light in
the darkness;
He is gracious, and full of compassion,
and righteous. Job 11:17
5 [R]A good man deals graciously and lends;
He will guide his affairs [R]with
discretion. [Luke 6:35] • [Eph. 5:15]
6 Surely he will never be shaken;
[R]The righteous will be in everlasting
remembrance. Prov. 10:7
7 [R]He will not be afraid of evil tidings;
His heart is steadfast, trusting in the
LORD. [Prov. 1:33]
8 His [R]heart *is* established;
[R]He will not be afraid,
Until he [R]sees *his desire* upon his
enemies. Heb. 13:9 • Prov. 1:33; 3:24 • Ps. 59:10

9 He has dispersed abroad,
He has given to the poor;
His righteousness endures forever;
His horn will be exalted with honor.
10 The wicked will see *it* and be grieved;
He will gnash his teeth and melt away;
The desire of the wicked shall perish.

PSALM 113

The Condescending Grace of God

PRAISE[T] the LORD! Heb. *Hallelujah*

Praise, O servants of the LORD,
Praise the name of the LORD!
2 Blessed be the name of the LORD
From this time forth and forevermore!
3 [R]From the rising of the sun to its going
down Is. 59:19
The LORD's name *is* to be praised.

4 The LORD *is* high above all nations,
And His glory above the heavens.
5 [R]Who *is* like the LORD our God,
Who dwells on high, [Is. 57:15]
6 [R]Who humbles Himself to behold
The things that are in the heavens and
in the earth? [Ps. 11:4]

7 [R]He raises the poor out of the dust,
And lifts the [R]needy out of the ash
heap, 1 Sam. 2:8 • Ps. 72:12
8 That He may [R]seat *him* with princes—
With the princes of His people. [Job 36:7]
9 [R]He grants the [T]barren woman a home,
Like a joyful mother of children.

Praise the LORD! 1 Sam. 2:5 • *childless*

PSALM 114

In Praise for the Exodus

WHEN Israel went out of Egypt,
The house of Jacob from a people [T]of
strange language, *who spoke unintelligibly*

2 [R]Judah became His sanctuary,
And Israel His dominion. Ex. 6:7; 19:6

3 [R]The sea saw *it* and fled;
[R]Jordan turned back. Ex. 14:21 • Josh. 3:13–16
4 [R]The mountains skipped like rams,
The little hills like lambs. Ps. 29:6
5 [R]What ails you, O sea, that you fled?
O Jordan, *that* you turned back? Hab. 3:8
6 O mountains, *that* you skipped like rams?
O little hills, like lambs?

7 Tremble, O earth, at the presence of the Lord,
At the presence of the God of Jacob,
8 [R]Who turned the rock *into* a pool of water, Ex. 17:6
The flint into a fountain of waters.

PSALM 115

To God Alone Be the Glory

NOT [R]unto us, O LORD, not unto us,
But to Your name give glory,
Because of Your mercy,
And because of Your truth. [Is. 48:11]
2 Why should the [T]Gentiles say, *nations*
[R]"Where now *is* their God?" Ps. 42:3, 10

3 [R]But our God *is* in heaven; [1 Chr. 16:26]
He does whatever He pleases.
4 [R]Their idols *are* silver and gold,
The work of men's hands. Jer. 10:3
5 They have mouths, but they do not speak;
Eyes they have, but they do not see;
6 They have ears, but they do not hear;
Noses they have, but they do not smell;
7 They have hands, but they do not handle;
Feet they have, but they do not walk;
Nor do they mutter through their throat.
8 Those who make them are like them;
So is everyone who trusts in them.

9 [R]O Israel, trust in the LORD; Ps. 118:2, 3
[R]He *is* their help and their shield. Ps. 33:20
10 O house of Aaron, trust in the LORD;
He *is* their help and their shield.
11 You who fear the LORD, trust in the LORD;
He *is* their help and their shield.

12 The LORD [T]has been mindful of *us;*
He will bless *us;* *has remembered us*
He will bless the house of Israel;
He will bless the house of Aaron.
13 [R]He will bless those who fear the LORD,
Both small and great. Ps. 128:1, 4

14 May the LORD give you increase more and more,
You and your children.
15 *May* you *be* blessed by the LORD,
[R]Who made heaven and earth. Gen. 1:1

16 The heaven, *even* the heavens, *are* the LORD's;
But the earth He has given to the children of men.
17 The dead do not praise the LORD,
Nor any who go down into silence.
18 [R]But we will bless the LORD
From this time forth and forevermore.

Praise the LORD! Dan. 2:20

PSALM 116

Love the Lord for What He Has Done

I [R]LOVE the LORD, because He has heard
My voice *and* my supplications. Ps. 18:1
2 Because He has inclined His ear to me,
Therefore I will call *upon Him* as long as I live.

3 The [T]pains of death encompassed me,
And the [T]pangs of Sheol [T]laid hold of me; Lit. *cords* • *distresses* • Lit. *found me*
I found trouble and sorrow.
4 Then I called upon the name of the LORD:
"O LORD, I implore You, deliver my soul!"

5 Gracious *is* the LORD, and [R]righteous;
Yes, our God *is* merciful. [Ezra 9:15]
6 The LORD preserves the simple;
I was brought low, and He saved me.
7 Return to your [R]rest, O my soul,
For [R]the LORD has dealt bountifully with you. [Jer. 6:16] • Ps. 13:6

8 [R]For You have delivered my soul from death,
My eyes from tears,
And my feet from falling. Ps. 56:13
9 I will walk before the LORD
[R]In the land of the living. Ps. 27:13
10 [R]I believed, therefore I spoke,
"I am greatly afflicted." 2 Cor. 4:13
11 [R]I said in my haste,
[R]"All men *are* liars." Ps. 31:22 • Rom. 3:4

12 What shall I render to the LORD
For all His benefits toward me?
13 I will take up the cup of salvation,
And call upon the name of the LORD.
14 [R]I will pay my vows to the LORD Ps. 116:18
Now in the presence of all His people.

15 [R]Precious in the sight of the LORD
Is the death of His saints. Ps. 72:14

16 O LORD, truly [R]I *am* Your servant;
I *am* Your servant, [R]the son of Your
maidservant; Ps. 119:125; 143:12 • Ps. 86:16
You have loosed my bonds.
17 I will offer to You [R]the sacrifice of
thanksgiving,
And will call upon the name of the
LORD. Lev. 7:12

18 I will pay my vows to the LORD
Now in the presence of all His people,
19 In the [R]courts of the LORD's house,
In the midst of you, O Jerusalem.

[T]Praise the LORD! Ps. 96:8 • Heb. *Hallelujah*

PSALM 117

The Praise of All Peoples

OH, praise the LORD, all you Gentiles!
[T]Laud Him, all you peoples! *Praise*
2 For His merciful kindness is great
toward us,
And [R]the truth of the LORD *endures*
forever.

Praise the LORD! [Ps. 100:5]

PSALM 118

Better to Trust God than Man

OH, [R]give thanks to the LORD, for *He is*
good! 1 Chr. 16:8, 34
Because His mercy *endures* forever.

2 [R]Let Israel now say,
"His mercy *endures* forever." [Ps. 115:9]
3 Let the house of Aaron now say,
"His mercy *endures* forever."
4 Let those who fear the LORD now say,
"His mercy *endures* forever."

5 [R]I called on the LORD in distress;
The LORD answered me *and* [R]*set me* in
a broad place. Ps. 120:1 • Ps. 18:19
6 [R]The LORD *is* on my side;
I will not fear.
What can man do to me? Ps. 27:1; 56:9
7 [R]The LORD is for me among those who
help me;
Therefore [R]I shall see *my desire* on
those who hate me. Ps. 54:4 • Ps. 59:10
8 [R]*It is* better to trust in the LORD
Than to put confidence in man. Ps. 40:4
9 [R]*It is* better to trust in the LORD Ps. 146:3
Than to put confidence in princes.

10 All nations surrounded me,
But in the name of the LORD I will
destroy them.
11 They [R]surrounded me,
Yes, they surrounded me;
But in the name of the LORD I will
destroy them. Ps. 88:17
12 They surrounded me [R]like bees;
They were quenched [R]like a fire of
thorns; Deut. 1:44 • Nah. 1:10
For in the name of the LORD I will
[T]destroy them. *cut them off*
13 You pushed me violently, that I might
fall,
But the LORD helped me.
14 [R]The LORD *is* my strength and song,
And He has become my salvation. Ex. 15:2

15 The voice of rejoicing and salvation
Is in the tents of the righteous;
The right hand of the LORD does
valiantly.
16 [R]The right hand of the LORD is exalted;
The right hand of the LORD does
valiantly. Ex. 15:6
17 [R]I shall not die, but live, Hab. 1:12
And declare the works of the LORD.
18 The LORD has chastened me severely,
But He has not given me over to death.

19 [R]Open to me the gates of righteousness;
I will go through them,
And I will praise the LORD. Is. 26:2
20 [R]This is the gate of the LORD,
[R]Through which the righteous shall
enter. Ps. 24:7 • Is. 35:8

21 I will praise You,
For You have [R]answered me,
And have become my salvation. Ps. 116:1

22 The stone *which* the builders rejected
Has become the chief cornerstone.
23 This [T]was the LORD's doing;
It *is* marvelous in our eyes. *is from the LORD*
24 This *is* the day *which* the LORD has
made;
We will rejoice and be glad in it.

25 Save now, I pray, O LORD;
O LORD, I pray, send now prosperity.
26 [R]Blessed *is* he who comes in the name of
the LORD!
We have blessed you from the house of
the LORD. Mark 11:9; Luke 19:38☆
27 God *is* the LORD,
And He has given us [R]light;
Bind the sacrifice with cords to the
horns of the altar. [1 Pet. 2:9]
28 You *are* my God, and I will praise You;
[R]*You are* my God, I will exalt You. Is. 25:1

29 Oh, give thanks to the LORD, for *He is*
good!
For His mercy *endures* forever.

PSALM 119

An Acrostic in Praise of the Scriptures

א ALEPH

BLESSED *are* the undefiled in the way,
Who walk in the law of the LORD!
2 Blessed *are* those who keep His testimonies,
Who seek Him with the whole heart!
3 [R]They also do no iniquity;
They walk in His ways. [1 John 3:9; 5:18]
4 You have commanded *us*
To keep Your precepts diligently.
5 Oh, that my ways were directed
To keep Your statutes!
6 [R]Then I would not be ashamed,
When I look into all Your commandments. Job 22:26
7 I will praise You with uprightness of heart,
When I learn Your righteous judgments.
8 I will keep Your statutes;
Oh, do not forsake me utterly!

ב BETH

9 How can a young man cleanse his way?
By taking heed according to Your word.
10 With my whole heart I have [R]sought You;
Oh, let me not wander from Your commandments! 2 Chr. 15:15
11 Your word I have hidden in my heart,
That I might not sin against You.
12 Blessed *are* You, O LORD!
Teach me Your statutes.
13 With my lips I have [R]declared Ps. 34:11
All the judgments of Your mouth.
14 I have rejoiced in the way of Your testimonies,
As *much as* in all riches.
15 I will meditate on Your precepts,
And [T]contemplate Your ways. *look into*
16 I will [R]delight myself in Your statutes;
I will not forget Your word. Ps. 1:2

ג GIMEL

17 Deal bountifully with Your servant,
That I may live and keep Your word.
18 Open my eyes, that I may see
Wondrous things from Your law.
19 [R]I *am* a stranger in the earth;
Do not hide Your commandments from me. Heb. 11:13
20 My soul [T]breaks with longing *is crushed*
For Your judgments at all times.
21 You rebuke the proud—the cursed,
Who stray from Your commandments.
22 [R]Remove from me reproach and contempt,
For I have kept Your testimonies. Ps. 39:8
23 Princes also sit *and* speak against me,
But Your servant meditates on Your statutes.
24 Your testimonies also *are* my delight
And my counselors.

ד DALETH

25 [R]My soul clings to the dust; Ps. 44:25
Revive me according to Your word.
26 I have declared my ways, and You answered me;
[R]Teach me Your statutes. Ps. 25:4; 27:11
27 Make me understand the way of Your precepts;
So [R]shall I meditate on Your wondrous works. Ps. 145:5, 6
28 My soul [T]melts from heaviness; Lit. *drops*
Strengthen me according to Your word.
29 Remove from me the way of lying,
And grant me Your law graciously.

119:9 God's Word Cleanses—One of the pieces of furniture in the Old Testament tabernacle was called the bronze laver (Page 111—Ex. 38:8). It consisted of a huge upright bronze bowl filled with water, resting upon a pedestal. The priests would often stop at this laver and wash. The Word of God may be thought of in terms of that laver, for it too has the power to cleanse. The Old Testament laver could only remove the physical dirt from human hands, but the Scriptures possess the ability to take away our moral filth (Page 1479—1 Pet. 1:22).

"If we confess our sins, He is faithful and just to forgive us *our* sins and to cleanse us from all unrighteousness" (Page 1494—1 John 1:9). What areas of my life can the Bible cleanse?

It can cleanse me from wrong thoughts. Sometimes we are tempted to think critically of others; God's Word can prevent this (Page 625—Ps. 1:2). On other occasions fearful thoughts may race through our minds; the Scriptures will prevent this also (Page 252—Josh. 1:8). In fact, the Bible will establish our total thought-life if we but allow it to do so (Page 1402—Phil. 4:8, 9; Page 1487—2 Pet. 1:5–10).

It can cleanse me from wrong words. Of all the Bible authors, James seems to be God's expert on the sins of the human tongue. In the first chapter of his book, he deals with this very thing and shows the absolute necessity of dependence upon the Scriptures to keep our words true (Page 1468—James 1:22–26). See also Psalm 119:172.

It can cleanse me from wrong actions. Jesus promised us this would be the case: "You are already clean because of the word which I have spoken to you" (Page 1258—John 15:3).

Finally, God's Word will keep us from wrong thoughts, words, and actions; or else wrong thoughts, words, and actions will keep us from God's Word.

Now turn to Page 1249—John 8:31: God's Word Confirms.

THE WORD OF THE LORD

In nearly every verse of Psalm 119, the author magnifies God's word. Following is a study of seven of the words he uses to represent God's word, in their order of appearance.

Law (*tôrah*)
Law (*tôrah*) occurs about 220 times in the Old Testament. It is perhaps unfortunate that "law" was chosen as the main translation of *tôrah.* The word is much broader than the legal implications that our word *law* might imply. The Jews refer to the first five books of the Old Testament as "the Torah." There is much more than legislation in these books, even in Exodus and Leviticus.

The basic meaning of *tôrah* is "teaching" or "instruction." Because God loves humankind, He has given a body of teaching and laws so that we can know what He expects from us and how we should live. "The [*tôrah*] of the LORD *is* perfect" (Ps. 19:7).

Testimony (*'ēdût*)
Testimony (*'ēdût,* v. 2) comes from the verb *'ûd,* "to bear witness," and is used nine times in Psalm 119. The word suggests not only corroboration by testimony, but sometimes includes a warning, as well. It is used in the Old Testament only with reference to God. His Word is His own testimony to Himself and, as such, should be accepted and acted upon.

Precepts (*piqqûdîm*)
Precepts (*piqqûdîm,* v. 4) always appears in the plural; and its twenty-four occurrences are all in Psalms, twenty-one in Psalm 119 alone. The noun is derived from the verb *pāqad* ("number," "reckon," "visit," "appoint," or "punish"). The precepts of God are those responsibilities that He has appointed for His people.

Statute (*hōq*)
Statute (*hōq,* v. 5) occurs 128 times and comes from the verb *hāqaq,* "engrave" or "write." In ancient times, statutes were engraved on metal or stone so that people could read and keep them. *Hōq* is a general term for laws imposed by God or man. The most common Hebrew word to be used with *hōq* is *shāmar* ("keep"). God's statutes are meant to be kept.

Another meaning of this word is "custom," such as in the custom in ancient Israel of women commemorating Jephthah's daughter (Judg. 11:39, 40).

Commandment (*mitzwah*)
Commandment (mitzwah, v. 6) is used to describe "The Ten Commandments" (Ex. 24:12). The noun is derived from the verb *tsāwah,* to "command" or "charge." God's commands are an expression of His Person and nature. Psalm 119 teaches that these revelations of God's will are "faithful" or reliable (v. 86), "truth" (v. 151), and "righteousness" (v. 172). Psalm 19:8 says they are also "pure." If we really love our Lord, we will keep His commandments, and they will not be burdensome.

Judgment (*mishpāt*)
Judgment (mishpāt, v. 7) is derived from the verb *shāphat,* "judge" or "govern," and occurs about four hundred times in the Old Testament, sixteen times in Psalm 119 alone. The general idea is one of justice, or specific ordinances to promote justice. There are many distinct usages of the noun in both secular and religious law. Each specific ordinance of the Pentateuch is called a *mishpāt* (Lev. 9:16; Deut. 33:21, e.g.).

"The LORD *is* a God of justice" (Is. 30:18) and "loves justice" (Ps. 37:28). His "judgments *are* a great deep" (Ps. 36:6). Because God is just in His judgments, so should we His people be.

Word (*dābār*)
Word (*dābār,* v. 9) is one of the great words of the Bible. It is such an idiomatic word in the Old Testament that the King James translators needed eighty-five different English words to translate it. The noun comes from the verb "to say" or "speak." The main idea is that whatever God says is His word.

30 I have chosen the way of truth;
Your judgments I have laid *before me.*
31 I cling to Your testimonies;
O LORD, do not put me to shame!
32 I will run in the way of Your
commandments,
For You shall [R]enlarge my heart. Is. 60:5

ה HE

33 [R]Teach me, O LORD, the way of Your
statutes,
And I shall keep it *to* the end. [Rev. 2:26]
34 [R]Give me understanding, and I shall keep
Your law;
Indeed, I shall observe it with *my* whole
heart. [Prov. 2:6]
35 Make me walk in the path of Your
commandments,
For I delight in it.
36 Incline my heart to Your testimonies,
And not to covetousness.
37 [R]Turn away my eyes from [R]looking at
worthless things, Is. 33:15 • Prov. 23:5
And revive me in Your way.
38 [R]Establish Your word to Your servant,
Who *is devoted* to fearing You. 2 Sam. 7:25
39 Turn away my reproach which I dread,
For Your judgments *are* good.
40 Behold, I long for Your precepts;
Revive me in Your righteousness.

ו WAW

41 Let Your mercies come also to me,
O LORD—
Your salvation according to Your word.
42 So shall I have an answer for him who
[T]reproaches me,
For I trust in Your word. *taunts*
43 And take not the word of truth utterly
out of my mouth,
For I have hoped in Your ordinances.
44 So shall I keep Your law continually,
Forever and ever.
45 And I will walk [T]at liberty,
For I seek Your precepts. *in a wide place*
46 [R]I will speak of Your testimonies also
before kings,
And will not be ashamed. Matt. 10:18
47 And I will delight myself in Your
commandments,
Which I love.
48 My hands also I will lift up to Your
commandments,
Which I love,
And I will meditate on Your statutes.

ז ZAYIN

49 Remember the word to Your servant,
Upon which You have caused me to
hope.
50 This *is* my comfort in my affliction,
For Your word has given me life.
51 The proud have me in great derision,
Yet I do not turn aside from Your law.
52 I remembered Your judgments of old,
O LORD,
And have comforted myself.
53 [R]Indignation has taken hold of me
Because of the wicked, who forsake
Your law. Ezra 9:3
54 Your statutes have been my songs
In the house of my pilgrimage.
55 [R]I remember Your name in the night,
O LORD,
And I keep Your law. Ps. 63:6
56 This has become mine,
Because I kept Your precepts.

ח HETH

57 [R]*You are* my portion, O LORD;
I have said that I would keep Your
words. Jer. 10:16
58 I entreated Your favor with *my* whole
heart;
Be merciful to me according to Your
word.
59 I [R]thought about my ways,
And turned my feet to Your
testimonies. Luke 15:17
60 I made haste, and did not delay
To keep Your commandments.
61 The cords of the wicked have bound
me,
But I have not forgotten Your law.
62 [R]At midnight I will rise to give thanks to
You, Acts 16:25
Because of Your righteous judgments.
63 I *am* a companion of all *those* who fear
You,
And of those who keep Your precepts.
64 [R]The earth, O LORD, is full of Your
mercy;
Teach me Your statutes. Ps. 33:5

ט TETH

65 You have dealt well with Your servant,
O LORD, according to Your word.
66 Teach me good judgment and
[R]knowledge, Phil. 1:9
For I believe Your commandments.
67 Before I was [R]afflicted I went astray,
But now I keep Your word. [Heb. 12:5-11]
68 You *are* [R]good, and do good;
Teach me Your statutes. [Matt. 19:17]
69 The proud have [R]forged[T] a lie against
me, Job 13:4 • Lit. *smeared me with a lie*
But I will keep Your precepts with *my*
whole heart.
70 Their heart is [T]as fat as grease,
But I delight in Your law. Insensible

71 *It is* good for me that I have been
afflicted,
That I may learn Your statutes.
72 [R]The law of Your mouth *is* better to me
Than thousands of *shekels of* gold and
silver. Ps. 19:10

 י YOD

73 [R]Your hands have made me and
fashioned me; Job 10:8; 31:15
Give me understanding, that I may
learn Your commandments.
74 [R]Those who fear You will be glad when
they see me, Ps. 34:2
Because I have hoped in Your word.
75 I know, O LORD, [R]that Your judgments
are [T]right,
And *that* in faithfulness You have
afflicted me. [Heb. 12:10] • Lit. *righteous*
76 Let, I pray, Your merciful kindness be
for my comfort,
According to Your word to Your
servant.
77 Let Your tender mercies come to me,
that I may live;
For Your law *is* my delight.
78 Let the proud [R]be ashamed, Ps. 25:3
For they treated me wrongfully with
falsehood;
But I will meditate on Your precepts.
79 Let those who fear You turn to me,
Those who know Your testimonies.
80 Let my heart be blameless regarding
Your statutes,
That I may not be ashamed.

כ KAPH

81 [R]My soul faints for Your salvation,
But I hope in Your word. Ps. 73:26; 84:2
82 My eyes fail *from seeking* Your word,
Saying, "When will You comfort me?"
83 For [R]I have become like a wineskin in
smoke, Job 30:30
Yet I do not forget Your statutes.
84 [R]How many *are* the days of Your
servant? Ps. 39:4
[R]When will You execute judgment on
those who persecute me? Rev. 6:10
85 [R]The proud have dug pits for me, Ps. 35:7
Which *is* not according to Your law.
86 All Your commandments *are* faithful;
They persecute me [R]wrongfully;
Help me! Ps. 35:19
87 They almost made an end of me on
earth,
But I did not forsake Your precepts.
88 Revive me according to Your
lovingkindness,
So that I may keep the testimony of
Your mouth.

ל LAMED

89 [R]Forever, O LORD, Matt. 24:35
Your word is settled in heaven.
90 Your faithfulness *endures* to all
generations;
You established the earth, and it
[T]abides. Lit. *stands*
91 They continue this day according to
[R]Your ordinances,
For all *are* Your servants. Jer. 33:25
92 Unless Your law *had been* my delight,
I would then have perished in my
affliction.
93 I will never forget Your precepts,
For by them You have given me life.
94 I *am* Yours, save me;
For I have sought Your precepts.
95 The wicked wait for me to destroy me,
But I will consider Your testimonies.
96 [R]I have seen the consummation of all
perfection,
But Your commandment *is* exceedingly
broad. Matt. 5:18

מ MEM

97 Oh, how I love Your law!
[R]It *is* my meditation all the day. Ps. 1:2
98 You, through Your commandments,
make me [R]wiser than my enemies;
For they *are* ever with me. Deut. 4:6
99 I have more understanding than all my
teachers,
[R]For Your testimonies *are* my
meditation. [2 Tim. 3:15]
100 I understand more than the [T]ancients,
Because I keep Your precepts. *aged*
101 I have restrained my feet from every
evil way,
That I may keep Your word.
102 I have not departed from Your
judgments,
For You Yourself have taught me.
103 How sweet are Your words to my taste,
Sweeter than honey to my mouth!
104 Through Your precepts I get
understanding;
Therefore I hate every false way.

נ NUN

105 [R]Your word *is* a lamp to my feet
And a light to my path. Prov. 6:23
106 [R]I have sworn and confirmed Neh. 10:29
That I will keep Your righteous
judgments.
107 I am afflicted very much;
Revive me, O LORD, according to Your
word.
108 Accept, I pray, [R]the freewill offerings of
my mouth, O LORD,
And teach me Your judgments. Hos. 14:2
109 My life *is* continually [T]in my hand,
Yet I do not forget Your law. In danger

110 [R]The wicked have laid a snare for me,
Yet I have not strayed from Your
precepts. Ps. 140:5
111 [R]Your testimonies I have taken as a
[T]heritage forever, Deut. 33:4 • *inheritance*
For they *are* the rejoicing of my heart.
112 I have inclined my heart to perform
Your statutes
Forever, to the very end.

ס SAMEK

113 I hate the double-minded,
But I love Your law.
114 [R]You *are* my hiding place and my shield;
I hope in Your word. [Ps. 32:7]
115 [R]Depart from me, you evildoers, Matt. 7:23
For I will keep the commandments of
my God!
116 Uphold me according to Your word,
that I may live;
And do not let me [R]be ashamed of my
hope. [Rom. 5:5; 9:33; 10:11]
117 [T]Hold me up, and I shall be safe,
And I shall observe Your statutes
continually. *Uphold me*
118 You reject all those who stray from
Your statutes,
For their deceit *is* falsehood.
119 You put away all the wicked of the
earth [R]*like* dross; Ezek. 22:18, 19
Therefore I love Your testimonies.
120 My flesh trembles for fear of You,
And I am afraid of Your judgments.

ע AYIN

121 I have done justice and righteousness;
Do not leave me to my oppressors.
122 Be surety for Your servant for good;
Do not let the proud oppress me.
123 My eyes fail *from seeking* Your
salvation
And Your righteous word.
124 Deal with Your servant according to
Your mercy,
And teach me Your statutes.
125 [R]I *am* Your servant; Ps. 116:16
Give me understanding,
That I may know Your testimonies.
126 *It is* time for *You* to act, O LORD,
For they have [T]regarded Your law as
void. *broken Your law*
127 Therefore I love Your commandments
More than gold, yes, than fine gold!
128 Therefore all *Your* precepts *concerning*
all *things*
I consider *to be* right;
I hate every false way.

פ PE

129 Your testimonies are wonderful;
Therefore my soul keeps them.
130 The entrance of Your words gives light;
It gives understanding to the simple.
131 I opened my mouth and [R]panted, Ps. 42:1
For I longed for Your commandments.
132 [R]Look upon me and be merciful to me,
[R]As Your custom *is* toward those who
love Your name. Ps. 106:4 • [2 Thess. 1:6]
133 [R]Direct my steps by Your word,
And [R]let no iniquity have dominion over
me. Ps. 17:5 • [Rom. 6:12]
134 [R]Redeem me from the oppression of
man, Luke 1:74
That I may keep Your precepts.
135 [R]Make Your face shine upon Your
servant, Ps. 4:6
And teach me Your statutes.
136 [R]Rivers of water run down from my
eyes, Jer. 9:1, 18; 14:17
Because *men* do not keep Your law.

צ TSADDE

137 [R]Righteous *are* You, O LORD, Neh. 9:33
And upright *are* Your judgments.
138 [R]Your testimonies, *which* You have
commanded, [Ps. 19:7–9]
Are righteous and very faithful.
139 [R]My zeal has [T]consumed me,
Because my enemies have forgotten
Your words. John 2:17 • *put an end to*
140 Your word *is* very [T]pure; Lit. *refined* or *tried*
Therefore Your servant loves it.
141 I *am* small and despised,
Yet I do not forget Your precepts.
142 Your righteousness *is* an everlasting
righteousness,
And Your law *is* [R]truth. [John 17:17]
143 Trouble and anguish have [T]overtaken
me, Lit. *found*
Yet Your commandments *are* my
delights.
144 The righteousness of Your testimonies
is everlasting;
Give me understanding, and I shall live.

ק QOPH

145 I cry out with *my* whole heart;
Hear me, O LORD!
I will keep Your statutes.
146 I cry out to You;
Save me, and I will keep Your
testimonies.
147 [R]I rise before the dawning of the
morning, Ps. 5:3
And cry for help;
I hope in Your word.
148 [R]My eyes are awake through the *night*
watches, Ps. 63:1, 6
That I may meditate on Your word.
149 Hear my voice according to Your
lovingkindness;

O LORD, revive me according to Your
justice.
150 They draw near who follow after
wickedness;
They are far from Your law.
151 You *are* [R]near, O LORD, [Ps. 145:18]
And all Your commandments *are* truth.
152 Concerning Your testimonies,
I have known of old that You have
founded them [R]forever. Luke 21:33

ר RESH

153 [R]Consider my affliction and deliver me,
For I do not forget Your law. Lam. 5:1
154 Plead my cause and redeem me;
Revive me according to Your word.
155 Salvation *is* far from the wicked,
For they do not seek Your statutes.
156 [T]Great *are* Your tender mercies, O LORD;
Revive me according to Your
judgments. Or *Many*
157 Many *are* my persecutors and my
enemies,
Yet I do not [R]turn from Your
testimonies. Ps. 44:18
158 I see the treacherous, and [R]am
disgusted, Ezek. 9:4
Because they do not keep Your word.
159 Consider how I love Your precepts;
Revive me, O LORD, according to Your
lovingkindness.
160 The entirety of Your word *is* truth,
And every one of Your righteous
judgments *endures* forever.

ש SHIN

161 [R]Princes persecute me without a cause,
But my heart stands in awe of Your
word. 1 Sam. 24:11; 26:18
162 I rejoice at Your word
As one who finds great treasure.
163 I hate and abhor lying,
But I love Your law.
164 Seven times a day I praise You,
Because of Your righteous judgments.
165 [R]Great peace have those who love Your
law, [Is. 26:3; 32:17]
And nothing causes them to stumble.
166 [R]LORD, I hope for Your salvation,
And I do Your commandments. Gen. 49:18
167 My soul keeps Your testimonies,
And I love them exceedingly.
168 I keep Your precepts and Your
testimonies,
[R]For all my ways *are* before You. Prov. 5:21

ת TAU

169 Let my cry come before You, O LORD;
[R]Give me understanding according to
Your word. Ps. 119:27, 144
170 Let my supplication come before You;
Deliver me according to Your word.
171 [R]My lips shall utter praise, Ps. 119:7
For You teach me Your statutes.
172 My tongue shall speak of Your word,
For all Your commandments *are*
righteousness.
173 Let Your hand become my help,
For I have chosen Your precepts.
174 [R]I long for Your salvation, O LORD,
And Your law *is* my delight. Ps. 119:166
175 Let my soul live, and it shall praise You;
And let Your judgments help me.
176 [R]I have gone astray like a lost sheep;
Seek Your servant, [Is. 53:6]
For I do not forget Your
commandments.

PSALM 120

A Cry in Distress

A Song of Ascents.

IN [R]my distress I cried to the LORD,
And He heard me. Jon. 2:2
2 Deliver my soul, O LORD, from lying lips
And from a deceitful tongue.

3 What shall be given to you,
Or what shall be done to you,
You false tongue?
4 Sharp arrows of the [T]warrior,
With coals of the broom tree! *mighty one*

5 Woe is me, that I sojourn in Meshech,
That I dwell among the tents of Kedar!
6 My soul has dwelt too long
With one who hates peace.
7 I *am for* peace;
But when I speak, they *are* for war.

PSALM 121

God Is Our Keeper

A Song of Ascents.

I [R]WILL lift up my eyes to the hills—
From whence comes my help? [Jer. 3:23]
2 [R]My help *comes* from the LORD,
Who made heaven and earth. [Ps. 124:8]

3 [R]He will not allow your foot to [T]be
moved; 1 Sam. 2:9 • *slip*
He who keeps you will not slumber.
4 Behold, He who keeps Israel
Shall neither slumber nor sleep.

5 The LORD *is* your [T]keeper;
The LORD *is* [R]your shade [R]at your right
hand. *protector* • Is. 25:4 • Ps. 16:8
6 [R]The sun shall not strike you by day,
Nor the moon by night. Is. 49:10

7 The LORD shall [T]preserve you from all
evil;
He shall [R]preserve your soul. *keep* • Ps. 41:2
8 The LORD shall [R]preserve[T] your going
out and your coming in
From this time forth, and even
forevermore. Deut. 28:6 • *keep*

PSALM 122

"Pray for the Peace of Jerusalem"

A Song of Ascents. Of David.

I WAS glad when they said to me,
"Let us go into the house of the LORD."
2 Our feet have been standing
Within your gates, O Jerusalem!

3 Jerusalem is built
As a city that is compact together,
4 [R]Where the tribes go up,
The tribes of the LORD,
[T]To the Testimony of Israel,
To give thanks to the name of the
LORD. Deut. 16:16 • Or *As a testimony to*
5 For thrones are set there for judgment,
The thrones of the house of David.

6 [R]Pray for the peace of Jerusalem:
"May they prosper who love you. Ps. 51:18
7 Peace be within your walls,
Prosperity within your palaces."
8 For the sake of my brethren and
companions,
I will now say, "Peace *be* within you."
9 Because of the house of the LORD our
God
I will [R]seek your good. Neh. 2:10

PSALM 123

Plea for the Mercy of God

A Song of Ascents.

UNTO You [R]I lift up my eyes, Ps. 121:1
O You who dwell in the heavens.
2 Behold, as the eyes of servants *look* to
the hand of their masters,
As the eyes of a maid to the hand of
her mistress,
[R]So our eyes *look* to the LORD our God,
Until He has mercy on us. Ps. 25:15

3 Have mercy on us, O LORD, have mercy
on us!
For we are exceedingly filled with
contempt.
4 Our soul is exceedingly filled
With the scorn of those who are at
ease,
With the contempt of the proud.

PSALM 124

God Is on Our Side

A Song of Ascents. Of David.

"IF it had not been the LORD who was
on our [R]side,"
[R]Let Israel now say— [Rom. 8:31] • Ps. 129:1
2 "If it had not been the LORD who was on
our side,
When men rose up against us,
3 Then they would have [R]swallowed us
alive,
When their wrath was kindled against
us; Prov. 1:12
4 Then the waters would have
overwhelmed us,
The stream would have [T]gone over our
soul; *swept over*
5 Then the swollen waters
Would have gone over our soul."

6 Blessed *be* the LORD,
Who has not given us *as* prey to their
teeth.
7 [R]Our soul has escaped [R]as a bird from
the snare of the [T]fowlers;
The snare is broken, and we have
escaped. Ps. 91:3 • Prov. 6:5 • *trappers of birds*
8 [R]Our help *is* in the name of the LORD,
Who made heaven and earth. [Ps. 121:2]

PSALM 125

Trust in the Lord and Abide Forever

A Song of Ascents.

THOSE who trust in the LORD
Are like Mount Zion,
Which cannot be moved, *but* abides
forever.
2 As the mountains surround Jerusalem,
So the LORD surrounds His people
From this time forth and forever.

3 For [R]the scepter of wickedness shall not
rest
On the land allotted to the righteous,
Lest the righteous reach out their hands
to iniquity. Prov. 22:8

4 Do good, O LORD, to *those who are*
good,
And to *those who are* upright in their
hearts.

5 As for such as turn aside to their
[R]crooked ways,
The LORD shall lead them away
With the workers of iniquity.

[R]Peace *be* upon Israel! Prov. 2:15 • [Gal. 6:16]

PSALM 126

"Sow in Tears . . . Reap in Joy"

A Song of Ascents.

WHEN the LORD brought back [T]the captivity of Zion, Those of the captivity
[R]We were like those who dream. Acts 12:9
2 Then [R]our mouth was filled with laughter,
And our tongue with singing.
Then they said among the [T]nations,
"The LORD has done great things for them." Job 8:21 • *Gentiles*
3 The LORD has done great things for us,
Whereof we are glad.

4 Bring back our captivity, O LORD,
As the streams in the South.

5 [R]Those who sow in tears
Shall reap in joy. Jer. 31:9
6 He who continually goes forth weeping,
Bearing [T]seed for sowing, Lit. *a bag of seed*
Shall doubtless come again [T]with [R]rejoicing, *with shouts of joy* • Is. 61:3
Bringing his sheaves *with him.*

PSALM 127

Children Are God's Heritage

A Song of Ascents. Of Solomon.

UNLESS the LORD builds the house,
They labor in vain who build it;
Unless the LORD guards the city,
The watchman stays awake in vain.
2 *It is* vain for you to rise up early,
To sit up late,
To eat the bread of sorrows;
For so He gives His beloved sleep.

3 Behold, [R]children *are* a heritage from the LORD, [Josh. 24:3, 4]
The fruit of the womb *is His* reward.
4 Like arrows in the hand of a warrior,
So *are* the children of one's youth.
5 [R]Happy *is* the man who has his quiver full of them;
[R]They shall not be ashamed,
But shall speak with their enemies in the gate. Ps. 128:2, 3 • Prov. 27:11

PSALM 128

Blessing on the House of the God-Fearing

A Song of Ascents.

BLESSED [R]*is* every one who fears the LORD,
Who walks in His ways. Ps. 119:1

2 [R]When you eat the [T]labor of your hands,
You *shall be* happy, and *it shall be* [R]well with you. Is. 3:10 • Fruit of the labor • Deut. 4:40
3 Your wife *shall be* [R]like a fruitful vine
In the very heart of your house,
Your [R]children like olive plants
All around your table. Ezek. 19:10 • Ps. 127:3–5
4 Behold, thus shall the man be blessed
Who fears the LORD.

5 [R]The LORD bless you out of Zion,
And may you see the good of Jerusalem
All the days of your life. Ps. 134:3
6 Yes, may you [R]see your children's children.

[R]Peace *be* upon Israel! Job 42:16 • Ps. 125:5

PSALM 129

Plea of the Persecuted

A Song of Ascents.

"MANY a time they have [T]afflicted me from my youth," *persecuted*
[R]Let Israel now say— Ps. 124:1
2 "Many a time they have afflicted me from my youth;
Yet they have not prevailed against me.
3 The plowers plowed on my back;
They made their furrows long."
4 The LORD *is* righteous;
He has cut in pieces the cords of the wicked.

5 Let all those who hate Zion
Be put to shame and turned back.
6 Let them be as the [R]grass *on* the housetops, Ps. 37:2
Which withers before it grows up,
7 With which the reaper does not fill his hand,
Nor he who binds sheaves, his arms.
8 Neither let those who pass by them say,
"The blessing of the LORD *be* upon you;
We bless you in the name of the LORD!"

PSALM 130

"My Soul Waits for the Lord"

A Song of Ascents.

OUT [R]of the depths I have cried to You, O LORD; Lam. 3:55
2 Lord, hear my voice!
Let Your ears be attentive
To the voice of my supplications.

3 If You, LORD, should [T]mark iniquities,
O Lord, who could stand? *take note of*
4 But *there is* forgiveness with You,
That [R]You may be feared. [1 Kin. 8:39, 40]

5 [R]I wait for the LORD, my soul waits,
And in His word I do hope. [Ps. 27:14]
6 [R]My soul *waits* for the Lord

More than those who watch for the
morning—
I say, more than those who watch for
the morning. Ps. 119:147

7 [R]O Israel, hope in the LORD; Ps. 131:3
For with the LORD *there is* mercy,
And with Him *is* abundant redemption.
8 And [R]He shall redeem Israel
From all his iniquities. [Ps. 103:3, 4]

PSALM 131

A Childlike Faith

A Song of Ascents. Of David.

LORD, my heart is not [T]haughty, Proud
Nor my eyes [T]lofty. Arrogant
[R]Neither do I [T]concern myself with great
matters, [Rom. 12:16] • Lit. *walk*
Nor with things too profound for me.

2 Surely I have calmed and quieted my
soul,
[R]Like a weaned child with his mother;
Like a weaned child *is* my soul within
me. [Matt. 18:3]

3 [R]O Israel, hope in the LORD [Ps. 130:7]
From this time forth and forever.

PSALM 132

Trust in the God of David

A Song of Ascents.

LORD, remember David
And all his afflictions;
2 How he swore to the LORD,
[R]*And* vowed to [R]the Mighty *God* of
Jacob: Ps. 65:1 • Gen. 49:24
3 "Surely I will not go into the chamber of
my house,
Or go up to the comfort of my bed;
4 I will [R]not give sleep to my eyes
Or slumber to my eyelids, Prov. 6:4
5 Until I [R]find a place for the LORD,
A dwelling place for the Mighty *God* of
Jacob." Acts 7:46

6 Behold, we heard of it in Ephrathah;
We found it in the fields of the woods.
7 Let us go into His tabernacle;
[R]Let us worship at His footstool. Ps. 99:5
8 Arise, O LORD, to Your resting place,
You and the ark of Your strength.
9 Let Your priests [R]be clothed with
righteousness, Job 29:14
And let Your saints shout for joy.

10 For Your servant David's sake,
Do not turn away the face of Your
[T]Anointed. *Commissioned One,* Heb. *Messiah*

11 [R]The LORD has sworn *in* truth to David;
He will not turn from it: [Ps. 89:3, 4, 33]
"I will set upon your throne [R]the [T]fruit of
your body. 2 Sam. 7:12 • *offspring*
12 If your sons will keep My covenant
And My testimony which I shall teach
them,
Their sons also shall sit upon your
throne forevermore."

13 [R]For the LORD has chosen Zion; [Ps. 48:1, 2]
He has desired *it* for His habitation:
14 "This *is* My resting place forever;
Here I will dwell, for I have desired it.
15 I will abundantly bless her [T]provision;
I will satisfy her poor with bread. *food*
16 I will also [R]clothe her priests with
salvation, 2 Chr. 6:41
And her saints shall shout aloud for joy.
17 [R]There I will make the horn of David
grow; Ezek. 29:21
I will prepare a lamp for My Anointed.
18 His enemies I will [R]clothe with shame,
But upon Himself His crown shall
flourish." Ps. 35:26

PSALM 133

Beauty of the Unity of the Brethren

A Song of Ascents. Of David.

BEHOLD, how good and how pleasant *it*
is
For [R]brethren to dwell together in
unity! Gen. 13:8

2 *It is* like the precious oil upon the head,
Running down on the beard,
The beard of Aaron,
Running down on the edge of his
garments.
3 *It is* like the dew of [R]Hermon,
Descending upon the mountains of
Zion;
For [R]there the LORD commanded the
blessing—
Life forevermore. Deut. 4:48 • Lev. 25:21

PSALM 134

Praise the Lord in the Evening

A Song of Ascents.

BEHOLD, bless the LORD,
All *you* servants of the LORD,
Who by night stand in the house of the
LORD!
2 [R]Lift up your hands *in* the sanctuary,
And bless the LORD. [1 Tim. 2:8]

3 The LORD who made heaven and earth
Bless you from Zion!

PSALM 135

God Has Done Great Things!

PRAISE the LORD!

Praise the name of the LORD;
Praise *Him*, O you servants of the LORD!
2 [R]You who stand in the house of the LORD, Luke 2:37
In the courts of the house of our God,
3 Praise the LORD, for [R]the LORD *is* good;
Sing praises to His name, [R]for *it is* pleasant. [Ps. 119:68] • Ps. 147:1
4 For [R]the LORD has chosen Jacob for Himself,
Israel for His special treasure. [Ex. 19:5]

5 For I know that [R]the LORD *is* great,
And our Lord *is* above all gods. Ps. 95:3
6 [R]Whatever the LORD pleases He does,
In heaven and in earth, Ps. 115:3
In the seas and in all deep places.
7 He causes the [T]vapors to ascend from the ends of the earth; Water vapor
[R]He makes lightning for the rain;
He brings the wind out of His [R]treasuries. Job 28:25, 26; 38:24–28 • Jer. 51:16

8 He destroyed the firstborn of Egypt,
[T]Both of man and beast. *From man to beast*
9 [R]He sent signs and wonders into the midst of you, O Egypt, Ex. 7:10
Upon Pharaoh and all his servants.
10 [R]He defeated many nations
And slew mighty kings— Num. 21:24
11 Sihon king of the Amorites,
Og king of Bashan,
And all the kingdoms of Canaan—
12 And gave their land *as* a [T]heritage,
A heritage to Israel His people. *inheritance*

13 [R]Your name, O LORD, *endures* forever,
Your fame, O LORD, throughout all generations. [Ex. 3:15]
14 [R]For the LORD will judge His people,
And He will have compassion on His servants. Deut. 32:36

15 [R]The idols of the nations *are* silver and gold,
The work of men's hands. [Ps. 115:4–8]
16 They have mouths, but they do not speak;
Eyes they have, but they do not see;
17 They have ears, but they do not hear;
Nor is there *any* breath in their mouths.
18 Those who make them are like them;
So is everyone who trusts in them.

19 Bless the LORD, O house of Israel!
Bless the LORD, O house of Aaron!
20 Bless the LORD, O house of Levi!
You who fear the LORD, bless the LORD!
21 Blessed be the LORD [R]out of Zion,
Who dwells in Jerusalem!

Praise the LORD! Ps. 134:3

PSALM 136

God's Mercy Endures Forever

OH, [R]give thanks to the LORD, for *He is* good! Ps. 106:1
For His mercy *endures* forever.
2 Oh, give thanks to the God of gods!
For His mercy *endures* forever.
3 Oh, give thanks to the Lord of lords!
For His mercy *endures* forever:

4 To Him [R]who alone does great wonders,
For His mercy *endures* forever; Ps. 72:18
5 [R]To Him who by wisdom made the heavens, Jer. 51:5
For His mercy *endures* forever;
6 [R]To Him who laid out the earth above the waters, Jer. 10:12
For His mercy *endures* forever;
7 To Him who made great lights,
For His mercy *endures* forever—
8 [R]The sun to rule by day, Gen. 1:16
For His mercy *endures* forever;
9 The moon and stars to rule by night,
For His mercy *endures* forever.

10 [R]To Him who struck Egypt in their firstborn, Ex. 12:29
For His mercy *endures* forever;
11 [R]And brought out Israel from among them, Ex. 12:51; 13:3, 16
For His mercy *endures* forever;
12 [R]With a strong hand, and with [T]an outstretched arm, Ex. 6:6 • Mighty power
For His mercy *endures* forever;
13 [R]To Him who divided the Red Sea in two, Ex. 14:21
For His mercy *endures* forever;
14 And made Israel pass through the midst of it,
For His mercy *endures* forever;
15 [R]But overthrew Pharaoh and his army in the Red Sea, Ex. 14:27
For His mercy *endures* forever;
16 [R]To Him who led His people through the wilderness, Ex. 13:18; 15:22
For His mercy *endures* forever;
17 To Him who struck down great kings,
For His mercy *endures* forever;
18 [R]And slew famous kings, Deut. 29:7
For His mercy *endures* forever—
19 [R]Sihon king of the Amorites, Num. 21:21
For His mercy *endures* forever;
20 [R]And Og king of Bashan, Num. 21:33
For His mercy *endures* forever—
21 And gave their land as a heritage,
For His mercy *endures* forever;

22 A heritage to Israel His servant,
For His mercy *endures* forever.

23 Who [R]remembered us in our lowly state,
For His mercy *endures* forever; Gen. 8:1
24 And [R]rescued us from our enemies,
For His mercy *endures* forever; Ps. 44:7
25 [R]Who gives food to all flesh, Ps. 104:27
For His mercy *endures* forever.

26 Oh, give thanks to the God of heaven!
For His mercy *endures* forever.

PSALM 137

Tears in Exile

BY the rivers of Babylon,
There we sat down, yea, we wept
When we remembered Zion.
2 We hung our harps
Upon the willows in the midst of it.
3 For there those who carried us away
captive [T]required of us a song,
And those who [R]plundered us *required of us* mirth,
Saying, "Sing us *one* of the songs of Zion!" *demanded* • Ps. 79:1

4 How shall we sing the LORD's song
In a foreign land?
5 If I forget you, O Jerusalem,
Let my right hand forget *her skill!*
6 If I do not remember you,
Let my [R]tongue cling to the roof of my mouth—
If I do not exalt Jerusalem
Above my chief joy. Ezek. 3:26

7 Remember, O LORD, against [R]the sons of Edom Jer. 49:7–22
The day of Jerusalem,
Who said, [T]"Raze *it*, raze *it*,
To its very foundation!" Lit. *Make it bare*

8 O daughter of Babylon, [R]who are to be destroyed, Is. 13:1–6; 47:1
Happy *shall he be* [R]who repays you as you have served us! Jer. 50:15
9 Happy *shall he be* who takes and [R]dashes
Your little ones against the rock. Is. 13:16

PSALM 138

God Answered My Prayer

A Psalm of David.

I WILL praise You with my whole heart;
[R]Before the gods I will sing praises to You. Ps. 119:46
2 [R]I will worship [R]toward Your holy temple, Ps. 28:2 • 1 Kin. 8:29
And praise Your name
For Your lovingkindness and Your truth;
For You have [R]magnified Your word above all Your name. Is. 42:21
3 In the day when I cried out, You answered me,
And made me bold *with* strength in my soul.

4 [R]All the kings of the earth shall praise You, O LORD,
When they hear the words of Your mouth. Ps. 102:15
5 Yes, they shall sing of the ways of the LORD,
For great *is* the glory of the LORD.
6 [R]Though the LORD *is* on high, [Ps. 113:4–7]
Yet [R]He regards the lowly; [James 4:6]
But the proud He knows from afar.

7 [R]Though I walk in the midst of trouble,
You will revive me; [Ps. 23:3, 4]
You will stretch out Your hand
Against the wrath of my enemies,
And Your right hand will save me.
8 [R]The LORD will [T]perfect *that which* concerns me; Ps. 57:2 • *complete*
Your mercy, O LORD, *endures* forever;
[R]Do not forsake the works of Your hands. Job 10:3, 8

PSALM 139

"Search Me, O God"

For the Chief Musician. A Psalm of David.

O LORD, [R]You have searched me and known *me*. Ps. 17:3
2 [R]You know my sitting down and my rising up; 2 Kin. 19:27
You understand my thought afar off.
3 [R]You [T]comprehend my path and my lying down, Job 14:16; 31:4 • Lit. *winnow*
And are acquainted with all my ways.
4 For *there is* not a word on my tongue,
But behold, O LORD, [R]You know it altogether. [Heb. 4:13]
5 You have [T]hedged me behind and before,
And laid Your hand upon me. *enclosed*
6 [R]*Such* knowledge *is* too wonderful for me;
It is high, I cannot *attain* it. Job 42:3

7 [R]Where can I go from Your Spirit?
Or where can I flee from Your presence? [Jer. 23:24]
8 [R]If I ascend into heaven, You *are* there;
[R]If I make my bed in [T]hell, behold, You *are there*. [Amos 9:2–4] • [Job 26:6] • Or *Sheol*
9 *If* I take the wings of the morning,
And dwell in the uttermost parts of the sea,

10 Even there Your hand shall lead me,
And Your right hand shall hold me.
11 If I say, "Surely the darkness shall *fall
on me,"
Even the night shall be light about me;
12 Indeed, [R]the darkness [T]shall not hide
from You,
But the night shines as the day;
The darkness and the light *are* both
alike *to You.* Job 26:6; 34:22 • Lit. *is not dark*

13 For You have formed my inward parts;
You have [T]covered me in my mother's
womb. *woven*

14 I will praise You, for I am fearfully *and*
wonderfully made;
Marvelous are Your works,
And *that* my soul knows very well.

15 [R]My [T]frame was not hidden from You,
When I was made in secret, Job 10:8, 9
And skillfully wrought in the lowest
parts of the earth. Lit. *bones were*
16 Your eyes saw my substance, being yet
unformed.
And in Your book they all were written,
The days fashioned for me,
When *as yet there were* none of them.

17 [R]How precious also are Your thoughts to
me, O God!
How great is the sum of them! [Ps. 40:5]
18 *If* I should count them, they would be
more in number than the sand;
When I awake, I am still with You.

19 Oh, that You would [R]slay the wicked,
O God! [Is. 11:4]
Depart from me, therefore, you
[T]bloodthirsty men. Lit. *men of bloodshed*
20 For they speak against You wickedly;
Your enemies take *Your name* in vain.
21 [R]Do I not hate them, O LORD, who hate
You?
And do I not loathe those who rise up
against You? 2 Chr. 19:2
22 I hate them with [T]perfect hatred;
I count them my enemies. *complete*

23 [R]Search me, O God, and know my heart;
Try me, and know my anxieties; Job 31:6
24 And see if *there is any* wicked way in
me,
And lead me in the way everlasting.

PSALM 140

Preserve Me from Violence

To the Chief Musician. A Psalm of David.

DELIVER me, O LORD, from evil men;
Preserve me from violent men,
2 Who plan evil things in *their* hearts;
[R]They continually gather together *for*
war. Ps. 56:6
3 They sharpen their tongues like a
serpent;
The [R]poison of asps *is* under their lips.
Selah Ps. 58:4

4 [R]Keep me, O LORD, from the hands of
the wicked;
Preserve me from violent men,
Who have purposed to make my steps
stumble. Ps. 71:4
5 The proud have hidden a [R]snare for me,
and cords; Jer. 18:22
They have spread a net by the wayside;
They have set traps for me. Selah

6 I said to the LORD: "You *are* my God;
Hear the voice of my supplications,
O LORD.
7 O GOD the Lord, the strength of my
salvation,
You have [T]covered my head in the day
of battle. *sheltered*
8 Do not grant, O LORD, the desires of the
wicked;

139:11 Vg., Symmachus *cover*

139:14 God's Work in Our Lives—All people possess an inward desire that their work should have meaning and permanence (Page 678—Ps. 90:16, 17). If man's work is not to be lost in the vastness of eternity, however, it must conform to the work God has designed for man. This work for the present day can be known only from God's Word.

According to the Word of God, the initial work of God is for us to believe in Jesus Christ (Page 1246—John 6:29; Page 1331—Rom. 6:17, 18). Apart from entering into this vital relationship with God, man cannot even begin to work for God. After coming to know Christ, the new Christian discovers God's program for the present from the Scriptures. It is, first of all, His work in the Christian himself. Regeneration is only the beginning of God's work in the believer. It actually introduces a process of becoming like Christ which God promises ultimately to bring to perfection (Page 1398—Phil. 1:6). The Christian's cheerful obedience to God's will as revealed in His Word helps speed this work along.

Second, no Christian can overlook God's work in the world. Jesus' command to spread the good news of the gospel to all men appears near the end of all four Gospels and at the beginning of the Book of Acts. God's method is that men proclaim the gospel and that the Holy Spirit convict (Page 1259—John 16:8–11).

Finally, God's work is in and through the church, the organism ordained by Christ for this age (Page 1136—Matt. 16:18). God works in the church through the Spirit and through spiritually gifted people to strengthen and bless it (Page 1390—Eph. 4:11–13).

Now turn to Page 7—Gen. 2:15–17: The Edenic Covenant.

Do not further his *wicked* scheme,
[R]*Lest* they be exalted. Selah Deut. 32:27

9 "*As for* the head of those who surround me,
Let the evil of their lips cover them;
10 [R]Let burning coals fall upon them;
Let them be cast into the fire,
Into deep pits, that they rise not up again. Ps. 11:6
11 Let not a slanderer be established in the earth;
Let evil hunt the violent man to overthrow *him*."

12 I know that the LORD will [R]maintain
The cause of the afflicted,
And justice for the poor. 1 Kin. 8:45
13 Surely the righteous shall give thanks to Your name;
The upright shall dwell in Your presence.

PSALM 141

"Set a Guard, O LORD, over My Mouth"

A Psalm of David.

LORD, I cry out to You;
Make haste to me!
Give ear to my voice when I cry out to You.
2 Let my prayer be set before You [R]*as* incense, [Rev. 5:8; 8:3, 4]
[R]The lifting up of my hands *as* [R]the evening sacrifice. [1 Tim. 2:8] • Ex. 29:39, 41

3 Set a guard, O LORD, over my mouth;
Keep watch over the door of my lips.
4 Do not incline my heart to any evil thing,
To practice wicked works
With men who work iniquity;
[R]And do not let me eat of their delicacies. Prov. 23:6

5 [R]Let the righteous strike me;
It shall be a kindness.
And let him reprove me;
It shall be as excellent oil;
Let my head not refuse it.

For still my prayer *is* against the deeds of the wicked. [Prov. 9:8]
6 Their judges are overthrown by the sides of the [T]cliff,
And they hear my words, for they are sweet. *rock*
7 Our bones are scattered at the mouth of the grave,
As when one plows and breaks up the earth.

8 But [R]my eyes *are* upon You, O GOD the Lord;
In You I take refuge;
Do not leave my soul destitute. Ps. 25:15
9 Keep me from [R]the snares *which* they have laid for me,
And from the traps of the workers of iniquity. Ps. 119:110
10 [R]Let the wicked fall into their own nets,
While I escape safely. Ps. 35:8

PSALM 142

"No One Cares for My Soul"

*A Contemplation of David.
A Prayer when he was in the cave.

I CRY out to the LORD with my voice;
With my voice to the LORD I make my supplication.
2 I pour out my complaint before Him;
I declare before Him my trouble.

3 When my spirit [T]was [R]overwhelmed within me, Lit. *fainted* • Ps. 77:3
Then You knew my path.
In the way in which I walk
They have secretly set a snare for me.
4 Look on *my* right hand and see,
For *there is* no one who acknowledges me;
Refuge has failed me;
No one cares for my soul.

5 I cried out to You, O LORD:
I said, "You *are* my refuge,
My portion in the land of the living.
6 [T]Attend to my cry,
For I am brought very low;
Deliver me from my persecutors,
For they are stronger than I. *Give heed*
7 Bring my soul out of prison,
That I may [R]praise Your name; Ps. 34:1, 2
The righteous shall surround me,
For You shall deal bountifully with me."

PSALM 143

"Teach Me to Do Your Will"

A Psalm of David.

HEAR my prayer, O LORD,
Give ear to my supplications!
In Your faithfulness answer me,
And in Your righteousness.
2 Do not enter into judgment with Your servant,
[R]For in Your sight no one living is righteous. [Gal. 2:16]

3 For the enemy has persecuted my soul;
He has crushed my life to the ground;

142:title, Heb. *Maschil*

He has made me dwell in darkness,
Like those who have long been dead.
4 [R]Therefore my spirit is overwhelmed within me;
My heart within me is distressed. Ps. 77:3

5 [R]I remember the days of old; Ps. 77:5, 10, 11
I meditate on all Your works;
I muse on the work of Your hands.
6 I spread out my hands to You;
[R]My soul *longs* for You like a thirsty land. Selah Ps. 63:1

7 Answer me speedily, O LORD;
My spirit fails!
Do not hide Your face from me,
[R]Lest I [T]be like those who [T]go down into the pit. Ps. 28:1 • *become* • Die
8 Cause me to hear Your lovingkindness [R]in the morning, Ps. 46:5
For in You do I trust;
[R]Cause me to know the way in which I should walk, Ps. 5:8
For [R]I lift up my soul to You. Ps. 25:1

9 Deliver me, O LORD, from my enemies;
*In You I take shelter.
10 [R]Teach me to do Your will, Ps. 25:4, 5
For You *are* my God;
[R]Your Spirit *is* good. Neh. 9:20
Lead me in the land of uprightness.

11 [R]Revive me, O LORD, for Your name's sake!
For Your righteousness' sake bring my soul out of trouble. Ps. 119:25
12 In Your mercy [R]cut[T] off my enemies,
And destroy all those who afflict my soul; Ps. 54:5 • *put an end to*
For I *am* Your servant.

PSALM 144

"What Is Man?"

A Psalm of David.

BLESSED *be* the LORD my Rock,
[R]Who trains my hands for war,
And my fingers for battle— 2 Sam. 22:35
2 My lovingkindness and my fortress,
My high tower and my deliverer,
My shield and *the One* in whom I take refuge,
Who subdues my people under me.

3 [R]LORD, what *is* man, that You take knowledge of him?
Or the son of man, that You are mindful of him? Heb. 2:6
4 [R]Man is like a breath; Ps. 39:11
His days *are* like a passing shadow.

5 [R]Bow down Your heavens, O LORD, and come down;
[R]Touch the mountains, and they shall smoke. Ps. 18:9 • Ps. 104:32
6 [R]Flash forth lightning and scatter them;
Shoot out Your arrows and destroy them. Ps. 18:13, 14
7 Stretch out Your hand from above;
Rescue me and deliver me out of great waters,
From the hand of foreigners,
8 Whose mouth [R]speaks [T]vain words,
And whose right hand *is* a right hand of falsehood. Ps. 12:2 • *empty* or *worthless*

9 I will [R]sing a new song to You, O God;
On a harp of ten strings I will sing praises to You, Ps. 33:2, 3; 40:3
10 *The One* who gives [T]salvation to kings,
[R]Who delivers David His servant
From the deadly sword. *deliverance* • Ps. 18:50

11 Rescue me and deliver me from the hand of foreigners,
Whose mouth speaks vain words,
And whose right hand *is* a right hand of falsehood—
12 That our sons *may be* [R]as plants grown up in their youth; Ps. 128:3
That our daughters *may be* as [T]pillars,
Sculptured in palace style; *corner pillars*
13 *That* our barns *may be* full,
Supplying all kinds of produce;
That our sheep may bring forth thousands
And ten thousands in our fields;
14 *That* our oxen *may be* well-laden;
That there be no [T]breaking in or going out; Lit. *breach*
That there be no outcry in our streets.
15 [R]Happy *are* the people who are in such a state;
Happy *are* the people whose God *is* the LORD! [Ps. 33:12]

PSALM 145

Testify to God's Great Acts

A Praise of David.

I WILL [T]extol You, my God, O King;
And I will bless Your name forever and ever. *praise*
2 Every day I will bless You,
And I will praise Your name forever and ever.
3 [R]Great *is* the LORD, and greatly to be praised; [Ps. 147:5]
And His greatness *is* unsearchable.

4 [R]One generation shall praise Your works to another, Is. 38:19
And shall declare Your mighty acts.

143:9 LXX, Vg. *To You I flee*

5 I will meditate on the glorious splendor
of Your majesty,
And on Your wondrous works.
6 *Men* shall speak of the might of Your
awesome acts,
And I will declare Your greatness.
7 They shall [T]utter the memory of Your
great goodness, *eagerly utter,* lit. *bubble forth*
And shall sing of Your righteousness.

8 [R]The LORD *is* gracious and full of
compassion, [Num. 14:18]
Slow to anger and great in mercy.
9 [R]The LORD *is* good to all,
And His tender mercies *are* over all His
works. Nah. 1:7

10 [R]All Your works shall praise You, O
LORD,
And Your saints shall bless You. Ps. 19:1
11 They shall speak of the glory of Your
kingdom,
And talk of Your power,
12 To make known to the sons of men His
mighty acts,
And the glorious majesty of His
kingdom.
13 [R]Your kingdom *is* an everlasting
kingdom,
And Your dominion *endures* throughout
all generations. [1 Tim. 1:17]

14 The LORD upholds all who fall,
And [R]raises up all *those who are* bowed
down. Ps. 146:8
15 [R]The eyes of all look expectantly to You,
And [R]You give them their food in due
season. Ps. 104:27 • Ps. 136:25
16 You open Your hand
[R]And satisfy the desire of every living
thing. Ps. 104:21, 28

17 The LORD *is* righteous in all His ways,
Gracious in all His works.
18 [R]The LORD *is* near to all who call upon
Him, [Deut. 4:7]
To all who call upon Him in truth.
19 He will fulfill the desire of those who
fear Him;
He also will hear their cry and save
them.
20 The LORD preserves all who love Him,
But all the wicked He will destroy.
21 My mouth shall speak the praise of the
LORD,
And all flesh shall bless His holy name
Forever and ever.

PSALM 146

"Do Not Put Your Trust in Princes"

PRAISE[T] the LORD! Heb. *Hallelujah*

Praise the LORD, O my soul!

2 [R]While I live I will praise the LORD;
I will sing praises to my God while I
have my being. Ps. 104:33

3 [R]Do not put your trust in princes,
Nor in [T]a son of man, in whom *there is*
no [T]help. [Is. 2:22] • A human being • *salvation*
4 [R]His spirit departs, he returns to his
earth; [Eccl. 12:7]
In that very day his plans perish.

5 [R]Happy *is he* who *has* the God of Jacob
for his help, Jer. 17:7
Whose hope *is* in the LORD his God,
6 [R]Who made heaven and earth,
The sea, and all that *is* in them;
Who keeps truth forever, Rev. 14:7
7 [R]Who executes justice for the oppressed,
[R]Who gives food to the hungry.
[R]The LORD gives freedom to the
prisoners. Ps. 103:6 • Ps. 107:9 • Ps. 107:10

8 [R]The LORD opens *the eyes of* the blind;
[R]The LORD raises those who are bowed
down; Matt. 9:30 • Luke 13:13
The LORD loves the righteous.
9 The LORD watches over the strangers;
He relieves the fatherless and widow;
[R]But the way of the wicked He [T]turns
upside down. Ps. 147:6 • Lit. *makes crooked*

10 [R]The LORD shall reign forever—
Your God, O Zion, to all generations.

Praise the LORD! Ex. 15:18

PSALM 147

God Heals the Brokenhearted

PRAISE[T] the LORD! Heb. *Hallelujah*
For [R]*it is* good to sing praises to our
God; Ps. 92:1
[R]For *it is* pleasant, *and* [R]praise is
beautiful. Ps. 135:3 • Ps. 33:1

2 The LORD [R]builds up Jerusalem;
[R]He gathers together the outcasts of
Israel. Ps. 102:16 • Deut. 30:3
3 [R]He heals the brokenhearted [Ps. 51:17]
And binds up their [T]wounds. Lit. *sorrows*
4 [R]He counts the number of the stars;
He calls them all by name. Is. 40:26
5 [R]Great *is* our Lord, and [R]mighty in
power; Ps. 48:1 • Nah. 1:3
[R]His understanding *is* infinite. Is. 40:28
6 [R]The LORD lifts up the humble;
He casts the wicked down to the
ground. Ps. 146:8, 9

7 Sing to the LORD with thanksgiving;
Sing praises on the harp to our God,

8 [R]Who covers the heavens with clouds,
Who prepares rain for the earth,
Who makes grass to grow on the
mountains. Job 38:26
9 [R]He gives to the beast its food, Job 38:41
And to the young ravens that cry.

10 [R]He does not delight in the strength of
the horse;
He takes no pleasure in the legs of a
man. Ps. 33:16, 17
11 The LORD takes pleasure in those who
fear Him,
In those who hope in His mercy.

12 Praise the LORD, O Jerusalem!
Praise your God, O Zion!
13 For He has strengthened the bars of
your gates;
He has blessed your children within
you.
14 He makes peace *in* your borders,
And fills you with the finest wheat.

15 [R]He sends out His command *to the* earth;
His word runs very swiftly. [Ps. 107:20]
16 [R]He gives snow like wool;
He scatters the frost like ashes; Job 37:6
17 He casts out His hail like [T]morsels;
Who can stand before His cold? *crumbs*
18 [R]He sends out His word and melts them;
He causes His wind to blow, *and* the
waters flow. Job 37:10

19 [R]He declares His word to Jacob,
[R]His statutes and His judgments to
Israel. Deut. 33:4 • Mal. 4:4
20 [R]He has not dealt thus with any nation;
And *as for His* judgments, they have
not known them.

[T]Praise the LORD! [Rom. 3:1, 2] • Heb. *Hallelujah*

PSALM 148

All Creation Praises the Lord

PRAISE[T] the LORD!

Praise the LORD from the heavens;
Praise Him in the heights! Heb. *Hallelujah*
2 Praise Him, all His angels;
Praise Him, all His hosts!
3 Praise Him, sun and moon;
Praise Him, all you stars of light!
4 Praise Him, you heavens of heavens,
And you waters above the heavens!

5 Let them praise the name of the LORD,
For [R]He commanded and they were
created. Gen. 1:1, 6
6 [R]He has also established them forever
and ever;
He has made a decree which shall not
pass away. Ps. 89:37

7 Praise the LORD from the earth,
[R]You great sea creatures and all the
depths; Is. 43:20
8 Fire and hail, snow and clouds;
Stormy wind, fulfilling His word;
9 [R]Mountains and all hills;
Fruitful trees and all cedars; Is. 44:23; 49:13
10 Beasts and all cattle;
Creeping things and flying fowl;
11 Kings of the earth and all peoples;
Princes and all judges of the earth;
12 Both young men and maidens;
Old men and children.

13 Let them praise the name of the LORD,
For His [R]name alone is exalted; Ps. 8:1
His glory *is* above the earth and heaven.
14 And He [R]has exalted the [T]horn of His
people, Ps. 75:10 • Strength or dominion
The praise of [R]all His saints—
Of the children of Israel,
[R]A people near to Him. Ps. 149:9 • Eph. 2:17

[T]Praise the LORD! Heb. *Hallelujah*

PSALM 149

"The LORD Takes Pleasure in His People"

PRAISE[T] the LORD! Heb. *Hallelujah*

[R]Sing to the LORD a new song,
And His praise in the congregation of
saints. Ps. 33:3

2 Let Israel rejoice in their Maker;
Let the children of Zion be joyful in
their [R]King. Zech. 9:9
3 [R]Let them praise His name with the
dance;
Let them sing praises to Him with the
timbrel and harp. Ps. 81:2
4 For [R]the LORD takes pleasure in His
people;
[R]He will beautify the [T]humble with
salvation. Ps. 35:27 • Ps. 132:16 • *meek*

5 Let the saints be joyful in glory;
Let them sing aloud on their beds.
6 *Let* the high praises of God *be* in their
mouth,
And a two-edged sword in their hand,
7 To execute vengeance on the nations,
And punishments on the peoples;
8 To bind their kings with chains,
And their nobles with fetters of iron;
9 [R]To execute on them the written
judgment— Deut. 7:1, 2
[R]This honor have all His saints.

[T]Praise the LORD! 1 Cor. 6:2 • Heb. *Hallelujah*

PSALM 150

"Praise the LORD"

PRAISE[R] the LORD! Ps. 145:5, 6

Praise God in His sanctuary;
Praise Him in His mighty firmament!

2 Praise Him for His mighty acts;
Praise Him according to His excellent
[R]greatness! Deut. 3:24

3 Praise Him with the sound of the
[T]trumpet;
Praise Him with the lute and harp! *cornet*
4 Praise Him with the timbrel and dance;
Praise Him with stringed instruments
and flutes!
5 Praise Him with loud cymbals;
Praise Him with clashing cymbals!

6 Let everything that has breath praise
the LORD.

[T]Praise the LORD! Heb. *Hallelujah*

150:1 Praise—To praise God is to acknowledge the glories of His excellent person. It differs somewhat from thanksgiving, which describes what God has done rather than what He is. Here are some facts about praise.

a. God alone is worthy of our praise (Page 634—Ps. 18:3; 113:3).
b. It is His will for us that we praise Him (Page 653—Ps. 50:23; Page 815—Is. 43:21).
c. This praise should be continuous (Page 643—Ps. 34:1; 71:6) and also public (Page 637—Ps. 22:25).
d. We are to praise God for His holiness (Page 520—2 Chr. 20:21), grace (Page 1387—Eph. 1:6), goodness (Page 703—Ps. 135:3), and kindness (Page 704—Ps. 138:2).
e. All nature praises God (Page 709—Ps. 148:7–10).
f. The sun, moon, and stars praise Him (Page 635—Ps. 19:1; 143:3).
g. The angels praise Him (Page 709—Ps. 148:2).

In fact, we are told that on occasion God uses even the wrath of men to praise Him (Page 668—Ps. 76:10). An example of this is seen in the selling of Joseph by his brothers into slavery (Page 49—Gen. 37:28). God later uses this cruel act to promote Joseph as second ruler over all Egypt. As Joseph would remind his brothers: "But as for you, you meant evil against me; *but* God meant it for good, in order to bring it about as *it is* this day, to save many people alive" (Page 64—Gen. 50:20).

Now turn to Page 1494—1 John 1:9: Confession.

THE BOOK OF

PROVERBS

THE BOOK OF PROVERBS

The key word in Proverbs is *wisdom,* "the ability to live life skillfully." A godly life in an ungodly world, however, is no simple assignment. Proverbs provides God's detailed instructions for His people to deal successfully with the practical affairs of everyday life: how to relate to God, parents, children, neighbors, and government. Solomon, the principal author, uses a combination of poetry, parables, pithy questions, short stories, and wise maxims to give in strikingly memorable form the common sense and divine perspective necessary to handle life's issues.

Because Solomon, the pinnacle of Israel's wise men, was the principal contributor, the Hebrew title of this book is *Mishle Shelomoh,* "Proverbs of Solomon" (1:1). The Greek title is *Paroimiai Salomontos,* "Proverbs of Solomon." The Latin title *Liber Proverbiorum,* "Book of Proverbs," combines the words *pro* "for" and *verba* "words" to describe the way the proverbs concentrate many words into a few. The Rabbinical writings called Proverbs *Sepher Hokhmah,* "Book of Wisdom."

THE AUTHOR OF PROVERBS

Solomon's name appears at the beginning of the three sections he wrote: 1:1 for chapters 1—9, 10:1 for chapters 10:1—22:16, and 25:1 for chapters 25—29. According to First Kings 4:32, he spoke 3,000 proverbs and 1,005 songs. Only about 800 of his 3,000 proverbs are included in the two Solomonic collections in this book. No man was better qualified than Solomon to be the principal contributor. He asked for wisdom (1 Kin. 3:5–9) and God granted it to him (1 Kin. 4:29–31) to such a degree that people from foreign lands came to hear him speak (1 Kin. 4:34; 10:1–13, 24). His breadth of knowledge, aptitude, skill, and perception were extraordinary. In every area Solomon brought prosperity and glory to Israel until his latter years (cf. 1 Kin. 11:4).

It is likely that Solomon collected and edited proverbs other than his own. According to Ecclesiastes 12:9, "he pondered and sought out *and* set in order many proverbs." The second collection of Solomonic proverbs in 25—29 was assembled by the scribes of King Hezekiah because of his interest in spiritually benefiting his subjects with the Word of God. The prophets Isaiah and Micah ministered during Hezekiah's time, and it has been suggested that they also might have been involved in this collection.

Proverbs 22:17—24:34 consists of "the words of the wise" (22:17; 24:23). Some of these sayings are quite similar to those found in The Wisdom of Amenemope, a document of teachings on civil service by an Egyptian who probably lived between 1000 B.C. and 600 B.C. Wise men of this period went to hear one another, and it is probable that Amenemope borrowed certain aphorisms from Hebrew literature. If the *hakhamim* ("wise men") lived before Solomon's time, he may have been the collector and editor of this series of wise sayings.

There is no biblical information about Agur (30) or Lemuel (31). Agur ben Jakeh (30:1) is simply called an oracle, and Lemuel is called a king and an oracle (31:1). Both have been identified with Solomon, but there is no basis for this suggestion.

THE TIME OF PROVERBS

Proverbs is a collection of topical maxims and is not a historical book. It is a product of the wisdom school in Israel. According to Jeremiah 18:18 and Ezekiel 7:26, three groups communicated to the people on behalf of God: the priests imparted the Law; the prophets communicated the divine word and visions; and the sages, or elders, gave counsel to the people. The sages provided the practical application of godly wisdom to specific problems and decisions. The "Preacher" of Ecclesiastes is a good example of the wisdom school (Eccl. 1:1, 12; 7:27; 12:8–10). *Qoheleth,* or "Preacher," meant "one who addresses an assembly": he presided over a "school" of wise men and "taught the people knowledge" (Eccl. 12:9). "My son" in Proverbs and Ecclesiastes evidently refers to the pupil. This was parallel to Samuel's role of heading Israel's school of prophets.

Wisdom literature is also found in other countries of the ancient Near East. In Egypt, written examples can be found as early as 2700 B.C. Although the style was similar to Israel's wisdom literature, the proverbs and sayings of these countries differed from those of Israel in content because they lacked the character of the righteous standards of the Lord.

Solomon's proverbs were written by 931 B.C., and his proverbs in chapters 25—29 were collected by Hezekiah about 230 years later (Hezekiah reigned from 715 to 686 B.C.). Under Solomon, Israel was at its spiritual, political, and economic summit. Solomon probably wrote his proverbs in his middle years, before his character began to decline into carnality, materialism, and idolatry.

THE CHRIST OF PROVERBS

In Proverbs 8, wisdom is personified and seen in its perfection. It is divine (8:22-31), it is the source of biological and spiritual life (8:35, 36; 3:18), it is righteous and moral (8:8, 9), and it is available to all who will receive it (8:1-6, 32-35). This wisdom became incarnate in Christ "in whom are hidden all the treasures of wisdom and knowledge" (Col. 2:3). "But of Him you are in Christ Jesus, who became for us wisdom from God—and righteousness and sanctification and redemption" (1 Cor. 1:30; cf. 1 Cor. 1:22-24).

KEYS TO PROVERBS

Key Word: Wisdom—Proverbs is one of the few biblical books that clearly spells out its purpose. The purpose statement in 1:2-6 is twofold: (1) to impart moral discernment and discretion (1:3-5), and (2) to develop mental clarity and perception (1:2, 6). The words "wisdom and instruction" in 1:2 complement each other because *wisdom (hokhmah)* means "skill" and *instruction (musar)* means "discipline." No skill is perfected without discipline, and when a person has skill he has freedom to create something beautiful. Proverbs deals with the most fundamental skill of all: practical righteousness before God in every area of life. This requires knowledge, experience, and a willingness to put God first (see 3:5-7). Chapters 1—9 are designed to create a felt need for wisdom, and Proverbs as a whole is designed both to prevent and to remedy ungodly life-styles. The book served as a manual to impart the legacy of wisdom, prudence, understanding, discretion, knowledge, guidance, competence, correction, counsel, and truth—from generation to generation.

Key Verses: Proverbs 1:5-7 and 3:5, 6—"A wise *man* will hear and increase learning, and a man of understanding will attain wise counsel, to understand a proverb and an enigma, the words of the wise and their riddles. The fear of the LORD *is* the beginning of knowledge, *but* fools despise wisdom and instruction" (1:5-7).

"Trust in the LORD with all your heart, and lean not on your own understanding; in all your ways acknowledge Him, and He shall direct your paths" (3:5, 6).

Key Chapter: Proverbs 31—The last chapter of Proverbs is unique in ancient literature, as it reveals a very high and noble view of women. The woman in these verses is: (1) a good woman (31:13, 15, 16, 19, 25), (2) a good wife (31:11, 12, 23, 24), (3) a good mother (31:14, 15, 18, 21, 27), and (4) a good neighbor (31:20-26). Her conduct, concern, speech, and life stand in sharp contrast to the woman pictured in Proverbs 7.

SURVEY OF PROVERBS

Proverbs is the most intensely practical book in the Old Testament because it teaches skillful living in the multiple aspects of everyday life. Its specific precepts include instruction on wisdom and folly, the righteous and the wicked, the tongue, pride and humility, justice and vengeance, the family, laziness and work, poverty and wealth, friends and neighbors, love and lust, anger and strife, masters and servants, life and death. Proverbs touches upon every facet of human relationships, and its principles transcend the bounds of time and culture.

The Hebrew word for "proverb" *(mashal)* means "comparison, similar, parallel." A proverb uses a comparison or figure of speech to make a pithy but poignant observation. Proverbs have been defined as simple illustrations that expose fundamental realities of life. These maxims are not theoretical but practical; they are easily memorized, based on real-life experience, and designed for use in the mainstream of life. The proverbs are general statements and illustrations of timeless truth, which allow for, but do not condone, exceptions to the rule. The key word is

FOCUS	PURPOSE OF PROVERBS	PROVERBS TO YOUTH	PROVERBS OF SOLOMON	PROVERBS OF SOLOMON (HEZEKIAH)	WORDS OF AGUR	WORDS OF LEMUEL
REFERENCE	1:1—	1:8—	10:1—	25:1—	30:1—	31:1—31:31
DIVISION	PURPOSE AND THEME	FATHER'S EXHORTATIONS	FIRST COLLECTION OF SOLOMON	SECOND COLLECTION OF SOLOMON	NUMERICAL PROVERBS	VIRTUOUS WIFE
TOPIC	PROLOGUE	PRINCIPLES OF WISDOM			EPILOGUE	
	COMMENDATION OF WISDOM	COUNSEL OF WISDOM			COMPARISONS OF WISDOM	
LOCATION	JUDAH					
TIME	c. 950 – 700 B.C.					

hokhmah, "wisdom": it literally means "skill" (in living). Wisdom is more than shrewdness or intelligence. Instead, it relates to practical righteousness and moral acumen. The Book of Proverbs may be divided into six segments: the purpose of Proverbs (1:1-7), the proverbs to the youth (1:8—9:18), the proverbs of Solomon (10:1—24:34), the proverbs of Solomon copied by Hezekiah's men (25:1—29:27), the words of Agur (30:1-33), and the words of King Lemuel (31:1-31).

The Purpose of Proverbs (1:1-7): The brief prologue states the author, theme, and purpose of the book.

The Proverbs to the Youth (1:8—9:18): Following the introduction, there is a series of ten exhortations, each beginning with "My son" (1:8—9:18). These messages introduce the concept of wisdom in the format of a father's efforts to persuade his son to pursue the path of wisdom in order to achieve godly success in life. Wisdom rejects the invitation of crime and foolishness, rewards seekers of wisdom on every level, and wisdom's discipline provides freedom and safety (1—4). Wisdom protects one from illicit sensuality and its consequences, from foolish practices and laziness, and from adultery and the lure of the harlot (5—7). Wisdom is to be preferred to folly because of its divine origin and rich benefits (8 and 9). There are four kinds of fools, ranging from those who are naive and uncommitted to scoffers who arrogantly despise the way of God. The fool is not mentally deficient; he is self-sufficient, ordering his life as if there were no God.

The Proverbs of Solomon (10:1—24:34): There is a minimal amount of topical arrangement in these chapters. There are some thematic clusters (e.g., 26:1-12, 13-16, 20-22), but the usual units are one-verse maxims. It is helpful to assemble and organize these proverbs according to such specific themes as money and speech. This Solomonic collection consists of 375 proverbs of Solomon. Chapters 10—15 contrast right and wrong in practice, and all but nineteen proverbs use antithetic parallelism, that is, parallels of paired opposite principles. Chapters 16:1—22:16 offer a series of self-evident moral truths and all but eighteen proverbs use synonymous parallelism, that is, parallels of paired identical or similar principles. The words of wise men (22:17—24:34) are given in two groups. The first group includes thirty distinct sayings (22:17—24:22), and six more are found in the second group (24:23-34).

The Proverbs of Solomon Copied by Hezekiah's Men (25:1—29:27): This second Solomonic collection was copied and arranged by "the men of Hezekiah" (25:1). These proverbs in chapters 25—29 further develop the themes in the first Solomonic collection.

The Words of Agur (30:1-33): The last two chapters of Proverbs form an appendix of sayings by two otherwise unknown sages, Agur and Lemuel. Most of Agur's material is given in clusters of numerical proverbs.

The Words of King Lemuel (31:1-31): The last chapter includes an acrostic of twenty-two verses (the first letter of each verse consecutively follows the complete Hebrew alphabet) portraying a virtuous wife (31:10-31).

OUTLINE OF PROVERBS

I. The Purpose of Proverbs 1:1-7

II. Proverbs to the Youth . . . . 1:8—9:18

- A. Obey Parents 1:8, 9
- B. Avoid Bad Company 1:10-19
- C. Seek Wisdom . . . . 1:20—2:22
- D. Benefits of Wisdom 3:1-26
- E. Be Kind to Others 3:27-35
- F. Father Says Get Wisdom 4:1-13
- G. Avoid the Wicked 4:14-22
- H. Keep Your Heart 4:23-27
- I. Do Not Commit Adultery 5:1-14
- J. Do Be Faithful to Your Spouse 5:15-23
- K. Avoid Surety 6:1-5
- L. Do Not Be Lazy 6:6-19
- M. Do Not Commit Adultery . . . . 6:20—7:27
- N. Praise of Wisdom . . . . 8:1—9:12
- O. Foolish Woman 9:13-18

III. Proverbs of Solomon . . . . 10:1—24:34

- A. Proverbs Contrasting the Godly and the Wicked . . . . 10:1—15:33
- B. Proverbs Encouraging Godly Lives . . . . 16:1—22:16
- C. Proverbs Concerning Various Situations . . . . 22:17—24:34

IV. Proverbs of Solomon Copied by Hezekiah's Men . . . . 25:1—29:27

- A. Proverbs Regulating Relationships with Others . . . . 25:1—26:28
  1. Relationships with Kings 25:1-7
  2. Relationships with Neighbors 25:8-20
  3. Relationships with Enemies 25:21-24
  4. Relationships with Yourself 25:25-28
  5. Relationships with Fools 26:1-12
  6. Relationships with Sluggards 26:13-16
  7. Relationships with Gossips 26:17-28
- B. Proverbs Regulating Various Activities . . . . 27:1—29:27

V. The Words of Agur 30:1-33

VI. The Words of King Lemuel 31:1-31

- A. Wisdom for Leaders 31:1-9
- B. Wise Woman 31:10-31

CHAPTER 1

The Purpose of Proverbs

THE Rproverbs of Solomon the son of
David, king of Israel: 1 Kin. 4:32

2 To know wisdom and instruction,
To Tperceive the words of
understanding, *understand* or *discern*
3 To receive the instruction of wisdom,
Justice, judgment, and equity;
4 To give prudence to the Rsimple,
To the young man knowledge and
discretion— Prov. 9:4
5 RA wise *man* will hear and increase
learning,
And a man of understanding will Tattain
wise counsel, Prov. 9:9 • *acquire*
6 To understand a proverb and an
enigma,
The words of the wise and their
Rriddles. Ps. 78:2

7 RThe fear of the LORD *is* the beginning of
knowledge,
But fools despise wisdom and
instruction. Job 28:28

Obey Parents

8 RMy son, hear the instruction of your
father,
And do not forsake the law of your
mother; Prov. 4:1
9 For they *will be* Rgraceful ornaments on
your head,
And chains about your neck. Prov. 3:22

Avoid Bad Company

10 My son, if sinners entice you,
RDo not consent. Gen. 39:7–10
11 If they say, "Come with us,
Let us Rlie in wait to *shed* blood;
Let us lurk secretly for the innocent
without cause; Jer. 5:26
12 Let us swallow them alive like TSheol,
And whole, Rlike those who go down to
the Pit; Or *the grave* • Ps. 28:1
13 We shall find all *kinds* of precious
Tpossessions, Lit. *wealth*
We shall fill our houses with spoil;
14 Cast in your lot among us,
Let us all have one purse"—
15 My son, Rdo not walk in the way with
them, Ps. 1:1
Keep your foot from their path;
16 RFor their feet run to evil, [Is. 59:7]
And they make haste to shed blood.
17 Surely, in Tvain the net is spread *futility*
In the sight of any Tbird; Lit. *lord of the wing*
18 But they lie in wait for their *own* blood,
They lurk secretly for their *own* lives.
19 RSo *are* the ways of everyone who is
greedy for gain; [1 Tim. 6:10]
It takes away the life of its owners.

Seek Wisdom

20 RWisdom calls aloud Toutside;
She raises her voice in the open
squares. [John 7:37] • *in the street*
21 She cries out in the chief concourses,
At the openings of the gates in the city
She speaks her words:
22 "How long, you Tsimple ones, will you
love Tsimplicity?
For scorners delight in their scorning,
And fools hate knowledge. *naive* • *naivete*
23 Turn at my reproof;
Surely I will pour out my spirit on you;
I will make my words known to you.
24 RBecause I have called and you refused,
I have stretched out my hand and no
one regarded, Jer. 7:13
25 Because you disdained all my counsel,
And would have none of my reproof,

1:8 The Role of Children—Both the Old and New Testaments agree that children have only one responsibility in the family—to obey their parents. The admonition of Solomon is more fully explained by Paul in Ephesians 6:1–3: "Children, obey your parents in the Lord, for this is right. 'Honor your father and mother,' which is the first commandment with promise: 'that it may be well with you and you may live long on the earth.'" "Children" is an inclusive term. It is not a matter of either sex or age that is involved.

Twice in Scripture God has intervened and directly stated what He would have children do. The last time was nearly two thousand years ago when He gave a revelation to Paul for the church. The first time was nearly thirty-four hundred years ago when He gave a revelation to Moses and Israel in which He commanded, "Honor your father and your mother." God's will for children is that they are to obey their parents. The expression "in the Lord" does not limit the responsibility only to the circumstances where the parents are believers. Colossians 3:20 clearly points out that children are to obey their parents "in all things," not just in those things pertaining to Christian living. "In the Lord" more properly is understood to mean by the Lord or because it is the Lord's directive (this is what God says children are to do). "For this is right" indicates that for children to obey their parents is righteous or godlike. Such obedience is perfectly illustrated by God the Son who was completely obedient to God the Father, even though that obedience resulted in His death (Page 1400—Phil. 2:6–8).

Two things are promised to children who obey their parents: it will be well with them—they will have a happy life; and they will have a long life. These are the two things that children want most, and obedience to parents is the only way to assure them. That is why this is the first commandment with promise; from it springs all the other important issues of life. The child who has not learned to obey his parents, who are God's representatives in the family, will not learn to obey God.

Now turn to Page 1392—Eph. 6:4: The Role of the Parents.

26 I also will laugh at your calamity;
I will mock when your terror comes,
27 When [R]your terror comes like a storm,
And your destruction comes like a whirlwind,
When distress and anguish come upon you. [Prov. 10:24, 25]

28 "Then[R] they will call on me, but I will not answer;
They will seek me diligently, but they will not find me. Is. 1:15
29 Because they [R]hated knowledge
And did not [R]choose the fear of the LORD, Job 21:14 • Ps. 119:173
30 [R]They would have none of my counsel
And despised all my reproof, Ps. 81:11
31 Therefore [R]they shall eat the fruit of their own way,
And be filled to the full with their own fancies. Job 4:8
32 For the [T]turning away of the simple will slay them,
And the complacency of fools will destroy them; *waywardness*
33 But whoever listens to me will dwell [R]safely,
And [R]will be [T]secure, without fear of evil." Prov. 3:24–26 • Ps. 112:7 • *at ease*

CHAPTER 2

MY son, if you receive my words,
And [R]treasure my commands within you, [Prov. 4:21]
2 So that you incline your ear to wisdom,
And apply your heart to understanding;
3 Yes, if you cry out for discernment,
And lift up your voice for understanding,
4 [R]If you seek her as silver,
And search for her as *for* hidden treasures; [Prov. 3:14]
5 [R]Then you will understand the fear of the LORD, [James 1:5, 6]
And find the knowledge of God.
6 [R]For the LORD gives wisdom;
From His mouth *come* knowledge and understanding; 1 Kin. 3:9, 12
7 He stores up sound wisdom for the upright;
[R]*He is* a shield to those who walk uprightly; [Ps. 84:11]
8 He guards the paths of justice,
And preserves the way of His saints.
9 Then you will understand righteousness and justice,
Equity *and* every good path.

10 When wisdom enters your heart,
And knowledge is pleasant to your soul,
11 Discretion will preserve you;
Understanding will keep you,
12 To deliver you from the way of evil,
From the man who speaks perverse things,
13 From those who leave the paths of uprightness
To walk in the ways of darkness;
14 [R]Who rejoice in doing evil,
And delight in the perversity of the wicked; [Rom. 1:32]
15 [R]Whose ways *are* crooked, Ps. 125:5
And *who are* devious in their paths;
16 To deliver you from [R]the immoral woman,
[R]From the seductress *who* flatters with her words, Prov. 5:20; 6:24; 7:5 • Prov. 5:3
17 Who forsakes the companion of her youth,
And forgets the covenant of her God.
18 For [R]her house [T]leads down to death,
And her paths to the dead; Prov. 7:27 • *sinks*
19 None who go to her return,
Nor do they regain the paths of life—
20 So you may walk in the way of goodness,
And keep *to* the paths of righteousness.
21 For the upright will dwell in the land,
And the blameless will remain in it;
22 But the wicked will be [T]cut off from the [T]earth,
And the unfaithful will be uprooted from it. *destroyed* • *land*

CHAPTER 3

Benefits of Wisdom

MY son, do not forget my law,
[R]But let your heart keep my commands; Deut. 8:1
2 For length of days and long life
And peace they will add to you.

3 Let not [T]mercy and truth forsake you;
Bind them around your neck, *lovingkindness*
Write them on the tablet of your heart,
4 [R]*And* so find favor and high esteem
In the sight of God and man. Rom. 14:18

5 [R]Trust in the LORD with all your heart,
[R]And lean not on your own understanding; [Ps. 37:3, 5] • [Jer. 9:23, 24]
6 In all your ways acknowledge Him,
And He shall [T]direct your paths. *smooth*

7 Do not be wise in your own eyes;
Fear the LORD and depart from evil.
8 It will be health to your [T]flesh, Lit. *navel*
And [T]strength to your bones. Lit. *drink*

9 [R]Honor the LORD with your possessions,
And with the firstfruits of all your increase; Ex. 22:29
10 [R]So your barns will be filled with plenty,

And your vats will overflow with new
wine. Deut. 28:8

11 [R]My son, do not despise the chastening
of the LORD,
Nor detest His correction; Job 5:17
12 For whom the LORD loves He corrects,
[R]Just as a father the son *in whom* he
delights. Deut. 8:5

13 Happy *is* the man *who* finds wisdom,
And the man *who* gains understanding;
14 [R]For her proceeds *are* better than the
profits of silver,
And her gain than fine gold. Job 28:13
15 She *is* more precious than rubies,
And [R]all the things you may desire
cannot compare with her. Matt. 13:44
16 Length of days *is* in her right hand,
In her left hand riches and honor.
17 [R]Her ways *are* ways of pleasantness,
And all her paths *are* peace. [Matt. 11:29]
18 She *is* [R]a tree of life to those who take
hold of her, Gen. 2:9
And happy *are all* who retain her.

19 [R]The LORD by wisdom founded the earth;
By understanding He established the
heavens; Ps. 104:24
20 By His knowledge the depths were
[R]broken up, Gen. 7:11
And clouds drop down the dew.

21 My son, let them not depart from your
eyes—
Keep sound wisdom and discretion;
22 So they will be life to your soul
And grace to your neck.
23 [R]Then you will walk safely in your way,
And your foot will not stumble. Prov. 10:9
24 When you lie down, you will not be
afraid;
Yes, you will lie down and your sleep
will be sweet.
25 [R]Do not be afraid of sudden terror,
Nor of trouble from the wicked when it
comes; Ps. 91:5
26 For the LORD will be your confidence,
And will keep your foot from being
caught.

Be Kind to Others

27 [R]Do not withhold good from [T]those to
whom it is due,
When it is in the power of your hand to
do *so*. Rom. 13:7 • Lit. *its owners*
28 [R]Do not say to your neighbor,
"Go, and come back,
And tomorrow I will give *it*,"
When *you have* it with you. Lev. 19:13
29 Do not devise evil against your
neighbor,
For he dwells by you for safety's sake.
30 [R]Do not strive with a man without
cause,
If he has done you no harm. [Rom. 12:18]

31 [R]Do not envy the oppressor,
And choose none of his ways; Ps. 37:1
32 For the perverse *person is* an
abomination to the LORD,
[R]But His secret counsel *is* with the
upright. Ps. 25:14
33 [R]The curse of the LORD *is* on the house
of the wicked,
But [R]He blesses the [T]habitation of the
just. Zech. 5:3, 4 • Ps. 1:3 • *dwelling place*
34 [R]Surely He scorns the scornful,
But gives grace to the humble. James 4:6
35 The wise shall inherit glory,
But shame shall be the legacy of fools.

CHAPTER 4

Father Says Get Wisdom

HEAR, [R]*my* children, the instruction of a
father,
And give attention to know
understanding; Ps. 34:11
2 For I give you good doctrine:
Do not forsake my law.
3 When I was my father's son,
[R]Tender and the only one in the sight of
my mother, 1 Chr. 29:1
4 He also taught me, and said to me:
"Let your heart retain my words;
[R]Keep my commands, and live. Prov. 7:2
5 [R]Get wisdom! Get understanding!
Do not forget, nor turn away from the
words of my mouth. Prov. 2:2, 3
6 Do not forsake her, and she will
preserve you;
Love her, and she will keep you.
7 [R]Wisdom *is* the principal thing;
Therefore get wisdom.
And in all your getting, get
understanding. Matt. 13:44
8 [R]Exalt her, and she will promote you;
She will bring you honor, when you
embrace her. 1 Sam. 2:30
9 She will place on your head [R]an
ornament of grace; Prov. 3:22
A crown of glory she will deliver to
you."

10 Hear, my son, and receive my sayings,
And the years of your life will be many.
11 I have [R]taught you in the way of
wisdom;
I have led you in right paths. 1 Sam. 12:23
12 When you walk, [R]your steps will not be
hindered,
[R]And when you run, you will not
stumble. Ps. 18:36 • [Ps. 91:11]

WISDOM

We tend to think of wisdom as being soundness of judgment or a right use of knowledge. But the Hebrew idea of wisdom is broader and deeper. It covers all of life.

Wisdom (*hokmah*)

The noun *hokmah* is derived from the verb *hākam*, "to be wise" or "to act wisely." All of the ancient near east was interested in being wise; hence, a large body of "wisdom literature" was built up in that part of the world. God gave great wisdom to King Solomon (1 Kin. 4:29, 30), and he is the author of much of the Old Testament's wisdom literature. The Hebrew wisdom literature is inspired by God, and includes Job, Proverbs, and Ecclesiastes, as well as other selections from the Old Testament. Biblical wisdom is ethical and spiritual because it is a reflection of the wisdom of a holy God.

Ethical Wisdom

Men and women cannot attain to ethical wisdom by themselves. They must first acknowledge the Lord in all their ways, and then He will direct their paths (Prov. 3:5, 6). Biblical wisdom is practical, not theoretical. Hence, the Book of Proverbs is filled with specific details on how to be a wise person. Wise people through the centuries have meditated upon this book and have practiced its precepts. Since there are thirty-one days in many months and thirty-one chapters in this supreme book of everyday wisdom, it is helpful discipline to read a chapter a day until, after years of study, one knows the book thoroughly.

The creation around us is evidence of God's wisdom since it was by wisdom that He founded the earth (Prov. 3:19).

Hokmah as Skill and Intelligence

Daniel and his friends were "gifted in all wisdom, possessing knowledge and quick to understand" (Dan. 1:4). The context suggests more intellectual ability than our usual idea of wisdom. But even the former is from God and can be improved and developed with divine help.

What we might call artistic talent or skill, the Hebrews called *hokmah:* God filled Bezaleel and Aholiab "with skill [*hokmah*] to do all manner of work of the engraver and the designer and the tapestry maker" (Ex. 35:35). God also filled Bezaleel "with the Spirit of God, in wisdom, in understanding, in knowledge" (Ex. 31:3). Then "artistic works" in metal, wood and jewel cutting are listed. "The spirit of wisdom" was needed to design and sew the priestly vestments for Aaron and his sons (Ex. 28:3). Military skill was also called *hokmah* in Hebrew (Is. 10:13).

Wisdom as Shrewdness

Some people are not wise in the Solomonic sense or even gifted to build, sew, create works of art, or excel in physical combat. But they are clever or shrewd. The woman who threw Sheba's head over the wall to Joab and saved her city was shrewd. Second Samuel 20:22 could well be translated "the woman in her shrewdness [*hokmah*] went to all the people."

Wisdom Personified

Hebrew, along with Greek, Latin, French, German, and many other languages, expresses gender in its nouns. That is, in learning the language a student has to memorize each word as to whether it is masculine or feminine. Hebrew has no neuter; hence, there is no word for "it" or "its." Thus, a masculine or feminine pronoun is used to express things or concepts, depending on the gender of the noun to which it refers. *Hokmah,* like many Hebrew nouns expressing such concepts as love, truth, justice, and wickedness, is a feminine noun. For this reason, wisdom is frequently referred to in Proverbs as "she" and "her." In poetry, when an abstract quality is presented as a person, the technique is called personification. Personification, while common in some languages, is rare in Hebrew.

Lady Wisdom is pictured as building a house, preparing a banquet, teaching in public, and crowning the wise. This personification of Wisdom in Proverbs is often seen as a foreshadowing of Christ, who is Himself "wisdom from God" (1 Cor. 1:30).

13 Take firm hold of instruction, do not let
go;
Keep her, for she *is* your life.

Avoid the Wicked

14 Do not enter the path of the wicked,
And do not walk in the way of evil.
15 Avoid it, do not travel on it;
Turn away from it and pass on.
16 [R]For they do not sleep unless they have
done evil; Ps. 36:4
And their sleep is [T]taken away unless
they make *someone* fall. Lit. *robbed*
17 For they eat the bread of wickedness,
And drink the wine of violence.

18 But the path of the just [R]*is* like the
shining [T]sun,
That shines ever brighter unto the
perfect day. 2 Sam. 23:4 • Lit. *light*
19 [R]The way of the wicked *is* like darkness;
They do not know what makes them
stumble. [Is. 59:9, 10]

20 My son, give attention to my words;
Incline your ear to my sayings.
21 Do not let them depart from your eyes;
Keep them in the midst of your heart;
22 For they *are* life to those who find
them,
And health to all their flesh.

Keep Your Heart

23 Keep your heart with all diligence,
For out of it *spring* the issues of life.
24 Put away from you a deceitful mouth,
And put perverse lips far from you.
25 Let your eyes look straight ahead,
And your eyelids look right before you.
26 Ponder the path of your [R]feet, Heb. 12:13
And let all your ways be established.
27 Do not turn to the right or the left;
Remove your foot from evil.

CHAPTER 5

Do Not Commit Adultery

MY son, pay attention to my wisdom;
Lend your ear to my understanding,
2 That you may [T]preserve discretion,
And *that* your lips [R]may keep
knowledge. *appreciate good judgment* • Mal. 2:7
3 [R]For the lips of [T]an immoral woman drip
honey, Prov. 2:16 • Lit. *a strange*
And her mouth *is* smoother than oil;
4 But in the end she is bitter as
wormwood,
Sharp as a two-edged sword.
5 Her feet go down to death,
Her steps lay hold of [T]hell. Or *Sheol*
6 Lest you ponder *her* path of life—
Her ways are unstable;
You do not know *them*.

7 Therefore hear me now, *my* children,
And do not depart from the words of
my mouth.
8 Remove your way far from her,
And do not go near the door of her
house,
9 Lest you give your [T]honor to others,
And your years to the cruel one; *vigor*
10 Lest aliens be filled with your [T]wealth,
And your labors *go* to the house of a
foreigner; Lit. *strength*
11 And you mourn at last,
When your flesh and your body are
consumed,
12 And say:
"How I have hated instruction,
And my heart despised reproof!
13 I have not obeyed the voice of my
teachers,
Nor inclined my ear to those who
instructed me!
14 I was on the verge of total ruin,
In the midst of the congregation and
assembly."

Do Be Faithful to Your Spouse

15 Drink water from your own cistern,
And running water from your own well.
16 Should your fountains be dispersed
abroad,
[T]Streams of water in the streets? *Channels*
17 Let them be only your own,
And not for strangers with you.
18 Let your fountain be blessed,
And rejoice with [R]the wife of your
youth. Mal. 2:14
19 [R]*As a* loving deer and a graceful doe,
Let her breasts satisfy you at all times;
And always be [T]enraptured with her
love. Song 2:9 • Lit. *intoxicated*
20 For why should you, my son, be
enraptured by [R]an immoral woman,
And be embraced in the arms of a
seductress? Prov. 2:16

21 [R]For the ways of man *are* before the
eyes of the LORD, Hos. 7:2
And He [T]ponders all his paths. Lit. *weighs*
22 [R]His own iniquities entrap the wicked
man, Num. 32:23
And he is caught in the cords of his sin.
23 [R]He shall die for lack of instruction,
And in the greatness of his folly he shall
go astray. Job 4:21

CHAPTER 6

Avoid Surety

MY son, [R]if you become [T]surety for your
friend, Prov. 11:15 • *guaranty* or *collateral*
If you have [T]shaken hands in pledge for
a stranger, Lit. *struck*
2 You are snared by the words of your
own mouth;

You are taken by the words of your
mouth.
3 So do this, my son, and deliver yourself;
For you have come into the hand of
your friend:
Go and humble yourself;
Plead with your friend.
4 [R]Give no sleep to your eyes,
Nor slumber to your eyelids. Ps. 132:4
5 Deliver yourself like a gazelle from the
hand *of the hunter*,
And like a bird from the hand of the
[T]fowler. *trapper of birds*

Do Not Be Lazy

6 [R]Go to the ant, you sluggard!
Consider her ways and be wise, Job 12:7
7 Which, having no [T]captain,
Overseer or ruler, Lit. *leader*
8 Provides her supplies in the summer,
And gathers her food in the harvest.
9 [R]How long will you [T]slumber, O
sluggard? Prov. 24:33, 34 • Lit. *lie down*
When will you rise from your sleep?
10 A little sleep, a little slumber,
A little folding of the hands to sleep—
11 [R]So shall your poverty come on you like
a robber, Prov. 10:4
And your need like an armed man.

12 A worthless person, a wicked man,
Walks with a perverse mouth;
13 [R]He [T]winks with his
eyes, Job 15:12 • *gives signals*
He [T]shuffles his feet, Lit. *scrapes*
He points with his fingers;
14 Perversity *is* in his heart,
[R]He devises evil continually,
[R]He sows discord. Mic. 2:1 • Prov. 6:19
15 Therefore his calamity shall come
[R]suddenly;
Suddenly he shall [R]be broken [R]without
remedy. Is. 30:13 • Jer. 19:11 • 2 Chr. 36:16

16 These six *things* the LORD hates,
Yes, seven *are* an abomination to Him:
17 [R]A[T] proud look, Ps. 101:5 • *Haughty eyes*
[R]A lying tongue, Ps. 120:2
[R]Hands that shed innocent blood, Is. 1:15
18 A heart that devises wicked plans,
Feet that are swift in running to evil,
19 [R]A false witness *who* speaks lies,
And one who [R]sows discord among
brethren. Ps. 27:12 • Prov. 6:14

Do Not Commit Adultery

20 [R]My son, keep your father's command,
And do not forsake the law of your
mother. Eph. 6:1
21 [R]Bind them continually upon your heart;
Tie them around your neck. Prov. 3:3
22 [R]When you roam, [T]they will lead you;
When you sleep, [R]they will keep you;
And *when* you awake, they will speak
with you. [Prov. 3:23] • Lit. *it* • Prov. 2:11

23 [R]For the commandment *is* a lamp,
And the law *is* light;
Reproofs of instruction *are* the way of
life, Ps. 19:8

24 [R]To keep you from the evil woman,
From the flattering tongue of a
seductress. Prov. 2:16
25 [R]Do not lust after her beauty in your
heart, Matt. 5:28
Nor let her allure you with her eyelids.
26 For [R]by means of a harlot Prov. 29:3
A man is reduced to a crust of bread;
And [T]an adulteress will prey upon his
precious life. Wife of another, lit. *a man's wife*
27 Can a man take fire to his bosom,
And his clothes not be burned?
28 Can one walk on hot coals,
And his feet not be seared?
29 So *is* he who goes in to his neighbor's
wife;
Whoever touches her shall not be
innocent.

30 *People* do not despise a thief
If he steals to satisfy himself when he is
starving.

6:23 Illumination of God's Word—Illumination is the last of three important steps taken by God in communicating His Word to us. The first step was revelation which occurred when God spoke to the Bible authors. The second step was inspiration, that process whereby God guided them in correctly writing or uttering His message. But now a third step is needed to provide understanding for men and women as they hear God's revealed and inspired message. This vital step is illumination, that divine process whereby God causes the written revelation to be understood by the human heart.

This third step is needed because unsaved man is blinded both by his fallen, fleshly nature (Page 1346—1 Cor. 2:14) and by Satan himself (Page 1367—2 Cor. 4:3, 4).

The Person behind this illumination is the Holy Spirit. Just prior to His crucifixion, Christ promised to send the Holy Spirit, who would illuminate both unsaved people (Page 1259—John 16:8–11) and Christians (Page 1258—John 14:26; 16:13, 14).

An important example of the Holy Spirit's using God's Word to illuminate sinners is seen at Pentecost, where three thousand people are saved after hearing Simon Peter preach about Christ and the Cross (Page 1274—Acts 2:36–41).

But Christians also need this illumination to help them fully grasp the marvelous message in God's Word. Paul tells us that the Holy Spirit will show these tremendous truths to us as we read the Scriptures (Page 1346—1 Cor. 2:10; Page 1367—2 Cor. 4:6).

Now turn to Page 565—Neh. 8:9: God's Word Convicts.

31 Yet *when* he is found, [R]he must restore
sevenfold;
He may have to give up all the
substance of his house. Ex. 22:1–4
32 Whoever commits adultery with a
woman [R]lacks understanding; Prov. 7:7
He *who* does so destroys his own soul.
33 Wounds and dishonor he will get,
And his reproach will not be wiped
away.
34 For [R]jealousy *is* a husband's fury;
Therefore he will not spare in the day
of vengeance. Song 8:6
35 He will [T]accept no recompense,
Nor will he be appeased though you
give many gifts. Lit. *lift up the face of any*

CHAPTER 7

MY son, keep my words,
And [R]treasure my commands within
you. Prov. 2:1
2 [R]Keep my commands and live, Lev. 18:5
And my law as the apple of your eye.
3 [R]Bind them on your fingers; Deut. 6:8
Write them on the tablet of your heart.
4 Say to wisdom, "You *are* my sister,"
And call understanding *your* nearest
kin,
5 [R]That they may keep you from the
immoral woman,
From the seductress *who* flatters with
her words. Prov. 2:16; 5:3

6 For at the window of my house
I looked through my lattice,
7 And saw among the simple,
I perceived among the [T]youths, Lit. *sons*
A young man [R]devoid[T] of
understanding, [Prov. 6:32; 9:4, 16] • *lacking*
8 Passing along the street near her
corner;
And he took the path to her house
9 [R]In the twilight, in the evening,
In the black and dark night. Job 24:15

10 And there a woman met him,
With the attire of a harlot, and a crafty
heart.
11 [R]She *was* loud and rebellious, Prov. 9:13
Her feet would not stay at home.
12 At times *she was* outside, at times in
the open square,
Lurking at every corner.
13 So she caught him and kissed him;
With an impudent face she said to him:
14 "*I have* peace offerings with me;
Today I have paid my vows.
15 So I came out to meet you,
Diligently to seek your face,
And I have found you.
16 I have spread my bed with tapestry,
Colored coverings of Egyptian linen.
17 I have perfumed my bed
With myrrh, aloes, and cinnamon.
18 Come, let us take our fill of love until
morning;
Let us delight ourselves with love.
19 For my husband *is* not at home;
He has gone on a long journey;
20 He has taken a bag of money [T]with
him,
And will come home [T]on the appointed
day." Lit. *in his hand* • *at the full moon*
21 With [T]her enticing speech she caused
him to yield, *By the greatness of her words*
[R]With her flattering lips she [T]seduced
him. Ps. 12:2 • *compelled*
22 Immediately he went after her, as an ox
goes to the slaughter,
Or *as a fool to the correction of the
[T]stocks, *shackles*
23 Till an arrow struck his liver.
[R]As a bird hastens to the snare, Eccl. 9:12
He did not know it *would take* his life.

24 Now therefore, listen to me, *my*
children;
Pay attention to the words of my
mouth:
25 Do not let your heart turn aside to her
ways,
Do not stray into her paths;
26 For she has cast down many wounded,
And [R]all who were slain by her were
strong *men*. Neh. 13:26
27 Her house *is* the way to [T]hell, Or *Sheol*
Descending to the chambers of death.

CHAPTER 8

Praise of Wisdom

DOES not [R]wisdom cry out, Prov. 1:20, 21
And understanding lift up her voice?
2 She takes her stand on the top of the
[T]high hill, Lit. *heights*
Beside the way, where the paths meet.
3 She cries out by the gates, at the entry
of the city,
At the entrance of the doors:
4 "To you, O men, I call,
And my voice *is* to the sons of men.
5 O you [T]simple ones, understand
prudence,
And you fools, be of an understanding
heart. *naive*
6 Listen, for I will speak of [R]excellent
things,
And from the opening of my lips *will
come* right things; Prov. 22:20
7 For my mouth will speak truth;
Wickedness *is* an abomination to my
lips.

7:22 LXX, Tg., Syr. *as a dog to bonds;* Vg. *as a lamb . . . to bonds*

8 All the words of my mouth *are* with
righteousness;
Nothing crooked or perverse *is* in them.
9 They *are* all plain to him who
understands,
And right to those who find knowledge.
10 Receive my instruction, and not silver,
And knowledge rather than choice gold;
11 [R]For wisdom *is* better than rubies,
And all the things one may desire
cannot be compared with her. Job 28:15

12 "I, wisdom, dwell with prudence,
And find out knowledge *and* discretion.
13 The fear of the LORD *is* to hate evil;
Pride and arrogance and the evil way
And the perverse mouth I hate.
14 Counsel *is* mine, and sound wisdom;
I *am* understanding, I have strength.
15 [R]By me kings reign,
And rulers decree justice. Rom. 13:1
16 By me princes rule, and nobles,
All the judges of *the earth.
17 [R]I love those who love me,
And [R]those who seek me diligently will
find me. [John 14:21] • James 1:5
18 [R]Riches and honor *are* with me, Prov. 3:16
Enduring riches and righteousness.
19 My fruit *is* better than gold, yes, than
fine gold,
And my revenue than choice silver.
20 I traverse the way of righteousness,
In the midst of the paths of justice,
21 That I may cause those who love me to
inherit wealth,
That I may fill their treasuries.

22 "The[R] LORD possessed me at the
beginning of His way,
Before His works of old. Prov. 3:19
23 [R]I have been established from
everlasting,
From the beginning, before there was
ever an earth. [Ps. 2:6]
24 When *there were* no depths I was
brought forth,
When *there were* no fountains
abounding with water.
25 Before the mountains were settled,
Before the hills, I was brought forth;
26 While as yet He had not made the earth
or the [T]fields, *outer places*
Or the primeval dust of the world.
27 When He prepared the heavens, I *was*
there,
When He drew a circle on the face of
the deep,
28 When He established the clouds above,
When He strengthened the fountains of
the deep,
29 [R]When He assigned to the sea its limit,
So that the waters would not transgress
His command,
When [R]He marked out the foundations
of the earth, Gen. 1:9, 10 • Job 28:4, 6
30 Then I was beside Him, *as* *a master
craftsman;
[R]And I was daily *His* delight, [Matt. 3:17]
Rejoicing always before Him,
31 Rejoicing in His inhabited world,
And [R]my delight *was* with the sons of
men. Ps. 16:3

32 "Now therefore, listen to me, *my*
children,
For [R]blessed *are those who* keep my
ways. Luke 11:28
33 Hear instruction and be wise,
And do not disdain *it*.
34 [R]Blessed is the man who listens to me,
Watching daily at my gates, Prov. 3:13, 18
Waiting at the posts of my doors.
35 For whoever finds me finds life,
And obtains favor from the LORD;
36 But he who sins against me [R]wrongs his
own soul; Prov. 20:2
All those who hate me love death."

CHAPTER 9

WISDOM has [R]built her house, [Matt. 16:18]
She has hewn out her seven pillars;
2 [R]She has slaughtered her meat,
She has mixed her wine, Matt. 22:4
She has also [T]furnished her table. *arranged*
3 She has sent out her maidens,
She cries out from the highest places of
the city,
4 "Whoever[R] *is* simple, let him turn in
here!"
As for him who lacks understanding,
she says to him, Ps. 19:7
5 "Come,[R] eat of my bread
And drink of the wine *which* I have
mixed. Is. 55:1
6 Forsake foolishness and live,
And go in the way of understanding.

7 "He who reproves a scoffer gets shame
for himself,
And he who rebukes a wicked *man gets*
himself a blemish.
8 [R]Do not reprove a scoffer, lest he hate
you;
[R]Rebuke a wise man, and he will love
you. Matt. 7:6 • Ps. 141:5
9 Give *instruction* to a wise *man*, and he
will be still wiser;
Teach a just *man*, [R]and he will increase
in learning. [Matt. 13:12]

10 "The[R] fear of the LORD *is* the beginning
of wisdom,

8:16 MT, Vg., Tg., Syr. *righteousness;* LXX, Bg., some mss. and editions *earth*
8:30 A Jewish tradition reads *one brought up*

And the knowledge of the Holy One *is*
understanding. Job 28:28
11 For by me your days will be multiplied,
And years of life will be added to you.
12 [R]If you are wise, you are wise for
yourself, Job 35:6, 7
And *if* you scoff, you alone will bear *it*."

Foolish Woman

13 A foolish woman is [T]clamorous; *boisterous*
She is simple, and knows nothing.
14 For she sits at the door of her house,
On a seat [R]*by* the highest places of the
city, Prov. 9:3
15 To call to those who pass by,
Who go straight on their way:
16 "Whoever[R] *is* [T]simple, let him turn in
here"; Prov. 7:7,8 • *naive*
And *as for* him who lacks
understanding, she says to him,
17 "Stolen[R] water is sweet, Prov. 20:17
And bread *eaten* in secret is pleasant."
18 But he does not know that [R]the dead
are there,
That her guests *are* in the depths of
[T]hell. Prov. 2:18; 7:27 • Or *Sheol*

CHAPTER 10

Proverbs Contrasting the Godly and the Wicked

THE proverbs of [R]Solomon: Prov. 1:1; 25:1
[R]A wise son makes a glad father,
But a foolish son *is* the grief of his
mother. Prov. 15:20; 17:21, 25; 19:13; 29:3, 15

2 Treasures of wickedness profit nothing,
But righteousness delivers from death.
3 [R]The LORD will not allow the righteous
soul to famish,
But He casts away the desire of the
wicked. Ps. 34:9, 10; 37:25

4 [R]He who deals *with* a slack hand
becomes poor,
But [R]the hand of the diligent makes *one*
rich. Prov. 19:15 • Prov. 12:24; 13:4; 21:5
5 He who gathers in [R]summer *is* a wise
son,
But he who sleeps in harvest *is* [R]a son
who causes shame. Prov. 6:8 • Prov. 19:26

6 Blessings *are* on the head of the
righteous,
But violence covers the mouth of the
wicked.
7 The memory of the righteous *is* blessed,
But the name of the wicked will rot.

8 The wise in heart will receive
commands,
But a prating fool will [T]fall. *be thrust down*

9 [R]He who walks with integrity walks
securely,
But he who perverts his ways will
become known. [Ps. 23:4]

10 He who winks with the eye causes
trouble,
But a prating fool will fall.

11 The mouth of the righteous *is* a well of
life,
But violence covers the mouth of the
wicked.

12 Hatred stirs up strife,
But [R]love covers all sins. [1 Cor. 13:4–7]

13 Wisdom is found on the lips of him who
has understanding,
But a rod *is* for the back of him who [T]is
devoid of understanding. *lacks heart*

14 Wise *people* store up knowledge,
But [R]the mouth of the foolish *is* near
destruction. Prov. 18:7

15 The [R]rich man's wealth *is* his strong
city;
The destruction of the poor *is* their
poverty. Job 31:24

16 The labor of the righteous *leads* to life,
The wages of the wicked to sin.

17 He who keeps instruction *is in* the way
of life,
But he who refuses reproof [T]goes
astray. *leads*

18 Whoever hides hatred *has* lying lips,
And whoever spreads slander *is* a fool.

19 [R]In the multitude of words sin is not
lacking, Eccl. 5:3
But he who restrains his lips *is* wise.
20 The tongue of the righteous *is* choice
silver;
The heart of the wicked *is worth* little.
21 The lips of the righteous feed many,
But fools die for lack of [T]wisdom. *heart*

22 [R]The blessing of the LORD makes *one*
rich, Gen. 24:35; 26:12
And He adds no sorrow with it.

23 [R]To do evil *is* like sport to a fool,
But a man of understanding has
wisdom. Prov. 2:14; 15:21
24 [R]The fear of the wicked will come upon
him,
And [R]the desire of the righteous will be
granted. Job 15:21 • Ps. 145:19

25 When the whirlwind passes by, [R]the
wicked *is* no *more,*
But [R]the righteous *has* an everlasting
foundation. Ps. 37:9, 10 • Ps. 15:5

26 As vinegar to the teeth and smoke to
the eyes,
So *is* the sluggard to those who send
him.

27 [R]The fear of the LORD prolongs days,
But [R]the years of the wicked will be
shortened. Prov. 9:11 • Job 15:32
28 The hope of the righteous *will be*
gladness,
But the [R]expectation of the wicked will
perish. Job 8:13
29 The way of the LORD *is* strength for the
upright,
But [R]destruction *will come* to the
workers of iniquity. Ps. 1:6

30 [R]The righteous will never be removed,
But the wicked will not inhabit the
[T]earth. Ps. 37:22 • *land*
31 [R]The mouth of the righteous brings forth
wisdom, Ps. 37:30
But the perverse tongue will be cut out.
32 The lips of the righteous know what is
acceptable,
But the mouth of the wicked *what is*
perverse.

CHAPTER 11

A [R]FALSE[T] balance *is* an abomination to
the LORD, Lev. 19:35, 36 • *deceptive*
But a just weight *is* His delight.

2 When pride comes, then comes shame;
But with the humble *is* wisdom.

3 The integrity of the upright will guide
[R]them,
But the perversity of the unfaithful will
destroy them. Prov. 13:6
4 Riches do not profit in the day of wrath,
But righteousness delivers from death.
5 The righteousness of the blameless will
[T]direct his way aright,
But the wicked will fall by his own
wickedness. *make his way smooth* or *straight*
6 The righteousness of the upright will
deliver them,
But the unfaithful will be taken by *their*
own lust.

7 When a wicked man dies, *his*
expectation will [R]perish, Prov. 10:28
And the hope of the unjust perishes.
8 The righteous is delivered from trouble,
And it comes to the wicked instead.

9 The hypocrite with *his* mouth destroys
his neighbor,
But through knowledge the righteous
will be delivered.
10 [R]When it goes well with the righteous,
the city rejoices;
And when the wicked perish, *there is*
shouting. Prov. 28:12
11 By the blessing of the upright the city is
[R]exalted,
But it is overthrown by the mouth of
the wicked. Prov. 14:34

12 He who [T]is devoid of wisdom despises
his neighbor,
But a man of understanding holds his
peace. Lit. *lacks heart*

13 [R]A talebearer reveals secrets,
But he who is of a faithful spirit
[R]conceals a matter. Lev. 19:16 • Prov. 19:11

14 [R]Where *there is* no counsel, the people
fall;
But in the multitude of counselors *there*
is safety. 1 Kin. 12:1

15 He who is [R]surety[T] for a stranger will
suffer *for it,* Prov. 6:1, 2 • *guaranty*
But one who hates [T]being surety is
secure. Lit. *those who strike hands*

16 A gracious woman retains honor,
But ruthless *men* retain riches.
17 [R]The merciful man does good for his
own soul,
But *he who is* cruel troubles his own
flesh. [Matt. 5:7; 25:34–36]
18 The wicked man does deceptive work,
But [R]to him who sows righteousness
will be a sure reward. Hos. 10:12
19 As righteousness *leads* to [R]life,
So he who pursues evil *pursues it* to his
own [R]death. Prov. 10:16; 12:28 • [Rom. 6:23]
20 Those who are of a perverse heart *are*
an abomination to the LORD,
But *such as are* blameless in their ways
are His delight.
21 *Though they join* [T]forces, the wicked
will not go unpunished;
But [R]the posterity of the righteous will
be delivered. Lit. *hand to hand* • Ps. 112:2

22 *As* a ring of gold in a swine's snout,
So is a lovely woman who lacks
[T]discretion. *taste*

23 The desire of the righteous *is* only good,
But the expectation of the wicked [R]*is*
wrath. Rom. 2:8, 9

24 There is *one* who [R]scatters, yet
increases more;

And there is *one* who withholds more
than is right,
But it *leads* to poverty. Ps. 112:9
25 [R]The generous soul will be made rich,
[R]And he who waters will also be watered
himself. [2 Cor. 9:6, 7] • [Matt. 5:7]
26 The people will curse [R]him who
withholds grain,
But [R]blessing *will be* on the head of him
who sells *it.* Amos 8:5, 6 • Job 29:13

27 He who diligently seeks good [T]finds
favor,
[R]But trouble will come to him who seeks
evil. Lit. *seeks* • Esth. 7:10

28 [R]He who trusts in his riches will fall,
But [R]the righteous will flourish like
foliage. Job 31:24 • Ps. 1:3

29 He who troubles his own house [R]will
inherit the wind,
And the fool *will be* [R]servant to the
wise of heart. Eccl. 5:16 • Prov. 14:19

30 The fruit of the righteous *is a* tree of
life,
And he who wins souls *is* wise.

31 [R]If the righteous will be [T]recompensed
on the earth,
How much more the wicked and the
sinner. Jer. 25:29 • *rewarded*

CHAPTER 12

WHOEVER loves instruction loves
knowledge,
But he who hates reproof *is* stupid.

2 A good *man* obtains favor from the
LORD,
But a man of wicked devices He will
condemn.

3 A man is not established by wickedness,
But the [R]root of the righteous cannot be
moved. [Prov. 10:25]

4 [R]An[T] excellent wife *is* the crown of her
husband, 1 Cor. 11:7 • Lit. *A woman of valor*
But she who causes shame *is* [R]like
rottenness in his bones. Prov. 14:30

5 The thoughts of the righteous *are* right,
But the counsels of the wicked *are*
deceitful.
6 [R]The words of the wicked *are*, "Lie in
wait for blood," Prov. 1:11, 18
[R]But the mouth of the upright will
deliver them. Prov. 14:3

7 [R]The wicked are overthrown and *are* no
more, Matt. 7:24–27
But the house of the righteous will
stand.

8 A man will be commended according to
his wisdom,
[R]But he who is of a perverse heart will
be despised. 1 Sam. 25:17

9 [R]Better *is the one* who is [T]slighted but
has a servant,
Than he who honors himself but lacks
bread. Prov. 13:7 • *lightly esteemed*

10 [R]A righteous *man* regards the life of his
animal, Deut. 25:4
But the tender mercies of the wicked
are cruel.

11 [R]He who [T]tills his land will be satisfied
with bread, Gen. 3:19 • *works* or *cultivates*
But he who follows [T]frivolity *is* devoid
of understanding. Lit. *vain things*

12 The wicked covet the catch of evil *men,*
But the root of the righteous yields
fruit.
13 [R]The wicked is ensnared by the
transgression of *his* lips,
[R]But the righteous will come through
trouble. Prov. 18:7 • [2 Pet. 2:9]
14 [R]A man will be satisfied with good by the
fruit of *his* mouth, Prov. 13:2; 15:23; 18:20
[R]And the recompense of a man's hands
will be rendered to him. [Is. 3:10, 11]

15 [R]The way of a fool *is* right in his own
eyes, Luke 18:11
But he who heeds counsel *is* wise.
16 A fool's wrath is known at once,
But a prudent *man* covers shame.

17 [R]He *who* speaks truth declares
righteousness, Prov. 14:5
But a false witness, deceit.
18 [R]There is one who speaks like the
piercings of a sword, Ps. 57:4
But the tongue of the wise *promotes*
health.
19 The truthful lip shall be established
forever,
But a lying tongue *is* but for a moment.
20 Deceit is in the heart of those who
devise evil,
But counselors of peace have joy.
21 [R]No grave [T]trouble will overtake the
righteous, 1 Pet. 3:13 • *harm*
But the wicked shall be filled with evil.
22 [R]Lying lips *are* an abomination to the
LORD, Rev. 22:15
But those who deal truthfully *are* His
delight.

23 [R]A prudent man conceals knowledge,

But the heart of fools proclaims
foolishness. Prov. 13:16

24 [R]The hand of the diligent will rule,
But the slothful will be put to forced
labor. Prov. 10:4

25 [R]Anxiety in the heart of man causes
depression, Prov. 15:13
But a good word makes it glad.

26 The righteous should choose his friends
carefully,
For the way of the wicked leads them
astray.

27 The slothful *man* does not roast what
he took in hunting,
But diligence *is* man's precious
possession.

28 In the way of righteousness *is* life,
And in *its* pathway *there is* no death.

CHAPTER 13

A WISE son *heeds* his father's instruction,
But a scoffer does not listen to rebuke.

2 [R]A man shall eat well by the fruit of *his*
mouth,
But the soul of the unfaithful feeds on
violence. Prov. 12:14

3 [R]He who guards his mouth preserves his
life,
But he who opens wide his lips shall
have destruction. Prov. 21:23

4 [R]The soul of a [T]sluggard desires, and *has*
nothing;
But the soul of the diligent shall be
made rich. Prov. 10:4 • *lazy man*

5 A righteous *man* hates lying,
But a wicked *man* is loathsome and
comes to shame.

6 [R]Righteousness keeps *him whose* way is
blameless, Prov. 11:3, 5, 6
But wickedness overthrows the sinner.

7 [R]There is one who makes himself rich,
yet *has* nothing;
And one who makes himself poor, yet
has great riches. [Prov. 11:24; 12:9]

8 The ransom of a man's life *is* his riches,
But the poor does not hear rebuke.

9 The light of the righteous rejoices,
[R]But the lamp of the wicked will be put
out. Prov. 24:20

10 By pride comes only contention,
But with the well-advised *is* wisdom.

11 [R]Wealth *gained by* dishonesty will be
diminished,
But he who gathers by labor will
increase. Prov. 10:2; 20:21

12 Hope deferred makes the heart sick,
But [R]*when* the desire comes, *it is* a tree
of life. Prov. 13:19

13 He who [R]despises the word will be
destroyed,
But he who fears the commandment
will be rewarded. Num. 15:31

14 [R]The law of the wise *is* a fountain of life,
To turn *one* away from [R]the snares of
death. Prov. 10:11; 14:27; 6:22 • 2 Sam. 22:6

15 Good understanding [T]gains favor, *gives*
But the way of the unfaithful *is* hard.

16 [R]Every prudent *man* acts with
knowledge,
But a fool lays open *his* folly. Prov. 12:23

17 A wicked messenger falls into trouble,
But [R]a faithful ambassador *brings*
health. Prov. 25:13

18 Poverty and shame *will come* to him
who [T]disdains correction,
But [R]he who regards reproof will be
honored. Lit. *ignores* • Prov. 15:5, 31, 32

19 A desire accomplished is sweet to the
soul,
But *it is* an abomination to fools to
depart from evil.

20 He who walks with wise *men* will be
wise,
But the companion of fools will be
destroyed.

21 [R]Evil pursues sinners,
But to the righteous, good shall be
repaid. Prov. 32:10

22 A good *man* leaves an inheritance to his
children's children,
But [R]the wealth of the sinner is stored
up for the righteous. [Eccl. 2:26]

23 [R]Much food *is in* the [T]fallow *ground* of
the poor, Prov. 12:11 • *uncultivated*
And for lack of justice there is waste.

24 [R]He who spares his rod hates his son,
But he who loves him disciplines him
[T]promptly. Prov. 19:18 • *early*

25 [R]The righteous eats to the satisfying of
his soul,
But the stomach of the wicked shall be
in want. Ps. 34:10

CHAPTER 14

EVERY wise woman builds her house,
But the foolish pulls it down with her hands.

2 He who walks in his uprightness fears the LORD,
[R]But *he who is* perverse in his ways despises Him. [Rom. 2:4]

3 In the mouth of a fool *is* a rod of pride,
[R]But the lips of the wise will preserve them. Prov. 12:6

4 Where no oxen *are*, the [T]trough *is* clean;
But much increase *comes* by the strength of an ox. *manger* or *feed trough*

5 A faithful witness does not lie,
But a false witness will utter lies.

6 A scoffer seeks wisdom and does not *find it*,
But [R]knowledge *is* easy to him who understands. Prov. 8:9; 17:24
7 Go from the presence of a foolish man,
When you do not perceive *in him* the lips of [R]knowledge. Prov. 23:9
8 The wisdom of the prudent *is* to understand his way,
But the folly of fools *is* deceit.

9 [R]Fools mock at [T]sin, Prov. 10:23 • Lit. *guilt*
But among the upright *there is* favor.

10 The heart knows its own bitterness,
And a stranger does not share its joy.

11 [R]The house of the wicked will be overthrown, Job 8:15
But the tent of the upright will flourish.

12 [R]There is a way *that seems* right to a man, Prov. 16:25
But its end *is* the way of death.

13 Even in laughter the heart may sorrow,
And the end of mirth *may be* grief.

14 The backslider in heart will be [R]filled with his own ways, Prov. 1:31; 12:15
But a good man *will be satisfied* [T]from [R]above. Lit. *from above himself* • Prov. 13:2; 18:20

15 The simple believes every word,
But the prudent *man* considers well his steps.
16 A wise *man* fears and departs from evil,
But a fool rages and is self-confident.
17 *He who is* quick-tempered acts foolishly,
And a man of wicked intentions is hated.

18 The simple inherit folly,
But the prudent are crowned with knowledge.
19 The evil will bow before the good,
And the wicked at the gates of the righteous.

20 [R]The poor *man* is hated even by his own neighbor, Prov. 19:7
But the rich *has* many [R]friends. Prov. 19:4
21 He who despises his neighbor sins;
[R]But he who has mercy on the poor, happy *is* he. Ps. 112:9

22 Do they not go astray who devise evil?
But mercy and truth *belong* to those who devise good.

23 In all labor there is profit,
But idle chatter *leads* only to poverty.

24 The crown of the wise is their riches,
But the foolishness of fools *is* folly.

25 A true witness [T]delivers souls, *saves lives*
But a deceitful *witness* speaks lies.

26 In the fear of the LORD *there is* strong confidence,
And His children will have a place of refuge.
27 [R]The fear of the LORD *is* a fountain of life,
To avoid the snares of death. Prov. 13:14

28 In a multitude of people *is* a king's honor,
But in the lack of people *is* the downfall of a prince.

29 [R]*He who is* slow to wrath has great understanding, James 1:19
But *he who is* impulsive exalts folly.

30 A sound heart *is* life to the body,
But envy *is* rottenness to the bones.

31 [R]He who oppresses the poor reproaches [R]his Maker,
But he who honors Him has mercy on the needy. Matt. 25:40 • [Prov. 22:2]

32 The wicked is banished in his wickedness,
But [R]the righteous has a refuge in his death. Job 13:15

33 Wisdom rests *quietly* in the heart of him who has understanding,
But [R]*what is* in the heart of fools is made known. Prov. 12:16

34 Righteousness exalts a [R]nation, Prov. 11:11
But sin *is* a reproach to *any* people.

35 [R]The king's favor *is* toward a wise
servant, Matt. 24:45–47
But his wrath *is against* him who
causes shame.

CHAPTER 15

A SOFT answer turns away wrath,
But a harsh word stirs up anger.
2 The tongue of the wise uses knowledge
rightly,
[R]But the mouth of fools pours forth
foolishness. Prov. 12:23

3 [R]The eyes of the LORD *are* in every place,
Keeping watch on the evil and the
good. Job 34:21

4 A wholesome tongue *is* a tree of life,
But perverseness in it breaks the spirit.

5 A fool despises his father's instruction,
But he who receives reproof is prudent.

6 *In* the house of the righteous *there is*
much treasure,
But in the revenue of the wicked is
trouble.

7 The lips of the wise [T]disperse
knowledge, *spread*
But the heart of the fool *does* not *do* so.

8 [R]The sacrifice of the wicked *is* an
abomination to the LORD,
But the prayer of the upright *is* His
delight. Is. 1:11
9 The way of the wicked *is* an
abomination to the LORD,
But He loves him who [R]follows
righteousness. Prov. 21:21

10 [R]Harsh correction *is* for him who
forsakes the way, 1 Kin. 22:8
And he who hates reproof will die.

11 [R]Hell[T] and [T]Destruction *are* before the
LORD; Job 26:6 • Or *Sheol* • Heb. *Abaddon*
So how much more [R]the hearts of the
sons of men. 2 Chr. 6:30

12 [R]A scoffer does not love one who
reproves him, Amos 5:10
Nor will he go to the wise.

13 [R]A merry heart makes a cheerful
[T]countenance, Prov. 12:25 • *face*
But [R]by sorrow of the heart the spirit is
broken. Prov. 17:22

14 The heart of him who has
understanding seeks knowledge,
But the mouth of fools feeds on
foolishness.

15 All the days of the afflicted *are* evil,
[R]But he who is of a merry heart *has* a
continual feast. Prov. 17:22

16 [R]Better *is* a little with the fear of the
LORD, Ps. 37:16
Than great treasure with trouble.
17 [R]Better *is* a dinner of [T]herbs where love
is, Prov. 17:1 • Or *vegetables*
Than a fatted calf with hatred.

18 [R]A wrathful man stirs up strife,
But *he who is* slow to anger allays
contention. Prov. 26:21

19 [R]The way of the [T]slothful *man is* like a
hedge of thorns, Prov. 22:5 • *lazy*
But the way of the upright *is* a
highway.

20 A wise son makes a father glad,
But a foolish man despises his mother.

21 [R]Folly *is* joy *to him who is* destitute of
[T]discernment, Prov. 10:23 • *heart*
[R]But a man of understanding walks
uprightly. Eph. 5:15

22 [R]Without counsel, plans go awry,
But in the multitude of counselors they
are established. Prov. 11:14

23 A man has joy by the answer of his
mouth,
And a word *spoken* [T]in due season, how
good *it is!* Lit. *in its time*

24 [R]The way of life *winds* upward for the
wise, Phil. 3:20
That he may [R]turn away from [T]hell
below. Prov. 14:16 • Or *Sheol*

25 [R]The LORD will destroy the house of the
proud, Prov. 12:7
But [R]He will establish the boundary of
the widow. Ps. 68:5, 6

26 [R]The thoughts of the wicked *are* an
abomination to the LORD, Prov. 6:16, 18
But *the words* of the pure *are* pleasant.

27 [R]He who is greedy for gain troubles his
own house, Is. 5:8
But he who hates bribes will live.

28 The heart of the righteous [R]studies how
to answer, 1 Pet. 3:15
But the mouth of the wicked pours
forth evil.

29 [R]The LORD *is* far from the wicked,
But [R]He hears the prayer of the righteous. Ps. 10:1; 34:16 • Ps. 145:18

30 The light of the eyes rejoices the heart,
And a good report makes the bones [T]healthy. Lit. *fat*

31 The ear that hears the reproof of life
Will abide among the wise.
32 He who disdains instruction despises his own soul,
But he who heeds reproof gets understanding.
33 [R]The fear of the LORD *is* the instruction of wisdom, Prov. 1:7
And [R]before honor *is* humility. Prov. 18:12

CHAPTER 16

Proverbs Encouraging Godly Lives

THE [R]preparations[T] of the heart *belong* to man, Jer. 10:23 • *plans*
[R]But the answer of the tongue *is* from the LORD. Matt. 10:19

2 All the ways of a man *are* pure in his own [R]eyes, Prov. 21:2
But the LORD weighs the spirits.

3 [R]Commit your works to the LORD, Ps. 37:5
And your thoughts will be established.

4 The [R]LORD has made all *things* for Himself, Is. 43:7
[R]Yes, even the wicked for the day of [T]doom. [Rom. 9:22] • Lit. *evil*

5 [R]Everyone *who is* proud in heart *is* an abomination to the LORD; Prov. 6:17; 8:13
Though they join [T]forces, none will go unpunished. Lit. *hand in hand*

6 [R]In mercy and truth Dan. 4:27
Atonement is provided for iniquity;
And [R]by the fear of the LORD *one* departs from evil. Prov. 8:13; 14:16

7 When a man's ways please the LORD,
He makes even his enemies to be at peace with him.

8 Better *is* a little with righteousness,
Than vast revenues without justice.

9 [R]A man's heart plans his way, Prov. 19:21
[R]But the LORD directs his steps. Jer. 10:23

10 *Even though* divination *is* on the lips of the king,
His mouth must not transgress in judgment.
11 [R]A just weight and balance *are* the LORD's; Lev. 19:36
All the weights in the bag *are* His [T]work. *concern*
12 *It is* an abomination for kings to commit wickedness,
For [R]a throne is established by righteousness. Prov. 25:5
13 [R]Righteous lips *are* the delight of kings,
And they love him who speaks *what is* right. Prov. 14:35
14 As messengers of death *is* the king's wrath,
But a wise man will appease it.
15 In the light of the king's face *is* life,
And his favor *is* like a [R]cloud of the latter rain. Zech. 10:1

16 [R]How much better *it is* to get wisdom than gold! Prov. 8:10, 11, 19
And to get understanding is to be chosen rather than silver.

17 The highway of the upright *is* to depart from evil;
He who keeps his way preserves his soul.

18 Pride *goes* before destruction,
And a haughty spirit before a fall.
19 Better *to be* of a humble spirit with the lowly,
Than to divide the [T]spoil with the proud. *plunder*

20 He who heeds the word wisely will find good,
And whoever [R]trusts in the LORD, happy *is* he. Ps. 34:8

16:3 Commitment—Dedication is the foundation of commitment. Without it the believer is unable to offer God anything else. Paul explains this dedication process in Romans 12:1 and 2. He emphasizes three things. First, it is our body which is to be dedicated as a living sacrifice to God. Second, we are to avoid being conformed to this world, but strive to be transformed by the Word. Finally, by doing this we can discover God's perfect will for our lives.

After the dedication of our bodies, what are we to commit? We are to commit our salvation to God (Page 1433—2 Tim. 1:12). Second, we are to commit our works (Prov. 16:3). Then, our goals in life are to be given to Him (Page 592—Job 5:8; Page 645—Ps. 37:5). It is difficult but vital to commit our suffering experiences to God (Page 1483—1 Pet. 4:19). Our Lord Jesus did this very thing when He was on earth (Page 1480—1 Pet. 2:23). Finally, in the hour of death we can with confidence commit our very souls to God (Page 641—Ps. 31:5). Paul the apostle assures us that any and all such commitments to the Lord will be accepted and honored. See First Corinthians 15:58.

Now turn to Page 1355—1 Cor. 12:1–10: Using Spiritual Gifts.

21 The wise in heart will be called prudent,
And sweetness of the lips increases learning.

22 Understanding *is* a wellspring of life to him who has it.
But the correction of fools *is* folly.

23 The heart of the wise teaches his mouth,
And adds learning to his lips.

24 Pleasant words *are like* a honeycomb,
Sweetness to the soul and health to the bones.

25 There is a way *that seems* right to a man,
But its end *is* the way of death.

26 The person who labors, labors for himself,
For his *hungry* mouth drives him *on.*

27 An ungodly man digs up evil,
And *it is* on his lips like a burning fire.
28 A perverse man sows strife,
And [R]a whisperer separates the best of friends. Prov. 17:9
29 A violent man entices his neighbor,
And leads him in a way *that is* not good.
30 He winks his eye to devise perverse things;
He [T]purses his lips *and* brings about evil. Lit. *compresses*

31 [R]The silver-haired head *is* a crown of glory, Prov. 20:29
If it is found in the way of righteousness.

32 [R]*He who is* slow to anger *is* better than the mighty, Prov. 14:29; 19:11
And he who rules his spirit than he who takes a city.

33 The lot is cast into the lap,
But its every decision *is* from the LORD.

CHAPTER 17

BETTER *is* [R]a dry morsel with quietness,
Than a house full of [T]feasting *with* strife. Prov. 15:17 • Or *sacrificial meals*

2 A wise servant will rule over [R]a son who causes shame,
And will share an inheritance among the brothers. Prov. 10:5

3 The refining pot *is* for silver and the furnace for gold,
[R]But the LORD tests the hearts. Jer. 17:10

4 An evildoer gives heed to false lips;
A liar listens eagerly to a [T]spiteful tongue. Lit. *destructive*

5 [R]He who mocks the poor reproaches his Maker;
[R]He who is glad at calamity will not go unpunished. Prov. 14:31 • Job 31:29

6 [R]Children's children *are* the crown of old men, [Ps. 127:3; 128:3]
And the glory of children *is* their father.

7 Excellent speech is not becoming to a fool,
Much less lying lips to a prince.

8 A present *is* a precious stone in the eyes of its possessor;
Wherever he turns, he prospers.

9 [R]He who covers a transgression seeks love, [Prov. 10:12]
But [R]he who repeats a matter separates *the best of* friends. Prov. 16:28

10 [R]Reproof is more effective for a wise man [Mic. 7:9]
Than a hundred blows on a fool.

11 An evil *man* seeks only rebellion;
Therefore a cruel messenger will be sent against him.

12 Let a man meet [R]a bear robbed of her cubs,
Rather than a fool in his folly. Hos. 13:8

13 Whoever rewards evil for good,
Evil will not depart from his house.

14 The beginning of strife *is like* releasing water;
Therefore [R]stop contention before a quarrel starts. [Prov. 20:3]

15 [R]He who justifies the wicked, and he who condemns the just,
Both of them alike *are* an abomination to the LORD. Ex. 23:7

16 Why *is there* in the hand of a fool the purchase price of wisdom,
Since *he has* no heart *for it*?

17 [R]A friend loves at all times, Ruth 1:16
And a brother is born for adversity.

18 A man devoid of [T]understanding shakes hands in a pledge, Lit. *heart*
And becomes surety for his friend.

19 He who loves transgression loves strife,
And [R]he who exalts his gate seeks destruction. Prov. 16:18

20 He who has a [T]deceitful heart finds no good,
And he who has [R]a perverse tongue falls into evil. *crooked* • James 3:8

21 He who begets a scoffer *does so* to his sorrow,
And the father of a fool has no joy.

22 A merry heart [T]does good, *like* medicine, Or *makes medicine even better*
But a broken spirit dries the bones.

23 A wicked *man* accepts a bribe [T]behind the back Under cover, lit. *from the bosom*
To pervert the ways of justice.

24 [R]Wisdom *is* in the sight of him who has understanding,
But the eyes of a fool *are* on the ends of the earth. Eccl. 2:14

25 A foolish son *is* a grief to his father,
And bitterness to her who bore him.

26 Also, to punish the righteous *is* not good,
Nor to strike princes for *their* uprightness.

27 [R]He who has knowledge spares his words,
And a man of understanding is of a calm spirit. James 1:19
28 [R]Even a fool is counted wise when he holds his peace; Job 13:5
When he shuts his lips, *he is considered* perceptive.

CHAPTER 18

A MAN who isolates himself seeks his own desire;
He rages against all wise judgment.

2 A fool has no delight in understanding,
But in expressing his own heart.

3 When the wicked comes, contempt comes also;
And with dishonor *comes* reproach.

4 [R]The words of a man's mouth *are* deep waters; Prov. 10:11
[R]The wellspring of wisdom *is* a flowing brook. [James 3:17]

5 *It is* not good to show partiality to the wicked,
Or to overthrow the righteous in [R]judgment. Prov. 17:15

6 A fool's lips enter into contention,
And his mouth calls for blows.
7 A fool's mouth *is* his destruction,
And his lips *are* the snare of his soul.
8 [R]The words of a [T]talebearer *are* like *tasty trifles, Prov. 12:18 • *gossip* or *slander*
And they go down into the [T]inmost body. Lit. *rooms of the belly*

9 He who is slothful in his work
Is a brother to him who is a great destroyer.

10 The name of the LORD *is* a strong [R]tower; 2 Sam. 22:2, 3, 33
The righteous run to it and are safe.
11 The rich man's wealth *is* his strong city,
And like a high wall in his own esteem.

12 [R]Before destruction the heart of a man is haughty, Prov. 15:33; 16:18
And before honor *is* humility.

13 He who answers a matter before he hears *it*,
It *is* folly and shame to him.

14 The spirit of a man will sustain him in sickness,
But who can bear a broken spirit?

15 The heart of the prudent acquires knowledge,
And the ear of the wise seeks knowledge.

16 A man's gift makes room for him,
And brings him before great men.

17 The first *one* to plead his cause *seems* right,
Until his neighbor comes and examines him.

18 Casting [R]lots causes contentions to cease, [Prov. 16:33]
And keeps the mighty apart.

19 A brother offended *is harder to win* than a strong city,
And contentions *are* like the bars of a castle.

20 [R]A man's stomach shall be satisfied from the fruit of his mouth, Prov. 12:14; 14:14
And from the produce of his lips he shall be filled.

18:8 A Jewish tradition reads *wounds*

21 [R]Death and life *are* in the power of the
tongue, Matt. 12:37
And those who love it will eat its fruit.

22 *He who* finds a wife finds a good *thing*,
And obtains favor from the LORD.

23 The poor *man* uses entreaties,
But the rich answers roughly.

24 A man *who has* friends *must himself
be friendly,
[R]But there is a friend *who* sticks closer
than a brother. Prov. 17:17

CHAPTER 19

BETTER [R]*is* the poor who walks in his
integrity
Than *one who is* perverse in his lips,
and is a fool. Prov. 28:6

2 Also it is not good *for* a soul *to be*
without knowledge,
And he sins who hastens with *his* feet.

3 The foolishness of a man twists his way,
And his heart frets against the LORD.

4 [R]Wealth makes many friends,
But the poor is separated from his
friend. Prov. 14:20

5 A false witness will not go unpunished,
And *he who* speaks lies will not escape.

6 Many entreat the favor of the nobility,
And every man *is* a friend to one who
gives gifts.
7 [R]All the brothers of the poor hate him;
How much more do his friends go [R]far
from him! Prov. 14:20 • Ps. 38:11
He may pursue *them with* words, *yet*
they [T]abandon *him*. Lit. *are not*

8 He who gets [T]wisdom loves his own
soul;
He who keeps understanding [R]will find
good. Lit. *heart* • Prov. 16:20

9 A false witness will not go unpunished,
And *he who* speaks lies shall perish.

10 Luxury is not fitting for a fool,
Much less [R]for a servant to rule over
princes. Prov. 30:21, 22

11 [R]The discretion of a man makes him
slow to anger,
[R]And *it is to* his glory to overlook a
transgression. James 1:19 • Eph. 4:32

12 [R]The king's wrath *is* like the roaring of a
lion, Prov. 16:14
But his favor *is* like dew on the grass.

13 A foolish son *is* the ruin of his father,
[R]And the contentions of a wife *are* a
continual [T]dripping. Prov. 21:9, 19 • Irritation

14 [R]Houses and riches *are* an inheritance
from fathers, 2 Cor. 12:14
But a prudent wife *is* from the LORD.

15 Slothfulness casts *one* into a deep sleep,
And an idle person will suffer hunger.

16 [R]He who keeps the commandment keeps
his soul,
But he who [T]is careless of his ways will
die. Luke 10:28; 11:28 • Is reckless, lit. *despises*

17 [R]He who has pity on the poor lends to
the LORD,
And He will pay back what he has
given. [2 Cor. 9:6–8]

18 [R]Chasten your son while there is hope,
And do not set your heart *on his
destruction. Prov. 13:24

19 *A man of* great wrath will suffer
punishment;
For if you deliver *him*, you will have to
do it again.

20 Listen to counsel and receive
instruction,
That you may be wise [R]in your latter
days. Ps. 37:37

21 There are many plans in a man's heart,
[R]Nevertheless the LORD's counsel—that
will stand. Heb. 6:17

22 What is desired in a man is kindness,
And a poor man is better than a liar.

23 [R]The fear of the LORD *leads* to life,
And *he who has it* will abide in
satisfaction; [1 Tim. 4:8]
He will not be visited with evil.

24 [R]A slothful *man* buries his hand in the
*bowl,
And will not so much as bring it to his
mouth again. Prov. 15:19

25 Strike a scoffer, and the simple [R]will
become wary; Deut. 13:11
[R]Reprove one who has understanding,
and he will discern knowledge. Prov. 9:8

26 He who mistreats *his* father *and* chases
away *his* mother

18:24 Tg., Syr., Gr. mss., Vg. *may come to ruin*
19:18 Lit. *to put to death*, A Jewish tradition reads *on his crying* **19:24** LXX, Syr. *bosom;* Tg., Vg. *armpit*

Is [R]a son who causes shame and brings
reproach. Prov. 17:2

27 Cease listening to instruction, my son,
And you will stray from the words of
knowledge.

28 A [T]disreputable witness scorns justice,
And the mouth of the wicked devours
iniquity. Lit. *witness of Belial, worthless witness*

29 Judgments are prepared for scoffers,
And beatings for the backs of fools.

CHAPTER 20

WINE [R]is a mocker, Gen. 9:21
Intoxicating drink arouses brawling,
And whoever is led astray by it is not
wise.

2 The [T]wrath of a king *is* like the roaring
of a lion; Lit. *fear* or *terror*
Whoever provokes him to anger sins
against his own life.

3 [R]*It is* honorable for a man to stop
striving, Prov. 17:14
Since any fool can start a quarrel.

4 [R]The sluggard will not plow because of
winter; Prov. 10:4
[R]*Therefore* he will beg during the harvest
And *have* nothing. Prov. 19:15

5 Counsel in the heart of man *is like* deep
water,
But a man of understanding will draw it
out.

6 Most men will proclaim each his own
[T]goodness, Lit. *lovingkindness*
But who can find a faithful man?

7 [R]The righteous *man* walks in his
integrity; 2 Cor. 1:12
His children *are* blessed after him.

8 A king who sits on the throne of
judgment
Scatters all evil with his eyes.

9 [R]Who can say, "I have made my heart
clean, [1 Kin. 8:46]
I am pure from my sin"?

10 [R]Diverse weights *and* diverse measures,
They *are* both alike, an abomination to
the LORD. Deut. 25:13

11 Even a child is [R]known by his deeds,
By whether what he does *is* pure and
right. Matt. 7:16

12 The hearing ear and the seeing eye,
The LORD has made both of them.

13 [R]Do not love sleep, lest you come to
poverty; Rom. 12:11
Open your eyes, *and* you will be
satisfied with bread.

14 "*It is* [T]good for nothing," cries the buyer;
But when he has gone his way, then he
boasts. Lit. *evil, evil*

15 There is gold and a multitude of rubies,
But [R]the lips of knowledge *are* a
precious jewel. [Prov. 3:13–15]

16 [R]Take the garment of one who is surety
for a stranger, Prov. 22:26
And hold it as a pledge *when it* is for a
seductress.

17 [R]Bread gained by deceit *is* sweet to a
man, Prov. 9:17
But afterward his mouth will be filled
with gravel.

18 [R]*Every* [T]purpose is established by
counsel; Prov. 24:6 • *plan*
[R]By wise counsel wage war. Luke 14:31

19 [R]He who goes about *as* a talebearer
reveals secrets; Prov. 11:13
Therefore do not associate with one
[R]who flatters with his lips. Rom. 16:18

20 [R]Whoever curses his father or his
mother, Matt. 15:4
[R]His lamp will be put out in deep
darkness. Job 18:5, 6

21 [R]An inheritance gained hastily at the
beginning Prov. 28:20
Will not be blessed at the end.

22 [R]Do not say, "I will [T]recompense evil";
[R]Wait for the LORD, and He will save
you. [Rom. 12:17–19] • *repay* • 2 Sam. 16:12

23 Diverse weights *are* an abomination to
the LORD,
And a false balance *is* not good.

24 A man's steps *are* of the LORD;
How then can a man understand his
own way?

25 *It is* a snare for a man to devote rashly
something as holy,
And afterward to reconsider *his* vows.

26 [R]A wise king sifts out the wicked,
And brings the threshing wheel over
them. Ps. 101:8

27 [R]The spirit of a man *is* the lamp of the LORD, 1 Cor. 2:11
Searching all the [T]inner depths of his heart. Lit. *rooms of the belly*

28 [R]Mercy and truth preserve the king,
And by [T]lovingkindness he upholds his throne. Prov. 21:21 • *mercy*

29 The glory of young men *is* their strength,
And [R]the splendor of old men *is* their gray head. Prov. 16:31

30 Blows that hurt cleanse away evil,
As *do* stripes the [T]inner depths of the heart. Lit. *rooms of the belly*

CHAPTER 21

THE king's heart *is* in the hand of the LORD,
Like the [T]rivers of water; *channels*
He turns it wherever He wishes.

2 [R]Every way of a man *is* right in his own eyes, Prov. 16:2
[R]But the LORD weighs the hearts. Prov. 24:12

3 [R]To do righteousness and justice
Is more acceptable to the LORD than sacrifice. 1 Sam. 15:22

4 [R]A haughty look, a proud heart, Prov. 6:17
And the plowing of the wicked *are* sin.

5 [R]The plans of the diligent *lead* surely to plenty, Prov. 10:4
But *those of* everyone *who is* hasty, surely to poverty.

6 [R]Getting treasures by a lying tongue
Is the fleeting fantasy of those who seek death. 2 Pet. 2:3

7 The violence of the wicked will [T]destroy them, Lit. *drag them away*
Because they refuse to do justice.

8 The way of a guilty man *is* perverse;
But *as for* the pure, his work *is* right.

9 *It is* better to dwell in a corner of a housetop,
Than in a house shared with [R]a contentious woman. Prov. 19:13

10 The soul of the wicked desires evil;
His neighbor finds no favor in his eyes.

11 When the scoffer is punished, the simple is made wise;
But when the [R]wise is instructed, he receives knowledge. Prov. 19:25

12 The righteous *God* wisely considers the house of the wicked,
Overthrowing the wicked for *their* wickedness.

13 [R]Whoever shuts his ears to the cry of the poor [Matt. 7:2; 18:30–34]
Will also cry himself and not be heard.

14 A gift in secret pacifies anger,
And a bribe [T]behind the back, strong wrath. Under cover, lit. *in the bosom*

15 *It is* a joy for the just to do justice,
But destruction *will come* to the workers of iniquity.

16 A man who wanders from the way of understanding
Will rest in the congregation of the [R]dead. Ps. 49:14

17 He who loves pleasure *will be* a poor man;
He who loves wine and oil will not be rich.

18 The wicked *shall be* a ransom for the righteous,
And the unfaithful for the upright.

19 *It is* better to dwell [T]in the wilderness,
Than with a contentious and angry woman. Lit. *in the land of the desert*

20 [R]*There is* desirable treasure, Ps. 112:3
And oil in the dwelling of the wise,
But a foolish man squanders it.

21 [R]He who follows righteousness and mercy Matt. 5:6
Finds life, righteousness and honor.

22 A [R]wise *man* [T]scales the city of the mighty, Prov. 24:5 • Climbs over the walls of
And brings down the trusted stronghold.

23 [R]Whoever guards his mouth and tongue
Keeps his soul from troubles. [James 3:2]

24 A proud *and* haughty *man*—"Scoffer" *is* his name;
He acts with arrogant pride.

25 The [R]desire of the slothful kills him,
For his hands refuse to labor. Prov. 13:4
26 He covets greedily all day long,
But the righteous [R]gives and does not spare. [Prov. 22:9]

27 [R]The sacrifice of the wicked *is* an
abomination; Jer. 6:20
How much more *when* he brings it with
wicked intent!

28 A false witness shall perish,
But the man who hears *him* will speak
endlessly.

29 A wicked man hardens his face,
But *as for* the upright, he *establishes
his way.

30 [R]*There is* no wisdom or understanding
Or counsel against the LORD. [Jer. 9:23, 24]

31 The horse *is* prepared for the day of
battle,
But [R]deliverance *is* of the LORD. Ps. 3:8

CHAPTER 22

A [R]*GOOD* name is to be chosen rather
than great riches, Eccl. 7:1
Loving favor rather than silver and
gold.

2 The [R]rich and the poor have this in
common, Prov. 29:13
The LORD *is* the maker of them all.

3 A prudent *man* foresees evil and hides
himself,
But the simple pass on and are
[R]punished. Prov. 27:12

4 By humility *and* the fear of the LORD
Are riches and honor and life.

5 Thorns *and* snares *are* in the way of the
perverse;
He who guards his soul will be far from
them.

6 [R]Train up a child in the way he should
go, Eph. 6:4
[T]And when he is old he will not depart
from it. *Even*

7 The [R]rich rules over the poor,
And the borrower *is* servant to the
lender. James 2:6

8 He who sows iniquity will reap
[R]sorrow,[T] Job 4:8 • *trouble*
And the rod of his anger will fail.

9 [R]He who has a [T]bountiful eye will be
[R]blessed, 2 Cor. 9:6 • Lit. *good* • [Prov. 19:17]
For he gives of his bread to the poor.

10 [R]Cast out the scoffer, and contention will
leave; Ps. 101:5
Yes, strife and reproach will cease.

11 [R]He who loves purity of heart Ps. 101:6
And has grace on his lips,
The king *will be* his friend.

12 The eyes of the LORD preserve
knowledge,

21:29 Qr., LXX *understands*

22:6 A Prescription for Rearing Children—This verse reveals two ingredients in the prescription for rearing children: first, the command, "Train up a child in the way he should go"; and second, the promise, "when he is old he will not depart from it."

The command involves three parts:

a. The concept of training—"Train up." This does not denote corporal punishment but rather includes three ideas: *Dedication*—this is the consistent meaning of the word in its other Old Testament occurrences (Page 230—Deut. 20:5; Page 404—1 Kin. 8:63; Page 509—2 Chr. 7:5). Child training must begin with dedication of the child to God; the parent must realize that the child belongs exclusively to God and is given to the parent only as a stewardship. *Instruction*—this is the meaning of this word as it is used in the Jewish writings; the parents are to instruct or cause their children to learn everything essential in pleasing God. *Motivation*—this is the meaning of the word in Arabic, as it is used to describe the action of a midwife who stimulates the palate of the newborn babe so it will take nourishment. Parents are to create a taste or desire within the child so that he is internally motivated (rather than externally compelled) to do what God wants him to do.
b. The recipient of training—"a child." This is one of seven Hebrew words translated by the English word *child* and would better be translated by our word *dependent*. As long as the child is dependent on his parents he is to be the recipient of training, regardless of his age.
c. The content of the training—"in the way that he should go." The thought is that at each stage of his development the parents or guardians are to dedicate, instruct, and motivate the child to do what God evidently has best equipped the child to do for Him. This is graphically illustrated by Joshua when he said, "But as for me and my house, we will serve the LORD" (Page 279—Josh. 24:15).

If the command has been kept, the promise can be claimed. The promise includes the time of realization—"when he is old"—this is best understood as being parallel with "a child," hence, "when he is independent," i.e., no longer economically dependent upon his parents, referring to the time when he leaves their home to establish his own. The promise includes the certainty of realization—"he will not depart from it." If the command has been kept, the promise will be realized. If the command has not been kept, the promise will not be realized. Rearing children is not an overnight occurrence; it takes careful forethought and conscious obedience on the part of the parents.

Now turn to Page 14—Gen. 9:5: The Origin of Human Government.

But He overthrows the words of the
faithless.

13 [R]The slothful *man* says, "*There is* a lion
outside! Prov. 26:13
I shall be slain in the streets!"

14 [R]The mouth of an immoral woman *is* a
deep pit; Prov. 2:16; 5:3; 7:5
[R]He who is abhorred of the LORD will fall
there. Eccl. 7:26

15 Foolishness *is* bound up in the heart of
a child,
But [R]the rod of correction will drive it
far from him. Prov. 13:24; 23:13, 14

16 He who oppresses the poor to increase
his *riches*,
And he who gives to the rich, *will*
surely *come* to poverty.

Proverbs Concerning Various Situations

17 Incline your ear and hear the words of
the wise,
And apply your heart to my knowledge;
18 For *it is* a pleasant thing if you keep
them within you;
Let them all be fixed upon your lips,
19 So that your trust may be in the LORD;
I have instructed you today, even you.
20 Have I not written to you excellent
things
Of counsels and knowledge,

21 That I may make you know the
certainty of the words of truth,
That you may answer words of truth
To those who [T]send to you? Or *send you*

22 Do not rob the [R]poor because he *is*
poor, Ex. 23:6
Nor oppress the afflicted at the gate;
23 [R]For the LORD will plead their cause,
And plunder the soul of those who
plunder them. 1 Sam. 24:12

24 Make no friendship with an angry man,
And with a furious man do not go,
25 Lest you learn his ways
And set a snare for your soul.

26 [R]Do not be one of those who [T]shakes
hands in a pledge, Prov. 11:15 • Lit. *strikes*
One of those who is surety for debts;
27 If you have nothing *with which* to pay,
Why should he take away your bed
from under you?

28 Do not remove the ancient [T]landmark
Which your fathers have set. *boundary*

29 Do you see a man *who* [T]excels in his
work? *is prompt in his business*
He will stand before kings;
He will not stand before [T]unknown
men. *obscure*

CHAPTER 23

WHEN you sit down to eat with a ruler,
Consider carefully what *is* before you;
2 And put a knife to your throat
If you *are* a man given to appetite.
3 Do not desire his delicacies,
For they *are* deceptive food.

4 [R]Do not overwork to be rich;
[R]Because of your own understanding,
cease! 1 Tim. 6:9, 10 • Rom. 12:16
5 Will you set your eyes on that which is
not?
For *riches* certainly make themselves
wings;
They fly away like an eagle *toward*
heaven.

6 Do not eat the bread of [R]a miser,
Nor desire his delicacies; Deut. 15:9
7 For as he thinks in his heart, so *is* he.
"Eat and drink!" [R]he says to you,
But his heart is not with you. Prov. 12:2

22:21 God's Word Equips—In a general sense it can be said that the Bible was written to convict sinners of sin and to equip believers for service.

a. It equips for evangelism. Philip the evangelist uses the fifty-third chapter of Isaiah to point the Ethiopian eunuch to Christ in Acts 8:26–35.

b. It equips for counseling others. In his two letters to Timothy, Paul constantly urges this young man to preach the Word of God (Page 1426—1 Tim. 1:3, 18; 4:13–15; Page 1434—2 Tim. 2:1, 2, 15). "If you instruct the brethren in these things, you will be a good minister of Jesus Christ, nourished in the words of faith and of the good doctrine which you have carefully followed" (Page 1429—1 Tim. 4:6).

c. It equips for using one's spiritual gifts from God. A spiritual gift is an ability given by the Holy Spirit to the believer for the purpose of edifying the church and glorifying God. In Ephesians 1:17–19 and 4:7, 11–14 Paul says a knowledge of God's Word will provide us with the maturity we need to use our gifts in the most effective way.

d. It equips us for doing battle with Satan. In Ephesians 6:10–17 Paul likens the believers' armor to that used by Roman foot soldiers. In this comparison the Word of God is likened to the soldier's sword (Page 1393—Eph. 6:17).

Now turn to Page 992—Dan. 11:32: We Know God Through His Word.

8 The morsel you have eaten, you will
vomit up,
And waste your pleasant words.

9 [R]Do not speak in the hearing of a fool,
For he will despise the wisdom of your
words. Matt. 7:6

10 Do not remove the ancient landmark,
Nor enter the fields of the fatherless;
11 [R]For their Redeemer *is* mighty; Prov. 22:23
He will plead their cause against you.

12 Apply your heart to instruction,
And your ears to words of knowledge.

13 [R]Do not withhold correction from a
child, Prov. 13:24
For *if* you beat him with a rod, he will
not die.
14 You shall beat him with a rod,
And deliver his soul from [T]hell. Or *Sheol*

15 My son, if your heart is wise,
My heart will rejoice—indeed, I myself;
16 Yes, my inmost being will rejoice
When your lips speak right things.

17 [R]Do not let your heart envy sinners,
But [R]in the fear of the LORD *continue* all
day *long*; Ps. 37:1 • Prov. 28:14
18 For surely there is a [T]hereafter, Future
And your hope will not be cut off.

19 Hear, my son, and be wise;
And guide your heart in the way.
20 [R]Do not mix with winebibbers, Is. 5:22
Or with gluttonous eaters of meat;
21 For the drunkard and the glutton will
come to poverty,
And drowsiness will clothe *a man* with
rags.

22 [R]Listen to your father who begot you,
And do not despise your mother when
she is old. Prov. 1:8

23 [R]Buy the truth, and do not sell *it*,
Also wisdom and instruction and
understanding. Matt. 13:44

24 [R]The father of the righteous will greatly
rejoice, Prov. 10:1
And he who begets a wise *child* will
delight in him.
25 Let your father and your mother be
glad,
And let her who bore you rejoice.

26 My son, give me your heart,
And let your eyes observe my ways.
27 [R]For a harlot *is* a deep pit, Prov. 22:14
And a seductress *is* a narrow well.
28 [R]She also lies in wait as *for* a victim,
And increases the unfaithful among
men. Prov. 7:12

29 [R]Who has woe? Is. 5:11, 22
Who has sorrow?
Who has contentions?
Who has complaints?
Who has wounds without cause?
Who [R]has redness of eyes? Gen. 49:12
30 Those who linger long at the wine,
Those who go in search of mixed wine.
31 Do not look on the wine when it is red,
When it sparkles in the cup,
When it swirls around smoothly;
32 At the last it bites like a serpent,
And stings like a viper.
33 Your eyes will see strange things,
And your heart will utter perverse
things.
34 Yes, you will be like one who lies down
in the [T]midst of the sea, Lit. *heart*
Or like one who lies at the top of the
mast, *saying*:
35 "They[R] have struck me, *but* I was not
hurt; Jer. 5:3
They have beaten me, but I did not feel
it.
When shall [R]I awake, that I may seek
another *drink*?" Eph. 4:19

CHAPTER 24

Do not be [R]envious of evil men,
Nor desire to be with them; Ps. 1:1; 37:1
2 For their heart devises violence,
And their lips talk of troublemaking.

3 Through wisdom a house is built,
And by understanding it is established;
4 By knowledge the rooms are filled
With all precious and pleasant riches.

5 [R]A wise man *is* strong, Prov. 21:22
Yes, a man of knowledge increases
strength;

6 [R]For by wise counsel you will wage your
own war, Luke 14:31
And in a multitude of counselors *there*
is safety.

24:6 Knowing the Will of God Through Circumstances and Counsel—While the Christian is to live above his circumstances, he is not to be unaware of them. God often works through circumstances in revealing His perfect will for us. Certainly Paul's wonderful statement, "all things work together for good to those who love God" (Page 1333—Rom. 8:28) takes into account our circumstances. A number of biblical examples can be given to illustrate this.

7 [R]Wisdom *is* too lofty for a fool; Ps. 10:5
He does not open his mouth in the gate.

8 He who [R]plots to do evil Rom. 1:30
Will be called a schemer.
9 The devising of foolishness *is* sin,
And the scoffer *is* an abomination to men.

10 *If* you [R]faint in the day of adversity,
Your strength *is* small. Heb. 12:3

11 [R]Deliver *those who* are drawn toward death, Ps. 82:4
And hold back *those* stumbling to the slaughter.
12 If you say, "Surely we did not know this,"
Does not [R]He who weighs the hearts consider *it?* Prov. 21:2
He who keeps your soul, does He *not* know *it?*
And will He *not* render to *each* man [R]according to his deeds? Ps. 62:12

13 My son, [R]eat honey because *it is* good,
And the honeycomb *which is* sweet to your taste; Song 5:1
14 [R]So *shall* the knowledge of wisdom *be* to your soul; Ps. 19:10; 58:11
If you have found *it,* there is a [T]prospect, Lit. *latter end*
And your hope will not be cut off.

15 Do not lie in wait, O wicked *man,* against the dwelling of the righteous;
Do not plunder his resting place;
16 [R]For a righteous *man* may fall seven times [Mic. 7:8]
And rise again,
But the wicked shall fall by calamity.

17 [R]Do not rejoice when your enemy falls,
And do not let your heart be glad when he stumbles; Obad. 12
18 Lest the LORD see *it,* and [T]it displease Him, Lit. *it is evil in His eyes*
And He turn away His wrath from him.

19 [R]Do not fret because of evildoers,
Nor be envious of the wicked; Ps. 37:1
20 For there will be no prospect for the evil *man;*
The lamp of the wicked will be put out.

21 My son, [R]fear the LORD and the king;
Do not associate with those given to change; [1 Pet. 2:17]
22 For their calamity will rise suddenly,
And who knows the ruin those two can bring?

23 These *things* also *belong* to the wise:

It is not good to [T]show partiality in judgment. Lit. *recognize faces*
24 [R]He who says to the wicked, "You *are* righteous," Is. 5:23
Him the people will curse;
Nations will abhor him.
25 But those who rebuke *the wicked* will have [R]delight, Prov. 28:23
And a good blessing will come upon them.

26 He who gives a right answer kisses the lips.

27 [R]Prepare your outside work, Prov. 27:23–27
Make it fit for yourself in the field;
And afterward build your house.

28 [R]Do not be a witness against your neighbor without cause, Eph. 4:25
*For would you deceive with your lips?
29 [R]Do not say, "I will do to him just as he has done to me; [Prov. 20:22]
I will render to the man according to his work."

30 I went by the field of the slothful,
And by the vineyard of the man devoid of understanding;
31 And there it was, [R]all overgrown with thorns; Gen. 3:18

24:28 LXX, Vg., *Do not deceive*

---

a. God directed Abraham to substitute a ram, whose horns had somehow become entangled in a thicket, for the life of Isaac (Page 30—Gen. 22:13).
b. God arranged for Pharaoh's daughter to be bathing in the river Nile at the exact time the baby Moses floated by in a little ark of bulrushes (Page 69—Ex. 2:1–10).
c. Paul's young nephew happened to overhear a plot to kill his famous uncle. He then reported it to the authorities, thus saving the apostle's life (Page 1307—Acts 23:12–22).

Surely the above circumstances were providentially arranged. So the Christian should ask, when attempting to discover God's will, Is the Lord showing me something through my circumstances?

Counselors also play an important role in finding God's will. "In a multitude of counselors *there is* safety" (Prov. 24:6). However, three things must be kept in mind at this point:

a. Counsel must come from a godly source. "Confidence in an unfaithful man in time of trouble *is like* a bad tooth and a foot out of joint" (Page 738—Prov. 25:19).
b. Sometimes even the godliest person can unknowingly give us wrong advice. Nathan the prophet did this when he encouraged David to build the temple (Page 365—2 Sam. 7:1–13).
c. In the final analysis, each person is responsible for knowing God's revealed purpose for his own life.

Now turn to Page 914—Lam. 5:20: Occasions of Doubt.

Its surface was covered with nettles;
Its stone wall was broken down.
32 When I saw *it*, I considered *it* well;
I looked on *it and* received instruction:
33 [R]A little sleep, a little slumber, Prov. 6:9, 10
A little folding of the hands to rest;
34 So your poverty will come *like* [T]a prowler, Lit. *one who walks about*
And your want like an armed man.

CHAPTER 25

Relationships with Kings

THESE[R] also *are* proverbs of Solomon which the men of Hezekiah king of Judah copied: 1 Kin. 4:32

2 [R]*It is* the glory of God to conceal a matter,
But the glory of kings *is* to search out a matter. Deut. 29:29

3 *As* the heavens for height and the earth for depth,
So the heart of kings *is* unsearchable.

4 [R]Take away the dross from silver,
And it will go to the silversmith *for* jewelry. 2 Tim. 2:21
5 Take away the wicked from before the king,
And his throne will be established in [R]righteousness. Prov. 16:12; 20:8

6 Do not exalt yourself in the presence of the king,
And do not stand in the place of great *men*;
7 [R]For *it is* better that he say to you,
"Come up here,"
Than that you should be put lower in the presence of the prince,
Whom your eyes have seen. Luke 14:7–11

Relationships with Neighbors

8 Do not go hastily to [T]court;
For what will you do in the end,
When your neighbor has put you to shame? Lit. *contend* or *bring a lawsuit*
9 [R]Debate your case with your neighbor *himself*,
And do not disclose the secret to another; [Matt. 18:15]
10 Lest he who hears *it* expose your shame,
And your reputation be ruined.

11 A word fitly [R]spoken *is like* apples of gold
In settings of silver. Prov. 15:23
12 *Like* an earring of gold and an ornament of fine gold
Is a wise reprover to an obedient ear.

13 [R]Like the cold of snow in time of harvest
Is a faithful messenger to those who send him, Prov. 13:17
For he refreshes the soul of his masters.

14 [R]Whoever falsely boasts of giving Prov. 20:6
Is like clouds and wind without rain.

15 [R]By long forbearance a ruler is persuaded, Prov. 15:1
And a gentle tongue breaks a bone.

16 Have you found honey?
Eat only as much as you need,
Lest you be filled with it and vomit.

17 Seldom set foot in your neighbor's house,
Lest he become weary of you and hate you.

18 [R]A man who bears false witness against his neighbor
Is like a club, a sword, and a sharp arrow. Ps. 57:4

19 Confidence in an unfaithful man in time of trouble
Is like a bad tooth and a foot out of joint.

20 *Like* one who takes away a garment in cold weather,
And like vinegar on soda,
Is one who [R]sings songs to a heavy heart. Dan. 6:18

Relationships with Enemies

21 [R]If your enemy is hungry, give him bread to eat;
And if he is thirsty, give him water to drink; Rom. 12:20
22 For *so* you will heap coals of fire on his head,
And the LORD will reward you.

23 The north wind brings forth rain,
And [R]a backbiting tongue an angry countenance. Ps. 101:5

24 [R]*It is* better to dwell in a corner of a housetop,
Than in a house shared with a contentious woman. Prov. 19:13

Relationships with Yourself

25 *As* cold water to a weary soul,
So *is* good news from a far country.

26 A righteous man who falters before the wicked

Is like a murky spring and a [T]polluted
well. *ruined*

27 It is not good to eat much honey;
So to seek one's own glory is not glory.

28 [R]Whoever has no rule over his own spirit
Is like a city broken down, without
walls. Prov. 16:32

CHAPTER 26

Relationships with Fools

AS snow in summer and rain in harvest,
So honor is not fitting for a fool.

2 Like a flitting sparrow, like a flying
swallow,
So [R]a curse without cause shall not
alight. Deut. 23:5

3 [R]A whip for the horse, Ps. 32:9
A bridle for the donkey,
And a rod for the fool's back.
4 Do not answer a fool according to his
folly,
Lest you also be like him.
5 Answer a fool according to his folly,
Lest he be wise in his own eyes.
6 He who sends a message by the hand of
a fool
Cuts off *his own* feet *and* drinks
violence.
7 *Like* the legs of the lame that hang limp
Is a proverb in the mouth of fools.
8 Like one who binds a stone in a sling
Is he who gives honor to a fool.
9 *Like* a thorn *that* goes into the hand of
a drunkard
Is a proverb in the mouth of fools.
10 *The great *God* who formed all *things*
Gives the fool *his* hire and the
transgressor *his* wages.
11 As a dog returns to his own vomit,
[R]*So* a fool repeats his folly. Ex. 8:15
12 [R]Do you see a man wise in his own eyes?
There is more hope for a fool than for
him. [Rev. 3:17]

Relationships with Sluggards

13 The slothful *man* says, "*There is* a lion
in the road!
A fierce lion *is* in the [T]streets!" *square*
14 *As* a door turns on its hinges,
So *does* the slothful *turn* on his bed.
15 The [R]slothful *man* buries his hand in the
*bowl; Prov. 19:24
It wearies him to bring it back to his
mouth.
16 The sluggard *is* wiser in his own eyes
Than seven men who can answer
sensibly.

Relationships with Gossips

17 He who passes by *and* meddles in a
quarrel not his own
Is like one who takes a dog by the ears.

18 Like a madman who throws firebrands,
arrows, and death,
19 *Is* the man *who* deceives his neighbor,
And says, [R]"I was only joking!" Eph. 5:4

20 Where *there is* no wood, the fire goes
out;
And where *there is* no [T]talebearer, strife
ceases. *gossip,* lit. *whisperer*
21 [R]*As* charcoal *is* to burning coals, and
wood to fire, Prov. 15:18
So *is* a contentious man to kindle strife.
22 The words of a [T]talebearer *are* like tasty
[T]trifles, *gossip* • Lit. *rooms of the belly*
And they go down into the *inmost
body.

23 Fervent lips with a wicked heart
Are like earthenware covered with
silver dross.

24 He who hates, disguises *it* with his lips,
And lays up deceit within himself;
25 [R]When [T]he speaks kindly, do not believe
him, Ps. 28:3 • Lit. *his voice is gracious*
For *there are* seven abominations in his
heart;
26 *Though his* hatred is covered by deceit,
His wickedness will be revealed before
the *whole* congregation.

27 [R]Whoever digs a pit will fall into it,
And he who rolls a stone will have it
roll back on him. Ps. 7:15

28 A lying tongue hates *those who are*
crushed by it,
And a flattering mouth works ruin.

CHAPTER 27

Proverbs Regulating Various Activities

DO[R] not boast about tomorrow,
For you do not know what a day may
bring forth. James 14:13–16

2 [R]Let another man praise you, and not
your own mouth; Prov. 25:27
A stranger, and not your own lips.

3 A stone *is* heavy and sand *is* weighty,
But a fool's wrath *is* heavier than both
of them.

26:10 Heb. difficult in v. 10; ancient and modern translators differ greatly
26:15 LXX, Syr. *bosom;* Tg., Vg. *armpit*
26:22 A Jewish tradition reads *wounds*

4 Wrath *is* cruel and anger a torrent,
But [R]who *is* able to stand before
jealousy? 1 John 3:12

5 [R]Open rebuke *is* better [Prov. 28:23]
Than love carefully concealed.

6 Faithful *are* the wounds of a friend,
But the kisses of an enemy *are*
[R]deceitful. Matt. 26:49

7 A satisfied soul [T]loathes the honeycomb,
But to a hungry soul every bitter thing
is sweet. Lit. *tramples on*

8 Like a bird that wanders from its nest
Is a man who wanders from his place.

9 Ointment and perfume delight the
heart,
And the sweetness of a man's friend
does so by hearty counsel.

10 Do not forsake your own friend or your
father's friend,
Nor go to your brother's house in the
day of your calamity;
For [R]better *is* a neighbor nearby than a
brother far away. Prov. 17:17; 18:24

11 My son, be wise, and make my heart
glad,
[R]That I may answer him who reproaches
me. Prov. 10:1; 23:15–26

12 A prudent *man* foresees evil *and* hides
himself;
The simple pass on *and* are punished.

13 Take the garment of him who is surety
for a stranger,
And hold it in pledge *when* he is surety
for a seductress.

14 He who blesses his friend with a loud
voice, rising early in the morning,
It will be counted a curse to him.

15 A [R]continual dripping on a very rainy
day Prov. 19:13
And a contentious woman are alike;
16 Whoever [T]restrains her restrains the
wind, *hides*
And grasps oil with his right hand.

17 *As* iron sharpens iron,
So a man sharpens the countenance of
his friend.

18 [R]Whoever [T]keeps the fig tree will eat its
fruit; [1 Cor. 3:8; 9:7–13] • *protects* or *tends*
So he who waits on his master will be
honored.

19 As in water face *reveals* face,
So a man's heart *reveals* the man.

20 Hell and Destruction are never full;
So the eyes of man are never satisfied.

21 [R]The refining pot *is* for silver and the
furnace for gold, Prov. 17:3
And a man *is valued* by what others say
of him.

22 [R]Though you grind a fool in a mortar
with a pestle along with crushed
grain, Jer. 5:3
Yet his foolishness will not depart from
him.

23 Be diligent to know the state of your
[R]flocks, Prov. 24:27
And attend to your herds;
24 For riches *are* not forever,
Nor does a crown *endure* to all
generations.
25 [R]*When* the hay is removed, and the
tender grass shows itself,
And the herbs of the mountains are
gathered in, Ps. 104:14
26 The lambs *will provide* your clothing,
And the goats the price of a field;
27 *You shall have* enough goats' milk for
your food,
For the food of your household,
And the nourishment of your
maidservants.

CHAPTER 28

THE wicked flee when no one pursues,
But the righteous are bold as a lion.

2 Because of the transgression of a land,
many *are* its princes;
But by a man of understanding *and*
knowledge
Right will be prolonged.

3 [R]A poor man who oppresses the poor
Is like a driving rain [T]which leaves no
food. Matt. 18:28 • Lit. *and there is no bread*

4 [R]Those who forsake the law praise the
wicked,
[R]But such as keep the law contend with
them. Ps. 49:18 • 1 Kin. 18:18

5 [R]Evil men do not understand justice,
But [R]those who seek the LORD
understand all. Ps. 92:6 • John 17:17

6 Better *is* the poor who walks in his
integrity
Than one perverse *in his* ways, though
he *be* rich.

HEBREW POETRY

The Bible is filled with poetic writings. In addition to entire books such as Psalms and Lamentations, which are written almost totally in poetic style, small sections of poetry are found in almost all the remaining books of the Bible.

As applied to the Bible, however, the word *poetry* means something different than the typical English-language structure to which we are accustomed. The main characteristic of Hebrew poetry is parallelism. This is a construction in which the content of one line is repeated, contrasted, or advanced by the content of the next—a type of sense rhythm characterized by thought arrangement rather than by word arrangement or rhyme.

There are three main types of parallelism in the Old Testament. Each is found in abundance in the Book of Psalms.

In **synonymous parallelism**, the second line of a poetic construction expresses essentially the same idea as the first: "The LORD of hosts *is* with us; / The God of Jacob *is* our refuge" (Ps. 46:11).

In **antithetic parallelism**, the second line introduces a thought that is the direct opposite of the first idea: "For the LORD knows the way of the righteous, / But the way of the ungodly shall perish" (Ps. 1:6).

In **progressive parallelism**, part of the first line of the poetic expression is repeated in the second line, but something more is added: "The floods have lifted up, O LORD, / The floods have lifted up their voice" (Ps. 93:3).

Another literary device the biblical writers used to give their psalms a peculiar style was the alphabetic acrostic. The best example of this technique is Psalm 119, which contains twenty-two different sections of eight verses each. Each major section of this psalm is headed by a different letter of the Hebrew alphabet. In the original language, each verse in these major divisions of the psalm begins with the Hebrew letter that appears as the heading for that section. Many modern translations of the Bible, including the New King James Version, print these Hebrew letters as headings throughout Psalm 119.

The flute was one of the musical instruments used to accompany psalms that were sung.

7 Whoever keeps the law *is* a discerning
son,
But a companion of gluttons shames his
father.

8 One who increases his possessions by
usury and extortion
Gathers it for him who will pity the
poor.

9 One who turns away his ear from
hearing the law,
[R]Even his prayer *shall be* an
abomination. Prov. 15:8

10 [R]Whoever causes the upright to go
astray in an evil way,
He himself will fall into his own pit;
[R]But the blameless will inherit good
things. Prov. 26:27 • [Matt. 6:33]

11 The rich man *is* wise in his own eyes,
But the poor who has understanding
searches him out.

12 When the righteous rejoice, *there is*
great [R]glory; Prov. 11:10; 29:2
But when the wicked arise, men [T]hide
themselves. Lit. *will be searched for*

13 [R]He who covers his sins will not prosper,
But whoever confesses and forsakes
them will have mercy. Ps. 32:3–5

14 Happy *is* the man who is always
reverent,
But he who hardens his heart will fall
into calamity.

15 *Like* a roaring lion and a charging bear
Is a wicked ruler over poor people.

16 A ruler who lacks understanding *is* a
great [R]oppressor,
But he who hates covetousness will
prolong *his* days. Eccl. 10:16

17 [R]A man burdened with bloodshed will
flee into a pit;
Let no one help him. Gen. 9:6

18 Whoever walks blamelessly will be
[T]saved,
But *he who is* perverse *in his* ways will
fall at once. *delivered*

19 [R]He who tills his land will have plenty of
bread,
But he who follows frivolity will have
poverty enough! Prov. 12:11; 20:13

20 A faithful man will abound with
blessings,
[R]But he who hastens to be rich will not
go unpunished. 1 Tim. 6:9

21 To [T]show partiality *is* not good,
[R]Because for a piece of bread a man will
transgress. Lit. *recognize faces* • Ezek. 13:19

22 A man with an evil eye hastens after
riches,
And does not consider that [R]poverty
will come upon him. Prov. 21:5

23 [R]He who rebukes a man will find more
favor afterward Prov. 27:5, 6
Than he who flatters with the tongue.

24 Whoever robs his father or his mother,
And says, "*It is* no transgression,"
The same *is* companion to a destroyer.

25 [R]He who is of a proud heart stirs up
strife,
[R]But he who trusts in the LORD will be
prospered. Prov. 13:10 • 1 Tim. 6:6

26 He who [R]trusts in his own heart is a
fool,
But whoever walks wisely will be
delivered. Prov. 3:5

27 [R]He who gives to the poor will not lack,
But he who hides his eyes will have
many curses. Deut. 15:7

28 When the wicked arise, [R]men hide
themselves;
But when they perish, the righteous
increase. Job 24:4

CHAPTER 29

HE[R] who is often reproved, *and* hardens
his neck,
Will suddenly be destroyed, and that
without remedy. 2 Chr. 36:16

2 When the righteous [T]are in authority,
the people rejoice; *become great*
But when a wicked *man* rules, [R]the
people groan. Esth. 4:3

3 Whoever loves wisdom makes his father
rejoice,
But a companion of harlots wastes *his*
wealth.

4 The king establishes the land by justice,
But he who receives bribes overthrows
it.

5 A man who [R]flatters his neighbor
Spreads a net for his feet. Prov. 26:28

6 By transgression an evil man is snared,
But the righteous sings and rejoices.

7 The righteous [R]considers the cause of the poor,
But the wicked does not understand *such* knowledge. Job 29:16

8 Scoffers [R]ensnare a city, Prov. 11:11
But wise *men* turn away wrath.

9 *If* a wise man contends with a foolish man,
[R]Whether [T]the fool rages or laughs, *there is* no peace. Matt. 11:17 • Lit. *he*

10 The bloodthirsty hate the blameless,
But the just seek his [T]well-being. Lit. *soul*

11 A fool vents all his [T]feelings, Lit. *spirit*
But a wise *man* holds them back.

12 If a ruler pays attention to lies,
All his servants *become* wicked.

13 The poor *man* and the oppressor have this in common:
[R]The LORD gives light to the eyes of both. [Matt. 5:45]

14 The king who judges the [R]poor with truth, Is. 11:4
His throne will be established forever.

15 The rod and reproof give [R]wisdom,
But a child left *to himself* brings shame to his mother. Prov. 22:15

16 When the wicked are multiplied, transgression increases;
But the righteous will see their fall.

17 Correct your son, and he will give you rest;
Yes, he will give delight to your soul.

18 Where *there is* no [T]revelation, the people cast off restraint; *prophetic vision*
But happy *is* he who keeps the law.

19 A servant will not be corrected by mere words;
For though he understands, he will not respond.

20 Do you see a man hasty in his words?
[R]*There is* more hope for a fool than for him. Prov. 26:12

21 He who pampers his servant from childhood
Will have him as a son in the end.

22 [R]An angry man stirs up strife,
And a furious man abounds in transgression. Prov. 26:21

23 [R]A man's pride will bring him low,
But the humble in spirit will retain honor. Is. 66:2

24 Whoever is a partner with a thief hates his own life;
He [T]swears to tell the truth, but reveals nothing. Lit. *hears the adjuration* or *oath*

25 [R]The fear of man brings a snare,
But whoever trusts in the LORD shall be [T]safe. Gen. 12:12; 20:2 • *secure,* lit. *set on high*

26 [R]Many seek the ruler's [T]favor,
But justice for man *comes* from the LORD. Ps. 20:9 • Lit. *face*

27 An unjust man *is* an abomination to the righteous,
And *he who is* upright in the way *is* an abomination to the wicked.

CHAPTER 30

The Words of Agur

THE words of Agur the son of Jakeh, *his* utterance. This man declared to Ithiel—to Ithiel and Ucal:

2 [R]Surely I *am* more stupid than *any* man,
And do not have the understanding of a man. Ps. 73:22

3 I neither learned wisdom
Nor have knowledge of the Holy One.

4 [R]Who has ascended into heaven, or descended? [John 3:13]
[R]Who has gathered the wind in His fists?
Who has bound the waters in a garment? Job 38:4
Who has established all the ends of the earth?
What *is* His name, and what *is* His Son's name,
If you know?

5 [R]Every word of God *is* [T]pure;
He *is* a shield to those who put their trust in Him. Ps. 12:6 • *tested, refined*

6 [R]Do not add to His words,
Lest He reprove you, and you be found a liar. Deut. 4:2; 12:32

7 Two *things* I request of You
(Deprive me not before I die):

8 Remove falsehood and lies far from me;
Give me neither poverty nor riches—
[R]Feed me with the food *You* prescribe for me; Matt. 6:11

9 [R]Lest I be full and deny *You*,
And say, "Who *is* the LORD?" Deut. 8:12–14
Or lest I be poor and steal,
And profane the name of my God.

10 Do not malign a servant to his master,
Lest he curse you, and you be found guilty.

11 *There is* a generation *that* curses its [R]father,
And does not bless its mother. Ex. 21:17
12 *There is* a generation [R]*that is* pure in its own eyes, Luke 18:11
Yet is not washed from its filthiness.
13 *There is* a generation—oh, how [R]lofty are their eyes! Prov. 6:17
And their eyelids are lifted up.
14 [R]*There is* a generation whose teeth *are like* swords, Job 29:17
And whose fangs *are like* knives,
[R]To devour the poor from off the earth,
And the needy from *among* men. Amos 8:4

15 The leech has two daughters,
Crying, "Give! Give!"

There are three *things that* are never satisfied,
Four *things* never say, "*It is* enough":
16 [R]The[T] grave,
The barren womb,
The earth *that* is not satisfied with water,
And the fire *that* never says, "*It is* enough." Prov. 27:20 • Or *Sheol*

17 [R]The eye *that* mocks *his* father, Gen. 9:22
And scorns obedience to *his* mother,
The ravens of the valley will pick it out,
And the young eagles will eat it.

18 There are three *things which* are too wonderful for me,
Yes, four *which* I do not understand:
19 The way of an eagle in the air,
The way of a serpent on a rock,
The way of a ship in the [T]midst of the sea, Lit. *heart*
And the way of a man with a virgin.

20 This *is* the way of an adulterous woman:
She eats and wipes her mouth,
And says, "I have done no wickedness."

21 For three *things* the earth is perturbed,
Yes, for four it cannot bear up:
22 [R]For a servant when he reigns, Prov. 19:10
A fool when he is filled with food,
23 A [T]hateful *woman* when she is married,
And a maidservant who succeeds her mistress. Or *hated*

24 There are four *things which* are little on the earth,
But they *are* exceedingly wise:
25 [R]The ants *are* a people not strong,
Yet they prepare their food in the summer; Prov. 6:6
26 The rock badgers are a feeble folk,
Yet they make their homes in the crags;
27 The locusts have no king,
Yet they all advance in ranks;
28 The [T]spider skillfully grasps with its hands,
And it is in kings' palaces. Or *lizard*

29 There are three *things which* are majestic in pace,
Yes, four *which* are stately in walk:
30 A lion, *which is* mighty among beasts
And does not turn away from any;
31 A [T]greyhound, Or perhaps *strutting rooster*
A male goat also,
And *a king *whose* troops *are* with him.

32 If you have been foolish in exalting yourself,
Or if you have devised evil, [R]*put your* hand on *your* mouth. Mic. 7:16
33 For *as* the churning of milk produces butter,
And *as* wringing the nose produces blood,
So the forcing of wrath produces strife.

CHAPTER 31

Wisdom for Leaders

THE words of King Lemuel, the utterance which his mother taught him:

2 What, my son?
And what, son of my womb?
And what, [R]son of my vows? Is. 49:15
3 [R]Do not give your strength to women,
Nor your ways [R]to that which destroys kings. Prov. 5:9 • Deut. 17:17

4 [R]*It is* not for kings, O Lemuel, Eccl. 10:17
It is not for kings to drink wine,
Nor for princes intoxicating drink;
5 [R]Lest they drink and forget the law,
And pervert the justice of all [T]the afflicted. Hos. 4:11 • Lit. *sons of affliction*
6 [R]Give strong drink to him who is perishing,
And wine to those who are bitter of heart. Ps. 104:15
7 Let him drink and forget his poverty,
And remember his misery no more.

8 [R]Open your mouth for the speechless,

30:31 A Jewish tradition reads *a king against whom there is no uprising*

In the cause of all *who are* [T]appointed
to die. Job 29:15, 16 • Lit. *sons of passing away*
9 Open your mouth, [R]judge righteously,
And [R]plead the cause of the poor and
needy. Lev. 19:15 • Jer. 22:16

Wise Woman

10 [R]Who can find a virtuous wife? Prov. 12:4
For her worth *is* far above rubies.
11 The heart of her husband safely trusts
her;
So he will have no lack of gain.
12 She does him good and not evil
All the days of her life.
13 She seeks wool and flax,
And willingly works with her hands.
14 She is like the merchant ships,
She brings her food from afar.
15 She also rises while it is yet night,
And provides food for her household,
And a portion for her maidservants.
16 She considers a field and buys it;
From her profits she plants a vineyard.
17 She girds herself with strength,
And strengthens her arms.
18 She perceives that her merchandise *is*
good,
And her lamp does not go out by night.
19 She stretches out her hands to the
distaff,
And her hand holds the spindle.
20 [R]She extends her hand to the poor,
Yes, she reaches out her hands to the
needy. Eph. 4:28
21 She is not afraid of snow for her
household,
For all her household *is* clothed with
scarlet.
22 She makes tapestry for herself;
Her clothing *is* fine linen and purple.
23 [R]Her husband is known in the gates,
When he sits among the elders of the
land. Prov. 12:4
24 She makes linen garments and sells
them,
And supplies sashes for the merchants.
25 Strength and honor *are* her clothing;
She shall rejoice in time to come.
26 She opens her mouth with wisdom,
And on her tongue *is* the law of
kindness.
27 She watches over the ways of her
household,
And does not eat the bread of idleness.
28 Her children rise up and call her
blessed;
Her husband *also*, and he praises her:
29 "Many daughters have done well,
But you excel them all."
30 Charm *is* deceitful and beauty *is* vain,
But a woman *who* fears the LORD, she
shall be praised.
31 Give her of the fruit of her hands,
And let her own works praise her in the
gates.

THE BOOK OF

ECCLESIASTES

THE BOOK OF ECCLESIASTES

The key word in Ecclesiastes is *vanity,* the futile emptiness of trying to be happy apart from God. The Preacher (traditionally taken to be Solomon—1:1, 12—the wisest, richest, most influential king in Israel's history) looks at life "under the sun" (1:9) and, from the human perspective, declares it all to be empty. Power, popularity, prestige, pleasure—nothing can fill the God-shaped void in man's life but God Himself! But once seen from God's perspective, life takes on meaning and purpose, causing Solomon to exclaim, "Eat . . . drink . . . rejoice . . . do good . . . live joyfully . . . fear God . . . keep His commandments!" Skepticism and despair melt away when life is viewed as a daily gift from God.

The Hebrew title *Qoheleth* is a rare term, found only in Ecclesiastes (1:1, 2, 12; 7:27; 12:8–10). It comes from the word *qahal,* "to convoke an assembly, to assemble." Thus, it means "one who addresses an assembly, a preacher." The Septuagint used the Greek word *Ekklesiastes* as its title for this book. Derived from the word *ekklesia,* "assembly, congregation, church," it simply means "preacher." The Latin *Ecclesiastes* means "speaker before an assembly."

THE AUTHOR OF ECCLESIASTES

There are powerful arguments that the author of Ecclesiastes was Solomon.

External Evidence: Jewish talmudic tradition attributes the book to Solomon but suggests that Hezekiah's scribes may have edited the text (see Prov. 25:1). Solomonic authorship of Ecclesiastes is the standard Christian position, although some scholars, along with the Talmud, believe the work was later edited during the time of Hezekiah or possibly Ezra.

Internal Evidence: The author calls himself "the son of David, king in Jerusalem" in 1:1, 12. Solomon was the best qualified Davidic descendant for the quest in this book. He was the wisest man who ever taught in Jerusalem (see 1:16; 1 Kin. 4:29, 30). The descriptions of Qoheleth's exploration of pleasure (2:1–3), impressive accomplishments (2:4–6), and unparalleled wealth (2:7–10) were fulfilled only by King Solomon. The proverbs in this book are similar to those in the Book of Proverbs (e.g., Eccl. 7; 10). According to 12:9, Qoheleth collected and arranged many proverbs, perhaps referring to the two Solomonic collections in Proverbs. The unity of authorship of Ecclesiastes is supported by the seven references to Qoheleth.

THE TIME OF ECCLESIASTES

Some scholars argue that the literary forms in Ecclesiastes are postexilic, but they are, in fact, unique, and cannot be used in dating this book. The phrase "all who were before me in Jerusalem" in 1:16 has been used to suggest a date after Solomon's time, but there were many kings and wise men in Jerusalem before the time of Solomon. However, Solomon was the only son of David who reigned over Israel from Jerusalem (1:12).

Ecclesiastes was probably written late in Solomon's life, about 935 B.C. If this is so, the great glory that Solomon ushered in early in his reign was already beginning to fade; and the disruption of Israel into two kingdoms would soon take place. Jewish tradition asserts that Solomon wrote Song of Solomon in his youthful years, Proverbs in his middle years, and Ecclesiastes in his latter years. This book may be expressing his regret for his folly and wasted time due to carnality and idolatry (cf. 1 Kin. 11).

There are no references to historical events other than to personal aspects of Qoheleth's life. The location was Jerusalem (1:1, 12, 16), the seat of Israel's rule and authority.

THE CHRIST OF ECCLESIASTES

Ecclesiastes convincingly portrays the emptiness and perplexity of life without a relationship with the Lord. Each person has eternity in his heart (3:11), and only Christ can provide ultimate satisfaction, joy, and wisdom. Man's highest good is found in the "one Shepherd" (12:11) who offers abundant life (John 10:9, 10).

KEYS TO ECCLESIASTES

Key Word: Vanity—Ecclesiastes reports the results of a diligent quest for purpose, meaning, and satisfaction in human life. The Preacher poignantly sees the emptiness and futility of power, popularity, prestige, and pleasure apart from God. The word *vanity* appears thirty-seven times to express the many things that cannot be understood about life. All earthly goals and ambitions when pursued as ends in themselves lead to dissatisfaction and frustration. Life "under the sun" (used twenty-nine times) seems to be filled with inequities, uncertainties, changes in fortune, and violations of justice. But Ecclesiastes does not give an answer of atheism or skepticism; God is referred to throughout. In fact, it claims that the search for man's *summum bonum* must end in God. Satisfaction in life can be found only by looking beyond this world. Ecclesiastes gives an analysis of negative themes but it also develops the positive theme of overcoming the vanities of life by fearing a God who is good, just, and sovereign (12:13, 14). Wisdom involves seeing life from a divine perspective and trusting God in the face of apparent futility and lack of purpose. Life is a daily gift from God and it should be enjoyed as much as possible (see 2:24–26; 3:12, 13, 22; 5:18–20; 8:15; 9:7–10; 11:8, 9). Our comprehension is indeed limited, but there are many things we can understand. Qoheleth recognized that ultimately God will judge all people. Therefore he exhorted: "Fear God and keep His commandments" (12:13).

Key Verses: Ecclesiastes 2:24 and 12:13, 14—"*There is* nothing better for a man *than* that he should eat and drink, and *that* his soul should enjoy good in his labor. This also, I saw, was from the hand of God" (2:24).

"Let us hear the conclusion of the whole matter: Fear God and keep His commandments, for this is the whole duty of man. For God will bring every work into judgment, including every secret thing, whether *it is* good or whether *it is* evil" (12:13, 14).

Key Chapter: Ecclesiastes 12—At the end of the Book of Ecclesiastes, the Preacher looks at life through "binoculars." On the other hand, from the perspective of the natural man who only sees life "under the sun," the conclusion is, "All *is* vanity." Life's every activity, even though pleasant for the moment, becomes purposeless and futile when viewed as an end in itself.

The Preacher carefully documents the latter view with a long list of his own personal pursuits in life. No amount of activities or possessions has satisfied the craving of his heart. Every earthly prescription for happiness has left the same bitter aftertaste. Only when the Preacher views his life from God's perspective "above the sun" does it take on meaning as a precious gift "from the hand of God" (2:24).

Chapter 12 resolves the book's extensive inquiry into the meaning of life with the single conclusion, "Fear God and keep His commandments, for this is the whole duty of man" (12:13).

SURVEY OF ECCLESIASTES

Ecclesiastes is a profound and problematic book. It is the record of an intense search for meaning and satisfaction in life on this earth, especially in view of all the iniquities and apparent absurdities that surround us. It takes the perspective of the greatest answers that wisdom under the sun can produce. If the Preacher is identified as Solomon, Ecclesiastes was written from a unique vantage point. Possessing the greatest mental, material, and political resources ever combined in one man, he was qualified beyond all others to write this book. Ecclesiastes is extremely difficult to synthesize, and several alternate approaches have been used. The one used here is: the thesis that "all *is* vanity" (1:1–11), the proof that "all *is* vanity" (1:12—6:12), the counsel for living with vanity (7:1—12:14).

The Thesis That "All Is Vanity" (1:1-11): After a one-verse introduction, the Preacher states his theme: "Vanity of vanities, all *is* vanity" (1:2). Life under the sun appears to be futile and perplexing. Verses 3–11 illustrate this theme in the endless and apparently meaningless cycles found in nature and history.

The Proof That "All Is Vanity" (1:12—6:12): The Preacher describes his multiple quest for meaning and satisfaction as he explores his vast personal resources. He begins with wisdom (1:12–18) but finds that "he who increases knowledge increases sorrow." Due to his intense perception of reality he experiences just the reverse of "ignorance is bliss." The Preacher moves from

FOCUS	THESIS: "ALL IS VANITY"		PROOF: "LIFE IS VAIN"		COUNSEL: "FEAR GOD"		
REFERENCE	1:1	1:4	1:12	3:1	7:1	10:1	12:9—12:14
DIVISION	INTRODUCTION OF VANITY	ILLUSTRATIONS OF VANITY	PROOF FROM SCRIPTURE	PROOF FROM OBSERVATIONS	COPING IN A WICKED WORLD	COUNSEL FOR UNCERTAINTY	CONCLUSION: FEAR AND OBEY GOD
TOPIC	DECLARATION OF VANITY		DEMONSTRATION OF VANITY		FROM VANITY		
	SUBJECT		SERMONS		SUMMARY		
LOCATION	UNIVERSE: "UNDER THE SUN"						
TIME	c. 935 B.C.						

wisdom to laughter, hedonism, and wine (2:1–3) and then turns to works, women, and wealth (2:4–11); but all lead to emptiness. He realizes that wisdom is far greater than foolishness, but both seem to lead to futility in view of the brevity of life and universality of death (2:12–17). He concludes by acknowledging that contentment and joy are found only in God.

At this point, Ecclesiastes turns from his situation in life to a philosophical quest; but the conclusion remains the same. The Preacher considers the unchanging order of events and the fixed laws of God. Time is short, and there is no eternity on earth (3:1–15). The futility of death seems to cancel the difference between righteousness and wickedness (3:16–22). Chapters 4 and 5 explore the futility in social relationships (oppression, rivalry, covetousness, power) and in religious relationships (formalism, empty prayer, vows). In addition, the world's offerings produce disappointment, not satisfaction. Ultimate meaning can be found only in God.

The Counsel for Living with Vanity (7:1—12:14): A series of lessons on practical wisdom is given in 7:1—9:12. Levity and pleasure-seeking are seen as superficial and foolish; it is better to have sober depth of thought. Wisdom and self-control provide perspective and strength in coping with life. One should enjoy prosperity and consider in adversity that God made both. Avoid the twin extremes of self-righteousness and immorality. Sin invades all men, and wisdom is cut short by evil and death. The human mind cannot grasp ultimate meaning. Submission to authority helps one avoid unnecessary hardship, but real justice is often lacking on earth. The uncertainties of life and certainty of the grave show that God's purposes and ways often cannot be grasped. One should, therefore, magnify opportunities while they last, because fortune can change suddenly.

Observations on wisdom and folly are found in 9:13—11:6. Wisdom, the most powerful human resource, is contrasted with the meaningless talk and effort of fools. In view of the unpredictability of circumstances, wisdom is the best course to follow in order to minimize grief and misfortune. Wisdom involves discipline and diligence. In 11:7—12:7 the Preacher offers exhortations on using life well. Youth is too brief and precious to be squandered in foolishness or evil. A person should live well in the fullness of each day before God and acknowledge Him early in life. This section closes with an exquisite allegory of old age (12:1–7).

The Preacher concludes that the "good life" is only attained by revering God. Those who fail to take God and His will seriously into account are doomed to lives of foolishness and futility. Life will not wait upon the solution of all its problems; nevertheless, real meaning can be found by looking not "under the sun" but beyond the sun to the "one Shepherd" (12:11).

OUTLINE OF ECCLESIASTES

Part One: The Thesis That "All Is Vanity" (1:1–11)

I. Introduction of Vanity **1:1–3**

II. Illustrations of Vanity **1:4–11**

Part Two: The Proof That "All Is Vanity" (1:12—6:12)

I. Proof of "All Is Vanity" from Experience .... **1:12—2:26**

A. Vanity of Striving After Wisdom 1:12–18
B. Vanity of Striving After Pleasure 2:1–3
C. Vanity of Great Accomplishments 2:4–17
D. Vanity of Hard Labor 2:18–23
E. Conclusion: Be Content 2:24–26

II. Proof of "All Is Vanity" from Observation .... **3:1—6:12**

A. Immutability of God's Program 3:1–22
1. God Predetermines the Events of Life 3:1–9
2. God Predetermines the Conditions of Life 3:10–15
3. God Judges All 3:16–22

B. Inequalities of Life 4:1–16
1. Evil Oppression.................. 4:1–3
2. Folly of Hard Work 4:4–12
3. Transience of Popularity 4:13–16

C. Insufficiencies of Human Religion 5:1–7
D. Insufficiencies of Wealth 5:8–20
1. Wealth Does Not Satisfy 5:8–12
2. Wealth Brings Difficulties 5:13–17
3. Wealth Comes Ultimately from God...................... 5:18–20

E. Inescapable Vanity of Life 6:1–12
1. No Satisfaction in Wealth 6:1, 2
2. No Satisfaction in Children 6:3–6
3. No Satisfaction in Labor 6:7, 8
4. No Satisfaction in the Future 6:9–12

Part Three: The Counsel for Living with Vanity (7:1—12:14)

I. Coping in a Wicked World .... 7:1—9:18
- A. Wisdom and Folly Contrasted 7:1–14
- B. Wisdom of Moderation 7:15–18
- C. Strength of Wisdom 7:19–29
- D. Submit to Authority 8:1–9
- E. Inability to Understand All God's Doing 8:10–17
- F. Judgment Comes to All Men 9:1–6
- G. Enjoy Life While You Have It 9:7–12
- H. Value of Wisdom 9:13–18

II. Counsel for the Uncertainties of Life .... 10:1—12:8
- A. Wisdom's Characteristics 10:1–15
- B. Wisdom Related to the King 10:16–20
- C. Wisdom Related to Business.......... 11:1–6
- D. Wisdom Related to the Youth..... 11:7—12:8
  - 1. Rejoice in Your Youth 11:7–10
  - 2. Remember God in Your Youth 12:1–8

III. Conclusion: "Fear God and Keep His Commandments" 12:9–14

CHAPTER 1

Introduction of Vanity

THE words of the Preacher, the son of
David, [R]king in Jerusalem. Prov. 1:1
2 "Vanity[T] of vanities," says the Preacher;
"Vanity of vanities, all *is* vanity." *Futility*

3 What profit has a man from all his labor
In which he [T]toils under the sun? *labors*

Illustrations of Vanity

4 *One* generation passes away, and
another generation comes;
[R]But the earth abides forever. Ps. 104:5
5 [R]The sun also rises, and the sun goes
down,
And [T]hastens to the place where it
arose. Ps. 19:4–6 • Is eager for, lit. *panting*
6 [R]The wind goes toward the south,
And turns around to the north;
The wind whirls about continually,
And comes again on its circuit. John 3:8
7 [R]All the rivers run into the sea,
Yet the sea *is* not full;
To the place from which the rivers
come,
There they return again. [Jer. 5:22]
8 All things *are* [T]full of labor; *wearisome*
Man cannot express *it*.
[R]The eye is not satisfied with seeing,
Nor the ear filled with hearing. Prov. 27:20

9 [R]That which has been *is* what will be,
That which *is* done is what will be
done,
And *there is* nothing new under the
sun. Eccl. 3:15
10 Is there anything of which it may be
said,
"See, this *is* new"?
It has already been in ancient times
before us.
11 *There is* [R]no remembrance of former
things,
Nor will there be any remembrance of
things that are to come
By *those* who will come after. Eccl. 2:16

Vanity of Striving After Wisdom

12 I, the Preacher, was king over Israel in
Jerusalem.
13 And I set my heart to seek and [R]search
out by wisdom concerning all that is done
under heaven; this grievous task God has
given to the sons of man, by which they may
be [T]exercised. [Eccl. 7:25; 8:16, 17] • Or *afflicted*
14 I have seen all the works that are done
under the sun; and indeed, all *is* vanity and
grasping for the wind.

15 [R]*What is* crooked cannot be made
straight,
And what is lacking cannot be
numbered. Eccl. 7:13

16 I communed with my heart, saying,
"Look, I have attained greatness, and have
gained more wisdom than all who were before me in Jerusalem. My heart has understood great wisdom and knowledge."
17 And I set my heart to know wisdom and
to know madness and folly. I perceived that
this also is grasping for the wind.

18 For [R]in much wisdom *is* much grief,
And he who increases knowledge
increases sorrow. Eccl. 12:12

CHAPTER 2

Vanity of Striving After Pleasure

I SAID in my heart, "Come now, I will test
you with mirth; therefore enjoy pleasure"; but surely, this also *was* vanity.
2 I said of laughter, "*It is* madness"; and of
mirth, "What does it accomplish?"
3 I searched in my heart *how* [T]to gratify
my flesh with wine, while guiding my heart
with wisdom, and how to lay hold on folly, till
I might see what *was* [R]good for the sons of
men to do under heaven all the days of their
lives. Lit. *to draw my flesh* • [Eccl. 3:12, 13; 5:18; 6:12]

VANITY OF VANITIES

"'Vanity of vanities,' says the Preacher; 'vanity of vanities, all *is* vanity.'" Twice the author of Ecclesiastes employs this now famous saying (1:2; 12:8). But what did he mean by *vanity*? The NKJV note gives "futility" as an alternative rendering.

Breath, vapor (*hebel*) is the literal meaning of the word translated "vanity." *Hebel* occurs seventy-one times in the Hebrew Bible, mostly with metaphorical meanings. Speaking of idols, Isaiah 57:13 uses the word literally: "A breath [*hebel*] will take *them*." In the New Testament, James wrote that our life is "a vapor that appears for a little time and then vanishes away" (James 4:14).

The second person born into the world was named Abel, which in the Hebrew is the same spelling as *Hebel*. This may be coincidental, but if his name was "Vapor" or "Breath" in Hebrew, it does fit with his life being cut short by murder.

Hebel in Ecclesiastes

Hebel occurs thirty-six times in Ecclesiastes; only chapter 10 does not use the word. The apparent futility of life "under the sun" is certainly one of the main themes of "The Preacher," if not his main idea.

Solomon was a great builder, skillful, creative, and wise. Yet he was frustrated by the emptiness of it all—including his gardens and building projects: "Then I looked on all the works that my hands had done and on the labor in which I had toiled; and indeed all *was* vanity and grasping for the wind" (Eccl. 2:11; see also vv. 19, 21, 23; 4:4, 8; 6:2).

King Solomon also found the apparent unfairness of life to be vanity. Actually, we might wonder what he had to complain about. God had granted him wisdom and wealth; his life was filled with plenty of "wine, women, and song," and yet he was not satisfied. His verdict: "There is a vanity which occurs on earth, that there are just *men* to whom it happens according to the work of the wicked; again, there are wicked *men* to whom it happens according to the work of the righteous. I said that this also *is* vanity" (Eccl. 8:14; see also vv. 10–13; 2:15; 6:7–9). It all seemed senseless and absurd.

This king, who had everything to live for materially, and in many other ways, was sad that life was so short. He wrote: "But if a man lives many years *and* rejoices in them all, yet let him remember the days of darkness, for they will be many. All that is coming *is* vanity" (Eccl. 11:8; see also v. 10; 3:19; 6:12).

Hebel as Idols

Since the Old Testament spares no expense in unmasking the absurdity of worshiping lifeless idols, we should not be surprised that they are called foolish idols in the Song of Moses (Deut. 32:21). Jeremiah concurs: He calls images "futile, a work of errors" (Jer. 10:15).

Many people would not think of worshiping literal images, yet have idols equally vain. The most common is "mammon," or money. To get really rich in a corrupt society nearly always involves some questionable dealings or "cutting corners." But Proverbs 13:11 warns us that "wealth *gained* by dishonesty [*hebel*]" rather than by hard work "will be diminished."

Hebel as an Adverbial Accusative

Sometimes the word *hebel* is used adverbially with the idea of "no purpose" or "no result": "For the Egyptians shall help in vain and to no purpose" (Is. 30:7).

Job laments, "*If* I am condemned, why then do I labor in vain [for no good purpose]?" (Job 9:29).

Elihu sums up Job's many speeches in a Solomonic style: "Therefore Job opens his mouth in vain; he multiplies words without knowledge" (Job 35:16).

Many people face times in their lives when negative and pessimistic thoughts such as those we find in Job and Ecclesiastes are all that can be entertained. But Christians should rejoice in the positive promise of the apostle Paul: "Therefore, my beloved brethren, be steadfast, immovable, always abounding in the work of the Lord, knowing that your labor is not in vain in the Lord" (1 Cor. 15:58).

Vanity of Great Accomplishments

4 I made my works great, I built myself
houses, and planted myself vineyards.
5 I made myself gardens and orchards, and
I planted all *kinds* of fruit trees in them.
6 I made myself waterpools from which to
[T]water the growing trees of the grove. *irrigate*
7 I acquired male and female servants, and
had servants born in my house. Yes, I had
greater possessions of herds and flocks than
all who were in Jerusalem before me.
8 [R]I also gathered for myself silver and
gold and the special treasures of kings and of
the provinces. I acquired male and female
singers, the delights of the sons of men, *and*
musical instruments of all kinds. 1 Kin. 9:28
9 So I became great and excelled more
than all who were before me in Jerusalem.
Also my wisdom remained with me.

10 Whatever my eyes desired I did not
keep from them.
I did not withhold my heart from any
pleasure,
For my heart rejoiced in all my labor;
And [R]this was my [T]reward from all my
labor. Eccl. 3:22; 5:18; 9:9 • Lit. *portion*
11 Then I looked on all the works that my
hands had done
And on the labor in which I had toiled;
And indeed all *was* [R]vanity and grasping
for the wind. Eccl. 1:3, 14
There was no profit under the sun.

12 Then I turned myself to consider
wisdom [R]and madness and folly;
For what *can* the man *do* who succeeds
the king?— Eccl. 1:17; 7:25
Only what he has already [R]done. Eccl. 1:9
13 Then I saw that wisdom [R]excels folly
As light excels darkness. Eccl. 7:11, 14, 19
14 [R]The wise man's eyes *are* in his head,
But the fool walks in darkness.
Yet I myself perceived
That [R]the same event happens to them
all. Prov. 17:24 • Ps. 49:10

15 So I said in my heart,
"As it happens to the fool,
It also happens to me,
And why was I then more wise?"
Then I said in my heart,
"This also *is* vanity."
16 For *there is* [R]no more remembrance of
the wise than of the fool forever,
Since all that now *is* will be forgotten in
the days to come.
And how does a wise *man* die?
As the fool! Eccl. 1:11; 4:16

17 Therefore I hated life because the work
that was done under the sun *was* grievous to
me, for all *is* vanity and grasping for the
wind.

Vanity of Hard Labor

18 Then I hated all my labor in which I had
toiled under the sun, because [R]I must leave it
to the man who will come after me. Ps. 49:10
19 And who knows whether he will be a
wise *man* or a fool? Yet he will rule over all
my labor in which I toiled and in which I
have shown myself wise under the sun. This
also *is* vanity.
20 Therefore I turned my heart and despaired of all the labor in which I had toiled
under the sun.
21 For there is a man whose labor *is* with
wisdom, knowledge, and skill; yet he must
leave his [T]heritage to a man who has not
labored for it. This also *is* vanity and a great
evil. Lit. *portion*
22 [R]For what has man for all his labor, and
for the striving of his heart with which he has
toiled under the sun? Eccl. 1:3; 3:9
23 For all his days *are* [R]sorrowful, and his
work grievous; even in the night his heart
takes no rest. This also is vanity. Job 5:7; 14:1

Conclusion: Be Content

24 *There is* nothing better for a man *than*
that he should eat and drink, and *that* his
soul should enjoy good in his labor. This also,
I saw, was from the hand of God.
25 For who can eat, or who can have enjoyment, *more than I?
26 For *God* gives [R]wisdom and knowledge
and joy to a man who *is* good in His sight; but
to the sinner He gives the work of gathering
and collecting, that [R]he may give to *him who*
is good before God. This also *is* vanity and
grasping for the wind. Prov. 2:6 • Prov. 28:8

CHAPTER 3

God Predetermines the Events of Life

TO everything *there is* a season,
A [R]time for every purpose under
heaven: Eccl. 3:17; 8:6

2 A time [T]to be born, Lit. *to bear*
And [R]a time to die; Heb. 9:27
A time to plant,
And a time to pluck *what is* planted;
3 A time to kill,
And a time to heal;
A time to break down,
And a time to build up;
4 A time to [R]weep,
And a time to laugh;
A time to mourn,
And a time to dance; Rom. 12:15
5 A time to cast away stones,
And a time to gather stones;
[R]A time to embrace,
And a time to refrain from
embracing; Joel 2:16

2:25 Some Heb. mss., LXX, Syr., Jerome, *without Him*

6 A time to gain,
And a time to lose;
A time to keep,
And a time to throw away;
7 A time to tear,
And a time to sew;
[R]A time to keep silence, Amos 5:13
And a time to [R]speak; Prov. 25:11
8 A time to love,
And a time to [R]hate;
A time of war,
And a time of peace. Luke 14:26

9 [R]What profit has the worker from that in
which he labors? Eccl. 1:3

God Predetermines the Conditions of Life

10 I have seen the God-given task with
which the sons of men are to be occupied.
11 He has made everything beautiful in its
time. Also He has put eternity in their hearts,
except that no one can find out the work that
God does from beginning to end.
12 I know that *there is* nothing [R]better for
them than to rejoice, and to do good in their
lives, Eccl. 2:3, 24
13 and also that [R]every man should eat and
drink and enjoy the good of all his labor—it *is*
the gift of God. Eccl. 2:24

14 I know that whatever God does,
It shall be forever.
[R]Nothing can be added to it,
And nothing taken from it.
God does *it,* that men should fear before
Him. James 1:17
15 [R]That which is has already been,
And what is to be has already been;
And God [T]requires an account of [T]what
is past. Eccl. 1:9 • Lit. *seeks* • *what is pursued*

God Judges All

16 Moreover [R]I saw under the sun: Eccl. 5:8

In the place of [T]judgment, *justice*
Wickedness *was* there;
And *in* the place of righteousness,
[T]Iniquity *was* there. *Wickedness*

17 I said in my heart,

[R]"God shall judge the righteous and the
wicked, [Rom. 2:6–10]
For *there shall be* a time there for every
[T]purpose and for every work." *desire*

18 I said in my heart, "Concerning the
estate of the sons of men, God tests them,
that they may see that they themselves are
like beasts."
19 [R]For what happens to the sons of men
also happens to beasts; one thing befalls
them: as one dies, so dies the other. Surely,
they all have one breath; man has no advantage over beasts, for all *is* vanity. [Eccl. 2:16]
20 All go to one place: [R]all are from the dust,
and all return to dust. Gen. 3:19
21 *Who knows the spirit of the sons of
men, which goes upward, and the spirit of the
beast, which goes down to the earth?
22 So I perceived that *there is* nothing
better than that a man should rejoice in his
own works, for [R]that *is* his [T]heritage. [R]For
who can bring him to see what will happen
after him? Eccl. 2:10 • *portion* or *lot* • Eccl. 6:12; 8:7

CHAPTER 4

Evil Oppression

THEN I returned and considered all the
[R]oppression that is done under the sun:

And look! The tears of the oppressed,
But they have no comforter—
[T]On the side of their oppressors *there*
was power, Eccl. 3:16; 5:8 • Lit. *At the hand*
But they have no comforter.
2 [R]Therefore I praised the dead who were
already dead, Job 3:17, 18
More than the living who are still alive.
3 [R]Yet, better than both *is he* who has
never existed,
Who has not seen the evil work that is
done under the sun. Job 3:11–22

Folly of Hard Work

4 Again, I saw that for all toil and every
skillful work a man is envied by his neighbor.
This also *is* vanity and grasping for the wind.

5 [R]The fool folds his hands Prov. 6:10; 24:33
And consumes his own flesh.
6 Better *is* a handful *with* quietness
Than both hands full, *together with* toil
and grasping for the wind.

7 Then I returned, and I saw vanity under
the sun:

8 There is one alone, without companion:
He has neither son nor brother.
Yet *there is* no end to all his labors,
Nor is his [R]eye satisfied with riches.
But [R]*he never asks,* [1 John 2:16] • Ps. 39:6
"For whom do I toil and deprive myself
of [R]good?" Eccl. 2:18–21
This also *is* vanity and a [T]grave
misfortune. Lit. *evil task*

9 Two *are* better than one,
Because they have a good reward for
their labor.

3:21 LXX, Tg., Syr., Vg. *Who knows whether . . . goes upward, and whether . . . goes downward to the earth?*

10 For if they fall, one will lift up his
companion.
But woe to him *who is* alone when he
falls,
For *he has* no one to help him up.
11 Again, if two lie down together, they
will keep warm;
But how can one be warm *alone?*
12 Though one may be overpowered by
another, two can withstand him.
And a threefold cord is not quickly
broken.

Transience of Popularity

13 Better *is* a poor and wise youth
Than an old and foolish king who will
be admonished no more.
14 For he comes out of prison to be king,
Although [T]he was born poor in his
kingdom. The youth
15 I saw all the living who walk under the
sun;
They were with the second youth who
stands in his place.
16 *There was* no end of all the people over
whom he was made king;
Yet those who come afterward will not
rejoice in him.
Surely this also *is* vanity and grasping
for the wind.

CHAPTER 5

Insufficiencies of Human Religion

WALK [R]prudently when you go to the
house of God; and draw near to hear
rather than to give the sacrifice of fools, for
they do not know that they do evil. Ex. 3:5

2 Do not be [R]rash with your mouth,
And let not your heart utter anything
hastily before God. Prov. 20:25
For God *is* in heaven, and you on earth;
Therefore let your words be few.
3 For a dream comes through much
activity,
And [R]a fool's voice *is known* by *his*
many words. Prov. 10:19

4 [R]When you make a vow to God, do not
delay to [R]pay it; Num. 30:2 • Ps. 66:13, 14
For *He has* no pleasure in fools.
Pay what you have vowed.
5 [R]*It is* better not to vow than to vow and
not pay. Acts 5:4

6 Do not let your [R]mouth cause your flesh
to sin, [R]nor say before the messenger *of God*
that it *was* an error. Why should God be
angry at your [T]excuse and destroy the work
of your hands? Prov. 6:2 • 1 Cor. 11:10 • Lit. *voice*
7 For in the multitude of dreams and many
words *there is* also vanity. But fear God.

Wealth Does Not Satisfy

8 If you [R]see the oppression of the poor,
and the violent [T]perversion of justice and
righteousness in a province, do not marvel at
the matter; for [R]high official watches over
high official, and higher officials are over
them. Eccl. 3:16 • *wresting* • [Ps. 12:5; 58:11; 82:1]
9 Moreover the profit of the land is for all;
the king *himself* is served from the field.

10 He who loves silver will not be satisfied
with silver;
Nor he who loves abundance, with
increase.
This also *is* vanity.

11 When goods increase,
They increase who eat them;
So what profit have the owners
Except to see *them* with their eyes?

12 The sleep of a laboring man *is* sweet,
Whether he eats little or much;
But the abundance of the rich will not
permit him to sleep.

Wealth Brings Difficulties

13 [R]There is a severe evil *which* I have seen
under the sun: Eccl. 6:1, 2
Riches kept for their owner to his hurt.
14 But those riches perish through
[T]misfortune;
When he begets a son, *there is* nothing
in his hand. Lit. *bad business*
15 [R]As he came from his mother's womb,
naked shall he return, 1 Tim. 6:7
To go as he came;
And he shall take nothing from his
labor
Which he may carry away in his hand.

16 And this also *is* a severe evil,
That just exactly as he came, so shall
he go.
And what profit has he [R]who has
labored for the wind? Prov. 11:29
17 All his days [R]he also eats in darkness,
And *he has* much sorrow and sickness
and anger. Ps. 127:2

Wealth Comes Ultimately from God

18 Here is what I have seen: *It is* good and
fitting *for one* to eat and drink, and to enjoy
the good of all his labor in which he toils
under the sun all the days of his life which
God gives him; for it *is* his heritage.
19 As for every man to whom God has
given riches and wealth, and given him
power to eat of it, to receive his heritage and
rejoice in his labor—this *is* the gift of God.
20 For he will not dwell unduly on the days
of his life, because God keeps *him* busy with
the joy of his heart.

CHAPTER 6

No Satisfaction in Wealth

THERE is an evil which I have seen under
the sun, and it *is* common among men:
2 A man to whom God has given riches
and wealth and honor, [R]so that he lacks
nothing for himself of all he desires; [R]yet God
does not give him power to eat of it, but a
foreigner consumes it. This *is* vanity, and it *is*
an evil [T]affliction. Job 21:10 • Luke 12:20 • *disease*

No Satisfaction in Children

3 If a man begets a hundred *children* and
lives many years, so that the days of his years
are many, but his soul is not satisfied with
goodness, or indeed he has no burial, I say
that a stillborn child *is* better than he—
4 for it comes in vanity and departs in
darkness, and its name is covered with darkness.
5 Though it has not seen the sun or known
anything, this has more rest than that man,
6 even if he lives a thousand years twice
over—but has not seen goodness. Do not all
go to one [R]place? Eccl. 2:14, 15

No Satisfaction in Labor

7 All the labor of man *is* for his mouth,
And yet the soul is not satisfied.
8 For what more has the wise *man* than
the fool?
What does the poor man have,
Who knows *how* to walk before the
living?

No Satisfaction in the Future

9 Better *is* [T]the [R]sight of the eyes than the
wandering of [T]desire.
This also *is* vanity and grasping for the
wind. What the eyes see • Eccl. 11:9 • Lit. *soul*

10 Whatever one is, he has been named
[R]already, Eccl. 1:9; 3:15
For it is known that he *is* man;
[R]And he cannot contend with Him who
is mightier than he. Job 9:32
11 Since there are many things that
increase vanity,
How *is* man the better?

12 For who knows what *is* good for man in
life, all the days of his vain life which he
passes like a shadow? Who can tell a man
what will happen after him under the sun?

CHAPTER 7

Wisdom and Folly Contrasted

A GOOD[R] name *is* better than precious
ointment,
And the day of death than the day of
one's [R]birth. Prov. 15:30; 22:1 • Eccl. 4:2
2 *It is* better to go to the house of
mourning
Than to go to the house of feasting,
For that *is* the end of all men;
And the living will take *it* to heart.
3 [T]Sorrow *is* better than laughter,
[R]For by a sad countenance the heart is
made better. *Vexation* or *Grief* • [2 Cor. 7:10]
4 The heart of the wise *is* in the house of
mourning,
But the heart of fools *is* in the house of
mirth.

5 [R]*It is* better to [T]hear the rebuke of the
wise
Than for a man to hear the song of
fools. Ps. 141:5 • *listen to*
6 [R]For like the [T]crackling of thorns under a
pot,
So *is* the laughter of the fool.
This also is vanity. Eccl. 2:2 • Lit. *sound*
7 Surely oppression destroys a wise *man's*
reason,
And a bribe [T]debases the heart. *destroys*

8 The end of a thing *is* better than its
beginning,
And [R]the patient in spirit *is* better than
the proud in spirit. Prov. 14:29
9 [R]Do not hasten in your spirit to be
angry, James 1:19
For anger rests in the bosom of fools.
10 Do not say,
"Why were the former days better than
these?"
For you do not inquire wisely
concerning this.

11 Wisdom *is* good with an inheritance,
And profitable [R]to those who see the
sun. Eccl. 11:7
12 For wisdom *is* [T]a defense *as* money *is* a
defense, A protective shade, lit. *shadow*
But the [T]excellence of knowledge *is that*
wisdom gives [R]life to those who have
it. *advantage* or *profit* • Prov. 3:18

13 Consider the work of God;
For [R]who can make straight what He
has made crooked? Job 12:14
14 [R]In the day of prosperity be joyful,
But in the day of adversity consider:
Surely God has appointed the one [T]as
well as the other,
So that man can find nothing *that will*
happen after him. Deut. 28:47 • *alongside*

Wisdom of Moderation

15 I have seen all *things* in my days of
vanity:

[R]There is a just *man* who perishes in his
righteousness, Eccl. 8:12–14

WISDOM LITERATURE

The wisdom literature of the Old Testament consists of the books of Job, Proverbs, and Ecclesiastes, as well as some of the Psalms. The Hebrew word for wisdom is translated "skill for living" (see word study on *hokmah*, p. 717), because the Jews regarded wisdom in very practical terms. This literature provided guidance for moral behavior and everyday living.

Hebrew wisdom literature, as distinguished from the wisdom writings of other cultures, was centered on God: "The fear of the LORD *is* the beginning of knowledge, *but* fools despise wisdom and instruction" (Prov. 1:7). In contrast, Egyptian wisdom, for example, focused on the wisdom of the sages and on disciplining oneself to accept the trials of life.

The three broad categories of wisdom literature in the Old Testament are (1) popular proverbs that express practical truths; (2) riddles or parables with a spiritual meaning; and (3) discussions of the problems of life.

The Book of Proverbs provides wise sayings and observations designed to develop proper attitudes and godly behavior. Ecclesiastes offers a philosophical discussion of the emptiness of life without God (Eccl. 1:2, 14). Job is a classic examination of the problems of evil and human suffering. Its conclusion is that people can understand only what God chooses to reveal to them (Job 28:20–28).

Many of the Psalms, including 1, 4, 10, 14, 18, 19, 37, 49, 73, 90, and 112, are regarded as wisdom literature. A recurring theme in these Psalms is the problem of the prosperity of the wicked while the godly suffer. But the wise psalmist often returns to this refrain: "For evildoers shall be cut off; but those who wait on the LORD, they shall inherit the earth" (Ps. 37:9).

Solomon, David's successor as king of Israel, was well known for his wisdom. God appeared to Solomon in a dream at the beginning of his reign and asked him what gift he wished above all else (1 Kin. 3:3–15; see illustration). Solomon chose wisdom. Solomon apparently wrote many of the sayings in the Book of Proverbs.

Solomon dreamed at Gibeon, and when the Lord asked him to choose a gift, he chose wisdom.

And there is a wicked *man* who
prolongs *his life* in his wickedness.

16 [R]Do not be overly righteous,
[R]Nor be overly wise: Prov. 25:16 • Rom. 12:3
Why should you destroy yourself?
17 Do not be overly wicked,
Nor be foolish:
Why should you die before your time?
18 *It is* good that you grasp this,
And also not remove your hand from
the other;
For he who fears God will [T]escape them
all. Lit. *come forth from all of them*

Strength of Wisdom

19 [R]Wisdom strengthens the wise Prov. 21:22
More than ten rulers of the city.

20 [R]For *there is* not a just man on earth
who does good
And does not sin. 1 John 1:8

21 Also do not take to heart everything
people say,
Lest you hear your servant cursing you.
22 For many times, also, your own heart
has known
That even you have cursed others.

23 All this I have [T]proved by wisdom.
[R]I said, "I will be wise";
But it *was* far from me. *tested* • Rom. 1:22
24 [R]As for that which is far off and
[R]exceedingly deep,
Who can find it out? 1 Tim. 6:16 • Rom. 11:33
25 [R]I applied my heart to know, Eccl. 1:17
To search and seek out wisdom and the
reason *of things*,
To know the wickedness of folly,
Even of foolishness *and* madness.
26 [R]And I find more bitter than death
The woman whose heart *is* snares and
nets, Prov. 5:3, 4
Whose hands *are* fetters.
[T]He who pleases God shall escape from
her, Lit. *He who is good before God*
But the sinner shall be taken by her.

27 "Here is what I have found," says [R]the
Preacher,
"*Adding* one thing to the other to find
out the reason, Eccl. 1:1, 2
28 Which my soul still seeks but I cannot
find:
[R]One man among a thousand I have
found,
But a woman among all these I have
not found. Job 33:23
29 Truly, this only I have found:
[R]That God made man upright,
But [R]they have sought out many
schemes." Gen. 1:27 • Gen. 3:6, 7

CHAPTER 8

Submit to Authority

WHO *is* like a wise *man*?
And who knows the interpretation of
a thing?
[R]A man's wisdom makes his face shine,
And [R]the [T]sternness of his face is
changed. Acts 6:15 • Deut. 28:50 • Lit. *strength*

2 I *counsel you*, "Keep the king's commandment for the sake of your oath to God.
3 "Do not be hasty to go from his presence.
Do not take your stand for an evil thing, for
he does whatever pleases him."

4 Where the word of a king *is, there is*
power;
And [R]who may say to him, "What are
you doing?" Job 34:18
5 He who keeps his command will
experience nothing harmful;
And a wise man's heart [T]discerns both
time and judgment, Lit. *knows*
6 Because [R]for every matter there is a
time and judgment,
Though the misery of man [T]increases
greatly. Eccl. 3:1, 17 • *is great upon him*
7 [R]For he does not know what will
happen; Eccl. 6:12
So who can tell him when it will occur?
8 [R]No one has power over the spirit to
retain the spirit, Ps. 49:6, 7
And no one has power in the day of
death.
There is [R]no discharge in that war,
And wickedness will not deliver those
who are given to it. Deut. 20:5–8

9 All this I have seen, and applied my heart
to every work that is done under the sun:

7:20 Individual Sin—Each individual man, woman, and child who composes mankind is a sinner. Paul points out in Romans 3:13–16 that "their throat *is* an open tomb . . . the poison of asps [a small, deadly poisonous snake] *is* under their lips; whose mouth *is* full of cursing and bitterness. Their feet *are* swift to shed blood [consider the high incidence of violent crime, murder, and abortion that infects our society]; destruction and misery *are* in their ways [whatever man touches he corrupts]." All of this shows that there is no person who seeks after God and no person does what is right (Page 1325—Rom. 3:10, 11). Each individual man, woman, and child needs the righteousness of God. Without God's righteousness no one can ever enter or stand in God's presence. Plainly, every man, woman, and child needs to have a new life because each is a sinner.

Now turn to Page 1331—Rom. 6:23: New Life: A Free Gift.

There is a time in which one man rules over
another to his own hurt.

Inability to Understand All God's Doing

10 Then I saw the wicked buried, who had
come and gone from the place of holiness,
and they were forgotten in the city where
they had so done. This also *is* vanity.
11 [R]Because the sentence against an evil
work is not executed speedily, therefore the
heart of the sons of men is fully set in them to
do evil. Is. 26:10
12 Though a sinner does evil a hundred
times, and his *days* are prolonged, yet I
surely know that [R]it will be well with those
who fear God, who fear before Him. [Is. 3:10]
13 But it will not be well with the wicked;
nor will he prolong *his* days, *which are* as a
shadow, because he does not fear before God.
14 There is a vanity which occurs on earth,
that there are just *men* to whom it [R]happens
according to the work of the wicked; again,
there are wicked *men* to whom it happens
according to the work of the righteous. I said
that this also *is* vanity. Ps. 73:14
15 [R]So I commended enjoyment, because a
man has nothing better under the sun than to
eat, drink, and be merry; for this will remain
with him in his labor *for* the days of his life
which God gives him under the sun. Eccl. 2:24
16 When I applied my heart to know wisdom and to see the business that is done on
earth, even though one sees no sleep day or
night,
17 then I saw all the work of God, that [R]a
man cannot find out the work that is done
under the sun. For though a man labors to
discover *it*, yet he will not find *it*; moreover,
though a wise *man* attempts to know *it*, he
will not be able to find *it*. Rom. 11:33

CHAPTER 9

Judgment Comes to All Men

FOR I [T]considered all this in my heart, so
that I could declare it all: that the righteous and the wise and their works *are* in the
hand of God. People know neither love nor
hatred *by* anything *that is* before them. *put*
2 [R]Everything *occurs* alike to all:

One event *happens* to the righteous and
the wicked;
To the good, the clean, and the unclean;
To him who sacrifices and him who
does not sacrifice.
As is the good, so *is* the sinner;
And he who takes an oath as *he* who
fears an oath. Mal. 3:15

3 This *is* an evil in all that is done under
the sun: that one thing *happens* to all. Truly
the hearts of the sons of men are full of evil;
madness *is* in their hearts while they live, and
after that *they* go to the dead.
4 But for him who is joined to all the living
there is hope, for a living dog is better than a
dead lion.

5 For the living know that they will die;
But [R]the dead know nothing, Is. 63:16
And they have no more reward,
For the memory of them is forgotten.
6 Also their love, their hatred, and their
envy have now perished;
Nevermore will they have a share
In anything done under the sun.

Enjoy Life While You Have It

7 Go, [R]eat your bread with joy,
And drink your wine with a merry
heart;
For God has already accepted your
works. Eccl. 8:15
8 Let your garments always be white,
And let your head lack no oil.

9 Live joyfully with the wife whom you
love all the days of your vain life which He
has given you under the sun, all your days of
vanity; for that *is* your portion in life, and in
the labor which you perform under the sun.
10 [R]Whatever your hand finds to do, do *it*
with your [R]might; for *there is* no work or
device or knowledge or wisdom in the grave
where you are going. [Col. 3:17] • Rom. 12:11
11 I returned [R]and saw under the sun that—

The race *is* not to the swift,
Nor the battle to the strong,
Nor bread to the wise,
Nor riches to men of understanding,
Nor favor to men of skill;
But time and [R]chance happen to them
all. Amos 2:14, 15 • 1 Sam. 6:9
12 For [R]man also does not know his time:
Like fish taken in a cruel net, Eccl. 8:7
Like birds caught in a snare,
So the sons of men *are* [R]snared in an
evil time, Prov. 29:6
When it falls suddenly upon them.

Value of Wisdom

13 This wisdom I have also seen under the
sun, and it *seemed* great to me:
14 *There was* a little city with few men in it;
and a great king came against it, besieged it,
and built great *snares around it.
15 Now there was found in it a poor wise
man, and he by his wisdom delivered the city.
Yet no one remembered that same poor man.
16 Then I said:

9:14 Or *siegeworks;* LXX, Syr., Vg. *bulwarks*

"Wisdom *is* better than [R]strength.
Nevertheless [R]the poor man's wisdom *is* despised, Eccl. 7:12, 19 • Mark 6:2, 3
And his words are not heard.
17 Words of the wise, *spoken* quietly, *should be* heard
Rather than the shout of a ruler of fools.
18 Wisdom *is* better than weapons of war;
But one sinner destroys much good."

CHAPTER 10

Wisdom's Characteristics

DEAD flies *putrefy the perfumer's ointment,
And cause it to give off a foul odor;
So does a little folly to one respected for wisdom *and* honor.
2 A wise man's heart *is* at his right hand,
But a fool's heart at his left.
3 Even when a fool walks along the way,
He lacks wisdom,
[R]And he shows everyone *that* he *is* a fool. Prov. 13:16; 18:2
4 If the spirit of the ruler rises against you,
[R]Do not leave your post; Eccl. 8:3
For conciliation pacifies great offenses.

5 There is an evil I have seen under the sun,
As an error proceeding from the ruler:
6 [R]Folly is set in great dignity, Esth. 3:1
While the rich sit in a lowly place.
7 I have seen servants [R]on horses,
While princes walk on the ground like servants. Prov. 19:10; 30:22

8 [R]He who digs a pit will fall into it,
And whoever breaks through a wall will be bitten by a serpent. Prov. 26:27
9 He who quarries stones may be hurt by them,
And he who splits wood may be endangered by it.
10 If the ax is dull,
And one does not sharpen the edge,
Then he must use more strength;
But wisdom brings success.

11 A serpent may bite
When *it is* not charmed;
The babbler is no different.
12 [R]The words of a wise man's mouth *are* gracious, Prov. 10:32
But [R]the lips of a fool shall swallow him up; Prov. 10:14
13 The words of his mouth begin with foolishness,
And the end of his talk *is* raving madness.
14 [R]A fool also multiplies words. [Prov. 15:2]
No man knows what is to be;
Who can tell him [R]what will be after him? Eccl. 3:22; 8:7
15 The labor of fools wearies them,
For they do not even know how to go to the city!

Wisdom Related to the King

16 [R]Woe to you, O land, when your king *is* a child, Is. 3:4, 5; 5:11
And your princes feast in the morning!
17 Blessed *are* you, O land, when your king *is* the son of nobles,
And your [R]princes feast at the proper time— Prov. 31:4
For strength and not for drunkenness!
18 Because of laziness the [T]building decays, Lit. *rafters sink*
And [R]through idleness of hands the house leaks. Prov. 24:30–34
19 A feast is made for laughter,
And [R]wine makes merry; Ps. 104:15
But money answers everything.

20 [R]Do not curse the king, even in your thought; Acts 23:5
Do not curse the rich, even in your bedroom;
For a bird of the air may carry your voice,
And a bird in flight may tell the matter.

CHAPTER 11

Wisdom Related to Business

CAST your bread upon the waters,
For you will find it after many days.
2 [R]Give a serving [R]to seven, and also to eight, [1 Tim. 6:18, 19] • Mic. 5:5
[R]For you do not know what evil will be on the earth. Eph. 5:16

3 If the clouds are full of rain,
They empty *themselves* upon the earth;
And if a tree falls to the south or the north,
In the place where the tree falls, there it shall lie.
4 He who observes the wind will not sow,
And he who regards the clouds will not reap.

5 As [R]you do not know what is the way of the [T]wind, John 3:8 • Or *spirit*
[R]*Or* how the bones *grow* in the womb of her who is with child, Ps. 139:14
So you do not know the works of God who makes all *things*.
6 In the morning sow your seed,
And in the evening do not withhold your hand;

10:1 Tg., Vg. omit *putrefy*

For you do not know which will
prosper,
Either this or that,
Or whether both alike *will be* good.

Rejoice in Your Youth

7 Truly the light is sweet,
And *it is* pleasant for the eyes [R]to
behold the sun; Eccl. 7:11
8 But if a man lives many years
And [R]rejoices in them all,
Yet let him [R]remember the days of
darkness, Eccl. 9:7 · Eccl. 12:1
For they will be many.
All that is coming *is* vanity.

9 Rejoice, O young man, in your youth,
And let your heart cheer you in the
days of your youth;
Walk in the ways of your heart,
And [T]in the sight of your eyes;
But know that for all these As you see best
God will bring you into judgment.
10 Therefore remove [T]sorrow from your
heart, *vexation*
And put away evil from your flesh,
For childhood and youth *are* vanity.

CHAPTER 12

Remember God in Your Youth

REMEMBER[R] *now* your Creator in the
days of your youth, Lam. 3:27
Before the [T]difficult days come, *evil*
And the years draw near [R]when you
say, 2 Sam. 19:35
"I have no pleasure in them":
2 While the sun and the light,
The moon and the stars,
Are not darkened,
And the clouds do not return after the
rain;
3 In the day when the keepers of the
house tremble,
And the strong men bow down;
When the grinders cease because they
are few,
And those that look through the
windows grow dim;
4 When the doors are shut in the streets,
And the sound of grinding is low;
When one rises up at the sound of a
bird,
And all [R]the daughters of music are
brought low; 2 Sam. 19:35
5 Also *when* they are afraid of height,
And of terrors in the way;
When the almond tree blossoms,
The grasshopper is a burden,
And desire fails.
For man goes to his eternal home,
And the mourners go about the streets.

6 *Remember your Creator* before the
silver cord is loosed,
Or the golden bowl is broken,
Or the pitcher shattered at the fountain,
Or the wheel broken at the well.
7 [R]Then the dust will return to the earth
as it was, Gen. 3:19
[R]And the spirit will return to God [R]who
gave it. Eccl. 3:21 · Job 34:14

8 "Vanity[R] of vanities," says the Preacher,
"All *is* vanity." Ps. 62:9

"Fear God and Keep His Commandments"

9 And moreover, because the Preacher was
wise, he still taught the people knowledge;
yes, he pondered and sought out *and* [R]set[T] in
order many proverbs. 1 Kin. 4:32 · *arranged*
10 The Preacher sought to find [T]acceptable
words; and *what was* written *was* upright—
words of truth. *delightful*
11 The words of the wise are like goads, and
the words of scholars are like well-driven
nails, given by one Shepherd.
12 And further, my son, be admonished by
these. Of making many books *there is* no
end, and [R]much study *is* wearisome to the
flesh. Eccl. 1:18
13 Let us hear the conclusion of the whole
matter:

Fear God and keep His commandments,
For this is the whole duty of man.
14 For [R]God will bring every work into
judgment, Matt. 12:36
Including every secret thing,
Whether *it is* good or whether *it is* evil.

THE SONG OF SOLOMON

THE BOOK OF SONG OF SOLOMON

The Song of Solomon is a love song written by Solomon and abounding in metaphors and oriental imagery. Historically, it depicts the wooing and wedding of a shepherdess by King Solomon, and the joys and heartaches of wedded love.

Allegorically, it pictures Israel as God's espoused bride (Hos. 2:19, 20), and the Church as the bride of Christ. As human life finds its highest fulfillment in the love of man and woman, so spiritual life finds its highest fulfillment in the love of God for His people and Christ for His Church.

The book is arranged like scenes in a drama with three main speakers: the bride (Shulamite), the king (Solomon), and a chorus (daughters of Jerusalem).

The Hebrew title *Shir Hashirim* comes from 1:1, "The song of songs." This is in the superlative and speaks of Solomon's most exquisite song. The Greek title *Asma Asmaton* and the Latin *Canticum Canticorum* also mean "Song of Songs" or "The Best Song." The name *Canticles* ("Songs") is derived from the Latin title. Because Solomon is mentioned in 1:1, the book is also known as the Song of Solomon.

THE AUTHOR OF SONG OF SOLOMON

Solomonic authorship is rejected by critics who claim it is a later collection of songs. Many take 1:1 to mean "which is about or concerning Solomon." But the internal evidence of the book strongly favors the traditional position that Solomon is its author. Solomon is specifically mentioned seven times (1:1, 5; 3:7, 9, 11; 8:11, 12), and he is identified as the groom. There is evidence of royal luxury and rich imported goods (e.g., 3:6–11). The king by this time also had sixty queens and eighty concubines (6:8). Solomon's harem at its fullest extent reached seven hundred queens and three hundred concubines (1 Kin. 11:3).

First Kings 4:32, 33 says that Solomon composed 1,005 songs and had intimate knowledge of the plant and animal world. This greatest of his songs alludes to twenty-one species of plants and fifteen species of animals. It cites geographical locations in the north and in the south, indicating that they were still one kingdom. For example, 6:4 mentions both Tirzah and Jerusalem, the northern and southern capitals (after Solomon's time, Samaria became the northern capital). Because of the poetic imagery, the Song of Solomon uses forty-nine words that occur nowhere else in Scripture.

THE TIME OF SONG OF SOLOMON

This song was written primarily from the point of view of the Shulamite, but Solomon was its author, probably early in his reign, about 965 B.C. There is a problem regarding how a man with a harem of 140 women (6:8) could extol the love of the Shulamite as though she were his only bride. It may be that Solomon's relationship with the Shulamite was the only pure romance he ever experienced. The bulk of his marriages were political arrangements. It is significant that the Shulamite was a vineyard keeper of no great means. This book was also written before Solomon plunged into gross immorality and idolatry. "For it was so, when Solomon was old, that his wives turned his heart after other gods; and his heart was not loyal to the LORD his God" (1 Kin. 11:4).

The Shulamite addresses the king as "my beloved" and the king addresses his bride as "my love." The daughters of Jerusalem were probably attendants to the Shulamite. The term *Shulamite* appears only in 6:13, and it may be derived from the town of Shunem which was southwest of the Sea of Galilee in the tribal area of Issachar. The song refers to fifteen geographic locations from Lebanon in the north to Egypt in the south: Kedar (1:5), Egypt (1:9), En Gedi (1:14), Sharon (2:1), Jerusalem (2:7), Lebanon (3:9), Mount Gilead (4:1), Amana (4:8), Senir (4:8), Hermon (4:8), Tirzah (6:4), Heshbon (7:4), Damascus (7:4), Carmel (7:5), and Baal Hamon (8:11).

THE CHRIST OF SONG OF SOLOMON

In the Old Testament, Israel is regarded as the bride of Yahweh (see Is. 54:5, 6; Jer. 2:2; Ezek. 16:8–14; Hos. 2:16–20). In the New Testament, the Church is seen as the bride of Christ (see 2 Cor. 11:2; Eph. 5:23–25; Rev. 19:7–9; 21:9). The Song of Solomon illustrates the former and anticipates the latter.

KEYS TO SONG OF SOLOMON

Key Word: Love in Marriage—The purpose of this book depends on the viewpoint taken as to its primary thrust. Is it fictional, allegorical, or historical?

(1) *Fictional:* Some hold that this song is a fictional drama that portrays Solomon's attraction and marriage to a poor but beautiful girl from the country. However, the book gives every indication that the story really happened.

(2) *Allegorical:* In this view, the primary purpose of the Song is to illustrate the truth of God's love for His people whether the events were

fictional or not. Some commentators insist that the book is indeed historical, but its primary purpose is typical, that is, to present God's love for His bride Israel or Christ's love for His Church. However, this interpretation is subjective and lacking in evidence. In other scriptures the husband and wife relationship is used symbolically (cf. Ezek. 16; 23; Hos. 1—3), but these are always indicated as symbols. This may be an application of the book, but it should not be the primary interpretation.

(3) *Historical:* The Song of Songs is a poetic record of Solomon's actual romance with a Shulamite woman. The various scenes in the book exalt the joys of love in courtship and marriage and teach that physical beauty and sexuality in marriage should not be despised as base or unspiritual. It offers a proper perspective of human love and avoids the extremes of lust and asceticism. Only when sexuality is viewed in the wrong way, as something akin to evil, is an attempt made to allegorize the book. But this is part of God's creation with its related desires and pleasures, and it is reasonable that He would provide us with a guide to a pure sexual relationship between a husband and wife. In fact, the union of the two sexes was originally intended to illustrate the oneness of the Godhead (see Gen. 1:27; 2:24; 1 Cor. 6:16–20). Thus, the Song is a bold and positive endorsement by God of marital love in all its physical and emotional beauty. This interpretation does not mean that the book has no spiritual illustrations and applications. It certainly illustrates God's love for His covenant people Israel, and anticipates Christ's love for His bride, the Church.

Key Verses: Song of Solomon 7:10 and 8:7—"I *am* my beloved's, and his desire *is* toward me" (7:10).

"Many waters cannot quench love, nor can the floods drown it. If a man would give for love all the wealth of his house, it would be utterly despised" (8:7).

Key Chapter: Song of Solomon—Since the whole book is a unity, there is no key chapter; rather, all eight chapters beautifully depict the love of a married couple.

SURVEY OF SONG OF SOLOMON

Solomon wrote 1,005 songs (1 Kin. 4:32), but this beautiful eulogy of love stood out among them as the "song of songs" (1:1). The great literary value of this song can be seen in its rich use of metaphor and oriental imagery as it extols the purity, beauty, and satisfaction of love. It is never crass, but often intimate, as it explores the dimensions of the relationship between two lovers: attraction, desire, companionship, pleasure, union, separation, faithfulness, and praise. Like Ecclesiastes, this little book is not easily outlined, and various schemes can be used. It abounds with sudden changes of speakers, and they are not identified. The beginning of love is seen in 1:1—5:1, and the broadening of love is found in 5:2—8:14.

The Beginning of Love (1:1—5:1): King Solomon has a vineyard in the country of the Shulamite (6:13; 8:11). The Shulamite must work in the vineyard with her brothers (1:6; 8:11, 12); and when Solomon visits the area, he wins her heart and eventually takes her to the palace in Jerusalem as his bride. She is tanned from hours of work outside in the vineyard, but she is "fairest among women" (1:6, 8).

This song is arranged like scenes in a one-act drama with three main speakers—the bride (the Shulamite), the king (Solomon), and a chorus (the daughters of Jerusalem). It is not always clear who is speaking, but this is a likely arrangement:

The bride: 1:2–4, 5–7, 12–14, 16, 17; 2:1, 3–6, 8–17; 3:1–4; 4:16; 5:2–8, 10–16; 6:2, 3, 11, 12; 7:9–13; 8:1–3, 6, 7, 10–12, 14.

FOCUS	BEGINNING OF LOVE		BROADENING OF LOVE	
REFERENCE	1:1——3:6	——5:2	——7:11	——8:14
DIVISION	FALLING IN LOVE	UNITED IN LOVE	STRUGGLING IN LOVE	GROWING IN LOVE
TOPIC	COURTSHIP	WEDDING	PROBLEM	PROGRESS
	FOSTERING OF LOVE	FULFILLMENT OF LOVE	FRUSTRATION OF LOVE	FAITHFULNESS OF LOVE
LOCATION	ISRAEL			
TIME	c. 1 YEAR			

The groom: 1:8–10, 15; 2:2, 7; 3:5; 4:1–15; 5:1; 6:4–10, 13; 7:1–9; 8:4, 5, 13.
The chorus: 1:4, 11; 3:6–11; 5:9; 6:1, 13; 8:5, 8, 9.

Chapters 1—3 give a series of recollections of the courtship: (1) the bride's longing for affection at the palace before the wedding (1:2–8), (2) expressions of mutual love in the banquet hall (1:9—2:7), (3) a springtime visit of the king to the bride's home in the country (2:8–17), (4) the Shulamite's dream of separation from her beloved (3:1–5), and (5) the ornate wedding procession from the bride's home to Jerusalem (3:6–11).

In 4:1—5:1, Solomon praises his bride from head to foot with a superb chain of similes and metaphors. Her virginity is compared to "a garden enclosed" (4:12), and the garden is entered when the marriage is consummated (4:16—5:1). The union is commended, possibly by God, in 5:1.

The Broadening of Love (5:2—8:14): Some time after the wedding, the Shulamite has a troubled dream (5:2) in the palace while Solomon is away. In her dream Solomon comes to her door, but she answers too late—he is gone. She panics and searches for him late at night in Jerusalem. Upon his return, Solomon assures her of his love and praises her beauty (6:4—7:10). The Shulamite begins to think of her country home and tries to persuade her beloved to return there with her (7:11—8:4). The journey takes place in 8:5–7 and their relationship continues to deepen. Their love will not be overthrown by jealousy or circumstances. At her homecoming (8:8–14) the Shulamite reflects on her brothers' care for her when she was young (8:8, 9). She remains virtuous ("I *am* a wall," 8:10) and is now in a position to look out for her brothers' welfare (8:11, 12). The song concludes with a dual invitation of lover and beloved (8:13, 14).

OUTLINE OF SONG OF SOLOMON

CHAPTER 1

Bride's Longing for Affection

THE song of songs, which *is* Solomon's.

THE SHULAMITE

2 Let him kiss me with the kisses of his mouth—
For your love *is* better than wine.
3 Because of the fragrance of your good ointments,
Your name *is* ointment poured forth;
Therefore the virgins love you.
4 [R]Lead[T] me away! Hos. 11:4 • Lit. *Draw me*

THE DAUGHTERS OF JERUSALEM

[R]We will run after you. Phil. 3:12–14

THE SHULAMITE

The king [R]has brought me into his chambers. Ps. 45:14, 15

THE DAUGHTERS OF JERUSALEM

We will be glad and rejoice in [T]you.
We will remember [T]your love more than wine. The Shulamite • The Beloved

THE SHULAMITE

Rightly do they love you.

5 I *am* dark, but lovely,
O daughters of Jerusalem,
Like the tents of Kedar,
Like the curtains of Solomon.
6 Do not look upon me, because I *am* dark,
Because the sun has tanned me.
My mother's sons were angry with me;
They made me the keeper of the vineyards,
But my own vineyard I have not kept.

(TO HER BELOVED)

7 Tell me, O you whom I love,
Where you feed *your flock*,

Where you make *it* rest at noon.
For why should I be as one who veils
herself
By the flocks of your companions?

THE BELOVED

8 If you do not know, [R]O fairest among
women, Song 5:9
[T]Follow in the footsteps of the flock,
And feed your little goats
Beside the shepherds' tents. Lit. *Go out*

Expressions of Mutual Love

9 I have compared you, my love,
To my filly among Pharaoh's chariots.
10 [R]Your cheeks are lovely with ornaments,
Your neck with chains *of gold*. Ezek. 16:11

THE DAUGHTERS OF JERUSALEM

11 We will make [T]you ornaments of gold
With studs of silver. The Shulamite

THE SHULAMITE

12 While the king *is* at his table,
My spikenard sends forth its fragrance.
13 A bundle of myrrh *is* my beloved to me,
That lies all night between my breasts.
14 My beloved *is* to me a cluster of henna
blooms
In the vineyards of En Gedi.

THE BELOVED

15 Behold, you *are* fair, my [T]love!
Behold, you *are* fair!
You *have* dove's eyes. *companion, friend*

THE SHULAMITE

16 Behold, you *are* [R]handsome, my
beloved! Song 5:10–16
Yes, pleasant!
Also our [T]bed *is* green. *couch*
17 The beams of our houses *are* cedar,
And our rafters of fir.

CHAPTER 2

I *AM* the rose of Sharon,
And the lily of the valleys.

THE BELOVED

2 Like a lily among thorns,
So is my love among the daughters.

THE SHULAMITE

3 Like an apple tree among the trees of
the woods,
So *is* my beloved among the sons.
I sat down in his shade with great
delight,
And his fruit *was* sweet to my taste.

THE SHULAMITE TO THE DAUGHTERS OF JERUSALEM

4 He brought me to the [T]banqueting
house, Lit. *house of wine*
And his banner over me *was* love.
5 Sustain me with cakes of raisins,
Refresh me with apples,
For I *am* lovesick.

6 [R]His left hand *is* under my head, Song 8:3
And his right hand embraces me.
7 [R]I [T]charge you, O daughters of
Jerusalem,
By the gazelles or by the does of the
field,
Do not stir up nor awaken love
Until it pleases. Song 3:5; 8:4 • *adjure*

Visit of the King to the Bride's Home

THE SHULAMITE

8 The voice of my beloved!
Behold, he comes
Leaping upon the mountains,
Skipping upon the hills.
9 [R]My beloved is like a gazelle or a young
stag.
Behold, he stands behind our wall;
He is looking through the windows,
Gazing through the lattice. Song 2:17

10 My beloved spoke, and said to me:
"Rise up, my love, my fair one,
And come away.
11 For lo, the winter is past,
The rain is over *and* gone.
12 The flowers appear on the earth;
The time of singing has come,
And the voice of the turtledove
Is heard in our land.
13 The fig tree puts forth her green figs,
And the vines *with* the tender grapes
Give a good smell.
Rise up, my love, my fair one,
And come away!

14 "O my dove, in the clefts of the rock,
In the secret *places* of the cliff,
Let me see your [T]countenance,
Let me hear your voice; Lit. *appearance*
For your voice *is* sweet,
And your countenance *is* lovely."

HER BROTHERS

15 Catch us [R]the foxes, Ezek. 13:4
The little foxes that spoil the vines,
For our vines *have* tender grapes.

THE SHULAMITE

16 My beloved *is* mine, and I *am* his.
He feeds *his flock* among the lilies.

(TO HER BELOVED)

17 [R]Until the day breaks Song 4:6
And the shadows flee away,
Turn, my beloved,
And be [R]like a gazelle Song 8:14
Or a young stag
Upon the mountains of Bether.

CHAPTER 3

Bride's Dream of Separation

THE SHULAMITE

BY [R]night on my bed I sought the one I
love; Is. 26:9
I sought him, but I did not find him.
2 "I will rise now," *I said,*
"And go about the city;
In the streets and in the squares
I will seek the one I love."
I sought him, but I did not find him.
3 [R]The watchmen who go about the city
found me,
To whom I said,
"Have you seen the one I love?" Song 5:7

4 Scarcely had I passed by them,
When I found the one I love.
I held him and would not let him go,
Until I had brought him to the [R]house
of my mother,
And into the [T]chamber of her who
conceived me. Song 8:2 • *room*

5 [R]I [T]charge you, O daughters of
Jerusalem,
By the gazelles or by the does of the
field,
Do not stir up nor awaken love
Until it pleases. Song 2:7; 8:4 • *adjure*

Wedding Procession

6 [R]Who *is* this coming out of the
wilderness
Like pillars of smoke,
Perfumed with myrrh and frankincense,
With all the merchant's fragrant
powders? Song 8:5
7 Behold, it *is* Solomon's couch,
With sixty valiant men around it,
Of the valiant of Israel.
8 They all hold swords,
Being expert in war.
Every man *has* his sword on his thigh
Because of fear in the night.

9 Of the wood of Lebanon
Solomon the King
Made himself a [T]palanquin: A portable chair
10 He made its pillars *of* silver,
Its support *of* gold,
Its seat *of* purple,
Its interior paved *with* love
By the daughters of Jerusalem.
11 Go forth, O daughters of Zion,
And see King Solomon with the crown
With which his mother crowned him
On the day of his [T]espousals, *engagement*
The day of the gladness of his heart.

CHAPTER 4

Bride's Beauty Is Praised

THE BELOVED

BEHOLD, [R]you *are* fair, my love!
Behold, you *are* fair! Song 1:15; 5:12
You *have* dove's eyes behind your veil.
Your hair *is* like a [R]flock of goats,
Going down from Mount Gilead. Song 6:5
2 [R]Your teeth *are* like a flock of shorn
sheep Song 6:6
Which have come up from the washing,
Every one of which bears twins,
And none *is* barren among them.
3 Your lips *are* like a strand of scarlet,
And your mouth is lovely.
[R]Your temples behind your veil
Are like a piece of pomegranate. Song 6:7
4 [R]Your neck *is* like the tower of David,
Built [R]for an armory, Song 7:4 • Neh. 3:19
On which hang a thousand [T]bucklers,
All shields of mighty men. Small shields
5 [R]Your two breasts *are* like two fawns,
Twins of a gazelle, Song 7:3
Which feed among the lilies.

6 [R]Until the day breaks Song 2:17
And the shadows flee away,
I will go my way to the mountain of
myrrh
And to the hill of frankincense.

7 [R]You *are* all fair, my love,
And *there is* no spot in you. Eph. 5:27
8 Come with me from Lebanon, *my*
spouse,
With me from Lebanon.
Look from the top of Amana,
From the top of Senir [R]and Hermon,
From the lions' dens, Deut. 3:9
From the mountains of the leopards.

9 You have ravished my heart,
My sister, *my* spouse;
You have ravished my heart
With one *look* of your eyes,
With one link of your necklace.
10 How fair is your love,
My sister, *my* spouse!
[R]How much better than wine is your
love,
And the [T]scent of your perfumes
Than all spices! Song 1:2, 4 • *fragrance*

11 Your lips, O *my* spouse,
Drip as the honeycomb;
Honey and milk *are* under your tongue;
And the fragrance of your garments
Is like the fragrance of Lebanon.

12 A garden [T]enclosed
Is my sister, *my* spouse,
A spring shut up,
A fountain sealed. *locked* or *barred*
13 Your plants *are* an orchard of
pomegranates
With pleasant fruits,
Fragrant henna with spikenard,
14 Spikenard and saffron,
Calamus and cinnamon,
With all trees of frankincense,
Myrrh and aloes,
With all the chief spices—
15 A fountain of gardens,
A well of [R]living waters, Zech. 14:8
And streams from Lebanon.

The Marriage Is Consummated

THE SHULAMITE

16 Awake, O north *wind*,
And come, O south!
Blow upon my garden,
That its spices may flow out.
[R]Let my beloved come to his garden
And eat its pleasant fruits. Song 5:1

CHAPTER 5

THE BELOVED

I [R]HAVE come to my garden, my [R]sister,
my spouse; Song 4:16 • Song 4:9
I have gathered my myrrh with my
spice;
[R]I have eaten my honeycomb with my
honey; Song 4:11
I have drunk my wine with my milk.

(TO HIS FRIENDS)

Eat, O [R]friends! Luke 15:7, 10
Drink, yes, drink deeply,
O beloved ones!

Bride's Second Dream of Separation

THE SHULAMITE

2 I sleep, but my heart is awake;
It is the voice of my beloved!
[R]He knocks, *saying*, Rev. 3:20
"Open for me, my sister, my love,
My dove, my perfect one;
For my head is covered with dew,
My locks with the drops of the night."

3 I have taken off my robe;
How can I put it on *again*?
I have washed my feet;
How can I [T]defile them? *dirty*
4 My beloved put his hand
By the [T]latch *of the door*,
And my heart yearned for him. *opening*
5 I arose to open for my beloved,
And my hands dripped *with* myrrh,
My fingers with liquid myrrh,
On the handles of the lock.

6 I opened for my beloved,
But my beloved had turned away *and*
was gone.
My [T]heart went out *to him* when he
spoke. Lit. *soul*
I sought him, but I could not find him;
I called him, but he gave me no answer.
7 [R]The watchmen who went about the city
found me.
They struck me, they wounded me;
The keepers of the walls
Took my veil away from me. Song 3:3

Bridegroom's Handsomeness Is Praised

8 I charge you, O daughters of Jerusalem,
If you find my beloved,
That you tell him I *am* lovesick!

THE DAUGHTERS OF JERUSALEM

9 What *is* your beloved
More than *another* beloved,
[R]O fairest among women? Song 1:8; 6:1
What *is* your beloved
More than *another* beloved,
That you so [T]charge us? *adjure*

THE SHULAMITE

10 My beloved *is* white and ruddy,
[T]Chief among ten thousand. *Distinguished*
11 His head *is like* the finest gold;
His locks *are* wavy,
And black as a raven.
12 [R]His eyes *are* like doves Song 1:15; 4:1
By the rivers of waters,
Washed with milk,
And [T]fitly set. *sitting in a setting*
13 His cheeks *are* like a bed of spices,
Like banks of scented herbs.
His lips *are* lilies,
Dripping liquid myrrh.

14 His hands *are* rods of gold
Set with beryl.
His body *is* carved ivory
Inlaid *with* sapphires.
15 His legs *are* pillars of marble
Set on bases of fine gold.
His countenance *is* like Lebanon,
Excellent as the cedars.
16 His mouth *is* most sweet,
Yes, he *is* altogether lovely.
This *is* my beloved,

And this *is* my friend,
O daughters of Jerusalem!

CHAPTER 6

THE DAUGHTERS OF JERUSALEM

WHERE has your beloved gone,
[R]O fairest among women? Song 1:8; 5:9
Where has your beloved turned aside,
That we may seek him with you?

THE SHULAMITE

2 My beloved has gone to his [R]garden,
To the beds of spices, Song 4:16; 5:1
To feed *his flock* in the gardens,
And to gather lilies.
3 [R]I *am* my beloved's, Song 2:16; 7:10
And my beloved *is* mine.
He feeds *his flock* among the lilies.

Bride's Beauty Is Praised

THE BELOVED

4 O my love, you *are as* beautiful as
Tirzah,
Lovely as Jerusalem,
Awesome as *an army* with banners!
5 Turn your eyes away from me,
For they have [T]overcome me. *overwhelmed*
Your hair *is* [R]like a flock of goats
Going down from Gilead. Song 4:1
6 [R]Your teeth *are* like a flock of sheep
Which have come up from the washing;
Every one bears twins, Song 4:2
And none *is* [T]barren among them. *bereaved*
7 [R]Like a piece of pomegranate Song 4:3
Are your temples behind your veil.

8 There are sixty queens
And eighty concubines,
And [R]virgins without number. Song 1:3
9 My dove, my [R]perfect one,
Is the only one,
The only one of her mother,
The favorite of the one who bore her.
The daughters saw her
And called her blessed,
The queens and the concubines,
And they praised her. Song 2:14; 5:2

10 Who is she *who* looks forth as the
morning,
Fair as the moon,
Clear as the sun,
Awesome as *an army* with banners?

THE SHULAMITE

11 I went down to the garden of nuts
To see the verdure of the valley,
To see whether the vine had budded
And the pomegranates had bloomed.
12 Before I was even aware,
My soul had made me
As the chariots of my noble people.

THE BELOVED AND HIS FRIENDS

13 Return, return, O Shulamite;
Return, return, that we may look upon
you!

THE SHULAMITE

What would you see in the Shulamite—
As it were, the dance of [T]the double
camp? Or *mahanaim*

CHAPTER 7

THE BELOVED

HOW beautiful are your feet in sandals,
[R]O prince's daughter!
The curves of your thighs *are* like
jewels,
The work of the hands of a skillful
workman. Ps. 45:13
2 Your navel *is* a rounded goblet
Which lacks no [T]blended beverage.
Your waist *is* a heap of wheat
Set about with lilies. Lit. *mixed* or *spiced drink*
3 [R]Your two breasts *are* like two fawns,
Twins of a gazelle. Song 4:5
4 [R]Your neck *is* like an ivory tower,
Your eyes *like* the pools in Heshbon
By the gate of Bath Rabbim.
Your nose *is* like the tower of Lebanon
Which looks toward Damascus. Song 4:4
5 Your head *crowns* you like *Mount*
Carmel,
And the hair of your head *is* like purple;
The king *is* held captive by *its* tresses.

6 How fair and how pleasant you are,
O love, with your delights!
7 This stature of yours is like a palm tree,
And your breasts *like* its clusters.
8 I said, "I will go up to the palm tree,
I will take hold of its branches."
Let now your breasts be like clusters of
the vine,
The fragrance of your [T]breath like
apples, Lit. *nose*
9 And the roof of your mouth like the
best wine.

THE SHULAMITE

[T]The wine goes *down* smoothly for my
beloved, Lit. *It*
Moving gently the lips of sleepers.
10 [R]I *am* my beloved's, Song 2:16; 6:3
And [R]his desire *is* toward me. Ps. 45:11

Bride's Desire to Visit Her Home

11 Come, my beloved,
Let us go forth to the field;
Let us lodge in the villages.
12 Let us get up early to the vineyards;
Let us [R]see *if* the vine has budded,
Whether the grape blossoms are open,
And the pomegranates are in bloom.
There I will give you my love. Song 6:11
13 The [R]mandrakes give off a fragrance,
And at our gates [R]*are* pleasant *fruits*,
All manner, new and old,
Which I have laid up for you, my
beloved. Gen. 30:14 • Matt. 13:52

CHAPTER 8

OH, that you *were* like my brother,
Who nursed at my mother's breasts!
If I should find you outside,
I would kiss you;
I would not be despised.
2 I would lead you *and* bring you
Into the [R]house of my mother,
She *who* used to instruct me.
I would cause you to drink of [R]spiced
wine, Song 3:4 • Prov. 9:2
Of the juice of my pomegranate.

(To the Daughters of Jerusalem)

3 His left hand *is* under my head,
And his right hand embraces me.
4 [R]I charge you, O daughters of Jerusalem,
Do not stir up nor awaken love
Until it pleases. Song 2:7; 3:5

Journey and Homecoming

A Relative

5 [R]Who *is* this coming up from the
wilderness, Song 3:6
Leaning upon her beloved?

I awakened you under the apple tree.
There your mother brought you forth;
There she *who* bore you brought *you*
forth.

The Shulamite to Her Beloved

6 [R]Set me as a seal upon your heart,
As a seal upon your arm; Jer. 22:24
For love *is as* strong as death,
Jealousy *as* [T]cruel as the grave;
Its flames *are* flames of fire,
A most vehement flame. *severe*

7 Many waters cannot quench love,
Nor can the floods drown it.
[R]If a man would give for love
All the wealth of his house, Prov. 6:35
It would be utterly despised.

The Shulamite's Brothers

8 [R]We have a little sister, Ezek. 23:33
And she has no breasts.
What shall we do for our sister
In the day when she is spoken for?
9 If she *is* a wall,
We will build upon her
A battlement of silver;
And if she *is* a door,
We will enclose her
With boards of cedar.

The Shulamite

10 I *am* a wall,
And my breasts like towers;
Then I became in his eyes
As one who found peace.
11 Solomon had a vineyard at Baal
Hamon;
He leased the vineyard to keepers;
Everyone was to bring for its fruit
A thousand *pieces* of silver.

(To Solomon)

12 My own vineyard *is* before me.
You, O Solomon, *may have* a thousand,
And those who keep its fruit two
hundred.

The Beloved

13 You who dwell in the gardens,
The companions listen for your voice—
[R]Let me hear it! Song 2:14

The Shulamite

14 [T]Make haste, my beloved, *Hurry*, lit. *Flee*
And [R]be like a gazelle Song 2:7, 9, 17
Or a young stag
On the mountains of spices.

THE BOOK OF

ISAIAH

THE BOOK OF ISAIAH

Isaiah is like a miniature Bible. The first thirty-nine chapters (like the thirty-nine books of the Old Testament) are filled with judgment upon immoral and idolatrous men. Judah has sinned; the surrounding nations have sinned; the whole earth has sinned. Judgment must come, for God cannot allow such blatant sin to go unpunished forever. But the final twenty-seven chapters (like the twenty-seven books of the New Testament) declare a message of hope. The Messiah is coming as a Savior and a Sovereign to bear a cross and to wear a crown.

Isaiah's prophetic ministry, spanning the reigns of four kings of Judah, covers at least forty years. *Yesha'yahu* and its shortened form *yeshaiah* mean "Yahweh Is Salvation." This name is an excellent summary of the contents of the book. The Greek form in the Septuagint is *Hesaias*, and the Latin form is *Esaias* or *Isaias*.

THE AUTHOR OF ISAIAH

Isaiah, the "St. Paul of the Old Testament," was evidently from a distinguished Jewish family. His education is evident in his impressive vocabulary and style. His work is comprehensive in scope and beautifully communicated. Isaiah maintained close contact with the royal court, but his exhortations against alliances with foreign powers were not always well received. This great poet and prophet was uncompromising, sincere, and compassionate. His wife was a prophetess and he fathered at least two sons (7:3; 8:3). He spent most of his time in Jerusalem, and talmudic tradition says his persecutors sawed him in two during the reign of Manasseh (cf. Heb. 11:37).

The unity of this book has been challenged by critics who hold that a "Deutero-Isaiah" wrote chapters 40—66 after the Babylonian captivity. They argue that 1—39 has an Assyrian background, while 40—66 is set against a Babylonian background. But Babylon is mentioned more than twice as often in 1—39 as in 40—66. The only shift is one of perspective from present time to future time. Critics also argue that there are radical differences in the language, style, and theology of the two sections. Actually, the resemblances between 1—39 and 40—66 are greater than the differences. These include similarities in thoughts, images, rhetorical ornaments, characteristic expressions, and local coloring. It is true that the first section is more terse and rational, while the second section is more flowing and emotional, but much of this is caused by the different subject matter, condemnation versus consolation. Critics often forget that content, time, and circumstances typically affect any author's style. In addition, there is no theological contradiction between the emphasis on the Messiah as King in 1—39 and as suffering Servant in 40—66. While the thrust is different, the Messiah is seen in both sections as Servant and King. Another critical argument is that Isaiah could not have predicted the Babylonian captivity and the return under Cyrus (mentioned by name in 44 and 45) 150 years in advance. This view is based on the mere assumption that divine prophecy is impossible, rejecting the predictive claims of the book (see 42:9). The theory cannot explain the amazing messianic prophecies of Isaiah that were literally fulfilled in the life of Christ (see "The Christ of Isaiah").

The unity of Isaiah is supported by the book of Ecclesiasticus, the Septuagint, and the Talmud. The New Testament also claims that Isaiah wrote both sections. John 12:37–41 quotes from Isaiah 6:9, 10 and 53:1 and attributes it all to Isaiah. In Romans 9:27 and 10:16–21, Paul quotes from Isaiah 10, 53, and 65 and gives the credit to Isaiah. The same is true of Matthew 3:3 and 12:17–21, Luke 3:4–6, and Acts 8:28.

If 40—66 was written by another prophet after the events took place, it is a misleading and deceptive work. Furthermore, it would lead to the strange conclusion that Israel's greatest prophet is the only writing prophet of the Old Testament to go unnamed.

THE TIME OF ISAIAH

Isaiah's long ministry ranged from about 740 to 680 B.C. (1:1). He began his ministry near the end of Uzziah's reign (790–739 B.C.) and continued through the reigns of Jotham (739–731 B.C.), Ahaz (731–715 B.C.), and Hezekiah (715–686 B.C.). Assyria was growing in power under Tiglath-Pileser who turned toward the west after his conquests in the east. He plucked up the small nations that dotted the Mediterranean coast including Israel and much of Judah. Isaiah lived during this time of military threat to Judah, and warned its kings against trusting in alliances with other countries rather than the power of Yahweh. As a contemporary of Hosea and Micah, he prophesied during the last years of the northern kingdom but ministered to the southern kingdom of Judah who was following the sins of her sister Israel. After Israel's demise in 722 B.C., he warned Judah of judgment not by Assyria but by Babylon, even though Babylon had not yet risen to power.

Isaiah ministered from the time of Tiglath-Pileser (745–727 B.C.) to the time of Sennacherib (705–681 B.C.) of Assyria. He outdated Hezekiah by a few years because 37:38 records the death of Sennacherib in 681 B.C. Hezekiah was succeeded by his wicked son Manasseh who overthrew the worship of Yahweh and no doubt opposed the work of Isaiah.

THE CHRIST OF ISAIAH

When he speaks about Christ, Isaiah sounds more like a New Testament writer than an Old Testament prophet. His messianic prophecies are clearer and more explicit than those in any other Old Testament book. They describe many aspects of the person and work of Christ in His first and second advents, and often blend the two together. Here are a few of the Christological prophecies with their New Testament fulfillments: 7:14 (Matt. 1:22, 23); 9:1, 2 (Matt. 4:12–16); 9:6 (Luke 2:11; Eph. 2:14–18); 11:1 (Luke 3:23, 32; Acts 13:22, 23); 11:2 (Luke 3:22); 28:16 (1 Pet. 2:4–6); 40:3–5 (Matt. 3:1–3); 42:1–4 (Matt. 12:15–21); 42:6 (Luke 2:29–32); 50:6 (Matt. 26:67; 27:26, 30); 52:14 (Phil. 2:7–11); 53:3 (Luke 23:18; John 1:11; 7:5); 53:4, 5 (Rom 5:6, 8); 53:7 (Matt. 27:12–14; John 1:29; 1 Pet. 1:18, 19); 53:9 (Matt. 27:57–60); 53:12 (Mark 15:28); 61:1, 2 (Luke 4:17–19, 21). The Old Testament has over three hundred prophecies about the first advent of Christ, and Isaiah contributes a number of them. The odds that even ten of them could be fulfilled by one person is a statistical marvel. Isaiah's messianic prophecies that await fulfillment in the Lord's second advent include: 4:2; 11:2–6, 10; 32:1–8; 49:7; 52:13, 15; 59:20, 21; 60:1–3; 61:2, 3.

Isaiah 52:13—53:12 is the central passage of the consolation section (40—66). Its five stanzas present five different aspects of the saving work of Christ: (1) 52:13–15—His wholehearted sacrifice (burnt offering); (2) 53:1–3—His perfect character (meal offering); (3) 53:4–6—He brought atonement that issues in peace with God (peace offering); (4) 53:7–9—He paid for the transgression of the people (sin offering); (5) 53:10–12—He died for the effects of sin (trespass offering).

KEYS TO ISAIAH

Key Word: Salvation Is of the Lord—The basic theme of this book is found in Isaiah's name: "Salvation Is of the Lord." The word *salvation* appears twenty-six times in Isaiah but only seven times in all the other prophets combined. Chapters 1—39 portray man's great need for salvation, and chapters 40—66 reveal God's great provision of salvation. Salvation is of God, not man; and He is seen as the supreme Ruler, the sovereign Lord of history, and the only Savior. Isaiah solemnly warns Judah of approaching judgment because of moral depravity, political corruption, social injustice, and especially spiritual idolatry. Because the nation does not turn away from its sinful practice, Isaiah announces the ultimate overthrow of Judah. Nevertheless, God will remain faithful to His covenant by preserving a godly remnant and promises salvation and deliverance through the coming Messiah. The Savior will come out of Judah and accomplish the dual work of redemption and restoration. The Gentiles will come to His light and universal blessing will finally take place.

Key Verses: Isaiah 9:6, 7 and 53:6—"For unto us a Child is born, unto us a Son is given; and the government will be upon His shoulder. And His name will be called Wonderful, Counselor, Mighty God, Everlasting Father, Prince of Peace. Of the increase of *His* government and peace *there will be* no end, upon the throne of David and over His kingdom, to order it and establish it with judgment and justice from that time for-

FOCUS	PROPHECIES OF CONDEMNATION				HISTORICAL PARENTHESIS	PROPHECIES OF COMFORT		
REFERENCE	1:1	13:1	24:1	28:1	36:1	40:1	49:1	58:1–66:24
DIVISION	PROPHECIES AGAINST		PROPHECIES OF		HEZEKIAH'S SALVATION, SICKNESS, AND SIN	ISRAEL'S DELIVERANCE	ISRAEL'S DELIVERER	ISRAEL'S GLORIOUS FUTURE
	JUDAH	THE NATIONS	DAY OF LORD	JUDGMENT & BLESSING				
TOPIC	PROPHETIC				HISTORIC	MESSIANIC		
	JUDGMENT				TRANSITION	HOPE		
LOCATION	ISRAEL AND JUDAH							
TIME	c. 740–680 B.C.							

ward, even forever. The zeal of the LORD of hosts will perform this" (9:6, 7).

"All we like sheep have gone astray; we have turned, every one, to his own way; and the LORD has laid on Him the iniquity of us all" (53:6).

Key Chapter: Isaiah 53—Along with Psalm 22, Isaiah 53 lists the most remarkable and specific prophecies of the atonement of the Messiah. Fulfilling each clear prophecy, the Jewish nation later proved the messiahship of Jesus.

SURVEY OF ISAIAH

Isaiah, the "Shakespeare of the prophets," has often been called the "evangelical prophet" because of his incredibly clear and detailed messianic prophecies. The "gospel according to Isaiah" has three major sections: prophecies of condemnation (1—35), historical parenthesis (36—39), and prophecies of comfort (40—66).

Prophecies of Condemnation (1—35): Isaiah's first message of condemnation is aimed at his own countrymen in Judah (1—12). Chapter 1 is a capsulized message of the entire book. Judah is riddled with moral and spiritual disease; the people are neglecting God as they bow to ritualism and selfishness. But Yahweh graciously invites them to repent and return to Him because this is their only hope of avoiding judgment. Isaiah's call to proclaim God's message is found in chapter 6, and this is followed by the book of Immanuel (7—12). These chapters repeatedly refer to the Messiah (see 7:14; 8:14; 9:2, 6, 7; 11:1, 2) and anticipate the blessing of His future reign.

The prophet moves from local to regional judgment as he proclaims a series of oracles against the surrounding nations (13—23). The eleven nations are Babylon, Assyria, Philistia, Moab, Damascus (Syria), Ethiopia, Egypt, Babylon (again), Edom, Arabia, Jerusalem (Judah), and Tyre. Isaiah's little apocalypse (24—27) depicts universal tribulation followed by the blessings of the kingdom. Chapters 28—33 pronounce six woes on Israel and Judah for specific sins. Isaiah's prophetic condemnation closes with a general picture of international devastation that will precede universal blessing (34 and 35).

Historical Parenthesis (36—39): This historical parenthesis looks back to the Assyrian invasion of Judah in 701 B.C. and anticipates the coming Babylonian invasion of Judah. Judah escapes captivity by Assyria (36 and 37; 2 Kin. 18 and 19), but they will not escape from the hands of Babylon (38 and 39; 2 Kin. 20). God answers King Hezekiah's prayers and delivers Judah from Assyrian destruction by Sennacherib. Hezekiah also turns to the Lord in his illness and is granted a fifteen-year extension of his life. But he foolishly shows all his treasures to the Babylonian messengers, and Isaiah tells him that the Babylonians will one day carry his treasure and descendants to their land.

Prophecies of Comfort (40—66): Having pronounced Judah's divine condemnation, Isaiah comforts them with God's promises of hope and restoration. The basis for this hope is the sovereignty and majesty of God (40—48). Of the 216 verses in these nine chapters, 115 speak of God's greatness and power. The Creator is contrasted with idols, the creations of men. His sovereign character is Judah's assurance of future restoration. Babylon will indeed carry them off; but Babylon will finally be judged and destroyed, and God's people will be released from captivity.

Chapters 49—57 concentrate on the coming Messiah who will be their Savior and suffering Servant. This rejected but exalted One will pay for their iniquities and usher in a kingdom of peace and righteousness throughout the earth. All who acknowledge their sins and trust in Him will be delivered (58—66). In that day Jerusalem will be rebuilt, Israel's borders will be enlarged, and the Messiah will reign in Zion. God's people will confess their sins and His enemies will be judged. Peace, prosperity, and justice will prevail, and God will make all things new.

OUTLINE OF ISAIAH

Part One: Prophecies of Condemnation (1:1—35:10)

I. Prophecies Against Judah . . . . 1:1—12:6

A. The Judgment of Judah 1:1-31
B. The Day of the Lord . . . . 2:1—4:6
C. The Parable of the Vineyard 5:1-30
D. The Commission of Isaiah 6:1-13
E. The Destruction of Israel by Assyria . . . . 7:1—10:4
1. Sign of Immanuel 7:1-25
2. Sign of Maher-Shalal-Hash-Baz 8:1-22
3. Prophecy of the Messiah's Birth 9:1-7
4. Judgment on Ephraim . . . . 9:8—10:4
F. The Destruction of Assyria by God . . . . 10:5—12:6
1. Destruction of Assyria 10:5-19
2. Remnant of Israel 10:20-34
3. Restoration of the Messiah's Kingdom 11:1-16
4. Thanksgiving in the Messiah's Kingdom 12:1-6

II. The Prophecies Against Other Nations . . . . 13:1—23:18

A. Prophecies Against Babylon . . . . . 13:1—14:23

CHAPTER 1

The Judgment of Judah

THE vision of Isaiah the son of Amoz,
which he saw concerning Judah and Jerusalem in the days of Uzziah, Jotham, Ahaz,
and Hezekiah, kings of Judah.

2 [R]Hear, O heavens, and give ear, O earth!
For the LORD has spoken: — Jer. 2:12
"I have nourished and brought up children,
And they have rebelled against Me;
3 [R]The ox knows its owner — Jer. 8:7
And the donkey its master's crib;
But Israel [R]does not know, — Jer. 9:3, 6
My people do not [T]consider." — *understand*

4 Alas, sinful nation,
A people [T]laden with iniquity, — *heavy*
A [T]brood of evildoers, — *offspring, seed*
Children who are corrupters!
They have forsaken the LORD,
They have provoked to anger
The Holy One of Israel,
They have turned away backward.

5 [R]Why should you be stricken again?
You will revolt more and more.

The whole head is sick,
And the whole heart faints. Jer. 5:3
6 From the sole of the foot even to the
head,
There is no soundness in it,
But wounds and bruises and putrefying
sores;
They have not been closed or bound up,
Or soothed with ointment.

7 [R]Your country *is* desolate,
Your cities *are* burned with fire;
Strangers devour your land in your
presence;
And *it is* desolate, as overthrown by
strangers. Deut. 28:51, 52
8 So the daughter of Zion is left [R]as a
[T]booth in a vineyard,
As a hut in a garden of cucumbers,
[R]As a besieged city. Job 27:18 • *shelter* • Jer. 4:17
9 [R]Unless the LORD of hosts
Had left to us a very small remnant,
We would have become like [R]Sodom,
We would have been made like
Gomorrah. Lam. 3:22 • Gen. 19:24

10 Hear the word of the LORD,
You rulers [R]of Sodom;
Give ear to the law of our God,
You people of Gomorrah: Deut. 32:32
11 "To what purpose *is* the multitude of
your [R]sacrifices to Me?"
Says the LORD.
"I have had enough of burnt offerings of
rams
And the fat of fed cattle.
I do not delight in the blood of bulls,
Or of lambs or goats. [1 Sam. 15:22]

12 "When you come [R]to appear before Me,
Who has required this from your hand,
To trample My courts? Ex. 23:17
13 Bring no more [R]futile[T] sacrifices;
Incense is an abomination to Me.
The New Moons, the Sabbaths, and [R]the
calling of assemblies—
I cannot endure iniquity and the sacred
meeting. Matt. 15:9 • *worthless* • Joel 1:14
14 Your [R]New Moons and your [R]appointed
feasts
My soul hates; Num. 28:11 • Lam. 2:6
They are a trouble to Me,
I am weary of bearing *them.*
15 When you [T]spread out your hands, Pray
I will hide My eyes from you;
[R]Even though you make many prayers,
I will not hear. Mic. 3:4
Your hands are full of [T]blood. *bloodshed*

16 "Wash[R] yourselves, make yourselves
clean;
Put away the evil of your doings from
before My eyes.
[R]Cease to do evil, Jer. 4:14 • Rom. 12:9
17 Learn to do good;
Seek justice,
Reprove *the oppressor;
[T]Defend the fatherless,
Plead for the widow. *Vindicate*

18 "Come now, and let us [R]reason
together,"
Says the LORD,
"Though your sins are like scarlet,
[R]They shall be as white as snow;
Though they are red like crimson,
They shall be as wool. Is. 43:26 • Ps. 51:7
19 If you are willing and obedient,
You shall eat the good of the land;
20 But if you refuse and rebel,
You shall be devoured by the sword";
For the mouth of the LORD has spoken.

21 [R]How the faithful city has become a
[T]harlot! Jer. 2:20 • Unfaithful
It was full of justice;
Righteousness lodged in it,
But now [R]murderers. Mic. 3:1–3
22 [R]Your silver has become dross,
Your wine mixed with water. Jer. 6:28
23 [R]Your princes *are* rebellious, Hos. 9:15
And [R]companions of thieves; Prov. 29:24
[R]Everyone loves bribes, Jer. 22:17
And follows after rewards.
They [R]do not defend the fatherless,
Nor does the cause of the widow come
before them. Jer. 5:28

24 Therefore the Lord says,
The LORD of hosts, the Mighty One of
Israel,
"Ah, [R]I will [T]rid Myself of My
adversaries, Deut. 28:63 • *be relieved of*
And take vengeance on My enemies.
25 I will turn My hand against you,
And [R]thoroughly[T] purge away your
dross, Mal. 3:3 • *refine with lye*
And take away all your alloy.
26 I will restore your judges [R]as at the
first, Jer. 33:7–11
And your counselors as at the
beginning.
Afterward you shall be called the city of
righteousness, the faithful city."

27 Zion shall be redeemed with justice,
And her penitents with righteousness.
28 The [R]destruction of transgressors and of
sinners *shall be* together,
And those who forsake the LORD shall
be consumed. [2 Thess. 1:8, 9]
29 For they shall be ashamed of the
[T]terebinth trees Sites of pagan worship
Which you have desired;
And you shall be embarrassed because
of the gardens

1:17 Some ancient vss. *the oppressed*

Which you have chosen.
30 For you shall be as a terebinth whose leaf fades,
And as a garden that has no water.
31 [R]The strong shall be as tinder, Ezek. 32:21
And the work of it as a spark;
Both will burn together,
And no one shall [R]quench *them*. Mark 9:43

CHAPTER 2

The Day of the Lord

THE word that Isaiah the son of Amoz saw concerning Judah and Jerusalem.

2 Now [R]it shall come to pass [R]in the latter days Mic. 4:1–3☆ • Gen. 49:1
[R]*That* the mountain of the LORD's house
Shall be established on the top of the mountains, Ps. 68:15
And shall be exalted above the hills;
And all nations shall flow to it.
3 Many people shall come and say,
[R]"Come, and let us go up to the mountain of the LORD,
To the house of the God of Jacob;
He will teach us His ways,
And we shall walk in His paths."
[R]For out of Zion shall go forth the law,
And the word of the LORD from Jerusalem. Jer. 50:5☆ • Is. 51:4, 5☆
4 He shall judge between the nations,
And shall rebuke many people;
[R]They shall beat their swords into plowshares, Is. 32:17, 18
And their spears into pruning [T]hooks;
Nation shall not lift up sword against nation, *knives*
Neither shall they learn war anymore.

5 O house of Jacob, come and let us [R]walk
In the light of the LORD. Eph. 5:8

6 For You have forsaken Your people, the house of Jacob,
Because they are filled [R]with eastern ways; Num. 23:7
They *are* [R]soothsayers like the Philistines, Deut. 18:14
[R]And they are pleased with the children of foreigners. Ps. 106:35
7 [R]Their land is also full of silver and gold,
And *there is no* end to their treasures;
Their land is also full of horses, Deut. 17:16
And *there is no* end to their chariots.
8 [R]Their land is also full of idols;
They worship the work of their own hands,
That which their own fingers have made. Jer. 2:28
9 People bow down,
And each man humbles himself;
Therefore do not forgive them.

10 [R]Enter into the rock, and hide in the dust, Rev. 6:15, 16
From the terror of the LORD
And the glory of His majesty.
11 The [T]lofty looks of man shall be [R]humbled,
The haughtiness of men shall be bowed down,
And the LORD alone shall be exalted [R]in that day. *proud* • Prov. 16:5 • Hos. 2:16

12 For the day of the LORD of hosts
Shall come upon everything proud and lofty,
Upon everything lifted up—
And it shall be brought low—
13 Upon all [R]the cedars of Lebanon *that are* high and lifted up, Zech. 11:1, 2
And upon all the oaks of Bashan;
14 [R]Upon all the high mountains, Is. 30:25
And upon all the hills *that are* lifted up;
15 Upon every high tower,
And upon every fortified wall;
16 [R]Upon all the ships of Tarshish, 1 Kin. 10:22
And upon all the beautiful sloops.
17 The [T]loftiness of man shall be bowed down,
And the haughtiness of men shall be brought low;
The LORD alone will be exalted in that day, *pride*
18 But the idols He shall utterly abolish.

19 They shall go into the [R]holes of the rocks, Hos. 10:8
And into the caves of the [T]earth,
[R]From the terror of the LORD
And the glory of His majesty,
When He arises [R]to shake the earth mightily. Lit. *dust* • [2 Thess. 1:9] • Hag. 2:6, 7

20 In that day a man will cast away his idols of silver
And his idols of gold,
Which they made, *each* for himself to worship,
To the moles and bats,
21 To go into the clefts of the rocks,
And into the crags of the rugged rocks,
From the terror of the LORD
And the glory of His majesty,
When He arises to shake the earth mightily.

22 Sever yourselves from such a man,
Whose [R]breath *is* in his nostrils;
For of what account is he? Job 27:3

CHAPTER 3

FOR behold, the Lord, the LORD of hosts,
[R]Takes away from Jerusalem and from
Judah Jer. 37:21
[T]The stock and the store, Every support
The whole supply of bread and the
whole supply of water;
2 [R]The mighty man and the man of war,
The judge and the prophet, 2 Kin. 24:14
And the diviner and the elder;
3 The captain of fifty and the [T]honorable
man, Eminent looking men
The counselor and the skillful artisan,
And the expert enchanter.

4 "I will give [T]children *to be* their princes,
And babes shall rule over them. *boys*
5 The people will be oppressed,
Every one by another and every one by
his neighbor;
The child will be insolent toward the
[T]elder, *aged*
And the base toward the honorable."

6 When a man takes hold of his brother
In the house of his father, *saying,*
"You have clothing;
You be our ruler,
And *let* these ruins *be* under your
hand,"
7 In that day he will protest, saying,
"I cannot cure *your* ills,
For in my house *is* neither food nor
clothing;
Do not make me a ruler of the people."

8 For [R]Jerusalem stumbled, Mic. 3:12
And Judah is fallen,
Because their tongue and their doings
Are against the LORD,
To provoke the eyes of His glory.
9 The look on their countenance
witnesses against them,
And they declare their sin as [R]Sodom;
They do not hide *it.*
Woe to their soul!
For they have brought evil upon
themselves. Gen. 13:13

10 "Say to the righteous [R]that *it shall be*
well *with them,*
[R]For they shall eat the fruit of their
doings. [Eccl. 8:12] • Ps. 128:2
11 Woe to the wicked! [R]*It shall be* ill *with*
him,
For the reward of his hands shall be
[T]given him. [Ps. 11:6] • *done to him*
12 *As for My* people, children *are* their
oppressors,
And women rule over them.
O My people! [R]Those who lead you
[T]cause *you* to err, Is. 9:16 • *lead you astray*
And destroy the way of your paths."

13 The LORD stands up to [T]plead, *contend*
And stands to judge the people.
14 The LORD will enter into judgment
With the elders of His people
And His princes:
"For you have [T]eaten up [R]the vineyard;
The plunder of the poor *is* in your
houses. *burned* • Matt. 21:33
15 What do you mean by [R]crushing My
people
And grinding the faces of the poor?"
Says the Lord GOD of hosts. Mic. 3:2, 3

16 Moreover the LORD says:

"Because the daughters of Zion are
haughty,
And walk with outstretched necks
And [T]wanton eyes, *seductive, ogling*
Walking and mincing *as* they go,
Making a jingling with their feet,
17 Therefore the Lord will strike with [R]a
scab
The crown of the head of the daughters
of Zion,
And the LORD will [R]uncover their secret
parts." Deut. 28:27 • Jer. 13:22

18 In that day the Lord will take away the
finery:
The jingling anklets, the [T]scarves, and
the [R]crescents; *headbands* • Judg. 8:21, 26
19 The pendants, the bracelets, and the
veils;
20 The headdresses, the leg ornaments,
and the headbands;
The perfume boxes, the charms,
21 and the rings;
The nose jewels,
22 the festal apparel, and the mantles;
The outer garments, the purses,
23 and the mirrors;
The fine linen, the turbans, and the
robes.

24 And so it shall be:

Instead of a sweet smell there will be a
stench;
Instead of a sash, a rope;
Instead of well-set hair, [R]baldness;
Instead of a rich robe, a girding of
sackcloth; Is. 22:12
And branding instead of beauty.
25 Your men shall fall by the sword,
And your [T]mighty in the war. Lit. *strength*

26 [R]Her gates shall lament and mourn,
And she *being* desolate [R]shall sit on the
ground. Jer. 14:2 • Lam. 2:10

CHAPTER 4

AND [R]in that day seven women shall take
hold of one man, saying, Is. 2:11, 17

"We will [R]eat our own food and wear our
own apparel; 2 Thess. 3:12
Only let us be called by your name,
To take away [R]our reproach." Luke 1:25

2 In that day [R]the Branch of the LORD
shall be beautiful and glorious;
And the fruit of the earth *shall be*
excellent and appealing [Jer. 23:5]
For those of Israel who have escaped.

3 And it shall come to pass that *he who is*
left in Zion and *he who* remains in Jerusalem
[R]will be called holy—everyone who is recorded among the living in Jerusalem. Is. 60:21
4 When [R]the Lord has washed away the
filth of the daughters of Zion, and purged
the [T]blood of Jerusalem from her midst, by
the spirit of judgment and by the spirit of
burning, Mal. 3:2, 3 • *bloodshed*
5 then the LORD will create above every
dwelling place of Mount Zion, and above her
assemblies, a cloud and smoke by day and the
shining of a flaming fire by night. For over all
the glory there *will be* a covering.
6 And there will be a tabernacle for shade
in the daytime from the heat, for a place of
refuge, and for a shelter from storm and rain.

CHAPTER 5

The Parable of the Vineyard

NOW let me sing to my Well-beloved
A song of my Beloved [R]regarding His
vineyard: Matt. 21:33

My Well-beloved has a vineyard
On a very fruitful hill.
2 He dug it up and cleared out its stones,
And planted it with the choicest vine.
He built a tower in its midst,
And also made a winepress in it;
[R]So He expected *it* to bring forth *good*
grapes, Deut. 32:6
But it brought forth wild grapes.

3 "And now, O inhabitants of Jerusalem
and men of Judah,
[R]Judge, please, between Me and My
vineyard. [Rom. 3:4]
4 What more could have been done to My
vineyard
That I have not done in [R]it?
Why then, when I expected *it* to bring
forth *good* grapes, 2 Chr. 36:15, 16
Did it bring forth wild grapes?
5 And now, please let Me tell you what I
will do to My vineyard:
[R]I will take away its hedge, and it shall
be burned;
And break down its wall, and it shall be
trampled down. Ps. 80:12; 89:40, 41

6 I will lay it [R]waste; 2 Chr. 36:19–21
It shall not be pruned or [T]dug, *hoed*
But there shall come up briers and
[R]thorns. Is. 7:19–25
I will also command the clouds
That they rain no rain on it."

7 For the vineyard of the LORD of hosts *is*
the house of Israel,
And the men of Judah are His pleasant
plant.
He looked for justice, but behold,
oppression;
For righteousness, but behold, weeping.

8 Woe to those who [T]join [R]house to
house, Accumulate houses • Mic. 2:2
Who add field to field,
Till *there is* no place
Where they may dwell alone in the
midst of the land!
9 [R]In my hearing the LORD of hosts *said,*
"Truly, many houses shall be desolate,
Great and beautiful ones, without
inhabitant. Is. 22:14
10 For [T]ten acres of vineyard shall yield
one [R]bath,[T] 6.81 acres • Ezek. 45:11 • 6 gal.
And a [T]homer of seed shall yield one
[T]ephah." 6.524 bu. • .65 bu.

11 [R]Woe to those who rise early in the
morning,
That they may [T]follow intoxicating
drink;
Who continue until night, *till* wine
inflames them! Prov. 23:29, 30 • *pursue*
12 [R]The harp and the strings,
The tambourine and flute,
And wine are in their feasts;
But [R]they do not regard the work of the
LORD,
Nor consider the operation of His
hands. Amos 6:5 • Job 34:27

13 [R]Therefore my people have gone into
captivity,
Because *they have* no [R]knowledge;
Their honorable men *are* famished,
And their multitude dried up with
thirst. 2 Kin. 24:14–16 • Hos. 4:6
14 Therefore Sheol has enlarged itself
And opened its mouth beyond measure;
Their glory and their multitude and
their pomp,
And he who is jubilant, shall descend
into it.
15 People shall be brought down,
[R]Each man shall be humbled,
And the eyes of the lofty shall be
humbled. Is. 2:9, 11
16 But the LORD of hosts shall be [R]exalted
in judgment,

MESSENGERS OF GOD

Most people would be amazed to learn that some church fathers believed that the last book of the Old Testament was written by an angel. This idea got started partly because Malachi names no father or grandfather, as most prophets do. But no doubt it was mostly due to his name. *Malachi* means "my messenger," the Hebrew word for "messenger" being *mal'āk*. But this is also the standard word for an angel, a messenger of God. The double meaning also exists in the Greek word *angelos*, whence English *angel*.

Angel, Messenger (*mal'āk*)

Mal'āk is used of both humans and angels, and suggests an envoy with a commission, not only carrying a message, though this is a primary function (e.g., Zech. 1:9; 5:5).

What traditional Christian art has done to angels is most unfortunate! They are presented as pale, anemic young men, usually with blond curls, snowy robes, and feathery wings. As someone has said, if you were to say "Boo!" to a Victorian angel, he (she?/it?) would run away in fear.

The tradition of "guardian angels" is biblical, since protection is one of their great ministries. Angels protected Israel in the Wilderness (Ex. 23:20). The Devil quoted Psalm 91:11 to our Lord in the temptation: "For He shall give His angels charge over you, to keep you in all your ways." Satan's angelology was accurate, but his aim was evil. Angels wrought deliverance, like Lot's rescue from Sodom (Gen. 19:12–17), and executed judgment (2 Sam. 24:17). Angels also are active in praising the Lord (Ps. 148:2).

The Angel of the LORD (*mal'āk YHWH*)

Also sometimes called "the Angel of God" (Judg. 13:6, 9), "the Angel of the LORD" fulfilled the same functions as other angels, but is presented on a higher plane than ordinary angels. For example, He spoke for God *in the first* person, as if He was divine (Gen. 16:10; Ex. 3:2, 6; Judg. 2:1). He was also recognized as God and received worship (Judg. 13:21, 22). Because He seemed to be God and yet, in a sense, distinct, as He interceded with God for men (for Jerusalem in Zech. 1:12 and 3:1–5), evangelical scholars have widely identified the Angel of the Lord as the preincarnate Christ.

Cherub (*kerûb*)

Actually, angels are powerful spirit-beings. The concept of a "cherub" as a rosy-faced little tyke on a pink cloud is even worse than the popular picture of angels in general. The origin of the word *cherub* is unknown, but the meaning of a cognate word in Akkadian, a language related to Hebrew, fits what we know about cherubim from the Bible: they praise, bless, and adore.

We first read of cherubim (plural) in Eden, as they guarded the way to the tree of life after the Fall (Gen. 3:24). Golden images of these mighty angelic beings were placed over the mercy seat on top of the ark of the covenant. Representations of cherubim were widely used in the decoration of the tabernacle and temple.

Ezekiel 10's description of cherubim with their several wings, four faces, and "throne" with wheels, is awesome, as befits worshipful guardians of God's glory.

Seraphim

Seraphim are mentioned only in Isaiah 6, when Isaiah received his commission from God. The word *seraphim* comes from the verb *sāraph* ("to burn") and appears in the context of holiness. Isaiah sensed his own lack of holiness in the light of the seraphim's ascription of praise to God: "Holy, holy, holy!" Seraphim are seen as burning with holiness. Some scholars believe cherubim and seraphim are not really that different. In fact, the living creatures in Revelation seem to have some characteristics of both.

In conclusion, it should be underscored that the study of angels is not theoretical; it should be practical and encouraging. Hebrews 1:14 gives believers a wonderful assurance: "Are they not all ministering spirits sent forth to minister for those who will inherit salvation?"

And God who is holy shall be hallowed
in righteousness. Is. 2:11
17 Then the lambs shall feed in their
pasture,
And in the waste places of the [T]fat ones
strangers shall eat. *fatlings,* rich ones

18 Woe to those who [T]draw iniquity with
cords of [T]vanity, *drag* • *emptiness* or *falsehood*
And sin as if with a cart rope;
19 [R]That say, "Let Him make speed *and*
hasten His work,
That we may see *it;*
And let the counsel of the Holy One of
Israel draw near and come,
That we may know *it.*" Jer. 17:15

20 Woe to those who call evil good, and
good evil;
Who put darkness for light, and light
for darkness;
Who put bitter for sweet, and sweet for
bitter!

21 Woe to *those who are* [R]wise in their
own eyes, Rom. 1:22; 12:16
And prudent in their own sight!

22 Woe to men mighty at drinking wine,
Woe to men valiant for mixing
intoxicating drink,
23 Who [R]justify the wicked for a bribe,
And take away justice from the
righteous man! Prov. 17:15

24 Therefore, [R]as the [T]fire devours the
stubble, Ex. 15:7 • Lit. *tongue of fire*
And the flame consumes the chaff,
So [R]their root will be as rottenness,
And their blossom will ascend like dust;
Because they have rejected the law of
the LORD of hosts, Job 18:16
And despised the word of the Holy One
of Israel.
25 [R]Therefore the anger of the LORD is
aroused against His people;
He has stretched out His hand against
them 2 Kin. 22:13, 17
And stricken them,
And [R]the hills trembled. Jer. 4:24
Their carcasses *were* as refuse in the
midst of the streets.

[R]For all this His anger is not turned
away, Is. 9:12, 17
But His hand *is* stretched out still.

26 [R]He will lift up a banner to the nations
from afar, Is. 11:10, 12
And will [R]whistle to them from [R]the end
of the earth; Is. 7:18 • Mal. 1:11
Surely [R]they shall come with speed,
swiftly. Joel 2:7
27 No one will be weary or stumble among
them,
No one will slumber or sleep;
Nor [R]will the belt on their loins be
loosed,
Nor the strap of their sandals be
broken; Dan. 5:6
28 [R]Whose arrows *are* sharp,
And all their bows bent;
Their horses' hooves will [T]seem like
flint, Jer. 5:16 • Lit. *be regarded as*
And their wheels like a whirlwind.
29 Their roaring *will be* like a lion,
They will roar like young lions;
Yes, they will roar
And lay hold of the prey;
They will carry *it* away safely,
And no one will deliver.
30 In that day they will roar against them
Like the roaring of the sea.
And if *one* [R]looks to the land, Is. 8:22
Behold, darkness *and* [T]sorrow; *distress*
And the light is darkened by the clouds.

CHAPTER 6

The Commission of Isaiah

IN the year that [R]King Uzziah died, I [R]saw
the Lord sitting on a throne, high and
lifted up, and the train of His *robe* filled the
temple. 2 Kin. 15:7 • John 12:41
2 Above it stood seraphim; each one had
six wings: with two he covered his face, with
two he covered his feet, and with two he flew.

3 And one cried to another and said:

"Holy, holy, holy *is* the LORD of hosts;
The whole earth *is* full of His glory!"

6:3 Holiness of God—Our greatest failing is in not realizing who God is and what His character is like. God is NOT human. He is God, and as such there is an infinite gap between the highest in us and the lowest in God. The gap between God and us is unbridgeable from our side. If the gap is to be bridged, it must be from God's side—for God is holy. To be holy means "to be set apart." God is set apart from the power, practice, and presence of sin, and is set apart to absolute righteousness and goodness. There is no sin in God and God can have nothing to do with sin. If we are to approach God, we must do so on God's terms. Somehow, we must be made holy—just as holy as God is. Any holiness which falls short of God's holiness will not be able to stand in the presence of God. Therefore, because of the holiness of God, we must have a new life in which our sins have been forgiven and done away with so that we actually can be as separated from sin as God is. This is the good news of the gospel—that Christ died for our sins, having taken them upon Himself, and has set us apart from them. This is

(continued on next page)

4 And the posts of the door were shaken
by the voice of him who cried out, and the
house was filled with smoke.

5 Then I said:

"Woe *is* me, for I am [T]undone!
Because I *am* a man of [R]unclean lips,
And I dwell in the midst of a people of
unclean lips; *destroyed, cut off* • Ex. 6:12, 30
For my eyes have seen the King,
The LORD of hosts."

6 Then one of the seraphim flew to me,
having in his hand a live coal *which* he had
taken with the tongs from [R]the altar. Rev. 8:3
7 And he [R]touched my mouth *with it*, and
said:

"Behold, this has touched your lips;
Your iniquity is taken away,
And your sin [T]purged." Jer. 1:9 • *atoned for*

8 Also I heard the voice of the Lord, saying:

"Whom shall I send,
And who will go for [R]Us?" Gen. 1:26

Then I said, "Here *am* I! Send me."

9 And He said, "Go, and tell this people:

[R]'Keep on hearing, but do not
understand; Matt. 13:14, 15☆
Keep on seeing, but do not perceive.'

10 "Make [R]the heart of this people dull,
And their ears heavy, Mark 6:1-6☆
And shut their eyes;
[R]Lest they see with their eyes, Jer. 5:21
And hear with their ears,
And understand with their heart,
And return and be healed."

11 Then I said, "Lord, how long?" And He
answered:

[R]"Until the cities are laid waste and
without inhabitant,
The houses are without a man,
The land is utterly desolate, Mic. 3:12
12 [R]The LORD has removed men far away,
And the forsaken places *are* many in
the midst of the land. 2 Kin. 25:21
13 But yet a tenth *will be* in it,
And will return and be for consuming,
As a terebinth tree or as an oak,
Whose stump *remains* when it is cut
down.
So the holy seed *shall be* its stump."

CHAPTER 7

Sign of Immanuel—2 Kin. 16:5; 2 Chr. 28:5-15

NOW it came to pass in the days of Ahaz
the son of Jotham, the son of Uzziah,
king of Judah, *that* Rezin king of Syria and
Pekah the son of Remaliah, king of Israel,
went up to Jerusalem to *make* war against it,
but could not prevail against it.
2 And it was told to the house of David,
saying, "Syria's forces are [T]deployed in
Ephraim." So his heart and the heart of his
people were moved as the trees of the woods
are moved with the wind. Lit. *settled upon*
3 Then the LORD said to Isaiah, "Go out
now to meet Ahaz, you and [T]Shear-Jashub
your son, at the end of the aqueduct from the

(continued from previous page)
our position before God which will never change. Because of what God has done, we can enter boldly into the presence of God.

Now turn to Page 8—Gen. 3:6, 7: Adam's Sin.

6:8 Knowing the Will of God Through Submission to the Spirit—The moment a repenting sinner receives Christ by faith into his heart the Holy Spirit immediately does five things for him:

a. He regenerates the believer, that is, He gives him a new nature (Page 1239—John 3:5, 6; Page 1442—Titus 3:5).
b. He baptizes the believer into the body of Christ (Page 1356—1 Cor. 12:13).
c. He indwells the believer (Page 1332—Rom. 8:9; Page 1351—1 Cor. 6:19).
d. He seals the believer (Page 1387—Eph. 1:13; 4:30).
e. He fills the believer (Page 1273—Acts 2:4; 4:8; 7:55; 13:52).

All five of these ministries often occur at conversion. The fifth ministry, however, should be asked for as needed. See Ephesians 5:18; Galatians 5:16. Actually the word *control* is a better term than *fill* in describing this fifth ministry. It does not mean that we get more of the Spirit, but rather that He gets more of us. The fifth ministry is lost when the believer either quenches (Page 1416—1 Thess. 5:19) or grieves (Page 1391—Eph. 4:30) the Holy Spirit. The fifth ministry can be regained by following the command of 1 John 1:9, "If we confess our sins, He is faithful and just to forgive us *our* sins and to cleanse us from all unrighteousness."

How can a Christian be certain that he is indeed controlled by the Holy Spirit on a daily basis? First, he must consecrate his body as a living sacrifice to the Holy Spirit (Page 1336—Rom. 12:1, 2). Second, he must depend upon the Holy Spirit to convict him of sin (Page 705—Ps. 139:23, 24; 19:12-14). Finally, he must look to the Holy Spirit for divine power in serving Christ (Page 1272—Acts 1:8; Page 1383—Gal. 5:16, 17; Page 1388—Eph. 3:16).

Now turn to Page 736—Prov. 24:6: Knowing the Will of God Through Circumstances and Counsel.

upper pool, on the highway to the Fuller's
Field, *Lit. A Remnant Shall Return*
4 "and say to him: [T]'Take heed, and [T]be
[R]quiet; do not fear or be fainthearted for
these two stubs of smoking firebrands, for the
fierce anger of Rezin and Syria, and the son
of Remaliah. *Be careful* • *be calm* • Is. 30:15
5 'Because Syria, Ephraim, and the son of
Remaliah [T]have taken evil counsel against
you, saying, Plotted
6 "Let us go up against Judah and [T]trouble
it, and let us make a gap in its wall for
ourselves, and set a king over them, the son
of Tabeel"— *cause a sickening dread*
7 'thus says the Lord GOD:

[R]"'It shall not stand,
Nor shall it come to pass. Is. 8:10
8 [R]For the head of Syria *is* Damascus,
And the head of Damascus *is* Rezin.
Within sixty-five years Ephraim will be
[T]broken, 2 Sam. 8:6 • Lit. *shattered*
So that it will not *be* a people.
9 The head of Ephraim *is* Samaria,
And the head of Samaria *is* Remaliah's
son.
[R]If you will not believe, 2 Chr. 20:20
Surely you shall not be established."' "

10 Moreover the LORD spoke again to Ahaz,
saying,
11 "Ask a sign for yourself from the LORD
your God; [T]ask it either in the depth or in the
height above." Lit. *make the request deep or high above*
12 But Ahaz said, "I will not ask, nor will I
test the LORD!"
13 Then he said, "Hear now, O house of
David! *Is it* a small thing for you to weary
men, but will you weary my God also?
14 "Therefore the Lord Himself will give
you a sign: [R]Behold, the virgin shall conceive
and bear a [R]Son, and shall call His name
Immanuel. Matt. 1:23; Luke 1:31, 34, 35 ☆ • [Is. 9:6]
15 "Curds and honey He shall eat, that He
may know to refuse the evil and choose the
good.
16 [R]"For before the Child shall know to
refuse the evil and choose the good, the land
that you dread will be forsaken by [R]both her
kings. Is. 8:4 • 2 Kin. 15:30
17 "The LORD will bring the king of Assyria
upon you and your people and your father's
house—days that have not come since the
day that Ephraim departed from Judah."

18 And it shall come to pass in that day
That the LORD [R]will whistle for the fly
That *is* in the farthest part of the rivers
of Egypt,
And for the bee that *is* in the land of
Assyria. Is. 5:26
19 They will come, and all of them will rest
In the desolate valleys and in [R]the clefts
of the rocks, Jer. 16:16
And on all thorns and in all pastures.
20 In the same day the Lord will shave
with a [R]hired razor, Is. 10:5, 15
With those from beyond [T]the River,
with the king of Assyria, The Euphrates
The head and the hair of the legs,
And will also remove the beard.

21 It shall be in that day
That a man will keep alive a young cow
and two sheep;
22 So it shall be, from the abundance of
milk they give,
That he will eat curds;
For curds and honey everyone will eat
who is left in the land.

23 It shall happen in that day,
That wherever there could be a
thousand vines
Worth a thousand *shekels* of silver,
[R]It will be for briers and thorns. Is. 5:6
24 With arrows and bows men will come
there,
Because all the land will become briers
and thorns.

25 And to any hill which could be dug
with the hoe,
You will not go there for fear of briers
and thorns;
But it will become a range for oxen
And a place for sheep to roam.

CHAPTER 8

Sign of Maher-Shalal-Hash-Baz

MOREOVER the LORD said to me, "Take
a large scroll, and [R]write on it with a
man's pen concerning [T]Maher-Shalal-Hash-
Baz. Hab. 2:2 • Lit. *Speed the Spoil, Hasten the Booty*
2 "And I will take for Myself faithful witnesses to record, [R]Uriah the priest and Zechariah the son of Jeberechiah." 2 Kin. 16:10
3 Then I went to the prophetess, and she
conceived and bore a son. Then the LORD said
to me, "Call his name Maher-Shalal-Hash-
Baz;
4 [R]"for before the child [T]shall have knowledge to cry 'My father' and 'My mother,' [R]the
riches of Damascus and the [T]spoil of Samaria
will be taken away before the king of As-
syria." 2 Kin. 17:6 • *knows how* • 2 Kin. 15:29 • *plunder*
5 The LORD also spoke to me again, saying:

6 "Inasmuch as these people refused
The waters of [R]Shiloah that flow softly,
And rejoice [R]in Rezin and in Remaliah's
son; John 9:7 • Is. 7:1, 2
7 Now therefore, behold, the Lord brings
up over them

The waters of [T]the River, strong and
mighty— The Euphrates
The king of Assyria and all his glory;
He will [T]go up over all his channels
And go over all his banks. Overflow
8 He will pass through Judah,
He will overflow and pass over,
[R]He will reach up to the neck; Is. 30:28
And the stretching out of his wings
Will [T]fill the breadth of Your land, O
[R]Immanuel. Lit. *be fullness of* • Is. 7:14

9 "Be[R] shattered, O you peoples, and be
broken in pieces!
Give ear, all you from far countries.
Gird yourselves, but be broken in
pieces;
Gird yourselves, but be broken in
pieces. Joel 3:9
10 [R]Take counsel together, but it will come
to nothing; Is. 7:7
Speak the word, but it will not stand,
For [T]God *is* with us." Heb. *Immanuel*

11 For the LORD spoke thus to me with a
strong hand, and instructed me that I should
not walk in the way of this people, saying:

12 "Do not say, 'A conspiracy,'
Concerning all that this people call a
conspiracy,
Nor be afraid of their [T]threats, nor be
[T]troubled. Lit. *fear* or *terror* • Lit. *in dread*
13 The LORD of hosts, Him you shall
hallow;
Let Him *be* your fear,
And *let* Him *be* your dread.
14 He will be as a [T]sanctuary, *holy abode*
But a [R]stone of stumbling and a rock of
[T]offense Luke 2:34; 20:17 ☆ • *stumbling over*
To both the houses of Israel,
As a trap and a snare to the inhabitants
of Jerusalem.
15 And many among them shall [R]stumble;
They shall fall and be broken,
Be snared and [T]taken." Matt. 21:44 • *captured*

16 Bind up the testimony,
Seal the law among my disciples.
17 And I will wait on the LORD,
Who [R]hides His face from the house of
Jacob;
And I [R]will hope in Him. Is. 54:8 • Hab. 2:3
18 [R]Here am I and the children whom the
LORD has given me! Heb. 2:13
We [R]*are* for signs and wonders in Israel
From the LORD of hosts, Ps. 71:7
Who dwells in Mount Zion.

19 And when they say to you, [R]"Seek those
who are mediums and wizards, [R]who whisper
and mutter," should not a people seek their
God? *Should they* [R]*seek* the dead on behalf of
the living? 1 Sam. 28:8 • Is. 29:4 • Ps. 106:28
20 To the law and to the testimony! If they
do not speak according to this word, *it is*
because [R]*there is* no light in them. Mic. 3:6
21 And they will pass through it hard
pressed and hungry; and it shall happen,
when they are hungry, that they will be
enraged and curse [T]their king and their God,
and look upward. Or *by their king and by their God*
22 Then they will look to the earth, and see
trouble and darkness, gloom of anguish; and
they will be driven into darkness.

CHAPTER 9

Prophecy of the Messiah's Birth

NEVERTHELESS [R]the gloom *will* not *be*
upon her who *is* distressed, Is. 8:22
As when at first He lightly esteemed
[R]The land of Zebulun and the land of
Naphtali, Matt. 4:13–16 ☆
And afterward more heavily oppressed
her,
By the way of the sea, beyond the
Jordan,
In Galilee of the Gentiles.
2 The [R]people who walked in darkness
Have seen a great light; Luke 1:79 ☆
Those who dwelt in the land of the
shadow of death,
Upon them a light has shined.

3 You have multiplied the nation
And [T]increased its joy;
They rejoice before You
According to the joy of harvest,
As *men* rejoice [R]when they divide the
spoil. Kt. *not increased* • Judg. 5:30
4 For You have broken the yoke of his
burden
And the staff of his shoulder,
The rod of his oppressor,
As in the day of [R]Midian. Judg. 7:22
5 For every warrior's [T]sandal from the
noisy battle,
And garments rolled in blood,
[R]Will be used for burning *and* fuel [T]of
fire. *boot* • Is. 66:15 • *for the fire*

6 [R]For unto us a Child is born,
Unto us a Son is given; [Is. 7:14; Luke 2:11] ☆
And [R]the government will be upon His
shoulder. [Matt. 28:18]

9:6 The Person of the Son of God—It is crucial to remember that the existence of the Son of God did not commence with His birth in Bethlehem. He is spoken of as the Son before He became a man (Is. 9:6; Page 1381—Gal. 4:4). Micah prophesies of His birth, but yet states that His "goings forth *have been* from of old, from everlasting" (Page 1039—Mic. 5:2). John says that He existed "in the beginning" before anything was created (Page 1236—John 1:1–3).

And His name will be called
Wonderful, Counselor, Mighty God,
Everlasting Father, Prince of Peace.

7 Of the increase of *His* government and
peace
[R]*There will be* no end,
Upon the throne of David and over His
kingdom, Dan. 2:44; Luke 1:32, 33 ☆
To order it and establish it with
judgment and justice
From that time forward, even forever.
The [R]zeal of the LORD of hosts will
perform this. Is. 37:32

Judgment on Ephraim

8 The LORD sent a word against [R]Jacob,
And it has fallen on Israel. Gen. 32:28
9 All the people will know—
Ephraim and the inhabitant of
Samaria—
Who say in pride and arrogance of
heart:
10 "The bricks have fallen down,
But we will rebuild with hewn stones;
The sycamores are cut down,
But we will replace *them* with cedars."
11 Therefore the LORD shall set up
The adversaries of Rezin against him,
And spur his enemies on,
12 The Syrians before and the Philistines
behind;
And they shall devour Israel with an
open mouth.

For all this His anger is not turned
away,
But His hand *is* stretched out still.

13 For the people do not turn to Him who
strikes them,
Nor do they seek the LORD of hosts.
14 Therefore the LORD will cut off head
and tail from Israel,
Palm branch and bulrush in one day.
15 The elder and honorable, he *is* the head;
The prophet who teaches lies, he *is* the
tail.
16 For [R]the leaders of this people cause
them to err,
And *those who are* led by them are
destroyed. Is. 3:12
17 Therefore the LORD [R]will have no joy in
their young men, Ps. 147:10
Nor have mercy on their fatherless and
widows;
For everyone *is* a hypocrite and an
evildoer,
And every mouth speaks folly.

[R]For all this His anger is not turned
away, Is. 5:25
But His hand *is* stretched out still.

18 For wickedness burns as the fire;
It shall devour the briers and thorns,
And kindle in the thickets of the forest;
They shall mount up *like* rising smoke.
19 Through the wrath of the LORD of hosts
[R]The land is burned up, Is. 8:22
And the people shall be as fuel for the
fire;
[R]No man shall spare his brother. Mic. 7:2, 6
20 And he shall [T]snatch on the right hand
And be hungry;
He shall devour on the left hand
[R]And not be satisfied;

Even before He was born of Mary, He appeared to men in the Old Testament as the "Angel of the LORD." It is clear that this Angel is no ordinary angel because He is identified as God (Page 70—Ex. 3:1, 4); He pardons sin (Page 94—Ex. 23:20, 21); and He is worshiped (Page 256—Josh. 5:13–15). While these passages do not say that this member of the Godhead was the preincarnate Christ, we may conclude that they are the same person since their work is the same.

While Christ was preexistent and appeared occasionally to men in the Old Testament, He took on a body permanently when He was conceived in Mary's womb. This incomparable event of God's becoming man in Jesus Christ is called the Incarnation. This miracle was prophesied hundreds of years previously (Page 779—Is. 7:14) and was fulfilled historically in Mary in whose womb the Holy Spirit's power conceived a child (Page 1116—Matt. 1:23; Page 1192—Luke 1:35). Thus Christ, the sinless God-man, was qualified to become our Redeemer (Page 1369—2 Cor. 5:21).

Having been born of a woman, Jesus Christ was fully man apart from sin (Page 1236—John 1:14). As a man He experienced the normal physical, mental, social, and spiritual growth as others did (Page 1194—Luke 2:52). He suffered pain, hunger, thirst, fatigue, temptation, pleasure, and rest. Because of His complete humanity He can be sympathetic and compassionate toward us (Page 1453—Heb. 4:15).

While Christ was fully man He was also fully God, as these facts indicate: He is called God (Page 1236—John 1:1; Page 1450—Heb. 1:8); He did works that only God could do, such as forgive sins (Page 1162—Mark 2:7) and create (Page 1406—Col. 1:16); He had attributes that only God could have, such as truth (Page 1258—John 14:6) and omniscience, all-knowing (Page 1239—John 2:24, 25); and He claimed equality with God (Page 1252—John 10:30).

The question may then be raised as to whether Christ lost anything of deity when He became a man (Page 1400—Phil. 2:6–8). While there is an inscrutable mystery involved in this unparalleled act of condescension, one can be certain that He lost none of God's attributes, because He was still God (Page 1265—John 20:28). He was fully God and fully man united in one person forever. Even now, at the right hand of God, He is the God-man (Page 1426—1 Tim. 2:5). The great condescension of the Son of God's becoming a man serves eternally as a perfect model of humility and self-giving love (Page 1400—Phil. 2:5).

Now turn to Page 1251—John 10:10: The Earthly Life of the Son of God.

[R]Every man shall eat the flesh of his own
arm. *slice off* or *tear* • Lev. 26:26 • Jer. 19:9
21 Manasseh *shall devour* Ephraim, and
Ephraim Manasseh,
And they together *shall be* [R]against
Judah. 2 Chr. 28:6, 8

[R]For all this His anger is not turned
away, Is. 9:12, 17
But His hand *is* stretched out still.

CHAPTER 10

"WOE to those who [R]decree Ps. 58:2
unrighteous decrees,
Who write misfortune,
Which they have prescribed
2 To rob the needy of justice,
And to take what is right from the poor
of My people,
That widows may be their prey,
And *that* they may rob the fatherless.
3 [R]What will you do in [R]the day of
punishment, Job 31:14 • Hos. 9:7
And in the desolation *which* will come
from [R]afar? Is. 5:26
To whom will you flee for help?
And where will you leave your glory?
4 Without Me they shall bow down
among the [R]prisoners, Is. 24:22
And they shall fall among the slain."

[R]For all this His anger is not turned
away, Is. 5:25
But His hand *is* stretched out still.

Destruction of Assyria

5 "Woe to Assyria, [R]the rod of My anger
And the staff in whose hand is My
indignation. Jer. 51:20
6 I will send him against [R]an ungodly
nation, Is. 9:17
And against the people of My wrath
I will [R]give him charge, Jer. 34:22
To seize the spoil, to take the prey,
And to tread them down like the mire
of the streets.
7 [R]Yet he does not mean so, Gen. 50:20
Nor does his heart think so;
But *it is* in his heart to destroy,
And cut off not a few nations.
8 [R]For he says, 2 Kin. 19:10
'*Are* not my princes altogether kings?
9 *Is* not [R]Calno like Carchemish?
Is not Hamath like Arpad? Amos 6:2
Is not Samaria [R]like Damascus? 2 Kin. 16:9
10 As my hand has found the kingdoms of
the idols,
Whose carved images excelled those of
Jerusalem and Samaria,
11 As I have done to Samaria and her
idols,
Shall I not do also to Jerusalem and her
idols?' "

12 Therefore it shall come to pass, when the
LORD has [T]performed all His work [R]on Mount
Zion and on Jerusalem, *that He will say,* [R]"I
will punish the fruit of the arrogant heart of
the king of Assyria, and the glory of his
haughty looks." *completed* • 2 Kin. 19:31 • Jer. 50:18
13 [R]For he says: Is. 37:24–27

"By the strength of my hand I have done
it,
And by my wisdom, for I am prudent;
Also I have removed the boundaries of
the people,
And have robbed their treasuries;
So I have put down the inhabitants like
a [T]valiant *man.* *mighty*
14 [R]My hand has found like a nest the
riches of the people, Job 31:25
And as one gathers eggs *that are* left,
I have gathered all the earth;
And there was no one who moved *his*
wing,
Nor opened *his* mouth with even a
peep."

15 Shall [R]the ax boast itself against him
who chops with it? Jer. 51:20
Or shall the saw magnify itself against
him who saws with it?
As if a rod could wield *itself* against
those who lift it up,
Or as if a staff could lift up, *as if it were*
not wood!
16 Therefore the Lord, the *Lord of hosts,
Will send leanness among his fat ones;
And under his glory
He will kindle a burning
Like the burning of a fire.
17 So the Light of Israel will be for a fire,
And his Holy One for a flame;
[R]It will burn and devour Is. 9:18
His thorns and his briers in one day.
18 And it will consume the glory of his
forest and of [R]his fruitful field,
Both soul and body; 2 Kin. 19:23
And they will be as when a sick man
wastes away.
19 Then the rest of the trees of his forest
Will be so few in number
That a child may write them.

Remnant of Israel

20 And it shall come to pass in that day
That the remnant of Israel,
And such as have escaped of the house
of Jacob,
[R]Will never again depend on him who
[T]defeated them, 2 Kin. 16:7 • *struck*

10:16 MT, DSS *YHWH, LORD*

THE REMNANT

The idea of the remnant is that a small nucleus of God's people, preserved by His unmerited grace, form a foundation for a new community devoted to His redemptive work. Long before the prophets, a type of remnant theology may be seen in God's preservation of Noah and his family from the great flood (Gen. 7:1). In the same way, God used Joseph in Egypt to sustain a remnant during the worldwide famine (Gen. 45:7).

Remnant theology is also evident in the Book of Deuteronomy, where Moses warned Israel that they would be scattered, but the obedient would eventually be restored to their homeland (Deut. 4:27–31). This concept was picked up by the prophets and applied to the Hebrew people when they were carried into captivity by the Assyrians and Babylonians.

In the eighth century B.C., the prophet Amos proclaimed Israel's doom (Amos 8:1, 2), but he also declared the possibility of deliverance for "the remnant of Joseph" (Amos 5:15). In Isaiah's vision of Judah's judgment, the prophet thundered, "Unless the LORD of hosts had left to us a very small remnant, we would have become like Sodom" (Is. 1:9). Isaiah even named one of his sons Shear-Jashub, meaning "A Remnant Shall Return" (Is. 7:3). He predicted that the nation of Judah would be overthrown by a foreign power but that a remnant would survive to serve as a witness to God's continuing work of world redemption (Is. 10:20–23). The prophet Micah, a contemporary of Isaiah, tied the restoration remnant to God's future reign in Zion (Mic. 2:12, 13).

In the New Testament, the apostle Paul applied remnant theology to the church, indicating that God's new people would include both believing Jews and Gentiles (Rom. 9:22–27). Alluding to the seven thousand who had not worshiped Baal in Elijah's time (1 Kin. 19:18), Paul declared, "Even so then, at this present time there is a remnant according to the election of grace" (Rom. 11:5).

Throughout history God has always preserved a remnant from among His people to serve as a lighthouse in the midst of a dark and sinful world.

Isaiah kneels in prayer.

But will depend on the LORD, the Holy One of Israel, in truth.
21 The remnant will return, the remnant of Jacob,
To the [R]Mighty God. [Is. 9:6]
22 [R]For though your people, O Israel, be as the sand of the sea, Rom. 9:27, 28
[R]*Yet* a remnant of them will return;
The destruction decreed shall overflow with righteousness. Is. 6:13
23 [R]For the Lord GOD of hosts Dan. 9:27
Will make a determined end
In the midst of all the land.

24 Therefore thus says the Lord GOD of
hosts: "O My people, who dwell in Zion, [R]do
not be afraid of the Assyrian. He shall strike
you with a rod and lift up his staff against
you, in the manner of Egypt. Is. 7:4; 12:2
25 "For yet a very little while [R]and the
indignation will cease, as will My anger in
their destruction." Dan. 11:36
26 And the LORD of hosts will [T]stir up [R]a
scourge for him like the slaughter of [R]Midian
at the rock of Oreb; [R]*as* His rod was on the
sea, so will He lift it up in the manner of
Egypt. *arouse* • 2 Kin. 19:35 • Is. 9:4 • Ex. 14:26, 27

27 It shall come to pass in that day
That his burden will be taken away from your shoulder,
And his yoke from your neck,
And the yoke will be destroyed because of [R]the anointing oil. Ps. 105:15

28 He has come to Aiath,
He has passed Migron;
At Michmash he has attended to his equipment.
29 They have gone [T]along [R]the ridge,
They have taken up lodging at Geba.
Ramah is afraid, Or *over the pass* • 1 Sam. 13:23
[R]Gibeah of Saul has fled. 1 Sam. 11:4
30 [T]Lift up your voice, Or *Cry shrilly*
O daughter [R]of Gallim! 1 Sam. 25:44
Cause it to be heard as far as [R]Laish—
O poor Anathoth! Judg. 18:7
31 [R]Madmenah has fled, Josh. 15:31
The inhabitants of Gebim seek refuge.
32 As yet he will remain at Nob that day;
He will [R]shake his fist at the mount of [R]the daughter of Zion,
The hill of Jerusalem. Is. 13:2 • Is. 37:22

33 Behold, the Lord,
The LORD of hosts,
Will lop off the bough with terror;
[R]Those of high stature *will be* hewn down, Amos 2:9
And the haughty will be humbled.
34 He will cut down the thickets of the forest with iron,
And Lebanon will fall by the Mighty One.

CHAPTER 11

Restoration of the Messiah's Kingdom

THERE [R]shall come forth a Rod from the stem of [R]Jesse, [Zech. 6:12] • [Acts 13:23] ☆
And [R]a Branch shall [T]grow out of his roots. Is. 4:2 • *be fruitful*
2 [R]The Spirit of the LORD shall rest upon Him,
The Spirit of wisdom and understanding,
The Spirit of counsel and might,
The Spirit of knowledge and of the fear of the LORD. [John 1:32] ☆

3 His delight *is* in the fear of the LORD,
[R]And He shall not judge by the sight of His eyes, John 2:25 ☆
Nor decide by the hearing of His ears;
4 But [R]with righteousness He shall judge the poor,
And decide with equity for the meek of the earth;
He shall [R]strike the earth with the rod of His mouth,
And with the breath of His lips He shall slay the wicked. Rev. 19:11 ☆ • Job 4:9
5 Righteousness shall be the belt of His loins,
And faithfulness the belt of His waist.

6 "The[R] wolf also shall dwell with the lamb, Hos. 2:18
The leopard shall lie down with the young goat,
The calf and the young lion and the fatling together;
And a little child shall lead them.
7 The cow and the bear shall graze;
Their young ones shall lie down together;
And the lion shall eat straw like the ox.
8 The nursing child shall play by the cobra's hole,
And the weaned child shall put his hand in the viper's den.
9 [R]They shall not hurt nor destroy in all My holy mountain, Job 5:23
For [R]the earth shall be full of the knowledge of the LORD Hab. 2:14
As the waters cover the sea.

10 "And[R] in that day [R]there shall be a [R]Root of Jesse, Is. 2:11 • Rom. 15:12 • Is. 11:1 ☆
Who shall stand as a [R]banner to the people; Is. 27:12, 13
For the Gentiles shall seek Him,
And His resting place shall be glorious."

11 It shall come to pass in that day

That the LORD shall set His hand again
the second time
To recover the remnant of His people
who are left,
[R]From Assyria and Egypt,
From Pathros and Cush,
From Elam and Shinar,
From Hamath and the [T]islands of the
sea. Zech. 10:10 • Or *coastlands*

12 He will set up a banner for the nations,
And will [T]assemble the outcasts of
Israel, *gather*
And gather together [R]the dispersed of
Judah John 7:35
From the four corners of the earth.
13 Also [R]the envy of Ephraim shall depart,
And the adversaries of Judah shall be
cut off; Jer. 3:18
Ephraim shall not envy Judah,
And Judah shall not harass Ephraim.
14 But they shall fly down upon the
shoulder of the Philistines toward the
west;
Together they shall plunder the [T]people
of the east;
[R]They shall lay their hand on Edom and
Moab;
And the people of Ammon shall obey
them. Lit. *sons* • Dan. 11:41
15 The LORD will utterly destroy the
tongue of the Sea of Egypt;
With His mighty wind He will shake His
fist over [T]the River, The Euphrates
And strike it in the seven streams,
And make *men* cross over dryshod.
16 [R]There will be a highway for the
remnant of His people
Who will be left from Assyria,
[R]As it was for Israel
In the day that he came up from the
land of Egypt. Is. 19:23 • Ex. 14:29

CHAPTER 12

Thanksgiving in the Messiah's Kingdom

AND [R]in that day you will say:

"O LORD, I will praise You;
Though You were angry with me,
Your anger is turned away, and You
comfort me. Is. 2:11
2 Behold, God *is* my salvation,
I will trust and not be afraid;
'For [R]YAH, the LORD, *is* my [R]strength
and *my* song; Ps. 83:18 • Ex. 15:2
He also has become my salvation.' "

3 Therefore with joy you will draw [R]water
From the wells of salvation. [John 4:10, 14]

4 And in that day you will say:

[R]"Praise the LORD, call upon His name;
[R]Declare His deeds among the peoples,
Make mention that His [R]name is
exalted. 1 Chr. 16:8 • Ps. 145:4–6 • Ps. 34:3
5 [R]Sing to the LORD,
For He has done excellent things;
This *is* known in all the earth. Ex. 15:1
6 [R]Cry out and shout, O inhabitant of
Zion,
For great *is* [R]the Holy One of Israel in
your midst!" Zeph. 3:14, 15 • Ps. 89:18

CHAPTER 13

Prophecies Against Babylon

THE [T]burden against Babylon which Isaiah
the son of Amoz saw. *oracle, prophecy*

2 "Lift[R] up a banner [R]on the high
mountain, Is. 18:3 • Jer. 51:25
Raise your voice to them;
[R]Wave your hand, that they may enter
the gates of the nobles. Is. 10:32
3 I have commanded My [T]sanctified ones;
I have also called [R]My mighty ones for
My anger— *consecrated* or *set apart* • Joel 3:11
Those who rejoice in My exaltation."

4 The [R]noise of a multitude in the
mountains,
Like that of many people!
A tumultuous noise of the kingdoms of
nations gathered together!
The LORD of hosts musters
The army for battle. Is. 17:12
5 They come from a far country,
From the end of heaven,
Even the [R]LORD and His [T]weapons of
indignation, Is. 42:13 • Or *instruments*
To destroy the whole land.

6 Wail, [R]for the day of the LORD *is* at
hand! Zeph. 1:7
[R]It will come as destruction from the
Almighty. Joel 1:15
7 Therefore all hands will be limp,
Every man's heart will melt,
8 And they will be afraid.
[R]Pangs[T] and sorrows will take hold of
them; Ps. 48:6 • *Sharp pains*
They will be in pain as a woman in
childbirth;
They will be amazed at one another;
Their faces *will be like* flames.

9 Behold, [R]the day of the LORD comes,
Cruel, with both wrath and fierce anger,
To lay the land desolate; Mal. 4:1
And He will destroy its sinners from it.
10 For the stars of heaven and their
constellations
Will not give their light;

The sun will be [R]darkened in its going
forth,
And the moon will not cause its light to
shine. Joel 2:31

11 "I will [R]punish the world for *its* evil,
And the wicked for their iniquity;
[R]I will halt the arrogance of the proud,
And will lay low the haughtiness of the
[T]terrible. Is. 26:21 • [Is. 2:17] • Or *tyrants*
12 I will make a mortal more rare than
fine gold,
A man more than the golden wedge of
Ophir.
13 [R]Therefore I will shake the heavens,
And the earth will move out of her
place, Hag. 2:6
In the wrath of the LORD of hosts
And in the day of His fierce anger.
14 It shall be as the hunted gazelle,
And as a sheep that no man takes up;
Every man will turn to his own people,
And everyone will flee to his own land.
15 Everyone who is found will be thrust
through,
And everyone who is captured will fall
by the sword.
16 Their children also will be [R]dashed to
pieces before their eyes; Nah. 3:10
Their houses will be plundered
And their wives [R]ravished. Zech. 14:2

17 "Behold,[R] I will stir up the Medes against
them,
Who will not [T]regard silver;
And *as for* gold, they will not delight in
it. Dan. 5:28, 31 • *esteem*
18 Also *their* bows will dash the young
men to pieces,
And they will have no pity on the fruit
of the womb;
Their eye will not spare children.
19 [R]And Babylon, the glory of kingdoms,
The beauty of the Chaldeans' pride,
Will be as when God overthrew [R]Sodom
and Gomorrah. Is. 14:4 • Gen. 19:24
20 [R]It will never be inhabited,
Nor will it be settled from generation to
generation;
Nor will the Arabian pitch tents there,
Nor will the shepherds make their
sheepfolds there. Jer. 50:3
21 [R]But wild beasts of the desert will lie
there, Is. 34:11–15
And their houses will be full of owls;
Ostriches will dwell there,
And wild goats will caper there.
22 The hyenas will howl in their citadels,
And jackals in their pleasant palaces.
[R]Her time *is* near to come, Jer. 51:33
And her days will not be prolonged."

CHAPTER 14

FOR the LORD [R]will have mercy on Jacob,
and will still choose Israel, and settle
them in their own land. [R]The strangers will be
joined with them, and they will cling to the
house of Jacob. Ps. 102:13 • Is. 60:4, 5, 10
2 Then people will take them [R]and bring
them to their place, and the house of Israel
will possess them for servants and maids in
the land of the LORD; they will take them
captive whose captives they were, [R]and rule
over their oppressors. Is. 49:22; 60:9; 66:20 • Is. 60:14
3 It shall come to pass in the day the LORD
gives you rest from your sorrow, and from
your fear and the hard bondage in which you
were made to serve,
4 that you [R]will take up this proverb
against the king of Babylon, and say: Hab. 2:6

"How the oppressor has ceased,
The [T]golden city ceased! Or *insolent*
5 The LORD has broken [R]the staff of the
wicked,
The scepter of the rulers; Ps. 125:3
6 He who struck the people in wrath with
a continual stroke,
He who ruled the nations in anger,
Is persecuted *and* no one hinders.
7 The whole earth is at rest *and* quiet;
They break forth into singing.
8 [R]Indeed the cypress trees rejoice over
you, Ezek. 31:16
And the cedars of Lebanon,
Saying, 'Since you were cut down,
No woodsman has come up against us.'

9 "Hell[R] from beneath is excited about
you, Ezek. 32:21
To meet *you* at your coming;
It stirs up the dead for you,
All the chief ones of the earth;
It has raised up from their thrones
All the kings of the nations.
10 They all shall [R]speak and say to you:
'Have you also become as weak as we?
Have you become like us? Ezek. 32:21
11 Your pomp is brought down to Sheol,
And the sound of your stringed
instruments;
The maggot is spread under you,
And worms cover you.'

12 "How you are fallen from heaven,
O [T]Lucifer, son of the morning!
How you are cut down to the ground,
You who weakened the nations! *Day Star*
13 For you have said in your heart:
[R]'I will ascend into heaven, Ezek. 28:2
[R]I will exalt my throne above the stars of
God; Dan. 8:10
I will also sit on the [R]mount of the
congregation Ezek. 28:14

[R]On the farthest sides of the north; Ps. 48:2
14 I will ascend above the heights of the
clouds,
[R]I will be like the Most High.' 2 Thess. 2:4
15 Yet you [R]shall be brought down to
Sheol, Matt. 11:23
To the [T]lowest depths of the Pit. *recesses*

16 "Those who see you will gaze at you,
And consider you, *saying*:
'*Is* this the man who made the earth
tremble,
Who shook kingdoms,
17 Who made the world as a wilderness
And destroyed its cities,
Who [T]did not open the house of his
prisoners?' Would not release

18 "All the kings of the nations,
All of them, sleep in glory,
Everyone in his own house;
19 But you are cast out of your grave
Like an [T]abominable branch,
Like the garment of those who are
slain, *despised*
[T]Thrust through with a sword, *Pierced*
Who go down to the stones of the pit,
Like a corpse trodden underfoot.
20 You will not be joined with them in
burial,
Because you have destroyed your land
And slain your people.
[R]The brood of evildoers shall never be
named. Ps. 21:10; 109:13
21 Prepare slaughter for his children
[R]Because of the iniquity of their fathers,
Lest they rise up and possess the land,
And fill the face of the world with
cities." Ex. 20:5

22 "For I will rise up against them," says
the LORD of hosts,
"And cut off from Babylon [R]the name
and [R]remnant,
[R]And offspring and posterity," says the
LORD. Prov. 10:7 • 1 Kin. 14:10 • Job 18:19
23 "I will also make it a possession for the
[R]porcupine, Zeph. 2:14
And marshes of muddy water;
I will sweep it with the broom of
destruction," says the LORD of hosts.

Prophecies Against Assyria

24 The LORD of hosts has sworn, saying,
"Surely, as I have thought, so it shall
come to pass,
And as I have purposed, *so* it shall
[R]stand: Is. 43:13
25 That I will break the [R]Assyrian in My
land,
And on My mountains tread him under
foot.
Then [R]his yoke shall be removed from
them,
And his burden removed from their
shoulders. Mic. 5:5, 6 • Is. 10:27
26 This *is* the [R]purpose that is purposed
against the whole earth,
And this *is* the hand that is stretched
out over all the nations. Is. 23:9
27 For the LORD of hosts has [R]purposed,
And who will annul *it?*
His hand *is* stretched out,
And who will turn it back?" Dan. 4:31, 35

Prophecies Against Philistia

28 This is the [T]burden which came in the
year that King Ahaz died. *oracle, prophecy*

29 "Do not rejoice, all you of Philistia,
[R]Because the rod that struck you is
broken;
For out of the serpent's roots will come
forth a viper,
[R]And its offspring *will be* a fiery flying
serpent. 2 Chr. 26:6 • 2 Kin. 18:8
30 The firstborn of the poor will feed,
And the needy will lie down in safety;
I will kill your roots with famine,
And it will slay your remnant.
31 Wail, O gate! Cry, O city!
All you of Philistia *are* dissolved;
For smoke will come from the north,
And no one *will be* alone in his
[T]appointed times." Or *ranks*

32 What will *one* then answer the
messengers of the nation?
That [R]the LORD has founded Zion,
And [R]the poor of His people shall take
refuge in it. Ps. 87:1, 5 • Zech. 11:11

CHAPTER 15

Prophecies Against Moab

THE [T]burden against Moab. *oracle, prophecy*

Because in the night [R]Ar of [R]Moab is
laid waste
And destroyed, Deut. 2:9 • Amos 2:1–3
Because in the night Kir of Moab is laid
waste
And destroyed,
2 He has gone up to the [T]temple and
Dibon, Heb. *bayith, house*
To the high places to weep.
Moab will wail over Nebo and over
Medeba;
[R]On all their heads *will be* baldness,
And every beard cut off. Lev. 21:5
3 In their streets they will clothe
themselves with sackcloth;
On the tops of their houses
And in their streets
Everyone will wail, weeping bitterly.

4 Heshbon and Elealeh will cry out,
Their voice shall be heard as far as
[R]Jahaz; Jer. 48:34
Therefore the armed soldiers of Moab
will cry out;
His life will be burdensome to him.

5 "My[R] heart will cry out for Moab; Jer. 48:31
His fugitives *shall flee* to Zoar,
Like a three-year-old heifer.
For [R]by the ascent of Luhith Jer. 48:5
They will go up with weeping;
For in the way of Horonaim
They will raise up a cry of destruction,
6 For the waters [R]of Nimrim will be
desolate, Num. 32:36
For the green grass has withered away;
The grass fails, there is nothing green.
7 Therefore the abundance they have
gained,
And what they have laid up,
They will carry away to the Brook of
the Willows.
8 For the cry has gone all around the
borders of Moab,
Its wailing to Eglaim
And its wailing to Beer Elim.
9 For the waters of Dimon will be full of
blood;
Because I will bring more upon Dimon,
[R]Lions upon him who escapes from
Moab, 2 Kin. 17:25
And on the remnant of the land."

CHAPTER 16

SEND the lamb to the ruler of the land,
From [T]Sela to the wilderness, Lit. *Rock*
To the mount of the daughter of Zion.
2 For it shall be as a [R]wandering bird
thrown out of the nest; Prov. 27:8
So shall be the daughters of Moab at
the fords of the [R]Arnon. Num. 21:13

3 "Take counsel, execute judgment;
Make your shadow like the night in the
middle of the day;
Hide the outcasts,
Do not betray him who escapes.
4 Let My outcasts dwell with you, O
Moab;
Be a shelter to them from the face of
the [T]spoiler.
For the extortioner is at an end,
Devastation ceases,
The oppressors are consumed out of the
land. *devastator*
5 In mercy [R]the throne will be
established; Dan. 7:14
And One will sit on it in truth, in the
tabernacle of David,
Judging and seeking justice and
hastening [R]righteousness." Is. 9:7

6 We have heard of the [R]pride of Moab—
He is very proud— Jer. 48:29
Of his haughtiness and his pride and his
wrath;
But his [T]lies *shall* not *be* so. Lit. *vain talk*
7 Therefore Moab shall [R]wail for Moab;
Everyone shall wail. Jer. 48:20
For the foundations [R]of Kir Hareseth
you shall mourn;
Surely *they are* stricken. 2 Kin. 3:25

8 For [R]the fields of Heshbon languish,
And [R]the vine of Sibmah;
The lords of the nations have broken
down its choice plants, Is. 24:7 • Is. 16:9
Which have reached to Jazer
And wandered through the wilderness.
Her branches are stretched out,
They are gone over the [R]sea. Jer. 48:32
9 Therefore I will bewail the vine of
Sibmah,
With the weeping of Jazer;
I will drench you with my tears,
[R]O Heshbon and Elealeh;
For [T]battle cries have fallen
Over your summer fruits and your
harvest. Is. 15:4 • Or *shouting has*

10 [R]Gladness is taken away, Is. 24:8
And joy from the plentiful field;
In the vineyards there will be no
singing,
Nor will there be shouting;
No treaders will tread out wine in *their*
presses;
I have made their shouting cease.
11 Therefore [R]my [T]heart shall resound like
a harp for Moab, Jer. 48:36 • Lit. *belly*
And my inner being for Kir Heres.

12 And it shall come to pass,
When it is seen that Moab is weary on
[R]the high place,
That he will come to his sanctuary to
pray;
But he will not prevail. Is. 15:2

13 This *is* the word which the LORD has
spoken concerning Moab since that time.
14 But now the LORD has spoken, saying,
"Within three years, [R]as the years of a hired
man, the glory of Moab will be despised with
all that great multitude, and the remnant *will
be* very small *and* feeble." Is. 21:16

CHAPTER 17

Prophecies Against Damascus and Samaria

THE [R]burden[T] against Damascus.
"Behold, Damascus will cease from *being*
a city, Zech. 9:1 • *oracle, prophecy*
And it will be a ruinous heap.

2 The cities of [R]Aroer *are* forsaken;
They will be for flocks
Which lie down, and [R]no one will make
them afraid. Num. 32:34 • Jer. 7:33
3 [R]The fortress also will cease from
Ephraim, Is. 7:16; 8:4
The kingdom from Damascus,
And the remnant of Syria;
They will be as the glory of the children
of Israel,"
Says the LORD of hosts.

4 "In that day it shall come to pass
That the glory of Jacob will wane,
And the fatness of his flesh grow lean.
5 [R]It shall be as when the harvester
gathers the grain,
And reaps the heads with his arm;
It shall be as he who gathers heads of
grain
In the Valley of Rephaim. Jer. 51:33
6 [R]Yet gleaning grapes will be left in it,
Like the shaking of an olive tree,
Two *or* three olives at the top of the
uppermost bough, Is. 24:13
Four *or* five in its most fruitful
branches,"
Says the LORD God of Israel.

7 In that day a man will [R]look to his
Maker, Mic. 7:7
And his eyes will have respect for the
Holy One of Israel.
8 He will not look to the altars,
The work of his hands;
He will not respect what his [R]fingers
have made, Is. 2:8; 31:7
Nor the [T]wooden images nor the
incense altars. *Asherim*, Canaanite gods

9 In that day his strong cities will be as a
forsaken bough
And an uppermost branch,
Which they left because of the children
of Israel;
And there will be desolation.

10 Because you have forgotten [R]the God of
your salvation, Ps. 68:19
And have not been mindful of the Rock
of your [T]stronghold, *refuge*
Therefore you will plant pleasant plants
And set out foreign seedlings;
11 In the day you will make your plant to
grow,
And in the morning you will make your
seed to flourish;
But the harvest *will be* a heap of ruins
In the day of grief and desperate
sorrow.

12 Woe to the multitude of many people
Who make a noise [R]like the roar of the
seas,
And to the rushing of nations
That make a rushing like the rushing of
mighty waters! Jer. 6:23
13 The nations will rush like the rushing of
many waters;
But *God* will [R]rebuke them and they
will flee far away,
And [R]be chased like the chaff of the
mountains before the wind,
Like a rolling thing before the
whirlwind. Ps. 9:5 • Hos. 13:3
14 Then behold, at eventide, trouble!
And before the morning, he *is* no more.
This *is* the portion of those who plunder
us,
And the lot of those who rob us.

CHAPTER 18

Prophecies Against Ethiopia

WOE [R]to the land shadowed with
buzzing wings, Zeph. 2:12; 3:10
Which *is* beyond the rivers of Ethiopia,
2 Which sends ambassadors by sea,
Even in vessels of reed on the waters,
saying,
"Go, swift messengers, to a nation tall
and smooth of skin,
To a people terrible from their
beginning onward,
A nation powerful and treading down,
Whose land the rivers divide."

3 All inhabitants of the world and
dwellers on the earth:
[R]When he lifts up a banner on the
mountains, you see *it*;
And when he blows a trumpet, you hear
it. Is. 5:26
4 For so the LORD said to me,
"I will take My rest,
And I will [T]look from My dwelling place
Like clear heat in sunshine,
Like a cloud of dew in the heat of
harvest." *watch*
5 For before the harvest, when the bud is
perfect
And the sour grape is ripening in the
flower,
He will both cut off the sprigs with
pruning hooks
And take away *and* cut down the
branches.
6 They will be left together for the
mountain birds of prey
And for the beasts of the earth;
The birds of prey will summer on them,
And all the beasts of the earth will
winter on them.

7 In that time [R]a present will be brought
to the LORD of hosts

From a people tall and smooth *of skin*,
And from a people terrible from their beginning onward,
A nation powerful and treading down,
Whose land the rivers divide—
To the place of the name of the LORD of hosts,
To Mount Zion. Zeph. 3:10

CHAPTER 19

Prophecies Against Egypt

THE [T]burden against Egypt. *oracle*

Behold, the LORD [R]rides on a swift cloud, Ps. 18:10; 104:3
And will come into Egypt;
[R]The idols of Egypt will [T]totter at His presence, Jer. 43:12 • Lit. *shake*
And the heart of Egypt will melt in its midst.

2 "I will [R]set Egyptians against Egyptians;
Everyone will fight against his brother,
And everyone against his neighbor,
City against city, kingdom against kingdom. Judg. 7:22
3 The spirit of Egypt will fail in its midst;
I will destroy their counsel,
And they will [R]consult the idols and the charmers, Is. 8:19; 47:12
The mediums and the sorcerers.
4 And the Egyptians I will give
Into the hand of a cruel master,
And a fierce king will rule over them,"
Says the Lord, the LORD of hosts.

5 [R]The waters will fail from the sea,
And the river will be wasted and dried up. Jer. 51:36
6 The rivers will turn foul,
And the brooks [R]of defense will be emptied and dried up; 2 Kin. 19:24
The reeds and rushes will wither.
7 The papyrus reeds by [T]the River, by the mouth of the River,
And everything sown by the River,
Will wither, be driven away, and be no more. The Nile
8 The fishermen also will mourn;
All those will lament who cast hooks into the River,
And they will languish who spread nets on the waters.
9 Moreover those who work in [R]fine flax
And those who weave fine fabric will be ashamed; Prov. 7:16
10 And its foundations will be broken.
All who make wages will be troubled of soul.

11 Surely the princes of [R]Zoan *are* fools;
Pharaoh's wise counselors give foolish counsel. Num. 13:22
[R]How do you say to Pharaoh, "I *am* the son of the wise, 1 Kin. 4:29, 30
The son of ancient kings?"
12 [R]Where *are* they? 1 Cor. 1:20
Where are your wise men?
Let them tell you now,
And let them know what the LORD of hosts has purposed against Egypt.
13 The princes of Zoan have become fools;
[R]The princes of [T]Noph are deceived;
They have also deluded Egypt,
Those who are the [T]mainstay of its tribes. Jer. 2:16 • Ancient Memphis • *cornerstone*
14 The LORD has mingled [R]a perverse spirit in her midst;
And they have caused Egypt to err in all her work,
As a drunken man staggers in his vomit. Is. 29:10
15 Neither will there be *any* work for Egypt,
Which [R]the head or tail, Is. 9:14–16
Palm branch or bulrush, may do.

16 In that day Egypt will [R]be like women,
and will be afraid and fear because of the
waving of the hand of the LORD of hosts,
[R]which He waves over it. Nah. 3:13 • Is. 11:15
17 And the land of Judah will be a terror to
Egypt; everyone who makes mention of it
will be afraid in himself, because of the
counsel of the LORD of hosts which He has
[R]determined against it. Dan. 4:35
18 In that day five cities in the land of
Egypt will speak the language of Canaan and
[R]swear by the LORD of hosts; one will be
called the City of Destruction. Is. 45:23
19 In that day there will be an altar to the
LORD in the midst of the land of Egypt, and a
pillar to the [R]LORD at its border. Ps. 68:31
20 And [R]it will be for a sign and for a
witness to the LORD of hosts in the land of
Egypt; for they will cry to the LORD because
of the oppressors, and He will send them a
[R]Savior and a Mighty One, and He will deliver
them. Josh. 4:20; 22:27 • Is. 43:11
21 Then the LORD will be known to Egypt,
and the Egyptians will [R]know the LORD in
that day, and [R]will make sacrifice and offering; yes, they will make a vow to the LORD
and perform *it*. [Is. 2:3, 4; 11:9] • Mal. 1:11
22 And the LORD will strike Egypt, He will
strike and [R]heal *it*; they will return to the
LORD, and He will be entreated by them and
heal them. Deut. 32:39
23 In that day there will be a highway from
Egypt to Assyria, and the Assyrian will come
into Egypt and the Egyptian into Assyria, and
the Egyptians will serve with the Assyrians.
24 In that day Israel will be one of three
with Egypt and Assyria, *even* a blessing in
the midst of the land,

25 whom the LORD of hosts shall bless,
saying, "Blessed *is* Egypt My people, and
Assyria [R]the work of My hands, and Israel
My inheritance." Is. 29:23

CHAPTER 20

IN the year that [R]Tartan[T] came to Ashdod,
when Sargon the king of Assyria sent
him, and he fought against Ashdod and took
it, 2 Kin. 18:17 • Or *the Commander in Chief*
2 at the same time the LORD spoke by
Isaiah the son of Amoz, saying, "Go, and
remove the sackcloth from your [T]body, and
take your sandals off your feet." And he did
so, walking naked and barefoot. Lit. *loins*
3 Then the LORD said, "Just as My servant
Isaiah has walked naked and barefoot three
years [R]*for* a sign and a wonder against Egypt
and Ethiopia, Is. 8:18
4 "so shall the [R]king of Assyria lead away
the Egyptians as prisoners and the Ethiopians
as captives, young and old, naked and barefoot, [R]with their buttocks uncovered, to the
shame of Egypt. Is. 19:4 • Jer. 13:22
5 [R]"Then they shall be afraid and ashamed
of Ethiopia their expectation and Egypt their
glory. 2 Kin. 18:21
6 "And the inhabitant of this territory will
say in that day, 'Surely such *is* our expectation, wherever we flee for [R]help to be delivered from the king of Assyria; and how shall
we escape?' " Is. 30:5, 7

CHAPTER 21

Prophecies Against Babylon

THE [T]burden against the Wilderness of the
Sea.

As [R]whirlwinds in the South pass
through,
So it comes from the desert, from a
terrible land. *oracle, prophecy* • Zech. 9:14
2 A distressing vision is declared to me;
[R]The treacherous dealer deals
treacherously,
And the plunderer plunders.
[R]Go up, O Elam!
Besiege, O Media! Is. 33:1 • Jer. 49:34
All its sighing I have made to cease.

3 Therefore my loins are filled with pain;
[R]Pangs have taken hold of me, like the
pangs of a woman in labor. Is. 13:8
I was [T]distressed when *I* heard *it;*
I was dismayed when *I* saw *it.* Lit. *bowed*
4 My heart wavered, fearfulness
frightened me;
[R]The night for which I longed He turned
into fear for me. Deut. 28:67
5 [R]Prepare the table,
Set a watchman in the tower,
Eat and drink.
Arise, you princes,
Anoint the shield! Dan. 5:5

6 For thus has the Lord said to me:
"Go, set a watchman,
Let him declare what he sees."
7 And he saw a chariot *with* a pair of
horsemen,
A chariot of donkeys, *and* a chariot of
camels,
And he listened diligently with great
care.
8 *Then he cried, "A lion, my Lord!
I stand continually on the [R]watchtower
in the daytime; Hab. 2:1
I have sat at my post every night.
9 And look, here comes a chariot of men
with a pair of horsemen!"
And he answered and said,
[R]"Babylon is fallen, is fallen! Jer. 51:8
And [R]all the carved images of her gods
He has broken to the ground." Is. 46:1

10 [R]Oh, my threshing and the grain of my
floor!
That which I have heard from the LORD
of hosts,
The God of Israel,
I have declared to you. Jer. 51:33

Prophecies Against Dumah (Edom)

11 The burden against Dumah.

He calls to me out of [R]Seir, Gen. 32:3
"Watchman, what of the night?
Watchman, what of the night?"
12 The watchman said,
"The morning comes, and also the night.
If you will inquire, inquire;
Return! Come back!"

Prophecies Against Arabia

13 The [T]burden against Arabia.

In the forest in Arabia you will lodge,
O you traveling companies [R]of
Dedanites. *oracle, prophecy* • 1 Chr. 1:9, 32
14 O inhabitants of the land of Tema,
Bring water to him who is thirsty;
With their bread they met him who
fled.
15 For they fled from the swords, from the
drawn sword,
From the bent bow, and from the
distress of war.

16 For thus the LORD has said to me:
"Within a year, according to the year of a
hired man, all the glory of Kedar will fail;
17 "and the remainder of the number of

21:8 DSS *Then the observer cried, "My Lord!*

archers, the mighty men of the people of Kedar, will be diminished; for the LORD God of Israel has spoken *it*."

CHAPTER 22

Prophecies Against Jerusalem

THE [T]burden against the Valley of Vision.

What ails you now, that you have all
gone up to the housetops, *oracle, prophecy*
2 You who are full of noise,
A [T]tumultuous city, [R]a joyous city?
Your slain *men are* not slain with the
sword,
Nor dead in battle. *boisterous* • Is. 32:13
3 All your rulers have fled together;
They are captured by the archers.
All who are found in you are bound
together,
Who have fled from afar.
4 Therefore I said, "Look away from me,
[R]I will weep bitterly;
Do not labor to comfort me
Because of the plundering of the
daughter of my people." Jer. 4:19

5 [R]For *it is* a day of trouble and treading
down and perplexity Is. 37:3
[R]By the Lord GOD of hosts Lam. 1:5; 2:2
In the Valley of Vision—
Breaking down the walls
And of crying to the mountain.
6 [R]Elam bore the quiver Jer. 49:35
With chariots of men *and* horsemen,
And [R]Kir uncovered the shield. Is. 15:1
7 It shall come to pass *that* your choicest
valleys
Shall be full of chariots,
And the horsemen shall set themselves
in array at the gate.

8 He removed the [T]protection of Judah.
You looked in that day to the armor of
the House of the Forest; Lit. *covering*
9 [R]You also saw the [T]damage to the city of
David, 2 Kin. 20:20 • Lit. *breaches* in the city walls
That it was great;
And you gathered together the waters
of the lower pool.
10 You numbered the houses of Jerusalem,
And the houses you broke down
To fortify the wall.
11 [R]You also made a reservoir between the
two walls Neh. 3:16
For the water of the old [R]pool.
But you did not look to its Maker,
Nor did you have respect for Him who
fashioned it long ago. 2 Chr. 32:3, 4

12 And in that day the Lord GOD of hosts
[R]Called for weeping and for mourning,
[R]For baldness and for girding with
sackcloth. Joel 1:13; 2:17 • Mic. 1:16
13 But instead, joy and gladness,
Slaying oxen and killing sheep,
Eating meat and [R]drinking wine:
[R]"Let us eat and drink, for tomorrow we
die!" Luke 17:26–29 • 1 Cor. 15:32

14 [R]Then it was revealed in my hearing by
the LORD of hosts,
"Surely for this iniquity there [R]will be no
atonement for you,
Even to your death," says the Lord GOD
of hosts. Is. 5:9 • Ezek. 24:13

15 Thus says the Lord GOD of hosts:

"Go, proceed to this steward,
To [R]Shebna, who *is* over the house, *and*
say: Is. 36:3
16 'What have you here, and whom have
you here,
That you have hewn a sepulcher here,
As he [R]who hews himself a sepulcher on
high,
Who carves a tomb for himself in a
rock? Matt. 27:60
17 Indeed, the LORD will throw you away
violently,
O mighty man,
[R]And will surely seize you. Esth. 7:8
18 He will surely turn violently and toss
you like a ball
Into a large country;
There you shall die, and there [R]your
glorious chariots
Shall be the shame of your master's
house. Is. 2:7
19 So I will drive you out of your office,
And from your position he will pull you
down.

20 'Then it shall be in that day,
That I will call My servant [R]Eliakim the
son of Hilkiah; 2 Kin. 18:18
21 I will clothe him with your robe
And strengthen him with your belt;
I will commit your responsibility into
his hand.
He shall be a father to the inhabitants
of Jerusalem
And to the house of Judah.
22 The key of the house of David
I will lay on his [R]shoulder;
So he shall [R]open, and no one shall
shut;
And he shall shut, and no one shall
open. Is. 9:6 • Rev. 3:7 ☆
23 I will fasten him *as* [R]a peg in a secure
place,
And he will become a glorious throne to
his father's house. Ezra 9:8

24 'They will hang on him all the glory of
his father's house, the offspring and the issue,
all vessels of small quantity, from the cups to
all the pitchers.
25 'In that day,' says the LORD of hosts, 'the
peg that is fastened in the secure place will
be removed and be cut down and fall, and the
burden that *was* on it will be cut off; for the
LORD has spoken.' "

CHAPTER 23

Prophecies Against Tyre

THE [R]burden against Tyre.

Wail, you ships of Tarshish!
For it is laid waste,
So that there is no house, no harbor;
From the land of [T]Cyprus it is revealed
to them. Zech. 9:2, 4 • Heb. *Kittim*

2 Be still, you inhabitants of the
coastland,
You merchants of Sidon,
Whom those who cross the sea have
filled.
3 And on great waters the grain of
Shihor,
The harvest of [T]the River, *is* her
revenue;
And [R]she is a marketplace for the
nations. The Nile • Ezek. 27:3–23

4 Be ashamed, O Sidon;
For the sea has spoken,
The strength of the sea, saying,
"I do not labor, nor bring forth children;
Neither do I rear young men,
Nor bring up virgins."
5 [R]When the report *comes to* Egypt,
They also will be in agony at the report
of Tyre. Is. 19:16

6 Cross over to Tarshish;
Wail, you inhabitants of the coastland!
7 *Is* this your [R]joyous *city*,
Whose antiquity *is* from ancient days,
Whose feet carried her far off to
sojourn? Is. 22:2; 32:13
8 Who has taken this counsel against
Tyre, [R]the crowning *city*,
Whose merchants *are* princes,
Whose traders *are* the honorable of the
earth? Ezek. 28:2, 12
9 The LORD of hosts has purposed it,
To [T]bring to dishonor the [R]pride of all
glory,
And to bring into contempt all the
honorable of the earth. *pollute* • Dan. 4:37

10 Overflow through your land like [T]the
River, The Nile
O daughter of Tarshish;
There is no more [T]strength. *restraint*
11 He stretched out His hand over the sea,
He shook the kingdoms;
The LORD has given a commandment
[R]against Canaan
To destroy its strongholds. Zech. 9:2–4
12 And He said, "You will rejoice no more,
O you oppressed virgin daughter of
Sidon.
Arise, [R]cross over to Cyprus; Rev. 18:22
There also you will have no rest."

13 Behold, the land of the [R]Chaldeans,
This people *which* was not;
Assyria founded it for [R]wild beasts of
the desert.
They set up its towers,
They raised up its palaces,
And brought it to ruin. Is. 47:1 • Ps. 72:9

14 [R]Wail, you ships of Tarshish! Ezek. 27:25–30
For your strength is laid waste.

15 Now it shall come to pass in that day
that Tyre will be forgotten seventy years,
according to the days of one king. At the end
of seventy years it will happen to Tyre as *in*
the song of the harlot:

16 "Take a harp, go about the city,
You forgotten harlot;
Make sweet melody, sing many songs,
That you may be remembered."

17 And it shall be, at the end of seventy
years, that the LORD will visit Tyre. She will
return to her pay, and [R]commit fornication
with all the kingdoms of the world on the
face of the earth. Rev. 17:2
18 Her gain and her pay [R]will be set apart
for the LORD; it will not be treasured nor laid
up, for her gain will be for those who dwell
before the LORD, to eat sufficiently, and for
[T]fine clothing. Zech. 14:20, 21 • *choice*

CHAPTER 24

Judgments of the Tribulation

BEHOLD, the LORD makes the earth
empty and makes it waste,
Distorts its surface
And scatters abroad its inhabitants.
2 And it shall be:
As with the people, so with the [R]priest;
As with the servant, so with his master;
As with the maid, so with her mistress;
[R]As with the buyer, so with the seller;
As with the lender, so with the
borrower; Hos. 4:9 • Ezek. 7:12, 13
As with the creditor, so with the debtor.
3 The land shall be entirely emptied and
utterly plundered,
For the LORD has spoken this word.

4 The earth mourns *and* fades away,
The world languishes *and* fades away;
The [R]haughty[T] people of the earth
languish. Is. 25:11 • *proud*
5 [R]The earth is also defiled under its
inhabitants,
Because they have [R]transgressed the
laws, Num. 35:33 • Is. 59:12
Changed the ordinance,
Broken the everlasting covenant.
6 Therefore [R]the curse has devoured the
earth, Mal. 4:6
And those who dwell in it are [T]desolate.
Therefore the inhabitants of the earth
are [R]burned, Or *held guilty* • Is. 9:19
And few men *are* left.

7 [R]The new wine fails, the vine languishes,
All the merry-hearted sigh. Joel 1:10, 12
8 The mirth [R]of the tambourine ceases,
The noise of the jubilant ends,
The joy of the harp ceases. Ezek. 26:13
9 They shall not drink wine with a song;
Strong drink is bitter to those who
drink it.
10 The city of confusion is broken down;
Every house is shut up, so that none
may go in.
11 *There is* a crying for wine in the streets,
All joy is darkened,
The mirth of the land is gone.
12 In the city desolation is left,
And the gate is stricken with
destruction.
13 When it shall be thus in the midst of
the land among the people,
[R]*It shall be* like the shaking of an olive
tree,
Like the gleaning of grapes when the
vintage is done. [Is. 17:5, 6; 27:12]

14 They shall lift up their voice, they shall
sing;
For the majesty of the LORD
They shall cry aloud from the sea.
15 Therefore [R]glorify the LORD in the
dawning light, Is. 25:3
[R]The name of the LORD God of Israel in
the coastlands of the sea. Mal. 1:11
16 From the ends of the earth we have
heard songs:
"Glory to the righteous!"
But I said, [T]"I am ruined, ruined!
Woe to me! Lit. *Leanness to me, leanness to me*
[R]The treacherous dealers have dealt
treacherously, Jer. 3:20; 5:11
Indeed, the treacherous dealers have
dealt very treacherously."

17 [R]Fear and the pit and the snare
Are upon you, O inhabitant of the
earth. Jer. 48:43
18 And it shall be
That he who flees from the noise of the
fear
Shall fall into the pit,
And he who comes up from the midst
of the pit
Shall be [T]caught in the snare;
For [R]the windows from on high are
open,
And [R]the foundations of the earth are
shaken. Lit. *taken* • Gen. 7:11 • Ps. 18:7; 46:2

19 [R]The earth is violently broken,
The earth is split open,
The earth is shaken exceedingly. Jer. 4:23
20 The earth shall [R]reel[T] to and fro like a
drunkard, Is. 19:14; 24:1; 28:7 • *stagger*
And shall totter like a hut;
Its transgression shall be heavy upon it,
And it will fall, and not rise again.

21 It shall come to pass in that day
That the LORD will punish on high the
host of exalted ones,
And on the earth [R]the kings of the
earth. Ps. 76:12
22 They will be gathered together,
As prisoners are gathered in the pit,
And will be shut up in the prison;
After many days they will be punished.
23 Then the [R]moon will be disgraced
And the sun ashamed; Is. 13:10; 60:19
For the LORD of hosts will reign
On Mount Zion and in Jerusalem
And before His elders, gloriously.

CHAPTER 25

Israel's Praise for Kingdom Blessings

O LORD, You *are* my God.
[R]I will exalt You,
I will praise Your name,
[R]For You have done wonderful *things*;
[R]*Your* counsels of old *are* faithfulness
and truth. Ex. 15:2 • Ps. 98:1 • Num. 23:19
2 For You have made [R]a city a ruin,
A fortified city a ruin,
A palace of foreigners to be a city no
more;
It will never be rebuilt. Jer. 51:37
3 Therefore the strong people will [R]glorify
You;
The city of the [T]terrible nations will fear
You. Is. 24:15 • *terrifying*
4 For You have been a strength to the
poor,
A strength to the needy in his distress,
[R]A refuge from the storm,
A shade from the heat;
For the blast of the terrible ones *is* as a
storm *against* the wall. Is. 4:6
5 You will reduce the noise of aliens,
As heat in a dry place;

As heat in the shadow of a cloud,
The song of the terrible ones will be
[T]diminished. *humbled*

6 And in [R]this mountain [Is. 2:2–4; 56:7]
[R]The LORD of hosts will make for [R]all
people Prov. 9:2 • [Dan. 7:14]
A feast of [T]choice pieces, Lit. *fat things*
A feast of wines on the lees,
Of fat things full of marrow,
Of well-refined wines on the lees.
7 And He will destroy on this mountain
The surface of the covering cast over all
people,
And [R]the veil that is spread over all
nations. [Eph. 4:18]
8 He will [R]swallow up death forever,
And the Lord GOD will [R]wipe away tears
from all faces; [Hos. 13:14] • Rev. 7:17; 21:4
The rebuke of His people
He will take away from all the earth;
For the LORD has spoken.

9 And it will be said in that day:
"Behold, this *is* our God;
[R]We have waited for Him, and He will
save us.
This *is* the LORD;
We have waited for Him;
[R]We will be glad and rejoice in His
salvation." Gen. 49:18 • Ps. 20:5

10 For on this mountain the hand of the
LORD will rest,
And [R]Moab shall be trampled down
under Him,
As straw is trampled down for the
refuse heap. Amos 2:1–3
11 And He will spread out His hands in
their midst
As he who swims spreads out *his hands*
to swim,
And He will bring down their [R]pride
Together with the trickery of their
hands. Is. 24:4; 26:5
12 The [R]fortress of the high fort of your
walls
He will bring down, lay low,
And bring to the ground, down to the
dust. Is. 26:5

CHAPTER 26

Israel's Kingdom Song

IN [R]that day this song will be sung in the
land of Judah:

"We have a strong city;
[R]*God* will appoint salvation *for* walls and
bulwarks. Is. 2:11; 12:1 • Is. 60:18
2 [R]Open the gates, Ps. 118:19, 20
That the righteous nation which [T]keeps
the truth may enter in. Or *remains faithful*
3 You will keep *him* in perfect [R]peace,
Whose mind *is* stayed *on You*,
Because he trusts in You. Is. 57:19
4 Trust in the LORD forever,
[R]For in YAH, the LORD, *is* [T]everlasting
strength. Is. 12:2; 45:17 • Or *Rock of Ages*
5 For He brings [T]down those who dwell
on high, *low*
[R]The lofty city; Is. 25:11, 12
He lays it low,
He lays it low to the ground,
He brings it down to the dust.
6 The foot shall [T]tread it down—
The feet of the poor
And the steps of the needy." *trample*

7 The way of the just *is* uprightness;
[R]O Most Upright, Ps. 37:23
You weigh the path of the just.
8 Yes, [R]in the way of Your judgments,
O LORD, we have waited for You;
The desire of *our* soul *is* for Your name
And for the remembrance of You. Is. 64:5
9 [R]With my soul I have desired You in the
night,
Yes, by my spirit within me I will seek
You early;
For when Your judgments *are* in the
earth,
The inhabitants of the world will learn
righteousness. Ps. 63:6

10 [R]Let grace be shown to the wicked,
Yet he will not learn righteousness;
In [R]the land of uprightness he will deal
unjustly,
And will not behold the majesty of the
LORD. [Rom. 2:4] • Ps. 143:10
11 LORD, *when* Your hand is lifted up,
[R]they will not see. Is. 5:12
But they will see and be ashamed
For [T]*their* envy of people;
Yes, the fire of Your enemies shall
devour them. Or *Your zeal for the people*

12 LORD, You will establish peace for us,
For You have also done all our works
[T]in us. Or *for us*
13 O LORD our God, [R]*other* masters besides
You
Have had dominion over us;
But by You only we make mention of
Your name. 2 Chr. 12:8
14 *They are* dead, they will not live;
They are deceased, they will not rise.
Therefore You have punished and
destroyed them,
And made all their memory to perish.
15 You have increased the nation, O LORD,
You have [R]increased the nation;
You are glorified;
You have expanded all the [T]borders of
the land. Is. 9:3 • Or *ends*

16 LORD, [R]in trouble they have visited You,
They poured out a prayer *when* Your
chastening *was* upon them. Hos. 5:15
17 As [R]a woman with child
Is in pain and cries out in her [T]pangs,
When she draws near the time of her
delivery, [John 16:21] • *sharp pains*
So have we been in Your sight, O LORD.
18 We have been with child, we have been
in pain;
We have, as it were, [T]brought forth
wind;
We have not accomplished any
deliverance in the earth,
Nor have [R]the inhabitants of the world
fallen. *given birth to* • Ps. 17:14

19 [R]Your dead shall live; [Ezek. 37:1–14] ☆
Together with my dead body they shall
arise.
Awake and sing, you who dwell in dust;
For your dew *is like* the dew of herbs,
And the earth shall cast out the dead.

20 Come, my people, [R]enter your
chambers,
And shut your doors behind you;
Hide yourself, as it were, [R]for a little
moment, Ex. 12:22, 23 • [Ps. 30:5]
Until the indignation is past.
21 For behold, the LORD [R]comes out of His
place Mic. 1:3
To punish the inhabitants of the earth
for their iniquity;
The earth will also disclose her blood,
And will no more cover her slain.

CHAPTER 27

Israel Blossoms in the Kingdom

IN that day the LORD with His severe
sword, great and strong,
Will punish Leviathan the fleeing
serpent,
[R]Leviathan that twisted serpent;
And He will slay [R]the reptile that *is* in
the sea. Ps. 74:13, 14 • Is. 51:9

2 In that day [R]sing to her, Is. 5:1
[R]"A vineyard of red wine! Is. 5:7
3 [R]I, the LORD, keep it, Is. 31:5
I water it every moment;
Lest any hurt it,
I keep it night and day.
4 Fury *is* not in Me.
Who would set [R]briers *and* thorns
Against Me in battle? 2 Sam. 23:6
I would go through them,
I would burn them together.
5 Or let him take hold of My strength,
That he may make peace with Me;
And he shall make peace with Me."

6 Those who come He shall cause [R]to
take root in Jacob; Is. 37:31
Israel shall blossom and bud,
And fill the face of the world with fruit.

7 [R]Has He struck [T]Israel as He struck
those who struck him?
Or has He been slain according to the
slaughter of those who were slain by
Him? Is. 10:12, 17; 30:30–33 • Lit. *him*
8 [R]In measure, by sending it away,
You contended with it. Job 23:6
[R]He removes *it* by His rough wind
In the day of the east wind. [Ps. 78:38]
9 Therefore by this the iniquity of Jacob
will be covered;
And this *is* all the fruit of taking away
his sin:
When he makes all the stones of the
altar
Like chalkstones that are beaten to
dust,
When [T]wooden images and incense
altars do not stand up. Or *Asherim*

10 Yet the fortified city *will be* [R]desolate,
The habitation forsaken and left like a
wilderness; Is. 5:6, 17; 32:14
There the calf will feed, and there it will
lie down
And consume its branches.
11 When its boughs are withered, they will
be broken off;
The women come *and* set them on fire.
For [R]it *is* a people of no understanding;
Therefore He who made them will [R]not
have mercy on them, Deut. 32:28 • Is. 9:17
And [R]He who formed them will show
them no favor. Deut. 32:18

12 And it shall come to pass in that day
That the LORD will thresh,
From the channel of [T]the River to the
Brook of Egypt; The Euphrates
And you will be [R]gathered one by one,
O you children of Israel. [Is. 11:11; 56:8]

13 [R]So it shall be in that day Is. 2:11
[R]*That* the great trumpet will be blown;
They will come, who are about to perish
in the land of Assyria, Rev. 11:15
And they who are outcasts in the land
of [R]Egypt, Is. 19:21, 22
And shall [R]worship the LORD in the holy
mount at Jerusalem. Zech. 14:16

CHAPTER 28

Woe to Ephraim

WOE to the crown of pride, to the
drunkards of Ephraim,
Whose glorious beauty *is* a fading
flower

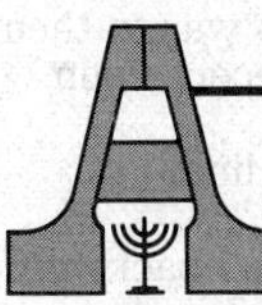

THE CITY OF SAMARIA

Samaria is probably best known as the setting for Jesus' visit with the woman at the well (John 4:5–42). But Samaria's importance as both a city and a region was well established long before the time of Jesus. This ancient city is second only to Jerusalem and Babylon in the number of times it is mentioned in the Bible.

One of the most striking features of Samaria was its hilltop location (see illustration). Built by King Omri about 880 B.C. as the capital of the northern kingdom of Israel, it contributed significantly to the history and culture of ancient Israel.

Samaria was one of the few major Jewish cities actually founded and built from the ground up by the Israelites. They took most of their cities from other nations and then either rebuilt or renovated them into distinctively Jewish population centers.

After succeeding Omri as king, Ahab (reigned 874–853 B.C.) remodeled and expanded Omri's beautiful palace in the city of Samaria. Some of Ahab's decorations, especially the expensive ivory with which he adorned his furniture and palace walls, have been discovered by archaeologists. But in spite of its wealth and splendor, the city fell to the Assyrians in 722 B.C., fulfilling Amos's prophecy of its destruction (Amos 3:11–15). The citizens of Samaria were carried away to Assyria as captives.

After its fall to the Assyrians, Samaria continued to be inhabited by several different groups under the successive authority of Assyria, Babylonia, Persia, Greece, and Rome. Herod the Great, Roman governor of Palestine (ruled 37 B.C.–A.D. 4), made many improvements to the city and renamed it Sebaste—the Greek term for Augustus—in honor of the emperor of Rome. This Herodian city is probably the "city of Samaria" mentioned in the Book of Acts (Acts 8:5).

Photo by Howard Vos

King Omri of the northern kingdom built the city of Samaria on this hill. It was the capital city of Israel until the nation fell in 722 B.C.

Which *is* at the head of the [T]verdant
valleys, Lit. *valleys of fatness*
To those who are overcome with wine!
2 Behold, the Lord has a mighty and
strong one,
[R]Like a tempest of hail and a destroying
storm,
Like a flood of mighty waters
overflowing,
Who will bring *them* down to the earth
with *His* hand. Ezek. 13:11
3 The crown of pride, the drunkards of
Ephraim,
Will be trampled underfoot;
4 And the glorious beauty is a fading
flower
Which *is* at the head of the [T]verdant
valley, Lit. *valley of fatness*
Like the first fruit before the summer,
Which an observer sees;
He eats it up while it is still in his hand.

5 In that day the LORD of hosts will be
For a crown of glory and a diadem of
beauty
To the remnant of His people,
6 For a spirit of justice to him who sits in
judgment,
And for strength to those who turn
back the battle at the gate.

7 But they also [R]have erred through wine,
And through intoxicating drink are out
of the way; Hos. 4:11
[R]The priest and the prophet have erred
through intoxicating drink, Is. 56:10, 12
They are swallowed up by wine,
They are out of the way through
intoxicating drink;
They err in vision, they stumble *in*
judgment.
8 For all tables are full of vomit *and*
filthiness,
So that no place *is clean.*

9 "Whom[R] will he teach knowledge?
And whom will he make to understand
the message? Jer. 6:10
Those *just* weaned from milk?
Those *just* drawn from the breasts?
10 [R]For precept *must be* upon precept,
precept upon precept,
Line upon line, line upon line,
Here a little, there a little." [2 Chr. 36:15]

11 For with [R]stammering lips and another
tongue
He will speak to this people, 1 Cor. 14:21
12 To whom He said, "This *is* the [R]rest
with which
You may cause the weary to rest,"
And, "This *is* the refreshing";
Yet they would not hear. Is. 30:15

13 But the word of the LORD was to them,
"Precept upon precept, precept upon
precept,
Line upon line, line upon line,
Here a little, there a little,"
That they might go and fall backward,
and be broken
And snared and caught.

14 Therefore hear the word of the LORD,
you scornful men,
Who rule this people who *are* in
Jerusalem,
15 Because you have said, "We have made
a covenant with death,
And with Sheol we are in agreement.
When the overflowing scourge passes
through,
It will not come to us,
[R]For we have made lies our refuge,
And under falsehood we have hidden
ourselves." Is. 9:15

16 Therefore thus says the Lord GOD:

"Behold, I lay in Zion [R]a stone for a
foundation, Matt. 21:42; 1 Pet. 2:6–8 ☆
A tried stone, a precious cornerstone, a
sure foundation;
Whoever believes will not act hastily.
17 Also I will make justice the measuring
line,
And righteousness the plummet;
The hail will sweep away the refuge of
lies,
And the waters will overflow the hiding
place.
18 Your covenant with death will be
annulled,
And your agreement with Sheol will not
stand;
When the overflowing scourge passes
through,
Then you will be trampled down by it.
19 As often as it goes out it will take you;
For morning by morning it will pass
over,
And by day and by night;
It will be a terror just to understand the
report."

20 For the bed is too short for *a man* to
stretch out *on*,
And the covering so narrow that he
cannot wrap himself *in it.*
21 For the LORD will rise up as *at* Mount
[R]Perazim, 2 Sam. 5:20
He will be angry as in the Valley of
[R]Gibeon—
That He may do His work, [R]His
awesome work,
And bring to pass His act, His [T]unusual
act. Josh. 10:10, 12 • [Lam. 3:33] • Lit. *foreign*

22 Now therefore, do not be mockers,
Lest your bonds be made strong;
For I have heard from the Lord GOD of
hosts,
[R]A [T]destruction determined even upon
the whole earth. Is. 10:22 • Lit. *complete end*
23 Give ear and hear my voice,
Listen and hear my speech.
24 Does the plowman keep plowing all day
to sow?
Does he keep turning his soil and
breaking the clods?
25 When he has leveled its surface,
Does he not sow the black cummin
And scatter the cummin,
Plant the wheat in rows,
The barley in the appointed place,
And the [T]spelt in its place? *rye*
26 For He instructs him in right judgment,
His God teaches him.

27 For the black cummin is not threshed
with a threshing sledge,
Nor is a cartwheel rolled over the
cummin;
But the black cummin is beaten out
with a stick,
And the cummin with a rod.
28 Bread *flour* must be ground;
Therefore he does not thresh it forever,
Break *it with* his cartwheel,
Or crush it *with* his horsemen.
29 This also comes from the LORD of hosts,
[R]*Who* is wonderful in counsel *and* Ps. 92:5
excellent in [T]guidance. *sound wisdom*

CHAPTER 29

Woe to Ariel (Jerusalem)

"WOE to [T]Ariel, to Ariel, the city
where David dwelt!
Add year to year; Jerusalem, lit. *Lion of God*
Let feasts come around.
2 Yet I will distress Ariel;
There shall be heaviness and sorrow,
And it shall be to Me as Ariel.
3 I will encamp against you all around,
I will lay siege against you with a
mound,
And I will raise siegeworks against you.
4 You shall be brought down,
You shall speak out of the ground;
Your speech shall be low, out of the
dust;
Your voice shall be like a medium's,
[R]out of the ground; Is. 8:19
And your speech shall whisper out of
the dust.

5 "Moreover the multitude of your [R]foes
Shall be like fine dust, Is. 25:5
And the multitude of the terrible ones
Shall be as chaff that passes away;
Yes, it shall be in an instant, suddenly.
6 [R]You will be punished by the LORD of
hosts Is. 28:2; 30:30
With thunder and [R]earthquake and
great noise, Rev. 16:18, 19
With storm and tempest
And the flame of devouring fire.
7 [R]The multitude of all the nations who
fight against [T]Ariel,
Even all who fight against her and her
fortress, Mic. 4:11, 12 • Jerusalem
And distress her,
Shall be as a dream of a night vision.
8 [R]It shall even be as when a hungry man
dreams,
And look—he eats;
But he awakes, and his soul is still
empty;
Or as when a thirsty man dreams,
And look—he drinks;
But he awakes, and indeed *he is* faint,
And his soul still craves:
So the multitude of all the nations shall
be,
Who fight against Mount Zion." Ps. 73:20

9 Pause and wonder!
Blind yourselves and be blind!
[R]They are drunk, [R]but not with wine;
They stagger, but not with intoxicating
drink. Is. 28:7, 8 • Is. 51:21
10 For [R]the LORD has poured out on you
The spirit of deep sleep, Rom. 11:8
And has [R]closed your eyes, namely, the
prophets; Ps. 69:23
And He has covered your heads,
namely, [R]the seers. Is. 44:18

11 The whole vision has become to you like
the words of a [T]book [R]that is sealed, which
men deliver to one who is literate, saying,
"Read this, please"; [R]and he says, "I cannot,
for it *is* sealed." *scroll* • Is. 8:16 • Dan. 12:4, 9
12 Then the book is delivered to one who [T]is
illiterate, saying, "Read this, please"; and he
says, "I am not literate." Lit. *does not know books*
13 Therefore the LORD said:

[R]"Inasmuch as these people draw near *to*
Me with their mouths Ezek. 33:31
And honor Me [R]with their lips, Col. 2:22
But have removed their hearts far from
Me,
And their fear toward Me is taught by
the commandment of men,
14 [R]Therefore, behold, I will again do a
marvelous work
Among this people,
A marvelous work and a wonder;
[R]For the wisdom of their wise men shall
perish,
And the understanding of their prudent
men shall be hidden." Hab. 1:5 • Jer. 49:7

15 [R]Woe to those who seek deep to hide
their counsel far from the LORD,
And their works are in the dark;
[R]They say, "Who sees us?" and, "Who
knows us?" Is. 30:1 • Ps. 10:11; 94:7
16 Surely you have things turned around!
Shall the potter be esteemed as the
clay;
For shall the [R]thing made say of him
who made it,
"He did not make me"?
Or shall the thing formed say of him
who formed it,
"He has no understanding"? Is. 45:9

17 *Is* it not yet a very little while
Till [R]Lebanon shall be turned into a
fruitful field,
And the fruitful field be esteemed as a
forest? Is. 32:15
18 [R]In that day the deaf shall hear the
words of the book, Is. 35:5
And the eyes of the blind shall see out
of obscurity and out of darkness.
19 [R]The humble also shall increase *their* joy
in the LORD, [Is. 11:4; 61:1]
And [R]the poor among men shall rejoice
In the Holy One of Israel. [James 2:5]
20 For the [T]terrible one is brought to
nothing,
[R]The scornful one is consumed,
And all who [R]watch for iniquity are cut
off— *terrifying* • Is. 28:14 • Mic. 2:1
21 Who make a man an offender by a
word,
And [R]lay a snare for him who reproves
in the gate,
And turn aside the just [R]for a thing of
naught. Amos 5:10, 12 • Prov. 28:21

22 Therefore thus says the LORD, [R]who redeemed Abraham, concerning the house of
Jacob: Josh. 24:3

"Jacob shall not now be [R]ashamed,
Nor shall his face now grow pale; Is. 45:17
23 But when he sees his children,
[R]The work of My hands, in his midst,
They will hallow My name,
And hallow the Holy One of Jacob,
And fear the God of Israel. [Is. 45:11]
24 These also [R]who erred in spirit will
come to understanding,
And those who murmured will learn
doctrine." Is. 28:7

CHAPTER 30

Woe to Egyptian Alliance

"WOE to the rebellious children," says
the LORD,
[R]"Who take counsel, but not of Me,
And who [T]devise plans, but not of My
Spirit, Is. 29:15 • Lit. *weave a web*
[R]That they may add sin to sin; Deut. 29:19
2 [R]Who walk to go down to Egypt,
And [R]have not asked My advice,
To strengthen themselves in the
strength of Pharaoh, Is. 31:1 • Josh. 9:14
And to trust in the shadow of Egypt!
3 [R]Therefore the strength of Pharaoh
Shall be your shame,
And trust in the shadow of Egypt
Shall be *your* humiliation. Is. 20:5
4 For his princes were at [R]Zoan, Is. 19:11
And his ambassadors came to Hanes.
5 [R]They were all ashamed of a people *who*
could not benefit them,
Or be help or benefit, Jer. 2:36
But a shame and also a reproach."

6 [R]The [T]burden against the beasts of the
South. Is. 57:9 • *oracle, prophecy*

Through a land of trouble and anguish,
From which *came* the lioness and lion,
[R]The viper and fiery flying serpent,
They will carry their riches on the
backs of young donkeys, Deut. 8:15
And their treasures on the humps of
camels,
To a people *who* shall not benefit *them;*
7 [R]For the Egyptians shall help in vain and
to no purpose. Jer. 37:7
Therefore I have called her
[T]Rahab-Hem-Shebeth. Lit. *Rahab Sits Idle*
8 Now go, [R]write it before them on a
tablet,
And note it on a scroll,
That it may be for time to come,
Forever and ever: Hab. 2:2
9 That [R]this *is* a rebellious people,
Lying children,
Children *who* will not hear the law of
the LORD; Is. 1:2, 4; 65:2
10 [R]Who say to the seers, "Do not see,"
And to the prophets, "Do not prophesy
to us right things;
[R]Speak to us smooth things, prophesy
deceits. Jer. 11:21 • 1 Kin. 22:8, 13
11 Get out of the way,
Turn aside from the path,
Cause the Holy One of Israel
To cease from before us."

12 Therefore thus says the Holy One of
Israel:

"Because you [R]despise this word,
And trust in oppression and perversity,
And rely on them, Is. 5:24
13 Therefore this iniquity shall be to you
[R]Like a breach ready to fall,
A bulge in a high wall,

ISRAEL AND THE EGYPTIANS

The history of Egypt stretches back to about 3000 B.C., at least a thousand years before the time of Abraham. During their formative years as a nation, the Hebrew people spent 430 years as slaves in Egypt (Ex. 12:40) before they were released miraculously through God's power under the leadership of Moses.

According to the table of nations in the Book of Genesis, Egypt was founded by Mizraim, one of the sons of Ham (Gen. 10:6, 13, 14). In the Old Testament, Egypt is referred to in a symbolic way as Mizraim (1 Chr. 1:8, 11).

Soon after arriving in the land of Canaan about 2000 B.C., Abraham migrated into Egypt for a time to escape a famine (Gen. 12:10). Still later, Joseph was sold into Egyptian slavery by his brothers (Gen. 37:12–36). Joseph rose to a position of prominence in the cabinet of the Egyptian Pharaoh (Gen. 41:37–46). This led Joseph's family to move to Egypt, and the Hebrew people were eventually enslaved when a new line of Pharaohs rose to power (Ex. 1:6–14).

After the Exodus of the Hebrews from Egypt, the once-powerful Egyptian Empire declined in strength and influence, becoming a second-rate political power. During the time of David and Solomon (about 1000 B.C.), Egypt's weakness and fragmentation contributed to the establishment of Israel as a strong nation. During Isaiah's time, about 730 B.C., the prophet warned the king of Judah about forming an alliance with Egypt against the Assyrians, predicting that "trust in the shadow of Egypt shall be *your* humiliation" (Is. 30:3).

The Egyptians worshiped many gods. Many of these were the personification of nature, including the earth, sun, and sky. Even the Nile River was thought to be divine, because its periodic flooding enriched the soil of the Nile delta for a premium agricultural harvest. Several of the plagues God sent upon the Egyptians (Ex. 7—12) affected the Nile, proving the weakness of the entire Egyptian religious system.

Great sphinx at Giza, Egypt.

Whose breaking [R]comes suddenly, in an
instant. Ps. 62:3, 4 • Is. 29:5
14 And [R]He shall break it like the breaking
of the potter's vessel, Jer. 19:11
Which is broken in pieces;
He shall not spare.
So there shall not be found among its
fragments
A shard to take fire from the hearth,
Or to take water from the cistern."

15 For thus says the Lord GOD, the Holy
One of Israel:

[R]"In returning and rest you shall be
saved;
In quietness and confidence shall be
your strength."
[R]But you would not, Is. 7:4; 28:12 • Matt. 23:37
16 And you said, "No, for we will flee on
horses"—
Therefore you shall flee!
And, "We will ride on swift *horses*"—
Therefore those who pursue you shall
be swift!

17 [R]One thousand *shall flee* at the threat of
one, Josh. 23:10
At the threat of five you shall flee,
Till you are left as a [T]pole on top of a
mountain A tree stripped of branches
And as a banner on a hill.

18 Therefore the LORD will wait, that He
may be [R]gracious to you; Is. 33:2
And therefore He will be exalted, that
He may have mercy on you.
For the LORD *is* a God of justice;
Blessed *are* all those who wait for Him.

19 For the people [R]shall dwell in Zion at
Jerusalem; Is. 65:9
You shall [R]weep no more. Is. 25:8
He will be very gracious to you at the
sound of your cry;
When He hears it, He will answer you.
20 And *though* the Lord gives you
[R]The bread of adversity and the water of
[T]affliction, 1 Kin. 22:27 • *oppression*
Yet [R]your teachers will not be moved
into a corner anymore, Amos 8:11
But your eyes shall see your teachers.
21 Your ears shall hear a word behind you,
saying,
"This *is* the way, walk in it,"
Whenever you [R]turn to the right hand
Or whenever you turn to the left. Josh. 1:7
22 [R]You will also defile the covering of your
graven images of silver, Is. 2:20; 31:7
And the ornament of your molded
images of gold.
You will throw them away as an
unclean thing;
You will say to them, "Get away!"

23 [R]Then He will give the rain for your seed
With which you sow the ground,
And bread of the increase of the earth;
It will be [T]fat and plenteous.
In that day your cattle will feed
In large pastures. [Matt. 6:33] • *rich*
24 Likewise the oxen and the young
donkeys that work the ground
Will eat cured fodder,
Which has been winnowed with the
shovel and fan.
25 There will be [R]on every high mountain
And on every high hill Is. 2:14, 15
Rivers *and* streams of waters,
In the day of the [R]great slaughter,
When the towers fall. Is. 2:10–21; 34:2
26 Moreover [R]the light of the moon will be
as the light of the sun, [Is. 60:19, 20]
And the light of the sun will be
sevenfold,
As the light of seven days,
In the day that the LORD binds up the
bruise of His people
And heals the stroke of their wound.

27 Behold, the name of the LORD comes
from afar,
Burning *with* His anger,
And *His* burden *is* heavy;
His lips are full of indignation,
And His tongue like a devouring fire;
28 [R]His breath is like an overflowing
stream, Is. 11:4
[R]Which reaches up to the neck,
To sift the nations with the sieve of
futility; Is. 8:8
And *there shall be* [R]a bridle in the jaws
of the people, Is. 37:29
Causing *them* to err.

29 You shall have a song
As in the night *when* a holy festival is
kept,
And gladness of heart as when one goes
with a flute,
To come into [R]the mountain of the
LORD, [Is. 2:3]
To [T]the Mighty One of Israel. Lit. *the Rock*
30 [R]The LORD will cause His glorious voice
to be heard,
And show the descent of His arm,
With the indignation of *His* anger
And the flame of a devouring fire,
With scattering, tempest, [R]and
hailstones. Is. 29:6 • Is. 28:2
31 For through the voice of the LORD
Assyria will be [T]beaten down, Lit. *shattered*
[R]*Who* struck with a rod. Is. 10:5, 24

32 And *in* every place where the staff of
punishment passes,
Which the LORD lays on him,
It will be with tambourines and harps;
And in battles of [R]brandishing He will
fight with it. Is. 11:15
33 [R]For Tophet *was* established of old,
Yes, for the king it is prepared.
He has made *it* deep and large;
Its pyre *is* fire with much wood;
The breath of the LORD, like a stream of
brimstone,
Kindles it. Jer. 7:31

CHAPTER 31

WOE to those [R]who go down to Egypt
for help, Is. 30:1, 2
And [R]rely on horses, Ps. 20:7
Who trust in chariots because *they are*
many,
And in horsemen because they are very
strong,
But who do not look to the Holy One of
Israel,
[R]Nor seek the LORD! Dan. 9:13
2 Yet He also *is* wise and will bring
disaster,
And [R]will not [T]call back His words,
But will arise against the house of
evildoers,
And against the help of those who work
iniquity. Num. 23:19 • Retract
3 Now the Egyptians *are* men, and not
God;
And their horses are flesh, and not
spirit.
When the LORD stretches out His hand,
Both he who helps will fall,
And he who is helped will fall down;
They all will perish [R]together. Is. 20:6

4 For thus the LORD has spoken to me:

[R]"As a lion roars, Hos. 11:10
And a young lion over his prey
(When a multitude of shepherds is
summoned against him,
He will not be afraid of their voice
Nor be disturbed by their noise),
So the LORD of hosts will come down
To fight for Mount Zion and for its hill.
5 [R]Like birds flying about, Deut. 32:11
So will the LORD of hosts defend
Jerusalem.
Defending, He will also deliver *it*;
Passing over, He will preserve *it*."

6 Return *to Him* against whom the children of Israel have [R]deeply revolted. Hos. 9:9
7 For in that day every man shall [R]throw
away his idols of silver and his idols of gold—
[R]sin, which your own hands have made for
yourselves. Is. 2:20; 30:22 • 1 Kin. 12:30

8 "Then Assyria shall [R]fall by a sword not
of man,
And a sword not of mankind shall
[R]devour him.
But he shall flee from the sword,
And his young men shall become forced
labor. 2 Kin. 19:35, 36 • Is. 37:36
9 [R]He shall cross over to his stronghold for
fear, Is. 37:37
And his princes shall be afraid of the
banner,"
Says the LORD,
Whose fire *is* in Zion
And whose furnace *is* in Jerusalem.

CHAPTER 32

Behold the Coming King

BEHOLD, [R]a king will reign in
righteousness, Ps. 45:1
And princes will rule with justice.
2 A man will be as a hiding place from
the wind,
And [R]a [T]cover from the tempest,
As rivers of water in a dry place,
As the shadow of a great rock in a
weary land. Is. 4:6 • *shelter*
3 [R]The eyes of those who see will not be
dim,
And the ears of those who hear will
listen. Is. 29:18; 35:5
4 Also the heart of the [T]rash will
[R]understand knowledge,
And the tongue of the stammerers will
be ready to speak plainly. *hasty* • Is. 29:24

5 The foolish person will no longer be
called [T]generous,
Nor the miser said *to be* bountiful; *noble*
6 For the foolish person will speak
foolishness,
And his heart will work [R]iniquity:
To practice ungodliness,
To utter error against the LORD,
To keep the hungry unsatisfied,
And he will cause the drink of the
thirsty to fail. Prov. 24:7–9
7 Also the schemes of the schemer *are*
evil;
He devises wicked plans
To destroy the poor with lying words,
Even when the needy speaks justice.
8 But a [T]generous man devises generous
things,
And by generosity he shall stand. *noble*

9 Rise up, you women [R]who are at ease,
Hear my voice;
You complacent daughters,
Give ear to my speech. Amos 6:1

10 In a year and *some* days
You will be troubled, you complacent women;
For the vintage will fail,
The gathering will not come.
11 Tremble, you *women* who are at ease;
Be troubled, you complacent ones;
Strip yourselves, make yourselves bare,
And gird *sackcloth* on *your* waists.

12 People shall mourn upon their breasts
For the pleasant fields, for the fruitful vine.
13 [R]On the land of my people will come up thorns *and* briers,
Yes, on all the happy homes *in* [R]the joyous city; Hos. 9:6 • Is. 22:2
14 [R]Because the palaces will be forsaken,
The bustling city will be deserted.
The forts and towers will become lairs forever,
A joy of wild donkeys, a pasture of flocks— Is. 27:10
15 Until [R]the Spirit is poured upon us from on high,
And [R]the wilderness becomes a fruitful field,
And the fruitful field is counted as a forest. [Joel 2:28] • Is. 29:17

16 Then justice will dwell in the wilderness,
And righteousness remain in the fruitful field.
17 [R]The work of righteousness will be peace, James 3:18
And the effect of righteousness, quietness and assurance forever.
18 My people will dwell in a peaceful habitation,
In secure dwellings, and in quiet [R]resting places, [Zech. 2:5; 3:10]
19 [R]Though hail comes down [R]on the forest,
And the city is brought low in humiliation. Is. 30:30 • Zech. 11:2

20 Blessed *are* you who sow beside all waters,
Who send out freely the feet of [R]the ox and the donkey. Is. 30:23, 24

CHAPTER 33

Woe to the Spoiler of Jerusalem (Assyria)

WOE to you [R]who plunder, though you *have* not *been* plundered; Hab. 2:8
And you who deal treacherously, though they have not dealt treacherously with you!
[R]When you cease plundering, Rev. 13:10
You will be [R]plundered; Is. 10:12; 14:25; 31:8
And when you make an end of dealing treacherously,
They will deal treacherously with you.

2 O LORD, be gracious to us;
[R]We have waited for You. Is. 25:9; 26:8
Be their arm every morning,
Our salvation also in the time of trouble.
3 At the noise of the tumult the people [R]shall flee;
When You lift Yourself up, the nations shall be scattered; Is. 17:13
4 And Your plunder shall be gathered
Like the gathering of the caterpillar;
As the running to and fro of locusts,
He shall run upon them.

5 [R]The LORD is exalted, for He dwells on high;
He has filled Zion with justice and righteousness. Ps. 97:9
6 Wisdom and knowledge will be the stability of your times,
And the strength of salvation;
The fear of the LORD *is* His treasure.

7 Surely their valiant ones shall cry outside,
[R]The ambassadors of peace shall weep bitterly. 2 Kin. 18:18, 37
8 [R]The highways lie waste,
The wayfaring man ceases.
[R]He has broken the covenant,
He has despised the cities,
He regards no man. Judg. 5:6 • 2 Kin. 18:13–17
9 [R]The earth mourns *and* languishes,
Lebanon is shamed *and* shriveled;
Sharon is like a wilderness,
And Bashan and Carmel shake off *their fruits.* Is. 24:4

10 "Now[R] I will rise," says the LORD;
"Now I will be exalted,
Now I will lift Myself up. Ps. 12:5
11 [R]You shall conceive chaff, [Ps. 7:14]
You shall bring forth stubble;
Your breath, *as* fire, shall devour you.
12 And the people shall be *like* the burnings of lime;
[R]*Like* thorns cut up they shall be burned in the fire. Is. 9:18
13 Hear, [R]you *who are* afar off, what I have done;
And you *who are* near, acknowledge My might." Is. 49:1

14 The sinners in Zion are afraid;
Fearfulness has seized the hypocrites:
"Who among us shall dwell with the devouring [R]fire?
Who among us shall dwell with everlasting burnings?" Heb. 12:29

15 He who [R]walks righteously and speaks
uprightly, Ps. 15:2; 24:3, 4
He who despises the gain of
oppressions,
Who gestures with his hands, refusing
bribes,
Who stops his ears from hearing of
bloodshed,
And shuts his eyes from seeing evil:
16 He will dwell on [T]high;
His place of defense *will be* the fortress
of rocks;
Bread will be given him,
His water *will be* sure. Lit. *heights*
17 Your eyes will see the King in His
[R]beauty;
They will see the land that is very far
off. Ps. 27:4
18 Your heart will meditate on terror:
[R]"Where *is* the scribe? 1 Cor. 1:20
Where *is* he who weighs?
Where *is* he who counts the towers?"
19 [R]You will not see a fierce people,
[R]A people of obscure speech, beyond
perception, 2 Kin. 19:32 • Jer. 5:15
Of a [T]stammering tongue *that you*
cannot understand. Unintelligible speech

20 [R]Look upon Zion, the city of our
appointed feasts; Ps. 48:12
Your eyes will see [R]Jerusalem, a quiet
habitation, Ps. 46:5; 125:1
A tabernacle *that* will not be taken
down;
[R]Not one of [R]its stakes will ever be
removed, Is. 37:33 • Is. 54:2
Nor will any of its cords be broken.
21 But there the majestic LORD *will be* for
us
A place of broad rivers *and* streams,
In which no [T]galley with oars will sail,
Nor majestic ships pass by *ship*
22 (For the LORD *is* our [R]Judge, [Acts 10:42]
The LORD *is* our [R]Lawgiver, James 4:12
[R]The LORD *is* our King; Ps. 89:18
He will save us);
23 Your tackle is loosed,
They could not strengthen their mast,
They could not spread the sail.

Then the prey of great plunder is
divided;
The lame take the prey.
24 And the inhabitant will not say, "I am
sick";
[R]The people who dwell in it *will be*
forgiven *their* iniquity. Is. 40:2

CHAPTER 34

Woe to the Nations

COME [R]near, you nations, to hear;
And heed, you people!
[R]Let the earth hear, and all that is in it,
The world and all things that come
forth from it. Ps. 49:1 • Deut. 32:1
2 For the indignation of the LORD *is*
against all nations,
And *His* fury against all their armies;
He has utterly destroyed them,
He has given them over to the
[R]slaughter. Is. 13:5
3 Also their slain shall be thrown out;
[R]Their stench shall rise from their
corpses,
And the mountains shall be melted with
their blood. Joel 2:20
4 [R]All the host of heaven shall be
dissolved, Is. 13:13
And the heavens shall be rolled up like
a scroll;
[R]All their host shall fall down Is. 14:12
As the leaf falls from the vine,
And as *fruit* falling from a fig tree.

5 "For [R]My sword shall be bathed in
heaven;
Indeed it [R]shall come down on Edom,
And on the people of My curse, for
judgment. Jer. 46:10 • Mal. 1:4
6 The [R]sword of the LORD is filled with
blood,
It is made [T]overflowing with fatness,
And with the blood of lambs and goats,
With the fat of the kidneys of rams.
For [R]the LORD has a sacrifice in Bozrah,
And a great slaughter in the land of
Edom. Is. 66:16 • Lit. *fat* • Zeph. 1:7
7 The wild oxen shall come down with
them,
And the young bulls with the mighty
bulls;
Their land shall be soaked with blood,
And their dust saturated with fatness."

8 For *it is* the day of the LORD's
[R]vengeance, Is. 63:4
The year of recompense for the cause of
Zion.
9 [R]Its streams shall be turned into pitch,
And its dust into brimstone; Deut. 29:23
Its land shall become burning pitch.
10 It shall not be quenched night or day;
[R]Its smoke shall ascend forever.
[R]From generation to generation it shall
lie waste;
No one shall pass through it forever and
ever. Rev. 14:11; 18:18; 19:3 • Mal. 1:3, 4
11 But the [T]pelican and the [T]porcupine
shall possess it, Or *owl* • Or *hedgehog*
Also the owl and the raven shall dwell
in it.
And [R]He shall stretch out over it Lam. 2:8
The line of confusion and the stones of
emptiness.
12 They shall call its nobles to the
kingdom,

But none *shall be* there, and all its
princes shall be nothing.

13 And [R]thorns shall come up in its
palaces, Is. 32:13
Nettles and brambles in its fortresses;
[R]It shall be a habitation of jackals,
A courtyard for ostriches. Is. 13:21
14 The wild beasts of the desert shall also
meet with the [T]jackals,
And the wild goat shall bleat to its
companion; Lit. *howling creatures*
Also the night creature shall rest there,
And find for herself a place of rest.
15 There the arrow snake shall make her
nest and lay *eggs*
And hatch, and gather *them* under her
shadow;
There also shall the hawks be gathered,
Every one with her mate.

16 "Search from [R]the book of the LORD, and
read: [Mal. 3:16]
Not one of these shall fail;
Not one shall lack her mate.
For My mouth has commanded it, and
His Spirit has gathered them.
17 He has cast the lot for them,
And His hand has divided it among
them with a measuring line.
They shall possess it forever;
From generation to generation they
shall dwell in it."

CHAPTER 35

Behold the Coming Kingdom

THE [R]wilderness and the [T]wasteland shall
be glad for them, Is. 32:15; 55:12 • *desert*
And the [R]desert[T] shall rejoice and
blossom as the rose; Is. 41:19 • Heb. *Arabah*
2 [R]It shall blossom abundantly and rejoice,
Even with joy and singing. Is. 32:15
The glory of Lebanon shall be given to
it,
The excellence of Carmel and Sharon.
They shall see the [R]glory of the LORD,
The excellency of our God. Is. 40:5

3 Strengthen the [T]weak hands, Lit. *sinking*
And make firm the feeble knees.
4 Say to those *who are* fearful-hearted,
"Be strong, do not fear!
Behold, your God will come *with*
[R]vengeance, Is. 34:8
With the recompense of God;
He will come and [R]save you." Is. 33:22☆

5 Then the [R]eyes of the blind shall be
opened,
And [R]the ears of the deaf shall be
unstopped. Is. 29:18; John 9:6, 7☆ • [Matt. 11:5]
6 Then the [R]lame shall leap like a deer,
And the [R]tongue of the dumb sing.
For [R]waters shall burst forth in the
wilderness, Matt. 15:30☆ • Is. 32:4 • [John 7:38]
And streams in the desert.
7 The parched ground shall become a
pool,
And the thirsty land springs of water;
In [R]the habitation of jackals, where
each lay, Is. 34:13
There shall be grass with reeds and
rushes.

8 A [R]highway shall be there, and a road,
And it shall be called the Highway of
Holiness. Is. 19:23
[R]The unclean shall not pass over it,
But it *shall be* for others. Joel 3:17
Whoever walks the road, although a
fool,
Shall not go astray.
9 [R]No lion shall be there, Lev. 26:6
Nor shall *any* ravenous beast go up on
it;
It shall not be found there.
But the redeemed shall walk *there*,
10 And the [R]ransomed of the LORD shall
return,
And come to Zion with singing,
With everlasting joy on their heads.
They shall obtain joy and gladness,
And [R]sorrow and sighing shall flee
away. Is. 51:11 • [Rev. 7:17; 21:4]

CHAPTER 36

Assyria Challenges God
2 Kin. 18:13–37; 2 Chr. 32:1–19

NOW it came to pass in the fourteenth
year of King Hezekiah *that* Sennacherib king of Assyria came up against all the
fortified cities of Judah and took them.
2 Then the king of Assyria sent *the* [T]Rab-
shakeh with a great army from Lachish to
King Hezekiah at Jerusalem. And he stood by
the aqueduct from the upper pool, on the
highway to the Fuller's Field. A title
3 And [R]Eliakim the son of Hilkiah, who
was over the household, [R]Shebna the scribe,
and Joah the son of Asaph, the recorder,
came out to him. Is. 22:20 • Is. 22:15
4 [R]Then *the* Rabshakeh said to them, "Say
now to Hezekiah, 'Thus says the great king,
the king of Assyria: "What confidence is this
in which you trust? 2 Kin. 18:19
5 "I say you speak of having counsel and
strength for war; but *they are* [T]vain words.
Now in whom do you trust, that you rebel
against me? Lit. *a word of the lips*
6 "Look! You are trusting in the [R]staff of
this broken reed, Egypt, on which if a man
leans, it will go into his hand and pierce it. So

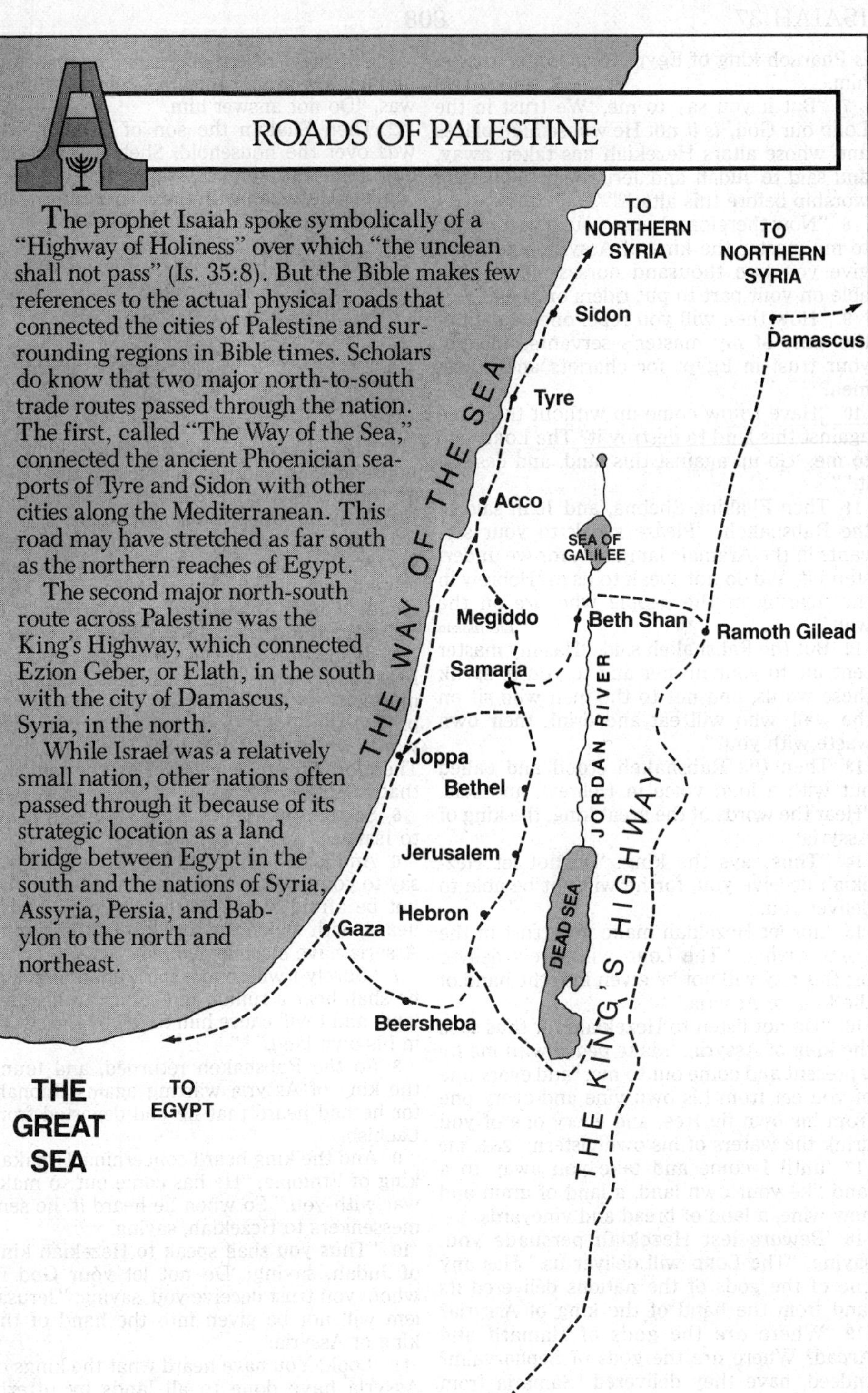

The prophet Isaiah spoke symbolically of a "Highway of Holiness" over which "the unclean shall not pass" (Is. 35:8). But the Bible makes few references to the actual physical roads that connected the cities of Palestine and surrounding regions in Bible times. Scholars do know that two major north-to-south trade routes passed through the nation. The first, called "The Way of the Sea," connected the ancient Phoenician seaports of Tyre and Sidon with other cities along the Mediterranean. This road may have stretched as far south as the northern reaches of Egypt.

The second major north-south route across Palestine was the King's Highway, which connected Ezion Geber, or Elath, in the south with the city of Damascus, Syria, in the north.

While Israel was a relatively small nation, other nations often passed through it because of its strategic location as a land bridge between Egypt in the south and the nations of Syria, Assyria, Persia, and Babylon to the north and northeast.

is Pharaoh king of Egypt to all who [R]trust in
him. Ezek. 29:6 • Ps. 146:3
7 "But if you say to me, 'We trust in the
LORD our God,' *is it* not He whose high places
and whose altars Hezekiah has taken away,
and said to Judah and Jerusalem, 'You shall
worship before this altar'?" '
8 "Now therefore, I urge you, give a pledge
to my master the king of Assyria, and I will
give you two thousand horses—if you are
able on your part to put riders on them!
9 "How then will you repel one captain of
the least of my master's servants, and put
your trust in Egypt for chariots and horsemen?
10 "Have I now come up without the LORD
against this land to destroy it? The LORD said
to me, 'Go up against this land, and destroy
it.' "
11 Then Eliakim, Shebna, and Joah said to
the Rabshakeh, "Please speak to your servants in the Aramaic language, for we understand *it*; and do not speak to us in [T]Hebrew in
the hearing of the people who *are* on the
wall." Lit. *Judean*
12 But *the* Rabshakeh said, "Has my master
sent me to your master and to you to speak
these words, and not to the men who sit on
the wall, who will eat and drink their own
waste with you?"
13 Then *the* Rabshakeh stood and called
out with a loud voice in Hebrew, and said,
"Hear the words of the great king, the king of
Assyria!
14 "Thus says the king: 'Do not let Hezekiah deceive you, for he will not be able to
deliver you;
15 'nor let Hezekiah make you trust in the
LORD, saying, "The LORD will surely deliver
us; this city will not be given into the hand of
the king of Assyria." '
16 "Do not listen to Hezekiah; for thus says
the king of Assyria: 'Make *peace* with me *by
a* present and come out to me; [R]and every one
of you eat from his own vine and every one
from his own fig tree, and every one of you
drink the waters of his own cistern; Zech. 3:10
17 'until I come and take you away to a
land like your own land, a land of grain and
new wine, a land of bread and vineyards.
18 '*Beware* lest Hezekiah persuade you,
saying, "The LORD will deliver us." Has any
one of the gods of the nations delivered its
land from the hand of the king of Assyria?
19 'Where *are* the gods of Hamath and
Arpad? Where *are* the gods of Sepharvaim?
Indeed, have they delivered [R]Samaria from
my hand? 2 Kin. 17:6
20 'Who among all the gods of these lands
have delivered their countries from my hand,
that the LORD should deliver Jerusalem from
my hand?' "
21 But they [T]held their peace and answered
him not a word; for the king's commandment
was, "Do not answer him." *were silent*
22 Then Eliakim the son of Hilkiah, who
was over the household, Shebna the scribe,
and Joah the son of Asaph, the recorder,
came to Hezekiah with *their* clothes torn, and
told him the words of *the* Rabshakeh.

CHAPTER 37

God Destroys Assyria—2 Kin. 19:1-37

AND [R]so it was, when King Hezekiah
heard *it*, that he tore his clothes, covered himself with sackcloth, and went into
the house of the LORD. 2 Kin. 19:1-37
2 Then he sent Eliakim, who *was* over the
household, Shebna the scribe, and the elders
of the priests, covered with sackcloth, to
Isaiah the prophet, the son of Amoz.
3 And they said to him, "Thus says Hezekiah: 'This day *is* a day of [R]trouble and
rebuke and [T]blasphemy; for the children have
come to birth, but *there is* no strength to
bring them forth. Is. 22:5; 26:16; 33:2 • *contempt*
4 'It may be that the LORD your God will
hear the words of *the* Rabshakeh, whom his
master the king of Assyria has sent to [R]re-
proach the living God, and will reprove the
words which the LORD your God has heard.
Therefore lift up *your* prayer for the remnant
that is left.' " Is. 36:15, 18, 20
5 So the servants of King Hezekiah came
to Isaiah.
6 And Isaiah said to them, "Thus shall you
say to your master, 'Thus says the LORD: "Do
not be afraid of the words which you have
heard, with which the servants of the king of
Assyria have blasphemed Me.
7 "Surely I will send a spirit upon him, and
he shall hear a rumor and return to his own
land; and I will cause him to fall by the sword
in his own land." ' "
8 So *the* Rabshakeh returned, and found
the king of Assyria warring against Libnah,
for he had heard that he had departed from
Lachish.
9 And the king heard concerning Tirhakah
king of Ethiopia, "He has come out to make
war with you." So when he heard *it*, he sent
messengers to Hezekiah, saying,
10 "Thus you shall speak to Hezekiah king
of Judah, saying: 'Do not let your God in
whom you trust deceive you, saying, "Jerusalem will not be given into the hand of the
king of Assyria."
11 'Look! You have heard what the kings of
Assyria have done to all lands by utterly
destroying them; and will you be delivered?
12 'Have the [R]gods of the nations delivered
those whom my fathers have destroyed, Gozan and Haran and Rezeph, and the people of
Eden who *were* in Telassar? Is. 36:18, 19

13 ‘Where *is* the king of [R]Hamath, the king
of Arpad, and the king of the city of Sepharvaim, Hena, and Ivah?’ ” Is. 49:23
14 And Hezekiah received the letter from
the hand of the messengers, and read it; and
Hezekiah went up to the house of the LORD,
and spread it before the LORD.
15 Then Hezekiah prayed to the LORD, saying:
16 “O LORD of hosts, God of Israel, *the One*
who dwells *between* the cherubim, You *are*
God, You alone, of all the kingdoms of the
earth. You have made heaven and earth.
17 [R]“Incline Your ear, O LORD, and hear;
open Your eyes, O LORD, and see; and [R]hear
all the words of Sennacherib, who has sent to
reproach the living God. Dan. 9:18 • Ps. 74:22
18 “Truly, LORD, the kings of Assyria have
laid waste all the nations and their lands,
19 “and have cast their gods into the fire;
for they *were* [R]not gods, but the work of
men’s hands—wood and stone. Therefore
they have destroyed them. Is. 40:19, 20
20 “Now therefore, O LORD our God, [R]save
us from his hand, that all the kingdoms of the
earth may [R]know that You *are* the LORD, You
alone.” Is. 33:22 • Ps. 83:18
21 Then Isaiah the son of Amoz sent to
Hezekiah, saying, “Thus says the LORD God
of Israel, ‘Because you have prayed to Me
against Sennacherib king of Assyria,
22 ‘this *is* the word which the LORD has
spoken concerning him:

“The virgin, the daughter of Zion,
Has despised you, laughed you to scorn;
The daughter of Jerusalem has shaken
her head behind your back!

23 “Whom have you reproached and
blasphemed?
Against whom have you raised *your*
voice,
And lifted up your eyes on high?
Against the Holy One of Israel.
24 By your servants you have reproached
the Lord,
And said, ‘By the multitude of my
chariots
I have come up to the height of the
mountains,
To the limits of Lebanon;
I will cut down its tall cedars
And its choice cypress trees;
I will enter its farthest height,
To its fruitful forest.
25 I have dug and drunk water,
And with the soles of my feet I have
dried up
All the brooks of [T]defense.’ Or perhaps *Egypt*

26 “Did you not hear [R]long ago
How I made it,
From ancient times that I formed it?
Now I have brought it to pass,
That you should be
For crushing fortified cities into heaps
of ruins. Is. 25:1; 40:21; 45:21
27 Therefore their inhabitants *had* little
power;
They were dismayed and confounded;
They were *as* the grass of the field
And *as* the green herb,
As the grass on the housetops
And *as grain* blighted before it is
grown.

28 “But I know your dwelling place,
Your going out and your coming in,
And your rage against Me.
29 Because your rage against Me and your
tumult
Have come up to My ears,
Therefore [R]I will put My hook in your
nose Is. 30:28
And My bridle in your lips,
And I will [R]turn you back Ezek. 38:4; 39:2
By the way which you came.” ’

30 “This *shall be* a sign to you:

You shall eat *this* year such as grows of
itself,
And the second year what springs from
the same;
Also in the third year sow and reap,
Plant vineyards, and eat the fruit of
them.
31 And the remnant who have escaped of
the house of Judah
Shall again take root downward,
And bear fruit upward.
32 For out of Jerusalem shall go a
remnant,
And those who escape from Mount
Zion.
The [R]zeal of the LORD of hosts will do
this. 2 Kin. 19:31

33 “Therefore thus says the LORD
concerning the king of Assyria:

‘He shall not come into this city,
Nor shoot an arrow there,
Nor come before it with shield,
Nor build a siege mound against it.
34 By the way that he came,
By the same shall he return;
And he shall not come into this city,’
Says the LORD.
35 ‘For I will [R]defend this city, to save it
For My own sake and for My servant
[R]David’s sake.’ ” Is. 31:5; 38:6 • 1 Kin. 11:13

36 Then the [T]angel of the LORD went out,
and killed in the camp of the Assyrians one
hundred and eighty-five thousand; and when

[T]people arose early in the morning, there
were the corpses—all dead. Or *Angel* • Lit. *they*
37 So Sennacherib king of Assyria departed
and went away, returned *home*, and remained at Nineveh.
38 Now it came to pass, as he was worshiping in the house of Nisroch his god, that
Adrammelech and Sharezer his sons struck
him down with the sword; and they escaped
into the land of Ararat. Then [R]Esarhaddon his
son reigned in his place. Ezra 4:2

CHAPTER 38

Hezekiah's Salvation from Sickness

IN those days Hezekiah was sick and near
death. And Isaiah the prophet, the son of
Amoz, went to him and said to him, "Thus
says the LORD: [R]'Set your house in order, for
you shall die and not live.' " 2 Sam. 17:23
2 Then Hezekiah turned his face toward
the wall, and prayed to the LORD,
3 and said, [R]"Remember now, O LORD, I
pray, how I have walked before You in truth
and with a [T]loyal heart, and have done *what*
is good in Your [R]sight." And Hezekiah wept
bitterly. Neh. 13:14 • *whole* or *peaceful* • 2 Kin. 18:5, 6
4 Then the word of the LORD came to
Isaiah, saying,
5 "Go and say to Hezekiah, 'Thus says the
LORD, the God of David your father: "I have
heard your prayer, I have seen your tears;
and I will add to your days fifteen years.
6 "I will deliver you and this city from the
hand of the king of Assyria, and [R]I will defend
this city." ' Is. 31:5; 37:35
7 "And this *is* [R]the sign to you from the
LORD, that the LORD will do this thing which
He has spoken: Is. 7:11
8 "Behold, I will bring the shadow on the
sundial, which has gone down with the sun
on the sundial of Ahaz, ten degrees backward." So the sun returned ten degrees on
the dial by which it had gone down.
9 This is the writing of Hezekiah king of
Judah, when he had been sick and had recovered from his sickness:

10 I said,
"In the prime of my life
I shall go to the gates of Sheol;
I am deprived of the remainder of my
years."
11 I said,
"I shall not see [T]YAH, Heb. *YAH-YAH*
The LORD [R]in the land of the living;
I shall observe man no more among the
inhabitants of the world. Ps. 27:13; 116:9
12 [R]My life span is gone,
Taken from me like a shepherd's tent;
I have cut off my life like a weaver.
He cuts me off from the loom;
From day until night You make an end
of me. Job 7:6
13 I have considered until morning—
Like a lion,
So He breaks all my bones;
From day until night You make an end
of me.
14 Like a crane *or* a swallow, so I
chattered;
[R]I mourned like a dove;
My eyes fail *from looking* upward.
O *LORD, I am oppressed;
[T]Undertake for me! Is. 59:11 • *Be my surety*

15 "What shall I say?
He has both spoken to me,
And He Himself has done *it*.
I shall walk carefully all my years
[R]In the bitterness of my soul. Job 7:11; 10:1
16 O LORD, by these *things men* live;
And in all these *things is* the life of my
spirit;
So You will restore me and make me
live.
17 Indeed *it was* for *my own* peace
That I had great bitterness;
But You have lovingly *delivered* my
soul from the pit of corruption,
For You have cast all my sins behind
Your back.
18 For [R]Sheol cannot thank You,
Death cannot praise You;
Those who go down to the pit cannot
hope for Your truth. Ps. 6:5; 30:9; 88:11
19 The living, the living man, he shall
praise You,
As I *do* this day;
[R]The father shall make known Your
truth to the children. Deut. 4:9; 6:7

20 "The LORD *was ready* to save me;
Therefore we will sing my songs with
stringed instruments
All the days of our life, in the house of
the LORD."

21 Now [R]Isaiah had said, "Let them take a
lump of figs, and apply *it* as a poultice on the
boil, and he shall recover." 2 Kin. 20:7
22 And [R]Hezekiah had said, "What *is* the
sign that I shall go up to the house of the
LORD?" 2 Kin. 20:8

CHAPTER 39

Hezekiah's Sin

AT that time Merodach-Baladan the son of
Baladan, king of Babylon, sent letters
and a present to Hezekiah, for he heard that
he had been sick and had recovered.

38:14 MT, DSS *Lord*

2 And Hezekiah was pleased with them,
and showed them the house of his treasures—the silver and gold, the spices and
precious ointment, and all his armory—all
that was found among his treasures. There
was nothing in his house or in all his dominion that Hezekiah did not show them.
3 Then Isaiah the prophet went to King
Hezekiah, and said to him, "What did these
men say, and from where did they come to
you?" And Hezekiah said, "They came to me
from a [R]far country, from Babylon." Deut. 28:49
4 And he said, "What have they seen in
your house?" So Hezekiah answered, "They
have seen all that *is* in my house; there is
nothing among my treasures that I have not
shown them."
5 Then Isaiah said to Hezekiah, "Hear the
word of the LORD of hosts:
6 'Behold, the days are coming [R]when all
that *is* in your house, and what your fathers
have accumulated until this day, shall be
carried to Babylon; nothing shall be left,' says
the LORD. Jer. 20:5
7 'And they shall take away *some* of your
[R]sons who will descend from you, whom you
will beget; and they shall be eunuchs in the
palace of the king of Babylon.' " Dan. 1:1–7
8 Then Hezekiah said to Isaiah, [R]"The
word of the LORD which you have spoken *is*
good!" For he said, "At least there will be
peace and truth in my days." 1 Sam. 3:18

CHAPTER 40

Comfort Because of Israel's Deliverance

"COMFORT, yes, comfort My people!"
Says your God.
2 "Speak [T]comfort to Jerusalem, and cry
out to her, Lit. *to the heart of*
That her warfare is ended,
That her iniquity is pardoned;
[R]For she has received from the LORD's
hand Is. 61:7
Double for all her sins."

3 [R]The voice of one crying in the
wilderness: Matt. 3:3 ☆
Prepare the way of the LORD;
[R]Make straight in the desert Ps. 68:4
A highway for our God.
4 Every valley shall be exalted,
And every mountain and hill shall be
made low;
[R]The crooked places shall be made
[T]straight, Is. 45:2 • Or *a plain*
And the rough places smooth;
5 The [R]glory of the LORD shall be
revealed, Is. 35:2
And all flesh shall see *it* together;
For the mouth of the LORD has
spoken."

6 The voice said, "Cry out!"
And he said, "What shall I cry?"

[R]"All flesh *is* grass, Job 14:2
And all its loveliness *is* like the flower
of the field.
7 The grass withers, the flower fades,
Because the breath of the LORD blows
upon it;
Surely the people *are* grass.
8 The grass withers, the flower fades,
But [R]the word of our God stands
forever." [John 12:34]

9 O Zion,
You who bring good tidings,
Get up into the high mountain;
O Jerusalem,
You who bring good tidings,
Lift up your voice with strength,
Lift *it* up, be not afraid;
Say to the cities of Judah, "Behold your
God!"

10 Behold, the Lord GOD shall come [R]with[T]
a strong *hand*, Is. 9:6, 7 • *in strength*
And His arm shall rule for Him;
Behold, His reward *is* with Him,
And His [T]work before Him. *recompense*
11 He will [R]feed His flock like a shepherd;
He will gather the lambs with His arm,
And carry *them* in His bosom,
And gently lead those who are with
young. Mic. 5:4; [John 10:11, 14–16] ☆

Comfort Because of God's Character

12 [R]Who has measured the waters in the
hollow of his hand, Prov. 30:4
Measured heaven with a span
And calculated the dust of the earth in
a measure?
Weighed the mountains in scales
And the hills in a balance?
13 [R]Who has directed the Spirit of the
LORD, [1 Cor. 2:16]
Or *as* His counselor has taught Him?
14 With whom did He take counsel, and
who instructed Him,
And [R]taught Him in the path of justice?
Who taught Him knowledge,
And showed Him the way of
understanding? Job 36:22, 23

15 Behold, the nations *are* as a drop in a
bucket,
And are counted as the small dust on
the balance;
Look, He lifts up the isles as a very
little thing.
16 And Lebanon *is* not sufficient to burn,
Nor its beasts sufficient for a burnt
offering.

17 All nations before Him *are* as nothing,
And [R]they are counted by Him less than
nothing and worthless. Ps. 62:9

18 To whom then will you [R]liken God?
Or what likeness will you compare to
Him? Is. 46:5
19 The workman molds a graven image,
The goldsmith overspreads it with gold,
And the silversmith casts silver chains.
20 Whoever *is* too impoverished for *such*
[T]a contribution
Chooses a tree *that* will not rot;
He seeks for himself a skillful workman
[R]To prepare a carved image *that* will not
totter. *an offering* • Is. 41:7; 46:7

21 [R]Have you not known?
Have you not heard?
Has it not been told you from the
beginning?
Have you not understood from the
foundations of the earth? Rom. 1:19
22 *It is* He who sits above the circle of the
earth,
And its inhabitants *are* like
grasshoppers,
Who [R]stretches out the heavens like a
curtain,
And spreads them out like a [R]tent to
dwell in. Jer. 10:12 • Ps. 19:4
23 He [T]brings the [R]princes to nothing;
He makes the judges of the earth
useless. *reduces* • Ps. 107:40

24 Scarcely shall they be planted,
Scarcely shall they be sown,
Scarcely shall their stock take root in
the earth,
When He will also blow on them,
And they will wither,
And the whirlwind will take them away
like stubble.

25 "To[R] whom then will you liken Me,
Or *to whom* shall I be equal?" says the
Holy One. Is. 40:18
26 Lift up your eyes on high,
And see who has created these *things*,
Who brings out their host by number;
[R]He calls them all by name,
By the greatness of His might
And the strength of *His* power;
Not one is missing. Ps. 147:4

27 [R]Why do you say, O Jacob,
And speak, O Israel:
"My way is hidden from the LORD,
And my just claim is passed over by my
God"? Is. 54:7, 8
28 Have you not known?
Have you not heard?
The everlasting God, the LORD,
The Creator of the ends of the earth,
Neither faints nor is weary.
[R]*There is* no searching of His
understanding. Rom. 11:33
29 He gives power to the weak,
And to *those who have* no might He
increases strength.
30 Even the youths shall faint and be
weary,
And the young men shall utterly fall,
31 But those who [R]wait on the LORD
[R]Shall renew *their* strength;
They shall mount up with wings like
eagles, Is. 30:15; 49:23 • Ps. 103:5
They shall run and not be weary,
They shall walk and not faint.

CHAPTER 41

Comfort Because of God's Greatness

"KEEP [R]silence before Me, O
coastlands,
And let the people renew *their* strength!
Let them come near, then let them
speak;
Let us [R]come near together for
judgment. Zech. 2:13 • Is. 1:18

2 "Who raised up one [R]from the east?
Who in righteousness called him to His
feet? Is. 46:11
Who [R]gave the nations before him,
And made *him* rule over kings?
Who gave *them* as the dust *to* his
sword, Is. 45:1, 13
As driven stubble to his bow?
3 Who pursued them, *and* passed [T]safely
By the way *that* he had not gone with
his feet? Lit. *in peace*
4 [R]Who has performed and done *it*,
Calling the generations from the
beginning? Is. 41:26
'I, the LORD, am [R]the first; Rev. 1:8, 17; 22:13
And with the last I *am* [R]He.' " Is. 43:10

5 The coastlands saw *it* and feared,
The ends of the earth were afraid;
They drew near and came.
6 [R]Everyone helped his neighbor,
And said to his brother,
[T]Be of good courage!" Is. 40:19 • Lit. *Be strong*
7 [R]So the craftsman encouraged the
[R]goldsmith,[T] Is. 44:13 • Is. 40:19 • *refined*
And he who smooths *with* the hammer
inspired him who strikes the anvil,
Saying, "It *is* ready for the soldering";
Then he fastened it with pegs,
[R]*That* it might not totter. Is. 40:20

8 "But you, Israel, *are* My servant,
Jacob, whom I have [R]chosen,
The descendants of Abraham My
[R]friend. Deut. 7:6; 10:15 • James 2:23

9 *You* whom I have taken from the ends
of the earth,
And called from its farthest regions,
And said to you,
'You *are* My servant,
I have chosen you and have not cast
you away:
10 [R]Fear not, [R]for I *am* with you;
Be not dismayed, for I *am* your God.
I will strengthen you,
Yes, I will help you,
I will uphold you with My righteous
right hand.' Is. 41:13, 14; 43:5 • [Deut. 31:6]

11 "Behold, all those who were incensed
against you
Shall be [R]ashamed and disgraced;
They shall be as nothing,
And those who strive with you shall
perish. Zech. 12:3
12 You shall seek them and not find
them—
[T]Those who contended with you.
Those who war against you
Shall be as nothing, Lit. *Men of your strife*
As a nonexistent thing.
13 For I, the LORD your God, will hold
your right hand,
Saying to you, 'Fear not, I will help
you.'

14 "Fear not, you [R]worm Jacob,
You men of Israel!
I will help you," says the LORD
And your Redeemer, the Holy One of
Israel. Job 25:6
15 "Behold, [R]I will make you into a new
threshing sledge with sharp teeth;
You shall thresh the mountains and
beat *them* small,
And make the hills like chaff. Mic. 4:13
16 You shall [R]winnow them, the wind shall
carry them away, Jer. 51:2
And the whirlwind shall scatter them;
You shall [R]rejoice in the LORD, Is. 25:9☆
And glory in the Holy One of Israel.

17 "*When* the poor and needy seek water,
and *there is* none,
And their tongues fail for thirst,
I, the LORD, will hear them;
I, the God of Israel, will not [R]forsake
them. Rom. 11:2
18 I will open [R]rivers in desolate heights,
And fountains in the midst of the
valleys;
I will make the [R]wilderness a pool of
water, Is. 35:6, 7; 43:19; 44:3 • Ps. 107:35
And the dry land springs of water.
19 I will plant in the wilderness the cedar
and the acacia tree,
The myrtle and the oil tree;
I will set in the [R]desert the cypress tree
and the pine
And the box tree together, Is. 35:1
20 [R]That they may see and know,
And consider and understand together,
That the hand of the LORD has done
this,
And the Holy One of Israel has created
it. Job 12:9

21 "Present your case," says the LORD.
"Bring forth your strong *reasons*," says
the [R]King of Jacob. Is. 43:15
22 "Let[R] them bring forth and show us what
will happen; Is. 45:21
Let them show the [R]former things, what
they *were*, Is. 43:9
That we may consider them,
And know the latter end of them;
Or declare to us things to come.
23 [R]Show the things that are to come
hereafter,
That we may know that you *are* gods;
Yes, [R]do good or do evil,
That we may be dismayed and see *it*
together. [John 13:19] • Jer. 10:5
24 Indeed [R]you *are* nothing, [1 Cor. 8:4]
And your work *is* nothing;
He who chooses you *is* an abomination.

25 "I have raised up one from the north,
And he shall come;
From the [T]rising of the sun [R]he shall
call on My name;
And he shall come against princes as
though mortar,
As the potter treads clay. East • Ezra 1:2
26 [R]Who has declared from the beginning,
that we may know?
And former times, that we may say, '*He
is* righteous'?
Surely *there is* no one who shows,
Surely *there is* no one who declares,
Surely *there is* no one who hears your
words. Is. 43:9
27 [R]The first time [R]*I said* to Zion,
'Look, there they are!'
And I will give to Jerusalem one who
brings good tidings. Is. 41:4 • Is. 40:9
28 [R]For I looked, and *there was* no man;
I looked among them, but *there was* no
counselor,
Who, when I asked of them, could
answer a word. Is. 63:5
29 [R]Indeed they *are* all worthless;
Their works *are* nothing;
Their molded images *are* wind and
confusion. Is. 41:24

CHAPTER 42

Comfort Because of God's Servant

"BEHOLD! [R]My Servant whom I
uphold, Luke 3:22☆

My [T]Elect One *in whom* My soul
[R]delights! *Chosen* • Matt. 3:17; 17:5
[R]I have put My Spirit upon Him;
He will bring forth justice to the
Gentiles. [Is. 11:2]
2 He will not cry out, nor raise *His voice*,
Nor cause His voice to be heard in the
street.
3 A bruised reed He will not break,
And smoking flax He will not quench;
He will bring forth justice for truth.
4 He will not fail nor be discouraged,
Till He has established justice in the
earth;
[R]And the coastlands shall wait for His
law." [Gen. 49:10] ☆

5 Thus says God the LORD,
[R]Who created the heavens and stretched
them out, Zech. 12:1
Who spread forth the earth and that
which comes from it,
Who gives breath to the people on it,
And spirit to those who walk on it:
6 "I,[R] the LORD, have called You in
[R]righteousness, Is. 43:1 • Jer. 23:5, 6 ☆
And will hold Your hand;
I will keep You [R]and give You as a
covenant to the people, Is. 49:8
As [R]a light to the Gentiles, Luke 2:32
7 [R]To open blind eyes,
To [R]bring out prisoners from the prison,
Those who sit in [R]darkness from the
prison house. Is. 35:5 ☆ • Luke 4:18 • Is. 9:2
8 I *am* the LORD, that *is* My name;
And My [R]glory I will not give to
another,
Nor My praise to graven images. Is. 48:11
9 Behold, the former things have come to
pass,
And new things I declare;
Before they spring forth I tell you of
them."

10 [R]Sing to the LORD a new song,
And His praise from the ends of the
earth, Ps. 33:3; 40:3; 98:1
[R]You who go down to the sea, and [T]all
that is in it,
You coastlands and you inhabitants of
them! Ps. 107:23 • Lit. *its fullness*
11 Let the wilderness and its cities lift up
their voice,
The villages *that* Kedar inhabits.
Let the inhabitants of Sela sing,
Let them shout from the top of the
mountains.
12 Let them give glory to the LORD,
And declare His praise in the
coastlands.
13 The LORD shall go forth like a mighty
man;
He shall stir up *His* zeal like a man of
war.
He shall cry out, yes, shout aloud;
He shall prevail against His enemies.

14 "I have held My peace a long time,
I have been still and restrained Myself.
Now I will cry like a woman in [T]labor,
I will pant and gasp at once. *childbirth*
15 I will lay waste the mountains and hills,
And dry up all their vegetation;
I will make the rivers coastlands,
And I will dry up the pools.
16 I will bring the blind by a way they did
not know;
I will lead them in paths they have not
known.
I will make darkness light before them,
And crooked places straight.
These things I will do for them,
And not forsake them.
17 They shall be [R]turned back,
They shall be greatly ashamed,
Who trust in carved images,
Who say to the molded images,
'You *are* our gods.' Ps. 97:7

18 "Hear, you deaf;
And look, you blind, that you may see.
19 [R]Who *is* blind but My servant, [John 9:39, 41]
Or deaf as My messenger *whom* I send?
Who *is* blind as *he who is* perfect,
And blind as the LORD's servant?
20 Seeing many things, [R]but you do not
observe;
Opening the ears, but he does not
hear." Rom. 2:21

21 The LORD is well pleased for His
righteousness' sake;
He will magnify the law and make *it*
honorable.
22 But this *is* a people robbed and
plundered;
All of them are [T]snared in holes,
And they are hidden in prison houses;
They are for prey, and no one delivers;
For plunder, and no one says,
"Restore!" Or *trapped in caves*

23 Who among you will give ear to this?
Who will listen and hear for the time to
come?
24 Who gave Jacob for plunder, and Israel
to the robbers?
Was it not the LORD,
He against whom we have sinned?
For they would not walk in His ways,
Nor were they obedient to His law.
25 Therefore He has poured on him the
fury of His anger
And the strength of battle;

[R]It has set him on fire all around,
[R]Yet he did not know; 2 Kin. 25:9 • Hos. 7:9
And it burned him,
Yet he did not take *it* to [R]heart. Is. 29:13

CHAPTER 43

Comfort Because of Israel's Restoration

BUT now, thus says the LORD, who
created you, O Jacob,
And He who formed you, O Israel:
"Fear not, [R]for I have redeemed you;
[R]I have called *you* by your name;
You *are* Mine. Is. 43:5; 44:6 • Is. 42:6; 45:4
2 [R]When you pass through the waters, [R]I
will be with you; [Ps. 91:3] • [Deut. 31:6]
And through the rivers, they shall not
overflow you.
When you [R]walk through the fire, you
shall not be burned, Dan. 3:25
Nor shall the flame scorch you.
3 For I *am* the LORD your God,
The Holy One of Israel, your Savior;
[R]I gave Egypt for your ransom, [Prov. 21:18]
Ethiopia and Seba in your place.
4 Since you were precious in My sight,
You have been honored,
And I have [R]loved you;
Therefore I will give men for you,
And people for your life. Is. 63:9
5 [R]Fear not, for I *am* with you; Is. 41:10; 44:2
I will bring your descendants from the
east,
And [R]gather you from the west; Is. 54:7
6 I will say to the [R]north, 'Give them up!'
And to the south, 'Do not keep them
back!'
Bring My sons from afar,
And My daughters from the ends of the
earth— Is. 49:12
7 Everyone who is [R]called by My name,
Whom [R]I have created for My glory;
I have formed him, yes, I have made
him." James 2:7 • 2 Cor. 5:17

8 [R]Bring out the blind people who have
eyes, Ezek. 12:2
And the [R]deaf who have ears. Is. 29:18
9 Let all the nations be gathered together,
And let the people be assembled.
[R]Who among them can declare this,
And show us former things?
Let them bring out their witnesses, that
they may be justified; Is. 41:21, 22, 26
Or let them hear and say, "*It is* truth."
10 "You *are* My witnesses," says the LORD,
"And My servant whom I have chosen,
That you may know and [R]believe Me,
And understand that I *am* He.
Before Me there was no God formed,
Nor shall there be after Me. Is. 41:4; 44:6
11 I, *even* I, [R]*am* the LORD, Hos. 13:4
And besides Me *there is* no savior.
12 I have declared and saved,
I have proclaimed,
And *there was* no [R]foreign *god* among
you; Deut. 32:16
[R]Therefore you *are* My witnesses,"
Says the LORD, "that I *am* God. Is. 44:8
13 [R]Indeed before the day *was*, I *am* He;
And *there is* no one who can deliver out
of My hand; Ps. 90:2
I work, and who will [R]reverse it?" Job 9:12

14 Thus says the LORD, your Redeemer,
The Holy One of Israel:
"For your sake I will send to Babylon,
And bring them all down as fugitives—
The Chaldeans, who rejoice in their
ships.
15 I *am* the LORD, your Holy One,
The Creator of Israel, your King."

16 Thus says the LORD, who [R]makes a way
in the sea Ex. 14:16, 21, 22
And a path through the mighty waters,
17 Who [R]brings forth the chariot and
horse,
The army and the power
(They shall lie down together, they shall
not rise;
They are extinguished, they are
quenched like a wick): Ex. 14:4–9, 25
18 "Do[R] not remember the former things,
Nor consider the things of old. Jer. 16:14
19 Behold, I will do a [R]new thing,
Now it shall spring forth;
Shall you not know it?
[R]I will even make a road in the
wilderness [2 Cor. 5:17] • Ex. 17:6
And rivers in the desert.
20 The beast of the field will honor Me,
The jackals and the ostriches,
Because [R]I give waters in the wilderness
And rivers in the desert, Is. 48:21
To give drink to My people, My chosen.
21 This people I have formed for Myself;
They shall declare My [R]praise. Jer. 13:11
22 "But you have not called upon Me, O
Jacob;
And you [R]have been weary of Me, O
Israel. Mal. 1:13; 3:14
23 [R]You have not brought Me the sheep for
your burnt offerings,
Nor have you honored Me with your
sacrifices.
I have not caused you to serve with
grain offerings,
Nor wearied you with incense. Amos 5:25
24 You have bought Me no sweet cane
with money,
Nor have you satisfied Me with the fat
of your sacrifices;
But you have burdened Me with your
sins,

You have [R]wearied Me with your
iniquities. Is. 1:14; 7:13
25 "I, *even* I, *am* He who blots out your
transgressions for My own sake;
And I will not remember your sins.
26 Put Me in remembrance;
Let us contend together;
State your *case*, that you may be
[T]acquitted. *justified*
27 Your first father sinned,
And your [T]mediators have transgressed
against Me. *interpreters*
28 Therefore I will profane the princes of
the sanctuary;
[R]I will give Jacob to the curse,
And Israel to reproaches. Dan. 9:11

CHAPTER 44

"YET hear now, O Jacob My servant,
And Israel whom I have chosen.
2 Thus says the LORD who made you
And formed you from the womb, *who*
will help you:
'Fear not, O Jacob My servant;
And you, Jeshurun, whom I have
chosen.
3 For I will pour water on him who is
thirsty,
And floods on the dry ground;
I will pour My Spirit on your
descendants,
And My blessing on your offspring;
4 They will spring up among the grass
Like willows by the watercourses.'
5 "One will say, 'I *am* the LORD's';
Another will call *himself* by the name of
Jacob;
Another will write *with* his hand, 'The
LORD's,'
And name *himself* by the name of
Israel.

6 "Thus says the LORD, the King of Israel,
And his Redeemer, the LORD of hosts:
[R]'I *am* the First and I *am* the Last;
Besides Me *there is* no God. Is. 41:4
7 And [R]who can proclaim as I do?
Then let him declare it and set it in
order for Me,
Since I appointed the ancient people.
And the things that are coming and
shall come, Is. 41:4, 22, 26
Let them show these to them.
8 Do not fear, nor be afraid;
[R]Have I not told you from that time, and
declared *it?* Is. 41:22
[R]You *are* My witnesses. Is. 43:10, 12
Is there a God besides Me?
Indeed [R]*there is* no other Rock; 1 Sam. 2:2
I know not *one.*'"

9 [R]Those who make a graven image, all of
them *are* useless,
And their precious things shall not
profit;
They *are* their own witnesses;
[R]They neither see nor know, that they
may be ashamed. Is. 41:24 • Ps. 115:4
10 Who would form a god or cast a graven
image
[R]*That* profits him nothing? Hab. 2:18
11 Surely all his companions would be
[R]ashamed;
And the workmen, they *are* mere men.
Let them all be gathered together,
Let them stand up;
Yet they shall fear,
They shall be ashamed together. Ps. 97:7

12 [R]The blacksmith with the tongs works
one in the coals, Jer. 10:3–5
Fashions it with hammers,
And works it with the strength of his
arms.
Even so, he is hungry, and his strength
fails;
He drinks no water and is faint.

13 The craftsman stretches out *his* rule,
He marks one out with chalk;
He fashions it with a plane,
He marks it out with the compass,
And makes it like the figure of a man,
According to the beauty of a man, that
it may remain in the house.
14 He hews down cedars for himself,
And takes the cypress and the oak;
He [T]secures *it* for himself among the
trees of the forest.
He plants a pine, and the rain nourishes
it. Lit. *appropriates*

15 Then it shall be for a man to burn,
For he will take some of it and warm
himself;
Yes, he kindles *it* and bakes bread;
Indeed he makes a god and worships *it*;
He makes it a carved image, and falls
down to it.
16 He burns half of it in the fire;
With this half he eats meat;
He roasts a roast, and is satisfied.
He even warms *himself* and says,
"Ah! I am warm,
I have seen the fire."
17 And the rest of it he makes into a god,
His carved image.
He falls down before it and worships *it*,
Prays to it and says,
"Deliver me, for you *are* my god."

18 [R]They do not know nor understand;
For He has shut their eyes, so that they
cannot see, Is. 45:20
And their hearts, so that they cannot
[R]understand. Jer. 10:14

19 And no one [R]considers in his heart,
Nor *is there* knowledge nor
understanding to say,
"I have burned half of it in the fire,
Yes, I have also baked bread on its
coals;
I have roasted meat and eaten *it;*
And shall I make the rest of it an
abomination?
Shall I fall down before a block of
wood?" Is. 46:8
20 He feeds on ashes;
[R]A deceived heart has turned him aside;
And he cannot deliver his soul,
Nor say, "*Is there* not a [R]lie in my right
hand?" 2 Thess. 2:11 • Rom. 1:25

21 "Remember these, O Jacob,
And Israel, for you *are* My servant;
I have formed you, you *are* My servant;
O Israel, you will not be [R]forgotten by
Me! Is. 49:15
22 [R]I have blotted out, like a thick cloud,
your transgressions,
And like a cloud, your sins.
Return to Me, for [R]I have redeemed
you." Is. 43:25 • 1 Cor. 6:20

23 [R]Sing, O heavens, for the LORD has done
it! Ps. 69:34
Shout, you lower parts of the earth;
Break forth into singing, you
mountains,
O forest, and every tree in it!
For the LORD has redeemed Jacob,
And [R]glorified Himself in Israel. Is. 60:21

24 Thus says the LORD, [R]your Redeemer,
And [R]He who formed you from the
womb:
"I *am* the LORD, who makes all *things,*
[R]Who stretches out the heavens [T]all
alone,
Who spreads abroad the earth by
Myself; Is. 43:14 • Is. 43:1 • Job 9:8 • By Himself
25 Who [R]frustrates the signs [R]of the
babblers, Is. 47:13 • Jer. 50:36
And drives diviners mad;
Who turns wise men backward,
And makes their knowledge foolishness;
26 [R]Who confirms the word of His servant,
And performs the counsel of His
messengers; Zech. 1:6
Who says to Jerusalem, 'You shall be
inhabited,'
To the cities of Judah, 'You shall be
built,'
And I will raise up her waste places;
27 [R]Who says to the deep, 'Be dry!
And I will dry up your rivers'; Jer. 50:38
28 Who says of [R]Cyrus, '*He is* My
shepherd,
And he shall perform all My pleasure,
Even saying to Jerusalem, [R]"You shall
be built,"
And to the temple, "Your foundation
shall be laid." ' Ezra 1:1 • Ezra 6:7

CHAPTER 45

Comfort Because of God's Use of Cyrus

"THUS says the LORD to His anointed,
To [R]Cyrus, whose right hand I have
[T]held— Is. 44:28 • *strengthened* or *sustained*
[R]To subdue nations before him Dan. 5:30
And [R]loose the armor of kings, Job 12:21
To open before him the double doors,
So that the gates will not be shut:
2 'I will go before you
[R]And make the crooked places straight;
[R]I will break in pieces the gates of
bronze Is. 40:4 • Ps. 107:16
And cut the bars of iron.
3 I will give you the treasures of darkness
And hidden riches of secret places,
[R]That you may know that I, the LORD,
Who [R]call *you* by your name,
Am the God of Israel. Is. 41:23 • Ex. 33:12
4 For [R]Jacob My servant's sake,
And Israel My elect,
I have even called you by your name;
I have named you, though you have not
known Me. Is. 44:1
5 I *am* the LORD, and [R]*there is* no other;
There is no God besides Me. Is. 45:14, 18
[R]I will gird you, though you have not
known Me, Ps. 18:32
6 That they may [R]know from the rising of
the sun to its setting [Is. 11:9; 52:10]
That *there is* none besides Me.
I *am* the LORD, and *there is* no other;
7 I form the light and create darkness,
I make peace and [R]create calamity;
I, the LORD, do all these *things.*' Amos 3:6

8 "Rain[R] down, you heavens, from above,
And let the skies pour down
righteousness; Ps. 85:11
Let the earth open, let them bring forth
salvation,
And let righteousness spring up
together.
I, the LORD, have created it.

9 "Woe to him who strives with [R]his
Maker!
Let the potsherd *strive* with the
potsherds of the earth.
[R]Shall the clay say to him who forms it,
'What are you making?'
Or shall your handiwork *say,* 'He has
no hands'? Is. 64:8 • Jer. 18:6
10 Woe to him who says to *his* father,
'What are you begetting?'

Or to the woman, 'What have you
brought forth?' "

11 Thus says the LORD,
The Holy One of Israel, and his Maker:
[R]"Ask Me of things to come concerning
[R]My sons; Is. 8:19 • Jer. 31:9
And concerning [R]the work of My hands,
you command Me. Is. 29:23; 60:21; 64:8
12 [R]I have made the earth, Is. 42:5
And [R]created man on it. Gen. 1:26
It was I—
My hands *that* stretched out the
heavens,
And all their host I have commanded.
13 [R]I have raised him up in righteousness,
And I will direct all his ways; Is. 41:2
He shall [R]build My city 2 Chr. 36:22
And let My exiles go free,
[R]Not for price nor reward," [Rom. 3:24]
Says the LORD of hosts.

14 Thus says the LORD:

[R]"The labor of Egypt and merchandise of
Cush Zech. 8:22, 23
And of the Sabeans, men of stature,
Shall come over to you, and they shall
be yours;
They shall walk behind you,
They shall come over in chains;
And they shall bow down to you.
They will make supplication to you,
saying, [R]'Surely God *is* in you,
And *there is* no other; 1 Cor. 14:25
[R]*There is* no other God.' " Is. 45:5

15 Truly You *are* God, [R]who hide Yourself,
O God of Israel, the Savior! Ps. 44:24
16 They shall be [R]ashamed
And also disgraced, all of them;
They shall go in confusion together,
Who are makers of idols. Is. 44:11
17 [R]*But* Israel shall be saved by the LORD
With an [R]everlasting salvation;
You shall not be ashamed or [R]disgraced
Forever and ever. Is. 26:4 • Is. 51:6 • Is. 29:22

18 For thus says the LORD,
[R]Who created the heavens,
Who is God, Is. 42:5
Who formed the earth and made it,
Who has established it,
Who did not create it [T]in vain, *a waste*
Who formed it to be [R]inhabited: Ps. 115:16
I *am* the LORD, and *there is* no other.
19 I have not spoken in [R]secret, Deut. 30:11
In a dark place of the earth;
I did not say to the seed of Jacob,
'Seek Me [T]in vain'; *in a waste place*
[R]I, the LORD, speak righteousness,
I declare things that are right. Ps. 19:8

20 "Assemble yourselves and come;
Draw near together,
You *who have* escaped from the
nations.
[R]They have no knowledge,
Who carry the wood of their carved
image, Is. 44:9; 46:7
And pray to a god *that* cannot save.
21 Tell and bring forth *your case;*
Yes, let them take counsel together.
[R]Who has declared this from ancient
time? Is. 41:22; 43:9
Who has told it from that time?
Have not I, the LORD?
[R]And *there is* no other God besides Me,
A just God and a Savior; Is. 44:8
There is none besides Me.

22 "Look to Me, and be saved,
[R]All you ends of the earth! Ps. 22:27; 65:5
For I *am* God, and *there is* no other.
23 [R]I have sworn by Myself; [Heb. 6:13]
The word has gone out of My mouth *in*
righteousness,
And shall not return,
That to Me every knee shall bow,
Every tongue shall take an oath.
24 He shall say,
Surely in the LORD I have
[R]righteousness and strength.
To Him *men* shall come, [1 Cor. 1:30]
And [R]all shall be ashamed Is. 41:11
Who are incensed against Him.
25 [R]In the LORD all the descendants of
Israel Is. 45:17
Shall be justified, and shall glory.' "

CHAPTER 46

Destruction of Babylon's Idols

BEL [R]bows down, Nebo stoops;
Their idols were on the beasts and on
the cattle. Jer. 50:2
Your carriages *were* heavily loaded,
[R]A burden to the weary *beast.* Jer. 10:5
2 They stoop, they bow down together;
They could not deliver the burden,
[R]But have themselves gone into
captivity. Jer. 48:7

3 "Listen to Me, O house of Jacob,
And all the remnant of the house of
Israel,
[R]Who have been upheld *by Me* from
[T]birth, Ps. 71:6 • Lit. *the belly*
Who have been carried from the womb:
4 Even to *your* old age, [R]I *am* He,
And *even* to gray hairs [R]I will carry
you! Mal. 3:6 • Ps. 48:14
I have made, and I will bear;
Even I will carry, and will deliver *you.*

5 "To[R] whom will you liken Me, and make
Me equal Is. 40:18, 25
And compare Me, that we should be
alike?
6 [R]They lavish gold out of the bag,
And weigh silver in the balance;
They hire a [R]goldsmith, and he makes it
a god;
They prostrate themselves, yes, they
worship. Is. 40:19; 41:6 • Is. 44:12
7 [R]They bear it on the shoulder, they carry
it Jer. 10:5
And set it in its place, and it stands;
From its place it shall not move.
Though [R]*one* cries out to it, yet it
cannot answer Is. 45:20
Nor save him out of his trouble.

8 "Remember this, and [T]show yourselves
men; *be men,* take courage
Recall to mind, O you transgressors.
9 Remember the former things of old,
For I *am* God, and *there is* no other;
I am God, and *there is* none like Me,
10 [R]Declaring the end from the beginning,
And from ancient times *things* that are
not *yet* done, Is. 45:21; 48:3
Saying, [R]'My counsel shall stand,
And I will do all My pleasure,' Ps. 33:11
11 Calling a bird of prey [R]from the east,
The man [R]who executes My counsel,
from a far country. Is. 41:2, 25 • Is. 44:28
Indeed [R]I have spoken *it;* Num. 23:19
I will also bring it to pass.
I have purposed *it;*
I will also do it.

12 "Listen to Me, you [R]stubborn-hearted,
Who *are* far from righteousness: Ps. 76:5
13 [R]I bring My righteousness near, it shall
not be far off; [Rom. 1:17]
My salvation shall not [T]linger. *delay*
And I will place [R]salvation in Zion,
For Israel My glory. Is. 62:11

CHAPTER 47

Destruction of Babylon

"COME [R]down and [R]sit in the dust,
O virgin daughter of Babylon;
Sit on the ground without a throne,
O daughter of the Chaldeans! Jer. 48:18
For you shall no more be called
Tender and [T]delicate. Is. 3:26 • *dainty*
2 [R]Take the millstones and grind meal.
Remove your veil,
Take off the skirt,
Uncover the thigh,
Pass through the rivers. Ex. 11:5
3 [R]Your nakedness shall be uncovered,
Yes, your shame will be seen; Is. 3:17; 20:4
[R]I will take vengeance, [Rom. 12:19]
And I will not arbitrate with a man."

4 *As for* [R]our Redeemer, the LORD of
hosts *is* His name, Jer. 50:34
The Holy One of Israel.

5 "Sit in [R]silence, and go into darkness,
O daughter of the Chaldeans; 1 Sam. 2:9
[R]For you shall no longer be called
The Lady of Kingdoms. [Dan. 2:37]
6 [R]I was angry with My people; 2 Sam. 24:14
[R]I have profaned My inheritance,
And given them into your hand.
You showed them no mercy;
[R]On the elderly you laid your yoke very
heavily. Is. 43:28 • Deut. 28:49, 50
7 And you said, 'I shall be [R]a lady
forever,' Rev. 18:7
So that you did not [R]take these *things*
to heart, Is. 42:25; 46:8
Nor remember the latter end of them.

8 "Therefore hear this now, *you who are*
given to pleasures,
Who dwell securely,
Who say in your heart,
'I *am*, and *there is* no one else besides
me;
I shall not sit *as* a widow,
Nor shall I know the loss of children';
9 But these two *things* shall come to you
[R]In a moment, in one day:
The loss of children, and widowhood.
They shall come upon you in their
fullness
Because of the multitude of your
sorceries,
For the great abundance of your
enchantments. 1 Thess. 5:3

10 "For you have trusted in your
wickedness;
You have said, 'No one [R]sees me';
Your wisdom and your knowledge have
[T]warped you;
And you have said in your heart,
'I *am*, and *there is* no one else besides
me.' Is. 29:15 • *led you astray*
11 Therefore evil shall come upon you;
You shall not know from where it
arises.
And trouble shall fall upon you;
You will not be able [T]to put it off.
And desolation shall come upon you
suddenly, Lit. *to cover it* or *atone for it*
Which you shall not know.

12 "Stand now with your enchantments
And the multitude of your sorceries,
In which you have labored from your
youth—
Perhaps you will be able to profit,
Perhaps you will prevail.
13 [R]You are wearied in the multitude of
your counsels; Is. 57:10

Let now [R]the[T] astrologers, the
stargazers,
And the monthly prognosticators
Stand up and save you
From *these things* that shall come upon
you. Dan. 2:2, 10 • Lit. *viewers of the heavens*
14 Behold, they shall be [R]as stubble,
The fire shall [R]burn them;
They shall not deliver themselves
From the power of the flame;
It shall not *be* a coal to be warmed by,
Nor a fire to sit before! Nah. 1:10 • Jer. 51:58
15 Thus shall they be to you
With whom you have labored,
[R]Your merchants from your youth;
They shall wander each one to his
[T]quarter. Rev. 18:11 • *own side* or *way*
No one shall save you.

CHAPTER 48

Declaration of Judah's Chastening

"HEAR this, O house of Jacob,
Who are called by the name of
Israel,
And have come forth from the
wellsprings of Judah;
Who swear by the name of the LORD,
And make mention of the God of Israel,
But not in truth or in righteousness;
2 For they call themselves [R]after the holy
city, Is. 52:1; 64:10
And [R]lean on the God of Israel; Mic. 3:11
The LORD of hosts *is* His name:

3 "I have [R]declared the former things from
the beginning; Is. 44:7, 8; 46:10
They went forth from My mouth, and I
caused them to hear it.
Suddenly I did *them,* [R]and they came to
pass. Josh. 21:45
4 Because I knew that you *were*
[T]obstinate, Heb. *hard*
And [R]your neck *was* an iron sinew,
And your brow bronze, Deut. 31:27
5 Even from the beginning I have
declared *it* to you;
Before it came to pass I proclaimed *it* to
you,
Lest you should say, 'My idol has done
them,
And my carved image and my molded
image
Have commanded them.'

6 "You have heard;
See all this.
And will you not declare *it?*
I have made you hear new things from
this time,
Even hidden things, and you did not
know them.
7 They are created now and not from the
beginning;
And before this day you have not heard
them,
Lest you should say, 'Of course I knew
them.'
8 Surely you did not hear,
Surely you did not know;
Surely from long ago your ear was not
opened.
For I knew that you would deal very
treacherously,
And were called [R]a transgressor from
the womb. Ps. 58:3

9 "For[R] My name's sake [R]I will [T]defer My
anger, Ezek. 20:9, 14, 22, 44 • Ps. 78:38 • *delay*
And *for* My praise I will restrain it from
you,
So that I do not cut you off.
10 Behold, [R]I have refined you, but not as
silver;
I have tested you in the [R]furnace of
affliction. Ps. 66:10 • Deut. 4:20
11 For My own sake, for My own sake, I
will do *it;*
For [R]how should *My name* be profaned?
And [R]I will not give My glory to
another. Ezek. 20:9 • Is. 42:8

12 "Listen to Me, O Jacob,
And Israel, My called:
I *am* He, [R]I *am* the [R]First,
I *am* also the Last. Deut. 32:39 • [Rev. 22:13]
13 Indeed [R]My hand has laid the
foundation of the earth,
And My right hand has stretched out
the heavens;
When [R]I call to them, Ps. 102:25 • Is. 40:26
They stand up together.

14 "All of you, assemble yourselves, and
hear!
Who among them has declared these
things?
[R]The LORD loves him;
[R]He shall do His pleasure on Babylon,
And His arm *shall be against* the
Chaldeans. Is. 45:1 • Is. 44:28; 47:1–15
15 I, *even* I, have spoken;
Yes, [R]I have called him,
I have brought him, and his way will
prosper. Is. 45:1, 2

16 "Come near to Me, hear this:
[R]I have not spoken in secret from the
beginning; Is. 45:19
From the time that it was, I *was* there.
And now the Lord GOD and His Spirit
[T]Have sent Me." Heb. verb is singular

17 Thus says [R]the LORD, your Redeemer,
The Holy One of Israel:

"I *am* the LORD your God,
Who teaches you to profit,
[R]Who leads you by the way you should go. Is. 43:14 • Ps. 32:8
18 [R]Oh, that you had heeded My commandments!
[R]Then your peace would have been like a river,
And your righteousness like the waves of the sea. Ps. 81:13 • Ps. 119:165
19 [R]Your descendants also would have been like the sand, Gen. 22:17
And the offspring of your body like the grains of sand;
His name would not have been cut off
Nor destroyed from before Me."

20 [R]Go forth from Babylon!
Flee from the Chaldees!
With a voice of singing,
Declare, proclaim this,
Utter it *even* to the end of the earth;
Say, "The LORD has [R]redeemed
His servant Jacob!" Zech. 2:6, 7 • [Ex. 19:4–6]
21 And they [R]did not thirst
When He led them through the deserts;
He [R]caused the waters to flow from the rock for them;
He also split the rock, and the waters gushed out. [Is. 41:17, 18] • Ex. 17:6

22 "*There*[R] *is* no peace," says the LORD, "for the wicked." [Is. 57:21]

CHAPTER 49

The Messiah's Mission

"LISTEN, [R]O coastlands, to Me,
And take heed, you peoples from afar! Is. 41:1
[R]The LORD has called Me from the womb; Jer. 1:5
From the [T]matrix of My mother He has made mention of My name. *inward parts*
2 And He has made [R]My mouth like a sharp sword; Rev. 1:16; 2:12 ☆
[R]In the shadow of His hand He has hidden Me, Is. 51:16
And made Me [R]a polished shaft; Ps. 45:5
In His quiver He has hidden Me."

3 "And He said to me,
[R]'You *are* My servant, O Israel, [Zech. 3:8]
[R]In whom I will be glorified.' Is. 44:23
4 [R]Then I said, 'I have labored in vain,
I have spent my strength for nothing and in vain; [Ezek. 3:19]
Yet surely my [T]just reward *is* with the LORD, *justice*
And my work with my God.' "

5 "And now the LORD says,
Who formed Me from the womb *to be* His Servant,
To bring Jacob back to Him,
So that Israel [R]is *gathered to Him
(For I shall be glorious in the eyes of the LORD, Matt. 23:37 ☆
And My God shall be My strength),
6 Indeed He says,
'It is too small a thing that You should be My Servant
To raise up the tribes of Jacob,
And to restore the preserved ones of Israel;
I will also give You as a [R]light to the Gentiles, [Luke 2:32] ☆
That You should be My salvation to the ends of the earth.' "

7 Thus says the LORD,
The Redeemer of Israel, [T]their Holy One, Lit. *his* or *its*
[R]To Him whom man despises,
To Him whom the nation abhors,
To the Servant of rulers: [Ps. 22:6–8] ☆
[R]"Kings shall see and arise, [Is. 52:15]
Princes also shall worship,
Because of the LORD who is faithful,
The Holy One of Israel;
And He has chosen You."

8 Thus says the LORD:

"In an [R]acceptable[T] time I have heard You, 2 Cor. 6:2 ☆ • *favorable*
And in the day of salvation I have helped You;
I will [T]preserve You [R]and give You
As a covenant to the people,
To restore the earth, *keep* • Is. 42:6
To cause them to inherit the desolate [T]heritages; *inheritances*
9 That You may say [R]to the prisoners, 'Go forth,' Is. 61:1; Luke 4:18 ☆
To those who *are* in darkness, 'Show yourselves.'

"They shall feed along the roads,
And their pastures *shall be* on all desolate heights.
10 They shall neither [R]hunger nor thirst,
[R]Neither heat nor sun shall strike them;
For He who has mercy on them [R]will lead them,
Even by the springs of water He will guide them. Rev. 7:16 ☆ • Ps. 121:6 • Ps. 23:2
11 [R]I will make each of My mountains a road, Is. 40:4
And My highways shall be elevated.
12 Surely [R]these shall come from afar;
Look! Those from the north and the west, Is. 43:5, 6

49:5 So with Qr., DSS, LXX; Kt. *not gathered*

And these from the land of Sinim."

13 [R]Sing, O heavens! Is. 44:23
Be joyful, O earth!
And break out in singing, O mountains!
For the LORD has comforted His people,
And will have mercy on His afflicted.

14 [R]But Zion said, "The LORD has forsaken
me,
And my Lord has forgotten me." Is. 40:27

15 "Can a woman forget her nursing child,
[T]And not have compassion on the son of
her womb? Lit. *From having compassion*
Surely they may forget,
[R]Yet I will not forget you. Rom. 11:29
16 See, [R]I have inscribed you on the palms
of My hands; Song 8:6
Your walls *are* continually before Me.
17 Your sons shall make haste;
Your destroyers and those who laid you
waste
Shall go away from you.
18 [R]Lift up your eyes, look around and see;
All these gather together *and* come to
you. Is. 60:4
As I live," says the LORD,
"You shall surely clothe yourselves with
them all [R]as an ornament, Prov. 17:6
And bind them *on you* as a bride *does*.

19 "For your waste and desolate places,
And the land of your destruction,
[R]Will even now be too small for the
inhabitants;
And those who swallowed you up will
be far away. Zech. 10:10
20 [R]The children you will have, Is. 60:4
[R]After you have lost the others,
Will say again in your ears, [Rom. 11:11]
'The place *is* too small for me;
Give me a place where I may dwell.'
21 Then you will say in your heart,
'Who has begotten these for me,
Since I have lost my children and am
desolate,
A captive, and wandering to and fro?
And who has brought these up?
There I was, left alone;
But these, where *were* they?' "

22 [R]Thus says the Lord GOD: Is. 60:4

"Behold, I will lift My hand in an oath to
the nations,
And set up My [T]*standard* for the
peoples; *banner*
They shall bring your sons in *their*
[T]arms,
And your daughters shall be carried on
their shoulders; Lit. *bosom*

23 [R]Kings shall be your foster fathers,
And their queens your nursing mothers;
They shall bow down to you with *their*
faces to the earth,
And [R]lick up the dust of your feet.
Then you will know that I *am* the
LORD,
[R]For they shall not be ashamed who wait
for Me." Is. 52:15 • Ps. 72:9 • [Rom. 5:5]

24 [R]Shall the prey be taken from the
mighty,
Or the captives of the righteous be
delivered? Luke 11:21, 22

25 But thus says the LORD:

"Even the captives of the mighty shall be
taken away,
And the prey of the terrible be
delivered;
For I will contend with him who
contends with you,
And I will save your children.
26 I will [R]feed those who oppress you with
their own flesh,
And they shall be drunk with their own
[R]blood as with sweet wine.
All flesh [R]shall know
That I, the LORD, *am* your Savior,
And your Redeemer, the Mighty One of
Jacob." Is. 9:20 • Rev. 14:20 • Ps. 9:16

CHAPTER 50

The Messiah's Obedience

THUS says the LORD:

"Where *is* [R]the certificate of your
mother's divorce, Deut. 24:1
Whom I have put away?
Or which of My [R]creditors *is it* to whom
I have sold you? Deut. 32:30
For your iniquities [R]you have sold
yourselves, Is. 52:3
And for your transgressions your
mother has been put away.
2 Why, when I came, *was there* no man?
Why, when I called, *was there* none to
answer?
Is My hand shortened at all that it
cannot redeem?
Or have I no power to deliver?
Indeed with My [R]rebuke I dry up the
sea,
I make the rivers a wilderness;
Their fish stink because *there is* no
water,
And die of thirst. Nah. 1:4
3 I clothe the heavens with blackness,
And I make sackcloth their covering."

4 "The[R] Lord GOD has given Me Ex. 4:11
The tongue of the learned,
That I should know how to speak
A word in season to *him who is* [R]weary.
He awakens Me morning by morning,
He awakens My ear Matt. 11:28
To hear as the learned.
5 The Lord GOD has opened My ear;
And I was not [R]rebellious,
Nor did I turn away. Matt. 26:39; John 14:31 ☆
6 [R]I gave My back to those who struck
Me, Matt. 27:26
And [R]My cheeks to those who plucked
out the beard; Matt. 26:67; 27:30 ☆
I did not hide My face from shame and
[R]spitting. Lam. 3:30

7 "For the Lord GOD will help Me;
Therefore I will not be disgraced;
Therefore [R]I have set My face like a
flint, Luke 9:51 ☆
And I know that I will not be ashamed.
8 [R]*He is* near who justifies Me; [Rom. 8:32–34]
Who will contend with Me?
Let us stand together.
Who *is* [T]My adversary?
Let him come near Me. *master of My judgment*
9 Surely the Lord GOD [R]will help Me;
Who *is* he *who* will condemn Me?
[R]Indeed they will all grow old like a
garment; Acts 2:24 ☆ • Job 13:28
[R]The moth will eat them up. Is. 51:6, 8

10 "Who among you fears the LORD?
Who obeys the voice of His Servant?
Who [R]walks in darkness Ps. 23:4
And has no light?
[R]Let him trust in the name of the LORD
And rely upon his God. 2 Chr. 20:20
11 Look, all you who kindle a fire,
Who encircle *yourselves* with sparks:
Walk in the light of your fire and in the
sparks you have kindled—
This you shall have from My hand:
You shall lie down [R]in torment. Ps. 16:4

CHAPTER 51

The Messiah's Encouragement to Israel

"LISTEN to Me, [R]you who [T]follow after
righteousness,
You who seek the LORD:
Look to the rock *from which* you were
hewn,
And to the hole of the pit *from which*
you were dug. [Rom. 9:30–32] • *pursue*
2 [R]Look to Abraham your father, Heb. 11:11
And to Sarah *who* bore you;
[R]For I called him alone, Gen. 12:1
And blessed him and increased him."

3 For the LORD will [R]comfort Zion,
He will comfort all her waste places;
He will make her wilderness like Eden,
And her desert [R]like the garden of the
LORD; Is. 40:1; 52:9 • Gen. 13:10
Joy and gladness will be found in it,
Thanksgiving and the voice of melody.

4 "Listen to Me, My people;
And give ear to Me, O My nation:
[R]For law will proceed from Me, Is. 2:3
And I will make My justice rest
[R]As a light of the peoples. Is. 42:6
5 [R]My righteousness *is* near, Is. 46:13
My salvation has gone forth,
And My arms will judge the peoples;
[R]The coastlands will wait upon Me,
And on My arm they will trust. Is. 60:9
6 [R]Lift up your eyes to the heavens,
And look on the earth beneath. Is. 40:26
For [R]the heavens will vanish away like
smoke, Matt. 24:35
[R]The earth will grow old like a garment,
And those who dwell in it will die in
like manner; Is. 24:19, 20; 50:9
But My salvation will be [R]forever,
And My righteousness will not be
[T]abolished. Is. 45:17 • *broken*

7 "Listen to Me, you who know
righteousness,
You people [R]in whose heart *is* My law:
Do not fear the reproach of men,
Nor be afraid of their revilings. Ps. 37:31
8 For [R]the moth will eat them up like a
garment, Is. 50:9
And the worm will eat them like wool;
But My righteousness will be forever,
And My salvation from generation to
generation."

9 [R]Awake, awake, [R]put on strength,
O arm of the LORD! Ps. 44:23 • Ps. 93:1
Awake [R]as in the ancient days,
In the generations of old. Ps. 44:1
[R]*Are* You not *the arm* that cut [R]Rahab
apart, Job 26:12 • Ps. 87:4
And wounded the [R]serpent? Ps. 74:13

10 *Are* You not *the One* who [R]dried up the
sea, Ex. 14:21
The waters of the great deep;
That made the depths of the sea a road
For the redeemed to cross over?
11 So [R]the ransomed of the LORD shall
return, Is. 35:10
And come to Zion with singing,
With everlasting joy on their heads;
They shall obtain joy and gladness,
And sorrow and sighing shall flee away.

12 "I, *even* I, *am* He [R]who comforts you.
Who *are* you that you should be afraid
[R]Of a man *who* will die, 2 Cor. 1:3 • Ps. 118:6
And of the son of a man *who* will be
made [R]like grass? Is. 40:6, 7

13 And [R]you forget the LORD your Maker,
Who stretched out the heavens Is. 17:10
And laid the foundations of the earth;
You have feared continually every day
Because of the fury of the oppressor,
When *he has* prepared to destroy.
And where *is* the fury of the oppressor?
14 The captive exile hastens, that he may
be loosed,
That he should not die in the pit,
And that his bread should not fail.
15 But I *am* the LORD your God,
Who [R]divided the sea whose waves
roared—
The LORD of hosts *is* His name. Job 26:12
16 And [R]I have put My words in your
mouth; Deut. 18:18
[R]I have covered you with the shadow of
My hand, Is. 49:2
That I may [T]plant the heavens, *establish*
Lay the foundations of the earth,
And say to Zion, 'You *are* My people.' "

17 [R]Awake, awake! Is. 52:1
Stand up, O Jerusalem,
You who [R]have drunk at the hand of
the LORD Job 21:20
The cup of His fury;
You have drunk the dregs of the cup of
trembling,
And drained *it* out.
18 *There is* no one to guide her
Among all the sons she has brought
forth;
Nor *is there any* who takes her by the
hand
Among all the sons she has brought up.
19 [R]These two *things* have come to you;
Who will be sorry for you?— Is. 47:9
Desolation and destruction, famine and
sword—
[R]By whom will I comfort you? Amos 7:2
20 [R]Your sons have fainted,
They lie at the head of all the streets,
Like an antelope in a net;
They are full of the fury of the LORD,
The rebuke of your God. Lam. 2:11

21 Therefore please hear this, you afflicted,
And drunk [R]but not with wine. Lam. 3:15
22 Thus says your Lord,
The LORD and your God,
Who [R]pleads the cause of His people:
"See, I have taken out of your hand
The cup of trembling,
The dregs of the cup of My fury;
You shall no longer drink it. Jer. 50:34
23 [R]*But I will put it into* the hand of those
who afflict you,
Who have said to [T]you,
'Lie down, that we may walk over you.'
And you have laid your body like the
ground,
And as the street, for those who walk
over." Zech. 12:2 • Lit. *your soul*

CHAPTER 52

AWAKE, awake!
Put on your strength, O Zion;
Put on your beautiful garments,
O Jerusalem, the holy city!
For the uncircumcised [R]and the unclean
Shall no longer come to you. [Rev. 21:2–27]
2 [R]Shake yourself from the dust, arise,
And sit down, O Jerusalem; Is. 3:26
[R]Loose yourself from the bonds of your
neck, Zech. 2:7
O captive daughter of Zion!

3 For thus says the LORD:

[R]"You have sold yourselves for nothing,
And you shall be redeemed [R]without
money." Ps. 44:12 • Is. 45:13

4 For thus says the Lord GOD:

"My people went down at first
Into [R]Egypt to [T]sojourn there;
Then the Assyrian oppressed them
without cause. Gen. 46:6 • Reside temporarily
5 Now therefore, what have I here," says
the LORD,
"That My people are taken away for
nothing?
Those who rule over them
Make them wail," says the LORD,
"And My name *is* [R]blasphemed
continually every day. Ezek. 36:20, 23
6 Therefore My people shall know My
name;
Therefore *they shall know* in that day
That I *am* He who speaks:
'Behold, *it is* I.' "

7 [R]How beautiful upon the mountains
Are the feet of him who brings good
news,
Who proclaims peace,
Who brings glad tidings of good *things*,
Who proclaims salvation,
Who says to Zion,
[R]"Your God reigns!" Rom. 10:15 • Ps. 93:1
8 Your watchmen shall lift up *their*
voices,
With their voices they shall sing
together;
For they shall see eye to eye
When the LORD brings back Zion.
9 Break forth into joy, sing together,
You waste places of Jerusalem!
For the LORD has comforted His people,
He has redeemed Jerusalem.
10 The LORD has made bare His holy arm
In the eyes of [R]all the nations; Luke 3:6

And all the ends of the earth shall see
The salvation of our God.

11 [R]Depart! Depart! Go out from there,
Touch no unclean *thing*;
Go out from the midst of her,
[R]Be clean, Is. 48:20 • Lev. 22:2
You who bear the vessels of the LORD.
12 For [R]you shall not go out with haste,
Nor go by flight;
[R]For the LORD will go before you,
[R]And the God of Israel *will be* your rear guard. Ex. 12:11, 33 • Mic. 2:13 • Ex. 14:19, 20

The Messiah's Atonement

13 Behold, [R]My Servant shall [T]deal prudently, Is. 42:1 • *prosper*
[R]He shall be exalted and [T]extolled and be very high. Phil. 2:9☆ • Lit. *be lifted up*
14 Just as many were astonished at you,
So His [R]visage[T] was marred more than any man,
And His form more than the sons of men; Ps. 22:6, 7; Is. 53:2, 3☆ • *appearance*
15 [R]So shall He [T]sprinkle many nations.
Kings shall shut their mouths at Him;
For [R]what had not been told them they shall see,
And what they had not heard they shall consider. 1 Pet. 1:2☆ • *startle* • Rom. 15:21☆

CHAPTER 53

WHO [R]has believed our report?
And to whom has the arm of the LORD been revealed? John 12:38; Rom. 10:16☆
2 For He shall grow up before Him as a tender plant,
And as a root out of dry ground.
He has no form or comeliness;
And [R]when we see Him, Mark 15:32☆
There is no [T]beauty that we should desire Him. Lit. *appearance*
3 [R]He is despised and rejected by men,
A Man of sorrows and acquainted with grief. Ps. 22:6; [Is. 49:7]☆
And we hid, as it were, *our* faces from Him;
He was despised, and [R]we did not esteem Him. [John 1:10, 11]☆

4 Surely [R]He has borne our griefs
And carried our sorrows; [Matt. 8:17]☆
Yet we esteemed Him stricken,
Smitten by God, and afflicted.
5 But He *was* [R]wounded for our transgressions, [Rom. 4:25; 1 Pet. 2:24, 25]☆
He was [T]bruised for our iniquities;
The chastisement for our peace *was* upon Him, *crushed*
And by His stripes we are healed.
6 All we like sheep have gone astray;
We have turned, every one, to his own way;
And the LORD has [R]laid on Him the iniquity of us all. Heb. 9:28☆

7 He was oppressed and He was afflicted,
Yet [R]He opened not His mouth;
[R]He was led as a lamb to the slaughter,
And as a sheep before its shearers is silent, Matt. 26:63; Mark 15:4, 5☆ • Acts 8:32☆
So He opened not his mouth.
8 He was [R]taken from [T]prison and from judgment, Luke 23:1-25 • *confinement*
And who will declare His generation?
For [R]He was cut off from the land of the living; [Dan. 9:26]
[R]For the transgressions of My people He was stricken. 1 Cor. 15:3☆
9 [R]And [T]they made His grave with the wicked— Matt. 27:38, 57-60☆ • Lit. *he* or *He*
But with the rich at His death,
Because He had done no violence,
Nor *was any* deceit in His mouth.

10 Yet it pleased the LORD to [T]bruise Him;
He has put *Him* to grief. *crush*
When You make His soul [R]an offering for sin, [John 1:29; 2 Cor. 5:21]☆
He shall see *His* seed, [R]He shall prolong *His* days, Acts 2:24☆
And the pleasure of the LORD shall prosper in His hand.
11 He shall see the [T]travail of His soul, *and* be satisfied. *distress*
[R]By His knowledge My righteous Servant shall justify many, Rom 5:18, 19☆
For He shall bear their iniquities.
12 [R]Therefore I will divide Him a portion with the great, Ps. 2:8
[R]And He shall divide the [T]spoil with the strong, Col. 2:15 • *plunder*
Because He [R]poured out His soul unto death, Is. 50:6
And He was [R]numbered with the transgressors, Matt. 27:38; Luke 22:37☆
And He bore the sin of many,
And [R]made intercession for the transgressors. Luke 23:34☆

CHAPTER 54

The Messiah's Promise of Israel's Restoration

"SING, O [R]barren,
You *who* have not borne!
Break forth into singing, and cry aloud,
You *who* have not travailed with child!
For more *are* the children of the desolate
Than the children of the married woman," says the LORD. Gal. 4:27
2 "Enlarge[R] the place of your tent,
And let them stretch out the curtains of your habitations;

MAJOR MESSIANIC PASSAGES

The Hebrew word *Messiah*, meaning "Anointed One," is translated "the Christ" in the Greek language. In the Old Testament, the word is often associated with the anointing of a prophet, a priest, king, or other ruler. God's promise to Abraham that in him and his descendants all the world would be blessed (Gen. 12:1–3) created the expectancy of a kingdom of God on earth among the Hebrew people. The reign of David as king of Judah further shaped popular messianic expectations that the coming kingdom would be one like King David's (2 Sam. 7).

As the Hebrew kingdom divided after Solomon's time, the idea of a messianic deliverer became popular. The people of Israel looked for a political ruler to deliver them from their enemies. The "salvation" spoken of in the Psalms and some prophecies of Isaiah and Jeremiah was interpreted as referring to deliverance from Israel's enemies, especially threatening world powers (Ps. 69:35; Is. 25:9; Jer. 42:11). The Hebrew people tended to overlook or ignore such prophecies as the suffering Servant message of Isaiah 53, which foretold that the Messiah would suffer and die.

Major Old Testament passages indicated that the Messiah would be born of a virgin (Is. 7:14), in Bethlehem (Mic. 5:2), and that He would be a descendant of the house of David (2 Sam. 7:12). He would be "a Man of sorrows" (Is. 53:3) who would suffer rejection by His own people (Ps. 69:8), followed by betrayal by a friend (Ps. 41:9), and crucifixion between two thieves (Is. 53:12). As the Messiah died, His spirit would be commended to His Father (Ps. 31:5). He would be raised from the dead (Ps. 16:10) to take His place at God's right hand (Ps. 110:1).

Jesus fulfilled these prophecies as Prophet, Priest, and King, but He came to deliver humankind from the reign of sin and bind us into God's family (Luke 4:18, 19; Acts 2:36–42). "My kingdom is not of this world" (John 18:36), He told Pilate. He ruled by serving (Matt. 20:25–28). As a priest, He offered not the blood of animals, but Himself, as a full and final sacrifice for sins (John 10:11–18; Heb. 9:12).

Old Testament prophecies foretold that the Messiah would suffer and die.

Do not spare;
Lengthen your cords,
And strengthen your stakes. Is. 49:19, 20
3 For you shall expand to the right and to the left,
And your descendants will [R]inherit the nations, Is. 14:2; 49:22, 23; 60:9
And make the desolate cities inhabited.

4 "Do[R] not fear, for you will not be ashamed; Is. 41:10
Nor be disgraced, for you will not be put to shame;
For you will forget the shame of your youth,
And will not remember the reproach of your widowhood anymore.
5 [R]For your Maker *is* your husband,
The LORD of hosts *is* His name;
And your Redeemer *is* the Holy One of Israel;
He is called [R]the God of the whole earth. Jer. 3:14 • Zech. 14:9
6 For the LORD [R]has called you
Like a woman forsaken and grieved in spirit,
Like a youthful wife when you were refused,"
Says your God. Is. 62:4
7 "For[R] a mere moment I have forsaken you,
But with great mercies [R]I will gather you. Is. 26:20; 60:10 • [Is. 43:5; 56:8]
8 With a little wrath I hid My face from you for a moment;
[R]But with everlasting kindness I will have mercy on you," Jer. 31:3
Says the LORD, your Redeemer.

9 "For this *is* like the waters of [R]Noah to Me; Gen. 8:21; 9:11
For as I have sworn
That the waters of Noah would no longer cover the earth,
So have I sworn
That I would not be angry with [R]you, nor rebuke you. Ezek. 39:29
10 For [R]the mountains shall depart
And the hills be removed, Is. 51:6
[R]But My kindness shall not depart from you, Ps. 89:33, 34
Nor shall My covenant of peace be removed,"
Says the LORD, who has mercy on you.

11 "O you afflicted one,
Tossed with tempest, *and* not comforted,
Behold, I will lay your stones with [R]colorful gems,
And lay your foundations with sapphires. Rev. 21:18, 19
12 I will make your pinnacles of rubies,
Your gates of crystal,
And all your walls of precious stones.
13 All your children *shall be* [R]taught by the LORD,
And [R]great *shall be* the peace of your children. [John 6:45] • Ps. 119:165
14 In righteousness you shall be established;
You shall be far from oppression, for you shall not fear;
And from terror, for it shall not come near you.
15 Indeed they shall surely assemble, *but* not because of Me.
Whoever assembles against you shall [R]fall for your sake. Is. 41:11-16

16 "Behold, I have created the blacksmith
Who blows the coals in the fire,
Who brings forth an [T]instrument for his work;
And I have created the [T]spoiler to destroy. Or *weapon* • *destroyer*
17 No weapon formed against you shall [R]prosper, Is. 17:12-14; 29:8
And every tongue *which* rises against you in judgment
You shall condemn.
This *is* the heritage of the servants of the LORD,
[R]And their righteousness *is* from Me,"
Says the LORD. Is. 45:24, 25; 54:14

CHAPTER 55

The Messiah's Invitation to the World

"HO! [R]Everyone who thirsts,
Come to the waters; [John 4:14; 7:37]
And you who have no money,
[R]Come, buy and eat. [Rev. 3:18]
Yes, come, buy wine and milk
Without money and without price.
2 Why do you [T]spend money for *what is* not bread,
And your wages for *what* does not satisfy?
Listen diligently to Me, and eat *what is* good,
And let your soul delight itself in abundance. Lit. *weigh out silver*
3 Incline your ear, and [R]come to Me.
Hear, and your soul shall live; Matt. 11:28
[R]And I will make an everlasting covenant with you— Jer. 32:40
The [R]sure mercies of David. 2 Sam. 7:8
4 Indeed I have given him *as* [R]a witness to the people, [Rev. 1:5]
A leader and commander for the people.
5 [R]Surely you shall call a nation you do not know, Is. 52:15; Eph. 2:11, 12☆
[R]And nations *who* do not know you shall run to you, Is. 60:5

Because of the LORD your God,
And the Holy One of Israel;
[R]For He has glorified you." Is. 60:9

6 [R]Seek the LORD while He may be found,
Call upon Him while He is near. [Heb. 3:13]
7 Let the [T]wicked forsake his way,
And the unrighteous man his thoughts;
Let him return to the LORD,
[R]And He will have mercy on him;
And to our God, Lit. *man of iniquity* • Jer. 3:12
For He will abundantly pardon.

8 "For[R] My thoughts *are* not your thoughts,
Nor *are* your ways My ways," says the LORD. 2 Sam. 7:19
9 "For[R] *as* the heavens are higher than the earth, Ps. 103:11
So are My ways higher than your ways,
And My thoughts than your thoughts.

10 "For [R]as the rain comes down, and the snow from heaven,
And do not return there,
But water the earth,
And make it bring forth and bud,
That it may give seed to the sower
And bread to the eater, Deut. 32:2
11 [R]So shall My word be that goes forth from My mouth; Is. 45:23
It shall not return to Me [T]void,
But it shall accomplish what I please,
And it shall [R]prosper *in the thing* for which I sent it. *empty* • Is. 46:9–11

12 "For[R] you shall go out with joy,
And be led out with peace;
The mountains and the hills
Shall [R]break forth into singing before you,
And [R]all the trees of the field shall clap *their* hands. Is. 35:10 • Ps. 98:8 • 1 Chr. 16:33
13 [R]Instead of [R]the thorn shall come up the cypress tree,
And instead of the brier shall come up the myrtle tree;
And it shall be to the LORD [R]for a name,
For an everlasting sign *that* shall not be cut off." Is. 41:19 • Mic. 7:4 • Jer. 13:11

CHAPTER 56

THUS says the LORD:

"Keep justice, and do righteousness,
For My salvation *is* about to come,
And My righteousness to be revealed.
2 Blessed *is* the man *who* does this,
And the son of man *who* lays hold on it;
[R]Who keeps from defiling the Sabbath,
And keeps his hand from doing any evil." Is. 58:13

3 Do not let [R]the son of the foreigner
Who has joined himself to the LORD
Speak, saying, [Eph. 2:12–19]
"The LORD has utterly separated me from His people";
Nor let the eunuch say,
"Here I am, a dry tree."
4 For thus says the LORD:
"To the eunuchs who keep My Sabbaths,
And choose what pleases Me,
And hold fast My covenant,
5 Even to them I will give in [R]My house
And within My walls a place [R]and a name 1 Tim. 3:15 • [1 John 3:1, 2]
Better than that of sons and daughters;
I will give them an everlasting name
That shall not be cut off.

6 "Also the sons of the foreigner
Who join themselves to the LORD, to serve Him,
And to love the name of the LORD, to be His servants—
Everyone who keeps from defiling the Sabbath,
And holds fast My covenant—
7 Even them I will [R]bring to My holy mountain, [Is. 2:2, 3; 60:11]
And make them joyful in My [R]house of prayer. Mark 11:17
[R]Their burnt offerings and their sacrifices
Will be accepted on My altar; [Rom. 12:1]
For My house shall be called a house of prayer [R]for all nations." [Mal. 1:11]
8 The Lord GOD, [R]who gathers the outcasts of Israel, says, Is. 11:12; 27:12
[R]"Yet I will gather to him [John 10:16]
Others besides those who are gathered to him."

The Messiah's Rebuke of the Wicked

9 [R]All you beasts of the field, come to devour,
All you beasts in the forest. Jer. 12:9
10 His watchmen *are* [R]blind, Matt. 15:14
They are all ignorant;
[R]They *are* all dumb dogs, Phil. 3:2
They cannot bark;
Sleeping, lying down, loving to slumber.
11 Yes, *they are* [R]greedy dogs [Mic. 3:5, 11]
Which [R]never have enough. Ezek. 34:2–10
And they *are* shepherds
Who cannot understand;
They all look to their own way,
Every one for his own gain,
From his *own* territory.
12 "Come," *one says*, "I will bring wine,
And we will fill ourselves with intoxicating [R]drink; Is. 28:7
Tomorrow will be [R]as today, 2 Pet. 3:4
And much more abundant."

CHAPTER 57

THE righteous perishes,
And no man takes *it* to heart;
[R]Merciful men *are* taken away,
[R]While no one considers
That the righteous is taken away from
[T]evil. Ps. 12:1 • 1 Kin. 14:13 • Lit. *the face of evil*
2 He shall enter into peace;
They shall rest in [R]their beds, 2 Chr. 16:14
Each one walking *in* his uprightness.

3 "But come here,
[R]You sons of the sorceress, Matt. 16:4
You offspring of the adulterer and the
harlot!
4 Whom do you ridicule?
Against whom do you make a wide
mouth
And stick out the tongue?
Are you not children of transgression,
Offspring of falsehood,
5 Inflaming yourselves with gods [R]under
every green tree, 2 Kin. 16:4
[R]Slaying the children in the valleys,
Under the clefts of the rocks? Jer. 7:31
6 Among the smooth [R]*stones* of the
stream Jer. 3:9
Is your portion;
They, they, *are* your lot!
Even to them you have poured a drink
offering,
You have offered a grain offering.
Should I receive comfort in these?

7 "On[R] a lofty and high mountain
You have set [R]your bed;
Even there you went up
To offer sacrifice. Ezek. 16:16 • Ezek. 23:41
8 Also behind the doors and their posts
You have set up your remembrance;
For you have uncovered yourself *to*
those other than Me,
And have gone up to them;
You have enlarged your bed
And [T]made *a covenant* with them;
You have loved their bed,
Where you saw *their* hand. Lit. *cut*
9 [R]You went to the king with ointment,
And increased your perfumes; Hos. 7:11
You sent your messengers far off,
And debased *yourself even* to Sheol.
10 You are wearied in the length of your
way;
Yet you did not say, 'There is no hope.'
You have found the life of your hand;
Therefore you were not grieved.

11 "And [R]of whom have you been afraid, or
feared, Is. 51:12, 13
That you have lied
And not remembered Me,
Nor taken *it* to your heart?
Is it not because [R]I have [T]held My peace
from of old Ps. 50:21 • *remained silent*
That you do not fear Me?
12 I will declare your righteousness
And your works,
For they will not profit you.
13 When you cry out,
Let your collection *of idols* deliver you.
But the wind will carry them all away,
A breath will take *them*.
But he who puts his trust in Me shall
possess the land,
And shall inherit My holy mountain."

14 And one shall say,
[R]"Heap it up! Heap it up!
Prepare the way,
Take the stumbling block out of the
way of My people." Is. 40:3; 62:10

15 For thus says the High and Lofty One
Who inhabits eternity, [R]whose name *is*
Holy: Job 6:10
[R]"I dwell in the high and holy *place*,
[R]With him *who* has a contrite and
humble spirit, Zech. 2:13 • Ps. 34:18; 51:17
[R]To revive the spirit of the humble,
And to revive the heart of the contrite
ones. Is. 61:1–3
16 [R]For I will not contend forever, [Mic. 7:18]
Nor will I always be angry;
For the spirit would fail before Me,
And the souls *which* I have made.
17 For the iniquity of [R]his covetousness
I was angry and struck him; Jer. 6:13
[R]I hid and was angry, Is. 8:17; 45:15; 59:2
[R]And he went on [T]backsliding in the way
of his heart. Is. 9:13 • Or *turning back*
18 I have seen his ways, and [R]will heal
him;
I will also lead him,
And restore comforts to him
And to [R]his mourners. Jer. 3:22 • Is. 61:2

19 "I create [R]the fruit of the lips:
Peace, peace [R]to *him who is* far off and
to *him who is* near,"
Says the LORD, Heb. 13:15 • Eph. 2:17
"And I will heal him."
20 [R]But the wicked *are* like the troubled
sea, Job 15:20
When it cannot rest,
Whose waters cast up mire and dirt.

21 "*There*[R] *is* no peace,"
Says my God, "for the wicked." Is. 48:22

CHAPTER 58

Blessings of True Worship

"CRY aloud, [T]spare not; *do not hold back*
Lift up your voice like a trumpet;

[R]Tell My people their
transgression, Mic. 3:8
And the house of Jacob their sins.
2 Yet they seek Me daily,
And delight to know My ways,
As a nation that did righteousness,
And did not forsake the ordinance of
their God.
They ask of Me the ordinances of
justice;
They take delight in approaching God.
3 'Why[R] have we fasted,' *they say*, 'and
You have not seen? Mal. 3:13–18
Why have we [R]afflicted our souls, and
You take no notice?' Lev. 16:29; 23:27

"In fact, in the day of your fast you find
pleasure,
And [T]exploit all your laborers. *drive hard*
4 [R]Indeed you fast for strife and debate,
And to strike with the fist of
wickedness. 1 Kin. 21:9
You will not fast as *you do* this day,
To make your voice heard on high.
5 Is [R]it a fast that I have chosen,
[R]A day for a man to afflict his soul?
Is it to bow down his head like a
bulrush, Zech. 7:5 • Lev. 16:29
And [R]to spread out sackcloth and
ashes? Esth. 4:3
Would you call this a fast,
And an acceptable day to the LORD?

6 "*Is* this not the fast that I have chosen:
To loose the bonds of wickedness,
[R]To undo the heavy burdens, Neh. 5:10–12
[R]To let the oppressed go free, Jer. 34:9
And that you break every yoke?
7 *Is it* not [R]to share your bread with the
hungry, Ezek. 18:7
And that you bring to your house the
poor who are [T]cast out; *wandering*
[R]When you see the naked, that you
cover him,
And not hide yourself from [R]your own
flesh? Job 31:19–22 • Neh. 5:5
8 [R]Then your light shall break forth like
the morning,
Your healing shall spring forth speedily,
And your righteousness shall go before
you;
[R]The glory of the LORD shall be your rear
guard. Job 11:17 • Ex. 14:19
9 Then you shall call, and the LORD will
answer;
You shall cry, and He will say, 'Here I
am.'

"If you take away the yoke from your
midst,
The [T]pointing of the finger, and
speaking wickedness, Lit. *sending out of*
10 *If* you extend your soul to the hungry
And satisfy the afflicted soul,
Then your light shall dawn in the
darkness,
And your [T]darkness shall *be* as the
noonday. Or *gloom*
11 The LORD will guide you continually,
And satisfy your soul in drought,
And strengthen your bones;
You shall be like a watered garden,
And like a spring of water, whose
waters do not fail.
12 Those from among you
[R]Shall build the old waste places;
You shall raise up the foundations of
many generations; Is. 61:4
And you shall be called the Repairer of
the Breach,
The Restorer of Streets to Dwell In.

13 "If [R]you turn away your foot from the
Sabbath, Is. 56:2, 4, 6
From doing your pleasure on My holy
day,
And call the Sabbath a delight,
The holy *day* of the LORD honorable,
And shall honor Him, not doing your
own ways,
Nor finding your own pleasure,
Nor speaking *your own* words,
14 [R]Then you shall delight yourself in the
LORD; Job 22:26
And I will cause you to [R]ride on the
high hills of the earth, Deut. 32:13; 33:29
And feed you with the heritage of Jacob
your father.
The mouth of the LORD has spoken."

CHAPTER 59

Sins of Israel

BEHOLD, the LORD's hand is not
[R]shortened,
That it cannot save;
Nor His ear heavy,
That it cannot hear. Num. 11:23

2 But your iniquities have separated you
from your God;

59:2 What Sin Does—Sin, regardless of its degree, always has an effect—separation. Sin separates one from God. This separation from God is death. Adam was told that if he ate of the tree of the knowledge of good and evil that he would die (Page 8—Gen. 3:3). Adam ate of the tree and immediately died spiritually—his soul was separated from God—and he began to die physically. The entrance of sin into the human race brought with it death (Page 1329—Rom. 5:12; 6:23). That man is a sinner is proven by the fact that he dies—where there is death, there is sin. Sin's penalty, death, can be remedied by

And your sins have hidden *His* face
from you,
So that He will [R]not hear. Is. 1:15

3 For [R]your hands are defiled with [T]blood,
And your fingers with iniquity; Ezek. 7:23
Your lips have spoken lies, *bloodshed*
Your tongue has muttered perversity.

4 No one calls for justice,
Nor does *any* plead for truth.
They trust in [R]empty words and speak
lies;
[R]They conceive [T]evil and bring forth
iniquity. Jer. 7:4 • Job 15:35 • *trouble*
5 They hatch vipers' eggs and weave the
spider's web;
He who eats of their eggs dies,
And *from* that which is crushed a viper
breaks out.

6 [R]Their webs will not become garments,
Nor will they cover themselves with
their works;
Their works *are* works of iniquity,
And the act of violence *is* in their
hands. Job 8:14
7 [R]Their feet run to evil, Rom. 3:15
And they make haste to shed [R]innocent
blood; Prov. 6:17
[R]Their thoughts *are* thoughts of iniquity;
Wasting and [R]destruction *are* in their
paths. Is. 55:7 • Rom. 3:16, 17
8 The way of [R]peace they have not
known,
And *there is* no justice in their ways;
[R]They have made themselves crooked
paths;
Whoever takes that way shall not know
peace. Is. 57:20, 21 • Prov. 2:15

9 Therefore justice is far from us,
Nor does righteousness overtake us;
[R]We look for light, but there is darkness!
For brightness, *but* we walk in
blackness! Jer. 8:15
10 We grope for the wall like the blind,
And we grope as if *we had* no eyes;
We stumble at noonday as at twilight;
We are as dead *men* in desolate places.
11 We all growl like bears,
And [R]moan sadly like doves; Ezek. 7:16
We look for justice, but *there is* none;
For salvation, *but* it is far from us.
12 For our [R]transgressions are multiplied
before You,
And our sins testify against us;
For our transgressions *are* with us,
And *as for* our iniquities, we know
them: Is. 24:5; 58:1
13 In transgressing and lying against the
LORD,
And departing from our God,
Speaking oppression and revolt,
Conceiving and uttering [R]from the heart
words of falsehood. Matt. 12:34
14 Justice is turned back,
And righteousness stands afar off;
For truth is fallen in the street,
And equity cannot enter.
15 So truth fails,
And he *who* departs from evil makes
himself a [R]prey. Is. 5:23; 10:2; 29:21; 32:7

Then the LORD saw *it*, and [T]it displeased
Him *Lit. it was evil in His eyes*
That *there was* no justice.
16 [R]He saw that *there was* no man,
And [R]wondered that *there was* no
intercessor;
[R]Therefore His own arm brought
salvation for Him;
And His own righteousness, it sustained
Him. Ezek. 22:30 • Mark 6:6 • Ps. 98:1
17 [R]For He put on righteousness as a
breastplate, Eph. 6:14, 17
And a helmet of salvation on His head;
He put on the garments of vengeance
for clothing,
And was clad with zeal as a cloak.
18 [R]According to *their* deeds, accordingly
He will repay, Is. 63:6
Fury to His adversaries,
Recompense to His enemies;
The coastlands He will fully repay.
19 [R]So shall they fear Mal. 1:11
The name of the LORD from the west,
And His glory from the rising of the
sun;
When the enemy comes in [R]like a flood,
The Spirit of the LORD will lift up a
standard against him. Rev. 12:15

---

life—union with God. This is achieved by belief in Jesus, who died to pay the penalty of man's sin (Page 1329—Rom. 5:21). For the one who believes in Jesus, the penalty of sin is broken. Yes, he will die physically (unless he is alive when Jesus returns to take all believers to heaven with Himself, Page 1416—1 Thess. 4:14–18), but physical death for him is only the doorway into the presence of God. Sin, however, does have an effect upon the believer, for it mars his fellowship with God. Sin in the believer's life is a terrible thing and is not to be tolerated. While it is probable that the believer will sin, it is never necessary for him to do so (Page 1494—1 John 2:1).

Now turn to Page 642—Ps. 32:5: What Should Be Done About Sin.

20 "The[R] Redeemer will come to Zion,
And to those who turn from
transgression in Jacob,"
Says the LORD. Rom. 11:26☆

21 "As[R] for Me," says the LORD, "this *is* My
covenant with them: My Spirit who *is* upon
you, and My words which I have put in your
mouth, shall not depart from your mouth, nor
from the mouth of your descendants, nor
from the mouth of your descendants' descendants," says the LORD, "from this time
and forevermore." [Heb. 8:10; 10:16]

CHAPTER 60

Glory of Israel in the Kingdom

ARISE, [R]shine;
For your light has come!
And [R]the glory of the LORD is risen
upon you. Eph. 5:14 • Mal. 4:2
2 For behold, the darkness shall cover the
earth,
And deep darkness the people;
But the LORD will arise over you,
And His glory will be seen upon you.
3 The [R]Gentiles shall come to your light,
And kings to the brightness of your
rising. Is. 49:6, 23; Rev. 21:24☆

4 "Lift[R] up your eyes all around, and see:
They all gather together, [R]they come to
you; Is. 49:18 • Is. 49:20–22
Your sons shall come from afar,
And your daughters shall be nursed at
your side.
5 Then you shall see and become radiant,
And your heart shall swell with joy;
Because [R]the abundance of the sea shall
be turned to you,
The wealth of the Gentiles shall come
to you. [Rom. 11:25–27]
6 The multitude of camels shall cover
your land,
The dromedaries of Midian and [R]Ephah;
All those from [R]Sheba shall come;
They shall bring [R]gold and incense,
And they shall proclaim the praises of
the LORD. Gen. 25:4 • Ps. 72:10 • Matt. 2:11
7 All the flocks of [R]Kedar shall be
gathered together to you,
The rams of Nebaioth shall minister to
you;
They shall ascend with [R]acceptance on
My altar,
And [R]I will glorify the house of My
glory. Gen. 25:13 • Is. 56:7 • Hag. 2:7, 9

8 "Who *are* these *who* fly like a cloud,
And like doves to their roosts?
9 [R]Surely the coastlands shall wait for Me;
And the ships of Tarshish *will come*
first, Ps. 72:10
[R]To bring your sons from afar, [Gal. 4:26]
[R]Their silver and their gold with them,
To the name of the LORD your God,
And to the Holy One of Israel, Jer. 3:17
[R]Because He has glorified you. Is. 55:5

10 "The[R] sons of foreigners shall build up
your walls, Zech. 6:15
And their kings shall minister to you;
For [R]in My wrath I struck you, Is. 57:17
[R]But in My favor I have had mercy on
you. Is. 54:7, 8
11 Therefore your gates [R]shall be open
continually; Rev. 21:25, 26
They shall not be shut day or night,
That *men* may bring to you the wealth
of the Gentiles,
And their kings in procession.
12 [R]For the nation and kingdom which will
not serve you shall perish,
And *those* nations shall be utterly
ruined. Zech. 14:17

13 "The[R] glory of Lebanon shall come to
you,

59:21 Inspiration of God's Word—The word *inspiration* is found but once in the New Testament. This occurs in Second Timothy 3:16, where Paul says "All Scripture *is* given by inspiration of God," literally "God-breathed." Divine inspiration logically follows divine revelation. In revelation God speaks to man's ear while by inspiration He guides the pen to ensure that the imparted message is correctly written down.

There are several ideas about the process of inspiration. One is called the natural theory. This says that the Bible authors were inspired in the same sense that William Shakespeare was inspired. Another theory, called the content theory, suggests that God merely gave the writer the main content or idea, allowing him to choose his own words to express that concept. In contrast Jesus Himself said that the very letters of the words were also chosen by God (Page 1120—see Matt. 5:18). This position is referred to as the plenary-verbal view, which says that all (plenary) the very words (verbal) of the Bible are inspired by God. Jesus once told the devil that the Christian is to live by each of these inspired words (Page 1118—Matt. 4:4). The Bible authors understood that their writings were being guided by the Spirit of God, even as they wrote them. Peter said this was true of the Old Testament authors (Page 1487—2 Pet. 1:20, 21). He then stated that his own letters (Page 1477—1 and 2 Pet.) were inspired by God (Page 1487—2 Pet. 3:1, 2). Finally, he pointed out that this was also true concerning Paul's writings (Page 1489—2 Pet. 3:15, 16).

One final thing should be said about inspiration. Plenary-verbal inspiration does not guarantee the inspiration of any translation, but only of the original Hebrew and Greek manuscripts.

Now turn to Page 719—Prov. 6:23: Illumination of God's Word.

The cypress, the pine, and the box tree
together,
To beautify the place of My sanctuary;
And I will make [R]the place of My feet
glorious. Is. 35:2 • 1 Chr. 28:2
14 Also the sons of those who afflicted you
Shall come [R]bowing to you, Is. 45:14
And all those who despised you shall
[R]fall prostrate at the soles of your
feet; Rev. 3:9
And they shall call you The City of the
LORD,
[R]Zion of the Holy One of Israel. [Heb. 12:22]

15 "Whereas you have been forsaken and
hated,
So that no one went through *you*,
I will make you an eternal excellence,
A joy of many generations.
16 You shall drink *dry* the milk of the
Gentiles,
[R]And shall milk the breast of kings;
You shall know that [R]I, the LORD, *am*
your Savior
And your Redeemer, the Mighty One of
Jacob. Is. 49:23 • Is. 43:3

17 "Instead of bronze I will bring gold,
Instead of iron I will bring silver,
Instead of wood, bronze,
And instead of stones, iron.
I will also make your officers peace,
And your magistrates righteousness.
18 Violence shall no longer be heard in
your land,
Neither [T]wasting nor destruction within
your borders;
But you shall call [R]your walls Salvation,
And your gates Praise. *devastation* • Is. 26:1

19 "The [R]sun shall no longer be your light
by day, Rev. 21:23; 22:5
Nor for brightness shall the moon give
light to you;
But the LORD will be to you an
everlasting light,
And [R]your God your glory. Zech. 2:5
20 [R]Your sun shall no longer go down,
Nor shall your moon withdraw itself;
For the LORD will be your everlasting
light,
And the days of your mourning shall be
ended. Amos 8:9
21 Also your people *shall* all *be* righteous;
[R]They shall inherit the land forever,
[R]The branch of My
planting, Ps. 37:11 • Is. 61:3
[R]The work of My hands, [Eph. 2:10]
That I may be glorified.
22 A little one shall become a thousand,
And a small one a strong nation.
I, the LORD, will hasten it in its time."

CHAPTER 61

Advents of the Messiah

"THE [R]Spirit of the Lord GOD *is* upon
Me, Is. 11:2; Luke 4:18 ☆
Because the LORD has anointed Me
To preach good tidings to the poor;
He has sent Me [R]to [T]heal the
brokenhearted, Ps. 147:3 • Lit. *bind up*
To proclaim [R]liberty to the captives,
And the opening of the prison to *those
who are* bound; Is. 42:7 ☆
2 [R]To proclaim the acceptable year of the
LORD, Lev. 25:9
And the day of vengeance of our God;
[R]To comfort all who mourn, Matt. 5:4
3 To [T]console those who mourn in Zion,
[R]To give them beauty for ashes,
The oil of joy for mourning,
The garment of praise for the spirit of
heaviness; Lit. *appoint* • Ps. 30:11
That they may be called trees of
righteousness,
[R]The planting of the LORD, [R]that He may
be glorified." Is. 60:21 • [John 15:8]

4 And they shall [R]rebuild the old ruins,
They shall raise up the former
desolations, Ezek. 36:33
And they shall repair the ruined cities,
The desolations of many generations.
5 [R]Strangers shall stand and feed your
flocks,
And the sons of the foreigner
Shall be your plowmen and your
vinedressers. [Eph. 2:12]
6 [R]But you shall be named the Priests of
the LORD, Ex. 19:6
Men shall call you the Servants of our
God.
You shall eat the riches of the Gentiles,
And in their glory you shall boast.
7 [R]Instead of your shame *you shall have*
double *honor*,
And *instead of* confusion they shall
rejoice in their portion.
Therefore in their land they shall
possess double;
Everlasting joy shall be theirs. Zech. 9:12

8 "For [R]I, the LORD, love justice; Ps. 11:7
[R]I hate robbery [T]for burnt offering;
I will direct their work in truth,
[R]And will make with them an everlasting
covenant. Is. 1:11, 13 • Or *in* • Is. 55:3
9 Their descendants shall be known
among the Gentiles,
And their offspring among the people.
All who see them shall acknowledge
them,
[R]That they *are* the posterity *whom* the
LORD has blessed." Is. 65:23

10 [R]I will greatly rejoice in the LORD,
My soul shall be joyful in my God;
For [R]He has clothed me with the garments of salvation,
He has covered me with the robe of righteousness,
[R]As a bridegroom decks *himself* with ornaments,
And as a bride adorns *herself* with her jewels. Hab. 3:18 • Ps. 132:9, 16 • Is. 49:18

11 For as the earth brings forth its bud,
As the garden causes the things that are sown in it to spring forth,
So the Lord GOD will cause righteousness and praise to spring forth before all the nations.

CHAPTER 62

Future of Jerusalem

FOR Zion's sake I will not [T]hold My peace, *keep silent*
And for Jerusalem's sake I will not rest,
Until her righteousness goes forth as brightness,
And her salvation as a lamp *that* burns.
2 [R]The Gentiles shall see your righteousness, Is. 60:3
And all [R]kings your glory. Ps. 102:15, 16
[R]You shall be called by a new name,
Which the mouth of the LORD will name. Is. 62:4, 12; 65:15
3 You shall also be [R]a crown of glory
In the hand of the LORD,
And a royal diadem
In the hand of your God. Zech. 9:16
4 You shall no longer be termed
[R]Forsaken,[T] Is. 49:14; 54:6, 7 • Heb. *Azubah*
Nor shall your land any more be termed
[R]Desolate;[T] Is. 54:1 • Heb. *Shemamah*
But you shall be called Hephzibah, and your land [T]Beulah; Lit. *Married*
For the LORD delights in you,
And your land shall be married.
5 For *as* a young man marries a virgin,
So shall your sons marry you;
And *as* the bridegroom rejoices over the bride,
So shall your God rejoice over you.

6 [R]I have set watchmen on your walls, O Jerusalem, Ezek. 3:17; 33:7
Who shall [T]never hold their peace day or night. *not be silent*
You who [T]make mention of the LORD, do not keep silent, *remember*
7 And give Him no rest till He establishes
And till He makes Jerusalem [R]a praise in the earth. Zeph. 3:19, 20

8 The LORD has sworn by His right hand
And by the arm of His strength:
"Surely I will no longer [R]give your grain
To be food for your enemies;
And the sons of the foreigner shall not drink your new wine, Deut. 28:31, 33
For which you have labored.
9 But those who have gathered it shall eat it,
And praise the LORD;
Those who have brought it together shall drink it in My holy courts."

10 Go through,
Go through the gates!
[R]Prepare the way for the people;
Build up, Is. 40:3; 57:14
Build up the highway!
Take out the stones,
[R]Lift up a banner for the peoples! Is. 11:12

11 Indeed the LORD has proclaimed
To the end of the world:
[R]"Say to the daughter of Zion, Zech. 9:9☆
'Surely your salvation is coming;
Behold, His reward *is* with Him,
And His [T]work before Him.' " *recompense*
12 And they shall call them The Holy People,
The Redeemed of the LORD;
And you shall be called Sought Out,
A City Not Forsaken.

61:10 Christ's Righteousness—One of the most awesome requirements of God made upon men and women is that they be righteous, that is, conform to His ethical and moral standards (Page 632—Ps. 15:2; Page 1041—Mic. 6:8). Since God is holy, He cannot allow sinners into His presence (Page 777—Is. 6:3–5). Since all persons are sinners, they could not be saved apart from the supernatural intervention of God (Page 1325—Rom 3:10, 23). The righteous demands of God coupled with the inability of man might present an insoluble dilemma. God Himself, however, has graciously solved the problem. He sent Christ, who never sinned, to die for our sins and thus satisfy His own wrath toward us. Simply put, it means that God, at the cross, treated Christ as though He had committed our sins even though He was righteous. On the other hand, when we believe in Christ, He treats us as though we were as righteous as Christ (Page 1369—2 Cor. 5:21). The Bible calls this type of righteousness "imputed righteousness" (Page 1327—Rom. 4:6). That simply means that God puts to our spiritual account the very worth of Christ, much as though He were a banker adding an inexhaustible deposit to our bank account. There are, sadly, many people who still refuse to believe that such an abundant blessing can be theirs as a free gift (Page 1387—Eph. 2:8, 9). Nevertheless, the Bible clearly urges all men to trust in Jesus Christ as Savior and thus be reckoned as righteous by God (Page 1329—Rom. 4:24).

Now turn to Page 1497—1 John 3:2: Placed into God's Family.

CHAPTER 63

Vengeance of God

WHO *is* this who comes from Edom,
With dyed garments from Bozrah,
This *One who is* [T]glorious in His
apparel, Or *adorned*
Traveling in the greatness of His
strength?—

"I who speak in righteousness, mighty to
save."

2 Why [R]*is* Your apparel red, [Rev. 19:13, 15] ☆
And Your garments like one who treads
in the winepress?

3 "I have [R]trodden the winepress alone,
And from the peoples no one *was* with
Me. Rev. 14:19, 20; 19:15 ☆
For I have trodden them in My anger,
And trampled them in My fury;
Their blood is sprinkled upon My
garments,
And I have stained all My robes.
4 For the [R]day of vengeance *is* in My
heart,
And the year of My redeemed has
come. Is. 34:8; 35:4; 61:2
5 [R]I looked, but [R]*there was* no one to help,
And I wondered Is. 41:28; 59:16 • [John 16:32]
That *there was* no one to uphold;
Therefore My own [R]arm brought
salvation for Me; Ps. 98:1
And My own fury, it sustained Me.
6 I have trodden down the peoples in My
anger,
Made them drunk in My fury,
And brought down their strength to the
earth."

Prayer of the Remnant

7 I will mention the lovingkindnesses of
the LORD
And the praises of the LORD,
According to all that the LORD has
bestowed on us,
And the great goodness toward the
house of Israel,
Which He has bestowed on them
according to His mercies,
According to the multitude of His
lovingkindnesses.
8 For He said, "Surely they *are* My
people,
Children *who* will not lie."
So He became their [R]Savior. Is. 60:16 ☆
9 [R]In all their affliction He was *afflicted,
[R]And the Angel of His Presence saved
them; Judg. 10:16 • Ex. 14:19
[R]In His love and in His pity He redeemed
them; Deut. 7:7
And [R]He bore them and carried them
All the days of old. Ex. 19:4
10 But they [R]rebelled and [R]grieved His
Holy Spirit; Ex. 15:24 • Ps. 78:40
[R]So He turned Himself against them as
an enemy, Ex. 23:21
And He fought against them.

11 Then he [R]remembered the days of old,
Moses *and* his people, *saying*: Ps. 106:44, 45
"Where *is* He who [R]brought them up out
of the sea Ex. 14:30
With the *shepherd of His flock?
[R]Where *is* He who put His Holy Spirit
within them, Num. 11:17, 25, 29
12 Who led *them* by the right hand of
Moses,
[R]With His glorious arm,
[R]Dividing the water before them
To make for Himself an everlasting
name, Ex. 15:6 • Ex. 14:21, 22
13 [R]Who led them through the deep,
As a horse in the wilderness,
That they might not stumble?" Ps. 106:9

14 As a beast goes down into the valley,
And the Spirit of the LORD causes him
to rest,
So You lead Your people,
To make Yourself a glorious name.

15 [R]Look down from heaven, Deut. 26:15
And see [R]from Your habitation, holy
and glorious. Ps. 33:14
Where *are* Your zeal and Your strength,
The yearning [R]of Your heart and Your
mercies toward me? Jer. 31:20
Are they restrained?
16 [R]Doubtless You *are* our Father,
Though Abraham [R]was ignorant of us,
And Israel does not acknowledge us.
You, O LORD, *are* our Father;
Our Redeemer from Everlasting *is* Your
name. Deut. 32:6 • Job 14:21
17 O LORD, why have You [R]made us stray
from Your ways,
And hardened our heart from Your
fear?
Return for Your servants' sake,
The tribes of Your inheritance. John 12:40
18 [R]Your holy people have possessed *it* but
a little while;
[R]Our adversaries have trodden down
Your sanctuary. Deut. 7:6 • Ps. 74:3–7
19 We have become *like* those of old, over
whom You never ruled,
Those who were never called by Your
name.

63:9 Kt., LXX, Syr. *not afflicted*
63:11 MT, Vg. *shepherds*

CHAPTER 64

OH, that You would [T]rend the heavens!
That You would come down!
That the mountains might shake at
Your [R]presence— *tear open* • Mic. 1:3, 4
2 As fire burns brushwood,
As fire causes water to boil—
To make Your name known to Your
adversaries,
That the nations may tremble at Your
presence!
3 When [R]You did awesome things *for
which* we did not look, Ex. 34:10
You came down,
The mountains shook at Your presence.
4 For since the beginning of the world
[R]*Men* have not heard nor perceived by
the ear, Ps. 31:19
Nor has the eye seen any God besides
You,
Who acts for the one who waits for
Him.
5 You meet him who rejoices and does
righteousness,
Who remembers You in Your ways.
You are indeed angry, for we have
sinned—
[R]In these ways we continue;
And we need to be saved. Mal. 3:6

6 But we are all like an unclean *thing*,
And all [R]our righteousnesses *are* like
[T]filthy rags; [Phil. 3:9] • Lit. *a filthy garment*
We all [R]fade as a leaf, Ps. 90:5, 6
And our iniquities, like the wind,
Have taken us away.
7 And *there is* no one who calls on Your
name,
Who stirs himself up to take hold of
You;
For You have hidden Your face from
us,
And have [T]consumed us because of our
iniquities. Lit. *caused us to melt*

8 But now, O LORD,
You *are* our Father;
We *are* the clay, and You our potter;
And all we *are* the work of Your hand.
9 Do not be furious, O LORD,
Nor remember iniquity forever;
Indeed, please look—we all *are* Your
people!
10 Your holy cities are a wilderness,
Zion is a wilderness,
Jerusalem a desolation.
11 Our holy and beautiful [T]temple,
Where our fathers praised You,
Is burned up with fire;
And all [R]our pleasant things are laid
waste. Lit. *house* • Ezek. 24:21
12 [R]Will You restrain Yourself because of
these *things*, O LORD? Is. 42:14
[R]Will You [T]hold Your peace, and afflict
us very severely? Ps. 83:1 • *keep silent*

CHAPTER 65

The Lord's Answer to the Remnant

"I WAS [R]sought by *those who* did not
ask *for Me*;
I was found by *those who* did not seek
Me.
I said, 'Here I am, here I am,'
To a nation *that* [R]was not called by My
name. Rom. 9:24; 10:20 • Is. 63:19
2 [R]I have stretched out My hands all day
long to a rebellious people, Rom. 10:21 ☆
Who [R]walk in a way *that is* not good,
According to their own thoughts; Is. 42:24
3 A people [R]who provoke Me to anger
continually to My face; Deut. 32:21
[R]Who sacrifice in gardens, Is. 1:29
And burn incense on altars of brick;
4 [R]Who sit among the graves, Deut. 18:11
And spend the night in the tombs;
[R]Who eat swine's flesh, Is. 66:17
And the broth of [T]abominable things is
in their vessels; Unclean meats, Lev. 7:18
5 [R]Who say, 'Keep to yourself, Matt. 9:11
Do not come near me,
For I am holier than you!'
These *are* smoke in My nostrils,
A fire that burns all the day.

6 "Behold, *it is* written before Me:
I will not keep silence, [R]but will repay—
Even repay into their bosom— Ps. 79:12
7 Your iniquities and [R]the iniquities of
your fathers together," Ex. 20:5
Says the LORD,
[R]"Who have burned incense on the
mountains Ezek. 18:6
[R]And blasphemed Me on the hills;
Therefore I will measure their former
work into their bosom." Ezek. 20:27, 28

8 Thus says the LORD:

"As the new wine is found in the cluster,
And *one* says, 'Do not destroy it,
For [R]a blessing *is* in it,' Joel 2:14
So will I do for My servants' sake,
That I may not destroy them all.
9 I will bring forth descendants from
Jacob,
And from Judah an heir of My
mountains;
My [R]elect shall inherit it, Matt. 24:22
And My servants shall dwell there.
10 [R]Sharon shall be a fold of flocks, Is. 33:9
And [R]the Valley of Achor a place for
herds to lie down, Josh. 7:24
For My people who have sought Me.

11 "But you *are* those who forsake the
LORD,
Who forget [R]My holy mountain, Is. 56:7
Who prepare a table for [T]Gad,
And who furnish a drink offering for
[T]Meni. Lit. *Fortune* • Lit. *Destiny*
12 Therefore I will number you for the
sword,
And you shall all bow down to the
slaughter;
[R]Because, when I called, you did not
answer;
When I spoke, you did not hear,
But did evil before My eyes,
And chose *that* in which I do not
delight." Prov. 1:24

13 Therefore thus says the Lord GOD:

"Behold, My servants shall eat,
But you shall be hungry;
Behold, My servants shall drink,
But you shall be thirsty;
Behold, My servants shall rejoice,
But you shall be ashamed;
14 Behold, My servants shall sing for joy of
heart,
But you shall cry for sorrow of heart,
And wail for [T]grief of spirit. *broken*
15 You shall leave your name [R]as a curse
to [R]My chosen; Jer. 29:22 • Is. 65:9, 22
For the Lord GOD will slay you,
And call His servants by another name;
16 [R]So that he who blesses himself in the
earth
Shall bless himself in the God of truth;
And [R]he who swears in the earth
Shall swear by the God of truth;
Because the former troubles are
forgotten,
And because they are hidden from My
eyes. Jer. 4:2 • Zeph. 1:5

Glorious Consummation of History

17 "For behold, I create [R]new heavens and a
new earth; Rev. 21:1
And the former shall not be
remembered or come to mind.
18 But be glad and rejoice forever in what
I create;
For behold, I create Jerusalem *as* a
rejoicing,
And her people a joy.
19 [R]I will rejoice in Jerusalem, Is. 62:4, 5
And joy in My people;
The [R]voice of weeping shall no longer
be heard in her, Rev. 7:17; 21:4
Nor the voice of crying.

20 "No more shall an infant from there *live
but a few* days,
Nor an old man who has not fulfilled
his days;
For the child shall die one hundred
years old,
[R]But the sinner *being* one hundred years
old shall be accursed. Eccl. 8:12, 13
21 [R]They shall build houses and inhabit
them;
They shall plant vineyards and eat their
fruit. Amos 9:14
22 They shall not build and another
inhabit;
They shall not plant and another eat;
For [R]as the days of a tree, *so shall be*
the days of My people, Ps. 92:12
And [R]My elect shall long enjoy the
work of their hands. Is. 65:9, 15
23 They shall not labor in vain,
Nor bring forth children for trouble;
For [R]they *shall be* the descendants of
the blessed of the LORD, Is. 61:9
And their offspring with them.

24 "It shall come to pass
That [R]before they call, I will answer;
And while they are still speaking, I will
[R]hear. Is. 58:9 • Dan. 9:20–23
25 The [R]wolf and the lamb shall feed
together,
The lion shall eat straw like the ox,
[R]And dust *shall be* the serpent's food.
They shall not hurt nor destroy in all
My holy mountain,"
Says the LORD. Is. 11:6–9 • Gen. 3:14

CHAPTER 66

THUS says the LORD:

[R]"Heaven *is* My throne, 1 Kin. 8:27
And earth *is* My footstool.
Where *is* the house that you will build
Me?
And where *is* the place of My rest?
2 For all those *things* My hand has made,
And all those *things* exist,"
Says the LORD.
[R]"But on this *one* will I look:
[R]On *him who is* poor and of a contrite
spirit, [Is. 57:15; 61:1] • Ps. 34:18; 51:17
And who trembles at My word.

3 "He[R] who kills a bull *is as if* he slays a
man; [Is. 1:10–17; 58:1–7]
He who sacrifices a lamb, *as if* he
[R]breaks a dog's neck; Deut. 23:18
He who offers a grain offering, *as if he
offers* swine's blood;
He who burns incense, *as if* he blesses
an idol.
Just as they have chosen their own
ways,
And their soul delights in their
abominations,

4 So will I choose their delusions,
And bring their fears on them;
RBecause, when I called, no one
answered,
When I spoke they did not hear;
But they did evil before My eyes,
And chose *that* in which I do not
delight." Is. 65:12

5 Hear the word of the LORD,
You who tremble at His word:
"Your brethren who Rhated you, Is. 60:15
Who cast you out for My name's sake,
said,
R'Let the LORD be glorified, Is. 5:19
That Rwe may see your joy.' [Titus 2:13]
But they shall be ashamed."

6 The sound of noise from the city!
A voice from the temple!
The voice of the LORD,
Who fully repays His enemies!

7 "Before she travailed, she gave birth;
Before her pain came,
She delivered a male child.
8 Who has heard such a thing?
Who has seen such things?
Shall the earth be made to give birth in
one day?
Or shall a nation be born at once?
For as soon as Zion travailed,
She gave birth to her children.
9 Shall I bring to the time of birth, and
not cause delivery?" says the LORD.
"Shall I who cause delivery shut up *the*
womb?" says your God.
10 "Rejoice with Jerusalem,
And be glad with her, all you who love
her;
Rejoice for joy with her, all you who
mourn for her;
11 That you may feed and be satisfied
With the consolation of her bosom,
That you may drink deeply and be
delighted
With the abundance of her glory."

12 For thus says the LORD:

"Behold, RI will extend peace to her like
a river, Is. 48:18; 60:5
And the glory of the Gentiles like a
flowing stream.
Then you shall Rfeed; Is. 60:16
On *her* sides shall you be carried,
And be dandled on *her* knees.
13 As one whom his mother comforts,
So I will Rcomfort you;
And you shall be comforted in
Jerusalem." Is. 51:3

14 When you see *this*, your heart shall
rejoice,
And Ryour bones shall flourish like
grass; Ezek. 37:1
The hand of the LORD shall be known
to His servants,
And *His* indignation to His enemies.
15 RFor behold, the LORD will come with fire
And with His chariots, like a whirlwind,
To render His anger with fury, Is. 9:5
And His rebuke with flames of fire.
16 For by fire and by RHis sword
The LORD will judge all flesh;
And the slain of the LORD shall be
Rmany. Is. 27:1 • Is. 34:6

17 "ThoseR who sanctify themselves and
purify themselves,
To go to the gardens
TAfter an *idol* in the midst,
Eating swine's flesh and the
abomination and the mouse,
Shall Tbe consumed together," says the
LORD. Is. 65:3–8 • Lit. *After one* • *come to an end*

18 "For I *know* their works and their
Rthoughts. It shall be that I will Rgather all
nations and tongues; and they shall come and
see My glory. Is. 59:7 • Jer. 3:17
19 "I will set a sign among them; and those
among them who escape I will send to the
nations: *to* Tarshish and Pul and Lud, who
draw the bow, and Tubal and Javan, *to* the
coastlands afar off who have not heard My
fame nor seen My glory. And they shall
declare My glory among the Gentiles.
20 "Then they shall Rbring all your brethren
Rfor an offering to the LORD out of all nations,
on horses and in chariots and in litters, on
mules and on camels, to My holy mountain
Jerusalem," says the LORD, "as the children of
Israel bring an offering in a clean vessel into
the house of the LORD. Is. 49:22 • [Rom. 15:16]
21 "And I will also take some of them for
Rpriests *and* Levites," says the LORD. Ex. 19:6

22 "For as Rthe new heavens and the new
earth
Which I will make shall remain before
Me," says the LORD,
"So shall your descendants and your
name remain. Rev. 21:1
23 And Rit shall come to pass Zech. 14:16
That from one New Moon to another,
And from one Sabbath to another,
RAll flesh shall come to worship before
Me," says the LORD. Zech. 14:17–21

24 "And they shall go forth and look
Upon the corpses of the men
Who have transgressed against Me.
For their Rworm does not die,
And their fire is not quenched.
They shall be an abhorrence to all
flesh." Mark 9:44, 46, 48

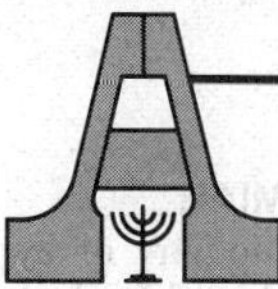

ISRAEL AND THE GREEKS

Greece was a nation of the ancient world, which rose to the status of a world power near the end of the Old Testament era. The Greeks exerted great influence on the Jewish people, particularly during the period between the Old and New Testaments. Greek culture also paved the way for the expansion of Christianity in the first century A.D.

Under the leadership of the great military conqueror Alexander the Great (ruled 336–323 B.C.; see illustration), the Greek Empire was extended through Asia Minor to Egypt and the borders of India. Alexander's conquests and his passion to spread Greek culture contributed to the advancement of Greek ideas throughout the ancient world. This adoption of Greek ideas by the rest of the world was known as Hellenism. So thoroughly did Greek ideas penetrate the other nations that the Greek language became the dominant language of the ancient world.

Since Greek was the universal language, the apostle Paul could communicate easily with the various nations and provinces he visited during his missionary journeys to spread the gospel. Paul visited such major cities as Philippi, Thessalonica, Athens, and Corinth, all of which retained distinct Greek cultural ideas, although they were ruled by the Romans in Paul's time. He showed a deep understanding of Greek thought and was able to communicate the gospel so the Greek mind could understand (Acts 17).

In the New Testament, the word "Greeks" refers to all people who have been influenced by Greek culture and who are not Jews (Mark 7:26). But the term "Hellenists" refers to Greek-speaking Jews (Acts 9:29) who lived in areas outside Palestine. Converts to Christianity included people from both these groups.

In the Old Testament, Greece is referred to as Javan (Is. 66:19). The rule of Greece was foretold by the prophet Daniel (Dan. 11:3–35).

Alexander the Great extended the Greek Empire through Asia Minor to Egypt and the borders of India.

THE BOOK OF

JEREMIAH

THE BOOK OF JEREMIAH

The Book of Jeremiah is the prophecy of a man divinely called in his youth from the priest-city of Anathoth. A heartbroken prophet with a heartbreaking message, Jeremiah labors for more than forty years proclaiming a message of doom to the stiff-necked people of Judah. Despised and persecuted by his countrymen, Jeremiah bathes his harsh prophecies in tears of compassion. His broken heart causes him to write a broken book, which is difficult to arrange chronologically or topically. But through his sermons and signs he faithfully declares that surrender to God's will is the only way to escape calamity.

Yirmeyahu or *Yirmeyah* literally means "Yahweh Throws," perhaps in the sense of laying a foundation. It may effectively mean "Yahweh establishes, appoints, or sends." The Greek form of the Hebrew name in the Septuagint is *Hieremias,* and the Latin form is *Jeremias.*

THE AUTHOR OF JEREMIAH

Jeremiah was the son of Hilkiah the priest and lived just over two miles north of Jerusalem in Anathoth. As an object lesson to Judah he was not allowed to marry (16:2). Because of his radical message of God's judgment through the coming Babylonian invasion, he led a life of conflict. He was threatened in his hometown of Anathoth, tried for his life by the priests and prophets of Jerusalem, put in stocks, forced to flee from King Jehoiakim, publicly humiliated by the false prophet Hananiah, and thrown into a cistern.

The book clearly states that Jeremiah is its author (1:1). Jeremiah dictated all his prophecies to his secretary Baruch from the beginning of his ministry until the fourth year of Jehoiakim. After this scroll was destroyed by the king, Jeremiah dictated a more complete edition to Baruch (see 36—38), and later sections were also composed. Only chapter 52 was evidently not written by Jeremiah. This supplement is almost identical to Second Kings 24:18—25:30, and it may have been added by Baruch.

Daniel alludes to Jeremiah's prophecy of the seventy-year captivity (25:11–14; 29:10; Dan. 9:2), and Jeremiah's authorship is also confirmed by Ecclesiasticus, Josephus, and the Talmud. The New Testament makes explicit and implicit references to Jeremiah's prophecy: Matthew 2:17, 18 (31:15); Matthew 21:13; Mark 11:17; Luke 19:4 (7:11); Romans 11:27 (31:33); and Hebrews 8:8–13 (31:31–34).

THE TIME OF JEREMIAH

Jeremiah was a contemporary of Zephaniah, Habakkuk, Daniel, and Ezekiel. His ministry stretched from 627 to about 580 B.C. Josiah, Judah's last good king (640–609 B.C.), instituted spiritual reforms when the Book of the Law was discovered in 622 B.C. Jeremiah was on good terms with Josiah and lamented when he was killed in 609 B.C. by Pharaoh Necho of Egypt. By this time, Babylon had already overthrown Nineveh, the capital city of Assyria (612 B.C.). Jehoahaz replaced Josiah as king of Judah, but reigned only three months before he was deposed and taken to Egypt by Necho. Jehoiakim (609–597 B.C.) was Judah's next king, but he reigned as an Egyptian vassal until 605 B.C., when Egypt was defeated by Babylon at Carchemish. Nebuchadnezzar took Palestine and deported key persons such as Daniel to Babylon. Judah's King Jehoiakim was now a Babylonian vassal, but he rejected Jeremiah's warnings in 601 B.C. and rebelled against Babylon. Jehoiachin became Judah's next king in 597 B.C., but was replaced by Zedekiah three months later when Nebuchadnezzar captured Jerusalem and deported Jehoiachin to Babylon. Zedekiah was the last king of Judah; his attempted alliance with Egypt led to Nebuchadnezzar's occupation and overthrow of Jerusalem in 586 B.C.

Thus, there were three stages in Jeremiah's ministry: (1) From 627 to 605 B.C. he prophesied while Judah was threatened by Assyria and Egypt. (2) From 605 to 586 B.C. he proclaimed God's judgment while Judah was threatened and besieged by Babylon. (3) From 586 to about 580 B.C. he ministered in Jerusalem and Egypt after Judah's downfall.

THE CHRIST OF JEREMIAH

The Messiah is clearly seen in 23:1–8 as the coming Shepherd and righteous Branch who "shall reign and prosper, and execute judgment and righteousness in the earth. In His days Judah will be saved, and Israel will dwell safely; now this *is* His name by which He will be called: THE LORD OUR RIGHTEOUSNESS" (23:5, 6). He will bring in the new covenant (31:31–34), which will fulfill God's covenants with Abraham (Gen. 12:1–3; 17:1–8), Moses and the people (Deut. 28—30), and David (2 Sam. 7:1–17).

The curse on Jehoiachin (Jeconiah, Coniah) in 22:28–30 meant that no physical descendant would succeed him to the throne. Matthew 1:1–17 traces the genealogy of Christ through Solomon and Jeconiah to His legal (but not His physical) father, Joseph. However, no son of

Joseph could sit upon the throne of David, for he would be under the curse of Jehoiachin. Luke 3:23–38 traces Christ's lineage backward from Mary (His physical parent) through David's other son, Nathan (3:31), thereby avoiding the curse. The righteous Branch will indeed reign on the throne of David.

KEYS TO JEREMIAH

Key Word: Judah's Last Hour—In Jeremiah, God is seen as patient and holy: He delays judgment and appeals to His people to repent before it is too late. As the object lesson at the potter's house demonstrates, a ruined vessel can be repaired while still wet (18:1–4); but once dried, a marred vessel is fit only for the garbage heap (19:10, 11). God's warning is clear: Judah's time for repentance will soon pass. Because they defy God's words and refuse to repent, the Babylonian captivity is inevitable. Jeremiah lists the moral and spiritual causes for their coming catastrophe, but he also proclaims God's gracious promise of hope and restoration. There will always be a remnant, and God will establish a new covenant.

Key Verses: Jeremiah 7:23, 24 and 8:11, 12—"But this is what I commanded them, saying, 'Obey My voice, and I will be your God, and you shall be My people. And walk in all the ways that I have commanded you, that it may be well with you.' Yet they did not obey or incline their ear, but walked in the counsels *and* in the imagination of their evil heart, and went backward and not forward" (7:23, 24).

"For they have healed the hurt of the daughter of My people slightly, saying, 'Peace, peace!' when *there is* no peace. Were they ashamed when they had committed abomination? No! They were not at all ashamed, nor did they know how to blush. Therefore they shall fall among those who fall; in the time of their punishment they shall be cast down, says the LORD" (8:11, 12).

Key Chapter: Jeremiah 31—Amid all the judgment and condemnation by Jeremiah are the wonderful promises of Jeremiah 31. Even though Judah has broken the covenants of her great King, God will make a new covenant when He will "put My law in their minds, and write it on their hearts; and I will be their God, and they shall be My people" (31:33). The Messiah instituted that new covenant with His death and resurrection (cf. Matt. 26:26–29).

SURVEY OF JEREMIAH

Jeremiah is a record of the ministry of one of Judah's greatest prophets during its darkest days. He is called as a prophet during the reign of Josiah, the last of Judah's good kings. But even Josiah's well-intentioned reforms cannot stem the tide of apostasy. The downhill slide of the nation continues virtually unabated through a succession of four godless kings during Jeremiah's ministry. The people wallow in apostasy and idolatry and grow even more treacherous than Israel was before its captivity (3:11). They pervert the worship of the true God and give themselves over to spiritual and moral decay. Because they refuse to repent or even listen to God's prophet, the divine cure requires radical surgery. Jeremiah proclaims an approaching avalanche of judgment. Babylon will be God's instrument of judgment, and this book refers to that nation 164 times, more references than the rest of the Bible.

Jeremiah faithfully proclaims the divine condemnation of rebellious Judah for forty years and is rewarded with opposition, beatings, isolations, and imprisonment. His sympathy and sensitivity cause him to grieve over the rebelliousness and imminent doom of his nation. He often desires to resign from his prophetic office because of the harshness of his message and his reception, but he

FOCUS	CALL OF JEREMIAH	PROPHECIES TO JUDAH				PROPHECIES TO THE GENTILES	FALL OF JERUSALEM
REFERENCE	1:1—	2:1—	26:1—	30:1—	34:1—	46:1—	52:1—52:34
DIVISION	PROPHETIC COMMISSION	CONDEMNATION OF JUDAH	CONFLICTS OF JEREMIAH	FUTURE RESTORATION OF JERUSALEM	PRESENT FALL OF JERUSALEM	CONDEMNATION OF NINE NATIONS	HISTORIC CONCLUSION
TOPIC	BEFORE THE FALL				THE FALL	AFTER THE FALL	
	CALL	MINISTRY					RETROSPECT
LOCATION	JUDAH					SURROUNDING NATIONS	BABYLON
TIME	c. 627–580 B.C.						

perseveres to Judah's bitter end. He is the weeping prophet (9:1; 13:17)—lonely, rejected, and persecuted.

Although Jeremiah is not easily arranged chronologically or thematically, its basic message is clear: surrender to God's will is the only way to escape calamity. Judgment cannot be halted, but promises of restoration are sprinkled through the book. Its divisions are: the call of Jeremiah (1); the prophecies to Judah (2—45); the prophecies to the Gentiles (46—51); and the fall of Jerusalem (52).

The Call of Jeremiah (1): Jeremiah is called and sanctified before birth to be God's prophet. This introductory chapter surveys the identification, inauguration, and instructions of the prophet.

The Prophecies to Judah (2—45): Jeremiah's message is communicated through a variety of parables, sermons, and object lessons. The prophet's life becomes a daily illustration to Judah, and most of the book's object lessons are found in this section (13:1-14; 14:1-9; 16:1-9; 18:1-8; 19:1-13; 24:1-10; 27:1-11; 32:6-15; 43:8-13). In a series of twelve graphic messages, Jeremiah lists the causes of Judah's coming judgment. The gentile nations are more faithful to their false gods than Judah is to God. They become a false vine by following idols and are without excuse. The people are condemned for their empty profession, disobedience to God's covenant, and spiritual harlotry. God has bound Judah to Himself; but like a rotten waistband, they have become corrupt and useless. Jeremiah offers a confession for the people, but their sin is too great; the prophet can only lament for them. As a sign of imminent judgment Jeremiah is forbidden to marry and participate in the feasts. Because the nation does not trust God or keep the Sabbath, the land will receive a sabbath rest when they are in captivity. Jerusalem will be invaded and the rulers and people will be deported to Babylon. Restoration will only come under the new Shepherd, the Messiah, the nation's future King. Jeremiah announces the duration of the captivity as seventy years, in contrast to the messages of the false prophets who insist it will not happen.

Because of his message (2:25), Jeremiah suffers misery and opposition (26—45). He is rejected by the prophets and priests who call for his death, but he is spared by the elders and officials. In his sign of the yoke he proclaims the unpopular message that Judah must submit to divine discipline. But he assures the nation of restoration and hope under a new covenant (30—33). A remnant will be delivered and there will be a coming time of blessing. Jeremiah's personal experiences and sufferings are the focal point of 34—45 as opposition against the prophet mounts. Since he is no longer allowed in the temple, he sends his assistant Baruch to read his prophetic warnings. His scroll is burned by Jehoiakim, and Jeremiah is imprisoned. After the destruction of the city, Jeremiah is taken to Egypt by fleeing Jews, but he prophesies that Nebuchadnezzar will invade Egypt as well.

The Prophecies to the Gentiles (46—51): These chapters are a series of prophetic oracles against nine nations: Egypt, Philistia, Moab, Ammon, Edom, Damascus (Syria), Arabia, Elam, and Babylon. Only Egypt, Moab, Ammon, and Elam are given a promise of restoration.

The Fall of Jerusalem (52): Jeremiah's forty-year declaration of doom was finally vindicated in an event so significant that it is recorded in detail four times in the Scriptures (2 Kin. 25; 2 Chr. 36; Jer. 39; 52). In this historical supplement, Jerusalem is captured, destroyed, and plundered. The leaders are killed and the captives taken to Babylon.

OUTLINE OF JEREMIAH

Part One: The Call of Jeremiah (1:1-19)

I. Jeremiah's Call **1:1-10**
II. Jeremiah's Signs **1:11-16**
III. Jeremiah's Assurance **1:17-19**

Part Two: The Prophecies to Judah (2:1—45:5)

I. The Condemnation of Judah .... **2:1—25:38**

A. Jeremiah's First Sermon: Judah Sinned Willfully............. 2:1—3:5
B. Jeremiah's Second Sermon: Judah to Be Judged .... 3:6—6:30
   1. Judah Ignores Israel's Example..... 3:6-10
   2. Judah Is Called from Backsliding 3:11—4:4
   3. Judah's Destruction from the North 4:5-31
   4. Judah's Sins..................... 5:1-31
   5. Jerusalem to Be Destroyed 6:1-30
C. Jeremiah's Third Sermon: Judah's Hypocrisy in Worship...................... 7:1—10:25
   1. Judah's Sin of External Religion 7:1—8:3

Part Three: The Prophecies to the Gentiles (46:1—51:64)

Part Four: The Fall of Jerusalem (52:1–34)

CHAPTER 1

Jeremiah's Call

THE words of Jeremiah the son of Hilkiah,
of the priests who *were* [R]in Anathoth in
the land of Benjamin, Josh. 21:18
2 to whom the word of the LORD came in
the days of Josiah the son of Amon, king of
Judah, in the thirteenth year of his reign.
3 It came also in the days of [R]Jehoiakim
the son of Josiah, king of Judah, [R]until the
end of the eleventh year of Zedekiah the son
of Josiah, king of Judah, [R]until the carrying
away of Jerusalem captive [R]in the fifth
month. 2 Kin. 23:34 • Jer. 39:2 • Jer. 52:12 • 2 Kin. 25:8
4 Then the word of the LORD came to me,
saying:

5 "Before I [R]formed you in the womb [R]I
knew you; Is. 49:1, 5 • Ex. 33:12
Before you were born I [R]sanctified[T] you;
And I [T]ordained you a prophet to the
nations." [Luke 1:15] • *set you apart* • *appointed*

6 Then said I:

[R]"Ah, Lord GOD!
Behold, I cannot speak, for I *am* a
youth." Ex. 4:10; 6:12, 30

7 But the LORD said to me:

"Do not say, 'I *am* a youth,'
For you shall go to all to whom I send
you,
And [R]whatever I command you, you
shall speak. Num. 22:20, 38
8 [R]Do not be afraid of their faces,
For [R]I *am* with you to deliver you," says
the LORD. Ezek. 2:6; 3:9 • Ex. 3:12

9 Then the LORD put forth His hand and
[R]touched my mouth, and the LORD said to me:

"Behold, I have [R]put My words in your
mouth. Is. 6:7 • Is. 51:16
10 See, I have this day set you over the
nations and over the kingdoms,
To [R]root out and to pull down,
To destroy and to throw down,
To build and to plant." [2 Cor. 10:4, 5]

Jeremiah's Signs

11 Moreover the word of the LORD came to
me, saying, "Jeremiah, what do you see?"
And I said, "I see a [T]branch of an almond
tree." Lit. *rod*
12 Then the LORD said to me, "You have
seen well, for I am [T]ready to perform My
word." Lit. *watching*
13 And the word of the LORD came to me
the second time, saying, "What do you see?"
And I said, "I see [R]a boiling pot, and it is
facing away from the north." Ezek. 11:3; 24:3
14 Then the LORD said to me:

"Out of the [R]north calamity shall break
forth Jer. 6:1
On all the inhabitants of the land.
15 For behold, I am [R]calling Jer. 6:22; 25:9
All the families of the kingdoms of the
north," says the LORD;
"They shall come and [R]each one set his
throne Jer. 39:3
At the entrance of the gates of
Jerusalem,
Against all its walls all around,
And against all the cities of Judah.
16 I will utter My judgments
Against them concerning all their
wickedness,
Because [R]they have forsaken Me,
Burned [R]incense to other gods,
And worshiped the works of their own
[R]hands. Deut. 28:20 • Jer. 7:9 • Is. 37:19

Jeremiah's Assurance

17 Therefore [R]prepare yourself and arise,
And speak to them all that I command
you. Job 38:3
[R]Do not be dismayed before their faces,
Lest I dismay you before them. Ezek. 2:6
18 For behold, I have made you this day
[R]A fortified city and an iron pillar,
And bronze walls against the whole
land— Is. 50:7
Against the kings of Judah,
Against its princes,
Against its priests,
And against the people of the land.
19 They will fight against you,
But they shall not prevail against you.
For I *am* with you," says the LORD, "to
deliver you."

CHAPTER 2

Jeremiah's First Sermon:
Judah Sinned Willfully

MOREOVER the word of the LORD came
to me, saying,
2 "Go and cry in the hearing of Jerusalem,
saying, 'Thus says the LORD:

"I remember you,
The kindness of your [R]youth, Ezek. 16:8
The love of your betrothal,
[R]When you [T]went after Me in the
wilderness, Deut. 2:7 • *followed*
In a land *that was* not sown.
3 [R]Israel *was* holiness to the LORD,
The firstfruits of His increase.
All that devour him will offend;
Disaster will [R]come upon them," says
the LORD.' " [Ex. 19:5, 6] • Is. 41:11

4 Hear the word of the LORD, O house of
Jacob and all the families of the house of
Israel.

5 Thus says the LORD:

[R]"What injustice have your fathers found
in Me, Is. 5:4
That they have gone far from Me,
Have followed [T]idols, *vanities* or *futilities*
And have become idolaters?
6 Neither did they say, 'Where *is* the
LORD,
Who [R]brought us up out of the land of
Egypt, Is. 63:11
Who led us through [R]the wilderness,
Through a land of deserts and pits,
Through a land of drought and the
shadow of death, Deut. 8:15; 32:10
Through a land that no one crossed
And where no one dwelt?'
7 I brought you into [R]a bountiful country,
To eat its fruit and its goodness.
But when you entered, you [R]defiled My
land Num. 13:27 • Num. 35:33
And made My heritage an abomination.
8 The priests did not say, 'Where *is* the
LORD?'
And those who handle the [R]law did not
know Me; Rom. 2:20
The rulers also transgressed against Me;
[R]The prophets prophesied by Baal,
And walked after *things that* do not
profit. Jer. 23:13

9 "Therefore [R]I will yet [T]bring charges
against you," says the LORD,
"And against your children's children I
will bring charges. Mic. 6:2 • *contend with*
10 For pass beyond the coasts of Cyprus
and see,
Send to Kedar and consider diligently,
And see if there has been such *a thing*.
11 [R]Has a nation changed *its* gods,
Which *are* [R]not gods?
[R]But My people have changed their
Glory Mic. 4:5 • Is. 37:19 • Rom. 1:23
For *what* does not profit.
12 Be astonished, O heavens, at this,
And be horribly afraid;
Be very desolate," says the LORD.
13 "For My people have committed two
evils:
They have forsaken Me, the [R]fountain
of living waters, Ps. 36:9
And hewn themselves cisterns—broken
cisterns that can hold no water.

14 "*Is* Israel [R]a servant?
Is he a homeborn *slave?*
Why is he plundered? [Ex. 4:22]
15 [R]The young lions roared at him, *and*
growled;
They made his land waste;
His cities are burned, without
inhabitant. Is. 1:7
16 Also the people of [T]Noph and
Tahpanhes Memphis in ancient Egypt
Have broken the crown of your head.
17 [R]Have you not brought this on yourself,
In that you have forsaken the LORD
your God Jer. 4:18
When [R]He led you in the way? Deut. 32:10
18 And now why take the road to Egypt,
To drink the waters of [R]Sihor? Josh. 13:3
Or why take the road to Assyria,
To drink the waters of the River?
19 Your own wickedness will [R]correct you,
And your backslidings will reprove you.
Know therefore and see that *it is* an
evil and bitter *thing* Jer. 4:18
That you have forsaken the LORD your
God,
And the [T]fear of Me *is* not in you,"
Says the Lord GOD of hosts. *dread*

20 "For of old I have [R]broken your yoke
and burst your bonds; Lev. 26:13
And [R]you said, 'I will not *transgress,'
When [R]on every high hill and under
every green tree Judg. 10:16 • Deut. 12:2
You lay down, playing the harlot.
21 Yet I had [R]planted you a noble vine, a
seed of highest quality.
How then have you turned before Me
Into [R]the degenerate plant of an alien
vine? Ex. 15:17 • Is. 5:4
22 For though you wash yourself with lye,
and use much soap,
Yet your iniquity is [T]marked before
Me," says the Lord GOD. *stained*

23 "How[R] can you say, 'I am not [T]polluted,
I have not gone after the Baals'?
See your way in the valley;
Know what you have done:
You are a swift dromedary breaking
loose in her ways, Prov. 30:12 • *defiled*
24 A wild donkey used to the wilderness,
That sniffs at the wind in her desire;
In her time of mating, who can turn her
away?
All those who seek her will not weary
themselves;
In her month they will find her.
25 Withhold your foot from being unshod,
and your throat from thirst.
But you said, [R]'There is no hope.
No! For I have loved [R]aliens, and after
them I will go.' Jer. 18:12 • Jer. 3:13

26 "As the thief is ashamed when he is
found out,

2:20 Kt. *serve*

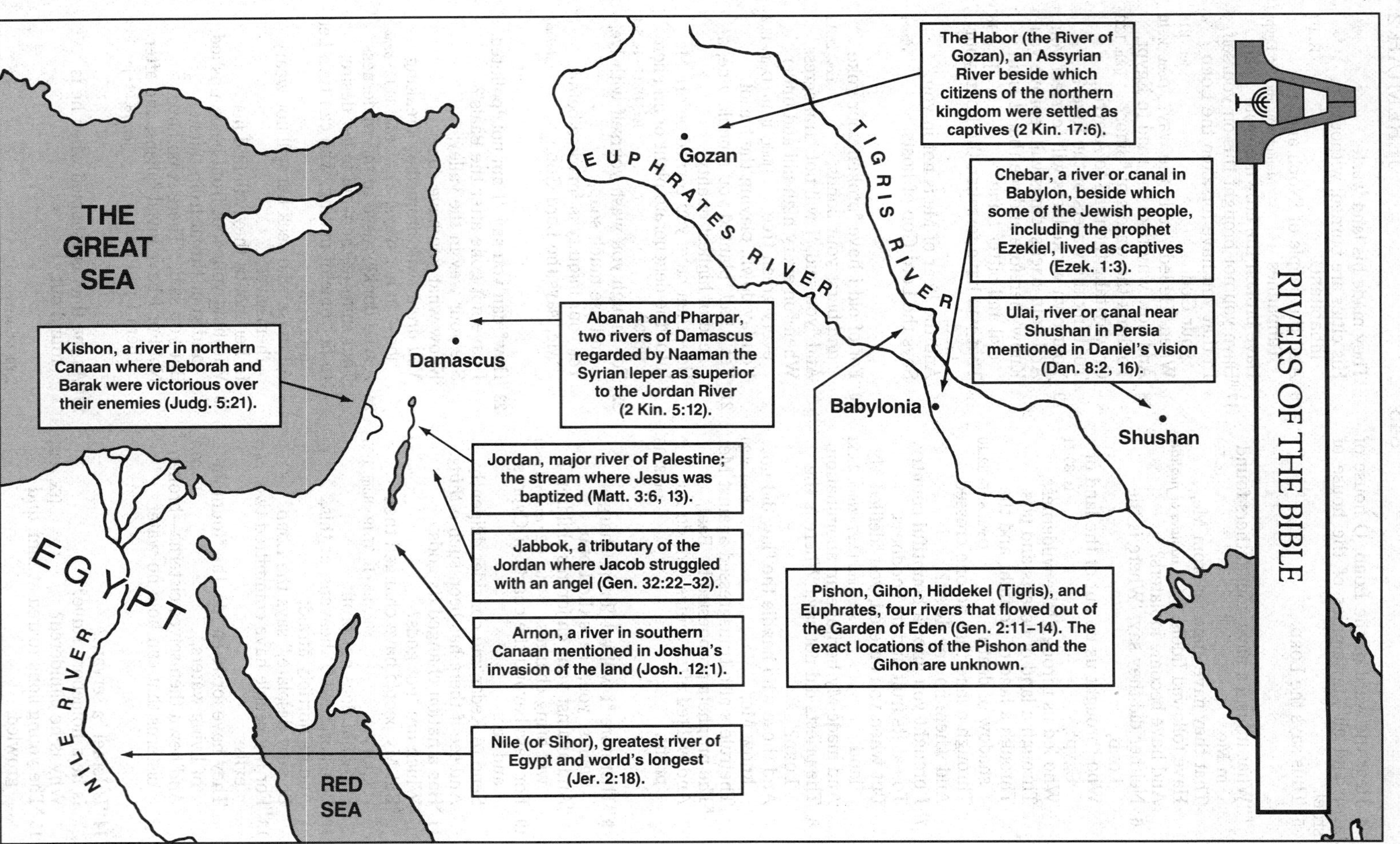
RIVERS OF THE BIBLE
THE GREAT SEA
Kishon, a river in northern Canaan where Deborah and Barak were victorious over their enemies (Judg. 5:21).
EGYPT
NILE RIVER
RED SEA
Damascus
Abanah and Pharpar, two rivers of Damascus regarded by Naaman the Syrian leper as superior to the Jordan River (2 Kin. 5:12).
Jordan, major river of Palestine; the stream where Jesus was baptized (Matt. 3:6, 13).
Jabbok, a tributary of the Jordan where Jacob struggled with an angel (Gen. 32:22–32).
Arnon, a river in southern Canaan mentioned in Joshua's invasion of the land (Josh. 12:1).
Nile (or Sihor), greatest river of Egypt and world's longest (Jer. 2:18).
Gozan
EUPHRATES RIVER
TIGRIS RIVER
The Habor (the River of Gozan), an Assyrian River beside which citizens of the northern kingdom were settled as captives (2 Kin. 17:6).
Chebar, a river or canal in Babylon, beside which some of the Jewish people, including the prophet Ezekiel, lived as captives (Ezek. 1:3).
Ulai, river or canal near Shushan in Persia mentioned in Daniel's vision (Dan. 8:2, 16).
Babylonia
Shushan
Pishon, Gihon, Hiddekel (Tigris), and Euphrates, four rivers that flowed out of the Garden of Eden (Gen. 2:11–14). The exact locations of the Pishon and the Gihon are unknown.

So is the house of Israel ashamed;
They and their kings and their princes,
and their priests and their prophets,
27 Saying to a tree, 'You *are* my father,'
And to a [R]stone, 'You gave birth to me.'
For they have turned *their* back to Me,
and not *their* face. Jer. 3:9
But in the time of their [R]trouble Is. 26:16
They will say, 'Arise and save us.'
28 But [R]where *are* your gods that you have
made for yourselves? Judg. 10:14
Let them arise,
If they [R]can save you in the time of
your [T]trouble; Is. 45:20 • Or *evil*
For [R]*according to* the number of your
cities Jer. 11:13
Are your gods, O Judah.

29 "Why will you plead with Me?
You all have transgressed against Me,"
says the LORD.
30 "In vain I have [R]chastened your children;
They received no correction. Is. 9:13
Your sword has [R]devoured your
prophets
Like a destroying lion. Neh. 9:26

31 "O generation, see the word of the LORD!
Have I been a wilderness to Israel,
Or a land of darkness?
Why do My people say, 'We are lords;
[R]We will come no more to You'? Deut. 32:15
32 Can a virgin forget her ornaments,
Or a bride her attire?
Yet My people [R]have forgotten Me days
without number. Ps. 106:21

33 "Why do you beautify your way to seek
love?
Therefore you have also taught
The wicked women your ways.
34 Also on your skirts is found
[R]The blood of the lives of the poor
innocents. Ps. 106:38
I have not found it by [T]secret search,
But plainly on all these things. *digging*
35 [R]Yet you say, 'Because I am innocent,
Surely His anger shall turn from me.'
Behold, [R]I will plead My case against
you, Jer. 2:23, 29 • Jer. 2:9
Because you say, 'I have not sinned.'
36 [R]Why do you gad about so much to
change your way? Hos. 5:13; 12:1
Also [R]you shall be ashamed of Egypt as
you were ashamed of Assyria. Is. 30:3
37 Indeed you will go forth from him
With your hands on [R]your head;
For the LORD has rejected your trusted
allies, 2 Sam. 13:19
And you will not prosper by them.

CHAPTER 3

"THEY say, 'If a man divorces his wife,
And she goes from him
And becomes another man's,
[R]May he return to her again?'
Would not that [R]land be greatly
polluted? Deut. 24:1–4 • Jer. 2:7
But you have [R]played the harlot with
many lovers; Ezek. 16:26
Yet return to Me," says the LORD.

2 "Lift up your eyes to [R]the desolate
heights and see: Deut. 12:2
Where have you not *lain *with men?*
[R]By the road you have sat for them
Like an Arabian in the wilderness;
[R]And you have polluted the land
With your harlotries and your
wickedness. Prov. 23:28 • Jer. 2:7
3 Therefore the [R]showers have been
withheld, Lev. 26:19
And there has been no latter rain.
You have had a [R]harlot's forehead;
You refuse to be ashamed. Zeph. 3:5
4 Will you not from this time cry to Me,
'My Father, You *are* [R]the guide of [R]my
youth? Prov. 2:17 • Jer. 2:2
5 [R]Will He remain angry forever?
Will He keep it to the end?'
Behold, you have spoken and done evil
things,
As you were able." [Is. 57:16]

Judah Ignores Israel's Example

6 The LORD said also to me in the days of
Josiah the king: "Have you seen what backsliding Israel has done? She has [R]gone up on
every high mountain and under every green
tree, and there played the harlot. Jer. 2:20
7 "And I said, after she had done all these
things, 'Return to Me.' But she did not return.
And her treacherous sister Judah saw it.
8 "Then I saw that [R]for all the causes for
which backsliding Israel had committed adultery, I had [R]put her away and given her a
certificate of divorce; [R]yet her treacherous
sister Judah did not fear, but went and played
the harlot also. Ezek. 23:9 • 2 Kin. 17:6 • Ezek. 23:11
9 "So it came to pass, through her casual
harlotry, that she defiled the land and committed adultery with stones and trees.
10 "And yet for all this her treacherous
sister Judah has not turned to Me with her
whole heart, but in pretense," says the LORD.

Judah Is Called from Backsliding

11 Then the LORD said to me, [R]"Backsliding
Israel has shown herself more righteous than
treacherous Judah. Ezek. 16:51, 52
12 "Go and proclaim these words toward
[R]the north, and say: 2 Kin. 17:6

3:2 Kt. *been violated*

'Return, backsliding Israel,' says the
LORD,
'*And* I will not cause My anger to fall on
you;
For I *am* merciful,' says the LORD,
'*And* I will not remain angry forever.
13 [R]Only acknowledge your iniquity,
That you have transgressed against the
LORD your God, Deut. 30:1, 2
And have [R]scattered your [T]charms
To [R]alien deities under every green
tree, Ezek. 16:15 • Lit. *ways* • Jer. 2:25
And you have not obeyed My voice,'
says the LORD.

14 "Return, O backsliding children," says
the LORD; "for I am married to you. I will
take you, one from a city and two from a
family, and I will bring you to Zion.
15 "And I will give you shepherds according
to My heart, who will [R]feed you with knowledge and understanding. Acts 20:28
16 "Then it shall come to pass, when you
are multiplied and [R]increased in the land in
those days," says the LORD, "that they will
say no more, 'The ark of the covenant of the
LORD.' [R]It shall not come to mind, nor shall
they remember it, nor shall they visit *it*, nor
shall it be made anymore. Is. 49:19 • Is. 65:17
17 "At that time Jerusalem shall be called
The Throne of the LORD, and all the nations
shall be gathered to it, to the name of the
LORD, to Jerusalem; they shall walk no more
after the stubbornness of their evil heart.
18 "In those days [R]the house of Judah shall
walk with the house of Israel, and they shall
come together out of the land of [R]the north to
[R]the land that I have given as an inheritance
to your fathers. Is. 11:13 • Jer. 31:8 • Amos 9:15
19 "But I said:

'How can I put you among the children
And give you [R]a pleasant land,
A beautiful heritage of the hosts of
nations?' Ps. 106:24

"And I said:

'You shall call Me, [R]"My Father,"
And not turn away from Me.' Is. 63:16
20 Surely, *as* a wife treacherously departs
from her [T]husband, Lit. *companion*
So [R]have you dealt treacherously with
Me, Is. 48:8
O house of Israel," says the LORD.

21 A voice was heard on [R]the desolate
heights,
Weeping *and* supplications of the
children of Israel;
For they have perverted their way,
And they have forgotten the LORD their
God. Is. 15:2

22 "Return, you backsliding children,
And I will [R]heal your backslidings."

"Indeed we do come to You, Hos. 6:1; 14:4
For You are the LORD our God.
23 [R]Truly, in vain *is salvation hoped for*
from the hills, Ps. 121:1, 2
And from the multitude of mountains;
[R]Truly, in the LORD our God Ps. 3:8
Is the salvation of Israel.
24 [R]For shame has devoured
The labor of our fathers from our
youth—
Their flocks and their herds,
Their sons and their daughters. Hos. 9:10
25 We lie down in our shame,
And our [T]reproach covers us. *disgrace*
[R]For we have sinned against the LORD
our God, Ezra 9:6, 7
We and our fathers,
From our youth even to this day,
And [R]have not obeyed the voice of the
LORD our God." Jer. 22:21

CHAPTER 4

"IF you will return, O Israel," says the
LORD,
[R]"Return to Me; Joel 2:12
And if you will put away your
abominations out of My sight,
Then you shall not be moved.
2 [R]And you shall swear, 'The LORD lives,'
[R]In truth, in [T]judgment, and in
righteousness; Deut. 10:20 • Zech. 8:8 • *justice*
[R]The nations shall bless themselves in
Him, [Gen. 22:18]
And in Him they shall [R]glory." 1 Cor. 1:31

3 For thus says the LORD to the men of
Judah and Jerusalem:

[R]"Break up your fallow ground, Hos. 10:12
And [R]do not sow among thorns. Matt. 13:7
4 [R]Circumcise yourselves to the LORD,
And take away the foreskins of your
hearts, Deut. 10:16; 30:6
You men of Judah and inhabitants of
Jerusalem,
Lest My fury come forth like fire,
And burn so that no one can quench *it*,
Because of the evil of your doings."

Judah's Destruction from the North

5 Declare in Judah and proclaim in Jerusalem, and say:

[R]"Blow the trumpet in the land;
Cry, 'Gather together,' Hos. 8:1
And say, [R]'Assemble yourselves, Jer. 8:14
And let us go into the fortified cities.'
6 Set up the [T]standard toward Zion.
Take refuge! Do not delay!

For I will bring disaster from the
[R]north, *banner* • Jer. 1:13–15; 6:1, 22; 50:17
And great destruction."

7 [R]The lion has come up from his thicket,
And [R]the destroyer of nations is on his
way. Dan. 7:4 • Jer. 25:9
He has gone forth from his place
[R]To make your land desolate. Is. 1:7; 6:11
Your cities will be laid waste,
Without inhabitant.
8 For this, [R]clothe yourself with
sackcloth, Is. 22:12
Lament and wail.
For the fierce anger of the LORD
Has not turned back from us.

9 "And it shall come to pass in that day,"
says the LORD,
"*That* the heart of the king shall perish,
And the heart of the princes;
The priests shall be astonished,
And the prophets shall wonder."

10 Then I said, "Ah, Lord GOD!
[R]Surely You have greatly deceived this
people and Jerusalem, Ezek. 14:9
[R]Saying, 'You shall have peace,'
Whereas the sword reaches to the
[T]heart." Jer. 5:12; 14:13 • *soul*

11 At that time it will be said
To this people and to Jerusalem,
[R]"A dry wind of the desolate heights
blows in the wilderness Hos. 13:15
Toward the daughter of My people—
Not to fan or to cleanse—
12 A wind too strong for these will come
for Me;
Now [R]I will also speak judgment
against them." Jer. 1:16

13 "Behold, he shall come up like clouds,
And his chariots like a whirlwind.
His horses are swifter than eagles.
Woe to us, for we are plundered!"

14 O Jerusalem, [R]wash your heart from
wickedness, James 4:8
That you may be saved.
How long shall your evil thoughts lodge
within you?
15 For a voice declares [R]from Dan
And proclaims [T]affliction from Mount
Ephraim: Jer. 8:16; 50:17 • Or *wickedness*
16 "Make mention to the nations,
Yes, proclaim against Jerusalem,
That watchers come from a [R]far
country Is. 39:3
And raise their voice against the cities
of Judah.
17 [R]Like keepers of a field they are against
her all around, 2 Kin. 25:1, 4
Because she has been rebellious against
Me," says the LORD.
18 "Your[R] ways and your doings Is. 50:1
Have procured these *things* for you.
This *is* your wickedness,
Because it is bitter,
Because it reaches to your heart."

19 O my [R]soul, my soul!
I am pained in my very heart!
My heart makes a noise in me;
I cannot hold my peace,
Because you have heard, O my soul,
The sound of the trumpet,
The alarm of war. Is. 15:5; 16:11; 21:3; 22:4
20 Destruction upon destruction is cried,
For the whole land is plundered.
Suddenly [R]my tents are plundered,
And my curtains in a moment. Jer. 10:20
21 How long will I see the standard,
And hear the sound of the trumpet?

22 "For My people *are* foolish,
They have not known Me.
They *are* [T]silly children, *foolish*
And they have no understanding.
[R]They *are* wise to do evil, Rom. 16:19
But to do good they have no
knowledge."

23 [R]I beheld the earth, and indeed *it was*
without form, and void; Is. 24:19
And the heavens, they *had* no light.
24 [R]I beheld the mountains, and indeed they
trembled, Ezek. 38:20
And all the hills moved back and forth.
25 I beheld, and indeed *there was* no man,
And [R]all the birds of the heavens had
fled. Zeph. 1:3
26 I beheld, and indeed the fruitful land
was a [R]wilderness, Jer. 9:10
And all its cities were broken down
At the presence of the LORD,
By His fierce anger.

27 For thus says the LORD:

"The whole land shall be desolate;
Yet I will not make a full end.
28 For this [R]shall the earth mourn,
And [R]the heavens above be black,
Because I have spoken. Hos. 4:3 • Is. 50:3
I have [R]purposed and will not relent,
Nor will I turn back from it. [Dan. 4:35]
29 The whole city shall flee from the noise
of the horsemen and bowmen.
They shall go into thickets and climb up
on the rocks.
Every city *shall be* forsaken,
And not a man shall dwell in it.

30 "And *when* you *are* plundered,
What will you do?
Though you clothe yourself with
crimson,
Though you adorn *yourself* with
ornaments of gold,
[R]Though you enlarge your eyes with
paint, 2 Kin. 9:30
In vain you will make yourself fair;
[R]*Your* lovers will despise you;
They will seek your life. Jer. 22:20, 22

31 "For I have heard a voice as of a woman
in [T]labor, *childbirth*
The anguish as of her who brings forth
her first child,
The voice of the daughter of Zion
bewailing herself,
Who [R]spreads her hands, *saying*,
'Woe *is* me now, for my soul is [T]weary
Because of murderers!' Lam. 1:17 • *faint*

CHAPTER 5

Judah's Sins

"RUN to and fro through the streets of
Jerusalem;
See now and know;
And seek in her open places
[R]If you can find a man, Ezek. 22:30
[R]If there is *anyone* who executes
[T]judgment, Gen. 18:23–32 • *justice*
Who seeks the truth,
[R]And I will pardon her. Gen. 18:26
2 Though they say, 'As [R]the LORD lives,'
Surely they [R]swear falsely." Jer. 4:2 • Jer. 7:9

3 O LORD, *are* not [R]Your eyes on the
truth? [2 Chr. 16:9]
You have [R]stricken them,
But they have not grieved;
You have consumed them,
But [R]they have refused to receive
correction. Is. 1:5; 9:13 • Zeph. 3:2
They have made their faces harder than
rock;
They have refused to return.

4 Therefore I said, "Surely these *are* poor.
They are foolish;
For [R]they do not know the way of the
LORD, Jer. 8:7
The judgment of their God.
5 I will go to the great men and speak to
them,
For [R]they have known the way of the
LORD, Mic. 3:1
The judgment of their God."

But these have altogether [R]broken the
yoke Ps. 2:3
And burst the bonds.

6 Therefore [R]a lion from the forest shall
slay them, Jer. 4:7
[R]A wolf of the deserts shall destroy
them; Zeph. 3:3
[R]A leopard will watch over their cities.
Everyone who goes out from there shall
be torn in pieces, Hos. 13:7
Because their transgressions are many;
Their backslidings have increased.

7 "How shall I pardon you for this?
Your children have forsaken Me
And [R]sworn by *those* [R]*that are* not gods.
When I had fed them to the full,
Then they committed adultery
And assembled themselves by troops in
the harlots' houses. Zeph. 1:5 • Deut. 32:21
8 [R]They were *like* well-fed lusty stallions;
Every one neighed after his neighbor's
wife. Ezek. 22:11
9 Shall I not punish *them* for these
things?" says the LORD.
"And shall I not [R]avenge Myself on such
a nation as this? Jer. 9:9

10 "Go up on her walls and destroy,
But do not make a [R]complete end.
Take away her branches, Jer. 4:27
For they *are* not the LORD's.
11 For [R]the house of Israel and the house
of Judah Jer. 3:6, 7, 20
Have dealt very treacherously with
Me," says the LORD.

12 They have lied about the LORD,
And said, [R]"*It is* not He. Jer. 23:17
Neither will evil come upon us,
Nor shall we see sword or famine.
13 And the prophets become wind,
For the word *is* not in them.
Thus shall it be done to them."

14 Therefore thus says the LORD God of
hosts:

"Because you speak this word,
[R]Behold, I will make My words in your
mouth fire, Jer. 1:9; 23:29
And this people wood,
And it shall devour them.
15 Behold, I will bring a [R]nation against
you [R]from afar, Deut. 28:49 • Jer. 4:16
O house of Israel," says the LORD.
"It *is* a mighty nation,
It *is* an ancient nation,
A nation whose language you do not
know,
Nor can you understand what they say.
16 Their quiver *is* like an open tomb;
They *are* all mighty men.
17 And they shall eat up your [R]harvest and
your bread, Lev. 26:16

Which your sons and daughters should eat.
They shall eat up your flocks and your herds;
They shall eat up your vines and your fig trees;
They shall destroy your fortified cities,
In which you trust, with the sword.

18 "Nevertheless in those days," says the
LORD, "I [R]will not [T]make a complete end of
you. Jer. 30:11 • *completely destroy*
19 "And it will be when you say, [R]'Why does
the LORD our God do all these *things* to us?'
then you shall answer them, 'Just as you
have [R]forsaken Me and served foreign gods in
your land, so you shall serve aliens in a land
that is not yours.' Deut. 29:24–29 • Jer. 1:16; 2:13

20 "Declare this in the house of Jacob
And proclaim it in Judah, saying,
21 'Hear this now, O foolish people,
Without [T]understanding, *heart*
Who have eyes and see not,
And who have ears and hear not:
22 [R]Do you not fear Me?' says the LORD.
'Will you not tremble at My presence,
Who have placed the sand as the [R]bound of the sea,
By a perpetual decree, that it cannot pass beyond it?
And though its waves toss to and fro,
Yet they cannot prevail;
Though they roar, yet they cannot pass over it. [Rev. 15:4] • Job 26:10
23 But this people has a defiant and rebellious heart;
They have revolted and departed.
24 They do not say in their heart,
"Let us now fear the LORD our God,
[R]Who gives rain, both the former and the latter, in its season. Acts 14:17
[R]He reserves for us the appointed weeks of the harvest." [Gen. 8:22]
25 [R]Your iniquities have turned these *things* away, Jer. 3:3
And your sins have withheld good *things* from you.

26 'For among My people are found wicked *men*;
They [R]lie in wait as one who sets snares; Hab. 1:15
They set a trap;
They catch men.
27 As a cage is full of birds,
So their houses *are* full of deceit.
Therefore they have become great and grown rich.
28 They have grown [R]fat, they are sleek;
Yes, they [T]surpass the deeds of the wicked; Deut. 32:15 • *pass over* or *overlook*
They do not plead [R]the cause,
The cause of the fatherless;
[R]Yet they prosper,
And the right of the needy they do not defend. Zech. 7:10 • Job 12:6
29 [R]Shall I not punish *them* for these *things*?' says the LORD. Mal. 3:5
'Shall I not avenge Myself on such a nation as this?'

30 "An astonishing and horrible thing
Has been committed in the land:
31 The prophets prophesy [R]falsely,
And the priests rule by their *own* power; Ezek. 13:6
And My people love *to have it* so.
But what will you do in the end?

CHAPTER 6

Jerusalem to Be Destroyed

"O YOU children of Benjamin,
Gather yourselves to flee from the midst of Jerusalem!
Blow the trumpet in Tekoa,
And set up a signal-fire in [R]Beth Haccerem; Neh. 3:14
[R]For disaster appears out of the north,
And great destruction. Jer. 4:6
2 I have likened the daughter of Zion
To a lovely and delicate woman.
3 The [R]shepherds with their flocks shall come to her. 2 Kin. 25:1–4
They shall pitch *their* tents against her all around.
Each one shall pasture in his own place."

4 "Prepare[R] war against her;
Arise, and let us go up [R]at noon.
Woe to us, for the day goes away,
For the shadows of the evening are lengthening. Joel 3:9 • Jer. 15:8
5 Arise, and let us go by night,
And let us destroy her palaces."

6 For thus has the LORD of hosts said:

"Hew down trees,
And build a mound against Jerusalem.
This *is* the city to be punished.
She *is* full of oppression in her midst.
7 [R]As a fountain [T]wells up with water,
So she wells up with her wickedness.
[R]Violence and plundering are heard in her. Is. 57:20 • *gushes* • Ps. 55:9
Before Me continually *are* [T]grief and wounds. *sickness*
8 Be instructed, O Jerusalem,
Lest [R]My soul depart from you;
Lest I make you desolate,
A land not inhabited." Hos. 9:12

9 Thus says the LORD of hosts:

"They shall thoroughly glean as a vine
the remnant of Israel;
As a grape-gatherer, put your hand
back into the branches."

10 To whom shall I speak and give
warning,
That they may hear?
Indeed their [R]ear *is* uncircumcised,
And they cannot give heed. [Acts 7:51]
Behold, [R]the word of the LORD is a
reproach to them; Jer. 8:9; 20:8
They have no delight in it.
11 Therefore I am full of the fury of the
LORD.
[R]I am weary of holding *it* in.
"I will pour it out [R]on the children
outside, Jer. 20:9 • Jer. 9:21
And on the assembly of young men
together;
For even the husband shall be taken
with the wife,
The aged with *him who is* full of days.
12 And [R]their houses shall be turned over
to others, Deut. 28:30
Fields and wives together;
For I will stretch out My hand
Against the inhabitants of the land,"
says the LORD.
13 "Because from the least of them even to
the greatest of them,
Everyone *is* given to [R]covetousness;
And from the prophet even to the
[R]priest, Is. 56:11 • Jer. 5:31; 23:11
Everyone deals falsely.
14 They have also healed the [T]hurt of My
people [T]slightly, Lit. *crushing* • Superficially
[R]Saying, 'Peace, peace!' Jer. 4:10; 23:17
When *there is* no peace.
15 Were they [R]ashamed when they had
committed abomination?
No! They were not at all ashamed;
Nor did they know how to blush.
Therefore they shall fall among those
who fall; Jer. 3:3; 8:12
At the time I punish them,
They shall be cast down," says the
LORD.

16 Thus says the LORD:

"Stand in the ways and see,
And ask for the [R]old paths, where the
good way *is*, Jer. 18:15
And walk in it;
Then you will find rest for your souls.
But they said, 'We will not walk *in it.*'
17 Also, I set watchmen over you, *saying*,
'Listen to the sound of the trumpet!'
But they said, 'We will not listen.'
18 Therefore hear, you nations,
And know, O congregation, what *is*
among them.
19 [R]Hear, O earth! Is. 1:2
Behold, I will certainly bring [R]calamity
on this people, Jer. 19:3, 15
Even [R]the fruit of their thoughts,
Because they have not heeded My
words, Prov. 1:31
Nor My law, but rejected it.
20 [R]For what purpose to Me Mic. 6:6, 7
Comes frankincense [R]from Sheba,
And sweet cane from a far country?
Your burnt offerings *are* not acceptable,
Nor your sacrifices sweet to Me." Is. 60:6

21 Therefore thus says the LORD:

"Behold, I will lay stumbling blocks
before this people,
And the fathers and the sons together
shall fall on them.
The neighbor and his friend shall
perish."

22 Thus says the LORD:

"Behold, a people comes from the [R]north
country, Jer. 1:15; 10:22; 50:41–43
And a great nation will be raised from
the farthest parts of the earth.
23 They will lay hold on bow and spear;
They *are* cruel and have no mercy;
Their voice [R]roars like the sea;
And they ride on horses, Is. 5:30
As men of war set in array against you,
O daughter of Zion."

24 We have heard the report of it;
Our hands grow feeble.
[R]Anguish has taken hold of us, Jer. 4:31
Pain as of a woman in [T]labor. *childbirth*
25 Do not go out into the field,
Nor walk by the way.
Because of the sword of the enemy,
Fear *is* on every side.
26 O daughter of my people,
[R]Clothe *yourself* with sackcloth,
[R]And roll about in ashes!
[R]Make mourning *as for* an only son,
most bitter lamentation;
For the plunderer will suddenly come
upon us. Jer. 4:8 • Mic. 1:10 • [Zech. 12:10]

27 "I have set you *as* an assayer *and* [R]a
fortress among My people, Jer. 1:18
That you may know and test their way.
28 [R]They *are* all stubborn rebels, [R]walking
as slanderers. Jer. 5:23 • Jer. 9:4
They are [R]bronze and iron, Ezek. 22:18
They *are* all corrupters;
29 The bellows blow fiercely,
The lead is consumed by the fire;

The smelter refines in vain,
For the wicked are not drawn off.
30 *People* will call them rejected silver,
Because the LORD has rejected them."

CHAPTER 7

Judah's Sin of External Religion

THE word that came to Jeremiah from the
LORD, saying,
2 "Stand in the gate of the LORD's house,
and proclaim there this word, and say, 'Hear
the word of the LORD, all *you of* Judah who
enter in at these gates to worship the LORD!' "
3 Thus says the LORD of hosts, the God of
Israel: "Amend your ways and your doings,
and I will cause you to dwell in this place.
4 [R]"Do not trust in these lying words,
saying, 'The temple of the LORD, the temple
of the LORD, the temple of the LORD *are*
these.' Mic. 3:11
5 "For if you thoroughly amend your ways
and your doings, if you thoroughly execute
judgment between a man and his neighbor,
6 "*if* you do not oppress the stranger, the
fatherless, and the widow, and do not shed
innocent blood in this place, [R]or walk after
other gods to your hurt, Deut. 6:14, 15
7 [R]"then I will cause you to dwell in this
place, in [R]the land that I gave to your fathers
forever and ever. Deut. 4:40 • Jer. 3:18
8 "Behold, you trust in [R]lying words that
cannot profit. Jer. 5:31; 14:13, 14
9 [R]"Will you steal, murder, commit adultery, swear falsely, burn incense to Baal, and
[R]walk after other gods whom you do not
know, 1 Kin. 18:21 • Ex. 20:3
10 [R]"and *then* come and stand before Me in
this house [R]which is called by My name, and
say, 'We are delivered to do all these abominations'? Ezek. 23:39 • Jer. 7:11, 14; 32:34; 34:15
11 "Has [R]this house, which is called by My
name, become a [R]den of thieves in your eyes?
Behold, I, even I, have seen *it*," says the
LORD. Is. 56:7 • Matt. 21:13
12 "But go now to [R]My place which *was* in
Shiloh, [R]where I set My name at the first, and
see what I did to it because of the wickedness
of My people Israel. Josh. 18:1 • Deut. 12:11
13 "And now, because you have done all
these works," says the LORD, "and I spoke to
you, [R]rising up early and speaking, but you
did not hear, and I [R]called you, but you did
not answer, 2 Chr. 36:15 • Prov. 1:24
14 "therefore I will do to *this* house which is
called by My name, in which you trust, and to
this place which I gave to you and your
fathers, as I have done to [R]Shiloh. 1 Sam. 4:10, 11
15 "And I will cast you out of My sight, [R]as
I have cast out all your brethren—[R]the whole
posterity of Ephraim. 2 Kin. 17:23 • Ps. 78:67
16 "Therefore do not pray for this people,
nor lift up a cry or prayer for them, nor make
intercession to Me; for I will not hear you.
17 "Do you not see what they do in the
cities of Judah and in the streets of Jerusalem?
18 [R]"The children gather wood, the fathers
kindle the fire, and the women knead *their*
dough, to make cakes for the queen of
heaven; and *they* [R]pour out drink offerings to
other gods, that they may provoke Me to
anger. Jer. 44:17 • Jer. 19:13
19 [R]"Do they provoke Me to anger?" says
the LORD. "*Do they* not *provoke* themselves,
to the shame of their own faces?" Deut. 32:16, 21
20 Therefore thus says the Lord GOD: "Behold, My anger and My fury will be poured
out on this place—on man and on beast, on
the trees of the field and on the fruit of the
ground. And it will burn and not be
quenched."
21 Thus says the LORD of hosts, the God of
Israel: [R]"Add your burnt offerings to your
sacrifices and eat meat. Jer. 6:20
22 [R]"For I did not speak to your fathers, or
command them in the day that I brought
them out of the land of Egypt, concerning
burnt offerings or sacrifices. [Hos. 6:6]
23 "But this is what I commanded them,
saying, 'Obey My voice, and [R]I will be your
God, and you shall be My people. And walk in
all the ways that I have commanded you,
that it may be well with you.' [Ex. 19:5, 6]
24 [R]"Yet they did not obey or incline their
ear, but walked in the counsels *and* in the
*imagination of their evil heart, and [T]went
backward and not forward. Ps. 81:11 • *they were*
25 "Since the day that your fathers came
out of the land of Egypt until this day, I have
even sent to you all My servants the prophets, daily rising up early and sending *them*.
26 [R]"Yet they did not obey Me or incline
their ear, but [R]stiffened their neck. They did
worse than their fathers. Jer. 11:8 • Neh. 9:17
27 "Therefore [R]you shall speak all these
words to them, but they will not obey you.
You shall also call to them, but they will not
answer you. Ezek. 2:7
28 "So you shall say to them, 'This *is* a
nation that does not obey the voice of the
LORD their God [R]nor receive correction.
[R]Truth has perished and has been cut off from
their mouth. Jer. 5:3 • Jer. 9:3
29 [R]'Cut off your hair and cast *it* away, and
take up a lamentation on the desolate
heights; for the LORD has rejected and forsaken the generation of His wrath.' Mic. 1:16
30 "For the children of Judah have done evil
in My sight," says the LORD. "They have set
their abominations in the house which is
called by My name, to [T]pollute it. *defile*
31 "And they have built the [R]high places of
Tophet, which *is* in the Valley of the Son of

7:24 Lit. *stubbornness;* LXX, Tg. *imagination*

Hinnom, to burn their sons and their daughters in the fire, which I did not command, nor
did it come into My heart. 2 Kin. 23:10
32 "Therefore behold, [R]the days are coming," says the LORD, "when it will no more be
called Tophet, or the Valley of the Son of
Hinnom, but the Valley of Slaughter; [R]for
they will bury in Tophet until there is no
room. Jer. 19:6 • 2 Kin. 23:10
33 "The [R]corpses of this people will be food
for the birds of the heaven and for the beasts
of the earth. And no one will frighten *them*
away. Jer. 9:22; 19:11
34 "Then I will cause to [R]cease from the
cities of Judah and from the streets of Jerusalem the voice of mirth and the voice of
gladness, the voice of the bridegroom and the
voice of the bride. For [R]the land shall be
desolate. Is. 24:7, 8 • Lev. 26:33

CHAPTER 8

"AT that time," says the LORD, "they
shall bring out the bones of the kings
of Judah, and the bones of its princes, and the
bones of the priests, and the bones of the
prophets, and the bones of the inhabitants of
Jerusalem, out of their graves.
2 "They shall spread them before the sun
and the moon and all the host of heaven,
which they have loved and which they have
served and after which they have walked,
which they have sought and [R]which they
have worshiped. They shall not be gathered
[R]nor buried; they shall be like refuse on the
face of the earth. 2 Kin. 23:5 • Jer. 22:19
3 "Then [R]death shall be chosen rather than
life by all the [T]residue of those who remain of
this evil family, who remain in all the places
where I have driven them," says the LORD of
hosts. Rev. 9:6 • *remnant*

Judah's Judgment Imminent

4 "Moreover you shall say to them, 'Thus
says the LORD:

"Will they fall and not rise?
Will one turn away and not return?
5 Why *then* has this people slidden back,
Jerusalem, in a perpetual backsliding?
[R]They hold fast to deceit,
[R]They refuse to return. Jer. 9:6 • Jer. 5:3
6 [R]I listened and heard, Ps. 14:2
But they do not speak aright.
[R]No man repented of his wickedness,
Saying, 'What have I done?' Mic. 7:2
Everyone turned to his own course,
As the horse rushes into the battle.

7 "Even [R]the stork in the heavens
Knows her appointed times;
And the turtledove, the swift, and the
swallow Song 2:12
Observe the time of their coming.
But [R]My people do not know the
judgment of the LORD. Jer. 5:4; 9:3

8 "How can you say, 'We *are* wise,
[R]And the law of the LORD *is* with us'?
Look, the false pen of the scribe
certainly works falsehood. Rom. 2:17
9 [R]The wise men are ashamed, Jer. 6:15
They are dismayed and taken.
Behold, they have rejected the word of
the LORD;
So [R]what wisdom do they have? Jer. 4:22
10 Therefore [R]I will give their wives to
others, Deut. 28:30
And their fields to those who will
inherit *them*;
Because from the least even to the
greatest
Everyone is given to [R]covetousness;
From the prophet even to the priest
Everyone deals falsely. Is. 56:11; 57:17
11 For they have healed the hurt of the
daughter of My people [T]slightly,
Saying, 'Peace, peace!'
When *there is* no peace. Superficially
12 Were they [R]ashamed when they had
committed abomination?
No! They were not at all ashamed,
Nor did they know how to blush.
Therefore they shall fall among those
who fall;
In the time of their punishment
They shall be cast down," says the
LORD. Jer. 3:3; 6:15

13 "I will surely [T]consume them," says the
LORD. Or *take them away*
"*There shall be* no grapes on the vine,
Nor figs on the [R]fig tree, Matt. 21:19
And the leaf shall fade;
And *the things* I have given them shall
pass away from them." ' "

14 "Why do we sit still?
[R]Assemble yourselves, Jer. 4:5
And let us enter the fortified cities,
And let us be silent there.
For the LORD our God has put us to
silence
And given us [R]water[T] of gall to drink,
Because we have sinned against the
LORD. Jer. 9:15 • Bitter or poisonous water

15 "*We* [R]looked for peace, but no good
came;
And for a time of health, and there was
trouble! Jer. 14:19
16 The snorting of His horses was heard
from [R]Dan. Jer. 4:15
The whole land trembled at the sound
of the neighing of His [R]strong ones;

For they have come and devoured the
land and all that is in it, Jer. 47:3
The city and those who dwell in it."

17 "For behold, I will send serpents among
you,
Vipers which cannot be charmed,
And they shall bite you," says the LORD.

Jeremiah's Lament for Judah

18 I would comfort myself in sorrow;
My heart *is* faint in me.
19 Listen! The voice,
The cry of the daughter of my people
From [R]a far country:
"*Is* not the LORD in Zion?
Is not her King in her?" Is. 39:3

"Why have they provoked Me to anger
With their carved images,
And with foreign idols?"

20 "The harvest is past,
The summer is ended,
And we are not saved!"

21 [R]For the hurt of the daughter of my
people I am hurt.
I am [R]mourning; Jer. 9:1 • Joel 2:6
Astonishment has taken hold of me.
22 *Is there* no [R]balm in Gilead,
Is there no physician there?
Why then is there no recovery
For the health of the daughter of my
people? Jer. 46:11

CHAPTER 9

OH, [R]that my head were waters,
And my eyes a fountain of tears,
That I might weep day and night
For the slain of the daughter of my
people! Is. 22:4
2 Oh, that I had in the wilderness
A lodging place for wayfaring men;
That I might leave my people,
And go from them!
For [R]they *are* all adulterers, Jer. 5:7, 8
An assembly of treacherous men.

3 "And *like* their bow [R]they have bent
their tongues *for* lies. Ps. 64:3
They are not valiant for the truth on
the earth.
For they proceed from [R]evil to evil,
And they [R]do not know Me," says the
LORD. Jer. 4:22; 13:23 • 1 Sam. 2:12
4 "Everyone[R] take heed to his [T]neighbor,
And do not trust any brother;
For every brother will utterly supplant,
And every neighbor will walk with
slanderers. Mic. 7:5, 6 • *friend*

5 Everyone will [R]deceive his neighbor,
And will not speak the truth;
They have taught their tongue to speak
lies,
And weary themselves to commit
iniquity. Is. 59:4
6 Your habitation *is* in the midst of
deceit;
Through deceit they refuse to know
Me," says the LORD.

7 Therefore thus says the LORD of hosts:

"Behold, [R]I will refine them and [T]try
them; Is. 1:25 • *test*
[R]For how shall I deal with the daughter
of My people? Hos. 11:8
8 Their tongue *is* an arrow shot out;
It speaks [R]deceit; Ps. 12:2
One speaks [R]peaceably to his neighbor
with his mouth,
But in his heart he lies in wait. Ps. 55:21

Judah's Judgment Is Described

9 [R]Shall I not punish them for these
things?" says the LORD.
"Shall I not avenge Myself on such a
nation as this?" Jer. 5:9, 29

10 I will take up a weeping and wailing for
the mountains,
And [R]for the [T]habitations of the
wilderness a lamentation,
Because they are burned up,
So that no one can pass through *them*;
Nor can *men* hear the voice of the
cattle. Hos. 4:3 • *pastures*
[R]Both the birds of the heavens and the
beasts have fled;
They are gone. Jer. 4:25

11 "I will make Jerusalem [R]a heap of ruins
and [R]a den of jackals.
I will make the cities of Judah desolate,
without an inhabitant." Is. 25:2 • Is. 13:22

12 [R]Who *is* the wise man who may understand this? And *who is he* to whom the
mouth of the LORD has spoken, that he may
declare it? Why does the land perish *and* burn
up like a wilderness, so that no one can pass
through? Hos. 14:9
13 And the LORD said, "Because they have
forsaken My law which I set before them,
and have [R]not obeyed My voice, nor walked
according to it, Jer. 3:25; 7:24
14 "but they have walked according to the
*imagination of their own heart and after the
Baals, which their fathers taught them,"
15 therefore thus says the LORD of hosts,
the God of Israel: "Behold, I will feed them,
this people, with wormwood, and give them
[T]water of gall to drink. Bitter or poisonous water

9:14 Lit. *stubbornness;* LXX, Tg. *imagination*

16 "I will scatter them also among the
Gentiles, whom neither they nor their fathers
have known. [R]And I will send a sword after
them until I have consumed them." Ezek. 5:2

17 Thus says the LORD of hosts:

"Consider and call for [R]the mourning
women, 2 Chr. 35:25
That they may come;
And send for skillful wailing women,
That they may come.
18 Let them make haste
And take up a wailing for us,
That our eyes may run with tears,
And our eyelids gush with water.
19 For a voice of wailing is heard from
Zion:
'How we are plundered!
We are greatly ashamed,
Because we have forsaken the land,
Because we have been cast out of [R]our
dwellings.' " Lev. 18:28

20 Yet hear the word of the LORD, O
women,
And let your ear receive the word of
His mouth;
Teach your daughters wailing,
And everyone her neighbor a
lamentation.
21 For death has come through our
windows,
Has entered our palaces,
To kill off the children—[T]*no longer to be*
outside! Lit. *from outside*
And the young men—[T]*no longer* on the
streets! Lit. *from the square*

22 Speak, "Thus says the LORD:

'Even the carcasses of men shall fall [R]as
refuse on the open field, Jer. 8:1, 2
Like cuttings after the harvester,
And no one shall gather *them*.' "

23 Thus says the LORD:

[R]"Let not the wise *man* glory in his
wisdom, [Eccl. 9:11]
Let not the mighty *man* glory in his
[R]might, Ps. 33:16–18
Nor let the rich *man* glory in his riches;
24 But [R]let him who glories glory in this,
That he understands and knows Me,
That I *am* the LORD, exercising
lovingkindness, judgment, and
righteousness in the earth. 1 Cor. 1:31
For in these I delight," says the LORD.

25 "Behold, the days are coming," says the
LORD, "that I will punish all *those who are*
circumcised with the uncircumcised—

26 "Egypt, Judah, Edom, the people of Ammon, Moab, and all *who are* in the [R]farthest
corners, who dwell in the wilderness. For all
these nations *are* uncircumcised, and all the
house of Israel *are* [R]uncircumcised in the
heart." Jer. 25:23 • [Rom. 2:28]

CHAPTER 10

Judah's Futile Idolatry

HEAR the word which the LORD speaks to
you, O house of Israel.
2 Thus says the LORD:

[R]"Do not learn the way of the Gentiles;
Do not be dismayed at the signs of
heaven, [Lev. 18:3; 20:23]
For the Gentiles are dismayed at them.
3 For the customs of the peoples *are*
[T]futile;
For [R]*one* cuts a tree from the forest,
The work of the hands of the workman,
with the ax. Lit. *vanity* • Is. 40:19; 45:20
4 They decorate it with silver and gold;
They [R]fasten it with nails and hammers
So that it will not topple. Is. 41:7
5 They *are* upright, like a palm tree,
And [R]they cannot speak; Ps. 115:5
They must be [R]carried, Ps. 115:7
Because they cannot go *by themselves*.
Do not be afraid of them,
For [R]they cannot do evil, Is. 41:23, 24
Nor can they do any good."

6 Inasmuch as *there is* none [R]like You, O
LORD
(You *are* great, and Your name *is* great
in might), Ex. 15:11
7 [R]Who would not fear You, O King of the
nations?
For this is Your rightful due.
For [R]among all the wise *men* of the
nations,
And in all their kingdoms,
There is none like You. Rev. 15:4 • Ps. 89:6
8 But they are altogether [R]dull-hearted
and foolish; Hab. 2:18
A wooden idol *is* a worthless doctrine.
9 Silver is beaten into plates;
It is brought from Tarshish,
And [R]gold from Uphaz, Dan. 10:5
The work of the craftsman
And of the hands of the metalsmith;
Blue and purple *are* their clothing;
They *are* all the work of skillful *men*.
10 But the LORD *is* the true God;
He *is* [R]the living God and the
[R]everlasting King. 1 Tim. 6:17 • Ps. 10:16
At His wrath the earth will tremble,
And the nations will not be able to
abide His indignation.

11 Thus you shall say to them: R"The gods
that have not made the heavens and the
earth Rshall perish from the earth and from
under these heavens." Ps. 96:5 • Zeph. 2:11

12 He Rhas made the earth by His power,
He has Restablished the world by His wisdom,
And Rhas stretched out the heavens at His discretion. Jer. 51:15 • Ps. 93:1 • Job 9:8
13 RWhen He utters His voice,
There is a Tmultitude of waters in the heavens:
"And RHe causes the vapors to ascend from the ends of the earth.
He makes lightning for the rain,
He brings the wind out of His treasuries." Job 38:34 • Or *noise* • Ps. 135:7

14 REveryone is Rdull-hearted, without knowledge; Jer. 51:17 • Prov. 30:2
REvery metalsmith is put to shame by the graven image; Is. 42:17; 44:11
RFor his molded image *is* falsehood,
And *there is* no breath in them. Hab. 2:18
15 They *are* futile, a work of errors;
In the time of their punishment they shall perish.
16 RThe Portion of Jacob *is* not like them,
For He *is* the Maker of all *things*,
And RIsrael *is* the tribe of His inheritance; Lam. 3:24 • Deut. 32:9
RThe LORD of hosts *is* His name. Is. 47:4

17 RGather up your wares from the land,
O inhabitant of the fortress! Jer. 6:1

18 For thus says the LORD:

"Behold, I will Rthrow out at this time
The inhabitants of the land,
And will distress them, 1 Sam. 25:29
RThat they may find *it so*." Ezek. 6:10

Jeremiah's Prayer for Correction

19 RWoe is me for my hurt! Jer. 8:21
My wound is severe.
But I say, R"Truly this *is* an infirmity,
And RI must bear it." Ps. 77:10 • Mic. 7:9
20 RMy tent is plundered,
And all my cords are broken;
My children have gone from me,
And they *are* Rno more.
There is no one to pitch my tent anymore,
Or set up my curtains. Jer. 4:20 • Jer. 31:15

21 For the shepherds have become dull-hearted,
And have not sought the LORD;
Therefore they shall not prosper,
And all their flocks shall be scattered.
22 Behold, the noise of the report has come,
And a great commotion out of the Rnorth country,
To make the cities of Judah desolate, a Rden of jackals. Jer. 5:15 • Jer. 9:11

23 O LORD, I know the Rway of man *is* not in himself;
It is not in man who walks to direct his own steps. Prov. 16:1; 20:24
24 O LORD, Rcorrect me, but with justice;
Not in Your anger, lest You bring me to nothing. Jer. 30:11
25 RPour out Your fury on the Gentiles,
Rwho do not know You,
And on the families who do not call on Your name; Ps. 79:6, 7 • Job 18:21
For they have eaten up Jacob,
Devoured him and consumed him,
And made his habitation desolate.

CHAPTER 11

Judah's Curse Because of the Broken Covenant

THE word that came to Jeremiah from the
LORD, saying,
2 "Hear the words of this covenant, and
speak to the men of Judah and to the inhabitants of Jerusalem;
3 "and say to them, 'Thus says the LORD
God of Israel: R"Cursed *is* the man who does
not obey the words of this covenant Deut. 27:26
4 "which I commanded your fathers in the
day *that* I brought them out of the land of
Egypt, Rfrom the iron furnace, saying, R'Obey
My voice, and do according to all that I
command you; so shall you be My people,
and I will be your God,' Deut. 4:20 • Lev. 26:3
5 "that I may establish the Roath which I
have sworn to your fathers, to give them a
land flowing with milk and honey, as *it is* this
day."'" Then I answered and said, T"So be it,
LORD." Ps. 105:9 • Heb. *Amen*
6 Then the LORD said to me, "Proclaim all
these words in the cities of Judah and in the
streets of Jerusalem, saying: 'Hear the words
of this covenant Rand do them. [Rom. 2:13]
7 'For I earnestly exhorted your fathers in
the day *that* I brought them up out of the
land of Egypt, until this day, Rrising early and
exhorting, saying, "Obey My voice." Jer. 35:15
8 'Yet they did not obey or incline their
ear, but everyone walked in the Timagination
of his evil heart; therefore I will bring upon
them all the words of this covenant, which I
commanded *them* to do, but *which* they have
not done.'" Lit. *stubbornness*, Jer. 7:24
9 And the LORD said to me, "A conspiracy
has been found among the men of Judah and
among the inhabitants of Jerusalem.

10 "They have turned back to [R]the iniquities
of their forefathers who refused to hear My
words, and they have gone after other gods
to serve them; the house of Israel and the
house of Judah have broken My covenant
which I made with their fathers." Ezek. 20:18
11 Therefore thus says the LORD: "Behold, I
will surely bring calamity on them which
they will not be able to escape; and though
they cry out to Me, I will not listen to them.
12 "Then the cities of Judah and the inhabitants of Jerusalem will go and [R]cry out to the
gods to whom they offer incense, but they
will not save them at all in the time of their
trouble. Deut. 32:37
13 "For *according to* the number of your
[R]cities were your gods, O Judah; and *according to* the number of the streets of Jerusalem
you have set up altars to *that* shameful thing,
altars to burn incense to Baal. Jer. 2:28
14 "Therefore [R]do not pray for this people,
or lift up a cry or prayer for them; for I will
not hear *them* in the time that they cry out to
Me because of their trouble. Ex. 32:10

15 "What[R] has My beloved to do in My
house, Ps. 50:16
Having [R]done lewd deeds with many?
And [R]the holy flesh has passed from
you. Ezek. 16:25 • [Titus 1:15]
When you do evil, then you rejoice.
16 The LORD called your name,
[R]Green Olive Tree, Lovely *and* of Good
Fruit.
With the noise of a great tumult
He has kindled fire on it,
And its branches are broken. Ps. 52:8

17 "For the LORD of hosts, [R]who planted
you, has pronounced doom against you for
the evil of the house of Israel and of the
house of Judah, which they have done
against themselves to provoke Me to anger in
offering incense to Baal." Is. 5:2

Anathoth's Conspiracy Against Jeremiah

18 Now the LORD gave me knowledge *of it*,
and I know *it*; for You showed me their
doings.
19 But I *was* like a docile lamb brought to
the slaughter; and I did not know that they
had devised schemes against me, *saying*, "Let
us destroy the tree with its fruit, and let us
cut him off from the land of the living, that
his name may be remembered no more."

20 But, O LORD of hosts,
You who judge righteously,
Testing the [T]mind and the heart, kidneys
Let me see Your vengeance on them,
For to You I have revealed my cause.

21 "Therefore thus says the LORD concerning the men of Anathoth who seek your life,
saying, [R]'Do not prophesy in the name of the
LORD, lest you die by our hand'— Mic. 2:6
22 "therefore thus says the LORD of hosts:
'Behold, I will punish them. The young men
shall die by the sword, their sons and their
daughters shall [R]die by famine; Jer. 9:21
23 'and there shall be no remnant of them,
for I will bring catastrophe on the men of
Anathoth, *even* [R]the year of their punishment.' " Jer. 23:12

CHAPTER 12

Jeremiah's Complaint to God

RIGHTEOUS [R]*are* You, O LORD, when I
plead with You;
Yet let me talk with You about *Your*
judgments.
[R]Why does the way of the wicked
prosper?
Why are those happy who deal so
treacherously? Ps. 51:14 • Mal. 3:15
2 You have planted them, yes, they have
taken root;
They grow, yes, they bear fruit.
[R]You *are* near in their mouth Matt. 15:8
But far from their [T]mind. Lit. *kidneys*

3 But You, O LORD, [R]know me;
You have seen me,
And You have [R]tested my heart toward
You.
Pull them out like sheep for the
slaughter,
And prepare them for [R]the day of
slaughter. Ps. 17:3 • Jer. 11:20 • James 5:5
4 How long will [R]the land mourn,
And the herbs of every field wither?
[R]The beasts and birds are consumed,
[R]For the wickedness of those who dwell
there,
Because they said, "He will not see our
final end." Hos. 4:3 • Jer. 9:10 • Ps. 107:34

God's Reply to Jeremiah

5 "If you have run with the footmen, and
they have wearied you,
Then how can you contend with
horses?
And *if* in the land of peace,
In which you trusted, *they wearied you*,
Then how will you do in [R]the flooding
of the Jordan? Josh. 3:15
6 For even [R]your brothers, the house of
your father, Jer. 9:4, 5
Even they have dealt treacherously
with you;
Yes, they have called [T]a multitude after
you. Or *abundantly*
[R]Do not believe them, Prov. 26:25
Even though they speak [T]smooth words
to you. Lit. *good*

7 "I have forsaken My house, I have left
My heritage;
I have given the dearly beloved of My
soul into the hand of her enemies.
8 My heritage is to Me like a lion in the
forest;
It cries out against Me;
Therefore I have [R]hated it. Hos. 9:15
9 My [T]heritage *is* to Me *like* a speckled
vulture; *inheritance*
The vultures all around *are* against her.
Come, assemble all the beasts of the
field,
[R]Bring them to devour! Lev. 26:22

10 "Many [T]rulers have destroyed [R]My
vineyard, Lit. *shepherds* or *pastors* • Is. 5:1–7
They have [R]trodden My portion under-
foot; Is. 63:18
They have made My [T]pleasant portion a
desolate wilderness. *desired portion* of land
11 They have made it [R]desolate;
Desolate, it mourns to Me; Jer. 10:22; 22:6
The whole land is made desolate,
Because no one takes *it* to heart.
12 The plunderers have come
On all the desolate heights in the
wilderness,
For the sword of the LORD shall devour
From *one* end of the land to the *other*
end of the land;
No flesh shall have peace.
13 [R]They have sown wheat but reaped
thorns;
They have [T]put themselves to pain *but*
do not profit.
But be ashamed of your harvest
Because of the fierce anger of the
LORD." Hag. 1:6 • Or *strained*

14 Thus says the LORD: "Against all My evil neighbors who [R]touch the inheritance which I have caused My people Israel to inherit—behold, I will [R]pluck them out of their land and pluck out the house of Judah from among them. Zech. 2:8 • Deut. 30:3

15 "Then it shall be, after I have plucked them out, that I will return and have compassion on them and bring them back, everyone to his heritage and everyone to his land.

16 "And it shall be, if they will diligently learn the ways of My people, to swear by My name, 'As the LORD lives,' as they taught My people to swear by Baal, then they shall be established in the midst of My people.

17 "But if they do not [R]obey, I will utterly pluck up and destroy that nation," says the LORD. Is. 60:12

CHAPTER 13

Sign of the Marred Sash

THUS the LORD said to me: "Go and get yourself a linen sash, and put it around your waist, but do not put it in water."

2 So I got a sash according to the word of the LORD, and put *it* around my waist.

3 And the word of the LORD came to me the second time, saying,

4 "Take the [T]sash that you acquired, which *is* [T]around your waist, and arise, go to the [T]Euphrates, and hide it there in a hole in the rock." *waistband* • Lit. *upon your loins* • Heb. *Perath*

5 So I went and hid it by the Euphrates, as the LORD commanded me.

6 And it came to pass after many days that the LORD said to me, "Arise, go to the Euphrates, and take from there the sash which I commanded you to hide there."

7 Then I went to the Euphrates and dug, and I took the [T]sash from the place where I had hidden it; and there was the sash, ruined. It was profitable for nothing. *waistband*

8 "Then the word of the LORD came to me, saying,

9 "Thus says the LORD: 'In this manner [R]I will ruin the pride of Judah and the great [R]pride of Jerusalem. Lev. 26:19 • Zeph. 3:11

10 'This evil people, who [R]refuse to hear My words, who walk in the imagination of their heart, and walk after other gods to serve them and worship them, shall be just like this sash which is profitable for nothing. Jer. 16:12

11 'For as the sash clings to the waist of a man, so I have caused the whole house of Israel and the whole house of Judah to cling to Me,' says the LORD, 'that they may become My people, for renown, for praise, and for glory; but they would not hear.'

Sign of the Wine Bottles

12 "Therefore you shall speak to them this word: 'Thus says the LORD God of Israel: "Every bottle shall be filled with wine." ' And they will say to you, 'Do we not certainly know that every bottle will be filled with wine?'

13 "Then you shall say to them, 'Thus says the LORD: "Behold, I will fill all the inhabitants of this land—even the kings who sit on David's throne, the priests, the prophets, and all the inhabitants of Jerusalem—[R]with drunkenness! Is. 51:17; 63:6

14 "And [R]I will dash them [T]one against another, even the fathers and the sons together," says the LORD. "I will not pity nor spare nor have mercy, but will destroy them." ' " Jer. 19:9–11 • Lit. *a man against his brother*

15 Hear and give ear:
Do not be proud,
For the LORD has spoken.
16 [R]Give glory to the LORD your God
Before He causes [R]darkness,
And before your feet stumble
On the dark mountains, Josh. 7:19 • Amos 8:9
And while you are looking for light,

He turns it into [R]the shadow of death
And makes *it* dense darkness. Ps. 44:19
17 But if you will not hear it,
My soul will [R]weep in secret for *your* pride;
My eyes will weep bitterly
And run down with tears,
Because the LORD's flock has been taken captive. Jer. 9:1; 14:17

18 Say to [R]the king and to the queen mother,
"Humble yourselves;
Sit down,
For your rule shall collapse, the crown of your glory." Jer. 22:26
19 The cities of the South shall be shut up,
And no one shall open *them*;
Judah shall be carried away captive, all of it;
It shall be wholly carried away captive.

20 Lift up your eyes and see
Those who come from the [R]north.
Where *is* the flock *that* was given to you,
Your beautiful sheep? Jer. 10:22; 46:20
21 What will you say when He punishes you?
For you have taught them
To be chieftains, to be head over you.
Will not [R]pangs seize you,
Like a woman in [T]labor? Jer. 6:24 • *childbirth*
22 And if you say in your heart,
"Why have these things come upon me?"
For the greatness of your iniquity
Your skirts have been uncovered,
Your heels [T]made bare. Lit. *suffer violence*
23 Can the Ethiopian change his skin or the leopard its spots?
Then may you also do good who are accustomed to do evil.

24 "Therefore I will [R]scatter them [R]like stubble
That passes away by the wind of the wilderness. Jer. 9:16 • Hos. 13:3
25 [R]This is your lot, Job 20:29
The portion of your measures from Me," says the LORD,
"Because you have forgotten Me
And trusted in [R]falsehood. Jer. 10:14
26 Therefore [R]I will uncover your skirts over your face,
That your shame may appear. Lam. 1:8
27 I have seen your adulteries
And your *lustful* [R]neighings,
The lewdness of your harlotry,
Your abominations [R]on the hills in the fields. Jer. 5:7, 8 • Is. 65:7
Woe to you, O Jerusalem!
Will you still not be made clean?"

CHAPTER 14

Judah's Drought Is Described

THE word of the LORD that came to Jeremiah concerning the droughts.

2 "Judah mourns,
And [R]her gates languish; Is. 3:26
They [R]mourn for the land, Jer. 8:21
And the cry of Jerusalem has gone up.
3 Their nobles have sent their lads for water;
They went to the cisterns *and* found no water.
They returned with their vessels empty;
They were ashamed and confounded
[R]And covered their heads. 2 Sam. 15:30
4 Because the ground is parched,
For there was [R]no rain in the land,
The plowmen were ashamed;
They covered their heads. Jer. 3:3
5 Yes, the deer also gave birth in the field,
But left because there was no grass.
6 And [R]the wild donkeys stood in the desolate heights; Jer. 2:24
They sniffed at the wind like jackals;
Their eyes failed because *there was* no grass."

Jeremiah's First Intercession

7 O LORD, though our iniquities testify against us,
Do it [R]for Your name's sake; Ps. 25:11
For our backslidings are many,
We have sinned against You.
8 [R]O the Hope of Israel, his Savior in time of trouble,
Why should You be like a stranger in the land,
And like a wayfaring man *who* turns aside to tarry for a night? Jer. 17:13
9 Why should You be like a man astonished,
Like a mighty one [R]*who* cannot save?
Yet You, O LORD, [R]*are* in our midst,
And we are called by Your name;
Do not leave us! Is. 59:1 • Ex. 29:45

10 Thus says the LORD to this people:

[R]"Thus they have loved to wander;
They have not restrained their feet.
Therefore the LORD does not accept them; Jer. 2:23–25
[R]He will remember their iniquity now,
And punish their sins." Hos. 8:13

11 Then the LORD said to me, [R]"Do not pray
for this people, for *their* good. Ex. 32:10
12 "When they fast, I will not hear their
cry; and when they offer burnt offering and

grain offering, I will not accept them. But [R]I will consume them by the sword, by the famine, and by the pestilence." Jer. 9:16

Jeremiah's Second Intercession

13 Then I said, "Ah, Lord GOD! Behold, the prophets say to them, 'You shall not see the sword, nor shall you have famine, but I will give you assured peace in this place.' "
14 And the LORD said to me, "The prophets prophesy lies in My name. I have not sent them, commanded them, nor spoken to them; they prophesy to you a false vision, [T]divination, a worthless thing, and the deceit of their heart. Telling the future by signs and omens
15 "Therefore thus says the LORD concerning the prophets who prophesy in My name, whom I did not send, [R]and who say, 'Sword and famine shall not be in this land'—'By sword and famine those prophets shall be consumed! Ezek. 14:10
16 'And the people to whom they prophesy shall be cast out in the streets of Jerusalem because of the famine and the sword; they will have no one to bury them—them nor their wives, their sons nor their daughters—for I will pour their wickedness on them.'
17 "Therefore you shall say this word to them:

[R]'Let my eyes flow with tears night and
day, Jer. 9:1; 13:17
And let them not cease;
[R]For the virgin daughter of my people
Has been broken with a mighty stroke,
with a very severe blow. Jer. 8:21
18 If I go out to [R]the field,
Then behold, those slain with the
sword! Ezek. 7:15
And if I enter the city,
Then behold, those sick from famine!
Yes, both prophet and [R]priest go about
in a land they do not know.' " Jer. 23:11

Jeremiah's Third Intercession

19 [R]Have You utterly rejected Judah?
Has Your soul loathed Zion?
Why have You stricken us so that
[R]*there is* no healing for us?
[R]We looked for peace, but *there was* no
good;
And for the time of healing, and there
was trouble. Lam. 5:22 • Jer. 15:18 • Jer. 8:15
20 We acknowledge, O LORD, our
wickedness
And the iniquity of our fathers,
For we have sinned against You.
21 Do not abhor *us*, for Your name's sake;
Do not disgrace the throne of Your
glory.
[R]Remember, do not break Your covenant
with us. Ps. 106:45
22 Are there any among the idols of the
nations that can cause [R]rain? Jer. 5:24
Or can the heavens give showers?
[R]*Are* You not He, O LORD our God?
Therefore we will wait for You,
Since You have made all these. Ps. 135:7

CHAPTER 15

THEN the LORD said to me, "Though Moses and [R]Samuel stood before Me, *yet* My [T]mind *could* not *be* favorable toward this people. Cast *them* out of My sight, and let them go forth. 1 Sam. 7:9 • Lit. *soul was not toward*
2 "And it shall be, if they say to you, 'Where should we go?' then you shall tell them, 'Thus says the LORD:

[R]"Such as *are* for death, to death;
And such as *are* for the sword, to the
sword;
And such as *are* for the famine, to the
famine;
And such as *are* for the [R]captivity, to
the captivity." ' Zech. 11:9 • Jer. 9:16; 16:13

3 "And I will [R]appoint over them four forms *of destruction*," says the LORD: "the sword to slay, the dogs to drag, [R]the birds of the heavens and the beasts of the earth to devour and destroy. Ezek. 14:21 • Jer. 7:33
4 "I will hand them over to [R]trouble, to all kingdoms of the earth, because of [R]Manasseh the son of Hezekiah, king of Judah, for what he did in Jerusalem. Deut. 28:25 • 2 Kin. 24:3, 4

5 "For who will have pity on you, O
Jerusalem?
Or who will bemoan you?
Or who will turn aside to ask how you
are doing?
6 [R]You have forsaken Me," says the LORD,
"You have gone backward.
Therefore I will stretch out My hand
against you and destroy you;
I am [T]weary of relenting! Jer. 2:13 • *tired*
7 And I will winnow them with a
winnowing fan in the gates of the
land;
I will [R]bereave *them* of children;
I will destroy My people,
Since they [R]do not return from their
ways. Jer. 18:21 • Is. 9:13
8 Their widows will be increased to Me
more than the sand of the seas;
I will bring against them,
Against the mother of the young men,
A plunderer at noonday;
I will cause anguish and terror to fall
on them [R]suddenly. Is. 29:5

9 "She[R] languishes who has borne seven;
She has breathed her last;

[R]Her sun has gone down
While *it was* yet day;
She has been ashamed and confounded.
And the remnant of them I will deliver
to the sword 1 Sam. 2:5 • Amos 8:9
Before their enemies," says the LORD.

God Encourages Jeremiah

10 [R]Woe is me, my mother, Job 3:1
That you have borne me,
A man of strife and a man of
contention to the whole [T]earth!
I have neither lent for interest,
Nor have men lent to me for interest.
Every one of them curses me. Or *land*

11 The LORD said:

"Surely it will be well with your
remnant;
Surely I will cause [R]the enemy to
intercede with you
In the time of adversity and in the time
of affliction. Jer. 40:4, 5
12 Can anyone break iron,
The northern iron and the bronze?
13 Your wealth and your treasures
I will give as [R]plunder without price,
Because of all your sins,
Throughout your territories. Ps. 44:12
14 And I will make *you* cross over with
your enemies
Into a land *which* you do not know;
For a [R]fire is kindled in My anger,
Which shall burn upon you." Deut. 32:22

15 O LORD, [R]You know; Jer. 12:3
Remember me and [T]visit me, *attend to*
And [R]take vengeance for me on my
persecutors. Jer. 20:12
Do not take me away in Your
longsuffering.
Know that [R]for Your sake I have
suffered rebuke. Ps. 69:7–9
16 Your words were found, and I [R]ate
them, Ezek. 3:1, 3
And [R]Your word was to me the joy and
rejoicing of my heart; [Job 23:12]
For I am called by Your name,
O LORD God of hosts.
17 [R]I did not sit in the assembly of the
mockers,
Nor did I rejoice;
I sat alone because of Your hand,
For You have filled me with
indignation. Ps. 26:4, 5
18 Why is my [R]pain perpetual Jer. 10:19; 30:15
And my wound incurable,
Which refuses to be healed?
Will You surely be to me [R]like an
unreliable stream, Job 6:15
As waters *that* [T]fail? Or *cannot be trusted*

19 Therefore thus says the LORD:

[R]"If you return,
Then I will bring you back;
You shall [R]stand before Me;
If you [R]take out the precious from the
vile, Zech. 3:7 • Jer. 15:1 • Ezek. 22:26; 44:23
You shall be as My mouth.
Let them return to you,
But you must not return to them.
20 And I will make you to this people a
fortified bronze [R]wall; Ezek. 3:9
And they will fight against you,
But [R]they shall not prevail against you;
For I *am* with you to save you
And deliver you," says the
LORD. Jer. 1:8, 19
21 "I will deliver you from the hand of the
wicked,
And I will redeem you from the grip of
the terrible."

CHAPTER 16

Jeremiah Is Not to Marry

THE word of the LORD also came to me,
saying,
2 "You shall not take a wife, nor shall you
have sons or daughters in this place."
3 For thus says the LORD concerning the
sons and daughters who are born in this
place, and concerning their mothers who
bore them and their fathers who begot them
in this land:
4 "They shall die gruesome deaths; they
shall not be lamented nor shall they be buried, *but* they shall be [R]like refuse on the face
of the earth. They shall be consumed by the
sword and by famine, and their [R]corpses shall
be meat for the birds of heaven and for the
beasts of the earth." Ps. 83:10 • Ps. 79:2
5 For thus says the LORD: [R]"Do not enter
the house of mourning, nor go to lament or
bemoan them; for I have taken away My
peace from this people," says the LORD,
"lovingkindness and mercies. Ezek. 24:17, 22, 23
6 "Both the great and the small shall die in
this land. They shall not be buried; neither
shall men lament for them, cut themselves,
nor make themselves bald for them.
7 "Nor shall *men* break *bread* in mourning
for them, to comfort them for the dead; nor
shall *men* give them the cup of consolation to
drink for their father or their mother.
8 "Also you shall not go into the house of
feasting to sit with them, to eat and drink."
9 For thus says the LORD of hosts, the God
of Israel: "Behold, [R]I will cause to cease from
this place, before your eyes and in your days,
the voice of [T]mirth and the voice of gladness, the voice of the bridegroom and the
voice of the bride. Rev. 18:23 • *rejoicing*

Judah's Idolatry

10 "And it shall be, when you show this
people all these words, and they say to you,
[R]'Why has the LORD pronounced all this great
disaster against us? Or what *is* our iniquity?
Or what *is* our sin that we have committed
against the LORD our God?' Deut. 29:24
11 "then you shall say to them, 'Because
your fathers have forsaken Me,' says the
LORD; 'they have walked after other gods and
have served them and worshiped them, and
have forsaken Me and not kept My law.
12 'And you have done worse than your
fathers, for behold, each one walks according
to the [T]imagination of his own evil heart, so
that no one listens to Me. Lit. *stubbornness*
13 'Therefore I will cast you out of this land
[R]into a land that you do not know, neither
you nor your fathers; and there you shall
serve other gods day and night, where I will
not show you favor.' Jer. 15:14

God's Promise of Judah's Restoration

14 "Therefore behold, the days are coming,"
says the LORD, "that it shall no more be said,
'The LORD lives who brought up the children
of Israel from the land of Egypt,'
15 "but, 'The LORD lives who brought up the
children of Israel from the land of the [R]north
and from all the lands where He had driven
them.' For I will bring them back into their
land which I gave to their fathers. Jer. 3:18
16 "Behold, I will send for many [R]fisher-
men," says the LORD, "and they shall fish
them; and afterward I will send for many
hunters, and they shall hunt them from every
mountain and every hill, and out of the holes
of the rocks. Amos 4:2
17 "For My [R]eyes *are* on all their ways; they
are not hidden from My face, nor is their
iniquity hidden from My eyes. Heb. 4:13
18 "And first I will repay [R]double for their
iniquity and their sin, because [R]they have
defiled My land; they have filled My inheritance with the carcasses of their detestable
and abominable idols." Jer. 17:18 • [Ezek. 43:7]

19 O LORD, [R]my strength and my fortress,
[R]My refuge in the day of affliction,
The Gentiles shall come to You
From the ends of the earth and say,
"Surely our fathers have inherited lies,
Worthlessness and [R]unprofitable
things." Ps. 18:1, 2 • Jer. 17:17 • Is. 44:10
20 Will a man make gods for himself,
[R]Which *are* not gods? Gal. 4:8

21 "Therefore behold, I will this once cause
them to know,
I will cause them to know
My hand and My might;
And they shall know that [R]My name *is*
the LORD. Amos 5:8

CHAPTER 17

Judah's Sins Are Listed

"THE sin of Judah *is* [R]written with a
[R]pen of iron; Jer. 2:22 • Job 19:24
With the point of a diamond *it is*
[R]engraved 2 Cor. 3:3
On the tablet of their heart,
And on the horns of your altars,
2 While their children remember
Their altars and their wooden images
By the green trees on the high hills.
3 O My mountain in the field,
I will give as plunder your wealth, all
your treasures,
And your high places of sin within all
your borders.
4 And you, even yourself,
Shall let go of your heritage which I
gave you;
And I will cause you to serve your
enemies
In the land which you do not know;
For you have kindled a fire in My anger
which shall burn forever."

5 Thus says the LORD:

"Cursed *is* the man who trusts in man
And makes flesh his [T]strength, Lit. *arm*
Whose heart departs from the LORD.
6 For he shall be [R]like a shrub in the
desert, Jer. 48:6
And [R]shall not see when good comes,
But shall inhabit the parched places in
the wilderness, Job 20:17
In a salt land *which is* not inhabited.

7 "Blessed[R] *is* the man who trusts in the
LORD,
And whose hope is the LORD. [Is. 30:18]
8 For he shall be [R]like a tree planted by
the waters, [Ps. 1:3]
Which spreads out its roots by the river,
And will not *fear when heat comes;
But its leaf will be green,
And will not be anxious in the year of
drought,
Nor will cease from yielding fruit.

9 "The heart *is* deceitful above all *things*,
And [T]desperately wicked; *incurably sick*
Who can know it?
10 I, the LORD, [R]search the heart, Rev. 2:23
I test the [T]mind, Most secret parts, lit. *kidneys*
[R]Even to give every man according to
his ways, Rom. 2:6
And according to the fruit of his doings.

11 "*As* a partridge that [T]broods but does not
hatch, Sits on eggs

17:8 Qr., Tg. *see*

So is he who gets riches, but not by right;
It [R]will leave him in the midst of his days, Ps. 55:23
And at his end he will be a fool."

12 A glorious high throne from the beginning
Is the place of our sanctuary.
13 O LORD, [R]the hope of Israel, Jer. 14:8
[R]All who forsake You shall be ashamed.

"Those who depart from Me [Is. 1:28]
Shall be [R]written in the earth, Luke 10:20
Because they have forsaken the LORD,
The [R]fountain of living waters." Jer. 2:13

14 Heal me, O LORD, and I shall be healed;
Save me, and I shall be saved,
For [R]You *are* my praise. Deut. 10:21
15 Indeed they say to me,
[R]"Where *is* the word of the LORD?
Let it come now!" Is. 5:19
16 As for me, [R]I have not hurried away
from *being* a shepherd *who* follows You,
Nor have I desired the woeful day;
You know what came out of my lips;
It was right there before You. Jer. 1:4–12
17 Do not be a terror to me;
You *are* my hope in the day of doom.
18 [R]Let them be ashamed who persecute me, Ps. 35:4; 70:2
But [R]do not let me be put to shame;
Let them be dismayed,
But do not let me be dismayed.
Bring on them the day of doom,
And [R]destroy[T] them with double destruction! Ps. 25:2 • Jer. 11:20 • Lit. *crush*

Jeremiah's Call for Sabbath Observance

19 Thus the LORD said to me: "Go and stand
in the gate of the children of the people, by
which the kings of Judah come in and by
which they go out, and in all the gates of
Jerusalem;
20 "and say to them, [R]'Hear the word of the
LORD, you kings of Judah, and all Judah, and
all the inhabitants of Jerusalem, who enter by
these gates. Jer. 19:3, 4
21 'Thus says the LORD: [R]"Take heed to
yourselves, and bear no burden on the Sabbath day, nor bring *it* in by the gates of
Jerusalem; Neh. 13:19
22 "nor carry a burden out of your houses
on the Sabbath day, nor do any work, but
hallow the Sabbath day, as I [R]commanded
your fathers. Ex. 20:8; 31:13
23 "But they did not obey nor incline their
ear, but made their neck stiff, that they might
not hear nor receive instruction.
24 "And it shall be, [R]if you diligently heed
Me," says the LORD, "to bring no burden
through the gates of this city on the [R]Sabbath
day, but hallow the Sabbath day, to do no
work in it, Jer. 11:4; 26:3 • Ex. 16:23–30; 20:8–10
25 [R]"then shall enter the gates of this city
kings and princes sitting on the throne of
David, riding in chariots and on horses, they
and their princes, accompanied by the men of
Judah and the inhabitants of Jerusalem; and
this city shall remain forever. Jer. 22:4
26 "And they shall come from the cities of
Judah and from the places around Jerusalem,
from the land of Benjamin and from the
lowland, from the mountains and from the
South, bringing burnt offerings and sacrifices,
grain offerings and incense, bringing sacrifices of praise to the house of the LORD.
27 "But if you will not heed Me to hallow
the Sabbath day, such as not carrying a
burden when entering the gates of Jerusalem
on the Sabbath day, then I will kindle a fire in
its gates, and it shall devour the palaces of
Jerusalem, and it shall not be quenched." ' "

CHAPTER 18

Sign of the Potter

THE word which came to Jeremiah from
the LORD, saying:
2 "Arise and go down to the potter's
house, and there I will cause you to hear My
words."
3 Then I went down to the potter's house,
and there he was, making something at the
[T]wheel. Potter's wheel
4 And the vessel that he [T]made of clay was
[T]marred in the hand of the potter; so he made
it again into another vessel, as it seemed good
to the potter to make. *was making • ruined*
5 Then the word of the LORD came to me,
saying:
6 "O house of Israel, can I not do with you
as this potter?" says the LORD. "Look, [R]as the
clay *is* in the potter's hand, so *are* you in My
hand, O house of Israel! Is. 64:8
7 "The instant I speak concerning a nation
and concerning a kingdom, to [R]pluck up, to
pull down, and to destroy *it*, Jer. 1:10
8 "if that nation against whom I have
spoken turns from its evil, I will relent of the
disaster that I thought to bring upon it.
9 "And the instant I speak concerning a
nation and concerning a kingdom, to build
and to plant *it*,
10 "if it does evil in My sight so that it does
not obey My voice, then I will relent concerning the good with which I said I would
benefit it.
11 "Now therefore, speak to the men of
Judah and to the inhabitants of Jerusalem,
saying, 'Thus says the LORD: "Behold, I am
fashioning a disaster and devising a plan
against you. [R]Return now every one from his

evil way, and make your ways and your
doings [R]good." ' " 2 Kin. 17:13 • Jer. 7:3–7
12 And they said, [R]"That is hopeless! So we
will walk according to our own plans, and we
will every one do the [T]imagination of his evil
heart." Jer. 2:25 • Lit. *stubbornness*, Jer. 7:24
13 Therefore thus says the LORD:

[R]"Ask now among the Gentiles,
Who has heard such things?
The virgin of Israel has done [R]a very
horrible thing. Jer. 2:10, 11 • Jer. 5:30
14 Will *a man* [T]leave the snow-water of
Lebanon,
Which comes from the rock of the field?
Will the cold flowing waters be forsaken
for strange waters? *forsake*

15 "Because My people have forgotten [R]Me,
They have burned incense to worthless
idols.
And they have caused themselves to
stumble in their ways,
From the [R]ancient paths,
To walk in pathways and not on a
highway, Jer. 2:13, 32 • Jer. 6:16
16 To make their land [R]desolate *and* a
perpetual [R]hissing;
Everyone who passes by it will be
astonished
And shake his head. Jer. 19:8 • 1 Kin. 9:8
17 [R]I will scatter them [R]as with an east
wind before the enemy;
[R]I will show them the back and not the
face Jer. 13:24 • Ps. 48:7 • Jer. 2:27
In the day of their calamity."

18 Then they said, "Come and let us devise
plans against Jeremiah; for the law shall not
perish from the priest, nor counsel from the
wise, nor the word from the prophet. Come
and let us attack him with the tongue, and let
us not give heed to any of his words."

19 Give heed to me, O LORD,
And listen to the voice of those who
contend with me!
20 Shall evil be repaid for good?
For they have [R]dug a pit for my life.
Remember that I [R]stood before You
To speak good [T]for them,
And to turn away Your wrath from
them. Jer. 5:26 • Jer. 14:7—15:1 • *concerning*
21 Therefore [R]deliver up their children to
the famine, Ps. 109:9–20
And pour out their *blood*
By the force of the sword;
Let their wives *become* widows
And [R]bereaved of their children.
Let their men be put to death,
Their young men *be* slain
By the sword in battle. Jer. 15:7, 8
22 Let a cry be heard from their houses,
When You bring a troop suddenly upon
them;
For they have dug a pit to take me,
And hidden snares for my feet.
23 Yet, LORD, You know all their counsel
Which is against me, to slay *me*.
[R]Provide no atonement for their iniquity,
Nor blot out their sin from Your sight;
But let them be overthrown before You.
Deal *thus* with them Ps. 35:14; 109:14
In the time of Your [R]anger. Jer. 7:20

CHAPTER 19

Sign of the Broken Flask

THUS says the LORD: "Go and get a potter's earthen flask, and *take* some of the
elders of the people and some of the elders of
the priests.
2 "And go out to [R]the Valley of the Son of
Hinnom, which *is* by the entry of the Potsherd Gate; and proclaim there the words
that I will tell you, Josh. 15:8
3 [R]"and say, 'Hear the word of the LORD, O
kings of Judah and inhabitants of Jerusalem.
Thus says the LORD of hosts, the God of
Israel: "Behold, I will bring such a catastrophe on this place, that whoever hears of it,
his ears will [R]tingle. Jer. 17:20 • 1 Sam. 3:11
4 "Because they [R]have forsaken Me and
made this an alien place, because they have
burned incense in it to other gods whom
neither they, their fathers, nor the kings of
Judah have known, and have filled this place
with the blood of the innocents Is. 65:11
5 "(they have also built the high places of
Baal, to burn their sons with fire *for* burnt
offerings to Baal, which I did not command
or speak, nor did it come into My mind),
6 "therefore behold, the days are coming,"
says the LORD, "that this place shall no more
be called Tophet or [R]the Valley of the Son of
Hinnom, but the Valley of Slaughter. Josh. 15:8
7 "And I will make void the counsel of
Judah and Jerusalem in this place, [R]and I will
cause them to fall by the sword before their
enemies and by the hands of those who seek
their lives; their [R]corpses I will give as meat
for the birds of the heaven and for the beasts
of the earth. Lev. 26:17 • Ps. 79:2
8 "I will make this city desolate and a
hissing; everyone who passes by it will be
astonished and hiss because of all its plagues.
9 "And I will cause them to eat the [R]flesh
of their sons and the flesh of their daughters,
and everyone shall eat the flesh of his friend
in the siege and in the desperation with
which their enemies and those who seek their
lives shall drive them to despair." ' Lev. 26:29
10 [R]"Then you shall break the flask in the
sight of the men who go with you, Jer. 51:63, 64

11 "and say to them, 'Thus says the LORD of
hosts: [R]"Even so I will break this people and
this city, as *one* breaks a potter's vessel,
which cannot be [T]made whole again; and
they shall [R]bury *them* in Tophet till *there is*
no place to bury. Is. 30:14 • *restored* • Jer. 7:32
12 "Thus I will do to this place," says the
LORD, "and to its inhabitants, and make this
city like Tophet.
13 "And the houses of Jerusalem and the
houses of the kings of Judah shall be defiled
like the place of Tophet, because of all the
houses on whose roofs they have burned
incense to all the host of heaven, and poured
out drink offerings to other gods."'"
14 Then Jeremiah came from Tophet, where
the LORD had sent him to prophesy; and he
stood in [R]the court of the Lord's house and
said to all the people, 2 Chr. 20:5
15 "Thus says the LORD of hosts, the God of
Israel: 'Behold, I will bring on this city and on
all her towns all the doom that I have pronounced against it, because [R]they have stif-
fened their necks that they might not hear
My words.'" Neh. 9:17, 29

CHAPTER 20

Jeremiah Is Persecuted by Pashhur

NOW [R]Pashhur the son of [R]Immer, the
priest who *was* also chief governor in
the house of the LORD, heard that Jeremiah
prophesied these things. Ezra 2:37, 38 • 1 Chr. 24:14
2 Then Pashhur struck Jeremiah the
prophet, and put him in the stocks that *were*
in the high [R]gate of Benjamin, which *was* by
the house of the LORD. Jer. 37:13
3 And it happened on the next day that
Pashhur brought Jeremiah out of the stocks.
Then Jeremiah said to him, "The LORD has
not called your name Pashhur, but [T]Magor-
Missabib. Lit. *Fear on Every Side*
4 "For thus says the LORD: 'Behold, I will
make you a terror to yourself and to all your
friends; and they shall fall by the sword of
their enemies, and your eyes shall see *it*. I will
give all Judah into the hand of the king of
Babylon, and he shall carry them captive to
Babylon and slay them with the sword.
5 'Moreover I [R]will deliver all the wealth of
this city, all its produce, and all its precious
things; all the treasures of the kings of Judah
I will give into the hand of their enemies,
who will plunder them, seize them, and
[R]carry them to Babylon. 2 Kin. 20:17 • Is. 39:6
6 'And you, Pashhur, and all who dwell in
your house, shall go into captivity. You shall
go to Babylon, and there you shall die, and be
buried there, you and all your friends, to
whom you have [R]prophesied lies.'" Jer. 14:13–15

Jeremiah Complains to God

7 O LORD, You [T]induced me, and I was
persuaded; *enticed* or *persuaded*
[R]You are stronger than I, and have
prevailed. Jer. 1:6, 7
I am [T]in derision daily;
Everyone mocks me. Lit. *a laughingstock*
8 For when I spoke, I cried out;
[R]I shouted, "Violence and plunder!"
Because the word of the LORD was
made to me
A reproach and a derision daily. Jer. 6:7
9 Then I said, "I will not make mention
of Him,
Nor speak anymore in His name."
But *His word* was in my heart like a
[R]burning fire
Shut up in my bones;
I was weary of holding *it* back,
And [R]I could not. Ps. 39:3 • Job 32:18
10 [R]For I heard many [T]mocking:
"Fear on every side!" Ps. 31:13 • *slandering*
"Report," *they say,* "and we will report
it!"
[R]All my acquaintances watched for my
stumbling, *saying,* Ps. 41:9; 55:13, 14
"Perhaps he can be induced;
Then we will prevail against him,
And we will take our revenge on him."

11 But the LORD *is* [R]with me as a mighty,
awesome one. Jer. 1:18, 19
Therefore my persecutors will stumble,
and will not [R]prevail. Jer. 15:20; 17:18
They will be greatly ashamed, for they
will not prosper.
Their [R]everlasting confusion will never
be forgotten. Jer. 23:40
12 But, O LORD of hosts,
You who [R]test the
righteous, [Jer. 11:20; 17:10]
And see the [T]mind and heart,
Let me see Your vengeance on them;
For I have pleaded my cause before
You. Most secret parts, lit. *kidneys*

13 Sing to the LORD! Praise the LORD!
For [R]He has delivered the life of the
poor Ps. 35:9, 10; 109:30, 31
From the hand of evildoers.

14 [R]Cursed *be* the day in which I was born!
Let the day not be blessed in which my
mother bore me! Job 3:3
15 Let the man *be* cursed
Who brought news to my father,
saying,
"A male child has been born to you!"
Making him very glad.
16 And let that man be like the cities
Which the LORD [R]overthrew, and did
not relent; Gen. 19:25

Let him [R]hear the cry in the morning
And the shouting at noon, Jer. 18:22
17 [R]Because he did not kill me from the womb,
That my mother might have been my grave,
And her womb always enlarged *with* me. Job 3:10, 11
18 [R]Why did I come forth from the womb
to [R]see [T]labor and sorrow,
That my days should be consumed with shame? Job 3:20 • Lam. 3:1 • *toil*

CHAPTER 21

Message Against Zedekiah

THE word which came to Jeremiah from
the LORD when [R]King Zedekiah sent to
him [R]Pashhur the son of Melchiah, and
[R]Zephaniah the son of Maaseiah, the priest,
saying, 2 Kin. 24:17, 18 • Jer. 38:1 • 2 Kin. 25:18
2 [R]"Please inquire of the LORD for us, for
Nebuchadnezzar king of Babylon makes war
against us. Perhaps the LORD will deal with us
according to all His wonderful works, that
the king may go away from us." Jer. 37:3, 7
3 Then Jeremiah said to them, "Thus you
shall say to Zedekiah,
4 'Thus says the LORD God of Israel: "Behold, I will turn back the weapons of war that
are in your hands, with which you fight
against the king of Babylon and the Chaldeans who besiege you outside the walls; and I
will assemble them in the midst of this city.
5 "I Myself will fight against you with an
outstretched hand and with a strong arm,
even in anger and fury and great wrath.
6 "I will strike the inhabitants of this city,
both man and beast; they shall die of a great
pestilence.
7 "And afterward," says the LORD, "I will
deliver Zedekiah king of Judah, his servants
and the people, and such as are left in this
city from the pestilence and the sword and
the famine, into the hand of Nebuchadnezzar
king of Babylon, into the hand of their enemies, and into the hand of those who seek
their life; and he shall strike them with the
edge of the sword. [R]He shall not spare them,
or have pity or mercy." ' 2 Chr. 36:17
8 "Now you shall say to this people, 'Thus
says the LORD: "Behold, [R]I set before you the
way of life and the way of death. Deut. 30:15, 19
9 "He who remains in this city shall die by
the sword, by famine, and by pestilence; but
he who goes out and [T]defects to the Chaldeans who besiege you, he shall live, and his life
shall be as a prize to him. Lit. *falls away*
10 "For I have [R]set My face against this city
for adversity and not for good," says the
LORD. [R]"It shall be given into the hand of the
king of Babylon, and he shall [R]burn it with
fire." ' Amos 9:4 • Jer. 38:3 • Jer. 34:2, 22; 37:10
11 "And concerning the house of the king
of Judah, *say*, 'Hear the word of the LORD,
12 'O house of David! Thus says the LORD:

"Execute judgment in the morning;
And deliver *him who is* plundered
Out of the hand of the oppressor,
Lest My fury go out like fire
And burn so that no one can quench *it*,
Because of the evil of your doings.

13 "Behold, [R]I *am* against you, O
[T]inhabitant of the valley,
And rock of the plain," says the LORD,
"Who say, [R]'Who shall come down
against us? [Ezek. 13:8] • *dweller* • Jer. 49:4
Or who shall enter our habitations?'
14 But I will punish you according to the
[R]fruit of your [T]doings," says the LORD;
"I will kindle a fire in its forest,
And [R]it shall devour all things around
it." ' " Is. 3:10, 11 • *deeds* • 2 Chr. 36:19

CHAPTER 22

THUS says the LORD: "Go down to the
house of the king of Judah, and there
speak this word,
2 "and say, [R]'Hear the word of the LORD, O
king of Judah, you who sit on the throne of
David, you and your servants and your people who enter these gates! Jer. 17:20
3 'Thus says the LORD: "Execute judgment
and righteousness, and deliver the plundered
out of the hand of the oppressor. Do no
wrong and do no violence to the stranger, the
[R]fatherless, or the widow, nor shed innocent
blood in this place. Jer. 7:6
4 "For if you indeed do this thing, [R]then
shall enter the gates of this house, riding on
horses and in chariots, accompanied by servants and people, kings who sit on the throne
of David. Jer. 17:25
5 "But if you will not [T]hear these words, I
swear by Myself," says the LORD, "that this
house shall become a desolation." ' " Obey
6 For thus says the LORD to the house of
the king of Judah:

"You *are* [R]Gilead to Me, Song 4:1
The head of Lebanon;
Yet I surely will make you a wilderness,
And cities *which* are not inhabited.
7 I will prepare destroyers against you,
Everyone with his weapons;
They shall cut down [R]your choice
cedars Is. 37:24
[R]And cast *them* into the fire. Jer. 21:14

8 "And many nations will pass by this city;
and everyone will say to his neighbor, 'Why
has the LORD done so to this great city?'
9 "Then they will answer, [R]'Because they
have forsaken the covenant of the LORD their

God, and worshiped other gods and served
them.' " 2 Chr. 34:25

Message Against Shallum

10 Weep not for [R]the dead, nor bemoan
him; 2 Kin. 22:20
But weep bitterly for him [R]who goes
away, Jer. 14:17; 22:11
For he shall return no more,
Nor see his native country.

11 For thus says the LORD concerning
[T]Shallum the son of Josiah, king of Judah,
who reigned instead of Josiah his father,
[R]who went from this place: "He shall not
return here anymore, Or *Jehoahaz* • 2 Kin. 23:34
12 "but he shall die in the place where they
have led him captive, and shall see this land
no more.

Message Against Jehoiakim

13 "Woe[R] to him who builds his house by
unrighteousness 2 Kin. 23:35
And his [T]chambers by injustice,
[R]*Who* uses his neighbor's service without
wages *roof chambers, upper chambers* • James 5:4
And gives him nothing for his work,
14 Who says, 'I will build myself a wide
house with spacious chambers,
And cut out windows for it,
Paneling *it* with cedar
And painting *it* with vermilion.'

15 "Shall you reign because you enclose
yourself in cedar?
Did not your father eat and drink,
And do justice and righteousness?
Then [R]*it was* well with him. Ps. 128:2
16 He [T]judged the cause of the poor and
needy;
Then *it was* well.
Was not this knowing Me?" says the
LORD. Defended
17 "Yet[R] your eyes and your heart *are* for
nothing but your covetousness,
For shedding innocent blood,
And practicing oppression and
violence." Ezek. 19:6

18 Therefore thus says the LORD concerning
Jehoiakim the son of Josiah, king of Judah:

[R]"They shall not lament for him,
Saying, [R]'Alas, my brother!' or 'Alas, my
sister!'
They shall not lament for him,
Saying, 'Alas, master!' or 'Alas, his
glory!' Jer. 16:4, 6 • 1 Kin. 13:30
19 [R]He shall be buried with the burial of a
donkey,
Dragged and cast out beyond the gates
of Jerusalem. Jer. 36:30

20 "Go up to Lebanon, and cry out,
And lift up your voice in Bashan;
Cry from Abarim,
For all your lovers are destroyed.
21 I spoke to you in your prosperity,
But you said, 'I will not hear.'
[R]This *has been* your manner from your
youth, Jer. 3:24, 25; 32:30
That you did not obey My voice.
22 The wind shall eat up all [R]your [T]rulers,
And your lovers shall go into captivity;
Surely then you will be ashamed and
humiliated Jer. 23:1 • Lit. *shepherds*
For all your wickedness.
23 O inhabitant of Lebanon,
Making your nest in the cedars,
How gracious will you be when pangs
come upon you,
Like the pain of a woman in labor?

Message Against Coniah (Jehoiachin)

24 "*As* I live," says the LORD, "though
[T]Coniah the son of Jehoiakim, king of Judah,
were the signet on My right hand, yet I
would pluck you off; Or *Jeconiah* or *Jehoiachin*
25 [R]"and I will give you into the hand of
those who seek your life, and into the hand
of those whose face you fear—the hand of
Nebuchadnezzar king of Babylon and the
hand of the [T]Chaldeans. Jer. 34:20 • Or *Babylonians*
26 "So I will cast you out, and your mother
who bore you, into another country where
you were not born; and there you shall die.
27 "But to the land to which they desire to
return, there they shall not return.

28 "Is this man [T]Coniah a despised, broken
idol?
Is he [R]a vessel in which *is* no pleasure?
Why are they cast out, he and his
descendants,
And cast into a land which they do not
know? *Jehoiachin,* v. 24 • Hos. 8:8
29 [R]O earth, earth, earth,
Hear the word of the LORD! Deut. 32:1
30 Thus says the LORD:
'Write this man down as [R]childless,
A man *who* shall not prosper in his
days; Matt. 1:12
For [R]none of his descendants shall
prosper, Jer. 36:30
Sitting on the throne of David,
And ruling anymore in Judah.' "

CHAPTER 23

Message of the Righteous King

"WOE [R]to the shepherds who destroy
and scatter the sheep of My pasture!" says the LORD. Jer. 10:21
2 Therefore thus says the LORD God of
Israel against the shepherds who feed My
people: "You have scattered My flock, driven

them away, and not attended to them. [R]Behold, I will attend to you for the evil of your doings," says the LORD. Ex. 32:34

3 "But [R]I will gather the remnant of My flock out of all countries where I have driven them, and bring them back to their folds; and they shall be fruitful and increase. Jer. 32:37

4 "I will set up [R]shepherds over them who will feed them; and they shall fear no more, nor be dismayed, nor shall they be lacking," says the LORD. Jer. 3:15

5 "Behold, [R]*the* days are coming," says the
LORD, Jer. 33:14
"That I [R]will raise to David a Branch of
righteousness; Matt. 1:1, 6☆
A King shall reign and prosper,
And execute [T]judgment and
righteousness in the [T]earth. *justice* • *land*
6 In His days Judah will be saved,
And Israel [R]will dwell safely;
Now [R]this *is* His name by which He will
be called: Jer. 32:37 • [1 Cor. 1:30]☆

THE LORD OUR RIGHTEOUSNESS.

7 "Therefore, behold, [R]*the* days are coming," says the LORD, "that they shall no longer say, 'As the LORD lives who brought up the children of Israel from the land of Egypt,' Jer. 16:14

8 but, 'As the LORD lives who brought up and led the descendants of the house of Israel from the north country and from all the countries where I had driven them.' And they shall dwell in their own land."

Jeremiah's Tenth Sermon: Against Judah's False Prophets

9 My heart within me is broken
Because of the prophets;
[R]All my bones shake.
I am like a drunken man,
And like a man whom wine has
overcome,
Because of the LORD,
And because of His holy words. Hab. 3:16
10 For [R]the land is full of adulterers;
For [R]because of a curse the land
mourns. Jer. 9:2 • Hos. 4:2
[R]The pleasant places of the wilderness
are dried up. Jer. 9:10
Their course of life is evil,
And their might *is* not right.

11 "For [R]both prophet and priest are
profane; Zeph. 3:4
Yes, [R]in My house I have found their
wickedness," says the LORD. Jer. 7:30
12 "Therefore[R] their way shall be to them
Like slippery *ways*;
In the darkness they shall be driven on
And fall in them;
For I [R]will bring disaster on them,
The year of their punishment," says the
LORD. [Prov. 4:19] • Jer. 11:23
13 "And I have seen [T]folly in the prophets
of Samaria: Lit. *distastefulness*
[R]They prophesied by Baal Jer. 2:8
And caused My people Israel to err.
14 Also I have seen a horrible thing in the
prophets of Jerusalem:
[R]They commit adultery and walk in lies;
They also [R]strengthen the hands of
evildoers, Jer. 29:23 • Ezek. 13:22, 23
So that no one turns back from his
wickedness.
All of them are like Sodom to Me,
And her inhabitants like Gomorrah.
15 Therefore thus says the LORD of hosts
concerning the prophets:
'Behold, I will feed them with
[R]wormwood,
And make them drink the water of gall;
For from the prophets of Jerusalem
[T]Profaneness has gone out into all the
land.' " Jer. 9:15 • Or *Pollution*

16 Thus says the LORD of hosts:

"Do not listen to the words of the
prophets who prophesy to you.
They make you worthless;
They speak a vision of their own heart,
Not from the mouth of the LORD.
17 They continually say to those who
despise Me,
'The LORD has said, [R]"You shall have
peace" '; Ezek. 13:10
And to everyone who walks according
to the imagination of his own heart,
[R]'No evil shall come upon you.' " Mic. 3:11

18 For [R]who has stood in the counsel of
the LORD,
And has perceived and heard His word?
Who has marked His word and heard
it? [1 Cor. 2:16]
19 Behold, a [R]whirlwind of the LORD has
gone forth in fury—
A violent whirlwind!
It will fall violently on the head of the
wicked. Amos 1:14
20 The [R]anger of the LORD will not turn
back
Until He has executed and performed
the thoughts of His heart.
[R]In the latter days you will understand it
perfectly. Jer. 30:24 • Gen. 49:1

21 "I[R] have not sent these prophets, yet
they ran.
I have not spoken to them, yet they
prophesied. Jer. 14:14; 23:32; 27:15
22 But if they had stood in My counsel,
And had caused My people to hear My
words,

Then they would have [R]turned them
from their evil way
And from the evil of their doings. Jer. 25:5

23 "*Am* I a God near at hand," says the
LORD,
"And not a God afar off?
24 Can anyone [R]hide himself in secret
places,
So I shall not see him?" says the LORD;
[R]"Do I not fill heaven and earth?" says
the LORD. [Ps. 139:7] • [1 Kin. 8:27]

25 "I have heard what the prophets have
said who prophesy lies in My name, saying, 'I
have dreamed, I have dreamed!'
26 "How long will *this* be in the heart of the
prophets who prophesy lies? Indeed *they are*
prophets of the deceit of their own heart,
27 "who try to make My people forget My
name by their dreams which everyone tells
his neighbor, [R]as their fathers forgot My
name for Baal. Judg. 3:7

28 "The prophet who has a dream, let him
tell a dream;
And he who has My word, let him
speak My word faithfully.
What *is* the chaff to the wheat?" says
the LORD.
29 "*Is* not My word like a [R]fire?" says the
LORD,
"And like a hammer *that* breaks the rock
in pieces? Jer. 5:14

30 "Therefore behold, [R]I *am* against the
prophets," says the LORD, "who steal My
words every one from his neighbor. Deut. 18:20
31 "Behold, I *am* [R]against the prophets,"
says the LORD, "who use their tongues and
say, 'He says.' Ezek. 13:9
32 "Behold, I *am* against those who prophesy false dreams," says the LORD, "and tell
them, and cause My people to err by their
[R]lies and by [R]their recklessness. Yet I did not
send them or command them; therefore they
shall not [R]profit this people at all," says the
LORD. Lam. 2:14; 3:37 • Zeph. 3:4 • Jer. 7:8
33 "So when these people or the prophet or
the priest ask you, saying, 'What is [R]the
[T]oracle of the LORD?' you shall then say to
them, 'What oracle?' I will even forsake you,"
says the LORD. Mal. 1:1 • *burden, prophecy*
34 "And *as for* the prophet and the priest
and the people who say, 'The [T]oracle of the
LORD!' I will even punish that man and his
house. *burden, prophecy*
35 "Thus every one of you shall say to his
neighbor, and every one to his brother, 'What
has the LORD answered?' and, 'What has the
LORD spoken?'
36 "And the [T]oracle of the LORD you shall
mention no more. For every man's word will
be his oracle, for you have [R]perverted the
words of the living God, the LORD of hosts,
our God. *burden, prophecy* • Deut. 4:2
37 "Thus you shall say to the prophet,
'What has the LORD answered you?' and,
'What has the LORD spoken?'
38 "But since you say, 'The [T]oracle of the
LORD!' therefore thus says the LORD: 'Because
you say this word, "The oracle of the LORD!"
and I have sent to you, saying, "Do not say,
'The oracle of the LORD!' " *burden, prophecy*
39 'therefore behold, I, even I, [R]will utterly
forget you and forsake you, and the city that
I gave you and your fathers, and *will cast you*
out of My presence. Hos. 4:6
40 'And I will bring [R]an everlasting reproach
upon you, and a perpetual [R]shame, which
shall not be forgotten.' " Jer. 20:11 • Mic. 3:5–7

CHAPTER 24

Jeremiah's Eleventh Sermon:
The Two Baskets of Figs

THE [R]LORD showed me, and there were
two baskets of figs set before the temple
of the LORD, after Nebuchadnezzar [R]king of
Babylon had carried away captive Jeconiah
the son of Jehoiakim, king of Judah, and the
princes of Judah with the craftsmen and
smiths, from Jerusalem, and had brought
them to Babylon. Amos 7:1, 4; 8:1 • 2 Kin. 24:12–16
2 One basket *had* very good figs, like the
figs *that are* first ripe; and the other basket
had very bad figs which could not be eaten,
they were so [R]bad. Jer. 29:17
3 Then the LORD said to me, "What do you
see, Jeremiah?" And I said, "Figs, the good
figs, very good; and the bad, very bad, which
cannot be eaten, they are so bad."
4 Again the word of the LORD came to me,
saying,
5 "Thus says the LORD, the God of Israel:
'Like these good figs, so will I [T]acknowledge
those who are carried away captive from
Judah, whom I have sent out of this place for
their own good, into the land of the Chaldeans. *regard*
6 'For I will set My eyes on them for good,
and I will bring them back to this land; I will
build them and not pull *them* down, and I will
plant them and not pluck *them* up.
7 'Then I will give them a heart to know
Me, that I *am* the LORD; and they shall be My
people, and I will be their God, for they shall
return to Me with their whole heart.
8 'And as the bad figs which cannot be
eaten, they are so bad'—surely thus says the
LORD—'so will I give up Zedekiah the king of
Judah, his princes, the residue of Jerusalem
who remain in this land, and [R]those who
dwell in the land of Egypt. Jer. 44:1, 26–30
9 'I will deliver them to trouble into all the
kingdoms of the earth, for *their* harm, *to be* a

reproach and a byword, a taunt and a curse,
in all places where I shall drive them.
10 'And I will send the sword, the famine,
and the pestilence among them, till they are
[T]consumed from the land that I gave to them
and their fathers.'" *destroyed*

CHAPTER 25

Jeremiah's Twelfth Sermon: The Seventy-Year Captivity

THE word that came to Jeremiah concerning all the people of Judah, [R]in the fourth
year of [R]Jehoiakim the son of Josiah, king of
Judah (which *was* the first year of Nebuchadnezzar king of Babylon), Jer. 36:1 • 2 Kin. 24:1, 2
2 which Jeremiah the prophet spoke to all
the people of Judah and to all the inhabitants
of Jerusalem, saying:
3 [R]"From the thirteenth year of Josiah the
son of Amon, king of Judah, even to this day,
this *is* the twenty-third year in which the
word of the LORD has come to me; and I have
spoken to you, rising early and speaking, [R]but
you have not listened. Jer. 1:2 • Jer. 7:13; 11:7, 8, 10
4 "And the LORD has sent to you all His
servants the prophets, [R]rising early and sending *them*, but you have not listened nor
inclined your ear to hear. Jer. 7:13, 25
5 "They said, [R]'Repent now everyone of his
evil way and his evil doings, and dwell in the
land that the LORD has given to you and your
fathers forever and ever. Jer. 18:11
6 'Do not go after other gods to serve them
and worship them, and do not provoke Me to
anger with the works of your hands; and I
will not harm you.'
7 "Yet you have not listened to Me," says
the LORD, "that you might [R]provoke Me to
anger with the works of your hands to your
own hurt. Deut. 32:21
8 "Therefore thus says the LORD of hosts:
'Because you have not heard My words,
9 'behold, I will send and take all the
families of the north,' says the LORD, 'and
Nebuchadnezzar the king of Babylon, My
servant, and will bring them against this land,
against its inhabitants, and against these
nations all around, and will utterly destroy
them, and [R]make them an astonishment, a
hissing, and perpetual desolations. Jer. 18:16
10 'Moreover I will [T]take from them the
voice of mirth and the voice of gladness, the
voice of the bridegroom and the voice of
the bride, the sound of the millstones and the
light of the lamp. Lit. *cause to perish from them*
11 'And this whole land shall be a desolation
and an astonishment, and these nations shall
serve the king of Babylon seventy years.
12 'Then it will come to pass, [R]when seventy
years are completed, *that* I will punish the
king of Babylon and that nation, the land of
the Chaldeans, for their iniquity,' says the
LORD; [R]'and I will make it a perpetual desolation. Ezra 1:1 • Is. 13:20
13 'So I will bring on that land all My words
which I have pronounced against it, all that is
written in this book, which Jeremiah has
prophesied concerning all the nations.
14 '(For many nations and great kings shall
[R]be served by them also; and I will repay
them according to their deeds and according
to the works of their own hands.)'" Jer. 27:7
15 For thus says the LORD God of Israel to
me: "Take this [R]wine cup of [T]fury from My
hand, and cause all the nations, to whom I
send you, to drink it. Rev. 14:10 • *wrath*
16 "And [R]they will drink and stagger and go
mad because of the sword that I will send
among them." Nah. 3:11
17 Then I took the cup from the LORD's
hand, and made all the nations drink, to
whom the LORD had sent me:
18 Jerusalem and the cities of Judah, its
kings and its princes, to make them [R]a desolation, an astonishment, a hissing, and [R]a curse,
as *it is* this day; Jer. 25:9, 11 • Jer. 24:9
19 Pharaoh king of Egypt, his servants, his
princes, and all his people;
20 all the mixed multitude, all the kings of
the land of Uz, all the kings of the land of the
Philistines (namely, Ashkelon, Gaza, Ekron,
and the remnant of Ashdod);
21 Edom, Moab, and the people of Ammon;
22 all the kings of [R]Tyre, all the kings of
Sidon, and the kings of the coastlands which
are across the [R]sea; Jer. 47:4 • Jer. 49:23
23 [R]Dedan, Tema, Buz, and all *who are* in
the farthest corners; Jer. 49:7, 8
24 all the kings of Arabia and all the kings
of the [R]mixed multitude who dwell in the
desert; Ezek. 30:5
25 all the kings of Zimri, all the kings of
Elam, and all the kings of the Medes;
26 [R]all the kings of the north, far and near,
one with another; and all the kingdoms of
the world which *are* on the face of the earth.
Also the king of [T]Sheshach shall drink after
them. Jer. 50:9 • Code word for *Babylon*, Jer. 51:41
27 "Therefore you shall say to them, 'Thus
says the LORD of hosts, the God of Israel:
[R]"Drink, [R]be drunk, and vomit! Fall and rise
no more, because of the sword which I will
send among you."' Hab. 2:16 • Is. 63:6
28 "And it shall be, if they refuse to take the
cup from your hand to drink, then you shall
say to them, 'Thus says the LORD of hosts:
"You shall certainly drink!
29 "For behold, [R]I begin to bring calamity
on the city [R]which is called by My name, and
should you be utterly unpunished? You shall
not be unpunished, for [R]I will call for a sword
on all the inhabitants of the earth," says the
LORD of hosts.' Ezek. 9:6 • Dan. 9:18 • Ezek. 38:21
30 "Therefore prophesy against them all
these words, and say to them:

'The LORD will [R]roar from on high,
And utter His voice from [R]His holy habitation; Amos 1:2 • Ps. 11:4
He will roar mightily against [R]His fold.
He will give [R]a shout, as those who tread *the grapes*, 1 Kin. 9:3 • Is. 16:9
Against all the inhabitants of the earth.
31 A noise will come to the ends of the earth—
For the LORD has [R]a controversy with the nations; Mic. 6:2
[R]He will plead His case with all flesh.
He will give those *who are* wicked to the sword,' says the LORD." Is. 66:16

32 Thus says the LORD of hosts:

"Behold, disaster shall go forth
From nation to nation,
And [R]a great whirlwind shall be raised up Jer. 23:19; 30:23
From the farthest parts of the earth.

33 "And at that day the slain of the LORD
shall be from *one* end of the earth even to the
other end of the earth. They shall not be
lamented, [R]or gathered, or buried; they shall
become refuse on the ground. Ps. 79:3

34 "Wail,[R] shepherds, and cry! Jer. 4:8; 6:26
Roll about *in the ashes*,
You leaders of the flock!
For the days of your slaughter and your dispersions are fulfilled;
You shall fall like a precious vessel.
35 And the shepherds will have no [T]way to flee, Or *refuge*,
Nor the leaders of the flock to escape.
36 A voice of the cry of the shepherds,
And a wailing of the leaders to the flock *will be heard*.
For the LORD has plundered their pasture,
37 And the peaceful habitations are cut down
Because of the fierce anger of the LORD.
38 He has left His lair like the lion;
For their land is desolate
Because of the fierceness of the Oppressor,
And because of His fierce anger."

CHAPTER 26

Conflict with the Nation

IN the beginning of the reign of Jehoiakim
the son of Josiah, king of Judah, this word
came from the LORD, saying,
2 "Thus says the LORD: 'Stand in [R]the
court of the LORD's house, and speak to all
the cities of Judah, which come to worship *in*
the LORD's house, [R]all the words that I command you to speak to them. [R]Do not diminish
a word. Jer. 19:14 • Matt. 28:20 • Acts 20:27
3 'Perhaps everyone will listen and turn
from his evil way, that I may relent concerning the calamity which I purpose to bring on
them because of the evil of their doings.'
4 "And you shall say to them, 'Thus says
the LORD: "If you will not listen to Me, to
walk in My law which I have set before you,
5 "to heed the words of My servants the
prophets [R]whom I sent to you, both rising up
early and sending *them* (but you have not
heeded), Jer. 25:4; 29:19
6 "then I will make this house like [R]Shiloh,
and will make this city [R]a curse to all the
nations of the earth." ' " 1 Sam. 4:10, 11 • Is. 65:15
7 So the priests and the prophets and all
the people heard Jeremiah speaking these
words in the house of the LORD.
8 Now it happened, when Jeremiah had
made an end of speaking all that the LORD
had commanded *him* to speak to all the
people, that the priests and the prophets and
all the people seized him, saying, "You will
surely die!
9 "Why have you prophesied in the name
of the LORD, saying, 'This house shall be like
Shiloh, and this city shall be [R]desolate, without an inhabitant'?" And all the people were
gathered against Jeremiah in the house of the
LORD. Jer. 9:11
10 When the princes of Judah heard these
things, they came up from the king's house to
the house of the LORD and sat down in the
entry of the New Gate of the LORD's *house*.
11 And the priests and the prophets spoke
to the princes and all the people, saying,
"This man deserves to [R]die! For he has prophesied against this city, as you have heard
with your ears." Jer. 38:4
12 Then Jeremiah spoke to all the princes
and all the people, saying: "The LORD sent me
to prophesy against this house and against
this city with all the words that you have
heard.
13 "Now therefore, [R]amend your ways and
your doings, and obey the voice of the LORD
your God; then the LORD will relent concerning the doom that He has pronounced against
you. Jer. 7:3
14 "As for me, here I am, in your hand; do
with me as seems good and proper to you.
15 "But know for certain that if you put me
to death, you will surely bring innocent blood
on yourselves, on this city, and on its inhabitants; for truly the LORD has sent me to you
to speak all these words in your hearing."
16 So the princes and all the people said to
the priests and the prophets, "This man does
not deserve to die. For he has spoken to us in
the name of the LORD our God."

17 [R]Then certain of the elders of the land rose up and spoke to all the assembly of the people, saying: Acts 5:34

18 [R]"Micah of Moresheth prophesied in the days of Hezekiah king of Judah, and spoke to all the people of Judah, saying, 'Thus says the LORD of hosts: Mic. 1:1

[R]"Zion shall be plowed *like* a field, Mic. 3:12
Jerusalem shall become heaps of ruins,
And the mountain of the temple
Like the bare hills of the forest." '

19 "Did Hezekiah king of Judah and all Judah ever put him to death? Did he not fear the LORD and seek the LORD's favor? And the Lord relented concerning the doom which He had pronounced against them. But we are doing great evil against ourselves."

20 Now there was also a man who prophesied in the name of the LORD, Urijah the son of Shemaiah of Kirjath Jearim, who prophesied against this city and against this land according to all the words of Jeremiah.

21 And when Jehoiakim the king, with all his mighty men and all the princes, heard his words, the king sought to put him to death; but when Urijah heard *it*, he was afraid and fled, and went to Egypt.

22 Then Jehoiakim the king sent men to Egypt: Elnathan the son of Achbor, and *other* men *who went* with him to Egypt.

23 And they brought Urijah from Egypt and brought him to Jehoiakim the king, who killed him with the sword and cast his dead body into the graves of the common people.

24 Nevertheless [R]the hand of Ahikam the son of Shaphan was with Jeremiah, so that they should not give him into the hand of the people to put him to death. 2 Kin. 22:12–14

CHAPTER 27

Conflict with the False Prophets

IN the beginning of the reign of Jehoiakim the son of Josiah, king of Judah, this word came to Jeremiah from the LORD, saying,

2 "Thus says the LORD to me: 'Make for yourselves bonds and yokes, [R]and put them on your neck, Jer. 28:10, 12

3 'and send them to the king of Edom, the king of Moab, the king of the Ammonites, the king of Tyre, and the king of Sidon, by the hand of the messengers who come to Jerusalem to Zedekiah king of Judah.

4 'And command them to say to their masters, "Thus says the LORD of hosts, the God of Israel—thus you shall say to your masters:

5 [R]'I have made the earth, the man and the beast that *are* on the ground, by My great power and by My outstretched arm, and [R]have given it to whom it seemed proper to Me. Is. 45:12 • Dan. 4:17, 25, 32

6 'And now I have given all these lands into the hand of Nebuchadnezzar the king of Babylon, My servant; and the beasts of the field I have also given him to serve him.

7 'So all nations shall serve him and his son and his son's son, until the time of his land comes; and then many nations and great kings shall make him serve them.

8 'And it shall be, *that* the nation and kingdom which will not serve Nebuchadnezzar the king of Babylon, and which will not put its neck under the yoke of the king of Babylon, that nation I will punish,' says the LORD, 'with the sword, the famine, and the pestilence, until I have consumed them by his hand.

9 'Therefore do not listen to your prophets, your diviners, your [T]dreamers, your soothsayers, or your sorcerers, who speak to you, saying, "You shall not serve the king of Babylon." Lit. *dreams*

10 'For they prophesy a [R]lie to you, to remove you far from your land; and I will drive you out, and you will perish. Jer. 23:16

11 'But the nations that bring their necks under the yoke of the king of Babylon and serve him, I will let them remain in their own land,' says the LORD, 'and they shall till it and dwell in it.' "

12 I also spoke to [R]Zedekiah king of Judah according to all these words, saying, "Bring your necks under the yoke of the king of Babylon, and serve him and his people, and live! Jer. 28:1; 38:17

13 [R]"Why will you die, you and your people, by the sword, by the famine, and by the pestilence, as the LORD has spoken against the nation that will not serve the king of Babylon? [Ezek. 18:31]

14 "Therefore [R]do not listen to the words of the prophets who speak to you, saying, 'You shall not serve the king of Babylon,' for they prophesy a lie to you; Jer. 23:16

15 "for I have [R]not sent them," says the LORD, "yet they prophesy a lie in My name, that I may drive you out, and that you may perish, you and the prophets who prophesy to you." Jer. 23:21; 29:9

16 Also I spoke to the priests and to all this people, saying, "Thus says the LORD: 'Do not listen to the words of your prophets who prophesy to you, saying, "Behold, [R]the vessels of the LORD's house will now shortly be brought back from Babylon"; for they prophesy a lie to you. Dan. 1:2

17 'Do not listen to them; serve the king of Babylon, and live! Why should this city be laid waste?

18 'But if they *are* prophets, and if the word of the LORD is with them, let them now make intercession to the LORD of hosts, that the

vessels which are left in the house of the LORD, *in* the house of the king of Judah, and at Jerusalem, do not go to Babylon.'

19 "For thus says the LORD of hosts [R]concerning the pillars, concerning the Sea, concerning the carts, and concerning the remainder of the vessels that remain in this city, 2 Kin. 25:13–17

20 "which Nebuchadnezzar king of Babylon did not take, when he carried away [R]captive Jeconiah the son of Jehoiakim, king of Judah, from Jerusalem to Babylon, and all the nobles of Judah and Jerusalem— Jer. 24:1

21 "yes, thus says the LORD of hosts, the God of Israel, concerning the vessels that remain in the house of the LORD, and in the house of the king of Judah and of Jerusalem:

22 'They shall be carried to Babylon, and there they shall be until the day that I visit them,' says the LORD. 'Then I will bring them up and restore them to this place.' "

CHAPTER 28

Conflict with Hananiah

AND it happened in the same year, at the beginning of the reign of Zedekiah king of Judah, in the fourth year *and* in the fifth month, *that* Hananiah the son of Azur the prophet, who *was* from Gibeon, spoke to me in the house of the LORD in the presence of the priests and of all the people, saying,

2 "Thus speaks the LORD of hosts, the God of Israel, saying: 'I have broken [R]the yoke of the king of Babylon. Jer. 27:12

3 [R]'Within two full years I will bring back to this place all the vessels of the LORD's house, that Nebuchadnezzar king of Babylon [R]took away from this place and carried to Babylon. Jer. 27:16 • Dan. 1:2

4 'And I will bring back to this place [R]Jeconiah the son of Jehoiakim, king of Judah, with all the captives of Judah who went to Babylon,' says the LORD, 'for I will break the yoke of the king of Babylon.' " 2 Kin. 24:12

5 Then the prophet Jeremiah spoke to the prophet Hananiah in the presence of the priests and in the presence of all the people who stood in the house of the LORD,

6 and the prophet Jeremiah said, [R]"Amen! The LORD do so; the LORD perform your words which you have prophesied, to bring back the vessels of the LORD's house and all who were carried away captive, from Babylon to this place. 1 Kin. 1:36

7 "Nevertheless hear now this word that I speak in your hearing and in the hearing of all the people:

8 "The prophets who have been before me and before you of old prophesied against many countries and great kingdoms—of war and disaster and pestilence.

9 "As for the prophet who prophesies of [R]peace, when the word of the prophet comes to pass, the prophet will be known *as* one whom the LORD has truly sent." Jer. 23:17

10 Then Hananiah the prophet took the [R]yoke off the prophet Jeremiah's neck and broke it. Jer. 27:2

11 And Hananiah spoke in the presence of all the people, saying, "Thus says the LORD: 'Even so I will break the yoke of Nebuchadnezzar king of Babylon from the neck of all nations within the space of two full years.' " And the prophet Jeremiah went his way.

12 Then the word of the LORD came to Jeremiah, after Hananiah the prophet had broken the yoke from the neck of the prophet Jeremiah, saying,

13 "Go and tell Hananiah, saying, 'Thus says the LORD: "You have broken the yokes of wood, but you have made in their place yokes of iron."

14 'For thus says the LORD of hosts, the God of Israel: [R]"I have put a yoke of iron on the neck of all these nations, that they may serve Nebuchadnezzar king of Babylon; and they shall serve him. [R]I have given him the beasts of the field also." ' " Deut. 28:48 • Jer. 27:6

15 Then the prophet Jeremiah said to Hananiah the prophet, "Hear now, Hananiah, the LORD has not sent you, but [R]you make this people trust in a [R]lie. Ezek. 13:22 • Jer. 27:10; 29:9

16 "Therefore thus says the LORD: 'Behold, I will cast you from the face of the earth. This year you shall die, because you have taught [R]rebellion against the LORD.' " Deut. 13:5

17 So Hananiah the prophet died the same year in the seventh month.

CHAPTER 29

First Letter to the Exiles

NOW these *are* the words of the letter that Jeremiah the prophet sent from Jerusalem to the remainder of the elders who were [R]carried away captive—to the priests, the prophets, and all the people whom Nebuchadnezzar had carried away captive from Jerusalem to Babylon. Jer. 27:20

2 (This happened after Jeconiah the king, the queen mother, the eunuchs, the princes of Judah and Jerusalem, the craftsmen, and the smiths had departed from Jerusalem.)

3 *The letter was sent* by the hand of Elasah the son of [R]Shaphan, and Gemariah the son of Hilkiah, whom Zedekiah king of Judah sent to Babylon, to Nebuchadnezzar king of Babylon, saying, 2 Chr. 34:8

4 Thus says the LORD of hosts, the God of
Israel, to all who were carried away
captive, whom I have caused to be
carried away from Jerusalem to
Babylon:

5 Build houses and dwell *in them*; plant
gardens and eat their fruit.
6 Take wives and beget sons and
daughters; and take wives for your sons
and give your daughters to husbands,
so that they may bear sons and
daughters—that you may be increased
there, and not diminished.
7 And seek the peace of the city where I
have caused you to be carried away
captive, and pray to the LORD for it; for
in its peace you will have peace.
8 For thus says the LORD of hosts, the
God of Israel: Do not let your prophets
and your diviners who are in your midst
[R]deceive you, nor listen to your dreams
which you cause to be dreamed. Eph. 5:6
9 For they prophesy [R]falsely to you in My
name; I have not sent them, says the
LORD. Jer. 28:15; 37:19
10 For thus says the LORD: After [R]seventy
years are completed at Babylon, I will
visit you and perform My good word
toward you, and cause you to [R]return to
this place. Dan. 9:2 • [Jer. 24:6, 7]
11 For I know the thoughts that I think
toward you, says the LORD, thoughts of
peace and not of evil, to give you a
future and a hope.
12 Then you will call upon Me and go and
pray to Me, and I will listen to you.
13 And [R]you will seek Me and find *Me*,
when you search for Me [R]with all your
heart. Deut. 30:1–3 • Jer. 24:7
14 I will be found by you, says the LORD,
and I will bring you back from your
captivity; I will gather you from all the
nations and from all the places where I
have driven you, says the LORD, and I
will bring you to the place from which I
cause you to be carried away captive.
15 Because you have said, "The LORD has
raised up prophets for us in Babylon"—
16 therefore thus says the LORD
concerning the king who sits on the
throne of David, concerning all the
people who dwell in this city, and
concerning your brethren who have not
gone out with you into captivity—
17 thus says the LORD of hosts: Behold, I
will send on them the sword, the
famine, and the pestilence, and will
make them like [R]rotten figs that cannot
be eaten, they are so bad. Jer. 24:3, 8–10
18 And I will pursue them with the sword,
with famine, and with pestilence; and I
[R]will deliver them to trouble among all
the kingdoms of the earth—to be [R]a
curse, an astonishment, a hissing, and a
reproach among all the nations where I
have driven them, Deut. 28:25 • Jer. 26:6; 42:18
19 because they have not heeded My
words, says the LORD, which I sent to
them by My servants the prophets,
rising up early and sending *them*;
neither would you heed, says the LORD.
20 Therefore hear the word of the LORD,
all you of the captivity, whom I have
sent from Jerusalem to Babylon.
21 Thus says the LORD of hosts, the God of
Israel, concerning Ahab the son of
Kolaiah, and Zedekiah the son of
Maaseiah, who prophesy a [R]lie to you in
My name: Behold, I will deliver them
into the hand of Nebuchadnezzar king
of Babylon, and he shall slay them
before your eyes. Lam. 2:14
22 [R]And because of them a curse shall be
taken up by all the captivity of Judah
who *are* in Babylon, saying, "The LORD
make you like Zedekiah and Ahab,
[R]whom the king of Babylon roasted in
the fire"; Is. 65:15 • Dan. 3:6, 21
23 because they have done disgraceful
things in Israel, have committed
adultery with their neighbors' wives,
and have spoken lying words in My
name, which I have not commanded
them. Indeed I [R]know, and *am* a
witness, says the LORD. [Prov. 5:21]

Letter from Shemaiah

24 You shall also speak to Shemaiah the
Nehelamite, saying,
25 Thus speaks the LORD of hosts, the God
of Israel, saying: You have sent letters
in your name to all the people who *are*
at Jerusalem, [R]to Zephaniah the son of
Maaseiah the priest, and to all the
priests, saying, Jer. 21:1
26 "The LORD has made you priest instead
of Jehoiada the priest, so that there
should be [R]officers *in* the house of the
LORD over every man *who* is [R]demented
and considers himself a prophet, that
you should [R]put him in prison and in
the stocks. Jer. 20:1 • John 10:20 • Jer. 20:1, 2
27 Now therefore, why have you not
reproved Jeremiah of Anathoth who
makes himself a prophet to you?
28 For he has sent to us *in* Babylon,
saying, 'This *captivity is* long; build
houses and dwell *in them*, and plant
gardens and eat their fruit.' "

29 Now Zephaniah the priest read this letter
in the hearing of Jeremiah the prophet.

Second Letter to the Exiles

30 Then the word of the LORD came to
Jeremiah, saying:
31 "Send to all those in captivity, saying,
'Thus says the LORD concerning Shemaiah
the Nehelamite: "Because Shemaiah has
prophesied to you, and I have not sent him,
and he has caused you to trust in a lie,"

32 'therefore thus says the LORD: "Behold, I
will punish Shemaiah the Nehelamite and his
[T]family: he shall not have anyone to dwell
among this people, nor shall he see the good
that I will do for My people," says the LORD,
[R]'"because he has taught rebellion against the
LORD."' " *descendants,* lit. *seed* • Jer. 28:16

CHAPTER 30

Restoration to the Land

THE word that came to Jeremiah from the
LORD, saying,
2 "Thus speaks the LORD God of Israel,
saying: 'Write in a book for yourself all the
words that I have spoken to you.
3 'For behold, the days are coming,' says
the LORD, 'that [R]I will bring back from captivity My people Israel and Judah,' says the
LORD. [R]'And I will cause them to return to the
land that I gave to their fathers, and they
shall possess it.' " Ezek. 39:25 • Jer. 16:15
4 Now these *are* the words that the LORD
spoke concerning Israel and Judah.
5 "For thus says the LORD:

'We have heard a voice of trembling,
Of [T]fear, and not of peace. *dread*
6 Ask now, and see,
Whether a [T]man is ever in labor with
child? Lit. *male can give birth*
So why do I see every man *with* his
hands on his loins
[R]Like a woman in labor,
And all faces turned pale? Jer. 4:31; 6:24
7 [R]Alas! For that day *is* great, Amos 5:18
[R]So that none *is* like it; Dan. 9:12; 12:1
And it *is* the time of Jacob's trouble,
But he shall be saved out of it.

8 'For it shall come to pass in that day,'
Says the LORD of hosts,
'*That* I will break his yoke from your
neck,
And will burst your bonds;
Foreigners shall no more enslave them.
9 But they shall serve the LORD their God,
And [R]David their king, [Luke 1:69] ☆
Whom I will raise up for them.

10 'Therefore [R]do not fear, O My servant
Jacob,' says the LORD,
'Nor be dismayed, O Israel;
For behold, I will save you from afar,
And your seed [R]from the land of their
captivity. Is. 41:13; 43:5; 44:2 • Jer. 3:18
Jacob shall return, have rest and be
quiet,
And no one shall make *him* afraid.
11 For I *am* with [R]you,' says the LORD, 'to
save you; [Is. 43:2–5]
[R]Though I make a full end of all nations
where I have scattered you, Amos 9:8
[R]Yet I will not make a complete end of
you. Jer. 4:27; 46:27, 28
But I will correct you [R]in justice,
And will not let you go altogether
unpunished.' Ps. 6:1

12 "For thus says the LORD:

[R]'Your affliction *is* incurable,
Your wound *is* severe. Jer. 15:18
13 *There is* no one to plead your cause,
That you may be bound up;
[R]You have no healing medicines. Jer. 8:22
14 [R]All your lovers have forgotten you;
They do not seek you; Lam. 1:2
For I have wounded you with the
wound [R]of an enemy, Job 13:24; 16:9; 19:11
With the chastisement of a cruel one,
For the multitude of your iniquities,
[R]*Because* your sins have increased. Jer. 5:6
15 Why [R]do you cry about your affliction?
Your sorrow *is* incurable. Jer. 15:18
Because of the multitude of your
iniquities,
Because your sins have increased,
I have done these things to you.

16 'Therefore all those who devour you
[R]shall be devoured; Jer. 10:25
And all your adversaries, every one of
them, shall go into [R]captivity; Is. 14:2
Those who plunder you shall become
[R]plunder, Ezek. 39:10
And all who prey upon you I will make
a [R]prey. Jer. 2:3
17 [R]For I will restore health to you
And heal you of your wounds,' says the
LORD,
'Because they called you an outcast
saying:
"This *is* Zion;
No one seeks her." ' Jer. 33:6

18 "Thus says the LORD:

'Behold, I will bring back the captivity
of Jacob's tents,
And [R]have mercy on his dwelling
places;
The city shall be built upon its own
[T]mound,
And the palace shall remain according
to its own plan. Ps. 102:13 • *ruins*
19 Then [R]out of them shall proceed
thanksgiving
And the voice of those who make
merry;
[R]I will multiply them, and they shall not
diminish;
I will also glorify them, and they shall
not be small. Is. 51:11 • Zech. 10:8

20 Their children also shall be [R]as before,
And their congregation shall be
established before Me; Is. 1:26
And I will punish all who oppress them.
21 Their nobles shall be from among them,
[R]And their governor shall come from
their midst; Gen. 49:10
Then I will [R]cause him to draw near,
And he shall approach Me; Num. 16:5
For who *is* this who pledged his heart
to approach Me?' says the LORD.
22 'You shall be [R]My people,
And I will be your God.' " Ezek. 36:28

23 Behold, the [R]whirlwind of the LORD
Goes forth with fury,
A [T]continuing whirlwind;
It will fall violently on the head of the
wicked. Jer. 23:19, 20; 25:32 • Or *sweeping*
24 The fierce anger of the LORD will not
return until He has done it,
And until He has performed the intents
of His heart.

In the latter days you will consider it.

CHAPTER 31

Israel Is Restored

"AT the same time," says the LORD, "I will be the God of all the families of Israel, and they shall be My people."

2 Thus says the LORD:

"The people who survived the sword
Found grace in the wilderness—
Israel, when I went to give him rest."

3 The LORD has appeared [T]of old to me,
saying: Lit. *from afar*
"Yes, [R]I have loved you with [R]an
everlasting love; Mal. 1:2 • Rom. 11:28
Therefore with lovingkindness I have
[R]drawn you. Hos. 11:4
4 Again [R]I will build you, and you shall be
rebuilt,
O virgin of Israel!
You shall again be adorned with your
[R]tambourines,
And shall go forth in the dances of
those who rejoice. Jer. 33:7 • Judg. 11:34
5 [R]You shall yet plant vines on the
mountains of Samaria; Amos 9:14
The planters shall plant and [T]eat *them*
as ordinary food. Lit. *treat them as common*
6 For there shall be a day
When the watchmen will cry on Mount
Ephraim,
[R]'Arise, and let us go up *to* Zion,
To the LORD our God.' " [Mic. 4:2]

7 For thus says the LORD:

[R]"Sing with gladness for Jacob,
And shout among the chief of the
nations;
Proclaim, give praise, and say,
'O LORD, save Your people,
The remnant of Israel!' Is. 12:5, 6
8 Behold, I will bring them [R]from the
north country, Jer. 3:12, 18; 23:8
And [R]gather them from the ends of the
earth, Ezek. 20:34, 41; 34:13
Among them the blind and the lame,
The woman with child
And the one who labors with child,
together;
A great throng shall return there.
9 [R]They shall come with weeping, [Jer. 50:4]
And with supplications I will lead them.
I will cause them to walk [R]by the rivers
of waters, Is. 35:8; 43:19; 49:10, 11
In a straight way in which they shall
not stumble;
For I am a Father to Israel,
And Ephraim *is* My [R]firstborn. Ex. 4:22

10 "Hear the word of the LORD, O nations,
And declare *it* in the [T]isles afar off, and
say,
'He who scattered Israel [R]will gather
him,
And keep him as a shepherd *does* his
flock.' Or *coastlands* • Is. 40:11
11 For the LORD has redeemed Jacob,
And ransomed him [R]from the hand of
one stronger than he. Is. 49:24
12 Therefore they shall come and sing in
[R]the height of Zion, Ezek. 17:23
Streaming to [R]the goodness of the
LORD— Hos. 3:5
For wheat and new wine and oil,
For the young of the flock and the
herd;
Their souls shall be like a [R]well-watered
garden, Is. 58:11
And they shall sorrow no more at all.

13 "Then shall the virgin rejoice in the
dance,
And the young men and the old,
together;
For I will turn their mourning to joy,
Will comfort them,
And make them rejoice rather than
sorrow.
14 I will [T]satiate the soul of the priests
with abundance, Fill to the full
And My people shall be satisfied with
My goodness, says the LORD."

15 Thus says the LORD:

"A voice was heard in Ramah,
Lamentation *and* bitter weeping,

Rachel weeping for her children,
Refusing to be comforted for her
[R]children, Gen. 42:13; Matt. 2:17☆
Because [R]they *are* no more." Jer. 10:20

16 Thus says the LORD:

"Refrain your voice from [R]weeping,
And your eyes from tears;
For your work shall be rewarded, says
the LORD,
And they shall come back from the land
of the enemy. [Is. 25:8; 30:19]
17 There is [R]hope in your future, says the
LORD,
That *your* children shall come back to
their own border. Jer. 29:11

18 "I have surely heard Ephraim bemoaning
himself:
'You have [R]chastised me, and I was
chastised, Ps. 94:12
Like an untrained bull;
[R]Restore me, and I will return, Lam. 5:21
For You *are* the LORD my God.
19 Surely, [R]after my turning, I repented;
And after I was instructed, I struck
myself on the thigh;
I was [R]ashamed, yes, even humiliated,
Because I bore the reproach of my
youth.' Deut. 30:2 • Ezek. 36:31
20 *Is* Ephraim My dear son?
Is he a pleasant child?
For though I spoke against him,
I earnestly remember him still;
Therefore My [T]heart yearns for him;
[R]I will surely have mercy on him, says
the LORD. Lit. *inward parts* • [Hos. 14:4]

21 "Set up signposts,
Make landmarks;
[R]Set your heart toward the highway,
The way in *which* you went. Jer. 50:5
[T]Turn back, O virgin of Israel, Or *Return*
Turn back to these your cities.

Judah Is Restored

22 "How long will you [R]gad about,
O you [R]backsliding daughter?
For the LORD has created a new thing
in the earth— Jer. 2:18, 23, 36 • Jer. 3:6, 8, 11
A woman shall encompass a man."

23 Thus says the LORD of hosts, the God of
Israel: "They shall again use this speech in
the land of Judah and in its cities, when I
bring back their captivity: [R]'The LORD bless
you, O habitation of justice, *and* [R]mountain
of holiness!' Is. 1:26 • [Zech. 8:3]
24 "And there shall dwell in Judah itself,
and [R]in all its cities together, farmers and
those going out with flocks. Jer. 33:12
25 "For I have satiated the weary soul, and
I have replenished every sorrowful soul."
26 After this I awoke and looked around,
and my sleep was [R]sweet to me. Prov. 3:24
27 "Behold, the days are coming, says the
LORD, that [R]I will sow the house of Israel and
the house of Judah with the seed of man and
the seed of beast. Ezek. 36:9–11
28 "And it shall come to pass, *that* as I have
watched over them [R]to pluck up, to break
down, to throw down, to destroy, and to
afflict, so I will watch over them [R]to build and
to plant, says the LORD. Jer. 1:10 • Jer. 24:6
29 [R]"In those days they shall say no more:

'The fathers have eaten sour grapes,
And the children's teeth are set on
edge.' Ezek. 18:2, 3

30 [R]"But every one shall die for his own
iniquity; every man who eats the sour grapes,
his teeth shall be set on edge. [Gal. 6:5, 7]

31 "Behold, the [R]days are coming, says the
LORD, when I will make a [R]new covenant
with the house of Israel and with the house
of Judah— Heb. 8:8–12; 10:16, 17 • [Luke 22:20]☆
32 "not according to the covenant that I
made with their fathers in the day *that* [R]I
took them by the hand to bring them out of
the land of Egypt, My covenant which they
broke, though I was a husband to them, says
the LORD. Deut. 1:31
33 "But this *is* the covenant that I will make
with the house of Israel after those days,
says the LORD: [R]I will put My law in their
minds, and write it on their [T]hearts; [R]and I

31:31–34 The New Covenant—The New Covenant is the fifth and last of the theocratic covenants (pertaining to the rule of God). Four provisions are made in this covenant: (1) regeneration—God will put His law in their inward parts and write it in their hearts, 31:33; (2) a national restoration—Yahweh will be their God and the nation will be His people, 31:33; (3) personal ministry of the Holy Spirit—they will all be taught individually by God, 31:34; and (4) full justification—their sins will be forgiven and completely removed, 31:34. The New Covenant is made sure by the blood that Jesus shed on Calvary's cross. That blood which guarantees to Israel its New Covenant also provides for the forgiveness of sins for the believers who comprise the church. Jesus' payment for sins is more than adequate to pay for the sins of all who will believe in Him. The New Covenant is called "new" in contrast to the covenant with Moses which is called "old" (Jer. 31:32; Page 1456—Heb. 8:6–13) because it actually accomplishes what the Mosaic Covenant could only point to, that is, the child of God living in a manner that is consistent with the character of God.

Now turn to Page 26—THE CHRISTIAN'S GUIDE: Understanding God's Being.

will be their God, and they shall be My people. Ps. 40:8 • Lit. *inward parts* • Heb. 10:15–17☆

34 "No more shall every man teach his neighbor, and every man his brother, saying, 'Know the LORD,' for [R]they all shall know Me, from the least of them to the greatest of them, says the LORD. For [R]I will forgive their iniquity, and their sin I will remember no more." [John 6:45] • Is. 11:9☆

35 Thus says the LORD,
[R]Who gives the sun for a light by day,
And the ordinances of the moon and
the stars for a light by night,
Who disturbs [R]the sea, Gen. 1:14–18 • Is. 51:15
And its waves roar
(The LORD of hosts *is* His name):

36 "If [R]those ordinances depart
From before Me, says the LORD,
Then the seed of Israel shall also cease
From being a nation before Me
forever." Ps. 148:6

37 Thus says the LORD:

[R]"If heaven above can be measured,
And the foundations of the earth
searched out beneath,
I will also [R]cast off all the seed of Israel
For all that they have done, says the
LORD. Jer. 33:22 • [Rom. 11:2–5, 26, 27]

38 "Behold, the days are coming, says the LORD, that the city shall be built for the LORD [R]from the Tower of Hananeel to the Corner Gate. Zech. 14:10

39 [R]"The surveyor's line shall again extend straight forward over the hill Gareb; then it shall turn toward Goath. Zech. 2:1, 2

40 "And the whole valley of the dead bodies and of the ashes, and all the fields as far as the Brook Kidron, [R]to the corner of the Horse Gate toward the east, [R]*shall be* holy to the LORD. It shall not be plucked up or thrown down anymore forever." Neh. 3:28 • [Joel 3:17]

CHAPTER 32

Rebuilding of Jerusalem

THE word that came to Jeremiah from the LORD [R]in the tenth year of Zedekiah king of Judah, which was the eighteenth year of Nebuchadnezzar. Jer. 39:1, 2

2 For then the king of Babylon's army besieged Jerusalem, and Jeremiah the prophet was shut up [R]in the court of the prison, which *was in* the king of Judah's house. Jer. 33:1; 37:21; 39:14

3 For Zedekiah king of Judah had shut him up, saying, "Why do you [R]prophesy and say, 'Thus says the LORD: [R]"Behold, I will give this city into the hand of the king of Babylon, and he shall take it; Jer. 26:8, 9 • Jer. 21:3–7; 34:2

4 "and Zedekiah king of Judah shall not escape from the hand of the Chaldeans, but shall surely be delivered into the hand of the king of Babylon, and shall speak with him face to face, and see him eye to eye;

5 "then he shall lead Zedekiah to Babylon, and there he shall be until I visit him," says the LORD; "though you fight with the Chaldeans, you shall not succeed" '?"

6 And Jeremiah said, "The word of the LORD came to me, saying,

7 'Behold, Hanameel the son of Shallum your uncle will come to you, saying, "Buy my field which *is* in Anathoth, for the [R]right of redemption *is* yours to buy *it*." ' Ruth 4:4

8 "Then Hanameel my uncle's son came to me in the court of the prison according to the word of the LORD, and said to me, 'Please buy my field that *is* in Anathoth, which *is* in the country of Benjamin; for the right of inheritance *is* yours, and the redemption yours; buy *it* for yourself.' Then I knew that this was the word of the LORD.

9 "So I bought the field from Hanameel, the son of my uncle who *was* in Anathoth, and [R]weighed *out to* him the money—[T]seventeen shekels of silver. Zech. 11:12 • $2,176

10 "And I signed the [T]deed and sealed *it*, took witnesses, and weighed the money in the balances. Lit. *book*

11 "So I took the purchase deed, *both* that which was sealed *according* to the law and custom, and that which was open;

12 "and I gave the purchase deed to Baruch the son of Neriah, son of Mahseiah, in the presence of Hanameel my uncle's *son*, and in the presence of the [R]witnesses who signed the purchase deed, before all the Jews who sat in the court of the prison. Is. 8:2

13 "Then I charged [R]Baruch before them, saying, Jer. 36:4

14 'Thus says the LORD of hosts, the God of Israel: "Take these deeds, both this purchase deed which is sealed and this deed which is open, and put them in an earthen vessel, that they may last many days."

15 'For thus says the LORD of hosts, the God of Israel: "Houses and fields and vineyards shall be possessed again in this land." '

16 "Now when I had delivered the purchase deed to Baruch the son of Neriah, I prayed to the LORD, saying:

17 'Ah, Lord GOD! Behold, You have made the heavens and the earth by Your great power and outstretched arm. [R]There is nothing too [T]hard for You. Luke 18:27 • *difficult*

18 'You show [R]lovingkindness to thousands, and repay the iniquity of the fathers into the bosom of their children after them—the Great, [R]the Mighty God, whose name *is* [R]the LORD of hosts. Deut. 5:9, 10 • [Is. 9:6] • Jer. 10:16

19 '*You are* [R]great in counsel and mighty in [T]work, for your [R]eyes *are* open to all the ways

of the sons of men, [R]to give everyone according to his ways and according to the fruit of
his doings. Is. 28:29 • *deed* • Prov. 5:21 • Jer. 17:10
20 'You have set signs and wonders in the
land of Egypt, to this day, and in Israel and
among *other* men; and You have made Yourself [R]a name, as it is this day. Is. 63:12
21 'You [R]have brought Your people Israel
out of the land of Egypt with signs and
wonders, with a strong hand and an outstretched arm, and with great terror; Ex. 6:6
22 'You have given them this land, of which
You swore to their fathers to give them— [R]"a
land flowing with milk and honey." Ex. 3:8, 17
23 'And they came in and took possession of
it, but [R]they have not obeyed Your voice or
walked in Your law. They have done nothing
of all that You commanded them to do;
therefore You have caused all this calamity
to come upon them. [Neh. 9:26]
24 'Look, the siege mounds! They have
come to the city to take it; and the city has
been given into the hand of the Chaldeans
who fight against it, because of the sword
and famine and pestilence. What You have
spoken has happened; there You see *it*!
25 'And You have said to me, O Lord GOD,
"Buy the field for money, and take witnesses"!—yet the city has been given into the
hand of the Chaldeans.' "
26 Then the word of the LORD came to
Jeremiah, saying,
27 "Behold, I *am* the LORD, the God of all
flesh. Is there anything too hard for Me?
28 "Therefore thus says the LORD: 'Behold, I
will give this city into the hand of the Chaldeans, into the hand of Nebuchadnezzar king of
Babylon, and he shall take it.
29 'And the Chaldeans who fight against
this city shall come and [R]set fire to this city
and burn it, with the houses [R]on whose roofs
they have offered incense to Baal and poured
out drink offerings to other gods, to provoke
Me to anger; 2 Chr. 36:19 • Jer. 19:13
30 'because the children of Israel and the
children of Judah have done only evil before
Me from their youth. For the children of
Israel have provoked Me only to anger with
the work of their hands,' says the LORD.
31 'For this city has been to Me *a provocation of* My anger and My fury from the day
that they built it, even to this day; [R]so I will
remove it from before My face 2 Kin. 23:27; 24:3
32 'because of all the evil of the children of
Israel and the children of Judah, which they
have done to provoke Me to anger—[R]they,
their kings, their princes, their priests, [R]their
prophets, the men of Judah, and the inhabitants of Jerusalem. Dan. 9:8 • Jer. 23:14
33 'And they have turned to Me the back,
and not the face; though I taught them,
rising up early and teaching *them*, yet they
have not listened to receive instruction.
34 'But they set their abominations in the
house which is called by My name, to defile it.
35 'And they built the high places of Baal
which *are* in the Valley of the Son of Hinnom, to cause their sons and their daughters
to pass through *the fire* to Molech, [R]which I
did not command them, nor did it come into
My mind that they should do this abomination, to cause Judah to sin.' Jer. 7:31
36 "Now therefore, thus says the LORD, the
God of Israel, concerning this city of which
you say, 'It shall be delivered into the hand of
the king of Babylon by the sword, by the
famine, and by the pestilence':
37 'Behold, I will [R]gather them out of all
countries where I have driven them in My
anger, in My fury, and in great wrath; I will
bring them back to this place, and I will
cause them [R]to dwell safely. Deut. 30:3 • Jer. 33:16
38 'They shall be [R]My people, and I will be
their God; [Jer. 24:7; 30:22; 31:33]
39 'then I will give them one heart and one
way, that they may fear Me forever, for the
good of them and their children after them.
40 'And [R]I will make an everlasting covenant with them, that I will not turn away
from doing them good; but [R]I will put My fear
in their hearts so that they will not depart
from Me. Is. 55:3 • [Jer. 31:33]
41 'Yes, I will rejoice over them to do them
good, and I will assuredly plant them in this
land, with all My heart and with all My soul.'
42 "For thus says the LORD: [R]'Just as I have
brought all this great calamity on this people,
so I will bring on them all the good that I
have promised them. Jer. 31:28
43 'And fields will be bought in this land [R]of
which you say, "*It is* desolate, without man
or beast; it has been given into the hand of
the Chaldeans." Jer. 33:10
44 'Men will buy fields for money, sign
deeds and seal *them*, and take witnesses, in
[R]the land of Benjamin, in the places around
Jerusalem, in the cities of Judah, in the cities
of the mountains, in the cities of the [T]low-
land, and in the cities of the [T]South; for I will
cause their captives to return,' says the
LORD." Jer. 17:26 • Heb. *Shephelah* • Heb. *Negev*

CHAPTER 33

Reconfirming the Covenant

MOREOVER the word of the LORD came
to Jeremiah a second time, while he
was still [R]shut up in the court of the prison,
saying, Jer. 32:2, 3
2 "Thus says the LORD [R]who made it, the
LORD who formed it to establish it [R](the
[T]LORD *is* His name): Is. 37:26 • Ex. 15:3 • Heb. *YHWH*
3 [R]'Call to Me, and I will answer you, and
show you great and [T]mighty things, which
you do not know.' Jer. 29:12 • *inaccessible*

4 "For thus says the LORD, the God of
Israel, concerning the houses of this city and
the houses of the kings of Judah, which have
been pulled down to *fortify against* [R]the siege
mounds and the sword: Is. 22:10
5 [R]'They come to fight with the Chaldeans,
but *only* to fill their places with the dead
bodies of men whom I will slay in My anger
and My fury, all for whose wickedness I have
hidden My face from this city. 2 Kin. 23:14
6 'Behold, [R]I will bring it health and healing; I will heal them and reveal to them the
abundance of peace and truth. Jer. 30:17
7 'And I will cause the captives of Judah
and the captives of Israel to return, and will
rebuild those places [R]as at the first. Is. 1:26
8 'I will [R]cleanse them from all their iniquity by which they have sinned against Me,
and I will pardon all their iniquities by which
they have sinned and by which they have
transgressed against Me. Zech. 13:1
9 [R] 'Then it shall be to Me a name of joy, a
praise, and an honor before all nations of the
earth, who shall hear all the good that I do to
them; they shall [R]fear and tremble for all the
goodness and all the prosperity that I provide
for it.' Is. 62:7 • Is. 60:5
10 "Thus says the LORD: 'Again there shall
be heard in this place—of which you say, "It
is desolate, without man and without beast"
—in the cities of Judah, in the streets of
Jerusalem that are desolate, without man and
without inhabitant and without beast,
11 'the [R]voice of joy and the voice of gladness, the voice of the bridegroom and the
voice of the bride, the voice of those who will
say: Rev. 18:23

[R]"Praise the LORD of hosts, Is. 12:4
For the LORD *is* good,
For His mercy *endures* forever"—

and of those *who will* bring [R]the sacrifice of
praise into the house of the LORD. For I will
cause the captives of the land to return as at
the first,' says the LORD. Lev. 7:12
12 "Thus says the LORD of hosts: [R]'In this
place which is desolate, without man and
without beast, and in all its cities, there shall
again be a habitation of shepherds causing
their flocks to lie down. Is. 65:10
13 'In the cities of the mountains, in the
cities of the lowland, in the cities of the
South, in the land of Benjamin, in the places
around Jerusalem, and in the cities of Judah,
the flocks shall again pass under the hands of
him who counts *them*,' says the LORD.
14 'Behold, the days are coming,' says the
LORD, 'that [R]I will perform that good thing
which I have promised to the house of Israel
and to the house of Judah: Jer. 29:10; 32:42

15 'In those days and at that time
I will cause to grow up to David
A [R]Branch of righteousness; Zech. 6:12, 13☆
He shall execute judgment and
righteousness in the earth.
16 In those days [R]Judah will be saved,
And Jerusalem will dwell safely.
And this *is the name* by which she will
be called: Is. 45:17, 22☆

THE LORD OUR RIGHTEOUSNESS.'

17 "For thus says the LORD: 'David shall
never [R]lack a man to sit on the throne of the
house of Israel; 2 Sam. 7:16
18 'nor shall the [R]priests, the Levites, lack a
man to [R]offer burnt offerings before Me, to
[T]kindle grain offerings, and to sacrifice continually.'" Ezek. 44:15 • [1 Pet. 2:5, 9] • *burn*
19 And the word of the LORD came to Jeremiah, saying,
20 "Thus says the LORD: 'If you can break
My covenant with the day and My covenant
with the night, so that there will not be day
and night in their season,
21 'then My covenant may also be broken
with David My servant, so that he shall not
have a son to reign on his throne, and with
the Levites, the priests, My ministers.
22 'As [R]the host of heaven cannot be numbered, nor the sand of the sea measured, so
will I [R]multiply the descendants of David My
servant and the [R]Levites who minister to
Me.'" Gen. 15:5; 22:17 • Jer. 30:19 • Is. 66:21
23 Moreover the word of the LORD came to
Jeremiah, saying,
24 "Have you not considered what these
people have spoken, saying, 'The two families
which the LORD has chosen, He has also cast
them off'? Thus they have [R]despised My
people, as if they should no more be a nation
before them. Esth. 3:6–8
25 "Thus says the LORD: 'If [R]My covenant *is*
not with day and night, *and if* I have not
[R]appointed the ordinances of heaven and
earth, Gen. 8:22 • Ps. 74:16; 104:19
26 'then I will cast away the descendants of
Jacob and David My servant, *so* that I will
not take *any* of his descendants *to be* rulers
over the descendants of Abraham, Isaac, and
Jacob. For I will cause their captives to
return, and will have mercy on them.'"

CHAPTER 34

Message to Zedekiah

THE word which came to Jeremiah from
the LORD, [R]when Nebuchadnezzar king of
Babylon and all his army, [R]all the kingdoms
of the earth under his dominion, and all the
people, fought against Jerusalem and all its
cities, saying, 2 Kin. 25:1 • Jer. 1:15; 25:9

2 "Thus says the LORD, the God of Israel: 'Go and speak to Zedekiah king of Judah and tell him, "Thus says the LORD: 'Behold, I will give this city into the hand of the king of Babylon, and he shall burn it with fire.

3 'And you shall not escape from his hand, but shall surely be taken and delivered into his hand; your eyes shall see the eyes of the king of Babylon, he shall speak with you [R]face to face,[T] and you shall go to Babylon.' " ' Jer. 32:4; 39:5, 6 • Lit. *mouth to mouth*

4 "Yet hear the word of the LORD, O Zedekiah king of Judah! Thus says the LORD concerning you: 'You shall not die by the sword.

5 '*But* you shall die in peace; as in the ceremonies of your fathers, the former kings who were before you, [R]so they shall burn incense for you and [R]lament for you, *saying,* "Alas, lord!" ' For I have pronounced the word," says the LORD. Dan. 2:46 • Jer. 22:18

6 Then Jeremiah the prophet spoke all these words to Zedekiah king of Judah in Jerusalem,

7 when the king of Babylon's army fought against Jerusalem and all the cities of Judah that were left, against Lachish and Azekah; for *only* [R]these fortified cities remained of the cities of Judah. 2 Kin. 18:13; 19:8

Message to the People

8 *This is* the word that came to Jeremiah from the LORD, after King Zedekiah had made a covenant with all the people who *were* at Jerusalem to proclaim [R]liberty to them: Ex. 21:2

9 [R]that every man should set free his male and female slave—a Hebrew man or woman—[R]that no one should keep a Jewish brother in bondage. Neh. 5:11 • Lev. 25:39–46

10 Now when all the princes and all the people, who had entered into the covenant, heard that everyone should set free his male and female slaves, that no one should keep them in bondage anymore, they obeyed and let *them* go.

11 But afterward they changed their minds and made the male and female slaves return, whom they had set free, and brought them into subjection as male and female slaves.

12 Therefore the word of the LORD came to Jeremiah from the LORD, saying,

13 "Thus says the LORD, the God of Israel: 'I made a covenant with your fathers in the day that I brought them out of the land of Egypt, out of the house of bondage, saying,

14 "At the end of [R]seven years let every man set free his Hebrew brother, who [T]has been sold to him; and when he has served you six years, you shall let him go free from you." But your fathers did not obey Me nor incline their ear. Deut. 15:12 • Or *sold himself*

15 'Then you [T]recently turned and did what was right in My sight—every man proclaiming liberty to his neighbor; and you [R]made a covenant before Me [R]in the house which is called by My name. Lit. *today* • Neh. 10:29 • Jer. 7:10

16 'Then you turned around and [R]profaned My name, and every one of you brought back his male and female slaves, whom he had set at liberty, at their pleasure, and brought them back into subjection, to be your male and female slaves.' Ex. 20:7

17 "Therefore thus says the LORD: 'You have not obeyed Me in proclaiming liberty, every one to his brother and every one to his neighbor. Behold, I proclaim liberty to you,' says the LORD—'to the sword, to pestilence, and to famine! And I will deliver you to trouble among all the kingdoms of the earth.

18 'And I will give the men who have transgressed My covenant, who have not performed the words of the covenant which they made before Me, when they cut the calf in two and passed between the parts of it—

19 'the princes of Judah, the princes of Jerusalem, the [T]eunuchs, the priests, and all the people of the land who passed between the parts of the calf— Or *officers*

20 'I will [R]give them into the hand of their enemies and into the hand of those who seek their life. Their [R]dead bodies shall be for meat for the birds of the heaven and the beasts of the earth. Jer. 22:25 • Jer. 7:33; 16:4; 19:7

21 'And I will give Zedekiah king of Judah and his princes into the hand of their enemies, into the hand of those who seek their life, and into the hand of the king of Babylon's army which has gone back from you.

22 [R]'Behold, I will command,' says the LORD, 'and cause them to return to this city. They will fight against it and take it and burn it with fire; and I will make the cities of Judah a desolation without inhabitant.' " Jer. 37:8, 10

CHAPTER 35

Message to the Rechabites

THE word which came to Jeremiah from the LORD in the days of Jehoiakim the son of Josiah, king of Judah, saying,

2 "Go to the house of the [R]Rechabites, speak to them, and bring them into the house of the LORD, into one of [R]the chambers, and give them wine to drink." 1 Chr. 2:55 • 1 Kin. 6:5, 8

3 Then I took Jaazaniah the son of Jeremiah, the son of Habazziniah, his brothers and all his sons, and the whole house of the Rechabites,

4 and I brought them into the house of the LORD, into the chamber of the sons of Hanan the son of Igdaliah, a man of God, which *was* by the chamber of the princes, above the chamber of Maaseiah the son of Shallum, the keeper of the [T]door. Lit. *threshold*

5 Then I set before the sons of the house of the Rechabites bowls full of wine, and cups; and I said to them, "Drink wine."

6 But they said, "We will drink no wine, for Jonadab the son of Rechab, our father, commanded us, saying, 'You shall drink [R]no wine, you nor your sons, forever. Luke 1:15

7 'You shall not build a house, sow seed, plant a vineyard, nor have *any of these;* but all your days you shall dwell in tents, [R]that you may live many days in the land where you are sojourners.' Ex. 20:12

8 "Thus we have [R]obeyed the voice of Jonadab the son of Rechab, our father, in all that he charged us, to drink no wine all our days, we, our wives, our sons, or our daughters, [Col. 3:20]

9 "nor to build ourselves houses to dwell in; nor do we have vineyard, field, or seed.

10 "But we have dwelt in tents, and have obeyed and done according to all that Jonadab our father commanded us.

11 "But it came to pass, when Nebuchadnezzar king of Babylon came up into the land, that we said, 'Come, let us [R]go to Jerusalem for fear of the army of the Chaldeans and for fear of the army of the Syrians.' So we dwell at Jerusalem." Jer. 4:5–7; 8:14

12 Then came the word of the LORD to Jeremiah, saying,

13 "Thus says the LORD of hosts, the God of Israel: 'Go and tell the men of Judah and the inhabitants of Jerusalem, "Will you not [R]receive instruction to [T]obey My words?" says the LORD. Jer. 6:10; 17:23; 32:33 • *listen to*

14 "The words of Jonadab the son of Rechab, which he commanded his sons, not to drink wine, are performed; for to this day they drink none, and obey their father's commandment. [R]But although I have spoken to you, [R]rising early and speaking, you did not [T]obey Me. 2 Chr. 36:15 • Jer. 7:13; 25:3 • *listen to*

15 "I have also sent to you all My servants the prophets, rising up early and sending *them,* saying, [R]'Turn now everyone from his evil way, amend your doings, and do not go after other gods to serve them; then you will [R]dwell in the land which I have given you and your fathers.' But you have not inclined your ear, nor obeyed Me. Jer. 18:11 • Jer. 7:7; 25:5, 6

16 "Surely the sons of Jonadab the son of Rechab have performed the commandment of their father, which he commanded them, but this people has not obeyed Me." '

17 "Therefore thus says the LORD God of hosts, the God of Israel: 'Behold, I will bring on Judah and on all the inhabitants of Jerusalem all the doom that I have pronounced against them; because I have spoken to them but they have not heard, and I have called to them but they have not answered.' "

18 And Jeremiah said to the house of the Rechabites, "Thus says the LORD of hosts, the God of Israel: 'Because you have obeyed the commandment of Jonadab your father, and kept all his precepts and done according to all that he commanded you,

19 'therefore thus says the LORD of hosts, the God of Israel: "Jonadab the son of Rechab shall not lack a man to [R]stand before Me forever." ' " Jer. 15:19

CHAPTER 36

Message of the Scroll

NOW it came to pass in the [R]fourth year of Jehoiakim the son of Josiah, king of Judah, *that* this word came to Jeremiah from the LORD, saying: Jer. 25:1, 3; 45:1

2 "Take a scroll of a book and write on it all the words that I have spoken to you against Israel, against Judah, and against all the nations, from the day I spoke to you, from the days of Josiah even to this day.

3 "It [R]may be that the house of Judah will hear all the adversities which I purpose to bring upon them, that everyone may [R]turn from his evil way, that I may forgive their iniquity and their sin." Jer. 26:3 • Jon. 3:8

4 Then Jeremiah [R]called Baruch the son of Neriah; and [R]Baruch wrote on a scroll of a book, [T]at the instruction of Jeremiah, all the words of the LORD which He had spoken to him. Jer. 32:12 • Jer. 45:1 • Lit. *from Jeremiah's mouth*

5 And Jeremiah commanded Baruch, saying, "I *am* confined, I cannot go into the house of the LORD.

6 "You go, therefore, and read from the scroll which you have written [T]at my instruction, the words of the LORD, in the hearing of the people in the LORD's house on [R]the day of fasting. And you shall also read them in the hearing of all Judah who come from their cities. Lit. *from my mouth* • Acts 27:9

7 "It may be that they will present their supplication before the LORD, and everyone will turn from his evil way. For great *is* the anger and the fury that the LORD has pronounced against this people."

8 And Baruch the son of Neriah did according to all that Jeremiah the prophet commanded him, reading from the book the words of the LORD in the LORD's house.

9 Now it came to pass in the fifth year of Jehoiakim the son of Josiah, king of Judah, in the ninth month, *that* they proclaimed a fast before the LORD to all the people in Jerusalem, and to all the people who came from the cities of Judah to Jerusalem.

10 Then Baruch read from the book the words of Jeremiah in the house of the LORD, in the chamber of Gemariah the son of Shaphan the scribe, in the upper court at the entry of the New Gate of the LORD's house, in the [T]hearing of all the people. Lit. *ears*

11 When Michaiah the son of Gemariah, the son of Shaphan, heard all the words of the LORD from the book,

12 he then went down to the king's house, into the scribe's chamber; and there all the princes were sitting—[R]Elishama the scribe, Delaiah the son of Shemaiah, [R]Elnathan the son of Achbor, Gemariah the son of Shaphan, Zedekiah the son of Hananiah, and all the princes. Jer. 41:1 • Jer. 26:22

13 Then Michaiah declared to them all the words that he had heard when Baruch read the book in the hearing of the people.

14 Therefore all the princes sent Jehudi the son of Nethaniah, the son of Shelemiah, the son of Cushi, to Baruch, saying, "Take in your hand the scroll from which you have read in the hearing of the people, and come." So Baruch the son of Neriah took the scroll in his hand and came to them.

15 And they said to him, "Sit down now, and read it in our hearing." So Baruch read *it* in their hearing.

16 Now it happened, when they had heard all the words, that they looked in fear from one to another, and said to Baruch, "We will surely tell the king of all these words."

17 And they asked Baruch, saying, "Tell us now, how did you write all these words—[T]at his instruction?" Lit. *with his mouth*

18 So Baruch answered them, "He proclaimed with his mouth all these words to me, and I wrote *them* with ink in the book."

19 Then the princes said to Baruch, "Go and hide, you and Jeremiah; and let no one know where you are."

20 And they went to the king, into the court; but they stored the scroll in the chamber of Elishama the scribe, and told all the words in the hearing of the king.

21 So the king sent Jehudi to bring the scroll, and he took it from Elishama the scribe's chamber. And Jehudi read it in the hearing of the king and in the hearing of all the princes who stood beside the king.

22 Now the king was sitting in [R]the winter house in the ninth month, with *a fire* burning on the hearth before him. Amos 3:15

23 And it happened, when Jehudi had read three or four columns, *that the king* cut it with the scribe's knife and cast *it* into the fire that *was* on the hearth, until all the scroll was consumed in the fire that *was* on the hearth.

24 Yet they were [R]not afraid, nor did they tear their garments, the king nor any of his servants who heard all these words. [Ps. 36:1]

25 Nevertheless Elnathan, Delaiah, and Gemariah implored the king not to burn the scroll; but he would not listen to them.

26 And the king commanded Jerahmeel [T]the king's son, Seraiah the son of Azriel, and Shelemiah the son of Abdeel, to seize Baruch the scribe and Jeremiah the prophet, but the LORD hid them. Heb. *Hammelech*

27 Now after the king had burned the scroll with the words which Baruch had written at the instruction of Jeremiah, the word of the LORD came to Jeremiah, saying:

28 "Take yet another scroll, and write on it all the former words that were in the first scroll which Jehoiakim the king of Judah has burned.

29 "And you shall say to Jehoiakim king of Judah, 'Thus says the LORD: "You have burned this scroll, saying, 'Why have you written in it that the king of Babylon will certainly come and destroy this land, and cause man and beast to cease from here?' "

30 'Therefore thus says the LORD concerning Jehoiakim king of Judah: "He shall have no one to sit on the throne of David, and his dead body shall be [R]cast out to the heat of the day and the frost of the night. Jer. 22:19

31 "I will punish him, his [T]family, and his servants for their iniquity; and I will bring on them, on the inhabitants of Jerusalem, and on the men of Judah all the doom that I have pronounced against them; but they did not heed." ' " Lit. *seed*

32 Then Jeremiah took another scroll and gave it to Baruch the scribe, the son of Neriah, who wrote on it [T]at the instruction of Jeremiah all the words of the book which Jehoiakim king of Judah had burned in the fire. And besides, there were added to them many similar words. Lit. *from Jeremiah's mouth*

CHAPTER 37

First Interview with Zedekiah
2 Kin. 24:17; 2 Chr. 36:10

THEN King Zedekiah the son of Josiah reigned instead of Coniah the son of Jehoiakim, whom Nebuchadnezzar king of Babylon made king in the land of Judah.

2 [R]But neither he nor his servants nor the people of the land gave heed to the words of the LORD which He spoke by the prophet Jeremiah. 2 Chr. 36:12–16

3 And Zedekiah the king sent Jehucal the son of Shelemiah, and [R]Zephaniah the son of Maaseiah, the priest, to the prophet Jeremiah, saying, [R]"Pray now to the LORD our God for us." Jer. 21:1, 2; 29:25; 52:24 • Jer. 42:2

4 Now Jeremiah was coming and going among the people, for they had not *yet* put him in prison.

5 Then [R]Pharaoh's army came up from Egypt; and when the Chaldeans who were besieging Jerusalem heard news of them, they departed from Jerusalem. Ezek. 17:15

6 And the word of the LORD came to the prophet Jeremiah, saying,

7 "Thus says the LORD, the God of Israel, 'Thus you shall say to the king of Judah, [R]who sent you to Me to inquire of Me: "Behold, Pharaoh's army which has come up to help you will return to Egypt, to their own land. Jer. 21:2

8 [R]"And the Chaldeans shall come back and fight against this city, and take it and burn it with fire." ' Jer. 34:22

9 "Thus says the LORD: 'Do not deceive yourselves, saying, "The Chaldeans will surely depart from us," for they will not depart.

10 'For though you had defeated the whole army of the Chaldeans who fight against you, and there remained *only* wounded men among them, they would rise up, every man in his tent, and burn the city with fire.' "

Jeremiah Is Imprisoned in a Dungeon

11 And it happened, when the army of the Chaldeans left *the siege* of Jerusalem for fear of Pharaoh's army,

12 that Jeremiah went out of Jerusalem to go into the land of Benjamin to claim his property there among the people.

13 And when he was in the Gate of Benjamin, a captain of the guard *was* there whose name *was* Irijah the son of Shelemiah, the son of Hananiah; and he seized Jeremiah the prophet, saying, "You are defecting to the Chaldeans!"

14 Then Jeremiah said, "*It is* [T]false! I am not defecting to the Chaldeans." But he did not listen to him. So Irijah seized Jeremiah and brought him to the princes. *a lie*

15 Therefore the princes were angry with Jeremiah, and they struck him [R]and put him in prison in the house of Jonathan the scribe. For they had made that the prison. Jer. 20:2

16 When Jeremiah entered [R]the dungeon and the cells, and Jeremiah had remained there many days, Jer. 38:6

Second Interview of Zedekiah

17 then Zedekiah the king sent and took him *out*. The king asked him secretly in his house, and said, "Is there *any* word from the LORD?" And Jeremiah said, "There is." Then he said, "You shall be [R]delivered into the hand of the king of Babylon!" Jer. 21:7

18 Moreover Jeremiah said to King Zedekiah, "What offense have I committed against you, against your servants, or against this people, that you have put me in prison?

19 "Where now *are* your prophets who prophesied to you, saying, 'The king of Babylon will not come against you or against this land?'

20 "Therefore please hear now, O my lord the king. Please, let my petition be accepted before you, and do not make me return to the house of Jonathan the scribe, lest I die there."

21 Then Zedekiah the king commanded that they should commit Jeremiah [R]to the court of the prison, and that they should give him daily a piece of bread from the bakers' street, [R]until all the bread in the city was gone. Thus Jeremiah remained in the court of the prison. Jer. 32:2; 38:13, 28 • Jer. 38:9; 52:6

CHAPTER 38

Jeremiah Is Imprisoned in a Cistern

NOW Shephatiah the son of Mattan, Gedaliah the son of Pashhur, Jucal the son of Shelemiah, and Pashhur the son of Malchiah heard the words that Jeremiah had spoken to all the people, saying,

2 "Thus says the LORD: [R]'He who remains in this city shall die by the sword, by famine,

---

37:15 Examples of Suffering—In the Word of God there are four great examples of believers suffering for the sake of righteousness. These are: Joseph, Job, Jeremiah, and Paul.

The sufferings of Joseph: he was hated by his brothers (Page 49—Gen. 37:4, 5, 8); he was sold into slavery (Page 49—Gen. 37:28); he was severely tempted (Page 51—Gen. 39:7); and he was imprisoned (Page 51—Gen. 39:20).

The sufferings of Job: his oxen and donkeys were stolen and his farmhands killed (Page 589—Job 1:14, 15); his sheep and herdsmen were burned by a fire (Page 589—Job 1:16); his camels were stolen and his servants killed (Page 589—Job 1:17); his sons and daughters died in a windstorm (Page 590—Job 1:18, 19); and he was struck with boils (Page 590—Job 2:7).

The sufferings of Jeremiah: he was persecuted by his own family (Page 858—Jer. 12:6); he was plotted against by his own hometown (Page 858—Jer. 11:18–23); he was rejected and ridiculed by his religious peers (Page 866—Jer. 20:1–3, 7–9); and he was arrested, beaten, and accused of treason (Jer. 37:11–16).

The sufferings of Paul: he was plotted against (Page 1286—Acts 9:23, 29; 20:3; 21:30; 23:10, 12; 25:3); he was stoned and left for dead (Page 1293—Acts 14:19); he was subjected to satanic pressure (Page 1415—1 Thess. 2:18); he was beaten and jailed at Philippi (Page 1295—Acts 16:19–24); he was ridiculed (Page 1297—Acts 17:16–18; 26:24); he was falsely accused (Page 1305—Acts 21:21, 28; 24:5–9); he endured a number of violent storms at sea (Page 1374—2 Cor. 11:25; Page 1314—Acts 27:14–20); he was bitten by a serpent (Page 1315—Acts 28:3, 4); and he was forsaken by all (Page 1436—2 Tim. 4:10, 16).

Now turn to Page 456—2 Kin. 23:3: Knowing the Will of God Through the Scriptures.

and by pestilence; but he who goes over to
the Chaldeans shall live; his life shall be as a
prize to him, and he shall live.' Jer. 21:9
3 "Thus says the LORD: 'This city shall
surely be given into the hand of the king of
Babylon's army, which shall take it.' "
4 Therefore the princes said to the king,
"Please, [R]let this man be put to death, for
thus he weakens the hands of the men of war
who remain in this city, and the hands of all
the people, by speaking such words to them.
For this man does not seek the welfare of this
people, but their harm." Jer. 26:11
5 Then Zedekiah the king said, "Look, he
is in your hand. For the king can *do* nothing
against you."
6 [R]So they took Jeremiah and cast him into
the dungeon of Malchiah the king's son,
which *was* in the court of the prison, and
they let Jeremiah down with ropes. And in
the dungeon *there was* no water, but mire. So
Jeremiah sank in the mire. Jer. 37:21
7 [R]Now Ebed-Melech the Ethiopian, one of
the [T]eunuchs, who was in the king's house,
heard that they had put Jeremiah in the
dungeon. When the king was sitting at the
Gate of Benjamin, Jer. 39:16 • Or *officers*
8 Ebed-Melech went out of the king's
house and spoke to the king, saying:
9 "My lord the king, these men have done
evil in all that they have done to Jeremiah the
prophet, whom they have cast into the dungeon, and he is likely to die from hunger in
the place where he is. For *there is* [R]no more
bread in the city." Jer. 37:21
10 Then the king commanded Ebed-Melech
the Ethiopian, saying, "Take from here thirty
men with you, and lift Jeremiah the prophet
out of the dungeon before he dies."
11 So Ebed-Melech took the men with him
and went into the house of the king under
the treasury, and took from there old clothes
and old rags, and let them down by ropes into
the dungeon to Jeremiah.
12 Then Ebed-Melech the Ethiopian said to
Jeremiah, "Please put these old clothes and
rags under your armpits, under the ropes."
And Jeremiah did so.
13 So they pulled Jeremiah up with ropes
and lifted him out of the dungeon. And
Jeremiah remained [R]in the court of the
prison. Jer. 37:21

Third Interview of Zedekiah

14 Then Zedekiah the king sent and had
Jeremiah the prophet brought to him at the
third entrance of the house of the LORD. And
the king said to Jeremiah, "I will ask you
something. Hide nothing from me."
15 Then Jeremiah said to Zedekiah, "If I
declare *it* to you, will you not surely put me
to death? And if I give you counsel, you will
not listen to me."
16 So Zedekiah the king swore secretly to
Jeremiah, saying, "*As* the LORD lives, [R]who
made our very souls, I will not put you to
death, nor will I give you into the hand of
these men who seek your life." Is. 57:16
17 Then Jeremiah said to Zedekiah, "Thus
says the LORD, the God of hosts, the God of
Israel: 'If you surely [T]surrender to the king of
Babylon's princes, then your soul shall live;
this city shall not be burned with fire, and
you and your house shall live. Lit. *go out*
18 'But if you do not [T]surrender to the king
of Babylon's princes, then this city shall be
given into the hand of the Chaldeans; they
shall burn it with fire, and you shall not
escape from their hand.' " Lit. *go out*
19 And Zedekiah the king said to Jeremiah,
"I am afraid of the Jews who have defected
to the Chaldeans, lest they deliver me into
their hand, and they [R]abuse me." 1 Sam. 31:4
20 But Jeremiah said, "They shall not deliver *you*. Please, obey the voice of the LORD
which I speak to you. So it shall be [R]well with
you, and your soul shall live. Jer. 40:9
21 "But if you refuse to surrender, this *is*
the word that the LORD has shown me:
22 'Now behold, all the [R]women who are left
in the king of Judah's house *shall be* surrendered to the king of Babylon's princes, and
those *women* shall say: Jer. 8:10

"Your close friends have [T]set upon you
And prevailed against you; Or *misled*
Your feet have sunk in the mire,
And they have turned away again."

23 'So they shall surrender all your wives
and [R]children to the Chaldeans. [R]You shall
not escape from their hand, but shall be
taken by the hand of the king of Babylon.
And you shall cause this city to be burned
with fire.' " Jer. 39:6; 41:10 • Jer. 39:5
24 Then Zedekiah said to Jeremiah, "Let no
one know of these words, and you shall not
die.
25 "But if the princes hear that I have
talked with you, and they come to you and
say to you, 'Declare to us now what you have
said to the king, and also what the king said
to you; do not hide *it* from us, and we will not
put you to death,'
26 "then you shall say to them, [R]'I presented
my request before the king, that he would
not make me return [R]to Jonathan's house to
die there.' " Jer. 37:20 • Jer. 37:15
27 Then all the princes came to Jeremiah
and asked him. And he told them according
to all these words that the king had commanded. So they stopped speaking with him,
for the conversation had not been heard.
28 Now [R]Jeremiah remained in the court of
the prison until the day that Jerusalem was
taken. And he was *there* when Jerusalem was
taken. Jer. 37:21; 39:14

CHAPTER 39

Jerusalem Falls—2 Kin. 25:1–12; Jer. 52:4–14

IN the ninth year of Zedekiah king of
Judah, in the tenth month, Nebuchadnezzar king of Babylon and all his army came
against Jerusalem, and besieged it.
2 In the eleventh year of Zedekiah, in the
fourth month, on the ninth *day* of the month,
the [T]city was penetrated. *city wall was breached*
3 Then all the princes of the king of Babylon came in and sat in the Middle Gate:
Nergal-Sharezer, Samgar-Nebo, Sarsechim,
Rabsaris, Nergal-Sarezer, Rabmag, with the
rest of the princes of the king of Babylon.
4 So it was, when Zedekiah the king of
Judah and all the men of war saw them, that
they fled and went out of the city by night, by
way of the king's garden, by the gate between the two walls. And he went out by way
of the [T]plain. Or *Arabah,* the Jordan Valley
5 But the Chaldean army pursued them
and overtook Zedekiah in the plains of Jericho. And when they had captured him, they
brought him up to Nebuchadnezzar king of
Babylon, to Riblah in the land of Hamath,
where he pronounced judgment on him.
6 Then the king of Babylon killed the sons
of Zedekiah before his [R]eyes in Riblah; the
king of Babylon also killed all the [R]nobles of
Judah. Deut. 28:34 • Jer. 34:19–21
7 Moreover [R]he put out Zedekiah's eyes,
and bound him with bronze [T]fetters to carry
him off to Babylon. Ezek. 12:13 • *chains*
8 And the Chaldeans burned the king's
house and the houses of the people with fire,
and broke down the walls of Jerusalem.
9 Then Nebuzaradan the captain of the
guard carried away captive to Babylon
the remnant of the people who remained
in the city and those who defected to him,
with the rest of the people who remained.
10 But Nebuzaradan the captain of the
guard left in the land of Judah the poor
people, who had nothing, and gave them
vineyards and fields at the same time.

Jeremiah Is Released

11 Now Nebuchadnezzar king of Babylon
gave charge concerning Jeremiah to Nebuzaradan the captain of the guard, saying,
12 "Take him and look after him, and do
him no [R]harm; but do to him just as he says
to you." Jer. 1:18, 19; 15:20, 21
13 So Nebuzaradan the captain of the
guard sent Nebushasban, Rabsaris, Nergal-
Sharezer, Rabmag, and all the king of Babylon's chief officers;
14 then they sent *someone* to take Jeremiah
from the court of the prison, and committed
him to Gedaliah the son of Ahikam, the son
of Shaphan, that he should take him home.
So he dwelt among the people.

Ebed-Melech Is Rewarded

15 Now the word of the LORD had come to
Jeremiah while he was shut up in the court of
the prison, saying,
16 "Go and speak to [R]Ebed-Melech the Ethiopian, saying, 'Thus says the LORD of hosts,
the God of Israel: "Behold, [R]I will bring My
words upon this city for adversity and not for
good, and they shall be *performed* in that day
before you. Jer. 38:7, 12 • [Dan. 9:12]
17 "But I will deliver you in that day," says
the LORD, "and you shall not be given into
the hand of the men of whom you *are* afraid.
18 "For I will surely deliver you, and you
shall not fall by the sword; but your life shall
be as a prize to you, [R]because you have put
your trust in Me," says the LORD.' " Ps. 37:40

CHAPTER 40

Ministry to Remnant in Judah

THE word that came to Jeremiah from the
LORD [R]after Nebuzaradan the captain of
the guard had let him go from Ramah, when
he had taken him bound in chains among all
who were carried away captive from Jerusalem and Judah, who were carried away captive to Babylon. Jer. 39:9, 11
2 And the captain of the guard took Jeremiah and said to him: "The LORD your God
has pronounced this doom on this place.
3 "Now the LORD has brought *it,* and has
done just as He said. [R]Because you *people*
have sinned against the LORD, and not
obeyed His voice, therefore this thing has
come upon you. Dan. 9:11
4 "And now look, I free you this day from
the chains that [T]*were* on your hand. If it
seems good to you to come with me to
Babylon, come, and I will look after you. But
if it seems wrong for you to come with me to
Babylon, remain here. See, all the land *is*
before you; wherever it seems good and
convenient for you to go, go there." Or *are*
5 Now while Jeremiah had not yet gone
back, *Nebuzaradan said,* "Go back to [R]Geda-
liah the son of Ahikam, the son of Shaphan,
[R]whom the king of Babylon has made governor over the cities of Judah, and dwell with
him among the people. Or go wherever it
seems convenient for you to go." So the
captain of the guard gave him rations and a
gift and let him go. Jer. 39:14 • Jer. 41:10
6 [R]Then Jeremiah went to Gedaliah the
son of Ahikam, to [R]Mizpah, and dwelt with
him among the people who were left in the
land. Jer. 39:14 • Judg. 20:1
7 [R]Now when all the captains of the armies
who *were* in the fields, they and their men,
heard that the king of Babylon had made
Gedaliah the son of Ahikam governor in the
land, and had committed to him men,

women, children, and [R]the poorest of the land
who had not been carried away captive to
Babylon, 2 Kin. 25:23, 24 • Jer. 39:10
8 then they came to Gedaliah at Mizpah—
Ishmael the son of Nethaniah, Johanan and
Jonathan the sons of Kareah, Seraiah the son
of Tanhumeth, the sons of Ephai the Netophathite, and [T]Jezaniah the son of a Maachathite, they and their men. *Jaazaniah,* 2 Kin. 25:23
9 And Gedaliah the son of Ahikam, the son
of Shaphan, took an oath before them and
their men, saying, "Do not be afraid to serve
the Chaldeans. Dwell in the land and serve
the king of Babylon, and it shall be [R]well with
you. Jer. 27:11; 38:17–20
10 "As for me, I will indeed dwell at Mizpah
and serve the Chaldeans who come to us. But
you, gather wine and summer fruit and oil,
put *them* in your vessels, and dwell in your
cities that you have taken."
11 Likewise, when all the Jews who *were* in
Moab, among the Ammonites, in Edom, and
who *were* in all the countries, heard that the
king of Babylon had left a remnant of Judah,
and that he had set over them Gedaliah the
son of Ahikam, the son of Shaphan,
12 then all the Jews [R]returned out of all
places where they had been driven, and came
to the land of Judah, to Gedaliah at Mizpah,
and gathered wine and summer fruit in abundance. Jer. 43:5
13 Moreover Johanan the son of Kareah
and all the captains of the forces that *were* in
the fields came to Gedaliah at Mizpah,
14 and said to him, [T]"Do you certainly know
that Baalis the king of the Ammonites has
sent Ishmael the son of Nethaniah to murder
you?" But Gedaliah the son of Ahikam did
not believe them. Or *Certainly you know that*
15 Then Johanan the son of Kareah spoke
secretly to Gedaliah in Mizpah, saying, "Let
me go, please, and I will kill Ishmael the son
of Nethaniah, and no one will know *it*. Why
should he murder you, so that all the Jews
who are gathered to you would be scattered,
and the [R]remnant in Judah perish?" Jer. 42:2
16 But Gedaliah the son of Ahikam said to
Johanan the son of Kareah, "You shall not do
this thing, for you speak falsely concerning
Ishmael."

CHAPTER 41

NOW it came to pass in the seventh month
that Ishmael the son of Nethaniah, the
son of Elishama, of the royal family and of
the officers of the king, came with ten men to
Gedaliah the son of Ahikam, at Mizpah. And
there they ate bread together in Mizpah.
2 Then Ishmael the son of Nethaniah, and
the ten men who were with him, arose and
[R]struck Gedaliah the son of [R]Ahikam, the son
of Shaphan, with the sword, and killed him
whom the king of Babylon had made [R]gover-
nor over the land. 2 Kin. 25:25 • Jer. 26:24 • Jer. 40:5
3 Ishmael also struck down all the Jews
who were with him, *that is*, with Gedaliah at
Mizpah, and the Chaldeans who were found
there, the men of war.
4 And it happened, on the second day after
he had killed Gedaliah, when as yet no one
knew *it*,
5 that certain men came from Shechem,
from Shiloh, and from Samaria, eighty men
[R]with their beards shaved and their clothes
torn, having cut themselves, with offerings
and incense in their hand, to bring *them* to
[R]the house of the LORD. Deut. 14:1 • 1 Sam. 1:7
6 Now Ishmael the son of Nethaniah went
out from Mizpah to meet them, weeping as
he went along; and it happened as he met
them that he said to them, "Come to Gedaliah the son of Ahikam!"
7 So it was, when they came into the midst
of the city, that Ishmael the son of Nethaniah
killed them *and cast them* into the midst of a
pit, he and the men who were with him.
8 But ten men were found among them
who said to Ishmael, "Do not kill us, for we
have treasures of wheat, barley, oil, and
honey in the field." So he desisted and did not
kill them among their brethren.
9 Now the [T]pit into which Ishmael had cast
all the dead bodies of the men whom he had
slain, because of Gedaliah, *was* [R]the same one
Asa the king had made for fear of Baasha
king of Israel. Ishmael the son of Nethaniah
filled it with *the* slain. Or *cistern* • 1 Kin. 15:22
10 Then Ishmael carried away captive all
the rest of the people who *were* in Mizpah,
the king's daughters and all the people who
remained in Mizpah, whom Nebuzaradan the
captain of the guard had committed to Gedaliah the son of Ahikam. And Ishmael the son
of Nethaniah carried them away captive and
departed to go over to the Ammonites.
11 But when [R]Johanan the son of Kareah
and all the captains of the forces that *were*
with him heard of all the evil that Ishmael
the son of Nethaniah had done, Jer. 40:7, 8, 13–16
12 they took all the men and went to fight
with Ishmael the son of Nethaniah; and they
found him by [R]the great pool that *is* in Gibeon. 2 Sam. 2:13
13 So it was, when all the people who *were*
with Ishmael saw Johanan the son of Kareah,
and all the captains of the forces who *were*
with him, that they were glad.
14 Then all the people whom Ishmael had
carried away captive from Mizpah turned
around and came back, and went to Johanan
the son of Kareah.
15 But Ishmael the son of Nethaniah escaped from Johanan with eight men and
went to the Ammonites.

THE GREAT POOL AT GIBEON

Photo by Howard Vos

This stairway of seventy-nine steps spirals down to the pool of Gibeon.

A battle between David's forces and Saul's son Ishbosheth began with a meeting "by the pool of Gibeon" (2 Sam. 2:13). The book of the prophet Jeremiah, written hundreds of years after David's time, also referred to "the great pool that *is* in Gibeon" (Jer. 41:12). What feature of this ancient city was so impressive that it rated these two references in the Bible?

Archaeologists believe they have found the answer with the discovery of a huge well dug through solid limestone at the site of the Old Testament city of Gibeon, located about seven miles north of Jerusalem. About 40 feet in diameter and 80 feet deep, this giant well apparently provided water for the Canaanite city of Gibeon as early as Joshua's time about 1400 B.C. (Josh. 9). It must have still been in use about eight centuries later during the ministry of the prophet Jeremiah, when the citizens of Judah occupied the site.

Digging a well like this with hand tools was a massive undertaking. But a dependable water supply was essential for ancient cities of Bible times. Access to the precious water was provided by a spiraling stairway cut into the rock around the edge of the shaft. The women of Gibeon made the long climb every day to bring up fresh water for their households.

In addition to this well at Gibeon, the wells dug by Isaac (Gen. 26:18–22) and Uzziah (2 Chr. 26:10) are also mentioned in the Bible. David longed for water from the well in his hometown of Bethlehem (2 Sam. 23:15, 16), and Jesus spoke about His free gift of unfailing water to the woman at the well in Samaria (John 4:1–26).

16 Then Johanan the son of Kareah, and all the captains of the forces that were with him, took from Mizpah all the [R]rest of the people whom he had recovered from Ishmael the son of Nethaniah after he had murdered Gedaliah the son of Ahikam—the mighty men of war and the women and the children and the eunuchs, whom he had brought back from Gibeon. Jer. 40:11, 12; 43:4–7

17 And they departed and dwelt in the habitation of Chimham, which is near Bethlehem, as they went on their way to Egypt,

18 because of the Chaldeans; for they were afraid of them, because Ishmael the son of Nethaniah had murdered Gedaliah the son of Ahikam, [R]whom the king of Babylon had made governor in the land. Jer. 40:5

CHAPTER 42

THEN all the captains of the forces, [R]Johanan the son of Kareah, Jezaniah the son of Hoshaiah, and all the people, from the least to the greatest, came near Jer. 40:8, 13; 41:11

2 and said to Jeremiah the prophet, "Please, let our petition be acceptable to you, and pray for us to the LORD your God, for all this remnant (since we are left *but* [R]a few of many, as you can see), Lev. 26:22

3 "that the LORD your God may show us [R]the way in which we should walk and the thing we should do." Ezra 8:21

4 Then Jeremiah the prophet said to them, "I have heard. Indeed, I will pray to the LORD your God according to your words, and it shall be, *that* whatever the LORD answers you, I will declare *it* to you. I will [R]keep nothing back from you." 1 Sam. 3:17, 18

5 Then they said to Jeremiah, "Let the LORD be a true and faithful witness between us, if we do not do according to everything which the LORD your God sends us by you.

6 "Whether *it is* [T]pleasing or [T]displeasing, we will [R]obey the voice of the LORD our God to whom we send you, [R]that it may be well with us when we obey the voice of the LORD our God." Lit. *good* • Lit. *evil* • Ex. 24:7 • Jer. 7:23

7 And it happened after ten days that the word of the LORD came to Jeremiah.

8 Then he called Johanan the son of Kareah, all the captains of the forces which *were* with him, and all the people from the least even to the greatest,

9 and said to them, "Thus says the LORD, the God of Israel, to whom you sent me to present your petition before Him:

10 'If you will still abide in this land, then [R]I will build you and not pull *you* down, and I will plant you and not pluck *you* up. For I [R]relent concerning the disaster that I have brought upon you. Jer. 24:6; 31:28; 33:7 • [Jer. 18:8]

11 'Do not be afraid of the king of Babylon, of whom you are afraid; do not be afraid of him,' says the LORD, 'for I *am* with you, to save you and deliver you from his hand.

12 'And [R]I will show you mercy, that he may have mercy on you and cause you to return to your own land.' Ps. 106:46

13 "But if [R]you say, 'We will not dwell in this land,' disobeying the voice of the LORD your God, Jer. 44:16

14 "saying, 'No, but we will go to the land of [R]Egypt where we shall see no war, nor hear the sound of the trumpet, nor be hungry for bread, and there we will dwell'— Jer. 41:17; 43:7

15 "Then hear now the word of the LORD, O remnant of Judah! Thus says the LORD of hosts, the God of Israel: 'If you [R]wholly[T] set [R]your faces to enter Egypt, and go to sojourn there, Deut. 17:16 • Or *surely* • Luke 9:51

16 'then it shall be *that* the [R]sword which you feared shall overtake you there in the land of Egypt; the famine of which you were afraid shall follow close after you there *in* Egypt; and there you shall die. Ezek. 11:8

17 'So shall it be with all the men who set their faces to go to Egypt to sojourn there. They shall die by the sword, by famine, and by pestilence. And [R]none of them shall remain or escape from the disaster that I will bring upon them.' Jer. 44:14, 28

18 "For thus says the LORD of hosts, the God of Israel: 'As My anger and My fury have been poured out on the inhabitants of Jerusalem, so will My fury be poured out on you when you enter Egypt. And you shall be an oath, an astonishment, a curse, and a reproach; and you shall see this place no more.'

19 "The LORD has said concerning you, O remnant of Judah, [R]'Do not go to Egypt!' Know certainly that I have [T]admonished you this day. Deut. 17:16 • *warned*

20 "For you were hypocrites in your hearts when you sent me to the LORD your God, saying, 'Pray for us to the LORD our God, and according to all that the LORD your God says, so declare to us and we will do *it*.'

21 "And I have this day declared *it* to you, but you have [R]not obeyed the voice of the LORD your God, or anything which He has sent you by me. Is. 30:1–7

22 "Now therefore, know certainly that you [R]shall die by the sword, by famine, and by pestilence in the place where you desire to go to sojourn." Ezek. 6:11

CHAPTER 43

Ministry to Remnant in Egypt

NOW it happened, when Jeremiah had stopped speaking to all the people all the [R]words of the LORD their God, for which the LORD their God had sent him to them, all these words, Jer. 42:9–18

2 that Azariah the son of Hoshaiah, Johanan the son of Kareah, and all the proud men

spoke, saying to Jeremiah, "You speak falsely! The LORD our God has not sent you to say, 'Do not go to Egypt to sojourn there.'

3 "But Baruch the son of Neriah has set you against us, to deliver us into the hand of the Chaldeans, that they may put us to death or carry us away captive to Babylon."

4 So Johanan the son of Kareah, all the captains of the forces, and all the people would [R]not obey the voice of the LORD, to remain in the land of Judah. 2 Kin. 25:26

5 But Johanan the son of Kareah and all the captains of the forces took [R]all the remnant of Judah who had returned to dwell in the land of Judah, from all nations where they had been driven— Jer. 40:11, 12

6 men, women, children, the king's daughters, [R]and every person whom Nebuzaradan the captain of the guard had left with Gedaliah the son of Ahikam, the son of Shaphan, and Jeremiah the prophet and Baruch the son of Neriah. Jer. 39:10; 40:7

7 [R]So they went to the land of Egypt, for they did not obey the voice of the LORD. And they went as far as Tahpanhes. Jer. 42:19

8 Then the [R]word of the LORD came to Jeremiah in Tahpanhes, saying, Jer. 44:1–30

9 "Take large stones in your hand, and hide them in the sight of the men of Judah, in the [T]clay in the brick courtyard which *is* at the entrance to Pharaoh's house in Tahpanhes; Or *mortar*

10 "and say to them, 'Thus says the LORD of hosts, the God of Israel: "Behold, I will send and bring Nebuchadnezzar the king of Babylon, My servant, and will set his throne above these stones that I have hidden. And he will spread his royal pavilion over them.

11 "When he comes, he shall strike the land of Egypt *and deliver* to death [R]*those appointed* for death, and to captivity *those appointed* for captivity, and to the sword *those appointed* for the sword. Jer. 15:2

12 "I will kindle a fire in the houses of [R]the gods of Egypt, and he shall burn them and carry them away captive. And he shall array himself with the land of Egypt, as a shepherd puts on his garment, and he shall go out from there in peace. Jer. 46:25

13 "He shall also break the sacred pillars of [T]Beth Shemesh that *are* in the land of Egypt; and the houses of the gods of the Egyptians he shall burn with fire." ' " Lit. *House of the Sun*

CHAPTER 44

THE word that came to Jeremiah concerning all the Jews who dwell in the land of Egypt, who dwell at Migdol, at Tahpanhes, at [R]Noph,[T] and in the country of [R]Pathros, saying, Is. 19:13 • Ancient Memphis • Ezek. 29:14; 30:14

2 "Thus says the LORD of hosts, the God of Israel: 'You have seen all the calamity that I have brought on Jerusalem and on all the cities of Judah; and behold, this day they *are* a desolation, and no one dwells in them,

3 'because of their wickedness which they have committed to provoke Me to anger, in that they went to burn incense *and* to [R]serve other gods whom they did not know, they nor you nor your fathers. Deut. 13:6; 32:17

4 'However [R]I have sent to you all My servants the prophets, rising early and sending *them,* saying, "Oh, do not do this abominable thing that I hate!" Jer. 7:25; 25:4; 26:5; 29:19

5 'But they did not listen or incline their ear to turn from their wickedness, to burn no incense to other gods.

6 'So My fury and My anger were poured out and kindled in the cities of Judah and in the streets of Jerusalem; and they are wasted *and* desolate, as it is this day.'

7 "Now therefore, thus says the LORD, the God of hosts, the God of Israel: 'Why do you commit *this* great evil against yourselves, to cut off from you man and woman, child and infant, out of Judah, leaving none to remain,

8 'in that you provoke Me to wrath with the works of your hands, burning incense to other gods in the land of Egypt where you have gone to dwell, that you may cut yourselves off and be a curse and a reproach among all the nations of the earth?

9 'Have you forgotten the wickedness of your fathers, the wickedness of the kings of Judah, the wickedness of their wives, your own wickedness, and the wickedness of your wives, which they committed in the land of Judah and in the streets of Jerusalem?

10 'They have not been [T]humbled, to this day, nor have they feared; they have not walked in My law or in My statutes that I set before you and your fathers.' Lit. *crushed*

11 "Therefore thus says the LORD of hosts, the God of Israel: 'Behold, [R]I will set My face against you for catastrophe and for [T]cutting off all Judah. Amos 9:4 • Destroying

12 'And I will take the remnant of Judah who have set their faces to go into the land of Egypt to sojourn there, and they shall all be consumed *and* fall in the land of Egypt. They shall be consumed by the sword *and* by famine. They shall die, from the least to the greatest, by the sword and by famine; and [R]they shall be an oath *and* an astonishment and a curse and a reproach! Is. 65:15

13 'For I will punish those who dwell in the land of Egypt, as I have punished Jerusalem, by the sword, by famine, and by pestilence,

14 'so that none of the remnant of Judah who have gone into the land of Egypt to sojourn there shall escape or survive, lest they return to the land of Judah, to which they desire to return and dwell. For none shall return except those who escape.' "

THE EGYPTIAN PHARAOH

Pharaoh was the title of the kings of Egypt. The word means "great house." Used originally to describe the king's palace, the term came to mean something like "his honor" or "his majesty."

The Egyptians believed their ruler was a god and the key to the nation's relationship to the cosmic gods of the universe. His word was law, and he owned everything in the land. When the Pharaoh died, he became the ruler of the underworld and those who live after death. The Egyptians took great pains to prepare their dead for the afterlife. They perfected the intricate process of mummification. In the lavish interiors of the great pyramids of Egypt the mummified bodies of royalty were buried, along with many of their earthly treasures (see illustration).

In all there were thirty dynasties of Pharaohs during Egypt's long history. Several different accounts in the Old Testament refer to a Pharaoh. Abraham's wife Sarah was summoned to the Pharaoh's palace (Gen. 12:14–20). Solomon married the daughter of a Pharaoh, who became a firm ally of the Hebrew monarch (1 Kin. 3:1). This Pharaoh later conquered the city of Gezer and gave it to his daughter as a dowry (1 Kin. 9:16). Jeroboam sought refuge in the court of the Pharaoh Shishak (1 Kin. 11:40).

The most famous Pharaoh in the Bible is the ruler of whom Moses asked permission to lead the Israelites out of Egypt. Scholars debate whether this was Amenhotep II (ruled 1450–1423 B.C.) or Raamses II (ruled 1301–1234). This Egyptian ruler repeatedly refused to release the people, in spite of the plagues God sent to break his will. Only when the Pharaoh's son was killed in the last plague did he submit to God's power and let the people go (Ex. 12:29–33).

During his ministry as a refugee in Egypt, the prophet Jeremiah predicted that Pharaoh Hophra, king of Egypt, would be overthrown by his enemies, just as the nation of Judah had been defeated by the Babylonians (Jer. 44:30).

Photo by Howard Vos

The gold mask buried with Pharaoh Tutankhamon of Egypt about 1350 B.C. illustrated the wealth of his kingdom.

15 Then all the men who knew that their
wives had burned incense to other gods, with
all the women who stood by, a great multitude, and all the people who dwelt in the land
of Egypt, in Pathros, answered Jeremiah,
saying:
16 "*As for* the word that you have spoken
to us in the name of the LORD, [R]we will not
listen to you! Jer. 6:16
17 "But we will certainly do whatever has
gone out of our own mouth, to burn incense
to the queen of heaven and pour out drink
offerings to her, as we have done, we and our
fathers, our kings and our princes, in the
cities of Judah and in the streets of Jerusalem. For *then* we had plenty of [T]food, were
well-off, and saw no trouble. Lit. *bread*
18 "But since we stopped burning incense
to the queen of heaven and pouring out drink
offerings to her, we have lacked everything
and have been consumed by the sword and
by famine."
19 *The women also said,* [R]"And when we
burned incense to the queen of heaven and
poured out drink offerings to her, did we
make cakes for her, to worship her, and pour
out drink offerings to her without our husbands' *permission?*" Jer. 7:18
20 Then Jeremiah spoke to all the people—
the men, the women, and all the people who
had given him *that* answer—saying:
21 "The incense that you burned in the
cities of Judah and in the streets of Jerusalem, you and your fathers, your kings and
your princes, and the people of the land, did
not the LORD remember them, and did it *not*
come into His mind?
22 "So the LORD could no longer bear *it,*
because of the evil of your doings *and* because of the abominations which you committed. Therefore your land is a desolation,
an astonishment, a curse, and without an
inhabitant, [R]as *it is* this day. Jer. 25:11, 18, 38
23 "Because you have burned incense and
because you have sinned against the LORD,
and have not obeyed the voice of the LORD or
walked in His law, in His statutes or in His
testimonies, [R]therefore this calamity has
happened to you, as *at* this day." Dan. 9:11, 12
24 Moreover Jeremiah said to all the people
and to all the women, "Hear the word of the
LORD, all Judah who *are* in the land of Egypt!
25 "Thus says the LORD of hosts, the God of
Israel, saying: 'You and your wives have
spoken with your mouths and fulfilled with
your hands, saying, "We will surely perform
our vows that we have made, to burn incense
to the queen of heaven and pour out drink
offerings to her." You will surely fulfill your
vows and perform your vows!'
26 "Therefore hear the word of the LORD, all
Judah who dwell in the land of Egypt: 'Behold, [R]I have sworn by My [R]great name,' says
the LORD, 'that [R]My name shall no more be
named in the mouth of any man of Judah in
all the land of Egypt, saying, "The Lord GOD
lives." Heb. 6:13 • Jer. 10:6 • Ezek. 20:39
27 'Behold, I will watch over them for adversity and not for good. And all the men of
Judah who *are* in the land of Egypt [R]shall be
consumed by the sword and by famine, until
there is an end to them. Ezek. 7:6
28 'Yet [R]a small number who escape the
sword shall return from the land of Egypt to
the land of Judah; and all the remnant of
Judah, who have gone to the land of Egypt to
sojourn there, shall know whose words will
stand, Mine or theirs. Is. 10:19; 27:12, 13
29 'And this *shall be* a sign to you,' says the
LORD, 'that I will punish you in this place,
that you may know that My words will surely
[R]stand against you for adversity.' [Ps. 33:11]
30 "Thus says the LORD: 'Behold, I will give
Pharaoh Hophra king of Egypt into the hand
of his enemies and into the hand of those
who seek his life, as I gave Zedekiah king of
Judah into the hand of Nebuchadnezzar king
of Babylon, his enemy who sought his life.' "

CHAPTER 45

Message to Baruch

THE word that Jeremiah the prophet spoke
to Baruch the son of Neriah, when he had
written these words in a book [T]at the instruction of Jeremiah, in the [R]fourth year of Jehoiakim the son of Josiah, king of Judah,
saying, Lit. *from Jeremiah's mouth* • Jer. 25:1; 36:1; 46:2
2 "Thus says the LORD, the God of Israel,
to you, O Baruch:
3 'You said, "Woe is me now! For the LORD
has added grief to my sorrow. I fainted in my
sighing, and I find no rest." '
4 "Thus you shall say to him, 'Thus says
the LORD: "Behold, [R]what I have built I will
break down, and what I have planted I will
pluck up, that is, this whole land. Is. 5:5
5 "And do you seek great things for yourself? Do not seek *them;* for behold, [R]I will
bring adversity on all flesh," says the LORD.
"But I will give your life to you as a prize in
all places, wherever you go." ' " Jer. 25:26

CHAPTER 46

Prophecies Against Egypt

THE word of the LORD which came to
Jeremiah the prophet against [R]the nations. Jer. 25:15
2 Against Egypt.
Concerning the army of Pharaoh Necho,
king of Egypt, which was by the River Euphrates in Carchemish, and which Nebuchadnezzar king of Babylon [R]defeated in the

[R]fourth year of Jehoiakim the son of Josiah, king of Judah: 2 Chr. 35:20 • Jer. 45:1

3 "Order the [T]buckler and shield,
And draw near to battle! A small shield
4 Harness the horses,
And mount up, you horsemen!
Stand forth with *your* helmets,
Polish the spears,
[R]Put on the armor! Jer. 51:11, 12
5 Why have I seen them dismayed *and*
turned back?
Their mighty ones are beaten down;
They have speedily fled,
And did not look back,
For [R]fear *was* all around," says the
LORD. Jer. 49:29
6 "Do not let the swift flee away,
Nor the mighty man escape;
They will [R]stumble and fall
Toward the north, by the River
Euphrates. Dan. 11:19

7 "Who *is* this coming up like a flood,
Whose waters move like the rivers?
8 Egypt rises up like a flood,
And *its* waters move like the rivers;
And he says, 'I will go up *and* cover the
earth,
I will destroy the city and its
inhabitants.'
9 Come up, O horses, and rage, O
chariots!
And let the mighty men come forth:
[T]The Ethiopians and [T]the Libyans who
handle the shield,
And the Lydians [R]who handle *and* bend
the bow. Heb. *Cush* • Heb. *Put* • Is. 66:19
10 For this *is* [R]the day of the Lord GOD of
hosts, Joel 1:15
A day of vengeance,
That He may avenge Himself on His
adversaries.
[R]The sword shall devour; Deut. 32:42
It shall be [T]satiated and made drunk
with their blood; Filled to the full
For the Lord GOD of hosts [R]has a
sacrifice Is. 34:6
In the north country by the River
Euphrates.

11 "Go up to Gilead and take balm,
[R]O virgin, the daughter of Egypt;
In vain you will use many medicines;
[R]You shall not be cured. Is. 47:1 • Ezek. 30:21
12 The nations have heard of your [R]shame,
And your cry has filled the land;
For the mighty man has stumbled
against the mighty;
They both have fallen together." Jer. 2:36

13 The word that the LORD spoke to Jeremiah the prophet, how Nebuchadnezzar king
of Babylon would come *and* [R]strike the land
of Egypt. Is. 19:1

14 "Declare in Egypt, and proclaim in
[R]Migdol; Jer. 44:1
Proclaim in Noph and in Tahpanhes;
Say, 'Stand fast and prepare yourselves,
For the sword devours all around you.'
15 Why are your valiant *men* swept away?
They did not stand
Because the LORD drove them away.
16 He made many fall;
Yes, [R]one fell upon another. Lev. 26:36, 37
And they said, 'Arise!
[R]Let us go back to our own people
And to the land of our nativity Jer. 51:9
From the oppressing sword.'
17 They cried there,
'Pharaoh, king of Egypt, *is but* a noise.
He has passed by the appointed time!'

18 "*As* I live," says the King,
[R]Whose name *is* the LORD of hosts,
"Surely as Tabor *is* among the
mountains
And as Carmel by the sea, *so* he shall
come. Jer. 48:15
19 O you daughter dwelling in Egypt,
Prepare yourself [R]to go into captivity!
For Noph shall be waste and be
desolate, without inhabitant. Is. 20:4

20 "Egypt *is like* a very pretty [R]heifer,
But destruction comes, it comes [R]from
the north. Hos. 10:11 • Jer. 1:14
21 Also her mercenaries are in her midst
like [T]fat bulls, Lit. *calves of the stall*
For they also are turned back,
They have fled away together.
They did not stand,
For [R]the day of their calamity had come
upon them, [Ps. 37:13]
The time of their punishment.
22 [R]Her noise shall go like a serpent,
For they shall march with an army
And come against her with axes,
Like those who chop wood. [Is. 29:4]

23 "They shall [R]cut down her forest," says
the LORD,
"Though it cannot be searched,
Because they *are* innumerable,
And more numerous than
[R]grasshoppers. Is. 10:34 • Judg. 6:5; 7:12
24 The daughter of Egypt shall be
ashamed;
She shall be delivered into the hand
Of [R]the people of the north." Jer. 1:15

25 The LORD of hosts, the God of Israel,
says: "Behold, I will bring punishment on
[T]Amon of No, and Pharaoh and Egypt, with

their gods and their kings—Pharaoh and
those who [R]trust in him. A sun god • Is. 30:1-5
26 [R]"And I will deliver them into the hand
of those who seek their lives, into the hand of
Nebuchadnezzar king of Babylon and the
hand of his servants. [R]Afterward it shall be
inhabited as in the days of old," says the
LORD. Ezek. 32:11 • Ezek. 29:8-14

27 "But[R] do not fear, O My servant Jacob,
And do not be dismayed, O Israel!
For behold, I will [R]save you from afar,
And your offspring from the land of
their captivity;
Jacob shall return, have rest and be at
ease; Is. 41:13, 14; 43:5; 44:2 • Is. 11:11
No one shall make *him* afraid.
28 Do not fear, O Jacob My servant," says
the LORD,
"For I *am* with you;
For I will make a complete end of all
the nations
To which I have driven you,
But I will not make [R]a complete end of
you.
I will rightly [R]correct you,
For I will not leave you wholly
unpunished." Amos 9:8, 9 • Jer. 30:11

CHAPTER 47

Prophecies Against Philistia

THE word of the LORD that came to Jeremiah the prophet against the Philistines,
[R]before Pharaoh attacked Gaza. Amos 1:6
2 Thus says the LORD:

"Behold, [R]waters rise [R]out of the north,
And shall be an overflowing flood;
They shall overflow the land and all
that is in it,
The city and those who dwell within;
Then the men shall cry,
And all the inhabitants of the land shall
wail. Is. 8:7, 8 • Jer. 1:14
3 At the [R]noise of the stamping hooves of
his strong horses, Jer. 8:16
At the rushing of his chariots,
At the rumbling of his wheels,
The fathers will not look back for *their*
children,
[T]Lacking courage, Lit. *From sinking hands*
4 Because of the day that comes to
plunder all the [R]Philistines, Is. 14:29-31
To cut off from [R]Tyre and Sidon every
helper who remains; Jer. 25:22
For the LORD shall plunder the
Philistines,
The remnant of the country of
[T]Caphtor. Cappadocia in Asia Minor
5 [R]Baldness has come upon Gaza, Mic. 1:16
[R]Ashkelon is cut off Jer. 25:20
With the remnant of their valley.
How long will you cut yourself?

6 "O you [R]sword of the LORD,
How long until you are quiet?
Put yourself up into your scabbard,
Rest and be still! Ezek. 21:3-5
7 How can [T]it be quiet, Lit. *you*
Seeing the LORD has [R]given it a charge
Against Ashkelon and against the
seashore? Ezek. 14:17
There He has [R]appointed it." Mic. 6:9

CHAPTER 48

Prophecies Against Moab

AGAINST [R]Moab. Is. 15:1—16:14; 25:10
Thus says the LORD of hosts, the God of
Israel:

"Woe to [R]Nebo! Is. 15:2
For it is plundered,
[R]Kirjathaim is shamed *and* taken;
[T]The high stronghold is shamed and
dismayed— Num. 32:37 • Or *Misgab*
2 [R]No more praise of Moab. Is. 16:14
In [R]Heshbon they have devised evil
against her: Jer. 49:3
'Come, and let us cut her off as a
nation.'
You also shall be cut down, O
[R]Madmen![T] Is. 10:31 • A city of Moab
The sword shall pursue you;
3 A voice of crying *shall be* from
[R]Horonaim: Is. 15:5
'Plundering and great destruction!'

4 "Moab is destroyed;
Her little ones have caused a cry to be
heard;
5 [R]For in the Ascent of Luhith they ascend
with continual weeping;
For in the descent of Horonaim the
enemies have heard a cry of
destruction. Is. 15:5

6 "Flee, save your lives!
And be like [T]the [R]juniper in the
wilderness. Or *Aroer*, a city of Moab • Jer. 17:6
7 For because you have trusted in your
works and your [R]treasures,
You also shall be taken.
And [R]Chemosh shall go forth into
captivity, Jer. 9:23 • Jer. 48:7
His priests and his princes together.
8 And [R]the plunderer shall come against
every city;
No one shall escape.
The valley also shall perish,
And the plain shall be destroyed,
As the LORD has spoken. Jer. 6:26

9 "Give[R] wings to Moab,
That she may flee and get away;
For her cities shall be desolate,
Without any to dwell in them. Ps. 55:6

10 [R]Cursed *is* he who does the work of the
LORD deceitfully,
And cursed *is* he who keeps back his
sword from blood. 1 Sam. 15:3

11 "Moab has been at ease from his youth;
He [R]has settled on his dregs,
And has not been emptied from vessel
to vessel, Zeph. 1:12
Nor has he gone into captivity.
Therefore his taste remained in him,
And his scent has not changed.

12 "Therefore behold, the days are coming,"
says the LORD,
"That I shall send him [T]wine-workers
Who will tip him over
And empty his vessels
And break the bottles. *tippers* of wine bottles
13 Moab shall be ashamed of Chemosh,
As the house of Israel [R]was ashamed of
Bethel, their confidence. Hos. 10:6

14 "How can you say, [R]'We *are* mighty
And strong men for the war'? Is. 16:6
15 Moab is plundered and gone up *from*
her cities;
Her chosen young men have [R]gone
down to the slaughter," says [R]the
King, Jer. 50:27 • Jer. 46:18; 51:57
Whose name *is* the LORD of hosts.

16 "The calamity of Moab *is* near at hand,
And his affliction comes quickly.
17 Bemoan him, all you who are around
him;
And all you who know his name,
Say, [R]'How the strong staff is broken,
The beautiful rod!' Is. 9:4; 14:4, 5

18 "O daughter[R] inhabiting [R]Dibon,
Come down from *your* glory,
And sit in thirst; Is. 47:1 • Is. 15:2
For the plunderer of Moab has come
against you,
He has destroyed your strongholds.
19 O inhabitant of [R]Aroer, Deut. 2:36
[R]Stand by the way and watch;
Ask him who flees 1 Sam. 4:13, 14, 16
And her who escapes;
Say, 'What has happened?'
20 Moab is shamed, for he is broken down.
[R]Wail and cry!
Tell it in [R]Arnon, that Moab is
plundered. Is. 16:7 • Num. 21:13

21 "And judgment has come on the plain
country:
On Holon and Jahzah and Mephaath,
22 On Dibon and Nebo and Beth
Diblathaim,
23 On Kirjathaim and Beth Gamul and
Beth Meon,
24 On [R]Kerioth and Bozrah,
On all the cities of the land of Moab,
Far or near. Amos 2:2
25 [R]The horn of Moab is cut off, Ps. 75:10
And his arm is broken," says the LORD.

26 "Make[R] him drunk, Jer. 25:15
For he magnified *himself* against the
LORD.
Moab shall wallow in his vomit,
And he shall also be in derision.
27 For was not Israel a derision to you?
[R]Was he found among thieves? Jer. 2:26
For whenever you speak of him,
You shake *your head in* [R]*scorn.* Lam. 2.15
28 You who dwell in Moab,
Leave the cities and [R]dwell in the rock,
And be like [R]the dove *which* makes her
nest Ps. 55:6, 7 • Song 2:14
In the sides of the cave's mouth.

29 "We have heard the [R]pride of Moab
(He *is* exceedingly proud),
Of his loftiness and arrogance and
[R]pride, Is. 16:6 • Jer. 49:16
And of the haughtiness of his heart."

30 "I know his wrath," says the LORD,
"But it *is* not right;
His lies have made nothing right.
31 Therefore I will wail for Moab,
And I will cry out for all Moab;
I will mourn for the men of Kir Heres.
32 [R]O vine of Sibmah! I will weep for you
with the weeping of Jazer. Is. 16:8, 9
Your plants have gone over the sea,
They reach to the sea of Jazer.
The plunderer has fallen on your
summer fruit and your vintage.
33 [R]Joy and gladness are taken
From the plentiful field
And from the land of Moab;
I have caused wine to [T]fail from the
winepresses;
No one will tread with joyous
shouting—
Not joyous shouting! Joel 1:12 • *cease*

34 "From[R] the cry of Heshbon to [R]Elealeh
and to Jahaz Is. 15:4–6 • Num. 32:3, 37
They have uttered their voice,
[R]From Zoar to Horonaim, Is. 15:5, 6
Like a three-year-old heifer;
For the waters of Nimrim also shall be
desolate.

35 "Moreover," says the LORD,
"I will cause to cease in Moab
The one who offers *sacrifices* in the
[T]high places Places for pagan worship
And burns incense to his gods.

36 Therefore [R]My heart shall wail like
flutes for Moab, Is. 15:5; 16:11
And like flutes My heart shall wail
For the men of Kir Heres.
Therefore [R]the riches they have
acquired have perished. Is. 15:7

37 "For [R]every head *shall be* bald, and every
beard clipped; Is. 15:2, 3
On all the hands *shall be* cuts, and [R]on
the loins sackcloth— Gen. 37:34
38 A general lamentation
On all the [R]housetops of Moab,
And in its streets;
For I have [R]broken Moab like a vessel
in which *is* no pleasure," says the
LORD. Is. 15:3 • Jer. 22:28
39 "They shall wail:
'How she is broken down!
How Moab has turned her back with
shame!'
So Moab shall be a derision
And a dismay to all those about her."

40 For thus says the LORD:

"Behold, one shall fly like an eagle,
And [R]spread his wings over Moab. Is. 8:8
41 Kerioth is taken,
And the strongholds are surprised;
[R]The mighty men's hearts in Moab on
that day shall be
Like the heart of a woman in birth
pangs. Is. 13:8; 21:3
42 And Moab shall be destroyed [R]as a
people,
Because he has magnified *himself*
against the LORD. Ps. 83:4
43 [R]Fear and the pit and the snare *shall be*
upon you, Is. 24:17, 18
O inhabitant of Moab," says the LORD.
44 "He who flees from the fear shall fall
into the pit,
And he who gets out of the pit shall be
caught in the [R]snare.
For upon Moab, upon it [R]I will bring
The year of their punishment," says the
LORD. Is. 24:18 • Jer. 11:23

45 "Those who fled stood under the shadow
of Heshbon
Because of exhaustion.
But a fire shall come out of Heshbon,
A flame from the midst of [R]Sihon,
And [R]shall devour the brow of Moab,
The crown of the head of the sons of
tumult. Ps. 135:11 • Num. 24:17
46 [R]Woe to you, O Moab!
The people of Chemosh perish;
For your sons have been taken captive,
And your daughters captive. Num. 21:29
47 "Yet I will bring back the captives of
Moab
In the latter days," says the LORD.

Thus far *is* the judgment of Moab.

CHAPTER 49

Prophecies Against Ammon

AGAINST the Ammonites.
Thus says the LORD:

"Has Israel no sons?
Has he no heir?
Why *then* does [T]Milcom inherit Gad,
And his people dwell in its cities? *Molech*
2 [R]Therefore behold, the days are coming,"
says the LORD, Amos 1:13–15
"That I will cause to be heard an alarm
of war
In [R]Rabbah of the Ammonites;
It shall be a desolate mound,
And her [T]villages shall be burned with
fire. Ezek. 25:5 • Lit. *daughters*
Then Israel shall take possession of his
inheritance," says the LORD.

3 "Wail, O Heshbon, for Ai is plundered!
Cry, you daughters of Rabbah,
Gird yourselves with sackcloth!
Lament and run to and fro by the walls;
For [T]Milcom shall go into captivity
With his priests and his princes
together. An Ammonite god, *Molech*
4 Why [R]do you glory in the valleys,
[T]Your flowing valley, O backsliding
daughter? Jer. 9:23 • Lit. *Your valley is flowing*
Who trusted in her treasures, [R]*saying*,
'Who will come against me?' Jer. 21:13
5 Behold, I will bring fear upon you,"
Says the Lord GOD of hosts,
"From all those who are around you;
You shall be driven out, everyone
headlong,
And no one will gather those who
wander off.
6 But [R]afterward I will bring back
The captives of the people of Ammon,"
says the LORD. Jer. 48:47

Prophecies Against Edom

7 [R]Against Edom. Ezek. 25:12–14; 35:1–15
Thus says the LORD of hosts:

"*Is* wisdom no more in Teman?
[R]Has counsel perished from the prudent?
Has their wisdom vanished? Is. 19:11
8 Flee, turn back, dwell in the depths, O
inhabitants of [R]Dedan! Jer. 25:23
For I will bring the calamity of Esau
upon him,
The time *that* I will punish him.

9 If [R]grape-gatherers came to you,
Would they not leave *some* gleaning grapes?
If thieves by night,
Would they not destroy until they have enough? Obad. 5, 6
10 [R]But I have made Esau bare;
I have uncovered his secret places,
And he shall not be able to hide himself.
His descendants are plundered,
His brethren and his neighbors,
And [R]he *is* no more. Mal. 1:3 • Is. 17:14
11 Leave your fatherless children,
I will preserve *them* alive;
And let your widows trust in Me."

12 For thus says the LORD: "Behold, [R]those
whose judgment *was* not to drink of the cup
have assuredly drunk. And *are* you the one
who will altogether go unpunished? You shall
not go unpunished, but you shall surely drink
of it. Jer. 25:29
13 "For I have sworn by Myself," says the
LORD, "that Bozrah shall become a desolation, a reproach, a waste, and a curse. And all
its cities shall be perpetual wastes."

14 I have heard a [R]message from the LORD,
And an ambassador has been sent to the nations:
"Gather together, come against her,
And rise up to battle! Obad. 1–4

15 "For indeed, I will make you small among nations,
Despised among men.
16 Your fierceness has deceived you,
The [R]pride of your heart, Jer. 48:29
O you who dwell in the clefts of the rock,
Who hold the height of the hill!
[R]Though you make your [R]nest as high as the eagle, Obad. 3, 4 • Job 39:27
[R]I will bring you down from there," says the LORD. Amos 9:2

17 "Edom also shall be an astonishment;
[R]Everyone who goes by it will be astonished Jer. 18:16; 49:13; 50:13
And will hiss at all its plagues.
18 [R]As in the overthrow of Sodom and Gomorrah Deut. 29:23
And their neighboring *cities*," says the LORD,
"No one shall abide there,
Nor shall a son of man dwell in it.

19 "Behold,[R] he shall come up like a lion
from [R]the flooding of the Jordan
Against the habitation of the strong;
But I will suddenly make him run away from her. Jer. 50:44 • Jer. 12:5
And who *is* a chosen *man that* I may appoint over her?
For [R]who *is* like Me? Ex. 15:11
Who will arraign Me?
And [R]who *is* that shepherd Job 41:10
Who will withstand Me?"

20 [R]Therefore hear the counsel of the LORD that He has taken against Edom,
And His purposes that He has proposed against the inhabitants of Teman:
Surely the least of the flock shall [T]draw them out; Jer. 50:45 • Or *drag them away*
Surely He shall make their habitations desolate with them.
21 [R]The earth shakes at the noise of their fall;
At the cry its noise is heard at the Red Sea. Jer. 50:46
22 Behold, [R]He shall come up and fly like the eagle,
And spread His wings over Bozrah;
The heart of the mighty men of Edom in that day shall be
Like the heart of a woman in birth pangs. Jer. 48:40, 41

Prophecies Against Damascus

23 [R]Against Damascus. Amos 1:3, 5

[R]"Hamath and Arpad are shamed,
For they have heard bad news.
They are fainthearted; Jer. 39:5
[R]*There is* [T]trouble on the sea;
It cannot be quiet. [Is. 57:20] • *anxiety*
24 Damascus has grown feeble
And turns to flee,
And fear has seized *her*.
[R]Anguish and sorrows have taken her like a woman in [T]labor. Is. 13:8 • *childbirth*
25 Why is [R]the city of praise not deserted, the city of My joy? Jer. 33:9
26 [R]Therefore her young men shall fall in her streets, Jer. 50:30
And all the men of war shall be cut off in that day," says the LORD of hosts.
27 "I will kindle a [R]fire in the wall of Damascus,
And it shall consume the palaces of Ben-Hadad." Amos 1:4

Prophecies Against Kedar and Hazor

28 [R]Against Kedar and against the kingdoms of Hazor, which Nebuchadnezzar king
of Babylon shall strike. Ezek. 27:21
Thus says the LORD:

"Arise, go up to Kedar,
And devastate the men of the East!
29 Their [R]tents and their flocks they shall take away.
They shall take for themselves their curtains,
All their vessels and their camels;

And they shall cry out to them,
R'Fear *is* on every side!' Ps. 120:5 • Jer. 46:5

30 "Flee, get far away! Dwell in the depths,
O inhabitants of Hazor!" says the LORD.
"For Nebuchadnezzar king of Babylon
has taken counsel against you,
And has conceived a plan against you.

31 "Arise, go up to Rthe wealthy nation that
dwells securely," says the LORD,
"Which has neither gates nor bars,
RDwelling alone. Ezek. 38:11 • Num. 23:9
32 Their camels shall be for booty,
And the multitude of their cattle for
plunder.
I will Rscatter to all winds those in the
farthest corners, Ezek. 5:10
And I will bring their calamity from all
its sides," says the LORD.
33 "Hazor Rshall be a dwelling for jackals, a
desolation forever;
No one shall reside there,
Nor son of man dwell in it." Mal. 1:3

Prophecies Against Elam

34 The word of the LORD that came to
Jeremiah the prophet against RElam, in the
Rbeginning of the reign of Zedekiah king of
Judah, saying, Jer. 25:25 • 2 Kin. 24:17, 18
35 "Thus says the LORD of hosts:

'Behold, I will break the Tbow of Elam,
The foremost of their might. Power
36 Against Elam I will bring the four winds
From the four quarters of heaven,
And scatter them toward all those
winds;
There shall be no nations where the
outcasts of Elam will not go.
37 For I will cause Elam to be dismayed
before their enemies
And before those who seek their life.
RI will bring disaster upon them,
My fierce anger,' says the LORD;
'And I will send the sword after them
Until I have consumed them. Jer. 9:16
38 I will Rset My throne in Elam, Jer. 43:10
And will destroy from there the king
and the princes,' says the LORD.

39 'But it shall come to pass Rin the latter
days:
I will bring back the captives of Elam,'
says the LORD." Jer. 48:47

CHAPTER 50

Babylon's Defeat

THE word that the LORD spoke Ragainst
Babylon *and* against the land of the Chaldeans by Jeremiah the prophet. Is. 13:1; 47:1

2 "Declare among the nations,
Proclaim, and Tset up a standard; lift
Proclaim, *and* do not conceal *it*—
Say, 'Babylon is taken, Bel is shamed.
TMerodach is broken in pieces; Marduk
RHer idols are humiliated, Jer. 43:12, 13
Her images are broken in pieces.'
3 RFor out of the north Ra nation comes up
against her, Jer. 51:48 • Is. 13:17, 18, 20
Which shall make her land desolate,
And no one shall dwell therein.
They shall Tmove, they shall depart,
Both man and beast. Or *wander*

4 "In those days and in that time," says
the LORD,
"The children of Israel shall come,
RThey and the children of Judah
together; Hos. 1:11
RWith continual weeping they shall
come, Ezra 3:12, 13
RAnd seek the LORD their God. Hos. 3:5
5 They shall ask the way to Zion,
With their faces toward it, *saying,*
'Come and let us join ourselves to the
LORD
In Ra perpetual covenant Jer. 31:31
That will not be forgotten.'

6 "My people have been Rlost sheep.
Their shepherds have led them astray;
They have turned them away *on* Rthe
mountains. Is. 53:6 • [Jer. 2:20; 3:6, 23]
They have gone from mountain to hill;
They have forgotten their resting place.
7 All who found them have Rdevoured
them; Ps. 79:7
And Rtheir adversaries said, R'We have
not offended, Zech. 11:5 • Jer. 2:3
Because they have sinned against the
LORD, the habitation of justice,
The LORD, the hope of their fathers.'

8 "Move from the midst of Babylon,
Go out of the land of the Chaldeans;
And be like the rams before the flocks.
9 RFor behold, I will raise and cause to
come up against Babylon
An assembly of great nations from the
north country, Jer. 15:14; 51:27
And they shall array themselves against
her;
From there she shall be captured.
Their arrows *shall be* like *those* of an
expert warrior;
RNone shall return in vain. 2 Sam. 1:22
10 And Chaldea shall become plunder;
RAll who plunder her shall be satisfied,"
says the LORD. [Rev. 17:16]

11 "BecauseR you were glad, because you
rejoiced, Is. 47:6

You destroyers of My heritage,
Because you have grown fat [R]like a
heifer threshing grain, Hos. 10:11
And you bellow like bulls,
12 Your mother shall be deeply ashamed;
She who bore you shall be ashamed.
Behold, the least of the nations *shall be*
a [R]wilderness,
A dry land and a desert. Jer. 51:43
13 Because of the wrath of the LORD
She shall not be inhabited,
[R]But she shall be wholly desolate.
[R]Everyone who goes by Babylon shall be
horrified Jer. 25:12 • Jer. 49:17
And hiss at all her plagues.

14 "Put[R] yourselves in array against
Babylon all around, Jer. 51:2
All you who bend the bow;
Shoot at her, spare no arrows,
For she has sinned against the LORD.
15 Shout against her all around;
She has [R]given her hand, Lam. 5:6
Her foundations have fallen,
[R]Her walls are thrown down; Jer. 51:58
For [R]it *is* the vengeance of the LORD.
Take vengeance on her. Jer. 51:6, 11
As she has done, so do to her.
16 Cut off the sower from Babylon,
And him who handles the sickle at
harvest time.
For fear of the oppressing sword
Everyone shall turn to his own people,
And everyone shall flee to his own land.

17 "Israel *is* like scattered sheep;
The lions have driven *him* away.
First the king of Assyria devoured him;
Now at last this Nebuchadnezzar king
of Babylon has broken his bones."

18 Therefore thus says the LORD of hosts, the God of Israel:

"Behold, I will punish the king of
Babylon and his land,
As I have punished the king of Assyria.
19 [R]But I will bring back Israel to his
habitation,
And he shall feed on Carmel and
Bashan;
His soul shall be satisfied on Mount
Ephraim and Gilead. Is. 65:10
20 In those days and in that time," says
the LORD,
[R]"The iniquity of Israel shall be sought,
but *there shall be* none;
And the sins of Judah, but they shall
not be found;
For I will pardon those [R]whom I
preserve. [Jer. 31:34] • Is. 1:9

Babylon's Desolation

21 "Go up against the land of Merathaim,
against it,
And against the inhabitants of Pekod.
[T]Waste and utterly destroy them," says
the LORD, Or *Attack* with the sword
"And do [R]according to all that I have
commanded you. 2 Sam. 16:11
22 [R]A sound of battle *is* in the land,
And of great destruction. Jer. 51:54
23 How [R]the hammer of the whole earth
has been cut apart and broken!
How Babylon has become a desolation
among the nations!
I have laid a snare for you; Jer. 51:20–24
24 You have indeed been [R]trapped, O
Babylon,
And you were not aware;
You have been found and also caught,
Because you have [R]contended against
the LORD. Dan. 5:30 • [Is. 45:9]
25 The LORD has opened His armory,
And has brought out [R]the weapons of
His indignation;
For this *is* the work of the Lord GOD of
hosts
In the land of the Chaldeans. Is. 13:5
26 Come against her from the farthest
border;
Open her storehouses;
Cast her up as heaps of ruins,
And destroy her utterly;
Let nothing of her be left.
27 Slay all her [R]bulls,
Let them go down to the slaughter.
Woe to them!
For their day has come, the time of
[R]their punishment. Is. 34:7 • Jer. 48:44
28 The voice of those who flee and escape
from the land of Babylon
[R]Declares in Zion the vengeance of the
LORD our God,
The vengeance of His temple. Jer. 51:10

29 "Call together the archers against
Babylon.
All you who bend the bow, encamp
against it all around;
Let none of them escape.
[R]Repay her according to her work;
According to all she has done, do to
her; Jer. 51:56
[R]For she has been proud against the
LORD, [Is. 47:10]
Against the Holy One of Israel.
30 [R]Therefore her young men shall fall in
the streets, Jer. 49:26; 51:4
And all her men of war shall be cut off
in that day," says the LORD.
31 "Behold, I *am* against you,
O you most proud!" says the Lord GOD
of hosts;

"For your day has come,
The time *that* I will punish you.
32 The most [R]proud shall stumble and fall,
And no one will raise him up; Mal. 4:1
[R]I will kindle a fire in his cities, Jer. 21:14
And it will devour all around him."

33 Thus says the LORD of hosts:

"The children of Israel *were* oppressed,
Along with the children of Judah;
All who took them captive have held them fast;
They have refused to let them go.
34 [R]Their Redeemer *is* strong; Rev. 18:8
[R]The LORD of hosts *is* His name. Is. 47:4
He will thoroughly plead their case,
That He may give rest to the land,
And disquiet the inhabitants of Babylon.

35 "A sword *is* against the Chaldeans," says the LORD,
"Against the inhabitants of Babylon,
And [R]against her princes and [R]her wise men. Dan. 5:30 • Is. 47:13
36 A sword *is* [R]against the soothsayers, and they will be fools.
A sword *is* against her mighty men, and they will be dismayed. Is. 44:25
37 A sword *is* against their horses,
Against their chariots,
And against all [R]the mixed peoples who *are* in her midst;
And [R]they will become like women.
A sword *is* against her treasures, and they will be robbed. Jer. 25:20 • Jer. 51:30
38 [R]A drought *is* against her waters, and they will be dried up. Rev. 16:12
For it *is* the land of carved images,
And they are insane with *their* idols.

39 "Therefore[R] the wild desert beasts shall dwell *there* with the jackals,
And the ostriches shall dwell in it.
[R]It shall be inhabited no more forever,
Nor shall it be dwelt in from generation to generation. Rev. 18:2 • Is. 13:20
40 [R]As God overthrew Sodom and Gomorrah Is. 13:19
And their neighboring *cities*," says the LORD,
"*So* no one shall reside there,
Nor son of man [R]dwell in it. Is. 13:20

41 "Behold,[R] a people shall come from the north,
And a great nation and many kings
Shall be raised up from the ends of the earth. Jer. 6:22; 25:14; 51:27
42 [R]They shall hold the bow and the lance;
[R]They *are* cruel and shall not show mercy. Jer. 6:23 • Is. 13:18
[R]Their voice shall roar like the sea;
They shall ride on horses, Is. 5:30
Set in array, like a man for the battle,
Against you, O daughter of Babylon.

43 "The king of Babylon has [R]heard the report about them, Jer. 51:31
And his hands grow feeble;
Anguish has taken hold of him,
Pangs as of a woman in childbirth.

44 "Behold,[R] he shall come up like a lion from the flooding of the Jordan
Against the habitation of the strong;
But I will make them suddenly run away from her. Jer. 49:19–21
And who *is* a chosen *man that* I may appoint over her?
For who *is* like Me?
Who will arraign Me?
And [R]who *is* that shepherd Job 41:10
Who will withstand Me?"

45 Therefore hear the counsel of the LORD that He has taken against Babylon,
And His [R]purposes that He has proposed against the land of the Chaldeans:
[R]Surely the least of the flock shall draw them out; Jer. 51:29 • Jer. 49:19, 20
Surely He will make their habitation desolate with them.
46 [R]At the noise of the taking of Babylon
The earth trembles, Rev. 18:9
And the cry is heard among the nations.

CHAPTER 51

Babylon's Destiny

THUS says the LORD:

"Behold, I will raise up against Babylon,
Against those who dwell in [T]Leb Kamai,
A destroying wind. A code word for *Chaldea*
2 And I will send [R]winnowers to Babylon,
Who shall winnow her and empty her land. Jer. 15:7
[R]For in the day of doom Jer. 50:14
They shall be against her all around.
3 Against *her* [R]let the archer bend his bow, Jer. 50:14, 29
And lift himself up against *her* in his armor.
Do not spare her young men;
[R]Utterly destroy all her army. Jer. 50:21
4 Thus the slain shall fall in the land of the Chaldeans,
And *those* thrust through in her streets.
5 For Israel is not forsaken, nor Judah,
By his God, the LORD of hosts,
Though their land was filled with sin against the Holy One of Israel."

6 [R]Flee from the midst of Babylon,
And every one save his life!

Do not be cut off in her iniquity,
For [R]this *is* the time of the LORD's vengeance; Rev. 18:4 • Jer. 50:15
[R]He shall recompense her. Jer. 25:14
7 [R]Babylon *was* a golden cup in the LORD's hand, Rev. 17:4
That made all the earth drunk.
[R]The nations drank her wine; Rev. 14:8
Therefore the nations are deranged.
8 Babylon has suddenly [R]fallen and been destroyed. Is. 21:9
[R]Wail for her! Rev. 18:9, 11, 19
[R]Take balm for her pain; Jer. 46:11
Perhaps she may be healed.

9 We would have healed Babylon,
But she is not healed.
Forsake her, and [R]let us go everyone to his own country; Is. 13:14
[R]For her judgment reaches to heaven and is lifted up to the skies. Rev. 18:5
10 The LORD has [R]revealed our righteousness. Ps. 37:6
Come and let us [R]declare in Zion the work of the LORD our God. Jer. 50:28

11 [T]Make the arrows bright! *Polish the arrows*
Gather the shields!
[R]The LORD has raised up the spirit of the kings of the Medes. Is. 13:17
[R]For His plan *is* against Babylon to destroy it, Jer. 50:45
Because it *is* [R]the vengeance of the LORD, Jer. 50:28
The vengeance for His temple.
12 [R]Set up the standard on the walls of Babylon;
Make the guard strong,
Set up the watchmen,
Prepare the ambushes.
For the LORD has both devised and done
What He spoke against the inhabitants of Babylon. Nah. 2:1; 3:14
13 [R]O you who dwell by many waters,
Abundant in treasures, Rev. 17:1, 15
Your end has come,
The measure of your covetousness.
14 [R]The LORD of hosts has sworn by Himself:
"Surely I will fill you with men, [R]as with locusts,
And they shall lift [R]up a shout against you." Jer. 49:13 • Nah. 3:15 • Jer. 50:15

15 [R]He has made the earth by His power;
He has established the world by His wisdom,
And [R]stretched out the heaven by His understanding. Gen. 1:1, 6 • Job 9:8
16 When He utters *His* voice—
There is a multitude of waters in the heavens:
[R]"He causes the vapors to ascend from the ends of the earth;
He makes lightnings for the rain;
He brings the wind out of His treasures." Ps. 135:7

17 [R]Everyone is dull-hearted, without knowledge; Jer. 10:14
Every metalsmith is put to shame by the carved image;
[R]For his molded image *is* falsehood,
And *there is* no breath in them. Jer. 50:2
18 They *are* futile, a work of errors;
In the time of their punishment they shall perish.
19 The Portion of Jacob *is* not like them,
For He *is* the Maker of all things;
And *Israel is* the tribe of His inheritance.
The LORD of hosts *is* His name.

20 "You[R] *are* My battle-ax *and* weapons of war: Is. 10:5, 15
For with you I will break the nation in pieces;
With you I will destroy kingdoms;
21 With you I will break in pieces the horse and its rider;
With you I will break in pieces the chariot and its rider;
22 With you also I will break in pieces man and woman;
With you I will break in pieces [R]old and young;
With you I will break in pieces the young man and the maiden; 2 Chr. 36:17
23 With you also I will break in pieces the shepherd and his flock;
With you I will break in pieces the farmer and his yoke of oxen;
And with you I will break in pieces governors and rulers.

24 "And[R] I will repay Babylon Jer. 50:15, 29
And all the inhabitants of Chaldea
For all the evil they have done
In Zion in your sight," says the LORD.

25 "Behold, I *am* against you, [R]O destroying mountain, Zech. 4:7
Who destroys all the earth," says the LORD.
"And I will stretch out My hand against you,
Roll you down from the rocks,
And make you a burnt mountain.
26 They shall not take from you a stone for a corner
Nor a stone for a foundation,
[R]But you shall be desolate forever," says the LORD. Jer. 50:26, 40

27 [R]Set up a banner in the land, Is. 13:2
Blow the trumpet among the nations!

[R]Prepare the nations against her,
Call [R]the kingdoms together against her: Jer. 25:14 • Jer. 50:41, 42
Ararat, Minni, and Ashkenaz.
Appoint a marshal against her;
Cause the horses to come up like the bristling locusts.
28 Prepare against her the nations,
With the kings of the Medes,
Its governors and all its rulers,
All the land of his dominion.
29 And the land will tremble and sorrow;
For every [R]purpose of the LORD shall be performed against Babylon, Jer. 50:45
[R]To make the land of Babylon a desolation without inhabitant. Jer. 50:13
30 The mighty men of Babylon have ceased fighting,
They have remained in their strongholds;
Their might has failed,
[R]They became *like* women; Is. 19:16
They have burned her dwelling places,
[R]The bars of her *gate* are broken. Lam. 2:9
31 [R]One runner will run to meet another,
And one messenger to meet another,
To show the king of Babylon that his city is taken on *all* sides; Jer. 50:24
32 [R]The passages are blocked, Jer. 50:38
The reeds they have burned with fire,
And the men of war are terrified.

33 For thus says the LORD of hosts, the God of Israel:

"The daughter of Babylon *is* [R]like a threshing floor Is. 21:10
When [R]*it is* time to thresh her;
Yet a little while Hab. 3:12
And the time of her harvest will come."

34 "Nebuchadnezzar the king of Babylon
Has [R]devoured me, he has crushed me;
He has made me an [R]empty vessel,
He has swallowed me up like a monster;
He has filled his stomach with my delicacies,
He has spit me out. Jer. 50:17 • Is. 24:1–3
35 Let the violence *done* to me and my flesh *be* upon Babylon,"
The inhabitant of Zion will say;
"And my blood be upon the inhabitants of Chaldea!"
Jerusalem will say.

36 Therefore thus says the LORD:

"Behold, [R]I will plead your case and take vengeance for you.
[R]I will dry up her sea and make her springs dry. Jer. 50:34 • Jer. 50:38
37 [R]Babylon shall become a heap, Is. 13:22
A dwelling place for jackals,
[R]An astonishment and a hissing,
Without an inhabitant. Jer. 25:9, 11
38 They shall roar together like lions,
They shall growl like lions' whelps.
39 In their excitement I will prepare their feasts;
[R]I will make them drunk, Jer. 51:57
That they may rejoice,
And sleep a perpetual sleep
And not awake," says the LORD.
40 "I will bring them down
Like lambs to the slaughter,
Like rams with male goats.

41 "Oh, how [T]Sheshach is taken!
Oh, how the praise of the whole earth is seized! A code word for *Babylon,* Jer. 25:26
How Babylon has become desolate among the nations!
42 [R]The sea has come up over Babylon;
She is covered with the multitude of its waves. Is. 8:7, 8
43 [R]Her cities are a desolation, Jer. 50:39, 40
A dry land and a wilderness,
A land where [R]no one dwells, Is. 13:20
Through which no son of man passes.
44 I will punish [T]Bel in Babylon,
And I will bring out of his mouth what he has swallowed; A Babylonian god
And the nations shall not stream to him anymore.
Yes, the wall of Babylon shall fall.

45 "My people, go out of the midst of her!
And let everyone deliver [T]himself from the fierce anger of the LORD. Lit. *his soul*
46 And lest your heart faint,
And you fear [R]for the rumor that *will be* heard in the land
(A rumor will come *one* year,
And after that, in *another* year
A rumor *will come,*
And violence in the land,
Ruler against ruler), 2 Kin. 19:7
47 Therefore behold, the days are coming
That I will bring judgment on the carved images of Babylon;
Her whole land shall be ashamed,
And all her slain shall fall in her midst.
48 Then [R]the heavens and the earth and all that *is* in them Is. 44:23; 48:20; 49:13
Shall sing joyously over Babylon;
For the plunderers shall come to her from the north," says the LORD.

49 As Babylon *has caused* the slain of Israel to fall,
So at Babylon the slain of all the earth shall fall.
50 [R]You who have escaped the sword,
Get away! Do not stand still! Jer. 44:28
Remember the LORD afar off,
And let Jerusalem come to your mind.

51 [R]We are ashamed because we have heard
reproach. Ps. 44:15; 79:4
Shame has covered our faces,
For strangers have come into the
sanctuaries of the LORD's house.

52 "Therefore behold, the days are coming,"
says the LORD,
"That I will bring judgment on her
carved images,
And throughout all her land the
wounded shall groan.
53 [R]Though Babylon were to [T]mount up to
heaven,
And though she were to fortify the
height of her strength,
Yet from Me plunderers would come to
her," says the LORD. Amos 9:2 • *ascend*

54 [R]The sound of a cry *comes* from
Babylon,
And great destruction from the land of
the Chaldeans, Jer. 50:22
55 Because the LORD is plundering Babylon
And silencing her loud voice,
Though her waves roar like great
waters,
And the noise of their voice is uttered,
56 Because the plunderer comes against
her, against Babylon,
And her mighty men are taken.
Every one of their bows is broken;
[R]For the LORD *is* the God of recompense,
He will surely repay. Jer. 50:29

57 "And I will make drunk
Her princes and [R]wise men,
Her governors, her deputies, and her
mighty men. Jer. 50:35
And they shall sleep a perpetual sleep
And not awake," says the King,
Whose name *is* the LORD of hosts.

58 Thus says the LORD of hosts:

"The broad walls of Babylon shall be
utterly [T]broken, Lit. *laid utterly bare*
And her high gates shall be burned with
fire;
[R]The people will labor in vain, Hab. 2:13
And the nations, because of the fire;
And they shall be weary."

59 The word which Jeremiah the prophet
commanded Seraiah the son of [R]Neriah, the
son of Mahseiah, when he went with Zedekiah the king of Judah to Babylon in the
fourth year of his reign. And Seraiah *was* the
quartermaster. Jer. 32:12
60 So Jeremiah wrote in a book all the evil
that would come upon Babylon, all these
words that are written against Babylon.
61 And Jeremiah said to Seraiah, "When
you arrive in Babylon and see it, and read all
these words,
62 "then you shall say, 'O LORD, You have
spoken against this place to cut it off, so that
none shall remain in it, neither man nor
beast, but it shall be desolate forever.'
63 "Now it shall be, when you have finished
reading this book, *that* you shall tie a stone to
it and throw it out into the Euphrates.
64 "Then you shall say, 'Thus Babylon shall
sink and not rise from the catastrophe that I
will bring upon her. And they shall be
weary.'" Thus far *are* the words of Jeremiah.

CHAPTER 52

The Capture of Jerusalem
2 Kin. 24:18—25:30; 2 Chr. 36:11–20; Jer. 39:1–8

ZEDEKIAH *was* [R]twenty-one years old
when he became king, and he reigned
eleven years in Jerusalem. His mother's name
was Hamutal the daughter of Jeremiah of
[R]Libnah. 2 Kin. 24:18 • Josh. 10:29
2 He also did evil in the sight of the LORD,
according to all that Jehoiakim had done.
3 For because of the anger of the LORD *this*
happened in Jerusalem and Judah, till He
finally cast them out from His presence. Then
Zedekiah [R]rebelled against the king of Babylon. 2 Chr. 36:13
4 Now it came to pass in the [R]ninth year of
his reign, in the tenth month, on the tenth
day of the month, *that* Nebuchadnezzar king
of Babylon and all his army came against
Jerusalem and encamped against it; and *they*
built a siege wall against it all around. Jer. 39:1
5 So the city was besieged until the eleventh year of King Zedekiah.
6 By the fourth month, on the ninth day of
the month, the famine had become so severe
in the city that there was no food for the
people of the land.
7 Then the city wall was broken through,
and all the men of war fled and went out of
the city at night by way of the gate between
the two walls, which *was* by the king's garden, even though the Chaldeans *were* near
the city all around. And they went by way of
the [T]plain. Or *Arabah*, the Jordan Valley
8 But the army of the Chaldeans pursued
the king, and they overtook Zedekiah in the
plains of Jericho. All his army was scattered
from him.
9 [R]So they took the king and brought him
up to the king of Babylon at Riblah in the
land of Hamath, and he pronounced judgment on him. Jer. 32:4; 39:5
10 [R]Then the king of Babylon killed the sons
of Zedekiah before his eyes. And he killed all
the princes of Judah in Riblah. Ezek. 12:13
11 He also put out the eyes of Zedekiah;
and the king of Babylon bound him in bronze
fetters, took him to Babylon, and put him in
prison till the day of his death.

The Destruction of Jerusalem

12 [R]Now in the fifth month, on the tenth
day of the month ([R]which *was* the nineteenth
year of King Nebuchadnezzar king of Babylon), [R]Nebuzaradan, the captain of the
guard, *who* served the king of Babylon, came
to Jerusalem. 2 Kin. 25:8–21 • Jer. 52:29 • Jer. 39:9
13 He burned the house of the LORD and the
king's house; all the houses of Jerusalem,
that is, all the houses of the great *men*, he
burned with fire.
14 And all the army of the Chaldeans who
were with the captain of the guard broke
down all the walls of Jerusalem all around.
15 [R]Then Nebuzaradan the captain of the
guard carried away captive *some* of the poor
people, the rest of the people who remained
in the city, the defectors who had deserted to
the king of Babylon, and the rest of the
craftsmen. Jer. 39:9
16 But Nebuzaradan the captain of the
guard left *some* of the poor of the land as
vinedressers and farmers.
17 [R]The bronze pillars that *were* in the
house of the LORD, and the carts and the
bronze Sea that *were* in the house of the
LORD, the Chaldeans broke in pieces, and
carried all their bronze to Babylon. Jer. 27:19
18 They also took away [R]the pots, the shovels, the trimmers, the [T]bowls, the spoons, and
all the bronze utensils with which the priests
ministered. Ex. 27:3 • *basins*
19 The basins, the firepans, the bowls, the
pots, the lampstands, the spoons, and the
cups, whatever *was* of solid gold and whatever *was* of solid silver, the captain of the
guard took away.
20 The two pillars, one Sea, the twelve
bronze bulls which *were* under *it, and* the
carts, which King Solomon had made for the
house of the LORD—[R]the bronze of all these
articles was beyond measure. 1 Kin. 7:47
21 Now *concerning* the [R]pillars: the height
of one pillar *was* [T]eighteen cubits, a measuring line of twelve cubits could measure its
circumference, and its thickness *was* [T]four
fingers; *it was* hollow. 2 Kin. 25:17 • 27 ft. • 3 in.
22 A capital of bronze *was* on it; and the
height of one capital *was* [T]five cubits, with a
network and pomegranates all around the
capital, all of bronze. The second pillar, with
pomegranates was the same. 7.5 ft.
23 There were ninety-six pomegranates on
the sides; [R]all the pomegranates, all around
on the network, *were* one hundred. 1 Kin. 7:20

The Exile to Babylon

24 The captain of the guard took Seraiah
the chief priest, [R]Zephaniah the second priest,
and the three doorkeepers. Jer. 21:1; 29:25
25 He also took out of the city an [T]officer
who had charge of the men of war, seven
men of the king's close associates who were
found in the city, the principal scribe of the
army who mustered the people of the land,
and sixty men of the people of the land who
were found in the midst of the city. Lit. *eunuch*
26 And Nebuzaradan the captain of the
guard took these and brought them to the
king of Babylon at Riblah.
27 Then the king of Babylon struck them
and put them to death at Riblah in the land of
Hamath. Thus Judah was carried away captive from its own land.
28 These *are* the people whom Nebuchadnezzar carried away captive: in the seventh
year, three thousand and twenty-three Jews;
29 [R]in the eighteenth year of Nebuchadnezzar he carried away captive from Jerusalem
eight hundred and thirty-two persons; Jer. 39:9
30 in the twenty-third year of Nebuchadnezzar, Nebuzaradan the captain of the
guard carried away captive of the Jews seven
hundred and forty-five persons. All the persons *were* four thousand six hundred.

The Liberation of Jehoiachin

31 Now it came to pass in the thirty-seventh
year of the captivity of Jehoiachin king of
Judah, in the twelfth month, on the twenty-
fifth *day* of the month, *that* Evil-Merodach
king of Babylon, in the first *year* of his reign,
lifted up the head of Jehoiachin king of Judah
and brought him out of prison.
32 And he spoke kindly to him and gave
him a more prominent seat than those of the
kings who *were* with him in Babylon.
33 So [T]Jehoiachin changed from his prison
garments, and he ate bread regularly before
the king all the days of his life. Lit. *he*
34 And as for his provisions, there was a
regular ration given him by the king of
Babylon, a portion for each day until the day
of his death, all the days of his life.

THE BOOK OF

LAMENTATIONS

THE BOOK OF LAMENTATIONS

Lamentations describes the funeral of a city. It is a tearstained portrait of the once proud Jerusalem, now reduced to rubble by the invading Babylonian hordes. In a five-poem dirge, Jeremiah exposes his emotions. A death has occurred; Jerusalem lies barren.

Jeremiah writes his lament in acrostic or alphabetical fashion. Beginning each chapter with the first letter *A* (aleph) he progresses verse by verse through the Hebrew alphabet, literally weeping from *A* to *Z*. And then, in the midst of this terrible holocaust, Jeremiah triumphantly cries out, "Great *is* Your faithfulness" (3:23). In the face of death and destruction, with life seemingly coming apart, Jeremiah turns tragedy into a triumph of faith. God has never failed him in the past. God has promised to remain faithful in the future. In the light of the God he knows and loves, Jeremiah finds hope and comfort.

The Hebrew title of this book comes from the first word of chapters 1, 2, and 4: *Ekah*, "Ah, how!" Another Hebrew word *Ginoth* ("Elegies" or "Lamentations") has also been used as the title because it better represents the contents of the book. The Greek title *Threnoi* means "Dirges" or "Laments," and the Latin title *Threni* ("Tears" or "Lamentations") was derived from this word. The subtitle in Jerome's Vulgate reads: *"Id est lamentationes Jeremiae prophetae,"* and this became the basis for the English title "The Lamentations of Jeremiah."

THE AUTHOR OF LAMENTATIONS

The author of Lamentations is unnamed in the book, but internal and external evidence is consistently in favor of Jeremiah.

External Evidence: The universal consensus of early Jewish and Christian tradition attributes this book to Jeremiah. The superscription to Lamentations in the Septuagint says: "And it came to pass, after Israel had been carried away captive, and Jerusalem had become desolate, that Jeremiah sat weeping, and lamented with this lamentation over Jerusalem, saying. . . ." This is also the position of the Talmud, the Aramaic Targum of Jonathan, and early Christian writers, such as Origen and Jerome. In addition, Second Chronicles 35:25 says that "Jeremiah also lamented for Josiah." This was an earlier occasion, but Jeremiah was obviously familiar with the lament form.

Internal Evidence: The scenes in this graphic book were clearly portrayed by an eyewitness to Jerusalem's siege and fall soon after the destruction took place (cf. 1:13–15; 2:6, 9; 4:1–12). Jeremiah witnessed the fall of Jerusalem and remained behind after the captives were deported (see Jer. 39). Although some critics claim that the style of Lamentations is different from the Book of Jeremiah, the similarities are, in fact, striking and numerous, especially in the poetic sections of Jeremiah. Compare these passages from Lamentations and Jeremiah: 1:2 (Jer. 30:14); 1:15 (Jer. 8:21); 1:16 and 2:11 (Jer. 9:1, 18); 2:22 (Jer. 6:25); 4:21 (Jer. 49:12). The same compassion, sympathy, and grief over Judah's downfall are evident in both books.

THE TIME OF LAMENTATIONS

The historical background of Lamentations can be found in "The Time of Jeremiah." The book was written soon after Jerusalem's destruction (Jer. 39; 52) at the beginning of the Exile. Nebuchadnezzar laid siege to Jerusalem from January 588 B.C. to July 586 B.C. It fell on July 19, and the city and temple were burned on August 15. Jeremiah probably wrote these five elegies before he was taken captive to Egypt by his disobedient countrymen not long after the destruction (Jer. 43:1–7).

THE CHRIST OF LAMENTATIONS

The weeping prophet Jeremiah is a type of Christ, the Prophet who wept over the same city six centuries later. "O Jerusalem, Jerusalem, the one who kills the prophets and stones those who are sent to her! How often I wanted to gather your children together, as a hen gathers her chicks under *her* wings, but you were not willing! See! Your house is left to you desolate" (Matt. 23:37, 38). Like Christ, Jeremiah identified himself personally with the plight of Jerusalem and with human suffering caused by sin.

Lamentations also includes elements that typify Christ's life and ministry as the man of sorrows who was acquainted with grief. He was afflicted (1:12; 3:19), despised, and derided by His enemies (2:15, 16; 3:14, 30).

KEYS TO LAMENTATIONS

Key Word: Lamentations—Three themes run through the five laments of Jeremiah. The most prominent is the theme of mourning over Jerusalem's holocaust. The Holy City has been laid waste and desolate: God's promised judgment for sin has come. In his sorrow, Jeremiah speaks for himself, for the captives, and sometimes for the personified city. The second theme is a confession of sin and an acknowledgment of God's righteous and holy judgment upon

Judah. The third theme is least prominent but very important: it is a note of hope in God's future restoration of His people. Yahweh has poured out His wrath, but in His mercy He will be faithful to His covenant promises.

Key Verses: Lamentations 2:5, 6 and 3:22, 23—"The Lord was like an enemy. He has swallowed up Israel, He has swallowed up all her palaces; He has destroyed her strongholds, and has increased mourning and lamentation in the daughter of Judah. He has done violence to His tabernacle, *as if it were* a garden; He has destroyed His place of assembly; the LORD has caused the appointed feasts and Sabbaths to be forgotten in Zion. In His burning indignation He has spurned the king and the priest" (2:5, 6).

"*Through* the LORD's mercies we are not consumed, because His compassions fail not. *They are* new every morning; great *is* Your faithfulness" (3:22, 23).

Key Chapter: Lamentations 3—In the midst of five chapters of ruin, destruction, and utter hopelessness, Jeremiah rises and grasps with strong faith the promises and character of God.

Lamentations 3:22–25 expresses a magnificent faith in the mercy of God—especially when placed against the dark backdrop of chapters 1, 2, 4, and 5.

SURVEY OF LAMENTATIONS

For forty years Jeremiah suffers rejection and abuse for his warnings of coming judgment. When Nebuchadnezzar finally comes and destroys Jerusalem in 586 B.C., a lesser man might say, "I told you so!" But Jeremiah compassionately identifies with the tragic overthrow of Jerusalem and composes five beautiful and emotional lament poems as a requiem for the once proud city. These dirges reflect the tender heart of the man who was divinely commissioned to communicate a harsh message to a sinful and stiff-necked people. The city, the temple, the palace, and the walls have been reduced to rubble and its inhabitants have been deported to distant Babylon. Jeremiah's five mournful poems can be entitled: the destruction of Jerusalem (1), the anger of Yahweh (2), the prayer for mercy (3), the siege of Jerusalem (4), and the prayer for restoration (5).

The Destruction of Jerusalem (1): This poem consists of a lamentation by Jeremiah (1:1–11) and a lamentation by the personified Jerusalem (1:12–22). The city has been left desolate because of its grievous sins, and her enemies "mocked at her downfall" (1:7). Jerusalem pleads with God to regard her misery and repay her adversaries.

The Anger of Yahweh (2): In his second elegy, Jeremiah moves from Jerusalem's desolation to a description of her destruction. Babylon has destroyed the city, but only as the Lord's instrument of judgment. Jeremiah presents an eyewitness account of the thoroughness and severity of Jerusalem's devastation. Through the Babylonians, God has terminated all religious observances, removed the priests, prophets, and kings, and razed the temple and palaces. Jeremiah grieves over the suffering the people brought on themselves through rebellion against God, and Jerusalem's supplications complete the lament.

The Prayer for Mercy (3): In the first eighteen verses, Jeremiah enters into the miseries and despair of his people and makes them his own. However, there is an abrupt turn in verses 19–39 as the prophet reflects on the faithfulness and loyal love of the compassionate God of Israel. These truths enable him to find comfort and hope in spite of his dismal circumstances. Jeremiah expresses his deep sorrow and petitions God for deliverance and for God to avenge Jerusalem's misery.

The Siege of Jerusalem (4): The prophet rehearses the siege of Jerusalem and remembers the suffering and starvation of rich and poor. He also reviews the causes of the siege, especially the sins of the prophets and priests and their foolish trust

FOCUS	DESTRUCTION OF JERUSALEM	ANGER OF JEHOVAH	PRAYER FOR MERCY	SIEGE OF JERUSALEM	PRAYER FOR RESTORATION
REFERENCE	1:1—	2:1—	3:1—	4:1—	5:1—5:22
DIVISION	MOURNING CITY	BROKEN PEOPLE	SUFFERING PROPHET	RUINED KINGDOM	PENITENT NATION
TOPIC	GRIEF	CAUSE	HOPE	REPENTANCE	PRAYER
LOCATION	JERUSALEM				
TIME	c. 586 B.C.				

in human aid. This poem closes with a warning to Edom of future punishment and a glimmer of hope for Jerusalem.

The Prayer for Restoration (5): Jeremiah's last elegy is a melancholy description of his people's lamentable state. Their punishment is complete, and Jeremiah prayerfully desires the restoration of his nation.

OUTLINE OF LAMENTATIONS

I. The Destruction of Jerusalem 1:1–22
- A. The Lament of the Prophet Jeremiah 1:1–11
  - 1. The Desolation of Jerusalem 1:1–7
  - 2. The Cause of Jerusalem's Desolation 1:8–11
- B. The Lament of the City Jerusalem ... 1:12–22
  - 1. The Contrition of Jerusalem 1:12–19
  - 2. The Confession of Jerusalem...... 1:20–22

II. The Anger of God.......................... 2:1–22
- A. The Anger of God.......................... 2:1–9
- B. The Agony of Jerusalem 2:10–17
- C. The Appeal of Jerusalem............. 2:18–22

III. The Prayer for Mercy.................... 3:1–66
- A. Jeremiah's Cry of Despair.............. 3:1–18
- B. Jeremiah's Confession of Faith....... 3:19–39
- C. Jeremiah's Condition of Need 3:40–54
- D. Jeremiah's Confidence in God 3:55–66

IV. The Siege of Jerusalem...................... 4:1–22
- A. The Conditions During the Siege...... 4:1–10
- B. The Cause of the Siege.................... 4:11–20
- C. The Consequences of the Siege...... 4:21, 22

V. The Prayer for Restoration.............. 5:1–22
- A. The Review of the Need for Restoration........................... 5:1–15
- B. The Repentance of Sin.................. 5:16–18
- C. The Request for Restoration........... 5:19–22

CHAPTER 1

The Desolation of Jerusalem

HOW lonely sits the city
That was full of people!
[R]*How* like a widow is she, Is. 47:7–9
Who *was* great among the nations!
The princess among the provinces
Has become a [T]slave! Lit. *forced laborer*

2 She [R]weeps bitterly in the [R]night,
Her tears *are* on her cheeks;
Among all her lovers
She has none to comfort *her.*
All her friends have dealt treacherously
with her; Jer. 13:17 • Job 7:3
They have become her enemies.

3 [R]Judah has gone into captivity, Jer. 52:27
Under affliction and hard servitude;
[R]She dwells among the [T]nations,
She finds no [R]rest;
All her persecutors overtake her in dire
straits. Lam. 2:9 • *Gentiles* • Deut. 28:65

4 The roads to Zion mourn
Because no one comes to the [T]set feasts.
All her gates are [R]desolate;
Her priests sigh,
Her virgins are afflicted,
And she *is* in bitterness. *appointed* • Is. 27:10

5 Her adversaries [R]have become [T]the
master, Deut. 28:43 • Lit. *her head*
Her enemies prosper;
For the LORD has afflicted her
[R]Because of the multitude of her
transgressions. Dan. 9:7, 16
Her [R]children have gone into captivity
before the enemy. Jer. 52:28

6 And from the daughter of Zion
All her splendor has departed.
Her princes have become like deer
That find no pasture,
That [T]flee without strength
Before the pursuer. Lit. *are gone*

7 In the days of her affliction and
roaming,
Jerusalem [R]remembers all her pleasant
things Ps. 137:1
That she had in the days of old.
When her people fell into the hand of
the enemy,
With no one to help her,
The adversaries saw her
And mocked at her *downfall.

The Cause of Jerusalem's Desolation

8 [R]Jerusalem has sinned grievously,
Therefore she has become *vile.
All who honored her despise her
Because they have seen her nakedness;
Yes, she sighs and turns away. [1 Kin. 8:46]

1:7 Vg. *Sabbaths* 1:8 LXX, Vg. *moved* or *removed*

9 Her uncleanness *is* in her skirts;
She [R]did not consider her destiny;
Therefore her collapse was awesome;
She had no comforter. Is. 47:7
"O LORD, behold my affliction,
For *the* enemy has magnified *himself!*"

10 The adversary has spread his hand
Over all her [T]pleasant things; *desirable*
For she has seen [R]the nations enter her
[T]sanctuary, Jer. 51:51 • *holy place,* The temple
Those whom You commanded
[R]Not to enter Your congregation. Deut. 23:3

11 All her people sigh,
[R]They [T]seek bread; Jer. 38:9; 52:6 • *hunt food*
They have given their [T]valuables for
food to restore life. *desirable things*
"See, O LORD, and consider,
For I am scorned."

The Contrition of Jerusalem

12 "*Is it* nothing to you, all you who pass
by?
Behold and see
[R]If there is any sorrow like my sorrow,
Which has been brought on me,
Which the LORD has inflicted *on me*
In the day of His fierce anger. Dan. 9:12

13 "From above He has sent fire into my
bones,
And it overpowered them;
He has [R]spread a net for my feet
And turned me back;
He has made me desolate
And faint all the day. Ezek. 12:13; 17:20

14 "The[R] yoke of my transgressions was
bound;
They were woven together by His
hands,
And thrust upon my neck.
He made my strength fail;
The Lord delivered me into the hands of
those whom I am not able to
withstand. Deut. 28:48

15 "The Lord has trampled underfoot all my
mighty *men* in my midst;
He has called an assembly against me
To crush my young men;
[R]The Lord trampled *as* in a winepress
The virgin daughter of Judah. [Rev. 14:19]

16 "For these *things* I weep;
My eye, [R]my eye overflows with water;
Because the comforter, who should
restore my life,
Is far from me.
My children are desolate
Because the enemy prevailed." Eccl. 4:1

17 [R]Zion [T]spreads out her hands,
But there is no one to comfort her;
The LORD has commanded concerning
Jacob
That those [R]around him *become* his
adversaries;
Jerusalem has become an unclean thing
among them. Jer. 4:31 • Prays • 2 Kin. 24:2–4

18 "The LORD is [R]righteous, Dan. 9:7, 14
For I rebelled against His
[T]commandment. Lit. *mouth*
Hear now, all peoples,
And behold my sorrow;
My virgins and my young men
Have gone into captivity.

19 "I called for my lovers,
But they deceived me;
My priests and my elders
Breathed their last in the city,
While they sought food
To restore their life.

The Confession of Jerusalem

20 "See, O LORD, that I *am* in distress;
My [T]soul is troubled; Lit. *inward parts*
My heart is overturned within me,
For I have been very rebellious.
[R]Outside the sword bereaves, Ezek. 7:15
At home *it is* like death.

21 "They have heard that I sigh,
With no one to comfort me.
All my enemies have heard of my
trouble;
They are [R]glad that You have done *it*.
Bring on [R]the day *that* You have
[T]announced, Ps. 35:15 • [Jer. 46] • *proclaimed*
That they may become like me.

22 "Let[R] all their wickedness come before
You,
And do to them as You have done to
me
For all my transgressions;
For my sighs *are* many,
And my heart *is* faint." Ps. 109:15; 137:7, 8

CHAPTER 2

The Anger of God

HOW the Lord has covered the daughter
of Zion
With a [R]cloud in His anger! [Lam. 3:44]
[R]He cast down from heaven to the earth
[R]The beauty of Israel, Matt. 11:23 • 2 Sam. 1:19
And did not remember [R]His footstool
In the day of His anger. Ps. 99:5

2 The Lord has swallowed up and has
[R]not pitied

All the habitations of Jacob.
He has thrown down in His wrath
The strongholds of the daughter of Judah;
He has brought *them* down to the ground;
[R]He has profaned the kingdom and its princes. Lam. 3:43 • Ps. 89:39, 40

3 He has cut off in fierce anger
Every [T]horn of Israel; Strength
[R]He has drawn back His right hand
From before the enemy. Ps. 89:46
[R]He has blazed against Jacob like a flaming fire Ps. 74:11
Which devours all around.

4 [R]Standing like an enemy, He has bent His bow; Is. 63:10
With His right hand, like an adversary,
He has slain [R]all *who were* pleasing to His eye; Ezek. 24:25
On the tent of the daughter of Zion,
He has poured out His fury like fire.

5 [R]The Lord was like an enemy.
He has swallowed up Israel,
He has swallowed up all her palaces;
[R]He has destroyed her strongholds,
And has increased mourning and lamentation Jer. 30:14 • Jer. 52:13
In the daughter of Judah.

6 He has done violence [R]to His [T]tabernacle, Ps. 80:12; 89:40 • Lit. *booth*
[R]*As if it were* a garden; Is. 1:8
He has destroyed His place of assembly;
The LORD has caused
The appointed feasts and Sabbaths to be forgotten in Zion.
In His burning indignation He has spurned the king and the priest.

7 The Lord has spurned His altar,
He has [R]abandoned His sanctuary;
He has [T]given up the walls of her palaces Ezek. 24:21 • *delivered*
Into the hand of the enemy.
[R]They have made a noise in the house of the LORD Ps. 74:3–8
As on the day of a set feast.

8 The LORD has [T]purposed to destroy
The [R]wall of the daughter of Zion.
[R]He has stretched out a line;
He has not withdrawn His hand from destroying; *determined* • Jer. 52:14 • [Is. 34:11]
Therefore He has caused the rampart and wall to lament;
They languished together.

9 Her gates have sunk into the ground;
He has destroyed and [R]broken her bars.
[R]Her king and her princes *are* among the [T]nations; Jer. 51:30 • Deut. 28:36 • *Gentiles*
[R]The Law *is* no *more*, 2 Chr. 15:3
And her [R]prophets find no [T]vision from the LORD. Ps. 74:9 • Prophetic revelation

The Agony of Jerusalem

10 The elders of the daughter of Zion
Sit on the ground *and* keep silence;
[T]They throw dust on their heads
And gird themselves with sackcloth.
The virgins of Jerusalem A sign of mourning
Bow their heads to the ground.

11 [R]My eyes fail with tears, Lam. 3:48
My [T]heart is troubled; Lit. *inward parts*
[R]My [T]bile is poured on the ground
Because of the destruction of the daughter of my people, Job 16:13 • Lit. *liver*
Because [R]the children and the infants
Faint in the streets of the city. Lam. 4:4

12 They say to their mothers,
"Where *is* grain and wine?"
As they swoon like the wounded
In the streets of the city,
As their life is poured out
In their mothers' bosom.

13 How shall I [T]console you?
To what shall I liken you,
O daughter of Jerusalem?
What shall I compare with you, that I may comfort you,
O virgin daughter of Zion?
For your ruin *is* spread wide as the sea;
Who can heal you? Or *bear witness to*

14 Your [R]prophets have seen for you
False and deceptive visions;
They have not [R]uncovered your iniquity, Jer. 2:8; 23:25–29 • Is. 58:1
To bring back your captives,
But have envisioned for you false [R]prophecies and delusions. Jer. 23:33–36

15 All who [T]pass by [R]clap *their* hands at you; Lit. *pass by this way* • Ezek. 25:6
They hiss [R]and shake their heads
At the daughter of Jerusalem: Ps. 44:14
"*Is* this the city that is called
[R]'The perfection of beauty, [Ps. 48:2; 50:2]
The joy of the whole earth'?"

16 [R]All your enemies have opened their mouth against you; Job 16:9, 10
They hiss and gnash *their* teeth.
They say, [R]"We have swallowed *her* up!
Surely this *is* the [R]day we have waited for; Ps. 56:2; 124:3 • Lam 1:21
We have found *it*, we have seen *it*."

17 The LORD has done what He [R]purposed;
He has fulfilled His word
Which He commanded in days of old.
He has thrown down and has not pitied,
And He has caused *your* enemy to
[R]rejoice over you;
He has exalted the [T]horn of your
adversaries. Lev. 26:16 • Ps. 38:16 • Strength

The Appeal of Jerusalem

18 Their heart cried out to the Lord,
"O wall of the daughter of Zion,
[R]Let tears run down like a river day and
night; Jer. 14:17
Give yourself no relief;
Give your eyes no rest.

19 "Arise, [R]cry out in the night, Ps. 119:147
At the beginning of the watches;
[R]Pour out your heart like water before
the face of the Lord. Ps. 42:4; 62:8
Lift your hands toward Him
For the life of your young children,
Who faint from hunger [R]at the head of
every street." Is. 51:20

20 "See, O LORD, and consider!
To whom have You done this?
[R]Should the women eat their offspring,
The children *they have cuddled?
Should the priest and prophet be slain
In the sanctuary of the Lord? Lev. 26:29

21 "Young[R] and old lie
On the ground in the streets;
My virgins and my young men
Have fallen by the [R]sword;
You have slain *them* in the day of Your
anger, 2 Chr. 36:17 • Jer. 18:21
You have slaughtered *and* not pitied.

22 "You have invited as to a feast day
[R]The terrors that surround me.
In the day of the LORD's anger
There was no refugee or survivor.
[R]Those whom I have borne and brought
up Ps. 31:13 • Hos. 9:12
My enemies have destroyed."

CHAPTER 3

Jeremiah's Cry of Despair

I *AM* the man *who* has seen affliction by
the rod of His wrath.
2 He has led me and made *me* walk
In darkness and not *in* light.
3 Surely He has turned His hand against
me
Time and time again throughout the
day.

4 He has aged [R]my flesh and my skin,
And [R]broken my bones. Job 16:8 • Ps. 51:8
5 He has besieged me
And surrounded *me* with bitterness and
[T]woe. *hardship* or *weariness*
6 [R]He has set me in dark places
Like the dead of long ago. [Ps. 88:5, 6; 143:3]

7 [R]He has hedged me in so that I cannot
get out;
He has made my chain heavy. Hos. 2:6
8 Even [R]when I cry and shout,
He shuts out my prayer. Job 30:20
9 He has blocked my ways with hewn
stone;
He has made my paths crooked.

10 [R]He *has been* to me *like* a bear lying in
wait, Is. 38:13
Like a lion in [T]ambush. Lit. *secret places*
11 He has turned aside my ways and [R]torn
me in pieces;
He has made me desolate. Hos. 6:1
12 He has bent His bow
And [R]set me up as a target for the
arrow. Job 7:20; 16:12

13 He has caused [R]the [T]arrows of His
quiver Job 6:4 • Lit. *sons of*
To pierce my [T]loins. Lit. *kidneys*
14 I have become the [R]ridicule of all my
people, Jer. 20:7
And their taunting song all the day.
15 [R]He has filled me with bitterness, Jer. 9:15
He has made me drink wormwood.

16 He has also broken my teeth [R]with
gravel, [Prov. 20:17]
And covered me with ashes.
17 You have moved my soul far from
peace;
I have forgotten [T]prosperity. Lit. *good*
18 [R]And I said, "My strength and my hope
Have perished from the LORD." Ps. 31:22

Jeremiah's Confession of Faith

19 Remember my affliction and roaming,
The wormwood and the [T]gall. *bitterness*
20 My soul still remembers
And [T]sinks within me. Lit. *bowed down*
21 This I recall to my mind,
Therefore I have [R]hope. Ps. 130:7

22 [R]*Through* the LORD's mercies we are not
consumed, [Mal. 3:6]
Because His compassions fail not.
23 *They are* new [R]every morning;
Great *is* Your faithfulness. Is. 33:2
24 "The LORD *is* my portion," says my soul,
"Therefore I [R]hope in Him!" Mic. 7:7

25 The LORD *is* good to those who [R]wait
for Him,
To the soul *who* seeks Him. Is. 30:18

2:20 Vg. *a span long*

26 *It is* good that *one* should [R]hope [R]and
wait quietly [Rom. 4:16–18] • Ps. 37:7
For the salvation of the LORD.
27 [R]*It is* good for a man to bear
The yoke in his youth. Ps. 94:12

28 Let him sit alone and keep silent,
Because [T]God has laid *it* on him; Lit. *He*
29 [R]Let him put his mouth in the dust—
There may yet be hope. Job 42:6
30 [R]Let him give *his* cheek to the one who
strikes him,
And be full of reproach. Is. 50:6

31 For the Lord will not cast off forever.
32 Though He causes grief,
Yet He will show compassion
According to the multitude of His
mercies.
33 For He does not afflict willingly,
Nor grieve the children of men.

34 To crush under His feet
All the prisoners of the earth,
35 To turn aside the justice *due* a man
Before the face of the Most High,
36 Or subvert a man in his cause—
[R]The Lord does not approve. [Hab. 1:13]

37 Who *is* he [R]*who* speaks and it comes to
pass, [Ps. 33:9–11]
When the Lord has not commanded *it*?
38 *Is it* not from the mouth of the Most
High
That woe and well-being proceed?
39 Why should a living man complain,
A man for the punishment of his sins?

Jeremiah's Condition of Need

40 Let us search out and examine our
ways,
And turn back to the LORD;
41 [R]Let us lift our hearts and hands
To God in heaven. Ps. 86:4
42 [R]We have transgressed and rebelled;
You have not pardoned. Dan. 9:5

43 You have covered *Yourself* with anger
And pursued us;
You have slain *and* not pitied.
44 You have covered Yourself with a
cloud,
That prayer should not pass through.
45 You have made us an [R]offscouring and
refuse
In the midst of the peoples. 1 Cor. 4:13

46 [R]All our enemies Lam. 2:16
Have opened their mouths against us.
47 Fear and a snare have come upon us,
[R]Desolation and destruction. Is. 51:19
48 [R]My eyes overflow with rivers of water
For the destruction of the daughter of
my people. Jer. 4:19; 14:17
49 [R]My eyes flow and do not cease,
Without interruption, Jer. 14:17
50 Till the LORD from heaven
[R]Looks down and sees. Is. 63:15
51 My eyes bring suffering to my soul
Because of all the daughters of my city.

52 My enemies [R]without cause
Hunted me down like a bird. Ps. 35:7, 19
53 They *silenced my life in the pit
And threw [T]stones at me. Lit. *a stone on*
54 [R]The waters flowed over my head;
[R]I said, "I am cut off!" Ps. 69:2 • Is. 38:10

Jeremiah's Confidence in God

55 [R]I called on Your name, O LORD,
From the lowest [R]pit. Ps. 130:1 • Jer. 38:6–13
56 [R]You have heard my voice:
"Do not hide Your ear
From my sighing, from my cry for
help." Ps. 3:4
57 You [R]drew near on the day I called on
You, James 4:8
And said, [R]"Do not fear!" Is. 41:10, 14

58 O Lord, You have [R]pleaded the case for
my soul; Jer. 51:36
[R]You have redeemed my life. Ps. 71:23
59 O LORD, You have seen [T]*how* I am
wronged;
[R]Judge my case. Lit. *my wrong* • Ps. 9:4
60 You have seen all their vengeance,
All their [R]schemes against me. Jer. 11:19

61 You have heard their reproach, O LORD,
All their schemes against me,
62 The lips of my enemies
And their whispering against me all the
day.
63 Look at their [R]sitting down and their
rising up;
I *am* their taunting song. Ps. 139:2

64 [R]Repay them, O LORD, Ps. 28:4
According to the work of their hands.
65 Give them a *veiled heart;
Your curse *be* upon them!
66 In Your anger,
Pursue and destroy them
From under the heavens of the LORD.

CHAPTER 4

The Conditions During the Siege

HOW the gold has become dim!
How changed the fine gold!
The stones of the sanctuary are
[T]scattered Lit. *poured out*
At the head of every street.

3:53 LXX *put to death*
3:65 A Jewish tradition reads *sorrow of*

2 The precious sons of Zion,
[T]Valuable as fine gold, Lit. *Weighed against*
How they are regarded as clay pots,
The work of the hands of the potter!

3 Even the jackals present their breasts
To nurse their young;
But the daughter of my people *has become* cruel,
Like ostriches in the wilderness.

4 The tongue of the infant clings
To the roof of its mouth for thirst;
[R]The young children ask for bread,
But no one breaks *it* for them. Ps. 22:15

5 Those who ate delicacies
Are desolate in the streets;
Those who were brought up in scarlet
[R]Embrace ash heaps. Job 24:8

6 The punishment of the iniquity of the daughter of my people
Is greater than the punishment of the [R]sin of Sodom, Ezek. 16:48
Which was [R]overthrown in a moment,
With no hand to help her! Gen. 19:25

7 Her [T]Nazirites were [T]brighter than snow
And whiter than milk; Or *nobles* • Or *purer*
They were more ruddy in body than rubies,
Like sapphire in their appearance.

8 *Now* their appearance is blacker than soot;
They go unrecognized in the streets;
[R]Their skin clings to their bones, Ps. 102:5
It has become as dry as wood.

9 *Those* slain by the sword are better off
Than *those* who die of hunger;
For these [R]pine away, Lev. 26:39
Stricken *for lack* of the fruits of the [R]field. Jer. 16:4

10 The hands of the [R]compassionate women Lam. 2:20
Have [T]cooked their [R]own children;
They became [R]food for them
In the destruction of the daughter of my people. *boiled* • Is. 49:15 • Deut. 28:57

The Cause of the Siege

11 The LORD has fulfilled His fury,
He has poured out His fierce anger.
[R]He kindled a fire in Zion, Deut. 32:22
And it has devoured its foundations.

12 The kings of the earth,
And all inhabitants of the world,
Would not have believed
That the adversary and the enemy
Could enter the gates of Jerusalem—

13 [R]Because of the sins of her prophets
And the iniquities of her priests,
[R]Who shed in her midst
The blood of the just. Jer. 5:31 • Matt. 23.31

14 They wandered blind in the streets;
[R]They have defiled themselves with blood, Jer. 2:34
[R]So that no one would touch their garments. Num. 19:16

15 They cried out to them,
"Go away, [R]unclean! Lev. 13:45, 46
Go away, go away,
Do not touch us!"
When they fled and wandered,
Those among the nations said,
"They shall no longer dwell *here*."

16 The *face of the LORD scattered them;
He no longer regards them.
[T]The people do not respect the priests
Nor show favor to the elders. Lit. *They*

17 Still [R]our eyes failed us, 2 Kin. 24:7
Watching vainly for our help;
In our watching we watched
For a nation *that* could not save *us*.

18 [R]They [T]tracked our steps
So that we could not walk in our streets. 2 Kin. 25:4 • Lit. *hunted*
[R]Our end was near; Ezek. 7:2, 3, 6
Our days were over,
For our end had come.

19 Our pursuers were [R]swifter Deut. 28:49
Than the eagles of the heavens.
They pursued us on the mountains
And lay in wait for us in the wilderness.

20 The [R]breath of our nostrils, the anointed of the LORD, Gen. 2:7
[R]Was caught in their pits, Jer. 52:9
Of whom we said, "Under his shadow
We shall live among the nations."

The Consequences of the Siege

21 Rejoice and be glad, O daughter of [R]Edom, Ps. 83:3–6
You who dwell in the land of Uz!
[R]The cup shall also pass over to you
And you shall become drunk and make yourself naked. Jer. 25:15

22 [R]*The punishment of* your iniquity [T]is accomplished, [Is. 40:2] • *has been completed*
O daughter of Zion;
He will no longer send you into captivity.

4:16 Tg. *anger*

[R]He will punish your iniquity, Ps. 137:7
O daughter of Edom;
He will uncover your sins!

CHAPTER 5

The Review of the Need for Restoration

REMEMBER, [R]O LORD, what has come
upon us; Ps. 89:50
Look, and behold our reproach!
2 [R]Our inheritance has been turned over to
aliens,
And our houses to foreigners. Ps. 79:1
3 We have become orphans and waifs,
Our mothers *are* like [R]widows. Jer. 15:8

4 We pay for the water we drink,
And our wood comes at a price.
5 *They* pursue at our [T]heels; Lit. *necks*
We labor *and* have no rest.
6 [R]We have given our hand [R]*to* the
Egyptians
And the [R]Assyrians, to be satisfied with
bread. Gen. 24:2 • Hos. 9:3; 12:1 • Hos. 5:13

7 [R]Our fathers sinned *and are* no more,
But we bear their iniquities. Jer. 31:29
8 Servants rule over us;
There is none to deliver *us* from their
hand.
9 We get our bread *at the risk* of our
lives,
Because of the sword in the wilderness.

10 Our skin is hot as an oven,
Because of the fever of famine.

11 They ravished the women in Zion,
The maidens in the cities of Judah.
12 Princes were hung up by their hands,
And elders were not respected.
13 Young men ground at the millstones;
Boys staggered under *loads of* wood.
14 The elders have ceased *gathering at* the
gate,
And the young men from their music.

15 The joy of our heart has ceased;
Our dance has turned into mourning.

The Repentance of Sin

16 [R]The crown has fallen *from* our head.
Woe to us, for we have sinned! Ps. 89:39
17 Because of this our heart is faint;
[R]Because of these *things* our eyes grow
dim; Ps. 6:7
18 Because of Mount Zion which is
[R]desolate,
With foxes walking about on it. Is. 27:10

The Request for Restoration

19 You, O LORD, [R]remain forever;
[R]Your throne from generation to
generation. Ps. 9:7 • Ps. 45:6

20 [R]Why do You forget us forever, Ps. 13:1
And forsake us for so long a time?

21 [R]Turn us back to You, O LORD, and we
will be [T]restored; Jer. 31:18 • *returned*
Renew our days as of old,
22 Unless You have utterly rejected us,
And are very angry with us!

5:20 Occasions of Doubt—Doubt may be defined as an uncertainty of belief or lack of confidence in something. Applied to the Christian life, doubt refers to the unbelief in God and His Word that Christians occasionally exhibit. It is possible that in a moment of infirmity a Christian may doubt the existence of God in spite of the fact that it is not reasonable for a person to disbelieve this obvious truth (Page 632—Ps. 14:1). A Christian is more likely to doubt his salvation after sinning or after a spiritual defeat. A misunderstanding of such verses as First John 3:9 contributes to this doubt: "Whoever has been born of God does not sin." It is crucial to note that this verse speaks of a life-style of sin, not instances of sin.

A Christian may also doubt God's sovereignty or His goodness. In such circumstances as sickness, suffering, injustice, opposition, economic problems, family problems, national calamity, or apparently unanswered prayer, a Christian may be tempted to doubt the goodness of God. One must remember that it is not always possible to discern God's good hand in the affairs of life. The person of faith believes God even when circumstances appear to the contrary.

All doubt may be traced ultimately to unbelief in the Word of God, which affirms beyond question the existence and character of God. To regard doubt as the sin of unbelief and then confess it to God as sin is therefore the first step toward conquering it.

Now turn to Page 1052—Hab. 1:2: Sources of Doubt.

THE BOOK OF

EZEKIEL

THE BOOK OF EZEKIEL

Ezekiel, a priest and a prophet, ministers during the darkest days of Judah's history: the seventy-year period of Babylonian captivity. Carried to Babylon before the final assault on Jerusalem, Ezekiel uses prophecies, parables, signs, and symbols to dramatize God's message to His exiled people. Though they are like dry bones in the sun, God will reassemble them and breathe life into the nation once again. Present judgment will be followed by future glory so that "you shall know that I *am* the LORD" (6:7).

The Hebrew name *Yehezke'l* means "God Strengthens" or "Strengthened by God." Ezekiel is indeed strengthened by God for the prophetic ministry to which he is called (3:8, 9). The name occurs twice in this book and nowhere else in the Old Testament. The Greek form in the Septuagint is *Iezekiel* and the Latin form in the Vulgate is *Ezechiel.*

THE AUTHOR OF EZEKIEL

Ezekiel, the son of Buzi (1:3), had a wife who died as a sign to Judah when Nebuchadnezzar began his final siege on Jerusalem (24:16–24). Like Jeremiah, he was a priest who was called to be a prophet of the Lord. His prophetic ministry shows a priestly emphasis in his concern with the temple, priesthood, sacrifices, and Shekinah (the glory of God). Ezekiel was privileged to receive a number of visions of the power and plan of God, and he was careful and artistic in his written presentation.

Some objections have been raised, but there is not a good reason to overthrow the strong evidence in favor of Ezekiel's authorship. The first person singular is used throughout the book, indicating that it is the work of a single personality. This person is identified as Ezekiel in 1:3 and 24:24, and internal evidence supports the unity and integrity of Ezekiel's prophetic record. The style, language, and thematic development are consistent throughout the book; and several distinctive phrases are repeated throughout, such as, "they shall know that I *am* the LORD," "Son of man," "the word of the LORD came to me," and the "glory of the LORD."

THE TIME OF EZEKIEL

Nebuchadnezzar destroyed Jerusalem in three stages. First, in 605 B.C., he overcame Jehoiakim and carried off key hostages including Daniel and his friends. Second, in 597 B.C., the rebellion of Jehoiakim and Jehoiachin brought further punishment; and Nebuchadnezzar made Jerusalem submit a second time. He carried off ten thousand hostages including Jehoiachin and Ezekiel. Third, in 586 B.C., Nebuchadnezzar destroyed the city after a long siege and disrupted all of Judah. If "thirtieth year" in 1:1 refers to Ezekiel's age, he was twenty-five years old when he was taken to Babylon and thirty years old when he received his prophetic commission (1:2, 3). This means he was about seventeen when Daniel was deported in 605 B.C., so that Ezekiel and Daniel were about the same age. Both men were about twenty years younger than Jeremiah who was ministering in Jerusalem. According to this chronology, Ezekiel was born in 622 B.C., deported to Babylon in 597 B.C., prophesied from 592 B.C. to at least 570 B.C., and died about 560 B.C. Thus, he overlapped the end of Jeremiah's ministry and the beginning of Daniel's ministry. By the time Ezekiel arrived in Babylon, Daniel was already well-known; and he is mentioned three times in Ezekiel's prophecy (14:14, 20; 28:3). Ezekiel's Babylonian home was at Tel Abib, the principal colony of Jewish exiles along the River Chebar, Nebuchadnezzar's "Grand Canal" (1:1; 3:15, 23).

From 592 to 586 B.C., Ezekiel found it necessary to convince the disbelieving Jewish exiles that there was no hope of immediate deliverance. But it was not until they heard that Jerusalem was destroyed that their false hopes of returning were abandoned.

Ezekiel no doubt wrote this book shortly after the incidents recorded in it occurred. His active ministry lasted for at least twenty-two years (1:2; 29:17), and his book was probably completed by 565 B.C.

THE CHRIST OF EZEKIEL

Ezekiel 17:22–24 depicts the Messiah as a tender twig that becomes a stately cedar on a lofty mountain, as He is similarly called the Branch in Isaiah (11:1), Jeremiah (23:5; 33:15), and Zechariah (3:8; 6:12). The Messiah is the King who has the right to rule (21:26, 27), and He is the true Shepherd who will deliver and feed His flock (34:11–31).

KEYS TO EZEKIEL

Key Word: The Future Restoration of Israel—The broad purpose of Ezekiel is to remind the generation born during the Babylonian exile of the cause of Israel's current destruction, of the coming judgment on the gentile nations, and of the coming national restoration of Israel. Central to that hope is the departure of the glory of God from Israel and the prediction of its ultimate return (43:2).

Key Verses: Ezekiel 36:24–26 and 36:33–35—"For I will take you from among the nations, gather you out of all countries, and bring you into your own land. Then I will sprinkle clean water on you, and you shall be clean; I will cleanse you from all your filthiness and from all your idols. I will give you a new heart and put a new spirit within you; I will take the heart of stone out of your flesh and give you a heart of flesh" (36:24–26).

"Thus says the Lord GOD: 'On the day that I cleanse you from all your iniquities, I will also enable *you* to dwell in the cities, and the ruins shall be rebuilt. The desolate land shall be tilled instead of lying desolate in the sight of all who pass by. So they will say, "This land that was desolate has become like the garden of Eden; and the wasted, desolate, and ruined cities *are now* fortified *and* are inhabited" ' " (36:33–35).

Key Chapter: Ezekiel 37—Central to the hope of the restoration of Israel is the vision of the valley of the dry bones. Ezekiel 37 outlines with clear steps Israel's future.

SURVEY OF EZEKIEL

Ezekiel prophesies among the Jewish exiles in Babylon during the last days of Judah's decline and downfall. His message of judgment is similar to that of his older contemporary Jeremiah, who has remained in Jerusalem. Judah will be judged because of her unfaithfulness, but God promises her future restoration and blessing. Like Isaiah and Jeremiah, Ezekiel proclaims a message of horror and hope, of condemnation and consolation. But Ezekiel places special emphasis on the glory of Israel's sovereign God who says, "They shall know that I *am* the LORD." The book breaks into four sections: the commission of Ezekiel (1—3), the judgment on Judah (4—24), the judgment on the Gentiles (25—32), and the restoration of Israel (33—48).

The Commission of Ezekiel (1—3): God gives Ezekiel an overwhelming vision of His divine glory and commissions him to be His prophet (cf. the experiences of Moses in Ex. 3:1–10, Isaiah in 6:1–10, Daniel in 10:5–14, and John in Rev. 1:12–19). Ezekiel is given instruction, enablement, and responsibility.

The Judgment on Judah (4—24): Ezekiel directs his prophecies against the nation God chose for Himself. The prophet's signs and sermons (4—7) point to the certainty of Judah's judgment. In 8—11, Judah's past sins and coming doom are seen in a series of visions of the abominations in the temple, the slaying of the wicked, and the departing glory of God. The priests and princes are condemned as the glory leaves the temple, moves to the Mount of Olives, and disappears in the east. Chapters 12—24 speak of the causes and extent of Judah's coming judgment through dramatic signs, powerful sermons, and parables. Judah's prophets are counterfeits and her elders are idolators. They have become a fruitless vine and an adulterous wife. Babylon will swoop down like an eagle and pluck them up, and they will not be aided by Egypt. The people are responsible for their own sins, and they are not being unjustly judged for the sins of their ancestors. Judah has been unfaithful, but God promises that her judgment ultimately will be followed by restoration.

The Judgment on the Gentiles (25—32): Judah's nearest neighbors may gloat over her destruction, but they will be next in line. They too will suffer the fate of siege and destruction by Babylon. Ezekiel shows the full circle of judgment on the nations that surround Judah by following them in a clockwise circuit: Ammon, Moab, Edom, Philistia, Tyre, and Sidon (25—28). He spends a disproportionate amount of time on Tyre, and many scholars believe that the "king of Tyre" in 28:11–19 may be Satan, the real power

FOCUS	COMMISSION OF EZEKIEL		JUDGMENT ON JUDAH	JUDGMENT ON GENTILES	RESTORATION OF ISRAEL	
REFERENCE	1:1—	2:1—	4:1—	25:1—	33:1—	40:1—48:35
DIVISION	EZEKIEL SEES THE GLORY	EZEKIEL IS COMMISSIONED TO THE WORK	SIGNS, MESSAGES, VISIONS, AND PARABLES OF JUDGMENT	JUDGMENT ON SURROUNDING NATIONS	RETURN OF ISRAEL TO THE LORD	RESTORATION OF ISRAEL IN THE KINGDOM
TOPIC	BEFORE THE SIEGE (c. 592-587 B.C.)			DURING THE SIEGE (c. 586 B.C.)	AFTER THE SIEGE (c. 585-570 B.C.)	
	JUDAH'S FALL			JUDAH'S FOES	JUDAH'S FUTURE	
LOCATION	BABYLON					
TIME	c. 592-570 B.C.					

behind the nation. Chapters 29—32 contain a series of oracles against Egypt. Unlike the nations in chapters 25—28 that were destroyed by Nebuchadnezzar, Egypt will continue to exist, but as "the lowliest of kingdoms" (29:15). Since that time it has never recovered its former glory or influence.

The Restoration of Israel (33—48): The prophecies in these chapters were given after the overthrow of Jerusalem. Now that the promised judgment has come, Ezekiel's message no longer centers on coming judgment but on the positive theme of comfort and consolation. Just as surely as judgment has come, blessing will also come; God's people will be regathered and restored. The mouth of Ezekiel, God's watchman, is opened when he is told that Jerusalem has been taken. Judah has had false shepherds (rulers), but the true Shepherd will lead them in the future. The vision of the valley of dry bones pictures the reanimation of the nation by the Spirit of God. Israel and Judah will be purified and reunited. There will be an invasion by the northern armies of Gog, but Israel will be saved because the Lord will destroy the invading forces.

In 572 B.C., fourteen years after the destruction of Jerusalem, Ezekiel returns in a vision to the fallen city and is given detailed specifications for the reconstruction of the temple, the city, and the land (40—48). After an intricate description of the new outer court, inner court, and temple (40—42), Ezekiel views the return of the glory of the Lord to the temple from the east. Regulations concerning worship in the coming temple (43—46) are followed by revelations concerning the new land and city (47 and 48).

OUTLINE OF EZEKIEL

Part One: The Commission of Ezekiel (1:1—3:27)

I. Ezekiel Sees the Glory of God.......... 1:1–28

- A. Time of the Vision.................... 1:1–3
- B. The Four Living Creatures.......... 1:4–14
- C. The Four Wheels.................. 1:15–21
- D. The Firmament 1:22–25
- E. The Appearance of a Man 1:26–28

II. Ezekiel Is Commissioned to the Word of God.......................... 2:1—3:27

- A. Ezekiel Is Sent to Israel........... 2:1—3:3
- B. Ezekiel Is Instructed About His Ministry 3:4–27

Part Two: Judgment on Judah (4:1—24:27)

I. Four Signs of Coming Judgment...... 4:1—5:17

- A. Sign of the Clay Tablet............. 4:1–3
- B. Sign of Ezekiel's Lying on His Side..... 4:4–8
- C. Sign of the Defiled Bread 4:9–17
- D. Sign of the Razor and Hair......... 5:1–4
- E. Explanation of the Signs.......... 5:5–17

II. Two Messages of Coming Judgment... 6:1—7:27

- A. Destruction Because of Idolatry...... 6:1–14
  1. Destruction of High Places 6:1–7
  2. Salvation of the Remnant 6:8–10
  3. Desolation of the Land 6:11–14
- B. Description of the Babylonian Conquest.......................... 7:1–27

III. Four-Part Vision of Coming Judgment......................... 8:1—11:25

- A. Vision of the Glory of God............ 8:1–4
- B. Vision of the Abominations in the Temple........................ 8:5–18
  1. Image of Jealousy................ 8:5, 6
  2. Paintings on the Wall............ 8:7–12
  3. Weeping for Tammuz 8:13, 14
  4. Sun Worship 8:15–18
- C. Vision of the Slaying in Jerusalem..... 9:1–11
  1. Call to the Six Men 9:1–3
  2. Command to Slay the Wicked 9:4–7
  3. Weeping of Ezekiel 9:8–11
- D. Departure of the Glory of God to the Threshold.................... 10:1–8
- E. Vision of the Wheels and Cherubim 10:9–22
- F. Vision of the Twenty-five Wicked Rulers........................... 11:1–12
- G. Promise of the Restoration of the Remnant.................... 11:13-21
- H. Departure of the Glory of God from the Mount of Olives.......... 11:22–25

IV. Signs, Parables, and Messages of Judgment .... 12:1—24:27

- A. Sign of Belongings for Removing...... 12:1–16
- B. Sign of Trembling 12:17–28
- C. Message Against the False Prophets 13:1–23
  1. Judgment upon False Prophets.... 13:1–16
  2. Judgment upon False Prophetesses 13:17–23
- D. Message Against the Elders 14:1–23
  1. Idolatry of the Elders............ 14:1–11
  2. Jerusalem to Be Destroyed 14:12–23
- E. Parable of the Vine 15:1–8
- F. Parable of Israel's Marriage 16:1–63
  1. God Has Mercy on Israel......... 16:1–14
  2. Israel Rejects God............... 16:15–34
  3. God Punishes Israel 16:35–59
  4. God Remembers His Covenant.... 16:60–63
- G. Parable of the Two Eagles 17:1–24

Part Three: Judgment on Gentiles (25:1—32:32)

Part Four: Restoration of Israel (33:1—48:35)

CHAPTER 1

Time of the Vision

NOW it came to pass in the thirtieth year, in the fourth *month*, on the fifth *day* of the month, as I *was* among the captives by the River Chebar, *that* the heavens were opened and I saw [R]visions of God. Ezek. 8:3

2 On the fifth *day* of the month, which *was* in the fifth year of King Jehoiachin's captivity,

3 the word of the LORD came expressly to Ezekiel the priest, the son of Buzi, in the land of the Chaldeans by the River Chebar; and the hand of the LORD was upon him there.

The Four Living Creatures

4 Then I looked, and behold, [R]a whirlwind was coming [R]out of the north, a great cloud with raging fire engulfing itself; and brightness *was* all around it and radiating out of its midst like the color of amber, out of the midst of the fire. Jer. 23:19; 25:32 • Jer. 1:14

5 Also from within it *came* the likeness of four living creatures. And this *was* their appearance: they had the likeness of a man.

6 Each one had four faces, and each one had four wings.

7 Their [T]legs *were* straight, and the soles of their feet *were* like the soles of calves' feet. They sparkled [R]like the color of burnished bronze. Lit. *feet* • Dan. 10:6

8 [R]*They had* the hands of a man under their wings on their four sides; and each of the four had faces and wings. Ezek. 10:8, 21

9 Their wings touched one another. *The creatures* did not turn when they went, but each one went straight [R]forward. Ezek. 1:12

10 As for the likeness of their faces, *each* had the face of a man, each of the four had the face of a lion on the right side, each of the four had the face of an ox on the left side, and each of the four had the face of an eagle.

11 Thus *were* their faces. Their wings *were* stretched upward; two *wings* of each one touched one another, and [R]two covered their bodies. Is. 6:2

12 And each one went straight forward; they went wherever the spirit wanted to go, and they did not turn when they went.

13 As for the likeness of the living creatures, their appearance *was* like burning coals of fire, *and* like the appearance of torches. *Fire* was going back and forth among the living creatures; the fire was bright, and out of the fire went lightning.

14 And the living creatures ran back and forth, in appearance like a flash of lightning.

The Four Wheels

15 Now as I looked at the living creatures, behold, a wheel *was* on the earth beside each living creature with its four faces.

16 [R]The appearance of the wheels and their works *was* [R]like the color of beryl, and all four had the same likeness. The appearance of their works *was*, as it were, a wheel in the middle of a wheel. Ezek. 10:9, 10 • Dan. 10:6

17 When they went, they went toward any one of four directions; they did not turn aside when they went.

18 As for their rims, they were so high they were awesome; and their rims *were* [R]full of eyes, all around the four of them. Ezek. 10:12

19 [R]When the living creatures went, the wheels went beside them; and when the living creatures were lifted up from the earth, the wheels were lifted up. Ezek. 10:16, 17

20 Wherever the spirit wanted to go, they went, *because* there the spirit went; and the wheels were lifted together with them, [R]for the spirit of the living creatures *was* in the wheels. Ezek. 10:17

21 When those went, *these* went; when those stood, *these* stood; and when those were lifted up from the earth, the wheels were lifted up together with them, for the spirit of the living creatures *was* in the wheels.

The Firmament

22 The likeness of the [T]firmament above the heads of the living creatures *was* like the color of an awesome [R]crystal, stretched out [R]over their heads. Or *expanse* • Rev. 4:6 • Ezek. 10:1

23 And under the firmament their wings *spread out* straight, one toward another. Each one had two which covered one side, and each one had two which covered the other side of the body.

24 When they went, I heard the noise of their wings, like the noise of many waters, like [R]the voice of the Almighty, a tumult like the noise of an army; and when they stood still, they let down their wings. Job 37:4, 5

25 A voice came from above the firmament that *was* over their heads; whenever they stood, they let down their wings.

The Appearance of a Man

26 And above the firmament over their heads *was* the likeness of a throne, in appearance like a sapphire stone; on the likeness of the throne *was* a likeness with the appearance of a man high above it.

27 Also from the appearance of His waist and upward I saw, as it were, the color of amber with the appearance of fire all around within it; and from the appearance of His waist and downward I saw, as it were, the appearance of fire with brightness all around.

28 [R]Like the appearance of a rainbow in a cloud on a rainy day, so *was* the appearance of the brightness all around it. [R]This *was* the appearance of the likeness of the glory of the LORD. Rev. 4:3; 10:1 • Ezek. 3:23; 8:4

So when I saw *it*, [R]I fell on my face, and I heard a voice of One speaking. Dan. 8:17

CHAPTER 2

Ezekiel Is Sent to Israel

AND He said to me, "Son of man, stand on your feet, and I will speak to you."

2 Then [R]the Spirit entered me when He spoke to me, and set me on my feet; and I heard Him who spoke to me. Ezek. 3:24

3 And He said to me: "Son of man, I am sending you to the children of Israel, to a rebellious nation that has rebelled against

Me; [R]they and their fathers have transgressed against Me to this very day. Jer. 3:25

4 "For *they are* impudent and stubborn children. I am sending you to them, and you shall say to them, 'Thus says the Lord GOD.'

5 "As for them, whether they hear or whether they refuse—for they *are* a rebellious house—yet they [R]will know that a prophet has been among them. Ezek. 33:33

6 "And you, son of man, do not be afraid of them nor be afraid of their words, though briers and thorns *are* with you and you dwell among scorpions; do not be afraid of their words or dismayed by their looks, [R]though they *are* a rebellious house. Ezek. 3:9, 26, 27

7 [R]"You shall speak My words to them, whether they hear or whether they refuse, for they *are* rebellious. Jer. 1:7, 17

8 "But you, son of man, hear what I say to you. Do not be rebellious like that rebellious house; open your mouth and [R]eat what I give you." Rev. 10:9

9 Now when I looked, there was [R]a hand stretched out to me; and behold, [R]a scroll of a book *was* in it. [Ezek. 8:3] • Ezek. 3:1

10 Then He spread it before me; and *there was* writing on the inside and on the outside, and written on it *were* lamentations and mourning and woe.

CHAPTER 3

MOREOVER He said to me, "Son of man, eat what you find; [R]eat this scroll, and go, speak to the house of Israel." Ezek. 2:8, 9

2 So I opened my mouth, and He caused me to eat that scroll.

3 And He said to me, "Son of man, feed your belly, and fill your stomach with this scroll that I give you." So I ate *it*, and it was in my mouth like honey in sweetness.

Ezekiel Is Instructed About His Ministry

4 And He said to me: "Son of man, go to the house of Israel and speak with My words to them.

5 "For you *are* not sent to a people of unfamiliar speech and of hard language, *but* to the house of Israel,

6 "not to many people of unfamiliar speech and of hard language, whose words you cannot understand. Surely, had I sent you to them, they would have listened to you.

7 "But the house of Israel will not listen to you, because they will not listen to Me; [R]for all the house of Israel *are* [T]impudent and hardhearted. Ezek. 2:4 • Lit. *strong of forehead*

8 "Behold, I have made your face strong against their faces, and your forehead strong against their foreheads.

9 [R]"Like adamant stone, harder than flint, I have made your forehead; do not be afraid of them, nor be dismayed at their looks, though they *are* a rebellious house." Mic. 3:8

10 Moreover He said to me: "Son of man, receive into your heart all My words that I speak to you, and hear with your ears.

11 "And go, get to the captives, to the children of your people, and speak to them and tell them, 'Thus says the Lord GOD,' whether they hear, or whether they refuse."

12 Then the Spirit lifted me up, and I heard behind me a great thunderous voice: "Blessed *is* the glory of the LORD from His place!"

13 *I* also *heard* the [R]noise of the wings of the living creatures that touched one another, and the noise of the wheels beside them, and a great thunderous noise. Ezek. 1:24; 10:5

14 So the Spirit lifted me up and took me away, and I went in bitterness, in the [T]heat of my spirit; but [R]the hand of the LORD was strong upon me. Or *anger* • 2 Kin. 3:15

15 Then I came to the captives at Tel Abib, who dwelt by the River Chebar; and [R]I sat where they sat, and remained there astonished among them seven days. Job 2:13

16 Now it [R]came to pass at the end of seven days that the word of the LORD came to me, saying, Jer. 42:7

17 [R]"Son of man, I have made you [R]a watchman for the house of Israel; therefore hear a word from My mouth, and give them [R]warning from Me: Ezek. 33:7–9 • Jer. 6:17 • [Lev. 19:17]

18 "When I say to the wicked, 'You shall surely die,' and you give him no warning, nor speak to warn the wicked from his wicked way, to save his life, that same wicked *man* [R]shall die in his iniquity; but his blood I will require at your hand. [John 8:21, 24]

19 "Yet, if you warn the wicked, and he does not turn from his wickedness, nor from his wicked way, he shall die in his iniquity; but you have delivered your soul.

20 "Again, when a [R]righteous *man* turns from his righteousness and commits iniquity, and I lay a stumbling block before him, he shall die; because you did not give him warning, he shall die in his sin, and his righteousness which he has done shall not be remembered; but his blood I will require at your hand. Ezek. 18:24; 33:18

21 "Nevertheless if you warn the righteous *man* that the righteous should not sin, and he does not sin, he shall surely live because he took warning; also you will have delivered your soul."

22 [R]Then the hand of the LORD was upon me there, and He said to me, "Arise, go out [R]into the plain, and there I shall talk with you." Ezek. 1:3 • Ezek. 8:4

23 So I arose and went out into the plain, and behold, the glory of the LORD stood there, like the glory which I saw by the River Chebar; and I fell on my face.

24 Then the Spirit entered me and set me on
my feet, and spoke with me and said to me:
"Go, shut yourself inside your house.
25 "And you, O son of man, surely they will
put ropes on you and bind you with them, so
that you cannot go out among them.
26 "I will make your tongue cling to the
roof of your mouth, so that you shall be mute
and [R]not be a reprover to them, [R]for they *are*
a rebellious house. Hos. 4:17 • Ezek. 2:5–7
27 "But when I speak with you, I will open
your mouth, and you shall say to them,
[R]'Thus says the Lord GOD.' He who hears, let
him hear; and he who refuses, let him refuse;
for they *are* a rebellious house. Ezek. 3:11

CHAPTER 4

Sign of the Clay Tablet

"YOU also, son of man, take a clay tablet
and lay it before you, and portray on it
a city, Jerusalem.
2 [R]"Lay siege against it, build a siege wall
against it, and heap up a [R]mound against it;
set camps against it also, and place battering
rams against it all around. Jer. 6:6 • 2 Kin. 25:1
3 "Moreover take for yourself an iron
plate, and set it *as* an iron wall between you
and the city. Set your face against it, and it
shall be [R]besieged, and you shall lay siege
against it. [R]This *will be* a sign to the house of
Israel. Jer. 39:1, 2 • Ezek. 12:6, 11; 24:24, 27

Sign of Ezekiel's Lying on His Side

4 "Lie also on your left side, and lay the
iniquity of the house of Israel upon it. *According* to the number of the days that you lie
on it, you shall bear their iniquity.
5 "For I have laid on you the years of their
iniquity, according to the number of the days,
three hundred and ninety days; so you shall
bear the iniquity of the house of Israel.
6 "And when you have completed them, lie
again on your right side; then you shall bear
the iniquity of the house of Judah forty days.
I have laid on you a day for each year.
7 "Therefore you shall set your face
toward the siege of Jerusalem; your arm *shall
be* uncovered, and you shall prophesy against
it.
8 "And surely I will constrain you so that
you cannot turn from one side to another till
you have ended the days of your siege.

Sign of the Defiled Bread

9 "Also take for yourself wheat, barley,
beans, lentils, millet, and spelt; put them into
one vessel, and make bread of them for
yourself. *During* the number of days that you
lie on your side, three hundred and ninety
days, you shall eat it.
10 "And your food which you eat *shall be*
by weight, [T]twenty shekels a day; from time
to time you shall eat it. 8 oz.
11 "You shall also drink water by measure,
[T]one-sixth of a hin; from time to time you
shall drink. 21.3 oz.
12 "And you shall eat it *as* barley cakes; and
bake it using fuel of human waste in their
sight."
13 Then the LORD said, "So [R]shall the children of Israel eat their defiled bread among
the Gentiles, where I will drive them." Hos. 9:3
14 So I said, "Ah, Lord GOD! Indeed I have
never defiled myself from my youth till now;
I have never eaten what died of itself or was
torn by beasts, nor has [T]abominable flesh
ever come into my mouth." Ritually unclean
15 Then He said to me, "See, I am giving
you cow dung instead of human waste, and
you shall prepare your bread over it."
16 Moreover He said to me, "Son of man,
surely I will cut off the [R]supply of bread in
Jerusalem; they shall eat bread by weight and
with anxiety, and shall [R]drink water by measure and with dread, Is. 3:1 • Ezek. 4:11
17 "that they may lack bread and water,
and be dismayed with one another, and waste
away because of their iniquity.

CHAPTER 5

Sign of the Razor and the Hair

"AND you, son of man, take a sharp
sword, take it as a barber's razor,
[R]and pass *it* over your head and your beard;
then take balances to weigh and divide the
hair. Is. 7:20
2 "You shall burn with fire one-third in the
midst of the city, when the days of the siege
are finished; then you shall take one-third
and strike around *it* with the sword, and one-
third you shall scatter in the wind: I will draw
out a sword after [R]them. Lev. 26:25
3 [R]"You shall also take a small number of
them and bind them in the edge of your
garment. Jer. 40:6; 52:16
4 "Then take some of them again and
throw them into the midst of the fire, and
burn them in the fire; *for* from there a fire will
go out into all the house of Israel.

Explanation of the Signs

5 "Thus says the Lord GOD: 'This *is* Jerusalem; I have set her in the midst of the nations
and the countries all around her.
6 'She has rebelled against My judgments
by doing wickedness more than the nations,
and against My statutes more than the countries that *are* all around her; for they have
refused My judgments, and they have not
walked in My statutes.'

7 "Therefore thus says the Lord GOD: 'Because you have [T]multiplied *disobedience* more than the nations that *are* all around you, *and* have not walked in My statutes, [R]nor kept My judgments, nor even done according to the judgments of the nations that *are* all around you,' Or *raged* • Jer. 2:10, 11

8 "therefore thus says the Lord GOD: 'Indeed I, even I, *am* against you and will execute judgments in your midst in the sight of the nations.

9 'And I will do among you what I have never done, and the like of which I will never do again, because of all your abominations.

10 'Therefore fathers [R]shall eat *their* sons in your midst, and sons shall eat their fathers; and I will execute judgments among you, and all of you who remain I will [R]scatter to all the winds. Jer. 19:9 • Zech. 2:6; 7:14

11 'Therefore, *as* I live,' says the Lord GOD, 'surely, because you have [R]defiled My sanctuary with all your [R]detestable things and with all your abominations, therefore I will also diminish *you*; My eye will not spare, nor will I have any pity. [Jer. 7:9–11] • Ezek. 11:21

12 [R]'One-third of you shall die of the pestilence, and be consumed with famine in your midst; and one-third shall fall by the sword all around you; and [R]I will scatter another third to all the winds, and I will draw out a sword after [R]them. Ezek. 6:12 • Jer. 9:16 • Jer. 43:10, 11; 44:27

13 'Thus shall My anger be spent, and I will cause My fury to rest upon them, and I will be avenged; [R]and they shall know that I, the LORD, have spoken *it* in My zeal, when I have spent My fury upon them. Ezek. 36:6; 38:19

14 'Moreover I will make you a waste and a reproach among the nations that *are* all around you, in the sight of all who pass by.

15 'So it shall be a [R]reproach, a taunt, a [R]lesson, and an astonishment to the nations that *are* all around you, when I execute judgments among you in anger and in fury and in [R]furious rebukes. I, the LORD, have spoken. Jer. 24:9 • [Is. 26:9] • Ezek. 5:8; 25:17

16 'When I send against them the terrible arrows of famine which shall be for *their* destruction, *and* which I will send to destroy you, I will increase the famine upon you and cut off your [R]supply of bread. Lev. 26:26

17 'So I will send against you famine and [R]wild beasts, and they will bereave you. [R]Pestilence and blood shall pass through you, and I will bring the sword against you. I, the LORD, have spoken.'" Lev. 26:22 • Ezek. 38:22

CHAPTER 6

Destruction of High Places

NOW the word of the LORD came to me, saying:

2 "Son of man, [R]set your face toward the [R]mountains of Israel, and prophesy against them, Ezek. 20:46; 21:2; 25:2 • Ezek. 36:1

3 "and say, 'O mountains of Israel, hear the word of the Lord GOD! Thus says the Lord GOD to the mountains, to the hills, to the ravines, and to the valleys: "Indeed I, *even* I, will bring a sword against you, and [R]I will destroy your high places. Lev. 26:30

4 "Then your altars shall be desolate, your incense altars shall be broken, and I will cast down your slain *men* before your idols.

5 "And I will lay the corpses of the children of Israel before their idols, and I will scatter your bones all around your altars.

6 "In all your dwelling places the cities shall be laid waste, and the [T]high places shall be desolate, so that your altars may be laid waste and made desolate, your idols may be broken and made to cease, your incense altars may be cut down, and your works may be abolished. Places for pagan worship

7 "The slain shall fall in your midst, and you shall know that I *am* the LORD.

Salvation of the Remnant

8 [R]"Yet I will leave a remnant, so that you may have *some* who escape the sword among the nations, when you are [R]scattered through the countries. Jer. 44:28 • Ezek. 5:12

9 "Then those of you who escape will remember Me among the nations where they are carried captive, because [R]I was crushed by their adulterous heart which has departed from Me, and by their eyes which play the harlot after their idols; they will loathe themselves for the evils which they committed in all their abominations. Ps. 78:40

10 "And they shall know that I *am* the LORD, *and that* I have not said in vain that I would bring this calamity upon them."

Desolation of the Land

11 'Thus says the Lord GOD: [T]"Pound your fists and stamp your feet, and say, 'Alas, for all the evil abominations of the house of Israel! For they shall fall by the sword, by famine, and by pestilence. Lit. *Strike your hands*

12 'He who is far off shall die by the pestilence, he who is near shall fall by the sword, and he who remains and is besieged shall die by the famine. [R]Thus will I spend My fury upon them. Ezek. 5:13

13 'Then you shall know that I *am* the LORD, when their slain *men* are among their idols all around their altars, [R]on every high hill, [R]on all the mountaintops, [R]under every green tree, and under every thick oak, wherever they offered sweet incense to all their idols. Jer. 2:20; 3:6 • Hos. 4:13 • Is. 57:5

14 'So I will [R]stretch out My hand against them and make the land desolate, yes, more desolate than the wilderness toward [R]Diblah,

in all their habitations. Then they shall know
that I *am* the LORD.' " ' " Is. 5:25 • Num. 33:46

CHAPTER 7

Description of the Babylonian Conquest

MOREOVER the word of the LORD came
to me, saying,
2 "And you, son of man, thus says the Lord
GOD to the land of Israel:

[R]'An end! The end has come upon the
four corners of the land. Amos 8:2, 10
3 Now the end *has come* upon you,
And I will send My anger against you;
I will judge you [R]according to your
ways,
And I will repay you for all your
abominations. [Rom. 2:6]
4 [R]My eye will not spare you,
Nor will I have pity;
But I will repay your ways,
And your abominations shall be in your
midst;
[R]Then you shall know that I *am* the
LORD!' Ezek. 5:11 • Ezek. 12:20

5 "Thus says the Lord GOD:

'A disaster, a singular [R]disaster;
Behold, it has come! 2 Kin. 21:12, 13
6 An end has come,
The end has come;
It has dawned for you;
Behold, it has come!
7 [R]Doom has come to you, you who dwell
in the land; Ezek. 7:10
[R]The time has come, Zeph. 1:14, 15
A day of trouble *is* near,
And not of rejoicing in the mountains.
8 Now upon you I will soon [R]pour out My
fury,
And spend My anger upon you;
I will judge you according to your
ways,
And I will repay you for all your
abominations. Ezek. 20:8, 21

9 'My eye will not spare,
Nor will I have pity;
I will [T]repay you according to your
ways,
And your abominations will be in your
midst.
Then you will know that I *am* the LORD
who strikes. Lit. *give*

10 'Behold, the day!
Behold, it has come!
[R]Doom has gone out;
The rod has blossomed,
Pride has budded. Ezek. 7:7
11 [R]Violence has risen up into a rod of
wickedness; Jer. 6:7
None of them *shall remain,*
None of their multitude,
None of [T]them; Or *their wealth*
Nor *shall there be* wailing for them.
12 The time has come,
The day draws near.

'Let not the buyer [R]rejoice, Prov. 20:14
Nor the seller [R]mourn, Is. 24:2
For wrath *is* on their whole multitude.
13 For the seller shall not return to what
has been sold,
Though he may still be alive;
For the vision concerns the whole
multitude,
And it shall not turn back;
No one will strengthen himself
Who lives in iniquity.

14 'They have blown the trumpet and made
everyone ready,
But no one goes to battle;
For My wrath *is* on all their multitude.
15 [R]The sword *is* outside, Jer. 14:18
And the pestilence and famine within.
Whoever *is* in the field
Will die by the sword;
And whoever *is* in the city,
Famine and pestilence will devour him.

16 'Those who [R]survive will escape and be
on the mountains
Like doves of the valleys,
All of them mourning,
Each for his iniquity. Ezek. 6:8; 14:22
17 Every [R]hand will be feeble,
And every knee will be *as* weak *as*
water. Is. 13:7
18 They will also [R]be girded with
sackcloth;
Horror will cover them;
Shame *will be* on every face,
Baldness on all their heads. Amos 8:10

19 'They will throw their silver into the
streets,
And their gold will be like refuse;
Their [R]silver and their gold will not be
able to deliver them
In the day of the wrath of the LORD;
They will not satisfy their souls,
Nor fill their stomachs,
Because it became their stumbling block
of iniquity. Zeph. 1:18

20 'As for the beauty of his ornaments,
He set it in majesty;
[R]But they made from it
The images of their abominations
And their detestable things;

Therefore I have made it
Like refuse to them. Jer. 7:30
21 I will give it as [R]plunder
Into the hands of strangers,
And to the wicked of the earth as spoil;
And they shall defile it. 2 Kin. 24:13
22 I will turn My face from them,
And they will defile My secret place;
For robbers shall enter it and defile it.

23 'Make a chain,
For [R]the land is filled with crimes of
blood, 2 Kin. 21:16
And the city is full of violence.
24 Therefore I will bring the [R]worst of the
Gentiles, Ezek. 21:31; 28:7
And they will possess their houses;
I will cause the pomp of the strong to
cease,
And their holy places shall be defiled.
25 Destruction comes;
They will seek peace, but *there shall be*
none.
26 [R]Disaster will come upon disaster,
And rumor will be upon rumor.
[R]Then they will seek a vision from a
prophet; Jer. 4:20 • Ps. 74:9
But the law will perish from the priest,
And counsel from the elders.

27 'The king will mourn,
The prince will be clothed with
desolation,
And the hands of the common people
will tremble.
I will do to them according to their
way,
And according to what they deserve I
will judge them;
Then they shall know that I *am* the
LORD!' "

CHAPTER 8

Vision of the Glory of God

AND it came to pass in the sixth year, in
the sixth *month*, on the fifth *day* of the
month, as I sat in my house with the elders of
Judah sitting before me, that [R]the hand of the
Lord GOD fell upon me there. Ezek. 1:3
2 Then I looked, and there was a likeness,
like the appearance of fire—from the appearance of His waist and downward, fire; and
from His waist and upward, like the appearance of brightness, like the color of amber.
3 He stretched out the form of a hand, and
took me by a lock of my hair; and the Spirit
lifted me up between earth and heaven, and
brought me in visions of God to Jerusalem, to
the door of the north gate of the inner *court*,
where the seat of the image of jealousy *was*,
which provokes to jealousy.
4 And behold, the [R]glory of the God of
Israel *was* there, like the vision that I [R]saw in
the plain. Ezek. 3:12; 9:3 • Ezek. 1:28; 3:22, 23

Image of Jealousy

5 Then He said to me, "Son of man, lift
your eyes now toward the north." So I lifted
my eyes toward the north, and there, north of
the altar gate, was this image of jealousy in
the entrance.
6 Furthermore He said to me, "Son of man,
do you see what they are doing, the great
[R]abominations that the house of Israel commits here, to make Me go far away from My
sanctuary? Now turn again, you will see
greater abominations." 2 Kin. 23:4, 5

Paintings on the Wall

7 So He brought me to the door of the
court; and when I looked, there was a hole in
the wall.
8 Then He said to me, "Son of man, dig
into the wall"; and when I dug into the wall,
there was a door.
9 And He said to me, "Go in, and see the
wicked abominations which they are doing
there."
10 So I went in and saw, and there—every
sort of creeping thing, abominable beasts,
and all the idols of the house of Israel, [T]por-
trayed all around on the walls. Or *carved*
11 And there stood before them seventy
men of the elders of the house of Israel, and
in their midst stood Jaazaniah the son of
Shaphan. Each man had a censer in his hand,
and a thick cloud of incense went up.
12 Then He said to me, "Son of man, have
you seen what the elders of the house of
Israel do in the dark, every man in the room
of his idols? For they say, 'The LORD does not
see us, the LORD has forsaken the land.' "

Weeping for Tammuz

13 And He said to me, "Turn again, *and* you
will see greater abominations that they are
doing."
14 So He brought me to the door of the
north gate of the LORD's house; and to my
dismay, women were sitting there weeping
for [T]Tammuz. A Sumerian god similar to Gr. god Adonis

Sun Worship

15 Then He said to me, "Have you seen *this*,
O son of man? Turn again, you will see
greater abominations than these."
16 So He brought me into the inner court of
the LORD's house; and there, at the door of
the temple of the LORD, [R]between the porch
and the altar, [R]*were* about twenty-five men
[R]with their backs toward the temple of the
LORD and their faces toward the east, and
they were worshiping [R]the sun toward the
east. Joel 2:17 • Ezek. 11:1 • Jer. 2:27; 32:33 • Deut. 4:19

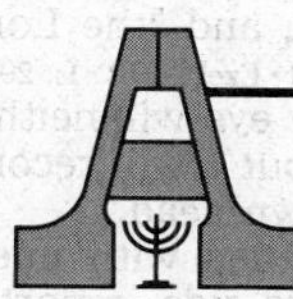

PAGAN GODS OF BIBLE TIMES

The Israelites were God's special people who followed the one true God. But they were surrounded by nations and cultures that worshiped heathen gods. The people of the covenant often gave in to the temptation to worship these pagan deities. Especially tempting in Old Testament times was the Canaanite fertility god known as Baal, who was thought to produce abundant crops and livestock. A fertility goddess of the New Testament era was Diana, or Artemis, of Ephesus (Acts 19:24–28), shown here with her many breasts, which were thought to provide succor for those who were born through her gift of fertility.

These gods and goddesses are the fruits of misguided human minds, which searched for meaning in the elementary forces of life. But real meaning and purpose are found only in the one true God and His Son Jesus Christ.

Listed below are other prominent pagan gods mentioned in the Old and New Testaments.

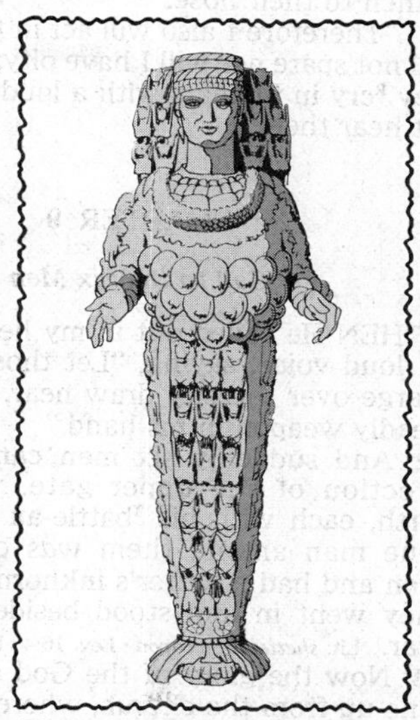

Diana, or Artemis, was a fertility goddess of the New Testament era.

Pagan God	Description	Biblical Reference
	OLD TESTAMENT	
Ashtaroth	Baal's wife or female counterpart	Judg. 2:13
Bel	A god identified with Merodach [Marduk], chief Babylonian god	Is. 46:1
Chemosh	God of the Moabites and Ammonites	Jer. 48:7, 13
Chiun	A star-god, identified with Saturn	Amos 5:26
Dagon	Chief Philistine god	1 Sam. 5:2–7
Merodach	Chief Babylonian god; connected with war. Also known as Marduk.	Jer. 50:2
Molech	Ammonite god; connected with child sacrifice	Lev. 18:21
Nebo	Babylonian god of wisdom and the arts	Is. 46:1
Rimmon	Syrian god of rain	2 Kin. 5:18
Tammuz	Babylonian fertility god	Ezek. 8:14
	NEW TESTAMENT	
Castor and Pollux	Twin sons of Zeus, chief Greek god	Acts 28:11
Zeus	Chief Greek god	Acts 14:12, 13
Hermes	The Greek god of commerce and speed	Acts 14:12, 13

17 Then He said to me, "Have you seen *this*, O son of man? Is it a trivial thing to the house of Judah to commit the abominations which they commit here? For they have [R]filled the land with violence; then they have returned to provoke Me to anger. Indeed they put the branch to their nose. Ezek. 9:9

18 "Therefore I also will act in fury. My eye will not spare nor will I have pity; and though they [R]cry in My ears with a loud voice, I will not hear them." Mic. 3:4

CHAPTER 9

Call to the Six Men

THEN He called out in my hearing with a loud voice, saying, "Let those who have charge over the city draw near, each *with* a [T]deadly weapon in his hand." Or *destroying*

2 And suddenly six men came from the direction of the upper gate, which faces north, each with his [T]battle-ax in his hand. [R]One man among them *was* clothed with linen and had a writer's inkhorn [T]at his side. They went in and stood beside the bronze altar. Lit. *shattering weapon* • Lev. 16:4 • Lit. *upon his loins*

3 Now the glory of the God of Israel had gone up from the cherub, where it had been, to the threshold of the [T]temple. And He called to the man clothed with linen, who *had* the writer's inkhorn at his side; Lit. *house*

Command to Slay the Wicked

4 and the LORD said to him, "Go through the midst of the city, through the midst of Jerusalem, and put a mark on the foreheads of the men who sigh and cry over all the abominations that are done within it."

5 To the others He said in my hearing, "Go after him through the city and kill; do not let your eye spare, nor have any pity.

6 "Utterly slay old *and* young men, maidens and little children and women; but do not come near anyone on whom *is* the mark; and begin at My sanctuary." So they began with the elders who *were* before the temple.

7 Then He said to them, "Defile the [T]temple, and fill the courts with the slain. Go out!" And they went out and killed in the city. Lit. *house*

Weeping of Ezekiel

8 So it was, that while they were killing them, I was left *alone*; and I fell on my face and cried out, and said, "Ah, Lord GOD! Will You destroy all the remnant of Israel in pouring out Your fury on Jerusalem?"

9 Then He said to me, "The iniquity of the house of Israel and Judah *is* exceedingly great, and [R]the land is full of bloodshed, and the city full of perversity; for they say, [R]'The LORD has forsaken the land, and [R]the LORD does not see!' 2 Kin. 21:16 • Ezek. 8:12 • Is. 29:15

10 "And as for Me also, My eye will neither spare, nor will I have pity, *but* I will recompense their deeds on their own head."

11 Just then, the man clothed with linen, who *had* the inkhorn at his side, reported back and said, "I have done as You commanded me."

CHAPTER 10

Departure of the Glory of God to the Threshold

AND I looked, and there in the [R]firmament[T] that was above the head of the cherubim, there appeared something like a sapphire stone, having the appearance of the likeness of a throne. Ezek. 1:22, 26 • *expanse*

2 [R]And He spoke to the man clothed with linen, and said, "Go in among the wheels, under the cherub, fill your hands with [R]coals of fire from among the cherubim, and [R]scatter *them* over the city." And he went in as I watched. Dan. 10:5 • Ezek. 1:13 • Rev. 8:5

3 Now the cherubim were standing on the south side of the temple when the man went in, and the cloud filled the inner court.

4 Then the glory of the LORD went up from the cherub, *and paused* over the threshold of the [T]temple; and the house was filled with the cloud, and the court was full of the brightness of the LORD's glory. Lit. *house*

5 And the [R]sound of the wings of the cherubim was heard *even* in the outer court, like [R]the voice of Almighty God when He speaks. Ezek. 1:24 • [Ps. 29:3]

6 Now it happened, when He commanded the man clothed in linen, saying, "Take fire from among the wheels, from among the cherubim," that he went in and stood beside the wheels.

7 And the cherub stretched out his hand from among the cherubim to the fire that *was* among the cherubim, and took *some of it* and put *it* into the hands of the *man* clothed with linen, who took *it* and went out.

8 The cherubim appeared to have the form of a man's hand under their wings.

Vision of the Wheels and Cherubim

9 [R]And when I looked, there were four wheels by the cherubim, one wheel by one cherub and another wheel by each other cherub; the wheels appeared *to have* the color of a [R]beryl stone. Ezek. 1:15 • Ezek. 1:16

10 *As for* their appearance, all four looked alike—as it were, a wheel in the middle of a wheel.

11 [R]When they went, they went toward *any of* their four directions; they did not turn aside when they went, but followed in the direction the head was facing. They did not turn aside when they went. Ezek. 1:17

12 And their whole body, with their back, their hands, their wings, and the wheels that the four had, *were* full of eyes all around.

13 As for the wheels, they were called in my [T]hearing, "Wheel." Lit. *ears*

14 [R]Each one had four faces: the first face *was* the face of a cherub, the second face the face of a man, the third the face of a lion, and the fourth the face of an eagle. Ezek. 1:6, 10, 11

15 And the cherubim were lifted up. This *was* [R]the living creature I saw by the River Chebar. Ezek. 1:3, 5

16 [R]When the cherubim went, the wheels went beside them; and when the cherubim lifted their wings to mount up from the earth, the same wheels also did not turn from beside them. Ezek. 1:19

17 When *the cherubim* stood still, *the wheels* stood still, and when *one* was lifted up, *the other* lifted itself up, for the spirit of the living creature *was* in them.

18 Then [R]the glory of the LORD [R]departed from the threshold of the [T]temple and stood over the cherubim. Ezek. 10:4 • Hos. 9:12 • Lit. *house*

19 And the cherubim lifted their wings and mounted up from the earth in my sight. When they went out, the wheels *were* beside them; and they stood at the door of the [R]east gate of the LORD's house, and the glory of the God of Israel *was* above them. Ezek. 11:1

20 [R]This *is* the living creature I saw under the God of Israel [R]by the River Chebar, and I knew they *were* cherubim. Ezek. 1:22 • Ezek. 1:1

21 [R]Each one had four faces and each one four wings, and the likeness of the hands of a man *was* under their wings. Ezek. 1:6, 8; 10:14

22 And the likeness of their faces *was* the same *as* the faces which I had seen by the River Chebar, their appearance and their persons. They each went straight forward.

CHAPTER 11

Vision of the Twenty-five Wicked Rulers

THEN [R]the Spirit lifted me up and brought me to [R]the east gate of the LORD's house, which faces eastward; and there [R]at the door of the gate were twenty-five men, among whom I saw Jaazaniah the son of Azzur, and Pelatiah the son of Benaiah, princes of the people. Ezek. 3:12, 14 • Ezek. 10:19 • Ezek. 8:16

2 And He said to me: "Son of man, these *are* the men who devise iniquity and give wicked [T]counsel in this city, Advice

3 "who say, '*The time is* not [R]near to build houses; [R]this *city is* the [T]caldron, and we *are* the meat.' 2 Pet. 3:4 • Jer. 1:13 • Pot

4 "Therefore prophesy against them, prophesy, O son of man!"

5 Then [R]the Spirit of the LORD fell upon me, and said to me, "Speak! 'Thus says the LORD: "Thus you have said, O house of Israel; for [R]I know the things that come into your mind. Ezek. 2:2; 3:24 • [Jer. 16:17; 17:10]

6 [R]"You have multiplied your slain in this city, and you have filled its streets with the slain." Ezek. 7:23; 22:2–6, 9, 12, 27

7 'Therefore thus says the Lord GOD: [R]"Your slain whom you have laid in its midst, they *are* the meat, and this *city is* the caldron; [R]but I shall bring you out of the midst of it. Mic. 3:2, 3 • Ezek. 11:9

8 "You have feared the sword; and I will bring a sword upon you," says the Lord GOD.

9 "And I will bring you out of its midst, and deliver you into the hands of strangers, and [R]execute judgments on you. Ezek. 5:8

10 "You shall fall by the sword. I will judge you at the border of Israel. [R]Then you shall know that I *am* the LORD. Ps. 9:16

11 "This *city* shall not be your [T]caldron, nor shall you be the meat in its midst. I will judge you at the border of Israel. Pot

12 "And you shall know that I *am* the LORD; for you have not walked in My statutes nor executed My judgments, but [R]have done according to the customs of the Gentiles which *are* all around you."'" Deut. 12:30, 31

Promise of the Restoration of the Remnant

13 Now it happened, while I was prophesying, that [R]Pelatiah the son of Benaiah died. Then [R]I fell on my face and cried with a loud voice, and said, "Ah, Lord GOD! Will You make a complete end of the remnant of Israel?" Acts 5:5 • Ezek. 9:8

14 Again the word of the LORD came to me, saying,

15 "Son of man, your brethren, your relatives, your kinsmen, and all the house of Israel in its entirety, *are* those about whom the inhabitants of Jerusalem have said, 'Get far away from the LORD; this land has been given to us as a possession.'

16 "Therefore say, 'Thus says the Lord GOD: "Although I have cast them far off among the Gentiles, and although I have scattered them among the countries, [R]yet I shall be a little [T]sanctuary for them in the countries where they have gone."' Is. 8:14 • *holy place*

17 "Therefore say, 'Thus says the Lord GOD: [R]"I will gather you from the peoples, assemble you from the countries where you have been scattered, and I will give you the land of Israel."' Jer. 3:12, 18; 24:5

18 "And they will go there, and they will take away all its [R]detestable things and all its abominations from there. Ezek. 37:23

19 "Then I will give them one heart, and I will put a new spirit within [T]them, and take [R]the stony heart out of their flesh, and give them a heart of flesh, Lit. *you* (pl.) • Zech. 7:12

20 "that they may walk in My statutes and keep My judgments and do them; and they shall be My people, and I will be their God.

21 "But *as for those* whose hearts walk
after the heart of their detestable things and
their abominations, [R]I will recompense their
deeds on their own heads," says the Lord
GOD. Ezek. 9:10

Departure of the Glory of God from the Mount of Olives

22 Then the cherubim lifted up their wings,
with the wheels beside them, and the glory of
the God of Israel *was* high above them.
23 And [R]the glory of the LORD went up from
the midst of the city and stood [R]on the
mountain, [R]which *is* on the east side of the
city. Ezek. 8:4; 9:3 • Zech. 14:4 • Ezek. 43:2
24 Then the Spirit took me up and brought
me in a vision by the Spirit of God into
Chaldea, to those in captivity. And the vision
that I had seen went up from me.
25 So I spoke to those in captivity of all the
things the LORD had shown me.

CHAPTER 12

Sign of Belongings for Removing

NOW the word of the LORD came to me,
saying:
2 "Son of man, you dwell in the midst of a
rebellious house, which has eyes to see but
does not see, and ears to hear but does not
hear; for they *are* a rebellious house.
3 "Therefore, son of man, prepare your
belongings for captivity, and go into captivity
by day in their sight. You shall go from your
place into captivity to another place in their
sight. It may be that they will consider,
though they *are* a rebellious house.
4 "By day you shall bring out your belongings in their sight, as though going into
captivity; and at evening you shall go in their
sight, like those who go into captivity.
5 "Dig through the wall in their sight, and
carry your belongings out through it.
6 "In their sight you shall bear *them* on
your shoulders *and* carry *them* out at twilight; you shall cover your face, so that you
cannot see the ground, [R]for I have made you
a sign to the house of Israel." Ezek. 4:3; 24:24
7 So I did as I was commanded. I brought
out my belongings by day, as though going
into captivity, and at evening I dug through
the wall with my hand. I brought *them* out at
twilight, *and* I bore *them* on *my* shoulder in
their sight.
8 And in the morning the word of the LORD
came to me, saying,
9 "Son of man, has not the house of Israel,
[R]the rebellious house, said to you, [R]'What are
you doing?' Ezek. 2:5 • Ezek. 17:12; 24:19
10 "Say to them, 'Thus says the Lord GOD:
"This [R]burden[T] *concerns* the prince in Jerusalem and all the house of Israel who are
among them." ' Mal. 1:1 • *oracle, prophecy*
11 "Say, [R]'I *am* a sign to you. As I have
done, so shall it be done to them; they shall
be carried away into captivity.' Ezek. 12:6
12 "And [R]the prince who *is* among them
shall bear *his belongings* on *his* shoulder at
twilight and go out. They shall dig through
the wall to carry *them* out through it. He
shall cover his face, so that he cannot see the
ground with *his* eyes. Jer. 39:4; 52:7
13 "I will also spread My [R]net over him, and
he shall be caught in My snare. [R]I will bring
him to Babylon, *to* the land of the Chaldeans;
yet he shall not see it, though he shall die
there. Jer. 52:9 • Jer. 52:11
14 "I will scatter to every wind all who *are*
around him to help him, and all his troops;
and I will draw out the sword after them.
15 [R]"Then they shall know that I *am* the
LORD, when I scatter them among the nations and disperse them throughout the
countries. Ezek. 6:7, 14; 12:16, 20
16 "But I will spare a few of their men from
the sword, from famine, and from pestilence,
that they may declare all their abominations
among the Gentiles wherever they go. Then
they shall know that I *am* the LORD."

Sign of Trembling

17 Moreover the word of the LORD came to
me, saying,
18 "Son of man, [R]eat your bread with [T]quak-
ing, and drink your water with trembling and
anxiety. Ezek. 4:16 • *shaking*
19 "And say to the people of the land, 'Thus
says the Lord GOD to the inhabitants of
Jerusalem *and* to the land of Israel: "They
shall eat their bread with anxiety, and drink
their water with dread, so that her land may
be emptied of all who are in it, because of the
violence of all those who dwell in it.
20 "Then the cities that are inhabited shall
be laid waste, and the land shall become
desolate; and you shall know that I *am* the
LORD." ' "
21 And the word of the LORD came to me,
saying,
22 "Son of man, what *is* this proverb *that*
you *people* have about the land of Israel,
which says, [R]'The days are prolonged, and
every vision fails'? Ezek. 11:3; 12:27
23 "Tell them therefore, 'Thus says the Lord
GOD: "I will lay this proverb to rest, and they
shall no more use it as a proverb in Israel."
But say to them, "The days are at hand, and
the [T]fulfillment of every vision. Lit. *word*
24 "For [R]no more shall there be any [R]false[T]
vision or flattering divination within the
house of Israel. Ezek. 13:6 • Lam. 2:14 • Lit. *vain*
25 "For I *am* the LORD. I speak, and the
word which I speak will come to pass; it will
no more be postponed; for in your days, O
rebellious house, I will say the word and
[R]perform it," says the Lord GOD.' " [Is. 14:24]

26 Again the word of the LORD came to me, saying,

27 [R]"Son of man, look, the house of Israel is saying, 'The vision that he sees *is* [R]for many days *from now*, and he prophesies of times far off.' Ezek. 12:22 • Dan. 10:14

28 "Therefore say to them, 'Thus says the Lord GOD: "None of My words will be postponed any more, but the word which I speak [R]will be done," says the Lord GOD.' " Jer. 4:7

CHAPTER 13

Judgment upon False Prophets

AND the word of the LORD came to me, saying,

2 "Son of man, prophesy against the prophets of Israel who prophesy, and say to those who prophesy out of their own heart, 'Hear the word of the LORD!' "

3 Thus says the Lord GOD: "Woe to the foolish prophets, who follow their own spirit and have [T]seen nothing! No vision

4 "O Israel, your prophets are [R]like foxes in the deserts. Song 2:15

5 "You [R]have not gone up into the [T]gaps to build a wall for the house of Israel to stand in battle on the day of the LORD. Ps. 106:23 • *breaches*

6 "They have envisioned futility and false divination, saying, 'Thus says the LORD!' But the LORD has not sent them; yet they hope that the word may [T]be confirmed. Come true

7 "Have you not seen a futile vision, and have you not spoken false divination? You say, 'The LORD says,' but I have not spoken."

8 Therefore thus says the Lord GOD: "Because you have spoken nonsense and envisioned lies, therefore I *am* indeed against you," says the Lord GOD.

9 "My hand will be against the prophets who envision futility and who divine lies; they shall not be in the assembly of My people, nor be written in the record of the house of Israel, [R]nor shall they enter into the land of Israel. [R]Then you shall know that I *am* the Lord GOD. Jer. 20:3–6 • Ezek. 11:10, 12

10 "Because, indeed, because they have seduced My people, saying, [R]'Peace!' when *there is* no peace—and one builds a *boundary* wall, and they [R]plaster[T] it with untempered *mortar*— Jer. 6:14; 8:11 • Ezek. 22:28 • Or *whitewash*

11 "say to those who plaster *it* with untempered *mortar*, that it will fall. [R]There will be flooding rain, and you, O great hailstones, shall fall; and a stormy wind shall tear *it* down. Ezek. 38:22

12 "Surely, when the wall has fallen, will it not be said to you, 'Where *is* the mortar with which you plastered *it*?' "

13 Therefore thus says the Lord GOD: "I will cause a stormy wind to break forth in My fury; and there shall be a flooding rain in My anger, and great hailstones in fury to consume *it*.

14 "So I will break down the wall you have plastered with untempered *mortar*, and bring it down to the ground, so that its foundation will be uncovered; it will fall, and you shall be consumed in the midst of it. [R]Then you shall know that I *am* the LORD. Ezek. 13:9, 21, 23; 14:8

15 "Thus will I accomplish My wrath on the wall and on those who have plastered it with untempered *mortar*; and I will say to you, 'The wall *is* no *more*, nor those who plastered it,

16 '*that is*, the prophets of Israel who prophesy concerning Jerusalem, and who [R]see visions of peace for her when *there is* no peace,' " says the Lord GOD. Jer. 6:14; 8:11; 28:9

Judgment upon False Prophetesses

17 "Likewise, son of man, [R]set your face against the daughters of your people, [R]who prophesy out of their own [T]heart; prophesy against them, Ezek. 20:46; 21:2 • Ezek. 13:2 • Inspiration

18 "and say, 'Thus says the Lord GOD: "Woe to the *women* who sew *magic* [T]charms on their sleeves and make veils for the heads of people of every height to hunt souls! Will you hunt the souls of My people, and keep yourselves alive? Lit. *bands on all joints of the hand*

19 "And will you profane Me among My people [R]for handfuls of barley and for pieces of bread, killing people who should not die, and keeping people alive who should not live, by your lying to My people who listen to lies?" Mic. 3:5

20 'Therefore thus says the Lord GOD: "Behold, I *am* against your *magic* charms by which you hunt souls there like [T]birds. I will tear them from your arms, and let the souls go, the souls you hunt like birds. Lit. *flying ones*

21 "I will also tear off your veils and deliver My people out of your hand, and they shall no longer be as prey in your hand. [R]Then you shall know that I *am* the LORD." ' ' Ezek. 13:9

22 "Because with lies you have made the heart of the righteous sad, whom I have not made sad; and you have strengthened the hands of the wicked, so that he does not turn from his wicked way to save his life.

23 "Therefore [R]you shall no longer envision futility nor practice divination; for I will deliver My people out of your hand, and you shall know that I *am* the LORD." ' ' Mic. 3:5, 6

CHAPTER 14

Idolatry of the Elders

NOW [R]some of the elders of Israel came to me and sat before me. Ezek. 8:1; 20:1; 33:31

2 And the word of the LORD came to me, saying,

3 "Son of man, these men have set up their
idols in their hearts, and put before them
[R]that which causes them to stumble into
iniquity. [R]Should I let Myself be inquired of at
all by them? Ezek. 7:19 • Ezek. 20:3, 31
4 "Therefore speak to them, and say to
them, 'Thus says the Lord GOD: "Everyone of
the house of Israel who sets up his idols in his
heart, and puts before him what causes him
to stumble into iniquity, and then comes to
the prophet, I the LORD will answer him who
comes, according to the multitude of his
idols,
5 "that I may seize the house of Israel by
their heart, because they are all estranged
from Me by their idols." '
6 "Therefore say to the house of Israel,
'Thus says the Lord GOD: "Repent, turn away
from your idols, and [R]turn your faces away
from all your abominations. Is. 2:20; 30:22; 55:6, 7
7 "For anyone of the house of Israel, or of
the strangers who sojourn in Israel, who
separates himself from Me and sets up his
idols in his heart and puts before him what
causes him to stumble into iniquity, then
comes to a prophet to inquire of him concerning Me, I the LORD will answer him by Myself.
8 "I will set My face against that man and
make him a sign and a proverb, and I will cut
him off from the midst of My people. Then
you shall know that I *am* the LORD.
9 "And if the prophet is induced to speak
anything, I the LORD [R]have induced that
prophet, and I will stretch out My hand
against him and destroy him from among My
people Israel. 2 Thess. 2:11
10 "And they shall bear their iniquity; the
punishment of the prophet shall be the same
as the punishment of the one who inquired,
11 "that the house of Israel may [R]no longer
stray from Me, nor be profaned anymore with
all their transgressions, [R]but that they may be
My people and I may be their God," says the
Lord GOD.' " 2 Pet. 2:15 • Ezek. 11:20; 37:27

Jerusalem to Be Destroyed

12 The word of the LORD came again to me,
saying:
13 "Son of man, when a land sins against
Me by persistent unfaithfulness, I will stretch
out My hand against it; I will cut off its
[R]supply of bread, send famine on it, and cut
off man and beast from it. Is. 3:1
14 [R]"*Though* these three men, Noah, Daniel,
and Job, *were* in it, they would deliver *only*
themselves [R]by their righteousness," says the
Lord GOD. Jer. 15:1 • [Prov. 11:4]
15 "If I cause wild beasts to pass through
the land, and they [T]empty it, and make it so
desolate that no man may pass through
because of the beasts, Lit. *bereave it* of children
16 "even *though* these three men *were* [T]in
it, *as* I live," says the Lord GOD, "they would
deliver neither sons nor daughters; only they
would be delivered, and the land would be
[R]desolate. Lit. *in the midst of it* • Ezek. 15:8; 33:28, 29
17 "Or *if* [R]I bring a sword on that land, and
say, 'Sword, go through the land,' and I [R]cut
off man and beast from it, Lev. 26:25 • Zeph. 1:3
18 "even [R]*though* these three men *were* in
it, *as* I live," says the Lord GOD, "they would
deliver neither sons nor daughters, but only
they themselves would be delivered. Ezek. 14:14
19 "Or *if* I send [R]a pestilence into that land
and [R]pour out My fury on it in blood, and cut
off from it man and beast, 2 Sam. 24:15 • Ezek. 7:8
20 "even [R]though Noah, Daniel, and Job
were in it, *as* I live," says the Lord GOD, "they
would deliver neither son nor daughter; they
would deliver *only* themselves by their righteousness." Ezek. 14:14
21 For thus says the Lord GOD: "How much
more it shall be when I send My four [T]severe
judgments on Jerusalem—the sword and
famine and wild beasts and pestilence—to cut
off man and beast from it? Lit. *evil*
22 [R]"Yet behold, there shall be left in it a
remnant who will be [R]brought out, *both* sons
and daughters; surely they will come out to
you, and [R]you will see their ways and their
doings. Then you will be comforted concerning the disaster that I have brought upon
Jerusalem, *indeed* all that I have brought
upon it. Ezek. 12:16; 36:20 • Ezek. 6:8 • Ezek. 20:43
23 "And they will comfort you, when you
see their ways and their doings; and you shall
know that I have done nothing [R]without
cause that I have done in it," says the Lord
GOD. Jer. 22:8, 9

CHAPTER 15

Parable of the Vine

THEN the word of the LORD came to me,
saying:
2 "Son of man, how is the wood of the vine
better than any other wood, the vine branch
which is among the trees of the forest?
3 "Is wood taken from it to make any
object? Or can *men* make a peg from it to
hang any vessel on?
4 "Instead, it is thrown into the fire for
fuel; the fire devours both ends of it, and its
middle is burned. Is it useful for *any* work?
5 "Indeed, when it was whole, no object
could be made from it. How much less will it
be useful for *any* work when the fire has
devoured it, and it is burned?
6 "Therefore thus says the Lord GOD: 'Like
the wood of the vine among the trees of the
forest, which I have given to the fire for fuel,
so I will give up the inhabitants of Jerusalem;
7 'and [R]I will set My face against them.
[R]They will go out from *one* fire, but *another*

fire shall devour them. [R]Then you shall know
that I *am* the LORD, when I set My face
against them. Ezek. 14:8 • Is. 24:18 • Ezek. 7:4
8 'Thus I will make the land desolate,
because they have persisted in unfaithfulness,' says the Lord GOD."

CHAPTER 16

God Has Mercy on Israel

AGAIN the word of the LORD came to me,
saying,
2 "Son of man, [R]cause Jerusalem to know
her abominations, Ezek. 20:4; 22:2
3 "and say, 'Thus says the Lord GOD to
Jerusalem: "Your birth and your nativity *are*
from the land of Canaan; your father *was* an
Amorite and your mother a Hittite.
4 "*As for* your nativity, [R]on the day you
were born your navel cord was not cut, nor
were you washed in water to cleanse *you*;
you were not rubbed with salt nor swathed in
swaddling cloths. Hos. 2:3
5 "No eye pitied you, to do any of these
things for you, to have compassion on you;
but you were thrown out into the open field,
when you yourself were [T]loathed on the day
you were born. *abhorred*
6 "And when I passed by you and saw you
struggling in your own blood, I said to you in
your blood, 'Live!' Yes, I said to you in your
blood, 'Live!'
7 "I made you thrive like a plant in the
field; and you grew, matured, and became
very beautiful. *Your* breasts were formed,
your hair grew, but you *were* naked and bare.
8 "When I passed by you again and looked
upon you, indeed your time *was* the time of
love; so I spread [T]My wing over you and
covered your nakedness. Yes, I swore an oath
to you and entered into a covenant with you,
and [R]you became Mine," says the Lord
GOD. Or *the corner of My garment* • [Ex. 19:5]
9 "Then I washed you in water; yes, I
thoroughly washed off your blood, and I
anointed you with oil.
10 "I clothed you in embroidered cloth and
gave you sandals of badger skin; I clothed
you with fine linen and covered you with silk.
11 "I adorned you with ornaments, [R]put
bracelets on your wrists, [R]and a chain on
your neck. Gen. 24:22, 47 • Prov. 1:9
12 "And I put a [T]jewel in your nose, earrings in your ears, and a beautiful crown on
your head. Lit. *ring*
13 "Thus you were adorned with gold and
silver, and your clothing *was of* fine linen,
silk, and embroidered cloth. You ate *pastry of*
fine flour, honey, and oil. You were exceedingly beautiful, and succeeded to royalty.
14 "Your fame went out among the nations
because of your beauty, for it *was* perfect
through My splendor which I had bestowed
on you," says the Lord GOD.

Israel Rejects God

15 [R]"But you trusted in your own beauty,
[R]played the harlot because of your fame, and
poured out your harlotry on everyone passing by who *would have* it. Mic. 3:11 • Is. 1:21; 57:8
16 [R]"You took some of your garments and
adorned multicolored high places for yourself, and played the harlot on them. *Such*
things should not happen, nor be. Ezek. 7:20
17 "You have also taken your beautiful
jewelry from My gold and My silver, which I
had given you, and made for yourself male
images and played the harlot with them.
18 "You took your embroidered garments
and covered them, and you set My oil and My
incense before them.
19 "Also My food which I gave you—the
pastry of fine flour, oil, and honey *which* I fed
you—you set it before them as sweet incense;
and *so* it was," says the Lord GOD.
20 [R]"Moreover you took your sons and your
daughters, whom you bore to Me, and these
you sacrificed to them to be devoured. *Were*
your *acts* of harlotry a small matter, Jer. 7:31
21 "that you have slain My children and
offered them up to them by causing them to
pass through *the* [R]*fire*? Jer. 19:5
22 "And in all your abominations and acts
of harlotry you did not remember the days of
your youth, [R]when you were naked and bare,
struggling in your blood. Ezek. 16:4–6
23 "Then it was so, after all your wickedness—'Woe, woe to you!' says the Lord
GOD—
24 "*that* you also built for yourself a shrine,
and [R]made a [T]high place for yourself in every
street. Jer. 2:20; 3:2 • Place for pagan worship
25 "You built your high places [R]at the head
of every road, and made your beauty to be
abhorred. You offered yourself to everyone
who passed by, and multiplied your acts of
harlotry. Prov. 9:14
26 "You also committed harlotry with [R]the
Egyptians, your very fleshly neighbors, and
increased your acts of harlotry to [R]provoke
Me to anger. Ezek. 16:26; 20:7, 8 • Deut. 31:20
27 "Behold, therefore, I stretched out My
hand against you, diminished your [T]allot-
ment, and gave you up to the will of those
who hate you, [R]the daughters of the Philistines, who were ashamed of your lewd behavior. Allowance of food • Ezek. 16:57
28 "You also played the harlot with the
[R]Assyrians, because you were insatiable;
indeed you played the harlot with them and
still were not satisfied. Jer. 2:18, 36
29 "Moreover you multiplied your acts of
harlotry as far as the land of the trader,
[R]Chaldea; and even then you were not satisfied. Ezek. 23:14–17

30 "How degenerate is your heart!" says the
Lord GOD, "seeing you do all these *things*, the
deeds of a brazen harlot.
31 "You erected your shrine at the head of
every road, and built your high place in every
street. Yet you were not like a harlot, because you scorned [R]payment. Is. 52:3
32 "*You are* an adulterous wife, *who* takes
strangers instead of her husband.
33 "Men make payment to all harlots, but
[R]you made your payments to all your lovers,
and [T]hired them to come to you from all
around for your harlotry. Hos. 8:9, 10 • Or *bribed*
34 "You are the opposite of *other* women in
your harlotry, because no one solicited you to
be a harlot. In that you gave payment but no
payment was given you, therefore you are
the opposite."

God Punishes Israel

35 'Now then, O harlot, hear the word of the
LORD!
36 'Thus says the Lord GOD: "Because your
filthiness was poured out and your nakedness
uncovered in your harlotry with your lovers,
and with all your abominable idols, and
because of [R]the blood of your children which
you gave to them, Jer. 2:34
37 "surely, therefore, [R]I will gather all your
lovers with whom you took pleasure, all
those you loved, *and* all those you hated; I
will gather them from all around against you
and will uncover your nakedness to them,
that they may see all your nakedness. Lam. 1:8
38 "And I will judge you as [R]women who
break wedlock or [R]shed blood are judged; I
will bring blood upon you in fury and jealousy. Lev. 20:10 • Gen. 9:6
39 "I will also give you into their hand, and
they shall throw down your shrines and
break down [R]your [T]high places. [R]They shall
also strip you of your clothes, take your
beautiful jewelry, and leave you naked and
bare. Ezek. 16:24, 31 • Places for pagan worship • Hos. 2:3
40 [R]"They shall also bring up an assembly
against you, [R]and they shall stone you with
stones and thrust you through with their
swords. Ezek. 23:45–47 • John 8:5, 7
41 "They shall burn your houses with fire,
and [R]execute judgments on you in the sight
of many women; and I will make you [R]cease
playing the harlot, and you shall no longer
hire lovers. Ezek. 5:8; 23:10, 48 • Ezek. 23:27
42 "So I will lay to rest My fury toward you,
and My jealousy shall depart from you. I will
be quiet, and be angry no more.
43 "Because you did not remember the days
of your youth, but agitated Me with all these
things, surely I will also recompense your
deeds on *your own* head," says the Lord GOD.
"And you shall not commit lewdness in addition to all your abominations.
44 "Indeed everyone who quotes proverbs
will use *this* proverb against you: 'Like
mother, like daughter!'
45 "You *are* your mother's daughter, [T]loath-
ing husband and children; and you *are* the
sister of your sisters, who loathed their husbands and children; your mother *was* a Hittite and your father an Amorite. *despising*
46 "Your elder sister *is* Samaria, who dwells
with her daughters to the north of you; and
[R]your younger sister, who dwells to the south
of you, *is* Sodom and her daughters. Is. 1:10
47 "You did not walk in their ways nor act
according to their abominations; but, as *if
that were* too little, [R]you became more corrupt than they in all your ways. Ezek. 5:6, 7
48 "*As* I live," says the Lord GOD, "neither
your sister Sodom nor her daughters have
done as you and your daughters have done.
49 "Look, this was the iniquity of your
sister Sodom: She and her daughter had
pride, [R]fullness of food, and abundance of
idleness; neither did she strengthen the hand
of the poor and needy. Gen. 13:10
50 "And they were haughty and committed
abomination before Me; therefore [R]I took
them away as I saw *fit*. Gen. 19:24
51 "Samaria did not commit [R]half of your
sins; but you have multiplied your abominations more than they, and [R]have justified
your sisters by all the abominations which
you have done. Ezek. 23:11 • Jer. 3:8–11
52 "You who judged your sisters, bear your
own shame also, because the sins which you
committed were more abominable than
theirs; they are more righteous than you.
Yes, be disgraced also, and bear your own
shame, because you justified your sisters.
53 [R]"When I bring back their captives, the
captives of Sodom and her daughters, and the
captives of Samaria and her daughters, then *I
will also bring back* [R]the captives of your
captivity among them, Is. 1:9 • Jer. 20:16
54 "that you may bear your own shame and
be disgraced by all that you did when [R]you
comforted them. Ezek. 14:22
55 "When your sisters, Sodom and her
daughters, return to their former state, and
Samaria and her daughters return to their
former state, then you and your daughters
will return to your former state.
56 "For your sister Sodom was not a byword in your mouth in the days of your pride,
57 "before your wickedness was uncovered.
It was like the time of the reproach of the
daughters of *Syria and all *who were* around
her, and of [R]the daughters of the Philistines,
who despise you everywhere. Ezek. 16:27
58 [R]"You have paid for your lewdness and
your abominations," says the LORD. Ezek. 23:49
59 'For thus says the Lord GOD: "I will deal

16:57 Heb. *Aram;* some mss., Syr. *Edom*

with you as you have done, who despised the
oath by breaking the covenant.

God Remembers His Covenant

60 "Nevertheless I will [R]remember My covenant with you in the days of your youth, and
I will establish [R]an everlasting covenant with
you. Ps. 106:45 • Is. 55:3
61 "Then you will remember your ways and
be ashamed, when you receive your older and
your younger sisters; for I will give them to
you for [R]daughters, [R]but not because of My
covenant with you. [Gal. 4:26] • Jer. 31:31
62 [R]"And I will establish My covenant with
you. Then you shall know that I *am* the
LORD, Hos. 2:19, 20
63 "that you may [R]remember and be
ashamed, [R]and never open your mouth anymore because of your shame, when I provide
you an atonement for all you have done,"
says the Lord GOD.' " Ezek. 36:31, 32 • [Rom. 3:19]

CHAPTER 17

Parable of the Two Eagles

AND the word of the LORD came to me,
saying,
2 "Son of man, pose a riddle, and speak a
[R]parable to the house of Israel, Ezek. 20:49; 24:3
3 "and say, 'Thus says the Lord GOD:

[R]"A great eagle with large wings and long
pinions,
Full of feathers of various colors,
Came to Lebanon
And [R]took from the cedar the highest
branch. Ezek. 17:12 • 2 Kin. 24:12
4 He cropped off its topmost young twig
And carried it to a land of trade;
He set it in a city of merchants.
5 Then he took some of the seed of the
land
And planted it in a fertile field;
He placed *it* by abundant waters
And set it [R]like a willow tree. Is. 44:4
6 And it grew and became a spreading
vine [R]of low stature; Ezek. 17:14
Its branches turned toward him,
But its roots were under it.
So it became a vine,
Brought forth branches,
And put forth shoots.

7 "But there was another great eagle with
large wings and many feathers;
And behold, [R]this vine bent its roots
toward him, Ezek. 17:15
And stretched its branches toward him,
From the garden terrace where it had
been planted,
That he might water it.
8 It was planted in [T]good soil by many
waters, Lit. *a good field*
To bring forth branches, bear fruit,
And become a majestic vine." '

9 "Say, 'Thus says the Lord GOD:

"Will it thrive?
[R]Will he not pull up its roots,
Cut off its fruit,
And leave it to wither?
All of its spring leaves will wither,
And no great power or many people
Will be needed to pluck it up by its
roots. 2 Kin. 25:7
10 Behold, *it is* planted,
Will it thrive?
[R]Will it not utterly wither when the east
wind touches it?
It will wither in the garden terrace
where it grew." ' " Hos. 13:15

11 Moreover the word of the LORD came to
me, saying,
12 "Say now to the rebellious house: 'Do
you not know what these *things mean*?' Tell
them, 'Indeed [R]the king of Babylon went to
Jerusalem and took its king and princes, and
led them with him to Babylon. 2 Kin. 24:11-16
13 [R]'And he took the king's offspring, made
a covenant with him, [R]and put him under
oath. He also took away the mighty of the
land, 2 Kin. 24:17 • 2 Chr. 36:13
14 'that the kingdom might be [R]abased and
not lift itself up, *but* that by keeping his
covenant it might stand. Ezek. 29:14
15 'But [R]he rebelled against him by sending
his ambassadors to Egypt, [R]that they might
give him horses and many people. [R]Will he
prosper? Will he who does such *things* escape? Can he break a covenant and still be
delivered? 2 Kin. 24:20 • Deut. 17:16 • Ezek. 17:9
16 '*As* I live,' says the Lord GOD, 'surely [R]in
the place *where* the king *dwells* who made
him king, whose oath he despised and whose
covenant he broke—with him in the midst of
Babylon he shall die. Ezek. 12:13
17 'Nor will Pharaoh with *his* mighty army
and great company do anything in the war,
when they heap up a siege mound and build
[T]a wall to cut off many persons. Or *siege wall*
18 'Since he despised the oath by breaking
the covenant, and in fact gave his hand and
still did all these *things*, he shall not escape.' "
19 Therefore thus says the Lord GOD: "*As* I
live, surely My oath which he despised, and
My covenant which he broke, I will recompense on his own head.
20 "I will spread My net over him, and he
shall be taken in My snare. I will bring him to
Babylon and try him there for the treason
which he committed against Me.
21 "All his fugitives with all his troops shall
fall by the sword, and those who remain

shall be scattered to every wind; and you shall know that I, the LORD, have spoken."

22 Thus says the Lord GOD: "I will take also *one* of the highest [R]branches of the high cedar and set *it* out. I will crop off from the topmost of its young twigs [R]a tender one, and will [R]plant *it* on a high and prominent mountain. [Zech. 3:8] • Is. 53:2 • [Ps. 2:6]

23 [R]"On the mountain height of Israel I will plant it; and it will bring forth boughs, and bear fruit, and be a majestic cedar. Under it will dwell birds of every sort; in the shadow of its branches they will dwell. [Is. 2:2, 3]

24 "And all the trees of the field shall know that I, the LORD, have brought down the high tree and exalted the low tree, dried up the green tree and made the dry tree flourish; I, the LORD, have spoken and have done *it*."

CHAPTER 18

Message of Personal Judgment for Personal Sin

THE word of the LORD came to me again, saying,

2 "What do you mean when you use this proverb concerning the land of Israel, saying:

'The [R]fathers have eaten sour grapes,
And the children's teeth are set on edge'? Lam. 5:7

3 "*As* I live," says the Lord GOD, "you shall no longer use this proverb in Israel.

4 "Behold, all souls are [R]Mine;
The soul of the father Num. 16:22; 27:16
As well as the soul of the son is Mine;
[R]The soul who sins shall die. [Rom. 6:23]
5 But if a man is just
And does what is lawful and right;
6 If he has not eaten [T]on the mountains,
Nor lifted up his eyes to the idols of the house of Israel, At the mountain shrines
Nor [R]defiled his neighbor's wife,
Nor approached [R]a woman during her impurity; Lev. 18:20; 20:10 • Lev. 18:19; 20:18
7 If he has not [R]oppressed anyone, Ex. 22:21
But has restored to the debtor his [R]pledge; Deut. 24:12
Has robbed no one by violence,
But has given his bread to the hungry
And covered the naked with clothing;
8 If he has not [T]exacted [R]usury
Nor taken any increase,
But has withdrawn his hand from iniquity Lent money at interest • Ex. 22:25
And [R]executed true [T]judgment between man and man; Zech. 8:16 • *justice*
9 *If* he has walked in My statutes
And kept My judgments faithfully—
He *is* just;
He shall surely [R]live!"
Says the Lord GOD. Amos 5:4

10 "If he begets a son *who is* a robber
Or [R]a shedder of blood,
Who does any of these *things* Num. 35:31
11 And does none of those *duties*,
But has eaten on the mountains
Or defiled his neighbor's wife;
12 If he has oppressed the poor and needy,
Robbed by violence,
Not restored the pledge,
Lifted his eyes to the idols,
Or [R]committed abomination; Ezek. 8:6, 17
13 If he has exacted usury
Or taken increase—
Shall he then live?
He shall not live!
If he has done any of these abominations,
He shall surely die;
His blood shall be upon him.

14 "*If*, however, he begets a son
Who sees all the sins which his father has done,
And considers but does not do likewise;
15 *Who* has not eaten [T]on the mountains,
Nor lifted his eyes to the idols of the house of Israel, At the mountain shrines
Nor defiled his neighbor's wife;
16 Has not oppressed anyone,
Nor withheld a pledge,
Nor robbed by violence,
But has given his bread to the hungry
And covered the naked with clothing;
17 *Who* has withdrawn his hand from the poor
And not received usury or increase,
But has executed My judgments
And walked in My statutes—
He shall not die for the iniquity of his father;
He shall surely live!

18 "*As for* his father,
Because he cruelly oppressed,
Robbed his brother by violence,
And did what *is* not good among his people,
Behold, he shall die for his iniquity.

19 "Yet you say, 'Why [R]should the son not
bear the guilt of the father?' Because the son
has done what is lawful and right, and has
kept all My statutes and done them, he shall
surely live. Ex. 20:5
20 "The soul who sins shall die. The son
shall not bear the guilt of the father, nor the
father bear the guilt of the son. [R]The righteousness of the righteous shall be upon
himself, [R]and the wickedness of the wicked
shall be upon himself. Is. 3:10, 11 • Rom. 2:6–9

SOUL

The crisp little telegraphic clicks went out over the icy waters of the North Atlantic that fateful night of April 14, 1912. For the first time in history the newly agreed upon international distress signal was used: "SOS—save our souls." The magnificent luxury liner *Titanic* was on her maiden voyage—and in great distress. When the supposedly unsinkable ship sank into the freezing depths of the ocean, she pulled down 2,207 "souls" with her, including nearly 900 crewmembers.

But what is a soul? Many have asked that question. The Hebrew word for soul has many meanings and seldom (some would say never!) equals what English-speaking Christians mean by the term.

Nephesh probably comes from the concept of breathing. Genesis 2:7 tells us that God "breathed into his [man's] nostrils the breath of life; and man became a living being [*nephesh*]." This shows that man's *nephesh* is from God. The KJV has over twenty different translations of this word, including "fish" (Is. 19:10).

Nephesh as Soul

The closest to our English concept of *soul*, that is, the inner, immaterial part of humankind (Greek *psychē*) as distinguished from the body, occurs in several passages. For example, in Genesis 35:18, we read of Rachel that "her soul was departing (for she died)." Job 14:22 presents body and soul as parts of one person: "But his flesh will be in pain over it, and his soul will mourn over it."

Nephesh as Life

Nephesh relating to life is used for both people and animals. This life is in the blood (Lev. 17:11). Therefore, Israel was not to drink blood, blood had sacrificial value, and purposeful bloodshed of another human being had to be punished by death.

Nephesh as the Person

Nephesh as the person is closest to the meaning of the "SOS" that the radio operator sent out from the *Titanic*. He did not mean "Save our immortal souls from perdition," but "Save our whole persons (or lives; see above)." When the newspapers reported how many "souls" were rescued, they were talking about how many people were saved. God told Abraham that if a male was not circumcised, "that person shall be cut off from his people" (Gen. 17:14). Sometimes *nephesh* is used like a reflexive pronoun: *myself* or *yourself*, for example. The elders in Jeremiah 26:19 complained, "we are doing great evil against ourselves."

Nephesh as a Personal Pronoun

This usage occurs especially in poetry. In Psalms, "my soul" (*naphshî*) is a very common expression, not always meaning much more than "I" or "me." (The examples from the Song of Songs below, under "the seat of feelings," can also go here.)

Nephesh as the Seat of Appetites

The hunger in Psalm 107:9 is not spiritual, but physical: "For He satisfies the longing soul, and fills the hungry soul with goodness."

In Proverbs 16:24, "soul" probably indicates physical taste ("the bones" suggests the body), although it may be referring to "spiritual" appreciation: "Pleasant words *are like* a honeycomb, sweetness to the soul and health to the bones."

Nephesh as the Seat of Feelings

Love, the strongest emotion, is understandably prominent in the Song of Songs. The Shulamite says, "my soul loveth" (KJV) in 1:7; 3:1, 2, 3, 4. Since in English the soul is not seen as the source of love, the NKJV updated this to simply "I love" (see *nephesh* as the person, above). The opposite emotion also occurs: "Has Your [God's] soul loathed Zion?" (Jer. 14:19). A soul may be troubled (Is. 19:10) or refreshed (Prov. 25:13).

Of course, the most famous poem in all literature includes the words, "He restores my soul [*naphshî*]." No matter which nuance of *nephesh* we may prefer here, the marvelous thing is that for the believer, the Lord restores every aspect we have discussed—plus several more.

21 "But [R]if a wicked man turns from all his
sins which he has committed, keeps all My
statutes, and does what is lawful and right, he
shall surely live; he shall not die. Ezek. 18:27
22 "None of the transgressions which he
has committed shall be remembered against
him; because of the righteousness which he
has done, he shall [R]live. [Ps. 18:20–24]
23 [R]"Do I have any pleasure at all that the
wicked should die?" says the Lord GOD, *"and*
not that he should turn from his ways and
live? [Ezek. 18:32; 33:11]
24 "But [R]when a righteous man turns away
from his righteousness and commits iniquity,
and does according to all the abominations
that the wicked *man* does, shall he live? [R]All
the righteousness which he has done shall
not be remembered; because of the unfaithfulness of which he is guilty and the sin
which he has committed, because of them he
shall die. Ezek. 3:20; 18:26; 33:18 • [2 Pet. 2:20]
25 "Yet you say, [R]'The way of the Lord is
not fair.' Hear now, O house of Israel, is it not
My way which is fair, and your ways which
are not fair? Ezek. 18:29; 33:17, 20
26 [R]"When a righteous *man* turns away
from his righteousness, commits iniquity, and
dies in it, it is because of the iniquity which
he has done that he dies. Ezek. 18:24
27 "Again, [R]when a wicked *man* turns away
from the wickedness which he committed,
and does what is lawful and right, he preserves himself alive. Ezek. 18:21
28 "Because he considers and turns away
from all the transgressions which he committed, he shall surely live; he shall not die.
29 [R]"Yet the house of Israel says, 'The way
of the Lord is not fair.' O house of Israel, is it
not My ways which are fair, and your ways
which are not fair? Ezek. 18:25
30 [R]"Therefore I will judge you, O house of
Israel, every one according to his ways," says
the Lord GOD. [R]"Repent, and turn from all
your transgressions, so that iniquity will not
be your ruin. Ezek. 7:3; 33:20 • Matt. 3:2
31 "Cast away from you all the transgressions which you have committed, and get
yourselves a new heart and a new spirit. For
why should you die, O house of Israel?
32 "For [R]I have no pleasure in the death of
one who dies," says the Lord GOD. "Therefore
turn and [R]live!" Lam. 3:33 • [Prov. 4:2, 5, 6]

CHAPTER 19

Lament for the Princes of Israel

"MOREOVER [R]take up a lamentation
for the princes of Israel, Ezek. 26:17
2 "and say:

'What *is* your mother? A lioness:
She lay down among the lions;
Among the young lions she nourished
her cubs.
3 She brought up one of her cubs,
And [R]he became a young lion;
He learned to catch prey,
And he devoured men. 2 Kin. 23:31, 32
4 The nations also heard of him;
He was trapped in their pit,
And they brought him with chains to
the land of [R]Egypt. 2 Kin. 33:33, 34

5 'When she saw that she waited, *that* her
hope was lost,
She took [R]another of her cubs *and*
made him a young lion. 2 Kin. 23:34
6 [R]He roved among the lions,
And [R]became a young lion;
He learned to catch prey;
He devoured men. Jer. 22:13–17 • Ezek. 19:3
7 He knew *their desolate places,
And laid waste their cities;
The land with its fullness was desolated
By the noise of his roaring.
8 Then the nations set against him from
the provinces on every side,
And spread their net over him;
[R]He was trapped in their pit. Ezek. 19:4
9 [R]They put him in a cage with [T]chains,
And brought him to the king of
Babylon; 2 Chr. 36:6 • Or *hooks*
They brought him in nets,
That his voice should no longer be
heard on the mountains of Israel.

Parable of the Withered Vine

10 'Your mother *was* [R]like a vine in your
bloodline, Ezek. 17:6
Planted by the waters,
[R]Fruitful and full of branches Deut. 8:7–9
Because of many waters.
11 She had strong branches for scepters of
rulers.
[R]She towered in stature above the thick
branches,
And was seen in her height amid the
[T]dense foliage. Dan. 4:11 • Or *many branches*
12 But she was [R]plucked up in fury,
She was cast down to the ground,
And the [R]east wind dried her fruit.
Her strong branches were broken and
withered; Jer. 31:27, 28 • Hos. 13:5
The fire consumed them.
13 And now she *is* planted in the
wilderness,
In a dry and thirsty land.
14 [R]Fire has come out from a rod of her
branches
And devoured her fruit,
So that she has no strong branch—a
scepter for ruling.' "

19:7 Lit. *its windows,* Tg. *their desolate palaces*

[R]This *is* a lamentation, and has become a lamentation. Judg. 9:15 • Lam. 2:5

CHAPTER 20

In Egypt

IT came to pass in the seventh year, in the fifth *month*, on the tenth *day* of the month, *that* [R]certain of the elders of Israel came to inquire of the LORD, and sat before me. Ezek. 8:1, 11, 12; 14:1

2 Then the word of the LORD came to me, saying,

3 "Son of man, speak to the elders of Israel, and say to them, 'Thus says the Lord GOD: "Have you come to inquire of Me? *As* I live," says the Lord GOD, [R]"I will not be inquired of by you." ' Ezek. 7:26; 14:3

4 "Will you judge them, son of man, will you judge *them*? Then make known to them the abominations of their fathers.

5 "Say to them, 'Thus says the Lord GOD: "On the day when [R]I chose Israel and lifted My hand in an oath to the descendants of the house of Jacob, and made Myself [R]known to them in the land of Egypt, I lifted My hand in an oath to them, saying, [R]'I *am* the LORD your God.' Ex. 6:6–8 • Deut. 4:34 • Ex. 20:2

6 "On that day I lifted My hand in an oath to them, [R]to bring them out of the land of Egypt into a land that I had searched out for them, flowing with milk and honey, [R]the glory of all lands. Jer. 32:22 • Jer. 11:5; 32:22

7 "Then I said to them, 'Each of you, [R]throw away [R]the abominations which are before his eyes, and do not defile yourselves with [R]the idols of Egypt. I *am* the LORD your God.' Ezek. 18:31 • 2 Chr. 15:8 • Lev. 18:3

8 "But they rebelled against Me and would not [T]obey Me. They did not all cast away the abominations which were before their eyes, nor did they forsake the idols of Egypt. Then I said, 'I will [R]pour out My fury on them and fulfill My anger against them in the midst of the land of Egypt.' Lit. *listen to* • Ezek. 7:8

9 "But I acted for My name's sake, that it should not be profaned before the Gentiles among whom they *were*, in whose sight I had made Myself [R]known to them, to bring them out of the land of Egypt. Josh. 2:10; 9:9, 10

In the Wilderness

10 "Therefore I [R]made them go out of the land of Egypt and brought them into the wilderness. Ex. 13:18

11 "And I gave them My statutes and showed them My judgments, [R]'which, *if* a man does, he shall live by them.' Lev. 18:5

12 "Moreover I also gave them My [R]Sabbaths, to be a sign between them and Me, that they might know that I *am* the LORD who sanctifies them. Deut. 5:12

13 "Yet the house of Israel rebelled against Me in the wilderness; they did not walk in My statutes; they despised My judgments, which, if a man does, he shall live by them; and they greatly [R]defiled My Sabbaths. Then I said I would pour out My fury on them in the wilderness, to consume them. Ex. 16:27

14 "But I acted for My name's sake, that it should not be profaned before the Gentiles, in whose sight I had brought them out.

15 "So [R]I also lifted My hand in an oath to them in the wilderness, that I would not bring them into the land which I had given *them*, flowing with milk and honey, [R]the glory of all lands, Num. 14:28 • Ezek. 20:6

16 [R]"because they despised My judgments and did not walk in My statutes, but profaned My Sabbaths; for [R]their heart went after their idols. Ezek. 20:13, 24 • Amos 5:25

17 [R]"Nevertheless My eye spared them from destruction. I did not make an end of them in the wilderness. [Ps. 78:38]

18 "But I said to their children in the wilderness, 'Do not walk in the statutes of your fathers, nor observe their judgments, nor defile yourselves with their idols.

19 'I *am* the LORD your God: Walk in My statutes, keep My judgments, and do them;

20 [R]'hallow My Sabbaths, and they will be a sign between Me and you, that you may know that I *am* the LORD your God.' Jer. 17:22

21 "Notwithstanding, [R]the children rebelled against Me; they did not walk in My statutes, and were not careful to observe My judgments, [R]'which, *if* a man does, he shall live by them'; but they profaned My Sabbaths. Then I said I would pour out My fury on them and fulfill My anger against them in the wilderness. Num. 25:1 • Lev. 18:5

22 "Nevertheless I withdrew My hand and acted for My name's sake, that it should not be profaned in the sight of the Gentiles, in whose sight I had brought them out.

23 "Also I lifted My hand in an oath to those in the wilderness, that [R]I would scatter them among the Gentiles and disperse them throughout the countries, Lev. 26:33

24 "because they had not executed My judgments, but had despised My statutes, profaned My Sabbaths, and [R]their eyes were fixed on their fathers' idols. Ezek. 6:9

25 "Therefore [R]I also gave them up to statutes *that were* not good, and judgments by which they could not live; Rom. 1:24

26 "and I pronounced them unclean because of their ritual gifts, in that they caused all their firstborn to pass through *the fire*, that I might make them desolate and that they might know that I am the LORD." '

In Canaan

27 "Therefore, son of man, speak to the house of Israel, and say to them, 'Thus says

the Lord GOD: "In this too your fathers have
blasphemed Me, by being unfaithful to Me.
28 "*For* when I brought them into the land
for which I had lifted My hand in an oath to
give them, and [R]they saw all the high hills
and all the thick trees, there they offered
their sacrifices and provoked Me with their
offerings. There they also sent up their
[R]sweet aroma and poured out their drink
offerings. Ezek. 6:13 • Ezek. 16:19

In Ezekiel's Time

29 "Then I said to them, 'What *is* this high
place to which you go?' So its name is called
[T]Bamah to this day."' Lit. *High Place*
30 "Therefore say to the house of Israel,
'Thus says the Lord GOD: "Are you defiling
yourselves in the manner of your [R]fathers,
and committing harlotry according to their
[R]abominations? Judg. 2:19 • Jer. 7:26; 16:12
31 "For when you offer your gifts and make
your sons pass through the fire, you defile
yourselves with all your idols, even to this
day. So shall I be inquired of by you, O house
of Israel? *As* I live," says the Lord GOD, "I
will not be inquired of by you.
32 [R]"What you have in your mind shall
never be, when you say, 'We will be like the
Gentiles, like the families in other countries,
serving wood and stone.' Ezek. 11:5

Message of God's Future Restoration of Israel

33 "*As* I live," says the Lord GOD, "surely
with a mighty hand, [R]with an outstretched
arm, and with fury poured out, I will rule
over you. Jer. 21:5
34 "I will bring you out from the peoples
and gather you out of the countries where
you are scattered, with a mighty hand, with
an outstretched arm, and with fury poured
out.
35 "And I will bring you into the wilderness
of the peoples, and there [R]I will plead My case
with you face to face. Jer. 2:9, 35
36 [R]"Just as I pleaded My case with your
fathers in the wilderness of the land of Egypt,
so I will plead My case with you," says the
Lord GOD. Num. 14:21–23, 28
37 "I will make you [R]pass under the rod,
and I will bring you into the bond of the
[R]covenant; Lev. 27:32 • Ps. 89:30–34
38 [R]"I will purge the rebels from among
you, and those who transgress against Me; I
will bring them out of the country where
they sojourn, but [R]they shall not enter the
land of Israel. Then you will know that I *am*
the LORD. Ezek. 34:17 • Jer. 44:14
39 "As for you, O house of Israel," thus says
the Lord GOD: [R]"Go, serve every one of you
his idols—and hereafter—if you will not obey
Me; [R]but profane My holy name no more with
your gifts and your idols. Amos 4:4 • Is. 1:13–15
40 "For on My holy mountain, on the
mountain height of Israel," says the Lord
GOD, "there all the house of Israel, all of them
in the land, shall serve Me; there I will accept
them, and there I will require your offerings
and the firstfruits of your [T]sacrifices, together
with all your holy things. *offerings*
41 "I will accept you as a [R]sweet aroma
when I bring you out from the peoples and
gather you out of the countries where you
have been scattered; and I will be hallowed in
you before the Gentiles. Phil. 4:18
42 "Then you shall know that I *am* the
LORD, when I bring you into the land of
Israel, into the country *for* which I lifted My
hand in an oath to give to your fathers.
43 "And there you shall remember your
ways and all your doings with which you
were defiled; and you shall [T]loathe yourselves
in your own sight because of all the evils that
you have committed. Or *despise*
44 "Then you shall know that I *am* the
LORD, when I have dealt with you for My
name's sake, not according to your wicked
ways nor according to your corrupt doings, O
house of Israel," says the Lord GOD.'"

Sign of the Forest Fire

45 Furthermore the word of the LORD came
to me, saying,
46 "Son of man, set your face toward the
south; preach against the south and prophesy
against the forest land, the South,
47 "and say to the forest of the South, 'Hear
the word of the LORD! Thus says the Lord
GOD: "Behold, I will kindle a fire in you, and
it shall devour every green tree and every dry
tree in you; the blazing flame shall not be
quenched, and all faces [R]from the south to
the north shall be scorched by it. Ezek. 21:4
48 "All flesh shall see that I, the LORD, have
kindled it; it shall not be quenched."'"
49 Then I said, "Ah, Lord GOD! They say of
me, 'Does he not speak parables?'"

CHAPTER 21

Sign of the Drawn Sword

AND the word of the LORD came to me,
saying,
2 "Son of man, set your face toward Jerusalem, [R]preach against the holy places, and
prophesy against the land of Israel; Amos 7:16
3 "and say to the land of Israel, 'Thus says
the LORD: "Behold, I *am* against you, and I
will draw My sword out of its sheath and cut
off both righteous and wicked from you.
4 "Because I will cut off both righteous
and wicked from you, therefore My sword
shall go out of its sheath against all flesh
[R]from south *to* north, Ezek. 20:47

WARFARE IN BIBLE TIMES

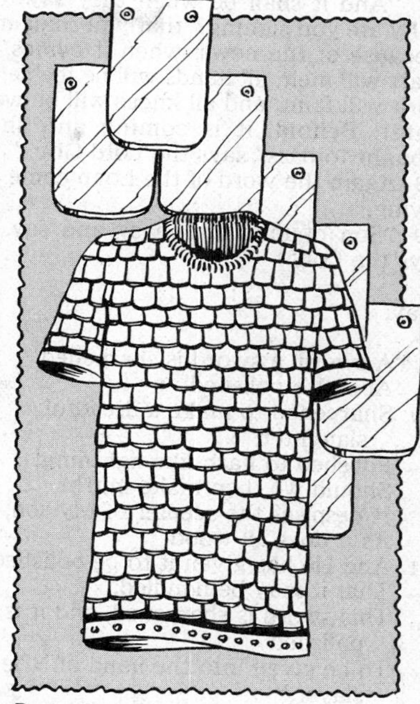

Protective armor.

In Old Testament times, the nation of Israel often waged war against its enemies. One notable example is the war of conquest led by Joshua to drive the Canaanites from the Land of Promise. To the Israelites, this was a "holy war" undertaken at God's command and carried out under His guidance and protection. Just before they attacked the city of Jericho, for example, Joshua issued this order to the priests and soldiers who were marching around the city walls: "Shout, for the LORD has given you the city!" (Josh. 6:16).

The weapons used by Joshua and his warriors were the simple arms of the time: the bow and arrow, the sling, the sword (see illustration), the spear or lance, the battle ax, and various pieces of protective armor (see illustration). His warfare techniques included threats, intimidation, ambush and surprise attack, siege warfare against walled cities, and hand-to-hand combat.

But there is a noticeable progression throughout Old Testament history in the types of weapons used and how warfare was carried out. By the time of Solomon, mounted warriors with more sophisticated weapons were a part of Israel's armed forces. Solomon also had a fleet of chariots at his command for swift attacks against enemy forces (1 Kin. 10:26).

As the nation of Israel increased its weaponry, it came to rely more on military might and less on God's guidance and protection as the key to victory in battle. Many of the prophets of the Old Testament condemned the kings of Israel and Judah for leading the people to place their trust in the sword rather than in the Word of God.

Some of the most striking warfare imagery in the Old Testament is found in the Book of Ezekiel. In a vision, the prophet saw the attack of Jerusalem by the Babylonians. He described how a besieging army gained entrance to a walled city. The king of Babylon gave orders for his army "to set battering rams against the gates, to heap up a *siege* mound, and to build a wall" (Ezek. 21:22).

Swords.

5 "that all flesh may know that I, the
LORD, have drawn My sword out of its
sheath; it shall not return anymore." '
6 "Sigh therefore, son of man, with [T]a
breaking heart, and sigh with bitterness
before their eyes. Lit. *the breaking of your loins*
7 "And it shall be when they say to you,
'Why are you sighing?' that you shall answer,
'Because of the news; when it comes, every
heart will melt, all hands will be feeble, every
spirit will faint, and all knees will be weak *as*
water. Behold, it is coming and shall be
brought to pass,' says the Lord GOD."
8 Again the word of the LORD came to me,
saying,
9 "Son of man, prophesy and say, 'Thus
says the LORD!

"Say:

[R]'A sword, a sword is sharpened
And also polished! Deut. 32:41
10 Sharpened to make a dreadful
slaughter,
Polished to flash like lightning!
Should we then make mirth?
It despises the scepter of My son,
As it does all wood.
11 And He has given it to be polished,
That it may be handled;
This sword is sharpened, and it is
polished
To be given into the hand of [R]the
slayer.' Ezek. 21:19

12 "Cry and wail, son of man;
For it will be against My people,
Against all the princes of Israel.
Terrors including the sword will be
against My people;
Therefore [R]strike *your* thigh. Jer. 31:19

13 "Because *it is* [R]a testing, Job 9:23
And what if *the sword* despises even
the scepter?
[R]*The scepter* shall be no *more*," Ezek. 21:27

says the Lord GOD.

14 "You therefore, son of man, prophesy,
And [R]strike *your* hands together.
The third time let the sword do double
damage. Num. 24:10
It is the sword *that* slays,
The sword that slays the great *men*,
That enters their private chambers.
15 I have set the point of the sword
against all their gates,
That the heart may melt and many may
stumble.
Ah! [R]*It is* made bright;
It is grasped for slaughter: Ezek. 21:10, 28

16 "Swords[R] at the ready! Ezek. 14:17
Thrust right!
Set your blade!
Thrust left—
Wherever your [T]edge is ordered! Lit. *face*

17 "I also will [R]beat My fists together,
And I will cause My fury to rest;
I, the LORD, have spoken." Ezek. 22:13

Sign of the Double Stroke of the Sword

18 The word of the LORD came to me again,
saying:
19 "And son of man, appoint for yourself
two ways for the sword of the king of Babylon to go; both of them shall go from the
same land. Make a sign; put *it* at the head of
the road to the city.
20 "Appoint a road for the sword to go to
[R]Rabbah of the Ammonites, and to Judah,
into fortified Jerusalem. Jer. 49:2
21 "For the king of Babylon stands at the
parting of the road, at the fork of the two
roads, to use divination: he shakes the arrows, he consults the [T]images, he looks at the
liver. Heb. *teraphim*
22 "In his right hand is the divination for
Jerusalem: to set up battering rams, to call
for a slaughter, to lift the voice with shouting, to set battering rams against the gates, to
heap up a *siege* mound, and to build a wall.
23 "And it will be to them like a false
divination in the eyes of those who [R]have
sworn oaths with them; but he will bring
their iniquity to remembrance, that they may
be taken. Ezek. 17:16, 18
24 "Therefore thus says the Lord GOD: 'Because you have made your iniquity to be
remembered, in that your transgressions are
uncovered, so that in all your doings your
sins appear—because you have come to remembrance, you shall be taken in hand.
25 'Now to you, O [R]profane, wicked prince
of Israel, [R]whose day has come, whose iniquity *shall* end, Jer. 52:2 • Ezek. 21:29
26 'thus says the Lord GOD:

"Remove the turban, and take off the
crown;
Nothing *shall remain* the same.
Exalt the lowly, and abase the exalted.
27 [T]Overthrown, overthrown, Or *Ruin*
I will make it overthrown!
[R]It shall be no *longer*, [Luke 1:32, 33]
Until He comes whose right it is,
And I will give it *to* [R]*Him*." ' [Jer. 23:5, 6]

28 "And you, son of man, prophesy and say,
'Thus says the Lord GOD [R]concerning the
Ammonites and concerning their reproach,'
and say:

'A sword, a sword *is* drawn,
Polished for slaughter,
For consuming, for flashing— Ezek. 25:1-7

29 While they [R]see vain visions for you,
While they divine a lie to you,
To bring you on the necks of the
wicked, the slain Ezek. 12:24; 13:6–9; 22:28
[R]Whose day has come, Job 18:20
Whose iniquity *shall* end.

30 'Return[R] *it* to its sheath. Jer. 47:6, 7
[R]I will judge you Gen. 15:14
In the place where you were created,
In the land of your [T]nativity. Or *origin*
31 I will [R]pour out My indignation on you;
I will [R]blow against you with the fire of
My wrath, Ezek. 7:8 • Ezek. 22:20, 21
And deliver you into the hands of brutal
men *who are* skillful to destroy.
32 You shall be fuel for the fire;
Your blood shall be in the midst of the
land.
[R]You shall not be remembered,
For I the LORD have spoken.' " Ezek. 25:10

CHAPTER 22

Message of Judgment on Jerusalem

MOREOVER the word of the LORD came
to me, saying,
2 "Now, son of man, [R]will you judge, will
you judge [R]the bloody city? Yes, show her all
her abominations! Ezek. 20:4 • Nah. 3:1
3 "Then say, 'Thus says the Lord GOD:
"The city sheds [R]blood in her own midst, that
her time may come; and she makes idols
within herself to defile herself. Ezek. 24:6, 7
4 "You have become guilty by the blood
which you have shed, and have defiled yourself with the idols which you have made. You
have caused your days to draw near, and
have come to *the end of* your years; therefore
I have made you a reproach to the nations,
and a mockery to all countries.
5 "*Those* near and *those* far from you will
mock you as infamous *and* full of tumult.
6 "Look, the princes of Israel: each one has
used his power to shed blood in you.
7 "In you they have made light of father
and mother; in your midst they have oppressed the stranger; in you they have mistreated the fatherless and the widow.
8 "You have despised My holy things and
[R]profaned My Sabbaths. Lev. 19:30
9 "In you are [R]men who slander to cause
bloodshed; [R]in you are those who eat on the
mountains; in your midst they commit lewdness. Lev. 19:16 • Ezek. 18:6, 11
10 "In you men uncover their fathers' nakedness; in you they violate women who are
set apart during their impurity.
11 "One commits abomination with his
neighbor's wife; another lewdly defiles his
daughter-in-law; and another in you violates
his sister, his father's [R]daughter. Lev. 18:9
12 "In you they take bribes to shed blood;
you take usury and increase; you have made
profit from your neighbors by extortion, and
have forgotten Me," says the Lord GOD.
13 "Behold, therefore, I beat My fists at the
dishonest profit which you have made, and at
the bloodshed which has been in your midst.
14 [R]"Can your heart endure, or can your
hands remain strong, in the days when I shall
deal with you? [R]I, the LORD, have spoken, and
will do *it*. Ezek. 21:7 • Ezek. 17:24
15 "I will scatter you among the nations,
disperse you throughout the countries, and
remove your filthiness completely from you.
16 "You shall defile yourself in the sight of
the nations; then [R]you shall know that I *am*
the LORD." ' " Ps. 9:16
17 The word of the LORD came to me, saying,
18 "Son of man, the house of Israel has
become dross to Me; they *are* all bronze, tin,
iron, and lead, in the midst of a [R]furnace; they
have become dross from silver. Prov. 17:3
19 "Therefore thus says the Lord GOD: 'Because you have all become dross, therefore
behold, I will gather you into the midst of
Jerusalem.
20 '*As men* gather silver, bronze, iron, lead,
and tin into the midst of a furnace, to blow
fire on it, to [R]melt *it*; so I will gather *you* in
My anger and in My fury, and I will leave *you*
there and melt you. Is. 1:25
21 'Yes, I will gather you and blow on you
with the fire of My wrath, and you shall be
melted in its midst.
22 'As silver is melted in the midst of a
furnace, so shall you be melted in its midst;
then you shall know that I, the LORD, have
[R]poured out My fury on you.' " Ezek. 20:8, 33
23 And the word of the LORD came to me,
saying,
24 "Son of man, say to her: 'You *are* a land
that is [R]not cleansed or rained on in the day
of indignation.' Ezek. 24:13
25 "The conspiracy of her prophets in her
midst is like a roaring lion tearing the prey;
they have devoured [T]people; they have taken
treasure and precious things; they have made
many widows in her midst. Lit. *souls*
26 "Her priests have violated My law and
profaned My holy things; they have not
[R]distinguished between the holy and unholy,
nor have they made known *the difference*
between the unclean and the clean; and they
have hidden their eyes from My Sabbaths, so
that I am profaned among them. Lev. 10:10
27 "Her princes in her midst *are* like wolves
tearing the prey, to shed blood, to destroy
people, and to get dishonest gain.
28 "Her prophets plastered them with untempered *mortar*, seeing false visions, and
divining lies for them, saying, 'Thus says the
Lord GOD,' when the LORD had not spoken.

29 "The people of the land have used oppressions, committed robbery, and mistreated the poor and needy; and they wrongfully [R]oppress the stranger. Ex. 23:9
30 "So I sought for a man among them who would make a wall, and stand in the gap before Me on behalf of the land, that I should not destroy it; but I found no one.
31 "Therefore I have [R]poured out My indignation on them; I have consumed them with the fire of My wrath; and I have recompensed [R]their deeds on their own heads," says the Lord GOD. Ezek. 22:22 • Ezek. 9:10

CHAPTER 23

Parable of Two Sisters

THE word of the LORD came again to me, saying:

2 "Son of man, there were two women,
The daughters of one mother.
3 [R]They committed harlotry in Egypt,
They committed harlotry in [R]their youth; Lev. 17:7 • Ezek. 16:22
Their breasts were there embraced,
Their virgin bosom was there pressed.
4 Their names: [T]Oholah the elder and Oholibah her sister; Lit. *Her Own Tabernacle*
[R]They were Mine, Ezek. 16:8, 20
And they bore sons and daughters.
As for their names,
Samaria *is* Oholah, and Jerusalem *is* Oholibah.

5 "Oholah played the harlot even though she was Mine;
And she lusted for her lovers, the neighboring [R]Assyrians, Hos. 5:13; 8:9, 10
6 *Who were* clothed in purple,
Captains and rulers,
All of them desirable young men,
Horsemen riding on horses.
7 Thus she committed her harlotry with them,
All of them choice men of Assyria;
And with all for whom she lusted,
With all their idols, she defiled herself.
8 She has never given up her harlotry *brought* [R]from Egypt,
For in her youth they had lain with her,
Pressed her virgin bosom,
And poured out their immorality upon her. Ezek. 23:3, 19

9 "Therefore I have delivered her
Into the hand of her lovers,
Into the hand of the [R]Assyrians,
For whom she lusted. 2 Kin. 17:3
10 They uncovered her nakedness,
Took away her sons and daughters,
And slew her with the sword;
She became a byword among women,
For they had executed judgment on her.

11 "Now although her sister Oholibah saw
this, [R]she became more corrupt in her inordinate love than she, and in her harlotry more
corrupt than her sister's harlotry. Jer. 3:8–11

12 "She lusted for the neighboring [R]Assyrians, 2 Kin. 16:27, 28
[R]Captains and rulers, Ezek. 23:6, 23
Clothed most gorgeously,
Horsemen riding on horses,
All of them desirable young men.
13 Then I saw that she was defiled;
Both *took* the same way.
14 But she increased her harlotry;
She looked at men portrayed on the wall,
Images of [R]Chaldeans portrayed in vermilion, Ezek. 8:10; 16:29
15 Girded with belts around their waists,
Flowing turbans on their heads,
All of them looking like captains,
In the manner of the Babylonians of Chaldea,
The land of their nativity.
16 [R]As soon as her eyes saw them,
She lusted for them
And sent [R]messengers to them in Chaldea. 2 Kin. 24:1 • Is. 57:9

17 "Then the [T]Babylonians came to her, into the bed of love, Lit. *sons of Babel*
And they defiled her with their immorality;
So she was defiled by them, and alienated herself from them.
18 She revealed her harlotry and uncovered her nakedness.
Then [R]I [R]alienated Myself from her,
As I had alienated Myself from her sister. Jer. 6:8 • Jer. 12:8

19 "Yet she multiplied her harlotry
In calling to remembrance the days of her youth,
[R]When she had played the harlot in the land of Egypt. Ezek. 23:2
20 For she lusted for her [T]paramours,
Whose flesh *is like* the flesh of donkeys,
And whose issue *is like* the issue of horses. Illicit lovers
21 Thus you called to remembrance the lewdness of your youth,
When the [R]Egyptians pressed your bosom Ezek. 16:26
Because of your youthful breasts.

22 "Therefore, Oholibah, thus says the Lord GOD:

[R]'Behold, I will stir up your lovers against you,

From whom you have alienated
yourself,
And I will bring them against you from
every side: Ezek. 16:37–41; 23:28
23 The Babylonians,
All the Chaldeans,
RPekod, Shoa, Koa, Jer. 50:21
RAll the Assyrians with them,
All of them desirable young men,
Governors and rulers, Ezek. 23:12
Captains and men of renown,
All of them riding on horses.
24 And they shall come against you
With chariots, wagons, and war-horses,
With a horde of people.
They shall array against you
Buckler, shield, and helmet all around.

'I will delegate judgment to them,
And they shall judge you according to
their judgments.
25 I will set My Rjealousy against you,
And they shall deal furiously with you;
They shall remove your nose and your
ears,
And your remnant shall fall by the
sword;
They shall take your sons and your
daughters,
And your remnant shall be devoured by
fire. Ex. 34:14
26 They shall also strip you of your clothes
And take away your beautiful jewelry.

27 'Thus RI will make you cease your
lewdness and your Rharlotry
Brought from the land of Egypt,
So that you will not lift your eyes to
them, Ezek. 16:41; 22:15 • Ezek. 23:3, 19
Nor remember Egypt anymore.'

28 "For thus says the Lord GOD: 'Surely I
will deliver you into the hand *of* R*those* whom
you hate, into the hand *of those* Rfrom whom
you alienated yourself. Ezek. 16:37–41 • Ezek. 23:17
29 R'They will deal hatefully with you, take
away all you have worked for, and Rleave you
naked and bare. The nakedness of your harlotry shall be uncovered, both your lewdness
and your harlotry. Deut. 28:48 • Ezek. 16:39
30 'I will do these *things* to you because you
have Rgone as a harlot after the Gentiles,
because you have become defiled by their
idols. Ezek. 6:9
31 'You have walked in the way of your
sister; therefore I will put her Rcup in your
hand.' Jer. 7:14, 15; 25:15
32 "Thus says the Lord GOD:

'You shall drink of your sister's cup,
The deep and wide one;
RYou shall be laughed to scorn
And held in derision;
It contains much. Ezek. 22:4, 5
33 You will be filled with drunkenness and
sorrow,
The cup of horror and desolation,
The cup of your sister Samaria.
34 You shall Rdrink and drain it, Is. 51:17
You shall break its Tshards,
And tear at your own breasts;
For I have spoken,'
Says the Lord GOD. Earthenware fragments

35 "Therefore thus says the Lord GOD:

'Because you Rhave forgotten Me and
cast Me behind your back, Jer. 3:21
Therefore you shall bear the *penalty*
Of your lewdness and your harlotry.' "

36 The LORD also said to me: "Son of man,
will you judge Oholah and Oholibah? Then
Rdeclare to them their abominations. Is. 58:1
37 "For they have committed adultery, and
Rblood *is* on their hands. They have committed adultery with their idols, and even
sacrificed their sons Rwhom they bore to Me,
passing them through *the fire,* to devour
them. Ezek. 16:38 • Ezek. 16:20, 21, 36, 45; 20:26, 31
38 "Moreover they have done this to Me:
They have defiled My sanctuary on the same
day and Rprofaned My Sabbaths. Ezek. 22:8
39 "For after they had slain their children
for their idols, on the same day they came
into My sanctuary to profane it; and indeed
Rthus they have done in the midst of My
house. 2 Kin. 21:2–8
40 "Furthermore you sent for men to come
from afar, to whom a messenger *was* sent;
and there they came. And you washed yourself for them, Rpainted your eyes, and
adorned yourself with ornaments. Jer. 4:30
41 "You sat on a stately Rcouch, with a
table prepared before it, Ron which you had
set My incense and My oil. Is. 57:7 • Prov. 7:17
42 "The sound of a carefree multitude *was*
with her, and TSabeans *were* brought from
the wilderness with men of the common sort,
who put bracelets on their Twrists and beautiful crowns on their heads. Or *drunkards* • Lit. *hands*
43 "Then I said concerning *her who had*
grown old in adulteries, 'Will they commit
harlotry with her now, and she *with them?*'
44 "Yet they went in to her, as men go in to
a woman who plays the harlot; thus they
went in to Oholah and Oholibah, the lewd
women.
45 "But righteous men will Rjudge them
after the manner of adulteresses, and after
the manner of women who shed blood, because they *are* adulteresses, and Rblood *is* on
their hands. Ezek. 16:38 • Ezek. 23:37
46 "For thus says the Lord GOD: R'Bring up
an assembly against them, give them up to
trouble and plunder. Ezek. 16:40

ISRAEL AND THE BABYLONIANS

Babylonia was an ancient pagan empire between the Tigris and Euphrates rivers in southern Mesopotamia. A long, narrow country, it was about forty miles wide at its widest point, covering an area of about eight thousand square miles. It was bordered on the north by Assyria, on the south and west by the Arabian desert, and on the southeast by the Persian Gulf.

The fortunes of the Babylonians rose and fell during the long sweep of Old Testament history. In its early history Hammurabi (probably reigned 1792–1750 B.C.) emerged as the ruler of the nation. He expanded the borders of the empire and organized its laws into a written system. This was about the time that Abraham's family left Ur, one of the ancient cities of lower Babylonia (Gen. 11:27–32).

During its long history, Babylonia was constantly at war with Assyria, its neighbor to the north. About 1270 B.C. the Assyrians overpowered Babylonia, reducing its power and influence so effectively that it remained a second-rate nation for the next six or seven centuries. But this began to change dramatically when Nebuchadnezzar became ruler of Babylonia about 605 B.C. During his reign of forty-four years, the Babylonians built an empire, which stretched from north of the Mediterranean Sea to south through Israel along the Red Sea to the Persian Gulf in the east (see map).

Because of his long reign and many military conquests, Nebuchadnezzar is mentioned several times in the Old Testament (2 Kin. 24:10–17; Dan. 1:1–3). In 586 B.C. the Babylonian army under Nebuchadnezzar's leadership destroyed Jerusalem and carried Israel's leading citizens to Babylon as captives (2 Chr. 36:6–13). This was a fulfillment of the warning of the prophets Jeremiah and Ezekiel that God would punish His people unless they turned from their idolatry to worship of the one true God (Jer. 27; Ezek. 23:17–21).

The Babylonians had a system of gods, each with a main temple in a particular city. The system included gods of heaven, air, the ocean, sun, moon, storms, love, and war. Their worship included elaborate festivals and many different types of priests, especially the exorcist and the diviner, whose function was to drive away evil spirits.

Babylonian literature was dominated by mythology and legends. Among them was a creation legend written to glorify a god known as Marduk, who created heaven and earth on a whim from the corpse of the goddess Tiamat. This is a dramatic contrast to the account of God's creation of the world in the Book of Genesis. The biblical writer declares that God created the world from nothing, and He did it with purpose and order in a cycle of six days, resting on the seventh (Gen. 1:1—2:3).

Babylonian dominance of the ancient world came to an end with the fall of their capital city, Babylon, to the Persians about 539 B.C. This was a clear fulfillment of the prophecies of Isaiah and Jeremiah. They predicted God would punish the Babylonians because of their destruction of Jerusalem and their deportation of the citizens of Judah into captivity (Is. 14:22; 21:9; 43:14; Jer. 50:9; 51:37).

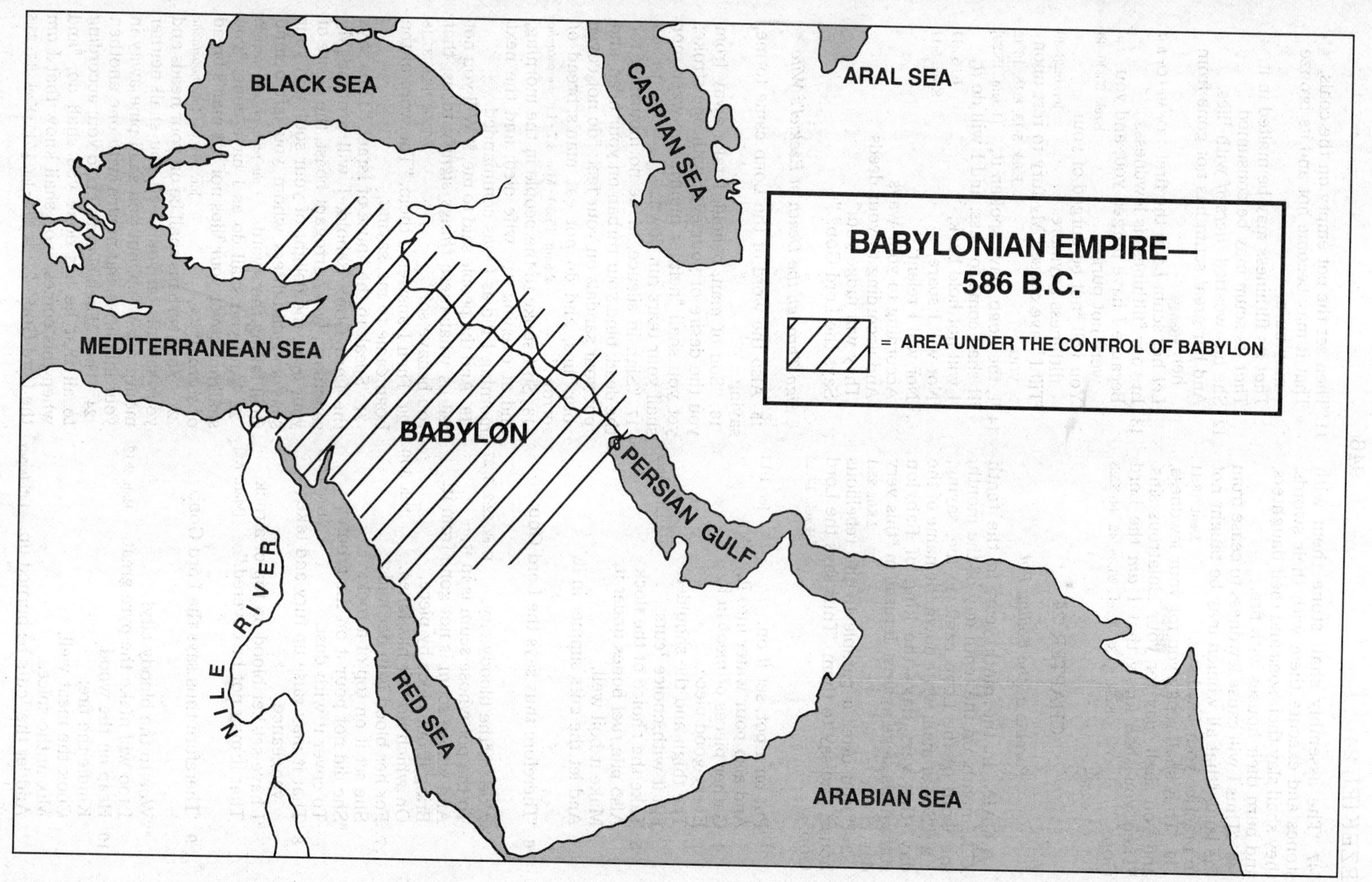
BABYLONIAN EMPIRE—
586 B.C.
= AREA UNDER THE CONTROL OF BABYLON
BLACK SEA
CASPIAN SEA
ARAL SEA
MEDITERRANEAN SEA
BABYLON
PERSIAN GULF
NILE RIVER
RED SEA
ARABIAN SEA

47 'The assembly shall stone them with
stones and execute them with their swords;
they shall slay their sons and their daughters,
and burn their houses with fire.
48 'Thus I will cause lewdness to cease from
the land, [R]that all women may be taught not
to practice your lewdness. Deut. 13:11
49 'They shall repay you for your lewdness,
and you shall [R]pay for your idolatrous sins.
[R]Then you shall know that I *am* the Lord
GOD.' " Ezek. 23:35 • Ezek. 20:38, 42, 44; 25:5

CHAPTER 24

Parable of the Boiling Pot

AGAIN, in the ninth year, in the tenth
month, on the tenth *day* of the month,
the word of the LORD came to me, saying,
2 "Son of man, write down the name of the
day, this very day—the king of Babylon
started his siege against Jerusalem [R]this very
day. 2 Kin. 25:1
3 [R]"And utter a parable to the rebellious
house, and say to them, 'Thus says the Lord
GOD: Ezek. 17:12

[R]"Put on a pot, set *it* on, Jer. 1:13
And also pour water into it.
4 Gather pieces *of meat* in it,
Every good piece,
The thigh and the shoulder.
Fill *it* with choice [T]cuts; Lit. *bones*
5 Take the choice of the flock.
Also pile *fuel* bones under it,
Make it boil well,
And let the cuts simmer in it."

6 'Therefore thus says the Lord GOD:

"Woe to [R]the bloody city, Ezek. 22:2, 3, 27
To the pot whose scum *is* in it,
And whose scum is not gone from it!
Bring it out piece by piece,
On which no [R]lot has fallen. Nah. 3:10
7 For her blood is in her midst;
She set it on top of a rock;
[R]She did not pour it on the ground,
To cover it with dust. Lev. 17:13
8 That it may raise up fury and take
vengeance,
[R]I have set her blood on top of a rock,
That it may not be covered." [Matt. 7:2]

9 'Therefore thus says the Lord GOD:

[R]"Woe to the bloody city!
I too will make the pyre great. Hab. 2:12
10 Heap on the wood,
Kindle the fire;
Cook the meat well,
Mix in the spices,
And let the [T]cuts be burned up. Lit. *bones*

11 "Then set the pot empty on the coals,
That it may become hot and its bronze
may burn,
That its filthiness may be melted in it,
That its scum may be consumed.
12 She has wearied [T]*herself* with [T]lies,
And her great scum has not gone from
her.
Let her scum *be* in the fire! Or *Me* • Or *toil*
13 In your [R]filthiness *is* lewdness.
Because I have purged you, and you
were not purged, Ezek. 23:36–48
You will [R]not be purged of your
filthiness anymore, Jer. 6:28–30
[R]Till I have caused My fury to rest upon
you. Ezek. 5:13; 8:18; 16:42
14 [R]I, the LORD, have spoken *it*; [1 Sam. 15:29]
[R]It shall come to pass, and I will do *it*;
I will not hold back, Is. 55:11
[R]Nor will I spare, Ezek. 5:11
Nor will I relent;
According to your ways
And according to your deeds
They will judge you,"
Says the Lord GOD.' "

Sign Through the Death of Ezekiel's Wife

15 Also the word of the LORD came to me,
saying,
16 "Son of man, behold, I take away from
you the desire of your eyes with one stroke;
yet you shall [R]neither mourn nor weep, nor
shall your tears run down. Jer. 16:5
17 "Sigh in silence, make no mourning for
the dead; bind your turban on your head, and
[R]put your sandals on your feet; [R]do not cover
your [T]lips, and do not eat man's bread *of
sorrow*." 2 Sam. 15:30 • Mic. 3:7 • Lit. *moustache*
18 So I spoke to the people in the morning,
and at evening my wife died; and the next
morning I did as I was commanded.
19 And the people said to me, [R]"Will you not
tell us what these *things signify* to us, that
you behave so?" Ezek. 12:9; 37:18
20 Then I answered them, "The word of the
LORD came to me, saying,
21 'Speak to the house of Israel, "Thus says
the Lord GOD: 'Behold, I will profane My
sanctuary, [T]your arrogant boast, the desire of
your eyes, the delight of your soul; and your
sons and daughters whom you left behind
shall fall by the sword. *the pride of your strength*
22 'And you shall do as I have done; [R]you
shall not cover *your* [T]lips nor eat man's bread
of sorrow. Jer. 16:6, 7 • Lit. *moustache*
23 'Your turbans shall be on your heads and
your sandals on your feet; you shall neither
mourn nor weep, but you shall pine away in
your iniquities and mourn with one another.
24 'Thus [R]Ezekiel is a sign to you; according
to all that he has done you shall do; [R]and
when this comes, [R]you shall know that I *am*
the Lord GOD.' " Is. 20:3 • Jer. 17:15 • Ezek. 6:7; 25:5

25 'And you, son of man—*will it* not *be* in the day when I take from them their stronghold, their joy and their glory, the desire of their eyes, and that on which they set their minds, their sons and their daughters:
26 'on that day one who escapes will come to you to let *you* hear *it* with *your* ears;
27 [R]'on that day your mouth will be opened to him who has escaped; you shall speak and no longer be mute. Thus you will be a sign to them, and they shall know that I *am* the LORD.' " Ezek. 3:26; 33:22

CHAPTER 25

Judgment on Ammon

THE word of the LORD came to me, saying,
2 "Son of man, set your face against the Ammonites, and prophesy against them.
3 "Say to the Ammonites, 'Hear the word of the Lord GOD! Thus says the Lord GOD: [R]"Because you said, 'Aha!' against My sanctuary when it was profaned, and against the land of Israel when it was desolate, and against the house of Judah when they went into captivity, Ezek. 26:2
4 "indeed, therefore, I will deliver you as a possession to the men of the East, and they shall set their encampments among you and make their dwellings among you; they shall eat your fruit, and they shall drink your milk.
5 "And I will make Rabbah a stable for camels and Ammon a resting place for flocks. Then you shall know that I *am* the LORD."
6 'For thus says the Lord GOD: "Because you [R]clapped *your* hands, stamped your feet, and [R]rejoiced in heart with all your disdain for the land of Israel, Job 27:23 • Ezek. 36:5
7 "indeed, therefore, I will [R]stretch out My hand against you, and give you as plunder to the nations; I will cut you off from the peoples, and I will cause you to perish from the countries; I will destroy you, and you shall know that I *am* the LORD." Ezek. 35:3

Judgment on Moab

8 'Thus says the Lord GOD: "Because Moab and [R]Seir say, 'Look! The house of Judah *is* like all the nations,' Ezek. 35:2, 5
9 "therefore, behold, I will clear the territory of Moab of cities, of the cities on its frontier, the glory of the country, Beth Jeshimoth, Baal Meon, and [R]Kirjathaim. Jer. 48:23
10 [R]"To the men of the East I will give it as a possession, together with the Ammonites, that the Ammonites [R]may not be remembered among the nations. Ezek. 25:4 • Ezek. 21:32
11 "And I will execute judgments upon Moab, and they shall know that I *am* the LORD."

Judgment on Edom

12 'Thus says the Lord GOD: [R]"Because of what Edom did against the house of Judah by taking vengeance, and has greatly offended by avenging itself on them," Obad. 10–14
13 'therefore thus says the Lord GOD: "I will also stretch out My hand against Edom, cut off man and beast from it, and make it desolate from Teman; [T]Dedan shall fall by the sword. Or *even to Dedan they shall fall*
14 [R]"I will lay My vengeance on Edom by the hand of My people Israel, that they may do in Edom according to My anger and according to My fury; and they shall know My vengeance," says the Lord GOD. Is. 11:14

Judgment on Philistia

15 'Thus says the Lord GOD: "Because the Philistines dealt vengefully and took vengeance with [T]a spiteful heart, to destroy because of the old hatred," Lit. *spite in soul*
16 'therefore thus says the Lord GOD: "I will stretch out My hand against the Philistines, and I will cut off the Cherethites and destroy the remnant of the seacoast.
17 "I will [R]execute great vengeance on them with furious rebukes; [R]and they shall know that I *am* the LORD, when I lay My vengeance upon them." ' " Ezek. 5:15 • Ps. 9:16

CHAPTER 26

Destruction of Tyre

AND it came to pass in the eleventh year, on the first *day* of the month, *that* the word of the LORD came to me, saying,
2 "Son of man, [R]because Tyre has said against Jerusalem, [R]'Aha! She is broken who *was* the gateway of the peoples; now she is turned over to me; I shall be filled; she is laid waste.' Jer. 25:22 • Ezek. 25:3
3 "Therefore thus says the Lord GOD: 'Behold, I *am* against you, O Tyre, and will cause many nations to come up against you, as the sea causes its waves to come up.
4 'And they shall destroy the walls of Tyre and break down her towers; I will also scrape her dust from her, and [R]make her like the top of a rock. Ezek. 26:14
5 'It shall be *a place for* spreading nets [R]in the midst of the sea, for I have spoken,' says the Lord GOD; 'it shall become plunder for the nations. Ezek. 27:32
6 'Also her daughter *villages* which *are* in the fields shall be slain by the sword. [R]Then they shall know that I am the LORD.' Ezek. 25:5
7 "For thus says the Lord GOD: 'Behold, I will bring against Tyre from the north Nebuchadnezzar king of Babylon, king of kings, with horses, with chariots, and with horsemen, and an army with many people.
8 'He will slay with the sword your daughter *villages* in the fields; he will heap up a siege mound against you, build a wall against you, and raise a [T]defense against you. *shield*

9 'He will direct his battering rams against
your walls, and with his axes he will break
down your towers.
10 'Because of the abundance of his horses,
their dust will cover you; your walls will
shake at the noise of the horsemen, the
wagons, and the chariots, when he enters
your gates, as men enter a city that has been
breached.
11 'With the hooves of his [R]horses he will
trample all your streets; he will slay your
people by the sword, and your strong pillars
will fall to the ground. Hab. 1:8
12 'They will plunder your riches and pillage
your merchandise; they will break down your
walls and destroy your pleasant houses; they
will lay your stones, your timber, and your
soil in the [R]midst of the water. Ezek. 27:27, 32
13 [R]'I will put an end to the sound of [R]your
songs, and the sound of your harps shall be
heard no more. Is. 14:11; 24:8 • Rev. 18:22
14 [R]'I will make you like the top of a rock;
you shall be *a place for* spreading nets, and
you shall never be rebuilt, for I the LORD have
spoken,' says the Lord GOD. Ezek. 26:4, 5
15 "Thus says the Lord GOD to Tyre: 'Will
the coastlands not shake at the sound of your
fall, when the wounded cry, when slaughter
is made in the midst of you?
16 'Then all the princes of the sea will come
down from their thrones, lay aside their
robes, and take off their embroidered garments; they will clothe themselves with trembling; they will sit on the ground, tremble
every moment, and be astonished at you.
17 'And they will take up a [R]lamentation for
you, and say to you:

"How you have perished,
O one inhabited by seafaring men,
O renowned city,
Who was [R]strong at sea,
She and her inhabitants,
Who caused their terror *to be* on all her
inhabitants! Ezek. 27:2–36 • Is. 23:4
18 Now [R]the coastlands tremble on the day
of your fall; Ezek. 26:15
Yes, the coastlands by the sea are
troubled at your departure." '

19 "For thus says the Lord GOD: 'When I
make you a desolate city, like cities that are
not inhabited, when I bring the deep upon
you, and great waters cover you,
20 'then I will bring you down with those
who descend into the Pit, to the people of old,
and I will make you dwell in the lowest part
of the earth, in places desolate from antiquity, with those who go down to the Pit, so
that you may never be inhabited; and I shall
establish glory in the land of the living.
21 [R]'I will make you a terror, and you *shall
be* no *more*; [R]though you are sought for, you
will never be found again,' says the Lord
GOD." Ezek. 27:36; 28:19 • Ps. 37:10, 36

CHAPTER 27

Lament over Tyre

THE word of the LORD came again to me,
saying,
2 "Now, son of man, [R]take up a lamentation for Tyre, Ezek. 26:17
3 "and say to Tyre, [R]'You who [T]are situated at the entrance of the sea, [R]merchant of
the peoples on many coastlands, thus says
the Lord GOD: Ezek. 26:17; 28:2 • Lit. *sit* or *dwell* • Is. 23:3

"O Tyre, you have said,
[R]'I *am* perfect in beauty.' Ezek. 28:12
4 Your borders *are* in the midst of the
seas.
Your builders have perfected your
beauty.
5 They [T]made all *your* planks of fir trees
from [R]Senir;
They took a cedar from Lebanon to
make you a mast. *built* • Deut. 3:9
6 *Of* oaks from Bashan they made your
oars;
The company of Ashurites have inlaid
your planks
With ivory from the coasts of Cyprus.
7 Fine embroidered linen from Egypt was
what you spread for your sail;
Blue and purple from the coasts of
Elishah was what covered you.

8 "Inhabitants of Sidon and Arvad were
your oarsmen;
Your *own* wise men, O Tyre, were in
you;
They became your pilots.
9 Elders of [R]Gebal and its wise men
Were in you to caulk your seams;
All the ships of the sea
And their oarsmen were in you
To market your merchandise. 1 Kin. 5:18

10 "Those from Persia, [T]Lydia, and [T]Libya
Were in your army as men of war;
They hung shield and helmet in you;
They gave splendor to you. *Lud* • *Put*
11 Men of Arvad with your army *were* on
your walls *all* around,
And the men of Gammad were in your
towers;
They hung their shields on your walls
all around;
They made your beauty perfect.

12 "Tarshish *was* your merchant because of
your many luxury goods. They gave you
silver, iron, tin, and lead for your goods.
13 "Javan, Tubal, and Meshech *were* your

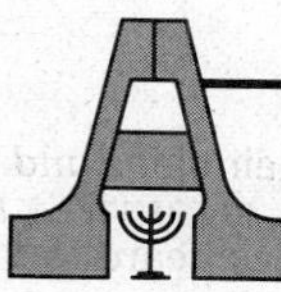

TYRE AND SIDON

Tyre and Sidon were two Phoenician seaport cities about twenty-five miles apart on the coast of the Mediterranean Sea. For the most part, Israel had a good relationship with these cities. The Phoenician king, Hiram, was a trading partner of both David and Solomon. He provided building materials, as well as skilled tradesmen to help build the temple and Solomon's palace complex in the city of Jerusalem.

Why, then, did the prophet Ezekiel utter such bitter words against Tyre (Ezek. 26)? It was probably because of the taunting attitude Tyre demonstrated when the nation of Judah was overrun by the Babylonians in 586 B.C. (Ezek. 26:2). Judah's collapse meant that Phoenicia was a region with little competition in central Palestine. Their trade monopoly complete, Tyre and Sidon rejoiced. Their insatiable greed and prideful attitude led Ezekiel to issue his bitter condemnation.

When Ezekiel spoke these words, the cities of Tyre and Sidon had no peers on the Mediterranean shores. As early as 1000 B.C. the two cities had emerged as important population centers. As the leader of a group of small city-states, Sidon first grew to prominence in trade. After a time, it was eclipsed by Tyre, which established an empire based on maritime trade. The ships of Tyre sailed as far away as Great Britain and North Africa on trading ventures.

As predicted by Ezekiel, the cities of Tyre and Sidon were eventually judged by God. Tyre was thought to be invincible because part of the city was located offshore, completely surrounded by the sea. But the Greek conqueror Alexander the Great built a causeway to the city and destroyed it in 332 B.C. After the Romans became the dominant world power, they rebuilt Tyre. The ruins of this city are visible today (see illustration).

Both Tyre and Sidon are mentioned in the New Testament. Jesus visited both cities during His ministry (Matt. 15:21–28). Paul also visited a Christian community in Tyre, staying with believers there for a week during his third missionary journey (Acts 21:1–6).

Photo by Howard Vos

Ruins of the city of Tyre from the Roman period.

traders. They bartered human lives and vessels of bronze for your merchandise.
14 "Those from the house of [R]Togarmah
traded for your wares with horses, steeds,
and mules. Gen. 10:3
15 "The men of [R]Dedan *were* your traders;
many isles *were* the market of your hand.
They brought you ivory tusks and ebony as
payment. Gen. 10:7
16 "Syria *was* your merchant because of the
abundance of goods you made. They gave
you for your wares emeralds, purple, embroidery, fine linen, corals, and rubies.
17 "Judah and the land of Israel *were* your
traders. They traded for your merchandise
wheat of [R]Minnith, millet, honey, oil, and
[R]balm. Judg. 11:33 • Jer. 8:22
18 "Damascus *was* your merchant because
of the abundance of goods you made, because
of your many luxury items, with the wine of
Helbon and with white wool.
19 "Dan and Javan paid for your wares,
*traversing back and forth. Wrought iron,
cassia, and cane were among your merchandise.
20 [R]"Dedan *was* your merchant in saddle-cloths for riding. Gen. 25:3
21 "Arabia and all the princes of [R]Kedar
were your regular merchants. They traded
with you in lambs, rams, and goats. Is. 60:7
22 "The merchants of [R]Sheba and Raamah
were your merchants. They traded for your
wares the choicest spices, all kinds of precious stones, and gold. Gen. 10:7
23 [R]"Haran, Canneh, Eden, the merchants
of [R]Sheba, Assyria, *and* Chilmad *were* your
merchants. 2 Kin. 19:12 • Gen. 25:3
24 "These *were* your merchants in choice
items—in purple clothes, in embroidered
garments, in chests of multicolored apparel,
in strong twined cords, which were in your
marketplace.

25 "The [R]ships of Tarshish were carriers of
your merchandise.
You were filled and very glorious [R]in
the midst of the seas. Is. 2:16 • Ezek. 27:4
26 Your oarsmen brought you into many
waters,
But [R]the east wind broke you in the
midst of the seas. Ps. 48:7

27 "Your [R]riches, wares, and merchandise,
Your mariners and pilots,
Your caulkers and merchandisers,
All your men of war who *are* in you,
And the entire company which *is* in
your midst,
Will fall into the midst of the seas on
the day of your ruin. [Prov. 11:4]
28 The common-land will shake at the
sound of the cry of your pilots.
29 "All [R]who handle the oar,
The mariners,
All the pilots of the sea
Will come down from their ships *and*
stand on the [T]shore. Rev. 18:17 • Lit. *land*
30 They will make their voice heard
because of you;
They will cry bitterly and [R]cast dust on
their heads; Rev. 18:19
They [R]will roll about in ashes; Jer. 6:26
31 They will [R]shave themselves completely
bald because of you,
Gird themselves with sackcloth,
And weep for you
With bitterness of heart *and* bitter
wailing. Ezek. 29:18
32 In their wailing for you
They will [R]take up a lamentation,
And lament for you, Ezek. 26:17
[R]'What *city is* like Tyre, Rev. 18:18
Destroyed in the midst of the sea?

33 'When[R] your wares went out by sea,
You satisfied many people;
You enriched the kings of the earth
With your many luxury goods and your
merchandise. Rev. 18:19
34 But *when* [R]you are broken by the seas
in the depths of the waters, Ezek. 26:19
Your merchandise and the entire
company will fall in your midst.
35 [R]All the inhabitants of the isles will be
astonished at you; Ezek. 26:15, 16
Their kings will be greatly afraid,
And *their* countenance will be troubled.
36 The merchants among the peoples [R]will
hiss at you; Jer. 18:16
[R]You will become a horror, and *be* no
[R]more forever.' " ' " Ezek. 26:2 • Ps. 37:10, 36

CHAPTER 28

Fall of the Prince of Tyre

THE word of the LORD came to me again,
saying,
2 "Son of man, say to the prince of Tyre,
'Thus says the Lord GOD:

"Because your heart *is* [R]lifted[T] up,
And you say, 'I *am* a god,
I sit *in* the seat of gods, Jer. 49:16 • Proud
[R]In the midst of the seas,' Ezek. 27:3, 4
[R]Yet you *are* a man, and not a god,
Though you set your heart as the heart
of a god Is. 31:3
3 (Behold, [R]you *are* wiser than Daniel!
There is no secret that can be hidden
from you! Dan. 1:20; 2:20–23, 28; 5:11, 12
4 With your wisdom and your
understanding

27:19 LXX, Syr. *from Uzal*

You have gained [R]riches for yourself,
And gathered gold and silver into your
treasuries; Zech. 9:1–3
5 [R]By your great wisdom in trade you have
increased your riches,
And your heart is lifted up because of
your riches)," Ps. 62:10

6 'Therefore thus says the Lord GOD:

"Because you have set your heart as the
heart of a god,
7 Behold, therefore, I will bring [R]strangers
against you, Ezek. 26:7
[R]The most terrible of the nations;
And they shall draw their swords
against the beauty of your wisdom,
And defile your splendor. Ezek. 7:24; 30:11
8 They shall throw you down into the
[R]Pit,
And you shall die the death of the slain
In the midst of the seas. Is. 14:15

9 "Will you still [R]say before him who slays
you, Ezek. 28:2
'I *am* a god'?
But you *shall be* a man, and not a god,
In the hand of him who slays you.
10 You shall die the death of [R]the
uncircumcised
By the hand of aliens;
For I have spoken," says the Lord
GOD.'" Ezek. 31:18; 32:19, 21, 25, 27

11 Moreover the word of the LORD came to
me, saying,
12 "Son of man, [R]take up a lamentation for
the king of Tyre, and say to him, 'Thus says
the Lord GOD: Ezek. 27:2

"You *were* the seal of perfection,
Full of wisdom and perfect in beauty.
13 You were in [R]Eden, the garden of God;
Every precious stone *was* your
covering: Ezek. 31:8, 9; 36:35
The sardius, topaz, and diamond,
Beryl, onyx, and jasper,
Sapphire, turquoise, and emerald with
gold.
The workmanship of [R]your timbrels and
pipes Ezek. 26:13
Was prepared for you on the day you
were created.

14 "You *were* the anointed [R]cherub who
covers;
I established you;
You were on [R]the holy mountain of
God;
You walked back and forth in the midst
of fiery stones. Ex. 25:20 • Ezek. 20:40
15 You *were* perfect in your ways from the
day you were created,
Till [R]iniquity was found in you. [Is. 14:12]

16 "By the abundance of your trading
You became filled with violence within,
And you sinned;
Therefore I cast you as a profane thing
Out of the mountain of God;
And I destroyed you, [R]O covering
cherub, Ezek. 28:14
From the midst of the fiery stones.

17 "Your [R]heart was [T]lifted up because of
your beauty; Ezek. 28:2, 5 • Proud
You corrupted your wisdom for the
sake of your splendor;
I cast you to the ground,
I laid you before kings,
That they might gaze at you.

18 "You defiled your sanctuaries
By the multitude of your iniquities,
By the iniquity of your trading;
Therefore I brought fire from your
midst;
It devoured you,
And I turned you to ashes upon the
earth
In the sight of all who saw you.
19 All who knew you among the peoples
are astonished at you;
[R]You have become a horror, Ezek. 26:21
And *shall be* no more forever."'"

Judgment on Sidon

20 Then the word of the LORD came to me,
saying,
21 "Son of man, [R]set your face toward Sidon, and prophesy against her, Ezek. 6:2
22 "and say, 'Thus says the Lord GOD:

[R]"Behold, I *am* against you, O Sidon;
I will be glorified in your midst;
And [R]they shall know that I *am* the
LORD, Ex. 14:4, 17 • Ps. 9:16
When I execute judgments in her and
am [R]hallowed in her. Ezek. 28:25
23 [R]For I will send pestilence upon her,
And blood in her streets;
The wounded shall be judged in her
midst
By the sword against her on every side;
Then they shall know that I *am* the
LORD. Ezek. 38:22

24 "And there shall no longer be a pricking
brier or a painful thorn for the house of Israel
from among all *who are* around them, who
[R]despise them. Then they shall know that I
am the Lord GOD." Ezek. 16:57; 25:6, 7
25 'Thus says the Lord GOD: "When I have
gathered the house of Israel from the peoples
among whom they are scattered, and am
[R]hallowed in them in the sight of the Gentiles,
then they will dwell in their own land which I
gave to My servant Jacob. Ezek. 28:22

26 "And they will [R]dwell [T]safely there, build
houses, and [R]plant vineyards; yes, they will
dwell securely, when I execute judgments on
all those around them who despise them.
Then they shall know that I *am* the LORD
their God." ' " Jer. 23:6 • *securely* • Jer. 31:5

CHAPTER 29

Egypt to Be Desolate

IN the tenth year, in the tenth *month*, on
the twelfth *day* of the month, the word of
the LORD came to me, saying,
2 "Son of man, [R]set your face against
Pharaoh king of Egypt, and prophesy against
him, and [R]against all Egypt. Ezek. 28:21 • Is. 19:1
3 "Speak, and say, 'Thus says the Lord
GOD:

[R]"Behold, I *am* against you, Jer. 44:30
O Pharaoh king of Egypt,
O great [R]monster who lies in the midst
of his rivers, Ps. 74:13, 14
Who has said, 'My [T]River *is* my own;
I have made *it* for myself.' The Nile
4 But [R]I will put hooks in your jaws,
And cause the fish of your rivers to
stick to your scales;
I will bring you up out of the midst of
your rivers,
And all the fish in your rivers will stick
to your scales. Ezek. 38:4
5 I will leave you in the wilderness,
You and all the fish of your rivers;
You shall fall on the open field;
[R]You shall not be picked up or gathered.
I have given you as food Jer. 8:2; 16:4; 25:33
To the beasts of the field
And to the birds of the heavens.

6 "Then all the inhabitants of Egypt
Shall know that I *am* the LORD,
Because they have been a [R]staff of reed
to the house of Israel. Is. 36:6
7 [R]When they took hold of you with the
hand,
You broke and tore all their shoulders;
When they leaned on you,
You broke and made all their loins
shake." Ezek. 17:17

8 'Therefore thus says the Lord GOD:
"Surely I will bring [R]a sword upon you and
cut off from you man and beast. Ezek. 14:17
9 "And the land of Egypt shall become
[R]desolate and waste; then they will know that
I *am* the LORD, because he said, 'The River *is*
mine, and I have made *it*.' Ezek. 30:7, 8
10 "Indeed, therefore, I *am* against you and
against your rivers, [R]and I will make the land
of Egypt utterly waste and desolate, [R]from
[T]Migdol *to* Syene, as far as the border of
Ethiopia. Ezek. 30:12 • Ezek. 30:6 • Or *the tower*
11 [R]"Neither foot of man shall pass through
it nor foot of beast pass through it, and it
shall be uninhabited forty years. Ezek. 32:13
12 "I will make the land of Egypt desolate
in the midst of the countries *that are* desolate; and among the cities *that are* laid waste,
her cities shall be desolate forty years; and I
will scatter the Egyptians among the nations
and disperse them throughout the countries."
13 'Yet, thus says the Lord GOD: "At the
[R]end of forty years I will gather the Egyptians
from the peoples among whom they were
scattered. Jer. 46:26
14 "I will bring back the captives of Egypt
and cause them to return to the land of
Pathros, to the land of their origin, and there
they shall be a [R]lowly kingdom. Ezek. 17:6, 14
15 "It shall be the lowliest of kingdoms; it
shall never again exalt itself above the nations, for I will diminish them so that they
will not rule over the nations anymore.
16 "No longer shall it be [R]the confidence of
the house of Israel, but will remind them of
their iniquity when they turned to follow
them. Then they shall know that I *am* the
Lord GOD." ' " Is. 30:2, 3; 36:4, 6

Egypt to Be Taken by Babylon

17 And it came to pass in the twenty-
seventh year, in the first *month*, on the first
day of the month, that the word of the LORD
came to me, saying,
18 "Son of man, Nebuchadnezzar king of
Babylon caused his army to labor strenuously
against Tyre; every head *was* made bald, and
every shoulder rubbed raw; yet neither he
nor his army received wages from Tyre, for
the labor which they expended on it.
19 "Therefore thus says the Lord GOD:
'Surely I will give the land of Egypt to [R]Nebu-
chadnezzar king of Babylon; he shall take
away her wealth, carry off her spoil, and
remove her pillage; and that will be the
wages for his army. Jer. 43:10–13
20 'I have given him the land of Egypt *for*
his labor, because they [R]worked for Me,' says
the Lord GOD. Jer. 25:9
21 'In that day I will cause the horn of the
house of Israel to spring forth, and I will open
your mouth to speak in their midst. Then
they shall know that I *am* the LORD.' "

CHAPTER 30

Egypt to Be Destroyed

THE word of the LORD came to me again,
saying,
2 "Son of man, prophesy and say, 'Thus
says the Lord GOD:

[R]"Wail, 'Woe to the day!' Is. 13:6; 15:2
3 For [R]the day *is* near,
Even the day of the LORD *is* near;

It will be a day of clouds, the time of
the Gentiles. Joel 2:1
4 The sword shall come upon Egypt,
And great anguish shall be in TEthiopia,
When the slain fall in Egypt, Heb. *Cush*
And they take away her wealth,
And her foundations are broken down.

5 "Ethiopia, TLibya, TLydia, Rall the mingled people, Chub, and the men of the lands
who are allied, shall fall with them by the
sword." Heb. *Put* • Heb. *Lud* • Jer. 25:20, 24
6 'Thus says the LORD:

"Those who uphold Egypt shall fall,
And the pride of her power shall come
down.
RFrom TMigdol *to* Syene
Those within her shall fall by the
sword,"
Says the Lord GOD. Ezek. 29:10 • Or *the tower*

7 "TheyR shall be desolate in the midst of
the desolate countries, Ezek. 29:12
And her cities shall be in the midst of
the cities *that are* laid waste.
8 Then they will know that I *am* the
LORD,
When I have set a fire in Egypt
And all her helpers are destroyed.
9 On that day Rmessengers shall go forth
from Me in ships Is. 18:1, 2
To make the Tcareless Ethiopians afraid,
And great anguish shall come upon
them, Or *secure*
As on the day of Egypt;
For indeed it is coming!"

10 'Thus says the Lord GOD:

R"I will also make a multitude of Egypt to
cease
By the hand of Nebuchadnezzar king of
Babylon. Ezek. 29:19
11 He and his people with him, Rthe most
terrible of the nations, Ezek. 28:7; 31:12
Shall be brought to destroy the land;
They shall draw their swords against
Egypt,
And fill the land with the slain.
12 RI will make the rivers dry, Is. 19:5, 6
And Rsell the land into the hand of the
wicked; Is. 19:4
I will make the land waste, and all that
is in it,
By the hand of aliens.
I, the LORD, have spoken."

13 'Thus says the Lord GOD:

"I will also Rdestroy the idols, Is. 19:1
And cause the images to cease from
TNoph; Ancient Memphis
RThere shall no longer be princes from
the land of Egypt; Zech. 10:11
I will put fear in the land of Egypt.
14 I will make RPathros desolate, Ezek. 29:14
Set fire to RZoan, Ps. 78:12, 43
And execute judgments in TNo. Thebes
15 I will pour My fury on TSin, the
strength of Egypt; Ancient Pelusium
RI will cut off the multitude of
No, Jer. 46:25
16 And Rset a fire in Egypt; Ezek. 30:8
Sin shall have great pain,
No shall be split open,
And Noph *shall be in* distress daily.
17 The young men of TAven and Pi Beseth
shall fall by the sword, Heliopolis
And these *cities* shall go into captivity.
18 RAt TTehaphnehes the day shall also be
darkened,
When I break the yokes of Egypt there.
And her arrogant strength shall cease in
her;
As for her, a cloud shall cover her,
And her daughters shall go into
captivity. Jer. 2:16 • *Tahpanhes*, Jer. 43:7
19 Thus I will Rexecute judgments on
Egypt,
Then they shall know that I *am* the
LORD." ' " [Ps. 9:16]

20 And it came to pass in the eleventh year,
in the first *month*, on the seventh *day* of the
month, *that* the word of the LORD came to
me, saying,
21 "Son of man, I have Rbroken the arm of
Pharaoh king of Egypt; and see, Rit has not
been bandaged for healing, nor a Tsplint put
on to bind it, to make it strong enough to
hold a sword. Jer. 48:25 • Jer. 46:11 • Lit. *bandage*
22 "Therefore thus says the Lord GOD:
'Surely I *am* against Pharaoh king of Egypt,
and will Rbreak his arms, both the strong one
and the one that was broken; and I will make
the sword fall out of his hand. Ps. 37:17
23 R'I will scatter the Egyptians among the
nations, and disperse them throughout the
countries. Ezek. 29:12; 30:17, 18, 26
24 'I will strengthen the arms of the king of
Babylon and put My sword in his hand; but I
will break Pharaoh's arms, and he will groan
before him with the groanings of a mortally
wounded *man*.
25 'Thus I will strengthen the arms of the
king of Babylon, but the arms of Pharaoh
shall fall down; Rthey shall know that I *am*
the LORD, when I put My sword into the hand
of the king of Babylon and he stretches it out
against the land of Egypt. Ps. 9:16
26 R'I will scatter the Egyptians among the
nations and disperse them throughout the
countries. Then they shall know that I *am*
the LORD.' " Ezek. 29:12

CHAPTER 31

Egypt Is Cut Down Like Assyria

NOW it came to pass in the [R]eleventh year,
in the third *month*, on the first *day* of
the month, *that* the word of the LORD came
to me, saying, Ezek. 30:20; 32:1
2 "Son of man, say to Pharaoh king of
Egypt and to his multitude:

'Whom are you like in your greatness?
3 [R]Indeed Assyria *was* a cedar in Lebanon,
With fine branches that shaded the forest,
And of high stature;
And its top was among the thick boughs. Dan. 4:10, 20–23
4 [R]The waters made it grow;
Underground waters gave it height,
With their rivers running around the place where it was planted,
And sent out [T]rivulets to all the trees of the field. Jer. 51:36 • Or *channels*

5 'Therefore [R]its height was exalted above all the trees of the field;
Its boughs were multiplied,
And its branches became long because of the abundance of water,
As it sent them out. Dan. 4:11
6 All the [R]birds of the heavens made their nests in its boughs; Dan. 4:12, 21
Under its branches all the beasts of the field brought forth their young;
And in its shadow all great nations [T]made their home. Lit. *dwelt*

7 'Thus it was beautiful in greatness and in the length of its branches,
Because its roots reached to abundant waters.
8 The cedars in the [R]garden of God could not hide it; Gen. 2:8, 9; 13:10
The fir trees were not like its boughs,
And the [T]chestnut trees were not like its branches; Or *plane*, Heb. *armon*
No tree in the garden of God was like it in beauty.
9 I made it beautiful with a multitude of branches,
So that all the trees of Eden envied it,
That *were* in the garden of God.'

10 "Therefore thus says the Lord GOD: 'Because you have increased in height, and it set
its top among the thick boughs, and [R]its heart
was [T]lifted up in its height, Dan. 5:20 • Proud
11 'therefore I will deliver it into the hand of
the [R]mighty one of the nations, and he shall
surely deal with it; I have driven it out for its
wickedness. Ezek. 30:10
12 'And aliens, the most terrible of the
nations, have cut it down and left it; its
branches have fallen [R]on the mountains and
in all the valleys; its boughs lie [R]broken by all
the rivers of the land; and all the peoples of
the earth have gone from under its shadow
and left it. Ezek. 32:5; 35:8 • Ezek. 30:24, 25

13 'On [R]its ruin will remain all the birds of the heavens,
And all the beasts of the field will come to its branches— Is. 18:6

14 'So that no trees by the waters may ever
again exalt themselves for their height, nor
set their tops among the thick boughs, that
no tree which drinks water may ever be high
enough to reach up to them.

'For [R]they have all been delivered to death,
[R]To the depths of the earth,
Among the children of men who go down to the Pit.' Ps. 82:7 • Ezek. 32:18

15 "Thus says the Lord GOD: 'In the day
when it went down to [T]hell, I caused mourning. I covered the deep because of it. I restrained its rivers, and the great waters were
held back. I caused Lebanon to [T]mourn for it,
and all the trees of the field wilted because of
it. Or *Sheol* • Lit. *be darkened*
16 'I made the nations shake at the sound of
its fall, when I cast it down to [T]hell together
with those who descend into the Pit; and all
the trees of Eden, the choice and best of
Lebanon, all that drink water, were comforted in the depths of the earth. Or *Sheol*
17 'They also went down to hell with it,
with those *slain* by the sword; and *those who*
were its *strong* arm [R]dwelt in its shadows
among the nations. Lam. 4:20
18 'To which of the trees in Eden will you
then be likened in glory and greatness? Yet
you shall be brought down with the trees of
Eden to the depths of the earth; you shall lie
in the midst of the uncircumcised, with *those*
slain by the sword. This *is* Pharaoh and all his
multitude,' says the Lord GOD."

CHAPTER 32

Egypt Is Lamented

AND it came to pass in the twelfth year, in
the [R]twelfth *month*, on the first *day* of
the month, *that* the word of the LORD came
to me, saying, Ezek. 31:1; 33:21
2 "Son of man, [R]take up a lamentation for
Pharaoh king of Egypt, and say to him:

[R]'You are like a young lion among the nations, Ezek. 27:2 • Ezek. 19:2–6
And you *are* like a monster in the seas,
[R]Bursting forth in your rivers, Jer. 46:7, 8

Troubling the waters with your feet,
And [R]fouling their rivers.' Ezek. 34:18

3 "Thus says the Lord GOD:

'I will therefore spread My net over you
with a company of many people,
And they will draw you up in My net.
4 Then I will leave you on the land;
I will cast you out on the open fields,
[R]And cause to [T]settle on you all the birds
of the heavens. Is. 18:6 • Lit. *sit* or *dwell*
And with you I will fill the beasts of the
whole earth.
5 I will lay your flesh on the mountains,
And fill the valleys with your carcass.

6 'I will also water the land with the flow
of your blood,
Even to the mountains;
And the riverbeds will be full of you.
7 When *I* put out your light,
[R]I will cover the heavens, and make its
stars dark; Rev. 6:12, 13; 8:12
I will cover the sun with a cloud,
And the moon shall not give her light.
8 All the [T]bright lights of the heavens I
will make dark over you,
And bring darkness upon your land,'
Says the Lord GOD. Or *shining*

9 'I will also trouble the hearts of many
peoples, when I bring your destruction
among the nations, into the countries which
you have not known.
10 'Yes, I will make many peoples astonished at you, and their kings shall be horribly
afraid of you when I brandish My sword
before them; and [R]they shall tremble *every*
moment, every man for his own life, in the
day of your fall.' Ezek. 26:16
11 [R]"For thus says the Lord GOD: 'The
sword of the king of Babylon shall come upon
you. Jer. 46:26
12 'By the swords of the mighty warriors,
all of them the most terrible of the nations,
I will cause your multitude to fall.

'They shall plunder the pomp of Egypt,
And all its multitude shall be destroyed.
13 Also I will destroy all its beasts
From beside its great waters;
[R]The foot of man shall muddy them no
more,
Nor shall the hooves of beasts muddy
them. Ezek. 29:11
14 Then I will make their waters [T]clear,
And make their rivers run like oil,'
Says the Lord GOD. Lit. *sink*, settle, grow clear

15 'When I make the land of Egypt
desolate,
And the country is destitute of all that
once filled it,
When I strike all who dwell in it,
[R]Then they shall know that I *am* the
LORD. Ps. 9:16

16 'This *is* the [R]lamentation
With which they shall lament her;
The daughters of the nations shall
lament her;
They shall lament for her, for Egypt,
And for all her multitude,'
Says the Lord GOD." Ezek. 26:17

Egypt in Sheol

17 It came to pass also in the twelfth year,
on the fifteenth *day* of the month, that the
word of the LORD came to me, saying:

18 "Son of man, wail over the multitude of
Egypt,
And [R]cast them down to the depths of
the earth, Ezek. 26:20; 31:14
Her and the daughters of the famous
nations,
With those who go down to the Pit:
19 'Whom [R]do you surpass in beauty?
[R]Go down, be placed with the
uncircumcised.' Ezek. 31:2, 18 • Ezek. 28:10

20 "They shall fall in the midst of *those*
slain by the sword;
She is delivered to the sword,
Drawing her and all her multitudes.
21 [R]The strong among the mighty
Shall speak to him out of the midst of
hell Is. 1:31; 14:9, 10
With those who help him:
'They have [R]gone down, Ezek. 32:19, 25
They lie with the uncircumcised, slain
by the sword.'

22 "Assyria *is* there, and all her company,
With their graves all around her,
All of them slain, fallen by the sword.
23 [R]Her graves are set in the recesses of the
Pit,
And her company is all around her
grave,
All of them slain, fallen by the sword,
Who [R]caused terror in the land of the
living. Is. 14:15 • Ezek. 32:24–27, 32

24 "There *is* [R]Elam and all her multitude,
All around her grave, Jer. 25:25; 49:34–39
All of them slain, fallen by the sword,
Who have gone down uncircumcised to
the lower parts of the earth,
[R]Who caused their terror in the land of
the living; Ezek. 32:23
Now they bear their shame with those
who go down to the Pit.

25 They have set her [R]bed in the midst of
the slain, Ps. 139:8
With all her multitude,
With her graves all around it,
All of them uncircumcised, slain by the
sword;
Though their terror was caused
In the land of the living,
Yet they bear their shame
With those who go down to the Pit;
It was put in the midst of the slain.

26 "There *are* [R]Meshech and Tubal and all
their multitudes,
With all their graves around it,
All of them [R]uncircumcised, slain by the
sword,
Though they caused their terror in the
land of the living. Gen. 10:2 • Ezek. 32:19
27 [R]They do not lie with the mighty
Who are fallen of the uncircumcised,
Who have gone down to hell with their
weapons of war;
They have laid their swords under their
heads,
But their iniquities will be on their
bones,
Because of the terror of the mighty in
the land of the living. Is. 14:18, 19
28 Yes, you shall be broken in the midst of
the uncircumcised,
And lie with *those* slain by the sword.

29 "There *is* [R]Edom, Ezek. 25:12–14
Her kings and all her princes,
Who despite their might
Are laid beside *those who were* slain by
the sword;
They shall lie with the uncircumcised,
And with those who go down to the Pit.
30 [R]There *are* the princes of the north,
All of them, and all the [R]Sidonians,
Who have gone down with the slain
In shame at the terror which they
caused by their might;
They lie uncircumcised with *those* slain
by the sword, Jer. 1:15; 25:26 • Ezek. 28:21–23
And bear their shame with those who
go down to the Pit.

31 "Pharaoh will see them
And be [R]comforted over all his
multitude,
Pharaoh and all his army,
Slain by the sword,"
Says the Lord GOD. Ezek. 14:22; 31:16

32 "For I have caused My terror in the land
of the living;
And he shall be placed in the midst of
the uncircumcised
With *those* slain by the sword,
Pharaoh and all his multitude,"
Says the Lord GOD.

CHAPTER 33

The Appointment of Ezekiel as Watchman

AGAIN the word of the LORD came to me,
saying,
2 "Son of man, speak to the children of
your people, and say to them: 'When I bring
the sword upon a land, and the people of the
land take a man from their territory and
make him their [R]watchman, 2 Sam. 18:24, 25
3 'when he sees the sword coming upon
the land, if he blows the trumpet and warns
the people,
4 'then whoever hears the sound of the
trumpet and does [R]not take warning, if the
sword comes and takes him away, [R]his blood
shall be on his *own* head. Zech. 1:4 • [Acts 18:6]
5 'He heard the sound of the trumpet, but
did not take warning; his blood shall be upon
himself. But he who takes warning will [T]save
his life. Or *deliver his soul*
6 'But if the watchman sees the sword
coming and does not blow the trumpet, and
the people are not warned, and the sword
comes and takes *any* person from among
them, [R]he is taken away in his iniquity; but
his blood I will require at the watchman's
hand.' Ezek. 33:8
7 [R]"So you, son of man: I have made you a
watchman for the house of Israel; therefore
you shall hear a word from My mouth and
warn them for Me. Is. 62:6
8 "When I say to the wicked, 'O wicked
man, you shall surely die!' and you do not
speak to warn the wicked from his way, that
wicked *man* shall die in his iniquity; but his
blood I will require at your hand.
9 "Nevertheless if you warn the wicked to
turn from his way, and he does not turn from
his way, he shall die in his iniquity; but you
have [T]delivered your soul. Or *saved your life*
10 "Therefore you, O son of man, say to the
house of Israel: 'Thus you say, "If our transgressions and our sins *lie* upon us, and we
[R]pine[T] away in them, [R]how can we then
live?" ' Ezek. 24:23 • Or *waste away* • Is. 49:14
11 "Say to them: '*As* I live,' says the Lord
GOD, 'I have no pleasure in the death of the
wicked, but that the wicked turn from his
way and live. Turn, turn from your evil ways!
For why should you die, O house of Israel?'
12 "Therefore you, O son of man, say to the
children of your people: 'The [R]righteousness
of the righteous man shall not deliver him in
the day of his transgression; as for the wickedness of the wicked, [R]he shall not fall because of it in the day that he turns from his
wickedness; nor shall the righteous be able to
live because of *his righteousness* in the day
that he sins.' Ezek. 3:20; 18:24, 26 • [2 Chr. 7:14]
13 "When I say to the righteous *that* he
shall surely live, [R]but he trusts in his own
righteousness and commits iniquity, none of

his righteous works shall be remembered; but because of the iniquity that he has committed, he shall die. Ezek. 3:20; 18:24

14 "Again, when I say to the wicked, 'You shall surely die,' if he turns from his sin and does [T]what is lawful and right, *justice*

15 "*if* the wicked restores the pledge, gives back what he has stolen, and walks in the statutes of life without committing iniquity, he shall surely live; he shall not die.

16 [R]"None of his sins which he has committed shall be remembered against him; he has done what is lawful and right; he shall surely live. [Is. 1:18; 43:25]

17 "Yet the children of your people say, 'The way of the LORD is not [T]fair.' But it is their way which is not fair! Or *equitable*

18 [R]"When the righteous turns from his righteousness and commits iniquity, he shall die because of it. Ezek. 18:26

19 "But when the wicked turns from his wickedness and does what is lawful and right, he shall live because of it.

20 "Yet you say, 'The way of the LORD is not fair.' O house of Israel, I will judge every one of you according to his own ways."

21 And it came to pass in the twelfth year of our captivity, in the tenth *month*, on the fifth *day* of the month, *that* one who had escaped from Jerusalem came to me and said, "The city has been [T]captured!" *struck down*

22 Now [R]the hand of the LORD had been upon me the evening before the man came who had escaped. And He had [R]opened my mouth; so when he came to me in the morning, my mouth was opened, and I was no longer mute. Ezek. 1:3; 8:1; 37:1 • Ezek. 24:27

23 Then the word of the LORD came to me, saying:

24 "Son of man, they who inhabit those ruins in the land of Israel are saying, 'Abraham was only one, and he inherited the land. [R]But we *are* many; the land has been given to us as a [R]possession.' [Matt. 3:9] • Ezek. 11:15

25 "Therefore say to them, 'Thus says the Lord GOD: "You eat *meat* with blood, you [R]lift up your eyes toward your idols, and [R]shed blood. Should you then possess the [R]land? Ezek. 18:6 • Ezek. 22:6, 9 • Deut. 29:28

26 "You rely on your sword, you commit abominations, and you defile one another's wives. Should you then possess the land?" '

27 "Say thus to them, 'Thus says the Lord GOD: "*As* I live, surely [R]those who *are* in the ruins shall fall by the sword, and the one who *is* in the open field [R]I will give to the beasts to be devoured, and those who *are* in the strongholds and [R]caves shall die of the pestilence. Ezek. 33:24 • Ezek. 39:4 • 1 Sam. 13:6

28 [R]"For I will make the land most desolate, her arrogant strength shall cease, and the mountains of Israel shall be so desolate that no one will pass through. Jer. 44:2, 6, 22

29 "Then they shall know that I *am* the LORD, when I have made the land most desolate because of all their abominations which they have committed." '

30 "As for you, son of man, the children of your people are talking about you beside the walls and in the doors of the houses; and they [R]speak to one another, everyone saying to his brother, 'Please come and hear what the word is that comes from the LORD.' Is. 29:13

31 "So they come to you as people do, they sit before you *as* My people, and they [R]hear your words, but they do not do them; for with their mouth they show much love, *but* their hearts pursue their *own* gain. Is. 58:2

32 "Indeed you *are* to them as a very lovely song of one who has a pleasant voice and can play well on an instrument; for they hear your words, but they do not do them.

33 "And when this comes to pass—surely it will come—then [R]they will know that a prophet has been among them." Ezek. 2:5

CHAPTER 34

The False Shepherds

AND the word of the LORD came to me, saying,

2 "Son of man, prophesy against the shepherds of Israel, prophesy and say to them, 'Thus says the Lord GOD to the shepherds: [R]"Woe to the shepherds of Israel who feed themselves! Should not the shepherds feed the flocks? Zech. 11:17

3 "You eat the fat and clothe yourselves with the wool; you [R]slaughter the fatlings, *but* you do not feed the flock. Ezek. 33:25, 26

4 "The weak you have not strengthened, nor have you healed those who were sick, nor bound up the broken, nor brought back what was driven away, nor [R]sought what was lost; but with [R]force and [T]cruelty you have ruled them. Luke 15:4 • [1 Pet. 5:3] • *harshness* or *rigor*

5 [R]"So they were [R]scattered because *there was* no shepherd; [R]and they became food for all the beasts of the field when they were scattered. Ezek. 33:21 • Matt. 9:36 • Is. 56:9

6 "My sheep [R]wandered through all the mountains, and on every high hill; yes, My flock was scattered over the whole face of the earth, and no one was seeking or searching *for them*." 1 Pet. 2:25

7 'Therefore, you shepherds, hear the word of the LORD:

8 "*as* I live," says the Lord GOD, "surely because My flock became a prey, and My flock [R]became food for every beast of the field, because *there was* no shepherd, nor did My shepherds search for My flock, [R]but the shepherds fed themselves and did not feed My flock"— Ezek. 34:5, 6 • Ezek. 34:2, 10

9 'therefore, O shepherds, hear the word of the LORD!

10 'Thus says the Lord GOD: "Behold, I *am*
against the shepherds, and I will require My
flock at their hand; I will cause them to cease
feeding the sheep, and the shepherds shall
feed themselves no more; for I will [R]deliver
My flock from their mouths, that they may
no longer be food for them." Ezek. 13:23

The True Shepherd

11 'For thus says the Lord GOD: "Indeed I
Myself will search for My sheep and seek
them out.
12 "As a [R]shepherd seeks out his flock on
the day he is among his scattered sheep, so
will I seek out My sheep and deliver them
from all the places where they were scattered
on [R]a cloudy and dark day. Jer. 31:10 • Ezek. 30:3
13 "And [R]I will bring them out from the
peoples and gather them from the countries,
and will bring them to their own land; I will
feed them on the mountains of Israel, [T]in the
valleys and in all the inhabited places of the
country. Jer. 23:3 • Or *by the streams*
14 [R]"I will feed them in good pasture, and
their fold shall be on the high mountains of
Israel. [R]There they shall lie down in a good
fold and feed in rich pasture on the mountains of Israel. [John 10:9] • Jer. 33:12
15 "I will feed My flock, and I will make
them lie down," says the Lord GOD.
16 [R]"I will seek what was lost and bring
back what was driven away, bind up the
broken and strengthen what was sick; but I
will destroy [R]the fat and the strong, and feed
them [R]in judgment." Mic. 4:6 • Is. 10:16 • Jer. 10:24
17 'And *as for* you, O My flock, thus says
the Lord GOD: [R]"Behold, I shall judge between sheep and sheep, between rams and
goats. [Matt. 25:32]
18 "*Is it* too little for you to have eaten up
the good pasture, that you must tread down
with your feet the residue of your pasture—
and to have drunk of the clear waters, that
you must foul the residue with your feet?
19 "And *as for* My flock, they eat what you
have trampled with your feet, and they drink
what you have fouled with your feet."
20 'Therefore thus says the Lord GOD to
them: [R]"Behold, I Myself will judge between
the fat and the lean sheep. Ezek. 34:17
21 "Because you have pushed with side and
shoulder, butted all the weak ones with your
horns, and scattered them abroad,
22 "therefore I will save My flock, and they
shall no longer be a prey; and I will judge
between sheep and sheep.
23 "I will establish one [R]shepherd over
them, and he shall feed them—[R]My servant
David. He shall feed them and be their shepherd. [Is. 40:11] • Jer. 30:9
24 "And [R]I, the LORD, will be their God, and
My servant David [R]a prince among them; I,
the LORD, have spoken. Ex. 29:45 • Ezek. 37:24, 25
25 "I will make a covenant of peace with
them, and cause wild beasts to cease from the
land; and they [R]will dwell safely in the wilderness and sleep in the woods. Jer. 23:6
26 "I will make them and the places all
around [R]My hill a blessing; and I will cause
showers to come down in their season; there
shall be [R]showers of blessing. Is. 56:7 • Ps. 68:9
27 "Then [R]the trees of the field shall yield
their fruit, and the earth shall yield her
increase. They shall be safe in their land; and
they shall know that I *am* the LORD, when I
have [R]broken the bands of their yoke and
delivered them from the hand of those who
[R]enslaved them. Is. 4:2 • Jer. 2:20 • Jer. 25:14
28 "And they shall no longer be a prey for
the nations, nor shall beasts of the land
devour them; but [R]they shall dwell safely, and
no one shall make *them* afraid. Jer. 30:10
29 "I will raise up for them a [R]garden of
renown, and they shall no longer be consumed with hunger in the land, nor bear the
shame of the Gentiles anymore. [Is. 11:1]
30 "Thus they shall know that [R]I, the LORD
their God, *am* with them, and *that* they, the
house of Israel, *are* [R]My people," says the
Lord GOD.'" Ezek. 34:24 • Ezek. 14:11; 36:28
31 "You are My [R]flock, the flock of My
pasture; you *are* men, *and* I *am* your God,"
says the Lord GOD.'" Ps. 100:3

CHAPTER 35

The Judgment of Edom

MOREOVER the word of the LORD came
to me, saying,
2 "Son of man, set your face against
Mount Seir and prophesy against it,
3 "and say to it, 'Thus says the Lord GOD:

"Behold, O Mount Seir, I *am* against
you;
[R]I will stretch out My hand against you,
And make you most desolate; Ezek. 6:14
4 I shall lay your cities waste,
And you shall be desolate.
Then you shall know that I *am* the
LORD.

5 "Because you have had an [T]ancient hatred, and have shed *the blood of* the children
of Israel by the power of the sword at the
time of their calamity, [R]*when* their iniquity
came to an end, Or *everlasting* • Ps. 137:7
6 "therefore, *as* I live," says the Lord GOD,
"I will prepare you for blood, and blood shall
pursue you; since you have not hated [T]blood,
therefore blood shall pursue you. Or *bloodshed*
7 "Thus I will make Mount Seir most
desolate, and cut off from it the [R]one who
leaves and the one who returns. Judg. 5:6
8 "And I will fill its mountains with the
slain; on your hills and in your valleys and in

all your ravines those who are slain by the
sword shall fall.
9 "I will make you perpetually desolate,
and your cities shall be uninhabited; then you
shall know that I *am* the LORD.
10 "Because you have said, 'These two nations and these two countries shall be mine,
and we will [R]possess them,' although [R]the
LORD was there, Ps. 83:4–12 • [Ps. 48:1–3; 132:13, 14]
11 "therefore, *as* I live," says the Lord GOD,
"I will do [R]according to your anger and
according to the envy which you showed in
your hatred against them; and I will make
Myself known among them when I judge
you. [James 2:13]
12 "Then you shall know that I *am* the
LORD. I have heard all your [R]blasphemies
which you have spoken against the mountains of Israel, saying, 'They are desolate;
they are given to us to consume.' Is. 52:5
13 "Thus with your mouth you have
boasted against Me and multiplied your
words against Me; I have heard *them*."
14 'Thus says the Lord GOD: "The whole
earth will rejoice when I make you desolate.
15 "As you rejoiced because the inheritance
of the house of Israel was desolate, so I will
do to you; you shall be desolate, O Mount
Seir, as well as all of Edom—all of it! Then
they shall know that I *am* the LORD." '

CHAPTER 36

Judgment on the Nations

"AND you, son of man, prophesy to the
[R]mountains of Israel, and say, 'O
mountains of Israel, hear the word of the
LORD! Ezek. 6:2, 3
2 'Thus says the Lord GOD: "Because the
enemy has said of you, 'Aha! The ancient
heights have become our possession,' " '
3 "therefore prophesy, and say, 'Thus says
the Lord GOD: "Because they made *you* desolate and swallowed you up on every side, so
that you became the possession of the rest of
the nations, and you are taken up by the lips
of talkers and slandered by the people"—
4 'therefore, O mountains of Israel, hear
the word of the Lord GOD! Thus says the Lord
GOD to the mountains, the hills, the [T]rivers,
the valleys, the desolate wastes, and the cities
that have been forsaken, which became plunder and [R]mockery to the rest of the nations
all around— Or *ravines* • Ps. 79:4
5 'therefore thus says the Lord GOD:
[R]"Surely I have spoken in My burning jealousy against the rest of the nations and
against all Edom, who gave My land to themselves as a possession, with whole-hearted
joy *and* spiteful minds, in order to plunder its
open country." ' Deut. 4:24
6 "Therefore prophesy concerning the land
of Israel, and say to the mountains, the hills,
the rivers, and the valleys, 'Thus says the
Lord GOD: "Behold, I have spoken in My
jealousy and My fury, because you have
[R]borne the shame of the nations." Ps. 74:10
7 'Therefore thus says the Lord GOD: "I
have [R]lifted My hand in an oath that surely
the nations that *are* around you shall [R]bear
their own shame. Ezek. 20:5 • Jer. 25:9, 15, 29

Israel Returns to the Lord

8 "But you, O mountains of Israel, you
shall shoot forth your branches and yield
your fruit to My people Israel, for they are
about to come.
9 "For indeed I *am* for you, and I will turn
to you, and you shall be tilled and sown.
10 "I will multiply men upon you, all the
house of Israel, all of it; and the cities shall be
inhabited and [R]the ruins rebuilt. Amos 9:14
11 "I will multiply upon you man and beast;
and they shall increase and [T]bear young; I
will make you inhabited as in former times,
and do [R]better *for you* than at your beginnings. [R]Then you shall know that I *am* the
LORD. Lit. *be fruitful* • Is. 51:3 • Ezek. 35:9; 37:6, 13
12 "Yes, I will cause men to walk on you,
My people Israel; [R]they shall take possession
of you, and you shall be their inheritance; no
more shall you [R]bereave them *of their children*." Obad. 17 • Jer. 15:7
13 'Thus says the Lord GOD: "Because they
say to you, [R]'You devour men and bereave
your nation *of children*,' Num. 13:32
14 "therefore you shall devour men no
more, nor bereave your nation anymore,"
says the Lord GOD.
15 [R]"Nor will I let you hear the taunts of the
nations anymore, nor bear the reproach of
the peoples anymore, nor shall you cause
your nation to stumble anymore," says the
Lord GOD.' " Ezek. 34:29
16 Moreover the word of the LORD came to
me, saying:
17 "Son of man, when the house of Israel
dwelt in their own land, [R]they defiled it by
their own ways and deeds; to Me their way
was like [R]the uncleanness of a woman in her
customary impurity. Jer. 2:7 • Lev. 15:19
18 "Therefore I poured out My fury on
them [R]for the blood they had shed on the
land, and for their idols *with which* they had
defiled it. Ezek. 16:36, 38; 23:37
19 "So I scattered them among the nations,
and they were dispersed throughout the
countries; I judged them [R]according to their
ways and their deeds. [Rom. 2:6]
20 "When they came to the nations, wherever they went, they [R]profaned My holy
name—when they said of them, 'These *are*
the people of the LORD, *and* yet they have
gone out of His land.' Rom. 2:24
21 "But I had concern for My holy name,

which the house of Israel had profaned
among the nations wherever they went.
22 "Therefore say to the house of Israel,
'Thus says the Lord GOD: "I do not do *this* for
your sake, O house of Israel, but for My holy
name's sake, which you have profaned
among the nations wherever you went.
23 "And I will sanctify My great name,
which has been profaned among the nations,
which you have profaned in their midst; and
the nations shall know that I *am* the LORD,"
says the Lord GOD, "when I am [R]hallowed in
you before their eyes. Ezek. 20:41; 28:22
24 "For [R]I will take you from among the
nations, gather you out of all countries, and
bring you into your own land. Ezek. 34:13; 37:21
25 [R]"Then I will sprinkle clean water on
you, and you shall be clean; I will cleanse you
[R]from all your filthiness and from all your
idols. Heb. 9:13, 19; 10:22 • Jer. 33:8
26 "I will give you a [R]new heart and put a
new spirit within you; I will take the heart of
stone out of your flesh and give you a heart
of flesh. Ezek. 11:19
27 "I will put My Spirit within you and
cause you to walk in My statutes, and you
will keep My judgments and do *them*.
28 "Then you shall dwell in the land that I
gave to your fathers; [R]you shall be My people,
and I will be your God. Jer. 30:22
29 "I will deliver you from all your unclean-
nesses. I will call for the grain and multiply it,
and bring no famine upon you.
30 [R]"And I will multiply the fruit of your
trees and the increase of your fields, so that
you need never again bear the reproach of
famine among the nations. Ezek. 34:27
31 "Then [R]you will remember your evil
ways and your deeds that *were* not good; and
you [R]will [T]loathe yourselves in your own
sight, for your iniquities and your abominations. Ezek. 16:61, 63 • Ezek. 6:9; 20:43 • *despise*
32 [R]"Not for your sake do I do *this*," says
the Lord GOD, "let it be known to you. Be
ashamed and confounded for your own ways,
O house of Israel!" Deut. 9:5
33 'Thus says the Lord GOD: "On the day
that I cleanse you from all your iniquities, I
will also enable *you* to dwell in the cities,
[R]and the ruins shall be rebuilt. Ezek. 36:10
34 "The desolate land shall be tilled instead
of lying desolate in the sight of all who pass
by.
35 "So they will say, 'This land that was
desolate has become like the garden of [R]Eden;
and the wasted, desolate, and ruined cities
are now fortified *and* inhabited.' Joel 2:3
36 "Then the nations which are left all
around you shall know that I, the LORD, have
rebuilt the ruined places *and* planted what
was desolate. [R]I, the LORD, have spoken *it*,
and I will do *it*." Ezek. 17:24; 22:14; 37:14
37 'Thus says the Lord GOD: [R]"I will also let
the house of Israel inquire of Me to do this
for them: I will [R]increase their men like a
flock. Ezek. 14:3; 20:3, 31 • Ezek. 36:10
38 "Like a [T]flock *offered as* holy *sacrifices*,
like the flock at Jerusalem on its [T]feast days,
so shall the ruined cities be filled with flocks
of men. Then they shall know that I *am* the
LORD."' " Lit. *holy flock* • *appointed feasts*

CHAPTER 37

Vision of Dry Bones

THE hand of the LORD came upon me and
brought me out [R]in the Spirit of the LORD,
and set me down in the midst of the valley;
and it *was* full of bones. Ezek. 3:14; 8:3; 11:24
2 Then He caused me to pass by them all
around, and behold, *there were* very many in
the open valley; and indeed *they were* very
dry.
3 And He said to me, "Son of man, can
these bones live?" So I answered, "O Lord
GOD, [R]You know." [1 Sam. 2:6]
4 Again He said to me, "Prophesy to these
bones, and say to them, 'O dry bones, hear
the word of the LORD!
5 'Thus says the Lord GOD to these bones:
"Surely I will [R]cause breath to enter into you,
and you shall live. Ps. 104:29, 30
6 "I will put sinews on you and bring flesh
upon you, cover you with skin and put breath
in you; and you shall live. [R]Then you shall
know that I *am* the LORD."' " Joel 2:27; 3:17
7 So I prophesied as I was commanded;
and as I prophesied, there was a noise, and
suddenly a rattling; and the bones came
together, bone to bone.
8 Indeed, as I looked, the sinews and the
flesh came upon them, and the skin covered
them over; but *there was* no breath in them.
9 Then He said to me, "Prophesy to the
breath, prophesy, son of man, and say to
the breath, 'Thus says the Lord GOD: "Come
from the four winds, O breath, and breathe
on these slain, that they may live."' "
10 So I prophesied as He commanded me,
[R]and [T]breath came into them, and they lived,
and stood upon their feet, an exceedingly
great army. Rev. 11:11 • Breath of life
11 Then He said to me, "Son of man, these
bones are the whole house of Israel. They
indeed say, [R]'Our bones are dry, our hope is
lost, and we ourselves are cut off!' Ps. 141:7
12 "Therefore prophesy and say to them,
'Thus says the Lord GOD: "Behold, [R]O My
people, I will open your graves and cause you
to come up from your graves, and [R]bring you
into the land of Israel. Is. 26:19; 66:14 • Ezek. 36:24
13 "Then you shall know that I *am* the
LORD, when I have opened your graves, O My
people, and brought you up from your graves.

14 "I [R]will put My Spirit in you, and you
shall live, and I will place you in your own
land. Then you shall know that I, the LORD,
have spoken *it* and performed *it*," says the
LORD.'" Ezek. 36:27

Sign of the Two Sticks

15 Again the word of the LORD came to me,
saying,
16 "As for you, son of man, [R]take a stick for
yourself and write on it: 'For Judah and for
the children of Israel, his companions.' Then
take another stick and write on it, 'For
Joseph, the stick of Ephraim, and *for* all the
house of Israel, his companions.' Num. 17:2, 3
17 "Then [R]join them one to another for
yourself into one stick, and they will become
one in your hand. Hos. 1:11
18 "And when the children of your people
speak to you, saying, [R]'Will you not show us
what you *mean* by these?'— Ezek. 12:9; 24:19
19 [R]"say to them, 'Thus says the Lord GOD:
"Surely I will take [R]the stick of Joseph, which
is in the hand of Ephraim, and the tribes of
Israel, his companions; and I will join them
with it, with the stick of Judah, and make
them one stick, and they will be one in My
hand."' Zech. 10:6 • Ezek. 37:16, 17
20 "And the sticks on which you write will
be in your hand [R]before their eyes. Ezek. 12:3
21 "Then say to them, 'Thus says the Lord
GOD: "Surely [R]I will take the children of
Israel from among the nations, wherever
they have gone, and will gather them from
every side and bring them into their own
land; Ezek. 36:24
22 "and I will make them one nation in the
land, on the mountains of Israel; and [R]one
king shall be king over them all; they shall no
longer be two nations, nor shall they ever be
divided into two kingdoms again. Ezek. 34:23
23 "They shall not defile themselves
anymore with their idols, nor with their
detestable things, nor with any of their transgressions; but I will deliver them from all
their dwelling places in which they have
sinned, and will cleanse them. Then they
shall be My people, and I will be their God.
24 [R]"David My servant *shall be* king over
them, and they shall all have one shepherd;
they shall also walk in My judgments and
observe My statutes, and do them. Is. 11:1 ☆
25 "Then they shall dwell in the land that I
have given to Jacob My servant, where your
fathers dwelt; and they shall dwell there,
they, their children, and their children's
children, forever; and [R]My servant David
shall be their prince forever. John 12:34 ☆
26 "Moreover I will [T]make a covenant of
peace with them, and it shall be an everlasting covenant with them; I will establish
them and multiply them, and I will set My
sanctuary in their midst forevermore. *cut*
27 [R]"My tabernacle also shall be with them;
indeed I will be [R]their God, and they shall be
My people. [John 1:14] • Ezek. 11:20
28 "The nations also will know that I, the
LORD, [R]sanctify Israel, when My sanctuary is
in their midst forevermore."'" Ezek. 20:12

CHAPTER 38

Attack by Gog

NOW the word of the LORD came to me,
saying,
2 "Son of man, set your face against [R]Gog,
of the land of [R]Magog, *the prince of Rosh,
[R]Meshech, and Tubal, and prophesy against
him, Rev. 20:8 • Gen. 10:2 • Ezek. 32:26
3 "and say, 'Thus says the Lord GOD: "Behold, I *am* against you, O Gog, the prince of
Rosh, Meshech, and Tubal.
4 "I will turn you around, put hooks into
your jaws, and lead you out, with all your
army, horses, and horsemen, all splendidly
clothed, a great company *with* bucklers and
shields, all of them handling swords.
5 "Persia, Ethiopia, and Libya are with
them, all of them *with* shield and helmet;
6 [R]"Gomer and all its troops; the house of
Togarmah *from* the far north and all its
troops—many people *are* with you. Gen. 10:2
7 [R]"Prepare yourself and be ready, you and
all your companies that are gathered about
you; and be a guard for them. Is. 8:9, 10
8 "After many days you will be visited. In
the latter years you will come into the land of
those brought back from the sword *and*
gathered from many people on [R]the mountains of Israel, which had long been desolate;
they were brought out of the nations, and
now all of them dwell safely. Ezek. 36:1, 4
9 "You will ascend, coming like a storm,
covering the land like a cloud, you and all
your troops and many peoples with you."
10 'Thus says the Lord GOD: "On that day it
shall come to pass *that* thoughts will arise in
your mind, and you will make an evil plan:
11 "You will say, 'I will go up against a land
of [R]unwalled villages; I will [R]go to a peaceful
people, [R]who dwell [T]safely, all of them dwelling without walls, and having neither bars
nor gates'— Zech. 2:4 • Jer. 49:31 • Ezek. 38:8 • *securely*
12 "to take plunder and to take booty, to
stretch out your hand against the waste
places *that are again* inhabited, [R]and against
a people gathered from the nations, who have
acquired livestock and goods, who dwell in
the midst of the land. Ezek. 38:8
13 "Sheba, [R]Dedan, the merchants [R]of Tarshish, and all [R]their young lions will say to
you, 'Have you come to take plunder? Have
you gathered your army to take booty, to

38:2 Tg., Vg., Aquila *the chief prince of Meshech,* also
v. 3

carry away silver and gold, to take away
livestock and goods, to take great plun-
der?' " ' Ezek. 27:15, 20 • Ezek. 27:12 • Ezek. 19:3, 5
14 "Therefore, son of man, prophesy and
say to Gog, 'Thus says the Lord GOD: [R]"On
that day when My people Israel [R]dwell safely,
will you not know *it*? Is. 4:1 • Ezek. 38:8, 11
15 [R]"Then you will come from your place
out of the far north, you and many peoples
with you, all of them riding on horses, a great
company and a mighty army. Ezek. 39:2
16 "You will come up against My people
Israel like a cloud, to cover the land. It will be
in the latter days that I will bring you against
My land, so that the nations may [R]know Me,
when I am [R]hallowed in you, O Gog, before
their eyes." Ezek. 35:11 • Ezek. 28:22

Judgment of God

17 'Thus says the Lord GOD: "Are *you* he of
whom I have spoken in former days by My
servants the prophets of Israel, who prophesied for years in those days that I would
bring you against them?
18 "And it will come to pass at the same
time, when Gog comes against the land of
Israel," says the Lord GOD, "*that* My fury will
show in My face.
19 "For in My jealousy [R]*and* in the fire of
My wrath I have spoken: [R]'Surely in that day
there shall be a great [T]earthquake in the land
of Israel, Ps. 89:46 • Rev. 16:8 • Lit. *shaking*
20 'so that the fish of the sea, the birds of
the heavens, the beasts of the field, all creeping things that creep on the earth, and all
men who *are* on the face of the earth shall
shake at My presence. The mountains
shall be thrown down, the steep places shall
fall, and every wall shall fall to the ground.'
21 "I will [R]call for [R]a sword against Gog
throughout all My mountains," says the Lord
GOD. [R]"Every man's sword will be against his
brother. Ps. 105:16 • Ezek. 14:17 • 1 Sam. 14:20
22 "And I will bring him to judgment with
pestilence and bloodshed; I will rain down on
him, on his troops, and on the many peoples
who *are* with him, flooding rain, great hailstones, fire, and brimstone.
23 "Thus I will magnify Myself and [R]sanc-
tify Myself, [R]and I will be known in the eyes
of many nations. Then they shall know that I
am the LORD." ' Ezek. 36:23 • Ezek. 37:28; 38:16

CHAPTER 39

"AND you, son of man, prophesy against
Gog, and say, 'Thus says the Lord
GOD: "Behold, I *am* against you, O Gog, the
chief *prince of Rosh, Meshech, and Tubal;
2 "and I will [R]turn you around and lead
you on, [R]bringing you up from the far north,
and bring you against the mountains of
Israel. Ezek. 38:8 • Ezek. 38:15
3 "Then I will knock the bow out of your
left hand, and cause the arrows to fall out of
your right hand.
4 "You shall [T]fall upon the mountains of
Israel, you and all your troops and the peoples who *are* with you; [R]I will give you to
birds of prey of every sort and *to* the beasts of
the field to be devoured. Be slain • Ezek. 33:27
5 "You shall [T]fall on the open field; for I
have spoken," says the Lord GOD. Be slain
6 "And I will send fire on Magog and on
those who live in security in the coastlands.
Then they shall know that I *am* the LORD.
7 "So I will make My holy name known in
the midst of My people Israel, and I will not
let them profane My holy name anymore.
[R]Then the nations shall know that *I am* the
LORD, the Holy One in Israel. Ezek. 38:16
8 "Surely it is coming, and it shall be
done," says the Lord GOD. "This *is* the day [R]of
which I have spoken. Ezek. 38:17
9 "Then those who dwell in the cities of
Israel will go out and set on fire and burn the
weapons, both the shields and bucklers, the
bows and arrows, the [T]javelins and spears;
and they will make fires with them for seven
years. Lit. *hand staffs*
10 "They will not take wood from the field
nor cut down *any* from the forests, because
they will make fires with the weapons; [R]and
they will plunder those who plundered them,
and pillage those who pillaged them," says
the Lord GOD. Is. 14:2; 33:1
11 "It will come to pass in that day *that* I
will give Gog a burial place there in Israel,
the valley of those who pass by east of the
sea; and it will obstruct travelers, because
there they will bury Gog and all his multitude. Therefore they will call *it* the Valley of
[T]Hamon Gog. Lit. *The Multitude of Gog*
12 "For seven months the house of Israel
will be burying them, [R]in order to cleanse the
land. Deut. 21:23
13 "Indeed all the people of the land will be
burying *them*, and they will gain [R]renown for
it on the day that [R]I am glorified," says the
Lord GOD. Zeph. 3:19, 20 • Ezek. 28:22
14 "They will set apart men regularly employed, with the help of [T]a search party, to
pass through the land and bury those bodies
remaining on the ground, in order [R]to cleanse
it. At the end of seven months they will make
a search. *those who pass through* • Ezek. 39:12
15 "The search party will pass through the
land; and *whenever anyone* sees a man's
bone, he shall [T]set up a marker by it, till the
buriers have buried it in the Valley of Hamon
Gog. *build*
16 "*The* name of *the* city *will* also *be*
[T]Hamonah. Thus they shall [R]cleanse the
land." ' Lit. *Multitude* • Ezek. 39:12

39:1 Tg., Vg., Aquila *the chief prince of Meshech*

17 "And as for you, son of man, thus says
the Lord GOD, [R]'Speak to every sort of bird
and to every beast of the field: Rev. 19:17, 18

[R]"Assemble yourselves and come; Is. 18:6
Gather together from all sides to My
[R]sacrificial meal Zeph. 1:7
Which I am sacrificing for you,
A great sacrificial meal [R]on the
mountains of Israel, Ezek. 39:4
That you may eat flesh and drink blood.
18 [R]You shall eat the flesh of the mighty,
Drink the blood of the princes of the
earth, Rev. 19:18
Of rams and lambs,
Of goats and bulls,
All of them fatlings of Bashan.
19 You shall eat fat till you are full,
And drink blood till you are drunk,
At My sacrificial meal
Which I am sacrificing for you.
20 [R]You shall be filled at My table
With horses and riders,
[R]With mighty men
And with all the men of war," says the
Lord GOD. Ps. 76:5, 6 • Rev. 19:18

21 [R]"I will set My glory among the nations;
all the nations shall see My judgment which I
have executed, and [R]My hand which I have
laid on them. Ezek. 36:23; 38:23 • Ex. 7:4
22 [R]"So the house of Israel shall know that I
am the LORD their God from that day forward. Ex. 39:7, 28
23 "The Gentiles shall know that the house
of Israel went into captivity for their iniquity;
because they were unfaithful to Me, therefore [R]I hid My face from them. I [R]gave them
into the hand of their enemies, and they all
fell by the sword. Is. 1:15; 59:2 • Lev. 26:25
24 "According to their uncleanness and
according to their transgressions I have dealt
with them, and hidden My face from them." '
25 "Therefore thus says the Lord GOD:
[R]'Now I will bring back the captives of Jacob,
and have mercy on the [R]whole house of
Israel; and I will be jealous for My holy
name— Ezek. 34:13; 36:24 • Hos. 1:11
26 [R]'after they have borne their shame, and
all their unfaithfulness in which they were
unfaithful to Me, when they [R]dwelt safely
in their *own* land and no one made *them*
afraid. Dan. 9:16 • Lev. 26:5, 6
27 'When I have brought them back from
the peoples and gathered them out of their
enemies' lands, and I [R]am hallowed in them in
the sight of many nations, Ezek. 36:23, 24; 38:16
28 [R]'then they shall know that I *am* the
LORD their God, who sent them into captivity
among the nations, but also brought them
back to their *own* land, and left none of them
[T]captive any longer. Ezek. 34:30 • Lit. *there*
29 [R]'And I will not hide My face from them
anymore; for I shall have [R]poured out My
Spirit on the house of Israel,' says the Lord
GOD." Is. 54:8, 9 • [Joel 2:28]

CHAPTER 40

Vision of the Man with the Measuring Rod

IN the twenty-fifth year of our captivity, at
the beginning of the year, on the tenth
day of the month, in the fourteenth year after
the city was [T]captured, on the very same day
[R]the hand of the LORD was upon me; and He
took me there. Lit. *struck* • Ezek. 1:3; 3:14, 22; 37:1
2 In the visions of God He took me into the
land of Israel and [R]set me on a very high
mountain; on it toward the south *was* something like the structure of a city. Rev. 21:10
3 He took me there, and behold, *there was*
a man whose appearance *was* like the appearance of bronze. [R]He had a line of flax
[R]and a measuring rod in his hand, and he
stood in the gateway. Ezek. 47:3 • Rev. 11:1
4 And the man said to me, "Son of man,
look with your eyes and hear with your ears,
and [T]fix your mind on everything I show you;
for you *were* brought here so that I might
show *them* to you. Declare to the house of
Israel everything you see." Lit. *set your heart*

The Outer Court

5 Now there was [R]a wall all around the
outside of the [T]temple. In the man's hand was
a measuring rod six cubits *long, each being a*
cubit and a handbreadth; and he measured
the width of the wall structure, one rod; and
the height, one rod. Ezek. 42:20 • Lit. *house*
6 Then he went to the gateway which
faced [R]east; and he went up its stairs and
measured the threshold of the gateway,
which was [T]one rod wide, and the other
threshold *was* one rod wide. Ezek. 43:1 • 10.5 ft.
7 Each gate chamber *was* one rod long and
one rod wide; between the gate chambers
was a space of [T]five cubits; and the threshold
of the gateway by the vestibule of the inside
gate *was* [T]one rod. 8.75 ft. • 10.5 ft.
8 He also measured the vestibule of the
inside gate, one rod.
9 Then he measured the vestibule of the
gateway, [T]eight cubits; and the gateposts,
[T]two cubits. The vestibule of the gate *was* on
the inside. 14 ft. • 42 in.
10 In the eastern gateway *were* three gate
chambers on one side and three on the other;
the three *were* all the same size; also the
gateposts were of the same size on this side
and that side.
11 He measured the width of the entrance
to the gateway, [T]ten cubits; *and* the length of
the gate, [T]thirteen cubits. 17.5 ft. • 22.75 ft.
12 *There was* a [T]space in front of the gate
chambers, [T]one cubit *on this side* and one
cubit on that side; the gate chambers *were*

[T]six cubits on this side and six cubits on that
side. Lit. *border* • 21 in. • 10.5 ft.
13 Then he measured the gateway from the
roof of *one* gate chamber to the roof of the
other; the width *was* [T]twenty-five cubits, as
door faces door. 43.75 ft.
14 He measured the gateposts, [T]sixty cubits
high, and the court all around the gateway
extended to the gatepost. 105 ft.
15 *From* the front of the entrance gate to
the front of the vestibule of the inner gate
was [T]fifty cubits. 87.5 ft.
16 *There were* [R]beveled window *frames* in
the gate chambers and in their intervening
archways on the inside of the gateway all
around, and likewise in the vestibules. *There*
were windows all around on the inside. And
on each gatepost *were* palm trees. 1 Kin. 6:4
17 Then he brought me into the outer court;
and *there were* chambers and a pavement
made all around the court; [R]thirty chambers
faced the pavement. Ezek. 45:5
18 The pavement was by the side of the
gateways, corresponding to the length of the
gateways; *this was* the lower pavement.
19 Then he measured the width from the
front of the lower gateway to the front of the
inner court exterior, [T]one hundred cubits
toward the east and the north. 175 ft.
20 On the outer court was also a gateway
facing north, and he measured its length and
its width.
21 Its gate chambers, three on this side and
three on that side, its gateposts and its archways, had the same measurements as the first
gate; its length *was* [T]fifty cubits and its width
[T]twenty-five cubits. 87.5 ft. • 43.75 ft.
22 Its windows and those of its archways,
and also its palm trees, *had* the same measurements as the gateway facing east; it was
ascended by seven steps, and its archway *was*
in front of it.
23 A gate of the inner court was opposite
the northern gateway, just as the eastern
gateway; and he measured from gateway to
gateway, [T]one hundred cubits. 175 ft.
24 After that he brought me toward the
south, and there a gateway was facing south;
and he measured its gateposts and archways
according to these same measurements.
25 *There were* windows in it and in its
archways all around like those windows; its
length *was* [T]fifty cubits and its width
[T]twenty-five cubits. 87.5 ft. • 43.75 ft.
26 Seven steps led up to it, and its archway
was in front of them; and it had palm trees on
its gateposts, one on this side and one on that
side.
27 *There was* also a gateway on the inner
court, facing south; and he measured from
gateway to gateway toward the south, [T]one
hundred cubits. 175 ft.

The Inner Court

28 Then he brought me to the inner court
through the southern gateway; he measured
the southern gateway according to these
same measurements.
29 Also its gate chambers, its gateposts, and
its archways *were* according to these same
measurements; *there were* windows in it and
in its archways all around; *it was* [T]fifty cubits
long and twenty-five cubits wide. 87.5 ft.
30 *There were* archways all around, twenty-
five cubits long and five cubits wide.
31 Its archways faced the outer court, palm
trees *were* on its gateposts, and going up to it
were eight steps.
32 Then he brought me into the inner court
facing east; he measured the gateway according to these same measurements.
33 Also its gate chambers, its gateposts, and
its archways *were* according to these same
measurements; and *there were* windows in it
and in its archways all around; *it was* fifty
cubits long and twenty-five cubits wide.
34 Its archways faced the outer court, and
palm trees *were* on its gateposts on this side
and on that side; and going up to it *were*
eight steps.
35 Then he brought me to the north gateway and measured *it* according to these same
measurements—
36 also its gate chambers, its gateposts, and
its archways. It had windows all around; its
length *was* fifty cubits and its width twenty-
five cubits.
37 Its gateposts faced the outer court, palm
trees *were* on its gateposts on this side and on
that side, and going up to it *were* eight steps.
38 *There was* a chamber and its entrance by
the gateposts of the gateway, where they
[R]washed the burnt offering. 2 Chr. 4:6
39 In the vestibule of the gateway *were* two
tables on this side and two tables on that side,
on which to slay the burnt offering, [R]the sin
offering, and the trespass offering. Lev. 4:2, 3
40 At the outer side of the vestibule, as one
goes up to the entrance of the northern
gateway, *were* two tables; and on the other
side of the vestibule of the gateway *were* two
tables.
41 Four tables *were* on this side and four
tables on that side, by the side of the gateway, eight tables on which they slaughtered
the sacrifices.
42 *There were* also four tables of hewn
stone for the burnt offering, [T]one cubit and a
half long, one cubit and a half wide, and [T]one
cubit high; on these they laid the instruments
with which they slaughtered the burnt offering and the sacrifice. 31.5 in. • 21 in.
43 Inside *were* hooks, a handbreadth wide,
fastened all around; and the flesh of the
sacrifices *was* on the tables.

44 Outside the inner gate *were* the chambers for [R]the singers in the inner court, one facing south at the side of the northern gateway, and the other facing north at the side of the southern gateway. 1 Chr. 6:31, 32

45 Then he said to me, "This chamber which faces south *is* for [R]the priests who have charge of the temple. Lev. 8:35

46 "The chamber which faces north *is* for the priests [R]who have charge of the altar; these *are* the sons of [R]Zadok, from the sons of Levi, who come near the LORD to minister to Him." Num. 18:5 • 1 Kin. 2:35

47 And he measured the court, [T]one hundred cubits long and one hundred cubits wide, foursquare. The altar *was* in front of the temple. 175 ft.

The Temple Vestibule

48 Then he brought me to the [R]vestibule of the temple and measured the doorposts of the vestibule, [T]five cubits on this side and five cubits on that side; and the width of the gateway was [T]three cubits on this side and three cubits on that side. 1 Kin. 6:3 • 8.75 ft. • 5.25 ft.

49 [R]The length of the vestibule *was* [T]twenty cubits, and the width eleven cubits; and by the steps which led up to it *there were* [R]pillars by the doorposts, one on this side and another on that side. 1 Kin. 6:3 • 35 ft. • 1 Kin. 7:15–22

CHAPTER 41

The Temple Itself

THEN he brought me into the sanctuary and measured the doorposts, six cubits wide on one side and six cubits wide on the other side—the width of the tabernacle.

2 The width of the entryway *was* [T]ten cubits, and the side walls of the entrance *were* five cubits on this side and five cubits on the other side; and he measured its length, forty cubits, and its width, twenty cubits. 17.5 ft.

3 Then he went inside and measured the doorposts, [T]two cubits; and the entrance, [T]six cubits *high*; and the width of the entrance, [T]seven cubits. 3.5 ft. • 10.5 ft. • 12.25 ft.

4 [R]He measured the length, [T]twenty cubits; and the width, twenty cubits, beyond the sanctuary; and he said to me, "This *is* the Most Holy *Place*." 1 Kin. 6:20 • 35 ft.

5 Next, he measured the wall of the [T]temple, [T]six cubits. The width of each side chamber all around the temple *was* [T]four cubits on every side. Lit. *house* • 10.5 ft. • 7 ft.

6 [R]The side chambers *were* in three stories, one above the other, thirty chambers in each story; they rested on [T]ledges which *were* for the side chambers all around, that they might be supported, but [R]not fastened to the wall of the temple. 1 Kin. 6:5–10 • Lit. *the wall* • 1 Kin. 6:6, 10

7 As one went up from story to story, the side chambers [R]became wider all around, because their supporting ledges in the wall of the temple ascended like steps; therefore the width of the structure increased as one went up *from* the lowest *story* to the highest by way of the middle one. 1 Kin. 6:8

8 I also saw an elevation all around the temple; it was the foundation of the side chambers, a full rod, *that is*, six cubits *high*.

9 The thickness of the outer wall of the side chambers *was* [T]five cubits, and so also the remaining terrace by the place of the side chambers of the [T]temple. 8.75 ft. • Lit. *house*

10 And between *it and* the *wall* chambers was a width of [T]twenty cubits all around the temple on every side. 35 ft.

11 The doors of the side chambers opened on the terrace, one door toward the north and another toward the south; and the width of the terrace *was* five cubits all around.

12 The building that fronted the separating courtyard at its western end *was* [T]seventy cubits wide; the wall of the building *was* [T]five cubits thick all around, and its length [T]ninety cubits. 122.5 ft. • 8.75 ft. • 157.5 ft.

13 So he measured the temple, [T]one [R]hundred cubits long; and the separating courtyard with the building and its walls *was* one hundred cubits long; 175 ft. • Ezek. 40:47

14 also the width of the eastern face of the temple, including the separating courtyard, *was* one hundred cubits.

15 He measured the length of the building behind it, facing the separating courtyard, with its galleries on the one side and on the other side, one hundred cubits, as well as the inner temple and the porches of the court,

16 their doorposts and the beveled window frames. And the galleries all around their three stories opposite the threshold were paneled with wood from the ground to the windows—the windows were covered—

17 from the space above the door, even to the inner [T]room, as well as outside, and on every wall all around, inside and outside, by measure. Lit. *house*, The Most Holy Place

18 And *it was* made with cherubim and palm trees, a palm tree between cherub and cherub. *Each* cherub had two faces,

19 [R]so that the face of a man *was* toward a palm tree on one side, and the face of a young lion toward a palm tree on the other side; thus *it was* made throughout the temple all around. Ezek. 1:10; 10:14

20 From the floor to the space above the door, and on the wall of the sanctuary, cherubim and palm trees *were* carved.

21 The [R]doorposts of the temple *were* square, *and so also* the front of the sanctuary; the appearance *of the one* was like the appearance *of the other*. 1 Kin. 6:33

22 [R]The altar *was* of wood, three cubits
high, and its length [T]two cubits. Its corners,
its length, and its sides *were* of wood; and he
said to me, "This *is* [R]the table that *is* [R]before
the LORD." Ex. 30:1–3 • 3.5 ft. • Ex. 25:23, 30 • Ex. 30:8
23 [R]The temple and the sanctuary had two
doors. 1 Kin. 6:31–35
24 The doors had two [R]panels *apiece,* two
folding panels: two *panels* for one door and
two panels for the other *door.* 1 Kin. 6:34
25 Cherubim and palm trees *were* carved on
the doors of the temple just as they *were*
carved on the walls. A wooden canopy *was*
on the front of the vestibule outside.
26 *There were* beveled window *frames* and
palm trees on one side and on the other, on
the sides of the vestibule—also on the side
chambers of the temple and on the canopies.

CHAPTER 42

The Chamber in the Outer Court

THEN he brought me out into the outer
court, by the way toward the north; and
he brought me into the chamber which *was*
opposite the separating courtyard, and which
was opposite the building toward the north.
2 Facing the length, *which was* [T]one hundred cubits (the width was [T]fifty cubits), was
the north door. 175 ft. • 87.5 ft.
3 Opposite the inner court of [T]twenty *cubits,* and opposite the [R]pavement of the outer
court, *was* [R]gallery against gallery in three
stories. 35 ft. • Ezek. 40:17 • Ezek. 41:15, 16; 42:5
4 In front of the chambers, toward the
inside, *was* a walk [T]ten cubits wide, at a
distance of [T]one cubit; and their doors faced
north. 17.5 ft. • 21 in.
5 Now the upper chambers *were* shorter,
because the galleries took away *space* from
them more than from the lower and middle
stories of the building.
6 For they *were* in three *stories* and did not
have pillars like the pillars of the courts;
therefore *the upper level* was [T]shortened
more than the lower and middle levels from
the ground up. Or *narrowed*
7 And a wall which *was* outside ran parallel to the chambers, at the front of the chambers, toward the outer court; its length *was*
[T]fifty cubits. 87.5 ft.
8 The length of the chambers toward the
outer court *was* fifty cubits, whereas that
facing the temple *was* one hundred cubits.
9 At the lower chambers *was* the entrance
on the east side, as one goes into them from
the outer court.
10 *There were* also chambers in the thickness of the wall of the court toward the east,
opposite the separating courtyard and opposite the building.
11 *There was* a walk in front of them also,
and their appearance *was* like the chambers
which *were* toward the north; they *were* as
long and as wide as the others, and all their
exits and entrances *were* according to plan.
12 And corresponding to the doors of the
chambers that *were* facing south, as one
enters them, *there was* a door in front of the
walk, the way directly in front of the wall
toward the east.
13 Then he said to me, "The north chambers *and* the south chambers, which *are*
opposite the separating courtyard, *are* the
holy chambers where the priests who approach the LORD [R]shall eat the most holy
offerings. There they shall lay the most holy
offerings—[R]the grain offering, the sin offering, and the trespass offering—for the place *is*
holy. Lev. 6:16, 26; 24:9 • Lev. 2:3, 10; 6:14, 17, 25
14 [R]"When the priests enter them, they
shall not go out of the holy *chamber* into the
outer court; but there they shall leave their
garments in which they minister, for they *are*
holy. They shall put on other garments; then
they may approach *that* which *is* for the
people." Ezek. 44:19

The Place of Separation

15 Now when he had finished measuring
the inner [T]temple, he brought me out through
the gateway that faces toward the [R]east, and
measured it all around. Lit. *house* • Ezek. 40:6; 43:1
16 He measured the east side with the measuring rod, [T]five hundred rods by the measuring rod all around. 1 mi.
17 He measured the north side, [T]five
hundred rods by the measuring rod all
around. 1 mi.
18 He measured the south side, [T]five hundred rods by the measuring rod. 1 mi.
19 He came around to the west side *and*
measured [T]five hundred rods by the measuring rod. 1 mi.
20 He measured it on the four sides; it had a
wall all around, [R]five hundred *cubits* long and
five hundred wide, to separate the holy areas
from the [T]common. Ezek. 45:2 • Or *profane*

CHAPTER 43

The Return of the Glory of God to the Temple

AFTERWARD he brought me to the gate,
the gate that faces toward the east.
2 And behold, the glory of the God of
Israel came from the way of the east. His
voice *was* like the sound of many waters; and
the earth shone with His glory.
3 *It was* like the appearance of the vision
which I saw—like the vision which I saw
when *I came to destroy the city. The visions
were like the vision which I saw by the River
Chebar; and I fell on my face.

43:3 Some mss., Vg. *He*

4 [R]And the glory of the LORD came into the [T]temple by way of the gate which faces toward the east. Ezek. 10:19; 11:23 • Lit. *house*

5 The Spirit lifted me up and brought me into the inner court; and behold, the glory of the LORD filled the [T]temple. Lit. *house*

6 Then I heard *Him* speaking to me from the temple, while a man stood beside me.

7 And He said to me, "Son of man, *this is* the place of My throne and the place of the soles of My feet, [R]where I will dwell in the midst of the children of Israel forever. [R]No more shall the house of Israel defile My holy name, they nor their kings, by their harlotry or with [R]the carcasses of their kings on their high places. Joel 3:17 • Ezek. 39:7 • Lev. 26:30

8 [R]"When they set their threshold by My threshold, and their doorpost by My doorpost, with a wall between them and Me, they defiled My holy name by the abominations which they committed; therefore I have consumed them in My anger. Ezek. 8:3

9 "Now let them put their harlotry and the carcasses of their kings far away from Me, and I will dwell in their midst forever.

10 "Son of man, [R]describe the [T]temple to the house of Israel, that they may be ashamed of their iniquities; and let them measure the pattern. Ezek. 40:4 • Lit. *house*

11 "And if they are ashamed of all that they have done, make known to them the design of the [T]temple and its arrangement, its exits and its entrances, its entire design and all its ordinances, all its forms and all its laws. Write *it* down in their sight, so that they may keep its whole design and all its ordinances, and [R]perform them. Lit. *house* • Ezek. 11:20

12 "This *is* the law of the [T]temple: The whole area surrounding [R]the mountaintop *shall be* most holy. Behold, this *is* the law of the temple. Lit. *house* • Ezek. 40:2

The Altar of Burnt Offerings

13 "These are the measurements of the altar in cubits (the *cubit is* one cubit and a handbreadth): the base one cubit high and one cubit wide, with a rim all around its edge of one span. This *is* the height of the altar:

14 "from the base on the ground to the lower ledge, [T]two cubits; the width of the ledge, [T]one cubit; from the smaller ledge to the larger ledge, [T]four cubits; and the width of the ledge, *one* cubit. 3.5 ft. • 21 in. • 7 ft.

15 "The altar hearth *is* four cubits high, with four [R]horns extending upward from the [T]hearth. Ex. 27:2 • Heb. *ariel*

16 "The altar hearth *is* twelve cubits long, twelve wide, square at its four corners;

17 "the ledge, fourteen *cubits* long and fourteen wide on its four sides, with a rim of half a cubit around it; its base, one cubit all around; and its steps face toward the east."

18 And He said to me, "Son of man, thus says the Lord GOD: 'These *are* the ordinances for the altar on the day when it is made, for sacrificing [R]burnt offerings on it, and for [R]sprinkling blood on it. Ex. 40:29 • Lev. 1:5, 11

19 'You shall give a young bull for a sin offering to the priests, the Levites, who are of the seed of Zadok, who approach Me to minister to Me,' says the Lord GOD.

20 'You shall take some of its blood and put *it* on the four horns of the altar, on the four corners of the ledge, and on the rim around it; thus you shall cleanse it and make atonement for it.

21 'Then you shall also take the bull of the sin offering, and burn it in the appointed place of the temple, outside the sanctuary.

22 'On the second day you shall offer a kid of the goats without blemish for a sin offering; and they shall cleanse the altar, as they cleansed *it* with the bull.

23 'When you have finished cleansing *it*, you shall offer a young bull without blemish, and a ram from the flock without blemish.

24 'When you offer them before the LORD, [R]the priests shall throw salt on them, and they will offer them up *as* a burnt offering to the LORD. Lev. 2:13

25 'Every day for [R]seven days you shall prepare a goat *for* a sin offering; they shall also prepare a young bull and a ram from the flock, both without blemish. Ex. 29:35

26 'Seven days they shall make atonement for the altar and purify it, and so [T]consecrate **it*. Lit. *fill its hands*

27 'When these days are over it shall be, on the eighth day and thereafter, that the priests shall offer your burnt offerings and your peace offerings on the altar; and I will [R]accept you,' says the Lord GOD." Ezek. 20:40, 41

CHAPTER 44

Duties of Temple Priests

THEN He brought me back to the outer gate of the sanctuary [R]which faces toward the east, but it *was* shut. Ezek. 43:1

2 And the LORD said to me, "This gate shall be shut; it shall not be opened, and no man shall enter by it, [R]because the LORD God of Israel has entered by it; therefore it shall be shut. Ezek. 43:2–4

3 "*As for* the [R]prince, *because* he *is* the prince, he may sit in it to [R]eat bread before the LORD; he shall enter by way of the vestibule of the gateway, and go out the same way." Gen. 31:54 • Ezek. 46:2, 8

4 Then He brought me by way of the north gate to the front of the temple; so I looked, and behold, the glory of the LORD filled the house of the LORD; and I fell on my face.

43:26 LXX, Syr. *themselves*

5 And the LORD said to me, "Son of man, mark well, see with your eyes and hear with your ears, all that I say to you concerning all the ordinances of the house of the LORD and all its laws. Mark well who may enter the house and all who go out from the sanctuary.

6 "Now say to the [R]rebellious, to the house of Israel, 'Thus says the Lord GOD: "O house of Israel, [R]let us have no more of all your abominations. Ezek. 2:5 • 1 Pet. 4:3

7 "When you brought in foreigners, uncircumcised in heart and uncircumcised in flesh, to be in My sanctuary to defile it—My house—and when you offered My food, the fat and the blood, then they broke My covenant because of all your abominations.

8 "And you have not [R]kept charge of My holy things, but you have set *others* to keep charge of My sanctuary for you." Lev. 22:2

9 'Thus says the Lord GOD: "No foreigner, uncircumcised in heart or uncircumcised in flesh, shall enter My sanctuary, including any foreigner who *is* among the children of Israel.

10 [R]"And the Levites who went far from Me, when Israel went astray, who strayed away from Me after their idols, they shall bear their iniquity. 2 Kin. 23:8

11 "Yet they shall be ministers in My sanctuary, *as* gatekeepers of the house and ministers of the house; [R]they shall slay the burnt offering and the sacrifice for the people, and [R]they shall stand before them to minister to them. 2 Chr. 29:34; 30:17 • Num. 16:9

12 "Because they ministered to them before their idols and caused the house of Israel to fall into iniquity, therefore I have lifted My hand in an oath against them," says the Lord GOD, "that they shall bear their iniquity.

13 [R]"And they shall not come near Me to minister to Me as priest, nor come near any of My holy things, nor into the Most Holy *Place*; but they shall [R]bear their shame and their abominations which they have committed. 2 Kin. 23:9 • Ezek. 32:30

14 "Nevertheless I will make them [R]keep charge of the temple, for all its work, and for all that has to be done in it. Num. 18:4

15 "But the priests, the Levites, [R]the sons of Zadok, who kept charge of My sanctuary [R]when the children of Israel went astray from Me, they shall come near Me to minister to Me; and they [R]shall stand before Me to offer to Me the [R]fat and the blood," says the Lord GOD. [1 Sam. 2:35] • Ezek. 44:10 • Deut. 10:8 • Ezek. 44:7

16 "They shall enter My sanctuary, and they shall come near My table to minister to Me, and they shall keep My charge.

17 "And it shall be, whenever they enter the gates of the inner court, that they shall put on linen garments; no wool shall come upon them while they minister within the gates of the inner court or within the house.

18 [R]"They shall have linen turbans on their heads and linen trousers on their bodies; they shall not clothe themselves with *anything that causes* sweat. Ex. 28:40; 39:28

19 "When they go out to the outer court, to the *outer* court to the people, they shall take off their garments in which they have ministered, leave them in the holy chambers, and put on other garments; and in their holy garments they shall not sanctify the people.

20 [R]"Nor shall they shave their heads, nor let their hair grow [R]long; but they shall keep their hair well trimmed. Lev. 21:5 • Num. 6:5

21 [R]"No priest shall drink wine when he enters the inner court. Lev. 10:9

22 "They shall not take as wife a [R]widow or a divorced woman, but take virgins of the descendants of the house of Israel, or widows of priests. Lev. 21:7, 13, 14

23 "And [R]they shall teach My people *the difference* between the holy and the unholy, and cause them to [R]discern between the unclean and the clean. Mal. 2:6–8 • Lev. 20:25

24 "In controversy they shall stand as judges, *and* judge it according to My judgments. They shall keep My laws and My statutes in all My appointed meetings, [R]and they shall hallow My Sabbaths. Ezek. 22:26

25 "They shall not defile *themselves* by coming near a dead person. Only for father or mother, for son or daughter, for brother or unmarried sister may they defile themselves.

26 [R]"After he is cleansed, they shall count seven days for him. Num. 6:10; 19:11, 13–19

27 "And on the day that he goes to the sanctuary to minister in the sanctuary, [R]he must offer his sin offering [R]in the inner court," says the Lord GOD. Lev. 5:3, 6 • Ezek. 44:17

28 "It shall be, in regard to their inheritance, *that* I [R]*am* their inheritance. You shall give them no [R]possession in Israel, for I *am* their possession. Num. 18:20 • Ezek. 45:4

29 "They shall eat the grain offering, the sin offering, and the trespass offering; every dedicated thing in Israel shall be theirs.

30 "The [T]best of all firstfruits of any kind, and every sacrifice of any kind from all your sacrifices, shall be the priest's; also you [R]shall give to the priest the first of your ground meal, [R]to cause a blessing to rest on your house. Lit. *first* • Neh. 10:37 • [Mal. 3:10]

31 "The priests shall not eat anything, bird or beast, that [R]died naturally or was torn *by wild animals*. Lev. 22:8

CHAPTER 45

Land of the Temple Priests

"MOREOVER, when you [R]divide the land by lot into inheritance, you shall [R]set apart a district for the LORD, a holy portion of the land; its length *shall be*

twenty-five thousand *cubits*, and the width
ten thousand. It *shall be* holy throughout its
territory all around. Ezek. 47:22 • Ezek. 48:8, 9
2 "Of this there shall be a square plot for
the sanctuary, [R]five hundred by five hundred
rods, with fifty cubits around it for an open
space. Ezek. 42:20
3 "So this is the district you shall measure:
[T]twenty-five thousand *cubits* long and [T]ten
thousand wide; [R]in it shall be the sanctuary,
the Most Holy *Place*. 8.3 mi. • 3.3 mi. • Ezek. 48:10
4 "It shall be [R]a holy *portion* of the land,
belonging to the priests, the ministers of the
sanctuary, who come near to minister to the
LORD; it shall be a place for their houses and a
holy place for the sanctuary. Ezek. 48:10, 11
5 "*An area* twenty-five thousand *cubits*
long and ten thousand wide shall belong to
the Levites, the ministers of the temple; they
shall have twenty chambers as a possession.
6 [R]"You shall appoint as the property of
the city *an area* [T]five thousand *cubits* wide
and twenty-five thousand long, adjacent to
the district of the holy *portion*; it shall belong
to the whole house of Israel. Ezek. 48:15 • 1.6 mi.
7 [R]"The prince shall have *a portion* on one
side and the other of the holy district and the
city's property; and bordering on the holy
district and the city's property, extending
westward on the west side and eastward on
the east side, the length *shall be* side by side
with one of the *tribal* portions, from the west
border to the east border. Ezek. 48:21
8 "The land shall be his possession in
Israel; and [R]My princes shall no more oppress
My people, but they shall give *the rest of* the
land to the house of Israel, according to their
tribes." Ezek. 22:27

Offerings of the Temple Priests

9 'Thus says the Lord GOD: [R]"Enough, O
princes of Israel! [R]Remove violence and plundering, execute justice and righteousness,
and stop dispossessing My people," says the
Lord GOD. Ezek. 44:6 • Jer. 22:3
10 "You shall have just [R]balances, a just
[T]ephah, and a just [T]bath. Lev. 19:36 • .65 bu. • 6 gal.
11 "The ephah and the bath shall be of the
same measure, so that the bath contains one-
tenth of a homer, and the ephah one-tenth of
a homer; their measure shall be according to
the [T]homer. 6.524 bu. or 60 gal.
12 "The [R]shekel *shall be* twenty gerahs;
twenty shekels, twenty-five shekels, *and*
fifteen shekels shall be your mina. Ex. 30:13
13 "This *is* the offering which you shall
offer: you shall give [T]one-sixth of an ephah
from a homer of wheat, and one-sixth of an
ephah from a homer of barley. 1.087 bu.
14 "The ordinance concerning oil, the bath
of oil, *is* one-tenth of a bath from a kor. A kor
is a homer or ten baths, for ten baths *are* a
homer.
15 "And one lamb shall be given from a
flock of two hundred, from the rich pastures
of Israel. These shall be for grain offerings,
burnt offerings, and peace offerings, to make
atonement for them," says the Lord GOD.
16 "All the people of the land shall give this
offering for the prince in Israel.
17 "Then it shall be the [R]prince's part *to give*
burnt offerings, grain offerings, and drink
offerings, at the feasts, the New Moons, the
Sabbaths, and at all the appointed seasons of
the house of Israel. He shall prepare the sin
offering, the grain offering, the burnt offering, and the peace offerings to make atonement for the house of Israel." Ezek. 46:4–12
18 'Thus says the Lord GOD: "In the first
month, on the first *day* of the month, you
shall take a young bull without blemish and
[R]cleanse the sanctuary. Lev. 16:16, 33
19 [R]"The priest shall take some of the blood
of the sin offering and put *it* on the doorposts
of the [T]temple, on the four corners of the
ledge of the altar, and on the gateposts of the
gate of the inner court. Ezek. 43:20 • Lit. *house*
20 "And so you shall do on the seventh *day*
of the month [R]for everyone who has sinned
unintentionally or in ignorance. Thus you
shall make atonement for the temple. Lev. 4:27
21 [R]"In the first *month*, on the fourteenth
day of the month, you shall observe the
Passover, a feast of seven days; unleavened
bread shall be eaten. Ex. 12:18
22 "And on that day the prince shall prepare for himself and for all the people of the
land [R]a bull *for* a sin offering. Lev. 4:14
23 "On the [R]seven days of the feast he shall
prepare a burnt offering to the LORD, seven
bulls and seven rams without blemish, daily
for seven days, and a kid of the goats daily *for*
a sin offering. Lev. 23:8
24 [R]"And he shall prepare a grain offering of
[T]one ephah for each bull and one ephah for
each ram, together with a [T]hin of oil for each
ephah. Ezek. 46:5, 7 • .65 bu. • 1 gal.
25 "In the seventh *month*, on the fifteenth
day of the month, at the [R]feast, he shall do
likewise for seven days, according to the sin
offering, the burnt offering, the grain offering, and the oil." Num. 29:12

CHAPTER 46

'THUS says the Lord GOD: "The gateway
of the inner court that faces toward the
east shall be shut the six working days; but
on the Sabbath it shall be opened, and on the
day of the New Moon it shall be opened.
2 [R]"The prince shall enter by way of the
vestibule of *that* gateway from the outside,
and stand by the gatepost. The priests shall
prepare his burnt offering and his peace
offerings. He shall worship at the threshold of
the gate. Then he shall go out, but the gate
shall not be shut until evening. Ezek. 44:3

3 "Likewise the people of the land shall
worship at the entrance to this gateway
before the LORD on the Sabbaths and the
New Moons.
4 "The burnt offering that [R]the prince
offers to the LORD on the [R]Sabbath day *shall*
be six lambs without blemish, and a ram
without blemish; Ezek. 45:17 • Num. 28:9, 10
5 "and the grain offering *shall be one*
ephah for a ram, and the grain offering for
the lambs, as much as he wants to give, as
well as a hin of oil with every ephah.
6 "On the day of the New Moon *it shall be*
a young bull without blemish, six lambs, and
a ram; they shall be without blemish.
7 "He shall prepare a grain offering of an
[T]ephah for a bull, an ephah for a ram, as
much as he wants to give for the lambs, and a
[T]hin of oil with every ephah. .65 bu. • 1 gal.
8 [R]"When the prince enters, he shall go in
by way of the vestibule of *that* gateway, and
go out the same way. Ezek. 44:3; 46:2
9 "But when the people of the land come
before the LORD on the appointed feast days,
whoever enters by way of the north [R]gate to
worship shall go out by way of the south
gate; and whoever enters by way of the south
gate shall go out by way of the north gate. He
shall not return by way of the gate through
which he came, but shall go out through the
opposite gate. Ezek. 48:31, 33
10 "The prince shall then be in their midst.
When they go in, he shall go in; and when
they go out, he shall go out.
11 "At the festivals and the appointed feast
days [R]the grain offering shall be an [T]ephah for
a bull, an ephah for a ram, as much as he
wants to give for the lambs, and a [T]hin of oil
with every ephah. Ezek. 46:5, 7 • .65 bu. • 1 gal.
12 "Now when the prince makes a voluntary burnt offering or voluntary peace offering to the LORD, the gate that faces toward
the east [R]shall then be opened for him; and he
shall prepare his burnt offering and his peace
offerings as he did on the Sabbath day. Then
he shall go out, and after he goes out the gate
shall be shut. Ezek. 44:3; 46:1, 2, 8
13 [R]"You shall daily make a burnt offering
to the LORD *of* a lamb of the first year without blemish; you shall prepare it [T]every morning. Num. 28:3–5 • Lit. *morning by morning*
14 "And you shall prepare a grain offering
with it every morning, a sixth of an ephah,
and a third of a hin of oil to moisten the fine
flour. This grain offering is a perpetual ordinance, to be made regularly to the LORD.
15 "Thus they shall prepare the lamb, the
grain offering, and the oil, *as* a [R]regular burnt
offering every morning." Ex. 29:42
16 'Thus says the Lord GOD: "If the prince
gives a gift *of some* of his inheritance to any
of his sons, it shall belong to his sons; it is
their possession by inheritance.
17 "But if he gives a gift of some of his
inheritance to one of his servants, it shall be
his until [R]the year of liberty, after which it
shall return to the prince. But his inheritance
shall belong to his sons; it shall become
theirs. Lev. 25:10
18 "Moreover [R]the prince shall not take any
of the people's inheritance by evicting them
from their property; he shall provide an
inheritance for his sons from his own property, so that none of My people may be
scattered from his property." ' " Ezek. 45:8
19 Then he brought me through the entrance, which *was* at the side of the gate, into
the holy chambers of the priests which face
toward the north; and there, a place *was*
situated at their extreme western end.
20 And he said to me, "This *is* the place
where the priests shall boil the trespass
offering and the sin offering, *and* where they
shall [R]bake the grain offering, so that they do
not bring *them* out into the outer court [R]to
sanctify the people." Lev. 2:4, 5, 7 • Ezek. 44:19
21 Then he brought me out into the outer
court and caused me to pass by the four
corners of the court; and in fact, in every
corner of the court *there was another* court.
22 In the four corners of the court *were*
enclosed courts, forty *cubits* long and thirty
wide; all four corners *were* the same size.
23 *There was* a row *of building stones* all
around in them, all around the four of them;
and [T]cooking hearths were made under the
rows of stones all around. Lit. *boiling places*
24 And he said to me, "These *are* the kitch-
ens where the ministers of the [T]temple shall
boil the sacrifices of the people." Lit. *house*

CHAPTER 47

River from the Temple

THEN he brought me back to the door of
the [T]temple; and there was [R]water, flowing from under the threshold of the temple
toward the east, for the front of the temple
faced east; the water was flowing from under
the right side of the temple, south of the
altar. Lit. *house* • Joel 3:18
2 He brought me out by way of the north
gate, and led me around on the outside to the
outer gateway that faces east; and there was
water, running out on the right side.
3 Then, when [R]the man went out to the
east with the line in his hand, he measured
[T]one thousand cubits, and he brought me
through the waters; the water *came up to my*
ankles. Ezek. 40:3 • 1750 ft.
4 Again he measured [T]one thousand and
brought me through the waters; the water
came up to my knees. Again he measured one
thousand and brought me through; the water
came up to my waist. 1750 ft.

5 Again he measured one thousand, *and it*
was a river that I could not cross; for the
water was too deep, water in which one must
swim, a river that could not be crossed.
6 He said to me, "Son of man, have you
seen *this*?" Then he brought me and returned
me to the bank of the river.
7 When I returned, there, along the bank
of the river, *were* very many [R]trees on one
side and the other. [Rev. 22:2]
8 Then he said to me: "This water flows
toward the eastern region, goes down into
the valley, and enters the sea. *When it*
reaches the sea, *its* waters are healed.
9 "And it shall be *that* every living thing
that moves, wherever [T]the rivers go, will live.
There will be a very great multitude of fish,
because these waters go there; for they will
be healed, and everything will live wherever
the river goes. Lit. *two rivers*
10 "It shall be *that* fishermen will stand by
it from En Gedi to En Eglaim; they will be
places for spreading their nets. Their fish will
be of the same kinds as the fish [R]of the Great
Sea, exceedingly many. Num. 34:3
11 "But its swamps and marshes will not be
healed; they will be given over to salt.
12 "Along the bank of the river, on this side
and that, will grow all *kinds of* trees used for
food; their leaves will not wither, and their
fruit will not fail. They will bear fruit every
month, because their water flows from the
sanctuary. Their fruit will be for food, and
their leaves for [R]medicine." [Rev. 22:2]

Boundaries of the Land

13 Thus says the Lord GOD: "These *are* the
borders by which you shall divide the land as
an inheritance among the twelve tribes of
Israel. Joseph *shall have two* portions.
14 "You shall inherit it equally with one
another; for I lifted My hand in an oath to
give it to your fathers, and this land shall [R]fall
to you as your inheritance. Ezek. 48:29
15 "This *shall be* the border of the land on
the north: from the Great Sea, *by* the road to
Hethlon, as one goes to [R]Zedad, Num. 34:7, 8
16 "Hamath, [R]Berothah, Sibraim (which *is*
between the border of Damascus and the
border of Hamath), to Hazar Hatticon (which
is on the border of Hauran). 2 Sam. 8:8
17 "Thus the boundary shall be from the
Sea to Hazar Enan, the border of Damascus;
and as for the north, northward, it is the
border of Hamath. *This is* the north side.
18 "On the east side you shall mark out the
border from between Hauran and Damascus,
and between Gilead and the land of Israel,
along the Jordan, and along the eastern side
of the sea. *This is* the east side.
19 "The south side, toward the South, *shall*
be from Tamar to the waters of Meribah by
Kadesh, along the brook to the Great Sea.
This is the south side, toward the South.
20 "The west side *shall be* the Great Sea,
from the *southern* boundary until one comes
to a point opposite Hamath. This *is* the west
side.
21 "Thus you shall divide this land among
yourselves according to the tribes of Israel.
22 "It shall be that you will divide it by lot
as an inheritance for yourselves, and for the
strangers who sojourn among you and who
bear children among you. [R]They shall be to
you as native-born among the children of
Israel; they shall have an inheritance with
you among the tribes of Israel. [Col. 3:11]
23 "And it shall be *that* in whatever tribe
the stranger sojourns, there you shall give
him his inheritance," says the Lord GOD.

CHAPTER 48

Divisions of the Land

"NOW these *are* the names of the tribes:
[R]From the northern border along the
road to Hethlon at the entrance of Hamath,
to Hazar Enan, the border of Damascus
northward, in the direction of Hamath, *there*
shall be one *portion for* [R]Dan from its east to
its west side; Ezek. 47:15 • Josh. 19:40–48
2 "by the border of Dan, from the east side
to the west, one *portion for* Asher;
3 "by the border of Asher, from the east
side to the west, one *portion for* Naphtali;
4 "by the border of Naphtali, from the east
side to the west, one *portion for* Manasseh;
5 "by the border of Manasseh, from the
east side to the west, one *portion for*
[R]Ephraim; Josh. 16:5–10; 17:8–10, 14–18
6 "by the border of Ephraim, from the east
side to the west, one *portion for* Reuben;
7 "by the border of Reuben, from the east
side to the west, one *portion for* Judah;
8 "by the border of Judah, from the east
side to the west, shall be the district which
you shall set apart, twenty-five thousand
cubits in width, and *in* length the same as one
of the *other* portions, from the east side to
the west, with the sanctuary in the center.
9 "The district that you shall set apart for
the LORD *shall be* twenty-five thousand *cu-*
bits in length and ten thousand in width.
10 "To these, *namely*, to the priests, shall
this holy district belong: on the north
[T]twenty-five thousand *cubits in length*, on
the west ten thousand in width, on the
east [T]ten thousand in width, and on the
south twenty-five thousand in length.
The sanctuary of the LORD shall be in the
center. 8.3 mi. • 3.3 mi.
11 [R]"*It shall be* for the priests of the sons of
Zadok, who are sanctified, who have kept My
charge, who did not go astray when the

children of Israel went astray, [R]as the Levites
went astray. Ezek. 40:46; 44:15 • Ezek. 44:10, 12
12 "And *this* district of land that is set apart
shall be to them a thing most [R]holy by the
border of the Levites. Ezek. 45:4
13 "Opposite the border of the priests, the
Levites *shall have an area* twenty-five thousand *cubits* in length and ten thousand in
width; its entire length *shall be* twenty-five
thousand and its width ten thousand.
14 "And they shall not sell or exchange any
of it; they may not alienate this best *part* of
the land, for *it is* holy to the LORD.
15 [R]"The five thousand *cubits* in width that
remain, along the edge of the twenty-five
thousand, shall be [R]for general use by the
city, for dwellings and common-land; and the
city shall be in the center. Ezek. 45:6 • Ezek. 42:20
16 "These *shall be* its measurements: the
north side four thousand five hundred *cubits*,
the south side four thousand five hundred,
the east side four thousand five hundred, and
the west side four thousand five hundred.
17 "The common-land of the city shall be:
to the north [T]two hundred and fifty *cubits*, to
the south two hundred and fifty, to the east
two hundred and fifty, and to the west two
hundred and fifty. 437.5 ft.
18 "The rest of the length, alongside the
district of the holy *portion*, *shall be* ten
thousand *cubits* to the east and ten thousand
to the west. It shall be adjacent to the district
of the holy *portion*, and its produce shall be
food for the workers of the city.
19 [R]"The workers of the city, from all the
tribes of Israel, shall cultivate it. Ezek. 45:6
20 "The entire district *shall be* twenty-five
thousand *cubits* by twenty-five thousand
cubits, foursquare. You shall set apart the
holy district with the property of the city.
21 "The rest *shall belong* to the prince, on
one side and on the other of the holy district
and of the city's property, next to the twenty-
five thousand *cubits* of the *holy* district as far
as the eastern border, and westward next to
the twenty-five thousand as far as the western border, adjacent to the *tribal* portions; *it
shall belong* to the prince. It shall be the holy
district, [R]and the sanctuary of the [T]temple
shall be in the center. Ezek. 48:8, 10 • Lit. *house*
22 "Moreover, apart from the possession of
the Levites and the possession of the city
which are in the midst of what *belongs* to the
prince, *the area* between the border of Judah
and the border of [R]Benjamin shall belong to
the prince. Josh. 18:21-28
23 "As for the rest of the tribes, from the
east side to the west, Benjamin *shall have*
one *portion*;
24 "by the border of Benjamin, from the
east side to the west, [R]Simeon *shall have* one
portion; Josh. 19:1-9
25 "by the border of Simeon, from the east
side to the west, [R]Issachar *shall have* one
portion; Josh. 19:17-23
26 "by the border of Issachar, from the east
side to the west, [R]Zebulun *shall have* one
portion; Josh. 19:10-16
27 "by the border of Zebulun, from the east
side to the west, Gad *shall have* one *portion*;
28 "by the border of Gad, on the south side,
toward the [T]South, the border shall be from
Tamar *to* the waters of Meribah *by* Kadesh,
along the brook to the Great Sea. *Negev*
29 [R]"This *is* the land which you shall divide
by lot as an inheritance among the tribes of
Israel, and these *are* their portions," says the
Lord GOD. Ezek. 47:14, 21, 22

Gates of the City

30 "These *are* the exits of the city. On the
north side, measuring [T]four thousand five
hundred *cubits* 1.5 mi.
31 [R]"(the gates of the city *shall be* named
after the tribes of Israel), the three gates
northward: one gate for Reuben, one gate for
Judah, and one gate for Levi; [Rev. 21:10-14]
32 "on the east side, [T]four thousand five
hundred *cubits*, three gates: one gate for
Joseph, one gate for Benjamin, and one gate
for Dan; 1.5 mi.
33 "on the south side, measuring [T]four
thousand five hundred *cubits*, three gates:
one gate for Simeon, one gate for Issachar,
and one gate for Zebulun; 1.5 mi.
34 "on the west side, [T]four thousand five
hundred *cubits* with their three gates: one
gate for Gad, one gate for Asher, and one
gate for Naphtali. 1.5 mi.

Name of the City

35 "All the way around *shall be* eighteen
thousand cubits; [R]and the name of the
city from *that* day *shall be*: [T]THE LORD *IS*
THERE." Joel 3:21 • Heb. *YHWH Shammah*

THE BOOK OF

DANIEL

THE BOOK OF DANIEL

Daniel's life and ministry bridge the entire seventy-year period of Babylonian captivity. Deported to Babylon at the age of sixteen, and handpicked for government service, Daniel becomes God's prophetic mouthpiece to the gentile and Jewish world declaring God's present and eternal purpose. Nine of the twelve chapters in his book revolve around dreams, including God-given visions involving trees, animals, beasts, and images. In both his personal adventures and prophetic visions, Daniel shows God's guidance, intervention, and power in the affairs of men.

The name *Daniye'l* or *Dani'el* means "God Is My Judge," and the book is, of course, named after the author and principal character. The Greek form *Daniel* in the Septuagint is the basis for the Latin and English titles.

THE AUTHOR OF DANIEL

Daniel and his three friends were evidently born into noble Judean families and were "young men in whom *there was* no blemish, but good-looking, gifted in all wisdom, possessing knowledge and quick to understand" (1:4). He was given three years of training in the best of Babylon's schools (1:5). As part of the reidentification process, he was given a new name that honored one of the Babylonian deities: *Belteshazzar* meant "Bel Protect His Life" (see 1:7; 4:8; Jer. 51:44). Daniel's wisdom and divinely given interpretive abilities brought him into a position of prominence, especially in the courts of Nebuchadnezzar and Darius. He is one of the few well-known Bible characters about whom nothing negative is ever written. His life was characterized by faith, prayer, courage, consistency, and lack of compromise. This "greatly beloved" man (9:23; 10:11, 19) was mentioned three times by his sixth-century B.C. contemporary Ezekiel as an example of righteousness.

Daniel claimed to write this book (12:4), and he used the autobiographical first person from 7:2 onward. The Jewish Talmud agrees with this testimony, and Christ attributed a quote from 9:27 to "Daniel the prophet" (Matt. 24:15).

THE TIME OF DANIEL

Babylon rebelled against the Assyrian Empire in 626 B.C. and overthrew the Assyrian capital of Nineveh in 612 B.C. Babylon became the master of the Middle East when it defeated the Egyptian armies in 605 B.C. Daniel was among those taken captive to Babylon that year when Nebuchadnezzar subdued Jerusalem. He ministered for the full duration of the Babylonian captivity as a prophet and a government official and continued on after Babylon was overcome by the Medes and Persians in 539 B.C. His prophetic ministry was directed to the gentile courts of Babylon (Nebuchadnezzar and Belshazzar) and Persia (Darius and Cyrus), as well as to his Jewish countrymen. Zerubbabel led a return of the Jews to Jerusalem in the first year of Cyrus, and Daniel lived and ministered at least until the third year of Cyrus (536 B.C.; 10:1). Daniel's book was no doubt written by Cyrus's ninth year (c. 530 B.C.). As he predicted, the Persian Empire continued until Alexander the Great (11:2, 3), who extended the boundaries of the Greek Empire as far east as India. The Romans later displaced the Greeks as rulers of the Middle East.

For various reasons, many critics have argued that Daniel is a fraudulent book that was written in the time of the Maccabees in the second century B.C., not the sixth century B.C. as it claims. But their arguments are not compelling:

(1) *The prophetic argument* holds that Daniel could not have made such accurate predictions; it must be a "prophecy after the events." Daniel 11 alone contains over one hundred specific prophecies of historical events that literally came true. The author, the critics say, must have lived at the time of Antiochus Epiphanes (175–163 B.C.) and probably wrote this to strengthen the faith of the Jews. But this argument was developed out of a theological bias that assumes true prophecy cannot take place. It also implies that the work was intentionally deceptive.

(2) *The linguistic argument* claims that the book uses a late Aramaic in 2—7 and that the Persian and Greek words also point to a late date. But recent discoveries show that Daniel's Aramaic is actually a form of the early Imperial Aramaic. Daniel's use of some Persian words is no argument for a late date since he continued living in the Persian period under Cyrus. The only Greek words are names of musical instruments in chapter 3, and this comes as no surprise since there were Greek mercenaries in the Assyrian and Babylonian armies. Far more Greek words would be expected if the book were written in the second century B.C.

(3) *The historical argument* asserts that Daniel's historical blunders argue for a late date. But recent evidence has demonstrated the historical accuracy of Daniel. Inscriptions found at Haran show that Belshazzar reigned in Babylon while his father Nabonidus was fighting the invading Persians. And Darius the Mede (5:31; 6:1) has been identified as Gubaru, a governor appointed by Cyrus.

THE CHRIST OF DANIEL

Christ is the Great Stone who will crush the kingdoms of this world (2:34, 35, 44), the Son of Man who is given dominion by the Ancient of Days (7:13, 14), and the coming Messiah who will be cut off (9:25, 26). It is likely that Daniel's vision in 10:5–9 was an appearance of Christ (cf. Rev. 1:12–16).

The vision of the sixty-nine weeks in 9:25, 26 pinpoints the coming of the Messiah. The decree of 9:25 took place on March 4, 444 B.C. (Neh. 2:1–8). The sixty-nine weeks of seven years equals 483 years, or 173,880 days (using 360-day prophetic years). This leads to March 29, A.D. 33, the date of the Triumphal Entry. This is checked by noting that 444 B.C. to A.D. 33 is 476 years, and 476 times 365.24219 days per year equals 173,855 days. Adding twenty-five days for the difference between March 4 and March 29 gives 173,880 days.

KEYS TO DANIEL

Key Word: God's Program for Israel—Daniel was written to encourage the exiled Jews by revealing God's sovereign program for Israel during and after the period of gentile domination. The "Times of the Gentiles" began with the Babylonian captivity, and Israel would suffer under gentile powers for many years. But this period is not permanent, and a time will come when God will establish the messianic kingdom which will last forever. Daniel repeatedly emphasizes the sovereignty and power of God over human affairs. "The Most High rules in the kingdom of men, and gives it to whomever He chooses" (4:25). The God who directs the forces of history has not deserted His people. They must continue to trust in Him, because His promises of preservation and ultimate restoration are as sure as the coming of the Messiah.

Key Verses: Daniel 2:20-22 and Daniel 2:44—"Daniel answered and said: 'Blessed be the name of God forever and ever, for wisdom and might are His. And He changes the times and the seasons; He removes kings and raises up kings; He gives wisdom to the wise and knowledge to those who have understanding. He reveals deep and secret things; He knows what *is* in the darkness, and light dwells with Him' " (2:20–22).

"And in the days of these kings the God of heaven will set up a kingdom which shall never be destroyed; and the kingdom shall not be left to other people; it shall break in pieces and consume all these kingdoms, and it shall stand forever" (2:44).

Key Chapter: Daniel 9—Daniel's prophecy of the seventy weeks (9:24–27) provides the chronological frame for messianic prediction from the time of Daniel to the establishment of the kingdom on earth. It is clear that the first sixty-nine weeks were fulfilled at Christ's first coming. Some scholars affirm that the last week has not yet been fulfilled because Christ relates its main events to His second coming (Matt. 24:6, 15). Others perceive these words of Christ as applying to the Roman desecration of the temple in A.D. 70.

SURVEY OF DANIEL

Daniel, the "Apocalypse of the Old Testament," presents a surprisingly detailed and comprehensive sweep of prophetic history. After an introductory chapter in Hebrew, Daniel switches to Aramaic in chapters 2—7 to describe the future course of the gentile world powers. Then in 8—12, Daniel reverts back to his native language to survey the future of the Jewish nation under gentile dominion. The theme of God's sovereign control in the affairs of world history clearly emerges and provides comfort to the future church, as well as to the Jews whose nation was destroyed by the Babylonians. The Babylonians, Persians, Greeks, and Romans will come and go, but God will establish His kingdom through His redeemed people forever. Daniel's three divisions are: the personal history of Daniel

FOCUS	HISTORY OF DANIEL	PROPHETIC PLAN FOR THE GENTILES				PROPHETIC PLAN OF ISRAEL		
REFERENCE	1:1—	2:1—	5:1—	6:1—	7:1—	8:1—	9:1—	10:1–12:13
DIVISION	PERSONAL LIFE OF DANIEL	VISIONS OF NEBUCHADNEZZAR	VISION OF BELSHAZZAR	DECREE OF DARIUS	FOUR BEASTS	VISION OF RAM AND HE-GOAT	VISION OF SEVENTY WEEKS	VISION OF ISRAEL'S FUTURE
TOPIC	DANIEL'S BACKGROUND	DANIEL INTERPRETS OTHERS' DREAMS				ANGEL INTERPRETS DANIEL'S DREAMS		
	HEBREW	ARAMAIC				HEBREW		
LOCATION	BABYLON OR PERSIA							
TIME	c. 605–536 B.C.							

(1), the prophetic plan for the Gentiles (2—7), and the prophetic plan for Israel (8—12).

The Personal History of Daniel (1): This chapter introduces the book by giving the background and preparation of the prophet. Daniel is deported along with other promising youths and placed in an intensive training program in Nebuchadnezzar's court. Their names and diets are changed so that they will lose their Jewish identification, but Daniel's resolve to remain faithful to the Lord is rewarded. He and his friends are granted wisdom and knowledge.

The Prophetic Plan for the Gentiles (2—7): Only Daniel can relate and interpret Nebuchadnezzar's disturbing dream of the great statue (2). God empowers Daniel to foretell the way in which He will sovereignly raise and depose four gentile empires. The Messiah's kingdom will end the times of the Gentiles. Because of his position revealed in the dream, Nebuchadnezzar erects a golden image and demands that all bow to it (3). The persecution and preservation of Daniel's friends in the fiery furnace again illustrate the power of God. After Nebuchadnezzar refuses to respond to the warning of his vision of the tree (4), he is humbled until he acknowledges the supremacy of God and the foolishness of his pride. The feast of Belshazzar marks the end of the Babylonian kingdom (5). Belshazzar is judged because of his arrogant defiance of God. In the reign of Darius, a plot against Daniel backfires when he is divinely delivered in the den of lions (6). Daniel's courageous faith is rewarded, and Darius learns a lesson about the might of the God of Israel. The vision of the four beasts (7) supplements the four-part statue vision of chapter 2 in its portrayal of the Babylonian, Persian, Greek, and Roman empires. But once again, "the saints of the Most High shall receive the kingdom, and possess the kingdom forever" (7:18).

The Prophetic Plan for Israel (8—12): The focus in chapter 8 narrows to a vision of the ram and goat that shows Israel under the Medo-Persian and Grecian empires. Alexander the Great is the large horn of 8:21 and Antiochus Epiphanes is the little horn of 8:9. After Daniel's prayer of confession for his people, he is privileged to receive the revelation of the seventy weeks, including the Messiah's atoning death (9). This gives the chronology of God's perfect plan for the redemption and deliverance of His people. Following is a great vision that gives amazing details of Israel's future history (10 and 11). Chapter 11 chronicles the coming kings of Persia and Greece, the wars between the Ptolemies of Egypt and the Seleucids of Syria, and the persecution led by Antiochus. God's people will be saved out of tribulation and resurrected (12).

OUTLINE OF DANIEL

Part One: The Personal History of Daniel (1:1-21)

I. The Deportation of Daniel to Babylon. 1:1-7

II. The Faithfulness of Daniel in Babylon. . . . 1:8-16

III. The Reputation of Daniel in Babylon . . . 1:17-21

Part Two: The Prophetic Plan for the Gentiles (2:1—7:28)

I. Nebuchadnezzar's Dream of the Great Image 2:1-49

A. Nebuchadnezzar Conceals His Dream 2:1-13
B. God Reveals the Dream 2:14-23
C. Daniel Interprets the Dream 2:24-45
D. Nebuchadnezzar Promotes Daniel . . . 2:46-49

II. Nebuchadnezzar's Image of Gold 3:1-30

A. Nebuchadnezzar's Image Is Erected 3:1-7
B. Daniel's Friends Refuse to Worship . . . 3:8-12
C. Daniel's Friends Trust God 3:13-18
D. Daniel's Friends Are Protected in the Furnace 3:19-25
E. Daniel's Friends Are Promoted 3:26-30

III. Nebuchadnezzar's Vision of a Great Tree 4:1-37

A. Nebuchadnezzar's Proclamation. 4:1-3
B. Nebuchadnezzar's Vision 4:4-18
C. Daniel's Interpretation of the Vision 4:19-27
D. Nebuchadnezzar's Humiliation. 4:28-33
E. Nebuchadnezzar's Restoration 4:34-37

IV. Belshazzar and the Handwriting on the Wall 5:1-31

A. Belshazzar Defiles the Temple Vessels 5:1-4
B. Belshazzar Sees the Handwriting. 5:5-9
C. Daniel Interprets the Handwriting . . . 5:10-29
D. Belshazzar Is Killed. 5:30, 31

V. Darius' Foolish Decree. 6:1-28

A. Daniel Is Promoted 6:1-3
B. Darius Signs the Foolish Decree 6:4-9
C. Daniel Prays Faithfully. 6:10-15
D. Daniel Is Saved in the Lions' Den. . . . 6:16-24
E. Darius's Wise Decree 6:25-28

VI. Daniel's Vision of the Four Beasts 7:1-28

A. The Revelation of the Vision 7:1-14
1. Four Beasts 7:1-8
2. "Ancient of Days" 7:9-14
B. The Interpretation of the Vision 7:15-28
1. Interpretation of the Four Beasts 7:15-22
2. Interpretation of the Fourth Beast 7:23-28

Part Three: The Prophetic Plan for Israel (8:1—12:13)

CHAPTER 1

The Deportation of Daniel to Babylon

IN the third year of the reign of Jehoiakim
king of Judah, Nebuchadnezzar king of
Babylon came to Jerusalem and besieged it.
2 And the Lord gave Jehoiakim king of
Judah into his hand, with some of the articles
of [T]the house of God, which he carried into
the land of Shinar to the house of his god;
and he brought the articles into the treasure
house of his god. The temple
3 Then the king instructed Ashpenaz, the
master of his eunuchs, to bring [R]some of the
children of Israel and some of the king's
descendants and some of the nobles, Is. 39:7
4 young men in whom *there was* no blemish,
but good-looking, gifted in all wisdom,
possessing knowledge and quick to understand,
who *had* ability to serve in the king's
palace, and whom they might teach the
language and literature of the Chaldeans.
5 And the king appointed for them a daily
provision of the king's delicacies and of the
wine which he drank, and three years of
training for them, so that at the end of *that*
time they might serve before the king.
6 Now from among those of the sons of
Judah were Daniel, Hananiah, Mishael, and
Azariah.
7 [R]To them the chief of the eunuchs gave
names: he gave Daniel *the name* Belteshazzar;
to Hananiah, Shadrach; to Mishael, Meshach;
and to Azariah, Abed-Nego. 2 Kin. 24:17

The Faithfulness of Daniel in Babylon

8 But Daniel purposed in his heart that he
would not defile himself [R]with the portion of
the king's delicacies, nor with the wine which
he drank; therefore he requested of the chief
of the eunuchs that he might not defile
himself. Hos. 9:3
9 Now [R]God had brought Daniel into the
favor and [T]good will of the chief of the
eunuchs. Gen. 39:21 • *kindness*
10 And the chief of the eunuchs said to
Daniel, "I fear my lord the king, who has
appointed your food and drink. For why
should he see your faces looking worse than
the young men who *are* your age? Then you
would endanger my head before the king."
11 So Daniel said to [T]the steward whom the
chief of the eunuchs had set over Daniel,
Hananiah, Mishael, and Azariah, Or *Melzar*
12 "Please test your servants for ten days,
and let them give us vegetables to eat and
water to drink.
13 "Then let our countenances be examined
before you, and the countenances of the
young men who eat the portion of the king's
delicacies; and as you see fit, *so* deal with
your servants."
14 So he consented with them in this matter,
and tested them ten days.
15 And at the end of ten days their countenance
appeared better and fatter in flesh than
all the young men who ate the portion of the
king's delicacies.

16 Thus [T]the steward took away their portion of delicacies and the wine that they were to drink, and gave them vegetables. Or *Melzar*

The Reputation of Daniel in Babylon

17 As for these four young men, [R]God gave them [R]knowledge and skill in all literature and wisdom; and Daniel had understanding in all visions and dreams. [James 1:5–7] • Acts 7:22

18 Now at the end of the days, when the king had said that they should be brought in, the chief of the eunuchs brought them in before Nebuchadnezzar.

19 Then the king [T]interviewed them, and among them all none was found like Daniel, Hananiah, Mishael, and Azariah; therefore they served before the king. Lit. *talked with*

20 [R]And in all matters of wisdom *and* understanding about which the king examined them, he found them ten times better than all the magicians *and* astrologers who *were* in all his realm. 1 Kin. 10:1

21 [R]Thus Daniel continued until the first year of King Cyrus. Dan. 6:28; 10:1

CHAPTER 2

Nebuchadnezzar Conceals His Dream

NOW in the second year of Nebuchadnezzar's reign, Nebuchadnezzar had dreams; [R]and his spirit was so troubled that [R]his sleep left him. Gen. 40:5–8; 41:1, 8 • Esth. 6:1

2 Then the king gave the command to call the magicians, the astrologers, the sorcerers, and the Chaldeans to tell the king his dreams. So they came and stood before the king.

3 And the king said to them, "I have had a dream, and my spirit is anxious to [T]know the dream." Or *understand*

4 Then the Chaldeans spoke to the king in Aramaic, [R]"O* king, live forever! Tell your servants the dream, and we will give the interpretation." Dan. 3:9; 5:10; 6:6, 21

5 *But* the king answered and said to the Chaldeans, "My decision is firm: if you do not make known the dream to me, and its interpretation, you shall be cut in pieces, and your houses shall be made an ash heap.

6 "However, if you tell the dream and its interpretation, you shall receive from me gifts, rewards, and great honor. Therefore tell me the dream and its interpretation."

7 They answered again and said, "Let the king tell his servants the dream, and we will give its interpretation."

8 The king answered and said, "I know for certain that you would gain time, because you see that my decision is firm:

9 "if you do not make known the dream to me, *there is only* one decree for you! For you have agreed to speak lying and corrupt words before me till the [T]time has changed. Therefore tell me the dream, and I shall know that you can give me its interpretation." Situation

10 The Chaldeans answered the king, and said, "There is not a man on earth who can tell the king's matter; therefore no king, lord, or ruler has *ever* asked such things of any magician, astrologer, or Chaldean.

11 "*It is* a [T]difficult thing that the king requires, and there is no other who can tell it to the king [R]except the gods, whose dwelling is not with flesh." Or *rare* • Dan. 5:11

12 For this reason the king was angry and very furious, and gave a command to destroy all the wise *men* of Babylon.

13 So the decree went out, and they began killing the wise *men*; and they sought [R]Daniel and his companions, to kill *them*. Dan. 1:19, 20

God Reveals the Dream

14 Then with counsel and wisdom Daniel answered Arioch, the captain of the king's guard, who had gone out to kill the wise *men* of Babylon;

15 he answered and said to Arioch the king's captain, "Why is the decree from the king so [T]urgent?" Then Arioch made the decision known to Daniel. Or *harsh*

16 So Daniel went in and asked the king to give him time, that he might tell the king the interpretation.

17 Then Daniel went to his house, and made the decision known to Hananiah, Mishael, and Azariah, his companions,

18 that they might seek mercies from the God of heaven concerning this secret, so that Daniel and his companions might not perish with the rest of the wise *men* of Babylon.

19 Then the secret was revealed to Daniel [R]in a night vision. So Daniel blessed the God of heaven. Job 33:15

20 Daniel answered and said:

[R]"Blessed be the name of God forever and
ever, Ps. 113:2
[R]For wisdom and might are His. [Jer. 32:19]
21 And He changes [R]the times and the
seasons; Esth. 1:13
[R]He removes kings and raises up kings;
[R]He gives wisdom to the wise
And knowledge to those who have
understanding. [Ps. 75:6, 7] • [James 1:5]
22 He reveals deep and secret things;
[R]He knows what *is* in the darkness,
And light dwells with Him. [Heb. 4:13]

23 "I thank You and praise You,
O God of my fathers;
You have given me wisdom and might,
And have now made known to me what
we [R]asked of You, Dan. 2:18, 29, 30
For You have made known to us the
king's [T]demand." Lit. *word*

2:4 The original language of Dan. 2:4b through 7:28 is Aramaic.

Daniel Interprets the Dream

24 Therefore Daniel went to Arioch, whom the king had appointed to destroy the wise *men* of Babylon. He went and said thus to him: "Do not destroy the wise *men* of Babylon; take me before the king, and I will tell the king the interpretation."

25 Then Arioch quickly brought Daniel before the king, and said thus to him, "I have found a man of the [T]captives of Judah, who will make known to the king the interpretation." Lit. *sons of the captivity*

26 The king answered and said to Daniel, whose name *was* Belteshazzar, "Are you able to make known to me the dream which I have seen, and its interpretation?"

27 Daniel answered in the presence of the king, and said, "The secret which the king has demanded, the wise *men*, the astrologers, the magicians, and the soothsayers cannot declare to the king.

28 "But there is a God in heaven who reveals secrets, and He has made known to King Nebuchadnezzar what will be in the latter days. Your dream, and the visions of your head upon your bed, were these:

29 "As for you, O king, thoughts came *to* your *mind while* on your bed, *about* what would come to pass after this; [R]and He who reveals secrets has made known to you what will be. [Dan. 2:22, 28]

30 [R]"But as for me, this secret has not been revealed to me because I have more wisdom than anyone living, but for *our* sakes who make known the interpretation to the king, [R]and that you may [T]know the thoughts of your heart. Acts 3:12 • Dan. 2:47 • Understand

31 "You, O king, were watching; and behold, a great image! This great image, whose splendor *was* excellent, stood before you; and its form *was* awesome.

32 [R]"This image's head *was* of fine gold, its chest and arms of silver, its belly and [T]thighs of bronze, Dan. 2:38, 45 • Or *sides*

33 "its legs of iron, its feet partly of iron and partly of [T]clay. Or *baked clay,* also vv. 34, 35, 42

34 "You watched while a stone was cut out [R]without hands, which struck the image on its feet of iron and clay, and broke them in pieces. [Zech. 4:6]

35 "Then the iron, the clay, the bronze, the silver, and the gold were crushed together, and became like chaff from the summer threshing floors; the wind carried them away so that no trace of them was found. And the stone that struck the image became a great mountain and filled the whole earth.

36 "This *is* the dream. Now we will tell the interpretation of it before the king.

37 [R]"You, O king, *are* a king of kings. [R]For the God of heaven has given you a kingdom, power, strength, and glory; Jer. 27:6, 7 • Ezra 1:2

38 [R]"and wherever the children of men dwell, or the beasts of the field and the birds of the heaven, He has given *them* into your hand, and has made you ruler over them all—[R]you *are* this head of gold. Dan. 4:21, 22 • Dan. 2:32

39 "But after you shall arise [R]another kingdom [R]inferior to yours; then another, a third kingdom of bronze, which shall rule over all the earth. Dan. 5:28, 31 • Dan. 2:32

40 "And [R]the fourth kingdom shall be as strong as iron, inasmuch as iron breaks in pieces and shatters all *things;* and like iron that crushes, *that kingdom* will break in pieces and crush all the others. Dan. 7:7, 23

41 "Whereas you saw the feet and toes, partly of potter's clay and partly of iron, the kingdom shall be divided; yet the strength of the iron shall be in it, just as you saw the iron mixed with ceramic clay.

42 "And *as* the toes of the feet *were* partly of iron and partly of clay, *so* the kingdom shall be partly strong and partly fragile.

43 "As you saw iron mixed with ceramic clay, they will mingle with the seed of men; but they will not adhere to one another, just as iron does not mix with clay.

44 "And in the days of these kings the God of heaven will [R]set up a kingdom which shall never be destroyed; and the kingdom shall not be left to other people; it shall break in pieces and [T]consume all these kingdoms, and it shall stand forever. Is. 9:7☆ • Lit. *put an end to*

45 [R]"Inasmuch as you saw that the stone was cut out of the mountain without hands, and that it broke in pieces the iron, the bronze, the clay, the silver, and the gold—the great God has made known to the king what will come to pass after this. The dream is certain, and its interpretation is sure."

Nebuchadnezzar Promotes Daniel

46 [R]Then King Nebuchadnezzar fell on his face, prostrate before Daniel, and commanded that they should present an offering [R]and incense to him. Acts 10:25; 14:13 • Ezra 6:10

47 The king answered Daniel, and said, "Truly your God *is* the God of [R]gods, the Lord of kings, and a revealer of secrets, since you could reveal this secret." [Deut. 10:17]

48 [R]Then the king promoted Daniel [R]and gave him many great gifts; and he made him ruler over the whole province of Babylon, and [R]chief administrator over all the wise *men* of Babylon. [Prov. 14:35; 21:1] • Dan. 2:6 • Dan. 4:9; 5:11

49 Also Daniel petitioned the king, and he set Shadrach, Meshach, and Abed-Nego over the affairs of the province of Babylon; but Daniel *sat* in the [T]gate of the king. Court

CHAPTER 3

Nebuchadnezzar's Image Is Erected

NEBUCHADNEZZAR the king made an image of gold, whose height *was* sixty

cubits *and* its width six cubits. He set it up in
the plain of Dura, in the province of Babylon.
2 And King Nebuchadnezzar sent *word* to
gather together the satraps, the administrators, the governors, the counselors, the treasurers, the judges, the magistrates, and all
the officials of the provinces, to come to the
dedication of the image which King Nebuchadnezzar had set up.
3 So the satraps, the administrators, the
governors, the counselors, the treasurers, the
judges, the magistrates, and all the officials of
the provinces gathered together for the dedication of the image that King Nebuchadnezzar had set up; and they stood before the
image that Nebuchadnezzar had set up.
4 Then a herald cried [T]aloud: "To you it is
commanded, [R]O peoples, nations, and languages, Lit. *with strength* • Dan. 4:1; 6:25
5 "*that* at the time you hear the sound of
the horn, flute, harp, lyre, *and* psaltery, in
symphony with all kinds of music, you shall
fall down and worship the gold image that
King Nebuchadnezzar has set up;
6 "and whoever does not fall down and
worship shall [R]be cast immediately into the
midst of a burning fiery furnace." Jer. 29:22
7 So at that time, when all the people
heard the sound of the horn, flute, harp, *and*
lyre, in symphony with all kinds of music, all
the people, nations, and languages fell down
and worshiped the gold image which King
Nebuchadnezzar had set up.

Daniel's Friends Refuse to Worship

8 Therefore at that time certain Chaldeans
came forward and accused the Jews.
9 They spoke and said to King Nebuchadnezzar, [R]"O king, live forever! Dan. 2:4; 5:10
10 "You, O king, have made a decree that
everyone who hears the sound of the horn,
flute, harp, lyre, *and* psaltery, in symphony
with all kinds of music, shall fall down and
worship the gold image;
11 "and whoever does not fall down and
worship shall be cast into the midst of a
burning fiery furnace.
12 [R]"There are certain Jews whom you have
set over the affairs of the province of Babylon: Shadrach, Meshach, and Abed-Nego;
these men, O king, have [R]not paid due regard
to you. They do not serve your gods or
worship the gold image which you have set
up." Dan. 2:49 • Dan. 1:8; 6:12, 13

Daniel's Friends Trust God

13 Then Nebuchadnezzar, in [R]rage and fury,
gave the command to bring Shadrach, Meshach, and Abed-Nego. So they brought these
men before the king. Dan. 2:12; 3:19
14 Nebuchadnezzar spoke, saying to them,
"*Is it* true, Shadrach, Meshach, and Abed-
Nego, *that* you do not serve my gods or
worship the gold image which I have set up?
15 "Now if you are ready at the time you
hear the sound of the horn, flute, harp, lyre,
and psaltery, in symphony with all kinds of
music, and you fall down and worship the
image which I have made, [R]*good!* But if you
do not worship, you shall be cast immediately
into the midst of a burning fiery furnace.
[R]And who *is* the god who will deliver you
from my hands?" Luke 13:9 • Ex. 5:2
16 Shadrach, Meshach, and Abed-Nego answered and said to the king, "O Nebuchadnezzar, [R]we have no need to answer you in
this matter. [Matt. 10:19]
17 "If that *is the case*, our [R]God whom we
serve is able to [R]deliver us from the burning
fiery furnace, and He will deliver *us* from
your hand, O king. [Is. 26:3, 4] • 1 Sam. 17:37
18 "But if not, let it be known to you, O
king, that we do not serve your gods, nor will
we [R]worship the gold image which you have
set up." Job 13:15

Daniel's Friends Are Protected in the Furnace

19 Then Nebuchadnezzar was full of fury,
and the expression on his face changed
toward Shadrach, Meshach, and Abed-Nego.
Therefore he spoke and commanded that
they heat the furnace seven times more than
it was usually heated.
20 And he commanded certain mighty men
of valor who *were* in his army to bind Shadrach, Meshach, and Abed-Nego, *and* cast
them into the burning fiery furnace.
21 Then these men were bound in their
coats, their trousers, their turbans, and their
other garments, and were cast into the midst
of the burning fiery furnace.
22 Therefore, because the king's command
was [T]urgent, and the furnace exceedingly
hot, the flame of the fire killed those men
who took up Shadrach, Meshach, and Abed-
Nego. Or *harsh*
23 And these three men, Shadrach, Meshach, and Abed-Nego, fell down bound into
the midst of the burning fiery furnace.
24 Then King Nebuchadnezzar was astonished; and he rose in haste *and* spoke, saying
to his [T]counselors, "Did we not cast three
men bound into the midst of the fire?" They
answered and said to the king, "True, O
king." High officials
25 "Look!" he answered, "I see four men
loose, walking in the midst of the fire; and
they are not hurt, and the form of the fourth
is like [T]the Son of God." Or *a son of the gods*

Daniel's Friends Are Promoted

26 Then Nebuchadnezzar went near the
[T]mouth of the burning fiery furnace *and*
spoke, saying, "Shadrach, Meshach, and
Abed-Nego, servants of the [R]Most High God,
come out, and come *here*." Then Shadrach,

Meshach, and Abed-Nego came from the
midst of the fire. Lit. *door* • [Dan. 4:2, 3, 17, 34, 35]
27 And the satraps, administrators, gover-
nors, and the king's counselors gathered
together, and they saw these men [R]on whose
bodies the fire had no power; the hair of their
head was not singed nor were their garments
affected, and the smell of fire was not on
them. Heb. 11:34
28 Nebuchadnezzar spoke, saying,
"Blessed be the God of Shadrach, Meshach,
and Abed-Nego, who sent His [R]Angel[T] and
delivered His servants who trusted in Him,
and they have frustrated the king's word, and
yielded their bodies, that they should not
serve nor worship any god except their own
God! [Ps. 34:7, 8] • Or *angel*
29 [R]"Therefore I make a decree that any
people, nation, or language which speaks
anything amiss against the God of Shadrach,
Meshach, and Abed-Nego shall be [R]cut in
pieces, and their houses shall be made an ash
heap; [R]because there is no other God who can
deliver like this." Dan. 6:26 • Dan. 2:5 • Dan. 6:27
30 Then the king [T]promoted Shadrach, Meshach, and Abed-Nego in the province of
Babylon. Lit. *caused to prosper*

CHAPTER 4

Nebuchadnezzar's Proclamation

NEBUCHADNEZZAR the king,
[R]To all peoples, nations and
languages that dwell in all the earth:
Peace be multiplied to you. Dan. 3:4; 6:25
2 I thought it good to declare the signs
and wonders [R]that the Most High God
has worked for me. Dan. 3:26

3 [R]How great *are* His signs, 2 Sam. 7:16
And how mighty His wonders!
His kingdom *is* [R]an everlasting
kingdom, [Dan. 2:44; 4:34; 6:26]
And His dominion *is* from generation to
generation.

Nebuchadnezzar's Vision

4 I, Nebuchadnezzar, was at rest in my
house, and flourishing in my palace.
5 I saw a dream which made me afraid,
and the thoughts on my bed and the
visions of my head [R]troubled me. Dan. 2:1
6 Therefore I issued a decree to bring in
all the wise *men* of Babylon before me,
that they might make known to me the
interpretation of the dream.
7 [R]Then the magicians, the astrologers,
the Chaldeans, and the soothsayers
came in, and I told them the dream; but
they did not make known to me its
interpretation. Dan. 2:2
8 But at last Daniel came before me (his
name *is* Belteshazzar, according to the
name of my god; [R]in him *is* the Spirit of
the Holy God), and I told the dream
before him, *saying*: Dan. 2:11; 4:18; 5:11, 14
9 "Belteshazzar, [R]chief of the magicians,
because I know that the Spirit of the
Holy God *is* in you, and no secret
troubles you, explain to me the visions
of my dream that I have seen, and its
interpretation. Dan. 2:48; 5:11
10 "These *were* the visions of my head
while on my bed:

I was looking, and behold,
[R]A tree in the midst of the earth,
And its height was great. Ezek. 31:3
11 The tree grew and became strong;
Its height reached to the heavens,
And it could be seen to the ends of all
the earth.
12 Its leaves *were* lovely,
Its fruit abundant,
And in it *was* food for all.
[R]The beasts of the field found shade
under it,
The birds of the heavens dwelt in its
branches,
And all flesh was fed from it. Lam. 4:20

13 "I saw in the visions of my head *while*
on my bed, and there was a watcher, a
holy one, coming down from heaven.
14 He cried aloud and said thus:

[R]'Chop down the tree and cut off its
branches, Ezek. 31:10–14
Strip off its leaves and scatter its fruit.
Let the beasts get out from under it,
And the birds from its branches.
15 Nevertheless leave the stump and roots
in the earth,
Bound with a band of iron and bronze,
In the tender grass of the field.
Let it be wet with the dew of heaven,
And *let* him graze with the beasts
On the grass of the earth.
16 Let his heart be changed from *that of* a
man,
Let him be given the heart of an
animal,
And let seven times pass over him.

17 'This decision *is* by the decree of the
watchers,
And the sentence by the word of the
holy ones,
In order [R]that the living may know
That the Most High rules in the
kingdom of men, Ps. 9:16; 83:18
[R]Gives it to whomever He will, Jer. 27:5–7
And sets over it the lowest of men.'

18 "This dream I, King Nebuchadnezzar,
have seen. Now you, Belteshazzar,

declare its interpretation, [R]since all the
wise *men* of my kingdom are not able
to make known to me the interpretation; but you *are* able, for the Spirit of
the Holy God *is* in you." Gen. 41:8, 15

Daniel's Interpretation of the Vision

19 Then Daniel, whose name was
Belteshazzar, was astonished for a time,
and his thoughts troubled him. *So* the
king spoke, and said, "Belteshazzar, do
not let the dream or its interpretation
trouble you." Belteshazzar answered
and said, "My lord, *may* the dream
concern those who hate you, and its
interpretation concern your enemies!
20 The[R] tree that you saw, which grew and
became strong, whose height reached to
the heavens and which *could be seen* by
all the earth, Dan. 4:10–12
21 whose leaves *were* lovely and its fruit
abundant, in which *was* food for all,
under which the beasts of the field
dwelt, and on whose branches the birds
of the heaven had their habitation—
22 it *is* you, O king, who have grown and
become strong; for your greatness has
grown and reaches to the heavens, and
your dominion to the end of the earth.
23 And[R] inasmuch as the king saw a
watcher, a holy one, coming down from
heaven and saying, 'Chop down the tree
and destroy it, but leave its stump and
roots in the earth, *bound* with a band of
iron and bronze in the tender grass of
the field; let it be wet with the dew of
heaven, [R]and let him graze with the
beasts of the field, till seven [T]times pass
over him'; Dan. 4:13–15 • Dan. 5:21 • Possibly *years*
24 this is the interpretation, O king, and
this is the decree of the Most High,
which has come upon my lord the king:
25 They shall drive you from men, your
dwelling shall be with the beasts of the
field, and they shall make you eat grass
like oxen. They shall wet you with the
dew of heaven, and seven [T]times shall
pass over you, till you know that the
Most High rules in the kingdom
of men, and gives it to whomever He
chooses. Possibly *years*
26 And inasmuch as they gave the
command to leave the stump *and* roots
of the tree, your kingdom shall be
assured to you, after you come to know
that [R]Heaven[T] rules. Matt. 21:25 • God
27 Therefore, O king, let my counsel be
acceptable to you; break off your sins
by *being* righteous, and your iniquities
by showing mercy to *the* poor.
Perhaps there may be [R]a [T]lengthening of
your prosperity." 1 Kin. 21:29 • *prolonging*

Nebuchadnezzar's Humiliation

28 All *this* came upon King
Nebuchadnezzar.
29 At the end of the twelve months he was
walking [T]about the royal palace of
Babylon. Or *upon*
30 The king [R]spoke, saying, "Is not this
great Babylon, that I have built for a
royal dwelling by my mighty power and
for the honor of my majesty?" Prov. 16:18
31 While the word *was still* in the king's
mouth, a voice fell from heaven: "King
Nebuchadnezzar, to you it is spoken:
the kingdom has departed from you!
32 And [R]they shall drive you from men,
and your dwelling *shall be* with the
beasts of the field. They shall make you
eat grass like oxen; and seven [T]times
shall pass over you, until you know that
the Most High rules in the kingdom of
men, and gives it to whomever He
chooses." [Dan. 4:25] • Possibly *years*
33 That very hour the word was fulfilled
concerning Nebuchadnezzar; he was
driven from men and ate grass like
oxen; his body was wet with the dew of
heaven till his hair had grown like
eagles' *feathers* and his nails like birds'
claws.

Nebuchadnezzar's Restoration

34 And [R]at the end of the [T]time I,
Nebuchadnezzar, lifted my eyes to
heaven, and my understanding returned
to me; and I blessed the Most High and
praised and honored Him [R]who lives
forever: Dan. 4:26 • Lit. *days* • [Rev. 4:10]

For His dominion *is* [R]an everlasting
dominion, [Luke 1:33]
And His kingdom *is* from generation to
generation.
35 [R]All the inhabitants of the earth *are*
reputed as nothing; Is. 40:15, 17
[R]He does according to His will in the
army of heaven Ps. 115:3; 135:6
And *among* the inhabitants of the earth.
[R]No one can restrain His hand Job 34:29
Or say to Him, [R]"What have You
done?" Rom. 9:20

36 At the same time my reason returned to
me, and for the glory of my kingdom,
my honor and splendor returned to me.
My counselors and nobles resorted to
me, I was restored to my kingdom, and
excellent majesty was added to me.
37 Now I, Nebuchadnezzar, praise and
extol and honor the King of heaven, [R]all
of whose works *are* truth, and His ways
justice. And those who walk in pride He
is able to [T]abase. [Ps. 33:4] • *humble*

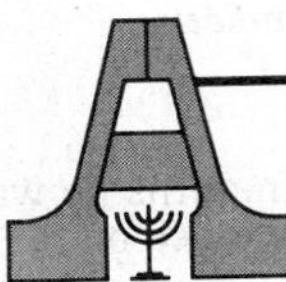

THE CITY OF BABYLON

Babylon, the ancient walled capital of the Babylonian Empire, was located between the Tigris and Euphrates rivers in southern Mesopotamia. The city was part of the empire of Nimrod referred to in Genesis 10:10.

While Babylon was an old city even when Abraham left southern Mesopotamia about 2000 B.C. (Gen. 11:27–31), it reached the height of its splendor under King Nebuchadnezzar II (ruled 605–562 B.C.). He enlarged the city to an area of about six square miles and beautified it with magnificent buildings.

In Nebuchadnezzar's time, eight major gates led into the city, whose double walls spanned both sides of the Euphrates River. The main gate, known as the Ishtar Gate, opened to a sacred processional way, which led to the temple of the pagan Babylonian god Marduk. The gate and the city walls were decorated with colored bricks, which featured drawings of lions, dragons, and bulls (see illustration).

The city also contained a palace complex, or residence for the king. The famous hanging gardens of Babylon, one of the seven wonders of the ancient world, were located near these buildings. According to tradition, Nebuchadnezzar built these gardens for one of his foreign wives to remind her of the scenery of her homeland.

Babylon is the city to which the citizens of Judah were carried as captives after the Babylonians overran their nation in 586 B.C. One of these captives, the prophet Daniel, interpreted a dream for King Nebuchadnezzar, making it clear that God would judge the Babylonians because of their mistreatment of God's people, as well as because of their paganism and idolatry (Dan. 4).

This happened as Daniel predicted in 539 B.C., when Babylonia fell to the Persians. Today the ruins of this ancient city are an eloquent testimony to the passing of mighty empires and the hand of God in human history.

The Ishtar Gate opened to a sacred processional way, which led to the temple of the Babylonian god Marduk.

CHAPTER 5

Belshazzar Defiles the Temple Vessels

BELSHAZZAR the king made a great feast for a thousand of his lords, and drank wine in the presence of the thousand.

2 While he tasted the wine, Belshazzar gave the command to bring the gold and silver vessels [R]which his [T]father Nebuchadnezzar had taken from the temple which *had been* in Jerusalem, that the king and his lords, his wives, and his concubines might drink from them. Dan. 1:2 • Or *ancestor*

3 Then they brought the gold [R]vessels that had been taken from the temple of the house of God which *had been* in Jerusalem; and the king and his lords, his wives, and his concubines drank from them. 2 Chr. 36:10

4 They drank wine, [R]and praised the gods of gold and silver, bronze and iron, wood and stone. Rev. 9:20

Belshazzar Sees the Handwriting

5 [R]In the same hour the fingers of a man's hand appeared and wrote opposite the lampstand on the plaster of the wall of the king's palace; and the king saw the part of the hand that wrote. Dan. 4:31

6 Then the king's countenance changed, and his thoughts troubled him, so that the joints of his hips were loosened and his [R]knees knocked against each other. Dan. 4:6

7 The king cried [T]aloud to bring in the astrologers, the Chaldeans, and the soothsayers. *And* the king spoke, saying to the wise *men* of Babylon, "Whoever reads this writing, and tells me its interpretation, shall be clothed with purple and *have* a chain of gold around his neck; [R]and he shall be the third ruler in the kingdom." Lit. *with* • Dan. 6:2, 3

8 Now all the king's wise *men* came, [R]but they could not read the writing, or make known to the king its interpretation. Dan. 2:27

9 Then King Belshazzar was greatly [R]troubled, his countenance was changed, and his lords were [T]astonished. Dan. 2:1; 5:6 • *perplexed*

Daniel Interprets the Handwriting

10 The queen, because of the words of the king and his lords, came to the banquet hall. *And* the queen spoke, saying, "O king, live forever! Do not let your thoughts trouble you, nor let your countenance change.

11 "There is a man in your kingdom in whom *is* the Spirit of the Holy God. And in the days of your father, light and understanding and wisdom, like the wisdom of the gods, were found in him; and King Nebuchadnezzar your father—your father the king—made him chief of the magicians, astrologers, Chaldeans, *and* soothsayers.

12 "Inasmuch as an excellent spirit, knowledge, understanding, interpreting dreams, solving riddles, and [T]explaining enigmas were found in this Daniel, whom the king named Belteshazzar, now let Daniel be called, and he will give the interpretation." Lit. *untying knots*

13 Then Daniel was brought in before the king. *And* the king spoke, and said to Daniel, "*Are* you that Daniel who is one of the captives from Judah, whom my [T]father the king brought from Judah? Or *ancestor*

14 "I have heard of you, that the Spirit of God *is* in you, and *that* light and understanding and excellent wisdom are found in you.

15 "Now [R]the wise *men,* the astrologers, have been brought in before me, that they should read this writing and make known to me its interpretation, but they could not give the interpretation of the thing. Dan. 5:7, 8

16 "And I have heard of you, that you can give interpretations and [T]explain enigmas. [R]Now if you can read the writing and make known to me its interpretation, you shall be clothed with purple and *have* a chain of gold around your neck, and shall be the third ruler in the kingdom." Lit. *untie knots* • Dan. 5:7, 29

17 Then Daniel answered, and said before the king, "Let your gifts be for yourself, and give your rewards to another; yet I will read the writing to the king, and make known to him the interpretation.

18 "O king, [R]the Most High God gave Nebuchadnezzar your [T]father a kingdom and majesty, glory and honor. Dan. 4:17 • Or *ancestor*

19 "And because of the majesty that He gave him, [R]all peoples, nations, and languages trembled and feared before him. Whomever he wished, he [R]executed; whomever he wished, he kept alive; whomever he wished, he set up; and whomever he wished, he put down. Jer. 27:7 • Dan. 2:12, 13; 3:6

20 [R]"But when his heart was lifted up, and his spirit was hardened in pride, he was deposed from his kingly throne, and they took his glory from him. Dan. 4:30, 37

21 "Then he was driven from the sons of men, his heart was made like the beasts, and his dwelling *was* with the wild donkeys. They fed him with grass like oxen, and his body was wet with the dew of heaven, [R]till he [T]knew that the Most High God rules in the kingdom of men, and appoints over it whomever He chooses. Ezek. 17:24 • Recognized

22 "But you his son, Belshazzar, [R]have not humbled your heart, although you knew all this. 2 Chr. 33:23; 36:12

23 And you have lifted yourself up against the Lord of heaven. They have brought the vessels of His house before you, and you and your lords, your wives and your concubines, have drunk wine from them. And you have praised the gods of silver and gold, bronze and iron, wood and stone, which do not see or hear or know; and the God who *holds* your breath in His hand and owns all your ways, you have not glorified.

24 "Then the fingers of the hand were sent
from Him, and this writing was written.
25 "And this is the inscription that was
written:

MENE, MENE, TEKEL, UPHARSIN.

26 "This *is* the interpretation of *each* word.
[T]MENE: God has numbered your kingdom,
and finished it; Lit. *a mina* (50 shekels)
27 [T]"TEKEL: You have been weighed in the
balances, and found wanting; Lit. *a shekel*
28 "PERES: Your kingdom has been divided,
and given to the Medes and Persians."
29 Then Belshazzar gave the command, and
they clothed Daniel with purple and *put* a
chain of gold around his neck, and made a
proclamation concerning him [R]that he should
be the third ruler in the kingdom. Dan. 5:7, 16

Belshazzar Is Killed

30 [R]That very night Belshazzar, king of the
Chaldeans, was slain. Jer. 51:31, 39, 57
31 And Darius the Mede received the kingdom, *being* about sixty-two years old.

CHAPTER 6

Daniel Is Promoted

IT pleased Darius to set over the kingdom
one hundred and twenty satraps, to be
over the whole kingdom;
2 and over these, three governors, of
whom Daniel *was* one, that the satraps might
give account to them, so that the king would
suffer no loss.
3 Then this Daniel distinguished himself
above the governors and satraps, because an
excellent spirit *was* in him; and the king gave
thought to setting him over the whole realm.

Darius Signs the Foolish Decree

4 [R]So the governors and satraps sought to
find *some* charge against Daniel concerning
the kingdom; but they could find no charge
or fault, because he *was* faithful; nor was
there any error or fault found in him. Eccl. 4:4
5 Then these men said, "We shall not find
any charge against this Daniel unless we find
it against him concerning the law of his
God."
6 So these governors and satraps thronged
before the king, and said thus to him: [R]"King
Darius, live forever! Neh. 2:3
7 "All the governors of the kingdom, the
administrators and satraps, the counselors
and advisors, have [R]consulted together to
establish a royal statute and to make a firm
decree, that whoever petitions any god or
man for thirty days, except you, O king, shall
be cast into the den of lions. Ps. 59:3; 62:4; 64:2–6
8 "Now, O king, establish the decree and
sign the writing, so that it cannot be
changed, according to the law of the Medes
and Persians, which does not alter."
9 Therefore King Darius signed the written
decree.

Daniel Prays Faithfully

10 Now when Daniel knew that the writing
was signed, he went home. And in his upper
room, with his windows open toward Jerusalem, he knelt down on his knees three times
that day, and prayed and gave thanks before
his God, as was his custom since early days.
11 Then these men assembled and found
Daniel praying and making supplication before his God.
12 And they went before the king, and
spoke concerning the king's decree: "Have
you not signed a decree that every man who
petitions any god or man within thirty days,
except you, O king, shall be cast into the den
of lions?" The king answered and said, "The
thing *is* true, according to the law of the
Medes and Persians, which does not alter."
13 So they answered and said before the
king, "That Daniel, who is [T]one of the captives from Judah, does not show due regard
for you, O king, or for the decree that you
have signed, but makes his petition three
times a day." Lit. *of the sons of the captivity*
14 And the king, when he heard *these*
words, [R]was greatly displeased with himself,
and set *his* heart on Daniel to deliver him;
and he [T]labored till the going down of the sun
to deliver him. Mark 6:26 • *strove*
15 Then these men [T]approached the king,
and said to the king, "Know, O king, that *it is*
[R]the law of the Medes and Persians that no
decree or statute which the king establishes
may be changed." Lit. *thronged before* • Dan. 6:8, 12

Daniel Is Saved in the Lions' Den

16 So the king gave the command, and they
brought Daniel and cast *him* into the den of
lions. *But* the king spoke, saying to Daniel,
"Your God, whom you serve continually, He
will deliver you."
17 Then a stone was brought and laid on
the mouth of the den, [R]and the king sealed it
with his own signet ring and with the signets
of his lords, that the purpose concerning
Daniel might not be changed. Matt. 27:66
18 Now the king went to his palace and
spent the night fasting; and no musicians
were brought before him. [R]Also his sleep
[T]went from him. Dan. 2:1 • Or *fled*
19 Then the [R]king arose very early in the
morning and went in haste to the den of
lions. Dan. 3:24
20 And when he came to the den, he cried
out with a [T]lamenting voice to Daniel. The
king spoke, saying to Daniel, "Daniel, servant
of the living God, [R]has your God, whom you

serve continually, been able to deliver you
from the lions?" Or *grieved* • Dan. 3:17
21 Then Daniel said to the king, R"O king,
live forever! Dan. 2:4; 6:6
22 R"My God sent His angel and Rshut the
lions' mouths, so that they have not hurt me,
because I was found innocent before Him;
and also, O king, I have done no wrong
before you." Dan. 3:28 • Heb. 11:33
23 Then the king was exceedingly glad for
him, and commanded that they should take
Daniel up out of the den. So Daniel was taken
up out of the den, and no injury whatever
was found on him, Rbecause he believed in his
God. Heb. 11:33
24 And the king gave the command, and
they brought those men who had accused
Daniel, and they cast *them* into the den of
lions—them, Rtheir children, and their wives;
and the lions overpowered them, and broke
all their bones in pieces before they ever
came to the bottom of the den. Deut. 24:16

Darius's Wise Decree

25 RThen King Darius wrote:

To all peoples, nations, and languages
that dwell in all the earth:
Peace be multiplied to you. Dan. 4:1
26 RI make a decree that in every Dan. 3:29
dominion of my kingdom *men must*
Rtremble and fear before the God of
Daniel. Ps. 99:1

RFor He *is* the living God, Dan. 4:34; 6:20
And steadfast forever;
His kingdom *is the one* which shall not
be Rdestroyed, Dan. 2:44; 4:3; 7:14, 27
And His dominion *shall endure* to the
end.
27 He delivers and rescues,
RAnd He works signs and wonders
In heaven and on earth,
Who has delivered Daniel from the
Tpower of the lions. Dan. 4:2, 3 • Lit. *hand*

28 So this Daniel prospered in the reign of
Darius Rand in the reign of RCyrus the Persian. Dan. 1:21 • Ezra 1:1, 2

CHAPTER 7

Four Beasts

IN the first year of Belshazzar king of
Babylon, RDaniel Thad a dream and Rvisions of his head *while* on his bed. Then he
wrote down the dream, telling Tthe main
facts. [Amos 3:7] • Lit. *saw* • [Dan. 2:28] • Lit. *the head*
2 Daniel spoke, saying, "I saw in my vision
by night, and behold, the four winds of
heaven were stirring up the Great Sea.
3 "And four great beasts came up from the
sea, each different from the other.
4 "The first *was* like a lion, and had eagle's
wings. I watched till its wings were plucked
off; and it was lifted up from the earth and
made to stand on two feet like a man, and a
man's heart was given to it.
5 R"And suddenly another beast, a second,
like a bear. It was raised up on one side, and
had three ribs in its mouth between its teeth.
And they said thus to it: 'Arise, devour much
flesh!' Dan. 2:39
6 "After this I looked, and there was another, like a leopard, which had on its back
four wings of a bird. The beast also had four
heads, and dominion was given to it.
7 "After this I saw in the night visions, and
behold, Ra fourth beast, dreadful and terrible,
exceedingly strong. It had huge iron teeth; it
was devouring, breaking in pieces, and trampling the residue with its feet. It *was* different
from all the beasts that *were* before it, Rand it
had ten horns. Dan. 2:40 • Rev. 12:3; 13:1
8 "I was considering the horns, and Rthere
was another horn, a little one, coming up
among them, before whom three of the first
horns were plucked out by the roots. And
there, in this horn, *were* eyes like the eyes Rof
a man, Rand a mouth speaking Tpompous
words. Dan. 8:9 • Rev. 9:7 • Rev. 13:5, 6 • Lit. *great things*

"Ancient of Days"

9 "IR watched till thrones were Tput in
place, [Rev. 20:4] • Or *set up*
And Rthe Ancient of Days was seated;
RHis garment *was* white as snow,
And the hair of His head *was* like pure
wool. Ps. 90:2 • Rev. 1:14
His throne *was* a fiery flame,
RIts wheels a burning fire; Ezek. 1:15
10 RA fiery stream issued
And came forth from before Him.
RA thousand thousands ministered to
Him; Is. 30:33; 66:15 • Rev. 5:11
Ten thousand times ten thousand stood
before Him.
RThe Tcourt was seated, [Rev. 20:11–15]
And the books were opened. Or *judgment*

11 "I watched then because of the sound of
the Tpompous words which the horn was
speaking; RI watched till the beast was slain,
and its body destroyed and given to the
burning flame. Lit. *great* • [Rev. 19:20; 20:10]
12 "As for the rest of the beasts, they had
their dominion taken away, yet their lives
were prolonged for a season and a time.

13 "I was watching in the night visions,
And behold, *One* like the Son of Man,
Coming with the clouds of heaven!
He came to the Ancient of Days,
And they brought Him near before Him.

14 [R]Then to Him was given dominion and
glory and a kingdom, [John 3:35, 36]
That all [R]peoples, nations, and
languages should serve Him. Dan. 3:4
His dominion *is* [R]an everlasting
dominion, Mic. 4:7; [Luke 1:33] ☆
Which shall not pass away,
And His kingdom *the one*
Which shall not be destroyed.

Interpretation of the Four Beasts

15 "I, Daniel, was grieved in my spirit
[T]within *my* body, and the visions of my head
troubled me. Lit. *in the midst of its sheath*
16 "I came near to one of those who stood
by, and asked him the truth of all this. So he
told me and made known to me the interpretation of these things:
17 'Those great beasts, which are four, *are*
four kings *which* arise out of the earth.
18 'But the saints of the Most High shall
receive the kingdom, and possess the kingdom forever, even forever and ever.'
19 "Then I wished to know the truth about
the fourth beast, which was different from all
the others, exceedingly dreadful, *with* its
teeth of iron and its nails of bronze, *which*
devoured, broke in pieces, and trampled the
residue with its feet;
20 "and about the ten horns that *were* on its
head, and *about* the other *horn* which came
up, before which three fell, namely, that horn
which had eyes and a mouth which spoke
[T]pompous words, whose appearance *was*
greater than his fellows. Lit. *great things*
21 "I was watching; [R]and the same horn
was making war against the saints, and
prevailing against them, Rev. 11:7; 13:7; 17:14
22 "until the Ancient of Days came, [R]and a
judgment was made *in favor* of the saints of
the Most High, and the time came for the
saints to possess the kingdom. [Rev. 1:6]

Interpretation of the Fourth Beast

23 "Thus he said:

'The fourth beast shall be
[R]A fourth kingdom on earth, Dan. 2:40
Which shall be different from all *other*
kingdoms,
And shall devour the whole earth,
Trample it and break it in pieces.
24 [R]The ten horns *are* ten kings Rev. 13:1
Who shall arise from this kingdom.
And another shall rise after them;
He shall be different from the first *ones*,
And shall subdue three kings.
25 [R]*He shall speak pompous* words against
the Most High, Rev. 13:1–6
Shall [R]persecute[T] the saints of the Most
High, Rev. 17:6 • Lit. *wear out*
And shall [R]intend to change times and
law. Dan. 2:21
Then [R]the[T] saints shall be given into his
hand Rev. 13:7; 18:24 • Lit. *they*
For a time and times and half a time.
26 'But[R] the court shall be seated,
And they shall [R]take away his
dominion, [Dan. 2:35; 7:10, 22] • Rev. 19:20
To consume and destroy *it* forever.
27 Then the [R]kingdom and dominion,
And the greatness of the kingdoms
under the whole heaven, Dan. 7:14, 18, 22
Shall be given to the people, the saints
of the Most High.
[R]His kingdom *is* an everlasting kingdom,
[R]And all dominions shall serve and obey
Him.' [Luke 1:33, 34] • Is. 60:12

28 "This *is* the end of the [T]account. As for
me, Daniel, my thoughts greatly troubled me,
and my countenance changed; but I kept the
matter in my heart." Lit. *word*

CHAPTER 8

The Ram

IN* the third year of the reign of King
Belshazzar a vision appeared *to* me—to
me, Daniel—after the one that appeared to
me [R]the first time. Dan. 7:1
2 I saw in the vision, and it so happened
while I was looking, that I *was* in [R]Shushan,[T]
the [T]citadel, which *is* in the province of Elam;
and I saw in the vision that I was by the
River Ulai. Esth. 1:2; 2:8 • *Susa* • Or *fortified palace*
3 Then I lifted my eyes and saw, and there,
standing beside the river, was a ram which
had two horns, and the two horns *were* high;
but one *was* [R]higher than the other, and the
higher *one* came up last. Dan. 7:5
4 I saw the ram pushing westward, northward, and southward, so that no beast could
[T]withstand him; nor *was there any* that could
deliver from his hand, but he did according to
his will and became great. Lit. *stand before*

The Male Goat

5 And as I was considering, suddenly a
male goat came from the west, across the
surface of the whole earth, without touching
the ground; and the goat *had* a notable [R]horn
between his eyes. Dan. 8:8, 21; 11:3
6 Then he came to the ram that had two
horns, which I had seen standing beside the
river, and ran at him with furious power.
7 And I saw him confronting the ram; he
was moved with rage against him, [T]attacked
the ram, and broke his two horns. There was
no power in the ram to withstand him, but he
cast him down to the ground and trampled
him; and there was no one that could deliver
the ram from his hand. Lit. *struck*

8:1 The Hebrew language resumes in Dan. 8:1.

8 Therefore the male goat grew very great;
but when he became strong, the large horn
was broken, and in place of it [R]four notable
ones came up toward the four winds of
heaven. Dan. 7:6; 8:22; 11:4

The Little Horn

9 [R]And out of one of them came a little
horn which grew exceedingly great toward
the south, [R]toward the east, and toward the
[R]Glorious *Land.* Dan. 11:21 • Dan. 11:25 • Ps. 48:2
10 [R]And it grew up to [R]the host of heaven;
and [R]it cast down *some* of the host and *some*
of the stars to the ground, and trampled
them. Dan. 11:28 • Is. 14:13 • Rev. 12:4
11 He even exalted *himself* as high as the
Prince of the host; and by him the daily
sacrifices were taken away, and the place of
[T]His sanctuary was cast down. The temple
12 Because of transgression, an army was
given over *to the horn* to oppose the daily
sacrifices; and he cast truth down to the
ground. He did *all this* and prospered.

The Length of the Vision

13 Then I heard [R]a holy one speaking; and
another holy one said to that certain *one* who
was speaking, "How long *will* the vision *be,*
concerning the daily *sacrifices* and the transgression [T]of desolation, the giving of both the
sanctuary and the host to be trampled underfoot?" Dan. 4:13, 23 • Or *making desolate*
14 And he said to me, "For two thousand
three hundred [T]days; then the sanctuary shall
be cleansed." Lit. *evening-mornings*

Interpretation of the Vision

15 Now it happened, when I, Daniel, had
seen the vision and was seeking the meaning,
that suddenly there stood before me [R]one
having the appearance of a man. Ezek. 1:26
16 And I heard a man's voice [R]between *the*
banks of the Ulai, who called, and said,
[R]"Gabriel, make this *man* understand the
vision." Dan. 12:6, 7 • Luke 1:19, 26
17 So he came near where I stood, and
when he came I was afraid and [R]fell on my
face; but he said to me, "Understand, son of
man, that the vision *refers* to the time of the
end." Rev. 1:17
18 Now, as he was speaking with me, I was
in a deep sleep with my face to the ground;
but he touched me, and stood me upright.
19 And he said, "Look, I am making known
to you what shall happen in the latter time of
the indignation; [R]for at the appointed time
the end *shall be.* Hab. 2:3

Interpretation of the Ram

20 "The ram which you saw, having the two
horns—*they are* the kings of Media and
Persia.

Interpretation of the Male Goat

21 "And the male goat *is* the [T]kingdom of
Greece. The large horn that *is* between its
eyes [R]*is* the first king. Lit. *king* • Dan. 11:3
22 [R]"As for the broken *horn* and the four
that stood up in its place, four kingdoms shall
arise out of that nation, but not with its
power. Dan. 11:4

Interpretation of the Little Horn

23 "And in the latter time of their kingdom,
When the transgressors have reached
their fullness,
A king shall arise,
Having fierce [T]features, Lit. *countenance*
Who understands sinister schemes.
24 His power shall be mighty, [R]but not by
his own power; Rev. 17:13
He shall destroy [T]fearfully, *extraordinarily*
[R]And shall prosper and thrive; Dan. 11:36
[R]He shall destroy the mighty, and *also*
the holy people. Dan. 7:25

25 "Through[R] his cunning Dan. 11:21
He shall cause deceit to prosper under
his hand;
[R]And he shall magnify *himself* in his
heart. Dan. 8:11–13; 11:36; 12:7
He shall destroy many in *their*
prosperity.
[R]He shall even rise against the Prince of
princes; Rev. 19:19
But he shall be [R]broken without *human*
hand. Job 34:20

26 "And the vision of the evenings and
mornings
Which was told is true;
[R]Therefore seal up the vision,
For *it refers* to many days *in the*
future." Ezek. 12:27

Response of Daniel

27 [R]And I, Daniel, fainted and was sick for
days; afterward I arose and went about the
king's business. I was astonished by the
vision, but no one understood it. Dan. 7:28

CHAPTER 9

The Understanding of Daniel

IN the first year [R]of Darius the son of
Ahasuerus, of the lineage of the Medes,
who was made king over the realm of the
Chaldeans— Dan. 1:21
2 in the first year of his reign I, Daniel,
understood by the books the number of the
years *specified* by the word of the LORD,
given through [R]Jeremiah the prophet, that He
would accomplish seventy years in the desolations of Jerusalem. 2 Chr. 36:21

The Intercession of Daniel

3 [R]Then I set my face toward the Lord God
to make request by prayer and supplications,
with fasting, sackcloth, and ashes. Neh. 1:4
4 And I prayed to the LORD my God, and
made confession, and said, "O Lord, great and
awesome God, who keeps His covenant and
mercy with those who love Him, and with
those who keep His commandments,

5 [R]"we have sinned and committed iniquity, we have done wickedly and rebelled,
even by departing from Your precepts and
Your judgments. 1 Kin. 8:47, 48
6 [R]"Neither have we heeded Your servants
the prophets, who spoke in Your name to our
kings and our princes, to our fathers and all
the people of the land. 2 Chr. 36:15
7 "O Lord, [R]righteousness *belongs* to You,
but to us shame of face, as *it is* this day—to
the men of Judah, to the inhabitants of
Jerusalem and all Israel, those near and those
far off in all the countries to which You have
driven them, because of the unfaithfulness
which they have committed against You.
8 "O Lord, to us *belongs* shame of face, to
our kings, our princes, and our fathers, because we have sinned against You.
9 [R]"To the Lord our God *belong* mercy and
forgiveness, though we have rebelled against
Him. [Ps. 130:4, 7]
10 "We have not obeyed the voice of the
LORD our God, to walk in His laws, which He
set before us by His servants the prophets.
11 "Yes, [R]all Israel has transgressed Your
law, and has departed so as not to obey Your
voice; therefore the curse and the oath written in the [R]Law of Moses the servant of God
have been poured out on us, because we have
sinned against Him. Is. 1:3–6 • Lev. 26:14
12 "And He has [R]confirmed His words,
which He spoke against us and against our
judges who judged us, by bringing upon us a
great disaster; [R]for under the whole heaven
such never has been done as what has been
done to Jerusalem. Zech. 1:6 • Lam. 1:12; 2:13
13 "As *it is* written in the Law of Moses, all
this disaster has come upon us; [R]yet we have
not made our prayer before the LORD our
God, that we might turn from our iniquities
and understand Your truth. Is. 9:13
14 "Therefore the LORD has [R]kept the disaster in mind, and brought it upon us; for [R]the
LORD our God *is* righteous in all the works
which He does, though we have not obeyed
His voice. Jer. 31:28; 44:27 • Neh. 9:33
15 "And now, O Lord our God, [R]who
brought Your people out of the land of Egypt
with a mighty hand, and made Yourself [R]a
name, as *it is* this day—we have sinned, we
have done wickedly! Neh. 1:10 • Neh. 9:10
16 "O Lord, according to all Your righteousness, I pray, let Your anger and Your fury be
turned away from Your city Jerusalem, Your
holy mountain; because for our sins, and for
the iniquities of our fathers, Jerusalem and
Your people [R]*have become* a reproach to all
who are around us. Ps. 79:4
17 "Now therefore, our God, hear the
prayer of Your servant, and his supplications,
and for the Lord's sake cause Your face to
shine on Your sanctuary, which is desolate.
18 "O my God, incline Your ear and hear;
open Your eyes and see our desolations, and
the city [R]which is called by Your name; for
we do not present our supplications before
You because of our righteous deeds, but
because of Your great mercies. Jer. 25:29
19 "O Lord, hear! O Lord, forgive! O Lord,
listen and act! Do not delay for Your own
sake, my God, for Your city and Your people
are called by Your name."

The Intervention of Gabriel

20 Now while I *was* speaking, praying, and
confessing my sin and the sin of my people

9:3, 4 Knowing the Will of God Through Prayer and Fasting—Soon after Israel had invaded Palestine in the days of Joshua, the Israelites were tricked into signing an unscriptural peace treaty with a group of deceitful pagans. The cause for this tragic error is clearly stated in God's Word, "Then the men . . . did not ask counsel of the LORD" (Page 261—Josh. 9:14). These pagans, the Gibeonites, brought only trouble to Israel. See Joshua 10:4–15; Second Samuel 21:1–14.

It therefore becomes immediately obvious that one of the most important factors in knowing God's will for our lives is to pray. "If any of you lacks wisdom, let him ask of God, who gives to all liberally and without reproach, and it will be given to him" (Page 1468—James 1:5). See also Psalm 143:8, 10; James 4:2.

In the light of these passages it is evident a Christian must pray to know God's will. In other Bible verses fasting is linked with prayer.

a. Meaning of fasting: to fast is to abstain for a period of time from some important and necessary activity in our lives.
b. Purpose of fasting: this is done that we might spend that time in prayer before God.
c. Kinds of fasting: one may, for a time, refrain from sleep (Page 1369—2 Cor. 6:5; 11:27), marital sex (Page 1351—1 Cor. 7:1–5), or food (Page 1117—Matt. 4:1, 2).
d. Examples of biblical fasting: Moses (Page 220—Deut. 9:9, 18, 25–29); Elijah (Page 418—1 Kin. 19:8); Daniel (Page 988—Dan. 9:3; 10:3); Ezra (Page 553—Ezra 10:6); Nehemiah (Page 558—Neh. 1:4); and Paul (Page 1369—2 Cor. 6:5; 11:27).

Now turn to Page 778—Is. 6:8: Knowing the Will of God Through Submission to the Spirit.

Israel, and presenting my supplication before
the LORD my God for the holy mountain of
my God,
21 yes, while I *was* speaking in prayer, the
man [R]Gabriel, whom I had seen in the vision
at the beginning, being caused to fly swiftly,
reached me about the time of the evening
offering. Dan. 8:16
22 And he informed *me*, and talked with
me, and said, "O Daniel, I have now come
forth to give you skill to understand.
23 "At the beginning of your supplications
the [T]command went out, and I have come to
tell *you*, for you *are* greatly [R]beloved; therefore [R]consider the matter, and understand the
vision: Lit. *word* • Dan. 10:11, 19 • Matt. 24:15

The Revelation of the Seventy Weeks

24 "Seventy [T]weeks are determined Lit. *sevens*
For your people and for your holy city,
To finish the transgression,
To make an end of sins,
[R]To make reconciliation for iniquity,
To bring in everlasting righteousness,
To seal up vision and prophecy, [Is. 53:10]
[R]And to anoint the Most Holy. Ps. 45:7

25 "Know therefore and understand,
That from the going forth of the
command
To restore and build Jerusalem
Until [R]Messiah [R]the Prince,
There shall be seven weeks and sixty-
two weeks; John 1:41; 4:25 ☆ • Is. 55:4
The [T]street shall be built again, and the
[T]wall, Or *open square* • Or *moat*
Even in troublesome times.

26 "And after the sixty-two weeks
[R]Messiah shall be cut off, [R]but not for
Himself; [Is. 53:8]; Matt. 27:50 ☆ • [1 Pet. 2:21]
And [R]the people of the prince who is to
come Matt. 22:7
[R]Shall destroy the city and the
sanctuary. Luke 19:43, 44
The end of it *shall be* with a flood,
And till the end of the war desolations
are determined.
27 Then he shall confirm a [T]covenant with
[R]many for one week; *treaty* • [Matt. 26:28]
But in the middle of the week
He shall bring an end to sacrifice and
offering.
And on the wing of abominations shall
be one who makes desolate,
[R]Even until the consummation, which is
determined, Dan. 11:36
Is poured out on the desolate."

CHAPTER 10

Time of the Vision

In the third year of Cyrus king of Persia a
message was revealed to Daniel, whose
[R]name was called Belteshazzar. The message
was true, but the appointed time *was* long;
and he understood the message, and had
understanding of the vision. Dan. 1:7
2 In those days I, Daniel, was mourning
three full weeks.
3 I ate no pleasant food, no meat or wine
came into my mouth, nor did I anoint myself
at all, till three whole weeks were fulfilled.
4 Now on the twenty-fourth day of the
first month, as I was by the side of the great
river, that *is*, the [T]Tigris, Heb. *Hiddekel*

Vision of the Heavenly Messenger

5 I lifted my eyes and looked, and behold, a
certain man clothed in linen, whose waist
was [R]girded with gold of Uphaz! Rev. 1:13
6 His body *was* like beryl, his face like the
appearance of lightning, his eyes like torches
of fire, his arms and feet like burnished
bronze in color, [R]and the sound of his words
like the voice of a multitude. [Rev. 1:15]
7 And I, Daniel, alone saw the vision, for
the men who were with me did not see the
vision; but a great terror fell upon them, so
that they fled to hide themselves.
8 Therefore I was left alone when I saw
this great vision, and no strength remained in
me; for my [T]vigor was turned to frailty in me,
and I retained no strength. Lit. *splendor*
9 Yet I heard the sound of his words; and
while I heard the sound of his words I was in
a deep sleep on my face, with my face to the
ground.

Touch of the Heavenly Messenger

10 [R]Then, suddenly, a hand touched me,
which made me tremble on my knees and *on*
the palms of my hands. Dan. 9:21
11 And he said to me, "O Daniel, man
greatly beloved, understand the words that I
speak to you, and stand upright, for I have
now been sent to you." While he was speaking this word to me, I stood trembling.
12 Then he said to me, "Do not fear, Daniel,
for from the first day that you set your heart
to understand, and to humble yourself before
your God, your words were heard; and I have
come because of your words.
13 [R]"But the prince of the kingdom of Persia
withstood me twenty-one days; and behold,
[R]Michael, one of the chief princes, came to
help me, for I had been left alone there with
the kings of Persia. Dan. 10:20 • Dan. 10:21; 12:1
14 "Now I have come to make you understand what will happen to your people [R]in the
latter days, [R]for the vision *refers* to *many*
days yet *to come*." Dan. 2:28 • Dan. 8:26; 10:1

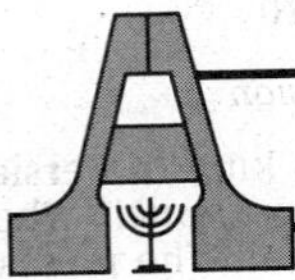

MESSIAH

Nearly everyone knows the Hebrew word *Messiah* (Hebrew spelling *Māshîah*). It is an important word for Orthodox Jews, but especially for Christians.

General Usage

Māshîah ("anointed" or "anointed one") is used about forty times in the Hebrew Bible, mostly in Samuel and Psalms. The word is a noun or adjective derived from the verb *māshah*, "to anoint" or "to spread a liquid upon." Most Christians are surprised to find out that the word is used much more frequently in the Old Testament for anointed figures other than *the* Messiah whom God told Moses would come to deliver His people (Deut. 18:18).

Occasionally *māshîah* is used for a high priest, since he was anointed when put into office. Generally, however, the king is meant. Even kings who turned out poorly were "messiahs" in the lesser sense of having been anointed into office. Sometimes the king was called "the anointed of the LORD [*māshîah YHWH*]."

The really amazing thing is that the Gentile King Cyrus is called "His anointed" or "His messiah" in Isaiah 45:1. Here it must mean that God had ordained this pagan king to do His bidding in world history in a way to benefit His chosen people. The blessing involved delivering Israel from the Babylonian captivity. Of course, deliverance is a standard messianic motif for the one we know as the Messiah.

The Messiah Par Excellence

Daniel wrote the following in his prophecy of the "Seventy Weeks": "Know therefore and understand, *that* from the going forth of the command to restore and build Jerusalem until Messiah the Prince, *there shall be* seven weeks and sixty-two weeks; . . . And after the sixty-two weeks Messiah shall be cut off, but not for Himself; and the people of the prince who is to come shall destroy the city and the sanctuary" (Dan. 9:25, 26). Sir Robert Anderson worked out a detailed chronology that shows that the Messiah in this passage must be the Christ of the New Testament, presenting Himself to Israel as their Messiah on that first Palm Sunday. Recent scholars, such as Harold Hoehner, have produced similar specific results. Some Jewish rabbis, such as Dr. Leopold Cohn, have been converted to Jesus as their Messiah through Daniel's chronology.

Another "messianic passage" in the modern Christian sense is Psalm 2:2, 3: "The kings of the earth set themselves, and the rulers take counsel together, against the LORD and against His Anointed, *saying*, 'Let us break Their bonds in pieces and cast away Their cords from us.'"

Of course, "Anointed" here is the Hebrew *māshîah*. The New Testament makes it clear that Jesus of Nazareth is meant here by quoting the passage in a prayer. The New Testament translates it with the Greek word for "Anointed": "against the LORD and against His Christ [*Christos*]" (Acts 4:26). The prayer goes on to use the Greek equivalent of the verb *māshah*: "For truly against Your holy Servant Jesus, whom You anointed [Greek *chriō*, see New Testament word study at 1 Peter 4]."

Messiah in the New Testament

In its translated form of *Christ* (*Christos*), the term occurs hundreds of times in the New Testament. However, twice in John, the actual Hebrew word *Messiah* is used.

In John 1:41, at the very beginning of our Lord's ministry to Israel, Andrew used the term in trying to interest his brother Peter in meeting Jesus: "He first found his own brother Simon, and said to him, 'We have found the Messiah' (which is translated, the Christ [Anointed])."

Moving out in the world to reach beyond Israel, Jesus had a religious dialog with a woman of the Samaritan community. The Samaritans had only the Pentateuch, but it is obvious that they did believe in the coming Anointed One, because the woman said to Jesus: "'I know that Messiah is coming' (who is called Christ). 'When He comes, He will tell us all things'" (John 4:25). She was right.

15 When he had spoken such words to me, [R]I [T]turned my face toward the ground and became speechless. Dan. 8:18; 10:9 • Lit. *set*

16 And suddenly, *one* having the likeness of the sons of men touched my lips; then I opened my mouth and spoke, saying to him who stood before me, "My lord, because of the vision my sorrows have overwhelmed me, and I have retained no strength.

17 "For how can this servant of my lord talk with you, my lord? As for me, no strength remains in me now, nor is any breath left in me."

Strengthening by the Heavenly Messenger

18 Then again, *the one* having the likeness of a man touched me and strengthened me.

19 And he said, "O man greatly beloved, [R]fear not! Peace *be* to you; be strong, yes, be strong!" So when he spoke to me I was strengthened, and said, "Let my lord speak, for you have strengthened me." Judg. 6:23

20 Then he said, "Do you know why I have come to you? And now I must return to fight [R]with the prince of Persia; and when I have gone forth, indeed the prince of Greece will come. Dan. 10:13

21 "But I will tell you what is noted in the Scripture of Truth. (No one upholds me against these, except Michael your prince.

CHAPTER 11

The Rule of Persia

"ALSO [R]in the first year of [R]Darius the Mede, I, *even* I, stood up to confirm and strengthen him.) Dan. 9:1 • Dan. 5:31

2 "And now I will tell you the truth: Behold, three more kings will arise in Persia, and the fourth shall be far richer than *them* all; by his strength, through his riches, he shall stir up all against the realm of Greece.

The Rule of Greece

3 "Then [R]a mighty king shall arise, who shall rule with great dominion, and [R]do according to his will. Dan. 7:6; 8:5 • Dan. 8:4; 10:16, 36

4 "And when he has arisen, his kingdom shall be broken up and divided toward the four winds of heaven, but not among his posterity nor according to his dominion with which he ruled; for his kingdom shall be uprooted, even for others besides these.

5 "Then the king of the South shall become strong, as well as *one* of his princes; and he shall gain power over him and have dominion. His dominion *shall be* a great dominion.

6 "And at the end of *some* years they shall join forces, for the daughter of the king of the South shall go to the king of the North to make an agreement; but she shall not retain the power of her [T]authority, and neither he nor his [T]authority shall stand; but she shall be given up, with those who brought her, and with him who begot her, and with him who strengthened her in *those* times. Lit. *arm*

7 "But from a branch of her roots *one* shall arise in his place, who shall come with an army, enter the fortress of the king of the North, and deal with them and prevail.

8 "And he shall also carry their gods captive to Egypt, with their [T]princes *and* their precious articles of silver and gold; and he shall continue *more* years than the king of the North. Or *molded images*

9 "Then [T]the king of the North shall come to the kingdom of the king of the South, but shall return to his own land. Lit. *he*

10 "However his sons shall stir up strife, and assemble a multitude of great forces; and *one* shall certainly come [R]and overwhelm and pass through; then he shall return [R]to his fortress and stir up strife. Is. 8:8 • Dan. 11:7

11 "And the king of the South shall be moved with rage, and go out and fight with him, with the king of the North, who shall muster a great multitude; but the multitude shall be given into the hand of his *enemy*.

12 "When he has taken away the multitude, his heart will be [T]lifted up; and he will cast down tens of thousands, but he will not prevail. Proud

13 "For the king of the North will return and muster a multitude greater than the former, and shall certainly come at the end of some years with a great army and much equipment.

14 "And in those times many shall rise up against the king of the South; also *certain* [T]violent men of your people shall exalt themselves [T]in fulfillment of the vision, but they shall fall. Lit. *sons of breakage* • Lit. *to establish*

15 "So the king of the North shall come and [R]build a siege mound, and take a fortified city; and the [T]forces of the South shall not withstand *him*. Even his choice troops *shall have* no strength to resist. Ezek. 4:2 • Lit. *arms*

16 "But he who comes against him shall do according to his own will, and no one shall stand against him. He shall stand in the Glorious Land with destruction in his power.

17 "He shall also [R]set his face to enter with the strength of his whole kingdom, and upright ones with him; thus shall he do. And he shall give him the daughter of women to destroy it; but she shall not stand *with him*, [R]or be for him. 2 Chr. 20:3 • Dan. 9:26

18 "After this he shall turn his face to the coastlands, and shall take many. But a ruler shall bring the reproach against them to an end; and with the reproach removed, he shall turn back on him.

19 "Then he shall turn his face toward the fortress of his own land; but he shall [R]stumble and fall, [R]and not be found. Jer. 46:6 • Ps. 37:36

20 "There shall arise in his place one who
imposes taxes *on* the glorious kingdom; but
within a few days he shall be destroyed, but
not in anger or in battle.
21 "And in his place [R]shall arise a vile
person, to whom they will not give the honor
of royalty; but he shall come in peaceably,
and seize the kingdom by intrigue. Dan. 7:8
22 "With the [T]force of a flood they shall be
swept away from before him and be broken,
and also the prince of the covenant. *arms*
23 "And after the league *is made* with him
[R]he shall act deceitfully, for he shall come up
and become strong with a small *number of*
people. Dan. 8:25
24 "He shall enter peaceably, even into the
richest places of the province; and he shall do
what his fathers have not done, nor his
forefathers: he shall disperse among them the
plunder, [T]spoil, and riches; and he shall devise
his plans against the strongholds, but *only* for
a time. *booty*
25 "He shall stir up his power and his courage against the king of the South with a great
army. And the king of the South shall be
stirred up to battle with a very great and
mighty army; but he shall not stand, for they
shall devise plans against him.
26 "Yes, those who eat of the portion of his
delicacies shall destroy him; his army shall
[T]be swept away, and many shall fall down
slain. Or *overflow*
27 "Both these kings' hearts *shall be* bent
on evil, and they shall speak lies at the same
table; but it shall not prosper, for the end *will*
still *be* at the [R]appointed time. Hab. 2:3
28 "While returning to his land with great
riches, his heart shall be *moved* against the
holy covenant; so he shall do *damage* and
return to his own land.
29 "At the appointed time he shall return
and go toward the south; but it shall not be
like the former or the latter.
30 "For ships from [T]Cyprus shall come
against him; therefore he shall be grieved,
and return in rage against the holy covenant,
and do *damage*. So he shall return and show
regard for those who forsake the holy covenant. Heb. *Kittim*, western lands, especially Cyprus
31 "And [T]forces shall be mustered by him,
[R]and they shall defile the sanctuary fortress;
then they shall take away the daily *sacrifices*,
and place *there* the abomination of desolation. Lit. *arms* • Dan. 8:11-13; 12:11

32 "Those who do wickedly against the
covenant he shall [T]corrupt with flattery; but
the people who know their God shall be
strong, and carry out *great exploits*. *pollute*

33 "And those of the people who understand shall instruct many; yet *for many* days
they shall fall by sword and flame, by captivity and plundering.
34 "Now when they fall, they shall be aided
with a little help; but many shall join with
them by [T]intrigue. Or *slipperiness, flattery*
35 "And *some* of those of understanding
shall fall, to refine them, purge *them*, and
make *them* white, *until* the time of the end;
because *it is* still for the appointed time.

Prophecy of the Willful King

36 "Then the king shall do according to his
own will: he shall [R]exalt and magnify himself
above every god, shall speak blasphemies
against the God of gods, and shall prosper till
the wrath has been accomplished; for what
has been determined shall be done. Dan. 7:8, 25

11:32 We Know God Through His Word—One of the most vital teachings of Scripture is that God can be known. The highest knowledge to which men and women can attain is a personal knowledge of God (Page 856—Jer. 9:24). People do not naturally possess this knowledge (Page 1325—Rom. 3:10, 11), even though they know that He exists (Page 632—Ps. 14:1; Page 1324—Rom. 1:19, 20). Knowing that God exists is not the same as knowing God personally, just as knowing about the President does not mean that you necessarily know him personally. This knowledge of God is crucial, however, since to know God personally is to be saved and have eternal life (Page 1261—John 17:3). People should rejoice in the fact that God earnestly wants them to attain this knowledge. That is why He has spoken to us in His Word, revealing Himself and disclosing the means by which we may know Him.

While God surely can be known, there is always more to be learned about Him. There are many Scriptures which teach that our knowledge of God is partial. It is said to be "too wonderful" (Page 704—Ps. 139:6), "unsearchable" (Page 707—Ps. 145:3; Page 1336—Rom. 11:33), and "infinite" (Page 708—Ps. 147:5). Since our knowledge of God is incomplete, we must increase it through spiritual growth. Paul, for example, prays to know God better (Page 1401—Phil. 3:10). We are even commanded to grow in the knowledge of Christ (Page 1490—2 Pet. 3:18). The development of one's intimate knowledge of God constitutes one of the greatest delights of the Christian life.

The Bible also reveals that God cannot be known personally apart from His Word. It contains the gospel which must be believed (Page 1387—Eph. 1:13), and the gospel brings forth saving faith in itself (Page 1335—Rom. 10:17). The gospel can therefore be called "the power of God to salvation" (Page 1324—Rom. 1:16). The part that the Scriptures and the gospel contained within them play in bringing men to know God is described in three important illustrations: the gospel is the agent of the new birth (Page 1468—James 1:18), that is, it is like the implanted seed without which the conception of new life cannot occur; it is also a cleansing agent through which God gives the believing sinner a spiritual bath that results in salvation (Page 1392—Eph. 5:26); the Scriptures are like an educator bringing the wisdom that leads to salvation (Page 1436—2 Tim. 3:15).

Now turn to Page 648—Ps. 40:8: We Know God's Will Through His Word.

37 "He shall regard neither the God of his
fathers nor the desire of women, [R]nor regard
any [T]god; for he shall magnify himself above
them all. Is. 14:13 • Or *gods*
38 "But in their place he shall honor a god
of fortresses; and a god which his fathers did
not know he shall honor with gold and silver,
with precious stones and pleasant things.
39 "Thus he shall act against the strongest
fortresses with a foreign god, which he shall
acknowledge, *and* advance *its* glory; and he
shall cause them to rule over many, and
divide the land for [T]gain. *profit*
40 "At the time of the end the king of the
South shall attack him; and the king of the
North shall come against him [R]like a whirlwind, with chariots, horsemen, and with
many ships; and he shall enter the countries,
overwhelm *them*, and pass through. Is. 21:1
41 "He shall also enter the Glorious Land,
and many *countries* shall be overthrown; but
these shall escape from his hand: Edom,
Moab, and the prominent people of Ammon.
42 "He shall stretch out his hand against
the countries, and the land of [R]Egypt shall
not escape. Joel 3:19
43 "He shall have power over the treasures
of gold and silver, and over all the precious
things of Egypt; also the Libyans and Ethiopians *shall follow* [R]at his heels. Ex. 11:8
44 "But news from the east and the north
shall trouble him; therefore he shall go out
with great fury to destroy and annihilate
many.
45 "And he shall plant the tents of his
palace between the seas and [R]the glorious
holy mountain; [R]yet he shall come to his end,
and no one will help him. Ps. 48:2 • Rev. 19:20

CHAPTER 12

Prophecy of the Great Time of Trouble

"AT that time Michael shall stand up,
The great prince who stands *watch*
over the sons of your people;
[R]And there shall be a time of trouble,
Such as never was since there was a
nation,
Even to that time.
And at that time your people [R]shall be
delivered,
Every one who is found [R]written in the
book. Jer. 30:7 • Rom. 11:26 • Ex. 32:32

Prophecy of the Resurrections

2 And many of those who sleep in the
dust of the earth shall awake,
[R]Some to everlasting life, [John 5:28, 29]
Some to shame [R]*and* everlasting
[T]contempt. [Is. 66:24] • Lit. *abhorrence*
3 Those who are wise shall [R]shine
Like the brightness of the firmament,
[R]And those who turn many to
righteousness Matt. 13:43 • [James 5:19, 20]
Like the stars forever and ever.

Sealing of the Book

4 "But you, Daniel, [R]shut up the words,
and seal the book until the time of the end;
many shall [R]run to and fro, and knowledge
shall increase." Rev. 22:10 • Amos 8:12

Questions Regarding the Great Time of Trouble

5 Then I, Daniel, looked; and there stood
two others, one on this riverbank and the
other on that [R]riverbank. Dan. 10:4
6 And *one* said to the man clothed in
[R]linen, who *was* above the waters of the river,
[R]"How long shall the fulfillment of these
wonders *be?*" Ezek. 9:2 • Dan. 8:13; 12:8
7 Then I heard the man clothed in linen,
who *was* above the waters of the river, when
he held up his right hand and his left hand to
heaven, and swore by Him who lives forever,
that *it shall be* for a time, times, and half *a*
time; and when the power of [R]the holy people
has been completely shattered, all these
things shall be finished. Dan. 8:24
8 Although I heard, I did not understand.
Then I said, "My lord, what *shall be* the end
of these *things?*"
9 And he said, "Go *your way*, Daniel, for
the words *are* closed up and sealed till the
time of the end.
10 "Many shall be purified, made white, and
refined, but the wicked shall do wickedly; and
none of the wicked shall understand, but the
wise shall understand.
11 "And from the time *that* the daily *sacri-*
fice is taken away, and the abomination of
desolation is set up, *there shall be* one thousand two hundred and ninety days.
12 "Blessed *is* he who waits, and comes to
the one thousand three hundred and thirty-
five days.
13 "But you, go *your way* till the end; [R]for
you shall rest, [R]and will arise to your inheritance at the end of the days." Rev. 14:13 • Ps. 1:5

THE BOOK OF

HOSEA

THE BOOK OF HOSEA

Hosea, whose name means "Salvation," ministers to the northern kingdom of Israel (also called Ephraim, after its largest tribe). Outwardly, the nation is enjoying a time of prosperity and growth; but inwardly, moral corruption and spiritual adultery permeate the people. Hosea, instructed by God to marry a woman named Gomer, finds his domestic life to be an accurate and tragic dramatization of the unfaithfulness of God's people. During his half century of prophetic ministry, Hosea repeatedly echoes his threefold message: God abhors the sins of His people; judgment is certain; but God's loyal love stands firm.

The names Hosea, Joshua, and Jesus are all derived from the same Hebrew root word. The word *hoshea* means "salvation," but "Joshua" and "Jesus" include an additional idea: "Yahweh Is Salvation" (see "The Book of Joshua"). As God's messenger, Hosea offers the possibility of salvation if only the nation will turn from idolatry back to God.

Israel's last king, Hoshea, has the same name as the prophet even though the English Bible spells them differently. Hosea in the Greek and Latin is *Osee.*

THE AUTHOR OF HOSEA

Few critics refute the claim in 1:1 that Hosea is the author of this book. His place of birth is not given, but his familiarity and obvious concern with the northern kingdom indicate that he lived in Israel, not Judah. This is also seen when he calls the king of Samaria "our king" (7:5). Hosea was the son of Beeri (1:1), husband of Gomer (1:3), and father of two sons and a daughter (1:4, 6, 9). Nothing more is known of him since he is not mentioned elsewhere in the Bible.

Hosea has a real compassion for his people, and his personal suffering because of Gomer gives him some understanding of God's grief over their sin. Thus, his words of coming judgment are passionately delivered but tempered with a heart of tenderness. He upbraids his people for their lying, murder, insincerity, ingratitude, idolatry, and covetousness with cutting metaphors and images; but his messages are punctuated with consolation and future hope.

THE TIME OF HOSEA

Hosea addressed the northern kingdom of Israel (5:1), often called Ephraim after the largest tribe (5:3, 5, 11, 13). According to 1:1, he ministered during the reigns of Uzziah (767–739 B.C.), Jotham (739–731 B.C.), Ahaz (731–715 B.C.), and Hezekiah (715–686 B.C.), kings of Judah. When Hosea began his ministry, Jeroboam II (782–753 B.C.) was still reigning in Israel. This makes Hosea a younger contemporary of Amos, another prophet to the northern kingdom. Hosea was also a contemporary of Isaiah and Micah who ministered to the southern kingdom. Hosea's long career continued after the time of Jeroboam II and spanned the reigns of the last six kings of Israel from Zechariah (753–752 B.C.) to Hoshea (732–722 B.C.). Hosea evidently compiled this book during the early years of Hezekiah, and his ministry stretched from about 755 B.C. to about 710 B.C. The Book of Hosea represents approximately forty years of prophetic ministry.

When Hosea began his ministry, Israel was enjoying a temporary period of political and economic prosperity under Jeroboam II. However, the nation began to crumble after Tiglath-Pileser III (745–727 B.C.) strengthened Assyria. The reigns of Israel's last six kings were relatively brief since four were murdered and a fifth was carried captive to Assyria. Confusion and decline characterized the last years of the northern kingdom, and her people refused to heed Hosea's warning of imminent judgment. The people were in a spiritual stupor, riddled with sin and idolatry.

THE CHRIST OF HOSEA

Matthew 2:15 applies Hosea 11:1 to Christ in Egypt: "When Israel *was* a child, I loved him, and out of Egypt I called My son." Matthew quotes the second half of this verse to show that the Exodus of Israel from Egypt as a new nation was a prophetic type of Israel's Messiah who was also called out of Egypt in His childhood. Both Israel and Christ left Palestine to take refuge in Egypt.

Christ's identification with our plight and His loving work of redemption can be seen in Hosea's redemption of Gomer from the slave market.

KEYS TO HOSEA

Key Word: The Loyal Love of God for Israel—The themes of chapters 1—3 echo throughout the rest of the book. The adultery of Gomer (1) illustrates the sin of Israel (4—7); the degradation of Gomer (2) represents the judgment of Israel (8—10); and Hosea's redemption of Gomer (3) pictures the restoration of Israel (11—14). More than any other Old Testament prophet, Hosea's personal experiences illustrate his prophetic message. In his relationship to Gomer, Hosea portrays God's faithfulness, justice, love, and forgiveness toward His people. The theme of God's holiness is developed in contrast to Israel's corruption and apostasy. Hosea utters about 150 statements concerning the sins of Israel, and more than half deal specifically with idolatry. The theme of God's justice is contrasted with Israel's lack of justice. There has never been a good king in Israel, and judgment is long overdue. The theme of God's love is seen in contrast to Israel's hardness and empty ritual. God's loyal love is unconditional and ceaseless; in spite of Israel's manifold sins, God tries every means to bring His people back to Himself. He pleads with the people to return to Him, but they will not. "O Israel, return to the LORD your God, for you have stumbled because of your iniquity" (14:1).

Key Verses: Hosea 4:1; 11:7-9—"Hear the word of the LORD, you children of Israel, for the LORD *brings* a charge against the inhabitants of the land: there is no truth or mercy or knowledge of God in the land" (4:1).

"My people are bent on backsliding from Me. Though they call to the Most High, none at all exalt *Him*. How can I give you up, Ephraim? *How* can I hand you over, Israel? How can I make you like Admah? *How* can I set you like Zeboiim? My heart churns within Me; My sympathy is stirred. I will not execute the fierceness of My anger; I will not again destroy Ephraim. For I *am* God, and not man, the Holy One in your midst; and I will not come with terror" (11:7–9).

Key Chapter: Hosea 4—The nation of Israel has left the knowledge of the truth and followed the idolatrous ways of their pagan neighbors. Central to the book is Hosea 4:6—"My people are destroyed for lack of knowledge. Because you have rejected knowledge, I also will reject you from being priest for Me; because you have forgotten the law of your God, I also will forget your children."

SURVEY OF HOSEA

Hosea is called by God to prophesy during Israel's last hours, just as Jeremiah will prophesy years later to the crumbling kingdom of Judah. As one commentator has noted, "What we see in the prophecy of Hosea are the last few swirls as the kingdom of Israel goes down the drain." This book represents God's last gracious effort to plug the drain. Hosea's personal tragedy is an intense illustration of Israel's national tragedy. It is a story of one-sided love and faithfulness that represents the relationship between Israel and God. As Gomer is married to Hosea, so Israel is betrothed to God. Both relationships gradually disintegrate—Gomer runs after other men, and Israel runs after other gods. Israel's spiritual adultery is illustrated in Gomer's physical adultery. The development of the book can be traced in two parts: the adulterous wife and faithful husband (1—3) and the adulterous Israel and faithful Lord (4—14).

The Adulterous Wife and Faithful Husband (1—3): Hosea marries a woman named Gomer who bears him three children appropriately named by God as signs to Israel. Jezreel, Lo-Ruhamah, and Lo-Ammi mean "God Scatters," "Not Pitied," and "Not My People." Similarly, God will judge and scatter Israel because of her sin.

Gomer seeks other lovers and deserts Hosea. In spite of the depth to which her sin carries her, Hosea redeems her from the slave market and restores her.

The Adulterous Israel and Faithful Lord (4—14): Because of his own painful experience, Hosea can feel some of the sorrow of God over the sinfulness of His people. His loyal love for Gomer is a reflection of God's concern for Israel. However, Israel has fallen into the dregs of sin and is hardened against God's gracious last appeal to return. The people have flagrantly violated all of God's commandments, and they are indicted by the holy God for their crimes. Even now God wants to heal and redeem them (7:1, 13), but in their arrogance and idolatry they rebel.

FOCUS	ADULTEROUS WIFE AND FAITHFUL HUSBAND			ADULTEROUS ISRAEL AND FAITHFUL LORD			
REFERENCE	1:1—	2:2—	3:1—	4:1—	6:4—	9:1—	11:1—14:9
DIVISION	PROPHETIC MARRIAGE	APPLICATION OF GOMER TO ISRAEL	RESTORATION OF GOMER	SPIRITUAL ADULTERY OF ISRAEL	REFUSAL OF ISRAEL TO REPENT	JUDGMENT OF ISRAEL BY GOD	RESTORATION OF ISRAEL TO GOD
TOPIC	MARRIAGE OF HOSEA			MESSAGE OF HOSEA			
	PERSONAL			NATIONAL			
LOCATION	NORTHERN KINGDOM OF ISRAEL						
TIME	c. 755–710 B.C.						

Chapters 9 and 10 give the verdict of the case God has just presented. Israel's disobedience will lead to her dispersion. "They sow the wind" (4—7), "and reap the whirlwind" (8—10). Israel spurns repentance, and the judgment of God can no longer be delayed.

God is holy (4—7) and just (8—10), but He is also loving and gracious (11—14). God must discipline, but because of His endless love, He will ultimately save and restore His wayward people. "How can I give you up, Ephraim? . . . I will heal their backsliding, I will love them freely, for My anger has turned away from him" (11:8; 14:4).

OUTLINE OF HOSEA

CHAPTER 1

The Introduction to the Book of Hosea

THE word of the LORD that came to Hosea
the son of Beeri, in the days of Uzziah,
[R]Jotham, [R]Ahaz, *and* Hezekiah, kings of Judah, and in the days of Jeroboam the son of
Joash, king of Israel. 2 Chr. 27 • 2 Chr. 28

Hosea's Marriage to Gomer

2 *When* the LORD began to speak by Hosea, the LORD said to Hosea:

[R]"Go, take yourself a wife of harlotry
And children of harlotry, Hos. 3:1
For [R]the land has committed great
[T]harlotry Jer. 2:13 • Spiritual adultery
By departing from the LORD."

The Children of Hosea and Gomer

3 So he went and took Gomer the daughter of Diblaim, and she conceived and bore
him a son.
4 Then the LORD said to him:

"Call his name Jezreel,
For in a little *while*
[R]I will avenge the bloodshed of Jezreel
on the house of Jehu, 2 Kin. 10:11
[R]And bring an end to the kingdom of the
house of Israel. 2 Kin. 15:8–10; 17:6, 23
5 [R]It shall come to pass in that day
That I will break the bow of Israel in
the Valley of Jezreel." 2 Kin. 15:29

6 And she conceived again and bore a
daughter. Then *God* said to him:

"Call her name [T]Lo-Ruhamah,
[R]For I will no longer have mercy on the
house of Israel, Lit. *No Mercy* • 2 Kin. 17:6
But I will utterly take them away.
7 [R]Yet I will have mercy on the house of
Judah, 2 Kin. 19:29–35
Will save them by the LORD their God,
And [R]will not save them by bow,
Nor by sword or battle,
By horses or horsemen." [Zech. 4:6]

8 Now when she had weaned Lo-Ruhamah, she conceived and bore a son.
9 Then *God* said:

"Call his name [T]Lo-Ammi, *Not My People*
For you *are* not My people,
And I will not be your *God.*

The Application of Future Restoration

10 "Yet [R]the number of the children of
Israel Gen. 22:17; 32:12
Shall be as the sand of the sea,
Which cannot be measured or
numbered.
[R]And it shall come to pass 1 Pet. 2:10
In the place where it was said to them,
'You *are* [T]not My people,' *Lo-Ammi*
There it shall be said to them,
'You *are* the sons of the living God.'
11 [R]Then the children of Judah and the
children of Israel Is. 11:11–13
Shall be gathered together,
And appoint for themselves one head;
And they shall come up out of the land,
For great *will be* the day of Jezreel!

CHAPTER 2

SAY to your brethren, 'My people,'
And to your sisters, 'Mercy *is shown.*'

Israel's Sin of Spiritual Adultery

2 "Bring[T] charges against your mother,
[T]bring charges; Or *Contend with* • Or *contend*
For [R]she *is* not My wife, nor *am* I her
Husband! Is. 50:1
Let her put away her [R]harlotries from
her sight, Ezek. 16:25
And her adulteries from between her
breasts;
3 Lest [R]I strip her naked Jer. 13:22, 26
And expose her, as in the day she was
[R]born, Ezek. 16:4–7, 22
And make her like a wilderness,
And set her like a dry land,
And slay her with [R]thirst. Amos 8:11–13

4 "I will not have mercy on her children,
For they *are* the children of harlotry.
5 For their mother has played the harlot;
She who conceived them has done
shamefully.
For she said, 'I will go after my lovers,
[R]Who give *me* my bread and my water,
My wool and my linen, Hos. 2:8, 12
My oil and my drink.'

Judgment of God

6 "Therefore, behold,
I will hedge up your way with thorns,
And [T]wall her in, Lit. *wall up her wall*
So that she cannot find her paths.
7 She will [T]chase her lovers, Or *pursue*
But not overtake them;
Yes, she will seek them, but not find
them.
Then she will say,
[R]'I will go and return to my [R]first
husband,
For then *it was* better for me than
now.' Luke 15:17, 18 • Ezek. 16:8; 23:4
8 For she did not [R]know Is. 1:3
That I gave her grain, new wine, and
oil,
And multiplied her silver and gold—
Which they prepared for Baal.

9 "Therefore I will return and take away
My grain in its time
And My new wine in its season,
And will take back My wool and My
linen,
Given to cover her nakedness.
10 Now [R]I will uncover her lewdness in the
sight of her lovers, Ezek. 16:37
And no one shall deliver her from My
hand.
11 [R]I will also cause all her mirth to cease,
Her feast days,
Her New Moons,
Her Sabbaths—
All her appointed feasts. Amos 5:21; 8:10

12 "And I will destroy her vines and her fig
trees,
Of which she has said,
'These *are* my rewards that my lovers
have given me.'
So I will make them a forest,
And the beasts of the field shall eat
them.
13 I will punish her
For the days of the Baals to which she
burned incense.
She decked herself with her earrings
and jewelry,
And went after her lovers.
Then she forgot Me," says the LORD.

Restoration of Israel

14 "Therefore, behold, I will allure her,
Will bring her into the wilderness,
And speak [T]comfort to her. Lit. *to her heart*
15 I will give her her vineyards from there,
And [R]the Valley of Achor as a door of
hope; Josh. 7:26
She shall sing there,
As in [R]the days of her youth,
[R]As in the day when she came up from
the land of Egypt. Ezek. 16:8–14 • Ex. 15:1

16 "And it shall be, in that day,"
Says the LORD,
"*That* you will call Me 'My Husband,'
And no longer call Me 'My Master,'
17 For [R]I will take from her mouth the
names of the Baals,

And they shall be remembered by their
name no more. Ex. 23:13
18 In that day I will make a [R]covenant for
them Job 5:23
With the beasts of the field,
With the birds of the air,
And *with* the creeping things of the
ground.
Bow and sword of battle [R]I will shatter
from the earth, Is. 2:4
To make them [R]lie down safely. Lev. 26:5

19 "I will betroth you to Me forever;
Yes, I will betroth you to Me
In righteousness and justice,
In lovingkindness and mercy;
20 I will betroth you to Me in faithfulness,
And you shall know the LORD.

21 "It shall come to pass in that day
That [R]I will answer," says the LORD;
"I will answer the heavens, Zech. 8:12
And they shall answer the earth.
22 The earth shall answer
With grain,
With new wine,
And with oil;
They shall answer [T]Jezreel. Lit. *God Will Sow*
23 Then [R]I will sow her for Myself in the
earth, Jer. 31:27
And I will have mercy on *her who had*
[T]not obtained mercy; Heb. *Lo-Ruhamah*
Then [R]I will say to *those who were* [T]not
My people, Hos. 1:10 • Heb. *Lo-Ammi*
'You *are* [T]My people!' Heb. *Ammi*
And they shall say, '*You are* my God!' "

CHAPTER 3

The Restoration of Gomer to Hosea

THEN the LORD said to me, "Go again, love
a woman *who is* loved by a [R]lover[T] and is
committing adultery, just like the love of the
LORD for the children of Israel, who look to
other gods and love *the* raisin cakes *of the*
pagans." Jer. 3:20 • Lit. *friend* or *husband*
2 So I bought her for myself for [T]fifteen
shekels of silver, and [T]one and one-half ho-
mers of barley. $1,920 • 9.786 bu.
3 And I said to her, "You shall [R]stay with
me many days; you shall not play the harlot,
nor shall you have a man; thus I *will* also *be*
toward you." Deut. 21:13
4 For the children of Israel shall abide
many days [R]without king or prince, without
sacrifice or sacred pillar, without [R]ephod or
[R]teraphim. Hos. 10:3 • Ex. 28:4–12 • Judg. 17:5; 18:14, 17
5 Afterward the children of Israel shall
return, seek the LORD their God and [R]David
their king, and fear the LORD and His goodness in the [R]latter days. Jer. 30:9 • [Is. 2:2, 3]

CHAPTER 4

Rejection of the Knowledge of God

HEAR the word of the LORD,
You children of Israel,
For the LORD *brings* a [R]charge against
the inhabitants of the land: Is. 1:18

"There is no truth or mercy
Or knowledge of God in the land.
2 *By* swearing and lying,
Killing and stealing and committing
adultery,
They break all restraint,
With bloodshed after bloodshed.
3 Therefore [R]the land will mourn;
And [R]everyone who dwells there will
waste away
With the beasts of the field
And the birds of the air;
Even the fish of the sea will be taken
away. Amos 5:16; 8:8 • Zeph. 1:3

4 "Now let no man contend, or reprove
another,
For your people *are* like those [R]who
contend with the priest. Deut. 17:12
5 Therefore you shall stumble [R]in the day;
The prophet also shall stumble with you
in the night;
And I will destroy your mother. Jer. 15:8
6 [R]My people are destroyed for lack of
knowledge. Is. 5:13
Because you have rejected knowledge,
I also will reject you from being priest
for Me;
[R]Because you have forgotten the law of
your God, Ezek. 22:26
I also will forget your children.

7 "The more they increased,
The more they sinned against Me;
I will change their glory into shame.
8 They eat up the sin of My people;
They set their heart on their iniquity.
9 And it shall be: like people, like priest.
So I will punish them for their ways,
And [T]reward them for their deeds. *repay*
10 For [R]they shall eat, but not have
enough;
They shall commit harlotry, but not
increase;
Because they have ceased obeying the
LORD. Lev. 26:26

11 "Harlotry, wine, and new wine [R]enslave
the heart. Is. 5:12; 28:7

Idolatry of Israel

12 My people ask counsel from their
[R]wooden *idols*, Jer. 2:27
And their [T]staff informs them.
For [R]the spirit of harlotry has caused
them to stray,

And they have played the harlot against
their God. Diviner's rod • Is. 44:19, 20
13 [R]They offer sacrifices on the
mountaintops,
And burn incense on the hills,
Under oaks, poplars, and terebinths,
Because their shade *is* good.
[R]Therefore your daughters commit
harlotry, Is. 1:29; 57:5, 7 • Amos 7:17
And your brides commit adultery.

14 "I will not punish your daughters when
they commit harlotry,
Nor your brides when they commit
adultery;
For *the men* themselves go apart with
harlots,
And offer sacrifices with a
[R]ritual harlot. Deut. 23:18
Therefore people *who* do not
understand will be trampled.

15 "Though you, Israel, play the harlot,
Let not Judah offend.
[R]Do not come up to Gilgal, Hos. 9:15; 12:11
Nor go up to [T]Beth Aven,
Nor swear an oath, *saying*, 'As the LORD
lives'— Lit. *House of Idolatry* or *Wickedness*

16 "For Israel [R]is stubborn
Like a stubborn calf; Jer. 3:6; 7:24; 8:5
Now the LORD will let them forage
Like a lamb in [T]open country. *a large place*

17 "Ephraim *is* joined to idols,
[R]Let him alone. Matt. 15:14
18 Their drink [T]is rebellion, Or *has turned aside*
They commit harlotry continually.
Her [T]rulers dearly love dishonor. *shields*
19 [R]The wind has wrapped her up in its
wings,
And [R]they shall be ashamed because of
their sacrifices. Jer. 51:1 • Is. 1:29

CHAPTER 5

Judgment on Israel

"HEAR this, O priests!
Take heed, O house of Israel!
Give ear, O house of the king!
For [T]yours *is* the judgment,
Because [R]you have been a snare to
Mizpah Or *to you* • Hos. 6:9
And a net spread on Tabor.
2 The revolters are [R]deeply involved in
slaughter,
Though I rebuke them all. Is. 29:15
3 [R]I know Ephraim,
And Israel is not hidden from Me;
For now, O Ephraim, [R]you commit
harlotry;
Israel is defiled. Amos 3:2; 5:12 • Hos. 4:17

4 "They[T] do not direct their deeds
Toward turning to their God,
For the spirit of harlotry is in their
midst, Or *Their deeds will not allow them to turn*
And they do not know the LORD.
5 The [R]pride of Israel testifies to his face;
Therefore Israel and Ephraim stumble
in their iniquity;
Judah also stumbles with them. Hos. 7:10

6 "With their flocks and herds
[R]They shall go to seek the LORD,
But they will not find *Him;* Prov. 1:28
He has withdrawn Himself from them.
7 They have [R]dealt treacherously with the
LORD, Jer. 3:20
For they have begotten [T]pagan children.
Now a New Moon shall devour them
and their heritage. Lit. *strange*

8 "Blow[R] the ram's horn in Gibeah,
The trumpet in Ramah! Joel 2:1
[R]Cry aloud *at* Beth Aven, Is. 10:30
'*Look* behind you, O Benjamin!'
9 Ephraim shall be desolate in the day of
rebuke;
Among the tribes of Israel I make
known what is sure.

10 "The princes of Judah are like those who
[R]remove a landmark;
I will pour out my wrath on them like
water. Deut. 19:14; 27:17
11 Ephraim is [R]oppressed *and* broken in
judgment,
Because he willingly walked by [R]*human*
precept. Deut. 28:33 • Mic. 6:16
12 Therefore I *will be* to Ephraim like a
moth,
And to the house of Judah [R]like
rottenness. Prov. 12:4

13 "When Ephraim saw his sickness,
And Judah *saw* his [R]wound, Jer. 30:12–15
Then Ephraim went [R]to Assyria
And sent to King Jareb;
Yet he cannot cure you,
Nor heal you of your wound. 2 Kin. 15:19
14 For [R]I *will be* like a lion to Ephraim,
And like a young lion to the house of
Judah.
[R]I, *even* I, will tear *them* and go away;
I will take *them* away, and no one shall
rescue. Lam. 3:10 • Ps. 50:22

Eventual Restoration of Israel

15 I will return again to My place
Till they [T]acknowledge their offense.
Then they will seek My face;
In their affliction they will diligently
seek Me." Lit. *become guilty*

CHAPTER 6

COME, and let us return to the LORD;
For He has torn, but He will heal us;
He has stricken, but He will bind us up.
2 [R]After two days He will revive us;
On the third day He will raise us up,
That we may live in His sight. [1 Cor. 15:4] ☆
3 [R]Let us know, Is. 54:13
Let us pursue the knowledge of the LORD.
His going forth is established [R]as the morning; 2 Sam. 23:4
[R]He will come to us [R]like the rain,
Like the latter *and* former rain to the earth. Ps. 72:6 • Job 29:23

Willful Transgression of the Covenant

4 "O Ephraim, what shall I do to you?
O Judah, what shall I do to you?
For your faithfulness is like a morning cloud,
And like the early dew it goes away.
5 Therefore I have hewn *them* by the prophets,
I have slain them by [R]the words of My mouth; [Jer. 23:29]
And [T]your judgments *are like* light *that* goes forth. Or *the judgments on you*
6 For I desire [T]mercy and not sacrifice,
And the knowledge of God more than burnt offerings. Or *faithfulness* or *loyalty*

7 "But like [T]men they transgressed the covenant; Or *Adam*
There they dealt treacherously with Me.
8 [R]Gilead *is* a city of evildoers, Hos. 12:11
And is [T]defiled with blood. Lit. *foot tracked*
9 As bands of robbers lie in wait for a man,
So the company of [R]priests [R]murder on the way to Shechem; Hos. 5:1 • Jer. 7:9, 10
Surely they commit lewdness.
10 I have seen a horrible thing in the house of Israel:
There *is* the [T]harlotry of Ephraim;
Israel is defiled. Spiritual adultery
11 Also, O Judah, a harvest is appointed for you,
When I return the captives of My people.

CHAPTER 7

Willful Refusal to Return to the Lord

"WHEN I would have healed Israel,
Then the iniquity of Ephraim was uncovered,
And the wickedness of Samaria.
For [R]they have committed fraud;
The thief comes in; Hos. 5:1
A band of robbers takes spoil outside.
2 They [T]do not consider in their hearts
That [R]I remember all their wickedness;
Now their own deeds have surrounded them; Lit. *do not say to* • Jer. 14:10; 17:1
They are before My face.
3 They make a [R]king glad with their wickedness, Hos. 1:1
And princes [R]with their lies. [Rom. 1:32]

4 "They[R] *are* all adulterers. Jer. 9:2; 23:10
Like an oven heated by a baker—
He ceases stirring *the fire* after kneading the dough,
Until it is leavened.
5 In the day of our king
Princes have made *him* sick, [T]inflamed with [R]wine; Lit. *with the heat of* • Is. 28:1, 7
He stretched out his hand with scoffers.
6 They prepare their heart like an oven,
While they lie in wait;
Their baker sleeps all night;
In the morning it burns like a flaming fire.
7 They are all hot, like an oven,
And have devoured their judges;
All their kings have fallen.
[R]*There is* none among them who calls upon Me. Is. 64:7

8 "Ephraim [R]has mixed himself among the peoples; Ps. 106:35
Ephraim is a cake unturned.
9 [R]Aliens have devoured his strength,
But he does not know *it;*
Yes, gray hairs are here and there on him,
Yet he does not know *it.* Hos. 8:7
10 And the [R]pride of Israel testifies to his face,
But [R]they do not return to the LORD their God,
Nor seek Him for all this. Hos. 5:5 • Is. 9:13

11 "Ephraim[R] also is like a silly dove, without [T]sense— Hos. 11:11 • Lit. *heart*
[R]They call to Egypt, Is. 30:3
They go to [R]Assyria. Hos. 5:13; 8:9
12 Wherever they go, I will [R]spread My net on them;
I will bring them down like birds of the air;
I will chastise them
[R]According to what their congregation has heard. Ezek. 12:13 • Lev. 26:14

13 "Woe to them, for they have fled from Me!
Destruction to them,
Because they have transgressed against Me!
Though [R]I redeemed them, Mic. 6:4
Yet they have spoken lies against Me.

14 [R]They did not cry out to Me with their
heart Job 35:9, 10
When they wailed upon their beds.

"They assemble together for grain and
new [R]wine,
They rebel against Me; Amos 2:8
15 Though I disciplined *and* strengthened
their arms,
Yet they devise evil against Me;
16 They return, *but* not [T]to the Most High;
They are like a deceitful bow. Or *upward*
Their princes shall fall by the sword
For the [R]cursings of their tongue.
This *shall be* their derision [R]in the land
of Egypt. Ps. 73:9 • Hos. 8:13; 9:3

CHAPTER 8

Willful Idolatry

"SET the [T]trumpet to your mouth!
He shall come like an eagle against
the house of the LORD,
Because they have transgressed My
covenant *ram's horn*, Heb. *shophar*
And rebelled against My law.
2 [R]Israel will cry to Me, Ps. 78:34
'My God, [R]we know You!' Titus 1:16
3 Israel has cast off the good;
The enemy will pursue him.

4 "They[R] set up kings, but not by Me;
They made princes, and I did not
acknowledge *it*.
From their silver and gold
They made idols for themselves—
That they might be cut off. 2 Kin. 15:23, 25
5 Your calf [T]is rejected, O Samaria!
My anger is aroused against them.
[R]How long *will it be* until they attain to
innocence? Or *has rejected you* • Jer. 13:27
6 For from Israel *is* even this:
A [R]workman made it, and it *is* not God;
But the calf of Samaria shall be broken
to pieces. Is. 40:19

7 "They[R] sow the wind, Prov. 22:8
And reap the whirlwind.
The stalk has no bud;
It shall never produce meal.
If it should produce,
[R]Aliens would swallow it up. Hos. 7:9
8 [R]Israel is swallowed up;
Now they are among the Gentiles
[R]Like a vessel in which *there is* no
pleasure. 2 Kin. 17:6 • Jer. 22:28; 25:34
9 For they have gone up to Assyria,
Like a wild donkey alone by itself;
Ephraim [R]has hired lovers. Ezek. 16:33, 34
10 Yes, though they have hired among the
nations,
Now [R]I will gather them; Ezek. 16:37; 22:20
And they shall sorrow a little,
Because of the [T]burden of [R]the king of
princes. Or *oracle* or *proclamation* • Is. 10:8

11 "Because Ephraim has made many altars
for sin,
They have become for him altars for
sinning.
12 I have written for him [R]the great things
of My law,
But they were considered a strange
thing. [Deut. 4:6–8]
13 *For* the sacrifices of My offerings [R]they
sacrifice flesh and eat *it*, Zech. 7:6
[R]*But* the LORD does not accept them.
[R]Now He will remember their iniquity
and punish their sins. Jer. 14:10 • Amos 8:7
They shall return to Egypt.

14 "For Israel has forgotten his Maker,
And has built [T]temples; Or *palaces*
Judah also has multiplied [R]fortified
cities; Jer. 17:27
But I will send fire upon his cities,
And it shall devour his [T]palaces." *citadels*

CHAPTER 9

Judgment of Dispersion

DO[R] not rejoice, O Israel, with joy like
other peoples,
For you have played the harlot against
your God.
You have loved *for* [R]reward on every
threshing floor. Is. 22:12, 13 • Jer. 44:17
2 The threshing floor and the winepress
Shall not feed them,
And the new wine shall fail in her.

3 They shall not dwell in [R]the LORD's
land, [Lev. 25:23]
[R]But Ephraim shall return to Egypt,
And [R]shall eat unclean *things* in
Assyria. Hos. 7:16; 8:13 • Ezek. 4:13
4 They shall not offer wine *offerings* to
the LORD,
Nor [R]shall their [R]sacrifices be pleasing
to Him.
It shall be like bread of mourners to
them;
All who eat it shall be defiled.
For their bread *shall be* for their life;
It shall not come into the house of the
LORD. Jer. 6:20 • Hos. 8:13

5 What will you do in the appointed day,
And in the day of the feast of the LORD?
6 For indeed they are gone because of
destruction.
Egypt shall gather them up;
Memphis shall bury them.
[R]Nettles shall possess their valuables of
silver; Is. 5:6; 7:23
Thorns *shall be* in their tents.

7 The days of punishment have come;
The days of recompense have come.
Israel [R]knows! Is. 10:3
The prophet *is* a [R]fool, Lam. 2:14
[R]The spiritual man *is* insane, Mic. 2:11
Because of the greatness of your
iniquity and great enmity.
8 The [R]watchman of Ephraim *is* with my
God;
But the prophet *is* a [T]fowler's snare in
all his ways, Ezek. 3:17; 33:7 • *bird trapper's*
And enmity in the house of his God.
9 [R]They are deeply corrupted, Hos. 10:9
As in the days of [R]Gibeah. Judg. 19:22
He will remember their iniquity;
He will punish their sins.

Judgment of Barrenness

10 "I found Israel
Like grapes in the [R]wilderness;
I saw your fathers Jer. 2:2
As the [R]firstfruits on the fig tree in its
first season. Is. 28:4
But they went to [R]Baal Peor, Num. 25:3
And [T]separated themselves *to that*
shame; Or *dedicated*
[R]They became an abomination like the
thing they loved. Ps. 81:12
11 *As for* Ephraim, their glory shall fly
away like a bird—
No birth, no pregnancy, and no
conception!
12 Though they bring up their children,
Yet I will bereave them to the last man.
Yes, [R]woe to them when I depart from
them! Deut. 31:17
13 Just [R]as I saw Ephraim like Tyre,
planted in a pleasant place,
So Ephraim will bring out his children
to the murderer." Ezek. 26—28

14 Give them, O LORD—
What will You give?
Give them [R]a miscarrying womb
And dry breasts. Luke 23:29

15 "All their wickedness *is* in [R]Gilgal,
For there I hated them. Hos. 4:15; 12:11
Because of the evil of their deeds
I will drive them from My house;
I will love them no more.
[R]All their princes *are* rebellious. Is. 1:23
16 Ephraim is [R]stricken,
Their root is dried up;
They shall bear no fruit.
Yes, were they to bear children,
I would kill the beloved *fruit* of their
womb." Hos. 5:11

17 My God will [R]cast them away,
Because they did not obey Him;
And they shall be [R]wanderers among
the nations. [Zech. 10:6] • Lev. 26:33

CHAPTER 10

Judgment of Destruction

ISRAEL [R]empties *his* vine;
He brings forth fruit for himself.
According to the multitude of his fruit
[R]He has increased the altars;
According to the bounty of his land
They have embellished *his* sacred
pillars. Nah. 2:2 • Jer. 2:28
2 Their heart is [T]divided; In loyalty
Now they are held guilty.
He will break down their altars;
He will ruin their sacred pillars.

3 For now they say,
"We have no king,
Because we did not fear the LORD.
And as for a king, what would he do for
us?"
4 They have spoken words,
Swearing falsely in making a covenant.
Thus judgment springs up [R]like Amos 5:7
hemlock in the furrows of the field.

5 The inhabitants of Samaria fear
Because of the [R]calf of Beth Aven.
For its people mourn for it, Hos. 8:5, 6
And its priests shriek for it—
Because its glory has departed from it.
6 *The idol* also shall be carried to Assyria
As a present for King [R]Jareb.
Ephraim shall receive shame,
And Israel shall be ashamed of his own
counsel. Hos. 5:13

7 *As for* Samaria, her king is cut off
Like a twig on the water.
8 Also the [R]high places of [T]Aven, [R]the sin
of Israel, Hos. 4:15 • Lit. *Idolatry* • 1 Kin. 13:34
Shall be destroyed.
The thorn and thistle shall grow on
their altars;
[R]They shall say to the mountains, "Cover
us!" Luke 23:30
And to the hills, "Fall on us!"

9 "O Israel, you have sinned from the days
of [R]Gibeah; Hos. 9:9
There they stood.
The battle in Gibeah against the
children of *iniquity
Did not [T]overtake them. Or *overcome*
10 When *it is* My desire, I will chasten
them.
Peoples shall be gathered against them
When I bind them [T]for their two
transgressions. Or *in their two habitations*
11 Ephraim *is* [R]a trained heifer [Mic. 4:13]
That loves to thresh *grain;*

10:9 So with many Heb. mss., LXX, Vg.; MT *unruliness*

But I harnessed her fair neck,
I will make Ephraim [T]pull *a plow*.
Judah shall plow; Lit. *to ride*
Jacob shall break his clods."

12 Sow for yourselves righteousness;
Reap in mercy;
[R]Break up your fallow ground,
For *it is* time to seek the LORD,
Till He [R]comes and rains righteousness
on you. Jer. 4:3 • Hos. 6:3

13 [R]You have plowed wickedness;
You have reaped iniquity. [Prov. 22:8]
You have eaten the fruit of lies,
Because you trusted in your own way,
In the multitude of your mighty men.
14 Therefore tumult shall arise among
your people,
And all your fortresses shall be
plundered
As Shalman plundered Beth Arbel in
the day of battle—
A mother dashed in pieces upon *her*
children.
15 Thus it shall be done to you, O Bethel,
Because of your great wickedness.
In a morning the king of Israel
Shall be cut off utterly.

CHAPTER 11

God's Love for Israel

"WHEN Israel *was* a [T]child, I loved
him, Or *youth*
And out of Egypt I called My son.
2 *As* they called them,
So they [R]went from them; 2 Kin. 17:13–15
They sacrificed to the Baals,
And burned incense to carved images.

3 "I[R] taught Ephraim to walk,
Taking them by their arms;
But they did not know that [R]I healed
them. Deut. 1:31; 32:10, 11 • Ex. 15:26
4 I drew them with [T]gentle cords,
With bands of love, Lit. *of a man*
And I was to them as those who take
the yoke from their [T]neck. Lit. *jaw*
[R]I stooped *and* fed them. Ps. 78:25

5 "He shall not return to the land of
Egypt;
But the Assyrian shall be his king,
Because they refused to repent.
6 And the sword shall slash in his cities,
Devour his districts,
And consume *them*,
Because of their own counsels.
7 My people are bent on [R]backsliding
from Me. Jer. 3:6, 7; 8:5
Though [T]they call to the Most High,
None at all exalt *Him*. The prophets

8 "How can I give you up, Ephraim?
How can I hand you over, Israel?
How can I make you like Admah?
How can I set you like Zeboiim?
My heart [T]churns within Me;
My sympathy is stirred. Lit. *turns over*
9 I will not execute the fierceness of My
anger;
I will not again destroy Ephraim.
[R]For I *am* God, and not man, Num. 23:19
The Holy One in your midst;
And I will not come with terror.

10 "They shall walk after the LORD.
[R]He will roar like a lion.
When He roars,
Then *His* sons shall come trembling
from the west; [Joel 3:16]
11 They shall come trembling like a bird
from Egypt,
[R]Like a dove from the land of Assyria.
[R]And I will let them dwell in their
houses,"
Says the LORD. Is. 11:11; 60:8 • Ezek. 28:25, 26
12 "Ephraim has encompassed Me with lies,
And the house of Israel with deceit;
But Judah still walks with God,
Even with the [T]Holy One *who is*
faithful. Or *holy ones*

CHAPTER 12

Israel's Continuing Sin

"EPHRAIM feeds on the wind,
And pursues the east wind;
He daily increases lies and [T]desolation.
[R]Also they make a [T]covenant with the
Assyrians, *ruin* • 2 Kin. 17:4 • Or *treaty*
And [R]oil is carried to Egypt. Is. 30:6

2 "The[R] LORD also *brings* a [T]charge against
Judah,
And will punish Jacob according to his
ways; Mic. 6:2 • A legal complaint
According to his deeds He will
recompense him.
3 He took his brother [R]by the heel in the
womb,
And in his strength he [R]struggled with
God. Gen. 25:26 • Gen. 32:24–28
4 Yes, he struggled with the Angel and
prevailed;
He wept, and sought favor from Him.
He found Him *in* [R]Bethel, [Gen. 28:12–19]
And there He spoke to us—
5 That is, the LORD God of hosts.
The LORD *is* His [R]memorial. Ex. 3:15
6 [R]So you, by *the help of* your God, return;
Observe mercy and justice, Mic. 6:8
And wait on your God continually.

7 "A cunning [T]Canaanite! Or *merchant*
[R]Deceitful scales *are* in his hand;
He loves to oppress. Amos 8:5
8 And Ephraim said,
'Surely[R] I have become rich, Rev. 3:17
I have found wealth for myself;
In all my labors
They shall find in me no iniquity that *is*
sin.'

9 "But I *am* the LORD your God,
Ever since the land of Egypt;
I will again make you dwell in tents,
As in the days of the appointed feast.
10 [R]I have also spoken by the prophets,
And have multiplied visions; 2 Kin. 17:13
I have given [T]symbols through the
witness of the prophets." Or *parables*

11 Though [R]Gilead *has* idols— Hos. 6:8
Surely they are [T]vanity— *worthless*
Though they sacrifice bulls in [R]Gilgal,
Indeed their altars *shall be* heaps in the
furrows of the field. Hos. 9:15

12 Jacob fled to the country of Syria;
[R]Israel served for a spouse, Gen. 29:20, 28
And for a wife he tended *sheep*.
13 [R]By a prophet the LORD brought Israel
out of Egypt, Ex. 12:50, 51; 13:3
And by a prophet he was preserved.
14 Ephraim [R]provoked *Him* to anger most
bitterly; Ezek. 18:10–13
Therefore his Lord will leave on him his
bloodguilt,
And return his reproach upon him.

CHAPTER 13

WHEN Ephraim spoke, trembling,
He exalted *himself* in Israel;
But when he offended in Baal, he died.
2 Now they sin more and more,
And have made for themselves molded
images,
Idols of their silver, according to their
skill;
All of it *is* the work of craftsmen.
They say of them,
"Let [T]the men who sacrifice kiss the
calves!" Or *those who offer human sacrifice*
3 Therefore they shall be like the morning
cloud
And like the early dew that passes
away,
[R]Like chaff blown off from a threshing
floor Dan. 2:35
And like smoke from a chimney.

4 "Yet [R]I *am* the LORD your God Is. 43:11
Ever since the land of Egypt,
And you shall know no God but Me;
For *there is* no savior besides Me.
5 I [T]knew you in the wilderness,
In the land of great drought. Cared for you
6 [R]When they had pasture, they were
filled; Deut. 8:12, 14; 32:13–15
They were filled and their heart was
exalted;
Therefore they forgot Me.

7 "So [R]I will be to them like a lion;
Like [R]a leopard by the road I will
observe *them;* Lam. 3:10 • Jer. 5:6
8 I will meet them [R]like a bear deprived
of her cubs;
I will tear open their rib cage,
And there I will devour them like a lion.
The wild beast shall tear them. 2 Sam. 17:8

9 "O Israel, you are destroyed,
But [T]your help *is* from Me. Lit. *in your help*
10 *I will be your King;
[R]Where *is any other,* Deut. 32:38
That he may save you in all your cities?
And your judges to whom [R]you said,
'Give me a king and princes'? 1 Sam. 8:5, 6
11 I gave you a king in My anger,
And took *him* away in My wrath.

12 "The[R] iniquity of Ephraim *is* bound up;
His sin *is* stored up. Deut. 32:34, 35
13 [R]The sorrows of a woman in childbirth
shall come upon him.
He *is* an unwise son,
For he should not stay long where
children are born. Is. 13:8

14 "I will ransom them from the [T]power of
[T]the grave; Lit. *hand* • Or *Sheol*
I will redeem them from death.
O Death, *I will be your plagues!
O Grave, *I will be your destruction!
[R]Pity is hidden from My eyes. Jer. 15:6

15 Though he is fruitful among *his*
brethren,
[R]An east wind shall come;
The wind of the LORD shall come up
from the wilderness.
Then his spring shall become dry,
And his fountain shall be dried up.
He shall plunder the treasury of every
desirable prize. Jer. 4:11, 12
16 Samaria *is held guilty,
For she has [R]rebelled against her God.
They shall fall by the sword,
Their infants shall be dashed in pieces,
And their women with child [R]ripped
open. 2 Kin. 8:12 • 2 Kin. 15:16

13:10 LXX, Syr., Tg., Vg. *Where is your king?*
13:14 LXX *Where is your punishment?*
13:14 LXX *Where is your sting?*
13:16 LXX *shall be disfigured*

CHAPTER 14

God's Promise to Restore Israel

O ISRAEL, [R]return to the LORD your God,
For you have stumbled because of your iniquity; [Joel 2:13]
2 Take words with you,
And return to the LORD.
Say to Him,
"Take away all iniquity;
Receive *us* graciously,
For we will offer the [R]sacrifices* of our lips. [Heb. 13:15]
3 Assyria shall [R]not save us,
We will not ride on horses, Hos. 7:11; 10:13
Nor will we say anymore to the work of our hands,
'*You are* our gods.'
For in You the fatherless finds mercy."

4 "I will heal their [R]backsliding,
I will [R]love them freely,
For My anger has turned away from him. Jer. 14:7 • [Eph. 1:6]
5 I will be like the [R]dew to Israel; Prov. 19:12
He shall [T]grow like the lily, Lit. *bud* or *sprout*
And lengthen his roots like Lebanon.
6 His branches shall [T]spread; Lit. *go*
His beauty shall be like an olive tree,
And his fragrance like Lebanon.
7 [R]Those who dwell under his shadow shall return; Dan. 4:12
They shall be revived *like* grain,
And [T]grow like the vine. Lit. *bud*
Their [T]scent *shall be* like the wine of Lebanon. Lit. *remembrance*

8 "Ephraim *shall say,*
'What have I to do anymore with idols?'
I have heard and observed him.
I *am* like a green cypress tree;
[R]Your fruit is found in Me." [John 15:4]

9 Who *is* wise?
Let him understand these things.
Who is prudent?
Let him know them.
For [R]the ways of the LORD *are* right;
The righteous walk in them, [Prov. 10:29]
But transgressors stumble in them.

14:2 Lit. *bull calves;* LXX *fruit*

THE BOOK OF
JOEL

THE BOOK OF JOEL

Disaster strikes the southern kingdom of Judah without warning. An ominous black cloud descends upon the land—the dreaded locusts. In a matter of hours, every living green thing has been stripped bare. Joel, God's spokesman during the reign of Joash (835–796 B.C.), seizes this occasion to proclaim God's message. Although the locust plague has been a terrible judgment for sin, God's future judgments during the day of the Lord will make that plague pale by comparison. In that day, God will destroy His enemies, but bring unparalleled blessing to those who faithfully obey Him.

The Hebrew name *Yo'el* means "Yahweh Is God." This name is appropriate to the theme of the book, which emphasizes God's sovereign work in history. The courses of nature and nations are in His hand. The Greek equivalent is *Ioel*, and the Latin is *Joel*.

THE AUTHOR OF JOEL

Although there are several other Joels in the Bible, the prophet Joel is known only from this book. In the introductory verse, Joel identifies himself as the son of Pethuel (1:1), meaning "Persuaded of God." His frequent references to Zion and the house of the Lord (1:9, 13, 14; 2:15–17, 23, 32; 3:1, 5, 6, 16, 17, 20, 21) suggest that he probably lived not far from Jerusalem. Because of his statements about the priesthood in 1:13, 14 and 2:17, some think Joel was a priest as well as a prophet. In any case, Joel was a clear, concise, and uncompromising preacher of repentance.

THE TIME OF JOEL

Since this book includes no explicit time references, it cannot be dated with certainty. Some commentators assign a late date (usually postexilic) to Joel for these reasons: (1) It does not mention the northern kingdom and indicates it was written after the 722 B.C. demise of Israel. (2) The references to priests but not kings fit the postexilic period. (3) Joel does not refer to Assyria, Syria, or Babylon, perhaps because these countries have already been overthrown. (4) If Joel 3:2 refers to the Babylonian captivity, this also supports the postexilic date. (5) The mention of the Greeks in 3:6 argues for a late date.

Commentators who believe Joel was written in the ninth century B.C. answer the above arguments in this way: (1) Joel's failure to mention the northern kingdom is an argument from silence. His prophecy was directed to Judah, not Israel. (2) Other early prophets omit references to a king (Obadiah, Jonah, Nahum, and Habakkuk). This also fits the political situation during 841–835 B.C. when Athaliah usurped the throne upon the death of her son Ahaziah. Joash, the legitimate heir to the throne, was a minor and protected by the high priest Jehoiada. When Athaliah was removed from power in 835, Joash came to the throne but ruled under the regency of Jehoiada. Thus, the prominence of the priests and lack of reference to a king in Joel fit this historical context. (3) It is true that Joel does not refer to Assyria or Babylon, but the countries Joel mentions are more crucial. They include Phoenicia, Philistia, Egypt, and Edom—countries prominent in the ninth century but not later. Assyria and Babylon are not mentioned because they had not yet reached a position of power. Also, if Joel was postexilic, a reference to Persia would be expected. (4) Joel 3:2 does not refer to the Babylonian captivity but to an event that has not yet occurred. (5) Greeks are mentioned in Assyrian records from the eighth century B.C. It is just an assumption to state that the Hebrews had no knowledge of the Greeks at an early time.

Evidence also points to a sharing of material between Joel and Amos (cf. Joel 3:16 and Amos 1:2; Joel 3:18 and Amos 9:13). The context of the books suggests that Amos, an eighth-century prophet, borrowed from Joel. Also, Joel's style is more like that of Hosea and Amos than of the postexilic writers. The evidence seems to favor a date of about 835 B.C. for Joel. Since Joel does not mention idolatry, it may have been written after the purge of Baal worship and most other forms of idolatry in the early reign of Joash under Jehoiada the priest. As an early prophet of Judah, Joel would have been a contemporary of Elisha in Israel.

THE CHRIST OF JOEL

Christ promised to send the Holy Spirit after His ascension to the Father (John 16:7–15; Acts 1:8). When this was fulfilled on the day of Pentecost, Peter said, "This is what was spoken by the prophet Joel" (Joel 2:28–32; Acts 2:16–21). Joel also portrays Christ as the One who will judge the nations in the Valley of Jehoshaphat in 3:2, 12.

KEYS TO JOEL

Key Word: The Great and Terrible Day of the Lord—The key theme of Joel is the day of the Lord in retrospect and prospect. Joel uses the terrible locust plague that has recently occurred in Judah to illustrate the coming day of judgment when God will directly intervene in human history to vindicate His righteousness. This will be a time of unparalleled retribution upon Israel (2:1–11) and the whole nation (3:1–17), but this time will culminate in great blessing and salvation for all who trust in the Lord (2:18–32; 3:18–21). "And it shall come to pass *that* whoever calls on the name of the LORD shall be saved" (2:32).

Joel is written as a warning to the people of Judah of their need to turn humbly to the Lord with penitent hearts (2:12–17) so that God can bless rather than buffet them. If they continue to spurn God's gracious call to repentance, judgment will be inevitable. Joel stresses the sovereign power of God over nature and nations, and points out how God uses nature to get the attention of people.

Key Verses: Joel 2:11, 28, 29—"The LORD gives voice before His army, for His camp is very great; for strong *is the One* who executes His word. For the day of the LORD *is* great and very terrible; who can abide it?" (2:11).

"And it shall come to pass afterward that I will pour out My Spirit on all flesh; your sons and your daughters shall prophesy, your old men shall dream dreams, your young men shall see visions; and also on *My* menservants and on *My* maidservants I will pour out My Spirit in those days" (2:28, 29).

Key Chapter: Joel 2—The prophet calls for Judah's repentance and promises God's repentance (2:13, 14) from His planned judgment upon Judah if they do indeed turn to Him. Though the offer is clearly given, Judah continues to rebel against the Lord, and judgment is to follow. In that judgment, however, is God's promise of His later outpouring, fulfilled initially on the day of Pentecost (Acts 2:16ff.) and ultimately when Christ returns for the culmination of the day of the Lord.

SURVEY OF JOEL

The brief book Joel develops the crucial theme of the coming day of the Lord (1:15; 2:1, 2, 11, 31; 3:14, 18). It is a time of awesome judgment upon people and nations that have rebelled against God. But it is also a time of future blessing upon those who have trusted in Him. The theme of disaster runs throughout the book (locust plagues, famine, raging fires, invading armies, celestial phenomena), but promises of hope are interspersed with the pronouncements of coming judgment. The basic outline of Joel is: the day of the Lord in retrospect (1:1–20) and the day of the Lord in prospect (2:1—3:21).

The Day of the Lord in Retrospect (1:1-20): Joel begins with an account of a recent locust plague that has devastated the land. The black cloud of insects has stripped the grapevines and fruit trees and ruined the grain harvest. The economy has been brought to a further standstill by a drought and the people are in a desperate situation.

The Day of the Lord in Prospect (2:1—3:21): Joel makes effective use of this natural catastrophe as an illustration of a far greater judgment to come. Compared to the terrible day of the Lord, the destruction by the locusts will seem insignificant. The land will be invaded by a swarming army; like locusts they will be speedy and voracious. The desolation caused by this army will be dreadful: "The day of the LORD *is* great and very terrible; who can endure it?" (2:11).

Even so, it is not too late for the people to avert disaster. The prophetic warning is designed to bring them to the point of repentance (2:12–17). " 'Now, therefore,' says the LORD, 'turn to me with all your heart, with fasting, with weeping, and with mourning' " (2:12). But God's gracious offer falls on deaf ears.

Ultimately, the swarming, creeping, stripping, and gnawing locusts (1:4; 2:25) will come again in a fiercer form. But God promises that judgment

FOCUS	DAY OF THE LORD IN RETROSPECT		DAY OF THE LORD IN PROSPECT	
REFERENCE	1:1	1:13	2:1	2:28 — 3:21
DIVISION	PAST DAY OF THE LOCUST	PAST DAY OF THE DROUGHT	IMMINENT DAY OF THE LORD	ULTIMATE DAY OF THE LORD
TOPIC	HISTORICAL INVASION		PROPHETIC INVASION	
	PAST JUDGMENT ON JUDAH		FUTURE JUDGMENT AND RESTORATION OF JUDAH	
LOCATION	SOUTHERN KINGDOM OF JUDAH			
TIME	c. 835 B.C.			

will be followed by great blessing in a material (2:18–27) and spiritual (2:28–32) sense.

These rich promises are followed by a solemn description of the judgment of all nations in the valley of decision (3:14) in the end times. The nations will give an account of themselves to the God of Israel who will judge those who have rebelled against Him. God alone controls the course of history. "So you shall know that I *am* the LORD your God, dwelling in Zion My holy mountain" (3:17). Joel ends with the kingdom blessings upon the remnant of faithful Judah: "But Judah shall abide forever, and Jerusalem from generation to generation" (3:20).

OUTLINE OF JOEL

I. The Day of the Lord in Retrospect....... 1:1–20

A. The Past Day of the Locust.......... 1:1–12
B. The Past Day of the Drought........ 1:13–20

II. The Day of the Lord in Prospect...... 2:1—3:21

A. The Imminent Day of the Lord....... 2:1–27
1. Prophecy of the Imminent Invasion of Judah.......................... 2:1–11
2. Conditional Promise of the Salvation of Judah.......................... 2:12–27
B. The Ultimate Day of the Lord .... 2:28—3:21
1. Last Events Before the Terrible Day of the Lord.......................... 2:28–32
2. Events of the Terrible Day of the Lord.......................... 3:1–21
a. Judgment on the Gentiles....... 3:1–15
b. Restoration of Judah........... 3:16–21

CHAPTER 1

The Past Day of the Locust

THE word of the LORD that came to [R]Joel
the son of Pethuel. Acts 2:16
2 Hear this, you elders,
And give ear, all you inhabitants of the land!
[R]Has *anything like* this happened in your days, Joel 2:2
Or even in the days of your fathers?
3 [R]Tell your children about it, Ps. 78:4
Let your children *tell* their children,
And their children another generation.

4 What the chewing locust left, the [R]swarming locust has eaten; Is. 33:4
What the swarming locust left, the crawling locust has eaten;
And what the crawling locust left, the consuming locust has eaten.

5 Awake, you [R]drunkards, and weep;
And wail, all you drinkers of wine,
Because of the new wine,
[R]For it has been cut off from your mouth. Is. 5:11; 28:1 • Is. 32:10
6 For [R]a nation has come up against My land, Joel 2:2, 11, 25
Strong, and without number;
[R]His teeth *are* the teeth of a lion, Rev. 9:8
And he has the fangs of a fierce lion.
7 He has [R]laid waste My vine, Is. 5:6
And [T]ruined My fig tree; Or *splintered*
He has stripped it bare and thrown *it* away;
Its branches are made white.

8 [R]Lament like a virgin girded with sackcloth Is. 22:12
For [R]the husband of her youth. Jer. 3:4
9 [R]The grain offering and the drink offering
Have been cut off from the house of the LORD;
The priests [R]mourn, who minister to the LORD. Joel 1:13; 2:14 • Joel 2:17
10 The field is wasted,
[R]The land mourns;
For the grain is ruined,
[R]The new wine is dried up,
The oil fails. Jer. 12:11 • Is. 24:7

11 [R]Be ashamed, you farmers,
Wail, you vinedressers,
For the wheat and the barley;
Because the harvest of the field has perished. Jer. 14:3, 4
12 [R]The vine has dried up,
And the fig tree has withered;
The pomegranate tree,
The palm tree also,
And the apple tree—
All the trees of the field are withered;
Surely [R]joy has withered away from the sons of men. Joel 1:10 • Jer. 48:33

The Past Day of the Drought

13 [R]Gird yourselves and lament, you priests;
Wail, you who minister before the altar;
Come, lie all night in sackcloth,
You who minister to my God;
For the grain offering and the drink offering
Are withheld from the house of your God. Jer. 4:8

14 [R]Consecrate a fast, Joel 2:15, 16
Call [R]a sacred assembly; Lev. 23:36
Gather the elders
And [R]all the inhabitants of the land
Into the house of the LORD your God,
And cry out to the LORD. 2 Chr. 20:13

15 [R]Alas for the day!
For [R]the day of the LORD *is* at hand;
It shall come as destruction from the
Almighty. [Jer. 30:7] • Is. 13:6
16 Is not the food [R]cut off before our eyes,
[R]Joy and gladness from the house of our
God? Is. 3:1 • Deut. 12:7
17 The seed *grain* shrivels under the clods,
Storehouses are in shambles;
Barns are broken down,
For the grain has withered.
18 How [R]the beasts groan! Hos. 4:3
The herds of cattle are restless,
Because they have no pasture;
Even the flocks of sheep *suffer *your*
punishment.

19 O LORD, [R]to You I cry out; [Ps. 50:15]
For fire has devoured the [T]open
pastures, Lit. *pastures of the wilderness*
And a flame has burned all the trees of
the field.
20 The beasts of the field also [R]cry out to
You, Ps. 104:21; 147:9
For [R]the water brooks are dried up,
And fire has devoured the open
pastures. 1 Kin. 17:7; 18:5

CHAPTER 2

Prophecy of the Imminent Invasion of Judah

BLOW [R]the [T]trumpet in Zion,
And [R]sound an alarm in My holy
mountain! Jer. 4:5 • *ram's horn* • Num. 10:5
Let all the inhabitants of the land
tremble;
For [R]the day of the LORD is coming,
For it is at hand: [Obad. 15]
2 [R]A day of darkness and gloominess,
A day of clouds and thick darkness,
Like the morning *clouds* spread over
the mountains. Amos 5:18
[R]A people *come*, great and strong,
[R]The like of whom has never been;
Nor will there ever be any *such* after
them, Joel 1:6; 2:11, 25 • Dan. 9:12; 12:1
Even for many successive generations.

3 A fire devours before them,
And behind them a flame burns;
The land *is* like [R]the Garden of Eden
before them, Is. 51:3
And behind them a desolate wilderness;
Surely nothing shall escape them.
4 [R]Their appearance is like the appearance
of horses;
And like swift steeds, so they run. Rev. 9:7
5 [R]With a noise like chariots Rev. 9:9
Over mountaintops they leap,
Like the noise of a flaming fire that
devours the stubble,
Like a strong people set in battle array.

6 Before them the people writhe in pain;
[R]All faces *are drained of color. Nah. 2:10
7 They run like mighty men,
They climb the wall like men of war;
Every one marches in formation,
And they do not break [R]ranks. Prov. 30:27
8 They do not push one another;
Every one marches in his own [T]column.
And *when* they lunge between the
weapons, Lit. *highway*
They are not [T]cut down. Halted by losses
9 They run to and fro in the city,
They run on the wall;
They climb into the houses,
They [R]enter at the windows [R]like a
thief. Jer. 9:21 • John 10:1

10 [R]The earth quakes before them, Ps. 18:7
The heavens tremble;
[R]The sun and moon grow dark, Is. 13:10
And the stars diminish their brightness.
11 [R]The LORD gives voice before His army,
For His camp is very great; Jer. 25:30
[R]For strong *is the One* who executes His
word. Rev. 18:8
For the [R]day of the LORD *is* great and
very terrible; Amos 5:18
[R]Who can endure it? [Mal. 3:2]

Conditional Promise of the Salvation of Judah

12 "Now, therefore," says the LORD,
[R]"Turn to Me with all your heart,
With fasting, with weeping, and with
mourning." Jer. 4:1
13 So [R]rend your heart, and not [R]your
garments; [Ps. 34:18; 51:17] • Gen. 37:34
Return to the LORD your God,
For He *is* [R]gracious and merciful,
Slow to anger, and of great kindness;
And He relents from doing harm. [Ex. 34:6]
14 [R]Who knows *if* He will turn and relent,
And leave [R]a blessing behind Him—
A grain offering and a drink offering
For the LORD your God? Jer. 26:3 • Hag. 2:19

15 Blow the [T]trumpet in Zion, *ram's horn*
[R]Consecrate a fast, Joel 1:14
Call a sacred assembly;
16 Gather the people,
[R]Sanctify the congregation,
Assemble the elders,

1:18 LXX, Vg. *are made desolate*
2:6 LXX, Tg., Vg. *gather blackness*

Gather the children and nursing babes;
[R]Let the bridegroom go out from his chamber, Ex. 19:10 • Ps. 19:5
And the bride from her dressing room.
17 Let the priests, who minister to the LORD,
Weep [R]between the porch and the altar;
Let them say, [R]"Spare Your people, O LORD, Matt. 23:35 • Ex. 32:11, 12
And do not give Your heritage to reproach,
That the nations should [T]rule over them. Or *speak a proverb against them*
[R]Why should they say among the peoples, Ps. 42:10
'Where *is* their God?' "

18 Then the LORD will [R]be zealous for His land,
And pity His people. [Is. 60:10; 63:9, 15]
19 The LORD will answer and say to His people,
"Behold, I will send you [R]grain and new wine and oil,
And you will be satisfied by them;
I will no longer make you a reproach among the nations. [Mal. 3:10]

20 "But [R]I will remove far from you [R]the northern *army*, Ex. 10:19 • Jer. 1:14, 15
And will drive him away into a barren and desolate land,
With his face toward the eastern sea
And his back [R]toward the western sea;
His stench will come up, Deut. 11:24
And his foul odor will rise,
Because he has done [T]monstrous things." Lit. *great*

21 Fear not, O land;
Be glad and rejoice,
For the LORD has done [T]marvelous things! Lit. *great*
22 Do not be afraid, you beasts of the field;
For [R]the open pastures are springing up,
And the tree bears its fruit;
The fig tree and the vine yield their strength. Joel 1:19
23 Be glad then, you children of Zion,
And [R]rejoice in the LORD your God;
For He has given you the former rain faithfully, Is. 41:16
And He [R]will cause the rain to come down for you— Lev. 26:4
The former rain,
And the latter rain in the first *month*.
24 The threshing floors shall be full of wheat,
And the vats shall overflow with new wine and oil.

25 "So I will restore to you the years that the swarming [T]locust has eaten,
The crawling locust,
The consuming locust,
And the chewing locust,
My great army which I sent among you. Exact identity of these locusts unknown
26 You shall [R]eat in plenty and be satisfied,
And praise the name of the LORD your God,
Who has dealt wondrously with you;
And My people shall never be put to [R]shame. Lev. 26:5 • Is. 45:17
27 Then you shall know that I *am* [R]in the midst of Israel, Lev. 26:11, 12
And *that* [R]I *am* the LORD your God
And there is no other. [Is. 45:5, 6]
My people shall never be put to shame.

Last Events Before the Terrible Day of the Lord

28 "And[R] it shall come to pass afterward
That [R]I will pour out My Spirit on all flesh; Ezek. 39:29 • Zech. 12:10
[R]Your sons and your [R]daughters shall prophesy, Is. 54:13 • Acts 21:9
Your old men shall dream dreams,
Your young men shall see visions;
29 And also on *My* [R]menservants and on *My* maidservants [Gal. 3:28]
I will pour out My Spirit in those days.

30 "And [R]I will show wonders in the heavens and in the earth: Matt. 24:29
Blood and fire and pillars of smoke.
31 [R]The sun shall be turned into darkness,
And the moon into blood, Is. 13:9, 10; 34:4
[R]Before the coming of the great and terrible day of the LORD. [Mal. 4:1, 5, 6]
32 And it shall come to pass
That [R]whoever calls on the name of the LORD Rom. 10:13
Shall be [T]saved. Or *delivered*
For [R]in Mount Zion and in Jerusalem there shall be [T]deliverance,
As the LORD has said, Is. 46:13 • Or *salvation*
Among [R]the remnant whom the LORD calls. [Mic. 4:7]

CHAPTER 3

Judgment on the Gentiles

"FOR behold, [R]in those days and at that time,
When I bring back the captives of Judah and Jerusalem, Jer. 30:3
2 [R]I will also gather all nations, Zech. 14:2
And bring them down to the Valley of Jehoshaphat;
And I [R]will enter into judgment with them there Is. 66:16
On account of My people, My heritage Israel,
Whom they have scattered among the nations;

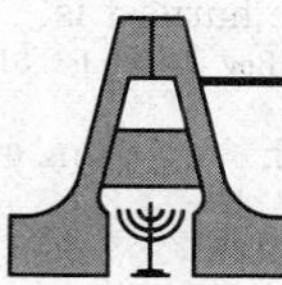

THE DAY OF THE LORD

The day of the Lord is a period at the end of human history when God's purpose for humankind will be fulfilled. The period will begin with the return of Christ and will end with the cleansing of the heavens and the earth with fire (2 Pet. 3:10–13; Rev. 21:1).

Some scholars believe the day of the Lord will be a long period of time. Others feel it will be an instantaneous event when Christ returns to earth to claim His own faithful believers and to consign unbelievers to eternal judgment (Rev. 20:14, 15).

The prophets of the Old Testament were the first to speak of the coming day of the Lord. This day "*will be* darkness, and not light," Amos warned the unsuspecting residents of Judah (Amos 5:18). Isaiah declared that the day of the Lord will come as "destruction from the Almighty" (Is. 13:6), and Jeremiah referred to it as "a day of vengeance" (Jer. 46:10). Along with judgment, the prophets emphasized the restorative and redemptive elements connected with the day of the Lord.

The prophet Joel envisioned God's Spirit being poured out "on all flesh" (2:28) just before the coming of the "great and terrible day of the LORD" (2:31). The occasion for Joel's prophecy was the invasion of Judah by a swarm of locusts, followed by a severe drought (Joel 1:1–4; see illustration). As tragic as this destruction was, Joel declared, it will be as nothing compared with the coming day of the Lord.

The New Testament emphasizes the suddenness of the Lord's coming (Luke 12:40; Rev. 3:3), the certainty of His judgment on unbelief (Matt. 25:32), and the restoration of heaven and earth by fire (2 Pet. 3:10). Christ will fulfill these prophecies on the day of the Lord as He judges all nations from the "throne of His glory" (Matt. 25:31).

Rather than speculating about the exact time of God's judgment, our pressing task is to proclaim His message of redemption to a lost world until the day of the Lord is fulfilled.

The occasion for Joel's prophecy was the invasion of Judah by a swarm of locusts.

They have also divided up My land.
3 They have [R]cast lots for My people,
Have given a boy *in exchange* for a
harlot, Nah. 3:10
And sold a girl for wine, that they may
drink.

4 "Indeed, what have you to do with Me,
[R]O Tyre and Sidon, and all the coasts of
Philistia? Amos 1:6–8
Will you retaliate against Me?
But if you [T]retaliate against Me, *repay me*
Swiftly and speedily I will return your
retaliation upon your own head;
5 Because you have taken My silver and
My gold,
And have carried into your temples My
[T]prized possessions. Lit. *precious good things*
6 Also the people of Judah and the people
of Jerusalem
You have sold to the Greeks,
That you may remove them far from
their borders.

7 "Behold, [R]I will raise them
Out of the place to which you have sold
them,
And will return your [T]retaliation upon
your own head. Jer. 23:8 • Or *repayment*
8 I will sell your sons and your daughters
Into the hand of the people of Judah,
And they will sell them to the
[R]Sabeans,[T] Ezek. 23:42 • Lit. *Shebaites*
To a people [R]far off; Jer. 6:20
For the LORD has spoken."

9 [R]Proclaim this among the nations:
"Prepare for war!
Wake up the mighty men,
Let all the men of war draw near,
Let them come up. Ezek. 38:7
10 [R]Beat your plowshares into swords [Is. 2:4]
And your pruninghooks into spears;
Let the weak say, 'I *am* strong.' "
11 Assemble and come, all you nations,
And gather together all around.
Cause [R]Your mighty ones to go down
there, O LORD. Is. 13:3

12 "Let the nations be wakened, and come
up to the Valley of Jehoshaphat;
For there I will sit to [R]judge all the
surrounding nations. Is. 2:4

13 [R]Put in the sickle, for [R]the harvest is
ripe. Rev. 14:15 • Jer. 51:33
Come, go down;
For the [R]winepress is full, [Is. 63:3]
The vats overflow—
For their wickedness *is* great."

14 Multitudes, multitudes in the valley of
decision!
For [R]the day of the LORD *is* near in the
valley of decision. Joel 2:1
15 The sun and moon will grow dark,
And the stars will diminish their
brightness.

Restoration of Judah

16 The LORD also will roar from Zion,
And utter His voice from Jerusalem;
The heavens and earth will shake;
[R]But the LORD will be a shelter for His
people,
And the strength of the children of
Israel. [Is. 51:5, 6]

17 "So you shall know that I *am* the LORD
your God,
Dwelling in Zion My [R]holy mountain.
Then Jerusalem shall be holy,
And no aliens shall ever pass through
her again." Zech. 8:3

18 And it will come to pass in that day
That the mountains shall drip with new
wine,
The hills shall flow with milk,
And all the brooks of Judah shall be
flooded with water;
A [R]fountain shall flow from the house of
the LORD Ezek. 47:1
And water the Valley of [T]Acacias. *Shittim*

19 "Egypt shall be a desolation,
And Edom a desolate wilderness,
Because of violence *against* the people
of Judah,
For they have shed innocent blood in
their land.
20 But Judah shall abide forever,
And Jerusalem from generation to
generation.
21 "For I will [R]acquit them of bloodguilt,
whom I had not acquitted;
For the LORD dwells in Zion." Is. 4:4

THE BOOK OF

AMOS

THE BOOK OF AMOS

Amos prophesies during a period of national optimism in Israel. Business is booming and boundaries are bulging. But below the surface, greed and injustice are festering. Hypocritical religious motions have replaced true worship, creating a false sense of security and a growing callousness to God's disciplining hand. Famine, drought, plagues, death, destruction—nothing can force the people to their knees.

Amos, the farmer-turned-prophet, lashes out at sin unflinchingly, trying to visualize the nearness of God's judgment and mobilize the nation to repentance. The nation, like a basket of rotting fruit, stands ripe for judgment because of its hypocrisy and spiritual indifference.

The name *Amos* is derived from the Hebrew root *amas,* "to lift a burden, to carry." Thus, his name means "Burden" or "Burden-Bearer." Amos lives up to the meaning of his name by bearing up under his divinely given burden of declaring judgment to rebellious Israel. The Greek and Latin titles are both transliterated in English as *Amos.*

THE AUTHOR OF AMOS

The only Old Testament appearance of the name *Amos* is in this book. (He should not be confused with Amoz, the father of Isaiah.) Concerning his background, Amos said, "I *was* no prophet, nor *was* I a son of a prophet, but I *was* a herdsman and a tender of sycamore fruit" (7:14). But he was gripped by God and divinely commissioned to bring his prophetic burden to Israel (3:8; 7:15). He came from the rural area of Tekoa in Judah, twelve miles south of Jerusalem, where he tended a special breed of small sheep that produced wool of the best quality. As a grower of sycamore figs, he had to puncture the fruit before it ripened to allow the insects inside to escape. Amos lived a disciplined life, and his knowledge of the wilderness often surfaces in his messages (cf. 3:4, 5, 12; 5:8, 19; 9:9). Amos was from the country, but he was well-educated in the Scriptures. His keen sense of morality and justice is obvious, and his objective appraisal of Israel's spiritual condition was not well received, especially since he was from Judah. He delivered his message in Bethel because it was the residence of the king of Israel and a center of idolatry. His frontal attack on the greed, injustice, and self-righteousness of the people of the northern kingdom made his words unpopular.

THE TIME OF AMOS

Amos prophesied "in the days of Uzziah king of Judah, and in the days of Jeroboam the son of Joash, king of Israel, two years before the earthquake" (1:1). Uzziah reigned from 767 to 739 B.C. and Jeroboam II reigned from 782 to 753 B.C., leaving an overlap from 767 to 753 B.C. Over two hundred years later, Zechariah referred to this earthquake in Uzziah's reign (Zech. 14:5). Amos 7:11 anticipates the 722 B.C. Assyrian captivity of Israel and indicates that at the time of writing, Jeroboam II was not yet dead. Thus, Amos prophesied in Bethel about 755 B.C. Astronomical calculations indicate that a solar eclipse took place in Israel on June 15, 763 B.C. This event was probably fresh in the minds of Amos's hearers (see 8:9).

Amos ministered after the time of Obadiah, Joel, and Jonah and just before Hosea, Micah, and Isaiah. At this time Uzziah reigned over a prosperous and militarily successful Judah. He fortified Jerusalem and subdued the Philistines, the Ammonites, and the Edomites. In the north, Israel was ruled by the capable King Jeroboam II. Economic and military circumstances were almost ideal, but prosperity only increased the materialism, immorality, and injustice of the people (2:6–8; 3:10; 4:1; 5:10–12; 8:4–6). During these years, Assyria, Babylon, Syria, and Egypt were relatively weak. Thus, the people of Israel found it hard to imagine the coming disaster predicted by Amos. However, it was only three decades until the downfall of Israel.

THE CHRIST OF AMOS

The clearest anticipation of Christ in Amos is found at the end of the book. He has all authority to judge (1:1—9:10), but He will also restore His people (9:11–15).

KEYS TO AMOS

Key Word: The Judgment of Israel—The basic theme of Amos is the coming judgment of Israel because of the holiness of Yahweh and the sinfulness of His covenant people. Amos unflinchingly and relentlessly visualizes the causes and course of Israel's quickly approaching doom. God is gracious and patient, but His justice and righteousness will not allow sin to go unpunished indefinitely. The sins of Israel are heaped as high as heaven: empty ritualism, oppression of the poor, idolatry, deceit, self-righteousness, arrogance, greed, materialism, and callousness. The people have repeatedly broken every aspect of their covenant relationship with God. Nevertheless, God's mercy and love are evident in His offer of deliverance if the people will only turn back to Him. God graciously sends Amos as a reformer to warn the people of Israel of their fate if they refuse to repent. But they reject his plea, and the course of judgment cannot be altered.

Key Verses: Amos 3:1, 2; 8:11, 12—"Hear this word that the LORD has spoken against you, O children of Israel, against the whole family which I brought up from the land of Egypt, saying: You only have I known of all the families of the earth; therefore I will punish you for all your iniquities" (3:1, 2).

" 'Behold, the days are coming,' says the Lord GOD, 'that I will send a famine on the land, not a famine of bread, nor a thirst for water, but of hearing the words of the LORD; they shall wander from sea to sea, and from north to east; they shall run to and fro, seeking the word of the LORD, but shall not find *it*' " (8:11, 12).

Key Chapter: Amos 9—Set in the midst of the harsh judgments of Amos are some of the greatest prophecies of restoration of Israel anywhere in Scripture. Within the scope of just five verses the future of Israel becomes clear, as the Abrahamic, Davidic, and Palestinian covenants are focused on their climactic fulfillment in the return of the Messiah.

SURVEY OF AMOS

Amos's message of the coming doom of the northern kingdom of Israel seems preposterous to the people. Unsurprisingly, Amos's earnest and forceful message against Israel's sins and abuses is poorly received. The prophet of Israel's Indian summer presents a painfully clear message: "prepare to meet your God, O Israel" (4:12). The four divisions of Amos are: the eight prophecies (1:1—2:16), the three sermons (3:1—6:14), the five visions (7:1—9:10), and the five promises (9:11-15).

The Eight Prophecies (1:1—2:16): Amos is called by God to the unenviable task of leaving his homeland in Judah to preach a harsh message of judgment to Israel. Each of his eight oracles in chapters 1 and 2 begins with the statement "For three transgressions of . . . and for four." The fourth transgression is equivalent to the last straw; the iniquity of each of the eight countries is full. Amos begins with the nations that surround Israel as his catalog of catastrophes gradually spirals in on Israel herself. Seven times God declares, "I will send a fire" (1:4, 7, 10, 12, 14; 2:2, 5), a symbol of judgment.

The Three Sermons (3:1—6:14): In these chapters, Amos delivers three sermons, each beginning with the phrase "Hear this word" (3:1; 4:1; 5:1). The first sermon (3) is a general pronouncement of judgment because of Israel's iniquities. The second sermon (4) exposes the crimes of the people and describes the ways God has chastened them in order to draw them back to Himself. Five times He says, "Yet you have not returned to Me" (4:6, 8, 9, 10, 11). The third sermon (5 and 6) lists the sins of the house of Israel and calls the people to repent. But they hate integrity, justice, and compassion, and their refusal to turn to Yahweh will lead to their exile. Although they arrogantly wallow in luxury, their time of prosperity will suddenly come to an end.

The Five Visions (7:1—9:10): Amos's three sermons are followed by five visions of coming judgment upon the northern kingdom. The first two judgments of locusts and fire do not come to pass because of Amos's intercession. The third vision of the plumb line is followed by the only narrative section in the book (7:10-17). Amaziah, the priest of Bethel, wants Amos to go back to Judah. The fourth vision pictures Israel as a basket of rotten fruit, overripe for judgment. The fifth vision is a relentless portrayal of Israel's unavoidable judgment.

The Five Promises (9:11-15): Amos has hammered upon the theme of divine retribution with oracles, sermons, and visions. Nevertheless, he

FOCUS	EIGHT PROPHECIES	THREE SERMONS	FIVE VISIONS	FIVE PROMISES
REFERENCE	1:1	3:1	7:1	9:11—9:15
DIVISION	JUDGMENT OF ISRAEL AND SURROUNDING NATIONS	SIN OF ISRAEL: PRESENT, PAST, AND FUTURE	PICTURES OF THE JUDGMENT OF ISRAEL	RESTORATION OF ISRAEL
TOPIC	PRONOUNCEMENTS OF JUDGMENT	PROVOCATIONS FOR JUDGMENT	FUTURE OF JUDGMENT	PROMISES AFTER JUDGMENT
	JUDGMENT			HOPE
LOCATION	SURROUNDING NATIONS	NORTHERN KINGDOM OF ISRAEL		
TIME	c. 760 – 753 B.C.			

ends his book on a note of consolation, not condemnation. God promises to reinstate the Davidic line, to renew the land, and to restore the people.

OUTLINE OF AMOS

CHAPTER 1

Introduction to Amos

THE words of Amos, who was among the herdsmen of Tekoa, which he saw concerning Israel in the days of [R]Uzziah king of Judah, and in the days of [R]Jeroboam the son of Joash, king of Israel, two years before the [R]earthquake. 2 Chr. 26:1–23 • Amos 7:10 • Zech. 14:5

2 And he said:

"The LORD [R]roars from Zion, Joel 3:16
And utters His voice from Jerusalem;
The pastures of the shepherds mourn,
And the top of Carmel withers."

Judgment on Damascus

3 Thus says the LORD:

"For three transgressions of [R]Damascus,
and for four, Is. 8:4; 17:1–3
I will not turn away its *punishment,*
Because they have [R]threshed Gilead
with implements of iron. 2 Kin. 10:32, 33
4 [R]But I will send a fire into the house of
Hazael,
Which shall devour the palaces of [R]Ben-
Hadad. Jer. 49:27; 51:30 • 2 Kin. 6:24
5 I will also break the *gate* [R]bar of
Damascus,
And cut off the inhabitant from the
Valley of Aven,
And the one who [T]holds the scepter
from [T]Beth Eden.
The people of Syria shall go captive to
Kir," Jer. 51:30 • Rules • Lit. *House of Eden*
Says the LORD.

Judgment on Gaza

6 Thus says the LORD:

"For three transgressions of [R]Gaza, and
for four,
I will not turn away its *punishment,*
Because they took captive the whole
captivity
To deliver *them* up to Edom. Jer. 47:1, 5
7 [R]But I will send a fire upon the wall of
Gaza,
Which shall devour its palaces. Jer. 47:1
8 I will cut off the inhabitant [R]from
Ashdod, Zeph. 2:4
And the one who holds the scepter from
Ashkelon;
I will [R]turn My hand against Ekron,
And [R]the remnant of the Philistines
shall perish," Ps. 81:14 • Ezek. 25:16
Says the Lord GOD.

Judgment on Tyre

9 Thus says the LORD:

"For three transgressions of [R]Tyre, and
for four,
I will not turn away its *punishment,*
Because they delivered up the whole
captivity to Edom,
And did not remember the covenant of
brotherhood. Is. 23:1–18

10 But I will send a fire upon the wall of
Tyre,
Which shall devour its palaces."

Judgment on Edom

11 Thus says the LORD:

"For three transgressions of [R]Edom, and
for four, Is. 21:11
I will not turn away its *punishment*,
Because he pursued his [R]brother with
the sword, Obad. 10–12
And cast off all pity;
His anger tore perpetually,
And he kept his wrath forever.
12 But [R]I will send a fire upon Teman,
Which shall devour the palaces of
Bozrah." Obad. 9, 10

Judgment on Ammon

13 Thus says the LORD:

"For three transgressions of [R]the people
of Ammon, and for four, Ezek. 25:2
I will not turn away its *punishment*,
Because they ripped open the women
with child in Gilead,
That they might enlarge their territory.
14 But I will kindle a fire in the wall of
[R]Rabbah,
And it shall devour its palaces,
[R]Amid shouting in the day of battle,
And a tempest in the day of the
whirlwind. Deut. 3:11 • Amos 2:2
15 [R]Their king shall go into captivity,
He and his princes together,"
Says the LORD. Jer. 49:3

CHAPTER 2

Judgment on Moab

THUS says the LORD:

[R]"For three transgressions of Moab, and
for four, Zeph. 2:8–11
I will not turn away its *punishment*,
Because he [R]burned the bones of the
king of Edom to lime. 2 Kin. 3:26, 27
2 But I will send a fire upon Moab,
And it shall devour the palaces of
[R]Kerioth; Jer. 48:24, 41
Moab shall die with tumult,
With shouting *and* trumpet sound.
3 And I will cut off [R]the judge from its
midst, Num. 24:17
And slay all its princes with him,"
Says the LORD.

Judgment on Judah

4 Thus says the LORD:

"For three transgressions of [R]Judah, and
for four, Hos. 12:2
I will not turn away its *punishment*,
[R]Because they have despised the law of
the LORD, Lev. 26:14
And have not kept His commandments.
[R]Their lies lead them astray, Jer. 16:19
Lies after which their fathers walked.
5 [R]But I will send a fire upon Judah,
And it shall devour the palaces of
Jerusalem." Hos. 8:14

Judgment on Israel

6 Thus says the LORD:

"For three transgressions of [R]Israel, and
for four, 2 Kin. 17:7–18; 18:12
I will not turn away its *punishment*,
Because [R]they sell the righteous for
silver, Is. 19:21
And the poor for a pair of sandals.
7 They [T]pant after the dust of the earth
which is on the head of the poor,
And [R]pervert the way of the humble.
[R]A man and his father go in to the *same*
girl, Or *trample on* • Amos 5:12 • Ezek. 22:11
[R]To defile My holy name. Lev. 20:3
8 They lie down by every altar on clothes
[R]taken in pledge, Ex. 22:26
And drink the wine of the condemned
in the house of their god.

9 "Yet *it was* I *who* destroyed the
[R]Amorite before them, Num. 21:25
Whose height *was* like the [R]height of
the cedars, Ezek. 31:3
And he *was as* strong as the oaks;
Yet I [R]destroyed his fruit above
And his roots beneath. [Mal. 4:1]
10 Also *it was* [R]I *who* brought you up from
the land of Egypt, Ex. 12:51
And [R]led you forty years through the
wilderness, Deut. 2:7
To possess the land of the Amorite.
11 I raised up some of your sons as
[R]prophets, Num. 12:6
And some of your young men as
[R]Nazirites. Num. 6:2, 3
Is it not so, O you children of Israel?"
Says the LORD.
12 "But you gave the Nazirites wine to
drink,
And commanded the prophets [R]saying,
'Do not prophesy!' Is. 30:10

13 "Behold, I am [T]weighed down by you,
As a cart [T]is weighed down *that is* full
of sheaves. *tottering under* • *totters*
14 [R]Therefore [T]flight shall perish from the
swift, Jer. 46:6 • Or *the place of refuge*
The strong shall not strengthen his
power,
Nor shall the mighty deliver himself;
15 He shall not stand who handles the
bow,

The swift of foot shall not [T]deliver
himself, Or *save*
Nor shall he who rides a horse deliver
himself.
16 The most courageous men of might
Shall flee naked in that day,"
Says the LORD.

CHAPTER 3

Israel's Judgment Is Deserved (Present)

HEAR this word that the LORD has spoken
against you, O children of Israel,
against the whole family which I brought up
from the land of Egypt, saying:

2 "You[R] only have I known of all the
families of the earth;
[R]Therefore I will punish you for all your
iniquities." [Deut. 7:6] · [Rom. 2:9]

3 Can two walk together, unless they are
agreed?
4 Will a lion roar in the forest, when he
has no prey?
Will a young lion [T]cry out of his den, if
he has caught nothing? Lit. *give his voice*
5 Will a bird fall into a snare on the
earth, where there is no [T]trap for it?
Will a snare spring up from the earth, if
it has caught nothing at all? Or *bait*
6 If a [T]trumpet is blown in a city, will not
the people be afraid? *ram's horn*
[R]If there is calamity in a city, will not
the LORD have done *it*? Is. 45:7

7 Surely the Lord GOD does nothing,
Unless [R]He reveals His secret to His
servants the prophets. [John 15:15]
8 A lion has roared!
Who will not fear?
The Lord GOD has spoken!
[R]Who can but prophesy? Acts 4:20

9 "Proclaim in the palaces at Ashdod,
And in the palaces in the land of Egypt,
and say:
'Assemble on the mountains of Samaria;
See great tumults in her midst,
And the [T]oppressed within her. *oppression*

10 For they [R]do not know to do right,'
Says the LORD,
'Who store up violence and [T]robbery in
their palaces.' " Jer. 4:22 · Or *devastation*

Israel's Judgment Is Described (Present)

11 Therefore thus says the Lord GOD:

"An adversary *shall be* all around the
land;
He shall sap your strength from you,
And your palaces shall be plundered."

12 Thus says the LORD:

"As a shepherd [T]takes from the mouth of
a lion Or *snatches*
Two legs or a piece of an ear,
So shall the children of Israel be taken
out
Who dwell in Samaria—
In the corner of a bed and [T]on the edge
of a couch! Uncertain, possibly *on the cover*
13 Hear and testify against the house of
Jacob,"
Says the Lord GOD, the God of hosts,
14 "That in the day I punish Israel for their
transgressions,
I will also visit *destruction* on the altars
of [R]Bethel;
And the horns of the altar shall be cut
off
And fall to the ground. Amos 4:4
15 I will [T]destroy the winter house along
with [R]the summer house;
The [R]houses of ivory shall perish,
And the great houses shall have an
end," Lit. *strike* · Judg. 3:20 · 1 Kin. 22:39
Says the LORD.

CHAPTER 4

Israel's Judgment Is Deserved (Past)

HEAR this word, you [R]cows of Bashan,
who *are* on the mountain of Samaria,
Who oppress the [R]poor, Ps. 22:12 · Amos 2:6
Who crush the needy,
Who say to [T]your husbands, "Bring
wine, let us drink!" Lit. *their masters* or *lords*

3:2 Selection of Israel—The selection of Israel as a special nation to God was part of God's plan (Page 1335—Rom. 11:2). Historically, the selection of Israel began with the Lord's promise to Abraham, "I will make you a great nation" (Page 18—Gen. 12:2). The name *Israel* actually is from the new name which God gave to Abraham's grandson, Jacob. It was occasioned by Jacob's spiritual victory at the ford of Jabbok (Page 44—Gen. 32:28). This fact explains why his descendants are often called the children of Israel.

The motivation for the Lord's choice of Israel as His select nation did not lie in any special attraction it possessed. Its people were, in fact, the least in number among all the nations (Page 217—Deut. 7:6–8). Rather, the Lord chose them because of His love for them and because of His covenant with Abraham. This fact does not mean that God did not love other nations, because it was through Israel that He intended to bring forth the Savior and to bless the entire world (Page 18—Gen. 12:3).

Now turn to Page 669—Ps. 78:4: History of Israel.

2 [R]The Lord GOD has sworn by His
holiness: Ps. 89:35
"Behold, the days shall come upon you
When He will take you away [R]with
fishhooks, Jer. 16:16
And your posterity with fishhooks.
3 [R]You will go out *through* broken *walls*,
Each one straight ahead of her,
And you will [T]be cast into Harmon,"
Says the LORD. Ezek. 12:5 • Or *cast them*

4 "Come to Bethel and transgress,
At Gilgal multiply transgression;
Bring your sacrifices every morning,
Your tithes every three [T]days. Or *years*
5 [R]Offer a sacrifice of thanksgiving with
leaven,
Proclaim *and* announce [R]the freewill
offerings;
For this you love,
You children of Israel!"
Says the Lord GOD. Lev. 7:13 • Lev. 22:18

Israel's Judgment Is Demonstrated (Past)

6 "Also I gave you [T]cleanness of teeth in
all your cities.
And lack of bread in all your places;
[R]Yet you have not returned to Me,"
Says the LORD. Hunger • Jer. 5:3

7 "I also withheld rain from you,
When *there were* still three months to
the harvest.
I made it rain on one city,
I withheld rain from another city.
One part was rained upon,
And where it did not rain the part
withered.
8 So two *or* three cities wandered to
another city to drink water,
But they were not satisfied;
Yet you have not returned to Me,"
Says the LORD.

9 "I[R] blasted you with blight and mildew.
When your gardens increased,
Your vineyards,
Your fig trees,
And your olive trees,
[R]The locust devoured *them;*
Yet you have not returned to Me,"
Says the LORD. Hag. 2:17 • Joel 1:4, 7

10 "I sent among you a plague [R]after the
manner of Egypt;
Your young men I killed with a sword,
Along with your captive horses;
I made the stench of your camps come
up into your nostrils;
Yet you have not returned to Me,"
Says the LORD. Ps. 78:50

11 "I overthrew *some* of you,
As God overthrew [R]Sodom and
Gomorrah,
And you were like a firebrand plucked
from the burning;
Yet you have not returned to Me,"
Says the LORD. Is. 13:19

Israel's Judgment Is Described (Past)

12 "Therefore thus will I do to you, O
Israel;
And because I will do this to you,
Prepare to meet your God, O Israel!"

13 For behold,
He who forms mountains,
And creates the [T]wind, Or *spirit*
[R]Who declares to man what [T]his thought
is, Ps. 139:2 • Or *His*
And makes the morning darkness,
[R]Who treads the high places of the
earth— Mic. 1:3
The LORD God of hosts *is* His name.

CHAPTER 5

Israel's Judgment Is Deserved (Future)

HEAR this word which I take up against
you, *this* lamentation, O house of Israel:

2 The virgin of Israel has fallen;
She will rise no more.
She lies forsaken on her land;
There is no one to raise her up.

3 For thus says the Lord GOD:

"The city that goes out by a thousand
Shall have a hundred left,
And that which goes out by a hundred
Shall have ten left to the house of
Israel."

4 For thus says the LORD to the house of
Israel:

[R]"Seek Me [R]and live; [Jer. 29:13] • [Is. 55:3]
5 But do not seek [R]Bethel, Amos 4:4
Nor enter Gilgal,
Nor pass over to [R]Beersheba; Amos 8:14
For Gilgal shall surely go into captivity,
And Bethel shall come to nothing.
6 [R]Seek the LORD and live, [Is. 55:3, 6, 7]
Lest He break out like fire *in* the house
of Joseph,
And devour *it*,
With no one to quench *it* in Bethel—
7 You who [R]turn justice to wormwood,
And lay righteousness to rest in the
earth!" Amos 6:12

8 He made the [R]Pleiades and Orion;
He turns the shadow of death into
morning Job 9:9; 38:31

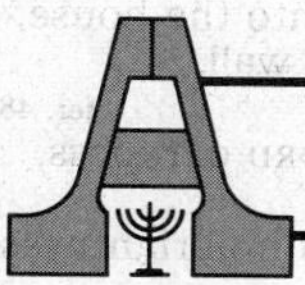

SODOM AND GOMORRAH

Located near the Dead Sea, Sodom and Gomorrah were two cities destroyed by God around 2000 B.C. because of their wickedness and depravity. These cities, along with Admah, Zeboiim, and Zoar, were known as the "cities of the plain" (Gen. 13:12; 19:25) in the rich, fertile flatlands south of the Dead Sea.

When Abraham gave his nephew Lot first choice of land in this area of Palestine, Lot chose the fertile, well-watered Jordan River Valley rather than the rocky hill country. Failing to consider the moral character of the inhabitants, Lot "pitched *his* tent even as far as Sodom" (Gen. 13:12).

Two angels were sent to warn Lot that God intended to destroy Sodom. A group of depraved citizens of Sodom wanted to abuse the two visitors sexually. The angels struck the Sodomites blind to save Lot (Gen. 19:1–11), and Lot and his family fled the doomed city. Fire and brimstone fell from heaven and consumed Sodom and Gomorrah, as well as Admah and Zeboiim (Deut. 29:23). Only Zoar escaped destruction (Gen. 19:30).

When Lot's wife looked back at the burning city of Sodom in disobedience of God's instructions, she was changed into a pillar of salt (Gen. 19:26). A formation of salt, traditionally referred to as "Lot's wife," may be seen today on the shores of the Dead Sea (see photo).

The destroyed cities of the plain were never rebuilt. Even Zoar eventually disappeared. Formations of salt, sulphur, and asphalt in the vicinity lead many scholars to believe that the cities of the plain are buried beneath the shallow waters of the southern end of the Dead Sea.

Before its destruction, this area was rich and productive. Today it is barren, with no plant life of any kind—an eloquent testimony of God's judgment. Many of the Old Testament prophets, including Amos, reminded the Israelites of the destruction of Sodom and Gomorrah to call the people back to worship of the one true God (Amos 4:11). In the New Testament, Paul quoted the prophet Isaiah's reference to the wickedness of the cities (Rom. 9:29).

A formation of salt, traditionally referred to as "Lot's wife."

[R]And makes the day dark as night;
He [R]calls for the waters of the sea
And pours them out on the face of the earth; Ps. 104:20 • Job 38:34
[R]The LORD *is* His name. [Amos 4:13]
9 He rains ruin upon the strong,
So that fury comes upon the fortress.

10 [R]They hate the one who rebukes in the gate,
And they [R]abhor the one who speaks uprightly. Is. 29:21; 66:5 • 1 Kin. 22:8
11 [R]Therefore, because you [T]tread down the poor Amos 2:6 • *trample*
And take grain [T]taxes from him, Or *tribute*
Though [R]you have built houses of hewn stone, Mic. 6:15
Yet you shall not dwell in them;
You have planted [T]pleasant vineyards,
But you shall not drink wine from them. *desirable*
12 For I [R]know your manifold transgressions
And your mighty sins.
[R]*You* afflict the just *and* take bribes;
You [R]divert the poor *from justice* at the gate. Hos. 5:3 • Amos 2:6 • Is. 29:21
13 Therefore [R]the prudent keep silent at that time,
For it *is* an evil time. Amos 6:10

14 Seek good and not evil,
That you may live;
So the LORD God of hosts will be with you,
[R]As you have spoken. Mic. 3:11
15 [R]Hate evil, love good;
Establish justice in the gate.
[R]It may be that the LORD God of hosts
Will be gracious to the remnant of Joseph. Rom. 12:9 • Joel 2:14

The First Woe of Judgment

16 Therefore the LORD God of hosts, the Lord, says this:

"*There shall be* wailing in all streets,
And they shall say in all the highways,
'Alas! Alas!'
They shall call the farmer to mourning,
[R]And skillful lamenters to wailing. Jer. 9:17
17 In all vineyards *there shall be* wailing,
For [R]I will pass through you,"
Says the LORD. Ex. 12:12

18 [R]Woe to you who desire the day of the LORD! Is. 5:19
For what good *is* [R]the day of the LORD to you?
It *will be* darkness, and not light. Joel 2:2
19 It *will be* [R]as though a man fled from a lion,
And a bear met him;
Or *as though* he went into the house,
Leaned his hand on the wall,
And a serpent bit him. Jer. 48:44
20 *Is* not the day of the LORD darkness, and not light?
Is it not very dark, with no brightness in it?

21 "I[R] hate, I despise your feast days,
And [R]I do not savor your sacred assemblies. Is. 1:11–16 • Lev. 26:31
22 [R]Though you offer Me burnt offerings and your grain offerings,
I will not accept *them,*
Nor will I regard your fattened peace offerings. Mic. 6:6, 7
23 Take away from Me the noise of your songs,
For I will not hear the melody of your stringed instruments.
24 But let justice run down like water,
And righteousness like a mighty stream.

25 "Did[R] you offer Me sacrifices and offerings
In the wilderness forty years, O house of Israel? Deut. 32:17
26 You also carried *Sikkuth your king
And [T]Chiun, your idols, A pagan deity
The star of your gods,
Which you made for yourselves.
27 Therefore I will send you into captivity [R]beyond Damascus,"
Says the LORD, [R]whose name *is* the God of hosts. 2 Kin. 17:6 • Amos 4:13

CHAPTER 6

The Second Woe of Judgment

WOE [R]to you *who are* at ease in Zion,
And trust in Mount Samaria, Luke 6:24
Notable persons in the chief nation,
To whom the house of Israel comes!
2 [R]Go over to [R]Calneh and see;
And from there go to [R]Hamath the great; Jer. 2:10 • Is. 10:9 • 2 Kin. 18:34
Then go down to Gath of the Philistines.
[R]*Are you* better than these kingdoms?
Or is their territory greater than your territory? Nah. 3:8

3 *Woe to* you who [R]put far off the day of [R]doom, Is. 56:12 • Amos 5:18
[R]Who cause [R]the seat of violence to come near; Amos 5:12 • Ps. 94:20
4 Who lie on beds of ivory,
Stretch out on your couches,
Eat lambs from the flock
And calves from the midst of the stall;

5:26 LXX, Vg. *tabernacle of Moloch*

5 [R]Who chant to the sound of stringed
instruments, Is. 5:12
And invent for yourselves musical
instruments [R]like David; 1 Chr. 23:5
6 Who [R]drink wine from bowls,
And anoint yourselves with the best
ointments,
[R]But are not grieved for the affliction of
Joseph. Amos 2:8; 4:1 • Gen. 37:25
7 Therefore they shall now go [R]captive as
the first of the captives, Amos 5:27
And those who recline at banquets shall
be removed.

8 [R]The Lord GOD has sworn by Himself,
The LORD God of hosts says: Jer. 51:14
"I abhor [R]the pride of Jacob, Amos 8:7
And hate his palaces;
Therefore I will deliver up *the* city
And all that is in it."

9 Then it shall come to pass, that if ten
men remain in one house, they shall die.
10 And when [T]a kinsman *of the dead,* with
one who will burn *the bodies,* picks up the
[T]bodies to take them out of the house, he will
say to one inside the house, "*Are there* any
more with you?" Then someone will say,
"None." And he will say, "Hold your tongue!
[R]For we dare not mention the name of the
LORD." Lit. *his uncle* • Lit. *bones* • Amos 8:3

11 For behold, [R]the LORD gives a
command: Is. 55:11
[R]He will break the great house into bits,
And the little house into pieces. Amos 3:15

12 Do horses run on rocks?
Does *one* plow *there* with oxen?
Yet [R]you have turned justice into gall,
And the fruit of righteousness into
wormwood, Hos. 10:4
13 You who rejoice over Lo Debar,
Who say, "Have we not taken [T]Karnaim
for ourselves Lit. *Horns,* a symbol of strength
By our own strength?"

14 "But, behold, [R]I will raise up a nation
against you, Jer. 5:15
O house of Israel,"
Says the LORD God of hosts;
"And they will afflict you from the
[R]entrance of Hamath 1 Kin. 8:65
To the Valley of the Arabah."

CHAPTER 7

Vision of the Locusts

THUS the Lord GOD showed me: Behold,
He formed locust swarms at the beginning of the late crop; indeed *it was* the late
crop after the king's mowings.

2 And so it was, when they had finished
eating the grass of the land, that I said:

"O Lord GOD, forgive, I pray!
[T]Oh, that Jacob may stand,
For he *is* small!" Or *How shall Jacob stand*
3 *So* [R]the LORD relented concerning this.
"It shall not be," said the LORD. Jon. 3:10

Vision of the Fire

4 Thus the Lord GOD showed me: Behold,
the Lord GOD called [T]for conflict by fire, and
it consumed the great deep and devoured the
[T]territory. *to contend* • Lit. *portion*
5 Then I said:

"O Lord GOD, cease, I pray!
[R]Oh, that Jacob may stand,
For he *is* small!" Amos 7:2, 3
6 *So* the LORD relented concerning this.
"This also shall not be," said the Lord
GOD.

Vision of the Plumb Line

7 Thus He showed me: Behold, the Lord
stood on a wall *made* with a plumb line, with
a plumb line in His hand.
8 And the LORD said to me, "Amos, what
do you see?" And I said, "A plumb line." Then
the Lord said:

"Behold, I am setting a plumb line
In the midst of My people Israel;
I will not pass by them anymore.
9 [R]The [T]high places of Isaac shall be
desolate, Gen. 46:1 • Places of pagan worship
And the [T]sanctuaries of Israel shall be
laid waste. Or *holy places*
[R]I will rise with the sword against the
house of Jeroboam." 2 Kin. 15:8–10

Opposition of Amaziah (Historical Parenthesis)

10 Then Amaziah the priest of [R]Bethel sent
to [R]Jeroboam king of Israel, saying, "Amos
has conspired against you in the midst of the
house of Israel. The land is not able to [T]bear
all his words. Amos 4:4 • 2 Kin. 14:23 • Or *endure*
11 "For thus Amos has said:

'Jeroboam shall die by the sword,
And Israel shall surely be led away
[R]captive
From their own land.'" Amos 5:27; 6:7

12 Then Amaziah said to Amos:

"Go, you seer!
Flee to the land of Judah.
There eat bread,
And there prophesy.

13 But [R]never again prophesy at Bethel,
For it *is* the king's sanctuary, Amos 2:12
And it *is* the royal [T]residence." Lit. *house*

14 Then Amos answered, and said to Amaziah:

"I *was* no prophet,
Nor *was* I a son of a prophet,
[R]But I *was* a herdsman Zech. 13:5
And a tender of sycamore fruit.
15 Then the LORD took me [T]as I followed the flock, Lit. *from behind*
And the LORD said to me,
'Go, prophesy to My people Israel.'
16 Now therefore, hear the word of the LORD:
You say, 'Do not prophesy against Israel,
And [R]do not [T]spout against the house of Isaac.' Ezek. 21:2 • Lit. *drip*

17 "Therefore[R] thus says the LORD:

[R]'Your wife shall be a harlot in the city;
Your sons and daughters shall fall by the sword; Jer. 28:12; 29:21, 32 • Zech. 14:2
Your land shall be divided by *survey* line;
You shall die in a [R]defiled land;
And Israel shall surely be led away captive Hos. 9:3
From his own land.'"

CHAPTER 8

Vision of the Summer Fruit

THUS the Lord GOD showed me: Behold, a basket of summer fruit.
2 And He said, "Amos, what do you see?"
So I said, "A basket of summer fruit." Then
the LORD said to me:

[R]"The end has come upon My people Israel; Ezek. 7:2
[R]I will not pass by them anymore. Amos 7:8
3 And [R]the songs of the temple Amos 5:23
Shall be wailing in that day,"
Says the Lord GOD—
"Many dead bodies everywhere,
They shall throw *them* out in silence."

4 Hear this, you who [T]swallow up the needy, Or *trample on,* Amos 2:7
And make the poor of the land fail,

5 Saying:

"When will the New Moon be past,
That we may sell grain?
And [R]the Sabbath, Neh. 13:15
That we may [T]trade *our* wheat? Lit. *open*
[R]Making the ephah small and the shekel large, Mic. 6:10, 11
Falsifying the balances by deceit,
6 That we may buy the poor for [R]silver,
And the needy for a pair of sandals—
Even sell the bad wheat?" Amos 2:6

7 The LORD has sworn by [R]the pride of Jacob: Amos 6:8
"Surely [R]I will never forget any of their works. Hos. 7:2; 8:13
8 [R]Shall the land not tremble for this,
And everyone mourn who dwells in it?
All of it shall swell like *the River,
Heave and subside
[R]Like the River of Egypt. Hos. 4:3 • Amos 9:5

9 "And it shall come to pass in that day," says the Lord GOD,
[R]"That I will make the sun go down at noon,
And I will darken the earth in [T]broad daylight; Job 5:14 • Lit. *a day of light*
10 I will turn your feasts into [R]mourning,
[R]And all your songs into lamentation;
[R]I will bring sackcloth on every waist,
And baldness on every head;
I will make it like mourning for an only son, Ezek. 7:18 • Ezek. 27:31 • [Zech. 12:10]
And its end like a bitter day.

11 "Behold, the days are coming," says the Lord GOD,
"That I will send a famine on the land,
Not a famine of bread,
Nor a thirst for water,
But of hearing the words of the LORD.
12 They shall wander from sea to sea,
And from north to east;
They shall run to and fro, seeking the word of the LORD,
But shall [R]not find *it*. Hos. 5:6

13 "In that day the fair virgins
And strong young men
Shall faint from thirst.
14 Those who [R]swear by the [T]sin of Samaria, Hos. 4:15 • Or *Ashima,* a Syrian goddess
Who say,
'As your god lives, O Dan!'
And, 'As the way of Beersheba lives!'
They shall fall and never rise again."

CHAPTER 9

Vision of the Stricken Doorposts

I SAW the Lord standing by the altar, and He said:

8:8 The Nile; So with Heb. mss., LXX, Tg., Syr., Vg. and Amos 9:5; MT *the light*

"Strike the [T]doorposts, that the
thresholds may shake, Capital of the pillars
And [R]break them on the heads of them
all. Hab. 3:13
I will slay the last of them with the
sword.
[R]He who flees from them shall not get
away, Amos 2:14
And he who escapes from them shall
not be delivered.

2 "Though they dig into [T]hell, Or *Sheol*
From there My hand shall take them;
[R]Though they climb up to heaven, Jer. 51:53
From there I will bring them down;
3 And though they [R]hide themselves on
top of Carmel,
From there I will search and take them;
Though they hide from My sight at the
bottom of the sea,
From there I will command the serpent,
and it shall bite them; Jer. 23:24
4 Though they go into captivity before
their enemies,
From there [R]I will command the sword,
And it shall slay them. Lev. 26:33
[R]I will set My eyes on them for harm
and not for good." Jer. 21:10; 39:16; 44:11

5 The Lord GOD of hosts,
He who touches the earth and it [R]melts,
And all who dwell there mourn; Mic. 1:4
All of it shall swell like the River,
And subside like the River of Egypt.
6 He who builds His [R]layers[T] in the sky,
And has founded His strata in the earth;
Who [R]calls for the waters of the sea,
And pours them out on the face of the
earth— Ps. 104:3, 13 • Or *stairs* • Amos 5:8
[R]The LORD *is* His name. Amos 4:13; 5:27

7 "*Are* you not like the [T]people of Ethiopia
to Me, Lit. *song of the Ethiopians*
O children of Israel?" says the LORD.
"Did I not bring up Israel from the land
of Egypt,
The Philistines from [T]Caphtor, Crete
And the Syrians from [R]Kir? Amos 1:5

8 "Behold, [R]the eyes of the Lord GOD *are*
on the sinful kingdom, Amos 9:4
And I [R]will destroy it from the face of
the earth; Jer. 5:10; 30:11
Yet I will not utterly destroy the house
of Jacob,"
Says the LORD.

9 "For surely I will command,
And will [T]sift the house of Israel among
all nations,
As *grain* is sifted in a sieve;
[R]Yet not the smallest [T]grain shall fall to
the ground. *shake* • [Is. 65:8–16] • Lit. *pebble*
10 All the sinners of My people shall die by
the sword,
[R]Who say, 'The calamity shall not
overtake *us*
Nor confront us.' Amos 6:3

The Five Promises of the Restoration of Israel

11 "On[R] that day I will raise up Acts 15:16–18
The [T]tabernacle of David, which has
fallen down, Lit. *booth*
And repair its damages;
I will raise up its ruins,
And rebuild it as in the days of old;
12 [R]That they may possess the remnant of
[R]Edom,* Obad. 19 • Num. 24:18
And all the Gentiles who are called by
My name,"
Says the LORD who does this thing.

13 "Behold, [R]the days are coming," says the
LORD,
"When the plowman shall overtake the
reaper,
And the treader of grapes him who
sows seed;
[R]The mountains shall drip with sweet
wine, Lev. 26:5 • Joel 3:18
And all the hills shall flow *with it.*
14 [R]I will bring back the captives of My
people Israel;
[R]They shall build the waste cities and
inhabit *them;*
They shall plant vineyards and drink
wine from them;
They shall also make gardens and eat
fruit from them. Jer. 30:3, 18 • Is. 61:4
15 I will plant them in their land,
[R]And no longer shall they be pulled up
From the land I have given them,"
Says the LORD your God. Ezek. 34:28; 37:25

9:12 LXX *mankind*

THE BOOK OF

OBADIAH

THE BOOK OF OBADIAH

A struggle that began in the womb between twin brothers, Esau and Jacob, eventuates in a struggle between their respective descendants, the Edomites and the Israelites. For the Edomites' stubborn refusal to aid Israel, first during the time of wilderness wandering (Num. 20:14–21) and later during a time of invasion, they are roundly condemned by Obadiah. This little-known prophet describes their crimes, tries their case, and pronounces their judgment: total destruction.

The Hebrew name *Obadyah* means "Worshiper of Yahweh" or "Servant of Yahweh." The Greek title in the Septuagint is *Obdiou*, and the Latin title in the Vulgate is *Abdias*.

THE AUTHOR OF OBADIAH

Obadiah was an obscure prophet who probably lived in the southern kingdom of Judah. Nothing is known of his hometown or family, but it is not likely that he came out of the kingly or priestly line, because his father is not mentioned (1:1). There are thirteen Obadiahs in the Old Testament, and some scholars have attempted to identify the author of this book with one of the other twelve. Four of the better prospects are: (1) the officer in Ahab's palace who hid God's prophets in a cave (1 Kin. 18:3); (2) one of the officials sent out by Jehoshaphat to teach the law in the cities of Judah (2 Chr. 17:7); (3) one of the overseers who took part in repairing the temple under Josiah (2 Chr. 34:12); or (4) a priest in the time of Nehemiah (Neh. 10:5).

THE TIME OF OBADIAH

Obadiah mentions no kings, so verses 10–14 provide the only historical reference point to aid in determining the book's time and setting. However, scholars disagree about which invasion of Jerusalem Obadiah had in mind. There are four possibilities: (1) In 926 B.C., Shishak of Egypt plundered the temple and palace of Jerusalem in the reign of Rehoboam (1 Kin. 14:25, 26). At this time, Edom was still subject to Judah. This does not fit Obadiah 10–14, which indicates that Edom was independent of Judah. (2) During the reign of Jehoram (848–841 B.C.), the Philistines and Arabians invaded Judah and looted the palace (2 Chr. 21:16, 17). Edom revolted during the reign of Jehoram and became a bitter antagonist (2 Kin. 8:20–22; 2 Chr. 21:8–20). This fits the description of Obadiah. (3) In 790 B.C., King Jehoash of Israel invaded Judah (2 Kin. 14; 2 Chr. 25). However, Obadiah in verse 11 calls the invaders "strangers." This would be an inappropriate term for describing the army of the northern kingdom. (4) In 586 B.C., Nebuchadnezzar of Babylon defeated and destroyed Jerusalem (2 Kin. 24 and 25).

The two best candidates are (2) and (4). Obadiah 10–14 seems to fit (2) better than (4) because it does not indicate the total destruction of the city, which took place when Nebuchadnezzar burned the palace and temple and razed the walls. And Nebuchadnezzar certainly would not have "cast lots for Jerusalem" (11) with anyone. Also, all of the other prophets who speak of the destruction of 586 B.C. identify Nebuchadnezzar and the Babylonians as the agents; but Obadiah leaves the enemy unidentified. For these and other reasons, it appears likely that the plundering of Jerusalem written of in Obadiah was by the Philistines between 848 and 841 B.C. This would make the prophet a contemporary of Elisha, and Obadiah would be the earliest of the writing prophets, predating Joel by a few years.

The history of Edom began with Esau who was given the name Edom ("Red") because of the red stew for which he traded his birthright. Esau moved to the mountainous area of Seir and absorbed the Horites, the original inhabitants. Edom refused to allow Israel to pass through their land on the way to Canaan. The Edomites opposed Saul and were subdued under David and Solomon. They fought against Jehoshaphat and successfully rebelled against Jehoram. They were again conquered by Judah under Amaziah, but they regained their freedom during the reign of Ahaz. Edom was later controlled by Assyria and Babylon; and in the fifth century B.C. the Edomites were forced by the Nabateans to leave their territory. They moved to the area of southern Palestine and became known as Idumeans. Herod the Great, an Idumean, became king of Judea under Rome in 37 B.C. In a sense, the enmity between Esau and Jacob was continued in Herod's attempt to murder Jesus. The Idumeans participated in the rebellion of Jerusalem against Rome and were defeated along with the Jews by Titus in A.D. 70. Ironically, the Edomites applauded the destruction of Jerusalem in 586 B.C. (see Ps. 137:7) but died trying to defend it in A.D. 70. After that time they were never heard of again. As Obadiah predicted, they would be "cut off forever" (10); "and no survivor shall *remain* of the house of Esau" (18).

THE CHRIST OF OBADIAH

Christ is seen in Obadiah as the Judge of the nations (15–16), the Savior of Israel (17–20), and the Possessor of the kingdom (21).

KEYS TO OBADIAH

Key Word: The Judgment of Edom—The major theme of Obadiah is a declaration of Edom's coming doom because of its arrogance and cruelty to Judah: "I will make you small among the nations" (2); "the pride of your heart has deceived you" (3); "how you will be cut off!" (5); "how Esau shall be searched out!" (6); "your mighty men, O Teman, shall be dismayed" (9); "shame shall cover you" (10); "you shall be cut off forever" (10); "as you have done, it shall be done to you" (15). Even the last few verses, which primarily deal with Israel, speak of Edom's downfall (17–21). The secondary theme of Obadiah is the future restoration of Israel and faithfulness of Yahweh to His covenant promises. God's justice will ultimately prevail.

Key Verses: Obadiah 10 and 21—"For *your* violence against your brother Jacob, shame shall cover you, and you shall be cut off forever" (10).

"Then saviors shall come to Mount Zion to judge the mountains of Esau, and the kingdom shall be the LORD's" (21).

SURVEY OF OBADIAH

Obadiah is the shortest book in the Old Testament (twenty-one verses), but it carries one of the strongest messages of judgment in the Old Testament. For Edom there are no pleas to return, no words of consolation or hope. Edom's fate is sealed, and there are no conditions for possible deliverance. God will bring total destruction upon Edom, and there will be no remnant. Obadiah is Edom's day in court, complete with Edom's arraignment, indictment, and sentence. This prophet of poetic justice describes how the Judge of the earth will overthrow the pride of Edom and restore the house of Jacob. The two sections of Obadiah are: the judgment of Edom (1–18) and the restoration of Israel (19–21).

The Judgment of Edom (1-18): The first section of Obadiah makes it clear that the coming overthrow of Edom is a certainty, not a condition. Edom is arrogant (3) because of its secure position in Mount Seir, a mountainous region south of the Dead Sea. Its capital city of Sela (Petra) is protected by a narrow canyon that prevents invasion by an army. But God says this will make no difference. Even a thief does not take everything, but when God destroys Edom it will be totally ransacked. Nothing will avert God's complete judgment. Verses 10–14 describe Edom's major crime of gloating over the invasion of Jerusalem. Edom rejoiced when foreigners plundered Jerusalem, and became as one of them. On the day when she should have been allies with Judah, she instead became an aggressor against Judah. Edom will eventually be judged during the coming day of the Lord when Israel "shall be a fire, . . . but the house of Esau *shall be* stubble" (18).

The Restoration of Israel (19-21): The closing verses give hope to God's people that they will possess not only their own land, but also that of Edom and Philistia.

FOCUS	JUDGMENT OF EDOM			RESTORATION OF ISRAEL
REFERENCE	1—	—10—	—15—	—19—21
DIVISION	PREDICTIONS OF JUDGMENT	REASONS FOR JUDGMENT	RESULTS OF JUDGMENT	POSSESSION OF EDOM BY ISRAEL
TOPIC	DEFEAT OF ISRAEL			VICTORY OF ISRAEL
	PREDICTION OF JUDGMENT			PREDICTION OF POSSESSION
LOCATION	EDOM AND ISRAEL			
TIME	c. 840 B.C.			

OUTLINE OF OBADIAH

I. The Predictions of Judgment on Edom . . . vv. 1–9

II. The Reasons for the Judgment on Edom . . . . vv. 10–14

III. The Results of the Judgment on Edom . . . . vv. 15–18

IV. The Possession of Edom by Israel . . . . . vv. 19–21

The Predictions of Judgment on Edom

THE vision of Obadiah.

Thus says the Lord GOD [R]concerning
Edom
[R](We have heard a report from the LORD,
And a messenger has been sent among
the nations, *saying,*
"Arise, and let us rise up against her for
battle"): Is. 21:11 • Jer. 49:14–16

2 "Behold, I will make you small among
the nations;
You shall be greatly despised.
3 The [R]pride of your heart has deceived
you,
You who dwell in the clefts of the rock,
Whose habitation is high;
[R]*You* who say in your heart,
'Who will bring me down to the
ground?' Jer. 49:16 • Rev. 18:7
4 [R]Though you exalt *yourself as* high as
the eagle, Job 20:6
And though you [R]set your nest among
the stars, Hab. 2:9
From there I will bring you down," says
the LORD.

5 "If [R]thieves had come to you,
If robbers by night— Jer. 49:9
Oh, how you will be cut off!—
Would they not have stolen till they
had enough?
If grape-gatherers had come to you,
[R]Would they not have left *some*
gleanings? Deut. 24:21

6 "Oh, how Esau shall be searched out!
How his hidden treasures shall be
sought after!
7 All the men in your confederacy
Shall force you to the border;
[R]The men at peace with you Jer. 38:22
Shall deceive you *and* prevail against
you.
Those who eat your bread shall lay a
[T]trap for you. Or *wound* or *plot*
[R]No one is aware of it. Is. 19:11

8 "Will[R] I not in that day," says the LORD,
"Even destroy the wise *men* from Edom,
And understanding from the mountains
of Esau? [Job 5:12–14]
9 Then your [R]mighty men, O [R]Teman,
shall be dismayed, Ps. 76:5 • Jer. 49:7
To the end that everyone from the
mountains of Esau
May be cut off by slaughter.

The Reasons for the Judgment on Edom

10 "For *your* [R]violence against your brother
Jacob, Gen. 27:41
Shame shall cover you,
And you shall be cut off forever.
11 In the day that you [R]stood on the other
side— Ps. 83:5–8
In the day that strangers carried
captive his forces,
When foreigners entered his gates
And [R]cast lots for Jerusalem—
Even you *were* as one of them. Nah. 3:10

12 But you should not have [R]gazed on the
day of your brother Mic. 4:11; 7:10
In the day of his captivity;
Nor should you have [R]rejoiced over the
children of Judah [Prov. 17:5]
In the day of their destruction;
Nor should you have spoken proudly
In the day of distress.
13 You should not have entered the gate
of My people
In the day of their calamity.
Indeed, you should not have [T]gazed on
their affliction
In the day of their calamity,
Nor laid *hands* on their substance
In the day of their calamity. Gloated over
14 You should not have stood at the
crossroads
To cut off those among them who
escaped;
Nor should you have [T]delivered up
those among them who remained
In the day of distress. To the enemy

The Results of the Judgment on Edom

15 "For[R] the day of the LORD upon all the
nations *is* near;
[R]As you have done, it shall be done to
you;
Your [T]reprisal shall return upon your
own head. Ezek. 30:3 • Hab. 2:8 • Or *reward*
16 [R]For as you drank on my holy mountain,
So shall all the nations drink
continually;
Yes, they shall drink, and swallow,
And they shall be as though they had
never been. Joel 3:17

17 "But on Mount Zion there [R]shall be
[T]deliverance,
And there shall be holiness;
The house of Jacob shall possess their
possessions. Amos 9:8 • Or *salvation*
18 The house of Jacob shall be a fire,
And the house of Joseph [R]a flame;
But the house of Esau *shall be* stubble;
They shall kindle them and devour
them,
And no survivor shall *remain* of the
house of Esau,"
For the LORD has spoken. Zech. 12:6

The Possession of Edom by Israel

19 *The inhabitants of* the [T]South
[R]Shall possess the mountains of Esau,
[R]And *the inhabitants of* the Philistine
lowland. Heb. *Negev* • Is. 11:14 • Zeph. 2:7
They shall possess the fields of Ephraim
And the fields of Samaria.
Benjamin *shall possess* Gilead.
20 And the captives of this host of the
children of Israel
Shall possess the land of the Canaanites
As [R]far as Zarephath. 1 Kin. 17:9
The captives of Jerusalem who are in
Sepharad
Shall possess the cities of the South.
21 Then [R]saviors[T] shall come to Mount
Zion [James 5:20] • Or *deliverers*
To judge the mountains of Esau,
And the kingdom shall be the LORD's.

THE BOOK OF

JONAH

THE BOOK OF JONAH

Nineveh is northeast; Tarshish is west. When God calls Jonah to preach repentance to the wicked Ninevites, the prophet knows that God's mercy may follow. He turns down the assignment and heads for Tarshish instead. But once God has dampened his spirits (by tossing him out of the boat and into the water) and has demonstrated His protection (by moving him out of the water and into the fish), Jonah realizes God is serious about His command. Nineveh must hear the word of the Lord; therefore Jonah goes. Although the preaching is a success, the preacher comes away angry and discouraged and he must learn firsthand of God's compassion for sinful men.

Yonah is the Hebrew word for "dove." The Septuagint hellenized this word into *Ionas,* and the Latin Vulgate used the title *Jonas.*

THE AUTHOR OF JONAH

The first verse introduces Jonah as "the son of Amittai." Nothing more would be known about him were it not for another reference to him in Second Kings 14:25 as a prophet in the reign of Jeroboam II of Israel. Under Jeroboam, the borders of Israel were expanded "according to the word of the LORD God of Israel, which He had spoken through His servant Jonah the son of Amittai, the prophet who *was* from Gath Hepher." Gath Hepher was three miles north of Nazareth in lower Galilee, making Jonah a prophet of the northern kingdom. The Pharisees were wrong when they said, "Search and look, for no prophet has arisen out of Galilee" (John 7:52), because Jonah was a Galilean. One Jewish tradition says that Jonah was the son of the widow of Zarephath whom Elijah raised from the dead (1 Kin. 17:8–24).

Some critics claim that Jonah was written during the fifth to third centuries B.C. as a historical fiction to oppose the "narrow nationalism" of Ezra and Nehemiah by introducing universalistic ideas. They say an anonymous writer created this work to counteract the Jewish practice of excluding the Samaritans from worship and of divorcing foreign wives. To support this view, it is noted that the book is written in the third person with no claim that Jonah wrote it. The use of Aramaic words and the statement that "Nineveh was an exceedingly great city" (3:3) indicate a late date after Nineveh's fall in 612 B.C.

Conservative scholars refute this claim with these arguments: (1) The idea of God's inclusion of the Gentiles in His program is found elsewhere in the Scripture (cf. Gen. 9:27; 12:3; Lev. 19:33, 34; 1 Sam. 2:10; Is. 2:2; Joel 2:28–32). (2) Aramaic words occur in early as well as late Old Testament books. Aramaic is found in Near Eastern texts as early as 1500 B.C. (3) The fact that the book does not explicitly say that it was written by Jonah is an argument from silence. (4) Use of the third-person style was common among biblical writers. (5) The text in 3:3 literally means "had become." At the time of the story, Nineveh had already become a very large city. (6) Jonah was a historical prophet (2 Kin. 14:25), and there are no hints that the book is fictional or allegorical. (7) Christ supported the historical accuracy of the book (Matt. 12:39–41).

THE TIME OF JONAH

Jonah was a contemporary of Jeroboam II of Israel (782–753 B.C.) who ministered after the time of Elisha and just before the time of Amos and Hosea. Israel under Jeroboam II was enjoying a period of resurgence and prosperity (see "The Time of Amos"). Conditions looked promising after many bleak years, and nationalistic fervor was probably high. During these years, Assyria was in a period of mild decline. Weak rulers had ascended the throne, but Assyria remained a threat. By the time of Jonah, Assyrian cruelty had become legendary. Graphic accounts of their cruel treatment of captives have been found in ancient Assyrian records, especially from the ninth and seventh centuries B.C. The repentance of Nineveh probably occurred in the reign of Ashurdan III (773–755 B.C.). Two plagues (765 and 759 B.C.) and a solar eclipse (763 B.C.) may have prepared the people for Jonah's message of judgment.

THE CHRIST OF JONAH

Jonah is the only prophet whom Jesus likened to Himself. "But He answered and said to them, 'An evil and adulterous generation seeks after a sign, and no sign will be given to it except the sign of the prophet Jonah. For as Jonah was three days and three nights in the belly of the great fish, so will the Son of Man be three days and three nights in the heart of the earth. The men of Nineveh will rise in the judgment with this generation and condemn it, because they repented at the preaching of Jonah; and indeed a greater than Jonah *is* here' " (Matt. 12:39–41). Jonah's experience is a type of the death, burial, and resurrection of Christ. (The Hebrew idiom, "three days and three nights," only requires a portion of the first and third days.)

KEYS TO JONAH

Key Word: The Revival in Nineveh—God's loving concern for the Gentiles is not a truth disclosed only in the New Testament. More than seven centuries before Christ, God commissioned the Hebrew prophet Jonah to proclaim a message of repentance to the Assyrians. Jewish nationalism, however, blinded both God's prophets and covenant people to God's worldwide purposes of salvation. The story of Jonah is one of the clearest demonstrations of God's love and mercy for all mankind in the entire Scriptures.

Key Verses: Jonah 2:8, 9; 4:2—"Those who regard worthless idols forsake their own Mercy. But I will sacrifice to You with the voice of thanksgiving; I will pay what I have vowed. Salvation *is* of the LORD" (2:8, 9).

"So he prayed to the LORD, and said, 'Ah, LORD, was not this what I said when I was still in my country? Therefore I fled previously to Tarshish; for I know that You *are* a gracious and merciful God, slow to anger and abundant in lovingkindness, One who relents from doing harm'" (4:2).

Key Chapter: Jonah 3—The third chapter of Jonah records perhaps the greatest revival of all time as the entire city of Nineveh "[believes] God, and [proclaims] a fast," and cries out to God.

SURVEY OF JONAH

Jonah is an unusual book because of its message and messenger. Unlike other Old Testament books, it revolves exclusively around a gentile nation. God is concerned for the Gentiles as well as for His covenant people Israel. But God's messenger is a reluctant prophet who does not want to proclaim his message for fear that the Assyrians will respond and be spared by the compassionate God of Israel. Of all the people and things mentioned in the book—the storm, the lots, the sailors, the fish, the Ninevites, the plant, the worm, and the east wind—only the prophet himself fails to obey God. All these were used to teach Jonah a lesson in compassion and obedience. The four chapters divide: the first commission of Jonah (1 and 2) and the second commission of Jonah (3 and 4).

The First Commission of Jonah (1 and 2): This chapter records the commission of Jonah (1:1, 2), the disobedience of Jonah (1:3), and the judgment on Jonah (1:4–17). Jonah does not want to see God spare the notoriously cruel Assyrians. To preach a message of repentance to them would be like helping Israel's enemy. In his patriotic zeal, Jonah put his country before his God and refused to represent Him in Nineveh. Instead of going five hundred miles northeast to Nineveh, Jonah attempts to go two thousand miles west to Tarshish (Spain). But the Lord uses a creative series of counter-measures to accomplish His desired result. Jonah's efforts to thwart God's plan are futile.

God prepares a "great fish" to preserve Jonah and deliver him on dry land. The fish and its divinely appointed rendezvous with the sinking prophet became a powerful reminder to Jonah of the sovereignty of God in every circumstance. While inside the fish (2), Jonah utters a declarative praise psalm which alludes to several psalms that were racing through his mind (Ps. 3:8; 31:22; 42:7; 69:1). In his unique "prayer closet," Jonah offers thanksgiving for his deliverance from drowning. When he acknowledges that "salvation *is* of the LORD" (2:9), he is finally willing to obey and be used by God. After he is cast up on the shore, Jonah has a long time to reflect on his experiences during his eastward trek of five hundred miles to Nineveh.

The Second Commission of Jonah (3 and 4): Jonah obeys his second commission to go to Nineveh (3:1–4) where he becomes "a sign to the

FOCUS	FIRST COMMISSION OF JONAH				SECOND COMMISSION OF JONAH			
REFERENCE	1:1—	1:4—	2:1—	2:10—	3:1—	3:5—	4:1—	4:4—4:11
DIVISION	DISOBEDIENCE TO THE FIRST CALL	JUDGMENT ON JONAH EXACTED	PRAYER OF JONAH IN THE FISH	DELIVERANCE OF JONAH FROM THE FISH	OBEDIENCE TO THE SECOND CALL	JUDGMENT ON NINEVEH AVERTED	PRAYER OF JONAH	REBUKE OF JONAH
TOPIC	GOD'S MERCY UPON JONAH				GOD'S MERCY UPON NINEVEH			
	"I WON'T GO."		"I WILL GO."		"I'M HERE."		"I SHOULDN'T HAVE COME."	
LOCATION	THE GREAT SEA				THE GREAT CITY			
TIME	c. 760 B.C.							

Ninevites" (Luke 11:30). The prophet is a walking object lesson from God, his skin no doubt bleached from his stay in the fish. As he proceeds through the city, his one-sentence sermon brings incredible results: it is the most responsive evangelistic effort in history. Jonah's words of coming judgment are followed by a proclamation by the king of the city to fast and repent. Because of His great mercy, God "relented from the disaster that He had said He would bring upon them" (3:10).

In the final chapter, God's love and grace are contrasted with Jonah's anger and lack of compassion. He is unhappy with the good results of his message because he knows God will now spare Nineveh. God uses a plant, a worm, and a wind to teach Jonah a lesson in compassion. Jonah's emotions shift from fierce anger (4:1), to despondency (4:3), then to great joy (4:6), and finally to despair (4:8). In a humorous but meaningful account, Jonah is forced to see that he has more concern for a plant than for hundreds of thousands of people (if 120,000 children are in mind in 4:11, the population of the area may have been 600,000). Jonah's lack of a divine perspective makes his repentance a greater problem than the repentance of Nineveh.

OUTLINE OF JONAH

I. The First Commission of Jonah . . . . 1:1—2:10

A. The Disobedience to the First Call 1:1–3
B. The Judgment on Jonah Is Exacted 1:4–17
  1. The Great Storm 1:4–16
  2. The Great Salvation of Jonah by the Fish 1:17
C. The Prayer of Jonah 2:1–9
D. The Deliverance of Jonah. 2:10

II. The Second Commission of Jonah . . . . . . 3:1—4:11

A. The Obedience to the Second Call 3:1–4
B. The Judgment of Nineveh Averted 3:5–10
  1. The Great Fast 3:5–9
  2. The Great Salvation of Nineveh by God 3:10
C. The Prayer of Jonah 4:1–3
D. The Rebuke of Jonah by God 4:4–11

CHAPTER 1

The Disobedience to the First Call

NOW the word of the LORD came to [R]Jo-
nah the son of Amittai, saying, 2 Kin. 14:25
2 "Arise, go to [R]Nineveh, that great city,
and cry out against it; for [R]their wickedness
has come up before Me." Is. 37:37 · Gen. 18:20
3 But Jonah arose to flee to Tarshish from
the presence of the LORD. He went down to
[R]Joppa, and found a ship going to Tarshish;
so he paid the fare, and went down into it, to
go with them to [R]Tarshish [R]from the presence
of the LORD. Josh. 19:46 · Is. 23:1 · Gen. 4:16

The Great Storm

4 But [R]the LORD [T]sent out a great wind on
the sea, and there was a mighty tempest on
the sea, so that the ship was about to be
broken up. Ps. 107:25 · Lit. *hurled*
5 Then the mariners were afraid; and every
man cried out to his god, and threw the cargo
that *was* in the ship into the sea, to lighten
[T]the load. But Jonah had gone down [R]into the
lowest parts of the ship, had lain down, and
was fast asleep. Lit. *from upon them* · 1 Sam. 24:3
6 So the captain came to him, and said to
him, "What do you mean, sleeper? Arise, call
on your God; perhaps your God will consider
us, so that we may not perish."
7 And they said to one another, "Come, let
us cast lots, that we may know for whose
cause this trouble *has come* upon us." So
they cast lots, and the lot fell on Jonah.
8 Then they said to him, [R]"Please tell us!
For whose cause *is* this trouble upon us?
What is your occupation? And where do you
come from? What is your country? And of
what people are you?" Josh. 7:19
9 And he said to them, "I *am* a Hebrew;
and I fear the LORD, the God of heaven, who
made the sea and the dry *land*."
10 Then the men were exceedingly afraid,
and said to him, "Why have you done this?"
For the men knew that he fled from the
presence of the LORD, because he had told
them.
11 Then they said to him, "What shall we do
to you that the sea may be calm for us?"—for
the sea was growing more tempestuous.
12 And he said to them, "Pick me up and
[T]throw me into the sea; then the sea will
become calm for you. For I know that this
great tempest *is* because of me." Lit. *hurl*
13 Nevertheless the men rowed hard to
bring *the ship* to land, [R]but they could not, for
the sea continued to grow more tempestuous
against them. [Prov. 21:30]
14 Therefore they cried out to the LORD and
said, "We pray, O LORD, please do not let us
perish for this man's life, and [R]do not charge
us with innocent blood; for You, O LORD,
have done as it pleased You." Deut. 21:8
15 So they picked up Jonah and threw him

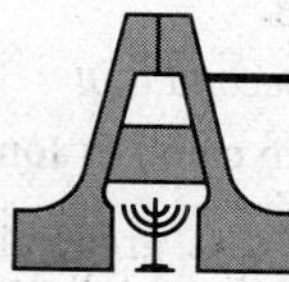

THE CITY OF NINEVEH

Founded by Nimrod, great-grandson of Noah (Gen. 10:6–12), Nineveh was for many years the capital city of the mighty Assyrian Empire.

At the height of its prosperity, Nineveh was a "great city" (Jon. 1:2; 3:2) with a population of 120,000 (Jon. 4:11). It would have taken a traveler three days to go around greater Nineveh, with its numerous outlying suburbs, and a day's journey to reach the center of the city (Jon. 3:4).

The most famous biblical personality connected with ancient Nineveh was the prophet Jonah. Assyrian kings were cruel and ruthless. This pagan nation had invaded and pillaged the homeland of the Israelites on numerous occasions when Jonah visited Nineveh about 760 B.C. The prophet wanted the city destroyed—not saved—because of its wickedness. But the people repented and were spared by a compassionate God (Jon. 3:10). God's love for a pagan people was deeper than His messenger could understand or accept.

Nineveh was eventually destroyed about 150 years after Jonah's visit—in 612 B.C. It fell after a long siege by an alliance of Medes, Babylonians, and Scythians. The attackers entered the city through walls made weak by a flooding of the Khosr and Tigris rivers. The sun-dried bricks of its buildings were also dissolved. This was a remarkable fulfillment of the prophecy of Nahum: "The gates of the rivers are opened, and the palace is dissolved" (Nah. 2:6).

Significant archaeological discoveries at Nineveh include the temples of Nabu and Ishtar, Assyrian gods, and the palaces of three Assyrian kings—Ashurbanipal, Ashurnasirpal, and Sennacherib (see map). One of the most important discoveries was the royal library of Ashurbanipal, which contained over sixteen thousand cuneiform tablets. These include Mesopotamian stories of creation and the flood, as well as many other religious and historical texts. It was to Nineveh that Sennacherib brought the tribute he exacted from King Hezekiah of Judah (2 Kin. 18:13–15).

Nineveh was one of the oldest cities of the ancient Near East. Excavations down to the virgin soil indicate the site was first occupied about 4500 B.C.

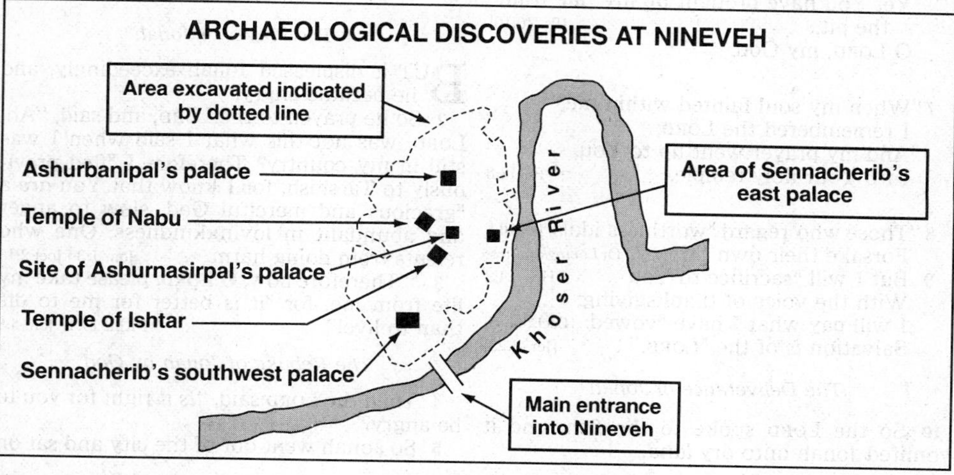

into the sea, [R]and the sea ceased from its
raging. [Ps. 89:9; 107:29]
16 Then the men [R]feared the LORD exceedingly, and offered a sacrifice to the LORD and
made vows. Acts 5:11

The Great Salvation of Jonah by the Fish

17 Now the LORD had prepared a great fish
to swallow Jonah. And Jonah was in the belly
of the fish three days and three nights.

CHAPTER 2

The Prayer of Jonah

THEN Jonah prayed to the LORD his God
from the fish's belly.
2 And he said:

"I [R]cried out to the LORD because of my
affliction, Ps. 120:1
[R]And He answered me. Ps. 65:2

"Out of the belly of Sheol I cried,
And You heard my voice.
3 [R]For You cast me into the deep,
Into the heart of the seas,
And the floods surrounded me;
[R]All Your billows and Your waves passed
over me. Ps. 88:6 • Ps. 42:7
4 [R]Then I said, 'I have been cast out of
Your sight;
Yet I will look again [R]toward Your holy
temple.' Ps. 31:22 • 1 Kin. 8:38
5 The [R]waters encompassed me, *even* to
my soul; Lam. 3:54
The deep closed around me;
Weeds were wrapped around my head.
6 I went down to the [T]moorings of the
mountains; *foundations* or *bases*
The earth with its bars *closed* behind
me forever;
Yet You have brought up my [R]life from
the pit, [Ps. 16:10]
O LORD, my God.

7 "When my soul fainted within me,
I remembered the LORD;
[R]And my prayer went *up* to You,
Into Your holy temple. Ps. 18:6

8 "Those who regard [R]worthless idols Jer. 10:8
Forsake their own [T]Mercy. Or *Lovingkindness*
9 But I will [R]sacrifice to You Hos. 14:2
With the voice of thanksgiving;
I will pay what I have [R]vowed. [Eccl. 5:4, 5]
Salvation *is* of the [R]LORD." [Jer. 3:23]

The Deliverance of Jonah

10 So the LORD spoke to the fish, and it
vomited Jonah onto dry *land*.

CHAPTER 3

The Obedience to the Second Call

NOW the word of the LORD came to Jonah
the second time, saying,
2 "Arise, go to Nineveh, that great city,
and preach to it the message that I tell you."
3 So Jonah arose and went to Nineveh,
according to the word of the LORD. Now
Nineveh was an exceedingly great city, [T]a
three-day journey *in extent*. Meaning unknown
4 And Jonah began to enter the city on the
first [T]day's walk. Then [R]he cried out and said,
"Yet forty days, and Nineveh shall be overthrown!" 20 mi. • [Deut. 18:22]

The Great Fast

5 So the [R]people of Nineveh believed God,
proclaimed a fast, and put on sackcloth, from
the greatest to the least of them. [Matt. 12:41]
6 Then word came to the king of Nineveh;
and he arose from his throne and laid aside
his robe, covered *himself* with sackcloth [R]and
sat in ashes. Job 2:8
7 And he caused *it* to be proclaimed and
published throughout Nineveh by the decree
of the king and his nobles, saying, "Let
neither man nor beast, herd nor flock, taste
anything; do not let them eat, or drink water.
8 "But let man and beast be covered with
sackcloth, and cry mightily to God; yes, let
every one turn from his evil way and from
[R]the violence that is in his hands. Is. 59:6
9 [R]"Who can tell *if* God will turn and
relent, and turn away from His fierce anger,
so that we may not perish?" Joel 2:14

The Great Salvation of Nineveh by God

10 [R]Then God saw their works, that they
turned from their evil way; and God relented
from the disaster that He had said He would
bring upon them, and He did not do it. Jer. 18:8

CHAPTER 4

The Prayer of Jonah

BUT it displeased Jonah exceedingly, and
he became angry.
2 So he prayed to the LORD, and said, "Ah,
LORD, was not this what I said when I was
still in my country? Therefore I [R]fled previously to Tarshish; for I know that You *are* a
[R]gracious and merciful God, slow to anger
and abundant in lovingkindness, One who
relents from doing harm. Jon. 1:3 • Joel 2:13
3 [R]"Therefore now, O LORD, please take my
life from me, for [R]*it is* better for me to die
than to live!" 1 Kin. 19:4 • Jon. 4:8

The Rebuke of Jonah by God

4 Then the LORD said, "*Is it* right for you to
be angry?"
5 So Jonah went out of the city and sat on

the east side of the city. There he made
himself a shelter and sat under it in the
shade, till he might see what would become
of the city.
6 And the LORD God prepared a ᵀplant and
made it come up over Jonah, that it might be
shade for his head to deliver him from his
misery. So Jonah was very grateful for the
plant. Heb. *kikayon*, exact identity unknown
7 But as morning dawned the next day
God prepared a worm, and it *so* damaged the
plant that it withered.
8 And it happened, when the sun arose,
that God prepared a vehement east wind; and
the sun beat on Jonah's head, so that he grew
faint. Then he wished death for himself, and
said, "*It is* better for me to die than to live."
9 Then God said to Jonah, "*Is it* right for
you to be angry about the plant?" And he
said, "*It is* right for me to be angry, even to
death!"
10 But the LORD said, "You have had pity
on the plant for which you have not labored,
nor made it grow, which ᵀcame up in a night
and perished in a night. Lit. *was a son of a night*
11 "And should I not pity Nineveh, that
great city, in which are more than one hundred and twenty thousand persons who cannot discern between their right hand and
their left, and *also* much livestock?"

THE BOOK OF

MICAH

THE BOOK OF MICAH

Micah, called from his rustic home to be a prophet, leaves his familiar surroundings to deliver a stern message of judgment to the princes and people of Jerusalem. Burdened by the abusive treatment of the poor by the rich and influential, the prophet turns his verbal rebukes upon any who would use their social or political power for personal gain. One-third of Micah's book exposes the sins of his countrymen; another third pictures the punishment God is about to send; and the final third holds out the hope of restoration once that discipline has ended. Through it all, God's righteous demands upon His people are clear: "to do justly, to love mercy, and to walk humbly with your God" (6:8).

The name *Michayahu* ("Who Is Like Yahweh?") is shortened to *Michaia.* In 7:18, Micah hints at his own name with the phrase "Who *is* a God like You?" The Greek and Latin titles of this book are *Michaias* and *Micha.*

THE AUTHOR OF MICAH

Micah's hometown of Moresheth Gath (1:14) was located about twenty-five miles southwest of Jerusalem on the border of Judah and Philistia, near Gath. Like Amos, Micah was from the country. His family and occupation are unknown, but Moresheth was in a productive agricultural belt. Micah was not as aware of the political situation as Isaiah or Daniel, but he showed a profound concern for the sufferings of the people. His clear sense of prophetic calling is seen in 3:8: "But truly I am full of power by the Spirit of the LORD, and of justice and might, to declare to Jacob his transgression and to Israel his sin."

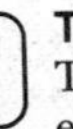

THE TIME OF MICAH

The first verse indicates that Micah prophesied in the days of Jotham (739–731 B.C.), Ahaz (731–715 B.C.), and Hezekiah (715–686 B.C.), kings of Judah. Although Micah deals primarily with Judah, he also addresses the northern kingdom of Israel and predicts the fall of Samaria (1:6). Much of his ministry, therefore, took place before the Assyrian captivity of Israel in 722 B.C. His strong denunciations of idolatry and immorality also suggest that his ministry largely preceded the sweeping religious reforms of Hezekiah. Thus, Micah's prophecies ranged from about 735 to 710 B.C. He was a contemporary of Hosea in the northern kingdom and of Isaiah in the court of Jerusalem.

After the prosperous reign of Uzziah in Judah (767–739 B.C.), his son, Jotham, came to power and followed the same policies (739–731 B.C.). He was a good king, although he failed to remove the idolatrous high places. Under the wicked King Ahaz (731–715 B.C.), Judah was threatened by the forces of Assyria and Syria. Hezekiah (715–686 B.C.) opposed the Assyrians and successfully withstood an Assyrian siege with the help of God. He was an unusually good king who guided the people of Judah back to a proper course in their walk with God.

During the ministry of Micah, the kingdom of Israel continued to crumble inwardly and outwardly until its collapse in 722 B.C. The Assyrian Empire under Tiglath-Pileser III (745–727 B.C.), Shalmaneser V (727–722 B.C.), Sargon II (722–705 B.C.), and Sennacherib (705–681 B.C.) reached the zenith of its power and became a constant threat to Judah. Babylon was still under Assyrian domination, and Micah's prediction of future Babylonian captivity for Judah (4:10) must have seemed unlikely.

THE CHRIST OF MICAH

Micah 5:2 is one of the clearest and most important of all Old Testament prophecies: "But you, Bethlehem Ephrathah, *though* you are little among the thousands of Judah, *yet* out of you shall come forth to Me the One to be ruler in Israel, whose goings forth *have been* from of old, from everlasting." This prophecy about the birthplace and eternity of the Messiah was made seven hundred years before His birth. The chief priests and scribes paraphrased this verse in Matthew 2:5, 6 when questioned about the birthplace of the Messiah. Micah 2:12, 13; 4:1–8; and 5:4, 5 offer some of the best Old Testament descriptions of the righteous reign of Christ over the whole world.

KEYS TO MICAH

Key Word: The Judgment and Restoration of Judah—Micah exposes the injustice of Judah and the righteousness and justice of Yahweh. About one-third of the book indicts Israel and Judah for specific sins, including oppression; bribery among judges, prophets, and priests; exploitation of the powerless; covetousness; cheating; violence; and pride. Another third of Micah predicts the judgment that will come as a result of those sins. The remaining third of the book is a message of hope and consolation. God's justice will triumph and the divine Deliverer will come. True peace and justice will prevail only when the Messiah reigns. The "goodness and severity of God" (Rom. 11:22) are illustrated in Micah's presentation of divine judgment and pardon. This book emphasizes the integral relationship between true spirituality and social ethics. Micah 6:8 summarizes what God wants to see in His people: justice and equity tempered with mercy and compassion, as the result of a humble and obedient relationship with Him.

Key Verses: Micah 6:8; 7:18—"He has shown you, O man, what *is* good; and what does the LORD require of you but to do justly, to love mercy, and to walk humbly with your God?" (6:8).

"Who *is* a God like You, pardoning iniquity and passing over the transgression of the remnant of His heritage? He does not retain His anger forever, because He delights *in* mercy" (7:18).

Key Chapters: Micah 6; 7—The closing section of Micah describes a courtroom scene. God has a controversy against His people, and He calls the mountains and hills together to form the jury as He sets forth His case. The people have replaced heartfelt worship with empty ritual, thinking that this is all God demands. They have divorced God's standards of justice from their daily dealings in order to cover their unscrupulous practices. They have failed to realize what the Lord requires of man. There can only be one verdict: guilty.

Nevertheless, the book closes on a note of hope. The same God who executes judgment also delights to extend mercy. "Who *is* a God like You, pardoning iniquity and passing over the transgression of the remnant of His heritage? He does not retain His anger forever, because He delights *in* mercy" (7:18). No wonder the prophet exclaims, "Therefore I will look to the LORD; I will wait for the God of my salvation; my God will hear me" (7:7).

SURVEY OF MICAH

Micah is the prophet of the downtrodden and exploited people of Judean society. He prophesies during a time of great social injustice and boldly opposes those who impose their power upon the poor and weak for selfish ends. Corrupt rulers, false prophets, and ungodly priests all become targets for Micah's prophetic barbs. Micah exposes judges who are bought by bribes and merchants who use deceptive weights. The pollution of sin has permeated every level of society in Judah and Israel. The whole earth is called to witness God's indictment against His people (1:2; 6:1, 2), and the guilty verdict leads to a sentence of destruction and captivity. However, while the three major sections begin with condemnation (1:2—2:11; 3:6), they all end on a clear note of consolation (2:12, 13; 4; 5; 7). After sin is punished and justice is established, "He will again have compassion on us, and will subdue our iniquities. You will cast all our sins into the depths of the sea" (7:19). The three sections of Micah are: the prediction of judgment (1—3), the prediction of restoration (4 and 5), and the plea for repentance (6 and 7).

The Prediction of Judgment (1—3): Micah begins by launching into a general declaration of the condemnation of Israel (Samaria) and Judah (Jerusalem). Both kingdoms will be overthrown because of their rampant treachery. Micah uses a series of wordplays on the names of several cities of Judah in his lamentation over Judah's coming destruction (1:10–16). This is followed by some of the specific causes for judgment: premeditated schemes, covetousness, and cruelty. Nevertheless, God will regather a remnant of His people (2:12, 13). The prophet then systematically condemns the princes (3:1–4) and the prophets (3:5–8) and concludes with a warning of coming judgment (3:9–12).

The Prediction of Restoration (4 and 5): Micah then moves into a two-chapter message of hope, which describes the reinstitution of the kingdom (4:1–5) and the intervening captivity of the kingdom (4:6—5:1), concluding with the coming

FOCUS	PREDICTION OF JUDGMENT		PREDICTION OF RESTORATION			PLEA FOR REPENTANCE		
REFERENCE	1:1———3:1———	4:1———	4:6———	5:2———	6:1———	6:10———	7:7———	7:20
DIVISION	JUDGMENT OF PEOPLE	JUDGMENT OF LEADERSHIP	PROMISE OF COMING KINGDOM	PROMISE OF COMING CAPTIVITIES	PROMISE OF COMING KING	FIRST PLEA OF GOD	SECOND PLEA OF GOD	PROMISE OF FINAL SALVATION
TOPIC	PUNISHMENT		PROMISE			PARDON		
	RETRIBUTION		RESTORATION			REPENTANCE		
LOCATION	JUDAH—ISRAEL							
TIME	c. 735–710 B.C.							

Ruler of the Kingdom (5:2–15). The prophetic focus gradually narrows from the nations to the remnant to the King.

The Plea for Repentance (6 and 7): In His two controversies with His people, God calls them into court and presents an unanswerable case against them. The people have spurned God's grace, choosing instead to revel in wickedness. Micah concludes with a sublime series of promises that the Lord will pardon their iniquity and renew their nation in accordance with His covenant.

OUTLINE OF MICAH

CHAPTER 1

Introduction to the Book of Micah

THE word of the LORD that came to Micah of Moresheth in the days of Jotham, Ahaz, *and* Hezekiah, kings of Judah, which he saw concerning Samaria and Jerusalem.

Judgment on Samaria

2 Hear, all you peoples!
Listen, O earth, and all that is in it!
Let the Lord GOD be a witness against you,
The Lord from [R]His holy temple. [Ps. 11:4]

3 For behold, the LORD is coming out of His place;
He will come down
And tread on the high places of the earth.
4 [R]The mountains will melt under Him, Amos 9:5
And the valleys will split
Like wax before the fire,
Like waters poured down a steep place.
5 All this is for the transgression of Jacob
And for the sins of the house of Israel.
What *is* the transgression of Jacob?
Is it not Samaria?
And what *are* the [R]high places of Judah?
Are they not Jerusalem? Deut. 32:13; 33:29

6 "Therefore I will make Samaria [R]a heap of ruins in the field, 2 Kin. 19:25
Places for planting a vineyard;
I will pour down her stones into the valley,
And I will uncover her foundations.
7 All her carved images shall be beaten to pieces,
And all her [R]pay as a harlot shall be burned with the fire;
All her idols I will lay desolate,
For she gathered *it* from the pay of a harlot,
And they shall return to the [R]pay of a harlot." Hos. 2:5 • Deut. 23:18

8 Therefore I will wail and howl,
I will go stripped and naked;
I will make a wailing like the jackals
And a mourning like the ostriches,

Judgment on Judah

9 For her wounds *are* incurable.
For [R]it has come to Judah;
It has come to the gate of My people,
Even to Jerusalem. 2 Kin. 18:13

10 [R]Tell *it* not in Gath, 2 Sam. 1:20
Weep not at all in [T]Beth Aphrah,
Roll yourself in the dust. Lit. *House of Dust*
11 Pass by in naked shame, you inhabitant of [T]Shaphir;
The inhabitant of [T]Zaanan does not go out.

Beth Ezel mourns;
Its place to stand is taken away from
you. Lit. *Beautiful* • Lit. *Going Out*

12 For the inhabitant of [T]Maroth [T]pined for
good, Lit. *Bitterness* • Lit. *was sick*
But [R]disaster came down from the LORD
To the gate of Jerusalem. Is. 59:9–11
13 O inhabitant of [R]Lachish,
Harness the chariot to the swift steeds
(She *was* the beginning of sin to the
daughter of Zion),
For the transgressions of Israel were
[R]found in you. Is. 36:2 • Ezek. 23:11

14 Therefore you shall give presents to
[T]Moresheth Gath; Lit. *Possession of Gath*
The houses of [R]Achzib[T] *shall be* a lie to
the kings of Israel. Josh. 15:44 • Lit. *Lie*
15 I will yet bring an heir to you, O
inhabitant of [T]Mareshah;
The glory of Israel shall come to
[T]Adullam. Lit. *Inheritance* • Lit. *Refuge*
16 Make yourself [R]bald and cut off your
hair,
Because of your [R]precious children;
Enlarge your baldness like an eagle,
For they shall go from you into
[R]captivity. Job 1:20 • Lam. 4:5 • Amos 7:11, 17

CHAPTER 2

Cause of the Judgment

WOE to those who devise iniquity,
And [T]work out evil on their beds! Plan
At morning light they practice it,
Because it is in the power of their hand.
2 They [R]covet fields and take *them* by
violence,
Also houses, and seize *them.*
So they oppress a man and his house,
A man and his inheritance. Is. 5:8

3 Therefore thus says the LORD:

"Behold, against this [R]family I am
devising [R]disaster,
From which you cannot remove your
necks;
Nor shall you walk haughtily,
For this *is* an evil time. Jer. 8:3 • Amos 5:13
4 In that day *one* shall take up a proverb
against you,
And [R]lament with a bitter lamentation,
and say: 2 Sam. 1:17
'We are utterly destroyed!
He has changed the [T]heritage of my
people; Lit. *portion*
How He has removed *it* from me!
To [T]a turncoat He has divided our
fields.' " Lit. *one turning back,* an apostate

5 Therefore you will have no one to
determine boundaries by lot
In the congregation of the LORD.

6 "Do not prattle," *you say to those* who
[T]prophesy. Or *preach,* lit. *drip* words
So they shall not prophesy to you;
*They shall not return insult for insult.
7 *You who are* named the house of Jacob:
"Is the Spirit of the LORD restricted?
Are these His doings?
Do not My words do good
To him who walks uprightly?

8 "Lately My people have risen up as an
enemy—
You pull off the robe with the garment
From those who trust *you,* as they pass
by,
Like men returned from war.
9 The women of My people you cast out
From their pleasant houses;
From their children
You have taken away My glory forever.

10 "Arise and depart,
For this *is* not *your* [R]rest;
Because it is [R]defiled, it shall destroy
you, Deut. 12:9 • Lev. 18:25
Even with utter destruction.
11 If a man should walk in a false spirit
And speak a lie, *saying,*
'I will [T]prophesy to you [T]of wine and
drink,' Or *preach,* lit. *drip* • *concerning*
Even he would be the [R]prattler of this
people. Is. 30:10

Promise of Future Restoration

12 "I[R] will surely assemble all of you, O
Jacob, [Mic. 4:6, 7]
I will surely gather the remnant of
Israel;
I will put them together [R]like sheep of
[T]the fold, Jer. 31:10 • Or *Bozrah*
Like a flock in the midst of their
pasture;
[R]They shall make a loud noise because of
so many men. Ezek. 33:22; 36:37
13 The one who breaks open will come up
before them;
They will break out,
Pass through the gate,
And go out by it;
[R]Their king will pass before them, [Hos. 3:5]
[R]With the LORD at their head." Is. 52:12

CHAPTER 3

Judgment on Princes

AND I said:
"Hear now, O heads of Jacob,

2:6 Vg. *He shall not take shame*

And you rulers of the house of Israel:
Is it not for you to know justice?
2 You who hate good and love evil;
Who strip the skin from [T]My people,
And the flesh from their bones; Lit. *them*
3 Who also [R]eat the flesh of My people,
Flay their skin from them, Ps. 14:4; 27:2
Break their bones,
And chop *them* in pieces
Like *meat* for the pot,
[R]Like flesh in the caldron." Ezek. 11:3, 6, 7

4 Then [R]they will cry to the LORD, Jer. 11:11
But He will not hear them;
He will even hide His face from them at that time,
Because they have been evil in their deeds.

Judgment on Prophets

5 Thus says the LORD [R]concerning the prophets Ezek. 13:10, 19
Who make my people stray;
Who chant [T]"Peace" All is well
While they chew with their teeth,
But who prepare war against him
Who puts nothing into their mouths:
6 "Therefore[R] you shall have night without [T]vision, Is. 8:20–22; 29:10–12 • Prophetic revelation
And you shall have darkness without divination;
The sun shall go down on the prophets,
And the day shall be dark for them.
7 So the seers shall be ashamed,
And the diviners abashed;
Indeed they shall all cover their lips;
For *there is* no answer from God."

8 But truly I am full of power by the Spirit of the LORD,
And of justice and might,
[R]To declare to Jacob his transgression
And to Israel his sin. Is. 58:1

Promise of Future Judgment

9 Now hear this,
You heads of the house of Jacob
And rulers of the house of Israel,
Who abhor justice
And [T]pervert all equity, Lit. *twist*
10 Who build up Zion with [R]bloodshed
And Jerusalem with iniquity: Hab. 2:12
11 [R]Her heads judge for a bribe, Is. 1:23
[R]Her priests teach for pay, Jer. 6:13
And her prophets divine for [T]money.
Yet they lean on the LORD, and say,
"Is not the LORD among us? Lit. *silver*
No harm can come upon us."
12 Therefore because of you
Zion shall be plowed *like* a field,
Jerusalem shall become heaps of ruins,
And the mountain of the [T]temple
Like the bare hills of the forest. Lit. *house*

CHAPTER 4

The Promise of the Coming Kingdom

NOW it shall come to pass [R]in the latter days
That the mountain of the LORD's house
Shall be established on the top of the mountains,
And shall be exalted above the hills;
And peoples shall flow to it. Is. 2:2–4
2 Many nations shall come and say,
"Come, and let us go up to the mountain of the LORD,
To the house of the God of Jacob;
He will teach us His ways,
And we shall walk in His paths."
For out of Zion the law shall go forth,
And the word of the LORD from Jerusalem.
3 He shall judge between many peoples,
And rebuke strong nations afar off;
They shall beat their swords into [R]plowshares, Is. 2:4
And their spears into [T]pruning hooks;
Nation shall not lift up sword against nation, *pruning knives*
Neither shall they learn war any more.

4 [R]But everyone shall sit under his vine and under his fig tree,
And no one shall make *them* afraid;
For the mouth of the LORD of hosts has spoken. Zech. 3:10
5 For all people walk each in the name of his god,
But [R]we will walk in the name of the LORD our God
Forever and ever. Zech. 10:12

The Promise of the Coming Captivities

6 "In that day," says the LORD,
[R]"I will assemble the lame, Ezek. 34:16
[R]I will gather the outcast Ps. 147:2
And those whom I have afflicted;
7 I will make the lame [R]a remnant,
And the outcast a strong nation;
So the LORD [R]will reign over them in Mount Zion Mic. 2:12 • [Is. 9:6; 24:23]
From now on, even forever.
8 And you, O tower of the flock,
The stronghold of the daughter of Zion,
To you shall it come,
Even the former dominion shall come,
The kingdom of the daughter of Jerusalem."

9 Now why do you cry aloud?
Is there no king in your midst?
Has your counselor perished?
For [R]pangs have seized you like a woman in [T]labor. Is. 13:8 • *childbirth*

10 Be in pain, and labor to bring forth,
O daughter of Zion,
Like a woman in birth pangs.
For now you shall go forth from the city,
You shall dwell in the field,
And you shall go *even* to [R]Babylon.
There you shall be delivered; Amos 5:27
There the [R]LORD will redeem you
From the hand of your enemies. [Is. 45:13]

11 [R]Now also many nations have gathered against you, Lam. 2:16
Who say, "Let her be defiled,
And let our eye look upon Zion."
12 But they do not know [R]the thoughts of the LORD,
Nor do they understand His counsel;
For He will gather them [R]like sheaves to the threshing floor. [Is. 55:8, 9] • Is. 21:10

13 "Arise and [R]thresh, O daughter of Zion;
For I will make your horn iron, Is. 41:15
And I will make your hooves bronze;
You shall [R]beat in pieces many peoples;
[R]I will consecrate their gain to the LORD,
And their substance to [R]the Lord of the whole earth." Dan. 2:44 • Is. 18:7 • Zech. 4:14

CHAPTER 5

NOW gather yourself in troops,
O daughter of troops;
He has laid siege against us;
They will [R]strike the judge of Israel
with a rod on the cheek. Mark 15:19☆

Birth of the Messiah

2 "But you, [R]Bethlehem Ephrathah,
Though you are little among the thousands of Judah, Luke 2:4–7☆
Yet out of you shall come forth to Me
The One to be [R]ruler in Israel,
[R]Whose goings forth *have been* from of old, Ex. 18:25 • [Is. 9:6]
From [T]everlasting." Lit. *the days of eternity*

Rejection of the Messiah

3 Therefore He shall give them up,
Until the time *that* [R]she who is in labor has given birth; Mic. 4:10
Then the remnant of His brethren
Shall return to the children of Israel.

Work of the Messiah

4 And He shall stand and [R]feed[T] *His flock*
In the strength of the LORD,
In the majesty of the name of the LORD
His God; [Is. 40:11; 49:9] • *shepherd*
And they shall abide,
For now He [R]shall be great Ps. 72:8
To the ends of the earth;
5 And this *One* [R]shall be peace. [Is. 9:6]
When the Assyrian comes into our land,
And when he treads in our palaces,
Then we will raise against him
Seven shepherds and eight princely men.
6 They shall [T]waste with the sword the land of Assyria, *devastate*
And the land of [R]Nimrod at its entrances; Gen. 10:8–11
Thus He shall [R]deliver *us* from the Assyrian, Is. 14:25
When he comes into our land
And when he treads within our borders.

7 Then [R]the remnant of Jacob Mic. 5:3
Shall be in the midst of many peoples,
[R]Like dew from the LORD, Deut. 32:2
Like showers on the grass,
That [T]tarry for no man *wait*
Nor [T]wait for the sons of men. *delay*
8 And the remnant of Jacob
Shall be among the Gentiles,
In the midst of many peoples,
Like a [R]lion among the beasts of the forest, Num. 24:9
Like a young lion among flocks of sheep,
Who, if he passes through,
Both treads down and tears in pieces,
And none can deliver.
9 Your hand shall be lifted against your adversaries,
And all your enemies shall be cut off.

10 "And it shall be in that day," says the LORD,
"That I will [R]cut[T] off your [R]horses from your midst Zech. 9:10 • *destroy* • Deut. 17:16
And destroy your [R]chariots. Is. 2:7; 22:18
11 I will cut off the cities of your land
And throw down all your strongholds.
12 I will cut off sorceries from your hand,
And you shall have no soothsayers.
13 [R]Your carved images I will also cut off,
And your sacred pillars from your midst;
You shall [R]no more worship the work of your hands; Zech. 13:2 • Is. 2:8
14 I will pluck your [T]wooden images from your midst; Or *Asherim*, Canaanite deities
Thus I will destroy your cities.
15 And I will [R]execute vengeance in anger and fury [2 Thess. 1:8]
On the nations that have not heard."

CHAPTER 6

God Pleads

HEAR now what the LORD says:

"Arise, plead your case before the mountains,
And let the hills hear your voice.

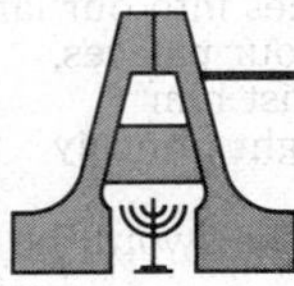

THE CITY OF BETHLEHEM

Located in the hill country of Judah in southern Palestine, the humble village of Bethlehem is famous as the home of David and the birthplace of Jesus Christ. Bethlehem is situated five miles south of Jerusalem.

The region around Bethlehem today is known for its fertile hills and valleys. Its busy marketplaces and religious shrines continue to attract tourists. Bethlehem's main attraction is the Church of Nativity, which is supposedly built over the birthplace of the Savior. Most scholars agree this is one of the best authenticated sites in the Holy Land. The present building, erected over the cave area, which served as a stable for the crowded inn, was built by the Roman emperor Justinian I in the sixth century A.D. The city and the church are especially popular as destinations for pilgrims during Christmas celebrations.

Bethlehem is also closely associated with King David, Israel's favorite king. Known as the city of David, Bethlehem is his ancestral home and the site where Samuel anointed David as Saul's successor. The prophet Micah foresaw the coming of a Ruler in the line of David who would be born in Bethlehem (Mic. 5:2). The city was the original home of Naomi, and it served as the setting for much of the Book of Ruth.

Other popular attractions at Bethlehem for Holy Land tourists are the fields of Boaz, where Ruth gleaned grain after the fields had been harvested, and Shepherds' Field, where the angels announced the birth of Jesus to the shepherds (Luke 2:8–18).

The name *Bethlehem* means "House of Bread," probably commemorating the reputation of the entire region as a grain-producing center in Old Testament times. How appropriate that Jesus Christ, who is the Bread of Life, was born in a town with such a name.

Church of the Nativity, Bethlehem.

2 [R]Hear, O you mountains, [R]the LORD's
complaint, Ps. 50:1, 4 • Hos. 12:2
And you strong foundations of the
earth;
For [R]the LORD has a complaint against
His people, [Is. 1:18]
And He will contend with Israel.

3 "O My people, what [R]have I done to
you?
And how have I [R]wearied you?
Testify against Me. Jer. 2:5, 31 • Is. 43:22, 23
4 [R]For I brought you up from the land of
Egypt,
I redeemed you from the house of
bondage;
And I sent before you Moses, Aaron,
and Miriam. [Deut. 4:20]
5 O My people, remember now
What [R]Balak king of Moab counseled,
And what Balaam the son of Beor
answered him, Num. 22:5, 6
From [T]Acacia Grove to Gilgal, Heb. *Shittim*
That you may know [R]the righteousness
of the LORD." Judg. 5:11

Micah Replies

6 With what shall I come before the
LORD,
And bow myself before the High God?
Shall I come before Him with burnt
offerings,
With calves a year old?
7 [R]Will the LORD be pleased with
thousands of rams Is. 1:11
Or ten thousand [R]rivers of oil? Job 29:6
[R]Shall I give my firstborn *for* my
transgression, 2 Kin. 16:3
[T]The fruit of my body *for* the sin of my
soul? My own child

8 He has [R]shown you, O man, what *is*
good; [Deut. 10:12]
And what does the LORD require of you
But [R]to do justly, Gen. 18:19
To love [T]mercy, Or *lovingkindness*
And to walk humbly with your God?

9 The LORD's voice cries to the city—
Wisdom shall see Your name:

"Hear the Rod!
Who has appointed it?

God Pleads

10 Are there yet the treasures of
wickedness
In the house of the wicked,
And the short measure *that is* an
abomination?
11 Shall I count pure *those* with [R]the
wicked [T]balances, Hos. 12:7 • Scales
And with the bag of deceitful weights?
12 For her rich men are full of [R]violence,
Her inhabitants have spoken lies,
And [R]their tongue is deceitful in their
mouth. Mic. 2:1, 2 • Jer. 9:2–6, 8

13 "Therefore I will also [R]make *you* sick by
striking you,
By making *you* desolate because of
your sins. Lev. 26:16
14 You shall eat, but not be satisfied;
[T]Hunger *shall be* in your midst.
*You may carry *some* away, but shall
not save *them;* Or *Emptiness* or *Humiliation*
And what you do rescue I will give over
to the sword.

15 "You shall [R]sow, but not reap;
You shall tread the olives, but not
anoint yourselves with oil;
And *make* sweet wine, but not drink
wine. Amos 5:11
16 For the statutes of Omri are [R]kept;
All the works of Ahab's house *are done;*
And you walk in their counsels, Hos. 5:11
That I may make you a [T]desolation,
And your inhabitants a hissing.
Therefore you shall bear the [R]reproach
of My people." Or *object of horror* • Is. 25:8

CHAPTER 7

Micah Replies

WOE is me!
For I am like those who gather
summer fruits,
Like those who [R]glean vintage grapes;
There is no cluster to eat
Of the first-ripe fruit *which* [R]my soul
desires. Is. 17:6 • Is. 28:4
2 The [R]faithful[T] *man* has perished from
the earth, Is. 57:1 • Or *loyal*
And *there is* no one upright among
men.
They all lie in wait for blood;
Every man hunts his brother with a net.

3 That they may successfully do evil with
both hands—
The prince asks *for gifts,*
The judge *seeks* a [R]bribe,
And the great *man* utters his evil desire;
So they scheme together. Mic. 3:11
4 The best of them *is* [R]like a brier;
The most upright *is sharper* than a
thorn hedge;
The day of your watchman and your
punishment comes;
Now shall be their perplexity. Ezek. 2:6

6:14 Tg., Vg., *You shall take hold*

5 [R]Do not trust in a friend;
Do not put your confidence in a companion; Jer. 9:4
Guard the doors of your mouth
From her who lies in your bosom.
6 For [R]son dishonors father,
Daughter rises against her mother,
Daughter-in-law against her mother-in-law;
A man's enemies *are* the men of his own house. Matt. 10:36

The Promise of Final Salvation

7 Therefore I will look to the LORD;
I will [R]wait for the God of my salvation;
My God will hear me. Is. 25:9

8 Do not rejoice over me, my enemy;
[R]When I fall, I will arise; [Prov. 24:16]
When I sit in darkness,
The LORD *will be* a light to me.
9 I will bear the indignation of the LORD,
Because I have sinned against Him,
Until He pleads my [R]case Jer. 50:34
And executes justice for me;
He will bring me forth to the light,
And I will see His righteousness.
10 Then *she who is* my enemy will see,
And [R]shame will cover her who said to me,
[R]"Where is the LORD your God?"
My eyes will see her;
Now she will be trampled down
Like mire in the streets. Ps. 35:26 • Ps. 42:3

11 *In* the day when your [R]walls are to be built, [Amos 9:11]
In that day [T]the decree shall go far and wide. Or *the boundary shall be extended*
12 *In* that day they shall come to you
From Assyria and the fortified cities,
From the [T]fortress to [T]the River,
From sea to sea, Possibly Egypt • The Euphrates
And mountain *to* mountain.

13 Yet the land shall be desolate
Because of those who dwell in it,
And for the fruit of their deeds.

14 Shepherd Your people with Your staff,
The flock of Your heritage,
Who dwell [T]solitarily *in* a [R]woodland,
In the midst of Carmel;
Let them feed *in* Bashan and Gilead,
As in days of old. Alone • Is. 37:24

15 "As[R] in the days when you came out of the land of Egypt, Ps. 68:22; 78:12
I will show them marvelous *things*."

16 The nations [R]shall see and be ashamed of all their might;
[R]They shall put *their* hand over *their* mouth;
Their ears shall be deaf. Is. 26:11 • Job 21:5
17 They shall lick the [R]dust like a serpent;
They shall crawl from their holes like [T]snakes of the earth. [Is. 49:23] • Lit. *crawlers*
[R]They shall be afraid of the LORD our God, Jer. 33:9
And shall fear because of You.
18 [R]Who *is* a God like You, Ex. 15:11
[R]Pardoning iniquity Ex. 34:6, 7, 9
And passing over the transgression of [R]the remnant of His heritage? Mic. 4:7

He does not retain His anger forever,
Because He delights *in* mercy.
19 He will again have compassion on us,
And will subdue our iniquities.

You will cast all [T]our sins
Into the depths of the sea. Lit. *their*
20 [R]You will give truth to Jacob
And [T]mercy to Abraham, Luke 1:72, 73 ☆
[R]Which You have sworn to our fathers
From days of old. Or *lovingkindness* • Ps. 105:9

THE BOOK OF NAHUM

THE BOOK OF NAHUM

"For everyone to whom much is given, from him much will be required" (Luke 12:48). Nineveh had been given the privilege of knowing the one true God. Under Jonah's preaching this great gentile city had repented, and God had graciously stayed His judgment. However, a hundred years later, Nahum proclaims the downfall of this same city. The Assyrians have forgotten their revival and have returned to their habits of violence, idolatry, and arrogance. As a result, Babylon will so destroy the city that no trace of it will remain—a prophecy fulfilled in painful detail.

The Hebrew word *nahum* ("comfort, consolation") is a shortened form of Nehemiah ("Comfort of Yahweh"). The destruction of the capital city of Assyria is a message of comfort and consolation to Judah and all who live in fear of the cruelty of the Assyrians. The title of this book in the Greek and Latin Bibles is *Naoum* and *Nahum.*

THE AUTHOR OF NAHUM

The only mention of Nahum in the Old Testament is found in 1:1 where he is called an Elkoshite. At least four locations have been proposed for Elkosh: (1) a sixteenth-century tradition identifies Elkosh with Al-Qush in Iraq, north of the site of Nineveh on the Tigris River. (2) Jerome believed that Elkesi, a city near Ramah in Galilee, was Elkosh because of the similarity of the consonants. (3) Capernaum means "City of Nahum" *(Kephar-Nahum),* and many believe that the name Elkosh was changed to Capernaum in Nahum's honor. (4) Most conservative scholars believe that Elkosh was a city of southern Judah (later called Elcesei) between Jerusalem and Gaza. This would make Nahum a prophet of the southern kingdom and may explain his interest in the triumph of Judah (1:15; 2:2).

THE TIME OF NAHUM

The fall of Nineveh to the Babylonians in 612 B.C. is seen by Nahum as a future event. Critics who deny predictive prophecy naturally date Nahum after 612 B.C., but this is not based upon exegetical or historical considerations. Nahum 3:8–10 refers to the fall of Thebes as a recent event, so this book must be dated after 664 B.C., the year when this took place. Thus, Nahum can safely be placed between 663 and 612 B.C. Thebes was restored a decade after its defeat, and Nahum's failure to mention this restoration has led several scholars to the conclusion that Nahum was written before 654 B.C. The fact that Nahum mentions no king in the introduction to his book (1:1) may point to the reign of the wicked King Manasseh (686–642 B.C.).

The conversion of the Ninevites in response to Jonah's message of judgment took place about 760 B.C. The revival was evidently short-lived, because the Assyrians soon returned to their ruthless practices. In 722 B.C., Sargon II of Assyria destroyed Samaria, the capital of the northern kingdom of Israel, and scattered the ten tribes. Led by Sennacherib, the Assyrians also came close to capturing Jerusalem in the reign of King Hezekiah in 701 B.C. By the time of Nahum (c. 660 B.C.), Assyria reached the peak of its prosperity and power under Ashurbanipal (669–633 B.C.). This king extended Assyria's influence farther than had any of his predecessors. Nineveh became the mightiest city on earth with walls 100 feet high and wide enough to accommodate three chariots riding abreast. Dotted around the walls were huge towers that stretched an additional 100 feet above the top of the walls. In addition, the walls were surrounded by a moat 150 feet wide and 60 feet deep. Nineveh appeared impregnable and could withstand a twenty-year siege. Thus, Nahum's prophecy of Nineveh's overthrow seemed unlikely indeed.

Assyrian power faded under Ashurbanipal's sons, Ashuretililani (633–629 B.C.) and Sinsharishkun (629–612 B.C.). Nahum predicted that Nineveh would end "with an overflowing flood" (1:8), and this is precisely what occurred. The Tigris River overflowed its banks and the flood destroyed part of Nineveh's wall. The Babylonians invaded through this breach in the wall, plundered the city, and set it on fire. Nahum also predicted that Nineveh would "be hidden" (3:11). After its destruction in 612 B.C. the site was not discovered until A.D. 1842.

THE CHRIST OF NAHUM

While there are no direct messianic prophecies in Nahum, the divine attributes in 1:2–8 are consistent with Christ's work as the Judge of the nations in His second advent.

KEYS TO NAHUM

Key Word: The Judgment of Nineveh—If ever a city deserved the title "Here to Stay," Nineveh was that city. The great city appeared invincible. But into the scene steps Nahum—a prophet of God's judgment—to declare that Nineveh will fall. Less than half a century later the prediction of God's spokesman comes true as the great city topples before the Babylonian onslaught, never again to be rebuilt.

Key Verses: Nahum 1:7, 8; 3:5–7—"The LORD *is* good, a stronghold in the day of trouble; and He knows those who trust in Him. But with an overflowing flood He will make an utter end of its place, and darkness will pursue His enemies" (1:7, 8).

"Behold, I *am* against you," says the LORD of hosts; "I will lift your skirts over your face, I will show the nations your nakedness, and the kingdoms your shame. I will cast abominable filth upon you, make you vile, and make you a spectacle. It shall come to pass *that* all who look upon you will flee from you, and say, 'Nineveh is laid waste! Who will bemoan her?' Where shall I seek comforters for you?" (3:5–7).

Key Chapter: Nahum 1—The first chapter of Nahum records the principles of divine judgment resulting in the decree of the destruction of Nineveh and the deliverance and celebration of Judah. Beginning with 1:9, the single thrust of Nahum's prophecy is the retribution of God upon the wickedness of Nineveh. Nineveh's judgment is irreversibly decreed by the righteous God who will no longer delay His wrath. Assyria's arrogance and cruelty to other nations will come to a sudden end: her power will be useless against the mighty hand of Yahweh.

Nahum 1:2–8 portrays the patience, power, holiness, and justice of the living God. He is slow to wrath, but God settles His accounts in full. This book concerns the downfall of Assyria, but it is written for the benefit of the surviving kingdom of Judah. (Israel had already been swallowed up by Assyria.) The people in Judah who trust in the Lord will be comforted to hear of God's judgment upon the proud and brutal Assyrians (1:15; 2:2).

SURVEY OF NAHUM

When God finally convinces His prophet Jonah to preach to the people of Nineveh, the whole city responds with repentance and Nineveh escapes destruction. The people humble themselves before the one true God, but their humility soon changes to arrogance as Assyria reaches its zenith as the most powerful empire in the world. About a century after the preaching of Jonah, God calls Nahum to proclaim the coming destruction of Nineveh. This time there will be no escape, because their measure of wickedness is full. Unlike Jonah, Nahum does not go to the city but declares his oracle from afar. There is no hope of repentance. Nineveh's destruction is decreed (1), described (2), and deserved (3).

The Destruction of Nineveh Is Decreed (1): Nahum begins with a very clear description of the character of Yahweh. Because of His righteousness, He is a God of vengeance (1:2). God is also characterized by patience (1:3) and power (1:3–6). He is gracious to all who respond to Him, but those who rebel against Him will be overthrown (1:7, 8). God is holy, and Nineveh stands condemned because of her sins (1:9–14). Nothing can stand in the way of judgment, and this is a message of comfort to the people of Judah (1:15). The threat of Assyrian invasion will soon be over.

The Destruction of Nineveh Is Described (2): Assyria will be conquered, but Judah will be restored (2:1, 2). Nahum's description of the siege of Nineveh (2:3–7) and the sack of Nineveh (2:8–13) is one of the most vivid portraits of battle in Scripture. The storming warriors and chariots can almost be seen as they enter the city through a breach in the wall. As the Ninevites flee in terror, the invading army plunders the treasures of the city. Nineveh is burned and cut off forever.

The Destruction of Nineveh Is Deserved (3): Nahum closes his brief book of judgment with God's reasons for Nineveh's coming overthrow. The city is characterized by cruelty and corruption (3:1–7). Just as Assyria crushed the Egyptian

FOCUS	DESTRUCTION OF NINEVEH DECREED		DESTRUCTION OF NINEVEH DESCRIBED		DESTRUCTION OF NINEVEH DESERVED	
REFERENCE	1:1	1:9	2:1	2:3	3:1	3:12 — 3:19
DIVISION	GENERAL PRINCIPLES OF DIVINE JUDGMENT	DESTRUCTION OF NINEVEH AND DELIVERANCE OF JUDAH	THE CALL TO BATTLE	DESCRIPTION OF THE DESTRUCTION OF NINEVEH	REASONS FOR THE DESTRUCTION OF NINEVEH	INEVITABLE DESTRUCTION OF NINEVEH
TOPIC	VERDICT OF VENGEANCE		VISION OF VENGEANCE		VINDICATION OF VENGEANCE	
	WHAT GOD WILL DO		HOW GOD WILL DO IT		WHY GOD WILL DO IT	
LOCATION	IN JUDAH AGAINST NINEVEH, CAPITAL OF ASSYRIA					
TIME	c. 660 B.C.					

capital city of Thebes (No Amon), Assyria's capital city will also be destroyed (3:8–10). Nineveh is fortified so well that defeat seems impossible, but God proclaims that its destruction is inevitable (3:11–19). None of its resources can deter divine judgment.

OUTLINE OF NAHUM

CHAPTER 1

God's Vengeance in Judgment

THE burden against Nineveh. The book of the vision of Nahum the Elkoshite.

2 God *is* [R]jealous, and the LORD avenges;
The LORD avenges and *is* furious.
The LORD will take vengeance on His adversaries, Ex. 20:5
And He reserves *wrath* for His enemies;

God's Power in Judgment

3 The LORD *is* [R]slow to anger and [R]great in power, Ex. 34:6, 7 • [Job 9:4]
And will not at all acquit *the wicked.*

[R]The LORD has His way Ps. 18:17
In the whirlwind and in the storm,
And the clouds *are* the dust of His feet.
4 [R]He rebukes the sea and makes it dry,
And dries up all the rivers. Matt. 8:26
[R]Bashan and Carmel wither, Is. 33:9
And the flower of Lebanon wilts.
5 The mountains quake before Him,
The hills melt,
And the earth *heaves at His presence,
Yes, the world and all who dwell in it.

6 Who can stand before His indignation?
And [R]who can endure the fierceness of His anger?
His fury is poured out like fire,
And the rocks are thrown down by Him. [Mal. 3:2]

7 [R]The LORD *is* good, [Jer. 33:11]
A stronghold in the day of trouble;
And He knows those who trust in Him.
8 But with an overflowing flood
He will make an utter end of its place,
And darkness will pursue His enemies.

The Destruction of Nineveh and Deliverance of Judah

9 [R]What do you [T]conspire against the LORD? Ps. 2:1 • Or *devise*
[R]He will make an utter end *of it.* 1 Sam. 3:12
Affliction will not rise up a second time.
10 For while tangled [R]*like* thorns,
[R]And while drunken *like* drunkards,
[R]They shall be devoured like stubble fully dried. 2 Sam. 23:6 • Nah. 3:11 • Mal. 4:1
11 From you comes forth *one*
Who plots evil against the LORD,
A [T]wicked counselor. Lit. *counselor of Belial*

12 Thus says the LORD:

"Though *they are* [T]safe, and likewise many, Or *at peace* or *complete*
Yet in this manner they will be [R]cut down [Is. 10:16–19, 33, 34]
When he passes through.
Though I have afflicted you,
I will afflict you no more;
13 For now I will break off his yoke from you,
And burst your bonds apart."

14 The LORD has given a command concerning you:
[T]"Your name shall be perpetuated no longer. Lit. *No more of your name shall be fruitful*
Out of the house of your gods

1:5 Tg. *burns*

ISRAEL AND THE ASSYRIANS

The Assyrians were a cruel and aggressive people who became one of the dominant nations of the ancient world from about 1300 to 600 B.C. During this long period, they often clashed with the Hebrew people. The ultimate outrage occurred in the eighth century when thousands of residents of the northern kingdom were carried to Assyria as captives and resettled in pagan territory.

The Assyrian Empire developed between the Tigris and Euphrates rivers in a region known as Upper Mesopotamia. The Assyrians defeated Babylon, their neighbors to the south, in 1300 B.C., a move that propelled them to the status of a world power. Assyria was actually the most powerful nation of the ancient world for two centuries—from about 850 to 650 B.C.

In 722 B.C., King Shalmaneser of Assyria began a long siege of Samaria, capital city of Israel, which resulted in complete destruction of this city. Thousands of Jews were deported to Assyrian territory, and most never returned. This was a blow from which the nation of Israel (northern kingdom) never recovered.

The southern kingdom also suffered from oppression by the Assyrians. King Ahaz of Judah appealed to King Tiglath-Pileser of Assyria for protection, in spite of the prophet Isaiah's warnings against such an alliance. Ahaz was eventually forced to pay tribute to Assyria and adopt some of the pagan nation's worship practices (2 Kin. 16).

Photo by Howard Vos

Winged bull, symbol of the Assyrian Empire.

Assyria emphasized the worship of nature, believing that the natural elements were possessed by a spirit. Along with the national deity, Assur, the Assyrian people worshiped Shemach, the sun god; Sin, the moon god; and Hadad, the god of thunder. The pagan worship of these people was soundly condemned by several prophets of the Old Testament (Is. 10:5, 6; Ezek. 16:28; Hos. 8:9).

The Assyrians were notorious for their savagery in warfare. They burned and looted cities and showed little mercy to their captives. In stone carvings discovered by

This carving from the palace of Ashurnasirpal at Nimrud shows this king of Assyria in a lion hunt.

archaeologists, Assyrian soldiers are shown torturing children, blinding warriors, chopping off hands, impaling victims on stakes, and beheading their enemies.

Because of the cruelty and paganism of the Assyrians, the Hebrew people harbored deep-seated resentment and hostility toward this nation. This attitude is revealed clearly in the Book of Jonah. When God instructed the prophet to preach to Nineveh, the capital of Assyria, Jonah refused and went in the opposite direction (Jon. 1:1–3). After he finally went to Nineveh, he was disappointed with God because He spared the city (Jon. 4:1–3).

The entire Book of Nahum is a prediction of God's judgment against the Assyrians. Nahum informed the nation that its days as a world power were drawing to a close. In an oracle of woe, the prophet described Nineveh as a "bloody city…full of lies *and* robbery" (Nah. 3:1). But soon the city of Nineveh would be laid waste, and Assyria would crumble before the judgment of God. This happened as Nahum prophesied when the Babylonians and Medians formed a coalition to defeat the Assyrians about 612 B.C.

I will cut off the carved image and the
molded image.
I will dig your [R]grave, Ezek. 32:22, 23
For you are [R]vile."[T] Nah. 3:6 • Or *contemptible*

15 Behold, on the mountains
The [R]feet of him who brings good
tidings, Rom. 10:15
Who proclaims peace!
O Judah, keep your appointed feasts,
Perform your vows.
For the [T]wicked one shall no more pass
through you; Lit. *one of Belial*
He is [R]utterly cut off. Is. 29:7, 8

CHAPTER 2

The Call to Battle

HE* who scatters has come up before
your face.
Man the fort!
Watch the road!
Strengthen *your* flanks!
Fortify *your* power mightily.

2 For the LORD will restore the excellence
of Jacob
Like the excellence of Israel,
For the emptiers have emptied them out
And ruined their vine branches.

The Destruction of Nineveh

3 The shields of his mighty men *are* made
red,
The valiant men *are* in scarlet.
The chariots *come* with flaming torches
In the day of his preparation,
And the spears are brandished.
4 The chariots rage in the streets,
They jostle one another in the broad
roads;
They seem like torches,
They run like lightning.

5 He remembers his worthies;
They stumble in their walk;
They make haste to her walls,
And the defense is prepared.
6 The gates of the rivers are opened,
And the palace is dissolved.
7 [T]It is decreed: Heb. *Huzzab*
She shall be led away captive,
She shall be brought up;
And her maidservants shall lead *her* as
with the voice of doves,
Beating their breasts.

8 Though Nineveh of old *was* like a pool
of water,
Now they flee away.
[T]"Halt! Halt!" *they cry*; Lit. *Stand*
But no one turns back.
9 [T]Take spoil of silver! *Plunder*
Take spoil of [R]gold! Zeph. 1:18
There is no end of treasure,
Or wealth of every desirable prize.
10 She is empty, desolate, and waste!
The heart melts, and the knees shake;
Much pain *is* in every side,
And all their faces *are drained of color.

11 Where *is* the dwelling of the [R]lions,
And the feeding place of the young
lions,
Where the lion walked, the lioness *and*
lion's cub,
And no one made *them* afraid? Job 4:10, 11
12 The lion tore in pieces enough for his
cubs,
[T]Killed for his lionesses, Lit. *Strangled*
[R]Filled his caves with prey, Jer. 51:34
And his dens with [T]flesh. *torn flesh*

13 "Behold, I *am* [R]against you," says the
LORD of hosts, "I will burn [T]your chariots in
smoke, and the sword shall devour your
young lions; I will cut off your prey from the
earth, and the voice of your messengers shall
be heard no more." Nah. 3:5 • Lit. *her*

CHAPTER 3

Nineveh's Great Ungodliness

WOE to the [R]bloody city! Hab. 2:12
It *is* all full of lies *and* robbery.
Its [T]victim never departs. Lit. *prey*
2 The noise of a whip
And the noise of rattling wheels,
Of galloping horses,
Of [T]clattering chariots! *bounding* or *jolting*
3 Horsemen charge with bright sword and
glittering spear.
There is a multitude of slain,
A great number of bodies,
Countless corpses—
They stumble over the corpses—
4 Because of the multitude of [T]harlotries
of the seductive harlot,
[R]The mistress of sorceries,
Who sells nations through her
harlotries, Spiritual unfaithfulness • Is. 47:9–12
And families through her sorceries.

5 "Behold, I *am* [R]against you," says the
LORD of hosts; Nah. 2:13
[R]"I will lift your skirts over your face,
I will show the nations your nakedness,
And the kingdoms your shame. Is. 47:2, 3
6 I will cast abominable filth upon you,
Make you [R]vile,[T] Nah. 1:14 • *despicable*
And make you [R]a spectacle. Heb. 10:33

2:1 Vg. *He who destroys*
2:10 LXX, Tg., Vg. *gather blackness;* Joel 2:6

7 It shall come to pass *that* all who look upon you
[R]Will flee from you, and say, Rev. 18:10
[R]'Nineveh is laid waste! Jon. 3:3; 4:11
[R]Who will bemoan her?' Jer. 15:5
Where shall I seek comforters for you?"

Comparison of Nineveh to No Amon

8 Are you better than *No Amon
That was situated by the River,
That had the waters around her,
Whose rampart *was like* the sea,
Whose wall *was like* the sea?
9 Ethiopia and Egypt *were* her strength,
And *it was* boundless;
Put and Lubim were *your helpers.
10 Yet she *was* carried away,
She went into captivity;
[R]Her young children also were dashed to pieces
[R]At the head of every street;
They [R]cast lots for her honorable men,
And all her great men were bound in chains. Hos. 13:16 • Lam. 2:19 • Joel 3:3
11 You also will be [R]drunk;
You will be hidden;
You also will seek refuge from the enemy. Nah. 1:10

Nineveh's Strongholds Are Weak

12 All your strongholds *are* [R]fig trees with ripened figs: Rev. 6:12, 13
If they are shaken,
They fall into the mouth of the eater.
13 Surely, [R]your people in your midst *are* women!
The gates of your land are wide open for your enemies;
Fire shall devour the [R]bars of your *gates*. Is. 19:16 • Jer. 51:30
14 Draw your water for the siege!
[R]Fortify your strongholds!
Go into the clay and tread the mortar!
Make strong the brick kiln! Nah. 2:1
15 There the fire will devour you,
The sword will cut you off;
It will eat you up like a [R]locust. Joel 1:4

Make yourself many—like the locust!
Make yourself many—like the *swarming* locusts!

Nineveh's Leaders Are Weak

16 You have multiplied your merchants more than the stars of heaven.
The locust plunders and flies away.
17 [R]Your commanders *are* like *swarming* locusts,
And your captains like great grasshoppers,
Which camp in the hedges on a cold day;
But when the sun rises they flee away,
And the place where they *are* is not known. Rev. 9:7
18 [R]Your shepherds slumber, O [R]king of Assyria; Ps. 76:5, 6 • Jer. 50:18
Your nobles rest *in the dust*.
Your people are [R]scattered on the mountains, 1 Kin. 22:17
And no one gathers them.
19 Your injury *has* no healing,
[R]Your wound is severe. Mic. 1:9
[R]All who hear news of you Lam. 2:15
Will clap *their* hands over you,
For upon whom has not your wickedness passed continually?

3:8 Ancient Thebes; Tg., Vg. *populous Alexandria*
3:9 LXX *her*

THE BOOK OF

HABAKKUK

THE BOOK OF HABAKKUK

Habakkuk ministers during the "death throes" of the nation of Judah. Although repeatedly called to repentance, the nation stubbornly refuses to change her sinful ways. Habakkuk, knowing the hardheartedness of his countrymen, asks God how long this intolerable condition can continue. God replies that the Babylonians will be His chastening rod upon the nation—an announcement that sends the prophet to his knees. He acknowledges that the just in any generation shall live by faith (2:4), not by sight. Habakkuk concludes by praising God's wisdom even though he doesn't fully understand God's ways.

Habaqquq is an unusual Hebrew name derived from the verb *habaq,* "embrace." Thus his name probably means "One Who Embraces" or "Clings." At the end of his book this name becomes appropriate because Habakkuk chooses to cling firmly to God regardless of what happens to his nation (3:16–19). The Greek title in the Septuagint is *Ambakouk,* and the Latin title in Jerome's Vulgate is *Habacuc.*

THE AUTHOR OF HABAKKUK

In the introduction to the book (1:1) and in the closing psalm (3:1), the author identifies himself as Habakkuk the prophet. This special designation seems to indicate that Habakkuk was a professional prophet. The closing statement at the end of the psalm "To the Chief Musician. With my stringed instruments" suggests that Habakkuk may have been a priest connected with the temple worship in Jerusalem. He mentions nothing of his genealogy or location, but speculative attempts have been made to identify him with certain unnamed Old Testament characters. In the apocryphal book of Bel and the Dragon, Daniel is rescued a second time by the prophet Habakkuk.

THE TIME OF HABAKKUK

The only explicit time reference in Habakkuk is to the Babylonian invasion as an imminent event (1:6; 2:1; 3:16). Some scholars suggest Habakkuk was written during the reign of Manasseh (686–642 B.C.) or Amon (642–640 B.C.) because of the list of Judah's sins in 1:2–4. However, the descriptions of the Chaldeans indicate that Babylon had become a world power; and this was not true in the time of Manasseh when Babylon was under the thumb of Assyria. It is also unlikely that this prophecy took place in the time of King Josiah (640–609 B.C.), because the moral and spiritual reforms of Josiah do not fit the situation in 1:2–4. The most likely date for the book is in the early part of Jehoiakim's reign (609–597 B.C.). Jehoiakim was a godless king who led the nation down the path of destruction (cf. 2 Kin. 23:34—24:5; Jer. 22:17).

The Babylonians began to rise in power during the reign of Nabopolassar (626–605 B.C.), and in 612 B.C. they destroyed the Assyrian capital of Nineveh. By the time of Jehoiakim, Babylon was the uncontested world power. Nabopolassar's successor, Nebuchadnezzar, came to power in 605 B.C. and carried out successful military expeditions in the west, advancing into Palestine and Egypt. Nebuchadnezzar's first invasion of Judah occurred in his first year, when he deported ten thousand of Jerusalem's leaders to Babylon. The nobles who oppressed and extorted from the poor were the first to be carried away. Since Habakkuk prophesied prior to the Babylonian invasion, the probable date for this book is about 607 B.C.

THE CHRIST OF HABAKKUK

The word *salvation* appears three times in 3:13, 18 and is the root word from which the name *Jesus* is derived (cf. Matt. 1:21). When He comes again, "the earth will be filled with the knowledge of the glory of the LORD, as the waters cover the sea" (2:14).

KEYS TO HABAKKUK

Key Word: "The Just Shall Live by His Faith"—The circumstances of life sometimes appear to contradict God's revelation concerning His power and purposes. Habakkuk struggles in his faith when he sees men flagrantly violate God's law and distort justice on every level, without fear of divine intervention. He wants to know why God allows this growing iniquity to go unpunished. When God reveals His intention to use Babylon as His rod of judgment, Habakkuk is even more troubled, because that nation is more corrupt than Judah. God's answer satisfies Habakkuk that he can trust Him even in the worst of circumstances because of His matchless wisdom, goodness, and power. God's plan is perfect, and nothing is big enough to stand in the way of its ultimate fulfillment. In spite of appearances to the contrary, God is still on the throne as the Lord of history and the Ruler of the nations. God may be slow to wrath, but all iniquity will be punished eventually. He is the worthiest object of faith, and the righteous man will trust in Him at all times.

Key Verses: Habakkuk 2:4; 3:17–19—"Behold the proud, his soul is not upright in him; but the just shall live by his faith" (2:4).

"Though the fig tree may not blossom, nor fruit be on the vines; though the labor of the olive may fail, and the fields yield no food; though the flock be cut off from the fold, and there be no herd in the stalls—yet I will rejoice in the LORD, I will joy in the God of my salvation. The LORD God is my strength; He will make my feet like deer's *feet*, and He will make me walk on my high hills. To the Chief Musician. With my stringed instruments" (3:17–19).

Key Chapter: Habakkuk 3—The Book of Habakkuk builds to a triumphant climax reached in the last three verses (3:17–19). The beginning of the book and the ending stand in stark contrast: mystery to certainty, questioning to affirming, and complaint to confidence. Chapter 3 is one of the most majestic of all Scripture and records the glory of God in past history and in future history (prophecy).

SURVEY OF HABAKKUK

Habakkuk is a freethinking prophet who is not afraid to wrestle with issues that test his faith. He openly and honestly directs his problems to God and waits to see how He will respond to his probing questions. After two rounds of dialogue with the Lord, Habakkuk's increased understanding of the person, power, and plan of God cause him to conclude with a psalm of unqualified praise. The more he knows about the Planner, the more he can trust His plans. No matter what God brings to pass, "the just shall live by his faith" (2:4). The two divisions of this book are: the problems of Habakkuk (1 and 2) and the praise of Habakkuk (3).

The Problems of Habakkuk (1 and 2): Habakkuk's first dialogue with God takes place in 1:1–11. In 1:1–4, the prophet asks God how long He will allow the wickedness of Judah to go unpunished. The people of Judah sin with impunity, and justice is perverted. God's startling answer is given in 1:5–11: He is raising up the fierce Babylonians as His rod of judgment upon sinful Judah. The Chaldeans will come against Judah swiftly, violently, and completely. The coming storm from the east will be God's answer to Judah's crimes.

This answer leads to Habakkuk's second dialogue with God (1:12—2:20). The prophet is more perplexed than ever and asks how the righteous God can punish Judah with a nation that is even more wicked (1:12—2:1). Will the God whose eyes are too pure to approve evil reward the Babylonians for their cruelty and idolatry? Habakkuk stands upon a watchtower to wait for God's reply. The Lord answers with a series of five woes—of greed and aggression (2:5–8), exploitation and extortion (2:9–11), violence (2:12–14), immorality (2:15–17), and idolatry (2:18–20). God is aware of the sins of the Babylonians, and they will not escape His terrible judgment. But Judah is guilty of the same offenses and stands under the same condemnation. Yahweh concludes His answer with a statement of His sovereign majesty: "But the LORD is in His holy temple. Let all the earth keep silence before Him" (2:20).

The Praise of Habakkuk (3): Habakkuk begins by questioning God, but he concludes his book with a psalm of praise for the person (3:1–3), power (3:4–12), and plan (3:13–19) of God. He now acknowledges God's wisdom in the coming invasion of Judah, and although it terrifies him, he will trust the Lord. God's creative and redemptive work in the past gives the prophet confidence in the divine purposes, and hope at a time when he would otherwise despair. "Yet I will rejoice in the LORD, I will joy in the God of my salvation" (3:18).

FOCUS	PROBLEMS OF HABAKKUK				PRAISE OF HABAKKUK
REFERENCE	1:1—	1:5—	1:12—	2:2—	3:1—3:19
DIVISION	FIRST PROBLEM OF HABAKKUK	FIRST REPLY OF GOD	SECOND PROBLEM OF HABAKKUK	SECOND REPLY OF GOD	PRAYER OF PRAISE OF HABAKKUK
TOPIC	FAITH TROUBLED				FAITH TRIUMPHANT
	WHAT GOD IS DOING				WHO GOD IS
LOCATION	THE NATION OF JUDAH				
TIME	c. 607 B.C.				

OUTLINE OF HABAKKUK

CHAPTER 1

The First Problem of Habakkuk

THE [T]burden which the prophet Habakkuk saw. *oracle, prophecy*

2 O LORD, how long shall I cry,
[R]And You will not hear? Lam. 3:8
Even cry out to You, "Violence!"
And You will [R]not save. [Job 21:5–16]

3 Why do You show me iniquity,
And cause *me* to see [T]trouble? Or *toil*
For plundering and violence *are* before me;
There is strife, and contention arises.
4 Therefore the law is powerless,
And justice never goes forth.
For the wicked surround the righteous;
Therefore perverse judgment proceeds.

God's First Reply

5 "Look[R] among the nations and watch—
Be utterly astounded!
For *I will* work a work in your days
Which you would not believe, though it were told *you*. Is. 29:14
6 For indeed I am [R]raising up the Chaldeans,
A bitter and hasty [R]nation
Which marches through the breadth of the earth,
To possess dwelling places *that are* not theirs. 2 Kin. 24:2 • Ezek. 7:24; 21:31
7 They are terrible and dreadful;
Their judgment and their dignity proceed from themselves.
8 Their horses also are [R]swifter than leopards, Jer. 4:13
And more fierce than evening wolves.
Their [T]chargers [T]charge ahead;
Their cavalry comes from afar;
They fly as the [R]eagle *that* hastens to eat. Lit. *horsemen* • Lit. *spring about* • Hos. 8:1

9 "They all come for violence;
Their faces are set *like* the east wind.
They gather captives like sand.
10 They scoff at kings,
And princes are scorned by them.
They deride every stronghold,
For they heap up *mounds of* earth and seize it.
11 Then *his* [T]mind changes, and he transgresses; Lit. *spirit* or *wind*
He commits offense,
[R]*Imputing* this power to his god." Dan. 5:4

The Second Problem of Habakkuk

12 Are You not [R]from everlasting,
O LORD my God, my Holy One?
We shall not die. Ps. 90:2; 93:2
O LORD, [R]You have appointed them for judgment;

1:2 Sources of Doubt—One of the most potent sources of doubt is introduced in the early chapters of Genesis. It is Satan himself who causes Eve to doubt God by questioning His Word: "Has God indeed said, 'You shall not eat of every tree of the garden'?" (Page 8—Gen. 3:1). Satan even tries to get the long-suffering Job to curse God (Page 589—Job 1:11). Satan is said to be seeking to devour Christians (Page 1483—1 Pet. 5:8). This statement must not be taken literally, but means that Satan wants to devour the Christian's commitment to God and testimony before others. One way he does this is by introducing doubt into the mind.

The world system is another source of doubt. Since it has its own set of values and objectives that are opposed to God, it also has its own worldly wisdom (Page 1346—1 Cor. 2:6). This wisdom stands in direct opposition to the wisdom of God taught by the Holy Spirit (Page 1346—1 Cor. 2:13). It is clearly revealed, for example, in the opposition of the evolutionary theory to the truth of the creation of man (Page 1430—1 Tim. 6:20).

Probably the greatest source of doubt Christians face is simply their own spiritual immaturity. James traces doubting in prayer to double-mindedness and instability (Page 1468—James 1:8). Paul explains that when Christians doubt sound doctrine, it is because they are children in the faith and thus are easily deceived (Page 1390—Eph. 4:14). Conquering this kind of doubt demands a growing, obedient relationship with God.

Now turn to Page 417—1 Kin. 18:21: Cure for Doubt.

O Rock, You have marked them for
[R]correction. Is. 10:5-7 • Jer. 25:9
13 *You are* of purer eyes than to behold
evil,
And cannot look on wickedness.
Why do You look on those who deal
treacherously,
And hold Your tongue when the wicked
devours
One more righteous than he?
14 *Why* do You make men like fish of the
sea,
Like creeping things *that have* no ruler
over them?

15 They take up all of them with a hook,
They catch them in their net,
And gather them in their dragnet.
Therefore they rejoice and are glad.
16 Therefore [R]they sacrifice to their net,
And burn incense to their dragnet;
Because by them their share *is*
[T]sumptuous Deut. 8:17 • Lit. *fat*
And their food plenteous.
17 Shall they therefore empty their net,
And continue to slay nations without
pity?

CHAPTER 2

I WILL [R]stand my watch
And set myself on the rampart,
And watch to see what He will say to
me,
And what I will answer when I am
reproved. Is. 21:8, 11

God's Second Reply

2 Then the LORD answered me and said:

[R]"Write the vision
And make *it* plain on tablets,
That he may run who reads it. Is. 8:1
3 For [R]the vision *is* yet for an appointed
time; Dan. 8:17, 19; 10:14
But at the end it will speak, and it will
[R]not lie. Ezek. 12:24, 25
[R]Though it tarries, wait for it;
Because it will [R]surely come,
It will not tarry. [Heb. 10:37, 38] • [2 Pet. 3:9]

4 "Behold the proud,
His soul is not upright in him;
But the just shall live by his faith.

5 "Indeed, because he transgresses by
wine,
He is a proud man,
And he does not stay at home.
Because he [R]enlarges his desire as [T]hell,
And he *is* like death, and cannot be
satisfied, Is. 5:11-15 • Or *sheol*
He gathers to himself all nations
And heaps up for himself all peoples.

6 "Shall not all these [R]take up a proverb
against him, Mic. 2:4
And a taunting riddle against him, and
say,
'Woe to him who increases
What is not his—how long?
And to him who loads himself with
*many pledges'?
7 Will not [T]your creditors rise up
suddenly? Lit. *those who bite you*
Will they not awaken who oppress you?
And you will become their booty.
8 [R]Because you have plundered many
nations, Is. 33:1
All the remnant of the people shall
plunder you,
Because of men's [T]blood Or *bloodshed*
And the violence of the land *and* the
city,
And of all who dwell in it.

9 "Woe to him who covets evil gain for his
house,
That he may [R]set his nest on high,
That he may be delivered from the
[T]power of disaster! Obad. 4 • Lit. *hand of evil*
10 You gave shameful counsel to your
house,
Cutting off many peoples,
And sinned *against* your soul.
11 For the stone will cry out from the wall,
And the beam from the timbers will
answer it.

12 "Woe to him who builds a town with
bloodshed,
Who establishes a city by iniquity!
13 Behold, *is it* not of the LORD of hosts
That the peoples labor to feed the fire,
And nations weary themselves in vain?
14 For the earth will be filled
With the knowledge of the glory of the
LORD,
As the waters cover the sea.

15 "Woe to him who gives drink to his
neighbor,
Pressing *him to* your [R]bottle, Hos. 7:5
Even to make *him* drunk,
That you may look on his nakedness!
16 You are filled with shame instead of
glory.
You also—drink!
And be exposed as uncircumcised!
The cup of the LORD's right hand *will
be* turned against you,
And utter shame will be on your glory.
17 For the violence *done to* Lebanon will
cover you,
And the plunder of beasts *which* made
them afraid,

2:6 Syr., Vg. *thick clay*

Because of men's blood
And the violence of the land *and* the city,
And of all who dwell in it.

18 "What profit is the image, that its maker should carve it,
The molded image, a teacher of lies,
That the maker of its mold should trust in it,
To make mute idols?
19 Woe to him who says to wood, 'Awake!'
To silent stone, 'Arise! It shall teach!'
Behold, it is overlaid with gold and silver,
And in it there is no breath at all.
20 [R]But the LORD is in His holy temple.
Let all the earth keep silence before Him." Zeph. 1:7

CHAPTER 3

Habakkuk Prays for God's Mercy

A PRAYER of Habakkuk the prophet, on [T]Shigionoth. Exact meaning unknown

2 O LORD, I have heard your speech *and* was afraid;
O LORD, revive Your work in the midst of the years!
In the midst of the years make *it* known;
In wrath remember mercy.

The Glory of the Person of God

3 God came from Teman,
The Holy One from Mount Paran. Selah

His glory covered the heavens,
And the earth was full of His praise.
4 *His* brightness was like the light;
He had rays *flashing* from His hand,
And there His power *was* hidden.

The Power of the Saving Acts of God

5 Before Him went pestilence,
And fever followed at His feet.

6 He stood and measured the earth;
He looked and startled the nations.
[R]And the everlasting mountains were scattered, Nah. 1:5
The perpetual hills bowed.
His ways *are* everlasting.
7 I saw the tents of Cushan in affliction;
The curtains of the land of Midian trembled.

8 O LORD, were *You* displeased with the rivers,
Was Your anger against the rivers,
Was Your wrath against the sea,
That You rode on Your horses,
Your chariots of salvation?
9 Your bow was made quite ready;
Oaths were sworn over *Your* arrows. Selah

You divided the earth with rivers.
10 The mountains saw You *and* trembled;
The overflowing of the water passed by.
The deep uttered its voice,
And [R]lifted its hands on high. Ex. 14:22
11 The [R]sun and moon stood still in their habitation; Josh. 10:12–14
At the light of Your arrows they went,
At the shining of Your glittering spear.

12 You marched through the land in indignation;
You trampled the nations in anger.
13 You went forth for the salvation of Your people,
For salvation with Your Anointed.
You struck the head from the house of the wicked,
By laying bare from foundation to neck. Selah

14 You thrust through with his own arrows
The head of his villages.
They came out like a whirlwind to scatter me;
Their rejoicing was like feasting on the poor in secret.
15 [R]You walked through the sea with Your horses, Ps. 77:19
Through the heap of great waters.

Habakkuk Trusts in God's Salvation

16 When I heard, [R]my body trembled;
My lips quivered at *the* voice;
Rottenness entered my bones;
And I trembled in myself, Ps. 119:120
That I might rest in the day of trouble.
When he comes up to the people,
He will invade them with his troops.

17 Though the fig tree may not blossom,
Nor fruit be on the vines;
Though the labor of the olive may fail,
And the fields yield no food;
Though the flock be cut off from the fold,
And there be no herd in the stalls—
18 Yet I will [R]rejoice in the LORD, Is. 61:10
I will joy in the God of my salvation.

19 [T]The LORD God is my strength;
He will make my feet like deer's *feet*,
And He will make me [R]walk on my high hills. Heb. *YHWH Adonai* • Deut. 32:13; 33:29

To the Chief Musician. With my stringed instruments.

THE BOOK OF

ZEPHANIAH

THE BOOK OF ZEPHANIAH

During Judah's hectic political and religious history, reform comes from time to time. Zephaniah's forceful prophecy may be a factor in the reform that occurs during Josiah's reign—a "revival" that produces outward change, but does not fully remove the inward heart of corruption which characterizes the nation. Zephaniah hammers home his message repeatedly that the day of the Lord, judgment day, is coming when the malignancy of sin will be dealt with. Israel and her gentile neighbors will soon experience the crushing hand of God's wrath. But after the chastening process is complete, blessing will come in the person of the Messiah, who will be the cause for praise and singing.

Tsephan-yah means "Yahweh Hides" or "Yahweh Has Hidden." Zephaniah was evidently born during the latter part of the reign of King Manasseh. His name may mean that he was "hidden" from Manasseh's atrocities. The Greek and Latin title is *Sophonias*.

THE AUTHOR OF ZEPHANIAH

The first verse is very unusual in that Zephaniah traces his lineage back four generations to Hezekiah. This is probably Hezekiah the king of Judah, since this would best explain the genealogy. If Zephaniah was the great-great-grandson of the godly King Hezekiah, he was the only prophet of royal descent. This may have given the prophet freer access to the court of King Josiah in whose reign he ministered. Because Zephaniah used the phrase "this place" (1:4) to refer to Jerusalem and was quite familiar with its features (cf. 1:9, 10; 3:1–7), he was probably an inhabitant of Judah's royal city.

THE TIME OF ZEPHANIAH

Zephaniah solves the dating problem by fixing his prophecy "in the days of Josiah the son of Amon, king of Judah" (1:1). Josiah reigned from 640 to 609 B.C., and 2:13 indicates that the destruction of Nineveh (612 B.C.) was still a future event. Thus, Zephaniah's prophecy can be dated between 640 and 612 B.C.

However, the sins cataloged in 1:3–13 and 3:1–7 indicate a date prior to Josiah's reforms when the sins from the reigns of Manasseh and Amon still predominated. It is therefore likely that Zephaniah's ministry played a significant role in preparing Judah for the revivals that took place in the reign of the nation's last righteous king. Josiah became king of Judah at the age of eight, and by the age of sixteen his heart had already begun to turn toward God. His first reform took place in the twelfth year of his reign (628 B.C.; 2 Chr. 34:3–7) when he tore down all the altars of Baal, destroyed the foreign incense altars, burned the bones of the false prophets on their altars, and broke the Asherim (carved images) and molten images in pieces. Six years later (622 B.C.), Josiah's second reform was kindled when Hilkiah the priest found the book of the law in the temple (2 Chr. 34:8—35:19). Thus, Zephaniah's prophecy can be dated more precisely as occurring between 630 and 625 B.C.

The evil reigns of Manasseh and Amon (a total of fifty-five years) had such a profound effect upon Judah that it never recovered. Josiah's reforms were too little and too late, and the people reverted to their crass idolatry and teaching soon after Josiah was gone. As a contemporary of Jeremiah and Habakkuk, Zephaniah was one of the eleventh-hour prophets to Judah.

THE CHRIST OF ZEPHANIAH

Jesus alluded to Zephaniah on two occasions (cf. Zeph. 1:3; Matt. 13:41 and cf. Zeph. 1:15; Matt. 24:29). Both of these passages about the day of the Lord are associated with Christ's second advent. Although the Messiah is not specifically mentioned in Zephaniah, it is clear that He is the One who will fulfill the great promises of 3:9–20. He will gather His people and reign in victory: "The LORD has taken away your judgments, He has cast out your enemy. The King of Israel, the LORD, *is* in your midst; you shall see disaster no more" (3:15).

KEYS TO ZEPHANIAH

Key Word: The Day of the Lord—Zephaniah discusses the day of the Lord and describes the coming day of judgment upon Judah and the nations. God is holy and must vindicate His righteousness by calling all the nations of the world into account before Him. The sovereign God will judge not only His own people but also the whole world: no one escapes from His authority and dominion. The day of the Lord will have universal impact. To some degree, that day has already come for Judah and all the nations mentioned in 2:4–15, but there is also a future aspect, when all the earth will be judged. Zephaniah 3:9–20 speaks of another side of the day of the Lord: it will be a day of blessing after the judgment is complete. A righteous remnant will survive and all who call upon Him, Jew or Gentile, will be blessed. God will regather and restore His people, and there will be worldwide rejoicing.

Zephaniah is also written as a warning to Judah and as a call to repentance (2:1–3). God wants to spare the people, but they ultimately reject Him.

His judgment will be great; but God promises His people a future day of hope and joy. Wrath and mercy, severity and kindness, cannot be separated in the character of God.

Key Verses: Zephaniah 1:14, 15; 2:3—"The great day of the LORD *is* near; *it is* near and hastens quickly. The noise of the day of the LORD is bitter; there the mighty men shall cry out. That day *is* a day of wrath, a day of trouble and distress, a day of devastation and desolation, a day of darkness and gloominess, a day of clouds and thick darkness" (1:14, 15).

"Seek the LORD, all you meek of the earth, who have upheld His justice. Seek righteousness, seek humility. It may be that you will be hidden in the day of the LORD's anger" (2:3).

Key Chapter: Zephaniah 3—The last chapter of Zephaniah records the two distinct parts of the day of the Lord: judgment and restoration. Following the conversion of the nation, Israel finally is fully restored. Under the righteous rule of God, Israel fully inherits the blessings contained in the biblical covenants.

SURVEY OF ZEPHANIAH

On the whole, Zephaniah is a fierce and grim book of warning about the coming day of the Lord. Desolation, darkness, and ruin will strike Judah and the nations because of the wrath of God upon sin. Zephaniah looks beyond judgment, however, to a time of joy when God will cleanse the nations and restore the fortunes of His people Israel. The book begins with God's declaration, "I will utterly consume all *things* from the face of the land" (1:2); but it ends with this promise, "At that time I will bring you back" and "return your captives before your eyes" (3:20). Zephaniah moves three times from the general to the specific: (1) from universal judgment (1:1–3) to judgment upon Judah (1:4—2:3); (2) from judgment upon surrounding nations (2:4–15) to judgment upon Jerusalem (3:1–7); (3) from judgment and cleansing of all nations (3:8–10) to restoration of Israel (3:11–20). The two broad divisions of the book are: the judgment in the day of the Lord (1:1—3:8), and the salvation in the day of the Lord (3:9–20).

The Judgment in the Day of the Lord (1:1—3:8): The prophetic oracle begins with an awesome statement of God's coming judgment upon the entire earth because of the sins of men (1:2, 3). Zephaniah then concentrates on the judgment of Judah (1:4–18), listing some of the offenses that will cause it to come. Judah is polluted with idolatrous priests who promote the worship of Baal and nature, and her officials and princes are completely corrupt. Therefore, the day of the Lord is imminent; and it will be characterized by terror, desolation, and distress. However, by His grace, Yahweh appeals to His people to repent and humble themselves to avert the coming disaster before it is too late (2:1–3).

Zephaniah pronounces God's coming judgment upon the nations that surround Judah (2:4–15). He looks in all four directions: Philistia (west), Moab and Ammon (east), Ethiopia (south), and Assyria (north). Then he focuses on Jerusalem, the center of God's dealings (3:1–7). Jerusalem is characterized by spiritual rebellion and moral treachery. "She has not obeyed *His* voice, she has not received correction; she has not trusted in the LORD; she has not drawn near to her God" (3:2).

The Salvation in the Day of the Lord (3:9–20): After a broad statement of the judgment of all nations (3:8), Zephaniah changes the tone of the remainder of his book to blessing; for this, too, is an aspect of the day of the Lord. The nation will be cleansed and will call on the name of the Lord (3:9, 10). The remnant of Israel will be regathered, redeemed, and restored (3:11–20). They will rejoice in their Redeemer, and He will be in their midst. Zephaniah opens with idolatry, wrath, and judgment, but closes with true worship, rejoicing, and blessing.

FOCUS	JUDGMENT IN THE DAY OF THE LORD					SALVATION IN THE DAY OF THE LORD	
REFERENCE	1:1—	1:4—	2:4—	3:1—	3:8—	3:9—	3:14—3:20
DIVISION	JUDGMENT ON THE WHOLE EARTH	JUDGMENT ON THE NATION OF JUDAH	JUDGMENT ON THE NATIONS SURROUNDING JUDAH	JUDGMENT ON THE CITY OF JERUSALEM	JUDGMENT ON THE WHOLE EARTH	PROMISE OF CONVERSION	PROMISE OF RESTORATION
TOPIC	DAY OF WRATH					DAY OF JOY	
	JUDGMENT ON JUDAH					RESTORATION FOR JUDAH	
LOCATION	JUDAH AND THE NATIONS						
TIME	c. 630 B.C.						

OUTLINE OF ZEPHANIAH

CHAPTER 1

The Judgment on the Whole Earth

THE word of the LORD which came to Zephaniah the son of Cushi, the son of Gedaliah, the son of Amariah, the son of Hezekiah, in the days of [R]Josiah the son of Amon, king of Judah. 2 Kin. 22:1, 2

2 "I will [T]utterly consume all *things*
From the face of the land,"
Says the LORD; Lit. *make a complete end of*
3 "I[R] will consume man and beast;
I will consume the birds of the heavens,
The fish of the sea,
And the [T]stumbling blocks along with the wicked.
I will cut off man from the face of the [T]land,"
Says the LORD. Hos. 4:3 • Idols • *ground*

Causes of the Judgment

4 "I will stretch out My hand against Judah,
And against all the inhabitants of Jerusalem.
[T]I will cut off every trace of Baal from this place, Fulfilled in 2 Kin. 23:4, 5
The names of the [T]idolatrous priests with the *pagan* priests— Heb. *chemarim*
5 Those [R]who worship the host of heaven on the housetops; 2 Kin. 23:12
Those who worship and swear *oaths* by the LORD,
But who *also* swear [R]by Milcom; Josh. 23:7
6 [R]Those who have turned back from *following* the LORD, Is. 1:4
And [R]have not sought the LORD, nor inquired of Him." Hos. 7:7

7 [R]Be silent in the presence of the Lord GOD; Zech. 2:13
For the day of the LORD *is* at hand,
For the LORD has prepared a sacrifice;
He has [T]invited His guests. Lit. *set apart*

8 "And it shall be,
In the day of the LORD's sacrifice,
That I will punish [R]the princes and the king's children,
And all such as are clothed with foreign apparel. Jer. 39:6
9 In the same day I will punish
All those who [R]leap over the threshold,
Who fill their masters' houses with violence and deceit. 1 Sam. 5:5

10 "And there shall be on that day," says the LORD,
"The sound of a mournful cry from [R]the Fish Gate, 2 Chr. 33:14
A wailing from the Second Quarter,
And a loud crashing from the hills.
11 Wail, you inhabitants of [T]Maktesh!
For all the merchant people are cut down; Lit. *Mortar,* a market district of Jerusalem
All those who handle money are cut off.

12 "And it shall come to pass at that time
That I will search Jerusalem with lamps,
And punish the men
Who are [R]settled in complacency,
[R]Who say in their heart, Jer. 48:11 • Ps. 94:7
'The LORD will not do good,
Nor will He do evil.'
13 Therefore their goods shall become booty,
And their houses a desolation;
They shall build houses, but not inhabit *them;*
They shall plant vineyards, but [R]not drink their wine." Deut. 28:39

Description of the Judgment

14 [R]The great day of the LORD *is* near;
It is near and hastens quickly.
The noise of the day of the LORD is bitter; Joel 2:1, 11
There the mighty men shall cry out.

15 [R]That day *is* a day of wrath, Is. 22:5
A day of trouble and distress,
A day of devastation and desolation,
A day of darkness and gloominess,
A day of clouds and thick darkness,
16 A day of [R]trumpet and alarm
Against the fortified cities
And against the high towers. Jer. 4:19

17 "I will bring distress upon men,
And they shall [R]walk like blind men,
Because they have sinned against the LORD;
Their blood shall be poured out like dust,
And their flesh like refuse." Deut. 28:29

18 [R]Neither their silver nor their gold
Shall be able to deliver them Ezek. 7:19
In the day of the LORD's wrath;
But the whole land shall be devoured
By the fire of His jealousy,
For He will make speedy riddance
Of all those who dwell in the land.

CHAPTER 2

Call to Repentance

GATHER[R] yourselves together, yes,
gather together, Joel 1:14; 2:16
O [T]undesirable nation, Or *shameless*
2 Before the decree is issued,
Before the day passes like chaff,
Before the LORD's fierce anger comes upon you,
Before the day of the LORD's anger comes upon you!
3 [R]Seek the LORD, [R]all you meek of the earth, Amos 5:6 • Ps. 76:9
Who have upheld His justice.
Seek righteousness, seek humility.
It may be that you will be hidden
In the day of the LORD's anger.

Judgment Against Philistia (West)

4 For [R]Gaza shall be forsaken,
And Ashkelon desolate;
They shall drive out Ashdod [R]at noonday, Zech. 9:5 • Jer. 6:4
And Ekron shall be uprooted.
5 Woe to the inhabitants of [R]the seacoast,
The nation of the Cherethites!
The word of the LORD *is* against you,
O [R]Canaan, land of the Philistines:
"I will destroy you; Ezek. 25:15–17 • Josh. 13:3
So there shall be no inhabitant."

6 The seacoast shall be pastures,
With [T]shelters for shepherds [R]and folds for flocks. Underground huts or cisterns • Is. 17:2
7 The coast shall be for [R]the remnant of the house of Judah; [Mic. 5:7, 8]
They shall feed *their* flocks there;
In the houses of Ashkelon they shall lie down at evening.
For the LORD their God will [R]intervene[T] for them, Luke 1:68 • Lit. *visit them*
And [R]return their captives. Jer. 29:14

Judgment Against Moab and Ammon (East)

8 "I[R] have heard the reproach of Moab,
And [R]the revilings of the people of Ammon, Jer. 48:27 • Ezek. 25:3
With which they have reproached My people,
And [R]made arrogant threats against their borders. Jer. 49:1
9 Therefore, as I live,"
Says the LORD of hosts, the God of Israel,
"Surely [R]Moab shall be like Sodom,
And [R]the people of Ammon like Gomorrah— Is. 15:1–9 • Amos 1:13
[R]Overrun with weeds and saltpits,
And a perpetual desolation;
The residue of My people shall plunder them,
And the remnant of My people shall possess them." Deut. 29:23

10 This they shall have [R]for their pride,
Because they have *reproached* and made arrogant threats Is. 16:6
Against the people of the LORD of hosts.
11 The LORD *will be* awesome to them,
For He will reduce to nothing all the gods of the earth;
[R]*People* shall worship Him, Mal. 1:11
Each one from his place,
Indeed all the shores of the nations.

Judgment Against Ethiopia (South)

12 "You[R] Ethiopians also, Is. 18:1–7
You shall be slain by My sword."

Judgment Against Assyria (North)

13 And He will stretch out His hand against the north,
[R]Destroy Assyria, Is. 10:5–27; 14:24–27
And make Nineveh a desolation,
As dry as the wilderness.
14 The herds shall lie down in her midst,
[R]Every beast of the nation. Is. 13:21
Both the [R]pelican and the bittern
Shall lodge on the capitals *of* her *pillars;* Is. 14:23; 34:11
Their voice shall sing in the windows;
Desolation *shall be* at the threshold;
For He will lay bare the cedar work.
15 This is the rejoicing city
[R]That dwelt securely, Is. 47:8
[R]That said in her heart, Rev. 18:7
"I *am it*, and *there is* none besides me."

How has she become a desolation,
A place for beasts to lie down!
Everyone who passes by her
Shall hiss and [R]shake his fist. Nah. 3:19

CHAPTER 3

Jerusalem's Injustice

WOE to her who is rebellious and polluted,
To the oppressing city!
2 She has not obeyed *His* voice,
She has not received correction;
She has not trusted in the LORD,
She has not drawn near to her God.

3 [R]Her princes in her midst *are* roaring lions; Ezek. 22:27
Her judges *are* [R]evening wolves Hab. 1:8
That leave not a bone till morning.
4 Her [R]prophets are insolent, treacherous people; Hos. 9:7
Her priests have [T]polluted the sanctuary, Or *profaned*
They have done violence to the law.

The Lord's Justice

5 The LORD *is* righteous,
He is in her midst,
He will do no unrighteousness.
[T]Every morning He brings His justice to light; Lit. *Morning by morning*
He never fails,
But [R]the unjust knows no shame. Jer. 3:3

6 "I have cut off nations,
Their fortresses are devastated;
I have made their streets desolate,
With none passing by.
Their cities are destroyed;
There is no one, no inhabitant.
7 [R]I said, 'Surely you will fear Me, Jer. 8:6
You will receive instruction'—
So that her dwelling would not be cut off,
Despite everything for which I punished her.
But [T]they rose early and [R]corrupted all their deeds. They were eager • Gen. 6:12

The Judgment on the Whole Earth

8 "Therefore [R]wait for Me," says the LORD,
"Until the day I rise up for plunder;
My determination *is* to [R]gather the nations Hab. 2:3 • Joel 3:2
To My assembly of kingdoms,
To pour on them My indignation,
All my fierce anger;
All the earth [R]shall be devoured
With the fire of My jealousy. Zeph. 1:18

The Promise of Conversion

9 "For then I will restore to the peoples [R]a pure [T]language, Is. 19:18; 57:19 • Lit. *lip*
That they all may call on the name of the LORD,
To serve Him with one accord.
10 [R]From beyond the rivers of Ethiopia
My worshipers,
The daughter of My dispersed ones,
Shall bring My offering. Ps. 68:31
11 In that day you shall not be shamed for any of your deeds
In which you transgress against Me;
For then I will take away from your midst
Those who [R]rejoice in your pride,
And you shall no longer be haughty
In My holy mountain. Is. 2:12; 5:15
12 I will leave in your midst
[R]A meek and humble people,
And they shall trust in the name of the LORD. Is. 14:32
13 [R]The remnant of Israel [R]shall do no unrighteousness [Mic. 4:7] • Is. 60:21
[R]And speak no lies, Rev. 14:5
Nor shall a deceitful tongue be found in their mouth;
For [R]they shall feed *their* flocks and lie down, Ezek. 34:13–15, 28
And no one shall make *them* afraid."

The Promise of Restoration

14 [R]Sing, O daughter of Zion!
Shout, O Israel!
Be glad and rejoice with all *your* heart,
O daughter of Jerusalem! Is. 12:6
15 The LORD has taken away your judgments,
He has cast out your enemy.
[R]The King of Israel, the LORD, [R]*is* in your midst; [John 1:49] • Ezek. 48:35
You shall *see disaster no more.

16 In that day [R]it shall be said to Jerusalem: Is. 35:3, 4
"Do not fear;
Zion, let not your hands be weak.
17 The LORD your God [R]in your midst,
The Mighty One, will save; Zeph. 3:5, 15
[R]He will rejoice over you with gladness,
He will quiet *you* in His love, Is. 62:5; 65:19
He will rejoice over you with singing."

18 "I will gather those who [R]sorrow over the appointed assembly, Lam. 2:6
Who are among you,
To whom its reproach *is* a burden.
19 Behold, at that time
I will deal with all who afflict you;

3:15 So with Heb. mss., LXX, Bg.; MT, Vg. *fear*

THE MIGHTY GOD

"In the beginning God [*'Elōhîm*, plural noun subject] created [singular verb] the heavens and the earth" (Gen. 1:1). With these simple yet majestic words the Word of God begins. Many believe that the very first verse in the Bible gives a strong hint (not "proves") of both the Trinity and the unity of the Godhead by using the plural form of God together with a singular verb. Others feel that this is a "plural of majesty," a form that isn't literally to be taken as referring to more than one person or thing, but put in the plural to stress the importance or grandeur of something or someone. A good example is the word *behēmôth*, a plural form of the word for animal (*behēmah*) to indicate a very large or impressive beast (see word study on p. 618).

Three Hebrew words (*'El, 'Elōah, 'Elōhîm*) are translated as "God" in the English Bible. It is debated whether these three forms for "God" in Hebrew all come from the same root or not. Other Semitic languages have related words meaning "God."

God, god, mighty one (*'El*)

This word is used both for pagan gods and the one true God, much like our English word. The term is also used at times to refer to angels or other important leaders.

The word *'El* or a very similar word occurs in nearly all the Semitic tongues and may be derived from the root idea of power or awe, but this is uncertain. Since other cultures had such a close cognate to the Hebrews' God—in name only!—it was crucial to distinguish Him from the grossly immoral gods of the heathen. Sometimes this was done by using His revealed covenantal name, *YHWH* or *Jehovah* (see word study on p. 71). When the actual word *'El* is used there are often adjectives modifying the word: "the great God" (*ha'El haggādôl*, Ps. 77:13); "the God of gods" (*'El 'ēlîm*, Dan. 11:36); "the God of heaven" (*'El hashshāmāyim*, Ps. 136:26); "God Most High" (*'El 'elyôn*, Gen. 14:18–20, 22); and in contrast to the lifeless idols of paganism, "the living God" (*'El hay*, Josh. 3:10). God's relationship to His chosen people appears in the title "God, the God of Israel" (*'El 'elōhê Yisrā'el*).

God, god (*'Elōah*)

'Elōah appears frequently in the Book of Job and also in other ancient poetry. It is believed to be a form that lost frequent use and then later was revived during the Exile and afterward. It is used chiefly for the one true God. This form of the word for God seems to stress the "mighty fortress" aspect of the Lord. It is used as a parallel for the words *Rock* (Deut. 32:15) and *shield* (Prov. 30:5) and for the idea of God's being a threat to His enemies (Ps. 50:22; 114:7; 139:19).

The word for "God" in biblical Aramaic is *'Elah*, which may have encouraged the revival of the term *'Elōah*.

God, gods, angels, judges (*'Elōhîm*)

'Elōhîm is much more commonly found in the Old Testament than either *'El* or *'Elōah*. It is used as a word for Deity some 2,570 times in the Hebrew Bible.

An interesting passage using *'Elōhîm* is Genesis 3:5, where Satan promises Eve that if she and Adam eat of the forbidden fruit they will be "as gods" (KJV) or "like God" (NKJV). Both translations are valid. Men and women prefer the idea of becoming gods to recognizing themselves as sinners. Since polytheism had not yet reared its ugly head, however, the rendering "God" is probably preferable here.

Many titles of God using *'Elōhîm* stress various aspects of His Person and work: Creator (Jon. 1:9); Savior (Ps. 18:46); Universal Sovereign (Gen. 24:3); Judge (Ps. 58:11); Personal God (Gen. 48:15; Ps. 23:1).

A few times the rendering "judges" (Ex. 22:8, 9, Septuagint) is preferred by many for this word.

For those who do not read Hebrew and yet would like to know which form (*'El, 'Elōah*, or *'Elohîm*) occurs in any given passage, J. N. Darby's *New Translation* marks the text to indicate the various words for "God."

I will save the [R]lame,
And gather those who were driven out;
I will appoint them for praise and fame
In every land where they were put to
shame. [Mic. 4:6, 7]
20 At that time [R]I will bring you back,
Even at the time I gather you;
For I will give you [T]fame and praise
Among all the peoples of the earth,
When I return your captives before
your eyes,"
Says the LORD.

Is. 11:12 • Lit. *a name*

THE BOOK OF

HAGGAI

THE BOOK OF HAGGAI

With the Babylonian exile in the past, and a newly returned group of Jews back in the land, the work of rebuilding the temple can begin. However, sixteen years after the process is begun, the people have yet to finish the project, for their personal affairs have interfered with God's business. Haggai preaches a fiery series of sermonettes designed to stir up the nation to finish the temple. He calls the builders to renewed courage in the Lord, renewed holiness of life, and renewed faith in God who controls the future.

The etymology and meaning of *haggay* is uncertain, but it is probably derived from the Hebrew word *hag,* "festival." It may also be an abbreviated form of *haggiah,* "festival of Yahweh." Thus, Haggai's name means "Festal" or "Festive," possibly because he was born on the day of a major feast, such as Tabernacles (Haggai's second message takes place during that feast, 2:1). The title in the Septuagint is *Aggaios* and in the Vulgate it is *Aggaeus.*

THE AUTHOR OF HAGGAI

Haggai's name is mentioned nine times (1:1, 3, 12, 13; 2:1, 10, 13, 14, 20); the authorship and date of the book are virtually uncontested. The unity of theme, style, and dating is obvious. Haggai is known only from this book and from two references to him in Ezra 5:1 and 6:14. There he is seen working alongside the younger prophet Zechariah in the ministry of encouraging the rebuilding of the temple. Haggai returned from Babylon with the remnant under Zerubbabel and evidently lived in Jerusalem. Some think 2:3 may mean that he was born in Judah before the 586 B.C. Captivity and was one of the small company who could remember the former temple before its destruction. This would mean Haggai was about seventy-five when he prophesied in 520 B.C. It is equally likely, however, that he was born in Babylon during the Captivity.

THE TIME OF HAGGAI

In 538 B.C. Cyrus of Persia issued a decree allowing the Jews to return to their land and rebuild their temple. The first return was led by Zerubbabel, and in 536 B.C. work on the temple began. Ezra 4—6 gives the background to the Book of Haggai and describes how the Samaritans hindered the building of the temple and wrote a letter to the Persian king. This opposition only added to the growing discouragement of the Jewish remnant. Their initial optimism upon returning to their homeland was dampened by the desolation of the land, crop failure, hard work, hostility, and other hardships. They gave up the relative comfort of Babylonian culture to pioneer in a land that seemed unproductive and full of enemies. Finding it easier to stop building than to fight their neighbors, the work on the temple ceased in 534 B.C. The pessimism of the people led to spiritual lethargy, and they became preoccupied with their own building projects. They used political opposition and a theory that the temple was not to be rebuilt until some later time (perhaps after Jerusalem was rebuilt) as excuses for neglecting the house of the Lord.

It was in this context that God called His prophets Haggai and Zechariah to the same task of urging the people to complete the temple. Both books are precisely dated: Haggai 1:1, September 1, 520 B.C.; Haggai 1:15, September 24, 520 B.C.; Haggai 2:1, October 21, 520 B.C.; Zechariah 1:1, November, 520 B.C.; Haggai 2:10, 20, December 24, 520 B.C.; Zechariah 1:7, February 24, 519 B.C.; Zechariah 7:1, December 4, 518 B.C. Zechariah's prophecy commenced between Haggai's second and third messages. Thus, after fourteen years of neglect, work on the temple was resumed in 520 B.C. and was completed in 516 B.C. (Ezra 6:15). The Talmud indicates that the ark of the covenant, the Shekinah glory, and the Urim and Thummim were not in the rebuilt temple.

Darius I (521–486 B.C.) was king of Persia during the ministries of Haggai and Zechariah. He was a strong ruler who consolidated his kingdom by defeating a number of revolting nations.

THE CHRIST OF HAGGAI

The promise of Haggai 2:9 points ahead to the crucial role the second temple is to have in God's redemptive plan. Herod the Great later spent a fortune on the project of enlarging and enriching this temple, and it was filled with the glory of God incarnate every time Christ came to Jerusalem.

The Messiah is also portrayed in the person of Zerubbabel: " 'I will take you, Zerubbabel . . . and I will make you as a signet *ring;* for I have chosen you' " (2:23). Zerubbabel becomes the center of the Messianic line and is like a signet ring, sealing both branches together.

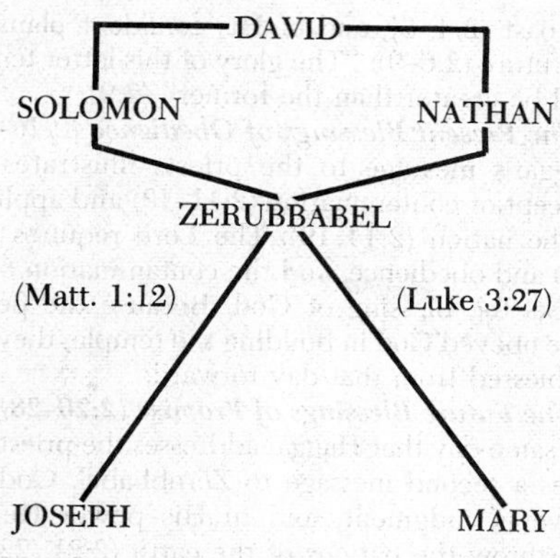

KEYS TO HAGGAI

Key Word: The Reconstruction of the Temple—Haggai's basic theme is clear: the remnant must reorder its priorities and complete the temple before it can expect the blessing of God upon its efforts. Because of spiritual indifference the people fail to respond to God's attempts to get their attention. In their despondency they do not realize that their hardships are divinely given symptoms of their spiritual disease. Haggai brings them to an understanding that circumstances become difficult when people place their own selfish interests before God's. When they put God first and seek to do His will, He will bring His people joy and prosperity.

Key Verses: Haggai 1:7, 8; 2:7–9—"Thus says the LORD of hosts: 'Consider your ways! Go up to the mountains, and bring wood and build the temple, that I may take pleasure in it and be glorified, says the LORD' " (1:7, 8).

" 'And I will shake all nations, and they shall come to the Desire of All Nations, and I will fill this temple with glory,' says the LORD of hosts. 'The silver *is* Mine, and the gold *is* Mine,' says the LORD of hosts. 'The glory of this latter temple shall be greater than the former,' says the LORD of hosts. 'And in this place I will give peace,' says the LORD of hosts" (2:7–9).

Key Chapter: Haggai 2—Verses 6–9 record some of the most startling prophecies in Scripture: "I will shake heaven and earth, the sea and dry land" (the tribulation) and "they shall come to the Desire of All Nations" and "in this place I will give peace" (the second coming of the Messiah).

SURVEY OF HAGGAI

Haggai is second only to Obadiah in brevity among Old Testament books, but this strong and frank series of four terse sermons accomplishes its intended effect. The work on the temple has ceased, and the people have become more concerned with the beautification of their own houses than with the building of the central sanctuary of God. Because of their misplaced priorities, their labor is no longer blessed by God. Only when the people put the Lord first by completing the task He has set before them will His hand of blessing once again be upon them. Haggai acts as God's man in God's hour, and his four messages are: the completion of the latter temple (1:1–15), the glory of the latter temple (2:1–9), the present blessings of obedience (2:10–19), and the future blessings of promise (2:20–23).

The Completion of the Latter Temple (1:1–15): When the remnant returns from Babylon under Zerubbabel, they begin to rebuild the temple of the Lord. However, the work soon stops and the people find excuses to ignore it as the years pass. They have no problem in building rich dwellings for themselves ("paneled houses," 1:4)

FOCUS	COMPLETION OF THE LATTER TEMPLE	GLORY OF THE LATTER TEMPLE	PRESENT BLESSING OF OBEDIENCE	FUTURE BLESSING THROUGH PROMISE
REFERENCE	1:1 —	2:1 —	2:10 —	2:20 — 2:23
DIVISION	"CONSIDER YOUR WAYS . . . MY HOUSE THAT IS IN RUINS."	"THE GLORY OF THIS LATTER TEMPLE SHALL BE GREATER."	"FROM THIS DAY FORWARD I WILL BLESS YOU."	"I WILL SHAKE HEAVEN AND EARTH."
TOPIC	THE TEMPLE OF GOD		THE BLESSINGS OF GOD	
	FIRST REBUKE (PRESENT)	FIRST ENCOURAGEMENT (FUTURE)	SECOND REBUKE (PRESENT)	SECOND ENCOURAGEMENT (FUTURE)
LOCATION	JERUSALEM			
TIME	SEPTEMBER 1 520 B.C.	OCTOBER 21 520 B.C.	DECEMBER 24 520 B.C.	DECEMBER 24 520 B.C.

while they claim that the time for building the temple has not yet come (1:2). God withdraws His blessing and they sink into an economic depression. However, they do not recognize what is happening because of their indifference to God and indulgence of self; so God communicates directly to the remnant through His prophet Haggai. Zerubbabel the governor, Joshua the high priest, and all the people respond; and twenty-three days later they again begin to work on the temple.

The Glory of the Latter Temple (2:1–9): In a few short weeks, the enthusiasm of the people sours into discouragement; the elders remember the glory of Solomon's temple and bemoan the puniness of the present temple (see Ezra 3:8–13). Haggai's prophetic word of encouragement reminds the people of God's covenant promises in the past (2:4, 5), and of His confident plans for the future (2:6–9): "The glory of this latter temple shall be greater than the former" (2:9).

The Present Blessings of Obedience (2:10–19): Haggai's message to the priests illustrates the concept of contamination (2:11–13) and applies it to the nation (2:14–19). The Lord requires holiness and obedience, and the contamination of sin blocks the blessing of God. Because the people have obeyed God in building the temple, they will be blessed from that day forward.

The Future Blessings of Promise (2:20–23): On the same day that Haggai addresses the priests, he gives a second message to Zerubbabel. God will move in judgment, and in His power He will overthrow the nations of the earth (2:21, 22). At that time, Zerubbabel, a symbol of the Messiah to come, will be honored.

OUTLINE OF HAGGAI

I. The Completion of the Latter Temple 1:1–15
- A. The Temple Is Not Complete 1:1–6
- B. The Temple Must Be Completed. 1:7–15

II. The Glory of the Latter Temple 2:1–9
- A. The Latter Temple Is Not as Glorious as the First 2:1–3
- B. The Latter Temple Will Be More Glorious than the First 2:4–9

III. The Present Blessings of Obedience 2:10–19
- A. The Disobedience of the Remnant . . . 2:10–14
- B. The Solution: The Obedience of the Remnant 2:15–19

IV. The Future Blessings Through Promise. . . 2:20-23
- A. The Future Destruction of the Nations 2:20–22
- B. The Future Recognition of Zerubbabel. . . 2:23

CHAPTER 1

The Temple Is Not Complete—Ezra 5:1

IN the second year of King Darius, in the
sixth month, on the first day of the
month, the word of the LORD came by [R]Haggai the prophet to [R]Zerubbabel the son of
Shealtiel, governor of Judah, and to [R]Joshua
the son of [R]Jehozadak, the high priest, saying, Ezra 5:1; 6:14 • Ezra 2:2 • Ezra 5:2, 3 • 1 Chr. 6:15
2 "Thus speaks the LORD of hosts, saying:
'This people says, "The time has not come,
the time that the LORD's house should be
built." ' "
3 Then the word of the LORD [R]came by
Haggai the prophet, saying, Ezra 5:1
4 "*Is it* [R]time for you yourselves to dwell in
your paneled houses, and this [T]temple *to lie* in
ruins?" 2 Sam. 7:2 • Lit. *house*
5 Now therefore, thus says the LORD of
hosts: [R]"Consider your ways! Lam. 3:40

6 "You have [R]sown much, and bring in
little;
You eat, but do not have enough;
You drink, but you are not filled with
drink;
You clothe yourselves, but no one is
warm;
And [R]he who earns wages,
Earns wages *to put* into a bag with
holes." Deut. 28:38–40 • Zech. 8:10

The Temple Must Be Completed

7 Thus says the LORD of hosts: "Consider
your ways!
8 "Go up to the mountains and bring wood
and build the temple, that I may take pleasure in it and be glorified," says the LORD.
9 "*You* looked for much, but indeed *it
came to* little; and when you brought it home,
I blew it away. Why?" says the LORD of hosts.
"Because of My house that *is in* ruins, while
every one of you runs to his own house.
10 "Therefore [R]the heavens above you withhold the dew, and the earth withholds its
fruit. Deut. 28:23
11 "For I called for a drought on the land
and the mountains, on the grain and the new
wine and the oil, on whatever the ground
brings forth, on men and livestock, and on
[R]all the labor of *your* hands." Hag. 2:17
12 [R]Then Zerubbabel the son of Shealtiel,
and Joshua the son of Jehozadak, the high

priest, with all the remnant of the people, obeyed the voice of the LORD their God, and the words of Haggai the prophet, as the LORD their God had sent him; and the people feared the presence of the LORD. Ezra 5:2

13 Then Haggai, the LORD's messenger, spoke the LORD's message to the people, saying, "I *am* with you, says the LORD."

14 So [R]the LORD stirred up the spirit of Zerubbabel the son of Shealtiel, [R]governor of Judah, and the spirit of Joshua the son of Jehozadak, the high priest, and the spirit of all the remnant of the people; [R]and they came and worked on the house of the LORD of hosts, their God, Ezra 1:1 • Hag. 2:21 • Ezra 5:2, 8

15 on the twenty-fourth day of the sixth month, in the second year of King Darius.

CHAPTER 2

The Latter Temple Is Not as Glorious as the First

IN the seventh *month*, on the twenty-first *day* of the month, the word of the LORD came by Haggai the prophet, saying:

2 "Speak now to Zerubbabel the son of Shealtiel, governor of Judah, and to Joshua the son of Jehozadak, the high priest, and to the remnant of the people, saying:

3 'Who is left among you who saw this [T]temple in its former glory? And how do you see it now? In comparison with it, [R]*is this* not in your eyes as nothing? Lit. *house* • Zech. 4:10

The Latter Temple Will Be More Glorious than the First

4 'Yet now [R]be strong, Zerubbabel,' says the LORD; 'and be strong, Joshua, son of Jehozadak, the high priest; and be strong, all you people of the land,' says the LORD, 'and work; for I *am* with you,' says the LORD of hosts. Zech. 8:9

5 [R]'*According to* the word that I covenanted with you when you came out of Egypt, so [R]My Spirit remains among you; do not fear!' Ex. 29:45, 46 • [Neh. 9:20]

6 "For thus says the LORD of hosts: "Once more (it *is* a little while) [R]I will shake heaven and earth, the sea and dry land; [Joel 3:16]

7 'and I will shake all nations, and they shall come to the [T]Desire of All Nations, and I will fill this [T]temple with glory,' says the LORD of hosts. Or *desire of all nations* • Lit. *house*

8 'The silver *is* Mine, and the gold *is* Mine,' says the LORD of hosts.

9 'The[R] glory of this latter temple shall be greater than the former,' says the LORD of hosts. 'And in this place I will give [R]peace,' says the LORD of hosts." [John 1:14] • Ps. 85:8, 9

The Disobedience of the Remnant

10 On the twenty-fourth *day* of the ninth *month*, in the second year of Darius, the word of the LORD came by Haggai the prophet, saying,

11 "Thus says the LORD of hosts: 'Now, [R]ask the priests *concerning the* law, saying, Mal. 2:7

12 "If one carries holy meat in the fold of his garment, and with the edge he touches bread or stew, wine or oil, or any food, will it become holy?" ' " Then the priests answered and said, "No."

13 And Haggai said, "If *one who is* [R]unclean *because* of a dead body touches any of these, will it be unclean?" So the priests answered and said, "It shall be unclean." Num. 19:11, 22

14 Then Haggai answered and said, " 'So is this people, and so is this nation before Me,' says the LORD, 'and so is every work of their hands; and what they offer there is unclean.

The Obedience of the Remnant

15 'And now, carefully consider from this day forward: from before stone was laid upon stone in the temple of the LORD—

16 'since those *days,* [R]when *one* came to a heap of twenty ephahs, there were *but* ten; when *one* came to the wine vat to draw out fifty baths from the press, there were *but* twenty. Zech. 8:10

17 'I struck you with blight and mildew and hail in all the labors of your hands; yet you did not *turn* to Me,' says the LORD.

18 'Consider now from this day forward, from the twenty-fourth day of the ninth month, from the day that the foundation of the LORD's temple was laid—consider it:

19 'Is the seed still in the barn? As yet the vine, the fig tree, the pomegranate, and the olive tree have not yielded *fruit. But* from this day *forward* I will bless *you.*' "

The Future Destruction of the Nations

20 And again the word of the LORD came to Haggai on the twenty-fourth day of the month, saying,

21 "Speak to Zerubbabel, [R]governor of Judah, saying: Zech. 4:6–10

[R]'I will shake heaven and earth. Hag. 2:6, 7
22 [R]I will overthrow the throne of
kingdoms; [Dan. 2:44]
I will destroy the strength of the
Gentile kingdoms.
[R]I will overthrow the chariots Mic. 5:10
And those who ride in them;
The horses and their riders shall come
down,
Every one by the sword of his brother.

The Future Recognition of Zerubbabel

23 'In that day,' says the LORD of hosts, 'I will take you, Zerubbabel My servant, the son of Shealtiel,' says the LORD, 'and will make you as a signet *ring*; for [R]I have chosen you,' says the LORD of hosts." Is. 42:1; 43:10

THE BOOK OF

ZECHARIAH

THE BOOK OF ZECHARIAH

For a dozen years or more, the task of rebuilding the temple has been half completed. Zechariah is commissioned by God to encourage the people in their unfinished responsibility. Rather than exhorting them to action with strong words of rebuke, Zechariah seeks to encourage them to action by reminding them of the future importance of the temple. The temple must be built, for one day the Messiah's glory will inhabit it. But future blessing is contingent upon present obedience. The people are not merely building a building; they are building the future. With that as their motivation, they can enter into the building project with wholehearted zeal, for their Messiah is coming.

Zekar-yah means "Yahweh Remembers" or "Yahweh Has Remembered." This theme dominates the whole book: Israel will be blessed because Yahweh remembers the covenant He made with the fathers. The Greek and Latin version of his name is *Zacharias*.

THE AUTHOR OF ZECHARIAH

Zechariah ("Yahweh Remembers") was a popular name shared by no fewer than twenty-nine Old Testament characters. It may have been given out of gratitude for God's gift of a baby boy. Like his predecessors, Jeremiah and Ezekiel, Zechariah was of priestly lineage as the son of Berechiah and grandson of Iddo (1:1, 7; Ezra 5:1; 6:14; Neh. 12:4, 16). He was born in Babylon and was brought by his grandfather to Palestine when the Jewish exiles returned under Zerubbabel and Joshua the high priest. If he was the "young man" of 2:4, he was called to prophesy at an early age in 520 B.C. According to Jewish tradition, Zechariah was a member of the Great Synagogue that collected and preserved the canon of revealed Scripture. Matthew 23:35 indicates he was "murdered between the temple and the altar" in the same way that an earlier Zechariah was martyred (see 2 Chr. 24:20, 21). The universal testimony of Jewish and Christian tradition affirms Zechariah as the author of the entire book.

THE TIME OF ZECHARIAH

Zechariah was a younger contemporary of Haggai the prophet, Zerubbabel the governor, and Joshua the high priest. The historical setting for chapters 1—8 (520–518 B.C.) is identical to that of Haggai (see "The Time of Haggai"). Work was resumed on the temple in 520 B.C., and the project was completed in 516 B.C. Chapters 9—14 are undated, but stylistic differences and references to Greece indicate a date of between 480 and 470 B.C. This would mean that Darius I (521–486 B.C.) had passed from the scene and had been succeeded by Xerxes (486–464 B.C.), the king who deposed Queen Vashti and made Esther queen of Persia.

THE CHRIST OF ZECHARIAH

Very clear messianic passages abound in this book. Christ is portrayed in His two advents as both Servant and King, Man and God. The following are a few of Zechariah's explicit anticipations of Christ: the angel of the Lord (3:1, 2); the righteous Branch (3:8; 6:12, 13), the stone with seven eyes (3:9); the King-Priest (6:13); the humble King (9:9, 10); the cornerstone, tent peg, and battle bow (10:4); the good Shepherd who is rejected and sold for thirty shekels of silver, the price of a slave (11:4–13); the pierced One (12:10); the cleansing fountain (13:1); the smitten Shepherd who is abandoned (13:7); the coming Judge and righteous King (14).

KEYS TO ZECHARIAH

Key Word: Prepare for the Messiah—The first eight chapters frequently allude to the temple and encourage the people to complete their great work on the new sanctuary. As they build the temple, they are building their future, because that very structure will be used by the Messiah when He comes to bring salvation. Zechariah eloquently attests to Yahweh's covenant faithfulness toward Israel through the work of the Messiah, especially in chapters 9—14. This book outlines God's program for His people during the times of the Gentiles until the Messiah comes to deliver them and reign upon the earth. This hope of glory provides a source of reassurance to the Jewish remnant at a time when circumstances are trying. Zechariah also seeks to promote spiritual revival so that the people will call upon the Lord with humble hearts and commit their ways to Him.

Key Verses: Zechariah 8:3; 9:9—"Thus says the LORD: 'I will return to Zion, and dwell in the midst of Jerusalem. Jerusalem shall be called the City of Truth, the Mountain of the LORD of hosts, the Holy Mountain' " (8:3).

"Rejoice greatly, O daughter of Zion! Shout, O daughter of Jerusalem! Behold, your King is coming to you; He *is* just and having salvation, lowly and riding on a donkey, a colt, the foal of a donkey" (9:9).

Key Chapter: Zechariah 14—Zechariah builds to a tremendous climax in the fourteenth chapter where he discloses the last siege of Jerusalem, the initial victory of the enemies of Israel, the cleaving of the Mount of Olives, the Lord's defense of Jerusalem with His visible appearance on Olivet, judgment on the confederated nations, the topographical changes in the land of Israel, the Feast of Tabernacles, and the ultimate holiness of Jerusalem and her people.

SURVEY OF ZECHARIAH

Zechariah uses a series of eight visions, four messages, and two burdens to portray God's future plans for His covenant people. The first eight chapters were written to encourage the remnant while they were rebuilding the temple; the last six chapters were written after the completion of the temple to anticipate Israel's coming Messiah. Zechariah moves from gentile domination to messianic rule, from persecution to peace, and from uncleanness to holiness. The book divides into: the eight visions (1—6), the four messages (7 and 8), and the two burdens (9—14).

The Eight Visions (1—6): The book opens with an introductory appeal to the people to repent and return to God, unlike their fathers who rejected the warnings of the prophets (1:1–6). A few months later, Zechariah has a series of eight night visions, evidently in one troubled night (February 15, 519 B.C.; 1:7). The angel who speaks with him interprets the visions, but some of the symbols are not explained. The visions mix the work of the Messiah in both advents, and like the other prophets, Zechariah sees only the peaks of God's program without the intervening valleys. The first five are visions of comfort, and the last three are visions of judgment: (1) The horseman among the myrtle trees—God will rebuild Zion and His people (1:7–17). (2) The four horns and craftsmen—Israel's oppressors will be judged (1:18–21). (3) The man with a measuring line—God will protect and glorify Jerusalem (2:1–13). (4) The cleansing of Joshua the high priest—Israel will be cleansed and restored by the coming Branch (3:1–10). (5) The golden lampstand—God's Spirit is empowering Zerubbabel and Joshua (4:1–14). (6) The flying scroll—individual sin will be judged (5:1–4). (7) The woman in the basket—national sin will be removed (5:5–11). (8) The four chariots—God's judgment will descend on the nations (6:1–8). The crowning of Joshua (6:9–15) anticipates the coming of the Branch who will be King and Priest (the composite crown).

The Four Messages (7 and 8): In response to a question about the continuation of the fasts (7:1–3), God gives Zechariah a series of four messages: (1) a rebuke of empty ritualism (7:4–7); (2) a reminder of past disobedience (7:8–14); (3) the restoration and consolation of Israel (8:1–17); and (4) the recovery of joy in the kingdom (8:18–23).

The Two Burdens (9—14): The first burden (9—11) concerns the first advent and rejection of Israel's coming King. Alexander the Great will conquer Israel's neighbors, but will spare Jerusalem (9:1–8) which will be preserved for her King (the Messiah; 9:9, 10). Israel will succeed against Greece (the Maccabean revolt; 9:11–17), and although they will later be scattered, the Messiah will bless them and bring them back (10:1—11:3). Israel will reject her Shepherd-King and be led astray by false shepherds (11:4–17). The second burden (12—14) concerns the second advent of Christ and the acceptance of Israel's King. The nations will attack Jerusalem, but the Messiah will come and deliver His people (12). They will be cleansed of impurity and falsehood (13), and the Messiah will come in power to judge the nations and reign in Jerusalem over the whole earth (14).

FOCUS	EIGHT VISIONS			FOUR MESSAGES	TWO BURDENS	
REFERENCE	1:1—	1:7—	6:9—	7:1—	9:1—	12:1—14:21
DIVISION	CALL TO REPENTANCE	EIGHT VISIONS	CROWNING OF JOSHUA	QUESTION OF THE FASTS	FIRST BURDEN: REJECTION OF THE MESSIAH	SECOND BURDEN: REIGN OF THE MESSIAH
TOPIC	PICTURES			PROBLEM	PREDICTION	
	ISRAEL'S FORTUNE			ISRAEL'S FASTINGS	ISRAEL'S FUTURE	
LOCATION	JERUSALEM					
TIME	WHILE BUILDING THE TEMPLE (520–518 B.C.)				AFTER BUILDING THE TEMPLE (c. 480–470 B.C.)	

OUTLINE OF ZECHARIAH

CHAPTER 1

The Call to Repentance—Ezra 5:1

IN the eighth month [R]of the second year of
Darius, the word of the LORD came [R]to
Zechariah the son of Berechiah, the son of
Iddo the prophet, saying, Zech. 7:1 • Matt. 23:35
2 "The LORD has been very angry with
your fathers.
3 "Therefore say to them, 'Thus says the
LORD of hosts: "Return [R]to Me," says the
LORD of hosts, "and I will return to you," says
the LORD of hosts. [Mal. 3:7–10]
4 "Do not be like your fathers, [R]to whom
the former prophets preached, saying, 'Thus
says the LORD of hosts: [R]"Turn now from
your evil ways and your evil deeds." ' But
they did not hear nor heed Me," says the
LORD. 2 Chr. 36:15, 16 • Is. 31:6

5 "Your fathers, where *are* they?
And the prophets, do they live forever?
6 Yet surely [R]My words and My statutes,
Which I commanded My servants the
prophets, [Is. 55:11]
Did they not overtake your fathers?"

"So they returned and said:

[R]'Just as the LORD of hosts determined to
do to us, Lam. 1:18; 2:17
According to our ways and according to
our deeds,
So He has dealt with us.' " ' "

The Horses Among the Myrtle Trees

7 On the twenty-fourth day of the eleventh
month, which is the month Shebat, in the
second year of Darius, the word of the LORD
came to Zechariah the son of Berechiah, the
son of Iddo the prophet:
8 I saw by night, and behold, a man riding
on a red horse, and it stood among the myrtle
trees in the hollow; and behind him *were*
[R]horses: red, sorrel, and white. [Zech. 6:2–7]
9 Then I said, "My lord, what *are* these?"
So the angel who talked with me said to me,
"I will show you what they *are*."
10 And the man who stood among the myrtle trees answered and said, [R]"These *are the*
ones whom the LORD has sent to walk to and
fro throughout the earth." [Heb. 1:14]
11 [R]So they answered the Angel of the
LORD, who stood among the myrtle trees, and
said, "We have walked to and fro throughout
the earth, and behold, all the earth is [T]resting
quietly." [Ps. 103:20, 21] • Lit. *sitting and quiet*
12 Then the Angel of the LORD answered
and said, "O LORD of hosts, [R]how long will
You not have mercy on Jerusalem and on the
cities of Judah, against which You were
angry these seventy years?" Ps. 74:10
13 And the LORD answered the angel who
talked to me, *with* [R]good *and* comforting
words. Jer. 29:10
14 So the angel who spoke with me said to
me, [T]"Proclaim, saying, 'Thus says the LORD
of hosts: Lit. *Cry out*

"I am [R]zealous for Jerusalem Zech. 8:2
And for Zion with great [T]zeal. Or *jealousy*

15 I am exceedingly angry with the
nations at ease;
For [R]I was a little angry, Is. 47:6
And they helped—*but* with evil *intent*."

16 'Therefore thus says the LORD:

[R]"I am returning to Jerusalem with
mercy; [Zech. 2:10; 8:3]
My [R]house [R]shall be built in it," says the
LORD of hosts, Ezra 6:14, 15 • Is. 44:28
"And [R]a *surveyor's* line shall be stretched
out over Jerusalem." ' Zech. 2:1–3

17 "Again proclaim, saying, 'Thus says the
LORD of hosts:

"My cities shall again [T]spread out
through prosperity; Or *overflow with good*
The LORD will again comfort Zion,
And will again choose Jerusalem." ' "

The Four Horns and Four Craftsmen

18 Then I raised my eyes and looked, and
there *were* four [R]horns. [Lam. 2:17]
19 And I said to the angel who talked with
me, "What *are* these?" So he answered me,
"These *are* the [T]horns that have scattered
Judah, Israel, and Jerusalem." Kingdoms
20 Then the LORD showed me four craftsmen.
21 And I said, "What are these coming to
do?" So he said, "These *are* the [R]horns that
scattered Judah, so that no one could lift up
his head; but the craftsmen are coming to
terrify them, to cast out the horns of the
nations that lifted up *their* horn against the
land of Judah to scatter it." [Ps. 75:10]

CHAPTER 2

The Man with the Measuring Line

THEN I raised my eyes and looked, and
behold, [R]a man with a measuring line in
his hand. Jer. 31:39
2 So I said, "Where are you going?" And
he said to me, "To measure Jerusalem, to see
what *is* its width and what *is* its length."
3 And there *was* the angel who talked with
me, going out; and another angel was coming
out to meet him,
4 who said to him, "Run, speak to this
young man, saying: 'Jerusalem shall be inhabited *as* towns without walls, because of
the multitude of men and livestock in it.
5 'For I,' says the LORD, 'will be [R]a wall of
fire all around her, [R]and I will be the glory in
her midst.' " [Is. 26:1] • [Is. 60:19]
6 "Up, up! Flee [R]from the land of the
north," says the LORD; "for I have [R]spread
you abroad like the four winds of heaven,"
says the LORD. Is. 48:20 • Deut. 28:64
7 "Up, Zion! [R]Escape, you who dwell with
the daughter of Babylon." Is. 48:20
8 For thus says the LORD of hosts: "He sent
Me after glory, to the nations which plunder
you; for he who [R]touches you touches the
[T]apple of His eye. Deut. 32:10 • Lit. *pupil*
9 "For surely I will shake My hand against
them, and they shall become [T]spoil for their
servants. Then you will know that the LORD
of hosts has sent Me. *booty*
10 [R]"Sing and rejoice, O daughter of Zion!
For behold, I am coming and I [R]will dwell in
your midst," says the LORD. Is. 12:6 • [Lev. 26:12]
11 [R]"Many nations shall be joined to the
LORD [R]in that day, and they shall become [R]My
people. And I will dwell in your midst. Then
you will know that the LORD of hosts has sent
Me to you. [Is. 2:2, 3] • Zech. 3:10 • Ex. 12:49
12 "And the LORD will [R]take possession of
Judah as His inheritance in the Holy Land,
and will again choose Jerusalem. [Deut. 32:9]
13 "Be silent, all flesh, before the LORD, for
He is aroused from His holy habitation!"

CHAPTER 3

The Cleansing of Joshua, the High Priest

THEN he showed me [R]Joshua the high
priest standing before the Angel of the
LORD, and [R]Satan[T] standing at his right hand
to oppose him. Hag. 1:1 • Ps. 109:6 • Lit. *the Adversary*
2 And the LORD said to Satan, "The LORD
rebuke you, Satan! The LORD who [R]has chosen Jerusalem rebuke you! *Is* this not a brand
plucked from the fire?" [Rom. 8:33]
3 Now Joshua was clothed with filthy garments, and was standing before the Angel.
4 Then He answered and spoke to those
who stood before Him, saying, "Take away
the filthy garments from him." And to him
He said, "See, I have removed your iniquity
from you, [R]and I will clothe you with rich
robes." Is. 61:10
5 And I said, "Let them put a clean [R]turban
on his head." So they put a clean turban on
his head, and they put the clothes on him.
And the Angel of the LORD stood by. Ex. 29:6
6 Then the Angel of the LORD admonished
Joshua, saying,
7 "Thus says the LORD of hosts:

'If you will walk in My ways,
And if you will [R]keep My command,
Then you shall also judge My house,
And likewise have charge of My courts;
I will give you places to walk Lev. 8:35
Among these who [R]stand here. Zech. 4:4

8 'Hear, O Joshua, the high priest,
You and your companions who sit
before you,
For they are [R]a wondrous sign;

For behold, I am bringing forth [R]My
Servant the BRANCH. Ps. 71:7 • Is. 42:1 ☆
9 For behold, the stone
That I have laid before Joshua:
[R]Upon the stone *are* seven eyes.
Behold, I will engrave its inscription,'
Says the LORD of hosts, [Zech. 4:10]
'And [R]I will remove the iniquity of that
land in one day. Jer. 31:34; 50:20
10 In that day,' says the LORD of hosts,
'Everyone will invite his neighbor
Under his vine and under his fig tree.' "

CHAPTER 4

The Golden Lampstand and Olive Trees

NOW [R]the angel who talked with me came
back and wakened me, [R]as a man who is
wakened out of his sleep. Zech. 1:9; 2:3 • Dan. 8:18
2 And he said to me, "What do you see?"
So I said, "I am looking, and there *is* [R]a
lampstand of solid gold with a bowl on top of
it, [R]and on the *stand* seven lamps with seven
pipes to the seven lamps. Rev. 1:12 • [Rev. 4:5]
3 "Two olive trees *are* by it, one at the
right of the bowl and the other at its left."
4 So I answered and spoke to the angel
who talked with me, saying, "What *are* these,
my lord?"
5 Then the angel who talked with me
answered and said to me, "Do you not know
what these are?" And I said, "No, my lord."
6 So he answered and said to me:

"This *is* the word of the LORD to
[R]Zerubbabel:
[R]'Not by might nor by power, but by My
Spirit,'
Says the LORD of hosts. Hag. 1:1 • Hos. 1:7
7 'Who *are* you, [R]O great mountain?
Before Zerubbabel *you shall become* a
plain! Jer. 51:25
And he shall bring forth the capstone
With shouts of "Grace, grace to it!" ' "

8 Moreover the word of the LORD came to
me, saying:

9 "The hands of Zerubbabel
[R]Have laid the foundation of this
[T]temple; Ezra 3:8–10; 5:16 • Lit. *house*
His hands [R]shall also finish *it*. Ezra 6:14, 15
Then [R]you will know Zech. 2:9, 11; 6:15
That the [R]LORD of hosts has sent Me to
you. [Is. 43:16]
10 For who has despised the day of [R]small
things? Hag. 2:3
For these seven rejoice to see
The [T]plumb line in the hand of
Zerubbabel. Lit. *plummet stone*
[R]They are the eyes of the LORD,
Which scan to and fro throughout the
whole earth." 2 Chr. 16:9

11 Then I answered and said to him, "What
are these two olive trees, *one* at the right of
the lampstand and *the other* at its left?"
12 And I further answered and said to him,
"What *are these* two olive branches that *drip*
into the [T]receptacles of the two gold pipes
from which the golden *oil* drains?" Lit. *hands*
13 Then he answered me and said, "Do you
not know what these *are*?" And I said, "No,
my lord."
14 So he said, "These *are* the two [T]anointed
ones, [R]who stand beside the Lord of the
whole earth." Lit. *sons of fresh oil* • Zech. 3:1–7

CHAPTER 5

The Flying Scroll

THEN I turned and raised my eyes, and
saw there a flying [R]scroll. Ezek. 2:9
2 And he said to me, "What do you see?"
So I answered, "I see a flying scroll. Its length
is [T]twenty cubits and its width [T]ten
cubits." 30 ft. • 15 ft.
3 Then he said to me, "This *is* the [R]curse
that goes out over the face of the whole
earth: 'Every thief shall be expelled,' according *to what is on* this side of *the scroll*; and,
'Every perjurer shall be expelled,' according
to what is on that side of it." Mal. 4:6

4 "I will send out *the curse*," says the
LORD of hosts;
"It shall enter the house of the [R]thief
And the house of [R]the one who swears
falsely by My name.
It shall remain in the midst of his house
And consume [R]it, with its timber and
stones." Ex. 20:15 • Lev. 19:12 • Lev. 14:34, 35

The Woman in the Basket

5 Then the angel who talked with me came
out and said to me, "Lift your eyes now, and
see what this *is* that goes forth."
6 So I asked, "What *is* it?" And he said, "It
is a [T]basket that is going forth." He also said,
"This *is* their resemblance throughout the
earth: Heb. *ephah*, a measuring container, and so elsewhere
7 "Here *is* a lead disc lifted up, and this *is* a
woman sitting inside the basket";
8 then he said, "This *is* Wickedness!" And
he thrust her down into the basket, and
threw the lead cover over its mouth.
9 Then I raised my eyes and looked, and
there *were* two women, coming with the
wind in their wings; for they had wings like
the wings of a [R]stork, and they lifted up the
basket between earth and heaven. Lev. 11:13, 19
10 So I said to the angel who talked with
me, "Where are they carrying the basket?"
11 And he said to me, "To build a house for
it in the land of [T]Shinar; when it is ready, *the*
basket will be set there on its base." Babylon

CHAPTER 6

The Four Chariots

THEN I turned and raised my eyes and looked, and behold, four chariots *were* coming from between two mountains, and the mountains *were* mountains of bronze.

2 With the first chariot *were* red horses, with the second chariot black horses,

3 with the third chariot white horses, and with the fourth chariot dappled horses—strong *steeds.*

4 Then I answered [R]and said to the angel who talked with me, "What *are* these, my lord?" Zech. 5:10

5 And the angel answered and said to me, [R]"These *are* four spirits of heaven, who go out from *their* [R]station before the Lord of all the earth. [Heb. 1:7, 14] • Dan. 7:10

6 [T]"The one with the black horses is going to [R]the north country, the white are going after them, and the dappled are going toward the south country." The chariot • Jer. 1:14

7 Then the strong *steeds* went out, eager to go, that they might walk to and fro throughout the earth. And He said, "Go, walk to and fro throughout the earth." So they walked to and fro throughout the earth.

8 And He called to me, and spoke to me, saying, "See, those who go toward the north country have given rest to My [R]Spirit in the north country." Eccl. 10:4

The Crowning of Joshua

9 Then the word of the LORD came to me, saying:

10 "Receive *the gift* from the captives—from Heldai, Tobijah, and Jedaiah, who have come from Babylon—and go the same day and enter the house of Josiah the son of Zephaniah.

11 "Take the silver and gold, make an elaborate crown, and set *it* on the head of Joshua the son of Jehozadak, the high priest.

12 "Then speak to him, saying, 'Thus says the LORD of hosts, saying:

"Behold, [R]the Man whose name *is* the
[R]BRANCH! John 1:45 • Is. 11:1 ☆
From His place He shall [T]branch out,
[R]And He shall build the temple of the
LORD; Lit. *sprout up* • [Eph. 2:20]
13 Yes, He shall build the temple of the
LORD.
He [R]shall bear the glory, Is. 22:24
And shall sit and rule on His throne;
So [R]He shall be a priest on His throne,
And the counsel of peace shall be
between them both."' [Ps. 110:4–7]

14 "Now the [T]elaborate crown shall be [R]for a memorial in the temple of the LORD for Helem, Tobijah, Jedaiah, and Hen the son of Zephaniah. Lit. *crowns* • Ex. 12:14

15 "Even [R]*those who* are far away shall come and build the temple of the LORD. Then you shall know that the LORD of hosts has sent Me to you. And *this* shall come to pass if you diligently obey the voice of the LORD your God." Is. 57:19

CHAPTER 7

The Question of Fasting

NOW in the fourth year of King Darius it came to pass *that* the word of the LORD came to Zechariah, on the fourth day of the ninth month, *which is* Chislev,

2 when the people sent Sherezer, with Regem-Melech and his men, *to* [T]the house of God, to pray before the LORD, Heb. *Bethel*

3 *and* to ask the priests who *were* in the house of the LORD of hosts, and the prophets, saying, "Should I weep in the fifth month and fast as I have done for so many years?"

Rebuke of Hypocrisy

4 Then the word of the LORD of hosts came to me, saying,

5 "Say to all the people of the land, and to the priests: 'When you [R]fasted and mourned in the fifth and seventh *months* [R]during those seventy years, did you really fast [R]for Me—for Me? [Is. 58:1–9] • Zech. 1:12 • [Rom. 14:6]

6 'When you eat and when you drink, do you not eat and drink *for yourselves?*

7 '*Should you* not *have obeyed* the words which the LORD proclaimed through the [R]former prophets when Jerusalem and the cities around it were inhabited and prosperous, and [R]the [T]South and the Lowland were inhabited?'" Zech. 1:4 • Jer. 17:26 • Heb. *Negev*

Repent of Disobedience

8 Then the word of the LORD came to Zechariah, saying,

9 "Thus says the LORD of hosts:

[R]'Execute true justice, Jer. 7:28
Show [T]mercy and compassion
Everyone to his brother. Or *lovingkindness*
10 [R]Do not oppress the widow or the
fatherless,
The alien or the poor.
[R]Let none of you plan evil in his heart
Against his brother.' Ex. 22:22 • Mic. 2:1

11 "But they refused to heed, [R]shrugged their shoulders, and [R]stopped their ears so that they could not hear. Neh. 9:29 • Jer. 17:23

12 "Yes, they made their hearts like flint, refusing to hear the law and the words which the LORD of hosts had sent by His Spirit through the former prophets. Thus great wrath came from the LORD of hosts.

13 "Therefore it happened, *that* just as He
proclaimed and they would not hear, so [R]they
called out and I would not listen," says the
LORD of hosts. Prov. 1:24–28
14 "But [R]I scattered them with a whirlwind
among all the nations which they had not
known. Thus the land became desolate after
them, so that no one passed through or
returned; for they made the pleasant land
desolate." Deut. 4:27; 28:64

CHAPTER 8

Restoration of Israel

AGAIN the word of the LORD of hosts came, saying,
2 "Thus says the LORD of hosts:

'I am zealous for Zion with great zeal;
With great fervor I am zealous for her.'

3 "Thus says the LORD:

[R]'I will return to Zion, Zech. 1:16
And [R]dwell in the midst of Jerusalem.
Jerusalem [R]shall be called the City of
Truth, Zech. 2:10, 11 • Is. 1:21
[R]The Mountain of the LORD of hosts,
[R]The Holy Mountain.' [Is. 2:2, 3] • Jer. 31:23

4 "Thus says the LORD of hosts:

[R]'Old men and old women shall again sit
In the streets of Jerusalem, Is. 65:20
Each one with his staff in his hand
Because of [T]great age. Lit. *many days*
5 The streets of the city
Shall be [R]full of boys and girls
Playing in its streets.' Jer. 30:19, 20

6 "Thus says the LORD of hosts:

'If it is [T]marvelous in the eyes of the
remnant of this people in these days,
Will it also be marvelous in My eyes?'
Says the LORD of hosts. Or *wonderful*

7 "Thus says the LORD of hosts:

'Behold, [R]I will save My people from the
land of the [T]east Is. 11:11 • Lit. *rising sun*
And from the land of the [T]west; *setting sun*
8 I will [R]bring them *back*, Zeph. 3:20
And they shall dwell in the midst of
Jerusalem.
[R]They shall be My people [Jer. 30:22; 31:1, 33]
And I will be their God,
[R]In truth and righteousness.' Jer. 4:2

9 "Thus says the LORD of hosts:

[R]'Let your hands be strong, Hag. 2:4
You who have been hearing in these
days
These words by the mouth of [R]the
prophets, Ezra 5:1, 2; 6:14
Who were in [R]the day Hag. 2:18
That the foundation was laid
For the house of the LORD of hosts,
That the temple might be built.
10 For before these days
There were no [R]wages for man nor any
hire for beast;
There was no peace from the enemy for
whoever went out or came in;
For I set all men, everyone, against his
neighbor. Hag. 1:6, 9

11 [R]'But now I *will* not *treat* the remnant of
this people as in the former days,' says the
LORD of hosts. Hag. 2:15–19

12 'For the [T]seed *shall be* prosperous,
The vine shall give its fruit, *seed of peace*
The ground shall give her increase,
And [R]the heavens shall give their dew.
I will cause the remnant of this people
To possess all these *things*. Hag. 1:10
13 And it shall come to pass
That just as you were [R]a curse among
the nations, Jer. 42:18
O house of Judah and house of Israel,
So I will save you, and [R]you shall be a
blessing.
Do not fear,
Let your hands be strong.' Gen. 12:2

14 "For thus says the LORD of hosts:

[R]'Just as I determined to [T]punish you
When your fathers provoked Me to
wrath,' Jer. 31:28 • Lit. *bring calamity to you*
Says the LORD of hosts,
[R]'And I would not relent, [2 Chr. 36:16]
15 So again in these days
I am determined to do good
To Jerusalem and to the house of
Judah.
Do not fear.
16 These *are* the things you shall [R]do:
[R]Speak each man the truth to his
neighbor; Zech. 7:9, 10 • [Eph. 4:25]
Give judgment in your gates for truth,
justice, and peace;
17 [R]Let none of you think evil in [T]your
heart against your neighbor;
And do not love a false oath.
For all these *are things* that I hate,'
Says the LORD." Prov. 3:29 • Lit. *his*

Rejoice in Israel's Future

18 Then the word of the LORD of hosts came
to me, saying,

19 "Thus says the LORD of hosts:

[R]'The fast of the fourth *month,* Jer. 52:6
[R]The fast of the fifth, Jer. 52:12
[R]The fast of the seventh, 2 Kin. 25:25
[R]And the fast of the tenth, Jer. 52:4
Shall be [R]joy and gladness and cheerful
feasts Esth. 8:17
For the house of Judah.
[R]Therefore love truth and peace.' Zech. 8:16

20 "Thus says the LORD of hosts:

'Peoples shall yet come,
Inhabitants of many cities;
21 The inhabitants of one *city* shall go to
another, saying,
[R]"Let us continue to go and pray before
the LORD,
And seek the LORD of hosts.
I myself will go also." [Is. 2:2, 3]
22 Yes, [R]many peoples and strong nations
Shall come to seek the LORD of hosts in
Jerusalem, Is. 60:3; 66:23
And to pray before the LORD.'

23 "Thus says the LORD of hosts: 'In those
days ten men from every language of the
nations shall [R]grasp the sleeve of a Jewish
man, saying, "Let us go with you, for we have
heard *that* God *is* with you." ' " [Is. 45:14]

CHAPTER 9

Judgment on Surrounding Nations

THE burden of the word of the LORD
Against the land of Hadrach,
And [R]Damascus its resting place
(For [R]the eyes of men Is. 17:1 • Amos 1:3–5
And all the tribes of Israel
Are on the LORD);
2 Also *against* [R]Hamath, which borders
on it, Jer. 49:23
And *against* [R]Tyre and [R]Sidon, though
they are very wise. Is. 23 • 1 Kin. 17:9

3 For Tyre built herself a tower,
Heaped up silver like the dust,
And gold like the mire of the streets.
4 Behold, [R]the LORD will cast her out;
He will destroy her power in the sea,
And she will be devoured by fire. Is. 23:1

5 Ashkelon shall see it and fear;
Gaza also shall be very sorrowful;
And [R]Ekron, for He dried up her
expectation. Zeph. 2:4, 5
The king shall perish from Gaza,
And Ashkelon shall not be inhabited.

6 "A mixed race shall settle [R]in Ashdod,
And I will cut off the pride of the
[R]Philistines. Amos 1:8 • Ezek. 25:15–17
7 I will take away the blood from his
mouth,
And the abominations from between his
teeth.
But he who remains, even he *shall be*
for our God,
And shall be like a leader in Judah,
And Ekron like a Jebusite.
8 [R]I will camp around My house [Ps. 34:7]
Because of the army,
Because of him who passes by and him
who returns.
No more shall an oppressor pass
through them,
For now I have seen with My eyes.

First Coming of the Messiah

9 "Rejoice [R]greatly, O daughter of Zion!
Shout, O daughter of Jerusalem!
Behold, your King is coming to you;
He *is* just and having salvation,
Lowly and riding on a donkey,
A colt, the foal of a donkey. Matt. 21:4, 5☆

Second Coming of the Messiah

10 I [R]will cut off the chariot from Ephraim
And the horse from Jerusalem;
The [R]battle bow shall be cut off.
He shall speak [R]peace to the nations;
His [R]dominion *shall be* 'from sea to sea,
And from the River to the ends of the
earth.' Hos. 1:7 • Hos. 2:18 • Mic. 4:2–4☆ • Ps. 72:8

11 "As for you also,
Because of the blood of your covenant,
I will set your [R]prisoners free from the
waterless pit. Is. 42:7
12 Return to the stronghold,
[R]You prisoners of hope. Is. 49:9
Even today I declare
That I will restore [R]double to you. Is. 61:7
13 For I have bent Judah, My *bow*,
Fitted the bow with Ephraim,
And raised up your sons, O Zion,
Against your sons, O Greece,
And made you like the sword of a
mighty man."

14 Then the LORD will be seen over them,
And [R]His arrow will go forth like
lightning.
The Lord GOD will blow the trumpet,
And go [R]with whirlwinds from the
south. Ps. 18:14 • Is. 21:1
15 The LORD of hosts will [R]defend them;
They shall devour and subdue with
sling stones. Zech. 12:8
They shall drink *and* roar as if with
wine;

They shall be filled *with blood* like
[T]basins, Sacrificial basins
Like the corners of the altar.
16 The LORD their God will [R]save them in
that day, Jer. 31:10, 11
As the flock of His people.
For [R]they *shall be like* the [T]jewels of a
crown, Is. 62:3 • Lit. *stones*
Lifted like a banner over His land—
17 For how great is [T]their goodness Lit. *his*
And how great their [R]beauty! Ps. 45:1–16
Grain shall make the young men thrive,
And new wine the young women.

CHAPTER 10

ASK the LORD for [R]rain [Deut. 11:13, 14]
In the time of the [T]latter rain. Spring
The LORD will make [T]flashing clouds;
He will give them showers of rain,
Grass in the field for everyone. Or *lightning*

2 For the idols speak delusion;
The diviners envision [R]lies,
And tell false dreams; Jer. 27:9
They [R]comfort in vain. Job 13:14
Therefore [T]the people wend their way
like [R]sheep; Lit. *they* • Jer. 50:6, 7
They are [T]in trouble [R]because *there is*
no shepherd. *afflicted* • Ezek. 34:5–8

3 "My anger is kindled against the
[R]shepherds, Jer. 25:34–36
[R]And I will punish the [T]goatherds.
For the LORD of hosts [R]will visit His
flock, Ezek. 34:17 • Leaders • Luke 1:68
The house of Judah,
And [R]will make them as His royal horse
in the battle. Song 1:9
4 From him comes [R]the cornerstone,
From him [R]the tent peg, Is. 28:16 • Is. 22:23
From him the battle bow,
From him every [T]ruler together. Or *despot*
5 They shall be like mighty *men*,
Who [R]tread down *their enemies*
In the mire of the streets in the battle.
They shall fight because the LORD is
with them,
And the riders on horses shall be put to
shame. Ps. 18:42

6 "I will strengthen the house of Judah,
And I will save the house of Joseph.
[R]I will bring them back, Jer. 3:18
Because I [R]have mercy on them. Hos. 1:7
They shall be as though I had not cast
them aside;
For I *am* the LORD their God,
And I [R]will hear them. Zech. 13:9
7 *Those of* Ephraim shall be like a mighty
man,
And their [R]heart shall rejoice as if with
wine. Ps. 104:15
Yes, their children shall see *it* and be
glad;
Their heart shall rejoice in the LORD.
8 I will [R]whistle for them and gather
them,
For I will redeem them;
[R]And they shall increase as they once
increased. Is. 5:26 • Ezek. 36:37

9 "I[R] will [T]sow them among the peoples,
And they shall [R]remember Me in far
countries; Hos. 2:23 • Or *scatter* • Deut. 30:1
They shall live, together with their
children,
And they shall return.
10 [R]I will also bring them back from the
land of Egypt, Is. 11:11
And gather them from Assyria.
I will bring them into the land of Gilead
and Lebanon,
Until no *more room* is found for them.
11 [R]He shall pass through the sea with
affliction, Is. 11:15
And strike the waves of the sea:
All the depths of [T]the River shall dry
up. The Nile
Then [R]the pride of Assyria shall be
brought down, Zeph. 2:13
And the scepter of Egypt shall depart.

12 "So I will strengthen them in the LORD,
And [R]they shall walk up and down in
His name,"
Says the LORD. Mic. 4:5

CHAPTER 11

Rejection of the Messiah

OPEN [R]your doors, O Lebanon, Zech. 10:10
That fire may devour your cedars.
2 Wail, O cypress, for the [R]cedar has
fallen, Ezek. 31:3
Because the mighty *trees* are ruined.
Wail, O oaks of Bashan,
For the thick forest has come down.
3 *There is* the sound of wailing
[R]shepherds! Jer. 25:34–36
For their glory is in ruins.
There is the sound of roaring lions!
For the pride of the Jordan is in ruins.

4 Thus says the LORD my God, "Feed the
flock for slaughter,
5 "whose owners slaughter them and [R]feel
no guilt; those who sell them [R]say, 'Blessed be
the LORD, for I am rich'; and their shepherds
do not pity them. [Jer. 2:3]; 50:7 • Hos. 12:8
6 "For I will no longer pity the inhabitants
of the land," says the LORD. "But indeed I will
give everyone into his neighbor's hand and
into the hand of his king. They shall [T]attack
the land, and I will not deliver *them* from
their hand." Lit. *strike*

7 So I fed the flock for slaughter, in particular [R]the poor of the flock. I took for myself two staffs: the one I called [T]Beauty, and the other I called [T]Bonds; and I fed the flock. Zeph. 3:12 • Or *Grace* • Or *Unity*

8 I [T]dismissed the three shepherds [R]in one month. My soul loathed them, and their soul also abhorred me. Or *destroyed,* lit. *cut off* • Hos. 5:7

9 Then I said, "I will not feed you. [R]Let what is dying die, and what is perishing perish. Let those that are left eat each other's flesh." Jer. 15:2

10 And I took my staff, [T]Beauty, and cut it in two, that I might break the covenant which I had made with all the peoples. Or *Grace*

11 So it was broken on that day. Thus the poor of the flock, who were watching me, knew that it *was* the word of the LORD.

12 Then I said to them, "If it is agreeable to you, give *me* my wages; and if not, refrain." So they [R]weighed out for my wages [T]thirty *pieces* of silver. Matt. 27:9 ☆ • $3,840

13 And the LORD said to me, "Throw it to the [R]potter"—that princely price they set on me. So I took the [T]thirty *pieces* of silver and threw them into the house of the LORD for the potter. Matt. 27:3–10 ☆ • $220

14 Then I cut in two my other staff, [T]Bonds, that I might break the brotherhood between Judah and Israel. Or *Unity*

15 And the LORD said to me, [R]"Next, take for yourself the implements of a foolish shepherd. Is. 56:11

16 "For indeed I will raise up a shepherd in the land *who* will not care for those who are cut off, nor seek the young, nor heal those that are broken, nor feed those that still stand. But he will eat the flesh of the fat and tear their hooves in [R]pieces. Ezek. 34:1–10

17 "Woe[R] to the worthless shepherd,
Who leaves the flock!
A sword *shall be* against his arm
And against his right eye;
His arm shall completely wither,
And his right eye shall be totally
blinded." Jer. 23:1

CHAPTER 12

Physical Salvation of Judah

THE [T]burden of the word of the LORD against Israel. Thus says the LORD, [R]who stretches out the heavens, lays the foundation of the earth, and [R]forms the spirit of man within him: *oracle, prophecy* • Is. 42:5; 44:24 • [Is. 57:16]

2 "Behold, I will make Jerusalem [R]a cup of [T]drunkenness to all the surrounding peoples, when they lay siege against Judah and Jerusalem. Is. 51:17 • Lit. *reeling*

3 "And it shall happen in that day that I will make Jerusalem [R]a very heavy stone for all peoples; all who would heave it away will surely be cut in pieces, though all nations of the earth are gathered against it. Matt. 21:44

4 "In that day," says the LORD, [R]"I will strike every horse with confusion, and its rider with madness; I will open My eyes on the house of Judah, and will strike every horse of the peoples with blindness. Ezek. 38:4

5 "And the governors of Judah shall say in their heart, 'The inhabitants of Jerusalem *are* my strength in the LORD of hosts, their God.'

6 "In that day I will make the governors of Judah like a firepan in the woodpile, and like a fiery torch in the sheaves; they shall devour all the surrounding peoples on the right hand and on the left, but Jerusalem shall be inhabited again in her own place—Jerusalem.

7 "The LORD will save the tents of Judah first, so that the glory of the house of David and the glory of the inhabitants of Jerusalem shall not become greater than that of Judah.

8 "In that day the LORD will defend the inhabitants of Jerusalem; the one who is feeble among them in that day shall be like David, and the house of David *shall be* like God, like the Angel of the LORD before them.

9 "It shall be in that day *that* I will seek to [R]destroy all the nations that come against Jerusalem. Hag. 2:22

Spiritual Salvation of Judah

10 [R]"And I will pour on the house of David and on the inhabitants of Jerusalem the Spirit of grace and supplication; then they will [R]look on Me whom they have pierced; they will mourn for Him as one mourns for *his* only *son,* and grieve for Him as one grieves for a firstborn. [Joel 2:28, 29] • John 19:34, 37; 20:27 ☆

11 "In that day there shall be a great mourning in Jerusalem, like the mourning at Hadad Rimmon in the plain of Megiddo.

12 [R]"And the land shall mourn, every family by itself: the family of the house of David by itself, and their wives by themselves; the family of the house of [R]Nathan by itself, and their wives by themselves; [Matt. 24:30] • Luke 3:31

13 "the family of the house of Levi by itself, and their wives by themselves; the family of Shimei by itself, and their wives by themselves;

14 "all the families that remain, every family by itself, and their wives by themselves.

CHAPTER 13

"IN that [R]day [R]a fountain shall be opened for the house of David and for the inhabitants of Jerusalem, for sin and for [R]uncleanness. [Rev. 21:6, 7] • [Heb. 9:14] • Ezek. 36:25

2 "It shall be in that day," says the LORD of hosts, "*that* I will [R]cut off the names of the idols from the land, and they shall no longer

be remembered. I will also cause [R]the prophets and the unclean spirit to depart from the
land. Ex. 23:13 • Jer. 23:14, 15
3 "It shall come to pass *that* if anyone still
prophesies, then his father and mother who
begot him will say to him, 'You shall not live,
because you have spoken lies in the name of
the LORD.' And his father and mother who
begot him [R]shall thrust him through when he
prophesies. Deut. 13:6–11
4 "And it shall be in that day *that* [R]every
prophet will be ashamed of his vision when
he prophesies; they will not wear [R]a robe of
coarse hair to deceive. [Mic. 3:6, 7] • 2 Kin. 1:8
5 [R]"But he will say, 'I *am* no prophet, I *am*
a farmer; for a man taught me to keep cattle
from my youth.' Amos 7:14
6 "And *someone* will say to him, [R]'What are
these wounds in your hands?' Then he will
answer, '*Those* with which I was wounded in
the house of my friends.' John 20:25, 27 ☆

7 "Awake, O sword, against [R]My Shepherd,
Against the Man [R]who is My
Companion," Is. 40:11 • [John 10:30]
Says the LORD of hosts.
[R]"Strike the Shepherd, Matt. 26:31, 56, 67 ☆
And the sheep will be scattered;
Then I will turn My hand against [R]the
little ones. Luke 12:32
8 And it shall come to pass in all the
land,"
Says the LORD,
"*That* [R]two-thirds in it shall be cut off
and die, Ezek. 5:2, 4, 12
[R]But *one*-third shall be left in it: [Rom. 11:5]
9 I will bring the *one*-third [R]through the
fire, Is. 48:10
Will [R]refine them as silver is refined,
And test them as gold is tested. 1 Pet. 1:6
[R]They will call on My name, Ps. 50:15
And I will answer them.
[R]I will say, 'This *is* My people'; Hos. 2:23
And each one will say, 'The LORD *is* my
God.' "

CHAPTER 14

Final Siege of Jerusalem

BEHOLD, [R]the day of the LORD is coming,
And your [T]spoil will be divided in your
midst. [Is. 13:6, 9] • *plunder* or *booty*
2 For [R]I will gather all the nations to
battle against Jerusalem; Zech. 12:2, 3
The city shall be taken,
The houses [T]rifled, *plundered*
And the women ravished.
Half of the city shall go into captivity,
But the *remnant* of the people shall not
be cut off from the city.

Second Coming of the Messiah

3 Then the LORD will go forth
And fight against those nations,
As He fights in the day of battle.
4 And in that day His feet will stand [R]on
the Mount of Olives, Ezek. 11:23
Which faces Jerusalem on the east.
And the Mount of Olives shall be split
in two,
From east to west,
[R]*Making* a very large valley; Joel 3:12
Half of the mountain shall move toward
the north
And half of it toward the south.
5 Then you shall flee *through* My
mountain valley,
For the mountain valley shall reach to
Azal.
Yes, you shall flee
As you fled from the [R]earthquake Amos 1:1
In the days of Uzziah king of Judah.
Thus the LORD my God will come,
And [R]all the saints with *You. Joel 3:11

6 It shall come to pass in that day
That there will be no light;
The [T]lights will diminish. Lit. *glorious ones*
7 It shall be one day
[R]Which is known to the LORD—
Neither day nor night. Matt. 24:36
But at [R]evening time it shall happen
That it will be light. Is. 30:26

8 And in that day it shall be
That living [R]waters shall flow from
Jerusalem, Ezek. 47:1–12
Half of them toward [T]the eastern sea
And half of them toward [T]the western
sea; Dead Sea • Mediterranean Sea
In both summer and winter it shall
occur.

Kingdom of the Messiah

9 And the LORD shall be [R]King over all
the earth.
In that day it shall be—
[R]"The LORD *is* one,"
And His name one. [Rev. 11:15] • Deut. 6:4

10 All the land shall be turned into a plain
from Geba to Rimmon south of Jerusalem.
[T]Jerusalem shall be raised up and [R]inhabited
in her place from Benjamin's Gate to the
place of the First Gate and the Corner Gate,
[R]and *from* the Tower of Hananeel to the
king's winepresses. Lit. *She* • Zech. 12:6 • Jer. 31:38

11 *The people* shall dwell in it;
And [R]no longer shall there be utter
destruction, Jer. 31:40
But Jerusalem shall be safely inhabited.

12 And this shall be the plague with which
the LORD will strike all the people who fought
against Jerusalem:

14:5 Some mss., vss. *Him*

Their flesh shall [T]dissolve while they
stand on their feet,
Their eyes shall dissolve in their
sockets,
And their tongues shall dissolve in their
mouths. Lit. *decay*

13 It shall come to pass in that day
That [R]a great panic from the LORD will
be among them.
Everyone will seize the hand of his
neighbor,
And raise [R]his hand against his
neighbor's hand; 1 Sam. 14:15, 20 • Judg. 7:22
14 Judah also will fight at Jerusalem.
[R]And the wealth of all the surrounding
nations
Shall be gathered together:
Gold, silver, and apparel in great
abundance. Ezek. 39:10, 17

15 [R]Such also shall be the plague
On the horse *and* the mule,
On the camel and the donkey,
And on all the cattle that will be in
those camps.
So *shall* this plague *be*. Zech. 14:12

16 And it shall come to pass *that* everyone
who is left of all the nations which came
against Jerusalem shall go up from year to
year to worship the King, the LORD of hosts,
and to keep the Feast of Tabernacles.
17 [R]And it shall be *that* whichever of the
families of the earth do not come up to
Jerusalem to worship the King, the LORD of
hosts, on them there will be no rain. Is. 60:12
18 If the family of Egypt will not come up
and enter in, [R]they *shall have* no *rain*; they
shall receive the plague with which the LORD
strikes the nations who do not come up to
keep the Feast of Tabernacles. Deut. 11:10
19 This shall be the [T]punishment of Egypt
and the punishment of all the nations that do
not come up to keep the Feast of Tabernacles. Lit. *sin*
20 In that day [R]"HOLINESS TO THE
LORD" shall be *engraved* on the bells of the
horses. The pots in the LORD's house shall be
like the bowls before the altar. Is. 23:18
21 Yes, every pot in Jerusalem and Judah
shall be holiness to the LORD of hosts. Everyone who sacrifices shall come and take them
and cook in them. In that day there shall no
longer be a Canaanite in the house of the
LORD of hosts.

THE BOOK OF
MALACHI

THE BOOK OF MALACHI

Malachi, a prophet in the days of Nehemiah, directs his message of judgment to a people plagued with corrupt priests, wicked practices, and a false sense of security in their privileged relationship with God. Using the question-and-answer method, Malachi probes deeply into their problems of hypocrisy, infidelity, mixed marriages, divorce, false worship, and arrogance. So sinful has the nation become that God's words to the people no longer have any impact. For four hundred years after Malachi's ringing condemnations, God remains silent. Only with the coming of John the Baptist (3:1) does God again communicate to His people through a prophet's voice.

The meaning of the name *Mal'aki* ("My Messenger") is probably a shortened form of *Mal'akya,* "Messenger of Yahweh," and it is appropriate to the book which speaks of the coming of the "messenger of the covenant" ("messenger" is mentioned three times in 2:7; 3:1). The Septuagint used the title *Malachias* even though it also translated it "by the hand of his messenger." The Latin title is *Maleachi.*

THE AUTHOR OF MALACHI

The only Old Testament mention of Malachi is in 1:1. The authorship, date, and unity of Malachi have never been seriously challenged. The unity of the book can be seen in the dialectic style that binds it together. Nothing is known of Malachi (not even his father's name), but a Jewish tradition says that he was a member of the Great Synagogue (see "The Author of Zechariah").

THE TIME OF MALACHI

Although an exact date cannot be established for Malachi, internal evidence can be used to deduce an approximate date. The Persian term for governor, *pechah* (1:8; cf. Neh. 5:14; Hag. 1:1, 14; 2:21), indicates that this book was written during the Persian domination of Israel (539–333 B.C.). Sacrifices were being offered in the temple (1:7–10; 3:8), which was rebuilt in 516 B.C. Evidently many years had passed since the offerings were instituted, because the priests had grown tired of them and corruptions had crept into the system. In addition, Malachi's oracle was inspired by the same problems that Nehemiah faced: corrupt priests (1:6—2:9; Neh. 13:1–9), neglect of tithes and offerings (3:7–12; Neh. 13:10–13), and intermarriage with pagan wives (2:10–16; Neh. 13:23–28). Nehemiah came to Jerusalem in 444 B.C. to rebuild the city walls, thirteen years after Ezra's return and reforms (457 B.C.). Nehemiah returned to Persia in 432 B.C., but came back to Palestine about 425 B.C. and dealt with the sins described in Malachi. It is therefore likely that Malachi proclaimed his message while Nehemiah was absent between 432 B.C. and 425 B.C., almost a century after Haggai and Zechariah began to prophesy (520 B.C.).

THE CHRIST OF MALACHI

The Book of Malachi is the prelude to four hundred years of prophetic silence, broken finally by the words of the next prophet, John the Baptist: "Behold! The Lamb of God who takes away the sin of the world!" (John 1:29). Malachi predicts the coming of the messenger who will clear the way before the Lord (3:1; cf. Is. 40:3). John the Baptist later fulfills this prophecy, but the next few verses (3:2–5) jump ahead to Christ in His second advent. This is also true of the prophecy of the appearance of "Elijah the prophet" (4:5). John the Baptist was this Elijah (Matt. 3:3; 11:10–14; 17:9–13; Mark 1:3; 9:10, 11; Luke 1:17; 3:4; John 1:23), but Elijah will also appear before the second coming of Christ.

KEYS TO MALACHI

Key Word: An Appeal to Backsliders—The divine dialogue in Malachi's prophecy is designed as an appeal to break through the barrier of Israel's disbelief, disappointment, and discouragement. The promised time of prosperity has not yet come, and the prevailing attitude that it is not worth serving God becomes evident in their moral and religious corruption. However, God reveals His continuing love in spite of Israel's lethargy. His appeal in this oracle is for the people and priests to stop and realize that their lack of blessing is not caused by God's lack of concern, but by their disobedience of the covenant law. When they repent and return to God with sincere hearts, the obstacles to the flow of divine blessing will be removed. Malachi also reminds the people that a day of reckoning will surely come when God will judge the righteous and the wicked.

Key Verses: Malachi 2:17—3:1; 4:5, 6—"You have wearied the LORD with your words; yet you say, 'In what way have we wearied *Him?*' In that you say, 'Everyone who does evil *is* good in the sight of the LORD, and He delights in them' or, 'Where *is* the God of justice?'

" 'Behold, I send My messenger, and he will prepare the way before Me. And the Lord, whom you seek, will suddenly come to His temple, even the Messenger of the covenant, in whom you delight. Behold, He is coming,' says the LORD of hosts" (2:17—3:1).

"Behold, I will send you Elijah the prophet before the coming of the great and dreadful day of the LORD. And he will turn the hearts of the fathers to the children, and the hearts of the children to their fathers, lest I come and strike the earth with a curse" (4:5, 6).

Key Chapter: Malachi 3—The last book of the Old Testament concludes with a dramatic prophecy of the coming of the Lord and John the Baptist: "I send My messenger, and he will prepare the way before Me" (3:1). Israel flocked to the Jordan four hundred years later when "the voice of one crying in the wilderness: 'Prepare the way of the LORD'" (Matt. 3:3) appeared, breaking the long silence of prophetic revelation. Malachi 3 and 4 record the coming of the Messiah and His forerunner.

SURVEY OF MALACHI

The great prophecies of Haggai and Zechariah are not yet fulfilled, and the people of Israel become disillusioned and doubtful. They begin to question God's providence as their faith imperceptibly degenerates into cynicism. Internally, they wonder whether it is worth serving God after all. Externally, these attitudes surface in mechanical observances, empty ritual, cheating on tithes and offerings, and crass indifference to God's moral and ceremonial law. Their priests are corrupt and their practices wicked, but they are so spiritually insensitive that they wonder why they are not being blessed by God.

Using a probing series of questions and answers, God seeks to pierce their hearts of stone. In each case the divine accusations are denied: How has God loved us? (1:2–5); How have we (priests) despised God's name? (1:6—2:9); How have we (people) profaned the covenant? (2:10–16); How have we wearied God? (2:17—3:6); How have we robbed God? (3:7–12); How have we spoken against God? (3:13–15). In effect, the people sneer, "Oh, come on now: it's not that bad!" However, their rebellion is quiet, not open. As their perception of God grows dim, the resulting materialism and externalism become settled characteristics that later grip the religious parties of the Pharisees and Sadducees. In spite of all this, God still loves His people and once again extends His grace to any who will humbly turn to Him. Malachi explores: the privilege of the nation (1:1–5), the pollution of the nation (1:6—3:15), and the promise to the nation (3:16—4:6).

The Privilege of the Nation (1:1–5): The Israelites blind themselves to God's love for them. Wallowing in the problems of the present, they are forgetful of God's works for them in the past. God gives them a reminder of His special love by contrasting the fates of Esau (Edom) and Jacob (Israel).

The Pollution of the Nation (1:6—3:15): The priests have lost all respect for God's name and in their greed offer only diseased and imperfect animals on the altar. They have more respect for the Persian governor than they do for the living God. Moreover, God is withholding His blessings from them because of their disobedience to God's covenant and because of their insincere teaching.

The people are indicted for their treachery in divorcing the wives of their youth in order to marry foreign women (2:10–16). In response to their questioning the justice of God, they receive a promise of the Messiah's coming but also a warning of the judgment that He will bring (2:17—3:6). The people have robbed God of the tithes and offerings due Him, but God is ready to bless them with abundance if they will put Him first (3:7–12). The final problem is the arrogant challenge to the character of God (3:13–15), and this challenge is answered in the remainder of the book.

FOCUS	PRIVILEGE OF THE NATION	POLLUTION OF THE NATION		PROMISE TO THE NATION		
REFERENCE	1:1—	1:6—	2:10—	3:16—	4:1—	4:4—4:6
DIVISION	LOVE OF GOD FOR THE NATION	SIN OF THE PRIESTS	SIN OF THE PEOPLE	BOOK OF REMEMBRANCE	COMING OF CHRIST	COMING OF ELIJAH
TOPIC	PAST	PRESENT		FUTURE		
	CARE OF GOD	COMPLAINT OF GOD		COMING OF GOD		
LOCATION	JERUSALEM					
TIME	c. 432–425 B.C.					

The Promise to the Nation (3:16—4:6): The Lord assures His people that a time is coming when the wicked will be judged and those who fear Him will be blessed. The day of the Lord will reveal that it is not "vain to serve God" (3:14).

Malachi ends on the bitter word curse. Although the people are finally cured of idolatry, there is little spiritual progress in Israel's history. Sin abounds, and the need for the coming Messiah is greater than ever.

OUTLINE OF MALACHI

CHAPTER 1

The Privilege of the Nation

THE [T]burden of the word of the LORD to Israel by Malachi. *oracle, prophecy*

2 "I[R] have loved you," says the LORD.
"Yet you say, 'In what way have You loved us?' Deut. 4:37; 7:8; 23:5
Was not Esau Jacob's brother?"
Says the LORD.
"Yet [R]Jacob I have loved; Rom. 9:13
3 But Esau I have hated,
And [R]laid waste his mountains and his heritage Jer. 49:18
For the jackals of the wilderness."

4 Even though Edom has said,
"We have been impoverished,
But we will return and build the desolate places,"

Thus says the LORD of hosts:

"They may build, but I will [R]throw down;
They shall be called the Territory of Wickedness, Jer. 49:16–18
And the people against whom the LORD will have indignation forever.
5 Your eyes shall see,
And you shall say,
[R]'The LORD is magnified beyond the border of Israel.' Ps. 35:27

The Priests Despise the Name of the Lord

6 "A son [R]honors *his* father, [Ex. 20:12]
And a servant *his* master.
[R]If then I am the Father, Luke 6:46
Where *is* My honor?
And if I *am* a Master,
Where *is* My reverence?
Says the LORD of hosts
To you priests who despise My name.
[R]Yet you say, 'In what way have we despised Your name?' Mal. 2:14

7 "*You* offer [R]defiled food on My altar.
But you say, Deut. 15:2
'In what way have we defiled You?'
By saying,
'The table of the LORD is contemptible.'
8 And [R]when you offer the blind as a sacrifice, Lev. 22:22
Is it not evil?
And when you offer the lame and sick,
Is it not evil?
Offer it then to your governor!
Would he be pleased with you?
Would he [T]accept you favorably?"
Says the LORD of hosts. Lit. *lift up your face*

9 "But now entreat God's favor,
That He may be gracious to us.
[R]*While* this is being *done* by your hands,
Will He accept you favorably?"
Says the LORD of hosts. Hos. 13:9
10 "Who *is there* even among you who would shut the doors,
[R]So that you would not kindle fire *on* My altar in vain?
I have no pleasure in you,"
Says the LORD of hosts,
[R]"Nor will I accept an offering from your hands. 1 Cor. 9:13 • Is. 1:11
11 For [R]from the rising of the sun, even to its going down, Is. 59:19

My name *shall be* great [R]among the
Gentiles; Is. 60:3, 5
[R]In every place [R]incense *shall be* offered
to My name, 1 Tim. 2:8 • Rev. 8:3
And a pure offering;
[R]For My name shall be great among the
nations," Is. 66:18, 19
Says the LORD of hosts.

12 "But you profane it,
In that you say,
[R]'The table of the *LORD is defiled; Mal. 1:7
And its fruit, its food, *is* contemptible.'
13 You also say,
'Oh, what a [R]weariness!'
And you sneer at it,"
Says the LORD of hosts.
"And you bring the stolen, the lame, and
the sick;
Thus you bring an offering!
[R]Should I accept this from your hand?"
Says the LORD. Is. 43:22 • Lev. 22:20
14 "But cursed *be* [R]the deceiver
Who has in his flock a male,
And makes a vow,
But sacrifices to the Lord [R]what is
blemished—
For [R]I *am* a great King,"
Says the LORD of hosts,
"And My name *is to be* feared among the
nations. Mal. 1:8 • Lev. 22:18–20 • Ps. 47:2

CHAPTER 2

The Lord Curses the Priests

"AND now, O [R]priests, this
commandment is for you. Mal. 1:6
2 [R]If you will not hear, [Deut. 28:15]
And if you will not take *it* to heart,
To give glory to My name,"
Says the LORD of hosts,
"I will send a curse upon you,
And I will curse your blessings.
Yes, I have cursed them [R]already, Mal. 3:9
Because you do not take *it* to heart.

3 "Behold, I will rebuke your descendants
And spread [R]refuse on your faces, Ex. 29:14
The refuse of your solemn feasts;
And *one* will take you away with it.
4 Then you shall know that I have sent
this commandment to you,
That My covenant with Levi may
continue,"
Says the LORD of hosts.
5 "My[R] covenant was with him, *one* of life
and peace, Num. 25:12
And I gave them to him [R]*that he might*
fear Me; Deut. 33:9
So he feared Me
And was reverent before My name.
6 [T]The law of truth was in his mouth,
And [T]injustice was not found on his
lips. Or *true instruction* • Or *unrighteousness*
He walked with Me in peace and equity,
And turned many away from iniquity.

7 "For[R] the lips of a priest should keep
knowledge,
And *people* should seek the law from
his mouth;
[R]For he is the messenger of the LORD of
hosts. Deut. 17:8–11 • [Gal. 4:14]
8 But you have departed from the way;
You [R]have caused many to stumble at
the law. Jer. 18:15
[R]You have corrupted the covenant of
Levi," Neh. 13:29
Says the LORD of hosts.
9 "Therefore [R]I also have made you
contemptible and base 1 Sam. 2:30
Before all the people,
Because you have not kept My ways
But have shown partiality in the law."

The People Commit Idolatry

10 [R]Have we not all one Father?
[R]Has not one God created us?
Why do we deal treacherously with one
another
By profaning the covenant of the
fathers? 1 Cor. 8:6 • Job 31:15

11 Judah has dealt treacherously,
And an abomination has been
committed in Israel and in Jerusalem,

1:12 MT *Lord*

2:10 God the Father of All—The Fatherhood of God applies in a general sense to everyone since all men and women are created by God in His image. Thus their creaturehood is derived from His Fatherhood. This fact is demonstrated by Hebrews 12:9, which speaks of God as "the Father of spirits" (cf. Page 180—Num. 16:22; Page 759—Eccl. 12:7). Paul even agrees with a heathen poet that all men are God's offspring (Page 1299—Acts 17:28). He does not mean, of course, that everyone will have eternal life but that all men and women are the offspring of God in their created natures. James says that men still bear this image (Page 1469—James 3:9).

God is also the Father of all as sustainer of life. Every person is an object of His fatherly care (Page 1138—Matt. 18:10) and a candidate for His kingdom (Page 1221—Luke 18:16). Furthermore, God is not willing that any should perish (Page 1138—Matt. 18:14; Page 1426—1 Tim. 2:4). Even when men and women reject God He still provides for them as He does believers with rain, fruitful seasons, food, and gladness (Page 1121—Matt. 5:45; Page 1293—Acts 14:17).

Now turn to Page 1117—Matt. 3:17: God the Father of Christ.

For Judah has [R]profaned
The LORD's holy *institution* which He
loves:
He has married the daughter of a
foreign god. Ezra 9:1, 2
12 May the LORD cut off from the tents of
Jacob
The man who does this, being *awake
and aware,
And [R]who brings an offering to the
LORD of hosts. Neh. 13:29

13 And this is the second thing you do:
You cover the altar of the LORD with
tears,
With weeping and crying;
So He does not regard the offering
anymore,
Nor receive *it* with good will from your
hands.

The People Divorce

14 Yet you say, "For what reason?"
Because the LORD has been witness
Between you and [R]the wife of your
youth, Mal. 3:5
With whom you have dealt
treacherously;
[R]Yet she is your companion Prov. 2:17
And your wife by covenant.
15 But [R]did He not make *them* one,
Having a remnant of the Spirit?
And why one? Matt. 19:4, 5
He seeks [R]godly offspring. [1 Cor. 7:14]
Therefore take heed to your spirit,
And let none deal treacherously with
the wife of his youth.

16 "For [R]the LORD God of Israel says
That He hates divorce,
For it covers one's garment with
violence," [Matt. 5:31; 19:6–8]
Says the LORD of hosts.
"Therefore take heed to your spirit,
That you do not deal treacherously."

The Lord Will Judge at His Coming

17 [R]You have wearied the LORD with your
words; Is. 43:22, 24
Yet you say,
"In what way have we wearied *Him?*"
In that you say,
[R]"Everyone who does evil Is. 5:20
Is good in the sight of the LORD,
And He delights in them,"
Or, "Where *is* the God of justice?"

CHAPTER 3

"BEHOLD, [R]I send My messenger,
And he will [R]prepare the way before
Me. Luke 1:76☆ · [Is. 40:3]
And the Lord, whom you seek,
Will suddenly come to His temple,
[R]Even the Messenger of the covenant,
In whom you delight. Is. 63:9
Behold, [R]He is coming," Hab. 2:7
Says the LORD of hosts.

2 "But who can endure [R]the day of His
coming? [Mal. 4:1]
And who can stand when He appears?
For [R]He *is* like a refiner's fire [Matt. 3:10–12]
And like [T]fullers' soap. *launderers' soap*
3 [R]He will sit as a refiner and a purifier of
silver; Is. 1:25
He will purify the sons of Levi,
And [T]purge them as gold and silver,
That they may offer to the LORD
An offering in righteousness. Or *refine*

4 "Then [R]the offering of Judah and
Jerusalem
Will be [T]pleasant to the LORD,
As in the days of old,
As in former years. Mal. 1:11 · *pleasing*
5 And I will come near you for judgment;
I will be a swift witness
Against sorcerers,
Against adulterers,
[R]Against perjurers, Zech. 5:4
Against those who [R]exploit wage
earners and [R]widows and the
fatherless, James 5:4 · Ex. 22:22
And against those who turn away an
alien—
Because they do not fear Me,"
Says the LORD of hosts.

The People Rob God

6 "For I *am* the LORD, [R]I do not change;
[R]Therefore you are not consumed, O
sons of Jacob. [Rom. 11:29] · [Lam. 3:22]
7 Yet from the days of [R]your fathers
You have gone away from My
ordinances Acts 7:51
And have not kept *them.*
[R]Return to Me, and I will return to you,"
Says the LORD of hosts. Zech. 1:3
[R]"But you said, Mal. 1:6
'In what way shall we return?'

8 "Will a man rob God?
Yet you have robbed Me!
But you say,
'In what way have we robbed You?'
[R]In tithes and offerings. Neh. 13:10–12
9 You are cursed with a curse,
For you have robbed Me,
Even this whole nation.
10 Bring all the tithes into the [R]storehouse,
That there may be food in My house,
And [T]prove Me now in this,"
Says the LORD of hosts, 1 Chr. 26:20 · Or *test*

2:12 Talmud, Vg. *teacher and student*

"If I will not open for you the [R]windows
of heaven Gen. 7:11
And [R]pour out for you *such* blessing
That *there will* not *be room* enough *to*
receive it. 2 Chr. 31:10

11 "And I will rebuke [R]the devourer for
your sakes,
So that he will not destroy the fruit of
your ground,
Nor shall the vine fail to bear fruit for
you in the field,"
Says the LORD of hosts; Amos 4:9
12 "And all nations will call you blessed,
For you will be [R]a delightful land,"
Says the LORD of hosts. Dan. 8:9

The People Doubt the Character of God

13 "Your[R] words have been [T]harsh against
Me," Mal. 2:17 • Lit. *strong*
Says the LORD,
"Yet you say,
'What have we spoken against You?'
14 [R]You have said,
'It is vain to serve God;
What profit *is it* that we have kept His
ordinance,
And that we have walked as mourners
Before the LORD of hosts? Job 21:14
15 So now [R]we call the proud blessed,
For those who do wickedness are
[T]raised up; Ps. 73:12 • Lit. *built*
Yes, *those who* tempt God go free.' "

The Rewards of the Book of Remembrance

16 Then those [R]who feared the LORD
[R]spoke to one another, Ps. 66:16 • Heb. 3:13
And the LORD listened and heard *them;*
So [R]a book of remembrance was written
before Him Ps. 56:8
For those who fear the LORD
And who [T]meditate on His name. Or *esteem*

17 "They[R] shall be Mine," says the LORD of
hosts, Ex. 19:5
"On the day that I make them My
[R]jewels.[T] Is. 62:3 • Lit. *special treasure*
And [R]I will spare them Ps. 103:13
As a man spares his own son who
serves him."
18 [R]Then you shall again discern
Between the righteous and the wicked,
Between one who serves God [Ps. 58:11]
And one who does not serve Him.

CHAPTER 4

The Rewards of the Coming of Christ

"FOR behold, [R]the day is coming,
Burning like an oven, [2 Pet. 3:7]
And all the proud, yes, all who do
wickedly will be [R]stubble. Obad. 18
And the day which is coming shall burn
them up,"
Says the LORD of hosts,
"That will [R]leave them neither root nor
branch. Amos 2:9
2 But to you who [R]fear My name Mal. 3:16
The [R]Sun of Righteousness shall arise
With healing in His wings; Luke 1:78
And you shall go out
And grow fat like stall-fed calves.
3 [R]You shall trample the wicked,
For they shall be ashes under the soles
of your feet
On the day that I do *this,*"
Says the LORD of hosts. Mic. 7:10

The Prophecy of the Coming of Elijah

4 "Remember the [R]Law of Moses, My
servant, Ex. 20:3
Which I commanded him in Horeb for
all Israel,
With the statutes and judgments.
5 Behold, I will send you [R]Elijah the
prophet [Matt. 11:14; 17:10–13] ☆
[R]Before the coming of the great and
dreadful day of the LORD. Joel 2:31
6 And he will turn
The hearts of the fathers to the
children,
And the hearts of the children to their
fathers,
Lest I come and [R]strike the earth with
[R]a curse." Is. 11:4 ☆ • Zech. 5:3

Old Testament Chronology

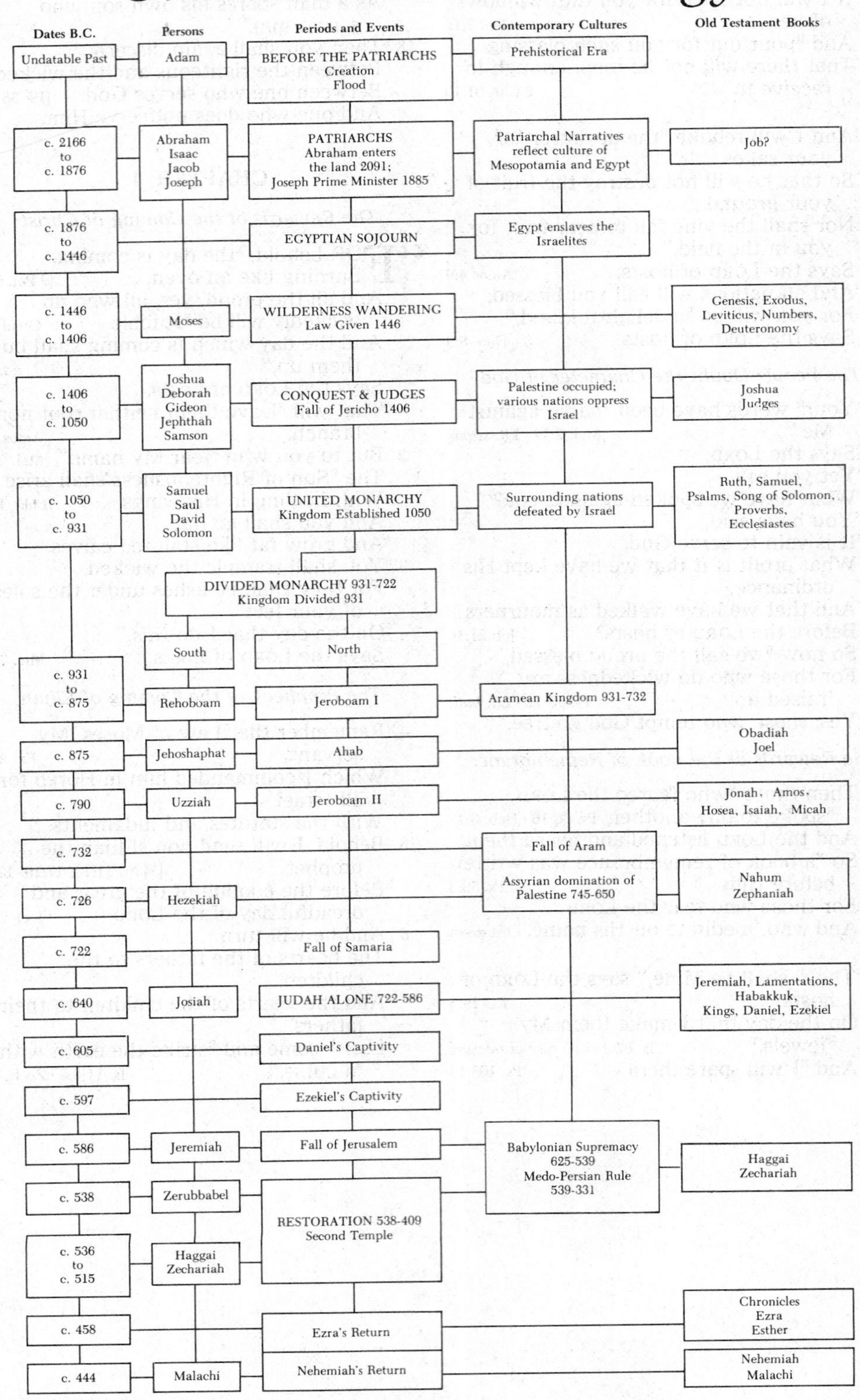

Dates B.C.
Persons
Periods and Events
Contemporary Cultures
Old Testament Books
Undatable Past
Adam
BEFORE THE PATRIARCHS Creation Flood
Prehistorical Era
c. 2166 to c. 1876
Abraham Isaac Jacob Joseph
PATRIARCHS Abraham enters the land 2091; Joseph Prime Minister 1885
Patriarchal Narratives reflect culture of Mesopotamia and Egypt
Job?
c. 1876 to c. 1446
EGYPTIAN SOJOURN
Egypt enslaves the Israelites
c. 1446 to c. 1406
Moses
WILDERNESS WANDERING Law Given 1446
Genesis, Exodus, Leviticus, Numbers, Deuteronomy
c. 1406 to c. 1050
Joshua Deborah Gideon Jephthah Samson
CONQUEST & JUDGES Fall of Jericho 1406
Palestine occupied; various nations oppress Israel
Joshua Judges
c. 1050 to c. 931
Samuel Saul David Solomon
UNITED MONARCHY Kingdom Established 1050
Surrounding nations defeated by Israel
Ruth, Samuel, Psalms, Song of Solomon, Proverbs, Ecclesiastes
DIVIDED MONARCHY 931-722 Kingdom Divided 931
South
North
c. 931 to c. 875
Rehoboam
Jeroboam I
Aramean Kingdom 931-732
c. 875
Jehoshaphat
Ahab
Obadiah Joel
c. 790
Uzziah
Jeroboam II
Jonah, Amos, Hosea, Isaiah, Micah
c. 732
Fall of Aram
c. 726
Hezekiah
Assyrian domination of Palestine 745-650
Nahum Zephaniah
c. 722
Fall of Samaria
c. 640
Josiah
JUDAH ALONE 722-586
Jeremiah, Lamentations, Habakkuk, Kings, Daniel, Ezekiel
c. 605
Daniel's Captivity
c. 597
Ezekiel's Captivity
c. 586
Jeremiah
Fall of Jerusalem
Babylonian Supremacy 625-539 Medo-Persian Rule 539-331
Haggai Zechariah
c. 538
Zerubbabel
RESTORATION 538-409 Second Temple
c. 536 to c. 515
Haggai Zechariah
c. 458
Ezra's Return
Chronicles Ezra Esther
c. 444
Malachi
Nehemiah's Return
Nehemiah Malachi

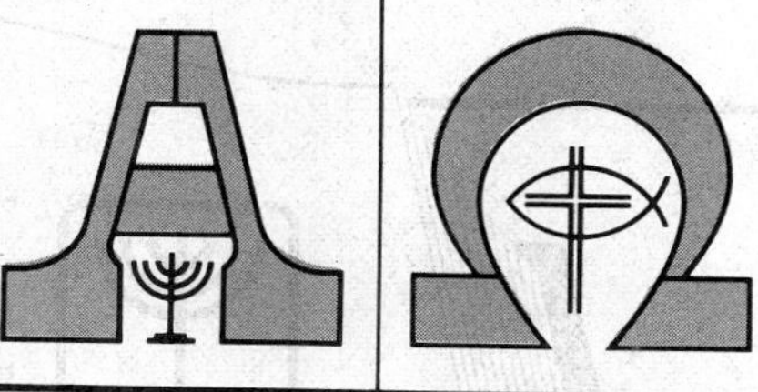

Introduction to the Visual Survey of the Bible

The book introductions in **The New Open Bible**™ provide background information and a survey of each book. But this Visual Survey of the Bible takes a further step by giving a perspective on the whole of Scripture.

Take a moment to familiarize yourself with the first chart, which compares the Old and New Testaments. Note particularly the time-line at the bottom of the page. This time-line divides the Old Testament into five periods and the New Testament into two. It is the key to the rest of the charts.

As you look through the following pages, notice that each chart has its own time-line containing both biblical and extrabiblical events. The maps portray the major movement of each period; the boxes persent the key topics. The charts also summarize the themes of the Old Testament poetic and prophetic books, and the themes of the New Testament Epistles.

The ten Life Applications are an important part of this Survey. Based on the flow of each period, they crystallize the central spiritual truths of Scripture. Each principle leads into the next, and all of them relate to your own life.

VISUAL SURVEY...

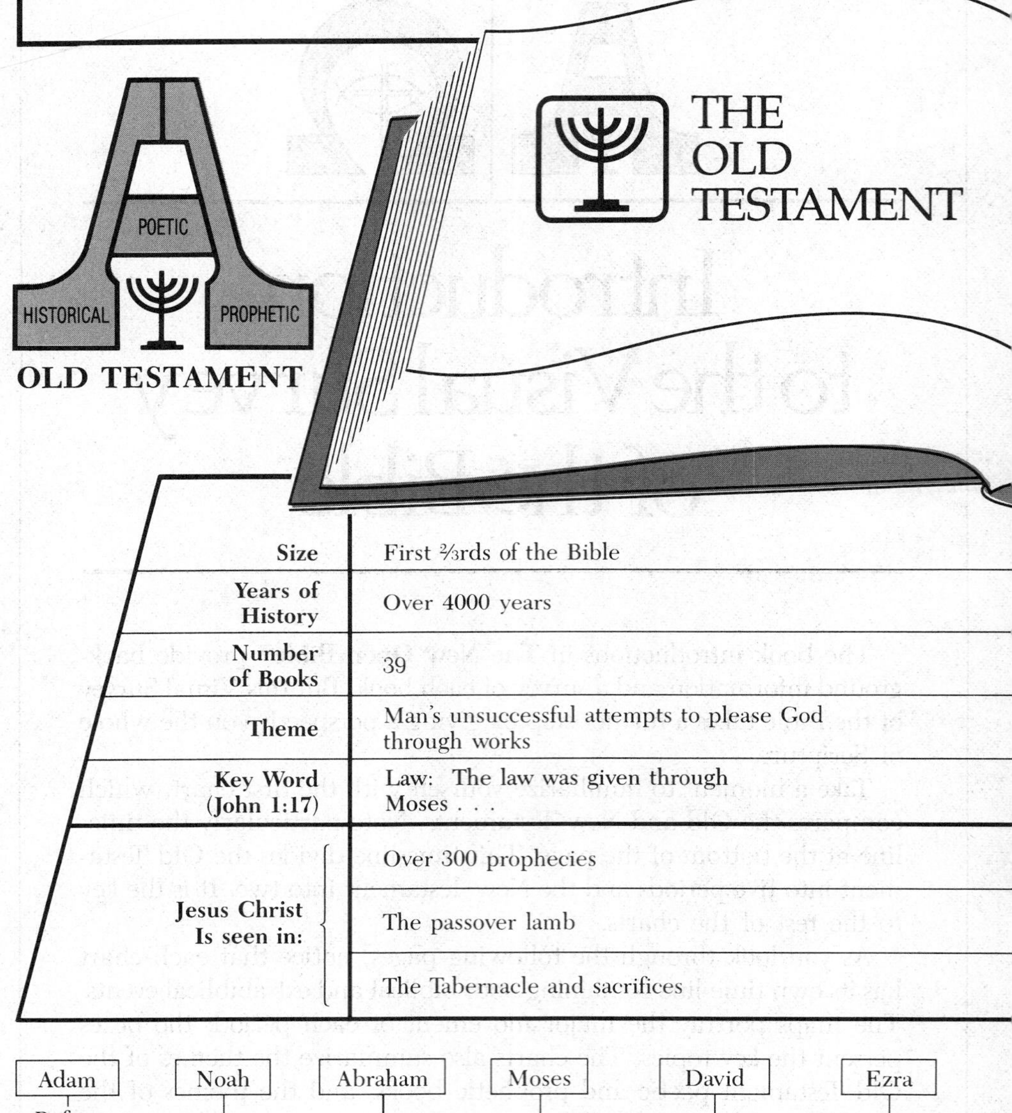

Size	First ⅔rds of the Bible
Years of History	Over 4000 years
Number of Books	39
Theme	Man's unsuccessful attempts to please God through works
Key Word (John 1:17)	Law: The law was given through Moses . . .
Jesus Christ Is seen in:	Over 300 prophecies
	The passover lamb
	The Tabernacle and sacrifices

Adam	Noah	Abraham	Moses	David	Ezra
Before 4000 B.C.	?	2000 B.C.	1500 B.C.	1000 B.C.	500 B.C.

History of the Early World		**History of Israel**			
Pre-Flood	After the Flood	The People	The Land	The Kingdom	The Remnant
11 Chapters (Gen. 1—11)		Over 38 Books (Gen. 12—Mal.)			

...OF THE BIBLE

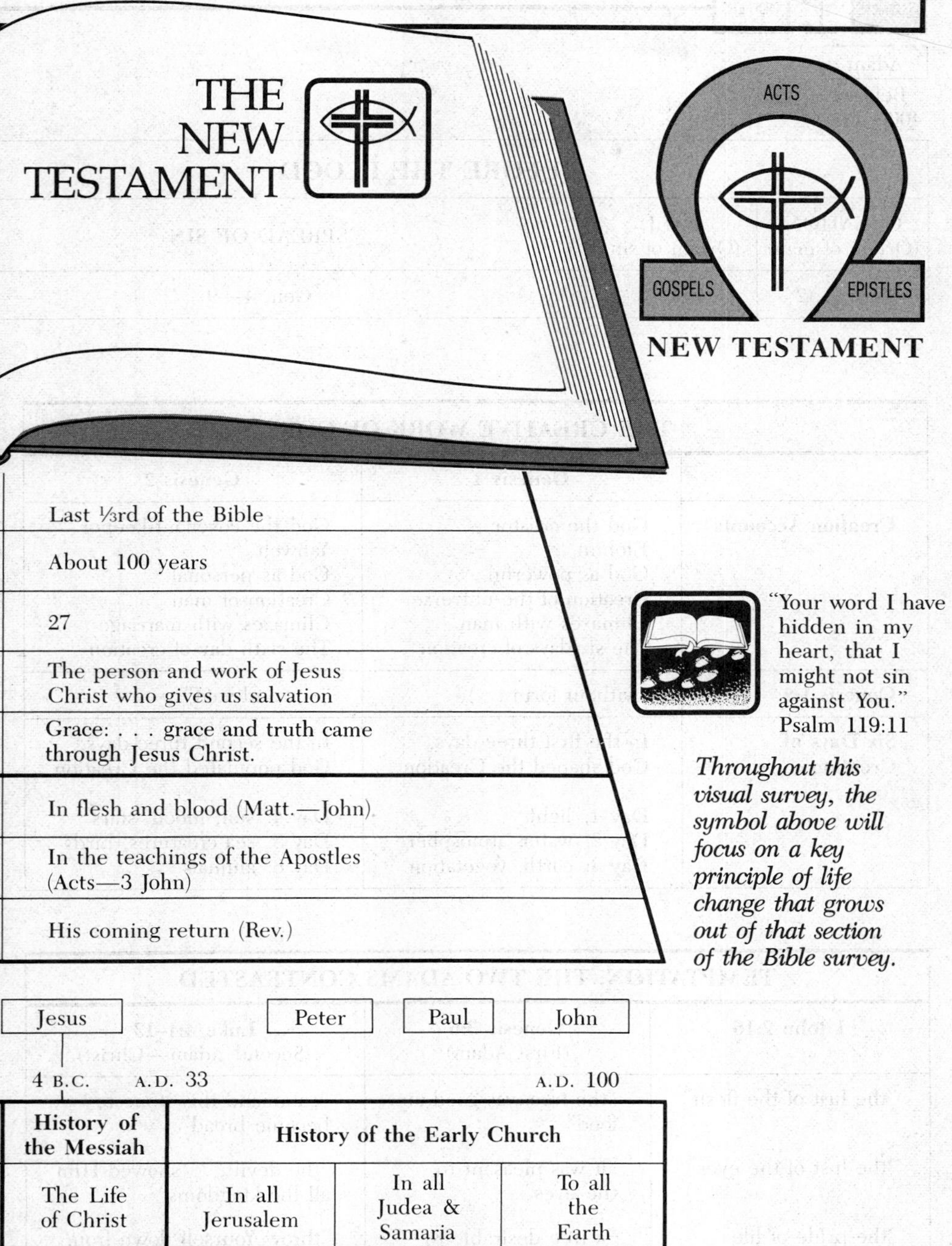

Last ⅓rd of the Bible
About 100 years
27
The person and work of Jesus Christ who gives us salvation
Grace: . . . grace and truth came through Jesus Christ.
In flesh and blood (Matt.—John)
In the teachings of the Apostles (Acts—3 John)
His coming return (Rev.)

"Your word I have hidden in my heart, that I might not sin against You."
Psalm 119:11

Throughout this visual survey, the symbol above will focus on a key principle of life change that grows out of that section of the Bible survey.

Jesus | Peter | Paul | John

4 B.C. | A.D. 33 | A.D. 100

History of the Messiah	History of the Early Church		
The Life of Christ	In all Jerusalem	In all Judea & Samaria	To all the Earth
(Matt.—John)	(Acts—Rev.)		

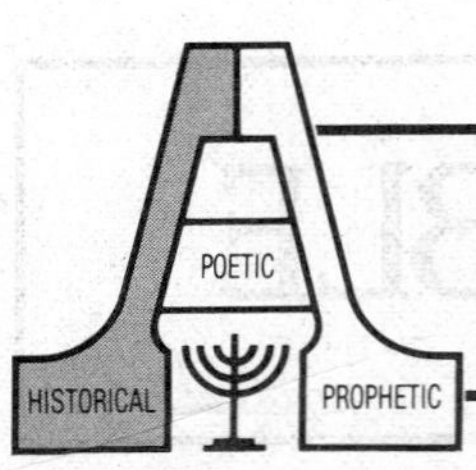

HISTORY OF THE EARLY WORLD

Adam
Before
4000 B.C.

BEFORE THE FLOOD		
CREATION (Origin of man)	FALL (Origin of sin)	SPREAD OF SIN
Gen. 1; 2	Gen. 3	Gen. 4—9

THE CREATIVE WORK OF GOD		
	Genesis 1	**Genesis 2**
Creation Accounts	God the creator Elohim God as powerful Creation of the universe Climaxes with man The six days of creation	God the covenant-keeper Yahweh God as personal Creation of man Climaxes with marriage The sixth day of creation
Genesis 1:2	"without form . . ."	". . . and void"
Six Days of Creation	In the first three days, God shaped the Creation Day 1: light Day 2: water, atmosphere Day 3: earth, vegetation	In the second three days, God populated the Creation Day 4: sun, moon, stars Day 5: sea creatures, birds Day 6: animals

TEMPTATION: THE TWO ADAMS CONTRASTED		
1 John 2:16	**Genesis 3:6** (First Adam)	**Luke 4:1–13** (Second Adam—Christ)
"the lust of the flesh"	"the tree was good for food"	"command this stone to become bread"
"the lust of the eyes"	"it was pleasant to the eyes"	"the devil . . . showed Him all the kingdoms"
"the pride of life"	"a tree desirable to make one wise"	"throw Yourself down from here"

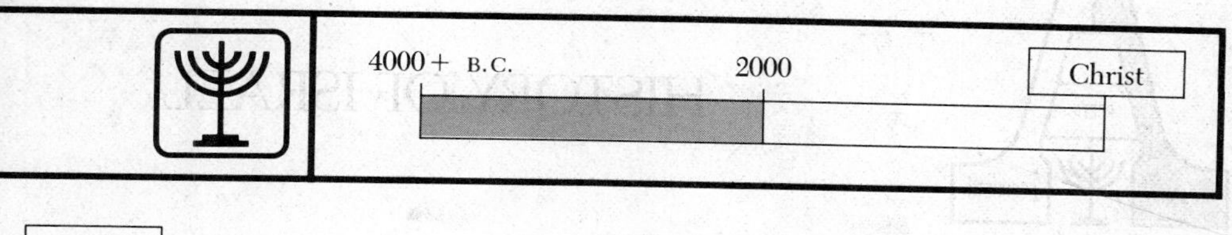

Noah		Abraham
2500 B.C. ?		2000 B.C.

AFTER THE FLOOD	
FLOOD (Judgment of sin)	SPREAD OF NATIONS
Gen. 6—9	Gen. 10—11

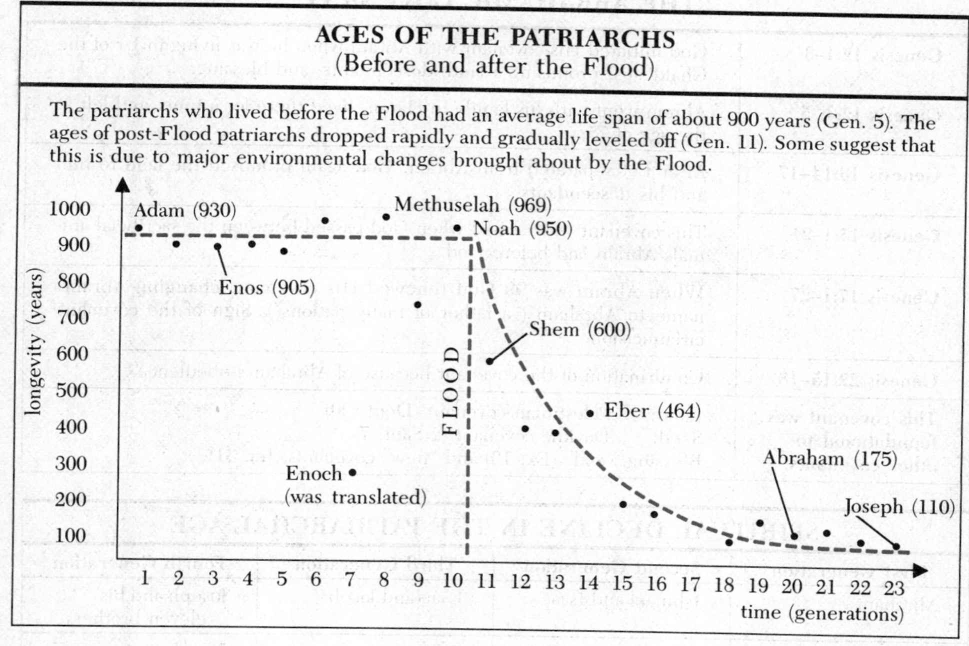

AGES OF THE PATRIARCHS
(Before and after the Flood)

The patriarchs who lived before the Flood had an average life span of about 900 years (Gen. 5). The ages of post-Flood patriarchs dropped rapidly and gradually leveled off (Gen. 11). Some suggest that this is due to major environmental changes brought about by the Flood.

Principle: Righteousness is creative; sin is destructive (Gen. 2:17; Rom. 6:23).

Practice: Genesis 1—11, the prologue not only to Genesis, but to the entire Bible, begins with the ordered and life-giving activity of the holy Creator. The fall of man and the consequent spread of sin stand in stark contrast to the work of God and illustrate the disorder and death that always accompanies rebellion against the purposes of the Lord. God is not mocked; in a moral and spiritual universe, sin must be judged. What must you do, according to Romans 3:21–26, to escape the condemnation of your Creator?

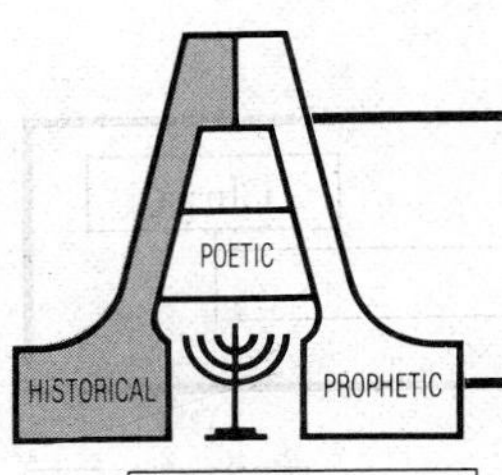

HISTORY OF ISRAEL:

Abraham	Joseph
2000 B.C.	1914 B.C.

THE PEOPLE

THE PATRIARCHS	BONDAGE IN EGYPT

2165	1991	Jacob	1790
Birth of Abraham	Beginning of Egyptian Middle Kingdom	Enters Egypt with His Family	Code of Hammurabi

THE ABRAHAMIC COVENANT	
Genesis 12:1–3	God initiated His covenant with Abram when he was living in Ur of the Chaldeans, promising a land, descendants, and blessing.
Genesis 12:4, 5	Abram went with his family to Haran, lived there for a time, and left at the age of 75.
Genesis 13:14–17	After Lot separated from Abram, God again promised the land to him and his descendants.
Genesis 15:1–21	This covenant was ratified when God passed between the sacrificial animals Abram laid before God.
Genesis 17:1–27	When Abram was 99 God renewed His covenant, changing Abram's name to Abraham ("a father of many nations"). Sign of the covenant: circumcision.
Genesis 22:15–18	Confirmation of the covenant because of Abraham's obedience.
This covenant was foundational to other covenants.	Land: Palestinian covenant (Deut. 30). Seed: Davidic covenant (2 Sam. 7). Blessing: "old" (Ex. 19) and "new" covenants (Jer. 31).

SPIRITUAL DECLINE IN THE PATRIARCHAL AGE			
First Generation	**Second Generation**	**Third Generation**	**Fourth Generation**
Abraham	Ishmael and Isaac	Esau and Jacob	Joseph and his eleven brothers
Abraham: man of faith believed God	Ishmael: not son of promise Isaac: called on God believed God	Esau: unspiritual little faith Jacob: at first compromised, later turned to the Lord	Joseph: man of God showed faith Brothers: treachery, immorality, lack of separation from Canaanites
Abraham: built altars to God (Gen. 12:7, 8; 13:4, 18; 22:9)	Isaac: built an altar to God (Gen. 26:25)	Jacob: built altars to God (Gen. 33:20; 35:1, 3, 7)	No altars were built to God in the fourth generation

THE PEOPLE

2000	1500	1000	500	Christ
People	Land	Kingdom	Remnant	

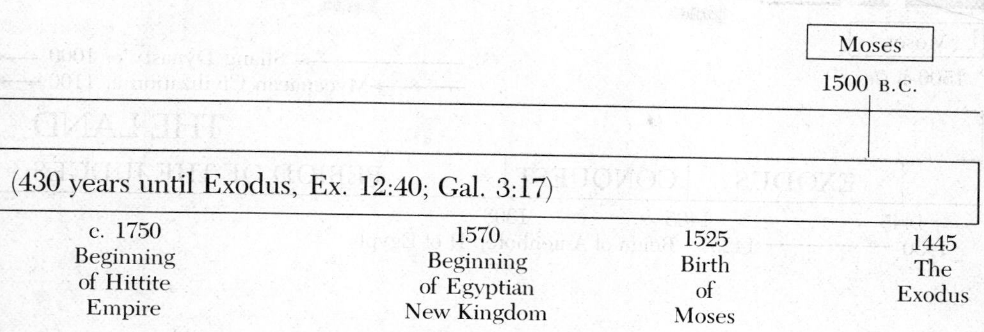

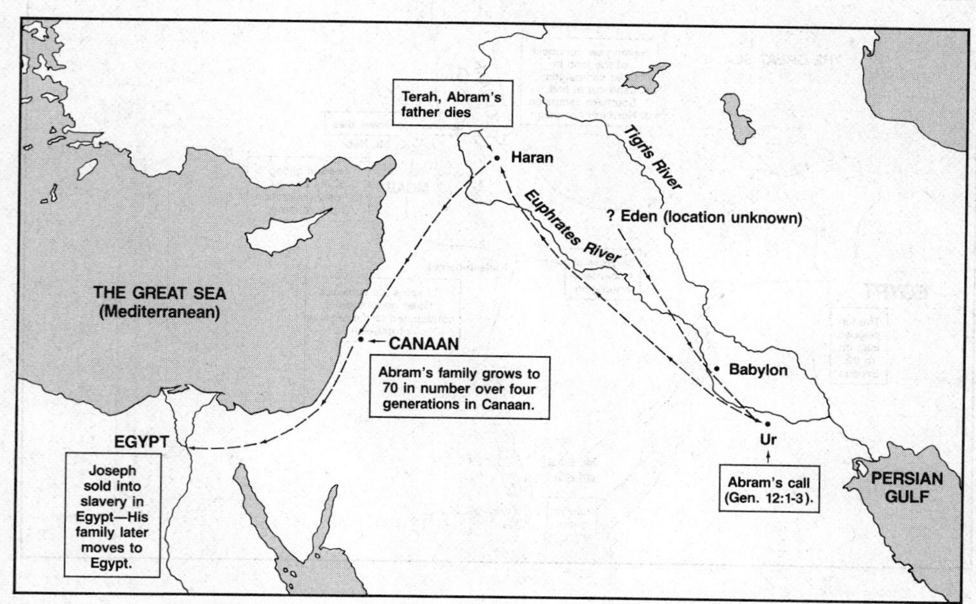

Principle: The destructiveness of sin is overcome by a faith that takes God at His word in spite of appearances and circumstances to the contrary (Gen. 15:6; John 3:16; Heb. 11:8–22).

Practice: Beginning in Genesis 12, God drew forth a man who would be the father of the people from whom and to whom the Messiah would come. Abraham became a friend of God through faith. In spite of appearances to the contrary, he went to a land he had not seen, believed God's promise of a son, and offered up that son at the same area where God's own Son would be crucified. Because he believed God, his faith was accounted to him for righteousness. In the same way, you can enter into a relationship with God by placing your trust in the person and work of His Son. Have you made that decision?

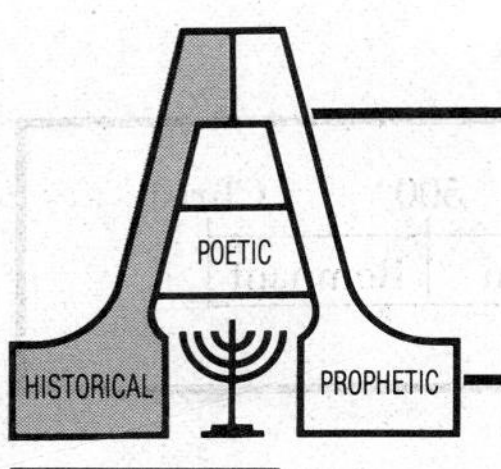
POETIC
HISTORICAL
PROPHETIC

HISTORY OF ISRAEL:

Moses			
1500 B.C.			

→ Shang Dynasty c. 1000 →
→ Mycenaean Civilization c. 1100 →

THE LAND		
EXODUS	CONQUEST	PERIOD OF THE JUDGES

1445 1405 1398

1450 —— 1423 Reign of Amenhotep II of Egypt

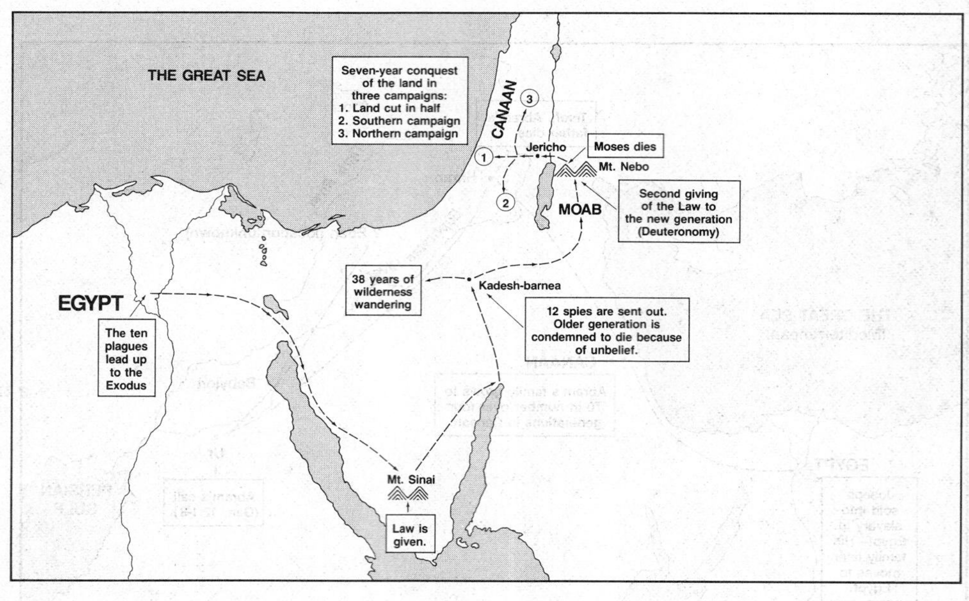
THE GREAT SEA
Seven-year conquest of the land in three campaigns:
1. Land cut in half
2. Southern campaign
3. Northern campaign
CANAAN
Jericho
Moses dies
Mt. Nebo
MOAB
Second giving of the Law to the new generation (Deuteronomy)
EGYPT
The ten plagues lead up to the Exodus
38 years of wilderness wandering
Kadesh-barnea
12 spies are sent out. Older generation is condemned to die because of unbelief.
Mt. Sinai
Law is given.

Principle: Revelation demands obedience, and obedience brings blessing (Deut. 6:1–15; Josh. 1:8; John 15:12–17).

Practice: After redeeming His people from bondage, the Lord spoke to them in power and glory at Mt. Sinai. The revelation of the Mosaic law required a response of obedience. Their success as individuals and as a nation would depend on the degree of their conformity to God's moral, civil, and ceremonial law. Likewise, disobedience would lead to disaster (e.g., the wilderness wandering and servitude in the time of the Judges). As believers in Christ, our success is measured by the degree of our conformity to His character. To what extent is Christ the Lord of your life?

THE LAND

2000	1500	1000	500	Christ
People	Land	Kingdom	Remnant	

Samuel 1105–1020

David 1000 B.C.

c. 1100 Greek Dark Ages →

1191
Gideon beats Midianites

1043
Saul anointed King

THE LAW After their deliverance from Egyptian bondage, the children of Israel needed to learn to walk with their God. The Law was given to instruct the people about the person and the ways of their Redeemer so that they could be set apart to a life of holiness and obedience, not to save anyone but to reveal the people's need to trust in the Lord. As Paul told the Galatians, "Therefore the law was our tutor *to bring us* to Christ, that we might be justified by faith" (Gal. 3:24).

The Law combines poetry, salvation history, legislation, and exhortation. The three major divisions of the Law (Deut. 4:44) are the testimonies (moral duties), the statutes (ceremonial duties), and the judgments or ordinances (civil and social duties). The moral portion of the Law is summarized in the Ten Commandments (Ex. 20:1–17; Deut. 5:6–21):

THE TEN COMMANDMENTS (Moral Law)		
1–4	Duties to God	"You shall love the LORD your God" (Matt. 22:37).
5–10	Duties to man	"You shall love your neighbor" (Matt. 22:39).

THE JUDGES: A CASE STUDY IN DISOBEDIENCE

Each of the seven cycles found in Judges 3:5—16:31 has five steps: sin, servitude, supplication, salvation, and silence. The cycles connect as a descending spiral of sin (2:19), with Israel vacillating between obedience and apostasy.

Cycle	Oppressor	Years of Oppression	Judge/Deliverer	Years of Peace
1. (3:7–11)	Mesopotamians	8	Othniel	40
2. (3:12–30)	Moabites	18	Ehud	80
(3:31)	Philistines		Shamgar	
3. (4:1—5:31)	Canaanites	20	Deborah/Barak	40
4. (6:1—8:32)	Midianites	7	Gideon	40
5. (8:33—10:5)	Abimelech	3	Tola/Jair	45
6. (10:6—12:15)	Ammonites	18	Jephthah/Ibzan/Elon/Abdon	6/7/10/8
7. (13:1—16:31)	Philistines	40	Samson	20

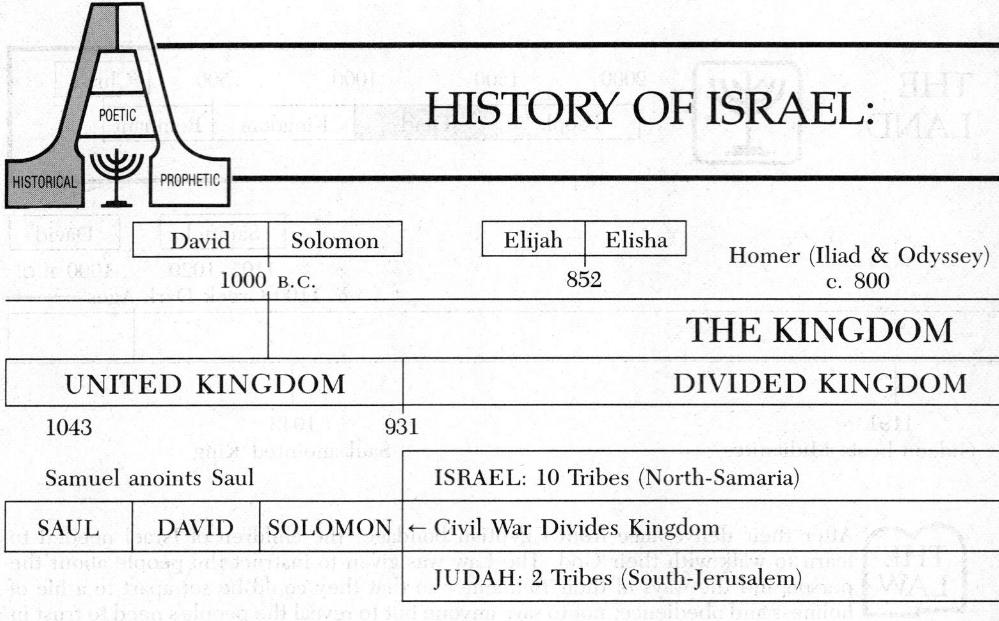

THE LIFE OF DAVID: A Man after God's own heart									
1041 B.C.				1011					971 B.C.
DAVID'S 70 YEARS									
David as Subject (30 Years)				David as King (40 Years)					
As a son to his father	As a servant to King Saul			King over the South		King over all 12 tribes			
	His rise over Saul	Rejected by Saul	Refuge with Philistines	Success → Growing		Growing → Crisis			
	17–18	19–26	27–31						
Psalms	1 Samuel			2 Samuel					1 Kings
23	17	19:1–10	31	7	11	14–18	24		2:10
David the Shepherd	Kills Goliath	Protected by Jonathan	Saul and Jonathan killed at Gilboa	Promise of Christ	Sins with Bathsheba	Absalom's Rebellion	David's Census		David Dies

Principle: Obedience grows out of a heart for God (Deut. 6:5; 1 Sam. 13:14; 1 Chr. 28:9; Acts 13:22).

Practice: Saul and David are a study in contrasts. The key to Saul's failure was his lack of a heart for God; the key to David's greatness was his obvious love for the Lord. David's relationship with God became the standard by which all the kings of Judah would be measured. To know God is to love Him, and to love Him is to desire to obey Him. Read Psalm 23 as a model of a man who was intimate with God. What are the things that may be hindering your growth in the knowledge of God?

2000	1500	1000	500	Christ
People	Land	Kingdom	Remnant	

Rome Founded 753

Births of Buddha, Confucius 563 551

Ezra 500 B.C.

	EXILE	RETURN
722	586	516

← Assyria Conquers Israel

Babylon Conquers Judah →

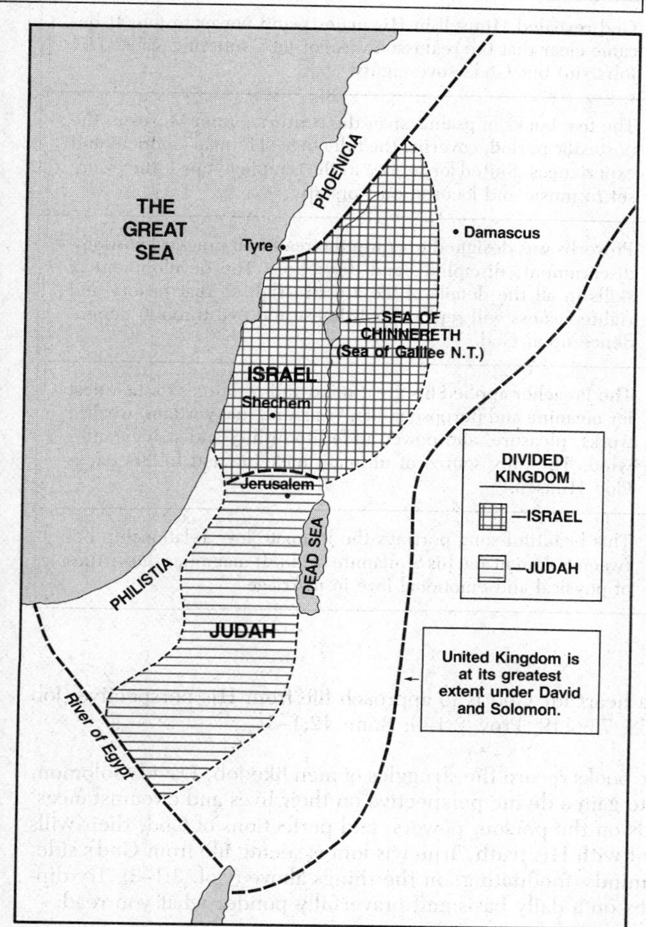

KINGS OF ISRAEL

1. Jeroboam I
2. Nadab
3. Baasha
4. Elah
5. Zimri
6. Omri
7. Ahab
8. Ahaziah
9. Jehoram
10. Jehu
11. Jehoahaz
12. Jehoash
13. Jeroboam II
14. Zechariah
15. Shallum
16. Menahem
17. Pekahiah
18. Pekah
19. Hoshea

KINGS OF JUDAH

1. Rehoboam
2. Abijam
3. Asa
4. Jehoshaphat
5. Jehoram
6. Ahaziah
7. Athaliah
8. Joash
9. Amaziah
10. Azariah
11. Jotham
12. Ahaz
13. Hezekiah
14. Manasseh
15. Amon
16. Josiah
17. Jehoahaz
18. Jehoiakim
19. Jehoiachin
20. Zedekiah

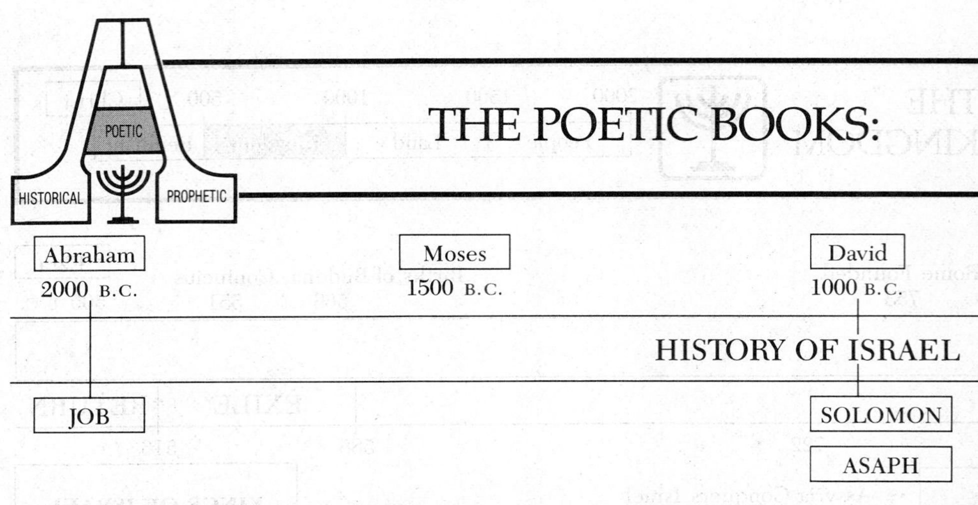

THEMES OF THE POETIC BOOKS		
BOOK	**KEY WORD**	**THEME**
Job	Sover-eignty	God revealed Himself in His majesty and power to Job. It became clear that the real issue was not Job's suffering (caused by Job's sin) but God's sovereignty.
Psalms	Worship	The five books of psalms span the centuries from Moses to the postexilic period, covering the full range of human emotions and experiences. Suited for service as the temple hymnal, they were set to music and focused on worship.
Proverbs	Wisdom	Proverbs was designed to equip the reader in practical wisdom, discernment, discipline, and discretion. The development of skills in all the details of life are stressed, so that beauty and righteousness will replace foolishness and evil through dependence upon God.
Ecclesi-astes	Vanity	The Preacher applied his great mind and resources to the quest for meaning and purpose in life. He found that wisdom, wealth, works, pleasure, and power all led to futility and striving after wind. The only source of ultimate meaning and fulfillment is God Himself.
Song of Solomon	Love in Marriage	This beautiful song portrays the intimate love relationship between Solomon and his Shulamite bride. It magnifies the virtues of physical and emotional love in marriage.

Principle: To have a heart for God is to approach life from His perspective (Job 42:1–6; Ps. 1; 19; 63; 73; 119; Prov. 2:1–9; Rom. 12:1–3).

Practice: The poetic books record the struggles of men like Job, David, Solomon, Asaph, and others to gain a divine perspective on their lives and circumstances. As they learned to set their minds on the person, powers, and perfections of God, their wills and emotions came into alignment with His truth. True wisdom is seeing life from God's side, and this is rooted in setting our minds (meditating) on the things above (Col. 3:1–3). Try dipping into the Psalms and Proverbs on a daily basis and prayerfully ponder what you read.

THE HEART OF THE JEWS

Ezra	Christ
500 B.C.	4 B.C.

THE PATH TO TRUE SUCCESS

Question	Principle
1. What is wisdom?	Wisdom is the key to a life of beauty, fulfillment, and purpose (Prov. 3:15–18). Wisdom is the skill in the art of living life with every area under the dominion of God. It is the ability to use the best means at the best time to accomplish the best ends.
2. How do we pursue wisdom?	The treasure of wisdom rests in the hands of God. Since it comes from above (Prov. 2:6; cf. James 3:17), we cannot attain it apart from Him.
3. What are the conditions for attaining wisdom?	True wisdom can only be gained by cultivating the fear of the Lord (Job 28:28; Ps. 86:11; 111:10; Prov. 1:7; 9:10).
4. What is the fear of the Lord?	To fear God is to have an attitude of awe and humility before Him (Prov. 15:33). It is to recognize Him as our Creator and our complete dependence upon Him in every activity of our lives.
5. Why have so few people developed this fear of God?	The temporal value system of this world is based on what is seen, while the eternal value system of Scripture is based on what is unseen (2 Cor. 4:16–18; 5:7). The former exerts a powerful influence upon us, and we struggle with giving up the seen for the unseen.
6. What can enable us to choose the eternal value system?	This choice is based on faith (believing God in spite of appearances and circumstances), and faith is based on trust.
7. How do we grow in faith?	Our ability to trust God is directly proportional to our knowledge of God. The better we know Him, the more we can trust Him.
8. How can we increase in our knowledge of God?	We become intimate with God as we talk with Him in prayer and listen to His voice in Scripture. The better we know God, the more we love Him and want to respond to His desires for our lives. Faith in God is simply trusting Him as a person, and trust is manifested in action.

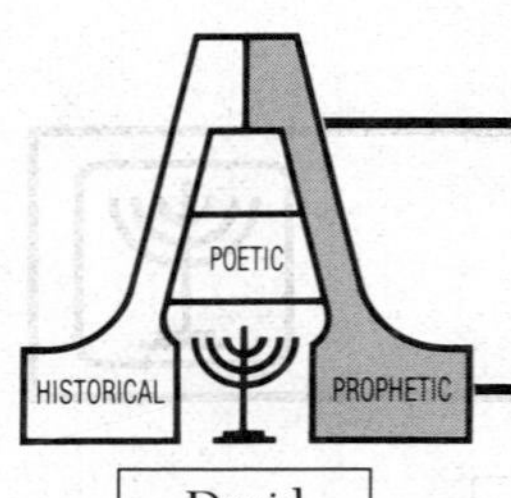

THE PROPHETIC BOOKS:

David	Elijah	Elisha	Zerubbabel	Ezra	Nehemiah
1000 B.C.	852		500		

THE KINGDOM			
UNITED KINGDOM	DIVIDED KINGDOM	EXILE	RETURN

UNITED KINGDOM	ISRAEL	← 722	70 Years in Babylon	3 stage return 1st Zerubbabel 2nd Ezra 3rd Nehemiah
	← 931	586 →		
	JUDAH			

PROPHETS BEFORE THE EXILE		EXILE PROPHETS	PROPHETS AFTER THE EXILE
To Israel: Amos (760) Hosea (755) To Nineveh: Jonah (760) Nahum (660) To Edom: Obadiah (840)	To Judah: Joel (835) Isaiah (740) Micah (735) Zephaniah (630) Jeremiah (627) Habakkuk (607) Lamentations (586)	To Jews in Babylon: Daniel (605) Ezekiel (592)	To the Remnant after returning: Haggai (520) Zechariah (520) Malachi (432)

Principle: God's disciplines are designed to restore a heart for Himself (Jer. 17:5, 7; Joel 2:12, 13; Heb. 12:5–11).

Practice: God had to discipline His people because of their moral and spiritual rebellion and their refusal to heed the warnings of His prophets. Reproof is designed to bring repentance and repentance brings restoration. The same prophets who pronounced the condemnation of God also announced the consolation of God. Similarly, because God loves us, He must sometimes chasten us as His children to train us in the ways of righteousness. How do you respond during these times? Are you teachable or intractable?

THE HOPE OF THE JEWS

Christ

4 B.C.

THE REMNANT

400 YEARS UNTIL CHRIST

415

THEMES OF THE PROPHETIC BOOKS

The Major Prophets

BOOK	KEY WORD	THEME
Isaiah	Salvation Is of the Lord	Twofold message of condemnation (1–39) and consolation (40–66). God's judgment on the sins of Judah, the surrounding nations, and the world, followed by future salvation and restoration.
Jeremiah	Judah's Last Hour	Declaration of certain judgment of God against Judah. God promises to establish a new covenant with His people.
Lamentations	Lamentations	This beautifully structured series of five lament poems is a funeral dirge for the fallen city of Jerusalem.
Ezekiel	Future Restoration	Ministry to the Jewish captives in Babylon before and after the fall of Jerusalem. The fate of Judah's foes and an apocalyptic vision of Judah's future.
Daniel	God's Program for Israel	Outlines God's plan for the gentile nations (2–7) and portrays Israel during the time of gentile domination (8–12).

The Minor Prophets

BOOK	KEY WORD	THEME
Hosea	God's Love for Israel	The story of Hosea and his faithless wife illustrates the loyal love of God and the spiritual adultery of Israel.
Joel	Day of the Lord	A recent locust plague illustrates the far more terrifying day of the Lord. God appeals to the people to repent in order to avert the coming disaster.
Amos	Judgment of Israel	In eight pronouncements of judgment, Amos spirals around the surrounding countries before landing on Israel. He lists the sins of Israel and calls for repentance.
Obadiah	Judgment of Edom	Condemns the nation of Edom (descended from Esau) for refusing to act as a brother toward Judah (descended from Jacob).
Jonah	Revival in Nineveh	The repentant response of the people of Nineveh to Jonah's one-line prophetic message caused the God of mercy to spare the city.
Micah	Judgment and Restoration of Judah	In spite of divine retribution against the corruption of Israel and Judah, God's covenant with them will be fulfilled in Messiah's future kingdom.
Nahum	Judgment of Nineveh	About 125 years after Nineveh repented under the preaching of Jonah, Micah predicted the destruction of the city because of its idolatry and brutality.
Habakkuk	Live by Faith	Troubled with God's plan to use the Babylonians as His rod of judgment on Judah, Habakkuk praises the Lord after gaining a better perspective on His power and purposes.
Zephaniah	Day of the Lord	The coming day of the Lord is a time of awesome judgment followed by great blessing. Judah stands condemned, but God will restore the fortunes of the remnant.
Haggai	Reconstruction of the Temple	After the Babylonian exile, Haggai urges the Jews to put God first and finish the Temple they had begun so that they can enjoy God's blessing.
Zechariah	Prepare for the Messiah	Like Haggai, Zechariah exhorts the Jews to complete the construction of the Temple. He relates it to the coming of Messiah in a series of visions and messianic prophecies.
Malachi	Appeal to Backsliders	The spiritual climate of the people had grown cold, and Malachi rebukes them for their religious and social compromise. If they return to God with sincere hearts, they will be blessed.

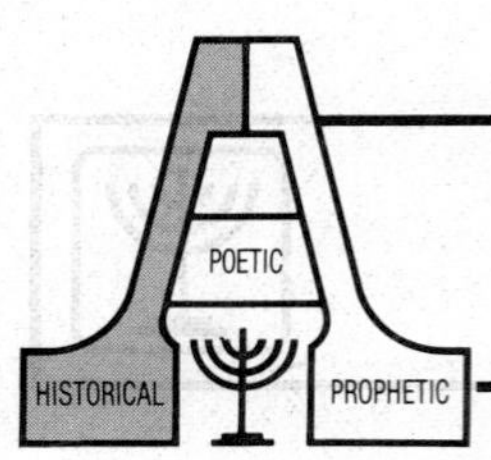

HISTORY OF ISRAEL: THE REMNANT

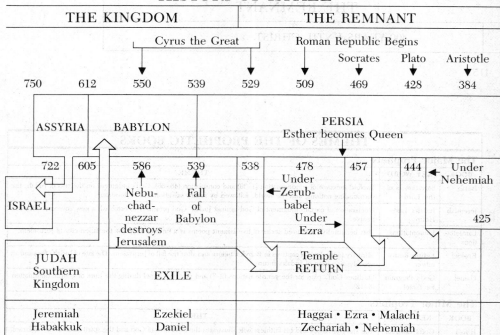

Ezra

500 B.C.

HISTORY OF ISRAEL

THE KINGDOM | THE REMNANT

Cyrus the Great (550, 529)

Roman Republic Begins (509)

Socrates (469) · Plato (428) · Aristotle (384)

750 · 612 · 550 · 539 · 529 · 509 · 469 · 428 · 384

ASSYRIA (750–612) · BABYLON (612–539) · PERSIA (539–)

Esther becomes Queen (478)

722 · 605 · 586 · 539 · 538 · 478 · 457 · 444 · 425

ISRAEL (722)

Nebuchadnezzar destroys Jerusalem (586)

Fall of Babylon (539)

Under Zerubbabel (538)

Under Ezra (457)

Under Nehemiah (444)

Temple RETURN

JUDAH Southern Kingdom	EXILE	Temple RETURN
Jeremiah Habakkuk	Ezekiel Daniel	Haggai • Ezra • Malachi Zechariah • Nehemiah

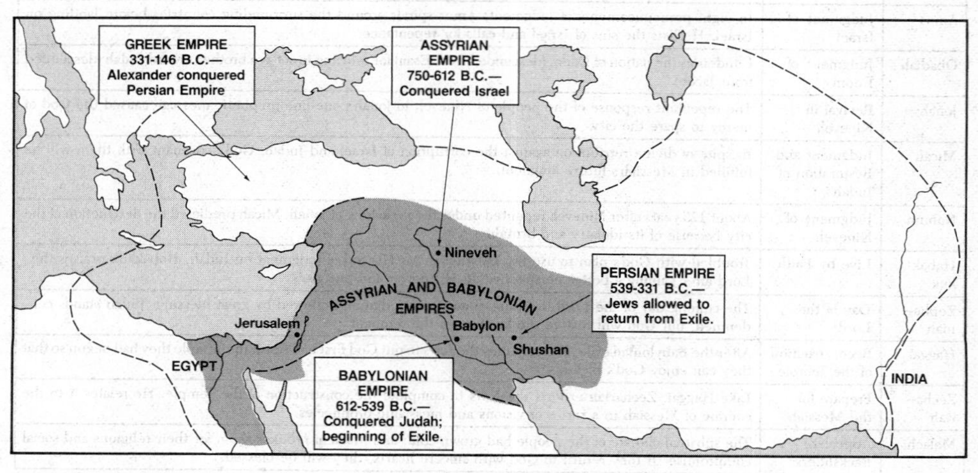

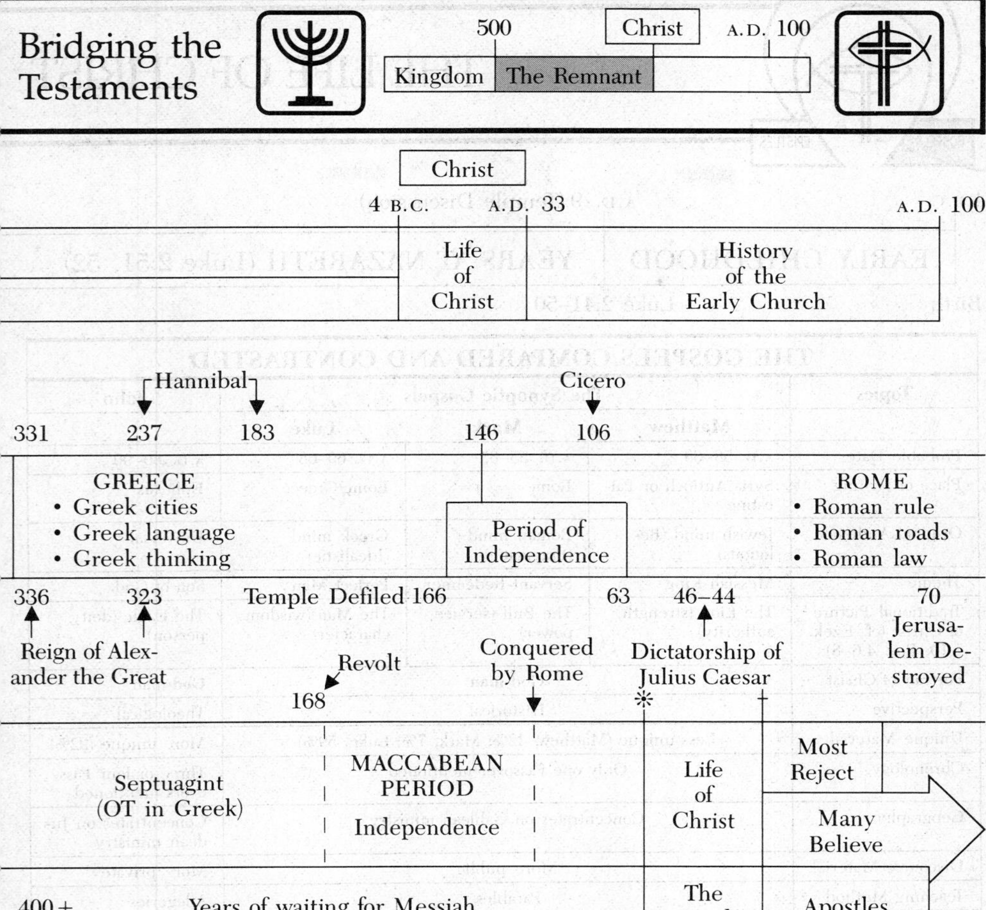

Principle: True restoration results from being molded by the Word within rather than the world without (Ezra 7:10; 9:10–15; Is. 46:3, 4; Acts 7:51–53).

Practice: Even after the chastening of the Exile, most of the returning Jews became enmeshed once again in the affairs of the world and neglected their relationship with God. For some, the problem was external religiosity without internal reality; for others, the problem was being more influenced by culture than Scripture. God has always had to work with a faithful minority who love Him enough to stand against the tide of the world system. Is your quality of life different from that of those who love the world more than the Lord?

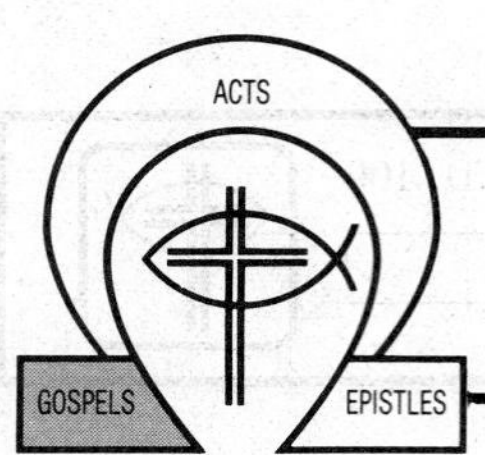

THE LIFE OF CHRIST

4 B.C. — A.D. 9 (Temple Discussion)

EARLY CHILDHOOD	YEARS AT NAZARETH (Luke 2:51, 52)
Birth	Luke 2:41–50

THE GOSPELS COMPARED AND CONTRASTED

Topics	The Synoptic Gospels			John
	Matthew	Mark	Luke	
Probable Date	A.D. 58–68	A.D. 55–65	A.D. 60–68	A.D. 80–90
Place of Writing	Syria Antioch or Palestine	Rome	Rome/Greece	Ephesus
Original Audience	Jewish mind (Religious)	Roman mind (Pragmatic)	Greek mind (Idealistic)	Universal
Theme	Messiah-King	Servant-Redeemer	Perfect Man	Son of God
Traditional Picture of Christ (cf. Ezek. 1:10; Rev. 4:6–8)	The Lion (strength, authority)	The Bull (service, power)	The Man (wisdom, character)	The Eagle (deity, person)
Portrait of Christ	**God-man**			**God**-man
Perspective	Historical			Theological
Unique Material	Less unique (Matthew, 42%; Mark, 7%; Luke, 59%)			More unique (92%)
Chronology	Only one Passover mentioned			Three or four Passovers mentioned
Geography	Concentrates on Galilean ministry			Concentrates on Judean ministry
Discourse Material	More public			More private
Teaching Method	Parables			Allegories
Teaching Emphasis	More on ethical, practical teachings			More on the person of Christ
Relationship to Other Gospels	Complementary			Supplementary

CHRIST'S PUBLIC MINISTRY

Masses drawn to His miracles and teachings

Popularity peaks

Leaders attribute His miracles

A.D. 29	30	31
Opening events	Early Judean ministry	Great Galilean ministry
Year of curious acceptance		Year of growing hostility

Baptized by John Matt. 3 — First miracle John 2 — Nicodemus learns of new birth John 3 — Woman at well John 4 — Rejected at Nazareth Luke 4 — Apostles selected Mark 3 — Sermon on Mount Matt. 5—7

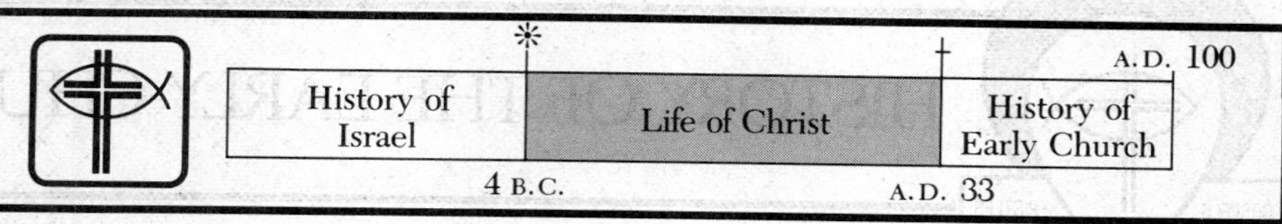

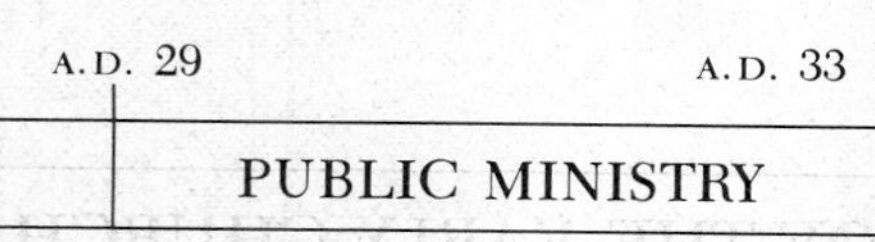

Principle: Jesus, the living Word, lives His life in and through us as we walk in dependence upon Him (John 1:11, 12; 10:10; 15:4, 5; Gal. 2:20).

Practice: In Christ, God personally revealed Himself in human flesh: to see Him is to see God (John 12:45; 14:9), to know Him is to know God (John 8:19), to receive Him is to receive God (Mark 9:37), to honor Him is to honor God (John 5:23), and to reject Him is to reject God (Luke 10:16). He is the vine, the source of life; we are the branches, the channels of life. It is only as we draw our life from Him that we bear lasting fruit. To what extent are you looking to Jesus as the true source of your security, significance, and fulfillment?

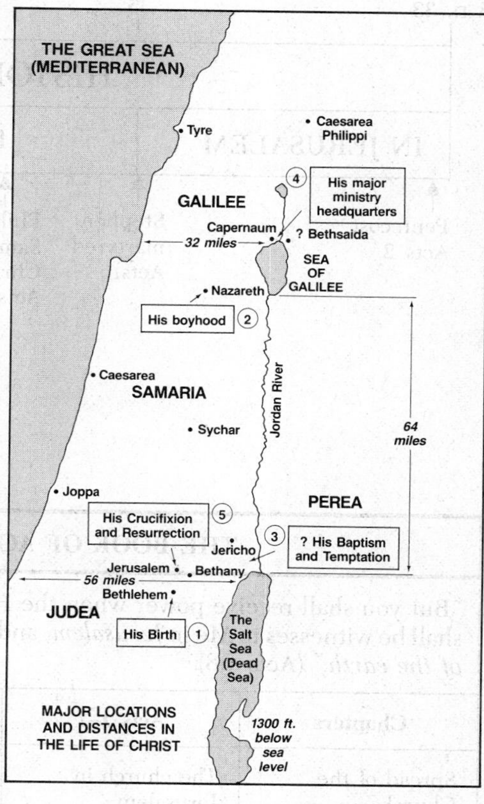

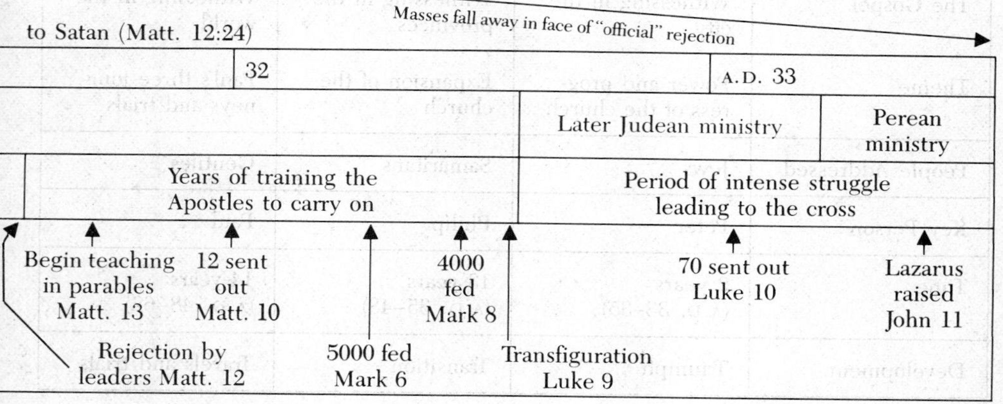

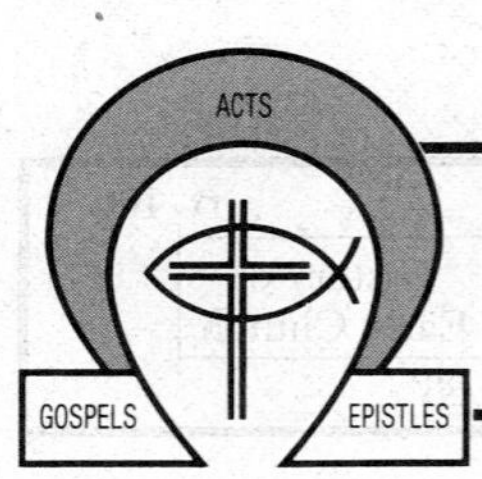

HISTORY OF THE EARLY CHURCH

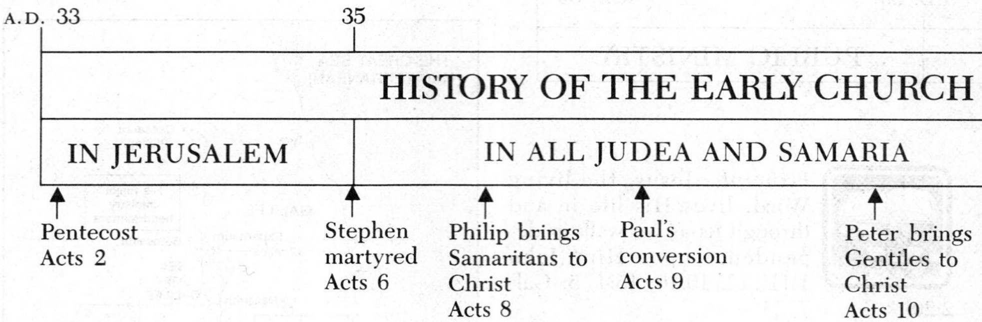

THE BOOK OF ACTS IN OVERVIEW

"But you shall receive power when the Holy Spirit has come upon you; and you shall be witnesses to Me in *Jerusalem*, and in all *Judea* and *Samaria*, and to the *end of the earth*" (Acts 1:8).

Chapters	Acts 1–7	Acts 8–12	Acts 13–28
Spread of the Church	The church in Jerusalem	The church in all Judea and Samaria	The church to all the earth
The Gospel	Witnessing in the city	Witnessing in the provinces	Witnessing in the world
Theme	Power and progress of the church	Expansion of the church	Paul's three journeys and trials
People Addressed	Jews	Samaritans	Gentiles
Key Person	Peter	Philip	Paul
Time	2 years (A.D. 33–35)	13 years (A.D. 35–48)	14 years (A.D. 48–62)
Development	Triumph	Transition	Travels and trials

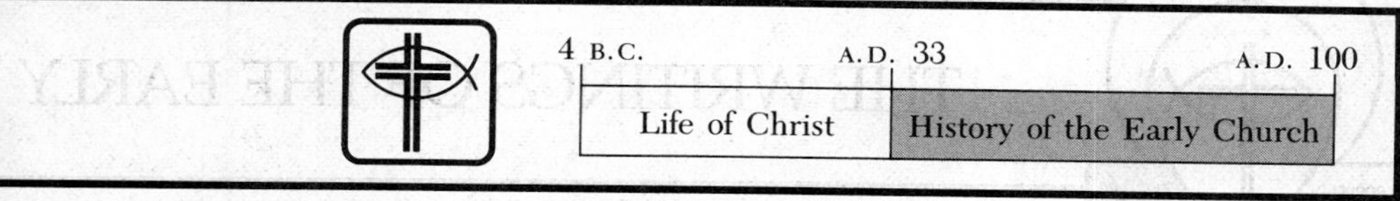

48 — 58 (Acts Ends) — 68 — 70 — A.D. 100

TO THE END OF THE EARTH

Missionary Journeys

Jerusalem Council
Acts 15

Paul Imprisoned

Peter Executed

Paul Executed

Jerusalem Destroyed

John Dies

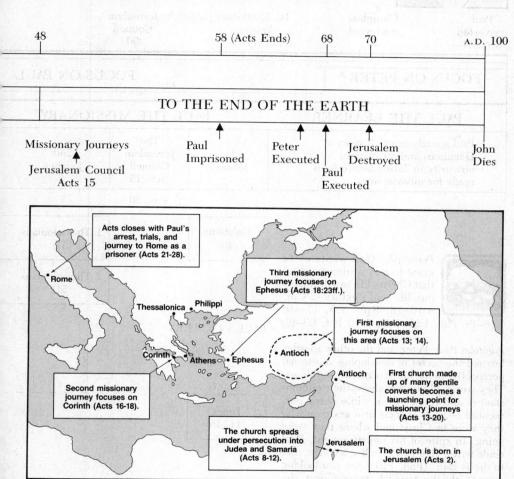

Acts closes with Paul's arrest, trials, and journey to Rome as a prisoner (Acts 21-28).

Rome

Thessalonica

Philippi

Third missionary journey focuses on Ephesus (Acts 18:23ff.).

First missionary journey focuses on this area (Acts 13; 14).

Antioch

Corinth

Athens

Ephesus

Antioch

First church made up of many gentile converts becomes a launching point for missionary journeys (Acts 13-20).

Second missionary journey focuses on Corinth (Acts 16-18).

The church spreads under persecution into Judea and Samaria (Acts 8-12).

Jerusalem

The church is born in Jerusalem (Acts 2).

Principle: Christ's life is reproduced in others when we take the initiative to witness in the power of the Holy Spirit (Matt. 28:18–20; Acts 1:8; Col. 4:2–6).

Practice: The Book of Acts records the spread of the gospel from the city of Jerusalem to the whole province of Judea and Samaria, and ultimately through the Roman Empire and beyond. These first-century Christians were sold out for the cause of Christ and transformed their world as their lives became living epistles of the Good News. God has called us to a life-style of evangelism in which we build relationships with non-Christians. These friendships in turn become natural bridges for communicating the gospel. Take a close look at Colossians 4:2–6 to learn how to become more effective as an instrument of the Holy Spirit to reproduce the life of Christ in others.

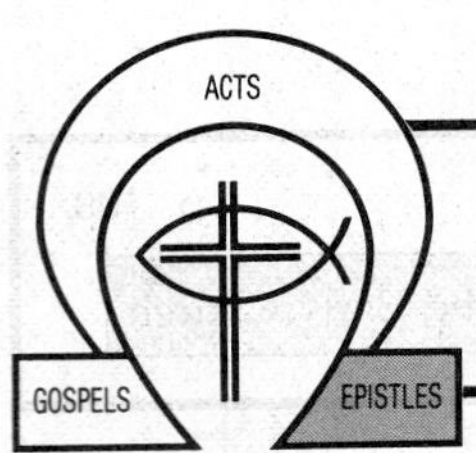

THE WRITINGS OF THE EARLY

Paul converted A.D. 34	Cornelius converted 40	1st Missionary Journey 48	Jerusalem Council 50

FOCUS ON PETER			FOCUS ON PAUL
PAUL THE LEARNER	PAUL THE MISSIONARY		
Paul spends nearly 3 years at Damascus and 10 years in obscurity in Tarsus before he is ready for mission work.	1st Journey	The Jerusalem Council Acts 15	2nd Journey
		A.D. 50	

PAUL'S LETTERS	Galatians (49)		1 Thessalonians (51) 2 Thessalonians (51)
LETTERS BY OTHERS	James (44, 45)		
GOSPELS & ACTS	Matthew (c. 40's)		

Principle: God wants us to grow in our understanding that Christ's life and destiny is our life and destiny (2 Cor. 4:16–18; Eph. 1:3, 17–19; 3:16–19; Phil. 1:21; 3:20, 21; 1 Pet. 1:3–9).

Practice: Paul, Peter, and the other apostles learned the secret of developing an eternal perspective in the midst of earthly problems. They were able to live above their circumstances and rejoice even while being persecuted because of their firm grasp on who they were in Christ and where they were going. In spite of his imprisonment, Paul could write, "For to me, to live is Christ, and to die is gain" (Phil. 1:21). Are you looking more at "the things which are seen" or at "the things which are not seen"? The former are temporary, but the latter are eternal (2 Cor. 4:18).

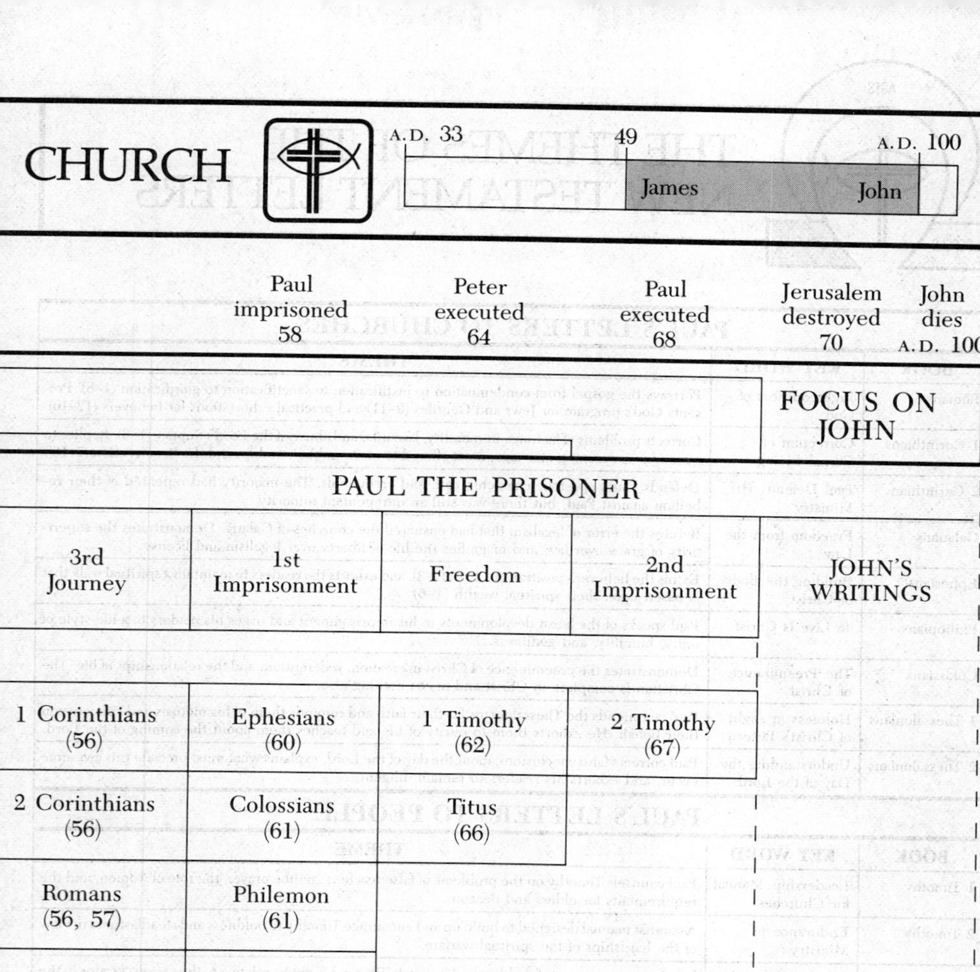
CHURCH
A.D. 33
49
A.D. 100
James
John
Paul imprisoned 58
Peter executed 64
Paul executed 68
Jerusalem destroyed 70
John dies A.D. 100
FOCUS ON JOHN
PAUL THE PRISONER
3rd Journey
1st Imprisonment
Freedom
2nd Imprisonment
JOHN'S WRITINGS
1 Corinthians (56)
Ephesians (60)
1 Timothy (62)
2 Timothy (67)
2 Corinthians (56)
Colossians (61)
Titus (66)
Romans (56, 57)
Philemon (61)
Philippians (62)
1 Peter (64)
Hebrews (66–69)
1 John (85–90)
2 Peter (64)
Jude (75)
2 John (85–90)
3 John (85–90)
Revelation (95–96)
Acts (62)
Luke (58–60)
Mark (60)
John (65–70)

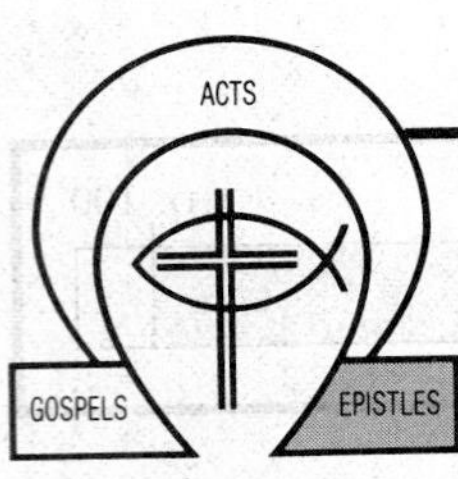

THE THEMES OF THE NEW TESTAMENT LETTERS

PAUL'S LETTERS TO CHURCHES

BOOK	KEY WORD	THEME
Romans	Righteousness of God	Portrays the gospel from condemnation to justification to sanctification to glorification (1–8). Presents God's program for Jews and Gentiles (9–11) and practical exhortations for believers (12–16).
1 Corinthians	Correction of Carnal Living	Corrects problems of factions, immorality, lawsuits, and abuse of the Lord's Supper (1–6). Replies to questions concerning marriage, meat offered to idols, public worship, and the Resurrection (7–16).
2 Corinthians	Paul Defends His Ministry	Defends Paul's apostolic character, call, and credentials. The majority had repented of their rebellion against Paul, but there was still an unrepentant minority.
Galatians	Freedom from the Law	Refutes the error of legalism that had ensnared the churches of Galatia. Demonstrates the superiority of grace over law, and magnifies the life of liberty over legalism and license.
Ephesians	Building the Body of Christ	Extols the believer's position in Christ (1–3), and exhorts the readers to maintain a spiritual walk that is based upon their spiritual wealth (4–6).
Philippians	To Live Is Christ	Paul speaks of the latest developments in his imprisonment and urges his readers to a life-style of unity, humility, and godliness.
Colossians	The Preeminence of Christ	Demonstrates the preeminence of Christ in creation, redemption, and the relationships of life. The Christian is complete in Christ and needs nothing else.
1 Thessalonians	Holiness in Light of Christ's Return	Paul commends the Thessalonians for their faith and reminds them of his motives and concerns on their behalf. He exhorts them to purity of life and teaches them about the coming of the Lord.
2 Thessalonians	Understanding the Day of the Lord	Paul corrects false conclusions about the day of the Lord, explains what must precede this awesome event, and exhorts his readers to remain diligent.

PAUL'S LETTERS TO PEOPLE

BOOK	KEY WORD	THEME
1 Timothy	Leadership Manual for Churches	Paul counsels Timothy on the problems of false teachers, public prayer, the role of women, and the requirements for elders and deacons.
2 Timothy	Endurance in Ministry	A combat manual designed to build up and encourage Timothy to boldness and steadfastness in view of the hardships of the spiritual warfare.
Titus	Conduct Manual for Churches	Lists the requirements for elders and instructs Titus in his duties relative to the various groups in the churches.
Philemon	Forgiveness from Slavery	Paul appeals to Philemon to forgive Onesimus and to regard him no longer as a slave but as a brother in Christ.

LETTERS FROM OTHERS

BOOK	KEY WORD	THEME
Hebrews	Superiority of Christ	Demonstrates the superiority of Christ's person, priesthood, and power over all that preceded Him to encourage the readers to mature and to become stable in their faith.
James	Faith that Works	A practical catalog of the characteristics of true faith written to exhort James' Hebrew-Christian readers to examine the reality of their own faith.
1 Peter	Suffering for Christ	Comfort and counsel to those who were being maligned for their faith in Christ. They are encouraged to develop an attitude of submission in view of their suffering.
2 Peter	Guard Against False Prophets	Copes with internal opposition in the form of false teachers who were enticing believers into their errors of belief and conduct. Appeals for growth in the true knowledge of Christ.
1 John	Fellowship with God	Explores the dimensions of fellowship between redeemed people and God. Believers must walk in His light, manifest His love, and abide in His life.
2 John	Avoid Fellowship with False Teachers	John commends his readers for remaining steadfast in apostolic truth and reminds them to walk in love and avoid false teachers.
3 John	Enjoy Fellowship with the Brethren	John thanks Gaius for his support of traveling teachers of the truth, in contrast to Diotrephes, who rejected them and told others to do the same.
Jude	Contend for the Faith	This exposé of false teachers reveals their conduct and character and predicts their judgment. Jude encourages his readers to build themselves up in the truth and contend earnestly for the faith.
Revelation	Revelation of the Coming Christ	The glorified Christ gives seven messages to the church (1–3). Visions of unparalleled judgment upon rebellious mankind are followed by the Second Advent (4–19). The Apocalypse concludes with a description of the new heaven and new earth and the marvels of the New Jerusalem (20–22).

The

New Testament

of

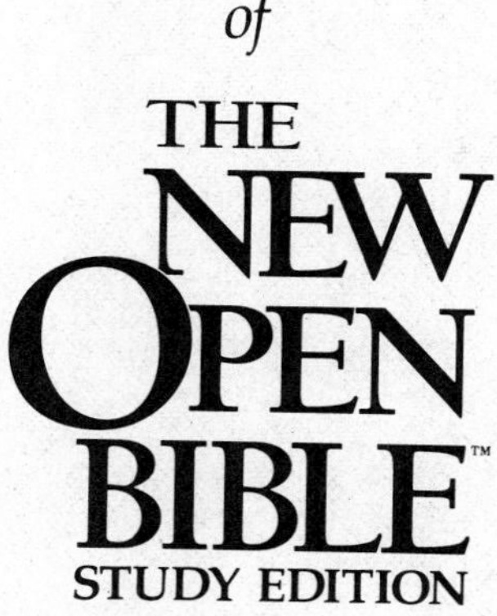

The New King James Version

THE GOSPEL ACCORDING TO

MATTHEW

THE BOOK OF MATTHEW

Matthew is the gospel written by a Jew to Jews about a Jew. Matthew is the writer, his countrymen are the readers, and Jesus Christ is the subject. Matthew's design is to present Jesus as the King of the Jews, the long-awaited Messiah. Through a carefully selected series of Old Testament quotations, Matthew documents Jesus Christ's claim to be Messiah. His genealogy, baptism, messages, and miracles all point to the same inescapable conclusion: Christ is King. Even in His death, seeming defeat is turned to victory by the Resurrection, and the message again echoes forth: the King of the Jews lives.

At an early date this gospel was given the title *Kata Matthaion,* "According to Matthew." As this title suggests, other gospel accounts were known at that time (the word *gospel* was added later). Matthew ("Gift of the Lord") was also surnamed Levi (Mark 2:14; Luke 5:27).

THE AUTHOR OF MATTHEW

The early church uniformly attributed this gospel to Matthew, and no tradition to the contrary ever emerged. This book was known early and accepted quickly. In his Ecclesiastical History (A.D. 323), Eusebius quoted a statement by Papias (c. A.D. 140) that Matthew wrote *logia* ("sayings") in Aramaic. No Aramaic gospel of Matthew has been found, and it is evident that Matthew is not a Greek translation of an Aramaic original. Some believe that Matthew wrote an abbreviated version of Jesus' sayings in Aramaic before writing his gospel in Greek for a larger circle of readers.

Matthew, the son of Alphaeus (Mark 2:14), occupied the unpopular post of tax collector in Capernaum for the Roman government. As a publican he was no doubt disliked by his Jewish countrymen. When Jesus called him to discipleship (9:9–13; Mark 2:14; Luke 5:27, 28), his quick response probably meant that he had already been stirred by Jesus' public preaching. He gave a large reception for Jesus in his house so that his associates could meet Jesus. He was chosen as one of the twelve apostles, and the last appearance of his name in the Bible is in Acts 1:13. Matthew's life from that point on is veiled in tradition.

THE TIME OF MATTHEW

Like all the gospels, Matthew is not easy to date: suggestions have ranged from A.D. 40 to 140. The two expressions "to this day" (27:8) and "until this day" (28:15) indicate that a substantial period of time has passed since the events described in the book, but they also point to a date prior to the destruction of Jerusalem in A.D. 70. The Olivet Discourse (24 and 25) also anticipates this event. The strong Jewish flavor of this gospel is another argument for a date prior to A.D. 70. If Matthew depended on Mark's gospel as a source, the date of Mark would determine the earliest date for Matthew. The likely time frame for this book is A.D. 58–68. It may have been written in Palestine or Syrian Antioch.

THE CHRIST OF MATTHEW

Matthew presents Jesus as Israel's promised messianic King (1:23; 2:2, 6; 3:17; 4:15–17; 21:5, 9; 22:44, 45; 26:64; 27:11, 27–37). The phrase "the kingdom of heaven" appears thirty-two times in Matthew but nowhere else in the New Testament. To show that Jesus fulfills the qualifications for the Messiah, Matthew uses more Old Testament quotations and allusions than any other book (almost 130). Often used in this gospel is the revealing phrase "that what was spoken through the prophet might be fulfilled," which appears nine times in Matthew and not once in the other gospels. Jesus is the climax of the prophets (12:39, 40; 13:13–15, 35; 17:5–13), "the Son of Man" (24:30ff.), the "Servant" of the Lord (12:17–21), and the "Son of David" (the Davidic reference occurs nine times in Matthew, but only six times in all of the other gospels).

KEYS TO MATTHEW

Key Word: Jesus the King—A Jewish tax collector named Matthew writes to a Jewish audience to convince them that the King of Jews has come. By quoting repeatedly from the Old Testament, Matthew validates Christ's claims that He is, in fact, the prophesied Messiah (the Anointed One) of Israel. Everything about this King is unique: His miraculous birth and obscure yet carefully prophesied birthplace, His flight into Egypt, His announcement by John, His battle with Satan in the wilderness, all support the only possible conclusion—Jesus is the culmination of promises delivered by the prophets over a period of a thousand years. Thus God's redemptive plan is alive and well, even after four hundred years of prophetic silence.

Key Verses: Matthew 16:16-19 and 28:18-20—"And Simon Peter answered and said, 'You are the Christ, the Son of the living God.' Jesus answered and said to him, 'Blessed are you, Simon Bar-Jonah, for flesh and blood has not revealed *this* to you, but My Father who is in heaven. And I also say to you, that you are Peter, and on this rock I will build My church, and the gates of Hades shall not prevail against it. And I will give you the keys of the kingdom of heaven, and whatever you bind on earth will be bound in heaven, and whatever you loose on earth will be loosed in heaven" (16:16–19).

"Then Jesus came and spoke to them, saying, 'All authority has been given to Me in heaven and on earth. Go therefore and make disciples of all the nations, baptizing them in the name of the Father and of the Son and of the Holy Spirit, teaching them to observe all things that I have commanded you; and lo, I am with you always, *even* to the end of the age.' Amen" (28:18–20).

Key Chapter: Matthew 12—The turning point of Matthew comes in the twelfth chapter when the Pharisees, acting as the leadership of the nation of Israel, formally reject Jesus Christ as the Messiah, saying that His power comes not from God but from Satan. Christ's ministry changes immediately with His new teaching of parables, increased attention given to His disciples, and His repeated statement that His death is now near.

SURVEY OF MATTHEW

The Old Testament prophets predicted and longed for the coming of the Anointed One who would enter history to bring redemption and deliverance. The first verse of Matthew succinctly announces the fulfillment of Israel's hope in the coming of Christ: "The book of the genealogy of Jesus Christ, the Son of David, the Son of Abraham." Matthew was placed first in the canon of New Testament books by the early church because it is a natural bridge between the Testaments. This gospel describes the person and work of Israel's messianic King. An important part of Matthew's structure is revealed in the phrase "when Jesus had ended" (7:28; 11:1; 13:53; 19:1; 26:1), which is used to conclude the five key discourses of the book: the Sermon on the Mount (5:3—7:27), Instruction of the Disciples (10:5–42), Parables of the Kingdom (13:3–52), Terms of Discipleship (18:3–35), and the Olivet Discourse (24:4—25:46). Matthew can be outlined as follows: the presentation of the King (1:1—4:11); the proclamation of the King (4:12—7:29); the power of the King (8:1—11:1); the progressive rejection of the King (11:2—16:12); the preparation of the King's disciples (16:13—20:28); the presentation and rejection of the King (20:29—27:66); the proof of the King (28:1–20).

The Presentation of the King (1:1—4:11): The promise to Abraham was that "in you all the families of the earth shall be blessed" (Gen. 12:3). Jesus Christ, the Savior of the world, is "the Son of Abraham" (1:1). However, He is also "the Son of David"; and as David's direct descendant, He is qualified to be Israel's King. The magi know that the "King of the Jews" (2:2) has been born and come to worship Him. John the Baptist, the messianic forerunner who breaks the four hundred years of prophetic silence, also bears witness of Him (cf. Mal. 3:1). The sinlessness of the King is proved when He overcomes the satanic temptations to disobey the will of the Father.

The Proclamation of the King (4:12—7:29): In this section, Matthew uses a topical rather than a chronological arrangement of his material in order to develop a crucial pattern in Christ's ministry. The words of the Lord are found in the Sermon on the Mount (5—7). This discourse requires less than fifteen minutes to read, but its brevity has not diminished its profound influence on the world. The Sermon on the Mount presents new laws and standards for God's people.

The Power of the King (8:1—11:1): The works of the Lord are presented in a series of ten miracles (8 and 9) that reveal His authority over every realm (disease, demons, death, and nature). Thus, the words of the Lord are supported by His works; His claims are verified by His credentials.

The Progressive Rejection of the King (11:2—16:12): Here we note a series of reactions to Christ's words and works. Because of increasing opposition, Jesus begins to spend

FOCUS	OFFER OF THE KING			REJECTION OF THE KING			
REFERENCE	1:1	4:12	8:1	11:2	16:13	20:29	28:1—28:20
DIVISION	PRESENTATION OF THE KING	PROCLAMATION OF THE KING	POWER OF THE KING	PROGRESSIVE REJECTION OF THE KING	PREPARATION OF THE KING'S DISCIPLES	PRESENTATION AND REJECTION OF THE KING	PROOF OF THE KING
TOPIC	TEACHING THE THRONGS				TEACHING THE TWELVE		
	CHRONOLOGICAL	THEMATIC		CHRONOLOGICAL			
LOCATION	BETHLEHEM AND NAZARETH	GALILEE				JUDEA	
TIME	C. 4 B.C.–A.D. 33						

proportionately more time with His disciples as He prepares them for His coming death and departure.

The Preparation of the King's Disciples (16:13—20:28): In a series of discourses, Jesus communicates the significance of accepting or rejecting His offer of righteousness. His teaching in 16:13—21:11 is primarily directed to those who accept Him.

The Presentation and Rejection of the King (20:29—27:66): The majority of Christ's words in this section are aimed at those who reject their King. The Lord predicts the terrible judgment that will fall on Jerusalem, resulting in the dispersion of the Jewish people. Looking beyond these events (fulfilled in A.D. 70), He also describes His second coming as the Judge and Lord of the earth.

The Proof of the King (28): Authenticating His words and works are the empty tomb, resurrection, and appearances, all proving that Jesus Christ is indeed the prophesied Messiah, the very Son of God.

Christ's final ministry in Judea (beginning in 19:1) reaches a climax at the cross as the King willingly gives up His life to redeem sinful persons. Jesus endures awesome human hatred in this great demonstration of divine love (cf. Rom. 5:7, 8). His perfect sacrifice is acceptable, and this gospel concludes with His glorious resurrection.

OUTLINE OF MATTHEW

Part One: The Presentation of the King (1:1—4:11)

I. The Advent of the King . . . . 1:1—2:23
- A. Genealogy of Christ 1:1–17
- B. Birth of Christ 1:18–25
- C. Visit of Wise Men 2:1–12
- D. Flight into Egypt 2:13–15
- E. Herod Kills the Children 2:16–18
- F. Jesus Returns to Nazareth 2:19–23

II. The Announcer of the King 3:1–12
- A. The Person of John the Baptist 3:1–6
- B. The Preaching of John the Baptist 3:7–12

III. The Approval of the King . . . . 3:13—4:11
- A. Baptism of Jesus 3:13–17
- B. Temptation of Jesus 4:1–11
  1. First Temptation 4:1–4
  2. Second Temptation 4:5–7
  3. Third Temptation 4:8–11

Part Two: The Proclamation of the King (4:12—7:29)

I. The Background for the Sermon 4:12–25
- A. Jesus Begins His Ministry 4:12–17
- B. Jesus Calls His First Disciples 4:18–22
- C. Jesus Ministers in Galilee 4:23–25

II. The Sermon on the Mount . . . . 5:1—7:29
- A. The Subjects of the Kingdom 5:1–16
  1. The Beatitudes 5:1–12
  2. The Similitudes 5:13–16
- B. The Relationship of Jesus to the Law . . . . 5:17—7:6
  1. Jesus Fulfills the Law 5:17–19
  2. Jesus Rejects Pharisaic Interpretation 5:20–48
     - a. Murder 5:20–26
     - b. Adultery 5:27–30
     - c. Divorce 5:31, 32
     - d. Oaths 5:33–37
     - e. Retaliation 5:38–42
     - f. Love 5:43–48
  3. Jesus Rejects Pharisaic Practices 6:1—7:6
     - a. Charitable Deeds 6:1–4
     - b. Prayer 6:5–15
     - c. Fasting 6:16–18
     - d. Wealth 6:19–34
     - e. Judging 7:1–6
- C. Jesus Instructs on Entering the Kingdom 7:7–27
  1. "Ask, and It Will Be Given" 7:7–11
  2. Golden Rule 7:12
  3. Two Ways of Life 7:13, 14
  4. False and True Teaching 7:15–20
  5. True Way into the Kingdom 7:21–23
  6. Parable of the Two Builders 7:24–27
- D. Response to the Sermon 7:28, 29

Part Three: The Power of the King (8:1—11:1)

I. The Demonstration of the King's Power . . . . 8:1—9:34
- A. Miracles of Healing 8:1–17
  1. The Leper Is Cleansed 8:1–4
  2. The Centurion's Servant Is Healed 8:5–13
  3. Peter's Mother-in-Law Is Healed . . . 8:14–17
- B. Demands of Discipleship 8:18–22
- C. Miracles of Power . . . . 8:23—9:8
  1. The Sea Is Stilled 8:23–27
  2. Demons Are Cast into Swine 8:28–34
  3. The Paralytic Is Forgiven 9:1–8
- D. Distinctions of Disciples 9:9–17
  1. Matthew Is Called 9:9
  2. The Disciples Eat with Sinners 9:10–13

3. The Disciples Do Not Fast 9:14–17
E. Miracles of Restoration 9:18–34
1. Life Is Restored 9:18–26
2. Sight Is Restored. 9:27–31
3. Speech Is Restored 9:32–34

II. The Delegation of the King's Power 9:35—11:1
A. The Need for Delegation of Power . . . 9:35–38
B. The Twelve Apostles Are Sent. 10:1–4
C. The Twelve Apostles Are Instructed. . . . . 10:5—11:1

Part Four: The Progressive Rejection of the King (11:2—16:12)

I. The Commencement of Rejection. 11:2–30
A. Rejection of John the Baptist 11:2–15
B. Rejection by Jesus' Generation. 11:16–19
C. Rejection of Chorazin, Bethsaida, and Capernaum 11:20–24
D. Invitation to Come to Jesus 11:25–30

II. The Rejection of Christ by the Pharisees 12:1–50
A. Controversy over Sabbath-Labor 12:1–8
B. Controversy over Sabbath-Healing. . . . 12:9–13
C. Pharisees Plan to Destroy Christ 12:14–21
D. Pharisees Blaspheme the Holy Spirit 12:22–30
E. Pharisees Commit the Unpardonable Sin 12:31–37
F. Pharisees Demand a Sign 12:38–45
G. Jesus and the True Brethren. 12:46–50

III. The Consequences of the Rejection 13:1–53
A. Parables Spoken to the Multitude 13:1–35
1. Parable of the Soils. 13:1–23
2. Parable of the Wheat and Tares 13:24–30
3. Parable of the Mustard Seed. 13:31, 32
4. Parable of the Leaven 13:33–35
B. Parables Spoken to the Disciples 13:36–53
1. Parable of the Tares Explained. . . 13:36–43
2. Parable of the Hidden Treasure 13:44
3. Parable of the Pearl of Great Price. 13:45, 46
4. Parable of the Dragnet. 13:47–50
5. Parable of the Householder 13:51–53

IV. The Continuing Rejection of the King . . . . 13:54—16:12
A. Rejection at Nazareth 13:54–58
B. Rejection by Herod 14:1–36
1. Reaction of Herod 14:1–12
a. Present Response to Jesus 14:1, 2
b. Recount of the Murder of John the Baptist 14:3–12
2. Withdrawal of Jesus 14:13–36
a. Jesus Feeds 5,000 . . . . 14:13–21
b. Jesus Walks on Water 14:22–33
c. Jesus Heals Many 14:34–36
C. Rejection by Scribes and Pharisees . . . 15:1–39
1. Debate over Tradition 15:1–20
2. Withdrawal of Jesus 15:21–39
a. Jesus Heals the Gentile Woman's Daughter. 15:21–28
b. Jesus Heals Many 15:29–31
c. Jesus Feeds 4,000 . . . . 15:32–39
D. Rejection by Pharisees and Sadducees 16:1–12
1. Debate over a Sign from Heaven . . . 16:1–4
2. Withdrawal of Jesus 16:5–12

Part Five: The Preparation of the King's Disciples (16:13—20:28)

I. The Revelation in View of Rejection. . . . . 16:13—17:13
A. Revelation of the Person of the King 16:13–17
B. Revelation of the Program of the King . . . . 16:18—17:13
1. Revelation of the Church. 16:18–20
2. Revelation of Jesus' Death. 16:21–23
3. Revelation of Jesus' Reward 16:24–26
4. The Prophecy of the Second Coming. 16:27, 28
5. The Transfiguration 17:1–13

II. The Instruction in View of Rejection. . . . . 17:14—20:28
A. Instruction About Faith 17:14–21
B. Instruction About Jesus' Death 17:22, 23
C. Instruction About Taxes 17:24–27
D. Instruction About Humility 18:1–5
E. Instruction About Causing Offense . . . 18:6–20
1. Punishment of Offenders 18:6–10
2. Parable of the Lost Sheep 18:11–14
3. The Offended Brother 18:15–20
F. Instruction About Forgiveness 18:21–35
G. Instruction About Divorce 19:1–15
H. Instruction About Wealth . . . . . . 19:16—20:16
1. Rich Young Ruler 19:16–26
2. The Apostles' Reward 19:27–30
3. Parable of the Laborers 20:1–16
I. Instruction About Jesus' Death 20:17–19
J. Instruction About Ambition 20:20–28

Part Six: The Presentation and Rejection of the King (20:29—27:66)

I. The Blind Men Recognize the King 20:29–34

II. The Public Presentation of the King 21:1–17
A. The Triumphal Entry 21:1–11
B. The Cleansing of the Temple. 21:12–17

III. The Nation Rejects the King . . . . . . 21:18—22:46
A. Cursing of the Fig Tree 21:18–22
B. Conflict with Priests and Elders 21:23—22:14
1. Question of Jesus' Authority 21:23–27
2. Parable of the Two Sons 21:28–32

3. Parable of the Landowner 21:33–46
4. Parable of the Marriage Feast 22:1–14
C. Conflict with Pharisees
and Herodians 22:15–22
D. Conflict with Sadducees 22:23–33
E. Conflict with Pharisees 22:34–46
1. The Greatest Commandment 22:34–40
2. The Son of David 22:41–46

IV. The King Rejects the Nation 23:1–39

A. Jesus Characterizes the Pharisees 23:1–12
B. Jesus Condemns the Pharisees 23:13–36
C. Jesus Laments over Jerusalem 23:37–39

**V. The Predictions of the King's
Second Coming . . . . 24:1—25:46**

A. The Temple to Be Destroyed 24:1, 2
B. The Disciples' Two Questions:
"When?" and "What?" 24:3
C. Jesus Answers the "What?" 24:4–31
1. The Tribulation 24:4–26
2. The Second Coming 24:27–31
D. Jesus Answers the "When?" 24:32–51
1. Parable of the Fig Tree 24:32–35
2. Illustration of the Days of Noah . . 24:36–44
3. Illustration of the Two Servants . . 24:45–51
E. Jesus Predicts Judgment
at His Coming 25:1–46
1. Parable of the Ten Virgins 25:1–13
2. Parable of the Talents 25:14–30
3. Judgment of the Gentiles 25:31–46

VI. The Passion of the King . . . . 26:1—27:66

A. The Religious Leaders Plot
to Kill Jesus 26:1–5
B. Mary Anoints Jesus for Burial 26:6–13
C. Judas Agrees to Betray Jesus 26:14–16
D. The Disciples Celebrate
the Passover 26:17–35
1. The Passover Is Prepared 26:17–19
2. The Passover Is Celebrated 26:20–25
3. The Lord's Supper Is Instituted 26:26–29
4. Peter's Denial Is Predicted 26:30–35
E. Jesus Is Arrested in Gethsemane 26:36–56
1. Jesus' Three Prayers 26:36–46
2. Jesus' Betrayal and Arrest 26:47–56
F. Jesus Is Tried . . . . 26:57—27:25
1. The Trial Before Caiaphas 26:57–75
a. Two False Witnesses 26:57–68
b. Three Denials of Peter 26:69–75
2. The Trial Before Pilate 27:1–25
a. Jesus Is Delivered to Pilate 27:1, 2
b. Judas Repents 27:3–10
c. Jesus Is Examined 27:11–14
d. Barabbas Is Freed 27:15–25
G. Jesus Is Crucified 27:26–56
1. Jesus Is Scourged 27:26–28
2. Jesus Is Led to Golgotha 27:29–33
3. Jesus Is Crucified 27:34–44
4. Jesus Dies 27:45–50
5. Signs Accompanying Jesus'
Death 27:51–56
H. Jesus Is Buried 27:57–66

Part Seven: The Proof of the King (28:1–20)

I. The Empty Tomb 28:1–8
**II. The Appearance of Jesus
to the Women 28:9, 10**
III. The Bribery of the Soldiers 28:11–15
**IV. The Appearance of Jesus
to the Disciples 28:16, 17**
V. The Great Commission 28:18–20

CHAPTER 1

Genealogy of Christ
Ruth 4:18–22; 1 Chr. 1:34, 2:1–15; Luke 3:31–34

THE book of the genealogy of Jesus
Christ, [R]the Son of David, [R]the Son of
Abraham: Ps. 132:11; Jer. 23:5★ · Gen. 12:3; 22:18
2 Abraham begot Isaac, Isaac begot Jacob,
and Jacob begot Judah and his brothers.
3 Judah begot Perez and Zerah by Tamar,
Perez begot Hezron, and Hezron begot Ram.
4 Ram begot Amminadab, Amminadab begot Nahshon, and Nahshon begot Salmon.
5 Salmon begot Boaz by Rahab, Boaz begot Obed by Ruth, Obed begot Jesse,
6 and [R]Jesse begot David the king.
David the king begot Solomon by her
who had been the wife of Uriah. Is. 11:1, 10★
7 Solomon begot Rehoboam, Rehoboam
begot Abijah, and Abijah begot *Asa.
8 Asa begot Jehoshaphat, Jehoshaphat
begot Joram, and Joram begot Uzziah.
9 Uzziah begot Jotham, Jotham begot
[R]Ahaz, and Ahaz begot Hezekiah. 2 Kin. 15:38
10 Hezekiah begot Manasseh, Manasseh
begot *Amon, and Amon begot Josiah.
11 Josiah begot [T]Jeconiah and his brothers
about the time they were [R]carried away to
Babylon. Or *Coniah* or *Jehoiachin* · 2 Kin. 24:14–16
12 And after they were brought to Babylon,
[R]Jeconiah begot Shealtiel, and Shealtiel begot
[R]Zerubbabel. 1 Chr. 3:17 · Ezra 3:2
13 Zerubbabel begot Abiud, Abiud begot
Eliakim, and Eliakim begot Azor.
14 Azor begot Zadok, Zadok begot Achim,
and Achim begot Eliud.
15 Eliud begot Eleazar, Eleazar begot Matthan, and Matthan begot Jacob.
16 And Jacob begot Joseph the husband of

1:7 NU *Asaph* **1:10** NU *Amos*

[R]Mary, of whom was born Jesus who is called
Christ. Matt. 13:55
17 So all the generations from Abraham to
David *are* fourteen generations, from David
until the captivity in Babylon *are* fourteen
generations, and from the captivity in Babylon until the Christ *are* fourteen generations.

Birth of Christ

18 Now the birth of Jesus Christ was as
follows: After His mother Mary was betrothed to Joseph, [R]before they came together, she was found with child of the Holy
Spirit. Is 7:14; 49:1, 5★
19 Then Joseph her husband, being [T]a just
man, and not wanting [R]to make her a public
example, was minded to put her away secretly. *an upright* • Deut. 24:1
20 But while he thought about these things,
behold, an angel of the Lord appeared to him
in a dream, saying, "Joseph, son of David, do
not be afraid to take to you Mary your wife,
[R]for that which is [T]conceived in her is of the
Holy Spirit. Luke 1:35 • Lit. *begotten*
21 "And she will bring forth a Son, and you
shall call His name JESUS, for He [R]will save
His people from their sins." Rom. 5:18, 19☆
22 Now all this was done that it might be
fulfilled which was spoken by the Lord
through the prophet, saying:
23 [R]*"Behold, a virgin shall be with child, and
bear a Son, and they shall call His name
Immanuel,"* which is translated, "God with
us." Is. 7:14★
24 Then Joseph, being aroused from sleep,
did as the angel of the Lord commanded him
and took to him his wife,
25 and did not know her till she had
brought forth her firstborn *Son. And he
[R]called His name JESUS. Luke 2:7, 21★

CHAPTER 2

Visit of Wise Men

NOW after [R]Jesus was [R]born in Bethlehem
of Judea in the days of Herod the king,
behold, [T]wise men from the East came to
Jerusalem, Luke 2:4–7 • Mic. 5:2★ • Gr. *magoi*
2 saying, "Where is He who has been born
King of the Jews? For we have seen His star
in the East and have come to worship Him."
3 When Herod the king heard *these things,*
he was troubled, and all Jerusalem with him.
4 And when he had gathered all [R]the chief
priests and [R]scribes of the people together,
[R]he inquired of them where the Christ was to
be born. 2 Chr. 36:14 • 2 Chr. 34:13 • Mal. 2:7
5 So they said to him, "In Bethlehem of
Judea, for thus it is written by the prophet:

6 *'But[R] you, Bethlehem, in the land of
Judah,* Mic. 5:2; John 7:42★
*Are not the least among the rulers of
Judah;
For out of you shall come a Ruler
Who will shepherd My people Israel.'* "

7 Then Herod, when he had secretly called
the [T]wise men, determined from them what
time the [R]star appeared. Gr. *magoi* • Num. 24:17
8 And he sent them to Bethlehem and said,
"Go and search diligently for the young
Child, and when you have found *Him,* bring
back word to me, that I may come and
worship Him also."
9 When they heard the king, they departed; and behold, the star which they had
seen in the East went before them, till it came
and stood over where the young Child was.
10 When they saw the star, they rejoiced
with exceedingly great joy.
11 And when they had come into the house,
they saw the young Child with Mary His
mother, and fell down and worshiped Him.
And when they had opened their treasures,
[R]they presented gifts to Him: gold, frankincense, and myrrh. Is. 60:6
12 Then, being divinely warned in a dream
that they should not return to Herod, they
departed for their own country another way.

Flight into Egypt

13 Now when they had departed, behold, an
angel of the Lord appeared to Joseph in a
dream, saying, "Arise, take the young Child
and His mother, flee to Egypt, and stay there
until I bring you word; for [R]Herod will seek
the young Child to destroy Him." Matt. 2:16☆
14 When he arose, he took the young Child
and His mother by night and departed for
Egypt,
15 and was there until the death of Herod,
that it might be fulfilled which was spoken by
the Lord through the prophet, saying, [R]*"Out
of Egypt I called My Son."* Hos. 11:1★

Herod Kills the Children

16 Then Herod, when he saw that he was
deceived by the wise men, was exceedingly
angry; and he sent forth and put to death all
the male children who were in Bethlehem
and in all its districts, from two years old and
under, according to the time which he had
determined from the wise men.
17 Then was fulfilled what was spoken by
[R]Jeremiah the prophet, saying: Jer. 31:15

18 *"A[R] voice was heard in Ramah,
Lamentation, weeping, and great
mourning,
Rachel weeping for her children,
Refusing to be comforted, because they
were no more."* Jer. 31:15★

1:25 NU *a Son*

Jesus Returns to Nazareth—Luke 2:39

19 But when Herod was dead, behold, an
angel of the Lord appeared in a dream to
Joseph in Egypt,
20 [R]saying, "Arise, take the young Child and
His mother, and go to the land of Israel, for
those who [R]sought the young Child's life are
dead." Luke 2:39 • Matt. 2:16
21 Then he arose, took the young Child and
His mother, and came into the land of Israel.
22 But when he heard that Archelaus was
reigning over Judea instead of his father
Herod, he was afraid to go there. And being
warned by God in a [R]dream, he turned aside
into the region of Galilee. Matt. 2:12, 13, 19
23 And he came and dwelt in a city called
[R]Nazareth, that it might be fulfilled [R]which
was spoken by the prophets, "He shall be
called a Nazarene." John 1:45, 46 • Judg. 13:5 ★

CHAPTER 3

The Person of John the Baptist
Mark 1:2–6; Luke 3:3–6

IN those days John the Baptist came
preaching in the wilderness of Judea,
2 and saying, "Repent, for [R]the kingdom of
heaven is at hand!" Dan. 2:44; Mal. 4:5, 6 ★
3 For this is he who was spoken of by the
prophet Isaiah, saying:

[R]*"The voice of one crying in the*
wilderness: Is. 40:3 ★
[R]*'Prepare the way of the* LORD,
Make His paths straight.'" Luke 1:76

4 And John himself was clothed in camel's
hair, with a leather belt around his waist; and
his food was locusts and wild honey.
5 Then Jerusalem, all Judea, and all the
region around the Jordan went out to him
6 [R]and were baptized by him in the Jordan,
confessing their sins. Acts 19:4, 18

The Preaching of John the Baptist
Mark 1:7–9; Luke 3:7–9, 16, 17

7 But when he saw many of the Pharisees
and Sadducees coming to his baptism, he said
to them, "Brood of vipers! Who has warned
you to flee from the wrath to come?
8 "Therefore bear fruits worthy of repentance,
9 "and do not think to say to yourselves,
[R]'We have Abraham as *our* father.' For I say
to you that God is able to raise up children to
Abraham from these stones. John 8:33
10 "And even now the ax is laid to the root
of the trees. [R]Therefore every tree which does
not bear good fruit is cut down and thrown
into the fire. Matt. 7:19
11 [R]"I indeed baptize you with water unto
repentance, but He who is coming after me is
mightier than I, whose sandals I am not
worthy to carry. He will baptize you with the
Holy Spirit *and fire. Acts 2:4, 33 ☆
12 [R]"His winnowing fan *is* in His hand, and
He will thoroughly [T]purge His threshing floor,
and gather His wheat into the barn; but He
will [R]burn up the chaff with unquenchable
fire." Mal. 3:3 • *clean out* • Matt. 13:30

Baptism of Jesus—Mark 1:9–11; Luke 3:21–23

13 Then Jesus came from Galilee to John at
the Jordan to be baptized by him.
14 And John *tried to* prevent Him, saying, "I
have need to be baptized by You, and are
You coming to me?"
15 But Jesus answered and said to him,
"Permit *it to be so* now, for thus it is fitting
for us to fulfill all righteousness." Then he
allowed Him.
16 Then Jesus, when He had been baptized,
came up immediately from the water; and
behold, the heavens were opened to Him, and
He saw the [R]Spirit of God descending like a
dove and alighting upon Him. Is. 11:2; 42:1 ★
17 [R]And suddenly a voice *came* from
heaven, saying, [R]"This is My beloved Son, in
whom I am well pleased." John 12:28 • Ps. 2:7

CHAPTER 4

First Temptation—Mark 1:12, 13; Luke 4:1–4

THEN Jesus was led up by the Spirit into
the wilderness to be tempted by the devil.
2 And when He had fasted forty days and
forty nights, afterward He was hungry.

3:11 M omits *and fire*

3:17 God the Father of Christ—Every new Christian eventually wonders in what sense God may be called the Father of Christ and Christ the Son of God. The answer to this question is not a simple one. First, one must recognize that the title *Son of God* does not speak of physical nature, for God is spirit (Page 1241—John 4:24), and Christ was the Son of God before He assumed a human body in Bethlehem (Page 1239—John 3:16; Page 1381—Gal. 4:4). Passages which use terms implying physical origin must be taken in a figurative sense (Page 1450—Heb. 1:5).

Second, the title expresses a unique relationship. Christ distinguished His sonship from that of His disciples (Page 1265—John 20:17). He is begotten of God in a sense that no one else is (Page 1236—John 1:14; 3:16). Some call it "eternal generation," signifying the timelessness of this "God from God" relationship.

(continued on next page)

3 Now when the tempter came to Him, he
said, "If You are the Son of God, command
that these stones become bread."
4 But He answered and said, "It is written,
[R]*'Man shall not live by bread alone, but by
every word that proceeds from the mouth of
God.'*" Deut. 8:3

Second Temptation—Luke 4:9-12

5 Then the devil took Him up [R]into the
holy city, set Him on the pinnacle of the
temple, Neh. 11:1, 18
6 and said to Him, "If You are the Son of
God, throw Yourself down. For it is written:

[R]*'He shall give His angels charge
concerning you,'* Ps. 91:11, 12★

and,

*'In their hands they shall bear you up,
Lest you dash your foot against a
stone.'*"

7 Jesus said to him, "It is written again,
'You shall not tempt the LORD your God.'"

Third Temptation—Mark 1:13; Luke 4:5–8, 13

8 Again, the devil took Him up on an
exceedingly high mountain, and [R]showed
Him all the kingdoms of the world and their
glory. [1 John 2:15–17]
9 And he said to Him, "All these things I
will give You if You will fall down and
worship me."
10 Then Jesus said to him, *"Away with
you, Satan! For it is written, [R]*'You shall
worship the LORD your God, and Him only
you shall serve.'*" Deut. 6:13; 10:20
11 Then the devil left Him, and behold,
angels came and ministered to Him.

*Jesus Begins His Ministry
Mark 1:14, 15; Luke 4:14, 31*

12 Now when Jesus heard that John had
been put in prison, He departed to Galilee.
13 And leaving Nazareth, He came and
dwelt in Capernaum, which is by the sea, in
the regions of Zebulun and Naphtali,
14 that it might be fulfilled which was spoken by Isaiah the prophet, saying:

15 *"The [R]land of Zebulun and the land of
Naphtali,
The way of the sea, beyond the Jordan,
Galilee of the Gentiles:* Is. 9:1, 2★
16 [R]*The people who sat in darkness saw a
great light,
And upon those who sat in the region
and shadow of death
Light has dawned."* Luke 2:32

17 [R]From that time Jesus began to preach
and to say, "Repent, for the kingdom of
heaven is [T]at hand." Mark 1:14, 15 • *has drawn near*

Jesus Calls His First Disciples—Mark 1:16-20

18 Now Jesus, walking by the Sea of Galilee, saw two brothers, Simon [R]called Peter,
and Andrew his brother, casting a net into
the sea; for they were fishermen. John 1:40–42
19 And He said to them, "Follow Me, and [R]I
will make you fishers of men." Luke 5:10
20 [R]Then they immediately left *their* nets
and followed Him. Mark 10:28
21 [R]And going on from there, He saw two
other brothers, James *the son* of Zebedee,
and John his brother, in the boat with Zebedee their father, mending their nets. And He
called them, Mark 1:19
22 and immediately they left the boat and
their father, and followed Him.

*Jesus Ministers in Galilee
Mark 1:39; Luke 4:44*

23 Now Jesus went about all Galilee,
[R]teaching in their synagogues, preaching [R]the
gospel of the kingdom, [R]and healing all kinds
of sickness and all kinds of disease among the
people. Ps. 22:22★ • [Matt. 24:14] • Mark 1:34
24 Then [T]His fame went throughout all
Syria; and they [R]brought to Him all sick
people who were afflicted with various diseases and torments, and those who were
demon-possessed, epileptics, and paralytics;
and He healed them. Lit. *the report of Him* • Luke 4:40
25 And great multitudes followed Him—
from Galilee, and *from* [T]Decapolis, Jerusalem,
Judea, and beyond the Jordan. Lit. *Ten Cities*

4:10 M *Get behind Me*

(continued from previous page)
Third, the title describes a relationship of equality. The Son of God is no less than God. When Jesus claimed to be "one" with the Father, He was speaking of a unity of "substance" with the Father and thus equality in all the attributes of deity (Page 1252—John 10:30). The Jews certainly understood this claim, for they took up stones to stone Him, protesting that "You . . . make Yourself God" (Page 1252—John 10:33).

Fourth, the title especially emphasizes Christ's role as the revealer of God. He alone possesses the knowledge of the Father (Page 1258—John 14:6-9; Page 1494—1 John 1:2) and He is the sole mediator of that knowledge (Page 1426—1 Tim. 2:5). Therefore no one can know the Father except through the Son (Page 1494—John 14:6). The narrowness of this way to God should be a sober incentive to take to all the world the message that the Son of God has come to impart to every person the life of the Father.

Now turn to Page 1332—Rom. 8:15: God the Father of Believers.

THE JORDAN RIVER

The Jordan River has such an important role in biblical history that many visitors to the Holy Land ask to be baptized in its waters near Jericho, where Jesus was baptized by John (Matt. 3:13; see photo).

This famous river begins as a small stream in the foothills of Mount Hermon near Caesarea Philippi (now called Banias), then passes through the Sea of Galilee, and finally ends in the Dead Sea in southern Palestine. Popularly, the name *Jordan* is thought to mean "Descender" or "The River That Rushes Down," which it does at the rate of 25 feet per mile along its twisting 100-mile journey. Its descent ranges from about 1,200 feet above sea level to about 1,286 feet below sea level. The place where it enters the Dead Sea is the lowest point on earth.

Through the centuries, the Jordan has served as a natural boundary between Palestine and other nations. In the period between the Old Testament and the New Testament, the Jordan River formed the main eastern boundary of the Persian and Greek province of Judea. The Decapolis, a federation of ten Greek cities, was formed on the eastern side of the Jordan in the Greek period.

The Old Testament speaks of the Jordan as the site of the land favored by Lot (Gen. 13:10, 11); the place where Israel would cross into the land of Canaan in Joshua's time (Deut. 3:20, 25, 27); and the scene of events in Elijah's and Elisha's lives (1 Kin. 17:2–5; 2 Kin. 2:13–15).

Because the Jordan is a short and rather shallow river, it was compared unfavorably by Naaman the leper to the two larger rivers in his homeland of Syria. When the prophet Elisha directed him to dip in the Jordan to be healed of his leprosy, he replied, "*Are* not the Abanah and the Pharpar, the rivers of Damascus, better than all the waters of Israel? Could I not wash in them and be clean?" (2 Kin. 5:12).

But his servants persuaded him to do as Elisha asked, and Naaman was healed.

Aerial view of the twisting Jordan River in which Jesus was baptized by John (Matt. 3:13).

CHAPTER 5

The Beatitudes—Luke 6:20–26

AND seeing the multitudes, [R]He went up
on a mountain, and when He was seated
His disciples came to Him. Mark 3:13
2 Then He opened His mouth and [R]taught
them, saying: [Matt. 7:29]

3 "Blessed[R] *are* the poor in spirit, Luke 6:20–23
For theirs is the kingdom of heaven.
4 [R]Blessed *are* those who mourn,
For they shall be comforted. Rev. 21:4
5 [R]Blessed *are* the meek, Ps. 37:11
For they shall inherit the earth.
6 Blessed *are* those who [R]hunger and
thirst for righteousness, Luke 1:53
[R]For they shall be filled. [Is. 55:1; 65:13]
7 Blessed *are* the merciful,
[R]For they shall obtain mercy. Ps. 41:1
8 [R]Blessed *are* the pure in heart, Ps. 15:2; 24:4
For [R]they shall see God. 1 Cor. 13:12
9 Blessed *are* the peacemakers,
For they shall be called sons of God.
10 [R]Blessed are those who are persecuted
for righteousness' sake, 1 Pet. 3:14
For theirs is the kingdom of heaven.

11 "Blessed are you when they revile and
persecute you, and say all kinds of [R]evil
against you falsely for My sake. 1 Pet. 4:14
12 [R]"Rejoice and be exceedingly glad, for
great *is* your reward in heaven, for [R]so they
persecuted the prophets who were before
you. 1 Pet. 4:13, 14 • Acts 7:52

The Similitudes

13 "You are the salt of the earth; [R]but if the
salt loses its flavor, how shall it be seasoned?
It is then good for nothing but to be thrown
out and trampled underfoot by men. Luke 14:34
14 [R]"You are the light of the world. A city
that is set on a hill cannot be hidden. [John 8:12]
15 "Nor do they light a lamp and put it
under a basket, but on a lampstand, and it
gives light to all *who are* in the house.
16 "Let your light so shine before men, that
they may see your good works and [R]glorify
your Father in heaven. [John 15:8]

Jesus Fulfills the Law

17 [R]"Do not think that I came to destroy
the Law or the Prophets. I did not come to
destroy but to fulfill. Rom. 10:4
18 "For assuredly, I say to you, [R]till heaven
and earth pass away, one jot or one [T]tittle
will by no means pass from the law till all is
fulfilled. Luke 16:17 • The smallest stroke in a Heb. letter
19 [R]"Whoever therefore breaks one of the
least of these commandments, and teaches
men so, shall be called least in the kingdom of
heaven; but whoever does and teaches *them*,
he shall be called great in the kingdom of
heaven. [James 2:10]

Murder

20 "For I say to you, that unless your righteousness exceeds [R]*the righteousness* of the
scribes and Pharisees, you will by no means
enter the kingdom of heaven. [Rom. 10:3]
21 "You have heard that it was said to those
of old, *'You shall not murder,'* and whoever
murders will be in danger of the judgment.
22 "But I say to you that whoever is angry
with his brother *without a cause shall be in
danger of the judgment. And whoever says to
his brother, 'Raca!' shall be in danger of the
council. But whoever says, 'You fool!' shall be
in danger of [T]hell fire. Gr. *Gehenna*
23 "Therefore [R]if you bring your gift to the
altar, and there remember that your brother
has something against you, Matt. 8:4
24 "leave your gift there before the altar,
and go your way. First be reconciled to your
brother, and then come and offer your gift.
25 [R]"Agree with your adversary quickly,
[R]while you are on the way with him, lest your
adversary deliver you to the judge, the judge
hand you over to the officer, and you be
thrown into prison. Luke 12:58, 59 • [Is. 55:6]
26 "Assuredly, I say to you, you will by no
means get out of there till you have paid the
last [T]penny. 50¢

Adultery

27 "You have heard that it was said *to
those of old, [R]*'You shall not commit adultery.'* Ex. 20:14; Deut. 5:18
28 "But I say to you that whoever [R]looks at
a woman to lust for her has already committed adultery with her in his heart. Prov. 6:25
29 "And if your right eye causes you to [T]sin,
[R]pluck it out and cast *it* from you; for it is
more profitable for you that one of your
members perish, than for your whole body to
be cast into hell. Lit. *stumble* or *offend* • [Col. 3:5]
30 "And if your right hand causes you to
[T]sin, cut it off and cast *it* from you; for it is
more profitable for you that one of your
members perish, than for your whole body to
be cast into hell. Lit. *stumble* or *offend*

Divorce

31 "Furthermore it has been said, [R]*'Whoever divorces his wife, let him give her a
certificate of divorce.'* Deut. 24:1
32 "But I say to you that [R]whoever divorces
his wife for any reason except sexual immorality causes her to commit adultery; and
whoever marries a woman who is divorced
commits adultery. [Luke 16:18]

5:22 NU omits *without a cause*
5:27 NU, M omit *to those of old*

Oaths

33 "Again you have heard that it was said
to those of old, 'You shall not swear falsely,
but shall perform your oaths to the Lord.'
34 "But I say to you, do not swear at all:
neither by heaven, for it is God's throne;
35 "nor by the earth, for it is His footstool;
nor by Jerusalem, for it is the city of [R]the
great King. Ps. 48:2
36 "Nor shall you swear by your head,
because you cannot make one hair white or
black.
37 [R]"But let [T]your 'Yes' be 'Yes,' and your
'No,' 'No.' For whatever is more than these is
from the evil one. [Col. 4:6] • Lit. *your word be yes yes*

Retaliation

38 "You have heard that it was said, *'An eye
for an eye and a tooth for a tooth.'*
39 "But I tell you not to resist an evil
person. [R]But whoever slaps you on your right
cheek, turn the other to him also. Is. 50:6
40 "If anyone wants to sue you and take
away your tunic, let him have *your* cloak
also.
41 "And whoever [R]compels you to go one
mile, go with him two. Matt. 27:32
42 "Give to him who asks you, and [R]from
him who wants to borrow from you do not
turn away. Luke 6:30–34

Love—Luke 6:27, 32

43 "You have heard that it was said, [R]'You
shall love your neighbor [R]and hate your
enemy.' cf. Lev. 19:18 • Deut. 23:3–6
44 *"But I say to you, love your enemies,
bless those who curse you, [R]do good to those
who hate you, and pray for those who spitefully use you and persecute you, [Rom. 12:20]
45 "that you may be sons of your Father in
heaven; for [R]He makes His sun rise on the
evil and on the good, and sends rain on the
just and on the unjust. Job 25:3
46 [R]"For if you love those who love you,
what reward have you? Do not even the tax
collectors do the same? Luke 6:32
47 "And if you greet your *brethren only,
what do you do more *than others?* Do not
even the *tax collectors do so?
48 "Therefore you shall be perfect, just [R]as
your Father in heaven is perfect. Eph. 5:1

CHAPTER 6

Charitable Deeds

"TAKE heed that you do not do your
charitable deeds before men, to be
seen by them. Otherwise you have no reward
from your Father in heaven.
2 "Therefore, [R]when you do a charitable
deed, do not sound a trumpet before you as
the hypocrites do in the synagogues and in
the streets, that they may have glory from
men. Assuredly, I say to you, they have their
reward. Rom. 12:8
3 "But when you do a charitable deed, do
not let your left hand know what your right
hand is doing,
4 "that your charitable deed may be in
secret; and your Father who sees in secret
[R]will Himself reward you openly. Luke 14:12–14

Prayer—Luke 11:2–4

5 "And when you pray, you shall not be
like the [T]hypocrites. For they love to pray
standing in the synagogues and on the corners of the streets, that they may be seen by
men. Assuredly, I say to you, they have their
reward. *pretenders*
6 "But you, when you pray, [R]go into your
room, and when you have shut your door,
pray to your Father who *is* in the secret
place; and your Father who sees in secret will
reward you openly. 2 Kin. 4:33
7 "But when you pray, [R]do not use vain
repetitions as the heathen *do*. [R]For they
think that they will be heard for their many
words. Eccl. 5:2 • 1 Kin. 18:26
8 "Therefore do not be like them. For your
Father [R]knows the things you have need of
before you ask Him. [Rom. 8:26, 27]
9 "In this manner, therefore, pray:

[R]Our Father in heaven, [Matt. 5:9, 16]
Hallowed be Your [R]name. Mal. 1:11
10 Your kingdom come.
[R]Your will be done Matt. 26:42
On earth [R]as *it is* in heaven. Ps. 103:20
11 Give us this day our daily bread.
12 And [R]forgive us our debts,
As we forgive our debtors. [Matt. 18:21, 22]
13 And do not lead us into temptation,
But deliver us from the evil one.
*For Yours is the kingdom and the
power and the glory forever. Amen.

14 "For if you forgive men their trespasses,
your heavenly Father will also forgive you.
15 "But [R]if you do not forgive men their
trespasses, neither will your Father forgive
your trespasses. Matt. 18:35

Fasting

16 "Moreover, [R]when you fast, do not be
like the hypocrites, with a sad countenance.
For they disfigure their faces that they may
appear to men to be fasting. Assuredly, I say
to you, they have their reward. Is. 58:3–7

5:44 NU *But I say to you, love your enemies and pray for those who persecute you*
5:47 M *friends* **5:47** NU *Gentiles*
6:13 NU omits rest of v. 13

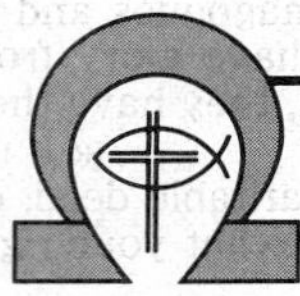

THE LORD'S PRAYER

The Lord's Prayer, or Model Prayer, is cherished by all Christians because of its simplicity, beautiful imagery, and instructive value. In contrast to the prayers of the heathen, Jesus emphasized that we should pray with faith and simplicity (Matt. 6:7, 8). Jesus drew great strength from His heavenly Father through prayer (see illustration), and it was only natural that He should teach His followers about the significance and meaning of prayer.

Matthew's account of the Lord's Prayer (6:9–13) comes from a portion of Jesus' Sermon on the Mount that warned against hypocrisy in prayer. Luke's version of the prayer consists of Jesus' response to a request from the disciples to "teach us to pray" (11:1). Consequently, the popular prayer might more accurately be called the "Disciple's Prayer," since it cannot be prayed in a meaningful way except by those who are disciples of Jesus.

The invocation of the prayer, "Our Father in heaven, hallowed be Your name" (Matt. 6:9), indicates the spirit of adoration and reverence in which the heavenly Father should be approached by His children.

"Your kingdom come. Your will be done on earth as *it is* in heaven" (6:10) expresses the longing for a society on earth where God's will is as perfectly done as it is in heaven. In our prayers, we should indicate our submission to the dominion and authority of God in our lives.

"Give us this day our daily bread" (6:11) addresses a loving Father who is concerned for our physical welfare, and it expresses our dependence on Him for our physical needs. "And forgive us our debts, as we forgive our debtors" (6:12) is a petition for pardon as we approach God in a spirit of forgiveness toward others. "And do not lead us into temptation, but deliver us from the evil one" (6:13) is a request for continual protection from the snares of Satan and all evil forces.

The prayer's closing doxology, "For Yours is the kingdom and the power and the glory forever" (6:13) appropriately attributes all power and glory to God for all eternity.

Jesus drew great strength from His heavenly Father through prayer.

17 "But you, when you fast, [R]anoint your head and wash your face, Ruth 3:3

18 "so that you do not appear to men to be fasting, but to your Father who *is* in the secret *place*; and your Father who sees in secret will reward you *openly.

Wealth—Luke 11:34–36; 12:22–34

19 [R]"Do not lay up for yourselves treasures on earth, where moth and rust destroy and where thieves break in and steal; Prov. 23:4

20 "but lay up for yourselves treasures in heaven, where neither moth nor rust destroys and where thieves do not break in and steal.

21 "For where your treasure is, there your heart will be also.

22 [R]"The lamp of the body is the eye. If therefore your eye is [T]good, your whole body will be full of light. Luke 11:34, 35 • Clear or healthy

23 "But if your eye is [T]bad, your whole body will be full of darkness. If therefore the light that is in you is darkness, how great *is* that darkness! Evil or unhealthy

24 [R]"No one can serve two masters; for either he will hate the one and love the other, or else he will be loyal to the one and despise the other. [R]You cannot serve God and [T]mammon. Luke 16:9, 11, 13 • [Gal. 1:10] • Lit., in Aram., *riches*

25 "Therefore I say to you, [R]do not worry about your life, what you will eat or what you will drink; nor about your body, what you will put on. Is not life more than food and the body more than clothing? Luke 12:22

26 [R]"Look at the birds of the air, for they neither sow nor reap nor gather into barns; yet your heavenly Father feeds them. Are you not of more value than they? Luke 12:24

27 "Which of you by worrying can add one [T]cubit to his [T]stature? 18 in. • *height*

28 "So why do you worry about clothing? Consider the lilies of the field, how they grow: they neither toil nor spin;

29 "and yet I say to you that even Solomon in all his glory was not [T]arrayed like one of these. *dressed*

30 "Now if God so clothes the grass of the field, which today is, and tomorrow is thrown into the oven, *will He* not much more *clothe* you, O you of little faith?

31 "Therefore do not worry, saying, 'What shall we eat?' or 'What shall we drink?' or 'What shall we wear?'

32 "For after all these things the Gentiles seek. For your heavenly Father knows that you need all these things.

33 "But [R]seek first the kingdom of God and His righteousness, and all these things shall be added to you. [1 Tim. 4:8]

34 "Therefore do not worry about tomorrow, for tomorrow will worry about its own things. Sufficient for the day *is* its own trouble.

CHAPTER 7

Judging—Luke 6:37–42

"JUDGE not, that you be not judged.

2 "For with what [T]judgment you judge, you will be judged; [R]and with the *same* measure you use, it will be measured back to you. Condemnation • Rom. 14:3

3 "And why do you look at the speck in your brother's eye, but do not consider the plank in your own eye?

4 "Or how can you say to your brother, 'Let me remove the speck out of your eye'; and look, a plank *is* in your own eye?

5 "Hypocrite! First remove the plank from your own eye, and then you will see clearly to remove the speck out of your brother's eye.

6 [R]"Do not give what is holy to the dogs; nor cast your pearls before swine, lest they trample them under their feet, and turn and tear you in pieces. Prov. 9:7, 8

"Ask, and It Will Be Given"—Luke 11:9–13

7 [R]"Ask, and it will be given to you; seek, and you will find; knock, and it will be opened to you. [Mark 11:24]

8 "For [R]everyone who asks receives, and he who seeks finds, and to him who knocks it will be opened. Prov. 8:17

9 [R]"Or what man is there among you who, if his son asks for bread, will give him a stone? Luke 11:11

10 "Or if he asks for a fish, will he give him a serpent?

11 "If you then, [R]being evil, know how to give good gifts to your children, how much more will your Father who is in heaven give good things to those who ask Him! Gen. 6:5

Golden Rule—Luke 6:31

12 "Therefore, [R]whatever you want men to do to you, do also to them, for [R]this is the Law and the Prophets. Luke 6:31 • Gal. 5:14

Two Ways of Life

13 [R]"Enter by the narrow gate; for wide *is* the gate and broad *is* the way that leads to destruction, and there are many who go in by it. Luke 13:24

14 *"Because narrow *is* the gate and [T]difficult *is* the way which leads to life, and there are few who find it. *confined*

False and True Teaching—Luke 6:43–45

15 [R]"Beware of false prophets, [R]who come to you in sheep's clothing, but inwardly they are ravenous wolves. Jer. 23:16 • Mic. 3:5

16 [R]"You will know them by their fruits. [R]Do men gather grapes from thornbushes or figs from thistles? Matt. 7:20; 12:33 • Luke 6:43

6:18 NU, M omit *openly* **7:14** NU, M *How narrow*

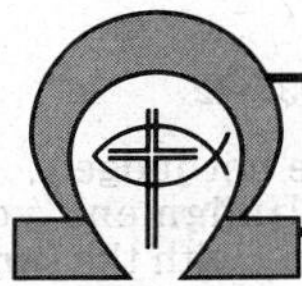

THE SERMON ON THE MOUNT

Jesus' long discourse known as the Sermon on the Mount (Matt. 5—7) is so named because He taught His disciples and the crowds that followed Him from a mountainside at the beginning of His public ministry (Matt. 5:1). The traditional site of the Sermon is marked today by a beautiful little church, the Chapel on the Mount of Beatitudes (see illustration), one of the major stopping points for tourists who visit the Holy Land.

The central theme of the Sermon is summarized in Matthew 5:48, "You shall be perfect, just as your Father in heaven is perfect." The word *perfect* does not refer to sinless or moral perfection. It indicates completeness, wholeness, maturity—being all that God wants a person to be. This goal, although we never attain it in this life, should continually challenge us to greater service for the Lord.

The ten major sections of the Sermon on the Mount are as follows:

1. The Beatitudes (5:3–12): The blessed rewards of living as citizens of Christ's kingdom.
2. The lessons of salt and light (5:13–16): The effects of Christian living on the world.
3. True righteousness (5:17–48): The deeper meaning of the law of God.
4. Practice without hypocrisy (6:1–18): The right motives for giving, praying, and fasting.
5. The Christian's concerns (6:19–34): Serving God with singleness of purpose and putting the concerns of His kingdom first are actions that free us from anxiety over lesser things.
6. Warning against judgment (7:1–6): The dangers of judging others harshly and carelessly.
7. Invitation to prayer (7:7–12): The blessings and privileges of prayer.
8. The two ways (7:13, 14): Choose the narrow way, not the broad way that leads to destruction.
9. A tree and its fruit (7:15–20): "By their fruits you will know them."
10. The importance of deeds (7:21–29): To obey God is far better than talking about your obedience.

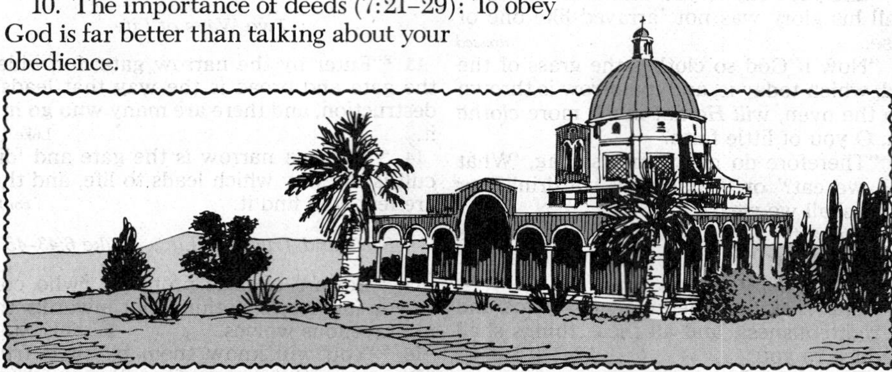

This chapel stands on the Mount of Beatitudes, from which Jesus delivered His Sermon on the Mount, according to many scholars.

17 "Even so, [R]every good tree bears good
fruit, but a bad tree bears bad fruit. Matt. 12:33
18 "A good tree cannot bear bad fruit, nor
can a bad tree bear good fruit.
19 "Every tree that does not bear good fruit
is cut down and thrown into the fire.
20 "Therefore by their fruits you will know
them.

True Way into the Kingdom—Luke 6:46

21 "Not everyone who says to Me, [R]'Lord,
Lord,' shall enter the kingdom of heaven, but
he who [R]does the will of My Father in
heaven. Luke 6:46 • Rom. 2:13
22 "Many will say to Me in that day, 'Lord,
Lord, have we [R]not prophesied in Your name,
cast out demons in Your name, and done
many wonders in Your name?' Num. 24:4
23 "And [R]then I will declare to them, 'I
never knew you; [R]depart from Me, you who
practice lawlessness!' [2 Tim. 2:19] • Ps. 5:5; 6:8 ☆

Parable of the Two Builders—Luke 6:47–49

24 "Therefore whoever hears these sayings
of Mine, and does them, I will liken him to a
wise man who built his house on the rock:
25 "and the rain descended, the floods
came, and the winds blew and beat on that
house; and it did not fall, for it was founded
on the rock.
26 "Now everyone who hears these sayings
of Mine, and does not do them, will be like a
foolish man who built his house on the sand:
27 "and the rain descended, the floods
came, and the winds blew and beat on that
house; and it fell. And great was its fall."

Response to the Sermon

28 And so it was, when Jesus had ended
these sayings, that [R]the people were astonished at His teaching, Matt. 13:54
29 [R]for He taught them as one having authority, and not as the scribes. [John 7:46]

CHAPTER 8

The Leper Is Cleansed
Mark 1:40–44; Luke 5:12–14

WHEN He had come down from the
mountain, great multitudes followed
Him.
2 [R]And behold, a leper came and [R]wor-
shiped Him, saying, "Lord, if You are willing,
You can make me clean." Mark 1:40–45 • John 9:38
3 Then Jesus put out *His* hand and
touched him, saying, "I am willing; be
cleansed." And immediately his leprosy [R]was
cleansed. Luke 4:27
4 And Jesus said to him, "See that you tell
no one; but go your way, show yourself to
the priest, and offer the gift that Moses
commanded, as a testimony to them."

The Centurion's Servant Is Healed
Luke 7:1–10

5 [R]Now when Jesus had entered Capernaum, a [R]centurion came to Him, pleading
with Him, Luke 7:1–3 • Matt. 27:54
6 saying, "Lord, my servant is lying at
home paralyzed, dreadfully tormented."
7 And Jesus said to him, "I will come and
heal him."
8 The centurion answered and said, "Lord,
I am not worthy that You should come under
my roof. But only [R]speak a word, and my
servant will be healed. Ps. 107:20
9 "For I also am a man under authority,
having soldiers under me. And I say to this
one, 'Go,' and he goes; and to another,
'Come,' and he comes; and to my servant, 'Do
this,' and he does *it*."
10 When Jesus heard *it*, He marveled, and
said to those who followed, "Assuredly, I say
to you, I have not found such great faith, not
even in Israel!
11 "And I say to you that [R]many will come
from east and west, and sit down with Abraham, Isaac, and Jacob in the kingdom of
heaven. Is. 49:12; 59:19; Mal. 1:11; Eph. 3:6 ☆
12 "But [R]the sons of the kingdom will be
cast out into outer darkness. There will be
weeping and gnashing of teeth." [Matt. 21:43]
13 Then Jesus said to the centurion, "Go
your way; and as you have believed, so let it
be done for you." And his servant was healed
that same hour.

Peter's Mother-in-Law Is Healed
Mark 1:29–34; Luke 4:38–41

14 [R]Now when Jesus had come into Peter's
house, He saw [R]his wife's mother lying sick
with a fever. Mark 1:29–31 • 1 Cor. 9:5
15 And He touched her hand, and the fever
left her. Then she arose and served *them.
16 [R]When evening had come, they brought
to Him many who were demon-possessed.
And He cast out the spirits with a word, and
healed all who were sick, Luke 4:40, 41
17 that it might be fulfilled which was spoken by Isaiah the prophet, saying:

[R]*"He Himself took our infirmities*
And bore our sicknesses." 1 Pet. 2:24 ★

Demands of Discipleship—Luke 9:57–62

18 Now when Jesus saw great multitudes
about Him, He gave a command to depart to
the other side.
19 [R]Then a certain scribe came and said to
Him, "Teacher, I will follow You wherever
You go." Luke 9:57, 58
20 And Jesus said to him, "Foxes have holes
and birds of the air *have* nests, but the Son of
Man has nowhere to lay *His* head."

8:15 NU, M *Him*

21 [R]Then another of His disciples said to
Him, "Lord, [R]let me first go and bury my
father." Luke 9:59, 60 • 1 Kin. 19:20
22 But Jesus said to him, "Follow Me, and
let the dead bury their own dead."

The Sea Is Stilled
Mark 4:35–41; Luke 8:22–25

23 Now when He got into a boat, His disciples followed Him.
24 [R]And suddenly a great tempest arose on
the sea, so that the boat was covered with the
waves. But He was asleep. Mark 4:37
25 Then His disciples came to *Him* and
awoke Him, saying, "Lord, save us! We are
perishing!"
26 But He said to them, "Why are you
fearful, O you of little faith?" Then [R]He arose
and rebuked the winds and the sea. And there
was a great calm. Ps. 65:7; 89:9; 107:29
27 And the men marveled, saying, [T]"Who
can this be, that even the winds and the sea
obey Him?" Lit. *What sort of man is this*

Demons Are Cast into Swine
Mark 5:1–17; Luke 8:26–37

28 [R]When He had come to the other side, to
the country of the *Gergesenes, there met
Him two demon-possessed *men*, coming out
of the tombs, exceedingly fierce, so that no
one could pass that way. Mark 5:1–4
29 And suddenly they cried out, saying,
"What have we to do with You, Jesus, You
Son of God? Have You come here to torment
us before the time?"
30 Now a good way off from them there was
a herd of many swine feeding.
31 So the demons begged Him, saying, "If
You cast us out, *permit us to go away into
the herd of swine."
32 And He said to them, "Go." So when
they had come out, they went into the herd
of swine. And suddenly the whole herd of
swine ran violently down the steep place into
the sea, and perished in the water.
33 Then those who kept *them* fled; and they
went away into the city and told everything,
including what *had happened* to the demon-
possessed *men*.
34 And behold, the whole city came out to
meet Jesus. And when they saw Him, they
begged *Him* to depart from their region.

CHAPTER 9

The Paralytic Is Forgiven
Mark 2:1–12; Luke 5:17–26

SO He got into a boat, crossed over, [R]and
came to His own city. Matt. 4:13; 11:23
2 And behold, they brought to Him a paralytic lying on a bed. And Jesus, seeing their
faith, said to the paralytic, "Son, be of good
cheer; your sins are forgiven you."
3 And at once some of the scribes said
within themselves, "This *Man* blasphemes!"
4 But Jesus, knowing their thoughts, said,
"Why do you think evil in your hearts?
5 "For which is easier, to say, '*Your* sins
are forgiven you,' or to say, 'Arise and walk'?
6 "But that you may know that the Son of
Man has power on earth to forgive sins"—
then He said to the paralytic, "Arise, take up
your bed, and go to your house."
7 And he arose and departed to his house.
8 Now when the multitudes saw *it*, they
[R]marveled* and glorified God, who had given
such power to men. John 7:15

Matthew Is Called—Mark 2:14; Luke 5:27, 28

9 [R]Then as Jesus passed on from there, He
saw a man named Matthew sitting at the tax
office. And He said to him, "Follow Me." And
he arose and followed Him. Luke 5:27

The Disciples Eat with Sinners
Mark 2:15–17; Luke 5:29–32

10 [R]And so it was, as Jesus sat at the table in
the house, *that* behold, many tax collectors
and sinners came and sat down with Him and
His disciples. Mark 2:15
11 And when the Pharisees saw *it*, they said
to His disciples, "Why does your Teacher eat
with tax collectors and [R]sinners?" [Gal. 2:15]
12 But when Jesus heard *that*, He said to
them, "Those who are well have no need of a
physician, but those who are sick.
13 "But go and learn what *this* means: [R]'*I
desire mercy and not sacrifice.*' For I did not
come to call the righteous, [R]but sinners, *to
repentance." Hos. 6:6 • 1 Tim. 1:15

The Disciples Do Not Fast
Mark 2:18–22; Luke 5:33–39

14 Then the disciples of John came to Him,
saying, "Why do we and the Pharisees fast
*often, but Your disciples do not fast?"
15 And Jesus said to them, "Can the friends
of the bridegroom mourn as long as the
bridegroom is with them? But the days will
come when the bridegroom will be taken
away from them, and then they will fast.
16 "No one puts a piece of unshrunk cloth
on an old garment; for [T]the patch pulls away
from the garment, and the tear is made
worse. Lit. *that which is put on*
17 "Nor do *people* put new wine into old
wineskins, or else the wineskins [T]break, the
wine is spilled, and the wineskins are ruined.
But they put new wine into new wineskins,
and both are preserved." *burst*

8:28 NU *Gadarenes* **8:31** NU *send us into*
9:8 NU *were afraid* **9:13** NU omits *to repentance*
9:14 NU brackets *often*

Life Is Restored—Mark 5:21–43; Luke 8:40–56

18 While He spoke these things to them,
behold, a ruler came and worshiped Him,
saying, "My daughter has just died, but come
and lay Your hand on her and she will live."
19 So Jesus arose and followed him, and so
did His [R]disciples. Matt. 10:2–4
20 And suddenly, a woman who had a flow
of blood for twelve years came from behind
and touched the hem of His garment;
21 for she said to herself, "If only I may
touch His garment, I shall be made well."
22 But Jesus turned around, and when He
saw her He said, "Be of good cheer, daughter;
your faith has made you well." And the
woman was made well from that hour.
23 [R]And when Jesus came into the ruler's
house, and saw [R]the flute players and the
noisy crowd wailing, Mark 5:38 • 2 Chr. 35:25
24 He said to them, [R]"Make room, for the
girl is not dead, but sleeping." And they
laughed Him to scorn. Acts 20:10
25 But when the crowd was put outside, He
went in and [R]took her by the hand, and the
girl arose. Mark 1:31
26 And the [R]report of this went out into all
that land. Matt. 4:24

Sight Is Restored

27 When Jesus departed from there, two
blind men followed Him, crying out and
saying, "Son of David, have mercy on us!"
28 And when He had come into the house,
the blind men came to Him. And Jesus said to
them, "Do you believe that I am able to do
this?" They said to Him, "Yes, Lord."
29 Then He touched their eyes, saying,
"According to your faith let it be to you."
30 And their eyes were opened. And Jesus
sternly warned them, saying, [R]"See *that* no
one knows *it*." Matt. 8:4
31 [R]But when they had departed, they
[T]spread the news about Him in all that [T]coun-
try. Mark 7:36 • Lit. *made Him known* • Lit. *land*

Speech Is Restored

32 As they went out, behold, they brought
to Him a man, mute and demon-possessed.
33 And when the demon was cast out, the
mute spoke. And the multitudes marveled,
saying, "It was never seen like this in Israel!"
34 But the Pharisees said, [R]"He casts out
demons by the ruler of the demons." Luke 11:15

The Need for Delegation of Power

35 And Jesus went about all the cities and
villages, [R]teaching in their synagogues,
preaching the gospel of the kingdom, and
healing every sickness and every disease
*among the people. Matt. 4:23
36 [R]But when He saw the multitudes, He
was moved with compassion for them, because they were *weary and scattered, like
sheep having no shepherd. Mark 6:34
37 Then He said to His disciples, [R]"The
harvest truly *is* plentiful, but the laborers *are*
few. Luke 10:2
38 "Therefore pray the Lord of the harvest
to send out laborers into His harvest."

CHAPTER 10

The Twelve Apostles Are Sent
Mark 6:7; Luke 9:1

AND when He had called His twelve disciples to *Him*, He gave them power *over*
unclean spirits, to cast them out, and to heal
all kinds of sickness and all kinds of disease.
2 Now the names of the twelve apostles
are these: first, Simon, [R]who is called Peter,
and Andrew his brother; James the *son* of
Zebedee, and John his brother; John 1:42
3 Philip and Bartholomew; Thomas and
Matthew the tax collector; James the *son* of
Alphaeus, and *Lebbaeus, whose surname
was Thaddaeus;
4 Simon the *Cananite, and Judas [R]Is-
cariot, who also betrayed Him. John 13:2, 26

The Twelve Apostles Are Instructed
Mark 6:8–13; Luke 9:2–6, 12:2–10

5 These twelve Jesus sent out and commanded them, saying: [R]"Do not go into the
way of the Gentiles, and do not enter a city of
[R]the Samaritans. Matt. 4:15 • John 4:9
6 [R]"But go rather to the [R]lost sheep of the
house of Israel. Matt. 15:24 • Jer. 50:6
7 [R]"And as you go, preach, saying, 'The
kingdom of heaven is at hand.' Luke 9:2
8 "Heal the sick, *cleanse the lepers, *raise
the dead, cast out demons. [R]Freely you have
received, freely give. [Acts 8:18]
9 [R]"Provide neither gold nor silver nor
[R]copper in your moneybelts, 1 Sam. 9:7 • Mark 6:8
10 "nor bag for *your* journey, nor two tunics, nor sandals, nor staffs; [R]for a worker is
worthy of his food. 1 Tim. 5:18
11 [R]"Now whatever city or town you enter,
inquire who in it is worthy, and stay there till
you go out. Luke 10:8
12 "And when you go into a household,
greet it.
13 [R]"If the household is worthy, let your
peace come upon it. [R]But if it is not worthy,
let your peace return to you. Luke 10:5 • Ps. 35:13
14 [R]"And whoever will not receive you nor
hear your words, when you depart from that
house or city, [R]shake off the dust from your
feet. Mark 6:11 • Acts 13:51

9:35 NU omits *among the people* **9:36** NU, M *harassed*
10:3 NU omits *Lebbaeus, whose surname was*
10:4 NU *Cananaean*
10:8 NU *raise the dead, cleanse the lepers*
10:8 M omits *raise the dead*

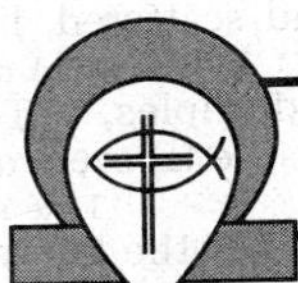

JESUS AND THE TWELVE

Jesus chose twelve apostles to serve with Him during His ministry and to provide leadership for the church after His ascension. Twelve probably were selected because this number corresponds to the twelve tribes of Old Testament Israel.

Chosen by Jesus after He prayed all night (Luke 6:12–16), the Twelve included two sets of fishermen brothers, a tax collector, and a traitor. Among the Twelve, Peter, James, and John were particularly close to the Master.

The terms *disciple* and *apostle* are often used interchangeably in referring to these men. But a disciple is a learner or follower, while an apostle generally refers to a person who is sent with a special message or commission (John 13:16). The Twelve were definitely apostles; when Jesus called them, He had a specific mission in mind for them—to carry on His work after He ended His earthly ministry.

The original twelve were chosen from among those people whom Jesus knew personally (Acts 1:21, 22). They had an inadequate understanding of Jesus' mission and the necessity for His death (Matt. 15:16). Jesus was patient with the immature apostles, although He occasionally rebuked them (Luke 9:55). After they were empowered by the Holy Spirit at Pentecost, the apostles were filled with new boldness and understanding. They became powerful witnesses in Jerusalem and surrounding regions, in spite of harsh persecution. Many were martyred for their faith.

As listed in Matthew 10:1–4 (also see Mark 3:13–19; Luke 6:12–16; Acts 1:13), the Twelve were: (1) Simon Peter (Cephas), leader of the apostles; (2) Andrew, brother of Simon; (3) James, son of Zebedee and brother of John; (4) John, the beloved apostle; (5) Philip, from Bethsaida; (6) Bartholomew (probably Nathanael), from Cana of Galilee; (7) Matthew (Levi), tax collector; (8) Thomas (Didymus, which means "Twin"), from Galilee; (9) Simon the Canaanite, probably Simon the Zealot, from Galilee; (10) James, the son of Alphaeus; (11) Lebbaeus, or Thaddaeus; and (12) Judas Iscariot, who betrayed Jesus.

Matthias was chosen by the apostles to replace Judas after the ascension of Jesus (Acts 1:26).

Jesus calls the disciples.

15 "Assuredly, I say to you, it will be more tolerable for the land of Sodom and Gomorrah in the day of judgment than for that city!

16 "Behold, I send you out as sheep in the midst of wolves. Therefore be wise as serpents and [R]harmless as doves. [Phil. 2:14–16]

17 "But beware of men, for [R]they will deliver you up to councils and [R]scourge you in their synagogues. Mark 13:9 • Acts 5:40; 22:19; 26:11

18 "And [R]you will be brought before governors and kings for My sake, as a testimony to them and to the Gentiles. 2 Tim. 4:16

19 [R]"But when they deliver you up, do not worry about how or what you should speak. For [R]it will be given to you in that hour what you should speak; Luke 12:11, 12; 21:14, 15 • Ex. 4:12

20 "for it is not you who speak, but the Spirit of your Father who speaks in you.

21 [R]"Now brother will deliver up brother to death, and a father *his* child; and children will rise up against parents and cause them to be put to death. Mic. 7:6

22 "And [R]you will be hated by all for My name's sake. [R]But he who endures to the end will be saved. Luke 21:17 • Mark 13:13

23 "But when they persecute you in this city, flee to another. For assuredly, I say to you, you will not have gone through the cities of Israel before the Son of Man comes.

24 [R]"A disciple is not above *his* teacher, nor a servant above his master. John 15:20

25 "It is enough for a disciple that he be like his teacher, and a servant like his master. If [R]they have called the master of the house *Beelzebub, how much more *will they call* those of his household! John 8:48, 52

26 "Therefore do not fear them. [R]For there is nothing covered that will not be revealed, and hidden that will not be known. Mark 4:22

27 "Whatever I tell you in the dark, [R]speak in the light; and what you hear in the ear, preach on the housetops. Acts 5:20

28 [R]"And do not fear those who kill the body but cannot kill the soul. But rather [R]fear Him who is able to destroy both soul and body in [T]hell. Luke 12:4 • Luke 12:5 • Gr. *Gehenna*

29 "Are not two sparrows sold for a copper coin? And not one of them falls to the ground apart from your Father's will.

30 [R]"But the very hairs of your head are all numbered. Luke 21:18

31 "Do not fear therefore; you are of more value than many sparrows.

32 [R]"Therefore whoever confesses Me before men, [R]him I will also confess before My Father who is in heaven. Luke 12:8 • [Rev. 3:5]

33 [R]"But whoever denies Me before men, him I will also deny before My Father who is in heaven. 2 Tim. 2:12

34 [R]"Do not think that I came to bring peace on earth. I did not come to bring peace but a sword. [Luke 12:49]

35 "For I have come to [T]'*set a man* [R]*against his father, a daughter against her mother, and a daughter-in-law against her mother-in-law.*' *alienate a man from* • Mic. 7:6☆

36 "And [R]'*a man's foes will be those of his own household.*' Ps. 41:9; John 13:18☆

37 [R]"He who loves father or mother more than Me is not worthy of Me. And he who loves son or daughter more than Me is not worthy of Me. Luke 14:26

38 "And he who does not take his cross and follow after Me is not worthy of Me.

39 "He who finds his life will lose it, and he who loses his life for My sake will find it.

40 [R]"He who receives you receives Me, and he who receives Me receives Him who sent Me. Luke 9:48

41 [R]"He who receives a prophet in the name of a prophet shall receive a prophet's reward. And he who receives a righteous man in the name of a righteous man shall receive a righteous man's reward. 1 Kin. 17:10

42 [R]"And whoever gives one of these little ones only a cup of cold *water* in the name of a disciple, assuredly, I say to you, he shall by no means lose his reward." Mark 9:41

CHAPTER 11

NOW it came to pass, when Jesus finished commanding His twelve disciples, that He departed from there to [R]teach and to preach in their cities. Luke 23:5

Rejection of John the Baptist—Luke 7:19–30

2 [R]And when John had heard [R]in prison about the works of Christ, he *sent two of his disciples Luke 7:18–35 • Matt. 4:12; 14:3

3 and said to Him, "Are You [R]the Coming One, or do we look for another?" John 6:14

4 Jesus answered and said to them, "Go and tell John the [R]things which you hear and see: Is. 29:18, 19; 35:4–6★

5 "*The* blind receive their sight and *the* lame walk; *the* lepers are cleansed and *the* deaf hear; *the* dead are raised up and *the* poor have the gospel preached to them.

6 "And blessed is he who is not [R]offended because of Me." [Rom. 9:32]

7 [R]As they departed, Jesus began to say to the multitudes concerning John: "What did you go out into the wilderness to see? [R]A reed shaken by the wind? Luke 7:24 • [Eph. 4:14]

8 "But what did you go out to see? A man clothed in soft garments? Indeed, those who wear soft *clothing* are in kings' houses.

9 "But what did you go out to see? A prophet? Yes, I say to you, [R]and more than a prophet. Luke 1:76; 20:6

10:25 NU, M *Beelzebul*, A Philistine deity, 2 Kin. 1:2, 3
11:2 NU *sent by his*

10 "For this is *he* of whom it is written:

R'*Behold, I send My messenger before*
Your face,
Who will prepare Your way before
You.' Mal. 3:1★

11 "Assuredly, I say to you, among those
born of women there has not risen one
greater than John the Baptist; but he who is
least in the kingdom of heaven is greater
than he.
12 "And from the days of John the Baptist
until now the kingdom of heaven suffers
violence, and the violent take it by force.
13 R"For all the prophets and the law prophesied until John. Mal. 4:4–6
14 "And if you are willing to receive *it*, he is
RElijah who is to come. Luke 1:17
15 "He who has ears to hear, let him hear!

Rejection by Jesus' Generation
Luke 7:31–35

16 R"But to what shall I liken this generation? It is like children sitting in the
marketplaces and calling to their companions, Luke 7:31
17 "and saying:

'We played the flute for you,
And you did not dance;
We mourned to you,
And you did not Tlament.' *beat your breast*

18 "For John came neither eating nor drinking, and they say, 'He has a demon.'
19 "The Son of Man came eating and drinking, and they say, 'Look, a gluttonous man
and a Twinebibber, Ra friend of tax collectors
and sinners!' RBut wisdom is justified by her
*children." *wine drinker* • Matt. 9:10 • Luke 7:35

Rejection of Chorazin, Bethsaida,
and Capernaum—Luke 10:12–15

20 Then He began to Tupbraid the cities in
which most of His mighty works had been
done, because they did not repent: *reproach*
21 "Woe to you, Chorazin! Woe to you,
Bethsaida! For if the mighty works which
were done in you had been done in Tyre and
Sidon, they would have repented long ago Rin
sackcloth and ashes. Jon. 3:6–8
22 "But I say to you, Rit will be more tolerable for Tyre and Sidon in the day of judgment than for you. Matt. 10:15; 11:24
23 "And you, Capernaum, Rwho* are exalted to heaven, will be brought down to
Hades; for if the mighty works which were
done in you had been done in Sodom, it
would have remained until this day. Is. 14:13
24 "But I say to you Rthat it shall be more
tolerable for the land of Sodom in the day of
judgment than for you." Matt. 10:15

Invitation to Come to Jesus

25 RAt that time Jesus answered and said, "I
thank You, Father, Lord of heaven and earth,
because RYou have hidden these things from
the wise and prudent Rand have revealed
them to babes. Luke 10:21, 22 • Ps. 8:2 • Matt. 16:17
26 "Even so, Father, for so it seemed good
in Your sight.
27 R"All things have been delivered to Me
by My Father, and no one knows the Son
except the Father. Nor does anyone know the
Father except the Son, and *he* to whom the
Son wills to reveal *Him*. Matt. 28:18
28 "Come to Me, all *you* who labor and are
heavy laden, and I will give you rest.
29 "Take My yoke upon you and learn from
Me, for I am Tgentle and lowly in heart, and
you will find rest for your souls. *meek*
30 R"For My yoke *is* easy and My burden is
light." [1 John 5:3]

CHAPTER 12

Controversy over Sabbath-Labor
Mark 2:23–28; Luke 6:1–5

AT that time RJesus went through the
grainfields on the Sabbath. And His
disciples were hungry, and began to Rpluck
heads of grain and to eat. Luke 6:1–5 • Deut. 23:25
2 But when the Pharisees saw *it*, they said
to Him, "Look, Your disciples are doing what
is not lawful to do on the Sabbath!"
3 Then He said to them, "Have you not
read Rwhat David did when he was hungry,
he and those who were with him: 1 Sam. 21:6
4 "how he entered the house of God and
ate Rthe showbread which was not lawful for
him to eat, nor for those who were with him,
Rbut only for the priests? Lev. 24:5 • Ex. 29:32
5 "Or have you not read in the law that on
the Sabbath the priests in the temple profane
the Sabbath, and are blameless?
6 "But I say to you that in this place there
is R*One* greater than the temple. [Is. 66:1, 2]
7 "But if you had known what *this* means,
R'*I desire mercy and not sacrifice,*' you would
not have condemned the guiltless. [Hos. 6:6]
8 "For the Son of Man is Lord *even of the
Sabbath."

Controversy over Sabbath-Healing
Mark 3:1–5; Luke 6:6–10

9 RNow when He had departed from there,
He went into their synagogue. Mark 3:1–6
10 And behold, there was a man who had a
withered hand. And they asked Him, saying,
R"Is it lawful to heal on the Sabbath?"—that
they might accuse Him. John 9:16

11:19 NU *works*
11:23 NU *will you be exalted to heaven? No, you will be*
12:8 NU, M omit *even*

11 Then He said to them, "What man is
there among you who has one sheep, and if it
falls into a pit on the Sabbath, will not lay
hold of it and lift *it* out?
12 "Of how much more value then is a man
than a sheep? Therefore it is lawful to do
good on the Sabbath."
13 Then He said to the man, "Stretch out
your hand." And he stretched *it* out, and it
was restored as whole as the other.

Pharisees Plan to Destroy Christ
Mark 3:6–12; Luke 6:11

14 Then [R]the Pharisees went out and took
counsel against Him, how they might destroy
Him. Mark 3:6
15 But when Jesus knew *it,* He withdrew
from there; [R]and great *multitudes followed
Him, and He healed them all. Matt. 19:2
16 And He [R]warned them not to make Him
known, Matt. 8:4; 9:30; 17:9
17 that it might be fulfilled which was spoken by Isaiah the prophet, saying:

18 *"Behold,*[R] *My Servant whom I have*
chosen,
My Beloved [R]*in whom My soul is well*
pleased;
I will put My Spirit upon Him,
And He will declare justice to the
Gentiles. Is. 42:1–4★ • Matt. 3:17; 17:5
19 *He will not quarrel nor cry out,*
Nor will anyone hear His voice in the
streets.
20 *A bruised reed He will not break,*
And smoking flax He will not quench,
Till He sends forth justice to victory.
21 *And in His name Gentiles will trust."*

Pharisees Blaspheme the Holy Spirit
Mark 3:22–27; Luke 11:17–23

22 [R]Then one was brought to Him who was
demon-possessed, blind and mute; and He
healed him, so that the *blind and mute man
both spoke and saw. Luke 11:14, 15
23 And all the multitudes were amazed and
said, "Could this be the Son of David?"
24 [R]But when the Pharisees heard *it* they
said, "This *fellow* does not cast out demons
except by *Beelzebub, the ruler of the demons." Matt. 9:34
25 But Jesus knew their thoughts, and said
to them: "Every kingdom divided against
itself is brought to desolation, and every city
or house divided against itself will not stand.
26 "And if Satan casts out Satan, he is
divided against himself. How then will his
kingdom stand?
27 "And if I cast out demons by Beelzebub,
by whom do your sons cast *them* out? Therefore they shall be your judges.
28 "But if I cast out demons by the Spirit of
God, [R]surely the kingdom of God has come
upon you. [Dan. 2:44; 7:14]
29 [R]"Or *else* how can one enter a strong
man's house and plunder his goods, unless he
first binds the strong man? And then he will
plunder his house. Is. 49:24
30 "He who is not with Me is against Me,
and he who does not gather with Me scatters
abroad.

Pharisees Commit the Unpardonable Sin
Mark 3:28, 29

31 "Therefore I say to you, [R]every sin and
blasphemy will be forgiven men, [R]but the
blasphemy *against* the Spirit will not be
forgiven men. Mark 3:28–30 • Acts 7:51
32 "Anyone who [R]speaks a word against the
Son of Man, [R]it will be forgiven him; but
whoever speaks against the Holy Spirit, it will
not be forgiven him, either in this age or in
the *age* to come. John 7:12, 52 • 1 Tim. 1:13
33 "Either make the tree good and its fruit
good, or else make the tree bad and its fruit
bad; for a tree is known by *its* fruit.
34 "Brood of vipers! How can you, being
evil, speak good things? For out of the abundance of the heart the mouth speaks.
35 "A good man out of the good treasure
*of his heart brings forth good things, and an
evil man out of the evil treasure brings forth
evil things.
36 "But I say to you that for every idle word
men may speak, they will give account of it
in the day of judgment.
37 "For by your words you will be justified,
and by your words you will be condemned."

Pharisees Demand a Sign
Luke 11:24–26, 29–32

38 [R]Then some of the scribes and Pharisees
answered, saying, "Teacher, we want to see a
sign from You." Mark 8:11
39 But He answered and said to them, "An
evil and [R]adulterous generation seeks after a
sign, and no sign will be given to it except the
sign of the prophet Jonah. Matt. 16:4
40 [R]"For as Jonah was three days and three
nights in the belly of the great fish, so will the
Son of Man be three days and three nights in
the heart of the earth. Jon. 1:17☆
41 [R]"The men of Nineveh will rise in the
judgment with this generation and [R]condemn
it, [R]because they repented at the preaching of
Jonah; and indeed a greater than Jonah *is*
here. Luke 11:32 • Jer. 3:11 • Jon. 3:5
42 "The queen of the South will rise up in
the judgment with this generation and con-

12:15 NU brackets *multitudes* **12:22** NU omits *blind and* **12:24** NU, M *Beelzebul,* A Philistine deity **12:35** NU, M omit *of his heart*

demn it, for she came from the ends of the
earth to hear the wisdom of Solomon; and
indeed a greater than Solomon *is* here.
43 [R]"When an unclean spirit goes out of a
man, [R]he goes through dry places, seeking
rest, and finds none. Luke 11:24–26 • [1 Pet. 5:8]
44 "Then he says, 'I will return to my house
from which I came.' And when he comes, he
finds it empty, swept, and put in order.
45 "Then he goes and takes with him seven
other spirits more wicked than himself, and
they enter and dwell there; and the last *state*
of that man is worse than the first. So shall it
also be with this wicked generation."

Jesus and the True Brethren—Mark 3:31–35

46 While He was still talking to the multitudes, behold, His mother and brothers stood
outside, seeking to speak with Him.
47 Then one said to Him, "Look, [R]Your
mother and Your brothers are standing outside, seeking to speak with You." Matt. 13:55, 56
48 But He answered and said to the one
who told Him, "Who is My mother and who
are My brothers?"
49 And He stretched out His hand toward
His disciples and said, "Here are My mother
and My [R]brothers! John 20:17
50 "For [R]whoever does the will of My Father in heaven is My brother and sister and
mother." John 15:14

CHAPTER 13

Parable of the Soils
Mark 4:1–20; Luke 8:4–15

ON the same day Jesus went out of the
house [R]and sat by the sea. Mark 4:1–12
2 [R]And great multitudes were gathered
together to Him, so that [R]He got into a boat
and sat; and the whole multitude stood on
the shore. Luke 8:4 • Luke 5:3
3 Then He spoke many things to them in
parables, saying: [R]"Behold, a sower went out
to sow. Luke 8:5
4 "And as he sowed, some *seed* fell by the
wayside; and the birds came and devoured
them.
5 "Some fell on stony places, where they
did not have much earth; and they immediately sprang up because they had no depth of
earth.
6 "But when the sun was up they were
scorched, and because they had no root they
withered away.
7 "And some fell among thorns, and the
thorns sprang up and choked them.
8 "But others fell on good ground and
yielded a crop: some [R]a hundredfold, some
sixty, some thirty. Gen. 26:12
9 "He who has ears to hear, let him hear!"
10 And the disciples came and said to Him,
"Why do You speak to them in parables?"
11 He answered and said to them, "Because
it has been given to you to know the [T]myster-
ies of the kingdom of heaven, but to them it
has not been given. *secret* or *hidden truths*
12 [R]"For whoever has, to him more will be
given, and he will have abundance; but whoever does not have, even what he has will be
taken away from him. Matt. 25:29
13 "Therefore I speak to them in parables,
because seeing they do not see, and hearing
they do not hear, nor do they understand.
14 "And in them the prophecy of Isaiah is
fulfilled, which says:

[R]*'Hearing you will hear and shall not*
understand,
And seeing you will see and not
[R]*perceive;* Is. 6:9, 10★ • [John 3:36]
15 *For the heart of this people has grown*
dull.
Their ears [R]*are hard of hearing,* Heb. 5:11
And their eyes they have [R]*closed,*
Lest they should see with their eyes and
hear with their ears, Luke 19:42
Lest they should understand with their
heart and turn,
*So that I *should heal them.'*

16 "But [R]blessed *are* your eyes for they see,
and your ears for they hear; Luke 10:23, 24
17 "for assuredly, I say to you [R]that many
prophets and righteous *men* desired to see
what you see, and did not see *it*, and to hear
what you hear, and did not hear *it*. Heb. 11:13
18 [R]"Therefore hear the parable of the
sower: Mark 4:13–20
19 "When anyone hears the word [R]of the
kingdom, and does not understand *it*, then
the wicked *one* comes and snatches away
what was sown in his heart. This is he who
received seed by the wayside. Matt. 4:23
20 "But he who received the seed on stony
places, this is he who hears the word and
immediately [R]receives it with joy; Is. 58:2
21 "yet he has no root in himself, but endures only for a while. For when [R]tribulation
or persecution arises because of the word,
immediately [R]he stumbles. [Acts 14:22] • Matt. 11:6
22 "Now [R]he who received seed [R]among the
thorns is he who hears the word, and the
cares of this world and the deceitfulness of
riches choke the word, and he becomes unfruitful. 1 Tim. 6:9 • Jer. 4:3
23 "But he who received seed on the good
ground is he who hears the word and understands *it*, who indeed bears [R]fruit and produces: some a hundredfold, some sixty, some
thirty." Col. 1:6

13:15 NU, M *would*

Parable of the Wheat and Tares

24 Another parable He put forth to them, saying: "The kingdom of heaven is like a man who sowed good seed in his field;
25 "but while men slept, his enemy came and sowed tares among the wheat and went his way.
26 "But when the grain had sprouted and produced a crop, then the tares also appeared.
27 "So the servants of the owner came and said to him, 'Sir, did you not sow good seed in your field? How then does it have tares?'
28 "He said to them, 'An enemy has done this.' The servants said to him, 'Do you want us then to go and gather them up?'
29 "But he said, 'No, lest while you gather up the tares you also uproot the wheat with them.
30 'Let both grow together until the harvest, and at the time of harvest I will say to the reapers, "First gather together the tares and bind them in bundles to burn them, but [R]gather the wheat into my barn." ' " Matt. 3:12

Parable of the Mustard Seed
Mark 4:30–32; Luke 13:18, 19

31 Another parable He put forth to them, saying: [R]"The kingdom of heaven is like a mustard seed, which a man took and sowed in his field, Luke 13:18, 19
32 "which indeed is the least of all the seeds; but when it is grown it is greater than the herbs and becomes a [R]tree, so that the birds of the air come and nest in its branches." Ezek. 17:22–24; 31:3–9

Parable of the Leaven—Luke 13:20, 21

33 Another parable He spoke to them: "The kingdom of heaven is like leaven, which a woman took and hid in three [T]measures of meal till it was all leavened." Gr. *saton*
34 [R]All these things Jesus spoke to the multitude in parables; and without a parable He did not speak to them, Mark 4:33, 34
35 that it might be fulfilled which was spoken by the prophet, saying:

[R]*"I will open My mouth in parables;*
[R]*I will utter things which have been kept*
secret from the foundation of the
world." Ps. 78:2 ★ • Eph. 3:9

Parable of the Tares Explained

36 Then Jesus sent the multitude away and went into the house. And His disciples came to Him, saying, "Explain to us the parable of the tares of the field."
37 He answered and said to them: "He who sows the good seed is the Son of Man.
38 [R]"The field is the world, the good seeds are the sons of the kingdom, but the tares are [R]the sons of the wicked *one.* Rom. 10:18 • John 8:44
39 "The enemy who sowed them is the devil, [R]the harvest is the end of the age, and the reapers are the angels. Rev. 14:15
40 "Therefore as the tares are gathered and burned in the fire, so it will be at the end of this age.
41 "The Son of Man will send out His angels, [R]and they will gather out of His kingdom all things that offend, and those who practice lawlessness, Matt. 18:7
42 [R]"and will cast them into the furnace of fire. [R]There will be wailing and gnashing of teeth. Rev. 19:20; 20:10 • Matt. 8:12; 13:50
43 "Then the righteous will shine forth as the sun in the kingdom of their Father. He who has ears to hear, let him hear!

Parable of the Hidden Treasure

44 "Again, the kingdom of heaven is like treasure hidden in a field, which a man found and hid; and for joy over it he goes and sells all that he has and [R]buys that field. [Is. 55:1]

Parable of the Pearl of Great Price

45 "Again, the kingdom of heaven is like a merchant seeking beautiful pearls,
46 "who, when he had found [R]one pearl of great price, went and sold all that he had and bought it. Prov. 2:4; 3:14, 15; 8:10, 19

Parable of the Dragnet

47 "Again, the kingdom of heaven is like a dragnet that was cast into the sea and [R]gathered some of every kind, Matt. 22:9, 10
48 "which, when it was full, they drew to shore; and they sat down and gathered the good into vessels, but threw the bad away.
49 "So it will be at the end of the age. The angels will come forth, [R]separate the wicked from among the just, Matt. 25:32
50 "and cast them into the furnace of fire. There will be wailing and gnashing of teeth."

Parable of the Householder

51 *Jesus said to them, "Have you understood all these things?" They said to Him, "Yes, *Lord."
52 Then He said to them, "Therefore every scribe instructed concerning the kingdom of heaven is like a householder who brings out of his treasure *things* new and old."
53 Now it came to pass, when Jesus had finished these parables, that He departed from there.

Rejection at Nazareth—Mark 6:1–6

54 [R]And when He had come to His own country, He [R]taught them in their synagogue, so that they were astonished and said, "Where did this *Man* get this wisdom and *these* mighty works? Luke 4:16 • Ps. 22:22 ★

13:51 NU omits *Jesus said to them*
13:51 NU omits *Lord*

55 "Is this not the carpenter's son? Is not His mother called Mary? And His brothers [R]James, *Joses, Simon, and Judas? Mark 15:40

56 "And His sisters, are they not all with us? Where then did this *Man* get all these things?"

57 So they [R]were offended at Him. But Jesus said to them, [R]"A prophet is not without honor except in his own country and in his own house." Matt. 11:6 • Luke 4:24

58 And [R]He did not do many mighty works there because of their unbelief. Mark 6:5, 6

CHAPTER 14

Present Response to Jesus
Mark 6:14–16; Luke 9:7–9

AT that time [R]Herod the tetrarch heard the report about Jesus Mark 6:14–29

2 and said to his servants, "This is John the Baptist; he is risen from the dead, and therefore these powers are at work in him."

Recount of the Murder of John the Baptist
Mark 6:17–29

3 For Herod had laid hold of John and bound him, and put *him* in prison for the sake of Herodias, his brother Philip's wife.

4 For John had said to him, [R]"It is not lawful for you to have her." Lev. 18:16; 20:21

5 And although he wanted to put him to death, he feared the multitude, [R]because they counted him as a prophet. Luke 20:6

6 But when Herod's birthday was celebrated, the daughter of Herodias danced before them and pleased Herod.

7 Therefore he promised with an oath to give her whatever she might ask.

8 So she, having been prompted by her mother, said, "Give me John the Baptist's head here on a platter."

9 And the king was sorry; nevertheless, because of the oaths and because of those who sat with him at the table, he commanded *it* to be given to *her.*

10 So he sent and had John beheaded in prison.

11 And his head was brought on a platter and given to the girl, and she brought *it* to her mother.

12 Then his disciples came and took away the body and buried it, and went and told Jesus.

Jesus Feeds 5,000
Mark 6:31–44; Luke 9:11–17; John 6:1–13

13 [R]When Jesus heard *it,* He departed from there by boat to a deserted place by Himself. But when the multitudes heard it, they followed Him on foot from the cities. John 6:1, 2

14 And when Jesus went out He saw a great multitude; and He [R]was moved with compassion for them, and healed their sick. Mark 6:34

15 [R]When it was evening, His disciples came to Him, saying, "This is a deserted place, and the hour is already late. Send the multitudes away, that they may go into the villages and buy themselves food." Luke 9:12

16 But Jesus said to them, "They do not need to go away. You give them something to eat."

17 And they said to Him, "We have here only five loaves and two fish."

18 He said, "Bring them here to Me."

19 Then He commanded the multitudes to sit down on the grass. And He took the five loaves and the two fish, and looking up to heaven, [R]He blessed and broke and gave the loaves to the disciples; and the disciples gave to the multitudes. Matt. 15:36; 26:26

20 So they all ate and were filled, and they took up twelve baskets full of the fragments that remained.

21 Now those who had eaten were about five thousand men, besides women and children.

Jesus Walks on Water
Mark 6:45–52; John 6:14–21

22 Immediately Jesus [T]made His disciples get into the boat and go before Him to the other side, while He sent the multitudes away. *strongly urged*

23 [R]And when He had sent the multitudes away, He went up on a mountain by Himself to pray. [R]And when evening had come, He was alone there. Mark 6:46 • John 6:16

24 But the boat was now *in the middle of the sea, tossed by the waves, for the wind was contrary.

25 Now in the fourth watch of the night Jesus went to them, walking on the sea.

26 And when the disciples saw Him [R]walking on the sea, they were troubled, saying, "It is a ghost!" And they cried out for fear. Job 9:8

27 But immediately Jesus spoke to them, saying, [T]"Be of good [R]cheer! [T]It is I; do not be afraid." *Take courage* • Acts 23:11; 27:22, 25, 36 • Lit. *I am*

28 And Peter answered Him and said, "Lord, if it is You, command me to come to You on the water."

29 So He said, "Come." And when Peter had come down out of the boat, he walked on the water to go to Jesus.

30 But when he saw *that the wind *was* boisterous, he was afraid; and beginning to sink he cried out, saying, "Lord, save me!"

31 And immediately Jesus stretched out *His* hand and caught him, and said to him, "O you of little faith, why did you doubt?"

32 And when they got into the boat, the wind ceased.

13:55 NU *Joseph*
14:24 NU *many furlongs away from the land*
14:30 NU brackets *that* and *boisterous*

33 Then those who were in the boat *came
and worshiped Him, saying, "Truly [R]You are
the Son of God." Ps. 2:7

Jesus Heals Many—Mark 6:53–56

34 [R]When they had crossed over, they came
*to the land of Gennesaret. Mark 6:53
35 And when the men of that place recognized Him, they sent out into all that surrounding region, brought to Him all who
were sick,
36 and begged Him that they might only
touch the hem of His garment. And as many
as touched it were made perfectly well.

CHAPTER 15

Debate over Tradition—Mark 7:1–23

THEN the scribes and Pharisees who were
from Jerusalem came to Jesus, saying,
2 [R]"Why do Your disciples transgress the
tradition of the elders? For they do not wash
their hands when they eat bread." Mark 7:5
3 But He answered and said to them, "Why
do you also transgress the commandment of
God because of your tradition?
4 "For God commanded, saying, [R]*'Honor
your father and your mother'*; and, [R]*'He who
curses father or mother, let him be put to
death.'* [Deut. 5:16] • Ex. 21:17
5 "But you say, 'Whoever says to *his* father or mother, [R]"Whatever profit you might
have received from me has been dedicated *to
the temple*"— Mark 7:11, 12
6 *'is released from* honoring his father *or
mother.' Thus you have made the *commandment of God of no effect by your tradition.
7 [R]"Hypocrites! Well did Isaiah prophesy
about you, saying: Mark 7:6

8 *'These[R] people *draw near to Me with*
their mouth, Is. 29:13
And honor Me with their lips,
But their heart is far from Me.
9 *And in vain they worship Me,*
[R]*Teaching as doctrines the*
commandments of men.'" [Col. 2:18–22]

10 [R]Then He called the multitude and said
to them, "Hear and understand: Mark 7:14
11 [R]"Not what goes into the mouth defiles a
man; but what comes out of the mouth, this
defiles a man." [Acts 10:15]
12 Then His disciples came and said to Him,
"Do You know that the Pharisees were offended when they heard this saying?"
13 But He answered and said, [R]"Every plant
which My heavenly Father has not planted
will be uprooted. [John 15:2]
14 "Let them alone. [R]They are blind leaders
of the blind. And if the blind leads the blind,
both will fall into a ditch." Luke 6:39
15 [R]Then Peter answered and said to Him,
"Explain this parable to us." Mark 7:17
16 So Jesus said, [R]"Are you also still without
understanding? Matt. 16:9
17 "Do you not yet understand that [R]what-
ever enters the mouth goes into the stomach
and is eliminated? [1 Cor. 6:13]
18 "But [R]those things which proceed out of
the mouth come from the heart, and they
defile a man. [James 3:6]
19 [R]"For out of the heart proceed evil
thoughts, murders, adulteries, fornications,
thefts, false witness, blasphemies. Prov. 6:14
20 "These are *the things* which defile a man,
but to eat with unwashed hands does not
defile a man."

Jesus Heals the Gentile Woman's Daughter Mark 7:24–30

21 Then Jesus went out from there and
departed to the region of Tyre and Sidon.
22 And behold, a woman of Canaan came
from that region and cried out to Him, saying, "Have mercy on me, O Lord, [R]Son of
David! My daughter is severely demon-
possessed." Matt. 1:1; 22:41, 42
23 But He answered her not a word. And
His disciples came and urged Him, saying,
"Send her away, for she cries out after us."
24 But He answered and said, [R]"I was not
sent except to the lost sheep of the house of
Israel." Matt. 10:5, 6
25 Then she came and worshiped Him, saying, "Lord, help me!"
26 But He answered and said, "It is not
good to take the children's bread and throw *it*
to the little [R]dogs." Matt. 7:6
27 And she said, "True, Lord, yet even the
little dogs eat the crumbs which fall from
their masters' table."
28 Then Jesus answered and said to her, "O
woman, [R]great *is* your faith! Let it be to you
as you desire." And her daughter was healed
from that very hour. Luke 7:9

Jesus Heals Many—Mark 7:31–37

29 [R]And Jesus departed from there, [R]skirted
the Sea of Galilee, and went up on the mountain and sat down there. Mark 7:31–37 • Matt. 4:18
30 [R]Then great multitudes came to Him,
having with them *those who were* lame,
blind, mute, [T]maimed, and many others; and
they laid them down at Jesus' [R]feet, and He
healed them. Is. 35:5, 6 • *crippled* • Luke 7:38; 8:41; 10:39
31 So the multitude marveled when they
saw *the* mute speaking, *the* maimed made
whole, *the* lame walking, and *the* blind seeing; and they glorified the God of Israel.

14:33 NU omits *came and* **14:34** NU *to land at* **15:6** NU omits *or mother* **15:6** NU *word* **15:8** NU omits *draw near to Me with their mouth, And*

Jesus Feeds 4,000—Mark 8:1-10

32 [R]Then Jesus called His disciples *to Him*
and said, "I have compassion on the multitude, because they have now continued with
Me three days and have nothing to eat. And I
do not want to send them away hungry, lest
they faint on the way." Mark 8:1–10
33 [R]Then His disciples said to Him, "Where
could we get enough bread in the wilderness
to fill such a great multitude?" 2 Kin. 4:43
34 Jesus said to them, "How many loaves do
you have?" And they said, "Seven, and a few
little fish."
35 And He commanded the multitude to sit
down on the ground.
36 And [R]He took the seven loaves and the
fish and [R]gave thanks, broke *them* and gave
them to His disciples; and the disciples *gave*
to the multitude. Matt. 14:19; 26:27 • Luke 22:19
37 So they all ate and were filled, and they
took up seven large baskets full of the fragments that were left.
38 Now those who ate were four thousand
men, besides women and children.
39 [R]And He sent away the multitude, got
into the boat, and came to the region of
*Magdala. Mark 8:10

CHAPTER 16

Debate over a Sign from Heaven
Mark 8:11, 12

THEN the [R]Pharisees and Sadducees came,
and testing Him asked that He would
show them a sign from heaven. Mark 8:11
2 He answered and said to them, "When it
is evening you say, '*It will be* fair weather, for
the sky is red';
3 "and in the morning, '*It will be* foul
weather today, for the sky is red and threatening.' *Hypocrites! You know how to discern the face of the sky, but you cannot
discern the signs of the times.
4 [R]"A wicked and adulterous generation
seeks after a sign, and no sign shall be given
to it except the sign of *the prophet Jonah."
And He left them and departed. Matt. 12:39

Withdrawal of Jesus—Mark 8:13–21

5 And when His disciples had come to the
other side, they had forgotten to take bread.
6 Then Jesus said to them, [R]"Take heed
and beware of the [T]leaven of the Pharisees
and the Sadducees." Luke 12:1 • *yeast*
7 And they reasoned among themselves,
saying, "*It is* because we have taken no
bread."
8 But when Jesus perceived it, He said to
them, "O you of little faith, why do you
reason among yourselves because you *have
brought no bread?
9 [R]"Do you not yet understand, or remember the five loaves of the five thousand and
how many baskets you took up? Matt. 14:15-21
10 [R]"Nor the seven loaves of the four thousand and how many large baskets you took
up? Matt. 15:32–38
11 "How is it you do not understand that I
did not speak to you concerning bread?—*but*
you should beware of the [T]leaven of the
Pharisees and Sadducees." *yeast*
12 Then they understood that He did not
tell *them* to beware of the leaven of bread,
but of the [T]doctrine of the Pharisees and
Sadducees. *teaching*

Revelation of the Person of the King
Mark 8:27–30; Luke 9:18–21

13 When Jesus came into the region of
Caesarea Philippi, He asked His disciples,
saying, [R]"Who do men say that I, the Son of
Man, am?" Luke 9:18
14 So they said, [R]"Some *say* John the Baptist, some Elijah, and others Jeremiah or [R]one
of the prophets." Matt. 14:2 • Matt. 21:11
15 He said to them, "But who do [R]you say
that I am?" John 6:67
16 And Simon Peter answered and said,
[R]"You are the Christ, the Son of the living
God." Acts 8:37; 9:20
17 Jesus answered and said to him, "Blessed
are you, Simon Bar-Jonah, [R]for flesh and
blood has not revealed *this* to you, but [R]My
Father who is in heaven. [Eph. 2:8] • Gal. 1:16

Revelation of the Church

18 "And I also say to you that you are
Peter, and [R]on this rock I will [R]build My
church, and the gates of Hades shall not
prevail against it. [Eph. 2:20] • Acts 2:41, 47 ☆

19 [R]"And I will give you the keys of the
kingdom of heaven, and whatever you bind
on earth will be bound in heaven, and whatever you loose on earth will be loosed in
heaven." Matt. 18:18

15:39 NU *Magadan* 16:3 NU omits *Hypocrites*
16:4 NU omits *the prophet* 16:8 NU *have no bread*

16:18 The Origin of the Church—The church was a mystery (i.e., hidden, not revealed) in the Old Testament. It was first prophesied in these words spoken to Peter, "on this rock I will build My church." In this prophecy there is a play on the word *rock* which also happens to be Peter's name. Jesus said, "you are Peter" (masculine, *petros*) and "on this rock [feminine, *petra*] I will build My church." But when did the church actually begin? Again, many suggestions are offered for varying reasons. The

20 [R]Then He commanded His disciples that
they should tell no one that He was Jesus the
Christ. Luke 9:21

Revelation of Jesus' Death
Mark 8:31–33; Luke 9:22

21 From that time Jesus began to show to
His disciples that He must go to Jerusalem,
and suffer many things from the elders and
chief priests and scribes, and be killed, and be
[R]raised again the third day. Acts 10:40; 1 Cor. 15:4☆
22 Then Peter took Him aside and began to
rebuke Him, saying, "Far be it from You,
Lord; this shall not happen to You!"
23 But He turned and said to Peter, "Get
behind Me, Satan! You are [T]an offense to Me,
for you are not mindful of the things of God,
but the things of men." *a stumbling block*

Revelation of Jesus' Reward
Mark 8:34–37; Luke 9:23–25

24 [R]Then Jesus said to His disciples, "If
anyone desires to come after Me, let him
deny himself, and take up his cross, and
[R]follow Me. [2 Tim. 3:12] • [1 Pet. 2:21]
25 "For [R]whoever desires to save his life will
lose it, and whoever loses his life for My sake
will find it. John 12:25
26 "For what is a man [R]profited if he gains
the whole world, and loses his own soul? Or
[R]what will a man give in exchange for his
soul? Luke 12:20, 21 • Ps. 49:7, 8

The Prophecy of the Second Coming
Mark 8:38—9:1; Luke 9:26, 27

27 "For [R]the Son of Man will come in the
glory of His Father [R]with His angels, [R]and
then He will reward each according to his
works. Mark 8:38 • [Dan. 7:10] • Rom. 2:6
28 "Assuredly, I say to you, [R]there are some
standing here who shall not taste death till
they see the Son of Man coming in His
kingdom." Luke 9:27

CHAPTER 17

The Transfiguration
Mark 9:2–13; Luke 9:28–36; 2 Pet. 1:17, 18

NOW after six days Jesus took Peter,
James, and John his brother, brought
them up on a high mountain by themselves,
2 and was transfigured before them. His
face shone like the sun, and His clothes
became as white as the light.
3 And behold, Moses and Elijah appeared
to them, talking with Him.
4 Then Peter answered and said to Jesus,
"Lord, it is good for us to be here; if You
wish, *let us make here three tabernacles:
one for You, one for Moses, and one for
Elijah."
5 While he was still speaking, behold, a
bright cloud overshadowed them; and suddenly a voice came out of the cloud, saying,
[R]"This is My beloved Son, in whom I am well
pleased. Hear Him!" Is. 42:1; 2 Pet. 1:17★
6 And when the disciples heard *it*, they fell
on their faces and were greatly afraid.
7 But Jesus came and [R]touched them and
said, "Arise, and do not be afraid." Dan. 8:18
8 And when they had lifted up their eyes,
they saw no one but Jesus only.
9 Now as they came down from the mountain, Jesus commanded them, saying, "Tell
the vision to no one until the Son of Man is
risen from the dead."
10 And His disciples asked Him, saying,
[R]"Why then do the scribes say that Elijah
must come first?" Mal. 4:5
11 Then Jesus answered and said to them,
"Elijah truly is coming *first and will [R]restore
all things. [Mal. 4:6]
12 [R]"But I say to you that Elijah has come
already, and they [R]did not know him but did
to him whatever they wished. Likewise [R]the
Son of Man is also about to suffer at their
hands." Mark 9:12, 13 • Matt. 14:3, 10 • Matt. 16:21
13 [R]Then the disciples understood that He
spoke to them of John the Baptist. Matt. 11:14

Instruction About Faith
Mark 9:14–29; Luke 9:37–42

14 [R]And when they had come to the multitude, a man came to Him, kneeling down to
Him and saying, Mark 9:14–28
15 "Lord, have mercy on my son, for he is
an epileptic and suffers severely; for he often
falls into the fire and often into the water.
16 "So I brought him to Your disciples, but
they could not cure him."
17 Then Jesus answered and said, "O [T]faith-
less and perverse generation, how long shall I
be with you? How long shall I bear with you?
Bring him here to Me." *unbelieving*
18 And Jesus [R]rebuked the demon, and he
came out of him; and the child was cured
from that very hour. Luke 4:41

17:4 NU *I will make* **17:11** NU omits *first*

---

simplest view is to understand the New Testament church as beginning on the Day of Pentecost in response to Peter's Pentecostal sermon when "that day about three thousand souls were added *to them* [i.e., the apostles]" (Page 1274—Acts 2:41). This group for the first time is called "the church" in Acts 2:47, and God added to their number daily those who were saved.

Now turn to Page 1388—Eph. 3:21: The Purpose of the Church.

19 Then the disciples came to Jesus privately and said, "Why could we not cast him
out?"
20 So Jesus said to them, "Because of your
*unbelief; for assuredly, I say to you, [R]if you
have faith as a mustard seed, you will say to
this mountain, 'Move from here to there,' and
it will move; and nothing will be impossible
for you. Luke 17:6
21 *"However, this kind does not go out
except by prayer and fasting."

Instruction About Jesus' Death
Mark 9:30–32; Luke 9:43–45

22 Now while they were *staying in Galilee,
Jesus said to them, "The Son of Man is about
to be betrayed into the hands of men,
23 "and they will [R]kill Him, and the third
day He will be raised up." And they were
exceedingly sorrowful. Mark 15:37; Acts 10:40☆

Instruction About Taxes

24 And when they had come to *Capernaum, those who received the [T]*temple* tax
came to Peter and said, "Does your Teacher
not pay the *temple* tax?" Lit. *double drachma*
25 He said, "Yes." And when he had come
into the house, Jesus anticipated him, saying,
"What do you think, Simon? From whom do
the kings of the earth take customs or taxes,
from their *own* sons or from strangers?"
26 Peter said to Him, "From strangers."
Jesus said to him, "Then the sons are free.
27 "Nevertheless, lest we offend them, go to
the sea, cast in a hook, and take the fish that
comes up first. And when you have opened
its mouth, you will find a [T]piece of money;
take that and give it to them for Me and
you." Gr. *stater*, the exact temple tax for two

CHAPTER 18

Instruction About Humility
Mark 9:33–37; Luke 9:46–48

AT [R]that time the disciples came to Jesus,
saying, "Who then is greatest in the
kingdom of heaven?" Luke 9:46–48; 22:24–27
2 And Jesus called a little [R]child to Him, set
him in the midst of them, Matt. 19:14
3 and said, "Assuredly, I say to you, [R]un-
less you are converted and become as little
children, you will by no means enter the
kingdom of heaven. Luke 18:16
4 [R]"Therefore whoever humbles himself as
this little child is the greatest in the kingdom
of heaven. [Matt. 20:27; 23:11]
5 "And [R]whoever receives one little child
like this in My name receives Me. [Matt. 10:42]

Punishment of Offenders—Mark 9:42–48

6 [R]"But whoever causes one of these little
ones who believe in Me to sin, it would be
better for him if a millstone were hung
around his neck, and he were drowned in the
depth of the sea. Mark 9:42
7 "Woe to the world because of [T]offenses!
For offenses must come, but woe to that man
by whom the offense comes! *enticements*
8 [R]"And if your hand or foot causes you to
sin, cut it off and cast *it* from you. It is better
for you to enter into life lame or maimed,
rather than having two hands or two feet, to
be cast into the everlasting fire. Matt. 5:29, 30
9 "And if your eye causes you to sin, pluck
it out and cast *it* from you. It is better for
you to enter into life with one eye, rather
than having two eyes, to be cast into [T]hell
fire. Gr. *Gehenna*
10 "Take heed that you do not despise one
of these little ones, for I say to you that in
heaven [R]their angels always see the face of
My Father who is in heaven. [Heb. 1:14]

Parable of the Lost Sheep—Luke 15:4–7

11 [R]"For* the Son of Man has come to save
that which was lost. Luke 9:56
12 [R]"What do you think? If a man has a
hundred sheep, and one of them goes astray,
does he not leave the ninety-nine and go to
the mountains to seek the one that is stray-
ing? Luke 15:4–7
13 "And if he should find it, assuredly, I say
to you, he rejoices more over that *sheep* than
over the ninety-nine that did not go astray.
14 "Even so it is not the [R]will of your Father
who is in heaven that one of these little ones
should perish. [1 Tim. 2:4]

The Offended Brother

15 "Moreover [R]if your brother sins against
you, go and tell him his fault between you
and him alone. If he hears you, [R]you have
gained your brother. Lev. 19:17 • [James 5:20]
16 "But if he will not hear *you*, take with
you one or two more, that [R]'*by the mouth of
two or three witnesses every word may be
established.*' Deut. 17:6; 19:15
17 "And if he refuses to hear them, tell *it* to
the church. But if he refuses even to hear the
church, let him be to you like a [R]heathen and
a tax collector. [2 Thess. 3:6, 14]
18 "Assuredly, I say to you, [R]whatever you
bind on earth will be bound in heaven, and
whatever you loose on earth will be loosed in
heaven. [John 20:22, 23]
19 [R]"Again* I say to you that if two of you
agree on earth concerning anything that they
ask, [R]it will be done for them by My Father in
heaven. [1 Cor. 1:10] • [1 John 3:22; 5:14]

17:20 NU *little faith* **17:21** NU omits v. 21
17:22 NU *gathering together*
17:24 NU *Capharnaum*, here and elsewhere
18:11 NU omits v. 11
18:19 NU, M *Again, assuredly, I say*

20 "For where two or three are gathered [R]together in My name, I am there in the midst of them." Acts 20:7

Instruction About Forgiveness

21 Then Peter came to Him and said, "Lord, how often shall my brother sin against me, and I forgive him? Up to seven times?"

22 Jesus said to him, "I do not say to you, [R]up to seven times, but up to seventy times seven. Col. 3:13

23 "Therefore the kingdom of heaven is like a certain king who wanted to settle accounts with his servants.

24 "And when he had begun to settle accounts, one was brought to him who owed him ten thousand talents.

25 "But as he was not able to pay, his master commanded [R]that he be sold, with his wife and children and all that he had, and that payment be made. 2 Kin. 4:1

26 "The servant therefore fell down before him, saying, 'Master, have patience with me, and I will pay you all.'

27 "Then the master of that servant was moved with compassion, released him, and forgave him the debt.

28 "But that servant went out and found one of his fellow servants who owed him a [T]hundred denarii; and he laid hands on him and took *him* by the throat, saying, 'Pay me what you owe!' 100 days' wages

29 "So his fellow servant fell down *at his feet and begged him, saying, 'Have patience with me, and I will pay you *all.'

30 "And he would not, but went and threw him into prison till he should pay the debt.

31 "So when his fellow servants saw what had been done, they were very grieved, and came and told their master all that had been done.

32 "Then his master, after he had called him, said to him, 'You wicked servant! I forgave you [R]all that debt because you begged me. Luke 7:41–43

33 'Should you not also have had compassion on your fellow servant, just as I had pity on you?'

34 "And his master was angry, and delivered him to the torturers until he should pay all that was due to him.

35 [R]"So My heavenly Father also will do to you if each of you, from his heart, does not forgive his brother *his trespasses." James 2:13

CHAPTER 19

Instruction About Divorce
Mark 10:1–16; Luke 18:15–17

NOW it came to pass, [R]when Jesus had finished these sayings, *that* He departed from Galilee and came to the region of Judea beyond the Jordan. Mark 10:1–12

2 [R]And great multitudes followed Him, and He healed them there. Matt. 12:15

3 The Pharisees also came to Him, testing Him, and saying to Him, "Is it lawful for a man to divorce his wife for *just* any reason?"

4 And He answered and said to them, [R]"Have you not read that He who *made *them* at the beginning *'made them male and female,'* Gen. 1:27; 5:2

5 "and said, [R]*'For this reason a man shall leave his father and mother and be joined to his wife, and* [R]*the two shall become one flesh'?* Gen. 2:24 • [1 Cor. 6:16; 7:2]

6 "So then, they are no longer two but one flesh. Therefore what God has joined together, let not man separate."

7 They said to Him, [R]"Why then did Moses command to give a certificate of divorce, and to put her away?" Deut. 24:1–4

8 He said to them, "Moses, because of the [R]hardness of your hearts, permitted you to divorce your [R]wives, but from the beginning it was not so. Heb. 3:15 • Mal. 2:16

9 [R]"And I say to you, whoever divorces his wife, except for sexual immorality, and marries another, commits adultery; and whoever marries her who is divorced commits adultery." [Matt. 5:32]

10 His disciples said to Him, [R]"If such is the case of the man with *his* wife, it is better not to marry." [Prov. 21:19]

11 But He said to them, [R]"All cannot accept this saying, but only *those* to whom it has been given: [1 Cor. 7:2, 7, 9, 17]

12 "For there are [T]eunuchs who were born thus from *their* mother's womb, and [R]there are eunuchs who were made eunuchs by men, and there are eunuchs who have made themselves eunuchs for the kingdom of heaven's sake. He who is able to accept *it*, let him accept *it*." Emasculated men • [1 Cor. 7:32]

13 Then little children were brought to Him that He might put *His* hands on them and pray, but the disciples rebuked them.

14 But Jesus said, "Let the little children come to Me, and do not forbid them; for [R]of such is the kingdom of heaven." Matt. 18:3, 4

15 And He laid *His* hands on them and departed from there.

Rich Young Ruler
Mark 10:17–27; Luke 18:18–27

16 Now behold, one came and said to Him, [R]"Good* Teacher, what good thing shall I do that I may have eternal life?" Luke 10:25

17 So He said to him, *"Why do you call Me good? *No one *is* [R]good but One, *that is*, God.

18:29 NU omits *at his feet* 18:29 NU, M omit *all*
18:35 NU omits *his trespasses* 19:4 NU *created*
19:16 NU omits *Good*
19:17 NU *Why do you ask Me about what is good?*
19:17 NU *There is One who is good. But*

But if you want to enter into life, [R]keep the
commandments." Nah. 1:7 • Lev. 18:5
18 He said to Him, "Which ones?" Jesus
said, [R]"*'You shall not murder,' 'You shall not*
commit adultery,' 'You shall not steal,' 'You
shall not bear false witness,' Ex. 20:13–16
19 [R]*'Honor your father and your mother,'*
and, [R]*'You shall love your neighbor as your-*
self.'" Ex. 20:12–16; Deut. 5:16–20 • Lev. 19:18
20 The young man said to Him, "All these
things I have [R]kept *from my youth. What do
I still lack?" [Phil. 3:6, 7]
21 Jesus said to him, "If you want to be
perfect, [R]go, sell what you have and give to
the poor, and you will have treasure in
heaven; and come, follow Me." Acts 2:45; 4:34, 35
22 But when the young man heard that
saying, he went away sorrowful, for he had
great possessions.
23 Then Jesus said to His disciples, "Assuredly, I say to you that it is hard for a rich
man to enter the kingdom of heaven.
24 "And again I say to you, it is easier for a
camel to go through the eye of a needle than
for a rich man to enter the kingdom of God."
25 When His disciples heard *it*, they were
exceedingly amazed, saying, "Who then can
be saved?"
26 But Jesus looked at *them* and said to
them, "With men this is impossible, but [R]with
God all things are possible." Jer. 32:17

The Apostles' Reward
Mark 10:28–30; Luke 18:28–30

27 Then Peter answered and said to Him,
"See, [R]we have left all and followed You.
Therefore what shall we have?" Deut. 33:9
28 So Jesus said to them, "Assuredly I say
to you, that in the regeneration, when the
Son of Man sits on the throne of His glory,
[R]you who have followed Me will also sit on
twelve thrones, judging the twelve tribes of
Israel. Luke 22:28–30
29 [R]"And everyone who has left houses or
brothers or sisters or father or mother *or
wife or children or [T]lands, for My name's
sake, shall receive a hundredfold, and inherit
everlasting life. Mark 10:29, 30 • Lit. *fields*
30 [R]"But many *who are* first will be last, and
the last first. Luke 13:30

CHAPTER 20

Parable of the Laborers—Mark 10:31

"FOR the kingdom of heaven is like a
landowner who went out early in the
morning to hire laborers for his vineyard.
2 "Now when he had agreed with the
laborers for a denarius a day, he sent them
into his vineyard.
3 "And he went out about the third hour
and saw others standing idle in the marketplace,
4 "and said to them, 'You also go into the
vineyard, and whatever is right I will give
you.' And they went.
5 "Again he went out about the sixth and
the ninth hour, and did likewise.
6 "And about the eleventh hour he went
out and found others standing *idle, and said
to them, 'Why have you been standing here
idle all day?'
7 "They said to him, 'Because no one hired
us.' He said to them, 'You also go into the
vineyard, *and whatever is right you will
receive.'
8 "So when evening had come, the owner
of the vineyard said to his steward, 'Call the
laborers and give them *their* wages, beginning with the last to the first.'
9 "And when those came who *were hired*
about the eleventh hour, they each received a
[T]denarius. 1 day's wage
10 "But when the first came, they supposed
that they would receive more; and they
likewise received each a denarius.
11 "And when they had received *it*, they
[T]murmured against the landowner, *grumbled*
12 "saying, 'These last *men* have worked
only one hour, and you made them equal to
us who have borne the burden and the heat
of the day.'
13 "But he answered one of them and said,
'Friend, I am doing you no wrong. Did you
not agree with me for a denarius?
14 'Take *what is* yours and go your way. I
wish to give to this last man *the same* as to
you.
15 [R]'Is it not lawful for me to do what I wish
with my own things? Or [R]is your eye evil
because I am good?' [Rom. 9:20, 21] • Deut. 15:9
16 "So the last will be first, and the first last.
*For many are called, but few chosen."

Instruction About Jesus' Death
Mark 10:32–34; Luke 18:31–34

17 [R]Then Jesus, going up to Jerusalem, took
the twelve disciples aside on the road and
said to them, Mark 10:32–34
18 "Behold, we are going up to Jerusalem,
and the Son of Man will be [R]betrayed to the
chief priests and to the scribes; and they will
condemn Him to death, Matt. 26:46, 66☆
19 [R]"and deliver Him to the Gentiles to
mock and to scourge and to crucify. And the
third day He will rise again." Acts 2:23, 24☆

Instruction About Ambition—Mark 10:35–45

20 [R]Then the mother of Zebedee's sons
came to Him with her sons, kneeling down
and asking something from Him. Mark 10:35–45

19:20 NU omits *from my youth*
19:29 NU omits *or wife*
20:6 NU omits *idle* **20:7** NU omits the rest of v. 7.
20:16 NU omits the rest of v. 16.

21 And He said to her, "What do you wish?"
She said to Him, "Grant that these two sons
of mine may sit, one on Your right hand and
the other on the left, in Your kingdom."
22 But Jesus answered and said, "You do
not know what you ask. Are you able to
drink [R]the cup that I am about to drink, *and
be baptized with [R]the baptism that I am
baptized with?" They said to Him, "We are
able." Luke 22:42 • Luke 12:50
23 So He said to them, [R]"You will indeed
drink My cup, *and be baptized with the
baptism that I am baptized with; but to sit on
My right hand and on My left is not Mine to
give, but *it is for those* for whom it is prepared by My Father." [Acts 12:2]
24 [R]And when the ten heard *it,* they were
moved with indignation against the two
brothers. Mark 10:41
25 But Jesus called them *to Himself* and
said, "You know that the rulers of the Gentiles lord it over them, and those who are
great exercise authority over them.
26 "Yet [R]it shall not be so among you; but
whoever desires to become great among you,
let him be your servant. [1 Pet. 5:3]
27 [R]"And whoever desires to be first among
you, let him be your slave— [Matt. 18:4]
28 "just as the Son of Man did not come to
be served, but to serve, and [R]to give His life a
ransom for many." Is. 53:12 ☆

The Blind Men Recognize the King
Mark 10:46–52; Luke 18:35–43

29 [R]Now as they departed from Jericho, a
great multitude followed Him. Mark 10:46–52
30 And behold, two blind men sitting by the
road, when they heard that Jesus was passing
by, cried out, saying, "Have mercy on us, O
Lord, [R]Son of David!" [Ezek. 37:21–25]
31 Then the multitude [R]warned them that
they should be quiet; but they cried out all
the more, saying, "Have mercy on us, O Lord,
Son of David!" Matt. 19:13
32 So Jesus stood still and called them, and
said, "What do you want Me to do for you?"
33 They said to Him, "Lord, that our eyes
may be opened."
34 So Jesus had compassion and touched
their eyes. And immediately their eyes received sight, and they followed Him.

CHAPTER 21

The Triumphal Entry
Mark 11:1–10; Luke 19:29–38; John 12:12–15

NOW when they drew near to Jerusalem,
and came to *Bethphage, at the Mount
of Olives, then Jesus sent two disciples,
2 saying to them, "Go into the village
opposite you, and immediately you will find a
donkey tied, and a colt with her. Loose *them*
and bring *them* to Me.
3 "And if anyone says anything to you,
you shall say, 'The Lord has need of them,'
and immediately he will send them."
4 *All this was done that it might be fulfilled which was spoken by the prophet,
saying:

5 *"Tell[R] the daughter of Zion,* Zech. 9:9 ★
'Behold, your King is coming to you,
Lowly, and sitting on a donkey,
A colt, the foal of a donkey.'"

6 [R]So the disciples went and did as Jesus
commanded them. Mark 11:4
7 They brought the donkey and the colt,
[R]laid their clothes on them, *and set *Him* on
them. 2 Kin. 9:13
8 And a very great multitude spread their
garments on the road; [R]others cut down
branches from the trees and spread *them* on
the road. Lev. 23:40
9 Then the multitudes who went before
and those who followed cried out, saying:

[R]"Hosanna to the Son of David!
[R]*'Blessed is He who comes in the name of*
the LORD!' Ps. 118:25, 26 ★ • Matt. 23:39
Hosanna in the highest!"

10 And when He had come into Jerusalem,
all the city was moved, saying, "Who is this?"
11 So the multitudes said, "This is Jesus, the
prophet from Nazareth of Galilee."

The Cleansing of the Temple
Mark 11:15–17; Luke 19:45, 46

12 [R]Then Jesus went into the temple *of
God and drove out all those who bought and
sold in the temple, and overturned the tables
of the [R]moneychangers and the seats of those
who sold doves. Mal. 3:1 ★ • Deut. 14:25
13 And He said to them, "It is written, *'My
house shall be called a house of prayer,'* but
you have made it a *'den of thieves.'"*
14 Then *the* blind and *the* lame came to
Him in the temple, and He healed them.
15 But when the chief priests and scribes
saw the wonderful things that He did, and the
children crying out in the temple and saying,
"Hosanna to the [R]Son of David!" they were
[T]indignant John 7:42 • *angry*
16 and said to Him, "Do You hear what
these are saying?" And Jesus said to them,
"Yes. Have you never read, [R]*'Out of the*

20:22 NU omits *and be baptized with the baptism that I am baptized with*
20:23 NU omits *and be baptized with the baptism that I am baptized with*
21:1 M *Bethsphage* **21:4** NU omits *All*
21:7 NU *and He sat* **21:12** NU omits *of God*

ABBA, FATHER! HOSANNA! MARANATHA!

As the everyday language of first-century Palestinian Jews—the language of Christ and the disciples—Aramaic is the first "Christian" language. This Semitic tongue, closely related to Hebrew, was soon to be superseded as such by the common (*Koinē*) Greek of the Roman Empire, especially in the East. As the Faith attracted more and more Gentiles, the Jewish and Aramaic flavor became more and more diluted. But a few early Aramaic expressions survived in the New Testament. These are well worth knowing.

ABBA

Abba is the most family-oriented of these terms. In the Old Testament, God was sometimes seen as the Father of the nation Israel, but it was Christ's revelation that all believers are individually children of God by redemption. In a lesser sense, all people are children of God by creation, but in the sense of the model prayer, the "Our Father," only believers can claim that revealed relationship.

Abba, Father occurs three times in the New Testament, the Aramaic term being used with a translation. *Abba* is the most intimate term for Father, the first word a child would learn for "Daddy." This word indicates how close the Father wants His children to feel toward Him.

Abba is used once in the Gospels and twice by Paul.

Mark 14:36. In the Garden of Gethsemane, His "soul... exceedingly sorrowful, *even* to death," Jesus prayed, "Abba, Father, all things *are* possible for You. Take this cup away from Me; nevertheless, not what I will, but what You *will*." At this crisis in His ministry, facing betrayal by Judas and shameful death on the cross, the Lord reverted to the tender word He had first used at Mary and Joseph's knees: *Abba*.

Romans 8:15. In one of the most beloved chapters in the Bible, Paul relates a word he no doubt learned at his own Jewish mother's knee to the believer's acceptance as a mature son by *adoption*, as well as a child by new *birth*. These blessings come through the third Person of the Trinity: "For as many as are led by the Spirit of God, these are sons of God. For you did not receive the spirit of bondage again to fear, but you received the Spirit of adoption by whom we cry out, 'Abba, Father.' The Spirit Himself bears witness with our spirit that we are children of God" (vv. 14–16).

Galatians 4:6. Paul's other use is similar, only here sonship is contrasted with slavery. We are not merely slaves of God, although we should serve on that level of submission; we are sons. As God's sons and daughters we can boldly say, "Abba, Father!"

HOSANNA

Hosanna is the Aramaic form of the Hebrew cry for help. It occurs six times in the gospel narratives of Christ's triumphal entry into Jerusalem. By the time of our Lord, the expression was more a shout of praise, but perhaps some of the more thoughtful remembered the words, "Save now, I pray, O LORD" (Ps. 118:25) as they waved their palm fronds and cried out: "Hosanna! 'Blessed *is* He who comes in the name of the LORD!' The King of Israel!" (John 12:13).

MARANATHA

Maranatha occurs only once in the Greek New Testament and the KJV. Because it sounds so much like the very negative word *anathema*, and most people misunderstand what it means, the NKJV translators decided to translate these words rather than leave the original words in the English text. The word can be divided two different ways. *Maran atha* ("Our Lord has come" or "Our Lord is coming") can refer to the incarnation or the Second Coming. *Marana tha* ("Our Lord, come!") is a plea for the Lord to come back. That many Christians have chosen *maranatha* as the name of their church probably indicates that most people see the expression as a plea, as did the translators of the NKJV: "If anyone does not love the Lord Jesus Christ, let him be accursed [*anathema*]. O Lord, come [*Marana tha*]!" (1 Cor. 16:22).

mouth of babes and nursing infants You have perfected praise'?" Ps. 8:2★
17 Then He left them and went out of the
city to Bethany, and He lodged there.

Cursing of the Fig Tree—Mark 11:11–14, 20–24

18 [R]Now in the morning, as He returned to
the city, He was hungry. Mark 11:12–14, 20–24
19 [R]And seeing a fig tree by the road, He
came to it and found nothing on it but leaves,
and said to it, "Let no fruit grow on you ever
again." And immediately the fig tree withered
away. Mark 11:13
20 [R]Now when the disciples saw *it*, they
marveled, saying, "How did the fig tree
wither away so soon?" Mark 11:20
21 So Jesus answered and said to them,
"Assuredly, I say to you, if you have faith and
do not doubt, you will not only do what was
done to the fig tree, [R]but also if you say to
this mountain, 'Be removed and be cast into
the sea,' it will be done. 1 Cor. 13:2
22 "And [R]all things, whatever you ask in
prayer, believing, you will receive." Matt. 7:7–11

Question of Jesus' Authority
Mark 11:27–33; Luke 20:1–18

23 [R]Now when He came into the temple, the
chief priests and the elders of the people
confronted Him as He was teaching, and
[R]said, "By what authority are You doing
these things? And who gave You this authority?" Luke 20:1–8 • Ex. 2:14
24 But Jesus answered and said to them, "I
also will ask you one thing, which if you tell
Me, I likewise will tell you by what authority
I do these things:
25 "The [R]baptism of John, where was it
from? From heaven or from men?" And they
reasoned among themselves, saying, "If we
say, 'From heaven,' He will say to us, 'Why
then did you not believe him?' [John 1:29–34]
26 "But if we say, 'From men,' we fear the
multitude, for all count John as a prophet."
27 So they answered Jesus and said, "We do
not know." And He said to them, "Neither
will I tell you by what authority I do these
things.

Parable of the Two Sons

28 "But what do you think? A man had two
sons, and he came to the first and said, 'Son,
go, work today in my [R]vineyard.' Matt. 20:1
29 "He answered and said, 'I will not,' but
afterward he regretted it and went.
30 "Then he came to the second and said
likewise. And he answered and said, 'I go, sir,'
but he did not go.
31 "Which of the two did the will of *his*
father?" They said to Him, "The first." Jesus
said to them, [R]"Assuredly, I say to you that
tax collectors and harlots enter the kingdom
of God before you. Luke 7:29, 37–50
32 "For John came to you in the way of
righteousness, and you did not believe him;
[R]but tax collectors and harlots believed him;
and when you saw *it*, you did not afterward
[T]relent and believe him. Luke 3:12, 13 • *regret it*

Parable of the Landowner
Mark 12:1–12; Luke 20:9–19

33 "Hear another parable: There was a certain landowner who planted a vineyard and
set a hedge around it, dug a winepress in it
and built a tower. And he leased it to vinedressers and went into a far country.
34 "Now when vintage-time drew near, he
sent his servants to the vinedressers, that
they might receive its fruit.
35 "And the vinedressers took his servants,
beat one, killed one, and stoned another.
36 "Again he sent other servants, more than
the first, and they did likewise to them.
37 "Then last of all he sent his [R]son to them,
saying, 'They will respect my son.' [John 3:16]
38 "But when the vinedressers saw the son,
they said among themselves, [R]'This is the
heir. [R]Come, let us kill him and seize his
inheritance.' [Heb. 1:2] • John 11:53
39 [R]"And they caught him, and cast *him* out
of the vineyard, and killed *him*. [Acts 2:23]
40 "Therefore, when the owner of the vineyard comes, what will he do to those vinedressers?"
41 They said to Him, "He will destroy those
wicked men miserably, and lease *his* vineyard
to other vinedressers who will [T]render to him
the fruits in their seasons." *give*
42 Jesus said to them, [R]"Did you never read
in the Scriptures: Ps. 118:22, 23★

'The stone which the builders rejected
Has become the chief cornerstone.
This was the LORD's doing,
And it is marvelous in our eyes'?

43 "Therefore I say to you, [R]the kingdom of
God will be taken from you and given to a
nation bearing the fruits of it. [Matt. 8:12]
44 "And [R]whoever falls on this stone will be
broken; but on whomever it falls, [R]it will
grind him to powder." Is. 8:14, 15★ • [Dan. 2:44]
45 Now when the chief priests and Pharisees heard His parables, they [T]perceived that
He was speaking of them. *knew*
46 But when they sought to lay hands on
Him, they feared the multitudes, because
[R]they took Him for a prophet. Matt. 21:11

CHAPTER 22

Parable of the Marriage Feast

AND Jesus answered [R]and spoke to them
again by parables and said: [Rev. 19:7–9]
2 "The kingdom of heaven is like a certain
king who arranged a marriage for his son,

3 "and sent out his servants to call those who were invited to the wedding; and they were not willing to come.

4 "Again, he sent out other servants, saying, 'Tell those who are invited, "See, I have prepared my dinner; [R]my oxen and fatted cattle *are* killed, and all things *are* ready. Come to the wedding." ' Prov. 9:2

5 "But they made light of it and went their ways, one to his own farm, another to his business.

6 "And the rest seized his servants, treated *them* [T]spitefully, and killed *them*. *insolently*

7 "But when the king heard *about it*, he was furious. And he sent out [R]his armies, destroyed those murderers, and burned up their city. [Dan. 9:26]

8 "Then he said to his servants, 'The wedding is ready, but those who were invited were not [R]worthy. Matt. 10:11

9 'Therefore go into the highways, and as many as you find, invite to the wedding.'

10 "So those servants went out into the highways and gathered together all whom they found, both bad and good. And the wedding *hall* was filled with guests.

11 "But when the king came in to see the guests, he saw a man there [R]who did not have on a wedding garment. [Col. 3:10, 12]

12 "So he said to him, 'Friend, how did you come in here without a wedding garment?' And he was [R]speechless. [Rom. 3:19]

13 "Then the king said to the servants, 'Bind him hand and foot, *take him away, and cast *him* into outer darkness; there will be weeping and gnashing of teeth.'

14 [R]"For many are called, but few *are* chosen." Matt. 20:16

Conflict with Pharisees and Herodians
Mark 12:13–17; Luke 20:20–26

15 Then the Pharisees went and plotted how they might entangle Him in *His* talk.

16 And they sent to Him their disciples with the Herodians, saying, "Teacher, we know that You are true, and teach the way of God in truth; nor do You care about anyone, for You do not regard the person of men.

17 "Tell us, therefore, what do You think? Is it lawful to pay taxes to Caesar, or not?"

18 But Jesus [T]perceived their wickedness, and said, "Why do you test Me, *you* hypocrites? *knew*

19 "Show Me the tax money." So they brought Him a [T]denarius. 1 day's wage

20 And He said to them, "Whose image and inscription *is* this?"

21 They said to Him, "Caesar's." And He said to them, [T]"Render therefore to Caesar the things that are [R]Caesar's, and to God the things that are God's." *Pay* • [Rom. 13:1–7]

22 When they had heard *these words*, they marveled, and left Him and went their way.

Conflict with Sadducees
Mark 12:18–27; Luke 20:27–40

23 [R]The same day the Sadducees, [R]who say there is no resurrection, came to Him and asked Him, Luke 20:27–40 • Acts 23:8

24 saying: "Teacher, [R]Moses said that if a man dies, having no children, his brother shall marry his wife and raise up offspring for his brother. Deut. 25:5

25 "Now there were with us seven brothers. The first died after he had married, and having no offspring, left his wife to his brother.

26 "Likewise the second also, and the third, even to the seventh.

27 "And last of all the woman died also.

28 "Therefore, in the resurrection, whose wife of the seven will she be? For they all had her."

29 Jesus answered and said to them, "You are [T]mistaken, [R]not knowing the Scriptures nor the power of God. *deceived* • John 20:9

30 "For in the resurrection they neither marry nor are given in marriage, but [R]are like angels *of God in heaven. [1 John 3:2]

31 "But concerning the resurrection of the dead, have you not read what was spoken to you by God, saying,

32 [R]'*I am the God of Abraham, the God of Isaac, and the God of Jacob*'? God is not the God of the dead, but of the living." Ex. 3:6, 15

33 And when the multitudes heard *this*, they were astonished at His teaching.

The Greatest Commandment—Mark 12:28–34

34 [R]But when the Pharisees heard that He had silenced the Sadducees, they gathered together. Mark 12:28–31

35 Then one of them, a lawyer, asked *Him a question*, testing Him, and saying,

36 "Teacher, which *is* the great commandment in the law?"

37 Jesus said to him, [R]" '*You shall love the* LORD *your God with all your heart, with all your soul, and with all your mind.*' Deut. 6:5

38 "This is *the* first and great commandment.

39 "And *the* second *is* like it: [R]'*You shall love your neighbor as yourself.*' Lev. 19:18

40 [R]"On these two commandments hang all the Law and the Prophets." [Matt. 7:12]

The Son of David
Mark 12:35–37: Luke 20:41–44

41 [R]While the Pharisees were gathered together, Jesus asked them, Luke 20:41–44

42 saying, "What do you think about the Christ? Whose Son is He?" They said to Him, "*The* [R]Son of David." Matt. 1:1; 21:9

43 He said to them, "How then does David in the Spirit call Him '*Lord*,' saying:

22:13 NU omits *take him away and*
22:30 NU omits *of God*

44 'The[R] LORD said to my Lord,
"Sit at My right hand,
Till I make Your enemies Your
footstool"'? Ps. 110:1

45 "If David then calls Him '*Lord*,' how is
He his Son?"
46 [R]And no one was able to answer Him a
word, [R]nor from that day on did anyone dare
question Him anymore. Luke 14:6 • Mark 12:34

CHAPTER 23

Jesus Characterizes the Pharisees
Mark 12:38–40; Luke 20:45–47

THEN Jesus spoke to the multitudes and to
His disciples,
2 saying: [R]"The scribes and the Pharisees
sit in Moses' seat. Neh. 8:4, 8
3 "Therefore whatever they tell you *to
observe, *that* observe and do, but do not do
according to their works; for [R]they say, and
do not do. [Rom. 2:19]
4 [R]"For they bind heavy burdens, hard to
bear, and lay *them* on men's shoulders; but
they *themselves* will not move them with one
of their fingers. Luke 11:46
5 "But all their works they do to be seen by
men. They make their phylacteries broad and
enlarge the borders of their garments.
6 "They love the [T]best places at feasts, the
best seats in the synagogues, Or *place of honor*
7 "greetings in the marketplaces, and to be
called by men, 'Rabbi, Rabbi.'
8 [R]"But you, do not be called 'Rabbi'; for
One is your [T]Teacher, *the Christ, and you
are all brethren. [James 3:1] • *Leader*
9 "Do not call anyone on earth your father; [R]for One is your Father, He who is in
heaven. [Mal. 1:6]
10 "And do not be called teachers; for One
is your Teacher, the Christ.
11 "But [R]he who is greatest among you shall
be your servant. Matt. 20:26, 27
12 [R]"And whoever exalts himself will be
[T]abased, and he who humbles himself will be
[T]exalted. Luke 14:11; 18:14 • *humbled* • *lifted up*

Jesus Condemns the Pharisees

13 "But [R]woe to you, scribes and Pharisees,
hypocrites! For you shut up the kingdom of
heaven against men; for you neither go in
yourselves, nor do you allow those who are
entering to go in. Luke 11:52
14 *"Woe to you, scribes and Pharisees,
hypocrites! For you devour widows' houses,
and for a pretense make long prayers. Therefore you will receive greater condemnation.
15 "Woe to you, scribes and Pharisees, hypocrites! For you travel land and sea to win
one proselyte, and when he is won, you make
him twice as much a son of [T]hell as yourselves. Gr. *Gehenna*
16 "Woe to you, blind guides, who say,
'Whoever swears by the temple, it is nothing;
but whoever swears by the gold of the temple, he is obliged *to perform it*.'
17 "Fools and blind! For which is greater,
the gold [R]or the temple that *sanctifies the
gold? Ex. 30:29
18 "And, 'Whoever swears by the altar, it is
nothing; but whoever swears by the gift that
is on it, he is obliged *to perform it*.'
19 "Fools and blind! For which is greater,
the gift or the altar that sanctifies the gift?
20 "Therefore he who [T]swears by the altar,
swears by it and by all things on it. Swears an oath
21 "He who swears by the temple, swears
by it and by Him who *dwells in it.
22 "And he who swears by heaven, swears
by [R]the throne of God and by Him who sits on
it. Matt. 5:34
23 "Woe to you, scribes and Pharisees, hypocrites! For you pay tithe of mint and anise
and cummin, and have neglected the weightier *matters* of the law: justice and mercy and
faith. These you ought to have done, without
leaving the others undone.
24 "Blind guides, who strain out a gnat and
swallow a camel!
25 "Woe to you, scribes and Pharisees, hypocrites! [R]For you cleanse the outside of the
cup and dish, but inside they are full of
extortion and *self-indulgence. Luke 11:39
26 "Blind Pharisee, first cleanse the inside of
the cup and dish, that the outside of them
may be clean also.
27 "Woe to you, scribes and Pharisees, hypocrites! [R]For you are like whitewashed tombs
which indeed appear beautiful outwardly, but
inside are full of dead *men's* bones and all
uncleanness. Acts 23:3
28 "Even so you also outwardly appear
righteous to men, but inside you are full of
hypocrisy and lawlessness.
29 [R]"Woe to you, scribes and Pharisees,
hypocrites! Because you build the tombs of
the prophets and [T]adorn the monuments of
the righteous, Luke 11:47, 48 • *decorate*
30 "and say, 'If we had lived in the days of
our fathers, we would not have been partakers with them in the blood of the prophets.'
31 "Therefore you are witnesses against
yourselves that [R]you are sons of those who
murdered the prophets. [Acts 7:51, 52]
32 [R]"Fill up, then, the measure of your
fathers' *guilt*. [1 Thess. 2:16]
33 "Serpents, brood of vipers! How can you
escape the condemnation of hell?

23:3 NU omits *to observe* **23:8** NU omits *the Christ*
23:14 NU omits v. 14 **23:17** NU *sanctified*
23:21 M *dwelt* **23:25** M *unrighteousness*

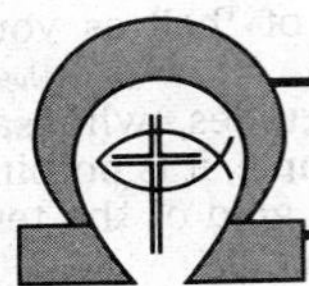

PHARISEES AND SADDUCEES

The Pharisees and Sadducees were two of the major sects or special-interest groups among the Jews in New Testament times. These groups stood for different principles, but Jesus clashed with both parties at different times during His ministry.

The word *Pharisee* means "separated." Their burning desire was to separate themselves from those people who did not observe the laws of tithing and ritual purity—matters they considered very important.

The Pharisees exerted strong influence in Jesus' time. They supported the scribes and rabbis in their interpretation of the Jewish law as handed down from the time of Moses. In Jesus' day, this interpretation of the law had become more authoritative and binding than the law itself. Jesus often challenged these traditional interpretations and the minute rules that had been issued to guide the people in every area of their behavior.

Jesus was also sensitive to the needs and hurts of individuals—an attitude that brought Him into conflict with the Pharisees. Matthew's gospel (23:1–36) contains Jesus' harsh words against the Pharisees. He believed they placed too much emphasis on minor details, while ignoring "the weightier *matters* of the law," such as "justice and mercy and faith" (Matt. 23:23).

The Pharisees often tried to trick Jesus into making statements that would be considered heretical or disloyal to Rome. On one occasion, Jesus used a denarius (see illustration), a common coin of the day, to show that citizens of His country had responsibilities to the civil ruling authorities, as well as to God (Matt. 22:15–22).

Not all Pharisees were legalistic and hypocritical, however. Three Pharisees favorably recognized in the New Testament are Joseph of Arimathea (Luke 23:50–53), Nicodemus (John 3:1–21), and Gamaliel (Acts 5:34–39).

The apostle Paul emphasized his own heritage as a Pharisee (Acts 22:3), but he also recognized the importance of abandoning this emphasis for the way of Christ (Phil. 3:1–14).

The Sadducees were the elite of Jewish society in the time of Jesus. As priests, merchants, and aristocrats, they supported the Roman authorities because they enjoyed a privileged status under Roman rule. In contrast to the Pharisees, they advocated loyalty to the original Law of Moses, insisting that interpretation of the Law could not be trusted. Also, unlike the Pharisees, they did not believe in the resurrection of the dead—a belief which Jesus challenged on one occasion (Mark 12:18–27).

The denarius coin was considered a day's wages for a laborer in the time of Jesus.

34 [R]"Therefore, indeed, I send you prophets, wise men, and scribes: *some* of them you will kill and crucify, and [R]*some* of them you will scourge in your synagogues and persecute from city to city, Luke 11:49 • 2 Cor. 11:24, 25

35 "that on you may come all the righteous blood shed on the earth, [R]from the blood of righteous Abel to the blood of Zechariah, son of Berechiah, whom you murdered between the temple and the altar. Gen. 4:8

36 "Assuredly, I say to you, all these things will come upon this generation.

Jesus Laments over Jerusalem

37 "O Jerusalem, Jerusalem, the one who kills the prophets and stones those who are sent to her! How often [R]I wanted to gather your children together, as a hen gathers her chicks under *her* wings, but you [R]were not willing! Deut. 32:11, 12 • Is. 49:5★

38 "See! Your house is left to you desolate;

39 "for I say to you, you shall see Me no more till you say, [R]*'Blessed is He who comes in the name of the* LORD*!'*" Ps. 118:26

CHAPTER 24

The Temple to Be Destroyed
Mark 13:1, 2; Luke 21:5, 6

THEN Jesus went out and departed from the temple, and His disciples came to *Him* to show Him the buildings of the temple.

2 And Jesus said to them, "Do you not see all these things? Assuredly, I say to you, [R]not one stone shall be left here upon another, that shall not be thrown down." Luke 19:44

The Disciples' Two Questions
Mark 13:3, 4; Luke 21:7

3 Now as He sat on the Mount of Olives, [R]the disciples came to Him privately, saying, [R]"Tell us, when will these things be? And what *will be* the sign of Your coming, and of the end of the age?" Mark 13:3 • [1 Thess. 5:1–3]

The Tribulation—Mark 13:5–23; Luke 21:5–24

4 And Jesus answered and said to them: "Take heed that no one deceives you.

5 "For many will come in My name, saying, 'I am the Christ,' and will deceive many.

6 "And you will hear of [R]wars and rumors of wars. See that you are not troubled; for *all *these things* must come to pass, but the end is not yet. [Rev. 6:2–4]

7 "For [R]nation will rise against nation, and kingdom against kingdom. And there will be [R]famines, *pestilences, and earthquakes in various places. Hag. 2:22 • Rev. 6:5, 6

8 "All these *are* the beginning of sorrows.

9 [R]"Then they will deliver you up to tribulation and kill you, and you will be hated by all nations for My name's sake. Matt. 10:17

10 "And then many will be offended, will betray one another, and will hate one another.

11 "Then [R]many false prophets will rise up and [R]deceive many. 2 Pet. 2:1 • [1 Tim. 4:1]

12 "And because lawlessness will abound, the love of many will grow [R]cold. [2 Thess. 2:3]

13 [R]"But he who endures to the end shall be saved. Matt. 10:22

14 "And this gospel of the kingdom will be preached in all the world as a witness to all the nations, and then the end will come.

15 "Therefore when you see the *'abomination of desolation,'* spoken of by Daniel the prophet, standing in the holy place" [R](whoever reads, let him understand), Dan. 9:23

16 "then let those who are in Judea flee to the mountains.

17 "Let him who is on the housetop not come down to take anything out of his house.

18 "And let him who is in the field not go back to get his clothes.

19 "But [R]woe to those who are pregnant and to those with nursing babies in those days! Luke 23:29

20 "And pray that your flight may not be in winter or on the Sabbath.

21 "For [R]then there will be great tribulation, such as has not been since the beginning of the world until this time, no, nor ever shall be. Dan. 9:26

22 "And unless those days were shortened, no flesh would be saved; but for the elect's sake those days will be shortened.

23 "Then if anyone says to you, 'Look, here *is* the Christ!' or 'There!' do not believe *it*.

24 "For false christs and false prophets will arise and show great signs and wonders, so as to deceive, if possible, even the elect.

25 "See, I have told you beforehand.

26 "Therefore if they say to you, 'Look, He is in the desert!' do not go out; *or* 'Look, *He is* in the inner rooms!' do not believe *it*.

The Second Coming
Mark 13:24–27; Luke 21:25–28

27 [R]"For as the lightning comes from the east and flashes to the west, so also will the coming of the Son of Man be. Luke 17:24

28 [R]"For wherever the carcass is, there the eagles will be gathered together. Luke 17:37

29 [R]"Immediately after the tribulation of those days [R]the sun will be darkened, and the moon will not give its light; the stars will fall from heaven, and the powers of the heavens will be shaken. [Dan. 7:11] • Ezek. 32:7

30 "Then the sign of the Son of Man will appear in heaven, [R]and then all the tribes of the earth will mourn, and they will see the Son of Man coming on the clouds of heaven with power and great glory. Rev. 1:7☆

24:6 NU omits *all* **24:7** NU omits *pestilences*

31 "And He will send His angels with a
great sound of a trumpet, and they will
gather together His elect from the four
winds, from one end of heaven to the other.

Parable of the Fig Tree
Mark 13:28–31; Luke 21:29–33

32 "Now learn [R]this parable from the fig
tree: When its branch has already become
tender and puts forth leaves, you know that
summer *is* near. Luke 21:29
33 "So you also, when you see all these
things, know [R]that [T]it is near, at the *very*
doors. [James 5:9] • Or *He*
34 "Assuredly, I say to you, [R]this generation
will by no means pass away till all these
things are fulfilled. [Matt. 10:23; 16:28; 23:36]
35 "Heaven and earth will pass away, but
My words will by no means pass away.

Illustration of the Days of Noah
Mark 13:32–37; Luke 21:34–36

36 [R]"But of that day and hour no one
knows, no, not even the angels of *heaven,
[R]but My Father only. Acts 1:7 • Zech. 14:7
37 "But as the days of Noah *were,* so also
will the coming of the Son of Man be.
38 [R]"For as in the days before the flood,
they were eating and drinking, marrying and
giving in marriage, until the day that Noah
entered the ark, [Gen. 6:3–5]
39 "and did not know until the flood came
and took them all away, so also will the
coming of the Son of Man be.
40 [R]"Then two *men* will be in the field: one
will be taken and the other left. Luke 17:34
41 "Two *women will be* grinding at the mill:
one will be taken and the other left.
42 [R]"Watch therefore, for you do not know
what *hour your Lord is coming. Matt. 25:13
43 [R]"But know this, that if the master of the
house had known what hour the thief would
come, he would have watched and not allowed his house to be broken into. Luke 12:39
44 [R]"Therefore you also be ready, for the
Son of Man is coming at an hour when you
do not expect *Him.* [1 Thess. 5:6]

Illustration of the Two Servants
Luke 12:41–48

45 "Who then is a faithful and wise servant,
whom his master made ruler over his household, to give them food in due season?
46 "Blessed *is* that servant whom his master, when he comes, will find so doing.
47 "Assuredly, I say to you that he will
make him ruler over all his goods.
48 "But if that evil servant says in his heart,
'My master is delaying *his coming,'
49 "and begins to beat *his* fellow servants,
and to eat and drink with the drunkards,
50 "the master of that servant will come on
a day when he is not looking for *him* and at
an hour that he is [R]not aware of, Mark 13:32
51 "and will cut him in two and appoint *him*
his portion with the hypocrites. There shall
be weeping and gnashing of teeth.

CHAPTER 25

Parable of the Ten Virgins

"THEN the kingdom of heaven shall be
likened to ten virgins who took their
lamps and went out to meet the bridegroom.
2 [R]"Now five of them were wise, and five
were foolish. Matt. 13:47; 22:10
3 "Those who *were* foolish took their
lamps and took no oil with them,
4 "but the wise took oil in their vessels
with their lamps.
5 "But while the bridegroom was delayed,
[R]they all slumbered and slept. 1 Thess. 5:6
6 "And at midnight [R]a cry was *heard:*
'Behold, the bridegroom *is coming; go out to
meet him!' [1 Thess. 4:16]
7 "Then all those virgins arose and
[R]trimmed their lamps. Luke 12:35
8 "And the foolish said to the wise, 'Give
us *some* of your oil, for our lamps are going
out.'
9 "But the wise answered, saying, '*No,* lest
there should not be enough for us and you;
but go rather to those who sell, and buy for
yourselves.'
10 "And while they went to buy, the bridegroom came, and those who were ready went
in with him to the wedding; and [R]the door
was shut. Luke 13:25
11 "Afterward the other virgins came also,
saying, [R]'Lord, Lord, open to us!' [Matt. 7:21–23]
12 "But he answered and said, 'Assuredly, I
say to you, [R]I do not know you.' [Hab. 1:13]
13 [R]"Watch therefore, for you [R]know neither the day nor the hour *in which the Son
of Man is coming. Mark 13:35 • Matt. 24:36, 42

Parable of the Talents

14 [R]"For *the kingdom of heaven is* [R]like a
man traveling to a far country, *who* called his
own servants and delivered his goods to
them. Luke 19:12–27 • Matt. 21:33
15 "And to one he gave [T]five talents, to
another two, and to another one, [R]to each
according to his own ability; and immediately
he went on a journey. $1,920,000 • [Rom. 12:6]
16 "Then he who had received the five
talents went and traded with them, and made
another five talents.
17 "And likewise he who *had received* two
gained two more also.

24:36 NU adds *nor the Son* **24:42** NU *day*
24:48 NU omits *his coming* **25:6** NU omits *is coming*
25:13 NU omits the rest of v. 13.

18 "But he who had received one went and dug in the ground, and hid his lord's money.

19 "After a long time the lord of those servants came and settled accounts with them.

20 "So he who had received five talents came and brought five other talents, saying, 'Lord, you delivered to me five talents; look, I have gained five more talents besides them.'

21 "His lord said to him, 'Well *done*, good and faithful servant; you were faithful over a few things, I will make you ruler over many things. Enter into the joy of your lord.'

22 "He also who had received two talents came and said, 'Lord, you delivered to me two talents; look, I have gained two more talents besides them.'

23 "His lord said to him, 'Well *done*, good and faithful servant; you have been faithful over a few things, I will make you ruler over many things. Enter into the joy of your lord.'

24 "Then he who had received the one talent came and said, 'Lord, I knew you to be a hard man, reaping where you have not sown, and gathering where you have not scattered seed.

25 'And I was afraid, and went and hid your talent in the ground. Look, *there* you have *what is* yours.'

26 "But his lord answered and said to him, 'You wicked and lazy servant, you knew that I reap where I have not sown, and gather where I have not scattered seed.

27 'Therefore you ought to have deposited my money with the bankers, and at my coming I would have received back my own with interest.

28 'Therefore take the talent from him, and give *it* to him who has ten talents.

29 [R]'For to everyone who has, more will be given, and he will have abundance; but from him who does not have, even what he has will be taken away. Matt. 13:12

30 'And cast the unprofitable servant into the outer darkness. [R]There will be weeping and [R]gnashing of teeth.' Matt. 24:51 • Ps. 112:10

Judgment of the Gentiles

31 "When the Son of Man comes in His glory, and all the *holy angels with Him, then He will sit on the throne of His glory.

32 "[R]All the nations will be gathered before Him, and [R]He will separate them one from another, as a shepherd divides *his* sheep from the goats. [2 Cor. 5:10] • Ezek. 20:38

33 "And He will set the [R]sheep on His right hand, but the goats on the left. [John 10:11, 27, 28]

34 "Then the King will say to those on His right hand, 'Come, you blessed of My Father, [R]inherit the kingdom prepared for you from the foundation of the world: [Rom. 8:17]

35 [R]'for I was hungry and you gave Me food; I was thirsty and you gave Me drink; I was a stranger and you took Me in; Is. 58:7

36 'I *was* [R]naked and you clothed Me; I was sick and you visited Me; [R]I was in prison and you came to Me.' [James 2:15, 16] • 2 Tim. 1:16

37 "Then the righteous will answer Him, saying, 'Lord, when did we see You hungry and feed *You*, or thirsty and give *You* drink?

38 'When did we see You a stranger and take *You* in, or naked and clothe *You*?

39 'Or when did we see You sick, or in prison, and come to You?'

40 "And the King will answer and say to them, 'Assuredly, I say to you, [R]inasmuch as you did *it* to one of the least of these My brethren, you did *it* to Me.' Mark 9:41

41 "Then He will also say to those on the left hand, [R]'Depart from Me, you cursed, [R]into the everlasting fire prepared for [R]the devil and his angels: Matt. 7:23 • Matt. 13:40, 42 • [2 Pet. 2:4]

42 'for I was hungry and you gave Me no food; I was thirsty and you gave Me no drink;

43 'I was a stranger and you did not take Me in, naked and you did not clothe Me, sick and in prison and you did not visit Me.'

44 "Then they also will answer *Him, saying, 'Lord, when did we see You hungry or thirsty or a stranger or naked or sick or in prison, and did not minister to You?'

45 "Then He will answer them, saying, 'Assuredly, I say to you, [R]inasmuch as you did not do *it* to one of the least of these, you did not do *it* to Me.' Prov. 14:31

46 "And [R]these will go away into everlasting punishment, but the righteous into eternal life." [Dan. 12:2]

CHAPTER 26

The Religious Leaders Plot to Kill Jesus Mark 14:1, 2; Luke 22:1, 2

NOW it came to pass, when Jesus had finished all these sayings, *that* He said to His disciples,

2 [R]"You know that after two days is the Passover, and the Son of Man will be delivered up to be crucified." Luke 22:1, 2

3 [R]Then the chief priests, *the scribes, and the elders of the people assembled at the palace of the high priest, who was called Caiaphas, John 11:47

4 and [R]plotted to take Jesus by [T]trickery and kill *Him*. Acts 4:25–28 • *deception*

5 But they said, "Not during the feast, lest there be an uproar among the people."

Mary Anoints Jesus for Burial Mark 14:3–9; John 12:2–8

6 And when Jesus was in [R]Bethany at the house of Simon the leper, Mark 14:3–9

25:31 NU omits *holy* **25:44** NU, M omit *Him*
26:3 NU omits *the scribes*

7 a woman came to Him having an alabaster flask of very costly fragrant oil, and she
poured it on His head as He sat *at the table.*
8 [R]But when His disciples saw *it,* they were
indignant, saying, "To what purpose *is* this
waste? John 12:4
9 "For this fragrant oil might have been
sold for much and given to *the* poor."
10 But when Jesus was aware of *it,* He said
to them, "Why do you trouble the woman?
For she has done a good work for Me.
11 "For you have the poor with you always,
but Me you do not have always.
12 "For in pouring this fragrant oil on My
body, she did *it* for My [R]burial. John 19:38–42
13 "Assuredly, I say to you, wherever this
gospel is preached in the whole world, what
this woman has done will also be told as a
memorial to her."

Judas Agrees to Betray Jesus
Mark 14:10, 11; Luke 22:3–6

14 Then one of the twelve, called [R]Judas
Iscariot, went to the chief priests Matt. 10:4
15 and said, "What are you willing to give
me if I deliver Him to you?" And they
counted out to him thirty pieces of silver.
16 So from that time he sought opportunity
to betray Him.

The Passover Is Prepared
Mark 14:12–16; Luke 22:7–13

17 Now on the first *day* of the *Feast of* the
Unleavened Bread the disciples came to
Jesus, saying to Him, "Where do You want us
to prepare for You to eat the Passover?"
18 And He said, "Go into the city to a
certain man, and say to him, 'The Teacher
says, "My time is at hand; I will keep the
Passover at your house with My disciples." ' "
19 So the disciples did as Jesus had directed
them; and they prepared the Passover.

The Passover Is Celebrated
Mark 14:17–21; Luke 22:14, 21–23;
John 13:21, 22

20 [R]Now when evening had come, He sat
down with the twelve. Mark 14:17–21
21 Now as they were eating, He said, "Assuredly, I say to you, one of you will [R]betray
Me." John 6:70, 71; 13:21
22 And they were exceedingly sorrowful,
and each of them began to say to Him, "Lord,
is it I?"
23 Then He answered and said, [R]"He who
dipped *his* hand with Me in the dish will
betray Me. Ps. 41:9★
24 "The Son of Man goes as it is written of
Him, but woe to that man by whom the Son
of Man is betrayed! It would have been good
for that man if he had not been born."
25 Then Judas, who was betraying Him,
answered and said, "Rabbi, is it I?" He said to
him, "You have said it."

The Lord's Supper Is Instituted
Mark 14:22–25; Luke 22:19, 20; 1 Cor. 11:23–26

26 [R]And as they were eating, [R]Jesus took
bread, *blessed *it* and broke *it,* and gave *it* to
the disciples and said, "Take, eat; [R]this is My
body." Mark 14:22–25 • 1 Cor. 11:23–25 • [1 Pet. 2:24]
27 Then He took the cup, and gave thanks,
and gave *it* to them, saying, [R]"Drink from it,
all of you. Mark 14:23
28 "For [R]this is My blood [R]of the *new
covenant, which is shed for many for the
[T]remission of sins. [Ex. 24:8] • Jer. 31:31 • *forgiveness*
29 "But [R]I say to you, I will not drink of this
fruit of the vine from now on [R]until that day
when I drink it new with you in My Father's
kingdom." Mark 14:25 • Acts 10:41

Peter's Denial Is Predicted
Mark 14:26–31; Luke 22:34, 39; John 13:37, 38

30 [R]And when they had sung a hymn, they
went out to the Mount of Olives. Mark 14:26–31
31 Then Jesus said to them, [R]"All of you will
[R]be made to stumble because of Me this
night, for it is written: John 16:32 • [Matt. 11:6]

[R]*'I will strike the Shepherd,*
And the sheep of the flock will be
scattered.' Zech. 13:7☆

32 "But after I have been raised, [R]I will go
before you to Galilee." Matt. 28:7, 10, 16☆
33 Peter answered and said to Him, "Even if
all are made to stumble because of You, I will
never be made to stumble."
34 Jesus said to him, [R]"Assuredly, I say to
you that this night, before the rooster crows,
you will deny Me three times." Matt. 26:74, 75☆
35 Peter said to Him, "Even if I have to die
with You, I will not deny You!" And so said
all the disciples.

Jesus' Three Prayers
Mark 14:32–42; Luke 22:40–46

36 Then Jesus came with them to a place
called Gethsemane, and said to the disciples,
"Sit here while I go and pray over there."
37 And He took with Him Peter and [R]the
two sons of Zebedee, and He began to be
sorrowful and deeply distressed. Matt. 4:21; 17:1
38 Then He said to them, [R]"My soul is
exceedingly sorrowful, even to death. Stay
here and watch with Me." John 12:27
39 He went a little farther and fell on His
face, and prayed, saying, "O My Father, if it is
possible, let this cup pass from Me; nevertheless, not as I will, but as You *will.*"
40 Then He came to the disciples and found
them asleep, and said to Peter, "What, could
you not watch with Me one hour?

26:26 M *gave thanks for* **26:28** NU omits *new*

41 R"Watch and pray, lest you enter into
temptation. RThe spirit indeed *is* willing, but
the flesh *is* weak." Luke 22:40, 46 • [Gal. 5:17]
42 He went away again a second time and
prayed, saying, "O My Father, *if this cup
cannot pass away from Me unless I drink it,
RYour will be done." Is. 50:5★
43 And He came and found them asleep
again, for their eyes were heavy.
44 So He left them, went away again, and
prayed the third time, saying the same words.
45 Then He came to His disciples and said to
them, "Are *you* still sleeping and resting?
Behold, the hour Tis at hand, and the Son of
Man is being Rbetrayed into the hands of
sinners. *has drawn near* • Matt. 17:22, 23; 20:18, 19
46 "Rise, let us be going. See, he who Rbe-
trays Me is at hand." Matt. 20:18; 26:21★

Jesus' Betrayal and Arrest
Mark 14:43–52; Luke 22:47–53; John 18:1–11

47 And Rwhile He was still speaking, behold,
Judas, one of the twelve, with a great multitude with swords and clubs, came from the
chief priests and elders of the people. Acts 1:16
48 Now His betrayer had given them a sign,
saying, "Whomever I kiss, He is the One;
seize Him."
49 Then immediately he went up to Jesus
and said, "Greetings, Rabbi!" Rand kissed
Him. 2 Sam. 20:9
50 And Jesus said to him, R"Friend, why
have you come?" Then they came and laid
hands on Jesus and took Him. Ps. 41:9; 55:13
51 And suddenly, Rone of those *who were*
with Jesus stretched out *his* hand and drew
his sword, struck the servant of the high
priest, and cut off his ear. John 18:10
52 Then Jesus said to him, "Put your sword
in its place, Rfor all who take the sword will
*perish by the sword. Rev. 13:10
53 "Or do you think that I cannot now pray
to My Father, and He will provide Me with
Rmore than twelve legions of angels? Dan. 7:10
54 "How then could the Scriptures be fulfilled, Rthat it must happen thus?" Is. 50:6
55 In that hour Jesus said to the multitudes,
"Have you come out, as against a robber,
with swords and clubs to take Me? I sat daily
with you, teaching in the temple, and you did
not seize Me.
56 "But all this was done that the Scriptures
of the prophets might be fulfilled." Then all
the disciples forsook Him and fled.

Two False Witnesses
Mark 14:53–65; Luke 22:54, 55, 63–65; John 18:12, 18, 24

57 RAnd those who had laid hold of Jesus
led *Him* away to Caiaphas the high priest,
where the scribes and the elders were assembled. John 18:12, 19–24
58 But Peter followed Him at a distance to
the high priest's courtyard. And he went in
and sat with the servants to see the end.
59 Now the chief priests, *the elders, and all
the council sought Rfalse testimony against
Jesus to put Him to death, Ps. 35:11
60 *but found none. Even though Rmany
false witnesses came forward, they found
none. But at last Rtwo *false witnesses came
forward Ps. 27:12★ • Deut. 19:15
61 and said, "This *fellow* said, R'I am able to
destroy the temple of God and to build it in
three days.'" John 2:19
62 RAnd the high priest arose and said to
Him, "Do You answer nothing? What *is it
that* these men testify against You?" Mark 14:60
63 But RJesus kept silent. And the high
priest answered and said to Him, R"I adjure
You by the living God that You tell us if You
are the Christ, the Son of God." Is. 53:7★ • Lev. 5:1
64 Jesus said to him, "*It is as* you said.
Nevertheless, I say to you, Rhereafter you will
see the Son of Man Rsitting at the right hand
of the Power, and coming on the clouds of
heaven." Dan. 7:13 • [Acts 7:55]
65 Then the high priest tore his clothes,
saying, "He has spoken blasphemy! What
further need do we have of witnesses? Look,
now you have heard His blasphemy!
66 "What do you think?" They answered
and said, "He is deserving of death."
67 RThen they spat in His face and beat
Him; and Rothers struck *Him* with Tthe palms
of their hands, Is. 50:6; 53:3★ • Luke 22:63–65 • *rods*
68 saying, R"Prophesy to us, Christ! Who is
the one who struck You?" Mark 14:65

Three Denials of Peter
Mark 14:66–72; Luke 22:55–62; John 18:15–18, 25–27

69 RNow Peter sat outside in the courtyard.
And a servant girl came to him, saying, "You
also were with Jesus of Galilee." John 18:17
70 But he denied it before *them* all, saying,
"I do not know what you are saying."
71 And when he had gone out to the gateway, another *girl* saw him and said to those
who were there, "This *fellow* also was with
Jesus of Nazareth."
72 But again he denied with an oath, "I do
not know the Man!"
73 And after a while those who stood by
came to *him* and said to Peter, "Surely you
also are *one* of them, because your Rspeech
betrays you." Luke 22:59
74 Then Rhe began to curse and swear,
saying, "I do not know the Man!" And immediately a rooster crowed. Matt. 26:34★

26:42 NU *if this may not pass away unless*
26:52 M *die*
26:59 NU omits *the elders*
26:60 NU *but found none, even though many false witnesses came forward.*
26:60 NU omits *false witnesses*

75 And Peter remembered the word of Jesus who had said to him, [R]"Before the rooster crows, you will deny Me three times." Then he went out and wept bitterly. Matt. 26:34

CHAPTER 27

Jesus Is Delivered to Pilate
Mark 15:1; Luke 22:66; 23:1; John 18:28

WHEN morning came, all the chief priests and elders of the people took counsel against Jesus to put Him to death.

2 And when they had bound Him, they led Him away and [R]delivered Him to *Pontius Pilate the governor. Luke 18:32; Acts 3:13★

Judas Repents—Acts 1:18, 19

3 Then Judas, His betrayer, seeing that He had been condemned, was remorseful and brought back the [T]thirty [R]pieces of silver to the chief priests and elders, $3,840 • Matt. 26:15

4 saying, "I have sinned by betraying innocent blood." And they said, "What *is that* to us? You see *to it!*"

5 Then he threw down the pieces of silver in the temple and [R]departed, and went and hanged himself. Matt. 18:7; 26:24★

6 But the chief priests took the silver pieces and said, "It is not lawful to put them into the treasury, because they are the price of blood."

7 And they took counsel and bought with them the potter's field, to bury strangers in.

8 Therefore that field has been called [R]the Field of Blood to this day. Acts 1:19

9 Then was fulfilled what was spoken by Jeremiah the prophet, saying, [R]*"And they took the* [T]*thirty pieces of silver, the value of Him who was priced,* whom they of the children of Israel priced, Zech. 11:12★ • $3,840

10 *"and gave them for the potter's field, as the* LORD [R]*directed me."* Jer. 32:6–9; Zech. 11:13★

Jesus Is Examined
Mark 15:2–5; Luke 23:2–5; John 18:29–38

11 Now Jesus stood before the governor. [R]And the governor asked Him, saying, "Are You the King of the Jews?" So Jesus said to him, [R]"*It is as* you say." Mark 15:2–5 • John 18:37

12 And while He was being accused by the chief priests and elders, [R]He answered nothing. John 19:9

13 Then Pilate said to Him, [R]"Do You not hear how many things they testify against You?" Matt. 26:62

14 And He answered him not one word, so that the governor marveled greatly.

Barabbas Is Freed
Mark 15:6–14; Luke 23:17–23; John 18:39, 40

15 [R]Now at the feast the governor was accustomed to releasing to the multitude one prisoner whom they wished. Luke 23:17–25

16 And they had then a notorious prisoner called *Barabbas.

17 Therefore, when they had gathered together, Pilate said to them, "Whom do you want me to release to you? Barabbas, or Jesus who is called Christ?"

18 For he knew that because of [R]envy they had delivered Him. Matt. 21:38

19 While he was sitting on the judgment seat, his wife sent to him, saying, "Have nothing to do with that just Man, for I have suffered many things today in a dream because of Him."

20 [R]But the chief priests and elders persuaded the multitudes that they should ask for Barabbas and destroy Jesus. Acts 3:14

21 The governor answered and said to them, "Which of the two do you want me to release to you?" They said, "Barabbas!"

22 Pilate said to them, "What then shall I do with Jesus who is called Christ?" *They* all said to him, "Let Him be crucified!"

23 Then the governor said, [R]"Why, what evil has He done?" But they cried out all the more, saying, "Let Him be crucified!" Acts 3:13

24 When Pilate saw that he could not prevail at all, but rather *that* a [T]tumult was rising, he [R]took water and washed *his* hands before the multitude, saying, "I am innocent of the blood of this *just Person. You see *to it.*" *an uproar* • Deut. 21:6–8

25 And all the people answered and said, "His blood *be* on us and on our children."

Jesus Is Scourged
Mark 15:15–17; Luke 23:24, 25; John 19:16

26 Then he released Barabbas to them; and when [R]he had scourged Jesus, he delivered *Him* to be crucified. [Is. 50:6; 53:5]★

27 Then the soldiers of the governor took Jesus into the Praetorium and gathered the whole [T]garrison around Him. *cohort*

28 And they [R]stripped Him and [R]put a scarlet robe on Him. John 19:2 • Luke 23:11

Jesus Is Lead to Golgotha
Mark 15:18–22; Luke 23:26–33; John 19:17

29 [R]When they had [T]twisted a crown of thorns, they put *it* on His head, and a reed in His right hand. And they bowed the knee before Him and mocked Him, saying, "Hail, King of the Jews!" Ps. 69:19; Is. 53:3★ • Lit. *woven*

30 Then [R]they spat on Him, and took the reed and struck Him on the head. Is. 50:6★

31 Then when they had mocked Him, they took the robe off Him, put His *own* clothes on Him, and led Him away to be crucified.

27:2 NU omits *Pontius* **27:16** NU *Jesus Barabbas*
27:24 NU omits *just*

NEW TESTAMENT EVENTS

BIRTH OF JESUS*	4 B.C.	Luke 2:1–20
JESUS' VISIT TO TEMPLE AS A BOY	A.D. 9	Luke 2:41–52
PERIOD OF JESUS' PUBLIC MINISTRY	A.D. 29–33	
JESUS' CRUCIFIXION AND RESURRECTION	A.D. 33	Matt. 27; 28
PENTECOST	A.D. 33	Acts 2
DEATH OF STEPHEN	A.D. 35	Acts 7
PAUL'S CONVERSION	A.D. 36	Acts 9
PHILIP PREACHES TO SAMARITANS	A.D. 38	Acts 8
PETER ACCEPTS GENTILE CONVERTS	A.D. 40	Acts 10
PAUL AND BARNABAS AT ANTIOCH	A.D. 42/43	Acts 11:19–30
PAUL'S FIRST MISSIONARY JOURNEY	A.D. 48–49	Acts 13; 14
MEETING OF JERUSALEM COUNCIL	A.D. 50	Acts 15
PAUL'S SECOND MISSIONARY TOUR	A.D. 51–53	Acts 15—18
PAUL'S THIRD MISSIONARY TOUR	A.D. 53–57	Acts 18—21
PAUL'S VOYAGE TO ROME	A.D. 59	Acts 27; 28
PAUL IMPRISONED AT ROME	A.D. 59–62	Acts 28
POSSIBLE DATE OF PETER'S EXECUTION	A.D. 64	
POSSIBLE DATE OF PAUL'S EXECUTION	A.D. 68	
WRITING OF JOHN'S EPISTLES	A.D. 85–90	
WRITING OF REVELATION	A.D. 95–96	
DEATH OF THE APOSTLE JOHN	A.D. 100	

***Pinning down exact dates for some of the events listed in this chart is difficult. Therefore, the dates given should be considered to be approximate.**

32 Now as they came out, [R]they found a
man of Cyrene, Simon by name. Him they
compelled to bear His cross. Mark 15:21
33 [R]And when they had come to a place
called Golgotha, that is to say, Place of a
Skull, John 19:17

Jesus Is Crucified
Mark 15:23–32; Luke 23:33–43; John 19:18–24

34 [R]they gave Him *sour wine mingled with
gall to drink. But when He had tasted *it*, He
would not drink. Ps. 69:21★
35 Then they crucified Him, and divided His
garments, casting lots, *that it might be
fulfilled which was spoken by the prophet:

[R]*"They divided My garments among*
them, Ps. 22:18★
And for My clothing they cast lots."

36 [R]Sitting down, they kept watch over Him
there. Ps. 22:17; Matt. 27:54★
37 And they [R]put up over His head the
accusation written against Him: John 19:19

THIS IS JESUS THE KING OF THE JEWS.

38 Then two robbers were crucified with
Him, one on the right and another on the left.
39 And [R]those who passed by blasphemed
Him, wagging their heads Ps. 22:7★
40 and saying, [R]"You who destroy the temple and build *it* in three days, save Yourself!
[R]If You are the Son of God, come down from
the cross." John 2:19 • Matt. 26:63
41 Likewise the chief priests, also [R]mocking
with the *scribes and elders, said, Matt. 20:19★
42 "He [R]saved others; Himself He cannot
save. [R]If* He is the King of Israel, let Him
now come down from the cross, and we will
believe *Him. [John 3:14, 15] • Ps. 22:6; 69:9★
43 [R]"He trusted in God; let Him deliver Him
now if He will have Him; for He said, 'I am
the Son of God.'" Ps. 22:8☆
44 Even the robbers who were crucified
with Him reviled Him with the same thing.

Jesus Dies
Mark 15:33–37; Luke 23:44–46; John 19:28–30

45 Now from the sixth hour until the ninth
hour there was darkness over all the land.
46 And about the ninth hour [R]Jesus cried
out with a loud voice, saying, "Eli, Eli, lama
sabachthani?" that is, [R]*"My God, My God,*
why have You forsaken Me?" [Heb. 5:7] • Ps. 22:1★
47 Some of those who stood there, when
they heard *that*, said, "This *Man* is calling for
Elijah!"
48 Immediately one of them ran and took a
sponge, [R]filled *it* with sour wine and put *it* on
a reed, and gave it to Him to drink. Ps. 69:21
49 The rest said, "Let Him alone; let us see if
Elijah will come to save Him."
50 Jesus, when He had cried out again with
a loud voice, yielded up His spirit.

Signs Accompanying Jesus' Death
Mark 15:38–41; Luke 23:45, 47–49

51 And behold, [R]the veil of the temple was
torn in two from top to bottom; and the earth
quaked, and the rocks were split, Zech. 11:10, 11★
52 and the graves were opened; and many
bodies of the saints who had fallen asleep
were raised;
53 and coming out of the graves after His
resurrection, they went into the holy city and
appeared to many.
54 [R]Now when the centurion and those with
him, who were guarding Jesus, saw the earthquake and the things that had happened,
they feared greatly, saying, [R]"Truly this was
the Son of God!" Mark 15:39 • Matt. 14:33
55 And many women [R]who followed Jesus
from Galilee, ministering to Him, were there
looking on from afar, Luke 8:2, 3
56 [R]among whom were Mary Magdalene,
Mary the mother of James and *Joses, and
the mother of Zebedee's sons. Mark 15:40, 47

Jesus Is Buried
Mark 15:42–47; Luke 23:50–55; John 19:38–42

57 Now [R]when evening had come, there
came a rich man from Arimathea, named
Joseph, who himself had also become a disciple of Jesus. John 19:38–42
58 This man went to Pilate and asked for
the body of Jesus. Then Pilate commanded
the body to be given to him.
59 And when Joseph had taken the body, he
wrapped it in a clean linen cloth,
60 and [R]laid it in his new tomb which he had
hewn out of the rock; and he rolled a large
stone against the door of the tomb, and
departed. Is. 53:9★
61 And Mary Magdalene was there, and the
other Mary, sitting opposite the tomb.
62 On the next day, which followed the Day
of Preparation, the chief priests and Pharisees
gathered together to Pilate,
63 saying, "Sir, we remember, while He was
still alive, how that deceiver said, [R]'After
three days I will rise.' Mark 8:31; 10:34
64 "Therefore command that the tomb be
made secure until the third day, lest His
disciples come *by night and steal Him *away*,
and say to the people, 'He has risen from the
dead.' So the last deception will be worse
than the first."
65 Pilate said to them, "You have a guard;
go your way, make *it* as secure as you know
how."

27:34 NU omits *sour*
27:35 NU, M omit the rest of v. 35.
27:41 M *scribes, the Pharisees, and the elders*
27:42 NU omits *If* **27:42** NU, M *in Him*
27:56 NU *Joseph* **27:64** NU omits *by night*

66 So they went and made the tomb secure,
sealing the stone and setting the guard.

CHAPTER 28

The Empty Tomb—Mark 16:1–8; Luke 24:1–11

NOW [R]after the Sabbath, as the first *day* of
the week began to dawn, Mary Magdalene [R]and the other Mary came to see the
tomb. Luke 24:1–10 • Matt. 27:56, 61
2 And behold, there was a great earthquake; for an angel of the Lord descended
from heaven, and came and rolled back the
stone *from the door, and sat on it.
3 [R]His countenance was like lightning, and
his clothing as white as snow. Dan. 7:9; 10:6
4 And the guards shook for fear of him,
and became like [R]dead *men*. Rev. 1:17
5 But the angel answered and said to the
women, "Do not be afraid, for I know that
you seek Jesus who was crucified.
6 "He is not here; [R]for He is risen, as He
said. Come, see the place where the Lord
lay. Matt. 12:40; 16:21 *
7 "And go quickly and tell His disciples
that He is risen from the dead, and indeed He
is going before you into Galilee; there you
will see Him. Behold, I have told you."
8 So they departed quickly from the tomb
with fear and great joy, and ran to bring His
disciples word.

The Appearance of Jesus to the Women

9 And *as they went to tell His disciples,
behold, [R]Jesus met them, saying, "Rejoice!"
And they came and held Him by the feet and
worshiped Him. John 20:14
10 Then Jesus said to them, "Do not be
afraid. Go *and* tell [R]My brethren to go to
Galilee, and there they will see Me." John 20:17

The Bribery of the Soldiers

11 Now while they were going, behold,
some of the guard came into the city and
reported to the chief priests all the things
that had happened.
12 When they had assembled with the elders and taken counsel, they gave a large
sum of money to the soldiers,
13 saying, "Tell them, 'His disciples came at
night and stole Him *away* while we slept.'
14 "And if this comes to the governor's ears,
we will appease him and make you secure."
15 So they took the money and did as they
were instructed; and this saying is commonly
reported among the Jews until this day.

The Appearance of Jesus to the Disciples

16 Then the eleven disciples went away into
Galilee, to the mountain [R]which Jesus had
appointed for them. Matt. 26:32; 28:7, 10
17 And when they saw Him, they worshiped
Him; but some [R]doubted. John 20:24–29

The Great Commission

18 Then Jesus came and spoke to them,
saying, [R]"All authority has been given to Me
in heaven and on earth. [Dan. 7:13, 14]
19 [R]"Go *therefore and [R]make disciples of
all the nations, baptizing them in the name of
the Father and of the Son and of the Holy
Spirit, Mark 16:15 • Luke 24:47
20 [R]"teaching them to observe all things
that I have commanded you; and lo, I am
[R]with you always, *even* to the end of the
age." *Amen. [Acts 2:42] • [Acts 4:31; 18:10; 23:11]

28:2 NU omits *from the door*
28:9 NU omits *as they went to tell His disciples*
28:19 M omits *therefore* 28:20 NU omits *Amen*

28:19 Sharing Our Faith: Why?—There are at least six compelling reasons for sharing our faith in Christ with those who have not experienced new life in Christ.

a. Because God has commanded us to do so. The final words of Jesus while on earth (Page 1272—Acts 1:8) and also the Bible (Page 1539—Rev. 22:17) speak concerning this.
b. Because it demonstrates our love for God. Christ said that if we truly loved Him we would keep His commandments (Page 1258—John 14:15).
c. Because all are lost (Page 1325—Rom. 3:10, 23).
d. Because our sharing is God's chosen method to tell all people. He could have used angels, but He didn't. Only redeemed sinners can tell lost sinners about Christ. See Romans 10:14–17; Acts 8:3.
e. Because God desires to save all people (Page 1276—Acts 4:12; Page 1486—2 Pet. 3:9; Page 1426—1 Tim. 2:4).
f. Because someone once shared his faith with us. It may have been a faithful Bible teacher, or a godly pastor, or a praying parent. In other words, they have the right to expect that we will do for others what they have done for us.

Now turn to Page 1359—1 Cor. 15:3, 4: Sharing Our Faith: What?

THE GOSPEL ACCORDING TO
MARK

THE BOOK OF MARK

The message of Mark's gospel is captured in a single verse: "For even the Son of Man did not come to be served, but to serve, and to give His life a ransom for many" (10:45). Chapter by chapter, the book unfolds the dual focus of Christ's life: service and sacrifice.

Mark portrays Jesus as a Servant on the move, instantly responsive to the will of the Father. By preaching, teaching, and healing, He ministers to the needs of others even to the point of death. After the resurrection, He commissions His followers to continue His work in His power—servants following in the steps of the perfect Servant.

The ancient title for this gospel was *Kata Markon,* "According to Mark." The author is best known by his Latin name *Marcus,* but in Jewish circles he was called by his Hebrew name *John.* Acts 12:12, 25 and 15:37 refer to him as "John, whose surname was Mark."

THE AUTHOR OF MARK

According to Acts 12:12, Mark's mother Mary had a large house that was used as a meeting place for believers in Jerusalem. Peter apparently went to this house often because the servant girl recognized his voice at the gate (Acts 12:13–16). Barnabas was Mark's cousin (Col. 4:10), but Peter may have been the person who led him to Christ (Peter called him "Mark my son," 1 Pet. 5:13). It was this close association with Peter that lent apostolic authority to Mark's gospel, since Peter was evidently Mark's primary source of information. It has been suggested that Mark was referring to himself in his account of "a certain young man" in Gethsemane (14:51, 52). Since all the disciples had abandoned Jesus (14:50), this little incident may have been a firsthand account.

Barnabas and Saul took Mark along with them when they returned from Jerusalem to Antioch (Acts 12:25) and again when they left on the first missionary journey (Acts 13:5). However, Mark left early and returned to Jerusalem (Acts 13:13). When Barnabas wanted to bring Mark on the second missionary journey, Paul's refusal led to a disagreement. The result was that Barnabas took Mark to Cyprus and Paul took Silas through Syria and Cilicia (Acts 15:36–41). Nevertheless, Paul wrote that Mark was with him during his first Roman imprisonment (Col. 4:10; Philem. 24) about twelve years later, so there must have been a reconciliation. In fact, at the end of his life Paul sent for Mark, saying, "he is useful to me for ministry" (2 Tim. 4:11).

The early church uniformly attested that Mark wrote this gospel. Papias, Irenaeus, Clement of Alexandria, and Origen are among the church fathers who affirmed Marcan authorship.

THE TIME OF MARK

Many scholars believe that Mark was the first of the four gospels, but there is uncertainty over its date. Because of the prophecy about the destruction of the temple (13:2), it should be dated before A.D. 70, but early traditions disagree as to whether it was written before or after the martyrdom of Peter (c. A.D. 64). The probable range for this book is A.D. 55–65.

Mark was evidently directed to a Roman readership and early tradition indicates that it originated in Rome. This may be why Mark omitted a number of items that would not have been meaningful to Gentiles, such as the genealogy of Christ, fulfilled prophecy, references to the Law, and certain Jewish customs that are found in other gospels. Mark interpreted Aramaic words (3:17; 5:41; 7:34; 15:22) and used a number of Latin terms in place of their Greek equivalents (4:21; 6:27; 12:14, 42; 15:15, 16, 39).

THE CHRIST OF MARK

The Lord is presented as an active, compassionate, and obedient Servant who constantly ministers to the physical and spiritual needs of others. Because this is the story of a Servant, Mark omits Jesus' ancestry and birth and moves right into His busy public ministry. The distinctive word of this book is *euthus,* translated "immediately" or "straightway," and it appears more often in this compact gospel (forty-two times) than in the rest of the New Testament. Christ is constantly moving toward a goal that is hidden to almost all. Mark clearly shows the power and authority of this unique Servant, identifying Him as no less than the Son of God (1:1, 11; 3:11; 5:7; 9:7; 13:32; 14:61; 15:39).

KEYS TO MARK

Key Word: Jesus the Servant—Even in the first verse it is obvious that this gospel centers on the person and mission of the Son of God. Mark's theme is captured well in 10:45 because Jesus is portrayed in this book as a Servant and as the Redeemer of men (cf. Phil. 2:5–11). Like the other gospels, Mark is not a biography but a topical narrative. Mark juxtaposes Christ's teachings and works to show how they authenticate each other. Miracles are predominant in this book (there are eighteen), and they are used to demonstrate not only the power of Christ but also His compassion. Mark shows his gentile readers how the Son of God—rejected by His own people—achieved ultimate victory through apparent defeat. There was no doubt an evangelistic purpose behind this gospel as Mark directed his words to a gentile audience that knew little about Old Testament theology.

Key Verses: Mark 10:43-45 and 8:34-37—"Yet it shall not be so among you; but whoever desires to become great among you shall be your servant. And whoever of you desires to be first shall be slave of all. For even the Son of Man did not come to be served, but to serve, and to give His life a ransom for many" (10:43–45).

"And when He had called the people *to Him*, with His disciples also, He said to them, 'Whoever desires to come after Me, let him deny himself, and take up his cross, and follow Me. For whoever desires to save his life will lose it, but whoever loses his life for My sake and the gospel's will save it. For what will it profit a man if he gains the whole world, and loses his own soul? Or what will a man give in exchange for his soul?' " (8:34–37).

Key Chapter: Mark 8—As in Matthew, Mark's gospel contains a pivotal chapter showing the change of emphasis in Jesus' ministry. In Matthew it is chapter 12; in Mark it is chapter 8. The pivotal event lies in Peter's confession, "You are the Christ." That faith-inspired response triggers a new phase in both the content and the course of Jesus' ministry. Until this point He has sought to validate His claims as Messiah. But now He begins to fortify His men for His forthcoming suffering and death at the hands of the religious leaders. Jesus' steps begin to take Him daily closer to Jerusalem—the place where the Perfect Servant will demonstrate the full extent of His servanthood.

SURVEY OF MARK

Mark, the shortest and simplest of the four gospels, gives a crisp and fast-moving look at the life of Christ. With few comments, Mark lets the narrative speak for itself as it tells the story of the Servant who constantly ministers to others through preaching, healing, teaching, and, ultimately, His own death. Mark traces the steady building of hostility and opposition to Jesus as He resolutely moves toward the fulfillment of His earthly mission. Almost forty percent of this gospel is devoted to a detailed account of the last eight days of Jesus' life, climaxing in His resurrection. The Lord is vividly portrayed in this book in two parts: to serve (1—10); to sacrifice (11—16).

To Serve (1—10): Mark passes over the birth and early years of Jesus' life and begins with the events that immediately precede the inauguration of His public ministry—His baptism by John and His temptation by Satan (1:1-13). The first four chapters emphasize the words of the Servant while chapters 5—7 accent His works. However, in both sections there is a frequent alternation between Christ's messages and miracles in order to reveal His person and power. Though He has come to serve others, Jesus' authority prevails over many realms.

Although Jesus has already been teaching and testing His disciples (see ch. 4), His ministry with them becomes more intense from this point on as He begins to prepare them for His departure. The religious leaders are growing more antagonistic, and Christ's "hour" is only about six months away. Mark 8:31 is the pivotal point in the gospel as the Son of Man speaks clearly to His disciples about His coming death and resurrection. The disciples struggle with this difficult revelation, but Jesus' steps head inexorably to Jerusalem.

To Sacrifice (11—16): Mark allots a disproportionate space to the last weeks of the Servant's redemptive ministry. During the last seven days in Jerusalem, hostility from the chief priests, scribes, elders, Pharisees, Herodians, and Saddu-

FOCUS	TO SERVE			TO SACRIFICE	
REFERENCE	1:1—	2:13—	8:27—	11:1—	16:1—16:20
DIVISION	PRESENTATION OF THE SERVANT	OPPOSITION TO THE SERVANT	INSTRUCTION BY THE SERVANT	REJECTION OF THE SERVANT	RESURRECTION OF THE SERVANT
TOPIC	SAYINGS AND SIGNS			SUFFERINGS	
	c. 3 YEARS		c. 6 MONTHS	8 DAYS	
LOCATION	GALILEE AND PERAEA			JUDEA AND JERUSALEM	
TIME	c. A.D. 29—33				

cees reaches crisis proportions as Jesus publicly refutes their arguments in the temple. After His last supper with the disciples, Jesus offers no resistance to His arrest, abuse, and agonizing crucifixion. His willingness to bear countless human sins is the epitome of servanthood.

OUTLINE OF MARK

Part One: The Presentation of the Servant (1:1—2:12)

I. The Forerunner of the Servant 1:1–8
II. The Baptism of the Servant 1:9–11
III. The Temptation of the Servant 1:12, 13
IV. The Mission of the Servant .... 1:14—2:12
A. The Work of the Servant 1:14, 15
B. The First Disciples Are Called 1:16–20
C. The First Miracles Are Performed 1:21—2:12
1. Demons Are Cast Out 1:21–28
2. Peter's Mother-in-Law Is Healed 1:29–31
3. Many Healings 1:32–39
4. A Leper Is Cleansed 1:40–45
5. A Paralytic Is Healed 2:1–12

Part Two: The Opposition to the Servant (2:13—8:26)

I. The Initial Opposition to the Servant 2:13—3:35
A. Controversy over Jesus' Friendship with Sinners 2:13–22
1. Call of Matthew 2:13–17
2. Parable of Cloth and Wineskins 2:18–22
B. Controversy over Sabbath-Work 2:23–28
C. Controversy over Sabbath-Healing 3:1–5
D. Pharisees Counsel to Destroy Jesus 3:6–12
E. Selection of the Twelve 3:13–19
F. Opposition of His Friends 3:20, 21
G. Scribes Commit the Unpardonable Sin 3:22–30
H. New Relationships Are Defined 3:31–35
II. The Parables of the Servant 4:1–34
A. Parable of the Soils 4:1–20
B. Parable of the Lamp 4:21–25
C. Parable of the Growing Seed 4:26–29
D. Parable of the Mustard Seed 4:30–34
III. The Miracles of the Servant .... 4:35—5:43
A. The Sea Is Stilled 4:35–41
B. Demons Are Cast into Swine 5:1–20
C. Jairus Pleads for His Daughter 5:21–24
D. A Woman with Issue Is Healed 5:25–34
E. Jairus's Daughter Is Healed 5:35–43
IV. The Growing Opposition to the Servant .... 6:1—8:26
A. Jesus Is Rejected at Nazareth 6:1–6
B. Twelve Are Sent to Serve 6:7–13
C. John the Baptist Is Murdered 6:14–29
D. Twelve Return 6:30, 31
E. Five Thousand Are Fed 6:32–44
F. Jesus Walks on Water 6:45–52
G. Jesus Heals at Gennesaret 6:53–56
H. Pharisees and Defilement 7:1–23
I. Withdrawal to the Gentiles .... 7:24—8:9
1. Syro-Phoenician's Daughter Is Healed 7:24–30
2. Deaf and Dumb Man Is Healed 7:31–37
3. Four Thousand Are Fed 8:1–9
J. Pharisees Seek a Sign 8:10–13
K. Disciples Do Not Understand 8:14–21
L. A Blind Man Is Healed 8:22–26

Part Three: The Instruction by the Servant (8:27—10:52)

I. Peter's Confession of Christ 8:27–33
II. Cost of Discipleship 8:34–38
III. The Transfiguration 9:1–13
IV. Demon-Possessed Son Is Delivered 9:14–29
V. Jesus Foretells His Death 9:30–32
VI. Jesus Teaches to Prepare the Disciples .... 9:33—10:45
A. Attitude of Servanthood 9:33–41
B. Warning About Hell 9:42–50
C. Marriage and Divorce 10:1–12
D. Children and the Kingdom 10:13–16
E. Wealth 10:17–31
1. Rich Young Ruler 10:17–22
2. Difficulty of Riches 10:23–27
3. Eternal Reward 10:28–31
F. Coming Crucifixion 10:32–34
G. "Whoever Desires to Become Great" 10:35–45
VII. Blind Bartimaeus Is Healed **10:46–52**

Part Four: The Rejection of the Servant (11:1—15:47)

I. The Formal Presentation of the Servant 11:1–19
A. The Triumphal Entry 11:1–11
B. A Fig Tree Is Cursed 11:12–14
C. The Temple Is Cleansed 11:15–19

CHAPTER 1

The Forerunner of the Servant
Matt. 3:1-11; Luke 3:3-16; John 1:19-34

THE beginning of the gospel of Jesus
Christ, [R]the Son of God. Matt. 14:33
2 As it is written in *the Prophets:

[R]*"Behold, I send My messenger before*
Your face, Mal. 3:1★
Who will prepare Your way before
You."
3 *"The[R] voice of one crying in the*
wilderness:
'Prepare the way of the LORD,
Make His paths straight.'" Is. 40:3★

4 [R]John came baptizing in the wilderness
and preaching a [R]baptism of repentance for
the remission of sins. Matt. 3:1 • Mal. 4:6★
5 [R]And all the land of Judea, and those
from Jerusalem, went out to him and were all
baptized by him in the Jordan River, confessing their sins. Matt. 3:5
6 Now John was [R]clothed with camel's hair
and with a leather belt around his waist, and
he ate locusts and wild honey. Matt. 3:4
7 And he preached, saying, [R]"There comes
One after me who is mightier than I, whose
sandal strap I am not worthy to stoop down
and loose. John 1:27
8 "I indeed baptized you with water, but
He will baptize you with the Holy Spirit."

The Baptism of the Servant
Matt. 3:13-17; Luke 3:21-23

9 [R]It came to pass in those days *that* Jesus
came from Nazareth of Galilee, and was
baptized by John in the Jordan. Matt. 3:13–17
10 And immediately, coming up *from the
water, He saw the heavens parting and the
Spirit descending upon Him like a dove.
11 Then a voice came from heaven, [R]"You
are My beloved Son, in whom I am well
pleased." Is. 42:1★

The Temptation of the Servant
Matt. 4:1-11; Luke 4:1-13

12 [R]And immediately the Spirit [T]drove Him
into the wilderness. Matt. 4:1–11 • *sent Him out*
13 And He was there in the wilderness forty
days, tempted by Satan, and was with the
wild beasts; [R]and the angels ministered to
Him. Matt. 4:10, 11

The Work of the Servant
Matt. 4:12-17; Luke 4:14, 15

14 [R]Now after John was put in prison, Jesus
came to Galilee, [R]preaching the gospel *of the
kingdom of God, Matt. 4:12 • Matt. 4:23
15 and saying, [R]"The time is fulfilled, and
the kingdom of God [T]is at hand. Repent, and
believe in the gospel." [Gal. 4:4] • *has drawn near*

1:2 NU *Isaiah the prophet* **1:10** NU *out of*
1:14 NU omits *of the kingdom*

THE CITY OF CAPERNAUM

One of the sites in modern Israel that stirs the soul of the Christian is the ruins of the synagogue that has been uncovered at Capernaum (see photo). Here, walking through the ruins, one can imagine Jesus healing the sick and teaching the people about the kingdom of God. This fishing town on the shores of the Sea of Galilee was the center of His activities soon after He began His public ministry.

Although the synagogue visited by tourists at Capernaum does not date to the time of Jesus, it was probably built in the second or third century A.D., and we may imagine Jesus ministering in just such a place (Mark 1:21). In Capernaum Jesus healed many people, including a centurion's paralyzed servant (Matt. 8:5–13), a paralyzed man carried by his friends (Mark 2:1–12), Peter's mother-in-law (Mark 1:29–31), and a nobleman's son (John 4:46–54).

While walking by the Sea of Galilee near Capernaum, Jesus called Peter, Andrew, James, and John to become His disciples (Mark 1:16–21). It was also at Capernaum that He called the tax collector Matthew (Mark 2:1, 13, 14). After the feeding of the five thousand, He delivered His discourse on the Bread of Life near this city (John 6:32–59).

Jesus was deeply concerned about the lack of belief demonstrated by the citizens of Capernaum. He pronounced a curse upon the city (Matt. 11:23, 24) and predicted its ruin (Luke 10:15). So strikingly did His prophecy come true that only recently has the site of Capernaum been positively identified.

The name *Capernaum* means "Village of Nahum." It was probably named for the man who owned the land where the village first grew up—an unknown person not to be confused with the prophet Nahum of the Old Testament.

Remains of a third-century synagogue at Capernaum.

Photo by Gustav Jeeninga

The First Disciples Are Called—Matt. 4:18–22

16 [R]And as He walked by the Sea of Galilee,
He saw Simon and Andrew his brother casting a net into the sea; for they were fishermen. Luke 5:2–11
17 Then Jesus said to them, "Come after
Me, and I will make you become [R]fishers of
men." Matt. 13:47, 48
18 And immediately [R]they left their nets and
followed Him. [Luke 14:26]
19 When He had gone a little farther from
there, He saw James the *son* of Zebedee, and
John his brother, who also *were* in the boat
mending their nets.
20 And immediately He called them, and
they left their father Zebedee in the boat with
the hired servants, and went after Him.

Demons Are Cast Out—Luke 4:31–37

21 [R]Then they went into Capernaum, and
immediately on the Sabbath He entered the
[R]synagogue and taught. Luke 4:31–37 • Matt. 4:23
22 [R]And they were astonished at His teaching, for He taught them as one having authority, and not as the scribes. Matt. 7:28, 29
23 Now there was a man in their synagogue
with an unclean spirit. And he cried out,
24 saying, "Let *us* alone! What have we to
do with You, Jesus of Nazareth? Did You
come to destroy us? I [R]know who You are—
the [R]Holy One of God!" James 2:19 • Ps. 16:10
25 But Jesus rebuked him, saying, [T]"Be
quiet, and come out of him!" Lit. *Be muzzled*
26 And when the unclean spirit [R]had convulsed him and cried out with a loud voice, he
came out of him. Mark 9:20
27 Then they were all amazed, so that they
questioned among themselves, saying,
*"What is this? What new [T]doctrine *is* this?
For with authority He commands even the
unclean spirits, and they obey Him." *teaching*
28 And immediately His fame spread
throughout all the region around Galilee.

Peter's Mother-in-Law Is Healed
Matt. 8:14, 15; Luke 4:38, 39

29 Now as soon as they had come out of the
synagogue, they entered the house of Simon
and Andrew, with James and John.
30 But Simon's wife's mother lay sick with a
fever, and they told Him about her at once.
31 So He came and took her by the hand
and lifted her up, and immediately the fever
left her. And she served them.

Many Healings
Matt. 8:16, 17, 4:23; Luke 4:40–44

32 [R]Now at evening, when the sun had set,
they brought to Him all who were sick and
those who were demon-possessed. Matt. 8:16, 17
33 And the whole city was gathered together at the door.
34 Then He healed many who were sick
with various diseases, and [R]cast out many
demons; and He did not allow the demons to
speak, because they knew Him. Luke 13:32
35 Now [R]in the morning, having risen a long
while before daylight, He went out and departed to a [T]solitary place; and there He
[R]prayed. Luke 4:42, 43 • *deserted* • Luke 5:16; 6:12; 9:28, 29
36 And Simon and those *who were* with
Him searched for Him.
37 When they found Him, they said to Him,
"Everyone [R]is looking for You." [Heb. 11:6]
38 But He said to them, "Let us go into the
next towns, that I may preach there also,
because for this purpose I have come forth."
39 [R]And He was preaching in their synagogues throughout all Galilee, and [R]casting
out demons. Matt. 4:23; 9:35 • Mark 5:8, 13; 7:29, 30

A Leper Is Cleansed
Matt. 8:1–4; Luke 5:12–16

40 [R]Then a leper came to Him, imploring
Him, kneeling down to Him and saying to
Him, "If You are willing, You can make me
clean." Luke 5:12–14
41 And Jesus, moved with [R]compassion, put
out *His* hand and touched him, and said to
him, "I am willing; be cleansed." Luke 7:13
42 As soon as He had spoken, immediately
the leprosy left him, and he was cleansed.
43 And He strictly warned him and sent him
away at once.
44 And He said to him, "See that you say
nothing to anyone; but go your way, show
yourself to the priest, and offer for your
cleansing those things [R]which Moses commanded, as a testimony to them." Lev. 14:1–32
45 [R]But he went out and began to proclaim
it freely, and to spread the matter, so that
Jesus could no longer openly enter the city,
but was outside in deserted places; and they
came to Him from every quarter. Luke 5:15

CHAPTER 2

A Paralytic Is Healed
Matt. 9:1–8; Luke 5:17–26

AND again [R]He entered Capernaum after
some days, and it was heard that He
was in the house. Matt. 9:1
2 *Immediately many gathered together,
so that there was no longer room to receive
them, not even near the door. And He
preached the word to them.
3 Then they came to Him, bringing a paralytic who was carried by four *men*.
4 And when they could not come near Him
because of the crowd, they uncovered the
roof where He was. And when they had

1:27 NU What is this? A new doctrine with authority. He **2:2** NU omits *immediately*

broken through, they let down the bed on
which the paralytic was lying.
5 When Jesus saw their faith, He said to
the paralytic, "Son, your sins are forgiven
you."
6 But some of the scribes were sitting
there and reasoning in their hearts,
7 "Why does this *Man* speak blasphemies
like this? [R]Who can forgive sins but God
alone?" Is. 43:25
8 And immediately, when Jesus perceived
in His spirit that they reasoned thus within
themselves, He said to them, "Why do you
reason about these things in your hearts?
9 [R]"Which is easier, to say to the paralytic,
'*Your* sins are forgiven you,' or to say, 'Arise,
take up your bed and walk'? Matt. 9:5
10 "But that you may know that the Son of
Man has [T]power on earth to forgive sins"—
He said to the paralytic, *authority*
11 "I say to you, arise, take up your bed,
and go your way to your house."
12 And immediately he arose, took up the
bed, and went out in the presence of them all,
so that all were amazed and glorified God,
saying, "We never saw *anything* like this!"

Call of Matthew—Matt. 9:9–13; Luke 5:27–32

13 [R]Then He went out again by the sea; and
all the multitude came to Him, and He taught
them. Matt. 9:9
14 And as He passed by, He saw Levi the
son of Alphaeus sitting at the tax office, and
said to him, [R]"Follow Me." And he arose and
[R]followed Him. John 1:43; 12:26; 21:22 • Luke 18:28
15 [R]Now it happened, as He was dining in
Levi's house, that many tax collectors and
sinners also sat together with Jesus and His
disciples; for there were many, and they
followed Him. Matt. 9:10
16 And when the scribes *and Pharisees
saw Him eating with the tax collectors and
sinners, they said to His disciples, "How *is it*
that He eats and drinks with tax collectors
and sinners?"
17 When Jesus heard *it*, He said to them,
[R]"Those who are well have no need of a
physician, but those who are sick. I did not
come to call *the* righteous, but sinners, *to
repentance." Matt. 9:12, 13; 18:11

Parable of Cloth and Wineskins
Matt. 9:14–17; Luke 5:33–39

18 [R]And the disciples of John and of the
Pharisees were fasting. And they came and
said to Him, "Why do the disciples of John
and of the Pharisees fast, but Your disciples
do not fast?" Luke 5:33–38
19 So Jesus said to them, "Can the friends
of the bridegroom fast while the bridegroom
is with them? As long as they have the
bridegroom with them they cannot fast.
20 "But the days will come when the bridegroom will be [R]taken away from them, and
then they will fast in those days. Acts 1:9
21 "No one sews a piece of unshrunk cloth
on an old garment; or else the new piece pulls
away from the old, and the tear is made
worse.
22 "And no one puts new wine into old
wineskins; or else the new wine bursts the
wineskins, the wine is spilled, and the wineskins are ruined. But new wine must be put
into new wineskins."

Controversy over Sabbath-Work
Matt. 12:1–8; Luke 6:1–5

23 [R]Now it happened that He went through
the grainfields on the Sabbath; and as they
went His disciples began [R]to pluck the heads
of grain. Luke 6:1–5 • Deut. 23:25
24 And the Pharisees said to Him, "Look,
why do they do what is [R]not lawful on the
Sabbath?" Ex. 20:10; 31:15
25 But He said to them, "Have you never
read what David did when he was in need
and hungry, he and those with him:
26 "how he went into the house of God *in
the days* of Abiathar the high priest, and ate
the showbread, [R]which is not lawful to eat,
except for the priests, and also gave some to
those who were with him?" Lev. 24:5–9
27 And He said to them, "The Sabbath was
made for man, and not man for the Sabbath.
28 "Therefore [R]the Son of Man is also Lord
of the Sabbath." Matt. 12:8

CHAPTER 3

Controversy over Sabbath-Healing
Matt. 12:9–13; Luke 6:6–10

AND [R]He entered the synagogue again,
and a man was there who had a withered hand. Luke 6:6–11
2 And they [R]watched Him closely, whether
He would heal him on the Sabbath, so that
they might accuse Him. Luke 14:1; 20:20
3 Then He said to the man who had the
withered hand, "Step forward."
4 And He said to them, "Is it lawful on the
Sabbath to do good or to do evil, to save life
or to kill?" But they kept silent.
5 So when He had looked around at them
with anger, being grieved by the hardness of
their hearts, He said to the man, "Stretch out
your hand." And he stretched *it* out, and his
hand was restored *as whole as the other.

Pharisees Counsel to Destroy Jesus
Matt. 12:14–16; Luke 6:11

6 [R]Then the Pharisees went out and imme-

2:16 NU *of the* 2:17 NU omits *to repentance*
3:5 NU omits *as whole as the other*

diately plotted with the Herodians against
Him, how they might destroy Him. Ps. 2:2 ★
7 But Jesus withdrew with His disciples to
the sea. And a great multitude from Galilee
followed Him, [R]and from Judea Luke 6:17
8 and Jerusalem and Idumea and beyond
the Jordan; and those from Tyre and Sidon, a
great multitude, when they heard how [R]many
things He was doing, came to Him. Mark 5:19
9 And He told His disciples that a small
boat should be kept ready for Him because of
the multitude, lest they should crush Him.
10 For He healed [R]many, so that as many as
had afflictions pressed about Him to [R]touch
Him. Luke 7:21 • Matt. 9:21; 14:36
11 [R]And the unclean spirits, whenever they
saw Him, fell down before Him and cried out,
saying, "You are the Son of God." Luke 4:41
12 But [R]He sternly warned them that they
should not make Him known. Mark 1:25, 34

Selection of the Twelve—Luke 6:12–16

13 [R]And He went up on the mountain and
called *to Him* those He Himself wanted. And
they came to Him. Luke 9:1
14 Then He appointed twelve, *that they
might be with Him and that He might send
them out to preach,
15 and to have [T]power *to heal sicknesses
and to cast out demons: *authority*
16 *Simon, [R]to whom He gave the name
Peter; John 1:42
17 James the *son* of Zebedee and John the
brother of James, to whom He gave the name
Boanerges, that is, "Sons of Thunder";
18 Andrew, Philip, Bartholomew, Matthew,
Thomas, James the *son* of Alphaeus, Thaddaeus, Simon the Cananite;
19 and Judas Iscariot, who also betrayed
Him. And they went into a house.

Opposition of His Friends

20 And the multitude came together again,
so that they could not so much as eat bread.
21 But when His [R]own people heard *about*
this, they went out to lay hold of Him, for
they said, "He is out of His mind." Mark 6:3

Scribes Commit the Unpardonable Sin
Matt. 12:24–32; Luke 11:17–23

22 And the scribes who came down from
Jerusalem said, [R]"He has Beelzebub," and,
"By the [R]ruler of the demons He casts out
demons." Matt. 9:34; 10:25 • [John 12:31; 14:30; 16:11]
23 [R]So He called them *to Him* and said to
them in parables: "How can Satan cast out
Satan? Matt. 12:25–29
24 "If a kingdom is divided against itself,
that kingdom cannot stand.
25 "And if a house is divided against itself,
that house cannot stand.
26 "And if Satan has risen up against himself, and is divided, he cannot stand, but has
an end.
27 [R]"No one can enter a strong man's house
and plunder his goods, unless he first binds
the strong man, and then he will plunder his
house. [Is. 49:24, 25]
28 [R]"Assuredly, I say to you, all sins will be
forgiven the sons of men, and whatever
blasphemies they may utter; Luke 12:10
29 "but he who blasphemes against the
Holy Spirit never has forgiveness, but is
subject to eternal condemnation"—
30 because they [R]said, "He has an unclean
spirit." Matt. 9:34

New Relationships Are Defined
Matt. 12:46–50; Luke 8:19–21

31 [R]Then His brothers and His mother
came, and standing outside they sent to Him,
calling Him. Matt. 12:46–50
32 And a multitude was sitting around Him;
and they said to Him, "Look, Your mother
and Your brothers *are outside seeking You."
33 But He answered them, saying, "Who is
My mother, or My brothers?"
34 And He looked around in a circle at
those who sat about Him, and said, "Here are
My mother and My brothers!
35 "For whoever does the [R]will of God is My
brother and My sister and mother." Eph. 6:6

CHAPTER 4

Parable of the Soils
Matt. 13:1–23; Luke 8:4–15

AND [R]again He began to teach by the sea.
And a great multitude was gathered to
Him, so that He got into a boat and sat *in it*
on the sea; and the whole multitude was on
the land facing the sea. Luke 8:4–10
2 Then He taught them many things by
parables, and said to them in His teaching:
3 "Listen! Behold, a sower went out to
sow.
4 "And it happened, as he sowed, *that*
some *seed* fell by the wayside; and the birds
*of the air came and devoured it.
5 "Some fell on stony ground, where it did
not have much earth; and immediately it
sprang up because it had no depth of earth.
6 "But when the sun was up it was
scorched, and because it had no root it withered away.
7 "And some *seed* fell among thorns; and
the thorns grew up and choked it, and it
yielded no [T]crop. Lit. *fruit*

3:14 NU adds *whom He also named apostles*
3:15 NU omits *to heal sicknesses and*
3:16 NU *and He appointed the twelve: Simon*
3:32 NU, M add *and your sisters*
4:4 NU, M omit *of the air*

8 "But other *seed* fell on good ground and
yielded a crop that sprang up, increased and
produced: some thirtyfold, some sixty,
and some a hundred."
9 And He said *to them, "He who has ears
to hear, let him hear!"
10 [R]But when He was alone, those around
Him with the twelve asked Him about the
parable. Luke 8:9
11 And He said to them, "To you it has been
given to [R]know the mystery of the kingdom
of God; but to those who are outside, all
things come in parables, [1 Cor. 2:10–16]
12 [R]"so that Is. 6:9, 10; 43:8

'Seeing they may see and not perceive,
And hearing they may hear and not
understand;
Lest they should turn,
and their sins be forgiven them.'"

13 And He said to them, "Do you not understand this parable? How then will you understand all the parables?
14 [R]"The sower sows the word. Matt. 13:18–23
15 "And these are the ones by the wayside
where the word is sown. And when they hear,
Satan comes immediately and takes away the
word that was sown in their hearts.
16 "These likewise are the ones sown on
stony ground who, when they hear the word,
immediately receive it with gladness;
17 "and they have no root in themselves,
and so endure only for a time. Afterward,
when tribulation or persecution arises for the
word's sake, immediately they stumble.
18 "Now these are the ones sown among
thorns; *they are* the ones who hear the word,
19 "and the [R]cares of this world, [R]the deceitfulness of riches, and the desires for other
things entering in choke the word, and it
becomes unfruitful. Luke 21:34 • 1 Tim. 6:9, 10, 17
20 "But these are the ones sown on good
ground, those who hear the word, [T]accept *it*,
and bear [R]fruit: some thirtyfold, some sixty,
and some a hundred." *receive* • [Rom. 7:4]

Parable of the Lamp—Luke 8:16–18

21 [R]And He said to them, "Is a lamp brought
to be put under a basket or under a bed? Is it
not to be set on a lampstand? Matt. 5:15
22 "For there is nothing hidden which will
not be revealed, nor has anything been kept
secret but that it should come to light.
23 [R]"If anyone has ears to hear, let him
hear." Matt. 11:15; 13:9, 43
24 And He said to them, "Take heed what
you hear. [R]With the same measure you use, it
will be measured to you; and to you who
hear, more will be given. Matt. 7:2
25 "For whoever has, to him more will be
given; but whoever does not have, even what
he has will be taken away from him."

Parable of the Growing Seed

26 And He said, "The kingdom of God is as
if a man should scatter seed on the ground,
27 "and should sleep by night and rise by
day, and the seed should sprout and [R]grow,
he himself does not know how. [2 Pet. 3:18]
28 "For the earth [R]yields crops by itself: first
the blade, then the head, after that the full
grain in the head. [John 12:24]
29 "But when the grain ripens, immediately
[R]he puts in the sickle, because the harvest has
come." Rev. 14:15

Parable of the Mustard Seed—Matt. 13:31–35

30 And He said, [R]"To what shall we liken
the kingdom of God? Or with what parable
shall we picture it? Matt. 13:31, 32
31 "*It is* like a mustard seed which, when it
is sown on the ground, is smaller than all the
seeds on earth;
32 "but when it is sown, it grows up and
becomes greater than all herbs, and shoots
out large branches, so that the birds of the air
may nest under its shade."
33 And with many such parables He spoke
the word to them as they were able to hear *it*.
34 But without a parable He did not speak
to them. And when they were alone, He
explained all things to His disciples.

The Sea Is Stilled
Matt. 8:23–27; Luke 8:22–25

35 [R]On the same day, when evening had
come, He said to them, "Let us cross over to
the other side." Luke 8:22, 25
36 Now when they had left the multitude,
they took Him along in the boat as He was.
And other little boats were also with Him.
37 And a great windstorm arose, and the
waves beat into the boat, so that it was
already filling.
38 But He was in the stern, asleep on a
pillow. And they awoke Him and said to Him,
[R]"Teacher, [R]do You not care that we are
perishing?" [Matt. 23:8–10] • Ps. 44:23
39 Then He arose and rebuked the wind,
and said to the sea, "Peace, be still!" And the
wind ceased and there was a great calm.
40 But He said to them, "Why are you so
fearful? *How *is it* that you have no faith?"
41 And they feared exceedingly, and said to
one another, "Who can this be, that even the
wind and the sea obey Him!"

CHAPTER 5

Demons Are Cast into Swine
Matt. 8:28–34; Luke 8:26–39

THEN they came to the other side of the
sea, to the country of the *Gadarenes.

4:9 NU, M omit *to them*
4:40 NU *Have you still no faith?* **5:1** NU *Gerasenes*

2 And when He had come out of the boat,
immediately there met Him out of the tombs
a man with an [R]unclean spirit, Mark 1:23; 7:25
3 who had *his* dwelling among the tombs;
and no one could bind *him, not even with
chains,
4 because he had often been bound with
shackles and chains. And the chains had been
pulled apart by him, and the shackles broken
in pieces; neither could anyone tame him.
5 And always, night and day, he was in the
mountains and in the tombs, crying out and
cutting himself with stones.
6 But when he saw Jesus from afar, he ran
and worshiped Him.
7 And he cried out with a loud voice and
said, "What have I to do with You, Jesus, Son
of the Most High God? I [T]implore You by God
that You do not torment me." *adjure*
8 For He said to him, [R]"Come out of the
man, unclean spirit!" Mark 1:25; 9:25
9 Then He asked him, "What *is* your
name?" And he answered, saying, "My name
is Legion; for we are many."
10 And he begged Him earnestly that He
would not send them out of the country.
11 Now a large herd of [R]swine was feeding
there near the mountains. Deut. 14:8
12 And all the demons begged Him, saying,
"Send us to the swine, that we may enter
them."
13 And *at once Jesus gave them permission. Then the unclean spirits went out and
entered the swine (there were about two
thousand); and the herd ran violently down
the steep place into the sea, and drowned in
the sea.
14 Now those who fed the swine fled, and
they told *it* in the city and in the country.
And they went out to see what it was that
had happened.
15 Then they came to Jesus, and saw the
one *who had been* demon-possessed and had
the legion, sitting and [R]clothed and in his
right mind. And they were afraid. [Is. 61:10]
16 And those who saw it told them how
it happened to him *who had been* demon-
possessed, and about the swine.
17 Then [R]they began to plead with Him to
depart from their region. Acts 16:39
18 And when He got into the boat, [R]he who
had been demon-possessed begged Him that
he might be with Him. Luke 8:38, 39
19 However, Jesus did not permit him, but
said to him, "Go home to your friends, and
tell them what great things the Lord has done
for you, and how He has had compassion on
you."
20 And he departed and began to proclaim
in [T]Decapolis all that Jesus had done for him;
and all [R]marveled. Lit. *Ten Cities* • Matt. 9:8, 33

Jairus Pleads for His Daughter
Matt. 9:18, 19; Luke 8:41, 42

21 Now when Jesus had crossed over again
by boat to the other side, a great multitude
gathered to Him; and He was by the sea.
22 [R]And behold, one of the rulers of the
synagogue came, Jairus by name. And when
he saw Him, he fell at His feet Matt. 9:18–26
23 and begged Him earnestly, saying, "My
little daughter lies at the point of death.
Come and [R]lay Your hands on her, that she
may be healed, and she will live." Acts 9:17; 28:8
24 So *Jesus* went with him, and a great
multitude followed Him and thronged Him.

A Woman with Issue Is Healed
Matt. 9:20–22; Luke 8:43–48

25 Now a certain woman [R]had a flow of
blood for twelve years, Lev. 15:19, 25
26 and had suffered many things from many
physicians. She had spent all that she had
and was no better, but rather grew worse.
27 When she heard about Jesus, she came
behind *Him* in the crowd and [R]touched His
garment; Matt. 14:35, 36
28 for she said, "If only I may touch His
clothes, I shall be made well."
29 Immediately the fountain of her blood
was dried up, and she felt in *her* body that she
was healed of the [T]affliction. *suffering*
30 And Jesus, immediately knowing in Himself that [R]power had gone out of Him, turned
around in the crowd and said, "Who touched
My clothes?" Luke 6:19; 8:46
31 But His disciples said to Him, "You see
the multitude thronging You, and You say,
'Who touched Me?' "
32 And He looked around to see her who
had done this thing.
33 But the woman, [R]fearing and trembling,
knowing what had happened to her, came
and fell down before Him and told Him the
whole truth. [Ps. 89:7]
34 And He said to her, "Daughter, your
faith has made you well. [R]Go in peace, and be
healed of your affliction." Luke 7:50; 8:48

Jairus's Daughter Is Healed
Matt. 9:23–26; Luke 8:49–56

35 [R]While He was still speaking, *some* came
from the ruler of the synagogue's *house* who
said, "Your daughter is dead. Why trouble
the Teacher any further?" Luke 8:49
36 As soon as Jesus heard the word that
was spoken, He said to the ruler of the
synagogue, "Do not be afraid; only believe."
37 And He permitted no one to follow Him
except Peter, James, and John the brother of
James.

5:3 NU adds *anymore* **5:13** NU *He gave*

38 Then He came to the house of the ruler of the synagogue, and saw [T]a tumult and those who wept and wailed loudly. *an uproar*

39 When He came in, He said to them, "Why make this commotion and weep? The child is not dead, but [R]sleeping." John 11:4, 11

40 And they laughed Him to scorn. [R]But when He had put them all out, He took the father and the mother of the child, and those *who were* with Him, and entered where the child was lying. Acts 9:40

41 Then He took the child by the hand, and said to her, "Talitha, cumi," which is translated, "Little girl, I say to you, arise."

42 Immediately the girl arose and walked, for she was twelve years *of age.* And they were overcome with great amazement.

43 But [R]He commanded them strictly that no one should know it, and said that *something* should be given her to eat. Matt. 8:4

CHAPTER 6

Jesus Is Rejected at Nazareth—Matt. 13:54–58

THEN [R]He went out from there and came to His own country, and His disciples followed Him. Matt. 13:54

2 And when the Sabbath had come, He began to teach in the synagogue. And many hearing *Him* were [R]astonished, saying, [R]"Where *did* this *Man get* these things? And what wisdom *is* this which is given to Him, that such mighty works are performed by His hands! Matt. 7:28 • John 6:42

3 "Is this not the carpenter, the Son of Mary, and brother of James, Joses, Judas, and Simon? And are not His sisters here with us?" And they were offended at Him.

4 But Jesus said to them, [R]"A prophet is not without honor except in his own country, among his own relatives, and in his own house." John 4:44

5 [R]Now He could do no mighty work there, except that He laid His hands on a few sick people and healed *them.* Gen. 19:22; 32:25

6 And [R]He marveled because of their unbelief. [R]Then He went about the villages in a circuit, teaching. Is. 59:16 • Matt. 9:35

Twelve Are Sent to Serve
Matt. 10:1–42; Luke 9:1–6

7 And He called the twelve *to Him,* and began to send them out two *by* two, and gave them power over unclean spirits.

8 He commanded them to take nothing for the journey except a staff—no bag, no bread, no copper in *their* money belts—

9 but [R]to wear sandals, and not to put on two tunics. [Eph. 6:15]

10 [R]Also He said to them, "In whatever place you enter a house, stay there till you depart from that place. Matt. 10:11

11 [R]"And *whoever will not receive you nor hear you, when you depart from there, [R]shake off the dust under your feet as a testimony against them. *Assuredly, I say to you, it will be more tolerable for Sodom and Gomorrah in the day of judgment than for that city!" Matt. 10:14 • Acts 13:51; 18:6

12 So they went out and preached that *people* should repent.

13 And they cast out many demons, [R]and anointed with oil many who were sick, and healed *them.* [James 5:14]

John the Baptist Is Murdered
Matt. 14:1–12; Luke 9:7–9

14 Now King Herod heard *of Him,* for His name had become well known. And he said, "John the Baptist is risen from the dead, and therefore these powers are at work in him."

15 [R]Others said, "It is Elijah." And others said, "It is the [R]Prophet, *or like one of the prophets." Mark 8:28 • Matt. 21:11

16 [R]But when Herod heard, he said, "This is John, whom I beheaded; he has been raised from the dead!" Luke 3:19

17 For Herod himself had sent and laid hold of John, and bound him in prison for the sake of Herodias, his brother Philip's wife; for he had married her.

18 For John had said to Herod, "It is not lawful for you to have your brother's wife."

19 Therefore Herodias held it against him and wanted to kill him, but she could not;

20 for Herod [R]feared John, knowing that he *was* a just and holy man, and he protected him. And when he heard him, he did many things, and heard him gladly. Matt. 14:5; 21:26

21 [R]Then an opportune day came when Herod [R]on his birthday gave a feast for his nobles, the high officers, and the chief *men* of Galilee. Matt. 14:6 • Gen. 40:20

22 And when Herodias' daughter herself came in and danced, and pleased Herod and those who sat with him, the king said to the girl, "Ask me whatever you want, and I will give *it* to you."

23 He also swore to her, [R]"Whatever you ask me, I will give you, up to half of my kingdom." Esth. 5:3, 6; 7:2

24 So she went out and said to her mother, "What shall I ask?" And she said, "The head of John the Baptist!"

25 Immediately she came in with haste to the king and asked, saying, "I want you to give me at once the head of John the Baptist on a platter."

26 [R]And the king was exceedingly sorry; *yet,* because of the oaths and because of those who sat with him, he did not want to refuse her. Matt. 14:9

6:11 NU *whatever place*
6:11 NU omits the rest of v. 11
6:15 NU, M omit *or*

27 And immediately the king sent an executioner and commanded his head to be brought. And he went and beheaded him in prison,
28 brought his head on a platter, and gave it to the girl; and the girl gave it to her mother.
29 And when his disciples heard *of it*, they came and [R]took away his corpse and laid it in a tomb. 1 Kin. 13:29, 30

Twelve Return—Luke 9:10

30 [R]Then the apostles gathered to Jesus and told Him all things, both what they had done and what they had taught. Luke 9:10
31 And He said to them, "Come aside by yourselves to a deserted place and rest a while." For there were many coming and going, and they did not even have time to eat.

Five Thousand Are Fed
Matt. 14:13–21; Luke 9:11–17; John 6:1–14

32 [R]So they departed to a deserted place in the boat by themselves. Matt. 14:13–21
33 But *the multitudes saw them departing, and many [R]knew Him and ran there on foot from all the cities. They arrived before them and came together to Him. [Col. 1:6]
34 And Jesus, when He came out, saw a great multitude and was moved with compassion for them, because they were like [R]sheep not having a shepherd. So [R]He began to teach them many things. Num. 27:17 • Luke 9:11
35 And when the day was now far spent, His disciples came to Him and said, "This is a deserted place, and already the hour *is* late.
36 "Send them away, that they may go into the surrounding country and villages and buy themselves *bread; for they have nothing to eat."
37 But He answered and said to them, "You give them something to eat." And they said to Him, [R]"Shall we go and buy two hundred denarii worth of bread and give them *something* to eat?" 2 Kin. 4:43
38 But He said to them, "How many loaves do you have? Go and see." And when they found out they said, "Five, and two fish."
39 Then He [R]commanded them to make them all sit down in groups on the green grass. Matt. 15:35
40 So they sat down in ranks, in hundreds and in fifties.
41 And when He had taken the five loaves and the two fish, He looked up to heaven, blessed and broke the loaves, and gave *them* to His disciples to set before them; and the two fish He divided among *them* all.
42 So they all ate and were filled.
43 And they took up twelve baskets full of fragments and of the fish.
44 Now those who had eaten the loaves were *about five thousand men.

Jesus Walks on Water
Matt. 14:22–33; John 6:15–21

45 [R]Immediately He [T]made His disciples get into the boat and go before Him to the other side, to Bethsaida, while He sent the multitude away. John 6:15–21 • *strongly urged*
46 And when He had sent them away, He [R]departed to the mountain to pray. Luke 5:16
47 Now when evening came, the boat was in the middle of the sea; and He *was* alone on the land.
48 Then He saw them straining at rowing, for the wind was against them. And about the fourth watch of the night He came to them, walking on the sea, and [R]would have passed them by. Luke 24:28
49 But when they saw Him walking on the sea, they supposed it was a [R]ghost, and cried out; Matt. 14:26
50 for they all saw Him and were troubled. And immediately He talked with them and said to them, [R]"Be[T] of good cheer! It is I; do not be [R]afraid." Matt. 9:2 • *Take courage* • Is. 41:10
51 Then He went up into the boat to them, and the wind [R]ceased. And they were greatly [R]amazed in themselves beyond measure, and marveled. Ps. 107:29 • Mark 1:27; 2:12; 5:42; 7:37
52 For they had not understood about the loaves, because their heart was hardened.

Jesus Heals at Gennesaret—Matt. 14:34–36

53 [R]When they had crossed over, they came to the land of Gennesaret and anchored there. Matt. 14:34–36
54 And when they came out of the boat, immediately the people recognized Him,
55 ran through that whole surrounding region, and began to carry about on beds those who were sick to wherever they heard He was.
56 Wherever He entered, into villages, cities, or the country, they laid the sick in the marketplaces, and begged Him that [R]they might just touch the [R]border of His garment. And as many as touched Him were made well. Matt. 9:20 • Num. 15:38, 39

CHAPTER 7

Pharisees and Defilement—Matt. 15:1–20

THEN [R]the Pharisees and some of the scribes came together to Him, having come from Jerusalem. Matt. 15:1–20
2 Now *when they saw some of His disciples eat bread with defiled, that is, with unwashed hands, *they found fault.

6:33 NU, M *they*
6:36 NU *something to eat* and omits the rest of v. 36.
6:44 NU, M omit *about* **7:2** NU omits *when*
7:2 NU omits *they found fault*

THE SEA OF GALILEE

The beautiful Sea of Galilee, also referred to in the Bible as the Sea of Tiberias (John 6:1), the Lake of Gennesaret (Luke 5:1), and the Sea of Chinnereth (Num. 34:11), was the geographical center of much of the ministry of Jesus. Almost thirteen miles long and about eight miles wide, the fresh-water lake is surrounded by high mountains. Interestingly, the Sea of Galilee is one of the lowest points on earth, standing 690 feet below sea level.

The region around the Sea of Galilee in the upper Jordan River valley in northern Palestine is a lush garden, with an abundance of fertile soil, water, fish, and a hot climate. About 200,000 people, mostly Gentiles, were scattered in the many towns along the shores of the lake and throughout the upper Jordan valley when Jesus taught and healed in Palestine.

Because of their openness to new ideas, Jesus appealed to the common people of Galilee, and many of them "heard Him gladly" (Mark 12:37). Jesus recruited eleven of His disciples from this area. Many of them, including brothers Peter and Andrew and brothers James and John, were fishermen who earned their livelihood from the waters of this lake. Settlements along the shores of Lake Galilee in the time of Jesus included Tiberias, Magdala, Capernaum, and Bethsaida (see map). In this region Jesus taught the multitudes and healed the sick (Mark 7:31–37).

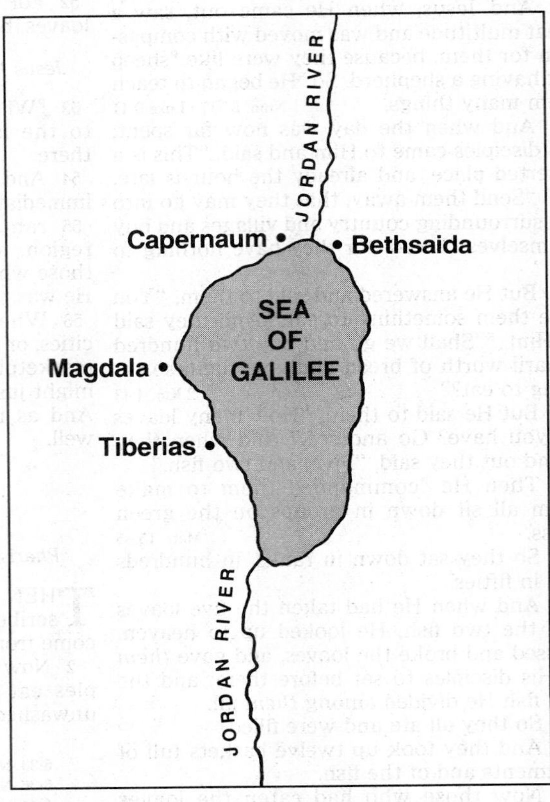

Powerful winds sometimes sweep down from the mountains along the shores of the lake, clashing with heat waves rising from the water's surface. The resulting turbulence creates sudden, violent storms. This is probably the type of storm that Jesus calmed on the lake in response to the pleas of His disciples. "Who can this be," the people marveled, "that even the winds and the sea obey Him?" (Matt. 8:27).

3 For the Pharisees and all the Jews do not
eat unless they wash *their* hands in a special
way, holding the tradition of the elders.
4 *When they come* from the marketplace,
they do not eat unless they wash. And there
are many other things which they have received and hold, *like* the washing of cups,
pitchers, copper vessels, and couches.
5 [R]Then the Pharisees and scribes asked
Him, "Why do Your disciples not walk according to the tradition of the elders, but eat
bread with unwashed hands?" Matt. 15:2
6 He answered and said to them, "Well did
Isaiah prophesy of you [R]hypocrites, as it is
written: Matt. 23:13–29

[R]*'This people honors Me with their lips,*
But their heart is far from Me. Is. 29:13 ★
7 *And in vain they worship Me,*
Teaching as doctrines the
commandments of men.'

8 "For laying aside the commandment of
God, you hold the tradition of men—*the
washing of pitchers and cups, and many
other such things you do."
9 And He said to them, "*All too* well [R]you
[T]reject the commandment of God, that you
may keep your tradition. Prov. 1:25 • *set aside*
10 "For Moses said, *'Honor your father and*
your mother'; and, [R]*'He who curses father or*
mother, let him be put to death.' Ex. 21:17
11 "But you say, 'If a man says to his father
or mother, [R]"Whatever profit you might have
received from me *is* Corban (that is, dedicated *to the temple*)"; Matt. 15:5; 23:18
12 "and you no longer let him do anything
for his father or his mother,
13 "making the word of God of no effect
through your tradition which you have
handed down. And many such things you
do."
14 And when He had called all the multitude *to Him*, He said to them, "Hear Me,
everyone, and [R]understand: Matt. 16:9, 11, 12
15 "There is nothing that enters a man from
outside which can defile him; but the things
which come out of him, those are the things
that [R]defile a man. Is. 59:3
16 [R]"If* anyone has ears to hear, let him
hear!" Matt. 11:15
17 [R]And when He had entered a house away
from the crowd, His disciples asked Him
concerning the parable. Matt. 15:15
18 So He said to them, [R]"Are you thus
without understanding also? Do you not
perceive that whatever enters a man from
outside cannot defile him, [Heb. 5:11–14]
19 "because it does not enter his heart but
his stomach, and is eliminated, *thus* *purifying all foods?"
20 And He said, [R]"What comes out of a
man, that defiles a man. Ps. 39:1
21 "For from within, out of the heart of
men, [R]proceed evil thoughts, [R]adulteries,
fornications, murders, [Gal. 5:19–21] • 2 Pet. 2:14
22 "thefts, covetousness, wickedness, deceit, [R]licentiousness, an evil eye, [R]blasphemy,
[R]pride, foolishness. 1 Pet. 4:3 • Rev. 2:9 • 1 John 2:16
23 "All these evil things come from within
and defile a man."

Syro-Phoenician's Daughter Is Healed
Matt. 15:21–28

24 And from there He arose and went to the
region of Tyre *and Sidon. And He entered a
house and wanted no one to know *it*, but He
could not be [R]hidden. Mark 2:1, 2
25 For a woman whose young daughter had
an unclean spirit heard about Him, and she
came and [R]fell at His feet. John 11:32
26 The woman was a Greek, a Syro-
Phoenician by birth, and she kept asking Him
to cast the demon out of her daughter.
27 But Jesus said to her, "Let the children
be filled first, for it is not good to take the
children's bread and throw *it* to the little
dogs."
28 And she answered and said to Him, "Yes,
Lord, yet even the little dogs under the table
eat from the children's crumbs."
29 Then He said to her, "For this saying go
your way; the demon has gone out of your
daughter."
30 And when she had come to her house,
she found the demon gone out, and her
daughter lying on the bed.

Deaf and Dumb Man Is Healed

31 [R]And again, departing from the region of
Tyre and Sidon, He came through the midst
of the region of Decapolis to the Sea of
Galilee. Matt. 15:29
32 Then they brought to Him one who was
deaf and had an impediment in his speech,
and they begged Him to put His hand on him.
33 And He took him aside from the multitude, and put His fingers in his ears, and [R]He
spat and touched his tongue. Mark 8:23
34 Then, [R]looking up to heaven, [R]He sighed,
and said to him, "Ephphatha," that is, "Be
opened." Mark 6:41 • John 11:33, 38
35 [R]Immediately his ears were opened, and
the [T]impediment of his tongue was loosed,
and he spoke plainly. Is. 35:5, 6 • Lit. *bond*
36 Then [R]He commanded them that they
should tell no one; but the more He commanded them, the more widely they proclaimed *it*. Mark 5:43
37 And they were [R]astonished beyond measure, saying, "He has done all things well. He

7:8 NU omits the rest of v. 8. **7:16** NU omits v. 16.
7:19 NU sets off the final phrase as Mark's comment that Jesus has declared all foods clean.
7:24 NU omits *and Sidon*

[R]makes both the deaf to hear and the mute to speak." Mark 6:51; 10:26 • Matt. 12:22

CHAPTER 8

Four Thousand Are Fed—Matt. 15:32–38

IN those days, the multitude being very great and having nothing to eat, Jesus called His disciples *to Him* and said to them,

2 "I have [R]compassion on the multitude, because they have now been with Me three days and have nothing to eat. Mark 1:41; 6:34

3 "And if I send them away hungry to their own houses, they will faint on the way; for some of them have come from afar."

4 Then His disciples answered Him, "How can one satisfy these people with bread here in the wilderness?"

5 [R]He asked them, "How many loaves do you have?" And they said, "Seven." Mark 6:38

6 And He commanded the multitude to sit down on the ground. And He took the seven loaves and gave thanks, broke *them* and gave *them* to His disciples to set before *them*; and they set *them* before the multitude.

7 And they had a few small fish; and [R]having blessed them, He said to set them also before *them*. Matt. 14:19

8 So they ate and were filled, and they took up seven large baskets of leftover fragments.

9 Now those who had eaten were about four thousand. And He sent them away.

10 And [R]immediately He got into the boat with His disciples and came to the region of Dalmanutha. Matt. 15:39

Pharisees Seek a Sign—Matt. 15:39—16:4

11 [R]And the Pharisees came out and began to dispute with Him, seeking from Him a sign from heaven, testing Him. Matt. 12:38; 16:1

12 But He [R]sighed deeply in His spirit, and said, "Why does this generation seek a sign? Assuredly, I say to you, [R]no sign shall be given to this generation." Mark 7:34 • Matt. 12:39

13 And He left them, and getting into the boat again, departed to the other side.

Disciples Do Not Understand—Matt. 16:5–12

14 [R]Now *the disciples had forgotten to take bread, and they did not have more than one loaf with them in the boat. Matt. 16:5

15 [R]Then He charged them, saying, "Take heed, beware of the [T]leaven of the Pharisees and the leaven of Herod." Luke 12:1 • *yeast*

16 So they reasoned among themselves, saying, *"It is* because we have no bread."

17 And Jesus, being aware of *it*, said to them, "Why do you reason because you have no bread? Do you not yet perceive nor understand? Is your heart *still hardened?

18 "Having eyes, do you not see? And having ears, do you not hear? And do you not remember?

19 [R]"When I broke the five loaves for the five thousand, how many baskets full of fragments did you take up?" They said to Him, "Twelve." Matt. 14:20

20 "And [R]when I broke the seven for the four thousand, how many large baskets full of fragments did you take up?" And they said, "Seven." Matt. 15:37

21 So He said to them, "How *is it* [R]you do not understand?" [Mark 6:52]

A Blind Man Is Healed

22 Then He came to Bethsaida; and they brought a [R]blind man to Him, and begged Him to [R]touch him. John 9:1 • Luke 18:15

23 So He took the blind man by the hand and led him out of the town. And when He had spit on his eyes and put His hands on him, He asked him if he saw anything.

24 And he looked up and said, "I see men like trees, walking."

25 Then He put *His* hands on his eyes again and made him look up. And he was restored and saw everyone clearly.

26 And He sent him away to his house, saying, *"Neither go into the town, [R]nor tell anyone in the town." Mark 5:43; 7:36

Peter's Confession of Christ
Matt. 16:13–23; Luke 9:18–22

27 [R]Now Jesus and His disciples went out to the towns of Caesarea Philippi; and on the road He asked His disciples, saying to them, "Who do men say that I am?" Luke 9:18–20

28 And they answered, [R]"John the Baptist; but some *say*, [R]Elijah; and others, one of the prophets." Matt. 14:2 • Luke 9:7, 8

29 He said to them, "But who do you say that I am?" And Peter answered and said to Him, [R]"You are the Christ." John 1:41; 4:42

30 [R]Then He charged them that they should tell no one about Him. Matt. 8:4; 16:20

31 And He began to teach them that the Son of Man must suffer many things, and be [R]rejected by the elders and chief priests and scribes, and be [R]killed, and after three days rise again. Mark 10:33 • Mark 9:31; 10:34; Luke 24:46 ☆

32 He spoke this word openly. And Peter took Him aside and began to rebuke Him.

33 But when He had turned around and looked at His disciples, He [R]rebuked Peter, saying, "Get behind Me, Satan! For you are not [T]mindful of the things of God, but the things of men." [Rev. 3:19] • *setting your mind on*

Cost of Discipleship
Matt. 16:24–27; Luke 9:22–26

34 And when He had called the people *to Him*, with His disciples also, He said to them,

8:14 NU, M *they* **8:17** NU omits *still*
8:26 NU *Do not even go into the town*

[R]"Whoever desires to come after Me, let him deny himself, and take up his cross, and follow Me. Luke 14:27

35 "For [R]whoever desires to save his life will lose it, but whoever loses his life for My sake and the gospel's will save it. John 12:25

36 "For what will it profit a man if he gains the whole world, and loses his own soul?

37 "Or what will a man give in exchange for his soul?

38 [R]"For whoever is ashamed of Me and My words in this adulterous and sinful generation, of him the Son of Man also will be ashamed when He comes in the glory of His Father with the holy angels." Matt. 10:33

CHAPTER 9

The Transfiguration
Matt. 16:28—17:3; Luke 9:27-36

AND He said to them, "Assuredly, I say to you that there are some standing here who will not taste death till they see the kingdom of God present with power."

2 [R]Now after six days Jesus took Peter, James, and John, and led them up on a high mountain apart by themselves; and He was transfigured before them. Matt. 17:1-8

3 His clothes became shining, exceedingly [R]white, like snow, such as no launderer on earth can whiten them. Dan. 7:9

4 And Elijah appeared to them with Moses, and they were talking with Jesus.

5 Then Peter answered and said to Jesus, "Rabbi, it is good for us to be here; and let us make three tabernacles: one for You, one for Moses, and one for Elijah"—

6 because he did not know what to say, for they were greatly afraid.

7 And a cloud came and overshadowed them; and a voice came out of the cloud, saying, "This is [R]My beloved Son. Hear Him!" Ps. 2:7; Is. 42:1; Luke 1:35★

8 Suddenly, when they had looked around, they saw no one anymore, but only Jesus with themselves.

9 Now as they came down from the mountain, He commanded them that they should tell no one the things they had seen, till the Son of Man had risen from the dead.

10 So they kept this word to themselves, questioning [R]what the rising from the dead meant. John 2:19-22

11 And they asked Him, saying, "Why do the scribes say that Elijah must come first?"

12 Then He answered and told them, "Elijah does come first, and restores all things. And [R]how is it written concerning the Son of Man, that He must suffer many things and be treated with contempt? Ps. 22:6; Is. 53:3☆

13 "But I say to you that [R]Elijah has also come, and they did to him whatever they wished, as it is written of him." Luke 1:17

Demon-Possessed Son Is Delivered
Matt. 17:14-21; Luke 9:37-42

14 [R]And when He came to the disciples, He saw a great multitude around them, and scribes disputing with them. Matt. 17:14-19

15 Immediately, when they saw Him, all the people were greatly amazed, and running to *Him*, greeted Him.

16 And He asked the scribes, "What are you discussing with them?"

17 Then [R]one from the multitude answered and said, "Teacher, I brought You my son, who has a mute spirit. Luke 9:38

18 "And wherever he seizes him, he throws him down; he foams at the mouth, gnashes his teeth, and becomes rigid. So I spoke to Your disciples, that they should cast him out, but they could not."

19 He answered him and said, "O [R]faithless[T] generation, how long shall I be with you? How long shall I [T]bear with you? Bring him to Me." John 4:48 • *unbelieving* • *put up with*

20 Then they brought him to Him. And [R]when he saw Him, immediately the spirit convulsed him, and he fell on the ground and wallowed, foaming at the mouth. Mark 1:26

21 So He asked his father, "How long has this been happening to him?" And he said, "From childhood.

22 "And often he has thrown him both into the fire and into the water to destroy him. But if You can do anything, have compassion on us and help us."

23 Jesus said to him, *"If you can believe, all things *are* possible to him who believes."

24 Immediately the father of the child cried out and said with tears, "Lord, I believe; [R]help my unbelief!" Luke 17:5

25 When Jesus saw that the people came running together, He [R]rebuked the unclean spirit, saying to him, "*You* deaf and dumb spirit, I command you, come out of him, and enter him no more!" Mark 1:25

26 Then *the spirit* cried out, convulsed him greatly, and came out of him. And he became as one dead, so that many said, "He is dead."

27 But Jesus took him by the hand and lifted him up, and he arose.

28 [R]And when He had come into the house, His disciples asked Him privately, "Why could we not cast him out?" Matt. 17:19

29 So He said to them, "This kind can come out by nothing but prayer *and fasting."

Jesus Foretells His Death
Matt. 17:22, 23; Luke 9:43-45

30 Then they departed from there and passed through Galilee, and He did not want anyone to know *it*.

9:23 NU *If you can! All things*
9:29 NU omits *and fasting*

31 [R]For He taught His disciples and said to
them, "The Son of Man is being delivered
into the hands of men, and they will kill Him.
And after He is killed, He will [R]rise the third
day." Luke 9:44 • Luke 24:46 ☆
32 But they [R]did not understand this saying,
and were afraid to ask Him. Luke 2:50; 18:34

Attitude of Servanthood
Matt. 18:1–5; Luke 9:46–50

33 [R]Then He came to Capernaum. And
when He was in the house He asked them,
"What was it you [T]disputed among yourselves on the road?" Matt. 18:1–5 • *discussed*
34 But they kept silent, for on the road they
had [R]disputed among themselves who *would*
be the [R]greatest. [Prov. 13:10] • Luke 22:24; 23:46; 24:46
35 And He sat down, called the twelve, and
said to them, "If anyone desires to be first, he
shall be last of all and servant of all."
36 Then He took a little child and set him in
the midst of them. And when He had taken
him in His arms, He said to them,
37 "Whoever receives one of these little
children in My name receives Me; and [R]who-
ever receives Me, receives not Me but Him
who sent Me." Matt. 10:40
38 [R]Now John answered Him, saying,
"Teacher, we saw someone who does not
follow us casting out demons in Your name,
and we forbade him because he does not
follow us." Num. 11:27–29
39 But Jesus said, "Do not forbid him, [R]for
no one who works a miracle in My name can
soon afterward speak evil of Me. 1 Cor. 12:3
40 "For [R]he who is not *against us is on our
side. [Matt. 12:30]
41 [R]"For whoever gives you a cup of water
to drink in My name, because you belong to
Christ, assuredly, I say to you, he will by no
means lose his reward. Matt. 10:42

Warning About Hell—Matt. 18:6–9

42 [R]"And whoever causes one of these little
ones who believe in Me [T]to stumble, it would
be better for him if a millstone were hung
around his neck, and he were thrown into the
sea. Luke 17:1, 2 • *to fall into sin*
43 [R]"And if your hand makes you sin, cut it
off. It is better for you to enter into life
[T]maimed, than having two hands, to go to
[T]hell, into the fire that shall never be
quenched— Matt. 5:29, 30 • *crippled* • Gr. *Gehenna*
44 [R]"where* *'their worm does not die and*
the fire is not quenched.' Is. 66:24
45 "And if your foot makes you sin, cut it
off. It is better for you to enter life lame, than
having two feet, to be cast into hell, *into the
fire that shall never be quenched—
46 [R]"where *'their worm does not die and the*
fire is not quenched.' Is. 66:24
47 "And if your eye makes you sin, pluck it
out. It is better for you to enter the kingdom
of God with one eye, than having two eyes, to
be cast into [T]hell fire— Gr. *Gehenna*
48 "where *'their* [R]*worm does not die and the*
[R]*fire is not quenched.'* Is. 66:24 • Jer. 7:20
49 "For everyone will be [R]seasoned with
fire, [R]and* every sacrifice will be seasoned
with salt. [Matt. 3:11] • Lev. 2:13
50 [R]"Salt *is* good, but if the salt loses its
flavor, how will you season it? [R]Have salt in
yourselves, and [R]have peace with one another." Matt. 5:13 • Col. 4:6 • Rom. 12:18; 14:19

CHAPTER 10

Marriage and Divorce—Matt. 19:1–9

THEN [R]He arose from there and came to
the region of Judea by the other side of
the Jordan. And the people gathered to Him
again, and as He was accustomed, He taught
them again. Matt. 19:1–9
2 [R]The Pharisees came and asked Him, "Is
it lawful for a man to divorce *his* wife?"
testing Him. Matt. 19:3
3 And He answered and said to them,
"What did Moses command you?"
4 They said, [R]"Moses permitted *a man* to
write a certificate of divorce, and to dismiss
her." Deut. 24:1–4
5 And Jesus answered and said to them,
"Because of the hardness of your heart he
wrote you this [T]precept. *command*
6 "But from the beginning of the creation,
God *'made them male and female.'*
7 *'For this reason a man shall leave his*
father and mother and be joined to his wife,
8 *'and the two shall become one flesh';* so
then they are no longer two, but one flesh.
9 "Therefore what God has joined together, let not man separate."
10 And in the house His disciples asked Him
again about the same *matter.*
11 So He said to them, [R]"Whoever divorces
his wife and marries another commits adultery against her. [Matt. 5:32; 19:9]
12 "And if a woman divorces her husband
and marries another, she commits adultery."

Children and the Kingdom
Matt. 19:13–15; Luke 18:15–17

13 Then they brought young children to
Him, that He might touch them; but the
disciples rebuked those who brought *them.*
14 But when Jesus saw *it,* He was greatly
displeased and said to them, "Let the little
children come to Me, and do not forbid them;
for [R]of such is the kingdom of God. [1 Pet. 2:2]

9:40 M *against you is on your side*
9:44 NU omits v. 44.
9:45 NU omits the rest of v. 45 and all of v. 46.
9:49 NU omits the rest of v. 49.

15 "Assuredly, I say to you, whoever does
not receive the kingdom of God as a little
child will Rby no means enter it." Luke 13:28
16 And He took them up in His arms, put
His hands on them, and blessed them.

Rich Young Ruler
Matt. 19:16–22; Luke 18:18–23

17 Now as He was going out on the road,
one came running, knelt before Him, and
asked Him, "Good Teacher, what shall I Rdo
that I may inherit eternal life?" John 6:28
18 So Jesus said to him, "Why do you call
Me good? No one *is* good but One, *that is,*
RGod. 1 Sam. 2:2
19 "You know the commandments: R*'Do
not commit adultery,' 'Do not murder,' 'Do
not steal,' 'Do not bear false witness,'* 'Do not
defraud,' *'Honor your father and your
mother.'* " Ex. 20:12–16; Deut. 5:16–20
20 And he answered and said to Him,
"Teacher, all these I have Robserved from my
youth." Phil. 3:6
21 Then Jesus, looking at him, loved him,
and said to him, "One thing you lack: Go
your way, Rsell whatever you have and give
to the poor, and you will have treasure in
heaven; and come, Rtake up the cross, and
follow Me." [Luke 12:33; 16:9] • [Mark 8:34]
22 But he was sad at this word, and went
away grieved, for he had great possessions.

Difficulty of Riches
Matt. 19:23–26; Luke 18:24–27

23 Then Jesus looked around and said to
His disciples, "How hard it is for those who
have riches to enter the kingdom of God!"
24 And the disciples were astonished at His
words. But Jesus answered again and said to
them, "Children, how hard it is *for those
Rwho trust in riches to enter the kingdom of
God! [1 Tim. 6:17]
25 "It is easier for a camel to go through the
eye of a needle than for a Rrich man to enter
the kingdom of God." [Matt. 13:22; 19:24]
26 And they were astonished beyond measure, saying among themselves, "Who then
can be saved?"
27 But looking at them, Jesus said, "With
men *it is* impossible, but not Rwith God; for
with God all things are possible." Jer. 32:17

Eternal Reward Matt. 19:27–30; Luke 18:28–30

28 RThen Peter began to say to Him, "See,
we have left all and followed You." Luke 18:28
29 So Jesus answered and said, "Assuredly,
I say to you, there is no one who has left
house or brothers or sisters or father or
mother *or wife or children or Tlands, for My
sake and the gospel's, Lit. *fields*
30 R"who shall not receive a hundredfold
now in this time—houses and brothers and
sisters and mothers and children and lands,
with Rpersecutions—and in the age to come,
eternal life. Luke 18:29, 30 • [1 Pet. 4:12, 13]
31 R"But many *who are* first will be last, and
the last first." Luke 13:30

Coming Crucifixion
Matt. 20:17–19; Luke 18:31–34

32 Now they were on the road, going up to
Jerusalem, and Jesus was going before them;
and they were amazed. And as they followed
they were afraid. RThen He took the twelve
aside again and began to tell them the things
that would happen to Him: Mark 8:31; 9:31
33 "Behold, we are going up to Jerusalem,
and the Son of Man will be Rdelivered to the
chief priests and to the scribes, and they will
condemn Him to death and deliver Him to
the Gentiles; Mark 14:53, 64 ☆
34 "and Rthey will mock Him, and scourge
Him, and spit on Him, and kill Him. And the
third day He will rise again." Luke 24:46 ☆

"Whoever Desires to Become Great"
Matt. 20:20–28

35 RThen James and John, the sons of Zebedee, came to Him, saying, "Teacher, we want
You to do for us whatever we ask." [James 4:3]
36 And He said to them, "What do you want
Me to do for you?"
37 They said to Him, "Grant us that we may
sit, one on Your right hand and the other on
Your left, in Your glory."
38 But Jesus said to them, "You do not
know what you ask. Can you drink the cup
that I drink, and be baptized with the Rbap-
tism that I am baptized with?" Luke 12:50
39 And they said to Him, "We can." And
Jesus said to them, R"You will indeed drink
the cup that I drink, and with the baptism I
am baptized with you will be baptized; Acts 12:2
40 "but to sit on My right hand and on My
left is not Mine to give, but *it is for those* Rfor
whom it is prepared." [Heb. 11:16]
41 And when the ten heard *it*, they began to
be greatly displeased with James and John.
42 But Jesus called them to *Himself* and
said to them, R"You know that those who are
considered rulers over the Gentiles lord it
over them, and their great ones exercise
authority over them. Luke 22:25
43 R"Yet it shall not be so among you; but
whoever desires to become great among you
shall be your servant. Mark 9:35
44 "And whoever of you desires to be first
shall be slave of all.

10:24 NU omits *for those who trust in riches*
10:29 NU omits *or wife*

45 "For even [R]the Son of Man did not come
to be served, but to serve, and [R]to give His life
a ransom for many." [Phil. 2:7, 8] • Is. 53:12 ☆

Blind Bartimaeus Is Healed
Matt. 20:29–34; Luke 18:35–43

46 [R]Then they came to Jericho. And as He
went out of Jericho with His disciples and a
great multitude, blind Bartimaeus, the son of
Timaeus, sat by the road begging. Luke 18:35–43
47 And when he heard that it was Jesus of
Nazareth, he began to cry out and say,
"Jesus, Son of David, have mercy on me!"
48 Then many warned him to be quiet; but
he cried out all the more, "Son of David, have
mercy on me!"
49 So Jesus stood still and commanded him
to be called. Then they called the blind man,
saying to him, "Be of good cheer. Rise, He is
calling you."
50 And throwing aside his garment, he rose
and came to Jesus.
51 And Jesus answered and said to him,
"What do you want Me to do for you?" The
blind man said to Him, [T]"Rabboni, that I may
receive my sight." Lit. *My Great One*
52 Then Jesus said to him, "Go your way;
[R]your faith has [T]made you well." And immediately he received his sight and followed
Jesus on the road. Matt. 9:22 • Lit. *saved you*

CHAPTER 11

The Triumphal Entry
Matt. 21:1–11; Luke 19:29–40

NOW when they came near Jerusalem, to
*Bethphage and Bethany, at the Mount
of Olives, He sent out two of His disciples;
2 and He said to them, "Go into the village
opposite you; and as soon as you have entered it you will find a colt tied, on which no
one has sat. Loose it and bring *it*.
3 "And if anyone says to you, 'Why are
you doing this?' say, 'The Lord has need of it,'
and immediately he will send it here."
4 So they went their way, and found *the
colt tied by the door outside on the street,
and they loosed it.
5 And some of those who stood there said
to them, "What are you doing, loosing the
colt?"
6 So they spoke to them just as Jesus had
commanded. And they let them go.
7 Then they brought the colt to Jesus and
threw their garments on it, and He sat on it.
8 And many spread their garments on the
road, and others cut down leafy branches
from the trees and spread *them* on the road.
9 Then those who went before and those
who followed [R]cried out, saying: Zech. 9:9 ☆

[R]"Hosanna!
'Blessed is He who comes in the name of
the LORD!' Ps. 118:26 ☆
10 Blessed *is* the kingdom of our father
David
That comes *in the name of the Lord!
[R]Hosanna in the highest!" Ps. 148:1

11 And Jesus went into Jerusalem and into
the temple. So when He had looked around at
all things, as the hour was already late, He
went out to Bethany with the twelve.

A Fig Tree Is Cursed—Matt. 21:18, 19

12 Now the next day, when they had come
out from Bethany, He was hungry.

11:1 M *Bethsphage* **11:4** NU, M *a*
11:10 NU omits *in the name of the Lord*

10:45 The Ministry of the Son of God—The ministry of Christ is threefold:

a. He is Savior. The title *Savior* implies many important and interrelated truths: the need of sinful men to be saved (Page 1426—1 Tim. 1:15); the qualifications of Christ as God-man to be our Savior (Page 1252—John 10:18); the humiliating death He experienced to become our Savior (Page 1264—John 19:18); the victorious, bodily resurrection He experienced as a sure guarantee of our salvation (Page 1359—1 Cor. 15:13–22); and the glorious results of salvation (Page 1243—John 5:24). It is no wonder that in light of these precious realities Paul speaks of Christ as "the great God and our Savior" (Page 1442—Titus 2:13).

b. He is High Priest. The high priest was of supreme importance in the Old Testament. It was on the basis of his mediation for the people before God on the Day of Atonement that they were brought near to God and protected from judgment (Page 139—Lev. 16:16). Therefore his qualifications were exacting: appointed by God, physically perfect, ceremonially pure, etc. (Page 143—Lev. 21). Jesus is eminently qualified to be our High Priest: He was appointed by God (Page 1453—Heb. 5:5); He is eternal (Page 1456—Heb. 7:24, 25); He is sinless (Page 1456—Heb. 7:26); His offering was final (Page 1457—Heb. 9:28); and His mediation is effective (Page 1333—Rom. 8:34; Page 1456—Heb. 7:25; Page 1494—1 John 2:1). As the only qualified High Priest for men and women, Jesus Christ thus constitutes the only way to God (Page 1426—1 Tim. 2:5).

c. He is King. The position of king implies sovereign authority and rule over all. The Scriptures clearly teach that this right belongs only to Jesus Christ, who is called "the King of Kings and Lord of Lords" (Page 1536—Rev. 19:16). This title means that He is destined to rule as king and that every knee must ultimately bow and acknowledge His authority (Page 1400—Phil. 2:10). Those who acknowledge Christ as King and Lord in this life will reign with Him; those who do not will be judged by Him (Page 1538—Rev. 20:11–15). The weight of eternity hangs on this solemn decision.

Now turn to Page 1390—Eph. 4:3: The Person of the Holy Spirit.

13 [R]And seeing from afar a fig tree having
leaves, He went to see if perhaps He would
find something on it. And when He came to
it, He found nothing but leaves, for it was not
the season for figs. Matt. 21:19
14 In response Jesus said to it, "Let no one
eat fruit from you ever again." And His
disciples heard *it.*

The Temple Is Cleansed
Matt. 21:12, 13; Luke 19:45, 46

15 So they came to Jerusalem. And Jesus
went into the temple and began to drive out
those who bought and sold in the temple, and
overturned the tables of the moneychangers
and the seats of those who sold doves.
16 And He would not allow anyone to carry
wares through the temple.
17 Then He taught, saying to them, "Is it
not written, *'My house shall be called a house
of prayer for all nations'?* But [R]you have
made it a *'den of thieves.'*" Jer. 7:11
18 And the scribes and chief priests heard it
and sought how they might destroy Him; for
they feared Him, because [R]all the people were
astonished at His teaching. Matt. 7:28
19 And when evening had come, He went
out of the city.

Power of Faith—Matt. 21:20–22

20 Now in the morning, as they passed by,
they saw the fig tree dried up from the roots.
21 And Peter, remembering, said to Him,
"Rabbi, look! The fig tree which You cursed
has withered away."
22 So Jesus answered and said to them,
"Have faith in God.
23 "For [R]assuredly, I say to you, whoever
says to this mountain, 'Be removed and be
cast into the sea,' and does not doubt in his
heart, but believes that those things he says
will come to pass, he will have whatever he
says. Matt. 17:20; 21:21
24 "Therefore I say to you, whatever things
you ask when you pray, believe that you
receive *them,* and you will have *them.*

Necessity of Forgiveness

25 "And whenever you stand praying, [R]if
you have anything against anyone, forgive
him, that your Father in heaven may also
forgive you your trespasses. [Col. 3:13]
26 *"But [R]if you do not forgive, neither will
your Father in heaven forgive your trespasses." Matt. 6:15; 18:35

Question of Authority
Matt. 21:23–27; Luke 20:1–8

27 Then they came again to Jerusalem.
[R]And as He was walking in the temple, the
chief priests, the scribes, and the elders came
to Him. Luke 20:1–8
28 And they said to Him, "By what authority are You doing these things? And who
gave You this authority to do these things?"
29 But Jesus answered and said to them, "I
will also ask you one question; then answer
Me, and I will tell you by what authority I do
these things:
30 "The baptism of John—was it from
heaven or from men? Answer Me."
31 And they reasoned among themselves,
saying, "If we say, 'From heaven,' He will
say, 'Why then did you not believe him?'
32 "But if we say, 'From men' "—they
feared the people, for [R]all counted John to
have been a prophet indeed. Matt. 3:5; 14:5
33 So they answered and said to Jesus, "We
do not know." And Jesus answered and said
to them, "Neither will I tell you by what
authority I do these things."

CHAPTER 12

Parable of the Vineyard Owner
Matt. 21:33–46; Luke 20:9–19

THEN He began to speak to them in parables: "A man planted a vineyard and set
a hedge around *it,* dug *a place for* the wine
vat and built a tower. And he leased it to
vinedressers and went into a far country.
2 "Now at vintage-time he sent a servant
to the vinedressers, that he might receive
some of the fruit of the vineyard from the
vinedressers.
3 "And they took *him* and beat him and
sent *him* away empty-handed.
4 "Again he sent them another servant,
*and at him they threw stones, wounded *him*
in the head, and sent *him* away shamefully
treated.
5 "And again he sent another, and him
they killed; and many others, [R]beating some
and killing some. 2 Chr. 36:16
6 "Therefore still having one son, his beloved, he also sent him to them last, saying,
'They will respect my son.'
7 "But those vinedressers said among
themselves, 'This is the heir. Come, let us kill
him, and the inheritance will be ours.'
8 "And they took him and [R]killed *him* and
cast *him* out of the vineyard. [Acts 2:23]
9 "Therefore what will the owner of the
vineyard do? He will come and destroy the
vinedressers, and give the vineyard to others.
10 "Have you not read this Scripture:

'The stone which the builders rejected
Has become the chief cornerstone.
11 [R]*This was the LORD's doing,* Ps. 118:22, 23 ★
And it is marvelous in our eyes'?"

11:26 NU omits v. 26.
12:4 NU omits *and at him they threw stones*

THE FOUR GOSPELS

Many readers of the New Testament wonder why it contains four different Gospels (accounts) of the one authentic gospel (the good news of salvation in Jesus Christ). Perhaps the main reason is that any one of these Gospels alone would not do justice to Jesus' life and ministry. Each Gospel writer wrote about Jesus to a different audience for a different purpose to give a unique perspective on His life. Together, the four Gospels give us a complete picture of who Jesus was and what He accomplished during His ministry.

Different symbols for the Gospels are often used to communicate the distinctives of each account. A lion, symbolizing Matthew, represents strength and royal authority; a bull, representing Mark, portrays service and power; the figure of a man, for Luke, stands for wisdom and character; and an eagle, John's symbol, represents deity. The following capsule summaries of the Gospels should help you understand the distinctives of each.

MATTHEW

—Written to a Jewish audience to show that Jesus was the promised Messiah of Old Testament prophecy; key expression is "that it might be fulfilled"; quotes more from the Old Testament than any other Gospel.

—Uses alternating sections of didactic and narrative material to emphasize Jesus as Teacher.

—A major theme is the kingdom of heaven or the kingdom of God—God's rule in the world and human hearts.

—Other dominant themes are the church (16:18; 18:19), the Second Coming of Jesus (ch. 25), and the ethical teachings of Jesus (chs. 5—7).

MARK

—Probably the first Gospel written; Matthew and Luke may have used Mark as a source.

—Focuses on Jesus as servant who ministers to the physical and spiritual needs of others.

—The shortest Gospel; written to a Gentile audience, particularly Roman citizens.

—Uses brevity in accounts, with rapid movement, to give a sense of urgency to the gospel message; key expression is "immediately."

—Mark's purpose was to show that Jesus was the Son of God; a Roman soldier's words at Jesus' death were, "Truly this Man was the Son of God!" (15:39).

LUKE

—Written by a Gentile writer, for Gentiles, to give the full story of Jesus' life, from His birth to the birth of the church.

—Records many of Jesus' parables not found in the other Gospels.

—Universal in outlook, portraying Jesus as the compassionate Savior of the world, with love for all people, whether rich or poor, Jew or Gentile; He reaches out especially to women and the poor and outcast of society.

—Emphasizes the work of the Holy Spirit and the central place of prayer in Jesus' life and ministry.

—Key expression is "it happened" or "it came to pass."

JOHN

—Focuses on the theological meaning of Jesus' actions, rather than on the actions themselves; emphasizes who Jesus is, rather than what He did.

—Includes many lengthy discourses of Jesus around which narrative is woven.

—Uses many key words, such as *life, light, believe, love, witness, glory, water,* and *truth,* to portray Jesus as God's eternal Son.

—Presents Jesus as God incarnate through seven miraculous signs; key expression is "believe."

—John's clear purpose in writing is "that you may believe that Jesus is the Christ, the Son of God, and that believing you may have life in His name" (20:31).

12 [R]And they sought to lay hold of Him, but
feared the multitude, for they knew He had
spoken the parable against them. So they left
Him and went away. John 7:25, 30, 44

Question of Taxes
Matt. 22:15–22; Luke 20:20–26

13 [R]Then they sent to Him some of the
Pharisees and the Herodians, to catch Him in
His words. Luke 20:20–26
14 When they had come, they said to Him,
"Teacher, we know that You are true, and
[T]care about no one; for You do not [T]regard
the person of men, but teach the way of God
in truth. Is it lawful to pay taxes to Caesar, or
not? Court no man's favor • Lit. *look at the face of men*
15 "Shall we pay, or shall we not pay?" But
He, knowing their [R]hypocrisy, said to them,
"Why do you test Me? Bring Me a [T]denarius
that I may see *it.*" Luke 12:1 • 1 day's wage
16 So they brought *it.* And He said to them,
"Whose image and inscription *is* this?" And
they said to Him, "Caesar's."
17 Then Jesus answered and said to them,
[T]"Render to Caesar the things that are Caesar's, and to [R]God the things that are God's."
And they marveled at Him. *Pay* • [Eccl. 5:4, 5]

Question of the Resurrection
Matt. 22:23–33; Luke 20:27–40

18 [R]Then *some* Sadducees, [R]who say there is
no resurrection, came to Him; and they asked
Him, saying: Luke 20:27–38 • Acts 23:8
19 "Teacher, [R]Moses wrote to us that if a
man's brother dies, and leaves *his* wife behind, and leaves no children, his brother
should take his wife and raise up offspring for
his brother. Deut. 25:5
20 "Now there were seven brothers. The
first took a wife; and dying, he left no offspring.
21 "And the second took her, and he died;
nor did he leave any offspring. And the third
likewise.
22 "So the seven had her and left no offspring. Last of all the woman died also.
23 "Therefore, in the resurrection, when
they rise, whose wife will she be? For all
seven had her as wife."
24 Jesus answered and said to them, "Are
you not therefore [T]mistaken, because you do
not know the Scriptures nor the power of
God? Or *deceived*
25 "For when they rise from the dead, they
neither marry nor are given in marriage, but
[R]are like angels in heaven. [1 Cor. 15:42, 49, 52]
26 "But concerning the dead, that they rise,
have you not read in the book of Moses, in
the *burning* bush *passage,* how God spoke to
him, saying, *'I am the God of Abraham, the
God of Isaac, and the God of Jacob'?*
27 "He is not the God of the dead, but the
God of the living. You are therefore greatly
[T]mistaken." Or *deceived*

Question of the Greatest Commandment
Matt. 22:34–40

28 [R]Then one of the scribes came, and having heard them reasoning together, *perceiv-
ing that He had answered them well, asked
Him, "Which is the [T]first commandment of
all?" Matt. 22:34–40 • *foremost*
29 Jesus answered him, "The [T]first of all the
commandments *is:* [R]*'Hear, O Israel, the* LORD
our God, the LORD *is one.* *foremost* • Deut. 6:4, 5
30 *'And you shall [R]love the* LORD *your God
with all your heart, with all your soul, with all
your mind, and with all your strength.'* *This
is the first commandment. [Deut. 10:12; 30:6]
31 "And the second, like *it, is* this: [R]*'You
shall love your neighbor as yourself.'* There
is no other commandment greater than
[R]these." Lev. 19:18 • [Rom. 13:9]
32 So the scribe said to Him, "Well *said,*
Teacher. You have spoken the truth, for
there is one God, [R]and there is no other but
He. Deut. 4:39
33 "And to love Him with all the heart, with
all the understanding, *with all the soul, and
with all the strength, and to love one's neighbor as oneself, [R]is more than all the whole
burnt offerings and sacrifices." [Hos. 6:6]
34 So when Jesus saw that he answered
wisely, He said to him, "You are not far from
the kingdom of God." [R]And after that no one
dared question Him. Matt. 22:46

Jesus Questions the Leaders
Matt. 22:41–45; Luke 20:41–44

35 [R]Then Jesus answered and said, while He
taught in the temple, "How *is it* that the
scribes say that the Christ is the Son of
David? Luke 20:41–44
36 "For David himself said [R]by the Holy
Spirit:

[R]*'The* LORD *said to my Lord,*
"Sit at My right hand,
Till I make Your enemies Your
footstool."' 2 Sam. 23:2 • Ps. 110:1

37 "Therefore David himself calls Him
'Lord'; how is He *then* his [R]Son?" And the
common people heard Him gladly. [Acts 2:29–31]

Jesus Condemns the Leaders
Matt. 23:1–14; Luke 20:45—21:4

38 Then [R]He said to them in His teaching,
[R]"Beware of the scribes, who desire to go
around in long robes, [R]*love* greetings in the
marketplaces, Mark 4:2 • Matt. 23:1–7 • Matt. 23:7

12:28 NU *seeing* **12:30** NU omits the rest of v. 30.
12:33 NU omits *with all the soul*

39 "the [R]best seats in the synagogues, and
the best places at feasts, Luke 14:7
40 [R]"who devour widows' houses, and for a
pretense make long prayers. These will receive greater condemnation." Matt. 23:14
41 [R]Now Jesus sat opposite the treasury and
saw how the people put money [R]into the
treasury. And many *who were* rich put in
much. Luke 21:1–4 • 2 Kin. 12:9
42 Then one poor widow came and threw in
two mites, which make a quadrans.
43 So He called His disciples *to Him* and said
to them, "Assuredly, I say to you that [R]this
poor widow has put in more than all those
who have given to the treasury; [2 Cor. 8:12]
44 "for they all put in out of their abundance, but she out of her poverty put in all
that she had, [R]her whole livelihood." Deut. 24:6

CHAPTER 13

Questions from the Disciples
Matt. 24:1–3; Luke 21:5–7

THEN [R]as He went out of the temple, one
of His disciples said to Him, "Teacher, see
what manner of stones and what buildings
are here!" Luke 21:5–36
2 And Jesus answered and said to him, "Do
you see these great buildings? [R]Not *one* stone
shall be left upon another, that shall not be
thrown down." Luke 19:44
3 Now as He sat on the Mount of Olives
opposite the temple, Peter, James, John, and
[R]Andrew asked Him privately, John 1:40
4 [R]"Tell us, when will these things be? And
what *will be* the sign when all these things
will be fulfilled?" Matt. 24:3

The Tribulation—Matt. 24:4–26; Luke 21:8–24

5 And Jesus, answering them, began to
say: "Take heed that no one deceives you.
6 "For many will come in My name, saying, 'I am *He*,' and will deceive many.
7 "And when you hear of wars and rumors
of wars, do not be troubled; for *such things*
must happen, but the end *is* not yet.
8 "For nation will rise against nation, and
kingdom against kingdom. And there will be
earthquakes in various places, and there will
be famines *and troubles. [R]These *are* the
beginnings of [T]sorrows. Matt. 24:8 • Lit. *birth pangs*
9 "But [R]watch out for yourselves, for they
will deliver you up to councils, and you will
be beaten in the synagogues. And you will
*be brought before rulers and kings for My
sake, for a testimony to them. Matt. 10:17, 18
10 "And [R]the gospel must first be preached
to all the nations. Matt. 24:14
11 "But when they arrest *you* and deliver
you up, do not worry beforehand, *or premeditate what you will speak. But whatever
is given you in that hour, speak that; for it is
not you who speak, but the Holy Spirit.
12 "Now [R]brother will betray brother to
death, and a father *his* child; and children will
rise up against parents and cause them to be
put to death. Mic. 7:6
13 [R]"And you will be hated by all *men* for
My name's sake. But he who [T]endures to the
end shall be saved. Luke 21:17 • *bears patiently*
14 "But when you see the *'abomination of
desolation,'* *spoken of by Daniel the
prophet, standing where it ought not" (let the
reader understand), "then [R]let those who are
in Judea flee to the mountains. Luke 21:21
15 "And let him who is on the housetop not
go down into the house, nor enter to take
anything out of his house.
16 "And let him who is in the field not go
back to get his garment.
17 [R]"But woe to those who are pregnant
and to those with nursing babies in those
days! Luke 21:23
18 "And pray that your flight may not be in
winter.
19 [R]"For *in* those days there will be tribulation, such as has not been from the beginning
of creation which God created until this time,
nor ever shall be. Dan. 9:26; 12:1
20 "And unless the Lord had shortened
those days, no flesh would be saved; but for
the elect's sake, whom He chose, He shortened the days.
21 [R]"Then if anyone says to you, 'Look, here
is the Christ!' or, 'Look, *He is* there!' do not
believe it. Luke 17:23; 21:8
22 "For false christs and false prophets will
rise and show signs and wonders to deceive,
if possible, even the [T]elect. *chosen ones*
23 "But [R]take heed; see, I have told you all
things beforehand. [2 Pet. 3:17]

The Second Coming
Matt. 24:29–31; Luke 21:25–28

24 [R]"But in those days, after that tribulation, the sun will be darkened, and the moon
will not give its light; Zeph. 1:15
25 "the stars of heaven will fall, and the
powers in heaven will be [R]shaken. Is. 13:10; 34:4
26 [R]"Then they will see the Son of Man
coming in the clouds with great power and
glory. [Dan. 7:13, 14; Matt. 16:27] ☆
27 "And then He will send His angels, and
gather together His [T]elect from the four
winds, from the farthest part of earth to the
farthest part of heaven. *chosen ones*

Parable of the Fig Tree—Matt. 24:32–35

28 [R]"Now learn this parable from the fig
tree: When its branch has already become

13:8 NU omits *and troubles* **13:9** NU, M *stand*
13:11 NU omits *or premeditate*
13:14 NU omits *spoken of by Daniel the prophet*

tender, and puts forth leaves, you know that
summer is near. Luke 21:29
29 "So you also, when you see these things
happening, know that [T]it is near, at the very
doors. Or *He*
30 "Assuredly, I say to you, this generation
will by no means pass away till all these
things take place.
31 "Heaven and earth will pass away, but
My words will by no means pass away.

Exhortation to Watch
Matt. 24:36–51; Luke 21:34–36

32 "But of that day and hour [R]no one
knows, neither the angels in heaven, nor the
Son, but only the [R]Father. Matt. 25:13 • Acts 1:7
33 [R]"Take heed, watch and pray; for you do
not know when the time is. 1 Thess. 5:6
34 "*It is* like a man going to a far country,
who left his house and gave authority to his
servants, and to each his work, and commanded the doorkeeper to watch.
35 [R]"Watch therefore, for you do not know
when the master of the house is coming—in
the evening, at midnight, at the crowing of
the rooster, or in the morning— Matt. 24:42, 44
36 "lest, coming suddenly, he find you
sleeping.
37 "And what I say to you, I say to all:
Watch!"

CHAPTER 14

Leaders Plot to Kill Jesus
Matt. 26:1–5; Luke 22:1, 2

AFTER [R]two days it was the Passover and
[R]*the Feast* of Unleavened Bread. And
the chief priests and the scribes sought how
they might take Him by [T]trickery and put
Him to death. Luke 22:1, 2 • Ex. 12:1–27 • *deception*
2 But they said, "Not during the feast, lest
there be an uproar of the people."

Mary Anoints Jesus
Matt. 26:6–13; John 12:2–8

3 [R]And being in Bethany at the house of
Simon the leper, as He sat at the table, a
woman came having an alabaster flask of
very costly oil of spikenard. And she broke
the flask and poured *it* on His head. Luke 7:37
4 But there were some who were indignant
among themselves, and said, "Why was this
fragrant oil wasted?
5 "For it might have been sold for more
than three hundred denarii and given to the
poor." And they criticized her sharply.
6 But Jesus said, "Let her alone. Why do
you trouble her? She has done a good work
for Me.
7 "For you have the poor with you always,
and whenever you wish you may do them
good; but Me you do not have always.
8 "She has done what she could. She has
come beforehand to anoint My body for
[R]burial. John 19:40–42 ☆
9 "Assuredly, I say to you, wherever this
gospel is [R]preached throughout the whole
world, what this woman did will also be
spoken of as a memorial to her." Luke 24:47

Judas Plans to Betray Jesus
Matt. 26:14–16; Luke 22:3–6

10 [R]Then Judas Iscariot, one of the twelve,
went to the chief priests to betray Him to
them. Matt. 10:2–4
11 So when they heard *it*, they were glad,
and promised to give him money. So he
sought how he might conveniently betray
Him.

The Passover Is Prepared
Matt. 26:17–19; Luke 22:7–13

12 [R]Now on the first day of Unleavened
Bread, when they [T]killed the Passover *lamb*,
His disciples said to Him, "Where do You
want us to go and prepare, that You may eat
the Passover?" Matt. 26:17–19 • *sacrificed*
13 So He sent out two of His disciples and
said to them, "Go into the city, and a man
will meet you carrying a pitcher of water;
follow him.
14 "And wherever he goes in, say to the
master of the house, 'The Teacher says,
"Where is the guest room in which I may eat
the Passover with My disciples?" '
15 "Then he will show you a large upper
room, furnished *and* prepared; there make
ready for us."
16 And His disciples went out, and came
into the city, and found it just as He had said
to them; and they prepared the Passover.

The Passover Is Celebrated
Matt. 26:20–25; Luke 22:14–16; John 13:21–30

17 [R]In the evening He came with the
twelve. Matt. 26:20–24
18 Now as they sat and ate, Jesus said,
"Assuredly, I say to you, [R]one of you who
eats with Me will betray Me." Ps. 41:9 ☆
19 And they began to be sorrowful, and to
say to Him one by one, "*Is* it I?" *And
another *said*, "*Is* it I?"
20 Then He answered and said to them, "*It*
is one of the twelve, who dips with Me in the
dish.
21 [R]"The Son of Man indeed goes just as it
is written of Him, but woe to that man by
whom the Son of Man is betrayed! It would
have been good for that man if he had never
been born." Luke 22:22

14:19 NU omits the rest of v. 19.

The Lord's Supper Is Instituted
Matt. 26:26–29; Luke 22:17–23

22 And as they were eating, Jesus took bread, blessed *it* and broke *it*, and gave *it* to them and said, "Take, *eat; this is My body."
23 Then He took the cup, and when He had given thanks He gave *it* to them, and they all drank from it.
24 And He said to them, "This is My blood of the *new covenant, which is shed for many.
25 "Assuredly, I say to you, I will no longer drink of the fruit of the vine until that day when I drink it new in the kingdom of God."

Jesus Predicts Peter's Denial
Matt. 26:30–35; Luke 22:31–39; John 13:36–38

26 And when they had sung [T]a hymn, they went out to the Mount of Olives. *Or hymns*
27 [R]Then Jesus said to them, "All of you will be made to stumble *because of Me this night, for it is written: Matt. 26:31–35

[R]*'I will strike the Shepherd,* Zech. 13:7
And the sheep will be scattered.'

28 "But [R]after I have been raised, I will go before you to Galilee." Mark 16:7
29 But Peter said to Him, "Even if all are made to stumble, yet I *will* not *be.*"
30 And Jesus said to him, "Assuredly, I say to you [R]that today, *even* this night, before the rooster crows twice, you will deny Me three times." Mark 14:72; Luke 22:61 ☆
31 But he spoke more vehemently, "If I have to die with You, I will not deny You!" And they all said likewise.

Jesus Prays in Gethsemane
Matt. 26:36–46; Luke 22:39–46

32 [R]Then they came to a place which was named Gethsemane; and He said to His disciples, "Sit here while I pray." Luke 22:40–46
33 And He [R]took Peter, James, and John with Him, and He began to be troubled and deeply distressed. Mark 5:37; 9:2; 13:3
34 Then He said to them, [R]"My soul is exceedingly sorrowful, *even* to death. Stay here and watch." John 12:27
35 He went a little farther, and fell on the ground, and prayed that if it were possible, the hour might pass from Him.
36 And He said, [R]"Abba, Father, [R]all things *are* possible for You. Take this cup away from Me; [R]nevertheless, not what I will, but what You *will*." Gal. 4:6 • [Heb. 5:7] • Is. 50:5 ★
37 Then He came and found them sleeping, and said to Peter, "Simon, are you sleeping? Could you not watch one hour?

38 [R]"Watch and pray, lest you enter into temptation. [R]The spirit truly *is* ready, but the flesh *is* weak." Luke 21:36 • [Rom. 7:18, 21–24]

39 Again He went away and prayed, and spoke the same words.
40 And when He returned, He found them asleep again, for their eyes were heavy; and they did not know what to answer Him.
41 Then He came the third time and said to them, "Are you still sleeping and resting? It is enough! [R]The hour has come; behold, the Son of Man is being betrayed into the hands of sinners. John 13:1; 17:1
42 [R]"Rise up, let us go. See, My [R]betrayer is at hand." John 13:21; 18:1, 2 • Matt. 20:18; 26:21 ★

Judas Betrays Jesus
Matt. 26:47–56; Luke 22:47–53; John 18:1–11

43 [R]And immediately, while He was still speaking, Judas, one of the twelve, with a great multitude with swords and clubs, came from the chief priests and the scribes and the elders. Luke 22:47–53
44 Now His betrayer had given them a signal, saying, "Whomever I kiss, He is the One; take Him and lead *Him* away safely."
45 And as soon as He had come, immediately he went up to Him and said to Him, "Rabbi, Rabbi!" and kissed Him.
46 Then they laid their hands on Him and took Him.

14:22 NU omits *eat* 14:24 NU omits *new*
14:27 NU omits *because of Me this night*

14:38 Temptation by the Flesh—*Flesh* in the Bible often means something other than the substance of the human body. It is used constantly to refer to the carnal, sinful principle within man that is opposed to God (Page 1332—Rom. 8:7). The actions produced by the flesh are given in detail in Galatians 5:19–21. Among these are all types of sexual immorality, impurity, hatred, anger, false religions, envy, and drunkenness. A person whose life is characterized by these sins cannot be a true Christian and is under the wrath of God (Page 1383—Gal. 5:21; Page 1387—Eph. 2:3).

Though the flesh is not eradicated for the Christian, he does not have to obey it (Page 1332—Rom. 7:15–25). He possesses a new nature empowered by the Holy Spirit. Since the flesh and the Spirit are totally opposed to each other, the one whom the believer allows to dominate him will take charge in his life and produce its own fruit. The solution to the urges of the flesh lies in acknowledging that the power of sin was nullified by Jesus' death (Page 1331—Rom. 6:11) and in living under the control of the Spirit's power (Page 1383—Gal. 5:16). The latter is a moment-by-moment dependence in faith on the Spirit's power. The believer must choose by an act of his will to benefit from the Spirit's enablement.

Now turn to Page 487—1 Chr. 21:1: Temptation by Satan.

47 And one of those who stood by drew his
sword and struck the servant of the high
priest, and cut off his ear.
48 [R]Then Jesus answered and said to them,
"Have you come out, as against a robber,
with swords and clubs to take Me? Matt. 26:55
49 "I was daily with you in the temple
[R]teaching, and you did not take Me. But [R]the
Scriptures must be fulfilled." Matt. 21:23 • Is. 53:7
50 Then they all forsook Him and fled.
51 Now a certain young man followed Him,
having a linen cloth thrown around *his* naked
body. And the young men laid hold of him,
52 and he left the linen cloth and fled from
them naked.

The Sanhedrin Tries Jesus
Matt. 26:57–68; Luke 22:54, 55, 63–65;
John 18:12, 18, 24

53 And they led Jesus away to the high
priest; and with him were assembled all the
chief priests, the elders, and the scribes.
54 But [R]Peter followed Him at a distance,
right into the courtyard of the high priest.
And he sat with the servants and warmed
himself at the fire. John 18:15
55 [R]And the chief priests and all the council
sought testimony against Jesus to put Him to
death, and found none. Matt. 26:59
56 For many bore false witness against Him,
but their testimonies did not agree.
57 And [R]some rose up and bore false witness
against Him, saying, Ps. 27:12; 35:11★
58 "We heard Him say, [R]'I will destroy this
temple that *is* made with hands, and within
three days I will build another made without
hands.'" John 2:19
59 But not even then did their testimony
agree.
60 [R]And the high priest stood up in the
midst and asked Jesus, saying, "Do You
answer nothing? What *is it* these men testify
against You?" Matt. 26:62
61 But [R]He kept silent and answered nothing. [R]Again the high priest asked Him, saying
to Him, "Are You the Christ, the Son of the
Blessed?" Is. 53:7 • Luke 22:67–71
62 And Jesus said, "I am. [R]And you will see
the Son of Man sitting at the right hand of
the Power, and coming with the clouds of
heaven." Luke 22:69
63 Then the high priest tore his clothes and
said, "What further need do we have of
witnesses?
64 "You have heard the blasphemy! What
do you think?" And they all [R]condemned Him
to be worthy of death. Matt. 20:18; Mark 10:33★
65 Then some began to [R]spit on Him, and to
blindfold Him, and to beat Him, and to say to
Him, "Prophesy!" And the officers *struck
Him with the palms of their hands. Is. 50:6★

Peter Denies Jesus
Matt. 26:69–75; Luke 22:55–62;
John 18:15–18, 25–27

66 [R]Now as Peter was below in the courtyard, one of the servant girls of the high
priest came. John 18:16–18, 25–27
67 And when she saw Peter warming himself, she looked at him and said, "You also
were with [R]Jesus of Nazareth." John 1:45
68 But he denied it, saying, "I neither know
nor understand what you are saying." And he
went out on the porch, and a rooster crowed.
69 [R]And the servant girl saw him again, and
began to say to those who stood by, "This is
one of them." Matt. 26:71
70 But he denied it again. And a little later
those who stood by said to Peter again,
"Surely you are *one* of them; for you are a
Galilean, *and your speech shows *it*."
71 But he began to curse and swear, "I do
not know this Man of whom you speak!"
72 And a second time *the* rooster crowed.
And Peter called to mind the word that Jesus
had said to him, "Before the rooster crows
twice, you will deny Me three times." And
when he thought about it, he wept.

CHAPTER 15

Pilate Tries Jesus
Matt. 27:1, 2, 11–23; Luke 23:1–5, 13–23;
John 18:28—19:15

IMMEDIATELY, in the morning, the chief
priests [R]held a consultation with the elders and scribes and the whole council; and
they bound Jesus, led *Him* away, and [R]deliv-
ered *Him* to Pilate. Ps. 2:2 • Is. 53:7★
2 [R]Then Pilate asked Him, "Are You the
King of the Jews?" And He answered and
said to him, "*It is as* you say." Matt. 27:11–14
3 And the chief priests accused Him of
many things, but He answered nothing.
4 [R]Then Pilate asked Him again, saying,
"Do You answer nothing? See how many
things *they testify against You!" Matt. 27:13
5 [R]But Jesus still answered nothing, so that
Pilate marveled. Ps. 38:13, 14; Is. 53:7; John 19:9★
6 Now [R]at the feast he was accustomed to
releasing one prisoner to them, whomever
they requested. Matt. 27:15–26
7 And there was one named Barabbas, *who
was* chained with his fellow insurrectionists;
they had committed murder in the insurrection.
8 Then the multitude, *crying aloud, began
to ask *him to do* just as he had always done
for them.

14:65 NU *received Him with slaps*
14:70 NU omits the rest of v. 70.
15:4 NU *of which they accuse You* 15:8 NU *going up*

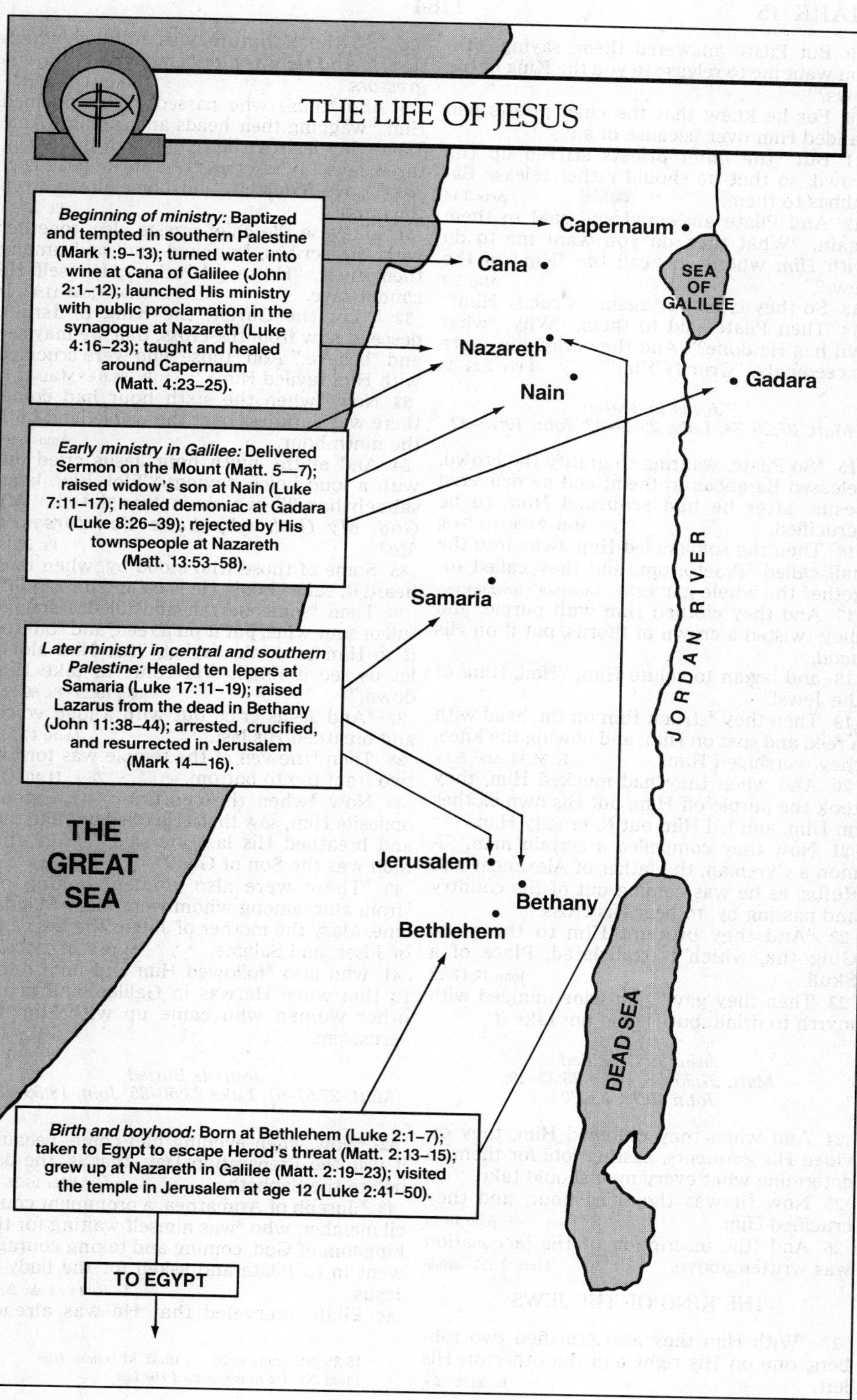
THE LIFE OF JESUS
Beginning of ministry: Baptized and tempted in southern Palestine (Mark 1:9–13); turned water into wine at Cana of Galilee (John 2:1–12); launched His ministry with public proclamation in the synagogue at Nazareth (Luke 4:16–23); taught and healed around Capernaum (Matt. 4:23–25).
Early ministry in Galilee: Delivered Sermon on the Mount (Matt. 5—7); raised widow's son at Nain (Luke 7:11–17); healed demoniac at Gadara (Luke 8:26–39); rejected by His townspeople at Nazareth (Matt. 13:53–58).
Later ministry in central and southern Palestine: Healed ten lepers at Samaria (Luke 17:11–19); raised Lazarus from the dead in Bethany (John 11:38–44); arrested, crucified, and resurrected in Jerusalem (Mark 14—16).
Birth and boyhood: Born at Bethlehem (Luke 2:1–7); taken to Egypt to escape Herod's threat (Matt. 2:13–15); grew up at Nazareth in Galilee (Matt. 2:19–23); visited the temple in Jerusalem at age 12 (Luke 2:41–50).
TO EGYPT
Capernaum
Cana
SEA OF GALILEE
Nazareth
Nain
Gadara
Samaria
JORDAN RIVER
Jerusalem
Bethany
Bethlehem
THE GREAT SEA
DEAD SEA

9 But Pilate answered them, saying, "Do
you want me to release to you the King of the
Jews?"
10 For he knew that the chief priests had
handed Him over because of envy.
11 But [R]the chief priests stirred up the
crowd, so that he should rather release Barabbas to them. Acts 3:14
12 And Pilate answered and said to them
again, "What then do you want me to do
with Him whom you call the [R]King of the
Jews?" Mic. 5:2
13 So they cried out again, "Crucify Him!"
14 Then Pilate said to them, "Why, [R]what
evil has He done?" And they cried out more
exceedingly, "Crucify Him!" 1 Pet. 2:21–23

Jesus Is Beaten
Matt. 27:26–34; Luke 23:24–32; John 19:16–22

15 [R]So Pilate, wanting to gratify the crowd,
released Barabbas to them; and he delivered
Jesus, after he had scourged *Him*, to be
[R]crucified. Matt. 27:26 • [Is. 53:8]
16 Then the soldiers led Him away into the
hall called [T]Praetorium, and they called together the whole garrison. Governor's headquarters
17 And they clothed Him with purple; and
they twisted a crown of thorns, put it on His
head,
18 and began to salute Him, "Hail, King of
the Jews!"
19 Then they [R]struck Him on the head with
a reed and spat on Him; and bowing the knee,
they worshiped Him. Is. 52:14; Mic. 5:1 ★
20 And when they had mocked Him, they
took the purple off Him, put His own clothes
on Him, and led Him out to crucify Him.
21 Now they compelled a certain man, Simon a Cyrenian, the father of Alexander and
Rufus, as he was coming out of the country
and passing by, to bear His cross.
22 [R]And they brought Him to the place
Golgotha, which is translated, Place of a
Skull. John 19:17–24
23 Then they gave Him wine mingled with
myrrh to drink, but He did not take *it*.

Jesus Is Crucified
Matt. 27:35–56; Luke 23:33–49;
John 19:18, 23–30

24 And when they crucified Him, they divided His garments, casting lots for them to
determine what every man should take.
25 Now [R]it was the third hour, and they
crucified Him. John 19:14
26 And [R]the inscription of His [T]accusation
was written above: Matt. 27:37 • *crime*

THE KING OF THE JEWS.

27 [R]With Him they also crucified two robbers, one on His right and the other on His
left. Is. 53:9, 12 ★
28 *So the Scripture was fulfilled which
says, [R]*"And He was numbered with the trans-*
gressors." Is. 53:12; Luke 22:37 ★
29 And [R]those who passed by blasphemed
Him, [R]wagging their heads and saying, "Aha!
[R]*You* who destroy the temple and build *it* in
three days, Ps. 22:6, 7; 69:7 ★ • Ps. 109:25 • John 2:19–21
30 [R]"save Yourself, and come down from
the cross!" Ps. 22:8 ★
31 Likewise the chief priests also, together
with the scribes, [R]mocked and said among
themselves, "He saved [R]others; Himself He
cannot save. Ps. 69:19 ★ • John 11:43, 44
32 [R]"Let the Christ, the King of Israel,
descend now from the cross, that we may see
and *believe." And [R]those who were crucified
with Him reviled Him. Ps. 22:8 ★ • Matt. 27:44
33 Now [R]when the sixth hour had come,
there was darkness over the whole land until
the ninth hour. Amos 8:9 ★
34 And at the ninth hour Jesus cried out
with a loud voice, saying, [R]"Eloi, Eloi, lama
sabachthani?" which is translated, *"My*
God, My God, why have You forsaken
Me?" Ps. 22:1 ★
35 Some of those who stood by, when they
heard *it*, said, "Look, He is calling for Elijah!"
36 Then [R]someone ran and filled a sponge
full of sour wine, put *it* on a reed, and [R]offered
it to Him to drink, saying, "Let Him alone;
let us see if Elijah will come to take Him
down." John 19:29 • Ps. 69:21 ★
37 [R]And Jesus cried out with a loud voice,
and breathed His last. Matt. 17:23 ★
38 Then [R]the veil of the temple was torn in
two from top to bottom. Zech. 11:10, 11 ★
39 Now [R]when the centurion, who stood
opposite Him, saw that *He cried out like this
and breathed His last, he said, "Truly this
Man was the Son of God!" Luke 23:47
40 [R]There were also women looking on
[R]from afar, among whom were Mary Magdalene, Mary the mother of James the Less and
of Joses, and Salome, Matt. 27:55 • Ps. 38:11
41 who also [R]followed Him and ministered
to Him when He was in Galilee; and many
other women who came up with Him to
Jerusalem. Luke 8:2, 3

Jesus Is Buried
Matt. 27:57–61; Luke 23:50–55; John 19:38–42

42 [R]Now when evening had come, because
it was the Preparation Day, that is, the day
before the Sabbath, John 19:38–42
43 [R]Joseph of Arimathea, a prominent council member, who [R]was himself waiting for the
kingdom of God, coming and taking courage,
went in to Pilate and asked for the body of
Jesus. Is. 53:9 ★ • Luke 23:51
44 Pilate marveled that He was already

15:28 NU omits v. 28. **15:32** M *believe Him*
15:39 NU *He thus breathed His last*

dead; and summoning the centurion, he
asked him if He had been dead for some time.
45 And when he found out from the centurion,
he granted the body to Joseph.
46 Then he bought fine linen, took Him
down, and wrapped Him in the linen. And he
[R]laid Him in a tomb which had been hewn out
of the rock, and rolled a stone against the
door of the tomb. Matt. 26:12; Mark 14:8*
47 And Mary Magdalene and Mary *the*
mother of Joses observed where He was laid.

CHAPTER 16

The Resurrection of Jesus
Matt. 28:1–8; Luke 24:1–9

NOW [R]when the Sabbath was past, Mary
Magdalene, Mary *the mother* of James,
and Salome [R]bought spices, that they might
come and anoint Him. John 20:1–8 • Luke 23:56
2 [R]Very early in the morning, on the first
day of the week, they came to the tomb when
the sun had risen. Luke 24:1
3 And they said among themselves, "Who
will roll away the stone from the door of the
tomb for us?"
4 But when they looked up, they saw that
the stone had been rolled away—for it was
very large.
5 [R]And entering the tomb, they saw a
young man clothed in a long white robe
sitting on the right side; and they were
alarmed. John 20:11, 12
6 But he said to them, "Do not be alarmed.
You seek Jesus of Nazareth, who was crucified.
He is [R]risen! He is not here. See the place
where they laid Him. Hos. 6:2*
7 "But go *and* tell His disciples—and Peter—that
He is going before you into Galilee;
there you will see Him, as He said to you."
8 And they went out *quickly and fled
from the tomb, for they trembled and were
amazed. [R]And they said nothing to anyone,
for they were afraid. Matt. 28:8

The Appearances of Jesus
Luke 24:13–48; John 20:1–10

9 Now when *He* rose early on the first *day*
of the week, He appeared first to Mary Magdalene,
[R]out of whom He had cast seven
demons. Luke 8:2
10 She went and told those who had been
with Him, as they mourned and wept.
11 [R]And when they heard that He was alive
and had been seen by her, they did not
believe. Luke 24:11, 41
12 After that, He appeared in another form
[R]to two of them as they walked and went into
the country. Luke 24:13–35
13 And they went and told *it* to the rest, *but*
they did not believe them either.
14 [R]Afterward He appeared to the eleven as
they sat at the table; and He rebuked their
unbelief and hardness of heart, because they
did not believe those who had seen Him after
He had risen. 1 Cor. 15:5
15 [R]And He said to them, "Go into all the
world [R]and preach the gospel to every creature.
Matt. 28:19 • [Col. 1:23]
16 [R]"He who believes and is baptized will be
saved; [R]but he who does not believe will be
condemned. [John 3:18, 36] • [John 12:48]
17 "And these signs will follow those who
believe: In My name they will cast out demons;
they will speak with new tongues;
18 [R]"they* will take up serpents; and if they
drink anything deadly, it will by no means
hurt them; [R]they will lay hands on the sick,
and they will recover." Acts 28:3–6 • James 5:14

The Ascension of Jesus
Luke 24:49–53; Acts 1:9

19 So then, after the Lord had spoken to
them, He was [R]received up into heaven, and
sat down at the right hand of God. Is. 9:7*
20 And they went out and preached everywhere,
the Lord working with *them* [R]and
confirming the word through the accompanying
signs. *Amen. [Heb. 2:4]

16:8 NU, M omit *quickly*
16:18 NU *and in their hands they will*
16:20 Vv. 9–20 are bracketed in NU as not original. They are lacking in Codex Sinaiticus and Codex Vaticanus, although nearly all other mss. of Mark contain them.

THE GOSPEL ACCORDING TO

LUKE

THE BOOK OF LUKE

Luke, a physician, writes with the compassion and warmth of a family doctor as he carefully documents the perfect humanity of the Son of Man, Jesus Christ. Luke emphasizes Jesus' ancestry, birth, and early life before moving carefully and chronologically through His earthly ministry. Growing belief and growing opposition develop side by side. Those who believe are challenged to count the cost of discipleship. Those who oppose will not be satisfied until the Son of Man hangs lifeless on a cross. But the resurrection insures that His purpose will be fulfilled: "to seek and to save that which was lost" (19:10).

Kata Loukon, "According to Luke," is the ancient title that was added to this gospel at a very early date. The Greek name *Luke* appears only three times in the New Testament (Col. 4:14; 2 Tim. 4:11; Philem. 24).

THE AUTHOR OF LUKE

It is evident from the prologues to Luke and Acts (Luke 1:1–4; Acts 1:1–5) that both books were addressed to Theophilus as a two-volume work (Luke is called "the former account"). Acts begins with a summary of Luke and continues the story from where the Gospel of Luke concludes. The style and language of both books are quite similar. The "we" portions of Acts (Acts 16:1–17; 20:5—21:18; 27:1—28:16) reveal that the author was a close associate and traveling companion of Paul. Because all but two of Paul's associates are named in the third person, the list can be narrowed to Titus and Luke. Titus has never been seriously regarded as a possible author of Acts, and Luke best fits the requirements. He was with Paul during his first Roman imprisonment, and Paul referred to him as "Luke the beloved physician" (Col. 4:14; cf. Philem. 24). During his second Roman imprisonment, Paul wrote "Only Luke is with me" (2 Tim. 4:11), an evidence of Luke's loyalty to the apostle in the face of profound danger.

Luke may have been a Hellenistic Jew, but it is more likely that he was a Gentile (this would make him the only gentile contributor to the New Testament). In Colossians 4:10–14, Paul lists three fellow workers who are "of the circumcision" (vv. 10, 11) and then includes Luke's name with two Gentiles (vv. 12–14). Luke's obvious skill with the Greek language and his phrase "their own language" in Acts 1:19 also imply that he was not Jewish. It has been suggested that Luke may have been a Greek physician to a Roman family who at some point was set free and given Roman citizenship. Another guess is that he was the "brother" referred to in Second Corinthians 8:18, 19. Ancient traditions (including the Muratorian Fragment, Irenaeus, Tertullian, Clement of Alexandria, Origen, Eusebius, and Jerome) strongly support Luke as the author of Luke and Acts. Tradition also says that Luke was from Syrian Antioch, remained unmarried, and died at the age of eighty-four.

THE TIME OF LUKE

Luke was not an eyewitness of the events in his gospel, but he relied on the testimony of eyewitnesses and written sources (1:1–4). He carefully investigated and arranged his material and presented it to Theophilus ("Friend of God"). The title "most excellent," or "most noble" (see Acts 23:26; 24:3; 26:25), indicates that Theophilus was a man of high social standing. He probably assumed responsibility for publishing Luke and Acts so that they would be available to gentile readers. Luke translates Aramaic terms with Greek words and explains Jewish customs and geography to make his gospel more intelligible to his original Greek readership. During Paul's two-year Caesarean imprisonment, Luke may have traveled in Palestine to gather information from eyewitnesses of Jesus' ministry. The date of this gospel depends on that of Acts since this was the first volume (see "The Time of Acts"). If Luke was written during Paul's first imprisonment in Rome it would be dated in the early 60s. However, it may have been given final form in Greece. In all probability, its publication preceded the destruction of Jerusalem (A.D. 70).

THE CHRIST OF LUKE

The humanity and compassion of Jesus are repeatedly stressed in Luke's gospel. Luke gives the most complete account of Christ's ancestry, birth, and development. He is the ideal Son of Man who identified with the sorrow and plight of sinful men in order to carry our sorrows and offer us the priceless gift of salvation. Jesus alone fulfills the Greek ideal of human perfection.

KEYS TO LUKE

Key Word: Jesus the Son of Man—Luke clearly states his purpose in the prologue of his gospel: "to write to you an orderly account . . . that you may know the certainty of those things in which you were instructed" (1:3, 4). Luke wanted to create an accurate, chronological, and comprehensive account of the unique life of Jesus the Christ to strengthen the faith of gentile believers and stimulate saving faith among nonbelievers. Luke also had another purpose, and that was to show that Christ was not only divine but also human. Luke portrays Christ in His fullest humanity by devoting more of his writing to Christ's feelings and humanity than any other gospel.

Key Verses: Luke 1:3, 4 and 19:10—"It seemed good to me also, having had perfect understanding of all things from the very first, to write to you an orderly account, most excellent Theophilus, that you may know the certainty of those things in which you were instructed" (1:3, 4).

" 'For the Son of Man has come to seek and to save that which was lost' " (19:10).

Key Chapter: Luke 15—Captured in the three parables of the Lost Sheep, Lost Coin, and Lost Son is the crux of this gospel: that God through Christ has come to seek and to save that which was lost.

SURVEY OF LUKE

Luke builds the gospel narrative on the platform of historical reliability. His emphasis on chronological and historical accuracy makes this the most comprehensive of the four gospels. This is also the longest and most literary gospel, and it presents Jesus Christ as the Perfect Man who came to seek and to save sinful men. This book can be divided into four sections: the introduction of the Son of Man (1:1—4:13); the ministry of the Son of Man (4:14—9:50); the rejection of the Son of Man (9:51—19:27); the crucifixion and resurrection of the Son of Man (19:28—24:53).

The Introduction of the Son of Man (1:1—4:13): Luke places a strong emphasis on the ancestry, birth, and early years of the Perfect Man and of His forerunner John the Baptist. Their infancy stories are intertwined as Luke records their birth announcements, advents, and temple presentations. Jesus prepares over thirty years (summarized in one verse, 2:52) for a public ministry of only three years. The ancestry of the Son of Man is traced back to the first man Adam, and His ministry commences after His baptism and temptation.

The Ministry of the Son of Man (4:14—9:50): The authority of the Son of Man over every realm is demonstrated in 4:14—6:49. In this section His authority over demons, disease, nature, the effects of sin, tradition, and all people is presented as a prelude to His diverse ministry of preaching, healing, and discipling (7:1—9:50).

The Rejection of the Son of Man (9:51—19:27): The dual response of growing belief and growing rejection has already been introduced in the gospel (cf. 4:14 and 6:11), but from this time forward the intensity of opposition to the ministry of the Son of Man increases. When the religious leaders accuse Him of being demonized, Jesus pronounces a series of divine woes upon them (11). Knowing that He is on His last journey to Jerusalem, Jesus instructs His disciples on a number of practical matters including prayer, covetousness, faithfulness, repentance, humility, discipleship, evangelism, money, forgiveness, service, thankfulness, the second advent, and salvation (12:1—19:27).

The Crucifixion and Resurrection of the Son of Man (19:28—24:53): After His triumphal entry into Jerusalem, Jesus encounters the opposition of the priests, Sadducees, and scribes and predicts the overthrow of Jerusalem (19:28—21:38). The Son of Man instructs His disciples for the last time before His betrayal in Gethsemane. The three religious and three civil trials culminate in His crucifixion. The glory and foundation of the Christian message is the historical resurrection of Jesus Christ. The Lord conquers the grave as He has promised, and appears on a number of occasions to His disciples before His ascension to the Father.

FOCUS	INTRODUCTION OF THE SON OF MAN	MINISTRY OF THE SON OF MAN	REJECTION OF THE SON OF MAN	CRUCIFIXION AND RESURRECTION OF THE SON OF MAN
REFERENCE	1:1	4:14	9:51	19:28—24:53
DIVISION	ADVENT	ACTIVITIES	ANTAGONISM AND ADMONITION	APPLICATION AND AUTHENTICATION
TOPIC	SEEKING THE LOST			SAVING THE LOST
	MIRACLES PROMINENT		TEACHING PROMINENT	
LOCATION	ISRAEL	GALILEE	ISRAEL	JERUSALEM
TIME	c. 4 B.C.–A.D. 33			

OUTLINE OF LUKE

Part One: The Introduction of the Son of Man (1:1—4:13)

Part Two: The Ministry of the Son of Man (4:14—9:50)

Part Three: The Rejection of the Son of Man (9:51—19:27)

6. Pilate Tries Christ Again 23:13–25
7. Christ Is Crucified 23:26–49
8. Christ Is Buried 23:50–55
F. Saturday: In the Grave 23:56

II. The Authentication of Christ 24:1–53

A. The Resurrection 24:1–12
B. Christ Appears on the Road to Emmaus 24:13–32
C. Christ Appears to the Eleven 24:33–53
1. The Proof of His Resurrection . . . 24:33–43
2. The Great Commission 24:44–48
3. The Ascension 24:49–53

CHAPTER 1

The Purpose and Method of Luke's Gospel

INASMUCH as many have taken in hand to set in order a narrative of those things which are most surely believed among us,

2 just as those who from the beginning were [R]eyewitnesses and ministers of the word [R]delivered them to us, Acts 1:2 • Heb. 2:3

3 it seemed good to me also, having [T]had perfect understanding of all things from the very first, to write to you an orderly account, most excellent Theophilus, *accurately followed*

4 that you may know the certainty of those things in which you were instructed.

Zacharias Ministers in the Temple

5 There was [R]in the days of Herod, the king of Judea, a certain priest named Zacharias, of the division of [R]Abijah. His [R]wife *was* of the daughters of Aaron, and her name *was* Elizabeth. Matt. 2:1 • Neh. 12:4 • Lev. 21:13, 14

6 And they were both righteous before God, walking in all the commandments and ordinances of the Lord blameless.

7 But they had no child, because Elizabeth was barren, and they were both well advanced in years.

8 So it was, that while he was serving as priest before God in the order of his division,

9 according to the custom of the priesthood, his lot fell [R]to burn incense when he went into the temple of the Lord. Ex. 30:7, 8

10 And the whole multitude of the people was praying outside at the hour of incense.

An Angel Announces the Birth of John the Baptist

11 Then an angel of the Lord appeared to him, standing on the right side of [R]the altar of incense. Ex. 30:1

12 And when Zacharias saw *him,* [R]he was troubled, and fear fell upon him. Luke 2:9

13 But the angel said to him, "Do not be afraid, Zacharias, for your prayer is heard; and your wife Elizabeth will bear you a son, and you shall call his name John.

14 "And you will have joy and gladness, and [R]many will rejoice at his birth. Luke 1:58

15 "For he will be great in the sight of the Lord, and shall drink neither wine nor strong drink. He will also be filled with the Holy Spirit, even from his mother's womb.

16 "And he will turn many of the children of Israel to the Lord their God.

17 [R]"He will also go before Him in the spirit and power of Elijah, *'to turn the hearts of the fathers to the children,'* and the disobedient to the wisdom of the just, to make ready a people prepared for the Lord." Mal. 4:5, 6 ☆

Zacharias Is Unable to Speak

18 And Zacharias said to the angel, [R]"How shall I know this? For I am an old man, and my wife is well advanced in years." Gen. 17:17

19 And the angel answered and said to him, "I am [R]Gabriel, who stands in the presence of God, and was sent to speak to you and bring you [T]these glad tidings. Dan. 8:16 • *this good news*

20 "But behold, you will be mute and not able to speak until the day these things take place, because you did not believe my words which will be fulfilled in their own time."

21 And the people waited for Zacharias, and marveled that he lingered so long in the temple.

22 But when he came out, he could not speak to them; and they perceived that he had seen a vision in the temple, for he beckoned to them and remained speechless.

23 And so it was, as soon as [R]the days of his service were completed, that he departed to his own house. 2 Kin. 11:5

24 Now after those days his wife Elizabeth conceived; and she hid herself five months, saying,

25 "Thus the Lord has dealt with me, in the days when He looked on *me,* to [R]take away my reproach among men." Gen. 30:23

Gabriel Announces Christ's Birth

26 Now in the sixth month the angel Gabriel was sent by God to a city of Galilee named Nazareth,

27 to a [R]virgin [R]betrothed to a man whose name was Joseph, of the house of David. The virgin's name *was* Mary. Is. 7:14★ • Matt. 1:18

28 And having come in, the angel said to her, "Rejoice, highly favored *one,* the Lord *is* with you; *blessed *are* you among women!"

29 But *when she saw *him,* [R]she was troubled at his saying, and considered what manner of greeting this was. Luke 1:12

1:28 NU omits *blessed are you among women*
1:29 NU omits *when she saw him*

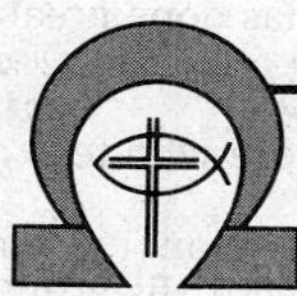

ANGELS IN THE NEW TESTAMENT

Angels are active throughout the New Testament as special messengers of God (Heb. 1:14). The news that she would give birth to the Messiah, the Savior of the world, was brought to Mary by the angel Gabriel (Luke 1:26–38). The New Testament also reveals that angels guide, instruct, and protect God's people. Angels still exist, but they are not as obviously active today as in New Testament times because of the larger role played by the Holy Spirit in the lives of Christians.

Following are other New Testament events in which angels played a significant role:

The angel Gabriel appears to Mary.

Personality	Angel's Action	Biblical Reference
Zacharias	Revealed to Zacharias the forthcoming birth of John the Baptist	Luke 1:11–20
Joseph	Assured Joseph of Mary's purity; warned him of Herod's plot; told Joseph about Herod's death	Matt. 1:20–25 Matt. 2:13 Matt. 2:19, 20
Shepherds	Announced Jesus' birth to them	Luke 2:8–15
Jesus	Ministered to Jesus during His temptations; strengthened Him in the Garden of Gethsemane; rolled away the stone from the tomb and announced His resurrection	Matt. 4:11 Luke 22:43 Matt. 28:2–6
Apostles	Predicted the Second Coming of Jesus; released the apostles from prison	Acts 1:10, 11 Acts 5:17–20
Philip	Sent Philip into the desert to meet the eunuch	Acts 8:26
Cornelius	Instructed Cornelius to send for Peter	Acts 10:3–8
Peter	Released Peter from prison	Acts 12:7
Herod	Judged Herod because of his blasphemy	Acts 12:23
Paul	Reassured Paul in a storm at sea	Acts 27:23, 24

30 Then the angel said to her, "Do not be
afraid, Mary, for you have found [R]favor with
God. Luke 2:52
31 [R]"And behold, you will conceive in your
womb and bring forth a Son, and [R]shall call
His name JESUS. Is. 7:14 • Matt. 1:21, 25; Luke 2:21 ☆
32 "He will be great, [R]and will be called
the Son of the Highest; and the Lord God
will give Him the throne of His father
David. Mark 5:7 ☆
33 [R]"And He will reign over the house of
Jacob [R]forever, and of His kingdom there will
be no end." [Dan. 2:44] • Ps. 89:36, 37 ☆

Mary Miraculously Conceives

34 Then Mary said to the angel, "How can
this be, since I do not know a man?"
35 And the angel answered and said to her,
"*The* Holy Spirit will come upon you, and the
power of the Highest will overshadow you;
therefore, also, that Holy One who is to be
born will be called the Son of God.
36 "Now indeed, Elizabeth your relative has
also conceived a son in her old age; and this is
now the sixth month for her who was called
barren.
37 "For [R]with God nothing will be impossible." Jer. 32:17
38 Then Mary said, "Behold the maidservant of the Lord! Let it be to me according to
your word." And the angel departed from her.

Mary Visits Elizabeth

39 Now Mary arose in those days and went
into the hill country with haste, [R]to a city of
Judah, Josh. 21:9
40 and entered the house of Zacharias and
greeted Elizabeth.
41 And it happened, when Elizabeth heard
the greeting of Mary, that the babe leaped in
her womb; and Elizabeth was [R]filled with the
Holy Spirit. Acts 6:3
42 Then she spoke out with a loud voice
and said, "Blessed *are* you among women,
and blessed *is* the fruit of your womb!
43 "But why *is* this *granted* to me, that the
mother of my Lord should come to me?
44 "For indeed, as soon as the voice of your
greeting sounded in my ears, the babe leaped
in my womb for joy.
45 [R]"Blessed *is* she who believed, for there
will be a fulfillment of those things which
were told her from the Lord." John 20:29
46 And Mary said:

[R]"My soul magnifies the Lord, 1 Sam. 2:1–10
47 And my spirit has [R]rejoiced in [R]God my
Savior. Hab. 3:18 • 1 Tim. 1:1; 2:3
48 For [R]He has regarded the lowly state of
His maidservant;
For behold, henceforth [R]all generations
will call me blessed. Ps. 138:6 • Luke 11:27
49 For He who is mighty [R]has done great
things for me, Ps. 71:19; 126:2, 3
And [R]holy *is* His name. Ps. 111:9
50 And [R]His mercy *is* on those who fear
Him
From generation to generation. Ps. 103:17
51 He has shown strength with His arm;
[R]He has scattered *the* proud in the
imagination of their hearts. [1 Pet. 5:5]
52 [R]He has put down the mighty from *their*
thrones,
And exalted *the* lowly. 1 Sam. 2:7, 8
53 He has [R]filled *the* hungry with good
things, [Matt. 5:6]
And *the* rich He has sent away empty.
54 He has helped His servant Israel,
[R]In remembrance of *His* mercy, [Jer. 31:3]
55 As He spoke to our [R]fathers, [Rom. 11:28]
To Abraham and to his seed forever."

56 And Mary remained with her about three
months, and returned to her house.

Elizabeth Gives Birth to John

57 Now Elizabeth's full time came for her to
be delivered, and she brought forth a son.
58 When her neighbors and relatives heard
how the Lord had shown great mercy to her,
they [R]rejoiced with her. [Rom. 12:15]
59 Now so it was, [R]on the eighth day, that
they came to circumcise the child; and they
would have called him by the name of his
father, Zacharias. Gen. 17:12
60 And his mother answered and said, [R]"No;
he shall be called John." Luke 1:13, 63
61 But they said to her, "There is no one
among your relatives who is called by this
name."
62 So they made signs to his father—what
he would have him called.
63 And he asked for a writing tablet, and
wrote, saying, "His name is John." And they
all marveled.
64 Immediately his mouth was opened and
his tongue *loosed*, and he spoke, praising
God.
65 Then fear came on all who dwelt around
them; and all these sayings were discussed
throughout all the hill country of Judea.
66 And all those who heard *them* [R]kept
them in their hearts, saying, "What kind of
child will this be?" And [R]the hand of the Lord
was with him. Luke 2:19 • Acts 11:21

Zacharias Prophesies of John's Ministry

67 Now his father Zacharias was filled with
the Holy Spirit, and prophesied, saying:

68 "Blessed[R] *is* the Lord God of Israel,
For [R]He has visited and redeemed His
people, 1 Kin. 1:48 • Ex. 3:16
69 [R]And has raised up a horn of salvation
for us Ps. 132:17

In the house of His servant David,
70 [R]As He spoke by the mouth of His holy prophets, Rom. 1:2
Who *have been* since the world began,
71 That we should be saved from our enemies
And from the hand of all who hate us,
72 [R]To perform the mercy *promised* to our fathers Lev. 26:42
And to remember His holy covenant,
73 [R]The oath which He swore to our father Abraham: Gen. 12:3; 22:16–18
74 To grant us that we,
Being delivered from the hand of our enemies,
Might [R]serve Him without fear, [Heb. 9:14]
75 [R]In holiness and righteousness before Him all the days of our life. [Eph. 4:24]
76 And you, child, will be called the [R]prophet of the Highest; Matt. 11:9, 10
For [R]you will go before the face of the Lord to prepare His ways, Is. 40:3
77 To give [R]knowledge of salvation to His people
By the remission of their sins, [Mark 1:4]
78 Through the tender mercy of our God,
With which the Dayspring from on high *has visited us;
79 [R]To give light to those who sit in darkness and the shadow of death,
To [R]guide our feet into the way of peace." Is. 9:2 • John 14:27; 16:33☆

80 So [R]the child grew and became strong in
spirit, and [R]was in the deserts till the day of
his manifestation to Israel. Luke 2:40 • Matt. 3:1

CHAPTER 2

Christ Is Born

AND it came to pass in those days *that* a
decree went out from Caesar Augustus
that all the world should be registered.
2 [R]This census first took place while Quirinius was governing Syria. Acts 5:37
3 So all went to be registered, everyone to
his own city.
4 And Joseph also went up from Galilee,
out of the city of Nazareth, into Judea, to
[R]the city of David, which is called [R]Bethle-
hem, [R]because he was of the house and
lineage of David, 1 Sam. 16:1 • Mic. 5:2★ • Matt. 1:16
5 to be registered with Mary, his betrothed
*wife, who was with child.
6 So it was, that while they were there, the
days were completed for her to be delivered.
7 And [R]she brought forth her firstborn Son,
and wrapped Him in swaddling cloths, and
laid Him in a [T]manger, because there was no
room for them in the inn. Matt. 1:25 • *feed trough*

The Angels Announce Jesus to the Shepherds

8 Now there were in the same country
shepherds living out in the fields, keeping
watch over their flock by night.
9 And *behold, an angel of the Lord stood
before them, and the glory of the Lord shone
around them, and they were greatly afraid.
10 Then the angel said to them, "Do not be
afraid, for behold, I bring you good tidings of
great joy which will be to all people.
11 [R]"For there is born to you this day in the
city of David [R]a Savior, [R]who is Christ the
Lord. Is. 9:6★ • Matt. 1:21 • Acts 2:36
12 "And this *will be* the sign to you: You
will find a Babe wrapped in swaddling cloths,
lying in a [T]manger." *feed trough*
13 [R]And suddenly there was with the angel
a multitude of the heavenly host praising God
and saying: Dan. 7:10

14 "Glory[R] to God in the highest,
And on earth [R]peace, [R]good* will toward men!" Luke 19:38 • Is. 57:19 • [Eph. 2:4, 7]

The Shepherds Visit Jesus

15 So it was, when the angels had gone
away from them into heaven, that the shepherds said to one another, "Let us now go to
Bethlehem and see this thing that has come
to pass, which the Lord has made known to
us."
16 And they came with haste and found
Mary and Joseph, and the Babe lying in a
manger.
17 Now when they had seen *Him*, they
made *widely known the saying which was
told them concerning this Child.
18 And all those who heard *it* marveled at
those things which were told them by the
shepherds.
19 [R]But Mary kept all these things and
pondered *them* in her heart. Gen. 37:11
20 Then the shepherds returned, glorifying
and praising God for all the things that they
had heard and seen, as it was told them.

Christ Is Circumcised

21 And when eight days were completed
*for the circumcision of the Child, His name
was called JESUS, the name given by the
angel before He was conceived in the womb.
22 Now when [R]the days of her purification
according to the law of Moses were completed, they brought Him to Jerusalem to
present *Him* to the Lord Lev. 12:2–8
23 (as it is written in the law of the Lord,
[R]*"Every male who opens the womb shall be
called holy to the LORD"*), Ex. 13:2, 12, 15

1:78 NU *shall visit* **2:5** NU omits *wife*
2:9 NU omits *behold*
2:14 NU *toward men of good will*
2:17 NU omits *widely* **2:21** NU *for His circumcision*

24 and to offer a sacrifice according to [R]what is said in the law of the Lord, *"A pair of turtledoves or two young pigeons."* Lev. 12:2, 8

Simeon's Prophecy

25 And behold, there was a man in Jerusalem whose name was Simeon, and this man was just and devout, [R]waiting for the Consolation of Israel, and the Holy Spirit was upon him. Mark 15:43

26 And it had been revealed to him by the Holy Spirit that he would not see death before he had seen the Lord's Christ.

27 So he came [R]by the Spirit into the temple. And when the parents brought in the Child Jesus, to do for Him according to the custom of the law, Matt. 4:1

28 he took Him up in his arms and blessed God and said:

29 "Lord, [R]now You are letting Your
servant depart in peace,
According to Your word; Gen. 46:30
30 For my eyes have seen Your salvation
31 Which You have prepared before the
face of all peoples,
32 [R]A light to *bring* revelation to the
Gentiles, Is. 9:2; 42:6☆
And the glory of Your people Israel."

33 *And Joseph and His mother marveled at those things which were spoken of Him.

34 Then Simeon blessed them, and said to Mary His mother, "Behold, this *Child* is destined for the [R]fall and rising of many in Israel, and for [R]a sign which will be spoken against Is. 8:14; [1 Pet. 2:7, 8]☆ • Acts 4:2; 17:32; 28:22

35 (yes, [R]a sword will pierce through your own soul also), that the thoughts of many hearts may be revealed." Ps. 42:10

Anna's Testimony

36 Now there was one, Anna, a prophetess, the daughter of Phanuel, of the tribe of [R]Asher. She was of a great age, and had lived with a husband seven years from her virginity; Josh. 19:24

37 and this woman *was* a widow *of about eighty-four years, who did not depart from the temple, but served *God* with fastings and prayers [R]night and day. 1 Tim. 5:5

38 And coming in that instant she gave thanks to *the Lord, and spoke of Him to all those who [R]looked for redemption in Jerusalem. Mark 15:43

Jesus Returns to Nazareth—Matt. 2:19–23

39 So when they had performed all things according to the law of the Lord, they returned to Galilee, to their *own* city, Nazareth.

40 [R]And the Child grew and became strong *in spirit, filled with wisdom; and the grace of God was upon Him. Luke 1:80; 2:52

Jesus Celebrates the Passover

41 His parents went to [R]Jerusalem every year at the Feast of the Passover. John 4:20

42 And when He was twelve years old, they went up to Jerusalem according to the [R]custom of the feast. Ex. 23:14, 15

43 When they had finished the [R]days, as they returned, the Boy Jesus lingered behind in Jerusalem. And *Joseph and His mother did not know *it;* Ex. 12:15

44 but supposing Him to have been in the company, they went a [T]day's journey, and sought Him among *their* relatives and acquaintances. 20 mi.

45 So when they did not find Him, they returned to Jerusalem, seeking Him.

46 Now so it was that after three days they found Him in the temple, sitting in the midst of the teachers, both listening to them and asking them questions.

47 And [R]all who heard Him were astonished at His understanding and answers. Matt. 7:28

48 So when they saw Him, they were amazed; and His mother said to Him, "Son, why have You done this to us? Look, Your father and I have sought You anxiously."

49 And He said to them, "Why *is it* that you sought Me? Did you not know that I must be about [R]My Father's business?" [Luke 4:22, 32]

50 But [R]they did not understand the statement which He spoke to them. John 7:15, 46

Jesus Grows in Wisdom

51 Then He went down with them and came to Nazareth, and was subject to them, but His mother kept all these things in her heart.

52 And Jesus increased in wisdom and stature, and in favor with God and men.

CHAPTER 3

The Ministry of John the Baptist
Matt. 3:1–12; Mark 1:2–8; John 1:19–31

NOW in the fifteenth year of the reign of Tiberius Caesar, [R]Pontius Pilate being governor of Judea, Herod being tetrarch of Galilee, his brother Philip tetrarch of Iturea and the region of Trachonitis, and Lysanias tetrarch of Abilene, Matt. 27:2

2 [R]Annas* and Caiaphas being high priests, the word of God came to [R]John the son of Zacharias in the wilderness. Acts 4:6 • Luke 1:13

3 And he went into all the region around the Jordan, preaching a baptism of repentance [R]for the remission of sins, Luke 1:17, 77★

2:33 NU *And His father and mother*
2:37 NU *until she was eighty-four*
2:38 NU *God* **2:40** NU omits *in spirit*
2:43 NU *His parents*
3:2 NU, M *in the high priesthood of Annas and Caiaphas*

4 as it is written in the book of the words of Isaiah the prophet, saying:

[R]*"The voice of one crying in the*
wilderness:
'Prepare the way of the LORD,
Make His paths straight. Is. 40:3★
5 [R]*Every valley shall be filled*
And every mountain and hill brought
low;
And the crooked places shall be made
straight Is. 40:4★
And the rough ways made smooth;
6 *And* [R]*all flesh shall see the salvation of*
God.'" Is. 40:5★

7 Then he said to the multitudes that came out to be baptized by him, [R]"Brood[T] of vipers! Who warned you to flee from the wrath to come? Matt. 3:7; 12:34; 23:33 • *Offspring*

8 "Therefore bear fruits [R]worthy of repentance, and do not begin to say to yourselves, 'We have Abraham as *our* father.' For I say to you that God is able to raise up children to Abraham from these stones. [2 Cor. 7:9–11]

9 "And even now the ax is laid to the root of the trees. Therefore [R]every tree which does not bear good fruit is cut down and thrown into the fire." Matt. 7:19

10 So the people asked him, saying, [R]"What shall we do then?" [Acts 2:37, 38; 16:30, 31]

11 He answered and said to them, [R]"He who has two tunics, let him give to him who has none; and he who has food, [R]let him do likewise." 2 Cor. 8:14 • Is. 58:7

12 Then [R]tax collectors also came to be baptized, and said to him, "Teacher, what shall we do?" Luke 7:29

13 And he said to them, [R]"Collect no more than what is appointed for you." Luke 19:8

14 Likewise the soldiers asked him, saying, "And what shall we do?" So he said to them, "Do not intimidate anyone or accuse falsely, and be content with your wages."

15 Now as the people were in expectation, and all reasoned in their hearts about John, whether he was the Christ or not,

16 John answered, saying to *them* all, "I indeed baptize you with water; but One mightier than I is coming, whose sandal strap I am not worthy to loose. He will baptize you with the Holy Spirit and with fire.

17 "His winnowing fan *is* in His hand, and He will thoroughly purge His threshing floor, and gather the wheat into His barn; but the chaff He will burn with unquenchable fire."

18 And with many other exhortations he preached to the people.

19 [R]But Herod the tetrarch, being rebuked by him concerning Herodias, his *brother Philip's wife, and for all the evils which Herod had done, Mark 6:17

20 also added this, above all, that he shut John up in prison.

The Baptism of Christ
Matt. 3:13–17; Mark 1:9–11; John 1:32–34

21 Now when all the people were baptized, it came to pass that Jesus also was baptized; and while He prayed, the heaven was opened.

22 And the Holy Spirit descended in bodily form like a dove upon Him, and a voice came from heaven which said, "You are My beloved Son; in You I am well pleased."

The Genealogy of Christ Through Mary
Gen. 5:1–32, 11:10–26; Ruth 4:18–22;
1 Chr. 1:1–4, 24–27, 34, 2:1–15; Matt. 1:2–6

23 Now Jesus Himself began *His ministry at* about thirty years of age, being (as was supposed) *the* son of Joseph, *the son* of Heli,

24 *the son* of Matthat, *the son* of Levi, *the son* of Melchi, *the son* of Janna, *the son* of Joseph,

25 *the son* of Mattathiah, *the son* of Amos, *the son* of Nahum, *the son* of Esli, *the son* of Naggai,

26 *the son* of Maath, *the son* of Mattathiah, *the son* of Semei, *the son* of Joseph, *the son* of Judah,

27 *the son* of Joannas, *the son* of Rhesa, *the son* of [R]Zerubbabel, *the son* of Shealtiel, *the son* of Neri, Ezra 2:2; 3:8

28 *the son* of Melchi, *the son* of Addi, *the son* of Cosam, *the son* of Elmodam, *the son* of Er,

29 *the son* of Jose, *the son* of Eliezer, *the son* of Jorim, *the son* of Matthat, *the son* of Levi,

30 *the son* of Simeon, *the son* of Judah, *the son* of Joseph, *the son* of Jonan, *the son* of Eliakim,

31 *the son* of Melea, *the son* of Menan, *the son* of Mattathah, *the son* of [R]Nathan, [R]*the son* of David, Zech. 12:12 • Is. 9:7★

32 [R]*the son* of Jesse, *the son* of Obed, *the son* of Boaz, *the son* of Salmon, *the son* of Nahshon, Is. 11:1, 10★

33 *the son* of Amminadab, *the son* of Ram, *the son* of Hezron, *the son* of Perez, [R]*the son* of Judah, Gen. 49:10★

34 *the son* of Jacob, *the son* of Isaac, *the son* of Abraham, [R]*the son* of Terah, *the son* of Nahor, Gen. 11:24, 26–30; 12:3

35 *the son* of Serug, *the son* of Reu, *the son* of Peleg, *the son* of Eber, *the son* of Shelah,

36 [R]*the son* of Cainan, *the son* of [R]Arphaxad, *the son* of Shem, *the son* of Noah, *the son* of Lamech, Gen. 11:12 • Gen. 10:22, 24; 11:10–13

37 *the son* of Methuselah, *the son* of Enoch, *the son* of Jared, *the son* of Mahalalel, *the son* of Cainan,

38 *the son* of Enos, *the son* of Seth, *the son* of Adam, [R]*the son* of God. Gen. 5:1, 2

3:19 NU *brother's wife*

THE HERODIAN DYNASTY

Herod was the family name of several Roman rulers who served as provincial governors of Palestine and surrounding regions during New Testament times.

The first Herod, known as Herod the Great, was the Roman ruler of Palestine during the days of the Roman Emperor Caesar Augustus when Jesus was born in Bethlehem (Matt. 2:1; Luke 3:1). All the other different Herods mentioned in the New Testament were the sons or grandsons of this Herod.

Herod the Great (ruled 37–4 B.C.), was known as a master builder, organizer, and developer, although his policies were considered cruel and ruthless by the Jewish people. His most notable achievement was the rebuilding of the temple in Jerusalem—a project that required almost fifty years. He also rebuilt and enlarged the city of Caesarea into a port city on the Mediterranean Sea. Caesarea served as the Roman provincial capital for Palestine during the New Testament era. The magnificent aqueducts that he built at this city are still visible today (see photo).

Herod's son Antipas succeeded him as Roman governor of Galilee and Perea (Matt. 14:1). Antipas was responsible for the imprisonment and death of John the Baptist (Luke 3:19, 20; Matt. 14:1–12).

Herod the Great's grandson Agrippa was named ruler over all of Palestine by the Roman emperor Caligula. Agrippa is known as a persecutor of early Christians. He had James put to death and had Peter arrested. Because of his cruelty

Photo by Gustav Jeeninga

This aqueduct at Caesarea Maritima illustrates the Romans' expertise at building water transportation systems.

and blasphemy, Agrippa was slain by an angel of the Lord (Acts 12).

In A.D. 50, Agrippa's son, known as Agrippa II, was made ruler of the king of Chalcis's territory. Later he was given Abilene, Trachonitis, Acra, and important parts of Galilee and Perea. The only reference to this Herod in the New Testament occurs in Acts 25:13—26:32, which deals with Paul's imprisonment in Caesarea. Agrippa listened to Paul's defense, but the apostle appealed to Rome. Agrippa had no power to set him free.

The other two Herods mentioned in the New Testament are Herod Archelaus (Matt. 2:22) and Herod Philip (Luke 3:1). Both of these rulers were sons of Herod the Great; they ruled parts of the territory previously administered by their father.

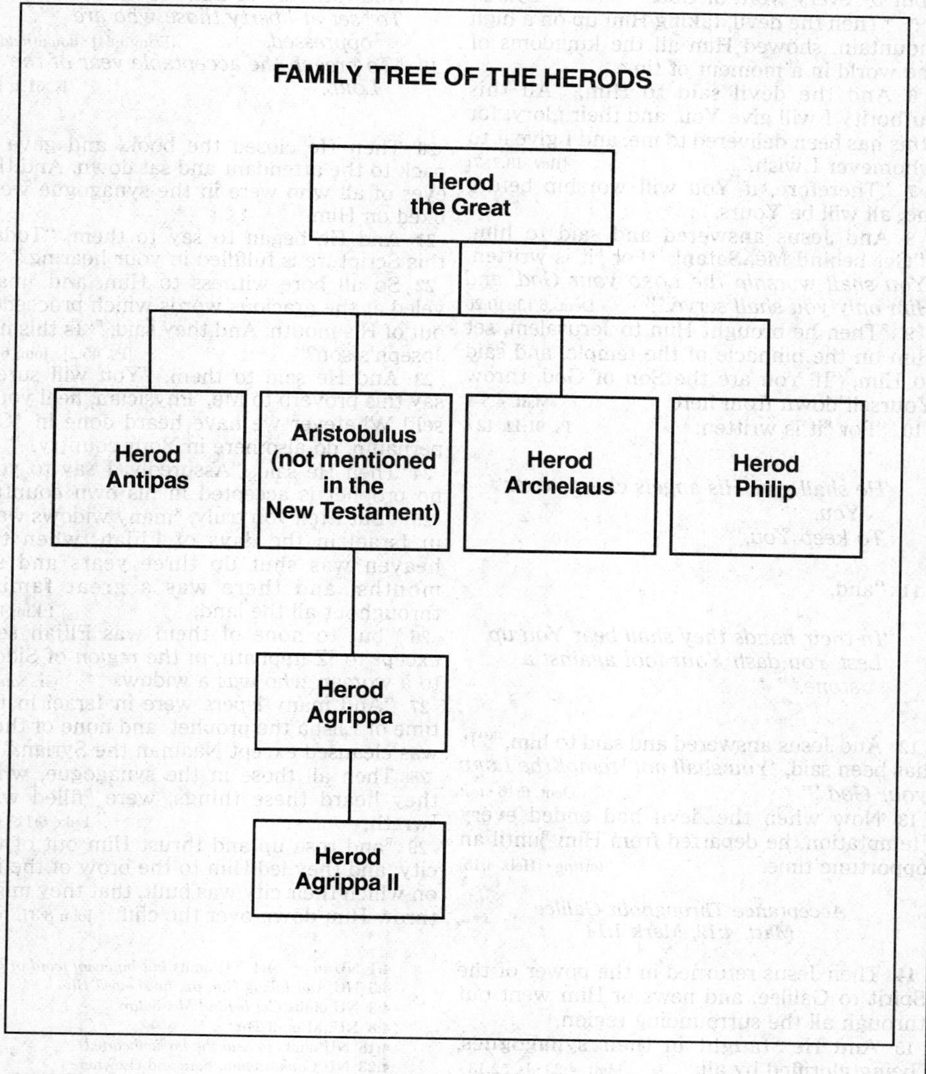

CHAPTER 4

The Temptation of Christ
Matt. 4:1–11; Mark 1:12, 13

THEN Jesus, being filled with the Holy
Spirit, returned from the Jordan and was
led by the Spirit *into the wilderness,
2 being [T]tempted for forty days by the
devil. And [R]in those days He ate nothing, and
afterward, when they had ended, He was
hungry. *tested* • Ex. 34:28
3 And the devil said to Him, "If You are
[R]the Son of God, command this stone to
become bread." John 20:31
4 But Jesus answered him, saying, [R]"It is
written, *'Man shall not live by bread alone,*
**but by every word of God.'*" Deut. 8:3
5 *Then the devil, taking Him up on a high
mountain, showed Him all the kingdoms of
the world in a moment of time.
6 And the devil said to Him, "All this
authority I will give You, and their glory; for
[R]*this* has been delivered to me, and I give it to
whomever I wish. [Rev. 13:2, 7]
7 "Therefore, if You will worship before
me, all will be Yours."
8 And Jesus answered and said to him,
*"Get behind Me, Satan! *For [R]it is written,
'You shall worship the LORD your God, and
Him only you shall serve.'" Deut. 6:13; 10:20
9 [R]Then he brought Him to Jerusalem, set
Him on the pinnacle of the temple, and said
to Him, "If You are the Son of God, throw
Yourself down from here. Matt. 4:5–7
10 "For [R]it is written: Ps. 91:11, 12 ★

'He shall give His angels charge over
You,
To keep You,'

11 "and,

'In their hands they shall bear You up,
Lest You dash Your foot against a
stone.'"

12 And Jesus answered and said to him, [R]"It
has been said, *'You shall not [T]tempt the LORD*
your God.'" Deut. 6:16 • *test*
13 Now when the devil had ended every
[T]temptation, he departed from Him [R]until an
opportune time. *testing* • [Heb. 4:15]

Acceptance Throughout Galilee
Matt. 4:12; Mark 1:14

14 Then Jesus returned in the power of the
Spirit to Galilee, and news of Him went out
through all the surrounding region.
15 And He [R]taught in their synagogues,
[R]being glorified by all. Matt. 4:23 • Is. 52:13 ★

Rejection at Nazareth

16 So He came to Nazareth, where He had
been brought up. And as His custom was, [R]He
went into the synagogue on the Sabbath day,
and stood up to read. Ps. 22:22 ★
17 And He was handed the book of the
prophet Isaiah. And when He had opened the
book, He found the place where it was written:

18 *"The Spirit of the LORD is upon Me,*
Because He has anointed Me to preach
the gospel to the poor.
*He has sent Me *to heal the*
brokenhearted,
To preach deliverance to the captives
And recovery of sight to the blind,
To [R]set at liberty those who are
[T]oppressed, [Dan. 9:24] • *downtrodden*
19 [R]*To preach the acceptable year of the*
LORD." Is. 61:1, 2 ★

20 Then He closed the book, and gave *it*
back to the attendant and sat down. And the
eyes of all who were in the synagogue were
fixed on Him.
21 And He began to say to them, "Today
this Scripture is fulfilled in your hearing."
22 So all bore witness to Him, and [R]mar-
veled at the gracious words which proceeded
out of His mouth. And they said, [R]"Is this not
Joseph's son?" [Ps. 45:2] • John 6:42
23 And He said to them, "You will surely
say this proverb to Me, 'Physician, heal yourself! Whatever we have heard done in *Capernaum, do also here in Your country.'"
24 Then He said, "Assuredly, I say to you,
no prophet is accepted in his own country.
25 "But I tell you truly, [R]many widows were
in Israel in the days of Elijah, when the
heaven was shut up three years and six
months, and there was a great famine
throughout all the land; 1 Kin. 17:9
26 "but to none of them was Elijah sent
except to [T]Zarephath, *in the region* of Sidon,
to a woman *who was* a widow. Gr. *Sarepta*
27 "And many lepers were in Israel in the
time of Elisha the prophet, and none of them
was cleansed except Naaman the Syrian."
28 Then all those in the synagogue, when
they heard these things, were [R]filled with
[T]wrath, Luke 6:11 • *rage*
29 [R]and rose up and thrust Him out of the
city; and they led Him to the brow of the hill
on which their city was built, that they might
throw Him down over the cliff. John 8:37; 10:31

4:1 NU *in* **4:4** NU omits *but by every word of God*
4:5 NU *And taking Him up, he showed Him*
4:8 NU omits *Get behind Me, Satan*
4:8 NU, M omit *For*
4:18 NU omits *to heal the brokenhearted*
4:23 NU *Capharnaum,* here and elsewhere

THE SYNAGOGUE

The synagogue as a Jewish religious institution probably arose after the Israelites returned from exile in Babylon. The public readings of the Law by Ezra the priest after the exiles resettled in Jerusalem (Neh. 8) may have signaled the beginning of the movement that led to the development of the synagogue system.

The synagogue, as distinguished from the tabernacle and temple with their sacrifices, was a local gathering place where Jews of all ages met for prayer and study of the Law of Moses. Scores of these synagogues sprang up in Jerusalem and surrounding cities during the two hundred years or so before the New Testament era. They were organized wherever ten or more men showed interest in preserving their Jewish customs and learning and obeying the Law.

Synagogue worship included readings from the Law, prayers, and a commentary or sermon on the Bible passage (see illustration). Any competent member of the congregation might be asked to read the Scriptures or bring the sermon. This privilege was apparently extended to Jesus in the synagogue at Nazareth early in His ministry. He read from the prophet Isaiah, identifying Himself as the Messiah whom Isaiah had prophesied hundreds of years before (Luke 4:16–30).

Several synagogue buildings, including one at the city of Capernaum, have been uncovered by archaeologists. These were generally rectangular structures with a large central seating area, much like a modern church building. The congregation sat on stone benches along the walls or cross-legged on the floor. The main piece of furniture in a synagogue was the ark, where the sacred scrolls with the Law were kept. The ark was placed along the wall nearest to the city of Jerusalem—the direction which the people faced during a synagogue service.

Synagogue life, as influenced by the rabbis who attached themselves to these local Jewish centers, came to dominate the religious thinking of the Jewish people during New Testament times. Each local synagogue had its own ruling group, which governed religious behavior among the Jews in that community.

The apostle Paul regularly proclaimed Christ at synagogues on his missionary journeys (Acts 13:5; 14:1). The emphasis of the synagogue on Scripture, prayer, and a sermon in worship has influenced the order of service used in most Christian churches today.

Reading of the Law in a Jewish synagogue.

30 Then [R]passing through the midst of
them, He went His way. John 8:59; 10:39

Demons Are Cast Out—Mark 1:21-28

31 Then [R]He went down to Capernaum, a
city of Galilee, and was teaching them on the
Sabbaths. Matt. 4:13
32 And they were astonished at His teaching, for His word was with authority.
33 [R]Now in the synagogue there was a man
who had a spirit of an unclean demon. And
he cried out with a loud voice, Mark 1:23
34 saying, "Let *us* alone! What have we to
do with You, Jesus of Nazareth? Did You
come to destroy us? [R]I know You, who You
are—[R]the Holy One of God!" Luke 4:41 • Ps. 16:10
35 But Jesus rebuked him, saying, "Be quiet,
and come out of him!" And when the demon
had thrown him in *their* midst, it came out of
him and did not hurt him.
36 So they were all amazed and spoke
among themselves, saying, "What a word this
is! For with authority and power He commands the unclean spirits, and they come
out."
37 And the report about Him went out into
every place in the surrounding region.

Peter's Mother-in-Law Is Healed
Matt. 8:14, 15; Mark 1:29-31

38 Now He arose from the synagogue and
entered Simon's house. But Simon's wife's
mother was sick with a high fever, and they
made request of Him concerning her.
39 So He stood over her and [R]rebuked the
fever, and it left her. And immediately she
arose and served them. Luke 8:24

Jesus Ministers Throughout Galilee
Matt. 4:23-25, 8:16, 17; Mark 1:32-39

40 Now when the sun was setting, all those
who had anyone sick with various diseases
brought them to Him; and He laid His hands
on every one of them and healed them.
41 And demons also came out of many,
crying out and saying, "You are *the Christ,
the Son of God!" And He, rebuking *them*, did
not allow them to [T]speak, for they knew that
He was the Christ. Or *say that they knew*
42 [R]Now when it was day, He departed and
went into a deserted place. And the crowd
sought Him and came to Him, and tried to
keep Him from leaving them; Mark 1:35-38
43 but He said to them, "I must preach the
kingdom of God to the other cities also,
because for this purpose I have been sent."
44 [R]And He was preaching in the synagogues of *Galilee. Matt. 4:23; 9:35

CHAPTER 5

The First Disciples Are Called

NOW so it was, as the multitude pressed
about Him to hear the word of God,
that He stood by the Lake of Gennesaret,
2 and saw two boats standing by the lake;
but the fishermen had gone from them and
were washing *their* nets.
3 Then He got into one of the boats, which
was Simon's, and asked him to put out a little
from the land. And He [R]sat down and taught
the multitudes from the boat. John 8:2
4 Now when He had stopped speaking, He
said to Simon, [R]"Launch out into the deep
and let down your nets for a catch." John 21:6
5 But Simon answered and said to Him,
"Master, we have toiled all night and caught
[R]nothing; nevertheless [R]at Your word I will
let down the net." John 21:3 • Ps. 33:9
6 And when they had done this, they
caught a great number of fish, and their net
was breaking.
7 So they signaled to *their* partners in the
other boat to come and help them. And they
came and filled both the boats, so that they
began to sink.
8 When Simon Peter saw *it*, he fell down at
Jesus' knees, saying, [R]"Depart from me, for I
am a sinful man, O Lord!" 1 Kin. 17:18
9 For he and all who were with him were
[R]astonished at the catch of fish which they
had taken; Mark 5:42; 10:24, 26
10 and so also *were* James and John, the
sons of Zebedee, who were partners with
Simon. And Jesus said to Simon, "Do not be
afraid. From now on you will catch men."
11 So when they had brought their boats to
land, they forsook all and followed Him.

A Leper Is Cleansed
Matt. 8:2-4; Mark 1:40-45

12 And it happened when He was in a certain city, that behold, a man who was full of
leprosy saw Jesus; and he fell on *his* face and
[T]implored Him, saying, "Lord, if You are
willing, You can make me clean." *begged*
13 Then He put out *His* hand and touched
him, saying, "I am willing; be cleansed." And
[R]immediately the leprosy left him. John 5:9
14 And He charged him to tell no one, "But
go and show yourself to the priest, and make
an offering for your cleansing, as a testimony
to them, just as Moses commanded."
15 Then [R]the report went around concerning Him all the more; and [R]great multitudes
came together to hear, and to be healed by
Him of their infirmities. Mark 1:45 • John 6:2

A Paralytic Is Healed
Matt. 9:1-8; Mark 2:1-12

16 [R]So He Himself *often* withdrew into the
wilderness and [R]prayed. Luke 9:10 • Matt. 14:23
17 Now it happened on a certain day, as He
was teaching, that there were Pharisees and
teachers of the law sitting by, who had come

4:41 NU omits *the Christ* **4:44** NU *Judea*

out of every town of Galilee, Judea, and
Jerusalem. And the power of the Lord was
present *to heal them.
18 Then behold, men brought on a bed a
man who was paralyzed. And they sought to
bring him in and lay *him* before Him.
19 And when they could not find how they
might bring him in, because of the crowd,
they went up on the housetop and let him
down with *his* bed through the tiling into the
midst [R]before Jesus. Matt. 15:30
20 So when He saw their faith, He said to
him, "Man, your sins are forgiven you."
21 [R]And the scribes and the Pharisees began
to reason, saying, "Who is this who speaks
blasphemies? [R]Who can forgive sins but God
alone?" Mark 2:6, 7 • Is. 43:25
22 But when Jesus perceived their thoughts,
He answered and said to them, "Why are you
reasoning in your hearts?
23 "Which is easier, to say, 'Your sins are
forgiven you,' or to say, 'Rise up and walk'?
24 "But that you may know that the Son of
Man has power on earth to forgive sins"—He
said to the man who was paralyzed, [R]"I say to
you, arise, take up your bed, and go to your
house." Luke 7:14
25 Immediately he rose up before them,
took up what he had been lying on, and
departed to his own house, glorifying God.
26 And they were all amazed, and they
glorified God and were filled with fear, saying, "We have seen strange things today!"

Matthew Is Called—Matt. 9:9; Mark 2:13, 14

27 After these things He went out and saw a
tax collector named Levi, sitting at the tax
office. And He said to him, "Follow Me."
28 And he left all, rose up, and [R]followed
Him. Mark 10:28

Jesus Eats with Sinners
Matt. 9:10–13; Mark 2:15–17

29 [R]Then Levi gave Him a great feast in his
own house. And [R]there were a great number
of tax collectors and others who sat down
with them. Matt. 9:9, 10 • Luke 15:1
30 *But their scribes and the Pharisees
[T]murmured against His disciples, saying,
[R]"Why do You eat and drink with tax collectors and sinners?" *grumbled* • Luke 15:2
31 And Jesus answered and said to them,
"Those who are well do not need a physician,
but those who are sick.
32 [R]"I have not come to call *the* righteous,
but sinners, to repentance." 1 Tim. 1:15

Jesus Teaches About Fasting
Matt. 9:14, 15; Mark 2:18–20

33 Then they said to Him, [R]"Why* do the
disciples of John fast often and make prayers,
and likewise those of the Pharisees, but
Yours eat and drink?" Matt. 9:14
34 And He said to them, "Can you make the
friends of the bridegroom fast while the
[R]bridegroom is with them? John 3:29
35 "But the days will come when the bridegroom will be taken away from them; then
they will fast in those days."

Parable of the Cloth and Wineskins
Matt. 9:16, 17; Mark 2:21, 22

36 [R]Then He spoke a parable to them: "No
one *puts a piece from a new garment on an
old one; otherwise the new makes a tear, and
also the piece that was *taken* out of the new
does not match the old. Mark 2:21, 22
37 "And no one puts new wine into old
wineskins; or else the new wine will burst the
wineskins and be spilled, and the wineskins
will be ruined.
38 "But new wine must be put into new
wineskins, *and both are preserved.
39 "And no one, having drunk old *wine*,
*immediately desires new; for he says, 'The
old is *better.'"

CHAPTER 6

Jesus Works on the Sabbath
Matt. 12:1–8; Mark 2:23–28

NOW [R]it happened *on the second Sabbath after the first that He went
through the grainfields. And His disciples
plucked the heads of grain and ate *them*,
rubbing *them* in *their* hands. Matt. 12:1–8
2 And some of the Pharisees said to them,
"Why are you doing [R]what is not lawful to do
on the Sabbath?" Ex. 20:10
3 But Jesus answering them said, "Have
you not even read this, [R]what David did when
he was hungry, he and those who were with
him: 1 Sam. 21:6
4 "how he went into the house of God,
took and ate the showbread, and also gave
some to those *who were* with him, which is
not lawful for any but the priests to eat?"
5 And He said to them, "The Son of Man is
also Lord of the Sabbath."

Jesus Heals on the Sabbath
Matt. 12:9–14; Mark 3:1–6

6 [R]Now it happened on another Sabbath,
also, that He entered the synagogue and
taught. And a man was there whose right
hand was withered. Mark 3:1–6
7 And the scribes and Pharisees watched
Him closely, whether He would [R]heal on the

5:17 NU *with Him to heal*
5:30 NU *But the Pharisees and their scribes*
5:33 NU omits *Why do,* making the verse a statement
5:36 NU *tears a piece from a new garment and puts it on an old one* **5:38** NU omits *and both are preserved*
5:39 NU omits *immediately* **5:39** NU *good*
6:1 NU *on a Sabbath that He went*

Sabbath, that they might find an [R]accusation
against Him. Luke 13:14; 14:1–6 • Luke 20:20
8 But He knew their thoughts, and said to
the man who had the withered hand, "Arise
and stand here." And he arose and stood.
9 Then Jesus said to them, "I will ask you
one thing: [R]Is it lawful on the Sabbath to do
good or to do evil, to save life or *to destroy
it?" John 7:23
10 And looking around at them all, He said
to *the man, "Stretch out your hand." And he
did so, and his hand was restored *as whole
as the other.
11 But they were filled with rage, and discussed with one another what they might do
to Jesus.

Selection of the Twelve Apostles
Mark 3:13–19

12 Now it came to pass in those days that
He went out to the mountain to pray, and
continued all night in [R]prayer to God. Mark 1:35
13 And when it was day, He called His
disciples *to Him*; and from them He chose
twelve whom He also named apostles:
14 Simon, [R]whom He also named Peter, and
Andrew his brother; James and John; Philip
and Bartholomew; John 1:42
15 Matthew and Thomas; James the *son* of
Alphaeus, and Simon called the Zealot;
16 Judas [R]*the son* of James, and Judas Iscariot who also became a traitor. Jude 1
17 And He came down with them and stood
on a level place with a crowd of His disciples
[R]and a great multitude of people from all
Judea and Jerusalem, and from the seacoast
of Tyre and Sidon, who came to hear Him
and be healed of their diseases, Mark 3:7, 8
18 as well as those who were tormented
with unclean spirits. And they were healed.
19 And the whole multitude sought to
[R]touch Him, for [R]power went out from Him
and healed *them* all. Mark 5:27, 28 • Luke 8:46

The Beatitudes—Matt. 5:1–12

20 Then He lifted up His eyes toward His
disciples, and said:

[R]"Blessed *are you* poor, Matt. 5:3–12
For yours is the kingdom of God.
21 Blessed *are you* who hunger now,
For you shall be [T]filled. *satisfied*
[R]Blessed *are you* who weep now,
For you shall [R]laugh. [Is. 61:3] • Ps. 126:5
22 Blessed are you when men hate you,
And when they [R]exclude you,
And revile *you*, and cast out your
name as evil, [John 16:2]
For the Son of Man's sake.
23 [R]Rejoice in that day and leap for joy!
For indeed your reward *is* great in
heaven,
For [R]in like manner their fathers did
to the prophets. James 1:2 • Acts 7:51
24 "But woe to you [R]who are rich,
For [R]you have received your
consolation. Luke 12:21 • Luke 16:25
25 [R]Woe to you who are full, [Is. 65:13]
For you shall hunger.
[R]Woe to you who laugh now, [Prov. 14:13]
For you shall mourn and weep.
26 [R]Woe *to you when *all men speak well
of you, [John 15:19]
For so did their fathers to the false
prophets.

Rules of Kingdom Life
Matt. 5:39–48, 7:1, 2, 12

27 "But I say to you who hear: Love your
enemies, do good to those who hate you,
28 "bless those who curse you, and [R]pray
for those who spitefully use you. Acts 7:60
29 [R]"To him who strikes you on the *one*
cheek, offer the other also. [R]And from him
who takes away your cloak, do not withhold
your tunic either. Matt. 5:39–42 • [1 Cor. 6:7]
30 [R]"Give to everyone who asks of you. And
from him who takes away your goods do not
ask *them* back. Deut. 15:7, 8
31 [R]"And just as you want men to do to
you, you also do to them likewise. Matt. 7:12
32 [R]"But if you love those who love you,
what credit is that to you? For even sinners
love those who love them. Matt. 5:45
33 "And if you do good to those who do
good to you, what credit is that to you? For
even sinners do the same.
34 [R]"And if you lend *to those* from whom
you hope to receive back, what credit is that
to you? For even sinners lend to sinners to
receive as much back. Matt. 5:42
35 "But [R]love your enemies, [R]do good, and
[R]lend, [T]hoping for nothing in return; and your
reward will be great, and you will be sons of
the Highest. For He is kind to the unthankful
and evil. [Rom. 13:10] • Heb. 13:16 • Ps. 37:26 • *expecting*
36 [R]"Therefore be merciful, just as your
Father also is merciful. Matt. 5:48
37 "Judge not, and you shall not be judged.
Condemn not, and you shall not be condemned. Forgive, and you will be forgiven.
38 "Give, and it will be given to you: good
measure, pressed down, shaken together, and
running over will be put into your bosom. For
[R]with the same measure that you use, it will
be measured back to you." James 2:13

Parable of the Blind Leading the Blind
Matt. 7:3–5, 16–18

39 And He spoke a parable to them: [R]"Can
the blind lead the blind? Will they not both
fall into the ditch? Matt. 15:14; 23:16

6:9 M *to kill* **6:10** NU, M *to him*
6:10 NU omits *as whole as the other*
6:26 NU, M omits *to you* **6:26** M omits *all*

40 [R]"A disciple is not above his teacher, but everyone who is perfectly trained will be like his teacher. [John 13:16; 15:20]

41 [R]"And why do you look at the speck in your brother's eye, but do not perceive the plank in your own eye? Matt. 7:3

42 "Or how can you say to your brother, 'Brother, let me remove the speck that *is* in your eye,' when you yourself do not see the plank that *is* in your own eye? Hypocrite! First remove the plank from your own eye, and then you will see clearly to remove the speck that is in your brother's eye.

43 "For a good tree does not bear bad fruit, nor does a bad tree bear good fruit.

44 "For [R]every tree is known by its own fruit. For *men* do not gather figs from thorns, nor do they gather grapes from a bramble bush. Matt. 12:33

45 [R]"A good man out of the good treasure of his heart brings forth good; and an evil man out of the evil *treasure of his heart brings forth evil. For out [R]of the abundance of the heart his mouth speaks. Matt. 12:35 • Matt. 12:34

Parable of the Two Foundations—Matt. 7:21–27

46 [R]"But why do you call Me 'Lord, Lord,' and do not do the things which I say? Mal. 1:6

47 [R]"Whoever comes to Me, and hears My sayings and does them, I will show you whom he is like: James 1:22–25

48 "He is like a man building a house, who dug deep and laid the foundation on the rock. And when the flood arose, the stream beat vehemently against that house, and could not shake it, for it was *founded on the rock.

49 "But he who heard and did nothing is like a man who built a house on the earth without a foundation, against which the stream beat vehemently; and immediately it *fell. And the ruin of that house was great."

CHAPTER 7

A Centurion's Servant Is Healed—Matt. 8:5–13

NOW when He concluded all His sayings in the hearing of the people, He [R]entered Capernaum. Matt. 8:5–13

2 And a certain centurion's servant, who was dear to him, was sick and ready to die.

3 So when he heard about Jesus, he sent elders of the Jews to Him, pleading with Him to come and heal his servant.

4 And when they came to Jesus, they begged Him earnestly, saying that the one for whom He should do this was worthy,

5 "for he loves our nation, and has built us a synagogue."

6 Then Jesus went with them. And when He was already not far from the house, the centurion sent friends to Him, saying to Him, "Lord, do not trouble Yourself, for I am not worthy that You should enter under my roof.

7 "Therefore I did not even think myself worthy to come to You. But [R]say the word, and my servant will be healed. Ps. 33:9; 107:20

8 "For I also am a man placed under [R]authority, having soldiers under me. And I say to one, 'Go,' and he goes; and to another, 'Come,' and he comes; and to my servant, 'Do this,' and he does *it*." [Mark 13:34]

9 When Jesus heard these things, He marveled at him, and turned around and said to the crowd that followed Him, "I say to you, I have not found such great faith, not even in Israel!"

10 And those who were sent, returning to the house, found the servant well *who had been sick.

A Widow's Son Is Raised

11 Now it happened, the day after, *that* He went into a city called Nain; and many of His disciples went with Him, and a large crowd.

12 And when He came near the gate of the city, behold, a dead man was being carried out, the only son of his mother; and she was a widow. And a large crowd from the city was with her.

13 When the Lord saw her, He had [R]compassion on her and said to her, [R]"Do not weep." John 11:35 • Luke 8:52

14 Then He came and touched the open coffin, and those who carried *him* stood still. And He said, "Young man, I say to you, [R]arise." Acts 9:40

15 And he who was dead [R]sat up and began to speak. And He [R]presented him to his mother. John 11:44 • 2 Kin. 4:36

16 Then fear [T]came upon all, and they glorified God, saying, [R]"A great prophet has risen up among us"; and, [R]"God has visited His people." *seized them all* • Luke 24:19 • Luke 1:68

John's Questions Are Answered—Matt. 11:2–6

17 And this report about Him went throughout all Judea and all the surrounding region.

18 [R]Then the disciples of John reported to him concerning all these things. Matt. 11:2–19

19 And John, calling two of his disciples to *him*, sent *them* to *Jesus, saying, "Are You [R]the Coming One, or [T]do we look for another?" [Zech. 9:9] • *should we expect*

20 When the men had come to Him, they said, "John the Baptist has sent us to You, saying, 'Are You the Coming One, or do we look for another?' "

6:45 NU omits *treasure of his heart*
6:48 NU *well built*
6:49 NU *collapsed* **7:10** NU omits *who had been sick*
7:19 NU *the Lord*

21 And that very hour He cured many *people* of *their* [T]infirmities, afflictions, and evil
spirits; and to many *who were* blind He gave
sight. *illnesses*
22 Then Jesus answered and said to them,
"Go and tell John the things you have seen
and heard: that [R]*the* blind see, *the* lame walk,
the lepers are cleansed, *the* deaf hear, *the*
dead are raised, *the* poor have the gospel
preached to them. Is. 35:5; 61:1 ★
23 "And [R]blessed is *he* who is not [T]offended
because of Me." Ps. 2:12 ★ • *caused to stumble*

Jesus Praises John—Matt. 11:7–15

24 [R]When the messengers of John had departed, He began to speak to the multitudes
concerning John: "What did you go out into
the wilderness to see? A reed shaken by the
wind? Matt. 11:7
25 "But what did you go out to see? A man
clothed in soft garments? Indeed those who
are gorgeously appareled and live in luxury
are in kings' courts.
26 "But what did you go out to see? A
prophet? Yes, I say to you, and more than a
prophet.
27 "This is *he* of whom it is written:

[R]*'Behold, I send My messenger before*
Your face,
Who will prepare Your way before
You.' Mal. 3:1 ★

28 "For I say to you, among those born of
women there is *not a greater prophet than
John the Baptist; but he who is least in the
kingdom of God is greater than he."
29 And when all the people heard *Him*, even
the tax collectors justified God, [R]having been
baptized with the baptism of John. Luke 3:12
30 But the Pharisees and lawyers rejected
[R]the counsel of God for themselves, not
having been baptized by him. Acts 20:27

Jesus Criticizes His Generation
Matt. 11:16–19

31 *And the Lord said, [R]"To what then shall
I liken the men of this generation, and what
are they like? Matt. 11:16
32 "They are like children sitting in the
marketplace and calling to one another,
saying:

'We played the flute for you,
And you did not dance;
We mourned to you,
And you did not weep.'

33 "For [R]John the Baptist came [R]neither
eating bread nor drinking wine, and you say,
'He has a demon.' Matt. 3:1 • Luke 1:15
34 "The Son of Man has come [R]eating and
drinking, and you say, 'Look, a glutton and a
[T]winebibber, a friend of tax collectors and
sinners!' Luke 15:2 • *An excessive drinker*
35 [R]"But wisdom is justified by all her children." Matt. 11:19

A Woman Anoints Jesus' Feet

36 [R]Then one of the Pharisees asked Him to
eat with him. And He went to the Pharisee's
house, and sat down to eat. John 11:2
37 And behold, a woman in the city who
was a sinner, when she knew that *Jesus* sat
at the table in the Pharisee's house, brought
an alabaster flask of fragrant oil,
38 and stood at His feet behind *Him* weeping; and she began to wash His feet with her
tears, and wiped *them* with the hair of her
head; and she kissed His feet and anointed
them with the fragrant oil.
39 Now when the Pharisee who had invited
Him saw *this*, he spoke to himself, saying,
"This man, if He were a prophet, would know
who and what manner of woman *this is* who
is touching Him, for she is a sinner."

The Parable of the Two Debtors

40 And Jesus answered and said to him,
"Simon, I have something to say to you."
And he said, "Teacher, say it."
41 "There was a certain creditor who had
two debtors. One owed five hundred [R]denarii,
and the other fifty. Matt. 18:28
42 "And when they had nothing with which
to repay, he freely forgave them both. Tell
Me, therefore, which of them will love him
more?"
43 Simon answered and said, "I suppose the
one whom he forgave more." And He said to
him, "You have rightly judged."
44 Then He turned to the woman and said
to Simon, "Do you see this woman? I entered
your house; you gave Me no [R]water for My
feet, but she has washed My feet with her
tears and wiped *them* with the hair of her
head. Gen. 18:4; 19:2; 43:24
45 "You gave Me no [R]kiss, but this woman
has not ceased to kiss My feet since the time
I came in. Rom. 16:16
46 [R]"You did not anoint My head with oil,
but this woman has anointed My feet with
fragrant oil. Ps. 23:5
47 [R]"Therefore I say to you, her sins, *which
are* many, are forgiven, for she loved much.
But to whom little is forgiven, *the same* loves
little." [1 Tim. 1:14]
48 And He said to her, [R]"Your sins are
forgiven." Matt. 9:2
49 And those who sat at the table with Him
began to say to themselves, [R]"Who is this
who even forgives sins?" Luke 5:21
50 Then He said to the woman, [R]"Your faith
has saved you. Go in peace." Matt. 9:22

7:28 NU *none greater than John;*
7:31 NU, M omit *And the Lord said*

CHAPTER 8

Certain Women Minister to Christ

NOW it came to pass, afterward, that He went through every city and village, preaching and [T]bringing the glad tidings of the kingdom of God. And the twelve *were* with Him, *proclaiming the good news*
2 and [R]certain women who had been healed of evil spirits and [T]infirmities—Mary called Magdalene, [R]out of whom had come seven demons, Matt. 27:55 • *sicknesses* • Mark 16:9
3 and Joanna the wife of Chuza, Herod's steward, and Susanna, and many others who provided for *Him from their substance.

Parable of the Soils
Matt. 13:1–23: Mark 4:1–20

4 [R]And when a great multitude had gathered, and *others* had come to Him from every city, He spoke by a parable: Mark 4:1–9
5 "A sower went out to sow his seed. And as he sowed, some fell by the wayside; and it was trampled down, and the birds of the air devoured it.
6 "Some fell on rock; and as soon as it sprang up, it withered away because it lacked moisture.
7 "And some fell among thorns, and the thorns sprang up with it and choked it.
8 "But others fell on good ground, sprang up, and yielded [T]a crop a hundredfold." When He had said these things He cried, "He who has ears to hear, let him hear!" *fruit*
9 [R]Then His disciples asked Him, saying, "What does this parable mean?" Matt. 13:10–23
10 And He said, "To you it has been given to know the mysteries of the kingdom of God, but to the rest *it is given* in parables, that

[R]'*Seeing they may not see,* Is. 6:9★
And hearing they may not understand.'

11 [R]"Now the parable is this: The seed is the [R]word of God. [1 Pet. 1:23] • Luke 5:1; 11:28
12 "Those by the wayside are the ones who hear; then the devil comes and takes away the word out of their hearts, lest they should believe and be saved.
13 "But the ones on the rock *are those* who, when they hear, receive the word with joy; and these have no root, who believe for a while and in time of temptation fall away.
14 "And the ones *that* fell among thorns are those who, when they have heard, go out and are choked with cares, riches, and pleasures of life, and bring no fruit to maturity.
15 "But the ones *that* fell on the good ground are those who, having heard the word with a noble and good heart, keep *it* and bear fruit with [R]patience.[T] [Heb. 10:36–39] • *endurance*

Parable of the Lamp—Mark 4:21–25

16 [R]"No one, when he has lit a lamp, covers it with a vessel or puts *it* under a bed, but sets *it* on a lampstand, that those who enter may see the [R]light. Luke 11:33 • Matt. 5:14
17 "For nothing is secret that will not be [R]revealed, nor *anything* hidden that will not be known and come to light. [2 Cor. 5:10]
18 "Therefore take heed how you hear. For whoever has, to him *more* will be given; and whoever does not have, even what he seems to have will be taken from him."

Christ's True Brethren
Matt. 12:46–50; Mark 3:31–35

19 [R]Then His mother and brothers came to Him, and could not approach Him because of the crowd. Mark 3:31–35
20 And it was told Him *by some,* who said, "Your mother and Your brothers are standing outside, desiring to see You."
21 But He answered and said to them, "My mother and My brothers are these who hear the word of God and do it."

The Storm Is Stilled
Matt. 8:23–27; Mark 4:35–41

22 Now it happened, on a certain day, that He got into a boat with His disciples. And He said to them, "Let us go over to the other side of the lake." And they launched out.
23 But as they sailed He fell asleep. And a windstorm came down on the lake, and they were filling *with water,* and were in [T]jeopardy. *danger*
24 And they came to Him and awoke Him, saying, "Master, Master, we are perishing!" Then He arose and rebuked the wind and the raging of the water. And they ceased, and there was a calm.
25 But He said to them, [R]"Where is your faith?" And they were afraid, and marveled, saying to one another, [R]"Who can this be? For He commands even the winds and water, and they obey Him!" Luke 9:41 • Luke 4:36; 5:26

Demons Are Cast into Swine
Matt. 8:28–34; Mark 5:1–20

26 Then they sailed to the country of the *Gadarenes, which is opposite Galilee.
27 And when He stepped out on the land, there met Him a certain man from the city who had demons *for a long time. And he wore no clothes, nor did he live in a house but in the tombs.
28 When he saw Jesus, he [R]cried out, fell down before Him, and with a loud voice said, [R]"What have I to do with [R]You, Jesus, Son of the Most High God? I beg You, do not torment me!" Mark 1:26; 9:26 • Mark 1:23, 24 • Luke 4:41

8:3 NU, M *them* **8:26** NU *Gerasenes*
8:27 NU *and for a long time wore no clothes*

29 For He had commanded the unclean
spirit to come out of the man. For it had often
seized him, and he was kept under guard,
bound with chains and shackles; and he
broke the bonds and was driven by the demon into the wilderness.
30 Jesus asked him, saying, "What is your
name?" And he said, "Legion," because many
demons had entered him.
31 And they begged Him that He would not
command them to go out into the abyss.
32 Now a herd of many [R]swine was feeding
there on the mountain. And they begged Him
that He would permit them to enter them.
And He permitted them. Lev. 11:7
33 Then the demons went out of the man
and entered the swine, and the herd ran
violently down the steep place into the lake
and drowned.
34 When those who fed *them* saw what had
happened, they fled and told *it* in the city and
in the country.
35 Then they went out to see what had
happened, and came to Jesus, and found the
man from whom the demons had departed,
sitting at the feet of Jesus, clothed and in his
right mind. And they were afraid.
36 They also who had seen *it* told them by
what means he who had been demon-
possessed was [T]healed. *delivered*
37 Then the whole multitude of the surrounding region of the *Gadarenes [R]asked
Him to [R]depart from them, for they were
seized with great [R]fear. And He got into the
boat and returned. Luke 4:34 • Acts 16:39 • Luke 5:26
38 Now the man from whom the demons
had departed begged Him that he might be
with Him. But Jesus sent him away, saying,
39 "Return to your own house, and tell
what great things God has done for you."
And he went his way and proclaimed
throughout the whole city what great things
Jesus had done for him.
40 So it was, when Jesus returned, that the
multitude welcomed Him, for they were all
waiting for Him.

A Woman Is Healed
Matt. 9:18–22; Mark 5:21–34

41 [R]And behold, there came a man named
Jairus, and he was a ruler of the synagogue.
And he fell down at Jesus' feet and begged
Him to come to his house, Mark 5:22–43
42 for he had an only daughter about
twelve years of age, and she was dying. But
as He went, the multitudes thronged Him.
43 [R]Now a woman, having a [R]flow of blood
for twelve years, who had spent all her livelihood on physicians and could not be healed
by any, Matt. 9:20 • Luke 15:19–22
44 came from behind and [R]touched the border of His garment. And immediately her flow
of blood stopped. Mark 6:56
45 And Jesus said, "Who touched Me?"
When all denied it, Peter *and those with him
said, "Master, the multitudes throng You and
press *You*, *and You say, 'Who touched
Me?' "
46 But Jesus said, "Somebody touched Me,
for I perceived power going out from Me."
47 Now when the woman saw that she was
not hidden, she came trembling; and falling
down before Him, she declared to Him in the
presence of all the people the reason she had
touched Him and how she was healed immediately.
48 And He said to her, "Daughter, *be of
good cheer; [R]your faith has made you well.
[R]Go in peace." Luke 7:50 • John 8:11

Jairus's Daughter Is Raised
Matt. 9:23–26; Mark 5:35–43

49 [R]While He was still speaking, someone
came from the ruler of the synagogue's
house, saying to him, "Your daughter is dead.
Do not trouble the *Teacher." Mark 5:35
50 But when Jesus heard *it*, He answered
him, saying, "Do not be afraid; [R]only believe,
and she will be made well." [Mark 11:22–24]
51 When He came into the house, He permitted no one to go *in except Peter, *James,
and John, and the father and mother of the
girl.
52 Now all wept and mourned for her; but
He said, [R]"Do not weep; she is not dead, [R]but
sleeping." Luke 7:13 • [John 11:11, 13]
53 And they laughed Him to scorn, knowing
that she was dead.
54 But He *put them all out, took her by the
hand and called, saying, "Little girl, arise."
55 Then her spirit returned, and she arose
immediately. And He commanded that she be
given *something* to eat.
56 And her parents were astonished, but
[R]He charged them to tell no one what had
happened. Matt. 8:4; 9:30

CHAPTER 9

Twelve Are Sent to Preach
Matt. 10:1–14, 14:1–14; Mark 6:7–16, 30–34

THEN He called His twelve disciples together and gave them power and authority over all demons, and to cure diseases.
2 [R]He sent them to preach the kingdom of
God and to heal the sick. Matt. 10:7, 8
3 [R]And He said to them, "Take nothing for
the journey, neither staffs nor bag nor bread

8:37 NU *Gerasenes*
8:45 NU omits *and those with him*
8:45 NU omits the rest of v. 45.
8:48 NU omits *be of good cheer*
8:49 NU adds *anymore* **8:51** NU adds *with Him*
8:51 NU, M *John and James*
8:54 NU omits *put them all out*

nor money; and do not have two tunics
apiece. Luke 10:4–12; 22:35
4 R"Whatever house you enter, stay there,
and from there depart. Mark 6:10
5 R"And whoever will not receive you,
when you go out of that city, Rshake off the
very dust from your feet as a testimony
against them." Matt. 10:14 • Acts 13:51
6 RSo they departed and went through the
towns, preaching the gospel and healing
everywhere. Mark 6:12
7 RNow Herod the tetrarch heard of all
that was done by Him; and he was perplexed,
because it was said by some that John had
risen from the dead, Matt. 14:1, 2
8 and by some that Elijah had appeared,
and by others that one of the old prophets
had risen again.
9 And Herod said, "John I have beheaded,
but who is this of whom I hear such things?"
RAnd he sought to see Him. Luke 23:8
10 RAnd the apostles, when they had returned, told Him all that they had done. RAnd
He took them and went aside privately into a
deserted place belonging to the city called
Bethsaida. Mark 6:30 • Matt. 14:13
11 But when the multitudes knew *it*, they
followed Him; and He received them and
spoke to them about the kingdom of God,
and healed those who had need of healing.

Five Thousand Are Fed
Matt. 14:15–21; Mark 6:35–44; John 6:1–14

12 RWhen the day began to wear away, the
twelve came and said to Him, "Send the
multitude away, that they may go into the
surrounding towns and country, and lodge
and get provisions; for we are in a deserted
place here." John 6:1, 5
13 But He said to them, "You give them
something to eat." And they said, "We have
no more than five loaves and two fish, unless
we go and buy food for all these people."
14 For there were about five thousand men.
And He said to His disciples, "Make them sit
down in groups of fifty."
15 And they did so, and made them all sit
down.
16 Then He took the five loaves and the two
fish, and looking up to heaven, He Rblessed
and broke *them*, and gave *them* to the disciples to set before the multitude. Luke 22:19; 24:30
17 So they all ate and were Tfilled, and
twelve baskets of the leftover fragments were
taken up by them. *satisfied*

Peter's Confession of Faith
Matt. 16:13–21; Mark 8:27–31

18 RAnd it happened, as He was alone praying, *that* His disciples joined Him, and He
asked them, saying, "Who do the crowds say
that I am?" Matt. 16:13–16
19 So they answered and said, "John the
Baptist, but some *say* Elijah; and others *say*
that one of the old prophets has risen again."
20 He said to them, "But who do you say
that I am?" RPeter answered and said, "The
Christ of God." John 6:68, 69
21 RAnd He strictly warned and commanded
them to tell this to no one, Matt. 8:4; 16:20
22 saying, R"The Son of Man must suffer
many things, and be rejected by the elders
and chief priests and scribes, and be killed,
and be raised the third day." John 19:7 ☆

True Cost of Discipleship
Matt. 16:24–27; Mark 9:34–38

23 RThen He said to *them* all, "If anyone
desires to come after Me, let him deny himself, and take up his cross *daily, and follow
Me. Matt. 10:38; 16:24
24 R"For whoever desires to save his life will
lose it, but whoever loses his life for My sake
will save it. [John 12:25]
25 R"For what Tadvantage is it to a man if he
gains the whole world, and is himself destroyed or lost? Mark 8:36 • *profit*
26 "For whoever is ashamed of Me and My
words, of him the Son of Man will be
ashamed when He comes in His *own* glory,
and *in His* Father's, and of the holy angels.

The Transfiguration
Matt. 16:28—17:9; Mark 9:1–9; 2 Pet. 1:17, 18

27 R"But I tell you truly, there are some
standing here who shall not taste death till
they see the kingdom of God." Acts 7:55, 56 ☆
28 RAnd it came to pass, about eight days
after these sayings, that He took Peter, John,
and James and went up on the mountain to
pray. Mark 9:2–8
29 And as He prayed, the appearance of His
face was altered, and His robe *became* white
and glistening.
30 Then behold, two men talked with Him,
who were Moses and RElijah, 2 Kin. 2:1–11
31 who appeared in glory and spoke of His
Tdecease which He was about to accomplish
at Jerusalem. *death*, lit. *departure*
32 But Peter and those with him Rwere
heavy with sleep; and when they were fully
awake, they saw His glory and the two men
who stood with Him. Dan. 8:18; 10:9
33 And it happened, as they were parting
from Him, *that* Peter said to Jesus, "Master, it
is good for us to be here; and let us make
three Ttabernacles: one for You, one for
Moses, and one for Elijah"—not knowing
what he said. *tents*
34 While he was saying this, a cloud came
and overshadowed them; and they were fearful as they entered the Rcloud. Ex. 13:21

9:23 M omits *daily*

35 Then a voice came out of the cloud,
saying, [R]"This is *My beloved Son. Hear
Him!" Ps. 2:7; Is. 42:1; Matt. 3:17★
36 And when the voice had ceased, Jesus
was found alone. [R]But they kept quiet, and
told no one in those days any of the things
they had seen. Matt. 17:9

Demoniac Son Is Healed
Matt. 17:14–18; Mark 9:14–27

37 [R]Now it happened on the next day, when
they had come down from the mountain, that
a great multitude met Him. Mark 9:14–27
38 Suddenly a man from the multitude cried
out, saying, "Teacher, I implore You, look on
my son, for he is my only child.
39 "And behold, a spirit seizes him, and he
suddenly cries out; it convulses him so that
he foams *at the mouth,* and bruising him, it
departs from him with great difficulty.
40 "So I implored Your disciples to cast it
out, but they could not."
41 Then Jesus answered and said, "O [T]faith-
less and perverse generation, how long shall I
be with you and [T]bear with you? Bring your
son here." *unbelieving • put up with*
42 And as he was still coming, the demon
threw him down and convulsed *him.* Then
Jesus rebuked the unclean spirit, healed the
child, and gave him back to his father.

Christ Prophesies His Coming Death
Matt. 17:22, 23; Mark 9:30–32

43 And they were all amazed at the majesty
of God. But while everyone marveled at all
the things which Jesus did, He said to His
disciples,
44 "Let these words sink down into your
ears, for the Son of Man is about to be
[R]delivered into the hands of men." Luke 22:54☆
45 [R]But they did not understand this saying,
and it was hidden from them so that they did
not perceive it; and they were afraid to ask
Him about this saying. Mark 9:32

True Greatness—Matt. 18:1–5; Mark 9:33–40

46 [R]Then a dispute arose among them as to
which of them would be greatest. Matt. 18:1–5
47 And Jesus, [R]perceiving the thought of
their heart, took a [R]little child and set him by
Him, Matt. 9:4 • Luke 18:17
48 and said to them, "Whoever receives this
little child in My name receives Me; and
[R]whoever receives Me [R]receives Him who
sent Me. [R]For he who is least among you all
will be great." John 12:44 • John 13:20 • Eph. 3:8
49 [R]Then John answered and said, "Master,
we saw someone casting out demons in Your
name, and we forbade him because he does
not follow with us." Mark 9:38–40
50 But Jesus said to him, "Do not forbid
him, for he who is not against *us is for *us."

Samaria Rejects Christ

51 Now it came to pass, when the time had
come for Him to be received up, that He
steadfastly set His face to go to Jerusalem,
52 and sent messengers before His face.
And as they went, they entered a village of
the Samaritans, to prepare for Him.
53 But they did not receive Him, because
His face was *set* for the journey to Jerusalem.
54 And when His disciples James and John
saw *this,* they said, "Lord, do You want us to
command fire to come down from heaven
and consume them, *just as Elijah did?"
55 But He turned and rebuked them, *and
said, "You do not know what manner of
[R]spirit you are of. [2 Tim. 1:7]
56 *"For [R]the Son of Man did not come to
destroy men's lives but to save *them.*" And
they went to another village. John 3:17; 12:47

True Cost of Discipleship—Matt. 8:18–22

57 Now it happened as they journeyed on
the road, *that* someone said to Him, "Lord, I
will follow You wherever You go."
58 And Jesus said to him, "Foxes have holes
and birds of the air *have* nests, but the Son of
Man has nowhere to lay *His* head."
59 [R]Then He said to another, "Follow Me."
But he said, "Lord, let me first go and bury
my father." Matt. 8:21, 22
60 Jesus said to him, "Let the dead bury
their own dead, but you go and preach the
kingdom of God."
61 And another also said, "Lord, [R]I will
follow You, but let me first go *and* bid them
farewell who are at my house." 1 Kin. 19:20
62 But Jesus said to him, "No one, having
put his hand to the plow, and looking back, is
[R]fit for the kingdom of God." 2 Tim. 4:10

CHAPTER 10

Mission of the Seventy

AFTER these things the Lord appointed
*seventy others also, and sent them two
by two before His face into every city and
place where He Himself was about to go.
2 Then He said to them, [R]"The harvest
truly *is* great, but the laborers *are* few; therefore [R]pray the Lord of the harvest to send out
laborers into His harvest. John 4:35 • 2 Thess. 3:1
3 "Go your way; [R]behold, I send you out as
lambs among wolves. Matt. 10:16
4 "Carry neither money bag, sack, nor
sandals; and greet no one along the road.

9:35 NU, *My Son, My Chosen One* **9:50** NU *you*
9:54 NU omits *just as Elijah did*
9:55 NU omits the rest of v. 55.
9:56 NU omits *For the Son of Man did not come to destroy men's lives but to save them.*
10:1 NU *seventy-two others*

5 [R]"But whatever house you enter, first
say, 'Peace to this house.' Matt. 10:12

6 "And if a son of peace is there, your
peace will rest on it; if not, it will return to
you.

7 [R]"And remain in the same house, eating
and drinking such things as they give, for
[R]the laborer is worthy of his wages. Do not go
from house to house. Matt. 10:11 • 1 Tim. 5:18

8 "Whatever city you enter, and they receive you, eat such things as are set before
you.

9 [R]"And heal the sick *who are* there, and
say to them, [R]'The kingdom of God has come
near to you.' Mark 3:15 • Matt. 3:2; 10:7

10 "But whatever city you enter, and they
do not receive you, go out into its streets and
say,

11 [R]'The very dust of your city which clings
to *us we wipe off against you. Nevertheless
know this, that the kingdom of God has come
near you.' Acts 13:51

12 *"But I say to you that [R]it will be more
tolerable in that day for Sodom than for that
city. Matt. 10:15; 11:24

13 "Woe to you, Chorazin! Woe to you,
Bethsaida! For if the mighty works which
were done in you had been done in Tyre and
Sidon, they would have repented a great
while ago, sitting in sackcloth and ashes.

14 "But it will be more tolerable for Tyre
and Sidon at the judgment than for you.

15 [R]"And you, Capernaum, *who are [R]ex-
alted to heaven, [R]will be thrust down to
Hades. Matt. 11:23 • Is. 14:13–15 • Ezek. 26:20

16 "He who hears you hears Me, he who
rejects you rejects Me, and [R]he who rejects
Me rejects Him who sent Me." John 5:23

Return of the Seventy

17 Then [R]the *seventy returned with joy,
saying, "Lord, even the demons are subject to
us in Your name." Luke 10:1

18 And He said to them, [R]"I saw Satan fall
like lightning from heaven. John 12:31

19 "Behold, [R]I give you the authority to
trample on serpents and scorpions, and over
all the power of the enemy, and nothing shall
by any means hurt you. Mark 16:18

20 "Nevertheless do not rejoice in this, that
the spirits are subject to you, but *rather
rejoice because [R]your names are written in
heaven." Is. 4:3

21 [R]In that hour Jesus rejoiced in the Spirit
and said, "I praise You, Father, Lord of
heaven and earth, that You have hidden
these things from *the* wise and prudent and
revealed them to babes. Even so, Father, for
so it seemed good in Your sight. Matt. 11:25–27

22 *"All things have been delivered to Me
by My Father, and [R]no one knows who the
Son is but the Father, and who the Father is
but the Son, and *the one* to whom the Son
wills to reveal *Him*." [John 1:18; 6:44, 46]

23 And He turned to *His* disciples and said
privately, [R]"Blessed *are* the eyes which see
the things you see; Matt. 13:16, 17

24 "for I tell you [R]that many prophets and
kings have desired to see what you see, and
have not seen *it*, and to hear what you hear,
and have not heard *it*." 1 Pet. 1:10, 11

How to Inherit Eternal Life

25 And behold, a certain [T]lawyer stood up
and tested Him, saying, "Teacher, what shall
I do to inherit eternal life?" *expert in the law*

26 He said to him, "What is written in the
law? What is your reading *of it*?"

27 So he answered and said, [R]" *'You shall
love the LORD your God with all your heart,
with all your soul, with all your strength, and
with all your mind,'* and [R]*'your neighbor as
yourself.'* " Deut. 6:5 • Lev. 19:18

28 And He said to him, "You have answered
rightly; do this and you will live."

Parable of the Good Samaritan

29 But he, wanting to [R]justify himself, said
to Jesus, "And who is my neighbor?" Luke 16:15

30 Then Jesus answered and said: "A certain *man* went down from Jerusalem to Jericho, and fell among [T]thieves, who stripped
him of his clothing, wounded *him*, and departed, leaving *him* half dead. *robbers*

31 "Now by chance a certain priest came
down that road. And when he saw him, [R]he
passed by on the other side. Ps. 38:11

32 "Likewise a Levite, when he arrived at
the place, came and looked, and passed by on
the other side.

33 "But a certain Samaritan, as he journeyed, came where he was. And when he saw
him, he had compassion *on him*,

34 "and went to *him* and bandaged his
wounds, pouring on oil and wine; and he set
him on his own animal, brought him to an
inn, and took care of him.

35 "On the next day, *when he departed, he
took out [T]two [R]denarii, gave *them* to the
innkeeper, and said to him, 'Take care of him;
and whatever more you spend, when I come
again, I will repay you.' 2 days' wages • Matt. 20:2

36 "So which of these three do you think
was neighbor to him who fell among the
thieves?"

37 And he said, "He who showed mercy on
him." Then Jesus said to him, [R]"Go and do
likewise." Prov. 14:21

10:11 NU *our feet* **10:12** NU, M omit *But*
10:15 NU *will you be exalted to heaven? You will be thrust down to Hades!*
10:17 NU *seventy-two* **10:20** NU, M omit *rather*
10:22 M *And returning to the disciples He said, "All*
10:35 NU omits *when he departed*

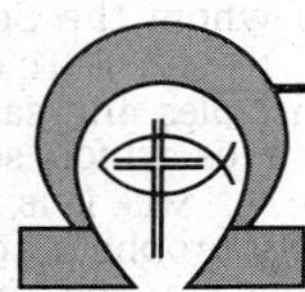

NEW TESTAMENT WOMEN

Mary, the virgin mother of Jesus, has a place of honor among the women of the New Testament. As the first member of the human race to accept Christ, she stands as the first of the redeemed throughout Christian history. She is an enduring example of faith, humility, and service (Luke 1:26–56).

Other notable women of the New Testament include the following:

Jesus visits with Mary and Martha.

Name	Description	Biblical Reference
Anna	Recognized Jesus as the long-awaited Messiah	Luke 2:36–38
Bernice	Sister of Agrippa before whom Paul made his defense	Acts 25:13
Candace	A queen of Ethiopia	Acts 8:27
Chloe	Woman who knew of divisions in the church at Corinth	1 Cor. 1:11
Claudia	Christian of Rome	2 Tim. 4:21
Damaris	Woman of Athens converted under Paul's ministry	Acts 17:34
Dorcas (Tabitha)	Christian in Joppa who was raised from the dead by Peter	Acts 9:36–41
Drusilla	Wife of Felix, governor of Judea	Acts 24:24
Elizabeth	Mother of John the Baptist	Luke 1:5, 13
Eunice	Mother of Timothy	2 Tim. 1:5
Herodias	Queen who demanded the execution of John the Baptist	Matt. 14:3–10
Joanna	Provided for the material needs of Jesus	Luke 8:3
Lois	Grandmother of Timothy	2 Tim. 1:5
Lydia	Convert under Paul's ministry in Philippi	Acts 16:14
Martha and Mary	Sisters of Lazarus; friends of Jesus	Luke 10:38–42
Mary Magdalene	Woman from whom Jesus cast out demons	Matt. 27:56–61; Mark 16:9
Phoebe	A servant, perhaps a deaconess, in the church at Cenchrea	Rom. 16:1, 2
Priscilla	Wife of Aquila; laborer with Paul at Corinth and Ephesus	Acts 18:2, 18, 19
Salome	Mother of Jesus' disciples James and John	Matt. 20:20–24
Sapphira	Held back goods from the early Christian community	Acts 5:1
Susanna	Provided for the material needs of Jesus	Luke 8:3

Mary and Martha Are Contrasted

38 Now it happened as they went that He
entered a certain village; and a certain
woman named [R]Martha welcomed Him into
her house. John 11:1; 12:2, 3
39 And she had a sister called Mary, who
also sat at *Jesus' feet and heard His word.
40 But Martha was distracted with much
serving, and she approached Him and said,
"Lord, do You not care that my sister has left
me to serve alone? Therefore tell her to help
me."
41 And *Jesus answered and said to her,
"Martha, Martha, you are worried and troubled about many things.
42 "But [R]one thing is needed, and Mary has
chosen that good part, which will not be
taken away from her." [Ps. 27:4]

CHAPTER 11

The Lord's Prayer—Matt. 6:9–13

AND it came to pass, as He was praying in
a certain place, when He ceased, *that*
one of His disciples said to Him, "Lord, teach
us to pray, as John also taught his disciples."
2 So He said to them, "When you pray,
say:

[R]Our* Father *in heaven, Matt. 6:9–13
Hallowed be Your name.
Your kingdom come.
*Your will be done
On earth as *it is* in heaven.
3 Give us day by day our daily bread.
4 And [R]forgive us our sins, [Eph. 4:32]
For we also forgive everyone who is
indebted to us.
And do not lead us into temptation,
*But deliver us from the evil one."

Parable of the Persistent Friend

5 And He said to them, "Which of you
shall have a friend, and go to him at midnight
and say to him, 'Friend, lend me three loaves;
6 'for a friend of mine has come to me on
his journey, and I have nothing to set before
him';
7 "and he will answer from within and say,
'Do not trouble me; the door is now shut, and
my children are with me in bed; I cannot rise
and give to you'?
8 "I say to you, [R]though he will not rise
and give to him because he is his friend, yet
because of his persistence he will rise and
give him as many as he needs. [Luke 18:1–5]
9 [R]"And I say to you, ask, and it will be
given to you; [R]seek, and you will find; knock,
and it will be opened to you. [John 15:7] • Is. 55:6
10 "For everyone who asks receives, and he
who seeks finds, and to him who knocks it
will be opened.

Parable of the Good Father—Matt. 7:7–11

11 [R]"If a son asks for *bread from any
father among you, will he give him a stone?
Or if *he asks* for a fish, will he give him a
serpent instead of a fish? Matt. 7:9
12 "Or if he asks for an egg, will he offer
him a scorpion?
13 "If you then, being evil, know how to
give [R]good gifts to your children, how much
more will *your* heavenly Father give the Holy
Spirit to those who ask Him!" James 1:17

Christ Heals the Demoniac

14 [R]And He was casting out a demon, and it
was mute. So it was, when the demon had
gone out, that the mute spoke; and the
multitudes marveled. Matt. 9:32–34; 12:22, 24

Christ's Power Not from Satan
Matt. 12:25–30, 43–45; Mark 3:22–27

15 But some of them said, [R]"He casts out
demons by *Beelzebub, the ruler of the demons." Matt. 9:34; 12:24
16 And others, testing *Him*, [R]sought from
Him a sign from heaven. Matt. 12:38; 16:1
17 [R]But [R]He, knowing their thoughts, said to
them: "Every kingdom divided against itself
is brought to desolation, and a house *divided*
against a house falls. Matt. 12:25–29 • John 2:25
18 "If Satan also is divided against himself,
how will his kingdom stand? Because you say
I cast out demons by Beelzebub.
19 "And if I cast out demons by Beelzebub,
by whom do your sons cast *them* out? Therefore they will be your judges.
20 "But if I cast out demons [R]with the finger
of God, surely the kingdom of God has come
upon you. Ex. 8:19
21 "When a strong man, fully armed, guards
his own palace, his goods are in peace.
22 "But [R]when a stronger than he comes
upon him and overcomes him, he takes from
him all his armor in which he trusted, and
divides his [T]spoils. [Is. 53:12] • *plunder*
23 "He who is not with Me is against Me,
and he who does not gather with Me scatters.
24 [R]"When an unclean spirit goes out of a
man, he goes through dry places, seeking
rest; and finding none, he says, 'I will return
to my house from which I came.' Matt. 12:43–45
25 "And when he comes, he finds *it* swept
and put in order.
26 "Then he goes and takes with *him* seven
other spirits more wicked than himself, and
they enter and dwell there; and [R]the last *state*
of that man is worse than the first." [2 Pet. 2:20]

10:39 NU *the Lord's* **10:41** NU *the Lord*
11:2 NU omits *Our* **11:2** NU omits *in heaven*
11:2 NU omits the rest of v. 2.
11:4 NU omits *But deliver us from the evil one*
11:11 NU omits *bread from any father among you, will he give him a stone? Or if he asks for*
11:15 NU, M *Beelzebul*

27 And it happened, as He spoke these
things, that a certain woman from the crowd
raised her voice and said to Him, R"Blessed *is*
the womb that bore You, and *the* breasts
which nursed You!" Luke 1:28, 48
28 But He said, R"More than that, blessed
are those who hear the word of God and keep
it!" [Luke 8:21]

Christ's Only Sign Is Jonah—Matt. 12:39–42

29 And while the crowds were thickly gathered together, He began to say, "This is an
evil generation. It seeks a sign, and no sign
will be given to it except Rthe sign of Jonah
*the prophet. Luke 24:46; Acts 10:40☆
30 "For as RJonah became a sign to the
Ninevites, Rso also the Son of Man will be to
this generation. Jon. 1:17; 2:10; 3:3–10 • 1 Cor. 15:4☆
31 R"The queen of the South will rise up in
the judgment with the men of this generation
and condemn them, for she came from the
ends of the earth to hear the wisdom of
Solomon; and indeed a Rgreater than Solomon *is* here. 1 Kin. 10:1–9 • [Rom. 9:5]
32 "The men of Nineveh will rise up in the
judgment with this generation and condemn
it, for Rthey repented at the preaching of
Jonah; and indeed a greater than Jonah *is*
here. Jon. 3:5

Parable of the Lighted Lamp

33 R"No one, when he has lit a lamp, puts *it*
in a secret place or under a Rbasket, but on a
lampstand, that those who come in may see
the light. Mark 4:21 • Matt. 5:15
34 "The lamp of the body is the eye. Therefore, when your eye is Tgood, your
whole body also is full of light. But when
your eye is Tbad, your body also *is* full of
darkness. Clear or healthy • Evil or unhealthy
35 "Therefore take heed that the light
which is in you is not darkness.
36 "If then your whole body *is* full of light,
having no part dark, *the* whole *body* will be
full of light, as when the bright shining of a
lamp gives you light."

"Woes" on the Pharisees

37 And as He spoke, a certain Pharisee
asked Him to dine with him. So He went in
and sat down to eat.
38 And Rwhen the Pharisee saw *it*, he marveled that He had not first washed before
dinner. Mark 7:2, 3
39 But the Lord said to him, "Now you
Pharisees make the outside of the cup and
dish clean, but your inward part is full of
Tgreed and wickedness. *eager grasping* or *robbery*
40 "Foolish ones! Did not RHe who made the
outside make the inside also? Gen. 1:26, 27
41 R"But rather give alms of Tsuch things as
you have; then indeed all things are clean to
you. [Luke 12:33; 16:9] • Or *what is inside*
42 "But woe to you Pharisees! For you tithe
mint and rue and all manner of herbs, and
Rpass by justice and the Rlove of God. These
you ought to have done, without leaving the
others undone. [Mic. 6:7, 8] • John 5:42
43 "Woe to you Pharisees! For you love the
Tbest seats in the synagogues and greetings in
the marketplaces. Or *places of honor*
44 R"Woe to you, *scribes and Pharisees,
hypocrites! For you are like graves which are
not seen, and the men who walk over *them*
are not aware *of them.*" Matt. 23:27

"Woes" on the Lawyers

45 Then one of the lawyers answered and
said to Him, "Teacher, by saying these things
You reproach us also."
46 And He said, "Woe to you also, *you*
lawyers! For you load men with burdens hard
to bear, and you yourselves do not touch the
burdens with one of your fingers.
47 "Woe to you! For you build the tombs of
the prophets, and your fathers killed them.
48 "In fact, you bear witness that you approve the deeds of your fathers; for they
indeed killed them, and you build their tombs.
49 "Therefore the wisdom of God also said,
'I will send them prophets and apostles, and
some of them they will kill and persecute,'
50 "that the blood of all the prophets which
was shed from the foundation of the world
may be required of this generation,
51 "from the blood of Abel to Rthe blood of
Zechariah who perished between the altar
and the temple. Yes, I say to you, it shall be
required of this generation. 2 Chr. 24:20, 21
52 R"Woe to you lawyers! For you have
taken away the key of knowledge. You did
not enter in yourselves, and those who were
entering in you hindered." Matt. 23:13
53 *And as He said these things to them, the
scribes and the Pharisees began to assail *Him*
vehemently, and to cross-examine Him about
many things,
54 lying in wait for Him, *and Rseeking to
catch Him in something He might say, *that
they might accuse Him. Mark 12:13

CHAPTER 12

Christ Warns About Hypocrisy—Matt. 10:26–33

IN Rthe meantime, when an innumerable
multitude of people had gathered together, so that they trampled one another, He
began to say to His disciples first *of all*,
R"Beware of the Tleaven of the Pharisees,
which is hypocrisy. Mark 8:15 • Matt. 16:12 • *yeast*

11:29 NU omits *the prophet*
11:44 NU omits *scribes and Pharisees, hypocrites*
11:53 NU *And when He left there*
11:54 NU omits *and seeking*
11:54 NU omits *that they might accuse Him*

HYPOCRITES AND HERETICS

What nasty words! And they are both Greek terms that have been taken over into English because we need such words to describe the all-too-common categories!

Hypocrite (*hypokritēs*)

"I could never join the church; it's full of hypocrites!" We have all heard that line! Unfortunately there are too many—but also in the club, the school, the political party, the lodge, the government, and even the home! Hypocrisy (*hypokrisis*) does not mean we don't measure up to our beliefs—we would all be hypocrites by that standard! *Hypocrisy* is pretending to be something we know we are not. The word comes from the Greek theater; literally used of an actor, it means "to answer (*krinomai*) from under (*hypo*) [a mask]." Someone has well said, "Hypocrisy is the compliment that vice pays to virtue." That means that the person recognizes a certain good category—such as that of a Christian gentleman, for example—and pretends to be one, knowing all the while that he is playacting. This is exactly what our Lord accused the Pharisees of: religious hypocrisy (Luke 20:20). Pretending to be righteous by keeping punctilious little traditions of hand washings and tithing mint, meanwhile they cheated widows out of their houses and violently opposed the only completely righteous Person who ever lived! Fourteen times in the Gospels *hypocrite* occurs, nearly always used by our Lord concerning the Pharisees!

Can a *real* Christian ever be guilty of hypocrisy? Unless we are prepared to read Peter and Barnabas out the Faith, the answer is yes! Six times in the New Testament *hypocrisy* occurs (seven if we accept the interesting textual variant in James 5:12; see the NKJV note there). Paul accused Peter of hypocrisy in Galatians 2 for eating with Gentile believers but then ceasing to do so when strict legalists showed up from Jerusalem who might criticize his (to them) too free life-style. Paul was shocked not so much that impulsive Peter erred here, but "that even Barnabas was carried away with their hypocrisy" (v. 13)! Sincerity was Barnabas's hallmark. So we all have to watch out for hypocrisy in our own lives.

James was strongly against a religion of all talk and no reality. "Religious phonies" is the slang term. As he ends his letter he pleads for sincerity: "But let your 'Yes' be 'Yes,' and *your* 'No,' 'No,' lest you fall into judgment" (5:12). Actually, a majority of manuscripts read "into hypocrisy" here, and since this also fits the context so well it may be what James originally wrote.

Heretic (*hairetikos*)

During the Middle Ages and after the Reformation, untold thousands were burned at the stake as heretics. That means they held views different from the ones taught by the established church. Sometimes this meant they were people who denied a major doctrine of the orthodox Christian Faith (such as the Trinity). Often it meant they went back to the Bible and believed doctrines that were no longer taught by the priestly authorities, but that were taught by Christ and the apostles. One example would be salvation by grace through faith, and not of works (Eph. 2:8, 9).

Titus 3:10 is the only place in the New Testament where *hairetikos* occurs; the KJV translates it as "a man that is an heretick." However, this is a later meaning of the word. The word comes from the verb "to choose," which occurs three times in the Greek New Testament. It means to choose one's own opinion, and it came to mean to cause a faction or split around that view. Hence, nearly all modern versions translate this verse much like NKJV: "Reject a divisive man after the first and second admonition, knowing that such a person is warped and sinning, being self-condemned" (Titus 3:10, 11). It is not necessary to teach a major heresy to split a church, school, or denomination. A divisive person can gather followers around any kind of minor detail of religion.

While we must maintain freedom of religion, we must also be submissive to the standard doctrines of God's Word. Otherwise, we can become guilty of starting a sect (Gr. *hairesis*, from which word we get *heresy*, though we have added the thought of false doctrine to the word).

2 [R]"For there is nothing covered that will
not be revealed, nor hidden that will not be
known. Matt. 10:26
3 "Therefore whatever you have spoken in
the dark will be heard in the light, and what
you have spoken in the ear in inner rooms
will be proclaimed on the housetops.
4 "And I say to you, My friends, do not be
afraid of those who kill the body, and after
that have no more that they can do.
5 "But I will show you whom you should
fear: Fear Him who, after He has killed, has
power to cast into hell; yes, I say to you, [R]fear
Him! Ps. 119:120
6 "Are not five sparrows sold for [T]two
copper coins? And [R]not one of them is forgotten before God. 1/8 day's wage • Matt. 6:26
7 "But the very hairs of your head are all
numbered. Do not fear therefore; you are of
more value than many sparrows.
8 "Also I say to you, whoever confesses
Me [R]before men, him the Son of Man also will
confess before the angels of God. Ps. 119:46
9 "But he who [R]denies Me before men will
be denied before the angels of God. Matt. 10:33
10 "And anyone who speaks a word against
the Son of Man, it will be forgiven him; but to
him who blasphemes against the Holy Spirit,
it will not be forgiven.
11 [R]"Now when they bring you to the synagogues and magistrates and authorities, do
not worry about how or what you should
answer, or what you should say. Mark 13:11
12 "For the Holy Spirit will teach you in
that very hour what you ought to say."

Parable of the Rich Fool

13 Then one from the crowd said to Him,
"Teacher, tell my brother to divide the inheritance with me."
14 But He said to him, "Man, who made Me
a judge or an arbitrator over you?"
15 And He said to them, [R]"Take heed and
beware of *covetousness, for one's life does
not consist in the abundance of the things he
possesses." [1 Tim. 6:6–10]
16 Then He spoke a parable to them, saying:
"The ground of a certain rich man yielded
plentifully.
17 "And he thought within himself, saying,
'What shall I do, since I have no room to
store my crops?'
18 "So he said, 'I will do this: I will pull
down my barns and build greater, and there I
will store all my crops and my goods.
19 'And I will say to my soul, "Soul, you
have many goods laid up for many years;
take your ease; eat, drink, *and* be merry."'
20 "But God said to him, '*You* fool! This
night [R]your soul will be required of you; [R]then
whose will those things be which you have
provided?' Ps. 52:7 • Ps. 39:6
21 "So *is* he who lays up treasure for himself, and is not rich toward God."

Seek the Kingdom of God—Matt. 6:25–33

22 And He said to His disciples, "Therefore I
say to you, [R]do not worry about your life,
what you will eat; nor about the body, what
you will put on. Matt. 6:25–33
23 "Life is more than food, and the body *is*
more than clothing.
24 "Consider the ravens, for they neither
sow nor reap, which have neither storehouse
nor barn; and God feeds them. Of how much
more value are you than the birds?
25 "And which of you by worrying can add
one cubit to his stature?
26 "If you then are not able to do *the* least,
why [T]are you anxious for the rest? *do you worry*
27 "Consider the lilies, how they grow: they
neither toil nor spin; and yet I say to you,
even [R]Solomon in all his glory was not [T]ar-
rayed like one of these. 1 Kin. 10:4–7 • *clothed*
28 "If then God so clothes the grass, which
today is in the field and tomorrow is thrown
into the oven, how much more *will He clothe*
you, O *you* of [R]little faith? Matt. 6:30; 8:26
29 "And do not seek what you should eat or
what you should drink, nor have an anxious
mind.
30 "For all these things the nations of the
world seek after, and your Father [R]knows
that you need these things. Matt. 6:31, 32
31 [R]"But seek *the kingdom of God, and all
these things shall be added to you. Matt. 6:33
32 "Do not fear, little [R]flock, for [R]it is your
Father's good pleasure to give you the kingdom. Is. 40:11; Zech. 13:7☆ • [Matt. 11:25, 26]
33 [R]"Sell what you have and give [R]alms;
[R]provide yourselves money bags which do
not grow old, a treasure in the heavens that
does not fail, where no thief approaches nor
moth destroys. Matt. 19:21 • Luke 11:41 • Matt. 6:20
34 "For where your treasure is, there your
heart will be also.

Parable of the Expectant Steward

35 [R]"Let your waist be girded and [R]*your*
lamps burning; [1 Pet. 1:13] • [Matt. 25:1–13]
36 "and you yourselves be like men who
wait for their master, when he will return
from the wedding, that when he comes and
knocks they may open to him immediately.
37 [R]"Blessed *are* those servants whom the
master, when he comes, will find watching.
Assuredly, I say to you that he will gird
himself and have them sit down *to eat,* and
will come and serve them. Matt. 24:46

12:15 NU *all covetousness*
12:31 NU *His kingdom, and these things*

38 "And if he should come in the second watch, or come in the third watch, and find *them* so, blessed are those servants.

39 [R]"But know this, that if the master of the house had known what hour the thief would come, he would *have watched and not allowed his house to be broken into. Rev. 3:3

40 [R]"Therefore you also be ready, for the Son of Man is coming at an hour you do not expect." Mark 13:33

Parable of the Faithful Steward
Matt. 24:45–51

41 Then Peter said to Him, "Lord, do You speak this parable *only* to us, or to all *people?*"

42 And the Lord said, "Who then is that faithful and wise steward, whom *his* master will make ruler over his household, to give *them their* portion of food in due season?

43 "Blessed *is* that servant whom his master will find so doing when he comes.

44 [R]"Truly, I say to you that he will make him ruler over all that he has. Matt. 24:47; 25:21

45 "But if that servant says in his heart, 'My master is delaying his coming,' and begins to beat the menservants and maidservants, and to eat and drink and be drunk,

46 "the master of that servant will come on a [R]day when he is not looking for *him*, and at an hour when he is not aware, and will cut him in two and appoint *him* his portion with the unbelievers. 1 Thess. 5:3

47 "And [R]that servant who [R]knew his master's will, and did not prepare *himself* or do according to his will, shall be beaten with many *stripes*. Deut. 25:2 • [James 4:17]

48 "But he who did not know, yet committed things worthy of stripes, shall be beaten with few. For everyone to whom much is given, from him much will be required; and to whom much has been committed, of him they will ask the more.

Christ Warns of the Costs of Discipleship

49 [R]"I came to send fire on the earth, and how I wish it were already kindled! Luke 12:51

50 "But [R]I have a baptism to be baptized with, and how distressed I am till it is [R]accomplished! Mark 10:38 • John 12:27; 19:30

51 [R]"Do *you* suppose that I came to give peace on earth? I tell you, not at all, [R]but rather division. Matt. 10:34–36 • John 7:43; 9:16; 10:19

52 [R]"For from now on five in one house will be divided: three against two, and two against three. Mark 13:12

53 [R]"Father will be divided against son and son against father, mother against daughter and daughter against mother, mother-in-law against her daughter-in-law and daughter-in-law against her mother-in-law." Matt. 10:21, 36

Christ Warns of Not Discerning the Times

54 Then He also said to the multitudes, [R]"When *you see* a cloud rising out of the west, immediately you say, 'A shower is coming'; and so it is. Matt. 16:2, 3

55 "And when you see the [R]south wind blow, you say, 'There will be hot weather'; and there is. Job 37:17

56 "Hypocrites! You can discern the face of the sky and of the earth, but how *is it* you do not discern [R]this time? Luke 19:41–44

57 "Yes, and why, even of yourselves, do you not judge what is right?

58 "When you go with your adversary to the magistrate, make every effort along the way to settle with him, lest he drag you to the judge, the judge deliver you to the officer, and the officer throw you into prison.

59 "I tell you, you shall not depart from there till you have paid the very last mite."

CHAPTER 13

Christ Teaches on Repentance

THERE were present at that season some who told Him about the Galileans whose blood Pilate had [T]mingled with their sacrifices. *mixed*

2 And Jesus answered and said to them, "Do you suppose that these Galileans were worse sinners than all *other* Galileans, because they suffered such things?

3 "I tell you, no; but unless you repent you will all likewise perish.

4 "Or those eighteen on whom the tower in Siloam fell and killed them, do you think that they were worse sinners than all *other* men who dwelt in Jerusalem?

5 "I tell you, no; but unless you repent you will all likewise perish."

6 He also spoke this parable: [R]"A certain *man* had a fig tree planted in his vineyard, and he came seeking fruit on it and found none. Matt. 21:19

7 "Then he said to the keeper of his vineyard, 'Look, for three years I have come seeking fruit on this fig tree and find none. Cut it down; why does it use up the ground?'

8 "But he answered and said to him, 'Sir, let it alone this year also, until I dig around it and fertilize *it*.

9 *'And if it bears fruit, *well*. But if not, after that you can [R]cut it down.'" [John 15:2]

Christ Heals the Crippled Woman

10 Now He was teaching in one of the synagogues on the Sabbath.

12:39 NU *not have allowed*
13:9 NU *And if it bears fruit after that, well. But if not, you can*

11 And behold, there was a woman who had a spirit of infirmity eighteen years, and was bent over and could in no way [T]raise *herself* up. *straighten up*

12 But when Jesus saw her, He called *her* to *Him* and said to her, "Woman, you are loosed from your [R]infirmity." Luke 7:21; 8:2

13 [R]And He laid *His* hands on her, and immediately she was made straight, and glorified God. Acts 9:17

14 But the ruler of the synagogue answered with indignation, because Jesus had healed on the Sabbath; and he said to the crowd, "There are six days on which men ought to work; therefore come and be healed on them, and [R]not on the Sabbath day." Mark 3:2

15 The Lord then answered him and said, *"Hypocrite! Does not each one of you on the Sabbath loose his ox or *his* donkey from the stall, and lead *it* away to water it?

16 "So ought not this woman, being a daughter of Abraham, whom Satan has bound—think of it—for eighteen years, be loosed from this bond on the Sabbath?"

17 And when He said these things, all His adversaries were put to shame; and all the multitude rejoiced for all the glorious things that were [R]done by Him. Mark 5:19, 20

Parable of the Mustard Seed
Matt. 13:31, 32; Mark 4:30–32

18 Then He said, "What is the kingdom of God like? And to what shall I compare it?

19 "It is like a mustard seed, which a man took and put in his garden; and it grew and became a *large tree, and the birds of the air nested in its branches."

Parable of the Leaven—Matt. 13:33–35

20 And again He said, "To what shall I liken the kingdom of God?

21 "It is like [T]leaven, which a woman took and hid in [T]three [R]measures of meal till it was all leavened." *yeast* • 6.524 bu. • Matt. 13:33

The Way into the Kingdom

22 [R]And He went through the cities and villages, teaching, and journeying toward Jerusalem. Mark 6:6

23 Then one said to Him, "Lord, are there few who are saved?" And He said to them,

24 [R]"Strive to enter through the narrow gate, for many, I say to you, will seek to enter and will not be able. [Matt. 7:13]

25 [R]"When once the Master of the house has risen up and shut the door, and you begin to stand outside and knock at the door, saying, 'Lord, Lord, open for us,' and He will answer and say to you, [R]'I do not know you, where you are from,' Is. 55:6 • Matt. 7:23; 25:12

26 "then you will begin to say, 'We ate and drank in Your presence, and You taught in our streets.'

27 "But He will say, 'I tell you I do not know you, where you are from. [R]Depart from Me, all you workers of iniquity.' Ps. 6:8

28 "There will be weeping and gnashing of teeth, [R]when you see Abraham and Isaac and Jacob and all the prophets in the kingdom of God, and yourselves thrust out. Matt. 8:11

29 "They will come from the east and the west, from the north and the south, and sit down in the kingdom of God.

30 "And indeed there are last who will be first, and there are first who will be last."

Christ Mourns over Jerusalem

31 *On that very day some Pharisees came, saying to Him, "Get out and depart from here, for Herod wants to kill You."

32 And He said to them, "Go, tell that fox, 'Behold, I cast out demons and perform cures today and tomorrow, and the [R]third *day* I shall be perfected.' Luke 24:46; Acts 10:40☆

33 "Nevertheless I must journey today, tomorrow, and the *day* following; for it cannot be that a prophet should perish outside of Jerusalem.

34 [R]"O Jerusalem, Jerusalem, the one who kills the prophets and stones those who are sent to her! How often I wanted to gather your children together, as a hen *gathers* her brood under *her* wings, but you were not willing! Matt. 23:37–39

35 [R]"See! [R]Your house is left to you desolate; and *assuredly, I say to you, you shall not see Me until *the time* comes when you say, [R]*'Blessed is He who comes in the name of the LORD!'*" Jer. 22:5☆ • Lev. 26:31, 32 • Ps. 118:26

CHAPTER 14

Instruction on the Sabbath

NOW it happened, as He went into the house of one of the rulers of the Pharisees to eat bread on the Sabbath, that they watched Him closely.

2 And behold, there was a certain man before Him who had dropsy.

3 And Jesus, answering, spoke to the lawyers and Pharisees, saying, [R]"Is it lawful to heal on the *Sabbath?" Matt. 12:10

4 But they kept silent. And He took *him* and healed him, and let him go.

5 Then He answered them, saying, [R]"Which of you, having a *donkey or an ox that has fallen into a pit, will not immediately pull him out on the Sabbath day?" [Ex. 23:5]

6 And they could not answer Him regarding these things.

13:15 NU, M *Hypocrites* **13:19** NU omits *large*
13:31 NU *In that very hour*
13:35 NU, M omit *assuredly*
14:3 NU adds *or not* **14:5** NU, M *son*

Parable of the Ambitious Guest

7 So He told a parable to those who were invited, when He noted how they chose the best places, saying to them:

8 "When you are invited by anyone to a wedding feast, do not sit down in the best place, lest one more honorable than you be invited by him;

9 "and he who invited you and him come and say to you, 'Give place to this man,' and then you begin with shame to take the lowest place.

10 [R]"But when you are invited, go and sit down in the lowest place, so that when he who invited you comes he may say to you, 'Friend, go up higher.' Then you will have glory in the presence of those who sit at the table with you. Prov. 25:6, 7

11 [R]"For whoever exalts himself will be [T]abased, and he who humbles himself will be exalted." Matt. 23:12 • *humbled*

12 Then He also said to him who invited Him, "When you give a dinner or a supper, do not ask your friends, your brothers, your relatives, nor *your* rich neighbors, lest they also invite you back, and you be repaid.

13 "But when you give a feast, invite *the* poor, *the* maimed, *the* lame, *the* blind.

14 "And you will be [R]blessed, because they cannot repay you; for you shall be repaid at the resurrection of the just." [Matt. 25:34–40]

Parable of the Great Supper

15 Now when one of those who sat at the table with Him heard these things, he said to Him, [R]"Blessed *is* he who shall eat *bread in the kingdom of God!" Rev. 19:9

16 Then He said to him, "A certain man gave a great supper and invited many,

17 "and [R]sent his servant at supper time to say to those who were invited, 'Come, for all things are now ready.' Prov. 9:2, 5

18 "But they all with one *accord* began to make excuses. The first said to him, 'I have bought a piece of ground, and I must go and see it. I ask you to have me excused.'

19 "And another said, 'I have bought five yoke of oxen, and I am going to test them. I ask you to have me excused.'

20 "Still another said, 'I have married a wife, and therefore I cannot come.'

21 "So that servant came and reported these things to his master. Then the master of the house, being angry, said to his servant, 'Go out quickly into the streets and lanes of the city, and bring in here *the* poor and *the* [T]maimed and *the* lame and *the* blind.' *crippled*

22 "And the servant said, 'Master, it is done as you commanded, and still there is room.'

23 "Then the master said to the servant, 'Go out into the highways and hedges, and compel *them* to come in, that my house may be filled.

24 'For I say to you that none of those men who were invited shall taste my supper.' "

Christ Teaches on Discipleship

25 And great multitudes went with Him. And He turned and said to them,

26 "If anyone comes to Me and does not hate his father and mother, wife and children, brothers and sisters, [R]yes, and his own life also, he cannot be My disciple. Rev. 12:11

27 "And whoever does not bear his cross and come after Me cannot be My disciple.

28 "For which of you, intending to build a tower, does not sit down first and count the cost, whether he has *enough* to finish *it*—

29 "lest, after he has laid the foundation, and is not able to finish *it*, all who see *it* begin to mock him,

30 "saying, 'This man began to build and was not able to finish.'

31 "Or what king, going to make war against another king, does not sit down first and consider whether he is able with ten thousand to meet him who comes against him with twenty thousand?

32 "Or else, while the other is still a great way off, he sends a delegation and asks conditions of peace.

33 "So likewise, whoever of you does not forsake all that he has cannot be My disciple.

34 [R]"Salt *is* good; but if the salt has lost its flavor, how shall it be seasoned? [Mark 9:50]

35 "It is neither fit for the land nor for the [T]dunghill, *but* men throw it out. He who has ears to hear, let him hear!" *rubbish heap*

CHAPTER 15

Parable of the Lost Sheep—Matt. 18:12–14

THEN all the tax collectors and the sinners drew near to Him to hear Him.

2 And the Pharisees and scribes murmured, saying, "This man [T]receives sinners [R]and eats with them." *welcomes* • Gal. 2:12

3 So He spoke this parable to them, saying:

4 "What man of you, having a hundred sheep, if he loses one of them, does not leave the ninety-nine in the wilderness, and go after the one which is lost until he finds it?

5 "And when he has found *it*, he lays *it* on his shoulders, rejoicing.

6 "And when he comes home, he calls together *his* friends and neighbors, saying to them, 'Rejoice with me, for I have found my sheep [R]which was lost!' [1 Pet. 2:10, 25]

7 "I say to you that likewise there will be more joy in heaven over one sinner who repents than over ninety-nine [T]just persons who [R]need no repentance. *upright* • [Mark 2:17]

14:15 M *the best*

Parable of the Lost Coin

8 "Or what woman, having ten silver
[T]coins, if she loses one coin, does not light a
lamp, sweep the house, and seek diligently
until she finds *it*? Gr. *drachma*, a valuable coin
9 "And when she has found *it*, she calls *her*
friends and neighbors together, saying, 'Rejoice with me, for I have found the piece
which I lost!'
10 "Likewise, I say to you, there is joy in
the presence of the angels of God over one
sinner who repents."

Parable of the Lost Son

11 Then He said: "A certain man had two
sons.
12 "And the younger of them said to *his*
father, 'Father, give me the portion of goods
that falls *to me*.' So he divided to them [R]*his*
livelihood. Mark 12:44
13 "And not many days after, the younger
son gathered all together, journeyed to a far
country, and there wasted his possessions
with [T]prodigal living. *wasteful*
14 "But when he had spent all, there arose a
severe famine in that land, and he began to
be in want.
15 "Then he went and joined himself to a
citizen of that country, and he sent him into
his fields to feed swine.
16 "And he would gladly have filled his
stomach with the [T]pods that the swine ate,
and no one gave him *anything*. *carob pods*
17 "But when he came to himself, he said,
'How many of my father's hired servants
have bread enough and to spare, and I perish
with hunger!
18 'I will arise and go to my father, and will
say to him, "Father, [R]I have sinned against
heaven and before you, 2 Sam. 12:13; 24:10, 17
19 and I am no longer worthy to be called
your son. Make me like one of your hired
servants." '
20 "And he arose and came to his father.
But when he was still a great way off, his
father saw him and had compassion, and ran
and fell on his neck and kissed him.
21 "And the son said to him, 'Father, I have
sinned against heaven and in your sight, and
am no longer worthy to be called your son.'
22 "But the father said to his servants,
*'Bring out the best robe and put *it* on him,
and put a ring on his hand and sandals on *his*
feet.
23 'And bring the fatted calf here and kill *it*,
and let us eat and be merry;
24 [R]'for this my son was dead and is alive
again; he was lost and is found.' And they
began to be merry. Luke 9:60; 15:32
25 "Now his older son was in the field. And
as he came and drew near to the house, he
heard music and dancing.
26 "So he called one of the servants and
asked what these things meant.
27 "And he said to him, 'Your brother has
come, and because he has received him safe
and sound, your father has killed the fatted
calf.'
28 "But he was angry and would not go in.
Therefore his father came out and pleaded
with him.
29 "So he answered and said to *his* father,
'Lo, these many years I have been serving
you; I never transgressed your commandment at any time; and yet you never gave me
a young goat, that I might make merry with
my friends.
30 'But as soon as this son of yours came,
who has devoured your livelihood with harlots, you killed the fatted calf for him.'
31 "And he said to him, 'Son, you are always with me, and all that I have is yours.
32 'It was right that we should make merry
and be glad, for your brother was dead and is
alive again, and was lost and is found.' "

CHAPTER 16

Parable of the Unjust Servant

AND He also said to His disciples: "There
was a certain rich man who had a steward, and an accusation was brought to him
that this man was wasting his goods.
2 "So he called him and said to him, 'What
is this I hear about you? Give an [R]account of
your stewardship, for you can no longer be
steward.' [Rom. 14:12]
3 "Then the steward said within himself,
'What shall I do? For my master is taking the
stewardship away from me. I cannot dig; I
am ashamed to beg.
4 'I have resolved what to do, that when I
am put out of the stewardship, they may
receive me into their houses.'
5 "So he called every one of his master's
debtors to *him*, and said to the first, 'How
much do you owe my master?'
6 "And he said, 'A [T]hundred measures of
oil.' So he said to him, 'Take your bill, and sit
down quickly and write fifty.' 600 gal.
7 "Then he said to another, 'And how
much do you owe?' So he said, 'A hundred
measures of wheat.' And he said to him,
'Take your bill, and write eighty.'
8 "So the master commended the unjust
steward because he had dealt shrewdly. For
the sons of this world are more shrewd in
their generation than the sons of light.
9 "And I say to you, make friends for
yourselves by unrighteous [T]mammon, that
when *you fail, they may receive you into
everlasting habitations. Lit., in Aram., *wealth*

15:22 NU *Quickly bring* **16:9** NU *it fails*

10 [R]"He who *is* faithful in *what is* least is faithful also in much; and he who is unjust in *what is* least is unjust also in much. Matt. 25:21

11 "Therefore if you have not been faithful in the unrighteous mammon, who will commit to your trust the true *riches?*

12 "And if you have not been faithful in what is another man's, who will give you what is your [R]own? [1 Pet. 1:3, 4]

13 [R]"No servant can serve two masters; for either he will hate the one and love the other, or else he will be loyal to the one and despise the other. You cannot serve God and mammon." Matt. 6:24

Christ Warns the Pharisees

14 Now the Pharisees, [R]who were lovers of money, also heard all these things, and they [T]derided Him. Matt. 23:14 • Lit. *turned up their nose at*

15 And He said to them, "You are those who justify yourselves [R]before men, but [R]God knows your hearts. For what is highly esteemed among men is an abomination in the sight of God. [Matt. 6:2, 5, 16] • Ps. 7:9

16 [R]"The law and the prophets *were* until John. Since that time the kingdom of God has been preached, and everyone is pressing into it. Matt. 3:1–12; 4:17; 11:12, 13

17 [R]"And it is easier for heaven and earth to pass away than for one [T]tittle of the law to fail. Is. 40:8; 51:6 • The smallest stroke in a Heb. letter

Christ Teaches on Divorce

18 [R]"Whoever divorces his wife and marries another commits adultery; and whoever marries her who is divorced from *her* husband commits adultery. 1 Cor. 7:10, 11

Parable of the Rich Man and Lazarus

19 "There was a certain rich man who was clothed in purple and fine linen and [T]fared sumptuously every day. *lived in luxury*

20 "But there was a certain beggar named Lazarus, full of sores, who was laid at his gate,

21 "desiring to be fed with *the crumbs which fell from the rich man's table. Moreover the dogs came and licked his sores.

22 "So it was that the beggar died, and was carried by the angels to Abraham's bosom. The rich man also died and was buried.

23 "And being in torments in Hades, he lifted up his eyes and saw Abraham afar off, and Lazarus in his bosom.

24 "Then he cried and said, 'Father Abraham, have mercy on me, and send Lazarus that he may dip the tip of his finger in water and [R]cool my tongue; for I [R]am tormented in this flame.' Zech. 14:12 • [Mark 9:42–48]

25 "But Abraham said, 'Son, remember that in your lifetime you received your good things, and likewise Lazarus evil things; but now he is comforted and you are tormented.

26 'And besides all this, between us and you there is a great gulf fixed, so that those who want to pass from here to you cannot, nor can those from there pass to us.'

27 "Then he said, 'I beg you therefore, father, that you would send him to my father's house,

28 'for I have five brothers, that he may testify to them, lest they also come to this place of torment.'

29 "Abraham said to him, 'They have Moses and the prophets; let them hear them.'

30 "And he said, 'No, father Abraham; but if one goes to them from the dead, they will repent.'

31 "But he said to him, 'If they do not hear Moses and the prophets, neither will they be persuaded though one rise from the dead.' "

CHAPTER 17

Christ Teaches on Offenses

THEN He said to the disciples, [R]"It is impossible that no [T]offenses should come, but [R]woe *to him* through whom they do come! [1 Cor. 11:19] • *stumbling blocks* • [2 Thess. 1:6]

2 "It would be better for him if a millstone were hung around his neck, and he were thrown into the sea, than that he should offend one of these little ones.

3 "Take heed to yourselves. If your brother sins *against you, [R]rebuke him; and if he repents, forgive him. [Prov. 17:10]

4 "And if he sins against you seven times in a day, and seven times in a day returns *to you, saying, 'I repent,' you shall forgive him."

5 And the apostles said to the Lord, "Increase our faith."

6 So the Lord said, "If you have faith as a mustard seed, you can say to this mulberry tree, 'Be pulled up by the roots and be planted in the sea,' and it would obey you.

7 "And which of you, having a servant plowing or tending sheep, will say to him when he has come in from the field, 'Come at once and sit down to eat'?

8 "But will he not rather say to him, 'Prepare something for my supper, and gird yourself and serve me till I have eaten and drunk, and afterward you will eat and drink'?

9 "Does he thank that servant because he did the things that were *commanded *him? I think not.

10 "So likewise you, when you have done all those things which you are commanded, say, 'We are [R]unprofitable servants. We have done what was our duty to do.' " Rom. 3:12; 11:35

16:21 NU *what fell* **17:3** NU omits *against you*
17:4 M omits *to you* **17:9** NU omits the rest of v. 9.
17:9 M omits *him*

Christ Cleanses Ten Lepers

11 Now it happened [R]as He went to Jerusalem that He passed through the midst of Samaria and Galilee. Luke 9:51, 52

12 Then as He entered a certain village, there met Him ten men who were lepers, [R]who stood afar off. Lev. 13:46

13 And they lifted up *their* voices and said, "Jesus, Master, have mercy on us!"

14 So when He saw *them*, He said to them, [R]"Go, show yourselves to the priests." And so it was that as they went, they were cleansed. Matt. 8:4

15 Now one of them, when he saw that he was healed, returned, and with a loud voice [R]glorified God, Luke 5:25; 18:43

16 and fell down on *his* face at His feet, giving Him thanks. And he was a [R]Samaritan. 2 Kin. 17:24

17 So Jesus answered and said, "Were there not ten cleansed? But where *are* the nine?

18 "Were there not any found who returned to give glory to God except this foreigner?"

19 [R]And He said to him, "Arise, go your way. Your faith has made you well." Matt. 9:22

Christ Teaches on the Second Coming

20 Now when He was asked by the Pharisees when the kingdom of God would come, He answered them and said, "The kingdom of God does not come with observation;

21 [R]"nor will they say, 'See here!' or 'See there!' For indeed, [R]the kingdom of God is [T]within you." Luke 17:23 • [Rom. 14:17] • *in your midst*

22 Then He said to the disciples, [R]"The days will come when you will desire to see one of the days of the Son of Man, and you will not see *it*. Matt. 9:15

23 [R]"And they will say to you, *'Look here!' or 'Look there!' Do not go after *them* or follow *them*. Matt. 24:23

24 [R]"For as the lightning that flashes out of one *part* under heaven shines to the other *part* under heaven, so also the Son of Man will be in His day. Matt. 24:27

25 "But first He must suffer many things and be [R]rejected by this generation. Luke 9:22

26 "And as it was in the days of Noah, so it will be also in the days of the Son of Man:

27 "They ate, they drank, they married wives, they were given in marriage, until the day that Noah entered the ark, and the flood came and [R]destroyed them all. Gen. 7:19–23

28 [R]"Likewise as it was also in the days of Lot: They ate, they drank, they bought, they sold, they planted, they built; Gen. 19

29 "but on [R]the day that Lot went out of Sodom it rained fire and brimstone from heaven and destroyed *them* all. Gen. 19:16, 24, 29

30 "Even so will it be in the day when the Son of Man [R]is revealed. [2 Thess. 1:7]

31 "In that day, he [R]who is on the housetop, and his [T]goods *are* in the house, let him not come down to take them away. And likewise the one who is in the field, let him not turn back. Mark 13:15 • *possessions*

32 [R]"Remember Lot's wife. Gen. 19:26

33 "Whoever seeks to save his life will lose it, and whoever loses his life will preserve it.

34 [R]"I tell you, in that night there will be two [T]*men* in one bed: the one will be taken and the other will be left. [1 Thess. 4:17] • Or *people*

35 "Two *women* will be grinding together: the one will be taken and the other left.

36 *"Two *men* will be in the field: the one will be taken and the other left."

37 And they answered and said to Him, [R]"Where, Lord?" So He said to them, "Wherever the body is, there the eagles will be gathered together." Matt. 24:28

CHAPTER 18

Parable of the Woman and the Judge

THEN He spoke a parable to them, that men [R]always ought to pray and not lose heart, Luke 11:5–10

2 saying: "There was in a certain city a judge who did not fear God nor regard man.

3 "Now there was a widow in that city; and she came to him, saying, [T]'Avenge me of my adversary.' *vindicate me against*

4 "And he would not for a while; but afterward he said within himself, 'Though I do not fear God nor regard man,

5 [R]'yet because this widow troubles me I will [T]avenge her, lest by her continual coming she weary me.'" Luke 11:8 • *vindicate*

6 Then the Lord said, "Hear what the unjust judge said.

7 "And [R]shall God not avenge His own elect who cry out day and night to Him, though He bears long with them? Rev. 6:10

8 "I tell you that He will avenge them speedily. Nevertheless, when the Son of Man comes, will He really find faith on the earth?"

Parable of the Pharisee and the Tax Collector

9 Also He spoke this parable to some [R]who trusted in themselves that they were righteous, and despised others: Luke 10:29; 16:15

10 "Two men went up to the temple to pray, one a Pharisee and the other a tax collector.

11 "The Pharisee stood and prayed thus with himself, 'God, I thank You that I am not like other men—extortioners, unjust, adulterers, or even as this tax collector.

12 'I fast twice a week; I give tithes of all that I possess.'

13 "And the tax collector, standing afar off, would not so much as raise *his* eyes to heaven, but beat his breast, saying, 'God be merciful to me a sinner!'

17:23 NU reverses *here* and *there*
17:36 NU, M omit v. 36.

14 "I tell you, this man went down to his
house justified *rather* than the other; for
everyone who exalts himself will be abased,
and he who humbles himself will be exalted."

Christ Blesses the Children
Matt. 19:13–15; Mark 10:13–16

15 Then they also brought infants to Him
that He might touch them; but when *His*
disciples saw *it*, they rebuked them.
16 But Jesus called them to *Him* and said,
"Let the little children come to Me, and do
not forbid them; for [R]of such is the kingdom
of God. 1 Pet. 2:2
17 [R]"Assuredly, I say to you, whoever does
not receive the kingdom of God as a little
child will by no means enter it." Mark 10:15

Rich Young Ruler
Matt. 19:16–26; Mark 10:17–27

18 [R]Now a certain ruler asked Him, saying,
"Good Teacher, what shall I do to inherit
eternal life?" Matt. 19:16–29
19 So Jesus said to him, "Why do you call
Me good? No one *is* good but [R]One, *that is*,
God. Ps. 86:5; 119:68
20 "You know the commandments: *'Do not
commit adultery,' 'Do not murder,' 'Do not
steal,' 'Do not bear false witness,'* [R]*'Honor
your father and your mother.'*" Eph. 6:2
21 And he said, "All [R]these I have kept from
my youth." Phil. 3:6
22 So when Jesus heard these things, He
said to him, "You still lack one thing. [R]Sell all
that you have and distribute to the poor, and
you will have treasure in heaven; and come,
follow Me." Matt. 6:19, 20; 19:21
23 But when he heard this, he became very
sorrowful, for he was very rich.
24 And when Jesus saw that he became
very sorrowful, He said, [R]"How hard it is for
those who have riches to enter the kingdom
of God! Mark 10:23
25 "For it is easier for a camel to go through
a needle's eye than for a rich man to enter
the kingdom of God."
26 And those who heard it said, "Who then
can be saved?"
27 But He said, "The things which are impossible with men are possible with God."

Christ Will Reward Sacrifice
Matt. 19:27–29; Mark 10:28–30

28 [R]Then Peter said, "See, we have left *all
and followed You." Matt. 19:27
29 So He said to them, "Assuredly, I say to
you, [R]there is no one who has left house or
parents or brothers or wife or children, for
the sake of the kingdom of God, Deut. 33:9
30 [R]"who shall not receive many times more
in this present time, and in the age to come
everlasting life." Job 42:10

Christ Foretells His Death and Resurrection
Matt. 20:17–19; Mark 10:32–34

31 [R]Then He took the twelve aside and said
to them, "Behold, we are going up to Jerusalem, and all things [R]that are written by the
prophets concerning the Son of Man will be
[T]accomplished. Matt. 16:21; 17:22 • Ps. 22 • *fulfilled*
32 "For [R]He will be delivered to the Gentiles
and will be mocked and insulted and spit
upon. Luke 23:1, 11, 36; Mark 15:19 ☆
33 "And [R]they will scourge *Him* and put
Him to death. And the third day He will rise
again." Luke 23:46; 24:46; John 19:1 ☆
34 [R]But they understood none of these
things; this saying was hidden from them,
and they did not know the things which were
spoken. Luke 2:50; 9:45

Christ Heals Bartimaeus
Matt. 20:29–34; Mark 10:46–52

35 [R]Then it happened, that as He was coming near Jericho, that a certain blind man sat
by the road begging. Matt. 20:29–34
36 And hearing a multitude passing by, he
asked what it meant.
37 So they told him that Jesus of Nazareth
was passing by.
38 And he cried out, saying, "Jesus, [R]Son of
David, have mercy on me!" Matt. 9:27
39 Then those who went before warned him
that he should be quiet; but he cried out all
the more, "Son of David, have mercy on me!"
40 So Jesus stood still and commanded him
to be brought to Him. And when he had come
near, He asked him,
41 saying, "What do you want Me to do for
you?" And he said, "Lord, that I may receive
my sight."
42 Then Jesus said to him, "Receive your
sight; [R]your faith has saved you." Luke 17:19
43 And immediately he received his sight,
and followed Him, [R]glorifying God. And all
the people, when they saw *it*, gave praise to
God. Luke 5:26

CHAPTER 19

Christ Abides with Zacchaeus

THEN *Jesus* entered and passed through
[R]Jericho. Josh. 6:26
2 Now behold, *there was* a man named
Zacchaeus who was a chief tax collector, and
he was rich.
3 And he sought to [R]see who Jesus was,
but could not because of the crowd, for he
was of short stature. John 12:21
4 So he ran ahead and climbed up into a
sycamore tree to see Him, for He was going
to pass that *way*.

18:28 NU *our own*

5 And when Jesus came to the place, He looked up *and saw him, and said to him, "Zacchaeus, [T]make haste and come down, for today I must stay at your house." *hurry*

6 So he [T]made haste and came down, and received Him joyfully. *hurried*

7 But when they saw *it,* they all [T]murmured, saying, "He has gone to be a guest with a man who is a sinner." *grumbled*

8 Then Zacchaeus stood and said to the Lord, "Look, Lord, I give half of my goods to the [R]poor; and if I have taken anything from anyone by [R]false accusation, [R]I restore fourfold." [Ps. 41:1] • Luke 3:14 • Ex. 22:1

9 And Jesus said to him, "Today salvation has come to this house, because [R]he also is [R]a son of Abraham; [Gal. 3:7] • [Luke 13:16]

10 [R]"for the Son of Man has come to seek and to save that which was lost." Matt. 18:11

Christ Gives the Parable of the Ten Minas

11 Now as they heard these things, He spoke another parable, because He was near Jerusalem and because they thought the kingdom of God would appear immediately.

12 [R]Therefore He said: "A certain nobleman went into a far country to receive for himself a kingdom and to return. Matt. 25:14–30

13 "So he called ten of his servants, delivered to them [T]ten minas, and said to them, 'Do business till I come.' *$64,000*

14 [R]"But his citizens hated him, and sent a delegation after him, saying, 'We will not have this *man* to reign over us.' [John 1:11]

15 "And so it was that when he returned, having received the kingdom, he then commanded these servants, to whom he had given the money, to be called to him, that he might know how much every man had gained by trading.

16 "Then came the first, saying, 'Master, your mina has earned ten minas.'

17 "And he said to him, 'Well *done,* good servant; because you were faithful in a very little, have authority over ten cities.'

18 "And the second came, saying, 'Master, your mina has earned five minas.'

19 "Likewise he said to him, 'You also be over five cities.'

20 "And another came, saying, 'Master, here is your mina, which I have kept put away in a handkerchief.

21 'For I feared you, because you are an austere man. You collect what you did not deposit, and reap what you did not sow.'

22 "And he said to him, [R]'Out of your own mouth I will judge you, *you* [R]wicked servant. You knew that I was an austere man, collecting what I did not deposit and reaping what I did not sow. Job 15:6 • Matt. 25:26

23 'Why then did you not put my money in the bank, that at my coming I might have collected it with interest?'

24 "And he said to those who stood by, 'Take the mina from him, and give *it* to him who has ten minas.'

25 ("But they said to him, 'Master, he has ten minas.')

26 'For I say to you, [R]that to everyone who has will be given; and from him who does not have, even what he has will be taken away from him. Luke 8:18

27 'But bring here those enemies of mine, who did not want me to reign over them, and slay *them* before me.' "

The Triumphal Entry
Matt. 21:1–9; Mark 11:1–10; John 12:12–19

28 When He had said this, [R]He went on ahead, going up to Jerusalem. Mark 10:32

29 [R]And it came to pass, when He came near to *Bethphage and [R]Bethany, at the mountain called [R]Olivet, *that* He sent two of His disciples, Matt. 21:1 • John 12:1 • Acts 1:12

30 saying, "Go into the village opposite *you,* where as you enter you will find a colt tied, on which no one has ever sat. Loose him and bring *him here.*

31 "And if anyone asks you, 'Why are you loosing *him?*' thus you shall say to him, 'Because the Lord has need of him.' "

32 So those who were sent departed and found *it* just as He had said to them.

33 But as they were loosing the colt, the owners of it said to them, "Why are you loosing the colt?"

34 And they said, "The Lord has need of him."

35 Then they brought him to Jesus. [R]And they threw their own garments on the colt, and they set Jesus on him. 2 Kin. 9:13

36 And as He went, they spread their clothes on the road.

37 Then, as He was now drawing near the descent of the Mount of Olives, the whole multitude of the disciples began to [R]rejoice and praise God with a loud voice for all the mighty works they had seen, Luke 13:17; 18:43

38 saying:

[R]" *'Blessed is the King who comes in the*
name of the LORD!'
[R]Peace in heaven and glory in the
highest!" Ps. 118:26★ • [Eph. 2:14]

39 And some of the Pharisees called to Him from the crowd, "Teacher, rebuke Your disciples."

40 But He answered and said to them, "I tell you that if these should keep silent, [R]the stones would immediately cry out." Hab. 2:11

41 Now as He drew near, He saw the city and [R]wept over it, John 11:35

19:5 NU omits *and saw him* **19:29** M *Bethsphage*

42 saying, "If you had known, even you,
especially in this your day, the things *that*
[R]*make* for your [R]peace! But now they are
hidden from your eyes. [Acts 10:36] • [Rom. 5:1]
43 "For *the* days will come upon you when
your enemies will [R]build an embankment
around you, surround you and close you in
on every side, Jer. 6:3, 6
44 "and level you, and your children within
you, to the ground; and they will not leave in
you one stone upon another, because you did
not know the time of your visitation."

Cleansing the Temple
Matt. 21:12, 13; Mark 11:15–17

45 [R]Then He went into the temple and began to drive out those who *bought and sold
in it, Mal. 3:1★
46 saying to them, [R]"It is written, *'My house*
**is a house of prayer,'* but [R]you have made it
a *'den of thieves.'* " Is. 56:7 • Jer. 7:11
47 And He [R]was teaching daily in the temple. But [R]the chief priests, the scribes, and
the leaders of the people sought to destroy
Him, Luke 21:37; 22:53 • John 7:19; 8:37
48 and were unable to do anything; for all
the people were very attentive to hear Him.

CHAPTER 20

Religious Leaders Question Christ's Authority—Matt. 21:23–27; Mark 11:27–33

NOW [R]it happened on one of those days,
as He taught the people in the temple
and preached the gospel, *that* the chief
priests and the scribes, together with the
elders, confronted *Him* Matt. 21:23–27
2 and spoke to Him, saying, "Tell us, by
what authority are You doing these things?
Or who is he who gave You this authority?"
3 But He answered and said to them, "I
will also ask you one thing, and answer Me:
4 "The [R]baptism of John—was it from
heaven or from men?" John 1:26, 31
5 And they reasoned among themselves,
saying, "If we say, 'From heaven,' He will
say, 'Why *then did you not believe him?'
6 "But if we say, 'From men,' all the people
will stone us, [R]for they are persuaded that
John was a prophet." Luke 7:24–30
7 So they answered that they did not know
where *it was* from.
8 And Jesus said to them, "Neither will I
tell you by what authority I do these things."

Parable of the Vineyard Owner
Matt. 21:33–44; Mark 12:1–11

9 Then He began to tell the people this
parable: "A certain man planted a vineyard,
leased it to [T]vinedressers, and went into a far
country for a long time. *tenant farmers*
10 "Now at [T]vintage-time he [R]sent a servant
to the vinedressers, that they might give him
some of the fruit of the vineyard. But the
vinedressers beat him and sent *him* away
empty-handed. Lit. *the season* • [1 Thess. 2:15]
11 "Again he sent another servant; and they
beat him also, treated *him* shamefully, and
sent *him* away empty-handed.
12 "And again he sent a third; and they
wounded him also and cast *him* out.
13 "Then the owner of the vineyard said,
'What shall I do? I will send my beloved son.
Probably they will respect *him* when they see
him.'
14 "But when the vinedressers saw him,
they reasoned among themselves, saying,
'This is the heir. Come, let us kill him, that
the inheritance may be [R]ours.' John 11:47, 48
15 "So they cast him out of the vineyard
and [R]killed *him*. Therefore what will the
owner of the vineyard do to them? Luke 23:33
16 "He will come and destroy those vinedressers and give the vineyard to [R]others."
And when they heard *it* they said, "Certainly
not!" Rom. 11:1, 11
17 And He looked at them and said, "What
then is this that is [R]written: Ps. 118:22★

'The stone which the builders rejected
Has become the chief cornerstone'?

18 "Whoever falls on that stone will be
broken; but [R]on whomever it falls, it will
grind him to powder." [Dan. 2:34, 35, 44, 45]

Herodians Question Tribute Money
Matt. 21:45, 46; 22:15–22; Mark 12:12–17

19 And the chief priests and the scribes that
very hour sought to lay hands on Him, but
they *feared the people—for they knew that
He had spoken this parable against them.
20 [R]So they watched *Him*, and sent spies
who pretended to be righteous, that they
might seize on His words, in order to deliver
Him to the power and the authority of the
governor. Matt. 22:15
21 And they asked Him, saying, [R]"Teacher,
we know that You say and teach rightly, and
You do not show personal favoritism, but
teach the way of God truly: Mark 12:14
22 "Is it lawful for us to pay taxes to Caesar
or not?"
23 But He perceived their craftiness, and
said to them, *"Why do you test Me?
24 "Show Me a denarius. Whose image and
inscription does it have?" They answered and
said, "Caesar's."

19:45 NU *were selling, saying* **19:46** NU *shall be*
20:5 NU, M omit *then* **20:19** M *were afraid—for*
20:23 NU omits *Why do you test Me?*

25 And He said to them, [T]"Render therefore
to Caesar the things that are Caesar's, and to
God the things that are God's." *Pay*
26 But they could not catch Him in His
words in the presence of the people. And they
marveled at His answer and kept silent.

Sadducees Question Resurrection
Matt. 22:23–32; Mark 12:18–27

27 [R]Then some of the Sadducees, [R]who deny
that there is a resurrection, came to *Him* and
asked Him, Mark 12:18–27 • Acts 23:6, 8
28 saying: "Teacher, Moses wrote to us *that*
if a man's brother dies, having a wife, and he
dies without children, his brother should take
his wife and raise up offspring for his brother.
29 "Now there were seven brothers. And
the first took a wife, and died without children.
30 "And the second *took her as wife, and
he died childless.
31 "Then the third took her, and in like
manner the seven *also; and they left no
children, and died.
32 "Last of all the woman died also.
33 "Therefore, in the resurrection, whose
wife does she become? For all seven had her
as wife."
34 And Jesus answered and said to them,
"The sons of this age marry and are given in
marriage.
35 "But those who are [R]counted worthy to
attain that age, and the resurrection from the
dead, neither marry nor are given in marriage; Phil. 3:11
36 "nor can they die anymore, for [R]they are
equal to the angels and are sons of God, being
sons of the resurrection. [1 John 3:2]
37 "Now even Moses showed in the *burning*
bush *passage* that the dead are raised, when
he called the Lord *'the God of Abraham, the
God of Isaac, and the God of Jacob.'*
38 "For He is not the God of the dead but of
the living, for [R]all live to Him." [Rom. 6:10, 11]

Christ Questions the Scribes
Matt. 22:41—23:14; Mark 12:35–40

39 Then some of the scribes answered and
said, "Teacher, You have spoken well."
40 But after that they dared not question
Him anymore.
41 And He said to them, "How can they say
that the Christ is David's Son?
42 "Now David himself said in the Book of
Psalms,

[R]*'The LORD said to my Lord,*
"Sit at My right hand, Ps. 110:1 ☆
43 *Till I make Your enemies Your*
footstool."'

44 "David therefore calls Him '*Lord*'; [R]how
is He then his Son?" Rom. 1:3; 9:4, 5

45 [R]Then, in the hearing of all the people,
He said to His disciples, Matt. 23:1–7
46 "Beware of the scribes, who desire to
walk in long robes, love greetings in the
marketplaces, the best seats in the synagogues, and the best places at feasts,
47 "who devour widows' houses, and for a
[R]pretense make long prayers. These will receive greater condemnation." [Matt. 6:5, 6]

CHAPTER 21

Christ Teaches on the Widow's Mites
Mark 12:41–44

THEN He looked up and saw the rich
putting their gifts into the treasury,
2 and He saw also a certain [R]poor widow
putting in [T]two mites. [2 Cor. 6:10] • $1
3 So He said, "Truly I say to you that this
poor widow has put in more than all;
4 "for all these out of their abundance
have put in offerings *for God, but she out of
her poverty has put in [R]all the livelihood that
she had." [2 Cor. 8:12]

The Disciples' Two Questions
Matt. 24:1–3; Mark 13:1–4

5 [R]Then, as some spoke of the temple, how
it was [T]adorned with beautiful stones and
donations, He said, Mark 13:1 • *decorated*
6 "*As for* these things which you see, the
days will come in which [R]not one stone shall
be left upon another that shall not be thrown
down." Luke 19:41–44
7 And they asked Him, saying, "Teacher,
but when will these things be? And what sign
will there be when these things are about to
take place?"

Signs of Christ's Coming
Matt. 24:4–13; Mark 13:5–13

8 And He said: [R]"Take heed that you not
be deceived. For many, will come in My
name, saying, 'I am *He*,' and, 'The time has
drawn near.' *Therefore do not [T]go after
them. Eph. 5:6 • *follow*
9 "But when you hear of [R]wars and com-
motions, do not be terrified; for these things
must come to pass first, but the end *will not
come* immediately." Rev. 6:4
10 [R]Then He said to them, "Nation will rise
against nation, and kingdom against kingdom. Matt. 24:7
11 "And there will be great [R]earthquakes in
various places, and famines and pestilences;
and there will be fearful sights and great
signs from heaven. Rev. 6:12
12 "But before all these things, they will lay
their hands on you and persecute *you*, deliv-

20:30 NU omits the rest of v. 30.
20:31 NU, M *also left no children*
21:4 NU omits *for God* **21:8** NU omits *Therefore*

ering *you* up to the synagogues and prisons,
and you will be brought before kings and
rulers for My name's sake.
13 "But [R]it will turn out for you as an
occasion for testimony. [Phil. 1:12–14, 28]
14 [R]"Therefore settle *it* in your hearts not to
meditate beforehand on what you will [T]answer; Luke 12:11 • *say in defense*
15 "for I will give you a mouth and wisdom
[R]which all your adversaries will not be able to
contradict or [T]resist. Acts 6:10 • *withstand*
16 "You will be betrayed even by parents
and brothers, relatives and friends; and they
will send *some* of you to *your* death.
17 "And [R]you will be hated by all for My
name's sake. Matt. 10:22
18 [R]"But not a hair of your head shall be
lost. Matt. 10:30
19 "In your patience possess your souls.

Destruction of Jerusalem
Matt. 24:15–21; Mark 13:14–19

20 [R]"But when you see Jerusalem surrounded by armies, then know that its desolation is near. Mark 13:14
21 "Then let those in Judea flee to the
mountains, let those who are in the midst of
her depart, and let not those who are in the
country enter her.
22 "For these are the days of vengeance,
that [R]all things which are written may be
fulfilled. [Dan. 9:24–27]
23 [R]"But woe to those who are pregnant
and to those who are nursing babies in those
days! For there will be great distress in the
land and wrath upon this people. Matt. 24:19
24 "And they will fall by the edge of the
sword, and be led away captive into all nations. And Jerusalem will be trampled by
Gentiles [R]until the times of the Gentiles are
fulfilled. [Dan. 9:27; 12:7]

The Second Coming
Matt. 24:29–31; Mark 13:24–27

25 [R]"And there will be signs in the sun, in
the moon, and in the stars; and on the earth
distress of nations, with perplexity, the sea
and the waves roaring; [2 Pet. 3:10–12]
26 "men's hearts failing them from fear and
the expectation of those things which are
coming on the earth, [R]for the powers of
heaven will be shaken. Matt. 24:29
27 "Then they will see the Son of Man
[R]coming in a cloud with power and great
glory. Rev. 1:7; 14:14
28 "Now when these things begin to happen, look up and lift up your heads, because
[R]your redemption draws near." [Rom. 8:19, 23]

Parable of the Fig Tree
Matt. 24:32–35; Mark 13:28–31

29 [R]And He spoke to them a parable: "Look
at the fig tree, and all the trees. Mark 13:28
30 "When they are already budding, you see
and know for yourselves that summer is now
near.
31 "So you, likewise, when you see these
things happening, know that the kingdom of
God is near.
32 "Assuredly, I say to you, this generation
will by no means pass away till all things are
fulfilled.
33 "Heaven and earth will pass away, but
My words will by no means pass away.

Warning to Watch for His Coming
Matt. 24:36–44; Mark 13:32–37

34 "But take heed to yourselves, lest your
hearts be weighed down with [T]carousing,
drunkenness, and cares of this life, and that
Day come on you unexpectedly. *dissipation*
35 "For it will come as a snare on all those
who dwell on the face of the whole earth.
36 "Watch therefore, and pray always that
you may *be counted worthy to escape all
these things that will come to pass, and [R]to
stand before the Son of Man." [Eph. 6:13]
37 And in the daytime He was teaching in
the temple, but at night He went out and
stayed on the mountain called Olivet.
38 Then early in the morning all the people
came to Him in the temple to hear Him.

CHAPTER 22

Judas Agrees to Betray Christ
Matt. 26:1–5, 14–16; Mark 14:1, 2, 10, 11

NOW the Feast of Unleavened Bread drew
near, which is called Passover.
2 And [R]the chief priests and the scribes
sought how they might kill Him, for they
feared the people. John 11:47
3 [R]Then Satan entered Judas, surnamed
Iscariot, who was numbered among the
[R]twelve. Mark 14:10, 11 • Matt. 10:2–4
4 So he went his way and conferred with
the chief priests and captains, how he might
betray Him to them.
5 And they were glad, and [R]agreed to give
him money. Zech. 11:12
6 Then he promised and sought opportunity to [R]betray Him to them in the absence of
the multitude. Ps. 41:9

The Upper Room Is Prepared
Matt. 26:17–19; Mark 14:12–16

7 Then came the Day of Unleavened
Bread, when the Passover must be killed.
8 And He sent Peter and John, saying, "Go
and prepare the Passover for us, that we may
eat."
9 So they said to Him, "Where do You
want us to prepare?"

21:36 NU *have strength to*

10 And He said to them, "Behold, when you
have entered the city, a man will meet you
carrying a pitcher of water; follow him into
the house which he enters.
11 "Then you shall say to the master of the
house, 'The Teacher says to you, "Where is
the guest room in which I may eat the Passover with My disciples?"'
12 "Then he will show you a large, furnished upper room; there make ready."
13 So they went and found it as He had said
to them, and they prepared the Passover.

The Passover Is Celebrated
Matt. 26:20, 29; Mark 14:17, 25

14 And when the hour had come, He sat
down, and the *twelve apostles with Him.
15 Then He said to them, "With *fervent*
desire I have desired to eat this Passover with
you before I suffer;
16 "for I say to you, I will no longer eat of it
until it is fulfilled in the kingdom of God."
17 Then He took the cup, and gave thanks,
and said, "Take this and divide *it* among
yourselves;
18 "for [R]I say to you, *I will not drink of the
fruit of the vine until the kingdom of God
comes." Mark 14:25

The Lord's Supper Is Instituted
Matt. 26:26–28; Mark 14:22–24

19 [R]And He took bread, gave thanks and
broke *it*, and gave *it* to them, saying, "This is
My [R]body which is given for you; do this in
remembrance of Me." Matt. 26:26 • [1 Pet. 2:24]
20 Likewise He also *took* the cup after
supper, saying, "This cup *is* the new covenant
in My blood, which is shed for you.

Christ Predicts His Betrayer
Matt. 26:21–25; Mark 14:18–21; John 13:21–26

21 [R]"But behold, the hand of My betrayer *is*
with Me on the table. Ps. 41:9 ☆
22 [R]"And truly the Son of Man goes [R]as it
has been determined, but woe to that man by
whom He is betrayed!" Matt. 26:24 • Acts 2:23
23 [R]Then they began to question among
themselves, which of them it was who would
do this thing. John 13:22, 25

The Disciples Argue over
Who Is the Greatest

24 [R]But there was also rivalry among them,
as to which of them should be considered the
greatest. Mark 9:34
25 [R]And He said to them, "The kings of the
Gentiles exercise lordship over them, and
those who exercise authority over them are
called 'benefactors.' Mark 10:42–45
26 [R]"But not so *among* you; on the contrary,
[R]he who is greatest among you, let him be as
the younger, and he who governs as he who
serves. [1 Pet. 5:3] • Luke 9:48
27 [R]"For who *is* greater, he who sits at the
table, or he who serves? *Is* it not he who sits
at the table? Yet [R]I am among you as the One
who serves. [Luke 12:37] • Phil. 2:7
28 "But you are those who have continued
with Me in [R]My trials. [Heb. 2:18; 4:15]
29 "And I bestow upon you a kingdom, just
as My Father bestowed *one* upon Me,
30 "that you may eat and drink at My table
*in My kingdom, [R]and sit on thrones judging
the twelve tribes of Israel." [Rev. 3:21]

Christ Predicts Peter's Denial
Matt. 26:31–35; Mark 14:27–31; John 13:36–38

31 *And the Lord said, "Simon, Simon!
Indeed, [R]Satan has asked for you, that he
may [R]sift *you* as wheat. 1 Pet. 5:8 • Amos 9:9
32 "But I have prayed for you, that your
faith should not fail; and when you have
returned to *Me*, strengthen your brethren."
33 But he said to Him, "Lord, I am ready to
go with You, both to prison and to death."
34 Then He said, "I tell you, Peter, the
rooster will not crow this day before you will
deny three times that you know Me."

Christ Predicts Coming Conflict

35 And He said to them, "When I sent you
without money bag, sack, and sandals, did
you lack anything?" So they said, "Nothing."
36 Then He said to them, "But now, he who
has a money bag, let him take *it*, and likewise
a sack; and he who has no sword, let him sell
his garment and buy one.
37 "For I say to you that this which is
written must still be [T]accomplished in Me:
[R]*'And He was numbered with the transgressors.'* For the things concerning Me have an
end." *fulfilled* • Is. 53:12; Luke 23:32; John 19:18 ☆
38 Then they said, "Lord, look, here *are* two
swords." And He said to them, "It is enough."

Christ Prays in Gethsemane
Matt. 26:36–46; Mark 14:32–42; John 18:1

39 [R]And coming out, [R]He went to the Mount
of Olives, as He was accustomed, and His
disciples also followed Him. John 18:1 • Luke 21:37
40 [R]When He came to the place, He said to
them, "Pray that you may not enter into
temptation." Mark 14:32–42
41 [R]And He was withdrawn from them
about a stone's throw, and He knelt down
and prayed, Matt. 26:39
42 saying, "Father, if it is Your will, remove
this cup from Me; nevertheless [R]not My will,
but Yours, be done." Is. 50:5 ☆
43 *Then [R]an angel appeared to Him from
heaven, strengthening Him. Matt. 4:11

22:14 NU omits *twelve* **22:18** NU adds *from now on*
22:30 M omits *in My kingdom*
22:31 NU omits *And the Lord said*
22:43 NU brackets vv. 43 and 44 as not in the original text.

EVENTS OF HOLY WEEK

The Gospel writers devoted many pages to the events leading up to the crucifixion of Jesus. The final week of His earthly ministry began with the triumphal entry into Jerusalem and the "Hosannas" from the crowd that changed to cries of "Crucify Him" before the week was over. Jesus apparently spent most of the week teaching in the temple area during the day. His evenings were spent in the home of Mary, Martha, and Lazarus in Bethany. Significant events during this week included the plot of the Sanhedrin, Jesus' betrayal and arrest, the trials of Jesus, His journey to Golgotha down the Jerusalem street, known today as the Via Dolorosa (see illustration), and the Resurrection. After His resurrection, Jesus ministered another forty days before His ascension.

Jesus walked to Golgotha down the Jerusalem street, known today as the Via Dolorosa.

Day	Event	Biblical Reference
Sunday	The triumphal entry into Jerusalem	Mark 11:1–11
Monday	Cleanses the temple in Jerusalem	Mark 11:15–19
Tuesday	The Sanhedrin challenges Jesus' authority	Luke 20:1–8
	Jesus foretells the destruction of Jerusalem and His Second Coming	Matt. 24; 25
	Mary anoints Jesus at Bethany	John 12:2–8
	Judas bargains with the Jewish rulers to betray Jesus	Luke 22:3–6
Thursday	Jesus eats the Passover meal with His disciples and institutes the Memorial Supper	John 13:1–30 Mark 14:22–26
	Prays in Gethsemane for His disciples	John 17
Friday	His betrayal and arrest in the Garden of Gethsemane	Mark 14:43–50
	Jesus questioned by Annas, the former high priest	John 18:12–24
	Condemned by Caiaphas and the Sanhedrin	Mark 14:53–65
	Peter denies Jesus three times	John 18:15–27
	Jesus is formally condemned by the Sanhedrin	Luke 22:66–71
	Judas commits suicide	Matt. 27:3–10
	The trial of Jesus before Pilate	Luke 23:1–5
	Jesus' appearance before Herod Antipas	Luke 23:6–12
	Formally sentenced to death by Pilate	Luke 23:13–25
	Jesus is mocked and crucified between two thieves	Mark 15:16–27
	The veil of the temple is torn as Jesus dies	Matt. 27:51–56
	His burial in the tomb of Joseph of Arimathea	John 19:31–42
Sunday	Jesus is raised from the dead	Luke 24:1–9

44 And being in agony, He prayed more
earnestly. And His sweat became like great
drops of blood falling down to the ground.
45 When He rose up from prayer, and had
come to His disciples, He found them sleeping
from sorrow.
46 Then He said to them, "Why [R]do you
sleep? Rise and [R]pray, lest you enter into
temptation." Luke 9:32 • Luke 22:40

Judas Betrays Christ
Matt. 26:47–56; Mark 14:43–50; John 18:2–11

47 And while He was still speaking, behold,
a multitude; and he who was called [R]Judas,
one of the twelve, went before them and
drew near to Jesus to kiss Him. Acts 1:16, 17
48 But Jesus said to him, "Judas, are you
betraying the Son of Man with a kiss?"
49 When those around Him saw what was
going to happen, they said to Him, "Lord,
shall we strike with the sword?"
50 And one of them struck the servant of
the high priest and cut off his right ear.
51 But Jesus answered and said, "Permit
even this." And He touched his ear and
healed him.
52 Then Jesus said to the chief priests,
captains of the temple, and the elders who
had come to Him, "Have you come out, as
against a robber, with swords and clubs?
53 "When I was with you daily in the temple, you did not try to seize Me. But this is
your hour, and the power of darkness."

Peter Denies Christ
Matt. 26:57, 58, 69–75; Mark 14:53, 54, 66–72; John 18:15–18, 25–27

54 Then, having arrested Him, they led *Him*
and brought Him into the high priest's house.
And Peter followed at a distance.
55 [R]Now when they had kindled a fire in the
midst of the courtyard and sat down together, Peter sat among them. Mark 14:66–72
56 And a certain servant girl, seeing him as
he sat by the fire, looked intently at him and
said, "This man was also with Him."
57 But he denied *Him, saying, "Woman, I
do not know Him."
58 [R]And after a little while another saw him
and said, "You also are of them." But Peter
said, "Man, I am not!" John 18:25
59 [R]Then after about an hour had passed,
another confidently affirmed, saying, "Surely
this *fellow* also was with Him, for he is a
[R]Galilean." Mark 14:70 • Acts 1:11; 2:7
60 But Peter said, "Man, I do not know
what you are saying!" And [R]immediately,
while he was still speaking, *the rooster
crowed. Luke 22:34; John 13:38★
61 And the Lord turned and looked at Peter.
And [R]Peter remembered the word of the
Lord, how He had said to him, [R]"Before the
rooster *crows, you will deny Me three
times." Matt. 26:75 • John 13:38
62 Then Peter went out and wept bitterly.

Christ Is Beaten—Matt. 26:67, 68; Mark 14:65

63 [R]Now the men who held Jesus mocked
Him and beat Him. Ps. 69:19; Is. 50:6; 52:14★
64 And having blindfolded Him, they
[R]struck* Him on the face and asked Him,
saying, "Prophesy! Who is it that struck
You?" Zech. 13:7
65 [R]And many other things they blasphe-
mously spoke against Him. Is. 53:3★

The Sanhedrin Tries Christ
Matt. 27:1; Mark 15:1

66 [R]As soon as it was day, [R]the elders of the
people, both chief priests and scribes, came
together and led Him into their council,
saying, Matt. 27:1 • Acts 4:26
67 [R]"If You are the Christ, tell us." But He
said to them, "If I tell you, you will [R]by no
means believe. Matt. 26:63–66 • Luke 20:5–7
68 "And if I *also ask *you*, you will by no
means answer *Me or let *Me* go.
69 "Hereafter the Son of Man will sit on the
right hand of the power of God."
70 Then they all said, "Are You then the
Son of God?" And He said to them, [R]"You
rightly say that I am." Luke 1:35★
71 [R]And they said, "What further testimony
do we need? For we have heard it ourselves
from His own mouth." Mark 14:63

CHAPTER 23

Pilate Tries Christ
Matt. 27:2, 11–14; Mark 15:1–5; John 18:28–38

THEN [R]the whole multitude of them arose
and led Him to Pilate. Luke 18:32★
2 And they began to accuse Him, saying,
"We found this *fellow* perverting *the nation,
and forbidding to pay taxes to Caesar, saying
that He Himself is Christ, a King."
3 [R]So Pilate asked Him, saying, "Are You
the King of the Jews?" And He answered him
and said, "*It is as* you say." 1 Tim. 6:13
4 Then Pilate said to the chief priests and
the crowd, "I find no fault in this Man."
5 But they were the more fierce, saying,
"He stirs up the people, teaching throughout
all Judea, beginning from [R]Galilee to this
place." John 7:41
6 When Pilate heard *of Galilee, he asked
if the Man were a Galilean.
7 And as soon as he knew that He belonged to [R]Herod's jurisdiction, he sent Him

22:57 NU *it* **22:60** NU, M *a rooster*
22:61 NU adds *today* **22:64** NU *asked Him.*
22:68 NU omits *also*
22:68 NU omits the rest of v. 68.
23:2 NU *our* **23:6** NU omits *of Galilee*

to Herod, who was also in Jerusalem at that
time. Luke 3:1; 9:7; 13:31

Herod Tries Christ

8 Now when Herod saw Jesus, [R]he was
exceedingly glad; for he had desired for a
long *time* to see Him, because [R]he had heard
many things about Him, and he hoped to see
some miracle done by Him. Luke 9:9 • Matt. 14:1
9 Then he questioned Him with many
words, but He answered him nothing.
10 And the chief priests and scribes stood
and vehemently accused Him.
11 [R]Then Herod, with his [T]men of war,
treated Him with contempt and mocked *Him*,
arrayed Him in a gorgeous robe, and sent
Him back to Pilate. Ps. 69:19; Is. 53:3 ★ • *troops*
12 That very day Pilate and Herod became
friends with each other, for before *that* they
had been at enmity with each other.

Pilate Tries Christ Again
Matt. 27:15–26; Mark 15:6–15;
John 18:39—19:16

13 [R]Then Pilate, when he had called together the chief priests, the rulers, and the
people, Mark 15:14
14 said to them, [R]"You have brought this
Man to me, as one who misleads the people.
And indeed, [R]having examined *Him* in your
presence, I have found no fault in this Man
concerning those things of which you accuse
Him; Luke 23:1, 2 • Luke 23:4
15 "no, neither did Herod, for *I sent you
back to him; and indeed nothing worthy of
death has been done by Him.
16 [R]"I will therefore chastise Him and release *Him*" John 19:1
17 [R](for* it was necessary for him to release
one to them at the feast). John 18:39
18 And [R]they all cried out at once, saying,
"Away with this *Man*, and release to us
Barabbas"— Is. 53:3; Acts 3:13–15 ★
19 who had been thrown into prison for a
certain insurrection made in the city, and for
murder.
20 Pilate, therefore, wishing to release
Jesus, again called out to them.
21 But they shouted, saying, "Crucify *Him*,
crucify Him!"
22 And he said to them the third time,
"Why, what evil has He done? I have found
no reason for death in Him. I will therefore
chastise Him and let *Him* go."
23 But they were insistent, demanding with
loud voices that He be crucified. And the
voices of these men *and of the chief priests
prevailed.
24 So [R]Pilate gave sentence that it should be
as they requested. Mark 15:15
25 [R]And he released *to them the one they
requested, who for insurrection and murder
had been thrown into prison; but he delivered
Jesus to their will. Is. 53:8

Christ Is Crucified
Matt. 27:31–56; Mark 15:20–41; John 19:16–30

26 [R]Now as they led Him away, they laid
hold of a certain man, Simon a Cyrenian, who
was coming from the country, and on him
they laid the cross that he might bear *it* after
Jesus. Matt. 27:32
27 And a great multitude of the people
followed Him, and women who also mourned
and lamented Him.
28 But Jesus, turning to them, said,
"Daughters of Jerusalem, do not weep for
Me, but weep for yourselves and for your
children.
29 [R]"For indeed the days are coming in
which they will say, 'Blessed *are* the barren,
the wombs that never bore, and *the* breasts
which never nursed!' Matt. 24:19
30 [R]"Then they will begin *'to say to the
mountains, "Fall on us!" and to the hills,
"Cover us!"'* Hos. 10:8; Rev. 6:16, 17; 9:6
31 [R]"For if they do these things in the green
wood, what will be done in the dry?" [Jer. 25:29]
32 [R]There were also two others, criminals,
led with Him to be put to death. Is. 53:9, 12
33 And [R]when they had come to the place
called Calvary, there they [R]crucified Him, and
the criminals, one on the right hand and the
other on the left. John 19:17–24 • Ps. 22:16–18 ★
34 *Then Jesus said, "Father, forgive them,
for they do not know what they do." And
they divided His garments and cast lots.
35 And [R]the people stood looking on. But
even the rulers with them sneered, saying,
"He saved others; let Him save Himself if He
is the Christ, the chosen of God." Ps. 22:7, 8 ★
36 And the soldiers also mocked Him, coming and offering Him [R]sour wine, Ps. 69:21
37 and saying, "If You are the King of the
Jews, save Yourself."
38 [R]And an inscription also was *written
over Him in letters of Greek, Latin, and
Hebrew: John 19:19

THIS IS THE KING OF THE JEWS.

39 Then one of the criminals who were
hanged blasphemed Him, [R]saying, *"If You
are the Christ, save Yourself and us." Ps. 22:8 ★
40 But the other, answering, rebuked him,
saying, "Do you not even fear God, seeing
you are under the same condemnation?
41 "And we indeed justly, for we receive the
due reward of our deeds; but this Man has
done [R]nothing wrong." [Heb. 7:26]
42 Then he said *to Jesus, "Lord, remember
me when You come into Your kingdom."

23:15 NU *he sent Him back to us*
23:17 NU omits v. 17.
23:23 NU omits *and of the chief priests*
23:25 NU, M omit *to them*
23:34 NU brackets the first sentence as a later addition.
23:38 NU omits *written* and *in letters of Greek, Latin, and Hebrew* **23:39** NU *Are You not the Christ? Save*
23:42 NU *"Jesus, remember me*

43 And Jesus said to him, "Assuredly, I say to you, today you will be with Me in [R]Paradise." [Rev. 2:7]

44 [R]And it *was about the sixth hour, and there was darkness over all the earth until the ninth hour. Amos 8:9★

45 Then the sun was *darkened, and [R]the veil of the temple was torn in two. Matt. 27:51

46 And when Jesus had cried out with a loud voice, He said, "Father, *'into Your hands I commend My spirit.'*" [R]And having said this, He breathed His last. Matt. 17:23★

47 [R]Now when the centurion saw what had happened, he glorified God, saying, "Certainly this was a righteous Man!" Mark 15:39

48 And the whole crowd who came together to that sight, seeing what had been done, beat their breasts and returned.

49 [R]But all His acquaintances, and the women who followed Him from Galilee, stood at a distance, watching these things. Ps. 38:11

Christ Is Buried
Matt. 27:57–61; Mark 15:42–47; John 19:38–42

50 [R]And behold, *there was* a man named Joseph, a council member, a good and just man. Matt. 27:57–61

51 He had not consented to their counsel and deed. *He was* from Arimathea, a city of the Jews, [R]who* himself was also waiting for the kingdom of God. Luke 2:25, 38

52 [R]This *man* went to Pilate and asked for the body of Jesus. Is. 53:9★

53 [R]Then he took it down, wrapped it in linen, and laid it in a tomb *that was* hewn out of the rock, where no one had ever lain before. Matt. 26:12; Mark 14:8★

54 That day was [R]the Preparation, and the Sabbath drew near. Matt. 27:62

55 And the women [R]who had come with Him from Galilee followed after, and [R]they observed the tomb and how His body was laid. Luke 8:2 • Mark 15:47

In the Grave

56 Then they returned and prepared spices and fragrant oils. And they rested on the Sabbath according to the commandment.

CHAPTER 24

The Resurrection
Matt. 28:1–8; Mark 16:1–8; John 20:1–10

NOW on the first *day* of the week, very early in the morning, they, *and certain *other women* with them, came to the tomb bringing the spices which they had prepared.

2 [R]But they found the stone rolled away from the tomb. Mark 16:4

3 [R]Then they went in and did not find the body of the Lord Jesus. Mark 16:5

4 And it happened, as they were *greatly perplexed about this, that [R]behold, two men stood by them in shining garments. John 20:12

5 Then, as they were afraid and bowed *their* faces to the earth, they said to them, "Why do you seek the living among the dead?

6 "He is not here, but is risen! [R]Remember how He spoke to you when He was still in Galilee, Matt. 16:21; Mark 8:31; Luke 9:22★

7 "saying, 'The Son of Man must be delivered into the hands of sinful men, and be crucified, and the third day rise again.' "

8 And they remembered His words.

9 [R]Then they returned from the tomb and told all these things to the eleven and to all the rest. Mark 16:10

10 It was Mary Magdalene, [R]Joanna, Mary *the mother* of James, and the other *women* with them, who told these things to the apostles. Luke 8:3

11 And their words seemed to them like idle tales, and they did not believe them.

12 But Peter arose and ran to the tomb; and stooping down, he saw the linen cloths *lying by themselves; and he departed, marveling to himself at what had happened.

Christ Appears on the Road to Emmaus
Mark 16:12, 13

13 [R]Now behold, two of them were traveling that same day to a village called Emmaus, which was *about* [T]seven miles from Jerusalem. Mark 16:12 • Lit. *60 stadia*

14 And they talked together of all these things which had happened.

15 So it was, while they conversed and reasoned, that [R]Jesus Himself drew near and went with them. [Matt. 18:20]

16 But [R]their eyes were restrained, so that they did not know Him. John 20:14; 21:4

17 And He said to them, "What kind of conversation *is* this that you have with one another as you *walk and are sad?"

18 Then the one [R]whose name was Cleopas answered and said to Him, "Are You the only stranger in Jerusalem, and have You not known the things which happened there in these days?" John 19:25

19 And He said to them, "What things?" And they said to Him, "The things concerning Jesus of Nazareth, [R]who was a Prophet [R]mighty in deed and word before God and all the people, Matt. 21:11 • Acts 7:22

20 [R]"and how the chief priests and our rulers delivered Him to be condemned to death, and crucified Him. Acts 13:27, 28

23:44 NU adds *now* **23:45** NU *obstructed*
23:51 NU *who was waiting*
24:1 NU omits *and certain other women with them*
24:4 NU omits *greatly* **24:12** NU omits *lying*
24:17 NU *walk? And they stood still, looking sad.*

21 "But we were hoping [R]that it was He
who was going to redeem Israel. Indeed,
besides all this, today is the third day since
these things happened. Luke 1:68; 2:38
22 "Yes, and [R]certain women of our company, who arrived at the tomb early, astonished us. Mark 16:10
23 "When they did not find His body, they
came saying that they had also seen a vision
of angels who said He was alive.
24 "And certain of those *who were* with us
went to the tomb and found *it* just as the
women had said; but Him they did not see."
25 Then He said to them, "O foolish ones,
and slow of heart to believe in all that the
prophets have spoken!
26 "Ought not the Christ to have suffered
these things and to enter into His glory?"
27 And beginning at Moses and all the
Prophets, He expounded to them in all the
Scriptures the things concerning Himself.
28 Then they drew near to the village where
they were going, and [R]He [T]indicated that He
would have gone farther. Mark 6:48 • *acted as if*
29 But [R]they constrained Him, saying,
[R]"Abide with us, for it is toward evening, and
the day is far spent." And He went in to stay
with them. Gen. 19:2, 3 • [John 14:23]
30 Now it came to pass, as [R]He sat at the
table with them, that He took bread, blessed
and broke *it*, and gave it to them. Matt. 14:19
31 Then their eyes were opened and they
knew Him; and He vanished from their sight.
32 And they said to one another, "Did not
our heart burn within us while He talked
with us on the road, and while He opened the
Scriptures to us?"

The Proof of His Resurrection
Mark 16:4; John 20:19–23; 1 Cor. 15:5

33 So they rose up that very hour and
returned to Jerusalem, and found the eleven
and those *who were* with them gathered
together,
34 saying, "The Lord is risen indeed, and
[R]has appeared to Simon!" 1 Cor. 15:5
35 And they told about the things *that had
happened* on the road, and how He was
known to them in the breaking of bread.
36 [R]Now as they said these things, Jesus
Himself stood in the midst of them, and said
to them, "Peace to you." Mark 16:14
37 But they were terrified and frightened,
and supposed they had seen [R]a spirit. Mark 6:49
38 And He said to them, "Why are you
troubled? And why do doubts arise in your
hearts?
39 "Behold My hands and My feet, that it is
I Myself. [R]Handle Me and see, for a [R]spirit
does not have flesh and bones as you see I
have." John 20:20, 27 • [1 Cor. 15:50]
40 *When He had said this, He showed
them His hands and His feet.
41 But while they still did not believe [R]for
joy, and marveled, He said to them, [R]"Have
you any food here?" Gen. 45:26 • John 21:5
42 So they gave Him a piece of a broiled fish
*and some honeycomb.
43 And He took *it* and ate in their presence.

The Great Commission—Acts 1:3–8

44 Then He said to them, "These *are* the
words which I spoke to you while I was still
with you, that all things must be fulfilled
which were written in the Law of Moses and
the Prophets and *the* Psalms concerning Me."
45 And He opened their understanding, that
they might comprehend the Scriptures.
46 Then He said to them, [R]"Thus it is written, *and thus it was necessary for the Christ
to suffer and to rise from the dead the third
day, Hos. 6:1, 2; Acts 17:3★
47 "and that repentance and remission of
sins should be preached in His name [R]to all
nations, beginning at Jerusalem. [Jer. 31:34]
48 "And you are witnesses of these things.

The Ascension—Mark 16:19; Acts 1:9

49 [R]"Behold, I send the Promise of My Father upon you; but tarry in the city *of
Jerusalem until you are endued with power
from on high." Is. 44:3; Joel 2:28; Acts 2:4☆
50 And He led them out as far as Bethany,
and He lifted up His hands and blessed them.
51 [R]Now it came to pass, while He blessed
them, that He was parted from them and
carried up into heaven. Ps. 68:18; 110:1★
52 [R]And they worshiped Him, and returned
to Jerusalem with great joy, Matt. 28:9
53 and were continually [R]in the temple
*praising and blessing God. *Amen. Acts 2:46

24:40 Some printed New Testaments omit v. 40. It is found in nearly all Gr. mss.
24:42 NU omits *and some honeycomb*
24:46 NU *that the Christ should suffer and rise*
24:49 NU omits *of Jerusalem*
24:53 NU omits *praising and* **24:53** NU omits *Amen.*

THE GOSPEL ACCORDING TO

JOHN

THE BOOK OF JOHN

Just as a coin has two sides, both valid, so Jesus Christ has two natures, both valid. Luke presents Christ in His humanity as the Son of Man; John portrays Him in His deity as the Son of God. John's purpose is crystal clear: to set forth Christ in His deity in order to spark believing faith in his readers. John's gospel is topical, not primarily chronological, and it revolves around seven miracles and seven "I am" statements of Christ.

Following an extended eyewitness description of the Upper Room meal and discourse, John records events leading up to the Resurrection, the final climactic proof that Jesus is who He claims to be—the Son of God.

The title of the Fourth Gospel follows the same format as the titles of the synoptic Gospels: *Kata Ioannen,* "According to John." As with the others, the word "Gospel" was later added. *Ioannes* is derived from the Hebrew name *Johanan,* "Yahweh Has Been Gracious."

THE AUTHOR OF JOHN

Jesus nicknamed John and his brother, James, "Sons of Thunder" (Mark 3:17). Their father was Zebedee; and their mother, Salome, served Jesus in Galilee and was present at His crucifixion (Mark 15:40, 41). John was evidently among the Galileans who followed John the Baptist until they were called to follow Jesus at the outset of His public ministry (1:19–51). These Galileans were later called to become full-time disciples of the Lord (Luke 5:1–11), and John was among the twelve men who were selected to be apostles (Luke 6:12–16). After Christ's ascension, John became one of the "pillars" of the church in Jerusalem along with James and Peter (Gal. 2:9). He is mentioned three times by name in Acts (3:1; 4:13; 8:14), each time in association with Peter. Tradition says that John later went to Ephesus (perhaps just before the destruction of Jerusalem). He was eventually exiled by the Romans for a time to the island of Patmos (Rev. 1:9).

The author of this gospel is identified only as the disciple "whom Jesus loved" (13:23; 19:26; 20:2; 21:7, 20). His knowledge of Palestinian geography and Jewish customs makes it clear that he was a Palestinian Jew, and his meticulous attention to numbers (2:6; 6:13, 19; 21:8, 11) and names (1:45; 3:1; 11:1; 18:10) indicates that he was an eyewitness. This fits his own claim to be a witness of the events he described (1:14; 19:35; 21:24, 25). The disciple "whom Jesus loved" was part of the inner circle of disciples and was closely associated with Peter. The synoptic Gospels name this inner circle as Peter, James, and John. Since Peter is separate from the beloved disciple, only James and John are left. James was martyred too early to be the author (Acts 12:1, 2), so the apostle John was the author of this gospel. This conclusion from internal evidence is consistent with the external testimony of the early church. Irenaeus (c. A.D. 185) was a disciple of Polycarp who was in turn a disciple of the apostle John. In his *Against Heresies,* Irenaeus bore witness to Johannine authorship of this gospel and noted that John lived until the time of the emperor Trajan (A.D. 98–117). Clement of Alexandria, Theophilus of Antioch, Origen, and others also ascribe this book to John.

THE TIME OF JOHN

In spite of the strong internal and external testimony supporting Johannine authorship of this gospel, theological assumptions have motivated a number of critics to deny this claim. Until recently it was popular to propose a second-century date for this book. The discovery of the John Rylands Papyrus 52 containing portions of John 18:31–33, 37, 38 has overthrown this conjecture. This fragment has been dated at about A.D. 135, and a considerable period of time must have been required for John's gospel to be copied and circulated before it reached Egypt, where this papyrus was found.

On the other hand, John was written after the last of the synoptic Gospels (c. A.D. 66–68). His familiarity with the topography of Jerusalem (e.g., 5:2; 19:13) does not necessarily require a date before A.D. 70. Since John's three epistles and Revelation were written after his gospel, the probable range for this work is A.D. 60–90. By this time, John would have been one of the last surviving eyewitnesses of the Lord. According to tradition, John wrote this gospel in Ephesus.

THE CHRIST OF JOHN

This book presents the most powerful case in all the Bible for the deity of the incarnate Son of God. "A Man called Jesus" (9:11) is also "Christ, the Son of the living God" (6:69). The deity of Christ can be seen in His seven "I am" statements: "I am the bread of life" (6:35, 48); "I am the light of the world" (8:12; 9:5); "I am the door" (10:7, 9); "I am the good shepherd" (10:11, 14); "I am the resurrection and the life" (11:25); "I am the way, the truth, and the life" (14:6); "I am the true vine" (15:1–5). The seven signs (1—12) and the five witnesses (5:30–40) also point to His divine character. On certain occasions, Jesus equates Himself with the Old Testament "I AM," or Yahweh (see 4:25, 26; 8:24, 28, 58; 13:19; 18:5, 6, 8). Some of the most crucial affirmations of His deity are in 1:1; 8:58; 10:30; 14:9; 20:28.

The Word was God (1:1), but the Word also became flesh (1:14). The humanity of Jesus can be seen in His weariness (4:6), thirst (4:7), dependence (5:19), grief (11:35), troubled soul (12:27), and His anguish and death (19).

KEYS TO JOHN

Key Word: Believe That Jesus Is the Son of God—The Fourth Gospel has the clearest statement of purpose in the Bible: "But these are written that you may believe that Jesus is the Christ, the Son of God, and that believing you may have life in His name" (20:31). John selected the signs he used for the specific purpose of creating intellectual ("that you may believe") and spiritual ("that believing you may have life") conviction about the Son of God. The key verb in John is "believe," and requires both knowledge (8:32; 10:38) and volition (1:12; 3:19; 7:17).

The predominant theme of this gospel is the dual response of faith and unbelief to the person of Jesus Christ. Those who place their faith in the Son of God have eternal life, but those who reject Him are under the condemnation of God (3:36; 5:24–29; 10:27–29): this is the basic issue. John 1:11, 12 summarizes the responses of accepting or rejecting the Son of God that are traced through the rest of the book. The rejection of Jesus by His own people can be seen over and over in chapters 2 through 19 ("His own did not receive Him"), but John also lists a number of men and women who believed in Him ("But as many as received Him").

Key Verses: John 1:11-13 and John 20:30, 31—"He came to His own, and His own did not receive Him. But as many as received Him, to them He gave the right to become children of God, *even* to those who believe in His name: who were born, not of blood, nor of the will of the flesh, nor of the will of man, but of God" (1:11–13).

"And truly Jesus did many other signs in the presence of His disciples, which are not written in this book; but these are written that you may believe that Jesus is the Christ, the Son of God, and that believing you may have life in His name" (20:30, 31).

Key Chapter: John 3—John 3:16 is without doubt the most quoted and preached verse in all of Scripture. Captured in it is the gospel in its clearest and simplest form: that salvation is a gift of God and is obtainable only through belief. The conversation with Nicodemus and the testimony of John the Baptist provide the setting that clearly points out that being "born again" is the only way to find the "kingdom of God."

SURVEY OF JOHN

This most unusual gospel, with its distinct content and style, serves as a supplement to the three synoptics. It is easily the simplest and yet the most profound of the gospels, and for many people it is the greatest and most powerful. John writes his gospel for the specific purpose of bringing people to spiritual life through belief in the person and work of Jesus Christ. The five basic sections of this gospel are: the incarnation of the Son of God (1:1–18); the presentation of the Son of God (1:19—4:54); the opposition to the Son of God (5:1—12:50); the preparation of the disciples by the Son of God (13:1—17:26); the crucifixion and resurrection of the Son of God (18:1—21:25).

The Incarnation of the Son of God (1:1-18): This prologue introduces the rest of the book and gives the background for the historical narrative that follows. It dates the nature of Jesus, introduces His forerunner, clarifies His mission, and

FOCUS	INCARNATION OF THE SON OF GOD	PRESENTATION OF THE SON OF GOD	OPPOSITION TO THE SON OF GOD	PREPARATION OF THE DISCIPLES	CRUCIFIXION AND RESURRECTION OF THE SON OF GOD
REFERENCE	1:1—	1:19—	5:1—	13:1—	18:1—21:25
DIVISION	INTRODUCTION TO CHRIST	REVELATION OF CHRIST	REJECTION OF CHRIST	REVELATION OF CHRIST	REJECTION OF CHRIST
TOPIC	SEVEN MIRACLES			UPPER ROOM DISCOURSE	SUPREME MIRACLE
	THAT YOU MIGHT BELIEVE			THAT YOU MIGHT HAVE LIFE	
LOCATION	ISRAEL				
TIME	A FEW YEARS			A FEW HOURS	A FEW WEEKS

notes the rejection and acceptance He will find during His ministry.

The Presentation of the Son of God (1:19—4:54): In this section Christ is under careful consideration and scrutiny by Israel. He is introduced by John the Baptist who directs his own disciples to Christ. Shortly the author begins listing the seven signs, which continue through the next section. John carefully selects seven miracles out of the many that Christ accomplished (cf. John 21:25) in order to build a concise case for His deity. They are called signs because they symbolize the life-changing results of belief in Jesus—(1) water to wine: the ritual of law is replaced by the reality of grace (2:1–11); (2) healing the nobleman's son: the gospel brings spiritual restoration (4:46–54); (3) healing the paralytic: weakness is replaced by strength (5:1–16); (4) feeding the multitude: Christ satisfies spiritual hunger (6:1–13); (5) walking on water: the Lord transforms fear to faith (6:16–21); (6) sight to the man born blind: Jesus overcomes darkness and brings in light (9:1–7); (7) raising of Lazarus: the gospel brings people from death to life (11:1–44). These signs combine to show that Jesus is indeed the Son of God.

The Opposition to the Son of God (5:1—12:50): John's unusual pattern in these chapters is to record the reactions of belief and disbelief after the performance of one miracle before moving to the next. In a series of growing confrontations, John portrays the intense opposition that will culminate in the Lord's final rejection on the cross. Even though many people received Him, the inevitable crucifixion is foreshadowed in several places (2:4, 21, 22; 7:6, 39; 11:51, 52; 12:16).

The Preparation of the Disciples by the Son of God (13:1—17:26): John surveys the incarnation and public ministry of Jesus in twelve chapters, but radically changes the pace in the next five chapters to give a detailed account of a few crucial hours. In this clear and vivid recollection of Jesus' last discourse to His intimate disciples, John captures the Lord's words of comfort and assurance to a group of fearful and confused followers. Jesus knows that in less than twenty-four hours He will be on the cross. Therefore, His last words speak of all the resources that will be at the disciples' disposal after His departure. They will be indwelled and empowered by the Triune Godhead. The Upper Room Discourse contains the message of the epistles in capsule form as it reveals God's pattern for Christian living. In it, the key themes of servanthood, the Holy Spirit, and abiding in Christ are developed.

The Crucifixion and Resurrection of the Son of God (18:1—21:25): After recording Christ's high priestly prayer on behalf of His disciples and all who believe in Him "through their word" (17:20), John immediately launches into a dramatic description of Christ's arrest and trials before Annas, Caiaphas, and Pilate. In His crucifixion, Jesus willingly fulfills John the Baptist's prophetic words: "Behold! The Lamb of God who takes away the sin of the world!" (1:29). John closes his profound gospel with a particularly detailed account of the post-resurrection appearances of the Lord. The Resurrection is the ultimate sign that points to Jesus as the Son of God.

OUTLINE OF JOHN

Part One: The Incarnation of the Son of God (1:1–18)

I. The Deity of Christ 1:1, 2
II. The Preincarnate Work of Christ 1:3–5
III. The Forerunner of Christ 1:6–8
IV. The Rejection of Christ 1:9–11
V. The Acceptance of Christ 1:12, 13
VI. The Incarnation of Christ 1:14–18

Part Two: The Presentation of the Son of God (1:19—4:54)

I. The Presentation of Christ by John the Baptist 1:19–34
- A. John's Witness to the Priests and Levites 1:19–28
- B. John's Witness at Christ's Baptism ... 1:29–34

II. The Presentation of Christ to John's Disciples 1:35–51
- A. Andrew and Peter Follow Christ 1:35–42
- B. Philip and Nathanael Follow Christ... 1:43–51

III. The Presentation of Christ in Galilee 2:1–12
- A. First Sign: Christ Changes Water to Wine 2:1–10
- B. The Disciples Believe 2:11, 12

IV. The Presentation of Christ in Judea 2:13—3:36
- A. Christ Cleanses the Temple 2:13–25
- B. Christ Witnesses to Nicodemus 3:1–21
- C. John the Baptist Witnesses Concerning Christ 3:22–36

Part Three: The Opposition to the Son of God (5:1—12:50)

Part Four: The Preparation of the Disciples by the Son of God (13:1—17:26)

Part Five: The Crucifixion and Resurrection of the Son of God (18:1—21:25)

I. The Rejection of Christ............ 18:1—19:16

A. The Arrest of Christ 18:1–11
B. The Trials of Christ .... 18:12—19:16
1. First Jewish Trial Before Annas 18:12–23
2. Second Jewish Trial
Before Caiaphas 18:24–27
3. First Roman Trial Before Pilate 18:28–38
4. Second Roman Trial
Before Pilate............... 18:39—19:16

II. The Crucifixion of Christ............ 19:17–37

A. Christ's Crucifixion 19:17, 18
B. Pilate's Inscription................ 19:19–22
C. Soldiers Cast Lots 19:23, 24
D. Mary's Committal 19:25–27
E. Christ's Death 19:28–37

III. The Burial of Christ 19:38–42

IV. The Resurrection of Christ............. 20:1–10

V. The Appearances of Christ .... 20:11—21:25

A. Christ Appears to Mary Magdalene 20:11–18
B. Christ Appears to the Disciples
(Thomas Absent) 20:19–25
C. Christ Appears to the Disciples
(Thomas Present)............... 20:26–29
D. The Purpose of John's Gospel 20:30, 31
E. Christ Appears to the Seven Disciples 21:1–14
F. Christ Speaks to Peter........... 21:15–23
G. The Conclusion of John's Gospel.... 21:24, 25

CHAPTER 1

The Deity of Christ

IN the beginning [R]was the Word, and the
[R]Word was [R]with God, and the Word was
[R]God. 1 John 1:1 • Rev. 19:13 • [John 17:5] • [1 John 5:20]
2 He was in the beginning with God.

The Preincarnate Work of Christ

3 [R]All things were made through Him, and
without Him nothing was made that was
made. [Col. 1:16, 17]
4 [R]In Him was life, and [R]the life was the
light of men. [1 John 5:11] • John 8:12; 9:5; 12:46
5 And the light shines in the darkness, and
the darkness did not comprehend it.

The Forerunner of Christ

6 There was a [R]man sent from God, whose
name *was* John. Matt. 3:1–17
7 This man came for a [R]witness, to bear
witness of the Light, that all through him
might [R]believe. John 3:25–36; 5:33–35 • [John 3:16]
8 He was not that Light, but *was sent* to
bear witness of that [R]Light. Is. 9:2; 49:6

The Rejection of Christ

9 *That was* the true Light which gives
light to every man who comes into the world.
10 He was in the world, and the world was
made through Him, and [R]the world did not
know Him. Heb. 1:2
11 [R]He came to His [T]own, and His [T]own did
not receive Him. [Luke 19:14] ☆ • place • people

The Acceptance of Christ

12 But as many as received Him, to them He
gave the right to become children of God, to
those who believe in His name:
13 [R]who were born, not of blood, nor of the
will of the flesh, nor of the will of man, but of
God. [1 Pet. 1:23]

The Incarnation of Christ

14 And the Word became flesh and dwelt
among us, and [R]we beheld His glory, the glory
as of the only begotten of the Father, [R]full of
grace and truth. Is. 40:5 • [John 8:32; 14:6; 18:37]
15 John bore witness of Him and cried out,
saying, "This was He of whom I said, 'He who
comes after me [T]is preferred before me, for
He was before me.' " *ranks higher than I*
16 *And of His [R]fullness we have all received, and grace for grace. [Col. 1:19; 2:9]
17 For the law was given through Moses,
but [R]grace and [R]truth came through Jesus
Christ. [Rom. 5:21; 6:14] • [John 8:32; 14:6; 18:37]
18 No one has seen God at any time. [R]The
only begotten *Son, who is in the bosom of
the Father, He has declared *Him*. Ps. 2:7 ★

John's Witness to the Priests and Levites
Matt. 3:1–12; Mark 1:2–8; Luke 3:3–16

19 Now this is [R]the testimony of John, when
the Jews sent priests and Levites from Jerusalem to ask him, "Who are you?" John 5:33
20 [R]He confessed, and did not deny, but
confessed, "I am not the Christ." Luke 3:15
21 And they asked him, "What then? Are
you Elijah?" He said, "I am not." "Are you
the Prophet?" And he answered, "No."
22 Then they said to him, "Who are you,
that we may give an answer to those who
sent us? What do you say about yourself?"
23 He said: "I *am*

[R]*'The voice of one crying in the*
wilderness: Is. 40:3 ★
"Make straight the way of the LORD,"'

as the prophet Isaiah said."
24 Now those who were sent were from the
Pharisees.

1:16 NU *For* **1:18** NU *God*

25 And they asked him, saying, "Why then do you baptize if you are not the Christ, nor Elijah, nor the Prophet?"

26 John answered them, saying, [R]"I baptize with water, [R]but there stands One among you whom you do not know. Matt. 3:11 • Mal. 3:1

27 [R]"It is He who, coming after me, [T]is preferred before me, whose sandal strap I am not worthy to loose." Acts 19:4 • *ranks higher than I*

28 These things were done [R]in *Bethabara beyond the Jordan, where John was baptizing. Judg. 7:24

John's Witness at Christ's Baptism
Matt. 3:13–17; Mark 1:9–11; Luke 3:21, 22

29 The next day John saw Jesus coming toward him, and said, "Behold! The Lamb of God who takes away the sin of the world!

30 "This is He of whom I said, 'After me comes a Man who [T]is preferred before me, for He was before me.' *ranks higher than I*

31 "I did not know Him; but that He should be revealed to Israel, [R]therefore I came baptizing with water." Matt. 3:6

32 [R]And John bore witness, saying, "I saw the Spirit descending from heaven like a dove, and He remained upon Him. Mark 1:10

33 "I did not know Him, but He who sent me to baptize with water said to me, 'Upon whom you see [R]the Spirit descending, and remaining on Him, this is He who baptizes with the Holy Spirit.' Is. 42:1; 61:1★

34 "And I have seen and testified that [R]this is the Son of God." Ps. 2:7; Luke 1:35★

Andrew and Peter Follow Christ

35 Again, the next day, John stood with two of his disciples.

36 And looking at Jesus as He walked, he said, [R]"Behold the Lamb of God!" John 1:29

37 The two disciples heard him speak, and they [R]followed Jesus. Matt. 4:20, 22

38 Then Jesus turned, and seeing them following, said to them, "What do you seek?" They said to Him, "Rabbi" (which is to say, when translated, Teacher), "where are You staying?"

39 He said to them, "Come and see." They came and saw where He was staying, and remained with Him that day (now it was about the tenth hour).

40 One of the two who heard John *speak,* and followed Him, was [R]Andrew, Simon Peter's brother. Matt. 4:18

41 He first found his own brother Simon, and said to him, "We have found the Messiah" (which is translated, the Christ).

42 And he brought him to Jesus. Now when Jesus looked at him, He said, "You are Simon the son of *Jonah. You shall be called Cephas" (which is translated, [T]A Stone). *Peter*

Philip and Nathanael Follow Christ

43 The following day Jesus wanted to go to Galilee, and He found [R]Philip and said to him, "Follow Me." John 6:5; 12:21, 22; 14:8, 9

44 Now [R]Philip was from Bethsaida, the city of Andrew and Peter. John 12:21

45 Philip found Nathanael and said to him, "We have found Him of whom Moses in the law, and also the prophets, wrote—Jesus [R]of Nazareth, the son of Joseph." [Matt. 2:23]

46 And Nathanael said to him, [R]"Can anything good come out of Nazareth?" Philip said to him, "Come and see." John 7:41, 42, 52

47 Jesus saw Nathanael coming toward Him, and said of him, "Behold, an Israelite indeed, in whom is no [T]guile!" *deceit*

48 Nathanael said to Him, "How do You know me?" Jesus answered and said to him, "Before Philip called you, when you were under the fig tree, I saw you."

49 Nathanael answered and said to Him, "Rabbi, [R]You are the Son of God! You are [R]the King of Israel!" Ps. 2:7★ • Matt. 21:5

50 Jesus answered and said to him, "Because I said to you, 'I saw you under the fig tree,' do you believe? You will see greater things than these."

51 And He said to him, "Most assuredly, I say to you, [R]hereafter* you shall see heaven open, and the angels of God ascending and descending upon the Son of Man." Gen. 28:12

CHAPTER 2

Christ Changes Water to Wine

ON the third day there was a [R]wedding in [R]Cana of Galilee, and the [R]mother of Jesus was there. [Heb. 13:4] • Josh. 19:28 • John 19:25

2 Now both Jesus and His disciples were invited to the wedding.

3 And when they ran out of wine, the mother of Jesus said to Him, "They have no wine."

4 Jesus said to her, [R]"Woman, [R]what does your concern have to do with Me? My hour has not yet come." John 19:26 • 2 Sam. 16:10

5 His mother said to the servants, "Whatever He says to you, do *it.*"

6 Now there were set there six waterpots of stone, [R]according to the manner of purification of the Jews, containing twenty or thirty gallons apiece. [Mark 7:3]

7 Jesus said to them, "Fill the waterpots with water." And they filled them up to the brim.

8 And He said to them, "Draw *some* out now, and take *it* to the master of the feast." And they took *it.*

9 When the master of the feast had tasted [R]the water that was made wine, and did not know where it came from (but the servants

1:28 NU, M *Bethany* **1:42** NU *John*
1:51 NU omits *hereafter*

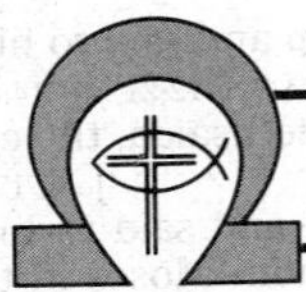

THE CITY OF NAZARETH

A town of lower Galilee where Jesus spent His boyhood years (Matt. 2:23), Nazareth is located about thirty miles from the Mediterranean Sea. Its mild climate and sheltered location in the hills of Galilee made Nazareth an ideal place to live.

Nazareth is not mentioned in the Old Testament, although artifacts discovered on the site indicate that Nazareth was a settled community at least 1,500 years before the New Testament era. In Jesus' time, the town apparently had a bad reputation in morals and religion. This may have prompted Nathanael, when he first learned of Jesus of Nazareth, to ask, "Can anything good come out of Nazareth?" (John 1:46).

The angel appeared to Mary at Nazareth and informed her of the coming birth of Jesus (Luke 1:26–38). After their sojourn in Egypt (Matt. 2:19–22), Joseph and Mary brought Jesus back to Nazareth where they had lived before His birth (Matt. 2:23). Here Jesus spent the greater part of His life (Luke 3:23). Apparently He was well received as a young man (Luke 2:42; 4:16), but His townspeople later rejected Him (Mark 6:1–6).

Because of His close association with the city, He became known as "Jesus of Nazareth" (John 1:45). There was also prophetic significance to His being known as a "Nazarene"—"that it might be fulfilled which was spoken by the prophets, 'He shall be called a Nazarene'" (Matt. 2:23).

Modern Nazareth, known as En-Nasira, is a city of about 30,000 people. Its location on the site of old Nazareth makes it impossible to conduct extensive archaeological excavations. The Church of the Annunciation, the major tourist attraction, has a special significance for all Bible students. This church contains a cave where, according to legend, the angel Gabriel appeared to Mary (Luke 1:26–31). Rebuilding and excavation work on this site has turned up evidence that a Christian church existed at this location as early as the fourth century A.D.

Photo by Howard Vos

Modern Nazareth is located on the site of old Nazareth where Jesus grew up (Luke 2:39; 4:16, 31–34).

who had drawn the water knew), the master
of the feast called the bridegroom. John 4:46
10 And he said to him, "Every man at the
beginning sets out the good wine, and when
the *guests* have well drunk, then that *which*
is inferior; *but* you have kept the good wine
until now."

The Disciples Believe

11 This beginning of signs Jesus did in Cana
of Galilee, and [T]manifested His glory; and His
disciples believed in Him. *revealed*
12 After this He went down to Capernaum,
He, His mother, His brothers, and His disciples; and they did not stay there many days.

Christ Cleanses the Temple

13 Now the Passover of the Jews was at
hand, and Jesus went up to Jerusalem.
14 [R]And He found in the temple those who
sold oxen and sheep and doves, and the
moneychangers doing business. Mal. 3:1 ★
15 When He had made a whip of cords, He
drove them all out of the temple, with the
sheep and the oxen, and poured out the
changers' money and overturned the tables.
16 And He said to those who sold doves,
"Take these things away! Do not make My
Father's house a house of merchandise!"
17 Then His disciples remembered that it
was written, [R]*"Zeal for Your house *has*
eaten Me up." Ps. 69:9 ★
18 So the Jews answered and said to Him,
[R]"What sign do You show to us, since You do
these things?" Matt. 12:38
19 Jesus answered and said to them, [R]"Destroy this temple, and in three days I will
raise it up." Matt. 26:61; 27:40; Acts 10:40 ☆
20 Then the Jews said, "It has taken forty-
six years to build this temple, and will You
raise it up in three days?"
21 But He was speaking [R]of the temple of
His body. [1 Cor. 3:16; 6:19]
22 Therefore, when He had risen from the
dead, His disciples remembered that He had
said this *to them; and they believed the
Scripture and the word which Jesus had said.
23 Now when He was in Jerusalem at the
[R]Passover, during the feast, many believed in
His name when they saw the signs which He
did. [Acts 2:22]
24 But Jesus did not commit Himself to
them, because He [R]knew all *men*, Rev. 2:23
25 and had no need that anyone should
testify of man, for [R]He knew what was in
man. Matt. 9:4

CHAPTER 3

Christ Witnesses to Nicodemus

THERE was a man of the Pharisees named
Nicodemus, a ruler of the Jews.
2 [R]This man came to Jesus by night and
said to Him, "Rabbi, we know that You are a
teacher come from God; for [R]no one can do
these signs that You do unless [R]God is with
him." John 7:50; 19:39 • John 9:16, 33 • [Acts 10:38]
3 Jesus answered and said to him, "Most
assuredly, I say to you, unless one is born
again, he cannot see the kingdom of God."
4 Nicodemus said to Him, "How can a man
be born when he is old? Can he enter a
second time into his mother's womb and be
born?"
5 Jesus answered, "Most assuredly, I say
to you, unless one is born of water and the
Spirit, he cannot enter the kingdom of God.
6 "That which is born of the flesh is flesh,
and that which is born of the Spirit is spirit.
7 "Do not marvel that I said to you, 'You
must be born again.'
8 [R]"The wind blows where it wishes, and
you hear the sound of it, but cannot tell
where it comes from and where it goes. So is
everyone who is born of the Spirit." Eccl. 11:5
9 Nicodemus answered and said to Him,
[R]"How can these things be?" John 6:52, 60
10 Jesus answered and said to him, "Are
you the teacher of Israel, and do not know
these things?
11 "Most assuredly, I say to you, We speak
what We know and testify what We have
seen, and you do not receive Our witness.
12 "If I have told you earthly things and
you do not believe, how will you believe if I
tell you heavenly things?
13 [R]"No one has ascended to heaven but He
who came down from heaven, *that is*, the
Son of Man *who is in heaven. Eph. 4:9
14 [R]"And as Moses lifted up the serpent in
the wilderness, even so [R]must the Son of Man
be lifted up, Num. 21:9 • John 8:28; 12:34; 19:18 ☆
15 "that whoever believes in Him should
*not perish but [R]have eternal life. John 3:36
16 [R]"For God so loved the world that He
gave His only begotten [R]Son, that whoever
believes in Him should not perish but have
everlasting life. Rom. 5:8 • [Is. 9:6]
17 "For God did not send His Son into the
world to condemn the world, but [R]that the
world through Him might be saved. Matt. 1:21 ☆
18 [R]"He who believes in Him is not condemned; but he who does not believe is
condemned already, because he has not believed in the name of the only begotten Son
of God. John 5:24; 6:40, 47; 20:31
19 "And this is the condemnation, [R]that the
light has come into the world, and men loved
darkness rather than light, because their
deeds were evil. [John 1:4, 9–11]
20 "For [R]everyone practicing evil hates the
light and does not come to the light, lest his
deeds should be exposed. Eph. 5:11, 13

2:17 NU, M *will eat* **2:22** NU, M omit *to them*
3:13 NU omits *who is in heaven*
3:15 NU omits *not perish but*

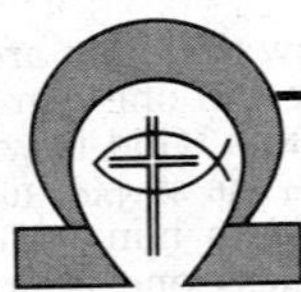

THE KINGDOM OF GOD

The kingdom of God refers to God's rule of grace in the world, a period foretold by the prophets of the Old Testament and identified by Jesus as beginning with His ministry.

A conquered and downtrodden Israel looked forward to the day when God, the King, would display His power and establish His kingdom of peace and righteousness (Zech. 9:9; Is. 24:23). His deliverance was often associated with the coming of a Davidic king (Is. 9:7).

In many striking ways Jesus proclaimed that He was the fulfillment of the Old Testament expectations of God's deliverance (Luke 4:17–21). One way He expressed this idea was by the phrase, "the kingdom of God." To Nicodemus He declared, "Unless one is born again, he cannot see the kingdom of God" (John 3:3). He made it clear to others that the kingdom was already present in His ministry (Matt. 12:28). He compared Himself to a sower scattering seed in a field, with the good seed taking root and growing among "the sons of the kingdom" (Matt. 13:38; see illustration).

Jesus also declared that a day was coming when the kingdom of God would be manifested in a different way, not yet seen, and that its coming would be soon (Matt. 16:28). He explained that the kingdom was present in an unexpected form, like a hidden treasure (Matt. 13:44). Although the Gospels focus on the present aspect of the kingdom, it is also clear that the kingdom will be realized perfectly only at the second coming of Christ.

In its spiritual nature, the kingdom of God is the salvation of His people, and the kingdom is His gift. It is also a gift of forgiveness of sin. Those who are forgiven must also forgive others (Matt. 18:35). Participation in the new reality of the kingdom involves the follower of Jesus in a call to the highest righteousness (Matt. 5:20).

Jesus compared Himself to a sower scattering seed in a field, with the good seed taking root and growing among "the sons of the kingdom" (Matt. 13:38).

21 "But he who does the truth comes to the light, that his deeds may be clearly seen, that they have been [R]done in God." 1 Cor. 15:10

John the Baptist Witnesses Concerning Christ

22 After these things Jesus and His disciples came into the land of Judea, and there He remained with them [R]and baptized. John 4:1, 2

23 Now John also was baptizing in Aenon near Salim, because there was much water there. And they came and were baptized.

24 For [R]John had not yet been thrown into prison. Matt. 4:12; 14:3

25 Then there arose a dispute between *some* of John's disciples and the Jews about purification.

26 And they came to John and said to him, "Rabbi, He who was with you beyond the Jordan, to whom you have testified—behold, He is baptizing, and all are coming to Him!"

27 John answered and said, [R]"A man can receive nothing unless it has been given to him from heaven. 1 Cor. 3:5, 6; 4:7

28 "You yourselves bear me witness, that I said, [R]'I am not the Christ,' but, [R]'I have been sent before Him.' John 1:19–27 • Mal. 3:1

29 [R]"He who has the bride is the bridegroom; but [R]the friend of the bridegroom, who stands and hears him, rejoices greatly because of the bridegroom's voice. Therefore this joy of mine is fulfilled. [2 Cor. 11:2] • Song 5:1

30 "He must increase, but I *must* decrease.

31 "He who comes from above is above all; [R]he who is of the earth is earthly and speaks of the earth. [R]He who comes from heaven is above all. 1 Cor. 15:47 • John 6:33

32 "And [R]what He has seen and heard, that He testifies; [R]and no one receives His testimony. John 3:11; 15:15 • Is. 53:1, 3★

33 "He who has received His testimony [R]has certified that God is true. 1 John 5:10

34 [R]"For He whom God has sent speaks the words of God, for God does not give the Spirit [R]by measure. Deut. 18:18★ • John 1:16

35 [R]"The Father loves the Son, and has given all things into His hand. [Heb. 2:8]

36 [R]"He who believes in the Son has everlasting life; and he who does not believe the Son shall not see life, but the [R]wrath of God abides on him." John 3:16, 17; 6:47 • Rom. 1:18

CHAPTER 4

Christ Witnesses to the Woman at the Well

THEREFORE, when the Lord knew that the Pharisees had heard that Jesus made and baptized more disciples than John

2 (though Jesus Himself did not baptize, but His disciples),

3 He left Judea and departed again to Galilee.

4 But He needed to go through Samaria.

5 So He came to a city of Samaria which is called Sychar, near the plot of ground that Jacob [R]gave to his son Joseph. Gen. 48:22

6 Now Jacob's well was there. Jesus therefore, being wearied from *His* journey, sat thus by the well. It was about the sixth hour.

7 A woman of Samaria came to draw water. Jesus said to her, "Give Me a drink."

8 For His disciples had gone away into the city to buy food.

9 Then the woman of Samaria said to Him, "How is it that You, being a Jew, ask a drink from me, a Samaritan woman?" For [R]Jews have no dealings with Samaritans. Acts 10:28

10 Jesus answered and said to her, "If you knew the [R]gift of God, and who it is who says to you, 'Give Me a drink,' you would have asked Him, and He would have given you [R]living water." [Rom. 5:15] • Is. 12:3; 44:3

11 The woman said to Him, "Sir, You have nothing to draw with, and the well is deep. Where then do You get that living water?

12 "Are You greater than our father Jacob, who gave us the well, and drank from it himself, as well as his sons and his livestock?"

13 Jesus answered and said to her, "Whoever drinks of this water will thirst again,

14 "but [R]whoever drinks of the water that I shall give him will never thirst. But the water that I shall give him [R]will become in him a fountain of water springing up into everlasting life." [John 6:35, 58] • John 7:37, 38

15 [R]The woman said to Him, "Sir, give me this water, that I may not thirst, nor come here to draw." John 6:34, 35; 17:2, 3

16 Jesus said to her, "Go, call your husband, and come here."

17 The woman answered and said, "I have no husband." Jesus said to her, "You have well said, 'I have no husband,'

18 "for you have had five husbands, and the one whom you now have is not your husband; in that you spoke truly."

19 The woman said to Him, "Sir, [R]I perceive that You are a prophet. Luke 7:16, 39; 24:19

20 "Our fathers worshiped on this mountain, and you *Jews* say that in Jerusalem is the place where one ought to worship."

21 Jesus said to her, "Woman, believe Me, the hour is coming [R]when you will neither on this mountain, nor in Jerusalem, worship the Father. 1 Tim. 2:8

22 "You worship [R]what you do not know; we know what we worship, for [R]salvation is of the Jews. [2 Kin. 17:28–41] • [Rom. 3:1; 9:4, 5]

23 "But the hour is coming, and now is, when the true worshipers will worship the Father in spirit [R]and truth; for the Father is seeking such to worship Him. [John 1:17]

24 "God *is* Spirit, and those who worship Him must worship in spirit and truth."

25 The woman said to Him, "I know that Messiah is coming" (who is called Christ). "When He comes, He will tell us all things."

26 Jesus said to her, [R]"I who speak to you
am *He*." Dan. 9:25; Matt. 26:63, 64; Mark 14:61, 62★

Christ Witnesses to the Disciples

27 And at this *point* His disciples came, and
they marveled that He talked with a woman;
yet no one said, "What do You seek?" or,
"Why are You talking with her?"
28 The woman then left her waterpot, went
her way into the city, and said to the men,
29 "Come, see a Man [R]who told me all
things that I ever did. Could this be the
Christ?" John 4:25
30 Then they went out of the city and came
to Him.
31 In the meantime His disciples urged Him,
saying, "Rabbi, eat."
32 But He said to them, "I have food to eat
of which you do not know."
33 Therefore the disciples said to one another, "Has anyone brought Him *anything* to
eat?"
34 Jesus said to them, [R]"My food is to do the
will of Him who sent Me, and to [R]finish His
work. Ps. 40:7, 8 • [John 6:38; 17:4; 19:30]
35 "Do you not say, 'There are still four
months and *then* comes [R]the harvest'? Behold, I say to you, lift up your eyes and look
at the fields, [R]for they are already white for
harvest! Gen. 8:22 • Matt. 9:37
36 [R]"And he who reaps receives wages, and
gathers fruit for eternal life, that [R]both he
who sows and he who reaps may rejoice
together. Dan. 12:3 • 1 Thess. 2:19
37 "For in this the saying is true: [R]'One sows
and another reaps.' 1 Cor. 3:5–9
38 "I sent you to reap that for which you
have not labored; [R]others have labored, and
you have entered into their labors." [1 Pet. 1:12]

Christ Witnesses to the Samaritans

39 And many of the Samaritans of that city
believed in Him [R]because of the word of the
woman who testified, "He told me all that I
ever did." John 4:29
40 So when the Samaritans had come to
Him, they urged Him to stay with them; and
He stayed there two days.
41 And many more believed because of His
own [R]word. Luke 4:32
42 Then they said to the woman, "Now we
believe, not because of what you said, for [R]we
have heard for ourselves and know that this
is indeed *the Christ, the Savior of the
world." 1 John 4:14

Christ Is Received by the Galileans

43 Now after the two days He departed
from there and went to Galilee.
44 For Jesus Himself testified that a prophet
has no honor in his own country.
45 So when He came to Galilee, the Galileans received Him, having seen all the things
He did in Jerusalem at the feast; [R]for they
also had gone to the feast. Deut. 16:16

Christ Heals the Nobleman's Son

46 So Jesus came again to Cana of Galilee
[R]where He had made the water wine. And
there was a certain [T]nobleman whose son
was sick at Capernaum. John 2:1, 11 • *royal official*
47 When he heard that Jesus had come out
of Judea into Galilee, he went to Him and
implored Him to come down and heal his son,
for he was at the point of death.
48 Then Jesus said to him, [R]"Unless you
people see signs and wonders, you will by no
means believe." 1 Cor. 1:22
49 The nobleman said to Him, "Sir, come
down before my child dies!"
50 Jesus said to him, "Go your way; your
son lives." So the man believed the word that
Jesus spoke to him, and he went his way.
51 And as he was now going down, his
servants met him and told *him*, saying, "Your
son lives!"
52 Then he inquired of them the hour when
he got better. And they said to him, "Yesterday at the seventh hour the fever left him."
53 So the father knew that *it was* at the
same hour in which Jesus said to him, "Your
son lives." And he himself believed, and his
whole household.
54 This again *is* the second sign *that* Jesus
did when He had come out of Judea into
Galilee.

CHAPTER 5

Christ Heals the Paralytic Man

AFTER this there was a feast of the Jews,
and Jesus went up to Jerusalem.
2 Now there is in Jerusalem [R]by the Sheep
Gate a pool, which is called in Hebrew, *Bethesda, having five porches. Neh. 3:1, 32; 12:39
3 In these lay a great multitude of sick
people, blind, lame, [T]paralyzed, *waiting for
the moving of the water. *withered*
4 For an angel went down at a certain time
into the pool and stirred up the water; then
whoever stepped in first, after the stirring of
the water, was made well of whatever disease
he had.
5 Now a certain man was there who had
an infirmity thirty-eight years.
6 When Jesus saw him lying there, and
knew that he already had been *in that condition* a long time, He said to him, "Do you
want to be made well?"
7 The sick man answered Him, "Sir, I have
no man to put me into the pool when the
water is stirred up; but while I am coming,
another steps down before me."

4:42 NU omits *the Christ* **5:2** NU *Bethzatha*
5:3 NU omits the rest of v. 3 and all of v. 4.

8 Jesus said to him, [R]"Rise, take up your
bed and walk." Luke 5:24
9 And immediately the man was made
well, took up his bed, and walked. And [R]that
day was the Sabbath. John 9:14

Christ Heals on the Sabbath

10 The Jews therefore said to him who was
cured, "It is the Sabbath; [R]it is not lawful for
you to carry *your* bed." Jer. 17:21, 22
11 He answered them, "He who made me
well said to me, 'Take up your bed and
walk.'"
12 Then they asked him, "Who is the Man
who said to you, 'Take up your bed and
walk'?"
13 But the one who was [R]healed did not
know who it was, for Jesus had withdrawn, a
multitude being in *that* place. Luke 13:14; 22:51
14 Afterward Jesus found him in the temple, and said to him, "See, you have been
made well. [R]Sin no more, lest a worse thing
come upon you." John 8:11
15 The man departed and told the Jews that
it was Jesus who had made him well.
16 For this reason the Jews persecuted
Jesus, *and sought to kill Him, because He
had done these things on the Sabbath.

Equality with God in Nature

17 But Jesus answered them, [R]"My Father
has been working until now, and I have been
working." [John 9:4; 17:4]
18 Therefore the Jews sought all the more
to kill Him, because He not only broke the
Sabbath, but also said that God was His
Father, making Himself equal with God.

Equality with God in Power

19 Then Jesus answered and said to them,
"Most assuredly, I say to you, [R]the Son can
do nothing of Himself, but what He sees the
Father do; for whatever He does, the Son also
does in like manner. John 5:30; 6:38; 8:28; 12:49; 14:10
20 "For the Father loves the Son, and
[R]shows Him all things that He Himself does;
and He will show Him greater works than
these, that you may marvel. [Matt. 11:27]

21 "For as the Father raises the dead and
gives life to *them*, [R]even so the Son gives life
to whom He will. [John 11:25]

Equality with God in Authority

22 "For the Father judges no one, but [R]has
committed all judgment to the Son, [Acts 17:31]
23 "that all should honor the Son just as
they honor the Father. [R]He who does not
honor the Son does not honor the Father who
sent Him. 1 John 2:23

24 Most assuredly, I say to you, [R]he who
hears My word and believes in Him who sent
Me has everlasting life, and shall not come
into judgment, [R]but has passed from death
into life. John 3:16, 18; 6:47 • [1 John 3:14]

25 "Most assuredly, I say to you, the hour is
coming, and now is, when [R]the dead will hear
the voice of the Son of God; and those who
hear will live. [Col. 2:13]
26 "For [R]as the Father has life in Himself, so
He has granted the Son to have [R]life in
Himself, Ps. 36:9 • 1 Cor. 15:45
27 "and [R]has given Him authority to execute judgment also, [R]because He is the Son
of Man. [Acts 10:42; 17:31] • Dan. 7:13
28 "Do not marvel at this; for the hour is
coming in which all who are in the graves
will [R]hear His voice [1 Thess. 4:15–17]
29 [R]"and come forth—[R]those who have
done good, to the resurrection of life, and
those who have done evil, to the resurrection
of condemnation. Is. 26:19 • Dan. 12:2
30 [R]"I can of Myself do nothing. As I hear, I
judge; and My judgment is righteous, because [R]I do not seek My own will but the will
of the Father who sent Me. John 5:19 • Matt. 26:39

Witness of John the Baptist

31 [R]"If I bear witness of Myself, My witness
is not [T]true. John 8:14 • *valid* as testimony
32 [R]"There is another who bears witness of
Me, and I know that the witness which He
witnesses of Me is true. [Matt. 3:17]

5:16 NU omits *and sought to kill Him*

5:24 Everlasting Life—One benefit of finding new life in Christ is called in the Bible "everlasting [eternal] life." The character of this great reality may be summarized by carefully looking at each word. The word *life* stresses the quality of this new relationship to God (Page 1251—John 10:10). It does not mean, of course, that we are not physically alive before salvation; it simply stresses the fact that we enter a new, personal relationship with God that gives us a fullness of spiritual vitality that we lacked before (Page 1261—John 17:3).

The word *everlasting* emphasizes life without end. Though it will not be completely fulfilled until our future bodily redemption (see Page 1333—Rom. 8:23), it is still a present possession that can never perish (Page 1252—John 10:28).

Everlasting life must not be conceived of as an exclusively future possession. Rather, its possession is clearly seen in our actions. Thus, "no murderer has eternal life abiding in him" (Page 1497—1 John 3:15). Indeed, love is the confirming evidence that we do, in fact, have eternal life (Page 1497—1 John 3:14).

The greatness of this spiritual reality constitutes a wonderful incentive to vigorously proclaim the gospel to those who are still "dead in trespasses and sins" (Page 1387—Eph. 2:1).

Now turn to Page 1368—2 Cor. 5:17: New Nature.

33 "You have sent to John, [R]and he has
borne witness to the truth. [John 1:15, 19, 27, 32]
34 "Yet I do not receive testimony from
man, but I say these things that you may be
saved.
35 "He was the burning and [R]shining lamp,
and [R]you were willing for a time to rejoice in
his light. 2 Pet. 1:19 • Mark 6:20

Witness of the Works of Christ

36 "But I have a greater witness than
John's; for [R]the works which the Father has
given Me to finish—the very [R]works that I
do—bear witness of Me, that the Father has
sent Me. John 3:2; 10:25; 17:4 • John 9:16; 10:38

Witness of the Father

37 "And the Father Himself, who sent Me,
has testified of Me. You have neither heard
His voice at any time, nor seen His form.
38 "But you do not have His word abiding
in you, because whom He sent, Him you do
not believe.

Witness of the Scriptures

39 "You search the Scriptures, for in them
you think you have eternal life; and [R]these
are they which testify of Me. Luke 24:27
40 [R]"But you are not willing to come to Me
that you may have life. [John 1:11; 3:19]
41 "I do not receive honor from men.
42 "But I know you, that you do not have
the love of God in you.
43 "I have come in My Father's name, and
you do not receive Me; if another comes in
his own name, him you will receive.
44 "How can you believe, who receive
honor from one another, and do not seek the
honor that *comes* from the only God?
45 "Do not think that I shall accuse you to
the Father; [R]there is *one* who accuses you—
Moses, in whom you trust. Rom. 2:12
46 "For if you believed Moses, you would
believe Me; for he wrote about Me.
47 "But if you [R]do not believe his writings,
how will you believe My words?" Luke 16:29, 31

CHAPTER 6

Christ Feeds 5,000
Matt. 14:13–21; Mark 6:31–44; Luke 9:11–17

AFTER [R]these things Jesus went over the
Sea of Galilee, which is *the Sea* of
[R]Tiberias. Mark 6:32 • John 6:23; 21:1
2 Then a great multitude followed Him,
because they saw His signs which He performed on those who were [T]diseased. *sick*
3 And Jesus went up on a mountain, and
there He sat with His disciples.
4 [R]Now the Passover, a feast of the Jews,
was near. Deut. 16:1
5 [R]Then Jesus lifted up *His* eyes, and seeing a great multitude coming toward Him, He
said to [R]Philip, "Where shall we buy bread,
that these may eat?" Matt. 14:14 • John 1:43
6 But this He said to test him, for He
Himself knew what He would do.
7 Philip answered Him, [R]"Two hundred
denarii worth of bread is not sufficient for
them, that every one of them may have a
little." Num. 11:21, 22
8 One of His disciples, [R]Andrew, Simon
Peter's brother, said to Him, John 1:40
9 "There is a lad here who has five barley
loaves and two small fish, [R]but what are they
among so many?" 2 Kin. 4:43
10 Then Jesus said, "Make the people sit
down." Now there was much grass in the
place. So the men sat down, in number about
five thousand.
11 And Jesus took the loaves, and when He
had given thanks He distributed *them* *to the
disciples, and the disciples to those sitting
down; and likewise of the fish, as much as
they wanted.
12 So when they were filled, He said to His
disciples, "Gather up the fragments that
remain, so that nothing is lost."
13 Therefore they gathered *them* up, and
filled twelve baskets with the fragments of
the five barley loaves which were left over by
those who had eaten.
14 Then those men, when they had seen the
sign that Jesus did, said, "This is truly the
Prophet who is to come into the world."

Christ Walks on the Water
Matt. 14:22–33; Mark 6:45–52

15 Therefore when Jesus perceived that
they were about to come and take Him by
force to make Him [R]king, He departed again
to a mountain by Himself alone. [John 18:36]
16 [R]And when evening came, His disciples
went down to the sea, Matt. 14:23
17 got into the boat, and went over the sea
toward Capernaum. And it was now dark,
and Jesus had not come to them.
18 Then the sea arose because a great wind
was blowing.
19 So when they had rowed about [T]three or
four miles, they saw Jesus walking on the sea
and drawing near the boat; and they were
[R]afraid. Lit. *25 or 30 stadia* • Matt. 17:6
20 But He said to them, [R]"It is I; do not be
afraid." Is. 43:1, 2
21 Then they willingly received Him into
the boat, and immediately the boat was at the
land where they were going.

"I Am the Bread of Life"

22 On the following day, when the people
who were standing on the other side of the
sea saw that there was no other boat there,

6:11 NU omits *to the disciples, and the disciples*

TITLES OF CHRIST

The two most popular titles or names Christians use in speaking of our Lord are *Jesus*, a transliteration of the Hebrew word *Joshua*, which means "Yahweh Is Salvation," and *Christ*, a translation of the Greek term *Christos*, meaning "Anointed One" or "Messiah." Following are some other significant names or titles for Christ used in the New Testament. Each title expresses a distinct truth about Jesus and His relationship to believers.

The Good Shepherd cares for His sheep.

Name or Title	Significance	Biblical Reference
Adam, Last Adam	First of the new race of the redeemed	1 Cor. 15:45
Alpha and Omega	The beginning and ending of all things	Rev. 21:6
Bread of Life	The one essential food	John 6:35
Chief Cornerstone	A sure foundation for life	Eph. 2:20
Chief Shepherd	Protector, sustainer, and guide	1 Pet. 5:4
Firstborn from the Dead	Leads us into resurrection and eternal life	Col. 1:18
Good Shepherd	Provider and caretaker	John 10:11
Great Shepherd of the Sheep	Trustworthy guide and protector	Heb. 13:20
High Priest	A perfect sacrifice for our sins	Heb. 3:1
Holy One of God	Sinless in His nature	Mark 1:24
Immanuel (God With Us)	Stands with us in all of life's circumstances	Matt. 1:23
King of Kings, Lord of Lords	The Almighty, before whom every knee will bow	Rev. 19:16
Lamb of God	Gave His life as a sacrifice on our behalf	John 1:29
Light of the World	Brings hope in the midst of darkness	John 9:5
Lord of Glory	The power and presence of the living God	1 Cor. 2:8
Mediator between God and Men	Brings us into God's presence redeemed and forgiven	1 Tim. 2:5
Only Begotten of the Father	The unique, one-of-a-kind Son of God	John 1:14
Prophet	Faithful proclaimer of the truths of God	Acts 3:22
Savior	Delivers from sin and death	Luke 1:47
Seed of Abraham	Mediator of God's covenant	Gal. 3:16
Son of Man	Identifies with us in our humanity	Matt. 18:11
The Word	Present with God at the creation	John 1:1

except *that one *which His disciples had
entered, and that Jesus had not entered the
boat with His disciples, but His disciples had
gone away alone—
23 however, other boats came from Tiberias, near the place where they ate bread
after the Lord had given thanks—
24 when the people therefore saw that Jesus
was not there, nor His disciples, they also got
into boats and came to Capernaum, [R]seeking
Jesus. Luke 4:42
25 And when they found Him on the other
side of the sea, they said to Him, "Rabbi,
when did You come here?"
26 Jesus answered them and said, "Most
assuredly, I say to you, you seek Me, not
because you saw the signs, but because you
ate of the loaves and were filled.
27 [R]"Do not labor for the food which perishes, but [R]for the food which endures to
everlasting life, which the Son of Man will
give you, [R]because God the Father has set His
seal on Him." Matt. 6:19 • John 4:14 • Acts 2:22
28 Then they said to Him, "What shall we
do, that we may work the works of God?"
29 Jesus answered and said to them, [R]"This
is the work of God, that you believe in Him
whom He sent." [1 John 3:23]
30 Therefore they said to Him, "What sign
will You perform then, that we may see it and
believe You? What work will You do?
31 [R]"Our fathers ate the manna in the desert; as it is written, [R]*'He gave them bread
from heaven to eat.'*" Ex. 16:15 • Ps. 78:24
32 Then Jesus said to them, "Most assuredly, I say to you, Moses did not give you
the bread from heaven, but [R]My Father gives
you the true bread from heaven. John 3:13, 16
33 "For the bread of God is He who comes
down from heaven and gives life to the
world."
34 [R]Then they said to Him, "Lord, give us
this bread always." John 4:15
35 And Jesus said to them, [R]"I am the bread
of life. [R]He who comes to Me shall never
hunger, and he who believes in Me shall
never [R]thirst. John 6:48, 58 • John 4:14; 7:37 • Is. 55:1, 2
36 "But I said to you that you have seen Me
and yet [R]do not believe. John 10:26
37 "All that the Father gives Me will come
to Me, and [R]the one who comes to Me I will
[T]by no means cast out. 2 Tim. 2:19 • *certainly not*
38 "For I have come down from heaven,
[R]not to do My own will, [R]but the will of Him
who sent Me. Matt. 26:39 • John 4:34
39 "This is the will of the Father who sent
Me, that of all He has given Me I should lose
nothing, but should raise it up at the last day.
40 "And this is the will of Him who sent Me,
[R]that everyone who sees the Son and believes
in Him may have everlasting life; and I will
raise him up at the last day." John 3:15, 16

41 The Jews then [T]murmured against Him,
because He said, "I am the bread which came
down from heaven." *grumbled*
42 And they said, [R]"Is not this Jesus, the son
of Joseph, whose father and mother we
know? How is it then that He says, 'I have
come down from heaven'?" Matt. 13:55
43 Jesus therefore answered and said to
them, "Do not murmur among yourselves.
44 "No one can come to Me unless the
Father who sent Me [R]draws him; and I will
raise him up at the last day. [Phil. 2:12, 13]
45 [R]"It is written in the prophets, *'And they
shall all be taught by God.'* [R]Therefore everyone who *has heard and learned from the
Father comes to Me. Is. 54:13 ★ • John 6:37
46 [R]"Not that anyone has seen the Father,
[R]except He who is from God; He has seen the
Father. John 1:18 • Matt. 11:27
47 "Most assuredly, I say to you, he who
believes *in Me has everlasting life.
48 [R]"I am the bread of life. John 6:33, 35
49 [R]"Your fathers ate the manna in the
wilderness, and are dead. John 6:31, 58
50 [R]"This is the bread which comes down
from heaven, that one may eat of it and not
die. John 6:51, 58
51 "I am the living bread [R]which came
down from heaven. If anyone eats of this
bread, he will live forever; and [R]the bread that
I shall give is My flesh, which I shall give for
the life of the world." John 3:13 • Heb. 10:5
52 The Jews therefore [R]quarreled among
themselves, saying, "How can this *Man* give
us *His* flesh to eat?" John 7:43; 9:16; 10:19
53 Then Jesus said to them, "Most assuredly, I say to you, unless [R]you eat the flesh
of the Son of Man and drink His blood, you
have no life in you. Matt. 26:26
54 [R]"Whoever eats My flesh and drinks My
blood has eternal life, and I will raise him up
at the last day. John 4:14; 6:27, 40
55 "For My flesh is *food indeed, and My
blood is *drink indeed.
56 "He who eats My flesh and drinks My
blood abides in Me, and I in him.
57 "As the living Father sent Me, and I live
because of the Father, so he who feeds on Me
will live because of Me.
58 [R]"This is the bread which came down
from heaven—not [R]as your fathers ate the
manna, and are dead. He who eats this bread
will live forever." John 6:49–51 • Ex. 16:14–35
59 These things He said in the synagogue as
He taught in Capernaum.

Rejection by Many Followers

60 [R]Therefore many of His disciples, when
they heard *this*, said, "This is a [T]hard saying;

6:22 NU omits *that*
6:22 NU omits *which His disciples had entered*
6:45 M *hears and has learned* **6:47** NU omits *in Me*
6:55 NU *true food* **6:55** NU *true drink*

who can understand it?" John 6:66 • *difficult*
61 When Jesus knew in Himself that His disciples murmured about this, He said to them, "Does this [T]offend you? *make you stumble*
62 [R]"*What* then if you should see the Son of Man ascend where He was before? Acts 1:9☆
63 [R]"It is the Spirit who gives life; the flesh profits nothing. The words that I speak to you are spirit, and *they* are life. 2 Cor. 3:6
64 "But there are some of you who do not believe." For [R]Jesus knew from the beginning who they were who did not believe, and who would betray Him. John 2:24, 25; 13:11
65 And He said, "Therefore I have said to you that no one can come to Me unless it has been granted to him by My Father."
66 From that *time* many of His disciples went back and walked with Him no more.

Confession by Peter

67 Then Jesus said to the twelve, "Do you also want to go away?"
68 Then Simon Peter answered Him, "Lord, to whom shall we go? You have [R]the words of eternal life. Acts 5:20
69 [R]"Also we have come to believe and know that You are the *Christ, the Son of the living God." Luke 9:20
70 Jesus answered them, "Did I not choose you, the twelve, and one of you is a devil?"
71 He spoke of Judas Iscariot, *the son* of Simon, for it was he who would [R]betray Him, being one of the twelve. Matt. 26:14–16

CHAPTER 7

Christ's Brothers Do Not Believe

AFTER these things Jesus walked in Galilee; for He did not want to walk in Judea, because the Jews sought to kill Him.
2 [R]Now the Jews' Feast of Tabernacles was at hand. Lev. 23:34
3 [R]His brothers therefore said to Him, "Depart from here and go into Judea, that Your disciples also may see the works that You are doing. Matt. 12:46
4 "For no one does anything in secret while he himself seeks to be known openly. If You do these things, show Yourself to the world."
5 For even His [R]brothers did not believe in Him. Ps. 69:8; Mic. 7:6; Mark 3:21★
6 Then Jesus said to them, "My time has not yet come, but your time is always ready.
7 [R]"The world cannot hate you, but it hates Me [R]because I testify of it that its works are evil. [John 15:19] • John 3:19
8 "You go up to this feast. I am not *yet going up to this feast, [R]for My time has not yet fully come." John 8:20
9 When He had said these things to them, He remained in Galilee.

Christ Secretly Goes to the Feast

10 But when His brothers had gone up, then He also went up to the feast, not openly, but as it were in secret.
11 Then [R]the Jews sought Him at the feast, and said, "Where is He?" John 11:56
12 And [R]there was much murmuring among the people concerning Him. [R]Some said, "He is good"; others said, "No, on the contrary, He deceives the people." John 9:16; 10:19 • Luke 7:16
13 However, no one spoke openly of Him [R]for fear of the Jews. [John 9:22; 12:42; 19:38]

Christ's Authority from the Father

14 Now about the middle of the feast [R]Jesus went up into the temple and taught. Ps. 22:22★
15 [R]And the Jews marveled, saying, "How does this Man know letters, having never studied?" Matt. 13:54
16 *Jesus answered them and said, "My doctrine is not Mine, but His who sent Me.
17 [R]"If anyone wants to do His will, he shall know concerning the doctrine, whether it is from God or *whether* I speak on My own *authority*. John 3:21; 8:43
18 [R]"He who speaks from himself seeks his own glory; but He who [R]seeks the glory of the One who sent Him is true, and [R]no unrighteousness is in Him. John 5:41 • John 8:50 • [2 Cor. 5:21]
19 [R]"Did not Moses give you the law, and *yet* none of you keeps the law? [R]Why do you seek to kill Me?" Deut. 33:4 • Matt. 12:14
20 The people answered and said, "You have a demon. Who is seeking to kill You?"
21 Jesus answered and said to them, "I did one work, and you all marvel.
22 [R]"Moses therefore gave you circumcision (not that it is from Moses, [R]but from the fathers), and you circumcise a man on the Sabbath. Lev. 12:3 • Gen. 17:9–14
23 "If a man receives circumcision on the Sabbath, so that the law of Moses should not be broken, are you angry with Me because I made a man completely well on the Sabbath?
24 "Do not judge according to appearance, but judge with righteous judgment."

Christ's Origin from the Father

25 Then some of them from Jerusalem said, "Is this not He whom they seek to kill?
26 "But look! He speaks boldly, and they say nothing to Him. [R]Do the rulers know indeed that this is *truly the Christ? John 7:48
27 [R]"However, we know where this Man is from; but when the Christ comes, no one knows where He is from." Luke 4:22
28 Then Jesus cried out, as He taught in the temple, saying, "You both know Me, and you know where I am from; and [R]I have not come

6:69 NU *Holy One of God* **7:8** NU omits *yet*
7:16 NU, M *So Jesus* **7:26** NU omits *truly*

of Myself, but He who sent Me [R]is true, whom
you do not know. John 5:43 • Rom. 3:4
29 *"But [R]I know Him, for I am from Him,
and He sent Me." Matt. 11:27
30 Then [R]they sought to take Him; but [R]no
one laid a hand on Him, because His hour had
not yet come. Mark 11:18 • John 7:32, 44; 8:20; 10:39
31 And [R]many of the people believed in
Him, and said, "When the Christ comes, will
He do more signs than these which this *Man*
has done?" Matt. 12:23

Christ's Departure to the Father

32 The Pharisees heard the crowd murmuring these things concerning Him, and the
Pharisees and the chief priests sent officers to
take Him.
33 Then Jesus said *to them, [R]"I shall be
with you a little while longer, and *then* I go
to Him who sent Me. Mark 16:19; Acts 1:9☆
34 "You will seek Me and not find *Me*, and
where I am you [R]cannot come." [Matt. 5:20]
35 Then the Jews said among themselves,
"Where does He intend to go that we shall
not find Him? Does He intend to go to [R]the
Dispersion among the Greeks and teach the
Greeks? James 1:1
36 "What is this thing that He said, 'You
will seek Me and not find Me, and where I am
you cannot come'?"

Christ Reveals the "Living Water"

37 On the last day, that great *day* of the
feast, Jesus stood and cried out, saying, "If
anyone thirsts, let him come to Me and drink.
38 [R]"He who believes in Me, as the Scripture has said, [R]out of his heart will flow rivers
of living water." Deut. 18:15 • Is. 12:3; 43:20; 44:3
39 [R]But this He spoke concerning the Spirit,
whom those *believing in Him would receive;
for the *Holy Spirit was not yet *given*, because Jesus was not yet glorified. Is. 44:3

Israel Is Divided over Christ

40 Therefore *many from the crowd, when
they heard this saying, said, "Truly this is
[R]the Prophet." Deut. 18:15, 18
41 Others said, "This is [R]the Christ," but
some said, "Will the Christ come out of
Galilee? John 4:42; 6:69
42 [R]"Has not the Scripture said that the
Christ comes from the seed of David and
from the town of Bethlehem, [R]where David
was?" Mic. 5:2 • 1 Sam. 16:1, 4
43 So [R]there was a division among the people because of Him. John 7:12
44 Now [R]some of them wanted to take Him,
but no one laid hands on Him. John 7:30

The Sanhedrin Is Confused over Christ

45 Then the officers came to the chief
priests and Pharisees, who said to them,
"Why have you not brought Him?"
46 The officers answered, [R]"No man ever
spoke like this Man!" Luke 4:22
47 Then the Pharisees answered them, "Are
you also deceived?
48 "Have any of the rulers or the Pharisees
believed in Him?
49 "But this crowd that does not know the
law is accursed."
50 Nicodemus (he who came to Jesus *by
night, being one of them) said to them,
51 "Does our law judge a man before it
hears him and knows what he is doing?"
52 They answered and said to him, "Are you
also from Galilee? Search and look, for [R]no
prophet *has arisen out of Galilee." [Is. 9:1, 2]
53 *And everyone went to his *own* house.

CHAPTER 8

A Woman Is Caught in Adultery

BUT Jesus went to the Mount of Olives.
2 But *early in the morning He came
again into the temple, and all the people
came to Him; and He sat down and taught
them.
3 Then the scribes and Pharisees brought
to Him a woman caught in adultery. And
when they had set her in the midst,
4 they said to Him, "Teacher, *this woman
was caught in adultery, in the very act.
5 [R]"Now *Moses, in the law, commanded
us *that such should be stoned. But what do
You *say?" Lev. 20:10
6 This they said, testing Him, that they
[R]might have *something* of which to accuse
Him. But Jesus stooped down and wrote on
the ground with *His* finger, *as though He did
not hear. Matt. 22:15
7 So when they continued asking Him, He
*raised Himself up and said to them, [R]"He
who is without sin among you, let him throw
a stone at her first." Deut. 17:7
8 And again He stooped down and wrote
on the ground.
9 Then those who heard *it*, [R]being* convicted by *their* conscience, went out one by
one, beginning with the oldest *even* to the
last. And Jesus was left alone, and the
woman standing in the midst. Rom. 2:22
10 When Jesus had raised Himself up *and
*saw no one but the woman, He said to her,

7:29 NU, M omits *But* **7:33** NU, M omit *to them*
7:39 NU *who believed* **7:39** NU omits *Holy*
7:40 NU *some* **7:50** NU *before*
7:52 NU *is to rise*
7:53 NU brackets 7:53 through 8:11 as not original. They are present in over 900 mss. **8:2** M *very early*
8:4 M *we found this woman*
8:5 M *in our law Moses commanded*
8:5 NU, M *to stone such* **8:5** M adds *about her*
8:6 NU, M omit *as though He did not hear*
8:7 M *He looked up*
8:9 NU, M omit *being convicted by their conscience*
8:10 NU omits *and saw no one but the woman*
8:10 M *He saw her and said,*

"Woman, where are those accusers *of
yours? Has no one condemned you?"
11 She said, "No one, Lord." And Jesus said
to her, [R]"Neither do I condemn you; go *and
[R]sin no more." [John 3:17] • [John 5:14]

"I Am the Light of the World"

12 Then Jesus spoke to them again, saying,
[R]"I am the light of the world. He who [R]follows
Me shall not walk in darkness, but have the
light of life." John 1:4; 9:5; 12:35 • 1 Thess. 5:5
13 The Pharisees therefore said to Him,
[R]"You bear witness of Yourself; Your witness
is not [T]true." John 5:31 • *valid* as testimony
14 Jesus answered and said to them, "Even
if I bear witness of Myself, My witness is true,
for I know where I came from and where I
am going; but [R]you do not know where I
come from and where I am going. John 7:28; 9:29
15 [R]"You judge according to the flesh; [R]I
judge no one. John 7:24 • [John 3:17; 12:47; 18:36]
16 "And yet if I do judge, My judgment is
true; for [R]I am not alone, but I *am* with the
Father who sent Me. John 16:32
17 [R]"It is also written in your law that the
testimony of two men is true. Deut. 17:6; 19:15
18 "I am One who bears witness of Myself,
and [R]the Father who sent Me bears witness of
Me." John 5:37
19 Then they said to Him, "Where is Your
Father?" Jesus answered, "You know neither
Me nor My Father. If you had known Me,
you would have known My Father also."
20 These words Jesus spoke in [R]the treasury, as He taught in the temple; and [R]no one
laid hands on Him, for [R]His hour had not yet
come. Mark 12:41, 43 • John 2:4; 7:30 • John 7:8
21 Then Jesus said to them again, "I am
going away, and [R]you will seek Me, and [R]will
die in your sin. [R]Where I go you cannot
come." John 7:34 • John 8:24 • Mark 16:19; Acts 1:9 ☆
22 So the Jews said, "Will He kill Himself,
because He says, 'Where I go you cannot
come'?"
23 And He said to them, [R]"You are from
beneath; I am from above. [R]You are of this
world; I am not of this world. John 3:31 • 1 John 4:5
24 [R]"Therefore I said to you that you will
die in your sins; for if you do not believe that
I am *He*, you will die in your sins." John 8:21
25 Then they said to Him, "Who are You?"
And Jesus said to them, "Just what I have
been saying to you from the beginning.
26 "I have many things to say and to judge
concerning you, but [R]He who sent Me is true;
and [R]I speak to the world those things which
I heard from Him." John 7:28 • John 3:32; 15:15
27 They did not understand that He spoke
to them of the Father.
28 Then Jesus said to them, "When you lift
up the Son of Man, [R]then you will know that
I am *He*, and [R]*that* I do nothing of Myself; but
as My Father taught Me, I speak these
things. [Rom. 1:4] • John 5:19, 30
29 "And [R]He who sent Me is with Me. The
Father has not left Me alone, for I always do
those things that please Him." John 14:10
30 As He spoke these words, [R]many believed in Him. John 7:31; 10:42; 11:45

31 Then Jesus said to those Jews who believed Him, "If you [R]abide in My word, you
are My disciples indeed. [John 14:15, 23]

32 "And you shall know the truth, and [R]the
truth shall make you free." [Rom. 6:14, 18, 22]
33 They answered Him, [R]"We are Abraham's descendants, and have never been in
bondage to anyone. How *can* you say, 'You
will be made free'?" [Matt. 3:9]
34 Jesus answered them, "Most assuredly, I
say to you, [R]whoever commits sin is a slave of
sin. 2 Pet. 2:19
35 "And [R]a slave does not abide in the house
forever, *but* a son abides forever. Gal. 4:30
36 [R]"Therefore if the Son makes you free,
you shall be free indeed. Gal. 5:1
37 "I know that you are Abraham's descendants, but [R]you seek to kill Me, because
My word has no place in you. John 7:19

8:10 NU, M omit *of yours*
8:11 NU, M add *from now on*

8:31 God's Word Confirms—To confirm means to fully establish a truth or fact. The Bible should be used to confirm the truth in our own hearts.

a. It confirms our salvation. Often Christians are troubled with doubts about their conversion experience. Did God really save them when they asked Him to do so? Are they still saved today? A number of verses may be used to confirm our salvation. One of the strongest is Jesus' own words in the gospel of John: "Most assuredly, I say to you, he who hears My word and believes in Him who sent Me has everlasting life, and shall not come into judgment, but has passed from death into life" (Page 1243—John 5:24). Compare John 3:16; 6:27, 35, 37, 40; 10:27–29; Romans 8:1.
b. It confirms the hand of God in all of life's bitter disappointments. Undoubtedly a most important verse of reassurance and comfort in the hour of great need is Romans 8:28: "And we know that all things work together for good to those who love God, to those who are the called according to *His* purpose."
c. It confirms our forgiveness when we sin. Sometimes believers carry with them an unnecessary burden of guilt over past sins and failures. Even though these have been confessed, they have difficulty believing God has truly forgiven and cleansed them. But time and again the Bible assures us that all confessed sin is instantly and eternally forgiven (Page 642—Ps. 32:5; 103:12; Page 810—Is. 38:17).

Now turn to Page 735—Prov. 22:21: God's Word Equips.

38 R"I speak what I have seen with My
Father, and you do what you have *seen with
your father." [John 3:32; 5:19, 30; 14:10, 24]
39 They answered and said to Him, R"Abraham is our father." Jesus said to them, R"If
you were Abraham's children, you would do
the works of Abraham. Matt. 3:9 • [Rom. 2:28]
40 "But now you seek to kill Me, a Man who
has told you the truth which I heard from
God. Abraham did not do this.
41 "You do the deeds of your father." Then
they said to Him, "We were not born of
fornication; we have one Father—God."
42 Jesus said to them, R"If God were your
Father, you would love Me, for I proceeded
forth and came from God; Rnor have I come
of Myself, but He sent Me. 1 John 5:1 • Gal. 4:4
43 R"Why do you not understand My
speech? Because you are not able to listen to
My word. [John 7:17]
44 "You are of *your* father the devil, and the
desires of your father you want to Rdo. He
was a murderer from the beginning, and
R*does not* stand in the truth, because there is
no truth in him. When he speaks a lie, he
speaks from his own *resources*, for he is a liar
and the father of it. [1 John 3:8–10, 15] • [Jude 6]
45 "But because I tell the truth, you do not
believe Me.
46 "Which of you convicts Me of sin? And if
I tell the truth, why do you not believe Me?
47 R"He who is of God hears God's words;
therefore you do not hear, because you are
not of God." 1 John 4:6
48 Then the Jews answered and said to
Him, "Do we not say rightly that You are a
Samaritan and Rhave a demon?" John 7:20; 10:20
49 Jesus answered, "I do not have a demon;
but I honor My Father, and Ryou dishonor
Me. John 5:41
50 "And RI do not seek My *own* glory; there
is One who seeks and judges. John 5:41; 7:18
51 "Most assuredly, I say to you, if anyone
keeps My word he shall never see death."
52 Then the Jews said to Him, "Now we
know that You Rhave a demon! RAbraham is
dead, and the prophets; and You say, 'If
anyone keeps My word he shall never taste
death.' John 7:20; 10:20 • Zech. 1:5
53 "Are You greater than our father Abraham, who is dead? And the prophets are dead.
Whom do You make Yourself out to be?"
54 Jesus answered, R"If I honor Myself, My
honor is nothing. RIt is My Father who honors Me, of whom you say that He is *your
God. John 5:31, 32 • Acts 3:13
55 "Yet Ryou have not known Him, but I
know Him. And if I say, 'I do not know Him,'
I shall be a liar like you; but I do know Him
and Rkeep His word. John 7:28, 29 • [John 15:10]
56 "Your father Abraham rejoiced to see
My day, and he saw *it* and was glad."
57 Then the Jews said to Him, "You are not
yet fifty years old, and have You seen Abraham?"
58 Jesus said to them, "Most assuredly, I
say to you, before Abraham was, I AM."
59 Then Rthey took up stones to throw at
Him; but Jesus hid Himself and went out of
the temple, Rgoing* through the midst of
them, and so passed by. John 10:31 • Luke 4:30

CHAPTER 9

Christ Heals the Blind Man

NOW as *Jesus* passed by, He saw a man
who was blind from birth.
2 And His disciples asked Him, saying,
"Rabbi, Rwho sinned, this man or his parents,
that he was born blind?" John 9:34
3 Jesus answered, "Neither this man nor
his parents sinned, Rbut that the works of
God should be revealed in him. John 11:4
4 R"I* must work the works of Him who
sent Me while it is day; *the* night is coming
when no one can work. [John 4:34; 5:19, 36; 17:4]
5 "As long as I am in the world, RI am the
light of the world." [John 1:5, 9; 3:19; 8:12; 12:35, 46]
6 When He had said these things, RHe spat
on the ground and made clay with the saliva;
and He anointed the eyes of the blind man
with the clay. Mark 7:33; 8:23
7 And He said to him, "Go, wash Rin the
pool of Siloam" (which is translated, Sent).
So Rhe went and washed, and came back
seeing. Neh. 3:15 • 2 Kin. 5:14
8 Therefore the neighbors and those who
previously had seen that he was *blind said,
"Is not this he who sat and begged?"
9 Some said, "This is he." Others *said*,
*"He is like him." He said, "I am *he*."
10 Therefore they said to him, "How were
your eyes opened?"
11 He answered and said, R"A Man called
Jesus made clay and anointed my eyes and
said to me, 'Go to *the pool of Siloam and
wash.' So I went and washed, and I received
sight." John 9:6, 7
12 Then they said to him, "Where is He?"
He said, "I do not know."
13 They brought him who formerly was
blind to the Pharisees.
14 Now it was a Sabbath when Jesus made
the clay and opened his eyes.
15 Then the Pharisees also asked him again
how he had received his sight. He said to
them, "He put clay on my eyes, and I washed,
and I see."
16 Therefore some of the Pharisees said,
"This Man is not from God, because He does
not keep the Sabbath." Others said, "How

8:38 NU *heard from* 8:54 NU, M *our*
8:59 NU omits the rest of v. 59. 9:4 NU *We*
9:8 NU *a beggar* 9:9 NU *No, but he is like him*
9:11 NU omits *the pool of*

can a man who is a sinner do such signs?"
And there was a division among them.
17 They said to the blind man again, "What
do you say about Him because He opened
your eyes?" He said, "He is a prophet."
18 But the Jews did not believe concerning
him, that he had been blind and received his
sight, until they called the parents of him
who had received his sight.
19 And they asked them, saying, "Is this
your son, who you say was born blind? How
then does he now see?"
20 His parents answered them and said,
"We know that this is our son, and that he
was born blind;
21 "but by what means he now sees we do
not know, or who opened his eyes we do not
know. He is of age; ask him. He will speak for
himself."
22 His parents said these *things* because
[R]they feared the Jews, for the Jews had
agreed already that if anyone confessed *that*
He *was* Christ, he [R]would be put out of the
synagogue. Acts 5:13 • John 16:2
23 Therefore his parents said, "He is of age;
ask him."
24 So they again called the man who was
blind, and said to him, "Give God the glory!
We know that this Man is a sinner."
25 He answered and said, "Whether He is a
sinner *or not* I do not know. One thing I
know: that though I was blind, now I see."
26 Then they said to him again, "What did
He do to you? How did He open your eyes?"
27 He answered them, "I told you already,
and you did not listen. Why do you want to
hear *it* again? Do you also want to become
His disciples?"
28 Then they reviled him and said, "You are
His disciple, but we are Moses' disciples.
29 "We know that God [R]spoke to [R]Moses; *as
for* this *fellow*, [R]we do not know where He is
from." Num. 12:6–8 • [John 5:45–47] • John 7:27, 28; 8:14
30 The man answered and said to them,
[R]"Why, this is a marvelous thing, that you do
not know where He is from, and *yet* He has
opened my eyes! John 3:10
31 "Now we know that [R]God does not hear
sinners; but if anyone is a worshiper of God
and does His will, He hears him. Zech. 7:13
32 "Since the world began it has been un-
heard of that anyone opened the eyes of one
who was born blind.
33 [R]"If this Man were not from God, He
could do nothing." John 3:2; 9:16
34 They answered and said to him, "You
were completely born in sins, and are you
teaching us?" And they cast him out.
35 Jesus heard that they had cast him out;
and when He had found him, He said to him,
"Do you believe in the Son of *God?"
36 He answered and said, "Who is He, Lord,
that I may believe in Him?"
37 And Jesus said to him, "You have both
seen Him and [R]it is He who is talking with
you." John 4:26
38 Then he said, "Lord, I believe!" And he
[R]worshiped Him. Matt. 8:2
39 And Jesus said, [R]"For judgment I have
come into this world, [R]that those who do not
see may see, and that those who see may be
made blind." [John 3:17; 5:22, 27; 12:47] • Matt. 13:13
40 Then *some* of the Pharisees who were
with Him heard these words, [R]and said to
Him, "Are we blind also?" [Rom. 2:19]
41 Jesus said to them, [R]"If you were blind,
you would have no sin; but now you say, 'We
see.' Therefore your sin remains. John 15:22, 24

CHAPTER 10

"I Am the Good Shepherd"

"MOST assuredly, I say to you, he who
does not enter the sheepfold by the
door, but climbs up some other way, the same
is a thief and a robber.
2 "But he who enters by the door is the
shepherd of the sheep.
3 "To him the doorkeeper opens, and the
sheep hear his voice; and he calls his own
sheep by [R]name and leads them out. John 20:16
4 "And when he brings out his own sheep,
he goes before them; and the sheep follow
him, for they know his voice.
5 "Yet they will by no means follow a
stranger, but will flee from him, for they do
not know the voice of strangers."
6 Jesus used this illustration, but they did
not understand the things which He spoke to
them.
7 Then Jesus said to them again, "Most
assuredly, I say to you, I am the door of the
sheep.
8 "All who *ever* came *before Me are
thieves and robbers, but the sheep did not
hear them.
9 [R]"I am the door. If anyone enters by Me,
he will be saved, and will go in and out and
find pasture. [Eph. 2:18]
10 "The thief does not come except to steal,
and to kill, and to destroy. I have come that

9:35 NU *Man* 10:8 M omits *before Me*

10:10 The Earthly Life of the Son of God—Since the gospel narratives are mainly concerned with Jesus' earthly ministry, it is important that the main aspects of His teaching be recognized. The most important of these are: the kingdom of God (Page 1120—Matt. 5—7; 24—25); His divine authority over men (Page 1125—Matt. 7:28, 29; Page 1162—Mark 2:10); His own role as God and Messiah demonstrated by miracles and signs (Page 1136—Matt. 16:15-20); the significance of His death and

(continued on next page)

they may have life, and that they may have *it*
more abundantly.

11 [R]"I am the good shepherd. The good
shepherd gives His life for the sheep. Is. 40:11
12 "But *he who is* a [T]hireling and not the
shepherd, one who does not own the sheep,
sees the wolf coming and [R]leaves the sheep
and flees; and the wolf catches the sheep and
scatters them. *hired man* • Zech. 11:16, 17
13 "The hireling flees because he is a hireling and does not care about the sheep.
14 "I am the good shepherd; and I know My
sheep, and am known by My own.
15 [R]"As the Father knows Me, even so I
know the Father; [R]and I lay down My life for
the sheep. Matt. 11:27 • Matt. 27:50☆
16 "And [R]other sheep I have which are not
of this fold; them also I must bring, and they
will hear My voice; [R]and there will be one
flock *and* one shepherd. Is. 42:6; 56:8★ • Eph. 2:13–18
17 "Therefore My Father [R]loves Me, [R]be-
cause I lay down My life that I may take it
again. John 5:20 • [Heb. 2:9]
18 "No one takes it from Me, but I lay it
down of Myself. I have power to lay it down,
and I have power to take it again. This
command I have received from My Father."
19 Therefore there was a division again
among the Jews because of these sayings.
20 And many of them said, [R]"He has a
demon and is [T]mad. Why do you listen to
Him?" John 7:20 • *insane*
21 Others said, "These are not the words of
one who has a demon. [R]Can a demon [R]open
the eyes of the blind?" [Ex. 4:11] • John 9:6, 7, 32, 33

The Opposition at the Feast of Dedication in Jerusalem

22 Now it was the Feast of Dedication in
Jerusalem, and it was winter.
23 And Jesus walked in the temple, [R]in
Solomon's porch. Acts 3:11; 5:12
24 Then the Jews surrounded Him and said
to Him, "How long do You keep us in [T]doubt?
If You are the Christ, tell us plainly." *suspense*
25 Jesus answered them, "I told you, and
you do not believe. The works that I do in My
Father's name, they bear witness of Me.
26 "But you do not believe, because you are
not of My sheep, *as I said to you.
27 [R]"My sheep hear My voice, and I know
them, and they follow Me. John 10:4, 14
28 "And I give them eternal life, and they
shall never perish; neither shall anyone
snatch them out of My hand.
29 "My Father, who has given *them* to Me,
is greater than all; and no one is able to
snatch *them* out of My Father's hand.
30 [R]"I and *My* Father are one." John 17:11
31 Then [R]the Jews took up stones again to
stone Him. John 8:59
32 Jesus answered them, "Many good
works I have shown you from My Father. For
which of those works do you stone Me?"
33 The Jews answered Him, saying, "For a
good work we do not stone You, but for
[R]blasphemy, and because You, being a Man,
[R]make Yourself God." John 5:18 • Matt. 9:3
34 Jesus answered them, [R]"Is it not written
in your law, *'I said, "You are gods"'?* Ps. 82:6
35 "If He called them gods, [R]to whom the
word of God came (and the Scripture [R]cannot
be broken), Matt. 5:17, 18 • 1 Pet. 1:25
36 "do you say of Him [R]whom the Father
sanctified and [R]sent into the world, 'You are
blaspheming,' [R]because I said, 'I am [R]the Son
of God'? John 6:27 • John 3:17 • John 5:17, 18 • Luke 1:35
37 [R]"If I do not do the works of My Father,
do not believe Me; John 10:25; 15:24
38 "but if I do, though you do not believe
Me, [R]believe the works, that you may know
and *believe [R]that the Father *is* in Me, and I
in Him." John 5:36 • John 14:10, 11

10:26 NU omits *as I said to you* **10:38** NU *understand*

(continued from previous page)
resurrection (Page 1137—Matt. 16:21; Page 1231—Luke 24:26); the relationship which His disciples and subsequent believers are to share with Him (Page 1257—John 13—16); and the urgency of His commission to believers to make disciples (Page 1155—Matt. 28:19, 20).

Of the many events of His earthly life the most significant, without a doubt, are His death and resurrection. On these two pivotal, historical incidents rests the validity of the entire Christian faith (Page 1359—1 Cor. 15:14). It is vital then to understand the nature of these two events. The death of Christ was first of all a humiliating physical death (Page 1264—John 19:18, 33). More than that, for a brief time it constituted a spiritual separation from God (Page 1154—Matt. 27:46). Within this moment there occurred the inexplicable mystery of the Father punishing the Son for the sins of the world (Page 1481—1 Pet. 3:18; Page 1369—2 Cor. 5:21). This event, though it was the greatest crime of human history, was in the plan of God (Page 1273—Acts 2:23), and thus became the basis of salvation for sinners (Page 825—Is. 53:5).

The power of the death of Christ would be nullified without His bodily resurrection. Though it does not justify us, the resurrection demonstrated that His death, by which believing sinners are justified, was valid (Page 1359—1 Cor. 15:12–20). While skeptics have denied the bodily resurrection of Christ, the historical evidence for it is overwhelming: the many separate accounts of post-resurrection appearances, the empty tomb, and the transformed disciples. Every life that has been dramatically and wonderfully changed by believing in Christ since the first century is a testimony to its historical reality. Furthermore, it is the power of the resurrection that marvelously empowers Christians today to live the Christian life (Page 1387—Eph. 1:19, 20; Page 1401—Phil. 3:10).

Now turn to page 1174—Mark 10:45: The Ministry of the Son of God.

39 Therefore they sought again to seize
Him, but He escaped out of their hand.
40 And He went away again beyond the
Jordan to the place [R]where John was baptizing at first, and there He stayed. John 1:28
41 Then many came to Him and said, "John
performed no sign, but all the things that
John spoke about this Man were true."
42 And many believed in Him there.

CHAPTER 11

Christ Raises Lazarus

NOW a certain *man* was sick, Lazarus of
Bethany, the town of [R]Mary and her
sister Martha. Luke 10:38, 39
2 It was *that* Mary who anointed the Lord
with fragrant oil and wiped His feet with her
hair, whose brother Lazarus was sick.
3 Therefore the sisters sent to Him, saying,
"Lord, behold, he whom You love is sick."
4 When Jesus heard *that*, He said, "This
sickness is not unto death, but for the glory
of God, that the Son of God may be glorified
through it."
5 Now Jesus loved Martha and her sister
and Lazarus.
6 So, when He heard that he was sick, [R]He
stayed two more days in the place where He
was. John 10:40
7 Then after this He said to *the* disciples,
"Let us go to Judea again."
8 *The* disciples said to Him, "Rabbi, lately
the Jews sought to [R]stone You, and are You
going there again?" John 8:59; 10:31
9 Jesus answered, "Are there not twelve
hours in the day? [R]If anyone walks in the day,
he does not stumble, because he sees the
[R]light of this world. John 9:4; 12:35 • Is. 9:2
10 "But [R]if one walks in the night, he stumbles, because the light is not in him." John 12:35
11 These things He said, and after that He
said to them, "Our friend Lazarus [R]sleeps, but
I go that I may wake him up." Matt. 9:24
12 Then His disciples said, "Lord, if he
sleeps he will get well."
13 However, Jesus spoke of his death, but
they thought that He was speaking about
taking rest in sleep.
14 Then Jesus said to them plainly, "Lazarus is dead.
15 "And I am glad for your sakes that I was
not there, that you may believe. Nevertheless
let us go to him."
16 Then [R]Thomas, who is called Didymus,
said to his fellow disciples, "Let us also go,
that we may die with Him." John 14:5; 20:26–28
17 So when Jesus came, He found that he
had already been in the tomb four days.
18 Now Bethany was near Jerusalem, about
[T]two miles away. Lit. *15 stadia*
19 And many of the Jews had joined the
women around Martha and Mary, to comfort
them concerning their brother.
20 Then Martha, as soon as she heard that
Jesus was coming, went and met Him, but
Mary was sitting in the house.
21 Then Martha said to Jesus, "Lord, if You
had been here, my brother would not have
died.
22 "But even now I know that whatever
You ask of God, God will give You."
23 Jesus said to her, "Your brother will rise
again."
24 Martha said to Him, [R]"I know that he
will rise again in the resurrection at the last
day." [John 5:29]
25 Jesus said to her, "I am the resurrection
and the life. He who believes in Me, though
he may [R]die, he shall live. 1 Cor. 15:22
26 "And whoever lives and believes in Me
shall never die. Do you believe this?"
27 She said to Him, "Yes, Lord, [R]I believe
that You are the Christ, the Son of God, who
is to come into the world." Matt. 16:16
28 And when she had said these things, she
went her way and secretly called Mary her
sister, saying, "The Teacher has come and is
calling for you."
29 As soon as she heard *that*, she arose
quickly and came to Him.
30 Now Jesus had not yet come into the
town, but *was in the place where Martha
met Him.
31 [R]Then the Jews who were with her in the
house, and comforting her, when they saw
that Mary rose up quickly and went out,
followed her, *saying, "She is going to the
tomb to weep there." John 11:19, 33
32 Then, when Mary came where Jesus was,
and saw Him, she fell down at His feet, saying
to Him, [R]"Lord, if You had been here, my
brother would not have died." John 11:21
33 Therefore, when Jesus saw her weeping,
and the Jews who came with her weeping, He
groaned in the spirit and was troubled.
34 And He said, "Where have you laid
him?" They said to Him, "Lord, come and
see."
35 [R]Jesus wept. Luke 19:41
36 Then the Jews said, "See how He loved
him!"
37 And some of them said, "Could not this
Man, [R]who opened the eyes of the blind, also
have kept this man from dying?" John 9:6, 7
38 Then Jesus, again groaning in Himself,
came to the tomb. It was a cave, and a [R]stone
lay against it. Matt. 27:60, 66
39 Jesus said, "Take away the stone." Martha, the sister of him who was dead, said to
Him, "Lord, by this time there is a stench, for
he has been *dead* four days."
40 Jesus said to her, "Did I not say to you

11:30 NU *was still*
11:31 NU *supposing that she was going*

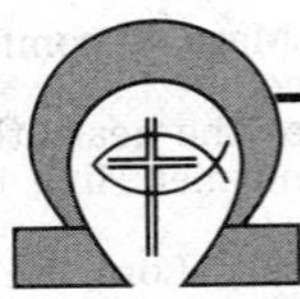

THE JEWISH SANHEDRIN

The Jewish Sanhedrin, also referred to as the Council, was the highest ruling body among the Jews in New Testament times. This group probably evolved from the council of advisors to the high priest during the years when the Jewish people lived under the domination of the Persians and the Greeks from about 500 to 150 B.C.

The Council originally was composed of leading priests and distinguished aristocrats among the Jewish people, but later scribes and Pharisees and Sadducees were added to the group.

With an assembly of seventy-one members, the Council was headed by the high priest. The body was granted limited authority over certain religious, civil, and criminal matters by the Romans during their years of dominance in Palestine. Most of the day-to-day business was left to the Sanhedrin, which was permitted to have its own police force. However, the Council was denied the right to exercise the death penalty (John 18:31). In spite of these restrictions, the Sanhedrin exercised considerable influence in religious matters.

The Council played a prominent role in the arrest and trial of Jesus, although it is not clear whether He was formally tried by the Council or given preliminary hearings. Christ was arrested by the temple police in the Garden of Gethsemane (Mark 14:43) and subjected to false accusations before the high priest (Matt. 26:59). Several of the apostles, including Peter, John, and Paul, were charged before the Sanhedrin (Acts 4:1–23; 5:17–41; 22—24) in later years.

Prominent members of the Sanhedrin mentioned in a favorable light in the New Testament were Joseph of Arimathea (Mark 15:43); Gamaliel (Acts 5:34); and Nicodemus (John 3:1; 7:50).

During most of its history, the Council met at Jerusalem. But after A.D. 150, it convened at Tiberias (see photo of modern Tiberias), a Roman city on the shores of the Sea of Galilee.

Photo by Howard Vos

After A.D. 150, the Council convened at Tiberias. Modern Tiberias, situated on the shores of the Sea of Galilee, is pictured here.

that if you would believe you would [R]see the glory of God?" [John 11:4, 23]
41 Then they took away the stone *from the place where the dead man was lying. And Jesus lifted up His eyes and said, "Father, I thank You that You have heard Me.
42 "And I know that You always hear Me, but [R]because of the people who are standing by I said this, that they may believe that You sent Me." John 12:30; 17:21
43 Now when He had said these things, He cried with a loud voice, "Lazarus, come forth!"
44 And he who had died came out bound hand and foot with graveclothes, and [R]his face was wrapped with a cloth. Jesus said to them, "Loose him, and let him go." John 20:7

The Pharisees Plan to Kill Christ

45 Then many of the Jews who had come to Mary, [R]and had seen the things Jesus did, believed in Him. John 2:23; 10:42; 12:11, 18
46 But some of them went away to the Pharisees and told them the things Jesus did.
47 [R]Then the chief priests and the Pharisees gathered a council and said, "What shall we do? For this Man works many signs. Ps. 2:2
48 "If we let Him alone like this, everyone will believe in Him, and the Romans will come and take away both our place and nation."
49 And one of them, [R]Caiaphas, being high priest that year, said to them, "You know nothing at all, Luke 3:2
50 [R]"nor do you consider that it is expedient for *us that one man should die for the people, and not that the whole nation should perish." John 18:14
51 Now this he did not say on his own *authority*; but being high priest that year he prophesied that Jesus would die for the nation,
52 and not for that nation only, but also that He would gather together in one the children of God who were scattered abroad.
53 Then from that day on they plotted to [R]put Him to death. Matt. 26:4
54 [R]Therefore Jesus no longer walked openly among the Jews, but went from there into the country near the wilderness, to a city called [R]Ephraim, and there remained with His disciples. John 4:1, 3; 7:1 • 2 Chr. 13:19
55 [R]And the Passover of the Jews was near, and many went from the country up to Jerusalem before the Passover, to [R]purify themselves. John 2:13; 5:1; 6:4 • Num. 9:10, 13; 31:19, 20
56 [R]Then they sought Jesus, and spoke among themselves as they stood in the temple, "What do you think—that He will not come to the feast?" John 7:11
57 Now both the chief priests and the Pharisees had given a command, that if anyone knew where He was, he should report *it*, that they might [R]seize Him. Matt. 26:14-16

CHAPTER 12

Mary Anoints Christ
Matt. 26:6-12; Mark 14:3-9

THEN, six days before the Passover, Jesus came to Bethany, [R]where Lazarus was *who had been dead, whom He had raised from the dead. John 11:1, 43
2 [R]There they made Him a supper; and Martha served, but Lazarus was one of those who sat at the table with Him. Mark 14:3
3 Then Mary took a pound of very costly oil of spikenard, anointed the feet of Jesus, and wiped His feet with her hair. And the house was filled with the fragrance of the oil.
4 Then one of His disciples, Judas Iscariot, Simon's *son*, who would betray Him, said,
5 "Why was this fragrant oil not sold for [T]three hundred denarii and given to the poor?" 1 year's wage
6 This he said, not that he cared for the poor, but because he was a thief, and [R]had the money box; and he used to take what was put in it. John 13:29
7 Then Jesus said, "Let her alone; *she has kept this for the day of My burial.
8 "For the poor you have with you always, but Me you do not have always."
9 Then a great many of the Jews knew that He was there; and they came, not for Jesus' sake only, but that they might also see Lazarus, whom He had raised from the dead.
10 But the chief priests took counsel that they might also put Lazarus to death,
11 because on account of him many of the Jews went away and believed in Jesus.

The Triumphal Entry
Matt. 21:1-9; Mark 11:1-10; Luke 19:29-38

12 [R]The next day a great multitude that had come to the feast, when they heard that Jesus was coming to Jerusalem, Matt. 21:4-9
13 took branches of palm trees and went out to meet Him, and cried out:

[R]"Hosanna!
'Blessed is He who comes in the name of the LORD!'
The King of Israel!" Ps. 118:26★

14 Then Jesus, when He had found a young donkey, sat on it; as it is written:

15 *"Fear[R] not, daughter of Zion;*
Behold, your King is coming,
Sitting on a donkey's colt." Zech. 9:9★

11:41 NU omits *from the place where the dead man was lying* **11:50** NU *you*
12:1 NU omits *who had been dead*
12:7 NU *that she may keep*

16 His disciples did not understand these
things at first; but when Jesus was glorified,
[R]then they remembered that these things
were written about Him and *that* they had
done these things to Him. [John 14:26]
17 Therefore the people, who were with
Him when He called Lazarus out of his tomb
and raised him from the dead, bore witness.
18 [R]For this reason the people also met Him,
because they heard that He had done this
sign. John 12:11
19 The Pharisees therefore said among
themselves, [R]"You see that you are accomplishing nothing. Look, the world has gone
after Him!" John 11:47, 48
20 Now there were certain Greeks among
those who came up to worship at the feast.
21 Then they came to Philip, [R]who was from
Bethsaida of Galilee, and asked him, saying,
"Sir, we wish to see Jesus." John 1:43, 44; 14:8–11
22 Philip came and told Andrew, and in turn
Andrew and Philip told Jesus.

The Messiah Teaches

23 But Jesus answered them, saying, [R]"The
hour has come [R]that the Son of Man should
be glorified. John 13:32 • Acts 3:13☆
24 "Most assuredly, I say to you, [R]unless a
grain of wheat falls into the ground and dies,
it remains alone; but if it dies, it produces
much [T]grain. 1 Cor. 15:36 • Lit. *fruit*
25 [R]"He who loves his life will lose it, and he
who hates his life in this world will keep it for
eternal life. Mark 8:35
26 "If anyone serves Me, let him [R]follow
Me; and [R]where I am, there My servant will
be also. If anyone serves Me, him *My* Father
will honor. [Matt. 16:24] • John 14:3; 17:24
27 "Now My soul is troubled, and what
shall I say? 'Father, save Me from this hour'?
But for this purpose I came to this hour.
28 "Father, glorify Your name." Then a
voice came from heaven, *saying*, "I have both
glorified *it* and will glorify *it* again."
29 Therefore the people who stood by and
heard *it* said that it had thundered. Others
said, "An angel has spoken to Him."
30 Jesus answered and said, "This voice did
not come because of Me, but for your sake.
31 "Now is the judgment of this world; now
the ruler of this world will be cast out.
32 "And I, if I am [T]lifted up from the earth,
will draw all *peoples* to Myself." Crucified
33 [R]This He said, signifying by what death
He would die. John 18:32; 21:19
34 The people answered Him, [R]"We have
heard from the law that the Christ remains
forever; and how *can* You say, 'The Son of
Man must be lifted up'? Who is this Son of
Man?" Mic. 4:7
35 Then Jesus said to them, "A little while
longer the light is with you. [R]Walk while you
have the light, lest darkness overtake you;
[R]he who walks in darkness does not know
where he is going. Eph. 5:8 • [1 John 2:9–11]
36 "While you have the light, believe in the
light, that you may become [R]sons of light."
These things Jesus spoke, and departed, and
[R]was hidden from them. Luke 16:8 • John 8:59
37 But although He had done so many
[R]signs before them, they did not believe in
Him, John 11:47
38 that the word of Isaiah the prophet
might be fulfilled, which he spoke:

> [R]*"Lord, who has believed our report?*
> *And to whom has the arm of the LORD*
> *been revealed?"* Is. 53:1★

39 Therefore they could not believe, because Isaiah said again:

> 40 *"He*[R] *has blinded their eyes and*
> *hardened their heart,*
> [R]*Lest they should see with their eyes*
> *And understand with their heart,*
> *Lest they should turn, so that I should*
> *heal them."* Is. 6:9, 10 • Matt. 13:14

41 [R]These things Isaiah said *when he saw
His glory and spoke of Him. Is. 6:10★
42 Nevertheless even among the rulers
many believed in Him, but because of the
Pharisees they did not confess *Him*, lest they
should be put out of the synagogue;
43 [R]for they loved the praise of men more
than the praise of God. John 5:41, 44
44 Then Jesus cried out and said, "He who
believes in Me, [R]believes not in Me [R]but in
Him who sent Me. [John 3:16, 18, 36] • [John 5:24]
45 "And [R]he who sees Me sees Him who
sent Me. [John 14:9]
46 [R]"I have come *as* a light into the world,
that whoever believes in Me should not abide
in darkness. John 1:4, 5; 8:12; 12:35, 36
47 "And if anyone hears My words and does
not *believe, [R]I do not judge him; for [R]I did
not come to judge the world but to save the
world. John 5:45 • John 3:17
48 [R]"He who rejects Me, and does not receive My words, has that which judges him—
[R]the word that I have spoken will judge him
in the last day. [Luke 10:16] • Deut. 18:18, 19
49 "For [R]I have not spoken on My own
authority; but the Father who sent Me gave
Me a command, [R]what I should say and what
I should speak. John 8:38 • Deut. 18:18
50 "And I know that His command is everlasting life. Therefore, whatever I speak, just
as the Father has told Me, so I speak."

12:41 NU *because* **12:47** NU *keep them*

CHAPTER 13

Christ Washes the Disciples' Feet

NOW before the feast of the Passover, when Jesus knew that His hour had come that He should depart from this world to the Father, having loved His own who were in the world, He loved them to the end.
2 And *supper being ended, the devil having already put it into the heart of Judas Iscariot, Simon's *son*, to betray Him,
3 Jesus, knowing that the Father had given all things into His hands, and that He had come from God and was going to God,
4 rose from supper and laid aside His garments, took a towel and girded Himself.
5 After that, He poured water into a basin and began to wash the disciples' feet, and to wipe *them* with the towel with which He was girded.
6 Then He came to Simon Peter. And *Peter* said to Him, [R]"Lord, are You washing my feet?" Matt. 3:14
7 Jesus answered and said to him, "What I am doing you [R]do not understand now, [R]but you will know after this." John 12:16 • John 13:19
8 Peter said to Him, "You shall never wash my feet!" Jesus answered him, "If I do not wash you, you have no part with Me."
9 Simon Peter said to Him, "Lord, not my feet only, but also *my* hands and *my* head!"
10 Jesus said to him, "He who is bathed needs only to wash *his* feet, but is completely clean; and you are clean, but not all of you."
11 For He knew who would betray Him; therefore He said, "You are not all clean."
12 So when He had washed their feet, taken His garments, and sat down again, He said to them, "Do you [T]know what I have done to you? *understand*
13 [R]"You call Me Teacher and Lord, and you say well, for *so* I am. Matt. 23:8, 10
14 [R]"If I then, *your* Lord and Teacher, have washed your feet, [R]you also ought to wash one another's feet. Luke 22:27 • [Rom. 12:10]
15 "For I have given you an example, that you should do as I have done to you.
16 "Most assuredly, I say to you, a servant is not greater than his master; nor is he who is sent greater than he who sent him.
17 [R]"If you know these things, happy are you if you do them. [James 1:25]
18 "I do not speak concerning all of you. I know whom I have chosen; but that the [R]Scripture may be fulfilled, [R]*'He who eats *bread with Me has lifted up his heel against Me.'* John 15:25; 17:12 • Ps. 41:9 ★
19 [R]"Now I tell you before it comes, that when it does come to pass, you may believe that I am *He*. John 14:29; 16:4
20 [R]"Most assuredly, I say to you, he who receives whomever I send receives Me; and he who receives Me receives Him who sent Me." Matt. 10:40

Christ Announces Judas, the Betrayer
Matt. 26:21, 22; Mark 14:18, 19; Luke 22:21–23

21 [R]When Jesus had said these things, [R]He was troubled in spirit, and testified and said, "Most assuredly, I say to you, [R]one of you will betray Me." Luke 22:21 • John 12:27 • John 18:2 ☆
22 Then the disciples looked at one another, perplexed about whom He spoke.
23 Now [R]there was [T]leaning on Jesus' bosom one of His disciples, whom Jesus loved. John 19:26; 20:2; 21:7, 20 • *reclining*
24 Simon Peter therefore motioned to him to ask who it was of whom He spoke.
25 Then, leaning *back on Jesus' breast, he said to Him, "Lord, who is it?"
26 Jesus answered, "It is he to whom I shall give a piece of bread when I have dipped *it*." And having dipped the bread, He gave *it* to [R]Judas Iscariot, *the son* of Simon. John 6:71
27 [R]Now after the piece of bread, Satan entered him. Then Jesus said to him, "What you do, do quickly." Luke 22:3
28 But no one at the table knew for what reason He said this to him.
29 For some thought, because Judas had the money box, that Jesus had said to him, "Buy *those things* we need for the feast," or that he should give something to the poor.
30 Having received the piece of bread, he then went out immediately. And it was night.

Christ Announces His Departure

31 So, when he had gone out, Jesus said, [R]"Now the Son of Man is glorified, and [R]God is glorified in Him. John 12:23 • [1 Pet. 4:11]
32 "If God is glorified in Him, God will also glorify Him in Himself, and [R]glorify Him immediately. John 12:23
33 "Little children, I shall be with you a little while longer. You will seek Me; and as I said to the Jews, 'Where I am going, you cannot come,' so now I say to you.
34 [R]"A new commandment I give to you, that you love one another; as I have loved you, that you also love one another. 1 Thess. 4:9
35 "By this all will know that you are My disciples, if you have love for one another."

Christ Foretells Peter's Denial
Matt. 26:34, 35; Mark 14:30, 31; Luke 22:33, 34

36 Simon Peter said to Him, "Lord, where are You going?" Jesus answered him, "Where I am going you cannot follow Me now, but you shall follow Me afterward."
37 Peter said to Him, "Lord, why can I not follow You now? I will [R]lay down my life for Your sake." Mark 14:29–31
38 Jesus answered him, "Will you lay down your life for My sake? Most assuredly, I say to you, the rooster shall not [R]crow till you have denied Me three times. John 18:25–27 ☆

13:2 NU *during supper* **13:18** NU *My bread has*
13:25 NU, M add *thus*

CHAPTER 14

Christ Comforts His Disciples

"LET not your heart be troubled; you
believe in God, believe also in Me.
2 "In My Father's house are many mansions; if *it were* not so, *I would have told
you. I go to prepare a place for you.
3 "And if I go and prepare a place for you,
I will come again and receive you to Myself;
that where I am, *there* you may be also.
4 "And where I go you know, and the way
you know."

Christ Answers Thomas

5 [R]Thomas said to Him, "Lord, we do not
know where You are going, and how can we
know the way?" Matt. 10:3
6 Jesus said to him, "I am the way, the
truth, and the life. No one comes to the
Father [R]except through Me. [John 10:7–9]
7 [R]"If you had known Me, you would have
known My Father also; and from now on you
know Him and have seen Him." John 8:19

Christ Answers Philip

8 Philip said to Him, "Lord, show us the
Father, and it is sufficient for us."
9 Jesus said to him, "Have I been with you
so long, and yet you have not known Me,
Philip? [R]He who has seen Me has seen the
Father; so how can you say, 'Show us the
Father'? Col. 1:15
10 "Do you not believe that I am in the
Father, and the Father in Me? The words that
I speak to you [R]I do not speak on My own
authority; but the Father who dwells in Me
does the works. Deut. 18:18; John 5:19; 14:24★
11 "Believe Me that I *am* in the Father and
the Father in Me, [R]or else believe Me for the
sake of the works themselves. John 5:36; 10:38
12 [R]"Most assuredly, I say to you, he who
believes in Me, the works that I do he will do
also; and greater *works* than these he will do,
because I go to My Father. Luke 10:17
13 [R]"And whatever you ask in My name,
that I will do, that the Father may be [R]glori-
fied in the Son. Matt. 7:7 • John 13:31
14 "If you *ask anything in My name, I will
do *it*.
15 [R]"If you love Me, *keep My commandments. 1 John 5:3
16 "And I will pray the Father, and [R]He will
give you another [T]Helper, that He may abide
with you forever, Acts 2:4, 33☆ • *Comforter*
17 "*even* the Spirit of truth, whom the
world cannot receive, because it neither sees
Him nor knows Him; but you know Him, for
He dwells with you and will be in you.
18 [R]"I will not leave you orphans; [R]I will
come to you. [Matt. 28:20] • [John 14:3, 28]
19 "A little while longer and the world will
see Me no more, but you will see Me. [R]Be-
cause I live, you will live also. [1 Cor. 15:20]
20 "At that day you will know that I *am* in
My Father, and you in Me, and I in you.
21 "He who has My commandments and
keeps them, it is he who loves Me. And he
who loves Me will be loved by My Father, and
I will love him and manifest Myself to him."

Christ Answers Judas

22 [R]Judas (not Iscariot) said to Him, "Lord,
how is it that You will manifest Yourself to
us, and not to the world?" Luke 6:16
23 Jesus answered and said to him, "If
anyone loves Me, he will keep My word; and
My Father will love him, and We will come to
him and make Our home with him.
24 "He who does not love Me does not keep
My words; and the word which you hear is
not Mine but the Father's who sent Me.
25 "These things I have spoken to you
while being present with you.
26 "But the Helper, the Holy Spirit, whom
the Father will send in My name, He will
teach you all things, and bring to your remembrance all things that I said to you.
27 [R]"Peace I leave with you, My peace I
give to you; not as the world gives do I give
to you. Let not your heart be troubled, neither let it be afraid. Luke 1:79; [Phil. 4:7]★
28 "You have heard Me [R]say to you, 'I am
going away and coming *back* to you.' If you
loved Me, you would rejoice because *I said,
[R]'I am going to the Father,' for [R]My Father is
greater than I. John 14:3, 18 • John 16:16 • [Phil. 2:6]
29 "And [R]now I have told you before it
comes, that when it does come to pass, you
may believe. John 13:19
30 "I will no longer talk much with you, [R]for
the ruler of this world is coming, and he has
[R]nothing in Me. [John 12:31] • [Heb. 4:15]
31 "But that the world may know that I
love the Father, and [R]as the Father gave Me
commandment, so I do. Arise, let us go from
here. Is. 50:5; John 10:18★

CHAPTER 15

The Relationship of Believers to Christ

"I AM the true vine, and My Father is the
vinedresser.
2 [R]"Every branch in Me that does not bear
fruit He takes away; and every *branch* that
bears fruit He prunes, that it may bear [R]more
fruit. Matt. 15:13 • [Matt. 13:12]
3 "You are already clean because of the
word which I have spoken to you.
4 [R]"Abide in Me, and I in you. As the
branch cannot bear fruit of itself, unless it
abides in the vine, neither can you, unless
you abide in Me. [Col. 1:23]

14:2 NU *would I have told you that I go* or *I would have told you; for I go* **14:14** NU *ask Me* **14:15** NU *you will keep* **14:28** NU omits *I said*

5 "I am the vine, you *are* the branches. He
who abides in Me, and I in him, bears much
fruit; for without Me you can do nothing.
6 "If anyone does not abide in Me, [R]he is
cast out as a branch and is withered; and they
gather them and throw *them* into the fire,
and they are burned. Matt. 3:10
7 "If you abide in Me, and My words abide
in you, [R]you* will ask what you desire, and it
shall be done for you. John 14:13; 16:23
8 "By this My Father is glorified, that you
bear much fruit; so you will be My disciples.
9 "As the Father [R]loved Me, I also have
loved you; abide in My love. John 5:20; 17:26
10 [R]"If you keep My commandments, you
will abide in My love, just as I have kept My
Father's commandments and abide in His
love. John 14:15
11 "These things I have spoken to you, that
My joy may remain in you, and [R]*that* your
joy may be full. 1 John 1:4

The Relationship of Believers to Each Other

12 "This is My commandment, that you
love one another as I have loved you.
13 [R]"Greater love has no one than this, than
to lay down one's life for his friends. 1 John 3:16
14 [R]"You are My friends if you do whatever
I command you. [Matt. 12:50; 28:20]
15 "No longer do I call you servants, for a
servant does not know what his master is
doing; but I have called you friends, [R]for all
things that I heard from My Father I have
made known to you. Gen. 18:17
16 "You did not choose Me, but I chose you
and [R]appointed you that you should go and
bear fruit, and *that* your fruit should remain,
that whatever you ask the Father in My
name He may give you. [Col. 1:6]
17 "These things I command you, that you
love one another.

The Relationship of Believers to the World

18 [R]"If the world hates you, you know that
it hated Me before *it hated* you. 1 John 3:13
19 "If you were of the world, the world
would love its own. Yet because you are not
of the world, but I chose you out of the
world, therefore the world hates you.
20 "Remember the word that I said to you,
[R]'A servant is not greater than his master.' If
they persecuted Me, they will also persecute
you. [R]If they kept My word, they will keep
yours also. John 13:16 • Ezek. 3:7
21 "But [R]all these things they will do to you
for My name's sake, because they do not
know Him who sent Me. Matt. 10:22; 24:9
22 [R]"If I had not come and spoken to them,
they would have no sin, [R]but now they have
no excuse for their sin. John 9:41; 15:24 • [James 4:17]
23 [R]"He who hates Me hates My Father
also. 1 John 2:23
24 "If I had not done among them [R]the
works which no one else did, they would
have no sin; but now they have seen and also
hated both Me and My Father. John 3:2
25 "But *this happened* that the word might
be fulfilled which is written in their law,
[R]*'They hated Me without a cause.'* Ps. 69:4 ★

The Promise of the Holy Spirit

26 "But when the [T]Helper comes, whom I
shall send to you from the Father, the Spirit
of truth who proceeds from the Father, He
will testify of Me. *Comforter,* Gr. *Parakletos*
27 "And [R]you also will bear witness, because [R]you have been with Me from the
beginning. Luke 24:48 • Luke 1:2

CHAPTER 16

"THESE things I have spoken to you,
that you [R]should not be made to
stumble. Matt. 11:6
2 [R]"They will put you out of the synagogues; yes, the time is coming [R]that whoever kills you will think that he offers God
service. John 9:22 • Acts 8:1
3 "And [R]these things they will do *to you
because they have not known the Father nor
Me. John 8:19; 15:21
4 "But these things I have told you, that
when *the time comes, you may remember
that I told you of them. And these things I
did not say to you at the beginning, because I
was with you.
5 "But now I [R]go away to Him who sent
Me, and none of you asks Me, 'Where are
You going?' John 7:33; 13:33; 14:28; 17:11
6 "But because I have said these things to
you, sorrow has filled your heart.
7 "Nevertheless I tell you the truth. It is to
your advantage that I go away; for if I do not
go away, the Helper will not come to you; but
[R]if I depart, I will send Him to you. Acts 2:33 ☆
8 "And when He has come, [R]He will convict the world of sin, and of righteousness,
and of judgment: Acts 1:8; 2:1–4, 37 ☆
9 [R]"of sin, because they do not believe in
Me; Acts 2:22
10 "of righteousness, [R]because I go to My
Father and you see Me no more; John 5:32
11 [R]"of judgment, because [R]the ruler of this
world is judged. Acts 26:18 • [Luke 10:18]
12 "I still have many things to say to you,
[R]but you cannot bear *them* now. Mark 4:33
13 "However, when He, the Spirit of truth,
has come, He will guide you into all truth; for
He will not speak on His own *authority,* but
whatever He hears He will speak; and [R]He
will tell you things to come. Acts. 11:28; Rev. 1:19 ☆
14 [R]"He will glorify Me, for He will take of
what is Mine and declare *it* to you. John 15:26
15 [R]"All things that the Father has are

15:7 NU omits *you will* **16:3** NU, M omit *to you*
16:4 NU *their*

THE TWO PARACLETES

One of the Greek verbs in the New Testament that is richly freighted with meaning is *parakaleō* (from *para*, "alongside," as in parallel lines, and *kaleō*, "call"). Its many occurrences are variously translated *exhort*, *comfort*, *console*, *encourage*, *entreat*, *beg*, and *beseech*, for no single English word covers its range of meanings. Three typical translations for the related noun *paraklēsis* are *comfort*, *encouragement*, and *exhortation*.

Paraclete (*Paraklētos*)

Paraklētos occurs five times in the Greek New Testament, four times in the Upper Room Discourse (John 13—17), and once in 1 John.

Many Christians know that the Holy Spirit is called "the Paraclete." What is perhaps less known is that Jesus Himself is called a Paraclete and that the Holy Spirit is "another Paraclete."

Christ the Paraclete

In 1 John 2:1, the apostle urges his readers not to sin. Yet being a realist, he knows that the most devout believers are subject to failure and do sin. So he adds a word of encouragement. "And if anyone sins, we have an Advocate [*Paraklētos*] with the Father, Jesus Christ the righteous. And He Himself is the propitiation [sacrifice that satisfies God] for our sins, and not for ours only but also for the whole world" (1 John 2:1, 2).

The translation "Advocate" in the KJV/NKJV comes from a Latin word *advocatus*. It is very similar to the Greek word in origin and meaning. The main part of the word (*-vocatus*) means "called," just like the *-klētos* part of *Paraclete*. Instead of *para* ("alongside"), however, the Latin calls someone "to" (*ad*) his side to help. The meanings are nearly the same. An advocate is someone who takes up your cause. For example, on a professional level he may be a lawyer.

Moulton and Milligan's valuable *The Vocabulary of the Greek Testament* gives the original idea as "one called in" to support, hence "advocate," "pleader," "a friend of the accused person, called to speak to his character, or otherwise enlist the sympathy of the judges" (p. 485). The word must have been popular because both the Hebrew and Aramaic languages borrowed the word.

Since we Christians cannot very well plead the merits of our "character" before God's throne (we have none!), Christ steps in with His own merits—the merits of His sacrifice on Calvary, which we appropriate by faith.

Another Paraclete (John 14:16)

While the Savior was here on earth the disciples could call Him aside at any time to answer a question or solve a problem. But in the Upper Room Discourse, He was preparing them for the time when He would not be personally present with them. Yes, He would be at God's right hand pleading their case and their needs, but He was going to leave Someone Else on earth for them (and for us) to turn to. This is His "Vicar," or Personal Representative on earth, the Holy Spirit.

In John 14:16, 17, our Lord made this promise: "And I will pray the Father, and He will give you another Helper [*Paraklētos*], that He may abide with you forever, *even* the Spirit of truth, whom the world cannot receive, because it neither sees Him nor knows Him; but you know Him, for He dwells with you and will be in you." He was predicting Pentecost, when the Spirit would come in a unique and new way that the Old Testament saints could not enjoy.

Precisely how to translate *Paraklētos* in this passage is difficult. No English word is a close match. The KJV has "Comforter." In 1611, this was a better rendering than it is today because then all educated Englishmen knew Latin and recognized the root *-fort* in "Comforter" as meaning "strong."

The NIV uses "Counselor" in John 14. The Living Bible retains the KJV "Comforter," but with "Helper" in a footnote. Twentieth Century, Moffatt, Basic English, Good News, and NKJV all use "Helper."

It is noteworthy that Jesus calls the Holy Spirit *another* Paraclete (*allos*, "another of the same kind"). He is like Jesus.

Mine. Therefore I said that He *will take of
Mine and declare *it* to you. Matt. 11:27

The Predictions of Christ's Death and Resurrection

16 "A [R]little while, and you will not see Me;
and again a little while, and you will see Me,
because I go to the Father." John 19:42; 20:19☆
17 **Then *some* of His disciples said among
themselves, "What is this that He says to us,
'A little while, and you will not see Me; and
again a little while, and you will see Me'; and,
'because I go to the Father'?"**
18 **They said therefore, "What is this that
He says, 'A little while'? We do not [T]know
what He is saying."** *understand*
19 **Now Jesus knew that they desired to ask
Him, and He said to them,** "Are you inquiring
among yourselves about what I said, 'A little
while, and you will not see Me; and again a
little while, and you will see Me'?
20 "Most assuredly, I say to you that you
will weep and [R]lament, but the world will
rejoice; and you will be sorrowful, but your
sorrow will be turned into joy. John 20:20☆
21 [R]"A woman, when she is in labor, has
sorrow because her hour has come; but as
soon as she has given birth to the child, she
no longer remembers the anguish, for joy
that a human being has been born into the
world. Is. 13:8; 26:17; 42:14
22 "Therefore you now have sorrow; but
I will see you again and [R]your heart will
rejoice, and your joy no one will take from
you. John 20:20; Acts 2:46; 13:52; 1 Pet. 1:8☆
23 "And in that day you will ask Me nothing. [R]Most assuredly, I say to you, whatever
you ask the Father in My name He will give
you. Matt. 7:7
24 "Until now you have asked nothing in
My name. Ask, and you will receive, [R]that
your joy may be [R]full. John 17:13 • John 15:11
25 "These things I have spoken to you in
figurative language; but the time is coming
when I will no longer speak to you in figurative language, but I will tell you [R]plainly
about the Father. John 7:13
26 "In that day you will ask in My name,
and I do not say to you that I shall pray the
Father for you;
27 [R]"for the Father Himself loves you, because you have loved Me, and have believed
that I came forth from God. [John 14:21, 23]
28 [R]"I came forth from the Father and have
come into the world. Again, I leave the world
and go to the Father." John 13:1, 3; 16:5, 10, 17
29 **His disciples said to Him, "See, now You
are speaking plainly, and using no figure of
speech!**
30 **"Now we are sure that [R]You know all
things, and have no need that anyone should
question You. By this [R]we believe that You
came forth from God."** John 21:17 • John 17:8

31 **Jesus answered them,** "Do you now believe?
32 [R]"Indeed the hour is coming, yes, has
now come, that you will be scattered, each to
[T]his own, and will leave Me alone. And yet I
am not alone, because the Father is with
Me. Matt. 26:31, 56; Mark 14:50☆ • *own things* or *place*
33 "These things I have spoken to you, that
in Me you may have peace. In the world you
*will have tribulation; but be of good cheer, I
have overcome the world."

CHAPTER 17

Christ Prays for Himself

**JESUS spoke these words, lifted up His eyes
to heaven, and said:** "Father, [R]the hour
has come. Glorify Your Son, that Your Son
also may glorify You, John 12:23
2 [R]"as You have given Him authority over
all flesh, that He *should give eternal life to
as many as You have given Him. John 3:35
3 "And this is eternal life, that they may
know You, the only true God, and Jesus
Christ [R]whom You have sent. John 3:34
4 [R]"I have glorified You on the earth. I
have finished the work which You have given
Me to do. Is. 49:3; 50:5; John 13:31★
5 "And now, O Father, glorify Me together
[T]with Yourself, with the glory which I had
with You before the world was. Lit. *alongside*

Christ Prays for His Disciples

6 "I have [T]manifested Your name to the
men whom You have given Me out of the
world. They were Yours, You gave them to
Me, and they have kept Your word. *revealed*
7 "Now they have known that all things
which You have given Me are from You.
8 "For [R]I have given to them the words
which You have given Me; and they have
received *them*, and have known surely that I
came forth from You; and they have believed
that You sent Me. Deut. 18:18★
9 "I pray for them. [R]I do not pray for the
world but for those whom You have given
Me, for they are Yours. [1 John 5:19]
10 "And all Mine are Yours, and [R]Yours are
Mine, and I am glorified in them. John 16:15
11 "Now I am no longer in the world, but
these are in the world, and I come to You.
Holy Father, [R]keep* through Your name
those whom You have given Me, that they
may be one [R]as We *are*. [1 Pet. 1:5] • John 10:30
12 "While I was with them *in the world, I
kept them in *Your name. Those whom You
gave Me I have kept; and none of them is lost

16:15 NU, M *takes of Mine and will declare*
16:33 NU, M omit *will* **17:2** M *shall*
17:11 NU, M *keep them through Your name which You have given Me* **17:12** NU omits *in the world*
17:12 NU *Your name which You gave Me. And I guarded them* (or *it.*);

except the son of [T]perdition, that the Scripture might be fulfilled. *destruction*

13 "But now I come to You, and these things I speak in the world, that they may have My joy fulfilled in themselves.

14 "I have given them Your word; and the world has hated them because they are not of the world, just as I am not of the world.

15 "I do not pray that You should take them out of the world, but [R]that You should keep them from the evil *one.* 1 John 5:18

16 "They are not of the world, just as I am not of the world.

17 [R]"Sanctify[T] them by Your truth. Your word is truth. [Eph. 5:26] • *Set them apart*

18 [R]"As You sent Me into the world, I also have sent them into the world. John 4:38; 20:21

19 "And for their sakes I sanctify Myself, that they also may be sanctified by the truth.

Christ Prays for All Believers

20 "I do not pray for these alone, but also for those who *will believe in Me through their word;

21 [R]"that they all may be one, as [R]You, Father, *are* in Me, and I in You; that they also may be one in Us, that the world may believe that You sent Me. [Gal. 3:28] • John 10:38; 17:11, 23

22 "And the [R]glory which You gave Me I have given them, [R]that they may be one just as We are one: 1 John 1:3 • [2 Cor. 3:18]

23 "I in them, and You in Me; that they may be made perfect in one, and that the world may know that You have sent Me, and have loved them as You have loved Me.

24 [R]"Father, I desire that they also whom You gave Me may be with Me where I am, that they may behold My glory which You have given Me; [R]for You loved Me before the foundation of the world. [1 Thess. 4:17] • John 17:5

25 "O righteous Father! The world has not known You, but I have known You; and these have known that You sent Me.

26 [R]"And I have declared to them Your name, and will declare *it,* that the love [R]with which You loved Me may be in them, and I in them." John 17:6 • John 15:9

CHAPTER 18

The Arrest of Christ
Matt. 26:47–56; Mark 14:43–52; Luke 22:47–53

WHEN Jesus had spoken these words, He went out with His disciples over the Brook Kidron, where there was a garden, which He and His disciples entered.

2 And Judas, who betrayed Him, also knew the place; [R]for Jesus often met there with His disciples. Luke 21:37; 22:39

3 [R]Then Judas, having received a detachment *of troops,* and officers from the chief priests and Pharisees, came there with lanterns, torches, and weapons. Luke 22:47–53

4 Jesus therefore, knowing all things that would come upon Him, went forward and said to them, "Whom are you seeking?"

5 They answered Him, [R]"Jesus [T]of Nazareth." Jesus said to them, "I am *He.*" And Judas, who [R]betrayed Him, also stood with them. Matt. 21:11 • Lit. *the Nazarene* • Ps. 41:9

6 Then—when He said to them, "I am *He,*"—they drew back and fell to the ground.

7 Then He asked them again, "Whom are you seeking?" And they said, "Jesus of Nazareth."

8 Jesus answered, "I have told you that I am *He.* Therefore, if you seek Me, let these go their way,"

9 that the saying might be fulfilled which He spoke, [R]"Of those whom You gave Me I have lost none." [John 6:39; 17:12]

10 [R]Then Simon Peter, having a sword, drew it and struck the high priest's servant, and cut off his right ear. The servant's name was Malchus. Matt. 26:51

11 Then Jesus said to Peter, "Put your sword into the sheath. Shall I not drink the cup which My Father has given Me?"

First Jewish Trial Before Annas
Matt. 26:69, 70; Mark 14:66–68; Luke 22:55–57

12 Then the detachment *of troops* and the captain and the officers of the Jews arrested Jesus and bound Him.

13 And they led Him away to Annas first, for he was the father-in-law of [R]Caiaphas who was high priest that year. Matt. 26:3

14 Now it was Caiaphas who gave counsel to the Jews that it was [T]expedient that one man should die for the people. *advantageous*

15 And Simon Peter followed Jesus, and so *did* *another disciple. Now that disciple was known to the high priest, and went with Jesus into the courtyard of the high priest.

16 But Peter stood at the door outside. Then the other disciple, who was known to the high priest, went out and spoke to her who kept the door, and brought Peter in.

17 Then the servant girl who kept the door said to Peter, "You are not also *one* of this Man's disciples, are you?" He said, "I am [R]not." Matt. 26:34

18 And the servants and officers who had made a fire of coals stood there, for it was cold, and they warmed themselves. And Peter stood with them and warmed himself.

19 The high priest then asked Jesus about His disciples and His doctrine.

20 Jesus answered him, "I spoke openly to the world. I always taught in synagogues and in the temple, where *the Jews always meet, and in secret I have said nothing.

21 "Why do you ask Me? Ask [R]those who

17:20 NU, M omit *will* **18:15** M *the other*
18:20 NU *all the Jews meet*

have heard Me what I said to them. Indeed they know what I said." Mark 12:37

22 And when He had said these things, one of the officers who stood by [R]struck Jesus with the palm of his hand, saying, "Do You answer the high priest like that?" Lam. 3:30★

23 Jesus answered him, "If I have spoken evil, bear witness of the evil; but if well, why do you strike Me?"

Second Jewish Trial Before Caiaphas
Matt. 26:57–68, 73–75; Mark 14:53–65, 70–72; Luke 22:59–65

24 [R]Then Annas sent Him bound to [R]Caiaphas the high priest. Matt. 26:57 • John 11:49

25 Now Simon Peter stood and warmed himself. [R]Therefore they said to him, "You are not also *one* of His disciples, are you?" He denied *it* and said, "I am not!" Luke 22:58–62

26 One of the servants of the high priest, a relative *of him* whose ear Peter cut off, said, "Did I not see you in the garden with Him?"

27 [R]Peter then denied again; and [R]immediately a rooster crowed. Matt. 26:34★ • John 13:38

First Roman Trial Before Pilate
Matt. 27:2, 11–14; Mark 15:1–5; Luke 23:1–5

28 [R]Then they led Jesus from Caiaphas to the Praetorium, and it was early morning. But they themselves did not go into the Praetorium, lest they should be defiled, but that they might eat the Passover. John 18:32★

29 [R]Pilate then went out to them and said, "What accusation do you bring against this Man?" Matt. 27:11–14

30 They answered and said to him, "If He were not [T]an evildoer, we would not have delivered Him up to you." *a criminal*

31 Then Pilate said to them, "You take Him and judge Him according to your law." Therefore the Jews said to him, "It is not lawful for us to put anyone to death,"

32 that the saying of Jesus might be fulfilled which He spoke, [R]signifying by what death He would die. John 3:14; 8:28; 12:32, 33

33 [R]Then Pilate entered the Praetorium again, called Jesus, and said to Him, "Are You the King of the Jews?" Matt. 27:11

34 Jesus answered him, "Are you speaking for yourself on this, or did others tell you this about Me?"

35 Pilate answered, "Am I a Jew? Your own nation and the chief priests have delivered You to me. What have You done?"

36 [R]Jesus answered, "My kingdom is not of this world. If My kingdom were of this world, My servants would fight, so that I should not be delivered to the Jews; but now My kingdom is not from here." 1 Tim. 6:13

37 Pilate therefore said to Him, "Are You a king then?" Jesus answered, "You say *rightly* that I am a king. For this cause I was born, and for this cause I have come into the world, [R]that I should bear [R]witness to the truth. Everyone who [R]is of the truth hears My voice." [Matt. 5:17; 20:28] • Is. 55:4 • [John 14:6]

38 Pilate said to Him, "What is truth?" And when he had said this, he went out again to the Jews, and said to them, [R]"I find no fault in Him *at all.* John 19:4, 6

Second Roman Trial Before Pilate
Matt. 27:15–31; Mark 15:6–20; Luke 23:13–25

39 [R]"But you have a custom that I should release someone to you at the Passover. Do you therefore want me to release to you the King of the Jews?" Luke 23:17–25

40 [R]Then they all cried again, saying, "Not this Man, but Barabbas!" [R]Now Barabbas was a robber. Is. 53:3; Acts 3:14★ • Luke 23:19

CHAPTER 19

SO then [R]Pilate took Jesus and scourged *Him.* Is. 50:6; Matt. 20:19; 27:26★

2 And the soldiers twisted a crown of thorns and put *it* on His head, and they put on Him a purple robe.

3 Then they *said, "Hail, King of the Jews!" And they [R]struck Him with their hands. Is. 50:6

4 Pilate then went out again, and said to them, "Behold, I am bringing Him out to you, [R]that you may know that I find no fault in Him." John 18:33, 38

5 Then Jesus came out, wearing the crown of thorns and the purple robe. And *Pilate* said to them, "Behold the Man!"

6 [R]Therefore, when the chief priests and officers saw Him, they cried out, saying, "Crucify *Him,* crucify *Him!*" Pilate said to them, "You take Him and crucify *Him,* for I find no fault in Him." Acts 3:13

7 The Jews answered him, [R]"We have a law, and according to *our law [R]He ought to die, because [R]He made Himself the Son of God." Lev. 24:16 • Matt. 20:18★ • Matt. 26:63–66

8 Therefore, when Pilate heard that saying, he was the more afraid,

9 and went again into the Praetorium, and said to Jesus, "Where are You from?" [R]But Jesus gave him no answer. Ps. 38:13, 14; Is. 53:7★

10 Then Pilate said to Him, "Are You not speaking to me? Do You not know that I have [T]power to crucify You, and [T]power to release You?" *authority*

11 Jesus answered, "You could have no power *at all* against Me unless it had been given you from above. Therefore the one who delivered Me to you has the greater sin."

12 From then on Pilate sought to release Him, but the Jews cried out, saying, "If you let this Man go, you are not Caesar's friend.

19:3 NU *came up to Him and said* **19:7** NU *the law*

[R]Whoever makes himself a king speaks
against Caesar." Luke 23:2
13 When Pilate therefore heard that saying,
he brought Jesus out and sat down in the
judgment seat in a place that is called *The*
Pavement, but in Hebrew, Gabbatha.
14 Now it was the Preparation Day of the
Passover, and about the sixth hour. And he
said to the Jews, "Behold your King!"
15 [R]But they cried out, "Away with *Him,*
away with *Him!* Crucify Him!" Pilate said to
them, "Shall I crucify your King?" The chief
priests answered, [R]"We have no king but
Caesar!" Is. 53:3★ • [Gen. 49:10]
16 [R]So he delivered Him to them to be
crucified. So they took Jesus *and led *Him*
away. Luke 23:24

The Crucifixion of Christ
Matt. 27:32–38, 48, 50; Mark 15:21–26, 36, 37;
Luke 23:26–33, 38, 46

17 And He, bearing His cross, [R]went out to a
place called *the Place* of a Skull, which is
called in Hebrew, Golgotha, Num. 15:36
18 where they [R]crucified Him, and two others with Him, one on either side, and Jesus in
the center. Ps. 22:16–18; Matt. 20:19; 26:2★
19 [R]Now Pilate wrote a title and put *it* on
the cross. And the writing was: Matt. 27:37

JESUS OF NAZARETH,
THE KING OF THE JEWS.

20 Then many of the Jews read this title, for
the place where Jesus was crucified was near
the city; and it was written in Hebrew, Greek,
and Latin.
21 Then the chief priests of the Jews said to
Pilate, "Do not write, 'The King of the Jews,'
but, 'He said, "I am the King of the Jews." ' "
22 Pilate answered, "What I have written, I
have written."
23 [R]Then the soldiers, when they had crucified Jesus, took His garments and made four
parts, to each soldier a part, and also the
tunic. Now the tunic was without seam,
woven from the top in one piece. Luke 23:34
24 They said therefore among themselves,
"Let us not tear it, but cast lots for it, whose
it shall be," that the Scripture might be
fulfilled which says:

[R]*"They divided My garments among*
them, Ps. 22:18★
And for My clothing they cast lots."

Therefore the soldiers did these things.
25 Now there stood by the cross of Jesus
His mother, and His mother's sister, Mary the
wife of Clopas, and Mary Magdalene.
26 When Jesus therefore saw His mother,
and [R]the disciple whom He loved standing by,
He said to His mother, [R]"Woman, behold
your son!" John 13:23; 20:2; 21:7, 20, 24 • John 2:4
27 Then He said to the disciple, "Behold
your mother!" And from that hour that disciple took her to his own *home.*
28 After this, Jesus, *knowing that all
things were now accomplished, [R]that
the Scripture might be fulfilled, said, "I
thirst!" Ps. 22:15★
29 Now a vessel full of sour wine was sitting
there; and [R]they filled a sponge with sour
wine, put *it* on hyssop, and put *it* to His
mouth. Ps. 69:21; Matt. 27:48, 50★
30 So when Jesus had received the sour
wine, He said, [R]"It is finished!" And bowing
His head, He gave up His spirit. Zech. 11:10, 11★
31 Therefore, because it was the Preparation *Day,* [R]that the bodies should not remain
on the cross on the Sabbath (for that Sabbath
was a [R]high day), the Jews asked Pilate that
their legs might be broken, and *that* they
might be taken away. Deut. 21:23 • Ex. 12:16
32 Then the soldiers came and broke the
legs of the first and of the other who was
crucified with Him.
33 But when they came to Jesus and saw
that He was already dead, [R]they did not break
His legs. Ps. 34:20★
34 But one of the soldiers pierced His side
with a spear, and immediately [R]blood and
water came out. [1 John 5:6, 8]
35 And he who has seen has testified, and
his testimony is true; and he knows that he is
telling the truth, so that you may believe.
36 For these things were done [R]that the
Scripture should be fulfilled, *"Not one of His*
bones shall be broken." Ps. 34:20★
37 And again another Scripture says,
[R]*"They shall look on Him whom they*
pierced." Zech. 12:10; 13:6★

The Burial of Christ
Matt. 27:57–60; Mark 15:42–46; Luke 23:50–54

38 [R]After this, Joseph of Arimathea, being a
disciple of Jesus, but secretly, [R]for fear of the
Jews, asked Pilate that he might take away
the body of Jesus; and Pilate gave *him* permission. So he came and took the body of
Jesus. Is. 53:9; Luke 23:50–56★ • [John 7:13; 9:22; 12:42]
39 And Nicodemus, who at first came to
Jesus by night, also came, bringing a mixture
of myrrh and aloes, about a hundred pounds.
40 Then they took the body of Jesus, and
[R]bound it in strips of linen with the spices, as
the custom of the Jews is to bury. John 20:5, 7
41 Now in the place where He was crucified
there was a garden, and in the garden a new
tomb in which no one had yet been laid.
42 So [R]there they laid Jesus, [R]because of the
Jews' Preparation *Day,* for the tomb was
nearby. Is. 53:9; Matt. 26:12; Mark 14:8★ • John 19:14, 31

19:16 NU omits *and led Him away* **19:28** M *seeing*

CHAPTER 20

The Resurrection of Christ
Matt. 28:1–8; Mark 16:1–8; Luke 24:1–12

ON the [R]first *day* of the week Mary Magdalene came to the tomb early, while it was still dark, and saw *that* the stone had been taken away from the tomb. Matt. 28:1–8

2 Then she ran and came to Simon Peter, and to the [R]other disciple, whom Jesus loved, and said to them, "They have taken away the Lord out of the tomb, and we do not know where they have laid Him." John 21:23, 24

3 [R]Peter therefore went out, and the other disciple, and were going to the tomb. Luke 24:12

4 So they both ran together, and the other disciple outran Peter and came to the tomb first.

5 And he, stooping down and looking in, saw [R]the linen cloths lying *there*; yet he did not go in. John 19:40

6 Then Simon Peter came, following him, and went into the tomb; and he saw the linen cloths lying *there*,

7 and the handkerchief that had been around His head, not lying with the linen cloths, but folded together in a place by itself.

8 Then the [R]other disciple, who came to the tomb first, went in also; and he saw and believed. John 21:23, 24

9 For as yet they did not know the Scripture, that He must rise again from the dead.

10 Then the disciples went away again to their own homes.

Christ Appears to Mary Magdalene

11 [R]But Mary stood outside by the tomb weeping, and as she wept she stooped down *and looked* into the tomb. Mark 16:5

12 And she saw two angels in white sitting, one at the head and the other at the feet, where the body of Jesus had lain.

13 Then they said to her, "Woman, why are you weeping?" She said to them, "Because they have taken away my Lord, and I do not know where they have laid Him."

14 Now when she had said this, she turned around and saw Jesus standing *there*, and [R]did not know that it was Jesus. John 21:4

15 Jesus said to her, "Woman, why are you weeping? Whom are you seeking?" She, supposing Him to be the gardener, said to Him, "Sir, if You have carried Him away, tell me where You have laid Him, and I will take Him away."

16 Jesus said to her, [R]"Mary!" She turned and said to *Him, "Rabboni!" (which is to say, Teacher). John 10:3

17 Jesus said to her, "Do not cling to Me, for I have not yet ascended to My Father; but go to My brethren and say to them, [R]'I am ascending to My Father and your Father, and to My God and your God.' " Mark 16:19; Acts 1:9☆

18 Mary Magdalene came and told the *disciples that she had seen the Lord, and *that* He had spoken these things to her.

Christ Appears to the Disciples (Thomas Absent)—Mark 16:14; Luke 24:36–43

19 Then, the same day at evening, being the first *day* of the week, when the doors were shut where the disciples were *assembled, for [R]fear of the Jews, [R]Jesus came and stood in the midst, and said to them, "Peace *be* with you." John 9:22; 19:38 • John 16:16★

20 Now when He had said this, He showed them *His* hands and His side. Then the disciples were glad when they saw the Lord.

21 Then Jesus said to them again, "Peace to you! [R]As the Father has sent Me, I also send you." John 17:18, 19

22 [R]And when He had said this, He breathed on *them*, and said to them, "Receive the Holy Spirit. John 16:20–22★

23 [R]"If you forgive the sins of any, they are forgiven them; if you retain the *sins* of any, they are retained." Matt. 16:19; 18:18

24 But Thomas, called Didymus, one of the twelve, was not with them when Jesus came.

25 The other disciples therefore said to him, "We have seen the Lord." But he said to them, "Unless I see in His hands the print of the nails, and put my finger into the print of the nails, and put my hand into His side, I will not believe."

Christ Appears to the Disciples (Thomas Present)—1 Cor. 15:5

26 And after eight days His disciples were again inside, and Thomas with them. Jesus came, the doors being shut, and stood in the midst, and said, "Peace to you!"

27 Then He said to Thomas, "Reach your finger here, and look at My hands; and reach your hand *here*, and put *it* into My side. Do not be unbelieving, but believing."

28 And Thomas answered and said to Him, "My Lord and my God!"

29 Jesus said to him, *"Thomas, because you have seen Me, you have believed. [R]Blessed *are* those who have not seen and *yet* have believed." 1 Pet. 1:8

The Purpose of John's Gospel

30 And [R]truly Jesus did many other signs in the presence of His disciples, which are not written in this book; John 21:25

31 but these are written that [R]you may believe that Jesus [R]is the Christ, the Son of God, [R]and that believing you may have life in His name. 1 John 5:13 • Luke 2:11 • John 3:15, 16; 5:24

20:16 NU adds *in Hebrew*
20:18 NU *disciples, "I have seen the Lord,"*
20:19 NU omits *assembled* **20:29** NU, M omit *Thomas*

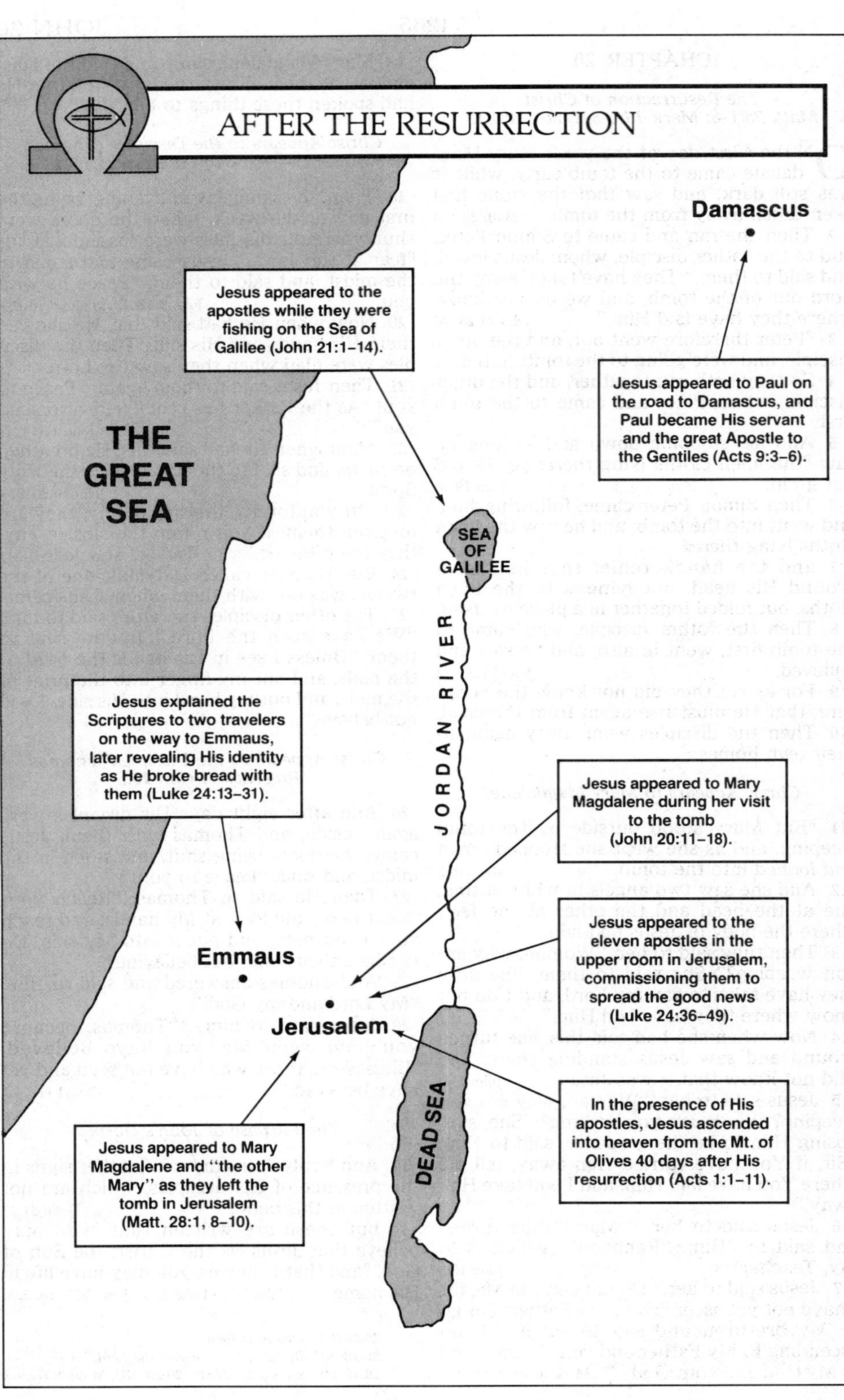

AFTER THE RESURRECTION
Damascus
Jesus appeared to the apostles while they were fishing on the Sea of Galilee (John 21:1–14).
Jesus appeared to Paul on the road to Damascus, and Paul became His servant and the great Apostle to the Gentiles (Acts 9:3–6).
THE GREAT SEA
SEA OF GALILEE
JORDAN RIVER
Jesus explained the Scriptures to two travelers on the way to Emmaus, later revealing His identity as He broke bread with them (Luke 24:13–31).
Jesus appeared to Mary Magdalene during her visit to the tomb (John 20:11–18).
Jesus appeared to the eleven apostles in the upper room in Jerusalem, commissioning them to spread the good news (Luke 24:36–49).
Emmaus
Jerusalem
DEAD SEA
In the presence of His apostles, Jesus ascended into heaven from the Mt. of Olives 40 days after His resurrection (Acts 1:1–11).
Jesus appeared to Mary Magdalene and "the other Mary" as they left the tomb in Jerusalem (Matt. 28:1, 8–10).

CHAPTER 21

Christ Appears to the Seven Disciples

AFTER these things Jesus showed Himself again to the disciples at the Sea of Tiberias, and in this way He showed *Himself*:

2 Simon Peter, [R]Thomas called Didymus, [R]Nathanael of [R]Cana in Galilee, [R]the *sons* of Zebedee, and two others of His disciples were together. John 20:24 • John 1:45–51 • John 2:1 • Matt. 4:21

3 Simon Peter said to them, "I am going fishing." They said to him, "We are going with you also." They went out and *immediately got into the boat, and that night they caught nothing.

4 But when the morning had now come, Jesus stood on the shore; yet the disciples [R]did not know that it was Jesus. John 20:14

5 Then [R]Jesus said to them, "Children, have you any food?" They answered Him, "No." Luke 24:41

6 And He said to them, [R]"Cast the net on the right side of the boat, and you will find *some*." So they cast, and now they were not able to draw it in because of the multitude of fish. Luke 5:4, 6, 7

7 Therefore that disciple whom Jesus loved said to Peter, "It is the Lord!" Now when Simon Peter heard that it was the Lord, he put on *his* outer garment (for he had removed it), and plunged into the sea.

8 But the other disciples came in the little boat (for they were not far from land, but about [T]two hundred cubits), dragging the net with fish. 300 ft.

9 Then, as soon as they had come to land, they saw a fire of coals there, and fish laid on it, and bread.

10 Jesus said to them, "Bring some of the fish which you have just caught."

11 Simon Peter went up and dragged the net to land, full of large fish, one hundred and fifty-three; and although there were so many, the net was not broken.

12 Jesus said to them, [R]"Come *and* eat breakfast." Yet none of the disciples dared ask Him, "Who are You?"—knowing that it was the Lord. Acts 10:41

13 Jesus then came and took the bread and gave it to them, and likewise the fish.

14 This *is* now [R]the third time Jesus showed Himself to His disciples after He was raised from the dead. John 20:19, 26

Christ Speaks to Peter

15 So when they had eaten breakfast, Jesus said to Simon Peter, "Simon, *son* of *Jonah, do you love Me more than these?" He said to Him, "Yes, Lord; You know that I love You." He said to him, "Feed My lambs."

16 He said to him again a second time, "Simon, *son* of *Jonah, do you love Me?" He said to Him, "Yes, Lord; You know that I love You." He said to him, "Tend My sheep."

17 He said to him the third time, "Simon, *son* of *Jonah, do you love Me?" Peter was grieved because He said to him the third time, "Do you love Me?" And he said to Him, "Lord, [R]You know all things; You know that I [T]love You." Jesus said to him, "Feed My sheep. John 2:24, 25; 16:30 • *have affection for*

18 [R]"Most assuredly, I say to you, when you were younger, you girded yourself and walked where you wished; but when you are old, you will stretch out your hands, and another will gird you and carry *you* where you do not wish." Acts 12:3, 4

19 This He spoke, signifying by what death he would glorify God. And when He had spoken this, He said to him, "Follow Me."

20 Then Peter, turning around, saw the disciple [R]whom Jesus loved following, [R]who also had leaned on His breast at the supper, and said, "Lord, who is the one who betrays You?" John 13:23; 20:2 • John 13:25

21 Peter, seeing him, said to Jesus, "But Lord, what *about* this man?"

22 Jesus said to him, "If I [T]will that he remain [R]till I come, what *is that* to you? You follow Me." *desire* • [Rev. 2:25; 3:11; 22:7, 20]

23 Then this saying went out among the brethren that this disciple would not die. Yet Jesus did not say to him that he would not die, but, "If I will that he remain till I come, what *is that* to you?"

The Conclusion of John's Gospel

24 This is the disciple who [R]testifies of these things, and wrote these things; and we know that his testimony is true. John 19:35

25 [R]And there are also many other things that Jesus did, which if they were written one by one, [R]I suppose that even the world itself could not contain the books that would be written. Amen. John 20:30 • Amos 7:10

21:3 NU omits *immediately* **21:15** NU *John* **21:16** NU *John* **21:17** NU *John*

THE ACTS

OF THE APOSTLES

THE BOOK OF ACTS

Jesus' last recorded words have come to be known as the Great Commission: "You shall be witnesses to Me in Jerusalem, and in all Judea and Samaria, and to the end of the earth" (1:8). The Book of Acts, written by Luke, is the story of the men and women who took that commission seriously and began to spread the news of a risen Savior to the most remote corners of the known world.

Each section of the book (1—7; 8—12; 13—28) focuses on a particular audience, a key personality, and a significant phase in the expansion of the gospel message.

As the second volume in a two-part work by Luke, this book probably had no separate title. But all available Greek manuscripts designate it by the title *Praxeis*, "Acts," or by an expanded title like "The Acts of the Apostles." *Praxeis* was commonly used in Greek literature to summarize the accomplishments of outstanding men. While the apostles are mentioned collectively at several points, this book really records the acts of Peter (1—12) and of Paul (13—28).

THE AUTHOR OF ACTS

Acts 1:1 refers Theophilus to "The former account," that is, the Gospel of Luke. (See "The Author of Luke" for the internal and external support for Lucan authorship of Luke.) Luke's source for the "we" sections in this book (16:10–17; 20:5—21:18; 27:1—28:16) was his own memory if not some kind of diary. For the remainder of this book, Luke no doubt followed the same careful investigative procedures that he used in writing his gospel (Luke 1:1–4). As a close traveling campanion of Paul, Luke had access to the principal eyewitness for chapters 13—28. It is also likely that he had opportunities to interview such key witnesses in Jerusalem as Peter and John for the information in chapters 1—12. Acts 15:23–29 and 23:26–30 indicate that Luke may have used written documents as well.

THE TIME OF ACTS

Suggested dates for the writing of Acts range from A.D. 62 to the middle of the second century. Twentieth-century archaeological discoveries have strikingly confirmed the trustworthiness and precision of Luke as a historian and show that his work should be dated in the first century. Luke's perplexingly abrupt ending with Paul awaiting trial in Rome has led many to believe that Acts was completed prior to Paul's trial (A.D. 62). If it was written after this crucial event, why didn't Luke mention the outcome? Luke may have had a reason, but the simplest explanation of his silence is that Paul had not yet stood before Caesar. Acts gives no hint of the persecution under Nero (A.D. 64), Paul's death (A.D. 68), or the destruction of Jerusalem (A.D. 70).

THE CHRIST OF ACTS

The resurrected Savior is the central theme of the sermons and defenses in Acts. The Old Testament Scriptures, the historical Resurrection, the apostolic testimony, and the convicting power of the Holy Spirit all bear witness that Jesus is both Lord and Christ (see Peter's sermons in 2:22–36 and 10:34–43). "To Him all the prophets witness that, through His name, whoever believes in Him will receive remission of sins" (10:43). "Nor is there salvation in any other, for there is no other name under heaven given among men by which we must be saved" (4:12).

KEYS TO ACTS

Key Word: The Growth of the Church—While there are four accounts of the life of Jesus, this is the only book that carries on the story from His ascension to the period of the New Testament epistles. Thus, Acts is the historical link between the gospels and the epistles. Because of Luke's strong emphasis on the ministry of the Holy Spirit, this book could be regarded as "the Acts of the Spirit of Christ working in and through the Apostles." As a missionary himself, Luke's interest in the progressive spread of the gospel is obviously reflected in this apostolic history. Luke was personally involved as a participant in this story, so it was not written from a detached point of view.

From a theological standpoint, Acts was written to trace the development of the body of Christ over the one-generation transition from a primarily Jewish to a predominantly gentile membership. This apologetic work presents Christianity as distinct from Judaism but also as its fulfillment.

Key Verses: Acts 1:8 and 2:42–47—"But you shall receive power when the Holy Spirit has come upon you; and you shall be witnesses to Me in Jerusalem, and in all Judea and Samaria, and to the end of the earth" (1:8).

"And they continued steadfastly in the apostles' doctrine and fellowship, in the breaking of bread, and in prayers. Then fear came upon every soul, and many wonders and signs were done through the apostles. Now all who believed were together, and had all things in common, and sold their possessions and goods, and divided them among all, as anyone had need. So continuing daily with one accord in the temple, and breaking bread from house to house, they ate their food with gladness and simplicity of heart, praising God and having favor with all the people. And the Lord added to the church daily those who were being saved" (2:42–47).

Key Chapter: Acts 2—Chapter 2 records the earth-changing events of the Day of Pentecost when the Holy Spirit comes, fulfilling Christ's promise to wait until the Holy Spirit arrives to empower and direct the witness. The Spirit transforms a small group of fearful men into a thriving, worldwide Church that is ever moving forward and fulfilling the Great Commission.

SURVEY OF ACTS

Luke begins the Book of Acts where he left off in his gospel. Acts records the initial fulfillment of the Great Commission of Matthew 28:19, 20 as it traces the beginning and growth of the New Testament church (this growth pattern can be seen in 1:15; 2:41, 47; 4:4; 5:14; 6:7; 9:31; 12:24; 13:49; 16:5; 19:20). Acts traces important events in the early history of Christianity from the ascension of Christ to the outpouring of the Holy Spirit to the rapid progress of the gospel, beginning in Jerusalem and spreading throughout the Roman Empire.

Acts is a pivotal book of transitions: from the gospels to the epistles (history), from Judaism to Christianity (religion), from law to grace (divine dealing), from Jews alone to Jews and Gentiles (people of God), and from kingdom to church (program of God).

The three movements in Acts follow its key verse (1:8): witness in Jerusalem (1:1—8:4); witness in Judea and Samaria (8:5—12:25); witness to the end of the earth (13—28).

Witness in Jerusalem (1:1—8:4): After appearing to His disciples for "forty days" (1:3), the Lord tells them to wait in Jerusalem for the fulfillment of His promise concerning the Holy Spirit. Ten days after His ascension, this promise is significantly fulfilled as the disciples are suddenly empowered and filled with the Holy Spirit. The disciples are transformed and filled with courage to proclaim the brand new message of the resurrected Savior. Peter's powerful sermon, like all the sermons in Acts, is built upon the Resurrection, and 3,000 persons respond with saving faith. After dramatically healing a man who was lame from birth, Peter delivers a second crucial message to the people of Israel resulting in thousands of additional responses. The religious leaders arrest the apostles, and this gives Peter an opportunity to preach a special sermon to them.

The enthusiasm and joy of the infant church are marred by internal and external problems. Ananias and Sapphira receive the ultimate form of discipline because of their treachery, and the apostles are imprisoned and persecuted because of their witness. Seven men, including Stephen and Philip, are selected to assist the apostles. Stephen is brought before the Sanhedrin; in his defense, Stephen surveys the Scriptures to prove that the Man they condemned and killed was the Messiah Himself. The members of the Sanhedrin react to Stephen's words by dragging him out of the city and making him the first Christian martyr.

Witness in Judea and Samaria (8:5—12:25): Philip goes to the province of Samaria and successfully proclaims the new message to a people hated by the Jews. Peter and John confirm his work and exercise their apostolic authority by imparting the Holy Spirit to these new members of the body of Christ. God sovereignly transforms Saul the persecutor into Paul the apostle to the Gentiles, but He uses Peter to introduce the gospel to the Gentiles. In a special vision Peter realizes that Christ has broken down the barrier between Jew and Gentile. After Cornelius and other Gentiles come to Christ through his preach-

FOCUS	WITNESS IN JERUSALEM		WITNESS IN JUDEA AND SAMARIA	WITNESS TO THE END OF THE EARTH	
REFERENCE	1:1 — 3:1	—	8:5 —	13:1 — 21:17	— 28:31
DIVISION	POWER OF THE CHURCH	PROGRESS OF THE CHURCH	EXPANSION OF THE CHURCH	PAUL'S THREE JOURNEYS	PAUL'S TRIALS
TOPIC	JEWS		SAMARITANS	GENTILES	
	PETER		PHILIP	PAUL	
LOCATION	JERUSALEM		JUDEA AND SAMARIA	UTTERMOST PART	
TIME	2 YEARS (A.D.33-35)		13 YEARS (A.D. 35-48)	14 YEARS (A.D. 48-62)	

ing, Peter convinces the Jewish believers in Jerusalem that "the Gentiles had also received the word of God" (11:1). Even while experiencing more and more persecution, the church continues to increase, spreading throughout the Roman Empire.

Witness to the End of the Earth (13—28): Beginning with chapter 13, Luke switches the focus of Acts from Peter to Paul. Antioch in Syria gradually replaces Jerusalem as the headquarters of the church, and all three of Paul's missionary journeys originate from that city. The first journey (A.D. 48–49) concentrates on the Galatian cities of Pisidian Antioch, Iconium, Lystra, and Derbe. After this journey, a council is held among the apostles and elders of the church in Jerusalem to determine that the gentile converts need not submit to the law of Moses. The second missionary journey (A.D. 50–52) brings Paul once again to the Galatian churches, and then for the first time on to Macedonia and Greece. Paul spends much of his time in the cities of Philippi, Thessalonica, and Corinth, and later returns to Jerusalem and Antioch. In his third missionary journey (A.D. 53–57), Paul spends almost three years in the Asian city of Ephesus before visiting Macedonia and Greece for the second time. Although he is warned not to go to Jerusalem, Paul cannot be dissuaded.

It is not long before Paul is falsely accused of bringing Gentiles into the temple. Only the Roman commander's intervention prevents his being killed by the mob. Paul's defense before the people and before the Sanhedrin evokes violent reactions. When the commander learns of a conspiracy to assassinate Paul, he sends his prisoner to Felix, the governor in Caesarea. During his two-year imprisonment there (A.D. 57–59), Paul defends the Christian faith before Felix, Festus, and Agrippa. His appeal to Caesar requires a long voyage to Rome, where he is placed under house arrest until his trial.

OUTLINE OF ACTS

Part One: The Witness in Jerusalem (1:1—8:4)

I. The Power of the Church . . . . 1:1—2:47

A. Prologue to Acts 1:1, 2
B. Appearances of the Resurrected Christ 1:3–8
C. Ascension of Christ 1:9–11
D. Anticipation of the Spirit 1:12–14
E. Appointment of Matthias 1:15–26
F. Filling with the Holy Spirit 2:1–4
G. Speaking with Other Tongues 2:5–13
H. Peter Explains Pentecost. 2:14–41
I. Practices of the Early Church 2:42–47

II. The Progress of the Church . . . . 3:1—8:4

A. Peter Heals the Lame Man. 3:1–11
B. Peter's Second Sermon 3:12–26
C. Peter and John Are Put into Custody 4:1–4
D. Peter Preaches to the Sanhedrin 4:5–12
E. Sanhedrin Commands Peter Not to Preach. 4:13–22
F. Apostles' Prayer for Boldness 4:23–31
G. Early Church Voluntarily Shares 4:32–37
H. Ananias and Sapphira Lie. 5:1–11
I. Apostles' Mighty Miracles. 5:12–16
J. Apostles' Persecution. 5:17–42
  1. Apostles Are Miraculously Freed from Prison 5:17–28
  2. Apostles Preach to the Council 5:29–32
  3. Gamaliel's Advice 5:33–39
  4. Apostles Are Beaten 5:40–42
K. Deacons Are Appointed 6:1–8
L. Stephen Is Martyred . . . . 6:9—7:60
  1. Stephen Is Brought Before the Council 6:9–15
  2. Stephen Preaches to the Council . . . 7:1–60
M. Saul Persecutes the Church 8:1–4

Part Two: The Witness in Judea and Samaria (8:5—12:25)

I. The Witness of Philip 8:5–40

A. Philip Witnesses to the Samaritans 8:5–25
B. Philip Witnesses to the Ethiopian Treasurer 8:26–40

II. The Conversion of Saul 9:1–31

A. Saul Is Converted and Blinded 9:1–9
B. Saul Is Filled with the Spirit 9:10–19
C. Saul Preaches at Damascus. 9:20–22
D. Saul Witnesses in Jerusalem 9:23–31

III. The Witness of Peter . . . . 9:32—11:18

A. Peter Heals Aeneas at Lydda 9:32–35
B. Peter Raises Dorcas at Joppa 9:36–43
C. Peter Witnesses to Cornelius at Caesarea . . . . 10:1—11:18
  1. Cornelius Sends for Peter 10:1–8
  2. Peter Sees the Great Sheet 10:9–22
  3. Peter Preaches to the Gentiles . . . 10:23–43
  4. Gentiles Are Converted and Speak in Tongues. 10:44–48
  5. Peter Defends His Ministry to the Gentiles. 11:1–18

IV. The Witness of the Early Church 11:19—12:25

A. The Witness of the Antioch Church 11:19–30
B. The Persecution by Herod 12:1–25
  1. Herod Kills James. 12:1, 2
  2. Peter Is Miraculously Released from Prison 12:3–19
  3. Herod Blasphemes and Dies 12:20–25

Part Three: The Witness to the End of the Earth (13:1—28:31)

I. The First Missionary Journey . . . . 13:1—14:28
- A. Barnabas and Saul Are Sent from Antioch 13:1–3
- B. Ministry at Cyprus 13:4–13
  - 1. Preaching in the Synagogues 13:4, 5
  - 2. Controversy with Bar-Jesus 13:6–13
- C. Ministry at Antioch 13:14–50
  - 1. Paul Preaches on First Sabbath 13:14–43
  - 2. Paul Preaches on Second Sabbath 13:44–50
- D. Ministry at Iconium . . . . 13:51—14:5
- E. Ministry at Lystra 14:6–20
  - 1. A Lame Man Is Healed 14:6–10
  - 2. Paul and Barnabas Are Deified 14:11–18
  - 3. Paul Is Stoned 14:19, 20
- F. Ministry on the Return Trip 14:21–25
- G. Report on the First Missionary Journey 14:26–28

II. The Jerusalem Council 15:1–35
- A. Debate over Gentiles Keeping the Law 15:1–5
- B. Peter Preaches Salvation Through Grace 15:6–11
- C. Paul and Barnabas Testify 15:12
- D. James Proves Gentiles Are Free from the Law 15:13–21
- E. The Council Sends an Official Letter 15:22–29
- F. Report to Antioch 15:30–35

III. The Second Missionary Journey . . . . 15:36—18:22
- A. Contention over John Mark 15:36–41
- B. Derbe and Lystra: Timothy Is Circumcised 16:1–5
- C. Troas: Macedonian Call 16:6–10
- D. Philippi: Extensive Ministry 16:11–40
  - 1. Lydia Is Converted 16:11–15
  - 2. A Spirit of Divination Is Cast Out 16:16–24
  - 3. Philippian Jailer Is Converted 16:25–34
  - 4. Paul Is Released from Prison 16:35–40
- E. Thessalonica: "Turned the World Upside Down" 17:1–9
- F. Berea: Many Receive the Word 17:10–15
- G. Athens: Paul's Sermon on Mars' Hill 17:16–34
- H. Corinth: One-and-a-half Years of Ministry 18:1–17
  - 1. Paul Works with Aquila and Priscilla 18:1–3
  - 2. Jews Reject Paul 18:4–6
  - 3. Crispus, the Gentile, Is Converted 18:7–11
  - 4. Gallio Will Not Try Paul 18:12–17
- I. Return Trip to Antioch 18:18–22

IV. The Third Missionary Journey . . . . . 18:23—21:16
- A. Galatia and Phrygia: Strengthening the Disciples 18:23
- B. Ephesus: Three Years of Ministry . . . . 18:24—19:41
  - 1. Apollos Teaches Effectively 18:24–28
  - 2. Disciples of John Receive the Holy Spirit 19:1–7
  - 3. Paul Teaches in Tyrannus's School 19:8–10
  - 4. Miracles Are Performed at Ephesus 19:11–20
  - 5. Timothy and Erastus Are Sent to Macedonia 19:21, 22
  - 6. Demetrius Causes Uproar at Ephesus 19:23–41
- C. Macedonia: Three Months of Ministry 20:1–5
- D. Troas: Eutychus Falls from Loft 20:6–12
- E. Miletus: Paul Bids Farewell to Ephesian Elders 20:13–38
- F. Tyre: Paul Is Warned About Jerusalem 21:1–6
- G. Caesarea: Agabus's Prediction 21:7–16

V. The Trip to Rome . . . . 21:17—28:31
- A. Paul Witnesses in Jerusalem . . . . 21:17—23:33
  - 1. Paul Conforms to Jewish Customs 21:17–26
  - 2. Paul's Arrest 21:27–39
  - 3. Paul's Defense Before the Crowd . . . . 21:40—22:23
  - 4. Paul's Defense Before the Centurion 22:24–29
  - 5. Paul's Defense Before the Sanhedrin . . . . 22:30—23:11
  - 6. Jews' Plan to Kill Paul 23:12–22
  - 7. Paul's Rescue 23:23–33
- B. Paul Witnesses in Caesarea . . . . 23:34—26:32
  - 1. Paul Is Tried Before Felix . . . . 23:34—24:27
  - 2. Paul Is Tried Before Festus 25:1–22
  - 3. Paul Is Tried Before Agrippa 25:23—26:32
- C. Paul Witnesses in Rome . . . . 27:1—28:31
  - 1. Paul's Witness During the Shipwreck 27:1–44
  - 2. Paul's Witness on Malta 28:1–15
  - 3. Paul's Witness in Rome 28:16–31

CHAPTER 1

Prologue to Acts

THE former account I made, O [R]Theophi-
lus, of all that Jesus began both to do and
teach, Luke 1:3
2 until the day in which [T]He was taken up,
after He through the Holy Spirit [R]had given
commandments to the apostles whom He had
chosen, He ascended into heaven. • Matt. 28:19

Appearances of the Resurrected Christ
Luke 24:44–49

3 [R]to whom He also presented Himself
alive after His suffering by many [T]infallible
proofs, being seen by them during forty days
and speaking of the things pertaining to the
kingdom of God. Mark 16:12, 14 • *unmistakable*
4 [R]And being assembled together with
them, He commanded them not to depart
from Jerusalem, but to wait for the Promise

of the Father, "which," *He said,* "you have
[R]heard from Me; Luke 24:49 • [John 14:16, 17, 26; 15:26]
5 "for John truly baptized with water, [R]but
you shall be baptized with the Holy Spirit not
many days from now." [Joel 2:28]
6 Therefore, when they had come together, they asked Him, saying, "Lord, will
You at this time restore the kingdom to
Israel?"
7 And He said to them, "It is not for you to
[R]know times or seasons which the Father has
put in His own authority. Matt. 24:36

8 [R]"But you shall receive power [R]when the
Holy Spirit has come upon you; and [R]you
shall be *witnesses to Me in Jerusalem, and in
all Judea and [R]Samaria, and to the end of the
earth." [Acts 2:1, 4] • Luke 24:49 • Luke 24:48 • Acts 8:1

Ascension of Christ
Mark 16:19; Luke 24:50, 51

9 Now when He had spoken these things,
while they watched, He was taken up, and a
cloud received Him out of their sight.
10 And while they looked steadfastly
toward heaven as He went up, behold, two
men stood by them [R]in white apparel, John 20:12
11 who also said, "Men of Galilee, why do
you stand gazing up into heaven? This *same*
Jesus, who was taken up from you into
heaven, [R]will so come in like manner as you
saw Him go into heaven." Dan. 7:13

Anticipation of the Spirit—Luke 24:52

12 [R]Then they returned to Jerusalem from
the mount called Olivet, which is near Jerusalem, a Sabbath day's journey. Luke 24:52
13 And when they had entered, they went
up into the upper room where they were
staying: Peter, James, John, and Andrew;
Philip and Thomas; Bartholomew and Matthew; James *the son* of Alphaeus and Simon
the Zealot; and Judas *the son* of James.
14 These all continued with one [T]accord in
prayer *and supplication, with [R]the women
and Mary the mother of Jesus, and with [R]His
brothers. *purpose* or *mind* • Luke 23:49, 55 • Matt. 13:55

Appointment of Matthias—Matt. 27:7, 8

15 And in those days Peter stood up in the
midst of the *disciples (altogether the number [R]of names was about a hundred and
twenty), and said, Rev. 3:4
16 "Men *and* brethren, this Scripture had to
be fulfilled, [R]which the Holy Spirit spoke
before by the mouth of David concerning
Judas, [R]who became a guide to those who
arrested Jesus; Ps. 41:9★ • Luke 22:47
17 "for he was numbered with us and obtained a part in [R]this ministry." Acts 1:25
18 (Now this man purchased a field with the
[T]wages of iniquity; and falling headlong, he
burst open in the middle and all his entrails
gushed out. *reward of unrighteousness*
19 And it became known to all those dwelling in Jerusalem; so that field is called in their
own language, Akel Dama, that is, Field of
Blood.)
20 "For it is written in the book of Psalms:

[R]*'Let his habitation be desolate,*
And let no one live in it'; Ps. 69:25

and,

[R]*'Let another take his office.'* Ps. 109:8★

21 "Therefore, of these men who have accompanied us all the time that the Lord Jesus
went in and out among us,
22 "beginning from the baptism of John to
that day when [R]He was taken up from us, one
of these must [R]become a witness with us of
His resurrection." Acts 1:9 • Acts 1:8; 2:32
23 And they proposed two: Joseph called
[R]Barsabas, who was surnamed Justus, and
Matthias. Acts 15:22
24 And they prayed and said, "You, O Lord,
[R]who know the hearts of all, show which of
these two You have chosen 1 Sam. 16:7

1:8 NU *My witnesses* **1:14** NU omits *and supplication*
1:15 NU *brethren*

1:8 Empowered by God—One of the most common excuses for not becoming a Christian is the fear of failure to live the Christian life. Besides overlooking the fact that men cannot be saved on the basis of good works (Page 1442—Titus 3:5), this objection neglects the truth that God provides the power to live the Christian life. Before Christ was crucified He promised the coming of the Holy Spirit to help believers (Page 1259—John 16:13, 14). The subsequent events of the Book of Acts supply ample evidence of the fulfillment of this prophecy (Page 1276—Acts 4:7, 33; 6:8).

The power of the Holy Spirit was not designed solely for the first-century church. Rather, all Christians are indwelt by the Spirit and thus have His power available (Page 1351—1 Cor. 6:19). However, living the Christian life under the Spirit's power must not be thought of as simply allowing the Spirit to take control while the believer does nothing. The believer still must live the Christian life, though he does it through the Spirit's power. Romans 8:13 says, "if by the Spirit you put to death the deeds of the body, you will live." It is you who are to put to death the sinful deeds of the body, but you are to do it through the Spirit's power.

The Christian who struggles in his own strength to live the Christian life will fail. He must by faith appropriate daily the power of the Holy Spirit (Page 1332—Rom. 8:4, 5). Described practically, this means that the believer trusts the Spirit to empower him in specific instances such as sharing his faith with others, resisting temptation, being faithful, etc. There is no *secret formula* that makes the Spirit's power available. It is simply a reliance on the Spirit to help.

Now turn to Page 1440—Titus 1:2: Promise of God.

25 "to take part in this ministry and apostleship from which Judas by transgression fell,
that he might go to his own place."
26 And they cast their lots, and the lot fell
on Matthias. And he was numbered with the
eleven apostles.

CHAPTER 2

Filling with the Holy Spirit

NOW when [R]the Day of Pentecost had
fully come, [R]they were all *with one
accord in one place. Lev. 23:15 • Acts 1:14
2 And suddenly there came a sound from
heaven, as of a rushing mighty wind, and [R]it
filled the whole house where they were sitting. Acts 4:31
3 Then there appeared to them *divided
tongues, as of fire, and *one* sat upon each of
them.
4 And they were all filled with the Holy
Spirit and began to speak with other tongues,
as the Spirit gave them utterance.

Speaking with Other Tongues

5 Now there were dwelling in Jerusalem
Jews, [R]devout men, from every nation under
heaven. Acts 8:2
6 And when this sound occurred, the [R]mul-
titude came together, and were confused,
because everyone heard them speak in his
own language. Acts 4:32
7 Then they were all amazed and marveled, saying to one another, "Look, are not
all these who speak [R]Galileans? Acts 1:11
8 "And how *is it that* we hear, each in our
own [T]language in which we were born? *dialect*
9 "Parthians and Medes and Elamites,
those dwelling in Mesopotamia, Judea and
[R]Cappadocia, Pontus and Asia, 1 Pet. 1:1
10 "Phrygia and Pamphylia, Egypt and the
parts of Libya adjoining Cyrene, visitors from
Rome, both Jews and proselytes,
11 "Cretans and [T]Arabs—we hear them
speaking in our own tongues the wonderful
works of God." *Arabians*
12 So they were all amazed and perplexed,
saying to one another, "Whatever could this
mean?"
13 Others mocking said, "They are full of
new wine."

Peter Explains Pentecost

14 But Peter, standing up with the eleven,
raised his voice and said to them, "Men of
Judea and all who dwell in Jerusalem, let this
be known to you, and heed my words.
15 "For these are not drunk, as you suppose, [R]since it is *only* [T]the third hour of the
day. 1 Thess. 5:7 • 9 A.M.
16 "But this is what was spoken by the
prophet Joel:

17 *'And[R] it shall come to pass in the last*
days, says God, Joel 2:28–32
[R]*That I will pour out of My Spirit on all*
flesh; Acts 10:45
Your sons and [R]*your daughters shall*
prophesy, Acts 21:9
Your young men shall see visions,
Your old men shall dream dreams.
18 *And on My menservants and on My*
maidservants
I will pour out My Spirit in those days;
[R]*And they shall prophesy.* 1 Cor. 12:10
19 [R]*I will show wonders in heaven above*
And signs in the earth beneath: Joel 2:30
Blood and fire and vapor of smoke.
20 [R]*The sun shall be turned into darkness,*
And the moon into blood,
Before the coming of the great and
notable day of the LORD. Matt. 24:29
21 *And it shall come to pass that* [R]*whoever*
calls on the name of the LORD shall
be saved.' Rom. 10:13

22 "Men of Israel, hear these words: Jesus
of Nazareth, [R]a Man attested by God to you
[R]by miracles, wonders, and signs which God
did through Him in your midst, as you yourselves also know— Is. 50:5★ • John 3:2; 5:6
23 "Him, [R]being delivered by the determined
counsel and foreknowledge of God, [R]you
*have taken by lawless hands, have crucified,
and put to death; Luke 22:22 • Acts 5:30
24 "whom God raised up, having [T]loosed the
pains of death, because it was not possible
that He should be held by it. *destroyed*
25 "For David says concerning Him:

[R]*'I foresaw the LORD always before my*
face,
For He is at my right hand, that I may
not be shaken; Ps. 16:8–11★
26 *Therefore my heart rejoiced, and my*
tongue was glad;
Moreover my flesh will also rest in
hope,
27 *Because You will not leave my soul in*
Hades,
Nor will You allow Your Holy One to
see [R]*corruption.* Acts 13:30–37
28 *You have made known to me the ways*
of life;
You will make me full of joy in Your
presence.'

29 "Men *and* brethren, let *me* speak freely
to you [R]of the patriarch David, that he is both
dead and buried, and his tomb is with us to
this day. Acts 13:36
30 "Therefore, being a prophet, [R]and knowing that God had sworn with an oath to him

2:1 NU *together*
2:3 Or *tongues as of fire, distributed and resting on each* **2:23** NU omits *have taken*
2:30 NU *He would seat one on his throne,*

that of the fruit of his body, *according to the
flesh, He would raise up the Christ to sit on
his throne, Ps. 132:11★
31 "he, foreseeing this, spoke concerning
the resurrection of the Christ, [R]that His soul
was not left in Hades, nor did His flesh see
corruption. Ps. 16:10; Acts 13:35★
32 [R]"This Jesus God has raised up, [R]of which
we are all witnesses. Ps. 68:18★ • Acts 1:8; 3:15
33 "Therefore being exalted to the right
hand of God, and having received from the
Father the promise of the Holy Spirit, He
poured out this which you now see and hear.
34 "For David did not ascend into the heavens, but he says himself:

[R]*'The LORD said to my Lord,*
"Sit at My right hand, Ps. 68:18; 110:1★
35 *Till I make Your enemies Your*
footstool."'

36 "Therefore let all the house of Israel
know assuredly that God has made this
Jesus, whom you crucified, both Lord and
Christ."
37 Now when they heard *this,* [R]they were
cut to the heart, and said to Peter and the
rest of the apostles, "Men *and* brethren, what
shall we do?" John 16:8★
38 Then Peter said to them, "Repent, and let
every one of you be baptized in the name of
Jesus Christ for the remission of sins; and you
shall receive the gift of the Holy Spirit.
39 "For the promise is to you and to your
children, and [R]to all who are afar off, as many
as the Lord our God will call." Eph. 2:13
40 And with many other words he testified
and exhorted them, saying, "Be saved from
this [T]perverse generation." *crooked*
41 Then those who *gladly received his
word were baptized; and that day about three
thousand souls were added *to them.*

Practices of the Early Church

42 And they continued steadfastly in the
apostles' [T]doctrine and fellowship, in the
breaking of bread, and in prayers. *teaching*
43 Then fear came upon every soul, and
[R]many wonders and signs were done through
the apostles. Acts 2:22
44 Now all who believed were together, and
[R]had all things in common, Acts 4:32, 34, 37; 5:2
45 and [T]sold their possessions and goods,
and [R]divided[T] them among all, as anyone had
need. *would sell* • Is. 58:7 • *distributed*
46 [R]So continuing daily with one accord [R]in
the temple, and breaking bread from house to
house, they ate their food with gladness and
simplicity of heart, Acts 1:14 • Luke 24:53
47 praising God and having favor with all
the people. And the Lord added *to the
church daily those who were being saved.

CHAPTER 3

Peter Heals the Lame Man

NOW Peter and John went up together [R]to
the temple at the hour of prayer, [R]the
[T]ninth *hour.* Acts 2:46 • Ps. 55:17 • 3:00 P.M.
2 And [R]a certain man lame from his mother's womb was carried, whom they laid daily
at the gate of the temple which is called
Beautiful, [R]to [T]ask alms from those who
entered the temple; Acts 14:8 • John 9:8 • Beg
3 who, seeing Peter and John about to go
into the temple, asked for alms.
4 And fixing his eyes on him, with John,
Peter said, "Look at us."
5 So he gave them his attention, expecting
to receive something from them.
6 Then Peter said, "Silver and gold I do not
have, but what I do have I give you: [R]In the
name of Jesus Christ of Nazareth, rise up and
walk." Acts 4:10
7 And he took him by the right hand and
lifted *him* up, and immediately his feet and
ankle bones received strength.
8 So he, [R]leaping up, stood and walked and
entered the temple with them—walking,
leaping, and praising God. Is. 35:6
9 [R]And all the people saw him walking and
praising God. Acts 4:16, 21
10 Then they knew that it was he who sat
begging alms at the Beautiful Gate of the
temple; and they were filled with wonder and
amazement at what had happened to him.
11 Now as the lame man who was healed
held on to Peter and John, all the people ran
together to them in the porch [R]which is called
Solomon's, greatly amazed. John 10:23

2:41 NU omits *gladly* **2:47** NU omits *to the church*

2:42–47 Benefits of Participation in the Local Church—The benefits of participation in a local church are immediately apparent. This passage records the first meeting of the first local church. From this passage seven benefits of participation in the local church are immediately apparent: instruction—"continued steadfastly in the apostles' doctrine"; fellowship—"and fellowship"; observance of the ordinances—"breaking of bread"; corporate prayer—"prayers"; effective outreach—"fear came upon every soul"; common cause—"had all things in common"; and mutual assistance—"divided them among all, as anyone had need." In addition to these, four other benefits of participation in the local church are clear: worship (Page 1302—Acts 20:7); discipline (Page 1138—Matt. 18:15–17; Page 1375—2 Cor. 13:1–10); pastoral oversight (Page 1483—1 Pet. 5:1–3); and obedience to God's command (Page 1458—Heb. 10:25). Participation in the local church is not optional for the child of God. It is imperative and yields eternal benefits.

Now turn to Page 1155—Matt. 28:19: Sharing Our Faith: Why?

THE NATIONS OF PENTECOST

Pentecost, a Jewish feast also known as the Feast of Weeks, marked the completion of the barley harvest. On this annual holiday about 50 days after the resurrection of Jesus, Jewish people from throughout the Roman Empire were gathered in the city of Jerusalem to observe this great religious holiday. When the Holy Spirit was poured out on the apostles, they began to speak with "other tongues," and these people from other nations understood them perfectly (Acts 2:5–13). This map shows the different regions of the Roman Empire represented in Jerusalem on the Day of Pentecost.

Peter's Second Sermon

12 So when Peter saw *it*, he responded to the people: "Men of Israel, why do you marvel at this? Or why look so intently at us, as though by our own power or godliness we had made this man walk?

13 "The God of Abraham, Isaac, and Jacob, the God of our fathers, glorified His Servant Jesus, whom you [R]delivered up and [R]denied in the presence of Pilate, when he was determined to let *Him* go. Matt. 27:2 • Matt. 27:20

14 "But you denied [R]the Holy One [R]and the Just, and [R]asked for a murderer to be granted to you, Mark 1:24 • Acts 7:52 • John 18:40

15 "and killed the [T]Prince of life, [R]whom God raised from the dead, [R]of which we are witnesses. Or *Originator* • Acts 2:24 • Acts 2:32

16 [R]"And His name, through faith in His name, has made this man strong, whom you see and know. Yes, the faith which *comes* through Him has given him this perfect soundness in the presence of you all. Matt. 9:22

17 "Yet now, brethren, I know that you did *it* in ignorance, as *did* also your rulers.

18 "But those things which God foretold by the mouth of all His prophets, that the Christ would suffer, He has thus fulfilled.

19 [R]"Repent therefore and be converted, that your sins may be blotted out, so that times of refreshing may come from the presence of the Lord, [Acts 2:38; 26:20]

20 "and that He may send *Jesus Christ, [R]who was preached to you before, Mal. 3:1 ★

21 "whom heaven must receive until the times of restoration of all things, which God has spoken by the mouth of all His holy prophets since [T]the world began. Or *time*

22 "For Moses truly said to the fathers, *'The* LORD *your God will raise up for you* [R]*a Prophet like me from your brethren. Him you shall hear in all things, whatever He says to you.* Deut. 18:15, 18, 19 ★

23 *'And it shall come to pass that every soul who will not hear that Prophet shall be utterly destroyed from among the people.'*

24 "Yes, and all the prophets, from Samuel and those who follow, as many as have spoken, have also *foretold these days.

25 [R]"You are sons of the prophets, and of the covenant which God made with our fathers, saying to Abraham, [R]*'And in your seed all the families of the earth shall be blessed.'* [Rom. 9:4, 8] • Gen. 12:3; 18:18 ★

26 "To you [R]first, God, having raised up His Servant Jesus, sent Him to bless you, [R]in turning away every one *of you* from your iniquities." [Rom. 1:16; 2:9] • Matt. 1:21 ★

CHAPTER 4

Peter and John Are Put into Custody

NOW as they spoke to the people, the priests, the captain of the temple, and the [R]Sadducees came upon them, Matt. 22:23

2 being greatly disturbed that they taught the people and preached in Jesus the resurrection from the dead.

3 And they laid hands on them, and put *them* in custody until the next day, for it was already evening.

4 However, many of those who heard the word believed; and the number of the men came to be about five thousand.

Peter Preaches to the Sanhedrin

5 And it came to pass, on the next day, that their rulers, elders, and scribes,

6 as well as [R]Annas the high priest, Caiaphas, John, and Alexander, and as many as were of the family of the high priest, were gathered together at Jerusalem. Luke 3:2

7 And when they had set them in the midst, they asked, [R]"By what power or by what name have you done this?" Matt. 21:23

8 [R]Then Peter, filled with the Holy Spirit, said to them, "Rulers of the people and elders of Israel: Luke 12:11, 12

9 "If we this day are judged for a good deed *done* to *the* helpless man, by what means he has been made well,

10 "let it be known to you all, and to all the people of Israel, that by the name of Jesus Christ of Nazareth, whom you crucified, [R]whom God raised from the dead, by Him this man stands here before you whole. Acts 2:24

11 [R]"This is the *'stone which was rejected by you builders, which has become the chief cornerstone.'* Ps. 118:22; Is. 28:16 ★

12 "Nor is there salvation in any other, for there is no other name under heaven given among men by which we must be saved."

Sanhedrin Commands Peter Not to Preach

13 Now when they saw the boldness of Peter and John, [R]and perceived that they were uneducated and untrained men, they marveled. And they realized that they had been with Jesus. [1 Cor. 1:27]

14 And seeing the man who had been healed [R]standing with them, they could say nothing against it. Acts 3:11

15 But when they had commanded them to go aside out of the council, they conferred among themselves,

16 saying, "What shall we do to these men? For, indeed, that a notable miracle has been done through them *is* evident to all who dwell in Jerusalem, and we cannot deny *it*.

17 "But so that it spreads no further among the people, let us severely threaten them, that from now on they speak to no man in this name."

18 [R]And they called them and commanded them not to speak at all nor teach in the name of Jesus. Acts 5:28, 40

3:20 NU, M *Christ Jesus, who was ordained for you before* **3:24** NU, M *proclaimed*

19 But Peter and John answered and said to
them, [R]"Whether it is right in the sight of
God to listen to you more than to God, you
judge. Acts 5:29
20 "For we cannot but speak the things
which we have seen and heard."
21 So when they had further threatened
them, they let them go, finding no way of
punishing them, [R]because of the people, since
they all [R]glorified God for [R]what had been
done. Acts 5:26 • Matt. 15:31 • Acts 3:7, 8
22 For the man was over forty years old on
whom this miracle of healing had been performed.

Apostles' Prayer for Boldness

23 And being let go, they went to their own
companions and reported all that the chief
priests and elders had said to them.
24 So when they heard that, they raised
their voice to God with one accord and said:
"Lord, You *are* God, who made heaven and
earth and the sea, and all that is in them,
25 "who *by the mouth of Your servant
David have said:

[R]*'Why did the nations rage,* Ps. 2:1, 2★
And the people plot vain things?
26 *The kings of the earth took their stand,*
And the rulers were gathered together
Against the LORD *and against His*
Christ.'

27 "For truly against Your holy Servant
Jesus, whom You anointed, both Herod and
Pontius Pilate, with the Gentiles and the
people of Israel, were gathered together
28 "to do whatever Your hand and Your
purpose determined before to be done.
29 "Now, Lord, look on their threats, and
grant to Your servants [R]that with all boldness
they may speak Your word, Acts 4:13, 31; 9:27
30 "by stretching out Your hand to heal,
[R]and that signs and wonders may be done
[R]through the name of [R]Your holy Servant
Jesus." Acts 2:43; 5:12 • Acts 3:6, 16 • Acts 4:27
31 And when they had prayed, [R]the place
where they were assembled together was
shaken; and they were all filled with the Holy
Spirit, [R]and they spoke the word of God with
boldness. Acts 2:2, 4; 16:26 • Acts 4:29

Early Church Voluntarily Shares

32 Now the multitude of those who believed
[R]were of one heart and one soul; [R]neither did
anyone say that any of the things he possessed was his own, but they had all things in
common. Rom. 15:5, 6 • Acts 2:44
33 And with great power the apostles gave
witness to the resurrection of the Lord Jesus.
And great grace was upon them all.
34 Nor was there anyone among them who
lacked; [R]for all who were possessors of lands
or houses sold them, and brought the proceeds of the things that were sold, Acts 2:45
35 and laid *them* at the apostles' feet; and
they distributed to each as anyone had need.
36 And *Joses, who was also named Barnabas by the apostles (which is translated Son
of [T]Encouragement), a Levite of the country
of Cyprus, Or *Consolation*
37 having land, sold *it*, and brought the
money and laid *it* at the apostles' feet.

CHAPTER 5

Ananias and Sapphira Lie

BUT a certain man named Ananias, with
Sapphira his wife, sold a possession.
2 And he kept back *part* of the proceeds,
his wife also being aware *of it*, and brought a
certain part and laid *it* at the apostles' feet.
3 [R]But Peter said, "Ananias, why has [R]Sa-
tan filled your heart to lie to the Holy Spirit
and keep back *part* of the price of the land for
yourself? Deut. 23:21 • Luke 22:3
4 "While it remained, was it not your own?
And after it was sold, was it not in your own
control? Why have you conceived this thing
in your heart? You have not lied to men but
to God."
5 Then Ananias, hearing these words, fell
down and breathed his last. So great fear
came upon all those who heard these things.
6 And the young men arose and wrapped
him up, carried *him* out, and buried *him*.
7 Now it was about three hours later when
his wife came in, not knowing what had
happened.
8 And Peter answered her, "Tell me
whether you sold the land for so much?" And
she said, "Yes, for so much."
9 Then Peter said to her, "How is it that
you have agreed together [R]to test the Spirit of
the Lord? Look, the feet of those who have
buried your husband *are* at the door, and
they will carry you out." Acts 5:3, 4
10 [R]Then immediately she fell down at his
feet and breathed her last. And the young
men came in and found her dead, and carrying *her* out, buried *her* by her husband. Acts 5:5
11 So great fear came upon all the church
and upon all who heard these things.

Apostles' Mighty Miracles

12 And through the hands of the apostles
many signs and wonders were done among
the people. [R]And they were all with one
accord in Solomon's Porch. Acts 3:11; 4:32
13 Yet none of the rest dared join them, but
the people esteemed them highly.
14 And believers were increasingly added to
the Lord, multitudes of both men and
women,

4:25 NU *through the Holy Spirit, by the mouth of our father, Your servant David,* **4:36** NU *Joseph*

15 so that they brought the sick out into the
streets and laid *them* on beds and couches,
[R]that at least the shadow of Peter passing by
might fall on some of them. Acts 19:12
16 Also a multitude gathered from the surrounding cities to Jerusalem, bringing sick
people and those who were tormented by
unclean spirits, and they were all healed.

Apostles Are Miraculously Freed from Prison

17 [R]Then the high priest rose up, and all
those who *were* with him (which is the sect
of the Sadducees), and they were filled with
[T]indignation, Acts 4:1, 2, 6 • *jealousy*
18 [R]and laid their hands on the apostles and
put them in the common prison. Luke 21:12
19 But at night [R]an angel of the Lord
opened the prison doors and brought them
out, and said, Acts 12:7; 16:26
20 "Go, stand in the temple and speak to
the people all the words of this life."
21 And when they heard *that,* they entered
the temple early in the morning and taught.
But the high priest and those with him came
and called the [T]council together, with all the
elders of the children of Israel, and sent to
the prison to have them brought. Sanhedrin
22 But when the officers came and did not
find them in the prison, they returned and
reported,
23 saying, "Indeed we found the prison shut
securely, and the guards standing *outside
before the doors; but when we opened them,
we found no one inside!"
24 Now when *the high priest, [R]the captain
of the temple, and the chief priests heard
these things, they wondered what the outcome would be. Acts 4:1; 5:26
25 Then one came and told them, *saying,
"Look, the men whom you put in prison are
standing in the temple and teaching the
people!"
26 Then the captain went with the officers
and brought them without violence, for they
feared the people, lest they should be stoned.
27 And when they had brought them, they
set *them* before the council. And the high
priest asked them,
28 saying, "Did we not strictly command
you not to teach in this name? And look, you
have filled Jerusalem with your doctrine, and
intend to bring this Man's blood on us!"

Apostles Preach to the Council

29 Then Peter and the *other* apostles answered and said: [R]"We ought to obey God
rather than men. Acts 4:19
30 "The God of our fathers raised up Jesus
whom you murdered by hanging on a tree.
31 "Him God has exalted to His right hand
to be Prince and Savior, [R]to give repentance
to Israel and forgiveness of sins. Luke 24:47
32 "And we are His witnesses to these
things, and *so* also *is* the Holy Spirit whom
God has given to those who obey Him."

Gamaliel's Advice

33 When they heard *this,* they were [R]furious
and took counsel to kill them. Acts 7:54
34 Then one in the council stood up, a
Pharisee named [R]Gamaliel, a teacher of the
law held in respect by all the people, and
commanded them to put the apostles outside
for a little while. Acts 22:3
35 And he said to them: "Men of Israel,
[T]take heed to yourselves what you intend to
do regarding these men. *be careful*
36 "For some time ago Theudas rose up,
claiming to be somebody. A number of men,
about four hundred, [T]joined him. He was
slain, and all who obeyed him were scattered
and came to nothing. *followed*
37 "After this man, Judas of Galilee rose up
in the days of the census, and drew away
many people after him. He also perished, and
all who obeyed him were dispersed.
38 "And now I say to you, keep away from
these men and let them alone; for if this plan
or this work is of men, it will come to nothing;
39 [R]"but if it is of God, you cannot overthrow it—lest you even be found [R]to fight
against God." 1 Cor. 1:25 • Acts 7:51; 9:5

Apostles Are Beaten

40 And they agreed with him, and when
they had called for the apostles and beaten
them, they commanded that they should not
speak in the name of Jesus, and let them go.
41 So they departed from the presence of
the council, [R]rejoicing that they were
counted worthy to suffer shame for *His
name. [1 Pet. 4:13–16]
42 And daily in the temple, and in every
house, [R]they did not cease teaching and
preaching Jesus *as* the Christ. Acts 4:20, 29

CHAPTER 6

Deacons Are Appointed

NOW in those days, when *the number of*
the disciples was multiplying, there
arose a murmuring against the Hebrews by
the Hellenists, because their widows were
neglected in the daily distribution.
2 Then the twelve summoned the multitude of the disciples and said, [R]"It is not
desirable that we should leave the word of
God and serve tables. Ex. 18:17
3 "Therefore, brethren, [R]seek out from
among you seven men of *good* reputation,
full of the Holy Spirit and wisdom, whom we
may appoint over this business; 1 Tim. 3:7

5:23 NU, M omit *outside* **5:24** NU omits *the high priest*
5:25 NU, M omit *saying*
5:41 NU *the name,* M *the name of Jesus*

4 "but we will give ourselves continually
to prayer and to the ministry of the word."
5 And the saying pleased the whole multitude. And they chose Stephen, a man full of
faith and the Holy Spirit, and Philip, Procho-
rus, Nicanor, Timon, Parmenas, and [R]Nicolas,
a proselyte from Antioch, Rev. 2:6, 15
6 whom they set before the apostles; and
[R]when they had prayed, [R]they laid hands on
them. Acts 1:24 • [2 Tim. 1:6]
7 And [R]the word of God spread, and the
number of the disciples multiplied greatly in
Jerusalem, and a great many [R]of the priests
were obedient to the faith. Acts 12:24 • John 12:42
8 And Stephen, full of *faith and power,
did great [R]wonders and signs among the
people. Acts 2:43; 5:12; 8:15; 14:3

Stephen Is Brought Before the Council

9 Then there arose some from what is
called the Synagogue of the Freedmen (Cyre-
nians, Alexandrians, and those from Cilicia
and Asia), disputing with Stephen.
10 And they were not able to resist the
wisdom and the Spirit by which he spoke.
11 [R]Then they secretly induced men to say,
"We have heard him speak blasphemous
words against Moses and God." 1 Kin. 21:10, 13
12 And they stirred up the people, the elders, and the scribes; and they came upon
him, seized him, and brought *him* to the
council.
13 They also set up false witnesses who
said, "This man does not cease to speak
*blasphemous words against this holy place
and the law;
14 [R]"for we have heard him say that this
Jesus of Nazareth will destroy this place and
change the customs which Moses delivered
to us." Acts 10:38; 25:8
15 And all who sat in the council, looking
steadfastly at him, saw his face as the face of
an angel.

CHAPTER 7

Stephen Preaches to the Council

THEN the high priest said, "Are these
things so?"
2 And he said, "Men and brethren and
fathers, listen: The [R]God of glory appeared to
our father Abraham when he was in Mesopotamia, before he dwelt in Haran, Ps. 29:3
3 "and said to him, [R]*'Get out of your country and from your relatives, and come to a
land that I will show you.'* Gen. 12:1
4 "Then he came out of the land of the
Chaldeans and dwelt in Haran. And from
there, when his father was dead, He moved
him to this land in which you now dwell.
5 "And *God* gave him no inheritance in it,
not even *enough* to set his foot on. But even
when *Abraham* had no child, [R]He promised to
give it to him for a possession, and to his
descendants after him. Gen. 12:7; 13:15; 15:3, 18
6 "But God spoke in this way: that his
descendants would sojourn in a foreign land,
and that they would bring them into bondage
and oppress *them* four hundred years.
7 [R]*'And the nation to whom they will be in
bondage I will [R]judge,'* said God, *'and after
that they shall come out and [R]serve Me in
this place.'* Gen. 15:14 • Ex. 14:13–31 • Ex. 3:12
8 "Then He gave him the covenant of
circumcision; [R]and so *Abraham* begot Isaac
and circumcised him on the eighth day; [R]and
Isaac *begot* Jacob, and Jacob *begot* the
twelve patriarchs. Gen. 21:1–5 • Gen. 25:21–26
9 [R]"And the patriarchs, becoming envious,
[R]sold Joseph into Egypt. [R]But God was with
him Gen. 37:4, 11, 28 • Gen. 37:28 • Gen. 39:2, 21, 23
10 "and delivered him out of all his troubles,
[R]and gave him favor and wisdom in the
presence of Pharaoh, king of Egypt; and he
made him governor over Egypt and all his
house. Gen. 41:38–44
11 "Now a famine and great [T]trouble came
over all the land of Egypt and Canaan, and
our fathers found no sustenance. *affliction*
12 "But when Jacob heard that there was
grain in Egypt, he sent out our fathers first.
13 "And the [R]second *time* Joseph was made
known to his brothers, and Joseph's family
became known to the Pharaoh. Gen. 45:4, 16
14 [R]"Then Joseph sent and called his father
Jacob and [R]all his relatives to *him*, seventy-
five people. Gen. 45:9, 27 • Deut. 10:22
15 [R]"So Jacob went down to Egypt; [R]and he
died, he and our fathers. Gen. 46:1–7 • Gen. 49:33
16 "And they were carried back to Shechem
and laid in [R]the tomb that Abraham bought
for a sum of money from the sons of Hamor,
the father of Shechem. Gen. 23:16
17 "But when the time of the promise drew
near which God had sworn to Abraham, the
people grew and multiplied in Egypt
18 "till another king [R]arose who did not
know Joseph. Ex. 1:8
19 "This man dealt treacherously with our
people, and oppressed our forefathers, [R]mak-
ing them expose their babies, so that they
might not live. Ex. 1:22
20 "At this time Moses was born, and was
well pleasing to God; and he was brought up
in his father's house for three months.
21 "But [R]when he was set out, [R]Pharaoh's
daughter took him away and brought him up
as her own son. Ex. 2:3, 4 • Ex. 2:5–10
22 "And Moses was learned in all the wisdom of the Egyptians, and was [R]mighty in
words and deeds. Luke 24:19
23 [R]"But when he was forty years old, it
came into his heart to visit his brethren, the
children of Israel. Ex. 2:11, 12

6:8 NU *grace* **6:13** NU omits *blasphemous*

SERMONS IN ACTS

Photo by Gustav Jeeninga

The Areopagus is a stony point overlooking the city of Athens. Paul may have delivered his speech to the Athenian philosophers on this hill (Acts 17).

One of the most eloquent sermons in the Book of Acts is Paul's speech to the Athenian philosophers from the Areopagus, or Mars' Hill, a stony point named for the Greek god of war Ares (Roman god Mars). This hill overlooked the city of Athens (see photo). In his speech, Paul declared that God will hold all people accountable for their response to His Son (Acts 17).

Several other important sermons and speeches, including the following, occur in the Book of Acts.

Speech	Theme	Biblical Reference
Peter to crowds at Pentecost	Peter's explanation of the meaning of Pentecost	Acts 2:14–40
Peter to crowds at the temple	The Jewish people should repent for crucifying the Messiah	Acts 3:12–26
Peter to the Sanhedrin	Testimony that a helpless man was healed by the power of Jesus	Acts 4:5–12
Stephen to the Sanhedrin	Stephen's rehearsal of Jewish history, accusing the Jews of killing the Messiah	Acts 7
Peter to Gentiles	Gentiles can be saved in the same manner as Jews	Acts 10:28–47
Peter to church at Jerusalem	Peter's testimony of his experiences at Joppa and a defense of his ministry to the Gentiles	Acts 11:4–18
Paul to synagogue at Antioch	Jesus was the Messiah in fulfillment of Old Testament prophecies	Acts 13:16–41
Peter to Jerusalem council	Salvation by grace available to all	Acts 15:7–11
James to Jerusalem council	Gentile converts do not require circumcision	Acts 15:13–21
Paul to Ephesian elders	Remain faithful in spite of false teachers and persecution	Acts 20:17–35
Paul to crowd at Jerusalem	Paul's statement of his conversion and his mission to the Gentiles	Acts 22:1–21
Paul to Sanhedrin	Paul's defense, declaring himself a Pharisee and a Roman citizen	Acts 23:1–6
Paul to King Agrippa	Paul's statement of his conversion and his zeal for the gospel	Acts 26
Paul to Jewish leaders at Rome	Paul's statement about his Jewish heritage	Acts 28:17–20

24 "And seeing one of *them* suffer wrong,
he defended and avenged him who was oppressed, and struck down the Egyptian.
25 "For he supposed that his brethren
would have understood that God would deliver them by his hand, but they did not
understand.
26 "And the next day he appeared to two of
them as they were fighting, and *tried to*
reconcile them, saying, 'Men, you are brethren; why do you wrong one another?'
27 "But he who did his neighbor wrong
pushed him away, saying, [R]*'Who made you a
ruler and a judge over us?* Ex. 2:14
28 *'Do you want to kill me as you did the
Egyptian yesterday?'*
29 [R]"Then, at this saying, Moses fled and
became a sojourner in the land of Midian,
where he had two sons. Heb. 11:27
30 [R]"And when forty years had passed, an
Angel *of the Lord appeared to him in a flame
of fire in a bush, in the wilderness of Mount
Sinai. Ex. 3:1–10
31 "When Moses saw *it*, he marveled at the
sight; and as he drew near to observe, the
voice of the Lord came to him,
32 *"saying, [R]'I am the God of your fathers—
the God of Abraham, the God of Isaac, and
the God of Jacob.'* And Moses trembled and
dared not look. Ex. 3:6, 15
33 [R]*'Then the* LORD *said to him, "Take your
sandals off your feet, for the place where you
stand is holy ground.* Ex. 3:5, 7, 8, 10
34 [R]*"I have certainly seen the oppression of
my people who are in Egypt; I have heard
their groaning and have come down to deliver them. And now come, I will [R]send you to
Egypt." '* Ex. 2:24, 25 • Ps. 105:26
35 "This Moses whom they rejected, saying,
[R]*'Who made you a ruler and a judge?'* is the
one God sent *to be* a ruler and a deliverer [R]by
the hand of the Angel who appeared to him
in the bush. Ex. 2:14 • Ex. 14:21
36 "He brought them out, after he had
shown wonders and signs in the land of
Egypt, [R]and in the Red Sea, [R]and in the
wilderness forty years. Ex. 14:21 • Ex. 16:1, 35

37 "This is that Moses who said to
the children of Israel, *'The* LORD *your
God will raise up for you [R]a Prophet like
me from your brethren. [R]Him* you shall
hear.'* Deut. 18:15★ • Matt. 17:5

38 "This is he who was in the [T]congregation
in the wilderness with the Angel who spoke
to him on Mount Sinai, and *with* our fathers,
the one who received the living [T]oracles to
give to us, *assembly* or *church* • *sayings*

39 "whom our fathers [R]would not obey, but
rejected. And in their hearts they turned
back to Egypt, Ps. 95:8–11
40 [R]"saying to Aaron, *'Make us gods to go
before us; as for this Moses who brought us
out of the land of Egypt, we do not know
what has become of him.'* Ex. 32:1, 23
41 "And they made a calf in those days,
offered sacrifices to the idol, and [R]rejoiced in
the works of their own hands. Ex. 32:6, 18, 19
42 "Then [R]God turned and gave them up to
worship the host of heaven, as it is written in
the book of the Prophets: [2 Thess. 2:11]

[R]*'Did you offer Me slaughtered animals
and sacrifices during forty years in
the wilderness,* Amos 5:25–27
O house of Israel?
43 *Yes, you took up the tabernacle of
Moloch,
And the star of your god Remphan,
Images which you made to worship;
And [R]I will carry you away beyond
Babylon.'* Jer. 25:9–12

44 "Our fathers had the tabernacle of witness in the wilderness, as He appointed,
instructing Moses [R]to make it according to
the pattern that he had seen, [Heb. 8:5]
45 [R]"which our fathers, having received it in
turn, also brought with Joshua into the land
possessed by the Gentiles, [R]whom God drove

7:30 NU omits *of the Lord*
7:37 NU, M omit *Him you shall hear*

7:38 The Meaning of the Church—In modern English the word *church* is used in five ways: (1) a building designated as a place of worship, i.e., a church building; (2) all who profess faith in Christ regardless of particular theological beliefs; (3) a denomination; (4) a single organized Christian group, i.e., a local church; and (5) the Body of Christ, i.e., the universal church. While all of these are legitimate uses for modern English, the word *church* is used in the New Testament in only the last two senses—a local church, or the Body of Christ, the universal church. At its root, the word *church* means a "called-out group." It is used of the nation Israel (Acts 7:38) which was a group of people who were called out of the rest of the people of the world to have a special national relationship to God. It is used of a local church (Page 1413—1 Thess. 1:1, church of the Thessalonians; Page 1519—Rev. 2:1, church of Ephesus, etc.), and of the universal church, the Body of Christ (Page 1406—Col. 1:18). The universal church comprises all believers from the Day of Pentecost until the time God takes the church out of the world, and at which time His program for the church will be complete. The local church is a local, visible, temporal manifestation of the universal church. At one point in history the local and universal churches were identical (Page 1274—Acts 2:41). The universal church will not meet until "we all get to heaven" and once in session will never cease.

Now turn to Page 1136—Matt. 16:18: The Origin of the Church.

out before the face of our fathers until the
[R]days of David, Josh. 3:14 • Ps. 44:2 • 2 Sam. 6:2–15
46 [R]"who found favor before God and
[R]asked to find a dwelling for the God of
Jacob. 2 Sam. 7:1–13 • 1 Chr. 22:7
47 "But Solomon built Him a house.
48 "However, [R]the Most High does not
dwell in temples made with hands, as the
prophet says: 1 Kin. 8:27

49 *'Heaven[R] is My throne,* Is. 66:1, 2
And earth is My footstool.
What house will you build for Me? says
the LORD,
Or what is the place of My rest?
50 *Has My hand not [R]made all these*
things?' Ps. 102:25

51 "*You* stiff-necked and uncircumcised in
heart and ears! You always resist the Holy
Spirit; as your fathers *did*, so *do* you.
52 [R]"Which of the prophets did your fathers
not persecute? And they killed those who
foretold the coming of [R]the Just One, of
whom you now have become the betrayers
and murderers, 2 Chr. 36:16 • Acts 3:14; 22:14
53 "who have received the law by the direction of angels and have not kept *it*."
54 [R]When they heard these things they
were [T]cut to the heart, and they gnashed at
him with *their* teeth. Acts 5:33 • *furious*
55 But he, being full of the Holy Spirit,
gazed into heaven and saw the glory of God,
and Jesus standing at the right hand of God,
56 and said, "Look! [R]I see the heavens
opened and the [R]Son of Man standing at the
right hand of God!" Matt. 3:16 • Dan. 7:13
57 Then they cried out with a loud voice,
stopped their ears, and ran at him with one
accord;
58 and they cast *him* out of the city and
stoned *him*. And [R]the witnesses laid down
their clothes at the feet of a young man
named Saul. Acts 22:20
59 And they stoned Stephen as he was
calling on *God* and saying, "Lord Jesus,
[R]receive my spirit." Ps. 31:5
60 Then he knelt down and cried out with a
loud voice, [R]"Lord, do not charge them with
this sin." And when he had said this, he fell
asleep. Matt. 5:44

CHAPTER 8

Saul Persecutes the Church

NOW Saul was consenting to his death. At
that time a great persecution arose
against the church which was at Jerusalem;
and [R]they were all scattered throughout the
regions of Judea and Samaria, except the
apostles. Acts 8:4; 11:19
2 And devout men carried Stephen *to his*
burial, and [R]made great lamentation over
him. Gen. 23:2
3 As for Saul, [R]he made havoc of the
church, entering every house, and dragging
off men and women, committing *them* to
prison. Phil. 3:6
4 Therefore those who were scattered
went everywhere preaching the word.

Philip Witnesses to the Samaritans

5 Then Philip went down to [T]the city of
Samaria and preached Christ to them. Or *a*
6 And the multitudes with one accord
heeded the things spoken by Philip, hearing
and seeing the miracles which he did.
7 For [R]unclean spirits, crying with a loud
voice, came out of many who were possessed;
and many who were paralyzed and lame were
healed. Mark 16:17
8 And there was great joy in that city.
9 But there was a certain man called Simon, who previously practiced sorcery in the
city and astonished the people of Samaria,
claiming that he was someone great,
10 to whom they all gave heed, from the
least to the greatest, saying, "This man is the
great power of God."
11 And they heeded him because he had
astonished them with his [T]sorceries for a long
time. *magic arts*
12 But when they believed Philip as he
preached the things [R]concerning the kingdom
of God and the name of Jesus Christ, both
men and women were baptized. Acts 1:3; 8:4
13 Then Simon himself also believed; and
when he was baptized he continued with
Philip, and was amazed, seeing the miracles
and signs which were done.
14 Now when the [R]apostles who were at
Jerusalem heard that Samaria had received
the word of God, they sent Peter and John to
them, Acts 5:12, 29, 40
15 who, when they had come down, prayed
for them [R]that they might receive the Holy
Spirit. Acts 2:38; 19:2
16 For [R]as yet He had fallen upon none of
them. [R]They had only been baptized in the
name of the Lord Jesus. Acts 19:2 • Matt. 28:19
17 Then [R]they laid hands on them, and they
received the Holy Spirit. Acts 6:6; 19:6
18 Now when Simon saw that through the
laying on of the apostles' hands the Holy
Spirit was given, he offered them money,
19 saying, "Give me this power also, that
anyone on whom I lay hands may receive the
Holy Spirit."
20 But Peter said to him, "Your money
perish with you, because [R]you thought that
[R]the gift of God could be purchased with
money! [Matt. 10:8] • [Acts 2:38; 10:45; 11:17]
21 "You have neither part nor portion in
this matter, for your [R]heart is not right in the
sight of God. Jer. 17:9
22 "Repent therefore of this your wickedness, and pray God [R]if perhaps the thought of
your heart may be forgiven you. 2 Tim. 2:25

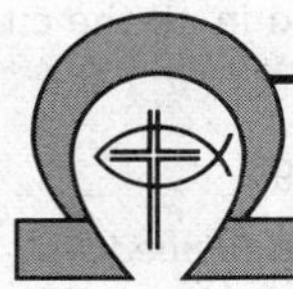

THE SPREAD OF THE GOSPEL

Philip and Peter, two of the original apostles of Jesus, were the first to preach the gospel throughout Palestine in the cities around Jerusalem in response to the command of Jesus, "You shall be witnesses to Me in Jerusalem, and in all Judea and Samaria, and to the end of the earth" (Acts 1:8). In later years, the apostle Paul became the great missionary to the Gentiles, proclaiming Christ in other nations throughout the Roman Empire.

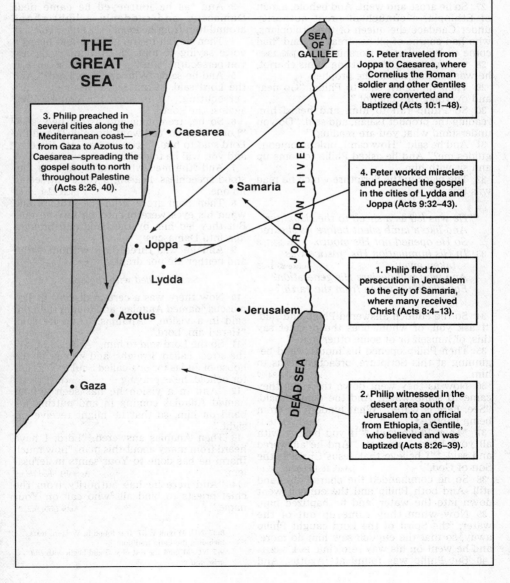

THE GREAT SEA

SEA OF GALILEE

JORDAN RIVER

DEAD SEA

Caesarea

Samaria

Joppa

Lydda

Jerusalem

Azotus

Gaza

1. Philip fled from persecution in Jerusalem to the city of Samaria, where many received Christ (Acts 8:4–13).

2. Philip witnessed in the desert area south of Jerusalem to an official from Ethiopia, a Gentile, who believed and was baptized (Acts 8:26–39).

3. Philip preached in several cities along the Mediterranean coast—from Gaza to Azotus to Caesarea—spreading the gospel south to north throughout Palestine (Acts 8:26, 40).

4. Peter worked miracles and preached the gospel in the cities of Lydda and Joppa (Acts 9:32–43).

5. Peter traveled from Joppa to Caesarea, where Cornelius the Roman soldier and other Gentiles were converted and baptized (Acts 10:1–48).

23 "For I see that you are [R]poisoned by
bitterness and bound by iniquity." Heb. 12:15
24 Then Simon answered and said, "Pray to
the Lord for me, that none of the things
which you have spoken may come upon me."
25 So when they had testified and preached
the word of the Lord, they returned to Jerusalem, preaching the gospel in many villages
of the Samaritans.

Philip Witnesses to the Ethiopian Treasurer

26 Now an angel of the Lord spoke to
[R]Philip, saying, "Arise and go toward the
south along the road which goes down from
Jerusalem to Gaza." This is desert. Acts 6:5
27 So he arose and went. And behold, a man
of Ethiopia, a eunuch of great authority
under Candace the queen of the Ethiopians,
who had charge of all her treasury, and [R]had
come to Jerusalem to worship, John 12:20
28 was returning. And sitting in his chariot,
he was reading Isaiah the prophet.
29 Then the Spirit said to Philip, "Go near
and overtake this chariot."
30 So Philip ran to him, and heard him
reading the prophet Isaiah, and said, "Do you
understand what you are reading?"
31 And he said, "How can I, unless someone
guides me?" And he asked Philip to come up
and sit with him.
32 The place in the Scripture which he read
was this:

[R]*"He was led as a sheep to the slaughter;*
And like a lamb silent before its shearer,
So He opened not His mouth. Is. 53:7, 8
33 *In His humiliation His* [R]*justice was*
taken away. Luke 23:1–25
And who will declare His generation?
For His life is taken from the earth."

34 So the eunuch answered Philip and said,
"I ask you, of whom does the prophet say
this, of himself or of some other man?"
35 Then Philip opened his mouth, [R]and beginning at this Scripture, preached Jesus to
him. Luke 24:27
36 Now as they went down the road, they
came to some water. And the eunuch said,
"See, *here is* water. [R]What hinders me from
being baptized?" Acts 10:47; 16:33
37 *Then Philip said, [R]"If you believe with
all your heart, you may." And he answered
and said, [R]"I believe that Jesus Christ is the
Son of God." [Mark 16:16] • Matt. 16:16
38 So he commanded the chariot to stand
still. And both Philip and the eunuch went
down into the water, and he baptized him.
39 Now when they came up out of the
water, [R]the Spirit of the Lord caught Philip
away, so that the eunuch saw him no more;
and he went on his way rejoicing. Ezek. 3:12, 14
40 But Philip was found at [T]Azotus. And
passing through, he preached in all the cities
till he came to Caesarea. Same as Heb. *Ashdod*

CHAPTER 9

Saul Is Converted and Blinded
Acts 22:4–11; 26:13–18

THEN [R]Saul, still breathing threats and
murder against the disciples of the Lord,
went to the high priest Acts 7:57; 8:1, 3; 26:10, 11
2 and asked [R]letters from him to the synagogues of Damascus, so that if he found any
who were of the Way, whether men or
women, he might bring them bound to Jerusalem. Acts 22:5
3 And [R]as he journeyed he came near
Damascus, and suddenly a light shone
around him from heaven. 1 Cor. 15:8
4 Then he fell to the ground, and heard a
voice saying to him, "Saul, Saul, [R]why are
you persecuting Me?" [Matt. 25:40]
5 And he said, "Who are You, Lord?" And
the Lord said, "I am Jesus, whom you are
persecuting. **It is* hard for you to kick
against the goads."
6 So he, trembling and astonished, said,
"Lord, what do You want me to do?" And the
Lord *said* to him, "Arise and go into the city,
and you will be told what you must do."
7 And [R]the men who journeyed with him
stood speechless, hearing a voice but seeing
no one. [Acts 22:9; 26:13]
8 Then Saul arose from the ground, and
when his eyes were opened he saw no one.
But they led him by the hand and brought
him into Damascus.
9 And he was three days without sight,
and neither ate nor drank.

Saul Is Filled with the Spirit

10 Now there was a certain disciple at Damascus [R]named Ananias; and to him the Lord
said in a vision, "Ananias." And he said,
"Here I am, Lord." Acts 22:12
11 So the Lord *said* to him, "Arise and go to
the street called Straight, and inquire at the
house of Judas for *one* called Saul [R]of Tarsus,
for behold, he is praying. Acts 21:39; 22:3
12 "And in a vision he has seen a man
named Ananias coming in and putting *his*
hand on him, so that he might receive his
sight."
13 Then Ananias answered, "Lord, I have
heard from many about this man, [R]how much
[T]harm he has done to Your saints in Jerusalem. Acts 9:1 • *bad things*
14 "And here he has authority from the
chief priests to bind all [R]who call on Your
name." Acts 7:59; 9:2, 21

8:37 NU, M omit v. 37. It is found in Western texts, including the Latin tradition.
9:5 NU, M omit the rest of v. 5 and begin with *But arise and go*

THE CITY OF DAMASCUS

Damascus is the oldest continually inhabited city in the world. As the current capital of Syria, the city is located on the border of some of the most important highways in the ancient Near Eastern world. Because of its ideal location, the city has always been an important trade center. Its name may be derived from a patterned cloth known as damask, its most important export item in Old Testament times (Ezek. 27:18).

According to Josephus, the founder of Damascus was Uz, grandson of Shem (Gen. 5:32; 10:21, 23). Its strategic location as a trading center brought Damascus into conflict with Israel on numerous occasions as it sought to regulate the flow of trade into all parts of the ancient Near East.

After periods of dominance by the Assyrians and the Persians, Damascus was conquered by Alexander the Great in 333 B.C. Later it became the capital of the Roman province of Syria. In the early years of Roman influence in Syria, many Jews from Judea moved to Damascus. The city had a large Jewish community during New Testament times.

All references to Damascus in the New Testament are associated with the apostle Paul's conversion and early ministry. He was blinded in a vision while traveling to Damascus to persecute early Christians (Acts 9:1–8). After his conversion, Paul went to the house of Judas on "Straight Street" in Damascus. There he met Ananias, a Christian citizen of the city who healed Paul's blindness (Acts 9:10–22). After regaining his sight, Paul preached in the Jewish synagogue in Damascus, astonishing those who remembered him as a persecutor of the Christian faith. Eventually Paul was forced to flee Damascus because of threats on his life.

Damascus is still a trading center filled with open-air markets and crowded streets, some of which are very similar to those which Paul might have visited.

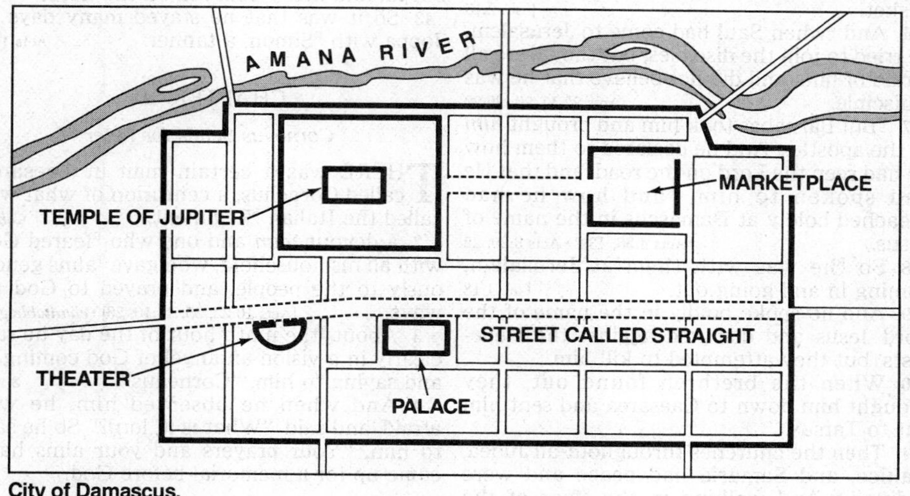

City of Damascus.

15 But the Lord said to him, "Go, for he is a chosen vessel of Mine to bear My name before Gentiles, [R]kings, and the [R]children[T] of Israel. Acts 25:22, 23; 26:1 • Rom. 1:16; 9:1–5 • Lit. *sons*
16 "For I will show him how many things he must suffer for My name's sake."
17 And Ananias went his way and entered the house; and [R]laying his hands on him he said, "Brother Saul, the Lord *Jesus, who appeared to you on the road as you came, has sent me that you may receive your sight and be filled with the Holy Spirit." Acts 8:17
18 Immediately there fell from his eyes *something* like scales, and he received his sight at once; and he arose and was baptized.
19 And when he had received food, he was strengthened. [R]Then Saul spent some days with the disciples at Damascus. Acts 26:20

Saul Preaches at Damascus

20 Immediately he preached *the Christ in the synagogues, that He is the Son of God.
21 Then all who heard were amazed, and said, "Is this not he who destroyed those who called on this name in Jerusalem, and has come here for that purpose, so that he might bring them bound to the chief priests?"
22 But Saul increased all the more in strength, [R]and confounded the Jews who dwelt in Damascus, proving that this *Jesus* is the Christ. Acts 18:28

Saul Witnesses in Jerusalem

23 Now after many days were past, [R]the Jews plotted to kill him. 2 Cor. 11:26
24 [R]But their plot became known to Saul. And they watched the gates day and night, to kill him. 2 Cor. 11:32
25 Then the disciples took him by night and [R]let *him* down through the wall in a large basket. Josh. 2:15
26 And [R]when Saul had come to Jerusalem, he tried to join the disciples; but they were all afraid of him, and did not believe that he was a disciple. Acts 22:17–20; 26:20
27 [R]But Barnabas took him and brought *him* to the apostles. And he declared to them how he had seen the Lord on the road, and that He had spoken to him, [R]and how he had preached boldly at Damascus in the name of Jesus. Acts 4:36; 13:2 • Acts 9:20, 22
28 So [R]he was with them at Jerusalem, coming in and going out. Gal. 1:18
29 And he spoke boldly in the name of the Lord Jesus and disputed against the Hellenists, but they attempted to kill him.
30 When the brethren found out, they brought him down to Caesarea and sent him out to Tarsus.
31 Then the churches throughout all Judea, Galilee, and Samaria had peace and were [R]edified.* And walking in the [R]fear of the Lord and in the comfort of the Holy Spirit, they were multiplied. [Eph. 4:16, 29] • Ps. 34:9

Peter Heals Aeneas at Lydda

32 Now it came to pass, as Peter went through all *parts of the country*, that he also came down to the saints who dwelt in Lydda.
33 There he found a certain man named Aeneas, who had been bedridden eight years and was paralyzed.
34 And Peter said to him, "Aeneas, [R]Jesus the Christ heals you. Arise and make your bed." Then he arose immediately. [Acts 4:10]
35 So all who dwelt at Lydda and Sharon saw him and [R]turned to the Lord. Acts 11:21

Peter Raises Dorcas at Joppa

36 At Joppa there was a certain disciple named Tabitha, which is translated [T]Dorcas. This woman was full of good works and charitable deeds which she did. *Gazelle*
37 But it happened in those days that she became sick and died. When they had washed her, they laid *her* in an upper room.
38 And since Lydda was near Joppa, and the disciples had heard that Peter was there, they sent two men to him, imploring *him* not to delay in coming to them.
39 Then Peter arose and went with them. When he had come, they brought *him* to the upper room. And all the widows stood by him weeping, showing the tunics and garments which Dorcas had made while she was with them.
40 But Peter put them all out, and knelt down and prayed. And turning to the body he said, "Tabitha, arise." And she opened her eyes, and when she saw Peter she sat up.
41 Then he gave her *his* hand and lifted her up; and when he had called the saints and widows, he presented her alive.
42 And it became known throughout all Joppa, and many believed on the Lord.
43 So it was that he stayed many days in Joppa with [R]Simon, a tanner. Acts 10:6

CHAPTER 10

Cornelius Sends for Peter

THERE was a certain man in Caesarea called Cornelius, a centurion of what was called the Italian [T]Regiment, *Cohort*
2 a devout *man* and one who [R]feared God with all his household, who gave [T]alms generously to the people, and prayed to God always. [Acts 10:22, 35; 13:16, 26] • *charitable gifts*
3 About [T]the ninth hour of the day he saw clearly in a vision an angel of God coming in and saying to him, "Cornelius!" 3 P.M.
4 And when he observed him, he was afraid, and said, "What is it, lord?" So he said to him, "Your prayers and your alms have come up for a memorial before God.

9:17 M omits *Jesus* **9:20** NU *Jesus*
9:31 NU *church . . . was edified*

5 "Now [R]send men to Joppa, and send for
Simon whose surname is Peter. Acts 11:13, 14
6 "He is lodging with [R]Simon, a tanner,
whose house is by the sea. [R]He* will tell you
what you must do." Acts 9:43 • Acts 11:14
7 And when the angel who spoke to him
had departed, Cornelius called two of his
household servants and a devout soldier from
among those who waited on him continually.
8 So when he had explained all *these*
things to them, he sent them to Joppa.

Peter Sees the Great Sheet

9 The next day, as they went on their
journey and drew near the city, [R]Peter went
up on the housetop to pray, about [T]the sixth
hour. Acts 10:9–32; 11:5–14 • Noon
10 Then he became very hungry and
wanted to eat; but while they made ready, he
fell into a trance
11 and saw heaven opened and an object
like a great sheet bound at the four corners,
descending to him and let down to the earth.
12 In it were all kinds of four-footed animals of the earth, wild beasts, creeping
things, and birds of the air.
13 And a voice came to him, "Rise, Peter;
kill and eat."
14 But Peter said, "Not so, Lord! [R]For I
have never eaten anything common or unclean." Deut. 14:3, 7
15 And a voice *spoke* to him again the
second time, "What God has [T]cleansed you
must not call common." *declared clean*
16 This was done three times. And the
object was taken up into heaven again.
17 Now while Peter [T]wondered within himself what this vision which he had seen
meant, behold, the men who had been sent
from Cornelius had made inquiry for Simon's
house, and stood before the gate. *was perplexed*
18 And they called and asked whether Simon, whose surname was Peter, was lodging
there.
19 While Peter thought about the vision,
[R]the Spirit said to him, "Behold, three men
are seeking you. Acts 11:12
20 [R]"Arise therefore, go down and go with
them, doubting nothing; for I have sent
them." Acts 15:7–9
21 Then Peter went down to the men *who
had been sent to him from Cornelius, and
said, "Yes, I am he whom you seek. For what
reason have you come?"
22 And they said, "Cornelius *the* centurion,
a just man, one who fears God and [R]has a
good reputation among all the nation of the
Jews, was divinely instructed by a holy angel
to summon you to his house, and to hear
words from you." Acts 22:12

Peter Preaches to the Gentiles

23 Then he invited them in and lodged
them. On the next day Peter went away with
them, [R]and some brethren from Joppa accompanied him. Acts 10:45; 11:12
24 And the following day they entered
Caesarea. Now Cornelius was waiting for
them, and had called together his relatives
and close friends.
25 As Peter was coming in, Cornelius met
him and fell down at his feet and worshiped
him.
26 But Peter lifted him up, saying, [R]"Stand
up; I myself am also a man." Acts 14:14, 15
27 And as he talked with him, he went in
and found many who had come together.
28 Then he said to them, "You know how
[R]unlawful it is for a Jewish man to keep
company with or go to one of another nation.
But God has shown me that I should not call
any man common or unclean. John 4:9; 18:28
29 "Therefore I came without objection as
soon as I was sent for. I ask, then, for what
reason have you sent for me?"
30 And Cornelius said, *"Four days ago I
was fasting until this hour; and at the ninth
hour I prayed in my house, and behold, a man
stood before me in bright clothing,
31 "and said, 'Cornelius, your prayer has
been heard, and [R]your [T]alms are remembered
in the sight of God. Heb. 6:10 • *charitable gifts*
32 'Send therefore to Joppa and call Simon
here, whose surname is Peter. He is lodging in
the house of Simon, a tanner, by the sea.
*When he comes, he will speak to you.'
33 "So I sent to you immediately, and you
have done well to come. Now therefore, we
are all present before God, to hear all the
things commanded you by God."
34 Then Peter opened *his* mouth and said:
[R]"In truth I perceive that God shows no
partiality. Deut. 10:17
35 "But in every nation whoever fears Him
and works righteousness is accepted by Him.
36 "The word which *God* sent to the [T]chil-
dren of Israel, preaching peace through Jesus
Christ—He is Lord of all— Lit. *sons*
37 "that word you know, which was proclaimed throughout all Judea, and [R]began
from Galilee after the baptism which John
preached: Luke 4:14
38 "how [R]God anointed Jesus of Nazareth
with the Holy Spirit and with power, who
[R]went about doing good and healing all who
were oppressed by the devil, [R]for God was
with Him. Luke 4:18 • Matt. 4:23 • John 3:2; 8:29
39 "And we are [R]witnesses of all things
which He did both in the land of the Jews and
in Jerusalem, whom *they [R]killed by hanging
on a tree. Acts 1:8 • Acts 2:23

10:6 NU, M omit the rest of v. 6.
10:21 NU, M omit *who had been sent to him from Cornelius*
10:30 NU *Four days ago to this hour, at the ninth hour*
10:32 NU omits the rest of v. 32. **10:39** NU, M add *also*

40 "Him [R]God raised up on the third day, and showed Him openly, Hos. 6:2; Matt. 12:39, 40 ★

41 [R]"not to all the people, but to witnesses chosen before by God, *even* to us [R]who ate and drank with Him after He arose from the dead. [John 14:17, 19, 22; 15:27] • Luke 24:30, 41–43

42 "And He commanded us to preach to the people, and to testify [R]that it is He who was ordained by God *to be* Judge [R]of the living and the dead. John 5:22, 27 • 1 Pet. 4:5

43 "To Him all the prophets witness that, through His name, whoever believes in Him will receive [T]remission of sins." *forgiveness*

Gentiles Are Converted and Speak in Tongues

44 While Peter was still speaking these words, [R]the Holy Spirit fell upon all those who heard the word. Acts 4:31

45 [R]And [T]those of the circumcision who believed were astonished, as many as came with Peter, [R]because the gift of the Holy Spirit had been poured out on the Gentiles also. Acts 10:23 • The Jews • Acts 11:18

46 For they heard them speak with tongues and magnify God. Then Peter answered,

47 "Can anyone forbid water, that these should not be baptized who have received the Holy Spirit [R]just as we *have?*" Acts 2:4; 10:44

48 And he commanded them to be baptized [R]in the name of the Lord. Then they asked him to stay a few days. Acts 2:38; 8:16; 19:5

CHAPTER 11

Peter Defends His Ministry to the Gentiles

NOW the apostles and brethren who were in Judea heard that the Gentiles had also received the word of God.

2 And when Peter came up to Jerusalem, [R]those of the circumcision contended with him, Acts 10:45

3 saying, [R]"You went in to uncircumcised men [R]and ate with them!" Acts 10:28 • Gal. 2:12

4 But Peter explained *it* to them [R]in order from the beginning, saying: Luke 1:3

5 [R]"I was in the city of Joppa praying; and in a trance I saw a vision, an object descending like a great sheet, let down from heaven by four corners; and it came to me. Acts 10:9

6 "When I observed it intently and considered, I saw four-footed animals of the earth, wild beasts, creeping things, and birds of the air.

7 "And I heard a voice saying to me, 'Rise, Peter; kill and eat.'

8 "But I said, 'Not so, Lord! For nothing common or unclean has at any time entered my mouth.'

9 "But the voice answered me again from heaven, 'What God has cleansed you must not call common.'

10 "Now this was done three times, and all were drawn up again into heaven.

11 "At that very moment, three men stood before the house where I was, having been sent to me from Caesarea.

12 "Then [R]the Spirit told me to go with them, doubting nothing. Moreover [R]these six brethren accompanied me, and we entered the man's house. [John 16:13] • Acts 10:23

13 [R]"And he told us how he had seen an angel standing in his house, who said to him, 'Send men to Joppa, and call for Simon whose surname is Peter, Acts 10:30

14 'who will tell you words by which you and all your household will be saved.'

15 "And as I began to speak, the Holy Spirit fell upon them, as upon us at the beginning.

16 "Then I remembered the word of the Lord, how He said, [R]'John indeed baptized with water, but [R]you shall be baptized with the Holy Spirit.' John 1:26, 33 • Is. 44:3

17 [R]"If therefore God gave them the same gift as *He gave* us when we believed on the Lord Jesus Christ, [R]who was I that I could withstand God?" [Acts 15:8, 9] • Acts 10:47

18 When they heard these things they became silent; and they glorified God, saying, [R]"Then God has also granted to the Gentiles repentance to life." Rom. 10:12, 13; 15:9, 16

The Witness of the Antioch Church

19 [R]Now those who were scattered after the persecution that arose over Stephen traveled as far as Phoenicia, Cyprus, and Antioch, preaching the word to no one but the Jews only. Acts 8:1, 4

20 But some of them were men from Cyprus and Cyrene, who, when they had come to Antioch, spoke to [R]the Hellenists, preaching the Lord Jesus. Acts 6:1; 9:29

21 And [R]the hand of the Lord was with them, and a great number believed and [R]turned to the Lord. Luke 1:66 • Acts 9:35; 14:1

22 Then news of these things came to the ears of the church in Jerusalem, and they sent out Barnabas to go as far as Antioch.

23 When he came and had seen the grace of God, he was glad, and [R]encouraged them all that with purpose of heart they should continue with the Lord. Acts 13:43; 14:22

24 For he was a good man, [R]full of the Holy Spirit and of faith. [R]And a great many people were added to the Lord. Acts 6:5 • Acts 5:14; 11:21

25 Then Barnabas departed for [R]Tarsus to seek Saul. Acts 9:11, 30

26 And when he had found him, he brought him to Antioch. So it was that for a whole year they assembled with the church and taught a great many people. And the disciples were first called Christians in Antioch.

27 And in these days [R]prophets came from Jerusalem to Antioch. 1 Cor. 12:28

28 Then one of them, named [R]Agabus, stood up and showed by the Spirit that there was going to be a great famine throughout all the world, which also happened in the days of [R]Claudius Caesar. Acts 21:10 • Acts 18:2

29 Then the disciples, each according to his ability, determined to send [R]relief to the brethren dwelling in Judea. 1 Cor. 16:1

30 This they also did, and sent it to the elders by the hands of Barnabas and Saul.

CHAPTER 12

Herod Kills James

NOW about that time Herod the king stretched out *his* hand to harass some from the church.

2 Then he killed James [R]the brother of John with the sword. Matt. 4:21; 20:23

Peter Is Miraculously Released from Prison

3 And because he saw that it pleased the Jews, he proceeded further to seize Peter also. Now it was *during* [R]the Days of Unleavened Bread. Ex. 12:15; 23:15

4 So when he had apprehended him, he put *him* in prison, and delivered *him* to four squads of soldiers to keep him, intending to bring him before the people after Passover.

5 Peter was therefore kept in prison, but *constant prayer was offered to God for him by the church.

6 And when Herod was about to bring him out, that night Peter was sleeping, bound with two chains between two soldiers; and the guards before the door were [T]keeping the prison. *guarding*

7 Now behold, [R]an angel of the Lord stood by *him,* and a light shone in the prison; and he struck Peter on the side and raised him up, saying, "Arise quickly!" And his chains fell off *his* hands. Acts 5:19

8 Then the angel said to him, "Gird yourself and tie on your sandals"; and so he did. And he said to him, "Put on your garment and follow me."

9 So he went out and followed him, and [R]did not know that what was done by the angel was real, but thought [R]he was seeing a vision. Ps. 126:1 • Acts 10:3, 17; 11:5

10 When they were past the first and the second guard posts, they came to the iron gate that leads to the city, [R]which opened to them of its own accord; and they went out and went down one street, and immediately the angel departed from him. Acts 5:19; 16:26

11 And when Peter had come to himself, he said, "Now I know for certain that [R]the Lord has sent His angel, and has delivered me from the hand of Herod and *from* all the expectation of the Jewish people." [Ps. 34:7]

12 So, when he had considered *this,* he came to the house of Mary, the mother of John whose surname was Mark, where many were gathered together praying.

13 And as Peter knocked at the door of the gate, a girl named Rhoda came to answer.

14 When she recognized Peter's voice, because of *her* gladness she did not open the gate, but ran in and announced that Peter stood before the gate.

15 But they said to her, "You are beside yourself!" Yet she kept insisting that it was so. So they said, [R]"It is his angel." [Matt. 18:10]

16 Now Peter continued knocking; and when they opened *the door* and saw him, they were astonished.

17 But [R]motioning to them with his hand to keep silent, he declared to them how the Lord had brought him out of the prison. And he said, "Go, tell these things to James and to the brethren." And he departed and went to another place. Acts 13:16; 19:33; 21:40

18 Then, as soon as it was day, there was no small [T]stir among the soldiers about what had become of Peter. *disturbance*

19 But when Herod had searched for him and not found him, he examined the guards and commanded that *they* should be put to death. And he went down from Judea to Caesarea, and stayed *there.*

Herod Blasphemes and Dies

20 Now Herod had been very angry with the people of Tyre and Sidon; but they came to him with one accord, and having made Blastus [T]the king's chamberlain their friend, they asked for peace, because their country was [T]supplied with food by the king's *country.* *who was in charge of the king's chamber* • Lit. *nourished*

21 So on a set day Herod, arrayed in royal apparel, sat on his throne and gave an oration to them.

22 And the people kept shouting, "The voice of a god and not of a man!"

23 Then immediately an angel of the Lord struck him, because he did not give glory to God. And he was eaten by worms and died.

24 But [R]the word of God grew and multiplied. Acts 6:7; 19:20

25 And [R]Barnabas and Saul returned *from Jerusalem when they had fulfilled *their* ministry, and they also took with them John whose surname was Mark. Acts 11:30

CHAPTER 13

Barnabas and Saul Are Sent from Antioch

NOW [R]in the church that was at Antioch there were certain prophets and teachers: [R]Barnabas, Simeon who was called Niger, [R]Lucius of Cyrene, Manaen who had been brought up with Herod the tetrarch, and Saul. Acts 14:26 • Acts 11:22 • Rom. 16:21

2 As they ministered to the Lord and fasted, the Holy Spirit said, [R]"Now separate to Me Barnabas and Saul for the work [R]to which I have called them." Gal. 1:15; 2:9 • Heb. 5:4

12:5 NU *constantly* or *earnestly* **12:25** NU, M *to*

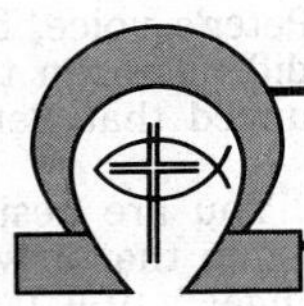

THE CITY OF ANTIOCH

Situated on the most important trade routes of the day, Antioch was an ideal city for a flourishing missions-minded church that was destined to play a key role in the expansion of early Christianity. Seleuchus I founded the city about 300 B.C. and named it for his father, Antiochus. Antioch served as the capital of the Roman province of Syria during the New Testament times.

Located on the east bank of the Orontes River, Antioch was about 16 miles from the Mediterranean Sea and about 300 miles north of Jerusalem. With a population of more than half a million, it was the third largest city of the Roman Empire, ranking behind only Rome and Alexandria.

Under the Roman rulers, Antioch became one of the most beautiful cities of the Roman Empire. Its main street, about two miles long, was paved with marble and flanked on both sides by hundreds of columns, which supported ornamented porches and balconies (see Street of Colonnades on map). Its cultural splendor and beautiful buildings, including the temple of Artemis, the amphitheater, and royal palaces, contributed to its reputation as the "Paris of the Ancient World" among scholars and researchers.

Antioch was also a city of many philosophies and cults. It prided itself on its toleration. But many citizens sought a more significant religious experience than the old Greek and Roman gods offered. Many accepted the gospel and committed themselves to Christ. Because this church was made up of both Gentiles and Jews, city officials sought a name that would distinguish them from other religious groups. They nicknamed them Christians, meaning "Christ Followers" or "People of Christ," and the name stuck. According to the Book of Acts, "the disciples were first called Christians in Antioch" (Acts 11:26).

Except for Jerusalem, Antioch played a larger part in the early life of the Christian church than any other city of the Roman Empire. It became the birthplace of foreign missions as Paul used the Antioch church as a base of operations for his missionary tours into Asia Minor.

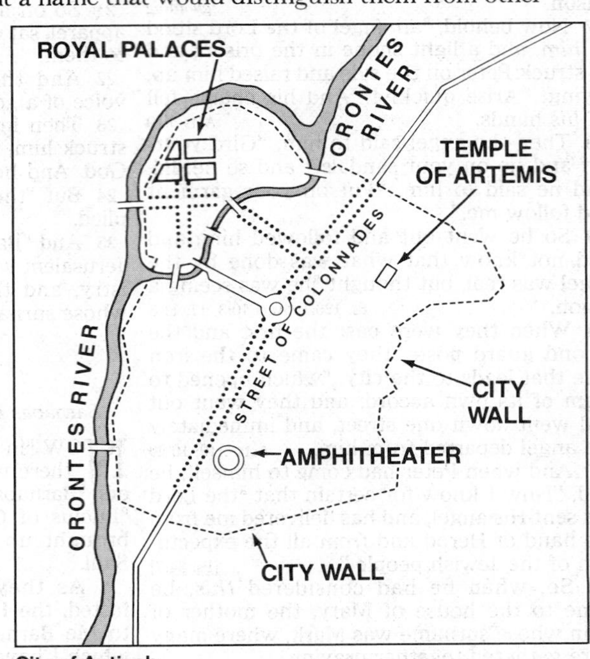

City of Antioch.

3 Then, having fasted and prayed, and laid
hands on them, they sent *them* away.

Preaching in the Synagogues

4 So, being sent out by the Holy Spirit,
they went down to Seleucia, and from there
they sailed to [R]Cyprus. Acts 4:36
5 And when they arrived in Salamis, [R]they
preached the word of God in the synagogues
of the Jews. They also had [R]John as *their*
assistant. [Acts 13:46] • Acts 12:25; 15:37

Controversy with Bar-Jesus

6 Now when they had gone through *the
island to Paphos, they found [R]a certain sorcerer, a false prophet, a Jew whose name *was*
Bar-Jesus, Acts 8:9
7 who was with the proconsul, Sergius
Paulus, an intelligent man. This man called
for Barnabas and Saul and sought to hear the
word of God.
8 But Elymas the sorcerer (for so his name
is translated) withstood them, seeking to turn
the proconsul away from the faith.
9 Then Saul, who also *is called* Paul, filled
with the Holy Spirit, looked intently at him
10 and said, "O full of all deceit and all
fraud, [R]*you* son of the devil, *you* enemy of all
righteousness, will you not cease perverting
the straight ways of the Lord? Matt. 13:38
11 "And now, indeed, the hand of the Lord
is upon you, and you shall be blind, not
seeing the sun for a time." And immediately a
dark mist fell on him, and he went around
seeking someone to lead him by the hand.
12 Then the proconsul believed, when he
saw what had been done, being astonished at
the teaching of the Lord.
13 Now when Paul and his party set sail
from Paphos, they came to Perga in Pamphylia; and [R]John, departing from them,
returned to Jerusalem. Acts 15:38

Paul Preaches on First Sabbath

14 But when they departed from Perga,
they came to Antioch in Pisidia, and [R]went
into the synagogue on the Sabbath day and
sat down. Acts 16:13
15 And [R]after the reading of the Law and
the Prophets, the rulers of the synagogue
sent to them, saying, "Men *and* brethren, if
you have [R]any word of [T]exhortation for the
people, say on." Luke 4:16 • Heb. 13:22 • *encouragement*
16 Then Paul stood up, and motioning with
his hand said, "Men of Israel, and [R]you who
fear God, listen: Acts 10:35
17 "The God of this people *Israel chose our
fathers, and exalted the people [R]when they
dwelt as strangers in the land of Egypt, and
with [T]an uplifted arm He [R]brought them out
of it. Acts 7:17 • Mighty power • Ex. 14:8
18 "Now for a time of about forty years He
put up with their ways in the wilderness.
19 "And when He had destroyed [R]seven
nations in the land of Canaan, He distributed
their land to them by allotment. Deut. 7:1
20 "After that [R]He gave *them* judges for
about four hundred and fifty years, [R]until
Samuel the prophet. Judg. 2:16 • 1 Sam. 3:20
21 "And afterward they asked for a king; so
God gave them Saul the son of Kish, a man of
the tribe of Benjamin, for forty years.
22 "And when He had removed him, He
raised up for them David as king, to whom
also He gave testimony and said, *'I have
found David* the *son* of Jesse, *a man after My
own heart,* who will do all My will.'
23 [R]"From this man's seed, according [R]to
the promise, God raised up for Israel [R]a*
Savior—Jesus— Is. 11:1 ★ • Ps. 132:11 • [Matt. 1:21]
24 [R]"after John had first preached, before
His coming, the baptism of repentance to all
the people of Israel. [Luke 3:3]
25 "And as John was finishing his course, he
said, [R]'Who do you think I am? I am not *He*.
But behold, [R]there comes One after me, the
sandals of whose feet I am not worthy to
loose.' Mark 1:7 • John 1:20, 27
26 "Men *and* brethren, sons of the [T]family
of Abraham, and [R]those among you who fear
God, [R]to you the [T]word of this salvation has
been sent. *stock* • Ps. 66:16 • Matt. 10:6 • *message*
27 "For those who dwell in Jerusalem, and
their rulers, [R]because they did not know Him,
nor even the voices of the Prophets which are
read every Sabbath, have fulfilled *them* in
condemning *Him*. Luke 23:34
28 [R]"And though they found no cause for
death *in Him*, they asked Pilate that He
should be put to death. Matt. 27:22, 23
29 "Now when they had fulfilled all that
was written concerning Him, they took *Him*
down from the tree and laid *Him* in a tomb.
30 "But God raised Him from the dead.
31 "He was seen for many days by those
who came up with Him from Galilee to Jerusalem, who are His witnesses to the people.
32 "And we declare to you glad tidings—
that promise which was made to the fathers.
33 "God has fulfilled this for us their children, in that He has raised up Jesus. As it is
also written in the second Psalm:

[R]*'You are My Son,* Ps. 2:7; Heb. 1:5★
Today I have begotten You.'

34 "And that He raised Him from the dead,
no more to return to [T]corruption, He has
spoken thus:

[R]*'I will give you the sure* [T]*mercies of
David.'* *the state of decay* • Is. 55:3★ • *blessings*

13:6 NU *the whole island* 13:17 M omits *Israel*
13:23 M *salvation, after*

35 "Therefore He also says in another *Psalm*:

[R]*'You will not allow Your Holy One to see corruption.'* Ps. 16:10★

36 "For David, after he had served [T]his own generation by the will of God, [R]fell asleep, was buried with his fathers, and [T]saw corruption; *in his* • Acts 2:29 • *underwent decay*
37 "but He whom God raised up [T]saw no corruption. *underwent no decay*
38 "Therefore let it be known to you, brethren, that [R]through this Man is preached to you the forgiveness of sins; Jer. 31:34
39 "and by Him everyone who believes is justified from all things from which you could not be justified by the law of Moses.
40 "Beware therefore, lest what has been spoken in the prophets come upon you:

41 *'Behold, you despisers,*
Marvel and perish;
For I work a work in your days,
A work which you will by no means believe,
Though one were to declare it to you.'"

42 *And when the Jews went out of the synagogue, the Gentiles begged that these words might be preached to them the next Sabbath.
43 Now when the congregation had broken up, many of the Jews and devout proselytes followed Paul and Barnabas, who, speaking to them, [R]persuaded them to continue in [R]the grace of God. Acts 11:23 • Titus 2:11

Paul Preaches on Second Sabbath

44 And the next Sabbath almost the whole city came together to hear the word of God.
45 But when the Jews saw the multitudes, they were filled with envy; and contradicting and blaspheming, they [R]opposed the things spoken by Paul. 1 Pet. 4:4
46 Then Paul and Barnabas grew bold and said, [R]"It was necessary that the word of God should be spoken to you first; but [R]since you reject it, and judge yourselves unworthy of everlasting life, behold, [R]we turn to the Gentiles. Rom. 1:16 • Ex. 32:10 • Acts 18:6
47 "For so the Lord has commanded us:

[R]*'I have set you to be a light to the Gentiles,*
That you should be for salvation to the ends of the earth.'" Is. 42:6; 49:6★

48 Now when the Gentiles heard this, they were glad and glorified the word of the Lord. [R]And as many as had been appointed to eternal life believed. [Acts 2:47]
49 And the word of the Lord was being spread throughout all the region.
50 But the Jews stirred up the devout and prominent women and the chief men of the city, [R]raised up persecution against Paul and Barnabas, and expelled them from their region. 2 Tim. 3:11

Ministry at Iconium

51 But they shook off the dust from their feet against them, and came to Iconium.
52 And the disciples [R]were filled with joy and with the Holy Spirit. John 16:22

CHAPTER 14

NOW it happened in Iconium that they went together to the synagogue of the Jews, and so spoke that a great multitude both of the Jews and of the Greeks believed.
2 But the unbelieving Jews stirred up the Gentiles and [T]poisoned their [T]minds against the brethren. *embittered* • Lit. *souls*
3 Therefore they stayed there a long time, speaking boldly in the Lord, who was bearing witness to the word of His grace, granting signs and wonders to be done by their hands.
4 But the multitude of the city was [R]divided: part sided with the Jews, and part with the [R]apostles. Luke 12:51 • Acts 13:2, 3
5 And when a violent attempt was made by both the Gentiles and Jews, with their rulers, [R]to abuse and stone them, 2 Tim. 3:11

A Lame Man Is Healed

6 they became aware of it and [R]fled to Lystra and Derbe, cities of Lycaonia, and to the surrounding region. Matt. 10:23
7 And they were preaching the gospel there.
8 And in Lystra a certain man without strength in his feet was sitting, a cripple from his mother's womb, who had never walked.
9 *This* man heard Paul speaking. [T]Paul, observing him intently and seeing that he had faith to be healed, Lit. *Who*
10 said with a loud voice, [R]"Stand up straight on your feet!" And he leaped and walked. [Is. 35:6]

Paul and Barnabas Are Deified

11 Now when the people saw what Paul had done, they raised their voices, saying in the Lycaonian *language*, "The gods have come down to us in the likeness of men!"
12 And Barnabas they called [T]Zeus, and Paul, [T]Hermes, because he was the chief speaker. Or *Jupiter* • Or *Mercury*
13 Then the priest of Zeus, whose temple was in front of their city, brought oxen and garlands to the gates, [R]intending to sacrifice with the multitudes. Dan. 2:46

13:42 Or *And when they went out of the synagogue of the Jews;* NU *And when they went out of the synagogue, they begged*

14 But when the apostles Barnabas and
Paul heard this, they tore their clothes and
ran in among the multitude, crying out
15 and saying, "Men, why are you doing
these things? We also are men with the same
nature as you, and preach to you that you
should turn from these vain things to the
living God, who made the heaven, the earth,
the sea, and all things that are in them,
16 [R]"who in bygone generations allowed all
nations to walk in their own ways. Ps. 81:12
17 "Nevertheless He did not leave Himself
without witness, in that He did good, gave us
rain from heaven and fruitful seasons, filling
our hearts with food and gladness."
18 And with these sayings they could
scarcely restrain the multitudes from sacrificing to them.

Paul Is Stoned

19 Then Jews from Antioch and Iconium
came there; and having persuaded the multitudes, they stoned Paul *and* dragged *him* out
of the city, supposing him to be dead.
20 However, when the disciples gathered
around him, he rose up and went into the
city. And the next day he departed with
Barnabas to Derbe.

Ministry on the Return Trip

21 And when they had preached the gospel
to that city and made many disciples, they
returned to Lystra, Iconium, and Antioch,
22 strengthening the souls of the disciples,
exhorting *them* to continue in the faith, and
saying, [R]"We must through many tribulations
enter the kingdom of God." [2 Tim. 2:12; 3:12]
23 So when they had [R]appointed elders in
every church, and prayed with fasting, they
commended them to the Lord in whom they
had believed. Titus 1:5
24 And after they had passed through Pisidia, they came to Pamphylia.
25 Now when they had preached the word
in Perga, they went down to Attalia.

Report on the First Missionary Journey

26 From there they sailed to Antioch, where
they had been commended to the grace of
God for the work which they had completed.
27 And when they had come and gathered
the church together, they reported all that
God had done with them, and that He had
opened the door of faith to the Gentiles.
28 So they stayed there a long time with the
disciples.

CHAPTER 15

Debate over Gentiles Keeping the Law

AND [R]certain *men* came down from Judea
and taught the brethren, [R]"Unless you
are circumcised according to the custom of
Moses, you cannot be saved." Gal. 2:12 • Phil. 3:2
2 Therefore, when Paul and Barnabas had
no small dissension and dispute with them,
they determined that [R]Paul and Barnabas and
certain others of them should go up to Jerusalem, to the apostles and elders, about this
question. Gal. 2:1
3 So, [R]being sent on their way by the
church, they passed through Phoenicia and
Samaria, [R]describing the conversion of the
Gentiles; and they caused great joy to all the
brethren. Rom. 15:24 • Acts 14:27; 15:4, 12
4 And when they had come to Jerusalem,
they were received by the church and the
apostles and the elders; and they reported all
things that God had done with them.
5 But some of the sect of the Pharisees
who believed rose up, saying, "It is necessary
to circumcise them, and to command *them* to
keep the law of Moses."

Peter Preaches Salvation Through Grace

6 So the apostles and elders came together
to consider this matter.
7 And when there had been much dispute,
Peter rose up and said to them: [R]"Men and
brethren, you know that a good while ago
God chose among us, that by my mouth the
Gentiles should hear the word of the gospel
and believe. Acts 10:20
8 "So God, who knows the heart, [T]ac-
knowledged them, by giving them the Holy
Spirit just as *He did* to us, *bore witness to*
9 "and made no distinction between us and
them, purifying their hearts by faith.
10 "Now therefore, why do you test God
[R]by putting a yoke on the neck of the disciples which neither our fathers nor we were
able to bear? Matt. 23:4
11 "But [R]we believe that through the grace
of the Lord Jesus *Christ we shall be saved in
the same manner as they." Rom. 3:4; 5:15

Paul and Barnabas Testify

12 Then all the multitude kept silent and
listened to Barnabas and Paul declaring how
many miracles and wonders God had worked
through them among the Gentiles.

James Proves Gentiles Are Free from the Law

13 And after they had [T]become silent,
[R]James answered, saying, "Men *and* brethren,
listen to me: *stopped speaking* • Acts 12:17
14 [R]"Simon has declared how God at the
first visited the Gentiles to take out of them a
people for His name. Acts 15:7
15 "And with this the words of the prophets
agree, just as it is written:

16 *'After[R] this I will return*
And will rebuild the tabernacle of David
which has fallen down.

15:11 NU, M omit *Christ*

I will rebuild its ruins,
And I will set it up, Amos 9:11, 12
17 *So that the rest of mankind may seek*
the LORD,
Even all the Gentiles who are called by
My name,
Says the *LORD *who does all these*
things.'

18 *"Known to God from eternity are all His
works.
19 "Therefore [R]I judge that we should not
trouble those from among the Gentiles who
[R]are turning to God, Acts 15:28; 21:25 • 1 Thess. 1:9
20 "but that we write to them to abstain
[R]from things polluted by idols, [R]*from* [T]sexual
immorality, *from* things strangled, and *from*
blood. [1 Cor. 8:1; 10:20, 28] • [1 Cor. 6:9] • *fornication*
21 "For Moses has had throughout many
generations those who preach him in every
city, [R]being read in the synagogues every
Sabbath." Acts 13:15, 27

The Council Sends an Official Letter

22 Then it pleased the apostles and elders,
with the whole church, to send chosen men
of their own company to Antioch with Paul
and Barnabas, *namely*, Judas who was also
named [R]Barsabas,* and Silas, leading men
among the brethren. Acts 1:23
23 They wrote this *letter* by them:

The apostles, the elders, and the
brethren,
To the brethren who are of the Gentiles
in Antioch, Syria, and Cilicia:
Greetings.
24 Since we have heard that [R]some who
went out from us have troubled you
with words, unsettling your souls,
*saying, '*You must* be circumcised and
keep the law'—to whom we gave no
such commandment— Titus 1:10, 11
25 it seemed good to us, being assembled
with one [T]accord, to send chosen men
to you with our beloved Barnabas and
Paul, *purpose* or *mind*
26 [R]men who have risked their lives for the
name of our Lord Jesus Christ. Acts 13:50
27 We have therefore sent Judas and Silas,
who will also report the same things by
word of mouth.
28 For it seemed good to the Holy Spirit,
and to us, to lay upon you no greater
burden than these necessary things:
29 that you abstain from things offered to
idols, [R]from blood, from things
strangled, and from [R]sexual[T] immorality.
If you keep yourselves from these, you
will do well.
Farewell. Lev. 17:14 • Col. 3:5 • *fornication*

Report to Antioch

30 So when they were sent off, they came to
Antioch; and when they had gathered the
multitude together, they delivered the letter.
31 When they had read it, they rejoiced
over its encouragement.
32 Now Judas and Silas, themselves being
[R]prophets also, exhorted the brethren with
many words and strengthened *them*. Eph. 4:11
33 And after they had stayed *there* for a
time, they were [R]sent back with greetings
from the brethren to *the apostles. Heb. 11:31
34 *However, it seemed good to Silas to
remain there.
35 [R]Paul and Barnabas also remained in
Antioch, teaching and preaching the word of
the Lord, with many others also. Acts 13:1

Contention over John Mark

36 Then after some days Paul said to Barnabas, "Let us now go back and visit our brethren in every city where we have preached the
word of the Lord, *and see* how they are
doing."
37 Now Barnabas [T]was determined to take
with them John called Mark. *resolved*
38 But Paul insisted that they should not
take with them [R]the one who had departed
from them in Pamphylia, and had not gone
with them to the work. Acts 13:13
39 Then the contention became so sharp
that they parted from one another. And so
Barnabas took Mark and sailed to Cyprus;
40 but Paul chose Silas and departed, [R]being
[T]commended by the brethren to the grace of
God. Acts 11:23; 14:26 • *committed*
41 And he went through Syria and Cilicia,
[R]strengthening the churches. Acts 16:5

CHAPTER 16

Derbe and Lystra: Timothy Is Circumcised

THEN he came to [R]Derbe and Lystra. And
behold, a certain disciple was there,
[R]named Timothy, [R]*the* son of a certain Jewish
woman who believed, but his father *was*
Greek. Acts 14:6 • Rom. 16:21 • 2 Tim. 1:5; 3:15
2 He was well spoken of by the brethren
who were at Lystra and Iconium.
3 Paul wanted to have him go on with him.
And he took *him* and circumcised him because of the Jews who were in that region,
for they all knew that his father was Greek.
4 And as they went through the cities,
they delivered to them the [R]decrees to keep,
[R]which were determined by the apostles and
elders at Jerusalem. Acts 15:19–21 • Acts 15:28, 29
5 So the churches were strengthened in
the faith, and increased in number daily.

Troas: Macedonian Call

6 Now when they had gone through
Phrygia and the region of [R]Galatia, they were

15:17 NU *Lord, who makes these things*
15:18 NU (continuing v. 17) *known from eternity (of old).'*
15:24 NU omits *saying, 'You must be circumcised and keep the law.'* **15:33** NU *those who had sent them*
15:34 NU, M omit v. 34.

forbidden by the Holy Spirit to preach the word in [T]Asia. Gal. 1:1, 2 • The Roman province of Asia

7 After they had come to Mysia, they tried to go into Bithynia, but the *Spirit did not permit them.

8 So passing by Mysia, they [R]came down to Troas. 2 Cor. 2:12

9 And a vision appeared to Paul in the night. A [R]man of Macedonia stood and pleaded with him, saying, "Come over to Macedonia and help us." Acts 10:30

10 Now after he had seen the vision, immediately we sought to go [R]to Macedonia, concluding that the Lord had called us to preach the gospel to them. 2 Cor. 2:13

Lydia Is Converted

11 Therefore, sailing from Troas, we ran a straight course to Samothrace, and the next *day* came to Neapolis,

12 and from there to [R]Philippi, which is the [T]foremost city of that part of Macedonia, a colony. And we were staying in that city for some days. Phil. 1:1 • Lit. *first*

13 And on the Sabbath day we went out of the city to the riverside, where prayer was customarily made; and we sat down and spoke to the women who met *there*.

14 Now a certain woman named Lydia heard *us*. She was a seller of purple from the city of [R]Thyatira, who worshiped God. [R]The Lord opened her heart to heed the things spoken by Paul. Rev. 1:11; 2:18, 24 • Luke 24:45

15 And when she and her household were baptized, she begged *us*, saying, "If you have judged me to be faithful to the Lord, come to my house and stay." And [R]she constrained us. Judg. 19:21

A Spirit of Divination Is Cast Out

16 Now it happened, as we went to prayer, that a certain slave girl possessed with a spirit of divination met us, who brought her masters much profit by fortune-telling.

17 This girl followed Paul and us, and cried out, saying, "These men are the servants of the Most High God, who proclaim to us the way of salvation."

18 And this she did for many days. But Paul, greatly [T]annoyed, turned and said to the spirit, "I command you in the name of Jesus Christ to come out of her." [R]And he came out that very hour. *distressed* • Mark 16:17

19 But [R]when her masters saw that their hope of profit was gone, they seized Paul and Silas and [R]dragged *them* into the marketplace to the authorities. Acts 16:16; 19:25, 26 • Matt. 10:18

20 And they brought them to the magistrates, and said, "These men, being Jews, [R]exceedingly trouble our city; Acts 17:8

21 "and they teach customs which are not lawful for us, being Romans, to receive or observe."

22 Then the multitude rose up together against them; and the magistrates tore off their clothes [R]and commanded *them* to be beaten with rods. 1 Thess. 2:2

23 And when they had laid many stripes on them, they threw *them* into prison, commanding the jailer to keep them securely.

24 Having received such a charge, he put them into the inner prison and fastened their feet in the stocks.

Philippian Jailer Is Converted

25 But at midnight Paul and Silas were praying and singing hymns to God, and the prisoners were listening to them.

26 Suddenly there was a great earthquake, so that the foundations of the prison were shaken; and immediately all the doors were opened and everyone's chains were loosed.

27 And the keeper of the prison, awaking from sleep and seeing the prison doors open, supposing the prisoners had fled, drew his sword and was about to kill himself.

28 But Paul called with a loud voice, saying, "Do yourself no harm, for we are all here."

29 Then he called for a light, ran in, and fell down trembling before Paul and Silas.

30 And he brought them out and said, "Sirs, what must I do to be saved?"

31 So they said, [R]"Believe on the Lord Jesus Christ, and you will be saved, you and your household." [John 3:16, 36; 6:47]

16:7 NU adds *of Jesus*

16:31 New Life: Received by Faith—The words spoken to the Philippian jailer are the best news human ears have ever heard, for they clearly tell how we receive God's gift of eternal life. When we receive God's gift of eternal life we are said to be "saved." The basic concept underlying "salvation" or "being saved" is deliverance. We are delivered from the penalty of sin (death, separation from God) and from the power of sin. Ultimately we will be delivered from the very presence of sin and will be delivered into the very presence of God. We receive new life by faith—believing that Jesus died for our sins, that His death was in our place, and that His payment for sin is fully acceptable in God's sight. Faith can be summarized in the acrostic:

F orsaking
A ll
I
T ake
H im

We are to forsake all (repent of our sins) and to take Him (by faith turn to God for our salvation) (Page 1303—Acts 20:21).

Now turn to Page 1243—John 5:24: Everlasting Life.

NEW TESTAMENT DELIVERANCES

Paul and Silas were beaten and imprisoned as troublemakers because of their preaching in Philippi.

In New Testament times Christian believers were often delivered from grim circumstances through a miraculous display of God's power. Paul and Silas, for example, were beaten and imprisoned as troublemakers because of their preaching in Philippi. While they prayed and sang during the night, the prison was shaken by an earthquake and they were released to continue their work (Acts 16:16–40). God's power to deliver is still available today for those who will exercise faith and seek His will in their lives.

Here are several other specific instances of God's miraculous deliverance of people of faith in New Testament times:

Name	God's Action	Biblical Reference
Gadarene with unclean spirit	Delivered from demon possession by Jesus	Mark 5:1–15
Lazarus	Raised from the dead by Jesus	John 11:38–44
Jesus	Raised from the dead after three days in the grave	Luke 24:1–7 John 20:1–10
Apostles	Freed from prison by an angel	Acts 5:17–20
Dorcas	Raised from the dead by Peter	Acts 9:36–41
Peter	Released from prison by an angel	Acts 12:1–11
Eutychus	Revived by Paul after his fall from a window	Acts 20:1–12
Paul	Delivered from a pressing burden (unnamed) in Asia	2 Cor. 1:8–11
Paul	Delivered unharmed to the island of Malta after a shipwreck	Acts 28:1

32 Then they spoke the word of the Lord to
him and to all who were in his house.
33 And he took them the same hour of the
night and washed *their* stripes. And immediately he and all his family were baptized.
34 Now when he had brought them into his
house, [R]he set food before them; and he
rejoiced, having believed in God with all his
household. Luke 5:29; 19:6

Paul Is Released from Prison

35 And when it was day, the magistrates
sent the officers, saying, "Let those men go."
36 So the keeper of the prison reported
these words to Paul, saying, "The magistrates
have sent to let you go. Now therefore depart, and go in peace."
37 But Paul said to them, "They have
beaten us openly, uncondemned Romans,
and have thrown *us* into prison. And now do
they put us out secretly? No indeed! Let them
come themselves and get us out."
38 And the officers told these words to the
magistrates, and they were afraid when they
heard that they were Romans.
39 Then they came and pleaded with them
and brought *them* out, and [R]asked *them* to
depart from the city. Matt. 8:34
40 So they went out of the prison [R]and
entered *the house of* Lydia; and when they
had seen the brethren, they encouraged them
and departed. Acts 16:14

CHAPTER 17

Thessalonica: "Turned the World Upside Down"

NOW when they had passed through Amphipolis and Apollonia, they came to
[R]Thessalonica, where there was a synagogue
of the Jews. 1 Thess. 1:1
2 Then Paul, as his custom was, [R]went in
to them, and for three Sabbaths reasoned
with them from the Scriptures, Luke 4:16
3 explaining and demonstrating [R]that the
Christ had to suffer and rise again from the
dead, and *saying*, "This Jesus whom I preach
to you is the Christ." Acts 18:5, 28
4 [R]And some of them were persuaded; and
a great multitude of the devout Greeks, and
not a few of the leading women, joined Paul
and [R]Silas. Acts 28:24 • Acts 15:22, 27, 32, 40
5 But the Jews *who were not persuaded,
*becoming envious, took some of the evil
men from the marketplace, and gathering a
mob, set all the city in an uproar and attacked the house of [R]Jason, and sought to
bring them out to the people. Rom. 16:21
6 But when they did not find them, they
dragged Jason and some brethren to the
rulers of the city, crying out, [R]"These who
have turned the world upside down have
come here too. [Acts 16:20]
7 "Jason has [T]harbored them, and these
are all acting contrary to the decrees of
Caesar, [R]saying there is another king—
Jesus." *welcomed* • 1 Pet. 2:13
8 And they troubled the crowd and the
rulers of the city when they heard these
things.
9 So when they had taken security from
Jason and the rest, they let them go.

Berea: Many Receive the Word

10 Then [R]the brethren immediately sent
Paul and Silas away by night to Berea. When
they arrived, they went into the synagogue of
the Jews. Acts 9:25; 17:14
11 These were more [T]fair-minded than those
in Thessalonica, in that they received the
word with all readiness, and [R]searched the
Scriptures daily *to find out* whether these
things were so. Lit. *noble* • John 5:39
12 Therefore many of them believed, and
also not a few of the Greeks, prominent
women as well as men.
13 But when the Jews from Thessalonica
learned that the word of God was preached
by Paul at Berea, they came there also and
stirred up the crowds.
14 [R]Then immediately the brethren sent
Paul away, to go to the sea; but both Silas
and Timothy remained there. Matt. 10:23
15 So those who conducted Paul brought
him to Athens; and [R]receiving a command for
Silas and Timothy to come to him with all
speed, they departed. Acts 18:5

Athens: Paul's Sermon on Mars' Hill

16 Now while Paul waited for them at Athens, [R]his spirit was provoked within him
when he saw that the city was [T]given over to
idols. 2 Pet. 2:8 • *full of idols*
17 Therefore he reasoned in the synagogue
with the Jews and with the *Gentile* worshipers, and in the marketplace daily with those
who happened to be there.
18 *Then certain Epicurean and Stoic philosophers encountered him. And some said,
"What does this [T]babbler want to say?"
Others said, "He seems to be a proclaimer of
foreign gods," because he preached to them
Jesus and the resurrection. Lit. *seed picker*
19 And they took him and brought him to
the Areopagus, saying, "May we know what
this new doctrine *is* of which you speak?
20 "For you are bringing some strange
things to our ears. Therefore we want to
know what these things mean."
21 For all the Athenians and the foreigners
who were there spent their time in nothing
else but either to tell or to hear some new
thing.

17:5 NU omits *who were not persuaded*
17:5 M omits *becoming envious* **17:18** NU, M *Also then*

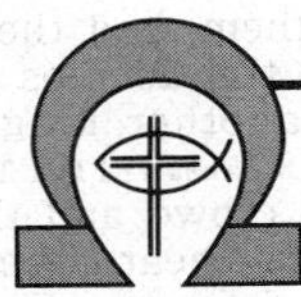

THE CITY OF ATHENS

As the capital city of the ancient Greek state of Attica, Athens dates to before 3000 B.C. It has a long history of famous and successful military campaigns. Athens was the center of art, architecture, literature, and politics during the "golden age" of the Greeks (fifth century B.C.). Many famous philosophers, playwrights, and other artists lived in Athens during this time. The city is recognized even today as the birthplace of western civilization and culture. Modern visitors to Athens are impressed by the city's ancient glory, with the ruins of the Parthenon and several other massive buildings that were devoted to pagan worship.

The apostle Paul visited Athens during his second missionary journey (Acts 17:15—18:1). While waiting in the city for Silas and Timothy, he spent some time sightseeing (Acts 17:23). He noticed the Athenians erected statues to all the gods, and even to "unknown" gods (Acts 17:23). Paul described Athens as a city "given over to idols" (Acts 17:16).

During his visit, Paul met "certain Epicurean and Stoic philosophers" (Acts 17:18) and preached to them about Jesus. This led them to bring him before the court of Areopagus—an institution revered from the city's earliest times. This court met upon the hill called Areopagus (Mars' Hill). Its purpose was to decide religious matters. Members of the court were curious about Paul's proclamation of the god they worshiped without knowing (Acts 17:23).

Paul's speech to the court (Acts 17:22–31) provides a model for communicating the gospel to a group that has no Bible background. He drew from his surroundings by mentioning the Athenians' love for religion, demonstrated by their many idols. He then made his plea for Christianity by declaring that God does not dwell in man-made temples.

In spite of this approach, most of the Athenians were not responsive to Paul's preaching. They could not accept Paul's statement about the resurrection of Jesus (Acts 17:32).

Photo by Gustav Jeeninga

The Porch of the Maidens, connected to the temple known as the Erechtheum in Athens.

22 Then Paul stood in the midst of the [T]Areopagus and said, "Men of Athens, I perceive that in all things you are very religious; Lit. *Hill of Ares*, or *Mars' Hill*

23 "for as I was passing through and considering the objects of your worship, I even found an altar with this inscription:

TO THE UNKNOWN GOD.

Therefore, the One whom you worship without knowing, Him I proclaim to you:

24 [R]"God, who made the world and everything in it, since He is [R]Lord of heaven and earth, [R]does not dwell in temples made with hands. Acts 14:15 • Matt. 11:25 • Acts 7:48–50

25 "Nor is He worshiped with men's hands, as though He needed anything, since He [R]gives to all life, breath, and all things. Is. 42:5

26 "And He has made from one *blood every nation of men to dwell on all the face of the earth, and has determined their preappointed times and the boundaries of their habitation,

27 [R]"so that they should seek the Lord, in the hope that they might grope for Him and find Him, [R]though He is not far from each one of us; [Rom. 1:20] • Jer. 23:23, 24

28 "for in Him we live and move and have our being, as also some of your own poets have said, 'For we are also His offspring.'

29 "Therefore, since we are the offspring of God, we ought not to think that the Divine Nature is like gold or silver or stone, something shaped by art and man's devising.

30 "Truly, [R]these times of ignorance God overlooked, but [R]now commands all men everywhere to repent, [Rom. 3:25] • [Titus 2:11, 12]

31 "because He has appointed a day on which [R]He will judge the world in righteousness by the Man whom He has ordained. He has given assurance of this to all by [R]raising Him from the dead." Acts 10:42 • Acts 2:24

32 And when they heard of the resurrection of the dead, some mocked, while others said, "We will hear you again on this *matter*."

33 So Paul departed from among them.

34 However, some men joined him and believed, among them Dionysius the Areopagite, a woman named Damaris, and others with them.

CHAPTER 18

Paul Works with Aquila and Priscilla

AFTER these things Paul departed from Athens and went to Corinth.

2 And he found a certain Jew named Aquila, born in Pontus, who had recently come from Italy with his wife Priscilla (because Claudius had commanded all the Jews to depart from Rome); and he came to them.

3 So, because he was of the same trade, he stayed with them [R]and worked; for by occupation they were tentmakers. Acts 20:34

Jews Reject Paul

4 [R]And he reasoned in the synagogue every Sabbath, and persuaded both Jews and Greeks. Acts 17:2

5 When Silas and Timothy had come from Macedonia, Paul was [R]constrained [T]by the Spirit, and testified to the Jews *that* Jesus *is* the Christ. Acts 18:28 • Or *in his spirit* or *in the Spirit*

6 But when they opposed him and blasphemed, [R]he shook *his* garments and said to them, [R]"Your blood *be* upon your *own* heads; [R]I *am* clean. From now on I will go to the Gentiles." Neh. 5:13 • 2 Sam. 1:16 • [Ezek. 3:18, 19]

Crispus, the Gentile, Is Converted

7 And he departed from there and entered the house of a certain *man* named *Justus, *one* who worshiped God, whose house was next door to the synagogue.

8 [R]Then Crispus, the ruler of the synagogue, believed on the Lord with all his household. And many of the Corinthians, hearing, believed and were baptized. 1 Cor. 1:14

9 Now [R]the Lord spoke to Paul in the night by a vision, "Do not be afraid, but speak, and do not keep silent; Acts 23:11

10 [R]"for I am with you, and no one will attack you to hurt you; for I have many people in this city." Jer. 1:18, 19

11 And he continued *there* a year and six months, teaching the word of God among them.

Gallio Will Not Try Paul

12 Now when Gallio was proconsul of Achaia, the Jews with one accord rose up against Paul and brought him to the [T]judgment seat, Gr. *bema*

13 saying, "This *fellow* persuades men to worship God contrary to the law."

14 And when Paul was about to open *his* mouth, Gallio said to the Jews, "If it were a matter of wrongdoing or wicked crimes, O Jews, there would be reason why I should bear with you.

15 "But if it is a [R]question of words and names and your own law, look *to it* yourselves; for I do not want to be a judge of such *matters*." Acts 23:29; 25:19

16 And he drove them from the judgment seat.

17 Then *all the Greeks took [R]Sosthenes, the ruler of the synagogue, and beat *him* before the judgment seat. But Gallio took no notice of these things. 1 Cor. 1:1

17:26 NU omits *blood* **18:7** NU *Titius Justus* **18:17** NU *they all*

Return Trip to Antioch

18 So Paul still remained [T]a good while.
Then he took leave of the brethren and sailed
for Syria, and Priscilla and Aquila *were* with
him. He had *his* hair cut off at Cenchrea, for
he had taken a vow. Lit. *many days*
19 And he came to Ephesus, and left them
there; but he himself entered the synagogue
and reasoned with the Jews.
20 When they asked *him* to stay a longer
time with them, he did not consent,
21 but took leave of them, saying, *"I must
by all means keep this coming feast in Jerusalem; but I will return again to you, God
willing." And he sailed from Ephesus.
22 And when he had landed at [R]Caesarea,
and [T]gone up and greeted the church, he
went down to Antioch. Acts 8:40 • To Jerusalem

Galatia and Phrygia: Strengthening the Disciples

23 After he had spent some time *there*, he
departed and went over *all* the region of
[R]Galatia and Phrygia [T]in order, strengthening
all the disciples. Gal. 1:2 • *successively*

Apollos Teaches Effectively

24 [R]Now a certain Jew named Apollos, born
at Alexandria, an eloquent man *and* mighty
in the Scriptures, came to Ephesus. Titus 3:13
25 This man had been instructed in the way
of the Lord; and being [R]fervent in spirit, he
spoke and taught accurately the things of the
Lord, [R]though he knew only the baptism of
John. Rom. 12:11 • Acts 19:3
26 So he began to speak boldly in the synagogue. When Aquila and Priscilla heard him,
they took him aside and explained to him the
way of God more accurately.
27 And when he desired to cross to Achaia,
the brethren wrote, exhorting the disciples to
receive him; and when he arrived, [R]he greatly
helped those who had believed through
grace; 1 Cor. 3:6
28 for he vigorously refuted the Jews publicly, [R]showing from the Scriptures that Jesus
is the Christ. Acts 9:22; 17:3; 18:5

CHAPTER 19

Disciples of John Receive the Holy Spirit

AND it happened, while Apollos was at
Corinth, that Paul, having passed
through [R]the upper regions, came to Ephesus.
And finding some disciples Acts 18:23
2 he said to them, "Did you receive the
Holy Spirit when you believed?" And they
said to him, [R]"We have not so much as heard
whether there is a Holy Spirit." 1 Sam. 3:7
3 And he said to them, "Into what then
were you baptized?" So they said, [R]"Into
John's baptism." Acts 18:25
4 Then Paul said, [R]"John indeed baptized
with a baptism of repentance, saying to the
people that they should believe on Him who
would come after him, that is, on Christ
Jesus." Matt. 3:11
5 When they heard *this*, they were baptized in the name of the Lord Jesus.
6 And when Paul had laid hands on them,
the Holy Spirit came upon them, and [R]they
spoke with tongues and prophesied. Acts 2:4
7 Now the men were about twelve in all.

Paul Teaches in Tyrannus's School

8 [R]And he went into the synagogue and
spoke boldly for three months, reasoning and
persuading [R]concerning the things of the
kingdom of God. Acts 17:2; 18:4 • Acts 1:3; 28:23
9 But when some were hardened and did
not believe, but spoke evil [R]of the Way before
the multitude, he departed from them and
withdrew the disciples, reasoning daily in the
school of Tyrannus. Acts 9:2; 19:23; 22:4; 24:14
10 And this continued for two years, so that
all who dwelt in Asia heard the word of the
Lord Jesus, both Jews and Greeks.

Miracles Are Performed at Ephesus

11 Now [R]God worked unusual miracles by
the hands of Paul, Mark 16:20
12 [R]so that even handkerchiefs or aprons
were brought from his body to the sick, and
the diseases left them and the evil spirits
went out of them. Acts 5:15
13 Then some of the itinerant Jewish exorcists took it upon themselves to call the name
of the Lord Jesus over those who had evil
spirits, saying, *"We adjure you by the Jesus
whom Paul preaches."
14 Also there were seven sons of Sceva, a
Jewish chief priest, who did so.
15 And the evil spirit answered and said,
"Jesus I know, and Paul I know; but who are
you?"
16 Then the man in whom the evil spirit
was leaped on them, *overpowered them, and
prevailed against *them, so that they fled out
of that house naked and wounded.
17 This became known both to all Jews and
Greeks dwelling in Ephesus; and [R]fear fell on
them all, and the name of the Lord Jesus was
magnified. Luke 1:65; 7:16
18 And many who had believed came [R]con-
fessing and telling their deeds. Matt. 3:6
19 Also, many of those who had practiced
magic brought their books together and
burned *them* in the sight of all. And they
counted up the value of them, and *it* totaled
[T]fifty thousand *pieces* of silver. $364,000
20 [R]So the word of the Lord grew mightily
and prevailed. Acts 6:7; 12:24

18:21 NU omits *I must by all means keep this coming feast in Jerusalem* **19:13** NU *I*
19:16 M *and they overpowered them*
19:16 NU *both of them*

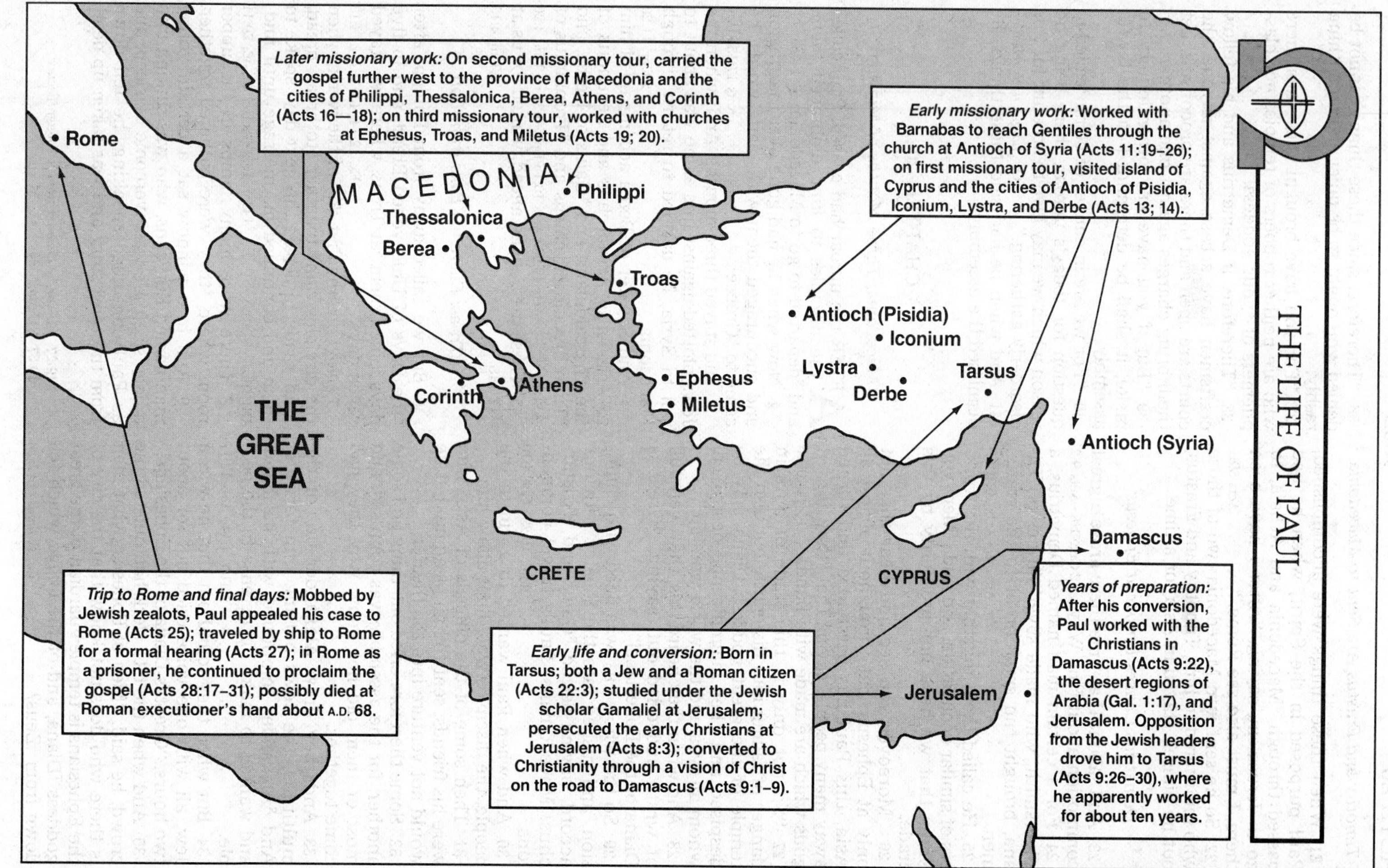
THE LIFE OF PAUL
Later missionary work: On second missionary tour, carried the gospel further west to the province of Macedonia and the cities of Philippi, Thessalonica, Berea, Athens, and Corinth (Acts 16—18); on third missionary tour, worked with churches at Ephesus, Troas, and Miletus (Acts 19; 20).
Early missionary work: Worked with Barnabas to reach Gentiles through the church at Antioch of Syria (Acts 11:19–26); on first missionary tour, visited island of Cyprus and the cities of Antioch of Pisidia, Iconium, Lystra, and Derbe (Acts 13; 14).
Rome
MACEDONIA
Philippi
Thessalonica
Berea
Troas
Antioch (Pisidia)
Iconium
Lystra
Derbe
Tarsus
Ephesus
Miletus
Corinth
Athens
THE GREAT SEA
Antioch (Syria)
CRETE
CYPRUS
Damascus
Jerusalem
Trip to Rome and final days: Mobbed by Jewish zealots, Paul appealed his case to Rome (Acts 25); traveled by ship to Rome for a formal hearing (Acts 27); in Rome as a prisoner, he continued to proclaim the gospel (Acts 28:17–31); possibly died at Roman executioner's hand about A.D. 68.
Early life and conversion: Born in Tarsus; both a Jew and a Roman citizen (Acts 22:3); studied under the Jewish scholar Gamaliel at Jerusalem; persecuted the early Christians at Jerusalem (Acts 8:3); converted to Christianity through a vision of Christ on the road to Damascus (Acts 9:1–9).
Years of preparation: After his conversion, Paul worked with the Christians in Damascus (Acts 9:22), the desert regions of Arabia (Gal. 1:17), and Jerusalem. Opposition from the Jewish leaders drove him to Tarsus (Acts 9:26–30), where he apparently worked for about ten years.

Timothy and Erastus Are Sent to Macedonia

21 When these things were accomplished,
Paul purposed in the Spirit, when he had
passed through [R]Macedonia and Achaia, to
go to Jerusalem, saying, "After I have been
there, I must also see Rome." Acts 20:1
22 So he sent into Macedonia two of those
who ministered to him, Timothy and Erastus,
but he himself stayed in Asia for a time.

Demetrius Causes Uproar at Ephesus

23 And [R]about that time there arose a great
commotion about [R]the Way. 2 Cor. 1:8 • Acts 9:2
24 For a certain man named Demetrius, a
silversmith, who made silver shrines of [T]Di-
ana, brought [R]no small profit to the craftsmen. Gr. *Artemis* • Acts 16:16,19
25 He called them together with the workers of similar occupation, and said: "Men, you
know that we have our prosperity by this
trade.
26 "Moreover you see and hear that not
only at Ephesus, but throughout almost all
Asia, this Paul has persuaded and turned
away many people, saying that [R]they are not
gods which are made with hands. Is. 44:10–20
27 "So not only is this trade of ours in
danger of falling into disrepute, but also the
temple of the great goddess Diana may be
despised and *her magnificence destroyed,
whom all Asia and the world worship."
28 And when they heard *this*, they were full
of wrath and cried out, saying, "Great *is*
Diana of the Ephesians!"
29 So the whole city was filled with confusion, and rushed into the theater with one
accord, having seized [R]Gaius and [R]Aristar-
chus, Macedonians, Paul's travel companions. Rom. 16:23 • Col. 4:10
30 And when Paul wanted to go in to the
people, the disciples would not allow him.
31 Then some of the officials of Asia, who
were his friends, sent to him pleading that he
would not venture into the theater.
32 Some therefore cried one thing and some
another, for the assembly was confused, and
most of them did not know why they had
come together.
33 And they drew Alexander out of the
multitude, the Jews putting him forward.
And [R]Alexander [R]motioned with his hand,
and wanted to make his defense to the people. 2 Tim. 4:14 • Acts 12:17
34 But when they found out that he was a
Jew, all with one voice cried out for about
two hours, "Great *is* Diana of the Ephesians!"
35 And when the city clerk had quieted the
crowd, he said: "Men of Ephesus, what man
is there who does not know that the city of
the Ephesians is temple guardian of the great
goddess [T]Diana, and of the *image* which fell
down from [T]Zeus? Gr. *Artemis* • *heaven*
36 "Therefore, since these things cannot be
denied, you ought to be quiet and do nothing
rashly.
37 "For you have brought these men here
who are neither robbers of temples nor blasphemers of *your goddess.
38 "Therefore, if Demetrius and his fellow
craftsmen have a case against anyone, the
courts are open and there are proconsuls. Let
them bring charges against one another.
39 "But if you have any other inquiry to
make, it shall be determined in the lawful
assembly.
40 "For we are in danger of being [T]called in
question for today's uproar, there being no
reason which we may give to account for this
disorderly gathering." Or *charged with rebellion*
41 And when he had said these things, he
dismissed the assembly.

CHAPTER 20

Macedonia: Three Months of Ministry

AFTER the uproar had ceased, Paul called
the disciples to *him*, embraced *them*,
and [R]departed to go to Macedonia. 1 Tim. 1:3
2 Now when he had gone over that region
and encouraged them with many words, he
came to [R]Greece Acts 17:15; 18:1
3 and stayed three months. And [R]when the
Jews plotted against him as he was about to
sail to Syria, he decided to return through
Macedonia. 2 Cor. 11:26
4 And Sopater of Berea accompanied him
to Asia—also Aristarchus and Secundus of
the Thessalonians, and [R]Gaius of Derbe, and
[R]Timothy, and [R]Tychicus and [R]Trophimus of
Asia. Acts 19:29 • Acts 16:1 • Eph. 6:21 • 2 Tim. 4:20
5 These men, going ahead, waited for us at
[R]Troas. 2 Tim. 4:13

Troas: Eutychus Falls from Loft

6 But we sailed away from Philippi after
[R]the Days of Unleavened Bread, and in five
days joined them [R]at Troas, where we stayed
seven days. Ex. 12:14, 15 • 2 Tim. 4:13
7 Now on [R]the first *day* of the week, when
the disciples came together [R]to break bread,
Paul, ready to depart the next day, spoke to
them and continued his message until midnight. 1 Cor. 16:2 • Acts 2:42, 46; 20:11
8 There were many lamps in the upper
room where *they were gathered together.
9 And in a window sat a certain young
man named Eutychus, who was sinking into
a deep sleep. He was overcome by sleep; and
as Paul continued speaking, he fell down
from the third story and was taken up dead.

19:27 NU *she be deposed from her magnificence*
19:37 NU *our* **20:8** NU, M *we*

10 But Paul went down, fell on him, and
embracing *him* said, [R]"Do not trouble yourselves, for his life is in him." Matt. 9:23, 24
11 Now when he had come up, had broken
bread and eaten, and talked a long while,
even till daybreak, he departed.
12 And they brought the young man in
alive, and they were not a little comforted.

Miletus: Paul Bids Farewell to Ephesian Elders

13 Then we went ahead to the ship and
sailed to Assos, there intending to take Paul
on board; for so he had [T]given orders, intending himself to go on foot. *arranged it*
14 And when he met us at Assos, we took
him on board and came to Mitylene.
15 We sailed from there, and the next *day*
came opposite Chios; the following *day* we
arrived at Samos and stayed at Trogyllium;
the next *day* we came to Miletus.
16 For Paul had decided to sail past Ephesus, so that he would not have to spend time
in Asia; for he was hurrying to be at Jerusalem, if possible, on the Day of Pentecost.
17 From Miletus he sent to Ephesus and
called for the elders of the church.
18 And when they had come to him, he said
to them: "You know, [R]from the first day that
I came to Asia, in what manner I always lived
among you, Acts 18:19; 19:1, 10; 20:4, 16
19 "serving the Lord with all humility, with
many tears and trials which happened to me
[R]by the plotting of the Jews; Acts 20:3
20 "*and* how I kept back nothing that was
helpful, but proclaimed it to you, and taught
you publicly and from house to house,
21 [R]"testifying to Jews, and also to Greeks,
[R]repentance toward God and faith toward our
Lord Jesus Christ. Acts 18:5; 19:10 • Mark 1:15
22 "And see, now [R]I go bound in the spirit
to Jerusalem, not knowing the things that
will happen to me there, Acts 19:21
23 "except that [R]the Holy Spirit testifies in
every city, saying that chains and tribulations
await me. Acts 21:4, 11
24 *"But [R]none of these things move me;
nor do I count my life dear to myself, [R]so that
I may finish my [T]race with joy, [R]and the
ministry [R]which I received from the Lord
Jesus, to testify to the gospel of the grace of
God. Acts 21:13 • 2 Tim. 4:7 • *course* • Acts 1:17 • Gal. 1:1
25 "And indeed, now I know that you all,
among whom I have gone preaching the
kingdom of God, will see my face no more.
26 "Therefore I testify to you this day that I
am innocent of the blood of all *men*.
27 "For I have not [T]shunned to declare to
you the whole counsel of God. *avoided*
28 "Therefore take heed to yourselves and
to all the flock, among which the Holy Spirit
[R]has made you overseers, to shepherd the
church of *God [R]which He purchased [R]with
His own blood. 1 Cor. 12:28 • Eph. 1:7, 14 • Heb. 9:14
29 "For I know this, that after my departure
[R]savage wolves will come in among you, not
sparing the flock. Matt. 7:15
30 "Also from among yourselves men will
rise up, speaking perverse things, to draw
away the disciples after themselves.
31 "Therefore watch, and remember that
[R]for three years I did not cease to warn
everyone night and day with tears. Acts 19:8
32 "And now, brethren, I commend you to
God and to the word of His grace, which is
able to build you up and give you an inheritance among all those who are sanctified.
33 "I have coveted no one's silver or gold or
apparel.
34 *"Yes, you yourselves know [R]that these
hands have provided for my necessities, and
for those who were with me. Acts 18:3
35 "I have shown you in every way, [R]by
laboring like this, that you must support the
weak. And remember the words of the Lord
Jesus, that He said, 'It is more blessed to give
than to receive.' " Rom. 15:1
36 And when he had said these things, he
knelt down and prayed with them all.
37 Then they all wept [T]freely, and fell on
Paul's neck and kissed him, Lit. *much*
38 sorrowing most of all for the words
which he spoke, that they would see his face
no more. And they accompanied him to the
ship.

CHAPTER 21

Tyre: Paul Is Warned About Jerusalem

NOW it came to pass, that when we had
departed from them and set sail, running a straight course we came to Cos, the
following *day* to Rhodes, and from there to
Patara.
2 And finding a ship sailing over to Phoenicia, we went aboard and set sail.
3 When we had sighted Cyprus, we passed
it on the left, sailed to Syria, and landed at
Tyre; for there the ship was to unload her
cargo.
4 And finding *disciples, we stayed there
seven days. [R]They told Paul through the
Spirit not to go up to Jerusalem. Acts 20:23
5 When we had come to the end of those
days, we departed and went on our way; and
they all accompanied us, with wives and
children, till *we were* out of the city. And we
knelt down on the shore and prayed.
6 When we had taken our leave of one
another, we boarded the ship, and they returned [R]home. John 1:11

20:24 NU *But I do not count my life of any value or dear to myself* **20:28** M *of the Lord and God* **20:34** NU, M omit *Yes* **21:4** NU *the disciples*

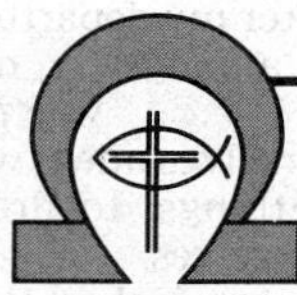

BISHOPS, PRESBYTERS, AND DEACONS

Bishops (*episkopoi*)

This word *bishop* was originally a secular word meaning "over-" (*epi-*) "seer" (*skopos*) or "superintendent," or "one who watches over (to protect)." The noun itself occurs only five times in the New Testament. The first time it is used it is a synonym for elder (compare v. 17 and v. 28 of Acts 20). Here the KJV translated it "overseer," though everywhere else as "bishop." The epistle to the church in Philippi (1:1) is addressed to three groups: "the saints" together with "the bishops and the deacons." The office was obviously plural, at least at that time and place.

The fifth New Testament occurrence of *bishop* is unique: "Jesus Christ is *episkopos* of our souls (1 Pet. 2:25), a phrase which suggests that *episkopos* was not yet in New Testament times exclusively a technical term for a definite office, as it became in the writings of the apostolic fathers" (Nigel Turner, *Christian Words*, p. 45).

Office of a Bishop (*episkopē*)

Episkopē is a noun meaning "a watching over." It occurs four times in the Greek New Testament, twice unrelated to the church, once related to a church office, and once where its connection is disputed.

First Timothy 3:1 gives the qualifications for a bishop and begins: "If a man desires the position of a bishop [*episkopē*], he desires a good work." A true overseer works hard, unlike some of the medieval ones who lived in splendor and were worldly and carnal.

Whether Judas's office [*episkopē*] in Acts 1:20 was apostleship or "bishoprick" (KJV) is disputed. Turner warns that "one must hesitate to deduce from this alone a close relationship between Apostle and Bishop" (*op. cit.*, p. 46).

Serve as a Bishop (*episkopeō*)

The verb form *episkopeō* occurs only twice in the New Testament. In Hebrews 12:15, it has a non-ecclesiastical sense, "looking diligently." Peter used it in the technical sense: "serving as overseers" (1 Pet. 5:2).

Elders (*Presbyteroi*)

If overseers and elders are the same office in the New Testament, why the double terms, one might ask? It is a matter of emphasis: *Bishop* or *overseer* stresses the office and what it entails; *presbyter* or *elder* stresses the maturity of the man holding that office.

English *elder* is an excellent translation of the Greek *presbyteros*, because it has the same double meaning: "older man" and "a church official." KJV translates 1 Timothy 5:1 with the word *elder* ("rebuke not an elder") although the context of different age groups suggests "older man" as the meaning. Of the many references that include this word, more than half do not refer to church elders. In the Gospels, elders of the Jews are usually meant or elders of the synagogue. Probably the first churches were organized much like the synagogues, which had a plurality of elders (cf. Acts 14:23). The Book of Revelation speaks of *presbyteroi* who may be angelic or other kinds of "elders."

In 1 Peter 5:1, 2, the apostle Peter nicely weaves all the church concepts together in one passage: "The elders [*presbyteroi*] who are among you I exhort, I who am a fellow elder [*sympresbyteros*] and a witness of the suffering of Christ, . . . Shepherd [*poimainō*] the flock of God which is among you, serving as overseers [*episkopeō*]."

Deacons (*diakonoi*)

Deacon is another word for servant. *Diakonos* is used in a general sense for ministry and in a technical sense for the office of deacon. In this latter sense, it occurs with *episkopos* in Philippians 1:1 and 1 Timothy 3:8, 12. Acts 6 is believed by many to be the origin of the office. While the seven chosen there are not called *diakonoi* as such, the verb form *diakoneō* is used (v. 2). The standards for deacons are nearly as strict as for elders, but nothing is said about their being able to teach. They did have to have a grasp of the Christian faith, however. Deacons generally have done practical service, under the leadership of elder-overseers.

Caesarea: Agabus's Prediction

7 And when we had finished *our* voyage
from Tyre, we came to Ptolemais, greeted the
brethren, and stayed with them one day.
8 On the next *day* we *who were Paul's
companions departed and came to [R]Caesarea,
and entered the house of Philip [R]the evangelist,
[R]who was *one* of the seven, and stayed
with him. Acts 8:40; 21:16 • Eph. 4:11 • Acts 6:5
9 Now this man had four virgin daughters
[R]who prophesied. Joel 2:28
10 And as we stayed many days, a certain
prophet named [R]Agabus came down from
Judea. Acts 11:28
11 When he had come to us, he took Paul's
belt, bound his *own* hands and feet, and said,
"Thus says the Holy Spirit, [R]'So shall the
Jews at Jerusalem bind the man who owns
this belt, and deliver *him* into the hands of
the Gentiles.'" Acts 20:23; 21:33; 22:25
12 And when we heard these things, both
we and those from that place pleaded with
him not to go up to Jerusalem.
13 Then Paul answered, [R]"What do you
mean by weeping and breaking my heart?
For I am ready not only to be bound, but also
to die at Jerusalem for the name of the Lord
Jesus." Acts 20:24, 37
14 So when he would not be persuaded, we
ceased, saying, [R]"The will of the Lord be
done." Luke 11:2; 22:42
15 And after those days we [T]packed and
went up to Jerusalem. *made preparations*
16 Also some of the disciples from Caesarea
went with us and brought with them one,
Mnason of Cyprus, an early disciple, with
whom we were to lodge.

Paul Conforms to Jewish Customs

17 [R]And when we had come to Jerusalem,
the brethren received us gladly. Acts 15:4
18 On the following *day* Paul went in with
us to James, and all the elders were present.
19 When he had greeted them, he told in
detail those things which God had done
among the Gentiles through his ministry.
20 And when they heard *it*, they glorified
the Lord. And they said to him, "You see,
brother, how many myriads of Jews there are
who have believed, and they are all [R]zealous
for the law; Acts 15:1; 22:3
21 "but they have been informed about you
that you teach all the Jews who are among
the Gentiles to forsake Moses, saying that
they ought not to circumcise *their* children
nor to walk according to the customs.
22 *"What then? The assembly must certainly
meet, for they will hear that you have
come.
23 "Therefore do what we tell you: We have
four men who have taken a vow.
24 "Take them and be purified with them,
and pay their expenses so that they may
[R]shave *their* heads, and that all may know
that those things of which they were informed
concerning you are nothing, but *that*
you yourself also walk orderly and keep the
law. Acts 18:18
25 "But concerning the Gentiles who believe,
we have written *and* decided *that they
should observe no such thing, except that
they should keep themselves from *things*
offered to idols, from blood, from things
strangled, and from sexual immorality."
26 Then Paul took the men, and the next
day, having been purified with them, entered
the temple to announce the expiration of the
days of purification, at which time an offering
should be made for each one of them.

Paul's Arrest

27 And when the seven days were almost
ended, [R]the Jews from Asia, seeing him in the
temple, stirred up the whole crowd and [R]laid
hands on him, Acts 20:19; 24:18 • Acts 26:21
28 crying out, "Men of Israel, help! This is
the man who teaches all *men* everywhere
against the people, the law, and this place;
and furthermore he also brought Greeks into
the temple and has defiled this holy place."
29 (For they had *previously seen [R]Trophimus
the Ephesian with him in the city, whom
they supposed that Paul had brought into the
temple.) Acts 20:4
30 And [R]all the city was disturbed; and the
people ran together, seized Paul, and dragged
him out of the temple; and immediately the
doors were shut. Acts 16:19; 26:21
31 Now as they were seeking to kill him,
news came to the commander of the garrison
that all Jerusalem was in an uproar.
32 [R]He immediately took soldiers and centurions,
and ran down to them. And when they
saw the commander and the soldiers, they
stopped beating Paul. Acts 23:27; 24:7
33 Then the [R]commander came near and
took him, and [R]commanded *him* to be bound
with two chains; and he asked who he was
and what he had done. Acts 24:7 • Acts 20:23; 21:11
34 And some among the multitude cried one
thing and some another. And when he could
not ascertain the truth because of the tumult,
he commanded him to be taken into the
barracks.
35 And when he reached the stairs, he had
to be carried by the soldiers because of the
violence of the mob.
36 For the multitude of the people followed
after, crying out, [R]"Away with him!" John 19:15
37 And as Paul was about to be led into the
barracks, he said to the commander, "May I

21:8 NU omits *who were Paul's companions*
21:22 NU *What then is to be done? They will certainly hear*
21:25 NU omits *that they should observe no such thing, except* **21:29** M omits *previously*

speak to you?" He replied, "Can you speak
Greek?
38 [R]"Are you not the Egyptian who some
time ago raised an insurrection and led the
four thousand assassins out into the wilderness?" Acts 5:36
39 But Paul said, [R]"I am a Jew from Tarsus,
in Cilicia, a citizen of no [T]mean city; and I
implore you, permit me to speak to the people." Acts 9:11; 22:3 • *insignificant*

Paul's Defense Before the Crowd
Acts 9:1–8, 17, 18; 26:13–18

40 So when he had given him permission,
Paul stood on the stairs and [R]motioned with
his hand to the people. And when there was a
great silence, he spoke to *them* in the [R]He-
brew language, saying, Acts 12:17 • Acts 22:2

CHAPTER 22

"MEN, [R]brethren, and fathers, hear my
defense before you now." Acts 7:2
2 And when they heard that he spoke to
them in the [R]Hebrew language, they kept all
the more silent. Then he said: Acts 21:40
3 [R]"I am indeed a Jew, born in Tarsus of
Cilicia, but brought up in this city at the feet
of Gamaliel, taught according to the strict-
ness of our fathers' law, and was zealous
toward God as you all are today. 2 Cor. 11:22
4 [R]"I persecuted this Way to the death,
binding and delivering into prisons both men
and women, 1 Tim. 1:13
5 "as also the high priest bears me witness,
and [R]all the council of the elders, [R]from whom
I also received letters to the brethren, and
went to Damascus [R]to bring in chains even
those who were there to Jerusalem to be
punished. Acts 23:14 • Luke 22:66 • Acts 9:2
6 "Now [R]it happened, as I journeyed and
came near Damascus at about noon, suddenly a great light from heaven shone around
me. Acts 9:3; 26:12, 13
7 "And I fell to the ground and heard a
voice saying to me, 'Saul, Saul, why are you
persecuting Me?'
8 "So I answered, 'Who are You, Lord?'
And He said to me, 'I am Jesus of Nazareth,
whom you are persecuting.'
9 "Now those who were with me indeed
saw the light *and were afraid, but they did
not hear the voice of Him who spoke to me.
10 "So I said, 'What shall I do, Lord?' And
the Lord said to me, 'Arise and go into Damascus, and there you will be told all things
which are appointed for you to do.'
11 "And since I could not see for the glory
of that light, being led by the hand of those
who were with me, I came into Damascus.
12 "Then [R]one, Ananias, a devout man according to the law, having a good testimony
with all the Jews who dwelt *there*, Acts 9:17
13 "came to me; and he stood and said to
me, 'Brother Saul, receive your sight.' And at
that same hour I looked up at him.
14 "Then he said, [R]'The God of our fathers
has chosen you that you should know His
will, and see the Just One, [R]and hear the voice
of His mouth. Acts 3:13; 5:30 • Gal. 1:12
15 [R]'For you will be His witness to all men
of what you have seen and heard. Acts 23:11
16 'And now why are you waiting? Arise
and be baptized, [R]and wash away your sins,
calling on the name of the Lord.' Heb. 10:22
17 "Then [R]it happened, when I returned to
Jerusalem and was praying in the temple,
that I was in a trance Acts 9:26; 26:20
18 "and [R]saw Him saying to me, [R]'Make
haste and get out of Jerusalem quickly, for
they will not receive your testimony concerning Me.' Acts 22:14 • Matt. 10:14
19 "So I said, 'Lord, [R]they know that in
every synagogue I imprisoned and beat those
who believe on You. Acts 8:3; 22:4
20 'And when the blood of Your martyr
Stephen was shed, I also was standing by
consenting *to his death, and guarding the
clothes of those who were killing him.'
21 "Then He said to me, 'Depart, for I will
send you far from here to the Gentiles.'"
22 And they listened to him until this word,
and *then* they raised their voices and said,
[R]"Away with such a *fellow* from the earth, for
[R]he is not fit to live!" Acts 21:36 • Acts 25:24
23 Then, as they cried out and [T]tore off *their*
clothes and threw dust into the air, Lit. *threw*

Paul's Defense Before the Centurion

24 the commander ordered him to be
brought into the barracks, and said that he
should be examined under scourging, so that
he might know why they shouted so against
him.
25 And as they bound him with thongs,
Paul said to the centurion who stood by, [R]"Is
it lawful for you to scourge a man who is a
Roman, and uncondemned?" Acts 16:37
26 When the centurion heard *that*, he went
and told the commander, saying, "Take care
what you do, for this man is a Roman."
27 Then the commander came and said to
him, "Tell me, are you a Roman?" He said,
"Yes."
28 And the commander answered, "With a
large sum I obtained this citizenship." And
Paul said, "But I was born *a citizen*."
29 Then immediately those who were about
to examine him withdrew from him; and the
commander was also afraid after he found
out that he was a Roman, and because he had
bound him.

22:9 NU omits *and were afraid*
22:20 NU omits *to his death*

Paul's Defense Before the Sanhedrin

30 The next day, because he wanted to
know for certain why he was accused by the
Jews, he released him from *his* bonds, and
commanded the chief priests and all their
council to appear, and brought Paul down
and set him before them.

CHAPTER 23

THEN Paul, looking earnestly at the council, said, "Men *and* brethren, [R]I have lived
in all good conscience before God until this
day." 2 Tim. 1:3
2 And the high priest Ananias commanded
those who stood by him [R]to strike him on the
mouth. John 18:22
3 Then Paul said to him, "God will strike
you, *you* whitewashed wall! For you sit to
judge me according to the law, and [R]do you
command me to be struck contrary to the
law?" Deut. 25:1, 2
4 And those who stood by said, "Do you
revile God's high priest?"
5 Then Paul said, [R]"I did not know, brethren, that he was the high priest; for it is
written, [R]*'You shall not speak evil of the ruler
of your people.'*" Lev. 5:17, 18 • Ex. 22:28
6 But when Paul perceived that one part
were Sadducees and the other Pharisees, he
cried out in the council, "Men *and* brethren,
[R]I am a Pharisee, the son of a Pharisee;
[R]concerning the hope and resurrection of the
dead I am being judged!" Phil. 3:5 • Acts 24:15, 21
7 And when he had said this, a dissension
arose between the Pharisees and the Sadducees; and the assembly was divided.
8 [R]For *the* Sadducees say that there is no
resurrection—and no angel or spirit; but the
Pharisees confess both. Matt. 22:23
9 Then there arose a loud outcry. And the
scribes *who were* of the Pharisees' party
arose and protested, saying, "We find no evil
in this man; *but if a spirit or an angel has
spoken to him, let us not fight against God."
10 And when there arose a great dissension,
the commander, fearing lest Paul might be
pulled to pieces by them, commanded the
soldiers to go down and take him by force
from among them, and bring *him* into the
barracks.
11 But the following night the Lord stood
by him and said, "Be of good cheer, Paul; for
as you have testified for Me in Jerusalem, so
you must also bear witness at Rome."

Jews' Plan to Kill Paul

12 And when it was day, [R]some of the Jews
banded together and bound themselves under
an oath, saying that they would neither eat
nor drink till they had killed Paul. Acts 23:21, 30
13 Now there were more than forty who
had formed this conspiracy.
14 They came to the chief priests and [R]el-
ders, and said, "We have bound ourselves
under a great oath that we will eat nothing
until we have killed Paul. Acts 4:5, 23; 6:12
15 "Now you, therefore, together with the
council, suggest to the commander that he be
brought down to you *tomorrow, as though
you were going to make further inquiries
concerning him; but we are ready to kill him
before he comes near."
16 And when Paul's sister's son heard of
their ambush, he went and entered the barracks and told Paul.
17 Then Paul called one of the centurions to
him and said, "Take this young man to the
commander, for he has something to tell
him."
18 So he took him and brought *him* to the
commander and said, "Paul the prisoner
called me to *him* and asked *me* to bring this
young man to you. He has something to say
to you."
19 Then the commander took him by the
hand, went aside and asked *him* privately,
"What is it that you have to tell me?"
20 And he said, [R]"The Jews have agreed to
ask that you bring Paul down to the council
tomorrow, as though they were going to
inquire more fully about him. Acts 23:12
21 "But do not yield to them, for more than
forty of them lie in wait for him, men who
have bound themselves by an oath that they
will neither eat nor drink till they have killed
him; and now they are ready, waiting for the
promise from you."
22 So the commander let the young man
depart, and commanded *him*, "Tell no one
that you have revealed these things to me."

Paul's Rescue

23 And he called for two centurions, saying,
"Prepare two hundred soldiers, seventy
horsemen, and two hundred spearmen to go
to Caesarea at the third hour of the night;
24 "and provide mounts to set Paul on, and
bring *him* safely to Felix the governor."
25 He wrote a letter in the following manner:

26 Claudius Lysias,
To the most excellent governor Felix:
Greetings.
27 This man was seized by the Jews and
was about to be killed by them.
Coming with the troops I rescued him,
having learned that he was a Roman.
28 [R]And when I wanted to know the
reason they accused him, I brought him
before their council. Acts 22:30

23:9 NU *what if a spirit or an angel has spoken to him?* omitting the last clause. **23:15** NU omits *tomorrow*

29 I found out that he was accused
[R]concerning questions of their law, but
had nothing charged against him
worthy of death or chains. Acts 18:15; 25:19
30 And [R]when it was told me that *the
Jews lay in wait for the man, I sent him
immediately to you, and [R]also
commanded his accusers to state before
you the charges against him.
Farewell. Acts 23:20 • Acts 24:8; 25:6

31 Then the soldiers, as they were commanded, took Paul and brought *him* by night
to Antipatris.
32 The next day they left the horsemen to
go on with him, and returned to the barracks.
33 When they came to [R]Caesarea and had
delivered the [R]letter to the governor, they
also presented Paul to him. Acts 8:40 • Acts 23:26–30

Paul Is Tried Before Felix

34 And when the governor had read *it*, he
asked what province he was from. And when
he understood that *he was* from Cilicia,
35 he said, [R]"I will hear you when your
accusers also have come." And he commanded him to be kept in [R]Herod's [T]Praeto-
rium. Acts 24:1, 10; 25:16 • Matt. 27:27 • Headquarters

CHAPTER 24

NOW after five days Ananias the high
priest came down with the elders and a
certain orator *named* Tertullus. These gave
evidence to the governor against Paul.
2 And when he was called upon, Tertullus
began his accusation, saying: "Seeing that
through you we enjoy great peace, and [T]pros-
perity is being brought to this nation by your
foresight, Or *reforms are*
3 "we accept *it* always and in all places,
most noble Felix, with all thankfulness.
4 "Nevertheless, not to be tedious to you
any further, I beg you to hear, by your
[T]courtesy, a few words from us. *graciousness*
5 [R]"For we have found this man a plague, a
creator of dissension among all the Jews
throughout the world, and a ringleader of the
sect of the Nazarenes. 1 Pet. 2:12, 15
6 [R]"He even tried to profane the temple,
and we seized him, *and wanted [R]to judge
him according to our law. Acts 21:28 • John 18:31
7 [R]"But the commander Lysias came by
and with great violence took *him* out of our
hands, Acts 21:33; 23:10
8 [R]"commanding his accusers to come to
you. By examining him yourself you may
ascertain all these things of which we accuse
him." Acts 23:30
9 And the Jews also *assented, maintaining that these things were so.
10 Then Paul, after the governor had
nodded to him to speak, answered: "Inasmuch as I know that you have been for many
years a judge of this nation, I do the more
cheerfully answer for myself,
11 "because you may ascertain that it is no
more than twelve days since I went up to
Jerusalem [R]to worship. Acts 21:15, 18, 26, 27; 24:17
12 [R]"And they neither found me in the
temple disputing with anyone nor inciting
the crowd, either in the synagogues or in the
city. Acts 25:8; 28:17
13 "Nor can they prove the things of which
they now accuse me.
14 "But this I confess to you, that according
to [R]the Way which they call a sect, so I
worship the [R]God of my fathers, believing all
things which are written in the Law and in
the Prophets. Acts 9:2; 24:22 • 2 Tim. 1:3
15 [R]"I have hope in God, which they themselves also accept, [R]that there will be a resurrection *of *the* dead, both of *the* just and *the*
unjust. Acts 23:6; 26:6, 7; 28:20 • [Dan. 12:2]
16 [R]"This *being* so, I myself always strive to
have a conscience without offense toward
God and men. Acts 23:1
17 "Now after many years [R]I came to bring
alms and offerings to my nation, Rom. 15:25–28
18 "in the midst of which some Jews from
Asia found me [R]purified in the temple, neither
with a multitude nor with tumult. Acts 21:26
19 [R]"They ought to have been here before
you to object if they had anything against
me. [Acts 23:30; 25:16]
20 "Or else let those who are *here* themselves say *if they found any wrongdoing in
me while I stood before the council,
21 "unless *it is* for this one statement which
I cried out, standing among them, [R]'Concerning the resurrection of the dead I am being
judged by you this day.'" [Acts 23:6; 24:15; 28:20]
22 But when Felix heard these things, having more accurate knowledge of *the* Way, he
adjourned the proceedings and said, "When
[R]Lysias the commander comes down, I will
make a decision on your case." Acts 23:26; 24:7
23 So he commanded the centurion to keep
Paul and to let *him* have liberty, and [R]told
him not to forbid any of his friends to provide
for or visit him. Acts 23:16; 27:3; 28:16
24 And after some days, when Felix came
with his wife Drusilla, who was Jewish, he
sent for Paul and heard him concerning the
[R]faith in Christ. [Rom. 10:9]
25 Now as he reasoned about righteousness,
self-control, and the judgment to come, Felix
was afraid and answered, "Go away for now;
when I have a convenient time I will call for
you."

23:30 NU *there would be a plot against the man*
24:6 NU ends the sentence here and omits the rest of v. 6, all of v. 7, and the first clause of v. 8.
24:9 NU, M *joined the attack*
24:15 NU omits *of the dead*
24:20 NU, M *what wrongdoing they have found*

PAUL'S ROMAN CITIZENSHIP

The apostle Paul was born at Tarsus, the chief city of the Roman province of Cilicia in southeast Asia Minor. While he was thoroughly Jewish by nationality, he was also born a Roman citizen (Acts 22:28), a privilege which worked to his advantage on several occasions during his ministry.

As the ruling world power of Paul's time, the Romans consolidated their empire by granting Roman citizenship to certain non-Romans. Paul's parents must have enjoyed this right before him, and he automatically became a Roman citizen at birth.

A Roman citizen could not be bound or imprisoned without a trial. Neither could he be beaten or scourged—the common form of torture used by the Romans to extract a confession from a prisoner. Finally, if a Roman citizen felt he was not receiving a fair trial under local authorities, he could appeal his cause to Rome.

Paul and his partner Silas were bound, beaten, and imprisoned by Roman authorities at Philippi. When Paul made it clear they were Roman citizens, the authorities quickly released them and begged them to leave town (Acts 16:12–40).

Later, in Jerusalem, Paul was taken into protective custody by Roman soldiers (see illustration) as a group of Jewish zealots threatened his life. He was spared a scourging by the soldiers and granted a hearing before their commander when he revealed his Roman citizenship (Acts 22:24–29). The soldiers also gave him safe passage out of Jerusalem when the zealots persisted in their threats against Paul (Acts 23:23, 24).

Imprisoned by Roman officials at Caesarea for two years, Paul finally appealed to Rome (Acts 25:11, 12). He was sent on a merchant ship to Rome (Acts 27), where he spent two years under house arrest. Here he was allowed to preach and make converts (Acts 28:30, 31).

Even the tradition that Paul was beheaded in Rome shows the influence of his Roman citizenship. Non-Roman criminals were generally crucified; beheading was a more honorable and merciful form of capital punishment reserved for Roman citizens.

Roman soldier.

26 Meanwhile he also hoped that [R]money
would be given him by Paul, *that he might
release him. Therefore he sent for him more
often and conversed with him. Ex. 23:8
27 But after two years Porcius Festus succeeded Felix; and Felix, [R]wanting to do the
Jews a favor, left Paul bound. Acts 12:3; 23:35

CHAPTER 25

Paul Is Tried Before Festus

NOW when Festus had come to the province, after three days he went up from
[R]Caesarea to Jerusalem. Acts 8:40; 25:4, 6, 13
2 [R]Then the *high priest and the chief men
of the Jews informed him against Paul; and
they petitioned him, Acts 24:1; 25:15
3 asking a favor against him, that he
would summon him to Jerusalem—while
they lay in ambush along the road to kill him.
4 But Festus answered that Paul should be
kept at Caesarea, and that he himself was
going *there* shortly.
5 "Therefore," he said, "let those who have
authority among you go down with *me* and
accuse this man, to see [R]if there is any fault in
him." Acts 18:14; 25:18
6 And when he had remained among them
more than ten days, he went down to Caesarea. And the next day, sitting on the judgment seat, he commanded Paul to be
brought.
7 When he had come, the Jews who had
come down from Jerusalem stood about [R]and
laid many serious complaints against Paul,
which they could not prove, Acts 24:5, 13
8 while he answered for himself, [R]"Neither
against the law of the Jews, nor against the
temple, nor against Caesar have I offended in
anything at all." Acts 6:13; 24:12; 28:17
9 But Festus, wanting to do the Jews a
favor, answered Paul and said, "Are you
willing to go up to Jerusalem and there be
judged before me concerning these things?"
10 Then Paul said, "I stand at Caesar's
judgment seat, where I ought to be judged.
To the Jews I have done no wrong, as you
very well know.
11 [R]"For if I am an offender, or have committed anything worthy of death, I do not
object to dying; but if there is nothing in
these things of which these men accuse me,
no one can deliver me to them. [R]I appeal to
Caesar." Acts 18:14; 23:29; 25:25; 26:31 • Acts 26:32; 28:19
12 Then Festus, when he had conferred
with the council, answered, "You have appealed to Caesar? To Caesar you shall go!"
13 And after some days King Agrippa and
Bernice came to Caesarea to greet Festus.
14 When they had been there many days,
Festus laid Paul's case before the king, saying: [R]"There is a certain man left a prisoner
by Felix, Acts 24:27
15 [R]"about whom the chief priests and the
elders of the Jews informed *me*, when I was
in Jerusalem, asking for a judgment against
him. Acts 24:1; 25:2, 3
16 [R]"To them I answered, 'It is not the
custom of the Romans to deliver any man *to
destruction before the accused meets the
accusers face to face, and has opportunity to
answer for himself concerning the charge
against him.' Acts 25:4, 5
17 "Therefore when they had come together, [R]without any delay, the next day I sat
on the judgment seat and commanded the
man to be brought in. Acts 25:6, 10
18 "When the accusers stood up, they
brought no accusation against him of such
things as I [T]supposed, *suspected*
19 [R]"but had some questions against him
about their own religion and about one,
Jesus, who had died, whom Paul affirmed to
be alive. Acts 18:14, 15; 23:29
20 "And because I was uncertain of such
questions, I asked whether he was willing to
go to Jerusalem and there be judged concerning these matters.
21 "But when Paul [R]appealed to be reserved
for the decision of Augustus, I commanded
him to be kept till I could send him to Caesar." Acts 25:11, 12
22 Then [R]Agrippa said to Festus, "I also
would like to hear the man myself." "Tomorrow," he said, "you shall hear him." Acts 9:15

Paul Is Tried Before Agrippa

23 So the next day, when Agrippa and Bernice had come with great [T]pomp, and had
entered the auditorium with the commanders
and the prominent men of the city, at Festus'
command Paul was brought in. *pageantry*
24 And Festus said: "King Agrippa and all
the men who are here present with us, you
see this man about whom [R]the whole assembly of the Jews petitioned me, both at Jerusalem and here, crying out that he was [R]not fit
to live any longer. Acts 25:2, 3, 7 • Acts 21:36; 22:22
25 "But when I found that [R]he had committed nothing worthy of death, [R]and that he
himself had appealed to Augustus, I decided
to send him. Acts 23:9, 29; 26:31 • Acts 25:11, 12
26 "I have nothing certain to write to my
lord concerning him. Therefore I have
brought him out before you, and especially
before you, King Agrippa, so that after the
examination has taken place I may have
something to write.
27 "For it seems to me unreasonable to send
a prisoner and not to specify the charges
against him."

24:26 NU omits *that he might release him*
25:2 NU *chief priests* **25:16** NU omits *to destruction*

THE CITY OF CAESAREA

Caesarea, a city in central Palestine on the Mediterranean Sea, served as the commercial port for the Roman-dominated Jewish territories during New Testament times. Built by the master Roman builder Herod the Great between 25 and 13 B.C., Caesarea was named for the Roman emperor Caesar Augustus. The city was known throughout the Roman world for its beauty as well as its spacious, well-protected harbor.

In addition to its commercial importance, Caesarea also served as Rome's administrative capital for the Jewish territories during the New Testament era. This is why Caesarea is mentioned so prominently in connection with the ministry of the apostle Paul and other New Testament personalities. Philip preached at Caesarea (Acts 8:40), and Peter was sent to this administrative capital to minister to Cornelius, the Roman centurion (Acts 10:24).

Paul made Caesarea his port of call after his second and third missionary journeys. A Roman official sent Paul to the Roman governor Felix for trial after he was charged with disturbing the peace in Jerusalem (Acts 23:23, 24, 30). The apostle spent two years in prison at Caesarea before making his celebrated defense before Festus and Agrippa (Acts 25). After his long Caesarean imprisonment, he finally sailed from the harbor in chains to appeal his case before the emperor in Rome (Acts 27:1).

Herod's seaport city was built on the site of an ancient Phoenician seaport city known as Strato's Tower. He constructed an impressive breakwater system, using massive stones 50 feet long. Even after hundreds of years, some of these stones are still visible today.

Other ruins on the site that demonstrate the splendor of ancient Caesarea are a large amphitheater and sections of an aqueduct, which was used to pipe water from the mountains to the coastal city.

Ruins of a large amphitheater and sections of an aqueduct demonstrate the splendor of ancient Caesarea.

CHAPTER 26

THEN Agrippa said to Paul, "You are
permitted to speak for yourself." So Paul
stretched out his hand and answered for
himself:
2 "I think myself happy, King Agrippa,
because today I shall answer [R]for myself
before you concerning all the things of which
I am accused by the Jews, [1 Pet. 3:15, 16]
3 "especially because you are expert in all
customs and questions which have to do with
the Jews. Therefore I beg you to hear me
patiently.
4 "My manner of life from my youth,
which was spent from the beginning among
my own nation at Jerusalem, all the Jews
know.
5 "They knew me from the first, if they
were willing to testify, that according to the
strictest sect of our religion I lived a Pharisee.
6 [R]"And now I stand and am judged for the
hope of [R]the promise made by God to our
fathers. Acts 23:6 • Acts 13:32
7 "To this *promise* [R]our twelve tribes, earnestly serving *God* night and day, [R]hope to
attain. For this hope's sake, King Agrippa, I
am accused by the Jews. James 1:1 • Phil. 3:11
8 "Why should it be thought incredible by
you that God raises the dead?
9 [R]"Indeed, I myself thought I must do
many things [T]contrary to the name of [R]Jesus
of Nazareth. 1 Tim. 1:12, 13 • *against* • Acts 2:22; 10:38
10 [R]"This I also did in Jerusalem, and many
of the saints I shut up in prison, having
received authority [R]from the chief priests;
and when they were put to death, I cast my
vote against *them*. Acts 8:1–3; 9:13 • Acts 9:14
11 [R]"And I punished them often in every
synagogue and compelled *them* to blaspheme; and being exceedingly enraged
against them, I persecuted *them* even to
foreign cities. Acts 22:19
12 [R]"While thus occupied, as I journeyed to
Damascus with authority and commission
from the chief priests, Acts 9:3–8; 22:6–11; 26:12–18
13 "at midday, O king, along the road I saw
a light from heaven, brighter than the sun,
shining around me and those who journeyed
with me.
14 "And when we all had fallen to the
ground, I heard a voice speaking to me and
saying in the Hebrew language, 'Saul, Saul,
why are you persecuting Me? *It is* hard for
you to kick against the goads.'
15 "So I said, 'Who are You, Lord?' And He
said, 'I am Jesus, whom you are persecuting.
16 'But rise and stand on your feet; for I
have appeared to you for this purpose, [R]to
make you a minister and a witness both of
the things which you have seen and of the
things which I will yet reveal to you. Acts 22:15
17 'I will [T]deliver you from the *Jewish* people, as well as *from* the Gentiles, [R]to whom I
*now send you, *rescue* • Acts 22:21
18 'to open their eyes *and to turn *them*
from darkness to light, and *from* the power of
Satan to God, that they may receive forgiveness of sins and an inheritance among those
who are [T]sanctified by faith in Me.' *set apart*
19 "Therefore, King Agrippa, I was not
disobedient to the heavenly vision,
20 "but declared first to those in Damascus
and in Jerusalem, and throughout all the
region of Judea, and *then* to the Gentiles,
that they should repent, turn to God, and do
[R]works befitting repentance. Matt. 3:8
21 "For these reasons the Jews seized me in
the temple and tried to kill *me*.
22 "Therefore, having obtained help from
God, to this day I stand, witnessing both to
small and great, saying no other things than
those [R]which the prophets and [R]Moses said
would come— Rom. 3:21 • John 5:46
23 [R]"that the Christ would suffer, that He
would be the first to rise from the dead, and
[R]would proclaim light to the *Jewish* people
and to the Gentiles." Luke 24:26 • Luke 2:32
24 Now as he thus made his defense, Festus
said with a loud voice, "Paul, you are beside
yourself! Much learning is driving you mad!"
25 But he said, "I am not [T]mad, most noble
Festus, but speak the words of truth and
reason. *out of my mind*
26 "For the king, before whom I also speak
freely, [R]knows these things; for I am convinced that none of these things escapes his
attention, since this thing was not done in a
corner. Acts 26:3
27 "King Agrippa, do you believe the prophets? I know that you do believe."
28 Then Agrippa said to Paul, "You almost
persuade me to become a Christian."
29 And Paul said, "I would to God that not
only you, but also all who hear me today,
might become both almost and altogether
such as I am, except for these chains."
30 When he had said these things, the king
stood up, as well as the governor and Bernice
and those who sat with them;
31 and when they had gone aside, they
talked among themselves, saying, "This man
is doing nothing worthy of death or chains."
32 Then Agrippa said to Festus, "This man
might have been set [R]free [R]if he had not
appealed to Caesar." Acts 28:18 • Acts 25:11

CHAPTER 27

Paul's Witness During the Shipwreck

AND when it was decided that we should
sail to Italy, they delivered Paul and
some other prisoners to *one* named Julius, a
centurion of the Augustan Regiment.

26:17 NU, M omit *now* **26:18** NU, M *in order*

NEW TESTAMENT JOURNEYS

The most famous traveler of the New Testament was the apostle Paul. The account of his journey to Rome in a Roman grain ship gives many insights into sea travel in New Testament times (Acts 27). Caught in a winter storm, the ship and its passengers ran aground on the island of Malta, or Melita, off the coast of Sicily. After three months and a break in the bad weather, they continued to Rome in a second ship which sailed from Alexandria, Egypt (Acts 28:11).

Other famous journeys of New Testament personalities include the following:

Personality	Description of Journey	Biblical Reference
Wise men	From the East (Persia?) to Bethlehem to worship the newborn Jesus	Matt. 2:1–12
Joseph and Mary	From Nazareth to Bethlehem, where Jesus was born	Luke 2:4
Mary, Joseph, and Jesus	Fled to Egypt to escape Herod's threat; returned to Nazareth after Herod's death	Matt. 2:13–23
Philip	From Jerusalem to Samaria to preach to the Samaritans; from Samaria into the desert to witness to the Ethiopian eunuch; from the desert to Caesarea	Acts 8:5 Acts 8:26 Acts 8:40
Paul	From Jerusalem to Damascus to arrest the early Christians	Acts 9
Peter	From Joppa to Caesarea to meet Cornelius and preach to the Gentiles	Acts 10
Barnabas	From Jerusalem to Antioch to work with the Gentile converts	Acts 11:19–26
Paul and Barnabas	Paul's first missionary tour from Antioch to numerous places, including the island of Cyprus and the cities of Attalia, Perga, Antioch of Pisidia, Iconium, Lystra, and Derbe	Acts 13; 14
Paul and Silas	Paul's second missionary tour from Antioch to numerous cities, including Tarsus, Troas, Neapolis, Philippi, Amphipolis, Thessalonica, Berea, Athens, Corinth, and Ephesus	Acts 15—18
Paul	Paul's third missionary tour from Antioch to numerous cities; new locations visited on this tour included Assos, Mitylene, Miletus, Cos, Patara, Myra, and the island of Rhodes in the Aegean Sea off the coast of Asia Minor	Acts 18—21

2 So, entering a ship of Adramyttium, we
put to sea, meaning to sail along the coasts of
Asia. [R]Aristarchus, a Macedonian of Thessalonica, was with us. Acts 19:29
3 And the next *day* we landed at Sidon.
And Julius treated Paul kindly and gave *him*
liberty to go to his friends and receive care.
4 When we had put to sea from there, we
sailed under *the shelter of* Cyprus, because
the winds were contrary.
5 And when we had sailed over the sea
which is off Cilicia and Pamphylia, we came
to Myra, *a city* of Lycia.
6 There the centurion found [R]an Alexandrian ship sailing to Italy, and he put us on
board. Acts 28:11
7 And when we had sailed slowly many
days, and arrived with difficulty off Cnidus,
the wind not permitting us to proceed, we
sailed under *the* shelter of [R]Crete off Sal-
mone. Titus 1:5, 12
8 Passing it with difficulty, we came to a
place called Fair Havens, near the city *of*
Lasea.
9 Now when much time had been spent,
and sailing was now dangerous because the
Fast was already over, Paul advised them,
10 saying, "Men, I perceive that this voyage
will end with disaster and much loss, not only
of the cargo and ship, but also our lives."
11 Nevertheless the centurion was more
persuaded by the helmsman and the owner of
the ship than by the things spoken by Paul.
12 And because the harbor was not suitable
to winter in, the majority advised to set sail
from there also, if by any means they could
reach Phoenix, a harbor of Crete opening
toward the southwest and northwest, *and*
winter *there*.
13 When the south wind blew softly, supposing that they had obtained *their* purpose,
putting out to sea, they sailed close by Crete.
14 But not long after, a tempestuous head
wind arose, called *Euroclydon.
15 So when the ship was caught, and could
not head into the wind, we let *her* drive.
16 And running under *the shelter of* an
island called *Clauda, we secured the skiff
with difficulty.
17 When they had taken it on board, they
used cables to undergird the ship; and fearing
lest they should run aground on the *Syrtis
Sands, they struck sail and so were driven.
18 And because we were exceedingly tem-
pest-tossed, the next *day* they lightened the
ship.
19 On the third *day* [R]we threw the ship's
tackle overboard with our own hands. Jon. 1:5
20 Now when neither sun nor stars appeared for many days, and no small tempest
beat on *us*, all hope that we would be saved
was finally given up.
21 But after long abstinence from food, then
Paul stood in the midst of them and said,
"Men, you should have listened to me, and
not have sailed from Crete and incurred this
disaster and loss.
22 "And now I urge you to take [T]heart, for
there will be no loss of life among you, but
only of the ship. *courage*
23 [R]"For there stood by me this night an
angel of the God to whom I belong and
[R]whom I serve, Acts 18:9; 23:11 • Dan. 6:16
24 "saying, 'Do not be afraid, Paul; you
must be brought before Caesar; and indeed
God has granted you all those who sail with
you.'
25 "Therefore take heart, men, for I believe
God that it will be just as it was told me.
26 "However, [R]we must run aground on a
certain island." Acts 28:1
27 But when the fourteenth night had
come, as we were driven up and down in the
Adriatic *Sea*, about midnight the sailors
sensed that they were drawing near some
land.
28 And they took soundings and found *it* to
be [T]twenty fathoms; and when they had gone
a little farther, they took soundings again and
found *it* to be [T]fifteen fathoms. 120 ft. • 90 ft.
29 Then, fearing lest we should run aground
on the rocks, they dropped four anchors from
the stern, and prayed for day to come.
30 And as the sailors were seeking to escape
from the ship, when they had let down the
skiff into the sea, under pretense of putting
out anchors from the prow,
31 Paul said to the centurion and the soldiers, "Unless these men stay in the ship, you
cannot be saved."
32 Then the soldiers cut away the ropes of
the skiff and let it fall off.
33 And as day was about to dawn, Paul
implored *them* all to take food, saying, "Today is the fourteenth day you have waited
and continued without food, and eaten nothing.
34 "Therefore I urge you to take nourishment, for this is for your survival, since not a
hair will fall from the head of any of you."
35 And when he had said these things, he
took bread and [R]gave thanks to God in the
presence of them all; and when he had broken *it* he began to eat. [1 Tim. 4:3, 4]
36 Then they were all encouraged, and also
took food themselves.
37 And in all we were two hundred and
seventy-six [R]persons on the ship. Acts 2:41; 7:14
38 So when they had eaten enough, they
lightened the ship and threw out the wheat
into the sea.
39 Now when it was day, they did not recognize the land; but they observed a bay with

27:14 A southeast wind that stirs up broad waves; NU *Euraquilon*, a northeaster **27:16** NU *Cauda* **27:17** M *Syrtes* **28:25** NU *your*

a beach, onto which they planned to run the
ship if possible.
40 And they [T]let go the anchors and left
them in the sea, meanwhile loosing the rudder ropes; and they hoisted the mainsail to
the wind and made for shore. *cast off*
41 But striking [T]a place where two seas met,
[R]they ran the ship aground; and the prow
stuck fast and remained immovable, but the
stern was being broken up by the violence of
the waves. A reef • 2 Cor. 11:25
42 Now the soldiers' plan was to kill the
prisoners, lest any of them should swim away
and escape.
43 But the centurion, wanting to save Paul,
kept them from *their* purpose, and commanded that those who could swim should
jump *overboard* first and get to land,
44 and the rest, some on boards and some
on *broken pieces* of the ship. And so it was
that they all escaped safely to land.

CHAPTER 28

Paul's Witness on Malta

NOW when they had escaped, they then
found out that [R]the island was called
Malta. Acts 27:26
2 And the [T]natives showed us unusual
kindness; for they kindled a fire and made us
all welcome, because of the rain that was
falling and because of the cold. Lit. *barbarians*
3 But when Paul had gathered a bundle of
sticks and laid *them* on the fire, a viper came
out because of the heat, and fastened on his
hand.
4 So when the natives saw the creature
hanging from his hand, they said to one
another, "No doubt this man is a murderer,
whom, though he has escaped the sea, yet
justice does not allow to live."
5 But he shook off the creature into the
fire and [R]suffered no harm. Mark 16:18
6 However, they were expecting that he
would swell up or suddenly fall down dead;
but after they had looked for a long time and
saw no harm come to him, they changed
their minds and said that he was a god.
7 Now in that region there was an estate of
the [T]leading citizen of the island, whose name
was Publius, who received us and entertained
us courteously for three days. Magistrate
8 And it happened that the father of Publius lay sick of a fever and dysentery. Paul
went in to him and [R]prayed, and he laid his
hands on him and healed him. [James 5:14, 15]
9 So when this was done, the rest of those
on the island who had diseases also came and
were healed.
10 They also honored us in many [R]ways;
and when we departed, they provided such
things as were [R]necessary. Matt. 15:6 • [Phil. 4:19]
11 After three months we sailed in an Alexandrian ship whose figurehead was the
[T]Twin Brothers, which had wintered at the
island. Gr. *Dioskouroi*, Zeus's sons Castor and Pollux
12 And landing at Syracuse, we stayed
three days.
13 From there we circled round and reached
Rhegium. And after one day the south wind
blew; and the next day we came to Puteoli,
14 where we found [R]brethren, and were
invited to stay with them seven days. And so
we went toward Rome. Rom. 1:8
15 And from there, when the brethren
heard about us, they came to meet us as far
as Appii Forum and Three Inns. When Paul
saw them, he thanked God and took courage.

Paul's Witness in Rome

16 Now when we came to Rome, the centurion delivered the prisoners to the captain
of the guard; but [R]Paul was permitted to
dwell by himself with the soldier who
guarded him. Acts 23:11; 24:25; 27:3
17 And it came to pass after three days that
Paul called the leaders of the Jews together.
So when they had come together, he said to
them: "Men *and* brethren, [R]though I have
done nothing against our people or the customs of our fathers, yet [R]I was delivered as a
prisoner from Jerusalem into the hands of the
Romans, Acts 23:29; 24:12, 13; 26:31 • Acts 21:33
18 "who, [R]when they had examined me,
wanted to let *me* go, because there was no
cause for putting me to death. Acts 22:24; 24:10
19 "But when the Jews spoke against *it*, I
was compelled to appeal to Caesar, not that I
had anything of which to accuse my nation.
20 "For this reason therefore I have called
for you, to see *you* and speak with *you*,
because [R]for the hope of Israel I am bound
with [R]this chain." Acts 26:6, 7 • Eph. 3:1; 4:1; 6:20
21 And they said to him, "We neither received letters from Judea concerning you,
nor have any of the brethren who came
reported or spoken any evil of you.
22 "But we desire to hear from you what
you think; for concerning this sect, we know
that it is spoken against everywhere."
23 So when they had appointed him a day,
many came to him at *his* lodging, to whom he
explained and solemnly testified of the kingdom of God, persuading them concerning
Jesus from both the Law of Moses and the
Prophets, from morning till evening.
24 And some were persuaded by the things
which were spoken, and some disbelieved.
25 So when they did not agree among themselves, they departed after Paul had said one
word: "The Holy Spirit spoke rightly through
Isaiah the prophet to *our fathers,

28:25 NU *your*

ROMAN ROADS IN PAUL'S TIME

The Romans were enthusiastic road builders. Across a period of about five centuries they completed roads that extended to every corner of their empire. This road system opened up areas to trade and allowed Rome to deploy troops to all the regions they controlled in the ancient world.

The Romans built their roads in straight lines as much as possible, often cutting tunnels through mountains. Trenches were dug the width of the road and four or five feet deep. Successive layers of large and small stones were added to the roadbed until it was even with the surrounding terrain. Then the roads were surfaced with a layer of gravel, although in high traffic areas they were often paved with volcanic sand or large stones carefully fitted together.

Mile markers along these routes (see photo) helped travelers keep track of the distances they traveled on their journeys and navigate from city to city.

One of the most famous Roman roads, the Appian Way, was named for the Roman censor Appius Claudius, who began its construction in 312 B.C. This road ran from just south of Rome along the coast of western Italy to the southernmost tip of Italy on the Adriatic Sea. The apostle Paul probably traveled this road to meet friends at Appii Forum, about forty miles south of Rome (Acts 28:15). It is one of the roads that continues to be used today.

Another road probably traveled by Paul on his missionary journeys was the route which ran from Antioch of Syria to Antioch of Pisidia. This road served Tarsus, Derbe, Lystra, and Iconium (Acts 14). On his travels still further west, Paul probably used another major Roman road, linking the cities of Berea, Thessalonica, Amphipolis, Philippi, and Neapolis (Acts 17:1–13).

Since nearly all important roads led to the city of Rome in Paul's time, this advanced transportation network helped Christianity spread to the far reaches of the Roman world.

Photo by Gustav Jeeninga

Roman milestones like this one stood along Roman highways and told travelers the distances to various cities along the way.

26 "saying,

[R]*'Go to this people and say:*
"Hearing you will hear, and shall not
understand;
And seeing you will see, and not
perceive; Is. 6:9, 10★
27 *For the heart of this people has grown*
dull.
Their ears are hard of hearing,
And their eyes they have closed,
Lest they should see with their eyes and
hear with their ears,
Lest they should understand with their
heart and turn,
So that I should heal them."'

28 "Therefore let it be known to you that
the salvation of God has been sent [R]to the
Gentiles, and they will hear it!" Is. 42:1; 49:6★
29 *And when he had said these words, the
Jews departed and had a great dispute among
themselves.
30 Then Paul dwelt two whole years in his
own rented house, and received all who came
to him,
31 [R]preaching the kingdom of God and
teaching the things which concern the Lord
Jesus Christ with all confidence, no one
forbidding him. Eph. 6:19

28:29 NU omits v. 29.

Jewish Feasts

Feast of	*Month on Jewish Calendar*	*Day*	*Corresponding Month*	*References*
Passover	Nisan	14	Mar.–Apr.	Ex. 12:1–14; Matt. 26:17–20
*Unleavened Bread	Nisan	15–21	Mar.–Apr.	Ex. 12:15–20
Firstfruits	Nisan or Sivan	16 6	Mar.–Apr. May–June	Lev. 23:9–14; Num. 28:26
*Pentecost (Harvest or Weeks)	Sivan	6 (50 days after barley harvest)	May–June	Deut. 16:9–12; Acts 2:1
Trumpets, *Rosh Hashanah*	Tishri	1, 2	Sept.–Oct.	Num. 29:1–6
Day of Atonement, *Yom Kippur*	Tishri	10	Sept.–Oct.	Lev. 23:26–32; Heb. 9:7
*Tabernacles (Booths or Ingathering)	Tishri	15–22	Sept.–Oct.	Neh. 8:13–18; John 7:2
Dedication (Lights), *Hanukkah*	Chislev	25 (8 days)	Nov.–Dec.	John 10:22
Purim (Lots)	Adar	14, 15	Feb.–Mar.	Esth. 9:18–32

*The three major feasts for which all males of Israel were required to travel to the Temple in Jerusalem (Ex. 23:14–19).

THE EPISTLE OF PAUL THE APOSTLE TO THE

ROMANS

THE BOOK OF ROMANS

Romans, Paul's greatest work, is placed first among his thirteen epistles in the New Testament. While the four Gospels present the words and works of Jesus Christ, Romans explores the significance of His sacrificial death. Using a question-and-answer format, Paul records the most systematic presentation of doctrine in the Bible. Romans is more than a book of theology; it is also a book of practical exhortation. The good news of Jesus Christ is more than facts to be believed; it is also a life to be lived—a life of righteousness befitting the person "justified freely by [God's] grace through the redemption that is in Christ Jesus" (3:24).

Although some manuscripts omit "in Rome" in 1:7, 15, the title *Pros Romaious,* "To the Romans," has been associated with the epistle almost from the beginning.

THE AUTHOR OF ROMANS

All critical schools agree on the Pauline authorship (1:1) of this foundational book. The vocabulary, style, logic, and theological development are consistent with Paul's other epistles. Paul dictated this letter to a secretary named Tertius (16:22), who was allowed to add his own greeting.

The problem arises not with the authorship but with the disunity of the epistle. Some Latin (but no Greek) manuscripts omit 15:1—16:24, and the closing doxology (16:25–27) is placed at the end of chapter 14 in some manuscripts. These variations have led some scholars to conclude that the last two chapters were not originally part of the epistle, or that Paul issued it in two editions. However, most scholars believe that chapter 15 fits in logically with the rest of the epistle. There is more debate over chapter 16, because Paul greets by name twenty-six persons in a church he has never visited. Some scholars contend that it was a separate letter, perhaps written to Ephesus, that was appended to this epistle. Such a letter would be surprising, to say the least (nothing but greetings), especially in the ancient world. It is simpler to understand the list of greetings as Paul's effort as a stranger to the Roman church to list his mutual friends. Paul met these people in the cities of his missionary journeys. Significantly, the only other Pauline epistle that lists individual greetings was addressed to the believers at Colosse, another church Paul had never visited. It may be that this portion was omitted from some copies of Romans because it did not seem relevant.

THE TIME OF ROMANS

Paul did not found the church at Rome, and the tradition that Peter was its founder is contrary to the evidence. It is possible that it began when some of the Jews and proselytes to Judaism who became followers of Christ on the day of Pentecost (cf. Acts 2:10) returned to Rome, but it is more likely that Christians from churches established by Paul in Asia, Macedonia, and Greece settled in Rome and led others to Christ. According to this epistle, Gentiles were predominant in the church at Rome (1:13; 11:13, 28–31; 15:15, 16), but there were also Jewish believers (2:17—3:8; 3:21—4:1; 7:1–14; 14:1—15:12).

Rome was founded in 753 B.C., and by the time of Paul it was the greatest city in the world with over one million inhabitants (one inscription says over four million). It was full of magnificent buildings, but the majority of people were slaves: opulence and squalor coexisted in the Imperial City. The church in Rome was well known (1:8), and it had been established for several years by the time of this letter (see 14:14; 15:23). The believers there were probably numerous, and evidently they met in several places (16:1–16). The historian Tacitus referred to the Christians who were persecuted under Nero in A.D. 64 as "an immense multitude." The gospel filled the gap left by the practically defunct polytheism of Roman religion.

Paul wrote Romans in A.D. 57, near the end of his third missionary journey (Acts 18:23—21:14; cf. Rom. 15:19). It was evidently written during his three-month stay in Greece (Acts 20:3–6), more specifically, in Corinth. Paul was staying with Gaius of Corinth (16:23; cf. 1 Cor. 1:14), and he also mentioned "Erastus, the treasurer of the city" (16:23). A first-century inscription in Corinth mentions him: "Erastus, the commissioner of public works, laid this pavement at his own expense." Paul's collection from the churches of Macedonia and Achaia for the needy Christians in Jerusalem was complete (15:26), and he was ready to deliver it (15:25). Instead of sailing directly to Jerusalem, Paul avoided a plot by the Jews by first going north to Philippi. He evidently gave this letter to Phoebe from the church at Cenchrea, near Corinth, and she carried it to Rome (16:1, 2).

THE CHRIST OF ROMANS

Paul presents Jesus Christ as the second Adam whose righteousness and substitutionary death have provided justification for all who place their faith in Him. He offers His righteousness as a gracious gift to sinful men, having borne God's condemnation and wrath for their sinfulness. His death and resurrection are the basis for the believer's redemption, justification, reconciliation, salvation, and glorification.

KEYS TO ROMANS

Key Word: The Righteousness of God—The theme of Romans is found in 1:16, 17: God offers the gift of His righteousness to everyone who comes to Christ by faith. Paul writes Romans to reveal God's sovereign plan of salvation (1—8), to show how Jews and Gentiles fit into that plan (9—11), and to exhort them to live righteous and harmonious lives (12—16). In his sweeping presentation of God's plan of salvation, Paul moves from condemnation to glorification and from positional truth to practical truth. Key words, such as *righteousness, faith, law, all,* and *sin* each appear at least sixty times in this epistle.

Key Verses: Romans 1:16, 17 and 3:21-25—"For I am not ashamed of the gospel of Christ, for it is the power of God to salvation for everyone who believes, for the Jew first and also for the Greek. For in it the righteousness of God is revealed from faith to faith; as it is written, 'The just shall live by faith' " (1:16, 17).

"But now the righteousness of God apart from the law is revealed, being witnessed by the Law and the Prophets, even the righteousness of God *which is* through faith in Jesus Christ to all and on all who believe. For there is no difference; for all have sinned and fall short of the glory of God, being justified freely by His grace through the redemption that is in Christ Jesus, whom God set forth *to be* a propitiation by His blood, through faith, to demonstrate His righteousness, because in His forbearance God had passed over the sins that were previously committed" (3:21-25).

Key Chapters: Romans 6—8—Foundational to all teaching on the spiritual life is the central passage of Romans 6—8. The answers to the questions of how to be delivered from sin, how to live a balanced life under grace, and how to live the victorious Christian life through the power of the Holy Spirit are all contained here. Many consider this to be the principal passage on conforming to the image of Jesus Christ.

SURVEY OF ROMANS

The poet Samuel Taylor Coleridge regarded Romans as "the most profound book in existence," and the commentator Godet called it "the cathedral of the Christian faith." Because of its majestic declaration of the divine plan of salvation, Martin Luther wrote: "This epistle is the chief part of the New Testament and the very purest gospel. . . . It can never be read or pondered too much, and the more it is dealt with the more precious it becomes, and the better it tastes." The four Gospels present the words and works of the Lord Jesus, but Romans, "the Gospel According to Paul," delves more into the significance of His death and resurrection. The theology of Romans is balanced by practical exhortation, because Paul sees the believer's position as the basis for his practice. The theme of righteousness that runs through the book is reflected in the following outline: the revelation of the righteousness of God (1—8); the vindication of the righteousness of God (9—11); the application of the righteousness of God (12—16).

The Revelation of the Righteousness of God (1—8): The prologue (1:1-17) consists of a salutation (1:1-7), a statement of Paul's desire to minister in Rome (1:8-15), and the theme of the book (1:16, 17). This two-verse theme is the basic text of Romans because it combines the three crucial concepts of salvation, righteousness, and faith.

FOCUS	REVELATION OF GOD'S RIGHTEOUSNESS			VINDICATION OF GOD'S RIGHTEOUSNESS			APPLICATION OF GOD'S RIGHTEOUSNESS	
REFERENCE	1:1—	3:21—	6:1—	9:1—	9:30—	11:1—	12:1—	14:1—16:27
DIVISION	NEED FOR GOD'S RIGHTEOUSNESS	IMPUTATION OF GOD'S RIGHTEOUSNESS	DEMONSTRATION OF GOD'S RIGHTEOUSNESS	ISRAEL'S PAST: ELECTION	ISRAEL'S PRESENT: REJECTION	ISRAEL'S FUTURE: RESTORATION	CHRISTIAN DUTIES	CHRISTIAN LIBERTIES
TOPIC	SIN	SALVATION	SANCTIFICATION	SOVEREIGNTY			SERVICE	
	DOCTRINAL						BEHAVIORAL	
LOCATION	PROBABLY WRITTEN IN CORINTH							
TIME	c. A.D. 57							

In 1:18—3:20, Paul builds a solid case for the condemnation of all people under the holy God. The Gentiles are without excuse because they have suppressed the knowledge of God they received from nature and their conscience (1:18–32; their seven-step regression is traced in 1:21–31). The Jews are also under the condemnation of God, and Paul overcomes every objection they could raise to this conclusion (2:1—3:8). God judges according to truth (2:2–5), works (2:6-10), and impartiality (2:11-16), and both the moral and religious Jews fail to meet His standard. Paul concludes his discussion of the reasons for the guilt of the Jews by reminding them they do not obey the Law (2:17–29) nor believe the Oracles of God (3:1–8). The divine verdict (3:9–20) is universal: "all have sinned and fall short of the glory of God" (3:23).

The section on justification (3:21—5:21) centers on and develops the theme of God's provision for man's need. The first eleven verses are the core of the book (3:21–31), revealing that in Christ, God is both Judge and Savior. Justification is by grace (the source of salvation; 3:21–24), by blood (the basis of salvation; 3:25, 26), and by faith (the condition of salvation; 3:27–31).

Chapter 4 illustrates the principle of justification by faith apart from works in the life of Abraham. Justification issues in reconciliation between God and man (5:1–11). It is brought about by the love of God which is causeless (5:6), measureless (5:7, 8), and ceaseless (5:9–11). In 5:12–21 Paul contrasts the two Adams and the opposite results of their two acts. The righteousness of the second Adam is imputed to all who trust in Him, leading to reconciliation.

Chapter 6 describes the believer's relationship to sin: in his position he is dead to the principle of sin (6:1–14) and the practice of sin (6:15–23). The reality of identification with Christ is the basis for the sanctified Christian life. After describing the Christian's emancipation from the Law (7), Paul looks at the work of the Holy Spirit who indwells and empowers every believer (8:1–17). The next major topic after condemnation, justification, and sanctification is glorification (8:18–39). All Christians can anticipate a time when they will be perfectly conformed to Jesus Christ not only in their position (present) but also in their practice (the future resurrection).

The Vindication of the Righteousness of God (9—11): It appears that God has rejected His people, Israel, but it is really Israel who has rejected her Messiah. God's rejection of Israel is only partial (there is a spiritual remnant that has trusted in Christ) and temporary (they will be grafted back; 11:23–27). Paul appropriately quotes frequently from the Old Testament in this section, and he emphasizes that God will be faithful to His covenant promises and restore Israel.

The Application of the Righteousness of God (12—16): Paul recognizes that behavior must be built upon belief, and this is why the practical exhortations of this epistle appear after his teaching on the believer's position in Christ. The salvation described in the first eleven chapters should transform a Christian's life in relation to God (12:1, 2), society (12:3–21), higher powers (13:1–7); and one's neighbors (13:8–14). In chapters 14 and 15 the apostle discusses the whole concept of Christian liberty, noting its principles (14) and its practice (15:1–13). A changed life is not a condition for salvation, but it should be the natural outcome of saving faith. The epistle closes with Paul's statement of his plans (15:14–33), a long series of personal greetings (16:1–16), and an admonition followed by a doxology (16:17–27).

OUTLINE OF ROMANS

Part One: The Revelation of the Righteousness of God (1:1—8:39)

I. Introduction **1:1–17**

II. Condemnation: The Need for God's Righteousness .... **1:18—3:20**

- A. Guilt of the Gentile 1:18–32
  1. Reason for Gentile Guilt 1:18–23
  2. Results of Gentile Guilt 1:24–32
- B. Guilt of the Jew .... 2:1—3:8
  1. Jews Are Judged According to Truth 2:1–5
  2. Jews Are Judged by Their Works 2:6–10
  3. Jews Are Judged with Impartiality 2:11–16
  4. Jews Do Not Obey the Law 2:17–29
  5. Jews Do Not Believe the Oracles 3:1–8
- C. Conclusion: All Are Guilty Before God 3:9–20

III. Justification: The Imputation of God's Righteousness .... **3:21—5:21**

- A. Description of Righteousness 3:21–31
- B. Illustration of Righteousness 4:1–25
  1. Abraham's Righteousness Apart from Works 4:1–8
  2. Abraham's Righteousness Apart from Circumcision 4:9–12
  3. Abraham's Righteousness Apart from the Law 4:13–15
  4. Abraham's Righteousness Was by Faith 4:16–25
- C. Benefits of Righteousness 5:1–11
  1. Peace with God 5:1, 2
  2. Joy in Tribulation 5:3–8
  3. Salvation from God's Wrath 5:9–11

CHAPTER 1

Introduction

PAUL, a [T]servant of Jesus Christ, [R]called *to*
be an apostle, [R]separated to the gospel of
God *slave* • 1 Tim. 1:11 • Acts 9:15; 13:2
2 which He promised before [R]through His
prophets in the Holy Scriptures, Gal. 3:8
3 concerning His Son Jesus Christ our
Lord, who [T]was [R]born of the seed of David
according to the flesh, *came* • Is. 9:7; Gal. 4:4★
4 and [R]declared *to be* the Son of God with
power, according to the Spirit of holiness, by
the resurrection from the dead, Ps. 2:7; 16:10, 11★
5 through whom we have received grace
and apostleship for obedience to the faith
among all nations [R]for His name, Acts 9:15
6 among whom you also are the called of
Jesus Christ;

7 To all who are in Rome, beloved of God,
[R]called *to be* saints: 1 Cor. 1:2, 24

[R]Grace to you and peace from God our
Father and the Lord Jesus Christ. 1 Cor. 1:3
8 First, I thank my God through Jesus
Christ for you all, that [R]your faith is spoken
of throughout the whole world. Rom. 16:19
9 For God is my witness, whom I serve
[T]with my spirit in the gospel of His Son, that
[R]without ceasing I make mention of you
always in my prayers, Or *in* • 1 Thess. 3:10
10 making request if, by some means, now
at last I may find a way in the will of God to
come to you.
11 For I long to see you, that [R]I may impart
to you some spiritual gift, so that you may be
established— Rom. 15:29
12 that is, that I may be encouraged together with you by [R]the mutual faith both of
you and me. Titus 1:4
13 Now I do not want you to be unaware,
brethren, that I often planned to come to you
(but [R]was hindered until now), that I might
have some fruit among you also, just as
among the other Gentiles. [1 Thess. 2:18]
14 I am a debtor both to Greeks and to
barbarians, both to wise and to unwise.
15 So, as much as is in me, *I am* ready to
preach the gospel to you who are in Rome
also.

THE CITY OF ROME

Seat of the mighty Roman Empire, Rome was the largest and most magnificent city of its day, with a population of more than 1,000,000 people in New Testament times. Situated near where the Tiber River meets the Mediterranean Sea, it was called *Urbs Septicollis* ("City of the Seven Hills") because of the seven hills upon which it was built.

When the apostle Paul entered Rome as a prisoner about A.D. 58, the city boasted of a history extending back more than 800 years. According to the legends of the Romans, the city was founded in 753 B.C. by Romulus, son of the Roman god Mars. The city grew across the years as the Roman Empire expanded its power and influence throughout the ancient world.

Rome reached the height of its splendor under the emperor Augustus. Especially notable was the Forum (see photo), the center of the city with roads (see photo) leading off in all directions, and the great outdoor theater known as the Colosseum, where Roman games and public events were held. The city featured more than 400 temples dedicated to worship of pagan gods. It was also noted for its public buildings, baths, aqueducts, arches, temples, and roads.

To keep from being killed by hostile Jews at Jerusalem, and because he was a Roman citizen (Acts 22:27), Paul appealed to Caesar, an act that ultimately brought him to Rome as a prisoner to await trial. Paul must have seen many of Rome's pagan temples and spectacular public buildings when he entered the city

Photo by Howard Vos

The Roman Forum looking toward the east, with the famous Colosseum of the city in the distance.

Photo by Ben Chapman

A section of the Roman road between Aleppo and Antioch.

on the famous road known as the Via Appia (Appian Way). He was kept at first under house arrest, and, later, according to tradition, as a condemned prisoner in a dungeon near the Forum.

The great missionary to the Gentiles proclaimed the gospel to all classes of people while in Rome, especially to Greek-speaking easterners (called "Greeks" in Romans 1:16) and Jews. According to tradition, he was executed outside the city at a spot on the Via Ostia about A.D. 68.

Paul's first known connection with Rome had occurred several years before he actually visited the city. During his ministry at Corinth, he worked with Priscilla and Aquila, who had left Rome when the emperor Claudius expelled all Jews from the city (Acts 18:2). An active Christian church also existed at Rome several years before Paul arrived in the city; these were the Christians to whom Paul addressed his letter known as the epistle to the Romans.

In Paul's time the houses of the wealthy people of Rome were elaborately constructed and situated on the various hills of the city. But the common people lived in tenements, much like the crowded inner city of a modern metropolis. Thousands of people were crowded into these tenements, which were surrounded by narrow, noisy streets with a constant flow of traffic.

The citizens of Rome received food and entertainment from the government. Wine was cheap and plentiful. Admission to the Roman games was free. Thousands of people attended these games, which included contests among the gladiators, chariot races, and theatrical performances.

Like Babylon, the city of Rome became a symbol of idolatry and paganism in the New Testament. The Book of Revelation contains several disguised references to the pagan city. Some scholars believe chapters 17 and 18 of Revelation should be interpreted as predictions of the fall of Rome.

16 For I am not ashamed of the gospel *of Christ, for [R]it is the power of God to salvation for everyone who believes, [R]for the Jew first and also for the Greek. 1 Cor. 1:18, 24 • Acts 3:26

17 For in it the righteousness of God is revealed from faith to faith; as it is written, [R]*"The just shall live by faith."* Hab. 2:4

Reason for Gentile Guilt

18 [R]For the wrath of God is revealed from heaven against all ungodliness and unrighteousness of men, who [T]suppress the truth in unrighteousness, [Acts 17:30] • *hold down*

19 because [R]what may be known of God is [T]manifest [T]in them, for [R]God has shown *it* to them. [Acts 14:17; 17:24] • *evident* • *among* • [John 1:9]

20 For since the creation of the world [R]His invisible *attributes* are clearly seen, being understood by the things that are made, *even* His eternal power and [T]Godhead, so that they are without excuse, Ps. 19:1–6 • *divine nature*

21 because, although they knew God, they did not glorify *Him* as God, nor were thankful, but [R]became futile in their thoughts, and their foolish hearts were darkened. Jer. 2:5

22 [R]Professing to be wise, they became fools, Jer. 10:14

23 and changed the glory of the incorruptible [R]God into an image made like [T]corruptible man—and birds and four-footed beasts and creeping things. Deut. 4:16–18 • *perishable*

Results of Gentile Guilt

24 Therefore God also gave them up to uncleanness, in the lusts of their hearts, to dishonor their bodies among themselves,

25 who exchanged [R]the truth of God [R]for the lie, and worshiped and served the creature rather than the Creator, who is blessed forever. Amen. 1 Thess. 1:9 • Is. 44:20

26 For this reason God gave them up to [R]vile passions. For even their [T]women exchanged the natural use for what is against nature. Lev. 18:22 • Lit. *females*

27 Likewise also the [T]men, leaving the natural use of the [T]woman, burned in their lust for one another, [T]men with [T]men committing what is shameful, and receiving in themselves the penalty of their error which was due. Lit. *males* • Lit. *female* • Lit. *males* • Lit. *males*

28 And even as they did not like to retain God in *their* knowledge, God gave them over to a debased mind, to do those things [R]which are not fitting; Eph. 5:4

29 being filled with all unrighteousness, *sexual immorality, wickedness, [T]covetousness, [T]maliciousness; full of envy, murder, strife, deceit, evil-mindedness; *they are* whisperers, *greed* • *malice*

30 backbiters, haters of God, violent, proud, boasters, inventors of evil things, disobedient to parents,

31 [T]undiscerning, untrustworthy, unloving, *unforgiving, unmerciful; *without understanding*

32 who, [R]knowing the righteous judgment of God, that those who practice such things [R]are worthy of death, not only do the same but also [R]approve of those who practice them. [Rom. 2:2] • [Rom. 6:21] • Hos. 7:3

CHAPTER 2

Jews Are Judged According to Truth

THEREFORE you are [R]inexcusable, O man, whoever you are who judge, [R]for in whatever you judge another you condemn yourself; for you who judge practice the same things. [Rom. 1:20] • [Matt. 7:1–5]

2 But we know that the judgment of God is according to truth against those who practice such things.

3 And do you think this, O man, you who judge those practicing such things, and doing the same, that you will escape the judgment of God?

4 Or do you despise [R]the riches of His goodness, [R]forbearance, and longsuffering, not knowing that the goodness of God leads you to repentance? [Eph. 1:7, 18; 2:7] • [Rom. 3:25]

5 But in accordance with your hardness and your [T]impenitent heart [R]you are [T]treasuring up for yourself wrath in the day of wrath and revelation of the righteous judgment of God, *unrepentant* • [Deut. 32:34] • *storing*

Jews Are Judged by Their Works

6 [R]who *"will render to each one according to his deeds"*: Ps. 62:12; Prov. 24:12

7 eternal life to those who by patient continuance in doing good seek for glory, honor, and immortality;

8 but to those who are self-seeking and [R]do not obey the truth, but obey unrighteousness—indignation and wrath, [2 Thess. 1:8]

9 tribulation and anguish, on every soul of man who does evil, of the Jew [R]first and also of the [T]Greek; 1 Pet. 4:17 • Gentile

10 [R]but glory, honor, and peace to everyone who works what is good, to the Jew first and also to the Greek. [1 Pet. 1:7]

Jews Are Judged with Impartiality

11 For there is no partiality with God.

12 For as many as have sinned without law will also perish without law, and as many as have sinned in the law will be judged by the law

13 (for [R]not the hearers of the law *are* just in the sight of God, but the doers of the law will be justified; [James 1:22, 25]

1:16 NU omits *of Christ*
1:29 *fornication,* NU omits *sexual immorality*
1:31 NU omits *unforgiving*

14 for when Gentiles, who do not have the
law, by nature do the things *contained* in
the law, these, although not having the law,
are a law to themselves,
15 who show the work of the law written in
their hearts, their conscience also bearing
witness, and between themselves *their*
thoughts accusing or else excusing *them*)
16 [R]in the day when God will judge the
secrets of men [R]by Jesus Christ, [R]according to
my gospel. [Matt. 25:31] • Acts 10:42; 17:31 • 1 Tim. 1:11

Jews Do Not Obey the Law

17 *Indeed you are called a Jew, and rest on
the law, and make your boast in God,
18 and [R]know *His* will, and [R]approve the
things that are excellent, being instructed out
of the law, Deut. 4:8 • Phil. 1:10
19 and [R]are confident that you yourself are
a guide to the blind, a light to those who are
in darkness, Matt. 15:14
20 an instructor of the foolish, a teacher of
babes, [R]having the form of knowledge and
truth in the law. [2 Tim. 3:5]
21 You, therefore, who teach another, do
you not teach yourself? You who preach that
a man should not steal, do you steal?
22 You who say, "Do not commit adultery,"
do you commit adultery? You who abhor
idols, [R]do you rob temples? Mal. 3:8
23 You who make your boast in the law, do
you dishonor God through breaking the law?
24 For *"The name of God is* [R]*blasphemed
among the Gentiles because of you,"* as it is
[R]written. Ezek. 16:27 • Is. 52:5; Ezek. 36:22
25 [R]For circumcision is indeed profitable if
you keep the law; but if you are a breaker of
the law, your circumcision has become uncircumcision. [Gal. 5:3]
26 Therefore, [R]if an uncircumcised man
keeps the righteous requirements of the law,
will not his uncircumcision be counted as
circumcision? [Acts 10:34]
27 And will not the physically uncircumcised, if he fulfills the law, judge you who,
even with *your* written *code* and circumcision, *are* a transgressor of the law?
28 For [R]he is not a Jew who *is one* outwardly, nor *is* that circumcision *which is*
outward in the flesh; [Gal. 6:15]
29 but *he is* a Jew [R]who *is one* inwardly, and
circumcision *is that* of the heart, in the Spirit,
and not in the letter; whose praise *is* not from
men but from God. [1 Pet. 3:4]

CHAPTER 3

Jews Do Not Believe the Oracles

WHAT advantage then has the Jew, or
what *is* the profit of circumcision?
2 Much in every way! Chiefly because to
them were committed the oracles of God.
3 For what if [R]some did not believe? [R]Will
their unbelief make the faithfulness of God
without effect? Heb. 4:2 • [2 Tim. 2:13]
4 Certainly not! Indeed, let [R]God be [T]true
but every man a liar. As it is written:

[R]*"That You may be justified in Your
words,* John 3:33 • Found true • Ps. 51:4
*And may overcome when You are
judged."*

5 But if our unrighteousness demonstrates
the righteousness of God, what shall we say?
Is God unjust who inflicts wrath? [R](I speak as
a man.) Gal. 3:15
6 Certainly not! For then [R]how will God
judge the world? [Gen. 18:25]
7 For if the truth of God has increased
through my lie to His glory, why am I also
still judged as a sinner?
8 And *why* not *say*, "Let us do evil that
good may come"?—as we are slanderously
reported and as some affirm that we say.
Their [T]condemnation is just. Lit. *judgment*

Conclusion: All Are Guilty Before God

9 What then? Are we better *than they?*
Not at all. For we have previously charged
both Jews and Greeks that [R]they are all under
sin. Gal. 3:22
10 As it is written:

"There is none righteous, no, not one;
11 *There is none who understands;*
There is none who seeks after God.
12 *They have all gone out of the way;*
*They have together become
unprofitable;*
*There is none who does good, no, not
one."*
13 *"Their*[R] *throat is an open* [T]*tomb;*
*With their tongues they have practiced
deceit";* Ps. 5:9 • *grave*
"The poison of asps is under their lips";
14 *"Whose*[R] *mouth is full of cursing and
bitterness."* Ps. 10:7
15 *"Their feet are swift to shed blood;*
16 *Destruction and misery are in their
ways;*
17 *And the way of peace they have not
known."*
18 *"There*[R] *is no fear of God before their
eyes."* Ps. 36:1

19 Now we know that whatever the law
says, it says to those who are under the law,
that every mouth may be stopped, and all the
world may become guilty before God.
20 Therefore [R]by the deeds of the law no
flesh will be justified in His sight, for by the
law *is* the knowledge of sin. [Gal. 2:16]

2:17 NU *But if*

SIN

In Romans 3, Paul proves that all humankind—Jew and Gentile, religious and pagan—have sinned. Both testaments have large and interesting vocabularies for the various forms of sin, showing how important a fact of human life sin really is.

The following paragraphs treat several of these words in the order of frequency of usage. Sin is seen as the following things.

Falling Short (*hamartia, hamartēma, hamartanō*, etc.)

This word-group is the broadest and most frequent in the New Testament, occurring over 250 times. The root idea is failing, missing the mark, "[falling] short of the glory of God" (Rom. 3:23). The most general word is *hamartia*, which can be sin in general or a specific act of sin. The similar word *hamartēma* stresses individual acts. The heretic Pelagius misquoted the golden-tongued preacher Chrysostom as saying that infants are without sin. He should have checked the original Greek of that great preacher. What he really said was "that infants were innocent of *hamartēmata*, individual acts of sin, and were not free from *hamartia*, which was sin in general" (Nigel Turner, *Christian Words*, p. 413).

Unrighteousness, Iniquity (*adikia, adikos*, etc.)

The basic meaning of these words is "injustice" or "dishonesty" in classical Greek, and the common translations of the verb *(adikeō)* are "to do wrong," "to be unjust," "to hurt." *Adikia* is the opposite of *uprightness*. A famous passage using this word is 1 John 1:9: "If we confess our sins, He is faithful and just to forgive us *our* sins and to cleanse us from all unrighteousness."

Trespass (*paraptōma*)

Trespass (*paraptōma*), occurring twenty-one times in the New Testament, is used in one popular rendition of the Lord's Prayer: "Forgive us our trespasses." It means to fall *(piptō)* when one should have resisted a temptation or maintained a spiritual walk. James tells us, "Confess *your* trespasses to one another and pray for one another" (5:16).

Iniquity (*anomia*)

Occurring fifteen times, *anomia* literally means "lawlessness," though the word is generally translated "iniquity" in the KJV tradition. First John 3:4 uses *anomia* as a definition of sin.

Transgression (*parabasis*)

Occurring only seven times, *parabasis* means "violating a specific law." *To transgress* is to cross a line that God has drawn; it is a specific disobedience of a command.

Ungodliness (*asebeia*, etc.)

The noun for *ungodliness* occurs six times, the verb twice, and the adjective ten times. Just as *eusebeia* (*eu*=good and *sebeia*=worship) means "piety," "godliness," or "religion," so this is the same root with the negative prefix *a-* (as in *atheist*—"no God"). *Asebeia* is the impiety and irreverence of the village atheist, living in rebellion against God and godly standards. It is irreligion in general. Jude, quoting an ancient prophecy of Enoch preserved by the Holy Spirit, uses all three forms of this word in a trenchant way (vv. 15–18).

Other Words for Sin

Debt (opheilēma) occurs in the sense of a sin in Matthew's version of the Lord's Prayer: "Forgive us our debts, as we forgive our debtors" (Matt. 6:12). Debts that we owe to God are sins.

Disobedience (*parakoē*) occurs three times, including the very central passage on how sin entered our world: by one man's disobedience (Rom. 5:19). The root idea is to neglect to hear and heed God's commands.

Ignorance (*agnoēma*), sins committed inadvertently (Heb. 9:7 only), nevertheless need atonement by blood. Ignorance is no excuse.

In face of all these words, which point out our shortcomings, we find the promise of 1 John 1:7 reassuring: "The blood of Jesus Christ His Son cleanses us from all sin."

Description of Righteousness

21 But now the righteousness of God apart from the law is revealed, being witnessed by the Law [R]and the Prophets, 1 Pet. 1:10

22 even the righteousness of God *which is* through faith in Jesus Christ to all *and on all who believe. For there is no difference;

23 for [R]all have sinned and fall short of the glory of God, Gal. 3:22

24 being justified [T]freely [R]by His grace [R]through the redemption that is in Christ Jesus, *without any cost* • [Eph. 2:8] • [Heb. 9:12, 15]

25 whom God set forth [R]*to be* a propitiation [R]by His blood, through faith, to demonstrate His righteousness, because in His forbearance God had passed over the sins that were previously committed, Lev. 16:15 • Col. 1:20

26 to demonstrate at the present time His righteousness, that He might be just and the justifier of the one who has faith in Jesus.

27 [R]Where *is* boasting then? It is excluded. By what law? Of works? No, but by the law of faith. [1 Cor. 1:29]

28 Therefore we conclude [R]that a man is [T]justified by faith apart from the deeds of the law. Gal. 2:16 • *declared righteous*

29 Or *is He* the God of the Jews only? *Is He* not also the God of the Gentiles? Yes, of the Gentiles also,

30 since [R]*there is* one God who will justify the circumcised by faith and the uncircumcised through faith. [Gal. 3:8, 20]

31 Do we then make void the law through faith? Certainly not! On the contrary, we establish the law.

CHAPTER 4

Abraham's Righteousness Apart from Works

WHAT then shall we say that Abraham our [T]father has found according to the flesh? Or *(fore)father according to the flesh has found*

2 For if Abraham was [R]justified by works, he has *something of which* to boast, but not before God. Rom. 3:20, 27

3 For what does the Scripture say? *"Abraham believed God, and it was* [T]*accounted to him for righteousness."* *imputed*

4 Now [R]to him who works, the wages are not counted as grace but as debt. Rom. 11:6

5 But to him who does not work but believes on Him who justifies the ungodly, his faith is accounted for righteousness,

6 just as David also describes the blessedness of the man to whom God imputes righteousness apart from works:

7 *"Blessed*[R] *are those whose lawless deeds*
are forgiven, Ps. 32:1, 2
And whose sins are covered;
8 *Blessed is the man to whom the* L*ORD*
shall not impute sin."

Abraham's Righteousness Apart from Circumcision

9 *Does* this blessedness then *come* upon the circumcised *only*, or upon the uncircumcised also? For we say that faith was accounted to Abraham for righteousness.

10 How then was it accounted? While he was circumcised, or uncircumcised? Not while circumcised, but while uncircumcised.

11 And he received the sign of circumcision, a seal of the righteousness of the faith which *he had while still* uncircumcised, that he might be the father of all those who believe, though they are uncircumcised, that righteousness might be imputed to them also,

12 and the father of circumcision to those who not only *are* of the circumcision, but who also walk in the steps of the faith which our father [R]Abraham *had while still* uncircumcised. Rom. 4:18–22

Abraham's Righteousness Apart from the Law

13 For the promise that he would be the [R]heir of the world *was* not to Abraham or to his seed through the law, but through the righteousness of faith. Gen. 17:4–6; 22:17

14 For [R]if those who are of the law *are* heirs, faith is made void and the promise made of no effect, Gal. 3:18

15 because [R]the law brings about wrath; for where there is no law *there is* no transgression. Rom. 3:20

Abraham's Righteousness Was by Faith

16 Therefore *it is* of faith that *it might be* [R]according to grace, [R]so that the promise might be sure to all the seed, not only to those who are of the law, but also to those who are of the faith of Abraham, [R]who is the father of us all [Rom. 3:24] • [Gal. 3:22] • Is. 51:2

17 (as it is written, *"I have made you a father of many nations"*) in the presence of Him whom he believed, *even* God, [R]who gives life to the dead and calls those things which do not exist as though they did; [Rom. 8:11]

18 who, contrary to hope, in hope believed, so that he became the father of many nations, according to what was spoken, [R]*"So shall your descendants be."* Gen. 15:5

19 And not being weak in faith, [R]he did not consider his own body, already dead (since he was about a hundred years old), [R]and the deadness of Sarah's womb. Gen. 17:17 • Heb. 11:11

20 He did not waver at the promise of God through unbelief, but was strengthened in faith, giving glory to God,

21 and being fully convinced that what He had promised He was also able to perform.

22 And therefore [R]*"it was accounted to him for righteousness."* Gen. 15:6

3:22 NU omits *and on all*

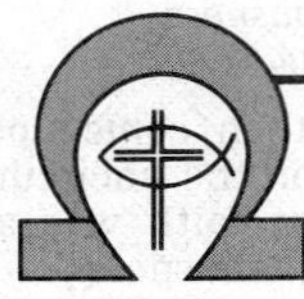

THE RITE OF CIRCUMCISION

Circumcision was a ritualistic operation that removed all or part of the foreskin from the male sex organ. The practice is of ancient origin, depicted on Egyptian tombs, and also practiced by African, Australian, Aztec, and American Indian tribes. It functioned in most cultures as a "rite of passage" or an initiation ceremony into manhood.

Circumcision of the Jewish male, however, was required as a visible, physical sign of the covenant between the Lord and His people. Any male not circumcised was to be "cut off from his people" (Gen. 17:14) and regarded as a covenant breaker (Ex. 12:48). In most cultures of the ancient world the ceremony was performed when the youth was about twelve, but among the Hebrews it occurred on the eighth day after birth (Gen. 17:12).

Although circumcision was required by the Mosaic Law, the rite was neglected during the days when the people of Israel wandered in the Wilderness. Perhaps this was a sign that the nation had broken their covenant with God through their disobedience. The rite was resumed when they entered the land of Canaan, with Joshua performing the ritual on the generation born in the Wilderness (Josh. 5:1–8).

Moses and the prophets used the term *circumcision* as a symbol for purity of heart and readiness to hear and obey. Through Moses the Lord challenged the Israelites to submit to "circumcision of the heart," a reference to their need for repentance. "If their uncircumcised hearts are humbled, and they accept their guilt," God declared, "then I will remember My covenant" (Lev. 26:41, 42; also Deut. 10:16). The prophet Jeremiah characterized rebellious Israel as having "uncircumcised" ears (6:10) and being "uncircumcised in the heart" (9:26).

The Hebrew people came to take great pride in their circumcision, and it became a badge of their spiritual and national superiority. Other peoples, such as the Philistines, were disdainfully called "the uncircumcised" (2 Sam. 1:20), and male converts to Judaism were required to be circumcised.

During New Testament times, a crisis erupted in the church at Antioch when the Judaizers taught, "Unless you are circumcised according to the custom of Moses, you cannot be saved" (Acts 15:1, 2). A council was convened at Jerusalem to resolve the issue (Acts 15:6–29).

The apostle Peter argued during this meeting that to insist on circumcision for the Gentiles would impose a burdensome yoke (Acts 15:10). Years later Paul reinforced this decision when he wrote that Abraham, "the father of circumcision" (Rom. 4:12), was saved by faith, long before the physical act of circumcision was required of Jewish males (Rom. 4:9–13).

Paul also spoke of the "circumcision of Christ" (Col. 2:11), referring to His atoning death which "condemned sin in the flesh" (Rom. 8:3) and nailed our sins "to the cross" (Col. 2:14). All that ultimately matters for both Jew and Gentile, Paul declared, is a changed nature, which comes only through faith and repentance as a person commits himself to Christ (Eph. 2:14–18).

23 Now [R]it was not written for his sake alone that it was imputed to him, Rom. 15:4

24 but also for us. It shall be imputed to us who believe [R]in Him who raised up Jesus our Lord from the dead, Acts 2:24

25 [R]who was delivered up because of our offenses, and [R]was raised because of our justification. Is. 53:4, 5 • [1 Cor. 15:17]

CHAPTER 5

Peace with God

THEREFORE, [R]having been justified by faith, we have [R]peace with God through our Lord Jesus Christ, Is. 32:17 • [Eph. 2:14]

2 through whom also we have access by faith into this grace in which we stand, and rejoice in hope of the glory of God.

Joy in Tribulation

3 And not only *that,* but we also glory in tribulations, [R]knowing that tribulation produces [T]perseverance; James 1:3 • *endurance*

4 [R]and perseverance, character; and [T]character, hope. [James 1:12] • *approved character*

5 Now hope does not disappoint, because the love of God has been poured out in our hearts by the Holy Spirit who was given to us.

6 For when we were still without strength, in due time Christ died for the ungodly.

7 For scarcely for a righteous man will one die; yet perhaps for a good man someone would even dare to die.

8 But [R]God demonstrates His own love toward us, in that while we were still sinners, Christ died for us. Is. 53:5; [John 3:16; 15:13] ★

Salvation from God's Wrath

9 Much more then, having now been justified [R]by His blood, we shall be saved [R]from wrath through Him. Eph. 2:13 • 1 Thess. 1:10

10 For [R]if when we were enemies we were reconciled to God through the death of His Son, much more, having been reconciled, we shall be saved by His life. [Rom. 8:32]

11 And not only *that,* but we also [R]rejoice in God through our Lord Jesus Christ, through whom we have now received the reconciliation. [Gal. 4:9]

Contrast of Righteousness and Condemnation

12 Therefore, just as [R]through one man sin entered the world, and [R]death through sin, and thus death spread to all men, because all sinned— [1 Cor. 15:21] • Gen. 2:17

13 (For until the law sin was in the world, but sin is not imputed when there is no law.

14 Nevertheless death reigned from Adam to Moses, even over those who had not sinned according to the likeness of the transgression of Adam, [R]who is a type of Him who was to come. [1 Cor. 15:21, 22]

15 But the free gift *is* not like the offense. For if by the one man's [T]offense many died, much more the grace of God and the gift by the grace of the one Man, Jesus Christ, abounded [R]to many. *trespass* or *false step* • [Is. 53:11]

16 And the gift *is* not like *that which came* through the one who sinned. For the judgment *which came* from one *offense resulted* in condemnation, but the free gift *which came* from many [T]offenses *resulted* in justification. *trespasses*

17 For if by the one man's [T]offense death reigned through the one, much more those who receive abundance of grace and of the gift of righteousness will reign in life through the One, Jesus Christ.) *trespass*

18 Therefore, as through one man's offense *judgment* came to all men, resulting in condemnation, even so [R]through one Man's righteous act *the free gift came* to all men, resulting in justification of life. Is. 53:11, 12 ★

19 For as by one man's disobedience many were made sinners, so also by one Man's obedience many will be made righteous.

20 Moreover the law entered that the offense might abound. But where sin abounded, grace abounded much more,

21 so that as sin reigned in death, even so grace might reign through righteousness to eternal life through Jesus Christ our Lord.

CHAPTER 6

Believer's Death to Sin in Principle

WHAT shall we say then? Shall we continue in sin that grace may abound?

2 Certainly not! How shall we who [R]died to sin live any longer in it? [Gal. 2:19]

3 Or do you not know that [R]as many of us as were baptized into Christ Jesus [R]were baptized into His death? [Gal. 3:27] • [1 Cor. 15:29]

4 Therefore we were buried with Him through baptism into death, that [R]just as Christ was raised from the dead by [R]the glory of the Father, [R]even so we also should walk in newness of life. 1 Cor. 6:14 • John 2:11 • [Gal. 6:15]

5 For if we have been united together in the likeness of His death, certainly we also shall be *in the likeness* of *His* resurrection,

6 knowing this, that our old man was crucified with *Him,* that the body of sin might be [T]done away with, that we should no longer be slaves of sin. *rendered inoperative*

7 For [R]he who has died has been [T]freed from sin. 1 Pet. 4:1 • *cleared*

8 Now [R]if we died with Christ, we believe that we shall also live with Him, 2 Tim. 2:11

9 knowing that [R]Christ, having been raised from the dead, dies no more. Death no longer has dominion over Him. Rev. 1:18

JUSTIFICATION

Paul's great discussion of sin and justification in Romans 5 is so crucial to Christian doctrine that it takes a great deal of time to comprehend it.

As with sanctification and faith, the doctrine of justification is made a little more difficult for users of English because roots that are the same in the original are different in English due to the dual origin of our tongue. Our words *just, justice, justify,* and *justification* are from the Latin; our words *righteous* and *righteousness* are from the Anglo-Saxon. All basically the same family of meanings, they translate the same Greek roots, however.

In Greek, the basic word root for *justice, justify, righteousness,* and so on is *dik-*.

Justify (*dikaioō*)

Justify is used thirty-nine times in the New Testament, fifteen times in Romans and eight times in Galatians alone.

But what does *justify* mean? The popular definition "just as if I'd never sinned" is easy to remember, but not very accurate. That definition would stress forgiveness—a subtraction of sin, while justification implies something more positive, namely that one is just or righteous in Christ Jesus.

The big question is: Does *justify* mean "to make righteous" or "to declare righteous"? The answer of the Reformers is that *justification* means "to declare righteous." For example, in Luke 7:29, the tax collectors are said to have "justified God." Obviously, it cannot mean they made Him righteous (He already was), so it must, here at least, mean "to declare righteous." (See also 1 Tim. 3:16, where Christ is said to be "justified in the Spirit.") "Making us righteous" is properly the doctrine of sanctification (see word study on p. 1478). In Romans 3:24, Paul writes that we are "justified freely by His grace" and in verse 28 that a person is "justified by faith." This is no contradiction—faith is the channel; grace is the source.

Not only are we justified by grace through faith, but the great apostle also tells us that "having now been justified by His blood, we shall be saved from wrath through Him" (Rom. 5:9).

This declaration by God is no legal fiction. He credits Christ's perfect righteousness to our spiritual account, having put our sin on His account. This is called *imputation*.

James 2 speaks of being justified by works, and some have said he is writing to contradict Paul. This is absurd. In the first place, nearly all scholars agree that James was written years before Romans. Actually, Paul and James are not contradictory—they simply are not talking about the same thing. Paul is writing about our being declared righteous before God; James is talking about being declared righteous before other people. Abraham (2:21) and Rahab (2:25) showed their faith in God by their actions. It was certainly not "justification by good works," since Abraham's "work" would have been human sacrifice, and Rahab the prostitute's work of hiding the spies was treason to her native city, Jericho.

Justification (*dikaiōsis*)

Dikaiōsis is used only twice in the Greek New Testament, and both examples are in Romans. Jesus our Lord "was delivered up because of our offenses, and was raised because of our justification" (Rom. 4:25). The same preposition (*dia* plus the accusative) is used in both clauses, and both are translated "because of" in the NKJV. If we take the verse as it stands, it means that Christ died for our sins (taught throughout the New Testament) and that God raised Him up because of His successful work of justifying believing sinners.

Romans 5:18 teaches that Adam's act of disobedience brought condemnation to all people and Christ's "righteous act" resulted in "justification of life."

To summarize, *to justify* in the New Testament theological sense is "to declare, to acknowledge, or to treat someone as righteous or just."

The result of justification and the One to whom credit is due for that justification are spelled out in Romans 5:1: "Therefore, having been justified by faith, we have peace with God through our Lord Jesus Christ."

10 For *the death* that He died, [R]He died to
sin once for all; but *the life* that He lives, [R]He
lives to God. Heb. 9:27 • Luke 20:38
11 Likewise you also, [T]reckon yourselves to
be dead indeed to sin, but [R]alive to God in
Christ Jesus our Lord. *consider* • [Gal. 2:19]
12 [R]Therefore do not let sin reign in your
mortal body, that you should obey it in its
lusts. Ps. 19:13
13 And do not present your members *as*
[T]instruments of unrighteousness to sin, but
present yourselves to God as being alive from
the dead, and your members *as* [T]instruments
of righteousness to God. Or *weapons*
14 For [R]sin shall not have dominion over
you, for you are not under law but under
grace. [Gal. 5:18]

Believer's Death to Sin in Practice

15 What then? Shall we sin [R]because we are
not under law but under grace? Certainly
not! 1 Cor. 9:21
16 Do you not know that [R]to whom you
present yourselves slaves to obey, you are
that one's slaves whom you obey, whether of
sin to death, or of obedience to righteousness? 2 Pet. 2:19
17 But God be thanked that *though* you
were slaves of sin, yet you obeyed from the
heart [R]that form of doctrine to which you
were [T]delivered. 2 Tim. 1:13 • *entrusted*
18 And [R]having been set free from sin, you
became slaves of righteousness. John 8:32
19 I speak in human *terms* because of the
weakness of your flesh. For just as you
presented your members *as* slaves of uncleanness, and of lawlessness *leading* to *more*
lawlessness, so now present your members *as*
slaves *of* righteousness for holiness.
20 For when you were [R]slaves of sin, you
were free in regard to righteousness. John 8:34
21 What fruit did you have then in the
things of which you are now ashamed? For
[R]the end of those things *is* death. Rom. 1:32
22 But now [R]having been set free from sin,
and having become slaves of God, you have
your fruit [T]to holiness, and the end, everlasting life. Rom. 6:18; 8:2 • *unto sanctification*

23 For [R]the wages of sin *is* death, but [R]the
[T]gift of God *is* eternal life in Christ Jesus our
Lord. Gen. 2:17 • 1 Pet. 1:4 • *free gift*

CHAPTER 7

Dead to the Law but Alive to God

OR do you not know, brethren (for I speak
to those who know the law), that the
law [T]has dominion over a man as long as he
lives? *rules*
2 For the woman who has a husband is
bound by the law to *her* husband as long as
he lives. But if the husband dies, she is
released from the law of *her* husband.
3 So then if, while *her* husband lives, she
marries another man, she will be called an
adulteress; but if her husband dies, she is free
from that law, so that she is no adulteress,
though she has married another man.
4 Therefore, my brethren, you also have
become dead to the law through the body of
Christ, that you may be married to another,
even to Him who was raised from the dead,
that we should [R]bear fruit to God. Gal. 5:22
5 For when we were in the flesh, the passions of sins which were aroused by the law
[R]were at work in our members [R]to bear fruit
to death. Rom. 6:13 • James 1:15
6 But now we have been delivered from
the law, having died to what we were held by,
so that we should serve in the newness of the
Spirit and not *in* the oldness of the letter.

Law Cannot Deliver from Sin

7 What shall we say then? *Is* the law sin?
Certainly not! On the contrary, I would not
have known sin except through the law. For I
would not have known covetousness unless
the law had said, *"You shall not covet."*
8 But sin, taking opportunity by the commandment, produced in me all *manner of evil*
desire. For apart from the law sin *was* dead.
9 I was alive once without the law, but
when the commandment came, sin revived
and I died.
10 And the commandment, [R]which *was* to
bring life, I found to *bring* death. Lev. 18:5
11 For sin, taking occasion by the commandment, deceived me, and by it killed *me*.
12 Therefore [R]the law *is* holy, and the commandment holy and just and good. Ps. 19:8
13 Has then what is good become death to
me? Certainly not! But sin, that it might
appear sin, was producing death in me
through what is good, so that sin through the
commandment might become exceedingly
sinful.

6:23 New Life: A Free Gift—You can work for sin but it is a cruel master. When it pays you off, its wage is death—separation from God forever. In stark contrast, God does not pay wages. He has a free gift to offer—eternal life. There is nothing that one can do to earn this gift. If one could earn it, it would not be a gift; it would be wages. Eternal life is just that—eternal—it never ceases. The basic concept underlying life is *union*. There are three kinds of life mentioned in the Bible: (1) physical life—union of the soul with the body; (2) spiritual life—union of the soul with God; and (3) eternal life— eternal union of the soul with God. Jesus said, "My sheep hear My voice . . . And I give them eternal life; and they shall never perish" (Page 1252—John 10:27, 28). The gift of God is eternal life. One receives this gift when he believes in Jesus as his own personal Savior. Having eternal life, he will never perish.

Now turn to Page 1406—Col. 1:22: New Life: Based on Christ's Death.

14 For we know that the law is spiritual, but I am carnal, [R]sold under sin. 2 Kin. 17:17

15 For what I am doing, I do not understand. [R]For what I will to do, that I do not practice; but what I hate, that I do. [Gal. 5:17]

16 If, then, I do what I will not to do, I agree with the law that *it is* good.

17 But now, *it is* no longer I who do it, but sin that dwells in me.

18 For I know that [R]in me (that is, in my flesh) nothing good dwells; for to will is present with me, but *how* to perform what is good I do not find. [Gen. 6:5; 8:21]

19 For the good that I will *to do*, I do not do; but the evil I will not *to do*, that I practice.

20 Now if I do what I will not *to do*, it is no longer I who do it, but sin that dwells in me.

21 I find then a law, that evil is present with me, the one who wills to do good.

22 For I [R]delight in the law of God according to [R]the inward man. Ps. 1:2 • [2 Cor. 4:16]

23 But [R]I see another law in [R]my members, warring against the law of my mind, and bringing me into captivity to the law of sin which is in my members. [Gal. 5:17] • Rom. 6:13, 19

24 O wretched man that I am! Who will deliver me from this body of death?

25 [R]I thank God—through Jesus Christ our Lord! So then, with the mind I myself serve the law of God, but with the flesh the law of sin. 1 Cor. 15:57

CHAPTER 8

The Spirit Delivers from the Power of the Flesh

THERE *is* therefore now no condemnation to those who are in Christ Jesus, [R]who* do not walk according to the flesh, but according to the Spirit. Gal. 5:16

2 For [R]the law of [R]the Spirit of life in Christ Jesus has made me free from [R]the law of sin and death. Rom. 6:18, 22 • [1 Cor. 15:45] • Rom. 7:24, 25

3 For [R]what the law could not do in that it was weak through the flesh, [R]God *did* by sending His own Son in the likeness of sinful flesh, on account of sin: He condemned sin in the flesh, Acts 13:39 • [2 Cor. 5:21]

4 that the righteous requirement of the law might be fulfilled in us who [R]do not walk according to the flesh but according to the Spirit. Gal. 5:16, 25

5 For those who live according to the flesh set their minds on the things of the flesh, but those *who live* according to the Spirit, [R]the things of the Spirit. [Gal. 5:22–25]

6 For to be carnally minded *is* death, but to be spiritually minded *is* life and peace.

7 Because the [T]carnal mind *is* enmity against God; for it is not subject to the law of God, [R]nor indeed can be. *fleshly* • 1 Cor. 2:14

8 So then, those who are in the flesh cannot please God.

9 But you are not in the flesh but in the Spirit, if indeed the Spirit of God dwells in you. Now if anyone does not have the Spirit of Christ, he is not His.

10 And if Christ *is* in you, the body *is* dead because of sin, but the Spirit *is* life because of righteousness.

11 But if the Spirit of [R]Him who raised Jesus from the dead dwells in you, [R]He who raised Christ from the dead will also give life to your mortal bodies [T]through His Spirit who dwells in you. Acts 2:24 • 1 Cor. 6:14 • Or *because of*

The Spirit Gives Sonship

12 Therefore, brethren, we are debtors—not to the flesh, to live according to the flesh.

13 For [R]if you live according to the flesh you will die; but if by the Spirit you put to death the deeds of the body, you will live. Gal. 6:8

14 For [R]as many as are led by the Spirit of God, these are sons of God. [Gal. 5:18]

15 For you did not receive the spirit of bondage again to fear, but you received the [R]Spirit of adoption by whom we cry out, "Abba,[T] Father." [Is. 56:5] • Lit., in Aram., *Father*

8:1 NU omits the rest of v. 1.

8:15 God the Father of Believers—God is the Father of all who believe in Christ in a special sense not shared by unbelievers. God is called their Father, first of all, because they have a new standing before Him. While unbelievers are the offspring of God because He created them (Page 1299—Acts 17:28, 29), they do not have the standing of sons. Their standing is rather as condemned sinners before God the Judge (Page 1239—John 3:18; Page 1538—Rev. 20:11). When a person believes in Christ as Savior, his estate is wonderfully changed from grim condemnation to privileged sonship. This new standing grants to all believers the legal right and spiritual privileges of divine sonship: "heirs of God and joint heirs with Christ" (Page 1333—Rom. 8:17).

God is the Father of believers also in the sense that He gives them new life (Page 1239—John 3:3). This relationship then is a family one involving many of the same realities that exist between an earthly father and child: birth of the child (Page 1239—John 3:3); partaking of the father's nature (Page 1487—2 Pet. 1:4); the father's care for the child (Page 1123—Matt. 6:32, 33; 7:9–11); and the father's discipline of the child (Page 1462—Heb. 12:6–8). Furthermore, this new Father-child relationship carries with it new brothers and sisters (Page 1463—Heb. 13:1).

To obtain God as Father is not a result of one's own merit but a result of Christ's. The one who believes in Christ as Savior enters into the blessed Father-child relationship with God solely on the grounds of Christ's sonship (Page 1333—Rom. 8:17; Page 1452—Heb. 2:17). It is the grand privilege and calling of those who know God as Father to graciously invite unbelievers to meet God as Father and not as Judge.

Now turn to Page 780—Is. 9:6: The Person of the Son of God.

16 [R]The Spirit Himself bears witness with our spirit that we are children of God, Eph. 1:13

17 and if children, then [R]heirs—heirs of God and joint heirs with Christ, [R]if indeed we suffer with *Him*, that we may also be glorified together. Acts 26:18 • Phil. 1:29

The Spirit Assures of Future Glory

18 For I consider that the sufferings of this present time are not worthy *to be compared* with the glory which shall be revealed in us.

19 For [R]the earnest expectation of the creation eagerly waits for the revealing of the sons of God. [2 Pet. 3:13]

20 For [R]the creation was subjected to futility, not willingly, but because of Him who subjected *it* in hope; Gen. 3:17–19

21 because the creation itself also will be delivered from the bondage of [T]corruption into the glorious [R]liberty of the children of God. *decay* • [2 Cor. 3:17]

22 For we know that the whole creation [R]groans and labors with birth pangs together until now. Jer. 12:4, 11

23 And not only *they*, but we also who have the firstfruits of the Spirit, [R]even we ourselves groan [R]within ourselves, eagerly waiting for the adoption, the [R]redemption of our body. 2 Cor. 5:2, 4 • [Luke 20:36] • Eph. 1:14; 4:30

24 For we were saved in this hope, but [R]hope that is seen is not hope; for why does one still hope for what he sees? Heb. 11:1

25 But if we hope for what we do not see, *then* we eagerly wait for *it* with perseverance.

26 Likewise the Spirit also helps in our weaknesses. For we do not know what we should pray for as we ought, but [R]the Spirit Himself makes intercession *for us with groanings which cannot be uttered. Eph. 6:18

27 Now [R]He who searches the hearts knows what the mind of the Spirit *is*, because He makes intercession for the saints [R]according to *the will of* God. 1 Chr. 28:9 • 1 John 5:14

28 And we know that all things work together for good to those who love God, to those [R]who are the called according to *His* purpose. 2 Tim. 1:9

29 For whom He foreknew, He also predestined [R]*to be* conformed to the image of His Son, [R]that He might be the firstborn among many brethren. [2 Cor. 3:18] • Heb. 1:6

30 Moreover whom He predestined, these He also [R]called; whom He called, these He also [R]justified; and whom He justified, these He also glorified. [1 Pet. 2:9; 3:9] • [Gal. 2:16]

The Spirit Assures of Final Victory

31 What then shall we say to these things? If God *is* for us, who *can be* against us?

32 He who did not spare His own Son, but delivered Him up for us all, how shall He not with Him also freely give us all things?

33 Who shall bring a charge against God's elect? [R]*It is* God who justifies. Is. 50:8, 9

34 Who *is* he who condemns? *It is* Christ who died, and furthermore is also risen, who is even at the right hand of God, [R]who also makes intercession for us. Heb. 7:25; 9:24

35 Who shall separate us from the love of Christ? *Shall* tribulation, or distress, or persecution, or famine, or nakedness, or peril, or sword?

36 As it is written:

> [R]*"For Your sake we are killed all day long;*
> *We are accounted as sheep for the slaughter."* Ps. 44:22

37 Yet in all these things we are more than conquerors through Him who loved us.

38 For I am persuaded that neither death nor life, nor angels nor [R]principalities nor powers, nor things present nor things to come, [Eph. 1:21]

39 nor height nor depth, nor any other created thing, shall be able to separate us from the love of God which is in Christ Jesus our Lord.

CHAPTER 9

Paul's Sorrow

I [R]TELL the truth in Christ, I am not lying, my conscience also bearing me witness in the Holy Spirit, 2 Cor. 1:23

2 [R]that I have great sorrow and continual grief in my heart. Rom. 10:1

3 For [R]I could wish that I myself were accursed from Christ for my brethren, my kinsmen according to the flesh, Ex. 32:32

4 who are Israelites, to whom *pertain* the adoption, the glory, [R]the covenants, [R]the giving of the law, [R]the service *of God*, and the promises; Acts 3:25 • Ps. 147:19 • Heb. 9:1, 6

5 [R]of whom *are* the fathers and from [R]whom, according to the flesh, Christ *came*, [R]who is over all, *the* eternally blessed God. Amen. Deut. 10:15 • [Luke 1:34, 35; 3:23] • Jer. 23:6

God's Sovereignty

6 [R]But it is not that the word of God has taken no effect. For [R]they *are* not all Israel who *are* of Israel, Num. 23:19 • [Gal. 6:16]

7 [R]nor *are they* all children because they are the seed of Abraham; but, *"In* [R]*Isaac your seed shall be called."* [Gal. 4:23] • Gen. 21:12

8 That is, those who *are* the children of the flesh, these *are* not the children of God; but [R]the children of the promise are counted as the seed. Gal. 4:28

9 For this *is* the word of promise: *"At this time I will come and Sarah shall have a son."*

10 And not only *this*, but when [R]Rebecca

8:26 NU omits *for us*

also had conceived by one man, *even* by our
father Isaac Gen. 25:21
11 (for *the children* not yet being born, nor
having done any good or evil, that the purpose of God according to election might
stand, not of works but of Him who calls),
12 it was said to her, [R]*"The older shall serve
the younger."* Gen. 25:23
13 As it is written, [R]*"Jacob I have loved, but
Esau I have hated."* Mal. 1:2, 3
14 What shall we say then? *Is there* unrighteousness with God? Certainly not!
15 For He says to Moses, [R]*"I will have
mercy on whomever I will have mercy, and I
will have compassion on whomever I will
have compassion."* Ex. 33:19
16 So then *it is* not of him who wills, nor of
him who runs, but of God who shows mercy.
17 For [R]the Scripture says to Pharaoh,
[R]*"Even for this same purpose I have raised
you up, that I might show My power in you,
and that My name might be declared in all
the earth."* Gal. 3:8 • Ex. 9:16
18 Therefore He has mercy on whom He
wills, and whom He wills He [R]hardens. Ex. 4:21
19 You will say to me then, "Why does He
still find fault? For [R]who has resisted His
will?" 2 Chr. 20:6
20 But indeed, O man, who are you to reply
against God? [R]Will the thing formed say to
him who formed *it,* "Why have you made me
like this?" Is. 29:16
21 Does not the potter have power over the
clay, from the same lump to make one vessel
for honor and another for dishonor?
22 *What* if God, wanting to show *His* wrath
and to make His power known, endured with
much longsuffering [R]the vessels of wrath
[R]prepared for destruction, [1 Thess. 5:9] • [1 Pet. 2:8]
23 and that He might make known [R]the
riches of His glory on the vessels of mercy,
which He had [R]prepared beforehand for
glory, [Col. 1:27] • [Rom. 8:28–30]
24 *even* us whom He called, not of the Jews
only, but also of the Gentiles?
25 As He says also in Hosea:

[R]*"I will call them My people, who were
not My people,
And her beloved, who was not
beloved."* Hos. 2:23
26 *"And[R] it shall come to pass in the place
where it was said to them,
'You are not My people,'
There they will be called sons of the
living God."* Hos. 1:10

27 Isaiah also cries out concerning Israel:

*"Though the number of the children of
Israel be as the sand of the sea,
[R]The remnant will be saved.* Rom. 11:5
28 *For He will finish the work and cut it
short in righteousness,
[R]Because the LORD will *make a short
work upon the earth."* Is. 10:23; 28:22

29 And as Isaiah said before:

[R]*"Unless the LORD of Sabaoth had left us
a seed,
[R]We would have become like Sodom,
And we would have been made like
Gomorrah."* Is. 1:9 • Is. 13:19

Israel Seeks Righteousness by Works

30 What shall we say then? [R]That Gentiles,
who did not pursue righteousness, have attained to righteousness, [R]even the righteousness of faith; Rom. 4:11 • Rom. 1:17; 3:21; 10:6
31 but Israel, [R]pursuing the law of righteousness, [R]has not attained to the law *of
righteousness. [Rom. 10:2–4] • [Gal. 5:4]
32 Why? Because *they did* not *seek it* by
faith, but as it were, *by the works of the law.
For they stumbled at that stumbling stone.
33 As it is written:

[R]*"Behold, I lay in Zion a stumbling stone
and rock of offense,
And whoever believes on Him will not
be put to shame."* Ps. 118:22; Is. 28:16 ★

CHAPTER 10

Israel Rejects Christ

BRETHREN, my heart's desire and prayer
to God for *Israel is that they may be
saved.
2 For I bear them witness [R]that they have
a zeal for God, but not according to knowledge. Acts 21:20
3 For they being ignorant of [R]God's righteousness, and seeking to establish their own
[R]righteousness, have not submitted to the
righteousness of God. [Rom. 1:17] • [Phil. 3:9]
4 For Christ *is* the end of the law for
righteousness to everyone who believes.
5 For Moses writes about the righteousness which is of the law, [R]*"The man who does
those things shall live by them."* Lev. 18:5
6 But the righteousness of faith speaks in
this way, [R]*"Do not say in your heart, 'Who
will ascend into heaven?' "* (that is, to bring
Christ down *from above*) Deut. 30:12–14
7 or, *" 'Who will descend into the abyss?' "*
(that is, to bring Christ up from the dead).
8 But what does it say? *"The word is near*

9:28 NU *finish the work and cut it short upon the earth*
9:31 NU omits *of righteousness*
9:32 NU *by works,* omitting *of the law* **10:1** NU *them*

you, even in your mouth and in your heart"
(that is, the word of faith which we preach):
9 that [R]if you confess with your mouth the
Lord Jesus and believe in your heart that God
has raised Him from the dead, you will be
saved. Luke 12:8
10 For with the heart one believes to righteousness, and with the mouth confession is
made to salvation.
11 For the Scripture says, *"Whoever believes on Him will not be put to shame."*
12 For there is no distinction between Jew
and Greek, for [R]the same Lord over all [R]is rich
to all who call upon Him. Acts 10:36 • Eph. 1:7
13 [R]For *"whoever calls* [R]*upon the name of
the* LORD *shall be saved."* Joel 2:32 • Acts 9:14
14 How then shall they call on Him in
whom they have not believed? And how shall
they believe in Him of whom they have not
heard? And how shall they hear [R]without a
preacher? Titus 1:3
15 And how shall they preach unless they
are sent? As it is written:

[R]*"How beautiful are the feet of those who*
**preach the gospel of peace,* Is. 52:7
Who bring glad tidings of good things!"

Israel Rejects the Prophets

16 But they have not all obeyed the gospel.
For Isaiah says, [R]*"Lord, who has believed our
report?"* Is. 53:1; John 12:38 ★
17 So then faith *comes* by hearing, and
hearing by the word of God.
18 But I say, have they not heard? Yes
indeed:

[R]*"Their sound has gone out to all the*
earth,
[R]*And their words to the ends of the*
world." Ps. 19:4 • 1 Kin. 18:10

19 But I say, did Israel not know? First
Moses says:

[R]*"I will provoke you to jealousy by those*
who are not a nation, Deut. 32:21
I will anger you by a foolish nation."

20 But Isaiah is very bold and says:

[R]*"I was found by those who did not seek*
Me;
I was made manifest to those who did
not ask for Me." Is. 65:1

21 But to Israel he says:

[R]*"All day long I have stretched out My*
hands Is. 65:2
To a disobedient and contrary people."

CHAPTER 11

Israel's Rejection Is Not Total

I SAY then, [R]has God cast away His people?
[R]Certainly not! For [R]I also am an Israelite,
of the seed of Abraham, *of* the tribe of Benjamin. Jer. 46:28 • 1 Sam. 12:22 • 2 Cor. 11:22
2 God has not cast away His people whom
[R]He foreknew. Or do you not know what the
Scripture says of Elijah, how he pleads with
God against Israel, saying, [Rom. 8:29]
3 [R]*"*LORD*, they have killed Your prophets
and torn down Your altars, and I alone am
left, and they seek my life"?* 1 Kin. 19:10, 14
4 But what does the divine response say to
him? [R]*"I have reserved for Myself seven
thousand men who have not bowed the knee
to Baal."* 1 Kin. 19:18
5 [R]Even so then, at this present time there
is a remnant according to the election of
grace. Rom. 9:27
6 And [R]if by grace, then *it is* no longer of
works; otherwise grace is no longer grace.
*But if *it is* of works, it is no longer grace;
otherwise work is no longer work. Rom. 4:4
7 What then? Israel has not obtained what
it seeks; but the elect have obtained it, and
the rest were [R]hardened. 2 Cor. 3:14
8 Just as it is written:

[R]*"God has given them a spirit of stupor,*
[R]*Eyes that they should not see*
And ears that they should not hear,
To this very day." Is. 29:10, 13 • Deut. 29:3, 4

9 And David says:

[R]*"Let their table become a snare and a*
trap,
A stumbling block and a recompense to
them; Ps. 69:22, 23 ★
10 *Let their eyes be darkened, that they*
may not see,
And bow down their back always."

Purpose of Israel's Rejection

11 I say then, have they stumbled that they
should fall? Certainly not! But through their
[T]fall, to provoke them to jealousy, salvation
has come to the Gentiles. *trespass*
12 Now if their fall *is* riches for the world,
and their failure [R]riches for the Gentiles, how
much more their fullness! Hos. 1:10; 2:23 ★
13 For I speak to you Gentiles; inasmuch as
[R]I am an apostle to the Gentiles, I magnify
my ministry, Acts 9:15; 22:21
14 if by any means I may provoke to jealousy *those who are* my flesh and [R]save some
of them. 1 Cor. 9:22

10:15 NU omits *preach the gospel of peace, Who*
11:6 NU omits the rest of v. 6.

15 For if their being cast away *is* the reconciling of the world, what *will* their acceptance
be [R]but life from the dead? [Is. 26:16–19]
16 For if [R]the firstfruit *is* holy, the lump *is*
also *holy*; and if the root *is* holy, so *are* the
branches. Lev. 23:10
17 And if [R]some of the branches were broken off, [R]and you, being a wild olive tree,
were grafted in among them, and with them
became a partaker of the root and [T]fatness of
the olive tree, Jer. 11:16 • [Eph. 2:12] • *richness*
18 do not boast against the branches. But if
you boast, *remember that* you do not support
the root, but the root supports you.
19 You will say then, "Branches were broken off that I might be grafted in."
20 Well *said.* Because of [R]unbelief they were
broken off, and you stand by faith. Do not be
haughty, but fear. Heb. 3:19
21 For if God did not spare the natural
branches, He may not spare you either.
22 Therefore consider the goodness and
severity of God: on those who fell, severity;
but toward you, *goodness, [R]if you continue
in *His* goodness. Otherwise [R]you also will be
cut off. 1 Cor. 15:2 • [John 15:2]
23 And they also, [R]if they do not continue in
unbelief, will be grafted in, for God is able to
graft them in again. [2 Cor. 3:16]
24 For if you were cut out of the olive tree
which is wild by nature, and were grafted
contrary to nature into a good olive tree, how
much more will these, who *are the* natural
branches, be grafted into their own olive
tree?

Promise of Israel's Restoration

25 For I do not desire, brethren, that you
should be ignorant of this mystery, lest you
should be [R]wise in your own [T]opinion, that
[R]hardening in part has happened to Israel
[R]until the fullness of the Gentiles has come
in. Rom. 12:16 • *estimation* • 2 Cor. 3:14 • Luke 21:24
26 And so all Israel will be saved, as it is
written:

[R]*"The Deliverer will come out of Zion,*
And He will turn away ungodliness
from Jacob; Is. 59:20, 21
27 [R]*For this is My covenant with them,*
When I take away their sins." Is. 27:9

28 Concerning the gospel *they are* enemies
for your sake, but concerning the election
they are beloved for the sake of the fathers.
29 For the gifts and the calling of God *are*
[R]irrevocable. Num. 23:19
30 For as you [R]were once disobedient to
God, yet have now obtained mercy through
their disobedience, [Eph. 2:2]
31 even so these also have now been disobedient, that through the mercy shown you
they also may obtain mercy.
32 For God has [T]committed them [R]all to
disobedience, that He might have mercy on
all. *shut them all up in* • [Gal. 3:22]

Israel's Restoration:
The Occasion for Glorifying God

33 Oh, the depth of the riches both of the
wisdom and knowledge of God! How unsearchable *are* His judgments and His ways
past finding out!

34 *"For who has known the [R]mind of the*
LORD? Is. 40:13; Jer. 23:18
Or who has become His counselor?"
35 *"Or[R] who has first given to Him*
And it shall be repaid to him?" Job 41:11

36 For [R]of Him and through Him and to Him
are all things, [R]to whom *be* glory forever.
Amen. Heb. 2:10 • Heb. 13:21

CHAPTER 12

Responsibilities Toward God

I BESEECH you therefore, brethren, by the
mercies of God, that you present your
bodies a living sacrifice, holy, acceptable to
God, *which is* your reasonable service.

11:22 NU adds *of God*

12:1 Walking in the Spirit: Yielding—Confession of sin in itself is not enough to enable the believer to automatically walk in the Spirit. He must then become a yielded instrument for God's service. What is to be yielded is simply himself (Page 1331—Rom. 6:13; Page 1471—James 4:7). This involves both the body (Rom. 12:1; Page 1351—1 Cor. 6:20) and the mind (Rom. 12:2), since it is with the body that actions conceived in the mind are carried out and with the mind that they are formulated. Stated another way, that which is conceived in the mind is carried out in the body; thus, one's whole being must be presented by a decisive act of the will to God for His service. Yielding must not be thought of simply as a willingness to do some specific thing. Rather, it consists of dedication by a person to do whatever God commands.

Yielding leads not only to dedication but also can result in separation: "do not be conformed to this world" (Rom. 12:2). Since the world is resolutely opposed to God, one cannot revel in its lusts and at the same time do the will of God (Page 1496—1 John 2:15–17). The same word translated "conformed" here is translated "fashioning" in First Peter 1:14. So the concept of separation involves being "unfashionable" in spirit, thought, values, and actions according to the world's standards.

Finally, yielding includes transformation of the mind. This work is said to be accomplished through a lifetime of "renewing" the mind. Man's mind has been darkened by sin (Page 1332—Rom. 8:7; Page 1406—Col. 1:21) and must be brought to the place where it thinks as God thinks (Page 1391—Eph.

2 And do not be conformed to this world,
but be transformed by the renewing of your
mind, that you may prove what *is* that good
and acceptable and perfect will of God.

Responsibilities Toward Society

3 For I say, through the grace given to me,
to everyone who is among you, not to think
of himself more highly than he ought to
think, but to think soberly, as God has dealt
to each one a measure of faith.
4 For [R]as we have many members in one
body, but all the members do not have the
same function, 1 Cor. 12:12–14
5 so [R]we, *being* many, are one body in
Christ, and individually members of one
another. [1 Cor. 10:17]
6 Having then gifts differing according to
the grace that is [R]given to us, *let us use them*:
if prophecy, *let us* [R]*prophesy* in proportion to
our faith; [John 3:27] • Acts 11:27
7 or ministry, *let us use it* in *our* ministering; [R]he who teaches, in teaching; Eph. 4:11
8 he who exhorts, in exhortation; [R]he who
gives, with liberality; [R]he who leads, with
diligence; he who shows mercy, [R]with cheerfulness. [Matt. 6:1–3] • [Acts 20:28] • 2 Cor. 9:7
9 *Let* love *be* without hypocrisy. [R]Abhor
what is evil. Cling to what is good. Ps. 34:14
10 [R]*Be* kindly affectionate to one another
with brotherly love, [R]in honor giving preference to one another; Heb. 13:1 • Phil. 2:3
11 not lagging in diligence, fervent in spirit,
serving the Lord;
12 rejoicing in hope, patient in tribulation,
continuing steadfastly in prayer;
13 distributing to the needs of the saints,
[R]given[T] to hospitality. 1 Tim. 3:2 • Lit. *pursuing*
14 [R]Bless those who persecute you; bless
and do not curse. [Matt. 5:44]
15 [R]Rejoice with those who rejoice, and
weep with those who weep. [1 Cor. 12:26]
16 [R]Be of the same mind toward one another. [R]Do not set your mind on high things,
but associate with the humble. Do not be
wise in your own opinion. [Phil. 2:2; 4:2] • Jer. 45:5
17 Repay no one evil for evil. Have regard
for good things in the sight of all men.
18 If it is possible, as much as depends on
you, [R]live peaceably with all men. Heb. 12:14
19 Beloved, [R]do not avenge yourselves, but
rather give place to wrath; for it is written,
[R]*"Vengeance is Mine, I will repay,"* says the
Lord. Lev. 19:18 • Deut. 32:35

20 *"Therefore* [R]*if your enemy hungers, feed him;*
If he thirsts, give him a drink;
For in so doing you will heap coals of fire on his head." Prov. 25:21, 22

21 Do not be overcome by evil, but [R]over-
come evil with good. [Rom. 12:1, 2]

CHAPTER 13

Responsibilities Toward Higher Powers

LET every soul be [R]subject to the governing
authorities. For there is no authority
except from God, and the authorities that
exist are appointed by God. 1 Pet. 2:13
2 Therefore whoever resists the authority
resists the ordinance of God, and those who
resist will bring judgment on themselves.
3 For rulers are not a terror to good works,
but to evil. Do you want to be unafraid of the
authority? [R]Do what is good, and you will
have praise from the same. 1 Pet. 2:14
4 For he is God's minister to you for good.
But if you do evil, be afraid; for he does not
bear the sword in vain; for he is God's minister, an avenger to *execute* wrath on him who
practices evil.

5 Therefore [R]*you* must be subject, not only
because of wrath [R]but also for conscience'
sake. Eccl. 8:2 • [1 Pet. 2:13, 19]

4:23). This renewing is said to come especially through prayer to God in everything (Page 1401—Phil. 4:6, 7) and through constant meditation on the Word of God (Page 694—Ps. 119:1). This transformation is a lifelong process that will not be completed until we are with Christ (Page 1398—Phil. 1:6; Page 1497—1 John 3:2). Along life's way, however, it brings a peace and delight that can only come from having embraced the mind of Christ.

Now turn to Page 1391—Eph. 5:18: Walking in the Spirit: Filling.

13:1–4 The Function of Human Government—The general function of human government, as instituted by God, may be said to be threefold: to protect, punish, and promote.

a. The Function of Protection: The moment Adam sinned it was obvious that civilizations would need some form of restraint and rule to protect citizens from themselves. An example of this function is seen in Acts 21:27-37 where Roman soldiers step in and save Paul from being murdered by his own enraged countrymen in Jerusalem.
b. The Function of Punishment: Both Paul and Peter bring this out. Paul writes that duly appointed human officials are to be regarded as God's servants to "bear the sword," that is, to impose punishment upon criminals (vv. 3, 4). Peter tells us that governors are "sent by him for the punishment of evildoers" (Page 1479—1 Pet. 2:13, 14).
c. The Function of Promotion: Human government is to promote the general welfare of the community where its laws are in effect. Paul commands us to pray for human leaders "that we may lead a quiet and peaceable life in all godliness and honesty" (Page 1426—1 Tim. 2:1, 2).

Now turn to Page 1479—1 Pet. 2:13: Our Responsibility to Human Government.

PAUL'S MAJOR TEACHINGS

Next to the Master Teacher Himself, the apostle Paul is probably the most eloquent and persuasive teacher in the Bible. Many of the doctrines he expounded are considered the hallmarks of the Christian faith.

Born a Jew in Tarsus, he was a Roman citizen, tentmaker, and a Pharisee, responsible for persecution of Christians before his conversion on the road to Damascus (Acts 9:1–9; see illustration). He became a faithful follower of Christ, a dedicated missionary, and a respected leader in the early church. Here are a few of his major teachings.

1. Justification by faith. According to Paul, God ushered in a new era through the death of His Son. Under the old covenant, people, such as Abraham, were justified by believing God, looking forward to the promise of the coming Messiah (see Gen. 15:6; Rom. 4:22). Now we are justified, or declared righteous before God, through faith in the Messiah, Jesus Christ, and His atoning death on our behalf. Our justification is based on the work of Christ, accomplished through His blood (Rom. 5:9), and brought to His people through His resurrection (Rom. 4:25).

2. Jesus Christ as the risen and living Son of God. From the moment Jesus appeared to Paul at his dramatic conversion, Paul never hesitated to proclaim Him as the mystery of the ages and the great Redeemer of sinful humanity (1 Cor. 15:1–20). To Paul, Jesus was the Messiah, God's Son, the center of the gospel, and the One through whom "all things were created" (Col. 1:16).

3. The church as the body of Christ. The only New Testament writer who speaks of the church as a body, Paul emphasized this fact in such passages as Ephesians 1:22, 23; 4:7–16; and 1 Corinthians 12. He also reminded Christians that their various gifts were to be used in building up the body of Christ and that they should work together for the common good of the Christian cause (Rom. 12:4, 5).

4. The power and influence of the Holy Spirit in the Christian's life. Paul taught that the Holy Spirit was a more effective power for holy living in the Christian's life than the old Jewish Law had ever been. The Law told people what to do, but it could not provide the will or the power to do it. But God's Spirit could provide the necessary power and motivation (Rom. 8:9–17; Gal. 5:16–25).

5. The Second Coming of Christ and the consummation of the kingdom of God as the redeemed are received into God's presence. Paul taught that Christ will return to earth at the end of this age and that all Christians will share in His glory in the age to come (1 Thess. 4:13–18; 1 Cor. 15:20–28).

Jesus speaks to Saul (Paul) on the road to Damascus (Acts 9:1–9).

6 For because of this you also pay taxes,
for they are God's ministers attending continually to this very thing.
7 [R]Render therefore to all their due: taxes
to whom taxes *are due*, customs to whom
customs, fear to whom fear, honor to whom
honor. Matt. 22:21

Responsibilities Toward Neighbors

8 Owe no one anything except to love one
another, for [R]he who loves another has fulfilled the law. [Gal. 5:13, 14]
9 For the commandments, *"You shall not*
commit adultery," "You shall not murder,"
"You shall not steal," **"You shall not bear*
false witness," "You shall not covet," and if
there is any other commandment, are *all*
summed up in this saying, namely, *"You shall*
love your neighbor as yourself."
10 Love does no harm to a neighbor; therefore love *is* the fulfillment of the law.
11 And *do* this, knowing the time, that now
it is high time [R]to awake out of sleep; for now
our salvation *is* nearer than when we *first*
believed. [1 Cor. 15:34]
12 The night is far spent, the day is at hand.
Therefore let us cast off the works of darkness, and let us put on the armor of light.
13 Let us walk [T]properly, as in the day, [R]not
in revelry and drunkenness, [R]not in licentiousness and lewdness, [R]not in strife and
envy. *decently* • Prov. 23:20 • [1 Cor. 6:9] • James 3:14
14 But [R]put on the Lord Jesus Christ, and
[R]make no provision for the flesh, to *fulfill its*
lusts. Gal. 3:27 • [Gal. 5:16]

CHAPTER 14

Principles of Christian Liberty

RECEIVE one who is weak in the faith,
but not to disputes over doubtful things.
2 For one believes he may eat all things,
but he who is weak eats *only* vegetables.
3 Let not him who eats despise him who
does not eat, and [R]let not him who does not
eat judge him who eats; for God has received
him. [Col. 2:16]
4 [R]Who are you to judge another's servant? To his own master he stands or falls.
Indeed, he will be made to stand, for God is
able to make him stand. James 4:11, 12
5 One person esteems *one* day above another; another esteems every day *alike*. Let
each be fully convinced in his own mind.
6 He who observes the day, observes *it* to
the Lord; *and he who does not observe the
day, to the Lord he does not observe *it*. He
who eats, eats to the Lord, for he gives God
thanks; and he who does not eat, to the Lord
he does not eat, and gives God thanks.
7 For [R]none of us lives to himself, and no
one dies to himself. [Gal. 2:20]
8 For if we live, we live to the Lord; and if
we die, we die to the Lord. Therefore,
whether we live or die, we are the Lord's.
9 For to this end Christ died *and rose and
lived again, that He might be [R]Lord of both
the dead and the living. Acts 10:36
10 But why do you judge your brother? Or
why do you show contempt for your brother?
For [R]we shall all stand before the judgment
seat of *Christ. 2 Cor. 5:10
11 For it is written:

[R]*"As I live, says the LORD,*
Every knee shall bow to Me,
And every tongue shall confess to
God." Is. 45:23

12 So then [R]each of us shall give account of
himself to God. 1 Pet. 4:5
13 Therefore let us not judge one another
[T]anymore, but rather resolve this, [R]not to put
a stumbling block or a cause to fall in *our*
brother's way. *any longer* • 1 Cor. 8:9
14 I know and am convinced by the Lord
Jesus [R]that *there is* nothing unclean of itself;
but to him who considers anything to be
unclean, to him *it is* unclean. 1 Cor. 10:25
15 Yet if your brother is grieved because of
your food, you are no longer walking in love.
[R]Do not destroy with your food the one for
whom Christ died. 1 Cor. 8:11
16 [R]Therefore do not let your good be spoken of as evil; [Rom. 12:17]
17 [R]for the kingdom of God is not food and
drink, but righteousness and [R]peace and joy
in the Holy Spirit. 1 Cor. 8:8 • [Rom. 8:6]
18 For he who serves Christ in *these things
is acceptable to God and approved by men.
19 Therefore let us pursue the things *which*
make for peace and the things by which one
may [T]edify another. *build up*
20 Do not destroy the work of God for the
sake of food. All things indeed *are* pure,
[R]but *it is* evil for the man who eats with
[T]offense. 1 Cor. 8:9–12 • A feeling of giving offense
21 *It is* good neither to eat meat nor drink
wine nor *do anything* by which your brother
stumbles *or is offended or is made weak.
22 *Do you have faith? Have *it* to yourself
before God. Happy *is* he who does not condemn himself in what he approves.
23 But he who doubts is condemned if he
eats, because *he does* not *eat* from faith; for
[R]whatever *is* not from faith is sin.* Titus 1:15

13:9 NU omits *"You shall not bear false witness,"*
14:6 NU omits the rest of this sentence.
14:9 NU omits *and rose* **14:10** NU *God*
14:18 NU *this thing* **14:21** NU omits the rest of v. 21.
14:22 NU *The faith which you have—have*
14:23 M adds Rom. 16:25–27 here.

CHAPTER 15

Practices of Christian Liberty

WE [R]then who are strong ought to bear
with the [T]scruples of the weak, and not
to please ourselves. [Gal. 6:1, 2] • *weaknesses*
2 Let each of us please *his* neighbor for *his*
good, leading to [T]edification. *building up*
3 For even Christ did not please Himself;
but as it is written, *"The [R]reproaches of those*
who reproached You fell on Me." Ps. 69:7, 9, 20 ★
4 For whatever things were written before
were written for our learning, that we
through the [T]patience and comfort of the
Scriptures might have hope. *perseverance*
5 [R]Now may the God of patience and comfort grant you to be like-minded toward one
another, according to Christ Jesus, 1 Cor. 1:10
6 that you may [R]with one mind *and* one
mouth glorify the God and Father of our Lord
Jesus Christ. Acts 4:24
7 Therefore receive one another, just as
Christ also received *us, to the glory of God.
8 Now I say that [R]Jesus Christ has become
a [T]servant to the circumcision for the truth of
God, [R]to confirm the promises *made* to the
fathers, Matt. 15:24 • *minister* • 2 Cor. 1:20
9 and [R]that the Gentiles might glorify God
for *His* mercy, as it is written: John 10:16

[R]*"For this reason I will confess to You*
among the Gentiles, 2 Sam. 22:50; Ps. 18:49
And sing to Your name."

10 And again he says:

"Rejoice, O Gentiles, with His people!"

11 And again:

[R]*"Praise the LORD, all you Gentiles!*
Laud Him, all you peoples!" Ps. 117:1

12 And again, Isaiah says:

[R]*"There shall be a root of Jesse;*
And He who shall rise to reign over the
Gentiles, Is. 11:10 ★
In Him the Gentiles shall hope."

13 Now may the God of hope fill you with
all [R]joy and peace in believing, that you may
abound in hope by the power of the Holy
Spirit. Rom. 12:12; 14:17

Paul's Purpose for Writing

14 Now I myself am confident concerning
you, my brethren, that you also are full of
goodness, [R]filled with all knowledge, able also
to admonish *one another. 1 Cor. 1:5; 8:1, 7, 10
15 Nevertheless, brethren, I have written
more boldly to you on *some* points, as reminding you, [R]because of the grace given to
me by God, Rom. 1:5; 12:3
16 that [R]I might be a minister of Jesus
Christ to the Gentiles, ministering the gospel
of God, that the [R]offering [T]of the Gentiles
might be acceptable, sanctified by the Holy
Spirit. Rom. 11:13 • [Is. 66:20] • Consisting of
17 Therefore I have reason to glory in
Christ Jesus [R]in the things *which pertain* to
God. Heb. 2:17; 5:1
18 For I will not dare to speak of any of
those things which Christ has not accomplished through me, in word and deed, [R]to
make the Gentiles obedient— Rom. 1:5
19 in mighty signs and wonders, by the
power of the Spirit of God, so that from
Jerusalem and round about to Illyricum I
have fully preached the gospel of Christ.
20 And so I have made it my aim to preach
the gospel, not where Christ was named, lest
I should build on another man's foundation,
21 but as it is written:

[R]*"To whom He was not announced, they*
shall see; Is. 52:15
And those who have not heard shall
understand."

Paul's Plans for Traveling

22 For this reason [R]I also have been much
hindered from coming to you. Rom. 1:13
23 But now no longer having a place in
these parts, and [R]having a great desire these
many years to come to you, Acts 19:21; 23:11
24 whenever I journey to Spain, *I shall
come to you. For I hope to see you on my
journey, [R]and to be helped on my way there
by you, if first I may [R]enjoy your *company*
for a while. Acts 15:3 • Rom. 1:12
25 But now [R]I am going to Jerusalem to
[T]minister to the saints. Acts 19:21 • *serve*
26 For [R]it pleased those from Macedonia
and Achaia to make a certain contribution
for the poor among the saints who are in
Jerusalem. 1 Cor. 16:1
27 It pleased them indeed, and they are
their debtors. For if the Gentiles have been
partakers of their spiritual things, their duty
is also to minister to them in material things.
28 Therefore, when I have performed this
and have sealed to them [R]this fruit, I shall go
by way of you to Spain. Phil. 4:17
29 [R]But I know that when I come to you, I
shall come in the fullness of the blessing *of
the gospel of Christ. [Rom. 1:11]
30 Now I beg you, brethren, through the
Lord Jesus Christ, and through the love of
the Spirit, [R]that you strive together with me
in *your* prayers to God for me, 2 Cor. 1:11
31 [R]that I may be delivered from those in
Judea who [T]do not believe, and that [R]my

15:7 NU, M *you* **15:14** M *others*
15:24 NU omits *I shall come to you* and joins *Spain* with the next sentence. **15:29** NU omits *of the gospel*

service for Jerusalem may be acceptable to
the saints, 2 Tim. 3:11; 4:17 • *are disobedient* • 2 Cor. 8:4
32 [R]that I may come to you with joy [R]by the
will of God, and may [R]be refreshed together
with you. Rom. 1:10 • Acts 18:21 • 1 Cor. 16:18
33 Now [R]the God of peace *be* with you all.
Amen. 1 Cor. 14:33

CHAPTER 16

Paul's Praise and Greetings

I COMMEND to you Phoebe our sister, who
is a servant of the church in Cenchrea,
2 [R]that you may receive her in the Lord [R]in
a manner worthy of the saints, and assist her
in whatever business she has need of you; for
indeed she has been a helper of many and of
myself also. Phil. 2:29 • Phil. 1:27
3 Greet [R]Priscilla and Aquila, my fellow
workers in Christ Jesus, Acts 18:2, 18, 26
4 who risked their own necks for my life,
to whom not only I give thanks, but also all
the churches of the Gentiles.

5 Likewise *greet* the church that is in their
house. Greet my beloved Epaenetus, who is
the firstfruits of *Achaia to Christ.

6 Greet Mary, who labored much for us.
7 Greet Andronicus and Junia, my kinsmen and my fellow prisoners, who are of note
among the [R]apostles, who also [R]were in
Christ before me. Acts 1:13, 26 • Gal. 1:22
8 Greet Amplias, my beloved in the Lord.
9 Greet Urbanus, our fellow worker in
Christ, and Stachys, my beloved.
10 Greet Apelles, approved in Christ. Greet
those who are of the *household* of Aristobulus.
11 Greet Herodion, my kinsman. Greet
those who are of the *household* of Narcissus
who are in the Lord.
12 Greet Tryphena and Tryphosa, who have
labored in the Lord. Greet the beloved Persis,
who labored much in the Lord.
13 Greet Rufus, [R]chosen in the Lord, and his
mother and mine. 2 John 1
14 Greet Asyncritus, Phlegon, Hermas, Pat-
robas, Hermes, and the brethren who are
with them.
15 Greet Philologus and Julia, Nereus and
his sister, and Olympas, and all the saints
who are with them.
16 [R]Greet one another with a holy kiss.
*The churches of Christ greet you. 1 Cor. 16:20
17 Now I urge you, brethren, note those
[R]who cause divisions and offenses, contrary
to the doctrine which you learned, and [R]avoid
them. [Acts 15:1] • [1 Cor. 5:9]
18 For those who are such do not serve our
Lord *Jesus Christ, but their own belly, and
[R]by smooth words and flattering speech deceive the hearts of the simple. Col. 2:4
19 For [R]your obedience has become known
to all. Therefore I am glad on your behalf; but
I want you to be wise in what is good, and
[T]simple concerning evil. Rom. 1:8 • *innocent*
20 And the God of peace will crush Satan
under your feet shortly. The grace of our
Lord Jesus Christ *be* with you. Amen.
21 [R]Timothy, my fellow worker, and [R]Lu-
cius, [R]Jason, and [R]Sosipater, my kinsmen,
greet you. Acts 16:1 • Acts 13:1 • Acts 17:5 • Acts 20:4
22 I, Tertius, who wrote *this* epistle, greet
you in the Lord.
23 [R]Gaius, my host and *the host* of the
whole church, greets you. [R]Erastus, the treasurer of the city, greets you, and Quartus, a
brother. 1 Cor. 1:14 • Acts 19:22
24 [R]The* grace of our Lord Jesus Christ *be*
with you all. Amen. 1 Thess. 5:28
25 *Now [R]to Him who is able to establish
you [R]according to my gospel and the preaching of Jesus Christ, according to the revelation of the mystery *which was* kept secret
since the world began [Eph. 3:20] • Rom. 2:16
26 but [R]now has been made manifest, and
by the prophetic Scriptures has been made
known to all nations, according to the commandment of the everlasting God, for [R]obedi-
ence to the faith— Eph. 1:9 • Rom. 1:5
27 to [R]God, alone wise, *be* glory through
Jesus Christ forever. Amen. Jude 25

16:5 NU *Asia* **16:16** NU *All the churches*
16:18 NU, M omit *Jesus* **16:24** NU omits v. 24.
16:25 M puts Rom. 16:25–27 after Rom. 14:23.

16:5 Definition of the Local Church—The local church is a geographically located, temporally limited, and visibly evident manifestation of the universal church, the body of Christ. In the early New Testament days the local church met in the Jewish synagogue and had a very simple organization (Page 1469—James 2:2). A little later the church met in the homes of believers (Rom. 16:5), and it was not uncommon to have a number of churches in an area (Page 1378—Gal. 1:2). The idea of meeting in a building constructed for that exclusive purpose is a post-New Testament idea. (For a more complete discussion of the church turn to Page 1281 and read Acts 7:38 and THE CHRISTIAN'S GUIDE: The Meaning of the Church.)

Now turn to Page 1458—Heb. 10:25: The Reason for Participation in the Local Church.

THE FIRST EPISTLE OF PAUL THE APOSTLE TO THE

CORINTHIANS

THE BOOK OF FIRST CORINTHIANS

Corinth, the most important city in Greece during Paul's day, was a bustling hub of worldwide commerce, degraded culture, and idolatrous religion. There Paul founded a church (Acts 18:1–17), and two of his letters are addressed "To the church of God which is at Corinth."

First Corinthians reveals the problems, pressures, and struggles of a church called out of a pagan society. Paul addresses a variety of problems in the life-style of the Corinthian church: factions, lawsuits, immorality, questionable practices, abuse of the Lord's Supper, and spiritual gifts. In addition to words of discipline, Paul shares words of counsel in answer to questions raised by the Corinthian believers.

The oldest recorded title of this epistle is *Pros Korinthious A*, in effect, the "First to the Corinthians." The *A* was no doubt a later addition to distinguish this book from Second Corinthians.

THE AUTHOR OF FIRST CORINTHIANS

Pauline authorship of First Corinthians is almost universally accepted. Instances of this widely held belief can be found as early as A.D. 95, when Clement of Rome wrote to the Corinthian church and cited this epistle in regard to their continuing problem of factions among themselves.

THE TIME OF FIRST CORINTHIANS

Corinth was a key city in ancient Greece until it was destroyed by the Romans in 146 B.C. Julius Caesar rebuilt it as a Roman colony in 46 B.C. and it grew and prospered, becoming the capital of the province of Achaia. Its official language was Latin, but the common language remained Greek. In Paul's day Corinth was the metropolis of the Peloponnesus, since it was strategically located on a narrow isthmus between the Aegean Sea and the Adriatic Sea that connects the Peloponnesus with northern Greece. Because of its two seaports it became a commercial center, and many small ships were rolled or dragged across the Corinthian isthmus to avoid the dangerous 200-mile voyage around southern Greece. Nero and others attempted to build a canal at the narrowest point, but this was not achieved until 1893. The city was filled with shrines and temples, but the most prominent was the Temple of Aphrodite on top of a 1,800-foot promontory called the Acrocorinthus. Worshipers of the "goddess of love" made free use of the 1,000 Hieroduli (consecrated prostitutes). This cosmopolitan center thrived on commerce, entertainment, vice, and corruption; pleasure-seekers came there to spend money on a holiday from morality. Corinth became so notorious for its evils that the term *Korinthiazomai* ("to act like a Corinthian") became a synonym for debauchery and prostitution.

In Paul's day the population of Corinth was approximately 700,000, about two-thirds of whom were slaves. The diverse population produced no philosophers, but Greek philosophy influenced any speculative thought that was there. In spite of these obstacles to the gospel, Paul was able to establish a church in Corinth on his second missionary journey (3:6, 10; 4:15; Acts 18:1–7). Persecution in Macedonia drove him south to Athens, and from there he proceeded to Corinth. He made tents with Aquila and Priscilla and reasoned with the Jews in the synagogue. Silas and Timothy joined him (they evidently brought a gift from Philippi; 2 Cor. 11:8, 9; Phil. 4:15), and Paul began to devote all his time to spreading the gospel. Paul wrote First and Second Thessalonians, moved his ministry from the synagogue to the house of Titius Justus because of opposition, and converted Crispus, the leader of the synagogue. Paul taught the Word of God in Corinth for eighteen months in A.D. 51 and 52. After Paul's departure, Apollos came from Ephesus to minister in the Corinthian church (3:6; Acts 18:24–28).

When Paul was teaching and preaching in Ephesus during his third missionary journey, he was disturbed by reports from the household of Chloe concerning quarrels in the church at Corinth (1:11). The church sent a delegation of three men (16:17), who apparently brought a letter that requested Paul's judgment on certain issues (7:1). Paul wrote this epistle as his response to the problems and questions of the Corinthians (he had already written a previous letter; 5:9). It may be that the men who came from Corinth took this letter back with them. Paul was planning to leave Ephesus (16:5–8), indicating that First Corinthians was written in A.D. 56.

THE CHRIST OF FIRST CORINTHIANS

This book proclaims the relevance of Christ Jesus to every area of the believer's life. He "became for us wisdom from God—and righteousness and sanctification and redemption—" (1:30), and these are the themes Paul addresses in this epistle.

KEYS TO FIRST CORINTHIANS

Key Word: Correction of Carnal Living—The basic theme of this epistle is the application of Christian principles to carnality in the individual as well as in the church. The cross of Christ is a message that is designed to transform the lives of believers and make them different as people and as a corporate body from the surrounding world. However, the Corinthians are destroying their Christian testimony because of immorality and disunity. Paul writes this letter as his corrective response to the news of problems and disorders among the Corinthians. It is designed to refute improper attitudes and conduct and to promote a spirit of unity among the brethren in their relationships and worship. Paul's concern as their spiritual father (4:14, 15) is tempered with love, and he wants to avoid visiting them "with a rod" (4:21).

Key Verses: First Corinthians 6:19, 20 and 10:12, 13—"Or do you not know that your body is the temple of the Holy Spirit *who is* in you, whom you have from God, and you are not your own? For you were bought at a price; therefore glorify God in your body and in your spirit, which are God's" (6:19, 20).

"Therefore let him who thinks he stands take heed lest he fall. No temptation has overtaken you except such as is common to man; but God *is* faithful, who will not allow you to be tempted beyond what you are able, but with the temptation will also make the way of escape, that you may be able to bear *it*" (10:12, 13).

Key Chapter: First Corinthians 13—Read at weddings and often the text for sermons, First Corinthians 13 has won the hearts of people across the world as the best definition of "love" ever penned. Standing in stark contrast to the idea that love is an emotion, that one can fall into or fall out of love, this chapter clearly reveals that true love is primarily an action. This is why when "God so loved the world that He gave" (John 3:16).

SURVEY OF FIRST CORINTHIANS

Through the missionary efforts of Paul and others, the church has been established in Corinth, but Paul finds it very difficult to keep Corinth out of the church. The pagan lifestyle of Corinth exerts a profound influence upon the Christians in that corrupt city—problems of every kind plague them. In this disciplinary letter, Paul is forced to exercise his apostolic authority as he deals firmly with problems of divisiveness, immorality, lawsuits, selfishness, abuses of the Lord's Supper and spiritual gifts, and denials of the Resurrection. This epistle is quite orderly in its approach as it sequentially addresses a group of problems that have come to Paul's attention. Paul also gives a series of perspectives on various questions and issues raised by the Corinthians in a letter. He uses the introductory words "Now concerning" or "Now" to delineate those topics (7:1, 25; 8:1; 11:2; 12:1; 15:1; 16:1). The three divisions of First Corinthians are: answer to Chloe's report of divisions (1—4); answer to report of fornication (5 and 6); and answer to letter of questions (7—16).

Answer to Chloe's Report of Divisions (1—4): Personality cults centering around Paul, Apollos, and Peter have led to divisions and false pride among the Corinthians (1). It is not their wisdom or cleverness that has brought them to Christ, because divine wisdom is contrary to human wisdom. The truth of the gospel is spiritually apprehended (2). Factions that exist among the saints at Corinth are indications of their spiritual immaturity (3). They should pride themselves in Christ, not in human leaders who are merely His servants (4).

Answer to Report of Fornication (5 and 6): The next problem Paul addresses is that of incest

FOCUS	ANSWER TO CHLOE'S REPORT OF DIVISIONS		ANSWER TO REPORT OF FORNICATION			ANSWER TO LETTER OF QUESTIONS				
REFERENCE	1:1—	1:18—	5:1—	6:1—	6:12—	7:1—	8:1—	11:2—	15:1—	16:1—16:24
DIVISION	REPORT OF DIVISIONS	REASON FOR DIVISIONS	INCEST	LITIGATION	IMMORALITY	MARRIAGE	OFFERINGS TO IDOLS	PUBLIC WORSHIP	RESUR-RECTION	COLLECTION FOR JERUSALEM
TOPIC	DIVISIONS IN THE CHURCH		DISORDER IN THE CHURCH			DIFFICULTIES IN THE CHURCH				
	CONCERN		CONDEMNATION			COUNSEL				
LOCATION	WRITTEN IN EPHESUS									
TIME	C. A.D. 56									

between a member of the church and his stepmother (5). The Corinthians have exercised no church discipline in this matter, and Paul orders them to remove the offender from their fellowship until he repents. Another source of poor testimony is the legal action of believer against believer in civil courts (6:1–8). They must learn to arbitrate their differences within the Christian community. Paul concludes this section with a warning against immorality in general (6:9–20).

Answer to Letter of Questions (7—16): In these chapters the apostle Paul gives authoritative answers to thorny questions raised by the Corinthians. His first counsel concerns the issues of marriage, celibacy, divorce, and remarriage (7). The next three chapters are related to the problem of meat offered to idols (8:1—11:1). Paul illustrates from his own life the twin principles of Christian liberty and the law of love, and he concludes that believers must sometimes limit their liberty for the sake of weaker brothers (cf. Rom. 14). The apostle then turns to matters concerning public worship, including improper observance of the Lord's Supper and the selfish use of spiritual gifts (11:2—14:40). Gifts are to be exercised in love for the edification of the whole body. The Corinthians also have problems with the Resurrection, which Paul seeks to correct (15). His historical and theological defense of the Resurrection includes teaching on the nature of the resurrected body. The Corinthians probably have been struggling over this issue because the idea of a resurrected body is disdainful in Greek thought. The epistle closes with Paul's instruction for the collection he will make for the saints in Jerusalem (16:1–4), followed by miscellaneous exhortations and greetings (16:5–24).

OUTLINE OF FIRST CORINTHIANS

Part One: In Answer to Chloe's Report of Divisions (1:1—4:21)

I. Introduction **1:1–9**

A. Greetings of Grace 1:1–3
B. Prayer of Thanksgiving 1:4–9

II. Report of Divisions **1:10–17**

III. Reasons for Divisions .... **1:18—4:21**

A. Misunderstanding of the Gospel Message .... 1:18—3:4
1. The Gospel Is Not Earthly Wisdom .... 1:18—2:5
2. The Gospel Is Heavenly Wisdom 2:6—3:4
B. Misunderstanding of the Gospel Messenger .... 3:5—4:5
1. Ministers Are Fellow Workers with God 3:5–17
2. Ministers Are Accountable to God .... 3:18—4:5
C. Misunderstanding of Paul's Ministry 4:6–21

Part Two: In Answer to Reports of Fornication (5:1—6:20)

I. On Incest **5:1–13**

A. Deliver the Fornicators for Discipline 5:1–8
B. Separate Yourselves from Immoral Believers 5:9–13

II. Concerning Litigation Between Believers 6:1–11

III. Warning Against Sexual Immorality **6:12–20**

Part Three: In Answer to the Letter of Questions (7:1—16:24)

I. Counsel Concerning Marriage **7:1–40**

A. Principles for Married Life 7:1–9
B. Principles for the Married Believer 7:10–16
C. Principle of Abiding in God's Call 7:17–24
D. Principles for the Unmarried 7:25–38
E. Principles for Remarriage 7:39, 40

II. Counsel Concerning Things Offered to Idols .... **8:1—11:1**

A. Principles of Liberty and the Weaker Brother 8:1–13
B. Illustration of Paul and His Liberty 9:1–27
1. Paul Lists His Rights as a Minister 9:1–14
2. Paul Limits His Rights for Ministry 9:15–27
C. Warning Against Forfeiting Liberty 10:1–13
D. Exhortation to Use Liberty to Glorify God .... 10:14—11:1

III. Counsel Concerning Public Worship 11:2—14:40

A. Principles of Public Prayer 11:2–16
B. Rebuke of Disorders at the Lord's Supper 11:17–34
C. Principles of Exercising Spiritual Gifts .... 12:1—14:40
1. Test of the Spirit's Control 12:1–3
2. Diversity of the Gifts 12:4–11
3. Importance of All Gifts 12:12–31
4. Exercise Gifts with Love 13:1–13
5. Superiority of Prophecy 14:1–6
6. Gift of Tongues 14:7–25
7. Exercising Gifts in Public Worship 14:26–40

IV. Counsel Concerning the Resurrection . . . **15:1–58**
A. Fact of Christ's Resurrection 15:1–11
B. Importance of Christ's Resurrection 15:12–19
C. Order of the Resurrections 15:20–28
D. Moral Implications of Christ's Resurrection 15:29–34
E. Bodies of the Resurrected Dead. 15:35–50
F. Bodies of the Translated Living 15:51–58

V. Counsel Concerning the Collection for Jerusalem **16:1–4**

VI. Conclusion **16:5–24**

CHAPTER 1

Greetings of Grace

PAUL, called *to be* an apostle of Jesus
Christ [R]through the will of God, and
[R]Sosthenes *our* brother, 2 Cor. 1:1 • Acts 18:17

2 To the church of God which is at Corinth, to those who are [T]sanctified in Christ
Jesus, called *to be* saints, with all who in
every place call on the name of Jesus Christ
our Lord, both theirs and ours: *set apart*

3 [R]Grace to you and peace from God our
Father and the Lord Jesus Christ. Rom. 1:7

Prayer of Thanksgiving

4 [R]I thank my God always concerning you
for the grace of God which was given to you
by Christ Jesus, Rom. 1:8
5 that you were enriched in everything by
Him in all utterance and all knowledge,
6 even as [R]the testimony of Christ was
confirmed [T]in you, 2 Tim. 1:8 • Or *among*
7 so that you come short in no gift, eagerly
[R]waiting for the revelation of our Lord Jesus
Christ, Phil. 3:20
8 [R]who will also confirm you to the end,
[R]*that you may be* blameless in the day of our
Lord Jesus Christ. 1 Thess. 3:13; 5:23 • Col. 1:22; 2:7
9 [R]God *is* faithful, by whom you were
called into [R]the fellowship of His Son, Jesus
Christ our Lord. Is. 49:7 • [John 15:4]

Report of Divisions

10 Now I plead with you, brethren, by the
name of our Lord Jesus Christ, that you all
speak the same thing, and *that* there be no
[T]divisions among you, but *that* you be perfectly joined together in the same mind and
in the same judgment. *schisms* or *dissensions*
11 For it has been declared to me concerning you, my brethren, by those of Chloe's
household, that there are [T]contentions among
you. *quarrels*
12 Now I say this, that each of you says, "I
am of Paul," or "I am of Apollos," or "I am of
[R]Cephas," or "I am of Christ." John 1:42
13 [R]Is Christ divided? Was Paul crucified for
you? Or were you baptized in the name of
Paul? 2 Cor. 11:4
14 I thank God that I baptized [R]none of you
except [R]Crispus and Gaius, John 4:2 • Acts 18:8
15 lest anyone should say that I had baptized in my own name.
16 Yes, I also baptized the household of
[R]Stephanas. Besides, I do not know whether I
baptized any other. 1 Cor. 16:15, 17
17 For Christ did not send me to baptize,
but to preach the gospel, [R]not with wisdom of
words, lest the cross of Christ should be made
of no effect. [1 Cor. 2:1, 4, 13]

The Gospel Is Not Earthly Wisdom

18 For the message of the cross is foolishness to those who are perishing, but to us
who are being saved it is the power of God.
19 For it is written:

[R]*"I will destroy the wisdom of the wise,*
And bring to nothing the understanding
of the prudent." Is. 29:14

20 Where *is* the wise? Where *is* the scribe?
Where *is* the disputer of this age? Has not
God made foolish the wisdom of this world?
21 For since, in the wisdom of God, the
world through wisdom did not know God, it
pleased God through the foolishness of the
message preached to save those who believe.
22 For [R]Jews request a sign, and Greeks
seek after wisdom; Matt. 12:38
23 but we preach Christ crucified, to the
Jews a [T]stumbling block and to the *Greeks
[R]foolishness, Gr. *skandalon, offense* • [1 Cor. 2:14]
24 but to those who are called, both Jews
and Greeks, Christ [R]the power of God and
[R]the wisdom of God. [Rom. 1:4] • Col. 2:3
25 Because the foolishness of God is wiser
than men, and the weakness of God is stronger than men.
26 For you see your calling, brethren, that
not many wise according to the flesh, not
many mighty, not many noble, *are called.*
27 But God has chosen the foolish things of
the world to put to shame the wise, and God
has chosen the weak things of the world to
put to shame the things which are mighty;
28 and the [T]base things of the world and the
things which are despised God has chosen,
and the things which are not, to bring to
nothing the things that are, *insignificant* or *lowly*
29 that no flesh should glory in His presence.
30 But of Him you are in Christ Jesus, who
became for us wisdom from God—and [R]righ-
teousness and sanctification and redemption— [2 Cor. 5:21]

1:23 NU *Gentiles*

31 that, as it is written, [R]*"He who glories, let him glory in the LORD."* Jer. 9:23, 24

CHAPTER 2

AND I, brethren, when I came to you, did
not come with excellence of speech or
of wisdom declaring to you the *testimony of
God.
2 For I determined not to know anything
among you [R]except Jesus Christ and Him
crucified. Gal. 6:14
3 [R]I was with you [R]in weakness, in fear,
and in much trembling. Acts 18:1 • [2 Cor. 4:7]
4 And my speech and my preaching [R]*were*
not with persuasive words of *human wisdom, [R]but in demonstration of the Spirit and
of power, 2 Pet. 1:16 • Rom. 15:19
5 that your faith should not be in the
wisdom of men but in the power of God.

The Gospel Is Heavenly Wisdom

6 However, we speak wisdom among those
who are mature, yet not the wisdom of this
age, nor of the rulers of this age, who are
coming to nothing.
7 But we speak the wisdom of God in a
mystery, the hidden *wisdom* which God ordained before the ages for our glory,
8 which none of the rulers of this age
knew; for [R]had they known, they would not
have crucified the Lord of glory. Luke 23:34
9 But as it is written:

[R]*"Eye has not seen, nor ear heard,*
Nor have entered into the heart of man
The things which God has prepared for
those who love Him." [Is. 64:4; 65:17]

10 But God has revealed *them* to us through
His Spirit. For the Spirit searches all things,
yes, the deep things of God.
11 For what man knows the things of a man
except the [R]spirit of the man which is in him?
[R]Even so no one knows the things of God
except the Spirit of God. [James 2:26] • Rom. 11:33
12 Now we have received, not the spirit of
the world, but [R]the Spirit who is from God,
that we might know the things that have
been freely given to us by God. [Rom. 8:15]
13 These things we also speak, not in words
which man's wisdom teaches but which the
*Holy Spirit teaches, comparing spiritual
things with spiritual.
14 But the natural man does not receive the
things of the Spirit of God, for they are
foolishness to him; nor can he know *them*,
because they are spiritually discerned.
15 But he who is spiritual judges all things,
yet he himself is *rightly* judged by no one.
16 [R]For *"Who has known the mind of the*
LORD that he may instruct Him?" [R]But we
have the mind of Christ. Is. 40:13 • [John 15:15]

CHAPTER 3

AND I, brethren, could not speak to you as
to spiritual *people* but as to carnal, as to
[R]babes in Christ. Heb. 5:13
2 I fed you with milk and not with solid
food; for until now you were not able *to*
receive it, and even now you are still not able;
3 for you are still carnal. For where *there*
are envy, strife, and divisions among you, are
you not carnal and behaving like *mere* men?
4 For when one says, "I am of Paul," and
another, "I *am* of Apollos," are you not
carnal?

Ministers Are Fellow Workers with God

5 Who then is Paul, and who *is* Apollos,
but [R]ministers through whom you believed,
as the Lord gave to each one? 2 Cor. 3:3, 6
6 I planted, [R]Apollos watered, [R]but God
gave the increase. Acts 18:24–27 • [2 Cor. 3:5]
7 So then [R]neither he who plants is anything, nor he who waters, but God who gives
the increase. [Gal. 6:3]
8 Now he who plants and he who waters
are one, [R]and each one will receive his own
reward according to his own labor. Ps. 62:12
9 For we are God's fellow workers; you are
God's field, *you are* God's building.
10 [R]According to the grace of God which
was given to me, as a wise master builder I
have laid [R]the foundation, and another builds
on it. But let each one take heed how he
builds on it. Rom. 1:5 • 1 Cor. 4:15
11 For no other foundation can anyone lay
than [R]that which is laid, [R]which is Jesus
Christ. Is. 28:16 • Eph. 2:20
12 Now if anyone builds on this foundation
with gold, silver, precious stones, wood, hay,
straw,
13 each one's work will become manifest;
for the Day will declare it, because [R]it will be
revealed by fire; and the fire will test each
one's work, of what sort it is. Luke 2:35
14 If anyone's work which he has built on *it*
endures, he will receive a reward.
15 If anyone's work is burned, he will suffer
loss; but he himself will be saved, yet so as
through fire.
16 [R]Do you not know that you are the
temple of God and *that* the Spirit of God
dwells in you? 2 Cor. 6:16
17 If anyone [T]defiles the temple of God, God
will destroy him. For the temple of God is
holy, which *temple* you are. *destroys*

Ministers Are Accountable to God

18 Let no one deceive himself. If anyone
among you seems to be wise in this age, let
him become a fool that he may become wise.

2:1 NU *mystery* **2:4** NU omits *human*
2:13 NU omits *Holy*

REWARDS AND PUNISHMENTS

God is "a rewarder of those who diligently seek Him" (Heb. 11:6). He also negatively "rewards" or recompenses those who run away from or reject Him and live sinful, selfish lives.

Reward (*misthos*)

Reward (*misthos*) is used in thirteen of the New Testament books. Significantly, Christ the rewarder uses the word first (Matt. 5:12) in promising great reward in heaven to those who are persecuted for His sake. At the very end of the Bible, He mentions that "My reward *is* with Me" (Rev. 22:12) to repay His people for their works.

Paul makes it clear that salvation is not a reward, but is reckoned to us by grace (Rom. 4:4). However, the apostle does promise that each one will be rewarded according to individual labor for the Lord (1 Cor. 3:8). This text has to do with rewards for Christians. The "fire" here (v. 13) tests the works to see if they are genuine. These are not fires to burn the Christian, but to burn away the dross of works done for the wrong reason (e.g., praise of men). The remaining works will receive a reward (v. 14).

The following words are used for both reward and punishment. Since they can be translated either in a negative or positive way, depending on context, they are only translated in the discussion.

Misthapodosia

Misthapodosia occurs three times in the Greek New Testament (all in Hebrews), twice for rewards, and once for punishment.

Reward (Heb. 10:35): "Therefore do not cast away your confidence, which has great reward." The author is encouraging his readers to remain steadfast in light of eternal reward. The context (v. 34) is largely one of temporal loss through persecution.

In the famous "faith chapter," Moses is praised for giving up the glamor and pleasure of the Egyptian court because he counted "the reproach of Christ greater riches than the treasures in Egypt; for he looked to the reward" (Heb. 11:26). He had his eye on eternity, not Egypt!

Punishment (Heb. 2:2–4): The author warns Christians not to think they will escape punishment when Old Testament law-breakers "receive a just reward."

Antapodoma

Antapodoma occurs twice, once positively and once negatively.

Reward (Luke 14:12–14): Christ warns of inviting only people who can invite you back so that you will "be repaid" (lit. "get a reward," *antapodoma*). Then He tells His people to show charity to the really unfortunate; then they will "be repaid" (verb forming this noun) "at the resurrection of the just." When Christians serve the poor, they serve Christ and will receive an eternal *apodoma*.

Punishment (Rom. 11:9): Paul quotes David from Psalm 69:22: "Let their table become a snare and a trap, a stumbling block and a recompense to them." He uses this verse to show that *unbelieving* Israelites, in contrast to the godly remnant, will be recompensed for their hard-heartedness.

Antimisthia

Antimisthia also is used twice, positively and negatively:

Reward (2 Cor. 6:13): The derivation of this word suggests give-and-take, and that is what Paul requests of the Corinthians: "Now in return [*antimisthia*] for the same (I speak as to children), you also be open." This speaks of everyday rewards between people.

Punishment (Rom. 1:26): The context is a detailed "sin catalog" of the Roman world. Now Paul writes that perverts will receive "in themselves a penalty [*antimisthia*] of their error which was due" (v. 27). This probably refers chiefly to the psychological and physical problems that perversion fosters. If they repent, of course, the penalty need not stretch into eternity.

The subject of rewards and punishments is both solemn and encouraging: solemn to those who either are rejecting God or frittering away their time, and encouraging to those who are working for the kingdom.

19 For the wisdom of this world is foolishness with God. For it is written, [R]*"He catches the wise in their own craftiness"*; Job 5:13
20 and again, *"The LORD knows the thoughts of the wise, that they are futile."*
21 Therefore let no one glory in men. For [R]all things are yours: [2 Cor. 4:5]
22 whether Paul or Apollos or Cephas, or the world or life or death, or things present or things to come—all are yours.
23 And [R]you *are* Christ's, and Christ *is* God's. 2 Cor. 10:7

CHAPTER 4

LET a man so consider us, as [R]servants of Christ [R]and stewards of the mysteries of God. Col. 1:25 • Titus 1:7
2 Moreover it is required in stewards that one be found faithful.
3 But with me it is a very small thing that I should be judged by you or by a human court. In fact, I do not even judge myself.
4 For I know nothing against myself, yet I am not justified by this; but He who judges me is the Lord.
5 Therefore judge nothing before the time, until the Lord comes, who will both bring to light the hidden things of darkness and reveal the counsels of the hearts; and then each one's praise will come from God.

Misunderstanding of Paul's Ministry

6 Now these things, brethren, I have figuratively transferred to myself and Apollos for your sakes, that you may learn in us not to think beyond what is written, that none of you may be [T]puffed up on behalf of one against the other. *arrogant*
7 For who [T]makes you differ *from another*? And [R]what do you have that you did not receive? Now if you did indeed receive *it*, why do you glory as if you had not received *it*? *distinguishes you* • John 3:27
8 You are already full! [R]You are already rich! You have reigned as kings without us—and indeed I could wish you did reign, that we also might reign with you! Rev. 3:17
9 For I think that God has displayed us, the apostles, last, as men condemned to death; for we have been made a spectacle to the world, both to angels and to men.
10 We *are* [R]fools for Christ's sake, but you *are* wise in Christ! [R]We *are* weak, but you *are* strong! You *are* distinguished, but we *are* dishonored! Acts 17:18; 26:24 • 2 Cor. 13:9
11 *Even* to the present hour we both hunger and thirst, and we are poorly clothed, and beaten, and homeless.
12 [R]And we labor, working with our own hands. [R]Being reviled, we bless; being persecuted, we endure *it*; Acts 18:3; 20:34 • Matt. 5:44
13 being defamed, we [T]entreat. We have been made as the filth of the world, the offscouring of all things until now. *exhort*
14 I do not write these things to shame you, but as my beloved children I warn *you*.
15 For though you might have ten thousand instructors in Christ, yet *you do* not *have* many fathers; for [R]in Christ Jesus I have begotten you through the gospel. Gal. 4:19
16 Therefore I urge you, imitate me.
17 For this reason I have sent [R]Timothy to you, who is my beloved and faithful son in the Lord, who will [R]remind you of my ways in Christ, as I [R]teach everywhere [R]in every church. Acts 19:22 • 1 Cor. 11:2 • 1 Cor. 7:17 • 1 Cor. 14:33
18 [R]Now some are [T]puffed up, as though I were not coming to you. 1 Cor. 5:2 • *arrogant*
19 But I will come to you shortly, if the Lord wills, and I will know, not the word of those who are puffed up, but the power.
20 For [R]the kingdom of God *is* not in word but in [R]power. 1 Thess. 1:5 • 1 Cor. 2:4
21 What do you want? [R]Shall I come to you with a rod, or in love and a spirit of gentleness? 2 Cor. 10:2

CHAPTER 5

Deliver the Fornicators for Discipline

IT is actually reported *that there is* sexual immorality among you, and such sexual immorality as is not even *named among the Gentiles—that a man has his father's wife!
2 And you are puffed up, and have not rather mourned, that he who has done this deed might be taken away from among you.
3 [R]For I indeed, as absent in body but present in spirit, have already judged, as though I were present, *concerning* him who has so done this deed. Col. 2:5
4 In the [R]name of our Lord Jesus Christ, when you are gathered together, along with my spirit, [R]with the power of our Lord Jesus Christ, [Matt. 18:20] • [John 20:23]
5 deliver such a one to Satan for the destruction of the flesh, that his spirit may be saved in the day of the Lord *Jesus.
6 [R]Your glorying *is* not good. Do you not know that [R]a little leaven leavens the whole lump? 1 Cor. 3:21 • Gal. 5:9
7 Therefore [T]purge out the old leaven, that you may be a new lump, since you truly are unleavened. For indeed [R]Christ, our Passover, was sacrificed *for us. *clean out* • Is. 53:7
8 Therefore let us keep the feast, not with old leaven, nor [R]with the leaven of malice and wickedness, but with the unleavened *bread* of sincerity and truth. Matt. 16:6

Separate Yourselves from Immoral Believers

9 I wrote to you in my epistle not to keep company with sexually immoral people.

5:1 NU omits *named* **5:5** NU omits *Jesus*
5:7 NU omits *for us*

10 Yet *I* certainly *did* not *mean* with the
sexually immoral people of this world, or with
the covetous, or extortioners, or idolaters,
since then you would need to go [R]out of the
world. John 17:15
11 But now I have written to you not to
[T]keep company [R]with anyone named a
brother, who is a fornicator, or covetous, or
an idolater, or a reviler, or a drunkard, or an
extortioner—[R]not even to eat with such a
person. *associate* • Matt. 18:17 • Gal. 2:12
12 For what *have* I *to do* with judging those
also who are outside? Do you not judge those
who are inside?
13 But those who are outside God judges.
Therefore [R]*"put away from yourselves that*
wicked person." Deut. 13:5; 17:7, 12; 19:19; 21:21

CHAPTER 6

Concerning Litigation Between Believers

DARE any of you, having a matter against
another, go to law before the unrighteous, and not before the [R]saints? Dan. 7:22
2 Do you not know that [R]the saints will
judge the world? And if the world will be
judged by you, are you unworthy to judge
the smallest matters? Ps. 49:14
3 Do you not know that we shall [R]judge
angels? How much more, things that pertain
to this life? 2 Pet. 2:4
4 If then you have [T]judgments concerning
things pertaining to this life, do you appoint
those who are least esteemed by the church
to judge? *courts*
5 I say this to your shame. Is it so, that
there is not a wise man among you, not even
one, who will be able to judge between his
brethren?
6 But brother goes to law against brother,
and that before unbelievers!
7 Now therefore, it is already an utter
failure for you that you go to law against one
another. [R]Why do you not rather accept
wrong? Why do you not rather *let yourselves*
be defrauded? [Prov. 20:22]
8 No, you yourselves do wrong and defraud, and *you do* these things *to your* brethren!
9 Do you not know that the unrighteous
will not inherit the kingdom of God? Do not
be deceived. Neither fornicators, nor idolaters, nor adulterers, nor [T]homosexuals, nor
sodomites, *catamites,* those submitting to homosexuals
10 nor thieves, nor covetous, nor drunkards,
nor revilers, nor extortioners will inherit the
kingdom of God.

11 And such were some of you. But you
were washed, but you were [T]sanctified, but
you were justified in the name of the Lord
Jesus and by the Spirit of our God. *set apart*

Warning Against Sexual Immorality

12 [R]All things are lawful for me, but all
things are not [T]helpful. All things are lawful
for me, but I will not be brought under the
power of [T]any. 1 Cor. 10:23 • *profitable* • Or *anything*
13 [R]Foods for the stomach and the stomach
for foods, but God will destroy both it and
them. Now the body *is* not for [R]sexual immorality but [R]for the Lord, [R]and the Lord for the
body. Matt. 15:17 • Gal. 5:19 • 1 Thess. 4:3 • [Eph. 5:23]
14 And God both raised up the Lord and will
also raise us up [R]by His power. Eph. 1:19
15 Do you not know that [R]your bodies are
members of Christ? Shall I then take the
members of Christ and make *them* members
of a harlot? Certainly not! Rom. 12:5
16 Or do you not know that he who is
joined to a harlot is one body *with her*? For
[R]*"The two,"* He says, *"shall become one*
flesh." Gen. 2:24
17 [R]But he who is joined to the Lord is one
spirit *with Him*. [John 17:21–23]
18 [R]Flee sexual immorality. Every sin that a
man does is outside the body, but he who
commits sexual immorality sins [R]against his
own body. Heb. 13:4 • Rom. 1:24

6:11 Changed Life—The first stanza of a famous Christian song begins: "What a wonderful change in my life has been wrought since Jesus came into my heart."

Without doubt the greatest proof of the new birth is a changed life. The child of God now suddenly loves the following:

a. He loves Jesus. Before conversion the sinner might hold Christ in high esteem, but after conversion he loves the Savior (Page 1498—1 John 5:1, 2).
b. He loves the Bible. We should love God's Word as the psalmist did in Psalm 119. He expresses his great love for God's Word no less than 17 times! See verses 24, 40, 47, 48, 72, 97, 103, 111, 113, 127, 129, 140, 143, 159, 162, 165, 168.
c. He loves other Christians. "We know that we have passed from death to life, because we love the brethren" (Page 1497—1 John 3:14).
d. He loves his enemies. See Matthew 5:43–45.
e. He loves the souls of all people. Like Paul, he too can cry out for the conversion of loved ones. "Brethren, my heart's desire and prayer to God for Israel is that they may be saved" (Page 1334—Rom. 10:1). See also Second Corinthians 5:14.
f. He loves the pure life. John says if one loves the world, the love of the Father is not in him (Page 1496—1 John 2:15–17). See also First John 5:4.
g. He loves to talk to God. "Speaking to one another in psalms and hymns and spiritual songs, singing and making melody in your heart to the Lord" (Page 1392—Eph. 5:19).

Now turn to Page 27—THE CHRISTIAN'S GUIDE: Growing in the New Life.

THE CITY OF CORINTH

Corinth was a busy commercial city in ancient Greece, strategically located on the narrow strip of land connecting the peninsula to the mainland. The city had two excellent harbors, Cenchrea and Lechaeum. A cosmopolitan center of about 500,000 people when Paul arrived, this metropolis has dwindled to only a small city in modern times.

In Paul's view, Corinth was an ideal city for a church. The constant movement of travelers, merchants, and pilgrims as they practiced their trades through Corinth made it possible for the gospel to influence people from every part of the Roman world.

In addition to its commercial importance, Corinth was a center of idolatry with numerous pagan temples dedicated to worship of the Greek and Roman gods. The infamous temple of Aphrodite, a fertility goddess, had a poisonous effect on the city's culture and morals. Paul must have been moved by the godless masses that were consumed with the pursuit of profit and pleasure.

With the Corinthian church made up of people from these backgrounds, learning to live together in harmony was most difficult. Paul's two letters to the young church at Corinth (1 and 2 Corinthians) contain instruction on Christian living in a pagan environment.

But along with these struggles, the Corinthian church also experienced significant Christian victories (Acts 18:8). One noted convert may have been the city treasurer, Erastus, mentioned in Romans 16:23. A bronze plaque, known as the Erastus Inscription (see illustration), found near the ruins of a large amphitheater, mentions a generous patron by this name.

Paul labored with the church at Corinth for about eighteen months. After he left the city, a Christian community apparently was established at Corinth's eastern port of Cenchrea (Rom. 16:1).

Photo by Gustav Jeeninga

A bronze plaque, known as the Erastus Inscription, found near the ruins of a large amphitheater in Corinth, mentions a generous patron named Erastus.

19 Or [R]do you not know that your body is
the temple of the Holy Spirit *who is* in you,
whom you have from God, [R]and you are not
your own? 2 Cor. 6:16 • Rom. 14:7

20 For [R]you were bought at a price; therefore glorify God in your body *and in your
spirit, which are God's. 2 Pet. 2:1

CHAPTER 7

Principles for Married Life

NOW concerning the things of which you
wrote to me: [R]*It is* good for a man not to
touch a woman. 1 Cor. 7:8, 26
2 Nevertheless, because of sexual immorality, let each man have his own wife, and let
each woman have her own husband.
3 [R]Let the husband render to his wife the
affection due her, and likewise also the wife
to her husband. Ex. 21:10
4 The wife does not have authority over
her own body, but the husband *does*. And
likewise the husband does not have authority
over his own body, but the wife *does*.
5 Do not deprive one another except with
consent for a time, that you may give yourselves to fasting and prayer; and come together again so that Satan does not tempt
you because of your lack of self-control.
6 But I say this as a concession, [R]not as a
commandment. 2 Cor. 8:8
7 For I wish that all men were even as I
myself. But each one has his own gift from
God, one in this manner and another in that.
8 But I say to the unmarried and to the
widows: [R]It is good for them if they remain
even as I am; 1 Cor. 7:1, 26
9 but [R]if they cannot exercise self-control,
let them marry. For it is better to marry than
to burn *with passion*. 1 Tim. 5:14

Principles for the Married Believer

10 Now to the married I command, *yet* not I
but the [R]Lord: [R]A wife is not to depart from
her husband. Mark 10:6–10 • [Matt. 5:32]
11 But even if she does depart, let her remain unmarried or be reconciled to *her* husband. And a husband is not to divorce *his*
wife.
12 But to the rest I, not the Lord, say: If any
brother has a wife who does not believe, and
she is willing to live with him, let him not
divorce her.
13 And a woman who has a husband who
does not believe, if he is willing to live with
her, let her not divorce him.
14 For the unbelieving husband is sanctified
by the wife, and the unbelieving wife is
sanctified by the husband; otherwise [R]your
children would be unclean, but now they are
holy. Mal. 2:15
15 But if the unbeliever departs, let him
depart; a brother or a sister is not under
bondage in such *cases*. But God has called us
[R]to peace. Rom. 12:18
16 For how do you know, O wife, whether
you will [R]save *your* husband? Or how do you
know, O husband, whether you will save *your*
wife? 1 Pet. 3:1

Principle of Abiding in God's Call

17 But as God has distributed to each one,
as the Lord has called each one, so let him
walk. And so I ordain in all the churches.
18 Was anyone called while circumcised?
Let him not become uncircumcised. Was
anyone called while uncircumcised? [R]Let him
not be circumcised. Acts 15:1
19 Circumcision is nothing and uncircumcision is nothing, but [R]keeping the commandments of God *is what matters*. [John 15:14]
20 Let each one remain in the same calling
in which he was called.
21 Were you called *while* a slave? Do not be
concerned about it; but if you can be made
free, rather use *it*.
22 For he who is called in the Lord *while* a

6:20 NU omits the rest of v. 20.

6:19 The Work of the Holy Spirit in Christian Living—As a loving and wise mother tenderly watches over her child, so the Holy Spirit cares for the children of God.

a. The Holy Spirit indwells Christians. The Bible teaches that all believers are indwelt by the Holy Spirit (1 Cor. 6:19). The purpose of this indwelling ministry is to control the newly created nature given at conversion (Page 1368—2 Cor. 5:17; Page 1388—Eph. 3:16).
b. The Holy Spirit fills believers. We are admonished to "be filled with the Spirit" (Page 1391—Eph. 5:18). The word "fill" means to be controlled. The filling does not mean that the Christian gets more of the Holy Spirit, but rather, He gets more of us!
c. The Holy Spirit sanctifies the believer (Page 1340—Rom. 15:16; Page 1421—2 Thess. 2:13).
d. The Holy Spirit produces fruit in the life of the believer. This fruit is described by Paul: "But the fruit of the Spirit is love, joy, peace, longsuffering, kindness, goodness, faithfulness, gentleness, self-control" (Page 1383—Gal. 5:22, 23).
e. The Holy Spirit imparts gifts to Christians (Page 1337—Rom. 12:6–8; Page 1355—1 Cor. 12:1–11; Page 1390—Eph. 4:7–12). A spiritual gift is an ability imparted to every Christian (Page 1351—1 Cor. 7:7; Page 1483—1 Pet. 4:10). The purpose of these gifts is twofold, namely, to glorify God (Page 1523—Rev. 4:11) and to edify the body of Christ (Page 1390—Eph. 4:12, 13).
f. The Holy Spirit teaches believers. He will instruct us in all spiritual things as we read the Word of God (Page 1258—John 14:26) and abide in the Son of God (Page 1496—1 John 2:24–27).

Now turn to Page 27—THE CHRISTIAN'S GUIDE: Beginning the New Life.

slave is the Lord's freedman. Likewise he who is called *while* free is Christ's slave.
23 [R]You were bought at a price; do not become slaves of men. 1 Pet. 1:18, 19
24 Brethren, let each one remain with God in that *calling* in which he was called.

Principles for the Unmarried

25 Now concerning virgins: [R]I have no commandment from the Lord; yet I give judgment as one whom the Lord in His mercy *has made* [R]trustworthy. 2 Cor. 8:8 • 1 Tim. 1:12
26 I suppose therefore that this is good because of the present distress—[R]that *it is* good for a man to remain as he is: 1 Cor. 7:1, 8
27 Are you bound to a wife? Do not seek to be loosed. Are you loosed from a wife? Do not seek a wife.
28 But even if you do marry, you have not sinned; and if a virgin marries, she has not sinned. Nevertheless such will have trouble in the flesh, but I would spare you.
29 But [R]this I say, brethren, the time *is* short, so that from now on even those who have wives should be as though they had none, 1 Pet. 4:7
30 those who weep as though they did not weep, those who rejoice as though they did not rejoice, those who buy as though they did not possess,
31 and those who use this world as not [R]misusing *it*. For [R]the form of this world is passing away. 1 Cor. 9:18 • [1 John 2:17]
32 But I want you to be without [T]care. [R]He who is unmarried [T]cares for the things *that belong* to the Lord—how he may please the Lord. *concern* • 1 Tim. 5:5 • *is concerned about*
33 But he who is married cares about the things of the world—how he may please *his* wife.
34 There *is a difference between a wife and a virgin. The unmarried woman [R]cares about the things of the Lord, that she may be holy both in body and in spirit. But she who is married cares about the things of the world—how she may please *her* husband. Luke 10:40
35 And this I say for your own profit, not that I may put a leash on you, but for what is proper, and that you may serve the Lord without distraction.
36 But if any man thinks he is behaving improperly toward his [T]virgin, if she is past the flower of *her* youth, and thus it must be, let him do what he wishes; he does not sin; let them marry. Or *virgin daughter*
37 Nevertheless he who stands steadfast in his heart, having no necessity, but has power over his own will, and has so determined in his heart that he will keep his [T]virgin, does well. Or *virgin daughter*
38 [R]So then he who gives **her* in marriage does well, but he who does not give *her* in marriage does better. Heb. 13:4

Principles for Remarriage

39 [R]A wife is bound by law as long as her husband lives; but if her husband dies, she is at liberty to be married to whom she wishes, [R]only in the Lord. Rom. 7:2 • 2 Cor. 6:14
40 But she is happier if she remains as she is, according to my judgment—and [R]I think I also have the Spirit of God. 1 Thess. 4:8

CHAPTER 8

Principles of Liberty and the Weaker Brother

NOW concerning things offered to idols: We know that we all have knowledge. Knowledge puffs up, but love edifies.
2 And [R]if anyone thinks that he knows anything, he knows nothing yet as he ought to know. [1 Cor. 13:8–12]
3 But if anyone loves God, this one is known by Him.
4 Therefore concerning the eating of things offered to idols, we know that [R]an idol *is* nothing in the world, [R]and that *there is* no other God but one. Is. 41:24 • Deut. 4:35, 39; 6:4
5 For even if there are [R]so-called gods, whether in heaven or on earth (as there are many gods and many lords), [John 10:34]
6 yet for us *there is only* one God, the Father, [R]of whom *are* all things, and we for Him; and [R]one Lord Jesus Christ, [R]through whom *are* all things, and [R]through whom we *live*. Acts 17:28 • John 13:13 • John 1:3 • Rom. 5:11
7 However, *there is* not in everyone that knowledge; for some, [R]with consciousness of the idol, until now eat *it* as a thing offered to an idol; and their conscience, being weak, is [R]defiled. [1 Cor. 10:28] • Rom. 14:14, 22
8 But [R]food does not commend us to God; for neither if we eat are we the better, nor if we do not eat are we the worse. [Rom. 14:17]
9 But beware lest somehow this liberty of yours become [R]a [T]stumbling block to those who are weak. Rom. 12:13, 21 • *cause of offense*
10 For if anyone sees you who have knowledge eating in an idol's temple, will not the conscience of him who is weak be emboldened to eat those things offered to idols?
11 And [R]because of your knowledge shall the weak brother perish, for whom Christ died? Rom. 14:15, 20
12 But [R]when you thus sin against the brethren, and wound their weak conscience, you sin against Christ. Matt. 25:40
13 Therefore, [R]if food makes my brother stumble, I will never again eat meat, lest I make my brother stumble. Rom. 14:21

7:34 NU *is also* 7:38 NU *his own virgin*

CHAPTER 9

Paul Lists His Rights as a Minister

AM [R]I not an apostle? Am I not free? Have I not seen Jesus Christ our Lord? Are you not my work in the Lord? Acts 9:15

2 If I am not an apostle to others, yet doubtless I am to you. For you are the [T]seal of my apostleship in the Lord. *certification*

3 My defense to those who examine me is this:

4 Do we have no right to eat and drink?

5 Do we have no right to take along a believing wife, as *do* also the other apostles, the brothers of the Lord, and Cephas?

6 Or *is it* only Barnabas and I [R]*who* have no right to refrain from working? Acts 4:36

7 Who ever goes to war at his own expense? Who plants a vineyard and does not eat of its fruit? Or who tends a flock and does not drink of the milk of the flock?

8 Do I say these things as a *mere* man? Or does not the law say the same also?

9 For it is written in the law of Moses, [R]*"You shall not muzzle an ox while it treads out the grain."* Is it oxen God is concerned about? Deut. 25:4

10 Or does He say *it* altogether for our sakes? For our sakes, no doubt, *this* is written, that [R]he who plows should plow in hope, and he who threshes in hope should be partaker of his hope. 2 Tim. 2:6

11 [R]If we have sown spiritual things for you, *is it* a great thing if we reap your material things? Rom. 15:27

12 If others are partakers of *this* right over you, *are* we not even more? Nevertheless we have not used this right, but endure all things lest we hinder the gospel of Christ.

13 Do you not know that those who minister the holy things eat *of the things* of the temple, and those who serve at the altar partake of *the offerings of* the altar?

14 Even so [R]the Lord has commanded [R]that those who preach the gospel should live from the gospel. Matt. 10:10 • Rom. 10:15

Paul Limits His Rights for Ministry

15 But [R]I have used none of these things, nor have I written these things that it should be done so to me; for [R]it *would be* better for me to die than that anyone should make my boasting void. Acts 18:3; 20:33 • 2 Cor. 11:10

16 For if I preach the gospel, I have nothing to boast of, for necessity is laid upon me; yes, woe is me if I do not preach the gospel!

17 For if I do this willingly, I have a reward; but if against my will, [R]I have been entrusted with a stewardship. Gal. 2:7

18 What is my reward then? That [R]when I preach the gospel, I may present the gospel *of Christ without charge, that I may not abuse my authority in the gospel. 1 Cor. 10:33

19 For though I am free from all *men*, [R]I have made myself a servant to all, [R]that I might win the more; Gal. 5:13 • Matt. 18:15

20 and [R]to the Jews I became as a Jew, that I might win Jews; to those *who are* under the law, as under the *law, that I might win those *who are* under the law; Acts 16:3; 21:23–26

21 to those *who are* without law, as without law [R](not being without *law toward God, but under *law toward Christ), that I might win those *who are* without law; [1 Cor. 7:22]

22 [R]to the weak I became *as weak, that I might win the weak. [R]I have become all things to all *men*, [R]that I might by all means save some. Rom. 14:1; 15:1 • 1 Cor. 10:33 • Rom. 11:14

23 Now this I do for the gospel's sake, that I may be partaker of it with *you*.

24 Do you not know that those who run in a race all run, but one receives the prize? Run in such a way that you may obtain *it*.

25 And everyone who competes *for the prize* [T]is temperate in all things. Now they *do it* to obtain a perishable crown, but we *for* [R]an imperishable *crown*. *exercises self-control* • James 1:12

26 Therefore I run thus: [R]not with uncertainty. Thus I fight: not as *one who* beats the air. 2 Tim. 2:5

27 But I discipline my body and bring *it* into subjection, lest, when I have preached to others, I myself should become disqualified.

CHAPTER 10

Warning Against Forfeiting Liberty

MOREOVER, brethren, I do not want you to be unaware that all our fathers were under the cloud, all passed through the sea,

2 all were baptized into Moses in the cloud and in the sea,

3 all ate the same [R]spiritual food, Ex. 16:4

4 and all drank the same spiritual drink. For they drank of that spiritual Rock that followed them, and that Rock was Christ.

5 But with most of them God was not well pleased, for *their bodies* [R]were scattered in the wilderness. Num. 14:29, 37; 26:65

6 Now these things became our examples, to the intent that we should not lust after evil things as [R]they also lusted. Num. 11:4, 34

7 [R]And do not become idolaters as *were* some of them. As it is written, [R]*"The people sat down to eat and drink, and rose up to play."* 1 Cor. 5:11; 10:14 • Ex. 32:6

8 Nor let us commit sexual immorality, as [R]some of them did, and [R]in one day twenty-three thousand fell; Num. 25:1–9 • Ps. 106:29

9 nor let us [T]tempt Christ, as [R]some of them also tempted, and [R]were destroyed by serpents; *test* • Ex. 17:2, 7 • Num. 21:6–9

9:18 NU omits *of Christ*
9:20 NU adds *though not being myself under the law*
9:21 NU *God's law* **9:21** NU *Christ's law*
9:22 NU omits *as*

10 nor murmur, as [R]some of them also murmured, and [R]were destroyed by [R]the destroyer. Ex. 16:2 • Num. 14:37 • Ex. 12:23
11 Now *all these things happened to them
as examples, and [R]they were written for our
[T]admonition, [R]on whom the ends of the ages
have come. Rom. 15:4 • *instruction* • Phil. 4:5
12 Therefore [R]let him who thinks he stands
take heed lest he fall. Rom. 11:20
13 No temptation has overtaken you except
such as is common to man; but God *is* faithful, who will not allow you to be tempted
beyond what you are able, but with the
temptation will also make the way of escape,
that you may be able to bear *it*.

Exhortation to Use Liberty to Glorify God

14 Therefore, my beloved, [R]flee from idolatry. 2 Cor. 6:17
15 I speak as to [R]wise men; judge for yourselves what I say. 1 Cor. 8:1
16 The cup of blessing which we bless, is it
not the [T]communion of the blood of Christ?
The bread which we break, is it not the
communion of the body of Christ? *sharing*
17 For [R]we, *being* many, are one bread *and*
one body; for we all partake of that one
bread. 1 Cor. 12:12, 27
18 Observe Israel after the flesh: [R]Are not
those who eat of the sacrifices [T]partakers of
the altar? Lev. 3:3; 7:6, 14 • *fellowshippers* or *sharers*
19 What am I saying then? [R]That an idol is
anything, or what is offered to idols is anything? 1 Cor. 8:4
20 But *I* say that the things which the
Gentiles sacrifice [R]they sacrifice to demons
and not to God, and I do not want you to
have fellowship with demons. Deut. 32:17
21 [R]You cannot drink the cup of the Lord
and [R]the cup of demons; you cannot partake
of the [R]Lord's table and of the table of demons. 2 Cor. 6:15, 16 • Deut. 32:38 • [1 Cor. 11:23–29]
22 Or do we provoke the Lord to jealousy?
[R]Are we stronger than He? Ezek. 22:14
23 All things are lawful *for me, but all
things are not helpful; all things are lawful
for me, but all things do not edify.
24 Let no one seek his own, but each one
[R]the other's *well-being*. Phil. 2:4
25 Eat whatever is sold in the meat market,
asking no questions for conscience' sake;
26 for [R]*"The earth is the* LORD*'s, and all its
fullness."* Ps. 24:1
27 If any of those who do not believe invites
you *to dinner*, and you desire to go, [R]eat
whatever is set before you, asking no question for conscience' sake. Luke 10:7, 8
28 But if anyone says to you, "This was
offered to idols," do not eat it [R]for the sake of
the one who told you, and for conscience'
sake; *for [R]*"The earth is the* LORD*'s, and all
its fullness."* [1 Cor. 8:7, 10, 12] • Ps. 24:1
29 Conscience, I say, not your own, but that
of the other. For [R]why is my liberty judged by
another *man's* conscience? Rom. 14:16
30 But if I partake with thanks, why am I
evil spoken of for *the food* [R]over which I give
thanks? Rom. 14:6
31 Therefore, whether you eat or drink, or
whatever you do, do all to the glory of God.
32 [R]Give no offense, either to the Jews or to
the Greeks or to the church of God, Rom. 14:13
33 just [R]as I also please all *men* in all *things*,
not seeking my own profit, but the *profit* of
many, that they may be saved. Rom. 15:2

CHAPTER 11

IMITATE me, just as I also *imitate* Christ.

Principles of Public Prayer

2 Now I praise you, brethren, that you
remember me in all things and keep the
traditions as I delivered *them* to you.
3 But I want you to know that the head of
every man is Christ, [R]the head of woman *is*
man, and the head of Christ *is* God. Gen. 3:16
4 Every man praying or prophesying, having *his* head covered, dishonors his head.
5 But every woman who prays or prophesies with *her* head uncovered dishonors her
head, for that is one and the same as if her
head were [R]shaved. Deut. 21:12
6 For if a woman is not covered, let her
also be shorn. But if it is [R]shameful for a
woman to be shorn or shaved, let her be
covered. Num. 5:18
7 For a man indeed ought not to cover *his*
head, since [R]he is the image and glory of God;
but woman is the glory of man. Gen. 1:26, 27
8 For man is not from woman, but woman
[R]from man. Gen. 2:21–23
9 Nor was man created for the woman, but
woman [R]for the man. Gen. 2:18
10 For this reason the woman ought to have
a symbol of authority on *her* head, because of
the angels.
11 Nevertheless, [R]neither *is* man independent of woman, nor woman independent of
man, in the Lord. [Gal. 3:28]
12 For as the woman *was* from the man,
even so the man also *is* through the woman;
but all things are from God.
13 Judge among yourselves. Is it proper for
a woman to pray to God with her head
uncovered?
14 Does not even nature itself teach you
that if a man has long hair, it is a dishonor to
him?
15 But if a woman has long hair, it is a glory
to her; for *her* hair is given *to her for a
covering.

10:11 NU omits *all* **10:23** NU omits *for me*
10:28 NU omits the rest of v. 28.
11:15 M omits *to her*

16 But [R]if anyone seems to be contentious,
we have no such custom, [R]nor *do* the
churches of God. 1 Tim. 6:4 • 1 Cor. 7:17

Rebuke of Disorders at the Lord's Supper

17 Now in giving these instructions I do not
praise *you*, since you come together not for
the better but for the worse.
18 For first of all, when you come together
as a church, I hear that there are divisions
among you, and in part I believe it.
19 For there must also be factions among
you, that those who are approved may be
[T]recognized among you. Lit. *evident, manifest*
20 Therefore when you come together in
one place, it is not to eat the Lord's Supper.
21 For in eating, each one takes his own
supper ahead of *others*; and one is hungry
and [R]another is drunk. Jude 12
22 What! Do you not have houses to eat
and drink in? Or do you despise the church of
God and [R]shame [T]those who have nothing?
What shall I say to you? Shall I praise you in
this? I do not praise *you*. James 2:6 • The poor
23 For [R]I received from the Lord that which
I also delivered to you: [R]that the Lord Jesus
on the *same* night in which He was betrayed
took bread; 1 Cor. 15:3 • Matt. 26:26–28
24 and when He had given thanks, He broke
it and said, *"Take, eat; this is My body
which is *broken for you; do this in remembrance of Me."
25 In the same manner *He* also *took* the cup
after supper, saying, "This cup is the new
covenant in My blood. This do, as often as
you drink *it*, in remembrance of Me."
26 For as often as you eat this bread and
drink this cup, you proclaim the Lord's death
[R]till He comes. John 14:3
27 Therefore whoever eats [R]this bread or
drinks *this* cup of the Lord in an unworthy
manner will be guilty of the body and *blood
of the Lord. [John 6:51]
28 But [R]let a man examine himself, and so
let him eat of *that* bread and drink of *that*
cup. 2 Cor. 13:5
29 For he who eats and drinks *in an unworthy manner eats and drinks judgment to
himself, not discerning the *Lord's body.
30 For this reason many *are* weak and sick
among you, and many [T]sleep. Are dead
31 For [R]if we would judge ourselves, we
would not be judged. [1 John 1:9]
32 But when we are judged, [R]we are chastened by the Lord, that we may not be condemned with the world. Ps. 94:12
33 Therefore, my brethren, when you come
together to eat, wait for one another.
34 But if anyone is hungry, let him eat at
home, lest you come together for judgment.
And the rest I will set in order when I come.

CHAPTER 12

Test of the Spirit's Control

NOW concerning spiritual *gifts*, brethren,
I do not want you to be ignorant:
2 You know [R]that* you were Gentiles,
carried away to these [R]dumb[T] idols, however
you were led. Eph. 2:11 • Ps. 115:5 • *mute, silent*
3 Therefore I make known to you that no
one speaking by the Spirit of God calls Jesus
[T]accursed, and no one can say that Jesus is
Lord except by the Holy Spirit. Gr. *anathema*

Diversity of the Gifts

4 Now there are [T]diversities of gifts, but
[R]the same Spirit. *allotments* or *various kinds* • Eph. 4:4
5 [R]There are differences of ministries, but
the same Lord. Rom. 12:6
6 And there are diversities of activities, but
it is the same God who works all in all.
7 But the manifestation of the Spirit is
given to each one for the profit *of all*:
8 for to one is given the word of wisdom
through the Spirit, to another [R]the word of
knowledge through the same Spirit, Rom. 15:14
9 to another faith by the same Spirit, to
another gifts of healings by *the same Spirit,
10 to another the working of miracles, to
another prophecy, to another discerning of
spirits, to another *different* kinds of tongues,
to another the interpretation of tongues.

11 But one and the same Spirit works all
these things, [R]distributing to each one individually [R]as He wills. Rom. 12:6 • [John 3:8]

Importance of All Gifts

12 For [R]as the body is one and has many
members, but all the members of that one

11:24 NU omits *Take, eat* **11:24** NU omits *broken*
11:27 NU, M *the blood*
11:29 NU omits *in an unworthy manner*
11:29 NU omits *Lord's* **12:2** NU, M *that when*
12:9 NU *one*

12:1–10 Using Spiritual Gifts—Spiritual gifts are discussed in detail in four passages of the New Testament: Romans 12:3–8; First Corinthians 12:1–10, 28–31; Ephesians 4:11, 12; and First Peter 4:10, 11. These lists are to be regarded as representative of spiritual gifts. Spiritual gifts are those gifts given by the Spirit of God for the accomplishment of God's purpose in the world and for the edification of the church, the body of Christ. Two things are important to remember concerning spiritual gifts: (1) every believer has been given spiritual gifts (Page 1337—Rom. 12:5, 6; 1 Cor. 12:7; Page 1483—1 Pet. 4:10); and (2) the gifts belong to God and are given for the believer to use for the glory of God (Page 1483—1 Pet. 4:11).

Now turn to Page 1382—Gal. 5:13: Serving.

body, being many, are one body, [R]so also *is*
Christ. Rom. 12:4, 5 • [Gal. 3:16]
13 For [R]by one Spirit we were all baptized
into one body—whether Jews or Greeks,
whether slaves or free—and have all been
made to drink *into one Spirit. [Rom. 6:5]
14 For in fact the body is not one member
but many.
15 If the foot should say, "Because I am not
a hand, I am not of the body," is it therefore
not of the body?
16 And if the ear should say, "Because I am
not an eye, I am not of the body," is it
therefore not of the body?
17 If the whole body *were* an eye, where
would be the hearing? If the whole *were*
hearing, where *would be* the smelling?
18 But now God has set the members, each
one of them, in the body just as He pleased.
19 And if they *were* all one member, where
would the body *be?*
20 But now indeed *there are* many members, yet one body.
21 And the eye cannot say to the hand, "I
have no need of you"; nor again the head to
the feet, "I have no need of you."
22 No, much rather, those members of the
body which seem to be weaker are necessary.
23 And those *members* of the body which
we think to be less honorable, on these we
bestow greater honor; and our unpresentable
parts have greater modesty,
24 but our presentable *parts* have no need.
But God composed the body, having given
greater honor to that *part* which lacks it,
25 that there should be no [T]schism in the
body, but *that* the members should have the
same care for one another. *division*
26 And if one member suffers, all the members suffer with *it;* or if one member is honored, all the members rejoice with *it*.
27 Now [R]you are the body of Christ, and
[R]members individually. Rom. 12:5 • Eph. 5:30
28 And God has appointed these in the
church: first [R]apostles, second [R]prophets,
third teachers, after that miracles, then gifts
of healings, helps, administrations, varieties
of tongues. [Eph. 2:20; 3:5] • Acts 13:1
29 *Are* all apostles? *Are* all prophets? *Are* all
teachers? *Are* all workers of miracles?
30 Do all have gifts of healings? Do all
speak with tongues? Do all interpret?
31 But earnestly desire the *best gifts. And
yet I show you a more excellent way.

CHAPTER 13

Exercise Gifts with Love

THOUGH I speak with the tongues of men
and of angels, but have not love, I have
become *as* sounding brass or a clanging
cymbal.
2 And though I have *the gift of* [R]prophecy,
and understand all mysteries and all knowledge, and though I have all faith, [R]so that I
could remove mountains, but have not love,
I am nothing. 1 Cor. 12:8–10, 28; 14:1 • Matt. 17:20
3 And [R]though I bestow all my goods to
feed *the poor*, and though I give my body *to
be burned, but have not love, it profits me
nothing. Matt. 6:1, 2
4 Love suffers long *and* is [R]kind; love [R]does
not envy; love does not parade itself, is not
[T]puffed up; Eph. 4:32 • Gal. 5:26 • *arrogant*
5 does not behave rudely, does not seek its
own, is not provoked, thinks no evil;
6 [R]does not rejoice in iniquity, but [R]rejoices
in the truth; Rom. 1:32 • 2 John 4
7 [R]bears all things, believes all things,
hopes all things, endures all things. Gal. 6:2
8 Love never fails. But whether *there are*
prophecies, they will fail; whether *there
are* tongues, they will cease; whether *there
is* knowledge, it will vanish away.
9 [R]For we know in part and we prophesy in
part. 1 Cor. 8:2; 13:12
10 But when that which is [T]perfect has
come, then that which is in part will be done
away. *complete*
11 When I was a child, I spoke as a child, I
understood as a child, I thought as a child;
but when I became a man, I put away childish things.
12 For now we see in a mirror, dimly, but
then face to face. Now I know in part, but
then I shall know just as I also am known.
13 And now abide faith, hope, love, these
three; but the greatest of these *is* love.

CHAPTER 14

Superiority of Prophecy

PURSUE love, and desire spiritual *gifts*, but
especially that you may prophesy.
2 For he who [R]speaks in a tongue does not
speak to men but to God, for no one understands *him*; however, in the spirit he speaks
mysteries. Acts 2:4; 10:46
3 But he who prophesies speaks edification
and exhortation and comfort to men.
4 He who speaks in a tongue edifies himself, but he who prophesies edifies the
church.
5 I wish you all spoke with tongues, but
even more that you prophesied; *for he who
prophesies *is* greater than he who speaks
with tongues, unless indeed he interprets,
that the church may receive edification.
6 But now, brethren, if I come to you
speaking with tongues, what shall I profit

12:13 NU omits *into* **12:31** NU *greater*
13:3 NU *so I may boast* **14:5** NU *and*

LOVE

What is love? The early Christians faced a problem similar to the one we face today in that the surrounding society was so corrupt that "love" often equaled sheer lust.

Fortunately, the language in which the New Testament was originally penned has four "L-words" to express various aspects of love. They are presented here in ascending order of Christian usage:

Physical Love (*erōs*)

The very common Greek family of words from which English derives *erotic* is not even used in the New Testament due to its bad connotations in pagan society. Forms of the word do occur in the Greek translation of the Old Testament, the Septuagint (LXX), but chiefly for "paramours" or "lovers." However, there is a valid place in Christian thinking for this love of physical attraction when it is between married couples (cf. Song of Solomon).

Family Love (*storgē*)

The Judeo-Christian tradition has always been strongly family-oriented. Today, as the Christian family is under constant attack by secular and humanistic forces, the fondness people share for their relatives, especially love between parents and children, is very crucial. Paul uses the negative form of the word in Romans 1:31 and 2 Timothy 3:3.

Another interesting form of *storgē* in the New Testament combines the "love-root" of this word with the next one we discuss. It forms the word *philostorgos*. Paul uses it to command us to be "kindly affectionate to one another" (Rom. 12:10).

Affectionate Love (*philia*)

Americans, especially Easterners, know this Greek root from the name of a great Pennsylvania city, Philadelphia, "the city of brotherly love." This city's name (from Rev. 3) speaks of warmhearted, spontaneous affection, liking, attractive appeal, and friendship.

Fortunately for us, God never commands us to have this kind of love for everyone, because our reactions to different types of people are often beyond our control. However, if we do obey the commands to choose to love (see below) we often end up liking and becoming fond of people who originally "turned us off."

God the Father loves the Son in both this affectionate way—He pleases Him so well (John 5:20)—and in the love of choice (John 3:35, see below).

Love of Choice (*agapē*)

Many Christians have heard of this Greek word. *Agapē* was practically "born within the bosom of revealed religion" (R.C. Trench), although it did occur a few times before Christians took it over and poured into it all the wonderful meanings of revelation.

Just because it is so popular a word, *agapē* has also been misunderstood by many. Commonly *agapē* is called "divine" love. This is misleading because it is used for love from man to God and from God to man. It is also used for love between people. It is divine in the sense that it is the love that God commands, the love of choice. Even if someone does not "appeal" to us we can still show *agapē* to that person—accept him, treat him right, and do all we can to help build up that person in the faith (if a believer) or to win him to the faith (if not).

The word *agapē* is used in 1 Corinthians 13. The King James translators, partly because the Latin Vulgate had *charitas* there, and partly, no doubt, in an effort to lift the concept above the carnal connotations of love in seventeenth-century England, chose "charity" to represent it. Unfortunately that word now has a restricted meaning that is most unsuitable for Christian love of the highest order. When we are told to love our neighbors as ourselves, the verb form of *agapē* is employed. John 13—17, the intimately Christian "Upper Room Discourse," is full of both *agapē* and *philia*.

In John 3:16, the verb "loved" expresses this concept of *agapē*. God (even in our sin) decided to love us, because it is His nature to love. In fact, while it is wrong to turn the verse around (as some do) and teach that "love is God," it is quite true that "God is love" (1 John 4:8).

you unless I speak to you either by [R]revelation, by knowledge, by prophesying, or by teaching? 1 Cor. 14:26

Gift of Tongues

7 Even things without life, whether flute or harp, when they make a sound, unless they make a distinction in the sounds, how will it be known what is piped or played?

8 For if the trumpet makes an uncertain sound, who will prepare himself for battle?

9 So likewise you, unless you utter by the tongue words easy to understand, how will it be known what is spoken? For you will be speaking into the air.

10 There are, it may be, so many kinds of languages in the world, and none of them *is* without [T]significance. *meaning*

11 Therefore, if I do not know the meaning of the language, I shall be a [T]foreigner to him who speaks, and he who speaks *will be* a foreigner to me. Lit. *barbarian*

12 Even so you, since you are zealous for spiritual *gifts*, *let it be* for the edification of the church *that* you seek to excel.

13 Therefore let him who speaks in a tongue pray that he may [R]interpret. 1 Cor. 12:10

14 For if I pray in a tongue, my spirit prays, but my understanding is unfruitful.

15 What is *the result* then? I will pray with the spirit, and I will also pray with the understanding. I will sing with the spirit, and I will also sing with the understanding.

16 Otherwise, if you bless with the spirit, how will he who occupies the place of the uninformed say "Amen" [R]at your giving of thanks, since he does not understand what you say? 1 Cor. 11:24

17 For you indeed give thanks well, but the other is not edified.

18 I thank my God I speak with tongues more than you all;

19 yet in the church I would rather speak five words with my understanding, that I may teach others also, than ten thousand words in a tongue.

20 Brethren, [R]do not be children in understanding; however, in malice [R]be babes, but in understanding be mature. Ps. 131:2 • [1 Pet. 2:2]

21 [R]In the law it is [R]written:

"With men of other tongues and other
lips
I will speak to this people;
And yet, for all that, they will not hear
Me," John 10:34 • Is. 28:11, 12

says the Lord.

22 Therefore tongues are for a [R]sign, not to those who believe but to unbelievers; but prophesying is not for unbelievers but for those who believe. Mark 16:17

23 Therefore if the whole church comes together in one place, and all speak with tongues, and there come in *those who are* uninformed or unbelievers, [R]will they not say that you are [T]out of your mind? Acts 2:13 • *insane*

24 But if all prophesy, and an unbeliever or an uninformed person comes in, he is convinced by all, he is judged by all.

25 *And thus the secrets of his heart are revealed; and so, falling down on *his* face, he will worship God and report [R]that God is truly among you. Is. 45:14

Exercising Gifts in Public Worship

26 How is it then, brethren? Whenever you come together, each of you has a psalm, has a teaching, has a tongue, has a revelation, has an interpretation. [R]Let all things be done for [T]edification. [2 Cor. 12:19] • *building up*

27 If anyone speaks in a tongue, *let there be* two or at the most three, *each* in turn, and let one interpret.

28 But if there is no interpreter, let him keep silent in church, and let him speak to himself and to God.

29 Let two or three prophets speak, and [R]let the others judge. 1 Cor. 12:10

30 But if *anything* is revealed to another who sits by, let the first keep silent.

31 For you can all prophesy one by one, that all may learn and all may be encouraged.

32 And [R]the spirits of the prophets are subject to the prophets. 1 John 4:1

33 For God is not *the author* of [T]confusion but of peace, [R]as in all the churches of the saints. *disorder* • 1 Cor. 11:16

34 [R]Let *your women keep silent in the churches, for they are not permitted to speak; but *they are* to be submissive, as the [R]law also says. 1 Tim. 2:11 • Gen. 3:16

35 And if they want to learn something, let them ask their own husbands at home; for it is shameful for women to speak in church.

36 Or did the word of God come *originally* from you? Or *was it* you only that it reached?

37 [R]If anyone thinks himself to be a prophet or spiritual, let him acknowledge that the things which I write to you are the commandments of the Lord. 2 Cor. 10:7

38 But *if anyone is ignorant, let him be ignorant.

39 Therefore, brethren, [R]desire earnestly to prophesy, and do not forbid to speak with tongues. 1 Cor. 12:31

40 [R]Let all things be done decently and in order. 1 Cor. 14:33

14:25 NU omits *And thus* **14:34** NU omits *your*
14:38 NU *If anyone does not recognize this, he is not recognized*

CHAPTER 15

Fact of Christ's Resurrection

MOREOVER, brethren, I declare to you the gospel [R]which I preached to you, which also you received and [R]in which you stand, [Gal. 1:11] • [Rom. 5:2; 11:20]

2 [R]by which also you are saved, if you hold fast that word which I preached to you—unless [R]you believed in vain. Rom. 1:16 • Gal. 3:4

3 For I delivered to you first of all that which I also received: that Christ died for our sins according to the Scriptures,

4 and that He was buried, and that He rose again the third day [R]according to the Scriptures, Ps. 16:10, 11; Is. 53:10; Luke 24:26; Acts 2:25 ★

5 [R]and that He was seen by [T]Cephas, then [R]by the twelve. Luke 24:34 • Peter • Matt. 28:17

6 After that He was seen by over five hundred brethren at once, of whom the greater part remain to the present, but some have [T]fallen asleep. Died

7 After that He was seen by James, then [R]by all the apostles. Acts 1:3, 4

8 [R]Then last of all He was seen by me also, as by one born out of due time. Acts 9:3–8

9 For I am the least of the apostles, who am not worthy to be called an apostle, because I persecuted the church of God.

10 But by the grace of God I am what I am, and His grace toward me was not in vain; but I labored more abundantly than they all, yet not I, but the grace of God *which was* with me.

11 Therefore, whether *it was* I or they, so we preach and so you believed.

Importance of Christ's Resurrection

12 Now if Christ is preached that He has been raised from the dead, how do some among you say that there is no resurrection of the dead?

13 But if there is no resurrection of the dead, [R]then Christ is not risen. [1 Thess. 4:14]

14 And if Christ is not risen, then our preaching *is* vain and your faith *is* also vain.

15 Yes, and we are found false witnesses of God, because [R]we have testified of God that He raised up Christ, whom He did not raise up—if in fact the dead do not rise. Acts 2:24

16 For if *the* dead do not rise, then Christ is not risen.

17 And if Christ is not risen, your faith *is* futile; [R]you are still in your sins! [Rom. 4:25]

18 Then also those who have [T]fallen [R]asleep in Christ have perished. Died • Job 14:12

19 If in this life only we have hope in Christ, we are of all men the most pitiable.

Order of the Resurrections

20 But now [R]Christ is risen from the dead, *and* has become [R]the firstfruits of those who have [T]fallen asleep. 1 Pet. 1:3 • Acts 26:23 • Died

21 For since by man *came* death, by Man also *came* the resurrection of the dead.

22 For as in Adam all die, even so in Christ all shall [R]be made alive. [John 5:28, 29]

23 But [R]each one in his own order: Christ the firstfruits, afterward those *who are* Christ's at His coming. [1 Thess. 4:15–17]

24 Then *comes* the end, when He delivers [R]the kingdom to God the Father, when He puts an end to all rule and all authority and power. [Dan. 2:44; 7:14, 27] ☆

25 For He must reign [R]till He has put all enemies under His feet. Ps. 110:1; Acts 2:34, 35 ☆

26 [R]The last enemy *that* will be destroyed *is* death. [2 Tim. 1:10; Rev. 20:14] ☆

27 For *"He* [R]*has put all things under His feet."* But when He says "all things are put under *Him," it is* evident that He who put all things under Him is excepted. Ps. 8:6 ☆

28 [R]Now when all things are made subject to Him, then the Son Himself will also be subject to Him who put all things under Him, that God may be all in all. [Phil. 3:21] ☆

Moral Implications of Christ's Resurrection

29 Otherwise, what will they do who are baptized for the dead, if the dead do not rise

---

15:3, 4 Sharing Our Faith: What?—Before discussing just what is to be shared concerning our faith, let us mention a few things we are not to do. We are not commanded to force Christian standards upon the unbelieving world (Page 1349—1 Cor. 5:12). We are not to confuse people by allowing them to believe that church membership, tithing, or any good works are somehow connected with becoming a Christian (Page 1387—Eph. 2:8–10).

Actually, we have but one thing to share with the unsaved, and that is the gospel of Christ. According to Paul it involves the death and resurrection of Christ (1 Cor. 15:1–4). A plan for sharing your faith might be as follows:

a. God's Word says all are sinners, condemned to hell (Page 825—Is. 53:6; Page 1325—Rom. 3:10, 11, 23; 5:8, 12; Page 1538—Rev. 20:15).

b. There is nothing a lost person can do on his own to save himself (Page 836—Is. 64:6; Page 1387—Eph. 2:9).

c. Christ was born, crucified, and resurrected to save lost people from their sin (Page 1239—John 3:16; Page 1426—1 Tim. 1:15).

d. To be saved a sinner must believe God's Word and invite Christ into his heart by faith (Page 1243—John 5:24; Page 1295—Acts 16:31).

Now turn to Page 1413—1 Thess. 1:5: Sharing Our Faith: How?

at all? Why then are they baptized for the
dead?
30 And [R]why do we stand in [T]jeopardy every
hour? 2 Cor. 11:26 • *danger*
31 I affirm, by the boasting in you which I
have in Christ Jesus our Lord, I die daily.
32 If, in the manner of men, [R]I have fought
with beasts at Ephesus, what advantage *is it*
to me? If *the* dead do not rise, *"Let us eat and*
drink, for tomorrow we die." 2 Cor. 1:8
33 Do not be deceived: [R]"Evil company
corrupts good habits." [1 Cor. 5:6]
34 Awake to righteousness, and do not sin;
[R]for some do not have the knowledge of God.
I speak *this* to your shame. [1 Thess. 4:5]

Bodies of the Resurrected Dead

35 But someone will say, [R]"How are the
dead raised up? And with what body do they
come?" Ezek. 37:3
36 Foolish one, [R]what you sow is not made
alive unless it dies. John 12:24
37 And what you sow, you do not sow that
body that shall be, but mere grain—perhaps
wheat or some other *grain.*
38 But God gives it a body as He pleases,
and to each seed its own body.
39 All flesh *is* not the same flesh, but *there*
is one *kind* *of flesh of men, another flesh of
beasts, another of fish, *and* another of birds.
40 *There are* also [T]celestial bodies and [T]ter-
restrial bodies; but the glory of the celestial *is*
one, and the *glory* of the terrestrial *is* another. *heavenly* • *earthly*
41 *There is* one glory of the sun, another
glory of the moon, and another glory of the
stars; for *one* star differs from *another* star in
glory.
42 [R]So also *is* the resurrection of the dead.
The body is sown in corruption, it is raised in
incorruption. [Dan. 12:3]
43 [R]It is sown in dishonor, it is raised in
glory. It is sown in weakness, it is raised in
power. [Phil. 3:21]
44 It is sown a natural body, it is raised a
spiritual body. There is a natural body, and
there is a spiritual body.
45 And so it is written, *"The first man Adam*
[R]*became a living being."* [R]The last Adam
became a life-giving spirit. Gen. 2:7 • [Rom. 5:14]
46 However, the spiritual is not first, but the
natural, and afterward the spiritual.
47 [R]The first man *was* of the earth, [R]*made*[T]
of dust; the second Man *is* *the Lord [R]from
heaven. John 3:31 • Gen. 2:7; 3:19 • *earthy* • John 3:13
48 As *was* the [T]*man* of dust, so also *are*
those *who are* [T]*made* of dust; [R]and as *is* the
heavenly *Man,* so also *are* those *who are*
heavenly. *earthy* • Phil. 3:20
49 And [R]as we have borne the image of the
man of dust, [R]we* shall also bear the image of
the heavenly *Man.* Gen. 5:3 • Rom. 8:29
50 Now this I say, brethren, that flesh and
blood cannot inherit the kingdom of God; nor
does corruption inherit incorruption.

Bodies of the Translated Living

51 Behold, I tell you a mystery: We shall not
all sleep, but we shall all be changed—
52 in a moment, in the twinkling of an eye,
at the last trumpet. [R]For the trumpet will
sound, and the dead will be raised incorruptible, and we shall be changed. Matt. 24:31
53 For this corruptible must put on incorruption, and [R]this mortal *must* put on immortality. 2 Cor. 5:4
54 So when this corruptible has put on
incorruption, and this mortal has put on
immortality, then shall be brought to pass the
saying that is written: [R]*"Death is swallowed*
up in victory." Is. 25:8

55 *"O** [R]*Death, where is your sting?* Hos. 13:14
O Hades, where is your victory?"

56 The sting of death *is* sin, and [R]the
strength of sin *is* the law. [Rom. 3:20; 4:15; 7:8]
57 But thanks *be* to God, who gives us the
victory through our Lord Jesus Christ.
58 Therefore, my beloved brethren, be
steadfast, immovable, always abounding in
the work of the Lord, knowing [R]that your
labor is not in vain in the Lord. [1 Cor. 3:8]

CHAPTER 16

Counsel Concerning the Collection
for Jerusalem

NOW concerning the collection for the
saints, as I have given orders to the
churches of Galatia, so you must do also:
2 [R]On the first *day* of the week let each one
of you lay something aside, storing up as he
may prosper, that there be no collections
when I come. Acts 20:7
3 And when I come, [R]whomever you approve by *your* letters I will send to bear your
gift to Jerusalem. 2 Cor. 3:1; 8:18
4 [R]But if it is fitting that I go also, they will
go with me. 2 Cor. 8:4, 19

Conclusion

5 Now I will come to you [R]when I pass
through Macedonia (for I am passing
through Macedonia). 2 Cor. 1:15, 16
6 But it may be that I will remain, or even
spend the winter with you, that you may
send me on my journey, wherever I go.

15:39 NU, M omit *of flesh* **15:47** NU omits *the Lord*
15:49 NU *let us also bear*
15:55 NU *O Death, where is your victory? O Death,*
where is your sting?

7 For I do not wish to see you now on the
way; but I hope to stay a while with you, [R]if
the Lord permits. James 4:15
8 But I will tarry in Ephesus until [R]Pente-
cost. Lev. 23:15–22
9 For [R]a great and effective door has
opened to me, and [R]*there are* many adversaries. Acts 14:27 • Acts 19:9
10 Now [R]if Timothy comes, see that he may
be with you without fear; for he does the
work of the Lord, as I also *do*. Acts 19:22
11 [R]Therefore let no one despise him. But
send him on his journey [R]in peace, that he
may come to me; for I am waiting for him
with the brethren. 1 Tim. 4:12 • Acts 15:33
12 Now concerning *our* brother [R]Apollos, I
strongly urged him to come to you with the
brethren, but he was quite unwilling to come
at this time; however, he will come when he
has a convenient time. 1 Cor. 1:12; 3:5
13 [R]Watch, [R]stand fast in the faith, be brave,
[R]be strong. Matt. 24:42 • Phil. 1:27; 4:1 • [Eph. 3:16; 6:10]
14 Let all *that* you *do* be done with love.
15 I urge you, brethren—you know the
household of Stephanas, that it is the firstfruits of Achaia, and *that* they have devoted
themselves to the ministry of the saints—
16 that you also submit to such, and to
everyone who works and labors with *us*.
17 I am glad about the coming of Stephanas, Fortunatus, and Achaicus, for what was
lacking on your part they supplied.
18 [R]For they refreshed my spirit and yours;
therefore acknowledge such men. Col. 4:8
19 The churches of Asia greet you. Aquila
and Priscilla greet you heartily in the Lord,
with the church that is in their house.
20 All the brethren greet you. [R]Greet one
another with a holy kiss. Rom. 16:16
21 [R]The salutation with my own hand—
Paul. Col. 4:18
22 If anyone does not love the Lord Jesus
Christ, let him be accursed. O Lord, come!
23 [R]The grace of our Lord Jesus Christ *be*
with you. Rom. 16:20
24 My love *be* with you all in Christ Jesus.
Amen.

THE SECOND EPISTLE OF PAUL THE APOSTLE TO THE

CORINTHIANS

THE BOOK OF SECOND CORINTHIANS

Since Paul's first letter, the Corinthian church had been swayed by false teachers who stirred the people against Paul. They claimed he was fickle, proud, unimpressive in appearance and speech, dishonest, and unqualified as an apostle of Jesus Christ. Paul sent Titus to Corinth to deal with these difficulties, and upon his return, rejoiced to hear of the Corinthians' change of heart. Paul wrote this letter to express his thanksgiving for the repentant majority and to appeal to the rebellious minority to accept his authority. Throughout the book he defends his conduct, character, and calling as an apostle of Jesus Christ.

To distinguish this epistle from First Corinthians, it was given the title *Pros Korinthious B*, the "Second to the Corinthians." The *A* and *B* were probably later additions to *Pros Korinthious.*

THE AUTHOR OF SECOND CORINTHIANS

External and internal evidence amply support the Pauline authorship of this letter. As with Romans, the problem of Second Corinthians is with its lack of unity, not with its authorship. Many critics theorize that chapters 10—13 were not a part of this letter in its original form because their tone contrasts with that of chapters 1—9. It is held that the sudden change from a spirit of joy and comfort to a spirit of concern and self-defense points to a "seam" between two different letters. Many hypotheses have been advanced to explain the problem, but the most popular is that chapters 10—13 belong to a lost letter referred to in 2:4. Several problems arise with these attempts to dissect Second Corinthians. Chapters 10—13 do not fit Paul's description of the "lost" letter of 2:4 because they are firm but not sorrowful and because they do not refer to the offender about whom that letter was written (2:5–11). Also, this earlier material would have been appended at the beginning of Second Corinthians, not at the end. There is simply no external (manuscripts, church fathers, tradition) or internal basis for challenging the unity of this epistle. The difference in tone between 1—9 and 10—13 is easily explained by the change of focus from the repentant majority to the rebellious minority.

THE TIME OF SECOND CORINTHIANS

Part of the background of Second Corinthians can be found in "The Time of First Corinthians." Paul was in Ephesus when he wrote First Corinthians and expected Timothy to visit Corinth and return to him (1 Cor. 16:10–11). Timothy apparently brought Paul a report of the opposition that had developed against him in Corinth, and Paul made a brief and painful visit to the Corinthians (this visit is not mentioned in Acts, but it can be inferred from 2 Cor. 2:1; 12:14; 13:1, 2). Upon returning to Ephesus, Paul regretfully wrote his sorrowful letter to urge the church to discipline the leader of the opposition (2:1–11; 7:8). Titus carried this letter. Paul, anxious to learn the results, went to Troas and then to Macedonia to meet Titus on his return trip (2:12, 13; 7:5–16). Paul was greatly relieved by Titus's report that the majority of the Corinthians had repented of their rebelliousness against Paul's apostolic authority. However, a minority opposition still persisted, evidently led by a group of Judaizers (10—13). There in Macedonia Paul wrote Second Corinthians and sent it with Titus and another brother (8:16–24). This took place late in A.D. 56, and the Macedonian city from which it was written may have been Philippi. Paul then made his third trip to Corinth (12:14; 13:1, 2; Acts 20:1–3) where he wrote his letter to the Romans.

There is an alternate view that the anguished letter of 2:4 and 7:8 is, in fact, First Corinthians and not a lost letter. This would require that the offender of Second Corinthians 2:5–11 and 7:12 be identified with the offender of First Corinthians 5.

THE CHRIST OF SECOND CORINTHIANS

Christ is presented as the believer's comfort (1:5), triumph (2:14), Lord (4:5), light (4:6), judge (5:10), reconciliation (5:19), substitute (5:21), gift (9:15), owner (10:7), and power (12:9).

KEYS TO SECOND CORINTHIANS

Key Word: Paul's Defense of His Ministry—The major theme of Second Corinthians is Paul's defense of his apostolic credentials and authority. This is especially evident in the portion directed to the still rebellious minority (10—13), but the theme of vindication is also clear in chapters 1—9. Certain false apostles had mounted an effective campaign against Paul in the church at Corinth, and Paul was forced to take a number of steps to overcome the opposition. This epistle expresses the apostle's joy over the triumph of the true gospel in Corinth (1—7), and it acknowledges the godly sorrow and repentance of the bulk of the believers. It also urges the Corinthians to fulfill their promise of making a liberal contribution for the poor among the Christians in Judea (8 and 9). This collection would not only assist the poor, but it would also demonstrate the concern of gentile Christians in Macedonia and Achaia for Jewish Christians in Judea, thus displaying the unity of Jews and Gentiles in the body of Christ.

The opposition addressed in chapters 10—13 apparently consists of Jews (Palestinean or Hellenistic; 11:22) who claim to be apostles (11:5, 13; 12:11) but who preach a false gospel (11:4) and are enslaving in their leadership (11:20). Chapters 10—13 are intended to expose these "false apostles" (11:13), and defend Paul's God-given authority and ministry as an apostle of Jesus Christ.

Key Verses: Second Corinthians 4:5, 6 and 5:17-19—"For we do not preach ourselves, but Christ Jesus the Lord, and ourselves your servants for Jesus' sake. For it is the God who commanded light to shine out of darkness who has shone in our hearts to *give* the light of the knowledge of the glory of God in the face of Jesus Christ" (4:5, 6).

"Therefore, if anyone *is* in Christ, *he is* a new creation; old things have passed away; behold, all things have become new. Now all things *are* of God, who has reconciled us to Himself through Jesus Christ, and has given us the ministry of reconciliation, that is, that God was in Christ reconciling the world to Himself, not imputing their trespasses to them, and has committed to us the word of reconciliation" (5:17-19).

Key Chapters: Second Corinthians 8 and 9—Chapters 8 and 9 are really one unit and comprise the most complete revelation of God's plan for giving found anywhere in the Scriptures. Contained therein are the principles for giving (8:1-6), the purposes for giving (8:7-15), the policies to be followed in giving (8:16—9:5), and the promises to be realized in giving (9:6-15).

SURVEY OF SECOND CORINTHIANS

Second Corinthians describes the anatomy of an apostle. The Corinthian church has been swayed by false teachers who have stirred the people against Paul, especially in response to First Corinthians, Paul's disciplinary letter. Throughout this letter (Second Corinthians) Paul defends his apostolic conduct, character, and call. The three major sections are: Paul's explanation of his ministry (1—7); Paul's collection for the saints (8 and 9); and Paul's vindication of his apostleship (10—13).

Paul's Explanation of His Ministry (1—7): After his salutation and thanksgiving for God's comfort in his afflictions and perils (1:1-11), Paul explains why he has delayed his planned visit to Corinth. It is not a matter of vacillation: the apostle wants them to have enough time to repent (1:12—2:4). Paul graciously asks them to restore the repentant offender to fellowship (2:5-13). At this point, Paul embarks on an extended defense of his ministry in terms of his message, circumstances, motives, and conduct (2:14—6:10). He then admonishes the believers to separate themselves from defilement (6:11—7:1), and expresses his comfort at Titus's news of their change of heart (7:2-16).

Paul's Collection for the Saints (8 and 9): This is the longest discussion of the principles and practice of giving in the New Testament. The example of the Macedonians' liberal giving for the needy brethren in Jerusalem (8:1-6) is followed by an appeal to the Corinthians to keep their promise by doing the same (8:7—9:15). In this connection, Paul commends the messengers he has sent to Corinth to make arrangements for the large gift they have promised. Their generosity will be more than amply rewarded by God.

Paul's Vindication of His Apostleship (10—13): Paul concludes this epistle with a defense of his apostolic authority and credentials that is

FOCUS	EXPLANATION OF PAUL'S MINISTRY			COLLECTION FOR THE SAINTS		VINDICATION OF PAUL'S APOSTLESHIP		
REFERENCE	1:1	2:14	6:11	8:1	8:7	10:1	11:1	12:14—13:14
DIVISION	HIS CHANGE OF PLANS	PHILOSOPHY OF MINISTRY	EXHORTATIONS TO THE CORINTHIANS	EXAMPLE OF THE MACEDONIANS	EXHORTATION TO THE CORINTHIANS	ANSWERS HIS ACCUSERS	DEFENDS HIS APOSTLESHIP	ANNOUNCES HIS UPCOMING VISIT
TOPIC	CHARACTER OF PAUL			COLLECTION FOR SAINTS		CREDENTIALS OF PAUL		
	EPHESUS TO MACEDONIA: CHANGE OF ITINERARY			MACEDONIA: PREPARATION FOR VISIT		TO CORINTH: IMMINENT VISIT		
LOCATION	WRITTEN IN MACEDONIA							
TIME	C. A.D. 56							

directed to the still rebellious minority in the Corinthian Church. His meekness in their presence in no way diminishes his authority as an apostle (10). To demonstrate his apostolic credentials, Paul is forced to boast about his knowledge, integrity, accomplishments, sufferings, visions, and miracles (11:1—12:13). He reveals his plans to visit them for the third time and urges them to repent so that he will not have to use severity when he comes (12:14—13:10). The letter ends with an exhortation, greetings, and a benediction (13:11-14).

OUTLINE OF SECOND CORINTHIANS

Part One: Paul's Explanation of His Ministry (1:1—7:16)

I. Introduction **1:1-11**
- A. Paul's Thanksgiving to God 1:1-7
- B. Paul's Trouble in Asia 1:8-11

II. Paul's Explanation of His Change of Plans .... **1:12—2:13**
- A. Paul's Original Plan 1:12-22
- B. Paul's Change of Plans .... 1:23—2:4
- C. Paul's Appeal to Forgive 2:5-13

III. Paul's Philosophy of Ministry .... **2:14—6:10**
- A. Christ Causes Us to Triumph 2:14-17
- B. Changed Lives Prove Ministry 3:1-5
- C. New Covenant Is the Basis of Ministry 3:6-18
- D. Christ Is the Theme of Ministry 4:1-7
- E. Trials Abound in the Ministry 4:8-15
- F. Motivation in the Ministry .... 4:16—5:21
  1. Motivation of External Perspective 4:16-18
  2. Motivation of the Future Presence of Christ 5:1-8
  3. Motivation of Future Reward 5:9, 10
  4. Motivation of the Love of Christ 5:11-16
  5. Motivation of the Message of Reconciliation 5:17-21
- G. Giving No Offense in the Ministry 6:1-10

IV. Paul's Exhortations to the Corinthians .... **6:11—7:16**
- A. Paul's Appeal for Reconciliation 6:11-13
- B. Paul's Appeal for Separation from Unbelievers .... 6:14—7:1
- C. Paul's Meeting with Titus 7:2-7
- D. Corinthians' Response to Paul's Letter 7:8-16

Part Two: Paul's Collection for the Saints (8:1—9:15)

I. Example of the Macedonians **8:1-6**

II. Exhortation to the Corinthians .... **8:7—9:15**
- A. Example of Christ 8:7-9
- B. Purpose of Giving 8:10-15
- C. Explanation of the Delegation .... 8:16—9:5
  1. Policies in Giving 8:16-24
  2. Readiness in Giving 9:1-5
- D. Exhortation to Giving 9:6-15
  1. Principles in Giving 9:6, 7
  2. Promises from Giving 9:8-15

Part Three: Paul's Vindication of His Apostleship (10:1—13:14)

I. Paul Answers His Accusers **10:1-18**
- A. The Charge of Cowardice Is Answered 10:1, 2
- B. The Charge of Walking in the Flesh Is Answered 10:3-9
- C. The Charge of Personal Weakness Is Answered 10:10-18

II. Paul Defends His Apostleship .... **11:1—12:13**
- A. Paul's Declaration of His Apostleship 11:1-15
- B. Paul's Sufferings Support His Apostleship 11:16-33
- C. Paul's Revelations Support His Apostleship 12:1-10
  1. Vision of Paradise 12:1-6
  2. Thorn in the Flesh 12:7-10
- D. Paul's Signs Support His Apostleship 12:11-13

III. Paul Announces His Upcoming Visit .... **12:14—13:10**
- A. Paul's Concern Not to Be a Financial Burden 12:14-18
- B. Paul's Concern Not to Find Them Carnal 12:19-21
- C. Paul's Warning to Examine Yourselves 13:1-10

IV. Conclusion **13:11-14**

CHAPTER 1

Paul's Thanksgiving to God

PAUL, [R]an apostle of Jesus Christ by the
will of God, and [R]Timothy *our* brother,
To the church of God which is at Corinth, [R]with all the saints who are in all
Achaia: 2 Tim. 1:1 • 1 Cor. 16:10 • Col. 1:2

2 [R]Grace to you and peace from God our
Father and the Lord Jesus Christ. Rom. 1:7

IMPORTANT CAPITAL CITIES

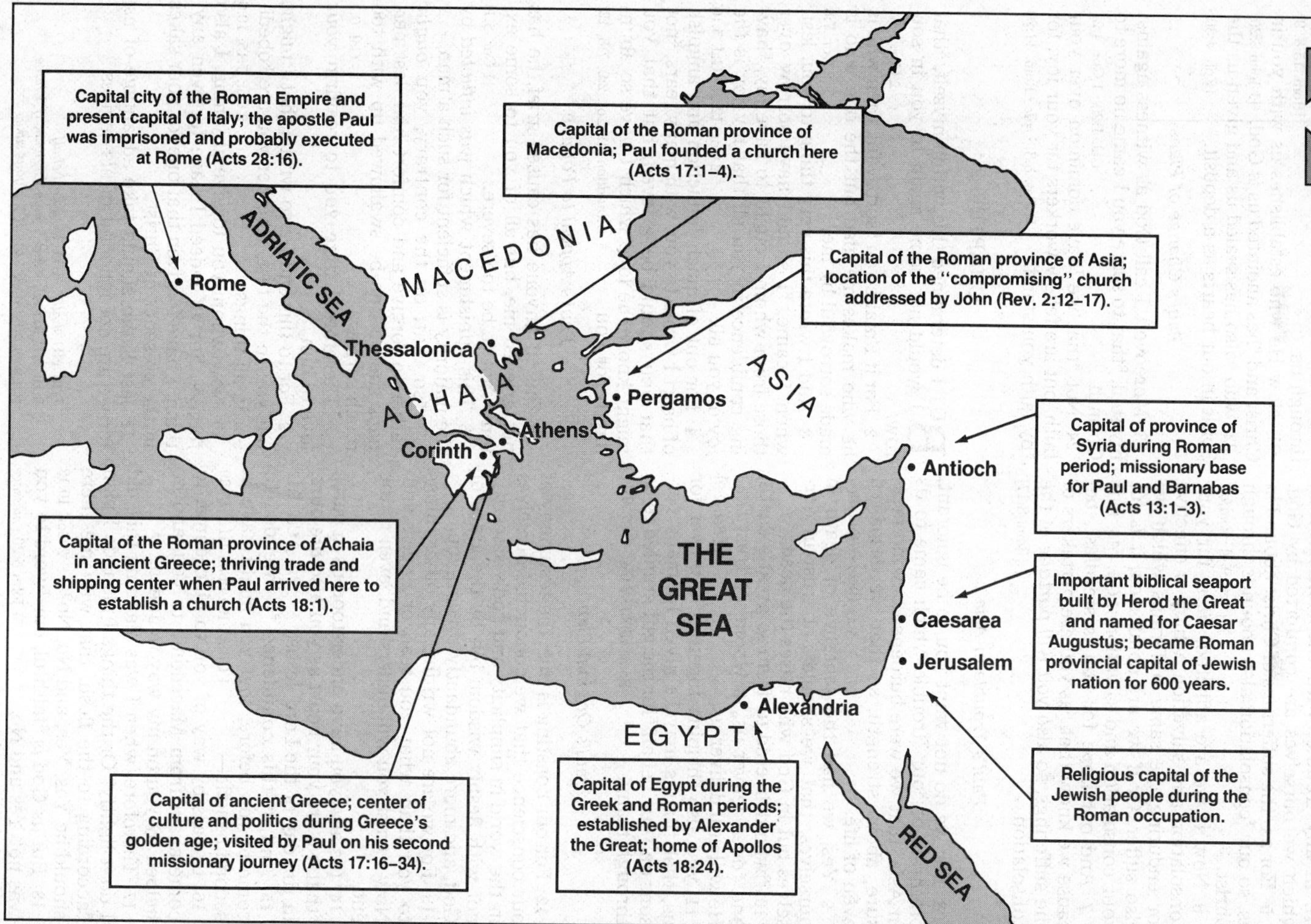

Capital city of the Roman Empire and present capital of Italy; the apostle Paul was imprisoned and probably executed at Rome (Acts 28:16).
Capital of the Roman province of Macedonia; Paul founded a church here (Acts 17:1–4).
Capital of the Roman province of Asia; location of the "compromising" church addressed by John (Rev. 2:12–17).
Rome
ADRIATIC SEA
MACEDONIA
Thessalonica
ACHAIA
ASIA
Pergamos
Athens
Corinth
Capital of province of Syria during Roman period; missionary base for Paul and Barnabas (Acts 13:1–3).
Antioch
Capital of the Roman province of Achaia in ancient Greece; thriving trade and shipping center when Paul arrived here to establish a church (Acts 18:1).
THE GREAT SEA
Important biblical seaport built by Herod the Great and named for Caesar Augustus; became Roman provincial capital of Jewish nation for 600 years.
Caesarea
Jerusalem
Alexandria
EGYPT
Capital of ancient Greece; center of culture and politics during Greece's golden age; visited by Paul on his second missionary journey (Acts 17:16–34).
Capital of Egypt during the Greek and Roman periods; established by Alexander the Great; home of Apollos (Acts 18:24).
Religious capital of the Jewish people during the Roman occupation.
RED SEA

3 [R]Blessed *be* the God and Father of our Lord Jesus Christ, the Father of mercies and God of all comfort, 1 Pet. 1:3

4 who comforts us in all our tribulation, that we may be able to comfort those who are in any trouble, with the comfort with which we ourselves are comforted by God.

5 For as [R]the sufferings of Christ abound in us, so our [T]consolation also abounds through Christ. [Acts 9:4] • *comfort*

6 Now if we are afflicted, [R]*it is* for your consolation and salvation, which is effective for enduring the same sufferings which we also suffer. Or if we are comforted, *it is* for your consolation and salvation. 2 Cor. 4:15; 12:15

7 And our hope for you *is* steadfast, because we know that [R]as you are partakers of the sufferings, so also *you will partake* of the consolation. [Rom. 8:17]

Paul's Trouble in Asia

8 For we do not want you to be ignorant, brethren, of [R]our [T]trouble which came to us in Asia: that we were burdened beyond measure, above strength, so that we despaired even of life. Acts 19:23 • *tribulation*

9 Yes, we had the sentence of death in ourselves, that we should not trust in ourselves but in God who raises the dead,

10 [R]who delivered us from so great a death, and *does deliver us; in whom we trust that He will still deliver *us,* [2 Pet. 2:9]

11 you also [R]helping together in prayer for us, that thanks may be given by many persons on *our behalf [R]for the gift *granted* to us through many. Rom. 15:30 • 2 Cor. 4:15; 9:11

Paul's Original Plan

12 For our boasting is this: the testimony of our conscience that we conducted ourselves in the world in simplicity and godly sincerity, not with fleshly wisdom but by the grace of God, and more abundantly toward you.

13 For we are not writing any other things to you than what you read or understand. Now I trust you will understand, even to the end

14 (as also you have understood us in part), [R]that we are your boast as you also *are* ours, in the day of the Lord Jesus. 2 Cor. 5:12

15 And in this confidence [R]I intended to come to you before, that you might have [R]a second benefit— 1 Cor. 4:19 • Rom. 1:11; 15:29

16 to pass by way of you to Macedonia, to come again from Macedonia to you, and be helped by you on my way to Judea.

17 Therefore, when I was planning this, did I do it lightly? Or the things I plan, do I plan [R]according to the flesh, that with me there should be Yes, Yes, and No, No? 2 Cor. 10:12

18 But *as* God *is* [R]faithful, our [T]word to you was not Yes and No. 1 John 5:20 • *message*

19 For [R]the Son of God, Jesus Christ, who was preached among you by us—by me, Silvanus, and Timothy—was not Yes and No, [R]but in Him was Yes. Mark 1:1 • [Heb. 13:8]

20 [R]For all the promises of God in Him *are* Yes, and in Him Amen, to the glory of God through us. [Rom. 15:8, 9]

21 Now He who establishes us with you in Christ and [R]has anointed us *is* God, [1 John 2:20]

22 who [R]also has sealed us and given us the Spirit in our hearts as a deposit. [Eph. 4:30]

Paul's Change of Plans

23 Moreover [R]I call God as witness against my soul, [R]that to spare you I came no more to Corinth. Gal. 1:20 • 1 Cor. 4:21

24 Not [R]that we [T]have dominion over your faith, but are fellow workers for your joy; for [R]by faith you stand. [1 Pet. 5:3] • *rule* • Rom. 11:20

CHAPTER 2

BUT I determined this within myself, [R]that I would not come again to you in sorrow. 2 Cor. 1:23

2 For if I make you [R]sorrowful, then who is he who makes me glad but the one who is made sorrowful by me? 2 Cor. 7:8

3 And I wrote this very thing to you, lest, when I came, [R]I should have sorrow over those from whom I ought to have joy, [R]having confidence in you all that my joy is *the joy* of you all. 2 Cor. 12:21 • Gal. 5:10

4 For out of much [T]affliction and anguish of heart I wrote to you, with many tears, [R]not that you should be grieved, but that you might know the love which I have so abundantly for you. *tribulation* • [2 Cor. 2:9; 7:8, 12]

Paul's Appeal to Forgive

5 But [R]if anyone has caused grief, he has not grieved me, but all of you to some extent—not to be too severe. [1 Cor. 5:1]

6 This punishment which *was inflicted* by the majority *is* sufficient for such a man,

7 [R]so that, on the contrary, you *ought* rather to forgive and comfort *him,* lest perhaps such a one be swallowed up with too much sorrow. Gal. 6:1

8 Therefore I urge you to reaffirm *your* love to him.

9 For to this end I also wrote, that I might put you to the test, whether you are [R]obedient in all things. 2 Cor. 7:15; 10:6

10 Now whom you forgive anything, I also *forgive.* For *if indeed I have forgiven anything, I have forgiven that one for your sakes in the presence of Christ,

11 lest Satan should take advantage of us; for we are not ignorant of his devices.

1:10 NU *shall* **1:11** M *your behalf*
2:10 NU *indeed, what I have forgiven, if I have forgiven anything, I did it for your sakes*

12 Furthermore, [R]when I came to Troas to
preach Christ's gospel, and a [T]door was
opened to me by the Lord, Acts 16:8 • Opportunity
13 I had no rest in my spirit, because I did
not find Titus my brother; but taking my
leave of them, I departed for Macedonia.

Christ Causes Us to Triumph

14 Now thanks *be* to God who always leads
us in triumph in Christ, and through us
[T]diffuses the fragrance of His knowledge in
every place. *manifests*
15 For we are to God the fragrance of
Christ among those who are being saved and
[R]among those who are perishing. [2 Cor. 4:3]
16 To the one *we are* the aroma of death to
death, and to the other the aroma of life to
life. And who *is* sufficient for these things?
17 For we are not, as *so many, [R]peddling[T]
the word of God; but as [R]of sincerity, but as
from God, we speak in the sight of God in
Christ. 2 Pet. 2:3 • *adulterating for gain* • 2 Cor. 1:12

CHAPTER 3

Changed Lives Prove Ministry

DO [R]we begin again to commend ourselves? Or do we need, as some *others*,
[R]epistles of commendation to you or *letters* of
commendation from you? 2 Cor. 5:12 • Acts 18:27
2 [R]You are our epistle written in our
hearts, known and read by all men; 1 Cor. 9:2
3 *you are* manifestly an epistle of Christ,
[R]ministered by us, written not with ink but by
the Spirit of the living God, not [R]on tablets of
stone but [R]on tablets of flesh, *that is*, of the
heart. 1 Cor. 3:5 • Ex. 24:12; 31:18; 32:15 • Ps. 40:8
4 And we have such trust through Christ
toward God.
5 [R]Not that we are sufficient of ourselves
to think of anything as *being* from ourselves,
but our sufficiency *is* from God, [John 15:5]

New Covenant Is the Basis of Ministry

6 who also made us sufficient as ministers
of the new covenant, not [R]of the letter but of
the [T]Spirit; for [R]the letter kills, [R]but the Spirit
gives life. Rom. 2:27 • Or *spirit* • Gal. 3:10 • John 6:63
7 But if [R]the ministry of death, [R]written
and engraved on stones, was glorious, [R]so
that the children of Israel could not look
steadily at the face of Moses because of the
glory of his countenance, which *glory* was
passing away, Rom. 7:10 • Ex. 34:1 • Ex. 34:29
8 how will [R]the ministry of the Spirit not
be more glorious? [Gal. 3:5]
9 For if the ministry of condemnation *had*
glory, the ministry [R]of righteousness exceeds
much more in glory. [Rom. 1:17; 3:21]
10 For even what was made glorious had no
glory in this respect, because of the glory that
excels.
11 For if what is passing away *was* glorious,
what remains *is* much more glorious.
12 Therefore, since we have such hope, [R]we
use great boldness of speech— Eph. 6:19
13 unlike Moses, [R]*who* put a veil over his
face so that the children of Israel could not
look steadily at [R]the end of what was passing
away. Ex. 34:33–35 • [Gal. 3:23]
14 [R]But their minds were hardened. For
until this day the same veil remains unlifted
in the reading of the Old Testament, because
the *veil* is taken away in Christ. Is. 29:10★
15 But even to this day, when Moses is read,
a veil lies on their heart.
16 Nevertheless [R]when one turns to the
Lord, [R]the veil is taken away. Rom. 11:23 • Is. 25:7
17 Now the Lord is the Spirit; and where the
Spirit of the Lord *is*, there *is* liberty.
18 But we all, with unveiled face, beholding
as in a mirror the glory of the Lord, [R]are
being transformed into the same image from
glory to glory, just as [T]by the Spirit of the
Lord. [Rom. 8:29, 30] • Or *from the Lord, the Spirit*

CHAPTER 4

Christ Is the Theme of Ministry

THEREFORE, since we have this ministry,
[R]as we have received mercy, we [R]do not
lose heart. 1 Cor. 7:25 • 2 Cor. 4:16
2 But we have renounced the hidden
things of shame, not walking in craftiness nor
[T]handling the word of God deceitfully, but by
manifestation of the truth [R]commending
ourselves to every man's conscience in the
sight of God. *adulterating the word of God* • 2 Cor. 5:11
3 But even if our gospel is veiled, [R]it is
veiled to those who are perishing, [1 Cor. 1:18]
4 whose minds the god of this age has
blinded, who do not believe, lest the light of
the gospel of the glory of Christ, who is the
image of God, should shine on them.
5 [R]For we do not preach ourselves, but
Christ Jesus the Lord, and [R]ourselves your
servants for Jesus' sake. 1 Cor. 1:13 • 1 Cor. 9:19
6 For it is the God who commanded light
to shine out of darkness who has shone in
our hearts to *give* the light of the knowledge
of the glory of God in the face of Jesus Christ.
7 But we have this treasure in earthen
vessels, [R]that the excellence of the power
may be of God and not of us. 1 Cor. 2:5

Trials Abound in the Ministry

8 *We are* [R]hard pressed on every side, yet
not crushed; *we are* perplexed, but not in
despair; 2 Cor. 1:8; 7:5
9 persecuted, but not [R]forsaken; [R]struck
down, but not destroyed— Ps. 37:24 • [Heb. 13:5]
10 always carrying about in the body the
dying of the Lord Jesus, that the life of Jesus
also may be manifested in our body.

2:17 M *the rest*

11 For we who live are always delivered to
death for Jesus' sake, that the life of Jesus
also may be manifested in our mortal flesh.
12 So then death is working in us, but life in
you.
13 But since we have [R]the same spirit of
faith, according to what is written, [R]*"I believed and therefore I spoke,"* we also believe
and therefore speak, 2 Pet. 1:1 • Ps. 116:10
14 knowing that [R]He who raised up the
Lord Jesus will also raise us up with Jesus,
and will present *us* with you. [Rom. 8:11]
15 For [R]all things *are* for your sakes, that
[R]grace, having spread through the many, may
cause thanksgiving to abound to the glory of
God. Col. 1:24 • 2 Cor. 1:11

Motivation of External Perspective

16 Therefore we do not lose heart. Even
though our outward man is perishing, yet the
inward *man* is being renewed day by day.
17 For our light affliction, which is but for a
moment, is working for us a far more exceeding *and* eternal weight of glory,
18 [R]while we do not look at the things
which are seen, but at the things which are
not seen. For the things which are seen *are*
temporary, but the things which are not seen
are eternal. [Heb. 11:1, 13]

CHAPTER 5

Motivation of the Future Presence of Christ

FOR we know that if our earthly [T]house,
this tent, is destroyed, we have a building
from God, a house [R]not made with hands,
eternal in the heavens. Physical body • Mark 14:58
2 For in this [R]we groan, earnestly desiring
to be clothed with our [T]habitation which is
from heaven, Rom. 8:23 • *dwelling*
3 if indeed, [R]having been clothed, we shall
not be found naked. Rev. 3:18
4 For we who are in *this* tent groan, being
burdened, not because we want to be unclothed, [R]but further clothed, that mortality
may be swallowed up by life. 1 Cor. 15:53
5 Now He who has prepared us for this
very thing *is* God, who also has given us the
Spirit as [T]a guarantee. *down payment, earnest*
6 Therefore *we are* always confident,
knowing that while we are at home in the
body we are absent from the Lord.
7 For we walk by faith, not by sight.
8 We are confident, yes, [R]well pleased
rather to be absent from the body and to be
present with the Lord. Phil. 1:23

Motivation of Future Reward

9 Therefore we make it our aim, whether
present or absent, to be well pleasing to Him.
10 [R]For we must all appear before the judgment seat of Christ, [R]that each one may
receive the things *done* in the body, according to what he has done, whether good or
bad. Rom. 2:16; 14:10, 12 • Gal. 6:7; Eph. 6:8 ☆

Motivation of the Love of Christ

11 Knowing, therefore, [R]the terror of the
Lord, we persuade men; but we are well
known to God, and I also trust are well
known in your consciences. [Heb. 10:31; 12:29]
12 For [R]we do not commend ourselves again
to you, but give you opportunity [R]to [T]glory on
our behalf, that you may have *something to answer* those who glory in appearance and
not in heart. 2 Cor. 3:1 • 2 Cor. 1:14 • *boast*
13 For if we are beside ourselves, *it is* for
God; or if we are of sound mind, *it is* for you.
14 For the love of Christ constrains us,
because we judge thus: that [R]if One died for
all, then all died; [Rom. 5:15; 6:6]
15 and He died for all, that those who live
should live no longer for themselves, but for
Him who died for them and rose again.
16 Therefore, from now on, we regard no
one according to the flesh. Even though we
have known Christ according to the flesh, yet
now we know *Him thus* no longer.

Motivation of the Message of Reconciliation

17 Therefore, if anyone *is* in Christ, *he is* a
new creation; old things have passed away;
behold, all things have become new.

5:17 New Nature—The term *new nature* refers to the spiritual transformation that occurs within the inner man when a person believes in Christ as Savior. The Christian is now a *new man* as opposed to the *old man* that he was before he became a Christian (Page 1329—Rom. 6:6; Page 1388—Eph. 2:15; 4:22–24; Page 1408—Col. 3:9, 10). This concept of *newness* may be traced to an important choice between two Greek words, both meaning "new." One word means "new" in the sense of renovation (to repair), the other in the sense of fresh existence. It is the latter that is used to describe the Christian. He is not the old man renovated or refreshed; he is a brand-new man with a new family, a new set of values, new motivations, and new possessions.

The old man is still present in the new life and expresses himself in corrupting deeds such as lying (Page 1391—Eph. 4:22; Page 1408—Col. 3:9). The new man, to be visible, must be *put on* as one would put on a new suit of clothes (Page 1408—Col. 3:10). In other words, the new nature must be cultivated or nurtured by spiritual decisiveness to grow in Christ. We must not revert to putting on the *old suit* of the former life; rather, we must continue to grow in this new life (Page 1391—Eph. 5:8).

The message of the new nature is a message of supreme hope: the Spirit of God can accomplish a life-changing transformation for all who will only believe in Christ.

Now turn to Page 834—Is. 61:10: Christ's Righteousness.

18 Now all things *are* of God, [R]who has reconciled us to Himself through Jesus Christ, and has given us the ministry of reconciliation, Rom. 5:10

19 that is, that [R]God was in Christ reconciling the world to Himself, not [T]imputing their trespasses to them, and has committed to us the word of reconciliation. [Rom. 3:24] • *reckoning*

20 Therefore we are [R]ambassadors for Christ, as though God were pleading through us: we implore *you* on Christ's behalf, be reconciled to God. Eph. 6:20

21 For [R]He made Him who knew no sin *to be* sin for us, that we might become the righteousness of God in Him. Is. 53:6, 9 ★

CHAPTER 6

Giving No Offense in the Ministry

WE then, *as* [R]workers together *with Him* also [R]plead with *you* not to receive the grace of God in vain. 1 Cor. 3:9 • 2 Cor. 5:20

2 For He says:

[R]*"In an acceptable time I have heard you,*
And in the day of salvation I have
helped you." Is. 49:8 ★

Behold, now *is* the accepted time; behold, now *is* the day of salvation.

3 [R]We give no offense in anything, that our ministry may not be blamed. Rom. 14:13

4 But in all *things* we commend ourselves as ministers of God: in much [T]patience, in tribulations, in needs, in distresses, *endurance*

5 in stripes, in imprisonments, in tumults, in labors, in sleeplessness, in fastings;

6 by purity, by knowledge, by longsuffering, by kindness, by the Holy Spirit, by [T]sincere love, Lit. *unhypocritical*

7 by the word of truth, by the power of God, by [R]the armor of righteousness on the right hand and on the left, 2 Cor. 10:4

8 by honor and dishonor, by evil report and good report; as deceivers, and *yet* true;

9 as unknown, and *yet* well known; [R]as dying, and behold we live; [R]as chastened, and *yet* not killed; 1 Cor. 4:9, 11 • Ps. 118:18

10 as sorrowful, yet always rejoicing; as poor, yet making many rich; as having nothing, and *yet* possessing all things.

Paul's Appeal for Reconciliation

11 O Corinthians! We have spoken openly to you, [R]our heart is wide open. 2 Cor. 7:3

12 You are not restricted by us, but [R]you are restricted by your *own* affections. 2 Cor. 12:15

13 Now in return for the same [R](I speak as to children), you also be open. 1 Cor. 4:14

Paul's Appeal for Separation from Unbelievers

14 Do not be unequally yoked together with unbelievers. For what fellowship has righteousness with lawlessness? And what communion has light with darkness?

15 And what accord has Christ with Belial? Or what part has a believer with an unbeliever?

16 And what agreement has the temple of God with idols? For [R]you* are the temple of the living God. As God has said: [1 Cor. 6:19]

[R]*"I will dwell in them* Ezek. 37:26, 27
And walk among them.
[R]*I will be their God,* Lev. 26:12; Jer. 31:33; 32:38
And they shall be My people."

17 Therefore

[R]*"Come out from among them*
And be separate, says the Lord.
Do not touch what is unclean,
And I will receive you." Is. 52:11

18 *"I* [R]*will be a Father to you,* Jer. 31:1, 9
And you shall be My [R]*sons and*
daughters, Rom. 8:14
Says the LORD *Almighty."*

CHAPTER 7

THEREFORE,[R] having these promises, beloved, let us cleanse ourselves from all filthiness of the flesh and spirit, perfecting holiness in the fear of God. [1 John 3:3]

Paul's Meeting with Titus

2 Open *your hearts* to us. We have wronged no one, we have corrupted no one, we have [T]defrauded no one. *taken advantage of*

3 I do not say *this* to condemn; for [R]I have said before that you are in our hearts, to die together and to live together. 2 Cor. 6:11, 12

4 Great *is* my boldness of speech toward you, [R]great *is* my boasting on your behalf. [R]I am filled with comfort. I am exceedingly joyful in all our tribulation. 1 Cor. 1:4 • Phil. 2:17

5 For indeed, when we came to Macedonia, our flesh had no rest, but [R]we were troubled on every side. [R]Outside *were* conflicts, inside *were* fears. 2 Cor. 4:8 • Deut. 32:25

6 Nevertheless [R]God, who comforts the downcast, comforted us by [R]the coming of Titus, 2 Cor. 1:3, 4 • 2 Cor. 2:13; 7:13

7 and not only by his coming, but also by the [T]consolation with which he was comforted in you, when he told us of your earnest desire, your mourning, your zeal for me, so that I rejoiced even more. *comfort*

Corinthians' Response to Paul's Letter

8 For even if I made you sorry with my letter, I do not regret it; [R]though I did regret it. For I perceive that the same epistle made you sorry, though only for a while. 2 Cor. 2:4

6:16 NU *we*

SALVATION AND REDEMPTION

Salvation

Save from Eternal Death. Of the numerous New Testament passages using *sōzō*, Matthew 1:21 gives a perfect illustration of salvation, God in Christ freely granting believers eternal life: "You shall call His name JESUS, for He will save His people from their sins." The name *Jesus* (*Yeshua*) comes from the Hebrew verb for "save." Among the typical verses presenting this most important meaning are "Believe on the Lord Jesus Christ, and you will be saved" (Acts 16:31) and "that the world through Him might be saved" (John 3:17).

Save from Danger or Death. Examples from the New Testament are Peter's plea to be saved from drowning (Matt. 14:30) and Paul and his fellow-passengers being saved from shipwreck (Acts 27:31).

Save from Disease, Heal. Jesus told the woman with the hemorrhage, "Daughter, your faith has made you well" (lit. "saved you," Mark 5:34). Here and elsewhere the physical healing and spiritual salvation may have taken place at the same time.

Save One's Life from Being Wasted. Because many people have a fixation on the word *saved* as only referring to escaping from hell, and of the word *soul* as only referring to the immortal part of man, this last usage has not been recognized by everyone. As we have seen, *sōzō* definitely has meanings other than "rescue from eternal destruction." So does *psychē* have meanings other than "soul" in the popular sense (see word studies on pp. 935 and 1417). The word *psychē* can just as easily mean "life" as "soul," and sometimes must mean that. The popular Christian expression "save a soul" has come to always equal meaning number one, above, but it is virtually never so used in the Scriptures.

Yet in Luke 9:24 and its parallel passages, our Lord appears to use *sōzō* and *psychē* to mean "save your Christian life from being wasted." There are other passages, such as in James, that in context would be better taken as referring to good works for rewards rather than to escaping from hell.

Redemption

There are several Greek words that mean "to purchase or redeem." The orthodox theological teaching is that at the Cross God paid a ransom price (the blood of Christ) to buy sinners from the slave market of sin.

Agorazō comes from the Greek word for market (*agora*) and is used thirty times in the New Testament, usually of simple buying. Three times in the KJV/NKJV, the word has the theological meaning "redeem," including the well-known text, "You [the Lamb]...have redeemed us to God by Your blood" (Rev. 5:9; cf. 14:3, 4).

Exagorazō is a strengthened form of the above, occurring four times, always translated "redeem." Twice it has the idea of Christ's redeeming us "from the curse of the law" (Gal. 3:13) and from "under the law" (Gal. 4:5).

Lutroō is a verb occurring three times in the New Testament and also translated "redeem." More specifically, it means "to set at liberty" upon receipt of a ransom (*lutron*). Peter tells us that the price was the precious blood of Christ (1 Pet. 1:18, 19). Paul says that the purpose of the ransom was to "redeem us from every lawless deed" to be "*His* own special people" (Titus 2:14).

Lutron is the noun for "ransom." In two parallel passages Christ says the reason He came was "to give His life a ransom for many" (Matt. 20:28; Mark 10:45).

Antilutron is a strengthened form of *lutron*. The prefix *anti-* emphasizes Christ's taking our place (1 Tim. 2:6).

Lutrosis occurs three times and is yet another word for "redemption." Hebrews 9:12 uses it to express redemption of transgressions under the old covenant to make way for the new.

Thus we see a general doctrine, salvation, using one verb *sōzō* for several different meanings, and a more specific doctrine, redemption (a subdivision of salvation), using many words to teach one general truth.

9 Now I rejoice, not that you were made
sorry, but that your sorrow led to repentance.
For you were made sorry in a godly manner,
that you might suffer loss from us in nothing.
10 For godly sorrow produces repentance to
salvation, not to be regretted; but the sorrow
of the world produces death.
11 For observe this very thing, that you
sorrowed in a godly manner: What diligence
it produced in you, *what* [R]clearing *of yourselves, what* indignation, *what* fear, *what*
vehement desire, *what* zeal, *what* vindication! In all *things* you proved yourselves to be
[R]clear in this matter. Eph. 5:11 • 2 Cor. 2:5–11
12 Therefore, although I wrote to you, *I did*
not *do it* for the sake of him who had done
the wrong, nor for the sake of him who
suffered wrong, but that our care for you in
the sight of God might appear to you.
13 Therefore we have been comforted in
your comfort. And we rejoiced exceedingly
more for the joy of Titus, because his spirit
[R]has been refreshed by you all. Rom. 15:32
14 For if in anything I have boasted to him
about you, I am not ashamed. But as we
spoke all things to you in truth, even so our
boasting to Titus was found true.
15 And his affections are greater for you as
he remembers the obedience of you all, how
with fear and trembling you received him.
16 Therefore I rejoice that [R]I have confidence in you in everything. 2 Thess. 3:4

CHAPTER 8

Example of the Macedonians

MOREOVER, brethren, we make known
to you the grace of God bestowed on
the churches of Macedonia:
2 that in a great trial of affliction the
abundance of their joy and their deep poverty
abounded in the riches of their liberality.
3 For I bear witness that according to *their*
ability, yes, and beyond *their* ability, *they
were* freely willing,
4 imploring us with much urgency *that
we would receive the [T]gift and the fellowship
of the ministering to the saints. Or *favor*
5 And *this they did*, not as we had hoped,
but first gave themselves to the Lord, and
then to us by the [R]will of God. [Eph. 6:6]
6 So [R]we urged Titus, that as he had begun, so he would also complete this grace in
you as well. 2 Cor. 8:17; 12:18

Example of Christ

7 But as [R]you abound in everything—in
faith, in speech, in knowledge, in all diligence,
and in your love for us—*see* that you abound
in this grace also. [1 Cor. 1:5; 12:13]
8 [R]I speak not by commandment, but I am
testing the sincerity of your love by the
diligence of others. 1 Cor. 7:6

9 For you know the grace of our Lord
Jesus Christ, that though He was rich, yet for
your sakes He became poor, that you through
His poverty might become rich.

Purpose of Giving

10 And in this [R]I give *my* advice: [R]It is to
your advantage not only to be doing what
you began and [R]were desiring to do a year
ago; 1 Cor. 7:25, 40 • [Heb. 13:16] • 2 Cor. 9:2
11 but now you also must complete the
doing *of it*; that as *there was* a readiness to
desire *it*, so *there* also *may be* a completion
out of what *you* have.
12 For if there is first a willing mind, *it is*
accepted according to what one has, *and* not
according to what he does not have.
13 For *I do* not *mean* that others should be
eased and you burdened;
14 but by an equality, *that* now at this time
your abundance may *supply* their lack, that
their abundance also may *supply* your lack—
that there may be equality.
15 As it is written, [R]*"He who gathered much
had nothing left over, and he who gathered
little had no lack."* Ex. 16:18

Policies in Giving

16 But thanks *be* to God who *puts the
same earnest care for you into the heart of
Titus.
17 For he not only accepted the exhortation, but being more diligent, he went to you
of his own accord.
18 And we have sent with him [R]the brother
whose praise *is* in the gospel throughout all
the churches, 2 Cor. 12:18
19 and not only *that*, but who was also
[R]chosen by the churches to travel with us
with this gift, which is administered by us [R]to
the glory of the Lord Himself and *to show*
your ready mind, 1 Cor. 16:3, 4 • 2 Cor. 4:15
20 avoiding this: that anyone should blame
us in this lavish gift which is administered by
us—
21 [R]providing honorable things, not only in
the sight of the Lord, but also in the sight of
men. Rom. 12:17
22 And we have sent with them our brother
whom we have often proved diligent in many
things, but now much more diligent, because
of the great confidence which *we have* in
you.
23 If *anyone inquires* about Titus, *he is* my
partner and fellow worker concerning you.
Or if our brethren *are inquired about, they
are* [R]messengers[T] of the churches, the glory of
Christ. Phil. 2:25 • Lit. *apostles,* "sent ones"
24 Therefore show to them, *and before the
churches, the proof of your love and of our
[R]boasting on your behalf. 2 Cor. 7:4, 14; 9:2

8:4 NU, M *for* and omit *we would receive*
8:16 NU *has put* **8:24** NU, M omit *and*

CHAPTER 9

Readiness in Giving

NOW concerning [R]the ministering to the
saints, it is superfluous for me to write
to you; Gal. 2:10
2 for I know your willingness, about which
I boast of you to the Macedonians, that
Achaia was ready a [R]year ago; and your zeal
has stirred up the majority. 2 Cor. 8:10
3 Yet I have sent the brethren, lest our
boasting of you should be in vain in this
respect, that, as I said, you may be ready;
4 lest if *some* Macedonians come with me
and find you unprepared, we (not to mention
you!) should be ashamed of this *confident
boasting.
5 Therefore I thought it necessary to exhort the brethren to go to you ahead of time,
and prepare your bountiful gift beforehand,
which *you had* previously promised, that it
may be ready as *a matter of* generosity and
not as a [T]grudging obligation. Lit. *covetousness*

Principles in Giving

6 But this *I say*: He who sows sparingly
will also reap sparingly, and he who sows
bountifully will also reap bountifully.
7 *So let* each one *give* as he purposes in his
heart, not grudgingly or of [T]necessity; for
God loves a cheerful giver. *compulsion*

Promises from Giving

8 [R]And God *is* able to make all grace
abound toward you, that you, always having
all sufficiency in all *things*, may have an
abundance for every good work. [Prov. 11:24]

9 As it is written:

[R]*"He has dispersed abroad,* Ps. 112:9
He has given to the poor;
His righteousness remains forever."

10 Now *may He who [R]supplies seed to the
sower, and bread for food, *supply and multiply the seed you have *sown* and increase the
fruits of your [R]righteousness, Is. 55:10 • Hos. 10:12
11 while *you are* enriched in everything for
all liberality, [R]which causes thanksgiving
through us to God. 2 Cor. 1:11
12 For the administration of this service not
only [R]supplies the needs of the saints, but also
is abounding through many thanksgivings to
God, 2 Cor. 8:14
13 while, through the proof of this ministry,
they glorify God for the obedience of your
confession to the gospel of Christ, and for
your liberal sharing with them and all *men*,
14 and by their prayer for you, who long for
you because of the exceeding [R]grace of God
in you. 2 Cor. 8:1
15 Thanks *be* to God [R]for His indescribable
gift! [James 1:17]

CHAPTER 10

The Charge of Cowardice Is Answered

NOW I, Paul, myself am pleading with you
by the meekness and gentleness of
Christ—who in presence *am* lowly among
you, but being absent am bold toward you.
2 But I beg *you* [R]that when I am present I
may not be bold with that confidence by
which I intend to be bold against some, who
think of us as if we walked according to the
flesh. 1 Cor. 4:21

The Charge of Walking in the Flesh Is Answered

3 For though we walk in the flesh, we do
not war according to the flesh.
4 [R]For the weapons of our warfare *are* not
[T]carnal but [R]mighty in God [R]for pulling down
strongholds, Eph. 6:13 • *of the flesh* • Acts 7:22 • Jer. 1:10
5 [R]casting down arguments and every high
thing that exalts itself against the knowledge
of God, bringing every thought into captivity
to the obedience of Christ, 1 Cor. 1:19
6 and being ready to punish all disobedience when your obedience is fulfilled.

9:4 NU *confidence* 9:10 NU omits *may*
9:10 NU *will supply*

9:6–8 Giving—There is no better indicator of growth in the new life than in the area of giving. This passage deals with the attitude one should have in his giving—it should be cheerful. When giving is cheerful, it will also be generous. The important rule of thumb is not how much is given, but how much is left after the giving. God is not primarily occupied with the amount of the gift, but with the motive that lies behind it. All the money in the world belongs to God. My gift to Him does not make Him any richer; it makes me richer spiritually because of the realization that everything I have is His and that I am giving because I love Him and want to give.

The formula for giving is found in First Corinthians 16:2 where three principles can be seen: (1) my giving is to be regular, "on the first *day* of the week"; (2) my giving is to be systematic, "let each one of you lay something aside"; and (3) my giving is to be proportionate, "as he may prosper."

Failure to give of the money which God has given is a serious matter. The person who fails to honor God with his money actually robs God (Page 1082—Mal. 3:8), not because it impoverishes God but because it denies the God-ordained means for the support of His work and His ministers. For the child of God who honors God with his money God promises abundant blessing (Page 1082—Mal. 3:10; Page 1202—Luke 6:38) and the provision of his every need (Page 1402—Phil. 4:19). Giving, then, is a key to growth in the new life.

Now turn to Page 483—1 Chr. 16:29: The Meaning of Worship.

7 Do you look at things according to the
outward appearance? If anyone is convinced
in himself that he is Christ's, let him again
consider this in himself, that just as he *is*
Christ's, even *so we *are* Christ's.
8 For even if I should boast somewhat
more about our authority, which the Lord
gave *us for edification and not for your
destruction, I shall not be ashamed—
9 lest I seem to terrify you by letters.

The Charge of Personal Weakness Is Answered

10 "For *his* letters," they say, "*are* weighty
and powerful, but [R]*his* bodily presence *is*
weak, and *his* speech contemptible." Gal. 4:13
11 Let such a person consider this, that
what we are in word by letters when we are
absent, such *we will* also *be* in deed when we
are present.
12 [R]For we dare not class ourselves or compare ourselves with those who commend
themselves. But they, measuring themselves
by themselves, and comparing themselves
among themselves, are not wise. 2 Cor. 5:12
13 [R]We, however, will not boast beyond
measure, but within the limits of the sphere
which God appointed us—a sphere which
especially includes you. 2 Cor. 10:15
14 For we are not extending ourselves beyond *our sphere* (thus not reaching you), [R]for
it was to you that we came with the gospel of
Christ; 1 Cor. 3:5, 6
15 not boasting of things beyond measure,
that is, in other men's labors, but having
hope, *that* as your faith is increased, we shall
be greatly enlarged by you in our sphere,
16 to preach the gospel in the *regions* beyond you, *and* not to boast in another man's
sphere of accomplishment.
17 [R]But *"He who glories, let him glory in the*
LORD." Jer. 9:24
18 For not he who commends himself is
approved, but whom the Lord commends.

CHAPTER 11

Paul's Declaration of His Apostleship

OH, that you would bear with me in a little
folly—and indeed you do bear with me.
2 For I am jealous for you with godly
jealousy. For I have betrothed you to one
husband, [R]that I may present *you* [R]*as* a
chaste virgin to Christ. Col. 1:28 • Lev. 21:13
3 But I fear, lest somehow, as [R]the serpent
deceived Eve by his craftiness, so your minds
[R]may be corrupted from the *simplicity that
is in Christ. Gen. 3:4, 13 • Eph. 6:24
4 For if he who comes preaches another
Jesus whom we have not preached, or *if* you
receive a different spirit which you have not
received, or a different gospel which you
have not accepted, you may well put up with
it.
5 For I consider that I am not at all inferior
to the most eminent apostles.
6 Even though [R]*I am* untrained in speech,
yet *I am* not [R]in knowledge. But [R]we have
*been thoroughly made manifest among you
in all things. [1 Cor. 1:17] • [Eph. 3:4] • [2 Cor. 12:12]
7 Did I commit sin in abasing myself that
you might be exalted, because I preached the
gospel of God to you free of charge?
8 I robbed other churches, taking wages
from them to minister to you.
9 And when I was present with you, and in
need, [R]I was a burden to no one, for what was
lacking to me [R]the brethren who came from
Macedonia supplied. And in everything I kept
myself from being burdensome to you, and so
I will keep *myself*. Acts 20:33 • Phil. 4:10
10 [R]As the truth of Christ is in me, [R]no one
shall stop me from this boasting in the regions of Achaia. Rom. 1:9; 9:1 • 1 Cor. 9:15
11 Why? [R]Because I do not love you? God
knows! 2 Cor. 6:11; 12:15
12 But what I do, I will also continue to do,
[R]that I may cut off the opportunity from
those who desire an opportunity to be regarded just as we are in the things of which
they boast. 1 Cor. 9:12
13 For such [R]*are* false apostles, [R]deceitful
workers, transforming themselves into apostles of Christ. Phil. 1:15 • Phil. 3:2
14 And no wonder! For Satan himself transforms himself into an angel of light.
15 Therefore *it is* no great thing if his ministers also transform themselves into ministers
of righteousness, [R]whose end will be according to their works. [Phil. 3:19]

Paul's Sufferings Support His Apostleship

16 I say again, let no one think me a fool. If
otherwise, at least receive me as a fool, that I
also may boast a little.
17 What I speak, [R]I speak not according to
the Lord, but as it were, foolishly, in this
confidence of boasting. 1 Cor. 7:6
18 Seeing that many boast according to the
flesh, I also will boast.
19 For you put up with fools gladly, [R]since
you *yourselves* are wise! 1 Cor. 4:10
20 For you put up with it [R]if one brings you
into bondage, if one devours *you*, if one takes
from you, if one exalts himself, if one strikes
you on the face. [Gal. 2:4; 4:3, 9; 5:1]
21 To *our* shame, I say that we were too
weak for that! But in whatever anyone is
bold—I speak foolishly—I am bold also.
22 Are they [R]Hebrews? So *am* I. Are they
Israelites? So *am* I. Are they the seed of
Abraham? So *am* I. Phil. 3:4–6
23 Are they ministers of Christ?—I speak as
a fool—I *am* more: in labors more abundant,

10:7 NU *as we are* **10:8** NU omits *us*
11:3 NU adds *and purity* **11:6** NU omits *been*

in stripes above measure, in prisons more
frequently, [R]in deaths often. 1 Cor. 15:30
24 From the Jews five times I received
[R]forty [R]*stripes* minus one. Deut. 25:3 • 2 Cor. 6:5
25 Three times I was [R]beaten with rods;
[R]once I was stoned; three times I [R]was shipwrecked; a night and a day I have been in the
deep; Acts 16:22, 23; 21:32 • Acts 14:5, 19 • Acts 27:1–44
26 *in* journeys often, *in* perils of waters, *in*
perils of robbers, *in* perils of *my own* countrymen, *in* perils of the Gentiles, *in* perils in the
city, *in* perils in the wilderness, *in* perils in the
sea, *in* perils among false brethren;
27 in weariness and toil, in sleeplessness
often, [R]in hunger and thirst, in fastings often,
in cold and nakedness— 1 Cor. 4:11
28 besides the other things, what comes
upon me daily: [R]my deep concern for all the
churches. Acts 20:18
29 [R]Who is weak, and I am not weak? Who
is made to stumble, and I do not burn with
indignation? [1 Cor. 8:9, 13; 9:22]
30 If I must boast, I will boast in the things
which concern my [T]infirmity. *weakness*
31 [R]The God and Father of our Lord Jesus
Christ, [R]who is blessed forever, knows that I
am not lying. 1 Thess. 2:5 • Rom. 9:5
32 [R]In Damascus the governor, under Aretas the king, was guarding the city of the
Damascenes with a garrison, desiring to
apprehend me; Acts 9:19–25
33 but I was let down in a basket through a
window in the wall, and escaped from his
hands.

CHAPTER 12

Vision of Paradise

IT is *doubtless not profitable for me to
boast. I will come to [R]visions and [R]revela-
tions of the Lord: Acts 16:9; 18:9 • [Gal. 1:12; 2:2]
2 I know a man [R]in Christ who fourteen
years ago—whether in the body I do not
know, or whether out of the body I do not
know, God knows—such a one [R]was caught
up to the third heaven. Rom. 16:7 • Acts 22:17
3 And I know such a man—whether in the
body or out of the body I do not know, God
knows—
4 how he was caught up into [R]Paradise and
heard inexpressible words, which it is not
lawful for a man to utter. Luke 23:43
5 Of such a one I will boast; yet of myself I
will not boast, except in my infirmities.
6 For though I might desire to boast, I will
not be a fool; for I will speak the truth. But I
forbear, lest anyone should think of me above
what he sees me *to be* or hears from me.

Thorn in the Flesh

7 And lest I should be exalted above measure by the abundance of the revelations, a
[R]thorn in the flesh was given to me, [R]a messenger of Satan to [T]buffet me, lest I be exalted above measure. Ezek. 28:24 • Job 2:7 • *beat*
8 [R]Concerning this thing I pleaded with
the Lord three times that it might depart
from me. Matt. 26:44
9 And He said to me, "My grace is sufficient for you, for My strength is made perfect
in weakness." Therefore most gladly I will
rather boast in my infirmities, that the power
of Christ may rest upon me.
10 Therefore [R]I take pleasure in infirmities,
in reproaches, in needs, in persecutions, in
distresses, for Christ's sake. For when I am
weak, then I am strong. [Rom. 5:3; 8:35]

Paul's Signs Support His Apostleship

11 I have become a fool *in boasting; you
have compelled me. For I ought to have been
commended by you; for [R]in nothing was I
behind the most eminent apostles, though [R]I
am nothing. 2 Cor. 11:5 • 1 Cor. 3:7; 13:2; 15:9
12 Truly the signs of an apostle were accomplished among you with all perseverance,
in signs and wonders and mighty deeds.
13 For what is it in which you were inferior
to other churches, except that I myself was
not burdensome to you? Forgive me this
wrong!

Paul's Concern Not to Be a Financial Burden

14 Now *for* the third time I am ready to
come to you. And I will not be burdensome to
you; for I do not seek yours, but you. For the
children ought not to lay up for the parents,
but the parents for the children.
15 And I will very gladly spend and be spent
[R]for your souls; though the more abundantly
I love you, the less I am loved. [2 Tim. 2:10]
16 But be that *as it may,* [R]I did not burden
you. Nevertheless, being crafty, I caught you
with guile! 2 Cor. 11:9
17 Did I take advantage of you by any of
those whom I sent to you?
18 I urged Titus, and sent our [R]brother with
him. Did Titus take advantage of you? Did we
not walk in the same spirit? Did *we* not *walk*
in the same steps? 2 Cor. 8:18

Paul's Concern Not to Find Them Carnal

19 *Again, do you think that we excuse
ourselves to you? [R]We speak before God in
Christ. [R]But *we do* all things, beloved, for
your edification. [Rom. 9:1, 2] • 1 Cor. 10:33
20 For I fear lest, when I come, I shall not
find you such as I wish, and *that* [R]I shall be
found by you such as you do not wish; lest
there be contentions, jealousies, outbursts of
wrath, selfish ambitions, backbitings, whisperings, conceits, tumults; 1 Cor. 4:21

12:1 NU *necessary, though not profitable, to boast*
12:11 NU omits *in boasting*
12:19 NU *You have been thinking for a long time that we*

21 *and* lest, when I come again, my God
[R]will humble me among you, and I shall
mourn for many [R]who have sinned before
and have not repented of the uncleanness,
[R]fornication, and licentiousness which they
have practiced. 2 Cor. 2:1, 4 • 2 Cor. 13:2 • 1 Cor. 5:1

CHAPTER 13

Paul's Warning to Examine Yourselves

THIS *will be* the third *time* I am coming to
you. *"By the mouth of two or three witnesses every word shall be established."*
2 I have told you before, and foretell as if I
were present the second time, and now being
absent *I write to those [R]who have sinned
before, and to all the rest, that if I come again
I will not spare— 2 Cor. 12:21
3 since you seek a proof of Christ [R]speak-
ing in me, who is not weak toward you, but
mighty [R]in you. Matt. 10:20 • [1 Cor. 9:2]
4 For though He was crucified in weakness, yet He lives by the power of God. For
we also are weak in Him, but we shall live
with Him by the power of God toward you.
5 Examine yourselves *as to* whether you
are in the faith. Prove yourselves. Do you not
know yourselves, that Jesus Christ is in
you?—unless indeed you are disqualified.
6 But I trust that you will know that we
are not disqualified.
7 Now *I pray to God that you do no evil,
not that we should appear approved, but that
you should do what is honorable, though [R]we
may seem disqualified. 2 Cor. 6:9
8 For we can do nothing against the truth,
but for the truth.
9 For we are glad when we are weak and
you are strong. And this also we pray, [R]that
you may be made complete. [1 Thess. 3:10]
10 [R]Therefore I write these things being
absent, lest being present I should use sharp-
ness, according to the [R]authority which the
Lord has given me for edification and not for
destruction. 1 Cor. 4:21 • 2 Cor. 10:8

Conclusion

11 Finally, brethren, farewell. Become complete. [R]Be of good comfort, be of one mind,
live in peace; and the God of love [R]and peace
will be with you. Rom. 12:16, 18 • Rom. 15:33
12 Greet one another with a holy kiss.
13 All the saints greet you.
14 The grace of the Lord Jesus Christ, and
the love of God, and the [T]communion of the
Holy Spirit *be* with you all. Amen. *fellowship*

13:2 NU omits *I write* 13:7 NU *we*

THE EPISTLE OF PAUL THE APOSTLE TO THE

GALATIANS

THE BOOK OF GALATIANS

The Galatians, having launched their Christian experience by faith, seem content to leave their voyage of faith and chart a new course based on works—a course Paul finds disturbing. His letter to the Galatians is a vigorous attack against the gospel of works and a defense of the gospel of faith.

Paul begins by setting forth his credentials as an apostle with a message from God: blessing comes from God on the basis of faith, not law. The law declares men guilty and imprisons them; faith sets men free to enjoy liberty in Christ. But liberty is not license. Freedom in Christ means freedom to produce the fruits of righteousness through a Spirit-led life-style.

The book is called *Pros Galatas,* "To the Galatians," and it is the only letter of Paul that is specifically addressed to a number of churches ("To the churches of Galatia," 1:2). The name *Galatians* was given to this Celtic people because they originally lived in Gaul before their migration to Asia Minor.

THE AUTHOR OF GALATIANS

The Pauline authorship and the unity of this epistle are virtually unchallenged. The first verse clearly identifies the author as "Paul, an apostle." Also in 5:2, we read, "Indeed I, Paul, say to you." In fact, Paul actually wrote Galatians (6:11) instead of dictating it to a secretary, as was his usual practice.

THE TIME OF GALATIANS

The term *Galatia* was used in an ethnographic sense (that is, cultural and geographic origin) and in a political sense. The original ethnographic sense refers to the central part of Asia Minor where these Celtic tribes eventually settled after their conflicts with the Romans and Macedonians. Later, in 189 B.C. Galatia came under Roman domination, and in 25 B.C. Augustus declared it a Roman province. The political or provincial Galatia included territory to the south that was not originally considered part of Galatia (for example, the cities of Pisidian Antioch, Iconium, Lystra, and Derbe). There are two theories regarding the date and setting of Galatians.

The *North Galatian Theory* holds that Paul was speaking of Galatia in its earlier, more restricted sense. According to this theory, the churches of Galatia were north of the cities Paul visited on his first missionary journey. Paul visited the ethnographic Galatia (the smaller region to the North) for the first time on his second missionary journey, probably while he was on his way to Troas (Acts 16:6). On his third missionary journey, Paul revisited the Galatian churches he had established (Acts 18:23) and wrote this epistle either in Ephesus (A.D. 53–56) or in Macedonia (A.D. 56).

According to the *South Galatian Theory,* Paul was referring to Galatia in its wider political sense as a province of Rome. This means that the churches he had in mind in this epistle were in the cities he evangelized during his first missionary journey with Barnabas (Acts 13:13—14:23). This was just prior to the Jerusalem Council (Acts 15), so the Jerusalem visit in Galatians 2:1–10 must have been the Acts 11:27–30 famine-relief visit. Galatians was probably written in Syrian Antioch in A.D. 49 just before Paul went to the Council in Jerusalem.

Paul wrote this epistle in response to a report that the Galatian churches were suddenly taken over by the false teaching of certain Judaizers who professed Jesus yet sought to place gentile converts under the requirements of the Mosaic Law (1:7; 4:17, 21; 5:2–12; 6:12, 13).

THE CHRIST OF GALATIANS

Christ has freed the believer from bondage to the law (legalism) and to sin (license) and has placed him in a position of liberty. The transforming cross provides for the believer's deliverance from the curse of sin, law, and self (1:4; 2:20; 3:13; 4:5; 5:24; 6:14).

KEYS TO GALATIANS

Key Word: Freedom from the Law—This epistle shows that the believer is no longer under the law but is saved by faith alone. It has been said that Judaism was the cradle of Christianity, but also that it was very nearly its grave as well. God raised up Paul as the Moses of the Christian church to deliver them from this bondage. Galatians is the Christian's Declaration of Independence. The power of the Holy Spirit enables the Christian to enjoy freedom within the law of love.

Key Verses: Galatians 2:20, 21 and 5:1—"I have been crucified with Christ; it is no longer I who live, but Christ lives in me; and the *life* which I now live in the flesh I live by faith in the Son of God, who loved me and gave Himself for me. I do not set aside the grace of God; for if righteousness *comes* through the law, then Christ died in vain" (2:20, 21).

"Stand fast therefore in the liberty by which Christ has made us free, and do not be entangled again with a yoke of bondage" (5:1).

Key Chapter: Galatians 5—The impact of the truth concerning freedom is staggering: freedom must not be used "as an opportunity for the flesh, but through love serve one another" (5:13). This chapter records the power, "Walk in the Spirit" (5:16), and the results, "the fruit of the Spirit" (5:22), of that freedom.

SURVEY OF GALATIANS

The Epistle to the Galatians has been called "the Magna Carta of Christian liberty." It is Paul's manifesto of justification by faith, and the resulting liberty. Paul directs this great charter of Christian freedom to a people who are willing to give up the priceless liberty they possess in Christ. The oppressive theology of certain Jewish legalizers has been causing the believers in Galatia to trade their freedom in Christ for bondage to the law. Paul writes this forceful epistle to do away with the false gospel of works and demonstrate the superiority of justification by faith. This carefully written polemic approaches the problem from three directions: the gospel of grace defended (1 and 2), the gospel of grace explained (3 and 4), and the gospel of grace applied (5 and 6).

The Gospel of Grace Defended (1 and 2): Paul affirms his divinely given apostleship and presents the gospel (1:1–5) because it has been distorted by false teachers among the Galatians (1:6–10). Paul launches into his biographical argument for the true gospel of justification by faith in showing that he received his message not from men but directly from God (1:11–24). When he submits his teaching of Christian liberty to the apostles in Jerusalem, they all acknowledge the validity and authority of his message (2:1–10). Paul also must correct Peter on the matter of freedom from the law (2:11–21).

The Gospel of Grace Explained (3 and 4): In this section Paul uses eight lines of reasoning to develop his theological defense of justification by faith: (1) The Galatians began by faith, and their growth in Christ must continue to be by faith (3:1–5). (2) Abraham was justified by faith, and the same principle applies today (3:6–9). (3) Christ has redeemed all who trust in Him from the curse of the law (3:10–14). (4) The promise made to Abraham was not nullified by the law (3:15–18). (5) The law was given to drive men to faith, not to save them (3:19–22). (6) Believers in Christ are adopted sons of God and are no longer bound by the law (3:23—4:7). (7) The Galatians must recognize their inconsistency and regain their original freedom in Christ (4:8–20). (8) Abraham's two sons allegorically reveal the superiority of the Abrahamic promise to the Mosaic Law (4:21–31).

The Gospel of Grace Applied (5 and 6): The Judaizers seek to place the Galatians under bondage to their perverted gospel of justification by law, but Paul warns them that law and grace are two contrary principles (5:1–12). So far, Paul has been contrasting the liberty of faith with the legalism of law, but at this point he warns the Galatians of the opposite extreme of license or antinomianism (5:13—6:10). The Christian is not only set free from bondage of law, but he is also free of the bondage of sin because of the power of the indwelling Spirit. Liberty is not an excuse to indulge in the deeds of the flesh; rather, it provides the privilege of bearing the fruit of the Spirit by walking in dependence upon Him. This letter closes with a contrast between the Judaizers—who are motivated by pride and a desire to avoid persecution—and Paul, who has suffered for the true gospel, but boasts only in Christ (6:11–18).

FOCUS	GOSPEL OF GRACE DEFENDED		GOSPEL OF GRACE EXPLAINED		GOSPEL OF GRACE APPLIED	
REFERENCE	1:1—	2:1—	3:1—	4:1—	5:1—	6:1—6:18
DIVISION	PAUL'S APOSTLESHIP	PAUL'S AUTHORITY	BONDAGE OF LAW	FREEDOM OF GRACE	FRUIT OF THE SPIRIT	FRUITS OF THE SPIRIT
TOPIC	BIOGRAPHICAL EXPLANATION		DOCTRINAL EXPOSITION		PRACTICAL EXHORTATION	
	AUTHENTICATION OF LIBERTY		ARGUMENTATION FOR LIBERTY		APPLICATION OF LIBERTY	
LOCATION	SOUTH GALATIAN THEORY: SYRIAN ANTIOCH NORTH GALATIAN THEORY: EPHESUS OR MACEDONIA					
TIME	SOUTH GALATIAN THEORY: A.D. 49 NORTH GALATIAN THEORY: A.D. 53–56					

OUTLINE OF GALATIANS

CHAPTER 1

Salutation: The Ground of Grace

PAUL, an apostle (not from men nor
through man, but [R]through Jesus Christ
and God the Father [R]who raised Him from
the dead), Acts 9:6 • Acts 2:24
2 and all the brethren who are with me,

To the churches of Galatia:

3 Grace to you and peace from God the
Father and our Lord Jesus Christ,
4 who gave Himself for our sins, that He
might deliver us from this present evil age,
according to the will of our God and Father,
5 to whom *be* glory forever and ever.
Amen.

Situation: The Departure from Grace

6 I marvel that you are turning away so
soon [R]from Him who called you in the grace
of Christ, to a different gospel, Gal. 1:15; 5:8
7 [R]which is not another; but there are
some who trouble you and want to [R]pervert[T]
the gospel of Christ. 2 Cor. 11:4 • 2 Cor. 2:17 • *distort*
8 But even if we, or an angel from heaven,
preach any other gospel to you than what we
have preached to you, let him be accursed.
9 As we have said before, so now I say
again, if anyone preaches any other gospel to
you [R]than what you have received, let him be
accursed. Deut. 4:2

Gospel of Grace Is Given by Divine Revelation

10 For [R]do I now [R]persuade men, or God?
Or [R]do I seek to please men? For if I still
pleased men, I would not be a servant of
Christ. 1 Thess. 2:4 • 1 Sam. 24:7 • 1 Thess. 2:4
11 [R]But I make known to you, brethren,
that the gospel which was preached by me is
not according to man. 1 Cor. 15:1
12 For I neither received it from man, nor
was I taught *it*, but *it came* [R]through the
revelation of Jesus Christ. [Eph. 3:3–5]
13 For you have heard of my former conduct in Judaism, how [R]I persecuted the
church of God beyond measure and [R]*tried to*
destroy it. Acts 9:1 • Acts 8:3; 22:4, 5
14 And I advanced in Judaism beyond many
of my contemporaries in my own nation,
[R]being more exceedingly zealous [R]for the
traditions of my fathers. Acts 26:9 • Jer. 9:14
15 But when it pleased God, [R]who separated
me from my mother's womb and called *me*
through His grace, Is. 49:1, 5
16 to reveal His Son in me, that I might
preach Him among the Gentiles, I did not
immediately confer with flesh and blood,
17 nor did I go up to Jerusalem to those
who were apostles before me; but I went to
Arabia, and returned again to Damascus.
18 Then after three years [R]I went up to
Jerusalem to see *Peter, and remained with
him fifteen days. Acts 9:26
19 But I saw none of the other apostles
except [R]James, the Lord's brother. Matt. 13:55
20 (Now *concerning* the things which I
write to you, indeed, before God, I do not lie.)

1:18 NU *Cephas*

GRACE AND MERCY

In his now dated but still valuable *Synonyms of the New Testament*, R. C. Trench chooses *grace (charis)* as one of the "Greek words taken up into Christian use" that are "glorified and transformed, seeming to have waited for this adoption of them, to come to their full rights, and to reveal all of the depth and the riches of meaning which they contained, or might be made to contain" (p. 156).

Since *grace* is the most characteristic of all Christian words, it is well worth our while to trace briefly its "glorification and transformation" from classical to Christian usage.

Grace (*charis*)

Grace (*charis*) is derived from the verb *rejoice* (*chairō*). Luke apparently makes a little play on this word in Acts 11:23: "When he [Barnabas] came and had seen the grace of God, he was glad [*echarē*]." To a Greek, anything of beauty, favor, or delight in which a person could rejoice spoke of *charis.* This usage, with no religious connotations, still exists today in our ideas of graceful beauty and gracious entertaining.

Those who are familiar with the rich and lovely Hebrew word *hesed* (see word study on p. 660) might expect that the translators of the Septuagint (LXX) would have chosen *charis* to translate it in the Greek Old Testament. In Esther 2:17, where *hesed* ("mercy," "lovingkindness," etc.) occurs, along with the somewhat similar word *hēn,* they are translated by *charis.* Generally, *charis* in the LXX renders *hēn*, not *hesed,* but a good argument could be made for translating *hesed* by "grace" in modern translations. This is because the concept that we associate with *charis*—divine favor that is completely undeserved by man—is not far from the meaning of *hesed* in many contexts.

In the New Testament itself (and those books, sermons, and hymns deeply rooted in that book), the word and message of *charis* come to full flower. Every New Testament book, except Matthew, Mark, and 1 John, uses *charis.* Common expressions include "the grace of God," "grace of the Lord," "the grace of Christ," and "the word [message] of grace."

It is fitting that the first New Testament use of "grace" is by the angel announcing the coming of the Messiah: "Do not be afraid, Mary, for you have found favor [*charis*] with God" (Luke 1:30). Then he goes on to predict the grace that the incarnation of God the Son would bring to the world. This is not to say that the Old Testament is without grace. God is always gracious. But only in the New Testament do we see the complete exposition of God's favor in the salvation freely offered by grace through faith to all who will believe. The Bible ends also on a "grace note." The last verse in God's Word reads: "The grace of our Lord Jesus *be* with you all" (Rev. 22:21).

Between Luke and Revelation, grace abounds (2 Cor. 9:14) and "superabounds" (1 Tim. 1:14).

Philip Doddridge captured the New Testament meaning of grace with these words:

Grace! 'tis a charming sound,
Harmonious to the ear;
Heav'n with the echo shall resound,
And all the earth shall hear.

Mercy (*eleos*)

Mercy (*eleos*) is closely related to grace. Man needs both mercy and grace in order to be saved. Logically, mercy precedes grace. The devout German scholar Bengel distinguished *grace* and *mercy* precisely in six Latin words: "Gratia tollit culpam, misericordia miseriam" ("Grace takes away the guilt; mercy [takes away] the misery").

From the human viewpoint, grace precedes mercy. We must accept God's grace through faith before we can have our misery removed. It is not surprising that this is the biblical order (Zech. 12:10; 1 Tim. 1:2; 2 Tim. 1:2; Titus 1:4; 2 John 3). Likewise, grace always precedes peace. We cannot have peace until we have experienced the forgiveness of our sins through God's unmerited favor to us—His *charis,* His grace.

21 [R]Afterward I went into the regions of
Syria and Cilicia; Acts 9:30
22 and I was unknown by face to the
churches of Judea which *were* in Christ.
23 But they were hearing only, "He who
formerly persecuted us now preaches the
faith which he once *tried to* destroy."
24 And they [R]glorified God in me. Acts 11:18

CHAPTER 2

Gospel of Grace Is Approved by Jerusalem Leadership

THEN after fourteen years [R]I went up
again to Jerusalem with Barnabas, and
also took Titus with *me*. Acts 15:2
2 And I went up by revelation, and communicated to them that gospel which I
preach among the Gentiles, but privately to
those who were of reputation, lest by any
means I might run, or had run, in vain.
3 Yet not even Titus who *was* with me,
being a Greek, was compelled to be circumcised.
4 But *this occurred* because of [R]false brethren secretly brought in (who came in by
stealth to spy out our [R]liberty which we have
in Christ Jesus, [R]that they might bring us into
bondage), Acts 15:1, 24 • Gal. 3:25; 5:1, 13 • Gal. 4:3, 9
5 to whom we did not yield submission
even for an hour, that [R]the truth of the gospel
might continue with you. [Gal. 1:6; 2:14; 3:1]
6 But from those who seemed to be something—whatever they were, it makes no
difference to me; [R]God shows personal favoritism to no man—for those who seemed *to be*
something added nothing to me. Acts 10:34
7 But on the contrary, when they saw that
the gospel for the uncircumcised [R]had been
committed to me, as *the gospel* for the circumcised *was* to Peter 1 Thess. 2:4
8 (for He who worked effectively in Peter
for the apostleship to the [R]circumcised [R]also
[R]worked effectively in me toward the Gentiles), 1 Pet. 1:1 • Acts 9:15 • [Gal. 3:5]
9 and when James, [T]Cephas, and John,
who seemed to be pillars, perceived [R]the
grace that had been given to me, they gave
me and Barnabas the right hand of fellowship, [R]that we *should* go to the Gentiles and
they to the circumcised. Peter • Rom. 1:5 • Acts 13:3
10 *They desired* only that we should remember the poor, [R]the very thing which I
also was eager to do. Acts 11:30

Gospel of Grace Is Vindicated by Rebuking Peter

11 [R]But when *Peter had come to Antioch, I
[T]withstood him to his face, because he was to
be blamed; Acts 15:35 • *opposed*
12 for before certain men came from James,
[R]he would eat with the Gentiles; but when
they came, he withdrew and separated himself, fearing [T]those who were of the circumcision. [Acts 10:28; 11:2, 3] • Jewish Christians
13 And the rest of the Jews also played the
hypocrite with him, so that even Barnabas
was carried away with their hypocrisy.
14 But when I saw that they were not
straightforward about the truth of the gospel,
I said to Peter before *them* all, "If you, being
a Jew, live in the manner of Gentiles and not
as the Jews, *why do you compel Gentiles to
live as [T]Jews? Some stop quotation here.
15 [R]"We *who are* Jews by nature, and not
[R]sinners of the Gentiles, [Acts 15:10] • Matt. 9:11
16 "knowing that a man is not justified by
the works of the law but by faith in Jesus
Christ, even we have believed in Christ Jesus,
that we might be justified by faith in Christ
and not by the works of the law; for by the
works of the law no flesh shall be justified.
17 "But if, while we seek to be justified by
Christ, we ourselves also are found [R]sinners,
is Christ therefore a minister of sin? Certainly
not! [1 John 3:8]
18 "For if I build again those things which I
destroyed, I make myself a transgressor.
19 "For I [R]through the law died to the law
that I might [R]live to God. Rom. 8:2 • [Rom. 6:11]
20 "I have been crucified with Christ; it is
no longer I who live, but Christ lives in me;
and the *life* which I now live in the flesh I live
by faith in the Son of God, who loved me and
[R]gave Himself for me. Is. 53:12 ★
21 "I do not set aside the grace of God; for
[R]if righteousness *comes* through the law,
then Christ died [T]in vain." Heb. 7:11 • *for nothing*

CHAPTER 3

Holy Spirit Is Given by Faith, Not by Works

O FOOLISH Galatians! Who has bewitched you *that you should not obey
the truth, before whose eyes Jesus Christ was
clearly portrayed *among you as crucified?
2 This only I want to learn from you: Did
you receive the Spirit by the works of the
law, [R]or by the hearing of faith? Rom. 10:16, 17
3 Are you so foolish? [R]Having begun in the
Spirit, are you now being made perfect by
[R]the flesh? [Gal. 4:9] • Heb. 7:16
4 Have you suffered so [T]many things in
vain—if indeed *it was* in vain? Or *great*
5 Therefore He who supplies the Spirit to
you and works miracles among you, *does He*
do it by the works of the law, or by the
hearing of faith?—

Abraham Was Justified by Faith, Not by Works

6 just as Abraham *"believed God, and it*
was accounted to him for righteousness."

2:11 NU *Cephas* **2:14** NU *how can you*
3:1 NU omits *that you should not obey the truth*
3:1 NU omits *among you*

7 Therefore know that *only* [R]those who are
of faith are sons of Abraham. John 8:39
8 And the Scripture, foreseeing that God
would justify the nations by faith, preached
the gospel to Abraham beforehand, *saying,*
"In you all the nations shall be blessed."
9 So then those who *are* of faith are
blessed with believing Abraham.

Christ Redeems Us from the Curse of the Law

10 For as many as are of the works of the
law are under the curse; for it is written,
[R]*"Cursed is everyone who does not continue*
in all things which are written in the book of
the law, to do them." Deut. 27:26
11 But that no one is [T]justified by the law in
the sight of God *is* evident, for [R]*"The just*
shall live by faith." *declared righteous* • Hab. 2:4
12 Yet the law is not of faith, but *"The man*
who does them shall live by them."
13 [R]Christ has redeemed us from the curse
of the law, having become a curse for us (for
it is written, [R]*"Cursed is everyone who hangs*
on a tree"), [Rom. 8:3] • Deut. 21:23
14 [R]that the blessing of Abraham might
come upon the Gentiles in Christ Jesus, that
we might receive [R]the promise of the Spirit
through faith. Is. 49:6; Rom. 4:9★ • Is. 32:15

Abrahamic Covenant Is Not Voided by the Law

15 Brethren, I speak in the manner of men:
Though *it is* only a man's covenant, yet *if it is*
confirmed, no one annuls or adds to it.
16 Now [R]to Abraham and his Seed were the
promises made. He does not say, "And to
seeds," as of many, but as of one, *"And to*
your Seed," who is Christ. Gen. 12:3★
17 And this I say, *that* the law, [R]which was
four hundred and thirty years later, cannot
annul the covenant that was confirmed before by God *in Christ, [R]that it should make
the promise of no effect. Ex. 12:40 • [Rom. 4:13]
18 For if [R]the inheritance *is* of the law, [R]*it is*
no longer of promise; but God gave *it* to
Abraham by promise. [Rom. 8:17] • Rom. 4:14

Law Given to Drive Us to Faith

19 What purpose then *does* the law *serve?* It
was added because of transgressions, till the
Seed should come to whom the promise was
made; *and it was* appointed through angels
by the hand [R]of a mediator. Ex. 20:19
20 Now a mediator does not *mediate* for one
only, [R]but God is one. [Rom. 3:29]
21 *Is* the law then against the promises of
God? Certainly not! For if there had been a
law given which could have given life, truly
righteousness would have been by the law.
22 But the Scripture has confined all under
sin, that the promise by faith in Jesus Christ
might be given to those who believe.

Believers Are Free from the Law

23 But before faith came, we were kept
under guard by the law, [T]kept for the faith
which would afterward be revealed. *confined*
24 Therefore the law was our tutor *to bring*
us to Christ, that we might be justified by
faith.
25 But after faith has come, we are no
longer under a tutor.
26 For you [R]are all sons of God through
faith in Christ Jesus. John 1:12
27 For [R]as many of you as were baptized
into Christ have put on Christ. [Rom. 6:3]
28 [R]There is neither Jew nor Greek, [R]there is
neither slave nor free, there is neither male
nor female; for you are all [R]one in Christ
Jesus. Col. 3:11 • [1 Cor. 12:13] • [Eph. 2:15, 16]
29 And [R]if you *are* Christ's, then you are
Abraham's [R]seed, and [R]heirs according to the
promise. Gen. 12:3; Heb. 11:18★ • Rom. 4:11 • Rom. 8:17

CHAPTER 4

NOW I say *that* the heir, as long as he is a
child, does not differ at all from a slave,
though he is master of all,
2 but is under guardians and stewards
until the time appointed by the father.
3 Even so we, when we were children,
[R]were in bondage under the elements of the
world. Col. 2:8, 20
4 But when the fullness of the time had
come, God sent forth His Son, [R]born of a
woman, born under the law, Is. 7:14★
5 [R]to redeem those who were under the
law, [R]that we might receive the adoption as
sons. [Matt. 20:28] • [John 1:12]
6 And because you are sons, God has sent
forth the Spirit of His Son into your hearts,
crying out, [T]"Abba, Father!" Aram., *Father*
7 Therefore you are no longer a slave but a
son, [R]and if a son, then an heir *of God
*through Christ. [Rom. 8:16, 17]
8 But then, indeed, [R]when you did not
know God, [R]you served those which by nature are not gods. Eph. 2:12 • Rom. 1:25
9 But now [R]after you have known God, or
rather are known by God, [R]how *is it that* you
turn again to [R]the weak and beggarly elements, to which you desire again to be in
bondage? [1 Cor. 8:3] • Col. 2:20 • Heb. 7:18
10 [R]You observe days and months and seasons and years. Rom. 14:5
11 I am afraid for you, [R]lest I have labored
for you in vain. 1 Thess. 3:5

Galatians Receive Blessing by Faith, Not by the Law

12 Brethren, I urge you to become as I *am,*
for I *am* as you *are.* [R]You have not injured
me at all. 2 Cor. 2:5

3:17 NU omits *in Christ* 4:7 NU *through God*
4:7 NU omits *through Christ*

13 You know that [R]because of physical
infirmity I preached the gospel to you at the
first. 1 Cor. 2:3
14 And my trial which was in my flesh you
did not despise or reject, but you received me
as an angel of God, *even* as Christ Jesus.
15 *What then was the blessing you *enjoyed?* For I bear you witness that, if possible,
you would have plucked out your own eyes
and given them to me.
16 Have I therefore become your enemy
because I tell you the truth?
17 They [R]zealously court you, *but* for no
good; yes, they want to exclude you, that you
may be zealous for them. Rom. 10:2
18 But it is good to be zealous in a good
thing always, and not only when I am present
with you.
19 My little children, for whom I labor in
birth again until Christ is formed in you,
20 I would like to be present with you now
and to change my tone; for I have doubts
about you.

Law and Grace Cannot Coexist

21 Tell me, you who desire to be under the
law, do you not hear the law?
22 For it is written that Abraham had two
sons: [R]the one by a bondwoman, [R]the other
by a freewoman. Gen. 16:15 · Gen. 21:2
23 But he *who was* of the bondwoman was
born according to the flesh, [R]and he of the
freewoman through promise, Heb. 11:11
24 which things are symbolic. For these are
*the two covenants: the one from Mount
[R]Sinai which gives birth to bondage, which is
Hagar— Deut. 33:2
25 for this Hagar is Mount Sinai in Arabia,
and corresponds to Jerusalem which now is,
and is in bondage with her children—
26 but the [R]Jerusalem above is free, which is
the mother of us all. [Is. 2:2]
27 For it is written:

[R]*"Rejoice, O barren,* Is. 54:1
You who do not bear!
Break forth and shout,
You who do not [T]travail! *have birth pangs*
For the desolate has many more
children
Than she who has a husband."

28 Now [R]we, brethren, as Isaac *was,* are
[R]children of promise. Gal. 3:29 · Acts 3:25
29 But, as he who was born according to the
flesh then persecuted him *who was born*
according to the Spirit, even so *it is* now.
30 Nevertheless what does the Scripture
say? *"Cast out the bondwoman and her son,
for the son of the bondwoman shall not be
heir with the son of the freewoman."*
31 So then, brethren, we are not children of
the bondwoman but of the free.

CHAPTER 5

Position of Liberty: "Stand Fast"

STAND* [R]fast therefore in the liberty by
which Christ has made us free, and do
not be entangled again with a [R]yoke of bondage. Phil. 4:1 · Acts 15:10
2 Indeed I, Paul, say to you that [R]if you
become circumcised, Christ will profit you
nothing. Acts 15:1
3 And I testify again to every man who
becomes circumcised [R]that he is [T]a debtor to
keep the whole law. [Rom. 2:25] · *obligated*
4 [R]You have become estranged from
Christ, you who *attempt to* be justified by
law; you have fallen from grace. [Rom. 9:31]
5 For we through the Spirit eagerly wait
for the hope of righteousness by faith.
6 For [R]in Christ Jesus neither circumcision
nor uncircumcision avails anything, but faith
working through love. [Gal. 6:15]
7 You [R]ran well. Who hindered you from
obeying the truth? 1 Cor. 9:24
8 This persuasion does not *come* from Him
who calls you.
9 A little leaven leavens the whole lump.
10 I have confidence in you, in the Lord,
that you will have no other mind; but he who
troubles you shall bear his judgment, whoever he is.
11 And I, brethren, if I still preach circumcision, why do I still suffer persecution? Then
the offense of the cross has ceased.
12 I could wish that those who trouble you
would even cut themselves off!

Practice of Liberty: Love One Another

13 For you, brethren, have been called to
liberty; only [R]do not *use* liberty as an [R]oppor-
tunity for the flesh, but [R]through love serve
one another. 1 Cor. 8:9 · 1 Pet. 2:16 · 1 Cor. 9:19

4:15 NU *Where* **4:24** NU, M omit *the*
5:1 NU *For freedom Christ has made us free; stand fast therefore, and*

5:13 Serving—God intended that the Christian life should be dynamic, not static. We should sit under the teaching of the Word of God, understand and apply its meaning and implications, and serve God and our fellow believers. The Spirit of God has given us spiritual gifts, but those gifts are worthless unless they are put to use in the service of God and His church. Paul often uses the figure of the human body to show the dependence of the members of the body upon one another and the importance of each member serving the other (Page 1337—Rom. 12:4, 5; Page 1355—1 Cor. 12:12–31). While some members of the body have more prominent places of service than others, all are equally important. The worst thing that can happen to the human body is for one of its members to become nonfunctioning.

14 For [R]all the law is fulfilled in one word, *even* in this: [R]*"You shall love your neighbor as yourself."* Matt. 7:12; 22:40 • Lev. 19:18

15 But if you bite and devour one another, beware lest you be consumed by one another!

Conflict Between the Spirit and the Flesh

16 I say then: [R]Walk in the Spirit, and you shall not fulfill the lust of the flesh. Rom. 6:12

17 For the flesh lusts against the Spirit, and the Spirit against the flesh; and these are contrary to one another, [R]so that you do not do the things that you wish. Rom. 7:15

18 But [R]if you are led by the Spirit, you are not under the law. [Rom. 6:14; 7:4; 8:14]

"Works of the Flesh"

19 Now [R]the works of the flesh are evident, which are: *adultery, [T]fornication, uncleanness, licentiousness, Eph. 5:3, 11 • *sexual immorality*

20 idolatry, sorcery, hatred, contentions, jealousies, outbursts of wrath, selfish ambitions, dissensions, heresies,

21 envy, *murders, drunkenness, revelries, and the like; of which I tell you beforehand, just as I also told *you* in time past, that [R]those who practice such things will not inherit the kingdom of God. 1 Cor. 6:9, 10

"Fruit of the Spirit"

22 But [R]the fruit of the Spirit is [R]love, joy, peace, longsuffering, kindness, [R]goodness, faithfulness, [John 15:2] • [Col. 3:12–15] • Rom. 15:14

23 [T]gentleness, self-control. [R]Against such there is no law. *meekness* • 1 Tim. 1:9

24 And those *who are* Christ's have crucified the flesh with its passions and desires.

25 [R]If we live in the Spirit, let us also walk in the Spirit. [Rom. 8:4, 5]

26 [R]Let us not become conceited, provoking one another, envying one another. Phil. 2:3

CHAPTER 6

"Bear One Another's Burdens"

BRETHREN, if a man is overtaken in any trespass, you who *are* spiritual restore such a one in a spirit of gentleness, considering yourself lest you also be tempted.

2 [R]Bear one another's burdens, and so fulfill [R]the law of Christ. Rom. 15:1 • [James 2:8]

3 For [R]if anyone thinks himself to be something, when [R]he is nothing, he deceives himself. Rom. 12:3 • [2 Cor. 3:5]

4 But let each one examine his own work, and then he will have rejoicing in himself alone, and [R]not in another. Luke 18:11

5 For each one shall bear his own load.

Do Not Be Weary While Doing Good

6 Let him who is taught the word share in all good things with him who teaches.

7 Do not be deceived, God is not mocked; for [R]whatever a man sows, that he will also reap. [Rom. 2:6]

8 For he who sows to his flesh will of the flesh reap corruption, but he who sows to the Spirit will of the Spirit reap everlasting life.

9 And [R]let us not grow weary while doing good, for in due season we shall reap [R]if we do not lose heart. 1 Cor. 15:58 • [James 5:7, 8]

10 Therefore, as we have opportunity, [R]let us do good to all, [R]especially to those who are of the household of faith. Titus 3:8 • Rom. 12:13

Motives of the Circumcised

11 See with what large letters I have written to you with my own hand!

12 As many as desire to make a good showing in the flesh, these *try to* compel you to be circumcised, [R]only that they may not suffer persecution for the cross of Christ. Gal. 5:11

13 For not even those who are circumcised keep the law, but they desire to have you circumcised that they may glory in your flesh.

Motives of the Apostle Paul

14 But God forbid that I should glory except in the cross of our Lord Jesus Christ, by [T]whom the world has been crucified to me, and [R]I to the world. Or *which,* the cross • Col. 2:20

15 For [R]in Christ Jesus neither circumcision nor uncircumcision avails anything, but a new creation. 1 Cor. 7:19

16 And as many as walk according to this rule, peace and mercy *be* upon them, and upon the Israel of God.

17 From now on let no one trouble me, for I bear in my body the marks of the Lord Jesus.

18 Brethren, the grace of our Lord Jesus Christ *be* with your spirit. Amen.

5:19 NU omits *adultery* **5:21** NU omits *murders*

Paralysis, sickness, deterioration, and sometimes death occur when a body member ceases to serve the other members of the body in the particular way that God intended. To maintain strength, health, and vitality, every member of the body must function and serve all the other members of the body. This is also true of the spiritual or new life. We will grow in the new life, become strong, and maintain good spiritual health as we use the talents and abilities that God has given us to meet the needs of the other members of the body.

Now turn to Page1372—2 Cor. 9:6–8: Giving.

THE EPISTLE OF PAUL THE APOSTLE TO THE

EPHESIANS

THE BOOK OF EPHESIANS

Ephesians is addressed to a group of believers who are rich beyond measure in Jesus Christ, yet living as beggars, and only because they are ignorant of their wealth. Since they have yet to accept their wealth, they relegate themselves to living as spiritual paupers. Paul begins by describing in chapters 1—3 the contents of the Christian's heavenly "bank account": adoption, acceptance, redemption, forgiveness, wisdom, inheritance, the seal of the Holy Spirit, life, grace, citizenship—in short, every spiritual blessing. Drawing upon that huge spiritual endowment, the Christian has all the resources needed for living "to the praise of the glory of His grace" (1:6). Chapters 4—6 resemble an orthopedic clinic, where the Christian learns a spiritual walk rooted in his spiritual wealth. "For we are His workmanship, created in Christ Jesus [1—3] for good works, . . . that we should walk in them [4—6]" (2:10).

The traditional title of this epistle is *Pros Ephesious,* "To the Ephesians." Many ancient manuscripts, however, omit *en Epheso,* "in Ephesus," in 1:1. This has led a number of scholars to challenge the traditional view that this message was directed specifically to the Ephesians. The encyclical theory proposes that it was a circular letter sent by Paul to the churches of Asia. It is argued that Ephesians is really a Christian treatise designed for general use: it involves no controversy and deals with no specific problems in any particular church. This is also supported by the formal tone (no terms of endearment) and distant phraseology ("after I heard of your faith," 1:15; if they "have heard" of his message, 3:2). These things seem inconsistent with the relationship Paul must have had with the Ephesians after a ministry of almost three years among them. On the other hand, the absence of personal greetings is not a support for the encyclical theory because Paul would have done this to avoid favoritism. The only letters that greet specific people are Romans and Colossians, and they were addressed to churches Paul had not visited. Some scholars accept an ancient tradition that Ephesians is Paul's letter to the Laodiceans (Col. 4:16), but there is no way to be sure. If Ephesians began as a circular letter, it eventually became associated with Ephesus, the foremost of the Asian churches. Another plausible option is that this epistle was directly addressed to the Ephesians, but written in such a way as to make it helpful for all the churches in Asia.

THE AUTHOR OF EPHESIANS

All internal (1:1) and external evidence strongly supports the Pauline authorship of Ephesians. In recent years, however, critics have turned to internal grounds to challenge this unanimous ancient tradition. It has been argued that the vocabulary and style are different from other Pauline epistles, but this overlooks Paul's flexibility under different circumstances (cf. Rom. and 2 Cor.). The theology of Ephesians in some ways reflects a later development, but this must be attributed to Paul's own growth and meditation on the church as the body of Christ. Since the epistle clearly names the author in the opening verse, it is not necessary to theorize that Ephesians was written by one of Paul's pupils or admirers, such as Timothy, Luke, Tychicus, or Onesimus.

THE TIME OF EPHESIANS

At the end of his second missionary journey, Paul visited Ephesus where he left Priscilla and Aquila (Acts 18:18–21). This strategic city was the commercial center of Asia Minor, but heavy silting required a special canal to be maintained so that ships could reach the harbor. Ephesus was a religious center as well, famous especially for its magnificent temple of Diana (Roman name) or Artemis (Greek name), a structure considered to be one of the seven wonders of the ancient world (cf. Acts 19:35). The practice of magic and the local economy were clearly related to this temple. Paul remained in Ephesus for nearly three years on his third missionary journey (Acts 18:23—19:41); the Word of God was spread throughout the province of Asia. Paul's effective ministry began to seriously hurt the traffic in magic and images, leading to an uproar in the huge Ephesian theater. Paul then left for Macedonia, but afterward he met with the Ephesian elders while on his way to Jerusalem (Acts 20:17–38).

Paul wrote the "Prison Epistles" (Ephesians, Philippians, Colossians, and Philemon) during his first Roman imprisonment in A.D. 60–62. These epistles all refer to his imprisonment (Eph. 3:1; 4:1; 6:20; Phil. 1:7, 13, 14; Col. 4:3, 10, 18; Philem. 9, 10, 13, 23), and fit well against the background in Acts 28:16–31. This is especially true of Paul's references to the palace guard (governor's official residential guard, Phil. 1:13) and "Caesar's household" (Phil. 4:22). Some commentators believe that the imprisonment in one or more of these epistles refers to Paul's Caesarean imprisonment or to a hypothetical

Ephesian imprisonment, but the weight of evidence favors the traditional view that they were written in Rome. Ephesians, Colossians, and Philemon were evidently written about the same time (cf. Eph. 6:21, 22 with Col. 4:7–9) in A.D. 60–61. Philippians was written in A.D. 62, not long before Paul's release.

THE CHRIST OF EPHESIANS

Paul's important phrase "in Christ" (or its equivalent) appears about thirty-five times, more than in any other New Testament book. The believer is in Christ (1:1), in the heavenly places in Christ (1:3), chosen in Him (1:4), adopted through Christ (1:5), in the Beloved (1:6), redeemed in Him (1:7), given an inheritance in Him (1:11), given hope in Him (1:12), sealed in Him (1:13), made alive together with Christ (2:5), raised and seated with Him (2:6), created in Christ (2:10), brought near by His blood (2:13), growing in Christ (2:21), a partaker of the promise in Christ (3:6), and given access through faith in Him (3:12).

KEYS TO EPHESIANS

Key Word: Building the Body of Christ—Ephesians focuses on the believer's responsibility to walk in accordance with his heavenly calling in Christ Jesus (4:1). Ephesians was not written to correct specific errors in a local church, but to prevent problems in the church as a whole by encouraging the body of Christ to maturity in Him. It was also written to make believers more aware of their position in Christ because this is the basis for their practice on every level of life.

Key Verses: Ephesians 2:8-10 and 4:1-3—"For by grace you have been saved through faith, and that not of yourselves; *it is* the gift of God, not of works, lest anyone should boast. For we are His workmanship, created in Christ Jesus for good works, which God prepared beforehand that we should walk in them" (2:8-10).

"I, therefore, the prisoner of the Lord, beseech you to have a walk worthy of the calling with which you were called, with all lowliness and gentleness, with longsuffering, bearing with one another in love, endeavoring to keep the unity of the Spirit in the bond of peace" (4:1-3).

Key Chapter: Ephesians 6—Even though the Christian is blessed "with every spiritual blessing in the heavenly *places* in Christ" (1:3), spiritual warfare is still the daily experience of the Christian while in the world. Chapter 6 is the clearest advice for how to "be strong in the Lord and in the power of His might" (6:10).

SURVEY OF EPHESIANS

Paul wrote this epistle to make Christians more aware of their position in Christ and to motivate them to draw upon their spiritual source in daily living: "walk worthy of the calling with which you were called" (4:1; see 2:10). The first half of Ephesians lists the believer's heavenly possessions: adoption, redemption, inheritance, power, life, grace, citizenship, and the love of Christ. There are no imperatives in chapters 1—3, which focus only on divine gifts. But chapters 4—6 include thirty-five directives in the last half of Ephesians that speak of the believer's responsibility to conduct himself according to his individual calling. So Ephesians begins in heaven, but concludes in the home and in all other relationships of daily life. The two divisions are: the position of the Christian (1:1—3:21) and the practice of the Christian (4:1—6:20).

The Position of the Christian (1:1—3:21): After a two-verse prologue, in one long Greek sentence Paul extols the triune God for the riches of redemption (1:3–14). This hymn to God's grace praises the Father for choosing us (1:3–6), the Son for redeeming us (1:7–12), and the Spirit for sealing us (1:13, 14). The saving work of each

FOCUS	THE POSITION OF THE CHRISTIAN				THE PRACTICE OF THE CHRISTIAN			
REFERENCE	1:1—	1:15—	2:1—	3:14—	4:1—	4:17—	5:22—	6:10—6:24
DIVISION	PRAISE FOR REDEMPTION	PRAYER FOR REVELATION	POSITION OF THE CHRISTIAN	PRAYER FOR REALIZATION	UNITY IN THE CHURCH	HOLINESS IN LIFE	RESPONSIBILITIES AT HOME AND WORK	CONDUCT IN THE CONFLICT
TOPIC	BELIEF				BEHAVIOR			
	PRIVILEGES OF THE CHRISTIAN				RESPONSIBILITIES OF THE CHRISTIAN			
LOCATION	ROME							
TIME	A.D. 60–61							

divine Person is to the praise of the glory of His grace (1:6, 12, 14). Before continuing, Paul offers the first of two very significant prayers (1:15–23; cf. 3:14–21). Here he asks that the readers receive spiritual illumination so that they may come to perceive what is, in fact, true. Next, Paul describes the power of God's grace by contrasting their former condition with their present spiritual life in Christ, a salvation attained not by human works but by divine grace (2:1–10). This redemption includes Jews, yet also extends to those Gentiles who previously were "strangers from the covenants of promise" (2:12). In Christ, the two for the first time have become members of one body (2:11–22). The truth that Gentiles would become "fellow heirs, of the same body" (3:6) was formerly a mystery that has now been revealed (3:1–13). Paul's second prayer (3:14–21) expresses his desire that the readers be strengthened with the power of the Spirit and fully apprehend the love of Christ.

The Practice of the Christian (4:1—6:20): The pivotal verse of Ephesians is 4:1, because it draws a sharp line between the doctrinal and the practical divisions of this book. There is a cause and effect relationship between chapters 1—3 and 4—6 because the spiritual walk of a Christian must be rooted in his spiritual wealth. As Paul emphasized in Romans, behavior does not determine blessing; instead, blessing should determine behavior.

Because of the unity of all believers in the body of Christ, growth and maturity come from "the effective working by which every part does its share" (4:16). This involves the exercise of spiritual gifts in love. Paul exhorts the readers to "put off, concerning your former conduct, the old man" (4:22) and "put on the new man" (4:24) that will be manifested by a walk of integrity in the midst of all people. They are also to maintain a walk of holiness as children of light (5:1–21). Every relationship (wives, husbands, children, parents, slaves, and masters) must be transformed by their new life in Christ (5:22—6:9). Paul's colorful description of the spiritual warfare and the armor of God (6:10–20) is followed by a word about Tychicus and then a benediction (6:21–24).

OUTLINE OF EPHESIANS

Part One: The Position of the Christian (1:1—3:21)

I. Praise for Redemption ... **1:1–14**
- A. Salutation from Paul ... 1:1, 2
- B. Chosen by the Father ... 1:3–6
- C. Redeemed by the Son ... 1:7–12
- D. Sealed by the Spirit ... 1:13, 14

II. Prayer for Revelation ... **1:15–23**

III. Position of the Christian ... **2:1—3:13**
- A. The Christian's Position Individually ... 2:1–10
  1. Old Condition: Dead to God ... 2:1–3
  2. New Condition: Alive to God ... 2:4–10
- B. The Christian's Position Corporately ... 2:11—3:13
  1. Reconciliation of Jews and Gentiles ... 2:11–22
  2. Revelation of the Mystery of the Church ... 3:1–13

IV. Prayer for Realization ... **3:14–21**

Part Two: The Practice of the Christian (4:1—6:24)

I. Unity in the Church ... **4:1–6**
- A. Exhortation to Unity ... 4:1–3
- B. Explanation of Unity ... 4:4–6
- C. Means for Unity: The Gifts ... 4:7–11
- D. Purpose of the Gifts ... 4:12–16

II. Holiness in Life ... **4:17—5:21**
- A. Put Off the Old Man ... 4:17–22
- B. Put On the New Man ... 4:23–29
- C. Grieve Not the Holy Spirit ... 4:30—5:12
- D. Walk as Children of Light ... 5:13–17
- E. Be Filled with the Spirit ... 5:18–21

III. Responsibilities in the Home and at Work ... **5:22—6:9**
- A. Wives: Submit to Your Husbands ... 5:22–24
- B. Husbands: Love Your Wives ... 5:25–33
- C. Children: Obey Your Parents ... 6:1–4
- D. Service on the Job ... 6:5–9

IV. Conduct in the Conflict ... **6:10–24**
- A. Put On the Armor of God ... 6:10–17
- B. Pray for Boldness ... 6:18–20
- C. Conclusion ... 6:21–24

CHAPTER 1

Salutation from Paul

PAUL, an apostle of Jesus Christ by the
will of God,

To the saints who are in Ephesus, and
faithful in Christ Jesus:

2 Grace to you and peace from God our
Father and the Lord Jesus Christ.

Chosen by the Father

3 [R]Blessed *be* the God and Father of our
Lord Jesus Christ, who has blessed us with
every spiritual blessing in the heavenly *places*
in Christ, 2 Cor. 1:3
4 just as He chose us in Him before the
foundation of the world, that we should be
holy and without blame before Him in love,
5 having predestined us to adoption as
sons by Jesus Christ to Himself, [R]according to
the good pleasure of His will, [1 Cor. 1:21]
6 to the praise of the glory of His grace,
[R]by which He has [T]made us accepted in the
Beloved. [Rom. 3:24] • Lit. *bestowed grace (favor) upon us*

Redeemed by the Son

7 In Him we have redemption through His
blood, the forgiveness of sins, according to
[R]the riches of His grace [Rom. 3:24, 25]
8 which He made to abound toward us in
all wisdom and [T]prudence, *understanding*
9 having made known to us the mystery of
His will, according to His good pleasure
[R]which He purposed in Himself, [2 Tim. 1:9]
10 that in the dispensation of the fullness of
the times He might gather together in one all
things in Christ, *both which are in heaven
and which are on earth—in Him,
11 in whom also we have obtained an inheritance, being predestined according to [R]the
purpose of Him who works all things according to the counsel of His will, Is. 46:10
12 that we who first trusted in Christ should
be to the praise of His glory.

Sealed by the Spirit

13 In Him you also *trusted*, after you heard
the word of truth, the gospel of your salvation; in whom also, having believed, you were
sealed with the Holy Spirit of promise,
14 *who is the guarantee of our inheritance
until the redemption of the purchased possession, to the praise of His glory.

Prayer for Revelation

15 Therefore I also, [R]after I heard of your
faith in the Lord Jesus and your love for all
the saints, Col. 1:4
16 [R]do not cease to give thanks for you,
making mention of you in my prayers: Rom. 1:9
17 that [R]the God of our Lord Jesus Christ,
the Father of glory, [R]may give to you the
spirit of wisdom and revelation in the knowledge of Him, John 20:17 • Col. 1:9
18 the eyes of your *understanding being
enlightened; that you may know what is the
hope of His calling, what are the riches of the
glory of His inheritance in the saints,
19 and what *is* the exceeding greatness of
His power toward us who believe, [R]according
to the working of His mighty power Col. 2:12
20 which He worked in Christ when He
raised Him from the dead and seated *Him* at
His right hand in the heavenly *places*,
21 far above all [T]principality and [T]power and
[T]might and dominion, and every name that is
named, not only in this age but also in that
which is to come. *rule • authority • power*
22 And [R]He put all *things* under His feet,
and gave Him [R]*to be* head over all *things* to
the church, Dan. 7:13, 14; Matt. 28:18 ☆ • Heb. 2:7
23 [R]which is His body, [R]the fullness of Him
[R]who fills all in all. Rom. 12:5 • Col. 2:9 • [1 Cor. 12:6]

CHAPTER 2

Old Condition: Dead to God

AND [R]you *He made alive*, [R]who were dead
in trespasses and sins, Col. 2:13 • Eph. 4:18
2 in which you once walked according to
the course of this world, according to the
prince of the power of the air, the spirit who
now works in the sons of disobedience,
3 [R]among whom also we all once conducted ourselves in [R]the lusts of our flesh,
fulfilling the desires of the flesh and of the
mind, and [R]were by nature children of wrath,
just as the others. 1 Pet. 4:3 • Gal. 5:16 • [Ps. 51:5]

New Condition: Alive to God

4 But God, who is rich in mercy, because
of His great love with which He loved us,
5 [R]even when we were dead in trespasses,
[R]made us alive together with Christ (by grace
you have been saved), Rom. 5:6, 8 • [Rom. 6:4, 5]
6 and raised *us* up together, and made *us*
sit together [R]in the heavenly *places* in Christ
Jesus, Eph. 1:20
7 that in the ages to come He might show
the exceeding riches of His grace in [R]*His*
kindness toward us in Christ Jesus. Titus 3:4
8 [R]For by grace you have been saved
through faith, and that not of yourselves; [R]*it*
is the gift of God, [2 Tim. 1:9] • [John 1:12, 13]
9 not of works, lest anyone should boast.
10 For we are [R]His workmanship, created in
Christ Jesus for good works, which God
prepared beforehand that we should walk in
them. Is. 19:25

1:10 NU, M omit *both* **1:14** NU *which*
1:18 NU, M *hearts*

Reconciliation of Jews and Gentiles

11 Therefore remember that you, once Gentiles in the flesh—who are called Uncircumcision by what is called [R]the Circumcision made in the flesh by hands— [Col. 2:11]

12 that at that time you were without Christ, being aliens from the commonwealth of Israel and strangers from the covenants of promise, having no hope and without God in the world.

13 But now in Christ Jesus you who once were far off have been made near by the blood of Christ.

14 [R]For He Himself is our peace, who has made both one, and has broken down the middle wall of division *between us,* Is. 9:6★

15 having abolished in His flesh the enmity, *that is,* the law of commandments *contained* in ordinances, so as to create in Himself one new man *from* the two, *thus* making peace,

16 and that He might reconcile them both to God in one body through the cross, thereby putting to death the enmity.

17 And He came and preached peace to you who were afar off and to those who were near.

18 For through Him we both have access [R]by one Spirit to the Father. 1 Cor. 12:13

19 Now, therefore, you are no longer strangers and foreigners, but fellow citizens with the saints and members of the household of God,

20 having been built on the foundation of the apostles and prophets, Jesus Christ Himself being the chief corner*stone,*

21 [R]in whom the whole building, being joined together, grows into [R]a holy temple in the Lord, Ps. 118:22★ • 1 Cor. 3:16, 17

22 in whom you also are being built together for a habitation of God in the Spirit.

CHAPTER 3

Revelation of the Mystery of the Church

FOR this reason I, Paul, the prisoner of Jesus Christ for you Gentiles—

2 if indeed you have heard of the [T]dispensation of the grace of God [R]which was given to me for you, *stewardship* • Acts 9:15

3 [R]how that by revelation [R]He made known to me the mystery (as I wrote before in a few words, Acts 22:17, 21 • [Rom. 11:25; 16:25]

4 by which, when you read, you may understand my knowledge in the mystery of Christ),

5 which in other ages was not made known to the sons of men, as it has now been revealed by the Spirit to His holy apostles and prophets:

6 that the Gentiles [R]should be fellow heirs, of the same body, and partakers of His promise in Christ through the gospel, Gal. 3:28, 29

7 of which I became a minister according to the gift of the grace of God given to me by the effective working of His power.

8 To me, [R]who am less than the least of all the saints, this grace was given, that I should preach among the Gentiles [R]the unsearchable riches of Christ, [1 Cor. 15:9] • [Col. 1:27; 2:2, 3]

9 and to make all *people* see what *is* the *fellowship of the mystery, which from the beginning of the ages has been hidden in God who [R]created all things *through Jesus Christ; Heb. 1:2

10 to the intent that now the [T]manifold wisdom of God might be made known by the church to the [T]principalities and powers in the heavenly *places,* *variegated* or *many-sided* • *rulers*

11 according to the eternal purpose which He accomplished in Christ Jesus our Lord,

12 in whom we have boldness and access with confidence through faith in Him.

13 [R]Therefore I ask that you do not lose heart at my tribulations for you, [R]which is your glory. Phil. 1:14 • 2 Cor. 1:6

Prayer for Realization

14 For this reason I bow my knees to the [R]Father *of our Lord Jesus Christ, Eph. 1:3

15 from whom the whole family in heaven and earth is named,

16 that He would grant you, [R]according to the riches of His glory, [R]to be strengthened with might through His Spirit in [R]the inner man, [Phil. 4:19] • Col. 1:11 • Rom. 7:22

17 [R]that Christ may dwell in your hearts through faith; that you, [R]being rooted and grounded in love, John 14:23 • Col. 1:23

18 [R]may be able to comprehend with all the saints [R]what *is* the width and length and depth and height— Eph. 1:18 • Rom. 8:39

19 to know the love of Christ which passes knowledge; that you may be filled [R]with all the fullness of God. Eph. 1:23

20 Now [R]to Him who is able to do exceedingly abundantly [R]above all that we ask or think, [R]according to the power that works in us, Rom. 16:25 • 1 Cor. 2:9 • Col. 1:29

21 [R]to Him *be* glory in the church by Christ Jesus throughout all ages, world without end. Amen. Rom. 11:36

3:9 NU, M *stewardship (dispensation)*
3:9 NU omits *through Jesus Christ*
3:14 NU omits *of our Lord Jesus Christ*

3:21 The Purpose of the Church—The ultimate purpose of the church is to bring honor and glory to its head, Jesus Christ. It does this as it fulfills its two purposes related to God's program for the world.

The one purpose of the church, as it relates to the world, is evangelism. This program is spelled out in the Great Commission (Page 1155—Matt. 28:19, 20), which has never been rescinded. The program is *(continued on page 1390)*

THE CITY OF EPHESUS

Ephesus was an important city on the western coast of Asia Minor where the apostle Paul founded a church. As the most favorable seaport in the Roman province of Asia, this city was the most important trade center west of Tarsus. Today the city lies in swampy ruins about six miles from the sea because of centuries of silting from the Cayster River.

During Paul's years in Ephesus, the city was a cultural center with a population of about 300,000 people. Ephesus boasted of a great amphitheater, which seated 25,000 people. The city also had a number of gymnasiums, baths, and impressive public buildings.

Religion was a prominent feature of life in Ephesus. The temple of Artemis (or Diana, her Roman name) ranked as one of the Seven Wonders of the Ancient World. As the daughter of Zeus, Artemis was variously known as the moon goddess, the goddess of hunting, and the patroness of young girls. The Ephesians took pride in the beautiful temple, which was supported by scores of stone columns (see map).

The church at Ephesus may have been established by Priscilla and Aquila (Acts 18:18). It was about two years old when Paul settled in the city. Timothy was also involved in ministry at Ephesus (1 Tim. 1:3). Paul taught daily in the lecture hall of Tyrannus (Acts 19:9). Influence from Paul's three-year ministry likely resulted in the planting of churches in the Lycus River Valley at Laodicea, Hierapolis, and Colosse. The apostle wrote 1 Corinthians during his Ephesian ministry.

Some time after Paul's ministry, the apostle John settled and ministered at Ephesus. Exiled on the Isle of Patmos off the coast of Ephesus, he addressed the Book of Revelation to the seven churches of Asia Minor, which included the congregation at Ephesus (Rev. 1:11; 2:1–7). The traditional tomb of John is located at the Church of St. John in Ephesus.

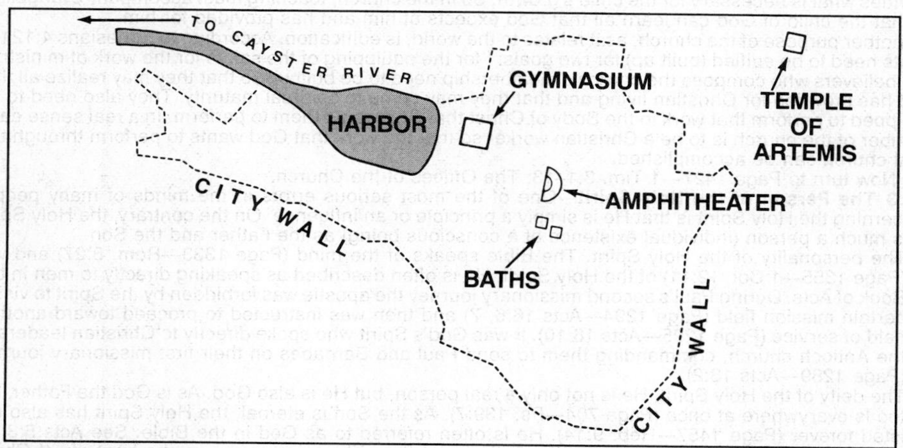

City of Ephesus.

CHAPTER 4

Exhortation to Unity

I THEREFORE, the prisoner of the Lord,
[T]beseech you to have a walk worthy of
the calling with which you were called, *exhort*
2 with all lowliness and gentleness, with
longsuffering, bearing with one another in
love,

3 endeavoring to keep the unity of the
Spirit [R]in the bond of peace. Col. 3:14

Explanation of Unity

4 *There is* one body and one Spirit, just as
you were called in one hope of your calling;
5 one Lord, one faith, one baptism;
6 one God and Father of all, who *is* above
all, and through all, and in *you all.

Means for Unity: The Gifts

7 But to each one of us grace was given
according to the measure of Christ's gift.
8 Therefore He says:

[R]*"When He ascended on high,*
He led captivity captive,
And gave gifts to men." Ps. 68:18☆

9 [R](Now this, *"He ascended"*—what does it
mean but that He also *first descended into
the lower parts of the earth? John 3:13; 20:17
10 He who descended is also the One [R]who
ascended far above all the heavens, that He
might fill all things.) John 20:17; Acts 1:9, 11★
11 And He Himself gave some *to be* apostles, some prophets, some evangelists, and
some pastors and teachers,

Purpose of the Gifts

12 for the equipping of the saints for the
work of ministry, [R]for the [T]edifying of [R]the
body of Christ, 1 Cor. 14:26 • *building up* • Col. 1:24
13 till we all come to the unity of the faith
[R]and the knowledge of the Son of God, to [R]a
perfect man, to the measure of the stature of
the fullness of Christ; Col. 2:2 • 1 Cor. 14:20
14 that we should no longer be [R]children,
tossed to and fro and carried about with
every wind of doctrine, by the trickery of
men, in the cunning craftiness [R]by which
they lie in wait to deceive, 1 Cor. 14:20 • Rom. 16:18
15 but, speaking the truth in love, may
grow up in all things into Him who is the
[R]head—Christ— Eph. 1:22
16 from whom the whole body, joined and
knit together by what every joint supplies,
according to the effective working by which
every part does its share, causes growth of
the body for the edifying of itself in love.

Put Off the Old Man

17 This I say, therefore, and testify in the
Lord, that you should [R]no longer walk as the

4:6 NU omits *you;* M *us* 4:9 NU omits *first*

(continued from page 1388)
to "make disciples of all the nations." The way this is to be done is twofold: by "baptizing them in the name of the Father and of the Son and of the Holy Spirit," and by "teaching them to observe all things that I have commanded you." Baptism is not an optional afterthought. It is a vital part of evangelism and making disciples. By baptism, one indicates that he has been identified with Christ in His death, burial, and resurrection (i.e., he is a member of the universal church, the Body of Christ) and wishes to be identified with the local church. A responsible parent not only brings a child into the world, but also provides what is necessary for the child's growth. So in the church, teaching must accompany evangelism so that the child of God can learn all that God expects of him and has provided for him.

Another purpose of the church, as it relates to the world, is edification. According to Ephesians 4:12 the saints need to be edified (built up) for two goals: "for the equipping of the saints for the work of ministry." The believers who compose the church's membership need to be built up so that they may realize all that God has provided for Christian living and that they may come to spiritual maturity. They also need to be equipped to perform that work in the Body of Christ that God wants them to perform. In a real sense each member of the church is to be a Christian worker so that the work that God wants to perform through the local church can be accomplished.

Now turn to Page 1427—1 Tim. 3:1-13: The Offices of the Church.

4:3 The Person of the Holy Spirit—One of the most serious errors in the minds of many people concerning the Holy Spirit is that He is simply a principle or an influence. On the contrary, the Holy Spirit is as much a person (individual existence of a conscious being) as the Father and the Son.

a. The personality of the Holy Spirit. The Bible speaks of the mind (Page 1333—Rom. 8:27) and will (Page 1355—1 Cor. 12:11) of the Holy Spirit. He is often described as speaking directly to men in the Book of Acts. During Paul's second missionary journey the apostle was forbidden by the Spirit to visit a certain mission field (Page 1294—Acts 16:6, 7) and then was instructed to proceed toward another field of service (Page 1295—Acts 16:10). It was God's Spirit who spoke directly to Christian leaders in the Antioch church, commanding them to send Paul and Barnabas on their first missionary journey (Page 1289—Acts 13:2).

b. The deity of the Holy Spirit. He is not only a real person, but He is also God. As is God the Father, He too is everywhere at once (Page 704—Ps. 139:7). As the Son is eternal, the Holy Spirit has also existed forever (Page 1457—Heb. 9:14). He is often referred to as God in the Bible. See Acts 5:3, 4. Finally, the Holy Spirit is equal with the Father and Son. This is seen during the baptism of Christ (Page 1117—Matt. 3:16, 17) and is mentioned by Jesus Himself just prior to His ascension from the Mount of Olives (Page 1155—Matt. 28:19, 20).

Now turn to Page 1442—Titus 3:5: The Work of the Holy Spirit in Salvation.

*rest of the Gentiles walk, in the futility of
their mind, Eph. 2:2; 4:22
18 having their understanding darkened,
being alienated from the life of God, because
of the ignorance that is in them, because of
the [R]hardening of their heart; Rom. 1:21
19 who, being past feeling, [R]have given
themselves over to licentiousness, to work all
uncleanness with greediness. 1 Pet. 4:3
20 But you have not so learned Christ,
21 if indeed you have heard Him and have
been taught by Him, as the truth is in Jesus:
22 that you [R]put off, concerning your former conduct, the old man which grows corrupt according to the deceitful lusts, Col. 3:8

Put On the New Man

23 and [R]be renewed in the spirit of your
mind, [Rom. 12:2]
24 and that you [R]put on the new man which
was created according to God, in righteousness and true holiness. [Rom. 6:4; 7:6; 12:2]
25 Therefore, putting away lying, [R]each one
speak truth with his neighbor, for [R]we are
members of one another. Zech. 8:16 • Rom. 12:5
26 [R]*"Be angry, and do not sin"*: do not let
the sun go down on your wrath, Ps. 4:4; 37:8
27 nor give [T]place to the devil. *opportunity*
28 Let him who stole steal no longer, but
rather [R]let him labor, working with *his* hands
what is good, that he may have something
[R]to give him who has need. Acts 20:35 • Luke 3:11
29 Let no corrupt communication proceed
out of your mouth, but what is good for
necessary [T]edification, [R]that it may impart
grace to the hearers. *building up* • Col. 3:16

Grieve Not the Holy Spirit

30 And [R]do not grieve the Holy Spirit of
God, by whom you were sealed for the day of
redemption. Is. 7:13
31 Let all bitterness, wrath, anger, [T]clamor,
and [R]evil speaking be put away from you,
[R]with all malice. *loud quarreling* • James 4:11 • Titus 3:3
32 And be kind to one another, tenderhearted, [R]forgiving one another, just as God
in Christ also forgave you. [Mark 11:25]

CHAPTER 5

THEREFORE[R] be followers of God as dear
[R]children. Luke 6:36 • 1 Pet. 1:14–16
2 And [R]walk in love, [R]as Christ also has
loved us and given Himself for us, an offering
and a sacrifice to God [R]for a sweet-smelling
aroma. 1 Thess. 4:9 • Gal. 1:4 • 2 Cor. 2:14, 15
3 But fornication and all [R]uncleanness or
covetousness, let it not even be named
among you, as is fitting for saints; Col. 3:5–7
4 neither filthiness, nor foolish talking, nor
coarse jesting, [R]which are not fitting, but
rather [R]giving of thanks. Rom. 1:28 • Phil. 4:6
5 For *this you know, that no fornicator,
unclean person, nor covetous man, who is an
idolater, has any [R]inheritance in the kingdom
of Christ and God. 1 Cor. 6:9, 10
6 Let no one deceive you with empty
words, for because of these things the wrath
of God comes upon the sons of disobedience.
7 Therefore do not be [R]partakers with
them. 1 Tim. 5:22
8 For you were once darkness, but now
you are [R]light in the Lord. Walk as children of
light 1 Thess. 5:5
9 (for [R]the fruit of the *Spirit *is* in all
goodness, righteousness, and truth), Gal. 5:22
10 proving what is acceptable to the Lord.
11 And have [R]no fellowship with the unfruitful works of darkness, but rather [T]expose
them. 2 Cor. 6:14 • *reprove*
12 For it is shameful even to speak of those
things which are done by them in secret.

Walk as Children of Light

13 But [R]all things that are [T]exposed are
made manifest by the light, for whatever
makes manifest is light. [John 3:20, 21] • *reproved*
14 Therefore He says:

[R]"Awake, you who sleep, [Is. 26:19; 60:1] *
Arise from the dead,
And Christ will give you light."

15 [R]See then that you walk [T]circumspectly,
not as fools but as wise, Col. 4:5 • *carefully*
16 [R]redeeming the time, [R]because the days
are evil. Col. 4:5 • Eccl. 11:2
17 [R]Therefore do not be unwise, but understand what the will of the Lord *is*. Col. 4:5

Be Filled with the Spirit

18 And [R]do not be drunk with wine, in
which is dissipation; but be filled with the
Spirit, Prov. 20:1; 23:31

4:17 NU omits *rest of the* **5:5** NU *know this*
5:9 NU *light*

5:18 Walking in the Spirit: Filling—To be filled with the Spirit is to be controlled by the Spirit and is therefore crucial to successfully living the Christian life. Unlike the indwelling of the Spirit, filling is a repeated experience. This is underscored by the use of the present tense ("be filled") as well as by biblical examples of Christians who were filled more than once (Page 1273—Acts 2:4; 4:31). Just as important, we must observe that filling is a command to be obeyed, not an option.

The next most important question is, How can someone be filled with the Spirit? The prerequisites are simply confession of sin and yielding to God. The former means to agree with God about the person's sin; the latter means primarily dedication of himself to God. As the believer chooses to obey in these areas, he is filled with the Spirit and enabled to manifest Christlike character. This obedience may be accompanied by prayer but is not necessarily so.

(continued on next page)

19 speaking to one another in psalms and
hymns and spiritual songs, singing and making melody in your heart to the Lord,
20 [R]giving thanks always for all things to
God the Father [R]in the name of our Lord
Jesus Christ, Ps. 34:1 • [1 Pet. 2:5]
21 [R]submitting to one another in the fear of
*God. [Phil. 2:3]

Wives: Submit to Your Husbands

22 Wives, [R]submit to your own husbands, as
to the Lord. Col. 3:18—4:1
23 For [R]the husband is head of the wife, as
also [R]Christ is head of the church; and He is
the Savior of the body. [1 Cor. 11:3] • Col. 1:18
24 Therefore, just as the church is subject
to Christ, so *let* the wives *be* to their own
husbands [R]in everything. Titus 2:4, 5

Husbands: Love Your Wives

25 [R]Husbands, love your wives, just as
Christ also loved the church and [R]gave Himself for it, Col. 3:19 • Acts 20:28
26 that He might sanctify and cleanse it
with the washing of water by the word,
27 [R]that He might present it to Himself a
glorious church, [R]not having spot or wrinkle
or any such thing, but that it should be holy
and without blemish. Col. 1:22 • Song 4:7
28 So husbands ought to love their own
wives as their own bodies; he who loves his
wife loves himself.
29 For no one ever hated his own flesh, but
nourishes and cherishes it, just as the Lord
does the church.
30 For [R]we are members of His body, *of His
flesh and of His bones. Gen. 2:23
31 *"For this reason a man shall leave his*
father and mother and be joined to his wife,
and the two shall become one flesh."
32 This is a great mystery, but I speak
concerning Christ and the church.
33 Nevertheless [R]let each one of you in
particular so love his own wife as himself,
and let the wife *see* that she [R]respects *her*
husband. Col. 3:19 • 1 Pet. 3:1, 6

CHAPTER 6

Children: Obey Your Parents

CHILDREN, [R]obey your parents in the
Lord, for this is right. Col. 3:20
2 *"Honor your father and mother,"* which
is the first commandment with promise:
3 *"that it may be well with you and you*
may live long on the earth."

4 And you, fathers, do not provoke your
children to wrath, but bring them up in the
training and admonition of the Lord.

5:21 NU *Christ* **5:30** NU omits the rest of v. 30.

(continued from previous page)

The certainty of being filled with the Spirit may be confirmed by the believer's faith and life. The believer must, of course, believe God's Word that meeting the conditions will result in the filling. The Spirit-filled person will exhibit the Christlike character described in Galatians 5:22, 23 as the fruit of the Spirit. Included in that list are all the vibrant, attractive qualities desired by all Christians. How delightful it is that any Christian may possess them and be transformed by the filling of the Spirit.

Now turn to Page 28—THE CHRISTIAN'S GUIDE: Facing Problems in the New Life.

5:25–29 The Relationship of the Church to Christ—The wonderful relationship that exists between Christ and the church was initiated by Christ who loved the church and gave Himself for it. The intimacies of that relationship are described with seven figures:

a. "The shepherd and the sheep" emphasizes both the warm leadership and protection of Christ and the helplessness and dependency of believers (Page 1251—John 10:1–18).
b. "The vine and the branches" points out the necessity for Christians to depend on Christ's sustaining strength for growth (Page 1258—John 15:1–8).
c. "Christ as high priest" and "the church as a kingdom of priests" stresses the joyful worship, fellowship, and service which the church can render to God through Christ (Page 1453—Heb. 5:1–10; 7:1; 8:6; Page 1479—1 Pet. 2:5–9; Page 1517—Rev. 1:6).
d. "The cornerstone and building stones" accents the foundational value of Christ to everything the church is and does, as well as Christ's value to the unity of believers. Love is to be the mortar which solidly holds the living stones together (Page 1346—1 Cor. 3:9; 13:1–13; Page 1388—Eph. 2:19–22; Page 1479—1 Pet. 2:5).
e. "The head and many-membered body" is frequently used in Scripture to illustrate several tremendous truths: the church is a vibrant organism, not merely an organization; it draws its vitality and direction from Christ, the head; and each believer has a unique and necessary place in its growth (Page 1355—1 Cor. 12:12, 13, 27; Page 1390—Eph. 4:4).
f. "The last Adam and new creation" presents Christ as the initiator of a new creation of believers as Adam was of the old creation (Page 1359—1 Cor. 15:22, 45; Page 1368—2 Cor. 5:17).
g. "The bridegroom and bride" beautifully emphasizes the intimate fellowship and co-ownership existing between Christ and the church (Eph. 5:25–33; Page 1536—Rev. 19:7, 8; 21:9).

You have now completed The Christian's Guide to the New Life.

6:4 The Role of the Parents—The father is the parent responsible for setting the pattern for the child's obedience in the family. Any disciplining the mother does is an extension of the father's authority in the home. The husband and father must take leadership in this area of the family, and the wife and mother must be in submission. The father's responsibility is set forth in two ways: First, what the father

Service on the Job

5 [R]Servants, be obedient to those who are
your masters according to the flesh, [R]with
fear and trembling, [R]in sincerity of heart, as
to Christ; [1 Tim. 6:1] • 2 Cor. 7:15 • 1 Chr. 29:17
6 [R]not with eyeservice, as men-pleasers,
but as servants of Christ, doing the will of
God from the heart, Col. 3:22
7 with good will doing service, as to the
Lord, and not to men,
8 [R]knowing that whatever good anyone
does, he will receive the same from the Lord,
whether *he is* a slave or free. Rom. 2:6
9 And you, masters, do the same things to
them, giving up threatening, knowing that
*your own Master also is in heaven, and
[R]there is no partiality with Him. Rom. 2:11

Put On the Armor of God

10 Finally, my brethren, be strong in the
Lord and in the power of His might.
11 [R]Put on the whole armor of God, that
you may be able to stand against the [T]wiles of
the devil. [2 Cor. 6:7] • *schemings*
12 For we do not wrestle against flesh and
blood, but against principalities, against powers, against [R]the rulers of *the darkness of
this age, against spiritual *hosts* of wickedness
in the heavenly *places*. Luke 22:53
13 Therefore take up the whole armor of
God, that you may be able to withstand in the
evil day, and having done all, to stand.
14 Stand therefore, [R]having girded your
waist with truth, [R]having put on the breastplate of righteousness, Is. 11:5 • Is. 59:17
15 [R]and having shod your feet with the
preparation of the gospel of peace; Is. 52:7
16 above all, taking [R]the shield of faith with
which you will be able to quench all the fiery
darts of the wicked one. 1 John 5:4
17 And [R]take the helmet of salvation, and
[R]the sword of the Spirit, which is the word of
God; 1 Thess. 5:8 • [Heb. 4:12]

Pray for Boldness

18 [R]praying always with all prayer and supplication in the Spirit, [R]being watchful to this
end with all perseverance and [R]supplication
for all the saints— Luke 18:1 • [Matt. 26:41] • Phil. 1:4
19 and for me, that utterance may be given
to me, that I may open my mouth boldly to
make known the mystery of the gospel,
20 for which [R]I am an ambassador in chains;
that in it I may speak boldly, as I ought to
speak. 2 Cor. 5:20

Conclusion

21 But that you also may know my affairs
and how I am doing, [R]Tychicus, a beloved
brother and faithful minister in the Lord, will
make all things known to you; Acts 20:4
22 whom I have sent to you for this very
purpose, that you may know our affairs, and
that he may [R]comfort your hearts. 2 Cor. 1:6
23 Peace to the brethren, and love with
faith, from God the Father and the Lord Jesus
Christ.
24 Grace *be* with all those who love our
Lord Jesus Christ in sincerity. Amen.

6:9 NU *He who is both their Master and yours is*
6:12 NU *this darkness*

---

is *not* to do—"do not provoke your children to wrath." He is not to over-discipline them or reign in terror, with the result that the child can only react in a blind outbreak or rage. Second, what the father *is* to do—"but bring them up in the training and admonition of the Lord." To "bring them up" involves three ideas:

a. It is a continuous job. As long as the child is a dependent, the father is to be responsible for providing for the child so that he becomes what God wants him to be.
b. It is a loving job. To "bring up" means literally *to nourish tenderly;* children should be objects of tender, loving care.
c. It is a twofold job involving nurture (lit., *child-training*)—all that a child needs for his development physically, mentally, and spiritually, and admonition (lit., *corrective* discipline) of the Lord.

The father is God's constituted home authority who is to discipline the child when he does not obey as God intends. The father who does not discipline his children is a father who is undisciplined himself and disobedient to God's will. A child's disobedience is not to be tolerated. See Exodus 21:15–17; Deuteronomy 21:18–21; Proverbs 13:24; 19:18; 22:15; 23:13, 14; 29:15–17.

Now turn to Page 734—Prov. 22:6: A Prescription for Rearing Children.

ISRAEL AND THE ROMANS

Modern Israel still bears many signs of the Roman occupation of that country. Ruins of the aqueduct and theater at Caesarea, the Roman encampment at Masada, and the Roman road at Emmaus bring to mind many mental pictures of what life under the Romans must have been like during New Testament times.

Rome was founded about 750 B.C., but it did not reach the status of a world power until several centuries later through victories over the Carthaginians and the Greeks. By New Testament times, the Romans were thoroughly entrenched as the ruling power of the ancient world.

Throughout the entire New Testament period, various emperors ruled over the Roman Empire. During the reign of Augustus, Christ was born (Luke 2:1). His crucifixion occurred during the reign of the succeeding emperor, Tiberius (Luke 3:1). The martyrdom of James, the brother of John, took place in the reign of the emperor Claudius (Acts 11:28; 12:1, 2). Paul appealed his case to the emperor Nero (Acts 25:11). The destruction of Jerusalem prophesied by Jesus (Luke 19:41–44) was accomplished in A.D. 70 by the Roman general Titus, who later became emperor. Thus, all of the New Testament story unfolded under the reign of Roman emperors.

The entire territory around the Mediterranean Sea ruled by the Romans enjoyed a time of peace and prosperity during New Testament times. The great Roman roads were built mainly as military routes from the capital city of Rome

Roman warship.

into the provinces and territories Rome controlled. A stable money system and improved methods of banking and credit encouraged economic expansion. Rome sent its merchant ships throughout the ancient world, trading in wine, olive oil, and grain.

The general stability of these times contributed to the spread of Christianity throughout the Roman world. Paul could travel easily from one Roman province to another over the great Roman roads and sea routes to spread the gospel. While the Romans themselves worshiped pagan gods, they were generally tolerant of all religions among the peoples and nations whom they controlled.

The Book of Acts shows how Christianity spread throughout the Roman Empire. Under Paul, the great missionary to the Gentiles, the gospel was preached as far west as the city of Rome and perhaps even into Spain (Rom. 15:28). By the time Paul wrote his Epistle to the Romans, a large Christian community existed in the capital city of Rome (Rom. 1:7).

In its early stages, Christianity was ignored by the Romans, because they thought it was a harmless sect of Judaism. But this apparently changed when Nero became emperor of Rome. Many Christians were arrested, tortured, crucified, and burned during his administration, seemingly in an attempt to blame them for the widespread rebellion and unrest that marked his years of rule. This persecution continued under the emperor Domitian. Many scholars believe the Book of Revelation was written by the apostle John during the Domitian persecutions.

The Romans worshiped many pagan gods: Jupiter, who was believed to control the universe; Mars, god of war; Juno, patron goddess of women; and Minerva, goddess of war, wisdom, and skill. The capital city of Rome was filled with shrines and temples devoted to worship of these pagan gods.

Because of its paganism and idolatry, the Roman Empire was singled out by New Testament writers as the very personification of the worldly evil forces that Christianity opposed. Many scholars believe the "beast rising up out of the sea" and the "beast coming up out of the earth" in the Revelation of John (ch. 13) are veiled references to the Roman Empire and the cult of emperor worship during the time of the Roman emperor Domitian about A.D. 90. John was confident that the forces of righteousness under the leadership of Jesus Christ would be victorious over these evil forces.

Bust of Augustus Caesar, first emperor of the Roman Empire.

THE EPISTLE OF PAUL THE APOSTLE TO THE

PHILIPPIANS

THE BOOK OF PHILIPPIANS

Paul writes a thank-you note to the believers at Philippi for their help in his hour of need, and he uses the occasion to send along some instruction on Christian unity. His central thought is simple: Only in Christ are real unity and joy possible. With Christ as your model of humility and service, you can enjoy a oneness of purpose, attitude, goal, and labor—a truth which Paul illustrates from his own life, and one the Philippians desperately need to hear. Within their own ranks, fellow workers in the Philippian church are at odds, hindering the work in proclaiming new life in Christ. Because of this, Paul exhorts the church to "stand fast . . . be of the same mind . . . rejoice in the Lord always . . . but in everything by prayer and supplication, with thanksgiving, let your requests be made known . . . and the peace of God, which surpasses all understanding, will guard your hearts and minds through Christ Jesus" (4:1, 2, 4, 6, 7).

This epistle is called *Pros Philippesious,* "To the Philippians." The church at Philippi was the first church Paul founded in Macedonia.

THE AUTHOR OF PHILIPPIANS

The external and internal evidence for the Pauline authorship of Philippians is very strong, and there is scarcely any doubt that anyone but Paul wrote it.

THE TIME OF PHILIPPIANS

In 356 B.C., King Philip of Macedonia (the father of Alexander the Great) took this town and expanded it, renaming it Philippi. The Romans captured it in 168 B.C.; and in 42 B.C., the defeat of the forces of Brutus and Cassius by those of Anthony and Octavian (later Augustus) took place outside the city. Octavian turned Philippi into a Roman colony (cf. Acts 16:12) and a military outpost. The citizens of this colony were regarded as citizens of Rome and given a number of special privileges. Because Philippi was a military city and not a commercial center, there were not enough Jews for a synagogue when Paul came (Acts 16:13).

Paul's "Macedonian Call" in Troas during his second missionary journey led to his ministry in Philippi with the conversion of Lydia and others. Paul and Silas were beaten and imprisoned, but this resulted in the conversion of the Philippian jailer. The magistrates were placed in a dangerous position by beating Roman citizens without a trial (Acts 16:37–40), and that embarrassment may have prevented future reprisals against the new Christians in Philippi. Paul visited the Philippians again on his third missionary journey (Acts 20:1, 6). When they heard of his Roman imprisonment, the Philippian church sent Epaphroditus with financial help (4:18); they had helped Paul in this way on at least two other occasions (4:16). Epaphroditus almost died of an illness, yet remained with Paul long enough for the Philippians to receive word of his malady. Upon his recovery, Paul sent this letter back with him to Philippi (2:25–30).

Silas, Timothy, Luke, and Paul first came to Philippi in A.D. 51, eleven years before Paul wrote this letter. Philippians 1:13 and 4:22 suggest that it was written from Rome, although some commentators argue for Caesarea or Ephesus. Paul's life was at stake, and he was evidently awaiting the verdict of the Imperial Court (2:20–26).

THE CHRIST OF PHILIPPIANS

The great *kenosis* passage is one of several portraits of Christ in this epistle. In chapter 1, Paul sees Christ as his life ("For to me, to live *is* Christ," 1:21). In chapter 2, Christ is the model of true humility ("Let this mind be in you which was also in Christ Jesus," 2:5). Chapter 3 presents Him as the One "who will transform our lowly body that it may be conformed to His glorious body" (3:21). In chapter 4, He is the source of Paul's power over circumstances ("I can do all things through Christ who strengthens me," 4:13).

KEYS TO PHILIPPIANS

Key Word: To Live Is Christ—Central to Philippians is the concept of "For to me, to live *is* Christ, and to die *is* gain" (1:21). Every chapter resounds with the theme of the centrality of Jesus in the Christian's life. High points include the following: "Let this mind be in you which was also in Christ Jesus" (2:5); "I also count all things loss for the excellence of the knowledge of Christ Jesus" (3:8); and "I can do all things through Christ who strengthens me" (4:13).

Key Verses: Philippians 1:21 and 4:12—"For to me, to live *is* Christ, and to die *is* gain" (1:21).

"I know how to be abased, and I know how to abound. Everywhere and in all things I have learned both to be full and to be hungry, both to abound and to suffer need" (4:12).

Key Chapter: Philippians 2—The grandeur of the truth of the New Testament seldom exceeds the revelation of the humility of Jesus Christ when He left heaven to become a servant of man. Christ is clearly the Christian's example, and Paul encourages "Let this mind be in you which was also in Christ Jesus" (2:5).

SURVEY OF PHILIPPIANS

Philippians is the epistle of joy and encouragement in the midst of adverse circumstances. Paul freely expresses his fond affection for the Philippians, appreciates their consistent testimony and support, and lovingly urges them to center their actions and thoughts on the pursuit of the person and power of Christ. Paul also seeks to correct the problems of disunity and rivalry (2:2–4) and to prevent the problems of legalism and antinomianism (3:1–19). Philippians focuses on: Paul's account of his present circumstances (1); Paul's appeal to have the mind of Christ (2); Paul's appeal to have the knowledge of Christ (3); Paul's appeal to have the peace of Christ (4).

Paul's Account of His Present Circumstances (1): Paul's usual salutation (1:1, 2) is followed by his thanksgiving, warm regard, and prayer on behalf of the Philippians (1:3–11). For years, they have participated in the apostle's ministry, and he prays for their continued growth in the real knowledge of Christ. Paul shares the circumstances of his imprisonment and rejoices in the spread of the gospel in spite of and because of his situation (1:12–26). As he considers the outcome of his approaching trial, he expresses his willingness to "depart and be with Christ" (1:23) or to continue in ministry. Paul encourages the Philippians to remain steadfast in the face of opposition and coming persecution (1:27–30).

Paul's Appeal to Have the Mind of Christ (2): Paul exhorts the Philippians to have a spirit of unity and mutual concern by embracing the attitude of humility (2:1–4), the greatest example of which is the incarnation and crucifixion of Christ (2:5–11). The *kenosis,* or "emptying," of Christ does not mean that He divested Himself of His deity, but that He withheld His preincarnate glory and voluntarily restricted His use of certain attributes (e.g., omnipresence and omniscience). Paul asks the Philippians to apply this attitude to their lives (2:12–18), and he gives two more examples of sacrifice, the ministries of Timothy and Epaphroditus (2:19–30).

Paul's Appeal to Have the Knowledge of Christ (3): It appears that Paul is about to close his letter ("Finally, my brethren," 3:1) when he launches into a warning about the continuing problem of legalism (3:1–9). Paul refutes this teaching with revealing autobiographical details about his previous attainments in Judaism. Compared to the goal of knowing Christ, those pursuits are as nothing. True righteousness is received through faith, not by mechanical obedience to any law. Paul yearns for the promised attainment of the resurrected body.

Paul's Appeal to Have the Peace of Christ (4): In a series of exhortations, Paul urges the Philippians to have peace with the brethren by living a life-style of unity, prayerful dependence, and holiness (4:13). In 4:4–9, Paul describes the secrets of having the peace of God as well as peace with God. He then rejoices over their gift, but explains that the power of Christ enables him to live above his circumstances (4:10–20). This joyous letter from prison closes with greetings and a benediction (4:21–23).

FOCUS	ACCOUNT OF CIRCUMSTANCES	THE MIND OF CHRIST	THE KNOWLEDGE OF CHRIST	THE PEACE OF CHRIST
REFERENCE	1:1—	2:1—	3:1—	4:1—4:23
DIVISION	PARTAKE OF CHRIST	PEOPLE OF CHRIST	PURSUIT OF CHRIST	POWER OF CHRIST
TOPIC	SUFFERING	SUBMISSION	SALVATION	SANCTIFICATION
	EXPERIENCE	EXAMPLES	EXHORTATION	
LOCATION	ROME			
TIME	C. A.D. 62			

OUTLINE OF PHILIPPIANS

CHAPTER 1

Paul's Prayer of Thanksgiving

PAUL and Timothy, servants of Jesus
Christ,

To all the saints in Christ Jesus who are
in Philippi, with the bishops and deacons:

2 Grace to you and peace from God our
Father and the Lord Jesus Christ.
3 [R]I thank my God upon every remembrance of you, 1 Cor. 1:4
4 always in [R]every prayer of mine making
request for you all with joy, Eph. 1:16
5 [R]for your fellowship in the gospel from
the first day until now, [Rom. 12:13]
6 being confident of this very thing, that
He who has begun a good work in you will
complete *it* until the day of Jesus Christ;
7 just as it is right for me to think this of
you all, because I have you in my heart,
inasmuch as both in my chains and in the
defense and confirmation of the gospel, you
all are partakers with me of grace.
8 For God is my witness, how greatly I
long for you all with the affection of Jesus
Christ.
9 And this I pray, that your love may
abound still more and more in knowledge and
all discernment,
10 that you may approve the things that are
excellent, that you may be sincere and without offense till the day of Christ,
11 being filled with the fruits of righteousness [R]which *are* by Jesus Christ, [R]to the glory
and praise of God. Col. 1:6 • John 15:8

Paul's Afflictions Promote the Gospel

12 But I want you to know, brethren, that
the things *which happened* to me have actually turned out for the furtherance of the
gospel,
13 so that it has become evident [R]to the
whole [T]palace guard, and to all the rest, that
my chains are in Christ; Phil. 4:22 • Or *praetorian*
14 and most of the brethren in the Lord,
having become confident by my chains, are
much more bold to speak the word without
fear.
15 Some indeed preach Christ even from
envy and strife, and some also from good will:
16 *The former preach Christ from selfish
ambition, not sincerely, supposing to add
affliction to my chains;
17 but the latter out of love, knowing that I
am appointed for the defense of the gospel.
18 What then? Only *that* in every way,
whether in pretense or in truth, Christ is
preached; and in this I rejoice, yes, and will
rejoice.

Paul's Afflictions Exalt the Lord

19 For I know that [R]this will turn out for my
salvation through your prayer and the supply
of the Spirit of Jesus Christ, Job 13:16, LXX
20 according to my earnest expectation and
hope that in nothing I shall be ashamed, but
that [R]with all boldness, as always, so now also
Christ will be magnified in my body, whether
by life [R]or by death. Eph. 6:19, 20 • [Rom. 14:8]
21 For to me, to live *is* Christ, and to die *is*
gain.
22 But if *I* live on in the flesh, this *will mean*
fruit from *my* labor; yet what I shall choose I
[T]cannot tell. *do not know*
23 *For I am hard pressed between the two,
having a [R]desire to depart and be with Christ,
which is [R]far better. [2 Cor. 5:2, 8] • [Ps. 16:11]
24 Nevertheless to remain in the flesh *is*
more needful for you.

1:16 NU reverses vv. 16 and 17. **1:23** NU, M *But*

THE CITY OF PHILIPPI

Philippi, known originally as Krenides (meaning "wells" or "springs"), was named after Philip II, father of the Greek conqueror Alexander the Great. This city of the Roman province of Macedonia was strategically located on the Egnatian Way, the main overland route between Asia and the West, making it an important bridge in the early spread of the gospel.

The ruins of the city bear the marks of a rich Roman history, including an agora, or marketplace, where trade took place, and the western arch, or "gate," of the city, described in Acts 16:13. The agora was an important discovery with its seat of judgment, library, and adjacent jail site, possibly the very place where Paul and Silas were imprisoned (Acts 16:23–40).

Paul founded the church at Philippi in the early fifties as the first church on European soil. Soon after he and Silas entered the city, they met with a group of women for prayer outside the city gate. This indicates that the city did not have a large Jewish population, since they generally preached at the local synagogue if one was available. When Paul and Silas removed a spirit from a slave girl, her angry owners took them to court. Beaten and jailed, they prayed and sang until an earthquake shook the jail during the night. The next day the magistrates were alarmed to discover that Paul and Silas were Roman citizens and should not have been beaten or jailed without a fair trial.

Lydia, a businesswoman, became the first Christian convert in all of Europe through the witness of Paul and Silas at Philippi (Acts 16:12–15, 40). Because of the influence of the church in this city, the way was opened for the gospel to spread to the rest of Europe. And it all began with a women's prayer group.

Photo by Howard Vos

Ruins of the agora, or marketplace, of Philippi, with pagan temple in the foreground.

25 And being confident of this, I know that
I shall remain and continue with you all for
your progress and joy of faith,
26 that [R]your rejoicing for me may be more
abundant in Jesus Christ by my coming to
you again. 2 Cor. 1:14

Paul's Exhortation to the Afflicted

27 Only [R]let your conduct be worthy of the
gospel of Christ, so that whether I come and
see you or am absent, I may hear of your
affairs, that you stand fast in one spirit, [R]with
one mind [R]striving together for the faith of
the gospel, Eph. 4:1 • Eph. 4:3 • Jude 3
28 and not in any way terrified by your
adversaries, which is to them a proof of
perdition, but *to you of salvation, and that
from God.
29 For to you it has been granted on behalf
of Christ, [R]not only to believe in Him, but also
to [R]suffer for His sake, Eph. 2:8 • [2 Tim. 3:12]
30 [R]having the same conflict which you saw
in me and now hear *is* in me. Col. 1:29

CHAPTER 2

Paul's Exhortation to Humility

THEREFORE if *there is* any [T]consolation in
Christ, if any comfort of love, if any
fellowship of the Spirit, if any [R]affection and
mercy, Or *encouragement* • Col. 3:12
2 [R]fulfill my joy [R]by being like-minded,
having the same love, *being* of [R]one accord,
of one mind. John 3:29 • Rom. 12:16 • Phil. 4:2
3 *Let* nothing *be done* through selfish ambition or conceit, but in lowliness of mind let
each esteem others better than himself.
4 [R]Let each of you look out not only for his
own interests, but also for the interests of
[R]others. 1 Cor. 13:5 • Rom. 15:1, 2

Christ's Example of Humility

5 [R]Let this mind be in you which was also
in Christ Jesus, [Matt. 11:29]
6 who, being in the form of God, did not
consider it robbery to be equal with God,
7 but [T]made Himself of no reputation,
taking the form of a servant, *and* coming in
the likeness of men. *emptied Himself* of His privileges
8 And being found in appearance as a man,
He humbled Himself and [R]became [R]obedient
to *the point of* death, even the death of the
cross. Matt. 26:39 • Heb. 5:8
9 [R]Therefore God also [R]has highly exalted
Him and [R]given Him the name which is above
every name, Heb. 2:9 • Ps. 68:18; Acts 2:33★ • Eph. 1:21
10 [R]that at the name of Jesus every knee
should bow, of those in heaven, and of those
on earth, and of those under the earth, Is. 45:23
11 and [R]*that* every tongue should confess
that Jesus Christ *is* Lord, to the glory of God
the Father. John 13:13

12 Therefore, my beloved, [R]as you have
always obeyed, not as in my presence only,
but now much more in my absence, [R]work
out your own salvation with [R]fear and trembling; Phil. 1:5, 6; 4:15 • John 6:27, 29 • Eph. 6:5
13 for it is God who works in you both to
will and to do for *His* good pleasure.
14 Do all things [R]without [T]murmuring and
[R]disputing,[T] 1 Pet. 4:9 • *grumbling* • Rom. 14:1 • *arguing*
15 that you may become blameless and
[T]harmless, children of God without fault in
the midst of a crooked and perverse generation, among whom you shine as [R]lights in the
world, *innocent* • Matt. 5:15, 16
16 holding fast the word of life, so that I
may rejoice in the day of Christ that [R]I have
not run in vain or labored in vain. Gal. 2:2

Paul's Example of Humility

17 Yes, and if [R]I am being poured out *as a
drink offering* on the sacrifice [R]and service of
your faith, [R]I am glad and rejoice with you
all. 2 Tim. 4:6 • Rom. 15:16 • 2 Cor. 7:4
18 For the same reason you also be glad and
rejoice with me.

Timothy's Example of Humility

19 But I trust in the Lord Jesus to send
Timothy to you shortly, that I also may be
encouraged when I know your state.
20 For I have no one [R]like-minded, who will
sincerely care for your state. 2 Tim. 3:10
21 For all seek their own, not the things
which are of Christ Jesus.
22 But you know his proven character,
[R]that as a son with *his* father he served with
me in the gospel. 1 Cor. 4:17
23 Therefore I hope to send him at once, as
soon as I see how it goes with me.
24 But I trust in the Lord that I myself shall
also come shortly.

Epaphroditus's Example of Humility

25 Yet I considered it necessary to send to
you [R]Epaphroditus, my brother, fellow
worker, and [R]fellow soldier, [R]but your messenger and [R]the one who ministered to my
need; Phil. 4:18 • Philem. 2 • 2 Cor. 8:23 • 2 Cor. 11:9
26 [R]since he was longing for you all, and
was distressed because you had heard that he
was sick. Phil. 1:8
27 For indeed he was sick almost unto
death; but God had mercy on him, and not
only on him but on me also, lest I should
have sorrow upon sorrow.
28 Therefore I sent him the more eagerly,
that when you see him again you may rejoice, and I may be less sorrowful.
29 Receive him therefore in the Lord with
all gladness, and hold such men in esteem;

1:28 NU *of your salvation*

30 because for the work of Christ he came
close to death, [T]not regarding his life, [R]to
supply what was lacking in your service
toward me. *risking* • 1 Cor. 16:17

CHAPTER 3

Warning Against Confidence in the Flesh

FINALLY, my brethren, rejoice in the
Lord. For me to write the same things to
you *is* not tedious, but for you *it is* safe.
2 Beware of dogs, beware of evil workers,
[R]beware of the mutilation! Rom. 2:28
3 For we are the circumcision, who worship *God in the Spirit, rejoice in Christ
Jesus, and have no confidence in the flesh,
4 though I also might have confidence in
the flesh. If anyone else thinks he may have
confidence in the flesh, I more so:
5 circumcised the eighth day, of the stock
of Israel, [R]*of* the tribe of Benjamin, [R]a Hebrew
of the Hebrews; concerning the law, [R]a Pharisee; Rom. 11:1 • 2 Cor. 11:22 • Acts 23:6
6 concerning zeal, [R]persecuting the
church; concerning the righteousness which
is in the law, blameless. Acts 8:3; 22:4, 5; 26:9–11
7 But [R]what things were gain to me, these
I have counted loss for Christ. Matt. 13:44
8 But indeed I also count all things loss
[R]for the excellence of the knowledge of Christ
Jesus my Lord, for whom I have suffered the
loss of all things, and count them as rubbish,
that I may gain Christ Jer. 9:23
9 and be found in Him, not having my own
righteousness, which *is* from the law, but that
which *is* through faith in Christ, the righteousness which is from God by faith;

Exhortation to Know Christ

10 that I may know Him and the power of
His resurrection, and the fellowship of His
sufferings, being conformed to His death,
11 if, by any means, I may [T]attain to the
resurrection from the dead. Lit. *arrive at*
12 Not that I have already [R]attained,[T] or am
already perfected; but I press on, that I may
lay hold of that for which Christ Jesus has
also laid hold of me. [1 Tim. 6:12, 19] • *obtained it*
13 Brethren, I do not count myself to have
apprehended; but one thing *I do*, forgetting
those things which are behind and reaching
forward to those things which are ahead,
14 I press toward the goal for the prize of
the upward call of God in Christ Jesus.
15 Therefore let us, as many as are mature,
have this mind; and if in anything you think
otherwise, God will reveal even this to you.
16 Nevertheless, to *the degree* that we have
already [T]attained, let us walk by the same
*rule, let us be of the same mind. *arrived*

Warning Against Living for the Flesh

17 Brethren, [R]join in following my example,
and note those who so walk, as [R]you have us
for a pattern. [1 Cor. 4:16; 11:1] • Titus 2:7, 8
18 For many walk, of whom I have told you
often, and now tell you even weeping, *that
they are* the enemies of the cross of Christ:
19 [R]whose end *is* destruction, [R]whose god *is
their* belly, and [R]*whose* glory *is* in their
shame—[R]who set their mind on earthly
things. 2 Cor. 11:15 • 1 Tim. 6:5 • Hos. 4:7 • Rom. 8:5
20 For our citizenship is in heaven, [R]from
which we also [R]eagerly wait for the Savior,
the Lord Jesus Christ, Acts 1:11 • 1 Cor. 1:7
21 who will transform our lowly body that it
may be conformed to His glorious body,
according to the working by which He is able
even to subdue all things to Himself.

CHAPTER 4

Peace with the Brethren

THEREFORE, my beloved and longed-for
brethren, [R]my joy and crown, so [R]stand
fast in the Lord, beloved. 2 Cor. 1:14 • Phil. 1:27
2 I implore Euodia and I implore Syntyche
to be of the same mind in the Lord.
3 *And I urge you also, true companion,
help these women who [R]labored with me in
the gospel, with Clement also, and the rest of
my fellow workers, whose names *are* in [R]the
Book of Life. Rom. 16:3 • Luke 10:20

Peace with the Lord

4 [R]Rejoice in the Lord always. Again I will
say, rejoice! Rom. 12:12
5 Let your [T]gentleness be known to all
men. The Lord *is* at hand. *graciousness*

6 [R]Be anxious for nothing, but in everything by prayer and supplication, with
[R]thanksgiving, let your requests be made
known to God; Matt. 6:25 • [1 Thess. 5:17, 18]

3:3 NU, M *in the Spirit of God*
3:16 NU omits *rule* and the rest of v. 16.
4:3 NU, M *Yes*

4:6 Thanksgiving—The importance and spiritual benefits of thanksgiving in our prayer life cannot be overemphasized. The Bible tells us God resists the proud, but gives grace to the humble (Page 1471—James 4:6). But the question is, How do you become humble? It is done by being thankful! A good rule is to be careful (worried) for nothing (Phil. 4:6), be prayerful in all things (Page 1416—1 Thess. 5:18), and be thankful for anything. It was the sin of thanklessness that caused the ancient world to plunge into the terrible depths of sexual depravity (Page 1324—Rom. 1:21). In the Old Testament a special
(continued on next page)

7 and [R]the peace of God, which surpasses
all understanding, will guard your hearts and
minds through Christ Jesus. [John 14:27]
8 Finally, brethren, whatever things are
true, whatever things are noble, whatever
things *are* [R]just, [R]whatever things *are* pure,
whatever things *are* [R]lovely, whatever things
are of good report, if *there is* any virtue and if
there is anything praiseworthy—meditate on
these things. Deut. 16:20 • 1 Thess. 5:22 • 1 Cor. 13:4–7
9 The things which you learned and re-
ceived and heard and saw in me, these do,
and the God of peace will be with you.

Peace in All Circumstances

10 But I rejoiced in the Lord greatly that
now at last your care for me has [T]flourished
again; though you surely did care, but you
lacked opportunity. *you have revived your care*
11 Not that I speak in regard to need, for I
have learned in whatever state I am, [R]to be
content: 1 Tim. 6:6, 8
12 I know how to be abased, and I know
how to abound. Everywhere and in all things
I have learned both to be full and to be
hungry, both to abound and to suffer need.
13 I can do all things [R]through *Christ who
strengthens me. John 15:5
14 Nevertheless you have done well that
[R]you shared in my distress. Phil. 1:7
15 Now you Philippians know also that in
the beginning of the gospel, when I departed
from Macedonia, [R]no church shared with me
concerning giving and receiving but you
only. 2 Cor. 11:8, 9
16 For even in Thessalonica you sent *aid*
once and again for my necessities.
17 Not that I seek the gift, but I seek [R]the
fruit that abounds to your account. Titus 3:14
18 Indeed I [T]have all and abound. I am full,
having received from Epaphroditus the
things *which were sent* from you, a sweet-
smelling aroma, [R]an acceptable sacrifice, well
pleasing to God. *Or have received all* • 2 Cor. 9:12
19 And my God [R]shall supply all your need
according to His riches in glory by Christ
Jesus. Ps. 23:1

Conclusion

20 [R]Now to our God and Father *be* glory
forever and ever. Amen. Rom. 16:27
21 Greet every saint in Christ Jesus. The
brethren [R]who are with me greet you. Gal. 1:2
22 All the saints greet you, but especially
those who are of Caesar's household.
23 The grace of our Lord Jesus Christ be
with *you all. Amen.

4:13 NU *Him who* **4:23** NU *your spirit*

(continued from previous page)
group of priests was appointed to do nothing else but praise and thank the Lord (Page 530—2 Chr. 31:2).

There are two main things we are to thank God for:

a. We are to thank Him for His work in Creation. David reminds us concerning this area of thanksgiving in Psalm 100. Later, John the apostle tells us we will thank God for His work in Creation throughout all eternity. Note the words of this song of praise: "You are worthy, O Lord, to receive glory and honor and power; for You created all things, and by Your will they exist and were created" (Page 1523—Rev. 4:11).

b. We are to thank Him for His work in redemption. John also informs us that our second song in heaven will feature thanksgiving for God's work in redemption: "And they sang a new song, saying, 'You are worthy to take the scroll, and to open its seals; for You were slain, and have redeemed us to God by Your blood'" (Page 1523—Rev. 5:9).

Now turn to Page 728—Prov. 16:3: Commitment.

THE EPISTLE OF PAUL THE APOSTLE TO THE

COLOSSIANS

THE BOOK OF COLOSSIANS

If Ephesians can be labeled the epistle portraying the "Church of Christ," then Colossians must surely be the "Christ of the Church." Ephesians focuses on the Body; Colossians focuses on the Head. Like Ephesians, the little Book of Colossians divides neatly in half with the first portion doctrinal (1 and 2) and the second practical (3 and 4). Paul's purpose is to show that Christ is preeminent—first and foremost in everything—and the Christian's life should reflect that priority. Because believers are rooted in Him, alive in Him, hidden in Him, and complete in Him, it is utterly inconsistent for them to live life without Him. Clothed in His love, with His peace ruling in their hearts, they are equipped to make Christ first in every area of life.

This epistle became known as *Pros Kolossaeis*, "To the Colossians," because of 1:2. Paul also wanted it to be read in the neighboring church at Laodicea (4:16).

THE AUTHOR OF COLOSSIANS

The external testimony to the Pauline authorship of Colossians is ancient and consistent, and the internal evidence also is very good. It not only claims to be written by Paul (1:1, 23; 4:18), but the personal details and close parallels with Ephesians and Philemon make the case even stronger. Nevertheless, the authenticity of this letter has been challenged on the internal grounds of vocabulary and thought. In its four chapters, Colossians uses fifty-five Greek words that do not appear in Paul's other epistles. However, Paul commanded a wide vocabulary; and the circumstances and subject of this epistle, especially the references to the Colossian heresy, account for these additional words. The high Christology of Colossians has been compared to John's later concept that Christ is the Logos (cf. 1:15–23 and John 1:1–18), with the conclusion that these concepts were too late for Paul's time. However, there is no reason to assume that Paul was unaware of Christ's work as Creator, especially in view of Philippians 2:5–11. It is also wrong to assume that the heresy refuted in Colossians 2 refers to the fully developed form of Gnosticism that did not appear until the second century. The parallels only indicate that Paul was dealing with an early form of Gnosticism.

THE TIME OF COLOSSIANS

Colosse was a minor city about one hundred miles east of Ephesus in the region of the seven Asian churches of Revelation 1—3. Located in the fertile Lycus Valley by a mountain pass on the road from Ephesus to the East, Colosse once was a populous center of commerce, famous for its glossy black wool. By the time of Paul, it had been eclipsed by its neighboring cities, Laodicea and Hierapolis (cf. 4:13), and was on the decline. Apart from this letter, Colosse exerted almost no influence on early church history. It is evident from 1:4–8 and 2:1 that Paul had never visited the church at Colosse, which was founded by Epaphras. On his third missionary journey, Paul devoted almost three years to an Asian ministry centered in Ephesus (cf. Acts 19:10; 20:31), and Epaphras probably came to Christ during this time. He carried the gospel to the cities in the Lycus Valley and years later came to visit Paul in his imprisonment (4:12, 13; Philem. 23).

Colossians, Philemon, and Ephesians were evidently written about the same time and under the same circumstances, judging by the overlapping themes and personal names (cf. Col. 4:9–17 and Philem. 2, 10, 23, 24). Although Caesarea and Ephesus have been suggested as the location of authorship, the bulk of the evidence indicates that Paul wrote all four Prison Epistles during his first Roman imprisonment (see "The Time of Ephesians" and "The Time of Philippians"). If so, Paul wrote it in A.D. 60 or 61 and sent it with Tychicus and the converted slave Onesimus to Colosse (4:7–9; see Eph. 6:21; Philem. 10–12).

Epaphras's visit and report about the conditions in Colosse prompted this letter. Although the Colossians had not yet succumbed (2:1–5), an encroaching heresy was threatening the predominantly gentile (1:21, 27; 2:13) Colossian church. The nature of this heresy can only be deduced from Paul's incidental references to it in his refutation in 2:8–23. It was apparently a religious system that combined elements from Greek speculation (2:4, 8–10), Jewish legalism (2:11–17), and Oriental mysticism (2:18–23). It involved a low view of the body (2:20–23) and probably nature as a whole. Circumcision, dietary regulations, and ritual observances were included in this system, which utilized asceticism, worship of angels as intermediaries, and mystical experiences as an approach to the spiritual realm. Any attempt to fit Christ into such a system would undermine His person and redemptive work.

THE CHRIST OF COLOSSIANS

This singularly Christological book is centered on the cosmic Christ—"the head of all principality and power" (2:10), the Lord of creation (1:16, 17), and the Author of reconciliation (1:20–22; 2:13–15). He is the basis for the believer's hope (1:5, 23, 27), the source of the believer's power for a new life (1:11, 29), the believer's Redeemer and Reconciler (1:14, 20–22; 2:11–15), the embodiment of full deity (1:15, 19; 2:9), the Creator and Sustainer of all things (1:16, 17), the Head of the church (1:18), the resurrected God-Man (1:18; 3:1), and the all-sufficient Savior (1:28; 2:3, 10; 3:1–4).

KEYS TO COLOSSIANS

Key Word: The Preeminence of Christ—The resounding theme in Colossians is the preeminence and sufficiency of Christ in all things. The believer is complete in Him alone and lacks nothing because "in Him dwells all the fullness of the Godhead bodily" (2:9); He has "all the treasures of wisdom and knowledge" (2:3). There is no need for speculation, mystical visions, or ritualistic regulations as though faith in Christ were insufficient. Paul's predominant purpose, then, is to refute a threatening heresy that is devaluing Christ. This false teaching is countered by a positive presentation of His true attributes and accomplishments. A proper view of Christ is the antidote for heresy. Paul also writes this epistle to encourage the Colossians to "continue in the faith, grounded and steadfast" (1:23), so that they will grow and bear fruit in the knowledge of Christ (1:10). A firm adherence to the true gospel will give them stability and resistance to opposing influences.

Key Verses: Colossians 2:9, 10 and 3:1, 2—"For in Him dwells all the fullness of the Godhead bodily; and you are complete in Him, who is the head of all principality and power" (2:9, 10).

"If then you were raised with Christ, seek those things which are above, where Christ is, sitting at the right hand of God. Set your mind on things above, not on things on the earth" (3:1, 2).

Key Chapter: Colossians 3—Chapter 3 links the three themes of Colossians (see "Key Word") together showing their cause and effect relationships. Because the believer is risen with Christ (3:1–4), he is to put off the old man and put on the new (3:5–17), which will result in holiness in all relationships (3:18–25).

SURVEY OF COLOSSIANS

Colossians is perhaps the most Christ-centered book in the Bible. In it Paul stresses the preeminence of the person of Christ and the completeness of the salvation He provides, in order to combat a growing heresy that is threatening the church at Colosse. This heresy seeks to devaluate Christ by elevating speculation, ritualism, mysticism, and asceticism. But Christ, the Lord of creation and Head of the Body, is completely sufficient for every spiritual and practical need of the believer. The last half of this epistle explores the application of these principles to daily life, because doctrinal truth (1 and 2) must bear fruit in practical conduct (3 and 4). The two major topics are: supremacy of Christ (1 and 2) and submission to Christ (3 and 4).

Supremacy of Christ (1 and 2): Paul's greeting (1:1, 2) is followed by an unusually extended thanksgiving (1:3–8) and prayer (1:9–14) on behalf of the believers at Colosse. Paul expresses his concern that the Colossians come to a deeper understanding of the person and power of Christ. Even here Paul begins to develop his major theme of the preeminence of Christ, but the most potent statement of this theme is in 1:15–23. He is supreme both in creation (1:15–18) and in redemption (1:19–23), and this majestic passage builds a positive case for Christ as the most effective refutation of the heresy that will be exposed in chapter 2. Paul describes his own ministry of proclaiming the mystery of "Christ in you, the hope of glory" (1:27) to the Gentiles and assures his readers that although he has not personally met them, he strongly desires that they become deeply rooted in Christ alone, who is preeminent in the Church (1:24—2:3). This is

FOCUS	SUPREMACY OF CHRIST			SUBMISSION TO CHRIST		
REFERENCE	1:1—	1:15—	2:4—	3:1—	3:5—	4:7—4:18
DIVISION	INTRODUCTION	PREEMINENCE OF CHRIST	FREEDOM IN CHRIST	POSITION OF THE BELIEVER	PRACTICE OF THE BELIEVER	CONCLUSION
TOPIC	DOCTRINAL			PRACTICAL		
	WHAT CHRIST DID FOR US			WHAT CHRIST DOES THROUGH US		
LOCATION	ROME					
TIME	A.D. 60–61					

especially important in view of false teachers who would defraud them through enticing rationalisms (2:4–7), vain philosophy (2:8–10), legalistic rituals (2:11–17), improper mysticism (2:18, 19), and useless asceticism (2:20–23). In each case, Paul contrasts the error with the corresponding truth about Christ.

Submission to Christ (3 and 4): The believer's union with Christ in His death, resurrection, and exaltation is the foundation upon which his earthly life must be built (3:1–4). Because of his death with Christ, the Christian must regard himself as dead to the old sins and put them aside (3:5–11); because of his resurrection with Christ, the believer must regard himself as alive to Him in righteousness and put on the new qualities that are prompted by Christian love (3:12–17). Turning from the inward life (3:1–17) to the outward life (3:18—4:6), Paul outlines the transformation that faith in Christ should make in relationships inside and outside the home. This epistle concludes with a statement concerning its bearers (Tychicus and Onesimus), greetings and instructions, and a farewell note (4:7–18).

OUTLINE OF COLOSSIANS

Part One: The Supremacy of Christ in the Church (1:1—2:23)

I. Introduction **1:1–14**
- A. Paul's Greeting to the Colossians 1:1, 2
- B. Paul's Thanksgiving for the Colossians 1:3–8
- C. Paul's Prayer for the Colossians 1:9–14

II. The Preeminence of Christ **1:15–2:3**
- A. Christ Is Preeminent in Creation 1:15–18
- B. Christ Is Preeminent in Redemption 1:19–23
- C. Christ Is Preeminent in the Church .... 1:24—2:3

III. The Freedom in Christ **2:4–23**
- A. Freedom from Enticing Words 2:4–7
- B. Freedom from Vain Philosophy 2:8–10
- C. Freedom from the Judgment of Men 2:11–17
- D. Freedom from Improper Worship 2:18, 19
- E. Freedom from the Doctrine of Men 2:20–23

Part Two: The Submission to Christ in the Church (3:1—4:18)

I. The Position of the Believer **3:1–4**

II. The Practice of the Believer **3:5–4:6**
- A. Put Off the Old Man 3:5–11
- B. Put On the New Man 3:12–17
- C. Personal Commands for Holiness .... 3:18—4:6
  1. Holiness in Family Life 3:18–21
  2. Holiness in Work Life .... 3:22—4:1
  3. Holiness in Public Life 4:2–6

III. Conclusion **4:7–18**
- A. Commendation of Tychicus 4:7–9
- B. Greetings from Paul's Friends 4:10–14
- C. Introductions Regarding This Letter 4:15–18

CHAPTER 1

Paul's Greeting to the Colossians

PAUL, an apostle of Jesus Christ by the
will of God, and Timothy our brother,

2 To the saints [R]and faithful brethren in
Christ *who are* in Colosse: 1 Cor. 4:17

[R]Grace to you and peace from God our
Father *and the Lord Jesus Christ. Gal. 1:3

Paul's Thanksgiving for the Colossians

3 [R]We give thanks to the God and Father
of our Lord Jesus Christ, praying always for
you, Phil. 1:3
4 since we heard of your faith in Christ
Jesus and of your love for all the saints;
5 because of the hope [R]which is laid up for
you in heaven, of which you heard before in
the word of the truth of the gospel, [1 Pet. 1:4]
6 which has come to you, as *it has* also in
all the world, and is bringing forth *fruit, as *it*
is also among you since the day you heard
and knew the grace of God in truth;
7 as you also learned from [R]Epaphras, our
dear fellow servant, who is a faithful minister
of Christ on your behalf, Philem. 23
8 who also declared to us your [R]love in the
Spirit. Rom. 15:30

Paul's Prayer for the Colossians

9 For this reason we also, since the day we
heard it, do not cease to pray for you, and to

1:2 NU omits *and the Lord Jesus Christ*
1:6 NU, M add *and growing*

ask that you may be filled with [R]the knowledge of His will [R]in all wisdom and spiritual
understanding; [Rom. 12:2] • Eph. 1:8
10 that you may have a walk worthy of the
Lord, fully pleasing *Him*, [R]being fruitful in
every good work and increasing in the
[R]knowledge of God; Heb. 13:21 • 2 Pet. 3:18
11 strengthened with all might, according
to His glorious power, [R]for all patience and
longsuffering [R]with joy; Eph. 4:2 • [Acts 5:41]
12 [R]giving thanks to the Father who has
qualified us to be partakers of the inheritance
of the saints in the light. [Eph. 5:20]
13 He has delivered us from the power of
darkness and [T]translated *us* into the kingdom
of the Son of His love, *transferred*
14 [R]in whom we have redemption *through
His blood, the forgiveness of sins. Eph. 1:7

Christ Is Preeminent in Creation

15 He is the image of the invisible God, [R]the
firstborn over all creation. Rev. 3:14
16 For by Him all things were created that
are in heaven and that are on earth, visible
and invisible, whether thrones or dominions
or [T]principalities or powers. All things were
created through Him and for Him. *rulers*
17 [R]And He is before all things, and in Him
[R]all things consist. [John 17:5] • Heb. 1:3
18 And [R]He is the head of the body, the
church, who is the beginning, [R]the firstborn
from the dead, that in all things He may have
the preeminence. Eph. 1:22 • Rev. 1:5

Christ Is Preeminent in Redemption

19 For it pleased *the Father that* [R]in Him all
the fullness should dwell, John 1:16
20 and by Him to reconcile all things to
Himself, by Him, whether things on earth or
things in heaven, [R]having made peace
through the blood of His cross. Eph. 1:10
21 And you, [R]who once were alienated and
enemies in your mind [R]by wicked works, yet
now He has reconciled [Eph. 2:1] • Titus 1:15

22 in the body of His flesh through death,
[R]to present you holy, and blameless, and
irreproachable in His sight— [Eph. 5:27]

23 if indeed you continue [R]in the faith,
grounded and steadfast, and are [R]not moved
away from the hope of the gospel which you
heard, [R]which was preached to every creature
under heaven, [R]of which I, Paul, became a
minister. Eph. 3:17 • [John 15:6] • Col. 1:6 • Col. 1:25

Christ Is Preeminent in the Church

24 I now rejoice in my sufferings for you,
and fill up in my flesh [R]what is lacking in the
afflictions of Christ, for [R]the sake of His body,
which is the church, [2 Cor. 1:5; 12:15] • Eph. 1:23
25 of which I became a minister according
to [R]the [T]stewardship from God which was
given to me for you, to fulfill the word of
God, Gal. 2:7 • *dispensation* or *administration*
26 the [T]mystery which has been hidden
from ages and from generations, but now has
been revealed to His saints. *hidden truth*
27 To them God willed to make known
what are [R]the riches of the glory of this
mystery among the Gentiles: *which is Christ
in you, the hope of glory. Rom. 9:23
28 Him we preach, [R]warning every man and
teaching every man in all wisdom, [R]that we
may present every man perfect in Christ
Jesus. Acts 20:20 • Eph. 5:27
29 To this *end* I also labor, striving according to His working which works in me
[R]mightily. Eph. 3:7

CHAPTER 2

FOR I want you to know what a great
[R]conflict[T] I have for you and those in
Laodicea, and *for* as many as have not seen
my face in the flesh, Phil. 1:30 • *struggle*
2 [R]that their hearts may be encouraged,
being knit together in love, and *attaining* to
all riches of the full assurance of understanding, to the knowledge of the mystery of God,
*both of the Father and of Christ, 2 Cor. 1:6
3 [R]in whom are hidden all the treasures of
wisdom and knowledge. 1 Cor. 1:24, 30

Freedom from Enticing Words

4 Now this I say [R]lest anyone should deceive you with persuasive words. Rom. 16:18
5 For though I am absent in the flesh, yet I
am with you in spirit, rejoicing [T]to see your
good order and the [R]steadfastness of your
faith in Christ. Lit. *and seeing* • 1 Pet. 5:9

1:14 NU, M omit *through His blood* **1:27** M *who*
2:2 NU omits *both of the Father and*

1:22 New Life: Based on Christ's Death—Salvation is free, but it is not cheap. Salvation is a gift and costs me nothing, but it cost God everything—it cost Jesus His life. The wages of sin is death (separation from God). God's gift is eternal life (eternal union of the soul with God). This is possible because of the death of Jesus on Calvary's cross (Page 1331—Rom. 6:23). Jesus actually took sin's penalty for every man, woman, and child who ever has lived or ever will live. As He hung upon the cross He cried, "Eli, Eli, lama sabachthani?" Being interpreted, He cried, "My God, My God, why have You forsaken Me?" (Page 1154—Matt. 27:46). Jesus was separated from God the Father so that you and I do not have to be. This is the heart of the atonement. The marvel of it all is that He did this while we were His enemies: "But God demonstrates His own love toward us, in that while we were still sinners, Christ died for us" (Page 1329—Rom. 5:8).

Now turn to Page 1295—Acts 16:31: New Life: Received by Faith.

THE CITY OF COLOSSE

Colosse was a city in the Roman province of Asia about a hundred miles east of Ephesus. Paul wrote a letter to the Christians in this city (his Epistle to the Colossians), but most scholars agree that he did not found the church.

During the fifth century B.C., Colosse was an important trading center on the Lycus River. By New Testament times, however, it had declined to the status of a small town, as its two neighbor cities, Laodicea and Hierapolis—about ten and twenty miles away, respectively—grew to the status of regional trading centers.

In A.D. 61 the city of Colosse suffered a devastating earthquake. It was rebuilt, only to be abandoned in the eighth century when the residents moved to a more suitable location at modern Honaz about three miles south. Only a mound of dirt and rubble remains today to mark the site of ancient Colosse.

Most scholars believe the church at Colosse was probably founded and nurtured during its early years by Paul's fellow laborer Epaphras (Col. 1:7; 4:12). Paul's reference to the Colossian Christians as among those who "have not seen my face in the flesh" (Col. 2:1) seems to indicate that he never visited the church.

Paul's letter to the Colossian Christians focuses on the person and work of Jesus Christ. It contains a majestic hymn to Christ, emphasizing His role in creation and redemption (Col. 1:9–23). Paul also warned the Colossians about false teachers who were apparently trying to add useless rules and regulations to the simple faith in Christ required by the gospel (Col. 2:11–23).

In this brief letter, Paul also mentioned ten of his friends (see chart), some of whom had connections with the city of Colosse. This indicates that Paul had numerous coworkers who helped him preach the gospel and nurture churches.

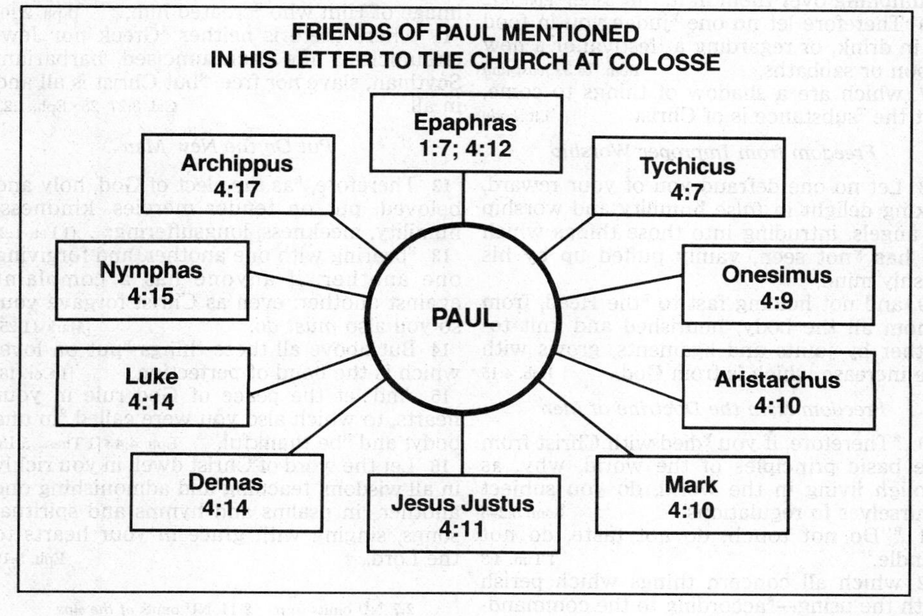

6 [R]As you have therefore received Christ
Jesus the Lord, so walk in Him, 1 Thess. 4:1
7 [R]rooted and built up in Him and established in the faith, as you have been taught,
abounding *in it with thanksgiving. Eph. 2:21

Freedom from Vain Philosophy

8 Beware lest anyone [T]cheat you through
philosophy and empty deceit, according to
[R]the tradition of men, according to the basic
principles of the world, and not according to
Christ. Lit. *plunder you* or *take you captive* • Gal. 1:14
9 For [R]in Him dwells all the fullness of the
Godhead [T]bodily; [John 1:14] • *in bodily form*
10 and you are complete in Him, who is the
head of all principality and power.

Freedom from the Judgment of Men

11 In Him you were also circumcised with
the circumcision made without hands, by
[R]putting off the body *of the sins of the flesh,
by the circumcision of Christ, Rom. 6:6; 7:24
12 [R]buried with Him in baptism, in which
you also were raised with *Him* through [R]faith
in the working of God, [R]who raised Him from
the dead. Rom. 6:4 • Eph. 1:19, 20 • Acts 2:24
13 And you, being dead in your trespasses
and the uncircumcision of your flesh, He has
made alive together with Him, having forgiven you all trespasses,
14 having wiped out the handwriting of
requirements that was against us, which was
contrary to us. And He has taken it out of the
way, having nailed it to the cross.
15 [R]Having disarmed [R]principalities and
powers, He made a public spectacle of them,
triumphing over them in it. [Is. 53:12] • Eph. 6:12
16 Therefore let no one [R]judge you in food
or in drink, or regarding a [T]festival or a new
moon or sabbaths, Rom. 14:3 • *feast day*
17 which are a shadow of things to come,
but the [T]substance is of Christ. Lit. *body*

Freedom from Improper Worship

18 Let no one defraud you of your reward,
taking delight in *false* humility and worship
of angels, intruding into those things which
he has *not seen, vainly puffed up by his
fleshly mind,
19 and not holding fast to [R]the Head, from
whom all the body, nourished and knit together by joints and ligaments, grows with
the increase *which is* from God. Eph. 4:15

Freedom from the Doctrine of Men

20 *Therefore, if you [R]died with Christ from
the basic principles of the world, why, as
though living in the world, do you subject
yourselves to regulations— Rom. 6:2–5
21 [R]"Do not touch, do not taste, do not
handle," 1 Tim. 4:3
22 which all concern things which perish
with the using—[R]according to the commandments and doctrines of men? Titus 1:14
23 These things indeed have an appearance
of wisdom in self-imposed religion, *false*
humility, and neglect of the body, *but are* of
no value against the indulgence of the flesh.

CHAPTER 3

The Position of the Believer

IF then you were raised with Christ, seek
those things which are above, where
Christ is, sitting at the right hand of God.
2 Set your mind on things above, not on
things on the [R]earth. [Matt. 6:19–21]
3 [R]For you died, [R]and your life is hidden
with Christ in God. [Rom. 6:2] • [2 Cor. 5:7]
4 When Christ *who is* our life appears,
then you also will appear with Him in glory.

Put Off the Old Man

5 [R]Therefore put to death [R]your members
which are on the earth: fornication, uncleanness, passion, evil desire, and covetousness,
which is idolatry. [Rom. 8:13] • [Rom. 6:13]
6 [R]Because of these things the wrath of
God is coming upon [R]the sons of disobedience, Rom. 1:18 • [Eph. 2:2]
7 [R]in which you also once walked when
you lived in them. 1 Cor. 6:11
8 [R]But now you must also put off all these:
anger, wrath, malice, blasphemy, filthy language out of your mouth. Eph. 4:22
9 Do not lie to one another, since you have
put off the old man with his deeds,
10 and have put on the new *man* who is
renewed in knowledge according to the
image of Him who [R]created him, [Eph. 2:10]
11 where there is neither [R]Greek nor Jew,
circumcised nor uncircumcised, barbarian,
Scythian, slave *nor* free, [R]but Christ *is* all and
in all. Gal. 3:27, 28 • Eph. 1:23

Put On the New Man

12 Therefore, [R]as *the* elect of God, holy and
beloved, put on tender mercies, kindness,
humility, meekness, longsuffering; [1 Pet. 1:2]
13 [R]bearing with one another, and forgiving
one another, if anyone has a complaint
against another; even as Christ forgave you,
so you also *must do.* [Mark 11:25]
14 But above all these things [R]put on love,
which is the bond of perfection. [1 Cor. 13]
15 And let the peace of God rule in your
hearts, to which also you were called [R]in one
body; and [R]be thankful. Eph. 4:4 • [1 Thess. 5:18]
16 Let the word of Christ dwell in you richly
in all wisdom, teaching and admonishing one
another [R]in psalms and hymns and spiritual
songs, singing with grace in your hearts to
the Lord. Eph. 5:19

2:7 NU omits *in it* **2:11** NU omits *of the sins*
2:18 NU omits *not* **2:20** NU, M omit *Therefore*

17 And *whatever* you do in word or deed, *do* all in the name of the Lord Jesus, giving thanks to God the Father through Him.

Holiness in Family Life

18 [R]Wives, submit to your own husbands, [R]as is fitting in the Lord. 1 Pet. 3:1 • [Eph. 5:22—6:9]

19 [R]Husbands, love your wives and do not be [R]bitter toward them. [Eph. 5:25] • Eph. 4:31

20 Children, obey your parents in all things, for this is well pleasing to the Lord.
21 [R]Fathers, do not provoke your children, lest they become discouraged. Eph. 6:4

Holiness in Work Life

22 [R]Servants, obey in all things your masters according to the flesh, not with eyeservice, as men-pleasers, but in sincerity of heart, fearing God. Eph. 6:5
23 [R]And whatever you do, do it heartily, as to the Lord and not to men, [Eccl. 9:10]
24 [R]knowing that from the Lord you will receive the reward of the inheritance; [R]for* you serve the Lord Christ. Eph. 6:8 • 1 Cor. 7:22
25 But he who does wrong will be repaid for *the wrong* which he has done, and [R]there is no partiality. Rom. 2:11

CHAPTER 4

MASTERS,[R] give your servants what is just and fair, knowing that you also have a Master in heaven. Eph. 6:9

Holiness in Public Life

2 [R]Continue earnestly in prayer, being vigilant in it with thanksgiving; Luke 18:1
3 [R]meanwhile praying also for us, that God would [R]open to us a door for the word, to speak the [T]mystery of Christ, for which I am also in chains, Eph. 6:19 • 1 Cor. 16:9 • *hidden truth*
4 that I may make it manifest, as I ought to speak.
5 Walk in [R]wisdom toward those *who are* outside, redeeming the time. [Matt. 10:16]
6 *Let* your speech always *be* [R]with grace, seasoned with salt, that you may know how you ought to answer each one. Eccl. 10:12

Commendation of Tychicus

7 Tychicus, *who is* a beloved brother, a faithful minister, and a fellow servant in the Lord, will tell you all the news about me.
8 [R]I am sending him to you for this very purpose, that *he may know your circumstances and comfort your hearts, Eph. 6:22
9 with [R]Onesimus, a faithful and beloved brother, who is *one* of you. They will make known to you all things which *are happening* here. Philem. 10

Greetings from Paul's Friends

10 Aristarchus my fellow prisoner greets you, with [R]Mark the cousin of Barnabas (about whom you received instructions: if he comes to you, welcome him), 2 Tim. 4:11
11 and Jesus who is called Justus. These *are my* only fellow workers for the kingdom of God who are of the circumcision; they have proved to be a comfort to me.
12 Epaphras, who is *one* of you, a servant of Christ, greets you, always laboring fervently for you in prayers, that you may stand perfect and *complete in all the will of God.
13 For I bear him witness that he has a great *zeal for you, and those who are in Laodicea, and those in Hierapolis.
14 [R]Luke the beloved physician and [R]Demas greet you. 2 Tim. 4:11 • 2 Tim. 4:10

3:24 NU omits *for*
4:8 NU *you may know our circumstances and he may comfort* **4:12** NU *fully assured* **4:13** NU *concern*

3:19 The Role of the Husband—Paul tells the husband to love his wife (Page 1392—Eph. 5:25), while Peter tells the husband to dwell together with his wife (Page 1480—1 Pet. 3:7). The husband cannot live with his wife as Peter says unless he loves her in the way Paul means. The love that the husband is commanded to have for the wife is not primarily sexual or emotional (though both of those concepts are involved); it is a love that loves in spite of the reponse (or lack of it) in the one loved. It is the kind of love that God has for the world (Page 1239—John 3:16) and is the fruit of the Spirit (Page 1383—Gal. 5:22). A husband can only love his wife properly if he is a Christian and under the control of the Holy Spirit.

The two responsibilities the husband has in the family are to dwell with his wife according to knowledge, and to render to his wife the honor which is due her because she is his wife. To "dwell together" with his wife means that the husband must take his wife into *every* aspect of his life. There are to be no areas of his life where there are signs that say, "Private, husband only—wife keep out."

The husband is to perform his two duties for a spiritual purpose: "that your prayers be not hindered." The man who is not taking his wife into every aspect of his life and rendering to her the honor which is due her because she is his wife cannot communicate with her in the way that God intended; hence, he cannot communicate with God either. To make sure that the channel of communication with God is open, the husband must make sure that the channel of communication with his wife is open. Only in this way can he truly love his wife as God intended and manifest his headship properly.

Now turn to Page 714—Prov. 1:8: The Role of Children.

Introductions Regarding This Letter

15 Greet the brethren who are in Laodicea,
and *Nymphas and [R]the church that *is* in *his
house. Rom. 16:5
16 Now when [R]this epistle is read among
you, see that it is read also in the church of
the Laodiceans, and that you likewise read
the epistle from Laodicea. 1 Thess. 5:27
17 And say to [R]Archippus, "Take heed to
the ministry which you have received in the
Lord, that you may fulfill it." Philem. 2
18 [R]This salutation by my own hand—Paul.
[R]Remember my chains. Grace *be* with you.
Amen. 1 Cor. 16:21 • Heb. 13:3

4:15 NU *Nympha* **4:15** NU *her*

THE FIRST EPISTLE OF PAUL THE APOSTLE TO THE

THESSALONIANS

THE BOOK OF FIRST THESSALONIANS

Paul has many pleasant memories of the days he spent with the infant Thessalonian church. Their faith, hope, love, and perseverance in the face of persecution are exemplary. Paul's labors as a spiritual parent to the fledgling church have been richly rewarded, and his affection is visible in every line of his letter.

Paul encourages them to excel in their newfound faith, to increase in their love for one another, and to rejoice, pray, and give thanks always. He closes his letter with instruction regarding the return of the Lord, whose advent signifies hope and comfort for believers both living and dead.

Because this is the first of Paul's two canonical letters to the church at Thessalonica, it received the title *Pros Thessalonikeis A*, the "First to the Thessalonians."

THE AUTHOR OF FIRST THESSALONIANS

First Thessalonians went unchallenged as a Pauline epistle until the nineteenth century, when radical critics claimed that its dearth of doctrinal content made its authenticity suspect. But this is a weak objection on two counts: (1) the proportion of doctrinal teaching in Paul's epistles varies widely, and (2) 4:13—5:11 is a foundational passage for New Testament eschatology (future events). Paul had quickly grounded the Thessalonians in Christian doctrine, and the only problematic issue when this epistle was written concerned the matter of Christ's return. The external and internal evidence points clearly to Paul.

THE TIME OF FIRST THESSALONIANS

In Paul's time, Thessalonica was the prominent seaport and the capital of the Roman province of Macedonia. This prosperous city was located on the Via Egnatia, the main road from Rome to the East, within sight of Mount Olympus, legendary home of the Greek pantheon. Cassander expanded and strengthened this site around 315 B.C. and renamed it after his wife, the half-sister of Alexander the Great. The Romans conquered Macedonia in 168 B.C. and organized it into a single province twenty-two years later with Thessalonica as the capital city. It became a "free city" under Augustus with its own authority to appoint a governing board of magistrates who were called "politarchs." The strategic location assured Thessalonica of commercial success, and it boasted a population of perhaps 200,000 in the first century. Thessalonica survives under the shortened name Salonika.

Thessalonica had a sizable Jewish population, and the ethical monotheism of Judaism attracted many Gentiles who had become disenchanted with Greek paganism. These God-fearers quickly responded to Paul's reasoning in the synagogue when he ministered there on his second missionary journey (Acts 17:10). The Jews became jealous of Paul's success and organized a mob to oppose the Christian missionaries. Not finding Paul and Silas, they dragged Jason, Paul and Silas's host, before the politarchs and accused him of harboring traitors of Rome. The politarchs extracted a pledge guaranteeing the departure of Paul and Silas, who left that night for Berea. After a time, the Thessalonian Jews raised an uproar in Berea so that Paul departed for Athens, leaving orders for Silas and Timothy to join him there (Acts 17:11–16). Because of Luke's account in Acts some scholars have reasoned that Paul was in Thessalonica for less than a month ("three Sabbaths," Acts 17:2), but other evidence suggests a longer stay: (1) Paul received two separate offerings from Philippi, 100 miles away, while he was in Thessalonica (Phil. 4:15, 16). (2) According to 1:9 and 2:14–16, most of the Thessalonian converts were Gentiles who came out of idolatry. This would imply an extensive ministry directed to the Gentiles after Paul's initial work with the Jews and gentile God-fearers. (3) Paul worked "night and day" (2:9; 2 Thess. 3:7–9) during his time there. He may have begun to work immediately, but Paul supported himself by tent-making, which took many hours away from his ministry, requiring a longer stay to accomplish the extensive ministry of evangelism and teaching that took place in that city. After Silas and Timothy met Paul in Athens (3:1, 2), he sent Timothy to Thessalonica (Silas also went back to Macedonia, probably Philippi), and his assistants later rejoined him in Corinth (Acts 18:5; cf. 1 Thess. 1:1 where Silas is called Silvanus). There he wrote this epistle in A.D. 51 as his response to Timothy's good report.

THE CHRIST OF FIRST THESSALONIANS

Christ is seen as the believer's hope of salvation both now and at His coming. When He returns, He will deliver (1:10; 5:4–11), reward (1:19), perfect (3:13), resurrect (4:13–18), and sanctify (5:23) all who trust Him.

KEYS TO FIRST THESSALONIANS

Key Word: Holiness in Light of Christ's Return—Throughout this letter is an unmistakable emphasis upon steadfastness in the

Lord (3:8) and a continuing growth in faith and love in view of the return of Christ (1:3–10; 2:12–20; 3:10–13; 4:1—5:28). The theme is not only the returning of Christ, but also the life of the believer in every practical relationship, each aspect of which can be transformed and illuminated by the glorious prospect of His eventual return.

Key Verses: First Thessalonians 3:12, 13 and 4:16–18—"And may the Lord make you increase and abound in love to one another and to all, just as we *do* to you, so that He may establish your hearts blameless in holiness before our God and Father at the coming of our Lord Jesus Christ with all His saints" (3:12, 13).

"For the Lord Himself will descend from heaven with a shout, with the voice of an archangel, and with the trumpet of God. And the dead in Christ will rise first. Then we who are alive *and* remain shall be caught up together with them in the clouds to meet the Lord in the air. And thus we shall always be with the Lord. Therefore comfort one another with these words" (4:16–18).

Key Chapter: First Thessalonians 4—Chapter 4 includes the central passage of the epistles on the coming of the Lord when the dead in Christ shall rise first, and those who remain are caught up together with them in the clouds.

SURVEY OF FIRST THESSALONIANS

After Paul's forced separation from the Thessalonians, he grows increasingly concerned about the progress of their faith. His great relief upon hearing Timothy's positive report prompts him to write this warm epistle of commendation, exhortation, and consolation. They are commended for remaining steadfast under afflictions, exhorted to excel still more in their Christian walk, and consoled concerning their loved ones who have died in Christ. The theme of the coming of the Lord recurs throughout this epistle, and 4:13—5:11 is one of the fullest New Testament developments of this crucial truth. The two major sections of First Thessalonians are: Paul's personal reflections of the Thessalonians (1—3) and Paul's instructions for the Thessalonians (4 and 5).

Paul's Personal Reflections on the Thessalonians (1—3): Paul's typical salutation in the first verse combines the customary Greek ("grace") and Hebrew ("peace") greetings of his day and enriches them with Christian content. The opening chapter is a declaration of thanksgiving for the Thessalonians' metamorphosis from heathenism to Christian hope. Faith, love, and hope (1:3) properly characterize the new lives of these believers. In 2:1–16, Paul reviews his brief ministry in Thessalonica and defends his conduct and motives, apparently to answer enemies who are trying to impugn his character and message. He sends Timothy to minister to them and is greatly relieved when Timothy reports the stability of their faith and love (2:17—3:10). Paul therefore closes this historical section with a prayer that their faith may continue to deepen (3:11–13).

Paul's Instructions to the Thessalonians (4 and 5): The apostle deftly moves into a series of exhortations and instructions by encouraging the Thessalonians to continue progressing. He reminds them of his previous teaching on sexual and social matters (4:1–12), since these gentile believers lack the moral upbringing in the Mosaic Law provided in the Jewish community. Now rooted in the Word of God (2:13), the readers must resist the constant pressures of a pagan society.

Paul has taught them about the return of Christ, and they have become distressed over the deaths of some among them. In 4:13–18, Paul comforts them with the assurance that all who die in Christ will be resurrected at His *parousia*

FOCUS	REFLECTIONS ON THE THESSALONIANS			INSTRUCTIONS TO THE THESSALONIANS			
REFERENCE	1:1——2:1	——2:17	——	4:1——4:13	——5:1	——5:12	——5:28
DIVISION	COMMENDATION FOR GROWTH	FOUNDING OF THE CHURCH	STRENGTHENING OF THE CHURCH	DIRECTION FOR GROWTH	THE DEAD IN CHRIST	THE DAY OF THE LORD	HOLY LIVING
TOPIC	PERSONAL EXPERIENCE			PRACTICAL EXHORTATION			
	LOOKING BACK			LOOKING FORWARD			
LOCATION	WRITTEN IN CORINTH						
TIME	C. A.D. 51						

("presence," "coming," or "advent"). The apostle continues his discourse on eschatology by describing the coming day of the Lord (5:1-11). In anticipation of this day, believers are to "watch and be sober" as "sons of light" who are destined for salvation, not wrath. Paul requests the readers to deal with integrity toward one another and to continue growing spiritually (5:12-22). The epistle closes with a wish for their sanctification, three requests, and a benediction (5:23-28).

OUTLINE OF FIRST THESSALONIANS

CHAPTER 1

Paul's Commendation for Their Growth

PAUL, [R]Silvanus, and Timothy, 1 Pet. 5:12

To the church of the [R]Thessalonians in
God the Father and the Lord Jesus Christ:

Grace to you and peace *from God our
Father and the Lord Jesus Christ. 1 Pet. 5:12
2 We give thanks to God always for you
all, making mention of you in our prayers,
3 remembering without ceasing [R]your
work of faith, [R]labor of love, and patience of
hope in our Lord Jesus Christ in the sight of
our God and Father, John 6:29 • Rom. 16:6
4 knowing, beloved brethren, [R]your election by God. Col. 3:12

5 For [R]our gospel did not come to you in
word only, but also in power, [R]and in the Holy
Spirit [R]and in much assurance, as you know
what kind of men we were among you for
your sake. Mark 16:20 • 2 Cor. 6:6 • Heb. 2:3
6 And you became followers of us and of
the Lord, having received the word in much
affliction, with joy of the Holy Spirit,
7 so that you became examples to all in
Macedonia and Achaia who believe.
8 For from you the word of the Lord [R]has
sounded forth, not only in Macedonia and
Achaia, but also [R]in every place. Your faith
toward God has gone out, so that we do not
need to say anything. Rom. 10:18 • Rom. 1:8; 16:19
9 For they themselves declare concerning
us what manner of entry we had to you, [R]and
how you turned to God from idols to serve
the living and true God, 1 Cor. 12:2
10 and to wait for His Son from heaven,
whom He raised from the dead, *even* Jesus
who delivers us from the wrath to come.

1:1 NU omits *from God our Father and the Lord Jesus Christ*

1:5 Sharing Our Faith: How?—In order to share our faith successfully, we must keep the following rules in mind.

a. First, we must be clean vessels. God reminds Isaiah the prophet of this, "Be clean, you who bear the vessels of the LORD" (Page 825—Is. 52:11). David the sinner prays for forgiveness and cleansing. Upon receiving this he states, "*Then* I will teach transgressors Your ways, and sinners shall be converted to You" (Page 654—Ps. 51:13). While God does not demand golden or silver vessels, He does require clean ones.
b. We must be able to clearly give out the simple facts of the gospel without getting bogged down with profound theological concepts. Philip the evangelist demonstrated how to do this when he dealt with a sinner in the desert. "Then Philip opened his mouth, and beginning at this Scripture, preached Jesus to him" (Page 1284—Acts 8:35).
c. We must avoid arguments and stick to the basic issues of man's sin and Christ's blood. Often unbelievers will attempt to sidestep the gospel by asking unrelated questions, such as "Where did Cain get his wife?"
d. We must use the Word of God. Paul's tremendous success as an evangelist can be linked directly to his constant use of God's Word. See Acts 17:2; 18:28; Second Timothy 2:15; 3:14-17.
e. We must depend upon the Spirit of God. See John 3:15; Acts 6:10; First Corinthians 2:4.

Now turn to Page 1436—2 Tim. 4:2: Sharing Our Faith: When?

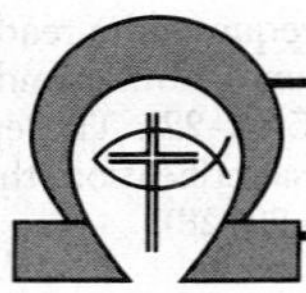

THE CITY OF THESSALONICA

Thessalonica was founded in 315 B.C. by the Macedonian king Cassander. He named the city after his wife Thessalonica, sister of the Greek military conqueror, Alexander the Great. The apostle Paul worked for several months in Thessalonica and later addressed two letters (1 and 2 Thessalonians) to the church in this city.

Paul visited Thessalonica in the early fifties during his second missionary journey through the Roman province of Macedonia (Acts 17:1–9). The church that he worked with here consisted of former members of the Jewish synagogue, as well as non-Jews from pagan backgrounds. The tender words with which Paul addressed the Thessalonians make it clear that he developed strong affection for the Thessalonian church (1 Thess. 2:1–12).

Thessalonica's natural harbor made it a vital trading center, which brought in people from many places. This may have been why it was selected as the site for a church. At the time of his visit, Thessalonica was the most populous city in the entire Roman province of Macedonia.

Roman influence on Thessalonica is evident in the city's physical structure. Vital to the city's prosperity was the Egnatian Way, a Roman military highway which provided a route to the empire's eastern provinces. This route still serves as one of the main streets for modern Thessalonica (known as Salonika). Roman arches stood at Thessalonica's two entrances to the Egnatian Way. The one built in A.D. 297 to honor the Roman emperor Galerius remains intact.

Thessalonica's importance is also demonstrated by the great wall that surrounded the city, portions of which are still standing. The modern wall was built after Paul's time, but it was constructed on the foundations of the old city wall from the New Testament era.

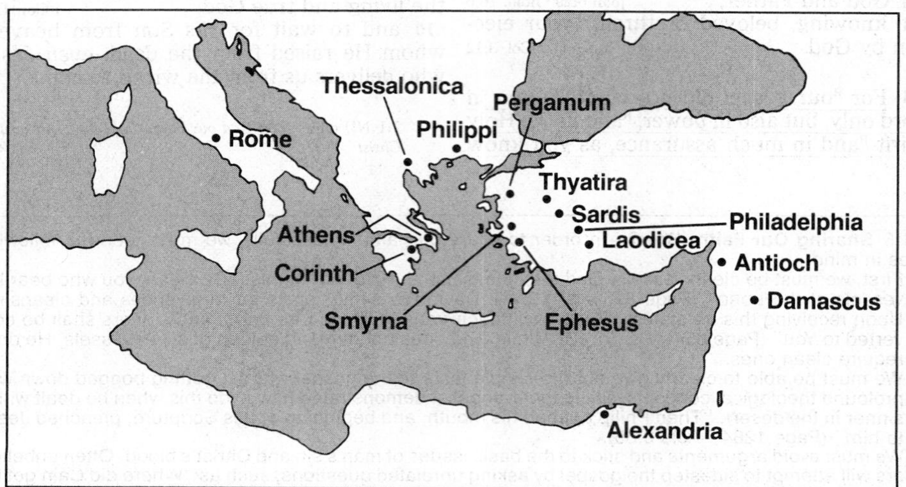

Thessalonica's natural harbor made it a vital trading center, which brought in people from many places.

CHAPTER 2

Paul's Founding of the Church

FOR you yourselves know, brethren, that our coming to you was not in vain.

2 But *even after we had suffered before and were spitefully treated at Philippi, as you know, we were bold in our God to speak to you the gospel of God in much conflict.

3 For our exhortation *did* not *come* from deceit or uncleanness, nor *was it* in guile.

4 But as we have been approved by God [R]to be entrusted with the gospel, even so we speak, [R]not as pleasing men, but God [R]who tests our hearts. Titus 1:3 • Gal. 1:10 • Prov. 17:3

5 For neither at any time did we use flattering words, as you know, nor a [T]cloak for covetousness—God *is* witness. *pretext*

6 Nor did we seek glory from men, either from you or from others, when we might have made demands as apostles of Christ.

7 But we were gentle among you, just as a nursing *mother* cherishes her own children.

8 So, affectionately longing for you, we were well pleased to impart to you not only the gospel of God, but also our own lives, because you had become dear to us.

9 For you remember, brethren, our labor and toil; for laboring night and day, that we might not be a burden to any of you, we preached to you the gospel of God.

10 You *are* witnesses, and God *also*, how devoutly and justly and blamelessly we behaved ourselves among you who believe;

11 as you know how we exhorted, and comforted, and *charged every one of you, as a father *does* his own children,

12 [R]that you would have a walk worthy of God [R]who calls you into His own kingdom and glory. Eph. 4:1 • 1 Cor. 1:9

13 For this reason we also thank God without ceasing, because when you received the word of God which you heard from us, you welcomed *it* not *as* the word of men, but as it is in truth, the word of God, which also effectively works in you who believe.

14 For you, brethren, became imitators [R]of the churches of God which are in Judea in Christ Jesus. For [R]you also suffered the same things from your own countrymen, just as they *did* from the Jews, Gal. 1:22 • Acts 17:5

15 [R]who killed both the Lord Jesus and their own prophets, and have persecuted us; and they do not please God [R]and are [T]contrary to all men, Acts 2:23 • Esth. 3:8 • *hostile*

16 forbidding us to speak to the Gentiles that they may be saved, so as always to fill up *the measure of* their sins; [R]but wrath has come upon them to the uttermost. Matt. 24:6

Satan Hinders Paul

17 But we, brethren, having been taken away from you for a short time [R]in presence, not in heart, endeavored more eagerly to see your face with great desire. 1 Cor. 5:3

18 Therefore we wanted to come to you—even I, Paul, time and again—but [R]Satan hindered us. Rom. 1:13; 15:22

19 For what *is* our hope, or joy, or crown of rejoicing? *Is it* not even you in the presence of our Lord Jesus Christ at His coming?

20 For you are our glory and joy.

CHAPTER 3

Paul Sends Timothy

THEREFORE, when we could no longer endure it, we thought it good to be left in Athens alone,

2 and sent [R]Timothy, our brother and minister of God, and our fellow laborer in the gospel of Christ, to establish you and encourage you concerning your faith, Rom. 16:21

3 [R]that no one should be shaken by these afflictions; for you yourselves know that [R]we are appointed to this. Eph. 3:13 • Acts 9:16; 14:22

4 For, in fact, we told you before when we were with you that we would suffer tribulation, just as it happened, and you know.

5 For this reason, when I could no longer endure it, I sent to know your faith, lest by some means the tempter had tempted you, and [R]our labor might be in vain. Gal. 2:2

Timothy's Encouraging Report

6 [R]But now that Timothy has come to us from you, and brought us good news of your faith and love, and that you always have good remembrance of us, greatly desiring to see us, [R]as we also *to see* you— Acts 18:5 • Phil. 1:8

7 therefore, brethren, in all our affliction and distress [R]we were comforted concerning you by your faith. 2 Cor. 1:4

8 For now we live, if you [R]stand fast in the Lord. Phil. 4:1

9 For what thanks can we render to God for you, for all the joy with which we rejoice for your sake before our God,

10 night and day praying exceedingly that we may see your face [R]and perfect what is lacking in your faith? 2 Cor. 13:9

Paul's Desire to Visit Them

11 Now may our God and Father Himself, and our Lord Jesus Christ, [R]direct our way to you. Mark 1:3

12 And may the Lord make you increase and [R]abound in love to one another and to all, just as we *do* to you, Phil. 1:9

13 so that He may establish [R]your hearts blameless in holiness before our God and Father at the coming of our Lord Jesus Christ with all His saints. 2 Thess. 2:17

2:2 NU, M omit *even* 2:11 NU, M *implored*

CHAPTER 4

Directions for Growth

FINALLY then, brethren, we urge and exhort in the Lord Jesus [R]that you should abound more and more, [R]just as you received from us how you ought to walk and to please God; 1 Cor. 15:58 • Phil. 1:27

2 for you know what commandments we gave you through the Lord Jesus.

3 For this is [R]the will of God, [R]your sanctification: [R]that you should abstain from sexual immorality; [Rom. 12:2] • Eph. 5:27 • [1 Cor. 6:15–20]

4 [R]that each of you should know how to possess his own vessel in sanctification and honor, Rom. 6:19

5 [R]not in passion of lust, like the Gentiles [R]who do not know God; Col. 3:5 • 1 Cor. 15:34

6 that no one should take advantage of and defraud his brother in this matter, because the Lord *is* the avenger of all such, as we also forewarned you and testified.

7 For God did not call us to uncleanness, [R]but in holiness. Lev. 11:44

8 [R]Therefore he who rejects *this* does not reject man, but God, [R]who* has also given us His Holy Spirit. Luke 10:16 • 1 Cor. 2:10

9 But concerning brotherly love you have no need that I should write to you, for [R]you yourselves are taught by God [R]to love one another; [Jer. 31:33, 34] • Matt. 22:39

10 and indeed you do so toward all the brethren who are in all Macedonia. But we urge you, brethren, [R]that you increase more and more; 1 Thess. 3:12

11 that you also aspire to lead a quiet life, to mind your own business, and to work with your own hands, as we commanded you,

12 [R]that you may walk properly toward those who are outside, and *that* you may lack nothing. Rom. 13:13

Revelation Concerning the Dead in Christ

13 But I do not want you to be ignorant, brethren, concerning those who have fallen [T]asleep, lest you sorrow [R]as others [R]who have no hope. Died • Lev. 19:28 • [Eph. 2:12]

14 For if we believe that Jesus died and rose again, even so God will bring with Him [R]those who *sleep in Jesus. 1 Cor. 15:20, 23

15 For this we say to you by the word of the Lord, that we who are alive *and* remain until the coming of the Lord will by no means precede those who are [T]asleep. Dead

16 For the Lord Himself will descend from heaven with a shout, with the voice of an archangel, and with the trumpet of God. And the dead in Christ will rise first.

17 Then we who are alive *and* remain shall be caught up together with them [R]in the clouds to meet the Lord in the air. And thus we shall always be with the Lord. Acts 1:9

18 [R]Therefore comfort one another with these words. 1 Thess. 5:11

CHAPTER 5

Description of the Day of the Lord

BUT concerning [R]the times and the seasons, brethren, you have no need that I should write to you. Matt. 24:3

2 For you yourselves know perfectly that [R]the day of the Lord so comes as a thief in the night. [2 Pet. 3:10]

3 For when they say, "Peace and safety!" then [R]sudden destruction comes upon them, [R]as labor pains upon a pregnant woman. And they shall not escape. Is. 13:6–9 • Hos. 13:13

4 [R]But you, brethren, are not in darkness, so that this Day should overtake you as a thief. 1 John 2:8

5 You are all sons of light and sons of the day. We are not of the night nor of darkness.

6 Therefore let us not sleep, as others *do*, but let us watch and be [T]sober. *self-controlled*

7 For those who sleep, sleep at night, and those who get drunk are drunk at night.

8 But let us who are of the day be sober, putting on the breastplate of faith and love, and *as* a helmet the hope of salvation.

9 For [R]God did not appoint us to wrath, [R]but to obtain salvation through our Lord Jesus Christ, Rom. 9:22 • [2 Thess. 2:13]

10 who died for us, that whether we wake or sleep, we should live together with Him.

11 Therefore comfort each other and edify one another, just as you also are doing.

Instruction for Holy Living

12 And we urge you, brethren, to recognize those who labor among you, and are over you in the Lord and [T]admonish you, *warn*

13 and to esteem them very highly in love for their work's sake. [R]Be at peace among yourselves. Mark 9:50

14 Now we [T]exhort you, brethren, warn those who are [T]unruly, comfort the fainthearted, uphold the weak, [R]be patient with all. *encourage* • *insubordinate* or *idle* • Gal. 5:22

15 See that no one renders evil for evil to anyone, but always [R]pursue what is good both for yourselves and for all. Gal. 6:10

16 [R]Rejoice always, [2 Cor. 6:10]

17 [R]pray without ceasing, Eph. 6:18

18 in everything give thanks; for this is the will of God in Christ Jesus for you.

19 [R]Do not quench the Spirit. Eph. 4:30

20 [R]Do not despise prophecies. 1 Cor. 14:1, 31

21 Test all things; hold fast what is good.

22 Abstain from every form of evil.

4:8 NU *who also gives* **4:14** Or *through Jesus sleep*

SPIRIT, SOUL, AND BODY

When the Bible says we were created in God's image, it does not mean God looks like us—a most carnal theory—for God in essence is Spirit (John 4:24). We are like God in creative personality, having intellect, sensibility, and will. Many believe this likeness also refers to the Trinity. God is one in essence but three in "Person"—the Father, the Son, and the Holy Spirit. A person also is a trinity of sorts, although the parallel is not exact. Many like to stress that a human being is composed of material (body) and immaterial (soul, spirit, mind, etc.) parts. This is a valid distinction.

In 1 Thessalonians 5:23, the apostle Paul differentiates among three components. People always put the body first and the spirit last. The popular expression is "body and soul," and the more biblically informed may add "and spirit." God's order, however, is just the opposite. These are not merely distinctions without a difference. Each component part must be separate in some way.

If, as many believe, there is analogy with the Holy Trinity, the spirit obviously would parallel the Holy Spirit. The body must parallel the Son, the member of the Godhead who assumed human flesh (and human spirit and soul, as well). This leaves the soul to parallel the Father, assuming the comparison is valid.

Spirit (*pneuma*)

Spirit (*pneuma*) has the same double meaning in both Testaments: Hebrew *rûah* and Greek *pneuma* both mean "wind" or "spirit." This explains Jesus' play on words in John 3 in His discussion on being born from above by the Spirit, and the wind blowing where it wills.

The spirit is that part of humans that differentiates us from animals. Animals obviously have bodies, and they also have "souls" in the sense of sentient life, but what animal has ever built a church or even prayed to God?

The spiritual aspect of human beings is the most important. Our spiritual growth and knowledge will last for all eternity.

Soul (*psychē*)

The Greek word *psychē* has spawned many an English derivative beginning with *psycho*. The main usages of *psychē* are "soul" (in its many meanings, including "person"; see word study on p. 935) and "life." There are passages where it is hard to know which of these is the better translation.

When Jesus asked "What shall a man give in exchange for his [*psychē*]?" He could have referred to man's soul or to his life here on earth and the rewards that come from living for God.

We are so used to using "saved" for eternal salvation (see word study on p. 1370) and "soul" for the personality that will last forever (see word study on p. 935) that we miss the meaning in some contexts of "make the most of your life [*psychē*] for the Lord." Saving our souls from hell is fundamental. If we are not believers we cannot serve God acceptably. However, since *psychē* also refers to our personality and our life on earth, we must also make the most of our lives so that we can have some reward for our labors in the Day of Christ.

Body (*sōma*)

There is far too much stress on the body in today's Western culture. Bodybuilding, the fitness craze, health food fads, and cosmetic treatments to improve physical appearance are all supported by gigantic industries. In reacting to this, however, we should not swing to the opposite extreme and neglect the body or even call it evil, as some of the ancient Greeks did. The human body is a masterpiece of divine engineering and should be properly maintained for health to serve God and our fellow man. In the resurrection, believers will receive perfect bodies with none of the weaknesses of mortality.

For our own tripartite personalities we can do no better than repeat Paul's prayer: "Now may the God of peace Himself sanctify you completely; and may your whole spirit, soul, and body be preserved blameless at the coming of our Lord Jesus Christ" (1 Thess. 5:23).

Conclusion

23 Now may the God of peace Himself
[R]sanctify[T] you completely; and may your
whole spirit, soul, and body [R]be preserved
blameless at the coming of our Lord Jesus
Christ. 1 Thess. 3:13 • *set you apart* • 1 Cor. 1:8, 9
24 He who calls you *is* [R]faithful, who also
will [R]do *it*. [1 Cor. 10:13] • Phil. 1:6

25 Brethren, pray for us.
26 Greet all the brethren with a holy kiss.
27 I charge you by the Lord that this epistle
be read to all the *holy brethren.
28 The grace of our Lord Jesus Christ *be*
with you. Amen.

5:27 NU omits *holy*

THE SECOND EPISTLE OF PAUL THE APOSTLE TO THE

THESSALONIANS

THE BOOK OF SECOND THESSALONIANS

Since Paul's first letter, the seeds of false doctrine have been sown among the Thessalonians, causing them to waver in their faith. Paul removes these destructive seeds and again plants the seeds of truth. He begins by commending the believers on their faithfulness in the midst of persecution and encouraging them that present suffering will be repaid with future glory. Therefore, in the midst of persecution, expectation can be high.

Paul then deals with the central matter of his letter: a misunderstanding spawned by false teachers regarding the coming day of the Lord. Despite reports to the contrary, that day has not yet come, and Paul recounts the events that must first take place. Laboring for the gospel, rather than lazy resignation, is the proper response.

As the second letter in Paul's Thessalonian correspondence, this was entitled *Pros Thessalonikeis B,* the "Second to the Thessalonians."

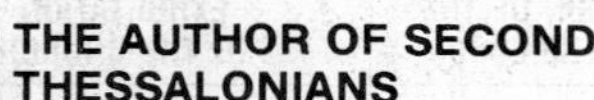

THE AUTHOR OF SECOND THESSALONIANS

The external attestation to the authenticity of Second Thessalonians as a Pauline epistle is even stronger than that for First Thessalonians. Internally, the vocabulary, style, and doctrinal content support the claims in 1:1 and 3:17 that it was written by Paul.

THE TIME OF SECOND THESSALONIANS

See "The Time of First Thessalonians" for the background to the Thessalonian correspondence. This letter was probably written a few months after First Thessalonians, while Paul was still in Corinth with Silas and Timothy (1:1; cf. Acts 18:5). The bearer of the first epistle may have brought Paul an update on the new developments, prompting him to write this letter. They were still undergoing persecution, and the false teaching about the day of the Lord led some of them to overreact by giving up their jobs. The problem of idleness recorded in First Thessalonians 4:11, 12 had become more serious (3:6–15). By this time, Paul was beginning to see the opposition he would face in his ministry in Corinth (3:2; see Acts 18:5–10).

THE CHRIST OF SECOND THESSALONIANS

The return of Christ is mentioned more times (318) in the New Testament than any other doctrine, and this is certainly the major concept in chapters 1 and 2 of this epistle. The return of the Lord Jesus is a reassuring and joyful hope for believers, but His revelation from heaven holds awesome and terrifying implications for those who have not trusted in Him (1:6–10; 2:8–12).

KEYS TO SECOND THESSALONIANS

Key Word: Understanding the Day of the Lord—The theme of this epistle is an understanding of the day of the Lord and the resulting lifestyle changes. The doctrinal error of chapter 2 has been causing the practical error that Paul seeks to overcome in chapter 3. Some of the believers have abandoned their work and have begun to live off others, apparently assuming that the end is at hand. Paul commands them to follow his example by supporting themselves and instructs the rest of the church to discipline them if they fail to do so.

Key Verses: Second Thessalonians 2:2, 3 and 3:5, 6—"Not to be soon shaken in mind or troubled, either by spirit or by word or by letter, as if from us, as though the day of Christ had come. Let no one deceive you by any means; for *that Day will not come* unless the falling away comes first, and the man of sin is revealed, the son of perdition" (2:2, 3).

"Now may the Lord direct your hearts into the love of God and into the patience of Christ. But we command you, brethren, in the name of our Lord Jesus Christ, that you withdraw from every brother who walks disorderly and not according to the tradition which he received from us" (3:5, 6).

Key Chapter: Second Thessalonians 2—The second chapter is written to correct the fallacious teaching that the day of the Lord has already come upon the Thessalonian church. This teaching, coupled with the afflictions they have been suffering, is causing a great disturbance among the believers who wonder when their "gathering together to Him" (2:1; 1 Thess. 4:13–18) will take place. Paul makes it clear that certain identifiable events will precede that day and that those events have not yet occurred.

SURVEY OF SECOND THESSALONIANS

This epistle is the theological sequel to First Thessalonians, which developed the theme of the coming day of the Lord (1 Thess. 5:1–11). However, not long after the Thessalonians receive that letter, they fall prey to false teaching or outright deception, thinking the day of the Lord has already begun. Paul writes this brief letter to correct the error and also to encourage those believers whose faith is being tested by the difficulties presented by persecution. He also reproves those who have decided to cease working because they believe the coming of Christ is near. Second Thessalonians deals with Paul's encouragement in persecution (1); Paul's explanation of the day of the Lord (2); and Paul's exhortation to the church (3).

Paul's Encouragement in Persecution (1): After his two-verse salutation, Paul gives thanks for the growing faith and love of the Thessalonians and assures them of their ultimate deliverance from those who are persecuting them (1:3–10). They are encouraged to patiently endure their afflictions, knowing that the Lord Jesus will judge their persecutors when He is "revealed from heaven with His mighty angels, in flaming fire" (1:7, 8). Before Paul moves to the next topic, he concludes this section with a prayer for the spiritual welfare of his readers (1:11, 12).

Paul's Explanation of the Day of the Lord (2): Because of the severity of their afflictions, the Thessalonians have become susceptible to false teaching (and possibly a fraudulent letter in the name of Paul), claiming that they are already in the day of the Lord (2:1, 2). This was particularly disturbing because Paul's previous letter had given them the comforting hope that they were not destined for the wrath of that day (1 Thess. 5:9). Paul therefore assures them that the day of the Lord is yet in the future and will not arrive unannounced (2:3–12). Paul then concludes with a word of encouragement and a benedictory prayer of comfort before moving to his next topic.

Paul's Exhortation to the Church (3:1–18): Paul requests the Thessalonian church to pray on his behalf and to wait patiently for the Lord (3:1–5). Having thus commended, corrected, and comforted his readers, the tactful apostle closes his letter with a sharp word of command to those who have been using the truth of Christ's return as an excuse for disorderly conduct (3:6–15; cf. 1 Thess. 4:11, 12). The doctrine of the Lord's return requires a balance between waiting and working. It is a perspective that should encourage holiness, not idleness. This final section, like the first two, closes on a benedictory note (3:16–18).

FOCUS	ENCOURAGEMENT IN PERSECUTION			EXPLANATION OF THE DAY OF THE LORD		EXHORTATION TO THE CHURCH	
REFERENCE	1:1	1:5	1:11	2:1	2:13	3:1	3:6 — 3:18
DIVISION	THANKSGIVING FOR GROWTH	ENCOURAGEMENT IN PERSECUTION	PRAYER FOR BLESSING	EVENTS PRECEDING	COMFORT OF THE BELIEVER	WAIT PATIENTLY	WITHDRAW
TOPIC	DISCOURAGED BELIEVERS			DISTURBED BELIEVERS		DISOBEDIENT BELIEVERS	
	THANKSGIVING FOR THEIR LIFE			INSTRUCTION OF THEIR DOCTRINE		CORRECTION OF THEIR BEHAVIOR	
LOCATION	WRITTEN IN CORINTH						
TIME	C. A.D. 51						

OUTLINE OF SECOND THESSALONIANS

I. Paul's Encouragement in Persecution 1:1–12

- A. Thanksgiving for Their Growth 1:1–4
- B. Encouragement in Their Persecution 1:5–10
- C. Prayer for God's Blessing 1:11, 12

II. Paul's Explanation of the Day of the Lord 2:1–17

- A. The Events Preceding the Day of the Lord 2:1–12
  1. First a Falling Away 2:1–3
  2. The Man of Sin Is Revealed 2:4, 5
  3. The Restrainer Is Taken Out of the Way 2:6, 7
  4. The Second Coming of Christ 2:8–12
- B. The Comfort of the Believer on the Day of the Lord 2:13–17

III. Paul's Exhortation to the Church 3:1–18

- A. Wait Patiently for Christ 3:1–5
- B. Withdraw from the Disorderly 3:6–15
- C. Conclusion 3:16–18

CHAPTER 1

Thanksgiving for Their Growth

PAUL, Silvanus, and Timothy,

To the church of the Thessalonians in God our Father and the Lord Jesus Christ:

2 [R]Grace to you and peace from God our Father and the Lord Jesus Christ. 1 Cor. 1:3

3 We are bound to thank God always for you, brethren, as it is fitting, because your faith grows exceedingly, and the love of every one of you all abounds toward each other,

4 so that we ourselves boast of you among the churches of God for your patience and faith in all your persecutions and [T]tribulations that you endure, *afflictions*

Encouragement in Their Persecution

5 *which is* [R]manifest[T] evidence of the righteous judgment of God, that you may be counted worthy of the kingdom of God, [R]for which you also suffer; Phil. 1:28 • *plain* • 1 Thess. 2:14

6 [R]since *it is* a righteous thing with God to repay with [T]tribulation those who trouble you, Rev. 6:10 • *affliction*

7 and to *give* you who are troubled rest with us when [R]the Lord Jesus is revealed from heaven with His mighty angels, Jude 14

8 in flaming fire taking vengeance on those who do not know God, and on those who do not obey the gospel of our Lord Jesus Christ.

9 These shall be punished with everlasting destruction from the presence of the Lord and [R]from the glory of His power, Deut. 33:2

10 when He comes, in that Day, to be glorified in His saints and to be admired among all those who *believe, because our testimony among you was believed.

Prayer for God's Blessing

11 Therefore we also pray always for you that our God would [R]count you worthy of *this* calling, and fulfill all the good pleasure of *His* goodness and [R]the work of faith with power, Col. 1:12 • 1 Thess. 1:3

12 [R]that the name of our Lord Jesus Christ may be glorified in you, and you in Him, according to the grace of our God and the Lord Jesus Christ. [Col. 3:17]

CHAPTER 2

The Events Preceding the Day of the Lord

NOW, brethren, concerning the coming of our Lord Jesus Christ and our gathering together to Him, we ask you,

2 [R]not to be soon shaken in mind or troubled, either by spirit or by word or by letter, as if from us, as though the day of *Christ had come. Matt. 24:4

3 Let no one deceive you by any means; for *that Day will not come* unless the falling away comes first, and the man of *sin is revealed, [R]the son of perdition, John 17:12

4 who opposes and exalts himself [R]above all that is called God or that is worshiped, so that he sits *as God in the temple of God, showing himself that he is God. 1 Cor. 8:5

5 Do you not remember that when I was still with you I told you these things?

6 And now you know what is restraining, that he may be revealed in his own time.

7 For the mystery of lawlessness is already at work; only He who now restrains *will do* so until He is taken out of the way.

8 And then the lawless one will be revealed, whom the Lord will consume with the breath of His mouth and destroy [R]with the brightness of His coming. Heb. 10:27

9 The coming of the *lawless one* is according to the working of Satan, with all power, [R]signs, and lying wonders, Deut. 13:1

10 and with all unrighteous deception among [R]those who perish, because they did not receive [R]the love of the truth, that they might be saved. 2 Cor. 2:15 • 1 Cor. 16:22

11 And for this reason God will send them strong delusion, that they should believe the lie,

12 that they all may be condemned who did not believe the truth but [R]had pleasure in unrighteousness. Rom. 1:32

The Comfort of the Believer on the Day of the Lord

13 But we are [T]bound to give thanks to God always for you, brethren beloved by the Lord, because God from the beginning chose you for salvation through sanctification by the Spirit and belief in the truth, *under obligation*

14 to which He called you by our gospel, for [R]the obtaining of the glory of our Lord Jesus Christ. 1 Pet. 5:10

15 Therefore, brethren, stand fast and hold the traditions which you were taught, whether by word or our [T]epistle. *letter*

16 Now may our Lord Jesus Christ Himself, and our God and Father, [R]who has loved us and given *us* everlasting consolation and [R]good hope by grace, [Rev. 1:5] • 1 Pet. 1:3

17 comfort your hearts and [T]establish you in every good word and work. *strengthen*

CHAPTER 3

Wait Patiently for Christ

FINALLY, brethren, pray for us, that the word of the Lord may have *free* course and be glorified, just as *it is* with you,

1:10 NU, M *have believed* **2:2** NU *the Lord*
2:3 NU *lawlessness* **2:4** NU omits *as God*

2 and [R]that we may be delivered from
unreasonable and wicked men; [R]for not all
have faith. Rom. 15:31 • Acts 28:24
3 But the Lord is faithful, who will establish you and guard *you* from the evil one.
4 And [R]we have confidence in the Lord
concerning you, both that you do and will do
the things we command you. 2 Cor. 7:16
5 Now may [R]the Lord direct your hearts
into the love of God and into the patience of
Christ. 1 Chr. 29:18

Withdraw from the Disorderly

6 But we command you, brethren, in the
name of our Lord Jesus Christ, that you
withdraw from every brother who walks
[R]disorderly and not according to the tradition
which *he received from us. 1 Thess. 4:11
7 For you yourselves know how you ought
to follow us, for we were not disorderly
among you;
8 nor did we eat anyone's bread [T]free of
charge, but worked with [R]labor and toil night
and day, that we might not be a burden to
any of you, Lit. *for nothing* • 1 Thess. 2:9
9 not because we do not have [R]authority,
but to make ourselves an example of how
you should follow us. 1 Cor. 9:4, 6–14
10 For even when we were with you, we
commanded you this: If anyone will not
work, neither shall he eat.
11 For we hear that there are some who
walk among you in a disorderly manner, not
working at all, but are [R]busybodies. 1 Pet. 4:15
12 Now those who are such we command
and [T]exhort through our Lord Jesus Christ
[R]that they work in quietness and eat their
own bread. *encourage* • Eph. 4:28
13 But *as for* you, brethren, [R]do not grow
weary *in* doing good. Gal. 6:9
14 And if anyone does not obey our word in
this [T]epistle, note that person and [R]do not
keep company with him, that he may be
ashamed. *letter* • Matt. 18:17
15 Yet do not count *him* as an enemy, [R]but
[T]admonish *him* as a brother. Titus 3:10 • *warn*

Conclusion

16 Now may [R]the Lord of peace Himself
give you peace always in every way. The
Lord *be* with you all. Rom. 15:33
17 [R]The salutation of Paul with my own
hand, which is a sign in every [T]epistle; so I
write. 1 Cor. 16:21 • *letter*
18 [R]The grace of our Lord Jesus Christ *be*
with you all. Amen. Rom. 16:20, 24

3:6 NU, M *they*

THE FIRST EPISTLE OF PAUL THE APOSTLE TO

TIMOTHY

THE BOOK OF FIRST TIMOTHY

Paul, the aged and experienced apostle, writes to the young pastor Timothy who is facing a heavy burden of responsibility in the church at Ephesus. The task is challenging: false doctrine must be erased, public worship safeguarded, and mature leadership developed. In addition to the conduct of the church, Paul talks pointedly about the conduct of the minister. Timothy must be on his guard lest his youthfulness become a liability, rather than an asset, to the gospel. He must be careful to avoid false teachers and greedy motives, pursuing instead righteousness, godliness, faith, love, perseverance, and the gentleness that befits a man of God.

The Greek title for this letter is *Pros Timotheon A*, the "First to Timothy." *Timothy* means "honoring God" or "honored by God," and probably was given to him by his mother Eunice.

THE AUTHOR OF FIRST TIMOTHY

Since the early nineteenth century, the Pastoral Epistles have been attacked more than any other Pauline epistles on the issue of authenticity. The similarity of these epistles requires that they be treated as a unit in terms of authorship because they stand or fall together.

The external evidence solidly supports the conservative position that Paul wrote the letters to Timothy and Titus. Postapostolic church fathers, such as Polycarp and Clement of Rome, allude to them as Paul's writing. In addition, these epistles are identified as Pauline by Irenaeus, Tertullian, Clement of Alexandria, and the Muratorian Canon. Only Romans and First Corinthians have better attestation among the Pauline epistles.

Suggestions of an author other than Paul are supported wholly on the basis of internal evidence. Even though these letters claim to be written by Paul (1:1; 2 Tim. 1:1; Titus 1:1), critics assert that they are "pious forgeries" that appeared in the second century. There are several problems with this: (1) Pseudonymous writing was unacceptable to Paul (see 2 Thess. 2:2; 3:17) and to the early church, which was very sensitive to the problem of forgeries. (2) The adjective *pious* should deceive no one: a forgery was as deliberately deceptive then as it is now. (3) The many personal facts and names that appear in the Pastoral Epistles would have been avoided by a forger who would have taken refuge in vagueness. Nor would a forger have used expressions like those in 1:13, 15 if he had been an admirer of Paul. The doctrinal teaching and autobiographical details (cf. 1:12–17; 2:7; 2 Tim. 1:8–12; 4:9–22; Titus 1:5; 3:12, 13) fit very well with "Paul, the aged" (Philem. 9). (4) What purpose or advantage would these epistles serve as forgeries written years later? There are too many personal elements, and the doctrinal refutations do not refer to second-century Gnosticism. (5) The style and content of the postapostolic writings or apocryphal books differ greatly with these three letters.

THE TIME OF FIRST TIMOTHY

Pauline authorship of the Pastoral Epistles requires Paul's release from his Roman imprisonment (Acts 28), the continuation of his missionary endeavors, and his imprisonment for a second time in Rome. Unfortunately, the order of events can only be reconstructed from hints, because there is no concurrent history paralleling Acts to chronicle the last years of the apostle. The following reconstruction, therefore, is only tentative:

As he anticipated in Philippians (1:19, 25, 26; 2:24), Paul was released from his first Roman imprisonment. It is possible that his Jewish accusers decided not to appear at his trial before Caesar. In fulfillment of his promise to the Philippians (Phil. 2:19–23), he sends Timothy to Philippi to relate the good news. Paul himself went to Ephesus (in spite of his earlier expectations in Acts 20:38) and to other Asian churches like Colosse (see Philem. 22). When Timothy rejoined him in Ephesus, Paul instructed his assistant to "remain in Ephesus" (1:3) while he journeyed to Macedonia. When he saw that he might be delayed in Macedonia, Paul wrote First Timothy, perhaps from Philippi (3:14, 15). After he saw Timothy in Ephesus, the apostle journeyed on to the island of Crete where, after a period of ministry, he left Titus to continue the work (Titus 1:5). In Corinth, Paul decided to write a letter to Titus because Zenas and Apollos were making a journey that would take them by way of Crete (Titus 3:13). He instructed Titus to join him in Nicopolis after the arrival of his replacement in Crete, Artemas or Tychicus (Titus 3:12).

If he went to Spain as he had planned (Rom. 15:24, 28), Paul probably departed with Titus for that western province after his winter in Nicopolis. Early church tradition holds that Paul did go to Spain. Before the end of the first century, Clement of Rome said that Paul "reached the limits of the West" (1 Clement 5:7). Since he was writing from Rome, he evidently had Spain in mind. Paul may have been in Spain from A.D. 64 to 66. He returned to Greece and Asia—to Corinth, Miletus, and Troas (2 Tim. 4:13, 20),—and may have been arrested in Troas where he left his valuable books and parchments (2 Tim. 4:13, 15).

Now that Christianity had become an illegal religion in the Empire (the burning of Rome took place in A.D. 64), Paul's enemies were able to successfully accuse him. He was imprisoned in A.D. 67 and wrote Second Timothy from his Roman cell after his first defense before the Imperial Court (2 Tim. 1:8, 17; 2:9; 4:16, 17). He was delivered from condemnation, but he held no hope of release and expected to be executed (2 Tim. 4:6–8, 18). He urged Timothy to come before that happened (2 Tim. 4:9, 21); and, according to tradition, the apostle was beheaded west of Rome on the Ostian Way.

Paul wrote First Timothy from Macedonia in A.D. 62 or 63 while Timothy was serving as his representative in Ephesus and perhaps in other churches in the province of Asia. Timothy was to appoint elders, combat false doctrine, and supervise church life as an apostolic representative.

THE CHRIST OF FIRST TIMOTHY

Christ is the "one Mediator between God and men" (2:5), and "God was manifested in the flesh, justified in the Spirit, seen by angels, preached among the Gentiles, believed on in the world, received up in glory" (3:16). He is the source of spiritual strength, faith, and love (1:12, 14). He "came into the world to save sinners" (1:15) and "gave Himself a ransom for all" (2:6) as "*the* Savior of all men, especially of those who believe" (4:10).

KEYS TO FIRST TIMOTHY

Key Word: Leadership Manual for Church Organization—The theme of this epistle is Timothy's organization and oversight of the Asian churches as a faithful minister of God. Paul writes this letter as a reference manual for leadership so that Timothy will have effective guidance for his work during Paul's absence in Macedonia (3:14, 15). Paul wants to encourage and exhort his younger assistant to become an example to others, exercise his spiritual gifts, and "fight the good fight of faith" (6:12; cf. 1:18; 4:12–16; 6:20). Timothy's personal and public life must be above reproach; and he must be ready to deal with matters of false teaching, organization, discipline, proclamation of the Scriptures, poverty and wealth, and the roles of various groups. Negatively, he is to refute error (1:7–11; 6:3–5); positively, he is to teach the truth (4:13–16; 6:2, 17, 18).

Key Verses: First Timothy 3:15, 16 and 6:11, 12—"But if I am delayed, *I write* so that you may know how you ought to conduct yourself in the house of God, which is the church of the living God, the pillar and ground of the truth. And without controversy great is the mystery of godliness: God was manifested in the flesh, justified in the Spirit, seen by angels, preached among the Gentiles, believed on in the world, received up in glory" (3:15, 16).

"But you, O man of God, flee these things and pursue righteousness, godliness, faith, love, patience, gentleness. Fight the good fight of faith, lay hold on eternal life, to which you were also called and have confessed the good confession in the presence of many witnesses" (6:11, 12).

Key Chapter: First Timothy 3—Listed in chapter 3 are the qualifications for the leaders of God's church, the elders and deacons. Notably absent are qualities of worldly success or position. Instead, Paul enumerates character qualities demonstrating that true leadership emanates from our walk with God rather than from achievements or vocational success.

SURVEY OF FIRST TIMOTHY

Paul's last three recorded letters, written near the end of his full and fruitful life, were addressed to his authorized representatives Timothy and Titus. These were the only letters Paul wrote exclusively to individuals (Philemon was addressed primarily to its namesake, but also to others), and they were designed to exhort and encourage Timothy and Titus in their ministry of solidifying the churches in Ephesus and Crete. In the eighteenth century, these epistles came to be known as the Pastoral Epistles even though they do not use any terms such as shepherd, pastor, flock, or sheep. Still, this title is appropriate for First Timothy and Titus, since they focus on the oversight of church life. It is less appropriate in the case of Second Timothy, which is a more personal than church-oriented letter. The Pastoral Epistles abound with principles for leadership and righteous living.

In his first letter to Timothy, Paul seeks to guide his younger and less experienced assistant in his weighty responsibility as the overseer of the work at Ephesus and other Asian cities. He writes, in effect, a challenge to Timothy to fulfill the task before him: combating false teaching with sound doctrine, developing qualified leadership, teaching God's Word, and encouraging Christian conduct. Because of the personal and conversational character of this letter, it is loosely structured around five clear charges that end each section (1:18–20; 3:14–16; 4:11–20; 5:21–25; 6:20, 21): Paul's charges concerning doctrine (1); Paul's charge concerning public worship (2 and 3); Paul's charge concerning false teachers (4); Paul's charge concerning church discipline (5); and Paul's charge concerning pastoral motives (6).

Paul's Charge Concerning Doctrine (1): After his greetings (1:1, 2), Paul warns Timothy about the growing problem of false doctrines, particularly as they relate to the misuse of the Mosaic Law (1:3–11). The aging apostle then recounts his radical conversion to Christ and subsequent calling to the ministry (1:12–17). Timothy, too, has received a divine calling, and Paul charges him to fulfill it without wavering in doctrine or conduct (1:18–20).

Paul's Charge Concerning Public Worship (2 and 3): Turning his attention to the church at large, Paul addresses the issues of church worship and leadership. Efficacious public prayer should be a part of worship, and Paul associates this with the role of men in the church (2:1–8). He then turns to the role of women (2:9–15), wherein he emphasizes the importance of the inner quality of godliness. In 3:1–7, Paul lists several qualifications for overseers or bishops. The word for "overseer" *(episkopos)* is used synonymously with the word for "elder" *(presbuteros)* in the New Testament, because both originally referred to the same office (see Acts 20:17, 28; Titus 1:5, 7). The qualifications for the office of deacon (*diakonos,* "servant") are listed in 3:8–13.

Paul's Charge Concerning False Teachers (4): Timothy obviously had difficulties with some of the older men (5:1) who had left the faith. Paul carefully advises on the issues of marriage, food, and exercise. The closing charge exhorts Timothy not to neglect the spiritual gift given to him.

Paul's Charge Concerning Church Discipline (5): One of the most difficult pastoral duties for the young minister is to lead in the exercise of church discipline. Commencing with the general advice of treating all members of the church as family (5:1, 2), Paul concentrates on the two special areas of widows and elders, focusing on Timothy's responsibility and providing practical instruction.

Paul's Charge Concerning Pastoral Duties (6): In addition, the insidious doctrine was being taught that godliness will eventually result in material blessing. Paul, in no uncertain terms, states "from such withdraw yourself" (6:5). The book closes with an extended charge (6:11–21), which is supplemented by an additional charge that Timothy is to give to the wealthy of this age (6:17–19).

FOCUS	DOCTRINE	PUBLIC WORSHIP	FALSE TEACHERS	CHURCH DISCIPLINE	PASTORAL MOTIVES
REFERENCE	1:1—	2:1—	4:1—	5:1—	6:1—6:21
DIVISION	PROBLEM OF FALSE DOCTRINE	PUBLIC WORSHIP AND LEADERSHIP	PRESERVE TRUE DOCTRINE	PRESCRIPTIONS FOR WIDOWS AND ELDERS	PASTORAL MOTIVATIONS
TOPIC	WARNING	WORSHIP	WISDOM	WIDOWS	WEALTH
	DANGERS OF FALSE DOCTRINE	DIRECTIONS FOR WORSHIP	DEFENSE AGAINST FALSE TEACHERS	DUTIES TOWARD OTHERS	DEALINGS WITH RICHES
LOCATION	WRITTEN IN MACEDONIA				
TIME	C. A.D. 62–63				

OUTLINE OF FIRST TIMOTHY

I. Paul's Charge Concerning Doctrine 1:1–20

A. Paul's Past Charge to Timothy 1:1–11
B. Christ's Past Charge to Paul 1:12–17
C. First Charge: "Wage the Good Warfare" 1:18–20

II. Paul's Charge Concerning Public Worship . . . . 2:1—3:16

A. Prayer in Public Worship 2:1–8
B. Women in Public Worship 2:9–15
C. Qualifications of Bishops 3:1–7
D. Qualifications of Deacons 3:8–13
E. Second Charge: "Conduct Yourself in the House of God" 3:14–16

III. Paul's Charge Concerning False Teachers . 4:1–16

A. Description of False Teachers 4:1–5
B. Instruction for the True Teacher 4:6–10
C. Third Charge: "Do Not Neglect the Gift" 4:11–16

IV. Paul's Charge Concerning Church Discipline 5:1–25

A. How to Treat All People 5:1, 2
B. How to Treat Widows 5:3–16
C. How to Treat Elders 5:17–20
D. Fourth Charge: "Observe These Things Without Prejudice" 5:21–25

CHAPTER 1

Paul's Past Charge to Timothy

PAUL, an apostle of Jesus Christ, by the
commandment of God our Savior and the
Lord Jesus Christ, our hope,
2 To Timothy, *my* true son in the faith:
[R]Grace, mercy, *and* peace from God our
Father and Jesus Christ our Lord. Gal. 1:3
3 As I urged you [R]when I went into Macedonia—remain in Ephesus that you may
[T]charge some [R]that they teach no other doctrine, Acts 20:1, 3 • *command* • Gal. 1:6, 7
4 nor give heed to fables and endless genealogies, which cause disputes rather than
godly edification which is in faith.
5 Now the purpose of the commandment is
love [R]from a pure heart, *from* a good conscience, and *from* sincere faith, Eph. 6:24
6 from which some, having strayed, have
turned aside to [R]idle talk, 1 Tim. 6:4, 20
7 desiring to be teachers of the law, understanding neither what they say nor the things
which they affirm.
8 But we know that the law *is* [R]good if one
uses it lawfully, Rom. 7:12, 16
9 knowing this: that the law is not made
for a righteous person, but for *the* lawless and
insubordinate, for *the* ungodly and for sinners, for *the* unholy and profane, for murderers of fathers and murderers of mothers, for
manslayers,
10 for fornicators, for sodomites, for kidnappers, for liars, for perjurers, and if there is any
other thing that is [T]contrary to sound doctrine, *opposed*
11 according to the glorious gospel of the
[R]blessed God which was [R]committed to my
trust. 1 Tim. 6:15 • 1 Cor. 9:17

Christ's Past Charge to Paul

12 And I thank Christ Jesus our Lord who
has enabled me, because He counted me
faithful, putting *me* into the ministry,
13 although [R]I was formerly a blasphemer, a
persecutor, and an [T]insolent man; but I obtained mercy because [R]I did *it* ignorantly in
unbelief. Acts 8:3 • *violently arrogant* • John 4:21
14 [R]And the grace of our Lord was exceedingly abundant, [R]with faith and love which
are in Christ Jesus. Rom. 5:20 • 2 Tim. 1:13; 2:22
15 [R]This *is* a faithful saying and worthy of
all acceptance, that [R]Christ Jesus came into
the world to save sinners, of whom I am
chief. 2 Tim. 2:11 • Is. 53:5; Matt. 1:21; 9:13 ★
16 However, for this reason I obtained
mercy, that in me first Jesus Christ might
show all longsuffering, as a pattern to those
who are going to believe on Him for everlasting life.
17 Now to the King eternal, immortal, invisible, to *God who alone is wise, *be* honor
and glory forever and ever. Amen.

First Charge: "Wage the Good Warfare"

18 This [T]charge I commit to you, son Timothy, according to the prophecies previously
made concerning you, that by them you may
wage the good warfare, *command*
19 having faith and a good conscience,
which some having rejected, concerning the
faith have suffered shipwreck,
20 of whom are Hymenaeus and Alexander,
whom I delivered to Satan that they may
learn not to [R]blaspheme. Acts 13:45

CHAPTER 2

Prayer in Public Worship

THEREFORE I [T]exhort first of all that
supplications, prayers, intercessions, *and*
giving of thanks be made for all men, *encourage*
2 for kings and [R]all who are in authority,
that we may lead a quiet and peaceable life in
all godliness and [T]reverence. [Rom. 13:1] • *dignity*
3 For this *is* [R]good and acceptable in the
sight [R]of God our Savior, Rom. 12:2 • 2 Tim. 1:9
4 who desires all men to be saved and to
come to the knowledge of the truth.
5 For *there is* one God and one Mediator
between God and men, *the* Man Christ Jesus,
6 [R]who gave Himself a ransom for all, to be
testified in due time, Mark 10:45
7 [R]for which I was appointed a preacher
and an apostle—I am speaking the truth *in
Christ *and* not lying—[R]a teacher of the Gentiles in faith and truth. Eph. 3:7, 8 • [Gal. 1:15, 16]
8 Therefore I desire that the men pray
[R]everywhere, [R]lifting up holy hands, without
wrath and doubting; Luke 23:34 • Ps. 134:2

Women in Public Worship

9 in like manner also, that the women
adorn themselves in modest apparel, with
propriety and moderation, not with braided
hair or gold or pearls or costly clothing,

1:17 NU *the only God* **2:7** NU omits *in Christ*

10 [R]but, which is proper for women professing godliness, with good works. 1 Pet. 3:4
11 Let a woman learn in silence with all
submission.
12 And [R]I do not permit a woman to teach
or to have authority over a man, but to be in
silence. 1 Cor. 14:34
13 For Adam was formed first, then Eve.
14 And Adam was not deceived, but the
woman being deceived, fell into transgression.
15 Nevertheless she will be saved in childbearing if they continue in faith, love, and
holiness, with self-control.

CHAPTER 3

Qualifications of Bishops

THIS *is* a faithful saying: If a man desires
the position of a *bishop, he desires a
good work.
2 A bishop then must be blameless, the
husband of one wife, temperate, sober-
minded, of good behavior, hospitable, able to
teach;
3 not [T]given to wine, not violent, *not
greedy for money, but gentle, not quarrelsome, not [T]covetous; *addicted* • *loving money*
4 one who rules his own house well, having *his* children in submission with all reverence
5 (for if a man does not know how to rule
his own house, how will he take care of the
church of God?);
6 not a [T]novice, lest being puffed up with
pride he fall into the *same* condemnation as
the devil. *new convert*
7 Moreover he must have a good testimony among those who are outside, lest he
fall into reproach and the snare of the devil.

Qualifications of Deacons

8 Likewise deacons *must be* reverent, not
double-tongued, [R]not given to much wine,
not greedy for money, Ezek. 44:21
9 holding the [T]mystery of the faith with a
pure conscience. *hidden truth*
10 But let these also first be [T]proved; then
let them serve as deacons, being *found*
blameless. *tested*
11 Likewise *their* wives *must be* reverent,
not [T]slanderers, temperate, faithful in all
things. *malicious gossips*
12 Let deacons be the husbands of one wife,
ruling *their* children and their own houses
well.
13 For those who have served well as deacons [R]obtain for themselves a good standing
and great boldness in the faith which is in
Christ Jesus. Matt. 25:21

Second Charge: "Conduct Yourself in the House of God"

14 These things I write to you, though I
hope to come to you shortly;
15 but if I am delayed, *I write* so that you
may know how you ought to conduct yourself in the house of God, which is the church
of the living God, the pillar and [T]ground of
the truth. *foundation, mainstay*
16 And without controversy great is the
[T]mystery of godliness: *hidden truth*

[R]God* was manifested in the flesh,
[R]Justified in the Spirit, [John 1:14] • [Matt. 3:16]
[R]Seen by angels, Matt. 28:2
[R]Preached among the Gentiles, Rom. 10:18
[R]Believed on in the world, Col. 1:6, 23
[R]Received up in glory. Luke 24:51

3:1 Lit. *overseer* 3:3 NU omits *not greedy for money*
3:16 NU *Who*

3:1–13 The Offices of the Church—The New Testament uses four terms to describe the leadership of the church: (1) "elder" (Gr., *presbuteros*) which places emphasis upon the authority that the leadership has to teach or rule in the church; (2) "bishop" (Gr., *episkopos*—overseer) which emphasizes the fact that the leadership is charged with overseeing the local church and as such is responsible for the spiritual well-being of those in the church; (3) "pastor" (Gr., *poimen*—shepherd) which places emphasis upon the responsibility of the leadership of the church to shepherd the flock. No shepherd has ever given birth to his sheep. It is the responsibility of those in leadership to do for the sheep what they cannot do for themselves and to make sure that they are in good spiritual condition so that they can do what comes naturally, that is, beget other sheep; (4) "deacon" (Gr., *diakonos*—minister) which places emphasis upon the attitude that the leaders are to have in their leading. They are not to "lord it over" the flock, but are to realize that they are the ministers or servants of those whom the Lord has put under their care.

The function of the office of elder is twofold: (1) teaching and (2) ruling (Page 1429—1 Tim. 5:17). An elder is to be able to teach his people what the Word of God teaches and to give direction as to how that is to be accomplished in and through the local church.

The qualifications for the office of deacon are essentially the same as those for the elder except that the deacon need not be "able to teach." The deacons are to be spiritual and in tune with the elders and seek to assist them in implementing the goals that the elders feel the Spirit of God is leading them to pursue through the local church.

Now turn to Page 1392—Eph. 5:25–29: The Relationship of the Church to Christ.

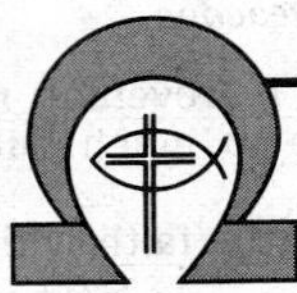

LAYING ON OF HANDS

The laying on of hands has great significance as a religious rite or ceremony in the Bible. This rite is associated with the bestowal of divine blessings upon a person, and it also is used as a special form of recognition for persons set apart for God's service.

On the Day of Atonement, the high priest placed his hands on the head of a goat before releasing it into the wilderness. Through this rite, he symbolically transferred the sins of the people to the scapegoat (Lev. 16:21).

Abraham and the other patriarchs placed hands on their descendants to confirm a birthright or to convey a special blessing, as when Jacob blessed the sons of Joseph (Gen. 48:14, 18). The ceremony sometimes implied the transfer of authority (Num. 27:18–20). Joshua was said to be "full of the spirit of wisdom, for Moses had laid his hands on him" (Deut. 34:9).

The laying on of hands apparently served also as a formal declaration of identification by the church at Antioch with Paul and Barnabas, whom they were sending out as missionaries (Acts 13:2, 3). This same sense of identification with sacrificial animals as a substitute for the people may be implied in the burnt offering presented by the priests in Old Testament times (Lev. 1:4).

Placing hands on persons in need of healing has a strong biblical precedent. The practice was used by Jesus during His healing ministry (Matt. 9:18) and when He blessed the children (Matt. 19:15). The apostles laid their hands on the sick (Acts 14:3) and on newly baptized persons (Acts 8:16, 17). There also appears to be a connection between the laying on of hands and the reception of the Holy Spirit (Acts 8:18).

The Levites were consecrated to service by the laying on of hands (Num. 8:10, 11). In the New Testament, the practice is associated with the ordination of deacons (Acts 6:6) and ministers (1 Tim. 4:14; 5:22) and the setting apart of missionaries for divine service (Acts 13:2, 3).

The laying on of hands has great significance as a religious rite or ceremony in the Bible.

CHAPTER 4

Description of False Teachers

NOW the Spirit [T]expressly says that in latter times some will depart from the faith, giving heed [R]to deceiving spirits and doctrines of demons, *explicitly* • Rev. 16:14

2 speaking lies in hypocrisy, having their own conscience seared with a hot iron,

3 forbidding to marry, *and commanding* to abstain from foods which God created to be received with thanksgiving by those who believe and know the truth.

4 For every creature of God *is* good, and nothing is to be refused if it is received with thanksgiving;

5 for it is [T]sanctified by the word of God and prayer. *set apart*

Instruction for the True Teacher

6 If you instruct the brethren in these things, you will be a good minister of Jesus Christ, [R]nourished in the words of faith and of the good doctrine which you have carefully followed. 2 Tim. 3:14

7 But reject profane and old wives' fables, and exercise yourself *rather* to godliness.

8 For [R]bodily exercise profits a little, but godliness is profitable for all things, [R]having promise of the life that now is and of that which is to come. 1 Cor. 8:8 • Ps. 37:9

9 This *is* a faithful saying and worthy of all acceptance.

10 For to this *end* *we both labor and suffer reproach, because we trust in the living God, [R]who is *the* Savior of all men, especially of those who believe. Ps. 36:6

Third Charge: "Do Not Neglect the Gift"

11 These things command and teach.

12 Let no one despise your youth, but be an example to the believers in word, in conduct, in love, *in spirit, in faith, in purity.

13 Till I come, give attention to reading, to exhortation, to [T]doctrine. *teaching*

14 Do not neglect the gift that is in you, which was given to you by prophecy with the laying on of the hands of the presbytery.

15 Meditate on these things; give yourself entirely to them, that your progress may be evident to all.

16 Take heed to yourself and to the doctrine. Continue in them, for in doing this you will save both yourself and those who hear you.

CHAPTER 5

How to Treat All People

DO not rebuke an older man, but exhort *him* as a father, *the* younger men as brothers,

2 *the* older women as mothers, *the* younger as sisters, with all purity.

How to Treat Widows

3 Honor widows who are really widows.

4 But if any widow has children or grandchildren, let them first learn to show piety at home and [R]to repay their parents; for this is *good and acceptable before God. Gen. 45:10

5 Now she who is really a widow, and left alone, trusts in God and continues in supplications and prayers [R]night and day. Acts 26:7

6 But she who lives in [T]pleasure is dead while she lives. *indulgence*

7 And these things command, that they may be blameless.

8 But if anyone does not provide for his own, [R]and especially for those of his household, [R]he has denied the faith [R]and is worse than an unbeliever. Is. 58:7 • 2 Tim. 3:5 • Matt. 18:17

9 Do not let a widow under sixty years old be taken into the number, *and not unless* she has been the wife of one man,

10 well reported for good works: if she has brought up children, if she has lodged strangers, if she has washed the saints' feet, if she has relieved the afflicted, if she has diligently followed every good work.

11 But refuse *the* younger widows; for when they have begun to grow wanton against Christ, they desire to marry,

12 having condemnation because they have cast off their first [T]faith. Or *solemn promise*

13 And besides they learn *to be* idle, wandering about from house to house, and not only idle but also gossips and busybodies, saying things which they ought not.

14 Therefore I desire that *the* younger *widows* marry, bear children, manage the house, give no opportunity to the adversary to speak reproachfully.

15 For some have already turned aside after Satan.

16 If any believing *man or woman has widows, let them [T]relieve them, and do not let the church be burdened, that it may relieve those who are really widows. *give aid to*

How to Treat Elders

17 Let the elders who rule well be counted worthy of double honor, especially those who labor in the word and doctrine.

18 For the Scripture says, *"You shall not muzzle an ox while it treads out the grain,"* and, "The laborer *is* worthy of his wages."

19 Do not receive an accusation against an elder except from two or three witnesses.

20 Those who are sinning rebuke in the presence of all, that the rest also may fear.

Fourth Charge: "Observe These Things Without Prejudice"

21 I charge *you* before God and the Lord Jesus Christ and the [T]elect angels that you

4:10 NU *we labor and strive,* **4:12** NU omits *in spirit*
5:4 NU, M omit *good and* **5:16** NU omits *man or*

observe these things without [R]prejudice,
doing nothing with partiality. *chosen* • Deut. 1:17
22 Do not lay hands on anyone hastily, nor
[R]share in other people's sins; keep yourself
pure. Eph. 5:6, 7
23 No longer drink only water, but use a
little wine for your stomach's sake and your
frequent [T]infirmities. *illnesses*
24 Some men's sins are [R]clearly evident,
preceding *them* to judgment, but those of
some *men* follow later. Gal. 5:19-21
25 Likewise, the good works *of some* are
clearly evident, and those that are otherwise
cannot be hidden.

CHAPTER 6

Exhortation to Servants

LET as many [R]servants as are under the
yoke count their own masters worthy of
all honor, so that the name of God and *His*
doctrine may not be blasphemed. Eph. 6:5
2 And those who have believing masters,
let them not despise *them* because they are
brethren, but rather serve *them* because
those who are benefited are believers and
beloved. Teach and exhort these things.

Exhortation to Godliness with Contentment

3 If anyone teaches otherwise and does
not consent to wholesome words, *even* the
words of our Lord Jesus Christ, and to the
doctrine which is according to godliness,
4 he is proud, knowing nothing, but is
obsessed with disputes and arguments over
words, from which come envy, strife, reviling,
evil suspicions,
5 *useless wranglings of men of corrupt
minds and destitute of the truth, who suppose that godliness is a *means of* gain. *From
[R]such withdraw yourself. 2 Tim. 3:5
6 Now godliness with [R]contentment is
great gain. Heb. 13:5
7 For we brought nothing into *this* world,
**and it is* certain we can carry nothing out.
8 And having food and clothing, with these
we shall be [R]content. Prov. 30:8, 9
9 But those who desire to be rich fall into
temptation and a snare, and *into* many foolish and harmful lusts which drown men in
destruction and perdition.
10 For the love of money is a root of all
kinds of evil, for which some have strayed
from the faith in their greediness, and pierced
themselves through with many sorrows.
11 But you, O man of God, flee these things
and pursue righteousness, godliness, faith,
love, patience, gentleness.
12 Fight the good fight of faith, lay hold on
eternal life, to which you were also called and
have confessed the good confession in the
presence of many witnesses.
13 I urge you in the sight of God who gives
life to all things, and *before* Christ Jesus [R]who
witnessed the good confession before Pontius
Pilate, John 18:36, 37
14 that you keep *this* commandment without spot, blameless until our Lord Jesus
Christ's appearing,
15 which He will manifest in His own time,
He who is the blessed and only [T]Potentate,
the King of kings and Lord of lords, *Sovereign*
16 who alone has immortality, dwelling in
[R]unapproachable light, [R]whom no man has
seen or can see, to whom *be* honor and
everlasting power. Amen. Dan. 2:22 • John 6:46

Exhortation to the Rich

17 Command those who are rich in this
present age not to be haughty, nor to trust in
uncertain [R]riches but in the living God, who
gives us richly all things to enjoy. Jer. 9:23
18 *Let them* do good, that they be rich in
good works, ready to give, willing to share,
19 [R]storing up for themselves a good foundation for the time to come, that they may
lay hold on eternal life. [Matt. 6:20, 21; 19:21]

Fifth Charge: "Guard What Was Committed"

20 O Timothy! Guard what was committed
to your trust, avoiding the profane *and* [T]vain
babblings and contradictions of what is
falsely called knowledge— *empty chatter*
21 by professing it, some have strayed concerning the faith. Grace *be* with you. Amen.

6:5 NU, M *constant friction* **6:5** NU omits the rest of v. 5. **6:7** NU omits *and it is certain*

THE SECOND EPISTLE OF PAUL THE APOSTLE TO

TIMOTHY

THE BOOK OF SECOND TIMOTHY

Prison is the last place from which to expect a letter of encouragement, but that is where Paul's second letter to Timothy originates. He begins by assuring Timothy of his continuing love and prayers, and reminds him of his spiritual heritage and responsibilities. Only the one who perseveres, whether as a soldier, athlete, farmer, or minister of Jesus Christ, will reap the reward. Paul warns Timothy that his teaching will come under attack as men desert the truth for ear "itching" words (4:3). But Timothy has Paul's example to guide him and God's Word to fortify him as he faces growing opposition and glowing opportunities in the last days.

Paul's last epistle received the title *Pros Timotheon B*, the "Second to Timothy." When Paul's epistles were collected together the *B* was probably added to distinguish this letter from the first letter he wrote to Timothy.

THE AUTHOR OF SECOND TIMOTHY

Since the Pastoral Epistles have to be treated as a unit on the matter of authorship, see "The Author of First Timothy" for comments on the origin of Second Timothy.

Timothy's name is found more often in the salutations of the Pauline epistles than any other (2 Cor.; Phil.; Col.; 1 and 2 Thess.; 1 and 2 Tim.; Philem.). His father was a Greek (Acts 16:1), but his Jewish mother Eunice and grandmother Lois reared him in the knowledge of the Hebrew Scriptures (1:5; 3:15). Timothy evidently became a convert of Paul (1 Cor. 4:17; 1 Tim. 1:2; 2 Tim. 1:2) when the apostle was in Lystra on his first missionary journey (Acts 14:8–20). When he visited Lystra on his second missionary journey, Paul decided to take Timothy along with him and circumcised him because of the Jews (Acts 16:1–3). Timothy was ordained to the ministry (1 Tim. 4:14; 2 Tim. 1:6) and served as a devoted companion and assistant to Paul in Troas, Berea, Thessalonica, and Corinth (Acts 16—18; 1 Thess. 3:1, 2). During the third missionary journey, Timothy labored with Paul and ministered for him as his representative in Ephesus, Macedonia, and Corinth. He was with Paul during his first Roman imprisonment and evidently went to Philippi (2:19–23) after Paul's release. Paul left him in Ephesus to supervise the work there (1 Tim. 1:3) and years later summoned him to Rome (4:9, 21). According to Hebrews 13:23, Timothy was imprisoned and released, but the passage does not say where. Timothy was sickly (1 Tim. 5:23), timid (2 Tim. 1:7), and youthful (1 Tim. 4:12), but he was a gifted teacher who was trustworthy and diligent.

THE TIME OF SECOND TIMOTHY

For a tentative reconstruction of the events following Paul's first Roman imprisonment, see "The Time of First Timothy." The cruel and unbalanced Nero, emperor of Rome from A.D. 54 to 68, was responsible for the beginning of the Roman persecution of Christians. Half of Rome was destroyed in July A.D. 64 by a fire, and mounting suspicion that Nero was responsible for the conflagration caused him to use the unpopular Christians as his scapegoat. Christianity thus became a *religio illicito,* and persecution of those who professed Christ became severe. By the time of Paul's return from Spain to Asia in A.D. 66, his enemies were able to use the official Roman position against Christianity to their advantage. Fearing for their own lives, the Asian believers failed to support Paul after his arrest (1:15) and no one supported him at his first defense before the Imperial Court (4:16). Abandoned by almost everyone (4:10, 11), the apostle found himself in circumstances very different from those of his first Roman imprisonment (Acts 28:16–31). At that time he was merely under house arrest, people could freely visit him, and he had the hope of release. Now he was in a cold Roman cell (4:13), regarded "as an evildoer" (2:9), and without hope of acquittal in spite of the success of his initial defense (4:6–8, 17, 18). Under these conditions, Paul wrote this epistle in the fall of A.D. 67, hoping that Timothy would be able to visit him before the approaching winter (4:21). Timothy evidently was in Ephesus at the time of this letter (see 1:18, 4:19), and on his way to Rome he would go through Troas (4:13) and Macedonia. Priscilla and Aquila (4:19) probably returned from Rome (Rom. 16:3) to Ephesus after the burning of Rome and the beginning of the persecution. Tychicus may have been the bearer of this letter (4:12).

THE CHRIST OF SECOND TIMOTHY

Christ Jesus appeared on earth, "abolished death and brought life and immortality to light through the gospel" (1:10). He rose from the dead (2:8) and provides salvation and "eternal glory" (2:10); for if believers "died with *Him*" they will "also live with *Him*" (2:11). All who love His appearing will receive "the crown of righteousness" (4:8) and "reign with *Him*" (2:12).

KEYS TO SECOND TIMOTHY

Key Word: Endurance in the Pastoral Ministry—In this letter, Paul commissions Timothy to faithfully endure and carry on the work that the condemned apostle must now relinquish. This set of instructions exhorts Timothy to use the Word of God constantly in order to overcome growing obstacles to the spread of the gospel. Timothy is in great need of encouragement because of the hardships he is facing, and Paul uses this letter to instruct him about handling persecution from the secular authorities and dissension and deception from within the church. As a spiritual father, Paul urges his young helper to overcome his natural timidity and boldly proclaim the gospel, even if it means that he will suffer for doing so.

Key Verses: Second Timothy 2:3, 4 and 3:14-17—"You therefore must endure hardship as a good soldier of Jesus Christ. No one engaged in warfare entangles himself with the affairs of *this* life, that he may please him who enlisted him as a soldier" (2:3, 4).

"But *as for* you, continue in the things which you have learned and have been assured of, knowing from whom you have learned *them*, and that from childhood you have known the Holy Scriptures, which are able to make you wise for salvation through faith which is in Christ Jesus. All Scripture *is* given by inspiration of God, and *is* profitable for doctrine, for reproof, for correction, for instruction in righteousness, that the man of God may be complete, thoroughly equipped for every good work" (3:14–17).

Key Chapter: Second Timothy 2—The second chapter of Second Timothy ought to be required daily reading for every pastor and full-time Christian worker. Paul lists the keys to an enduring successful ministry: (1) a reproducing ministry (1 and 2), an enduring ministry (3—13), a studying ministry (14—18), and a holy ministry (19—26).

SURVEY OF SECOND TIMOTHY

Paul knows as he writes this final epistle that his days on earth are quickly drawing to a close. About to relinquish his heavy burdens, the godly apostle seeks to challenge and strengthen his somewhat timid but faithful associate, Timothy, in his difficult ministry in Ephesus. In spite of Paul's bleak circumstances, this is a letter of encouragement that urges Timothy on to steadfastness in the fulfillment of his divinely appointed task. Paul calls Timothy a "good solider of Jesus Christ" (2:3), and it is clear from the sharp imperatives that this letter is really a combat manual for use in the spiritual warfare: "stir up" (1:6); "do not be ashamed" (1:8, 12, 13); "share with me in the sufferings" (1:8); "Hold fast . . . sound words" (1:13); "That good thing . . . keep" (1:14); "be strong" (2:1); "endure hardship" (2:3); "Be diligent to present yourself approved" (2:15); "Flee . . . pursue" (2:22); "avoid" (2:23); "You . . . must beware" (4:15). Central to everything in Second Timothy is the sure foundation of the Word of God. Paul focuses on the need to persevere in present testing (1 and 2), and to endure in future testing (3 and 4).

Persevere in Present Testing (1 and 2): After his salutation to his "beloved son" (1:2), Paul expresses his thanksgiving for Timothy's "genuine faith" (1:5). He then encourages Timothy to stand firm in the power of the gospel and to overcome any fear in the face of opposition. At personal risk, Onesiphorus boldly sought out Paul in Rome, but most of the Asian Christians failed to stand behind Paul at the time of his arrest. Timothy must remain faithful and not fear possible persecution. Paul then exhorts his spiritual son to reproduce in the lives of others what he has received in Christ (four generations are mentioned in 2:2). He is responsible to work hard and discipline himself like a teacher, a soldier, a farmer, a workman, a vessel, and a servant, following the example of Paul's perseverance (2:1-13). In his dealings with others, Timothy must not become entangled in false speculation, foolish quarrels, or youthful lusts, which would hamper his effectiveness. As he pursues "righ-

FOCUS	PERSEVERE IN PRESENT TESTINGS			ENDURE IN FUTURE TESTINGS		
REFERENCE	1:1—	1:6—	2:1—	3:1—	4:1—	4:6—4:22
DIVISION	THANKSGIVING FOR TIMOTHY'S FAITH	REMINDER OF TIMOTHY'S RESPONSIBILITY	CHARACTERISTICS OF A FAITHFUL MINISTER	APPROACHING DAY OF APOSTASY	CHARGE TO PREACH THE WORD	APPROACHING DEATH OF PAUL
TOPIC	POWER OF THE GOSPEL		PERSEVERANCE OF THE GOSPEL	PROTECTOR OF THE GOSPEL	PROCLAMATION OF THE GOSPEL	
	REMINDER		REQUIREMENTS	RESISTANCE	REQUESTS	
LOCATION	ROMAN PRISON					
TIME	c. A.D. 67					

teousness, faith, love, peace" (2:22), he must know how to graciously overcome error.

Endure in Future Testing (3 and 4): Paul anticipates a time of growing apostasy and wickedness when men and women will be increasingly susceptible to empty religiosity and false teaching (3:1–9). Arrogance and godlessness will breed further deception and persecution, but Timothy must not waver in using the Scripture to combat doctrinal error and moral evil (3:10–17). The Scriptures are inspired ("God-breathed") and with them Timothy is equipped to carry out the ministry to which he was called. Paul's final exhortation to Timothy (4:1–5) is a classic summary of the task of the man of God to proclaim the gospel in spite of opposing circumstances. This very personal letter closes with an update of Paul's situation in Rome along with certain requests (4:6–22). Paul longs to see Timothy before the end, and he also needs certain articles, especially "the parchments" (probably portions of the Old Testament Scriptures).

OUTLINE OF SECOND TIMOTHY

I. Persevere in Present Testings .... 1:1—2:26
- A. Thanksgiving for Timothy's Faith 1:1–5
- B. Reminder of Timothy's Responsibility 1:6–18
- C. Characteristics of a Faithful Minister 2:1–26
  1. Discipling Teacher 2:1, 2
  2. Single-Minded Soldier 2:3–5
  3. Enduring Farmer 2:6–13
  4. Diligent Workman 2:14–19
  5. Sanctified Vessel 2:20–23
  6. Gentle Servant 2:24–26

II. Endure in Future Testings .... 3:1—4:22
- A. Approaching Day of Apostasy 3:1–17
  1. Coming of Apostasy 3:1–9
  2. Confronting Apostasy 3:10–17
- B. Charge to Preach the Word 4:1–5
- C. Approaching Death of Paul 4:6–22
  1. Paul's Hope in Death 4:6–8
  2. Paul's Situation in Prison 4:9–18
  3. Paul's Closing Greetings 4:19–22

CHAPTER 1

Thanksgiving for Timothy's Faith

PAUL, an apostle of *Jesus Christ by the
will of God, according to the [R]promise of
life which is in Christ Jesus, Titus 1:2

2 To Timothy, *my* [R]beloved son:

Grace, mercy, *and* peace from God the
Father and Christ Jesus our Lord. 1 Tim. 1:2
3 I thank God, whom I serve with a pure
conscience, as *my* [R]forefathers *did*, as without ceasing I remember you in my prayers
night and day, Acts 24:14
4 greatly desiring to see you, being mindful
of your tears, that I may be filled with joy,
5 when I call to remembrance the genuine
faith that is in you, which dwelt first in your
grandmother Lois and your mother Eunice,
and I am persuaded is in you also.

Reminder of Timothy's Responsibility

6 Therefore I remind you [R]to stir up the
gift of God which is in you through the laying
on of my hands. 1 Tim. 4:14
7 For [R]God has not given us a spirit of fear,
[R]but of power and of love and of a sound
mind. Rom. 8:15 • [Acts 1:8]
8 Therefore do not be ashamed of the
testimony of our Lord, nor of me His prisoner, but share with me in the sufferings for
the gospel according to the power of God,
9 who has saved us and called *us* with a
holy calling, [R]not according to our works, but
[R]according to His own purpose and grace
which was given to us in Christ Jesus [R]before
time began, [Rom. 3:20] • Rom. 8:28 • Rom. 16:25
10 but [R]has now been revealed by the appearing of our Savior Jesus Christ, *who* has
abolished death and brought life and immortality to light through the gospel, Eph. 1:9
11 to which I was appointed a preacher, an
apostle, and a teacher *of the Gentiles.
12 For this reason I also suffer these things;
nevertheless I am not ashamed, [R]for I know
whom I have believed and am persuaded that
He is able to keep what I have committed to
Him until that Day. 1 Pet. 4:19
13 Hold fast the pattern of [R]sound words
which you have heard from me, in faith and
love which are in Christ Jesus. 1 Tim. 6:3
14 That good thing which was committed to
you, keep by the Holy Spirit who dwells in us.
15 This you know, that all those in Asia
have turned away from me, among whom are
Phygellus and Hermogenes.
16 The Lord grant mercy to the [R]household
of Onesiphorus, for he often refreshed me,
and was not ashamed of my chain; 2 Tim. 4:19
17 but when he arrived in Rome, he sought
me out very diligently and found *me*.

1:1 NU, M *Christ Jesus* 1:11 NU omits *of the Gentiles*

18 The Lord grant to him that he may find
mercy from the Lord [R]in that Day—and you
know very well how many ways he [R]minis-
tered to me at Ephesus. 2 Thess. 1:10 • Heb. 6:10

CHAPTER 2

Discipling Teacher

YOU therefore, my son, [R]be strong in the
grace that is in Christ Jesus. Eph. 6:10
2 And the things that you have heard from
me among many witnesses, commit these to
faithful men who will be able to teach others
also.

Single-Minded Soldier

3 You therefore must *endure hardship
[R]as a good soldier of Jesus Christ. 1 Tim. 1:18
4 No one engaged in warfare entangles
himself with the affairs of *this* life, that he
may please him who enlisted him as a soldier.
5 And also [R]if anyone competes in athletics, he is not crowned unless he competes
according to the rules. [1 Cor. 9:25]

Enduring Farmer

6 The hard-working farmer must be first to
partake of the crops.
7 Consider what I say, and *may the Lord
give you understanding in all things.
8 Remember that Jesus Christ, [R]of the seed
of David, [R]was raised from the dead [R]accord-
ing to my gospel, Rom. 1:3, 4 • 1 Cor. 15:4 • Rom. 2:16
9 [R]for which I suffer trouble as an evildoer,
[R]*even* to the point of chains; [R]but the word of
God is not chained. Acts 9:16 • Eph. 3:1 • Acts 28:31
10 Therefore [R]I endure all things for the
sake of the [T]elect, [R]that they also may obtain
the salvation which is in Christ Jesus with
eternal glory. Eph. 3:13 • *chosen ones* • 2 Cor. 1:6
11 *This is* a faithful saying:

For [R]if we died with *Him*,
We shall also live with *Him*. Rom. 6:5, 8
12 [R]If we endure, [Rom. 5:17; 8:17]
We shall also reign with *Him*.
[R]If we deny *Him*,
He also will deny us. Matt. 10:33
13 If we are faithless,
He remains faithful;
He [R]cannot deny Himself. Num. 23:19

Diligent Workman

14 Remind *them* of these things, charging
them before the Lord not to strive about
words to no profit, to the ruin of the hearers.
15 Be diligent to present yourself approved
to God, a worker who does not need to be
ashamed, rightly dividing the word of truth.
16 But shun profane *and* vain babblings, for
they will increase to more ungodliness.
17 And their message will spread like cancer. [R]Hymenaeus and Philetus are of this
sort, 1 Tim. 1:20
18 who have strayed concerning the truth,
saying that the resurrection is already past;
and they overthrow the faith of some.
19 Nevertheless [R]the solid foundation of
God stands, having this seal: "The Lord
[R]knows those who are His," and, "Let everyone who names the name of *Christ depart
from iniquity." [1 Cor. 3:11] • [Nah. 1:7]

Sanctified Vessel

20 But in a great house there are not only
[R]vessels of gold and silver, but also of wood
and clay, some for honor and some for dishonor. Rom. 9:21
21 Therefore if anyone cleanses himself
from the latter, he will be a vessel for honor,
[T]sanctified and useful for the Master, [R]pre-
pared for every good work. *set apart* • 2 Tim. 3:17
22 Flee also youthful lusts; but pursue righteousness, faith, love, peace with those who
call on the Lord out of a pure heart.
23 But avoid foolish and ignorant disputes,
knowing that they generate strife.

Gentle Servant

24 And [R]a servant of the Lord must not
quarrel but be gentle to all, [R]able to teach,
[R]patient, Titus 3:2 • Titus 1:9 • 1 Tim. 3:3
25 [R]in humility correcting those who are in
opposition, [R]if God perhaps will grant them
repentance, [R]so that they may know the
truth, Gal. 6:1 • Acts 8:22 • 1 Tim. 2:4
26 and *that* they may come to their senses
and escape the snare of the devil, having
been taken captive by him to *do* his will.

CHAPTER 3

Coming of Apostasy

BUT know this, that in the last days [T]peril-
ous times will come: *times of stress*
2 For men will be lovers of themselves,
lovers of money, boasters, proud, blasphemers, disobedient to parents, unthankful, unholy,
3 unloving, unforgiving, slanderers, without self-control, brutal, despisers of good,
4 [R]traitors, headstrong, haughty, lovers of
pleasure rather than lovers of God, 2 Pet. 2:10
5 having a form of godliness but denying
its power. And from such people turn away!
6 For [R]of this sort are those who creep into
households and make captives of gullible
women loaded down with sins, led away by
various lusts, Matt. 23:14
7 always learning and never able [R]to come
to the knowledge of the truth. 1 Tim. 2:4
8 [R]Now as Jannes and Jambres resisted
Moses, so do these also resist the truth: [R]men

2:3 NU *share* 2:7 NU *the Lord will give you*
2:19 NU, M *the Lord*

REPENTANCE, REMORSE, CONVERSION

Repent (*metanoeō*)

The word *repent* literally means "to change the mind," "to have second thoughts" or "to regret." The basic meaning of "a change of mind" still exists in New Testament usage, but in a context of accepting Christ by faith. For example: "Testifying to Jews, and also to Greeks, repentance [*metanoia*] toward God and faith toward our Lord Jesus Christ" (Acts 20:21). Repentance is so closely related to believing that many view it as the reverse side of "the coin of faith." That is, one cannot truly believe in Christ as Savior without changing one's mind about one's relationship to Him.

The Christian era started when John the Baptist, the Messiah's forerunner, called on Israel, saying, "Repent, for the kingdom of heaven is at hand" (Matt. 3:2). He added, "Therefore bear fruits worthy of repentance" (v. 8). The change should be visible to others. After being tempted by Satan in the wilderness, our Lord repeats the same message: "Repent, for the kingdom of heaven is at hand" (Matt. 4:17).

At Pentecost Peter opened the Christian era with a call to Israel to repent of crucifying the Messiah and to express that change by being baptized with water (Acts 2:38). God is good to us in order to lead us to repentance (Rom. 2:4). God's desire is "that all should come to repentance" (2 Pet. 3:9).

Repentance is prominent in Revelation, especially in the letters to the churches. People in churches often desperately need to repent. Hardened latter-day sinners undergoing God's wrath against a Christ-rejecting world are four times said not to repent (Rev. 9:20, 21; 16:9, 11).

Remorse

To have remorse (*metamelomai*) is similar in both Greek and English to repenting. It is used only five times in the New Testament, once for God (Heb. 7:21) in an Old Testament quotation. The NKJV "relent" is an improvement over the KJV "repent," since God only appears to change; it is really His invariable reaction to our change of mind. Jesus used this verb twice in His parable of the two sons. The son who said he would not work in his father's vineyard later changed his mind and "regretted [*metamelomai*] it and went" (Matt. 21:29). Jesus applied this to the chief priests and elders for not relenting (NKJV) and believing when they saw tax collectors and harlots accepting the Baptist's message. Judas is a clear example of the difference between repentance and remorse: "His betrayer, seeing that He had been condemned, was remorseful [*metamelomai*] and brought back the thirty pieces of silver to the chief priests and elders, saying, 'I have sinned by betraying innocent blood'" (Matt. 27:3, 4). Judas was sorry for his mistake, but he did not repent and seek forgiveness. Paul uses both concepts: "For godly sorrow produces repentance [*metanoia*] to salvation, not to be regretted [*ametamelētos*]" (2 Cor. 7:10). No one who truly repents will ever regret it.

Convert (*strephō*, *epistrephō*)

Convert (*strephō*, *epistrephō*) means "to turn," as when we say "She turned Protestant," meaning she converted from some other belief. People raised in Christian homes often find it hard to conceive of being "converted" to Christ since they learned to know Him gradually. However, whether one knows the time or not, there must be a point when one turns from self and sin to accept the Lord Jesus. "Unless you are converted (*strephō*) and become as little children, you will by no means enter the kingdom of heaven" (Matt. 18:3). Children don't have to become like adults to come to Christ—just the opposite!

Epistrephō is translated "convert" more frequently, although it often means simply "turn" (Rev. 1:12, e.g.).

In his defense before Agrippa, Paul spoke of both repentance and conversion. "They [Paul's hearers] should repent [*metanoeō*], turn to [*epistrephō*] God, and do works befitting repentance" (Acts 26:20).

What Paul told his hearers to do, all should do by coming to faith in the Lord Jesus Christ.

of corrupt minds, [R]disapproved concerning
the faith; Ex. 7:11, 12, 22; 8:7 • 1 Tim. 6:5 • Rom. 1:28
9 but they will progress no further, for
their folly will be manifest to all, [R]as theirs
also was. Ex. 7:11, 12; 8:18; 9:11

Confronting Apostasy

10 [R]But you have carefully followed my
doctrine, manner of life, purpose, faith, longsuffering, love, perseverance, 1 Tim. 4:6
11 persecutions, afflictions, which happened to me at Antioch, at Iconium, at Lystra—what persecutions I endured. And out of
them all the Lord delivered me.
12 Yes, and [R]all who desire to live godly in
Christ Jesus will suffer persecution. [Ps. 34:19]
13 [R]But evil men and impostors will grow
worse and worse, deceiving and being deceived. 2 Thess. 2:11
14 But *as for* you, continue in the things
which you have learned and been assured of,
knowing from whom you have learned *them*,
15 and that from childhood you have
known [R]the Holy Scriptures, which are able
to make you wise for salvation through faith
which is in Christ Jesus. John 5:39
16 [R]All Scripture *is* given by inspiration of
God, [R]and *is* profitable for doctrine, for reproof, for correction, for [T]instruction in righteousness, [2 Pet. 1:20] • Rom. 15:4 • *training, discipline*
17 that the man of God may be complete,
thoroughly equipped for every good work.

CHAPTER 4

Charge to Preach the Word

I [R]CHARGE *you* *therefore before God and
the Lord Jesus Christ, [R]who will judge the
living and the dead *at His appearing and His
kingdom: 1 Tim. 5:21 • Acts 10:42

2 Preach the word! Be ready in season *and*
out of season. [R]Convince, rebuke, exhort,
with all longsuffering and teaching. Titus 2:15

3 [R]For the time will come when they will
not endure [R]sound doctrine, [R]but according to
their own desires, *because* they have itching
ears, they will heap up for themselves teachers; 2 Tim. 3:1 • 1 Tim. 1:10 • 2 Tim. 3:6
4 and they will turn *their* ears away from
the truth, and be turned aside to fables.
5 But you be watchful in all things, [R]en-
dure afflictions, do the work of [R]an evangelist, fulfill your ministry. 2 Tim. 1:8 • Acts 21:8

Paul's Hope in Death

6 For [R]I am already being poured out *as a
drink offering*, and the time of [R]my departure
is at hand. Phil. 2:17 • [Phil. 1:23]
7 I have fought the good fight, I have
finished the race, I have kept the faith.
8 Finally, there is laid up for me the crown
of righteousness, which the Lord, the righteous [R]Judge, will give to me [R]on that Day,
and not to me only but also to all who have
loved His appearing. John 5:22 • 2 Tim. 1:12

Paul's Situation in Prison

9 Be diligent to come to me quickly;
10 for [R]Demas has forsaken me, [R]having
loved this present world, and has departed for
Thessalonica—Crescens for Galatia, Titus for
Dalmatia. Col. 4:14 • 1 John 2:15
11 Only Luke is with me. Get [R]Mark and
bring him with you, for he is useful to me for
ministry. Acts 12:12, 25; 15:37–39
12 And Tychicus I have sent to Ephesus.
13 Bring the cloak that I left with Carpus at
Troas when you come—and the books, especially the parchments.
14 [R]Alexander the coppersmith did me
much harm. May the Lord repay him according to his works. 1 Tim. 1:20
15 You also must beware of him, for he has
greatly resisted our words.
16 At my first defense no one stood with
me, but all forsook me. [R]May it not be
charged against them. Acts 7:60
17 But the Lord stood with me and
strengthened me, so that the message might
be preached fully through me, and *that* all
the Gentiles might hear. And I was delivered
[R]out of the mouth of the lion. 1 Sam. 17:37

4:1 NU omits *therefore* **4:1** NU *and by*

4:2 Sharing Our Faith: When?—A famous evangelist once ended a revival meeting in Chicago by advising the unbelievers who were present that night to go home and seriously consider the claims of the gospel, and then return on the following night prepared to make a decision for Christ. But on that same night, October 8, 1871, the tragic Chicago fire broke out. Before it was finally extinguished nearly four miles of buildings were consumed, along with 250 human fatalities. The evangelist then vowed never to end a service without giving an invitation to accept Christ immediately.

The question as to when we should share our faith is directly tied to when a sinner should accept Christ. *The Bible is clear that God's accepted time is today.* See Hebrews 3:15; 4:7; Second Corinthians 6:2; Isaiah 55:6. The reason for this is very simple—a sinner has no assurance whatsoever that he will live to see tomorrow. See Proverbs 27:1; Luke 12:19; James 4:13–15.

Thus, we are to witness any time, all the time, in any place and in all places. The apostle Paul shows us how this should be done. He witnesses everywhere, in a prison at midnight (Page 1295—Acts 16:25–31), and even on a sinking ship during a dark and stormy day (Page 1314—Acts 27:20–25).

Now turn to Page 666—Ps. 73:1: Walking in the Spirit: Confession.

18 [R]And the Lord will deliver me from every
evil work and preserve *me* for His heavenly
kingdom. [R]To Him *be* glory forever and ever.
Amen! Ps. 121:7 • Rom. 11:36

Paul's Closing Greetings

19 Greet [R]Prisca and Aquila, and the household of [R]Onesiphorus. Acts 18:2 • 2 Tim. 1:16

20 Erastus stayed in Corinth, but [R]Trophi-
mus I have left in Miletus sick. Acts 20:4; 21:29
21 Do your utmost to come before winter.
Eubulus greets you, as well as Pudens, Linus,
Claudia, and all the brethren.
22 The Lord *Jesus Christ be with your
spirit. Grace be with you. Amen.

4:22 NU omits *Jesus Christ*

THE EPISTLE OF PAUL THE APOSTLE TO

TITUS

THE BOOK OF TITUS

Titus, a young pastor, faces the unenviable assignment of setting in order the church at Crete. Paul writes advising him to appoint elders, men of proven spiritual character in their homes and businesses, to oversee the work of the church. But elders are not the only individuals in the church who are required to excel spiritually. Men and women, young and old, each have their vital functions to fulfill in the church if they are to be living examples of the doctrine they profess. Throughout his letter to Titus, Paul stresses the necessary, practical working out of salvation in the daily lives of both the elders and the congregation. Good works are desirable and profitable for all believers.

This third Pastoral Epistle is simply titled *Pros Titon,* "To Titus." Ironically, this was also the name of the Roman general who destroyed Jerusalem in A.D. 70 and succeeded his father Vespasian as emperor.

THE AUTHOR OF TITUS

Since the Pastoral Epistles have to be treated as a unit on the matter of authorship, see "The Author of First Timothy" for the authorship of Titus.

Titus is not mentioned in Acts, but the thirteen references to him in the Pauline epistles make it clear that he was one of Paul's closest and most trusted companions. This convert of Paul ("*my* true son in *our* common faith," 1:4) was probably from Syrian Antioch, if he was one of the disciples of Acts 11:26. Paul brought this uncircumcised Greek believer to Jerusalem (Gal. 2:3) where he became a test case on the matter of Gentiles and liberty from the law. Years later when Paul set out from Antioch on his third missionary journey (Acts 18:22), Titus must have accompanied him because he was sent by the apostle to Corinth on three occasions during that time (2 Cor. 2:12, 13; 7:5–7, 13–15; 8:6, 16–24). He is not mentioned again until Paul leaves him in Crete to carry on the work (Titus 1:5). He was with Paul during his second Roman imprisonment but left to go to Dalmatia (2 Tim. 4:10), possibly on an evangelistic mission. Paul spoke of this reliable and gifted associate as his "brother" (2 Cor. 2:13), his "partner and fellow worker" (2 Cor. 8:23), and his "son" (1:4). He lauded Titus's character and conduct in Second Corinthians 7:13–15 and 8:16, 17.

THE TIME OF TITUS

For a tentative reconstruction of the events following Paul's first Roman imprisonment, see "The Time of First Timothy."

The Mediterranean island of Crete is 156 miles long and up to 30 miles wide, and its first-century inhabitants were notorious for untruthfulness and immorality (1:12, 13). "To act the Cretan" became an idiom meaning "to play the liar." A number of Jews from Crete were present in Jerusalem at the time of Peter's sermon on the day of Pentecost (Acts 2:11), and some of them may have believed in Christ and introduced the gospel to their countrymen. Certainly Paul would not have had opportunity to do evangelistic work during his brief sojourn in Crete while he was en route to Rome (Acts 27:7–13). The apostle spread the gospel in the cities of Crete after his release from Roman imprisonment and left Titus there to finish organizing the churches (1:5). Because of the problem of immorality among the Cretans, it was important for Titus to stress the need for righteousness in Christian living. False teachers, especially "those of the circumcision" (1:10), were also misleading and divisive. Paul wrote this letter about A.D. 63, perhaps from Corinth, taking advantage of the journey of Zenas and Apollos (3:13), whose destination would take them by way of Crete. Paul was planning to spend the winter in Nicopolis (western Greece), and he urged Titus in this letter to join him there upon his replacement by Artemas or Tychicus (3:12). Paul may have been planning to leave Nicopolis for Spain in the spring, and he wanted his useful companion Titus to accompany him.

THE CHRIST OF TITUS

The deity and redemptive work of Christ are beautifully stated in 2:13, 14: "Looking for the blessed hope and glorious appearing of our great God and Savior Jesus Christ, who gave Himself for us, that He might redeem us from every lawless deed and purify for Himself *His* own special people, zealous of good works."

KEYS TO TITUS

Key Word: Conduct Manual for Church Living—This brief letter focuses on Titus's role and responsibility in the organization and supervision of the churches in Crete. It is written to strengthen and exhort Titus to firmly exercise his authority as an apostolic representative to churches that need to be put in order, refuting false teachers and dissenters and replacing immoral behavior with good deeds. Paul uses this letter to remind Titus of some of the details related to his task, including the qualifications for elders and the behavior expected of various groups in the churches. Paul includes three doctrinal sections in this letter to stress that proper belief (orthodoxy) gives the basis for proper behavior (orthopraxy).

Key Verses: Titus 1:5 and 3:8—"For this reason I left you in Crete, that you should set in order the things that are lacking, and appoint elders in every city as I commanded you—" (1:5).

"This is a faithful saying, and these things I want you to affirm constantly, that those who have believed in God should be careful to maintain good works. These things are good and profitable to men" (3:8).

Key Chapter: Titus 2—Summarized in Titus 2 are the key commands to be obeyed which insure godly relationships within the church. Paul includes all categories of people instructing them to show "all good fidelity, that they may adorn the doctrine of God our Savior in all things" (2:10).

SURVEY OF TITUS

Titus, like First Timothy, was written by Paul after his release from Roman imprisonment and was also written to an associate who was given the task of organizing and supervising a large work as an apostolic representative. Paul left Titus on the island of Crete to "set in order the things that are lacking, and appoint elders in every city" (1:5). Not long after Paul's departure from Crete, he wrote this letter to encourage and assist Titus in his task. It stresses sound doctrine and warns against those who distort the truth, but it also is a conduct manual that emphasizes good deeds and the proper conduct of various groups within the churches. This epistle falls into two major sections: appoint elders (1); set things in order (2 and 3).

Appoint Elders (1): The salutation to Titus is actually a compact doctrinal statement, which lifts up "His word" as the source of the truth that reveals the way to eternal life (1:1–4). Paul reminds Titus of his responsibility to organize the churches of Crete by appointing elders (also called overseers; see 1:7) and rehearses the qualifications these spiritual leaders must meet (1:5–9). This is especially important in view of the disturbances that are being caused by false teachers who are upsetting a number of the believers with their Judaic myths and commandments (1:10–16). The natural tendency toward moral laxity among the Cretans coupled with that kind of deception is a dangerous force that must be overcome by godly leadership and sound doctrine.

Set Things in Order (2 and 3): Titus is given the charge to "speak the things which are proper for sound doctrine" (2:1), and Paul delineates Titus's role with regard to various groups in the church, including older men, older women, young women, young men, and servants (2:2–10). The knowledge of Christ must effect a transformation in each of these groups so that their testimony will "adorn the doctrine of God" (2:10). The second doctrinal statement of Titus (2:11–14) gives the basis for the appeals Paul has just made for righteous living. God in His grace redeems believers from being slaves of sin, assuring them the "blessed hope" of the coming of Christ that will eventually be realized. Paul urges Titus to authoritatively proclaim these truths (2:15).

In chapter 3, Paul moves from conduct in groups (2:1–10) to conduct in general (3:1–11). The behavior of believers as citizens must be different than the behavior of unbelievers because of their regeneration and renewal by the Holy Spirit. The third doctrinal statement in this book (3:4–7) emphasizes the kindness, love, and mercy of God who saves us "not by works of righteousness which we have done" (3:5). Nevertheless, the need for good deeds as a result of salvation is stressed six times in the three chapters of Titus (1:16; 2:7, 14; 3:1, 8, 14). Paul exhorts Titus to deal firmly with dissenters who would cause factions and controversies (3:9–11) and closes the letter with three instructions, a greeting, and a benediction (3:12–15).

FOCUS	APPOINT ELDERS		SET THINGS IN ORDER	
REFERENCE	1:1—	1:10—	2:1—	3:1—3:15
DIVISION	ORDAIN QUALIFIED ELDERS	REBUKE FALSE TEACHERS	SPEAK SOUND DOCTRINE	MAINTAIN GOOD WORKS
TOPIC	PROTECTION OF SOUND DOCTRINE		PRACTICE OF SOUND DOCTRINE	
	ORGANIZATION	OFFENDERS	OPERATION	OBEDIENCE
LOCATION	PROBABLY WRITTEN IN CORINTH			
TIME	c. A.D. 63			

OUTLINE OF TITUS

CHAPTER 1

Introduction

PAUL, a servant of God and an apostle of
Jesus Christ, according to the faith of
God's elect and the acknowledgment of the
truth which is according to godliness,

2 in hope of eternal life which God, who
cannot lie, promised before time began,

3 but has in due time manifested His word
through preaching, which was committed to
me according to the commandment of God
our Savior;

4 To [R]Titus, *my* true son in *our* common
faith: 2 Cor. 2:13; 8:23

Grace, mercy, *and* peace from God the
Father and *the Lord Jesus Christ our Savior.

Ordain Qualified Elders

5 For this reason I left you in Crete, that
you should [R]set in order the things that are
lacking, and appoint elders in every city as I
commanded you— 1 Cor. 11:34
6 if a man is blameless, the husband of one
wife, having faithful children not accused of
[T]dissipation or insubordination. *incorrigibility*
7 For a *bishop must be blameless, as a
steward of God, not self-willed, not quick-
tempered, [R]not given to wine, not violent, not
greedy for money, Lev. 10:9
8 but hospitable, a lover of what is good,
sober-minded, just, holy, self-controlled,
9 holding fast the faithful word as he has
been taught, that he may be able, by sound
doctrine, both to exhort and convict those
who contradict.

Rebuke False Teachers

10 For there are many insubordinate, both
idle [R]talkers and deceivers, especially those of
the circumcision, James 1:26
11 whose mouths must be stopped, who
subvert whole households, teaching things
which they ought not, [R]for the sake of dishonest gain. 1 Tim. 6:5
12 [R]One of them, a prophet of their own,
said, "Cretans *are* always liars, evil beasts,
lazy gluttons." Acts 17:28
13 This testimony is true. [R]Therefore rebuke
them sharply, that they may be sound in the
faith, 2 Cor. 13:10
14 not giving heed to Jewish fables and
[R]commandments of men who turn from the
truth. Is. 29:13
15 [R]To the pure all things are pure, but to
those who are defiled and unbelieving nothing is pure; but even their mind and conscience are defiled. 1 Cor. 6:12
16 They profess to know God, but in works
they deny Him, being abominable, disobedient, and disqualified for every good work.

CHAPTER 2

Speak Sound Doctrine

BUT as for you, speak the things which are
proper for sound doctrine:
2 that the older men be sober, reverent,
temperate, sound in faith, in love, in patience;
3 the older women likewise, that they be
reverent in behavior, not slanderers, not
given to much wine, teachers of good
things—

1:4 NU *Christ Jesus* **1:7** Lit. *overseer*

1:2 Promise of God—Often the Christian will doubt his salvation simply because he doesn't feel saved, not understanding that the basis for that salvation is the promise of God and not emotional feelings. In fact, the entire Trinity is involved in this.

a. The promise and work of the Father in our salvation. He has promised to graciously accept in Christ all repenting sinners (Page 1387—Eph. 1:6; Page 1408—Col. 3:3). This means a Christian has the right to be in heaven someday, for he is in Christ. God guarantees to us that He will work out all things for our good (Page 1333—Rom. 8:28).
b. The promise and work of the Son. He has promised us eternal life (Page 1243—John 5:24) and abundant life (Page 1251—John 10:10). This covers not only our final destiny in heaven, but also our present Christian service here on earth. He is, in fact, right now praying for us and ministering to us at His Father's right hand (Page 1456—Heb. 8:1; 9:24).
c. The promise and work of the Holy Spirit. The Holy Spirit is said to indwell the believer (Page 1258—John 14:16). In addition, He places all believing sinners into the body of Christ, thus assuring us of union with God Himself (Page 1356—1 Cor. 12:13).

Now turn to Page 1498—1 John 3:24: Witness of the Spirit.

PAUL'S PASTORAL EPISTLES

The last three letters written by the apostle Paul are known as the pastoral epistles—so named because they deal with matters pertaining to pastors and their congregations. The epistles of 1 Timothy and Titus are our earliest guides to church organization; they are noted for their lists of qualifications for pastors and deacons in the early church. All three of these epistles emphasize sound doctrine, challenging believers to good works.

First Timothy was written from Macedonia to remind Paul's young preacher friend and colleague, who was ministering in Ephesus, to preach sound doctrine (1:3–11) and avoid false teaching (6:20, 21). The epistle emphasized the conduct of public worship (2:8–15) and gave instructions to both servants and the wealthy. Paul also urged Timothy to be diligent and faithful (4:11–16).

Second Timothy was written several years later during Paul's final Roman imprisonment. The apostle encouraged Timothy to be trustworthy in carrying out his responsibilities (2:1–13), even in times of hardship, and to preach the Word faithfully in the future when additional testings were sure to come (3:1–9). Even as he praised Timothy, Paul warned him of pitfalls that could be hindrances to his ministry (4:1–5).

The letter to Titus, a Greek who had become a believer under Paul's ministry (Gal. 2:3), was written at about the same time as 1 Timothy. Paul had left Titus on the island of Crete in the Mediterranean Sea (see photo) to supervise a large ministry. He encouraged Titus to organize the church carefully—to ordain qualified persons (1:5–16), rebuke false teachers (3:9–11), preach sound doctrine, and encourage good works (3:1–8).

These letters contained important messages for early Christian churches, and they also serve as a model for effective church life today.

Photo by Howard Vos

Paul left Titus on the island of Crete in the Mediterranean Sea to supervise a large ministry.

4 that they admonish the young women to
love their husbands, to love their children,
5 to be discreet, chaste, homemakers,
good, obedient to their own husbands, that
the word of God may not be blasphemed.
6 Likewise exhort the young men to be
sober-minded,
7 in all things showing yourself *to be* a
pattern of good works; in doctrine *showing*
integrity, reverence, *incorruptibility,
8 sound speech that cannot be condemned,
that one who is an opponent may be
ashamed, having nothing evil to say of *you.
9 *Exhort* [R]servants to be obedient to their
own masters, to be well pleasing in all *things*,
not answering back, 1 Tim. 6:1
10 not [T]pilfering, but showing all good [T]fi-
delity, that they may adorn the doctrine of
God our Savior in all things. *thieving • honesty*
11 For [R]the grace of God that brings salvation has appeared to all men, [Rom. 5:15]
12 teaching us that, denying ungodliness
and worldly lusts, we should live soberly,
righteously, and godly in the present age,
13 [R]looking for the blessed [R]hope and glorious appearing of our great God and Savior
Jesus Christ, 1 Cor. 1:7 • [Col. 3:4]
14 [R]who gave Himself for us, that He might
redeem us from every lawless deed and purify
for Himself *His* own special people, zealous
for good works. Is. 53:12; Gal. 1:4★
15 Speak these things, exhort, and rebuke
with all authority. Let no one despise you.

CHAPTER 3

Maintain Good Works

REMIND them [R]to be subject to rulers and
authorities, to obey, [R]to be ready for
every good work, 1 Pet. 2:13 • Col. 1:10
2 to speak evil of no one, to be peaceable,
gentle, showing all humility to all men.
3 For [R]we ourselves were also once foolish,
disobedient, deceived, serving various lusts
and pleasures, living in malice and envy,
hateful and hating one another. 1 Cor. 6:11
4 But when the kindness and the love of
God our Savior toward man appeared,

5 not by works of righteousness which we
have done, but according to His mercy He
saved us, through [R]the washing of regeneration and renewing of the Holy Spirit, John 3:3

6 [R]whom He poured out on us abundantly
through Jesus Christ our Savior, Ezek. 36:25
7 that having been justified by His grace
[R]we should become heirs according to the
hope of eternal life. [Rom. 8:17, 23, 24]
8 [R]This is a faithful saying, and these
things I want you to affirm constantly, that
those who have believed in God should be
careful to maintain good works. These things
are good and profitable to men. 1 Tim. 1:15
9 But [R]avoid foolish disputes, genealogies,
contentions, and strivings about the law; for
they are unprofitable and useless. 2 Tim. 2:23
10 [R]Reject a divisive man after the first and
second [T]admonition, Matt. 18:17 • *warning*
11 knowing that such a person is warped
and sinning, being self-condemned.

Conclusion

12 When I send Artemas to you, or Tychicus, be diligent to come to me at Nicopolis,
for I have decided to spend the winter there.
13 Send Zenas the lawyer and [R]Apollos on
their journey with haste, that they may lack
nothing. Acts 18:24
14 And let our *people* also learn to maintain
good works, to *meet* urgent needs, that they
may not be unfruitful.
15 All who *are* with me greet you. Greet
those who love us in the faith. Grace *be* with
you all. Amen.

2:7 NU omits *incorruptibility* 2:8 NU, M *us*

3:5 The Work of the Holy Spirit in Salvation—There are three wonderful works performed by the Holy Spirit in preparing unsaved people to become Christians.

a. The work of the Holy Spirit in restraining. Satan would enjoy nothing more than to destroy people before they make their decision to accept Christ as Savior. But the Holy Spirit prevents this from occurring (Page 831—Is. 59:19).
b. The work of the Holy Spirit in convicting. Mankind's sin and righteousness are exposed by the Holy Spirit (Page 1259—John 16:8). There are two well-known examples of sinners being convicted by the Holy Spirit in the Book of Acts. Felix, a Roman governor, actually trembles under conviction as he hears Paul preach (Page 1308—Acts 24:25). The other case involves King Agrippa who responds to a gospel message by saying: "'You almost persuade me to become a Christian'" (Page 1312—Acts 26:28).
c. The work of the Holy Spirit in regenerating. When a repenting sinner accepts Christ as Savior he is given a new nature by the Holy Spirit. See Second Corinthians 5:17. Jesus carefully explained this ministry of the Holy Spirit to Nicodemus (Page 1239—John 3:3–7).

Now turn to Page 1351—1 Cor. 6:19: The Work of the Holy Spirit in Christian Living.

THE EPISTLE OF PAUL THE APOSTLE TO

PHILEMON

THE BOOK OF PHILEMON

Does Christian brotherly love really work, even in situations of extraordinary tension and difficulty? Will it work, for example, between a prominent slave owner and one of his runaway slaves? Paul has no doubt! He writes a "postcard" to Philemon, his beloved brother and fellow worker, on behalf of Onesimus—a deserter, thief, and formerly worthless slave, but now Philemon's brother in Christ. With much tact and tenderness, Paul asks Philemon to receive Onesimus back with the same gentleness with which he would receive Paul himself. Any debt Onesimus owes, Paul promises to make good. Knowing Philemon, Paul is confident that brotherly love and forgiveness will carry the day.

Since this letter is addressed to Philemon in verse 1, it becomes known as *Pros Philemona*, "To Philemon." Like First and Second Timothy and Titus, it is addressed to an individual, but unlike the Pastoral Epistles, Philemon is also addressed to a family and a church (v. 2).

THE AUTHOR OF PHILEMON

The authenticity of Philemon was not called into question until the fourth century, when certain theologians concluded that its lack of doctrinal content made it unworthy of the apostle Paul. But men like Jerome and Chrysostom soon vindicated this epistle, and it was not challenged again until the nineteenth century. Some radical critics who denied the authenticity of Colossians also turned against the Pauline authorship of Philemon because of the close connection between the two epistles (e.g., the same people are associated with Paul in both letters: cf. Col. 4:9, 10, 12, 14 with Philem. 10, 23, 24). The general consensus of scholarship, however, recognized Philemon as Paul's work. There could have been no doctrinal motive for its forgery, and it is supported externally by consistent tradition and internally by no less than three references to Paul (vv. 1, 9, 19).

THE TIME OF PHILEMON

Reconstructing the background of this letter, it appears that a slave named Onesimus had robbed or in some other way wronged his master Philemon and had escaped. He had made his way from Colosse to Rome where he had found relative safety among the masses in the Imperial City. Somehow Onesimus had come into contact with Paul: it is possible that he had even sought out the apostle for help. (Onesimus no doubt had heard Philemon speak of Paul.) Paul had led him to Christ (v. 10), and although Onesimus had become a real asset to Paul, both knew that as a Christian, Onesimus had a responsibility to return to Philemon. That day came when Paul wrote his epistle to the Colossians. Tychicus was the bearer of that letter. Paul decided to send Onesimus along with Tychicus to Colosse (Col. 4:7–9; Philem. 12), knowing that it would be safer, in view of slave-catchers, to send Onesimus with a companion.

Philemon is one of the four Prison Epistles (see Ephesians, Philippians, and especially "The Time of Colossians" for background). It was written in A.D. 60 or 61 and dispatched at the same time as Colossians during Paul's first Roman imprisonment (see vv. 1, 9, 10, 13, 23). Philemon 22 reflects Paul's confident hope of release: "prepare a guest room for me, for I trust that through your prayers I shall be granted to you."

Philemon was a resident of Colosse (Col. 4:9, 17; Philem. 1, 2) and a convert of Paul (v. 19), perhaps through an encounter with Paul in Ephesus during Paul's third missionary journey. Philemon's house was large enough to serve as the meeting place for the church there (v. 2). He was benevolent to other believers (vv. 5–7), and his son Archippus evidently held a position of leadership in the church (Col. 4:17; Philem. 2). Philemon may have had other slaves in addition to Onesimus, and he was not alone as a slave owner among the Colossian believers (Col. 4:1). Thus this letter and his response would provide guidelines for other master-slave relationships.

According to Roman law, runaway slaves such as Onesimus could be severely punished or condemned to a violent death. It is doubtful that Onesimus would have returned to Philemon even with this letter if he had not become a believer in Christ.

THE CHRIST OF PHILEMON

The forgiveness that the believer finds in Christ is beautifully portrayed by analogy in Philemon. Onesimus, guilty of a great offense (vv. 11, 18), is motivated by Paul's love to intercede on his behalf (vv. 10–17). Paul lays aside his rights (v. 8) and becomes Onesimus's substitute by assuming his debt (vv. 18, 19). By Philemon's gracious act, Onesimus is restored and placed in a new relationship (vv. 15, 16). In this analogy, we are as Onesimus. Paul's advocacy before Philemon is parallel to Christ's work of mediation before the Father. Onesimus was condemned by law but saved by grace.

KEYS TO PHILEMON

Key Word: Forgiveness from Slavery—Philemon develops the transition from bondage to brotherhood that is brought about by

Christian love and forgiveness. Just as Philemon was shown mercy through the grace of Christ, so he must graciously forgive his repentant runaway who has returned as a brother in Christ. Paul writes this letter as his personal appeal that Philemon receive Onesimus even as he would receive Paul. This letter is also addressed to other Christians in Philemon's circle, because Paul wants it to have an impact on the Colossian church as a whole.

Key Verses: Philemon 16, 17—"No longer as a slave but more than slave, *as* a beloved brother, especially to me but how much more to you, both in the flesh and in the Lord. If then you count me as a partner, receive him as *you would* me" (vv. 16, 17).

SURVEY OF PHILEMON

This briefest of Paul's epistles (only 334 words in the Greek text) is a model of courtesy, discretion, and loving concern for the forgiveness of one who would otherwise face the sentence of death. This tactful and highly personal letter can be divided into three components: prayer of thanksgiving for Philemon (vv. 1–7); petition of Paul for Onesimus (vv. 8–16); promise of Paul to Philemon (vv. 17–25).

Prayer of Thanksgiving for Philemon (vv. 1-7): Writing this letter as a "prisoner of Christ Jesus," Paul addresses it personally to Philemon (a Christian leader in Colosse), to Apphia and Archippus (evidently Philemon's wife and son), as well as to the church that meets in Philemon's house. The main body of this compact letter begins with a prayer of thanksgiving for Philemon's faith and love.

Petition of Paul for Onesimus (vv. 8-16): Basing his appeal on Philemon's character, Paul refuses to command Philemon to pardon and receive Onesimus. Instead, Paul seeks to persuade his friend of his Christian responsibility to forgive even as he was forgiven by Christ. Paul urges Philemon not to punish Onesimus but to receive him "no longer as a slave" but as "a beloved brother" (v. 16).

Promise of Paul to Philemon (vv. 17-25): Paul places Onesimus's debt on his account, but then reminds Philemon of the greater spiritual debt which Philemon himself owes as a convert to Christ (vv. 17–19).

Paul closes this effective epistle with a hopeful request (v. 22), greetings from his companions (vv. 23, 24), and a benediction (v. 25). The fact that it was preserved indicates Philemon's favorable response to Paul's pleas.

FOCUS	PRAYER OF THANKSGIVING	PETITION FOR ONESIMUS	PROMISE TO PHILEMON
REFERENCE	1——————8	——————17	——————25
DIVISION	COMMENDATION OF PHILEMON'S LOVE	INTERCESSION FOR ONESIMUS	CONFIDENCE IN PHILEMON'S OBEDIENCE
TOPIC	PRAISE OF PHILEMON	PLEA OF PAUL	PLEDGE OF PAUL
	CHARACTER OF PHILEMON	CONVERSION OF ONESIMUS	CONFIDENCE OF PAUL
LOCATION		ROME	
TIME		c. A.D. 60 – 61	

OUTLINE OF PHILEMON

The Prayer of Thanksgiving for Philemon

PAUL, a [R]prisoner of Christ Jesus, and
Timothy *our* brother,

To Philemon our beloved *friend* and
fellow laborer, Eph. 3:1
2 to *the beloved Apphia, [R]Archippus our
fellow soldier, and to the church in your
house: Col. 4:17

3 Grace to you and peace from God our
Father and the Lord Jesus Christ.
4 [R]I thank my God, making mention of you
always in my prayers, 2 Thess. 1:3
5 [R]hearing of your love and faith which
you have toward the Lord Jesus and toward
all the saints, Col. 1:4
6 that the sharing of your faith may become effective [R]by the acknowledgment of
[R]every good thing which is in *you in Christ
Jesus. Phil. 1:9 • [1 Thess. 5:18]
7 For we *have great *joy and consolation
in your love, because the hearts of the saints
have been refreshed by you, brother.

The Petition of Paul for Onesimus

8 Therefore, though I might be very bold
in Christ to command you what is fitting,
9 *yet* for love's sake I rather appeal *to
you*—being such a one as Paul, the aged, and
now also a prisoner of Jesus Christ—
10 I appeal to you for my son Onesimus,
whom I have begotten *while* in my chains,
11 who once was unprofitable to you, but
now is profitable to you and to me.
12 I am sending him *back. You therefore
receive him, that is, my own heart,
13 whom I wished to keep with me, that on
your behalf he might minister to me in my
chains for the gospel.
14 But without your consent I wanted to do
nothing, that your good deed might not be by
compulsion, as it were, but voluntary.
15 For perhaps he departed for a while for
this *purpose*, that you might receive him
forever,
16 no longer as a slave but more than a
slave, *as* a beloved brother, especially to me
but how much more to you, both in the [R]flesh
and in the Lord. Col. 3:22

The Promise of Paul to Philemon

17 If then you count me as a partner, receive him as *you would* me.
18 But if he has wronged you or owes *you*
anything, put that on my account.
19 I, Paul, am writing with my own [R]hand. I
will repay—not to mention to you that you
owe me even your own self besides. 1 Cor. 16:21
20 Yes, brother, let me have joy from you in
the Lord; refresh my heart in the Lord.
21 [R]Having confidence in your obedience, I
write to you, knowing that you will do even
more than I say. 2 Cor. 7:16
22 But, meanwhile, also prepare a guest
room for me, for I trust that [R]through your
prayers I shall be granted to you. 2 Cor. 1:11
23 [R]Epaphras, my fellow prisoner in Christ
Jesus, greets you, Col. 1:7; 4:12
24 *as do* Mark, Aristarchus, [R]Demas, [R]Luke,
my fellow laborers. Col. 4:14 • 2 Tim. 4:11
25 [R]The grace of our Lord Jesus Christ *be*
with your spirit. Amen. 2 Tim. 4:22

1:2 NU *our sister Apphia* **1:6** NU, M *us*
1:7 NU *had* **1:7** M *thanksgiving*
1:12 NU *back to you in person, that is, my own heart*

THE EPISTLE TO THE

HEBREWS

THE BOOK OF HEBREWS

Many Jewish believers, having stepped out of Judaism into Christianity, want to reverse their course in order to escape persecution by their countrymen. The writer of Hebrews exhorts them to "go on to perfection" (6:1). His appeal is based on the superiority of Christ over the Judaic system. Christ is better than the angels, for they worship Him. He is better than Moses, for He created him. He is better than the Aaronic priesthood, for His sacrifice was once for all time. He is better than the Law, for He mediates a better covenant. In short, there is more to be gained in Christ than to be lost in Judaism. Pressing on in Christ produces tested faith, self-discipline, and a visible love seen in good works.

Although the King James Version uses the title "The Epistle of Paul the Apostle to the Hebrews," there is no early manuscript evidence to support it. The oldest and most reliable title is simply *Pros Ebraious*, "To Hebrews."

THE AUTHOR OF HEBREWS

Like the ancestry of Melchizedek, the origin of Hebrews is unknown. Uncertainty plagues not only its authorship, but also where it was written, its date, and its readership. The question of authorship delayed its recognition in the West as part of the New Testament canon in spite of early support by Clement of Rome. Not until the fourth century was it generally accepted as authoritative in the Western church, when the testimonies of Jerome and Augustine settled the issue. In the Eastern church, there was no problem of canonical acceptance because it was regarded as one of the "fourteen" epistles of Paul. The issue of its canonicity was again raised during the Reformation, but the spiritual depth and quality of Hebrews bore witness to its inspiration, despite its anonymity.

Hebrews 13:18–24 tells us that this book was not anonymous to the original readers; they evidently knew the author. For some reason, however, early church tradition is divided over the identity of the author. Part of the church attributed it to Paul; others preferred Barnabas, Luke, or Clement; and some chose anonymity. Thus, external evidence will not help determine the author.

Internal evidence must be the final court of appeal, but here, too, the results are ambiguous. Some aspects of the language, style, and theology of Hebrews are very similar to Paul's epistles, and the author also refers to Timothy (13:23). However, significant differences have led the majority of biblical scholars to reject Pauline authorship of this book: (1) The Greek style of Hebrews is far more polished and refined than that found in any of Paul's recognized epistles. (2) In view of Paul's consistent claims to be an apostle and an eyewitness of Christ, it is very doubtful that he would have used the phraseology found in 2:3: "which at the first began to be spoken by the Lord, and was confirmed to us by those who heard *Him*." (3) The lack of Paul's customary salutation, which includes his name, goes against the firm pattern found in all his other epistles. (4) While Paul used both the Hebrew text and the Septuagint to quote from the Old Testament, the writer of Hebrews apparently did not know Hebrew and quoted exclusively from the Septuagint. (5) Paul's common use of compound titles to refer to the Son of God is not followed in Hebrews, which usually refers to Him as Christ, Jesus, and Lord. (6) Hebrews concentrates on Christ's present priestly ministry, but Paul's writings have very little to say about the present work of Christ. Thus, Hebrews appears not to have been written by Paul although the writer shows a Pauline influence. The authority of Hebrews in no way depends upon Pauline authorship, especially since it does not claim to have been written by Paul.

Tertullian referred to Barnabas as the author of Hebrews, but it is unlikely that this resident of Jerusalem (Acts 4:36, 37) would include himself as one of those who relied on others for eyewitness testimony about Jesus (2:3). Other suggestions include Luke, Clement of Rome, Apollos, Silvanus (Silas), Philip, and even Priscilla. Some of these are possibilities, but we must agree with the third-century theologian Origen who wrote: "Who it was that really wrote the Epistle, God only knows."

THE TIME OF HEBREWS

Because of the exclusive use of the Septuagint (Greek translation of the Hebrew Old Testament) and the elegant Greek style found in Hebrews, some recent scholars have argued that this book was written to a gentile readership. However, the bulk of the evidence favors the traditional view that the original recipients of this letter were Jewish Christians. In addition to the ancient title "To Hebrews," there is also the frequent use of the Old Testament as an unquestioned authority, the assumed knowledge of the sacrificial ritual, and the many contrasts between Christianity and Judaism, which are designed to prevent the readers from lapsing into Judaism.

Many places have been suggested for the locality of the readers, but this letter's destination cannot be determined with any certainty. In the past, Jerusalem was most frequently suggested, but this view is hindered by four problems: (1) It is unlikely that a book addressed to Palestineans would quote exclusively from the Septuagint rather than the Hebrew Old Testament. (2) Palestinean believers were poor (Rom. 15:26), but these readers were able to financially assist other Christians (6:10). (3) Residents of Jerusalem would not be characterized by the description in 2:3 because some would have been eyewitnesses of the ministry of Christ. (4) "You have not yet resisted to bloodshed" (12:4) does not fit the situation in Jerusalem. The majority view today is that the recipients of Hebrews probably lived in Rome. The statement "Those from Italy greet you" in 13:24 seems to suggest that Italians away from Italy are sending their greetings home.

The recipients of this letter were believers (3:1) who had come to faith through the testimony of eyewitnesses of Christ (2:3). They were not novices (5:12), and they had successfully endured hardships because of their stand for the gospel (10:32–34). Unfortunately, they had become "dull of hearing" (5:11) and were in danger of drifting away (2:1; 3:12). This made them particularly susceptible to the renewed persecutions that were coming upon them (12:4–12), and the author found it necessary to check the downward spiral with "the word of exhortation" (13:22). While there is disagreement over the specific danger involved, the classic position that the readers were on the verge of lapsing into Judaism to avoid persecution directed at Christians seems to be supported by the whole tenor of the book. Hebrews' repeated emphasis on the superiority of Christianity over Judaism would have been pointless if the readers were about to return to Gnosticism or heathenism.

The place of writing is unknown, but a reasonable estimate of the date can be made. Hebrews was quoted in A.D. 95 by Clement of Rome, but its failure to mention the ending of the Old Testament sacrificial system with the destruction of Jerusalem in A.D. 70 indicates that it was written prior to that date. Timothy was still alive (13:23), persecution was mounting, and the old Jewish system was about to be removed (12:26, 27). All this suggests a date between A.D. 64 and 68.

THE CHRIST OF HEBREWS

Christ is our eternal High Priest according to the order of Melchizedek. He identified with man in His incarnation and offered no less a sacrifice than Himself on our behalf.

Hebrews presents Christ as the divine-human Prophet, Priest, and King. His deity (1:1–3, 8) and humanity (2:9, 14, 17, 18) are asserted with equal force, and over twenty titles are used to describe His attributes and accomplishments (e.g., Heir of all things, Apostle and High Priest, Mediator, Author and Perfecter of faith). He is superior to all who went before and offers the supreme sacrifice, priesthood, and covenant.

KEYS TO HEBREWS

Key Word: The Superiority of Christ—The basic theme of Hebrews is found in the word *better,* describing the superiority of Christ in His person and work (1:4; 6:9; 7:7, 19, 22; 8:6; 9:23; 10:34; 11:16, 35, 40; 12:24). The words *perfect* and *heavenly* are also prominent. He offers a better revelation, position, priesthood, covenant, sacrifice, and power. The writer develops this theme to prevent the readers from giving up the substance for the shadow by abandoning Christianity and retreating into the old Judaic system. This epistle is also written to exhort them to become mature in Christ and to put away their spiritual dullness and degeneration. Thus, it places heavy stress on doctrine, concentrating on Christology and soteriology (the study of salvation).

Key Verses: Hebrews 4:14–16 and 12:1, 2—"Seeing then that we have a great High Priest who has passed through the heavens, Jesus the Son of God, let us hold fast *our* confession. For we do not have a High Priest who cannot sympathize with our weaknesses, but was in all *points* tempted as *we are, yet* without sin. Let us therefore come boldly to the throne of grace, that we may obtain mercy and find grace to help in time of need" (4:14–16).

"Therefore we also, since we are surrounded by so great a cloud of witnesses, let us lay aside every weight, and the sin which so easily ensnares *us,* and let us run with endurance the race that is set before us, looking unto Jesus, the author and finisher of *our* faith, who for the joy that was set before Him endured the cross, despising the shame, and has sat down at the right hand of the throne of God" (12:1, 2).

Key Chapter: Hebrews 11—The hall of fame of the Scriptures is located in Hebrews 11 and records those who willingly took God at His word even when there was nothing to cling to but His promise. Inherent to all those listed is the recognition that "without faith *it is* impossible to please *Him,* for he who comes to God must believe that He is, and *that* He is a rewarder of those who diligently seek Him" (Heb. 11:6).

SURVEY OF HEBREWS

Hebrews stands alone among the New Testament Epistles in its style and approach, and it is the only New Testament book whose authorship remains a real mystery. This profound work builds a case for the superiority of Christ through a cumulative argument in which Christ is presented as "better" in every respect.

In His person He is better than the angels, Moses, and Joshua; and in His performance He provides a better priesthood, covenant, sanctuary, and sacrifice. Evidently, the readers are in danger of reverting to Judaism because of the suffering they are beginning to experience for their faith in Christ. However, by doing so, they would be retreating from the substance back into the shadow. In addition to his positive presentation of the supremacy of Christ, the writer intersperses five solemn warnings about the peril of turning away from Christ (2:1–4; 3:7—4:13; 5:11—6:20; 10:19–39; 12:25–29). These parenthetical warnings include cautions against neglect (2:1–4) and refusal (12:25–29). After using the Old Testament to demonstrate the superiority of Christ's person (1:1—4:13) and the superiority of Christ's work (4:14—10:18), the writer applies these truths in a practical way to show the superiority of the Christian's walk of faith (10:19—13:25).

The Superiority of Christ's Person (1:1—4:13): Instead of the usual salutation, this epistle immediately launches into its theme—the supremacy of Christ even over the Old Testament prophets (1:1–3). Christianity is built upon the highest form of divine disclosure: the personal revelation of God through His incarnate Son. Christ is therefore greater than the prophets, and He is also greater than the angels, the mediators of the Mosaic Law (1:4—2:18; see Acts 7:53; Heb. 2:2). This is seen in His name, His position, His worship by the angels, and His incarnation. The Son of God partook of flesh and blood and was "made like *His* brethren" in all things (2:17) in order to bring "many sons to glory" (2:10). Christ is also superior to Moses (3:1–6), for Moses was a servant in the house of God, but Christ is the Son over God's household. Because of these truths, the readers are exhorted to avoid the divine judgment that is visited upon unbelief (3:7—4:13). Their disbelief had prevented the generation of the Exodus from becoming the generation of the conquest, and the rest that Christ offers is so much greater than what was provided by Joshua. The readers are therefore urged to enter the eternal rest that is possessed by faith in Christ.

The Superiority of Christ's Work (4:14—10:18): The high priesthood of Christ is superior to the Aaronic priesthood (4:14—7:28). Because of His incarnation, Christ can "sympathize with our weaknesses," having been "in all *points* tempted as *we are, yet* without sin" (4:15). Christ was not a Levite, but He qualified for a higher priesthood according to the order of Melchizedek. The superiority of Melchizedek to Levi is seen in the fact that Levi, in effect, paid tithes through Abraham to Melchizedek (7:9–10). Abraham was blessed by Melchizedek, and "the lesser is blessed by the better" (7:7). The parenthetical warning in 5:11—6:20 exhorts the readers to "go on to perfection" by moving beyond the basics of salvation and repentance.

By divine oath (7:21), Christ has become a permanent and perfect high priest and the "Mediator of a better covenant" (8:6). The new covenant has made the old covenant obsolete (8:6–13). Our great high priest similarly ministers in "the greater and more perfect tabernacle not made with hands, that is, not of this creation" (9:11). And unlike the former priests, He offers Himself as a sinless and voluntary sacrifice once and for all (9:1—10:18).

The Superiority of the Christian's Walk of Faith (10:19—13:25): The author applies what he has been saying about the superiority of Christ by warning his readers of the danger of discarding their faith in Christ (10:19–39). The faith that the readers must maintain is defined in 11:1–3 and illustrated in 11:4–40. The triumphs and accomplishments of faith in the lives of Old Testament believers should encourage the recipients of "something better" (11:40) in Christ to look

FOCUS	CHRIST'S PERSON			CHRIST'S WORK			THE WALK OF FAITH		
REFERENCE	1:1—	1:4—	3:1—	4:14—	8:1—	9:1—	10:19—	12:1—	13:1–13:25
DIVISION	CHRIST OVER PROPHETS	CHRIST OVER ANGELS	CHRIST OVER MOSES	PRIEST-HOOD	COVENANT	SANCTUARY AND SACRIFICE	ASSURANCE OF FAITH	ENDURANCE OF FAITH	EXHORTATION TO LOVE
TOPIC	MAJESTY OF CHRIST			MINISTRY OF CHRIST			MINISTERS FOR CHRIST		
	DOCTRINE						DISCIPLINE		
LOCATION	PLACE OF WRITING UNKNOWN								
TIME	c. A.D. 64–68								

"unto Jesus, the author and finisher of *our* faith" (12:2). Just as Jesus endured great hostility, those who believe in Him will sometimes have to endure divine discipline for the sake of holiness (12:1–29). The readers are warned not to turn away from Christ during such times, but to place their hope in Him. The character of their lives must be shaped by their dedication to Christ (13:1–19), and this will be manifested in their love of each other through their hospitality, concern, purity, contentment, and obedience. The author concludes this epistle with one of the finest benedictions in Scripture (13:20, 21) and some personal words (13:22–25).

OUTLINE OF HEBREWS

Part One: The Superiority of Christ's Person (1:1—4:13)

I. The Superiority of Christ over the Prophets. . . . 1:1–3

II. The Superiority of Christ over the Angels. . . . 1:4—2:18

A. Christ Is Superior Because of His Deity 1:4–14
B. First Warning: Danger of Neglect 2:1–4
C. Christ Is Superior Because of His Humanity 2:5–18

III. The Superiority of Christ over Moses . . . . 3:1—4:13

A. Christ Is Superior to Moses in His Work 3:1–4
B. Christ Is Superior to Moses in His Person 3:5, 6
C. Second Warning: Danger of Unbelief. . . . 3:7—4:13
1. Danger of Hardening the Heart 3:7–19
2. Challenge to Enter His Rest 4:1–13

Part Two: The Superiority of Christ's Work (4:14—10:18)

I. The Superiority of Christ's Priesthood. 4:14—7:28

A. Christ Is Superior in His Position 4:14–16
B. Christ Is Superior in His Qualifications. 5:1–10
1. Aaronic Priesthood 5:1–4
2. Melchizedekian Priesthood 5:5–10
C. Third Warning: Danger of Not Maturing . . . . 5:11—6:20
1. Dullness of Hearing 5:11–14
2. Need for Maturity 6:1–8
3. Exhortation to Maturity. . . . 6:9–20
D. Christ Is Superior in His Priestly Order 7:1–28
1. Description of Melchizedek. . . . 7:1–3
2. Superiority of Melchizedek 7:4–10
3. Imperfection of Aaronic Priesthood 7:11–28

II. The Superiority of Christ's Covenant 8:1–13

A. A Better Covenant. . . . 8:1–6
B. A New Covenant. . . . 8:7–13

III. The Superiority of Christ's Sanctuary and Sacrifice . . . . 9:1—10:18

A. Old Covenant's Sanctuary and Sacrifice. . . . 9:1–10
1. Old Covenant's Sanctuary. . . . 9:1–5
2. Old Covenant's Sacrifice 9:6–10
B. New Covenant's Sanctuary and Sacrifice . . . . 9:11—10:18
1. New Covenant's Sanctuary 9:11
2. New Covenant's Sacrifice . . . . 9:12—10:18

Part Three: The Superiority of the Christian's Walk of Faith (10:19—13:25)

I. Exhortation to Full Assurance of Faith . . . . 10:19—11:40

A. Hold Fast the Confession of Faith 10:19–25
B. Fourth Warning: Danger of Drawing Back 10:26–39
C. Definition of Faith. . . . 11:1–3
D. Examples of Faith 11:4–40
1. Abel 11:4
2. Enoch 11:5, 6
3. Noah. . . . 11:7
4. Abraham and Sarah 11:8–19
5. Isaac. . . . 11:20
6. Jacob 11:21
7. Joseph 11:22
8. Moses' Parents 11:23
9. Moses. . . . 11:24–29
10. Joshua and Rahab. . . . 11:30, 31
11. Many Other Heroes of Faith. . . . 11:32–40

II. Endurance of Faith. . . . 12:1–29

A. Example of Christ's Endurance 12:1–4
B. Exhortation to Endure God's Chastening. . . . 12:5–24
C. Fifth Warning: Danger of Refusing God. . . . 12:25–29

III. Exhortation to Love 13:1–17

A. Love in the Social Realm 13:1–6
B. Love in the Religious Realm. . . . 13:7–17

IV. Conclusion 13:18–25

CHAPTER 1

The Superiority of Christ over the Prophets

GOD, who [T]at various times and in different ways spoke in time past to the fathers by the prophets, Or *in many portions*

2 has in these last days spoken to us by *His* Son, whom He has appointed heir of all things, through whom also He made the [T]worlds; Or *ages*, Gr. *aiones*, aeons

3 who being the brightness of *His* glory and the express image of His person, and upholding all things by the word of His power, when He had *by Himself [T]purged *our sins, [R]sat down at the right hand of the Majesty on high, *cleansed* • Ps. 68:18; 110:1 ⋆

Christ Is Superior Because of His Deity

4 having become so much better than the angels, as [R]He has by inheritance obtained a more excellent name than they. [Phil. 2:9, 10]

5 For to which of the angels did He ever say:

[R]*"You are My Son,* Ps. 2:7
Today I have begotten You"?

And again:

[R]*"I will be to Him a Father,* 2 Sam. 7:14
And He shall be to Me a Son"?

6 But when He again brings [R]the firstborn into the world, He says: [Rom. 8:29]

**"Let all the angels of God worship Him."*

7 And of the angels He says:

[R]*"Who makes His angels spirits* Ps. 104:4
And His ministers a flame of fire."

8 But to the Son *He says:*

[R]*"Your throne, O God, is forever and*
ever; Deut. 33:27; Ps. 45:6 ⋆
A [T]scepter of righteousness is the
scepter of Your Kingdom. A ruler's staff
9 *You have loved righteousness and*
hated lawlessness;
Therefore God, Your God, [R]has anointed
You Ps. 45:7; Is. 61:3 ⋆
With the oil of gladness more than
Your companions."

10 And:

[R]*"You, LORD, in the beginning laid the*
foundation of the earth,
And the heavens are the work of Your
hands; Ps. 102:25–27
11 [R]*They will perish, but You remain;*
And [R]they will all grow old like a
garment; [Is. 34:4] • Is. 50:9; 51:6
12 *Like a cloak You will fold them up,*
And they will be changed.
But You are the [R]same,
And Your years will not fail." Heb. 13:8

13 But to which of the angels has He ever said:

[R]*"Sit at My right hand,*
Till I make Your enemies Your
footstool"? Ps. 110:1

14 [R]Are they not all ministering spirits sent forth to minister for those who will [R]inherit salvation? Ps. 103:20 • Rom. 8:17

CHAPTER 2

First Warning: Danger of Neglect

THEREFORE we must give [T]the more earnest heed to the things we have heard, lest we drift away. *all the more careful attention*

2 For if the word spoken through angels proved steadfast, and every transgression and disobedience received a just reward,

3 how shall we escape if we neglect so great a salvation, which at the first began to be spoken by the Lord, and was [R]confirmed to us by those who heard *Him,* Luke 1:2

4 [R]God also bearing witness [R]both with signs and wonders, with various miracles, and [T]gifts of the Holy Spirit, according to His own will? Mark 16:20 • Acts 2:22, 43 • *distributions*

Christ Is Superior Because of His Humanity

5 For He has not put the world to come, of which we speak, in subjection to angels.

6 But one testified in a certain place, saying:

[R]*"What is man that You are mindful of*
him,
Or the son of man that You take care
of him? Ps. 8:4–6
7 *You made him [T]a little lower than the*
angels; Or *for a little while*
You crowned him with glory and honor,
**And set him over the works of Your*
hands.
8 [R]*You have put all things in subjection*
under his feet." Matt. 28:18

For in that He put all in subjection under him, He left nothing *that is* not put under him. But now [R]we do not yet see all things put under him. 1 Cor. 15:25, 27

9 But we see Jesus, who was made [T]a little lower than the angels, for the suffering of death crowned with glory and honor, that He, by the grace of God, might taste death [R]for everyone. Or *for a little while* • [John 3:16]

1:3 NU omits *by Himself* 1:3 NU omits *our*
1:6 Deut. 32:43, LXX, DSS; Ps. 97:7
2:7 NU, M omit the rest of v. 7.

SATISFACTION AND RECONCILIATION

The cofounder and first president of a leading seminary detailed thirty-three separate things that happen to a person who accepts Christ as Savior. He or she is saved, redeemed, justified, sealed by the Spirit, and receives twenty-nine other blessings! In this word study, we investigate two of these blessings: that God is *satisfied* and we are *reconciled*.

Satisfaction

There is a very interesting and theologically important cluster of three related Greek words in the New Testament, each one occurring twice. All three start with the same root, *hilas-*.

Make propitiation (*hilaskomai*) occurs first in Luke 18:13 in a very famous passage. Our Lord tells the story of two men who went up to the temple to pray. The Pharisee praised himself and his own record in his "prayer." The tax collector dared not lift his eyes, but beat his breast and said, "God be merciful [a form of this verb] to me, a sinner!" He, not the self-righteous religionist, went away justified. A more literal rendering of his prayer would be, "God be propitiated with me, the sinner!" *To propitiate* means "to satisfy the demands of," in this case, an offended Deity. Sacrifice for sins is the method God chose to make satisfaction for sins. In the Old Testament, animal sacrifices were pictures looking forward to the once-for-all infinite sacrifice of the Lamb of God. *God is satisfied with the sacrifice of His Son.* We do not have to plead with Him to accept us. He loves us and desires that we put our faith in His Son.

The other use of *hilaskomai* is in Hebrews 2:17: "Therefore, in all things He had to be made like *His* brethren, that He might be a merciful and faithful High Priest in things *pertaining* to God, to make propitiation for the sins of the people." The Lord Jesus became Man to meet the needs of humankind and died on the cross to satisfy God's righteous demands against sinners. He propitiated, or made satisfaction for, the sins of His people.

Propitiation (*hilasmos*), a noun form, occurs twice, both in 1 John. In 1 John 2:2, an important doctrinal verse, we read: "And He Himself is the propitiation for our sins, and not for ours only but also for the whole world." Christ Himself is the satisfaction or satisfying sacrifice for sins. The New Testament concept of propitiation is not at all like the pagan idea of appeasing a cruel deity. Propitiation in the New Testament is a result of God's love (1 John 4:10).

Mercy seat (*hilastērion*) occurs twice, once meaning the cover of the ark of the covenant (Heb. 9:5) and once translated the same as *hilasmos*. The mercy seat is "the place where propitiation is made." Like so much in the tabernacle, it pictured Christ and His work on the cross. The main teaching of these three terms is that not only is God satisfied with the Person and work of His Son, but through faith in Him, we can be reconciled to God.

Reconciliation (*katallagē*)

Many people who have studied Greek think the King James translators were in error in Romans 5:11 when they had Paul write: "by whom we have now received the atonement [*katallagē*, the standard Greek word for "reconciliation"]." Atonement, today at least, refers to the entire work that Christ performed on the cross. Actually, the KJV scholars, brilliant linguists that they were, did choose the right word for 1611. In 1611, *atonement* meant "at-one-ment," that is, coming from a position of enmity to one of friendship, becoming "at one" with each other. That is what reconciliation is.

Reconcile (*katallassō*) comes from the verb *allassō*, "to change." With the prefix, it means "to change completely." By faith in Christ, a person's spiritual relationship with God is thoroughly changed (*katallassō*). He or she is reconciled to God.

The verb occurs six times and the noun four, all but one in Romans 5 and 2 Corinthians 5. For a good understanding of reconciliation, read 2 Corinthians 5:18–20, thinking in terms of a complete change of relationship.

10 For it was fitting for Him, [R]for whom *are* all things and by whom *are* all things, in bringing many sons to glory, to make the author of their salvation [R]perfect through sufferings. Col. 1:16 • Heb. 5:8, 9; 7:28

11 For [R]both He who [T]sanctifies and those who are being sanctified [R]*are* all of one, for which reason [R]He is not ashamed to call them brethren, Heb. 10:10 • *sets apart* • Acts 17:26 • Matt. 28:10

12 saying:

[R]*"I will declare Your name to My*
brethren;
In the midst of the congregation I will
sing praise to You." Ps. 22:22

13 And again:

[R]*"I will put My trust in Him."*

And again: 2 Sam. 22:3; Is. 8:17

[R]*"Here am I and the children whom God*
has given Me." Is. 8:18

14 Inasmuch then as the children have partaken of flesh and blood, He Himself likewise shared in the same, [R]that through death He might destroy him who had the power of death, that is, the devil, Col. 2:15

15 and [R]release those who [R]through fear of death were all their lifetime subject to bondage. Is. 42:7; 49:9; 61:1 ★ • [Luke 1:74]

16 For indeed He does not [T]give aid to angels, but He does give aid to the seed of Abraham. Lit. *take hold of*

17 Therefore, in all things He had [R]to be made like *His* brethren, that He might be [R]a merciful and faithful High Priest in things *pertaining* to God, to make propitiation for the sins of the people. Phil. 2:7 • [Heb. 4:15; 5:1–10]

18 [R]For in that He Himself has suffered, being [T]tempted, He is able to aid those who are tempted. [Heb. 4:15, 16] • *tested*

CHAPTER 3

Christ Is Superior to Moses in His Work

THEREFORE, holy brethren, partakers of the heavenly calling, consider the Apostle and [R]High Priest of our confession, Christ Jesus, Ps. 110:4★

2 who was faithful to Him who appointed Him, as [R]Moses also *was faithful* in all His house. Num. 12:7

3 For this One has been counted worthy of more glory than Moses, inasmuch as [R]He who built the house has more honor than the house. Zech. 6:12, 13

4 For every house is built by someone, but [R]He who built all things *is* God. [Eph. 2:10]

Christ Is Superior to Moses in His Person

5 And Moses indeed *was* faithful in all His house as a servant, for a testimony of those things which would be spoken *afterward*,

6 but Christ as [R]a Son over His own house, [R]whose house we are [R]if we hold fast the confidence and the rejoicing of the hope *firm to the end. Heb. 1:2 • [1 Cor. 3:16] • [Matt. 10:22]

Danger of Hardening the Heart

7 Therefore, as the Holy Spirit says:

"Today, if you will hear His voice,
8 *Do not harden your hearts as in the*
rebellion,
In the day of trial in the wilderness,
9 *Where your fathers tested Me, proved*
Me,
And saw My works forty years.
10 *Therefore I was angry with that*
generation,
And said, 'They always go astray in
their heart,
And they have not known My ways.'
11 *So I swore in My wrath,*
'They shall not enter My rest.'"

12 Beware, brethren, lest there be in any of you an evil heart of unbelief in departing from the living God;

13 but [T]exhort one another daily, while it is called *"Today,"* lest any of you be hardened through the deceitfulness of sin. *encourage*

14 For we have become partakers of Christ if we hold the beginning of our confidence steadfast to the end,

15 while it is said:

[R]*"Today, if you will hear His voice,*
Do not harden your hearts as in the
rebellion." Ps. 95:7, 8

16 [R]For who, having heard, rebelled? Indeed, *was it* not all who came out of Egypt, *led* by Moses? Num. 14:2, 11, 30

17 Now with whom was He angry forty years? *Was it* not with those who sinned, whose corpses fell in the wilderness?

18 And [R]to whom did He swear that they would not enter His rest, but to those who did not obey? Num. 14:30

19 So we see that they could not enter in because of [R]unbelief. 1 Cor. 10:11, 12

CHAPTER 4

Challenge to Enter His Rest

THEREFORE, since a promise remains of entering His rest, [R]let us fear lest any of you seem to have come short of it. Heb. 12:15

2 For indeed the gospel was preached to us as well as to them; but the word which they

3:6 NU omits *firm to the end*

heard did not profit them, *not being mixed
with faith in those who heard *it*.
3 For we who have believed do enter that
rest, as He has said:

[R]*"So I swore in My wrath,*
They shall not enter My rest," Ps. 95:11

although the works were finished from the
foundation of the world.
4 For He has spoken in a certain place of
the seventh *day* in this way: [R]*"And God*
rested on the seventh day from all His
works"; Gen. 2:2
5 and again in this *place*: [R]*"They shall not*
enter My rest." Ps. 95:11
6 Since therefore it remains that some
must enter it, and those to whom it was first
preached did not enter because of disobedience,
7 again He designates a certain day, saying
in David, *"Today,"* after such a long time, as
it has been said:

[R]*"Today, if you will hear His voice,*
Do not harden your hearts." Ps. 95:7, 8

8 For if [T]Joshua had [R]given them rest, then
He would not afterward have spoken of
another day. Gr. *Jesus,* same as Heb. *Joshua* • Josh. 22:4
9 There remains therefore a rest for the
people of God.
10 For he who has entered His rest has
himself also ceased from his works as God *did*
from His.
11 [R]Let us therefore be diligent to enter that
rest, lest anyone fall after the same example
of disobedience. 2 Pet. 1:10
12 For the word of God *is* [R]living and powerful, and [R]sharper than any [R]two-edged
sword, piercing even to the division of soul
and spirit, and of joints and marrow, and is [R]a
discerner of the thoughts and intents of the
heart. Ps. 147:15 • Is. 49:2 • Eph. 6:17 • 1 Cor. 14:24, 25
13 [R]And there is no creature hidden from
His sight, but all things *are* [R]naked and open
to the eyes of Him to whom we *must give*
account. Ps. 33:13–15; 90:8 • Job 26:6

Christ Is Superior in His Position

14 Seeing then that we have a great [R]High
Priest who has passed through the heavens,
Jesus the Son of God, [R]let us hold fast *our*
confession. Heb. 2:17; 7:26 • Heb. 10:23
15 For [R]we do not have a High Priest who
cannot sympathize with our weaknesses, but
[R]was in all *points* tempted as *we are,* [R]*yet*
without sin. Is. 53:3–5 • Luke 22:28 • 2 Cor. 5:21
16 Let us therefore come boldly to the
throne of grace, that we may obtain mercy
and find grace to help in time of need.

CHAPTER 5

Aaronic Priesthood

FOR every high priest taken from among
men [R]is appointed for men in things *per-*
taining to God, that he may offer both gifts
and sacrifices for sins. Heb. 2:17; 8:3
2 He can have compassion on those who
are ignorant and going astray, since he himself is also [T]beset by weakness. *subject to*
3 Because of this he is required as for the
people, so also for himself, to offer for sins.
4 And no man takes this honor to himself,
but he who is called by God, just as [R]Aaron
was. Ex. 28:1

Melchizedekian Priesthood

5 [R]So also Christ did not glorify Himself to
become High Priest, *but it* was He who said
to Him: John 8:54

[R]*"You are My Son,*
Today I have begotten You." Ps. 2:7★

6 As *He* also *says* in another *place*:

[R]*"You are a priest forever*
According to the order of
Melchizedek"; Ps. 110:4★

7 who, in the days of His flesh, when He
had offered up prayers and supplications,
with vehement cries and tears to Him who
was able to save Him from death, and was
heard [R]because of His godly fear, Matt. 26:37
8 though He was a Son, *yet* He learned
obedience by the things which He suffered.
9 And [R]having been perfected, He became
the author of eternal salvation to all who
obey Him, Heb. 2:10
10 [R]called by God as High Priest *"according*
to the order of Melchizedek," Ps. 110:4★

Dullness of Hearing

11 of whom [R]we have much to say, and hard
to explain, since you have become [R]dull of
hearing. [John 16:12] • [Matt. 13:15]
12 For though by this time you ought to be
teachers, you need *someone* to teach you
again the first principles of the [T]oracles of
God; and you have come to need [R]milk and
not solid food. *sayings,* Scriptures • 1 Cor. 3:1–3
13 For everyone who partakes *only* of milk
is unskilled in the word of righteousness, for
he is [R]a babe. Eph. 4:14
14 But solid food belongs to those who are
[T]of full age, *that is,* those who by reason of
[T]use have their senses exercised [R]to discern
both good and evil. *mature* • *practice* • Is. 7:15

4:2 NU, M *since they were not united by faith with those*

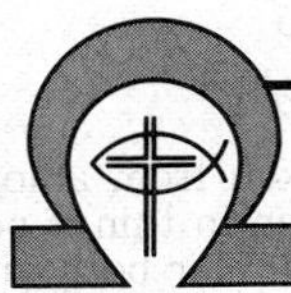

ROMAN CRUCIFIXION

Crucifixion, a method of torture and execution, was used many centuries before the time of Jesus by several nations of the ancient world, including the Assyrians, the Medes, and the Persians. Adopted by the Romans as their most severe form of capital punishment, it was reserved for criminals and slaves. No Roman citizen could be crucified.

Crucifixion involved attaching the victim with nails through the wrists or with leather thongs to a crossbeam attached to a vertical stake (see illustration). At times the feet also were nailed to the vertical stake. As the victim hung dangling by the arms, blood could not circulate to his vital organs. He died of suffocation or exhaustion, normally after a long period of agonizing pain.

Usually the victim was beaten before his crucifixion. Jesus' flogging must have been severe, since He could not carry His cross afterward (Matt. 27:26; Mark 15:21). This also may explain His relatively quick death on the cross. By the ninth hour, probably 3:00 P.M., and only six hours after He was placed on the cross, Jesus was dead. There was no need for the soldiers to break His legs to hasten His death (Mark 15:33–37; John 19:31–33).

Jesus' body was not left to decompose in disgrace as was the case with most crucifixion victims. The followers of Jesus were able to secure Pilate's permission to give Him a proper burial (Matt. 27:57–60).

The cross has been a major stumbling block for many people, preventing the Jewish nation from accepting Jesus as the Messiah. According to Jewish teaching, a person who had been killed "by hanging on a tree"—or crucifixion—was "accursed of God" (Deut. 21:23; Acts 5:30; Gal. 3:13). This form of death was so repulsive to the Jewish people that they refused to discuss it in polite society.

For Christians, the apostle Paul best summarized the importance of the crucifixion: "We preach Christ crucified, to the Jews a stumbling block and to the Greeks foolishness, but to those who are called, both Jews and Greeks, Christ the power of God and the wisdom of God" (1 Cor. 1:23, 24). Other New Testament references to His crucifixion include Romans 6:6; 1 Corinthians 2:2; and Hebrews 6:6.

A victim is crucified on a "t"-shaped cross.

CHAPTER 6

Need for Maturity

THEREFORE, leaving the discussion of the elementary *principles* of Christ, let us go on to [T]perfection, not laying again the foundation of repentance from [R]dead works and of faith toward God, *maturity* • [Heb. 9:14]

2 of the doctrine of baptisms, [R]of laying on of hands, of resurrection of the dead, [R]and of eternal judgment. [Acts 8:17] • Acts 24:25

3 And this *we will do if God permits.

4 For *it is* impossible for those who were once enlightened, and have tasted [R]the heavenly gift, and [R]have become partakers of the Holy Spirit, [John 4:10] • [Gal. 3:2, 5]

5 and have tasted the good word of God and the powers of the age to come,

6 if they fall away, to renew them again to repentance, [R]since they crucify again for themselves the Son of God, and put *Him* to an open shame. Heb. 10:29

7 For the earth which drinks in the rain that often comes upon it, and bears herbs useful for those by whom it is cultivated, [R]receives blessing from God; Ps. 65:10

8 [R]but if it bears thorns and briars, *it is* rejected and near to being cursed, whose end *is* to be burned. Is. 5:6

Exhortation to Maturity

9 But, beloved, we are confident of better things concerning you, yes, things that accompany salvation, though we speak in this manner.

10 For God *is* not unjust to forget your work and *labor of love which you have shown toward His name, *in that* you have ministered to the saints, and do minister.

11 And we desire that each one of you show the same diligence [R]to the full assurance of hope until the end, Col. 2:2

12 that you do not become [T]sluggish, but imitate those who through faith and patience [R]inherit the promises. *lazy* • Heb. 10:36

13 For when God made a promise to Abraham, because He could swear by no one greater, [R]He swore by Himself, Gen. 22:16, 17

14 saying, *"Surely blessing I will bless you, and multiplying I will multiply you."*

15 And so, after he had patiently endured, he obtained the [R]promise. Gen. 12:4; 21:5

16 For men indeed swear by the greater, and [R]an oath for confirmation *is* for them an end of all dispute. Ex. 22:11

17 Thus God, determining to show more abundantly to the heirs of promise the [T]immutability of His counsel, [T]confirmed *it* by an oath, *unchangeableness of His purpose* • *guaranteed*

18 that by two immutable things, in which it *is* impossible for God to lie, we *might have strong consolation, who have fled for refuge to lay hold of the hope set before *us*.

19 This *hope* we have as an anchor of the soul, both sure and steadfast, [R]and which enters the Presence *behind* the veil, Lev. 16:2, 15

20 where the forerunner has entered for us, *even* Jesus, having become High Priest forever according to the order of Melchizedek.

CHAPTER 7

Description of Melchizedek

FOR this [R]Melchizedek, king of Salem, priest of the Most High God, who met Abraham returning from the slaughter of the kings and blessed him, Gen. 14:18–20

2 to whom also Abraham gave a tenth part of all, first being translated "king of righteousness," and then also king of Salem, meaning "king of peace,"

3 without father, without mother, without genealogy, having neither beginning of days nor end of life, but made like the Son of God, remains a priest continually.

Superiority of Melchizedek

4 Now consider how great this man *was*, to whom even the patriarch Abraham gave a tenth of the [T]spoils. *plunder*

5 And indeed [R]those who are of the sons of Levi, who receive the priesthood, have a commandment to receive tithes from the people according to the law, that is, from their brethren, though they have come from the loins of Abraham; Num. 18:21–26

6 but he whose genealogy is not derived from them received tithes from Abraham and blessed him who had the promises.

7 Now beyond all contradiction the lesser is blessed by the better.

8 Here mortal men receive tithes, but there he *receives them*, [R]of whom it is witnessed that he lives. Heb. 5:6; 6:20

9 Even Levi, who receives tithes, paid tithes through Abraham, so to speak,

10 for he was still in the loins of his father when Melchizedek met him.

Imperfection of Aaronic Priesthood

11 [R]Therefore, if perfection were through the Levitical priesthood (for under it the people received the law), what further need *was there* that another priest should rise according to the order of Melchizedek, and not be called according to the order of Aaron? Heb. 7:18; 8:7

12 For the priesthood being changed, of necessity there is also a change of the law.

13 For He of whom these things are spoken

6:3 M *let us do* **6:10** NU omits *labor of*
6:18 M omits *might*

belongs to another tribe, from which no man
has [T]officiated at the altar. *served*
14 For *it is* evident that [R]our Lord arose
from Judah, of which tribe Moses spoke
nothing concerning *priesthood. Is. 1:1★
15 And it is yet far more evident if, in the
likeness of Melchizedek, there arises another
priest
16 who has come, not according to the law
of a fleshly commandment, but according to
the power of an endless life.
17 For *He testifies:

[R]*"You are a priest forever*
According to the order of
Melchizedek." Ps. 110:4★

18 For on the one hand there is an annulling
of the former commandment because of [R]its
weakness and unprofitableness, [Rom. 8:3]
19 for [R]the law made nothing [T]perfect; on
the other hand, *there is the* bringing in of [R]a
better hope, through which [R]we draw near to
God. [Acts 13:39] • *complete* • Heb. 6:18, 19 • Rom. 5:2
20 And inasmuch as *He was* not *made*
priest without an oath
21 (for they have become priests without an
oath, but He with an oath by Him who said to
Him:

[R]*"The LORD has sworn* Ps. 110:4
And will not relent,
*'You are a priest *forever*
According to the order of
Melchizedek' "),

22 by so much more Jesus has become a
[T]surety of a [R]better covenant. *guarantee* • Heb. 8:6
23 And there were many priests, because
they were prevented by death from continuing.
24 But He, because He continues forever,
has an unchangeable priesthood.
25 Therefore He is also [R]able to save [T]to the
uttermost those who come to God through
Him, since He ever lives [R]to make interces-
sion for them. Jude 24 • *completely* or *forever* • Rom. 8:34
26 For such a High Priest was fitting for us,
[R]*who is* holy, [T]harmless, undefiled, separate
from sinners, [R]and has become higher than
the heavens; Heb. 4:15 • *innocent* • Eph. 1:20
27 who does not need daily, as those high
priests, to offer up sacrifices, first for His
[R]own sins and then for the people's, for this
He did once for all when He offered up
Himself. Lev. 9:7; 16:6
28 For the law appoints as high priests men
who have weakness, but the word of the
oath, which came after the law, *appoints* the
Son who has been perfected forever.

CHAPTER 8

A Better Covenant

NOW *this is* the main point of the things
we are saying: We have such a High
Priest, [R]who is seated at the right hand of the
throne of the Majesty in the heavens, Col. 3:1
2 a Minister of [R]the [T]sanctuary and of [R]the
true tabernacle which the Lord erected, and
not man. Heb. 9:8, 12 • Lit. *holies* • Heb. 9:11, 24
3 For [R]every high priest is appointed to
offer both gifts and sacrifices. Therefore [R]*it is*
necessary that this One also have something
to offer. Heb. 5:1; 8:4 • [Eph. 5:2]
4 For if He were on earth, He would not be
a priest, since there are priests who offer the
gifts according to the law;
5 who serve the copy and [R]shadow of the
heavenly things, as Moses was divinely instructed when he was about to make the
tabernacle. [R]For He said, *"See that you make*
all things according to the pattern shown you
on the mountain." Col. 2:17 • Ex. 25:40
6 But now [R]He has obtained a more excellent ministry, inasmuch as He is also Mediator of a [R]better covenant, which was established on better promises. [2 Cor. 3:6–8] • Heb. 7:22

A New Covenant

7 For if that [R]first *covenant* had been faultless, then no place would have been sought
for a second. Ex. 3:8; 19:5
8 Because finding fault with them, He says:
[R]*"Behold, the days are coming, says the LORD,*
when I will make a new covenant with the
house of Israel and with the house of Ju-
dah— Jer. 31:31–34★
9 *"not according to the covenant that I*
made with their fathers in the day when I
took them by the hand to lead them out of
the land of Egypt; because they did not
continue in My covenant, and I disregarded
them, says the LORD.
10 *"For this is the covenant that I will make*
with the house of Israel after those days, says
the LORD: I will put My laws in their mind
and write them on their hearts; and I will be
their God, and they shall be My people.
11 *"None of them shall teach his neighbor,*
and none his brother, saying, 'Know the
[R]*LORD,' for all shall know Me, from the least*
of them to the greatest of them. Jer. 31:34
12 *"For I will be merciful to their unrigh-*
teousness, [R]*and their sins *and their lawless*
deeds I will remember no more." Rom. 11:27
13 [R]In that He says, *"A new covenant,"* He
has made the first obsolete. Now what is
becoming obsolete and growing old is ready
to vanish away. [2 Cor. 5:17]

7:14 NU *priests* **7:17** NU *it is testified*
7:21 NU ends the quotation after *forever.*
8:12 NU omits *and their lawless deeds*

CHAPTER 9

Old Covenant's Sanctuary

THEN indeed, even the first *covenant* had ordinances of divine service and [R]the earthly sanctuary. Ex. 25:8

2 For a tabernacle was prepared: the first *part,* in which *was* the lampstand, the table, and the showbread, which is called the [T]sanctuary; *holy place,* lit. *holies*

3 [R]and behind the second veil, the part of the tabernacle which is called the Holiest of All, Ex. 26:31–35; 40:3

4 which had the golden altar of incense and the ark of the covenant overlaid on all sides with gold, in which *were* the golden pot that had the manna, Aaron's rod that budded, and the tablets of the covenant;

5 and [R]above it were the cherubim of glory overshadowing the mercy seat. Of these things we cannot now speak in detail. Lev. 16:2

Old Covenant's Sacrifice

6 Now when these things had been thus prepared, [R]the priests always went into the first part of the tabernacle, performing *the services.* Num. 18:2–6; 28:3

7 But into the second part the high priest *went* alone once a year, not without blood, which he offered for himself and *for* the people's sins *committed* in ignorance;

8 the Holy Spirit indicating this, that [R]the way into the Holiest of All was not yet made manifest while the first tabernacle was still standing. [John 14:6]

9 It *was* symbolic for the present time in which both gifts and sacrifices are offered which cannot make him who performed the service perfect in regard to the conscience—

10 *concerned* only with foods and drinks, various washings, and fleshly ordinances imposed until the time of reformation.

New Covenant's Sanctuary

11 But Christ came *as* High Priest of [R]the good things *to come, with the greater and more perfect tabernacle not made with hands, that is, not of this creation. Heb. 10:1

New Covenant's Sacrifice

12 Not with the blood of goats and calves, but with His own blood He entered the Most Holy Place [R]once for all, [R]having obtained eternal redemption. Zech. 3:9 • [Dan. 9:24]★

13 For if the blood of bulls and goats and the ashes of a heifer, sprinkling the unclean, sanctifies for the purifying of the flesh,

14 how much more shall the blood of Christ, who through the eternal Spirit [R]offered Himself without [T]spot to God, [T]purge your conscience from [R]dead works [R]to serve the living God? Is. 53:12★ • *blemish* • *cleanse* • Heb. 6:1 • Luke 1:74

15 And for this reason [R]He is the Mediator of the new covenant, by means of death, for the redemption of the transgressions under the first covenant, that [R]those who are called may receive the promise of the eternal inheritance. Rom. 3:25 • Heb. 3:1

16 For where there *is* a testament, there must also of necessity be the death of the testator.

17 For [R]a testament *is* in force after men are dead, since it has no power at all while the testator lives. Gal. 3:15

18 [R]Therefore not even the first *covenant* was dedicated without blood. Ex. 24:6

19 For when Moses had spoken every precept to all the people according to the law, he took the blood of calves and goats, with water, scarlet wool, and hyssop, and sprinkled both the book itself and all the people,

20 saying, *"This is the blood of the covenant which God has commanded you."*

21 Then likewise [R]he sprinkled with blood both the tabernacle and all the vessels of the ministry. Ex. 29:12, 36

22 And according to the law almost all things are purged with blood, and without shedding of blood there is no remission.

23 Therefore *it was* necessary that the copies of the things in the heavens should be purified with these, but the heavenly things themselves with better sacrifices than these.

24 For Christ has not entered the holy places made with hands, *which are* copies of the true, but into heaven itself, now to appear in the presence of God for us;

25 not that He should offer Himself often, as [R]the high priest enters the Most Holy Place every year with blood of another— Heb. 9:7

26 He then would have had to suffer often since the foundation of the world; but now, once at the end of the ages, He has appeared to put away sin by the sacrifice of Himself.

27 [R]And as it is appointed for men to die once, but after this the judgment, Gen. 3:19

28 so [R]Christ was offered once to bear the sins of many. To those who eagerly wait for Him He will appear a second time, apart from sin, for salvation. Is. 53:12; Rom. 6:10★

CHAPTER 10

FOR the law, having a shadow of the good things to come, *and* not the very image of the things, can never with these same sacrifices, which they offer continually year by year, make those who approach perfect.

2 For then would they not have ceased to be offered? For the worshipers, once [T]purged, would have had no more consciousness of sins. *cleansed*

3 But in those *sacrifices there is* a reminder of sins every year.

9:11 NU *that have come*

4 For *it is* not possible that the blood of
bulls and goats could take away sins.
5 Therefore, when He came into the world,
He said:

[R]*"Sacrifice and offering You did not*
desire, Ps. 40:6–8★
But a body You have prepared for Me.
6 *In burnt offerings and sacrifices for sin*
You had no pleasure.
7 *Then I said, 'Behold, I have come—*
In the volume of the book it is written
of Me—
To do Your will, O God.' "

8 Previously saying, *"Sacrifice and offer-*
ing, burnt offerings, and offerings for sin You
did not desire, nor had pleasure in them"
(which are offered according to the law),
9 then He said, *"Behold, I have come to do*
*Your will, *O God."* He takes away the first
that He may establish the second.
10 [R]By that will we have been [T]sanctified
[R]through the offering of the body of Jesus
Christ once *for all.* Is. 53:12 • *set apart* • [Heb. 9:12]★
11 And every priest stands ministering daily
and offering repeatedly the same sacrifices,
which can never take away sins.
12 [R]But this Man, after He had offered one
sacrifice for sins forever, sat down [R]at the
right hand of God, Ps. 68:18; Col. 3:1★ • Ps. 110:1
13 from that time waiting [R]till His enemies
are made His footstool. Ps. 110:1★
14 For by one offering He has perfected
forever those who are being sanctified.
15 And the Holy Spirit also witnesses to us;
for after He had said before,
16 *"This is the covenant that I will make*
with them after those days, says the [R]*LORD: I*
will put My laws into their hearts, and in
their minds I will write them," Jer. 31:33, 34★
17 then *He adds, "Their sins and their law-*
less deeds I will remember no more."
18 Now where there is [T]remission of these,
there is no longer an offering for sin. *forgiveness*

Hold Fast the Confession of Faith

19 Therefore, brethren, having boldness to
enter the Holiest by the blood of Jesus,
20 by a new and [R]living way which He
consecrated for us, through the veil, that is,
His flesh, John 14:6
21 and *having* a [R]High Priest over the house
of God, Ps. 110:4★
22 let us draw near with a true heart [R]in full
assurance of faith, having our hearts sprinkled from an evil conscience and our bodies
washed with pure water. Eph. 3:12
23 Let us hold fast the confession of *our*
hope without wavering, for [R]He who promised *is* faithful. 1 Cor. 1:9; 10:13
24 And let us consider one another in order
to stir up love and good works,

25 not forsaking the assembling of ourselves together, as *is* the manner of some, but
exhorting *one another,* and so much the more
as you see the Day approaching.

Fourth Warning: Danger of Drawing Back

26 For if we sin willfully after we have
received the knowledge of the truth, there no
longer remains a sacrifice for sins,
27 but a certain fearful expectation of judgment, and [R]fiery indignation which will devour the adversaries. Zeph. 1:18
28 Anyone who has rejected Moses' law
dies without mercy on the testimony of two
or three [R]witnesses. Deut. 17:2–6; 19:15
29 Of how much worse punishment, do you
suppose, will he be thought worthy who has
trampled the Son of God underfoot, counted
the blood of the covenant by which he was
sanctified a common thing, [R]and insulted the
Spirit of grace? [Matt. 12:31]
30 For we know Him who said, [R]*"Ven-*
*geance is Mine, I will repay," **says the Lord.
And again, [R]*"The LORD will judge His peo-*
ple." Deut. 32:35 • Deut. 32:36
31 [R]It is a fearful thing to fall into the hands
of the living God. [Luke 12:5]
32 But recall the former days in which, after
you were [T]illuminated, you endured a great
struggle with sufferings: *enlightened*
33 partly while you were made [R]a spectacle
both by reproaches and tribulations, and
partly while [R]you became companions of
those who were so treated; 1 Cor. 4:9 • Phil. 1:7
34 for you had compassion on *me in my
chains, and [R]joyfully accepted the plundering
of your [T]goods, knowing that [R]you have a
better and an enduring possession for yourselves *in heaven. Matt. 5:12 • *possessions* • Matt. 6:20
35 Therefore do not cast away your confi-
dence, [R]which has great reward. Matt. 5:12

10:9 NU, M omit *O God* **10:30** NU omits *says the Lord*
10:34 NU *the prisoners* instead of *me in my chains*
10:34 NU omits *in heaven*

10:25 The Reason for Participation in the Local Church—The ultimate reason that we should participate in a local church is because it is specifically commanded by God. Even in New Testament days there were those who yielded to the temptation of absenting themselves from the worship services of the local church. The writer of Hebrews points out that members of a local church have an obligation to one another. They are to provoke one another to good works and to exhort one another to live consistent lives worthy of God. This can best be done within the context of a local church; so believers are commanded not to forsake the assembling of themselves together.

Now turn to Page 1274—Acts 2:42–47: Benefits of Participation in the Local Church.

THE SACRIFICIAL SYSTEM

Sacrifice was a ritual through which the Hebrew people offered the blood or flesh of an animal to God in payment for their sins. Sacrifice originated in the Garden of Eden, when God killed animals and made tunics for Adam and Eve (Gen. 3:21). God's provision of this covering symbolized that sinful man could come before God without fear of death.

When Noah left the ark, his first act was to build an altar and sacrifice animals to God (Gen. 8:20). Abraham regularly worshiped God by offering sacrifices to Him (Gen. 12:7).

In the Mosaic Law, sacrifice had three central ideas: consecration, expiation (covering of sin), and propitiation (satisfaction of divine anger). Sacrifice as worship required man to give back to God what God had given to him.

Some specific sacrificial offerings called for in the Mosaic Law included the burnt offering, which pointed to Christ's atoning death for sinners (2 Cor. 5:21) and His total consecration to God (Luke 2:49); the meal offering, which symbolically presented the best fruits of human living to God (Heb. 10:5–10); the peace offering, which celebrated the covering of sin, forgiveness by God, and the restoration of a right relationship with God (Judg. 20:26); and the sin offering, in which guilt for the worshiper's sin was transferred symbolically to the animal through the laying on of the offerer's hands (Lev. 16:8–10).

Both Old and New Testaments confirm that sacrifices were symbolic. Because of their sins, the Hebrews presented offerings by which they gave another life in place of their own. These substitutes pointed forward to the ultimate sacrifice, Jesus Christ (Heb. 10:1–18), who laid down His life for the sins of all people.

Priest offers a sacrifice in the tabernacle in the Wilderness.

36 [R]For you have need of endurance, so that
after you have done the will of God, [R]you
may receive the promise: Luke 21:19 · [Col. 3:24]

37 *"For [R]yet a little while,* Luke 18:8
And [R]He who is coming will come and
will not [T]tarry. Hab. 2:3, 4☆ · *delay*
38 *Now [R]the* just shall live by faith;*
But if anyone draws back, Rom. 1:17
My soul has no pleasure in him."

39 But we are not of those [R]who draw back
to [T]perdition, but of those who [R]believe to the
saving of the soul. 2 Pet. 2:20 · *destruction* · Acts 16:31

CHAPTER 11

Definition of Faith

NOW faith is the [T]substance of things
hoped for, the [T]evidence [R]of things not
seen. *realization* · Or *confidence* · Rom. 8:24
2 For by it the elders obtained a *good*
testimony.
3 By faith we understand that the [T]worlds
were framed by the word of God, so that the
things which are seen were not made of
things which are visible. Or *ages,* Gr. *aiones,* aeons

Abel

4 By faith [R]Abel offered to God a more
excellent sacrifice than Cain, through which
he obtained witness that he was righteous,
God testifying of his gifts; and through it he
being dead still [R]speaks. Gen. 4:3–5 · Heb. 12:24

Enoch

5 By faith [R]Enoch was translated so that
he did not see death, *"and was not found*
because God had translated him"; for before
his translation he had this testimony, that he
pleased God. Gen. 5:21–24
6 But without faith *it is* impossible to
please *Him,* for he who comes to God must
believe that He is, and *that* He is a rewarder
of those who diligently seek Him.

Noah

7 By faith Noah, being divinely warned of
things not yet seen, moved with godly fear,
[R]prepared an ark for the saving of his household, by which he condemned the world and
became heir of [R]the righteousness which is
according to faith. 1 Pet. 3:20 · Rom. 3:22

Abraham and Sarah

8 By faith Abraham obeyed when he was
called to go out to the place which he would
afterward receive as an inheritance. And he
went out, not knowing where he was going.
9 By faith he sojourned in the land of
promise as *in* a foreign country, dwelling in
tents with Isaac and Jacob, [R]the heirs with
him of the same promise; Heb. 6:17
10 for he waited for [R]the city which has
foundations, [R]whose builder and maker *is*
God. [Heb. 12:22; 13:14] · [Rev. 21:10]
11 By faith Sarah herself also received
strength to conceive seed, and *she bore a
child when she was past the age, because she
judged Him faithful who had promised.
12 Therefore from one man, and him as
good as dead, were born *as many* as the stars
of the sky in multitude—innumerable as the
sand which is by the seashore.
13 These all died in faith, not having received the promises, but having seen them
afar off *were assured of *them,* embraced
them, and [R]confessed that they were strangers and pilgrims on the earth. Ps. 39:12
14 For those who say such things [R]declare
plainly that they seek a homeland. Heb. 13:14
15 And truly if they had called to mind that
country from which they had come out, they
would have had opportunity to return.
16 But now they desire a better, that is, a
heavenly *country.* Therefore God is not
ashamed [R]to be called their God, for He has
[R]prepared a city for them. Ex. 3:6 · [Rev. 21:2]
17 By faith Abraham, when he was tested,
offered up Isaac, and he who had received the
promises offered up his only begotten *son,*
18 [T]of whom it was said, [R]*"In Isaac your*
seed shall be called," *to* · Gen. 21:12★
19 accounting that God *was* able to raise
him up, even from the dead, from which he
also received him in a figurative sense.

Isaac

20 By faith [R]Isaac blessed Jacob and Esau
concerning things to come. Gen. 27:26–40

Jacob

21 By faith Jacob, when he was dying,
blessed each of the sons of Joseph, and
worshiped, *leaning* on the top of his staff.

Joseph

22 By faith [R]Joseph, when he was dying,
made mention of the departure of the children of Israel, and gave instructions concerning his bones. Gen. 50:24, 25

Moses' Parents

23 By faith Moses, when he was born, was
hidden three months by his parents, because
they saw *he was* a beautiful child; and they
were not afraid of the king's command.

Moses

24 By faith [R]Moses, when he became of age,
refused to be called the son of Pharaoh's
daughter, Ex. 2:11–15
25 choosing rather to suffer affliction with

10:38 NU *my just one*
11:11 NU omits *she bore a child*
11:13 NU, M omit *were assured of them*

FAITH TO BELIEVE

There are three main words in the Greek New Testament about faith and believing: *pistis*, a noun, *pisteuō*, a verb, and *pistos*, an adjective.

Faith (*pistis*)

Faith (*pistis*) is defined in a practical way in Hebrews 11:1: "Now faith is the substance [or substantiation] of things hoped for, the evidence of things not seen." The writer of Hebrews goes on for thirty-nine additional verses to illustrate these who took God at His word and had faith in what He said. They were not all outstanding believers. Jacob, Gideon, and Samson were all too human in their failure, and even father Abraham slipped up a few times. But they were believers.

What is faith? It is confidence that someone or something is reliable. Our whole life is based on faith. Without it, banks and post offices would not be possible. Paper money and credit cards (the very word *credit* is from the Latin verb "to believe") would never be accepted.

We must have some content to our Christianity. Paul puts the facts of the faith in a nutshell: "That Christ died for our sins according to the Scriptures, and that He was buried, and that He rose again the third day according to the Scriptures" (1 Cor. 15:3, 4).

Faith can also refer to the body of beliefs, as in "the Christian faith." Paul uses it this way in 1 Timothy 5:8: "But if anyone does not provide for his own, and especially for those of his household, he has denied the faith and is worse than an unbeliever."

Believe (*pisteuō*)

Believe (*pisteuō*) is a prominent verb in the New Testament. Many people think Acts 16:31 is too easy and simple a method of salvation: "Believe on the Lord Jesus Christ, and you will be saved." Actually, simply believing is very hard for most people. If salvation consisted of faith, plus giving $100 to the church, most people would prefer it. But God does not want human boasting, so salvation is "by grace," and "through faith," "not of works" (Eph. 2:8, 9).

Believing is intellectual in the sense that faith has to have some facts to rest upon. We must believe what God says in His Word. But believing also involves deciding either for or against Christ and His offer of salvation (Rom. 6:23).

The verb *pisteuō* can be used with different prepositions. It is often used with *in* (*en*, probably influenced by the Hebrew expression with the same preposition). The most beloved Gospel verse in the New Testament uses this expression (John 3:16). It means "to confide in someone or something."

Pisteuō is also used with *on* (*epi*), as in Acts 16:31. This stresses laying hold upon the object of faith.

Sometimes this verb is followed not by a preposition, but by a clause or clauses: "If you confess with your mouth the Lord Jesus and believe in your heart that God has raised Him from the dead, you will be saved" (Rom. 10:9).

To make belief in Christ clearer, since it is the most important step in one's spiritual life, the New Testament uses several terms that are practically synonymous with "believe" when used in the context of faith: "Receive" (John 1:12), "ask" (John 4:10), "confess" (Rom. 10:9), and "call upon" (Rom. 10:13).

Faithful, Believing (*pistos*)

The usual translation of *pistos* is "faithful" but it can mean "believing" (a believer, whether faithful or not). In Titus 1:6, a qualification for an elder is that his children be *pistos*. It might make a difference here which is meant, since some elders might have children who were believers but (at least for a time) not faithful Christians. Another translation of *pistos* is "reliable" or "trustworthy," especially when talking about words or sayings (e.g., Titus 3:8; Rev. 21:5).

The importance of having faith to believe can hardly be overstated: "But without faith *it is* impossible to please *Him*, for he who comes to God must believe that He is, and *that* He is a rewarder of those who diligently seek Him" (Heb. 11:6).

the people of God than to enjoy the [T]passing
pleasures of sin, *temporary*
26 esteeming the [T]reproach of Christ
greater riches than the treasures *in Egypt;
for he looked to the reward. *reviling because of*
27 By faith [R]he forsook Egypt, not fearing
the wrath of the king; for he endured as
seeing Him who is invisible. Ex. 10:28
28 By faith [R]he kept the Passover and the
sprinkling of blood, lest he who destroyed the
firstborn should touch them. Ex. 12:21
29 By faith they passed through the Red Sea
as by dry *land, whereas* the Egyptians, attempting *to do* so, were drowned.

Joshua and Rahab

30 By faith the walls of Jericho fell down
after they were encircled for seven days.
31 By faith the harlot Rahab did not perish
with those who did not believe, when [R]she
had received the spies with peace. Josh. 2:1

Many Other Heroes of Faith

32 And what more shall I say? For the time
would fail me to tell of Gideon and [R]Barak
and Samson and Jephthah, also *of* David and
Samuel and the prophets: Judg. 4:6–24
33 who through faith subdued kingdoms,
worked righteousness, obtained promises,
[R]stopped the mouths of lions, Dan. 6:22
34 [R]quenched the violence of fire, escaped
the edge of the sword, out of weakness were
made strong, became valiant in battle, turned
to flight the armies of the aliens. Dan. 3:23–28
35 [R]Women received their dead raised to life
again. And others were [R]tortured, not accepting deliverance, that they might obtain a
better resurrection. 1 Kin. 17:22 • Acts 22:25
36 Still others had trial of mockings and
scourgings, yes, and [R]of chains and imprisonment. Gen. 39:20
37 [R]They were stoned, they were sawn in
two, *were tempted, were slain with the
sword. [R]They wandered about [R]in sheepskins
and goatskins, being destitute, afflicted, tormented— 1 Kin. 21:13 • 2 Kin. 1:8 • Zech. 13:4
38 of whom the world was not worthy.
They wandered in deserts and mountains, [R]*in*
dens and caves of the earth. 1 Kin. 18:4, 13; 19:9
39 And all these, [R]having obtained a good
testimony through faith, did not receive the
promise, Heb. 11:2, 13
40 God having provided something better
for us, that they should not be [R]made [T]perfect
apart from us. Heb. 5:9 • *complete*

CHAPTER 12

Example of Christ's Endurance

THEREFORE we also, since we are surrounded by so great a cloud of witnesses,
let us lay aside every weight, and the sin
which so easily ensnares *us*, and let us run
with endurance the race that is set before us,
2 looking unto Jesus, the author and finisher of *our* faith, who for the joy that was set
before Him [R]endured the cross, despising the
shame, and has sat down at the right hand of
the throne of God. Ps. 68:18; 69:7, 19 ★
3 [R]For consider Him who endured such
hostility from sinners against Himself, [R]lest
you become weary and discouraged in your
souls. Matt. 10:24 • Gal. 6:9
4 [R]You have not yet resisted to bloodshed,
striving against sin. [1 Cor. 10:13]

Exhortation to Endure God's Chastening

5 And you have forgotten the exhortation
which speaks to you as to sons:

[R]*"My son, do not despise the* [T]*chastening*
of the LORD,
Nor be discouraged when you are
rebuked by Him; Prov. 3:11, 12 • *discipline*
6 *For* [R]*whom the LORD loves He chastens,*
And scourges every son whom He
receives." Rev. 3:19

7 [R]If* you endure chastening, God deals
with you as with sons; for what son is there
whom a father does not chasten? Deut. 8:5
8 But if you are without chastening, [R]of
which all have become partakers, then you
are illegitimate and not sons. 1 Pet. 5:9
9 Furthermore, we have had human fathers who corrected *us*, and we paid *them*
respect. Shall we not much more readily be
in subjection to [R]the Father of spirits and
live? [Job 12:10]
10 For they indeed for a few days chastened
us as seemed *best* to them, but He for *our*
profit, [R]that *we* may be partakers of His
holiness. Lev. 11:44
11 Now no [T]chastening seems to be joyful
for the present, but grievous; nevertheless,
afterward it yields [R]the peaceable fruit of
righteousness to those who have been trained
by it. *discipline* • James 3:17, 18
12 Therefore [R]strengthen the hands which
hang down, and the feeble knees, Is. 35:3
13 and make straight paths for your feet, so
that what is lame may not be *dislocated*, but
rather be healed.
14 Pursue peace with all *men*, and holiness,
without which no one will see the Lord:
15 looking diligently lest anyone [R]fall short
of the grace of God; lest any [R]root of bitterness springing up cause trouble, and by this
many become defiled; Heb. 4:1 • Deut. 29:18
16 lest there *be* any [R]fornicator or [T]profane

11:26 NU, M *of* **11:37** NU omits *were tempted*
12:7 NU, M *It is for discipline that you endure*

person like Esau, who for one morsel of food sold his birthright. [1 Cor. 6:13–18] · *godless*

17 For you know that afterward, when he wanted to inherit the blessing, he was rejected, for he found no place for repentance, though he sought it diligently with tears.

18 For you have not come *to [R]the mountain that may be touched and that burned with fire, and to blackness and *darkness and tempest, Deut. 4:11; 5:22

19 and the sound of a trumpet and the voice of words, so that those who heard *it* [R]begged that the word should not be spoken to them anymore. Ex. 20:18–26

20 (For they could not endure what was commanded: [R]*"And if so much as a beast touches the mountain, it shall be stoned *or thrust through with an arrow."* Ex. 19:12, 13

21 And so terrifying was the sight *that* Moses said, [R]*"I am exceedingly afraid* and trembling.") Deut. 9:19

22 But you have come to Mount Zion and to the city of the living God, the heavenly Jerusalem, to an innumerable company of angels,

23 to the [T]general assembly and church of the firstborn *who are* registered in heaven, to God the Judge of all, to the spirits of just men [R]made [T]perfect, *festal gathering* · Phil. 3:12 · *complete*

24 to Jesus the Mediator of the new covenant, and to the blood of sprinkling that speaks better things than *that of* Abel.

Fifth Warning: Danger of Refusing God

25 See that you do not refuse Him who speaks. For [R]if they did not escape who refused Him who spoke on earth, much more *shall we not escape* if we turn away from Him who *speaks* from heaven, Heb. 2:2, 3

26 whose voice then shook the earth; but now He has promised, saying, [R]*"Yet once more I *shake not only the earth, but also heaven."* Hag. 2:6

27 Now this, *"Yet once more,"* indicates the removal of those things that are being shaken, as of things that are made, that the things which cannot be shaken may remain.

28 Therefore, since we are receiving [R]a kingdom which cannot be shaken, let us have grace, by which we *may serve God acceptably with reverence and godly fear. [Dan. 2:44] ☆

29 For [R]our God *is* a consuming fire. Ex. 24:17

CHAPTER 13

Love in the Social Realm

LET [R]brotherly love continue. Rom. 12:10

2 [R]Do not forget to entertain strangers, for by so *doing* [R]some have unwittingly entertained angels. Matt. 25:35 · Gen. 18:1–22; 19:1

3 Remember the prisoners as if chained with them, *and* those who are mistreated, since you yourselves are in the body also.

4 [R]Marriage *is* honorable among all, and the bed undefiled; [R]but fornicators and adulterers God will judge. Prov. 5:18, 19 · 1 Cor. 6:9

5 *Let your* conduct *be* without covetousness, *and be* content with such things as you have. For He Himself has said, [R]*"I will never leave you nor forsake you."* Deut. 31:6, 8; Josh. 1:5

6 So we may boldly say:

[R]*"The LORD is my helper;* Ps. 27:1; 118:6
I will not fear.
What can man do to me?"

Love in the Religious Realm

7 Remember those who [T]rule over you, who have spoken the word of God to you, whose faith follow, considering the outcome of *their* conduct. *lead*

8 Jesus Christ *is* [R]the same yesterday, today, and forever. Heb. 1:12

9 Do not be carried *about with various and strange doctrines. For *it is* good that the heart be established by grace, not with foods which have not profited those who have been occupied with them.

10 We have an altar from which those who serve the tabernacle have no right to eat.

11 For the bodies of those beasts, whose blood is brought into the sanctuary by the high priest for sin, are burned outside the camp.

12 Therefore Jesus also, that He might [T]sanctify the people with His own blood, suffered outside the gate. *set apart*

13 Therefore let us go forth to Him, outside the camp, bearing [R]His reproach. 1 Pet. 4:14

14 For here we have no continuing city, but we seek the one to come.

15 [R]Therefore by Him let us continually offer [R]the sacrifice of praise to God, that is, [R]the fruit of *our* lips, [T]giving thanks to His name. Eph. 5:20 · Lev. 7:12 · Hos. 14:2 · Lit. *confessing*

12:18 NU *to that which* **12:18** NU *gloom*
12:20 NU, M omit the rest of v. 20.
12:26 NU *will shake*
12:28 M omits *may* **13:9** NU, M *away*

13:15 The Expressions of Worship—Since worship encompasses thought, feeling, and deed, there are many expressions of it. Worship especially includes praise and thanksgiving which may be expressed privately or publicly, either by grateful declarations (Heb. 13:15) or by joyful singing (Page 681—Ps. 100:2; Page 1392—Eph. 5:19; Page 1408—Col. 3:16). Portions of early Christian hymns of worship actually may be preserved in the New Testament (Page 1427—1 Tim. 3:16; Page 1434—2 Tim. 2:11–13).

(continued on next page)

16 [R]But do not forget to do good and to
share, for [R]with such sacrifices God is well
pleased. Rom. 12:13 • Phil. 4:18
17 Obey those who [T]rule over you, and be
submissive, for they watch out for your souls,
as those who must give account. Let them do
so with joy and not with grief, for that would
be unprofitable for you. *lead*

Conclusion

18 [R]Pray for us; for we are confident that we
have [R]a good conscience, in all things desiring to live honorably. Eph. 6:19 • Acts 23:1
19 But I especially urge *you* to do this, that
I may be restored to you the sooner.
20 Now may the God of peace [R]who
brought up our Lord Jesus from the dead,
that great Shepherd of the sheep, through the
blood of the everlasting covenant, Hos. 6:2 ★
21 make you complete in every good work
to do His will, working in *you what is well
pleasing in His sight, through Jesus Christ, to
whom *be* glory forever and ever. Amen.
22 And I appeal to you, brethren, bear with
the word of exhortation, for I have written to
you in few words.
23 Know that *our* brother Timothy has been
set free, with whom I shall see you if he
comes shortly.
24 Greet all those who [T]rule over you, and
all the saints. Those from Italy greet you. *lead*
25 Grace *be* with you all. Amen.

13:21 NU, M *us*

(continued from previous page)

One very important expression of worship for the church is remembering the death of Christ through the Lord's Supper (Page 1355—1 Cor. 11:26). The Lord's Supper was instituted by Christ Himself (Page 1150—Matt. 26:26–28) and judged by Paul not to be taken lightly (Page 1355—1 Cor. 11:28–32).

Since worship means giving something to God, the cheerful giving of money to God's work is certainly an act of worship (Page 1372—2 Cor. 9:7). The giving of one's time to the Lord's work may be considered worship as well. The use of one's spiritual gifts in ministry to the body of Christ constitutes an example of worship as service (Page 1355—1 Cor. 12), as does faithfully occupying a church office (Page 1390—Eph. 4:11; Page 1427—1 Tim. 3:1–13; Page 1440—Titus 1:5–9). Ministry in edifying saints and evangelizing sinners both likewise constitute services of worship.

The single most important act of worship for the Christian is the unqualified presentation of himself to God as an obedient servant. This dedication involves the body and the mind (Page 1336—Rom. 12:1, 2): the body because it contains the tools by which the will of God is carried out; the mind because it coordinates the actions to be executed by the body. When these are gladly devoted to God, they become instruments by which He effects His will on the earth. Such faithful and joyous service makes one's entire life a performance of worship.

Now turn to Page 508—2 Chr. 7:3: The Reasons for Worship.

THE EPISTLE OF

JAMES

THE BOOK OF JAMES

Faith without works cannot be called faith. Faith without works is dead, and a dead faith is worse than no faith at all. Faith must work; it must produce; it must be visible. Verbal faith is not enough; mental faith is insufficient. Faith must be there, but it must be more. It must inspire action. Throughout his epistle to Jewish believers, James integrates true faith and everyday practical experience by stressing that true faith must manifest itself in works of faith.

Faith endures trials. Trials come and go, but a strong faith will face them head-on and develop endurance. Faith understands temptations. It will not allow us to consent to our lust and slide into sin. Faith obeys the Word. It will not merely hear and not do. Faith produces doers. Faith harbors no prejudice. For James, faith and favoritism cannot coexist. Faith displays itself in works. Faith is more than mere words; it is more than knowledge; it is demonstrated by obedience; and it overtly responds to the promises of God. Faith controls the tongue. This small but immensely powerful part of the body must be held in check. Faith can do it. Faith acts wisely. It gives us the ability to choose wisdom that is heavenly and to shun wisdom that is earthly. Faith produces separation from the world and submission to God. It provides us with the ability to resist the devil and humbly draw near to God. Finally, faith waits patiently for the coming of the Lord. Through trouble and trial it stifles complaining.

The name *Iakobos* (James) in 1:1 is the basis for the early title *Iakobou Epistole,* "Epistle of James." *Iakobos* is the Greek form of the Hebrew name Jacob, a Jewish name common in the first century.

THE AUTHOR OF JAMES

Four men are named James in the New Testament: (1) James, the father of Judas (not Iscariot), is mentioned twice (Luke 6:16; Acts 1:13) as the father of one of the twelve disciples, but is otherwise completely unknown. (2) James, the son of Alphaeus (Matt. 10:3; Mark 3:18; Luke 6:15; Acts 1:13), elsewhere called James the Less (Mark 15:40), was one of the twelve disciples. Apart from being listed with the other disciples, this James is completely obscure, and it is doubtful that he is the authoritative figure behind the epistle. Some attempts have been made to identify this James with the Lord's brother (Gal. 1:19), but this view is difficult to reconcile with the gospel accounts. (3) James, the son of Zebedee and brother of John (Matt. 4:21; 10:2; 17:1; Mark 3:17; 10:35; 13:3; Luke 9:54; Acts 1:13), was one of Jesus' intimate disciples, but his martyrdom by A.D. 44 (Acts 12:2) makes it very unlikely that he wrote this epistle. (4) James, the Lord's brother (Matt. 13:55; Mark 6:3; Gal. 1:19), was one of the "pillars" in the church in Jerusalem (Acts 12:17; 15:13–21; 21:18; Gal. 2:9, 12). Tradition points to this prominent figure as the author of the epistle, and this best fits the evidence of Scripture. There are several clear parallels between the language of the letter drafted under his leadership in Acts 15:23–29 and the epistle of James (e.g., the unusual word *chairein,* "greeting," is found only in Acts 15:23; 23:26; and James 1:1). The Jewish character of this epistle with its stress upon the law, along with the evident influence by the Sermon on the Mount (e.g., 4:11, 12; 5:12), complement what we know about James "the Just" from Scripture and early tradition.

It has been argued that the Greek of this epistle is too sophisticated for a Galilean such as James, but this assumes that he never had the opportunity or aptitude to develop proficiency in Koine ("common") Greek. As a prominent church leader, it would have been to his advantage to become fluent in the universal language of the Roman Empire.

For various reasons, some assert that James was a stepbrother of Jesus by a previous marriage of Joseph, or that the "brothers" of Jesus mentioned in Matthew 13:55 and Mark 6:3 were really His cousins. However, the most natural understanding of the gospel accounts is that James was the half-brother of Jesus, being the offspring of Joseph and Mary after the birth of Jesus (Matt. 1:24, 25). He apparently did not accept the claims of Jesus until the Lord appeared to him after His resurrection (1 Cor. 15:7). He and his brothers were among the believers who awaited the coming of the Holy Spirit on the day of Pentecost (Acts 1:14). It was not long before he became an acknowledged leader of the Jerusalem church (Acts 12:17; Gal. 2:9, 12), and he was a central figure in the Jerusalem Council in Acts 15. Even after Paul's third missionary journey, James continued to observe the Mosaic Law as a testimony to other Jews (Acts 21:18–25). Early tradition stresses his Jewish piety and his role in bringing others to an understanding of Jesus as the Messiah. He suffered a violent martyr's death not long before the fall of Jerusalem.

The brevity and limited doctrinal emphasis of James kept it from wide circulation; and by the time it became known in the church as a whole, there was uncertainty about the identity of the James in 1:1. Growing recognition that it was written by the Lord's brother led to its acceptance as a canonical book.

THE TIME OF JAMES

James is addressed "to the twelve tribes which are scattered abroad" (1:1), and it is apparent from verses like 1:19 and 2:1, 7 that this greeting refers to Hebrew Christians outside of Palestine. Their place of meeting is called a "synagogue" in the Greek text of 2:2, and the whole epistle reflects Jewish thought and expressions (e.g., 2:19, 21; 4:11, 12; 5:4, 12). There are no references to slavery or idolatry, and this also fits an originally Jewish readership.

These Jewish believers were beset with problems that were testing their faith, and James was concerned that they were succumbing to impatience, bitterness, materialism, disunity, and spiritual apathy. As a resident of Jerusalem and a leader of the church, James no doubt had frequent contact with Jewish Christians from a number of Roman provinces. He therefore felt a responsibility to exhort and encourage them in their struggles of faith.

According to Josephus, James was martyred in A.D. 62 (Hegesippus, quoted in Eusebius, fixed the date of James's death at A.D. 66). Those who accept him as the author of this epistle have proposed a date of writing ranging from A.D. 45 to the end of his life. However, several factors indicate that this letter may have been the earliest writing of the New Testament (c. A.D. 46–49): (1) There is no mention of gentile Christians or their relationship to Jewish Christians as would be expected in a later epistle. (2) Apart from references to the person of Christ, there is practically no distinctive theology in James, suggesting an early date when Christianity was viewed in terms of Messianic Judaism. (3) The allusions to the teachings of Christ have such little verbal agreement with the synoptic Gospels that they probably preceded them. (4) James uses the word "synagogue" (assembly, 2:2) in addition to "church" and indicates a very simple organization of elders and masters, that is, teachers (3:1; 5:14), which was patterned after the early synagogue. (5) James does not mention the issues involved in the Acts 15 Council in Jerusalem (A.D. 49).

THE CHRIST OF JAMES

In 1:1 and 2:1 James refers to the "Lord Jesus Christ," and in 5:7, 8 he anticipates "the coming of the Lord." Compared to other New Testament writers, James says little about Christ, and yet his speech is virtually saturated with allusions to the teaching of Christ. The Sermon on the Mount is especially prominent in James's thinking (there are c. fifteen indirect references; e.g., James 1:2 and Matt. 5:10–12; James 1:4 and Matt. 5:48; James 2:13 and Matt. 6:14, 15; James 4:11 and Matt. 7:1, 2; James 5:2 and Matt. 6:19). This epistle portrays Christ in the context of early Messianic Judaism.

KEYS TO JAMES

Key Word: Faith That Works—Throughout his epistle, James develops the theme of the characteristics of true faith. He effectively uses these characteristics as a series of tests to help his readers evaluate the quality of their relationship to Christ. The purpose of this work is not doctrinal or apologetic but practical. James seeks to challenge these believers to examine the quality of their daily lives in terms of attitudes and actions. A genuine faith will produce real changes in a person's conduct and character, and the absence of change is a symptom of a dead faith.

Key Verses: James 1:19–22 and 2:14–17—"Therefore, my beloved brethren, let every man be swift to hear, slow to speak, slow to wrath; for the wrath of man does not produce the righteousness of God. Therefore lay aside all filthiness and overflow of wickedness, and receive with meekness the implanted word, which is able to save your souls. But be doers of the word, and not hearers only, deceiving yourselves" (1:19–22).

"What *does it* profit, my brethren, if someone says he has faith but does not have works? Can faith save him? If a brother or sister is naked and destitute of daily food, and one of you says to them, 'Depart in peace, be warmed and filled,' but you do not give them the things which are needed for the body, what *does it* profit? Thus also faith by itself, if it does not have works, is dead" (2:14-17).

Key Chapter: James 1—One of the most difficult areas of the Christian life is that of testings and temptations. James reveals our correct response to both: to testings, count them all joy; to temptations, realize that God is not their source.

SURVEY OF JAMES

James is the Proverbs of the New Testament because it is written in the terse moralistic style of wisdom literature. It is evident that James was profoundly influenced by the Old Testament (especially by its wisdom literature) and by the Sermon on the Mount. But James's impassioned preaching against inequity and social injustice also earns him the title of the Amos of the New Testament. Because of the many subjects in this epistle, it is difficult to outline; suggestions have ranged from no connection between the various topics to a unified scheme. The outline used here is: the test of faith (1:1–18); the characteristics of faith (1:19—5:6); and the triumph of faith (5:7–20).

The Test of Faith (1:1-18): The first part of this epistle develops the qualities of genuine faith in regard to trials and temptations. After a one-verse salutation to geographically dispersed Hebrew Christians (1:1), James quickly introduces his first subject, outward tests of faith (1:2–12). These trials are designed to produce mature endurance and a sense of dependence upon God, to whom the believer turns for wisdom and enablement. Inward temptations (1:13–18) do not come from the One who bestows "every good gift" (1:17). These solicitations to evil must be checked at an early stage or they may result in disastrous consequences.

The Characteristics of Faith (1:19—5:6): A righteous response to testing requires that one be "swift to hear, slow to speak, slow to wrath" (1:19), and this broadly summarizes the remainder of the epistle. Quickness of hearing involves an obedient response to God's Word (1:19–27). True hearing means more than mere listening; the Word must be received and applied. After stating this principle (1:21, 22), James develops it with an illustration (1:23–25) and an application (1:26, 27). A genuine faith should produce a change in attitude from partiality to the rich to a love for the poor as well as the rich (2:1–13). True faith should also result in actions (2:14–26). In Romans 4, Paul used the example of Abraham to show that justification is by faith, not by works. But James says that Abraham was justified by works (2:21). In spite of the apparent contradiction, Romans 4 and James 2 are really two sides of the same coin. In context, Paul is writing about justification before God while James writes of the evidence of justification before men. A faith that produces no change is not saving faith.

Moving from works to words, James shows how a living faith controls the tongue ("slow to speak," 1:19). The tongue is small, but it has the power to accomplish great good or equally great evil. Only the power of God applied by an active faith can tame the tongue (3:1–12). Just as there are wicked and righteous uses of the tongue, so there are demonic and divine manifestations of wisdom (3:13–18). James contrasts seven characteristics of human wisdom with seven qualities of divine wisdom.

The strong pulls of worldliness (4:1–12) and wealth (4:13—5:6) create conflicts that are harmful to the growth of faith. The world system is at enmity with God, and the pursuit of its pleasures produces covetousness, envy, fighting, and arrogance (4:1–6). The believer's only alternative is submission to God out of a humble and repentant spirit. This will produce a transformed attitude toward others as well (4:7–12). This spirit of submission and humility should be applied to any attempts to accrue wealth (4:13–17), especially because wealth can lead to pride, injustice, and selfishness (5:1–6).

The Triumph of Faith (5:7–20): James encourages his readers to patiently endure the sufferings of the present life in view of the future prospect of the coming of the Lord (5:7–12). They may be oppressed by the rich or by other circumstances, but as the example of Job teaches, believers can be sure that God has a gracious purpose in His dealings with them. James concludes his epistle with some practical words on prayer and restoration (5:13–20). The prayers of righteous men (e.g., elders in local churches) are efficacious for the healing and restoration of believers. When sin is not dealt with, it can contribute to illness and even death.

FOCUS	TEST OF FAITH		CHARACTERISTICS OF FAITH	TRIUMPH OF FAITH		
REFERENCE	1:1—	1:13—	1:19—	5:7—	5:13—	5:19—5:20
DIVISION	PURPOSE OF TESTS	SOURCE OF TEMPTATION	OUTWARD DEMONSTRATION OF INNER FAITH	ENDURES WAITING	PRAYS FOR AFFLICTED	CONFRONTS SIN
TOPIC	DEVELOPMENT OF FAITH		WORKS OF FAITH	POWER OF FAITH		
	RESPONSE OF FAITH		REALITY OF FAITH	REASSURANCE OF FAITH		
LOCATION	PROBABLY JERUSALEM					
TIME	c. A.D. 46–49					

OUTLINE OF JAMES

I. The Test of Faith 1:1–18
- A. The Purpose of Tests.................. 1:1–12
- B. The Source of Temptations 1:13–18

II. The Characteristics of Faith .... 1:19—5:6
- A. Faith Obeys the Word 1:19–27
- B. Faith Removes Discrimination......... 2:1–13
- C. Faith Proves Itself by Works 2:14–26
- D. Faith Controls the Tongue............. 3:1–12
- E. Faith Produces Wisdom 3:13–18
- F. Faith Produces Humility............. 4:1–12
- G. Faith Produces Dependence on God .... 4:13—5:6

III. The Triumph of Faith 5:7–20
- A. Faith Endures Awaiting Christ's Return 5:7–12
- B. Faith Prays for the Afflicted.......... 5:13–18
- C. Faith Confronts the Erring Brother 5:19–20

CHAPTER 1

The Purpose of Tests

JAMES, [R]a servant of God and of the Lord
Jesus Christ, Acts 12:17

To the twelve tribes which are scattered
abroad:

Greetings.
2 My brethren, [R]count it all joy [R]when you
fall into various trials, Acts 5:41 • 2 Pet. 1:6
3 knowing that the testing of your faith
produces [T]patience. *endurance* or *perseverance*
4 But let patience have *its* perfect work,
that you may be [T]perfect and complete, lacking nothing. *mature*
5 If any of you lacks wisdom, let him ask
of God, who gives to all liberally and without
reproach, and it will be given to him.
6 But let him ask in faith, with no doubting, for he who doubts is like a wave of the
sea driven and tossed by the wind.
7 For let not that man suppose that he will
receive anything from the Lord;
8 *he is* [R]a double-minded man, unstable in
all his ways. James 4:8
9 Let the lowly brother glory in his exaltation,
10 but the rich in his humiliation, because
as a flower of the field he will pass away.
11 For no sooner has the sun risen with a
burning heat than it withers the grass; its
flower falls, and its beautiful appearance
perishes. So the rich man also will fade away
in his pursuits.
12 Blessed *is* the man who endures temptation; for when he has been proved, he will
receive the crown of life [R]which the Lord has
promised to those who love Him. Matt. 10:22

The Source of Temptations

13 Let no one say when he is tempted, "I
am tempted by God"; for God cannot be
tempted by evil, nor does He Himself tempt
anyone.
14 But each one is tempted when he is
drawn away by his own desires and enticed.
15 Then, when desire has conceived, it gives
birth to sin; and sin, when it is full-grown,
[R]brings forth death. [Rom. 5:12; 6:23]
16 Do not be deceived, my beloved brethren.
17 [R]Every good gift and every perfect gift is
from above, and comes down from the Father
of lights, [R]with whom there is no variation or
shadow of turning. John 3:27 • Num. 23:19
18 Of His own will He brought us forth by
the word of truth, [R]that we might be a kind of
firstfruits of His creatures. [Eph. 1:12, 13]

Faith Obeys the Word

19 *Therefore, my beloved brethren, let
every man be swift to hear, [R]slow to speak,
[R]slow to wrath; Prov. 10:19; 17:27 • Prov. 14:17; 16:32
20 for the wrath of man does not produce
the righteousness of God.
21 Therefore [R]lay aside all filthiness and
[T]overflow of wickedness, and receive with
meekness the implanted word, [R]which is able
to save your souls. Col. 3:8 • *abundance* • Acts 13:26
22 But [R]be doers of the word, and not hearers only, deceiving yourselves. Matt. 7:21-28
23 For [R]if anyone is a hearer of the word
and not a doer, he is like a man observing his
natural face in a mirror; Luke 6:47
24 for he observes himself, goes away, and
immediately forgets what kind of man he
was.
25 But he who looks into the perfect law of
liberty and continues *in it*, and is not a
forgetful hearer but a doer of the work, this
one will be blessed in what he does.
26 If anyone *among you thinks he is religious, and [R]does not bridle his tongue but
deceives his own heart, this one's religion *is*
useless. Ps. 34:13
27 Pure and undefiled religion before God
and the Father is this: [R]to visit orphans and
widows in their trouble, [R]*and* to keep oneself
unspotted from the world. Is. 1:17 • [Rom. 12:2]

1:19 NU *Know (this)* or *(This) you know*
1:26 NU omits *among you*

CHAPTER 2

Faith Removes Discrimination

MY brethren, do not hold the faith of our Lord Jesus Christ, [R]*the Lord* of glory, with [R]partiality. 1 Cor. 2:8 • Lev. 19:15

2 For if there should come into your assembly a man with gold rings, in [T]fine apparel, and there should also come in a poor man in [T]filthy clothes, *bright* • *vile*

3 and you [T]pay attention to the one wearing the fine clothes and say to him, "You sit here in a good place," and say to the poor man, "You stand there," or, "Sit here at my footstool," Lit. *look upon*

4 have you not [T]shown partiality among yourselves, and become judges with evil thoughts? *differentiated*

5 Listen, my beloved brethren: Has God not chosen the poor of this world *to be* rich in faith and heirs of the kingdom [R]which He promised to those who love Him? Ex. 20:6

6 But [R]you have dishonored the poor man. Do not the rich oppress you [R]and drag you into the courts? 1 Cor. 11:22 • Acts 13:50

7 Do they not blaspheme that noble name by which you are [R]called? 1 Pet. 4:16

8 If you really fulfill *the* royal law according to the Scripture, [R]*"You shall love your neighbor as yourself,"* you do well; Lev. 19:18

9 but if you [T]show partiality, you commit sin, and are convicted by the law as [R]transgressors. Lit. *to receive the face* • Deut. 1:17

10 For whoever shall keep the whole law, and yet [R]stumble in one *point*, [R]he is guilty of all. Gal. 3:10 • Deut. 27:26

11 For He who said, *"Do not commit adultery,"* also said, *"Do not murder."* Now if you do not commit adultery, but you do murder, you have become a transgressor of the law.

12 So speak and so do as those who will be judged by [R]the law of liberty. James 1:25

13 For judgment is without mercy to the one who has shown no [R]mercy. [R]Mercy triumphs over judgment. Mic. 7:18 • Rom. 12:8

Faith Proves Itself by Works

14 [R]What *does it* profit, my brethren, if someone says he has faith but does not have works? Can faith save him? Matt. 7:21–23, 26

15 [R]If a brother or sister is naked and destitute of daily food, Luke 3:11

16 and [R]one of you says to them, "Depart in peace, be warmed and filled," but you do not give them the things which are needed for the body, what *does it* profit? [1 John 3:17, 18]

17 Thus also faith by itself, if it does not have works, is dead.

18 But someone will say, "You have faith, and I have works." [R]Show me your faith without *your works, [R]and I will show you my faith by *my works. Heb. 6:10 • James 3:13

19 You believe that there is one God. You do well. Even the demons believe—and tremble!

20 But do you want to know, O foolish man, that faith without works is *dead?

21 Was not Abraham our father justified by works [R]when he offered Isaac his son on the altar? Gen. 22:9, 10, 12, 16–18

22 Do you see [R]that faith was working together with his works, and by [R]works faith was made [T]perfect? Heb. 11:17 • John 8:39 • *complete*

23 And the Scripture was fulfilled which says, *"Abraham believed God, and it was* [T]*accounted to him for righteousness."* And he was called the friend of God. *credited*

24 You see then that a man is justified by works, and not by faith only.

25 Likewise, was not Rahab the harlot also justified by works when she received the messengers and sent *them* out another way?

26 For as the body without the spirit is dead, so faith without works is dead also.

CHAPTER 3

Faith Controls the Tongue

MY brethren, [R]let not many of you become teachers, knowing that we shall receive a stricter judgment. [Matt. 23:8]

2 For [R]we all stumble in many things. [R]If anyone does not stumble in word, [R]he *is* a [T]perfect man, able also to bridle the whole body. 1 Kin. 8:46 • Ps. 34:13 • [Matt. 12:34–37] • *mature*

3 *Indeed, [R]we put bits in horses' mouths that they may obey us, and we turn their whole body. Ps. 32:9

4 Look also at ships: although they are so large and are driven by fierce winds, they are turned by a very small rudder wherever the pilot desires.

5 Even so the tongue is a little member and [R]boasts great things. See how great a forest a little fire kindles! Ps. 12:3; 73:8

6 And the tongue *is* a fire, a world of [T]iniquity. The tongue is so set among our members that it defiles the whole body, and sets on fire the course of [T]nature; and it is set on fire by [T]hell. *unrighteousness* • *existence* • Gr. *Gehenna*

7 For every kind of beast and bird, of reptile and creature of the sea, is tamed and has been tamed by mankind.

8 But no man can tame the tongue. *It is* an unruly evil, [R]full of deadly poison. Ps. 140:3

9 With it we bless our God and Father, and with it we curse men, who have been made [R]in the [T]similitude of God. Gen. 1:26; 5:1 • *likeness*

10 Out of the same mouth proceed blessing and cursing. My brethren, these things ought not to be so.

11 Does a spring send forth fresh *water* and bitter from the same opening?

2:18 NU omits *your* **2:18** NU omits *my*
2:20 NU *useless* **3:3** NU *Now if*

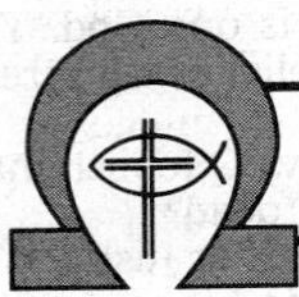

WATCH YOUR TONGUE

James warns us sharply of the sins of the tongue in his very practical (and convicting!) epistle: "And the tongue *is* a fire, a world of iniquity. The tongue is so set among our members that it defiles the whole body, and sets on fire the course of nature; and it is set on fire by hell" (3:6).

Both Greek (and English) have vocabularies rich in words that express the sins of the tongue. Here are just a few.

Blasphemy (*blasphēmia*)

Christians use the word *blasphemy* primarily to mean "harsh (*blas-*) speech (*-phēmia*) against God or sacred persons or things." In secular Greek, the word was originally used more widely, including to slander other people. Most, but not all, New Testament usages refer to defaming sacred things. The adjective *blasphēmos* occurs four times, once used by Paul in describing his pre-conversion days as a blasphemer and a persecutor (1 Tim. 1:13). The Pharisees accused Christ (e.g., Matt. 9:3; 26:65) and the early Christians (e.g., Acts 6:11, 13) of blasphemy. Actually, it was they who were guilty of blasphemy against the Holy Spirit in attributing our Lord's gracious miracles of healing to Satan. Some sensitive Christians fear they have committed this, the "unpardonable sin." Many believe it is not possible to commit it today since we have never witnessed Christ performing miracles. But if it is possible, a person who is concerned about it is not brazen and callous enough to be guilty of it. The very concern shows this.

Evil-speaking (*katalalia*)

Evil-speaking (*katalalia*) occurs twice in this noun form, five times as a verb, and once as an adjective used as a noun. It is easy to see how *kata* ("down") *lalia* ("speech") was formed and it closely parallels the modern expression to "put someone down." Three times in one verse James uses this word: "Do not speak evil of one another, brethren. He who speaks evil of a brother and judges his brother, speaks evil of the law and judges the law. But if you judge the law, you are not a doer of the law but a judge" (4:11). Other translations of these words include "backbite," "revile," "defame," "slander" (2 Cor. 12:20).

Whisperers (*psithyristēs*)

Whisperers (*psithyristēs*) sounds like what it describes. The Greeks pronounced both the *p* and the *s* sounds in words beginning with their letter *psi*. Whispering is not wrong, unless one whispers gossip, evil or other unsavory things—the meaning here. Paul uses it in Romans 1:30 in his catalog of the sins of the Greco-Roman world. He uses the related word *psithyrismos* in 2 Corinthians 12:20 (both times next to the previous root *katalal-*). Here he fears to find the same dreadful sins of "backbitings and whisperings" among the not-so-saintly saints at Corinth. The difference between these last two words (*katalalos* and *psithyristēs*) is that the whisperers are secret slanderers and backbiters are more public in their evil-speaking.

Complaining (*gongysmos*)

The words in the Greek New Testament that mean "murmur," "complain," "grumble," "gripe," and so on, like the previous word, sound like what they represent. Say the word *gongysmos*, and it suggests the grumbling undertones of complaint. (The English word *murmur* does the same, but unfortunately it has lost some of its "bite" due to poetic associations with brooks and trees and the soothing sounds they make.) The verb occurs eight times, the abstract noun occurs four times, and the word for "grumbler" once (Jude 16, of the apostates).

It is easy for us to sneer at the Pharisees for murmuring against the Lord Jesus (Luke 5:30). But even the disciples complained. It is easy to put down the ancient Jews in the Wilderness for grumbling against Moses, but Paul warns us not to do the same (1 Cor. 10:10).

Paul commands Christians to "do all things without murmuring and disputing" (Phil. 2:14) and Peter tells us to "be hospitable to one another without grumbling" (1 Pet. 4:9). Apparently these two apostles knew human nature only too well.

12 Can a [R]fig tree, my brethren, bear olives,
or a grapevine bear figs? *Thus no spring *can*
yield both salt water and fresh. Matt. 7:16–20

Faith Produces Wisdom

13 Who *is* wise and understanding among
you? Let him show by good conduct *that* his
works *are done* in the meekness of wisdom.
14 But if you have bitter envy and [T]self-
seeking in your hearts, [R]do not boast and lie
against the truth. *selfish ambition* • Rom. 2:17
15 This wisdom does not descend from
above, but *is* earthly, sensual, demonic.
16 For where envy and self-seeking *exist*,
confusion and every evil thing *will be* there.
17 But the wisdom that is from above is first
pure, then peaceable, gentle, willing to yield,
full of mercy and good fruits, without partiality [R]and without hypocrisy. Rom. 12:9
18 [R]Now the fruit of righteousness is sown
in peace by those who make peace. Prov. 11:18

CHAPTER 4

Faith Produces Humility

WHERE do [T]wars and fights *come* from
among you? Do *they* not *come* from
your *desires for* pleasure [R]that war in your
members? *battles* • Rom. 7:23
2 You lust and do not have. You murder
and covet and cannot obtain. You fight and
[T]war. *Yet you do not have because you do
not ask. *battle*
3 [R]You ask and do not receive, [R]because
you ask amiss, that you may spend *it* on your
pleasures. Job 27:8, 9 • [Ps. 66:18]
4 *Adulterers and adulteresses! Do you not
know that [R]friendship with the world is
enmity with God? [R]Whoever therefore wants
to be a friend of the world makes himself an
enemy of God. 1 John 2:15 • Gal. 1:4
5 Or do you think that the Scripture says
in vain, [R]"The Spirit who dwells in us yearns
jealously"? Gen. 6:5
6 But He gives more grace. Therefore He
says:

[R]*"God resists the proud,* Prov. 3:34
But gives grace to the humble."

7 Therefore submit to God. [R]Resist the
devil and he will flee from you. [Eph. 4:27; 6:11]
8 [R]Draw near to God and He will draw
near to you. [R]Cleanse *your* hands, *you* sinners; and [R]purify *your* hearts, *you* double-
minded. 2 Chr. 15:2 • Is. 1:16 • 1 Pet. 1:22
9 [R]Lament and mourn and weep! Let your
laughter be turned to mourning and *your* joy
to gloom. Matt. 5:4
10 [R]Humble yourselves in the sight of the
Lord, and He will lift you up. Job 22:29
11 Do not speak evil of one another, brethren. He who speaks evil of a brother and
judges his brother, speaks evil of the law and
judges the law. But if you judge the law, you
are not a doer of the law but a judge.
12 There is one *Lawgiver, [R]who is able to
save and to destroy. [R]Who* are you to judge
*another? [Matt. 10:28] • Rom. 14:4

Faith Produces Dependence on God

13 Come now, you who say, "Today or
tomorrow *we will go to such and such a
city, spend a year there, buy and sell, and
make a profit";
14 whereas you do not know what *will
happen* tomorrow. For what *is* your life? [R]It is
even a vapor that appears for a little time and
then vanishes away. Job 7:7
15 Instead you *ought* to say, "If the Lord
wills, we shall live and do this or that."
16 But now you boast in your arrogance.
[R]All such boasting is evil. 1 Cor. 5:6
17 Therefore, to him who knows to do good
and does not do *it*, to him it is sin.

CHAPTER 5

COME now, *you* [R]rich, weep and howl for
your miseries that are coming upon
you! [Luke 6:24]
2 Your riches [T]are corrupted, and [R]your
garments are moth-eaten. *have rotted* • Job 13:28
3 Your gold and silver are corroded, and
their corrosion will be a witness against you
and will eat your flesh like fire. [R]You have
heaped up treasure in the last days. Rom. 2:5
4 Indeed the wages of the laborers who
mowed your fields, which you kept back by
fraud, cry out; and the cries of the reapers
have reached the ears of the Lord of Sabaoth.
5 You have lived on the earth in pleasure
and [T]luxury; you have [T]fattened your hearts
*as in a day of slaughter. *indulgence* • *nourished*
6 You have condemned, you have mur-
dered the just; he does not resist you.

Faith Endures Awaiting Christ's Return

7 Therefore be patient, brethren, until the
coming of the Lord. See *how* the farmer waits
for the precious fruit of the earth, waiting
patiently for it until it receives the early and
latter rain.
8 You also be patient. Establish your
hearts, for the coming of the Lord is at hand.
9 Do not [T]grumble against one another,
brethren, lest you be *condemned. Behold,
the Judge is standing at the door! Lit. *groan*
10 [R]My brethren, take the prophets, who
spoke in the name of the Lord, as an example
of suffering and [R]patience. Matt. 5:12 • Heb. 10:36

3:12 NU *Neither can a salty spring produce fresh water*
4:2 NU, M omit *Yet* **4:4** NU omits *Adulterers and*
4:12 NU adds *and Judge* **4:12** NU, M *But who*
4:12 NU *a neighbor* **4:13** M *let us*
5:5 NU omits *as* **5:9** NU, M *judged*

ANOINTING IN THE BIBLE

Anointing, or the pouring of oil on a person's head, was a common practice in Bible times. A guest in a home was anointed, partly as a token of honor and esteem and partly to moisten the skin after the visitor had been exposed to the hot, dry climate of Palestine.

Anointing was also a distinct religious rite among the Jewish people. A person was sometimes anointed to set him apart for a particular work or service. Saul was anointed when the Israelites demanded a king (1 Sam. 8:4–22; 10:1). Samuel anointed David as king of Israel (1 Sam. 16:1–13), and Solomon was also anointed as David's successor (1 Kin. 1:39).

These kings, called "anointed ones," were anointed by prophets acting on God's behalf. They ruled as God's representatives to the people and were to rely on God's wisdom as leaders and rulers.

During an anointing, the person customarily knelt while the oil was poured over his head. The substance used was olive oil, myrrh, or sweet cinnamon.

Jesus was God's "anointed one," or the Messiah, who had been foretold by the prophets of the Old Testament (Ps. 45:7; Is. 61:1). A woman poured perfume on Jesus' head as an anointing before His death (Mark 14:3–9). This showed that Jesus had fulfilled His purpose as God's special messenger.

Anointing also refers to a spiritual process in which the Holy Spirit empowers a person's heart and mind with God's truth and love (1 John 2:20, 27). On the Day of Pentecost, after Jesus' ascension, the disciples of Jesus were anointed for special service in a great outpouring of His Holy Spirit on believers (Acts 2:1–4). The apostle Paul declared that all followers of Christ are anointed as God's very own and set apart to His service.

In the New Testament, anointing was also frequently used in connection with healing. Jesus' disciples anointed the sick (Mark 6:13), and James instructed the elders of the church to anoint the sick with oil (James 5:14). This anointing was for the purpose of healing.

The olive tree was one source for the oil used in anointing.

11 Indeed [R]we count them blessed who
[R]endure. You have heard of [R]the perseverance of Job and seen the end *intended by* the
Lord—that the Lord is very compassionate
and merciful. [Ps. 94:12] • [James 1:12] • Job 1:22; 2:10
12 But above all, my brethren, [R]do not
swear, either by heaven or by earth or with
any other oath. But let your "Yes" be "Yes,"
and *your* "No," "No," lest you fall into *judgment. Matt. 5:34–37

Faith Prays for the Afflicted

13 Is anyone among you suffering? Let him
[R]pray. Is anyone cheerful? [R]Let him sing
psalms. Ps. 50:14, 15 • Eph. 5:19
14 Is anyone among you sick? Let him call
for the elders of the church, and let them
pray over him, [R]anointing him with oil in the
name of the Lord. Mark 6:13; 16:18
15 And the prayer of faith will save the sick,
and the Lord will raise him up. [R]And if he has
committed sins, he will be forgiven. Is. 33:24
16 *Confess *your* trespasses to one another,
and pray for one another, that you may be
healed. The effective, [T]fervent prayer of a
righteous man avails much. *supplication*
17 Elijah was a man with a nature like ours,
and [R]he prayed earnestly that it would not
rain; and it did not rain on the land for three
years and six months. 1 Kin. 17:1; 18:1
18 And he prayed again, and the heaven
gave rain, and the earth produced its fruit.

Faith Confronts the Erring Brother

19 Brethren, if anyone among you wanders
from the truth, and someone [R]turns him
back, Gal. 6:1
20 let him know that he who turns a sinner
from the error of his way will save *a soul
from death and cover a multitude of sins.

5:12 M *hypocrisy* 5:16 NU *Therefore confess your sins*
5:20 NU *his soul*

THE FIRST EPISTLE OF

PETER

THE BOOK OF FIRST PETER

Persecution can cause either growth or bitterness in the Christian life. Response determines the result. In writing to Jewish believers struggling in the midst of persecution, Peter encourages them to conduct themselves courageously for the Person and program of Christ. Both their character and conduct must be above reproach. Having been born again to a living hope, they are to imitate the Holy One who has called them. The fruit of that character will be conduct rooted in submission: citizens to government, servants to masters, wives to husbands, husbands to wives, and Christians to one another. Only after submission is fully understood does Peter deal with the difficult area of suffering. The Christians are not to think it "strange concerning the fiery trial which is to try you, as though some strange thing happened to you" (4:12), but are to rejoice as partakers of the suffering of Christ. That response to life is truly the climax of one's submission to the good hand of God.

This epistle begins with the phrase *Petros apostolos Iesou Christou*, "Peter, an apostle of Jesus Christ." This is the basis of the early title *Petrou A*, the "First of Peter."

THE AUTHOR OF FIRST PETER

The early church universally ackowledged the authenticity and authority of First Peter. The internal evidence supports this consistent external testimony in several ways. The apostle Peter's name is given in 1:1, and there are definite similarities between certain phrases in this letter and Peter's sermons as recorded in the Book of Acts (cf. 1 Pet. 1:20 and Acts 2:23; 1 Pet. 4:5 and Acts 10:42). Twice in Acts Peter used the Greek word *xylon*, "wood, tree," to speak of the cross, and this distinctive use is also found in First Peter (see Acts 5:30; 10:39; 1 Pet. 2:24). The epistle contains a number of allusions to events in the life of Christ that held special significance for Peter (e.g., 2:23; 3:18; 4:1; 5:1; cf. 5:5 and John 13:4).

Nevertheless, critics since the nineteenth century have challenged the authenticity of First Peter on several grounds. Some claim that 1:1, 2 and 4:12—5:14 were later additions that turned an anonymous address or a baptismal sermon into a Petrine epistle. Others argue that the sufferings experienced by readers of this letter must refer to the persecution of Christians that took place after the time of Peter in the reigns of the emperors Domitian (A.D. 81–96) and Trajan (A.D. 98–117). There is no basis for the first argument, and the second argument falsely assumes that Christians were not being reviled for their faith during the life of Peter. Another challenge asserts that the quality of the Greek of this epistle is too high for a Galilean like Peter. But Galileans were bilingual (Aramaic and Greek), and writers such as Matthew and James were skillful in their use of Greek. It is also likely that Peter used Silvanus as his scribe (5:12; Paul calls him Silvanus in 2 Cor. 1:19; 1 Thess. 1:1; 2 Thess. 1:1; Luke calls him Silas in Acts 15:40—18:5), and Silvanus may have smoothed out Peter's speech in the process.

THE TIME OF FIRST PETER

This letter is addressed "to the strangers scattered," or more literally, "pilgrims of the Dispersion" (1:1). This, coupled with the injunction to keep their behavior "honorable among the Gentiles" (2:12), gives the initial appearance that the bulk of the readers are Hebrew Christians. A closer look, however, forms the opposite view that most of these believers were Gentiles. They were called "out of darkness" (2:9), and they "once *were* not a people but *are* now the people of God" (2:10). Their former "aimless conduct *received* by tradition from [their] fathers" was characterized by ignorance and futility (1:14, 18; cf. Eph. 4:17). Because they no longer engage in debauchery and idolatry, they are maligned by their countrymen (4:3, 4). These descriptions do not fit a predominantly Hebrew Christian readership. Though Peter was an apostle "to the circumcised" (Gal. 2:8), he also ministered to Gentiles (Acts 10:34–48; Gal. 2:12), and a letter like this would not be beyond the scope of his ministry.

This epistle was addressed to Christians throughout Asia Minor, indicating the spread of the gospel in regions not evangelized when Acts was written (Pontus, Cappadocia, Bithynia; 1:1). It is possible that Peter visited and ministered in some of these areas, but there is no evidence. He wrote this letter in response to the news of growing opposition to the believers in Asia Minor (1:6; 3:13–17; 4:12–19; 5:9, 10). Hostility and suspicion were mounting against Christians in the empire, and they were being reviled and abused for their life-styles and subversive talk about another Kingdom. Christianity had not yet received the official Roman ban, but the stage was being set for the persecution and martyrdom of the near future.

Peter's life was dramatically changed after the Resurrection, and he occupied a central role in the early church and in the spread of the gospel to the Samaritans and Gentiles (Acts 2—10). After the Jerusalem Council in Acts 15, little is recorded of Peter's activities. He evidently traveled extensively with his wife (1 Cor. 9:5) and ministered in various Roman provinces. According to tradition, Peter was crucified upside down in Rome prior to Nero's death in A.D. 68.

This epistle was written from Babylon (5:13), but scholars are divided as to whether this refers literally to Babylon in Mesopotamia or symbolically to Rome. There is no tradition that Peter went to Babylon, and in his day it had few inhabitants. On the other hand, tradition consistently indicates that Peter spent the last years of his life in Rome. As a center of idolatry, the term "Babylon" was an appropriate figurative designation for Rome (cf. the later use of Babylon in Rev. 17; 18). Peter used other figurative expressions in this epistle, and it is not surprising that he would do the same with Rome. His mention of Mark (5:13) also fits this view because Mark was in Rome during Paul's first imprisonment (Col. 4:10). This epistle was probably written shortly before the outbreak of persecution under Nero in A.D. 64.

THE CHRIST OF FIRST PETER

This epistle presents Christ as the believer's example and hope in times of suffering in a spiritually hostile world. He is the basis for the Christian's "living hope" and "inheritance" (1:3, 4), and the love relationship available with Him by faith is a source of inexpressible joy (1:8). His suffering and death provide redemption for all who trust in Him: "who Himself bore our sins in His own body on the tree, that we, having died to sins, might live for righteousness—by whose stripes you were healed" (2:24; cf. 1:18, 19; 3:18). Christ is the Chief Shepherd and Overseer of believers (2:25; 5:4), and when He appears, those who know Him will be glorified.

KEYS TO FIRST PETER

Key Word: Suffering for the Cause of Christ—The basic theme of First Peter is the proper response to Christian suffering. Knowing that his readers will be facing more persecution than ever before, Peter writes this letter to give them a divine perspective on these trials so that they will be able to endure them without wavering in their faith. They should not be surprised at their ordeal because the One they follow also suffered and died (2:21; 3:18; 4:1, 12–14). Rather, they should count it a privilege to share the sufferings of Christ. Peter therefore exhorts them to be sure that their hardships are not being caused by their own wrongdoings, but for their Christian testimony. They are not the only believers who are suffering (5:9), and they must recognize that God brings these things into the lives of His children, not as a punishment but as a stimulus to "perfect *you*" in Christ (5:10). Peter wants to overcome the attitudes of bitterness and anxiety, replacing them with dependence on and confidence in God.

Another theme is stated in 5:12: "I have written to you briefly, exhorting and testifying that this is the true grace of God." In this epistle, Peter frequently speaks of the believer's position in Christ and future hope, and he does so to remind his readers that they are merely sojourners on this planet: their true destiny is eternal glory "when His glory is revealed" (4:13). The grace of God in their salvation (1:1—2:10) shall give them an attitude of submission (2:11—3:12) in the context of suffering for the name of Christ (3:13—5:14).

Key Verses: First Peter 1:10–12 and 4:12, 13—"Of this salvation the prophets have inquired and searched diligently, who prophesied of the grace *that would come* to you, searching what, or what manner of time, the Spirit of Christ who was in them was indicating when He testified beforehand the sufferings of Christ and the glories that would follow. To them it was revealed that, not to themselves, but to us they were ministering the things which now have been reported to you through those who have preached the gospel to you by the Holy Spirit sent from heaven—things which angels desire to look into" (1:10–12).

"Beloved, do not think it strange concerning the fiery trial which is to try you, as though some strange thing happened to you; but rejoice to the extent that you partake of Christ's sufferings, that when His glory is revealed, you may also be glad with exceeding joy" (4:12, 13).

Key Chapter: First Peter 4—Central in the New Testament revelation concerning how to handle persecution and suffering caused by one's Christian testimony is First Peter 4. Not only is Christ's suffering to be our model (4:1, 2), but also we are to rejoice in that we can share in His suffering (4:12–14).

SURVEY OF FIRST PETER

Peter addresses this epistle to "pilgrims" in a world that is growing increasingly hostile to Christians. These believers are beginning to suffer because of their stand for Christ, and Peter uses this letter to give them counsel and comfort by stressing the reality of their living hope in the Lord. By standing firm in the grace of God (5:12) they will be able to endure their "fiery trial" (4:12), knowing that there is a divine purpose behind their pain. This letter logically proceeds through the themes of the salvation of the believer (1:1—2:12); the submission of the believer (2:13—3:12); and the suffering of the believer (3:13—5:14).

The Salvation of the Believer (1:1—2:12): Addressing his letter to believers in several Roman provinces, Peter briefly describes the saving work of the triune Godhead in his salutation (1:1, 2). He then extols God for the riches of this salvation by looking in three temporal directions (1:3–12). First, Peter anticipates the future realization of the Christian's manifold inheritance (1:3–5). Second, he looks at the present joy that this living hope produces in spite of various trials (1:6–9). Third, he reflects upon the prophets of the past who predicted the gospel of God's grace in Christ (1:10–12).

The proper response to this salvation is the pursuit of sanctification or holiness (1:13—2:10). This involves a purifying departure from conformity with the world to godliness in behavior and love. With this in mind, Peter exhorts his readers to "desire the pure milk of the word, that [they] may grow" (2:2) by applying "the word of God which lives and abides forever"(1:23) and acting as a holy priesthood of believers.

The Submission of the Believer (2:13—3:12): Peter turns to the believer's relationships in the world and appeals for an attitude of submission as the Christlike way to harmony and true freedom. Submission for the Lord's sake to those in governmental (2:13–17) and social (2:18–20) authority will foster a good testimony to outsiders. Before moving on to submission in marital relationships (3:1–7), Peter again picks up the theme of Christian suffering (mentioned in 1:6, 7 and 2:12, 18–20) and uses Christ as the supreme model: He suffered sinlessly, silently, and as a substitute for the salvation of others (2:21–25; cf. Is. 52:13—53:12). Peter summarizes his appeal for Christlike submission and humility in 3:8–12.

The Suffering of the Believer (3:13—5:14): Anticipating that growing opposition to Christianity will require a number of his readers to defend their faith and conduct, Peter encourages them to be ready to do so in an intelligent and gracious way (3:13–16). Three times he tells them that if they must suffer, it should be for righteousness' sake and not as a result of sinful behavior (3:17; see 2:20; 4:15, 16). The end of this chapter (3:18–22) is an extremely difficult passage to interpret, and several options have been offered. Verses 19 and 20 may mean that Christ, during the period between His death and resurrection, addressed demonic spirits or the spirits of those who were alive before the Flood. Another interpretation is that Christ preached through Noah to his pre-Flood contemporaries.

As believers in Christ, the readers are no longer to pursue the lusts of the flesh as they did formerly, but rather the will of God (4:1–6). In view of the hardships that they may suffer, Peter exhorts them to be strong in their mutual love and to exercise their spiritual gifts in the power of God so that they will be built up (4:7–11). They should not be surprised when they are slandered and reviled for their faith because the sovereign God has a purpose in all things, and the time of judgment will come when His name and all who trust in Him will be vindicated (4:12–19). They must therefore "commit their souls *to Him* in doing good" (4:19).

In a special word to the elders of the churches in these Roman provinces, Peter urges them to be diligent but gentle shepherds over the flocks that have been divinely placed under their care (5:1–4). The readers as a whole are told to clothe themselves with humility toward one another and toward God who will exalt them at the proper time (5:5–7). They are to resist the adversary in the sure knowledge that their calling to God's eternal glory in Christ will be realized (5:8–11). Peter ends his epistle by stating his theme ("the true grace of God") and conveying greetings and a benediction (5:12–14).

FOCUS	SALVATION OF THE BELIEVER		SUBMISSION OF THE BELIEVER	SUFFERING OF THE BELIEVER			
REFERENCE	1:1	1:13	2:13	3:13	3:18	4:7	5:1—5:14
DIVISION	SALVATION OF THE BELIEVER	SANCTIFICATION OF THE BELIEVER	GOVERNMENT, BUSINESS, MARRIAGE, AND ALL OF LIFE	CONDUCT IN SUFFERING	CHRIST'S EXAMPLE OF SUFFERING	COMMANDS IN SUFFERING	MINISTER IN SUFFERING
TOPIC	BELIEF OF CHRISTIANS		BEHAVIOR OF CHRISTIANS	BUFFETING OF CHRISTIANS			
	HOLINESS		HARMONY	HUMILITY			
LOCATION	EITHER ROME OR BABYLON						
TIME	C. A.D. 63-64						

OUTLINE OF FIRST PETER

CHAPTER 1

Salutation

PETER, an apostle of Jesus Christ,

To the pilgrims of the Dispersion in Pontus,
Galatia, Cappadocia, Asia, and Bithynia,
2 elect [R]according to the foreknowledge of
God the Father, in sanctification of the Spirit,
for obedience and [R]sprinkling of the blood of
Jesus Christ: [Rom. 8:29] • Is. 52:15★

Grace to you and peace be multiplied.

Hope for the Future

3 Blessed *be* the God and Father of our
Lord Jesus Christ, who according to His
abundant mercy [R]has begotten us again to a
living hope through the resurrection of Jesus
Christ from the dead, [John 3:3, 5]
4 to an inheritance [T]incorruptible and undefiled and that does not fade away, [R]re-
served in heaven for you, *imperishable* • Col. 1:5

Trials for the Present

5 [R]who are kept by the power of God
through faith for salvation ready to be revealed in the last time. John 10:28
6 In this you greatly rejoice, though now
for a little while, if need be, [R]you have been
[T]grieved by various trials, James 1:2 • *distressed*
7 that the genuineness of your faith, *being*
much more precious than gold that perishes,
though [R]it is tested by fire, [R]may be found to
praise, honor, and glory at the revelation of
Jesus Christ, Job 23:10 • [Rom. 2:7]
8 [R]whom having not *seen you love.
[R]Though now you do not see *Him*, yet believing, you rejoice with joy inexpressible and
full of glory, 1 John 4:20 • John 20:29
9 receiving the end of your faith—the
salvation of *your* souls.

Anticipation in the Past

10 Of this salvation the prophets have inquired and searched diligently, who prophesied of the grace *that would come* to you,
11 searching what, or what manner of time,
[R]the Spirit of Christ who was in them was
indicating when He testified beforehand the
sufferings of Christ and the glories that
would follow. 2 Pet. 1:21
12 To them it was revealed that, not to
themselves, but to *us they were ministering
the things which now have been reported to
you through those who have preached the
gospel to you by the Holy Spirit sent from
heaven—things which [R]angels desire to look
into. Eph. 3:10

"Be Holy"

13 Therefore gird up the loins of your mind,
be sober, and rest *your* hope fully upon the
grace that is to be brought to you at the
revelation of Jesus Christ;
14 as obedient children, not [R]conforming
yourselves to the former lusts, *as* in your
ignorance; [Rom. 12:2]
15 [R]but as He who called you *is* holy, you
also be holy in all *your* conduct, [2 Cor. 7:1]

1:8 M *known* 1:12 NU, M *you*

SANCTIFICATION

Bible sanctification is a very basic and thorough-going work of grace. In the Old Testament, especially Leviticus, the Holy Spirit stresses the importance of holiness in everyday life. Peter quotes Leviticus 11:44, "Be holy, for I am holy," as crucial to a true Christian walk (1 Pet. 1:16).

Holy, Saint (*hagios*)

Holy, Saint (*hagios*) was a very rare word in classical Greek, but is an important part of the New Testament vocabulary. R. C. Trench defines *hagios* as follows: "Its fundamental idea is separation, and so to speak, consecration and devotion to the service of Deity" (*Synonyms of the New Testament*, pp. 309, 310).

The word is first used in the New Testament for the Holy Spirit (Matt. 1:18), and also many times after. We find "Holy Father" in John 17:11 and "Your holy Servant Jesus" in Acts 4:27. Because God is thrice holy Himself (Is. 6:3), He wants His people to be holy, too.

Sometimes the word *hagios* is used as a noun, and then it is translated "saint." In the New Testament, it is always plural (*hagioi*, "saints") in this sense. "Saint John" and "Saint Mary" are postbiblical expressions. For example, 2 Corinthians is addressed to "all the saints who are in all Achaia" (1:1). In New Testament times, all Christians were called saints. How can this be when we know of the very unsaintly goings-on at the Corinthian congregation? The answer is that sanctification has a positional, as well as a practical aspect. All believers are set apart by the Holy Spirit as soon as they believe. They become saints. That is *positional sanctification*. But these saints should also be constantly growing more holy in actual lifestyle. That is *practical* or *progressive sanctification*. There is also a *future, final sanctification* when we will be delivered from the very presence of sin.

When set apart for God's use, even things can be holy, such as "the holy city" (Matt. 4:5), "the holy place" (Matt. 24:15), "His holy covenant" (Luke 1:72), "a holy kiss" (1 Thess. 5:26), and "holy faith" (Jude 20).

Sanctify, Hallow (*hagiazō*)

Sanctify, hallow (*hagiazō*) is used twenty-eight times, always translated "sanctify," except in the Lord's Prayer (Matt. 6:9; Luke 11:2), where it is rendered "hallowed." The meaning "set apart" is especially prominent in the verb form. For example, when Paul wrote that "the unbelieving husband is sanctified by the wife, and the unbelieving wife is sanctified by the husband" (1 Cor. 7:14), he did not mean that the non-Christian spouse of a believer will definitely come to experience the sanctification that accompanies salvation. Rather, he or she is set apart by God with special privileges for the sake of the family. Often, of course, this does lead to salvation.

Holiness (*hagiōsynē*)

Holiness (*hagiōsynē*) is the abstract noun form of *hagios* and occurs three times, all in Paul's Epistles. Christ is "declared *to be* the Son of God with power, according to the Spirit of holiness" (Rom. 1:4), probably referring to the Holy Spirit. The Corinthians were urged to join Paul in practical sanctification, "perfecting holiness in the fear of God" (2 Cor. 7:1). Paul prayed that God would establish the Thessalonians' "hearts blameless in holiness" (1 Thess. 3:13).

Sanctification, Holiness (*hagiasmos*)

Sanctification, holiness (*hagiasmos*) is a similar word but stresses the "process, or more often, its result (the state of being made holy)" (Arndt, Gingrich, Danker, *A Greek-English Lexicon of the New Testament*, p. 9). It is a word unique to Christianity and is used ten times in the New Testament, eight times by Paul, once in Hebrews, and once by Peter.

Christ Himself is our sanctification (1 Cor. 1:30), and sanctification is God's will for us (1 Thess. 4:3). The great importance of being sanctified is clearly stated in Hebrews 12:14: "Pursue peace with all *men*, and holiness, without which no one will see the Lord."

16 because it is written, [R]*"Be holy, for I am
holy."* Lev. 11:44, 45; 19:2; 20:7
17 And if you call on the Father, who [R]with-
out partiality judges according to each one's
work, conduct yourselves throughout the
time of your sojourning *here* in fear; Acts 10:34
18 knowing that you were not [R]redeemed
with [T]corruptible things, *like* silver or gold,
from your aimless conduct *received* by tradition from your fathers, Is. 52:3 ★ • *perishable*
19 but [R]with the precious blood of Christ,
[R]as of a lamb without blemish and without
spot. Acts 20:28 • Ex. 12:5; Is. 53:7 ★
20 [R]He indeed was foreordained before the
foundation of the world, but was manifest [R]in
these last times for you Rom. 3:25 • Gal. 4:4
21 who through Him believe in God, [R]who
raised Him from the dead and [R]gave Him
glory, so that your faith and hope are in
God. Acts 2:24 • Acts 2:33

"Love One Another"

22 Since you [R]have purified your souls in
obeying the truth *through the Spirit in
sincere love of the brethren, love one another
fervently with a pure heart, Acts 15:9
23 having been born again, not of corruptible seed but incorruptible, through the word
of God which lives and abides *forever,
24 because

[R]*"All flesh is as grass,* Is. 40:6–8
*And all *the glory of man as the flower*
of the grass.
The grass withers,
And its flower falls away,
25 [R]*But the word of the LORD endures*
forever." Is. 40:8

[R]Now this is the word which by the gospel
was preached to you. [John 1:1]

CHAPTER 2

"Desire the Pure Milk of the Word"

THEREFORE, [R]laying aside all malice, all
guile, hypocrisy, envy, and all evil speaking, Heb. 12:1
2 as newborn babes, desire the pure milk of
the word, that you may grow *thereby,
3 if indeed you have [R]tasted that the Lord
is gracious. Heb. 6:5

"Offer Up Spiritual Sacrifices"

4 Coming to Him *as to* a living stone,
[R]rejected indeed by men, but chosen by God
and precious, Ps. 118:22
5 you also, as living stones, are being built
up a spiritual house, a holy priesthood, to
offer up spiritual sacrifices acceptable to God
through Jesus Christ.
6 Therefore it is also contained in the
Scripture,

[R]*"Behold, I lay in Zion*
A chief cornerstone, elect, precious,
And he who believes on Him will by no
means be put to shame." Is. 28:16 ★

7 Therefore, to you who believe, *He is*
precious; but to those who *are disobedient,

"The stone which the builders rejected
Has become the chief cornerstone,"

8 and

[R]*"A stone of stumbling*
And a rock of offense." Ps. 118:22; Is. 8:14 ★

They stumble, being disobedient to the word,
to which they also were appointed.
9 But you *are* a chosen generation, a royal
priesthood, a holy nation, His own special
people, that you may proclaim the praises of
Him who called you out of [R]darkness into His
marvelous light; [Acts 26:18]
10 who once *were* not a people but *are* now
the people of God, who had not obtained
mercy but now have obtained mercy.

"Abstain from Fleshly Lusts"

11 Beloved, I beg *you* as sojourners and
pilgrims, abstain from fleshly lusts [R]which
war against the soul, James 4:1
12 [R]having your conduct honorable among
the Gentiles, that when they speak against
you as evildoers, [R]they may, by *your* good
works which they observe, glorify God in the
day of visitation. Phil. 2:15 • Matt. 5:16; 9:8

Submission to the Government

13 Therefore submit yourselves to every
[T]ordinance of man for the Lord's sake,
whether to the king as supreme, *institution*

1:22 NU omits *through the Spirit*
1:23 NU omits *forever* **1:24** NU *its glory as*
2:2 NU adds *up to salvation* **2:7** NU *disbelieve*

2:13 Our Responsibility to Human Government—It is impossible for a believer to be a good Christian and a bad citizen at the same time. As children of God our responsibility to human government is threefold.

a. We are to recognize and accept that the powers that be are ordained by God. "Let every soul be subject to the governing authorities. For there is no authority except from God, and the authorities that exist are appointed by God" (Page 1337—Rom. 13:1). This truth applies even to atheistic human governments unless, of course, the law is anti-scriptural. In that situation the believer must obey God rather than man (Page 1276—Acts 4:18–20). In fact, when Paul wrote those words in Romans 13:1, the evil emperor Nero was on the throne. See also Titus 3:1.

(continued on next page)

14 or to governors, as to those who are sent
by him for the punishment of evildoers and
for the praise of those who do good.
15 For this is the will of God, that by doing
good you may put to silence the ignorance of
foolish men—
16 as free, yet not using *your* liberty as a
cloak for vice, but as servants of God.
17 Honor all *people*. Love the brotherhood.
Fear [R]God. Honor the king. Prov. 24:21

Submission in Business

18 [R]Servants, *be* submissive to *your* masters
with all fear, not only to the good and gentle,
but also to the harsh. Eph. 6:5–8
19 For this *is* [R]commendable, if because of
conscience toward God one endures grief,
suffering wrongfully. Matt. 5:10
20 For [R]what credit *is it* if, when you are
beaten for your faults, you take it patiently?
But when you do good and suffer *for it*, if you
take it patiently, this *is* commendable before
God. Luke 6:32–34
21 For to this you were called, because
Christ also suffered for *us, leaving *us an
example, that you should follow His steps:

22 *"Who[R] committed no sin,* Is. 53:9★
Nor was guile found in His mouth";

23 [R]who, when He was reviled, did not revile
in return; when He suffered, He did not
threaten, but [R]committed *Himself* to Him
who judges righteously; Is. 53:7★ • Luke 23:46
24 who Himself bore our sins in His own
body on the tree, that we, having died to sins,
might live for righteousness—[R]by whose
[T]stripes you were healed. Is. 53:5★ • *wounds*
25 For you were like sheep going astray, but
have now returned [R]to the Shepherd and
*Overseer of your souls. [Ezek. 34:23]; Zech. 13:7★

CHAPTER 3

Submission in Marriage

LIKEWISE *you* wives, *be* submissive to
your own husbands, that even if some do
not obey the word, they, without a word, may
be won by the conduct of their wives,
2 [R]when they observe your chaste conduct
accompanied by fear. 1 Pet. 2:12; 3:6
3 Do not let your beauty be that outward
adorning of arranging the hair, of wearing
gold, or of putting on *fine* apparel;
4 but *let it be* [R]the hidden person of the
heart, with the [T]incorruptible *ornament* of a
gentle and quiet spirit, which is very precious
in the sight of God. Rom. 2:29 • *imperishable*
5 For in this manner, in former times, the
holy women who trusted in God also adorned
themselves, being submissive to their own
husbands,
6 as Sarah obeyed Abraham, [R]calling him
lord, whose daughters you are if you do good
and are not afraid with any terror. Gen. 18:12

7 [R]Likewise *you* husbands, dwell with
them with understanding, giving honor to the
wife, as to the weaker vessel, and as *being*
heirs together of the grace of life, that your
prayers may not be hindered. [Eph. 5:25]
8 Finally, all of *you be* of one mind, having
compassion for one another; love as brothers,
be tenderhearted, *be* *courteous;

2:21 NU *you* **2:21** NU, M *you* **2:25** Gr. *Episkopon* **3:8** NU *humble*

(continued from previous page)

b. We are to pay our taxes to human government (see Page 1138—Matt. 17:24–27; 22:21; Page 1339—Rom. 13:7).
c. We are to pray for the leaders in human government. "Therefore I exhort first of all that supplications, prayers, intercessions, *and* giving of thanks be made for all men, for kings and all who are in authority, that we may lead a quiet and peaceable life in all godliness and reverence. For this *is* good and acceptable in the sight of God our Savior" (Page 1426—1 Tim. 2:1–3).

Paul exhorts us to pray for those who are in authority that we may lead a quiet life. We are to pray that they hold their offices in godliness and honesty (Page 1426—1 Tim. 2:1–3).

Now turn to Page 1017—Amos 3:2: Selection of Israel.

3:1–6 The Role of the Wife—This passage describes "subjection" to her husband as a fundamental responsibility of the married woman. (Other roles for women are covered in such passages as Prov. 31:10–31—Page 745 and Titus 2:3–5—Page 1440.) The wife is to submit to the authority of her husband, not to mankind in general. This does not mean the wife is by nature inferior to the husband. In marriage two people become one through the joining of their intellects, their emotions, and their wills. To keep their special union from fracturing and destroying itself, one member is charged to lead and one to submit.

The wife's submission to her husband is her "adorning," which makes her truly beautiful (3:3). This inner beauty is of great value in God's sight (3:4). The believing women of the Old Testament who hoped to be the human channel for the Messiah to come into the world made themselves beautiful by being in subjection to their own husbands. This is supremely illustrated in the relationship between Sarah and Abraham. Wives are exhorted to do what Sarah did, to be in subjection to their husbands, letting the consequences rest with God, and thus become Sarah's daughters (3:6). For the wife who will do this God promises that, if her husband is either an unbeliever or out of fellowship with God, her subjection can be the very means God will use to bring her husband into a proper relationship with God (3:1, 2). The wife's subjection may lead to the husband's salvation.

Now turn to Page 1409—Col. 3:19: The Role of the Husband.

Submission in All of Life

9 [R]not returning evil for evil or reviling for
reviling, but on the contrary [R]blessing, knowing that you were called to this, that you may
inherit a blessing. [Prov. 17:13] • Matt. 5:44
10 For

[R]*"He who would love life* Ps. 34:12–16
And see good days,
Let him refrain his tongue from evil,
And his lips from speaking [T]*guile;* deceit
11 *Let him* [R]*turn away from evil and do*
good; Ps. 37:27
Let him seek peace and pursue it.
12 *For the eyes of the* LORD *are on the*
righteous,
[R]*And his ears are open to their prayers;*
But the face of the LORD *is against*
those who do evil." John 9:31

Conduct in Suffering

13 [R]And who *is* he who will harm you if you
become followers of what is good? Prov. 16:7
14 [R]But even if you should suffer for righteousness' sake, *you are* blessed. [R]*"And do*
not be afraid of their threats, nor be trou-
bled." James 1:12 • Is. 8:12
15 But sanctify *the Lord God in your
hearts, and always *be* ready to *give* a defense
to everyone who asks you a reason for the
hope that is in you, with meekness and fear;
16 [R]having a good conscience, that when
they defame you as evildoers, those who
revile your good conduct in Christ may be
ashamed. Heb. 13:18

17 For *it is* better, if it is the will of God, to
suffer for doing good than for doing evil.

Christ's Example of Suffering

18 For Christ also suffered once for sins, the
just for the unjust, that He might bring *us to
God, being put to death in the flesh but made
alive by the Spirit,
19 by whom also He went and preached to
the spirits in prison,
20 who formerly were disobedient, when
once the longsuffering of God *waited in the
days of Noah, while *the* ark was being prepared, in which a few, that is, eight souls,
were saved through water.
21 There is also an antitype which now
saves us, *namely* baptism (not the removal of
the filth of the flesh, [R]but the answer of a
good conscience toward God), through the
resurrection of Jesus Christ, [Rom. 10:10]
22 who has gone into heaven and [R]is at the
right hand of God, [R]angels and authorities
and powers having been made subject to
Him. Ps. 110:1 • Rom. 8:38

CHAPTER 4

THEREFORE, since Christ suffered *for us
in the flesh, arm yourselves also with the
same mind, for he who has suffered in the
flesh has ceased from sin,
2 that he no longer should live the rest of
his time in the flesh for the lusts of men, [R]but
for the will of God. John 1:13
3 For we *have spent* enough of our past
*lifetime in doing the will of the Gentiles—
when we walked in licentiousness, lusts,
drunkenness, revelries, drinking parties, and
abominable idolatries.
4 In regard to these, they think it strange
that you do not run with *them* in the same
flood of dissipation, speaking evil of *you.*
5 They will give an account to Him who is
ready to judge the living and the dead.
6 For this reason the gospel was preached
also to those who are dead, that they might
be judged according to men in the flesh, but
[R]live according to God in the spirit. [Rom. 8:9, 13]

Commands in Suffering

7 But [R]the end of all things is at hand;
therefore be serious and watchful in your
prayers. Rom. 13:11

3:15 NU *Christ as Lord* **3:18** NU, M *you*
3:20 NU, M *waited patiently* **4:1** NU omits *for us*
4:3 NU *time*

3:17 Kinds of Suffering—There are three basic kinds of suffering, all of which can bring about much pain and discomfort to the believer.

a. Physical suffering. This, of course, occurs when a part of our body is injured or begins to malfunction, resulting in a disharmony between it and the rest of the body. Several factors can be involved in physical suffering. It can be caused by an accident or by carelessness (Page 363—2 Sam. 4:4). It can be due to birth deformities (Page 1250—John 9:1). It can result from internal disorders (Page 1206—Luke 8:43). Finally, physical suffering may actually be caused by Satan (Page 590—Job 2:7; Page 1216—Luke 13:16).

b. Mental suffering. In many ways this suffering is even more intense than physical suffering. Justified or unjustified concern over some matter can easily produce mental anguish. Paul himself experienced "fear and trembling" and "anguish of heart" (Page 1346—1 Cor. 2:3; Page 1366—2 Cor. 1:8; 2:4, 13; 7:5).

c. Spiritual suffering. Spiritual suffering can come from the world (Page 1496—1 John 2:15–17), the flesh (Page 1332—Rom. 7:18–24), or the devil. Often it is the latter. See Acts 13:8–11; 16:16–18; First Thessalonians 2:18.

Now turn to Page 590—Job 2:7: Purposes of Suffering.

CHRIST, THE ANOINTED ONE

Anoint (*chriō*)

The verb from which the following word studies are derived means "to pour oil on" or "anoint," and is used five times in the New Testament. Twice it appears in a quotation from an Old Testament passage, in which the original Hebrew has the word *māshah,* whence "Messiah" (see the word study on p. 990). Our Lord read Isaiah 61:1 in His hometown synagogue: "He has anointed Me to preach the gospel to *the* poor" (Luke 4:18). In his long chain of Old Testament quotations in chapter 1, the author of Hebrews includes the address of the Father to the Son: "Therefore God, Your God, has anointed You with the oil of gladness more than Your companions" (Heb. 1:9). Two of the other uses deal with God's anointing Jesus as His Servant (Acts 4:27) and with the Holy Spirit and power (Acts 10:38) in Peter's sermon at Cornelius's house. Paul only uses the word once in all his thirteen letters, and there with regard to Christians: "He who… has anointed us *is* God, who also has sealed us and given us the Spirit in our hearts as a deposit" (2 Cor. 1:21, 22).

Christ (*Christos*)

The Messiah, or Anointed One, is so called in the New Testament only twice—once by the early disciples (John 1:41) and once by the woman of Samaria (John 4:25). We begin to feel the impact of the title "Christ" on the original audiences if we sometimes substitute the word "Messiah" for "Christ" when we read passages with Jewish connotations. Saying "Jesus Christ" is the same as saying, "Yeshua of Nazareth is the Messiah," anointed by God to be the Savior of the world.

Antichrist (*Antichristos*)

The apostle John used this very negative title five times in his first two epistles. He is the only New Testament writer to use the word and may well have coined it. English has taken over one of the main meanings of the Greek preposition *anti-,* namely, "against." The Antichrist (and the "many antichrists" that John warns us of in 1 John 2:18) is definitely against Jesus as the Messiah. But a second meaning of *anti-* in Greek is "instead of" or "in place of." The historical figure predicted in the Bible who will appear on the scene to oppose our Lord and His Kingdom will also be trying to take Christ's rightful place as anointed deliverer.

Anointing, Unction, "Chrism" (*chrisma*)

The word *chrisma* is not an active noun, but means "the result of being anointed." It is used only three times and all by John in his first epistle. After mentioning the deceiving Antichrist and the many antichrists in 2:18, John gives as an antidote to antichrist delusions the anointing that Christians have "from the Holy One" (v. 20). This unction abiding in us teaches us all the truth that we need to know to withstand error (vv. 26, 27).

Christian (*Christianos*)

In the original Greek and in precise translations, "Christian" occurs only three times.

We do not often have an authoritative history of the origin of a word. However, in Acts 11:26, we have the inspired record of the Antiochians coining the word *Christian.* Antiochians were witty, worldly, and rather wicked. There is no reason to believe that they were being complimentary when they used the term *Christian* to describe followers of Jesus. It was no doubt like *Quaker* or *Methodist*—a term of reproach, which became a badge of honor.

Second, "Christian" is used in an evangelistic context, Paul witnessing to the Jewish ruler Agrippa (Acts 26:28). Whether "almost persuaded" to be a Christian is a sincere remark or (as many think) a cynical one is not certain. At any rate, *Christian* was by then becoming the standard word to describe those who follow Jesus as their Messiah.

Third, suffering and Christianity were closely related in the early church and still are in many countries. Hence, Peter tells believers that there is no shame in suffering as a Christian, but it is a shame to suffer for wrongdoing (1 Pet. 4:16).

8 And above all things have fervent love
for one another, for [R]*"love will cover a multitude of sins."* [Prov. 10:12]
9 [R]*Be* hospitable to one another [R]without
grumbling. Heb. 13:2 • 2 Cor. 9:7
10 [R]As each one has received a gift, minister
it to one another, as good stewards of [R]the
manifold grace of God. Rom. 12:6–8 • [1 Cor. 12:4]
11 [R]If anyone speaks, *let him speak* as [T]the
oracles of God. If anyone ministers, *let him
do it* as with the ability which God supplies,
that in all things God may be glorified
through Jesus Christ, to whom belong the
glory and the [T]dominion forever and ever.
Amen. Eph. 4:29 • *utterances* • *sovereignty*
12 Beloved, do not think it strange concerning the fiery trial which is to try you, as
though some strange thing happened to you;
13 but rejoice [R]to the extent that you partake of Christ's sufferings, that [R]when His
glory is revealed, you may also be glad with
exceeding joy. James 1:2 • 2 Tim. 2:12
14 If you are [T]reproached for the name of
Christ, [R]blessed *are you*, for the Spirit of glory
and of God rests upon you. *On their part He
is blasphemed, [R]but on your part He is glorified. *insulted* or *reviled* • Matt. 5:11 • Matt. 5:16
15 But let none of you suffer as a murderer,
a thief, an evildoer, or as a [T]busybody in other
people's matters. *meddler*
16 Yet if *anyone suffers* as a Christian, let
him not be ashamed, but let him glorify God
in this *matter.
17 For the time *has come* [R]for judgment to
begin at the house of God; and if *it begins*
with us first, what will *be* the end of those
who do not obey the gospel of God? Is. 10:12
18 Now

[R]*"If the righteous one is scarcely saved,*
Where will the ungodly and the sinner
appear?" Prov. 11:31

19 Therefore let those who suffer according
to the will of God commit their souls *to Him*
in doing good, as to a faithful Creator.

CHAPTER 5

Elders, Shepherd the Flock

THE elders who are among you I exhort, I
who am a fellow elder and a [R]witness of
the sufferings of Christ, and also a partaker of
the glory that will be revealed: Matt. 26:37
2 [R]Shepherd the flock of God which is
among you, serving as overseers, [R]not by
[T]constraint but *willingly, not for dishonest
gain but eagerly; Acts 20:28 • 1 Cor. 9:17 • *compulsion*
3 nor as [R]being [T]lords over [R]those entrusted to you, but [R]being examples to the
flock; Ezek. 34:4 • *masters* • Ps. 33:12 • Phil. 3:17
4 and when [R]the Chief Shepherd appears,
you will receive [R]the crown of glory that does
not fade away. Heb. 13:20 • 2 Tim. 4:8

Saints, Humble Yourselves

5 Likewise you younger people, submit
yourselves to *your* elders. Yes, [R]all of *you* be
submissive to one another, and be clothed
with humility, for Eph. 5:21

[R]*"God resists the proud,* Prov. 3:34
But [R]*gives grace to the humble."* Is. 57:15

6 Therefore humble yourselves under the
mighty hand of God, that He may exalt you
in due time,
7 casting all your care upon Him, for He
cares for you.
8 Be sober, be [T]vigilant; *because your
adversary the devil walks about like a roaring
lion, seeking whom he may devour. *watchful*
9 Resist him, steadfast in the faith, knowing that the same sufferings are experienced
by your brotherhood in the world.

Benediction

10 But *may the God of all grace, [R]who
called *us to His eternal glory by Christ
Jesus, after you have suffered a while,
*perfect, establish, strengthen, and settle
you. 1 Cor. 1:9
11 [R]To Him *be* the glory and the dominion
forever and ever. Amen. Rev. 1:6
12 By Silvanus, our faithful brother as I
consider him, I have written to you briefly,
exhorting and testifying [R]that this is the true
grace of God in which you stand. Acts 20:24
13 She who is in Babylon, elect together
with *you*, greets you; and *so does* [R]Mark my
son. Acts 12:12, 25; 15:37, 39
14 Greet one another with a kiss of love.
Peace to you all who are in Christ Jesus.
Amen.

4:14 NU omits the rest of v. 14. **4:16** NU *name*
5:2 NU adds *according to God*
5:8 NU, M omit *because*
5:10 NU *the God of all Grace*
5:10 NU, M *you* **5:10** NU *will perfect*

THE SECOND EPISTLE OF

PETER

THE BOOK OF SECOND PETER

First Peter deals with problems from the outside; Second Peter deals with problems from the inside. Peter writes to warn the believers about the false teachers who are peddling damaging doctrine. He begins by urging them to keep close watch on their personal lives. The Christian life demands diligence in pursuing moral excellence, knowledge, self-control, perseverance, godliness, brotherly kindness, and selfless love. By contrast, the false teachers are sensual, arrogant, greedy, and covetous. They scoff at the thought of future judgment and live their lives as if the present would be the pattern for the future. Peter reminds them that although God may be longsuffering in sending judgment, ultimately it will come. In view of that fact, believers should live lives of godliness, blamelessness, and steadfastness.

The statement of authorship in 1:1 is very clear: "Simon Peter, a servant and apostle of Jesus Christ." To distinguish this epistle from the first by Peter it was given the Greek title *Petrou B*, "Second of Peter."

THE AUTHOR OF SECOND PETER

No other book in the New Testament poses as many problems of authenticity as does Second Peter. Unlike First Peter, this letter has very weak external testimony, and its genuineness is hurt by internal difficulties as well. Because of these obstacles, many scholars reject the Petrine authorship of this epistle, but this does not mean that there is no case for the opposite position.

External Evidence: The external testimony for the Petrine authorship of Second Peter is weaker than that for any other New Testament book, but by the fourth century it became generally recognized as an authentic work of the apostle Peter. There are no undisputed second-century quotations from Second Peter, but in the third century it is quoted in the writings of several church fathers, notably Origen and Clement of Alexandria. Third-century writers were generally aware of Second Peter and respected its contents, but it was still cataloged as a disputed book. The fourth century saw the official acknowledgment of the authority of Second Peter in spite of some lingering doubts. For several reasons Second Peter was not quickly accepted as a canonical book: (1) Slow circulation kept it from being widely known. (2) Its brevity and contents greatly limited the number of quotations from it in the writings of early church leaders. (3) The delay in recognition meant that Second Peter had to compete with several later works which falsely claimed to be Petrine (e.g., the Apocalypse of Peter). (4) Stylistic differences between First and Second Peter also raised doubts.

Internal Evidence: On the positive side, Second Peter bears abundant testimony to its apostolic origin. It claims to be by "Simon Peter" (1:1), and 3:1 says "Beloved, I now write to you this second epistle." The writer refers to the Lord's prediction about the apostle's death in 1:14 (cf. John 21:18, 19) and says he was an eyewitness of the Transfiguration (1:16–18). As an apostle (1:1), he places himself on an equal level with Paul (3:15). There are also distinctive words that are found in Second Peter and in Peter's sermons in Acts, as well as unusual words and phrases shared by First and Second Peter.

On the negative side, a number of troublesome areas challenge the traditional position: (1) There are differences between the style and vocabulary of First and Second Peter. The Greek of Second Peter is rough and awkward compared to that of First Peter, and there are also differences in informality and in the use of the Old Testament. But these differences are often exaggerated, and they can be explained by Peter's use of Silvanus as his secretary for First Peter and his own hand for Second Peter. (2) It is argued that Second Peter used a passage from Jude to describe false teachers, and that Jude was written after Peter's death. However, this is a debated issue, and it is possible that Jude quoted from Peter or that both used a common source (see "The Author of Jude"). (3) The reference to a collection of Paul's letters (3:15, 16) implies a late date for this epistle. But it is not necessary to conclude that all of Paul's letters were in mind here. Peter's contact with Paul and his associates no doubt made him familiar with several Pauline epistles. (4) Some scholars claim that the false teaching mentioned in Second Peter was a form of Gnosticism that emerged after Peter's day, but there is insufficient evidence to support this stand.

The alternative to Petrine authorship is a later forgery done in the name of Peter. Even the claim that Second Peter was written by a disciple of Peter cannot overcome the problem of misrepresentation. In addition Second Peter is clearly superior to any pseudonymous writings. In spite of the external and internal problems, the traditional position of Petrine authorship overcomes more difficulties than any other option.

THE TIME OF SECOND PETER

Most scholars regard 3:1 ("Beloved, I now write to you this second epistle") as a reference to First Peter. If this is so, Peter had the same readers of Asia Minor in mind (see "The Time of First Peter"), although the more general salutation in 1:1 would also allow for a wider audience. Peter wrote this epistle in response to the spread of heretical teachings which were all the more insidious because they emerged from within the churches. These false teachers perverted the doctrine of justification and promoted a rebellious and immoral way of life.

This epistle was written just before the apostle's death (1:14), probably from Rome. His martyrdom took place between A.D. 64 and 66 (if Peter were alive in 67 when Paul wrote Second Timothy during his second Roman imprisonment, it is likely that Paul would have mentioned him).

THE CHRIST OF SECOND PETER

Apart from the first verse of his epistle, Peter employs the title *Lord* every time he names the Savior. The Lord Jesus Christ is the source of full knowledge and power for the attainment of spiritual maturity (1:2, 3, 8; 3:18). Peter recalls the glory of His transfiguration on the holy mountain and anticipates His *parousia*, "coming," when the whole world, not just three men on a mountain, will behold His glory.

KEYS TO SECOND PETER

Key Word: Guard Against False Teachers—The basic theme that runs through Second Peter is the contrast between the knowledge and practice of truth versus falsehood. This epistle is written to expose the dangerous and seductive work of false teachers, and to warn believers to be on their guard so that they will not be "led away with the error of the wicked" (3:17). It is also written to exhort the readers to "grow in the grace and knowledge of our Lord and Savior Jesus Christ" (3:18), because this growth into Christian maturity is the best defense against spiritual counterfeits. This letter serves to remind its readers of the foundational elements in the Christian life from which they must not waver (1:12, 13; 3:1, 2). This includes the certainty of the Lord's return in power and judgment.

Key Verses: Second Peter 1:20, 21 and 3:9–11—"Knowing this first, that no prophecy of Scripture is of any private interpretation, for prophecy never came by the will of man, but holy men of God spoke *as they were* moved by the Holy Spirit" (1:20, 21).

"The Lord is not slack concerning *His* promise, as some count slackness, but is longsuffering toward us, not willing that any should perish but that all should come to repentance. But the day of the Lord will come as a thief in the night, in which the heavens will pass away with a great noise, and the elements will melt with fervent heat; both the earth and the works that are in it will be burned up. Therefore, since all these things will be dissolved, what manner *of persons* ought you to be in holy conduct and godliness" (3:9–11).

Key Chapter: Second Peter 1—The Scripture clearest in defining the relationship between God and man on the issue of inspiration is contained in 1:19–21. Three distinct principles surface: (1) that the interpretation of Scriptures is not limited to a favored elect but is open for all who "rightly [divide] the word of truth" (2 Tim. 2:15); (2) that the divinely inspired prophet did not initiate the Scripture himself; and (3) that the Holy Spirit (not the emotion or circumstances of the moment) moved holy men.

SURVEY OF SECOND PETER

Peter wrote his first epistle to encourage his readers to respond properly to external opposition. His second epistle focuses on internal opposition caused by false teachers whose "destructive heresies" (2:1) can seduce believers into error and immorality. While First Peter speaks of the new birth through the living Word, Second Peter stresses the need for growth in the grace and knowledge of Christ. The best antidote for error is a mature understanding of the truth. Second Peter divides into three parts: cultivation of Christian character (1); condemnation of false teachers (2); and confidence of Christ's return (3).

Cultivation of Christian Character (1): Peter's salutation (1:1, 2) is an introduction to the major theme of chapter 1, that is, the true knowledge of Jesus Christ. The readers are reminded of the "great and precious promises" that are theirs because of their calling to faith in Christ (1:3, 4). They have been called away from the corruption of the world to conformity with Christ, and Peter urges them to progress by forging a chain of eight Christian virtues from faith to love (1:5–7). If a believer does not transform profession into practice, he becomes spiritually useless, perverting the purpose for which he was called (1:8–11).

This letter was written not long before Peter's death (1:14) to remind believers of the riches of their position in Christ and their responsibility to hold fast to the truth (1:12–21). Peter knew that his departure from this earth was imminent, and he left this letter as a written legacy. As an eyewitness of the life of Christ (he illustrates this with a portrait of the Transfiguration in 1:16–18), Peter affirms the authority and reliability of the prophetic word. The clearest biblical description of the divine-human process of inspiration is found in 1:21: "but holy men of God spoke *as they were* moved by the Holy Spirit."

Condemnation of False Teachers (2): Peter's discussion of true prophecy leads him to an extended denunciation of false prophecy in the churches. These false teachers were especially dangerous because they arose within the church and undermined the confidence of believers (2:1–3). Peter's extended description of the characteristics of these false teachers (2:10–22) exposes the futility and corruption of their strategies. Their teachings and life-styles reek of arrogance and selfishness, but their crafty words are capable of enticing immature believers.

Confidence of Christ's Return (3): Again Peter states that this letter is designed to stir up the minds of his readers "by way of reminder" (3:1; cf. 1:13). This very timely chapter is designed to remind them of the certain truth of the imminent *parousia* (this Greek word, used in 3:4, 12, refers to the second coming or advent of Christ) and to refute those mockers who will deny this doctrine in the last days. These scoffers will claim that God does not powerfully intervene in world affairs, but Peter calls attention to two past and one future divinely induced catastrophic events: the Creation, the Flood, and the dissolution of the present heavens and earth (3:1–7). It may appear that the promise of Christ's return will not be fulfilled, but this is untrue for two reasons: God's perspective on the passing of time is quite unlike that of men, and the apparent delay in the *parousia* is due to His patience in waiting for more individuals to come to a knowledge of Christ (3:8, 9). Nevertheless, the day of consummation will come, and all the matter of this universe will evidently be transformed into energy from which God will fashion a new cosmos (3:10–13).

In light of this coming day of the Lord, Peter exhorts his readers to live lives of holiness, steadfastness, and growth (3:14–18). He mentions the letters of "our beloved brother Paul" and significantly places them on a level with the Old Testament Scriptures (3:15, 16). After a final warning about the danger of false teachers, the epistle closes with an appeal to growth, and a doxology.

FOCUS	CULTIVATION OF CHRISTIAN CHARACTER		CONDEMNATION OF FALSE TEACHERS			CONFIDENCE IN CHRIST'S RETURN	
REFERENCE	1:1	1:15	2:1	2:4	2:10	3:1	3:8 — 3:18
DIVISION	GROWTH IN CHRIST	GROUNDS OF BELIEF	DANGER	DESTRUCTION	DESCRIPTION	MOCKERY IN THE LAST DAYS	DAY OF THE LORD
TOPIC	TRUE PROPHECY		FALSE PROPHETS			PROPHECY: DAY OF THE LORD	
	HOLINESS		HERESY			HOPE	
LOCATION	PROBABLY ROME						
TIME	c. A.D. 64–66						

OUTLINE OF SECOND PETER

I. Cultivation of Christian Character 1:1–21
- A. Salutation 1:1, 2
- B. Growth in Christ 1:3–14
- C. Grounds of Belief 1:15–21
  - 1. Experience of the Transfiguration 1:15–18
  - 2. Certainty of the Scriptures 1:19–21

II. Condemnation of False Teachers 2:1–22
- A. Danger of False Teachers 2:1–3
- B. Destruction of False Teachers 2:4–9
- C. Description of False Teachers 2:10–22

III. Confidence of Christ's Return 3:1–18
- A. Mockery in the Last Days 3:1–7
- B. Manifestation of the Day of the Lord 3:8–10
- C. Maturity in View of the Day of the Lord 3:11–18

CHAPTER 1

Salutation

SIMON PETER, a servant and [R]apostle of Jesus Christ, Gal. 2:8

To those who have [T]obtained like precious faith with us by the righteousness of our God and Savior Jesus Christ: *received*

2 Grace and peace be multiplied to you in the knowledge of God and of Jesus our Lord,

Growth in Christ

3 as His [R]divine power has given to us all things that *pertain* to life and godliness, through the knowledge of Him [R]who called us by glory and virtue, 1 Pet. 1:5 • 1 Thess. 2:12

4 by which have been given to us exceedingly great and precious promises, that through these you may be partakers of the divine nature, having escaped the [T]corruption *that is* in the world through lust. *depravity*

5 But also for this very reason, [R]giving all diligence, add to your faith virtue, to virtue [R]knowledge, 2 Pet. 3:18 • 1 Pet. 3:7

6 to knowledge self-control, to self-control perseverance, to perseverance godliness,

7 to godliness brotherly kindness, and [R]to brotherly kindness love. Gal. 6:10

8 For if these things are yours and abound, *you will be* neither barren nor unfruitful in the knowledge of our Lord Jesus Christ.

9 For he who lacks these things is shortsighted, even to blindness, and has forgotten that he was purged from his old sins.

10 Therefore, brethren, be even more diligent [R]to make your calling and election sure, for if you do these things you will never stumble; 1 John 3:19

11 for so an entrance will be supplied to you abundantly into the everlasting kingdom of our Lord and Savior Jesus Christ.

12 Therefore [R]I will not be negligent to remind you always of these things, [R]though you know *them*, and *are* established in the present truth. Phil. 3:1 • 1 Pet. 5:12

13 Yes, I think it is right, as long as I am in this tent, to stir you up by reminding *you*,

14 [R]knowing that shortly I *must* [T]put off my tent, just as our Lord Jesus Christ showed me. [2 Tim. 4:6] • Die and leave this body

Experience of the Transfiguration
Matt. 17:5; Mark 9:7; Luke 9:35

15 Moreover I will be careful to ensure that you always have a reminder of these things after my [T]decease. Lit. *exodus, departure*

16 For we did not follow cunningly devised fables when we made known to you the power and coming of our Lord Jesus Christ, but were eyewitnesses of His majesty.

17 For He received from God the Father honor and glory when such a voice came to Him from the Excellent Glory: "This is My beloved Son, in whom I am well pleased."

18 And we heard this voice which came from heaven when we were with Him on [R]the holy mountain. Matt. 17:1

Certainty of the Scriptures

19 We also have the prophetic word [T]made more sure, which you do well to heed as a [R]light that shines in a dark place, until the day dawns and the morning star rises in your hearts; Or *which is even more sure than this* • [John 1:4, 5, 9]

20 knowing this first, that no prophecy of Scripture is of any private interpretation,

21 for [R]prophecy never came by the will of man, but *holy men of God spoke *as they were* moved by the Holy Spirit. [2 Tim. 3:16]

CHAPTER 2

Danger of False Teachers

BUT there were also false prophets among the people, even as there will be [R]false teachers among you, who will secretly bring in destructive heresies, even denying the Lord who bought them, *and* bring on themselves swift destruction. 1 Tim. 4:1, 2

2 And many will follow their destructive ways, because of whom the way of truth will be blasphemed.

3 By covetousness they will exploit you with deceptive words; for a long time their judgment has not been idle, and their destruction *does not slumber.

Destruction of False Teachers

4 For if God did not spare the angels who sinned, but cast *them* down to [T]hell and delivered *them* into chains of darkness, to be reserved for judgment; Lit. *Tartarus*

5 and did not spare the ancient world, but saved Noah, *one of* eight *people*, a preacher of righteousness, bringing in the flood on the world of the ungodly;

6 and turning the cities of Sodom and Gomorrah into ashes, condemned *them* to destruction, making *them* an example to those who afterward would live ungodly;

7 and [R]delivered righteous Lot, *who was* oppressed with the filthy conduct of the wicked Gen. 19:16, 29

8 (for that righteous man, dwelling among them, [R]tormented *his* righteous soul from day to day by seeing and hearing *their* lawless deeds)— Ps. 119:139

9 *then* [R]the Lord knows how to deliver the godly out of temptations and to reserve the unjust under punishment for the day of judgment, Ps. 34:15–19

1:21 NU *men spoke from God* **2:3** M *will not*

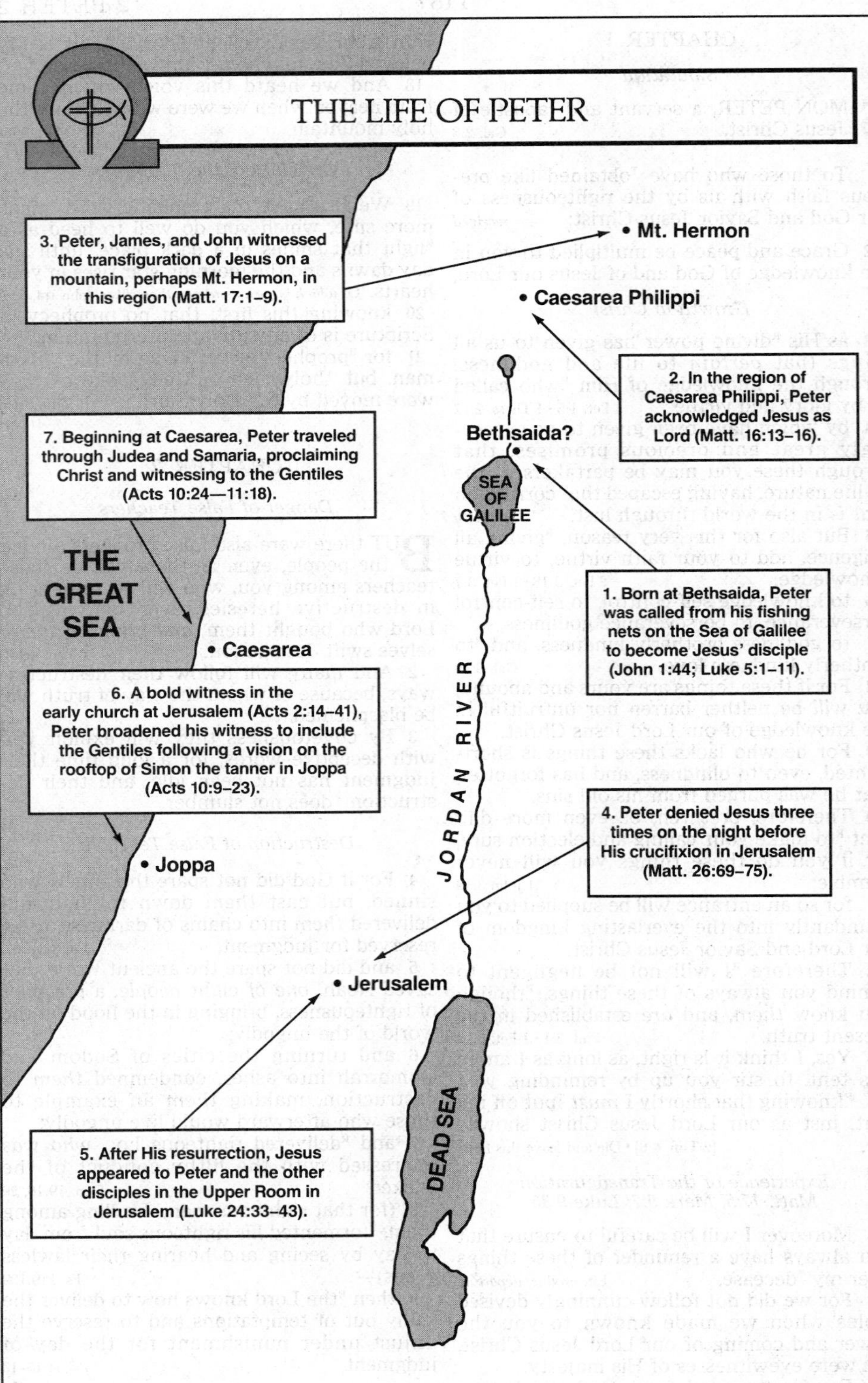

THE LIFE OF PETER
3. Peter, James, and John witnessed the transfiguration of Jesus on a mountain, perhaps Mt. Hermon, in this region (Matt. 17:1–9).
Mt. Hermon
Caesarea Philippi
2. In the region of Caesarea Philippi, Peter acknowledged Jesus as Lord (Matt. 16:13–16).
7. Beginning at Caesarea, Peter traveled through Judea and Samaria, proclaiming Christ and witnessing to the Gentiles (Acts 10:24—11:18).
Bethsaida?
SEA OF GALILEE
THE GREAT SEA
1. Born at Bethsaida, Peter was called from his fishing nets on the Sea of Galilee to become Jesus' disciple (John 1:44; Luke 5:1–11).
Caesarea
6. A bold witness in the early church at Jerusalem (Acts 2:14–41), Peter broadened his witness to include the Gentiles following a vision on the rooftop of Simon the tanner in Joppa (Acts 10:9–23).
JORDAN RIVER
4. Peter denied Jesus three times on the night before His crucifixion in Jerusalem (Matt. 26:69–75).
Joppa
Jerusalem
DEAD SEA
5. After His resurrection, Jesus appeared to Peter and the other disciples in the Upper Room in Jerusalem (Luke 24:33–43).

Description of False Teachers

10 and especially [R]those who walk according to the flesh in the lust of uncleanness and despise authority. [R]*They are* presumptuous, self-willed; they are not afraid to speak evil of [T]dignitaries, Jude 4, 7, 8 • Jude 8 • *glorious ones*, lit. *glories*

11 whereas angels, who are greater in power and might, do not bring a reviling accusation against them before the Lord.

12 But these, [R]like natural brute beasts made to be caught and destroyed, speak evil of the things they do not understand, and will utterly perish in their own corruption, Jude 10

13 *and* will receive the wages of unrighteousness, *as* those who count it pleasure to [T]carouse in the daytime. *They are* spots and blemishes, [T]carousing in their own deceptions while they feast with you, *revel* • *reveling*

14 having eyes full of adultery and that cannot cease from sin, [T]beguiling unstable souls. *They have* a heart trained in covetous practices, *and are* accursed children. *enticing*

15 They have forsaken the right way and gone astray, following the way of [R]Balaam the *son* of Beor, who loved the wages of unrighteousness; Num. 22:5, 7

16 but he was rebuked for his iniquity: a dumb donkey speaking with a man's voice restrained the madness of the prophet.

17 [R]These are wells without water, *clouds carried by a tempest, to whom the gloom of darkness is reserved *forever. Jude 12, 13

18 For when they speak great swelling *words* of emptiness, they allure through the lusts of the flesh, through licentiousness, the ones who *have actually escaped from those who live in error.

19 While they promise them liberty, they themselves are slaves of [T]corruption; [R]for by whom a person is overcome, by him also he is brought into [T]bondage. *depravity* • John 8:34 • *slavery*

20 For if, after they [R]have escaped the pollutions of the world through the knowledge of the Lord and Savior Jesus Christ, they are [R]again entangled in them and overcome, the latter end is worse for them than the beginning. Matt. 12:45 • [Heb. 6:4–6]

21 For [R]it would have been better for them not to have known the way of righteousness, than having known *it*, to turn from the holy commandment delivered to them. Luke 12:47

22 But it has happened to them according to the true proverb: [R]*"A dog returns to his own vomit,"* and, "a sow, having washed, to her wallowing in the mire." Prov. 26:11

CHAPTER 3

Mockery in the Last Days

BELOVED, I now write to you this second epistle (in *both of* which [R]I stir up your pure minds by way of reminder), 2 Pet. 1:13

2 that you may be mindful of the words which were spoken before by the holy prophets, [R]and of the commandment of *us the apostles of the Lord and Savior, Jude 17

3 knowing this first: that scoffers will come in the last days, [R]walking according to their own lusts, 2 Pet. 2:10

4 and saying, "Where is the promise of His coming? For since the fathers fell asleep, all things continue as *they were* from the beginning of [R]creation." Gen. 6:1–7

5 For this they willfully forget: that by the word of God the heavens were of old, and the earth standing out of water and in the water,

6 [R]by which the world *that* then existed perished, being flooded with water. Gen. 7:11

7 But the heavens and the earth *which* now *exist* are kept in store by the same word, reserved for fire until the day of judgment and [T]perdition of ungodly men. *destruction*

Manifestation of the Day of the Lord

8 But, beloved, do not forget this one thing, that with the Lord one day *is* as a thousand years, and [R]a thousand years as one day. Ps. 90:4

9 The Lord is not slack concerning *His* promise, as some count slackness, but [R]is longsuffering toward *us, [R]not willing that any should perish but [R]that all should come to repentance. Is. 30:18 • Ezek. 33:11 • [Rom. 2:4]

10 But [R]the day of the Lord will come as a thief in the night, in which [R]the heavens will pass away with a great noise, and the elements will melt with fervent heat; both the earth and the works that are in it will be *burned up. Matt. 24:43 ☆ • Ps. 102:25, 26

Maturity in View of the Day of the Lord

11 Therefore, since all these things will be dissolved, what manner *of persons* ought you to be [R]in holy conduct and godliness, 1 Pet. 1:15

12 looking for and hastening the coming of the day of God, because of which the heavens will be dissolved being on fire, and the elements will melt with fervent heat?

13 Nevertheless we, according to His promise, look for new heavens and a [R]new earth in which righteousness dwells. Rev. 21:1

14 Therefore, beloved, looking forward to these things, be diligent to be found by Him in peace, without spot and blameless;

15 and account *that* [R]the longsuffering of our Lord *is* salvation—as also our beloved brother Paul, according to the wisdom given to him, has written to you, Rom. 2:4

16 as also in all his [R]epistles, speaking in

2:17 NU *and mists* **2:17** NU omits *forever*
2:18 NU *are barely escaping*
3:2 NU, M *the apostles of your Lord and Savior* or *your apostles of the Lord and Savior* **3:9** NU *you*
3:10 NU *laid bare*, lit. *found*

them of these things, in which are some
things hard to understand, which those *who*
are untaught and unstable twist to their own
destruction, as *they do* also the [R]rest of the
Scriptures. 1 Cor. 15:24 • 2 Tim. 3:16
17 You therefore, beloved, since you know
these things beforehand, beware lest you also
fall from your own steadfastness, being led
away with the error of the wicked;
18 but grow in the grace and knowledge of
our Lord and Savior Jesus Christ. To Him *be*
the glory both now and forever. Amen.

THE FIRST EPISTLE OF

JOHN

THE BOOK OF FIRST JOHN

God is light; God is love; and God is life. John is enjoying a delightful fellowship with that God of light, love, and life, and he desperately desires that his spiritual children enjoy the same fellowship.

God is light. Therefore, to engage in fellowship with Him we must walk in light and not in darkness. As we walk in the light, we will regularly confess our sins, allowing the blood of Christ to continually cleanse us. Christ will act as our defense attorney before the Father. Proof of our "walk in the light" will be keeping the commandments of God and replacing any hatred we have toward our brother with love. Two major roadblocks to hinder this walk will be falling in love with the world and falling for the alluring lies of false teachers.

God is love. Since we are His children we must walk in love. In fact, John says that if we do not love, we do not know God. Additionally, our love needs to be practical. Love is more than just words; it is actions. Love is giving, not getting. Biblical love is unconditional in its nature. It is an "in spite of" love. Christ's love fulfilled those qualities and when that brand of love characterizes us, we will be free of self-condemnation and experience confidence before God.

God is life. Those who fellowship with Him must possess His quality of life. Spiritual life begins with spiritual birth. Spiritual birth occurs through faith in Jesus Christ. Faith in Jesus Christ infuses us with God's life—eternal life. Therefore, one who walks in fellowship with God will walk in light, love, and life.

Although the apostle John's name is not found in this book, it was given the title *Ioannou A*, "First of John."

THE AUTHOR OF FIRST JOHN

The external evidence for the authorship of First John shows that from the beginning it was universally received without dispute as authoritative. It was used by Polycarp (who knew John in his youth) and Papias in the early second century, and later in that century Irenaeus (who knew Polycarp in his youth) specifically attributed it to the apostle John. All the Greek and Latin church fathers accepted this epistle as Johannine.

The internal evidence supports this universal tradition because the "we" (apostles), "you" (readers), and "they" (false teachers) phraseology places the writer in the sphere of the apostolic eyewitnesses (cf. 1:1–3; 4:14). John's name was well known to the readers, and it was unnecessary for him to mention it. The style and vocabulary of First John are so similar to those of the Fourth Gospel that most scholars acknowledge these books to be by the same hand (see "The Author of John"). Both share many distinctively Johannine phrases, and the characteristics of limited vocabulary and frequent contrast of opposites are also common to them. Even so, some critics have assailed this conclusion on various grounds, but the theological and stylistic differences are not substantial enough to overcome the abundant similarities.

The traditional view is also rejected by those who hold that the Fourth Gospel and these three epistles were written by John the "elder" or "presbyter," who is to be distinguished from John the apostle. But the only basis for this distinction is Eusebius's interpretation in his *Ecclesiastical History* (A.D. 323) of a statement by Papias. Eusebius understood the passage to refer to two distinct Johns, but the wording does not require this; the elder John and the apostle John may be one and the same. Even if they were different, there is no evidence for contradicting the consistent acknowledgment by the early church that this book was written by the apostle John.

THE TIME OF FIRST JOHN

In Acts 8:14, John is associated with "the apostles who were at Jerusalem," and Paul calls him one of the "pillars" of the Jerusalem church in Galatians 2:9. Apart from Revelation 1, the New Testament is silent about his later years, but early Christian tradition uniformly tells us that he left Jerusalem (probably not long before its destruction in A.D. 70) and that he ministered in and around Ephesus. The seven churches in the Roman province of Asia, mentioned in Revelation 2 and 3, were evidently a part of this ministry. Although there is no address in First John, it is likely that the apostle directed this epistle to the Asian churches that were within the realm of his oversight.

The believers in these congregations were well established in Christian truth, and John wrote to them not as novices but as brethren grounded in apostolic doctrine (2:7, 18–27; 3:11). The apostle does not mention his own affairs, but his use of such terms of address as "beloved" and "my little children" gives this letter a personal touch that reveals his close relationship to the original recipients. First John was probably written in Ephesus after the Gospel of John, but the date cannot be fixed with certainty. No persecution is mentioned, suggesting a date prior to A.D. 95 when persecution broke out during the end of Domitian's reign (A.D. 81–96).

Advanced in years, John wrote this fatherly epistle out of loving concern for his "children," whose steadfastness in the truth was being threatened by the lure of worldliness and the guile of false teachers. The Gnostic heresy taught that matter is inherently evil, and a divine being therefore could not take on human flesh. This resulted in the distinction between the man Jesus and the spiritual Christ who came upon Jesus at His baptism but departed prior to His crucifixion. Another variation was Docetism (from *dokeo*, "to seem"), the doctrine that Christ only seemed to have a human body. The result in both cases was the same—a flat denial of the incarnation.

The Gnostics also believed that their understanding of the hidden knowledge *(gnosis)* made them a kind of spiritual elite, who were above the normal distinctions of right and wrong. This led in most cases to deplorable conduct and complete disregard for Christian ethics.

THE CHRIST OF FIRST JOHN

The present ministry of Christ is portrayed in 1:5—2:22. His blood continually cleanses the believer from all sin, and He is our righteous Advocate before the Father. This epistle places particular stress on the incarnation of God the Son and the identity of Jesus as the Christ (2:22; 4:2, 3), in refutation of Gnostic doctrine. Jesus Christ "came by water and blood" (5:6). He was the same indivisible person from the beginning (His baptism) to the end (His crucifixion) of His public ministry.

KEYS TO FIRST JOHN

Key Word: Fellowship with God—The major theme of First John is fellowship with God. John wants his readers to have assurance of the indwelling God through their abiding relationship with Him (2:28; 5:13). Belief in Christ should be manifested in the practice of righteousness and love for the brethren, which in turn produces joy and confidence before God. John writes this epistle to encourage this kind of fellowship and to emphasize the importance of holding fast to apostolic doctrine.

First John is also written to refute the destructive teachings of the Gnostics by stressing the reality of the incarnation and the emptiness of profession without practice. These antichrists fail the three tests of righteous living, love for the brethren, and belief that Jesus is the Christ, the incarnate God-man.

Key Verses: First John 1:3, 4 and 5:11–13—"That which we have seen and heard we declare to you, that you also may have fellowship with us; and truly our fellowship *is* with the Father and with His Son Jesus Christ. And these things we write to you that your joy may be full" (1:3, 4).

"And this is the testimony: that God has given us eternal life, and this life is in His Son. He who has the Son has life; he who does not have the Son of God does not have life. These things I have written to you who believe in the name of the Son of God, that you may know that you have eternal life, and that you may *continue to* believe in the name of the Son of God" (5:11–13).

Key Chapter: First John 1—The two central passages for continued fellowship with God are John 15 and First John 1. John 15 relates the positive side of fellowship, that is, abiding in Christ. First John 1 unfolds the other side, pointing out that when Christians do not abide in Christ, they must seek forgiveness before fellowship can be restored.

SURVEY OF FIRST JOHN

John writes his first epistle at a time when apostolic doctrine is being challenged by a proliferation of false teachings. Like Second Peter and Jude, First John has a negative and a positive thrust: it refutes erroneous doctrine and encourages its readership to walk in the knowledge of the truth. John lists the criteria and characteristics of fellowship with God and shows that those who abide in Christ can have confidence and assurance before Him. This simply written but profound work develops the meaning of fellowship in the basis of fellowship (1:1—2:27) and the behavior of fellowship (2:28—5:21).

The Basis of Fellowship (1:1—2:27): John's prologue (1:1–4) recalls the beginning of apostolic contact with Christ. It relates his desire to transmit this apostolic witness to his readers so that they may share the same fellowship with Jesus Christ, the personification of life. This proclamation is followed by a description of the conditions of fellowship (1:5—2:14).

The readers' sins have been forgiven and they enjoy fellowship with God. As a result, they know "Him *who is* from the beginning" and are strengthened to overcome the temptations of the evil one (2:12–14). The cautions to fellowship are both practical (the lusts of the corrupt world system which opposes God, 2:15–17) and doctrinal (the teachings of those who differentiate between Jesus and the Christ, 2:18–23). In contrast to these antichrists, the readers have the knowledge of the truth and an anointing from the Holy One. Therefore, it would be foolish for them to turn away from the teachings of the apostles to the innovations of the antichrists. The antidote to these heretical teachings is abiding in the apostolic truths that they "heard from the beginning," which are authenticated by the anointing they have received (2:24–27).

The Behavior of Fellowship (2:28—5:21): The basic theme of First John is summarized in 2:28—assurance through abiding in Christ. The next verse introduces the motif of regeneration, and

2:29—3:10 argues that regeneration is manifested in the practice of righteousness. Because we are children of God through faith in Christ, we have a firm hope of being fully conformed to Him when He appears (3:1-3). Our present likeness to Christ places us in a position of incompatibility with sin, because sin is contrary to the person and work of Christ (3:4-6). The concept in 3:6 does not contradict 1:8 because it is saying that the abider, insofar as he abides, does not sin. When the believer sins, he does not reflect the regenerate new man but Satan, the original sinner (3:7-10).

Regeneration is shown in righteousness (2:29—3:10), and righteousness is manifested in love (3:10-23). The apostle uses the example of Cain to illustrate what love is not: hatred is murdering in spirit, and it arises from the worldly sphere of death. John then uses the example of Christ to illustrate what love is: love is practiced in self-sacrifice, not mere profession. This practical expression of love results in assurance before God and answered prayers because the believer is walking in obedience to God's commands to believe in Christ and love one another.

In 3:24 John introduces two important motifs, which are developed in 4:1-16: the indwelling God, and the Spirit as a mark of this indwelling. The Spirit of God confesses the incarnate Christ and confirms apostolic doctrine (4:1-6). The mutual abiding of the believer in God and God in the believer is manifested in love for others, and this love produces a divine and human fellowship that testifies to and reflects the reality of the incarnation (4:7-16). It also anticipates the perfect fellowship to come and creates a readiness to face the One from whom all love is derived (4:17-19).

John joins the concepts he has presented into a circular chain of six links that begins with love for the brethren (4:20—5:17): (1) Love for believers is the inseparable product of love for God (4:20—5:1). (2) Love for God arises out of obedience to His commandments (5:2, 3). (3) Obedience to God is the result of faith in His Son (5:4, 5). (4) This faith is in Jesus, who was the Christ not only at His baptism (the water), but also at His death (the blood; 5:6-8). (5) The divine witness to the person of Christ is worthy of complete belief (5:9-13). (6) This belief produces confident access to God in prayer (5:14-17). Since intercessory prayer is a manifestation of love for others, the chain has come full circle.

The epilogue (5:18-21) summarizes the conclusions of the epistle in a series of three certainties: (1) Sin is a threat to fellowship, and it should be regarded as foreign to the believer's position in Christ (cf. Rom. 6). (2) The believer stands with God against the satanic world system. (3) The incarnation produces true knowledge and communion with Christ. Since He is the true God and eternal life, the one who knows Him should avoid the lure of any substitute.

FOCUS	BASIS OF FELLOWSHIP		BEHAVIOR OF FELLOWSHIP	
REFERENCE	1:1 — 2:15	— 2:28	— 5:4	— 5:21
DIVISION	CONDITIONS FOR FELLOWSHIP	CAUTIONS TO FELLOWSHIP	CHARACTERISTICS OF FELLOWSHIP	CONSEQUENCES OF FELLOWSHIP
TOPIC	MEANING OF FELLOWSHIP		MANIFESTATIONS OF FELLOWSHIP	
	ABIDING IN GOD'S LIGHT		ABIDING IN GOD'S LOVE	
LOCATION	WRITTEN IN EPHESUS			
TIME	c. A.D. 90			

OUTLINE OF FIRST JOHN

Part One: The Basis of Fellowship (1:1—2:27)

I. Introduction **1:1-4**

II. The Conditions for Fellowship .... **1:5—2:14**

A. Walk in the Light 1:5-7
B. Confession of Sin .... 1:8—2:2
C. Obedience to His Commandments 2:3-6
D. Love for One Another 2:7-14

III. The Cautions to Fellowship **2:15-27**

A. Love of the World 2:15-17
B. Spirit of the Antichrist 2:18-27

Part Two: The Behavior of Fellowship (2:28—5:21)

CHAPTER 1

Introduction

THAT which was from the beginning,
which we have heard, which we have
seen with our eyes, which we have looked
upon, and [R]our hands have handled, concerning the [R]Word of life— Luke 24:39 • [John 1:1, 4, 14]
2 the life was manifested, and we have
seen, and bear witness, and declare to you
that eternal life which was [R]with the Father
and was manifested to us— [John 1:1, 18; 16:28]
3 that which we have seen and heard we
declare to you, that you also may have fellowship with us; and truly our fellowship *is*
[R]with the Father and with His Son Jesus
Christ. 1 Cor. 1:9
4 And these things we write to you [R]that
*your joy may be full. John 15:11; 16:24

Walk in the Light

5 This is the message which we have heard
from Him and declare to you, that God is
light and in Him is no darkness at all.
6 [R]If we say that we have fellowship with
Him, and walk in darkness, we lie and do not
practice the truth. [1 John 2:9–11]
7 But if we [R]walk in the light as He is in the
light, we have fellowship with one another,
and [R]the blood of Jesus Christ His Son
cleanses us from all sin. Is. 2:5 • [1 Cor. 6:11]

Confession of Sin

8 If we say that we have no sin, we deceive
ourselves, and the truth is not in us.
9 If we confess our sins, He is [R]faithful and
just to forgive us *our* sins and to cleanse us
from all unrighteousness. [Rom. 3:24–26]

10 If we say that we have not sinned, we
make Him a liar, and His word is not in us.

CHAPTER 2

MY little children, these things I write to
you, that you may not sin. And if
anyone sins, [R]we have an Advocate with the
Father, Jesus Christ the righteous. Heb. 7:25
2 And [R]He Himself is the propitiation for
our sins, and not for ours only but [R]also for
the whole world. [Rom. 3:25] • John 1:29

Obedience to His Commandments

3 Now by this we know that we know
Him, if we keep His commandments.
4 He who says, "I know Him," and does
not keep His commandments, is a [R]liar, and
the truth is not in him. Rom. 3:4
5 But whoever keeps His word, truly the
love of God [T]is perfected in him. By this we
know that we are in Him. *has been completed*
6 He who says he abides in Him ought
himself also to walk just as He walked.

Love for One Another

7 *Brethren, I write no new commandment to you, but an old commandment which

1:4 NU, M *our* 2:7 NU *Beloved*

1:9 Confession—One of the most remarkable chapters in the Old Testament is Psalm 51. This Psalm contains the actual words of confession uttered by King David after his great sins of adultery and murder (Page 369—2 Sam. 11).

This prayer can serve as a pattern to the Christian when he is guilty of sin in his life today.

a. David begins his prayer by freely admitting his sin (Page 654—Ps. 51:3, 4). This honesty is vital in our confession. God will graciously forgive all our sins, but not on account of our excuses.
b. He then displays real sorrow over his sin (Page 654—Ps. 51:17). Paul writes (Page 1371—2 Cor. 7:10) that the main characteristic of true confession is godly sorrow.
c. He asks God's forgiveness (Page 653—Ps. 51:1, 7–9).
d. He believes that God has heard him and will restore him (Page 654—Ps. 51:12–15).

In the New Testament the most important single verse concerning confession is First John 1:9. In essence John tells us the means of forgiveness and cleansing is the blood of Christ, while the method of this forgiveness and cleansing is the confession of the Christian.

Like David, we must admit our sin, regret the actions of our sin, plead the blood of Christ, and believe that God has indeed done what He promised, namely, to cleanse us from sin and restore us to fellowship and service.

Now turn to Page 321—1 Sam. 1:17: Petition.

THE WORLD, THE FLESH, AND THE DEVIL

Three powerful enemies are constantly trying to defeat the Christian's testimony and spiritual success: the world, the flesh, and the Devil. The key to conquering the world is the love of the Father. Victory over the flesh is through the Holy Spirit. Power over the Devil is in the Son of God, who came to "destroy the works of the devil" (1 John 3:8).

The World (*kosmos*)

The root meaning of *kosmos* is "order" or "arrangement," hence beauty (cf. *cosmetics* and the *cosmos* flower). The main meaning of *kosmos* is the organized system that is under the Devil's control and leaves out God and Christ. *Kosmos* is a major New Testament word, with over half of its occurrences in John's Gospel, where it is one of the evangelist's key terms. His verdict: "the whole world lies *under the sway of* the wicked one" (1 John 5:19).

Kosmos does not always have a negative connotation. John 3:16 uses the word for the people that "God so loved." This meaning also occurs in the expression "Savior of the world" (John 4:42). Paul uses *kosmos* for the created planet in his sermon on Mars' Hill (Acts 17:24).

Two related words are *kosmikos* (cf. English *cosmic*), "worldly" or "pertaining to this earth," and *kosmoskratōr*. "Worldly" in an evil sense are the "lusts" or strong desires that Paul teaches us to deny (Titus 2:12). The morally neutral sense merely describes "the earthly sanctuary" (Heb. 9:1).

The "rulers" ("cosmocrats," used only in Eph. 6:12) are evil forces the believer has to contend with. When they are demonic, they work through flesh-and-blood enemies.

The Flesh (*sarx*)

The literal meaning of *flesh* is found in expressions like "flesh and blood" and "flesh and bones." Christianity does not teach that the human body is evil, but that it can be used for evil. The expression "vile body" (Phil. 3:21, KJV) is misleading because today it suggests moral evil. The meaning is "lowly" (NKJV).

As a destructive influence, the flesh can be our most insidious enemy because it is inside the believer and ever present with its depraved cravings. Even sincere and devout Christians (including the apostle Paul) can have terrific struggles with the flesh. One should not think that he or she is not a true believer because of such temptations. Unfortunately, in a certain sense, as long as we live in the body we will have to contend with the flesh. The whole terrible catalog of the works of the flesh is recounted in Galatians 5:19–21.

The secret of victory over the flesh is to be led by the Holy Spirit: "Walk [i.e., "live your life"] in the Spirit, and you shall not fulfill the lust of the flesh" (Gal. 5:16).

The Devil (*diabolos*)

Devil (*diabolos*) is simply an anglicized form of the Greek word that suggests hurling (slander) back and forth. He is an accuser of the brethren (Zech. 3:1; Rev. 12:10). The Devil is a personal enemy who is opposed to God, His people, and His plans.

An ancient secular usage of this word is "slanderer," and Paul uses it just so in warning older women not to become a *diabolos* (1 Tim. 3:11). Our Lord calls Judas a *diabolos* in John 6:70. He was not a misunderstood follower who had good intentions as some writers like to paint him.

The vast majority of New Testament examples of *diabolos* refer to Satan (Heb. for "adversary"). In the Greek version of the Old Testament (LXX), *diabolos* is the translation of this word over a dozen times. Jesus was not tempted by an evil influence, but by a personal fallen angel who can cite Scripture to his purpose. The Christian's defense against the Devil is "the whole armor of God" (Eph. 6:10–17). The Devil is a defeated foe—Christ bested him at Calvary. Nevertheless, he will remain active in the world until he is locked up for one thousand years (Rev. 20). The Devil's ultimate doom is the lake of fire (Rev. 20:10). While Christians should not fear the Devil, they should, like Michael the archangel, treat him with respect (Jude 9).

you have had [R]from the beginning. The old
commandment is the word which you heard
*from the beginning. 1 John 3:11, 23; 4:21
8 Again, a new commandment I write to
you, which thing is true in Him and in you,
[R]because the darkness is passing away, and
the true light is already shining. Rom. 13:12
9 [R]He who says he is in the light, and hates
his brother, is in darkness until now. [1 Cor. 13:2]
10 [R]He who loves his brother abides in the
light, and [R]there is no cause for stumbling in
him. [1 John 3:14] • 2 Pet. 1:10
11 But he who [R]hates his brother is in darkness and walks in darkness, and does not
know where he is going, because the darkness has blinded his eyes. [1 John 2:9; 3:15; 4:20]

12 I write to you, little children,
Because [R]your sins are forgiven you
for His name's sake. [1 Cor. 6:11]
13 I write to you, fathers,
Because you have known Him *who is*
[R]from the beginning. John 1:1
I write to you, young men,
Because you have overcome the
wicked one.
I write to you, little children,
Because you have known the Father.
14 I have written to you, fathers,
Because you have known Him *who is*
from the beginning.
I have written to you, young men,
Because [R]you are strong, and the
word of God abides in you, Eph. 6:10
And you have overcome the wicked
one.

Love of the World

15 [R]Do not love the world or the things in
the world. If anyone loves the world, the love
of the Father is not in him. [Rom. 12:2]

16 For all that *is* in the world—the lust of
the flesh, [R]the lust of the eyes, and the pride
of life—is not of the Father but is of the
world. [Eccl. 5:10, 11]

17 And [R]the world is passing away, and the
lust of it; but he who does the will of God
abides forever. 1 Cor. 7:31

Spirit of the Antichrist

18 [R]Little children, [R]it is the last hour; and
as you have heard that [R]the* Antichrist is
coming, [R]even now many antichrists have
come, by which we know that it is the last
hour. John 21:5 • 1 Pet. 4:7 • 2 Thess. 2:3 • 2 John 7
19 [R]They went out from us, but they were
not of us; for [R]if they had been of us, they
would have continued with us; but *they went*
out that they might be made manifest, that
none of them were of us. Deut. 13:13 • Matt. 24:24
20 But you have an anointing [R]from the
Holy One, and *you know all things. Acts 3:14
21 I have not written to you because you do
not know the truth, but because you know it,
and that no lie is of the truth.
22 Who is a liar but he who denies that
[R]Jesus is the Christ? He is antichrist who
denies the Father and the Son. 1 John 4:3
23 [R]Whoever denies the Son does not have
the [R]Father either; he who acknowledges the
Son has the Father also. John 15:23 • John 5:23
24 Therefore let that abide in you which
you heard from the beginning. If what you
heard from the beginning abides in you, you
also will abide in the Son and in the Father.
25 [R]And this is the promise that He has
promised us—eternal life. John 3:14–16; 6:40; 17:2, 3
26 These *things* I have written to you concerning those who *try to* deceive you.
27 But the anointing which you have received from Him abides in you, and you do
not need that anyone teach you; but as the
same anointing teaches you concerning all
things, and is true, and is not a lie, and just as
it has taught you, you *will abide in Him.

2:7 NU omits *from the beginning* **2:18** NU omits *the*
2:20 NU *you all know* **2:27** NU omits *will*

2:15 Temptation by the World—The term *world* does not always refer to the universe as created by God. It often is used to describe the community of sinful humanity that possesses a spirit of rebellion against God (Page 1499—1 John 5:19). Because of its opposition to God, the world values those things which are contrary to God's will: "the lust of the flesh, and the lust of the eyes, and the pride of life" (1 John 2:16). Its temptations to the believer are thus twofold: lust for the sensual and pride in mastery of his own life.

The attraction of the world is amplified by Satan who is head of its system. He is called the "prince of this world" (Page 1256—John 12:31; 14:30; 16:11), and the whole world is said to be under his power (see Page 1499—1 John 5:19, where "wickedness" can also be translated "wicked one").

Some of the tragic effects that love of the world will produce in the believer's life are:

a. A turning away from the Lord's work and other believers (Page 1436—2 Tim. 4:10);
b. Alienation from God (Page 1471—James 4:4);
c. Corrupting sins (Page 1487—2 Pet. 1:4; 1 John 2:15–17);
d. Deception by false teachers (Page 1498—1 John 4:1; Page 1502—2 John 7).

The solution to the love of the world is to have a greater love for the Father (1 John 2:15). The Christian who seeks daily to please God in everything and who strives for spiritual growth through prayer, study of God's Word, and witnessing need not fall prey to the temptations of the world.

Now turn to Page 1181—Mark 14:38: Temptation by the Flesh.

Purity of Life

28 And now, little children, abide in Him,
that *when He appears, we may have [R]confi-
dence and not be ashamed before Him at His
coming. 1 John 3:21; 4:17; 5:14
29 [R]If you know that He is righteous, you
know that [R]everyone who practices righteousness is born of Him. Acts 22:14 • 1 John 3:7, 10

CHAPTER 3

BEHOLD [R]what manner of love the Father
has bestowed on us, that [R]we should be
called children of *God! Therefore the world
does not know *us, [R]because it did not know
Him. [1 John 4:10] • [John 1:12] • John 15:18, 21; 16:3

2 Beloved, now we are children of God;
and [R]it has not yet been revealed what we
shall be, but we know that when He is revealed, we shall be like Him, for [R]we shall see
Him as He is. [Rom. 8:18, 19, 23] • [Ps. 16:11]

3 [R]And everyone who has this hope in Him
purifies himself, just as He is pure. 1 John 4:17

Practice of Righteousness

4 Whoever commits sin also commits lawlessness, and [R]sin is lawlessness. Rom. 4:15
5 And you know [R]that He was manifested
[R]to take away our sins, and [R]in Him there is
no sin. 1 John 1:2; 3:8 • John 1:29 • [2 Cor. 5:21]
6 Whoever abides in Him does not sin.
Whoever sins has neither seen Him nor
known Him.
7 Little children, let no one deceive you.
He who practices righteousness is righteous,
just as He is righteous.
8 He who sins is of the devil, for the devil
has sinned from the beginning. For this purpose the Son of God was manifested, that He
might destroy the works of the devil.
9 Whoever has been born of God does not
sin, for His seed remains in him; and he
cannot sin, because he has been born of God.
10 In this the children of God and the children of the devil are manifest: Whoever does
not practice righteousness is not of God, nor
is he who does not love his brother.
11 For this is the message that you heard
from the beginning, [R]that we should love one
another, [John 13:34; 15:12]
12 not as [R]Cain *who* was of the wicked one
and murdered his brother. And why did he
murder him? Because his works were evil and
his brother's righteous. Gen. 4:4, 8

Love in Deed and Truth

13 Do not marvel, my brethren, if [R]the
world hates you. [John 15:18; 17:14]
14 We know that we have passed from
death to life, because we love the brethren.
He who does not love *his* brother abides in
death.
15 Whoever hates his brother is a murderer,
and you know that [R]no murderer has eternal
life abiding in him. [Gal. 5:20, 21]
16 By this we know love, because He laid
down His life for us. And we also ought to lay
down *our* lives for the brethren.
17 But [R]whoever has this world's goods, and
sees his brother in need, and shuts up his
heart from him, how does the love of God
abide in him? Deut. 15:7
18 My little children, let us not love in word
or in tongue, but in deed and in truth.
19 And by this we *know [R]that we are of
the truth, and shall [T]assure our hearts before
Him. John 18:37 • *persuade, set at rest*
20 For if our heart condemns us, God is
greater than our heart, and knows all things.
21 Beloved, if our heart does not condemn
us, we have confidence toward God.

2:28 NU *if* **3:1** NU adds *And we are*
3:1 M *you* **3:14** NU omits *his brother*
3:19 NU *shall know*

3:2 Placed into God's Family—In a general sense all men and women are the offspring of God in that He is the Creator (Page 1299—Acts 17:28, 29). This relationship, however, is not sufficient to offset the penalty of sin, because all persons are sinners separated from God (Page 1327—Rom. 3:23). Therefore, for a sinful person to become a child of God, a miraculous transformation must take place. The Bible refers to this change as being "born again" (Page 1239—John 3:3). When an individual places his faith in Christ as Savior, he is born again into a new, spiritual, family relationship with God (Page 1381—Gal. 3:26). He gains God as Father (Page 1390—Eph. 4:6) and other Christians as brothers and sisters (Page 1452—Heb. 3:1). It is significant to note that the term "brotherly love," which Christians are commanded to have for each other (Page 1463—Heb. 13:1), is never used in the Greek language to refer to loving others as though they were your brothers. Rather, it is always used of loving those who actually are your brothers. So it is in the Christian faith: we actually are brothers and sisters with other Christians.

Not only are Christians the children of God by spiritual birth; they are adopted as well (Page 1387—Eph. 1:5). This figure implies a dramatic transformation of status from slave to son (Page 1381—Gal. 4:1–5). One is no longer in bondage to the master but becomes a free son possessing all the rights and privileges of sonship. One of these benefits is the right to call God *Abba,* an affectionate term meaning "father" (Page 1332—Rom. 8:15). This marvelous relationship carries responsibilities with it, as well as privileges. Everyone who has the hope of having his sonship perfected someday is presently purifying his own life. Since he bears the family relationship to God, he must also exhibit the family character.

Now turn to Page 1272—Acts 1:8: Empowered by God.

22 And [R]whatever we ask we receive from
Him, because we keep His commandments
[R]and do those things that are pleasing in His
sight. Ps. 34:15 • John 8:29
23 And this is His commandment: that we
should believe on the name of His Son Jesus
Christ [R]and love one another, as He gave *us
commandment. Matt. 22:39

24 Now [R]he who keeps His commandments
abides in Him, and He in him. And [R]by this we
know that He abides in us, by the Spirit
whom He has given us. John 14:23 • Rom. 8:9, 14, 16

CHAPTER 4

Testing the Spirits

BELOVED, do not believe every spirit, but
[R]test the spirits, whether they are of
God; because [R]many false prophets have
gone out into the world. 1 Cor. 14:29 • Matt. 24:5
2 By this you know the Spirit of God:
[R]Every spirit that confesses that Jesus Christ
has come in the flesh is of God, 1 Cor. 12:3
3 and every spirit that does not confess
*that Jesus *Christ has come in the flesh is
not of God. And this is the *spirit* of the
Antichrist, which you have heard was coming, and is now already in the world.
4 You are of God, little children, and have
overcome them, because He who is in you is
greater than he who is in the world.
5 [R]They are of the world. Therefore they
speak *as* of the world, and [R]the world hears
them. John 3:31 • John 15:19; 17:14
6 We are of God. He who knows God hears
us; he who is not of God does not hear us. [R]By
this we know the spirit of truth and the spirit
of error. [1 Cor. 2:12–16]

Love as Christ Loved

7 Beloved, let us love one another, for love
is of God; and everyone who [R]loves is born of
God and knows God. 1 Thess. 4:9
8 He who does not love does not know
God, for God is love.
9 [R]In this the love of God was manifested
toward us, that God has sent His only begotten [R]Son into the world, that we might live
through Him. Rom. 5:8 • John 3:16
10 In this is love, [R]not that we loved God,
but that He loved us and sent His Son [R]*to be*
the propitiation for our sins. Titus 3:5 • 1 John 2:2
11 Beloved, [R]if God so loved us, we also
ought to love one another. Matt. 18:33
12 [R]No one has seen God at any time. If we
love one another, God abides in us, and His
love has been perfected in us. John 1:18
13 [R]By this we know that we abide in Him,
and He in us, because He has given us of His
Spirit. John 14:20
14 And [R]we have seen and testify that [R]the
Father has sent the Son *as* Savior of the
world. John 1:14 • John 3:17; 4:42; 1 John 2:2
15 Whoever confesses that Jesus is the Son
of God, God abides in him, and he in God.
16 And we have known and believed the
love that God has for us. God is love, and [R]he
who abides in love abides in God, and God [R]in
him. [1 John 3:24] • [John 14:23]
17 Love has been perfected among us in
this: that [R]we may have boldness in the day
of judgment; because as He is, so are we in
this world. 1 John 2:28
18 There is no fear in love; but perfect love
casts out fear, because fear involves torment.
But he who fears has not been made perfect
in love.
19 We love *Him because He first loved us.
20 If someone says, "I love God," and hates
his brother, he is a liar; for he who does not
love his brother whom he has seen, *how can
he love God whom he has not seen?
21 And [R]this commandment we have from
Him: that he who loves God *must* love his
brother also. [Matt. 5:43, 44; 22:37]

CHAPTER 5

WHOEVER believes that [R]Jesus is the
Christ is [R]born of God, and everyone
who loves Him who begot also loves him who
is begotten of Him. 1 John 2:22; 4:2, 15 • John 1:13
2 By this we know that we love the children of God, when we love God and [R]keep His
commandments. John 15:10

3:23 M omits *us* **4:3** NU omits *that*
4:3 NU omits *Christ has come in the flesh*
4:19 NU omits *Him* **4:20** NU *he cannot*

3:24 Witness of the Spirit—While it is true that one need not always feel spiritual to have new life in Christ, nevertheless, feelings and emotions do play a vital role in our salvation. Both Paul (Page 1333—Rom. 8:16) and John (1 John 3:24) inform us we can experience that inner witness of the Holy Spirit to our spirit. What does this mean? It means we can enjoy the quiet confidence given by the Spirit that we have indeed passed from death unto life. It means we can now approach the mighty Creator of the vast universe and refer to Him as Abba, Father (Page 1332—Rom. 8:15). *Abba* is a very personal and intimate term for one's father. Prior to Pentecost only Christ had used the title for God (Page 1181—Mark 14:36). It is almost akin to our modern title *daddy,* or *papa*. It not only means we can approach the throne of grace with a holy boldness (Page 1453—Heb. 4:16), but we can also experience the blessing of knowing that the Father will hear and answer our prayers (1 John 3:22).

The apostle Paul experiences this witness during a crisis in his life while preaching in Corinth. See Acts 18:9, 10.

Now turn to Page 1349—1 Cor. 6:11: Changed Life.

3 [R]For this is the love of God, that we keep His commandments. And His commandments are not burdensome. John 14:15

Victory over the World

4 For [R]whatever is born of God overcomes the world. And this is the victory that has overcome the world—*our faith. John 16:33

5 Who is he who overcomes the world, but [R]he who believes that Jesus is the Son of God? 1 Cor. 15:57

Assurance of Salvation

6 This is He who came by water and blood—Jesus Christ; not only by water, but by water and blood. And it is the Spirit who bears witness, because the Spirit is truth.

7 For there are three who bear *witness in heaven: the Father, [R]the Word, and the Holy Spirit; and these three are one. [John 1:1]

8 And there are three that bear witness on earth: [R]the Spirit, the water, and the blood; and these three agree as one. John 15:26

9 If we receive [R]the witness of men, the witness of God is greater; [R]for this is the witness of *God which He has testified of His Son. John 5:34, 37; 8:17, 18 • [Matt. 3:16, 17]

10 He who believes in the Son of God [R]has the witness in himself; he who does not believe God [R]has made Him a liar, because he has not believed the testimony that God has given of His Son. [Rom. 8:16] • John 3:18, 33

11 And this is the testimony: that God has given us eternal life, and this life is in His Son.

12 [R]He who has the Son has [T]life; he who does not have the Son of God does not have [T]life. [John 3:15, 36; 6:47; 17:2, 3] • Or *the life*

13 These things I have written to you who believe in the name of the Son of God, that you may know that you have eternal life, *and that you may *continue to* believe in the name of the Son of God.

Guidance in Prayer

14 Now this is the confidence that we have in Him, that [R]if we ask anything according to His will, He hears us. [1 John 2:28; 3:21, 22]

15 And if we know that He hears us, whatever we ask, we know that we have the petitions that we have asked of Him.

16 If anyone sees his brother sinning a sin *which does* not *lead* to death, he will ask, and [R]He will give him life for those who commit sin not *leading* to death. [R]There is sin *leading* to death. [R]I do not say that he should pray about that. Job 42:8 • [Matt. 12:31] • Jer. 7:16; 14:11

17 [R]All unrighteousness is sin, and there is sin not *leading* to death. 1 John 3:4

Freedom from Habitual Sin

18 We know that [R]whoever is born of God does not sin; but he who has been born of God [T]keeps *himself, and the wicked one does not touch him. [1 Pet. 1:23] • *guards*

19 We know that we are of God, and [R]the whole world lies *under the sway of* the wicked one. Gal. 1:4

20 And we know that the Son of God has come and has given us an understanding, that we may know Him who is true; and we are in Him who is true, in His Son Jesus Christ. This is the true God and eternal life.

21 Little children, keep yourselves from idols. Amen.

5:4 M *your*
5:7 NU, M omit the rest of v. 7 and through *on earth* of v. 8, a passage found in only 4 or 5 very late *Greek* mss.
5:9 NU *God, that* **5:13** NU omits the rest of v. 13.
5:18 NU *him*

THE SECOND EPISTLE OF

JOHN

THE BOOK OF SECOND JOHN

"Let him who thinks he stands take heed lest he fall" (1 Cor. 10:12). These words of the apostle Paul could well stand as a subtitle for John's little epistle. The recipients, a chosen lady and her children, were obviously standing. They were walking in truth, remaining faithful to the commandments they had received from the Father. John is deeply pleased to be able to commend them. But he takes nothing for granted. Realizing that standing is just one step removed from falling, he hesitates not at all to issue a reminder: love one another. The apostle admits that this is not new revelation, but he views it sufficiently important to repeat. Loving one another, he stresses, is equivalent to walking according to God's commandments.

John indicates, however, that this love must be discerning. It is not a naive, unthinking, open to anything and anyone kind of love. Biblical love is a matter of choice; it is dangerous and foolish to float through life with undiscerning love. False teachers abound who do not acknowledge Christ as having come in the flesh. It is false charity to open the door to false teaching. We must have fellowship with God. We must have fellowship with Christians. But we must not have fellowship with false teachers.

The "elder" of verse 1 has been traditionally identified with the apostle John, resulting in the Greek title *Ioannou B*, "Second of John."

THE AUTHOR OF SECOND JOHN

Because of the similarity of the contents and circumstances of Second and Third John, the authorship of both will be considered here. These letters were not widely circulated at the beginning because of their brevity and their specific address to a small number of people. This limited circulation, combined with the fact that they have few distinctive ideas to add that are not found in First John, meant that they were seldom quoted in the patristic writings of the early church. Their place in the canon of New Testament books was disputed for a time, but it is significant that there was no question in the minds of those church fathers who lived closest to the time of John that these two epistles were written by the apostle. The second-century writers Irenaeus and Clement of Alexandria entertained no other view. Only as the details of their origin were forgotten did doubts arise, but the positive evidence in their favor eventually won for them the official recognition of the whole church.

It is obvious that the recipients of Second and Third John well knew the author's identity, although he did not use his name. Instead, he designated himself in the first verse of both letters as "the elder." This is not an argument against the Johannine authorship of Second and Third John, since the context of these epistles reveals that his authority was far greater than that of an elder in a local church. The apostle Peter also referred to himself as an elder (1 Pet. 5:1), and John uses the distinguishing term "the elder."

The similarity of style, vocabulary, structure, and mood between Second and Third John makes it clear that these letters were written by the same author. In addition, both (especially Second John) bear strong resemblances to First John and to the Fourth Gospel. Thus, the external and internal evidence lends clear support to the traditional view that these epistles were written by the apostle John.

THE TIME OF SECOND JOHN

The identification of the original readers of this epistle is difficult because of disagreement regarding the interpretation of "the elect lady and her children" (v. 1). Some scholars believe the address should be taken literally to refer to a specific woman and her children, while others prefer to take it as a figurative description of a local church.

The evidence is insufficient for a decisive conclusion, but in either case, the readers were well-known to John and probably lived in the province of Asia, not far from Ephesus. If the figurative view is taken, "the children of your elect sister" (v. 13) refers to the members of a sister church.

In his first epistle, John wrote that a number of false teachers had split away from the church ("they went out from us, but they were not of us," 1 John 2:19). Some of these became traveling teachers who depended on the hospitality of individuals while they sought to infiltrate churches with their teachings.

Judging by the content and circumstances of Second John, it was evidently contemporaneous with First John or was written slightly later. It was probably written about A.D. 90. All three of John's epistles may have been written in Ephesus (see "The Time of First John").

THE CHRIST OF SECOND JOHN

John refutes the same error regarding the person of Christ in this epistle as he did in his first epistle. Again he stresses that those "who do not confess Jesus Christ *as* coming in the flesh" (v. 7) are deceivers who must be avoided. One must abide "in the doctrine of Christ" (v. 9) to have a relationship with God. The doctrine of the person and work of Jesus Christ affects every other area of theology.

KEYS TO SECOND JOHN

Key Word: Avoid Fellowship with False Teachers—The basic theme of this brief letter is steadfastness in the practice and purity of the apostolic doctrine that the readers "have heard from the beginning" (v. 6). John writes it as a reminder to continue walking in obedience to God's commandment to love one another (practical exhortation, vv. 4–6). His primary purpose is to deliver a warning not to associate with or assist teachers who do not acknowledge the truth about Jesus Christ (doctrinal exhortation, vv. 7–11).

It has been suggested that Second and Third John were written as cover letters for First John to provide a personal word to a church (2 John) and to Gaius (3 John) that would supplement the longer epistle. However, there is no way to be sure.

Key Verses: Second John 9, 10—"Whoever transgresses and does not abide in the doctrine of Christ does not have God. He who abides in the doctrine of Christ has both the Father and the Son. If anyone comes to you and does not bring this doctrine, do not receive him into your house nor greet him" (vv. 9, 10).

SURVEY OF SECOND JOHN

This brief letter has much in common with First John, including a warning about the danger of false teachers who deny the incarnation of Jesus Christ. John encourages the readers to continue walking in love but exhorts them to be discerning in their expression of love. Second John breaks with two parts: abide in God's commandments (vv. 1–6) and abide not with false teachers (vv. 7–13).

Abide in God's Commandments (vv. 1–6): The salutation (vv. 1–3) centers on the concept of abiding in the truth (mentioned four times in these three verses). The recipients are loved for their adherence to the truth by "all those who have known the truth." The apostle commends his readers on their walk in truth in obedience to God's commandment (v. 4), and reminds them that this commandment entails the practice of love for one another (vv. 5, 6). The divine command is given in verse 5 and the human response follows in verse 6.

Abide Not with False Teachers (vv. 7–13): Moving from the basic test of Christian behavior (love for the brethren) to the basic test of Christian belief (the person of Christ), John admonishes the readers to beware of deceivers "who do not confess Jesus Christ *as* coming in the flesh" (vv. 7–9). In no uncertain terms, the apostle enjoins the readers to deny even the slightest assistance or encouragement to itinerant teachers who promote an erroneous view of Christ (and hence of salvation; vv. 10, 11).

This letter closes with John's explanation of its brevity: he anticipates a future visit during which he will be able to "speak face to face" with his readers (v. 12). The meaning of the greeting in verse 13 relates to the interpretation of verse 1.

FOCUS	ABIDE IN GOD'S COMMANDMENTS			ABIDE NOT WITH FALSE TEACHERS		
REFERENCE	1—	4—	5—	7—	10—	12—13
DIVISION	SALUTATION	WALK IN TRUTH	WALK IN LOVE	DOCTRINE OF FALSE TEACHERS	AVOID THE FALSE TEACHERS	BENEDICTION
TOPIC	WALK IN COMMANDMENTS			WATCH FOR COUNTERFEITS		
	PRACTICE THE TRUTH			PROTECT THE TRUTH		
LOCATION	WRITTEN IN EPHESUS					
TIME	c. A.D. 90					

OUTLINE OF SECOND JOHN

I. Abide in God's Commandments 1–6
- A. Salutation 1–3
- B. Walk in Truth 4
- C. Walk in Love 5, 6

II. Abide Not with False Teachers 7–13
- A. Doctrine of the False Teachers 7–9
- B. Avoid the False Teachers 10, 11
- C. Benediction 12, 13

Salutation

THE ELDER,
To the [T]elect lady and her children,
whom I love in truth, and not only I, but also
all those who have known the truth, *chosen*
2 because of the truth which abides in us
and will be with us forever:

3 [R]Grace, mercy, *and* peace will be with
*you from God the Father and from the Lord
Jesus Christ, the Son of the Father, in truth
and love. 1 Tim. 1:2

Walk in Truth

4 I rejoiced greatly that I have found *some*
of your children walking in truth, as we
received commandment from the Father.

Walk in Love

5 And now I plead with you, lady, not as
though I wrote a new commandment to you,
but that which we have had from the beginning: [R]that we love one another. John 13:34
6 This is love, that we walk according to
His commandments. This is the commandment, that [R]as you have heard from the
beginning, you should walk in it. 1 John 2:24

Doctrine of the False Teachers

7 For [R]many deceivers have gone out into
the world [R]who do not confess Jesus Christ *as*
coming in the flesh. [R]This is a deceiver and an
antichrist. 1 John 2:19; 4:1 • 1 John 4:2 • 1 John 2:22
8 [R]Look to yourselves, [R]that *we do not
lose those things we worked for, but *that* we
may receive a full reward. Mark 13:9 • Gal. 3:4
9 [R]Whoever *transgresses and does not
abide in the doctrine of Christ does not have
God. He who abides in the doctrine of Christ
has both the Father and the Son. John 7:16

Avoid the False Teachers

10 If anyone comes to you and [R]does not
bring this doctrine, do not receive him into
your house nor greet him; Rom. 16:17
11 for he who greets him shares in his evil
deeds.

Benediction

12 [R]Having many things to write to you, I
did not wish *to do so* with paper and ink; but
I hope to come to you and speak face to face,
[R]that our joy may be full. 3 John 13, 14 • John 17:13
13 [R]The children of your elect sister greet
you. Amen. 1 Pet. 5:13

1:3 NU, M *us* 1:8 NU *you* 1:9 NU *goes ahead*

THINGS IN COMMON

The cluster of Greek words based on the root *koin-* ("common") is so rich that English needs to use several different vocabulary entries to cover the concepts. Such words as *common, share, fellowship, communion*, and *partner* are needed.

Common (*koinos*)

Common (*koinos*) occurs fourteen times in the Greek New Testament. This adjective can mean "common" in the sense of defiled or unclean, as, for example, "unwashed hands" (Mark 7:2) or non-kosher food (Acts 10:14).

A more positive meaning of *koinos* is "common" in the sense of widely shared. The very name of the language in which the New Testament was originally written is called "the common dialect" (*hē koinē dialektos*). The earliest Christians shared "all things in common" (Acts 2:44; 4:32). This was not communism, but a voluntary sharing as needs arose. Paul called Titus "a true son in *our* common faith" (Titus 1:4), and Jude wrote to the saints about "our common salvation" (Jude 3).

Partake, Share (*koinōneō*)

Partake, share (*koinōneō*), a verb built on this root, is used eight times. Twice it has a negative context of sharing in other people's "sins" (1 Tim. 5:22) or "evil deeds" (2 John 11). Paul used this verb for "distributing to the needs of the saints" (Rom. 12:13), the Gentiles' being "partakers of their [the Jews'] spiritual things" (Rom. 15:27), and to command Christians who are taught the Scriptures to "share in all good things with him who teaches" (Gal. 6:6).

Partaker, Partner (*koinōnos*)

Partaker, partner (*koinōnos*) occurs ten times. It is used twice in the Gospels: the scribes and Pharisees denied that they would have "been partakers" with their ancestors in murdering the prophets (Matt. 23:30). Luke used the word in a business sense by telling us that James and John "were partners" with Simon Peter in the fishing trade (Luke 5:10).

Paul used *koinōnos* five times, twice translated "partner"—once in reference to Titus (2 Cor. 8:23) and once to himself as Philemon's partner (Philem. 17). The original recipients of the Epistle to the Hebrews were companions of those who were suffering for Christ (10:33).

Peter used the word twice, calling himself "a partaker of the glory that will be revealed" (1 Pet. 5:1), and prayed that his readers "may be partakers of the divine nature" (2 Pet. 1:4).

The compound form of this noun (*synkoinōnos*) occurs four times with the same general meanings. The compound verb *synkoinōneō* occurs three times and is translated about the same. The prefix *syn-* slightly strengthens the "sharing" motif. Paul used the noun in Philippians 1:7 regarding his original readers' partaking of grace with him; in 4:14 he used the verb to commend them for sharing in his distress.

Fellowship, Sharing, Communion (*koinōnia*)

Fellowship, sharing, communion (*koinōnia*) occurs nineteen times. This beautiful Greek word has become almost as popular in English-speaking congregations as the well-known *agapē* (see word study at 1 Cor. 13). Fellowship groups and Bible classes are sometimes called "koinonias." Fellowship is one of the four staples of the New Testament church, along with the apostles' doctrine, prayer, and the breaking of bread (Acts 2:42). The breaking of bread is *koinōnia* ("communion") of the body and blood of Christ. We can have *koinōnia* with God "the Father and with His Son Jesus Christ" and with the apostles (1 John 1:3), with one another (1 John 1:7), with the Spirit (Phil. 2:1), and with Christ's sufferings.

Even such mundane things as money and goods become *koinōnia* when shared for Christ's sake, making the contribution itself "fellowship" (Rom. 15:26; 2 Cor. 9:13; Phil. 1:5).

Paul ends 2 Corinthians on this widely quoted note of fellowship: "The grace of the Lord Jesus Christ, and the love of God, and the communion of the Holy Spirit *be* with you all. Amen" (2 Cor. 13:14).

THE THIRD EPISTLE OF

JOHN

THE BOOK OF THIRD JOHN

In First John the apostle discusses fellowship with God; in Second John he forbids fellowship with false teachers; and in Third John he encourages fellowship with Christian brothers. Following his expression of love for Gaius, John assures him of his prayers for his health and voices his joy over Gaius's persistent walk in truth and for the manner in which he shows hospitality and support for missionaries who have come to his church. The phrase "send them forward on their journey" means to provide help for the missionaries' endeavors. Included in this help can be food, money, arrangements for companions, and means of travel. By supporting these men who are ministering for Christ, Gaius has become a fellow worker of the truth.

But not everyone in the church feels the same way. Diotrephes' heart is one hundred and eighty degrees removed from Gaius's heart. He is no longer living in love. Pride has taken precedence in his life. He has refused a letter John has written for the church, fearing that his authority might be superseded by that of the apostle. He also has accused John of evil words and refused to accept missionaries. He forbids others to do so and even expels them from the church if they disobey him. John uses this negative example as an opportunity to encourage Gaius to continue his hospitality. Demetrius has a good testimony and may even be one of those turned away by Diotrephes. He is widely known for his good character and his loyalty to the truth. Here he is well commended by John and stands as a positive example for Gaius.

The Greek titles of First, Second, and Third John are *Ioannou A, B,* and *G.* The *G* is gamma, the third letter of the Greek alphabet; *Ioannou G* means "Third of John."

THE AUTHOR OF THIRD JOHN

The authorship of Second and Third John was considered together because the contents and circumstances of both books are similar (see "The Author of Second John"). Although the external evidence for Second and Third John is limited (there is even less for Third John than for Second John), what little there is consistently points to the apostle John as author. The internal evidence is stronger, and it, too, supports the apostolic origin of both letters.

THE TIME OF THIRD JOHN

The parallels between Second and Third John suggest that these epistles were written at about the same time (A.D. 90). Early Christian writers are unified in their testimony that the headquarters of John's later ministry was in Ephesus, the principal city of the Roman province of Asia (see "The Time of First John"). John evidently commissioned a number of traveling teachers to spread the gospel and to solidify the Asian churches, and these teachers were supported by believers who received them into their homes.

Third John, probably delivered by Demetrius, was occasioned by the report of some of these emissaries (called "brethren" in this letter), who returned to the apostle and informed him of the hospitality of Gaius and the hostility of Diotrephes. The arrogant Diotrephes seized the reins of an Asian church and vaunted himself as its preeminent authority. He maligned John's authority and rejected the teachers sent out by John, expelling those in his church who wanted to receive them.

Gaius was a common name in the Roman Empire, and three other men by that name are mentioned in the New Testament: (1) Gaius, one of Paul's traveling companions from Macedonia (Acts 19:29); (2) Gaius of Derbe (Acts 20:4); and (3) Gaius, Paul's host in Corinth, one of the few Corinthians Paul baptized (Rom. 16:23; 1 Cor. 1:14). The Gaius of Third John evidently lived in Asia, and it is best to distinguish him from these other men.

In verse 9, John alludes to a previous letter that Diotrephes had spurned. This may have been First or Second John, but it is more likely a letter that has been lost or perhaps destroyed by Diotrephes.

THE CHRIST OF THIRD JOHN

Unlike First and Second John, Third John makes no mention of the name of Jesus Christ. But verse 7 says "they went forth for His name's sake," an indirect reference to our Lord (cf. Acts 5:41, where the identical Greek construction is used to refer back to "the name of Jesus" in Acts 5:40). The concept of truth runs throughout this letter, and Christ is the source and incarnation of truth, as is obvious from John's other writings.

KEYS TO THIRD JOHN

Key Word: Enjoy Fellowship with the Brethren—The basic theme of this letter is to enjoy and continue to have fellowship (hospitality) with fellow believers, especially full-time Christian workers. This is contrasted between the truth and servanthood of Gaius and the error and selfishness of Diotrephes. Moving through Third John, five specific purposes can be discerned from its contents: (1) to commend Gaius for his adherence to the truth and his hospitality to the emissaries sent out by John (vv. 1–6); (2) to encourage Gaius to continue his support of these brethren (vv. 6–8); (3) to rebuke Diotrephes for his pride and misconduct (vv. 9–11); (4) to provide a recommendation for Demetrius (v. 12); and (5) to inform Gaius of John's intention to visit and straighten out the difficulties (vv. 10, 13, 14).

Key Verse: Third John 11—"Beloved, do not imitate what is evil, but what is good. He who does good is of God, but he who does evil has not seen God" (v. 11).

SURVEY OF THIRD JOHN

Third John is the shortest book in the Bible, but it is very personal and vivid. It offers a stark contrast between two men who respond in opposite ways to the itinerant teachers who have been sent out by the apostle. The faithful Gaius responds with generosity and hospitality, but the faithless Diotrephes responds with arrogance and opposition. Thus, John writes this letter to commend Gaius for walking in the truth (vv. 1–8) and to condemn Diotrephes for walking in error (vv. 9–14).

Commendation of Gaius (vv. 1–8): The "elder" writes to one of his beloved "children" whose godly behavior has given the apostles great joy (vv. 1–4). The "brethren," upon returning to John, have informed him of Gaius's faithfulness, love, and generosity in their behalf. The apostle acknowledges these actions and urges Gaius to continue supporting traveling teachers and missionaries who go out "for His [Jesus'] name's sake" (vv. 5–8).

Condemnation of Diotrephes (vv. 9–14): The epistle suddenly shifts to a negative note as John describes a man whose actions are diametrically opposed to those of Gaius (vv. 9–11). Diotrephes boldly rejects John's apostolic authority and refuses to receive the itinerant teachers sent out by the apostle. Diotrephes evidently has been orthodox in his doctrine, but his evil actions indicate a blindness to God in his practice.

By contrast, John gives his full recommendation to Demetrius, another emissary and probably the bearer of this letter to Gaius (v. 12). John expresses his hope of a personal visit in the closing remarks (vv. 13, 14), as he does in Second John.

FOCUS	COMMENDATION OF GAIUS			CONDEMNATION OF DIOTREPHES		
REFERENCE	1 —	2 —	5 —	9 —	12 —	13 — 14
DIVISION	SALUTATION	GODLINESS OF GAIUS	GENEROSITY OF GAIUS	PRIDE OF DIOTREPHES	PRAISE FOR DEMETRIUS	BENEDICTION
TOPIC	SERVANTHOOD			SELFISHNESS		
	DUTY OF HOSPITALITY			DANGER OF HAUGHTINESS		
LOCATION	WRITTEN IN EPHESUS					
TIME	C. A.D. 90					

OUTLINE OF THIRD JOHN

I. The Commendation of Gaius 1–8
- A. Salutation. 1
- B. Godliness of Gaius 2–4
- C. Generosity of Gaius 5–8

II. The Condemnation of Diotrephes 9–14
- A. Pride of Diotrephes 9–11
- B. Praise for Demetrius 12
- C. Benediction. 13, 14

Salutation

THE ELDER,
To the beloved Gaius, [R]whom I love in
truth: 2 John 1

Godliness of Gaius

2 Beloved, I pray that you may prosper in
all things and be in health, just as your soul
prospers.
3 For I [R]rejoiced greatly when brethren
came and testified of the truth *that is* in you,
just as you walk in the truth. 2 John 4
4 I have no greater joy than to hear that
[R]my children walk in *truth. [1 Cor. 4:15]

Generosity of Gaius

5 Beloved, you do faithfully whatever you
do for the brethren *and for strangers,
6 who have borne witness of your love
before the church. *If* you send them forward
on their journey in a manner worthy of God,
you will do well,
7 because they went forth for His name's
sake, taking nothing from the Gentiles.
8 We therefore ought to [R]receive* such,
that we may become fellow workers for the
truth. Matt. 10:40

Pride of Diotrephes

9 I wrote to the church, but Diotrephes,
who loves to have the preeminence among
them, does not receive us.
10 Therefore, if I come, I will call to mind
his deeds which he does, [T]prating against us
with malicious words. And not content with
that, he himself does not receive the brethren, and forbids those who wish to, putting
them out of the church. *talking nonsense*
11 Beloved, do not imitate what is evil, but
what is good. He who does good is of God,
*but he who does evil has not seen God.

Praise for Demetrius

12 Demetrius [R]has a *good* testimony from
all, and from the truth itself. And we also
[T]bear witness, [R]and you know that our testimony is true. 1 Tim. 3:7 • *testify* • John 19:35; 21:24

Benediction

13 [R]I had many things to write, but I do not
wish to write to you with pen and ink; 2 John 12
14 but I hope to see you shortly, and we
shall speak face to face. Peace to you. Our
friends greet you. Greet the friends by name.

1:4 NU *the truth* **1:5** NU *and especially for*
1:8 NU *support* **1:11** NU, M omit *but*

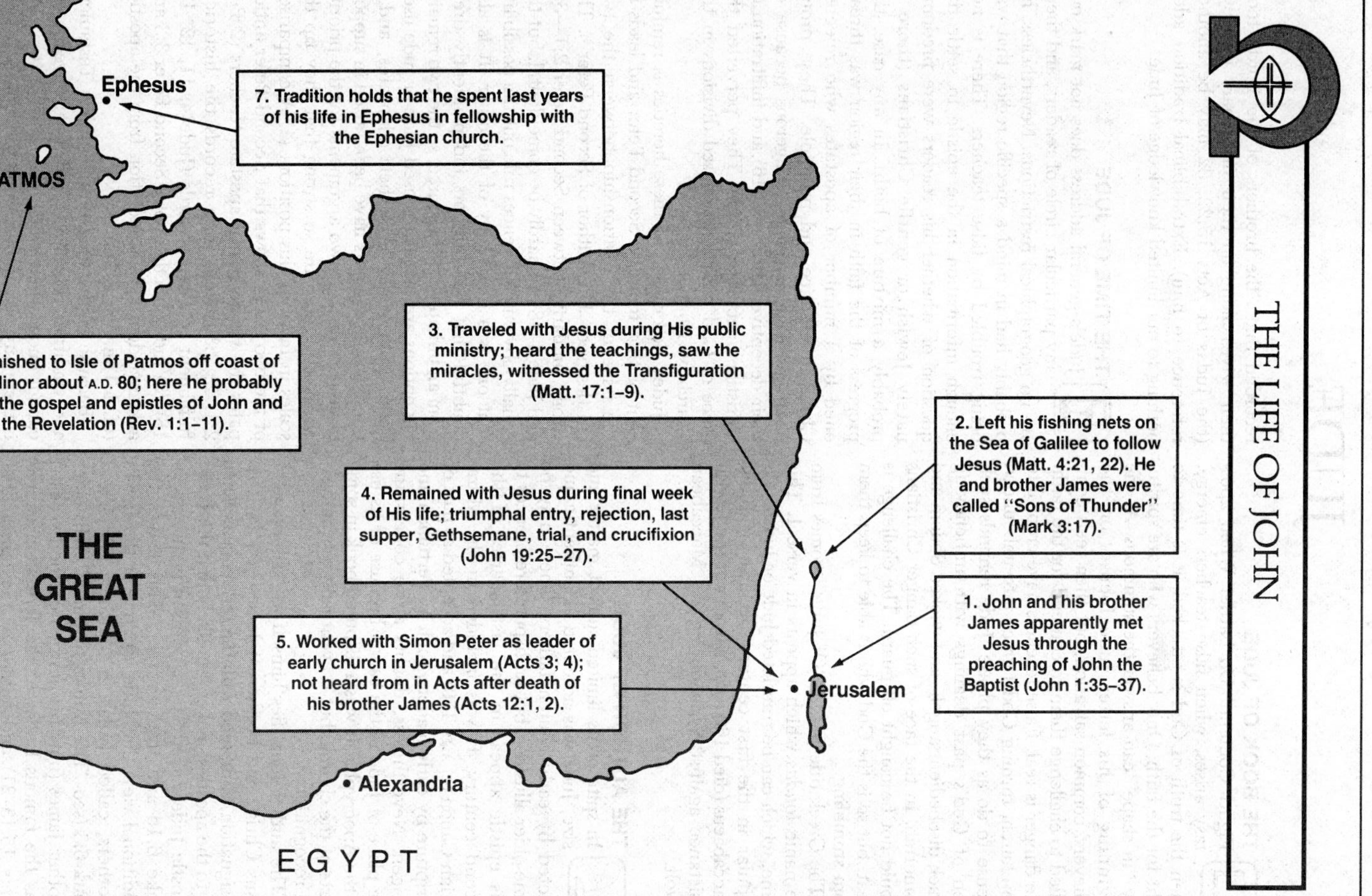
THE LIFE OF JOHN
1. John and his brother James apparently met Jesus through the preaching of John the Baptist (John 1:35–37).
2. Left his fishing nets on the Sea of Galilee to follow Jesus (Matt. 4:21, 22). He and brother James were called "Sons of Thunder" (Mark 3:17).
3. Traveled with Jesus during His public ministry; heard the teachings, saw the miracles, witnessed the Transfiguration (Matt. 17:1–9).
4. Remained with Jesus during final week of His life; triumphal entry, rejection, last supper, Gethsemane, trial, and crucifixion (John 19:25–27).
5. Worked with Simon Peter as leader of early church in Jerusalem (Acts 3; 4); not heard from in Acts after death of his brother James (Acts 12:1, 2).
6. Banished to Isle of Patmos off coast of Asia Minor about A.D. 80; here he probably wrote the gospel and epistles of John and the Revelation (Rev. 1:1–11).
7. Tradition holds that he spent last years of his life in Ephesus in fellowship with the Ephesian church.
Ephesus
PATMOS
THE GREAT SEA
Jerusalem
Alexandria
EGYPT

THE EPISTLE OF

JUDE

THE BOOK OF JUDE

Fight! Contend! Do battle! When apostasy arises, when false teachers emerge, when the truth of God is attacked, it is time to fight for the faith. Only believers who are spiritually "in shape" can answer the summons. At the beginning of his letter Jude focuses on the believers' common salvation, but then feels compelled to challenge them to contend for the faith. The danger is real. False teachers have crept into the church, turning God's grace into unbounded license to do as they please. Jude reminds such men of God's past dealings with unbelieving Israel, disobedient angels, and wicked Sodom and Gomorrah. In the face of such danger Christians should not be caught off guard. The challenge is great, but so is the God who is able to keep them from stumbling.

The Greek title *Iouda,* "Of Jude," comes from the name *Ioudas* which appears in verse 1. This name, which can be translated Jude or Judas, was popular in the first century because of Judas Maccabaeus (died 160 B.C.), a leader of the Jewish resistance against Syria during the Maccabean revolt.

THE AUTHOR OF JUDE

In spite of its limited subject matter and size, Jude was accepted as authentic and quoted by early church fathers. There may be some older allusions, but undisputed references to this epistle appear in the last quarter of the second century. It was included in the Muratorian Canon (c. A.D. 170) and accepted as part of Scripture by early leaders, such as Tertullian and Origen. Nevertheless, doubts arose concerning the place of Jude in the canon because of its use of the Apocrypha. It was a disputed book in some parts of the church, but it eventually won universal recognition.

The author identifies himself as "a servant of Jesus Christ, and brother of James" (v. 1). This designation, combined with the reference in verse 17 to the apostles, makes it unlikely that this is the apostle Jude, called "Judas *the son* of James" in Luke 6:16 and in Acts 1:13. This leaves the traditional view that Jude was one of the Lord's brothers, called Judas in Matthew 13:55 and Mark 6:3 (see "The Author of James"). His older brother James (note his position on the two lists) was the famous leader of the Jerusalem church (Acts 15:13–21) and author of the epistle that bears his name. Like his brothers, Jude did not believe in Jesus before the Resurrection (John 7:1–9; Acts 1:14). The only other biblical allusion to him is in First Corinthians 9:5 where it is recorded that "the brothers of the Lord" took their wives along on their missionary journeys (the Judas of Acts 15:22, 32 may be another reference to him). Extrabiblical tradition adds nothing to our limited knowledge of Jude.

THE TIME OF JUDE

Jude's general address does not mark out any particular circle of readers, and there are no geographical restrictions. Nevertheless, he probably had in mind a specific region that was being troubled by false teachers. There is not enough information in the epistle to settle the question of whether his readers were predominately Jewish or gentile Christians (there is probably a mixture of both). In any case, the progress of the faith in their region was threatened by a number of apostates who rejected Christ in practice and principle. These proud libertines were especially dangerous because of their deceptive flattery (v. 16) and infiltration of Christian meetings (v. 12). They perverted the grace of God (v. 4) and caused divisions in the church (v. 19).

Jude's description of these heretics is reminiscent of that found in Second Peter and leads to the issue of the relationship between the two epistles (see "The Author of Second Peter"). The strong similarity between Second Peter 2:1—3:4 and Jude 4–18 can hardly be coincidental, but the equally obvious differences rule out the possibility that one is a mere copy of the other. It is also doubtful that both authors independently drew from an unknown third source, so the two remaining options are that Peter used Jude or Jude used Peter. Both views have their advocates, and a number of arguments have been raised in support of either side. But two arguments for the priority of Second Peter are so strong that they tip the scales in favor of this position: (1) A comparison of the two books shows that Second Peter anticipates the future rise of apostate teachers (2 Pet. 2:1, 2; 3:3) while Jude records the historical fulfillment of Peter's words (Jude 4, 11, 12, 17, 18); (2) Jude directly quotes Second Peter 3:3 and acknowledges it as a quotation from the apostles (cf. 1 Tim. 4:1; 2 Tim. 3:1).

Because of the silence of the New Testament and tradition concerning Jude's later years, we cannot know where this epistle was written. Nor is there any way to be certain of its date. Assuming the priority of Second Peter (A.D. 64–66), the probable range is A.D. 66-80. (Jude's silence concerning the destruction of Jerusalem does not prove that he wrote this letter before A.D. 70.)

THE CHRIST OF JUDE

In contrast to those who stand condemned by their licentiousness and denial of Christ (v. 4), the believer is "preserved in Jesus Christ" (v. 1). Jude tells his readers to "keep yourselves in the love of God, looking for the mercy of our Lord Jesus Christ unto eternal life" (v. 21). But at the same time, the Lord "is able to keep you from stumbling, and to present *you* faultless before the presence of His glory with exceeding joy" (v. 24).

KEYS TO JUDE

Key Word: Contend for the Faith—This epistle is intensely concerned with the threat of heretical teachers in the church and the believer's proper response to that threat. The contents reveal two major purposes: first, to condemn the practices of the ungodly libertines who were infesting the churches and corrupting believers; and second, to counsel the readers to stand firm, grow in their faith, and contend for the truth. Jude says little about the actual doctrines of these "raging waves of the sea," but they may have held to an antinomian version of Gnosticism (see "The Time of First John"). The readers are encouraged to reach out to those who have been misled by these men.

Key Verse: Jude 3—"Beloved, while I was very diligent to write to you concerning our common salvation, I found it necessary to write to you exhorting you to contend earnestly for the faith which was once for all delivered to the saints" (v. 3).

SURVEY OF JUDE

A surprisingly large number of the Pauline and non-Pauline epistles confront the problem of false teachers, and almost all of them allude to it. But Jude goes beyond all other New Testament epistles in its relentless and passionate denunciation of the apostate teachers who have "crept in unnoticed." With the exception of its salutation (vv. 1, 2) and doxology (vv. 24, 25), the entire epistle revolves around this alarming problem. Combining the theme of Second Peter with the style of James, Jude is potent in spite of its brevity. This urgent letter has four major sections: purpose of Jude (vv. 1–4); description of false teachers (vv. 5–16); defense against false teachers (vv. 17-23); and doxology of Jude (vv. 24, 25).

Purpose of Jude (vv. 1-4): Jude addresses his letter to believers who are "called," "sanctified," and "preserved," and wishes for them the threefold blessing of mercy, peace, and love (vv. 1, 2). Grim news about the encroachment of false teachers in the churches has impelled Jude to put aside his commentary on salvation to write this timely word of rebuke and warning (vv. 3, 4). In view of apostates who turn "the grace of our God into licentiousness" and deny Christ, it is crucial that believers "contend earnestly for the faith."

Description of False Teachers (vv. 5-16): Jude begins his extended exposé of the apostate teachers by illustrating their ultimate doom with three examples of divine judgment from the Pentateuch (vv. 5–7).

Like unreasoning animals, these apostates are ruled by the things they revile, and they are destroyed by the things they practice (vv. 8–10). Even the archangel Michael is more careful in his dealings with superhuman powers than are these arrogant men. He compares these men to three spiritually rebellious men from Genesis (Cain) and Numbers (Balaam and Korah) who incurred the condemnation of God (v. 11). Verses 12 and 13 succinctly summarize their character with five highly descriptive metaphors taken from nature. After affirming the judgment of God upon such ungodly men with a quote from the noncanonical Book of Enoch (vv. 14, 15), Jude catalogs some of their practices (v. 16).

FOCUS	PURPOSE	DESCRIPTION OF FALSE TEACHERS			DEFENSE AGAINST FALSE TEACHERS	DOXOLOGY
REFERENCE	1—	5—	8—	14—	17—	24—25
DIVISION	INTRODUCTION	PAST JUDGMENT	PRESENT CHARACTERISTICS	FUTURE JUDGMENT	DUTY OF BELIEVERS	CONCLUSION
TOPIC	REASON TO CONTEND				HOW TO CONTEND	
	ANATOMY OF APOSTASY				ANTIDOTE FOR APOSTASY	
LOCATION	UNKNOWN					
TIME	c. A.D. 66-80					

Defense Against False Teachers (vv. 17–23): This letter has been exposing apostate teachers (vv. 8, 10, 12, 14, 16), but now Jude directly addresses his readers ("But you, beloved, remember" v. 17). He reminds them of the apostolic warning that such men would come (vv. 17–19) and encourages them to protect themselves against the onslaught of apostasy (vv. 20, 21). The readers must become mature in their own faith so that they will be able to rescue those who are enticed or already ensnared by error (vv. 22, 23).

Doxology of Jude (vv. 24, 25): Jude closes with one of the greatest doxologies in the Bible. It emphasizes the power of Christ to keep those who trust in Him from being overthrown by error.

OUTLINE OF JUDE

Purpose of Jude

JUDE, a servant of Jesus Christ, and
[R]brother of James,

To those who are [R]called, *sanctified by
God the Father, and [R]preserved in Jesus
Christ: Acts 1:13 • Rom. 1:7 • John 17:1
2 Mercy, [R]peace, and love be multiplied to
you. 1 Pet. 1:2
3 Beloved, while I was very diligent to
write to you [R]concerning our common salvation, I found it necessary to write to you
exhorting [R]you to contend earnestly for the
faith which was once for all delivered to the
saints. Titus 1:4 • Phil. 1:27
4 For certain men have crept in unnoticed,
who long ago were marked out for this condemnation, ungodly men, who turn the grace
of our God into licentiousness and deny the
only Lord *God and our Lord Jesus Christ.

Past Judgment of False Teachers

5 But I want to remind you, though you
once knew this, that the Lord, having saved
the people out of the land of Egypt, afterward
destroyed those who did not believe.
6 And the angels who did not keep their
proper domain, but left their own habitation,
He has reserved in everlasting chains under
darkness for the judgment of the great day;
7 as [R]Sodom and Gomorrah, and the cities
around them in a similar manner to these,
having given themselves over to sexual immorality and gone after strange flesh, are set
forth as an example, suffering the [T]vengeance
of eternal fire. Gen. 19:24 • *punishment*

Present Characteristics of False Teachers

8 Likewise also these dreamers defile the
flesh, reject authority, and [R]speak evil of
[T]dignitaries. Ex. 22:28 • *glorious ones*, lit. *glories*
9 Yet Michael the archangel, in [T]contending with the devil, when he disputed about
the body of Moses, dared not bring against
him a reviling accusation, but said, [R]"The
Lord rebuke you!" *arguing* • Zech. 3:2
10 [R]But these speak evil of whatever they
do not know; and whatever they know naturally, like brute beasts, in these things they
corrupt themselves. 2 Pet. 2:12
11 Woe to them! For they have gone in the
way of Cain, [R]have run greedily in the error
of Balaam for profit, and perished [R]in the
rebellion of Korah. 2 Pet. 2:15 • Num. 16:1–3, 31–35
12 These are [T]spots in your love feasts,
while they feast with you without fear, serving *only* themselves; *they are* clouds without
water, carried *about by the winds; late
autumn trees without fruit, twice dead,
pulled up by the roots; *hidden reefs* or *stains*
13 raging waves of the sea, foaming up their
own shame; wandering stars for whom is
reserved the blackness of darkness forever.

Future Judgment of False Teachers

14 [R]Now Enoch, the seventh from Adam,
prophesied about these men also, saying,
"Behold, the Lord comes with ten thousands
of His saints, Gen. 5:18; Dan. 7:10; Zech. 14:5 ☆
15 [R]"to execute judgment on all, to convict
all who are ungodly among them of all their
ungodly deeds which they have committed in
an ungodly way, and of all the [R]harsh things
which ungodly sinners have spoken against
Him." 2 Pet. 2:6 ☆ • 1 Sam. 2:3

1:1 NU *beloved* 1:4 NU omits *God*
1:12 NU, M *along*

JESUS IS LORD

Lord, Master (*Kyrios*)

Lord or *Master* (*Kyrios*) is a most important New Testament word. In secular usage, the word meant "master," "guardian," or "trustee." This ancient usage still occurs in New Testament passages, such as Ephesians 6:5 and Colossians 4:1, regarding masters and servants.

In the Septuagint, *Kyrios* was chosen as the translation of the Hebrew *Adonai* ("Lord"). Since *Yahweh* (or *Jehovah*) was read aloud as *Adonai*, it also stands for that personal name of God. In many Bibles the difference in the original is indicated by capitalizing only the first letter in *Lord* when it stands for *Adonai*, and capitalizing the whole word *LORD* when it translates *Yahweh*.

Kyrios can also mean "Sir," just as in Spanish *Señor* can be used for "Mister" or for "Lord" (*El Señor Jesucristo*). In the Gospels, we cannot always be sure how the speaker regards our Lord. When Thomas, after seeing the risen Lord, exclaimed, "My Lord and my God!" (John 20:28), there can be no doubt he recognized Christ's Lordship. When the Samaritan woman in John 4 addressed Him as an unknown traveler from a rival ethnic group, the KJV translation "Sir" is, no doubt, correct. But there are doubtful passages. For example, in Matthew 8:2, 6, were the leper and the centurion aware of who Jesus was (KJV, NKJV, NIV: "Lord"), or were they just being polite (Moffat: "Sir")?

Jesus is Lord of His Church and should receive the service and homage He deserves. We who know Him as Savior and Lord do well to address Him often as "Lord Jesus."

Jesus is also Lord of the Sabbath, Lord of His Day, Sunday, literally the "Lordly [*kyriakē*, "belonging to the Lord"] day" (Rev. 1:10), and Lord of His worship service, literally the "Lordly [*kyriakē*] Supper" (1 Cor. 11:20).

Ancient pagan kings liked to call themselves "king of kings," a Semitic expression meaning "greatest king." Those despots earned their titles chiefly by their cruelty and absolutism. Jesus, however, fully deserves His title "Lord of lords" (1 Tim. 6:15 and Rev. 11:15).

Finally, and most important, Jesus is Lord in His deity. Matthew 3:3, among other New Testament passages, quotes the Old Testament with the word *Kyrios* representing Yahweh (Jehovah): "Prepare the way of the LORD." This must refer to John the Baptist as the forerunner of Christ.

In the temptation account (Matt. 4:7), Jesus rebukes Satan with, "You shall not tempt the LORD your God." This is often taken to mean Jesus would not tempt God the Father by throwing Himself down from the top of the temple. But is there not also a direct rebuke to Satan for tempting Jesus, who is Himself God the Son?

Lord (*Despotēs*)

Despotēs, like *Kyrios*, means "Lord." In fact, in Jude 4, both words are used to condemn "ungodly men, who . . . deny the only Lord [*Despotēs*] God and our Lord [*Kyrios*] Jesus Christ." *Despotēs*, however, stresses the absolute sovereignty of the Lord. In fact, in ancient times, the Greeks used *despotai* to refer to their gods. Philo maintained that a *despotēs* was a lord, but a lord to be feared. A person who used this word would be admitting his total prostration before God's majesty and power.

Christ as *Despotēs*

Archbishop Trench believed that in Jude 4 both *Kyrios* and *Despotēs* refer to Christ. He criticized Erasmus for applying the stronger word only to the Father. Trench felt that Erasmus did not do this on linguistic grounds, but from a "latent Arianism [i.e., Unitarianism] of which, perhaps, he was scarcely conscious to himself" (*Synonyms of the New Testament*, p. 92).

In 2 Peter 2:1, it seems clear that the word *Despotēs* refers to Christ. Peter refers to "false teachers," who deny "the Lord [*Despotēs*] who bought them." Surely this must speak of the redemption effected by Jesus Christ the Son of God.

Truly, in light of all these usages and passages, we can say: "Jesus is Lord!"

16 These are murmurers, complainers,
walking according to their own lusts; and
they [R]mouth great swelling *words*, [R]flattering
people to gain advantage. 2 Pet. 2:18 • Prov. 28:21

Defense Against False Teachers

17 [R]But you, beloved, remember the words
which were spoken before by the apostles of
our Lord Jesus Christ: 2 Pet. 3:2
18 how they told you that there would be
mockers in the last time who would walk
according to their own ungodly lusts.
19 These are [T]sensual persons, who cause
divisions, not having the Spirit. *soulish* or *worldly*
20 But you, beloved, [R]building yourselves up
on your most holy faith, [R]praying in the Holy
Spirit, Col. 2:7 • [Rom. 8:26]
21 keep yourselves in the love of God,
[R]looking for the mercy of our Lord Jesus
Christ unto eternal life. Titus 2:13
22 And on some have compassion, *making
a distinction;
23 but others save *with fear, [R]pulling *them*
out of the *fire, hating even [R]the garment
defiled by the flesh. Amos 4:11 • [Zech. 3:4, 5]

Doxology of Jude

24 [R]Now to Him who is able to keep *you
from stumbling,
And [R]to present *you* faultless
Before the presence of His glory with
exceeding joy, [Eph. 3:20] • Col. 1:22
25 To *God our Savior,
*Who alone is wise,
Be glory and majesty,
Dominion and *power,
Both now and forever.
Amen.

1:22 NU *who are doubting (or making distinctions)*
1:23 NU omits *with fear*
1:23 NU adds *and on some have mercy with fear*
1:24 M *them*
1:25 NU *the only God our*
1:25 NU *Through Jesus Christ our Lord, Be glory*
1:25 NU adds *Before all time,*

Measures of Length

Unit	*Length*	*Equivalents*	*Translations*
Day's journey	c. 20 miles		day's journey
Roman mile	4,854 feet	8 stadia	mile
Sabbath day's journey	3,637 feet	6 stadia	Sabbath day's journey
Stadion	606 feet	⅛ Roman mile	furlong
Rod	9 feet (10.5 feet in Ezekiel)	3 paces; 6 cubits	measuring reed, reed
Fathom	6 feet	4 cubits	fathom
Pace	3 feet	⅓ rod; 2 cubits	pace
Cubit	18 inches	½ pace; 2 spans	cubit
Span	9 inches	½ cubit; 3 handbreadths	span
Handbreadth	3 inches	⅓ span; 4 fingers	handbreadth
Finger	.75 inches	¼ handbreadth	finger

THE REVELATION

OF JESUS CHRIST

THE BOOK OF REVELATION

Just as Genesis is the book of beginnings, Revelation is the book of consummation. In it, the divine program of redemption is brought to fruition, and the holy name of God is vindicated before all creation. Although there are numerous prophecies in the Gospels and Epistles, Revelation is the only New Testament book that focuses primarily on prophetic events. Its title means "unveiling" or "disclosure." Thus, the book is an unveiling of the character and program of God. Penned by John during his exile on the island of Patmos, Revelation centers around visions and symbols of the resurrected Christ, who alone has authority to judge the earth, to remake it, and to rule it in righteousness.

The title of this book in the Greek text is *Apokalypsis Ioannou,* "Revelation of John." It is also known as the Apocalypse, a transliteration of the word *apokalypsis,* meaning "unveiling," "disclosure," or "revelation." Thus, the book is an unveiling of that which otherwise could not be known. A better title comes from the first verse: *Apokalypsis Iesou Christou,* "Revelation of Jesus Christ." This could be taken as a revelation which came from Christ or as a revelation which is about Christ—both are appropriate. Because of the unified contents of this book, it should not be called Revelations.

THE AUTHOR OF REVELATION

The style, symmetry, and plan of Revelation show that it was written by one author, four times named "John" (1:1, 4, 9; 22:8; see "The Author of John"). Because of its contents and its address to seven churches, Revelation quickly circulated and became widely known and accepted in the early church. It was frequently mentioned and quoted by second- and third-century Christian writers and was received as part of the canon of New Testament books. From the beginning, Revelation was considered an authentic work of the apostle John, the same John who wrote the gospel and three epistles. This was held to be true by Justin Martyr, the Shepherd of Hermas, Melito, Irenaeus, the Muratorian Canon, Tertullian, Clement of Alexandria, Origen, and others.

This view was seldom questioned until the middle of the third century when Dionysius presented several arguments against the apostolic authorship of Revelation. He observed a clear difference in style and thought between Revelation and the books that he accepted as Johannine, and he concluded that the Apocalypse must have been penned by a different John. Indeed, the internal evidence does pose some problems for the traditional view: (1) The Greek grammar of Revelation is not on par with the Fourth Gospel or the Johannine Epistles. (2) There are also differences in vocabulary and expressions used. (3) The theological content of this book differs from John's other writings in emphasis and presentation. (4) John's other writings avoid the use of his name, but it is found four times in this book. While these difficulties exist, two things should be kept in mind: (1) There are a number of remarkable similarities between the Apocalypse and the other books traditionally associated with the apostle John (e.g., the distinctive use of terms, such as *word, lamb,* and *true,* and the careful development of conflicting themes, such as light and darkness, love and hatred, good and evil). (2) Many of the differences can be explained by the unusual circumstances surrounding this book. The apocalyptic subject matter demands a different treatment, and John received the contents not by reflection but by a series of startling and ecstatic visions. It is also possible that John used a secretary who smoothed out the Greek style of his other writings, and that his exile on Patmos prevented the use of such a scribe when he wrote Revelation.

Thus, the internal evidence, while problematic, need not overrule the early and strong external testimony to the apostolic origin of this important book. The author was obviously well-known to the recipients in the seven Asian churches, and this fits the unqualified use of the name John and the uniform tradition about his ministry in Asia. Alternate suggestions, such as John the Elder or a prophet named John, create more problems than they solve.

THE TIME OF REVELATION

John directed this prophetic word to seven selected churches in the Roman province of Asia (1:3, 4). The messages to these churches in chapters 2 and 3 begin with Ephesus, the most prominent, and continue in a clockwise direction until Laodicea is reached. It is likely that this book was initially carried along this circular route. While each of these messages had particular significance for these churches, they were also relevant for the church as a whole ("He who has an ear, let him hear what the Spirit says to the churches").

John's effective testimony for Christ led the Roman authorities to exile him to the small, desolate island of Patmos in the Aegean Sea (1:9). This island of volcanic rock was one of several places to which the Romans banished criminals and political offenders.

Revelation was written at a time when Roman

hostility to Christianity was erupting into overt persecution (1:9; 2:10, 13). Some scholars believe that it should be given an early date during the persecution of Christians under Nero after the A.D. 64 burning of Rome. The Hebrew letters for Nero Caesar (*Neron Kesar*) add up to 666, the number of the beast (13:18), and there was a legend that Nero would reappear in the East after his apparent death (cf. Rev. 13:3, 12, 14). This kind of evidence is weak, and a later date near the end of the reign of the emperor Domitian (A.D. 81–96) is preferable for several reasons: (1) This was the testimony of Irenaeus (disciple of Polycarp who was a disciple of John) and other early Christian writers. (2) John probably did not move from Jerusalem to Ephesus until about A.D. 67, shortly before the Roman destruction of Jerusalem in A.D. 70. The early dating would not give him enough time to have established an ongoing ministry in Asia by the time he wrote this book. (3) The churches of Asia appear to have been in existence for a number of years, long enough for some to reach a point of complacency and decline (cf. 2:4; 3:1, 15–18). (4) The deeds of Domitian are more relevant than those of Nero to the themes of the Apocalypse. Worship of deceased emperors had been practiced for years, but Domitian was the first emperor to demand worship while he was alive. This led to a greater clash between the state and the church, especially in Asia, where the worship of Caesar was widely practiced. The persecution under Domitian presaged the more severe persecutions to follow.

Thus, it is likely that John wrote this book in A.D. 95 or 96. The date of his release from Patmos is unknown, but he was probably allowed to return to Ephesus after the reign of Domitian. Passages such as 1:11; 22:7, 9, 10, 18, 19 suggest that the book was completed before John's release.

THE CHRIST OF REVELATION

Revelation has much to say about all three persons of the Godhead, but it is especially clear in its presentation of the awesome resurrected Christ who has received all authority to judge the earth. He is called Jesus Christ (1:1), the faithful witness, the firstborn from the dead, the ruler over the kings of the earth (1:5), the First and the Last (1:17), He who lives (1:18), the Son of God (2:18), holy and true (3:7), the Amen, the Faithful and True Witness, the Beginning of the creation of God (3:14), the Lion of the tribe of Judah, the Root of David (5:5), a Lamb (5:6), Faithful and True (19:11), The Word of God (19:13), KING OF KINGS, AND LORD OF LORDS (19:16), Alpha and Omega (22:13), the Bright and Morning Star (22:16), and the Lord Jesus Christ (22:21).

This book is indeed "The Revelation of Jesus Christ" (1:1) since it comes from Him and centers on Him. It begins with a vision of His glory, wisdom, and power (1), and portrays His authority over the entire church (2; 3). He is the Lamb who was slain and declared worthy to open the book of judgment (5). His righteous wrath is poured out upon the whole earth (6—18), and He returns in power to judge His enemies and to reign as the Lord over all (19; 20). He will rule forever over the heavenly city in the presence of all who know Him (21; 22).

The Scriptures close with His great promise: " 'Behold, I am coming quickly' " (22:7, 12). " 'Surely I am coming quickly.' Amen. Even so, come, Lord Jesus" (22:20).

KEYS TO REVELATION

Key Word: The Revelation of the Coming of Christ—The purposes for which Revelation was written depend to some extent on how the book as a whole is interpreted. Because of its complex imagery and symbolism, Revelation is the most difficult biblical book to interpret, and there are four major alternatives: (1) The symbolic or idealist view maintains that Revelation is not a predictive prophecy, but a symbolic portrait of the cosmic conflict of spiritual principles. (2) The preterist view (the Latin word *praeter* means "past") maintains that it is a symbolic description of the Roman persecution of the church, emperor worship, and the divine judgment of Rome. (3) The historicist view approaches Revelation as an allegorical panorama of the history of the (Western) church from the first century to the Second Advent. (4) The futurist view acknowledges the obvious influence that the first-century conflict between Roman power and the church had upon the themes of this book. It also accepts the bulk of Revelation (4—22) as an inspired look into the time immediately preceding the Second Advent (the "Tribulation," usually seen as seven years; 6—18), and extending from the return of Christ to the creation of the new cosmos (19—22).

Advocates of all four interpretive approaches to Revelation agree that it was written to assure the recipients of the ultimate triumph of Christ over all who rise up against Him and His saints. The readers were facing dark times of persecution, and even worse times would follow. Therefore they needed to be encouraged to persevere by standing firm in Christ in view of God's plan for the righteous and the wicked. This plan is especially clear in the stirring words of the epilogue (22:6–21). The book was also written to challenge complacent Christians to stop compromising with the world. According to futurists, Revelation serves the additional purpose of providing a perspective on end-time events that would have meaning and relevance to the spiritual lives of all succeeding generations of Christians.

Key Verses: Revelation 1:19 and 19:11-15—" 'Write the things which you have seen, and the things which are, and the things which will take place after this' " (1:19).

"Then I saw heaven opened, and behold, a white horse. And He who sat on him *was* called Faithful and True, and in righteousness He judges and makes war. His eyes *were* like a flame of fire, and on His head *were* many crowns. He had a name written that no one knew except Himself. He *was* clothed with a robe dipped in blood, and His name is called The Word of God. And the armies in heaven, clothed in fine linen, white and clean, followed Him upon white horses. Now out of His mouth goes a sharp sword, that with it He should strike the nations. And He Himself will rule them with a rod of iron. He Himself treads the winepress of the fierceness and wrath of Almighty God" (19:11–15).

Key Chapters: Revelation 19—22—When the end of history is fully understood, its impact radically affects the present. In Revelation 19—22 the plans of God for the last days and for all of eternity are recorded in explicit terms. Careful study of and obedience to them will bring the blessings that are promised (1:3). Uppermost in the mind and deep in the heart should be guarded the words of Jesus, "Behold, I am coming quickly."

SURVEY OF REVELATION

Revelation is written in the form of apocalyptic literature (cf. Daniel and Zechariah) by a prophet (10:11; 22:9) and refers to itself as a prophetic book (1:3; 22:7, 10, 18, 19). The three major movements in this profound unveiling are captured in 1:19: "the things which you have seen" (1); "the things which are" (2 and 3); and "the things which will take place after this" (4—22).

"The Things Which You Have Seen" (1): Revelation contains a prologue (1:1–3) before the usual salutation (1:4–8). The Revelation was received by Christ from the Father and communicated by an angel to John. This is the only biblical book that specifically promises a blessing to those who read it (1:3), but it also promises a curse to those who add to or detract from it (22:18, 19). The salutation and closing benediction show that it was originally written as an epistle to seven Asian churches.

A rich theological portrait of the triune God (1:4–8) is followed by an overwhelming theophany (visible manifestation of God) in 1:9–20. The omnipotent and omniscient Christ who will subjugate all things under His authority is the central figure in this book.

"The Things Which Are" (2 and 3): The messages to the seven churches (2, 3) refer back to an aspect of John's vision of Christ and contain a command, a commendation and/or condemnation, a correction, and a challenge.

"The Things Which Will Take Place After This" (4—22): John is translated into heaven where he is given a vision of the divine majesty. In it, the Father ("*One* sat on the throne") and the Son (The Lion/Lamb) are worshiped by the twenty-four elders, the four living creatures, and the angelic host because of who they are and what they have done (creation and redemption; 4 and 5).

Three cycles of seven judgments in chapters 6—16 consist of seven seals, seven trumpets, and seven bowls. There is a prophetic insert between the sixth and seventh seal and trumpet judgments and an extended insert between the trumpet and bowl judgments. Because of the similarity of the seventh judgment in each series, it is possible that the three sets of judgments take place concurrently or with some overlap so that they all terminate with the return of Christ. An alternate approach views them as three consecutive series of judgments, so that the seventh seal is the seven trumpets and the seventh trumpet is the seven bowls.

FOCUS	"THINGS WHICH YOU HAVE SEEN"	"THINGS WHICH ARE"	"THINGS WHICH WILL TAKE PLACE"				
REFERENCE	1:1—	2:1—	4:1—	6:1—	19:7—	20:1—	21:1—22:21
DIVISION	THE LORD JESUS CHRIST	SEVEN CHURCHES	THE JUDGE	TRIBULATION	SECOND COMING	MILLENNIUM	ETERNAL STATE
TOPIC	VISION OF CHRIST		VISION OF CONSUMMATION				
	THEOPHANY	TALKS	TRIBULATIONS		TRUMPETS		TOGETHER
LOCATION	WRITTEN ON THE ISLAND OF PATMOS						
TIME	c. A.D. 95–96						

The seven seals (6:1—8:5) include war, the famine and death that are associated with war, and persecution. The prophetic insert between the sixth and seventh seals (7) describes the protective sealing of 144,000 "children of Israel," 12,000 from every tribe. It also looks ahead to the multitudes from every part of the earth who come "out of the great tribulation." The catastrophic events in most of the trumpet judgments are called "woes" (8:2—11:19). The prophetic interlude between the sixth and seventh trumpets (10:1—11:14) adds more details about the nature of the tribulation period and mentions a fourth set of seven judgments (the "seven thunders"), which would have extended it if they had not been withdrawn. Two unnamed witnesses minister during three-and-a-half years of the tribulation (forty-two months or 1,260 days). At the end of their ministry they are overcome by the beast, but their resurrection and ascension confound their enemies.

Chapters 12—14 contain a number of miscellaneous prophecies that are inserted between the trumpet and bowl judgments to give further background on the time of tribulation. In chapter 12 a woman gives birth to a male child, who is caught up to God. The woman flees into the wilderness and is pursued by a dragon, who is cast down to earth. Chapter 13 gives a graphic description of the beast and his false prophet, both empowered by the dragon. The first beast is given political, economic, and religious authority; and because of his power and the lying miracles performed by the second beast, he is worshiped as the ruler of the earth. Chapter 14 contains a series of visions including the 144,000 at the end of the tribulation, the fate of those who follow the beast, and the outpouring of the wrath of God.

The seven bowl judgments of chapter 16 are prefaced by a heavenly vision of the power, holiness, and glory of God in chapter 15.

Chapters 17 and 18 anticipate the final downfall of Babylon, the great harlot sitting upon a scarlet-colored beast.

The marriage banquet of the Lamb is ready and the King of Kings, Lord of Lords leads the armies of heaven into battle against the beast and his false prophet. They are cast into a lake of fire (19).

In chapter 20 the dragon—Satan—is bound for a thousand years. He is cast into a bottomless pit. During this one thousand-year period Christ reigns over the earth with His resurrected saints, but by the end of this millennium, many have been born who refuse to submit their hearts to Christ. At the end of the thousand years, Satan is released and a final battle ensues. This is followed by the judgment at the great white throne.

A new universe is created, this time unspoiled by sin, death, pain, or sorrow. The new Jerusalem, described in 21:9—22:5, is shaped like a gigantic cube, 1,500 miles in length, width, and height (the most holy place in the Old Testament tabernacle and the temple was also a perfect cube). Its multicolored stones will reflect the glory of God, and it will continually be filled with light. But the greatest thing of all is that believers will be in the presence of God and "they shall see His face."

Revelation concludes with an epilogue (22:6–21), which reassures the readers that Christ is coming quickly (22:7, 12, 20) and invites all who wish to "take the water of life freely" (22:17) to come to the Alpha and Omega, the Bright and Morning Star.

OUTLINE OF REVELATION

Part One: "The Things Which You Have Seen" (1:1–20)

I. Introduction **1:1–8**

II. Revelation of Christ **1:9–20**

Part Two: "The Things Which Are" (2:1—3:22)

I. Message to Ephesus **2:1–7**

II. Message to Smyrna **2:8–11**

III. Message to Pergamos **2:12–17**

IV. Message to Thyatira **2:18–29**

V. Message to Sardis **3:1–6**

VI. Message to Philadelphia **3:7–13**

VII. Message to Laodicea **3:14–22**

Part Three: "The Things Which Will Take Place After This" (4:1—22:21)

I. Person of the Judge .... **4:1—5:14**

A. The Throne of God 4:1–11
B. The Sealed Book 5:1–14

II. Prophecies of Tribulation .... **6:1—19:6**

A. Seven Seals of Judgment .... 6:1—8:5
1. First Seal 6:1, 2

2. Second Seal 6:3, 4
3. Third Seal.......................... 6:5, 6
4. Fourth Seal 6:7, 8
5. Fifth Seal 6:9–11
6. Sixth Seal 6:12–17
7. 144,000 Jews 7:1–8
8. Great Multitude of Gentiles 7:9–17
9. Seventh Seal........................ 8:1–5

B. Seven Trumpets of Judgment .... 8:6—11:19
1. First Trumpet 8:6, 7
2. Second Trumpet...................... 8:8, 9
3. Third Trumpet...................... 8:10, 11
4. Fourth Trumpet 8:12, 13
5. Fifth Trumpet 9:1–12
6. Sixth Trumpet 9:13–21
7. Little Book 10:1–11
8. Two Witnesses...................... 11:1–14
9. Seventh Trumpet................... 11:15–19

C. Explanatory Prophecies......... 12:1—14:20
1. The Woman 12:1–6
2. The War in Heaven.............. 12:7–12
3. The War on Earth................ 12:13–17
4. The Beast Out of the Sea 13:1–10
5. The Beast Out of the Earth 13:11–18
6. The 144,000 .... 14:1–5
7. The Three Angels' Announcements 14:6–13
8. The Harvest Judgment 14:14–20

D. Seven Bowls of Judgment........ 15:1—19:6
1. Preparation for the Bowl Judgments 15:1–8
2. First Bowl 16:1, 2
3. Second Bowl.......................... 16:3
4. Third Bowl.......................... 16:4–7
5. Fourth Bowl........................ 16:8, 9
6. Fifth Bowl 16:10, 11
7. Sixth Bowl 16:12–16
8. Seventh Bowl................... 16:17–21
9. Overthrow of the Great Harlot ... 17:1–18
   a. Great Harlot Is Described...... 17:1–6
   b. Great Harlot Is Destroyed..... 17:7–18
10. Overthrow of Babylon the Great................. 18:1—19:6
   a. Babylon the Great Is Destroyed.............. 18:1–8
   b. Earth Mourns Babylon's Destruction 18:9–19
   c. Heaven Rejoices Babylon's Destruction .... 18:20—19:6

III. Prophecies of the Second Coming 19:7–21

A. Marriage Supper of the Lamb....... 19:7–10
B. Second Coming of Christ 19:11–21

IV. Prophecies of the Millennium.......... 20:1–15

A. Satan Is Bound 1,000 Years.......... 20:1–3
B. Saints Reign 1,000 Years 20:4–6
C. Satan Is Released and Leads Rebellion 20:7–9
D. Satan Is Tormented Forever 20:10
E. Great White Throne Judgment..... 20:11–15

V. Prophecies of the Eternal State...... 21:1—22:5

A. New Heaven and Earth Are Created.... 21:1
B. New Jerusalem Descends............. 21:2–8
C. New Jerusalem Is Described ..... 21:9—22:5

VI. Conclusion 22:6–21

CHAPTER 1

Introduction

THE Revelation of Jesus Christ, [R]which
God gave Him to show His servants—
things which must [T]shortly take place. And
[R]He sent and signified *it* by His angel to His
servant John, John 3:32 • *quickly* or *swiftly* • Rev. 22:6
2 [R]who bore witness to the word of God,
and to the testimony of Jesus Christ, and to
all things [R]that he saw. 1 Cor. 1:6 • 1 John 1:1
3 [R]Blessed *is* he who reads and those who
hear the words of this prophecy, and keep
those things which are written in it; for [R]the
time *is* near. Luke 11:28 • James 5:8
4 John, to the seven churches which are in
Asia:

Grace to you and peace from Him [R]who
is and [R]who was and who is to come, [R]and
from the seven Spirits who are before His
throne, Ex. 3:14 • John 1:1 • [Is. 11:2]
5 and from Jesus Christ, [R]the faithful [R]wit-
ness, the firstborn from the dead, and [R]the
ruler over the kings of the earth. To Him who
*loved us and washed us from our sins in His
own blood, John 8:14 • Is. 55:4 • Ps. 89:27★
6 and has made us *kings and priests to
His God and Father, [R]to Him *be* glory and
dominion forever and ever. Amen. 1 Tim. 6:16
7 Behold, He is coming with clouds, and
every eye will see Him, and they *also* who
pierced Him. And all the tribes of the earth
will mourn because of Him. Even so, Amen.
8 [R]"I am the Alpha and the Omega, **the*
Beginning and *the* End," says the *Lord,
[R]"who is and who was and who is to come,
the [R]Almighty." Is. 41:4 • Rev. 4:8; 11:17 • Is. 9:6

Revelation of Christ

9 I, John, both your brother and companion in tribulation, and [R]in the kingdom and
patience of Jesus Christ, was on the island
that is called Patmos for the word of God and
for the testimony of Jesus Christ. [2 Tim. 2:12]
10 [R]I was in the Spirit on [R]the Lord's Day,
and I heard behind me [R]a loud voice, as of a
trumpet, Acts 10:10 • Acts 20:7 • Rev. 4:1
11 saying, *"I am the Alpha and the Omega,
the First and the Last," and, "What you see,
write in a book and send *it* to the seven
churches *which are in Asia: to Ephesus, to

1:5 NU, M *loves us and freed*
1:6 NU, M *a kingdom*
1:8 NU, M omit *the Beginning and the End*
1:8 NU, M *Lord God*
1:11 NU, M omit *I am the Alpha and Omega, the First and the Last, and*
1:11 NU, M omit *which are in Asia*

THE SEVEN CHURCHES

Revelation 2; 3

The Book of Revelation contains special messages directed to churches in seven specific cities throughout the Roman province of Asia. These cities were important trade and communication centers, which were connected by major roads in New Testament times. Notice that John addressed the churches in exactly the order shown on this map—from Ephesus north to Pergamos, then south all the way to Laodicea. Some scholars believe Revelation was a circular letter that would have been read first by the Ephesian church, then passed on to the next church on the route.

John received his vision and wrote the Revelation while in exile on this island in the Aegean Sea (Rev. 1:1, 9).

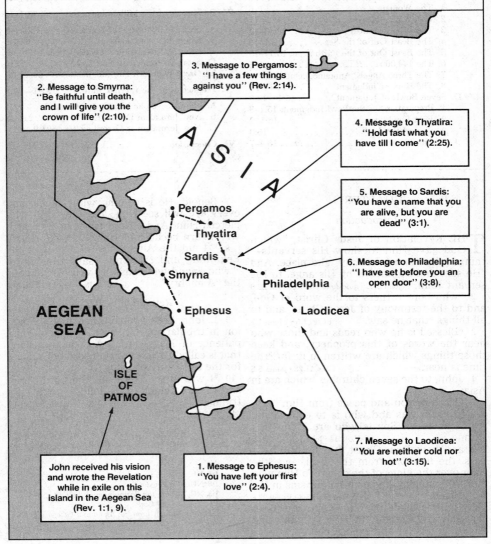

Smyrna, to Pergamos, to Thyatira, to Sardis, to Philadelphia, and to Laodicea."

12 Then I turned to see the voice that spoke with me. And having turned [R]I saw seven golden lampstands, Ex. 25:37; 37:23

13 [R]and in the midst of the seven lampstands *One* like the Son of Man, clothed with a garment down to the feet and girded about the chest with a golden band. Rev. 2:1

14 His head and [R]*His* hair *were* white like wool, as white as snow, and [R]His eyes like a flame of fire; Dan. 7:9 • Dan. 7:9; 10:6

15 [R]His feet *were* like fine brass, as if refined in a furnace, and [R]His voice as the sound of many waters; Ezek. 1:7 • Ezek. 1:24; 43:2

16 He had in His right hand seven stars, [R]out of His mouth went a sharp two-edged sword, and His countenance *was* like the sun shining in its strength. Is. 49:2 ★

17 And [R]when I saw Him, I fell at His feet as dead. But He laid His right hand on me, saying *to me, "Do not be afraid; [R]I am the First and the Last. Ezek. 1:28 • Is. 41:4; 44:6; 48:12

18 "I *am* He who lives, and was dead, and behold, I am alive forevermore. Amen. And I have the keys of Hades and of Death.

19 *"Write the things which you have seen, and the things which are, and the things which will take place after this.

20 "The [T]mystery of the seven stars which you saw in My right hand, and the seven golden lampstands: The seven stars are the [T]angels of the seven churches, and [R]the seven lampstands *which you saw are the seven churches. *hidden truth* • Or *messengers* • Zech. 4:2

CHAPTER 2

Message to Ephesus

"TO the [T]angel of the church of Ephesus write, Or *messenger*

'These things says He who holds the seven stars in His right hand, who walks in the midst of the seven golden lampstands:

2 "I know your works, your labor, your [T]patience, and that you cannot [T]bear those who are evil. And you have tested those who say they are apostles and are not, and have found them liars; *perseverance* • *endure*

3 "and you have persevered and have patience, and have labored for My name's sake and have [R]not become weary. Gal. 6:9

4 "Nevertheless I have *this* against you, that you have left your first love.

5 "Remember therefore from where you have fallen; repent and do the first works, [R]or else I will come to you quickly and remove your lampstand from its place—unless you repent. Matt. 21:41

6 "But this you have, that you hate the deeds of the Nicolaitans, which I also hate.

7 [R]"He who has an ear, let him hear what the Spirit says to the churches. To him who overcomes I will give [R]to eat from [R]the tree of life, which is in the midst of the Paradise of God."' Matt. 11:15 • [Rev. 22:2, 14] • [Gen. 2:9; 3:22]

Message to Smyrna

8 "And to the [T]angel of the church in Smyrna write, Or *messenger*

'These things says [R]the First and the Last, who was dead, and came to life: Rev. 1:8

9 "I know your works, tribulation, and poverty (but you are rich); and *I know* the blasphemy of those who say they are Jews and are not, but *are* a synagogue of Satan.

10 "Do not fear any of those things which you are about to suffer. Indeed, the devil is about to throw *some* of you into prison, that you may be tested, and you will have tribulation ten days. Be faithful until death, and I will give you [R]the crown of life. James 1:12

11 [R]"He who has an ear, let him hear what the Spirit says to the churches. He who overcomes shall not be hurt by [R]the second death."' Rev. 13:9 • [Rev. 20:6, 14; 21:8]

Message to Pergamos

12 "And to the [T]angel of the church in Pergamos write, Or *messenger*

'These things says [R]He who has the sharp two-edged sword: Is. 49:2 ☆

13 "I know your works, and where you dwell, where Satan's throne *is*. And you hold fast to My name, and did not deny My faith even in the days in which Antipas *was* My faithful martyr, who was killed among you, where Satan dwells.

14 "But I have a few things against you, because you have there those who hold the doctrine of Balaam, who taught Balak to put a stumbling block before the children of Israel, to eat things sacrificed to idols, [R]and to commit sexual immorality. 1 Cor. 6:13

15 "Thus you also have those who hold the doctrine of the Nicolaitans, *which thing I hate.

16 'Repent, or else I will come to you quickly and [R]will fight against them with the sword of My mouth. 2 Thess. 2:8

17 "He who has an ear, let him hear what the Spirit says to the churches. To him who overcomes I will give some of the hidden [R]manna to eat. And I will give him a white stone, and on the stone [R]a new name written which no one knows except him who receives *it*."' Ex. 16:33, 34 • Rev. 3:12

Message to Thyatira

18 "And to the [T]angel of the church in Thyatira write, Or *messenger*

1:17 NU, M omit *to me*
1:19 NU, M *Therefore, write*
1:20 NU, M omit *which you saw*
2:15 NU, M *likewise* for *which thing I hate*

THE CITY OF PERGAMOS

Pergamos (or Pergamum) was a city in northwest Asia Minor where one of the seven churches addressed by the apostle John in the Book of Revelation (Rev. 2:12–17) was located. The city was a center of Greek culture for many years; its magnificent library contained more than 200,000 volumes. Parchment, a superior writing material, was developed and manufactured at Pergamos.

John issued the church at Pergamos a stern warning against compromise with evil (Rev. 2:16). As capital of the Roman province of Asia, the city became the first site where the cult of emperor worship was practiced, beginning in 29 B.C. This shameful distinction may have caused John to identify Pergamos as the site "where Satan's throne is" (Rev. 2:13). Refusal to burn incense before the Roman emperor's statue brought charges of disloyalty and possibly death. Antipas, a Christian leader, was martyred, perhaps for his refusal to worship the emperor (Rev. 2:13).

Pergamos was also a center of other types of idolatry and pagan worship. The city featured temples dedicated to worship of the chief pagan god Zeus and to Aesculapius, Greco-Roman god of healing.

The Christian community in Pergamos was too tolerant of evil. Some church teachers apparently advised Christians to participate in immoral sexual practices, as well as pagan worship (Rev. 2:14, 15). John commanded, on behalf of the Lord, "Repent, or else I will come to you quickly and will fight against them with the sword of My mouth" (Rev. 2:16). Choice spiritual blessings were promised to those Christians who were faithful witnesses (Rev. 2:17).

The Pergamos of New Testament times has disappeared, although the site is occupied today by the town of Bergama in modern Turkey. Excavation of the old city has uncovered the ruins of the temple where the Roman emperor was worshiped and the huge temple of Zeus (see photo).

Photo by Howard Vos

Remains of the altar for worship of the pagan god Zeus at Pergamos.

'These things says the Son of God, [R]who has eyes like a flame of fire, and His feet like fine brass: Rev. 1:14, 15

19 "I know your works, love, service, faith, and your [T]patience; and *as* for your works, the last *are* more than the first. *perseverance*

20 "Nevertheless I have *a few things against you, because you allow *that woman [R]Jezebel, who calls herself a prophetess, *to teach and beguile My servants [R]to commit sexual immorality and to eat things sacrificed to idols. 1 Kin. 16:31; 21:25 • Ex. 34:15

21 "And I gave her time to *repent of her sexual immorality, and she did not repent.

22 "Indeed I will cast her into a sickbed, and those who commit adultery with her into great tribulation, unless they repent of *their deeds.

23 "And I will kill her children with death. And all the churches shall know that I am He who [R]searches[T] the minds and hearts. And I will give to each one of you according to your works. Jer. 11:20; 17:10 • *examines*

24 "But to you I say, and to the rest in Thyatira, as many as do not have this doctrine, and who have not known the [R]depths of Satan, as they call *them*, [R]I will put on you no other burden. 2 Tim. 3:1–9 • Acts 15:28

25 "But hold fast [R]what you have till I come. Rev. 3:11

26 "And he who overcomes, and keeps [R]My works until the end, [R]to him I will give power over the nations— [John 6:29] • [Matt. 19:28]

27 *'He[R] shall rule them with a rod of iron;*
As the potter's vessels shall be broken
to pieces'— Ps. 2:8, 9☆

as I also have received from My Father;

28 "and I will give him the morning star.

29 "He who has an ear, let him hear what the Spirit says to the churches." '

CHAPTER 3

Message to Sardis

"AND to the [T]angel of the church in Sardis write, Or *messenger*

'These things says He who [R]has the seven Spirits of God and the seven stars: "I know your works, that you have a name that you are alive, but you are dead. Rev. 1:4, 16

2 "Be watchful, and strengthen the things which remain, that are ready to die, for I have not found your works perfect before *God.

3 "Remember therefore how you have received and heard; hold fast and repent. Therefore if you will not watch, I will come upon you [R]as a thief, and you will not know what hour I will come upon you. [Rev. 16:15]

4 *"You have [R]a few names *even in Sardis who have not [R]defiled their garments; and they shall walk with Me [R]in white, for they are worthy. Acts 1:15 • [Jude 23] • Rev. 4:4; 6:11

5 "He who overcomes [R]shall be clothed in white garments, and I will not [R]blot out his name from the [R]Book of Life; but I will confess his name before My Father and before His angels. [Rev. 19:8] • Ex. 32:32 • Phil. 4:3

6 [R]"He who has an ear, let him hear what the Spirit says to the churches." ' Rev. 2:7

Message to Philadelphia

7 "And to the [T]angel of the church in Philadelphia write, Or *messenger*

'These things says He who is holy, He who is true, "*He who has* [R]*the key of David,* [R]*He who opens and no one shuts, and shuts and no one opens*": Is. 9:7; 22:22 • [Matt. 16:19]

8 [R]"I know your works. See, I have set before you [R]an open door, and no one can shut it; for you have a little strength, have kept My word, and have not denied My name. Rev. 3:1 • 1 Cor. 16:9

9 "Indeed I will make [R]*those* of the synagogue of Satan, who say they are Jews and are not, but lie—indeed I will make them come and worship before your feet, and to know that I have loved you. Rev. 2:9

10 "Because you have kept [T]My command to persevere, I also will keep you from the hour of trial which shall come upon [R]the whole world, to test those who dwell [R]on the earth. Lit. *the word of My patience* • Luke 2:1 • Is. 24:17

11 *"Behold, [R]I come quickly! [R]Hold fast what you have, that no one may take [R]your crown. Phil. 4:5 • Rev. 2:25 • [Rev. 2:10]

12 "He who overcomes, I will make him a pillar in the temple of My God, and he shall go out no more. And I will write on him the name of My God and the name of the city of My God, the New Jerusalem, which [R]comes down out of heaven from My God. And *I will write on him* My new name. Rev. 21:2

13 [R]"He who has an ear, let him hear what the Spirit says to the churches." ' Rev. 2:7

Message to Laodicea

14 "And to the [T]angel of the church *of the Laodiceans write, Or *messenger*

'These things says the Amen, [R]the Faithful and True Witness, [R]the Beginning of the creation of God: Rev. 1:5; 3:7; 19:11 • [Col. 1:15]

15 [R]"I know your works, that you are neither cold nor hot. I could wish you were cold or hot. Rev. 3:1

2:20 NU, M *against you that you put up with*
2:20 M *your wife Jezebel*
2:20 NU, M *and teaches and beguiles*
2:21 NU, M *repent, and she does not want to repent of her sexual immorality* 2:22 NU, M *her*
3:2 NU, M *My God* 3:4 NU, M *Nevertheless you*
3:4 NU, M omit *even* 3:11 NU, M omit *Behold*
3:14 NU, M *in Laodicea*

THE CITY OF LAODICEA

In New Testament times, Laodicea was the most important city in the Roman province of Phrygia in central Asia Minor. Located about ninety miles east of Ephesus and about ten miles west of Colosse, Laodicea stood on the banks of the Lycus River. It served as an important commercial center at a major crossroads in this part of the Roman Empire.

This city was known throughout the ancient world for its beautiful black wool, which was woven into fine, expensive garments. It was populated by a number of wealthy and socially prominent citizens, many of whom earned their livelihood by raising the sheep which produced this wool.

Although it had many natural advantages, Laodicea had one serious shortcoming—lack of good drinking water. Nearly all the streams in the area come from hot springs, which are filled with impurities. When the apostle John addressed the Christians at Laodicea, he referred to them as "lukewarm," and "neither cold nor hot" (Rev. 3:16). Could this be a reference to Laodicea's thermal springs? John's statement "I will spew you out of My mouth" (Rev. 3:16) also brings to mind a mouthful of warm water, which is not a pleasant way to quench one's thirst!

Excavations at Laodicea have revealed that the city apparently tried to solve its water supply problem by bringing water in through stone pipes from an outside source. But these pipes contain limestone deposits, a sign that this water was not much better than the supply from Laodicea's hot springs.

This water problem may have led to the eventual decline of Laodicea. The site is easily recognized today from the remains of the huge city gate (see photo) in the walls that surrounded the city.

The apostle Paul evidently wrote a letter to the Laodiceans (Col. 4:16), but it has apparently been lost. His fellow worker Epaphras worked for a while with the Christians in this city (Col. 4:12, 13).

Photo by Gustav Jeeninga

Ruins of the city gate in the wall of ancient Laodicea.

16 "So then, because you are lukewarm,
and neither cold nor hot, I will [T]spew you out
of My mouth. *spit* or *vomit*
17 "Because you say, [R]'I am rich, have
become wealthy, and have need of nothing'—
and do not know that you are wretched,
miserable, poor, blind, and naked— Hos. 12:8
18 "I counsel you [R]to buy from Me gold
refined in the fire, that you may be rich; and
[R]white garments, that you may be clothed,
that the shame of your nakedness may not be
revealed; and anoint your eyes with eye
salve, that you may see. Is. 55:1 • 2 Cor. 5:3
19 "As many as I love, I rebuke and chasten. Therefore be zealous and repent.
20 "Behold, I stand at the door and knock.
[R]If anyone hears My voice and opens the
door, [R]I will come in to him and dine with
him, and he with Me. Luke 12:36, 37 • [John 14:23]
21 "To him who overcomes I will grant to
sit with Me on My throne, as I also overcame
and sat down with My Father on His throne.
22 [R]"He who has an ear, let him hear what
the Spirit says to the churches." ' " Rev. 2:7

CHAPTER 4

The Throne of God

AFTER these things I looked, and behold, a
door *standing* [R]open in heaven. And the
first voice which I heard *was* like a [R]trumpet
speaking with me, saying, "Come up here,
and I will show you things which must take
place after this." Ezek. 1:1 • Rev. 1:10
2 Immediately [R]I was in the Spirit; and
behold, [R]a throne set in heaven, and *One* sat
on the throne. Rev. 1:10 • Is. 6:1
3 *And He who sat there was [R]like a jasper
and a sardius stone in appearance; [R]and *there*
was a rainbow around the throne, in appearance like an emerald. Rev. 21:11 • Ezek. 1:28
4 Around the throne *were* twenty-four
thrones, and on the thrones I saw twenty-
four elders sitting, clothed in white robes; and
they had crowns of gold on their heads.
5 And from the throne proceeded lightnings, thunderings, and voices. And *there*
were seven lamps of fire burning before the
throne, which are *the seven Spirits of God.
6 Before the throne *there* **was* [R]a sea of
glass, like crystal. [R]And in the midst of the
throne, and around the throne, *were* four
living creatures full of eyes in front and in
back. Rev. 15:2 • Ezek. 1:5
7 [R]The first living creature *was* like a lion,
the second living creature like a calf, the
third living creature had a face like a man,
and the fourth living creature *was* like a
flying eagle. Ezek. 1:10; 10:14
8 And *the* four living creatures, each having [R]six wings, were full of eyes around and
within. And they do not rest day or night,
saying: Is. 6:2

[R]"Holy,* holy, holy, Is. 6:3
[R]Lord God Almighty, Rev. 1:8
[R]Who was and is and is to come!" Rev. 1:4

9 Whenever the living creatures give glory
and honor and thanks to Him who sits on the
throne, [R]who lives forever and ever, Rev. 1:18
10 [R]the twenty-four elders fall down before
Him who sits on the throne and worship Him
who lives forever and ever, and cast their
crowns before the throne, saying: Rev. 5:8, 14

11 "You[R] are worthy, *O Lord, Rev. 1:6; 5:12
To receive glory and honor and power;
[R]For You created all things, Gen. 1:1
And by [R]Your will they *exist and were
created." Col. 1:16

CHAPTER 5

The Sealed Book

AND I saw in the right *hand* of Him who
sat on the throne a scroll written inside
and on the back, sealed with seven seals.
2 Then I saw a strong angel proclaiming
with a loud voice, [R]"Who is worthy to open
the scroll and to loose its seals?" Rev. 4:11; 5:9
3 And no one in heaven or on the earth or
under the earth was able to open the scroll, or
to look at it.
4 So I wept much, because no one was
found worthy to open *and read the scroll, or
to look at it.
5 But one of the elders said to me, "Do not
weep. Behold, the Lion of the tribe of Judah,
the Root of David, has prevailed to open the
scroll and *to loose its seven seals."
6 And I looked, *and behold, in the midst
of the throne and of the four living creatures,
and in the midst of the elders, stood a Lamb
as though it had been slain, having seven
horns and seven eyes, which are the seven
Spirits of God sent out into all the earth.
7 Then He came and took the scroll out of
the right hand of Him who sat on the throne.
8 Now when He had taken the scroll, the
four living creatures and the twenty-four
elders fell down before the Lamb, each having a harp, and golden bowls full of incense,
which are the [R]prayers of the saints. Rev. 8:3
9 And [R]they sang a new song, saying:

[R]"You are worthy to take the scroll,
And to open its seals;
For You were slain, Rev. 14:3 • Rev. 4:11

4:3 M omits *And He who sat there was,* making the following a description of the throne.
4:5 M omits *the* 4:6 NU, M add *something like*
4:8 M has *holy* nine times.
4:11 NU, M *Our Lord and God*
4:11 NU, M *existed* 5:4 NU, M omit *and read*
5:5 NU, M omit *to loose*
5:6 NU, M omit *and behold*

And [R]have redeemed us to God [R]by
Your blood John 1:29 • [Heb. 9:12]
Out of every tribe and tongue and
people and nation,
10 And have made *us [R]kings* and [R]priests
to our God; Ex. 19:6 • Is. 61:6
And *we shall reign on the earth."

11 Then I looked, and I heard the voice of
many angels around the throne, the living
creatures, and the elders; and the number of
them was ten thousand times ten thousand,
and thousands of thousands,
12 saying with a loud voice:

"Worthy is the [R]Lamb who was slain
To receive power and riches and
wisdom,
And strength and honor and glory and
blessing!" Is. 53:7 ★

13 And [R]every creature which is in heaven
and on the earth and under the earth and
such as are in the sea, and all that are in
them, I heard saying: Phil. 2:10

"Blessing and honor and glory and power
Be to Him who sits on the throne,
And to the Lamb, forever and *ever!"

14 Then the four living creatures said,
"Amen!" And the *twenty-four elders fell
down and worshiped *Him who lives forever
and ever.

CHAPTER 6

First Seal

NOW [R]I saw when the Lamb opened one
of the *seals; and I heard one of the
four living creatures saying with a voice like
thunder, "Come and see." [Rev. 5:5–7, 12; 13:8]
2 And I looked, and behold, a white horse.
And he who sat on it had a bow; and a crown
was given to him, and he went out [R]conquer-
ing and to conquer. Matt. 24:5

Second Seal

3 When He opened the second seal, [R]I
heard the second living creature saying,
"Come *and see." Rev. 4:7
4 [R]And another horse, fiery red, went out.
And it was granted to the one who sat on it to
[R]take peace from the earth, and that *people*
should kill one another; and there was given
to him a great sword. Zech. 1:8; 6:2 • Matt. 24:6, 7

Third Seal

5 When He opened the third seal, [R]I heard
the third living creature say, "Come and see."
And I looked, and behold, [R]a black horse, and
he who sat on it had a pair of [R]scales[T] in his
hand. Rev. 4:7 • Zech. 6:2, 6 • Matt. 24:7 • *balances*

6 And I heard a voice in the midst of the
four living creatures saying, "A [T]quart of
wheat for a denarius, and three quarts of
barley for a denarius; and [R]do not harm the
oil and the wine." Gr. *choinix* • Rev. 7:3; 9:4

Fourth Seal

7 When He opened the fourth seal, [R]I
heard the voice of the fourth living creature
saying, "Come and see." Rev. 4:7
8 And I looked, and behold, a pale horse.
And the name of him who sat on it was
Death, and Hades followed with him. And
power was given to them over a fourth of the
earth, to kill with sword, with hunger, with
death, and by the beasts of the earth.

Fifth Seal

9 When He opened the fifth seal, I saw
under [R]the altar [R]the souls of those who had
been slain for the word of God and for the
testimony which they held. Rev. 8:3 • [Rev. 20:4]
10 And they cried with a loud voice, saying,
"How long, O Lord, [R]holy and true, [R]until You
judge and avenge our blood on those who
dwell on the earth?" Rev. 3:7 • Rev. 11:18
11 And a [R]white robe was given to each of
them; and it was said to them [R]that they
should rest a little while longer, until both *the*
number of their fellow servants and their
brethren, who would be killed as they *were*,
was completed. Rev. 3:4, 5; 7:9 • Heb. 11:40

Sixth Seal

12 I looked when He opened the sixth seal,
and *behold, there was a great earthquake;
and the sun became black as sackcloth of
hair, and the *moon became like blood.
13 [R]And the stars of heaven fell to the earth,
as a fig tree drops its late figs when it is
shaken by a mighty wind. Rev. 8:10; 9:1
14 Then the sky [T]receded as a scroll when it
is rolled up, and every mountain and island
was moved out of its place. *split apart*
15 And the [R]kings of the earth, the great
men, the rich men, the commanders, the
mighty men, every slave and every free man,
[R]hid themselves in the caves and in the rocks
of the mountains, Ps. 2:2–4 • Is. 2:10, 19, 21; 24:21
16 [R]and said to the mountains and rocks,
"Fall on us and hide us from the face of Him
who [R]sits on the throne and from the wrath
of the Lamb! Luke 23:29, 30 • Rev. 20:11
17 "For the great day of His wrath has
come, [R]and who is able to stand?" Zeph. 1:14

5:10 NU, M *them* **5:10** NU *a kingdom*
5:10 NU, M *they* **5:13** M adds *Amen*
5:14 NU, M omit *twenty-four*
5:14 NU, M omit *Him who lives forever and ever*
6:1 NU, M *seven seals* **6:3** NU, M omit *and see*
6:12 NU, M omit *behold* **6:12** NU, M *whole moon*

CHAPTER 7

144,000 Jews

AFTER these things I saw four angels
standing at the four corners of the
earth, holding the four winds of the earth,
[R]that the wind should not blow on the earth,
on the sea, or on any tree. Rev. 7:3; 8:7; 9:4
2 Then I saw another angel ascending
from the east, having the seal of the living
God. And he cried with a loud voice to the
four angels to whom it was granted to harm
the earth and the sea,
3 saying, [R]"Do not harm the earth, the sea,
or the trees till we have sealed the servants of
our God [R]on their foreheads." Rev. 6:6 • Rev. 22:4
4 And I heard the number of those who
were sealed. [R]One hundred *and* forty-four
thousand [R]of all the tribes of the children of
Israel *were* sealed: Rev. 14:1, 3 • Gen. 49:1–27

5 of the tribe of Judah
twelve thousand *were* sealed;
of the tribe of Reuben
twelve thousand *were* *sealed;
of the tribe of Gad
twelve thousand *were* sealed;
6 of the tribe of Asher
twelve thousand *were* sealed;
of the tribe of Naphtali
twelve thousand *were* sealed;
of the tribe of Manasseh
twelve thousand *were* sealed;
7 of the tribe of Simeon
twelve thousand *were* sealed;
of the tribe of Levi
twelve thousand *were* sealed;
of the tribe of Issachar
twelve thousand *were* sealed;
8 of the tribe of Zebulun
twelve thousand *were* sealed;
of the tribe of Joseph
twelve thousand *were* sealed;
of the tribe of Benjamin
twelve thousand *were* sealed.

Great Multitude of Gentiles

9 After these things I looked, and behold, a
great multitude which no one could number,
[R]of all nations, tribes, peoples, and tongues,
standing before the throne and before the
Lamb, clothed with white robes, with palm
branches in their hands, Rev. 5:9
10 and crying out with a loud voice, saying,
[R]"Salvation *belongs* to our God [R]who sits on
the throne, and to the Lamb!" Ps. 3:8 • Rev. 5:13
11 [R]And all the angels stood around the
throne and the elders and the four living
creatures, and fell on their faces before the
throne and [R]worshiped God, Rev. 4:6 • Rev. 4:11
12 [R]saying:
"Amen! Blessing and glory and wisdom,
Thanksgiving and honor and power and
might,
Be to our God forever and ever.
Amen." Rev. 5:13, 14

13 Then one of the elders answered, saying
to me, "Who are these arrayed in white robes,
and where did they come from?"
14 And I said to him, "Sir, you know." So he
said to me, [R]"These are the ones who come
out of the great tribulation, and [R]washed
their robes and made them white in the blood
of the Lamb. Rev. 6:9 • [Heb. 9:14]
15 "Therefore they are before the throne of
God, and serve Him day and night in His
temple. And He who sits on the throne will
[R]dwell among them. Is. 4:5, 6
16 [R]"They shall neither hunger anymore nor
thirst anymore; [R]the sun shall not strike
them, nor any heat; Is. 49:10 ☆ • Ps. 121:6
17 "for the Lamb who is in the midst of the
throne will shepherd them and lead them to
*living fountains of waters. And God will
wipe away every tear from their eyes."

CHAPTER 8

Seventh Seal

WHEN[R] He opened the seventh seal,
there was silence in heaven for about
half an hour. Rev. 6:1
2 [R]And I saw the seven angels who stand
before God, [R]and to them were given seven
trumpets. [Matt. 18:10] • 2 Chr. 29:25–28
3 Then another angel, having a golden
censer, came and stood at the altar. And he
was given much incense, that he should offer
it with the prayers of all the saints upon the
golden altar which was before the throne.
4 And [R]the smoke of the incense, with the
prayers of the saints, ascended before God
from the angel's hand. Ps. 141:2
5 Then the angel took the censer, filled it
with fire from the altar, and threw *it* to the
earth. And there were noises, thunderings,
lightnings, [R]and an earthquake. 2 Sam. 22:8

First Trumpet

6 So the seven angels who had the seven
trumpets prepared themselves to sound.
7 The first angel sounded: [R]And hail and
fire followed, mingled with blood, and they
were thrown [R]to the *earth; and a third of the
trees were burned up, and all green grass was
burned up. Ezek. 38:22 • Rev. 16:2

Second Trumpet

8 Then the second angel sounded: And
something like a great mountain burning

7:5 NU, M omit *sealed* in vv. 5b–8c
7:17 NU, M *fountains of the waters of life*
8:7 NU, M add *and a third of the earth was burned up*

with fire was thrown into the sea, and a third of the sea [R]became blood; Ezek. 14:19

9 [R]and a third of the living creatures in the sea died, and a third of the ships were destroyed. Rev. 16:3

Third Trumpet

10 Then the third angel sounded: [R]And a great star fell from heaven, burning like a torch, [R]and it fell on a third of the rivers and on the springs of water; Is. 14:12 • Rev. 14:7; 16:4

11 [R]and the name of the star is Wormwood; [R]and a third of the waters became wormwood; and many men died from the water, because it was made bitter. Ruth 1:20 • Ex. 15:23

Fourth Trumpet

12 Then the fourth angel sounded: And a third of the sun was struck, a third of the moon, and a third of the stars, so that a third of them were darkened; and a third of the day did not shine, and likewise the night.

13 And I looked, [R]and I heard an *angel flying through the midst of heaven, saying with a loud voice, "Woe, woe, woe to the inhabitants of the earth, because of the remaining blasts of the trumpet of the three angels who are about to sound!" Rev. 14:6

CHAPTER 9

Fifth Trumpet

THEN the fifth angel sounded: [R]And I saw a star fallen from heaven to the earth. And to him was given the key to [R]the [T]bottomless pit. Rev. 8:10 • Luke 8:31 • Lit. *shaft of the abyss*

2 And he opened the bottomless pit, and smoke arose out of the pit like the smoke of a great furnace. And the sun and the air were darkened because of the smoke of the pit.

3 Then out of the smoke locusts came upon the earth. And to them was given power, [R]as the scorpions of the earth have power. Judg. 7:12

4 They were commanded not to harm the grass of the earth, or any green thing, or any tree, but only those men who do not have the seal of God on their foreheads.

5 And they were not given *authority* to kill them, but to torment them *for* five months. And their torment *was* like the torment of a scorpion when it strikes a man.

6 In those days [R]men will seek death and will not find it; they will desire to die, and death will flee from them. Jer. 8:3

7 And the shape of the locusts was like horses prepared for battle; and on their heads were crowns of something like gold, and their faces *were* like the faces of men.

8 They had hair like women's hair, and [R]their teeth were like lions' *teeth*. Joel 1:6

9 And they had breastplates like breastplates of iron, and the sound of their wings *was* [R]like the sound of chariots with many horses running into battle. Joel 2:5–7

10 They had tails like scorpions, and there were stings in their tails. And their power *was* to hurt men five months.

11 And they had as king over them the angel of the bottomless pit, whose name in Hebrew *is* [T]Abaddon, but in Greek he has the name [T]Apollyon. Lit. *Destruction* • Lit. *Destroyer*

12 [R]One woe is past. Behold, still two more woes are coming after these things. Rev. 8:13

Sixth Trumpet

13 Then the sixth angel sounded: And I heard a voice from the four horns of the [R]golden altar which is before God, Rev. 8:3

14 saying to the sixth angel who had the trumpet, "Release the four angels who are bound at the great river Euphrates."

15 So the four angels, who had been prepared for the hour and day and month and year, were released to kill a [R]third of mankind. Rev. 8:7–9; 9:18

16 Now the number of the army [R]of the horsemen *was* two hundred million, [R]and I heard the number of them. Ezek. 38:4 • Rev. 7:4

17 And thus I saw the horses in the vision: those who sat on them had breastplates of fiery red, hyacinth blue, and sulfur yellow; [R]and the heads of the horses *were* like the heads of lions; and out of their mouths came fire, smoke, and brimstone. Is. 5:28, 29

18 By these three *plagues* a third of mankind was killed—by the fire and the smoke and the brimstone which came out of their mouths.

19 For *their power is in their mouth and in their tails; for their tails *are* like serpents, having heads; and with them they do harm.

20 But the rest of mankind, who were not killed by these plagues, did not repent of the works of their hands, that they should not worship [R]demons, [R]and idols of gold, silver, brass, stone, and wood, which can neither see nor hear nor walk; 1 Cor. 10:20 • Dan. 5:23

21 and they did not repent of their murders [R]or their *sorceries or their sexual immorality or their thefts. Rev. 21:8; 22:15

CHAPTER 10

Little Book

AND I saw still another mighty angel coming down from heaven, clothed with a cloud. [R]And a rainbow *was* on [R]his head, his face *was* like the sun, and [R]his feet like pillars of fire. Rev. 4:3 • Rev. 1:16 • Rev. 1:15

2 And he had a little book open in his hand. [R]And he set his right foot on the sea and *his* left *foot* on the land, Matt. 28:18

8:13 NU, M *eagle*
9:19 NU, M *the power of the horses*
9:21 NU, M *drugs*

NAMES FOR SATAN

Satan, or Adversary, is the most frequently used name for the Devil in the New Testament, appearing over fifty times. Devil, or Slanderer, is used over thirty times. Satan, the personification of evil in this world, is the great superhuman enemy of God, His people, and all that is good. His character is vile and evil, and he is portrayed as the great deceiver. So sly is Satan in his deception that he sometimes transforms himself into an angel of light (2 Cor. 11:14).

Regarded by many scholars as a fallen angel, Satan has a continuing ambition to replace God and have others worship him (Matt. 4:8, 9). He constantly tempts people to try to entice them into sin (1 Thess. 3:5). In falling from God's favor, Satan persuaded other angels to join him in his rebellion (Rev. 12:9). When Christ returns, Satan will be defeated and ultimately cast into the lake of fire (Rev. 20:1–10).

The following names or titles for Satan in the New Testament throw further light on the Devil's character.

Title	Biblical Reference
Beelzebub, ruler of demons	Matt. 12:24
The wicked one	Matt. 13:19
The enemy	Matt. 13:39
Murderer	John 8:44
A liar	John 8:44
Ruler of this world	John 12:31; 14:30
God of this age	2 Cor. 4:4
Prince of the power of the air	Eph. 2:2
Ruler of darkness	Eph. 6:12
The tempter	1 Thess. 3:5
The king of death	Heb. 2:14
A roaring lion	1 Pet. 5:8
Adversary	1 Pet. 5:8
Angel of the bottomless pit	Rev. 9:11
Abaddon (Destruction)	Rev. 9:11
Apollyon (Destroyer)	Rev. 9:11
The dragon	Rev. 12:7
Accuser of our brethren	Rev. 12:10
Serpent of old	Rev. 20:2
The deceiver	Rev. 20:10

3 and cried with a loud voice, as *when* a
lion roars. And when he cried out, [R]seven
thunders uttered their voices. Ps. 29:3–9
4 Now when the seven thunders uttered
their voices, I was about to write; but I heard
a voice from heaven saying *to me, [R]"Seal up
the things which the seven thunders uttered,
and do not write them." Dan. 8:26; 12:4, 9
5 And the angel whom I saw standing on
the sea and on the land [R]lifted up his *hand to
heaven Dan. 12:7
6 and swore by Him who lives forever and
ever, who created heaven and the things that
are in it, the earth and the things that are in
it, and the sea and the things that are in it,
that there should be delay no longer,
7 but in the days of the sounding of the
seventh angel, when he is about to sound, the
mystery of God would be finished, as He
declared to His servants the prophets.
8 Then the voice which I heard from
heaven spoke to me again and said, "Go, take
the little book which is open in the hand of
the angel who stands on the sea and on the
earth."
9 And I went to the angel and said to him,
"Give me the little book." And he said to me,
[R]"Take and eat it; and it will make your
stomach bitter, but it will be as sweet as
honey in your mouth." Jer. 15:16
10 And I took the little book out of the
angel's hand and ate it, and it was as sweet as
honey in my mouth. But when I had eaten it,
[R]my stomach became bitter. Ezek. 2:10
11 And *he said to me, "You must prophesy
again about many peoples, nations, tongues,
and kings."

CHAPTER 11

Two Witnesses

THEN I was given a [T]reed like a measuring
rod. *And the angel stood, saying, [R]"Rise
and measure the temple of God, the altar, and
those who worship there. 10.5 ft. • Num. 23:18
2 "But leave out the court which is outside
the temple, and do not measure it, [R]for it has
been given to the Gentiles. And they will
[R]tread the holy city underfoot *for* [R]forty-two
months. Ps. 79:1 • Dan. 8:10 • Rev. 12:6; 13:5
3 "And I will give *power* to my two [R]wit-
nesses, [R]and they will prophesy [R]one thousand two hundred and sixty days, clothed in
sackcloth." Rev. 20:4 • Rev. 19:10 • Rev. 12:6
4 These are the [R]two olive trees and the
two lampstands standing before the *God of
the earth. Zech. 4:2, 3, 11, 14
5 And if anyone wants to harm them, fire
proceeds from their mouth and devours their
enemies. And if anyone wants to harm them,
he must be killed in this manner.
6 These [R]have power to shut heaven, so
that no rain falls in the days of their prophecy; and they have power over waters to turn
them to blood, and to strike the earth with all
plagues, as often as they desire. 1 Kin. 17:1
7 Now when they finish their testimony,
the beast that ascends [R]out of the bottomless
pit [R]will make war against them, overcome
them, and kill them. Rev. 9:1, 2 • Dan. 7:21
8 And their dead bodies *will lie* in the
street of [R]the great city which spiritually is
called Sodom and Egypt, [R]where also *our
Lord was crucified. Rev. 14:8 • Heb. 13:12
9 Then *those* from the peoples, tribes,
tongues, and nations will see their dead
bodies three and a half days, and not allow
their dead bodies to be put into graves.
10 [R]And those who dwell on the earth will
rejoice over them, make merry, [R]and send
gifts to one another, [R]because these two
prophets tormented those who dwell on the
earth. Rev. 12:12 • Esth. 9:19, 22 • Rev. 16:10
11 [R]Now after the three and a half days [R]the
breath of life from God entered them, and
they stood on their feet, and great fear fell on
those who saw them. Rev. 11:9 • Ezek. 37:5, 9, 10
12 And *they heard a loud voice from
heaven saying to them, "Come up here."
[R]And they ascended to heaven [R]in a cloud,
and their enemies saw them. Is. 14:13 • Acts 1:9
13 In the same hour there was a great
earthquake, [R]and a tenth of the city fell. In
the earthquake seven thousand men were
killed, and the rest were afraid and gave glory
to the God of heaven. Rev. 16:19
14 [R]The second woe is past. Behold, the
third woe is coming quickly. Rev. 8:13; 9:12

Seventh Trumpet

15 Then the seventh angel sounded: And
there were loud voices in heaven, saying,
"The *kingdoms of this world have become
the kingdoms of our Lord and of His Christ,
and He shall reign forever and ever!"
16 And the twenty-four elders who sat before God on their thrones fell on their faces
and [R]worshiped God, Rev. 4:11; 5:9, 12, 14; 7:11
17 saying:

"We give You thanks, O Lord God
Almighty,
The One [R]who is and who was *and
who is to come,
Because You have taken Your great
power [R]and reigned. Rev. 16:5 • Rev. 19:6
18 The nations were [R]angry, and Your
[T]wrath has come,
And the time of the [R]dead, that they
should be judged,

10:4 NU, M omit *to me* **10:5** NU, M *right hand*
10:11 NU, M *they*
11:1 NU, M omit *And the angel stood*
11:4 NU, M *Lord* **11:8** NU, M *their*
11:15 NU, M *kingdom . . . has* **11:12** M *I*
11:17 NU, M omit *and who is to come*

And that You should reward Your
servants the prophets and the saints,
And those who fear Your name, small
and great,
And should destroy those who destroy
the earth." Ps. 2:1 • *anger* • Dan. 7:10

19 Then [R]the temple of God was opened in
heaven, and the ark of *His covenant was
seen in His temple. And [R]there were lightnings, noises, thunderings, an earthquake,
[R]and great hail. Rev. 4:1; 15:5, 8 • Rev. 8:5 • Rev. 16:21

CHAPTER 12

The Woman

NOW a great sign appeared in heaven: a
woman clothed with the sun, with the
moon under her feet, and on her head a
garland of twelve stars.
2 Then being with child, she cried out [R]in
labor and in pain to give birth. Is. 26:17; 66:6–9
3 And another sign appeared in heaven:
behold, [R]a great, fiery red dragon having
seven heads and ten horns, and seven diadems on his heads. Rev. 13:1; 17:3, 7, 9
4 His tail drew a third of the stars of
heaven and threw them to the earth. And the
dragon stood [R]before the woman who was
ready to give birth, [R]to devour her Child as
soon as it was born. Rev. 12:2 • Matt. 2:16
5 And she bore a male Child [R]who was to
rule all nations with a rod of iron. And her
Child was [R]caught up to God and *to* His
throne. Ps. 2:9; Rev. 19:15☆ • Acts 1:9–11
6 Then [R]the woman fled into the wilderness, where she has a place prepared by God,
that they should feed her there one thousand
two hundred and sixty days. Rev. 12:4

The War in Heaven

7 And war broke out in heaven: Michael
and his angels fought against the dragon; and
the dragon and his angels fought,
8 but they did not prevail, nor was a place
found for *them in heaven any longer.
9 So [R]the great dragon was cast out, [R]that
serpent of old, called the Devil and Satan,
[R]who deceives the whole world; [R]he was cast
to the earth, and his angels were cast out
with him. John 12:31 • Gen. 3:1, 4 • Rev. 20:3 • Rev. 9:1
10 Then I heard a loud voice saying in
heaven, "Now salvation, and strength, and
the kingdom of our God, and the power of
His Christ have come, for the accuser of our
brethren, [R]who accused them before our God
day and night, has been cast down. Zech. 3:1
11 "And [R]they overcame him by the blood
of the Lamb and by the word of their testimony, [R]and they did not love their lives to the
death. Rom. 16:20 • Luke 14:26
12 "Therefore rejoice, O heavens, and you
who dwell in them! Woe to the inhabitants of
the earth and the sea! For the devil has come
down to you, having great wrath, because he
knows that he has a short time."

The War on Earth

13 Now when the dragon saw that he had
been cast to the earth, he persecuted the
woman who gave birth to the male *Child.*
14 But the woman was given two wings of a
great eagle, that she might fly [R]into the
wilderness to her place, where she is nourished for a time and times and half a time,
from the presence of the serpent. Rev. 17:3
15 So the serpent [R]spewed water out of his
mouth like a flood after the woman, that he
might cause her to be carried away by the
flood. Is. 59:19
16 But the earth helped the woman, and the
earth opened its mouth and swallowed up the
flood which the dragon had spewed out of his
mouth.
17 And the dragon was enraged with the
woman, and he went to make war with the
rest of her offspring, who keep the commandments of God and have the testimony of
Jesus *Christ.

CHAPTER 13

The Beast Out of the Sea

THEN *I stood on the sand of the sea. And
I saw a beast rising up out of the sea,
[R]having seven heads and ten horns, and on
his horns ten crowns, and on his heads a
[R]blasphemous name. Rev. 12:3 • Rev. 17:3
2 Now the beast which I saw was like a
leopard, his feet were like *the feet of* a bear,
and his mouth like the mouth of a lion. And
the [R]dragon gave him his power, his throne,
and great authority. Rev. 12:3, 9; 13:4, 12
3 I saw one of his heads [R]as if it had been
mortally wounded, and his deadly wound was
healed. And [R]all the world marveled and
followed the beast. Rev. 13:12, 14 • Rev. 17:8
4 So they worshiped the dragon who gave
authority to the beast; and they worshiped
the beast, saying, [R]"Who *is* like the beast?
Who is able to make war with him?" Rev. 18:18
5 And he was given [R]a mouth speaking
great things and blasphemies, and he was
given authority to *continue for [R]forty-two
months. Dan. 7:8, 11, 20, 25; 11:36 • Rev. 11:2
6 Then he opened his mouth in blasphemy
against God, to blaspheme His name, His
tabernacle, and those who dwell in heaven.
7 And it was granted to him [R]to make war
with the saints and to overcome them. And
[R]authority was given him over every *tribe,
tongue, and nation. Dan. 7:21 • Rev. 11:18

11:19 M *the covenant of the Lord* **12:8** M *him*
12:17 NU, M omit *Christ* **13:1** NU *he*
13:5 M *make war* **13:7** NU, M add *and people*

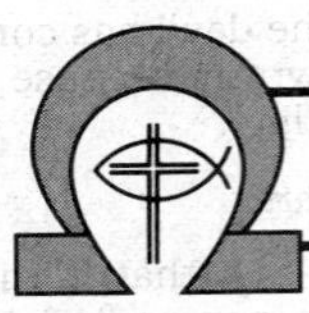

NEW TESTAMENT DREAMS

In New Testament times, God often used dreams (when a person was asleep) and visions (when a person was awake) to make His will known. The apostle John, exiled on the Isle of Patmos, received a series of seven visions from God, which he faithfully recorded for future generations in the Book of Revelation. Dreams and visions were also prominently associated with the birth of Jesus and the conversion and ministry of the apostle Paul.

Does God still speak today through visions and dreams? Some scholars believe He does; while others insist there is no need for such revelation today, since God communicates with all believers directly through His Holy Spirit.

Other significant dreams and visions in the New Testament include the following:

DREAMS

Personality	Message of Dream	Biblical Reference
Joseph	Three separate dreams: (1) assured of Mary's purity (2) warned to flee to Egypt (3) told to return to Nazareth	 Matt. 1:20 Matt. 2:13 Matt. 2:19–23
Wise men	Warned of Herod's plot against the baby Jesus	Matt. 2:12

VISIONS

Personality	Message of Vision	Biblical Reference
Paul	Converted to Christianity in a blinding vision of Christ on the Damascus road	Acts 9:3–9
Ananias	Instructed to minister to Saul in Damascus	Acts 9:10–16
Cornelius	Instructed to ask Peter to come to Joppa	Acts 10:3–6
Peter	Told to eat unclean animals—a message to accept the Gentiles	Acts 10:9–18, 28
Paul	Beckoned to do missionary work in the province of Macedonia	Acts 16:9
Paul	Assured of God's presence in Corinth	Acts 18:9, 10
Paul	Promised God's presence during his trip to Rome	Acts 23:11
Paul	Viewed the glories of the third heaven	2 Cor. 12:1–4

8 And all who dwell on the earth will
worship him, whose names have not been
written in the Book of Life of the Lamb slain
[R]from the foundation of the world. Rev. 17:8
9 If anyone has an ear, let him hear.
10 He who leads into captivity shall go into
captivity; he who kills with the sword must
be killed with the sword. Here is the patience
and the faith of the saints.

The Beast Out of the Earth

11 Then I saw another beast [R]coming up out
of the earth, and he had two horns like a
lamb and spoke like a dragon. Rev. 11:7
12 And he exercises all the authority of the
first beast in his presence, and causes the
earth and those who dwell in it to worship
the first beast, [R]whose deadly wound was
healed. Rev. 13:3, 4
13 He performs great signs, [R]so that he even
makes fire come down from heaven on the
earth in the sight of men. 1 Kin. 18:38
14 [R]And he deceives *those who dwell on
the earth [R]by those signs which he was
granted to do in the sight of the beast, telling
those who dwell on the earth to make an
image to the beast who was wounded by the
sword [R]and lived. Rev. 12:9 • 2 Thess. 2:9 • 2 Kin. 20:7
15 He was granted *power* to give breath to
the image of the beast, that the image of the
beast should both speak [R]and cause as many
as would not worship the image of the beast
to be killed. Rev. 16:2
16 And he causes all, both small and great,
rich and poor, free and slave, [R]to receive a
mark on their right hand or on their foreheads, Rev. 7:3; 14:9; 20:4
17 and that no one may buy or sell except
one who has the mark or the name of the
beast, [R]or the number of his name. Rev. 15:2
18 Here is wisdom. Let him who has [R]under-
standing calculate [R]the number of the beast,
[R]for it is the number of a man: His number *is*
666. [1 Cor. 2:14] • Rev. 15:2 • Rev. 21:17

CHAPTER 14

The 144,000

THEN I looked, and behold, *a [R]Lamb
standing on Mount Zion, and with Him
[R]one hundred *and* forty-four thousand, *having His Father's name [R]written on their
foreheads. Rev. 5:6 • Rev. 7:4; 14:3 • Rev. 7:3; 22:4
2 And I heard a voice from heaven, like the
voice of many waters, and like the voice of
loud thunder. And I heard the sound of
[R]harpists playing their harps. Rev. 5:8
3 And they sang as it were a new song
before the throne, before the four living
creatures, and the elders; and no one could
learn that song [R]except the hundred *and*
forty-four thousand who were redeemed
from the earth. Rev. 5:9
4 These are the ones who were not defiled
with women, [R]for they are virgins. These are
the ones [R]who follow the Lamb wherever He
goes. These [R]were *redeemed from *among*
men, [R]*being* firstfruits to God and to the
Lamb. [2 Cor. 11:2] • Rev. 3:4; 7:17 • Rev. 5:9 • James 1:18
5 And [R]in their mouth was found no
[T]guile,* for [R]they are without fault *before
the throne of God. Ps. 32:2 • *deceit* • Eph. 5:27

The Three Angels' Announcements

6 Then I saw another angel [R]flying in the
midst of heaven, [R]having the everlasting
gospel to preach to those who dwell on the
earth—[R]to every nation, tribe, tongue, and
people— Rev. 8:13 • Eph. 3:9 • Rev. 13:7
7 saying with a loud voice, [R]"Fear God and
give glory to Him, for the hour of His judgment has come; [R]and worship Him who made
heaven and earth, the sea and springs of
water." Rev. 11:18 • Neh. 9:6
8 And another angel followed, saying,
*"Babylon is fallen, *is fallen, that great city,
because she has made all nations drink of the
wine of the wrath of her fornication."
9 Then a third angel followed them, saying
with a loud voice, "If anyone worships the
beast and his image, and receives *his* [R]mark
on his forehead or on his hand, Rev. 13:16
10 "he himself shall also drink of the wine
of the wrath of God, which is poured out full
strength into the cup of His indignation. And
he shall be tormented with [R]fire and brimstone in the presence of the holy angels and
in the presence of the Lamb. 2 Thess. 1:7
11 "And [R]the smoke of their torment ascends forever and ever; and they have no rest
day or night, who worship the beast and his
image, and whoever receives the mark of his
name." Is. 34:8–10
12 Here is the patience of the saints; *here
are those who keep the commandments of
God and the faith of Jesus.
13 Then I heard a voice from heaven saying
*to me, "Write: 'Blessed *are* the dead who die
in the Lord from now on.'" "Yes," says the
Spirit, "that they may rest from their labors,
and their works follow them."

The Harvest Judgment

14 And I looked, and behold, a white cloud,
and on the cloud sat *One* like the Son of Man,
having on His head a golden crown, and in
His hand a sharp sickle.
15 And another angel came out of the temple, crying with a loud voice to Him who sat

13:14 M *my own people* **14:1** NU, M *the*
14:1 NU, M add *His name and*
14:4 M adds *by Jesus* **14:5** NU, M *falsehood*
14:5 NU, M omit the rest of v. 5.
14:8 NU, M add *the great*
14:8 NU, M omit *is fallen, the great city, because*
14:12 NU, M omit *here are those*
14:13 NU, M omit *to me*

on the cloud, "Thrust in Your sickle and reap,
for the time has come *for You to reap, for
the harvest of the earth is ripe."
16 So He who sat on the cloud thrust in His
sickle on the earth, and the earth was reaped.
17 Then another angel came out of the
temple which is in heaven, he also having a
sharp sickle.
18 And another angel came out from the
altar, who had power over fire, and he cried
with a loud cry to him who had the sharp
sickle, saying, [R]"Thrust in your sharp sickle
and gather the clusters of the vine of the
earth, for her grapes are fully ripe." Joel 3:13
19 So the angel thrust his sickle into the
earth and gathered the vine of the earth, and
threw *it* into [R]the great winepress of the
wrath of God. Rev. 19:15
20 And the winepress was trampled outside
the city, and blood came out of the winepress,
[R]up to the horses' bridles, for [T]one thousand
six hundred furlongs. Is. 34:3 • 184 mi.

CHAPTER 15

Preparation for the Bowl Judgments

THEN [R]I saw another sign in heaven, great
and marvelous: [R]seven angels having the
seven last plagues, [R]for in them the wrath of
God is complete. Rev. 12:1, 3 • Rev. 21:9 • Rev. 14:10
2 And I saw *something* like [R]a sea of glass
[R]mingled with fire, and those who have the
victory over the beast, [R]over his image and
*over his mark *and* over the number of his
name, standing on the sea of glass, having
harps of God. Rev. 4:6 • [Matt. 3:11] • Rev. 13:14, 15
3 And they sing [R]the song of Moses, the
servant of God, and the song of the [R]Lamb,
saying: Ex. 15:1–21 • Rev. 15:3

[R]"Great and marvelous *are* Your works,
Lord God Almighty! Deut. 32:3, 4
[R]Just and true *are* Your ways,
O King of the *saints! Ps. 145:17
4 [R]Who shall not fear You, O Lord, and
glorify Your name?
For *You* alone *are* [R]holy.
For [R]all nations shall come and worship
before You,
For Your judgments have been
manifested." Ex. 15:14 • Lev. 11:44 • Is. 66:23

5 After these things I looked, and *behold,
the [T]temple of the tabernacle of the testimony in heaven was opened. The inner shrine
6 And out of the [T]temple came the seven
angels having the seven plagues, clothed in
pure bright linen, and having their chests
girded with golden bands. The inner shrine
7 [R]Then one of the four living creatures
gave to the seven angels seven golden bowls
full of the wrath of God [R]who lives forever
and ever. Rev. 4:6 • 1 Thess. 1:9
8 The temple was filled with smoke from
the glory of God and from His power, and no
one was able to enter the temple till the seven
plagues of the seven angels were completed.

CHAPTER 16

First Bowl

THEN I heard a loud voice from the temple
saying [R]to the seven angels, "Go and pour
out the *bowls [R]of the wrath of God on the
earth." Rev. 15:1 • Rev. 14:10
2 So the first went and poured out his bowl
[R]upon the earth, and a [T]foul and [R]loathsome
sore came upon the men who had the mark
of the beast and those who worshiped his
image. Rev. 8:7 • Lit. *bad and evil* • Ex. 9:9–11

Second Bowl

3 Then the second angel poured out his
bowl [R]on the sea, and [R]it became blood as of a
dead *man*; [R]and every living creature in the
sea died. Rev. 8:8; 11:6 • Ex. 7:17–21 • Rev. 8:9

Third Bowl

4 Then the third angel poured out his bowl
[R]on the rivers and springs of water, [R]and they
became blood. Rev. 8:10 • Ex. 7:17–20
5 And I heard the angel of the waters
saying:

[R]"You are righteous, *O Lord,
The One [R]who is and who was and who
is to be, Rev. 15:3, 4 • Rev. 1:4, 8
Because You have judged these things.
6 For [R]they have shed the blood [R]of saints
and prophets,
[R]And You have given them blood to
drink. Matt. 23:34 • Rev. 11:18 • Is. 49:26
For it is their just due."

7 And I heard *another from the altar
saying, "Even so, [R]Lord God Almighty, true
and righteous *are* Your judgments." Rev. 15:3

Fourth Bowl

8 Then the fourth angel poured out his
bowl on the sun, [R]and power was given to
him to scorch men with fire. Rev. 9:17, 18
9 And men were scorched with great heat,
and they blasphemed the name of God who
has power over these plagues; and they did
not repent [R]and give Him glory. Rev. 11:13

Fifth Bowl

10 Then the fifth angel poured out his bowl
on the throne of the beast, and his kingdom
became full of darkness; [R]and they gnawed
their tongues because of the pain. Rev. 11:10

14:15 NU, M omit *for You*
15:2 NU, M omit *over his mark* 15:3 NU, M *nations*
15:5 NU, M omit *behold* 16:1 NU, M *seven bowls*
16:5 NU, M omit *O Lord*
16:7 NU, M omit *another from*

11 And they blasphemed the God of heaven
because of their pains and their sores, and did
not repent of their deeds.

Sixth Bowl

12 Then the sixth angel poured out his bowl
[R]on the great river Euphrates, and its water
was dried up, so that the way of the kings
from the east might be prepared. Rev. 9:14
13 And I saw three unclean spirits like frogs
coming out of the mouth of the dragon, out
of the mouth of the beast, and out of the
mouth of the false prophet.
14 For they are spirits of demons, [R]perform-
ing signs, *which* go out to the kings *of the
earth [R]and of the whole world, to gather
them to [R]the battle of that great day of God
Almighty. 2 Thess. 2:9 • Luke 2:1 • Rev. 17:14; 19:19; 20:8
15 [R]"Behold, I am coming as a thief. Blessed
is he who watches, and keeps his garments, lest he walk naked and they see his
shame." Matt. 24:43 ☆
16 And they gathered them together to the
place called in Hebrew, *Armageddon.

Seventh Bowl

17 Then the seventh angel poured out his
bowl into the air, and a loud voice came out
of the temple of heaven, from the throne,
saying, [R]"It is done!" Rev. 10:6; 21:6
18 And [R]there were noises and thunderings
and lightnings; [R]and there was a great earthquake, such a mighty and great earthquake
[R]as had not occurred since men were on the
earth. Rev. 4:5 • Rev. 11:13 • Dan. 12:1
19 Now the great city was divided into three
parts, and the cities of the nations fell. And
great Babylon [R]was remembered before God,
[R]to give her the cup of the wine of the
fierceness of His wrath. Rev. 14:8; 18:5 • Is. 51:17
20 Then [R]every island fled away, and the
mountains were not found. Rev. 6:14; 20:11
21 And great hail from heaven fell upon
men, *every hailstone* about the weight of a
[T]talent. And men blasphemed God because of
the plague of the hail, since that plague was
exceedingly great. 75 lb.

CHAPTER 17

Great Harlot Is Described

THEN one of the seven angels who had the
seven bowls came and talked with me,
saying *to me, "Come, [R]I will show you the
judgment of [R]the great harlot [R]who sits on
many waters, Rev. 16:19 • Nah. 3:4 • Jer. 51:13
2 [R]"with whom the kings of the earth
committed fornication, and [R]the inhabitants
of the earth were made drunk with the wine
of her fornication." Rev. 2:22; 18:3, 9 • Jer. 51:7
3 So he carried me away in the Spirit [R]into
the wilderness. And I saw a woman sitting
[R]on a scarlet beast *which was* full of [R]names
of blasphemy, having seven heads and ten
horns. Rev. 12:6, 14; 21:10 • Rev. 12:3 • Rev. 13:1
4 The woman was arrayed in purple and
scarlet, and adorned with gold and precious
stones and pearls, having in her hand a
golden cup [R]full of abominations and the
filthiness of *her fornication. Rev. 14:8
5 And on her forehead a name *was* written:

[R]MYSTERY, 2 Thess. 2:7
BABYLON THE GREAT,
THE MOTHER OF HARLOTS AND OF THE
ABOMINATIONS OF THE EARTH.

6 And I saw the woman, drunk with the
blood of the saints and with the blood of [R]the
martyrs of Jesus. And when I saw her, I
marveled with great amazement. Rev. 6:9, 10

Great Harlot Is Destroyed

7 But the angel said to me, "Why did you
marvel? I will tell you the mystery of the
woman and of the beast that carries her,
which has the seven heads and the ten horns.
8 "The beast that you saw was, and is not,
and will ascend out of the bottomless pit and
go to perdition. And those who dwell on the
earth [R]will marvel, whose names are not
written in the Book of Life from the foundation of the world, when they see the beast
that was, and is not, and *yet is. Rev. 13:3
9 [R]"Here *is* the mind which has wisdom:
[R]The seven heads are seven mountains on
which the woman sits. Rev. 13:18 • Rev. 13:1
10 There are also seven kings. Five have
fallen, one is, *and* the other has not yet come.
And when he comes, he must [R]continue a
short time. Rev. 13:5
11 "And the [R]beast that was, and is not, is
himself also the eighth, and is of the seven,
and is going to [T]perdition. Rev. 13:3 • *destruction*
12 "And [R]the ten horns which you saw are
ten kings who have received no kingdom as
yet, but they receive authority for one hour
as kings with the beast. Dan. 7:20
13 "These are of one mind, and they will
give their power and authority to the beast.
14 [R]"These will make war with the Lamb,
and the Lamb will [R]overcome them, [R]for He is
Lord of lords and King of kings; and those
who are with Him *are* called, chosen, and
faithful." Rev. 16:14; 19:19 • Rev. 19:20 • 1 Tim. 6:15
15 And he said to me, "The waters which
you saw, where the harlot sits, [R]are peoples,
multitudes, nations, and tongues. Rev. 13:7
16 "And the ten horns which you saw on
the beast, these will hate the harlot, make her

16:14 NU, M omit *of the earth and*
16:16 Lit. *Mount Megiddo*, M *Megiddo*
17:1 NU, M omit *to me*
17:4 M *the fornication of the earth*
17:8 NU, M *shall be present*

THE CITY OF MEGIDDO

Megiddo, a walled city in the Carmel Mountains, was the most strategic city in Palestine. All major traffic through the nation traveled past the city, making it an important military stronghold where many major battles were fought.

Megiddo is first mentioned in the Old Testament as a site where Joshua conquered one of thirty-one Canaanite kings (Josh. 12:21). During the period of the judges, the forces of Deborah and Barak defeated the army of Sisera "in Taanach, by the waters of Megiddo" (Judg. 5:19).

In spite of these minor victories, Megiddo did not become firmly occupied by the Israelites until the time of Solomon, who reconstructed the city as one of his storage cities (1 Kin. 9:15–19). This scale model of Megiddo (see illustration) shows that the original walls of the city were about thirteen feet thick, and they were apparently enlarged and reinforced at selected points to twice this thickness.

Zechariah prophesied that great mourning would take place "in the plain of Megiddo" (Zech. 12:11). The fulfillment of this prophecy is to be at the end of time in the Battle of Armageddon. The word *Armageddon* means "mountain of Megiddo" in Hebrew. At the end of time God will destroy the armies of the Beast and the False Prophet (Rev. 16:13–16), and the King of kings and Lord of lords will reign forever and ever (Rev. 11:15; 19:16).

Photo by Howard Vos

A model of the walled city of Megiddo.

desolate [R]and naked, eat her flesh and [R]burn
her with fire. Ezek. 16:37, 39 • Rev. 18:8
17 [R]"For God has put it into their hearts to
fulfill His purpose, to be of one mind, and to
give their kingdom to the beast, [R]until the
words of God are fulfilled. 2 Thess. 2:11 • Rev. 10:7
18 "And the woman whom you saw [R]is that
great city [R]which reigns over the kings of the
earth." Rev. 11:8; 16:19 • Rev. 12:4

CHAPTER 18

Babylon the Great Is Destroyed

AFTER[R] these things I saw another angel
coming down from heaven, having
great authority, [R]and the earth was illuminated with his glory. Rev. 17:1, 7 • Ezek. 43:2
2 And he cried *mightily with a loud voice,
saying, "Babylon the great is fallen, is fallen,
and has become a habitation of demons, a
prison for every foul spirit, and [R]a cage for
every unclean and hated bird! Is. 14:23
3 "For all the nations have drunk of the
wine of the wrath of her fornication, the
kings of the earth have committed fornication with her, [R]and the merchants of the
earth have become rich through the [T]abundance of her luxury." Is. 47:15 • Lit. *strengths*
4 And I heard another voice from heaven
saying, [R]"Come out of her, my people, lest
you share in her sins, and lest you receive of
her plagues. Is. 48:20
5 "For her sins have *reached to heaven,
and God has remembered her iniquities.
6 [R]"Render to her just as she rendered *to
you, and repay her double according to her
works; [R]in the cup which she has mixed, [R]mix
for her double. Ps. 137:8 • Rev. 14:10 • Rev. 16:19
7 "In the measure that she glorified herself
and lived [T]luxuriously, in the same measure
give her torment and sorrow; for she says in
her heart, 'I sit *as* queen, and am no widow,
and will not see sorrow.' *sensually*
8 "Therefore her plagues will come [R]in one
day—death and mourning and famine. And
she will be utterly burned with fire, for strong
is the Lord God who *judges her. Rev. 18:10

Earth Mourns Babylon's Destruction

9 "And the kings of the earth who committed fornication and lived luxuriously with
her will weep and lament for her, [R]when they
see the smoke of her burning, Rev. 19:3
10 "standing at a distance for fear of her
torment, saying, [R]'Alas, alas, that great city
Babylon, that mighty city! [R]For in one hour
your judgment has come.' Is. 21:9 • Rev. 18:17, 19
11 "And [R]the merchants of the earth will
weep and mourn over her, for no one buys
their merchandise anymore: Ezek. 27:27–34
12 [R]"merchandise of gold and silver, precious stones and pearls, fine linen and purple,
silk and scarlet, every kind of citron wood,
every kind of object of ivory, every kind of
object of most precious wood, bronze, iron,
and marble; Rev. 17:4
13 "and cinnamon and incense, fragrant oil
and frankincense, wine and oil, fine flour and
wheat, cattle and sheep, horses and chariots,
and bodies and [R]souls of men. Ezek. 27:13
14 "And the fruit that your soul longed for
has gone from you, and all the things which
are rich and splendid have *gone from you,
and you shall find them no more at all.
15 "The merchants of these things, who
became rich by her, will stand at a distance
for fear of her torment, weeping and wailing,
16 "and saying, 'Alas, alas, [R]that great city
[R]that was clothed in fine linen, purple, and
scarlet, and adorned with gold and precious
stones and pearls! Rev. 17:18 • Rev. 17:4
17 'For in one hour such great riches came
to nothing.' And [R]every shipmaster, all who
travel by ship, sailors, and as many as trade
on the sea, stood at a distance Is. 23:14
18 [R]"and cried out when they saw the
smoke of her burning, saying, [R]'What *is* like
this great city?' Ezek. 27:30 • Rev. 13:4
19 "And [R]they threw dust on their heads
and cried out, weeping and wailing, and
saying, 'Alas, alas, that great city, in which all
who had ships on the sea became rich by her
wealth! [R]For in one hour she [T]is made desolate.' Josh. 7:6 • Rev. 18:8 • *has been laid waste*

Heaven Rejoices Babylon's Destruction

20 [R]"Rejoice over her, O heaven, and *you*
*holy apostles and prophets, for [R]God has
avenged you on her!" Jer. 51:48 • Luke 11:49
21 Then a mighty angel took up a stone like
a great millstone and threw *it* into the sea,
saying, [R]"Thus with violence the great city
Babylon shall be thrown down, and [R]shall not
be found anymore. Jer. 51:63, 64 • Rev. 12:8; 16:20
22 [R]"The sound of harpists, musicians, flutists, and trumpeters shall not be heard in you
anymore. And no craftsman of any craft
shall be found in you anymore. And the
sound of a millstone shall not be heard in you
anymore. Jer. 7:34; 16:9; 25:10
23 "And the light of a lamp shall not shine
in you anymore. And the voice of bridegroom
and bride shall not be heard in you anymore.
For your merchants were the great men of
the earth, [R]for by your sorcery all the nations
were deceived. 2 Kin. 9:22
24 "And [R]in her was found the blood of
prophets and saints, and of all who [R]were
slain on the earth." Rev. 16:6; 17:6 • Jer. 51:49

CHAPTER 19

AFTER these things I heard a loud voice of
a great multitude in heaven, saying,

18:2 NU, M omit *mightily*
18:5 NU, M *been heaped up*
18:6 NU, M omit *to you* **18:8** NU, M *has judged*
18:14 NU, M *been lost to you*
18:20 NU, M *saints and apostles*

"Alleluia! [R]Salvation and glory and honor and
power to *the Lord our God! Rev. 4:11
2 "For true and righteous *are* His judgments, because He has judged the great harlot who corrupted the earth with her fornication; and He has avenged on her the blood of His servants *shed* by her."
3 Again they said, "Alleluia! [R]And her
smoke rises up forever and ever!" Is. 34:10
4 And [R]the twenty-four elders and the four living creatures fell down and worshiped God who sat on the throne, saying, [R]"Amen! Alleluia!" Rev. 4:4, 6, 10 • 1 Chr. 16:36
5 Then a voice came from the throne, saying, [R]"Praise our God, all you His servants and those who fear Him, [R]both small and great!" Ps. 134:1 • Rev. 11:18
6 [R]And I heard, as it were, the voice of a great multitude, as the sound of many waters and as the sound of mighty thunderings, saying, "Alleluia! For [R]the Lord God Omnipotent reigns! Ezek. 1:24 • Rev. 11:15

Marriage Supper of the Lamb

7 "Let us be glad and rejoice and give Him glory, for the marriage of the Lamb has come, and His wife has made herself ready."
8 And to her it was granted to be arrayed in fine linen, clean and bright, for the fine linen is the righteous acts of the saints.
9 Then he said to me, "Write: 'Blessed *are* those who are called to the marriage supper of the Lamb!' " And he said to me, [R]"These are the true sayings of God." Rev. 22:6
10 And I fell at his feet to worship him. But he said to me, "See *that you* do not *do that!* I am your [R]fellow servant, and of your brethren [R]who have the testimony of Jesus. Worship God! For the testimony of Jesus is the spirit of prophecy." [Heb. 1:14] • 1 John 5:10

Second Coming of Christ

11 Then I saw heaven opened, and behold, a white horse. And He who sat on him *was* called Faithful and True, and [R]in righteousness He judges and makes war. Is. 11:4
12 [R]His eyes *were* like a flame of fire, and on His head *were* many crowns. [R]He *had a name written that no one knew except Himself. Rev. 1:14☆ • Rev. 2:17; 19:16
13 [R]He *was* clothed with a robe dipped in blood, and His name is called [R]The Word of God. Is. 63:2, 3☆ • [John 1:1, 14]
14 [R]And the armies in heaven, [R]clothed in fine linen, white and clean, followed Him on white horses. Rev. 14:20 • Matt. 28:3
15 Now [R]out of His mouth goes a *sharp sword, that with it He should strike the nations. And [R]He Himself will rule them with a rod of iron. [R]He Himself treads the winepress of the fierceness and wrath of Almighty God. Is. 11:4 • Ps. 2:8, 9 • Is. 63:3–6
16 And [R]He has on *His* robe and on His thigh a name [R]written: Rev. 2:17 • Dan. 2:47

KING OF KINGS
AND LORD OF LORDS.

17 Then I saw an angel standing in the sun; and he cried with a loud voice, saying to all the birds that fly in the midst of heaven, [R]"Come and gather together for the *supper of the great God, Ezek. 39:17
18 [R]"that you may eat the flesh of kings, the flesh of captains, the flesh of mighty men, the flesh of horses and of those who sit on them, and the flesh of all *people,* free and slave, both small and great." Ezek. 39:18–20
19 [R]And I saw the beast, the kings of the earth, and their armies, gathered together to make war against Him who sat on the horse and against His army. Rev. 16:13–16☆
20 Then the beast was captured, and with him the false prophet who worked signs in his presence, by which he deceived those who received the mark of the beast and [R]those who worshiped his image. [R]These two were cast alive into the lake of fire [R]burning with brimstone. Rev. 13:8, 12, 13 • Dan. 7:11 • Rev. 14:10
21 And the rest were killed with the sword which proceeded from the mouth of Him who sat on the horse. [R]And all the birds [R]were filled with their flesh. Rev. 19:17, 18 • Rev. 17:16

CHAPTER 20

Satan Is Bound 1,000 Years

THEN I saw an angel coming down from heaven, having the key to the bottomless pit and a great chain in his hand.
2 He laid hold of [R]the dragon, that serpent of old, who is *the* Devil and Satan, and bound him for a thousand years; 2 Pet. 2:4
3 and he cast him into the bottomless pit, and shut him up, and [R]set a seal on him, [R]so that he should deceive the nations no more till the thousand years were finished. But after these things he must be released for a little while. Dan. 6:17 • Rev. 12:9; 20:8, 10

Saints Reign 1,000 Years

4 And I saw [R]thrones, and they sat on them, and [R]judgment was committed to them. And *I saw* [R]the souls of those who had been beheaded for their witness to Jesus and for the word of God, who had not worshiped the beast or his image, and had not received *his* mark on their foreheads or on their hands. And they lived and reigned with Christ for *a thousand years. Dan. 7:9 • [1 Cor. 6:2, 3] • Rev. 6:9
5 But the rest of the dead did not live again until the thousand years were finished. This *is* the first resurrection.

19:1 NU, M omit *the Lord*
19:12 M adds *names written, and*
19:15 M *sharp two-edged*
19:17 NU, M *great supper of God* **20:4** M *the*

THE MILLENNIUM

The Millennium, a term meaning "thousand," refers to the thousand-year reign of Christ in connection with His return to earth. Some Christians believe the Millennium will be an age of blessedness on the earth. Some believe the Millennium is the present church age—a period of indefinite length. Still others regard the Millennium as a way of referring to the ages of eternity.

The Bible's only specific mention of the Millennium is in the twentieth chapter of Revelation, a book of visions and prophecies written by the apostle John while in exile on the Isle of Patmos off the coast of Asia Minor (see tomb of John at Ephesus in photo below). Many Old Testament passages also seem to point to a millennial reign (Is. 11:4; Jer. 3:17; Zech. 14:9).

Interpreters differ greatly in their understanding of the Millennium and when and how it will occur.

Postmillennialists expect Christ's visible return to earth *after* the Millennium. They look for teaching and preaching to usher in a thousand years of peace and righteousness before Christ's return. Some postmillennialists believe this "golden age" has already begun, without our being able to mark a specific date when it started.

Premillennialists, on the other hand, believe that Christ will return *before* the Millennium. Interpreting Revelation 20 literally, they hold that Christ will reign on earth (probably in Jerusalem) for a literal thousand years. According to this view, God's promises made to the nation of Israel will be fulfilled. Satan will be bound and cast into a bottomless pit during Christ's reign (Rev. 20:2, 3). All believers will be raised before the Millennium to share Christ's reign (Rev. 5:10; 20:4). The remaining dead will wait for the second resurrection (Rev. 20:5). Premillennialists also believe that after the Millennium Satan will be released for a season but ultimately will be thrown into a "lake of fire" (Rev. 20:7, 10).

Amillennialists interpret Christ's millennial reign in a spiritual sense. While believing in the Lord's return, they reject a literal thousand-year reign on earth. Some see Christ's reign as having begun in His life or at the time of His resurrection. They cite Peter's declaration that Christ now rules from the right hand of God (Acts 2:33–36). The kingdom promises to Israel are viewed symbolically by amillennialists and are applied either to the church age or to the ages of eternity.

Whatever our view of the Millennium, we should focus on preparing for the Lord's Second Coming and His eternal reign (Heb. 10:13; 1 Cor. 15:25–27).

Photo by Howard Vos

Traditional tomb of the apostle John in the Church of St. John at Ephesus.

6 Blessed and holy *is* he who has part in
the first resurrection. Over such [R]the second
death has no power, but they shall be [R]priests
of God and of Christ, and shall reign with
Him a thousand years. [Rev. 2:11; 20:14] • Is. 61:6

Satan Is Released and Leads Rebellion

7 Now when the thousand years have expired, Satan will be released from his prison
8 and will go out [R]to deceive the nations
which are in the four corners of the earth,
[R]Gog and Magog, [R]to gather them together to
battle, whose number *is* as the sand of the
sea. Rev. 12:9; 20:3, 10 • Ezek. 38:2; 39:1, 6 • Rev. 16:14
9 They went up on the breadth of the earth
and surrounded the camp of the saints and
the beloved city. And fire came down from
God out of heaven and devoured them.

Satan Is Tormented Forever

10 And the devil, who deceived them, was
cast into the lake of fire and brimstone
[R]where the beast and the false prophet *are.*
And they [R]will be tormented day and night
forever and ever. Rev. 19:20; 20:14, 15 • Rev. 14:10

Great White Throne Judgment

11 Then I saw a great white throne and Him
who sat on it, from whose face [R]the earth and
the heaven fled away. [R]And there was found
no place for them. 2 Pet. 3:7 • Dan. 2:35
12 And I saw the dead, small and great,
standing before *God, and books were
opened. And another book was opened,
which is *the Book* of Life. And the dead were
judged according to their works, by the
things which were written in the books.
13 The sea gave up the dead who were in it,
and Death and Hades delivered up the dead
who were in them. [R]And they were judged,
each one according to his works. Rev. 2:23
14 Then Death and Hades were cast into the
lake of fire. This is the second *death.
15 And anyone not found written in the
Book of Life was cast into the lake of fire.

CHAPTER 21

New Heaven and Earth Are Created

AND [R]I saw a new heaven and a new earth,
[R]for the first heaven and the first earth
had passed away. Also there was no more
sea. [2 Pet. 3:13] • Rev. 20:11

New Jerusalem Descends

2 Then I, *John, saw [R]the holy city, New
Jerusalem, coming down out of heaven from
God, prepared [R]as a bride adorned for her
husband. Is. 52:1 • 2 Cor. 11:2
3 And I heard a loud voice from heaven
saying, "Behold, [R]the tabernacle of God *is*
with men, and He will dwell with them, and
they shall be His people, and God Himself will
be with them *and be* their God. Lev. 26:11
4 [R]"And God will wipe away every tear
from their eyes; there shall be no more death,
[R]nor sorrow, nor crying; and there shall be no
more pain, for the former things have passed
away." Is. 25:8☆ • Is. 35:10☆
5 Then [R]He who sat on the throne said,
[R]"Behold, I make all things new." And He
said *to me, "Write, for [R]these words are true
and faithful." Rev. 20:11 • Is. 43:19 • Rev. 19:9; 22:6
6 And He said to me, *"It is done! I am the
Alpha and the Omega, the Beginning and the
End. I will give of the fountain of the water of
life freely to him who thirsts.
7 "He who overcomes *shall inherit all
things, and [R]I will be his God and he shall be
My son. Zech. 8:8☆
8 "But the cowardly, *unbelieving, abominable, murderers, sexually immoral, sorcerers, idolaters, and all liars shall have their
part in the lake which burns with fire and
brimstone, which is the second death."

New Jerusalem Is Described

9 Then one of [R]the seven angels who had
the seven bowls filled with the seven last
plagues came *to me and talked with me,
saying, "Come, I will show you [R]the *bride,
the Lamb's wife." Rev. 15:1 • Rev. 19:7; 21:2
10 And he carried me away [R]in the Spirit to
a great and high mountain, and showed me
the *great city, the *holy Jerusalem, descending out of heaven from God, Rev. 1:10
11 [R]having the glory of God. And her light
was like a most precious stone, like a jasper
stone, clear as crystal. Rev. 15:8; 21:23; 22:5
12 Also she had a great and high wall with
[R]twelve gates, and twelve angels at the gates,
and names written on them, which are *the
names* of the twelve tribes of the children of
Israel: Ezek. 48:31–34
13 [R]three gates on the east, three gates on
the north, three gates on the south, and three
gates on the west. Ezek. 48:31–34
14 Now the wall of the city had twelve
foundations, and [R]on them were the *names
of the twelve apostles of the Lamb. Eph. 2:20
15 And he who talked with me [R]had a gold
[T]reed to measure the city, its gates, and its
wall. Ezek. 40:3 • 10.5 ft.
16 And the city is laid out as a square, and
its length is as great as its breadth. And he
measured the city with the reed: twelve
thousand [T]furlongs. Its length, breadth, and
height are equal. 1377 mi.
17 Then he measured its wall: [T]one hundred

20:12 NU, M *the throne*
20:14 NU, M *death, the lake of fire.*
21:2 NU, M omit *John* **21:5** NU, M omit *to me*
21:6 M omits *It is done*
21:7 M *I shall give him these things*
21:8 M adds *and sinners,* **21:9** NU, M omit *to me*
21:9 NU, M *woman, the Lamb's bride*
21:10 NU, M omit *great*
21:10 NU, M *holy city, Jerusalem*
21:14 NU, M *twelve names*

and forty-four cubits, *according* to the measure of a man, that is, of an angel. 216 ft.

18 And the construction of its wall was *of* jasper; and the city *was* pure gold, like clear glass.

19 [R]And the foundations of the wall of the city *were* adorned with all kinds of precious stones: the first foundation *was* jasper, the second sapphire, the third chalcedony, the fourth emerald, Is. 54:11

20 the fifth sardonyx, the sixth sardius, the seventh chrysolite, the eighth beryl, the ninth topaz, the tenth chrysoprase, the eleventh jacinth, and the twelfth amethyst.

21 And the twelve gates *were* twelve [R]pearls: each individual gate was of one pearl. [R]And the street of the city *was* pure gold, like transparent glass. Matt. 13:45, 46 • Rev. 22:2

22 But I saw no temple in it, for the Lord God Almighty and the Lamb are its temple.

23 [R]And the city had no need of the sun or of the moon to shine *in it, for the *glory of God illuminated it, and the Lamb *is* its light. Is. 24:23; John 4:23☆

24 And the nations *of those who are saved shall walk in its light, and the kings of the earth bring their glory and honor *into it.

25 Its gates shall not be shut at all by day [R](there shall be no night there). Is. 60:20

26 [R]And they shall bring the glory and the honor of the nations into *it. Rev. 21:24

27 But [R]there shall by no means enter it anything *that defiles, or causes an abomination or a lie, but only those who are written in the Lamb's [R]Book of Life. Joel 3:17 • Phil. 4:3

CHAPTER 22

AND he showed me a *pure river of water of life, clear as crystal, proceeding from the throne of God and of the Lamb.

2 [R]In the middle of its street, and on either side of the river, *was* the tree of life, which bore twelve fruits, each *tree* yielding its fruit every month. And the leaves of the tree *were* for the healing of the nations. Ezek. 47:12☆

3 And there shall be no more curse, but the throne of God and of the Lamb shall be in it, and His servants shall serve Him.

4 [R]They shall see His face, and [R]His name *shall be* on their foreheads. [Matt. 5:8]☆ • Rev. 14:1

5 And there shall be no night there: They need no lamp nor light of the sun, for [R]the Lord God gives them light. [R]And they shall reign forever and ever. Ps. 36:9 • Dan. 7:18, 27

Conclusion

6 Then he said to me, [R]"These words *are* faithful and true." And the Lord God of the *holy prophets [R]sent His angel to show His servants the things which must [R]shortly take place. Rev. 19:9 • Rev. 1:1 • Heb. 10:37

7 [R]"Behold, I am coming quickly! [R]Blessed *is* he who keeps the words of the prophecy of this book." [Rev. 3:11] • Rev. 1:3

8 Now I, John, *saw and heard these things. And when I heard and saw, [R]I fell down to worship before the feet of the angel who showed me these things. Rev. 19:10

9 Then he said to me, [R]"See *that you do* not *do that*. For I am your fellow servant, and of your brethren the prophets, and of those who keep the words of this book. Worship God." Rev. 19:10

10 [R]And he said to me, "Do not seal the words of the prophecy of this book, [R]for the time is at hand. Dan. 8:26 • Rev. 1:3

11 "He who is unjust, let him be unjust still; he who is filthy, let him be filthy still; he who is righteous, let him *be righteous still; he who is holy, let him be holy still."

12 "And behold, I am coming quickly, and [R]My reward *is* with Me, [R]to give to every one according to his work. Is. 40:10☆ • Rev. 20:12

13 [R]"I am the Alpha and the Omega, *the* *Beginning and *the* End, the First and the Last." Is. 41:4

14 Blessed *are* those who *do His commandments, that they may have the right [R]to the tree of life, [R]and may enter through the gates into the city. [Prov. 11:30] • Rev. 21:27

15 But outside *are* dogs and sorcerers and sexually immoral and murderers and idolaters, and whoever loves and practices a lie.

16 "I, Jesus, have sent My angel to testify to you these things in the churches. [R]I am the Root and the Offspring of David, [R]the Bright and Morning Star." Rev. 5:5 • Num. 24:17

17 And the Spirit and [R]the bride say, "Come!" And let him who hears say, "Come!" [R]And let him who thirsts come. And whoever desires, let him take the water of life freely. [Rev. 21:2, 9] • Is. 55:1

18 For I testify to everyone who hears the words of the prophecy of this book: If anyone adds to these things, *God will add to him the plagues that are written in this book;

19 and if anyone takes away from the words of the book of this prophecy, [R]God* shall take away his part from the *Book of Life, from the holy city, and *from* the things which are written in this book. Ex. 32:33

20 He who testifies to these things says, "Surely I am coming quickly." Amen. Even so, come, Lord Jesus!

21 The grace of our Lord Jesus Christ *be* *with you all. Amen.

21:23 NU, M omit *in it* **21:23** M *very glory*
21:24 NU, M omit *of those who are saved*
21:24 M *of the nations to Him*
21:26 M adds *that they may enter in.*
21:27 NU, M *profane nor one who causes*
22:1 NU, M omit *pure*
22:6 NU, M *spirits of the prophets*
22:8 NU, M *am the one who heard and saw*
22:11 NU, M *do righteousness*
22:13 NU, M *First and the Last, the Beginning and the End* **22:14** NU *wash their robes* **22:18** M *may God*
22:19 M *may God take away* **22:19** NU, M *tree*
22:21 NU *with all,* M *with all the saints*

Harmony of the Gospels

Date	Event	Location	Matthew	Mark	Luke	John	Related References
	Luke's Introduction				1:1–4		Acts 1:1
	Pre-fleshly state of Christ					1:1–18	Heb. 1:1–14
	Genealogy of Jesus Christ		1:1–17		3:23–38		Ruth 4:18–22 1 Chr. 1:1–4

BIRTH, INFANCY, AND ADOLESCENCE OF JESUS AND JOHN THE BAPTIST IN 17 EVENTS

Date	Event	Location	Matthew	Mark	Luke	John	Related References
7 B.C.	(1) Announcement of Birth of John	Jerusalem (Temple)			1:5–25		Num. 6:3
7 or 6 B.C.	(2) Announcement of Birth of Jesus to the Virgin	Nazareth			1:26–38		Is. 7:14
c. 5 B.C.	(3) Song of Elizabeth to Mary	Hill Country of Judea			1:39–45		
	(4) Mary's Song of Praise				1:46–56		Ps. 103:17
5 B.C.	(5) Birth, Infancy, and Purpose for Future of John the Baptist	Judea			1:57–80		Mal. 3:1
	(6) Announcement of Jesus' Birth to Joseph	Nazareth	1:18–25				Is. 9:6, 7
5–4 B.C.	(7) Birth of Jesus Christ	Bethlehem	1:24, 25		2:1–7		Is. 7:14
	(8) Proclamation by the Angels	Near Bethlehem			2:8–14		1 Tim. 3:16
	(9) The Visit of Homage by Shepherds	Bethlehem			2:15–20		
	(10) Jesus' Circumcision	Bethlehem			2:21		Lev. 12:3
4 B.C.	(11) First Temple Visit with Acknowledgments by Simeon and Anna	Jerusalem			2:22–38		Ex. 13:2 Lev. 12
	(12) Visit of the Wise Men	Jerusalem & Bethlehem	2:1–12				Num. 24:17
	(13) Flight into Egypt and Massacre of Innocents	Bethlehem, Jerusalem & Egypt	2:13–18				Jer. 31:15
	(14) From Egypt to Nazareth with Jesus		2:19–23		2:39		
Afterward	(15) Childhood of Jesus	Nazareth			2:40, 51		
A.D. 7–8	(16) Jesus, 12 Years Old, Visits the Temple	Jerusalem			2:41–50		Deut. 16:1–8
Afterward	(17) 18-Year Account of Jesus' Adolescence and Adulthood	Nazareth			2:51, 52		1 Sam. 2:26

TRUTHS ABOUT JOHN THE BAPTIST

Date	Event	Location	Matthew	Mark	Luke	John	Related References
c. A.D. 25–27	John's Ministry Begins	Judean Wilderness	3:1	1:1–4	3:1, 2	1:19–28	Mal. 3:1
	Man and Message		3:2–12	1:2–8	3:3–14		Is. 40:3
	His Picture of Jesus		3:11, 12	1:7, 8	3:15–18	1:26, 27	Acts 2:38
	His Courage		14:4–12		3:19, 20		

BEGINNING OF JESUS' MINISTRY IN 12 EVENTS

Date	Event	Location	Matthew	Mark	Luke	John	Related References
c. A.D. 27	(1) Jesus Baptized	Jordan River	3:13–17	1:9–11	3:21–23	1:29–34	Ps. 2:7
	(2) Jesus Tempted	Wilderness	4:1–11	1:12, 13	4:1–13		Ps. 91:11
	(3) Calls First Disciples	Beyond Jordan				1:35–51	
	(4) The First Miracle	Cana in Galilee				2:1–11	
	(5) First Stay in Capernaum	(Capernaum is "His" city)				2:12	
A.D. 27	(6) First Cleansing of the Temple	Jerusalem				2:13–22	Ps. 69:9
	(7) Received at Jerusalem	Judea				2:23–25	
	(8) Teaches Nicodemus about Second Birth	Judea				3:1–21	Num. 21:8, 9
	(9) Co-Ministry with John	Judea				3:22–30	

Date	Event	Location	Matthew	Mark	Luke	John	Related References
A.D. 27	(10) Leaves for Galilee	Judea	4:12	1:14	4:14	4:1–4	
	(11) Samaritan Woman at Jacob's Well	Samaria				4:5–42	Josh. 24:32
	(12) Returns to Galilee			1:15	4:15	4:43–45	
A.D. 27–29	**THE GALILEAN MINISTRY OF JESUS IN 55 EVENTS**						
A.D. 27	(1) Healing of the Nobleman's Son	Cana				4:46–54	
	(2) Rejected at Nazareth	Nazareth			4:16–30		Is. 61:1, 2
	(3) Moved to Capernaum	Capernaum	4:13–17				Is. 9:1, 2
	(4) Four Become Fishers of Men	Sea of Galilee	4:18–22	1:16–20	5:1–11		Ps. 33:9
	(5) Demoniac Healed on the Sabbath Day	Capernaum		1:21–28	4:31–37		
	(6) Peter's Mother-in-Law Cured, Plus Others	Capernaum	8:14–17	1:29–34	4:38–41		Is. 53:4
c. A.D. 27	(7) First Preaching Tour of Galilee	Galilee	4:23–25	1:35–39	4:42–44		
	(8) Leper Healed and Response Recorded	Galilee	8:1–4	1:40–45	5:12–16		Lev. 13:49
	(9) Paralytic Healed	Capernaum	9:1–8	2:1–12	5:17–26		Rom. 3:23
	(10) Matthew's Call and Reception Held	Capernaum	9:9–13	2:13–17	5:27–32		Hos. 6:6
	(11) Disciples Defended via a Parable	Capernaum	9:14–17	2:18–22	5:33–39		
A.D. 28	(12) Goes to Jerusalem for Second Passover; Heals Lame Man	Jerusalem				5:1–47	Ex. 20:10
	(13) Plucked Grain Precipitates Sabbath Controversy	En Route to Galilee	12:1–8	2:23–28	6:1–5		Deut. 5:14
	(14) Withered Hand Healed Causes Another Sabbath Controversy	Galilee	12:9–14	3:1–6	6:6–11		
	(15) Multitudes Healed	Sea of Galilee	12:15–21	3:7–12	6:17–19		
	(16) Twelve Apostles Selected After a Night of Prayer	Near Capernaum		3:13–19	6:12–16		
	(17) Sermon on the Mt.	Near Capernaum	5:1—7:29		6:20–49		
	(18) Centurion's Servant Healed	Capernaum	8:5–13		7:1–10		Is. 49:12, 13
	(19) Raises Widow's Son from Dead	Nain			7:11–17		Job 19:25
	(20) Jesus Allays John's Doubts	Galilee	11:2–19		7:18–35		Mal. 3:1
	(21) Woes Upon the Privileged		11:20–30				Gen. 19:24
	(22) A Sinful Woman Anoints Jesus	Simon's House, Capernaum			7:36–50		
	(23) Another Tour of Galilee	Galilee			8:1–3		
	(24) Jesus Accused of Blasphemy	Capernaum	12:22–37	3:20–30	11:14–23		
	(25) Jesus' Answer to a Demand for a Sign	Capernaum	12:38–45		11:24–26, 29–36		
	(26) Mother, Brothers Seek Audience	Capernaum	12:46–50	3:31–35	8:19–21		
	(27) Famous Parables of Sower, Seed, Tares, Mustard Seed, Leaven, Treasure, Pearl, Dragnet, Lamp Told	By Sea of Galilee	13:1–52	4:1–34	8:4–18		Joel 3:13
	(28) Sea Made Serene	Sea of Galilee	8:23–27	4:35–41	8:22–25		
	(29) Gadarene Demoniac Healed	E. Shore of Galilee	8:28–34	5:1–20	8:26–39		
	(30) Jairus' Daughter Raised and Woman with Hemorrhage Healed		9:18–26	5:21–43	8:40–56		
	(31) Two Blind Men's Sight Restored		9:27–31				

Date	Event	Location	Matthew	Mark	Luke	John	Related References
A.D. 28	(32) Mute Demoniac Healed		9:32–34				
	(33) Nazareth's Second Rejection of Christ	Nazareth	13:53–58	6:1–6			
	(34) Twelve Sent Out		9:35—11:1	6:6–13	9:1–6		1 Cor. 9:14
	(35) Fearful Herod Beheads John	Galilee	14:1–12	6:14–29	9:7–9		
Spring A.D. 29	(36) Return of 12, Jesus Withdraws, 5000 Fed	Near Bethsaida	14:13–21	6:30–44	9:10–17	6:1–14	
	(37) Walks on the Water	Sea of Galilee	14:22–33	6:45–52		6:15–21	
	(38) Sick of Gennesaret Healed	Gennesaret	14:34–36	6:53–56			
	(39) Peak of Popularity Passes in Galilee	Capernaum				6:22–71 7:1	Is. 54:13
A.D. 29	(40) Traditions Attacked		15:1–20	7:1–23			Ex. 21:17
	(41) Aborted Retirement in Phoenicia: Syro-Phoenician Healed	Phoenicia	15:21–28	7:24–30			
	(42) Afflicted Healed	Decapolis	15:29–31	7:31–37			
	(43) 4000 Fed	Decapolis	15:32–39	8:1–9			
	(44) Pharisees Increase Attack	Magdala	16:1–4	8:10–13			
	(45) Disciples' Carelessness Condemned; Blind Man Healed		16:5–12	8:14–26			Jer. 5:21
	(46) Peter Confesses Jesus Is the Christ	Near Caesarea Philippi	16:13–20	8:27–30	9:18–21		
	(47) Jesus Foretells His Death	Caesarea Philippi	16:21–26	8:31–37	9:22–25		
	(48) Kingdom Promised		16:27, 28	9:1	9:26, 27		Prov. 24:12
	(49) The Transfiguration	Mountain Unnamed	17:1–13	9:2–13	9:28–36		Is. 42:1
	(50) Epileptic Healed	Mt. of Transfiguration	17:14–21	9:14–29	9:37–42		
	(51) Again Tells of Death, Resurrection	Galilee	17:22, 23	9:30–32	9:43–45		
	(52) Taxes Paid	Capernaum	17:24–27				Ex. 30:11–15
	(53) Disciples Contend About Greatness; Jesus Defines; also Patience, Loyalty, Forgiveness	Capernaum	18:1–35	9:33–50	9:46–62		
	(54) Jesus Rejects Brothers' Advice	Galilee				7:2–9	
c. Sept. A.D. 29	(55) Galilee Departure and Samaritan Rejection		19:1		9:51–56	7:10	

A.D. 29–30 LAST JUDEAN AND PEREAN MINISTRY OF JESUS IN 42 EVENTS

Date	Event	Location	Matthew	Mark	Luke	John	Related References
Oct. A.D. 29	(1) Feast of Tabernacles	Jerusalem				7:2, 11–52	
	(2) Forgiveness of Adulteress	Jerusalem				7:53—8:11	Lev. 20:10
A.D. 29	(3) Christ—the Light of the World	Jerusalem				8:12–20	
	(4) Pharisees Can't Meet the Prophecy Thus Try to Destroy the Prophet	Jerusalem—Temple				8:12–59	Is. 6:9
	(5) Man Born Blind Healed; Following Consequences	Jerusalem				9:1–41	
	(6) Parable of the Good Shepherd	Jerusalem				10:1–21	
	(7) The Service of the Seventy	Probably Judea			10:1–24		
	(8) Lawyer Hears the Story of the Good Samaritan	Judea (?)			10:25–37		
	(9) The Hospitality of Martha and Mary	Bethany			10:38–42		
	(10) Another Lesson on Prayer	Judea (?)			11:1–13		

Date	Event	Location	Matthew	Mark	Luke	John	Related References
A.D. 29	(11) Accused of Connection with Beelzebub				11:14–36		
	(12) Judgment Against Lawyers and Pharisees				11:37–54		Mic. 6:8
	(13) Jesus Deals with Hypocrisy, Covetousness, Worry, and Alertness				12:1–59		Mic. 7:6
	(14) Repent or Perish				13:1–5		
	(15) Barren Fig Tree				13:6–9		
	(16) Crippled Woman Healed on Sabbath				13:10–17		Deut. 5:12–15
	(17) Parables of Mustard Seed and Leaven	Probably Perea			13:18–21		
Winter A.D. 29	(18) Feast of Dedication	Jerusalem				10:22–39	Ps. 82:6
	(19) Withdrawal Beyond Jordan					10:40–42	
	(20) Begins Teaching Return to Jerusalem with Special Words About Herod	Perea			13:22–35		Ps. 6:8
	(21) Meal with a Pharisee Ruler Occasions Healing Man with Dropsy; Parables of Ox, Best Places, and Great Supper				14:1–24		
	(22) Demands of Discipleship	Perea			14:25–35		
	(23) Parables of Lost Sheep, Coin, Son				15:1–32		1 Pet. 2:25
	(24) Parables of Unjust Steward, Rich Man and Lazarus				16:1–31		
	(25) Lessons on Service, Faith, Influence				17:1–10		
	(26) Resurrection of Lazarus	Perea to Bethany				11:1–44	
	(27) Reaction to It: Withdrawal of Jesus					11:45–54	
A.D. 30	(28) Begins Last Journey to Jerusalem via Samaria & Galilee	Samaria, Galilee			17:11		
	(29) Heals Ten Lepers				17:12–19		Lev. 13:45, 46
	(30) Lessons on the Coming Kingdom				17:20–37		Gen. 6—7
	(31) Parables: Persistent Widow, Pharisee and Tax Collector				18:1–14		
	(32) Doctrine on Divorce		19:1–12	10:1–12			Deut. 24:1–4 Gen. 2:23–25
	(33) Jesus Blesses Children: Objections	Perea	19:13–15	10:13–16	18:15–17		Ps. 131:2
	(34) Rich Young Ruler	Perea	19:16–30	10:17–31	18:18–30		Ex. 20:1–17
	(35) Laborers of the 11th Hour		20:1–16				
	(36) Foretells Death and Resurrection	Near Jordan	20:17–19	10:32–34	18:31–34		Ps. 22
	(37) Ambition of James and John		20:20–28	10:35–45			
	(38) Blind Bartimaeus Healed	Jericho		10:46–52	18:35–43		
	(39) Interview with Zacchaeus	Jericho			19:1–10		
	(40) Parable: the Minas	Jericho			19:11–27		
	(41) Returns to Home of Mary and Martha	Bethany				11:55—12:1	
	(42) Plot to Kill Lazarus	Bethany				12:9–11	
Spring A.D. 30	**JESUS' FINAL WEEK OF WORK AT JERUSALEM IN 41 EVENTS**						
Sunday	(1) Triumphal Entry	Bethany, Jerusalem, Bethany	21:1–9	11:1–11	19:28–44	12:12–19	Zech. 9:9

Date	Event	Location	Matthew	Mark	Luke	John	Related References
Monday	(2) Fig Tree Cursed and Temple Cleansed	Bethany to Jerusalem	21:10–19	11:12–18	19:45–48		Jer. 7:11
	(3) The Attraction of Sacrifice	Jerusalem				12:20–50	Is. 6:10
Tuesday	(4) Withered Fig Tree Testifies	Bethany to Jerusalem	21:20–22	11:19–26			
	(5) Sanhedrin Challenges Jesus. Answered by Parables: Two Sons, Wicked Vinedressers and Marriage Feast	Jerusalem	21:23—22:14	11:27—12:12	20:1–19		Is. 5:1, 2
	(6) Tribute to Caesar	Jerusalem	22:15–22	12:13–17	20:20–26		
	(7) Sadducees Question the Resurrection	Jerusalem	22:23–33	12:18–27	20:27–40		Ex. 3:6
	(8) Pharisees Question Commandments	Jerusalem	22:34–40	12:28–34			
	(9) Jesus and David	Jerusalem	22:41–46	12:35–37	20:41–44		Ps. 110:1
	(10) Jesus' Last Sermon	Jerusalem	23:1–39	12:38–40	20:45–47		
	(11) Widow's Mite	Jerusalem		12:41–44	21:1–4		Lev. 27:30
	(12) Jesus Tells of the Future	Mt. Olives	24:1–51	13:1–37	21:5–36		Dan. 12:1
	(13) Parables: Ten Virgins, Talents. The Day of Judgment	Mt. Olives	25:1–46				Zech. 14:5
	(14) Jesus Tells Date of Crucifixion		26:1–5	14:1, 2	22:1, 2		
	(15) Anointing by Mary at Simon's Feast	Bethany	26:6–13	14:3–9		12:2–8	
	(16) Judas Contracts the Betrayal		26:14–16	14:10, 11	22:3–6		Zech. 11:12
Thursday	(17) Preparation for the Passover	Jerusalem	26:17–19	14:12–16	22:7–13		Ex. 12:14–28
Thursday P.M.	(18) Passover Eaten, Jealousy Rebuked	Jerusalem	26:20	14:17	22:14–16, 24–30		
	(19) Feet Washed	Upper Room				13:1–20	
	(20) Judas Revealed, Defects	Upper Room	26:21–25	14:18–21	22:21–23	13:21–30	Ps. 41:9
	(21) Jesus Warns About Further Desertion; Cries of Loyalty	Upper Room	26:31–35	14:27–31	22:31–38	13:31–38	Zech. 13:7
	(22) Institution of the Lord's Supper	Upper Room	26:26–29	14:22–25	22:17–20		1 Cor. 11:23–34
	(23) Last Speech to the Apostles and Intercessory Prayer	Jerusalem				14:1—17:26	Ps. 35:19
Thursday-Friday	(24) The Grief of Gethsemane	Mt. Olives	26:30, 36–46	14:26, 32–42	22:39–46	18:1	Ps. 42:6
Friday	(25) Betrayal, Arrest, Desertion	Gethsemane	26:47–56	14:43–52	22:47–53	18:2–12	
	(26) First Examined by Annas	Jerusalem				18:12–14, 19–23	
	(27) Trial by Caiaphas and Council; Following Indignities	Jerusalem	26:57, 59–68	14:53, 55–65	22:54, 63–65	18:24	Lev. 24:16
	(28) Peter's Triple Denial	Jerusalem	26:58, 69–75	14:54, 66–72	22:54–62	18:15–18, 25–27	
	(29) Condemnation by the Council	Jerusalem	27:1	15:1	22:66–71		Ps. 110:1
	(30) Suicide of Judas	Jerusalem	27:3–10				Acts 1:18, 19
	(31) First Appearance Before Pilate	Jerusalem	27:2, 11–14	15:1–5	23:1–7	18:28–38	
	(32) Jesus Before Herod	Jerusalem			23:6–12		
	(33) Second Appearance Before Pilate	Jerusalem	27:15–26	15:6–15	23:13–25	18:39—19:16	Deut. 21:6–9
	(34) Mockery by Roman Soldiers	Jerusalem	27:27–30	15:16–19			
	(35) Led to Golgotha	Jerusalem	27:31–34	15:20–23	23:26–33	19:16, 17	Ps. 69:21
	(36) 6 Events of First 3 Hours on Cross	Calvary	27:35–44	15:24–32	23:33–43	19:18–27	Ps. 22:18
	(37) Last 3 Hours on Cross	Calvary	27:45–50	15:33–37	23:44–46	19:28–30	Ps. 22:1
	(38) Events Attending Jesus' Death		27:51–56	15:38–41	23:45, 47–49		
	(39) Burial of Jesus	Jerusalem	27:57–60	15:42–46	23:50–54	19:31–37	Ex. 12:46
Friday-Saturday	(40) Tomb Sealed	Jerusalem	27:61–66		23:55, 56		Ex. 20:8–11
	(41) Women Watch	Jerusalem		15:47			

Date	Event	Location	Matthew	Mark	Luke	John	Related References
A.D. 30	**THE RESURRECTION THROUGH THE ASCENSION IN 12 EVENTS**						
Dawn of First Day (Sunday, "Lord's Day")	(1) Women Visit the Tomb	Near Jerusalem	28:1–10	16:1–8	24:1–11		
	(2) Peter and John See the Empty Tomb				24:12	20:1–10	
	(3) Jesus' Appearance to Mary Magdalene	Jerusalem		16:9–11		20:11–18	
	(4) Jesus' Appearance to the Other Women	Jerusalem	28:9, 10				
	(5) Guards' Report of the Resurrection		28:11–15				
Sunday Afternoon	(6) Jesus' Appearance to Two Disciples on Way to Emmaus			16:12, 13	24:13–35		1 Cor. 15:5
Late Sunday	(7) Jesus' Appearance to Ten Disciples Without Thomas	Jerusalem		16:14	24:36–43	20:19–25	
One Week Later	(8) Appearance to Disciples with Thomas	Jerusalem				20:26–31	
During 40 Days until Ascension	(9) Jesus' Appearance to Seven Disciples by Sea of Galilee	Galilee				21:1–25	
	(10) Appearance to 500	Mt. in Galilee					1 Cor. 15:6
	(11) Great Commission		28:16–20	16:15–18	24:44–49		
	(12) The Ascension	Mt. Olivet		16:19, 20	24:50–53		Acts 1:4–11

The Jewish Calendar

The Jews used two kinds of calendars:
Civil Calendar—official calendar of kings, childbirth, and contracts.
Sacred Calendar—from which festivals were computed.

NAMES OF MONTHS	CORRESPONDS WITH	NO. OF DAYS	MONTH OF CIVIL YEAR	MONTH OF SACRED YEAR
TISHRI	Sept.–Oct.	30 days	1st	7th
HESHVAN	Oct.–Nov.	29 or 30	2nd	8th
CHISLEV	Nov.–Dec.	29 or 30	3rd	9th
TEBETH	Dec.–Jan.	29	4th	10th
SHEBAT	Jan.–Feb.	30	5th	11th
ADAR	Feb.–Mar.	29 or 30	6th	12th
NISAN	Mar.–Apr.	30	7th	1st
IYAR	Apr.–May	29	8th	2nd
SIVAN	May–June	30	9th	3rd
TAMMUZ	June–July	29	10th	4th
AB	July–Aug.	30	11th	5th
***ELUL**	Aug.–Sept.	29	12th	6th

The Jewish day was from sunset to sunset, in 8 equal parts:

FIRST WATCH . . . .SUNSET TO 9 P.M.
SECOND WATCH . .9 P.M. TO MIDNIGHT
THIRD WATCH . . .MIDNIGHT TO 3 A.M.
FOURTH WATCH . .3 A.M. TO SUNRISE

FIRST HOUR . . . . .SUNRISE TO 9 A.M.
THIRD HOUR . . . . .9 A.M. TO NOON
SIXTH HOUR . . . . .NOON TO 3 P.M.
NINTH HOUR . . . . .3 P.M. TO SUNSET

*Hebrew months were alternately 30 and 29 days long. Their year, shorter than ours, had 354 days. Therefore, about every 3 years (7 times in 19 years) an extra 29-day-month, VEADAR, was added between ADAR and NISAN.

TEACHINGS AND ILLUSTRATIONS OF CHRIST

Subject	*Reference*
Abiding in Christ	John 15:4–10
Ability	Matt. 25:14, 15
Ablution	Matt. 6:17, 18
Abode	John 14:23
Abraham	John 8:37, 56
Abstinence	Luke 21:34
Abundant life	John 10:10
Access to God	John 10:7, 9
Accountability	Luke 12:47, 48
Accusation, false	Matt. 5:11
Adultery	Matt. 5:27, 28
Adversity	Luke 24:46
Affliction	Matt. 24:7–12
Agreement	Matt. 18:19
Altar	Matt. 23:18, 19
Ambition	Luke 22:25–30
Angels	Matt. 13:39, 41
Anger	Matt. 5:22
Anxiety	Luke 12:22–31
Apostasy	Matt. 13:18–22 Luke 8:13
Apostles	Luke 11:49
Appearance	Matt. 6:16
Appearance, outward	Matt. 23:27, 28
Authority	Matt. 21:24 Luke 10:19
Avarice	Luke 12:16–21
Backsliding	Luke 9:62
Baptism	Acts 1:5 Matt. 28:19
Beatitudes	Matt. 5:3–11
Beelzebub	Matt. 10:25
Begging	Luke 16:3
Beneficence	Matt. 5:42
Betrayal	Matt. 26:21
Bigotry	Luke 18:9–14
Birds	Matt. 8:20
Blasphemy	Matt. 12:31, 32
Blessings	Matt. 5:3–11
Blind guides	Matt. 15:14
Borrowing	Matt. 5:42
Bread of life	John 6:32–35
Brothers	Matt. 23:8
Builders	Luke 6:47–49 Matt. 7:24
Burdens	Luke 11:46
Burial	Matt. 8:22
Caesar	Matt. 22:21
Call of God	Matt. 20:16
Called ones	Matt. 22:14
Capital and labor	Matt. 20:1–15
Capital punishment	Matt. 26:52
Care of God	Matt. 6:30, 33
Caution	Mark 4:24
Celibacy	Matt. 19:11, 12
Character	John 1:47
Charity	Luke 12:33
Cheating	Mark 10:19
Chosen	Matt. 22:14
Church	Matt. 18:17
Circumcision	John 7:22, 23
Cleansing	John 15:3
Coin	Matt. 22:19–21
Coldness	Matt. 24:12
Communication	Luke 24:17
Compassion	Matt. 15:32 Luke 10:33
Compromise	Matt. 5:25, 26
Conceit	Luke 18:10–12
Conduct, Christian	Matt. 5:16
Confessing Christ	Matt. 10:32, 33
Confession of sin	Luke 18:13, 14
Confidence	Mark 10:24
Conflict	Matt. 10:34–36
Conscience	John 8:7–9
Contention	Matt. 18:15–17
Contentment	John 6:43
Conversion	Matt. 13:15
Convict	John 16:8
Corruption, moral	Luke 11:39
Courage	Matt. 9:22
Covenant	Mark 14:24
Coveting	Mark 7:21, 22
Cross-bearing	Matt. 10:38
Crucifixion	Luke 9:22
Cup of water	Matt. 10:42
Dancing	Luke 15:25–27
Daniel	Matt. 24:15
Darkness	Luke 11:35
David	Matt. 12:3
Day	John 11:9
Deaf	Matt. 13:13–15
Death	Luke 9:22 John 8:51
Debts	Matt. 18:24
Deceivers	Matt. 24:4, 5
Decision	Matt. 6:24
Defilement	Matt. 15:11, 18, 19
Devil	Matt. 13:38, 39
Diligence	John 9:4
Disbelief	John 5:38
Discernment	Matt. 16:2, 3
Discipleship	Luke 14:33
Disputes	Mark 9:33, 34
Distress	Luke 21:23, 25
Divorce	Matt. 5:31, 32
Doctrine	Mark 7:7
Doubt	Matt. 21:21
Drunkard	Luke 7:34
Drunkenness	Luke 21:34
Dullness	Matt. 13:13
Duty	Luke 17:10
Dwelling places	John 14:2, 3
Earth	Matt. 5:18
Earthquakes	Mark 13:8
Economy	Matt. 15:37 John 6:12
Elect	Matt. 24:24, 31
Election	Matt. 25:34
Elijah	Matt. 17:11, 12
Employer	Matt. 20:1–16
Encouragement	Matt. 9:2
Endowments	Matt. 25:14, 15
Endurance	Matt. 10:22 Luke 21:19
Enemies	Matt. 5:43, 44
Eternal life	Matt. 19:29
Eternal sin	Mark 3:29
Etiquette	Luke 10:8
Evil	Matt. 15:19
Exaltation	Matt. 23:12
Example	John 13:15
Excuses	Luke 14:18–20
Extravagance	Luke 15:11–14
Fainting	Mark 8:2, 3
Faith	Matt. 6:25 Mark 11:22 Luke 7:50
Faithfulness	Matt.25:21
Faithlessness	Matt 25:24–30
False prophets	Matt. 24:11
False witness	Matt. 19:18
Farm	Matt. 22:2–6
Fasting	Matt. 6:16–18
Faultfinding	Matt. 7:3–5
Faults	Matt. 18:15
Fear of God	Matt. 10:28
Feast	Luke 14:8
Feet washing	John 13:12–15
Fellowship	Matt. 8:11
Flattery	Luke 6:26
Flesh	John 6:53
Flock	Matt. 26:31
Following Christ	Matt. 10:37, 38
Food	Matt. 6:11 Matt. 6:25 John 6:27
Fool	Matt. 5:22
Formalism	Matt. 23:23–28
Forsaking all	Luke 14:33
Foxes	Luke 9:58
Friends	Luke 11:5–8
Frugality	John 6:12
Fruitfulness	Matt. 13:23
Fruitlessness	Luke 13:6–9
Generosity	Matt. 25:34–40
Gentiles	Matt. 10:5–7

Subject	*Reference*
Gentleness	Matt. 5:5
Giving	Luke 6:38
Gladness	Luke 15:32
Glorifying God	Matt. 5:16
Gluttony	Luke 21:34
God	Matt. 19:17, 26
Godlessness	John 5:42, 44
Golden Rule	Matt. 7:12
Gospel	Luke 4:18
Grace	2 Cor. 12:9
Greatness	Matt. 5:19
Grumble	John 6:43
Guidance	John 16:13
Hairs numbered	Matt. 10:30
Hand of God	John 10:27–29
Happiness	Matt. 5:12
	John 13:16, 17
Harlots	Matt. 21:31
Harvest	Matt. 9:37, 38
Hatred	John 15:18, 19
Healing	Matt. 10:7, 8
	Mark 2:17
Heart	Matt. 13:19
Heaven	Luke 16:17
	John 3:13
Hell	Matt. 5:22
	Matt. 10:28
Helper	John 14:16
	John 15:26
Helpless	John 6:44
Hireling	John 10:11–13
Holy Spirit	John 14:26
Home	Mark 5:19
Honesty	Luke 8:15
	Mark 10:19
Honor of men	Matt. 6:2
Honor of parents	Matt. 15:3–6
Hospitality	Luke 14:12–14
Humility	John 13:14
	Matt. 11:29
Hunger, spiritual	Luke 6:21
	Matt. 5:6
Hypocrisy	Matt. 6:5
	Luke 6:42
Ignorance	Matt. 22:29
Immortality	Matt. 25:46
	John 11:25, 26
Impartiality of God	Matt. 5:45
Inconsistency	Matt. 7:3–5
	Luke 6:41, 42
Indecision	Luke 9:62
Indifference	Matt. 24:12
Industry	John 4:36
Infidelity	John 3:18
Influence	Matt. 5:13
Ingratitude	Luke 17:17, 18
Innocence	Matt. 10:16
Insincerity	Luke 16:15
Inspiration	Luke 12:12
Instability	Matt. 7:26, 27
Instruction	John 6:45
Insufficiency	Mark 10:21
Integrity	Luke 16:10
Intercession	John 17:9
Investment	Matt. 6:19, 20
Jealousy	Luke 15:25–30
John the Baptist	Luke 7:24–28
Jonah	Matt. 12:39–41
Joy	Matt. 25:21
	Luke 15:7, 10
Judge not	Matt. 7:1, 2
Judgment	Matt. 11:24
Judgment day	Matt. 25:31–46
Justice	John 5:30
Justification, self	Luke 16:15
Killing	Matt. 5:21, 22
Kindness	Luke 10:30–35
Kingdom	Luke 7:28
	John 18:36
Kiss	Luke 7:45
Knowledge	John 8:31, 32
Labor	Matt. 20:1–14
Laughter	Luke 6:21
Law	Luke 16:16
Lawsuit	Matt. 5:25, 40
Lawyers	Luke 11:46
Leaven	Matt. 16:6
	Luke 13:20, 21
Lending	Luke 6:34, 35
Lepers	Matt. 10:7, 8
Levite	Luke 10:30–32
Liars	John 8:44, 45
Liberality	Luke 6:30, 38
Liberty	Luke 4:18
Life	Matt. 6:25
	John 5:40
Light	Luke 11:33
	John 8:12
Living water	John 4:10
Log	Luke 6:41, 42
Loneliness	John 16:32
Lord's Supper	Matt. 26:26–29
Loss of soul	Matt. 16:25, 26
Lost opportunity	Matt. 25:7–12
Love	Matt. 22:37–40
Lukewarmness	Matt. 26:40, 41
Lunatic	Matt. 17:14, 15
Lust	Mark 4:18, 19
Magistrates	Luke 12:11, 58
Mammon	Matt. 6:24
Marriage	Matt. 19:4–6
	Mark 12:25
Martyrdom	John 16:1–3
Mary's choice	Luke 10:41, 42
Memorial	Matt. 26:13
Mercy	Matt. 5:7
	Luke 16:24
Minister	Luke 10:2
Miracles	Matt. 12:28
Money lender, creditor	Luke 7:41, 42
Moses	Matt. 19:8
Moses' Law	John 7:19
Mother	Matt. 10:37
Mourn	Matt. 5:4
Murder	Matt. 15:19
Mysteries of Heaven	Matt. 13:11
Narrow way	Matt. 7:13, 14
Neglect	Luke 12:47
Neighbor	Matt. 19:19
Neutrality	Matt. 12:30
New birth	John 3:3, 5–8
Noah	Luke 17:26, 27
Oath	Matt. 5:33–37
Obedience	Matt. 12:50
Offering	Matt. 5:25
Offerings	Luke 21:3, 4
Opportunity	Matt. 5:25
Parables	Mark 4:11, 12
Paradise	Luke 23:43
Pardoning	Luke 6:37
Parents	Matt. 10:21
Patriotism	Matt. 22:21
Peace	Mark 9:50
Peacemakers	Matt. 5:9
Penitence	Luke 18:13
Perception	John 8:43
Perfection	Matt. 5:48
Persecution	Matt. 24:9
Perseverance	Matt. 10:22
Pharisaism	Matt. 23:2–33
Pharisee and tax collector	Luke 18:10–14
Pharisees	Matt. 5:20
Philanthropy	Luke 11:41
Physician	Matt. 9:12
Piety	John 1:47
Pleasing God	John 8:29
Pleasures	Luke 8:14
Poison	Mark 16:17, 18
Poll tax	Matt. 22:19–21
Polygamy	Matt. 19:8, 9
Poor	Mark 14:7
Power	Matt. 6:13
Prayer	Matt. 7:7–11
	Matt. 6:9–13
Preaching	Mark 16:15, 16
Procrastination	Matt. 25:3
Profit and loss	Matt. 16:26
Prophets	Matt. 10:41
	Matt. 7:15
Proselyte	Luke 23:15
Protection	Luke 18:3
Providence	Matt. 6:25–33
Prudence	Matt. 10:16–20
Punishment	Matt. 21:41
Purity	Matt. 5:8
Ransom	Matt. 20:28
Reaping	John 4:35–38
Receiving Christ	Mark 9:37
Reconciliation	Matt. 5:23, 24
Regeneration	Matt. 19:28
Rejecting Christ	John 3:18
Rejoicing	Luke 10:20
Release	Luke 4:18
Religion	Mark 7:6–8
	Matt. 25:34–36

Subject	*Reference*
Repentance	Matt. 11:21
	Luke 13:28
Reproof	Matt. 11:21–23
Resignation	Matt. 26:39
Responsibility	Luke 12:47, 48
Rest	Matt. 26:45
	Matt. 11:28–30
Resurrection	John 6:40
Retaliation	Matt. 5:39–44
Retribution	Matt. 23:34, 35
Reward	Matt. 10:42
Riches	Mark 4:19
Righteousness	Matt. 5:6, 20
	John 16:10
Robbers	Luke 10:30
	John 10:1
Robbery	Matt. 23:25
Sabbath	Matt. 12:5–8
Sackcloth	Matt. 11:21
Sacrifice	Matt. 12:7
Sacrilege	Matt. 21:13
Sadducees	Matt. 16:6
Salt	Matt. 5:13
	Mark 9:50
Salvation	Luke 19:19
	John 4:22
Samaritan	Luke 10:30–35
Sanctification	John 17:17
Satan	Matt. 4:10
	Mark 4:15
Scripture	Matt. 21:42
	Luke 4:21
Secrecy	Luke 12:2, 3
Security	Luke 6:47, 48
Seduction	Mark 13:22
Seeking the kingdom	Matt. 6:19, 20
Self-condemnation	Matt. 23:29–32
	Luke 19:20–24
Self-control	Matt. 5:21
Self-deception	Luke 12:16–21
Self-denial	Matt. 16:24–26
Self-exaltation	Matt. 23:12
Self-examination	Matt. 7:3–5
Selfishness	Luke 6:32–35
Self-righteousness	Matt. 23:23–27
Self-sacrifice	Matt. 16:25
Serpents	Matt. 23:33
	John 3:14
Service	Luke 22:27
Sheep	Luke 15:4–7
Shepherd	John 10:1–18
Sickness	Matt. 10:8
Signs	John 4:48
	Luke 11:16
Silence	Matt. 17:9
Sin	John 8:34
	Matt. 26:28
Sincerity	Matt. 5:13–16
Skepticism	John 20:27, 29
Slaves	Matt. 18:23
	John 15:15
Sleep	Mark 4:26, 27
	Mark 13:35, 36
Slothfulness	Matt. 25:26–30
Son of Man	Luke 9:22
Sorrow	Matt. 19:22
	John 16:6
Soul	Matt. 10:28
	Luke 12:19, 20
Soul winners	Matt. 4:19
Sowing	Mark 4:14
Speech	John 8:43
Spirit	Matt. 26:41
	Mark 5:8
Statement	Matt. 5:37
Steadfastness	Matt. 10:22
Stealing	Matt. 19:18
Steward	Luke 12:42, 43
	Luke 16:1–8
Stewardship	Luke 19:13–27
Stomach	Matt. 15:17
Strife	Luke 22:24
Stubbornness	John 5:40
Stumbling block	Matt. 23:13
Submission	Matt. 26:39, 42
Suffering	Matt. 26:38
Supper, The Lord's	Luke 22:14–20
Swearing	Matt. 23:16–22
Talents	Matt. 18:24
Taxes	Matt. 22:19–21
Tax collectors	Matt. 5:46, 47
Teaching	Matt. 28:19, 20
	John 13:13–15
Temperance	Luke 21:34
Temptations	Matt. 4:1–11
	Luke 8:13
Thieves	Matt. 6:19
	John 10:1, 8
Timidness	Mark 4:40
Tithes	Luke 18:11, 12
Traditions	Mark 7:9, 13
Transgressions	Matt. 15:2
Treasures	Matt. 6:19–21
Tribulation	Matt. 24:9
	John 16:33
Truth	John 14:6
Unbelievers	Luke 12:46
Uncharitableness	John 7:24
Unchastity	Matt. 5:31, 32
Uncleanness	Matt. 23:27
Unity	John 17:20, 21
Unpardonable sin	Matt. 12:31, 32
Vengeance	Matt. 5:39, 40
Vine	John 15:1, 4, 5
Visions	Matt. 17:9
Walks of Life	John 12:35
	John 8:12
War	Matt. 24:26
Watchfulness	Matt. 24:42, 44
	Luke 12:37–40
Wedding	Luke 14:8–10
Widow	Mark 12:43, 44
Wine	Luke 5:37–39
Wisdom	Luke 21:15
Witness	John 8:14
Witness, false	Matt. 19:18
Witnessing	Acts 1:8
Wives	Luke 14:20, 26
Worker	Matt. 10:10
Worldliness	Luke 21:34
Worm	Mark 9:43–48
Worries of the world	Matt. 13:22
Worship	Matt. 4:10
Yoke	Matt. 11:28, 29
Zacchaeus	Luke 19:5
Zeal	John 2:17

PROPHECIES OF THE MESSIAH FULFILLED IN JESUS CHRIST

Presented Here in Their Order of Fulfillment

PROPHETIC SCRIPTURE	SUBJECT	FULFILLED
Gen. 3:15, p. 9 "And I will put enmity between you and the woman, and between your seed and her Seed; He shall bruise your head, and you shall bruise His heel."	**seed of a woman**	*Gal. 4:4, p. 1381* "But when the fullness of the time had come, God sent forth His Son, born of a woman, born under the law,"
Gen. 12:3, p. 18 "I will bless those who bless you, and I will curse him who curses you; And in you all the families of the earth shall be blessed."	**descendant of Abraham**	*Matt. 1:1, p. 1115* "The book of the genealogy of Jesus Christ, the Son of David, the Son of Abraham:"
Gen. 17:19, p. 24 "Then God said, 'No, Sarah your wife shall bear you a son, and you shall call his name Isaac; I will establish My covenant with him for an everlasting covenant, *and* with his descendants after him.'"	**descendant of Isaac**	*Luke 3:34, p. 1195* "*the son* of Jacob, *the son* of Isaac, *the son* of Abraham, *the son* of Terah, *the son* of Nahor,"
Num. 24:17, p. 189 "I see Him, but not now; I behold Him, but not near; a Star shall come out of Jacob; a Scepter shall rise out of Israel, and batter the brow of Moab, and destroy all the sons of tumult."	**descendant of Jacob**	*Matt. 1:2, p. 1115* "Abraham begot Isaac, Isaac begot Jacob, and Jacob begot Judah and his brothers."
Gen. 49:10, p. 63 "The scepter shall not depart from Judah, nor a lawgiver from between his feet, until Shiloh comes; and to Him *shall be* the obedience of the people."	**from the tribe of Judah**	*Luke 3:33, p. 1195* "*the son* of Amminadab, *the son* of Ram, *the son* of Hezron, *the son* of Perez, *the son* of Judah."
Is. 9:7, p. 781 "Of the increase of *His* government and peace *there will be* no end, upon the throne of David and over His kingdom, to order it and establish it with judgment and justice from that time forward, even forever. The zeal of the LORD of hosts will perform this."	**heir to the throne of David**	*Luke 1:32, 33, p. 1192* "He will be great, and will be called the Son of the Highest; and the Lord God will give Him the throne of His father David. And He will reign over the house of Jacob forever, and of His kingdom there will be no end."
Ps. 45:6, 7, p. 651; 102:25–27, p. 683 "Your throne, O God, *is* forever and ever; a scepter of righteousness *is* the scepter of Your kingdom. You love righteousness and hate wickedness; therefore God, Your God, has anointed You with the oil of gladness more than Your companions." "Of old You laid the foundation of the earth, and the heavens *are* the work of Your hands. They will perish, but You will endure; yes, all of them will grow old like a garment; like a cloak You will change them, and they will be changed. But You *are* the same, and Your years will have no end."	**anointed and eternal**	*Heb. 1:8–12, p. 1450* "But to the Son *He says: 'Your throne, O God, is forever and ever; a scepter of righteousness is the scepter of Your kingdom. You have loved righteousness and hated lawlessness; therefore God, Your God, has anointed You with the oil of gladness more than Your companions.'* And: *'You, LORD, in the beginning laid the foundation of the earth, and the heavens are the work of Your hands; they will perish, but You remain; and they will all grow old like a garment; like a cloak You will fold them up, and they will be changed. But You are the same, and Your years will not fail.'*"

PROPHETIC SCRIPTURE	SUBJECT	FULFILLED
Mic. 5:2, p. 1039 "But you, Bethlehem, Ephrathah, *though* you are little among the thousands of Judah, *yet* out of you shall come forth to Me the One to be ruler in Israel, whose goings forth *have been* from of old, from everlasting."	**born in Bethlehem**	*Luke 2:4, 5, 7, p. 1193* "And Joseph also went up from Galilee, out of the city of Nazareth, into Judea, to the city of David, which is called Bethlehem, because he was of the house and lineage of David, to be registered with Mary, his betrothed wife, who was with child. . . . And she brought forth her firstborn Son, and wrapped Him in swaddling cloths, and laid Him in a manger, because there was no room for them in the inn."
Dan. 9:25, p. 989 "Know therefore and understand, *that* from the going forth of the command to restore and build Jerusalem until Messiah the Prince, *there shall be* seven weeks and sixty-two weeks; the street shall be built again, and the wall, even in troublesome times."	**time for His birth**	*Luke 2:1, 2, p. 1193* "And it came to pass in those days *that* a decree went out from Caesar Augustus that all the world should be registered. This census first took place while Quirinius was governing Syria."
Is. 7:14, p. 779 "Therefore the Lord Himself will give you a sign: Behold, the virgin shall conceive and bear a Son, and shall call His name Immanuel."	**to be born of a virgin**	*Luke 1:26, 27, 30, 31, p. 1190* "Now in the sixth month the angel Gabriel was sent by God to a city of Galilee named Nazareth, to a virgin betrothed to a man whose name was Joseph, of the house of David. The virgin's name *was* Mary. . . . Then the angel said to her, 'Do not be afraid, Mary, for you have found favor with God. And behold, you will conceive in your womb and bring forth a Son, and shall call His name JESUS.'"
Jer. 31:15, p. 877 "Thus says the LORD: 'A voice was heard in Ramah, lamentation *and* bitter weeping, Rachel weeping for her children, refusing to be comforted for her children, because they *are* no more.'"	**slaughter of children**	*Matt. 2:16–18, p. 1116* "Then Herod, when he saw that he was deceived by the wise men, was exceedingly angry; and he sent forth and put to death all the male children who were in Bethlehem and in all its districts, from two years old and under, according to the time which he had determined from the wise men. Then was fulfilled what was spoken by Jeremiah the prophet, saying: '*A voice was heard in Ramah, lamentation, weeping, and great mourning, Rachel weeping for her children, refusing to be comforted, because they were no more*.'"
Hos. 11:1, p. 1003 "When Israel *was* a child, I loved him, and out of Egypt I called My son."	**flight to Egypt**	*Matt. 2:14, 15, p. 1116* "When he arose, he took the young Child and His mother by night and departed for Egypt, and was there until the death of Herod, that it might be fulfilled which was spoken by the Lord through the prophet, saying, '*Out of Egypt I called My Son*.'"
Is. 40:3–5, p. 811 "The voice of one crying in the wilderness: 'Prepare the way of the LORD; make straight in the desert a highway for our God. Every valley shall be exalted, and every mountain and hill shall be made low; the crooked places shall be made straight, and the rough places smooth; the glory of the LORD shall be revealed, and all flesh shall see *it* together; for the mouth of the LORD has spoken.'"	**the way prepared**	*Luke 3:3–6, p. 1194* "And he went into all the region around the Jordan, preaching a baptism of repentance for the remission of sins, as it is written in the book of the words of Isaiah the prophet, saying: '*The voice of one crying in the wilderness: "Prepare the way of the LORD, make His paths straight. Every valley shall be filled and every mountain and hill brought low; and the crooked places shall be made straight and the rough ways made smooth; and all flesh shall see the salvation of God.*"'"

PROPHETIC SCRIPTURE	SUBJECT	FULFILLED
Mal 3:1, p. 1082 "'Behold, I send My messenger, and he will prepare the way before Me. And the Lord, whom you seek, will suddenly come to His temple, even the messenger of the covenant, in whom you delight. Behold, He is coming,' says the LORD of hosts."	**preceded by a forerunner**	***Luke 7:24, 27, p. 1204*** "When the messengers of John had departed, He began to speak to the multitudes concerning John: 'What did you go out into the wilderness to see? A reed shaken by the wind? . . . This is *he* of whom it is written: *"Behold, I send My messenger before Your face, who will prepare Your way before You."'*"
Mal. 4:5, 6, p. 1083 "Behold I will send you Elijah the prophet before the coming of the great and dreadful day of the LORD. And he will turn the hearts of the fathers to the children, and the hearts of the children to their fathers, lest I come and strike the earth with a curse."	**preceded by Elijah**	***Matt. 11:13, 14, p. 1130*** "For all the prophets and the law prophesied until John. And if you are willing to receive *it*, he is Elijah who is to come."
Ps. 2:7, p. 625 "I will declare the decree: the LORD has said to Me, "You *are* My Son, today I have begotten You."	**declared the Son of God**	***Matt. 3:17, p. 1117*** "And suddenly a voice *came* from heaven, saying, 'This is My beloved Son, in whom I am well pleased.'"
Is. 9:1, 2, p. 780 "Nevertheless the gloom *will* not *be* upon her who *is* distressed, as when at first He lightly esteemed the land of Zebulun and the land of Naphtali, and afterward more heavily oppressed *her*, *by* the way of the sea, beyond the Jordan, in Galilee of the Gentiles. The people who walked in darkness have seen a great light; those who dwelt in the land of the shadow of death, upon them a light has shined."	**Galilean ministry**	***Matt. 4:13–16, p. 1118*** "And leaving Nazareth, He came and dwelt in Capernaum, which is by the sea, in the regions of Zebulun and Naphtali, that it might be fulfilled which was spoken by Isaiah the prophet, saying: *'The land of Zebulun and the land of Naphtali, the way of the sea, beyond the Jordan, Galilee of the Gentiles: The people who sat in darkness saw a great light, and upon those who sat in the region and shadow of death light has dawned.'*"
Ps. 78:2–4, p. 669 "I will open my mouth in a parable; I will utter dark sayings of old, which we have heard and known, and our fathers have told us. We will not hide *them* from their children, telling to the generation to come the praises of the LORD, and His strength and His wonderful works that He has done."	**speaks in parables**	***Matt. 13:34, 35, p. 1133*** "All these things Jesus spoke to the multitude in parables; and without a parable He did not speak to them that it might be fulfilled which was spoken by the prophet, saying: *'I will open My mouth in parables; I will utter things which have been kept secret from the foundation of the world.'*"
Deut. 18:15, p. 229 "The LORD your God will raise up for you a Prophet like me from your midst, from your brethren. Him you shall hear."	**a prophet**	***Acts 3:20, 22, p. 1276*** "And that He may send Jesus Christ, who was preached to you before, . . . For Moses truly said to the fathers, *'The LORD your God will raise up for you a Prophet like me from your brethren. Him you shall hear in all things, whatever He says to you.'*"
Is. 61:1, 2, p. 833 "The Spirit of the Lord GOD *is* upon Me, because the LORD has anointed Me to preach good tidings to the poor; He has sent Me to heal the brokenhearted, to proclaim liberty to the captives, and the opening of the prison to *those who are* bound; to proclaim the acceptable year of the LORD, and the day of vengeance of our God; to comfort all who mourn."	**to bind up the brokenhearted**	***Luke 4:18, 19, p. 1198*** *"The Spirit of the LORD is upon Me, because He has anointed Me to preach the gospel to the poor. He has sent Me to heal the brokenhearted, to preach deliverance to the captives and recovery of sight to the blind, to set at liberty those who are oppressed, to preach the acceptable year of the LORD."*
Is. 53:3, p. 825 "He is despised and rejected by men, a man of sorrows and acquainted with grief. And we hid, as it were, *our* faces from Him; He was despised, and we did not esteem Him."	**rejected by His own people, the Jews**	***John 1:11, p. 1236*** "He came to His own, and His own did not receive Him." ***Luke 23:18, p. 1229*** "And they all cried out at once, saying, 'Away with this *Man*, and release to us Barabbas'"—

PROPHETIC SCRIPTURE	SUBJECT	FULFILLED
Ps. 110:4, p. 689 "The LORD has sworn and will not relent, 'You *are* a priest forever according to the order of Melchizedek.'"	**priest after order of Melchizedek**	*Heb. 5:5, 6, p. 1453* "So also Christ did not glorify Himself to become High Priest, *but it* was He who said to Him: '*You are My Son, today I have begotten You*.' As *He* also *says* in another *place: 'You are a priest forever according to the order of Melchizedek*.'"
Zech. 9:9, p. 1073 "Rejoice greatly, O daughter of Zion! Shout, O daughter of Jerusalem! Behold, your King is coming to you; He *is* just and having salvation, lowly and riding on a donkey, a colt, the foal of a donkey."	**triumphal entry**	*Mark 11:7, 9, 11, p. 1174* "Then they brought the colt to Jesus and threw their garments on it, and He sat on it. . . . Then those who went before and those who followed cried out, saying: 'Hosanna! *Blessed is He who comes in the name of the LORD!*' . . . And Jesus went into Jerusalem and into the temple. So when He had looked around at all things, as the hour was already late, He went out to Bethany with the twelve."
Ps. 8:2, p. 630 "Out of the mouth of babes and infants You have ordained strength, because of Your enemies, that You may silence the enemy and the avenger."	**adored by infants**	*Matt. 21:15, 16, p. 1141* "But when the chief priests and scribes saw the wonderful things that He did, and the children crying out in the temple and saying, 'Hosanna to the Son of David!' they were indignant and said to Him, 'Do You hear what these are saying?' And Jesus said to them, 'Yes. Have you never read, "*Out of the mouth of babes and nursing infants You have perfected praise*"?'"
Is. 53:1, p. 825 "Who has believed our report? And to whom has the arm of the LORD been revealed?"	**not believed**	*John 12:37, 38, p. 1256* "But although He had done so many signs before them, they did not believe in Him, that the word of Isaiah the prophet might be fulfilled, which he spoke: '*Lord, who has believed our report? And to whom has the arm of the LORD been revealed?*'"
Ps. 41:9, p. 649 "Even my own familiar friend in whom I trusted, who ate my bread, has lifted up *his* heel against me."	**betrayed by a close friend**	*Luke 22:47, 48, p. 1228* "And while He was still speaking, behold, a multitude; and he who was called Judas, one of the twelve, went before them and drew near to Jesus to kiss Him. But Jesus said to him, 'Judas, are you betraying the Son of Man with a kiss?'"
Zech. 11:12, p. 1075 "Then I said to them, 'If it is agreeable to you, give *me* my wages; and if not, refrain.' So they weighed out for my wages thirty *pieces* of silver."	**betrayed for thirty pieces of silver**	*Matt. 26:14, 15, p. 1150* "Then one of the twelve, called Judas Iscariot, went to the chief priests and said, 'What are you willing to give me if I deliver Him to you?' And they counted out to him thirty pieces of silver."
Ps. 35:11, p. 644 "Fierce witnesses rise up; they ask me *things* that I do not know."	**accused by false witnesses**	*Mark 14:57, 58, p. 1182* "And some rose up and bore false witness against Him, saying, 'We heard Him say, "I will destroy this temple that *is* made with hands, and within three days I will build another made without hands."'"
Is. 53:7, p. 825 "He was oppressed and He was afflicted, yet He opened not His mouth; He was led as a lamb to the slaughter, and as a sheep before its shearers is silent, so He opened not His mouth."	**silent to accusations**	*Mark 15:4, 5, p. 1182* "Then Pilate asked Him again, saying, 'Do You answer nothing? See how many things they testify against You!' But Jesus still answered nothing, so that Pilate marveled."

PROPHETIC SCRIPTURE	SUBJECT	FULFILLED
Is. 50:6, p. 823 "I gave My back to those who struck *Me*, and My cheeks to those who plucked out the beard; I did not hide My face from shame and spitting."	**spat on and struck**	***Matt. 26:67, p. 1151*** "Then they spat in His face and beat Him; and others struck *Him* with the palms of their hands,"
Ps. 35:19, p. 644 "Let them not rejoice over me who are wrongfully my enemies; nor let them wink with the eye who hate me without a cause."	**hated without reason**	***John 15:24, 25, p. 1259*** "If I had not done among them the works which no one else did, they would have no sin; but now they have seen and also hated both Me and My Father. But *this happened* that the word might be fulfilled which is written in their law, *'They hated Me without a cause.'*"
Is. 53:5, p. 825 "But He *was* wounded for our transgressions, *He was* bruised for our iniquities; the chastisement for our peace *was* upon Him, and by His stripes we are healed."	**vicarious sacrifice**	***Rom. 5:6, 8, p. 1329*** "For when we were still without strength, in due time Christ died for the ungodly. . . . But God demonstrates His own love toward us, in that while we were still sinners, Christ died for us."
Is. 53:12, p. 825 "Therefore I will divide Him a portion with the great, and He shall divide the spoil with the strong, because He poured out His soul unto death, and He was numbered with the transgressors, and He bore the sin of many, and made intercession for the transgressors."	**crucified with malefactors**	***Mark 15:27, 28, p. 1184*** "With Him they also crucified two robbers, one on His right and the other on His left. So the Scripture was fulfilled which says, *'And He was numbered with the transgressors.'*"
Zech. 12:10, p. 1075 "And I will pour on the house of David and on the inhabitants of Jerusalem the Spirit of grace and supplication; then they will look on Me whom they have pierced; they will mourn for Him as one mourns for *his* only *son,* and grieve for Him as one grieves for a firstborn."	**pierced through hands and feet**	***John 20:27, p. 1265*** "Then He said to Thomas, 'Reach your finger here, and look at My hands; and reach your hand *here,* and put *it* into My side. Do not be unbelieving, but believing.'"
Ps. 22:7, 8, p. 637 "All those who see Me laugh Me to scorn; they shoot out the lip, they shake the head, *saying,* 'He trusted in the LORD, let Him rescue Him; let Him deliver Him, since He delights in Him!'"	**sneered and mocked**	***Luke 23:35, p. 1229*** "And the people stood looking on. But even the rulers with them sneered, saying, 'He saved others; let Him save Himself if He is the Christ, the chosen of God.'"
Ps. 69:9, p. 663 "Because zeal for Your house has eaten me up, and the reproaches of those who reproach You have fallen on me."	**was reproached**	***Rom. 15:3, p. 1340*** "For even Christ did not please Himself; but as it is written, *'The reproaches of those who reproached You fell on Me.'*"
Ps. 109:4, p. 688 "In return for my love they are my accusers, but I *give myself to* prayer."	**prayer for His enemies**	***Luke 23:34, p. 1229*** "Then Jesus said, 'Father, forgive them, for they do not know what they do.' And they divided His garments and cast lots."
Ps. 22:17, 18, p. 637 "I can count all My bones. They look *and* stare at Me. They divide My garments among them, and for My clothing they cast lots."	**soldiers gambled for His clothing**	***Matt. 27:35, 36, p. 1154*** "Then they crucified Him, and divided His garments, casting lots, that it might be fulfilled which was spoken by the prophet: *'They divided My garments among them, and for My clothing they cast lots.'* Sitting down, they kept watch over Him there."
Ps. 22:1, p. 636 "My God, My God, why have You forsaken Me? *Why are You so* far from helping Me, *and from* the words of My groaning?"	**forsaken by God**	***Matt. 27:46, p. 1154*** "And about the ninth hour Jesus cried out with a loud voice, saying, 'Eli, Eli, lama sabachthani?' that is, *'My God, My God, why have You forsaken Me?'*"

PROPHETIC SCRIPTURE	SUBJECT	FULFILLED
Ps. 34:20, p. 644 "He guards all his bones; not one of them is broken."	**no bones broken**	***John 19:32, 33, 36, p. 1264*** "Then the soldiers came and broke the legs of the first and of the other who was crucified with Him. But when they came to Jesus and saw that He was already dead, they did not break His legs. . . . For these things were done that the Scripture should be fulfilled, *'Not one of His bones shall be broken.'*"
Zech. 12:10, p. 1075 "And I will pour on the house of David and on the inhabitants of Jerusalem the Spirit of grace and supplication; then they will look on Me whom they have pierced; they will mourn for Him as one mourns for *his* only *son,* and grieve for Him as one grieves for a firstborn."	**His side pierced**	***John 19:34, p. 1264*** "But one of the soldiers pierced His side with a spear, and immediately blood and water came out."
Is. 53:9, p. 825 "And they made His grave with the wicked—but with the rich at His death, because He had done no violence, nor *was any* deceit in His mouth."	**buried with the rich**	***Matt. 27:57–60, p. 1154*** "Now when evening had come, there came a rich man from Arimathea, named Joseph, who himself had also become a disciple of Jesus. This man went to Pilate and asked for the body of Jesus. Then Pilate commanded the body to be given to him. And when Joseph had taken the body, he wrapped it in a clean linen cloth, and laid it in his new tomb which he had hewn out of the rock; and he rolled a large stone against the door of the tomb, and departed."
Ps. 16:10, p. 633 "For You will not leave my soul in Sheol, nor will You allow Your Holy One to see corruption." ***Ps. 49:15, p. 653*** "But God will redeem my soul from the power of the grave, for He shall receive me. Selah"	**to be resurrected**	***Mark 16:6, 7, p. 1185*** "But he said to them, 'Do not be alarmed. You seek Jesus of Nazareth, who was crucified. He is risen! He is not here. See the place where they laid Him. But go *and* tell His disciples—and Peter—that He is going before you into Galilee; there you will see Him, as He said to you.'"
Ps. 68:18, p. 662 "You have ascended on high, You have led captivity captive; You have received gifts among men; even *among* the rebellious, that the LORD God might dwell *there.*"	**His ascension to God's right hand**	***Mark 16:19, p. 1185*** "So then after the Lord had spoken to them, He was received up into heaven, and sat down at the right hand of God." ***1 Cor. 15:4, p. 1231*** "And that He was buried, and that He rose again the third day according to the Scriptures." ***Eph. 4:8, p. 1390*** "Therefore He says: *'When He ascended on high, He led captivity captive, and gave gifts to men.'*"

THE PARABLES OF JESUS CHRIST

Parable	*Matthew*	*Mark*	*Luke*
1. Lamp Under a Basket	5:14–16	4:21, 22	8:16, 17 11:33–36
2. A Wise Man Builds on Rock and a Foolish Man Builds on Sand	7:24–27		6:47–49
3. Unshrunk (New) Cloth on an Old Garment	9:16	2:21	5:36
4. New Wine in Old Wineskins	9:17	2:22	5:37, 38
5. The Sower	13:3–23	4:2–20	8:4–15
6. The Tares (Weeds)	13:24–30		
7. The Mustard Seed	13:31, 32	4:30–32	13:18, 19
8. The Leaven	13:33		13:20, 21
9. The Hidden Treasure	13:44		
10. The Pearl of Great Price	13:45, 46		
11. The Dragnet	13:47–50		
12. The Lost Sheep	18:12–14		15:3–7
13. The Unforgiving Servant	18:23–35		
14. The Workers in the Vineyard	20:1–16		
15. The Two Sons	21:28–32		
16. The Wicked Vinedressers	21:33–45	12:1–12	20:9–19
17. The Wedding Feast	22:2–14		
18. The Fig Tree	24:32–44	13:28–32	21:29–33
19. The Wise and Foolish Virgins	25:1–13		
20. The Talents	25:14–30		
21. The Growing Seed		4:26–29	
22. The Absent Householder		13:33–37	
23. The Creditor and Two Debtors			7:41–43
24. The Good Samaritan			10:30–37
25. A Friend in Need			11:5–13
26. The Rich Fool			12:16–21
27. The Faithful Servant and the Evil Servant			12:35–40
28. Faithful and Wise Steward			12:42–48
29. The Barren Fig Tree			13:6–9
30. The Great Supper			14:16–24
31. Building a Tower and a King Making War			14:25–35
32. The Lost Coin			15:8–10
33. The Lost Son			15:11–32
34. The Unjust Steward			16:1–13
35. The Rich Man and Lazarus			16:19–31
36. Unprofitable Servants			17:7–10
37. The Persistent Widow			18:1–8
38. The Pharisee and the Tax Collector			18:9–14
39. The Minas (Pounds)			19:11–27

THE MIRACLES OF JESUS CHRIST

Miracle	*Matthew*	*Mark*	*Luke*	*John*
1. Cleansing a Leper	8:2	1:40	5:12	
2. Healing a Centurion's Servant (of paralysis)	8:5		7:1	
3. Healing Peter's Mother-in-law	8:14	1:30	4:38	
4. Healing the Sick at Evening	8:16	1:32	4:40	
5. Stilling the Storm	8:23	4:35	8:22	
6. Demons Entering a Herd of Swine	8:28	5:1	8:26	
7. Healing a Paralytic	9:2	2:3	5:18	
8. Raising the Ruler's Daughter	9:18, 23	5:22, 35	8:40, 49	
9. Healing the Hemorrhaging Woman	9:20	5:25	8:43	
10. Healing Two Blind Men	9:27			
11. Curing a Demon-possessed, Mute Man	9:32			
12. Healing a Man's Withered Hand	12:9	3:1	6:6	
13. Curing a Demon-possessed, Blind and Mute Man	12:22		11:14	
14. Feeding the Five Thousand	14:13	6:30	9:10	6:1
15. Walking on the Sea	14:25	6:48		6:19
16. Healing the Gentile Woman's Daughter	15:21	7:24		
17. Feeding the Four Thousand	15:32	8:1		
18. Healing the Epileptic Boy	17:14	9:17	9:38	
19. Temple Tax in the Fish's Mouth	17:24			
20. Healing Two Blind Men	20:30	10:46	18:35	
21. Withering the Fig Tree	21:18	11:12		
22. Casting Out an Unclean Spirit		1:23	4:33	
23. Healing a Deaf Mute		7:31		
24. Healing a Blind Paralytic at Bethsaida		8:22		
25. Escape from the Hostile Multitude			4:30	
26. Draught of Fish			5:1	
27. Raising of a Widow's Son at Nain			7:11	
28. Healing the Infirm, Bent Woman			13:11	
29. Healing the Man with Dropsy			14:1	
30. Cleansing the Ten Lepers			17:11	
31. Restoring a Servant's Ear			22:51	
32. Turning Water into Wine				2:1
33. Healing the Nobleman's Son (of fever)				4:46
34. Healing an Infirm Man at Bethesda				5:1
35. Healing the Man Born Blind				9:1
36. Raising of Lazarus				11:43
37. Second Draught of Fish				21:1

THE SCARLET THREAD OF REDEMPTION

Introduction

The Bible is a book of redemption. It is that or nothing at all. It is not merely a book of history, or of science, or of anthropology, or of cosmogony. It is a book of salvation and deliverance for lost mankind.

The idea in the word "redemption" is twofold: it refers to a deliverance; and it refers to the price paid for that deliverance, a ransom. We are redeemed from the penalty of sin, from the power of Satan and evil, by the price Jesus paid on the cross for us; and we are redeemed to a new freedom from sin, a new relationship to God, and a new life of love by the appropriation of that atonement for our sins.

The whole of the Bible, whether the Old Testament or the New Testament, looks to the mighty, redemptive atonement of Christ. His blood sacrifice is the ransom paid for our deliverance. He took our sinful nature upon Himself in order that He might satisfy the demands of the law. His sacrifice is accepted as the payment for the debt the sinner owes to God, and His death is accepted as the full payment for man's deliverance.

Our Lord's redemptive work for us is threefold: First, it is closely associated with forgiveness, since we receive forgiveness through the redemptive price of Christ's death. Second, it involves justification, since the deliverance establishes us in a restored position of favor before God. Third, it promises final deliverance from the power of sin at the coming of the Lord. This redemption is "The Scarlet Thread."

The Creation and the Fall

When God made the heavens and the earth, they must have been beautiful, perfect, and pure.

In the Garden of Eden, however, through a denial of the Word of God and through a deception of the woman, our first parents fell. Eve was deceived, but Adam chose to die by the side of the woman whom God had created and placed in his arms. When the Lord came to visit the man and his wife in the cool of the day, He could not find them. They were afraid and hid themselves from the Lord because they were naked and ashamed. To hide their guilt, they made for themselves aprons of fig leaves, but when God looked upon the covering, He said, "This will not do." Covering for sin (atonement for sin) cannot be woven by human hands. Therefore, somewhere in the Garden of Eden, the Lord took an innocent animal, and before the eyes of Eve and Adam, God slew that innocent animal as the ground drank up its blood. This is the beginning of "The Scarlet Thread of Redemption." Through the slaughter of an innocent victim, God took coats of skin and covered over the shame and the nakedness of the man and his wife. This is the first sacrifice, and it was offered by the hand of Almighty God. When Adam saw the gasping, spent life of that innocent creature, and when he saw the crimson stain which soiled the ground, it was his first experience of knowing what it meant to die because of sin. So the story of atonement and sacrifice begins and unfolds throughout the Word of God until finally in glory we shall see great throngs of the saints who have washed their robes and made them white in the blood of the Lamb. This is "The Scarlet Thread of Redemption."

From the Seventh Day in Eden to the Call of Abraham

In the Garden of Eden, as the Lord covered over the nakedness of the man and the woman, He turned to Satan and said, "And I will put enmity between you and the woman, and between your seed and her Seed; He shall bruise your head, and you shall bruise His heel" (Gen. 3:15). For centuries the rabbis studied that word of Jehovah God to Satan. The Seed of the woman. Seed is masculine. The rabbis contemplated the promise of God that the "Seed" of the woman would bruise Satan's head. We now know that the promise is related to the long conflict and struggle betwen the hatred of Lucifer and the love of God in Christ Jesus. It speaks of Jesus at Calvary. Jesus suffered. His heel was bruised. But in that bruising, He defeated once and for all the power of that old serpent, the devil. He bruised his head.

As the man Adam and his wife, Eve, made their first home in earth cursed for their sakes, after a time there were born to them two sons. One was named Cain and the other Abel. In jealousy and insane fury, the older brother killed the younger brother. But the seed of God would be preserved. The Lord, therefore, gave to Eve another son, named Seth. Seth was a man of faith, as Cain was a man of the world. When the children of Seth, the godly remnant, intermarried with the children of Cain, the people of the world, the result was a fallen progeny that filled the earth with violence. Finally, God said it was enough. One hundred twenty years later, He would destroy the world by a flood. But a member of the line of Seth found grace in the sight of the Lord. His name was Noah. To preserve the righteous seed, God told Noah to build an ark; and into that ark of safety, salvation, and hope Noah brought his family. After the passing of the awesome judgment of the flood, the earth once again began its story of redemption through the life of this one man and his three sons.

It was not long, however, until the ravages of sin began to waste the select family of God. Instead of carrying out the great commission of the Lord for mankind to inhabit the whole earth, the people drew together into one plain and announced their purpose to build a tower around which they were to center their civilization and their collective, communal unity. When God looked down and saw their pride, He confused their speech and caused them to "babble." From this "Tower of Babel," therefore, the different parts of the human race, being unable to understand each other, scattered in different directions and so fathered the nations of the earth that grew up from those three great family lines of Noah.

From the Call of Abraham Through the Times of the Judges

We begin the story of Abraham in a dark era. The whole world had been plunged into abysmal idolatry, but God called out this man to leave his home, his place, his country, and his family to go into another country which he would afterward receive for an inheritance. In obedience, Abraham left the Mesopotamian valley and came as a pilgrim, a stranger, and a sojourner into the land of Canaan. There he dwelt, and there God gave him two sons. But the Lord God said to Abraham that Ishmael, the son of a slave woman, would not be the promised seed. When Abraham was a hundred years old and Sarah was ninety years old, God miraculously placed in the arms of the parents the child of promise, whom they named Isaac. Isaac was the father of two sons, Esau and Jacob. The Lord, refusing Esau, chose Jacob whom He renamed, after a deep conversion experience, the "prince of God" or "Israel."

Because of a severe famine in Canaan and because Jacob's son, Joseph, was in Egypt, the entire household of Jacob went down to live in the land of the Nile. Later, there arose a Pharaoh who "did not know" Joseph. The chosen family became slaves to this new ruler of Egypt, and their heavy groaning mounted up to the ears of the Lord God in heaven. The Lord, therefore, raised up the mighty prophet, Moses, to deliver his people from the bondage and slavery of the Egyptians. God worked this deliverance by a miracle called the Passover. For the Lord had said, "When I see the blood, I will pass over you and will spare you and your home." This way of salvation, through the blood, is once again "The Scarlet Thread of Redemption."

After the Lord God delivered the chosen family from Egypt, He brought them by the leadership of Moses through the parting of the Red Sea into the Sinaitic Peninsula to the base of Mount Horeb. There, for forty days and forty nights, Moses was with God, and there the Lord gave to Moses the pattern of the tabernacle, the ritual instructions of holy worship, and all of the other marvelous things in the Book of Leviticus that portray and prophesy the sacrifice of the Son of God.

After the death of Moses, Joshua went over Jordan and led the wars of conquest. In the first confrontation, at Jericho, an incident happened which gave rise to the title of this summary. The scouts sent out by Joshua to spy out Jericho were saved by the faith and kindness of Rahab. The men of Israel promised life and safety, both for her and her father's house, if she would bind a scarlet thread in her window. This she did, and, when Jericho fell into the hands of Joshua by the intervention of God, Rahab and her family were spared because of that scarlet line, "The Scarlet Thread of Redemption."

After the conquest of Canaan, under Joshua, we have the story of the Judges. The difference between a judge and a king was that a king gave to his son his throne by inheritance, but a judge was raised up in a crisis and endowed with special gifts from God for a period of time. The days of the Judges end with the birth of Samuel.

From the First of the Prophets to the Founding of the Kingdom

During the time of Samuel, the people began to cry for a king. It was the purpose of God in the beginning for the children of Israel to have a king (Deut. 17:14–20), but it hurt the heart of the Lord that the request should come in so vain and rebellious a way as they presented it to Samuel. But according to the word and instruction of God, Samuel anointed Saul to be king over Israel. In his beginning ministry, Saul was a mighty man and carried out the mandates of heaven, but he soon fell away from the instruction of Samuel and fell into gross disobedience to the will of God. The Word of the Lord, therefore, came to Samuel that he must anoint a man after God's own heart. That anointing was directed toward a lad from the shepherd field, a son of Jesse by the name of David.

David and the Kingdoms of Israel and Judah

The first part of David's life as king of Israel was magnificent. Then, in the very prime of his life, at the very height of his glory, he turned aside from the will of God and became self-indulgent and lustful like other Oriental kings. This brought to David an infinite tragedy, one by which the name of God was blasphemed. Nevertheless, God forgave the sin of David and chose him to be the father of that marvelous Son who would sit upon His throne as King forever. A type of that glorious Son of David, was the *immediate* son of David, called Solomon. Solomon also began his reign gloriously and triumphantly, but like his father, Solomon also fell into tragic decline. Upon his death, the kingdom was divided.

Thereafter, the people of God were divided into two kingdoms: that of the north was called the kingdom of Israel, and that of the south was called the kingdom of Judah. The northern kingdom of Israel was taken away into captivity by the cruel and ruthless Assyrians in 722 B.C. The southern kingdom was carried away into Babylonian captivity in 587 B.C. In the days of the Babylonian captivity, Jeremiah prophesied in Jerusalem while Daniel, the prophet-statesman, and Ezekiel, the holy seer, comforted and strengthened the people of God in Mesopotamia.

Out of the Babylonian captivity came three great establishments by which God has blessed our world. First, the Jews were never idolatrous again. Second, the synagogue was born, and from the synagogue came the church. The services of the synagogue are the same type of services we have today. Third, from the captivity came the canon of the Holy Scriptures. Out of tears and suffering came our greatest blessing, "The Scarlet Thread of Redemption."

From the Prophets to the Christ to the Preaching of Paul

Out of the agonies of the days of the kingdoms of Israel and of Judah came the predictions by the prophets of a more glorious Savior and King, whom God would send to His people. When we read a passage like the twenty-second Psalm or the fifty-third chapter of Isaiah, we seem to be standing by the cross of the Son of God. More and more, the great spiritual leaders of Israel and of Judah began to depict the coming of a Redeemer who would save His people from their sins and bring to them the everlasting hope and righteousness of God. This messianic hope became stronger and more gloriously received as the centuries passed.

In 536 B.C. Cyrus the Persian gave the people the right to return from the Babylonian captivity to their homeland in Judah and to build their holy temple in Jerusalem. Thus, the remnant of the captivity returned under Zerubbabel, the political leader; under Joshua, the priestly leader; under Ezra, the scribe; and under Nehemiah, who had been the prime minister at the court of Shushan, the Persian capital. This holy remnant, thus seeking to restore the worship of the true God in Jerusalem and to recreate the political life of Judah, was encouraged by God's messengers, Haggai, Zechariah, and Malachi.

Of the three great restoration prophets, Zechariah is by far the greatest. Zechariah spoke much about Israel, about the end of time, and about the conversion of the people of the Lord. The last prophet is Malachi. He delivered his message from about 450 B.C. to about 425 B.C.

The four-hundred-year period between the Old Testament and the New Testament marks the rise of the Hellenistic empire. God used Alexander the Great to spread abroad throughout the civilized world one culture and one language, which made possible the later preaching of Christ to all men everywhere.

In that inter-biblical period also arose the might of the Roman Empire. When Augustus Caesar was the Roman emperor, and when Rome had the entire world in her hand, the great prophecies of Isaiah, Micah, Nathan to David, Jacob to his son Judah, and the great promise of God Almighty to Eve in the Garden of Eden, came to pass. In the seed progeny of the woman and through the seed of Abraham, all the families of the earth were to be blessed—and our Savior was thus born into the world. "The Scarlet Thread of Redemption" has led us to the birth of Him who has come to redeem the human race from their fallen estate.

In His ministry Jesus early began to teach His disciples that He should suffer and die. When He was transfigured, there appeared Moses and Elijah talking to Him about His death, which He should accomplish in Jerusalem. When He was anointed by Mary of Bethany, He said it was for His burial. When the Greeks came to see Him from afar He said, "And I, if I am lifted up from the earth, will draw all *peoples* to Myself" (John 12:32). At the last supper He said, "This is My body; eat in remembrance of Me." And again He said, "This is My blood; drink in remembrance of Me." Before He went to the cross, He gave Himself in Gethsemane in travail of soul for our redemption (Is. 53:11). And when He bowed His head and died He said, "It is finished!" (John 19:30). When we preach the cross, when we preach the blood, when we preach the sacrificial death of Christ, we are preaching the meaning of His coming into the world. The sacrifice of Christ consummated the great redemptive plan and purpose of God on the earth. This is "The Scarlet Thread of Redemption."

After the resurrection of our Lord, after the giving of the Great Commission to the apostles, and after the ascension of our Savior into heaven, the Lord poured out His Holy Spirit upon His church in Jerusalem on the day of Pentecost. Then the disciples of Jesus began to make known throughout the earth the Good News of our hope and salvation.

The epistles of Paul are divided into four distinct groups. The first group he wrote on his second missionary journey from Athens and Corinth. They are First and Second Thessalonians. The second group of letters was born in his third missionary journey. While he was in Ephesus, he wrote First Corinthians. Somewhere between

Ephesus and Corinth, he wrote Second Corinthians in Macedonia. Then, either in Antioch or on his way to Antioch, he wrote Galatians and Romans. First and Second Corinthians, Galatians, and Romans, therefore, center around the city of Ephesus. The third group of epistles Paul wrote from the prison in Rome, during his first Roman imprisonment. They are Ephesians, Philippians, Colossians, and Philemon. The fourth and last group of his epistles, written after his first Roman imprisonment were First Timothy, Titus, and Second Timothy, called the pastoral epistles. In all of Paul's letters, there is the constant theme of redemptive love. It is a part of "The Scarlet Thread of Redemption."

The Apocalypse and the Consummation of the Age

We come now to the conclusion of the Bible.

On the Isle of Patmos, a rocky little point in the Mediterranean Sea, several miles southwest of Ephesus, John was exiled to die of exposure and starvation. But there the Lord appears to John in a glorious vision. The vision is called the Revelation, that is, "the unveiling." "The Apocalypse," the unveiling of Jesus Christ in His glory, in His majesty, and in His kingdom, is the reward that God gave to Jesus for saving us, Adam's fallen children, from our sins.

After the vision of the exalted and glorified Christ in chapter one, and after the prophetic words in chapters two and three, John is taken up through an open door into heaven. While John, the translated saint, is with the Savior in heaven, the judgments of Almighty God are poured out on the earth. They are depicted in the opening of the seven seals, the seven trumpets, and the seven bowls. In those dark days John sees a vision in Revelation, chapter seven, concerning the blood-washed redeemed souls in glory. Announcement is made to him through one of the elders that these are they who have come out of the great tribulation and have washed their robes and made them white in the blood of the Lamb. This is "The Scarlet Thread of Redemption" that began with the blood of covering in the Garden of Eden and finds its ultimate and final consummation in the blood-washed throng before the throne of God in glory.

After the seven seals and the judgments, the seven trumpets and the judgments, the seven bowls and the judgments, and the seven personages and the judgments, we come to the final great Judgment Day of Almighty God. The anti-Christ, who professes to be the leader of the nations of the world, is seen gathering the armies of the entire earth together. They are converging from the north, from the east, from the south, from the west, and from the islands of the sea. They are converging for that great day of the Lord. That is the Battle of Armageddon, the last great war the world is going to fight. At Megiddo, the armies of the earth by the millions will converge to face that rendezvous with God. In the midst of this holocaust, Christ will intervene in human history. He comes with His saints. He will deliver His people, shut up in the holy city, and take Satan and bind him for a thousand years in the bottomless pit.

After the binding of Satan for a thousand years, which is called the millennium, Satan is released and thereafter goes forth once again to lead men in rebellion against God. This is the final conflict which ends forever man's refusal to accept the will of God for their lives. At the end time, in the final resurrection of the wicked dead and the great white throne judgment, the books are opened, and those whose names are not found written in the Lamb's Book of Life are cast out and rewarded according to their deeds. Into the abyss of hell are flung Satan and his angels, along with those who choose Satan and his way of life, plus death and the grave—all are hurled into the fiery flames where the Beast and the False Prophet have already been for a thousand years.

After the purging of the earth of Satan and his minions, and after the judgment upon those who reject Christ and His grace, and after cleansing the earth of the heartache and tears of sickness, sin, death, and the grave, will come the renovation of earth and heaven. It is a new creation with a glorious new heaven and new earth. In it is the holy city, the heavenly Jerusalem, and in it is the dwelling place of God Himself. Tears, death, sorrow, pain, and crying are passed away. There are no graves on the hillsides of glory and no funeral wreaths on the doors of those mansions in the sky.

The book closes with the incomparable message of the hope, salvation, and redemption accomplished in the person and work of the Lord Christ.

FIRST MENTIONED THINGS IN THE BIBLE

Subject	*Reference*	*Page*
Adultery	Ex. 20:14	90
Altar	Gen. 8:20	14
Angel	Gen. 16:7	23
Archer	Gen. 21:20	30
Bird	Gen. 1:21	4
Camp	Gen. 32:2	43
Cave dweller	Gen. 19:30	28
Chariot	Gen. 41:43	54
Child	Gen. 11:30	18
Child named before birth	Gen. 16:11	23
City builder	Gen. 4:17	10
Coffin	Gen. 50:26	64
Command	Gen. 1:3	4
Congregation	Ex. 12:3	80
Dancing	Ex. 15:20	86
Darkness	Gen. 1:2	4
Death	Gen. 24:67	33
Dew	Gen. 27:28	37
Disaster	Gen. 19:19	28
Dream	Gen. 20:3	29
Drunk	Gen. 9:21	15
Dungeon	Gen. 40:15	52
Earth	Gen. 1:1	4
Emancipator	Ex. 3:7–22	70
Embalming	Gen. 50:2	63
Execution	Gen. 40:20–22	52
Family	Gen. 8:19	14
Farmer	Gen. 4:2	9
Father	Gen. 2:24	8
Fear	Gen. 9:2	14
Food	Gen. 1:29	7
Food control	Gen. 41:25–27	52
Forgiveness	Gen. 50:17	64
Friend	Gen. 38:12	50
Game	Gen. 25:28	34
Gardener	Gen. 2:15	7
Gift	Gen. 9:3	14
God	Gen. 1:1	4
Gold	Gen. 2:11	7
Grace of God	Ezra 9:8	551
Grave	Gen. 23:6	31
Guilt	Gen. 26:10	34
Harlot	Gen. 34:31	46
Hate	Gen. 24:60	33
Healing	Deut. 32:39	245
Heart	Gen. 6:5	11
Heavens	Gen. 1:1	4
Heir	Gen. 15:2	21
Home	Gen. 27:5	36
Hunter	Gen. 10:8, 9	16
Husband	Gen. 3:6	8
Idols	Gen. 31:19	42
Jail	Gen. 39:20	51
Joy	Gen. 31:27	42
Kill	Gen. 4:8	10
King	Gen. 14:1	21
Kiss	Gen. 27:26	37
Man to interpret	Gen. 41:15	52
Man to wear a ring	Gen. 41:42	54
Murderer	Gen. 4:8	10
Oath	Gen. 21:23, 24	30
Pilgrim	Gen. 12:1–8	18
Prayer	Gen. 4:26	10
Preacher to become drunk	Gen. 9:20, 21	15
Prophecy	Gen. 3:15	9
Purchase of land	Gen. 23:3–20	31
Question	Gen. 3:1	8
Rain	Gen. 7:1–12	12
Rainbow	Gen. 9:13	15
Saddle	Gen. 22:3	30
Scribe	Ex. 24:4	95
Shipbuilder	Gen. 6:14, 22	11
Sin	Gen. 3:1–24	8
Snake	Gen. 49:17	63
Sword	Gen. 3:24	9
Temptation	Gen. 3:1–6	8
Tower	Gen. 11:4, 5	16
Veil	Gen. 24:65	33
Violence	Gen. 6:11	11
Wage contract	Gen. 29:15–20	40
War	Gen. 14:2	21
Wealth	Gen. 31:1	42
Well	Gen. 16:14	23
Wife	Gen. 2:24	8
Wind	Gen. 8:1	12
Wine	Gen. 9:21	15
Wish	Gen. 23:8	31
Witness	Gen. 21:30	30
Woman thief	Gen. 31:19	42
Words spoken to man	Gen. 1:28	7
Worship	Gen. 4:3–5	9

PRAYERS OF THE BIBLE

Subject	*Reference*
Abijah's army—for victory	2 Chr. 13:14
Abraham—for a son	Gen. 15:1–6
Abraham—for Ishmael	Gen. 17:18–21
Abraham—for Sodom	Gen. 18:20–32
Abraham—for Abimelech	Gen. 20:17
Abraham's servant—for guidance	Gen. 24:12–52
Asa—for victory	2 Chr. 14:11
Cain—for mercy	Gen. 4:13–15
Centurion—for his servant	Matt. 8:5–13
Christians—for Peter	Acts 12:5–12
Christians—for kings in authority	1 Tim. 2:1, 2
Corinthians—for Paul	2 Cor. 1:9–11
Cornelius—for enlightenment	Acts 10:1–33
Criminal—for salvation	Luke 23:42, 43
Daniel—for the Jews	Dan. 9:3–19
Daniel—for knowledge	Dan. 2:17–23
David—for blessing	2 Sam. 7:18–29
David—for help	1 Sam. 23:10–13
David—for guidance	2 Sam. 2:1
David—for grace	Ps. 25:16
David—for justice	Ps. 9:17–20
Disciples—for boldness	Acts 4:24–31
Elijah—for drought and rain	James 5:17, 18
Elijah—for the raising to life of the widow's son	1 Kin. 17:20–23
Elijah—for triumph over Baal	1 Kin. 18:36–38
Elijah—for death	1 Kin. 19:4
Elisha—for blindness and sight	2 Kin. 6:17–23
Ezekiel—for undefilement	Ezek. 4:12–15
Ezra—for the sins of the people	Ezra 9:6–15
Gideon—for proof of his call	Judg. 6:36–40
Habakkuk—for deliverance	Hab. 3:1–19
Habakkuk—for justice	Hab. 1:1–4
Hagar—for consolation	Gen. 21:14–20
Hannah—for a son	1 Sam. 1:10–17
Hezekiah—for deliverance	2 Kin. 19:15–19
Hezekiah—for health	2 Kin. 20:1–11
Holy Spirit—for Christians	Rom. 8:26, 27
Isaac—for children	Gen. 25:21, 24–26
Israelites—for deliverance	Ex. 2:23–25 Ex. 3:7–10
Jabez—for prosperity	1 Chr. 4:10
Jacob—all night	Gen. 32:24–30
Jacob—for deliverance from Esau	Gen. 32:9–12
Jehoahaz—for victory	2 Kin. 13:1–5
Jehoshaphat—for protection	2 Chr. 20:5–12, 27
Jehoshaphat—for victory	2 Chr. 18:31
Jeremiah—for Judah	Jer. 42:1–6
Jeremiah—for mercy	Jer. 14:7–10
Jesus—Lord's Prayer	Matt. 6:9–13
Jesus—praise for revelation to babes	Matt. 11:25, 26
Jesus—at Lazarus' tomb	John 11:41, 42
Jesus—for the Father's glory	John 12:28
Jesus—for the Church	John 17:1–26
Jesus—for deliverance	Matt. 26:39, 42, 44 Matt. 27:46
Jesus—for forgiveness for others	Luke 23:34
Jesus—in submission	Luke 23:46
Jews—for safe journey	Ezra 8:21, 23
Jonah—for deliverance from the fish	Jon. 2:1–10
Joshua—for help and mercy	Josh. 7:6–9
Leper—for healing	Matt. 8:2, 3
Manasseh—for deliverance	2 Chr. 33:12, 13
Manoah—for guidance	Judg. 13:8–15
Moses—for Pharaoh	Ex. 8:9–13
Moses—for water	Ex. 15:24, 25
Moses—for Israel	Ex. 32:31–35
Moses—for Miriam	Num. 12:11–14
Moses—that he might see the Promised Land	Deut. 3:23–25 Deut. 34:1–4
Moses—for a successor	Num. 27:15–17
Nehemiah—for the Jews	Neh. 1:4–11
Paul—for the healing of Publius' father	Acts 28:8
Paul—for the Ephesians	Eph. 3:14–21
Paul—for grace	2 Cor. 12:8, 9
People of Judah—for a covenant	2 Chr. 15:12–15
Peter—for the raising of Dorcas	Acts 9:40
Priests—for blessing	2 Chr. 30:27
Rebekah—for understanding	Gen. 25:22, 23
Reubenites—for victory	1 Chr. 5:18–20
Samson—for water	Judg. 15:18, 19
Samson—for strength	Judg. 16:29, 30
Samuel—for Israel	1 Sam. 7:5–12
Solomon—for wisdom	1 Kin. 3:6–14
Tax collector—for mercy	Luke 18:13
Zechariah—for a son	Luke 1:13

THE GREATEST ARCHAEOLOGICAL DISCOVERIES

and Their Effects on the Bible

I
Introduction

Definition and Importance of Biblical Archaeology

The last 150 years have witnessed the birth, growth, and phenomenal development of the science of biblical archaeology. This new science has performed many wonders in furnishing background material and in illustrating, illuminating, and in many cases authenticating the message and meaning of the Old and New Testament Scriptures.

Biblical archaeology may be defined as a study based on the excavation, decipherment, and critical evaluation of the records of the past as they affect the Bible. While the general field of archaeology is fascinating, much more so is the study of biblical archaeology, since it deals with the Holy Scriptures. This is the reason for the growing enthusiasm for biblical archaeology. The attraction lies in the supreme importance of the message and meaning of the Bible. The Scriptures, by virtue of their character as the inspired revelation of God to man and meeting man's deepest need, today as in the past, have naturally held a paramount place in the interest and affection of mankind. Biblical archaeology, illustrating the Bible in its historical background and contemporary life, attracts a measure of the interest that lies in the Bible itself. Accordingly, this science has a worthy ministry of expanding biblical horizons on the human plane.

No field of research has offered greater challenge and promise than that of biblical archaeology. Until the beginning of the 19th century very little was known of biblical times and biblical backgrounds, except what appeared on the pages of the Old Testament or what happened to be preserved in the writings of classical antiquity. This was considerable for the New Testament era but very little indeed for the Old Testament period. The reason for this is that Greek and Latin historians catalogued very little information before the 5th century B.C. As a result, the Old Testament period was very little known extrabiblically, and what was known was confined to what the Bible gave. This from the viewpoint of contemporary secular history was sparse. The result was that before the beginning of the science of modern archaeology there was practically nothing available to authenticate Old Testament history and literature. One can therefore imagine the fervor aroused among serious Bible students by illuminating discoveries in Bible lands, especially from c. 1800 to the present. In fact, modern archaeology may be said to have had its beginning in 1798, when the rich antiquities of the Nile Valley were opened up to scientific study by Napoleon's Egyptian Expedition.

II
Foundational Discoveries of the Nineteenth Century

Although the most notable discoveries affecting the Bible and particularly the Old Testament were not made until the 20th century, foundational discoveries were made in the 19th century and prepared the way for the modern era.

1. The Rosetta Stone—Key to Egypt's Splendid Past

This very important monument was discovered in 1798 at *Rosetta* (Rashid), near the westernmost mouth of the Nile River, by an officer in Napoleon's Expedition to Egypt. It was a slab of black basalt trilingually inscribed, which may be said to be the key that unlocked the door to knowledge of the language and literature of ancient Egypt and turned out to be the inscription that opened the modern era of scientific biblical archaeology.

The three languages in which this monument was found to be inscribed were the Greek of 200 B.C., two forms of Egyptian writing—the older, more complicated hieroglyphic script and the later simplified and more popular demotic writing, which was the common language of the people. The Greek could at once be read and provided the clue to the decipherment of the other two ancient Egyptian scripts. Sylvester de Sacy of France and J. D. Akerblad of Sweden succeeded in unraveling the demotic Egyptian by identifying the Greek personal names it contained, namely Ptolemy, Arsinoe, and Berenike. Thomas Young of England then proceeded to identify the name of Ptolemy in the hieroglyphic portion, where groups of characters enclosed in oval frames, called cartouches, had already been surmised to be royal names. From this point on, the young Frenchman Jean François Champollion, 1790–1832, was able to decipher the hieroglyphics of the monument, show the true nature of this script, make a dictionary, formulate a grammar, and translate numerous Egyptian texts, from the year 1818 to 1832.

Champollion's achievement formally opened up the science of Egyptology. Scholars from henceforth were able to read Egyptian monumental inscriptions and reliefs. From that time forth the literary treasures of the Nile Valley have been opened to scholarly study. Today many universities maintain chairs in the language and culture of ancient Egypt. These studies have opened up vistas of history hitherto unknown so that, from the beginning of Egypt. c. 2800 B.C. to 63 B.C. when Rome took over, the entire history of the land of the Nile can fairly well be traced.

All of this has tremendous bearing on the background of the Bible. Egypt figures largely in the patriarchal narratives and the Book of Exodus and all through the Pentateuch. As a result, the background of the story of Joseph and of the sojourn of the children of Israel in Egypt, their deliverance under Moses, and much of their sojourn in the desert and later history in Canaan can now be set in the general framework of Egyptian history. It can be said that the whole context of Old Testament history, in its broad span from Abraham to Christ, is made immeasurably clearer because of the vast strides in our knowledge of Egypt. That great nation of antiquity interacted with the mighty Assyro-Babylonian empires on the Tigris-Euphrates and with the Hittite power on the Halys across the tiny bridge that was ancient Palestine.

2. The Behistun Inscription—Gateway to Assyrian-Babylonian Antiquity

This famous monument was the key to the languages of Assyria and Babylonia. It consists of a large relief panel containing numerous columns of inscription, which was boldly carved on the face of a mountain about 500 feet above the surrounding plain of Karmanshah on the old caravan route from Babylon to Ecbatana. Unlike the Rosetta Stone written in ancient Egyptian hieroglyphics, and later in popular demotic and in the Greek of the 3rd century B.C., the ***Behistun Inscription*** was written in the wedge-shaped characters of ancient Assyria-Babylonia. It contained about 1200 lines of inscription. The three languages in which it was inscribed were all written in cuneiform characters, consisting of Old Persian, Elamite, and Akkadian. The third language, the Akkadian, was the wedge-shaped language of ancient Assyria and Babylonia, in which thousands upon thousands of clay tablets discovered in the Tigris-Euphrates region are inscribed.

Early excavations revealed a mass of material on which this curious wedge-shaped Babylonian-Akkadian writing appeared. But it was an unsolved riddle. Practically no progress was made until a young English officer in the Persian army, Henry C. Rawlinson, in 1835 and the following years made the dangerous climb to the Behistun inscription and made copies and plaster of paris impressions of it. Rawlinson knew modern Persian and set to work to decipher the old Persian, the cuneiform part of the inscription. After a decade of labor, he finally succeeded in translating the five columns, nearly 400 lines of the old Persian portion of the Behistun Inscription, and sent it to Europe in 1845. The text translation and commentary on it were published in 1847 in the ***Journal of the Royal Asiatic Society***.

In conjunction with the literary part of the monument was a life-sized figure with numerous individuals bowing before it. This person turned out to be Darius the Great (522–486 B.C.), the Achemenid prince who saved the Persian Empire from a rebellion. The scene depicts the king, as Rawlinson's translation of the Persian portion of the inscription shows, receiving the submission of the rebels. The emperor is portrayed at the top of the relief accompanied by two attendants. His foot is placed upon the prostrate form of a leading rebel. The king's left hand holds a bow, while his right hand is lifted toward the winged disc symbolizing Ahura-Mazda, the spirit of good, whom Darius, an ardent follower of Zoroaster, worshiped. Behind the rebel stands a procession of rebel leaders, roped together by their necks. Beside and beneath the sculptured panel the numerous columns of the inscription appear, relating in three languages how Darius defended the throne and crushed the revolt.

Working on the supposition that the other inscriptions told the same story, scholars were soon enabled to read the second language, which was the Elamite or Susian. Then last, but most important, they could decipher the Akkadian or Assyro-Babylonian. This was a great discovery, for this wedge-shaped character of writing is recorded on numerous literary remains from the Tigris-Euphrates Valley. It opened up a vast new field of biblical background, so that today, as in the case of the Rosetta Stone opening up the science of Egyptology, the Behistun Inscription has given birth to the science of Assyriology. Moreover, both Egyptology and Assyriology offers great help in understanding biblical backgrounds and biblical history. No Bible dictionary, Bible handbook or commentary that is up to date can ignore the great findings of these sciences.

The task of deciphering cuneiform is increasing with every decade. Numerous cuneiform libraries have been discovered from antiquity. Two at Nineveh were unearthed. These contained thousands of clay tablets. ***The library of Ashurbanipal*** (669–625 B.C.) contained some 22,000 tablets. Among the tablets unearthed in this collection and sent to the British Museum were Assyrian copies of the Babylonian creation and flood stories. The identification and decipherment of these particular tablets by George Smith in 1872

A gateway into Nebuchadnezzar's Palace in Babylon.
Matson Photo Service

produced great excitement in the archaeological world.

Not only in Babylonia but in many other places large bodies of cuneiform literature have been uncovered. For example, the famous ***Amarna Letters*** from Egypt were discovered in 1886 at Tell el-Amarna about 200 miles south of modern Cairo. These Amarna Tablets proved to be diplomatic correspondence of petty princes of Palestine in the 14th century B.C. with the Egyptian court at Amarna. The Amarna Letters give an inside glance into conditions in Palestine just before the conquest by Joshua and the Israelites. Many scholars actually think that they describe aspects of that invasion. One of the documents from the governor of Jerusalem (Urusalim) tells Amenophis IV that the "Habiru" (perhaps the Hebrews) were overrunning many Palestine cities and could not be held back.

Other important bodies of cuneiform literature bearing upon the Bible have been retrieved from Boghaz-Keui and Kanish in Asia Minor. Others come from Susa and Elam, others from the city of Mari on the middle Euphrates, others from Ras Shamra (ancient Ugarit), mentioned in the Amarna Letters and located in North Syria. Others stem from various sites within and without Babylonia. Of first-rate importance then is the Rosetta Stone from Egypt and the Behistun Inscription from Babylonia. These two monuments may be said to have laid the foundation for the key discoveries of the 20th century.

3. The Moabite Stone—A Sensational Literary Find

This important inscription, found in 1868, offers another example of the discoveries of the 19th century that prepared the way for the great finds of the 20th century. The inscription dates from c. 850 B.C. It was erected by Mesha, king of Moab, and is often styled the ***Mesha Stone***. It tells of the wars of Mesha of Moab with Omri, king of Israel, and Omri's successors. It also tells of Mesha's wars with the Edomites. The material recorded on the ***Moabite Stone*** parallels biblical history recorded in Second Kings, chapters 1 and 3. Numerous places mentioned in the Old Testament occur on the stele (inscribed monument). Among them are Arnon (Num. 21:13; Deut. 2:24), Ataroth (Num. 32:34), Baal Meon or Beth Baal Meon (Josh. 13:17), Beth Bamoth or Bamoth Baal (Josh. 13:17), Beth Diblathaim (Jer. 48:22), Bezer (Josh. 20:8), Dibon (Num. 32:34), Jahaza (Josh. 13:18), Medeba (Josh. 13:9), and Nebo (Num. 32:38).

This inscribed monument or stele measures 3 feet 8½ inches in height, 2 feet 3½ inches in width, and 1 foot 1¾ inches in thickness. Its 34 lines constitute the longest single literary inscription yet recovered extrabiblically dealing with Palestine in the period 900–600 B.C. It records that Moab had been conquered by Omri and his son Ahab but was set free from the Israelite yoke

A replica of the Moabite Stone. *Matson Photo Service*

by Mesha's god Chemosh. This deity is represented as commanding King Mesha to go to war against Israel, who, according to Second Kings 3:27, offered up his eldest son as a burnt offering upon the wall to propitiate the god Chemosh and to secure his favor.

The Moabite Stone is written in the language of Moab, which was very similar to the Hebrew of the time of Omri and Ahab. This inscription, therefore, has great value in tracing the development of early Hebrew through the centuries. When it was discovered, the Mesha Stone was not only the longest and oldest Phoenician-Hebrew inscription then in existence, it was the only one. Now the ***Gezer Calendar*** is known and it dates from c. 925 B.C. It is a school boy's exercise written in perfect classical Hebrew. This small limestone tablet, found at ancient Gezer, gives an incidental sidelight on Palestinian agriculture as well as on ancient Hebrew writing. Such discoveries as the Gezer Calendar and the Mesha Stone not only give glimpses into the background of the Bible but form important links in the culture and history of the people outside the pale of Israel.

III
Great Discoveries of the Twentieth Century

Although such discoveries as the Rosetta Stone, the Behistun Inscription, the Mesha Stone, and the Siloam Inscription are important for their time and laid the foundations of scientific archaeology in the 19th century, it remained for the 20th century to produce the most thrilling and outstanding archaeological finds. During this period biblical archaeology came to be a refined and precise science, adding to the frontiers of biblical knowledge on the human plane and making tremendous contributions to the background, historical and cultural, of the written Word of God.

1. The Code of Hammurabi—Light on Mosaic Laws

A slab of black diorite, over 7 feet tall and some 6 feet wide, was discovered in 1901. This record of the past contains engraved upon it almost 300 paragraphs of legal provision dealing with the commercial, social, domestic, and moral life of the Babylonians of King Hammurabi's time (1728–1676 B.C.). A copy of this code was found by Jacques de Morgan at Susa in Elam, where it had been carried off by the Elamites from Babylon. At the top of the stele the king is shown receiving the laws from the sun god Shamash, patron of law and justice. At some time when Babylon was weak, an Elamite conqueror carried away the monument to Susa. Its finding was one of the most startling legal discoveries in history.

The code is important in furnishing background material for comparison with other ancient bodies of law. It is also natural that it should offer comparative data for the study of the laws of the Pentateuch. The fact that the code is older by over three centuries than the laws of Moses has disposed of some untenable theories of the critics and given rise to others. For instance, the old critical view that detailed codes of law like those recorded in the Pentateuch are anachronistic for such an early period has been exploded by the discovery of Hammurabi's laws and much earlier codes in Mesopotamia.

A discovery of this sort illustrates how archaeology purges out radical critical views, which used to place the origin of many of the laws ascribed to Moses to much later times, such as the 9th, 8th, and 7th centuries B.C., or even later. These erroneous theories had to be drastically revised or entirely rejected. On the other hand, the discovery of the early extrabiblical legal material has led many to adopt an equally faulty view that Hebrew legislation is merely a selection and adaptation of Babylonian law. The only position that is valid as the two bodies of legal material are studied is that the Mosaic code is neither borrowed from, nor dependent upon, the Babylonian. It is divinely given, as it claims to be, and unique in those features that met Israel's peculiar need as an elect, theocratic nation.

The resemblances between the ***Mosaic laws*** and the ***Code of Hammurabi*** are clearly due to similarity of antecedents and general intellectual and cultural heritage. It is natural that in codes dealing with peoples in somewhat similar conditions, related racially and culturally, there should be some likeness in the incidents leading to litigation and likewise in the penalties imposed for infringement of common statutes. A striking difference, however, is obtained. These clearly demonstrate that there is no direct borrowing and that the Mosaic law, although later by three centuries, is in no sense dependent upon the Babylonian.

The biblical law of divorce (Deut. 24:1), for instance, permits the man to put away his wife but does not extend the same right to the wife, as does the Babylonian code. Again the so-called ***Lex Talionis*** is a primitive Semitic law and would be expected to be reflected in various Semitic legal codes. Mosaic injunctions (Ex. 21:23–25; Deut. 19:21) state precisely the same principle of retaliation upon which a number of Hammurabi's laws are based, namely "life for life, eye for eye, tooth for tooth, hand for hand, foot for foot, burning for burning, wound for wound, stripe for stripe."

The Mosaic and Hammurabi codes are ***different in content***. The Hebrew code contains many purely religious injunctions and ritual regulations. The Code of Hammurabi, on the other hand, is civil.

However, the priestly laws of Leviticus contain many points of similarity with priestly ritual and practice in western Asia, whether in Canaan or Phoenicia or Mesopotamia. But this in no sense casts doubt on the fact that Israel's religious practices as recorded in the Pentateuch are divinely given and uniquely invested with significance to fit a nation divinely called to serve the one God. In some cases similar cultic practice among surrounding peoples was divinely given to Israel. But at the same time it was invested with a special significance for the worship of the Lord.

The two codes, of course, are ***different in their origin***. The Babylonian laws are alleged to have been received by Hammurabi from the sun god Shamash. Moses received his laws directly from the Lord. Hammurabi, despite his reported reception from Shamash, takes credit for them in both the prologue and epilogue of the code. He, not Shamash, established order and equity throughout the land. Moses, in contrast, is only an instrument. The legislation is "Thus saith the LORD."

The two codes govern a ***different type of society***. Hammurabi's laws are fitted to the irrigation culture and highly commercialized urban society of Mesopotamia. The Mosaic injunctions, on the other hand, suit a simple, agricultural, pastoral people of a dry land like Palestine much less advanced in social and commercial development, but keenly conscious of their divine calling in all phases of their living.

The two codes ***differ in their morality***. From the ethical and spiritual standpoint the Mosaic legislation, as would be expected, offers a considerable advance over the Babylonian code. Hammurabi's laws, for example, enumerate at least ten varieties of bodily mutilation prescribed for various offenses. If a doctor performs an operation that is unsuccessful, his hand is to be cut off. In the Mosaic legislation only one instance of mutilation occurs where a wife's hand is to be severed (Deut. 25:11, 12). Also in the Hebrew laws a greater value is set upon human life. A stricter regard for the honor of womanhood is seen and more humane treatment of slaves is enjoined. In addition, the Babylonian code has nothing in it corresponding to that twofold golden thread running through the Mosaic legislation, namely, love to God and love to one's neighbor (Matt. 22:37–40).

Elephantine Island seen from across the Nile. *Matson Photo Service*

The Israelite Torah and the Babylonian code may be contrasted as follows: In the Babylonian code there is no control of lust, no limitation of selfishness. The postulate of charity cannot be found. The religious motif is absent, which recognizes sin as the destruction of the people because it is in opposition to the fear of God. In the Hammurabi code every trace of religious thought is absent. Behind the Israelite laws stands the ruling will of a holy God. The laws are stamped throughout with a divine character.

2. The Elephantine Papyri—Light on the Ezra-Nehemiah Era

Discovered in 1903 on the island of Elephantine at the First Cataract of the Nile in Egypt, these important documents give an interesting glimpse of one of the outlying regions of the Persian Empire in the latter part of the 5th century B.C. ***The Elephantine Papyri*** come from a Jewish military colony which was settled at that place. Inscribed in Aramaic, the language of diplomacy and trade throughout western Asia in the Persian period, and which was gradually replacing Hebrew as the everyday tongue of the Jewish people, the contents are varied, ranging from the copy of the Behistun Inscription of Darius to such a document as a Jewish marriage contract. The letters tell us about the sacking of a Jewish temple at Elephantine in an anti-Jewish persecution about 411 B.C. The Jews at this far-off colony worshiped the Lord whom they referred to by the name of Yahu.

Other letters from Elephantine which have in recent years become known and have been published by the Brooklyn Museum demonstrate that the temple was rebuilt after its destruction. They contain mention of Yahu as "the god who dwells in Yeb, the fortress." Compare Psalm 31:3. These new papyri demonstrate that Egypt was still under the authority of Persia in the first years of Artaxerxes II (404–359 B.C.).

The Elephantine Papyri therefore illuminate the general background of the period of Ezra-Nehemiah and the earlier Persian period. They shed important light on the life of the Jewish dispersion in a remote frontier place such as Elephantine in Egypt. They also are invaluable in giving the scholar a knowledge of the Aramaic language of that period, and many of the customs and names that appear in the Bible are illustrated by these important literary finds.

3. The Hittite Monuments from Boghaz-Keui—Mementos of an Imperial People

In 1906 Professor Hugo Winkler of Berlin began excavations at Boghaz-Keui, a site which lies 90 miles east of Ankara in the great bend of the Halys River in Asia Minor. It was discovered that this was an ancient Hittite capital. Numerous clay tablets were dug up written in texts containing six different languages. A large number of these were inscribed in the cuneiform characters of the Hittite language. Eventually deciphered through the labors of three men and particularly of the Czech

The city ruins at Ur. *Matson Photo Service*

The Ziggurat at Ur. *Matson Photo Service*

scholar Friedrich Hrozny, this language proved to be the key to a great deal of background of interest to the biblical student.

Before the Boghaz-Keui tablets revealed the Hittites to be an ancient people, the biblical references to them used to be regarded in critical circles as historically worthless. In the five books of Moses, references to the Hittites as inhabiting the land of Canaan and as among those whom the Israelites drove out occur in several places (Ex. 33:2; Deut. 7:1, 20:17; Josh. 3:10, 24:11). In the various lists the order varies, and there is not an inkling that one reference might be the name of a powerful imperial people and the other a small local tribe. Less than a century ago the "Hittites" meant little more to the reader of the Bible than the "Hivite" or the "Perizzite" still does.

It was commonly known from the biblical record that when Abraham settled in Hebron he had Hittites as neighbors. It was everyday knowledge that one of David's eminent soldiers was Uriah, a Hittite. But who would have expected that "Hittites" were more prominent than "Gadites" or "Beerothites"?

Now it is known that two great periods of Hittite power are to be noted. The first goes back to c. 1800 B.C., and the second is dated from c. 1400–1200 B.C. In this latter period of Hittite supremacy the powerful rulers reigned at Boghaz-Keui. One of these was named Subbiluliuma. This great conqueror extended his empire to the confines of Syria-Palestine. The great Rameses II of Egypt, in the famous battle of Kadesh, collided with Hittite power. A Hittite treaty of peace with the Pharaoh in the 21st year of the latter's reign was confirmed by a royal marriage.

About 1200 B.C. the great Hittite Empire collapsed, and the Hittite city of Boghaz-Keui fell. However, important centers of Hittite power remained at Carchemish, Sengirli, Hamath, and other places in north Syria. As a result of the excavation and decipherment of various Hittite monuments, the whole context of the ancient biblical world has been illuminated.

Because of this increased background knowledge, such allusions as those to the "kings of the Hittites" (1 Kin. 10:29; 2 Chr. 1:17) are much better understood. Also Ezekiel's reference to unfaithful Jerusalem as having an Amorite for a father and a Hittite for a mother (Ezek. 16:45) are now comprehensible. The manner in which archaeology has brought to light the ancient Hittites furnishes a good example of the way this important science is expanding biblical horizons.

4. The City of Ur—Abraham's Home

An important metropolis of the ancient world, Ur was located on the Euphrates River in lower Mesopotamia, present-day Iraq. Several centuries before Abraham lived there as a boy and grew up there as a young man, this place was a very important city under the 2nd and 3rd dynasties of Ur, an important line of kings. But the glory of the city was suddenly destroyed in the period from c. 1960–1830 B.C. Foreigners stormed down from the surrounding hills and took the reigning king, Ibi-Sin, a captive and reduced the capital ***city of Ur*** to ruins. So complete was the eclipse of the city that it lay buried in oblivion for centuries until, like Nineveh, it was resurrected in modern times by the work of archaeologists.

So thoroughly was the ancient city blotted out

that when it was referred to in Genesis 11:28–31 and 15:7 as Abraham's ancestral home and the place from which he started on his trek to Palestine, some scribe later had to append the descriptive phrase "*of the Chaldeans*" to the name of the city to give later readers some idea of where it had been located.

The long-lost and buried city was brought to the light of modern study by the work of numerous archaeologists, particularly by the work of Sir Leonard Woolley (1922–1934). Until the year 1854, the site of the ancient city was completely unknown. The Arabs used to call the location ***Al-muqayyer, "Mount of bitumen."*** It was a forbidding place in a climate of terrific heat and surrounded by intense desolation. In 1854, J. E. Taylor, an English archaeologist, assisted by others, made some preliminary excavations. Some cylinders turned up inscribed in cuneiform characters declaring that King Nabonidus of Babylon (556–539 B.C.) had restored the famous ziggurat of Ur-Nammu.

Later explorations were made by Campbell Thompson in 1918. H. R. Hall in 1918 continued other excavations, but it was left for the pivotal work of Sir Leonard Woolley, undertaken in 1922 as a joint expedition of the British Museum, the University of Pennsylvania, and the University Museum, to give a complete history and description of the city. The expedition completed twelve very successful archaeological campaigns, and by 1934 the long-lost and buried city of Ur, vanished from the pages of history, had become one of the best-known sites in all the ancient Near East.

Abraham's Native Town. Abraham lived in the city of Ur at the height of its splendor under the 3rd dynasty of kings. This is indicated if we follow the chronology of the Masoretic text of the Hebrew Bible. According to this system of reckoning, Abraham was born c. 2161 B.C. and entered Canaan c. 2086 B.C. Under this time arrangement, the patriarch left the city when it was near the acme of its prosperity. He entered Canaan precisely when Ur reached the pinnacle of its power, for the 3rd dynasty of kings (c. 2070–1969 B.C.) lifted the city to great prominence.

The first king was Ur-Nammu. This monarch had the title of "King of Sumer and Akkad." He built a splendid temple tower or ziggurat at this site. Today this is still preserved as the best monument of its type in all the flat alluvial territory of Lower Mesopotamia, the basin of Tigris-Euphrates rivers. It was this structure that Nabonidus, the last of the Babylonian kings, restored in the 6th century B.C.

In the famous ***monument of Ur-Nammu*** there is extant a contemporary record of the construction of the ziggurat at Ur. This stele is a slab of white limestone measuring 5 feet across and 10 feet in height. At the top of the monument the king is standing in an attitude of prayer. An account of the building of the monument is given, and scenes are inscribed denoting the actual construction. In the days of Ur-Nammu other buildings were built around the ziggurat, and the entire sacred area was dedicated to Nannar, the moon god (patron deity of the city) and his consort, whose name was Nin-Gal.

A king by the name of Dungi succeeded Ur-Nammu, whom Nabonidus declared completed the ziggurat. Dungi was a great ruler who built a magnificent mortuary temple and tomb for himself. His son Bur-Sin succeeded him. He was followed on the throne at Ur by Gimil-Sin and then by Ibi-Sin.

Ur and Abraham. When Abraham lived in the city before he left for Haran and Canaan, Ur was a center of religion and industry. The city was wholly given over to the worship of the moon god cult. The Babylonians were devotees of many deities. But at Ur the moon god Sin was supreme.

Sir Leonard Woolley's lengthy excavations in twelve highly rewarding campaigns have revealed the splendor and the size of the city and also have given details of the *temonos* or the religious section of the city. In other words, Abraham was surrounded on all sides by idolatry. This we have recorded in the Bible in Joshua 24:2. "Your fathers, *including* Terah, the father of Abraham and the father of Nahor, dwelt on the other side of the River in old times; and they served other gods."

The moon god Sin was given such epithets as "the exalted lord" and "the beautiful lord who shines in the heavens." The immense temple tower, built like a mountain with various stages, contained the holy chamber of Nannar on its uppermost level. Here in this lofty Babylonian temple mystic ritual in honor of the deity was conducted. In front of the immense ziggurat and on the lower level was an open court, a kind of holy market where the people brought their gifts and paid their taxes to the king, who was also their landlord. Accordingly, the city was a kind of theocracy centered in the moon deity.

The sacred area was called the *temenos*. In it were located other sacred buildings and shrines, including houses for the priests and priestesses of Nannar. To the west the river Euphrates flowed near the city walls, and there were canals running around and through the city. In Abraham's day instead of being a hot, forbidding, desert-like region, Ur was a flourishing and beautiful city because of irrigation and civilization. It was surrounded by fertile farms and a busy populace engaged in agriculture and in woolen and textile industries. All of this commerce was centered in religion.

The houses of Ur have been excavated and examined. It is conceivable that Abraham grew up as a lad in one of these residences. There is presumptive evidence that Terah's father worshiped the moon god and was a devotee of Nannar and Nin-Gal. In one of the dwellings, there is a small domestic chapel with altar niche and family burial vault. It is very likely that Terah worshiped at such an altar.

It is out of this polluted atmosphere of polytheism that God's sovereign grace called Abraham to begin a new line that was to be separated from idolatry and through which Messiah was to come, who would deliver the world from sin and idolatry.

The City Before the Time of Abraham. Ur existed as a brilliant city many hundreds of years before Abraham appeared on the scene. The lower regions of the Tigris-Euphrates basin with its flat land and very fertile soil have been the seat of many ancient empires—Sumer, Babylonia, Assyria, and Chaldea. The first of these civilizations was Sumer, one of the oldest civilized countries in the world. Wrapped in obscurity is the story of the beginnings of Sumer. At least by 3500 B.C. the Sumerians, that is the natives of the flat, alluvial lower courses of the Tigris-Euphrates plain, were advancing in civilization.

In the next thousand years the ***Sumerian Empire*** diffused culture and civilization over most of western Asia. The extreme southern part of Sumer was called the land of Shinar. It was a flat, mud plain, immensely rich, formed by the sediment of the Tigris-Euphrates River. As these mighty streams flowed into the lower part of the Fertile Crescent, their current slackened, and they deposited huge amounts of a rich, sandy loam and formed a region which today is called Iraq, which is about as large as New Jersey.

With a network of canals running through this rich territory, this region blossomed like a rose.

The Euphrates River. *Matson Photo Service*

More than 150 years ago, travelers began to wonder about the strange mounds or hillocks of earth which dotted this flat region. What could they possibly be? Now and then antiquarian bits of carved marble or other remnants of bygone civilizations were exposed by the weather. Archaeologists began to dig beneath the truncated hillocks, and it was discovered that they were long-lost and buried cities.

One of these mounds proved to be the city of Ur of biblical fame. From these regions many tablets have been resurrected with cuneiform or wedge-shaped writing on them. These tablets were made of soft mud from the riverbank and carefully inscribed with a flat pen and set out in the sun to dry, or put in the fire to bake in a more firm form. And so, under these truncated mounds were not only buried artifacts and remnants of ancient civilizations but, what is most arresting, there are vast quantities of practically indestructible materials, all inscribed on clay tablets. These have been the basis of resurrecting the history and the civilization of Bible lands in Lower Mesopotamia in the land of Sumer.

The First Dynasty of Ur. In an ancient list of kings called the Sumerian King List in ***The Oxford Edition of Cuneiform Texts II***, 1923, by F. Langdon, an interesting story is told of the early rulers of Sumer. Among the line of kings who reigned at Kish, Uruk (biblical Erech, Gen. 10:10), Awan, Adap, Mari, and Akshak are listed several dynasties who ruled at Ur. The first kings at Ur witnessed the culminating phase of the early dynastic period in Mesopotamia (c. 2800–2360 B.C.).

The King List goes on to say, "Uruk was smitten with weapons. Its kingship was carried to Ur. Mes-Anne-pada became king and ruled 80 years. A-Anne-pada, a son of Mes-Anne-pada, reigned . . . years. Meskiag-Nanna, a son of Mes-Anne-pada became king and reigned 36 years. Elulu reigned 25 years. Balulu reigned 36 years. Four kings reigned 177 years. Ur was smitten with weapons."

This line of kings was very powerful and lifted the city-state, since Ur was more than a city, to a high level of culture. This is demonstrated in the discoveries of the royal tombs by Sir Leonard Woolley, dating from c. 2500 B.C. These consisted of rooms and vaults built of brick and stone. Among one of the most interesting finds was the tomb of an important lady named ***Shubad of Ur.*** Her name is identified by an inscribed cylinder of lapis lazuli. Near her hand was a gold cup. Her lovely artistic headdress contained 9 yards of gold band.

Another exquisite find was the so-called "***Standard of Ur.***" This was a wooden panel, 22 inches long by 9 inches wide, skillfully inlaid with mosaic work on both sides depicting scenes of war and peace. In the war panel the king is seen receiving captives. In another the phalanx of the royal army advances. Scenes of fighting with chariots and javelins are depicted. The panel of peace presents a royal family feast. Musicians entertain while servants wait in the banquet hall and bring in spoils captured from the enemy.

Certainly the archaeological resurrection of Abraham's ancient city of Ur has greatly illuminated the Bible references to the patriarch and given a much wider view of the historical horizons c. 2000 B.C. The early civilization of the Tigris-Euphrates Valley is becoming better known year after year. Bible dictionaries, encyclopedias, commentaries, and biblical works of every description are highly indebted to the restless and productive spade of the archaeologist. Certainly God has blessed, enabling scholars in our day to study these monuments and other remains of antiquity. The result is greater appreciation of the Bible on the human plane.

It must always be remembered that the Word of God is not only divine but human. It is God's Book for man. On the human side, God has so ordained that the horizons of biblical knowledge may be expanded and increased that we may on the spiritual plane better comprehend the Word of God. How unfortunate it is when the spiritual is divorced from the historical and archaeological, or vice versa, when the historical and archaeological are divorced from the spiritual. The two work hand in hand and help one another. Happy is the student of the Bible who will combine both of these disciplines in a better understanding of the Word of God.

5. The Religious Texts from Ras Shamra (Ugarit)—Canaanite Cults Exposed

One of the most important discoveries of the 20th century was the recovery of hundreds of clay tablets which have been housed in a library situated between two great temples, one dedicated to Baal and another dedicated to Dagon, in the city of ***Ugarit***—modern ***Ras Shamra*** in north Syria. These clay tablets date from the 15th to early 14th centuries B.C. They are inscribed in the earliest-known alphabet written in wedge-shaped signs. Professor H. Bower of the University of Halle recognized this new writing as Semitic. Numbers of scholars such as E. Dhorme and Charles Virolleaud began working on the decipherment of this new Semitic language.

The tablets turned out to be religious and cultic in nature and inscribed in a dialect that was closely akin to biblical Hebrew and Phoenician. Although Semitic in form, this new writing displayed evidences of Akkadian influence, since Mesopotamians wrote on clay tablets with wedge-shaped characters from left to right. First intimations of the archaeological importance of the ancient city of Ugarit, which was unknown until 1928, came in the spring of that year when a Syrian peasant plowing in his field a little north of present-day Minet el-Beida suddenly came across some antiquities. On April 2, 1929, work began at Minet el-Beida under the direction of Claude F. Schaffer. After a month's work he changed to the nearby tell of Ras Shamra. Only a few days' work demonstrated the importance of the new location. On May 20th the first tablets were uncovered. Schaffer continued excavations from 1929 to 1937. Between 1929 and 1933, the bulk of significant religious texts were recovered in the royal library in the area. Many of these were inscribed in an early Canaanite dialect, roughly contemporary with the Mosaic age.

The City of Ugarit. This flourishing second-millennium city, which had been known by scholars from Egyptian inscriptions from the ***Tell el Amarna Letters*** and ***Hittite documents***, was located on the north Syrian coast opposite the island of Cyprus, about 8 miles north of Latakia and 50 miles southwest of Antioch. It was situated on a bay and had a port which could be used by seagoing trade ships. It was a harbor town known in Greek times as Leukos Limen, the white harbor. It is now called ***Ras Shamra***, ***"hill of fennel,"*** because fennel grows there.

The hill which comprises the ruin of the ancient city has the form of a trapezium with the long side about 670 yards north and south and the longer diagonal about 1,100 yards. The hill is about 22 yards high. The site was located on the important trade route along the coast from Egypt to Asia Minor, which was connected by a road with Aleppo, Mari on the Euphrates, and Babylon. The sea route from Ugarit to Alashiya—that is, Cyprus—was a short one.

Very early, Ugarit struck up a brisk trade with the Aegean Islands. It became an important harbor. One of the main exported articles was copper, which was used in the production of bronze. Copper was imported from Asia Minor and Cyprus. Bronze was produced in Ugarit. Being a Phoenician town, Ugarit, like its sister cities, delivered timber to Egypt. Not only cedars from the interior were exported but other kinds of wood as well. There were also purple dye factories, great heaps of murex shells indicate this. These shells, abundantly found along the east Mediterranean coast, produced a famous dye of antiquity.

Literary Importance of the Texts. After preliminary work by many scholars, Cyrus Gordon worked out a **Ugaritic Grammar** and later put out an edition of the texts called **Ugaritic Literature.** The decipherment of the texts showed the important parallels between Ugaritic and Hebrew literary style and vocabulary. By 1936 H. L. Ginsberg had made some far-reaching observations with regard to common structural elements. Ginsberg's study showed that Canaanite poetry, like Hebrew, was basically accentual, that is, consisted of numbers of feet, each of which was accented. A good example of the survival of Canaanite literary elements in Hebrew religious literature is the following tricolon (unit of three lines) from the ***Baal Epic of Ras Shamra:***

"Behold, thine enemies, O Baal;
Behold, thine enemies shalt thou crush;
Behold, thou shalt smite thy foes."

In ***Psalm 92:9*** there is a striking parallel to this.

"For behold, Your enemies, O LORD,
For behold, Your enemies shall perish;
All the workers of iniquity shall be scattered."

The following tricolon occurs frequently in the ***Aqhat Epic:***

"Do thou ask for life, O lad Aqhat;
Do thou ask for life, I'll grant it thee,
Eternal life, and I'll accord it thee."

A similar literary device is found in the ***Song of Deborah*** (Judg. 5:30).

"For Sisera, plunder of dyed garments,
Plunder of garments embroidered and dyed,
Two pieces of dyed embroidery for the neck of the looter?"

Background material such as this is an invaluable aid in the study of Hebrew poetry and the general literary qualities of style and vocabulary in Old Testament Hebrew. Since the Ugaritic language is very closely connected with biblical Hebrew, much light has been shed upon Hebrew lexicography. Any recent lexicon of Hebrew must take into consideration the vocabulary used at Ugarit. Future Hebrew dictionaries will include many words hitherto misunderstood or only partially known.

For example, the word *beth-heber* (Prov. 21:9; 25:24) hitherto rendered "house" has been shown from Ugaritic and Assyrian to mean specifically "a storehouse." These verses must then be rendered "*It is* better to dwell in a corner of the housetop, than with a brawling woman and in a storehouse." It is of interest to note that the Egyptian proverbs of Amenemope, which have many parallels to the biblical Book of Proverbs, employs a word for "storehouse" in exactly the same sense.

Religious Significance of the Ugaritic Inscriptions. By far the most important contribution of the religious texts from Ras Shamra (Ugarit) is in giving the Bible student background material for the study of Old Testament religions. The epics set forth very clearly the ***Canaanite pantheon.*** We now know that this pantheon of the Canaanites was headed up by the god El, the supreme Canaanite deity. This is also a name by which God is known in the Old Testament (cf. Gen. 33:20). This name, El, often occurs in Old Testament poetry (Ps. 18:31, 32; Job 8:3). It occurs frequently also in prose in compound names, for example, El Elyon, the God Most High (Gen. 14:18); El Shaddai, Almighty God (Gen. 17:1); El Hai, the living God (Josh. 3:10). This, however, does not mean any connection, of course, with Canaanite mythology. El is simply the common Semitic word for God. In Ugaritic, El was a bloody, lustful tyrant. The description of him, as well as of other Canaanite gods, fully substantiates the testimony of the Old Testament with regard to the degeneracy and polluting influence of Canaanite religion.

Baal was the son of El. He was the active king of the gods in the Canaanite pantheon and dominated the entire list of gods. He was the deity of the storm and the rain. Thunder was thought to be the reverberation of his voice in the heavens. At Ras Shamra a stele was discovered depicting Baal holding a stylized thunderbolt. Three of the Ugaritic poems concern Baal. Baalism, the worship of this god, was one of the most debilitating and destructive influences which threatened the Hebrews in Palestine and against which they had to be continually on guard.

As the giver of rain and all fertility, Baal figures very prominently in Canaanite mythology. He struggles with Mot, the god of death and the god of drought. In the fight Baal is slain. As a consequence, the seasonal drought occurs from June to late October. Then Anath, sister and lover of Baal, goes out in search of him, discovers his body, and slays his enemy, Mot. Baal is then brought back to life, thus ensuring the revival of vegetation for a seven-year period. The great Baal Epic of Ugarit finds in this representation a central theme.

The Phoenicians at Ugarit not only had gods who were polluted and immoral but also goddesses. Three of these who are prominent are Anath, Astarte, and Asherah. They are patronesses of war and sex. Their character, like that of El and Baal, bears out the pollution and damaging effects of Canaanite religion, since they portray war in its aspect of violence and murder and sex mainly in its lustful connotation of indulgence.

The new knowledge of Canaanite religion aids the Bible student correctly to evaluate the testimony of the Old Testament to the Canaanites. Higher criticism has impugned the morality of the Old Testament writers in such episodes as the divine command to exterminate these cults. Examples are the extermination of the people of Jericho, Saul's extermination of the Amalekites, and the driving out of the Canaanites in general. All of these examples appear in a different view when adjudged in the light of the vileness of Canaanite religion. In Genesis 15:16 the Lord declares, "the iniquity of the Amorites" was not yet "full" in Abraham's day. But archaeology shows Canaanite religious immorality was complete in

Joshua's day, 400 years later, and had to be destroyed.

Now, as a result of the Ras Shamra literature, the nature of Canaanite religion comes before the scholar in its real light. No longer do we have to rely on the witness of early church fathers such as Eusebius, who quotes an earlier authority, or Philo of Byblos, who in turn goes back to a much earlier authority named Sanchuniathon. No longer must we doubt the veracity of this extrabiblical witness or doubt the authenticity of the Old Testament witness. Now, as a result of archaeology, an independent witness to the effete and degenerate nature of Canaanite cults is available. No longer can critics isolate the Old Testament and accuse it of a low morality in ordering the extermination of the Canaanites. The truth is, archeology points out that the people had become so immoral, so honeycombed with the sins of violence and sexual immorality, that had Joshua and the children of Israel not appeared to take over the land, these people would have perished under the weight of their own iniquity.

"***Like priest, like people***" is an old adage. Never in all the annals of history was there such a mixture of violence and lust as was combined and made an intricate part of Canaanite cults. So the Scriptures stand as a warning, corroborated by archaeology, of the judgment of God falling upon apostate and sinful religionism. Archaeology helps us to see this in an entirely different light in regard to the Canaanites.

This is especially true when we consider the low moral tone of Canaanite goddesses and gods. El was a brutal and lustful tyrant who was guilty of incest and murder. Baal also was guilty of enormous crimes. How could people worship such deities and not themselves be polluted? No wonder the warning of God was issued again and again for separation from Baalism. No wonder the history of Baal contamination of Israel is a long story of woe and suffering, as God's people were trapped into complicity with Phoenician cults.

The era of Ahab and Jezebel, and the importation of Canaanite fertility cults and intermarriage with the Canaanites, show the devastating effect of such disobedience to the plain warning of God. Exterminating the Canaanite in the time of Joshua was not a question of destroying innocent people. It was a question of destroying or being destroyed, separating or being contaminated, being quarantined from the plague or having the plague destroy everyone.

Later Excavations at Ugarit. During World War II excavations at Ras Shamra were discontinued. They were resumed in 1948 and have been going on regularly. Work under the direction of C. F. Schaffer has been centered upon uncovering the great palace. The most important discoveries in connection with this structure were the royal archives. These archives, discovered in the palace, were of a historical nature in contrast to the mythological ritual texts of the early years, 1929–1937. The archives in the west wing of the building contained administrative documents to a large degree relating to the royal estates. Those in the east wing had documents relating to the capital city. Those in the central archive were mainly legal finds. Almost all documents were inscribed in the common language of these centuries, namely Akkadian. A few were written in Hurrian and Ugaritic. The names of twelve Ugaritic kings were found in the documents which date from the 18th to the 13th centuries B.C. The seals of the royal acts are remarkable as they all are identical in design at the top, without regard to the name of the reigning king. The motif is well known from Babylonian glyptic art and shows homage being paid to the deified king.

Numbers of fine objects have been recovered from the palace, especially pieces from the king's bedroom. Especially noteworthy was the large ivory foot panel of the royal bedstead, perhaps the largest single piece of ivory carving yet recovered in the Near East. Another remarkable piece found in the campaign of 1952–1953 is the ancient Ugaritic alphabet of thirty letters. This piece is now housed in the National Museum at Damascus.

6. The Nuzi Tablets and the Biblical Horites

From this city east of ancient Asshur and a short distance west of Arrapkha, which flourished in the middle centuries of the 2nd millennium B.C., have come several thousand cuneiform texts. These texts have proved of immense value, illustrating the rise of the Hurrians and patriarchal customs. The present site of Nuzi is Yoghlan-Tepe. It is a mound 150 miles north of Baghdad near the foothills of southern Khurdistan. Nuzi was excavated in 1925–1931 by the American School of Oriental Research in Baghdad and Harvard University. The name "Nuzi" was used during its occupation by the Hurrians.

Before the time of the Hurrian settlement the site of Nuzi was occupied by a different ethnic group, called the Subarians. In this older period, the city bore the name of Gasur, and its earliest occupation goes back to prehistoric times. But the vital interest in the town stems from its occupation by the Hurrians and the cuneiform texts which have been excavated from it and from nearby Arrapkha, modern Kirkuk, some 9 miles to the east.

The Nuzi Tablets and the Hurrians. Modern archaeology has not only resurrected the ancient Hittites, who were for centuries practically unknown except for sporadic references on the pages of the Bible, but also the enigmatic Horites. In the books of the Pentateuch there are numbers of references to a perplexing people called Horites. These people were defeated by Chedorlaomer and the invading Mesopotamian army (Gen. 14:6). They were governed by chiefs (Gen. 36:20–30). They are said to have been destroyed by Esau's descendants (Deut. 2:12, 22).

This unknown people used to be thought of as a very local, restricted group of cave dwellers. The name "Horite" was thought to be derived from the Hebrew *hor,* "hole" or "cave." Other than this etymological description the Horites remained completely obscure, not appearing outside the Pentateuch or in extrabiblical literature. Within the last 35 years, however, archaeology has performed a miracle in resurrecting the ancient Hurrians, the biblical Horites. They are known not to be a local, restricted group but to be a prominent people who took a preeminent place on the stage of ancient history. It is now known that they not only existed but played a far-reaching role in ancient Near Eastern cultural history. As a result of the discovery of the Hurrians, the popular etymology which connects them with "cave dwellers" has had to be abandoned.

The Hurrians or Horites were non-Semitic peoples who, before the beginning of the 2nd millennium B.C., migrated into northeastern Mesopotamia. Their homeland was in the region south of the Caucasus. They appear first upon the horizon of history c. 2400 B.C. in the Zagros Mountains east of the Tigris River. In the period c. 2000–1400 B.C., the Hurrians were very common and widespread in Upper Mesopotamia.

The Nuzi Tablets and the Patriarchs. The main interest of the Nuzi Tablets lies in the illumination of patriarchal times and customs. In the patriarchal narratives, many local practices have been quite obscure to the modern reader. Numerous clay tablets from Nuzi and nearby Arrapkha have in many cases illuminated these customs, so that now we see them as they existed in the general historical background of the time. Although the Nuzi Tablets are to be dated in the 15th and 14th centuries B.C., sometime after the patriarchal period (c. 2000–1800 B.C.), nevertheless, they illustrate the times of the patriarchs. The reason is that when the patriarchs came out of Ur, they sojourned in Haran and mingled in west Hurrian society. But the same customs prevailed by extension among the west Hurrians as among the east Hurrians at Nuzi and Arrapkha. Hence, the results obtained at Nuzi are valid by extension for the west Hurrians, as well as for a period considerably later than the patriarchs.

In Genesis 15:2 Abraham laments his childless condition and the fact that his servant Eliezer was to be his heir. In the light of this situation, God assures the patriarch that he is to have a son of his own to inherit his property. The Nuzi Tablets explain this difficult matter. They tell how a trusted servant, an apparent outsider, could be heir. At ancient Nuzi, it was customary in Hurrian society for a couple who did not have a child to adopt a son to take care of his foster parents as long as they lived, take over when they died, and then in return for his filial duty to become their heir. But it is important to note that if a natural son was born, this agreement was nullified, at least in part, and the natural son became heir. Eliezer was plainly Abraham's adopted son. But the miraculous birth of Isaac, as the promised posterity, altered Eliezer's status as heir.

At Nuzi a marriage contract occasionally included the statement that a given slave girl is presented outright to a new bride, exactly as in the marriage of Leah (Gen. 29:24) and Rachel (29:29). Other marriage provisions specify that a wife of the upper classes who was childless was to furnish her husband with a slave girl as a concubine. In such a case, however, the wife was entitled to treat the concubine's offspring as her own. This last provision illuminates the difficult statement in Genesis 16:2 with its punning: "I shall obtain children by her," which means "I may be built up through her." It is interesting to note that the related law of Hammurabi, paragraph 144, offers no complete parallel. There the wife is a priestess and is not entitled to claim the children of the concubine for herself.

It is thus seen that in Nuzian law and society in which the patriarchs moved for a time, marriage was regarded primarily for bearing children and not mainly for companionship. In one way or another, it was considered necessary for the family to procreate. After Isaac's birth, Abraham's reluctance to comply with Sarah's demand that Hagar's child be driven out is illustrated by local practice at Nuzi. In the event the slave wife should have a son, that son must not be expelled. In Abraham's case, only a divine dispensation overruled human law and made the patriarch willing to comply.

Cases involving rights of the firstborn occurring in Genesis are also illustrated. In the Bible Esau sells his birthright to Jacob. In the Nuzi Tablets one brother sells a grove which he has inherited for three sheep. Evidently this in value is quite comparable to the savory food for which Esau sold his right.

In Hurrian society birthright was not so much the matter of being the firstborn as of paternal decree. Such decrees were binding above all others when handed down in the form of a deathbed declaration introduced by the following formula: "Behold now, I am old." This situation helps to illuminate Genesis 27, the chapter that tells of Jacob stealing the family blessing.

The obscure ***teraphim*** are also explained in Nuzian law. We now know that the teraphim were small household deities. Possession of them implied headship of family. In the case of a married daughter, they assured her husband the right to her father's property. Laban had sons of his own when Jacob left for Canaan. They alone had the right to their father's gods. The theft of these important household idols by Rachel was a notorious offense (Gen. 31:19, 30; 35). She aimed at nothing less than to preserve for her husband the chief title to Laban's estate.

The texts from Arrapkha and Nuzi have at last supplied details for explaining these difficult customs. In special circumstances the property could pass to a daughter's husband, but only if the father had handed over his household gods to his son-in-law as a formal token that the arrangement had proper sanction.

Another custom illuminated is that found in Genesis 12:10–20; 20:2–6; 26:1–11, where the wife of a patriarch is introduced as his sister with no apparent worthy reason. The texts from Nuzi, however, show that among the Hurrians marriage bonds were most solemn, and the wife had legally, although not necessarily through ties of blood, the simultaneous status of sister, so that the term "sister" and "wife" could be interchangeable in an official use under certain circumstances. Thus, in resorting to the wife-sister relationship, both Abraham and Isaac were availing themselves of the strongest safeguards the law, as it existed then, could afford them.

Critical Value. Discoveries such as those at Nuzi and Arrapkha are forcing higher critics to abandon many radical and untenable theories. For example, not long ago it was customary for critics to view the patriarchal stories as retrojections from a much later period and not as authentic stories from the Mosaic age, namely, the 15th century B.C. But now the question rises, How could such authentic local color be retrojected from a later age? The Nuzi Letters have done a great service to students of early Bible history in not only attesting the influence of social customs in the patriarchal age and in the same portion of Mesopotamia from which the patriarchs come, but also have demonstrated these narratives are authentic to their time. Such discoveries add greatly to our historical background and enable us in our modern day to reveal them in their genuine local color and historical setting.

7. The Mari Letters—Light on the World of the Patriarchs

One of the most historically and archaeologically rewarding sites that has been discovered in Mesopotamia and Bible lands is the city of ***Mari,*** modern Tell el-Hariri on the Middle Euphrates, about 7 miles northwest of Abu-

The excavated ruins of the capital city of Babylon. *D. J. Wiseman*

Kemal, a small town on the Syrian side of the Syro-Iraq frontier. The ancient city owed its importance to being a focal point on caravan routes crossing the Syrian desert and linking the city with Syria and the Mediterranean coast and with the civilizations of Assyria and Babylonia. This site was further identified by William Foxwell Albright in 1932.

Mari began to be excavated in 1933 by Andre Parrot under the auspices of the Musee du Louvre. The results were the digging up of an ancient imperial city of great importance and splendor. World War II interrupted excavations in 1939, after six highly successful campaigns had taken place. In 1951 this work was resumed. After four further campaigns it was broken off in 1956, as a result of the trouble over the Suez Canal.

Among the most important discoveries at Mari was the great ***temple of Ishtar,*** for the Babylonian goddess of propagation, and a temple tower or ziggurat. The temple itself had courts of the Sumerian type, columns, and a cella. The ziggurat or temple tower was similar to that at Ur and other Mesopotamian sites. Statuettes were uncovered to illustrate the popularity of the Ishtar fertility cult. One of the palace murals depicts the fact that the ruling monarch at Mari was believed to have received his staff and ring, the emblems of his authority, from Ishtar.

Another important discovery at Mari was the ***royal palace.*** A sprawling structure contemporary with the 1st dynasty of Babylon, it was built in the center of the mound and contained almost 300 rooms. The throne room furnished some rare specimens of well-preserved wall paintings. This huge building with its beautifully colored mural paintings, its royal apartments, administrative offices, and scribal school is considered one of the best preserved palaces of the Middle East. The structure was built by later Amorites, who worshiped the deities Adad and Dagon. In the postwar campaign the excavation centered mainly around the older strata going back to buildings of the pre-Sargonic period from the time of the dynasty of Akkad.

The Royal Archives. The most interesting finds, however, were the so-called ***Mari Letters,*** some 20,000 clay tablets dug up and which have revolutionized knowledge of the ancient biblical world. These documents were written in the dialect of Old Babylonian. They date from the era of Hammurabi, c. 1700 B.C., the same monarch whose code was discovered in 1901 at Susa. These records constitute memoranda of the king and governors of the city-state of Mari, and belong to the time of the kings Yasmah-Adad, under whose reign the construction of the palace was begun, and Zimri-Lim, under whom it was completed. Some of the correspondence is that of King Yasmah-Adad with his father, the powerful empire builder King Shamshi-Adad I of Assyria, as well as with the representatives of the provinces of his realm. King Zimri-Lim's correspondence also figures in exchanges of diplomatic correspondence with King Hammurabi of Babylon, as well as with the king of Aleppo and other vassals. Two letters dispatched from Aleppo to Zimri-Lim deal with prophetic utterances delivered in the name of the god Adad of Aleppo. The subject and tenor of these remind one of biblical prophecies.

Biblical Value of the Mari Texts. These records are of great value to biblical students because they stem from the region which was the home of the Hebrew patriarchs for a number of years before going on to Canaan. However, Abraham's migration from Ur, according to preserved biblical chronology, apparently took place some 400 years before the era of Zimri-Lim and the fall of Mari. At this time of the 3rd dynasty of Ur, Mari was ruled by the governors of the kings of Ur. Eventually, however, a prince of Mari, Ishbi-Irra, who had brought the city-state of Isin under his dominion c. 2021 B.C., was instrumental in bringing about the downfall of the city of Ur.

Nahor, which figures prominently in the patriarchal narratives (Gen. 24:10), is mentioned quite often in the Mari Letters. One letter from Nahor is sent from a woman of that town to the king and runs as follows:

> **To my lord say, Thus Inib-Sharrim, thy maid servant. How long must I remain in Nahor? Peace is established and the road is unobstructed. Let my lord write and let me be brought that I may see the face of my lord from whom I am separated. Further, let my lord send me an answer to my tablet.**

The term "Habiru," very important since Abraham is the first individual in the Bible to be named a "Hebrew" (Gen. 14:13), is found frequently in the Mari Letters, as is also the case in the Nuzi Letters. In both instances the term apparently means "a wanderer," "one who crosses over," or "one who passes from one place to another." This explanation fits Abraham and the early patriarchs very well since they were nomadic travelers.

When Abraham left Ur in southern Mesopotamia to migrate to Canaan, he no doubt passed through the magnificent city of Mari. There can be little doubt that he and Terah with their families put up in one of the caravansaries there. Perhaps they spent days or weeks in the famous city and went sightseeing in the palace traces of whose grandeur are still visible to the eye of the modern archaeologist.

The city of Mari was idolatrous and in it there was the widespread practice of divination. A diviner was an important official in all phases of daily life at Mari. People went to him for advice in ordinary difficulties of life. Commanders saw him for help in the movement of their troops.

The patriarchs were remarkably free from occult practices and contamination from paganism and divinatory phenomena in general. This fact is true despite the teraphim (household gods) of Rachel and despite the "foreign gods" which Jacob ordered put away and which he hid under a terebinth tree in Shechem (Gen. 35:2–4).

Interestingly, the Mari Letters refer to "sons of the right," that is, "sons of the south," since the directions were taken as one faced the east, and the south would be on one's right hand. These were a fierce tribe of wanderers and called Benjaminites, but they have no connection with the "Benjamites" of the Bible. The name "Benjamin," "son of the south," that is, "southerner," was a term suited to occur in various places, especially in Mari, where the parallel term "sons of the left," that is, "sons of the north," is found.

The Bible presents Benjamin as being of Palestinian birth after Jacob's return from Mesopotamia. He is set forth as never having been in Mesopotamia at all. Genesis 49:27 describes Benjamin as a ravenous wolf. This fits the description of the veteran tribe at Mari remarkably well. Any connection, however, is obviously dubious and purely imaginary.

Another interesting sidelight is the fact that the word translated "chieftain," with reference to the plundering Benjaminites, is *dawidum*, meaning "leader." This sheds light on the etymology of the name of Israel's most renowned king, who evidently had a name meaning "the leader."

Historical Value of the Mari Letters. These documents establish that Shamshi-Adad I of Assyria, who ruled c. 1748–1716 B.C., and Hammurabi the Great of Babylon, were contemporaries. With these facts and other details furnished by the Mari documents, the date of Hammurabi can be fixed c. 1728–1676 B.C. This and other evidence have forced scholars to give up identifying Hammurabi of Babylon with Amraphel (Gen. 14:1). The high antiquity of Genesis 14 has been vindicated, but archaeology has not yet succeeded in furnishing the background of the four Mesopotamian kings who invaded the Trans-Jordanic country in the days of Abraham.

Hammurabi was a strong military leader and a great administrator. He was a member of the strong 1st dynasty of Babylon which reigned from 1830 to c. 1550 B.C. The power of this dynasty reached its height under Hammurabi's rule. He was the greatest of all Babylonian rulers. Hammurabi defeated Rim-Sin of Larsa and established himself over all the city-states of Lower Babylonia. His expanding military machine enabled him to destroy Mari. It was his code of laws, as we have seen, that was discovered at Susa in 1901. This famous codification has remained classic in illustrating and illuminating Israelite laws.

It was during the reign of Hammurabi that the Babylonian story of creation was composed. The poem glorified Marduk, the patron god of Babylon, whom Hammurabi established as the national god of Babylonia. In this period, the early Sumerian language became an antiquity and Semitic-Babylonian came into common usage.

The Mari Letters and the Amorites. About 2000 B.C. the Semitic-nomadic peoples, who lived along the desert fringes of the Fertile Crescent, invaded the centers of established civilization. Known as "Westerners," they are preserved in the Old Testament as "Amorites." Amorite states came into existence all over the Mesopotamian area. Nahor, Haran, Mari, Qatna, and Ugarit all appear as Amorite cities with Amorite kings. Babylon itself became the capital of an Amorite state under Hammurabi. This important historical fact is clearly reflected in the Mari Letters and in the peoples known as "Amorites" or "Westerners." In such a manner archaeology is slowly but surely outlining the historical frame work of the patriarchal age. Such discoveries as the Mari Letters prove of incalculable assistance to the historian of the ancient biblical world.

8. The Lachish Ostraca—Jeremiah's Age Lives Again

In the excavations of Lachish, a southwestern Palestinian city, the most astonishing finds were some letters embedded in a layer of burnt charcoal and ashes. They were eighteen in number and were in Hebrew writing done in the ancient Phoenician script. Three more of these letters were discovered in later campaigns in 1938.

Almost all of the letters were written by one named Hoshiah, who was stationed at some military outpost, to Jaosh, who was evidently a high ranking officer in the garrison at Lachish. It was the era of the Babylonian overrunning of Palestine several years before the fall of Jerusalem in 587 B.C. The Babylonians had attacked and partly burned Lachish some ten years before in the reign of Jehoiakim. These particular letters were in the layer of ashes which represent the final destruction of the city. Accordingly, they are to be dated from 588 B.C., when Nebuchadnezzar was making the final siege of Jerusalem and also of Lachish and Azekah.

Identification of Lachish. This large mound, one of the largest occupied in Palestine, is located 30 miles southwest of Jerusalem, 20 miles inland from the Mediterranean and 50 miles west of Hebron. It is mentioned in the Amarna Letters and in earlier Egyptian sources. Its strategic importance is attested by its being on the main route from central Palestine to Egypt. It overlooked the rich Shephelah (terrain which descended to the coastal lowland). The fortress city was an ideal barrier between the Philistine plains and the elevated Judaean country. It was one of the principal fortified cities of Judah and one of the bastions taken by the Israelites in their conquest of Palestine (Josh. 10:31–35). The site of Umm-Lakis was first thought to be Lachish. Then the location was sought at Tell el-Hesy by Sir Flinders Petrie, a pioneer archaeologist. William Foxwell Albright finally identified it correctly with the large mound of Tell el-Duweir.

Nebuchadnezzar captured Lachish in 588–586 B.C. (Jer. 34:7). Marks of a huge conflagration on the road leading up to the gate and on the adjacent wall display that the attackers relied largely upon fire, for which felled olive trees not yet harvested supplied the fuel.

Excavations at Lachish. The Wellcome-Marston Archaeological Expedition in 1933 commenced work there, under the direction of J. L. Starkey. In 1938 Starkey was killed by Arab brigands, and the work was carried on by Lankester Harding and Charles H. Inge.

The Results of the Excavation. Besides evidences of earlier occupation, Lachish disclosed settlement by the Hyksos c. 1720–1550 B.C. These people overran Egypt during this period. A typical Hyksos defense ditch or *fosse*, with a ramp of clay and lime that apparently provided an enclosure for their horses, was brought to light. In the fosse three Canaanite Egyptian temples built between 1450 and 1225 B.C. were excavated. A Persian temple of a much later period was also found. Cemeteries at Lachish yielded a great quantity of pottery, jewelry, scarabs, and skeletal evidence.

A well, 200 feet deep, was located within the city, the remains of a tremendous engineering excavation for water storage, which was not completed. A shaft about 85 feet terminates in a rectangle 80 x 70 feet cut to a depth of 80 feet. The aim was a water system which would have been much larger than that provided by Hezekiah for Jerusalem in the Siloam Tunnel and comparable to similar systems at Gezer and Megiddo.

A good quantity of inscribed material has been removed from the Lachish excavations. A bronze dagger from c. 1700 B.C. contains four pictographic signs, samples of the early script. A bowl and a ewer contain specimens of the same early writing as that found at Serabit el-Khadem. The name "Gedaliah" was found on a jar handle and may be the official whom Nebuchadnezzar set over the land after the fall of Jerusalem (cf. Jer. 40—42).

Contents of the Lachish Letters. But of all the epigraphic discoveries at Lachish, the most important are the Lachish Letters. These letters may be briefly described as follows: Letter 1 lists names, the majority of which are found in the Old

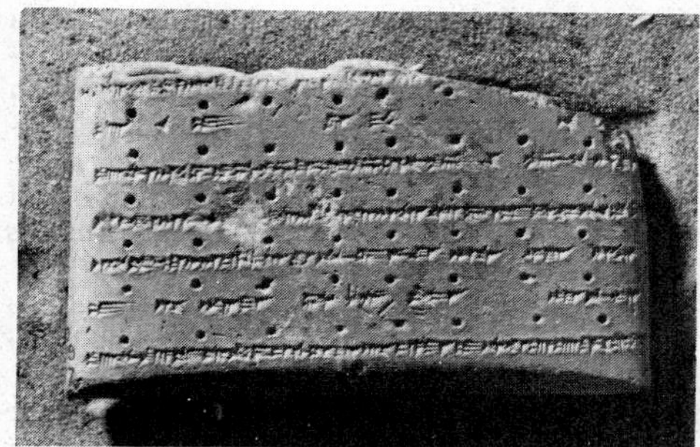

A clay tablet showing the colophon at the end of a typical Assyrian library tablet. Found at Nineveh. *British Museum*

Testament. Letters 2 and 5 consist largely of greetings. Letter 3, the longest, contains the most information. This concerns movements of Jewish troops and also makes an interesting note to an unnamed prophet and his word of warning. Letter 4 states that Hoshiah, though observing the signals of Lachish, cannot see those of Azekah. Azekah may well have fallen earlier, for this letter states, "We are watching for the signal station at Lachish according to all the signals you are giving, because we cannot see the signals of Azekah." Letter 6 contains the biblical expression, "to weaken the hands of the people." This recalls Jeremiah, who uses a similar expression (Jer. 38:4).

Historical Importance of the Letters. The Lachish Letters give us an independent view of conditions in Judah in the last days before the fall of Jerusalem. As the Neo-Babylonian army advanced, the doom of Jerusalem was sealed, in contrast to its deliverance under the Assyrian, Sennacherib, as Isaiah had predicted (2 Kin. 19:20, 32–36). Relentlessly, Nebuchadnezzar advanced on the city after a terrible eighteen-month siege, 587 B.C. The walls of the city were broken down, the houses and the temple burned, and the people carried away to exile (2 Kin. 25:1–12).

Jeremiah conducted his difficult ministry in these agonizing times. His reference to Azekah and Lachish is most interesting. "When the king of Babylon's army fought against Jerusalem and all the cities of Judah that were left, against Lachish and Azekah; for *only* these fortified cities remained of the cities of Judah" (Jer. 34:7).

Tell Zakariya in the Shephelah region has been identified as Azekah. In 1898 it was excavated by Frederick K. Bliss of the Palestine Exploration Fund. It had a strong inner fortress buttressed with eight large towers.

The Lachish Letters concern the time just prior to the fall of the city and present the same conditions of turmoil and confusion that are revealed in the Book of Jeremiah. Numerous place names that occur in the Bible are found in the letters, as well as personal names. Hoshaiah appears in Jeremiah 42:1 and Nehemiah 12:32. God is referred to by the four-letter word YHWH, which are the consonants of the name "Jehovah" or "Yahweh." It is also interesting to note that many of the men's names have Yahweh endings. A prophet like Jeremiah is referred to in the letters. But this is most probably not Jeremiah himself.

So complete was the destruction by the Babylonians that it took many centuries for Judah to recover. The returned remnant was tiny and weak. The small Jewish state stamped its coins with the name "Yehud," that is, Judah, but not until after 300 B.C. do substantial archaeological remains appear, and then they are not abundant. Certainly the Babylonians did a thorough job of destroying Jewish power for many centuries.

The Paleographic Importance of the Letters. Being inscribed in biblical Hebrew, in which the Old Testament Scriptures were written, and with stylistic and vocabulary similarities to the Book of Jeremiah, these letters are of great paleographic importance. They help the scholar to trace the evolution of the Hebrew alphabet, noting the formation of the letters and their style. They also enable him to see how the Old Testament Scriptures, which were then written, appeared.

Surely research of this type, that makes it possible for the scholar to look back, to resurrect the past, and to see how the language of the Old Testament developed, is fascinating. Great strides are being made in this field of enquiry. It is the one truly bright spot in original biblical studies. This type of study is of immense value in expanding historical backgrounds and illuminating Holy Scripture on the human plane.

9. The Dead Sea Scrolls

The middle of the 20th century saw the greatest manuscript discovery of modern times. In 1947 a young Bedouin shepherd stumbled upon a cave south of Jericho, containing many leather scrolls of Hebrew and Aramaic writing and about 600 fragmentary inscriptions. Great excitement prevailed in the archaeological world. In 1952 new caves containing fragments of later scrolls in Hebrew, Greek, and Aramaic were found. These and other startling manuscript discoveries have been followed by news of additional manuscripts found in other caves in the Dead Sea area.

A. The Date of the Scrolls. After intensive study of the manscripts from the Dead Sea area, scholars define three periods: 1. The Archaic Period c. 200–150 B.C. 2. The Hasmonaean Period c. 150–30 B.C. 3. The Herodian Period c. 30 B.C. to A.D. 70. The great majority originated in the 2nd and 3rd periods, especially the last half of the 2nd period and last half of the 3rd period.

Although attacks have been made against the antiquity and authenticity of these manuscripts, two lines of evidence substantiate their antiquity. **The evidence of radiocarbon count.** This scien-

The area near the Dead Sea where the Qumran scrolls were found. *Matson Photo Service*

tific method of dating places the linen in which the scrolls were wrapped in the general era of c. 175 B.C. to A.D. 225. **Paleographic evidence.** Scholars conversant in this science date these documents by the form of the letters and the way they are written in comparison with other eras of writing. They are able to demonstrate that they come in the intermediate period between the script of the 3rd century B.C. and of the middle of the 1st century A.D. W. F. Albright observes, "All competent students of writing conversant with the available material and with paleographic method date the scrolls in the 250 years before A.D. 70."

B. The Contents of the Scrolls. The Dead Sea cave manuscripts contain material partly biblical and partly intertestamental. The biblical includes two scrolls of Isaiah, one complete, and most of the first two chapters of Habakkuk, and fragments of all Old Testament books except Esther. Large numbers of fragmentary manuscripts have been recovered from the Pentateuchal books and Isaiah. Fragments of Psalms, Jeremiah, and Daniel are numerous.

The scroll of ***Isaiah,*** in the initial finds from the site of Qumran, has remained the best known of the discoveries. It was the first major biblical manuscript of great antiquity to be recovered. It is earlier by a millennium than the oldest Hebrew text preserved in the Masoretic Hebrew Bible. This Masoretic Hebrew Bible is the basis of all recent translations and does not go back any earlier than A.D. 900.

This fact of the antiquity of the Hebrew text of Isaiah, dating as early as 150–125 B.C., constitutes these discoveries as the greatest of modern times. They are the oldest existing manuscripts of the Bible in any language.

In the original group of manuscripts of 1947 were a commentary on Habakkuk and so-called ***Manual of Discipline*** of pre-Christian Jewish sect of Essenes. Of unusual interest were manuscripts later purchased by the Hebrew University of Jerusalem, containing a later Isaiah scroll more conformed to the traditional Hebrew, and a document of great interest called ***"The War Between the Children of Light and Darkness."*** This composition evidently issued from the Maccabaean struggles against Greek paganism in 158–137 B.C.

In winter, 1949, the first manuscript-bearing cave was excavated by two well-known Palestinian archaeologists, Pierre de Vaux and Lankester Harding. Recovered were fragments of Genesis, Deuteronomy, and Judges with a fragment of Leviticus in Old Hebrew script. Nonbiblical finds included a fragment of the ***Book of Jubilees,*** a work related to the Enoch literature, and some unknown material.

C. Other Manuscript-Yielding Sites. In 1952 a cave was uncovered at Murabbaat in another part of the desert. This yielded manuscripts chiefly from the 2nd century A.D. in Hebrew, Greek, and Aramaic, including a few texts of Genesis, Exodus, Deuteronomy, and Isaiah. Several Hebrew letters were discovered from the period of Simon ben Keseba, that is, Bar Cocheba, who led the revolt in 132–135. A notable exception to the 2nd century A.D. date of this material is an archaic Hebrew papyrus piece, a palimpsest, a list of names and numbers, dated in the 6th century B.C.

In the same general area, other caves have been found, one group in Khirbet Mird, northeast of the monastery of Mar Saba. These contain Arabic papyri, Greek and Christo-Palestinian-Syrian documents, with fragments of biblical codices, all late Byzantine and early Arabic. Another group of manuscripts date from the period of the bulk of the Murabbaat material. Among them is a version of the minor prophets in Greek and a corpus of Nabataean papyri, both of great biblical and historical importance.

D. Excavations at Khirbet Qumran. Khirbet Qumran was excavated between 1951 and 1954. This Essene community, with the nearby caves, proved to be the richest manuscript-yielding center. Members of this Essenic community copied these manuscripts and preserved them by hiding them in the caves. The Essenes at Khirbet Qumran, 7 miles south of Jericho near the shores of the Dead Sea, were next to the Pharisees and Sadducees in importance in sectarian Judaism. This site has become one of the most publicized places in Palestine because of the phenomenal manuscript finds in the cave-dotted cliffs.

Excavations at Khirbet Qumran have fully authenticated this site as the center of Essenic Judaism. As the result of the recovery of coins, pottery, and architectural remains, the story of Qumran's occupation can now be told. Four periods in the later history of the site are traced.

Period 1 extends from its founding c. 110 B.C. under John Hyrcanus. Numerous coins of this ruler were dug up, as well as of other Hasmonaean rulers including Antigonus, 40–37 B.C., the last ruler of this line, to the seventh year of Herod, 31 B.C. At this time an earthquake apparently leveled the site. Indications are that during Herod's reign the place was abandoned because of his antagonism.

Period 2 at Qumran dates from rebuilding and enlargement c. A.D. 1 and Roman destruction in June A.D. 68. During this era in the lifetime of Jesus, John the Baptist, and the early Christian apostles, Qumran flourished, influencing Judaism and the early Christian church. Coins have been found dating from the reign of Archelaus, 4 B.C. to A.D. 6, and from the time of the Roman procurators down to the second year of the first Jewish revolt in A.D. 66–70.

The Roman army, which took Jericho in June, A.D. 68, evidently likewise captured Qumran. One coin, marked with an X, belonged to the Tenth Legion. Iron arrowheads were found in a layer of burned ash in the excavation.

Qumran fell to Roman occupation. Some coins describe *Judaea Capta*. These date in the reign of Titus, A.D. 79–81, and mark **Period 3** as the Roman occupation after Jerusalem's destruction in A.D. 70. Evidence that Qumran structures were converted into army barracks indicates that a Roman garrison was stationed there from A.D. 68–c. A.D. 100. At this time the site apparently was abandoned.

Period 4. Qumran is distinguished by reoccupation of the site during the 2nd Jewish revolt, A.D. 132–135. Coins dating from this era indicate that here the Jews made their last stand to drive the Romans from their country. After that Qumran sank into obscurity.

Architectural Remains at Qumran. The main edifice at Qumran is 100 feet by 120 and formed the communal center and hub of the complex. At the northwest corner was a massive defense tower with thick walls enforced by stone embankments. Some coins from the time of the 2nd Jewish revolt (A.D. 132–135) attest its use as a fortress against Roman power.

Alongside the general meeting room is the largest hall of the main building. Here was located the scriptorium. Several inkwells of the Roman period, and even some dried ink, indicate that the manuscripts had been copied by the community's scribes.

Also in the complex were two cisterns (artificial reservoirs) carefully plastered. There were installations for ablutions and baptisms. Of the possibly 40 cisterns and reservoirs, the bulk of them must have been used for storage of water in the very hot, dry climate.

Of great interest is the cemetery, containing about 1,000 burial places. De Vaux excavated many of these tombs. They are noted for their lack of jewelry and any evidences of luxury.

E. Khirbet Qumran and the Essenes. Not only do the excavations at Khirbet Qumran demonstrate that it was the headquarters of Essenic Judaism but three authorities who were contemporary witnesses attest the same fact, namely, Josephus, Philo, and Pliny. Pliny, for example, locates the Essenes at precisely the spot where Qumran is situated, namely, "on the west side of the Dead Sea." He also designates the town of En-Gedi as situated "below the Essenes."

Josephus relates their unselfish character, industry, and communal life. He extols their love for common toil, says they dressed in white, and describes their three-year probationary period before admission to the sect, and other phases of discipline. He also mentions their various lustrations and says that they numbered about 4,000. He comments on their celibacy, piety, convictions concerning immortality, and their belief in rewards for righteousness.

Philo gives a similar description of this group in Judaism. The library at Qumran attests their delight in the Bible and literature. This is reflected in information given by Philo and Josephus. The Essenes carefully copied Holy Scripture and took pains to preserve it.

There are difficulties in equating the Essenes at Qumran with the sect described by Philo, Pliny, and Josephus. Nevertheless, the likenesses far outweigh the differences. The evidence would seem to equate Qumran with the Essenes of the 1st century A.D.

F. The Essenes at Qumran and John the Baptist. Concerning John, Luke wrote: "So the child grew, and became strong in spirit, and was in the deserts till the day of his manifestation to Israel" (Luke 1:80). The home of John the Baptist's parents was in the hill country of Judea (Luke 1:39, 40, 65). Although nothing is known definitely, it is easy to believe that John the Baptist did in some way come in contact with the Essenes. There are many characteristics in his own life that parallel theirs.

Both John and the Qumranites feature Isaiah 40:3 with regard to preparing "the way of the LORD." But John must have early realized that there were some features of the Essenes that were not conducive to preparing the nation for the advent of the Messiah, and so if he ever had a connection with them, he must have broken with them, giving himself to an active ministry of preaching repentance and baptizing in the Jordan Valley.

John's message featured repentance (Matt. 3:2; Mark 1:4; Luke 3:3). Repentance was also a vital note in Qumran theology. They belonged to a "covenant of repentance" and they called themselves "the penitents of Israel." The baptism of repentance, which John administered, was also paralleled by the Essenes who practiced water baptism. John's baptism was an outer indication of inward spirital renovation, enabling the recipients to recognize the Messiah when He came.

Baptism among the Qumranites, however, was purely ritual, and the recipients were enjoined to separate themselves rigidly from any who did not belong to their community. The severe indictment of the Jewish nation, which was characteristic of John, was also characteristic of the Essenes. They looked upon those not belonging to their sect as "sons of darkness" connected with Belial. They regarded themselves as true Israel, living in accordance with the law. For them alone the baptismal rite could have meaning.

John featured the baptism "with the Holy Spirit and fire" (Matt. 3:11), the baptism with fire being the judgment upon the unrepentant in an eschatological sense. Such judgment of fire is described in a Qumran hymn under the figure of a fiery river overflowing in wrath "on the outcasts" and in "the time of fury for all Belial."

The baptism of the Holy Spirit, on the other hand, is prophesied by John to be the portion of those who would repent and receive the coming Messiah (John 1:33). In Qumran literature not only does God "sprinkle upon him," the Messiah, the spirit of truth as purifying water to cleanse Him from all abominations of falsehood and from the spirit of impurity, but the Messiah sprinkles His people with His Holy Spirit, constituting them His anointed ones.

John the Baptist was intensely missionary and evangelistic in his message. The Qumranites were self-centered, strictly sectarian, and did not spread their convictions. They did adopt children to train in their ways.

John the Baptist was vouchsafed the honor of preparing the way for the Messiah and being His forerunner. The Qumran community did not recognize the Messiah when He came. Their asceticism led to a deadend. It never conducted them to Him who would take away the sin of the world (John 1:29).

G. The Essenes and Jesus the Messiah. Although the Qumran community had a messianic hope, it was strikingly different from that of the Old Testament. They could not comprehend the combination of King and Priest in *one* Person (Zech. 6:9–15). Neither could they comprehend in the union of the same Person the additional office of a Prophet, although they did feature in their writings the messianic prophecy of "a Prophet" (Deut. 18:18, 19).

Their great priest was Messiah of Aaron. Their great military leader, Messiah of Israel; their prophet comprehended in the rule of the community is set down alongside the "messiahs of Aaron and Israel," apparently as a separate messianic figure.

There are other similarities between the orgaization and teachings of the Qumran group and the teachings of Jesus and the formation of the Christian church. The passage in Matthew 18:15–17 has a striking parallel in Qumran literature.

It is easily seen that with this new material the background of the gospel stories is much more richly illustrated. The Last Supper, the Sermon on the Mount, and numerous other aspects of the earthly life and ministry of Jesus are fitted into a larger framework of historical background material, and to that extent are understood on the

Jerusalem Temple inscription warning Gentiles against intrusion.
Matson Photo Service

human side. However, it is transparently clear that the ministries of John the Baptist and Jesus remain unique. Qumran literature in no sense casts any shadow upon the unique Person and work of Jesus Christ. Christianity stands as authentically growing out of the Old Testament and not connected with later Gnosticism in a post-apostolic era that would jeopardize its historical genuineness.

H. The Dead Sea Scrolls and Literary Criticism of the New Testament. The Dead Sea material has had a stabilizing effect upon New Testament criticism. In the light of the new material, the New Testament appears as a Jewish book with a Christian theology with less Greek influence in its formation than Jewish, and there is reason to date the ***synoptic gospels***, beginning with ***Mark***, between A.D. 60 and 65.

Especially interesting is the dating of the ***Gospel of John***. A radical criticism customarily dated this Gospel about A.D. 150 or later. Thus it was removed from apostolic tradition and treated more as an apocryphal book. Now it is well known that the Fourth Gospel reflects the genuine Jewish background of John the Baptist and Jesus and not a later 2nd-century Gnostic milieu. This is clearly attested by the parallels to the conceptual imagery of John's Gospel in the Essenic literature from Qumran.

There is every evidence to believe in the authenticity of John's Gospel, and there is not the slightest reason critically to date the Gospel after A.D. 90. Indeed, it may be quite a bit earlier. Thus the Dead Sea discoveries and the excavations at Qumran not only give additional background material to the inter-biblical and New Testament period but also help to stabilize higher criticism and purge out radical views that are now shown to be untenable.

The ***Book of Hebrews*** also is interesting. This is certainly to be definitely dated before the destruction of Jerusalem in 70 A.D. The treatise apparently was planned to offset the Essenic idea of "two anointed ones," one a prince and the other a priest. It was designed to present the Christian and Old Testament doctrine (cf. Zech. 6:9, 15; Ps. 110:1) that Messiah would be *both King and Priest in one Person*. Also the ***Book of the Revelation*** was doubtless penned toward the end of the 1st century, and, in the light of the Dead Sea Scrolls, may now possibly be dated earlier, that is before A.D. 70. This conclusion is based on its Hebraic background, being illuminated by the evidence from the Dead Sea manuscripts.

10. Jerusalem

Probably no excavation ever carried out has been as important as that carried on by Israeli institutions at the western and southern walls of the temple mountain in Jerusalem. The actual steps and entrances of Herod's temple have been uncovered as have the tiny shops and narrow streets where the merchants must have hawked their wares. The giant stone blocks from the top of the wall, which were thrown down into the streets by Titus' troops in A.D. 70, were found where they fell. In a grave in another part of the city was found the remains of a Jew who had been crucified by the Romans, the first physical evidence of this form of execution ever found. So extensive were these finds that it will be a generation before they are all deciphered and integrated into the historical framework of the Roman Age.

11. Ebla

The modern Arabic name for this 140-acre mound in the Northwest corner of Syria is Tell Mardikh. Archaeologists of the University of Rome began digging this mound in 1964 and found an inscription in 1968 that identified this site as ancient Ebla. They uncovered portions of impressive ***buildings from the time of the biblical Patriarchs*** (1900–1700 B.C.); and beneath these were palaces and temples of the Early Bronze Age (2400–2250 B.C.). This was the discovery of an early but advanced civilization which was previously unknown.

In 1974, 1975, and 1976, three rooms of one palace yielded almost 7000 well-preserved ***clay tablets*** and about 13,000 fragments of other tablets ***with cuneiform writing on them.*** This archive of ***ancient Sumerian and Canaanite literature*** is very important. The tablets contain economic, political, and legal records of Ebla. (Understanding the cultures of Israel's neighbors aids biblical interpretation.) They show that Ebla was a merchant empire. Its rulers controlled trade routes that reached into the Mesopotamian Valley, into the mountains of modern-day Turkey, and to the edge of the Nile Valley.

But more importantly, some tablets are ***dictionaries***—the earliest known—providing the meanings of words used in both the Sumerian and early Canaanite (Eblaite) languages. (Languages help archaeologists understand the cultures.) Many Canaanite words at Ugarit and ***Hebrew words in the Old Testament*** can be understood more accurately because they also occur on these early tablets.

Many ***place names*** occur in the Ebla records, including those familiar to readers of the Bible: Haran, Damascus, Hazor, Beth-shan, Shechem, Joppa, Eshkelon, Jerusalem, Dor—and some scholars believe also Sodom and Gommorah. Since the Bible itself presents these as real places, the Ebla tablets help support its historical reliability.

About 10,000 names of people are found on the tablets. Among them are ***biblical names*** such as Adam, Eve, Noah, Jubal, Abram. Ishmael, Hagar, Keturah, Bilhah, Israel, Micah, Michael, Saul, David, Jehorum, and Jonah. Although these names do not refer to the biblical personages, they establish that the names in Scripture are authentic.

Sometimes, however, the tablets contain mythic and legendary stories which conflict with the Scriptures (e.g., different creation accounts). Such cases illumine the biblical authors' polemics against pagan worldviews.

The excavation project continues until the present and may be expected to cast more light on the Bible's meaning and reliability.

The thrilling story of biblical archaeology is not yet completed. Other great discoveries as a result of continuous research in Bible lands promise even greater contributions to biblical studies in future years. For example, the recovery of thirteen Coptic codices from Nag Hammadi in Upper Egypt, since 1945, have almost rivaled the Dead Sea Scrolls in actual biblical importance. These even include the apocryphal "Gospel of Thomas" and are of inestimable value, especially from a critical standpoint in dating New Testament literature.

What new and exciting discovery affecting the Bible may we not expect the archaeologist's spade to turn up next? The prospect should engender a love for the Scriptures and a desire to study them employing history, linguistics, and archaeology as the means under the Holy Spirit to a more accurate understanding of the Bible's message to mankind.

Acknowledgements: The publisher gratefully acknowledges the cooperation of these sources, whose photographs appear in this article:

British Museum (80-7-19, 277)
G. Eric Matson Collection, The Episcopal House
Professor D. J. Wiseman

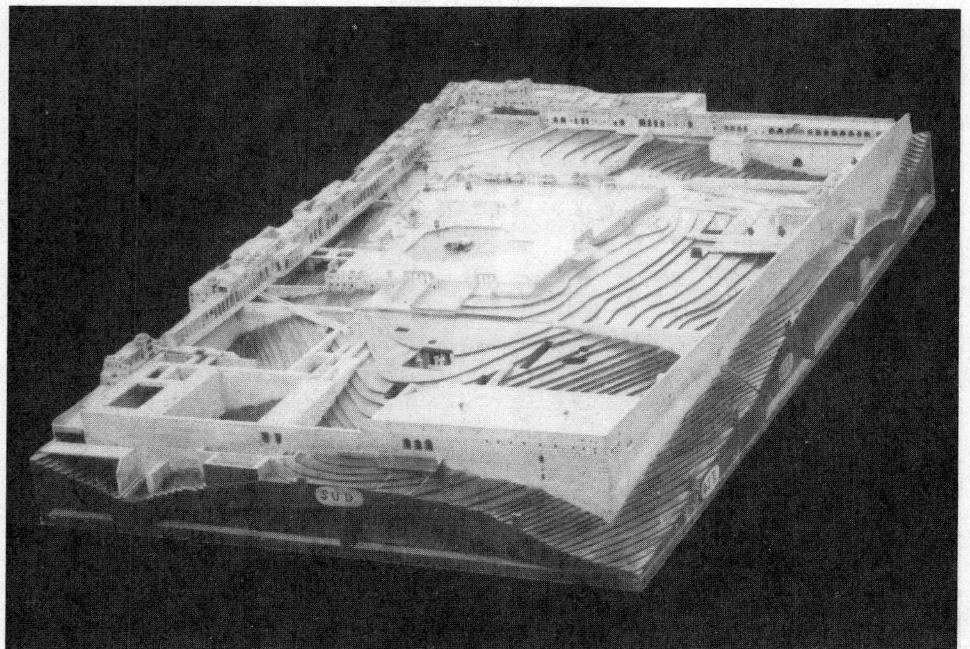

The Temple area in Jerusalem, showing the slope of the hill. *Matson Photo Service*

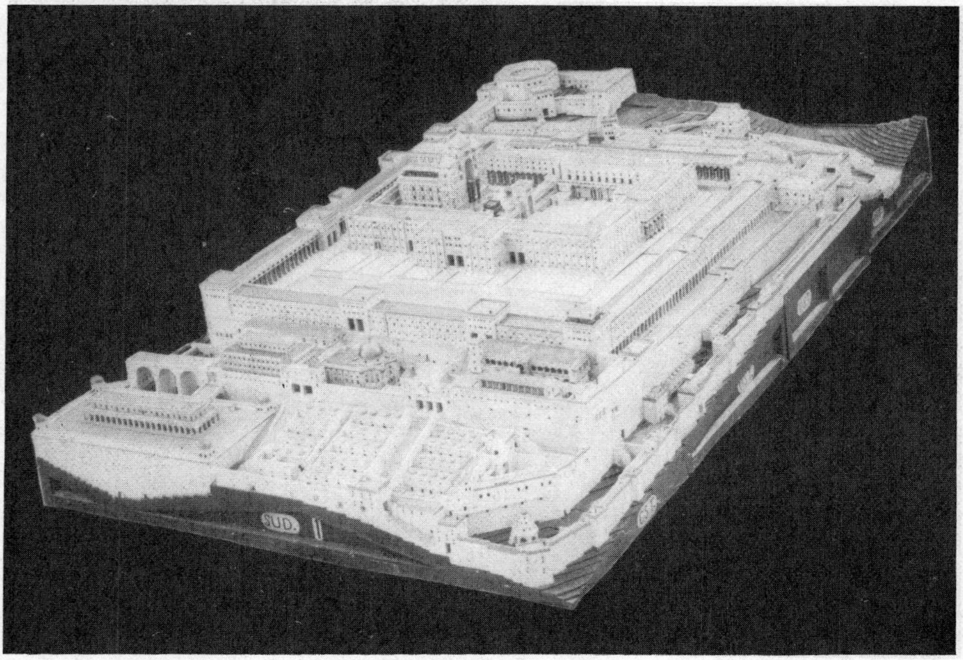

Model of the Temple of Solomon in Jerusalem. *Matson Photo Service*

Model of the Temple of Zerubbabel in Jerusalem. *Matson Photo Service*

Model of the Temple of Herod in Jerusalem. *Matson Photo Service*

A GUIDE TO CHRISTIAN WORKERS

I. Commission

Give us a watchword for the hour,
A thrilling word, a word of power;
A battle cry, a flaming breath,
A call to conquest or to death;
A word to rouse the church from rest,
To heed the Master's high behest.
The call is given, ye hosts arise,
The watchword is EVANGELIZE!
To fallen men, a dying race,
Make known the gift of gospel grace.
The world that now in darkness lies,
O Church of Christ, EVANGELIZE!

"Then Jesus came and spoke to them, saying, 'All authority has been given to Me in heaven and on earth. Go therefore and make disciples of all the nations, baptizing them in the name of the Father and of the Son and of the Holy Spirit, teaching them to observe all things that I have commanded you; and lo, I am with you always, *even* to the end of the age.' Amen" (Matt. 28:18–20).

"But you shall receive power when the Holy Spirit has come upon you; and you shall be witnesses to Me in Jerusalem, and in all Judea and Samaria, and to the end of the earth" (Acts 1:8).

"So you, son of man: I have made you a watchman for the house of Israel; therefore you shall hear a word from My mouth and warn them for Me. When I say to the wicked, 'O wicked *man,* you shall surely die!' and you do not speak to warn the wicked from his way, that wicked *man* shall die in his iniquity; but his blood I will require at your hand" (Ezek. 33:7, 8).

"You are the salt of the earth; but if the salt loses its flavor, how shall it be seasoned? It is then good for nothing but to be thrown out and trampled under foot by men. You are the light of the world. A city that is set on a hill cannot be hidden. Nor do they light a lamp and put it under a basket, but on a lampstand, and it gives light to all *who are* in the house. Let your light so shine before men, that they may see your good works and glorify your Father in heaven" (Matt. 5:13–16).

II. Compassion

The story is told that Martinelli received $25,000 for singing only twice. Paul and Silas sang one night in a prison. Their song was not rendered with the skill or harmony of that of Martinelli's, but its tenderness touched the heart of the keeper of the prison and echoed through the angel-crowded streets of heaven; and the listening King of kings rewarded those who sang with crowns of glory that will gleam in beauty throughout eternal ages.

An immortal soul is beyond all price. There is no trouble too great, no humiliation too deep, no suffering too severe, no love too strong, no labor too hard, no expense too large, but that it is worth it, if it is spent in the effort to win a soul.

God loves the soul more than all creation. He fashioned it after His own image, and made it like unto Himself. Every soul has departed from God and gone astray, and God has bought the soul back again with a price.

That price was in, and through, and by Jesus Christ. God loves the soul with an everlasting love.

Satan hates the soul. In Satan's enmity toward God he is using all his energy, using every snare, his utmost cunning, employing every means *with the single purpose of ruining the soul of man.*

When a million eternities have each lived their endless ages and have rolled by into the unthinkable past and time is no more, the soul will still be living, *a conscious personality* endowed with perpetual life reunited with the body.

God has said: "And he who wins souls *is* wise" (Prov. 11:30).

The Bible says: "Those who are wise shall shine like the brightness of the firmament, and those who turn many to righteousness like the stars forever and ever" (Dan. 12:3).

Compassion was the heartbeat of our Savior's ministry. "But when He saw the multitudes, He was moved with compassion for them, because they were weary and scattered, like sheep having no shepherd" (Matt. 9:36). "But You, O Lord, *are* a God full of compassion and gracious, longsuffering and abundant in mercy and truth" (Ps. 86:15).

Heaven is geared for redemption. "I say to you that likewise there will be more joy in heaven over one sinner who repents than over ninety-nine just persons who need no repentance" (Luke 15:7).

No man who ever had a glimpse of hell would ever want a fellow human being to go there (see Luke 16:28).

"Those who sow in tears shall reap in joy. He who continually goes forth weeping, bearing seed for sowing, shall doubtless come again with rejoicing, Bringing his sheaves *with him*" (Ps. 126:5, 6).

III. Concern

One of the first questions raised in recorded history was, "*Am* I my brother's keeper?" (Gen. 4:9). ***Do I have moral obligations toward others?*** "So I sought for a man among them who would make a wall, and stand in the gap before Me on behalf of the land, that I should not destroy it; but I found no one" (Ezek. 22:30).

"My sheep wandered through all the mountains, and on every high hill; yes, My flock was scattered over the whole face of the earth, and no one was seeking or searching *for them*" (Ezek. 34:6).

"*If* you extend your soul to the hungry and satisfy the afflicted soul, then your light shall dawn in the darkness, and your darkness shall *be* as the noonday"(Is. 58:10).

"I tell the truth in Christ, I am not lying, my conscience also bearing me witness in the Holy Spirit, that I have great sorrow and continual grief in my heart. For I could wish that I myself were accursed from Christ for my brethren, my kinsmen according to the flesh" (Rom. 9:1–3). See also Psalms 106:23; Luke 19:41; Acts 20:31.

Intercession is the way that leads to the winning of souls. No church can prosper without it. No Christian can grow without it. The law of life demands reproduction—that kind should beget kind.

Jesus interceded for each of us. "Therefore I will divide Him a portion with the great, and He shall divide the spoil with the strong, Because He poured out His soul unto death, And He was numbered with the transgressors, And He bore the sin of many, And made intercession for the transgressors" (Is. 53:12).

Christ left this command to us: "Therefore pray the Lord of the harvest to send out laborers into His harvest" (Matt. 9:38).

IV. Contact

It began with ***personal contact***.

"He first found his own brother Simon, and said to him, 'We have found the Messiah,' (which is translated, the Christ)" (John 1:41).

With Christ came the emphasis of *seeking the lost*. "For the Son of Man has come to seek and to save that which was lost" (Luke 19:10).

The movement of Christianity in this world is scripturally based on personal contact. Anyone who really knows Jesus will want others to know Him.

The secret is in the words of Andrew, "We have *found*." The search for satisfaction in a man's soul is completed in a living knowledge of Jesus Christ. Personal evangelism is sharing this discovery.

"And he brought him to Jesus" (John 1:42).

How is this accomplished? Christ gives the answer. "Follow Me, and I will make you fishers of men" (Matt. 4:19). ***A love for Christ produces a love for mankind.***

We are to be workmen "who [do] not need to be ashamed" (2 Tim. 2:15). Lives today are complicated by sin. They need more than slogans and formulas. They need personal help. A conscientious doctor must deal with each patient separately and so must a conscientious soul-winner.

These guidelines must be kept in mind:

1. I MUST LIVE IT. I can't say to others, "Do as I *say*, but don't do as I *do*." They must see Christ in me (1 Cor. 4:9). My strongest testimony is my daily life.

2. I MUST LOVE PEOPLE. I cannot pretend. The other person knows my motive immediately. The power of evangelism is described in Revelation 22:17, "And the Spirit and the bride say, 'Come!'" When my *concern* for others is in keeping with the concern of the Holy Spirit toward mankind, there is a community of interest in the individual that results in *compulsion*.

3. I MUST MEET THE PUBLIC. Jesus was heaven's artist at this. He never met a stranger. Paul testified, "I have become all things to all *men*, that I might by all means save some" (1 Cor. 9:22).

Kindness will open doors (Eph. 4:32). It will bring an affirmative response.

4. I MUST LOOK FOR NEED. Jesus said, "Those who are well have no need of a physician, but those who are sick. I did not come to call *the* righteous, but sinners, to repentance" (Mark 2:17).

You will be surprised how many people are ready to talk. They simply need someone in whom they can have confidence. Zacchaeus was in trouble. Uninvited, he talked about his sin. *That is my point of contact—human need*.

5. I MUST COMMUNICATE. Keep away from technicalities. Refuse to become involved in debate. The Samaritan woman quibbled: "Our fathers worshiped on this mountain, and you *Jews* say that in Jerusalem is the place where one ought to worship" (John 4:20). It wasn't her *head* that was troubling her. It was her *heart*. She needed Christ before she needed a church; a Redeemer before she needed a ritual. "I know that Messiah is coming" (who is called Christ). "When He comes, He will tell us all things." Jesus said to her, "I who speak to you am *He*" (John 4:25, 26).

6. I MUST CONCENTRATE ON CHRIST. I can get so much "I" into my testimony that spiritual pride will offend the person to whom I am witnessing. The rule of the great Baptist still holds: "He must increase, but I *must* decrease." (John 3:30). *My business is to present Jesus* (John 12:32). Christ is the attraction.

7. I MUST USE TACT. This suggests a sensitivity to the other man's feelings. It is a spirit of discernment. "If any of you lacks wisdom, let him ask of God, who gives to all liberally and without reproach, and it will be given to him" (James 1:5). Be natural. Be courteous. Be a good listener. Ask wise questions.

8. I MUST BRING A PERSON TO A DECI-

SION. This can only be accomplished through the power and presence of the Holy Spirit (John 16:8).

The chance may never come again. *Opportunity is God-given*. Don't gamble with it. Press for a decision. "Yet you do not have because you do not ask" (James 4:2). Don't let people say of you at Judgment Day, "He never asked me to be a Christian!"

9. I MUST TEACH THEM TO LISTEN TO GOD'S VOICE. It is my business to *introduce* them to the Savior. So often the worker only introduces himself. "Now acquaint yourself with Him, and be at peace; Thereby good will come to you" (Job 22:21). Let the person with whom you are dealing hear for the first time the voice of God speaking to him or her in reassurance and comfort, and you have built strength.

This is done by teaching the person two or three primary verses of Scripture. Tie the seeker to God's Word. Let your friend know before you leave him that God has spoken these words to him. These words carry a guarantee.

Here is an *example*:

"Most assuredly, I say to you, he who hears My word and believes in Him who sent Me has everlasting life, and shall not come into judgment, but has passed from death into life" (John 5:24).

These are the words of the Son of God. They are spoken to *you*. They are spoken with finality and authority.

10. I MUST MAKE IT CRYSTAL CLEAR THAT THERE IS A DIFFERENCE BETWEEN KNOWING GOD AND KNOWING ABOUT GOD. Hearsay is not enough. *Birth is not something that is second-hand*. "And when he brings out his own sheep, he goes before them; and the sheep follow him, for they know his voice. Yet they will by no means follow a stranger, but will flee from him, for they do not know the voice of strangers" (John 10:4, 5).

I know God when I get down to business with Him. "Draw near to God, and He will draw near to you" (James 4:8). God has expressed His willingness in a covenant, contract, or testament. It bears His signature in the death and resurrection of Jesus Christ. ***The moment I exercise faith toward this written word and become personally involved in agreement, that very moment the entire contract, or covenant, is in force toward me.***

If I do not associate the seeker with the Word of God, that person will miss his way. The devil will deceive the inquirer before breakfast. He will lie so cleverly that the inquirer will apologize to worldly associates before the day is over.

Remember! The authority is in the Word of God.

V. A Conversation

Dr. R. G. Lee calls this two-way conversation "convincing confutation." The following are answers to some excuses as Dr. Lee sets them forth.

1. Excuse: *"I want to get established in business first. After that I will be a Christian."*

Answer: No business should be allowed to cheat one out of heaven's blessings. Property should not kill the privilege of being a child of God. "For what will it profit a man if he gains the whole world, and loses his own soul?" (Mark 8:36). God called one man a fool to his face. "But God said to him, '*You* fool! This night your soul will be required of you; then whose will those things be which you have provided?'" (Luke 12:20). He was the man who neglected his soul's welfare by building barns, enlarging crops, and feeding his soul on corn.

Further Scriptures which may be used: Matthew 6:33, Psalms 1:1, 2, Proverbs 29:25, Mark 10:29, 30.

2. Excuse: *"I am not a sinner."*

Answer: But God says "*There is none righteous, no, not one*" (Rom. 3:10). "But the Scripture has confined all under sin" (Gal. 3:22). If you are not a sinner, are you keeping God's commands? What about Matthew 22:37? "Jesus said to him, 'You shall love the LORD your God with all your heart, with all your soul, and with all your mind.'"

3. Excuse: *"I have no encouragement at home."*

Answer: Without families we came. Without our families we go. Guilt is personal. Then, too, if you have praying parents, a saintly wife or husband, and godly children, and you continue your selfish resistance to their accepted and your rejected Savior, your guilt is deeper.

4. Excuse: *"I am good enough as I am."*

Answer: God says you are bad enough—by nature. Man in his natural state does wicked deeds, thinks evil thoughts, goes to bad places, rejects Jesus Christ—because he has an evil heart. No one is naturally good. If you are good, why not become acquainted with Jesus, who is supremely good?

5. Excuse: *"I am as good as others."*

Answer: Violin players do not take their tones from each other, but from the piano. Builders are constantly using the plumb line, the level, and the square. We need to live by standards—not comparisons. Nobody can claim health because he is better than another diabetic or stronger than another cancer victim. Measure yourself by Jesus if you want to know how good or bad you are. Do not be too sure you are better than many within the Church. They have confessed Jesus before men—as Jesus asked. You have not. Moreover, you are forbidden to judge to justify yourself. You are not saved or lost by the deeds of others.

6. Excuse: *"I have no feeling."*

Answer: The world isn't run by feeling. Washington did not live at Valley Forge because he felt like it. Most people do most of their worthy acts contrary to feeling. The doctor does not deal with diseases because of feeling but because of necessity.

Scriptures which may be used: Revelation 3:20, John 3:36, Ephesians 1:13, First Peter 1:8.

7. Excuse: *"I am so weak."*

Answer: "You will keep *him* in perfect peace, *whose* mind *is* stayed *on You,* because he trusts in You. Trust in the LORD forever, for in YAH, the LORD, *is* everlasting strength" (Is. 26:3, 4). Who will keep? The Almighty God. How? "In perfect peace." On what condition? "Whose mind is stayed" on God—not on self, nor circumstances, failures, successes, nor on others. Trust—not try or worry, but trust. In whom? God. How long? All the time. Why? For God is everlasting strength.

Further Scriptures which may be used: Jude 24, First Corinthians 10:13, Philippians 1:6, Isaiah 41:10, 13, 14, Second Timothy 1:12.

8. Excuse: *"I am doing the best I can."*

Answer: How long have you been doing your best? Have you succeeded? How long will it take you to make yourself fit for heaven? Suppose you die now? The best you can do is to acknowledge you cannot do anything to save yourself—except believe.

9. Excuse: *"I am too big a sinner."*

Answer: Jesus came to save *all* sinners. "This *is* a faithful saying and worthy of all acceptance, that Christ Jesus came into the world to save sinners, of whom I am chief" (1 Tim. 1:15). Are your sins scarlet? "Come now, and let us reason together," Says the Lord, 'Though your sins are like scarlet, they shall be as white as snow; though they are red like crimson, they shall be as wool'" (Is. 1:18). Are you lost? "For the Son of Man has come to seek and to save that which was lost" (Luke 19:10). Are you without strength? "For when we were still without strength, in due time Christ died for the ungodly. For scarcely for a righteous man will one die; yet perhaps for a good man someone would even dare to die. But God demonstrates His own love toward us, in that while we were still sinners, Christ died for us" (Rom. 5:6–8). "All that the Father gives Me will come to Me, and the one who comes to Me I will by no means cast out" (John 6:37).

Further Scriptures which may be used: Matthew 9:13, Hebrews 7:25, Luke 23:39–43.

10. Excuse: *"There are too many hypocrites."*

Answer: Hypocrites are lost. If you let hypocrites keep you from being saved, you will spend eternity in hell with them. Besides, you have to be smaller than what you hide behind. If you hide behind a hypocrite, you must be smaller than a hypocrite.

Further Scriptures which may be used: Zechariah 13:6, Acts 1:6, Hebrews 12:2, Acts 17:30, 31, Romans 2:1–6; 14:12, Matthew 7:1–5, First Samuel 16:7.

11. Excuse: *"A professing Christian wronged me."*

Answer: Granted. But is that any reason why you should wrong God and insult Christ, who loved you and gave Himself for you? "He who believes in the Son has everlasting life; and he who does not believe the Son shall not see life, but the wrath of God abides on him" (John 3:36).

12. Excuse: *"There is too much to give up."*

Answer: Better give up everything than lose the soul. Put Christ and your soul ahead of all else. Is it too much to give up paste pearls for glittering gems? Dirt for diamonds? Is it too much to give up rags for riches?

Further Scriptures which may be used: Psalms 16:11; 84:11, Proverbs 3:17; 13:15, Matthew 11:30, Isaiah 57:21, Romans 8:32, Mark 8:36, 37, Luke 18:29, 30.

13. Excuse: *"I cannot understand."*

Answer: Why let mystery cause you to refuse the Master? Do you understand the chemistry of digestion? Does your ignorance of it keep you from eating steak? Can you understand why the same sun and the same soil and the same rain get sweetness into the orange and sourness into the lemon and bitterness into the persimmon?

Lay aside your excuse of mystery and trust God as you trust the telephone to transmit your voice.

Further Scriptures which may be used: Romans 11:33, First Corinthians 1:8; 2:14.

14. Excuse: *"God is unjust."*

Answer: Who is God? Who are you? Injustice is sin. Do you mean to accuse God of sin? God is so just that He never demands two payments for one debt. Jesus paid your sin debt on the Cross—all of it. Therefore, when you accept Christ, you do not have that sin debt to pay.

15. Excuse: *"Folks would laugh."*

Answer: Better let them laugh than to have God laugh. "I also will laugh at your calamity; I will mock when your terror comes" (Prov. 1:26). Shun evil companions. "Do not enter the path of the wicked. And do not walk in the way of evil. The way of the wicked *is* like darkness; they do not know what makes them stumble" (Prov. 4:14, 19). Do not be ashamed of Christ. "Therefore whoever confesses Me before men, him I will also confess before My Father who is in heaven. But whoever denies Me before men, him I will also deny before My Father who is in heaven" (Matt. 10:32, 33).

16. Excuse: *"Not now."*

Answer: Every time you say no, it is more difficult to say yes. The time and day is *now.* "For He says: 'In an acceptable time I have heard you, and in the day of salvation I have helped you'" (2 Cor. 6:2).

Seek the Lord while He may be found. Delay is decision for the wrong way. "Today—if you will," says the Lord. Tomorrow is the day when the idle man works, the thief becomes honest, the drunkard sober. Tomorrow is a period nowhere to be found except, perhaps, in the fool's calendar. God's call is not a call for tomorrow, but for *today*.

Dr. Lee says of the above, "In this manner do I deal with excuse-makers. With many excuse-makers I have had success. With some, I have not."

Further Scriptures which may be used: Proverbs 27:1; 29:1, Isaiah 55:6, Hebrews 2:3.

Some other common excuses and questions are:

17. Excuse: *"I think you are making too big a fuss about this."*

Answer: Why is Calvary such a big date in history? "But God demonstrates His own love toward us, in that while we were still sinners, Christ died for us" (Rom. 5:8).

Isn't your soul important? "For what is a man profited if he gains the whole world, and loses his own soul? Or what will a man give in exchange for his soul?" (Matt. 16:26).

Isn't life uncertain? "But God said to him, '*You* fool! This night your soul will be required of you; then whose will those things be which you have provided?'" (Luke 12:20).

Death, judgment, and hell lie ahead (Gal. 6:7, Heb. 9:27).

The Son of God asks for your decision (Rev. 3:20).

18. Excuse: *"I will take my chances."*

Answer: God always has the last word. "So he said to him, 'Friend, how did you come in here without a wedding garment?' And he was speechless. Then the king said to the servants, 'Bind him hand and foot, take him away, and cast *him* into outer darkness; there will be weeping and gnashing of teeth'" (Matt. 22:12, 13).

Nebuchadnezzar gave this testimony, "That the Most High rules in the kingdom of men, gives it to whomever He will" (Dan. 4:17). "All the inhabitants of the earth *are* reputed as nothing; He does according to His will in the army of heaven and *among* the inhabitants of the earth. No one can restrain His hand or say to Him, 'What have you done?'" (Dan. 4:35).

God's Word has eternal force (Is. 55:11).

A judgment must be rendered on each life lived (John 5:27–29).

19. Excuse: *"My friends mean so much to me."*

Answer: Are they your friends or your enemies? "Adulterers and adulteresses! Do you not know that friendship with the world is enmity with God? Whoever therefore wants to be a friend of the world makes himself an enemy of God" (James 4:4).

Do your friends care for your soul? "But when he had spent all, there arose a severe famine in that land, and he began to be in want. Then he went and joined himself to a citizen of that country, and he sent him into his fields to feed swine. And he would gladly have filled his stomach with the pods that the swine ate, and no one gave him *anything*" (Luke 15:14–16).

You will gain a greater Friend and friends (John 15:15, Matt. 19:29).

Your example can lead your unsaved friends to Christ (John 1:45).

20. Excuse: *"I am going to have a good time in this world and let the next world take care of itself."*

Answer: Others have followed this course before. "Son, remember that in your lifetime you received your good things, and likewise Lazarus evil things; but now he is comforted and you are tormented" (Luke 16:25).

Your life can prove to be a *charade* (Luke 12:15).

Opportunity brings responsibility (Eccl. 11:9).

21. Excuse: *"Please do not talk to me about it."*

Answer: I am simply bringing God's message to you. "Therefore prepare yourself and arise, and speak to them all that I command you. Do not be dismayed before their faces, lest I dismay you before them" (Jer. 1:17). "And go, get to the captives, to the children of your people, and speak to them and tell them, 'Thus says the Lord GOD,' whether they hear, or whether they refuse" (Ezek. 3:11).

My business is to *witness* (2 Cor. 2:15, 16).

22. Excuse: *"I am my own boss."*

Answer: Wise men and women receive *counsel*. "There is a way which seems right to a man, but its end *is* the way of death" (Prov. 14:12).

The straight way is the best way (Matt. 7:13, 14).

The easiest thing in the world to get is *a wrong answer*.

23. Excuse: *"Frankly, I am skeptical about the whole matter."*

Answer: Are you honestly looking for *answers*? Will you accept evidence as it would be accepted before a court of law? Are you an *inquirer* or a *spiritual subversive* "who exchanged the truth of God for the lie, and worshiped and served the creature rather than the Creator" (Rom. 1:25). "And even as they did not like to retain God in *their* knowledge, God gave them over to a debased mind, to do those things which are not fitting" (Rom. 1:28).

Jesus Christ threw out this challenge: "He who is of God hears God's words; therefore you do not hear, because you are not of God" (John 8:47).

You can *doubt* to your own peril (2 Thess. 2:10, 12).

The way to find out whether or not a thing is true and worthy of one's acceptance is to put it to *a personal test* (Ps. 34:8).

24. Excuse: *"I want to be absolutely neutral about this matter."*

Answer: There are some things you can't be neutral about—food, drink, sleep, light, for instance. That is why Christ likened Himself to the *necessities* of life. "I am the bread of life" (John 6:48). "I am the light of the world. He who follows Me shall not walk in darkness, but have the light of life" (John 8:12).

Jesus said, "He who is not with Me is against Me, and he who does not gather with Me scatters abroad (Matt. 12:30).

25. Excuse: *"I believe God is too good to damn anyone."*

Answer: That is not what the Bible says. "Therefore the ungodly shall not stand in the judgment, nor sinners in the congregation of the righteous. For the LORD knows the way of the righteous, but the way of the ungodly shall perish" (Ps. 1:5, 6).

God bases your salvation or damnation on your acceptance or rejection of Jesus Christ (John 12:48).

It is not God that is hard. It is you! "But in accordance with your hardness and your impenitent heart you are treasuring up for yourself wrath in the day of wrath and revelation of the righteous judgment of God" (Rom. 2:5).

Every agency of God seeks to lead you to repentance (2 Pet. 3:9).

26. Excuse: *"How can I reconcile the doctrine of hell with the Christian's God of salvation?"*

Answer: "Then He will also say to those on the left hand, 'Depart from Me, you cursed, into the everlasting fire prepared for the devil and his angels'" (Matt. 25:41).

"Judas by transgression fell, that he might go to his own place" (Acts 1:25).

"The Lord is not slack concerning *His* promise, as some count slackness, but is longsuffering toward us, not willing that any should perish but that all should come to repentance" (2 Pet. 3:9).

"Do I have any pleasure at all that the wicked should die?" says the Lord GOD, "*and* not that he should turn from his ways and live?" (Ezek. 18:23).

"And these will go away into everlasting punishment, but the righteous into eternal life" (Matt. 25:46).

"Son, remember that in your lifetime you received your good things, and likewise Lazarus evil things; but now he is comforted and you are tormented" (Luke 16:25).

"Serpents, brood of vipers! How can you escape the condemnation of hell?" (Matt. 23:33).

"And do not fear those who kill the body but cannot kill the soul. But rather fear Him who is able to destroy both soul and body in hell" (Matt. 10:28).

"Therefore Sheol has enlarged itself and opened its mouth beyond measure; their glory and their multitude and their pomp, and he who is jubilant, shall descend into it. People shall be brought down, each man shall be humbled, and the eyes of the lofty shall be humbled. But the LORD of hosts shall be exalted in judgment, and God who is holy shall be hallowed in righteousness" (Is. 5:14–16).

27. Excuse: *"I am religious."*

Answer: Religion is often something that is on the outside. "Many will say to Me in that day, 'Lord, Lord, have we not prophesied in Your name, cast out demons in Your name, and done many wonders in Your name?' And then I will declare to them, 'I never knew you; depart from Me, you who practice lawlessness!'" (Matt. 7:22, 23).

No man was more religious than Paul (Gal. 1:14, Phil. 3:6, 1 Tim. 1:13, 15).

Cornelius was a religious man who needed to be saved (Acts 11:14).

28. Excuse: *"I am trying to be a Christian."*

Answer: It is not *trying*, it is *trusting* that counts. A drowning man tries with all his might and perishes, but when he trusts in the saving power of another he is rescued. "Behold, God *is* my salvation, I will trust and not be afraid; 'For YAH, the LORD, *is* my strength and *my* song; He also has become my salvation'" (Is. 12:2).

Ishmael was Abraham's fleshly attempt to fulfill the promise of God (he tried). Isaac was God's provision (he trusted) (Rom. 4:3, 5).

No work that you can do for yourself can ever substitute in merit for the work that Jesus has done for you on the Cross (Eph. 2:9).

"But we are all like an unclean *thing*, and all our righteousnesses *are* like filthy rags; we all fade as a leaf, and our iniquities, like the wind, have taken us away" (Is. 64:6). To try is to fail! "For whoever shall keep the whole law, and yet stumble in one *point*, he is guilty of all" (James 2:10).

29. Excuse: *"What is sin?"*

Answer: Sin is breaking God's law (1 John 3:10). All unrighteousness is sin, and there is no sin not *leading* to death (1 John 5:17).

Unbelief is sin (John 16:8, 9).

Questionable indulgences are sin (Rom. 14:23).

Missing the mark is sin (Rom. 3:23).

Undone duty is sin (James 4:17).

30. Excuse: *"My sins are small, so why worry?"*

Answer: Because any sin torments. "*There is* no peace," says the LORD, "for the wicked" (Is. 48:22).

Because any sin separates you from God (Is. 59:2).

Because any sin enslaves you (John 8:34).

Because any sin excludes from heaven (1 Cor. 6:9).

Because any sin ends in death (Rom. 6:23).

31. Excuse: *"I may be punished but not eternally."*

Answer: If God is eternal and heaven is eternal—hell will be eternal also. "Then He will also say to those on the left hand, 'Depart from Me, you cursed, into the everlasting fire prepared for the devil and his angels'" (Matt. 25:41).

There is "a resurrection of condemnation" (John 5:28, 29).

Don't forget there is the "second death" (Rev. 20:13–15).

32. Excuse: *"I am too old now to become a Christian."*

Answer: There is no age limit (2 Cor. 6:2).

God has foreseen your problem. "But from there you will seek the LORD your God, and you will find *Him* if you seek Him with all your heart and with all your soul. When you are in distress, and all these things come upon you in the latter days, when you turn to the LORD your God and obey His voice (for the LORD your God *is* a merciful God), He will not forsake you nor destroy you, nor forget the covenant of your fathers which He swore to them" (Deut. 4:29–31).

33. Excuse: *"I do not think I am old enough to make a decision."*

Answer: You have reached an age of accountability if you sense Christ's approach to your life. "Remember *now* your Creator in the days of your youth, before the difficult days come, and the years draw near when you say, 'I have no pleasure in them'" (Eccl. 12:1).

The time to make a decision is when your conscience is tender (2 Sam. 19:35).

The best time is *now* (Heb. 3:13).

34. Excuse: *"I intend to before I die."*

Answer: Can you determine the hour of your death? *Nothing is so uncertain as life* (Prov. 29:1, Job 34:20).

God warns against *presumption* (James 4:13–17).

There is no time like the present. "Seek the LORD while He may be found, call upon Him while He is near" (Is. 55:6).

35. Excuse: *"I am afraid I cannot hold out."*

Answer: Jesus not only saves but He keeps. He is the Good Shepherd (John 10:11, 14).

The same One who convicts you is concerned about you. "He who calls you *is* faithful, who also will do *it*" (1 Thess. 5:24).

Paul gives his experience. "And He said to me, My grace is sufficient for you, for My strength is made perfect in weakness. Therefore most gladly I will rather boast in my infirmities, that the power of Christ may rest upon me" (2 Cor. 12:9).

God has made an investment in you and He will work to protect that investment (Phil. 1:6).

To know Him is to have assurance. Commit your entire life to His care. Leave the future in your Master's hands (2 Tim. 1:12).

36. Excuse: *"I am afraid of persecution."*

Answer: It is a cowardly thing to deny Jesus Christ. "But the cowardly, unbelieving, abominable, murderers, sexually immoral, sorcerers, idolaters, and all liars shall have their part in the lake which burns with fire and brimstone, which is the second death" (Rev. 21:8).

"For whoever is ashamed of Me and My words in this adulterous and sinful generation, of him the Son of Man also will be ashamed when he comes in the glory of His Father with the holy angels" (Mark 8:38).

So little is asked for so much in return. "For I consider that the sufferings of this present time are not worthy *to be compared* with the glory which shall be revealed in us" (Rom. 8:18).

It is all or nothing. "If we endure, we shall also reign with *Him*, if we deny *Him*, He also will deny us" (2 Tim. 2:12).

You join a select company. It is a chance of a lifetime to do something worthwhile. "Blessed are you when men hate you, and when they exclude you, and revile *you*, and cast out your name as evil, for the Son of Man's sake. Rejoice in that day and leap for joy! For indeed your reward *is* great in heaven, for in like manner their fathers did to the prophets" (Luke 6:22, 23).

He does not ask you to do anything for Him that He did not do for you (Heb. 12:2).

37. Excuse: *"I think that Jesus Christ is only one of the great men in history."*

Answer: He claimed to be God. ". . . Who, being in the form of God, did not consider it robbery to be equal with God" (Phil. 2:6). He was put to death for this claim (Matt. 26:63–65). The resurrection substantiated this claim: "Whom God raised up, having loosed the pains of death, because it was not possible that He should be held by it" (Acts 2:24).

The moral grandeur of His life surpasses anything on record. "Which of you convicts Me of sin? And if I tell the truth, why do you not believe Me?" (John 8:46).

No one has so influenced history (Luke 2:34).

There is the repeated testimony of personal experience. "Now we believe, not because of what you said, for we have heard for ourselves and know that this is indeed the Christ, the Savior of the world" (John 4:42).

There is the open challenge to prove His divinity for yourself. "If anyone wants to do His will, he shall know concerning the doctrine, whether it is from God or *whether* I speak on My own *authority*" (John 7:17).

38. Question: *"Why does God allow evil in this world?"*

Answer: Freedom of choice is the Creator's great gift to the human race. "I call heaven and earth as witnesses today against you, *that* I have set before you life and death, blessing and cursing; therefore choose life, that both you and your descendants may live" (Deut. 30:19).

Sin originated in man, not in God. God prevents sin's dominion (Rom. 6:14).

God has, at His own cost, provided a remedy. "I am the way, the truth, and the life. No one comes to the Father except through Me" (John 14:6).

39. Excuse: *"There is so much suffering."*

Answer: This is not the world as God planned it—the world that He said was "very good" (Gen. 1:31). It is the world in which man has spread his sin. "Even as I have seen, those who plow iniquity and sow trouble reap the same" (Job 4:8).

God has provided an alternative. "For the wages of sin *is* death, but the gift of God *is* eternal life in Christ Jesus our Lord" (Rom. 6:23).

It is not the world that God intends to establish (Is. 65:20).

40. Question: *"Does this have to be done publicly?"*

Answer: God makes the rules. He has undertaken our salvation completely; therefore He has the right to say how we are to receive it. "Therefore whoever confesses Me before men, him I will also confess before My Father who is in heaven. But whoever denies Me before men, him I *will* also deny before My Father who is in heaven" (Matt. 10:32, 33). "For with the heart one believes to righteousness, and with the mouth confession is made to salvation" (Rom. 10:10).

Like a true marriage—a miracle of trust happens in the heart first; then an open acknowledgment, through proper ordinances, is made to the public.

"For whoever is ashamed of Me and My words in this adulterous and sinful generation, of him the Son of Man also will be ashamed when He comes in the glory of His Father with the holy angels" (Mark 8:38).

"Also I say to you, whoever confesses Me before men, him the Son of Man also will confess before the angels of God. But he who denies Me before men will be denied before the angels of God" (Luke 12:8, 9).

"Nevertheless even among the rulers many believed in Him, but because of the Pharisees they did not confess *Him,* lest they should be put out of the synagogue; for they loved the praise of men more than the praise of God" (John 12:42, 43).

41. Question: *What about baptism?"*

Answer: Baptism like Communion "shows the Lord's death." It is faith you show publicly when you are baptized.

"Or do you not know that as many of us as were baptized into Christ Jesus were baptized into His death? Therefore we were buried with Him through baptism into death, that just as Christ was raised from the dead by the glory of the Father, even so we also should walk in newness of life" (Rom. 6:3–5).

Baptism is our open profession before the world that we are now living a miracle, supernatural life of Christian grace by the quickening, regenerating power of God in us.

You should be baptized because like your Lord it fulfills " . . . all righteousness. . . ." It keeps setting forth the gospel of Jesus before this world. Baptism is one of the first tests of obedience.

42. Excuse: *"I cannot break with my sins."*

Answer: Salvation is a life-and-death choice. "I tell you, no; but unless you repent you will all likewise perish" (Luke 13:3).

You cannot live one way and die another way. "For he who sows to his flesh will of the flesh reap corruption, but he who sows to the Spirit will of the Spirit reap everlasting life" (Gal. 6:8, cf. Rev. 21:8).

You cannot do it in your own strength. "Therefore if the Son makes you free, you shall be free indeed" (John 8:36). "I can do all things through Christ who strengthens me" (Phil. 4:13).

Christ can reach you where you are (Heb. 7:25).

43. Excuse: *"I see no harm in worldly amusements."*

Answer: The approach to this question should always be *positive,* and not negative. Instead of asking, "What *harm* is there in it?" I should ask, "What *good* is there in it?"

"And *whatever* you do in word or deed, *do* all in the name of the Lord Jesus, giving thanks to God the Father through Him" (Col. 3:17).

"Therefore, whether you eat or drink, or whatever you do, do all to the glory of God" (1 Cor. 10:31).

"All things are lawful for me, but all things are not helpful. All things are lawful for me, but I will not be brought under the power of any" (1 Cor. 6:12).

As a Christian, I am responsible to use my body and my mind in trust for God's glory (1 Cor. 6:19, 20).

Sharp warnings appear in the New Testament: "If anyone defiles the temple of God, God will destroy him. For the temple of God is holy, which *temple* you are" (1 Cor. 3:17). "Therefore come out from among them and be separate, says the Lord. Do not touch what is unclean, and I will receive you" (2 Cor. 6:17). "They profess to know God, but in works they deny Him, being abominable, disobedient, and disqualified for every good work" (Titus 1:16).

My aim should always be to give my utmost for His highest (2 Tim. 2:4).

44. Excuse: *"I am not respectable enough to be a Christian."*

Answer: It is your saving, active faith in Christ that counts, "And he arose and came to his father. But when he was still a great way off, his father saw him and had compassion, and ran and fell on his neck and kissed him. And the son said to him, 'Father, I have sinned against heaven and in your sight, and am no longer worthy to be called your son.' But the father said to his servants, 'Bring out the best robe and put *it* on him, and put a ring on his hand and sandals on *his* feet. And bring the fatted calf here and kill *it,* and let us eat and be merry; for this my son was dead and is alive again;

he was lost and is found.' And they began to be merry" (Luke 15:20–24). See also Luke 18:10–14.

We can never make ourselves good enough. "But to him who does not work but believes on Him who justifies the ungodly, his faith is accounted for righteousness" (Rom. 4:5). See also Isaiah 41:13.

45. Excuse: *"I am afraid Jesus will not receive me."*

Answer: You have His word on it. "All that the Father gives Me will come to Me, and the one who comes to Me I will by no means cast out" (John 6:37).

God is no respector of persons (Rom. 10:13, Luke 15:2). See also Revelation 22:17.

46. Excuse: *"I have tried before and failed."*

Answer: One failure need not mean final defeat. *Upon whom did you depend?* Did you make a complete surrender? Did you keep something back? Did you confess Christ publicly? Were you faithful in prayer? Did you seek guidance from the Word? "These were more fair-minded than those in Thessalonica, in that they received the word with all readiness, and searched the Scriptures daily *to find out* whether these things were so" (Acts 17:11). Did you go to work for Christ? (Luke 11:24–26). See also First Peter 2:2.

Make a full surrender. "I beseech you therefore, brethren, by the mercies of God, that you present your bodies a living sacrifice, holy, acceptable to God, *which is* your reasonable service" (Rom. 12:1).

Keep in touch! "Watch and pray, lest you enter into temptation. The spirit indeed *is* willing, but the flesh *is* weak" (Matt. 26:41).

Be present in church (Heb. 10:25).

47. Excuse: *"I think I have committed the unpardonable sin."*

Answer: You will *know* if you have committed this sin. The desire to be a Christian will be forever past. No spiritual impression will ever again come to your soul. *A hardening process will have taken place*.

"Therefore I say to you, every sin and blasphemy will be forgiven men, but the blasphemy *against* the Spirit will not be forgiven men. Anyone who speaks a word against the Son of Man, it will be forgiven him; but whoever speaks against the Holy Spirit, it will not be forgiven him, either in this age or in the *age* to come" (Matt. 12:31, 32).

In another passage we read: "but he who blasphemes against the Holy Spirit never has forgiveness, but is subject to eternal condemnation" (Mark 3:29).

The tragedy lies in *the eternally unforgiven soul*. Since the Holy Spirit is the agent in conviction and conversion, there can be no rebirth without the Holy Spirit. To sin against the Holy Spirit is to sin against your own soul. To blaspheme against the Holy Spirit is to shut yourself off forever from access to God.

"If anyone sees his brother sinning a sin *which does* not *lead* to death, he will ask, and He will give him life for those who commit sin not *leading* to death" (1 John 5:16).

You will *know* if you cross this line. Those who have committed this sin are completely given over to Satan and have not the slightest interest in spiritual matters. Paul describes it as being "past feeling" (Eph. 4:19).

On the other hand, Satan, *the deceiver*, will lie to you and tell you that you are unpardonable. God makes no exceptions in His offer of salvation.

"And by Him everyone who believes is justified from all things from which you could not be justified by the law of Moses" (Acts 13:39).

Murder is not unpardonable. David confessed his sin and was forgiven (Ps. 32:5).

Theft is not unpardonable. The penitent thief on the cross was pardoned (Luke 23:43).

Blasphemy is not unpardonable. Paul was a blasphemer, and he was pardoned (1 Tim. 1:13).

Adultery is not unpardonable. The woman of Samaria was saved (John 4:18).

One of the amazing records of forgiveness is found in First Corinthians 6:9–11.

The person who sincerely asks for pardon will never be refused. "Let the wicked forsake his way, and the unrighteous man his thoughts; let him return to the LORD, and He will have mercy on him; and to our God, for He will abundantly pardon" (Is. 55:7).

"'Come now, and let us reason together,' says the LORD, 'though your sins are like scarlet, they shall be as white as snow; though they are red like crimson, they shall be as wool'" (Is. 1:18). See also Acts 10:43.

Paul was a great sinner, but he obtained salvation (1 Tim. 1:15, 16).

48. Question: *"Would not suicide be the best way out of my trouble?"*

Answer: There is only one solution for guilt consciousness—forgiveness and cleansing (Job 15:20, 1 John 1:9).

Self-murder only hastens judgment. "So then each of us shall give account of himself to God" (Rom. 14:12).

A correct relationship with Christ brings a new approach to living. "Therefore, if anyone *is* in Christ, *he is* a new creation; old things have passed away; behold, all things have become new" (2 Cor. 5:17).

Get the *sin-problem* settled first, and then the *trouble-problem* can be settled (Matt. 6:33).

49. Excuse: *"I am seeking but I cannot find Christ."*

Answer: Christ is not distant. His presence is noticeable, "so that they should seek the Lord, in the hope that they might grope for Him and find

Him, though He is not far from each one of us; for in Him we live and move and have our being, as also some of your own poets have said, 'For we are also His offspring'" (Acts 17:27, 28).

Paul says that Christ makes Himself real to a person through the exercise of faith (Rom. 10:6–11).

Be sure you are looking in the right direction! "And you will seek Me and find *Me*, when you search for Me with all your heart" (Jer. 29:13).

50. Excuse: *"I am ashamed to come to Christ."*

Answer: "But when Jesus heard *that*, He said to them, 'Those who are well have no need of a physician, but those who are sick. But go and learn what *this* means: *"I desire mercy and not sacrifice."* For I did not come to call the righteous, but sinners, to repentance'" (Matt. 9:12, 13).

Salvation is for the *lost*. "For when we were still without strength, in due time Christ died for the ungodly. For scarcely for a righteous man will one die; yet perhaps for a good man someone would even dare to die. But God demonstrates His own love toward us, in that while we were still sinners, Christ died for us" (Rom. 5:6–8).

51. Excuse: *"I would like to be a Christian, but I cannot forgive my enemies."*

Answer: Through God's help you can do what you cannot do otherwise. "With men this is impossible, but with God all things are possible" (Matt. 19:26).

I become a recipient of God's *grace*. "And God *is* to make all grace abound toward you, that you, always having all sufficiency in all *things*, have an abundance for every good work" (2 Cor. 9:8). See also Second Corinthians 12:9.

Tell God only that *you are willing to be made willing* (Matt. 6:14, 15).

52. Excuse: *"I want to be saved, but I cannot believe."*

Answer: *Whom* does the Bible ask you to believe? "Believe on the Lord Jesus Christ, and you will be saved, you and your household" (Acts 16:31).

Do you believe that God has saved *others*? Do you believe that He wants to save *you*? Do you believe that He *can* save you? Will you trust Him to save you *now*?

You are saved through the Word which is God's contract with you, and because God wants you to be saved (John 5:24). "But as many as received Him, to them He gave the right to become children of God, *even* to those who believe in His name: who were born, not of blood, nor of the will of the flesh, nor of the will of man, but of God" (John 1:12, 13).

Use the faith that God gives you! "For by grace you have been saved through faith, and that not of yourselves; *it is* the gift of God" (Eph. 2:8). See also Romans 5:1.

53. Question: *"Does not the Bible have inconsistencies and contradictions in it?"*

Answer: Where are they? The Bible is *revelation*. "'For My thoughts *are* not your thoughts, nor *are* your ways My ways,' says the LORD. 'For *as* the heavens are higher than the earth, so are My ways higher than your ways, and My thoughts than your thoughts" (Is. 55:8, 9).

The Bible is a *locked book* to a *locked heart*.

"Many shall be purified, made white, and refined, but the wicked shall do wickedly; and none of the wicked shall understand, but the wise shall understand" (Dan. 12:10). "But the natural man does not receive the things of the Spirit of God, for they are foolishness to him; nor can he know *them*, because they are spiritually discerned" (1 Cor. 2:14).

Certainly there are mysteries presented in God's Word! "As also in all his epistles, speaking in them of these things, in which are some things hard to understand, which those *who are* untaught and unstable twist to their own destruction, as *they do* also the rest of the Scriptures. You therefore, beloved, since you know *these things* beforehand, beware lest you also fall from your own steadfastness, being lead away with the error of the wicked; but grow in the grace and knowledge of our Lord and Savior Jesus Christ. To Him *be* the glory both now and forever. Amen" (2 Pet. 3:16–18).

Know Him and you will know His book!

54. Question: *"How can I know there is a God?"*

Answer: There are *three sources* of material. First, there is the Bible. Second, there is nature. Third, there is man. These point to the Creator. None are possible by happenstance. None could have been produced by accident.

"Because what may be known of God is manifest in them, for God has shown *it* to them" (Rom. 1:19).

"When I consider Your heavens, the work of Your fingers, the moon and the stars, which You have ordained" (Ps. 8:3).

"By the word of the LORD the heavens were made, and all the host of them by the breath of His mouth" (Ps. 33:6).

55. Question: *"Why do I need the blood?"*

Answer: "For the life of the flesh *is* in the blood, and I have given it to you upon the altar to make atonement for your souls; for it *is* the blood *that* makes atonement for the soul" (Lev. 17:11).

Jesus died for you and me (Matt. 26:28).

"And according to the law almost all things are purged with blood, and without shedding of blood there is no remission" (Heb. 9:22).

He tasted death for me. Thus He bore the supreme penalty of my sins (Rom. 5:9, 10).

It took the greatest price in the universe. "Knowing that you were not redeemed with corruptible things, *like* silver or gold, from your aimless conduct *received* by tradition from your fathers, but with the precious blood of Christ, as of a lamb without blemish and without spot" (1 Pet. 1:18, 19).

56. Question: *"Why should I accept the Bible as the final authority?"*

Answer: *The Bible has survived all unbelievers*. "For what if some did not believe? Will their unbelief make the faithfulness of God without effect? Certainly not! Indeed, let God be true but every man a liar" (Rom. 3:3, 4).

"All Scripture *is* given by inspiration of God, and *is* profitable for doctrine, for reproof, for correction, for instruction in righteousness" (2 Tim. 3:16).

God's character rests upon the authenticity and authority of the Bible (Mark 13:31).

57. Question: *"What must I do to be saved?"*

Answer: God, through Jesus Christ, His Son, has provided a way for you (Is. 53:5, 6). That sixth verse begins and ends with the same word, "all." It is a universal salvation for a universal need.

Your part is to "receive," God's part is to give you "power to become." "But as many as received Him, to them He gave the right to become children of God, *even* to those who believe in His name" (John 1:12).

Conversion and regeneration go together. When you have turned to God (conversion), He will turn over your life (regeneration). God's part is as essential as your part (John 3:7).

Saving faith reaches out and believes what God's Word says about you. "Most assuredly, I say to you, he who hears My word and believes in Him who sent Me has everlasting life, and shall not come into judgment, but has passed from death into life" (John 5:24).

Your salvation is in your acceptance of what Christ has done for you. Did He, or did He not, die for you? (Acts 16:31).

Outward form is useless until something has happened within your life. Salvation is like marriage. All the ceremony involved can't really marry a couple unless first of all something real toward each other has happened in each of their hearts. When that occurs, they want the whole world to know (Rom. 10:9–19).

God saves sinners only. Are you a sinner? Do you need two things—(1) FORGIVENESS and (2) CLEANSING?

What God has done for others, He will do for you. "For *'whoever calls upon the name of the* LORD *shall be saved'*" (Rom. 10:13).

Jesus foretold that excuses and alibis would be given. *Excuses* are never *reasons*.

"Then He said to him, 'A certain man gave a great supper and invited many, and sent his servant at supper time to say to those who were invited, 'Come, for all things are now ready.' But they all with one *accord* began to make excuses. The first said to him, 'I have bought a piece of ground, and I must go and see it. I ask you to have me excused.' And another said, 'I have bought five yoke of oxen, and I am going to test them. I ask you to have me excused.' Still another said, 'I have married a wife, and therefore I cannot come.' So that servant came and reported these things to his master. Then the master of the house, being angry, said to his servant, 'Go out quickly into the streets and lanes of the city, and bring in here *the* poor, and *the* maimed and *the* lame and *the* blind.' And the servant said, 'Master, it is done as you commanded, and still there is room.' Then the master said to the servant, 'Go out into the highways and hedges, and compel *them* to come in, that my house may be filled. For I say to you that none of those men who were invited shall taste my supper'" (Luke 14:16–24).

> Let not conscience make you linger,
> Nor of fitness fondly dream;
> All the fitness he requireth
> Is to feel your need of Him.
>
> —Joseph Hart

VI. Conversion

Steps to the Christian Life:

1. REPENT. Turn around. Change your mind. "I tell you, no; but unless you repent you will all likewise perish" (Luke 13:3).

2. RECEIVE HIM. You need the Savior. Accept Him. "But as many as received Him, to them He gave the right to become children of God, *even* to those who believe in His name" (John 1:12).

3. BE "BORN AGAIN." This is what God does for you. This is the New Birth—a miracle of spiritual life performed by the Holy Spirit. "Who were born, not of blood, nor of the will of the flesh, nor of the will of man, but of God" (John 1:13). See also John 11:25.

4. REJOICE PUBLICLY. Make your testimony for Christ, "that if you confess with your mouth the Lord Jesus and believe in your heart that God has raised Him from the dead, you will be saved. For with the heart one believes to righteousness, and with the mouth confession is made to salvation" (Rom. 10:9, 10). See also Matthew 10:32, 33.

5. REQUEST WATER BAPTISM. This is an outward testimony to an inward transaction. "He who believes and is baptized will be saved; but he who does not believe will be condemned" (Mark 16:16).

6. READ THE WORD. The Word is the source of your faith. "These things I have written to you who believe in the name of the Son of God, that you may know that you have eternal life, and that you may *continue to* believe in the name of the Son of God" (1 John 5:13). See also Romans 10:17, Psalms 119:105.

The Bible can never be the private and exclusive property of any one religion. God gave it to the world. It cannot be copyrighted. It is not man's product. Therefore, look for your eternal assurance from the Bible. *It is what God says that counts*.

7. REACH GOD IN PRAYER. Prayer is conversation with God. Life is sustained by union and communion (Eph. 6:18, James 4:2). "Now this is the confidence that we have in Him, that if we ask anything according to His will, He hears us. And if we know that He hears us, whatever we ask, we know that we have the petitions that we have asked of Him" (1 John 5:14, 15).

8. RELATE YOUR EXPERIENCE TO OTHERS. You maintain strength by exercise. "Nevertheless if you warn the wicked to turn from his way, and he does not turn from his way, he shall die in his inquity; but you have delivered your soul. Therefore you, O son of man, say to the house of Israel: 'Thus you say, "If our transgressions and our sins *lie* upon us, and we pine away in them, how can we then live?"'" (Ezek. 33:9, 10).

9. RESIST THE DEVIL. Temptation is not sin. It is yielding to temptation that is sin. "That the genuineness of your faith, *being* much more precious than gold that perishes, though it is tested by fire, may be found to praise, honor, and glory at the revelation of Jesus Christ" (1 Pet. 1:7).

"For we do not have a High Priest who cannot sympathize with our weaknesses, but was in all *points* tempted as *we are, yet* without sin" (Heb. 4:15).

10. RESTITUTION. Your guilt is gone, and you can convert your influence for good. "Then Zacchaeus stood and said to the Lord, 'Look, Lord, I give half of my goods to the poor; and if I have taken anything from anyone by false accusation, I restore fourfold'" (Luke 19:8).

"This *being* so, I myself always strive to have a conscience without offense toward God and men" (Acts 24:16).

11. "RENDER . . . TO GOD THE THINGS THAT ARE GOD'S." Start tithing your income immediately. "Will a man rob God? Yet you have robbed Me! But you say, 'In what way have we robbed You?' In tithes and offerings. Bring all the tithes into the storehouse, That there may be food in My house, And prove Me now in this," Says the LORD of hosts, "If I will not open for you the windows of heaven and pour out for you *such* blessing that *there will* not *be room* enough *to receive it*" (Mal. 3:8, 10). See also First Corinthians 16:2.

12. REGULARLY ATTEND CHURCH AND SUNDAY SCHOOL. Associate yourself immediately with God's people. Become a church member (Heb. 10:25).

"So He came to Nazareth, where He had been brought up. And as His custom was, He went into the synagogue on the Sabbath day, and stood up to read" (Luke 4:16).

"As His divine power has given to us all things that *pertain* to life and godliness, through the knowledge of Him who called us by glory and virtue" (2 Pet. 1:3).

VII. Convincement

"In Him was life, and the life was the light of men" (John 1:4).

"But that you may know that the Son of Man has power on earth to forgive sins" (Luke 5:24).

It is too late in another world. Forgiveness of sins must be received on this side (1 John 3:2).

What is this assurance? How can I know for certain?

There are second chances in health, money, championships, and education; but when a man passes from this life, he cannot return for a second chance. *Your religion must furnish your proof.* You have a right to demand it.

Calvary is ridiculous if your life can be changed and you do not know it. Something you may have and not know it, is something you can lose and never miss. ***The proof of your salvation is not by sensation. It is by Scripture.***

Certain evidences must be manifested in our lives immediately. These evidences are recorded in the Bible.

1. THERE IS AN INFALLIBLE INSIDE WITNESS. "He who believes in the Son of God has the witness in himself; he who does not believe God has made Him a liar, because he has not believed the testimony that God has given of His Son" (1 John 5:10). The preacher and the church may tell you that you are all right. But you, *yourself,* are the final judge in that matter.

Christ asked Peter about this. He said, "do you love Me more than these?" (John 21:15). There was no doubt in Peter's mind about his relationship to Jesus.

2. THERE IS A FAMILY RELATIONSHIP. "We know that we have passed from death to life, because we love the brethren" (1 John 3:14). ***You sense a different and vital relationship with God's children.*** You are at home with spiritual things. It is a tie stronger than any family background in this world (Gal. 6:10).

3. THERE IS A NEW IMAGE. "Therefore, if anyone *is* in Christ, ***he is*** a new creation; old things have passed away; behold, all things have become new" (2 Cor. 5:17). A New Testament Christian is not a patched-up job, a reformed sinner. There is a new will; there are new affections; there is a new purpose because there is a new nature.

The emptiest and unhappiest occupation in the world is trying to act like a Christian when you are not a Christian. You do not gradually stop stealing. You stop stealing. It is miracle, not magic.

4. THERE IS A RESPONSE OF VICTORY. "For whatever is born of God overcomes the world. And this is the victory that has overcome the world—our faith." (1 John 5:4). See also John 17:15, 16. ***The born-again man or woman is not motivated by this world-system.***

Fancy yourself on the farm. It is hot midsummer. Nearby is a big mud wallow. Here comes a pig. He grunts with contentment as he wades into the slime. You say, "Mr. Hog, why do you want to submerge in that filth? Why do you not seek a cleaner environment?" That pig has not the slightest interest in your ideas for his betterment. He loves the mud.

Now watch a sheep with long white wool. The moment a sheep notices mud it heads toward safer ground. The sheep has a different nature. So has a New Testament Christian.

These are Bible proofs. "These things I have written to you who believe in the name of the Son of God, that you may know that you have eternal life, and that you may *continue to* believe in the name of the Son of God" (1 John 5:13).

Paul testified on two continents (2 Tim. 3:11).

VIII. Camouflage

Today is a day of *substitutes*. Nylon has been substituted for silk. Oleomargarine has been substituted for butter. There also are many substitutes offered for salvation. Beware.

1. SERVICE IS NOT SALVATION. "Woe to you, scribes and Pharisees, hypocrites! For you travel land and sea to win one proselyte, and when he is won, you make him twice as much a son of hell as yourselves" (Matt. 23:15). How can you lead others to Christ when you do not know Christ yourself?

2. TURNING OVER A NEW LEAF IS NOT SALVATION. Man does not get saved by *reforming*, saying, "I will clean up my life, and begin life anew."

"But we are all like an unclean *thing*, And all our righteousnesses *are* like filthy rags; We all fade as a leaf, And our iniquities, like the wind, Have taken us away" (Is. 64:6). "How you turned to God from idols to serve the living and true God" (1 Thess. 1:9). *Notice the direction!* They did not turn from idols to God. The new birth is a divine miracle.

3. ASSERTING ONE'S MANHOOD IS NOT SALVATION. Men "dead in trespasses and sins" (Eph. 2:1) cannot throw back their shoulders and assert their manhood for righteousness. The cross of Christ does not call upon men to assert their manhood. ***The cross of Christ exposes men's degradation.*** That is part of the "offense of the cross" (Gal. 5:11). It does not appeal to man's pride. It unsparingly shows man that he cannot do anything for himself. He has no righteousness or decency to offer to God.

4. RIGHT THINKING IS NOT SALVATION. It is not cultivating and concentrating on a "divine spark" that is within you. "Behold, I was brought forth in iniquity, And in sin my mother conceived me" (Ps. 51:5). It is not keeping a picture of your mother, sweetheart, or your wife in your billfold, and looking at it frequently. ***It is not thinking high thoughts*** (Is. 55:8, 9). ***How can you think high thoughts with a base nature?***

5. DENYING THE EXISTENCE OF SIN IS NOT SALVATION. God does not deny sin. ***Calvary is God's recognition of sin.*** "And the LORD has laid on Him the iniquity of us all" (Is. 53:6). "But the Scripture has confined all under sin" (Gal. 3:22). One of the first steps toward salvation is to recognize your sin—not deny it.

6. TO DENY SELF IS NOT SALVATION. The heathen are masters at this. They practice all kinds of asceticism (1 Cor. 13:3). ***You are not saved by crucifying yourself.*** It is not proving to yourself that you can do hard things.

7. SACRIFICE IS NOT SALVATION. Dying for a great cause—the supreme sacrifice—is not salvation. ***Discipline does not cleanse a man from sin.*** If that were true, then everybody who entered a penitentiary would become a Christian. Paying for wrongdoing does not make a person a Christian (1 Sam. 15:22).

There is no *side door* into heaven. Jesus said, "I am the door. If anyone enters by Me, he will be saved" (John 10:9).

"He who does not enter the sheepfold by the door, but climbs up some other way, the same is a thief and a robber" (John 10:1). You cannot steal your way into heaven.

IX. Christ

The Master has not asked us to do what He did not do constantly during His ministry upon earth. He says, "Follow Me, and I will make you fishers of men" (Matt. 4:19).

His record is one of personal contact from when He said to Andrew, "Come and see" to His assurance to the penitent thief, "Today you will be with Me in Paradise."

He is clear and concise about God's plan of salvation.

1. He came to meet a human need. "I have not come to call ***the*** righteous, but sinners . . ." (Luke 5:32). Salvation is for sinners only.

2. He came to be the sinner's substitute. "The good shepherd gives His life for the sheep" (John 10:11).

3. He came to do what none other can do. "I am the way, the truth, and the life. No one comes to the Father except through Me" (John 14:6).

4. He came to provide assurance to the trusting sinner. "Your sins are forgiven . . . go in peace" (Luke 7:48–50).

James remembers emphatically the passion that his brother manifested toward the lost. He reflects this when he says, "let him know that he who turns a sinner from the error of his way will save a soul from death and cover a multitude of sins" (James 5:20).

X. *Condensation*

The story of salvation can be told in four words:

Sin
Calvary
Faith
Life

1. Salvation is needed. "For all have sinned and fall short of the glory of God" (Rom. 3:23).

2. Salvation is provided. "Who Himself bore our sins in His own body on the tree, that we, having died to sins, might live for righteousness—by whose stripes you were healed" (1 Pet. 2:24).

3. Salvation is offered. "For by grace you have been saved through faith, and that not of yourselves; *it is* the gift of God" (Eph. 2:8).

4. Salvation accepted. "He who has the Son has life; he who does not have the Son of God does not have life" (1 John 5:12).

There is a time, we know not when,
A place, we know not where;
Which marks the destiny of men
To glory or despair.

There is a line, by us unseen,
Which crosses every path,
Which marks the boundary between
God's mercy and his wrath.

To pass that limit is to die,
To die as if by stealth;
It does not dim the beaming eye,
Nor pale the glow of health.

The conscience may be still at ease,
The spirit light and gay;
And that which pleases still may please,
And care be thrust away.

But on that forehead God hath set
Indelibly a mark;
Unseen by man, for man as yet,
Is blind and in the dark.

He feels perchance that all is well
And every fear is calmed;
He lives, he dies, he walks in hell,
Not only doomed, but damned!

O, Where is that mysterious line
That may by men be crossed,
Beyond which God himself hath sworn,
That he who goes is lost?

An answer from the skies repeats,
"Ye who from God depart."
TODAY, O hear His voice,
TODAY repent and harden not your heart.

—Joseph Addison Alexander

CONCORDANCE

— A —

ABASED
himself will be *a*............ Matt 23:12
I know how to be *a*.........Phil 4:12

ABBA
And He said, "*A*............ Mark 14:36
whom we cry out, "*A*...... Rom 8:15
crying out, "*A*............... Gal 4:6

ABHOR
A what is evil.................Rom 12:9

ABIDE
Lord, who may *a*........... Ps 15:1
the Most High Shall *a*.......Ps 91:1
Him, "If you *a*.............. John 8:31
And a slave does not *a*.... John 8:35
Helper, that He may *a*......John 14:16
"*A* in Me....................... John 15:4
"If you *a* in Me.............. John 15:7
a in My love.................... John 15:9
And now *a* faith............. 1 Co 13:13
does the love of God *a*.... 1 Jn 3:17
this we know that we *a*.... 1 Jn 4:13

ABIDES
He who *a* in Me............. John 15:5
lives and *a* forever.......... 1 Pe 1:23
will of God *a* forever........1 Jn 2:17

ABIDING
do not have His word *a*... John 5:38
has eternal life *a*............ 1 Jn 3:15

ABILITY
and beyond their *a*..........2 Co 8:3

ABLE
shall give as he is *a*........ Deut 16:17
"The LORD is *a*................ 2 Ch 25:9
God whom we serve is *a*.. Dan 3:17
God is *a* to raise up........ Matt 3:9
believe that I am *a*..........Matt 9:28
fear Him who is *a*........... Matt 10:28
Are you *a* to drink the.... Matt 20:22
beyond what you are *a*.... 1 Co 10:13
And God is *a* to make......2 Co 9:8
may be *a* to comprehend.. Eph 3:18
persuaded that He is *a*.....2 Ti 1:12
learning and never *a*.......2 Ti 3:7
being tempted, He is *a*.... Heb 2:18
that God was *a* to............ Heb 11:19
to Him who is *a*.............. Jude 24
has come, and who is *a*....Rev 6:17

ABOLISHED
your works may be *a*....... Ezek 6:6
having *a* in His flesh........Eph 2:15
Christ, who has *a*............2 Ti 1:10

ABOMINATION
yes, seven are an *a*...........Prov 6:16
wickedness is an *a*...........Prov 8:7
false balance is an *a*........ Prov 11:1
An unjust man is an *a*..... Prov 29:27
and place there the *a*....... Dan 11:31
the *a* of desolation.......... Dan 12:11
when you see the '*a*......... Matt 24:15

ABOMINATIONS
to follow the *a*................Deut 18:9
you will see greater *a*...... Ezek 8:6
a golden cup full of *a*...... Rev 17:4
Harlots and of the *A*....... Rev 17:5

ABOUND
lawlessness will *a*........... Matt 24:12
the offense might *a*......... Rom 5:20
sin that grace may *a*......... Rom 6:1
thanksgiving to *a*............2 Co 4:15
to make all grace *a*......... 2 Co 9:8
and I know how to *a*....... Phil 4:12
things are yours and *a*..... 2 Pe 1:8

ABOUNDED
But where sin *a*.............. Rom 5:20

ABOUNDING
immovable, always *a*........1 Co 15:58

ABOVE
that is in heaven *a*.......... Ex 20:4
"He who comes from *a*.... John 3:31
I am from *a*.................... John 8:23
the name which is *a*........ Phil 2:9
things which are *a*........... Col 3:1
perfect gift is from *a*........Jas 1:17

ABSENT
For I indeed, as *a*........... 1 Co 5:3
in the body we are *a*....... 2 Co 5:6

ABSTAIN
we write to them to *a*...... Acts 15:20
A from every form.......... 1 Th 5:22
and commanding to *a*...... 1 Ti 4:3
and pilgrims, *a*............... 1 Pe 2:11

ABUNDANCE
is the sound of *a*............. 1 Ki 18:41
For out of the *a*..............Matt 12:34
put in out of their *a*....... Mark 12:44
not consist in the *a*..........Luke 12:15
above measure by the *a*... 2 Co 12:7

ABUNDANT
slow to anger and *a*..........Jon 4:2
a mercy has begotten.......1 Pe 1:3

ABUNDANTLY
a satisfied with the.......... Ps 36:8
may have it more *a*......... John 10:10
to do exceedingly *a*......... Eph 3:20
to show more *a* to the..... Heb 6:17

ACCEPTABLE
sought to find *a*.............. Eccl 12:10
a time I have heard.......... Is 49:8
preach the a year........... Luke 4:19
is that good and *a*............ Rom 12:2
proving what is *a*............. Eph 5:10
For this is good and *a*...... 1 Ti 2:3
spiritual sacrifices *a*........ 1 Pe 2:5

ACCEPTED
"Behold, now is the *a*.......2 Co 6:2
which He has made us *a*.. Eph 1:6

ACCESS
whom also we have *a*...... Rom 5:2
we have boldness and *a*... Eph 3:12

ACCOMPLISHED
today the LORD has *a*....... 1 Sa 11:13
A desire *a* is sweet to...... Prov 13:19
all things were now *a*.......John 19:28

ACCORD
and Israel with one *a*.......Josh 9:2
serve Him with one *a*....... Zeph 3:9
continued with one *a*....... Acts 1:14
daily with one *a*..............Acts 2:46
a has Christ with.............2 Co 6:15
love, being of one *a*......... Phil 2:2

ACCOUNT
they will give *a*............... Matt 12:36
The former *a* I made........ Acts 1:1
of us shall give *a*............. Rom 14:12
put that on my *a*............. Phm 18
those who must give *a*...... Heb 13:17

ACCOUNTED
his faith is *a*................... Rom 4:5
a as sheep for the...........Rom 8:36
God, and it was a........... Gal 3:6
God, and it was a........... Jas 2:23

ACCURSED
he who is hanged is *a*........ Deut 21:23
regarding the *a*.................Josh 7:1
not know the law is *a*...... John 7:49
that I myself were *a*......... Rom 9:3
of God calls Jesus *a*......... 1 Co 12:3
to you, let him be *a*......... Gal 1:8

ACCUSATION
over His head the *a*..........Matt 27:37
they might find an *a*........ Luke 6:7
Do not receive an *a*......... 1 Ti 5:19
not bring a reviling *a*.......2 Pe 2:11

ACCUSE
anyone or *a* falsely.......... Luke 3:14
they began to *a* Him........ Luke 23:2
think that I shall *a*.......... John 5:45

ACCUSED
while He was being *a*....... Matt 27:12

ACCUSER
have come, for the *a*........ Rev 12:10

ACKNOWLEDGE
a my transgressions......... Ps 51:3
in all your ways *a*........... Prov 3:6

ACKNOWLEDGED
of Israel, and God *a*......... Ex 2:25
a my sin to You............... Ps 32:5

ACQUAINTED
lying down, And are *a*..... Ps 139:3
a man of sorrows and *a*... Is 53:3

ACQUIT
at all *a* the wicked.......... Nah 1:3

ACTS
LORD, the righteous *a*.......Judg 5:11
to Moses, His *a*.............. Ps 103:7
declare Your mighty *a*...... Ps 145:4

ADD
"You shall not *a*............... Deut 4:2
Do not *a* to His words..... Prov 30:6

ADDED
things shall be *a*.............. Matt 6:33
And the Lord *a* to the...... Acts 2:47
It was *a* because of.......... Gal 3:19

ADMONISH
also to *a* one another....... Rom 15:14
a him as a brother........... 2 Th 3:15

ADMONITION
were written for our *a*...... 1 Co 10:11
in the training and *a*........ Eph 6:4

ADOPTION
the Spirit of *a*................. Rom 8:15
waiting for the *a*.............. Rom 8:23
we might receive the *a*......Gal 4:5
a as sons by Jesus........... Eph 1:5

ADORN
also, that the women *a*.... 1 Ti 2:9

ADORNED
temple, how it was *a*....... Luke 21:5
God also *a* themselves....... 1 Pe 3:5
prepared as a bride *a*.......Rev 21:2

ADULTERERS
nor idolaters, nor *a*......... 1 Co 6:9

a God will judge............Heb 13:4
A and adulteresses.........Jas 4:4

ADULTEROUS
a generation..................Matt 12:39

ADULTERY
You shall not commit *a*....Ex 20:14
already committed *a*........Matt 5:28
is divorced commits *a*......Matt 5:32
another commits *a*...........Mark 10:11
a woman caught in *a*........John 8:3

ADVANTAGE
"For what *a* is it to.........Luke 9:25
Satan should take *a*.........2 Co 2:11
no one should take *a*.......1 Th 4:6

ADVERSARIES
The *a* of the LORD..........1 Sa 2:10
terrified by your *a*..........Phil 1:28
will devour the *a*............Heb 10:27

ADVERSARY
"Agree with your *a*.........Matt 5:25
opportunity to the *a*........1 Ti 5:14
a the devil walks............1 Pe 5:8

ADVERSITY
brother is born for *a*........Prov 17:17
you the bread of *a*..........Is 30:20

ADVOCATE
sins, we have an *A*..........1 Jn 2:1

AFAR
and worship from *a*.........Ex 24:1
sons shall come from *a*....Is 60:4
And not a God *a*.............Jer 23:23
and saw Abraham *a*.........Luke 16:23
to all who are *a*..............Acts 2:39
to you who were *a*..........Eph 2:17

AFFAIRS
He will guide his *a*..........Ps 112:5
I may hear of your *a*.......Phil 1:27
himself with the *a*...........2 Ti 2:4

AFFECTION
to his wife the *a*.............1 Co 7:3
for you all with the *a*.......Phil 1:8
the Spirit, if any *a*..........Phil 2:1

AFFECTIONATE
Be kindly *a* to one..........Rom 12:10

AFFLICTED
"Why have You *a*...........Num 11:11
and the Almighty has *a*....Ruth 1:21
To him who is *a*.............Job 6:14
hears the cry of the *a*......Job 34:28
How You *a* the peoples...Ps 44:2
a I went astray..............Ps 119:67
smitten by God, and *a*.....Is 53:4
oppressed and He was *a*...Is 53:7
she has relieved the *a*......1 Ti 5:10
being destitute, *a*............Heb 11:37

AFFLICTION
is, the bread of *a*...........Deut 16:3
is my comfort in my *a*.....Ps 119:50
a He was afflicted..........Is 63:9
refuge in the day of *a*......Jer 16:19
For our light *a*...............2 Co 4:17
supposing to add *a*..........Phil 1:16
the word in much *a*.........1 Th 1:6

AFRAID
garden, and I was *a*........Gen 3:10
saying, "Do not be *a*......Gen 15:1
his face, for he was *a*......Ex 3:6
I will not be *a*.................Ps 3:6
Whenever I am *a*.............Ps 56:3
a conspiracy, nor be *a*.....Is 8:12
one will make them *a*......Is 17:2
that you should be *a*........Is 51:12
do not be *a*.....................Matt 14:27
if you do evil, be *a*.........Rom 13:4
do good and are not *a*.....1 Pe 3:6

AFTERWARD
A he will let you go........Ex 11:1
a we will speak..............Job 18:2
a receive me to glory.......Ps 73:24
you shall follow Me *a*......John 13:36
the firstfruits, *a*..............1 Co 15:23

AGAIN
day He will rise *a*...........Matt 20:19
'You must be born *a*.......John 3:7
to renew them *a*.............Heb 6:6
having been born *a*.........1 Pe 1:23

AGAINST
his hand shall be *a*..........Gen 16:12
'I will set My face *a*........Lev 20:3
come to '*set a man a*.......Matt 10:35
or house divided *a*..........Matt 12:25
Me is *a* Me.....................Matt 12:30
a the Spirit will not.........Matt 12:31
For nation will rise *a*.......Matt 24:7
I have sinned *a*...............Luke 15:18
lifted up his heel a..........John 13:18
LORD and a His Christ....Acts 4:26
to kick *a* the goads..........Acts 9:5
let us not fight *a*.............Acts 23:9
a the promises of God.....Gal 3:21
we do not wrestle *a*.........Eph 6:12
I have a few things *a*.......Rev 2:20

AGE
the grave at a full *a*.........Job 5:26
and in the *a* to come........Mark 10:30
who are of full *a*.............Heb 5:14
the powers of the *a*.........Heb 6:5

AGES
ordained before the *a*......1 Co 2:7
a was not made known....Eph 3:5
at the end of the *a*..........Heb 9:26

AGONY
And being in *a*...............Luke 22:44

AGREE
that if two of you *a*.........Matt 18:19
and these three *a*............1 Jn 5:8

AGREED
unless they are *a*.............Amos 3:3

AGREEMENT
what *a* has the temple......2 Co 6:16

AIR
of the *a* have nests..........Luke 9:58
as one who beats the *a*....1 Co 9:26
be speaking into the *a*.....1 Co 14:9
of the power of the *a*......Eph 2:2
meet the Lord in the *a*....1 Th 4:17

ALIENATED
a herself from them.........Ezek 23:17
darkened, being *a*...........Eph 4:18
you, who once were *a*......Col 1:21

ALIENS
For we are *a* and............1 Ch 29:15
For I have loved *a*..........Jer 2:25
Christ, being *a*...............Eph 2:12

ALIVE
in the ark remained *a*......Gen 7:23
with them went down *a*....Num 16:33
I kill and I make *a*..........Deut 32:39
Let them go down *a*........Ps 55:15
heard that He was *a*........Mark 16:11
son was dead and is *a*......Luke 15:24
presented Himself *a*.........Acts 1:3
indeed to sin, but *a*.........Rom 6:11
I was *a* once without.......Rom 7:9
all shall be made *a*..........1 Co 15:22
trespasses, made us *a*.......Eph 2:5
flesh, He has made *a*.......Col 2:13
that we who are *a*............1 Th 4:15
the flesh but made *a*........1 Pe 3:18
and behold, I am *a*..........Rev 1:18
These two were cast *a*.....Rev 19:20

ALLOW
a Your Holy One.............Acts 2:27
who will not *a*.................1 Co 10:13

ALMOST
for me, my feet had *a*......Ps 73:2
a persuade me to............Acts 26:28

ALPHA
"I am the *A* and the.......Rev 1:8
"I am the *A* and the.......Rev 22:13

ALTAR
Then Noah built an *a*......Gen 8:20
it to you upon the *a*........Lev 17:11
"Go up, erect an *a*..........2 Sa 24:18
day there will be an *a*......Is 19:19
Lord has spurned His *a*....Lam 2:7
you cover the *a*...............Mal 2:13
your gift to the *a*............Matt 5:23
the offerings of the *a*.......1 Co 9:13
partakers of the *a*............1 Co 10:18
which had the golden *a*....Heb 9:4
We have an *a* from..........Heb 13:10
Isaac his son on the *a*......Jas 2:21
and stood at the *a*...........Rev 8:3

ALTARS
a Hezekiah has taken.......2 Ki 18:22
Even Your *a*, O LORD.....Ps 84:3
on the horns of your *a*.....Jer 17:1
and torn down Your a.....Rom 11:3

ALWAYS
delight, rejoicing *a*..........Prov 8:30
the poor with you *a*.........Matt 26:11
lo, I am with you *a*.........Matt 28:20
Rejoice in the Lord *a*......Phil 4:4
thus we shall *a*...............1 Th 4:17
a be ready to give a........1 Pe 3:15

AM
to Moses, "I *A* WHO I...Ex 3:14
First and I *a* the Last.....Is 44:6
in My name, I *a*.............Matt 18:20
a the bread of life...........John 6:35
a the light of the.............John 8:12
I *a* from above.................John 8:23
Abraham was, I *A*..........John 8:58
"I *a* the door...................John 10:9
a the good shepherd........John 10:11
a the resurrection............John 11:25
to him, "I *a* the way.......John 14:6
of God I *a* what I *a*........1 Co 15:10
a, for I *a* as you are........Gal 4:12

ANGEL
Now the *A* of the LORD...Gen 16:7
"Behold, I send an *A*......Ex 23:20
the donkey saw the *A*......Num 22:23
standing before the *A*......Zech 3:3
like God, like the *A*.........Zech 12:8
things, behold, an *a*.........Matt 1:20
for an *a* of the Lord.......Matt 28:2
Then an *a* of the Lord.....Luke 1:11
And behold, an *a*............Luke 2:9
a appeared to Him from..Luke 22:43
For an *a* went down at....John 5:4
But at night an *a*............Acts 5:19
A who appeared to him...Acts 7:35
and no *a* or spirit............Acts 23:8
a has spoken to him........Acts 23:9
by me this night an *a*.......Acts 27:23
himself into an *a*.............2 Co 11:14
Then I saw a strong *a*......Rev 5:2

ANGELS
if He charges His *a*.........Job 4:18
lower than the *a*.............Ps 8:5
give His a charge............Matt 4:6
but are like *a*..................Matt 22:30
no, not even the *a*...........Matt 24:36
and all the holy *a*............Matt 25:31
twelve legions of *a*..........Matt 26:53
the presence of the *a*.......Luke 15:10
And she saw two *a*..........John 20:12

took them up in His *a*..... Mark 10:16
took Him up in his *a*....... Luke 2:28

AROMA
smelled a soothing *a*........ Gen 8:21
the one we are the *a*....... 2 Co 2:16
for a sweet-smelling *a*...... Eph 5:2
a sweet-smelling *a*.......... Phil 4:18

ARROW
deliverance and the *a*.......2 Ki 13:17
a cannot make him flee....Job 41:28
make ready their *a*.......... Ps 11:2
a that flies by day.......... Ps 91:5
Their tongue is an *a*........ Jer 9:8

ARROWS
a pierce me deeply............Ps 38:2
There He broke the *a*.........Ps 76:3
He has caused the *a*........ Lam 3:13

ASCEND
Who may *a* into the.......... Ps 24:3
If I *a* into heaven............Ps 139:8
'I will *a* into heaven........ Is 14:13
see the Son of Man *a*...... John 6:62

ASCENDED
Who has *a* into heaven.... Prov 30:4
"No one has *a*...............John 3:13
"*When He a on high*....... Eph 4:8
And they *a* to heaven...... Rev 11:12

ASCENDING
angels of God were *a*...... Gen 28:12
the angels of God *a*.........John 1:51

ASCRIBE
a greatness to our God.... Deut 32:3
a righteousness............... Job 36:3
A strength to God............Ps 68:34

ASHAMED
all my enemies be *a*........ Ps 6:10
Let me not be *a*.............. Ps 25:2
forsake You shall be *a*.....Jer 17:13
For whoever is *a*..............Mark 8:38
am not *a* of the gospel.....Rom 1:16
nothing I shall be *a*.......... Phil 1:20
Therefore God is not *a*.... Heb 11:16
in Christ may be *a*.......... 1 Pe 3:16
let him not be *a*..............1 Pe 4:16
and not be *a* before.........1 Jn 2:28

ASHES
become like dust and *a*.... Job 30:19
sackcloth and sat in *a*...... Jon 3:6
in sackcloth and *a*.......... Luke 10:13

ASIDE
of you lay something *a*......1 Co 16:2
lay *a* all filthiness..............Jas 1:21
Therefore, laying *a*..........1 Pe 2:1

ASK
when your children *a*.......Josh 4:6
A a sign for yourself..........Is 7:11
things, whatever you *a*...... Matt 21:22
a, and it will be.................Luke 11:9
that whatever You *a*.........John 11:22
a anything in My name.... John 14:14
in that day you will *a*...... John 16:23
something, let them *a*...... 1 Co 14:35
above all that we *a*...........Eph 3:20
wisdom, let him *a*........... Jas 1:5
But let him *a* in faith.......Jas 1:6
because you do not *a*........Jas 4:2
us, whatever we *a*........... 1 Jn 5:15

ASKS
For everyone who *a*........ Matt 7:8
you who, if his son *a*........Matt 7:9
Or if he *a* for a fish........ Luke 11:11

ASLEEP
down, and was fast *a*........Jon 1:5
But He was *a*.................Matt 8:24
but some have fallen *a*.....1 Co 15:6
those who are *a*..............1 Th 4:15
the fathers fell *a*............. 2 Pe 3:4

ASSEMBLING
not forsaking the *a*.........Heb 10:25

ASSEMBLY
praise Him in the *a*......... Ps 107:32
to the general *a*.............. Heb 12:23

ASSURANCE
night, and have no *a*....... Deut 28:66
riches of the full *a*...........Col 2:2
Spirit and in much *a*.........1 Th 1:5
to the full *a* of hope..........Heb 6:11
a true heart in full *a*.........Heb 10:22

ASTONISHED
Just as many were *a*......... Is 52:14
that the people were *a*......Matt 7:28
who heard Him were *a*..... Luke 2:47

ASTRAY
and one of them goes *a*... Matt 18:12
'*They always go a*........... Heb 3:10
like sheep going *a*........... 1 Pe 2:25

ATONEMENT
a year he shall make *a*......Ex 30:10
priest shall make *a*......... Lev 16:30
the blood that makes *a*.... Lev 17:11
for it is the Day of *A*...... Lev 23:28
what shall I make *a*.........2 Sa 21:3
offerings to make *a*......... Neh 10:33
a is provided for............. Prov 16:6
I provide you an *a*.......... Ezek 16:63

ATTAIN
It is high, I cannot *a*....... Ps 139:6
by any means, I may *a*.... Phil 3:11

ATTENTION
My son, give *a* to my...... Prov 4:20
Till I come, give *a*......... 1 Ti 4:13

AUTHOR
For God is not the *a*....... 1 Co 14:33
He became the *a*.............Heb 5:9
unto Jesus, the *a*.............Heb 12:2

AUTHORITIES
a that exist are............... Rom 13:1
of God, angels and *a*........1 Pe 3:22

AUTHORITY
the righteous are in *a*...... Prov 29:2
them as one having *a*........Matt 7:29
All *a* has been given.........Matt 28:18
a I will give You..............Luke 4:6
and has given Him *a*........ John 5:27
You have given Him *a*.....John 17:2
has put in His own *a*....... Acts 1:7
For there is no *a*..............Rom 13:1
to have a symbol of *a*....... 1 Co 11:10
and all who are in *a*.........1 Ti 2:2
and rebuke with all *a*.......Tit 2:15
the flesh, reject *a*.............Jude 8

AVAILS
nor uncircumcision *a*........Gal 5:6
of a righteous man *a*....... Jas 5:16

AVENGE
for He will *a* the............Deut 32:43
A me of my adversary..... Luke 18:3
Beloved, do not *a*.......... Rom 12:19
a our blood on those....... Rev 6:10

AVENGER
'The *a* of blood............. Num 35:19
the enemy and the *a*.........Ps 8:2
God's minister, an *a*........Rom 13:4
the Lord is the *a*............1 Th 4:6

AWAKE
be satisfied when I *a*........ Ps 17:15
A, lute and harp............ Ps 108:2
My eyes are *a* through..... Ps 119:148
but my heart is *a*............ Song 5:2
of the earth shall *a*.........Dan 12:2
it is high time to *a*......... Rom 13:11
A to righteousness........... 1 Co 15:34
"*A*, you who sleep.......... Eph 5:14

AWAY
the wind drives *a*...............Ps 1:4
Do not cast me *a*............Ps 51:11
a time to cast *a* stones..... Eccl 3:5
and earth will pass *a*........Matt 24:35
of God who takes *a*.........John 1:29
they cried out, "*A*.........John 19:15
"They have taken *a*.........John 20:2
crying out, "*A*.................. Acts 21:36
the veil is taken *a*........... 2 Co 3:14
unless the falling *a*.......... 2 Th 2:3
heard, lest we drift *a*....... Heb 2:1
if they fall *a*.................. Heb 6:6
which can never take *a*.... Heb 10:11
that does not fade *a*....... 1 Pe 5:4
the world is passing *a*...... 1 Jn 2:17
if anyone takes *a*............. Rev 22:19

AWESOME
a thing that I will do....... Ex 34:10
God, the great and *a*....... Deut 7:21
God, mighty and *a*.......... Deut 10:17
Angel of God, very *a*...... Judg 13:6
a deeds for Your land.......2 Sa 7:23
heaven, O great and *a*.....Neh 1:5
hand shall teach You *a*.... Ps 45:4
By *a* deeds in................... Ps 65:5
a are Your works............. Ps 66:3
O God, You are more *a*.. Ps 68:35
He is *a* to the kings..........Ps 76:12
Your great and *a* name.... Ps 99:3
of the might of Your *a*..... Ps 145:6
When You did *a* things.... Is 64:3
with me as a mighty, *a*.... Jer 20:11
"O Lord, great and *a*....... Dan 9:4

AX
And even now the *a*.......Matt 3:10

— B —

BABBLINGS
the profane and vain *b*.....1 Ti 6:20

BABE
You will find a *B*............Luke 2:12
for he is a *b*...................Heb 5:13

BABES
b shall rule over them.......Is 3:4
revealed them to *b*.......... Matt 11:25
Out of the mouth of b..... Matt 21:16
as to carnal, as to *b*........ 1 Co 3:1
as newborn *b*................. 1 Pe 2:2

BACK
but a rod is for the *b*.......Prov 10:13
for the fool's *b*.................Prov 26:3
I gave My *b* to those.......Is 50:6
plow, and looking *b*........ Luke 9:62
someone turns him *b*........Jas 5:19

BACKSLIDINGS
b will reprove you............Jer 2:19
and I will heal your *b*.......Jer 3:22
b have increased..............Jer 5:6
for our *b* are many...........Jer 14:7

BALM
Is there no *b* in.............. Jer 8:22

BANQUETING
He brought me to the *b*... Song 2:4

BAPTISM
coming to his *b*...............Matt 3:7
b that I am baptized........Matt 20:22
"The *b* of John.................Matt 21:25
"But I have a *b*.............Luke 12:50
said, "Into John's *b*..........Acts 19:3
with Him through *b*..........Rom 6:4
Lord, one faith, one *b*..... Eph 4:5
buried with Him in *b*.......Col 2:12
now saves us, namely *b*....1 Pe 3:21

BAPTISMS
of the doctrine of *b*.........Heb 6:2

BAPTIZE
"I indeed *b* you with....... Matt 3:11
"Why then do you *b*....... John 1:25
Himself did not *b*..........John 4:2
did not send me to *b*....... 1 Co 1:17

BAPTIZED
"I have need to be *b*....... Matt 3:14
b will be saved.............. Mark 16:16
b more disciples.............John 4:1
every one of you be *b*..... Acts 2:38
all his family were *b*......... Acts 16:33
believed and were *b*........ Acts 18:8
Arise and be *b*.............. Acts 22:16
were *b* into Christ........... Rom 6:3
I thank God that I *b*....... 1 Co 1:14
all were *b* into Moses...... 1 Co 10:2
Spirit we were all *b*......... 1 Co 12:13
who are *b* for the dead.... 1 Co 15:29
of you as were *b*............ Gal 3:27

BAPTIZING
b them in the name of..... Matt 28:19
therefore I came *b*.......... John 1:31

BARNS
b will be filled............... Prov 3:10
b are broken down............ Joel 1:17
reap nor gather into *b*..... Matt 6:26
I will pull down my *b*...... Luke 12:18

BARREN
But Sarai was *b*............. Gen 11:30
b has borne seven........... 1 Sa 2:5
He grants the *b*............. Ps 113:9
"Sing, O *b*...................... Is 54:1
'Blessed are the *b*........... Luke 23:29
"*Rejoice, O b*................. Gal 4:27
you will be neither *b*....... 2 Pe 1:8

BASKET
and put it under a *b*....... Matt 5:15
I was let down in a *b*...... 2 Co 11:33

BASKETS
they took up twelve *b*...... Matt 14:20
up seven large *b*............. Matt 15:37

BATHED
My sword shall be *b*........ Is 34:5
to him, "He who is *b*....... John 13:10

BATTLE
b is the LORD's................1 Sa 17:47
strength for the *b*............Ps 18:39
for the day of *b*..............Prov 21:31
the *b* to the strong.......... Eccl 9:11
A sound of *b* is in the...... Jer 50:22
prepare himself for *b*....... 1 Co 14:8
became valiant in *b*......... Heb 11:34
gather them to the *b*....... Rev 16:14

BEAR
They shall *b* you up in..... Ps 91:12
b their iniquities............ Is 53:11
He shall *b* the glory........ Zech 6:13
child, and b a Son........... Matt 1:23
A good tree cannot *b*....... Matt 7:18
How long shall I *b*........... Matt 17:17
And whoever does not *b*.. Luke 14:27
in Me that does not *b*....... John 15:2
are strong ought to *b*....... Rom 15:1
you may be able to *b*...... 1 Co 10:13
B one another's.............. Gal 6:2
I *b* in my body the.......... Gal 6:17
b the sins of many.......... Heb 9:28

BEARING
goes forth weeping, *B*...... Ps 126:6
And He, *b* His cross....... John 19:17
b with one another.......... Col 3:13
the camp, *b* His reproach Heb 13:13

BEARS
every branch that *b*......... John 15:2
b all things.................... 1 Co 13:7
it is the Spirit who *b*....... 1 Jn 5:6

BEAST
b touches the mountain.... Heb 12:20
And I saw a *b* rising......... Rev 13:1
Then I saw another *b*...... Rev 13:11
the mark of the *b*............ Rev 19:20

BEASTS
like the *b* that perish....... Ps 49:12
I have fought with *b*........ 1 Co 15:32
like brute *b*.................... Jude 10

BEAT
You shall *b* him with a.... Prov 23:14
b their swords into.......... Is 2:4
spat in His face and *b*..... Matt 26:67
but *b* his breast.............. Luke 18:13

BEATEN
and you will be *b*........... Mark 13:9
Three times I was *b*........ 2 Co 11:25
it if, when you are *b*....... 1 Pe 2:20

BEAUTIFUL
but Rachel was *b*............ Gen 29:17
B in elevation................. Ps 48:2
has made everything *b*...... Eccl 3:11
my love, you are as *b*...... Song 6:4
of the LORD shall be *b*.... Is 4:2
How *b* upon the............. Is 52:7
indeed appear *b*.............. Matt 23:27
they saw he was a *b*....... Heb 11:23

BEAUTY
for glory and for *b*......... Ex 28:2
"The *b* of Israel is.......... 2 Sa 1:19
To behold the *b*.............. Ps 27:4
and *b* is vain................... Prov 31:30
see the King in His *b*...... Is 33:17
no *b* that we should......... Is 53:2
Do not let your *b*............ 1 Pe 3:3

BED
remember You on my *b*... Ps 63:6
If I make my *b* in hell..... Ps 139:8
Arise, take up your *b*...... Matt 9:6
and the *b* undefiled......... Heb 13:4

BEGGARLY
weak and *b* elements....... Gal 4:9

BEGINNING
b God created the........... Gen 1:1
Though your *b* was.......... Job 8:7
of the LORD is the *b*...... Ps 111:10
that God does from *b*...... Eccl 3:11
who made them at the *b*.. Matt 19:4
In the *b* was the Word..... John 1:1
This *b* of signs Jesus........ John 2:11
a murderer from the *b*..... John 8:44
with Me from the *b*......... John 15:27
the *b*, the firstborn.......... Col 1:18
having neither *b*.............. Heb 7:3
True Witness, the *B*........ Rev 3:14
and the Omega, the *B*..... Rev 21:6

BEGOTTEN
I have *b* You................. Ps 2:7
glory as of the only *b*...... John 1:14
Christ Jesus I have *b*....... 1 Co 4:15
abundant mercy has *b*...... 1 Pe 1:3
loves him who is *b*.......... 1 Jn 5:1

BEGUN
Having *b* in the Spirit...... Gal 3:3
that He who has *b*.......... Phil 1:6

BEHAVIOR
of good *b*, hospitable......... 1 Ti 3:2
they be reverent in *b*....... Tit 2:3

BEHOLD
the eyes to *b* the sun....... Eccl 11:7
B, you are fair................ Song 1:15
B, the virgin shall........... Is 7:14
Judah, "*B* your God.......... Is 40:9
B the Lamb of God.......... John 1:36
I am, that they may *b*...... John 17:24
to them, "*B* the Man........ John 19:5
B what manner of love.... 1 Jn 3:1

BEING
man became a living *b*..... Gen 2:7
God while I have my *b*.... Ps 104:33
move and have our *b*........ Acts 17:28
who, *b* in the form of...... Phil 2:6

BELIEVE
B in the LORD your......... 2 Ch 20:20
tears, "Lord, I *b*............ Mark 9:24
b that you receive........... Mark 11:24
because they did not *b*..... Mark 16:14
have no root, who *b*........ Luke 8:13
and slow of heart to *b*..... Luke 24:25
even to those who *b*........ John 1:12
how will you *b*................ John 3:12
sent, Him you do not *b*... John 5:38
we may see it and *b*........ John 6:30
to him, "Do you *b*.......... John 9:35
this, that they may *b*....... John 11:42
you *b* in God.................. John 14:1
written that you may *b*.... John 20:31
the Lord Jesus and *b*....... Rom 10:9
And how shall they *b*....... Rom 10:14
a wife who does not *b*..... 1 Co 7:12
I spoke," we also *b*......... 2 Co 4:13
given to those who *b*........ Gal 3:22
Christ, not only to *b*........ Phil 1:29
comes to God must *b*...... Heb 11:6
Even the demons *b*.......... Jas 2:19
Beloved, do not *b*............ 1 Jn 4:1

BELIEVED
And he *b* in the LORD..... Gen 15:6
Who has *b* our report....... Is 53:1
of that city *b* in Him........ John 4:39
seen Me, you have *b*....... John 20:29
who heard the word *b*..... Acts 4:4
of those who *b* were of.... Acts 4:32
Holy Spirit when you *b*.... Acts 19:2
"*Abraham b God*............. Rom 4:3
I know whom I have *b*.... 2 Ti 1:12

BELIEVES
The simple *b* every.......... Prov 14:15
"He who *b* and is........... Mark 16:16
that whoever *b* in Him..... John 3:16
"He who *b* in the Son...... John 3:36
with the heart one *b*....... Rom 10:10
b all things.................... 1 Co 13:7

BELIEVING
you ask in prayer, *b*........ Matt 21:22
blessed with *b* Abraham... Gal 3:9

BELLY
on your *b* you shall go..... Gen 3:14
And Jonah was in the *b*.... Jon 1:17
three nights in the *b*........ Matt 12:40
whose god is their *b*....... Phil 3:19

BELONG
To the Lord our God *b*..... Dan 9:9
My name, because you *b*.. Mark 9:41

BELOVED
My *b* is mine.................. Song 2:16
a song of my *B*.............. Is 5:1
for you are greatly *b*........ Dan 9:23
"This is My *b*................ Matt 3:17
election they are *b*.......... Rom 11:28
us accepted in the *B*........ Eph 1:6
"This is My *b*................ 2 Pe 1:17
our *b* brother Paul........... 2 Pe 3:15

BENEATH
and on the earth *b*.......... Deut 4:39
"You are from *b*.............. John 8:23

BESEECH
Return, we *b* You............ Ps 80:14
b you therefore............... Rom 12:1

BESIDE
He leads me *b* the.......... Ps 23:2

BEST
earnestly desire the *b*....... 1 Co 12:31

BESTOWED
love the Father has *b*........1 Jn 3:1

BETRAY
you, one of you will *b*..... Matt 26:21
"Now brother will *b*........ Mark 13:12

BETRAYED
Man is about to be *b*.......Matt 17:22
in which He was *b*..... 1 Co 11:23

BETRAYING
"Judas, are you *b*........... Luke 22:48

BETRAYS
See, he who *b* Me is at....Matt 26:46
who is the one who *b*...... John 21:20

BETROTHED
to a virgin *b* to a man..... Luke 1:27
For I have *b* you to.........2 Co 11:2

BETTER
b than sacrifice............. 1 Sa 15:22
It is *b* to trust in............Ps 118:8
B is a little with the......... Prov 15:16
B is a dry morsel............ Prov 17:1
B is the poor who........... Prov 19:1
It is *b* to dwell in............Prov 21:19
b is a neighbor.............. Prov 27:10
B is a handful with..........Eccl 4:6
Two are *b* than one..........Eccl 4:9
B is a poor and wise....... Eccl 4:13
were the former days *b*.... Eccl 7:10
For it is *b* to marry......... 1 Co 7:9
Christ, which is far *b*.......Phil 1:23
b than the angels........... Heb 1:4
b things concerning......... Heb 6:9
b things than that...........Heb 12:24

BEWARE
"*B* of false prophets........ Matt 7:15
b of evil workers.............Phil 3:2
B lest anyone cheat.........Col 2:8

BEWITCHED
b you that you should......Gal 3:1

BIRDS
b will eat your flesh........ Gen 40:19
b make their nests..........Ps 104:17
"Look at the *b*.............. Matt 6:26
Foxes have holes and *b*....Matt 8:20

BIRTH
heaven, who gives it *b*.....Job 38:29
makes the deer give *b*......Ps 29:9
the day of one's *b*...........Eccl 7:1
Now the *b* of Jesus......... Matt 1:18
will rejoice at his *b*......... Luke 1:14
conceived, it gives *b*........Jas 1:15

BIRTHRIGHT
"Sell me your *b*............. Gen 25:31
according to his *b*........... Gen 43:33
of food sold his *b*...........Heb 12:16

BISHOP
the position of a *b*.......... 1 Ti 3:1
b must be blameless........ Tit 1:7

BITTER
and do not be *b*.............Col 3:19
But if you have *b*...........Jas 3:14

BITTERNESS
heart knows its own *b*......Prov 14:10
all my years in the *b*....... Is 38:15
you are poisoned by *b*..... Acts 8:23
b springing up cause........Heb 12:15

BLACKNESS
whom is reserved the *b*.... Jude 13

BLAME
be holy and without *b*......Eph 1:4

BLAMELESS
"You shall be *b*............. Deut 18:13
when You speak, And *b*.. Ps 51:4
Let my heart be *b*..........Ps 119:80
end, that you may be *b*....1 Co 1:8
which is in the law, *b*...... Phil 3:6
you holy, and *b*............. Col 1:22
your hearts *b* in.............1 Th 3:13
body be preserved *b*........1 Th 5:23
bishop then must be *b*..... 1 Ti 3:2
deacons, being found *b*.... 1 Ti 3:10
without spot and *b*......... 2 Pe 3:14

BLASPHEME
b Your name forever....... Ps 74:10
compelled them to *b*........Acts 26:11
may learn not to *b*.......... 1 Ti 1:20
b that noble name...........Jas 2:7
God, to *b* His name........ Rev 13:6

BLASPHEMED
a foolish people has *b*......Ps 74:18
who passed by *b* Him.........Matt 27:39
who were hanged *b*.......... Luke 23:39
The name of God is b......Rom 2:24
doctrine may not be *b*..... 1 Ti 6:1
On their part He is *b*...... 1 Pe 4:14
great heat, and they *b*..... Rev 16:9

BLASPHEMER
I was formerly a *b*.......... 1 Ti 1:13

BLASPHEMERS
boasters, proud, *b*..........2 Ti 3:2

BLASPHEMES
b the name of the LORD.. Lev 24:16
"This Man *b*................. Matt 9:3

BLASPHEMIES
false witness, *b*.............. Matt 15:19
is this who speaks *b*........ Luke 5:21
great things and *b*.......... Rev 13:5

BLASPHEMY
men, but the *b* against..... Matt 12:31
"He has spoken *b*........... Matt 26:65
was full of names of *b*..... Rev 17:3

BLEMISH
shall be without *b*........... Ex 12:5
LORD, a ram without *b*.... Lev 6:6
be holy and without *b*......Eph 5:27
as of a lamb without *b*.....1 Pe 1:19

BLEMISHED
to the Lord what is *b*...... Mal 1:14

BLESS
b those who *b* you.......... Gen 12:3
You go unless You *b*........Gen 32:26
"The LORD *b* you and.....Num 6:24
b the LORD at all............Ps 34:1
b You while I live...........Ps 63:4
b His holy name.............Ps 103:1
b the house of Israel....... Ps 115:12
b you in the name of.......Ps 129:8
I will abundantly *b*..........Ps 132:15
b those who curse........... Luke 6:28
B those who persecute..... Rom 12:14
Being reviled, we *b*......... 1 Co 4:12
With it we *b* our God.......Jas 3:9

BLESSED
And God *b* them............ Gen 1:22
the earth shall be *b*......... Gen 12:3
b be those who............... Gen 27:29
B is he who.................. Num 24:9
B shall be the................Deut 28:4
You have *b* the work of....Job 1:10
B is the man Who walks.. Ps 1:1
B is the man to whom.... Ps 32:2
B is the nation whose...... Ps 33:12
B are those who keep......Ps 106:3
rise up and call her *b*...... Prov 31:28
will call you *b*................ Mal 3:12
B are the poor in............Matt 5:3
B are you when they....... Matt 5:11
b is He who comes.......... Matt 21:9
hand, 'Come, you *b*........ Matt 25:34
b are you among women.. Luke 1:28
B are those who have...... John 20:29
It is more *b* to give......... Acts 20:35
the Creator, who is *b*...... Rom 1:25
all, the eternally *b*...........Rom 9:5
B be the God and............Eph 1:3
b God which was............ 1 Ti 1:11
this one will be *b*............Jas 1:25
B is he who reads........... Rev 1:3
B are the dead who.........Rev 14:13
B is he who watches........Rev 16:15
B are those who are........ Rev 19:9
B and holy is he who...... Rev 20:6
B is he who keeps the..... Rev 22:7
B are those who do His... Rev 22:14

BLESSING
and you shall be a *b*........Gen 12:2
I will command My *b*...... Lev 25:21
before you today a *b*........ Deut 11:26
Your *b* is upon Your....... Ps 3:8
The *b* of the LORD.......... Prov 10:22
shall be showers of *b*........ Ezek 34:26
and you shall be a *b*........Zech 8:13
b which we bless............1 Co 10:16
that the *b* of Abraham..... Gal 3:14
with every spiritual *b*.......Eph 1:3
to inherit the *b*.............. Heb 12:17
honor and glory and *b*..... Rev 5:12

BLIND
To open *b* eyes...............Is 42:7
b receive their sight......... Matt 11:5
b leads the *b*.................. Matt 15:14
of sight to the b.............. Luke 4:18
to Him, "Are we *b*.......... John 9:40
miserable, poor, *b*........... Rev 3:17

BLINDED
b their eyes and............ John 12:40
of this age has *b*............. 2 Co 4:4
the darkness has *b*.......... 1 Jn 2:11

BLOOD
b shall be shed............... Gen 9:6
b that makes atonement... Lev 17:11
hands are full of *b*.......... Is 1:15
and the moon into *b*........Joel 2:31
For this is My *b*..............Matt 26:28
called the Field of *B*........Matt 27:8
His *b* be on us and......... Matt 27:25
new covenant in My *b*..... Luke 22:20
were born, not of *b*.........John 1:13
b has eternal life.............John 6:54
b every nation of men..... Acts 17:26
with His own *b*............... Acts 20:28
propitiation by His *b*....... Rom 3:25
justified by His *b*........... Rom 5:9
through His *b*.................Eph 1:7
made near by the *b*..........Eph 2:13
against flesh and *b*.......... Eph 6:12
peace through the *b*........ Col 1:20
"*This is the b*................. Heb 9:20
of *b* there is no............. Heb 9:22
the Holiest by the *b*........ Heb 10:19
sprinkling of the *b*...........1 Pe 1:2
with the precious *b*...........1 Pe 1:19
b of Jesus Christ His....... 1 Jn 1:7
our sins in His own *b*...... Rev 1:5
us to God by Your *b*.......Rev 5:9
them white in the *b*........Rev 7:14
overcame him by the *b*.... Rev 12:11
a robe dipped in *b*.......... Rev 19:13

BLOODGUILTINESS
Deliver me from *b*.......... Ps 51:14

BLOSSOM
Israel shall *b* and bud...... Is 27:6
and *b* as the rose............ Is 35:1
the fig tree may not *b*......Hab 3:17

BLOT
from my sins, And *b*....... Ps 51:9
and I will not *b*.............. Rev 3:5

BLOTTED
Let them be *b* out of...... Ps 69:28
I have *b* out.................... Is 44:22
your sins may be *b*..........Acts 3:19

everything that has *b*....... Ps 150:6
from it, Who gives *b*....... Is 42:5
Surely I will cause *b*........ Ezek 37:5
God who holds your *b*..... Dan 5:23
gives to all life, *b*............ Acts 17:25
consume with the *b*......... 2 Th 2:8
power to give *b*............. Rev 13:15

BRETHREN
and you are all *b*........... Matt 23:8
least of these My *b*......... Matt 25:40
Go and tell My *b*............ Matt 28:10
firstborn among many *b*... Rom 8:29
to judge between his *b*..... 1 Co 6:5
thus sin against the *b*....... 1 Co 8:12
over five hundred *b*.......... 1 Co 15:6
perils among false *b*......... 2 Co 11:26
to be made like His *b*...... Heb 2:17
sincere love of the *b*........ 1 Pe 1:22
because we love the *b*....... 1 Jn 3:14
does not receive the *b*..... 3 Jn 10
of your *b* the prophets..... Rev 22:9

BRIBE
you shall take no *b*......... Ex 23:8
b blinds the eyes............. Deut 16:19
b debases the heart......... Eccl 7:7

BRIBES
hand is full of *b*.............. Ps 26:10
but he who hates *b*......... Prov 15:27
but he who receives *b*...... Prov 29:4

BRIDE
them on you as a *b*......... Is 49:18
"He who has the *b*.......... John 3:29
I will show you the *b*....... Rev 21:9
the Spirit and the *b*......... Rev 22:17

BRIDEGROOM
righteousness, as a *b*........ Is 61:10
and as the *b* rejoices........ Is 62:5
mourn as long as the *b*.... Matt 9:15
went out to meet the *b*.... Matt 25:1
b fast while the............... Mark 2:19
the friend of the *b*.......... John 3:29

BRIGHTNESS
From the *b* before Him..... 2 Sa 22:13
and kings to the *b*........... Is 60:3
goes forth as *b*............... Is 62:1
very dark, with no *b*........ Amos 5:20
who being the *b*.............. Heb 1:3

BRIMSTONE
Then the LORD rained *b*.. Gen 19:24
B is scattered on his......... Job 18:15
fire, smoke, and *b*........... Rev 9:17
the lake of fire and *b*....... Rev 20:10

BRING
LORD your God will *b*..... Deut 30:3
Lord said, "I will *b*......... Ps 68:22
"And she will *b*.............. Matt 1:21
Who shall *b* a charge....... Rom 8:33
b Christ down from......... Rom 10:6
even so God will *b*.......... 1 Th 4:14

BROAD
b is the way that............ Matt 7:13

BROKE
b them at the foot of....... Ex 32:19
covenant which they *b*..... Jer 31:32
He blessed and *b*........... Matt 14:19
b the legs of the............ John 19:32

BROKEN
he has *b* My covenant...... Gen 17:14
I am like a *b* vessel......... Ps 31:12
their bows shall be *b*....... Ps 37:15
He has *b* his covenant..... Ps 55:20
heart the spirit is *b*.......... Prov 15:13
b spirit dries the............ Prov 17:22
but who can bear a *b*...... Prov 18:14
heart within me is *b*........ Jer 23:9
is oppressed and *b*......... Hos 5:11
this stone will be *b*.......... Matt 21:44
Scripture cannot be *b*...... John 10:35
is My body which is *b*...... 1 Co 11:24
vessels shall be b............ Rev 2:27

BROKENHEARTED
He heals the *b* And......... Ps 147:3

BRONZE
So Moses made a *b*......... Num 21:9
b serpent that Moses....... 2 Ki 18:4
a third kingdom of *b*....... Dan 2:39
make your hooves *b*........ Mic 4:13
were mountains of *b*........ Zech 6:1

BROOD
"*B* of vipers..................... Matt 12:34
as a hen gathers her *b*..... Luke 13:34

BROTHER
Where is Abel your *b*...... Gen 4:9
and a *b* is born for.......... Prov 17:17
b offended is harder........ Prov 18:19
and do not trust any *b*.... Jer 9:4
Was not Esau Jacob's *b*... Mal 1:2
b will deliver up.............. Matt 10:21
how often shall my *b*....... Matt 18:21
b will rise again.............. John 11:23
do you judge your *b*........ Rom 14:10
b goes to law against....... 1 Co 6:6
shall the weak *b*............. 1 Co 8:11
slave, as a beloved *b*....... Phm 16
He who loves his *b*.......... 1 Jn 2:10
and murdered his *b*.......... 1 Jn 3:12
b sinning a sin which....... 1 Jn 5:16

BROTHER'S
Am I my *b* keeper......... Gen 4:9
at the speck in your *b*..... Matt 7:3

BROTHERHOOD
the covenant of *b*........... Amos 1:9
I might break the *b*......... Zech 11:14
Love the *b*...................... 1 Pe 2:17
experienced by your *b*..... 1 Pe 5:9

BROTHERLY
to one another with *b*...... Rom 12:10
b love continue............... Heb 13:1

BROTHERS
is My mother, or My *b*.... Mark 3:33
b are these who hear....... Luke 8:21
b did not believe............ John 7:5
love as *b*....................... 1 Pe 3:8

BRUISE
He shall *b* your head....... Gen 3:15
LORD binds up the *b*....... Is 30:26
the LORD to *b* Him......... Is 53:10

BRUISED
He was *b* for our............ Is 53:5
b reed He will not.......... Matt 12:20

BUILD
"Would you *b* a house..... 2 Sa 7:5
b a house for the name.... 1 Ki 8:17
that the LORD will *b*........ 1 Ch 17:10
Solomon who shall *b*....... 1 Ch 28:6
able to *b* Him a temple.... 2 Ch 2:6
labor in vain who *b*......... Ps 127:1
down, and a time to *b*..... Eccl 3:3
house that you will *b*....... Is 66:1
Who *b* up Zion with........ Mic 3:10
What house will you b..... Acts 7:49
b you up and give you..... Acts 20:32
named, lest I should *b*..... Rom 15:20

BUILDER
me, as a wise master *b*.... 1 Co 3:10
foundations, whose *b*....... Heb 11:10

BUILDING
field, you are God's *b*...... 1 Co 3:9
destroyed, we have a *b*.... 2 Co 5:1
in whom the whole *b*....... Eph 2:21
But you, beloved, *b*........ Jude 20

BUILDS
Every wise woman *b*....... Prov 14:1
one take heed how he *b*... 1 Co 3:10

BUILT
Wisdom has *b* her house.. Prov 9:1
to a wise man who *b*....... Matt 7:24
work which he has *b*....... 1 Co 3:14
having been *b* on the....... Eph 2:20
rooted and *b* up in Him... Col 2:7
For every house is *b*........ Heb 3:4
stones, are being *b*.......... 1 Pe 2:5

BURDEN
one knows his own *b*....... 2 Ch 6:29
Cast your *b* on the.......... Ps 55:22
easy and My *b* is light..... Matt 11:30
as it may, I did not *b*...... 2 Co 12:16
we might not be a *b*........ 1 Th 2:9
on you no other *b*........... Rev 2:24

BURDENS
and looked at their *b*....... Ex 2:11
For they bind heavy *b*...... Matt 23:4
Bear one another's *b*....... Gal 6:2

BURDENSOME
I myself was not *b*......... 2 Co 12:13
commandments are not *b* 1 Jn 5:3

BURIAL
she did it for My *b*.......... Matt 26:12
for the day of My *b*........ John 12:7

BURIED
and there will I be *b*...... Ruth 1:17
away the body and *b*....... Matt 14:12
Therefore we were *b*....... Rom 6:4
and that He was *b*.......... 1 Co 15:4
b with Him in baptism.... Col 2:12

BURN
the bush does not *b*......... Ex 3:3
that My wrath may *b*....... Ex 32:10
"Did not our heart *b*....... Luke 24:32

BURNED
If anyone's work is *b*....... 1 Co 3:15
I give my body to be *b*.... 1 Co 13:3
whose end is to be *b*...... Heb 6:8
are *b* outside the camp.... Heb 13:11
in it will be *b*................ 2 Pe 3:10

BURNING
b torch that passed.......... Gen 15:17
on his lips like a *b*.......... Prov 16:27
b fire shut up in my........ Jer 20:9
b jealousy against the...... Ezek 36:5
plucked from the *b*.......... Amos 4:11
a great mountain *b*.......... Rev 8:8

BURY
and let the dead *b*........... Matt 8:22

BUSH
from the midst of a *b*...... Ex 3:2
Him who dwelt in the *b*... Deut 33:16
to him in the *b*.............. Acts 7:35

BUSINESS
in ships, Who do *b*......... Ps 107:23
farm, another to his *b*...... Matt 22:5
about My Father's *b*........ Luke 2:49

BUSYBODIES
at all, but are *b*............. 2 Th 3:11
but also gossips and *b*...... 1 Ti 5:13

BUY
B the truth.................... Prov 23:23
Yes, come, *b* wine and.... Is 55:1
that we may *b* the poor... Amos 8:6
b food for all these......... Luke 9:13
B those things we.......... John 13:29
"I counsel you to *b*......... Rev 3:18

— C —

CALAMITY
for the day of their *c*....... Deut 32:35
will laugh at your *c*......... Prov 1:26
c shall come suddenly...... Prov 6:15
If there is *c* in a............ Amos 3:6

CALF
and made a molded *c*..... Ex 32:4
They made a *c* in Horeb.. Ps 106:19
is, than a fatted *c*............Prov 15:17
like a stubborn *c*............Hos 4:16
Your *c* is rejected.......... Hos 8:5
And bring the fatted *c*..... Luke 15:23

CALL
I will *c* to the LORD........ 1 Sa 12:17
c their lands after............Ps 49:11
c upon Him while He....... Is 55:6
'*C* to Me...................... Jer 33:3
Arise, *c* on your God...... Jon 1:6
They will *c* on My name.. Zech 13:9
c His name JESUS............Matt 1:21
c the righteous................Matt 9:13
Lord our God will *c*........ Acts 2:39
c them My people.......... Rom 9:25
How then shall they *c*......Rom 10:14
For God did not *c*............1 Th 4:7

CALLED
"I, the LORD, have *c*.......Is 42:6
I have *c* you by your....... Is 43:1
The LORD has *c* Me .... Is 49:1
"*Out of Egypt I c*........... Matt 2:15
For many are *c*...............Matt 20:16
to those who are the *c*...... Rom 8:28
these He also *c*..............Rom 8:30
But God has *c* us to........1 Co 7:15
praises of Him who *c*.......1 Pe 2:9
knowledge of Him who *c* 2 Pe 1:3
that we should be *c*.......... 1 Jn 3:1

CALLING
the gifts and the *c*........... Rom 11:29
For you see your *c*..........1 Co 1:26
remain in the same *c*....... 1 Co 7:20
a walk worthy of the *c*.....Eph 4:1
us with a holy *c*..............2 Ti 1:9
of the heavenly *c*............ Heb 3:1
to make your *c* and.........2 Pe 1:10

CALLS
c them all by name......... Ps 147:4
there is no one who *c*.......Is 64:7
c his own sheep...............John 10:3
For "*whoever c*..............Rom 10:13

CAMEL
it is easier for a *c*...........Matt 19:24
and swallow a *c*...............Matt 23:24

CAMP
"This is God's *c*...............Gen 32:2
who went before the *c*...... Ex 14:19
to Him, outside the *c*...... Heb 13:13

CAPTIVE
and be led away *c*............Luke 21:24
He led captivity c............Eph 4:8

CAPTIVES
will bring back the *c*.........Amos 9:14
and return their *c*.............Zeph 2:7
households and make *c*... 2 Ti 3:6

CAPTIVITY
bring you back from *c*..... Deut 30:3
from David until the *c*..... Matt 1:17
and bringing me into *c*.....Rom 7:23
every thought into *c*........ 2 Co 10:5
on high, He led c............Eph 4:8

CARCASS
For wherever the *c*.........Matt 24:28

CARE
you to be without *c*..........1 Co 7:32
who will sincerely *c*..........Phil 2:20
how will he take *c*............1 Ti 3:5
casting all your *c*.............1 Pe 5:7

CAREFULLY
c keep all these............. Deut 11:22

CARELESS
but he who is *c*...............Prov 19:16

CARES
and are choked with *c*..... Luke 8:14
He who is unmarried *c*.....1 Co 7:32
for He *c* for you.............1 Pe 5:7

CARNAL
spiritual, but I am *c*........ Rom 7:14
c mind is enmity............ Rom 8:7
for you are still *c*............1 Co 3:3
our warfare are not *c*.......2 Co 10:4

CARNALLY
c minded is death............Rom 8:6

CAROUSE
count it pleasure to *c*.......2 Pe 2:13

CARRIED
the LORD your God *c*........Deut 1:31
and *c* our sorrows............ Is 53:4
parted from them and *c*... Luke 24:51
c me away in the............. Rev 17:3

CARRY
their hands cannot *c*........Job 5:12
c them away like a..........Ps 90:5
I am not worthy to *c*....... Matt 3:11
for you to *c* your bed...... John 5:10
it is certain we can *c*....... 1 Ti 6:7

CASE
c that is too hard........... Deut 1:17
I have prepared my *c*...... Job 13:18
"Present your *c*.............. Is 41:21
Festus laid Paul's *c*.......... Acts 25:14

CAST
When they *c* you down.... Job 22:29
c away Their.................Ps 2:3
Why are you *c* down....... Ps 42:5
But You have *c* us off...... Ps 44:9
and the earth shall *c*........Is 26:19
C away from you all.........Ezek 18:31
brought Daniel and *c*.........Dan 6:16
c all our sins into............Mic 7:19
whole body to be *c*......... Matt 5:29
the kingdom will be *c*...... Matt 8:12
spirits, to *c* them out....... Matt 10:1
In My name they will *c*.....Mark 16:17
I will by no means *c*.........John 6:37
c away His people............Rom 11:1
c away your confidence.... Heb 10:35
c their crowns before....... Rev 4:10
the great dragon was *c*..... Rev 12:9

CASTING
nation which I am *c*........ Lev 20:23
Andrew his brother, *c*......Matt 4:18
c down arguments........... 2 Co 10:5
c all your care................1 Pe 5:7

CATCH
in wait to *c* the poor....... Ps 10:9
c Him in His words.......... Mark 12:13
down your nets for a *c*.....Luke 5:4
From now on you will *c*... Luke 5:10

CAUGHT
behind him was a ram *c*... Gen 22:13
and that night they *c*........ John 21:3
Spirit of the Lord *c*......... Acts 8:39
And her Child was *c*....... Rev 12:5

CAUSE
c His face to shine......... Ps 67:1
C me to know the way...... Ps 143:8
God, *Who* pleads the *c*.... Is 51:22
hated Me without a c........John 15:25
For this *c* I was born.......John 18:37

CEASE
and night shall not *c*........Gen 8:22
Why should the work *c*.....Neh 6:3
There the wicked *c*...........Job 3:17
He makes wars *c*............. Ps 46:9
C listening to.................Prov 19:27
C to do evil.....................Is 1:16
tongues, they will *c*.......... 1 Co 13:8
do not *c* to pray for......... Col 1:9

CEDAR
dwell in a house of *c*.......2 Sa 7:2
He shall grow like a *c*......Ps 92:12
of our houses are *c*......... Song 1:17
it, paneling it with *c*........ Jer 22:14

CEDARS
the LORD breaks the *c*.....Ps 29:5
c of Lebanon which He....Ps 104:16

CHAFF
c which the wind.............Ps 1:4
He will burn up the *c*...... Matt 3:12

CHAINS
their kings with *c*............Ps 149:8
your neck with *c*.............Song 1:10
And his *c* fell off............. Acts 12:7
am, except for these *c*..... Acts 26:29
Remember my *c*............... Col 4:18
minister to me in my *c*......Phm 13
delivered them into *c*........2 Pe 2:4

CHANGE
a cloak You will *c*............Ps 102:26
with those given to *c*....... Prov 24:21
Can the Ethiopian *c*......... Jer 13:23
c times and law............... Dan 7:25
c their glory into..............Hos 4:7
the LORD, I do not *c*........Mal 3:6
now and to *c* my tone......Gal 4:20
there is also a *c*.............. Heb 7:12

CHARACTER
and *c*, hope......................Rom 5:4

CHARIOT
He took off their *c*..........Ex 14:25
makes the clouds His *c*.... Ps 104:3
and overtake this *c*.......... Acts 8:29

CHARM
C is deceitful and............Prov 31:30

CHASTEN
C your son while there.... Prov 19:18
is My desire, I will *c*........ Hos 10:10
a father does not *c*..........Heb 12:7
I love, I rebuke and *c*.......Rev 3:19

CHASTENED
c my soul with fasting......Ps 69:10
c every morning..............Ps 73:14
The LORD has *c* me........ Ps 118:18
In vain I have *c*..............Jer 2:30
c us as seemed best.........Heb 12:10

CHASTENING
have not seen the *c*......... Deut 11:2
do not despise the *c*........ Job 5:17
'I have borne *c*................Job 34:31
a prayer when Your *c*......Is 26:16
if you are without *c*.........Heb 12:8

CHASTENS
the LORD loves He c........ Heb 12:6

CHASTISEMENT
the *c* for our peace..........Is 53:5

CHEEK
on your right *c*................ Matt 5:39

CHEEKS
c are lovely with............. Song 1:10
struck Me, and My *c*....... Is 50:6

CHEERFUL
for God loves a *c*............2 Co 9:7
Is anyone *c*....................Jas 5:13

CHERUBIM
and He placed *c*............ Gen 3:24
dwell between the *c*.........Ps 80:1
fire from among the *c*......Ezek 10:2
above it were the *c*......... Heb 9:5

CHILD
Like a weaned *c*..............Ps 131:2
c is known by his.............Prov 20:11
Train up a *c* in the..........Prov 22:6
For unto us a *C*...............Is 9:6

c shall lead them............Is 11:6
When Israel was a *c*........ Hos 11:1
virgin shall be with c....... Matt 1:23
He took a little *c*........... Mark 9:36
of God as a little *c*.........Mark 10:15
kind of *c* will this be....... Luke 1:66
So the *c* grew and.......... Luke 1:80
When I was a *c*............. 1 Co 13:11
And she bore a male *C*....Rev 12:5

CHILDBEARING
she will be saved in *c*...... 1 Ti 2:15

CHILDREN
c are a heritage............. Ps 127:3
c rise up and call her.......Prov 31:28
c are their oppressors...... Is 3:12
they are My people, *c*......Is 63:8
c will rise up against........Matt 10:21
and become as little *c*.......Matt 18:3
"Let the little *c*............. Matt 19:14
the right to become *c*...... John 1:12
you were Abraham's *c*..... John 8:39
spirit that we are *c*.......... Rom 8:16
c ought not to lay up.......2 Co 12:14
and were by nature *c*......Eph 2:3
Walk as *c* of light............. Eph 5:8
and harmless, *c*..............Phil 2:15
now we are *c* of God.......1 Jn 3:2

CHOOSE
therefore *c* life................Deut 30:19
c none of his ways.......... Prov 3:31
evil and *c* the good......... Is 7:15
"You did not *c*...............John 15:16
yet what I shall *c*........... Phil 1:22

CHOSE
just as He *c* us in Him.....Eph 1:4
from the beginning *c*....... 2 Th 2:13

CHOSEN
of Jacob, His *c*.............. 1 Ch 16:13
people whom He has *c*.... Ps 33:12
a covenant with My *c*...... Ps 89:3
c the way of truth........... Ps 119:30
servant whom I have *c*.....Is 43:10
c that good part.............Luke 10:42
I know whom I have *c*.....John 13:18
c you that you should...... Acts 22:14
c the foolish things.........1 Co 1:27
Has God not *c* the poor...Jas 2:5
But you are a *c*............. 1 Pe 2:9

CHRIST
genealogy of Jesus *C*....... Matt 1:1
Jesus who is called *C*.......Matt 1:16
"You are the *C*............. Matt 16:16
if You are the *C*............ Matt 26:63
a Savior, who is *C*.......... Luke 2:11
It is *C* who died............ Rom 8:34
C did not please............ Rom 15:3
Is *C* divided?..................1 Co 1:13
to be justified by *C*......... Gal 2:17
been crucified with *C*.......Gal 2:20
but *C* lives in me........... Gal 2:20
your Seed," who is *C*...... Gal 3:16
C may dwell in your........Eph 3:17
C will give you.............. Eph 5:14
C is head of the church....Eph 5:23
to me, to live is *C*...........Phil 1:21
confess that Jesus *C*........ Phil 2:11
through *C* who.............. Phil 4:13
which is *C* in you...........Col 1:27
C who is our life............Col 3:4
C is all and in all...........Col 3:11
and men, the Man *C*....... 1 Ti 2:5
Jesus *C* is the same......... Heb 13:8
C His Son cleanses us......1 Jn 1:7
that Jesus is the *C*...........1 Jn 5:1
of His *C* have come........ Rev 12:10
and reigned with *C*.........Rev 20:4

CHRISTIAN
me to become a *C*........... Acts 26:28
anyone suffers as a *C*...... 1 Pe 4:16

CHRISTIANS
were first called *C*..........Acts 11:26

CHURCH
rock I will build My *c*......Matt 16:18
c daily those who were.... Acts 2:47
also loved the *c*............. Eph 5:25
as the Lord does the *c*.....Eph 5:29
body, which is the *c*......... Col 1:24
and do not let the *c*........ 1 Ti 5:16
general assembly and *c*.... Heb 12:23
To the angel of the *c*.......Rev 2:1

CHURCHES
strengthening the *c*.......... Acts 15:41
John, to the seven *c*........ Rev 1:4
angels of the seven *c*....... Rev 1:20
these things in the *c*........ Rev 22:16

CIRCUMCISE
c the foreskin of your...... Deut 10:16
LORD your God will *c*..... Deut 30:6
C yourselves to the.......... Jer 4:4
is necessary to *c* them......Acts 15:5

CIRCUMCISED
among you shall be *c*.......Gen 17:10
who will justify the *c*........ Rom 3:30
While he was *c*................Rom 4:10
the gospel for the *c*.......... Gal 2:7
if you become *c*............... Gal 5:2
c the eighth day...............Phil 3:5
In Him you were also *c*... Col 2:11

CIRCUMCISION
him the covenant of *c*.......Acts 7:8
c is that of the heart........Rom 2:29
C is nothing and............1 Co 7:19
Christ Jesus neither *c*.......Gal 5:6
circumcised with the *c*.......Col 2:11

CITIES
He overthrew those *c*...... Gen 19:25
repair the ruined *c*.......... Is 61:4
c are a wilderness.......... Is 64:10
c will be laid waste..........Jer 4:7
three parts, and the *c*...... Rev 16:19

CITY
And he built a *c*............ Gen 4:17
the LORD guards the *c*.....Ps 127:1
after the holy *c*.............Is 48:2
How lonely sits the *c*....... Lam 1:1
Nineveh, that great *c*.......Jon 4:11
c that dwelt securely........Zeph 2:15
to the oppressing *c*.......... Zeph 3:1
c called Nazareth........... Matt 2:23
c that is set on a...........Matt 5:14
He has prepared a *c*.......Heb 11:16
Zion and to the *c*..........Heb 12:22
fallen, that great *c*...........Rev 14:8
and the beloved *c*........... Rev 20:9
John, saw the holy *c*........Rev 21:2
the gates into the *c*.......... Rev 22:14

CLAY
have made me like *c*....... Job 10:9
pit, Out of the miry *c*...... Ps 40:2
Shall the *c* say to him......Is 45:9
we are the *c*....................Is 64:8
iron and partly of *c*......... Dan 2:33
blind man with the *c*........ John 9:6
have power over the *c*..... Rom 9:21

CLEAN
seven each of every *c*...... Gen 7:2
between unclean and *c*.....Lev 10:10
wash in them and be *c*.....2 Ki 5:12
Who can bring a *c*........... Job 14:4
He who has *c* hands and.. Ps 24:4
Then I will sprinkle *c*...... Ezek 36:25
You can make me *c*........ Matt 8:2
all things are *c*................Luke 11:41

"You are not all *c*..........John 13:11
"You are already *c*.........John 15:3
in fine linen, *c*.................Rev 19:8

CLEANSE
You shall *c* the altar........Ex 29:36
C me from secret............Ps 19:12
And *c* me from my sin.....Ps 51:2
How can a young man *c*.. Ps 119:9
c the lepers, raise............Matt 10:8
might sanctify and *c*........ Eph 5:26
us our sins and to *c*.........1 Jn 1:9

CLEAR
c shining after rain.......... 2 Sa 23:4
yourselves to be *c*.............2 Co 7:11
like a jasper stone, *c*........ Rev 21:11
of life, *c* as crystal...........Rev 22:1

CLINGS
And My tongue *c*...........Ps 22:15
My soul *c* to the dust...... Ps 119:25

CLOAK
c You will change them... Ps 102:26
let him have your *c*......... Matt 5:40
c You will fold them...... Heb 1:12
your liberty as a *c*.......... 1 Pe 2:16

CLOTH
a piece of unshrunk *c*...... Matt 9:16
in a clean linen *c*........... Matt 27:59

CLOTHED
of skin, and *c* them......... Gen 3:21
off my sackcloth and *c*..... Ps 30:11
The pastures are *c*...........Ps 65:13
The LORD is *c*................ Ps 93:1
You are *c* with honor...... Ps 104:1
c himself with cursing...... Ps 109:18
Let Your priests be *c*........Ps 132:9
all her household is *c*........Prov 31:21
c you with fine linen........Ezek 16:10
A man *c* in soft..............Matt 11:8
I was naked and you *c*.....Matt 25:36
And they *c* Him with.......Mark 15:17
desiring to be *c*..............2 Co 5:2
that you may be *c*............ Rev 3:18
a woman *c* with the sun... Rev 12:1

CLOTHES
c became shining............Mark 9:3
they spread their *c*.......... Luke 19:36
a poor man in filthy *c*......Jas 2:2

CLOTHING
to you in sheep's *c*.......... Matt 7:15
those who wear soft *c*...... Matt 11:8
c as white as snow.......... Matt 28:3
c they cast lots..............John 19:24
before me in bright *c*....... Acts 10:30

CLOTHS
wrapped in swaddling *c*.... Luke 2:12
in, saw the linen *c*...........John 20:5

CLOUD
c covered the mountain.... Ex 24:15
c descended and stood..... Ex 33:9
of Man coming in a *c*...... Luke 21:27
c received Him out of......Acts 1:9
were under the *c*..............1 Co 10:1
great a *c* of witnesses.......Heb 12:1

CLOUDS
of Man coming on the *c*...Matt 24:30
He is coming with *c*........ Rev 1:7

COLD
and harvest, and *c*...........Gen 8:22
can stand before His *c*..... Ps 147:17
c water to a weary.......... Prov 25:25
c water in the name of.....Matt 10:42
of many will grow *c*.........Matt 24:12
that you are neither *c*...... Rev 3:15

COME
You all flesh will *c*.......... Ps 65:2
He will *c* and save you.... Is 35:4

who have no money, *c*.....Is 55:1
Your kingdom *c*.............Matt 6:10
"*C* to Me.......................Matt 11:28
For many will *c*.............Matt 24:5
Israel, let Him now *c*.......Matt 27:42
If anyone desires to *c*...... Luke 9:23
kingdom of God has *c*...... Luke 10:9
thirsts, let him *c*............ John 7:37
c that they may have....... John 10:10
c as a light into the......... John 12:46
I will *c* to you................ John 14:18
"If I had not *c*................ John 15:22
savage wolves will *c*..........Acts 20:29
O Lord, *c*.......................1 Co 16:22
"Behold, I *c* quickly........ Rev 3:11
the door, I will *c*............ Rev 3:20
the bride say, "*C*........... Rev 22:17

COMES
Who is this who *c*........... Is 63:1
'Come,' and he *c*............ Matt 8:9
Lord's death till He *c*...... 1 Co 11:26
Then *c* the end...............1 Co 15:24

COMFORT
with him, and to *c* him.... Job 2:11
and Your staff, they *c*......Ps 23:4
yes, *c* My people............ Is 40:1
For the LORD will *c*.........Is 51:3
c all who mourn............. Is 61:2
she has none to *c* her....... Lam 1:2
the LORD will again *c*...... Zech 1:17
and God of all *c*.............. 2 Co 1:3
trouble, with the *c*........... 2 Co 1:4
in Christ, if any *c*.............Phil 2:1
c each other and edify..... 1 Th 5:11

COMFORTS
I, even I, am He who *c*... Is 51:12
who *c* us in all our..........2 Co 1:4
who *c* the downcast...........2 Co 7:6

COMING
your salvation is *c*............Is 62:11
behold, the day is *c*.........Mal 4:1
but He who is *c*..............Matt 3:11
"Are You the *C* One...... Matt 11:3
be the sign of Your *c*...... Matt 24:3
is delaying his *c*............. Matt 24:48
see the Son of Man *c*........ Mark 13:26
mightier than I is *c*..........Luke 3:16
are Christ's at His *c*........ 1 Co 15:23
to you the power and *c*....2 Pe 1:16
the promise of His *c*........2 Pe 3:4
"Behold, I am *c*............ Rev 22:7

COMMAND
"The LORD will *c*...........Deut 28:8
c His lovingkindness........Ps 42:8
C victories for Jacob........Ps 44:4
to all that I *c*................ Jer 11:4
if it is You, *c*.................. Matt 14:28
c fire to come down......... Luke 9:54
And I know that His *c*.....John 12:50
if you do whatever I *c*..... John 15:14
do the things we *c*...........2 Th 3:4

COMMANDED
"Have you *c* the..............Job 38:12
it is the God who *c*......... 2 Co 4:6
not endure what was *c*..... Heb 12:20

COMMANDMENT
The *c* of the LORD is.......Ps 19:8
c is exceedingly broad......Ps 119:96
For the *c* is a lamp.........Prov 6:23
which is the great *c*......... Matt 22:36
"A new *c* I give to..........John 13:34
the Father gave Me *c*...... John 14:31
law, but when the *c*..........Rom 7:9
which is the first *c*............Eph 6:2
c is the word which...........1 Jn 2:7
And this is His *c*..............1 Jn 3:23
as we received *c*............. 2 Jn 4

COMMANDMENTS
covenant, the Ten *C*........Ex 34:28
myself in Your *c*.............Ps 119:47
Your *c* are faithful.......... Ps 119:86
as doctrines the c............ Matt 15:9
c hang all the Law.......... Matt 22:40
"He who has My *c*..........John 14:21
according to the *c*........... Col 2:22
Now he who keeps His *c*..1 Jn 3:24

COMMEND
into Your hands I *c*.........Luke 23:46
But food does not *c*........ 1 Co 8:8

COMMIT
"You shall not *c*............ Ex 20:14
C your works to the........ Prov 16:3
But Jesus did not *c*.......... John 2:24
c sexual immorality........ 1 Co 10:8
c these to faithful............2 Ti 2:2
c their souls to Him........ 1 Pe 4:19
c sin not leading............. 1 Jn 5:16

COMMITTED
For My people have *c*......Jer 2:13
"*Who c no sin*................1 Pe 2:22
c Himself to Him who..... 1 Pe 2:23

COMMON
of the *c* people sins......... Lev 4:27
poor have this in *c*.......... Prov 22:2
c people heard Him........ Mark 12:37
had all things in *c*........... Acts 2:44
never eaten anything *c*..... Acts 10:14
not call any man *c*........... Acts 10:28

COMMUNION
bless, is it not the *c*.........1 Co 10:16
c has light with...............2 Co 6:14
c of the Holy Spirit.......... 2 Co 13:14

COMPANION
a man my equal, My *c*.....Ps 55:13
I am a *c* of all those........Ps 119:63
the Man who is My *C*......Zech 13:7
your brother and *c*........... Rev 1:9

COMPANY
Great was the *c*...............Ps 68:11
epistle not to keep *c*.........1 Co 5:9
c corrupts good habits......1 Co 15:33
and do not keep *c*............2 Th 3:14
to an innumerable *c*......... Heb 12:22

COMPASSION
show you mercy, have *c*... Deut 13:17
His people and have *c*..... Deut 32:36
He, being full of *c*.......... Ps 78:38
are a God full of *c*...........Ps 86:15
will return and have *c*......Jer 12:15
yet He will show *c*........... Lam 3:32
Show *c* everyone to his.... Zech 7:9
He was moved with *c*....... Matt 9:36
"I have *c* on the............ Mark 8:2
whomever I will have c...... Rom 9:15
He can have *c* on those... Heb 5:2
And on some have *c*......... Jude 22

COMPASSIONS
because His *c* fail...........Lam 3:22

COMPEL
c them to come in...........Luke 14:23

COMPLETE
that you may be made *c*...2 Co 13:9
work in you will *c*........... Phil 1:6
and you are *c* in Him...... Col 2:10
of God may be *c*............ 2 Ti 3:17
make you *c* in every........ Heb 13:21
the wrath of God is *c*...... Rev 15:1

COMPREHEND
which we cannot *c*..........Job 37:5
c my path and my lying... Ps 139:3
the darkness did not *c*..... John 1:5
may be able to *c*.............Eph 3:18

CONCEIVE
the virgin shall *c*............. Is 7:14
And behold, you will *c*.... Luke 1:31

CONCEIVED
in sin my mother *c*..........Ps 51:5
when desire has *c*............Jas 1:15

CONDEMN
world to *c* the world........John 3:17
her, "Neither do I *c*......... John 8:11
judge another you *c*........ Rom 2:1
our heart does not *c*.........1 Jn 3:21

CONDEMNATION
will receive greater *c*....... Matt 23:14
can you escape the *c*....... Matt 23:33
subject to eternal *c*..........Mark 3:29
And this is the *c*.............John 3:19
the resurrection of *c*........ John 5:29
Their *c* is just.................Rom 3:8
therefore now no *c*..........Rom 8:1
having *c* because they...... 1 Ti 5:12
marked out for this *c*.......Jude 4

CONDUCT
c yourself in the.............1 Ti 3:15
c that his works are.........Jas 3:13
to each one's work, *c*...... 1 Pe 1:17
may be won by the *c*........ 1 Pe 3:1

CONFESS
that if you *c* with........... Rom 10:9
every tongue shall c.......... Rom 14:11
C your trespasses............ Jas 5:16
If we *c* our sins.............. 1 Jn 1:9
but I will *c* his name....... Rev 3:5

CONFESSED
c that He was Christ........John 9:22
c the good confession...... 1 Ti 6:12

CONFESSES
prosper, but whoever *c*.... Prov 28:13
c that Jesus is the.......... 1 Jn 4:15

CONFESSION
of Israel, and make *c*.......Josh 7:19
with the mouth *c*............ Rom 10:10
confessed the good *c*....... 1 Ti 6:12
High Priest of our *c*........ Heb 3:1
let us hold fast our *c*....... Heb 4:14

CONFIDENCE
You who are the *c*........... Ps 65:5
the LORD Than to put *c*...Ps 118:8
c shall be your................Is 30:15
Jesus, and have no *c*....... Phil 3:3
if we hold fast the *c*........ Heb 3:6
appears, we may have *c*... 1 Jn 2:28

CONFIRMED
covenant that was *c*.........Gal 3:17
by the Lord, and was *c*....Heb 2:3
c it by an oath.................Heb 6:17

CONFORMED
predestined to be *c*..........Rom 8:29
And do not be *c*.............Rom 12:2
sufferings, being *c*........... Phil 3:10
body that it may be *c*....... Phil 3:21

CONGREGATION
Nor sinners in the *c*..........Ps 1:5
c I will praise You........... Ps 22:22
I have hated the *c*............Ps 26:5
God stands in the *c*..........Ps 82:1
also in the *c* of the...........Ps 89:5
will rest in the *c*............ Prov 21:16
people, sanctify the *c*.......Joel 2:16
c I will sing praise...........Heb 2:12

CONQUERORS
we are more than *c*......... Rom 8:37

CONSCIENCE
convicted by their *c*.........John 8:9
strive to have a *c*............ Acts 24:16

I am not lying, my *c*........Rom 9:1
wrath but also for *c*........Rom 13:5
no questions for *c*........1 Co 10:25
faith with a pure *c*........1 Ti 3:9
having their own *c*........1 Ti 4:2
to God, purge your *c*........Heb 9:14
from an evil *c* and our........Heb 10:22
having a good *c*........1 Pe 3:16

CONSIDER
When I *c* Your heavens........Ps 8:3
My people do not *c*........Is 1:3
C the lilies of the........Matt 6:28
"*C* the ravens........Luke 12:24
Let a man so *c* us........1 Co 4:1
c how great this man........Heb 7:4
c one another in order........Heb 10:24
c Him who endured........Heb 12:3

CONSIST
in Him all things *c*........Col 1:17

CONSOLATION
waiting for the *C*........Luke 2:25
have received your *c*........Luke 6:24
abound in us, so our *c*........2 Co 1:5
if there is any *c*........Phil 2:1
given us everlasting *c*........2 Th 2:16
we might have strong *c*........Heb 6:18

CONSTRAINS
the love of Christ *c*........2 Co 5:14

CONSUMED
but the bush was not *c*........Ex 3:2
For we have been *c*........Ps 90:7
mercies we are not *c*........Lam 3:22
beware lest you be *c*........Gal 5:15

CONSUMING
the LORD was like a *c*........Ex 24:17
before you as a *c*........Deut 9:3
For our God is a *c*........Heb 12:29

CONTEMPTIBLE
of the LORD is *c*........Mal 1:7
also have made you *c*........Mal 2:9
and his speech *c*........2 Co 10:10

CONTEND
show me why You *c*........Job 10:2
Will you *c* for God........Job 13:8
let us *c* together........Is 43:26
for I will *c* with him........Is 49:25
then how can you *c*........Jer 12:5
c earnestly for the........Jude 3

CONTENT
state I am, to be *c*........Phil 4:11
these we shall be *c*........1 Ti 6:8
covetousness, and be *c*........Heb 13:5

CONTENTMENT
c is great gain........1 Ti 6:6

CONTINUAL
a merry heart has a *c*........Prov 15:15
in wrath with a *c*........Is 14:6
c coming she weary me........Luke 18:5
c grief in my heart........Rom 9:2

CONTINUALLY
heart was only evil *c*........Gen 6:5
His praise shall *c*........Ps 34:1
of God endures *c*........Ps 52:1
I keep Your law *c*........Ps 119:44
Before Me *c* are grief........Jer 6:7
and wait on your God *c*........Hos 12:6
will give ourselves *c*........Acts 6:4
remains a priest *c*........Heb 7:3
c offer the sacrifice........Heb 13:15

CONTINUE
persuaded them to *c*........Acts 13:43
Shall we *c* in sin that........Rom 6:1
who does not c in all........Gal 3:10
C earnestly in prayer........Col 4:2
because they did not c........Heb 8:9

CONTINUED
c steadfastly in the........Acts 2:42
us, they would have *c*........1 Jn 2:19

CONTRITE
saves such as have a *c*........Ps 34:18
A broken and a *c*........Ps 51:17
with him who has a *c*........Is 57:15
poor and of a *c* spirit........Is 66:2

CONVERSION
describing the *c*........Acts 15:3

CONVERTED
unless you are *c*........Matt 18:3

CONVICT
He has come, He will *c*........John 16:8
c those who........Tit 1:9
c all who are........Jude 15

CONVICTS
"Which of you *c*........John 8:46

COOL
in the garden in the *c*........Gen 3:8
water and *c* my tongue........Luke 16:24

CORD
this line of scarlet *c*........Josh 2:18
and a threefold *c*........Eccl 4:12
before the silver *c*........Eccl 12:6

CORNER
was not done in a *c*........Acts 26:26

CORNERSTONE
Or who laid its *c*........Job 38:6
stone, a precious *c*........Is 28:16
Has become the chief c........Matt 21:42
in Zion a chief c........1 Pe 2:6

CORRECT
with rebukes You *c*........Ps 39:11
C your son........Prov 29:17
But I will *c* you in........Jer 30:11

CORRECTION
nor detest His *c*........Prov 3:11
Harsh *c* is for him who........Prov 15:10
the rod of *c*........Prov 22:15
Do not withhold *c*........Prov 23:13
for reproof, for *c*........2 Ti 3:16

CORRUPT
have together become *c*........Ps 14:3
old man which grows *c*........Eph 4:22
men of *c* minds........2 Ti 3:8
in these things they *c*........Jude 10

CORRUPTED
for all flesh had *c*........Gen 6:12
no one, we have *c*........2 Co 7:2
so your minds may be *c*........2 Co 11:3
Your riches are *c*........Jas 5:2
the great harlot who *c*........Rev 19:2

CORRUPTIBLE
For this *c* must put on........1 Co 15:53
redeemed with *c* things........1 Pe 1:18

CORRUPTION
Your Holy One to see *c*........Ps 16:10
God raised up saw no *c*........Acts 13:37
from the bondage of *c*........Rom 8:21
The body is sown in *c*........1 Co 15:42
c inherit incorruption........1 Co 15:50
of the flesh reap *c*........Gal 6:8
having escaped the *c*........2 Pe 1:4
perish in their own *c*........2 Pe 2:12

COUNSEL
and strength, He has *c*........Job 12:13
the *c* of the wicked is........Job 21:16
is this who darkens *c*........Job 38:2
Who walks not in the *c*........Ps 1:1
We took sweet *c*........Ps 55:14
guide me with Your *c*........Ps 73:24
have none of my *c*........Prov 1:30
Where there is no *c*........Prov 11:14
C in the heart of man........Prov 20:5
chief priests took *c*........John 12:10
by the determined *c*........Acts 2:23
according to the *c*........Eph 1:11
immutability of His *c*........Heb 6:17
"I *c* you to buy from........Rev 3:18

COUNSELOR
be called Wonderful, *C*........Is 9:6
but there was no *c*........Is 41:28
Has your *c* perished........Mic 4:9
who has become His c........Rom 11:34

COUNSELORS
c there is safety........Prov 11:14

COUNT
c the people of Israel........2 Sa 24:4
c my life dear to........Acts 20:24
c me as a partner........Phm 17
His promise, as some *c*........2 Pe 3:9

COUNTED
Even a fool is *c*........Prov 17:28
c as the small dust........Is 40:15
the wages are not *c*........Rom 4:4
He *c* me faithful........1 Ti 1:12
who rule well be *c*........1 Ti 5:17

COUNTENANCE
the LORD lift up His *c*........Num 6:26
up the light of Your *c*........Ps 4:6
His *c* was like........Matt 28:3
of the glory of his *c*........2 Co 3:7
sword, and His *c*........Rev 1:16

COUNTRY
"Get out of your *c*........Gen 12:1
good news from a far *c*........Prov 25:25
and went into a far *c*........Matt 21:33
as in a foreign *c*........Heb 11:9
that is, a heavenly *c*........Heb 11:16

COURAGE
strong and of good *c*........Deut 31:6
thanked God and took *c*........Acts 28:15

COURT
appoint my day in *c*........Job 9:19
by you or by a human *c*........1 Co 4:3
They zealously *c*........Gal 4:17

COURTEOUS
be tenderhearted, be *c*........1 Pe 3:8

COURTS
he may dwell in Your *c*........Ps 65:4
even faints For the *c*........Ps 84:2
flourish in the *c*........Ps 92:13
And into His *c*........Ps 100:4
drink it in My holy *c*........Is 62:9

COVENANT
I will establish My *c*........Gen 6:18
day the LORD made a *c*........Gen 15:18
for Me, behold, My *c*........Gen 17:4
as a perpetual *c*........Ex 31:16
it is a *c* of salt........Num 18:19
Remember His *c* always........1 Ch 16:15
"I have made a *c*........Job 31:1
will show them His *c*........Ps 25:14
c shall stand firm........Ps 89:28
sons will keep My *c*........Ps 132:12
I might break the *c*........Zech 11:10
the Messenger of the *c*........Mal 3:1
This cup is the new *c*........Luke 22:20
c that was confirmed........Gal 3:17
Mediator of a better *c*........Heb 8:6
He says, "*A new c*........Heb 8:13
Mediator of the new *c*........Heb 12:24
of the everlasting *c*........Heb 13:20

COVER
c Yourself with light........Ps 104:2
LORD as the waters *c*........Is 11:9
not to *c* his head........1 Co 11:7
c a multitude of sins........Jas 5:20

COVERED
c my transgressions as......Job 31:33
Whose sin is *c*................Ps 32:1
c all their sin.................Ps 85:2
You have *c* me in my......Ps 139:13
with two he *c* his face......Is 6:2
of Jacob will be *c*............Is 27:9
For there is nothing *c*......Matt 10:26

COVERING
spread a cloud for a *c*......Ps 105:39
make sackcloth their *c*.....Is 50:3
given to her for a *c*.........1 Co 11:15

COVET
"You shall not *c*............Ex 20:17
c fields and take them.....Mic 2:2
You murder and *c*...........Jas 4:2

COVETOUSNESS
but he who hates *c*..........Prov 28:16
for nothing but your *c*.....Jer 22:17
heed and beware of *c*......Luke 12:15
would not have known *c*..Rom 7:7
all uncleanness or *c*.........Eph 5:3
conduct be without *c*.......Heb 13:5

CRAFTINESS
not walking in *c*..............2 Co 4:2
deceived Eve by his *c*......2 Co 11:3
in the cunning *c*..............Eph 4:14

CREAM
she brought out *c*............Judg 5:25
were bathed with *c*..........Job 29:6

CREATED
So God *c* man in His.......Gen 1:27
Spirit, they are *c*.............Ps 104:30
and see who has *c*...........Is 40:26
For the LORD has *c*..........Jer 31:22
Has not one God *c*..........Mal 2:10
Nor was man *c* for the.....1 Co 11:9
c in Christ Jesus.............Eph 2:10
hidden in God who *c*........Eph 3:9
new man which was *c*......Eph 4:24
Him all things were *c*......Col 1:16
from foods which God *c*...1 Ti 4:3
for You *c* all things.........Rev 4:11

CREATION
c which God...................Mark 13:19
c was subjected..............Rom 8:20
Christ, he is a new *c*.......2 Co 5:17
anything, but a new *c*......Gal 6:15
firstborn over all *c*..........Col 1:15

CREATOR
Remember now your *C*....Eccl 12:1
God, the LORD, the *C*.....Is 40:28
rather than the *C*...........Rom 1:25
to a faithful *C*...............1 Pe 4:19

CREATURE
the gospel to every *c*.......Mark 16:15
For every *c* of God is......1 Ti 4:4
no *c* hidden from His......Heb 4:13
And every *c* which is.......Rev 5:13
and every living *c*...........Rev 16:3

CREATURES
created great sea *c*..........Gen 1:21
firstfruits of His *c*............Jas 1:18
were four living *c*............Rev 4:6

CRIMINALS
also two others, *c*............Luke 23:32

CROOKED
whose ways are *c*.............Prov 2:15
c places straight..............Is 45:2
c places shall be made.....Luke 3:5
in the midst of a *c*..........Phil 2:15

CROSS
does not take his *c*..........Matt 10:38
to bear His *c*....................Matt 27:32
come down from the *c*.....Matt 27:40
lest the *c* of Christ..........1 Co 1:17
persecution for the *c*........Gal 6:12
glory except in the *c*........Gal 6:14
one body through the *c*....Eph 2:16
the enemies of the *c*........Phil 3:18
Him endured the *c*...........Heb 12:2

CROWN
c the year with Your.......Ps 65:11
The *c* of the wise is.........Prov 14:24
head is a *c* of glory.........Prov 16:31
Woe to the *c* of pride......Is 28:1
c has fallen from our.......Lam 5:16
they had twisted a *c*........Matt 27:29
obtain a perishable *c*.......1 Co 9:25
brethren, my joy and *c*....Phil 4:1
laid up for me the *c*........2 Ti 4:8
he will receive the *c*........Jas 1:12
no one may take your *c*...Rev 3:11
on His head a golden *c*....Rev 14:14

CROWNED
athletics, he is not *c*........2 Ti 2:5
You c him with glory.......Heb 2:7

CROWNS
and they had *c* of gold.....Rev 4:4
on his horns ten *c*...........Rev 13:1
His head were many *c*.....Rev 19:12

CRUCIFIED
"Let Him be *c*................Matt 27:22
Calvary, there they *c*.......Luke 23:33
lawless hands, have *c*.......Acts 2:23
that our old man was *c*....Rom 6:6
Was Paul *c* for you.........1 Co 1:13
Jesus Christ and Him *c*....1 Co 2:2
they would not have *c*.....1 Co 2:8
though He was *c*.............2 Co 13:4
"I have been *c*...............Gal 2:20

CRUCIFY
out again, "*C* Him..........Mark 15:13
I have power to *c* You......John 19:10
since they *c* again...........Heb 6:6

CRUEL
wrath, for it is *c*.............Gen 49:7
spirit and *c* bondage.......Ex 6:9
hate me with *c* hatred.....Ps 25:19
of the wicked are *c*.........Prov 12:10

CRUELTY
of *c* are in their..............Gen 49:5
the habitations of *c*.........Ps 74:20
c you have ruled.............Ezek 34:4

CRUSHED
every side, yet not *c*........2 Co 4:8

CRY
and their *c* came up to.....Ex 2:23
of oppressions they *c*.......Job 35:9
heart and my flesh *c*........Ps 84:2
I *c* out with my whole.....Ps 119:145
Does not wisdom *c*..........Prov 8:1
"What shall I *c*...............Is 40:6
c mightily to God............Jon 3:8
at midnight a *c*...............Matt 25:6
His own elect who *c*........Luke 18:7

CRYING
"*The voice of one c*.........Matt 3:3
nor sorrow, nor *c*............Rev 21:4

CRYSTAL
of an awesome *c*.............Ezek 1:22
a sea of glass, like *c*........Rev 4:6

CUBIT
shall finish it to a *c*........Gen 6:16
worrying can add one *c*....Matt 6:27

CUNNING
the serpent was more *c*....Gen 3:1
c comes quickly..............Job 5:13
c craftiness by which........Eph 4:14

CUP
My *c* runs over...............Ps 23:5
I will take up the *c*.........Ps 116:13
the dregs of the *c*............Is 51:17
"Take this wine *c*............Jer 25:15
The *c* of the LORD's........Hab 2:16
make Jerusalem a *c*.........Zech 12:2
little ones only a *c*.........Matt 10:42
Then He took the *c*.........Matt 26:27
possible, let this *c*..........Matt 26:39
c is the new covenant......Luke 22:20
You cannot drink the *c*....1 Co 10:21
c is the new covenant......1 Co 11:25
to give her the *c*.............Rev 16:19

CURSE
c the ground for man's.....Gen 8:21
'You shall not *c*..............Lev 19:14
c this people for me........Num 22:6
your God turned the *c*.....Deut 23:5
C God and die................Job 2:9
Do not *c* the king...........Eccl 10:20
do not *c* the rich.............Eccl 10:20
"I will send a *c*...............Mal 2:2
are cursed with a *c*..........Mal 3:9
law are under the *c*..........Gal 3:10

CURSED
c more than all cattle.......Gen 3:14
Depart from Me, you *c*....Matt 25:41
and near to being *c*..........Heb 6:8

CURSES
I will curse him who *c*.....Gen 12:3
For everyone who *c*.........Lev 20:9
c his father or his............Prov 20:20

CUSTOM
to me, As Your *c*............Ps 119:132
according to the *c*...........Acts 15:1
we have no such *c*...........1 Co 11:16

CUT
evildoers shall be *c*..........Ps 37:9
the wicked will be *c*.........Prov 2:22
causes you to sin, *c*.........Matt 5:30
"and will *c* him in...........Matt 24:51
him whose ear Peter *c*.....John 18:26
He had his hair *c*............Acts 18:18

CYMBAL
or a clanging *c*................1 Co 13:1

— D —

DAILY
much as they gather *d*.....Ex 16:5
Give us this day our *d*.....Matt 6:11
I sat *d* with you.............Matt 26:55
take up his cross *d*..........Luke 9:23
the Scriptures *d*..............Acts 17:11
our Lord, I die *d*.............1 Co 15:31
stands ministering *d*.........Heb 10:11

DANCE
and their children *d*.........Job 21:11
mourn, and a time to *d*....Eccl 3:4
And you did not *d*..........Matt 11:17

DANCED
Then David *d* before........2 Sa 6:14
daughter of Herodias *d*....Matt 14:6

DANCING
saw the calf and the *d*....Ex 32:19
me my mourning into *d*...Ps 30:11
he heard music and *d*......Luke 15:25

DARK
I am *d*..........................Song 1:5
d place of the earth.........Is 45:19
and makes the day *d*.......Amos 5:8
and the day shall be *d*.....Mic 3:6
I tell you in the *d*............Matt 10:27
while it was still *d*...........John 20:1
shines in a *d* place..........2 Pe 1:19

DARKNESS
d He called Night...........Gen 1:5
shall enlighten my *d*.........2 Sa 22:29
Those who sat in *d*..........Ps 107:10
d shall not hide...............Ps 139:12
d have seen a..................Is 9:2

I will make *d* light... Is 42:16
body will be full of *d*... Matt 6:23
cast out into outer *d*... Matt 8:12
and the power of *d*... Luke 22:53
d rather than light... John 3:19
d does not know... John 12:35
For you were once *d*... Eph 5:8
the rulers of the *d*... Eph 6:12
us from the power of *d*... Col 1:13
of the night nor of *d*... 1 Th 5:5
and to blackness and *d*... Heb 12:18
called you out of *d*... 1 Pe 2:9
d is reserved... 2 Pe 2:17
and in Him is no *d*... 1 Jn 1:5
d is passing away... 1 Jn 2:8
blackness of *d* forever... Jude 13

DARTS
quench all the fiery *d*... Eph 6:16

DASH
You shall *d* them in... Ps 2:9
lest you d your foot... Matt 4:6

DAUGHTER
Rejoice greatly, O *d*... Zech 9:9
"*Fear not, d of Zion*... John 12:15
the son of Pharaoh's *d*... Heb 11:24

DAUGHTERS
he begot sons and *d*... Gen 5:4
of God saw the *d*... Gen 6:2
d shall prophesy... Acts 2:17
man had four virgin *d*... Acts 21:9
shall be My sons and d... 2 Co 6:18

DAY
God called the light *D*... Gen 1:5
and *d* and night... Gen 8:22
shall observe this *d*... Ex 12:17
Remember the Sabbath *d* Ex 20:8
and cursed the *d*... Job 3:1
D unto *d* utters speech... Ps 19:2
For a *d* in Your courts... Ps 84:10
d which the LORD has... Ps 118:24
not strike you by *d*... Ps 121:6
night shines as the *d*... Ps 139:12
do not know what a *d*... Prov 27:1
For the *d* of the LORD... Joel 2:11
for the *d* of the LORD... Zeph 1:7
who has despised the *d*... Zech 4:10
who can endure the *d*... Mal 3:2
d our daily bread... Matt 6:11
and Gomorrah in the *d*... Matt 10:15
sent Me while it is *d*... John 9:4
great and notable d... Acts 2:20
person esteems one *d*... Rom 14:5
D will declare it... 1 Co 3:13
again the third *d*... 1 Co 15:4
perfectly that the *d*... 1 Th 5:2
and sons of the *d*... 1 Th 5:5
with the Lord one *d*... 2 Pe 3:8

DAYS
d are swifter than a... Job 7:6
of woman is of few *d*... Job 14:1
The *d* of our lives are... Ps 90:10
for length of *d*... Prov 3:2
before the difficult *d*... Eccl 12:1
had shortened those *d*... Mark 13:20
raise it up in three *d*... John 2:20
You observe *d* and... Gal 4:10
life and see good d... 1 Pe 3:10

DAYSPRING
with which the *D*... Luke 1:78

DEACONS
with the bishops and *d*... Phil 1:1
d be the husbands... 1 Ti 3:12

DEAD
"We shall all be *d*... Ex 12:33
he stood between the *d*... Num 16:48
work wonders for the *d*... Ps 88:10
but the *d* know nothing... Eccl 9:5
shall cast out the *d*... Is 26:19
d bury their own *d*... Matt 8:22
d are raised up and... Matt 11:5
not the God of the *d*... Matt 22:32
for this my son was *d*... Luke 15:24
d will hear the voice... John 5:25
was raised from the *d*... Rom 6:4
yourselves to be *d*... Rom 6:11
from the law sin was *d*... Rom 7:8
be Lord of both the *d*... Rom 14:9
resurrection of the *d*... 1 Co 15:12
baptized for the *d*... 1 Co 15:29
made alive, who were *d*... Eph 2:1
And the *d* in Christ... 1 Th 4:16
d while she lives... 1 Ti 5:6
without works is *d*... Jas 2:26
d did not live again... Rev 20:5
And the *d* were judged... Rev 20:12

DEADLY
they drink anything *d*... Mark 16:18
evil, full of *d* poison... Jas 3:8
d wound was healed... Rev 13:3

DEAF
makes the mute, the *d*... Ex 4:11
d shall hear the words... Is 29:18
d shall be unstopped... Is 35:5
d as My messenger... Is 42:19
d who have ears... Is 43:8
their ears shall be *d*... Mic 7:16
are cleansed and the *d*... Matt 11:5

DEATH
Let me die the *d*... Num 23:10
d parts you and me... Ruth 1:17
and the shadow of *d*... Job 10:21
For in *d* there is no... Ps 6:5
I sleep the sleep of *d*... Ps 13:3
of the shadow of *d*... Ps 23:4
house leads down to *d*... Prov 2:18
D and life are in the... Prov 18:21
no pleasure in the *d*... Ezek 18:32
who shall not taste *d*... Matt 16:28
but has passed from *d*... John 5:24
he shall never see *d*... John 8:51
Nevertheless *d* reigned... Rom 5:14
as sin reigned in *d*... Rom 5:21
D no longer has... Rom 6:9
the wages of sin is *d*... Rom 6:23
to bear fruit to *d*... Rom 7:5
proclaim the Lord's *d*... 1 Co 11:26
since by man came *d*... 1 Co 15:21
D is swallowed up in... 1 Co 15:54
The sting of *d* is sin... 1 Co 15:56
we are the aroma of *d*... 2 Co 2:16
d is working in us... 2 Co 4:12
the world produces *d*... 2 Co 7:10
to the point of *d*... Phil 2:8
taste *d* for everyone... Heb 2:9
who had the power of *d*... Heb 2:14
that he did not see *d*... Heb 11:5
brings forth *d*... Jas 1:15
to God, being put to *d*... 1 Pe 3:18
is sin leading to *d*... 1 Jn 5:16
Be faithful until *d*... Rev 2:10
Over such the second *d*... Rev 20:6
shall be no more *d*... Rev 21:4
which is the second *d*... Rev 21:8

DEBTORS
As we forgive our *d*... Matt 6:12
brethren, we are *d*... Rom 8:12
and they are their *d*... Rom 15:27

DECEIT
nor was any *d* in His... Is 53:9
"O full of all *d*... Acts 13:10
philosophy and empty *d*... Col 2:8

DECEITFUL
of the wicked are *d*... Prov 12:5
"The heart is *d*... Jer 17:9
are false apostles, *d*... 2 Co 11:13

DECEITFULLY
an idol, Nor sworn *d*... Ps 24:4
the word of God *d*... 2 Co 4:2

DECEIVE
'Do not *d* yourselves... Jer 37:9
rise up and *d* many... Matt 24:11
wonders, so as to *d*... Matt 24:24
Let no one *d* himself... 1 Co 3:18
they lie in wait to *d*... Eph 4:14
Let no one *d* you with... Eph 5:6
we have no sin, we *d*... 1 Jn 1:8

DECEIVED
"The serpent *d*... Gen 3:13
d heart has turned him... Is 44:20
by the commandment, *d*... Rom 7:11
as the serpent *d*... 2 Co 11:3
but the woman being *d*... 1 Ti 2:14
deceiving and being *d*... 2 Ti 3:13

DECEIVER
But cursed be the *d*... Mal 1:14
how that *d* said... Matt 27:63
This is a *d* and an... 2 Jn 7

DECENTLY
all things be done *d*... 1 Co 14:40

DECISION
but its every *d*... Prov 16:33
in the valley of *d*... Joel 3:14

DECLARE
The heavens *d* the... Ps 19:1
d that the LORD is... Ps 92:15
d His generation... Is 53:8
"*I will d Your name*... Heb 2:12
seen and heard we *d*... 1 Jn 1:3

DECLARED
the Father, He has *d*... John 1:18
and *d* to be the Son of... Rom 1:4

DECREE
I will declare the *d*... Ps 2:7
in those days that a *d*... Luke 2:1

DEDICATION
sacrifices at the *d*... Ezra 6:17
it was the Feast of *D*... John 10:22

DEED
d has been done... Judg 19:30
you do a charitable *d*... Matt 6:2
you do in word or *d*... Col 3:17

DEEDS
Declare His *d* among... Ps 9:11
vengeance on their *d*... Ps 99:8
declare His *d* among... Is 12:4
they surpass the *d*... Jer 5:28
because their *d*... John 3:19
"You do the *d*... John 8:41
one according to his d... Rom 2:6
you put to death the *d*... Rom 8:13
shares in his evil *d*... 2 Jn 11

DEEP
LORD God caused a *d*... Gen 2:21
D calls unto *d*... Ps 42:7
In His hand are the *d*... Ps 95:4
put out in *d* darkness... Prov 20:20
led them through the *d*... Is 63:13
d closed around me... Jon 2:5
d uttered its voice... Hab 3:10
Launch out into the *d*... Luke 5:4
I have been in the *d*... 2 Co 11:25

DEFEND
'For I will *d* this... 2 Ki 19:34
d my own ways before... Job 13:15
D the poor and... Ps 82:3
d the fatherless... Is 1:17
of hosts *d* Jerusalem... Is 31:5

DEFENSE
For wisdom is a *d*... Eccl 7:12
am appointed for the *d*... Phil 1:17

d no one stood with me... 2 Ti 4:16
be ready to give a *d*........ 1 Pe 3:15

DEFILED
lest they should be *d*....... John 18:28
to those who are *d*.......... Tit 1:15
even the garment *d*......... Jude 23

DEFILES
mouth, this *d* a man........ Matt 15:11
d the temple of God........ 1 Co 3:17
it anything that *d*.......... Rev 21:27

DEFRAUD
'You shall not *d*............. Lev 19:13
d his brother in this......... 1 Th 4:6

DEFRAUDED
let yourselves be *d*.......... 1 Co 6:7
no one, we have *d*.......... 2 Co 7:2

DEGREES
go forward ten *d*............ 2 Ki 20:9

DELIGHT
But his *d* is in the.......... Ps 1:2
D yourself also in the...... Ps 37:4
I *d* to do Your will.......... Ps 40:8
Your law had been my *d*.. Ps 119:92
d ourselves with love....... Prov 7:18
and I was daily His *d*...... Prov 8:30
call the Sabbath a *d*........ Is 58:13
For I *d* in the law of....... Rom 7:22

DELIVER
Let Him *d* Him.............. Ps 22:8
I will *d* him and honor..... Ps 91:15
d you from the immoral... Prov 2:16
wickedness will not *d*....... Eccl 8:8
have I no power to *d*....... Is 50:2
we serve is able to *d*....... Dan 3:17
into temptation, but *d*...... Matt 6:13
let Him *d* Him now if...... Matt 27:43
d such a one to Satan...... 1 Co 5:5
And the Lord will *d*......... 2 Ti 4:18
d the godly out of.......... 2 Pe 2:9

DELIVERANCE
d He gives to His king..... Ps 18:50
but *d* is of the LORD....... Prov 21:31
to preach d to the.......... Luke 4:18
not accepting *d*............. Heb 11:35

DELIVERED
All things have been *d*..... Matt 11:27
who was *d* up because..... Rom 4:25
But now we have been *d*.. Rom 7:6
who *d* us from so great.... 2 Co 1:10
was once for all *d*.......... Jude 3

DELIVERER
the LORD raised up a *d*.... Judg 3:9
LORD gave Israel a *d*....... 2 Ki 13:5
D will come out of......... Rom 11:26

DELUSION
send them strong *d*.......... 2 Th 2:11

DEMON
Jesus rebuked the *d*......... Matt 17:18
you say, 'He has a *d*....... Luke 7:33
Samaritan and have a *d*... John 8:48

DEMONIC
is earthly, sensual, *d*........ Jas 3:15

DEMONS
They sacrificed to *d*......... Deut 32:17
authority over all *d*......... Luke 9:1
even the *d* are subject..... Luke 10:17
Lord and the cup of *d*..... 1 Co 10:21
Even the *d* believe.......... Jas 2:19
a habitation of *d*............ Rev 18:2

DEN
in the viper's *d*.............. Is 11:8
cast him into the *d*.......... Dan 6:16
it a '*d of thieves*............ Matt 21:13

DENARIUS
the laborers for a *d*........ Matt 20:2
they brought Him a *d*...... Matt 22:19
quart of wheat for a *d*..... Rev 6:6

DENIED
before men will be *d*....... Luke 12:9
Peter then *d* again.......... John 18:27
d the Holy One and the... Acts 3:14
things cannot be *d*........... Acts 19:36
household, he has *d*........ 1 Ti 5:8
word, and have not *d*...... Rev 3:8

DENY
Lest I be full and *d*........ Prov 30:9
let him *d* himself............ Matt 16:24
He cannot *d* Himself....... 2 Ti 2:13
in works they *d*............. Tit 1:16

DENYING
but *d* its power.............. 2 Ti 3:5
d ungodliness and.......... Tit 2:12
d the Lord who bought.... 2 Pe 2:1

DEPART
scepter shall not *d*.......... Gen 49:10
they say to God, '*D*........ Job 21:14
D from evil.................. Ps 34:14
fear the LORD and *d*....... Prov 3:7
the mountains shall *d*....... Is 54:10
on the left hand, '*D*........ Matt 25:41
times some will *d*........... 1 Ti 4:1

DEPOSIT
in our hearts as a *d*........ 2 Co 1:22

DEPTH
because they had no *d*..... Matt 13:5
nor height nor *d*............ Rom 8:39
Oh, the *d* of the............ Rom 11:33
width and length and *d*.... Eph 3:18

DEPTHS
d have covered them....... Ex 15:5
The *d* also trembled........ Ps 77:16
my soul from the *d*......... Ps 86:13
led them through the *d*.... Ps 106:9
go down again to the *d*.... Ps 107:26
d I was brought forth...... Prov 8:24
our sins into the *d*.......... Mic 7:19
have not known the *d*...... Rev 2:24

DESCEND
d now from the cross....... Mark 15:32
Lord Himself will *d*......... 1 Th 4:16
This wisdom does not *d*... Jas 3:15

DESCENDANTS
All you *d* of Jacob.......... Ps 22:23
d shall inherit the........... Ps 25:13
In the LORD all the *d*...... Is 45:25
"We are Abraham's *d*...... John 8:33

DESCENDING
were ascending and *d*....... Gen 28:12
"I saw the Spirit *d*.......... John 1:32
of God ascending and *d*.. John 1:51
the holy Jerusalem, *d*...... Rev 21:10

DESIRE
d shall be for your......... Gen 3:16
Behold, You *d* truth in.... Ps 51:6
The *d* of the wicked......... Ps 112:10
And satisfy the *d*............ Ps 145:16
The *d* of the slothful....... Prov 21:25
"Father, I *d* that............ John 17:24
all manner of evil *d*........ Rom 7:8
Brethren, my heart's *d*..... Rom 10:1
d the best gifts.............. 1 Co 12:31
passion, evil *d*.............. Col 3:5
d has conceived............. Jas 1:15

DESIRED
d are they than gold........ Ps 19:10
One thing I have *d*.......... Ps 27:4
Whatever my eyes *d*........ Eccl 2:10

DESIRES
shall give you the *d*........ Ps 37:4
the devil, and the *d*......... John 8:44
fulfilling the *d*............... Eph 2:3

DESOLATE
on me, For I am *d*.......... Ps 25:16
any more be termed *D*.... Is 62:4
to make your land *d*........ Jer 4:7
house is left to you *d*....... Matt 23:38
one hour she is made *d*.... Rev 18:19

DESOLATION
the '*abomination of d*.... Matt 24:15
then know that its *d*....... Luke 21:20

DESPISE
if you *d* My statutes....... Lev 26:15
d Me shall be lightly........ 1 Sa 2:30
d your mother when she.. Prov 23:22
d your feast days........... Amos 5:21
to you priests who *d*........ Mal 1:6
one and *d* the other........ Matt 6:24
d the riches of His.......... Rom 2:4
d the church of God........ 1 Co 11:22

DESPISES
d the word will be........... Prov 13:13
d his neighbor sins.......... Prov 14:21
but a foolish man *d*......... Prov 15:20
d the scepter of My......... Ezek 21:10

DESPISING
the cross, *d* the shame..... Heb 12:2

DESTROY
d the righteous............... Gen 18:23
d all the wicked............. Ps 101:8
the wicked He will *d*....... Ps 145:20
shall not hurt nor *d*......... Is 11:9
have mercy, but will *d*..... Jer 13:14
I did not come to *d*......... Matt 5:17
Him who is able to *d*....... Matt 10:28
d this temple that is........ Mark 14:58
to save life or to *d*.......... Luke 6:9
d men's lives but to......... Luke 9:56
d the work of God for..... Rom 14:20
d the wisdom of the........ 1 Co 1:19
able to save and to *d*....... Jas 4:12

DESTRUCTION
not be afraid of *d*........... Job 5:21
d that lays waste............ Ps 91:6
your life from *d*.............. Ps 103:4
Pride goes before *d*......... Prov 16:18
called the City of *D*........ Is 19:18
wrath prepared for *d*....... Rom 9:22
one to Satan for the *d*..... 1 Co 5:5
whose end is *d*............... Phil 3:19
then sudden *d*................ 1 Th 5:3
with everlasting *d*............ 2 Th 1:9
which drown men in *d*..... 1 Ti 6:9
twist to their own *d*......... 2 Pe 3:16

DESTRUCTIVE
bring in *d* heresies............ 2 Pe 2:1

DETERMINED
Since his days are *d*......... Job 14:5
"Seventy weeks are *d*...... Dan 9:24
d their preappointed........ Acts 17:26
For I *d* not to know........ 1 Co 2:2

DEVICES
not ignorant of his *d*........ 2 Co 2:11

DEVIL
to be tempted by the *d*.... Matt 4:1
prepared for the *d*........... Matt 25:41
forty days by the *d*.......... Luke 4:2
then the *d* comes and...... Luke 8:12
and one of you is a *d*...... John 6:70
of your father the *d*......... John 8:44
d having already put........ John 13:2
give place to the *d*.......... Eph 4:27
the wiles of the *d*........... Eph 6:11
the snare of the *d*........... 2 Ti 2:26
Resist the *d* and he......... Jas 4:7
the works of the *d*........... 1 Jn 3:8
contending with the *d*...... Jude 9
Indeed, the *d* is about..... Rev 2:10

DEVISES
d wickedness on his......... Ps 36:4
he *d* evil continually........ Prov 6:14
But a generous man *d*..... Is 32:8

DEVOUR
A fire shall *d* before........Ps 50:3
For you *d* widows'.......... Matt 23:14
bite and *d* one another.... Gal 5:15
seeking whom he may *d*...1 Pe 5:8
d her Child as............... Rev 12:4

DEVOURED
Some wild beast has *d*..... Gen 37:20
rebel, you shall be *d*........Is 1:20
the curse has *d*...............Is 24:6
For shame has *d*.............Jer 3:24
have *d* their judges..........Hos 7:7
trees, The locust *d*.........Amos 4:9
birds came and *d* them.... Matt 13:4
of heaven and *d* them......Rev 20:9

DEVOUT
man was just and *d*........ Luke 2:25
d men carried................Acts 8:2
d soldier from among...... Acts 10:7
d proselytes....................Acts 13:43

DIADEM
LORD, and a royal *d*........Is 62:3

DIADEMS
ten horns, and seven *d*......Rev 12:3

DIE
it you shall surely *d*........Gen 2:17
but a person shall *d*.........2 Ch 25:4
sees that wise men *d*........ Ps 49:10
I shall not *d*.....................Ps 118:17
who are appointed to *d*...Prov 31:8
how does a wise man *d*...Eccl 2:16
born, and a time to *d*.......Eccl 3:2
why should you *d*..............Eccl 7:17
wicked way, he shall *d*.....Ezek 3:19
"Even if I have to *d*........Matt 26:35
"nor can they *d*...............Luke 20:36
eat of it and not *d*.......... John 6:50
to you that you will *d*......John 8:24
though he may *d*................John 11:25
that one man should *d*.....John 11:50
our law He ought to *d*.....John 19:7
the flesh you will *d*......... Rom 8:13
For as in Adam all *d*.......1 Co 15:22
and to *d* is gain.............Phil 1:21
for men to *d* once...........Heb 9:27
are the dead who *d*......... Rev 14:13

DIED
And all flesh *d*............... Gen 7:21
"Oh, that we had *d*.........Ex 16:3
was that the beggar *d*...... Luke 16:22
in due time Christ *d*........ Rom 5:6
Christ *d* for us................Rom 5:8
For he who has *d*.............Rom 6:7
sin revived and I *d*..........Rom 7:9
that if One *d* for all........ 2 Co 5:14
and He *d* for all............. 2 Co 5:15
through the law *d*........... Gal 2:19
who *d* for us.................. 1 Th 5:10
For if we *d* with Him...... 2 Ti 2:11
These all *d* in faith.........Heb 11:13
having *d* to sins............. 1 Pe 2:24

DILIGENT
And my spirit makes *d*.... Ps 77:6
of the *d* will rule.............Prov 12:24
d shall be made rich.........Prov 13:4
Let us therefore be *d*.......Heb 4:11

DILIGENTLY
If you *d* obey My............Deut 11:13
d followed every good..... 1 Ti 5:10
d lest anyone fall............ Heb 12:15

DIM
His eyes were not *d*........ Deut 34:7
the windows grow *d*......... Eccl 12:3
the gold has become *d*.....Lam 4:1

DIPPED
d his finger in the........... Lev 9:9
of bread when I have *d*....John 13:26
clothed with a robe *d*...... Rev 19:13

DISCERN
Can I *d* between the........2 Sa 19:35
Then you shall again *d*.....Mal 3:18
d the face of the sky........ Matt 16:3
senses exercised to *d*....... Heb 5:14

DISCERNED
they are spiritually *d*........1 Co 2:14

DISCERNER
d of the thoughts............ Heb 4:12

DISCIPLE
d is not above his........... Matt 10:24
in the name of a *d*.......... Matt 10:42
he cannot be My *d*..........Luke 14:26
d whom Jesus loved......... John 21:7

DISCIPLES
but Your *d* do not fast.....Matt 9:14
d transgress the.............. Matt 15:2
took the twelve *d*............Matt 20:17
My word, you are My *d*...John 8:31
to become His *d*.............John 9:27
but we are Moses' *d*........John 9:28
so you will be My *d*........ John 15:8

DISCRETION
d will preserve you..........Prov 2:11
out knowledge and *d*....... Prov 8:12
woman who lacks *d*.........Prov 11:22
The *d* of a man makes.....Prov 19:11
the heavens at His *d*........Jer 10:12

DISHONOR
d Who wish me evil........ Ps 40:14
d the pride of all............ Is 23:9
My Father, and you *d* Me John 8:49
d their bodies among....... Rom 1:24
and another for *d*............Rom 9:21
It is sown in *d*................1 Co 15:43
honor and some for *d*......2 Ti 2:20

DISOBEDIENT
out My hands to a d........Rom 10:21
d, deceived, serving.........Tit 3:3
They stumble, being *d*..... 1 Pe 2:8
who formerly were *d*....... 1 Pe 3:20

DISPUTES
d rather than godly.......... 1 Ti 1:4
but is obsessed with *d*...... 1 Ti 6:4
foolish and ignorant *d*......2 Ti 2:23
But avoid foolish *d*..........Tit 3:9

DISQUALIFIED
myself should become *d*... 1 Co 9:27
indeed you are *d*.............2 Co 13:5
though we may seem *d*.... 2 Co 13:7

DISSOLVED
of heaven shall be *d*........ Is 34:4
the heavens will be *d*........2 Pe 3:12

DISTRESS
me in the day of my *d*..... Gen 35:3
"When you are in *d*........ Deut 4:30
my life from every *d*........1 Ki 1:29
d them in His deep.......... Ps 2:5
on the LORD in *d*..............Ps 118:5
a whirlwind, when *d*.........Prov 1:27
and on the earth *d*.......... Luke 21:25
tribulation, or *d*..............Rom 8:35
of the present *d*..............1 Co 7:26

DIVIDE
D the living child............ 1 Ki 3:25
d their tongues................ Ps 55:9
d the spoil with the......... Prov 16:19
d the inheritance.............Luke 12:13
"Take this and *d*.............Luke 22:17

DIVIDED
and the waters were *d*..... Ex 14:21
death they were not *d*......2 Sa 1:23
"Every kingdom *d*...........Matt 12:25
and a house *d* against...... Luke 11:17
in one house will be *d*..... Luke 12:52
appeared to them *d*......... Acts 2:3
d them among all............Acts 2:45
Is Christ *d*...................... 1 Co 1:13
the great city was *d*......... Rev 16:19

DIVIDING
rightly *d* the word of....... 2 Ti 2:15

DIVINATION
shall you practice *d*......... Lev 19:26
Even though *d* is on......... Prov 16:10
darkness without *d*.......... Mic 3:6
a spirit of *d* met us.......... Acts 16:16

DIVINE
futility and who *d*........... Ezek 13:9
and her prophets *d*..........Mic 3:11
d service and the............ Heb 9:1
d power has given........... 2 Pe 1:3

DIVISIONS
note those who cause *d*.... Rom 16:17
and that there be no *d*.....1 Co 1:10
envy, strife, and *d*...........1 Co 3:3
hear that there are *d*....... 1 Co 11:18
persons, who cause *d*.......Jude 19

DIVISIVE
Reject a *d* man after....... Tit 3:10

DIVORCE
her a certificate of *d*........Deut 24:1
of your mother's *d*.......... Is 50:1
a certificate of *d*............ Mark 10:4

DO
I will also *d* it................ Is 46:11
men to *d* to you, *d*..........Matt 7:12
d this and you will.......... Luke 10:28
without Me you can *d*......John 15:5
d evil that good may....... Rom 3:8
good that I will to *d*........ Rom 7:19
or whatever you *d*, *d*.......1 Co 10:31
d all things through.......... Phil 4:13

DOCTRINE
said, 'my *d* is pure........... Job 11:4
for I give you good *d*...... Prov 4:2
of bread, but of the *d*......Matt 16:12
What new *d* is this.......... Mark 1:27
"My *d* is not Mine...........John 7:16
Jerusalem with your *d*......Acts 5:28
heart that form of *d*......... Rom 6:17
with every wind of *d*........ Eph 4:14
is contrary to sound *d*...... 1 Ti 1:10
followed my *d*................. 2 Ti 3:10
is profitable for *d*............2 Ti 3:16
not endure sound *d*......... 2 Ti 4:3
in *d* showing................... Tit 2:7
they may adorn the *d*...... Tit 2:10

DOERS
of God, but the *d*........... Rom 2:13
But be *d* of the word.......Jas 1:22

DOG
to David, "Am I a *d*....... 1 Sa 17:43
They growl like a *d*.........Ps 59:6
d is better than a........... Eccl 9:4
d returns to his own....... 2 Pe 2:22

DOGS
what is holy to the *d*....... Matt 7:6
d eat the crumbs which....Matt 15:27
Moreover the *d* came....... Luke 16:21
But outside are *d*........... Rev 22:15

DOMINION
let them have *d*.............. Gen 1:26
"*D* and fear belong......... Job 25:2
made him to have *d*........ Ps 8:6
Let them not have *d*........Ps 19:13
d is an everlasting.......... Dan 4:34
sin shall not have *d*......... Rom 6:14
Not that we have *d*......... 2 Co 1:24
glory and majesty, *d*........Jude 25

DONKEY
d saw the Angel........ Num 22:23
d its master's crib............ Is 1:3
colt, the foal of a d......... Matt 21:5
He had found a young *d*.. John 12:14
d speaking with a............ 2 Pe 2:16

DOOR
sin lies at the *d*.............. Gen 4:7
Keep watch over the *d*..... Ps 141:3
d turns on its hinges........ Prov 26:14
stone against the *d*.......... Matt 27:60
to you, I am the *d*.......... John 10:7
and effective *d*............... 1 Co 16:9
d was opened to me by.... 2 Co 2:12
would open to us a *d*......... Col 4:3
is standing at the *d*.......... Jas 5:9
before you an open *d*...... Rev 3:8
I stand at the *d*............... Rev 3:20
and behold, a *d*............... Rev 4:1

DOORKEEPER
I would rather be a *d*...... Ps 84:10
"To him the *d*............... John 10:3

DOORPOSTS
write them on the *d*........ Deut 6:9
"Strike the *d*.................. Amos 9:1

DOUBLE
from the LORD's hand *d*... Is 40:2
first I will repay *d*........... Jer 16:18
worthy of *d* honor............ 1 Ti 5:17
and repay her *d*............... Rev 18:6

DOUBLE-MINDED
I hate the *d*..................... Ps 119:113
he is a *d* man.................. Jas 1:8
your hearts, you *d*........... Jas 4:8

DOUBTS
And why do *d* arise in..... Luke 24:38
for I have *d* about you..... Gal 4:20
doubting, for he who *d*.... Jas 1:6

DOVE
d found no resting........... Gen 8:9
I had wings like a *d*........ Ps 55:6
also is like a silly *d*........ Hos 7:11
descending like a *d*.......... Matt 3:16

DOWNCAST
who comforts the *d*......... 2 Co 7:6

DRAGON
a great, fiery red *d*.......... Rev 12:3
they worshiped the *d*....... Rev 13:4
He laid hold of the *d*....... Rev 20:2

DRANK
them, and they all *d*........ Mark 14:23
d the same spiritual......... 1 Co 10:4

DRAW
d honey from the rock..... Deut 32:13
me to *d* near to God....... Ps 73:28
and the years *d* near........ Eccl 12:1
with joy you will *d*........... Is 12:3
"*D* some out now........... John 2:8
You have nothing to *d*..... John 4:11
will *d* all peoples............. John 12:32
let us *d* near with a......... Heb 10:22
D near to God and He.... Jas 4:8

DREAM
Now Joseph dreamed a *d* Gen 37:5
will fly away like a *d*....... Job 20:8
As a *d* when one awakes.. Ps 73:20
like those who *d*.............. Ps 126:1
For a *d* comes through..... Eccl 5:3
her, shall be as a *d*......... Is 29:7
prophet who has a *d*........ Jer 23:28
do not let the *d*............... Dan 4:19
to Joseph in a *d*.............. Matt 2:13
things today in a *d*.......... Matt 27:19
your old men shall d....... Acts 2:17

DRINK
"What shall we *d*........... Ex 15:24
gave me vinegar to *d*....... Ps 69:21
D water from your own... Prov 5:15
mocker, intoxicating *d*..... Prov 20:1
Give strong *d* to him........ Prov 31:6
Bring wine, let us *d*........ Amos 4:1
to you of wine and *d*........ Mic 2:11
and you gave Me no *d*..... Matt 25:42
that day when I *d*........... Matt 26:29
mingled with gall to *d*...... Matt 27:34
with myrrh to *d*.............. Mark 15:23
to her, "Give Me a *d*...... John 4:7
him come to Me and *d*.... John 7:37
d wine nor do anything.... Rom 14:21
do, as often as you *d*....... 1 Co 11:25
all been made to *d*.......... 1 Co 12:13
No longer *d* only water.... 1 Ti 5:23
has made all nations *d*..... Rev 14:8

DROVE
So He *d* out the man....... Gen 3:24
temple of God and *d*....... Matt 21:12
a whip of cords, He *d*...... John 2:15

DRUNK
of the wine and was *d*..... Gen 9:21
the guests have well *d*...... John 2:10
For these are not *d*......... Acts 2:15
and another is *d*.............. 1 Co 11:21
And do not be *d*.............. Eph 5:18
and those who get *d*......... 1 Th 5:7
the earth were made *d*...... Rev 17:2

DRUNKARD
d could be included......... Deut 29:19
d is a proverb in the....... Prov 26:9
to and fro like a *d*........... Is 24:20
or a reviler, or a *d*.......... 1 Co 5:11

DRUNKENNESS
will be filled with *d*........ Ezek 23:33
Jerusalem a cup of *d*........ Zech 12:2
with carousing, *d*............. Luke 21:34
not in revelry and *d*........ Rom 13:13
envy, murders, *d*.............. Gal 5:21
lusts, *d*........................... 1 Pe 4:3

DULL
heart of this people *d*...... Is 6:10
people has grown d......... Matt 13:15
you have become *d*.......... Heb 5:11

DUMB
the tongue of the *d*.......... Is 35:6
You deaf and *d* spirit...... Mark 9:25

DUST
formed man of the *d*....... Gen 2:7
d you shall return........... Gen 3:19
descendants as the *d*....... Gen 13:16
"Who can count the *d*..... Num 23:10
and repent in *d*............... Job 42:6
that we are *d*.................. Ps 103:14
counted as the small *d*..... Is 40:15
They shall lick the *d*........ Mic 7:17
city, shake off the *d*........ Matt 10:14
image of the man of *d*..... 1 Co 15:49

DWELL
Who may *d* in Your holy Ps 15:1
D in the land.................. Ps 37:3
the LORD God might *d*.... Ps 68:18
of my God than *d*............ Ps 84:10
he will *d* on high............ Is 33:16
"I *d* in the high and........ Is 57:15
They shall no longer *d*..... Lam 4:15
"*I will d in them*............. 2 Co 6:16
that Christ may *d*............. Eph 3:17
the fullness should *d*........ Col 1:19
the word of Christ *d*......... Col 3:16
men, and He will *d*.......... Rev 21:3

DWELLS
He who *d* in the secret.... Ps 91:1
Father who *d* in Me......... John 14:10
do it, but sin that *d*......... Rom 7:17
the Spirit of God *d*.......... Rom 8:9
the Spirit of God *d*.......... 1 Co 3:16
d all the fullness............ Col 2:9
which righteousness *d*...... 2 Pe 3:13
you, where Satan *d*.......... Rev 2:13

DWELT
became flesh and *d*......... John 1:14

— E —

EAGLE
As an *e* stirs up its.......... Deut 32:11
e swooping on its prey..... Job 9:26
fly away like an *e*............ Prov 23:5
the way of an *e*.............. Prov 30:19
nest as high as the *e*........ Jer 49:16
had the face of an *e*........ Ezek 1:10
like a flying *e*................. Rev 4:7
two wings of a great *e*..... Rev 12:14

EAGLES
how I bore you on *e*........ Ex 19:4
up with wings like *e*........ Is 40:31
are swifter than *e*............ Jer 4:13
e will be gathered............ Matt 24:28

EAR
shall pierce his *e*............. Ex 21:6
Bow down Your *e*............ Ps 31:2
what you hear in the *e*..... Matt 10:27
cut off his right *e*........... John 18:10
not seen, nor e heard....... 1 Co 2:9
if the *e* should say........... 1 Co 12:16
"He who has an *e*........... Rev 2:7

EARNESTLY
He prayed more *e*........... Luke 22:44
in this we groan, *e*.......... 2 Co 5:2
e that it would not.......... Jas 5:17
you to contend *e*............. Jude 3

EARS
Whoever shuts his *e*......... Prov 21:13
and hear with their *e*....... Is 6:10
"He who has *e*................ Matt 11:15
e are hard of hearing...... Matt 13:15
they have itching *e*.......... 2 Ti 4:3

EARTH
coming to judge the *e*...... 1 Ch 16:33
he hangs the *e* on............ Job 26:7
e is the LORD's............... Ps 24:1
You had formed the *e*...... Ps 90:2
Let the *e* be moved.......... Ps 99:1
wisdom founded the *e*...... Prov 3:19
e abides forever.............. Eccl 1:4
for the meek of the *e*....... Is 11:4
e is My footstool............. Is 66:1
shall inherit the *e*............ Matt 5:5
heaven and *e* pass away... Matt 5:18
e as it is in heaven......... Matt 6:10
treasures on *e*................. Matt 6:19
then shook the *e*............. Heb 12:26
"Do not harm the *e*........ Rev 7:3
from whose face the *e*...... Rev 20:11
new heaven and a new *e*.. Rev 21:1

EARTHLY
If I have told you *e*......... John 3:12
we know that if our *e*...... 2 Co 5:1
their mind on *e* things...... Phil 3:19
from above, but is *e*........ Jas 3:15

EARTHQUAKE
after the wind an *e*.......... 1 Ki 19:11
there was a great *e*......... Matt 28:2
there was a great *e*......... Rev 6:12

EARTHQUAKES
And there will be *e*......... Mark 13:8

EASIER
"Which is *e*..................... Mark 2:9
"It is *e* for a camel.......... Mark 10:25

EAST
goes toward the *e*............ Gen 2:14
As far as the *e*................ Ps 103:12
descendants from the *e*.... Is 43:5

wise men from the *E*....... Matt 2:1
many will come from *e*.... Matt 8:11
will come from the *e*....... Luke 13:29
e might be prepared........ Rev 16:12

EAT
you may freely *e*............ Gen 2:16
up my people as they *e*.... Ps 53:4
good to *e* much honey..... Prov 25:27
e this scroll.................... Ezek 3:1
e the flesh of My............ Mic 3:3
life, what you will *e*.........Matt 6:25
You to *e* the Passover......Matt 26:17
give us His flesh to *e*.......John 6:52
one believes he may *e*......Rom 14:2
e meat nor drink wine..... Rom 14:21
I will never again *e*......... 1 Co 8:13
neither shall he *e*............ 2 Th 3:10
e your flesh like fire........Jas 5:3

EATS
receives sinners and *e*...... Luke 15:2
"Whoever *e* My flesh.......John 6:54
e this bread will live........ John 6:58
e despise him who does....Rom 14:3
He who *e*, *e* to the..........Rom 14:6
an unworthy manner *e*..... 1 Co 11:29

EDIFICATION
his good, leading to *e*...... Rom 15:2
prophesies speaks *e*......... 1 Co 14:3
things be done for *e*........ 1 Co 14:26
has given me for *e*.......... 2 Co 13:10
rather than godly *e*..........1 Ti 1:4

EDIFIES
puffs up, but love *e*.........1 Co 8:1
he who prophesies *e*........ 1 Co 14:4

EDIFY
all things do not *e*...........1 Co 10:23
and *e* one another...........1 Th 5:11

ELDER
The *e* and honorable....... Is 9:15
against an *e* except.......... 1 Ti 5:19
I who am a fellow *e*........ 1 Pe 5:1

ELDERS
and seventy of the *e*........ Ex 24:1
the tradition of the *e*....... Matt 15:2
be rejected by the *e*........ Luke 9:22
they had appointed *e*....... Acts 14:23
and called for the *e*......... Acts 20:17
e who rule well be.......... 1 Ti 5:17
lacking, and appoint *e*......Tit 1:5
e obtained a good.......... Heb 11:2
Let him call for the *e*...... Jas 5:14
e who are among you I.... 1 Pe 5:1
I saw twenty-four *e*......... Rev 4:4

ELECT
whom I uphold, My *E*...... Is 42:1
and Israel My *e*............. Is 45:4
gather together His *e*....... Matt 24:31
e have obtained it........... Rom 11:7
e according to the........... 1 Pe 1:2
a chief cornerstone, e....... 1 Pe 2:6

ELECTION
e they are beloved...........Rom 11:28
calling and *e* sure............2 Pe 1:10

ELEMENTS
weak and beggarly *e*........Gal 4:9
e will melt with..............2 Pe 3:10

ELOQUENT
O my Lord, I am not *e*....Ex 4:10
an *e* man and mighty in... Acts 18:24

EMPTY
appear before Me *e*......... Ex 23:15
e things which................ 1 Sa 12:21
not listen to *e* talk...........Job 35:13
LORD makes the earth *e*...Is 24:1
comes, he finds it *e*......... Matt 12:44

He has sent away *e*......... Luke 1:53
you with *e* words............ Eph 5:6

END
make me to know my *e*... Ps 39:4
e is the way of death....... Prov 14:12
Declaring the *e*...............Is 46:10
what shall be the *e*...........Dan 12:8
e has come upon my.........Amos 8:2
the harvest is the *e*..........Matt 13:39
to pass, but the *e*............Matt 24:6
always, even to the *e*....... Matt 28:20
He loved them to the *e*....John 13:1
For Christ is the *e*...........Rom 10:4
ages, world without *e*........Eph 3:21
the hope firm to the *e*..... Heb 3:6
but now, once at the *e*.....Heb 9:26
But the *e* of all...............1 Pe 4:7
the latter *e* is worse.........2 Pe 2:20
Beginning and the *E*.........Rev 22:13

ENDS
All the *e* of the world......Ps 22:27
she came from the *e*........ Matt 12:42
to the e of the earth........Acts 13:47
their words to the e..........Rom 10:18

ENDURANCE
For you have need of *e*....Heb 10:36
e the race that................ Heb 12:1

ENDURES
And His truth *e*..............Ps 100:5
For His mercy *e*..............Ps 136:1
But he who *e* to the.........Matt 10:22
e only for a while............Matt 13:21
for the food which *e*........John 6:27

ENEMIES
me wiser than my *e*......... Ps 119:98
I count them my *e*.......... Ps 139:22
to you, love your *e*..........Matt 5:44
be saved from our *e*......... Luke 1:71
e we were reconciled...... Rom 5:10
till He has put all *e*......... 1 Co 15:25
and devours their *e*......... Rev 11:5

ENEMY
If your *e* is hungry.......... Prov 25:21
and hate your *e*..............Matt 5:43
last *e* that will be............ 1 Co 15:26
become your *e* because.... Gal 4:16
not count him as an *e*......2 Th 3:15
makes himself an *e*..........Jas 4:4

ENJOY
e its sabbaths as long.......Lev 26:34
therefore *e* pleasure"........Eccl 2:1
richly all things to *e*.........1 Ti 6:17
than to *e* the passing....... Heb 11:25

ENJOYMENT
So I commended *e*.......... Eccl 8:15

ENMITY
And I will put *e*..............Gen 3:15
the carnal mind is *e*.........Rom 8:7
putting to death the *e*...... Eph 2:16
with the world is *e*.......... Jas 4:4

ENTER
E into His gates..............Ps 100:4
Do not *e* into judgment... Ps 143:2
you will by no means *e*.... Matt 5:20
"*E* by the narrow............Matt 7:13
e the kingdom of God..... Matt 19:24
E into the joy of your..... Matt 25:21
and pray, lest you *e*.........Matt 26:41
you, he who does not *e*....John 10:1
who have believed do *e*....Heb 4:3
e the Holiest by the.........Heb 10:19
e through the gates..........Rev 22:14

ENTERED
Then Satan *e* Judas......... Luke 22:3
through one man sin *e*..... Rom 5:12
ear heard, nor have e...... 1 Co 2:9

the forerunner has *e*........ Heb 6:20
e the Most Holy Place..... Heb 9:12

ENTREAT
E me not to leave you..... Ruth 1:16
But now *e* God's favor.....Mal 1:9
being defamed, we *e*........1 Co 4:13

ENVY
not in strife and *e*........... Rom 13:13
love does not *e*...............1 Co 13:4
living in malice and *e*.......Tit 3:3
For where *e* and............ Jas 3:16

EPISTLE
You are our *e* written...... 2 Co 3:2
are manifestly an *e*.......... 2 Co 3:3
by word or our *e*............ 2 Th 2:15
is a sign in every *e*.......... 2 Th 3:17

EPISTLES
e of commendation to...... 2 Co 3:1
as also in all his *e*........... 2 Pe 3:16

EQUAL
it was you, a man my *e*....Ps 55:13
and you made them *e*...... Matt 20:12
making Himself *e*.............John 5:18
it robbery to be *e*............Phil 2:6

ERROR
a sinner from the *e*..........Jas 5:20
led away with the *e*......... 2 Pe 3:17
and the spirit of *e*........... 1 Jn 4:6
run greedily in the *e*........Jude 11

ESCAPE
E to the mountains......... Gen 19:17
and they shall not *e*.........Job 11:20
speaks lies will not *e*........Prov 19:5
and how shall we *e*..........Is 20:6
e all these things.............Luke 21:36
same, that you will *e*....... Rom 2:3
also make the way of *e*.... 1 Co 10:13
how shall we *e* if we........Heb 2:3
e who refused Him who... Heb 12:25

ESTABLISH
to *e* them forever............2 Ch 9:8
'Your seed I will *e*.......... Ps 89:4
e the work of our............Ps 90:17
e an everlasting...............Ezek 16:60
seeking to *e* their own..... Rom 10:3
faithful, who will *e*.......... 2 Th 3:3
E your hearts..................Jas 5:8
a while, perfect, *e*........... 1 Pe 5:10

ESTABLISHED
built up in Him and *e*......Col 2:7
covenant, which was *e*..... Heb 8:6
that the heart be *e*.......... Heb 13:9

ESTEEM
and we did not *e*.............Is 53:3
e others better than.........Phil 2:3
and hold such men in *e*....Phil 2:29
e them very highly......... 1 Th 5:13

ESTEEMS
One person *e* one day......Rom 14:5

ETERNAL
e God is your refuge....... Deut 33:27
For man goes to his *e*...... Eccl 12:5
I do that I may have *e*.....Matt 19:16
in the age to come, *e*.......Mark 10:30
not perish but have *e*.......John 3:15
you think you have *e*.......John 5:39
And I give them *e* life..... John 10:28
that He should give *e*...... John 17:2
"And this is *e* life.......... John 17:3
e life to those who by...... Rom 2:7
the gift of God is *e*......... Rom 6:23
e weight of glory............2 Co 4:17
are not seen are *e*...........2 Co 4:18
not made with hands, *e*....2 Co 5:1
lay hold on *e* life............ 1 Ti 6:12
e life which God............Tit 1:2

and of *e* judgment..........Heb 6:2
e life which was.............1 Jn 1:2
that no murderer has *e*.... 1 Jn 3:15
God has given us *e*..........1 Jn 5:11
that you have *e* life.........1 Jn 5:13
Jesus Christ unto *e*..........Jude 21

EUNUCH
of Ethiopia, a *e*............. Acts 8:27

EUNUCHS
have made themselves *e*... Matt 19:12

EVANGELIST
of Philip the *e*................ Acts 21:8
do the work of an *e*........ 2 Ti 4:5

EVANGELISTS
some prophets, some *e*.....Eph 4:11

EVERLASTING
God of Israel from *e*....... 1 Ch 16:36
Your kingdom is an *e*...... Ps 145:13
from *E* is Your name...... Is 63:16
awake, some to *e* life.........Dan 12:2
and inherit *e* life............Matt 19:29
not perish but have *e*........John 3:16
endures to *e* life.............John 6:27
in Him may have *e*...........John 6:40
believes in Me has *e*........John 6:47
of the Spirit reap *e*...........Gal 6:8

EVIDENCE
e of things not seen.........Heb 11:1

EVIDENT
of some are clearly *e*....... 1 Ti 5:25
e that our Lord arose...... Heb 7:14

EVIL
of good and *e*...................Gen 2:9
knowing good and *e*......... Gen 3:5
his heart was only *e*.........Gen 6:5
rebellious and *e* city........ Ezra 4:12
e shall touch you..............Job 5:19
I will fear no *e*................ Ps 23:4
e shall befall you..............Ps 91:10
e will bow before the.......Prov 14:19
Whoever rewards *e*..........Prov 17:13
to those who call *e*..........Is 5:20
of peace and not of *e*...... Jer 29:11
Seek good and not *e*..........Amos 5:14
deliver us from the *e*........ Matt 6:13
If you then, being *e*.........Matt 7:11
Why do you think *e*.......... Matt 9:4
everyone practicing *e*........John 3:20
e I will not to do............. Rom 7:19
Repay no one *e* for...........Rom 12:17
not be overcome by *e*......Rom 12:21

EVILDOER
If He were not an *e*........ John 18:30
suffer trouble as an *e*.......2 Ti 2:9
a thief, an *e*.................. 1 Pe 4:15

EVILDOERS
Depart from me, you *e*.... Ps 119:115
against you as *e*.............. 1 Pe 2:12

EXALT
e His name together........Ps 34:3
are my God, I will *e*........Ps 118:28
into heaven, I will *e*........ Is 14:13

EXALTED
Let God be *e*.................. 2 Sa 22:47
name, which is *e*.............Neh 9:5
When vileness is *e*............Ps 12:8
I will be *e* among the...... Ps 46:10
His name alone is *e*.........Ps 148:13
LORD alone shall be *e*......Is 2:11
valley shall be *e*.............Is 40:4
"Him God has *e*..............Acts 5:31
also has highly *e*.............Phil 2:9

EXALTS
Righteousness *e*.............Prov 14:34
e himself above all..........2 Th 2:4

EXAMINE
But let a man *e*..............1 Co 11:28
But let each one *e*...........Gal 6:4

EXAMPLE
to make her a public *e*.....Matt 1:19
I have given you an *e*...... John 13:15
in following my *e*............ Phil 3:17
to make ourselves an *e*...... 2 Th 3:9
youth, but be an *e*........... 1 Ti 4:12
us, leaving us an *e*.......... 1 Pe 2:21
making them an *e*............2 Pe 2:6
are set forth as an *e*........ Jude 7

EXAMPLES
happened to them as *e*.......1 Co 10:11
so that you became *e*........1 Th 1:7
to you, but being *e*...........1 Pe 5:3

EXCEEDING
He might show the *e*........ Eph 2:7

EXCEEDINGLY
"Rejoice and be *e*...........Matt 5:12

EXCELLENT
He is *e* in power............Job 37:23
For He has done *e*.......... Is 12:5
in counsel and *e*..............Is 28:29
"Inasmuch as an *e*...........Dan 5:12
the things that are *e*......... Rom 2:18
the things that are *e*......... Phil 1:10
e sacrifice than Cain........ Heb 11:4
came to Him from the *E*.. 2 Pe 1:17

EXCHANGED
nor can it be *e*................Job 28:17
e the truth of God for..... Rom 1:25
For even their women *e*... Rom 1:26

EXCUSE
God be angry at your *e*....Eccl 5:6
but now they have no *e*... John 15:22
they are without *e*...........Rom 1:20
do you think that we *e*.....2 Co 12:19

EXERCISE
those who are great *e*...... Matt 20:25
e profits a little...............1 Ti 4:8

EXHORT
such we command and *e*.. 2 Th 3:12
e him as a father..............1 Ti 5:1
and *e* these things........... 1 Ti 6:2
doctrine, both to *e*.......... Tit 1:9
Speak these things, *e*....... Tit 2:15
e one another...................Heb 3:13

EXHORTATION
you have any word of *e*... Acts 13:15
he who exhorts, in *e*........Rom 12:8
to reading, to *e*...............1 Ti 4:13
with the word of *e*.......... Heb 13:22

EXPECTATION
The *e* of the poor............ Ps 9:18
God alone, For my *e*........Ps 62:5
the people were in *e*........Luke 3:15
a certain fearful *e*...........Heb 10:27

EXPLAIN
was no one who could *e*...Gen 41:24
E this parable to us.........Matt 15:15
to say, and hard to *e*....... Heb 5:11

EXPOSED
his deeds should be *e*.......John 3:20
all things that are *e*......... Eph 5:13

EXPOUNDED
He *e* to them in all.......... Luke 24:27

EXTOL
I will *e* You.................... Ps 30:1
E Him who rides............. Ps 68:4

EXTOLLED
shall be exalted and *e*...... Is 52:13

EYE
"*e* for *e*.......................... Ex 21:24
guide you with My *e*........Ps 32:8
He who formed the *e*...... Ps 94:9
and the seeing *e*..............Prov 20:12
who has a bountiful *e*...... Prov 22:9
A man with an evil *e*.......Prov 28:22
e that mocks his..............Prov 30:17
e is not satisfied..............Eccl 1:8
the apple of His *e*.......... Zech 2:8
if your right *e*.................Matt 5:29
it was said, '*An e*............Matt 5:38
plank in your own *e*....... Matt 7:3
e causes you to sin......... Matt 18:9
Or is your *e* evil..............Matt 20:15
through a needle's *e*........ Luke 18:25
Because I am not an *e*.....1 Co 12:16
the twinkling of an *e*....... 1 Co 15:52
every *e* will see Him........Rev 1:7

EYES
e will be opened............ Gen 3:5
The *e* of the LORD are.....Ps 34:15
I will lift up my *e*............Ps 121:1
e look straight ahead....... Prov 4:25
Who has redness of *e*...... Prov 23:29
be wise in his own *e*...... Prov 26:5
The wise man's *e*.............Eccl 2:14
You have dove's *e*.............Song 1:15
e have seen the King........ Is 6:5
who have *e* and see not... Jer 5:21
e will weep bitterly...........Jer 13:17
rims were full of *e*...........Ezek 1:18
full of *e* all around......... Ezek 10:12
horn between his *e*.......... Dan 8:5
But blessed are your *e*..... Matt 13:16
"He put clay on my *e*...... John 9:15
plucked out your own *e*... Gal 4:15
have seen with our *e*....... 1 Jn 1:1
the lust of the *e*.............1 Jn 2:16
as snow, and His *e*.......... Rev 1:14
and anoint your *e*............Rev 3:18
creatures full of *e*........... Rev 4:6
horns and seven *e*........... Rev 5:6
tear from their *e*............. Rev 21:4

EYEWITNESSES
the beginning were *e*....... Luke 1:2
e of His majesty.............. 2 Pe 1:16

— F —

FABLES
nor give heed to *f*........... 1 Ti 1:4
be turned aside to *f*.........2 Ti 4:4
cunningly devised *f*...........2 Pe 1:16

FACE
For I have seen God *f*..... Gen 32:30
f shone while he.............. Ex 34:29
he put a veil on his *f*....... Ex 34:33
the LORD make His *f*...... Num 6:25
curse You to Your *f*.........Job 1:11
me, I will see Your *f*........ Ps 17:15
Why do You hide Your *f* Ps 44:24
sins have hidden His *f*..... Is 59:2
before Your f, who............Matt 11:10
f shone like the sun...........Matt 17:2
dimly, but then *f*..............1 Co 13:12
with unveiled *f*................ 2 Co 3:18
his natural *f* in a..............Jas 1:23
but the f of the LORD...... 1 Pe 3:12
They shall see His *f*.........Rev 22:4

FADE
we all *f* as a leaf............ Is 64:6
and the leaf shall *f*..........Jer 8:13
rich man also will *f*..........Jas 1:11
and that does not *f*..........1 Pe 1:4

FADES
withers, the flower *f*........ Is 40:7

FAIL
flesh and my heart *f*.........Ps 73:26
tittle of the law to *f*.........Luke 16:17
faith should not *f*............Luke 22:32
prophecies, they will *f*......1 Co 13:8
Your years will not f....... Heb 1:12

FAILS
My strength f because...... Ps 31:10
My spirit f...... Ps 143:7
and every vision f...... Ezek 12:22
Love never f...... 1 Co 13:8

FAINT
shall walk and not f...... Is 40:31
my heart is f in me...... Jer 8:18

FAIR
Behold, you are f...... Song 1:15
to a place called F...... Acts 27:8
what is just and f...... Col 4:1

FAITH
shall live by his f...... Hab 2:4
you, O you of little f...... Matt 6:30
not found such great f...... Matt 8:10
f as a mustard seed...... Matt 17:20
it that you have no f...... Mark 4:40
"Increase our f...... Luke 17:5
will He really find f...... Luke 18:8
are sanctified by f...... Acts 26:18
for obedience to the f...... Rom 1:5
God is revealed from f...... Rom 1:17
God which is through f...... Rom 3:22
f apart from the deeds...... Rom 3:28
his f is accounted for...... Rom 4:5
f comes by hearing...... Rom 10:17
and you stand by f...... Rom 11:20
in proportion to our f...... Rom 12:6
though I have all f...... 1 Co 13:2
And now abide f...... 1 Co 13:13
For we walk by f...... 2 Co 5:7
the flesh I live by f...... Gal 2:20
or by the hearing of f...... Gal 3:2
f are sons of Abraham...... Gal 3:7
the law is not of f...... Gal 3:12
f working through love...... Gal 5:6
been saved through f...... Eph 2:8
one Lord, one f...... Eph 4:5
to the unity of the f...... Eph 4:13
taking the shield of f...... Eph 6:16
ceasing your work of f...... 1 Th 1:3
for not all have f...... 2 Th 3:2
having f and a good...... 1 Ti 1:19
he has denied the f...... 1 Ti 5:8
I have kept the f...... 2 Ti 4:7
not being mixed with f...... Heb 4:2
f is the substance...... Heb 11:1
without f it is...... Heb 11:6
Show me your f...... Jas 2:18
f will save the sick...... Jas 5:15
add to your f virtue...... 2 Pe 1:5
on your most holy f...... Jude 20

FAITHFUL
God, He is God, the f...... Deut 7:9
f disappear from among... Ps 12:1
LORD preserves the f...... Ps 31:23
but who can find a f...... Prov 20:6
the Holy One who is f...... Hos 11:12
"Who then is a f...... Matt 24:45
good and f servant...... Matt 25:23
"He who is f in what...... Luke 16:10
God is f...... 1 Co 1:9
is my beloved and f...... 1 Co 4:17
But as God is f...... 2 Co 1:18
He who calls you is f...... 1 Th 5:24
This is a f saying and...... 1 Ti 1:15
f High Priest in...... Heb 2:17
as Moses also was f...... Heb 3:2
He who promised is f...... Heb 10:23
He is f and just to...... 1 Jn 1:9
Be f until death...... Rev 2:10
words are true and f...... Rev 21:5

FAITHFULNESS
I have declared Your f...... Ps 40:10
And Your f every night... Ps 92:2
f endures to all...... Ps 119:90
In Your f answer me...... Ps 143:1
great is Your f...... Lam 3:23

FAITHLESS
"O f generation...... Mark 9:19
If we are f...... 2 Ti 2:13

FALL
a deep sleep to f...... Gen 2:21
Yes, all kings shall f...... Ps 72:11
a righteous man may f...... Prov 24:16
digs a pit will f...... Prov 26:27
men shall utterly f...... Is 40:30
And great was its f...... Matt 7:27
the blind, both will f...... Matt 15:14
the stars will f...... Matt 24:29
"I saw Satan f...... Luke 10:18
take heed lest he f...... 1 Co 10:12
with pride he f...... 1 Ti 3:6
if they f away...... Heb 6:6
lest anyone f short of...... Heb 12:15
it all joy when you f...... Jas 1:2
and rocks, "F on us...... Rev 6:16

FALLEN
"Babylon is f...... Is 21:9
you have f from grace...... Gal 5:4
And I saw a star f...... Rev 9:1
"Babylon is f...... Rev 14:8

FALLING
f away comes first...... 2 Th 2:3

FALLS
who is alone when he f...... Eccl 4:10
"And whoever f...... Matt 21:44
master he stands or f...... Rom 14:4
its flower f...... Jas 1:11
so that no rain f...... Rev 11:6

FALSE
You shall not bear f...... Ex 20:16
I hate every f way...... Ps 119:104
gives heed to f lips...... Prov 17:4
f witness shall perish...... Prov 21:28
and do not love a f...... Zech 8:17
Beware of f prophets...... Matt 7:15
f christs and f...... Matt 24:24
and we are found f...... 1 Co 15:15
among f brethren...... 2 Co 11:26
of f brethren...... Gal 2:4
f prophets have gone...... 1 Jn 4:1
mouth of the f prophet...... Rev 16:13

FAMILIES
in you all the f...... Gen 12:3
And makes their f...... Ps 107:41
the God of all the f...... Jer 31:1
in your seed all the f...... Acts 3:25

FAMINE
Now there was a f...... Gen 12:10
keep them alive in f...... Ps 33:19
send the sword, the f...... Jer 24:10
I will increase the f...... Ezek 5:16
there arose a severe f...... Luke 15:14

FAR
removed my brothers f...... Job 19:13
Be not f from Me...... Ps 22:11
those who are f...... Ps 73:27
The LORD is f from the... Prov 15:29
removed their hearts f...... Is 29:13
Those near and those f...... Ezek 22:5
their heart is far f...... Matt 15:8
going to a f country...... Mark 13:34
though He is not f...... Acts 17:27
you who once were f...... Eph 2:13

FARMER
The hard-working f...... 2 Ti 2:6
See how the f waits...... Jas 5:7

FAST
f that I have chosen...... Is 58:5
Moreover, when you f...... Matt 6:16
disciples do not f...... Matt 9:14
'I f twice a week...... Luke 18:12

FASTED
'Why have we f...... Is 58:3
'When you f and...... Zech 7:5
And when He had f...... Matt 4:2

FASTING
humbled myself with f...... Ps 35:13
are weak through f...... Ps 109:24
house on the day of f...... Jer 36:6
except by prayer and f...... Matt 17:21
give yourselves to f...... 1 Co 7:5

FATHER
man shall leave his f...... Gen 2:24
and you shall be a f...... Gen 17:4
'You are my f...... Job 17:14
I was a f to the poor...... Job 29:16
A f of the fatherless...... Ps 68:5
f pities his children...... Ps 103:13
the instruction of a f...... Prov 4:1
God, Everlasting F...... Is 9:6
You, O LORD, are our F Is 63:16
for I am a F to Israel...... Jer 31:9
"A son honors his f...... Mal 1:6
Have we not all one F...... Mal 2:10
Our F in heaven...... Matt 6:9
"He who loves f...... Matt 10:37
does anyone know the F.. Matt 11:27
'*He who curses f*...... Matt 15:4
for One is your F...... Matt 23:9
F will be divided...... Luke 12:53
F loves the Son...... John 3:35
F has been working...... John 5:17
F raises the dead...... John 5:21
F judges no one...... John 5:22
He has seen the F...... John 6:46
F who sent Me bears...... John 8:18
we have one F...... John 8:41
of your f the devil...... John 8:44
"I and My F are one...... John 10:30
and believe that the F...... John 10:38
'I am going to the F...... John 14:28
came forth from the F...... John 16:28
that he might be the f...... Rom 4:11
"*I have made you a f*...... Rom 4:17
"*I will be a F*...... 2 Co 6:18
one God and F of all...... Eph 4:6
but exhort him as a f...... 1 Ti 5:1
I will be to Him a F...... Heb 1:5
comes down from the F... Jas 1:17
if you call on the F...... 1 Pe 1:17
and testify that the F...... 1 Jn 4:14

FATHERS
the LORD God of our f...... Ezra 7:27
f trusted in You...... Ps 22:4
have sinned with our f...... Ps 106:6
f ate the manna...... John 6:31
of whom are the f...... Rom 9:5
you do not have many f... 1 Co 4:15
unaware that all our f...... 1 Co 10:1

FATTED
f cattle are...... Matt 22:4
has killed the f...... Luke 15:27

FAVOR
granted me life and f...... Job 10:12
His f is for life...... Ps 30:5
A good man obtains f...... Prov 12:2
but his f is like dew...... Prov 19:12
and seek the LORD's f...... Jer 26:19
and stature, and in f...... Luke 2:52
God and having f...... Acts 2:47
to do the Jews a f...... Acts 24:27

FAVORITISM
do not show personal f...... Luke 20:21
God shows personal f...... Gal 2:6

FEAR
f the LORD your God...... Deut 6:2
they are in great f...... Ps 14:5
The f of the LORD is...... Ps 19:9
of death, I will f...... Ps 23:4
Whom shall I f...... Ps 27:1
Oh, f the LORD...... Ps 34:9

There is no *f* of God ... Ps 36:1
The *f* of the LORD is ... Ps 111:10
f the LORD and depart ... Prov 3:7
The *f* of man brings a ... Prov 29:25
F God and keep His ... Eccl 12:13
"Be strong, do not *f* ... Is 35:4
f Him who is able ... Matt 10:28
"Do not *f* ... Luke 12:32
a judge who did not *f* ... Luke 18:2
"Do you not even *f* ... Luke 23:40
And walking in the *f* ... Acts 9:31
the rest also may *f* ... 1 Ti 5:20
given us a spirit of *f* ... 2 Ti 1:7
because of His godly *f* ... Heb 5:7
love casts out *f* ... 1 Jn 4:18
"Do not *f* any of ... Rev 2:10

FEAST
Then he made them a *f* ... Gen 19:3
and you shall keep a *f* ... Num 29:12
f is made for laughter ... Eccl 10:19
f day the terrors that ... Lam 2:22
hate, I despise your *f* ... Amos 5:21
every year at the *F* ... Luke 2:41
when you give a *f* ... Luke 14:13
Now the Passover, a *f* ... John 6:4
great day of the *f* ... John 7:37
let us keep the *f* ... 1 Co 5:8

FEED
ravens to *f* you there ... 1 Ki 17:4
Death shall *f* on them ... Ps 49:14
to him, "*F* My lambs ... John 21:15
your enemy hungers, f ... Rom 12:20
my goods to *f* the poor ... 1 Co 13:3

FEET
So she lay at his *f* ... Ruth 3:14
all things under his *f* ... Ps 8:6
You have set my *f* ... Ps 31:8
f had almost stumbled ... Ps 73:2
Her *f* go down to death ... Prov 5:5
place of My *f* glorious ... Is 60:13
began to wash His *f* ... Luke 7:38
also sat at Jesus' *f* ... Luke 10:39
wash the disciples' *f* ... John 13:5
at the apostles' *f* ... Acts 4:35
f are swift to shed ... Rom 3:15
beautiful are the f ... Rom 10:15
all things under His f ... 1 Co 15:27
and having shod your *f* ... Eph 6:15
fell at His *f* as dead ... Rev 1:17

FELLOW
f servants who owed ... Matt 18:28
begins to beat his *f* ... Matt 24:49
f worker concerning ... 2 Co 8:23
f citizens with the ... Eph 2:19
Gentiles should be *f* ... Eph 3:6
rest of my *f* workers ... Phil 4:3
that we may become *f* ... 3 Jn 8
I am your *f* servant ... Rev 19:10

FELLOWSHIP
doctrine and *f* ... Acts 2:42
were called into the *f* ... 1 Co 1:9
not want you to have *f* ... 1 Co 10:20
the right hand of *f* ... Gal 2:9
And have no *f* with the ... Eph 5:11
your *f* in the gospel ... Phil 1:5
of love, if any *f* ... Phil 2:1
and the *f* of His ... Phil 3:10
also may have *f* ... 1 Jn 1:3

FERVENT
and being *f* in spirit ... Acts 18:25
f prayer of a ... Jas 5:16
all things have *f* love ... 1 Pe 4:8
will melt with *f* heat ... 2 Pe 3:10

FEW
f and evil have been ... Gen 47:9
f days and full of ... Job 14:1
Let his days be *f* ... Ps 109:8
let your words be *f* ... Eccl 5:2
and there are *f* ... Matt 7:14
but the laborers are *f* ... Matt 9:37
called, but *f* chosen ... Matt 20:16
"Lord, are there *f* ... Luke 13:23
prepared, in which a *f* ... 1 Pe 3:20
I have a *f* things ... Rev 2:20

FIELD
"The *f* is the world ... Matt 13:38
and buys that *f* ... Matt 13:44
f has been called the ... Matt 27:8
you are God's *f* ... 1 Co 3:9

FIELDS
f yield no food ... Hab 3:17
living out in the *f* ... Luke 2:8
eyes and look at the *f* ... John 4:35

FIERY
So the LORD sent *f* ... Num 21:6
of a burning *f* furnace ... Dan 3:6
concerning the *f* trial ... 1 Pe 4:12
f red dragon having ... Rev 12:3

FIG
f leaves together ... Gen 3:7
f tree may not blossom ... Hab 3:17
"Look at the *f* ... Luke 21:29
I saw you under the *f* ... John 1:50
Can a *f* tree ... Jas 3:12
f tree drops its late ... Rev 6:13

FIGHT
"The LORD will *f* ... Ex 14:14
Our God will *f* for us ... Neh 4:20
My servants would *f* ... John 18:36
let us not *f* against God ... Acts 23:9
F the good *f* ... 1 Ti 6:12
have fought the good *f* ... 2 Ti 4:7
You *f* and war ... Jas 4:2

FIGS
puts forth her green *f* ... Song 2:13
men do not gather *f* ... Luke 6:44
or a grapevine bear *f* ... Jas 3:12

FILL
f the earth and subdue ... Gen 1:28
"do I not *f* heaven ... Jer 23:24
F the waterpots ... John 2:7
that He might *f* ... Eph 4:10

FILLED
the whole earth be *f* ... Ps 72:19
for they shall be *f* ... Matt 5:6
he would gladly have *f* ... Luke 15:16
being *f* with all ... Rom 1:29
full of goodness, *f* ... Rom 15:14
that you may be *f* ... Eph 3:19
but be *f* with the ... Eph 5:18
being *f* with the ... Phil 1:11
peace, be warmed and *f* ... Jas 2:16

FILTH
has washed away the *f* ... Is 4:4
been made as the *f* ... 1 Co 4:13
the removal of the *f* ... 1 Pe 3:21

FILTHINESS
ourselves from all *f* ... 2 Co 7:1
lay aside all *f* ... Jas 1:21
abominations and the *f* ... Rev 17:4

FILTHY
malice, blasphemy, *f* ... Col 3:8
poor man in *f* clothes ... Jas 2:2
oppressed with the *f* ... 2 Pe 2:7

FIND
sure your sin will *f* ... Num 32:23
seek, and you will *f* ... Matt 7:7
for My sake will *f* ... Matt 10:39
when he comes, will *f* ... Matt 24:46
f a Babe wrapped ... Luke 2:12
f no fault in this Man ... Luke 23:4
f grace to help in ... Heb 4:16

FINDS
f me *f* life ... Prov 8:35
f a wife *f* a good ... Prov 18:22
Whatever your hand *f* ... Eccl 9:10
f his life will lose ... Matt 10:39
and he who seeks *f* ... Luke 11:10

FINE
gold, Yea, than much *f* ... Ps 19:10
set on bases of *f* gold ... Song 5:15
rings, in *f* apparel ... Jas 2:2

FINGER
the ground with His *f* ... John 8:6
"Reach your *f* ... John 20:27

FINGERS
the work of Your *f* ... Ps 8:3

FINISHED
f the work which You ... John 17:4
He said, "It is *f* ... John 19:30
I have *f* the race ... 2 Ti 4:7
thousand years were *f* ... Rev 20:3

FIRE
rained brimstone and *f* ... Gen 19:24
LORD was not in the *f* ... 1 Ki 19:12
I was musing, the *f* ... Ps 39:3
f goes before Him ... Ps 97:3
says the LORD, whose *f* ... Is 31:9
you walk through the *f* ... Is 43:2
like a refiner's *f* ... Mal 3:2
the Holy Spirit and *f* ... Matt 3:11
f is not quenched ... Mark 9:44
"I came to send *f* ... Luke 12:49
tongues, as of *f* ... Acts 2:3
f taking vengeance ... 2 Th 1:8
and that burned with *f* ... Heb 12:18
And the tongue is a *f* ... Jas 3:6
vengeance of eternal *f* ... Jude 7
f came down from God ... Rev 20:9
into the lake of *f* ... Rev 20:14

FIREBRAND
f plucked from the ... Amos 4:11

FIRM
f the feeble knees ... Is 35:3
of the hope *f* to the ... Heb 3:6

FIRMAMENT
Thus God made the *f* ... Gen 1:7
f shows His handiwork ... Ps 19:1
brightness of the *f* ... Dan 12:3

FIRST
f father sinned ... Is 43:27
desires to be *f* ... Matt 20:27
And the gospel must *f* ... Mark 13:10
evil, of the Jew *f* ... Rom 2:9
f man Adam became a ... 1 Co 15:45
that we who *f* trusted ... Eph 1:12
For Adam was formed *f* ... 1 Ti 2:13
love Him because He *f* ... 1 Jn 4:19
I am the *F* and the ... Rev 1:17
you have left your *f* ... Rev 2:4
is the *f* resurrection ... Rev 20:5

FIRSTBORN
LORD struck all the *f* ... Ex 12:29
I will make him My *f* ... Ps 89:27
Shall I give my *f* ... Mic 6:7
brought forth her *f* ... Matt 1:25
that He might be the *f* ... Rom 8:29
invisible God, the *f* ... Col 1:15
the beginning, the *f* ... Col 1:18
witness, the *f* from ... Rev 1:5

FIRSTFRUITS
and with the *f* ... Prov 3:9
also who have the *f* ... Rom 8:23
and has become the *f* ... 1 Co 15:20
might be a kind of *f* ... Jas 1:18
among men, being *f* ... Rev 14:4

FISH
f taken in a cruel net ... Eccl 9:12
had prepared a great *f* ... Jon 1:17
do You make men like *f* ... Hab 1:14
Or if he asks for a *f* ... Matt 7:10

belly of the great *f*.........Matt 12:40
five loaves and two *f*.......Matt 14:17
and likewise the *f*...........John 21:13

FISHERS
and I will make you *f*......Matt 4:19

FIVE
f smooth stones.............1 Sa 17:40
about *f* thousand men......Matt 14:21
and *f* were foolish..........Matt 25:2

FLAME
appeared to him in a *f*.....Ex 3:2
f will dry out his............Job 15:30
f consumes the chaff........Is 5:24
and tempest And the *f*.....Is 29:6
nor shall the *f*...............Is 43:2
behind them a *f*.............Joel 2:3
am tormented in this *f*.....Luke 16:24
and His ministers a f.......Heb 1:7
and His eyes like a *f*.......Rev 1:14

FLATTERING
f mouth works ruin.........Prov 26:28
f speech deceive.............Rom 16:18
any time did we use *f*......1 Th 2:5
swelling words, *f*............Jude 16

FLEE
f away secretly...............Gen 31:27
those who hate You *f*......Num 10:35
such a man as I *f*...........Neh 6:11
who see me outside *f*.......Ps 31:11
Or where can I *f*.............Ps 139:7
and the shadows *f*..........Song 2:17
who are in Judea *f*.........Matt 24:16
F sexual immorality.........1 Co 6:18
devil and he will *f*..........Jas 4:7

FLESH
bone of my bones and *f*...Gen 2:23
f had corrupted their.......Gen 6:12
f I shall see God.............Job 19:26
My *f* also will rest in.......Ps 16:9
is wearisome to the *f*.......Eccl 12:12
and all *f* shall see it.........Is 40:5
"All *f* is grass.................Is 40:6
out My Spirit on all *f*......Joel 2:28
Simon Bar-Jonah, for *f*....Matt 16:17
two shall become one f....Matt 19:5
were shortened, no *f*.......Matt 24:22
two shall become one f....Mark 10:8
And the Word became *f*..John 1:14
I shall give is My *f*.........John 6:51
unless you eat the *f*.........John 6:53
f profits nothing.............John 6:63
when we were in the *f*.....Rom 7:5
on the things of the *f*.......Rom 8:5
you are not in the *f*.........Rom 8:9
to the *f* you will die........Rom 8:13
f should glory in His........1 Co 1:29
"*shall become one f*.........1 Co 6:16
there is one kind of *f*.......1 Co 15:39
For the *f* lusts...............Gal 5:17
have crucified the *f*.........Gal 5:24
good showing in the *f*......Gal 6:12
f has ceased from sin.......1 Pe 4:1
the lust of the *f*.............1 Jn 2:16
has come in the *f*...........1 Jn 4:2
dreamers defile the *f*.......Jude 8

FLOCK
Your people like a *f*........Ps 77:20
the footsteps of the *f*.......Song 1:8
He will feed His *f*...........Is 40:11
Do not fear, little *f*.........Luke 12:32
there will be one *f*.........John 10:16
Shepherd the *f* of God.....1 Pe 5:2
examples to the *f*............1 Pe 5:3

FLOOD
the waters of the *f*..........Gen 7:10
sat enthroned at the *F*.....Ps 29:10
the days before the *f*.......Matt 24:38

FLOWER
comes forth like a *f*.........Job 14:2
As a *f* of the field..........Ps 103:15
beauty is a fading *f*.........Is 28:4
grass withers, the *f*.........Is 40:7
of man as the f...............1 Pe 1:24

FLOWING
'a land *f* with milk.........Deut 6:3

FOLD
are not of this *f*.............John 10:16
a cloak You will f..........Heb 1:12

FOLLOW
f what is altogether.........Deut 16:20
to Me, you who *f*............Is 51:1
f You wherever You go...Matt 8:19
He said to him, "*F*..........Matt 9:9
up his cross, and *f*...........Mark 8:34
someone who does not *f*..Mark 9:38
will by no means *f*..........John 10:5
serves Me, let him *f*........John 12:26
those of some men *f*.........1 Ti 5:24
f the Lamb wherever He..Rev 14:4
and their works *f*............Rev 14:13

FOOD
that there may be *f*.........Mal 3:10
and you gave Me *f*..........Matt 25:35
and he who has *f*............Luke 3:11
have you any *f*...............John 21:5
they ate their *f*...............Acts 2:46
our hearts with *f*.............Acts 14:17
destroy with your *f*..........Rom 14:15
f makes my brother.........1 Co 8:13
the same spiritual *f*.........1 Co 10:3
sower, and bread for *f*.....2 Co 9:10
And having *f* and...........1 Ti 6:8
and not solid *f*................Heb 5:12
of *f* sold his...................Heb 12:16
destitute of daily *f*...........Jas 2:15

FOOL
f has said in his.............Ps 14:1
is like sport to a *f*...........Prov 10:23
f will be servant..............Prov 11:29
f is right in his own.........Prov 12:15
f lays open his folly.........Prov 13:16
is too lofty for a *f*...........Prov 24:7
whoever says, 'You *f*.......Matt 5:22
I speak as a *f*.................2 Co 11:23
I have become a *f*...........2 Co 12:11

FOOLISHNESS
Forsake *f* and live...........Prov 9:6
F is bound up in the........Prov 22:15
devising of *f* is sin...........Prov 24:9
person will speak *f*..........Is 32:6
of the cross is *f*...............1 Co 1:18
Because the *f* of God......1 Co 1:25

FOOLS
f despise wisdom............Prov 1:7
folly of *f* is deceit...........Prov 14:8
has no pleasure in *f*.........Eccl 5:4
We are *f* for Christ's.......1 Co 4:10

FOOT
will not allow your *f*........Ps 121:3
f will not stumble............Prov 3:23
From the sole of the *f*.....Is 1:6
f causes you to sin.........Matt 18:8
You dash Your f against..Luke 4:11
If the *f* should say...........1 Co 12:15

FOOTSTOOL
Your enemies Your f.......Matt 22:44
"Sit here at my *f*...........Jas 2:3

FOREHEADS
put a mark on the *f*.........Ezek 9:4
seal of God on their *f*......Rev 9:4
his mark on their *f*..........Rev 20:4

FOREKNEW
For whom He *f*.............Rom 8:29
His people whom He *f*.....Rom 11:2

FOREKNOWLEDGE
counsel and *f* of God.......Acts 2:23
according to the *f*...........1 Pe 1:2

FOREORDAINED
He indeed was *f*.............1 Pe 1:20

FOREVER
and eat, and live *f*..........Gen 3:22
to our children *f*.............Deut 29:29
has loved Israel *f*............1 Ki 10:9
I would not live *f*............Job 7:16
from this generation *f*......Ps 12:7
LORD sits as King *f*.........Ps 29:10
Do not cast us off *f*.........Ps 44:23
"You are a priest *f*..........Ps 110:4
His mercy endures *f*........Ps 136:1
will bless Your name *f*.....Ps 145:1
Who keeps truth *f*...........Ps 146:6
The LORD shall reign *f*....Ps 146:10
for riches are not *f*..........Prov 27:24
Trust in the LORD *f*.........Is 26:4
of our God stands *f*.........Is 40:8
My salvation will be *f*......Is 51:6
will not cast off *f*...........Lam 3:31
be the name of God *f*......Dan 2:20
like the stars *f*...............Dan 12:3
of the LORD our God *f*....Mic 4:5
and the glory *f*...............Matt 6:13
the Christ remains *f*........John 12:34
who is blessed *f*.............2 Co 11:31
to whom be glory *f*..........Gal 1:5
and Father be glory *f*.......Phil 4:20
throne, O God, is f.........Heb 1:8
has been perfected *f*........Heb 7:28
lives and abides *f*............1 Pe 1:23
of darkness *f*..................Jude 13
power, both now and *f*....Jude 25
And they shall reign *f*......Rev 22:5

FORGAVE
f the iniquity of my........Ps 32:5
to repay, he freely *f*........Luke 7:42
God in Christ also *f*........Eph 4:32
even as Christ *f*..............Col 3:13

FORGET
For God has made me *f*...Gen 41:51
f the covenant of your.....Deut 4:31
f the LORD who brought..Deut 6:12
f the works of God.........Ps 78:7
I will not *f* Your word.....Ps 119:16
If I *f* you.......................Ps 137:5
My son, do not *f*............Prov 3:1
f your work and labor......Heb 6:10

FORGETS
and immediately *f*...........Jas 1:24

FORGIVE
f their sin and heal..........2 Ch 7:14
And *f* us our debts..........Matt 6:12
Father will also *f*............Matt 6:14
his heart, does not *f*........Matt 18:35
Who can *f* sins but God...Mark 2:7
f the sins of any..............John 20:23
you ought rather to *f*.......2 Co 2:7
F me this wrong............2 Co 12:13
f us our sins and to.........1 Jn 1:9

FORGIVEN
transgression is *f*............Ps 32:1
sins be f them................Mark 4:12
to whom little is *f*...........Luke 7:47
indeed I have *f*...............2 Co 2:10
f you all trespasses..........Col 2:13
sins, he will be *f*............Jas 5:15
your sins are *f*...............1 Jn 2:12

FORGIVENESS
But there is *f* with..........Ps 130:4
God belong mercy and *f*..Dan 9:9
preached to you the *f*......Acts 13:38
they may receive *f*...........Acts 26:18
His blood, the *f*.............Eph 1:7

— G —

GARMENTS
g did not wear out on.......Deut 8:4
They divide My *g*..........Ps 22:18
g always be white..........Eccl 9:8
from Edom, with dyed *g*.. Is 63:1
man clothed in soft *g*.......Matt 11:8
spread their *g* on the.......Matt 21:8
and divided His *g*...........Matt 27:35
by them in shining *g*........Luke 24:4
be clothed in white *g*.......Rev 3:5

GATE
by the narrow *g*...............Matt 7:13
suffered outside the *g*......Heb 13:12
each individual *g*.............Rev 21:21

GATES
up your heads, O you *g*... Ps 24:7
and the *g* of Hades.......... Matt 16:18
wall with twelve *g*............ Rev 21:12
g were twelve pearls........Rev 21:21
g shall not be shut..........Rev 21:25

GAVE
to be with me, she *g*....... Gen 3:12
g you this authority.........Matt 21:23
that He *g* His only...........John 3:16
Those whom you *g*...........John 17:12
but God *g* the increase.... 1 Co 3:6
g Himself for our sins......Gal 1:4
g Himself for me.............Gal 2:20
g Himself for it...............Eph 5:25
The sea *g* up the dead.....Rev 20:13

GENEALOGIES
fables and endless *g*.........1 Ti 1:4

GENERATION
One *g* passes away.........Eccl 1:4
who will declare His *g*..... Is 53:8
and adulterous *g*.............Matt 12:39
this *g* will by no..............Matt 24:34
from this perverse *g*........Acts 2:40
But you are a chosen *g*.... 1 Pe 2:9

GENTILES
G were separated..........Gen 10:5
as a light to the *G*.........Is 42:6
the riches of the *G*..........Is 61:6
all these things the *G*...... Matt 6:32
into the way of the *G*.......Matt 10:5
revelation to the *G*..........Luke 2:32
G are fulfilled.................Luke 21:24
bear My name before *G*...Acts 9:15
poured out on the *G*.......Acts 10:45
to be a light to the G......Acts 13:47
blasphemed among the G Rom 2:24
also the God of the *G*.....Rom 3:29
mystery among the *G*......Col 1:27
a teacher of the *G*...........1 Ti 2:7
nothing from the *G*...........3 Jn 7

GENTLE
from Me, for I am *g*.........Matt 11:29
But we were *g* among......1 Th 2:7
to be peaceable, *g*...........Tit 3:2
only to the good and *g*.... 1 Pe 2:18
ornament of a *g*...............1 Pe 3:4

GENTLENESS
g has made me great....... Ps 18:35
love and a spirit of *g*....... 1 Co 4:21
g, self-control.................Gal 5:23
all lowliness and *g*...........Eph 4:2
Let your *g* be known to... Phil 4:5
love, patience, *g*.............1 Ti 6:11

GIFT
If you knew the *g*...........John 4:10
But the free *g* is not........Rom 5:15
but the *g* of God is..........Rom 6:23
each one has his own *g*.... 1 Co 7:7
though I have the *g*.........1 Co 13:2
it is the *g* of God..............Eph 2:8
Not that I seek the *g*.......Phil 4:17
Do not neglect the *g*....... 1 Ti 4:14
you to stir up the *g*.........2 Ti 1:6
tasted the heavenly *g*....... Heb 6:4
Every good *g* and every... Jas 1:17

GIFTS
how to give good *g*......... Matt 7:11
rich putting their *g*.......... Luke 21:1
are diversities of *g*..........1 Co 12:4
and desire spiritual *g*.........1 Co 14:1
captive, and gave g..........Eph 4:8

GIVE
g me wisdom and............2 Ch 1:10
G ear to my prayer.........Ps 17:1
G to them according.........Ps 28:4
g you the desires.............Ps 37:4
G me understanding........Ps 119:34
g me your heart...............Prov 23:26
"*G* to him who asks.........Matt 5:42
G us this day our............Matt 6:11
what you have and *g*.......Matt 19:21
authority I will *g*.............Luke 4:6
g them eternal life...........John 10:28
A new commandment I *g* John 13:34
but what I do have I *g*.....Acts 3:6
g us all things.................Rom 8:32
g him who has need........ Eph 4:28
g thanks to God always....2 Th 2:13
g yourself entirely........... 1 Ti 4:15
good works, ready to *g*.... 1 Ti 6:18

GLAD
I will be *g* and..................Ps 9:2
Be *g* in the LORD and..... Ps 32:11
streams shall make *g*....... Ps 46:4
And wine that makes *g*.... Ps 104:15
I was *g* when they said.... Ps 122:1
he saw it and was *g*.........John 8:56

GLADNESS
in the day of your *g*........ Num 10:10
You have put *g* in my......Ps 4:7
me to hear joy and *g*........Ps 51:8
Serve the LORD with *g*.....Ps 100:2
shall obtain joy and *g*...... Is 35:10
over you with *g*...............Zeph 3:17
receive it with *g*..............Mark 4:16

GLASS
there was a sea of *g*........ Rev 4:6
like transparent *g*............Rev 21:21

GLORIFIED
and they *g* the God of..... Matt 15:31
Jesus was not yet *g*......... John 7:39
when Jesus was *g*.............John 12:16
By this My Father is *g*.....John 15:8
"I have *g* You on the...... John 17:4
g His Servant Jesus......... Acts 3:13
these He also *g*.................Rom 8:30
things God may be *g*.........1 Pe 4:11

GLORIFY
"Father, *g* Your name..... John 12:28
"He will *g* Me.................John 16:14
And now, O Father, *g*......John 17:5
what death he would *g*......John 21:19
also Christ did not *g*.........Heb 5:5

GLORIOUS
daughter is all *g*..............Ps 45:13
And blessed be His *g*...... Ps 72:19
G things are spoken........ Ps 87:3
it to Himself a *g*............. Eph 5:27
be conformed to His *g*.....Phil 3:21
g appearing of our.......... Tit 2:13

GLORY
Please, show me Your *g*...Ex 33:18
g has departed from........ 1 Sa 4:21
You who set Your *g*........Ps 8:1
Who is this King of *g*...... Ps 24:8
The *g* of young men is.....Prov 20:29
It is the *g* of God to........Prov 25:2
He shall bear the *g*......... Zech 6:13
the power and the *g*.........Matt 6:13
Man will come in the *g*....Matt 16:27
with power and great *g*.... Matt 24:30
"*G* to God in the............Luke 2:14
and we beheld His *g*........John 1:14
and manifested His *g*.......John 2:11
I do not seek My own *g*...John 8:50
"Give God the *g*..............John 9:24
g which I had with You... John 17:5
he did not give *g*............ Acts 12:23
doing good seek for *g*...... Rom 2:7
fall short of the *g*.............Rom 3:23
the adoption, the *g*..........Rom 9:4
the riches of His *g*........... Rom 9:23
God, alone wise, be *g*......Rom 16:27
who glories, let him g...... 1 Co 1:31
Therefore let no one *g*.....1 Co 3:21
but woman is the *g*......... 1 Co 11:7
of the gospel of the *g*...... 2 Co 4:4
eternal weight of *g*.......... 2 Co 4:17
that they may *g*............... Gal 6:13
forbid that I should *g*...... Gal 6:14
to His riches in *g*............ Phil 4:19
appear with Him in *g*...... Col 3:4
For you are our *g*............ 1 Th 2:20
to whom belong the *g*......1 Pe 4:11
for the Spirit of *g*.............1 Pe 4:14
the presence of His *g*.......Jude 24

GO
'Let My people *g*............Ex 5:1
for wherever you *g*...........Ruth 1:16
"Look, I *g* forward...........Job 23:8
For I used to *g*................Ps 42:4
Those who *g* down to...... Ps 107:23
Where can I *g* from.........Ps 139:7
G to the ant....................Prov 6:6
All *g* to one place............Eccl 3:20
do not *g* out....................Matt 24:26
He said to them, "*G*....... Mark 16:15
to whom shall we *g*.........John 6:68
g you cannot come..........John 8:21
I *g* to prepare a place......John 14:2
will do, because I *g*.........John 14:12

GOAL
I press toward the *g*........ Phil 3:14

GOD
G created the heavens..... Gen 1:1
Abram of *G* Most High... Gen 14:19
and I will be their *G*....... Gen 17:8
the *G* of Abraham........ Ex 3:6
I am the LORD your *G*.... Ex 20:2
"*G* is not a man............. Num 23:19
G is a consuming fire...... Deut 4:24
great and awesome *G*...... Deut 7:21
my people, and your *G*.... Ruth 1:16
know that there is a *G*.....1 Sa 17:46
G is greater than all........ 2 Ch 2:5
"Behold, *G* is mighty...... Job 36:5
"Behold, *G* is great.........Job 36:26
Where is your *G*..............Ps 42:3
G is our refuge................Ps 46:1
me a clean heart, O *G*.....Ps 51:10
Our *G* is the *G*..............Ps 68:20
Who is so great a *G*........Ps 77:13
You alone are *G*..............Ps 86:10
Yes, our *G* is merciful..... Ps 116:5
give thanks to the *G*........Ps 136:26
Counselor, Mighty *G*.......Is 9:6
G is my salvation............Is 12:2
Behold, this is our *G*........Is 25:9
"Behold your *G*...............Is 40:9
Is there a *G* besides........ Is 44:8
and I will be their *G*....... Jer 31:33
and I saw visions of *G*..... Ezek 1:1
"*G with us*......................Matt 1:23
in *G* my Savior..................Luke 1:47
the Word was with *G*...... John 1:1
"For *G* so loved the........John 3:16
"*G* is Spirit......................John 4:24
"My Lord and my *G*.......John 20:28
Christ is the Son of *G*..... Acts 8:37
to the unknown *G*............Acts 17:23
Indeed, let *G* be true....... Rom 3:4

If *G* is for us... Rom 8:31
G is faithful... 1 Co 1:9
us there is only one *G*... 1 Co 8:6
G shall supply all... Phil 4:19
G is a consuming fire... Heb 12:29
G is greater than our... 1 Jn 3:20
for *G* is love... 1 Jn 4:8
No one has seen *G*... 1 Jn 4:12
G Himself will be... Rev 21:3
and I will be his *G*... Rev 21:7

GODHEAD
eternal power and *G*... Rom 1:20
the fullness of the *G*... Col 2:9

GODLINESS
is the mystery of *g*... 1 Ti 3:16
g is profitable... 1 Ti 4:8
But *g* with contentment... 1 Ti 6:6
having a form of *g*... 2 Ti 3:5
pertain to life and *g*... 2 Pe 1:3
to perseverance *g*... 2 Pe 1:6

GODLY
who desire to live *g*... 2 Ti 3:12

GODS
He judges among the *g*... Ps 82:1
If He called them *g*... John 10:35
g have come down to us.. Acts 14:11

GOLD
a mercy seat of pure *g*... Ex 25:17
Yea, than much fine *g*... Ps 19:10
is like apples of *g*... Prov 25:11
g I do not have... Acts 3:6
with braided hair or *g*... 1 Ti 2:9
a man with *g* rings... Jas 2:2
Your *g* and silver are... Jas 5:3
more precious than *g*... 1 Pe 1:7
like silver or *g*... 1 Pe 1:18
of the city was pure *g*... Rev 21:21

GOOD
God saw that it was *g*... Gen 1:10
but God meant it for *g*... Gen 50:20
Who will show us any *g*... Ps 4:6
is none who does *g*... Ps 14:1
Truly God is *g* to... Ps 73:1
g man obtains favor... Prov 12:2
on the evil and the *g*... Prov 15:3
A merry heart does *g*... Prov 17:22
learn to do *g*... Is 1:17
they may see your *g*... Matt 5:16
No one is *g* but One... Matt 19:17
For she has done a *g*... Matt 26:10
behold, I bring you *g*... Luke 2:10
"Can anything *g*... John 1:46
who went about doing *g*... Acts 10:38
g man someone would... Rom 5:7
in my flesh) nothing *g*... Rom 7:18
overcome evil with *g*... Rom 12:21
fruitful in every *g*... Col 1:10
know that the law is *g*... 1 Ti 1:8
For this is *g* and... 1 Ti 2:3
bishop, he desires a *g*... 1 Ti 3:1
for this is *g* and... 1 Ti 5:4
be rich in *g* works... 1 Ti 6:18
prepared for every *g*... 2 Ti 2:21
and have tasted the *g*... Heb 6:5
Every *g* gift and every... Jas 1:17
to suffer for doing *g*... 1 Pe 3:17

GOODNESS
I will make all My *g*... Ex 33:19
and abounding in *g*... Ex 34:6
Surely *g* and mercy... Ps 23:6
That I would see the *g*... Ps 27:13
how great is Your *g*... Ps 31:19
The *g* of God endures... Ps 52:1
the riches of His *g*... Rom 2:4
consider the *g* and... Rom 11:22
kindness, *g*... Gal 5:22

GOODS
and plunder his *g*... Matt 12:29
ruler over all his *g*... Matt 24:47
Soul, you have many *g*... Luke 12:19
man was wasting his *g*... Luke 16:1
I give half of my *g*... Luke 19:8
has this world's *g*... 1 Jn 3:17

GOSPEL
The beginning of the *g*... Mark 1:1
and believe in the *g*... Mark 1:15
g must first be... Mark 13:10
to testify to the *g*... Acts 20:24
not ashamed of the *g*... Rom 1:16
should live from the *g*... 1 Co 9:14
if our *g* is veiled... 2 Co 4:3
to a different *g*... Gal 1:6
the mystery of the *g*... Eph 6:19
g which you heard... Col 1:23
the everlasting *g*... Rev 14:6

GOSSIPS
only idle but also *g*... 1 Ti 5:13

GOVERNMENT
and the *g* will be upon... Is 9:6

GRACE
But Noah found *g*... Gen 6:8
G is poured upon Your... Ps 45:2
The LORD will give *g*... Ps 84:11
and the *g* of God was... Luke 2:40
g and truth came... John 1:17
G to you and peace... Rom 1:7
g is no longer *g*... Rom 11:6
The *g* of our Lord... Rom 16:20
For you know the *g*... 2 Co 8:9
My *g* is sufficient... 2 Co 12:9
The *g* of the Lord... 2 Co 13:14
you have fallen from *g*... Gal 5:4
to the riches of His *g*... Eph 1:7
g you have been saved... Eph 2:8
dispensation of the *g*... Eph 3:2
g was given according... Eph 4:7
But He gives more *g*... Jas 4:6
this is the true *g*... 1 Pe 5:12
but grow in the *g*... 2 Pe 3:18

GRACIOUS
I will be *g* to whom I... Ex 33:19
know that You are a *g*... Jon 4:2
at the *g* words which... Luke 4:22
that the Lord is *g*... 1 Pe 2:3

GRAIN
Israel went to buy *g*... Gen 42:5
him who withholds *g*... Prov 11:26
be revived like *g*... Hos 14:7
unless a *g* of wheat... John 12:24
it treads out the g... 1 Co 9:9

GRAPES
in the blood of *g*... Gen 49:11
their *g* are *g*... Deut 32:32
vines have tender *g*... Song 2:15
brought forth wild *g*... Is 5:2
have eaten sour *g*... Ezek 18:2
Do men gather *g*... Matt 7:16
g are fully ripe... Rev 14:18

GRASS
his days are like *g*... Ps 103:15
The *g* withers... Is 40:7
"*All flesh is as g*... 1 Pe 1:24

GRASSHOPPERS
inhabitants are like *g*... Is 40:22
captains like great *g*... Nah 3:17

GRAVE
my soul up from the *g*... Ps 30:3
or wisdom in the *g*... Eccl 9:10
And they made His *g*... Is 53:9
the power of the *g*... Hos 13:14

GRAY
would bring down my *g*... Gen 42:38
of old men is their *g*... Prov 20:29

GREAT
and make your name *g*... Gen 12:2
For the LORD is *g*... 1 Ch 16:25
G men are not always... Job 32:9
in the *g* congregation... Ps 22:25
g are Your works... Ps 92:5
my God, You are very *g*.. Ps 104:1
"The LORD has done *g*... Ps 126:2
g is the sum of them... Ps 139:17
And do you seek *g*... Jer 45:5
g is Your faithfulness... Lam 3:23
The *g* day of the LORD... Zeph 1:14
he shall be called *g*... Matt 5:19
one pearl of *g* price... Matt 13:46
desires to become *g*... Matt 20:26
G is Diana of the... Acts 19:28
with contentment is *g*... 1 Ti 6:6
appearing of our *g*... Tit 2:13
Mystery, Babylon the *G*... Rev 17:5
Then I saw a *g* white... Rev 20:11

GREATER
kingdom of heaven is *g*... Matt 11:11
place there is One *g*... Matt 12:6
g than Jonah is here... Matt 12:41
g things than these... John 1:50
g than our father... John 4:12
a servant is not *g*... John 13:16
G love has no one... John 15:13
'A servant is not *g*... John 15:20
he who prophesies is *g*... 1 Co 14:5
swear by no one *g*... Heb 6:13
condemns us, God is *g*... 1 Jn 3:20

GREATEST
little child is the *g*... Matt 18:4
be considered the *g*... Luke 22:24
but the *g* of these is... 1 Co 13:13

GREEK
written in Hebrew, *G*... John 19:20
and also for the *G*... Rom 1:16
with me, being a *G*... Gal 2:3
is neither Jew nor *G*... Gal 3:28

GREW
And the Child *g*... Luke 2:40
But the word of God *g*... Acts 12:24

GRIEF
Though I speak, my *g*... Job 16:6
observe trouble and *g*... Ps 10:14
of mirth may be *g*... Prov 14:13
much wisdom is much *g*... Eccl 1:18
and acquainted with *g*... Is 53:3
joy and not with *g*... Heb 13:17

GRIEVE
g the children of men... Lam 3:33
g the Holy Spirit... Eph 4:30

GROUND
"Cursed is the *g*... Gen 3:17
you stand is holy *g*... Ex 3:5
others fell on good *g*... Matt 13:8
bought a piece of *g*... Luke 14:18

GROUNDED
being rooted and *g*... Eph 3:17

GROW
the earth will *g*... Is 51:6
you shall go out and *g*... Mal 4:2
truth in love, may *g*... Eph 4:15
but *g* in the grace and... 2 Pe 3:18

GRUDGINGLY
in his heart, not *g*... 2 Co 9:7

GUARANTEE
us the Spirit as a *g*... 2 Co 5:5
who is the *g* of our... Eph 1:14

GUARD
will be your rear *g*... Is 52:12
we were kept under *g*... Gal 3:23
G what was committed... 1 Ti 6:20

GUIDE
LORD He will be our *g*... Ps 48:14
father, You are the *g*... Jer 3:4
g our feet into the... Luke 1:79

has come, He will *g*........ John 16:13
Judas, who became a *g*.... Acts 1:16
you yourself are a *g*........ Rom 2:19

GUILE
spirit there is no *g*.......... Ps 32:2
from speaking *g*.............. Ps 34:13
in whom is no *g*.............. John 1:47
no sin, nor was g........... 1 Pe 2:22
mouth was found no *g*...... Rev 14:5

GUILTY
"We are truly *g*.............. Gen 42:21
we have been very *g*........ Ezra 9:7
the world may become *g*.. Rom 3:19
in one point, he is *g*........ Jas 2:10

— H —

HABITATION
their *h* be desolate.......... Ps 69:25
from His holy *h*.............. Zech 2:13
'*Let his h be*................. Acts 1:20
built together for a *h*....... Eph 2:22
but left their own *h*......... Jude 6

HADES
be brought down to *H*..... Matt 11:23
gates of *H* shall not........ Matt 16:18
being in torments in *H*..... Luke 16:23
not leave my soul in H.... Acts 2:27
I have the keys of *H*....... Rev 1:18
H were cast into the........ Rev 20:14

HAIL
cause very heavy *h*.......... Ex 9:18
of the plague of the *h*...... Rev 16:21

HAIR
bring down my gray *h*...... Gen 42:38
Your *h* is like a flock...... Song 4:1
you cannot make one *h*.... Matt 5:36
"But not a *h* of your....... Luke 21:18
if a woman has long *h*..... 1 Co 11:15
not with braided *h*.......... 1 Ti 2:9
h like women's *h*........... Rev 9:8

HALLOWED
the Sabbath day and *h*..... Ex 20:11
but I will be *h*................ Lev 22:32
who is holy shall be *h*...... Is 5:16
heaven, *h* be Your name.. Matt 6:9

HAND
tooth for tooth, *h*............ Ex 21:24
the *h* of God was very..... 1 Sa 5:11
and strengthened his *h*..... 1 Sa 23:16
Uzzah put out his *h*......... 2 Sa 6:6
h has held me up............ Ps 18:35
My times are in Your *h*... Ps 31:15
Let Your *h* be upon the... Ps 80:17
days is in her right *h*....... Prov 3:16
heart is in the *h*.............. Prov 21:1
Whatever your *h*............. Eccl 9:10
His left *h* is under my...... Song 8:3
Behold, the LORD's *h*........ Is 59:1
of heaven is at *h*............ Matt 3:2
if your right *h*................ Matt 5:30
do not let your left *h*....... Matt 6:3
h makes you sin............. Mark 9:43
sitting at the right *h*........ Mark 14:62
at the right *h* of God....... Acts 7:55
is even at the right *h*....... Rom 8:34
to you with my own *h*..... Gal 6:11
The Lord is at *h*............ Phil 4:5
"*Sit at My right h*.......... Heb 1:13
down at the right *h*......... Heb 10:12
stars in His right *h*.......... Rev 2:1

HANDIWORK
firmament shows His *h*.... Ps 19:1

HANDS
the *h* are the *h*.............. Gen 27:22
took his life in his *h*........ 1 Sa 19:5
put my life in my *h*......... 1 Sa 28:21
but His *h* make whole..... Job 5:18
h have made me and....... Job 10:8
They pierced My *h*.......... Ps 22:16
h formed the dry land...... Ps 95:5
stretches out her *h*.......... Prov 31:19
these wounds in your *h*.... Zech 13:6
than having two *h*........... Matt 18:8
"Behold My *h* and My.... Luke 24:39
only, but also my *h*......... John 13:9
h the print of the........... John 20:25
know that these *h*........... Acts 20:34
lifting up holy *h*............ 1 Ti 2:8
the laying on of the *h*...... 1 Ti 4:14
to fall into the *h*............ Heb 10:31

HAPPY
H are the people who...... Ps 144:15
trusts in the LORD, *h*....... Prov 16:20
h is he who keeps........... Prov 29:18
know these things, *h*........ John 13:17
H is he who does not...... Rom 14:22

HARD
"Is anything too *h*........... Gen 18:14
I knew you to be a *h*....... Matt 25:24
This is a *h* saying............ John 6:60
are some things *h*............ 2 Pe 3:16

HARDENED
But Pharaoh *h* his........... Ex 8:32
Who has *h* himself........... Job 9:4
their heart was *h*............ Mark 6:52
eyes and h their heart...... John 12:40
and the rest were *h*......... Rom 11:7
lest any of you be *h*........ Heb 3:13

HARDSHIP
h that has befallen us...... Num 20:14
h as a good soldier.......... 2 Ti 2:3

HARLOT
of a *h* named Rahab........ Josh 2:1
h is a deep pit................ Prov 23:27
h is one body with her..... 1 Co 6:16
h Rahab did not perish.... Heb 11:31
of the great *h* who.......... Rev 17:1

HARLOTRY
through her casual *h*........ Jer 3:9
the lewdness of your *h*..... Jer 13:27
are the children of *h*........ Hos 2:4
for the spirit of *h*........... Hos 5:4

HARVEST
seedtime and *h*............... Gen 8:22
"The *h* is past................ Jer 8:20
pray the Lord of the *h*...... Matt 9:38
already white for *h*.......... John 4:35

HATE
love the LORD, *h* evil...... Ps 97:10
love, and a time to *h*....... Eccl 3:8
either he will *h*............... Matt 6:24

HATES
six things the LORD *h*...... Prov 6:16
lose it, and he who *h*....... John 12:25
"If the world *h*............... John 15:18
h his brother is.............. 1 Jn 2:11

HAUGHTY
Your eyes are on the *h*.... 2 Sa 22:28
bring down *h* looks.......... Ps 18:27
my heart is not *h*............ Ps 131:1
h spirit before a fall........ Prov 16:18
A proud and *h* man........ Prov 21:24
Do not be *h*................... Rom 11:20
age not to be *h*............... 1 Ti 6:17

HEAD
He shall bruise your *h*..... Gen 3:15
The whole *h* is sick......... Is 1:5
could lift up his *h*........... Zech 1:21
you swear by your *h*........ Matt 5:36
having his *h* covered........ 1 Co 11:4
and gave Him to be *h*...... Eph 1:22
For the husband is *h*....... Eph 5:23
His *h* and His hair.......... Rev 1:14

HEADS
Him, wagging their *h*...... Matt 27:39
dragon having seven *h*...... Rev 12:3

HEAL
I wound and I *h*............. Deut 32:39
O LORD, *h* me................ Ps 6:2
h your backslidings.......... Jer 3:22
"*H* the sick..................... Matt 10:8
Physician, *h* yourself........ Luke 4:23

HEALED
and return and be *h*......... Is 6:10
His stripes we are *h*......... Is 53:5
h the hurt of My............. Jer 6:14
When I would have *h*...... Hos 7:1
and He *h* them............... Matt 4:24
he had faith to be *h*......... Acts 14:9
that you may be *h*........... Jas 5:16
his deadly wound was *h*... Rev 13:3

HEALINGS
to another gifts of *h*........ 1 Co 12:9
Do all have gifts of *h*...... 1 Co 12:30

HEALS
h all your diseases........... Ps 103:3
Jesus the Christ *h*............ Acts 9:34

HEAR
"*H*, O Israel.................. Deut 6:4
Him you shall *h*.............. Deut 18:15
H me when I call............. Ps 4:1
O You who *h* prayer........ Ps 65:2
ear, shall He not *h*.......... Ps 94:9
H, O heavens.................. Is 1:2
Let the earth *h*................ Is 34:1
I spoke, you did not *h*..... Is 65:12
"*Hearing you will h*.......... Matt 13:14
if he will not *h*............... Matt 18:16
ears, do you not *h*.......... Mark 8:18
And how shall they *h*...... Rom 10:14
man be swift to *h*............ Jas 1:19
h what the Spirit says...... Rev 2:7

HEARD
h the sound of the.......... Gen 3:8
h their cry because of....... Ex 3:7
Have you not *h*............... Is 40:21
h the word believed......... Acts 4:4
I say, have they not *h*...... Rom 10:18
not seen, nor ear h.......... 1 Co 2:9
h inexpressible................ 2 Co 12:4
things that you have *h*..... 2 Ti 2:2
the things we have *h*....... Heb 2:1
the word which they *h*...... Heb 4:2
Lord's Day, and I *h*........ Rev 1:10

HEARERS
for not the *h* of the.......... Rom 2:13
impart grace to the *h*....... Eph 4:29
of the word, and not *h*.... Jas 1:22

HEARING
and read in the *h*............ Ex 24:7
Book of Moses in the *h*... Neh 13:1
h they do not................. Matt 13:13
and h they may............... Mark 4:12
or by the *h* of faith......... Gal 3:2
have become dull of *h*..... Heb 5:11

HEARS
for Your servant *h*.......... 1 Sa 3:9
He who *h* you *h* Me........ Luke 10:16
of God *h* God's words..... John 8:47
"And if anyone *h*............ John 12:47
who is of the truth *h*....... John 18:37
He who knows God *h*...... 1 Jn 4:6
And let him who *h*.......... Rev 22:17

HEART
h was only evil............... Gen 6:5
great searchings of *h*........ Judg 5:16
h rejoices in the LORD..... 1 Sa 2:1
LORD looks at the *h*........ 1 Sa 16:7
My *h* also instructs me..... Ps 16:7
h is overflowing............. Ps 45:1

My *h* is steadfast...... Ps 57:7
My *h* and my flesh cry...... Ps 84:2
h shall depart from me...... Ps 101:4
with my whole *h*...... Ps 111:1
The king's *h* is in the...... Prov 21:1
as he thinks in his *h*...... Prov 23:7
trusts in his own *h*...... Prov 28:26
The *h* of the wise is...... Eccl 7:4
h yearned for him...... Song 5:4
the yearning of Your *h*...... Is 63:15
h is deceitful above...... Jer 17:9
I will give them a *h*...... Jer 24:7
therefore My *h* yearns...... Jer 31:20
and take the stony *h*...... Ezek 11:19
are the pure in *h*...... Matt 5:8
is, there your *h*...... Matt 6:21
of the *h* proceed evil...... Matt 15:19
h will flow rivers...... John 7:38
"Let not your *h*...... John 14:1
believed were of one *h*...... Acts 4:32
Satan filled your *h*...... Acts 5:3
h is not right in the...... Acts 8:21
in sincerity of *h*...... Eph 6:5
and shuts up his *h*...... 1 Jn 3:17
if our *h* condemns us...... 1 Jn 3:20

HEARTILY
you do, do it *h*...... Col 3:23

HEARTS
God tests the *h*...... Ps 7:9
And he will turn the *h*...... Mal 4:6
h failing them from...... Luke 21:26
purifying their *h*...... Acts 15:9
will guard your *h*...... Phil 4:7
of God rule in your *h*...... Col 3:15

HEATHEN
repetitions as the *h*...... Matt 6:7
him be to you like a *h*...... Matt 18:17

HEAVEN
called the firmament *H*...... Gen 1:8
LORD looks down from *h* Ps 14:2
word is settled in *h*...... Ps 119:89
For God is in *h*...... Eccl 5:2
"*H* is My throne...... Is 66:1
come to know that *H*...... Dan 4:26
for the kingdom of *h*...... Matt 3:2
your Father in *h*...... Matt 5:16
on earth as it is in *h*...... Matt 6:10
"*H* and earth will...... Matt 24:35
from Him a sign from *h*...... Mark 8:11
have sinned against *h*...... Luke 15:18
you shall see *h*...... John 1:51
one has ascended to *h*...... John 3:13
the true bread from *h*...... John 6:32
a voice came from *h*...... John 12:28
the whole family in *h*...... Eph 3:15
laid up for you in *h*...... Col 1:5
there was silence in *h*...... Rev 8:1
sign appeared in *h*...... Rev 12:1
And I saw a new *h*...... Rev 21:1

HEAVENLY
your *h* Father will...... Matt 6:14
h host praising God...... Luke 2:13
if I tell you *h* things...... John 3:12
blessing in the *h*...... Eph 1:3
and have tasted the *h*...... Heb 6:4
h things themselves...... Heb 9:23
a better, that is, a *h*...... Heb 11:16

HEAVENS
I will make your *h*...... Lev 26:19
and the highest *h*...... Deut 10:14
h cannot contain...... 1 Ki 8:27
the LORD made the *h*...... 1 Ch 16:26
in the *h* shall laugh...... Ps 2:4
h declare the glory...... Ps 19:1
Let the *h* declare His...... Ps 50:6
The *h* are Yours...... Ps 89:11
For as the *h* are high...... Ps 103:11
When He prepared the *h* Prov 8:27
h are higher than the...... Is 55:9
behold, I create new *h*...... Is 65:17
and behold, the *h*...... Matt 3:16
h will be shaken...... Matt 24:29
h are the work of Your...... Heb 1:10
h will pass away...... 2 Pe 3:10

HEED
By taking *h* according...... Ps 119:9
and let us not give *h*...... Jer 18:18
nor give *h* to fables...... 1 Ti 1:4

HEEL
you shall bruise His *h*...... Gen 3:15
Me has lifted up his h...... John 13:18

HEIGHT
nor *h* nor depth...... Rom 8:39
length and depth and *h*...... Eph 3:18

HEIR
if a son, then an *h*...... Gal 4:7
He has appointed *h*...... Heb 1:2

HEIRS
of God and joint *h*...... Rom 8:17
should be fellow *h*...... Eph 3:6
vessel, and as being *h*...... 1 Pe 3:7

HELL
shall be turned into *h*...... Ps 9:17
go down alive into *h*...... Ps 55:15
house is the way to *h*...... Prov 7:27
his soul from *h*...... Prov 23:14
H and Destruction are...... Prov 27:20
"*H* from beneath is...... Is 14:9
be in danger of *h* fire...... Matt 5:22
to be cast into *h*...... Matt 18:9
the condemnation of *h*...... Matt 23:33
power to cast into *h*...... Luke 12:5
it is set on fire by *h*...... Jas 3:6

HELMET
And take the *h* of...... Eph 6:17
and love, and as a *h*...... 1 Th 5:8

HELP
the shield of your *h*...... Deut 33:29
Is my *h* not within me...... Job 6:13
"There is no *h*...... Ps 3:2
He is our *h* and our...... Ps 33:20
A very present *h*...... Ps 46:1
God, make haste to *h*...... Ps 71:12
the LORD had been my *h* Ps 94:17
there was none to *h*...... Ps 107:12
He is their *h* and...... Ps 115:9
h my unbelief...... Mark 9:24
and find grace to *h*...... Heb 4:16

HELPER
I will make him a *h*...... Gen 2:18
Behold, God is my *h*...... Ps 54:4
give you another *H*...... John 14:16
"But when the *H*...... John 15:26
"*The LORD is my h*...... Heb 13:6

HELPS
the Spirit also *h*...... Rom 8:26
gifts of healings, *h*...... 1 Co 12:28

HERESIES
dissensions, *h*...... Gal 5:20
in destructive *h*...... 2 Pe 2:1

HIDDEN
Your word I have *h*...... Ps 119:11
h that will not...... Matt 10:26
the *h* wisdom which God...... 1 Co 2:7
let it be the *h* person...... 1 Pe 3:4
some of the *h* manna...... Rev 2:17

HIDE
H me under the shadow...... Ps 17:8
O God, And do not *h*...... Ps 55:1
You *h* Your face...... Ps 104:29
darkness shall not *h*...... Ps 139:12
You are God, who *h*...... Is 45:15
h yourself from your...... Is 58:7
"Fall on us and *h*...... Rev 6:16

HIGH
priest of God Most *H*...... Gen 14:18
For the LORD Most *H*...... Ps 47:2
the LORD is on *h*...... Ps 138:6
know that the Most *H*...... Dan 4:17
up on a *h* mountain by...... Matt 17:1
your mind on *h* things...... Rom 12:16
h thing that exalts...... 2 Co 10:5
and faithful *H* Priest...... Heb 2:17

HINDERED
prayers may not be *h*...... 1 Pe 3:7

HOLIEST
the way into the *H*...... Heb 9:8
to enter the *H* by the...... Heb 10:19

HOLINESS
You, glorious in *h*...... Ex 15:11
I have sworn by My *h*...... Ps 89:35
H adorns Your house...... Ps 93:5
to the Spirit of *h*...... Rom 1:4
be partakers of His *h*...... Heb 12:10

HOLY
where you stand is *h*...... Ex 3:5
priests and a *h* nation...... Ex 19:6
day, to keep it *h*...... Ex 20:8
distinguish between *h*...... Lev 10:10
LORD your God am *h*...... Lev 19:2
God, In His *h* mountain...... Ps 48:1
"*H*, *h*, *h*...... Is 6:3
child of the *H* Spirit...... Matt 1:18
baptize you with the *H*...... Mark 1:8
who speak, but the *H*...... Mark 13:11
H Spirit will come...... Luke 1:35
H Spirit descended...... Luke 3:22
Father give the *H*...... Luke 11:13
H Spirit will teach...... Luke 12:12
H Spirit was not...... John 7:39
all filled with the *H*...... Acts 2:4
apostles' hands the *H*...... Acts 8:18
to speak, the *H* Spirit...... Acts 11:15
receive the *H* Spirit...... Acts 19:2
peace and joy in the *H*...... Rom 14:17
H Spirit teaches...... 1 Co 2:13
that we should be *h*...... Eph 1:4
were sealed with the *H*...... Eph 1:13
partakers of the *H*...... Heb 6:4
He who called you is *h*...... 1 Pe 1:15
it is written, "*Be h*...... 1 Pe 1:16
moved by the *H* Spirit...... 2 Pe 1:21
is *h*, let him be *h*...... Rev 22:11

HOME
LORD has brought me *h*...... Ruth 1:21
sparrow has found a *h*...... Ps 84:3
to his eternal *h*...... Eccl 12:5
said to him, "Go *h*...... Mark 5:19
to him and make Our *h*...... John 14:23
took her to his own *h*...... John 19:27
own husbands at *h*...... 1 Co 14:35
that while we are at *h*...... 2 Co 5:6
to show piety at *h*...... 1 Ti 5:4

HOMEMAKERS
be discreet, chaste, *h*...... Tit 2:5

HONEY
What is sweeter than *h*...... Judg 14:18
And with *h* from the...... Ps 81:16
h and milk are under...... Song 4:11
was locusts and wild *h*...... Matt 3:4

HONOR
both riches and *h*...... 1 Ki 3:13
the king delights to *h*...... Esth 6:6
Sing out the *h* of His...... Ps 66:2
H and majesty are...... Ps 96:6
H the LORD with your...... Prov 3:9
before *h* is humility...... Prov 15:33
h is not fitting...... Prov 26:1
Father, where is My *h*...... Mal 1:6
is not without *h*...... Matt 13:57
H your father and your...... Matt 15:4
h the Son just as they...... John 5:23

"I do not receive *h*........ John 5:41
but I *h* My Father.......... John 8:49
him My Father will *h*....... John 12:26
make one vessel for *h*...... Rom 9:21
worthy of double *h*......... 1 Ti 5:17
no man takes this *h*........ Heb 5:4
H the king................. 1 Pe 2:17
from God the Father *h*...... 2 Pe 1:17
give glory and *h*........... Rev 4:9

HONORABLE
providing *h* things......... 2 Co 8:21
Marriage is *h* among........ Heb 13:4
having your conduct *h*...... 1 Pe 2:12

HOPE
also will rest in *h*........ Ps 16:9
heart, All you who *h*....... Ps 31:24
My *h* is in You............. Ps 39:7
For You are my *h*........... Ps 71:5
I *h* in Your word........... Ps 119:147
O Israel, *h* in the......... Ps 130:7
There is more *h*............ Prov 26:12
the living there is *h*...... Eccl 9:4
O the *H* of Israel.......... Jer 14:8
good that one should *h*..... Lam 3:26
"I have *h* in God........... Acts 24:15
to *h*, in *h* believed...... Rom 4:18
h does not disappoint...... Rom 5:5
h that is seen is.......... Rom 8:24
And now abide faith, *h*..... 1 Co 13:13
life only we have *h*........ 1 Co 15:19
may know what is the *h*..... Eph 1:18
were called in one *h*....... Eph 4:4
h which is laid............ Col 1:5
Christ in you, the *h*....... Col 1:27
For what is our *h*.......... 1 Th 2:19
others who have no *h*....... 1 Th 4:13
and as a helmet the *h*...... 1 Th 5:8
Jesus Christ, our *h*........ 1 Ti 1:1
in *h* of eternal life........ Tit 1:2
for the blessed *h*.......... Tit 2:13
to lay hold of the *h*....... Heb 6:18
in of a better *h*........... Heb 7:19
us again to a living *h*..... 1 Pe 1:3
you a reason for the *h*..... 1 Pe 3:15
who has this *h* in Him...... 1 Jn 3:3

HORN
My shield and the *h*........ Ps 18:2
h will be exalted.......... Ps 112:9
goat had a notable *h*....... Dan 8:5
and has raised up a *h*...... Luke 1:69

HORSE
The *h* and its rider He..... Ex 15:1
h is a vain hope........... Ps 33:17
and behold, a white *h*...... Rev 6:2
and behold, a white *h*...... Rev 19:11

HOSANNA
H in the highest........... Matt 21:9

HOSPITABLE
of good behavior, *h*........ 1 Ti 3:2
Be *h* to one another........ 1 Pe 4:9

HOSTS
name of the LORD of *h*...... 1 Sa 17:45
As the LORD of *h* lives..... 1 Ki 18:15
The LORD of *h* is with...... Ps 46:7
LORD, all you His *h*........ Ps 103:21
Praise Him, all His *h*...... Ps 148:2
word of the LORD of *h*...... Is 39:5
LORD of *h* is His name...... Is 47:4
against spiritual *h*........ Eph 6:12

HOUR
day and *h* no one knows..... Matt 24:36
Man is coming at an *h*...... Matt 24:44
Behold, the *h* is at........ Matt 26:45
But this is your *h*......... Luke 22:53
h has not yet come......... John 2:4
"But the *h* is coming....... John 4:23
save Me from this *h*........ John 12:27
"Father, the *h*............. John 17:1
keep you from the *h*........ Rev 3:10

HOUSE
from your father's *h*....... Gen 12:1
But as for me and my *h*..... Josh 24:15
the goodness of Your *h*..... Ps 65:4
for her *h* leads down....... Prov 2:18
better to go to the *h*...... Eccl 7:2
to the *h* of the God of..... Is 2:3
'Set your *h* in order....... Is 38:1
and beat on that *h*......... Matt 7:25
h divided against.......... Matt 12:25
h shall be called a........ Matt 21:13
h may be filled............ Luke 14:23
not make My Father's *h*..... John 2:16
h are many mansions........ John 14:2
publicly and from *h*........ Acts 20:20
who rules his own *h*........ 1 Ti 3:4
the church in your *h*....... Phm 2
For every *h* is built........ Heb 3:4
him into your *h*............ 2 Jn 10

HOUSEHOLD
"If the *h* is worthy........ Matt 10:13
be those of his own h...... Matt 10:36
saved, you and your *h*...... Acts 16:31
also baptized the *h*........ 1 Co 1:16

HOVERING
Spirit of God was *h*........ Gen 1:2

HUMBLE
man Moses was very *h*....... Num 12:3
h you and test you......... Deut 8:2
who is proud, and *h*........ Job 40:11
the cry of the *h*........... Ps 9:12
Do not forget the *h*........ Ps 10:12
h He guides in justice..... Ps 25:9
h shall hear of it and..... Ps 34:2
LORD lifts up the *h*........ Ps 147:6
h spirit with the.......... Prov 16:19
contrite and *h* spirit...... Is 57:15
a meek and *h* people........ Zeph 3:12
associate with the *h*....... Rom 12:16
gives grace to the h....... Jas 4:6
H yourselves in the........ Jas 4:10
gives grace to the h....... 1 Pe 5:5
h yourselves under the..... 1 Pe 5:6

HUMILIATION
h His justice was.......... Acts 8:33
but the rich in his *h*...... Jas 1:10

HUMILITY
the Lord with all *h*........ Acts 20:19
delight in false *h*......... Col 2:18
gentle, showing all *h*...... Tit 3:2
and be clothed with *h*...... 1 Pe 5:5

HUNGER
you, allowed you to *h*...... Deut 8:3
lack and suffer *h*.......... Ps 34:10
They shall neither *h*....... Is 49:10
likely to die from *h*....... Jer 38:9
are those who *h*............ Matt 5:6
For you shall *h*............ Luke 6:25
to Me shall never *h*........ John 6:35
They shall neither *h*....... Rev 7:16

HUNGRY
bread from the *h*........... Job 22:7
And fills the *h*............ Ps 107:9
gives food to the *h*........ Ps 146:7
your soul to the *h*......... Is 58:10
'for I was *h* and you....... Matt 25:35
and one is *h* and........... 1 Co 11:21
to be full and to be *h*..... Phil 4:12

HUSBAND
She also gave to her *h*..... Gen 3:6
h safely trusts her........ Prov 31:11
woman have her own *h*....... 1 Co 7:2
For the unbelieving *h*...... 1 Co 7:14
betrothed you to one *h*..... 2 Co 11:2
For the *h* is head of....... Eph 5:23
the *h* of one wife.......... 1 Ti 3:2

HUSBANDS
them ask their own *h*....... 1 Co 14:35
H, love your wives......... Eph 5:25
Let deacons be the *h*....... 1 Ti 3:12

HYMN
when they had sung a *h*..... Matt 26:30

HYPOCRISY
you are full of *h*.......... Matt 23:28
Pharisees, which is *h*...... Luke 12:1
Let love be without *h*...... Rom 12:9
malice, all guile, *h*....... 1 Pe 2:1

HYPOCRITES
"But the *h* in heart........ Job 36:13
not be like the *h*.......... Matt 6:5
do you test Me, you *h*...... Matt 22:18
and Pharisees, *h*........... Matt 23:13

HYSSOP
Purge me with *h*............ Ps 51:7
sour wine, put it on *h*..... John 19:29

— I —

IDLE
i word men may speak....... Matt 12:36
saw others standing *i*...... Matt 20:3
they learn to be *i*......... 1 Ti 5:13
both *i* talkers and......... Tit 1:10

IDOL
if he blesses an *i*......... Is 66:3
thing offered to an *i*...... 1 Co 8:7
That an *i* is anything...... 1 Co 10:19

IDOLATERS
fornicators, nor *i*......... 1 Co 6:9
immoral, sorcerers, *i*...... Rev 21:8
and murderers and *i*........ Rev 22:15

IDOLS
stolen the household *i*..... Gen 31:19
This was offered to *i*...... 1 Co 10:28
keep yourselves from *i*..... 1 Jn 5:21
worship demons, and *i*...... Rev 9:20

IGNORANT
I was so foolish and *i*..... Ps 73:22
though Abraham was *i*....... Is 63:16
But if anyone is *i*......... 1 Co 14:38
on those who are *i*......... Heb 5:2

ILLEGITIMATE
then you are *i*............. Heb 12:8

IMAGE
Us make man in Our *i*....... Gen 1:26
yourselves a carved *i*...... Deut 4:16
shall despise their *i*...... Ps 73:20
the king made an *i*......... Dan 3:1
to them, "Whose *i*.......... Matt 22:20
since he is the *i*.......... 1 Co 11:7
He is the *i* of the......... Col 1:15
the beast and his *i*........ Rev 14:9
who worshiped his *i*........ Rev 19:20

IMITATE
I urge you, *i* me........... 1 Co 4:16
as I also *i* Christ......... 1 Co 11:1
i those who through........ Heb 6:12

IMMORALITY
except sexual *i*............ Matt 5:32
i as is not even named..... 1 Co 5:1
abstain from sexual *i*...... 1 Th 4:3

IMMORTAL
to the King eternal, *i*..... 1 Ti 1:17

IMMORTALITY
glory, honor, and *i*........ Rom 2:7
mortal must put on *i*....... 1 Co 15:53
who alone has *i*............ 1 Ti 6:16
and brought life and *i*..... 2 Ti 1:10

- then how will God *j* ... Rom 3:6
- Therefore let us not *j* ... Rom 14:13
- Christ, who will *j* ... 2 Ti 4:1
- Lord, the righteous *J* ... 2 Ti 4:8
- heaven, to God the *J* ... Heb 12:23
- are you to *j* another ... Jas 4:12

JUDGES
- *j* who delivered ... Judg 2:16
- in the days when the *j* ... Ruth 1:1
- Surely He is God who *j* ... Ps 58:11
- For the Father *j* ... John 5:22
- he who is spiritual *j* ... 1 Co 2:15
- *j* me is the Lord ... 1 Co 4:4
- Him who *j* righteously ... 1 Pe 2:23

JUDGMENT
- show partiality in *j* ... Deut 1:17
- Teach me good *j* ... Ps 119:66
- from prison and from *j* ... Is 53:8
- I will also speak *j* ... Jer 4:12
- be in danger of the *j* ... Matt 5:21
- will rise up in the *j* ... Matt 12:42
- shall not come into *j* ... John 5:24
- and My *j* is righteous ... John 5:30
- if I do judge, My *j* ... John 8:16
- "Now is the *j* ... John 12:31
- the righteous *j* ... Rom 1:32
- *j* which came from one ... Rom 5:16
- all stand before the *j* ... Rom 14:10
- eats and drinks *j* ... 1 Co 11:29
- appear before the *j* ... 2 Co 5:10
- after this the *j* ... Heb 9:27
- receive a stricter *j* ... Jas 3:1
- time has come for *j* ... 1 Pe 4:17
- a long time their *j* ... 2 Pe 2:3
- darkness for the *j* ... Jude 6

JUDGMENTS
- The *j* of the LORD are ... Ps 19:9
- I dread, For Your *j* ... Ps 119:39
- unsearchable are His *j* ... Rom 11:33
- righteous are His *j* ... Rev 19:2

JUST
- Noah was a *j* man ... Gen 6:9
- Hear a *j* cause ... Ps 17:1
- It is a joy for the *j* ... Prov 21:15
- For there is not a *j* ... Eccl 7:20
- her husband, being a *j* ... Matt 1:19
- resurrection of the *j* ... Luke 14:14
- *j* persons who need no ... Luke 15:7
- the Holy One and the *J* ... Acts 3:14
- dead, both of the *j* ... Acts 24:15
- *j shall live by faith* ... Rom 1:17
- that He might be *j* ... Rom 3:26
- whatever things are *j* ... Phil 4:8
- *j* men made perfect ... Heb 12:23
- have murdered the *j* ... Jas 5:6
- He is faithful and *j* ... 1 Jn 1:9
- *J* and true are Your ... Rev 15:3

JUSTICE
- for all His ways are *j* ... Deut 32:4
- the Almighty pervert *j* ... Job 8:3
- *j* as the noonday ... Ps 37:6
- Do *j* to the afflicted ... Ps 82:3
- the LORD is a God of *j* ... Is 30:18
- *J* is turned back ... Is 59:14
- I, the LORD, love *j* ... Is 61:8
- observe mercy and *j* ... Hos 12:6
- 'Execute true *j* ... Zech 7:9
- Where is the God of *j* ... Mal 2:17
- *and He will declare j* ... Matt 12:18
- *His humiliation His j* ... Acts 8:33

JUSTIFICATION
- because of our *j* ... Rom 4:25
- offenses resulted in *j* ... Rom 5:16

JUSTIFIED
- Me that you may be *j* ... Job 40:8
- words you will be *j* ... Matt 12:37
- But wisdom is *j* ... Luke 7:35
- *j* rather than the ... Luke 18:14
- who believes is *j* ... Acts 13:39
- "*That You may be j* ... Rom 3:4
- law no flesh will be *j* ... Rom 3:20
- *j* freely by His grace ... Rom 3:24
- having been *j* by ... Rom 5:1
- these He also *j* ... Rom 8:30
- but you were *j* ... 1 Co 6:11
- no flesh shall be *j* ... Gal 2:16
- who attempt to be *j* ... Gal 5:4
- *j* in the Spirit ... 1 Ti 3:16
- then that a man is *j* ... Jas 2:24
- the harlot also *j* ... Jas 2:25

JUSTIFIES
- He who *j* the wicked ... Prov 17:15
- It is God who *j* ... Rom 8:33

JUSTIFY
- *j* the wicked for a ... Is 5:23
- wanting to *j* himself ... Luke 10:29
- "You are those who *j* ... Luke 16:15
- is one God who will *j* ... Rom 3:30
- that God would *j* ... Gal 3:8

— K —

KEEP
- day, to *k* it holy ... Ex 20:8
- Do not *k* silence ... Ps 35:22
- *k* them in the midst of ... Prov 4:21
- a time to *k* silence ... Eccl 3:7
- Let all the earth *k* ... Hab 2:20
- *k* the commandments ... Matt 19:17
- If you love Me, *k* ... John 14:15
- *k* through Your name ... John 17:11
- Let your women *k* ... 1 Co 14:34
- *k* the unity of the ... Eph 4:3
- *k* yourself pure ... 1 Ti 5:22
- *k* His commandments ... 1 Jn 2:3
- *k* you from stumbling ... Jude 24
- *k* those things ... Rev 1:3

KEEPER
- Am I my brother's *k* ... Gen 4:9
- The LORD is your *k* ... Ps 121:5

KEPT
- vineyard I have not *k* ... Song 1:6
- *k* back part of the ... Acts 5:2
- I have *k* the faith ... 2 Ti 4:7
- who are *k* by the power ... 1 Pe 1:5

KEYS
- I will give you the *k* ... Matt 16:19
- And I have the *k* ... Rev 1:18

KILL
- *k* the Passover ... Ex 12:21
- I *k* and I make alive ... Deut 32:39
- "Am I God, to *k* ... 2 Ki 5:7
- a time to *k* ... Eccl 3:3
- to save life or to *k* ... Mark 3:4
- of them they will *k* ... Luke 11:49
- afraid of those who *k* ... Luke 12:4
- Why do you seek to *k* ... John 7:19
- *k* and eat ... Acts 10:13

KILLED
- Abel his brother and *k* ... Gen 4:8
- For I have *k* a man for ... Gen 4:23
- "Your servant has *k* ... 1 Sa 17:36
- and scribes, and be *k* ... Matt 16:21
- *k* the Prince of life ... Acts 3:15
- *For Your sake we are k* ... Rom 8:36
- who *k* both the Lord ... 1 Th 2:15
- martyr, who was *k* ... Rev 2:13

KIND
- animals after their *k* ... Gen 6:20
- For He is *k* to the ... Luke 6:35
- suffers long and is *k* ... 1 Co 13:4
- And be *k* to one ... Eph 4:32

KINDNESS
- may the LORD show *k* ... 2 Sa 2:6
- anger, abundant in *k* ... Neh 9:17
- me His marvelous *k* ... Ps 31:21
- For His merciful *k* ... Ps 117:2
- tongue is the law of *k* ... Prov 31:26
- *k* shall not depart ... Is 54:10
- I remember you, the *k* ... Jer 2:2
- by longsuffering, by *k* ... 2 Co 6:6
- longsuffering, *k* ... Gal 5:22
- But when the *k* and the ... Tit 3:4
- and to brotherly *k* ... 2 Pe 1:7

KING
- Then Melchizedek *k* ... Gen 14:18
- days there was no *k* ... Judg 17:6
- said, "Give us a *k* ... 1 Sa 8:6
- they anointed David *k* ... 2 Sa 2:4
- Yet I have set My *K* ... Ps 2:6
- The LORD is *K* forever ... Ps 10:16
- And the *K* of glory ... Ps 24:7
- For God is my *K* ... Ps 74:12
- In the year that *K* ... Is 6:1
- the LORD is our *K* ... Is 33:22
- the LORD shall be *K* ... Zech 14:9
- He who has been born *K* ... Matt 2:2
- This Is Jesus the *K* ... Matt 27:37
- by force to make Him *k* ... John 6:15
- "Behold your *K* ... John 19:14
- there is another *k* ... Acts 17:7
- Now to the *K* eternal ... 1 Ti 1:17
- only Potentate, the *K* ... 1 Ti 6:15
- this Melchizedek, *k* ... Heb 7:1
- Honor the *k* ... 1 Pe 2:17
- *K* of Kings and Lord of ... Rev 19:16

KINGDOM
- you shall be to Me a *k* ... Ex 19:6
- LORD has torn the *k* ... 1 Sa 15:28
- Yours is the *k* ... 1 Ch 29:11
- *k* is the LORD's ... Ps 22:28
- the scepter of Your *k* ... Ps 45:6
- in heaven, And His *k* ... Ps 103:19
- is an everlasting *k* ... Ps 145:13
- *k* which shall never be ... Dan 2:44
- High rules in the *k* ... Dan 4:17
- *k* shall be the LORD's ... Obad 21
- "Repent, for the *k* ... Matt 3:2
- for Yours is the *k* ... Matt 6:13
- But seek first the *k* ... Matt 6:33
- the mysteries of the *k* ... Matt 13:11
- of such is the *k* ... Matt 19:14
- are not far from the *k* ... Mark 12:34
- back, is fit for the *k* ... Luke 9:62
- he cannot see the *k* ... John 3:3
- If My *k* were of this ... John 18:36
- for the *k* of God is ... Rom 14:17
- will not inherit the *k* ... Gal 5:21
- *the scepter of Your K* ... Heb 1:8
- into the everlasting *k* ... 2 Pe 1:11

KINGDOMS
- showed Him all the *k* ... Matt 4:8
- have become the *k* ... Rev 11:15

KINGS
- The *k* of the earth set ... Ps 2:2
- *k* shall fall down ... Ps 72:11
- By me *k* reign ... Prov 8:15
- He will stand before *k* ... Prov 22:29
- that which destroys *k* ... Prov 31:3
- *K* shall be your foster ... Is 49:23
- before governors and *k* ... Matt 10:18
- *k* have desired to see ... Luke 10:24
- You have reigned as *k* ... 1 Co 4:8
- and has made us *k* ... Rev 1:6
- that the way of the *k* ... Rev 16:12
- may eat the flesh of *k* ... Rev 19:18

KISS
- *K* the Son ... Ps 2:12
- Let him *k* me with the ... Song 1:2
- "You gave Me no *k* ... Luke 7:45
- another with a holy *k* ... Rom 16:16

KISSED
- And they *k* one another ... 1 Sa 20:41
- and *k* Him ... Matt 26:49
- and she *k* His feet and ... Luke 7:38

KNEE
And they bowed the *k*..... Matt 27:29
have not bowed the k...... Rom 11:4
every k shall bow to....... Rom 14:11
of Jesus every *k*.............Phil 2:10

KNEES
make firm the feeble *k*.... Is 35:3
this reason I bow my *k*.... Eph 3:14
and the feeble *k*............ Heb 12:12

KNEW
Adam *k* Eve his wife........Gen 4:1
in the womb I *k*............ Jer 1:5
to them, 'I never *k*.........Matt 7:23
k what was in man..........John 2:25
For He made Him who *k* 2 Co 5:21

KNOCK
k, and it will be............Matt 7:7
at the door and *k*...........Rev 3:20

KNOW
k good and evil............. Gen 3:22
k that I am the LORD...... Ex 6:7
k that there is no God..... 2 Ki 5:15
k that my Redeemer........Job 19:25
'What does God *k*............Job 22:13
k that I am God............ Ps 46:10
make me to *k* wisdom..... Ps 51:6
Who can *k* it..................Jer 17:9
saying, '*K* the LORD........Jer 31:34
k what hour your Lord.... Matt 24:42
an oath, "I do not *k*........Matt 26:72
the world did not *k*........ John 1:10
We speak what We *k*...... John 3:11
k what we worship.......... John 4:22
hear My voice, and I *k*.... John 10:27
If you *k* these things........John 13:17
we are sure that You *k*.... John 16:30
k that I love You.............John 21:15
k times or seasons..........Acts 1:7
nor can he *k* them........... 1 Co 2:14
For we *k* in part and....... 1 Co 13:9
k a man in Christ who..... 2 Co 12:2
k the love of Christ......... Eph 3:19
k whom I have believed... 2 Ti 1:12
so that they may *k*........... 2 Ti 2:25
this we *k* that we *k*......... 1 Jn 2:3
and you *k* all things......... 1 Jn 2:20
By this we *k* love............ 1 Jn 3:16
k that He abides............. 1 Jn 3:24
k that we are of God....... 1 Jn 5:19
"I *k* your works.............. Rev 2:2

KNOWLEDGE
and the tree of the *k*....... Gen 2:9
LORD is the God of *k*...... 1 Sa 2:3
Can anyone teach God *k*..Job 21:22
unto night reveals *k*......... Ps 19:2
k is too wonderful............ Ps 139:6
Wise people store up *k*.... Prov 10:14
and he who increases *k*.... Eccl 1:18
k is that wisdom.............. Eccl 7:12
no work or device or *k*.... Eccl 9:10
k shall increase............... Dan 12:4
you have rejected *k*.......... Hos 4:6
having the form of *k*........ Rom 2:20
by the law is the *k*......... Rom 3:20
K puffs up..................... 1 Co 8:1
whether there is *k*........... 1 Co 13:8
Christ which passes *k*.......Eph 3:19
is falsely called *k*............ 1 Ti 6:20

KNOWN
In Judah God is *k*.......... Ps 76:1
my mouth will I make *k*... Ps 89:1
If you had *k* Me............ John 8:19
My sheep, and am *k*........John 10:14
The world has not *k*........ John 17:25
peace they have not k...... Rom 3:17
I would not have *k*..........Rom 7:7
"*For who has k*.............. Rom 11:34
after you have *k* God...... Gal 4:9
k the Holy Scriptures....... 2 Ti 3:15

KNOWS
"For God *k* that in......... Gen 3:5
and hour no one *k*.......... Matt 24:36
k who the Son is............Luke 10:22
but God *k* your hearts..... Luke 16:15
searches the hearts *k*....... Rom 8:27
k the things of God......... 1 Co 2:11
k those who are His........ 2 Ti 2:19
to him who *k* to do......... Jas 4:17
and *k* all things............... 1 Jn 3:20
written which no one *k*.... Rev 2:17

— L —

LABOR
Six days you shall *l*......... Ex 20:9
to Me, all you who *l*....... Matt 11:28
"Do not *l* for the.............John 6:27
knowing that your *l*.......... 1 Co 15:58
but rather let him *l*......... Eph 4:28
mean fruit from my *l*....... Phil 1:22
your work of faith, *l*......... 1 Th 1:3
forget your work and *l*......Heb 6:10
your works, your *l*........... Rev 2:2

LABORED
l more abundantly than.... 1 Co 15:10
for you, lest I have *l*....... Gal 4:11

LABORERS
but the *l* are few.............Matt 9:37

LABORS
The person who *l*............Prov 16:26
is no end to all his *l*........ Eccl 4:8
entered into their *l*.......... John 4:38
creation groans and *l*....... Rom 8:22
l more abundant............... 2 Co 11:23
may rest from their *l*....... Rev 14:13

LACK
the LORD shall not *l*........ Ps 34:10
to the poor will not *l*....... Prov 28:27
What do I still *l*.............. Matt 19:20
"One thing you *l*............ Mark 10:21

LACKING
the things that are *l*......... Tit 1:5

LADDER
and behold, a *l*................. Gen 28:12

LADEN
nation, a people *l*............. Is 1:4
and are heavy *l*................ Matt 11:28

LAID
the place where they *l*..... Mark 16:6
Where have you *l*............ John 11:34

LAKE
cast alive into the *l*.......... Rev 19:20

LAMB
but where is the *l*............ Gen 22:7
took the poor man's *l*....... 2 Sa 12:4
shall dwell with the *l*....... Is 11:6
He was led as a *l*............. Is 53:7
l shall feed together......... Is 65:25
The *L* of God who takes.. John 1:29
of Christ, as of a *l*........... 1 Pe 1:19
"Worthy is the *L*............. Rev 5:12
by the blood of the *L*...... Rev 12:11
Book of Life of the *L*...... Rev 13:8
supper of the *L*................ Rev 19:9

LAME
l shall leap like a............ Is 35:6
when you offer the *l*......... Mal 1:8
their sight and the *l*......... Matt 11:5
And a certain man *l*......... Acts 3:2
so that what is *l*.............. Heb 12:13

LAMENTATION
was heard in Ramah, l.... Matt 2:18
and made great *l*.............. Acts 8:2

LAMP
For You are my *l*............ 2 Sa 22:29
You will light my *l*.......... Ps 18:28
Your word is a *l*.............. Ps 119:105
the *l* of the wicked........... Prov 13:9
his *l* will be put out......... Prov 20:20
Nor do they light a *l*........ Matt 5:15
"The *l* of the body........... Matt 6:22
They need no *l* nor........... Rev 22:5

LAMPS
he made its seven *l*......... Ex 37:23
and trimmed their *l*.......... Matt 25:7
And there were seven *l*.... Rev 4:5

LAMPSTAND
branches of the *l*.............. Ex 25:32
and there is a *l*................ Zech 4:2
and remove your *l*........... Rev 2:5

LAND
l that I will show you...... Gen 12:1
l flowing with milk.......... Ex 3:8
is heard in our *l*.............. Song 2:12
Bethlehem, in the l.......... Matt 2:6

LANGUAGE
whole earth had one *l*...... Gen 11:1
is no speech nor *l*............ Ps 19:3
speak in his own *l*........... Acts 2:6
blasphemy, filthy *l*........... Col 3:8

LAST
He shall stand at *l*........... Job 19:25
First and I am the *L*........ Is 44:6
l will be first................... Matt 20:16
children, it is the *l*.......... 1 Jn 2:18
the First and the *L*........... Rev 1:11

LAUGH
Why did Sarah *l*.............. Gen 18:13
"God has made me *l*....... Gen 21:6
All those who see Me *l*.... Ps 22:7
You, O LORD, shall *l*...... Ps 59:8
Woe to you who *l*........... Luke 6:25

LAUGHS
he *l* at the threat of......... Job 41:29
The Lord *l* at him............ Ps 37:13

LAW
stones a copy of the *l*..... Josh 8:32
The *l* of the LORD is........ Ps 19:7
The *l* of his God is in...... Ps 37:31
l is my delight.................. Ps 119:77
Oh, how I love Your *l*..... Ps 119:97
And Your *l* is truth.......... Ps 119:142
and the *l* is light.............. Prov 6:23
for this is the *L*.............. Matt 7:12
"The *l* and the................ Luke 16:16
because the *l* brings......... Rom 4:15
when there is no *l*........... Rom 5:13
you are not under *l*......... Rom 6:14
Is the *l* sin...................... Rom 7:7
For what the *l* could........ Rom 8:3
l is fulfilled in one........... Gal 5:14
l is not made for a.......... 1 Ti 1:9
into the perfect *l*............. Jas 1:25
fulfill the royal *l*............. Jas 2:8

LAWFUL
doing what is not *l*.......... Matt 12:2
Is it *l* to pay taxes........... Matt 22:17
All things are *l*................ 1 Co 6:12

LAWLESS
l one will be revealed...... 2 Th 2:8
and hearing their *l*.......... 2 Pe 2:8

LAWLESSNESS
Me, you who practice *l*.... Matt 7:23
l is already at work......... 2 Th 2:7
and hated l...................... Heb 1:9
and sin is *l*...................... 1 Jn 3:4

LAY
nowhere to *l* His head..... Matt 8:20
l hands may receive......... Acts 8:19

Do not *l* hands on..........1 Ti 5:22
l aside all......................Jas 1:21

LEAD
Your hand shall *l*............Ps 139:10
And do not *l* us into.........Matt 6:13
"Can the blind *l*............Luke 6:39

LEADS
He *l* me in the paths.......Ps 23:3
And if the blind *l*...........Matt 15:14
by name and *l* them out...John 10:3
the goodness of God *l*.....Rom 2:4

LEAF
plucked olive *l*................Gen 8:11

LEAN
all your heart, and *l*........Prov 3:5
yet they *l* on the LORD....Mic 3:11

LEANING
Then, *l* back on Jesus'.....John 13:25
l on the top of his..........Heb 11:21

LEARN
l Your statutes...............Ps 119:71
neither shall they *l*..........Is 2:4
My yoke upon you and *l*..Matt 11:29
Let a woman *l* in............1 Ti 2:11
let our people also *l*........Tit 3:14

LEARNED
who has heard and *l*........John 6:45
have not so *l* Christ.........Eph 4:20
in all things I have *l*........Phil 4:12
l obedience by the..........Heb 5:8

LEARNING
hear and increase *l*.........Prov 1:5
l is driving you mad........Acts 26:24
were written for our *l*......Rom 15:4

LEAST
Judah, are not the l..........Matt 2:6
so, shall be called *l*.........Matt 5:19
For I am the *l* of the.......1 Co 15:9

LEAVE
a man shall *l* his............Gen 2:24
For You will not *l*...........Ps 16:10
Do not *l* me nor.............Ps 27:9
"*I will never l*................Heb 13:5

LEAVEN
day you shall remove *l*.....Ex 12:15
of heaven is like *l*...........Matt 13:33
and beware of the *l*.........Matt 16:6
know that a little *l*..........1 Co 5:6
l leavens the whole..........Gal 5:9

LEAVES
and they sewed fig *l*........Gen 3:7
nothing on it but *l*...........Matt 21:19
And the *l* of the tree.......Rev 22:2

LED
so the LORD alone *l*........Deut 32:12
l them forth by the..........Ps 107:7
l them by the right..........Is 63:12
For as many as are *l*........Rom 8:14
l captivity captive...........Eph 4:8
l away by various............2 Ti 3:6

LEFT
l hand know what your....Matt 6:3
"See, we have *l*..............Matt 19:27

LEGS
Like the *l* of the lame......Prov 26:7
l are pillars of...............Song 5:15
did not break His *l*..........John 19:33

LENDS
ever merciful, and *l*.........Ps 37:26
deals graciously and *l*......Ps 112:5
has pity on the poor *l*......Prov 19:17

LENGTH
The *l* of the ark shall.......Gen 6:15
is your life and the *l*.......Deut 30:20

L of days is in her.........Prov 3:16
l is as great as its...........Rev 21:16

LEOPARD
the *l* shall lie down..........Is 11:6
or the *l* its spots............Jer 13:23

LETTER
the oldness of the *l*.........Rom 7:6
for the *l* kills...................2 Co 3:6
you sorry with my *l*..........2 Co 7:8
or by word or by *l*...........2 Th 2:2

LETTERS
to you or *l* of...................2 Co 3:1
"For his *l*........................2 Co 10:10
with what large *l*.............Gal 6:11

LEVIATHAN
"Can you draw out *L*......Job 41:1
L Which You have made. Ps 104:26

LEVITE
"Is not Aaron the *L*........Ex 4:14
a *L* of the country of.......Acts 4:36

LIAR
for he is a *l* and the........John 8:44
but every man a *l*..............Rom 3:4
we make Him a *l*..............1 Jn 1:10
Who is a *l* but he who.....1 Jn 2:22
his brother, he is a *l*........1 Jn 4:20
God has made Him a *l*....1 Jn 5:10

LIARS
"All men are *l*.................Ps 116:11
Cretans are always *l*........Tit 1:12
and have found them *l*.....Rev 2:2
l shall have their.............Rev 21:8

LIBERALITY
he who gives, with *l*........Rom 12:8
the riches of their *l*.........2 Co 8:2

LIBERTY
year, and proclaim *l*........Lev 25:10
And I will walk at *l*..........Ps 119:45
to proclaim *l* to the..........Is 61:1
into the glorious *l*...........Rom 8:21
For why is my *l*...............1 Co 10:29
Lord is, there is *l*............2 Co 3:17
therefore in the *l*............Gal 5:1
l as an opportunity..........Gal 5:13
the perfect law of *l*..........Jas 1:25
yet not using your *l*.........1 Pe 2:16

LIE
man, that He should *l*......Num 23:19
I will not *l* to David........Ps 89:35
Do not *l* to one.............Col 3:9
God, who cannot *l*...........Tit 1:2
do not boast and *l*...........Jas 3:14
know it, and that no *l*......1 Jn 2:21
an abomination or a *l*......Rev 21:27

LIES
sin *l* at the door.............Gen 4:7
and he who speaks *l*........Prov 19:5
speaking *l* in....................1 Ti 4:2

LIFE
the breath of *l*................Gen 2:7
l was also in the.............Gen 2:9
then you shall give *l*........Ex 21:23
'For the *l* of the..............Lev 17:11
before you today *l*...........Deut 30:15
You have granted me *l*....Job 10:12
In whose hand is the *l*.....Job 12:10
with the light of *l*...........Job 33:30
He will redeem their *l*.....Ps 72:14
word has given me *l*........Ps 119:50
regain the paths of *l*........Prov 2:19
She is a tree of *l*.............Prov 3:18
finds me finds *l*...............Prov 8:35
is that wisdom gives *l*......Eccl 7:12
I have cut off my *l*...........Is 38:12
not worry about your *l*.....Matt 6:25
l does not consist...........Luke 12:15

l was the light................John 1:4
so the Son gives *l*...........John 5:21
as the Father has *l*..........John 5:26
spirit, and they are *l*........John 6:63
have the light of *l*...........John 8:12
and I lay down My *l*........John 10:15
resurrection and the *l*......John 11:25
even God, who gives *l*.....Rom 4:17
that pertain to this *l*........1 Co 6:3
l which I now live...........Gal 2:20
l is hidden with...............Col 3:3
of God who gives *l*..........1 Ti 6:13
For what is your *l*...........Jas 4:14
that pertain to *l*..............2 Pe 1:3
l was manifested.............1 Jn 1:2
and the pride of *l*............1 Jn 2:16
who has the Son has *l*......1 Jn 5:12
the Lamb's Book of *L*......Rev 21:27
right to the tree of *l*........Rev 22:14
the water of *l* freely........Rev 22:17
from the Book of *L*........Rev 22:19

LIFT
I will *l* up my eyes to......Ps 121:1
l up your voice like a......Is 58:1
Lord, and He will *l*.........Jas 4:10

LIFTED
in Hades, he *l* up his.......Luke 16:23
the Son of Man be *l*........John 3:14
"And I, if I am *l*.............John 12:32

LIGHT
"Let there be *l*...............Gen 1:3
"The *l* of the wicked.......Job 18:5
The LORD is my *l*............Ps 27:1
Oh, send out Your *l*........Ps 43:3
And He has given us *l*.....Ps 118:27
And a *l* to my path.........Ps 119:105
Truly the *l* is sweet.........Eccl 11:7
let us walk in the *l*..........Is 2:5
l shall break forth...........Is 58:8
For your *l* has come........Is 60:1
"You are the *l*................Matt 5:14
"Let your *l* so shine........Matt 5:16
body will be full of *l*.......Matt 6:22
than the sons of *l*............Luke 16:8
and the life was the *l*.......John 1:4
That was the true *L*.........John 1:9
darkness rather than *l*......John 3:19
truth comes to the *l*.........John 3:21
saying, "I am the *l*..........John 8:12
believe in the *l*...............John 12:36
"I have come as a *l*.........John 12:46
l the hidden....................1 Co 4:5
God who commanded *l*....2 Co 4:6
Walk as children of *l*.......Eph 5:8
You are all sons of *l*........1 Th 5:5
into His marvelous *l*........1 Pe 2:9
to you, that God is *l*.......1 Jn 1:5
l as He is in the..............1 Jn 1:7
says he is in the *l*............1 Jn 2:9
and the Lamb is its *l*.......Rev 21:23

LIGHTNING
"For as the *l*...................Matt 24:27
countenance was like *l*.....Matt 28:3
saw Satan fall like *l*........Luke 10:18

LIGHTS
"Let there be *l*...............Gen 1:14
Him who made great *l*.....Ps 136:7
whom you shine as *l*........Phil 2:15
from the Father of *l*........Jas 1:17

LIKE-MINDED
grant you to be *l*.............Rom 15:5
For I have no one *l*.........Phil 2:20

LIKENESS
according to Our *l*...........Gen 1:26
carved image, or any *l*.....Ex 20:4
when I awake in Your *l*...Ps 17:15
His own Son in the *l*.......Rom 8:3
and coming in the *l*.........Phil 2:7

MEDITATE
Isaac went out to *m*........ Gen 24:63
but you shall *m*............. Josh 1:8
M within your heart on.... Ps 4:4
I *m* within my heart........ Ps 77:6
I will *m* on Your........... Ps 119:15
Your heart will *m*.......... Is 33:18
m beforehand on what..... Luke 21:14
m on these things...........Phil 4:8

MEDITATION
of my mouth and the *m*... Ps 19:14
It is my *m* all the day...... Ps 119:97

MEEK
with equity for the *m*.......Is 11:4
Blessed are the *m*........... Matt 5:5

MEET
For You *m* him with the.. Ps 21:3
prepare to *m* your God.... Amos 4:12
go out to *m* him............ Matt 25:6
m the Lord in the air...... 1 Th 4:17

MELT
man's heart will *m*.......... Is 13:7
the elements will *m*.........2 Pe 3:10

MEMBER
the body is not one *m*..... 1 Co 12:14
tongue is a little *m*..........Jas 3:5

MEMBERS
you that one of your *m*....Matt 5:29
do not present your *m*..... Rom 6:13
that your bodies are *m*.....1 Co 6:15
neighbor, for we are *m*.... Eph 4:25

MEN
m began to call on the.....Gen 4:26
saw the daughters of *m*.....Gen 6:2
you shall die like *m*..........Ps 82:7
the Egyptians are *m*..........Is 31:3
make you fishers of *m*..... Matt 4:19
good will toward *m*......... Luke 2:14
from heaven or from *m*....Luke 20:4
Likewise also the *m*.........Rom 1:27
let no one glory in *m*........1 Co 3:21
the Lord, and not to *m*....Eph 6:7
between God and *m*........1 Ti 2:5

MENSERVANTS
and on My m and on My Acts 2:18

MERCHANDISE
perceives that her *m*........ Prov 31:18
house a house of *m*.........John 2:16

MERCIES
for His *m* are great......... 2 Sa 24:14
And His tender *m*...........Ps 145:9
give you the sure m.........Acts 13:34
the Father of *m*.............. 2 Co 1:3

MERCIFUL
God be *m* to us and........Ps 67:1
Blessed are the *m*............ Matt 5:7
saying, 'God be *m*...........Luke 18:13
For I will be m.............. Heb 8:12
compassionate and *m*.......Jas 5:11

MERCY
but showing *m* to........... Ex 20:6
and abundant in *m*..........Num 14:18
m endures forever...........1 Ch 16:34
You, O Lord, belongs *m*..Ps 62:12
M and truth have met......Ps 85:10
M shall be built.............. Ps 89:2
M and truth go before..... Ps 89:14
m is everlasting..............Ps 100:5
For Your *m* is great........ Ps 108:4
is full of Your *m*.............Ps 119:64
do justly, to love *m*.........Mic 6:8
'*I desire m and not*.........Matt 9:13
And His *m* is on those.....Luke 1:50
"*I will have m*............... Rom 9:15
of God who shows *m*.......Rom 9:16
that He might have *m*......Rom 11:32
m has made trustworthy...1 Co 7:25
as we have received *m*.....2 Co 4:1
God, who is rich in *m*..... Eph 2:4
but I obtained *m*.............1 Ti 1:13
him that he may find *m*... 2 Ti 1:18
that we may obtain *m*......Heb 4:16
judgment is without *m*..... Jas 2:13

MERRY
m heart makes a............Prov 15:13
eat, drink, and be *m*....... Eccl 8:15
that we should make *m*....Luke 15:32

MESSIAH
until *M* the Prince..........Dan 9:25
"We have found the *M*....John 1:41

MIDST
God is in the *m*..............Ps 46:5
that I am in the *m*...........Joel 2:27
I am there in the *m*.........Matt 18:20

MIGHT
the greatness of His *m*..... Is 40:26
man glory in his *m*..........Jer 9:23
'Not by *m* nor by............Zech 4:6
in the power of His *m*..... Eph 6:10
greater in power and *m*....2 Pe 2:11
honor and power and *m*... Rev 7:12

MIGHTIER
coming after me is *m*.......Matt 3:11

MIGHTY
He was a *m* hunter......... Gen 10:9
for they are too *m*.......... Num 22:6
How the *m* have fallen....2 Sa 1:19
The LORD *m* in battle......Ps 24:8
their Redeemer is *m*........Prov 23:11
Woe to men *m* at........... Is 5:22
great in counsel and *m*.....Jer 32:19
He has put down the *m*... Luke 1:52
the flesh, not many *m*.......1 Co 1:26
the working of His *m*...... Eph 1:19
from heaven with His *m*...2 Th 1:7

MILK
honey and *m* are under....Song 4:11
shall flow with *m*............Joel 3:18
have come to need *m*...... Heb 5:12
desire the pure *m*............1 Pe 2:2

MIND
perfect peace, whose *m*.... Is 26:3
Be of the same *m*............Rom 12:16
convinced in his own *m*....Rom 14:5

MINISTER
to make you a *m*............ Acts 26:16
for he is God's *m*............Rom 13:4
you will be a good *m*.......1 Ti 4:6
a *M* of the sanctuary....... Heb 8:2

MINISTERS
angels spirits, His *m*........ Ps 104:4
for they are God's *m*........ Rom 13:6
commend ourselves as *m*.. 2 Co 6:4
Are they *m* of Christ........ 2 Co 11:23

MINISTRY
I magnify my *m*.............. Rom 11:13
But if the *m* of death...... 2 Co 3:7
for the work of *m*............ Eph 4:12
a more excellent *m*...........Heb 8:6

MIRACLES
is a sinner do such *m*.......John 9:16
God worked unusual *m*.... Acts 19:11
the working of *m*............. 1 Co 12:10
with various *m*................Heb 2:4

MIRTH
I will test you with *m*...... Eccl 2:1
is in the house of *m*......... Eccl 7:4
joy is darkened, the *m*.....Is 24:11

MITES
widow putting in two *m*... Luke 21:2

MOCKED
at noon, that Elijah *m*..... 1 Ki 18:27
"I am one *m* by his.........Job 12:4
knee before Him and *m*... Matt 27:29
deceived, God is not *m*.... Gal 6:7

MOCKER
Wine is a *m*................... Prov 20:1

MOMENT
face from you for a *m*..... Is 54:8
in a *m*, in the.................1 Co 15:52
which is but for a *m*........2 Co 4:17

MONEY
be redeemed without *m*... Is 52:3
and you who have no *m*... Is 55:1
and hid his lord's *m*........ Matt 25:18
promised to give him *m*... Mark 14:11
"Carry neither *m*............ Luke 10:4
I sent you without *m*....... Luke 22:35
be purchased with *m*........ Acts 8:20
not greedy for *m*............. 1 Ti 3:3
m is a root of all............ 1 Ti 6:10

MONEYCHANGERS
the tables of the *m*..........Matt 21:12
m doing business.............John 2:14

MOON
Until the *m* is no more.... Ps 72:7
morning, fair as the *m*..... Song 6:10
sun and *m* grow dark.......Joel 2:10
m will not give its........... Mark 13:24

MORNING
the eyelids of the *m*........ Job 41:18
Evening and *m* and at..... Ps 55:17
the wings of the *m*.......... Ps 139:9
looks forth as the *m*........ Song 6:10
Lucifer, son of the *m*....... Is 14:12
very early in the *m*.......... Luke 24:1
the Bright and *M* Star..... Rev 22:16

MOTH
where *m* and rust............Matt 6:19

MOTHER
because she was the *m*.....Gen 3:20
leave his father and m..... Matt 19:5
"Behold your *m*..............John 19:27
the *M* of Harlots.............Rev 17:5

MOUNT
come up to *M* Sinai.........Ex 19:23
you like *M* Carmel............Song 7:5
they shall *m* up with........Is 40:31
for this Hagar is *M*......... Gal 4:25

MOUNTAIN
let us go up to the *m*.......Is 2:3
image became a great *m*.. Dan 2:35
you will say to this *m*...... Matt 17:20
with Him on the holy *m*...2 Pe 1:18

MOUNTAINS
m melt like wax at the.....Ps 97:5
m skipped like rams........ Ps 114:4
m surround Jerusalem......Ps 125:2
m shall depart and the..... Is 54:10
in Judea flee to the *m*..... Matt 24:16
that I could remove *m*..... 1 Co 13:2
m were not found........... Rev 16:20

MOURN
a time to *m*.....................Eccl 3:4
are those who *m*............. Matt 5:4
Lament and *m* and weep..Jas 4:9
of the earth will *m*.......... Rev 1:7

MOURNING
This is a grievous *m*........ Gen 50:11
m all the day long...........Ps 38:6
m shall be ended............ Is 60:20

I will turn their *m*.......... Jer 31:13
shall be a great *m*.......... Zech 12:11
be turned to *m* and.......... Jas 4:9

MOUTH
Who has made man's *m*... Ex 4:11
Out of the *m* of babes..... Ps 8:2
m speaking pompous....... Dan 7:8
m defiles a man.............. Matt 15:11
m I will judge you......... Luke 19:22
spew you out of My *m*..... Rev 3:16

MOVE
and the earth will *m*........ Is 13:13
in Him we live and *m*...... Acts 17:28

MULTIPLY
"Be fruitful and *m*.......... Gen 1:22
m your descendants.......... Gen 16:10
m my days as the............ Job 29:18
m the descendants............ Jer 33:22

MULTITUDE
In the *m* of words sin...... Prov 10:19
compassion on the *m*....... Matt 15:32
with the angel a *m*.......... Luke 2:13
"*love will cover a m*........ 1 Pe 4:8
and behold, a great *m*...... Rev 7:9

MURDER
'*You shall not m*............ Matt 5:21
threats and *m* against....... Acts 9:1
You *m* and covet and...... Jas 4:2

MURDERER
He was a *m* from the...... John 8:44
and asked for a *m*........... Acts 3:14
of you suffer as a *m*........ 1 Pe 4:15
his brother is a *m*........... 1 Jn 3:15

MURMURED
"and you *m* in your......... Deut 1:27
But *m* in their tents......... Ps 106:25
as some of them also *m*... 1 Co 10:10

MURMURING
all things without *m*......... Phil 2:14

MUZZLE
"*You shall not m*............ 1 Ti 5:18

MYSTERIES
to you to know the *m*...... Matt 13:11
and understand all *m*....... 1 Co 13:2
the spirit he speaks *m*...... 1 Co 14:2

MYSTERY
given to know the *m*....... Mark 4:11
wisdom of God in a *m*..... 1 Co 2:7
Behold, I tell you a *m*..... 1 Co 15:51
made known to us the *m*.. Eph 1:9
This is a great *m*............ Eph 5:32
m which has been........... Col 1:26
the *m* of godliness........... 1 Ti 3:16

— N —

NAILED
n it to the cross.............. Col 2:14

NAKED
And they were both *n*..... Gen 2:25
knew that they were *n*..... Gen 3:7
N I came from my.......... Job 1:21
'I was *n* and you............ Matt 25:36
and fled from them *n*...... Mark 14:52
poor, blind, and *n*........... Rev 3:17

NAKEDNESS
of Canaan, saw the *n*..... Gen 9:22
or famine, or *n*.............. Rom 8:35
often, in cold and *n*........ 2 Co 11:27
n may not be revealed..... Rev 3:18

NAME
Abram called on the *n*..... Gen 13:4
This is My *n* forever........ Ex 3:15
shall not take the *n*......... Ex 20:7
excellent is Your *n*.......... Ps 8:1
He calls them all by *n*..... Ps 147:4
The *n* of the LORD is a.... Prov 18:10
A good *n* is to be.......... Prov 22:1
They will call on My *n*..... Zech 13:9
n shall be great.............. Mal 1:11
to you who fear My *n*...... Mal 4:2
hallowed be Your *n*......... Matt 6:9
prophesied in Your *n*....... Matt 7:22
righteous man in the *n*..... Matt 10:41
together in My *n*............ Matt 18:20
many will come in My *n*.. Matt 24:5
"My *n* is Legion............ Mark 5:9
"His *n* is John................ Luke 1:63
who believe in His *n*....... John 1:12
comes in his own *n*......... John 5:43
his own sheep by *n*......... John 10:3
through faith in His *n*...... Acts 3:16
there is no other *n*.......... Acts 4:12
suffer shame for His *n*..... Acts 5:41
which is above every *n*..... Phil 2:9
deed, do all in the *n*........ Col 3:17
reproached for the *n*........ 1 Pe 4:14
you hold fast to My *n*...... Rev 2:13
n that you are alive......... Rev 3:1
having His Father's *n*....... Rev 14:1
and glorify Your *n*........... Rev 15:4
n written that no one........ Rev 19:12

NARROW
"Enter by the *n* gate....... Matt 7:13
n is the gate and............ Matt 7:14

NATION
make you a great *n*......... Gen 12:2
up sword against *n*.......... Is 2:4
I will make them one *n*... Ezek 37:22
n will rise against........... Matt 24:7
for he loves our *n*........... Luke 7:5
those who are not a n..... Rom 10:19
tribe, tongue, and *n*........ Rev 13:7

NATIONS
itself among the *n*........... Num 23:9
Why do the *n* rage.......... Ps 2:1
I will give You The *n*...... Ps 2:8
is high above all *n*.......... Ps 113:4
disciples of all the *n*........ Matt 28:19
who was to rule all *n*...... Rev 12:5
the healing of the *n*......... Rev 22:2

NATURAL
women exchanged the *n*... Rom 1:26
the men, leaving the *n*.... Rom 1:27
did not spare the *n*......... Rom 11:21
n man does not receive.... 1 Co 2:14
It is sown a *n* body......... 1 Co 15:44

NATURE
for what is against *n*........ Rom 1:26
n itself teach you............ 1 Co 11:14
We who are Jews by *n*...... Gal 2:15
n children of wrath.......... Eph 2:3
of the divine *n*................ 2 Pe 1:4

NEAR
that has God so *n*........... Deut 4:7
The LORD is *n* to all....... Ps 145:18
upon Him while He is *n*... Is 55:6
know that it is *n*............. Matt 24:33
kingdom of God is *n*........ Luke 21:31
"*The word is n*.............. Rom 10:8
to those who were *n*........ Eph 2:17
for the time is *n*............. Rev 1:3

NEED
in nakedness, and in *n*..... Deut 28:48
the things you have *n*...... Matt 6:8
'The Lord has *n*.............. Matt 21:3
each as anyone had *n*...... Acts 4:35
hand, "I have no *n*.......... 1 Co 12:21
who ministered to my *n*... Phil 2:25
supply all your *n*............ Phil 4:19
to help in time of *n*......... Heb 4:16
sees his brother in *n*........ 1 Jn 3:17
And the city had no *n*..... Rev 21:23

NEGLECT
n the gift that is............. 1 Ti 4:14
if we *n* so great a........... Heb 2:3

NEIGHBOR
For better is a *n*............ Prov 27:10
every man teach his *n*...... Jer 31:34
gives drink to his *n*......... Hab 2:15
You shall love your n...... Matt 5:43
And who is my *n*............ Luke 10:29
You shall love your n...... Rom 13:9

NET
have hidden their *n*......... Ps 35:7
They have prepared a *n*... Ps 57:6
catch them in their *n*........ Hab 1:15
I will let down the *n*........ Luke 5:5
to them, "Cast the *n*....... John 21:6

NEVER
in Me shall *n* thirst.......... John 6:35
in Me shall *n* die............ John 11:26
Love *n* fails.................... 1 Co 13:8
n take away sins............. Heb 10:11
"*I will n leave you*.......... Heb 13:5
for prophecy *n* came by... 2 Pe 1:21

NEW
Now there arose a *n*......... Ex 1:8
the LORD creates a *n*....... Num 16:30
They chose *n* gods.......... Judg 5:8
and there is nothing *n*...... Eccl 1:9
n every morning............. Lam 3:23
wine into *n* wineskins...... Matt 9:17
of the *n* covenant............ Matt 26:28
n commandment I give.... John 13:34
he is a *n* creation............ 2 Co 5:17
n man who is renewed..... Col 3:10
when I will make a n..... Heb 8:8
n heavens and a *n*........... 2 Pe 3:13
n name written which...... Rev 2:17
And they sang a *n*.......... Rev 5:9
And I saw a *n* heaven..... Rev 21:1

NIGHT
darkness He called *N*....... Gen 1:5
It is a *n* of solemn........... Ex 12:42
pillar of fire by *n*........... Ex 13:22
and the *n* be ended......... Job 7:4
gives songs in the *n*......... Job 35:10
n reveals knowledge......... Ps 19:2
awake through the *n*........ Ps 119:148
and stars to rule by *n*...... Ps 136:9
desired You in the *n*....... Is 26:9
and perished in a *n*......... Jon 4:10
and continued all *n*......... Luke 6:12
man came to Jesus by *n*... John 3:2
n is coming when no....... John 9:4
came to Jesus by *n*......... John 19:39
The *n* is far spent........... Rom 13:12
as a thief in the *n*........... 1 Th 5:2
We are not of the *n*......... 1 Th 5:5
there shall be no *n*.......... Rev 22:5

NINETY-NINE
he not leave the *n*........... Matt 18:12
n just persons................. Luke 15:7

NOISE
The *n* of a multitude....... Is 13:4
They have made a *n*......... Lam 2:7
away with a great *n*......... 2 Pe 3:10

NOSTRILS
n the breath of life.......... Gen 2:7
breath of God in my *n*..... Job 27:3
breath is in his *n*............ Is 2:22

NOTHING
"It is good for *n*............ Prov 20:14
before Him are as *n*......... Is 40:17
I can of Myself do *n*........ John 5:30
Me you can do *n*............ John 15:5

OVERTAKEN
No temptation has *o*........1 Co 10:13
if a man is *o* in any.........Gal 6:1

OVERTHROW
you shall utterly *o*........... Ex 23:24
o the righteous in............Prov 18:5
o the faith of some..........2 Ti 2:18

OVERTHROWN
Their judges are *o*...........Ps 141:6
I will make it *o*.............. Ezek 21:27
and Nineveh shall be *o*.... Jon 3:4

OVERTURNED
my heart is *o* within........ Lam 1:20
o the tables of the...........Matt 21:12

OVERWHELMED
When my heart is *o*...........Ps 61:2
o their enemies...............Ps 78:53
waters would have *o*.........Ps 124:4
my spirit is *o* within........ Ps 143:4

OWED
o him ten thousand.......... Matt 18:24
o five hundred denarii..... Luke 7:41

OWN
He came to His *o*........... John 1:11
having loved His *o*.......... John 13:1
world would love its *o*...... John 15:19
and you are not your *o*....1 Co 6:19
But each one has his *o*.... 1 Co 7:7
For all seek their *o*......... Phil 2:21
from our sins in His *o*..... Rev 1:5

OX
Sabbath loose his *o*......... Luke 13:15
shall not muzzle an o....... 1 Co 9:9

— P —

PAIN
p you shall bring............Gen 3:16
p as a woman in............. Is 13:8
are filled with *p*.............. Is 21:3
before her *p* came........... Is 66:7
Why is my *p* perpetual......Jer 15:18
shall be no more *p*.......... Rev 21:4

PALACE
enter the King's *p*........... Ps 45:15
a *p* of foreigners............. Is 25:2
guards his own *p*.............Luke 11:21
evident to the whole *p*..... Phil 1:13

PALACES
Out of the ivory *p*...........Ps 45:8
God is in her *p*................Ps 48:3
has entered our *p*............Jer 9:21

PALE
behold, a *p* horse............Rev 6:8

PANTS
As the deer *p* for the...... Ps 42:1

PARADISE
will be with Me in *P*....... Luke 23:43
was caught up into *P*....... 2 Co 12:4
in the midst of the *P*....... Rev 2:7

PARDON
p your transgressions....... Ex 23:21
O LORD, *P* my iniquity.... Ps 25:11
He will abundantly *p*....... Is 55:7
p all their iniquities......... Jer 33:8

PARENTS
will rise up against *p*....... Matt 10:21
has left house or *p*.......... Luke 18:29
disobedient to *p*..............Rom 1:30
to lay up for the *p*.......... 2 Co 12:14

PART
You have no *p* in the...... Josh 22:25
has chosen that good *p*.... Luke 10:42
you, you have no *p*......... John 13:8
For we know in *p*........... 1 Co 13:9
p has a believer............. 2 Co 6:15
shall take away his *p*....... Rev 22:19

PARTAKER
And have been a *p*......... Ps 50:18
in hope should be *p*........ 1 Co 9:10
Christ, and also a *p*.........1 Pe 5:1

PARTAKERS
Gentiles have been *p*....... Rom 15:27
of the sacrifices *p*............1 Co 10:18
know that as you are *p*.... 2 Co 1:7
gospel, you all are *p*........Phil 1:7
qualified us to be *p*......... Col 1:12
For we have become *p*.....Heb 3:14

PARTIALITY
'You shall not show *p*......Deut 1:17
unjustly, And show *p*...... Ps 82:2
is not good to show *p*......Prov 18:5
but have shown *p*.............Mal 2:9
that God shows no *p*....... Acts 10:34
For there is no *p*............ Rom 2:11
doing nothing with *p*....... 1 Ti 5:21
but if you show *p*.............Jas 2:9
good fruits, without *p*...... Jas 3:17

PARTS
anything but death *p*....... Ruth 1:17
in the inward *p*................Ps 51:6
Shout, you lower *p*..........Is 44:23
but our presentable *p*...... 1 Co 12:24
into the lower p.............. Eph 4:9

PASS
I will *p* over you.............Ex 12:13
of the sea That *p*............ Ps 8:8
When you *p* through the.. Is 43:2
"I will make you *p*.......... Ezek 20:37
and earth will *p*............. Matt 24:35

PASSED
And behold, the LORD *p*..1 Ki 19:11
forbearance God had *p*.... Rom 3:25
High Priest who has *p*..... Heb 4:14
We know that we have *p* 1 Jn 3:14

PASSES
For the wind *p* over it..... Ps 103:16
of Christ which *p*............ Eph 3:19

PASSOVER
It is the LORD's *P*........... Ex 12:11
I will keep the *P*.............Matt 26:18
indeed Christ, our *P*........1 Co 5:7
By faith he kept the *P*..... Heb 11:28

PAST
My days are *p*................ Job 17:11
lo, the winter is *p*........... Song 2:11
and His ways *p* finding.... Rom 11:33
ways spoke in time *p*....... Heb 1:1

PASTURE
the people of His *p*..........Ps 95:7
feed them in good *p*......... Ezek 34:14
in and out and find *p*...... John 10:9

PASTURES
to lie down in green *p*..... Ps 23:2

PATHS
He leads me in the *p*........Ps 23:3
Teach me Your *p*.............Ps 25:4
and all her *p* are.............Prov 3:17
p they have not............... Is 42:16
themselves crooked *p*.......Is 59:8
make His p straight.......... Matt 3:3
and make straight *p*..........Heb 12:13

PATIENCE
'Master, have *p*.............. Matt 18:26
and bear fruit with *p*....... Luke 8:15
Now may the God of *p*.... Rom 15:5
labor of love, and *p*......... 1 Th 1:3
faith, love, *p*.................. 1 Ti 6:11
p have its perfect............Jas 1:4
in the kingdom and *p*...... Rev 1:9
Here is the *p* and the...... Rev 13:10

PAY
with me, and I will *p*.......Matt 18:26
p taxes to Caesar............Matt 22:17
For you *p* tithe of...........Matt 23:23

PEACE
you, and give you *p*........ Num 6:26
both lie down in *p*.......... Ps 4:8
Seek *p*............................ Ps 34:14
For He will speak *p*......... Ps 85:8
Pray for the *p* of..............Ps 122:6
P be upon Israel..............Ps 125:5
war, and a time of *p*....... Eccl 3:8
Father, Prince of *P*.......... Is 9:6
keep him in perfect *p*...... Is 26:3
slightly, saying, '*P*............Jer 6:14
they will seek *p*............... Ezek 7:25
is worthy, let your *p*........Matt 10:13
that I came to bring *p*..... Matt 10:34
and on earth *p*................ Luke 2:14
that make for your *p*....... Luke 19:42
I leave with you, My *p*.... John 14:27
in Me you may have *p*.....John 16:33
Grace to you and *p*.......... Rom 1:7
by faith, we have *p*.......... Rom 5:1
God has called us to *p*.....1 Co 7:15
p will be with you.............2 Co 13:11
Spirit is love, joy, *p*........ Gal 5:22
He Himself is our *p*......... Eph 2:14
and the *p* of God.............Phil 4:7
heaven, having made *p*.... Col 1:20
And let the *p* of God...... Col 3:15
Be at *p* among................ 1 Th 5:13
faith, love, *p*................... 2 Ti 2:22
meaning "king of *p*,"........Heb 7:2
is sown in *p* by those.......Jas 3:18
p be multiplied.................2 Pe 1:2

PEACEMAKERS
Blessed are the *p*............ Matt 5:9

PEARLS
nor cast your *p*................Matt 7:6
hair or gold or *p*..............1 Ti 2:9
gates were twelve *p*......... Rev 21:21

PEOPLE
p shall be my *p*.............. Ruth 1:16
p who know the joyful..... Ps 89:15
We are His *p* and the...... Ps 100:3
and they shall be My *p*.... Jer 24:7
for you are not My *p*...... Hos 1:9
like *p*, like priest............ Hos 4:9
to make ready a *p*............Luke 1:17
take out of them a *p*....... Acts 15:14
who were not My p......... Rom 9:25
and they shall be My p.... 2 Co 6:16
His own special *p*............Tit 2:14
LORD will judge His p..... Heb 10:30
but are now the *p*........... 1 Pe 2:10
tribe and tongue and *p*.... Rev 5:9
they shall be His *p*.......... Rev 21:3

PERDITION
except the son of *p*......... John 17:12
to them a proof of *p*....... Phil 1:28
revealed, the son of *p*......2 Th 2:3
who draw back to *p*........ Heb 10:39
day of judgment and *p*.....2 Pe 3:7

PERFECT
Noah was a just man, *p*... Gen 6:9
one who is *p* in............. Job 36:4
for God, His way is *p*......Ps 18:30
You were *p* in your.........Ezek 28:15
Father in heaven is *p*.......Matt 5:48
"If you want to be *p*....... Matt 19:21
they may be made *p*........John 17:23
and *p* will of God........... Rom 12:2
when that which is *p*....... 1 Co 13:10

present every man *p*........ Col 1:28
the law made nothing *p*... Heb 7:19
of just men made *p*......... Heb 12:23
good gift and every *p*...... Jas 1:17
in word, he is a *p*........... Jas 3:2
p love casts out fear......... 1 Jn 4:18

PERFECTED
third day I shall be *p*...... Luke 13:32
or am already *p*............. Phil 3:12
the Son who has been *p*... Heb 7:28
the love of God is *p*........ 1 Jn 2:5

PERISH
All flesh would *p*............ Job 34:15
very day his plans *p*........ Ps 146:4
so that we may not *p*....... Jon 1:6
little ones should *p*.......... Matt 18:14
will all likewise *p*............ Luke 13:3
in Him should not *p*......... John 3:16
and they shall never *p*...... John 10:28
concern things which *p*..... Col 2:22
among those who *p*......... 2 Th 2:10
that any should *p*............ 2 Pe 3:9

PERMIT
the Spirit did not *p*......... Acts 16:7
And I do not *p* a woman 1 Ti 2:12

PERSECUTE
p me as God does........... Job 19:22
p me wrongfully.............. Ps 119:86
when they revile and *p*.... Matt 5:11
Bless those who *p*........... Rom 12:14

PERSECUTED
p the poor and needy...... Ps 109:16
p the prophets who......... Matt 5:12
If they *p* Me.................. John 15:20
p the church of God......... 1 Co 15:9
p, but not forsaken.......... 2 Co 4:9
p us now preaches the..... Gal 1:23

PERSEVERANCE
tribulation produces *p*...... Rom 5:3
to this end with all *p*....... Eph 6:18
longsuffering, love, *p*....... 2 Ti 3:10
to self-control *p*.............. 2 Pe 1:6

PERSON
do not regard the *p*......... Matt 22:16
express image of His *p*..... Heb 1:3
let it be the hidden *p*....... 1 Pe 3:4

PERSUADE
"You almost *p* me............ Acts 26:28
the Lord, we *p* men........ 2 Co 5:11
For do I now *p* men......... Gal 1:10

PERSUADED
a ruler is *p*..................... Prov 25:15
neither will they be *p*...... Luke 16:31
p that He is able............ 2 Ti 1:12

PERSUASIVE
p words of human........... 1 Co 2:4
you with *p* words............ Col 2:4

PERVERSE
because your way is *p*...... Num 22:32
for the *p* person is an...... Prov 3:32
p lips far from you.......... Prov 4:24
p heart will be................ Prov 12:8
p man sows strife............ Prov 16:28
but he who is *p*............... Prov 28:18
from this *p* generation..... Acts 2:40

PERVERT
"You shall not *p* justice... Deut 16:19
and *p* all equity.............. Mic 3:9
p the gospel of Christ...... Gal 1:7

PERVERTING
We found this fellow *p*.... Luke 23:2
will you not cease *p*........ Acts 13:10

PHILOSOPHERS
p encountered him......... Acts 17:18

PHYLACTERIES
They make their *p*.......... Matt 23:5

PHYSICIAN
Gilead, is there no *p*....... Jer 8:22
have no need of a *p*........ Matt 9:12
Luke the beloved *p* .... Col 4:14

PIECES
they took the thirty p....... Matt 27:9
shall be broken to p........ Rev 2:27

PIERCE
a sword will *p*............... Luke 2:35

PIERCED
p My hands and My feet.. Ps 22:16
on Me whom they have *p* Zech 12:10
of the soldiers *p*............. John 19:34
p themselves through....... 1 Ti 6:10
and they also who *p*........ Rev 1:7

PIERCING
p even to the division...... Heb 4:12

PIETY
first learn to show *p*........ 1 Ti 5:4

PILGRIMAGE
heart is set on *p*............. Ps 84:5
In the house of my *p*....... Ps 119:54

PILGRIMS
we are aliens and *p*......... 1 Ch 29:15
were strangers and *p*....... Heb 11:13

PILLAR
and she became a *p*......... Gen 19:26
and by night in a *p*......... Ex 13:21
the living God, the *p*....... 1 Ti 3:15

PILLARS
break their sacred *p*........ Ex 34:13
I set up its *p* firmly......... Ps 75:3
out her seven *p*.............. Prov 9:1
blood and fire and *p*........ Joel 2:30
and his feet like *p*........... Rev 10:1

PILOT
rudder wherever the *p*..... Jas 3:4

PIT
cast him into some *p*....... Gen 37:20
who go down to the *p*...... Ps 28:1
a harlot is a deep *p*......... Prov 23:27
fall into his own *p*........... Prov 28:10
who descend into the *P*.... Ezek 31:16
up my life from the *p*...... Jon 2:6
if it falls into a *p*........... Matt 12:11
into the bottomless *p*....... Rev 20:3

PITIABLE
of all men the most *p*...... 1 Co 15:19

PITY
"Have *p* on me............. Job 19:21
for someone to take *p*..... Ps 69:20
He who has *p* on the....... Prov 19:17
And should I not *p*......... Jon 4:11
just as I had *p*............... Matt 18:33

PLACE
p know him anymore....... Job 7:10
Come, see the *p*............. Matt 28:6
My word has no *p*........... John 8:37
I go to prepare a *p*......... John 14:2
might go to his own *p*...... Acts 1:25

PLACES
set them in slippery *p*...... Ps 73:18
dark *p* of the earth.......... Ps 74:20
and the rough *p*.............. Is 40:4
They love the best *p*........ Matt 23:6
in the heavenly *p*........... Eph 1:3

PLAGUES
I will send all My *p*......... Ex 9:14
p that are written........... Rev 22:18

PLAINLY
the Christ, tell us *p*......... John 10:24
now You are speaking *p*.. John 16:29
such things declare *p*....... Heb 11:14

PLANK
First remove the *p*.......... Matt 7:5

PLANS
He makes the *p* of the..... Ps 33:10
A man's heart *p*............. Prov 16:9

PLANT
a time to *p*.................... Eccl 3:2
Him as a tender *p*........... Is 53:2
they shall *p* vineyards...... Is 65:21
into the degenerate *p*....... Jer 2:21
p which My heavenly....... Matt 15:13

PLANTED
shall be like a tree *P*....... Ps 1:3
shall they be *p*................ Is 40:24
by the roots and be *p*...... Luke 17:6
I *p*, Apollos watered....... 1 Co 3:6

PLANTS
our sons may be as *p*....... Ps 144:12
neither he who *p*............. 1 Co 3:7

PLAY
P skillfully with a........... Ps 33:3
nursing child shall *p*....... Is 11:8
and rose up to p............. 1 Co 10:7

PLEAD
Oh, that one might *p*....... Job 16:21
p my cause against an....... Ps 43:1
p with your friend........... Prov 6:3

PLEASANT
food, that it was *p*.......... Gen 3:6
how good and how *p*........ Ps 133:1
and knowledge is *p*......... Prov 2:10
P words are like a.......... Prov 16:24
p places of the.............. Jer 23:10
Is he a *p* child............... Jer 31:20
I ate no *p* food.............. Dan 10:3

PLEASE
When a man's ways *p*...... Prov 16:7
do those things that *p*...... John 8:29
in the flesh cannot *p*........ Rom 8:8
how he may *p* the Lord.... 1 Co 7:32
Or do I seek to *p* men..... Gal 1:10
is impossible to *p* Him..... Heb 11:6

PLEASED
Then You shall be *p*........ Ps 51:19
Would he be *p* with you.. Mal 1:8
in whom I am well *p*....... Matt 3:17
God was not well *p*......... 1 Co 10:5
testimony, that he *p*........ Heb 11:5

PLEASURE
not a God who takes *p*.... Ps 5:4
p will be a poor man....... Prov 21:17
for He has no *p*.............. Eccl 5:4
shall perform all My *p*..... Is 44:28
"Do I have any *p*........... Ezek 18:23
I have no *p* in you.......... Mal 1:10
your Father's good *p*....... Luke 12:32
to the good *p* of His........ Eph 1:5
fulfill all the good *p*........ 2 Th 1:11
for sin you had no p....... Heb 10:6
back, my soul has no p.... Heb 10:38

PLEASURES
Your right hand are *p*...... Ps 16:11
cares, riches, and *p*......... Luke 8:14
to enjoy the passing *p*...... Heb 11:25

PLENTIFUL
You, O God, sent a *p*...... Ps 68:9
The harvest truly is *p*...... Matt 9:37

PLOTTED
and *p* to take Jesus by..... Matt 26:4

PREACHER
The words of the *P*........ Eccl 1:1
they hear without a *p*...... Rom 10:14
I was appointed a *p*.........1 Ti 2:7
of eight people, a *p*.........2 Pe 2:5

PREACHES
the Jesus whom Paul *p*.... Acts 19:13
p another Jesus whom..... 2 Co 11:4
p the faith which he........ Gal 1:23

PRECEDE
p those who are asleep.... 1 Th 4:15

PRECEPT
p must be upon *p*.......... Is 28:10

PRECIOUS
because my life was *p*......1 Sa 26:21
P in the sight of the........ Ps 116:15
How *p* also are Your.......Ps 139:17
She is more *p* than..........Prov 3:15
Since you were *p*............ Is 43:4
If you take out the *p*.......Jer 15:19
being much more *p*......... 1 Pe 1:7
who believe, He is *p*....... 1 Pe 2:7
which is very *p*.............. 1 Pe 3:4

PREDESTINED
He foreknew, He also *p*... Rom 8:29
having *p* us to................ Eph 1:5
inheritance, being *p*........Eph 1:11

PREEMINENCE
He may have the *p*......... Col 1:18
loves to have the *p*..........3 Jn 9

PREPARATION
Now it was the *P*............John 19:14
your feet with the *p*........ Eph 6:15

PREPARE
p a table before me in..... Ps 23:5
P the way of the LORD.... Mark 1:3
will, and did not *p*.......... Luke 12:47
p a place for you............ John 14:2

PREPARED
place which I have *p*....... Ex 23:20
You *p* room for it........... Ps 80:9
for whom it is *p*..............Matt 20:23
things which God has p....1 Co 2:9
Now He who has *p*.......... 2 Co 5:5
p beforehand that we.......Eph 2:10
God, for He has *p*.......... Heb 11:16

PRESBYTERY
of the hands of the *p*.......1 Ti 4:14

PRESENCE
themselves from the *p*......Gen 3:8
went out from the *p*........ Gen 4:16
P will go with you...........Ex 33:14
p is fullness of joy...........Ps 16:11
shall dwell in Your *p*....... Ps 140:13
shall shake at My *p*..........Ezek 38:20
Be silent in the *p*............Zeph 1:7
full of joy in Your p........ Acts 2:28
but his bodily *p*.............. 2 Co 10:10
obeyed, not as in my *p*.... Phil 2:12

PRESENT
we are all *p* before..........Acts 10:33
a law, that evil is *p*.........Rom 7:21
p your bodies a living.....Rom 12:1
absent in body but *p*........ 1 Co 5:3
not only when I am *p*......Gal 4:18
that He might *p*...............Eph 5:27
to *p* yourself................... 2 Ti 2:15
p you faultless................Jude 24

PRESERVE
before you to *p* life......... Gen 45:5
You shall *p* me from....... Ps 32:7
The LORD shall *p*.............Ps 121:8
children, I will *p*.............Jer 49:11
pardon those whom I *p*....Jer 50:20

loses his life will *p*.......... Luke 17:33
every evil work and *p*......2 Ti 4:18

PRESERVES
For the LORD *p* the.........Ps 31:23
p the souls of His........... Ps 97:10
The LORD *p* the simple.....Ps 116:6
who guards his mouth *p*...Prov 13:3
he who keeps his way *p*...Prov 16:17

PRESS
I *p* toward the goal......... Phil 3:14

PREVAIL
our tongue we will *p*....... Ps 12:4
but they shall not *p*.........Jer 1:19
of Hades shall not *p*........Matt 16:18

PREVAILED
hand, that Israel *p*..........Ex 17:11
with the Angel and *p*.......Hos 12:4
grew mightily and *p*.........Acts 19:20

PRICE
one pearl of great *p*........ Matt 13:46
back part of the *p*...........Acts 5:3
you were bought at a *p*....1 Co 6:20

PRIDE
p and arrogance and........Prov 8:13
By *p* comes only...............Prov 13:10
P goes before...................Prov 16:18
p will bring him low........ Prov 29:23
p He is able to abase........Dan 4:37
p he fall into the.............1 Ti 3:6
of the eyes, and the *p*......1 Jn 2:16

PRIEST
he was the *p* of God....... Gen 14:18
so He shall be a *p*...........Zech 6:13
and faithful High *P*.......... Heb 2:17
we have a great High *P*... Heb 4:14
p forever according...........Heb 5:6
Christ came as High *P*.......Heb 9:11

PRIESTHOOD
has an unchangeable *p*.....Heb 7:24
house, a holy *p*................1 Pe 2:5
generation, a royal *p*....... 1 Pe 2:9

PRIESTS
to Me a kingdom of *p*..... Ex 19:6
her *p* teach for pay......... Mic 3:11
made us kings and *p*.........Rev 1:6
but they shall be *p*...........Rev 20:6

PRINCE
"Who made you a *p*........Ex 2:14
everlasting Father, *P*....... Is 9:6
until Messiah the *P*......... Dan 9:25
except Michael your *p*..... Dan 10:21
according to the *p*............Eph 2:2

PRINCES
He is not partial to *p*.......Job 34:19
to put confidence in *p*......Ps 118:9
children to be their *p*.........Is 3:4
He brings the *p*................ Is 40:23

PRISON
and put him into the *p*.....Gen 39:20
Bring my soul out of *p*.... Ps 142:7
John had heard in *p*........ Matt 11:2
I was in *p* and you..........Matt 25:36
to the spirits in *p*............ 1 Pe 3:19

PRISONERS
gives freedom to the *p*..... Ps 146:7
the stronghold, you *p*...... Zech 9:12
Remember the *p* as if....... Heb 13:3

PRIZE
life shall be as a *p*...........Jer 21:9
but one receives the *p*..... 1 Co 9:24
the goal for the *p*............Phil 3:14

PROCEEDS
by every word that p....... Matt 4:4
Spirit of truth who *p*....... John 15:26
back part of the *p*........... Acts 5:2

PROCLAIM
began to *p* it freely......... Mark 1:45
knowing, Him I *p*........... Acts 17:23
drink this cup, you *p*....... 1 Co 11:26

PROCLAIMED
p the good news............ Ps 40:9
company of those who *p*.. Ps 68:11
he went his way and *p*..... Luke 8:39
inner rooms will be *p*...... Luke 12:3

PRODIGAL
with *p* living....................Luke 15:13

PROFANE
and offered *p* fire............Lev 10:1
and priest are *p*.............. Jer 23:11
"But you *p* it...................Mal 1:12
tried to *p* the temple........ Acts 24:6
But reject *p* and old........1 Ti 4:7
p person like Esau.......... Heb 12:16

PROFIT
p is there in my blood..... Ps 30:9
p has a man from all....... Eccl 1:3
there was no *p* under.......Eccl 2:11
for they will not *p*...........Is 57:12
words that cannot *p*.........Jer 7:8
p which you have made... Ezek 22:13
p is it that we have......... Mal 3:14
For what will it *p*............Mark 8:36
her masters much *p*..........Acts 16:16
not seeking my own *p*......1 Co 10:33
Christ will *p* you.............Gal 5:2
about words to no *p*........2 Ti 2:14
them, but He for our *p*....Heb 12:10
What does it *p*................Jas 2:14
and sell, and make a *p*.... Jas 4:13

PROFITABLE
things are good and *p*...... Tit 3:8
to you, but now is *p*.........Phm 11

PROMISE
of all His good *p*............ 1 Ki 8:56
Behold, I send the *P*....... Luke 24:49
but to wait for the *P*....... Acts 1:4
"For the *p* is to you......... Acts 2:39
for the hope of the *p*.......Acts 26:6
is made void and the *p*.... Rom 4:14
it is no longer of *p*.......... Gal 3:18
Therefore, since a *p*.........Heb 4:1
p the immutability............Heb 6:17
did not receive the *p*....... Heb 11:39

PROMISED
bless you as He has *p*...... Deut 1:11
Him faithful who had *p*....Heb 11:11

PROMISES
For all the *p* of God........2 Co 1:20
his Seed were the *p*..........Gal 3:16
patience inherit the *p*........Heb 6:12
having received the *p*........Heb 11:13
great and precious *p*.........2 Pe 1:4

PROPHECY
miracles, to another *p*.......1 Co 12:10
for *p* never came by the....2 Pe 1:21
is the spirit of *p*..............Rev 19:10
of the book of this *p*........ Rev 22:19

PROPHESIED
upon them, that they *p*.... Num 11:25
Lord, have we not *p*........Matt 7:22
prophets and the law *p*..... Matt 11:13
virgin daughters who *p*..... Acts 21:9

PROPHESY
prophets, "Do not *p*........Is 30:10
the prophets *p* falsely....... Jer 5:31
Who can but *p*................ Amos 3:8
saying, "*P* to us...............Matt 26:68
your daughters shall p...... Acts 2:17
if prophecy, let us *p*........ Rom 12:6

know in part and we *p*.....1 Co 13:9
desire earnestly to *p*........1 Co 14:39

PROPHET
shall be your *p*..............Ex 7:1
raise up for you a *P*........Deut 18:15
arisen in Israel a *p*..........Deut 34:10
"I alone am left a *p*..........1 Ki 18:22
send you Elijah the *p*......Mal 4:5
p shall receive a..............Matt 10:41
p is not without honor.....Matt 13:57
it cannot be that a *p*........Luke 13:33
Nazareth, who was a *P*....Luke 24:19
"Are you the *P*..............John 1:21
"This is truly the *P*.........John 6:14
with him the false *p*........Rev 19:20

PROPHETS
Saul also among the *p*.....1 Sa 10:12
the Law or the *P*............Matt 5:17
is the Law and the *P*.......Matt 7:12
or one of the *p*...............Matt 16:14
the tombs of the *p*..........Matt 23:29
indeed, I send you *p*.......Matt 23:34
Then many false *p*..........Matt 24:11
have Moses and the *p*......Luke 16:29
You are sons of the *p*......Acts 3:25
p did your fathers not......Acts 7:52
To Him all the *p*.............Acts 10:43
do you believe the *p*........Acts 26:27
before through His *p*........Rom 1:2
by the Law and the *P*......Rom 3:21
have killed Your p..........Rom 11:3
p are subject to the.........1 Co 14:32
to be apostles, some *p*.....Eph 4:11
brethren, take the *p*........Jas 5:10
were also false *p*.............2 Pe 2:1
because many false *p*.......1 Jn 4:1
blood of saints and *p*.......Rev 16:6

PROPITIATION
set forth to be a *p*...........Rom 3:25
to God, to make *p*..........Heb 2:17
He Himself is the *p*.........1 Jn 2:2
His Son to be the *p*.........1 Jn 4:10

PROSPER
made all he did to *p*........Gen 39:3
they *p* who love you........Ps 122:6
his sins will not *p*............Prov 28:13
of the LORD shall *p*..........Is 53:10
storing up as he may *p*....1 Co 16:2
I pray that you may *p*......3 Jn 2

PROSPERITY
p all your days..............Deut 23:6
p exceed the fame..........1 Ki 10:7
spend their days in *p*.......Job 36:11
Now in my *p* I said.........Ps 30:6
has pleasure in the *p*.......Ps 35:27
When I saw the *p*...........Ps 73:3
I pray, send now *p*..........Ps 118:25
the day of *p* be joyful......Eccl 7:14

PROUD
tongue that speaks *p*........Ps 12:3
does not respect the *p*.....Ps 40:4
a haughty look and a *p*....Ps 101:5
the house of the *p*...........Prov 15:25
Everyone who is *p*..........Prov 16:5
by wine, he is a *p*...........Hab 2:5
he has scattered the *p*.......Luke 1:51
"*God resists the p*..........1 Pe 5:5

PROVE
p yourself a man............1 Ki 2:2
does your arguing *p*.........Job 6:25
p Me now in this............Mal 3:10
mind, that you may *p*......Rom 12:2
P yourselves...................2 Co 13:5

PROVIDE
"My son, God will *p*.......Gen 22:8
Can He *p* meat for His....Ps 78:20
"*P* neither gold nor.........Matt 10:9
if anyone does not *p*........1 Ti 5:8

PROVOKE
do not *p* Him................Ex 23:21
"Do they *p* Me to..........Jer 7:19
p them to jealousy..........Rom 11:11
you, fathers, do not *p*......Eph 6:4

PROVOKED
Thus they *p* Him to.........Ps 106:29
his spirit was *p*..............Acts 17:16
seek its own, is not *p*......1 Co 13:5

PRUDENT
p man covers shame........Prov 12:16
A *p* man conceals...........Prov 12:23
The wisdom of the *p*.......Prov 14:8
p man considers well.......Prov 14:15
p wife is from the...........Prov 19:14
p man foresees evil.........Prov 22:3
perished from the *p*.........Jer 49:7
Therefore the *p*..............Amos 5:13
from the wise and *p*........Matt 11:25

PSALMS
Sing to Him, sing *p*.........1 Ch 16:9
to one another in *p*.........Eph 5:19
Let him sing *p*................Jas 5:13

PUNISH
p the righteous is............Prov 17:26
"I will *p* the world..........Is 13:11
p your iniquity.................Lam 4:22
So I will *p* them for........Hos 4:9

PUNISHED
You our God have *p*.......Ezra 9:13
because He has not *p*......Job 35:15
p them often in every......Acts 26:11
These shall be *p*.............2 Th 1:9

PUNISHMENT
p is greater than I..........Gen 4:13
you do in the day of *p*.....Is 10:3
days of *p* have come.........Hos 9:7
not turn away its *p*..........Amos 1:3
into everlasting *p*............Matt 25:46
p which was inflicted.......2 Co 2:6
Of how much worse *p*.....Heb 10:29
sent by him for the *p*.......1 Pe 2:14
the unjust under *p*..........2 Pe 2:9

PURE
a mercy seat of *p* gold.....Ex 25:17
Can a man be more *p*......Job 4:17
'My doctrine is *p*............Job 11:4
the heavens are not *p*......Job 15:15
the stars are not *p*..........Job 25:5
of the LORD are *p*...........Ps 12:6
will show Yourself *p*........Ps 18:26
To such as are *p*.............Ps 73:1
of the *p* are pleasant.......Prov 15:26
ways of a man are *p*........Prov 16:2
things indeed are *p*..........Rom 14:20
whatever things are *p*......Phil 4:8
keep yourself *p*...............1 Ti 5:22
p all things are *p*...........Tit 1:15
above is first *p*...............Jas 3:17
babes, desire the *p*..........1 Pe 2:2
just as He is *p*................1 Jn 3:3

PURGE
P me with hyssop............Ps 51:7
p them as gold and.........Mal 3:3
p His threshing floor.......Matt 3:12
p your conscience...........Heb 9:14

PURGED
away, and your sin *p*.......Is 6:7
and you were not *p*.........Ezek 24:13
He had by Himself *p*.......Heb 1:3
all things are *p*..............Heb 9:22

PURIFY
p the sons of Levi...........Mal 3:3
and *p* your hearts............Jas 4:8

PURPLE
who was clothed in *p*.......Luke 16:19
they put on Him a *p*.......John 19:2
She was a seller of *p*.......Acts 16:14

PURPOSE
And fulfill all your *p*.......Ps 20:4
p is established..............Prov 20:18
a time for every *p*...........Eccl 3:1
But for this *p* I came.......John 12:27
to the eternal *p*...............Eph 3:11
Now the *p* of the............1 Ti 1:5
to fulfill His *p*................Rev 17:17

PURPOSED
For the LORD had *p*........2 Sa 17:14
LORD of hosts has *p*........Is 23:9
But Daniel *p* in his.........Dan 1:8
pleasure which He *p*........Eph 1:9

PURSUE
And will You *p* dry.........Job 13:25
p my honor as the wind...Job 30:15
The sword shall *p*...........Jer 48:2
but their hearts *p*...........Ezek 33:31
Let us know, let us *p*.......Hos 6:3
p righteousness...............Rom 9:30
P love...........................1 Co 14:1
p righteousness...............1 Ti 6:11
him seek peace and p......1 Pe 3:11

— Q —

QUARREL
see how he seeks a *q*.......2 Ki 5:7
any fool can start a *q*......Prov 20:3
He will not q nor cry.......Matt 12:19
of the Lord must not *q*....2 Ti 2:24

QUEEN
Q Vashti also made a......Esth 1:9
"The *q* of the South........Matt 12:42
under Candace the *q*.......Acts 8:27

QUENCH
Many waters cannot *q*......Song 8:7
so that no one can *q*.......Jer 4:4
flax He will not q...........Matt 12:20
q all the fiery.................Eph 6:16
Do not *q* the Spirit.........1 Th 5:19

QUENCHED
LORD, the fire was *q*.......Num 11:2
They were *q* like a..........Ps 118:12
and the fire is not q........Mark 9:44
q the violence of fire.......Heb 11:34

QUICKLY
with your adversary *q*......Matt 5:25
"What you do, do *q*........John 13:27
"Behold, I come *q*..........Rev 3:11
Surely I am coming *q*......Rev 22:20

QUIET
warned him to be *q*........Mark 10:48
aspire to lead a *q*............1 Th 4:11
we may lead a *q* and.......1 Ti 2:2
a gentle and *q* spirit........1 Pe 3:4

QUIETNESS
will give peace and *q*.......1 Ch 22:9
When He gives *q*............Job 34:29
is a handful with *q*..........Eccl 4:6
in *q* and confidence.........Is 30:15
of righteousness, *q*..........Is 32:17
that they work in *q*.........2 Th 3:12

QUIVER
q rattles against him........Job 39:23
the man who has his *q*.....Ps 127:5
q He has hidden Me........Is 49:2
Their *q* is like an...........Jer 5:16

— R —

REIGN
but a king shall *r* ... 1 Sa 12:12
"And He will *r* ... Luke 1:33
not have this man to *r* ... Luke 19:14
righteousness will *r* ... Rom 5:17
do not let sin *r* ... Rom 6:12
For He must *r* till He ... 1 Co 15:25
and we shall *r* on the ... Rev 5:10
of Christ, and shall *r* ... Rev 20:6

REJECTED
He is despised and *r* ... Is 53:3
r has become the chief ... Matt 21:42
many things and be *r* ... Luke 17:25
This Moses whom they *r* .. Acts 7:35
to a living stone, *r* ... 1 Pe 2:4
r has become the chief ... 1 Pe 2:7

REJOICE
let the field *r* ... 1 Ch 16:32
and let Your saints *r* ... 2 Ch 6:41
R in the LORD ... Ps 33:1
The righteous shall *r* ... Ps 58:10
of Your wings I will *r* ... Ps 63:7
Let them *r* before God ... Ps 68:3
Let the heavens *r* ... Ps 96:11
Let the earth *r* ... Ps 97:1
righteous see it and *r* ... Ps 107:42
We will *r* and be glad ... Ps 118:24
who *r* in doing evil ... Prov 2:14
R, O young man ... Eccl 11:9
We will be glad and *r* ... Song 1:4
I will greatly *r* ... Is 61:10
your heart shall *r* ... Is 66:14
'Yes, I will *r* ... Jer 32:41
but the world will *r* ... John 16:20
and your heart will *r* ... John 16:22
R with those who ... Rom 12:15
R in the Lord always ... Phil 4:4
R always ... 1 Th 5:16
yet believing, you *r* ... 1 Pe 1:8

REJOICED
and my spirit has *r* ... Luke 1:47
In that hour Jesus *r* ... Luke 10:21
Your father Abraham *r* ... John 8:56

REJOICING
His works with *r* ... Ps 107:22
The voice of *r* and ... Ps 118:15
For they are the *r* ... Ps 119:111
come again with *r* ... Ps 126:6
r in His inhabited ... Prov 8:31
he went on his way *r* ... Acts 8:39
yet always *r* ... 2 Co 6:10
or joy, or crown of *r* ... 1 Th 2:19
confidence and the *r* ... Heb 3:6

RELENT
and will not *r* ... Jer 4:28
then the LORD will *r* ... Jer 26:13
if He will turn and *r* ... Joel 2:14
sworn and will not r ... Heb 7:21

RELENTED
So the LORD *r* from the ... Ex 32:14
the LORD looked and *r* ... 1 Ch 21:15
and God *r* from the ... Jon 3:10

RELIGION
about their own *r* ... Acts 25:19
in self-imposed *r* ... Col 2:23
and undefiled *r* ... Jas 1:27

RELIGIOUS
things you are very *r* ... Acts 17:22
you thinks he is *r* ... Jas 1:26

REMAIN
shall let none of it *r* ... Ex 12:10
r angry forever ... Jer 3:5
and this city shall *r* ... Jer 17:25
that if ten men *r* ... Amos 6:9
you, that My joy may *r* ... John 15:11
your fruit should *r* ... John 15:16
If I will that he *r* ... John 21:22
Nevertheless to *r* ... Phil 1:24
we who are alive and *r* ... 1 Th 4:15
the things which *r* ... Rev 3:2

REMEMBER
"But *r* me when it is ... Gen 40:14
R the Sabbath day ... Ex 20:8
R His marvelous works ... 1 Ch 16:12
But we will *r* the name ... Ps 20:7
r the sins of my youth ... Ps 25:7
R now your Creator ... Eccl 12:1
r the former things ... Is 43:18
and their sin I will *r* ... Jer 31:34
r the covenant of ... Amos 1:9
in wrath *r* mercy ... Hab 3:2
and to *r* His holy ... Luke 1:72
"*R* Lot's wife ... Luke 17:32
R my chains ... Col 4:18
R that Jesus Christ ... 2 Ti 2:8
R those who rule ... Heb 13:7

REMEMBERED
Then God *r* Noah ... Gen 8:1
r His covenant with ... Ex 2:24
r His covenant forever ... Ps 105:8
yea, we wept When we *r* .. Ps 137:1
And Peter *r* the word ... Matt 26:75
r the word of the Lord ... Acts 11:16

REMEMBRANCE
Put Me in *r* ... Is 43:26
do this in *r* of Me ... Luke 22:19
do this in *r* of Me ... 1 Co 11:24

REMISSION
repentance for the *r* ... Mark 1:4
Jesus Christ for the *r* ... Acts 2:38
where there is *r* ... Heb 10:18

REMNANT
to us a very small *r* ... Is 1:9
The *r* will return ... Is 10:21
I will gather the *r* ... Jer 23:3
and all the *r* of Judah ... Jer 44:28
Yet I will leave a *r* ... Ezek 6:8
r whom the LORD calls ... Joel 2:32
I will not treat the *r* ... Zech 8:11
time there is a *r* ... Rom 11:5

REMOVE
r your foot from evil ... Prov 4:27
r falsehood and lies ... Prov 30:8
r this cup from Me ... Luke 22:42
r your lampstand ... Rev 2:5

REMOVED
Though the earth be *r* ... Ps 46:2
r our transgressions ... Ps 103:12
will never be *r* ... Prov 10:30
and the hills be *r* ... Is 54:10
this mountain, 'Be *r* ... Matt 21:21

RENDER
What shall I *r* to the ... Ps 116:12
who will *r* to him the ... Matt 21:41
R therefore to Caesar ... Matt 22:21

RENEWED
that your youth is *r* ... Ps 103:5
inward man is being *r* ... 2 Co 4:16
and be *r* in the spirit ... Eph 4:23
the new man who is *r* ... Col 3:10

RENEWING
transformed by the *r* ... Rom 12:2
of regeneration and *r* ... Tit 3:5

REPAY
again, I will *r* ... Luke 10:35
because they cannot *r* ... Luke 14:14
R no one evil for evil ... Rom 12:17
is Mine, I will r ... Rom 12:19
r their parents ... 1 Ti 5:4

REPENT
I abhor myself, and *r* ... Job 42:6
R, for the kingdom ... Matt 3:2
said to them, "*R* ... Acts 2:38
men everywhere to *r* ... Acts 17:30
be zealous and *r* ... Rev 3:19

REPENTANCE
you with water unto *r* ... Matt 3:11
a baptism of *r* for the ... Mark 1:4
persons who need no *r* ... Luke 15:7
sorrow produces *r* ... 2 Co 7:10
will grant them *r* ... 2 Ti 2:25
renew them again to *r* ... Heb 6:6
found no place for *r* ... Heb 12:17
all should come to *r* ... 2 Pe 3:9

REPETITIONS
r as the heathen do ... Matt 6:7

REPORT
circulate a false *r* ... Ex 23:1
who has believed our r ... Rom 10:16
things are of good *r* ... Phil 4:8

REPROACH
r me as long as I live ... Job 27:6
does he take up a *r* ... Ps 15:3
You make us a *r* ... Ps 44:13
R has broken my heart ... Ps 69:20
nation, but sin is a *r* ... Prov 14:34
with dishonor comes *r* ... Prov 18:3
do not fear the *r* ... Is 51:7
bring an everlasting *r* ... Jer 23:40
because I bore the *r* ... Jer 31:19
you shall bear the *r* ... Mic 6:16
these things You *r* ... Luke 11:45
lest he fall into *r* ... 1 Ti 3:7
esteeming the *r* ... Heb 11:26
and without *r* ... Jas 1:5

REPROOF
but he who hates *r* ... Prov 12:1
R is more effective ... Prov 17:10
for doctrine, for *r* ... 2 Ti 3:16

REPROVE
He will surely *r* ... Job 13:10
And let him *r* me ... Ps 141:5
Do not *r* a scoffer ... Prov 9:8
r the oppressor ... Is 1:17

REPUTATION
seven men of good *r* ... Acts 6:3
to those who were of *r* ... Gal 2:2
made Himself of no *r* ... Phil 2:7

REQUEST
For Jews *r* a sign ... 1 Co 1:22
of mine making *r* ... Phil 1:4

REQUESTS
r be made known ... Phil 4:6

REQUIRE
the LORD your God *r* ... Deut 10:12
a foreigner you may *r* ... Deut 15:3
"You will not *r* ... Ps 10:13
offering You did not *r* ... Ps 40:6
what does the LORD *r* ... Mic 6:8

REQUIRED
your soul will be *r* ... Luke 12:20
him much will be *r* ... Luke 12:48

RESERVED
Which I have *r* for the ... Job 38:23
"*I have r for Myself* ... Rom 11:4
r in heaven for you ... 1 Pe 1:4
of darkness, to be *r* ... 2 Pe 2:4
habitation, He has *r* ... Jude 6

RESIST
r an evil person ... Matt 5:39
r the Holy Spirit ... Acts 7:51
R the devil and he ... Jas 4:7

RESISTED
For who has *r* His will ... Rom 9:19
Jannes and Jambres *r* ... 2 Ti 3:8

R and justice are the....... Ps 97:2
And he who does *r*......... Ps 106:3
r endures forever........... Ps 111:3
r delivers from death....... Prov 10:2
r leads to life................ Prov 11:19
the way of *r* is life......... Prov 12:28
R exalts a nation............Prov 14:34
found in the way of *r*...... Prov 16:31
r He shall judge.............Is 11:4
and *r* the plummet.......... Is 28:17
r will be peace................Is 32:17
in the LORD I have *r*.......Is 45:24
I will declare your *r*........ Is 57:12
r as a breastplate........... Is 59:17
r goes forth as............... Is 62:1
The Lord Our *R*.............Jer 23:6
to David a Branch of *r*.... Jer 33:15
The *r* of the righteous......Ezek 18:20
who turn many to *r*......... Dan 12:3
to fulfill all *r*.................. Matt 3:15
exceeds the *r* of the.........Matt 5:20
to you in the way of *r*..... Matt 21:32
in holiness and *r*............ Luke 1:75
even the *r* of God.......... Rom 3:22
accounted to him for r..... Rom 4:22
is life because of *r*...........Rom 8:10
who did not pursue *r*.......Rom 9:30
ignorant of God's *r*.......... Rom 10:3
we might become the *r*.... 2 Co 5:21
r comes through the........ Gal 2:21
the breastplate of *r*..........Eph 6:14
not having my own *r*....... Phil 3:9
r which we have............ Tit 3:5
r which is according.........Heb 11:7
does not produce the *r*.....Jas 1:20
should suffer for *r*.......... 1 Pe 3:14
a preacher of *r*.............. 2 Pe 2:5
a new earth in which *r*.....2 Pe 3:13
who practices *r*............... 1 Jn 2:29
He who practices *r*.......... 1 Jn 3:7

RIGHTLY
R do they love you........ Song 1:4
"You have answered *r*..... Luke 10:28
r dividing the word..........2 Ti 2:15

RISE
is vain for you to *r*..........Ps 127:2
"Now I will *r*................. Is 33:10
for He makes His sun *r*... Matt 5:45
of Nineveh will *r*.............Matt 12:41
third day He will *r*......... Matt 20:19
persuaded though one *r*... Luke 16:31
third day He will *r*......... Luke 18:33
had to suffer and *r*.......... Acts 17:3
be the first to *r*..............Acts 26:23
fact the dead do not *r*......1 Co 15:15
in Christ will *r*................1 Th 4:16

RISEN
of the LORD is *r*............ Is 60:1
women there has not *r*.....Matt 11:11
disciples that He is *r*........Matt 28:7
"The Lord is *r*................Luke 24:34
furthermore is also *r*........Rom 8:34
then Christ is not *r*..........1 Co 15:13
if Christ is not *r*..............1 Co 15:17
But now Christ is *r*......... 1 Co 15:20

RIVER
Indeed the *r* may rage..... Job 40:23
them drink from the *r*......Ps 36:8
r whose streams shall.......Ps 46:4
The *r* of God is full.........Ps 65:9
went through the *r*.......... Ps 66:6
peace to her like a *r*........Is 66:12
in the Jordan *R*.............. Mark 1:5
he showed me a pure *r*.... Rev 22:1

RIVERS
He turns *r* into a............ Ps 107:33
R of water run down....... Ps 119:136
By the *r* of Babylon........ Ps 137:1

All the *r* run into the...... Eccl 1:7
us a place of broad *r*....... Is 33:21
the wilderness and *r*........ Is 43:19
the sea, I make the *r*.......Is 50:2
his heart will flow *r*.........John 7:38

ROAR
Let the sea *r*.................. 1 Ch 16:32
Though its waters *r*......... Ps 46:3
The young lions *r*............Ps 104:21
'The LORD will *r*.............Jer 25:30
He will *r* like a lion.........Hos 11:10
Will a lion *r* in the.......... Amos 3:4

ROARING
Like a *r* lion and a.........Prov 28:15
and the waves *r*..............Luke 21:25
walks about like a *r*..........1 Pe 5:8

ROB
"Will a man *r* God..........Mal 3:8
do you *r* temples.............Rom 2:22

ROBBERS
and Israel to the *r*...........Is 42:24
also crucified two *r*..........Mark 15:27
Me are thieves and *r*....... John 10:8
here who are neither *r*..... Acts 19:37
waters, in perils of *r*........2 Co 11:26

ROBE
covered me with the *r*......Is 61:10
'Bring out the best *r*.........Luke 15:22
on Him a purple *r*............John 19:2
And a white *r* was.......... Rev 6:11

ROBES
have stained all My *r*.......Is 63:3
clothe you with rich *r*...... Zech 3:4
to walk in long *r*..............Luke 20:46
clothed with white *r*........ Rev 7:9

ROCK
you shall strike the *r*....... Ex 17:6
and struck the *r*..............Num 20:11
R who begot you............ Deut 32:18
For their *r* is not.............Deut 32:31
nor is there any *r*.............1 Sa 2:2
"The LORD is my *r*......... 2 Sa 22:2
away, and as a *r*..............Job 14:18
set me high upon a *r*........ Ps 27:5
For You are my *r*............ Ps 31:3
r that is higher than......... Ps 61:2
And my God the *r*............Ps 94:22
Who turned the *r*.............Ps 114:8
been mindful of the *R*..... Is 17:10
shadow of a great *r*......... Is 32:2
his house on the *r*............Matt 7:24
r I will build My..............Matt 16:18
"Some fell on *r*................ Luke 8:6
stumbling stone and r...... Rom 9:33
R that followed them.......1 Co 10:4

ROD
And Moses took the *r*..... Ex 4:20
chasten him with the *r*.....2 Sa 7:14
Your *r* and Your staff......Ps 23:4
The *r* and reproof give.....Prov 29:15
shall come forth a *R*.........Is 11:1
you pass under the *r*........Ezek 20:37
I come to you with a *r*.....1 Co 4:21
rule them with a r.............Rev 2:27

ROOM
you a large upper *r*......... Mark 14:15
no *r* for them in the........ Luke 2:7
still there is *r*................. Luke 14:22
into the upper *r*..............Acts 1:13

ROOSTER
him, "Before the *r*.......... Matt 26:75

ROOT
r bearing bitterness..........Deut 29:18
day there shall be a *R*..... Is 11:10
because they had no *r*......Matt 13:6

and if the *r* is holy......... Rom 11:16
of money is a *r*...............1 Ti 6:10
lest any *r* of..................... Heb 12:15
I am the *R* and the......... Rev 22:16

ROOTED
that you, being *r*.............Eph 3:17
r and built up in Him...... Col 2:7

ROSE
I am the *r* of Sharon....... Song 2:1
and blossom as the *r*....... Is 35:1
end Christ died and *r*...... Rom 14:9
buried, and that He *r*...... 1 Co 15:4
that Jesus died and *r*....... 1 Th 4:14

RUBIES
of wisdom is above *r*....... Job 28:18
more precious than *r*....... Prov 3:15
is better than *r*................ Prov 8:11
worth is far above *r*.........Prov 31:10
your pinnacles of *r*.......... Is 54:12

RULE
and he shall *r*................. Gen 3:16
A wise servant will *r*....... Prov 17:2
puts an end to all *r*......... 1 Co 15:24
us walk by the same *r*......Phil 3:16
let the peace of God *r*..... Col 3:15
Let the elders who *r*........1 Ti 5:17
Remember those who *r*....Heb 13:7

RULER
to Me the One to be *r*.....Mic 5:2
by Beelzebub, the *r*.........Matt 12:24
I will make you *r*............Matt 25:21
the *r* of this world...........John 12:31
because the *r* of this.......John 16:11
'*Who made you a r*......... Acts 7:27
speak evil of the r...........Acts 23:5

RULERS
And the *r* take counsel.... Ps 2:2
"You know that the *r*...... Matt 20:25
"Have any of the *r*..........John 7:48
which none of the *r*.........1 Co 2:8
powers, against the *r*....... Eph 6:12
to be subject to *r*............Tit 3:1

RULES
'He who *r* over men........2 Sa 23:3
them know that God *r*.... Ps 59:13
He *r* by His power............Ps 66:7
r his spirit than he........... Prov 16:32
that the Most High *r*....... Dan 4:17
r his own house well........1 Ti 3:4
according to the *r*........... 2 Ti 2:5

RUN
I will *r* in the way of....... Ps 119:32
r and not be weary...........Is 40:31
many shall *r* to and.........Dan 12:4
Therefore I *r* thus............1 Co 9:26
I might *r*, or had *r*......... Gal 2:2
that I have not *r*............. Phil 2:16
us, and let us *r*...............Heb 12:1

— S —

SABAOTH
S had left us a.............. Rom 9:29
ears of the Lord of *S*.......Jas 5:4

SABBATH
'Tomorrow is a *S*............ Ex 16:23
"Remember the *S*........... Ex 20:8
S was made for man........Mark 2:27
is also Lord of the *S*........Mark 2:28
not only broke the *S*....... John 5:18

SABBATHS
S you shall keep............ Ex 31:13
The New Moons, the *S*.... Is 1:13
also gave them My *S*....... Ezek 20:12

SACRIFICE
S and offering You did.... Ps 40:6
But I will *s* to You..........Jon 2:9

offer the blind as a *s*....... Mal 1:8
desire mercy and not s..... Matt 9:13
s will be seasoned........... Mark 9:49
an offering and a *s*.......... Eph 5:2
aroma, an acceptable *s*..... Phil 4:18
put away sin by the *s*....... Heb 9:26
He had offered one *s*....... Heb 10:12
no longer remains a *s*...... Heb 10:26
God a more excellent *s*..... Heb 11:4
offer the *s* of praise......... Heb 13:15

SACRIFICES
The *s* of God are a......... Ps 51:17
by him the daily *s*........... Dan 8:11
burnt offerings and s........ Mark 12:33
priests, to offer up *s*........ Heb 7:27
s God is well pleased....... Heb 13:16
offer up spiritual *s*........... 1 Pe 2:5

SAINTS
ten thousands of *s*.......... Deut 33:2
puts no trust in His *s*....... Job 15:15
s who are on the earth..... Ps 16:3
"Gather My *s*................ Ps 50:5
Is the death of His *s*........ Ps 116:15
war against the *s*............ Dan 7:21
Jesus, called to be *s*........ 1 Co 1:2
the least of all the *s*........ Eph 3:8
Christ with all His *s*........ 1 Th 3:13
be glorified in His *s*......... 2 Th 1:10
all delivered to the *s*........ Jude 3
shed the blood of *s*.......... Rev 16:6
the camp of the *s*............ Rev 20:9

SALT
shall season with *s*........... Lev 2:13
"You are the *s*............... Matt 5:13
s loses its flavor............. Mark 9:50

SALVATION
still, and see the *s*........... Ex 14:13
the good news of His *s*.... 1 Ch 16:23
S belongs to the LORD..... Ps 3:8
is my light and my *s*........ Ps 27:1
God is the God of *s*........ Ps 68:20
And Your *s* all the day.... Ps 71:15
Surely His *s* is near......... Ps 85:9
And He has become my *s* Ps 118:14
with an everlasting *s*......... Is 45:17
for My *s* is about to........ Is 56:1
call your walls *S*............ Is 60:18
s as a lamp that burns..... Is 62:1
joy in the God of my *s*.... Hab 3:18
is just and having *s*......... Zech 9:9
raised up a horn of *s*....... Luke 1:69
eyes have seen Your *s*..... Luke 2:30
what we worship, for *s*..... John 4:22
"Nor is there *s*.............. Acts 4:12
you should be for s............ Acts 13:47
the power of God to *s*..... Rom 1:16
s is nearer than................ Rom 13:11
now is the day of *s*.......... 2 Co 6:2
work out your own *s*......... Phil 2:12
wrath, but to obtain *s*..... 1 Th 5:9
chose you for *s*.............. 2 Th 2:13
also may obtain the *s*....... 2 Ti 2:10
of God that brings *s*........ Tit 2:11
neglect so great a *s*......... Heb 2:3
s the prophets have......... 1 Pe 1:10

SAMARITAN
But a certain *S*............. Luke 10:33
a drink from me, a *S*....... John 4:9

SANCTIFICATION
righteousness and *s*......... 1 Co 1:30
will of God, your *s*.......... 1 Th 4:3

SANCTIFIED
s this house which you..... 1 Ki 9:3
you were born I *s*........... Jer 1:5
Him whom the Father *s*... John 10:36
they also may be *s*.......... John 17:19
might be acceptable, *s*..... Rom 15:16
to those who are *s*.......... 1 Co 1:2
washed, but you were *s*.... 1 Co 6:11
husband is *s* by the........ 1 Co 7:14
for it is *s* by the............. 1 Ti 4:5
those who are being *s*...... Heb 2:11
will we have been *s*......... Heb 10:10
who are called, *s*............. Jude 1

SANCTIFY
"*S* to Me all the............ Ex 13:2
therefore *s* yourselves...... Lev 11:44
s My great name............ Ezek 36:23
S them by Your truth...... John 17:17
that He might *s*............. Eph 5:26

SANCTUARY
let them make Me a *s*...... Ex 25:8
I went into the *s*............ Ps 73:17
set fire to Your *s*........... Ps 74:7
O God, is in the *s*.......... Ps 77:13
He will be as a *s*............ Is 8:14
He has abandoned His *s*.. Lam 2:7
I shall be a little *s*.......... Ezek 11:16
to shine on Your *s*.......... Dan 9:17
and the earthly *s*............ Heb 9:1

SAND
descendants as the *s*......... Gen 32:12
in number than the *s*....... Ps 139:18
innumerable as the *s*........ Heb 11:12

SATAN
S stood up against.......... 1 Ch 21:1
before the LORD, and *S*... Job 1:6
And the LORD said to *S*... Zech 3:2
"Away with you, *S*.......... Matt 4:10
"Get behind Me, *S*......... Matt 16:23
"How can *S* cast out....... Mark 3:23
to them, "I saw *S*........... Luke 10:18
S has asked for you......... Luke 22:31
S filled your heart........... Acts 5:3
such a one to *S*.............. 1 Co 5:5
For *S* himself.................. 2 Co 11:14
to the working of *S*.......... 2 Th 2:9
are a synagogue of *S*....... Rev 2:9
you, where *S* dwells........ Rev 2:13
known the depths of *S*..... Rev 2:24
called the Devil and *S*..... Rev 12:9
years have expired, *S*....... Rev 20:7

SATISFIED
I shall be *s* when I.......... Ps 17:15
a good man will be *s*....... Prov 14:14
that are never *s*.............. Prov 30:15
of His soul, and be *s*....... Is 53:11
but they were not *s*......... Amos 4:8
and cannot be *s*.............. Hab 2:5

SATISFIES
s your mouth with good... Ps 103:5
s the longing soul............ Ps 107:9

SATISFY
s us early with Your........ Ps 90:14
long life I will *s*............ Ps 91:16
for what does not *s*......... Is 55:2

SAVE
there was none to *s*......... 2 Sa 22:42
that it cannot *s*............... Is 59:1
mighty to *s*..................... Is 63:1
O LORD, *s* Your people... Jer 31:7
JESUS, for He will *s*......... Matt 1:21
s his life will.................. Matt 16:25
s that which was............. Matt 18:11
s life or to kill................ Mark 3:4
let Him *s* Himself if........ Luke 23:35
You are the Christ, *s*....... Luke 23:39
'Father, *s* Me from.......... John 12:27
but to *s* the world........... John 12:47
and *s* some of them......... Rom 11:14
the world to *s* sinners...... 1 Ti 1:15
doing this you will *s*........ 1 Ti 4:16
able to *s* your souls......... Jas 1:21
Can faith *s* him............... Jas 2:14

SAVED
and we are not *s*............. Jer 8:20
"Who then can be *s*........ Matt 19:25
"He *s* others.................. Matt 27:42
that we should be *s*......... Luke 1:71
"Your faith has *s*............ Luke 7:50
through Him might be *s*... John 3:17
them, saying, "Be *s*......... Acts 2:40
what must I do to be *s*.... Acts 16:30
is that they may be *s*...... Rom 10:1
all Israel will be *s*.......... Rom 11:26
his spirit may be *s*.......... 1 Co 5:5
which also you are *s*........ 1 Co 15:2
those who are being *s*...... 2 Co 2:15
grace you have been *s*..... Eph 2:8
she will be *s* in.............. 1 Ti 2:15
to His mercy He *s*........... Tit 3:5
eight souls, were *s*.......... 1 Pe 3:20
of those who are *s*.......... Rev 21:24

SAVIOR
forgot God their *S*.......... Ps 106:21
He will send them a *S*..... Is 19:20
of Israel, your *S*............ Is 43:3
Me, a just God and a *S*... Is 45:21
I, the LORD, am your *S*... Is 60:16
So He became their *S*...... Is 63:8
for there is no *s*............. Hos 13:4
rejoiced in God my *S*...... Luke 1:47
the city of David a *S*...... Luke 2:11
the Christ, the *S*............ John 4:42
to be Prince and *S*.......... Acts 5:31
up for Israel a *S*............. Acts 13:23
and He is the *S*.............. Eph 5:23
of God our *S* and the...... 1 Ti 1:1
God, who is the *S*........... 1 Ti 4:10
of our *S* Jesus Christ....... 2 Ti 1:10
God and *S* Jesus Christ.... Tit 2:13

SAYING
cannot accept this *s*........ Matt 19:11
"This is a hard *s*............ John 6:60
This is a faithful *s*.......... 1 Ti 1:15

SCARLET
s cord in the window....... Josh 2:18
are like a strand of *s*....... Song 4:3
your sins are like *s*.......... Is 1:18
s beast which was full...... Rev 17:3

SCATTERED
lest we be *s* abroad......... Gen 11:4
of iniquity shall be *s*........ Ps 92:9
"You have *s* My flock..... Jer 23:2
s Israel will gather........... Jer 31:10
Israel is like *s* sheep........ Jer 50:17
they were weary and *s*..... Matt 9:36
the sheep will be s......... Mark 14:27
that you will be *s*............ John 16:32

SCEPTER
s shall not depart............ Gen 49:10
S shall rise out of........... Num 24:17
a s of righteousness........ Heb 1:8

SCOFFER
"He who reproves a *s*...... Prov 9:7
s does not listen............. Prov 13:1
s seeks wisdom and......... Prov 14:6
s is an abomination......... Prov 24:9

SCORCHED
sun was up they were *s*.... Matt 13:6
And men were *s* with...... Rev 16:9

SCORPIONS
on serpents and *s*........... Luke 10:19
They had tails like *s*........ Rev 9:10

SCOURGE
up to councils and *s*........ Matt 10:17
will mock Him, and *s*...... Mark 10:34

SCRIBES
and not as the *s*............. Matt 7:29
"But woe to you, *s*.......... Matt 23:13
"Beware of the *s*............ Mark 12:38

SCRIPTURE
what is noted in the S... Dan 10:21
S was fulfilled which... Mark 15:28
"Today this S... Luke 4:21
S cannot be broken... John 10:35
S has confined all... Gal 3:22
All S is given by... 2 Ti 3:16
that no prophecy of S... 2 Pe 1:20

SCRIPTURES
not knowing the S... Matt 22:29
S must be fulfilled... Mark 14:49
and mighty in the S... Acts 18:24
also the rest of the S... 2 Pe 3:16

SCROLL
In the s of the Book... Ps 40:7
saw there a flying s... Zech 5:1
was able to open the s... Rev 5:3
the sky receded as a s... Rev 6:14

SEA
drowned in the Red S... Ex 15:4
who go down to the s... Ps 107:23
to the s its limit... Prov 8:29
the waters cover the s... Hab 2:14
and the s obey Him... Matt 8:27
throne there was a s... Rev 4:6
there was no more s... Rev 21:1

SEAL
Set me as a s upon... Song 8:6
of circumcision, a s... Rom 4:11
stands, having this s... 2 Ti 2:19
He opened the second s... Rev 6:3

SEANCE
"Please conduct a s... 1 Sa 28:8

SEARCH
"Can you s out the... Job 11:7
Would not God s... Ps 44:21
glory of kings is to s... Prov 25:2
found it by secret s... Jer 2:34
I, the LORD, s the... Jer 17:10
s the Scriptures... John 5:39

SEARCHES
for the LORD s all... 1 Ch 28:9
For the Spirit s... 1 Co 2:10
that I am He who s... Rev 2:23

SEASONS
days and months and s... Gal 4:10
the times and the s... 1 Th 5:1

SEAT
shall make a mercy s... Ex 25:17
sit in Moses' s... Matt 23:2
before the judgment s... 2 Co 5:10
the mercy s... Heb 9:5

SECRET
s things belong... Deut 29:29
The s of the LORD is... Ps 25:14
In the s place of His... Ps 27:5
When I was made in s... Ps 139:15
do not disclose the s... Prov 25:9
I have not spoken in s... Is 45:19
Father who is in the s... Matt 6:6
are done by them in s... Eph 5:12

SEDUCED
flattering lips she s... Prov 7:21

SEE
in my flesh I shall s... Job 19:26
lest they s with their... Is 6:10
for they shall s God... Matt 5:8
seeing they do not s... Matt 13:13
s greater things than... John 1:50
rejoiced to s My day... John 8:56
we wish to s Jesus... John 12:21
and the world will s... John 14:19
Him, for we shall s... 1 Jn 3:2
They shall s His face... Rev 22:4

SEED
He shall see His s... Is 53:10
you a noble vine, a s... Jer 2:21
s is the word of God... Luke 8:11
had left us a s... Rom 9:29
to each s its own body... 1 Co 15:38
you are Abraham's s... Gal 3:29
Jesus Christ, of the s... 2 Ti 2:8
of corruptible s... 1 Pe 1:23
not sin, for His s... 1 Jn 3:9

SEEK
will find Him if you s... Deut 4:29
and pray and s My face... 2 Ch 7:14
You said, "S My face... Ps 27:8
Early will I s You... Ps 63:1
the Gentiles shall s... Is 11:10
S the LORD while He... Is 55:6
Yet they s Me daily... Is 58:2
s great things for... Jer 45:5
"S Me and live... Amos 5:4
things the Gentiles s... Matt 6:32
s, and you will find... Matt 7:7
s diligently until she... Luke 15:8
of Man has come to s... Luke 19:10
because I do not s... John 5:30
"You will s Me and... John 7:34
Because they did not s... Rom 9:32
Let no one s his own... 1 Co 10:24
for I do not s yours... 2 Co 12:14
For all s their own... Phil 2:21
s those things which... Col 3:1
s the one to come... Heb 13:14

SEEMS
There is a way which s... Prov 14:12
have, even what he s... Luke 8:18
If anyone among you s... 1 Co 3:18

SEEN
s God face to face... Gen 32:30
All this I have s... Eccl 8:9
s the one I love... Song 3:3
Who has s such things... Is 66:8
No one has s God at... John 1:18
time, nor s His form... John 5:37
I speak what I have s... John 8:38
s Me has s the... John 14:9
things which we have s... Acts 4:20
s Jesus Christ our... 1 Co 9:1
things which are not s... 2 Co 4:18
whom no man has s... 1 Ti 6:16
heard, which we have s... 1 Jn 1:1

SELF-CONTROL
about righteousness, s... Acts 24:25
they cannot exercise s... 1 Co 7:9
gentleness, s... Gal 5:23
slanderers, without s... 2 Ti 3:3
to knowledge s... 2 Pe 1:6

SELL
said, "S me your... Gen 25:31
s Your people for... Ps 44:12
s the righteous... Amos 2:6
s whatever you have... Mark 10:21
no sword, let him s... Luke 22:36
no one may buy or s... Rev 13:17

SEND
He shall s from heaven... Ps 57:3
"Whom shall I s... Is 6:8
s them a Savior... Is 19:20
"Behold, I s you out... Matt 10:16
The Son of Man will s... Matt 13:41
s Lazarus that he... Luke 16:24
whom the Father will s... John 14:26
has sent Me, I also s... John 20:21

SENSUAL
but is earthly, s... Jas 3:15
These are s persons... Jude 19

SENT
and His Spirit have s... Is 48:16
s these prophets... Jer 23:21
As the Father has s... John 20:21
unless they are s... Rom 10:15
s His Son to be the... 1 Jn 4:10

SEPARATE
'he shall s himself... Num 6:3
s yourselves from the... Ezra 10:11
let not man s... Matt 19:6
Who shall s us from... Rom 8:35
harmless, undefiled, s... Heb 7:26

SERAPHIM
Above it stood s... Is 6:2

SERPENT
s was more cunning... Gen 3:1
"Make a fiery s... Num 21:8
like the poison of a s... Ps 58:4
s you shall trample... Ps 91:13
air, the way of a s... Prov 30:19
s may bite when it is... Eccl 10:11
be a fiery flying s... Is 14:29
and wounded the s... Is 51:9
will he give him a s... Matt 7:10
Moses lifted up the s... John 3:14
was cast out, that s... Rev 12:9

SERVANT
a s of servants he... Gen 9:25
s will rule over a son... Prov 17:2
Who is blind but My s... Is 42:19
"Is Israel a s... Jer 2:14
and a s his master... Mal 1:6
you, let him be your s... Matt 20:26
good and faithful s... Matt 25:21
that s who knew his... Luke 12:47
s does not know what... John 15:15
against Your holy S... Acts 4:27

SERVANTS
puts no trust in His s... Job 4:18
shall call you the S... Is 61:6
We are unprofitable s... Luke 17:10
longer do I call you s... John 15:15
so consider us, as s... 1 Co 4:1
S, be obedient to... Eph 6:5
Masters, give your s... Col 4:1
s shall serve Him... Rev 22:3

SERVE
LORD your God and s... Deut 6:13
land, so you shall s... Jer 5:19
s Him with one accord... Zeph 3:9
You cannot s God and... Matt 6:24
to be served, but to s... Matt 20:28
but through love s... Gal 5:13
s the Lord Christ... Col 3:24
s the living God... Heb 9:14
s Him day and night in... Rev 7:15

SERVICE
do you mean by this s... Ex 12:26
that he offers God s... John 16:2
is your reasonable s... Rom 12:1

SEVEN
S times a day I praise... Ps 119:164
s other spirits more... Luke 11:26
s times in a day... Luke 17:4
out from among you s... Acts 6:3
s churches which are... Rev 1:4

SEVENTY
S weeks are... Dan 9:24
up to s times seven... Matt 18:22
Then the s returned... Luke 10:17

SHADOW
walks about like a s... Ps 39:6
like a passing s... Ps 144:4
in the s of His hand... Is 49:2
which are a s of... Col 2:17
the law, having a s... Heb 10:1
is no variation or s... Jas 1:17

SHAKE
s the earth... Is 2:19
and the knees s... Nah 2:10

I will *s* all nations.......... Hag 2:7
s not only the earth........ Heb 12:26

SHAME
you turn my glory to *s*..... Ps 4:2
let them be put to *s*........ Ps 83:17
s who serve carved......... Ps 97:7
hate Zion Be put to *s*...... Ps 129:5
is a son who causes *s*....... Prov 10:5
hide My face from *s*........ Is 50:6
S has covered our.......... Jer 51:51
their glory into *s*........... Hos 4:7
never be put to *s*............ Joel 2:26
the unjust knows no *s*...... Zeph 3:5
worthy to suffer *s*........... Acts 5:41
will not be put to s.......... Rom 9:33
to put to *s* the wise.......... 1 Co 1:27
I say this to your *s*.......... 1 Co 6:5
glory is in their *s*........... Phil 3:19
put Him to an open *s*....... Heb 6:6

SHAMEFUL
committing what is *s*........ Rom 1:27
for it is *s* for women........ 1 Co 14:35
For it is *s* even to........... Eph 5:12

SHARE
a stranger does not *s*....... Prov 14:10
s your bread with the...... Is 58:7
is taught the word *s*......... Gal 6:6
to give, willing to *s*......... 1 Ti 6:18
to do good and to *s*......... Heb 13:16

SHED
which is *s* for many......... Matt 26:28

SHEDDING
blood, and without *s*........ Heb 9:22

SHEEP
astray like a lost *s*........... Ps 119:176
slaughter, and as a *s*........ Is 53:7
have been lost *s*.............. Jer 50:6
s will be scattered........... Zech 13:7
rather to the lost *s*.......... Matt 10:6
I send you out as *s*.......... Matt 10:16
And He will set the *s*....... Matt 25:33
having a hundred *s*........... Luke 15:4
and I know My *s*............ John 10:14
s I have which are not..... John 10:16
"*He was led as a s*.......... Acts 8:32
like *s* going astray........... 1 Pe 2:25

SHEOL
down to the gates of *S*..... Job 17:16
not leave my soul in *S*..... Ps 16:10
S laid hold of me............ Ps 116:3
the belly of *S* I cried....... Jon 2:2

SHEPHERD
s My people Israel.......... 2 Sa 5:2
The LORD is my *s*........... Ps 23:1
His flock like a *s*............ Is 40:11
of Cyrus, 'He is My *s*...... Is 44:28
I will establish one *s*........ Ezek 34:23
to the worthless *s*............ Zech 11:17
'*I will strike the S*........... Matt 26:31
"I am the good *s*............ John 10:11
s the church of God......... Acts 20:28
the dead, that great *S*...... Heb 13:20
S the flock of God.......... 1 Pe 5:2
when the Chief *S*............ 1 Pe 5:4
of the throne will *s*.......... Rev 7:17

SHEPHERDS
your sons shall be *s*......... Num 14:33
And they are *s* who......... Is 56:11
And I will give you *s*....... Jer 3:15
s who destroy and........... Jer 23:1
s have led them astray..... Jer 50:6
s fed themselves.............. Ezek 34:8
in the same country *s*...... Luke 2:8

SHIELD
I am your *s*..................... Gen 15:1
he is a *s* to all who......... 2 Sa 22:31
My *s* and the horn of...... Ps 18:2
God is a sun and *s*.......... Ps 84:11
truth shall be your *s*........ Ps 91:4
all, taking the *s*............... Eph 6:16

SHINE
LORD make His face *s*..... Num 6:25
cause His face to *s*.......... Ps 67:1
Make Your face *s*............ Ps 119:135
who are wise shall *s*........ Dan 12:3
the righteous will *s*.......... Matt 13:43
among whom you *s*........... Phil 2:15

SHINING
the earth, by clear *s*........ 2 Sa 23:4
His clothes became *s*....... Mark 9:3
light is already *s*............. 1 Jn 2:8
was like the sun *s*........... Rev 1:16

SHIPS
down to the sea in *s*........ Ps 107:23
like the merchant *s*.......... Prov 31:14
Look also at *s*.................. Jas 3:4

SHIPWRECK
faith have suffered *s*........ 1 Ti 1:19

SHOUT
S joyfully to the LORD..... Ps 98:4
Make a joyful *s*.............. Ps 100:1
from heaven with a *s*........ 1 Th 4:16

SHOW
a land that I will *s*.......... Gen 12:1
S me Your ways.............. Ps 25:4
s Him greater works........ John 5:20
s us the Father................ John 14:8

SHOWBREAD
you shall set the *s*........... Ex 25:30
s which had been taken.... 1 Sa 21:6
s which was not lawful..... Matt 12:4

SHOWERS
make it soft with *s*.......... Ps 65:10
s have been withheld....... Jer 3:3
can the heavens give *s*...... Jer 14:22
from the LORD, like *s*....... Mic 5:7

SHUTS
s his ears to the cry......... Prov 21:13
s his eyes from seeing...... Is 33:15
brother in need, and *s*..... 1 Jn 3:17
who opens and no one s..... Rev 3:7

SICK
have made him *s*............. Hos 7:5
I was *s* and you.............. Matt 25:36
he whom You love is *s*.... John 11:3
many are weak and *s*....... 1 Co 11:30
have left in Miletus *s*....... 2 Ti 4:20
faith will save the *s*......... Jas 5:15

SICKLE
Put in the *s*.................... Joel 3:13
"Thrust in Your *s*........... Rev 14:15

SIGHT
and see this great *s*......... Ex 3:3
seemed good in Your *s*.... Matt 11:26
by faith, not by *s*............ 2 Co 5:7

SIGN
Show me a *s* for good...... Ps 86:17
will give you a *s*............. Is 7:14
for an everlasting *s*.......... Is 55:13
we want to see a *s*.......... Matt 12:38
And what will be the *s*.... Matt 24:3
s which will be spoken..... Luke 2:34
again is the second *s*........ John 4:54
For Jews request a *s*........ 1 Co 1:22
Now a great *s* appeared... Rev 12:1

SIGNS
and let them be for *s*....... Gen 1:14
you not know their *s*....... Job 21:29

They performed His *s*...... Ps 105:27
We are for *s* and.............. Is 8:18
How great are His *s*........ Dan 4:3
cannot discern the *s*......... Matt 16:3
the accompanying *s*......... Mark 16:20
s Jesus did in Cana of...... John 2:11
no one can do these *s*...... John 3:2
you people see *s*............ John 4:48
because you saw the *s*...... John 6:26
this Man works many *s*.... John 11:47
Jesus did many other *s*..... John 20:30
demons, performing *s*...... Rev 16:14

SILENT
season, and am not *s*....... Ps 22:2
Let your women keep *s*... 1 Co 14:34

SILVER
and your precious *s*......... Job 22:25
Though he heaps up *s*..... Job 27:16
s tried in a furnace.......... Ps 12:6
have refined us as *s*......... Ps 66:10
than the profits of *s*......... Prov 3:14
chosen rather than *s*........ Prov 16:16
refining pot is for *s*......... Prov 17:3
He who loves *s* will......... Eccl 5:10
s has become dross.......... Is 1:22
call them rejected *s*......... Jer 6:30
may buy the poor for *s*.... Amos 8:6
him thirty pieces of *s*....... Matt 26:15

SIMPLE
making wise the *s*........... Ps 19:7
LORD preserves the *s*....... Ps 116:6
s believes every word....... Prov 14:15
the hearts of the *s*.......... Rom 16:18

SIN
and be sure your *s*.......... Num 32:23
to death for his own *s*...... Deut 24:16
all this Job did not *s*........ Job 2:10
Be angry, and do not *s*.... Ps 4:4
in *s* my mother............... Ps 51:5
soul an offering for *s*....... Is 53:10
who believe in Me to *s*.... Matt 18:6
who takes away the *s*....... John 1:29
S no more....................... John 5:14
"He who is without *s*....... John 8:7
convict the world of *s*...... John 16:8
they are all under *s*......... Rom 3:9
s entered the world.......... Rom 5:12
s that grace may............. Rom 6:1
died to *s* once for all....... Rom 6:10
s shall not have.............. Rom 6:14
Shall we *s* because we..... Rom 6:15
s that dwells in me.......... Rom 7:17
made Him who knew no *s* 2 Co 5:21
man of *s* is revealed........ 2 Th 2:3
we are, yet without *s*....... Heb 4:15
appeared to put away *s*.... Heb 9:26
s willfully after we........... Heb 10:26
it gives birth to *s*............ Jas 1:15
do it, to him it is *s*.......... Jas 4:17
"*Who committed no s*...... 1 Pe 2:22
say that we have no *s*...... 1 Jn 1:8
that you may not *s*.......... 1 Jn 2:1
s is lawlessness.............. 1 Jn 3:4
in Him there is no *s*........ 1 Jn 3:5
and he cannot *s*.............. 1 Jn 3:9
unrighteousness is *s*......... 1 Jn 5:17

SINCERE
Holy Spirit, by *s* love...... 2 Co 6:6
and from *s* faith............. 1 Ti 1:5
s love of the brethren...... 1 Pe 1:22

SING
"*S* to the LORD............. Ex 15:21
the widow's heart to *s*...... Job 29:13
I will *s* of mercy and....... Ps 101:1
S us one of the songs...... Ps 137:3
I will *s* with the............. 1 Co 14:15
congregation I will s........ Heb 2:12
Let him *s* psalms............. Jas 5:13

SINGING
His presence with *s*......... Ps 100:2
And our tongue with *s*..... Ps 126:2
the time of *s* has come..... Song 2:12
break forth into *s*........... Is 14:7
come to Zion with *s*........ Is 35:10
and spiritual songs, *s*....... Eph 5:19

SINNED
You only, have I *s*.......... Ps 51:4
Jerusalem has *s*.............. Lam 1:8
Our fathers *s* and are...... Lam 5:7
"Father, I have *s*............ Luke 15:18
"Rabbi, who *s*................ John 9:2
For as many as have *s*..... Rom 2:12
for all have *s* and........... Rom 3:23
marries, she has not *s*...... 1 Co 7:28
say that we have not *s*..... 1 Jn 1:10
for the devil has *s*.......... 1 Jn 3:8

SINNER
s destroys much good...... Eccl 9:18
the city who was a *s*........ Luke 7:37
s who repents than.......... Luke 15:7
can a man who is a *s*....... John 9:16
the ungodly and the s...... 1 Pe 4:18

SINNERS
in the path of *s*.............. Ps 1:1
son, if *s* entice you.......... Prov 1:10
the righteous, but *s*......... Matt 9:13
tax collectors and *s*.......... Matt 11:19
s love those who love...... Luke 6:32
Galileans were worse *s*..... Luke 13:2
God does not hear *s*........ John 9:31
while we were still *s*........ Rom 5:8
many were made *s*.......... Rom 5:19
the ungodly and for *s*...... 1 Ti 1:9
the world to save *s*.......... 1 Ti 1:15
separate from *s*............... Heb 7:26
such hostility from *s*........ Heb 12:3
things which ungodly *s*..... Jude 15

SINS
my iniquities and *s*.......... Job 13:23
from presumptuous *s*........ Ps 19:13
You, Our secret *s*........... Ps 90:8
but he who *s* against........ Prov 8:36
s have hidden His face..... Is 59:2
the soul who *s* shall......... Ezek 18:4
to make an end of *s*......... Dan 9:24
if your brother *s*........... Matt 18:15
I take away their s.......... Rom 11:27
s according to the........... 1 Co 15:3
are still in your *s*........... 1 Co 15:17
the forgiveness of *s*......... Eph 1:7
s are clearly evident........ 1 Ti 5:24
once to bear the *s*........... Heb 9:28
If we confess our *s*.......... 1 Jn 1:9
propitiation for our *s*....... 1 Jn 2:2
Whoever *s* has neither..... 1 Jn 3:6

SIT
but to *s* on My right........ Matt 20:23
and the Pharisees *s*.......... Matt 23:2
"*S at My right hand*....... Heb 1:13
say to him, "You *s*.......... Jas 2:3
I will grant to *s*............. Rev 3:21
heart, 'I *s* as queen......... Rev 18:7

SKIN
God made tunics of *s*...... Gen 3:21
LORD and said, "*S*.......... Job 2:4
have escaped by the *s*...... Job 19:20
Ethiopian change his *s*..... Jer 13:23

SKULL
to say, Place of a *S*......... Matt 27:33

SLACK
s hand becomes poor....... Prov 10:4
The Lord is not *s*............ 2 Pe 3:9

SLAIN
s his thousands.............. 1 Sa 18:7
beauty of Israel is *s*......... 2 Sa 1:19
the dead, Like the *s*........ Ps 88:5
I shall be *s* in the........... Prov 22:13
no more cover her *s*........ Is 26:21
and night for the *s*.......... Jer 9:1
Those *s* by the sword....... Lam 4:9
the prophets, I have *s*...... Hos 6:5
is the Lamb who was *s*.... Rev 5:12

SLANDERERS
be reverent, not *s*........... 1 Ti 3:11
unforgiving, *s*................ 2 Ti 3:3
in behavior, not *s*........... Tit 2:3

SLAUGHTER
led as a lamb to the *s*...... Is 53:7
but the Valley of *S*.......... Jer 7:32
Feed the flock for *s*......... Zech 11:4
as sheep for the s.......... Rom 8:36

SLAVE
that you were a *s*............ Deut 15:15
commits sin is a *s*........... John 8:34
you called while a *s*......... 1 Co 7:21
you are no longer a *s*...... Gal 4:7

SLAY
s the righteous................ Gen 18:25
s a righteous nation........ Gen 20:4
Evil shall *s* the............... Ps 34:21
Oh, that You would *s*...... Ps 139:19
s them before me........... Luke 19:27

SLEEP
God caused a deep *s*....... Gen 2:21
my eyes, Lest I *s*............ Ps 13:3
neither slumber nor *s*....... Ps 121:4
He gives His beloved *s*.... Ps 127:2
s will be sweet................ Prov 3:24
A little *s*....................... Prov 6:10
among you, and many *s*... 1 Co 11:30
We shall not all *s*........... 1 Co 15:51
"Awake, you who *s*......... Eph 5:14

SLEEPING
is not dead, but *s*........... Matt 9:24

SLEEPS
Our friend Lazarus *s*....... John 11:11

SLIPPERY
way be dark and *s*........... Ps 35:6
set them in *s* places......... Ps 73:18

SLOW
but I am *s* of speech........ Ex 4:10
He who is *s* to wrath....... Prov 14:29
hear, *s* to speak, *s*........... Jas 1:19

SLUGGARD
will you slumber, O *s*...... Prov 6:9
soul of a *s* desires........... Prov 13:4
s is wiser in his own........ Prov 26:16

SMALL
I will make you *s*............ Jer 49:15
I will make you *s*............ Obad 2
And I saw the dead, *s*..... Rev 20:12

SMITTEN
Him stricken, *s*............... Is 53:4

SMOKE
s shall ascend forever....... Is 34:10
vanish away like *s*........... Is 51:6
s arose out of the pit....... Rev 9:2
was filled with *s*............. Rev 15:8
And her *s* rises up........... Rev 19:3

SMOOTH
speak to us *s* things......... Is 30:10
and the rough places *s*..... Is 40:4
though they speak *s*......... Jer 12:6
the rough ways made s..... Luke 3:5

SMOOTH-SKINNED
man, and I am a *s*.......... Gen 27:11

SNARE
as a bird from the *s*......... Ps 124:7
birds caught in a *s*........... Eccl 9:12
I have laid a *s*................ Jer 50:23
it will come as a *s*........... Luke 21:35
temptation and a *s*.......... 1 Ti 6:9
and escape the *s*............. 2 Ti 2:26

SNARES
The *s* of death................ Ps 18:5

SNATCH
neither shall anyone *s*...... John 10:28

SNATCHES
s away what was............. Matt 13:19

SNIFFED
they *s* at the wind........... Jer 14:6

SNOW
and heat consume the *s*.... Job 24:19
For He says to the *s*........ Job 37:6
the treasury of *s*............. Job 38:22
shall be whiter than *s*...... Ps 51:7
He gives *s* like wool........ Ps 147:16
As *s* in summer and........ Prov 26:1
She is not afraid of *s*....... Prov 31:21
shall be as white as *s*....... Is 1:18
garment was white as *s*.... Dan 7:9
clothing as white as *s*...... Matt 28:3
wool, as white as *s*.......... Rev 1:14

SOBER
the older men be *s*.......... Tit 2:2

SOBERLY
think, but to think *s*........ Rom 12:3
we should live *s*.............. Tit 2:12

SODOMITES
nor homosexuals, nor *s*.... 1 Co 6:9
for fornicators, for *s*........ 1 Ti 1:10

SOJOURNED
By faith he *s* in the......... Heb 11:9

SOJOURNER
am a foreigner and a *s*..... Gen 23:4
fled and became a *s*........ Acts 7:29

SOJOURNERS
are strangers and *s*.......... Lev 25:23
I beg you as *s*................ 1 Pe 2:11

SOJOURNING
the time of your *s*.......... 1 Pe 1:17

SOLD
s his birthright................ Gen 25:33
s all that he had............. Matt 13:46
they bought, they *s*.......... Luke 17:28
s their possessions........... Acts 2:45
but I am carnal, *s*........... Rom 7:14

SOLDIER
hardship as a good *s*........ 2 Ti 2:3

SOLDIERS
sum of money to the *s*..... Matt 28:12
And the *s* also mocked..... Luke 23:36
s twisted a crown............ John 19:2

SOMETHING
thinks himself to be *s*...... Gal 6:3

SON
s makes a glad father....... Prov 10:1
s is a grief to his............. Prov 17:25
is born, unto us a *S*......... Is 9:6
heaven, O Lucifer, *s*......... Is 14:12
fourth is like the *S*.......... Dan 3:25
will bring forth a *S*.......... Matt 1:21
This is My beloved *S*....... Matt 3:17
Jesus, You *S* of God....... Matt 8:29
not the carpenter's *s*....... Matt 13:55
You are the *S* of God...... Matt 14:33
are the Christ, the *S*....... Matt 16:16
Lord,' how is He his *S*.... Matt 22:45
coming of the *S* of Man... Matt 24:37
I am the *S* of God........ Matt 27:43
Truly this was the *S*....... Matt 27:54
called the *S* of the.......... Luke 1:32

to be called your *s*.......... Luke 15:19
The only begotten *S*........ John 1:18
that this is the *S*............. John 1:34
of the only begotten *S*..... John 3:18
S can do nothing............. John 5:19
s abides forever.............. John 8:35
you believe in the *S*........ John 9:35
I said, 'I am the *S*........... John 10:36
Woman, behold your *s*..... John 19:26
Jesus Christ is the *S*........ Acts 8:37
declared to be the *S*........ Rom 1:4
by sending His own *S*...... Rom 8:3
not spare His own *S*......... Rom 8:32
live by faith in the *S*........ Gal 2:20
God sent forth His *S*........ Gal 4:4
the knowledge of the *S*.... Eph 4:13
"*You are My S*.............. Heb 1:5
but Christ as a *S*............. Heb 3:6
though He was a *S*........... Heb 5:8
but made like the *S*......... Heb 7:3
This is My beloved *S*........ 2 Pe 1:17
Whoever denies the *S*....... 1 Jn 2:23
God has given of His *S*.... 1 Jn 5:10
One like the *S* of Man..... Rev 1:13

SONG
is my strength and *s*........ Ex 15:2
Sing to Him a new *s*......... Ps 33:3
He has put a new *s*........... Ps 40:3
in the night His *s*............ Ps 42:8
I will sing a new *s*........... Ps 144:9
to my Well-beloved a *s*..... Is 5:1
and their taunting *s*......... Lam 3:14
as a very lovely *s*............ Ezek 33:32
And they sang a new *s*..... Rev 5:9
And they sing the *s*.......... Rev 15:3

SONGS
my Maker, Who gives *s*... Job 35:10
have been my *s* In the..... Ps 119:54
Sing us one of the *s*......... Ps 137:3
and spiritual *s*................. Eph 5:19

SONS
He will purify the *s*......... Mal 3:3
and you will be *s*............. Luke 6:35
that you may become *s*.... John 12:36
"You are *s* of the............ Acts 3:25
of God, these are *s*.......... Rom 8:14
who are of faith are *s*...... Gal 3:7
the adoption as *s*............. Gal 4:5
You are all *s* of light........ 1 Th 5:5
in bringing many *s*.......... Heb 2:10
illegitimate and not *s*....... Heb 12:8

SORCERER
omens, or a *s*................. Deut 16:10
But Elymas the *s*............ Acts 13:8

SORCERERS
soothsayers, or your *s*...... Jer 27:9
outside are dogs and *s*...... Rev 22:15

SORCERESS
shall not permit a *s*.......... Ex 22:18

SORCERY
For there is no *s*............. Num 23:23
idolatry, *s*....................... Gal 5:20

SORES
and putrefying *s*.............. Is 1:6
Lazarus, full of *s*............. Luke 16:20

SORROW
multiply your *s*................ Gen 3:16
I found trouble and *s*....... Ps 116:3
and He adds no *s*............. Prov 10:22
the heart may *s*.............. Prov 14:13
S is better than................ Eccl 7:3
Therefore remove *s*.......... Eccl 11:10
you shall cry for *s*........... Is 65:14
to see labor and *s*........... Jer 20:18
them sleeping from *s*....... Luke 22:45
s will be turned................ John 16:20
that I have great *s*........... Rom 9:2
s produces repentance...... 2 Co 7:10
lest I should have *s*.......... Phil 2:27
s as others who have....... 1 Th 4:13
no more death, nor *s*....... Rev 21:4

SORROWFUL
were exceedingly *s*.......... Matt 17:23
saying, he went away *s*.... Matt 19:22
soul is exceedingly *s*....... Matt 26:38
and you will be *s*............ John 16:20

SORROWS
the *s* of Sheol.................. 2 Sa 22:6
s shall be multiplied........ Ps 16:4
by men, a man of *s*.......... Is 53:3
are the beginning of *s*...... Matt 24:8
through with many *s*........ 1 Ti 6:10

SORRY
s that He had made man.. Gen 6:6
who will be *s* for you....... Is 51:19
And the king was *s*.......... Matt 14:9
For you were made *s*........ 2 Co 7:9

SOUGHT
I *s* the LORD..................... Ps 34:4
whole heart I have *s*........ Ps 119:10
s the one I love................ Song 3:1
"So I *s* for a man............ Ezek 22:30
s it diligently.................. Heb 12:17

SOUL
was knit to the *s*............. 1 Sa 18:1
"My *s* loathes life........... Job 10:1
s draws near the Pit......... Job 33:22
will not leave my *s*.......... Ps 16:10
converting the *s*.............. Ps 19:7
He restores my *s*............. Ps 23:3
you cast down, O my *s*.... Ps 42:5
s knows very well............ Ps 139:14
No one cares for my *s*..... Ps 142:4
so destroys his own *s*...... Prov 6:32
When You make His *s*...... Is 53:10
able to destroy both *s*...... Matt 10:28
and loses his own *s*......... Matt 16:26
with all your s................. Matt 22:37
Now My *s* is troubled...... John 12:27
of one heart and one *s*..... Acts 4:32
your whole spirit, *s*......... 1 Th 5:23
to the saving of the *s*...... Heb 10:39

SOULS
And will save the *s*......... Ps 72:13
and he who wins *s*.......... Prov 11:30
s shall be like a.............. Jer 31:12
unsettling your *s*............. Acts 15:24
is able to save your *s*....... Jas 1:21

SOUND
s heart is life.................. Prov 14:30
one rises up at the *s*........ Eccl 12:4
voice was like the *s*......... Ezek 43:2
s an alarm in My holy....... Joel 2:1
do not *s* a trumpet........... Matt 6:2
s words which you............ 2 Ti 1:13
that they may be *s*.......... Tit 1:13

SOUNDNESS
There is no *s* in my......... Ps 38:3

SOW
s trouble reap.................. Job 4:8
Those who *s* in tears....... Ps 126:5
ground, and do not *s*....... Jer 4:3
"They *s* the wind............ Hos 8:7
S for yourselves.............. Hos 10:12

SOWER
may give seed to the *s*..... Is 55:10
"Behold, a *s* went........... Matt 13:3

SOWN
a land that was not *s*....... Jer 2:2
"You have *s* much.......... Hag 1:6
It is *s* in weakness.......... 1 Co 15:43
of righteousness is *s*......... Jas 3:18

SOWS
s righteousness will......... Prov 11:18
s the good seed is the....... Matt 13:37
'One *s* and another......... John 4:37
s sparingly will............... 2 Co 9:6
for whatever a man *s*....... Gal 6:7

SPARE
The LORD would not *s*..... Deut 29:20
hand, but *s* his life.......... Job 2:6
s the poor and needy........ Ps 72:13
I will not pity nor *s*......... Jer 13:14
say, "*S* Your people........ Joel 2:17
s them as a man spares.... Mal 3:17
He who did not *s*............ Rom 8:32
s the natural branches...... Rom 11:21
flesh, but I would *s*........ 1 Co 7:28
if God did not *s*.............. 2 Pe 2:4

SPARES
s his rod hates his........... Prov 13:24

SPARKLES
it is red, when it *s*.......... Prov 23:31

SPARKS
to trouble, as the *s*......... Job 5:7
s you have kindled.......... Is 50:11

SPARROWS
more value than many *s*... Matt 10:31

SPAT
Then they *s* on Him......... Matt 27:30
in his ears, and He *s*....... Mark 7:33

SPEAK
oh, that God would *s*...... Job 11:5
and a time to *s*.............. Eccl 3:7
s anymore in His name.... Jer 20:9
s each man the truth....... Zech 8:16
or what you should *s*....... Matt 10:19
to you when all men *s*..... Luke 6:26
s what I have seen.......... John 8:38
He hears He will *s*.......... John 16:13
Spirit and began to *s*....... Acts 2:4
Do all *s* with tongues....... 1 Co 12:30
I would rather *s*.............. 1 Co 14:19

SPEAKS
to face, as a man *s*......... Ex 33:11
He whom God has sent *s*. John 3:34
When he *s* a lie.............. John 8:44
he being dead still *s*........ Heb 11:4
of sprinkling that *s*......... Heb 12:24

SPEAR
His side with a *s*............. John 19:34

SPEARS
Whose teeth are *s*........... Ps 57:4
and their *s* into............... Is 2:4
pruninghooks into *s*......... Joel 3:10

SPECK
do you look at the *s*........ Matt 7:3

SPECTACLE
we have been made a *s*.... 1 Co 4:9
He made a public *s*......... Col 2:15
you were made a *s*.......... Heb 10:33

SPEECH
one language and one *s*.... Gen 11:1
There is no *s* nor............ Ps 19:3
not understand My *s*........ John 8:43
and his *s* contemptible..... 2 Co 10:10
I am untrained in *s*......... 2 Co 11:6
s always be with grace...... Col 4:6

SPEEDILY
judgment be executed *s*.... Ezra 7:26
I call, answer me *s*.......... Ps 102:2

SPEND
I will very gladly *s*.......... 2 Co 12:15
amiss, that you may *s*...... Jas 4:3

SPENT
in vain, I have *s*............ Is 49:4
"But when he had *s*........ Luke 15:14

SPEW
nor hot, I will *s*............. Rev 3:16

SPIRIT
And the *S* of God was..... Gen 1:2
S shall not strive............ Gen 6:3
there was no more *s*........ 2 Ch 9:4
Then a *s* passed before.... Job 4:15
The *S* of God has made... Job 33:4
hand I commit my *s*........ Ps 31:5
You send forth Your *S*.... Ps 104:30
The *s* of a man is the...... Prov 20:27
Who knows the *s*............ Eccl 3:21
s will return to God....... Eccl 12:7
S has gathered them........ Is 34:16
I have put My *S*............. Is 42:1
and His *S* have sent Me... Is 48:16
S entered me when He.... Ezek 2:2
the *S* lifted me up.......... Ezek 3:12
new heart and a new *s*..... Ezek 18:31
"I will put My *S*............ Ezek 36:27
and He saw the *S*.......... Matt 3:16
I will put My S............ Matt 12:18
S descending upon Him... Mark 1:10
And immediately the *S*... Mark 1:12
in the power of the *S*..... Luke 4:14
manner of *s* you are of..... Luke 9:55
hands I commend My *s*.... Luke 23:46
"God is *S*..................... John 4:24
I speak to you are *s*........ John 6:63
"even the *S* of truth........ John 14:17
when He, the *S*............. John 16:13
but if a *s* or an angel....... Acts 23:9
according to the *S*.......... Rom 8:5
what the mind of the *S*.... Rom 8:27
to us through His *S*......... 1 Co 2:10
gifts, but the same *S*....... 1 Co 12:4
but the *S* gives life.......... 2 Co 3:6
Having begun in the *S*..... Gal 3:3
has sent forth the *S*......... Gal 4:6
he who sows to the *S*...... Gal 6:8
the unity of the *S*............ Eph 4:3
stand fast in one *s*.......... Phil 1:27
yet I am with you in *s*..... Col 2:5
and may your whole *s*...... 1 Th 5:23
S expressly says that....... 1 Ti 4:1
division of soul and *s*....... Heb 4:12
through the eternal *S*....... Heb 9:14
S who dwells in us.......... Jas 4:5
do not believe every *s*...... 1 Jn 4:1
has given us of His *S*....... 1 Jn 4:13
S who bears witness........ 1 Jn 5:6
I was in the *S* on the....... Rev 1:10
And the *S* and the.......... Rev 22:17

SPIRITS
Who makes His angels *s*.. Ps 104:4
power over unclean *s*....... Matt 10:1
heed to deceiving *s*.......... 1 Ti 4:1
not all ministering *s*......... Heb 1:14
to the Father of *s*............ Heb 12:9
and preached to the *s*...... 1 Pe 3:19
spirit, but test the *s*......... 1 Jn 4:1

SPIRITUAL
s judges all things........... 1 Co 2:15
s people but as to........... 1 Co 3:1
to be a prophet or *s*........ 1 Co 14:37
However, the *s* is not...... 1 Co 15:46
s restore such a one........ Gal 6:1

SPIRITUALLY
s minded is life.............. Rom 8:6

SPITEFULLY
for those who *s*.............. Matt 5:44

SPOILER
I have created the *s*........ Is 54:16

SPOKE
"No man ever *s*............. John 7:46
"We know that God *s*..... John 9:29
I was a child, I *s*............ 1 Co 13:11
in different ways *s*........... Heb 1:1
s as they were moved...... 2 Pe 1:21

SPOKEN
'just as you have *s*......... Num 14:28
God has *s* once.............. Ps 62:11
I have not *s* in secret....... Is 45:19
'What have we *s*............ Mal 3:13
why am I evil *s*.............. 1 Co 10:30

SPOT
and there is no *s*............. Song 4:7
church, not having *s*........ Eph 5:27
commandment without *s*... 1 Ti 6:14
Himself without *s*............ Heb 9:14

SPREAD
They have *s* a net by....... Ps 140:5
Then He *s* it before me.... Ezek 2:10
And the word of God *s*... Acts 6:7
their message will *s*......... 2 Ti 2:17

SPRING
Truth shall *s* out of......... Ps 85:11
is like a murky *s*............ Prov 25:26
sister, my spouse, a *s*....... Song 4:12
s forth I tell you............ Is 42:9
of Israel to *s* forth.......... Ezek 29:21
s shall become dry.......... Hos 13:15
s send forth fresh........... Jas 3:11

SPRINGING
a fountain of water *s*....... John 4:14
root of bitterness *s*.......... Heb 12:15

SPRINGS
Have you entered the *s*.... Job 38:16
He sends the *s* into......... Ps 104:10
and the thirsty land *s*....... Is 35:7
and the dry land *s*........... Is 41:18

SPRINKLE
He *s* many nations.......... Is 52:15
"Then I will *s*................ Ezek 36:25

SPRINKLED
s dust on his head........... Job 2:12
and hyssop, and *s*........... Heb 9:19
having our hearts *s*.......... Heb 10:22

SPRINKLING
s that speaks.................. Heb 12:24
for obedience and *s*......... 1 Pe 1:2

SQUARES
voice in the open *s*.......... Prov 1:20
s I will seek the one........ Song 3:2

STAFF
this Jordan with my *s*...... Gen 32:10
Your rod and Your *s*....... Ps 23:4
LORD has broken the *s*.... Is 14:5
on the top of his *s*.......... Heb 11:21

STAGGER
and He makes them *s*....... Job 12:25
they will drink and *s*........ Jer 25:16

STAGGERS
as a drunken man *s*......... Is 19:14

STAMMERING
For with *s* lips and.......... Is 28:11
s tongue that you............ Is 33:19

STAND
one shall be able to *s*...... Deut 7:24
"Who is able to *s*............ 1 Sa 6:20
lives, and He shall *s*.......... Job 19:25
ungodly shall not *s*........... Ps 1:5
Why do You *s* afar off........ Ps 10:1
Or who may *s* in His....... Ps 24:3
but she shall not *s*........... Dan 11:17
And who can *s* when He.. Mal 3:2
that kingdom cannot *s*..... Mark 3:24
he will be made to *s*....... Rom 14:4
Watch, *s* fast in the......... 1 Co 16:13
for by faith you *s*........... 2 Co 1:24
having done all, to *s*....... Eph 6:13
s fast in the Lord............ Phil 4:1
"Behold, I *s* at the.......... Rev 3:20

STANDARD
LORD will lift up a *s*........ Is 59:19
Set up the *s* toward......... Jer 4:6

STANDING
the LORD, and Satan *s*..... Zech 3:1
they love to pray *s*.......... Matt 6:5
and the Son of Man *s*...... Acts 7:56
Then I saw an angel *s*...... Rev 19:17

STANDS
The LORD *s* up to plead... Is 3:13
him who thinks he *s*........ 1 Co 10:12

STAR
S shall come out of......... Num 24:17
For we have seen His *s*.... Matt 2:2
for one *s* differs from...... 1 Co 15:41
give him the morning *s*.... Rev 2:28
And a great *s* fell............ Rev 8:10
Bright and Morning *S*...... Rev 22:16

STARS
He made the *s* also......... Gen 1:16
s are not pure in His....... Job 25:5
when the morning *s*......... Job 38:7
The moon and the *s*......... Ps 8:3
Praise Him, all you *s*....... Ps 148:3
born as many as the *s*...... Heb 11:12
wandering *s* for whom..... Jude 13
a garland of twelve *s*....... Rev 12:1

STATE
man at his best *s*............ Ps 39:5
and the last *s* of that....... Matt 12:45
learned in whatever *s*....... Phil 4:11

STATURE
add one cubit to his *s*...... Matt 6:27
in wisdom and *s*.............. Luke 2:52
the measure of the *s*........ Eph 4:13

STATUTES
The *s* of the LORD are..... Ps 19:8
Teach me Your *s*............ Ps 119:12

STAY
S here and watch with..... Matt 26:38
for today I must *s*........... Luke 19:5

STEADFAST
O God, my heart is *s*...... Ps 57:7
His heart is *s*................. Ps 112:7
God, and *s* forever.......... Dan 6:26
beloved brethren, be *s*..... 1 Co 15:58
faith, grounded and *s*....... Col 1:23
angels proved *s*............... Heb 2:2
of our confidence *s*......... Heb 3:14
soul, both sure and *s*....... Heb 6:19
Resist him, *s* in the......... 1 Pe 5:9

STEAL
"You shall not *s*............. Ex 20:15
s My words every one...... Jer 23:30
thieves break in and *s*...... Matt 6:19
night and *s* Him away...... Matt 27:64
murder,' 'Do not s.......... Mark 10:19
not come except to *s*........ John 10:10
Let him who stole *s*......... Eph 4:28

STEPS
and count all my *s*.......... Job 31:4
and He sees all his *s*........ Job 34:21
The *s* of a good man....... Ps 37:23
of his *s* shall slide........... Ps 37:31
s had nearly slipped......... Ps 73:2
the LORD directs his *s*...... Prov 16:9
A man's *s* are of the....... Prov 20:24
should follow His *s*.......... 1 Pe 2:21

STEWARD
faithful and wise *s*...Luke 12:42
commended the unjust *s*...Luke 16:8
be blameless, as a *s*...Tit 1:7

STEWARDS
one another, as good *s*...1 Pe 4:10

STIFFNECKED
"Now do not be *s*...2 Ch 30:8
"You *s* and...Acts 7:51

STILL
on your bed, and be *s*...Ps 4:4
s the noise of the...Ps 65:7
earth feared and was *s*...Ps 76:8
that its waves are *s*...Ps 107:29
When I awake, I am *s*...Ps 139:18
time, I have been *s*...Is 42:14
rest and be *s*...Jer 47:6
sea, "Peace, be *s*...Mark 4:39
let him be holy *s*...Rev 22:11

STIR
that he would dare *s*...Job 41:10
S up Yourself...Ps 35:23
I remind you to *s*...2 Ti 1:6
another in order to *s*...Heb 10:24

STIRS
and the innocent *s*...Job 17:8
it *s* up the dead for...Is 14:9
on Your name, who *s*...Is 64:7

STOIC
and *S* philosophers...Acts 17:18

STOMACH
mouth goes into the *s*...Matt 15:17
Foods for the *s*...1 Co 6:13

STONE
s shall be a witness...Josh 24:27
heart is as hard as *s*...Job 41:24
I lay in Zion a *s*...Is 28:16
take the heart of *s*...Ezek 36:26
will give him a *s*...Matt 7:9
secure, sealing the *s*...Matt 27:66
s which the builders...Luke 20:17
you, let him throw a *s*...John 8:7
those works do you *s*...John 10:32
Jews sought to *s* You...John 11:8
Him as to a living *s*...1 Pe 2:4
give him a white *s*...Rev 2:17
angel took up a *s*...Rev 18:21
like a jasper *s*...Rev 21:11

STONED
s Stephen as he was...Acts 7:59
once I was *s*...2 Co 11:25
They were *s*...Heb 11:37

STONES
I will lay your *s*...Is 54:11
Among the smooth *s*...Is 57:6
Abraham from these *s*...Matt 3:9
command that these *s*...Matt 4:3
see what manner of *s*...Mark 13:1
also, as living *s*...1 Pe 2:5
kinds of precious *s*...Rev 21:19

STONY
Some fell on *s* ground...Mark 4:5

STORK
s has her home in the...Ps 104:17
"Even the *s* in the...Jer 8:7

STORM
terror comes like a *s*...Prov 1:27
a refuge from the *s*...Is 25:4
coming like a *s*...Ezek 38:9
whirlwind and in the *s*...Nah 1:3

STRAIGHT
Make Your way *s*...Ps 5:8
for who can make *s*...Eccl 7:13
make *s* in the desert a...Is 40:3
LORD, make His paths s...Luke 3:4
to the street called *S*...Acts 9:11
and make *s* paths for...Heb 12:13

STRANGE
"We have seen *s*...Luke 5:26
these, they think it *s*...1 Pe 4:4

STRANGER
but he acted as a *s*...Gen 42:7
"I have been a *s*...Ex 2:22
neither mistreat a *s*...Ex 22:21
and loves the *s*...Deut 10:18
I have become a *s*...Ps 69:8
s will suffer for it...Prov 11:15
s does not share its...Prov 14:10
should You be like a *s*...Jer 14:8
I was a *s* and you took...Matt 25:35
"Are You the only *s*...Luke 24:18

STRANGERS
know the voice of *s*...John 10:5
of Israel and *s*...Eph 2:12
that they were *s*...Heb 11:13
forget to entertain *s*...Heb 13:2

STRAW
They are like *s*...Job 21:18
stones, wood, hay, *s*...1 Co 3:12

STRAYED
Yet I have not *s*...Ps 119:110
for which some have *s*...1 Ti 6:10
who have *s* concerning...2 Ti 2:18

STREAM
like a flowing *s*...Is 66:12

STREAMS
He dams up the *s*...Job 28:11
O LORD, As the *s*...Ps 126:4

STREET
s called Straight...Acts 9:11
And the *s* of the city...Rev 21:21
In the middle of its *s*...Rev 22:2

STREETS
the corners of the *s*...Matt 6:5
You taught in our *s*...Luke 13:26

STRENGTH
my soul, march on in *s*...Judg 5:21
a man is, so is his *s*...Judg 8:21
the God of my *s*...2 Sa 22:3
have armed me with *s*...2 Sa 22:40
Him are wisdom and *s*...Job 12:13
You have ordained *s*...Ps 8:2
love You, O LORD, my *s* Ps 18:1
The LORD is the *s*...Ps 27:1
is our refuge and *s*...Ps 46:1
I will go in the *s*...Ps 71:16
But God is the *s*...Ps 73:26
They go from *s* to...Ps 84:7
the glory of their *s*...Ps 89:17
S and beauty are in...Ps 96:6
knowledge increases *s*...Prov 24:5
S and honor are her...Prov 31:25
for *s* and not for...Eccl 10:17
him take hold of My *s*...Is 27:5
might He increases *s*...Is 40:29
O LORD, my *s* and my...Jer 16:19
were still without *s*...Rom 5:6
s is made perfect...2 Co 12:9
you have a little *s*...Rev 3:8

STRENGTHEN
And He shall *s*...Ps 27:14
S the weak hands...Is 35:3
"So I will *s* them in...Zech 10:12
s your brethren...Luke 22:32
s the hands...Heb 12:12
s the things...Rev 3:2

STRENGTHENED
unbelief, but was *s*...Rom 4:20
of His glory, to be *s*...Eph 3:16
stood with me and *s*...2 Ti 4:17

STRETCH
said to the man, "*S*...Matt 12:13

STRETCHED
I have *s* out my hands...Ps 88:9
His wisdom, And has *s*...Jer 10:12
All day long I have s...Rom 10:21

STRICKEN
yet we esteemed Him *s*...Is 53:4
You have *s* them...Jer 5:3

STRIFE
let there be no *s*...Gen 13:8
at the waters of *s*...Ps 106:32
Hatred stirs up *s*...Prov 10:12
transgression loves *s*...Prov 17:19
borne me, a man of *s*...Jer 15:10
even from envy and *s*...Phil 1:15
which come envy, *s*...1 Ti 6:4

STRIKE
The sun shall not *s*...Ps 121:6
S a scoffer...Prov 19:25
s the waves of the sea...Zech 10:11
s the earth with a...Mal 4:6
I will s the Shepherd...Matt 26:31
the sun shall not *s*...Rev 7:16

STRIP
s yourselves...Is 32:11
s her naked and expose...Hos 2:3

STRIPES
s we are healed...Is 53:5
be beaten with many *s*...Luke 12:47
I received forty *s*...2 Co 11:24
s you were healed...1 Pe 2:24

STRIVE
My Spirit shall not *s*...Gen 6:3
He will not always *s*...Ps 103:9
Let the potsherd *s*...Is 45:9
"*S* to enter through...Luke 13:24

STRONG
"Be *s* and conduct...1 Sa 4:9
The LORD *s* and mighty...Ps 24:8
bring me into the *s*...Ps 60:9
S is Your hand...Ps 89:13
A wise man is *s*...Prov 24:5
s shall be as tinder...Is 1:31
the weak say, 'I am *s*...Joel 3:10
"When a *s* man...Luke 11:21
We then who are *s*...Rom 15:1
are weak and you are *s*...2 Co 13:9
my brethren, be *s*...Eph 6:10
weakness were made *s*...Heb 11:34
s is the Lord God...Rev 18:8

STRUCK
s the rock twice...Num 20:11
Behold, He *s* the rock...Ps 78:20
in My wrath I *s*...Is 60:10
took the reed and *s*...Matt 27:30
Him, they *s* Him on the...Luke 22:64

STUMBLE
your foot will not *s*...Prov 3:23
we *s* at noonday as at...Is 59:10
you will be made to *s*...Matt 26:31
immediately they *s*...Mark 4:17
who believe in Me to *s*...Mark 9:42
whole law, and yet *s*...Jas 2:10
For we all *s* in many...Jas 3:2

STUMBLES
word, immediately he *s*...Matt 13:21

STUMBLING
but a stone of *s*...Is 8:14
it became their *s*...Ezek 7:19
I lay in Zion a s...Rom 9:33
this, not to put a *s*...Rom 14:13
to the Jews a *s*...1 Co 1:23
and "*A stone of s*...1 Pe 2:8
is no cause for *s*...1 Jn 2:10
to keep you from *s*...Jude 24

STUPID
and regarded as *s*............Job 18:3
who hates reproof is *s*......Prov 12:1

SUBDUE
s the peoples under us..... Ps 47:3
shall *s* three kings........... Dan 7:24
s our iniquities................Mic 7:19
s all things to................. Phil 3:21

SUBJECT
for it is not *s*.................Rom 8:7
Let every soul be *s*..........Rom 13:1
all things are made *s*.........1 Co 15:28
Remind them to be *s*.......Tit 3:1
all their lifetime *s*...........Heb 2:15
having been made *s*..........1 Pe 3:22

SUBJECTION
put all things in s............Heb 2:8
more readily be in *s*........... Heb 12:9

SUBMISSIVE
you wives, be *s*...............1 Pe 3:1
Yes, all of you be *s*...........1 Pe 5:5

SUBMIT
Wives, *s* to your own.......Eph 5:22
Therefore *s* to God.........Jas 4:7
s yourselves to every....... 1 Pe 2:13
you younger people, *s*......1 Pe 5:5

SUCCESS
please give me *s*............ Gen 24:12
but wisdom brings *s*.........Eccl 10:10

SUDDENLY
whom you seek, will *s*..... Mal 3:1
s there was with the........ Luke 2:13

SUFFER
for a stranger will *s*......... Prov 11:15
for the Christ to *s*........... Luke 24:46
Christ, if indeed we *s*...... Rom 8:17
all the members *s*...........1 Co 12:26
that they may not *s*......... Gal 6:12
s trouble as an................2 Ti 2:9
when you do good and *s*.. 1 Pe 2:20
the will of God, to *s*.........1 Pe 3:17
s as a murderer............. 1 Pe 4:15
you are about to *s*...........Rev 2:10

SUFFERED
for whom I have *s*...........Phil 3:8
with His own blood, *s*......Heb 13:12
because Christ also *s*....... 1 Pe 2:21
For Christ also *s*.............1 Pe 3:18
since Christ *s*..................1 Pe 4:1
after you have *s*...............1 Pe 5:10

SUFFERING
Is anyone among you *s*.... Jas 5:13

SUFFERINGS
I consider that the *s*........ Rom 8:18
share with me in the *s*..... 2 Ti 1:8
perfect through *s*.............Heb 2:10
beforehand the *s*..............1 Pe 1:11

SUFFERS
Love *s* long and is...........1 Co 13:4

SUFFICIENCY
ourselves, but our *s*.........2 Co 3:5
always having all *s*.......... 2 Co 9:8

SUFFICIENT
S for the day is its.......... Matt 6:34
by the majority is *s*......... 2 Co 2:6
Not that we are *s*............2 Co 3:5

SUMMER
heat, and winter and *s*..... Gen 8:22
into the drought of *s*....... Ps 32:4
You have made *s*............. Ps 74:17
you know that *s*..............Matt 24:32

SUN
So the *s* stood still......... Josh 10:13
the LORD God is a *s*....... Ps 84:11
s shall not strike you....... Ps 121:6
The *s* to rule by day........Ps 136:8
while the *s* and the..........Eccl 12:2
s returned ten degrees..... Is 38:8
The *s* and moon stood..... Hab 3:11
for He makes His *s*......... Matt 5:45
the *s* was darkened..........Luke 23:45
is one glory of the *s*........ 1 Co 15:41
do not let the *s*...............Eph 4:26
s became black as........... Rev 6:12
s shall not strike.............Rev 7:16
had no need of the *s*........ Rev 21:23

SUPPER
to eat the Lord's *S*.......... 1 Co 11:20
took the cup after *s*.........1 Co 11:25
together for the *s*........... Rev 19:17

SUPPLICATION
LORD has heard my *s*...... Ps 6:9
Let my *s* come before......Ps 119:170
with all prayer and *s*........Eph 6:18
by prayer and *s*.............. Phil 4:6

SUPPLY
s what was lacking.......... Phil 2:30
And my God shall *s*......... Phil 4:19

SURE
s your sin will find.......... Num 32:23
calling and election *s*....... 2 Pe 1:10
word made more *s*.......... 2 Pe 1:19

SURROUNDED
their own deeds have *s*.... Hos 7:2
and the floods *s*...............Jon 2:3
also, since we are *s*......... Heb 12:1

SUSTAIN
You will *s* him on his...... Ps 41:3
S me with cakes of..........Song 2:5

SWADDLING
thick darkness its *s*..........Job 38:9
Him in *s* cloths............... Luke 2:7

SWALLOW
s observe the time...........Jer 8:7
great fish to *s* Jonah........Jon 1:17
a gnat and *s* a camel....... Matt 23:24

SWEAR
'You shall not *s*.............. Matt 5:33
began to curse and *s*........Matt 26:74
because He could *s*......... Heb 6:13
my brethren, do not *s*.......Jas 5:12

SWEARS
He who *s* to his own....... Ps 15:4
Everyone who *s* by Him...Ps 63:11
but whoever *s* by the.......Matt 23:18

SWEAT
In the *s* of your face........Gen 3:19
And His *s* became like.....Luke 22:44

SWEET
Though evil is *s*...............Job 20:12
s are Your words............ Ps 119:103
His mouth is most *s*........ Song 5:16
but it will be as *s*...........Rev 10:9

SWIFT
s as the eagle flies..........Deut 28:49
pass by like *s* ships..........Job 9:26
let every man be *s*.......... Jas 1:19

SWIM
night I make my bed *s*.....Ps 6:6

SWORD
s which turned every....... Gen 3:24
The *s* of the LORD is....... Is 34:6
will die by the *s*..............Ezek 7:15
a *s* is sharpened..............Ezek 21:9
to bring peace but a *s*......Matt 10:34
for all who take the *s*...... Matt 26:52
s will pierce through........Luke 2:35
the *s* of the Spirit............Eph 6:17
than any two-edged *s*.......Heb 4:12
a sharp two-edged *s*.........Rev 1:16
mouth goes a sharp *s*.......Rev 19:15

SWORDS
Yet they were drawn *s*.....Ps 55:21
shall beat their *s*............. Is 2:4
look, here are two *s*........ Luke 22:38

SWORE
So I s in My wrath...........Heb 3:11
and *s* by Him who lives... Rev 10:6

SWORN
By Myself I have *s*.......... Gen 22:16
The LORD has *s* in.......... Ps 132:11
I have *s* by Myself.......... Is 45:23
"*The LORD has s*............ Heb 7:21

SYMPATHIZE
Priest who cannot *s*......... Heb 4:15

SYNAGOGUE
He went into the *s*.......... Luke 4:16
but are a *s* of Satan.........Rev 2:9

— T —

TABERNACLE
you shall make the *t*......... Ex 26:1
t He shall hide me.......... Ps 27:5
I will abide in Your *t*.......Ps 61:4
How lovely is Your *t*....... Ps 84:1
quiet habitation, a *t*.........Is 33:20
Yes, you took up the t..... Acts 7:43
and will rebuild the t....... Acts 15:16
and more perfect *t*.......... Heb 9:11
"Behold, the *t*................Rev 21:3

TABERNACLES
us make here three *t*....... Matt 17:4
Feast of *T* was at hand.... John 7:2

TABLE
prepare a *t* before me...... Ps 23:5
dogs under the *t*............ Mark 7:28
of the Lord's *t*................1 Co 10:21

TABLES
and overturned the *t*.........Matt 21:12
of God and serve *t*.......... Acts 6:2

TAIL
the head and not the *t*..... Deut 28:13
t drew a third of the.........Rev 12:4

TAKE
T your sandal off your.....Josh 5:15
t Your Holy Spirit...........Ps 51:11
T words with you............Hos 14:2
T My yoke upon you and.Matt 11:29
and *t* up his cross...........Mark 8:34
T this cup away.............Mark 14:36
My life that I may *t*..........John 10:17
I urge you to *t* heart..........Acts 27:22

TAKEN
one will be *t* and the....... Matt 24:40
what he has will be *t*....... Mark 4:25
He was *t* up.................... Acts 1:9
until He is *t* out of..........2 Th 2:7

TALENT
went and hid your *t*.........Matt 25:25

TALK
entangle Him in His *t*...... Matt 22:15
"I will no longer *t*............John 14:30
turned aside to idle *t*....... 1 Ti 1:6

TALKED
within us while He *t*........ Luke 24:32

TALKERS
both idle *t* and................Tit 1:10

TARES
the *t* also appeared..........Matt 13:26

TASTE
and its *t* was like the....... Num 11:8
Oh, *t* and see that the..... Ps 34:8

THIEVES
and companions of *t*........ Is 1:23
destroy and where *t*.........Matt 6:19
before Me are *t*............. John 10:8

THINGS
evil, speak good *t*...........Matt 12:34
kept all these *t*.............. Luke 2:51

THINK
t you have eternal........... John 5:39
not to *t* of himself........... Rom 12:3
all that we ask or *t*.......... Eph 3:20

THINKS
Yet the LORD *t* upon me..Ps 40:17
for as he *t* in his............ Prov 23:7
t that he knows..............1 Co 8:2
t he stands take heed.......1 Co 10:12
For if anyone *t*.............. Gal 6:3
t he is religious.............. Jas 1:26

THIRST
tongues fail for *t*............ Is 41:17
those who hunger and *t*....Matt 5:6
in Me shall never *t*.......... John 6:35
said, "I *t*!"..................... John 19:28
we both hunger and *t*...... 1 Co 4:11
anymore nor *t* anymore.... Rev 7:16

THIRSTS
My soul *t* for God........... Ps 42:2
saying, "If anyone *t*......... John 7:37
freely to him who *t*......... Rev 21:6

THIRSTY
I was *t* and you gave....... Matt 25:35

THISTLES
t grow instead of............ Job 31:40
or figs from *t*................. Matt 7:16

THORN
t shall come up the.......... Is 55:13
a *t* in the flesh was.......... 2 Co 12:7

THORNS
Both *t* and thistles it........ Gen 3:18
all overgrown with *t*......... Prov 24:31
Like a lily among *t*.......... Song 2:2
and do not sow among *t*...Jer 4:3
wheat but reaped *t*........... Jer 12:13
And some fell among *t*..... Matt 13:7
wearing the crown of *t*..... John 19:5

THOUGHT
You understand my *t*....... Ps 139:2
I *t* as a child.................. 1 Co 13:11

THOUGHTS
the intent of the *t*........... 1 Ch 28:9
is in none of his *t*............ Ps 10:4
t which are toward us...... Ps 40:5
t will be established......... Prov 16:3
For My *t* are not your..... Is 55:8
long shall your evil *t*........ Jer 4:14
they do not know the *t*.... Mic 4:12
Jesus, knowing their *t*...... Matt 9:4
heart proceed evil *t*......... Matt 15:19
futile in their *t*................ Rom 1:21
The LORD knows the t..... 1 Co 3:20

THREATEN
suffered, He did not *t*...... 1 Pe 2:23

THREATS
Lord, look on their *t*....... Acts 4:29
still breathing *t*.............. Acts 9:1

THREE
you will deny Me *t*......... Matt 26:34
hope, love, these *t*.......... 1 Co 13:13
and these *t* are one......... 1 Jn 5:7

THROAT
put a knife to your *t*........ Prov 23:2
unshod, and your *t*.......... Jer 2:25
t is an open tomb........... Rom 3:13

THRONE
LORD sitting on His *t*....... 1 Ki 22:19
has established His *t*........ Ps 103:19
Lord sitting on a *t*........... Is 6:1
"Heaven is My *t*............. Is 66:1
shall be called The *T*....... Jer 3:17
t was a fiery flame.......... Dan 7:9
sit and rule on His *t*........ Zech 6:13
will give Him the *t*.......... Luke 1:32
Your t, O God, is............ Heb 1:8
come boldly to the *t*......... Heb 4:16
where Satan's *t*................ Rev 2:13
My Father on His *t*.......... Rev 3:21
I saw a great white *t*........ Rev 20:11

THRONES
also sit on twelve *t*......... Matt 19:28
mighty from their *t*......... Luke 1:52
t I saw twenty-four.......... Rev 4:4

THROW
t Yourself down.............. Matt 4:6
children's bread and *t*...... Matt 15:26

THUNDER
But the *t* of His power..... Job 26:14
The voice of Your *t*......... Ps 77:18
that is, "Sons of *T*"........ Mark 3:17
the voice of loud *t*........... Rev 14:2

THUNDERED
"The LORD *t* from.......... 2 Sa 22:14
The LORD also *t*............. Ps 18:13

THUNDERINGS
people witnessed the *t*...... Ex 20:18
the sound of mighty *t*...... Rev 19:6

THUNDERS
t marvelously with His..... Job 37:5
The God of glory *t*.......... Ps 29:3

TIDINGS
I bring you good *t*.......... Luke 2:10
who bring glad t.............. Rom 10:15

TIME
pray to You In a *t*.......... Ps 32:6
how short my *t* is............ Ps 89:47
A *t* to be born................. Eccl 3:2
but *t* and chance............. Eccl 9:11
t has not yet come........... John 7:6
I have a convenient *t*....... Acts 24:25
for the *t* is near.............. Rev 1:3

TIMES
t are in Your hand.......... Ps 31:15
the signs of the *t*............ Matt 16:3
Gentiles until the *t*.......... Luke 21:24
not for you to know *t*...... Acts 1:7
their preappointed *t*......... Acts 17:26
last days perilous *t*.......... 2 Ti 3:1
God, who at various *t*...... Heb 1:1

TITHE
For you pay *t* of mint...... Matt 23:23

TITHES
I give *t* of all that I........ Luke 18:12
to receive *t* from the........ Heb 7:5

TITHING
which is the year of *t*....... Deut 26:12

TITTLE
away, one jot or one *t*..... Matt 5:18

TODAY
the grass, which *t*........... Luke 12:28
t you will be with Me...... Luke 23:43
t I have begotten You...... Heb 1:5
"*T, if you will hear*......... Heb 3:7
the same yesterday, *t*........ Heb 13:8

TOIL
t you shall eat of............ Gen 3:17
they neither *t* nor........... Matt 6:28

TOLD
things which were *t*......... Luke 2:18

so, I would have *t*........... John 14:2
And now I have *t*........... John 14:29

TOLERABLE
you, it will be more *t*....... Matt 10:15

TOMB
in the garden a new *t*....... John 19:41
throat is an open t........... Rom 3:13

TOMBS
like whitewashed *t*........... Matt 23:27

TOMORROW
t is thrown into the......... Matt 6:30
do not worry about *t*....... Matt 6:34
drink, for t we die.......... 1 Co 15:32

TONGUE
hides it under his *t*......... Job 20:12
Keep your *t* from evil...... Ps 34:13
Lest I sin with my *t*......... Ps 39:1
but the perverse *t*............ Prov 10:31
forever, but a lying *t*....... Prov 12:19
t should confess that........ Phil 2:11
does not bridle his *t*........ Jas 1:26
And the *t* is a fire........... Jas 3:6
no man can tame the *t*..... Jas 3:8
every nation, tribe, *t*........ Rev 14:6

TONGUES
From the strife of *t*......... Ps 31:20
will speak with new *t*...... Mark 16:17
to them divided *t*............ Acts 2:3
and they spoke with *t*...... Acts 19:6
I speak with the *t*............ 1 Co 13:1
Therefore *t* are for a....... 1 Co 14:22

TOPHET
T was established............ Is 30:33
the high places of *T*........ Jer 7:31
make this city like *T*........ Jer 19:12

TORMENT
"How long will you *t*....... Job 19:2
shall lie down in *t*........... Is 50:11
You come here to *t*.......... Matt 8:29
to this place of *t*............ Luke 16:28
fear involves *t*................. 1 Jn 4:18
t ascends forever.............. Rev 14:11

TORN
of the temple was *t*......... Matt 27:51

TORTURED
And others were *t*........... Heb 11:35

TOSSED
t with tempest................ Is 54:11
t to and fro and.............. Eph 4:14

TOUCH
seven no evil shall *t*........ Job 5:19
t no unclean thing........... Is 52:11
If only I may *t*................ Matt 9:21
that they might only *t*...... Matt 14:36
a man not to *t* a woman... 1 Co 7:1
wicked one does not *t*...... 1 Jn 5:18

TOUCHED
whose hearts God had *t*... 1 Sa 10:26
t my mouth with it.......... Is 6:7
hand and *t* my mouth...... Jer 1:9
mountain that may be *t*.... Heb 12:18

TOWER
t whose top is in the........ Gen 11:4
for me, And a strong *t*..... Ps 61:3
my fortress, My high *t*..... Ps 144:2
like an ivory *t*................. Song 7:4
in it and built a *t*............ Matt 21:33

TRADERS
are princes, whose *t*......... Is 23:8

TRADITION
according to the *t*............ Col 2:8
t which he received.......... 2 Th 3:6
conduct received by *t*....... 1 Pe 1:18

TRADITIONS
zealous for the *t*..............Gal 1:14
t which you were..........2 Th 2:15

TRAIN
T up a child in the.........Prov 22:6
t of His robe filled...........Is 6:1

TRAINED
who is perfectly *t*............Luke 6:40
those who have been *t*.....Heb 12:11

TRAINING
bring them up in the *t*.....Eph 6:4

TRAITOR
also became a *t*..............Luke 6:16

TRAMPLE
You shall *t* the wicked.....Mal 4:3
swine, lest they *t*.............Matt 7:6

TRAMPLED
t them in My fury..........Is 63:3
Jerusalem will be *t*........Luke 21:24
worthy who has *t*.............Heb 10:29

TRANCE
he fell into a *t*..............Acts 10:10
t I saw a vision..............Acts 11:5

TRANSFIGURED
and was *t* before them.....Matt 17:2

TRANSFORMED
this world, but be *t*.........Rom 12:2

TRANSGRESSED
t My covenant..................Josh 7:11
their fathers have *t*.........Ezek 2:3
Yes, all Israel has *t*.........Dan 9:11

TRANSGRESSION
Make me know my *t*.......Job 13:23
be innocent of great *t*.....Ps 19:13
He who covers a *t*...........Prov 17:9
He who loves *t* loves.......Prov 17:19
tell My people their *t*.......Is 58:1
deceived, fell into *t*.........1 Ti 2:14

TRANSGRESSIONS
if I have covered my *t*...Job 31:33
"I will confess my *t*.........Ps 32:5
mercies, Blot out my *t*.....Ps 51:1
For I acknowledge my *t*...Ps 51:3
has He removed our *t*.......Ps 103:12
who blots out your *t*........Is 43:25
was wounded for our *t*.....Is 53:5
from you all the *t*.............Ezek 18:31
was added because of *t*....Gal 3:19
redemption of the *t*..........Heb 9:15

TRANSGRESSORS
Then I will teach *t*..........Ps 51:13
numbered with the t........Mark 15:28

TRANSLATED
of darkness and *t*............Col 1:13
By faith Enoch was *t*........Heb 11:5

TRAVAIL
He shall see the *t*............Is 53:11

TREACHEROUSLY
and you who deal *t*.........Is 33:1
"This man dealt *t*............Acts 7:19

TREAD
it is He who shall *t*..........Ps 60:12
You shall *t* upon the........Ps 91:13
And they will *t*..............Rev 11:2

TREADS
like one who *t* in the.......Is 63:2
t the winepress...............Rev 19:15

TREASURE
to you His good *t*............Deut 28:12
one who finds great *t*......Ps 119:162
"For where your *t*............Matt 6:21
t brings forth evil............Matt 12:35
and you will have *t*..........Matt 19:21
So is he who lays up *t*.....Luke 12:21
You have heaped up *t*.....Jas 5:3

TREASURER
Erastus, the *t* of the........Rom 16:23

TREASURES
it more than hidden *t*.......Job 3:21
her as for hidden *t*..........Prov 2:4
for yourselves *t*...............Matt 6:19
are hidden all the *t*..........Col 2:3
riches than the *t*..............Heb 11:26

TREATY
Now Solomon made a *t*....1 Ki 3:1

TREE
"but of the *t*....................Gen 2:17
you eaten from the *t*........Gen 3:11
t Planted by the...............Ps 1:3
Like an apple *t*..................Song 2:3
for as the days of a *t*.......Is 65:22
t bears good fruit............Matt 7:17
His own body on the *t*.....1 Pe 2:24
give to eat from the *t*......Rev 2:7
the river, was the *t*..........Rev 22:2

TREES
t once went forth............Judg 9:8
Also he spoke of *t*...........1 Ki 4:33
Then all the *t* of the.........Ps 96:12
The *t* of the LORD are.......Ps 104:16
they may be called *t*.........Is 61:3
"I see men like *t*..............Mark 8:24
late autumn *t* without......Jude 12
the sea, or the *t*................Rev 7:3

TREMBLE
T before Him....................1 Ch 16:30
that the nations may *t*.......Is 64:2
'Will you not *t*.................Jer 5:22
wrath the earth will *t*.......Jer 10:10
my kingdom men must *t*...Dan 6:26

TREMBLED
Then everyone who *t*........Ezra 9:4
the earth shook and *t*.......Ps 18:7

TREMBLING
it was a very great *t*.......1 Sa 14:15
in fear, and in much *t*......1 Co 2:3
flesh, with fear and *t*.......Eph 6:5
with fear and *t*................Phil 2:12

TRESPASSES
still goes on in His *t*........Ps 68:21
forgive men their *t*...........Matt 6:14
not imputing their *t*.........2 Co 5:19
who were dead in *t*...........Eph 2:1

TRIAL
in the day of t..................Heb 3:8
concerning the fiery *t*.......1 Pe 4:12
t which shall come...........Rev 3:10

TRIBE
belongs to another *t*.........Heb 7:13
the Lion of the *t*...............Rev 5:5
blood out of every *t*.........Rev 5:9

TRIBES
to raise up the *t*...............Is 49:6
t which are scattered........Jas 1:1

TRIBULATION
there will be great *t*.........Matt 24:21
world you will have *t*.......John 16:33
in hope, patient in *t*.........Rom 12:12
and you will have *t*...........Rev 2:10
with her into great *t*.........Rev 2:22
out of the great *t*..............Rev 7:14

TRIBULATIONS
t enter the kingdom..........Acts 14:22
but we also glory in *t*.......Rom 5:3
not lose heart at my *t*.......Eph 3:13
t that you endure..............2 Th 1:4

TRIED
You have *t* me and have..Ps 17:3
a *t* stone, a precious.......Is 28:16

TRIUMPH
Let not my enemies *t*........Ps 25:2
I will *t* in the works.........Ps 92:4
always leads us in *t*.........2 Co 2:14

TRIUMPHED
the LORD, for He has *t*.....Ex 15:1

TROUBLE
few days and full of *t*.......Job 14:1
t He shall hide me..........Ps 27:5
O LORD, for I am in *t*.....Ps 31:9
will be with him in *t*.........Ps 91:15
is delivered from *t*............Prov 11:8
Savior in time of *t*............Jer 14:8
there are some who *t*.......Gal 1:7

TROUBLED
Your face, and I was *t*.....Ps 30:7
Your face, they are *t*.......Ps 104:29
you are worried and *t*......Luke 10:41
to give you who are *t*......2 Th 1:7
shaken in mind or *t*.........2 Th 2:2

TROUBLES
my soul is full of *t*...........Ps 88:3
will be famines and *t*.......Mark 13:8

TRUE
and Your words are *t*......2 Sa 7:28
But the LORD is the *t*.......Jer 10:10
"Let the LORD be a *t*........Jer 42:5
we know that You are *t*...Matt 22:16
He who sent Me is *t*.........John 7:28
Indeed, let God be *t*.........Rom 3:4
whatever things are *t*.........Phil 4:8
may know Him who is *t*...1 Jn 5:20
is holy, He who is *t*...........Rev 3:7
"These are the *t*.............Rev 19:9
for these words are *t*........Rev 21:5

TRUMPET
deed, do not sound a *t*.....Matt 6:2
t makes an uncertain.......1 Co 14:8
For the *t* will sound..........1 Co 15:52
loud voice, as of a *t*........Rev 1:10

TRUST
T in the LORD..................Ps 37:3
T in the LORD with all.....Prov 3:5
Do not *t* in a friend.........Mic 7:5

TRUSTED
"He *t* in the LORD...........Ps 22:8
"He *t* in God....................Matt 27:43
that we who first *t*...........Eph 1:12

TRUSTS
But he who *t* in the.........Ps 32:10
He who *t* in his own.........Prov 28:26

TRUTH
Behold, You desire *t*.......Ps 51:6
T shall spring out of........Ps 85:11
t shall be your shield.......Ps 91:4
And Your law is *t*.............Ps 119:142
not valiant for the *t*..........Jer 9:3
called the City of *T*...........Zech 8:3
speak each man the *t*........Zech 8:16
you shall know the *t*.........John 8:32
"I am the way, the *t*........John 14:6
He, the Spirit of *t*.............John 16:13
speak the words of *t*.........Acts 26:25
who suppress the *t*...........Rom 1:18
but, speaking the *t*...........Eph 4:15
your waist with *t*...............Eph 6:14
the love of the *t*...............2 Th 2:10
they may know the *t*.........2 Ti 2:25
the knowledge of the *t*......2 Ti 3:7
that we are of the *t*...........1 Jn 3:19
the Spirit is *t*....................1 Jn 5:6
t that is in you..................3 Jn 3

TUNICS
the LORD God made *t*..... Gen 3:21
not to put on two *t*......... Mark 6:9

TURN
Yet I do not *t*................ Ps 119:51
T at my reproof............. Prov 1:23
yes, let every one *t*.......... Jon 3:8
T now from your evil...... Zech 1:4
on your right cheek, *t*...... Matt 5:39
t the hearts of the........... Luke 1:17
t them from darkness....... Acts 26:18
let him t away from......... 1 Pe 3:11

TURNED
The wicked shall be *t*......Ps 9:17
Let them be *t* back and.....Ps 70:2
of Israel, they have *t*....... Is 1:4
number believed and *t*..... Acts 11:21
to you, and how you *t*..... 1 Th 1:9

TURNING
marvel that you are *t*....... Gal 1:6
or shadow of *t*................ Jas 1:17

TURNS
A soft answer *t*...............Prov 15:1
him know that he who *t*... Jas 5:20

TUTOR
the law was our *t*............ Gal 3:24
no longer under a *t*......... Gal 3:25

TWIST
All day they *t* my............Ps 56:5
and unstable *t* to............2 Pe 3:16

TWO
the ark to Noah, *t*...........Gen 7:15
T are better than one....... Eccl 4:9
t shall become one........... Matt 19:5
t young pigeons.............. Luke 2:24
one new man from the *t*...Eph 2:15

TYPE
of Adam, who is a *t*........ Rom 5:14

— U —

UNAFRAID
Do you want to be *u*....... Rom 13:3

UNBELIEF
because of their *u*........... Matt 13:58
help my *u*........................ Mark 9:24
and He rebuked their *u*... Mark 16:14
did it ignorantly in *u*....... 1 Ti 1:13
you an evil heart of *u*...... Heb 3:12
enter in because of *u*....... Heb 3:19

UNBELIEVERS
who believe but to *u*....... 1 Co 14:22
yoked together with *u*......2 Co 6:14

UNBELIEVING
Do not be *u*.....................John 20:27
u Jews stirred up the....... Acts 14:2
For the *u* husband is....... 1 Co 7:14
u nothing is pure............ Tit 1:15

UNCIRCUMCISED
You stiff-necked and *u*.....Acts 7:51
by faith and the *u*........... Rom 3:30

UNCLEAN
of animals that are *u*....... Gen 7:2
who touches any *u*........... Lev 7:21
I am a man of *u* lips....... Is 6:5
u shall no longer come.......Is 52:1
He commands even the *u* Mark 1:27
any man common or *u*....... Acts 10:28
there is nothing *u*.............Rom 14:14
Do not touch what is u.... 2 Co 6:17
that no fornicator, *u*........ Eph 5:5

UNCLEANNESS
men's bones and all *u*...... Matt 23:27
members as slaves of *u*.... Rom 6:19
did not call us to *u*..........1 Th 4:7
flesh in the lust of *u*........2 Pe 2:10

UNDEFILED
Blessed are the *u*............ Ps 119:1
all, and the bed *u*.......... Heb 13:4
incorruptible and *u*..........1 Pe 1:4

UNDERSTAND
if there are any who *u*..... Ps 14:2
is to *u* his way................Prov 14:8
hearing, but do not *u*...... Is 6:9
set your heart to *u*.......... Dan 10:12
u shall instruct many....... Dan 11:33
people who do not *u*....... Hos 4:14
Why do you not *u*............John 8:43
u what you are reading.... Acts 8:30
lest they should u............Acts 28:27
u all mysteries................. 1 Co 13:2
some things hard to *u*......2 Pe 3:16

UNDERSTANDING
Almighty gives him *u*........Job 32:8
Your precepts I get *u*...... Ps 119:104
His *u* is infinite................Ps 147:5
apply your heart to *u*........Prov 2:2
lean not on your own *u*... Prov 3:5
Spirit of wisdom and *u*.....Is 11:2
the heaven by His *u*.........Jer 51:15
also still without *u*..........Matt 15:16
And He opened their *u*....Luke 24:45
also pray with the *u*........ 1 Co 14:15
and spiritual *u*.................Col 1:9
the Lord give you *u*........ 2 Ti 2:7
Who is wise and *u*.......... Jas 3:13

UNDERSTANDS
is easy to him who *u*....... Prov 14:6
there is none who u..........Rom 3:11

UNDERSTOOD
Then I *u* their end.......... Ps 73:17
Have you not *u* from.........Is 40:21
u all these things.............Matt 13:51
clearly seen, being *u*........Rom 1:20

UNDONE
Woe is me, for I am *u*.....Is 6:5
leaving the others *u*.........Matt 23:23

UNEDUCATED
that they were *u*.............. Acts 4:13

UNFORGIVING
unloving, *u*...................... Rom 1:31

UNFORMED
substance, being yet *u*......Ps 139:16

UNGODLINESS
heaven against all *u*.........Rom 1:18
He will turn away u.........Rom 11:26

UNGODLY
u shall not stand.............. Ps 1:5
who justifies the *u*............Rom 4:5
Christ died for the *u*.........Rom 5:6
and perdition of *u* men.... 2 Pe 3:7
convict all who are *u*....... Jude 15

UNHOLY
between the holy and *u*....Ezek 22:26
for sinners, for the *u*....... 1 Ti 1:9

UNITY
to dwell together in *u*...... Ps 133:1
to keep the *u* of the........ Eph 4:3
we all come to the *u*....... Eph 4:13

UNJUST
hope of the *u* perishes..... Prov 11:7
u knows no shame.......... Zeph 3:5
master commended the *u* Luke 16:8
of the just and the *u*....... Acts 24:15
u who inflicts wrath.........Rom 3:5
For God is not *u*............. Heb 6:10
the just for the *u*............ 1 Pe 3:18
let him be *u* still............. Rev 22:11

UNKNOWN
not stand before *u*...........Prov 22:29
to the *u* God.....................Acts 17:23

UNLEAVENED
the Feast of *U* Bread.......Ex 12:17
since you truly are *u*........1 Co 5:7

UNLOVING
untrustworthy, *u*.............. Rom 1:31

UNPROFITABLE
'And cast the *u*...............Matt 25:30
We are *u* servants........... Luke 17:10
have together become u... Rom 3:12
for that would be *u*......... Heb 13:17

UNQUENCHABLE
up the chaff with *u*..........Matt 3:12

UNRIGHTEOUS
u man his thoughts...........Is 55:7
u will not inherit the....... 1 Co 6:9

UNRIGHTEOUSNESS
Him is true, and no *u*......John 7:18
the truth, but obey *u*....... Rom 2:8
Is there *u* with God.........Rom 9:14
cleanse us from all *u*....... 1 Jn 1:9
All *u* is sin......................1 Jn 5:17

UNSEARCHABLE
heart of kings is *u*........... Prov 25:3
u are His judgments........ Rom 11:33

UNSPOTTED
to keep oneself *u*............ Jas 1:27

UNTRUSTWORTHY
undiscerning, *u*............... Rom 1:31

UNWORTHY
and judge yourselves *u*.....Acts 13:46
u manner will be.............1 Co 11:27

UPHOLD
U me according to Your.. Ps 119:116
My Servant whom I *u*......Is 42:1
there was no one to *u*......Is 63:5

UPHOLDING
u all things by the...........Heb 1:3

UPPER
show you a large *u*...........Mark 14:15
went up into the *u*.......... Acts 1:13

UPRIGHT
righteous and *u* is He...... Deut 32:4
where were the *u*............Job 4:7
Good and *u* is the LORD.. Ps 25:8
u shall have dominion...... Ps 49:14
u will be blessed............. Ps 112:2
is strength for the *u*.........Prov 10:29
u will guide them............ Prov 11:3
u is His delight............... Prov 15:8
of the *u* is a highway....... Prov 15:19
that God made man *u*...... Eccl 7:29

URIM
of judgment the *U*.......... Ex 28:30
Thummim and Your *U*.... Deut 33:8

US
"*God with u*..................Matt 1:23
who is not against *u*........ Mark 9:40
If God is for *u*................ Rom 8:31
They went out from *u*.......1 Jn 2:19

USE
who spitefully *u* you........ Matt 5:44
u this world as not.......... 1 Co 7:31
u liberty as an................ Gal 5:13
u a little wine..................1 Ti 5:23

USELESS
all of them are *u*..............Is 44:9
are unprofitable and *u*..... Tit 3:9
one's religion is *u*.............Jas 1:26

USING
u no figure of speech.......John 16:29
perish with the *u*...........Col 2:22
u your liberty as a..........1 Pe 2:16

UTTERANCE
the Spirit gave them *u*..... Acts 2:4
u may be given to me......Eph 6:19

UTTERED
The deep *u* its voice........Hab 3:10
which cannot be *u*............Rom 8:26
the seven thunders *u*....... Rev 10:4

UTTERMOST
upon them to the *u*.......... 1 Th 2:16
u those who come............Heb 7:25

UTTERS
Day unto day *u* speech.... Ps 19:2
u His voice from..............Amos 1:2
and the great man *u*.........Mic 7:3

— V —

VAGABOND
v you shall be on the.......Gen 4:12

VAIN
the people plot a *v*..........Ps 2:1
'I have labored in *v*.........Is 49:4
you believed in *v*............ 1 Co 15:2

VALLEY
I walk through the *v*........Ps 23:4
pass through the *V*..........Ps 84:6
v shall be exalted.............Is 40:4
in the midst of the *v*........Ezek 37:1
v shall be filled..............Luke 3:5

VALUE
does not know its *v*.........Job 28:13
of more *v* than they........ Matt 6:26
they counted up the *v*....... Acts 19:19

VANISH
For the heavens will *v*..... Is 51:6
knowledge, it will *v*.........1 Co 13:8
old is ready to v away..... Heb 8:13

VANISHED
and He *v* from their........ Luke 24:31

VANITY
of vanities, all is *v*...........Eccl 1:2

VAPOR
best state is but *v*............Ps 39:5
It is even a *v* that.......... Jas 4:14

VARIATION
whom there is no *v*......... Jas 1:17

VEIL
he put a *v* on his face......Ex 34:33
v of the temple was.........Matt 27:51
Moses, who put a *v*..........2 Co 3:13
Presence behind the *v*......Heb 6:19

VENGEANCE
'You shall not take *v*.......Lev 19:18
spare in the day of *v*....... Prov 6:34
God will come with *v*...... Is 35:4
on the garments of *v*....... Is 59:17
let me see Your *v*........... Jer 11:20
are the days of *v*.............Luke 21:22
written, "*V is Mine*........ Rom 12:19
flaming fire taking *v*........ 2 Th 1:8
suffering the *v*................Jude 7

VESSEL
like a potter's *v*.............. Ps 2:9
v that he made of clay.....Jer 18:4
for he is a chosen *v*.........Acts 9:15
lump to make one *v*........ Rom 9:21
to possess his own *v*........ 1 Th 4:4
to the weaker *v*................ 1 Pe 3:7

VESSELS
longsuffering the *v*......... Rom 9:22
treasure in earthen *v*....... 2 Co 4:7
as the potter's v.............Rev 2:27

VICE
as a cloak for *v*............. 1 Pe 2:16

VICTORY
who gives us the *v*.......... 1 Co 15:57
v that has overcome........ 1 Jn 5:4

VIGILANT
in prayer, being *v*.......... Col 4:2
Be sober, be *v*................1 Pe 5:8

VILE
sons made themselves *v*... 1 Sa 3:13
"Behold, I am *v*............. Job 40:4
them up to *v* passions...... Rom 1:26

VINDICATED
know that I shall be *v*......Job 13:18

VINE
planted you a noble *v*......Jer 2:21
shall sit under his *v*......... Mic 4:4
of this fruit of the *v*........ Matt 26:29
"I am the true *v*............. John 15:1

VINEDRESSER
and My Father is the *v*.... John 15:1

VINES
foxes that spoil the *v*....... Song 2:15
nor fruit be on the *v*....... Hab 3:17

VINEYARD
laborers for his *v*............ Matt 20:1
Who plants a *v* and.......... 1 Co 9:7

VIOLENCE
was filled with *v*............. Gen 6:11
You save me from *v*.........2 Sa 22:3
from oppression and *v*..... Ps 72:14
He had done no *v*............Is 53:9
way and from the *v*.......... Jon 3:8
rich men are full of *v*...... Mic 6:12
For plundering and *v*....... Hab 1:3
one's garment with *v*....... Mal 2:16
of heaven suffers *v*.......... Matt 11:12

VIOLENT
me from the *v* man......... Ps 18:48
Let evil hunt the *v*.......... Ps 140:11
violence, and the *v*..........Matt 11:12
haters of God, *v*............. Rom 1:30
given to wine, not *v*........ 1 Ti 3:3

VIPER
and stings like a *v*.......... Prov 23:32
which is crushed a *v*........ Is 59:5

VIPERS
to them, "Brood of *v*...... Matt 3:7

VIRGIN
v daughter of my............Jer 14:17
"*Behold, a v shall*...........Matt 1:23

VIRGINS
v who took their lamps.... Matt 25:1
women, for they are *v*..... Rev 14:4

VIRTUE
if there is any *v*............. Phil 4:8
us by glory and *v*...........2 Pe 1:3
to your faith *v*................2 Pe 1:5

VISAGE
v was marred more than.. Is 52:14

VISIBLE
that are on earth, *v*........ Col 1:16
of things which are *v*....... Heb 11:3

VISION
the Valley of *V*...............Is 22:1
her prophets find no *v*..... Lam 2:9
they had also seen a *v*..... Luke 24:23
in a trance I saw a *v*....... Acts 11:5

VISIONS
thoughts from the *v*.........Job 4:13
young men shall see *v*......Joel 2:28
I will come to *v*..............2 Co 12:1

VISIT
but God will surely *v*.......Gen 50:24
in the day when I *v*.........Ex 32:34
Oh, *v* me with Your........Ps 106:4
v orphans and widows......Jas 1:27

VISITATION
the time of your *v*..........Luke 19:44
God in the day of *v*........ 1 Pe 2:12

VISITING
v the iniquity of the
fathers..............................Ex 20:5

VOICE
"I heard Your *v*............ Gen 3:10
fire a still small *v*............1 Ki 19:12
you thunder with a *v*....... Job 40:9
He uttered His *v*..............Ps 46:6
for your *v* is sweet........... Song 2:14
A *v* from the temple........ Is 66:6
v was heard in Ramah..... Matt 2:18
"*The v of one crying*....... Matt 3:3
And suddenly a *v*............Matt 3:17
will anyone hear His v..... Matt 12:19
for they know his *v*.......... John 10:4
the truth hears My *v*....... John 18:37
the *v* of an archangel....... 1 Th 4:16
whose *v* then shook the... Heb 12:26
If anyone hears My *v*...... Rev 3:20

VOID
they are a nation *v*.........Deut 32:28
the LORD had made a *v*...Judg 21:15
regarded Your law as *v*...Ps 119:126
Do we then make *v*.........Rom 3:31
heirs, faith is made *v*.......Rom 4:14
make my boasting *v*........ 1 Co 9:15

VOLUME
in the v of the book........Heb 10:7

VOMIT
returns to his own v........ 2 Pe 2:22

VOWS
you will pay your *v*......... Job 22:27
I will pay My *v*...............Ps 22:25
V made to You are...........Ps 56:12

— W —

WAGES
I will give you your *w*......Ex 2:9
the *w* of the wicked.........Prov 10:16
and he who earns *w*........ Hag 1:6
to you, give me my *w*......Zech 11:12
and give them their *w*......Matt 20:8
be content with your *w*.... Luke 3:14
him who works, the *w*...... Rom 4:4
For the *w* of sin is.......... Rom 6:23
is worthy of his w........... 1 Ti 5:18
Indeed the *w* of the.........Jas 5:4

WAILING
of heart and bitter *w*....... Ezek 27:31
There will be *w*.............. Matt 13:42

WAIT
W on the LORD............. Ps 27:14
My eyes fail while I *w*..... Ps 69:3
And I will *w* on the........ Is 8:17
those who *w* on the.........Is 40:31
w quietly for the............. Lam 3:26
then we eagerly *w*...........Rom 8:25
we also eagerly *w*............Phil 3:20
and to *w* for His Son....... 1 Th 1:10
To those who eagerly *w*... Heb 9:28

WAITING
w at the posts of my........Prov 8:34
w for the Consolation...... Luke 2:25

who himself was also *w*....Luke 23:51
ourselves, eagerly *w*........ Rom 8:23
from that time *w*............Heb 10:13

WAITS
my soul silently *w*.......... Ps 62:1
the creation eagerly *w*......Rom 8:19

WALK
w before Me and be........Gen 17:1
Yea, though I *w*............ Ps 23:4
I will *w* before the........... Ps 116:9
"This is the way, *w*.......... Is 30:21
be weary, they shall *w*...... Is 40:31
w in the light of your...... Is 50:11
w humbly with your God Mic 6:8
take up your bed and *w*... John 5:8
W while you have the...... John 12:35
so we also should *w*........ Rom 6:4
Let us *w* properly........... Rom 13:13
For we *w* by faith........... 2 Co 5:7
W in the Spirit.............. Gal 5:16
And *w* in love................ Eph 5:2
W as children of light...... Eph 5:8
that you may have a *w*.... Col 1:10
Jesus the Lord, so *w*....... Col 2:6
us how you ought to *w*.... 1 Th 4:1

WALKED
Methuselah, Enoch *w*...... Gen 5:22
by His light I *w*.............. Job 29:3
He *w* with Me in peace....Mal 2:6
in which you once *w*........Eph 2:2
to walk just as He *w*....... 1 Jn 2:6

WALKING
of the LORD God *w*........ Gen 3:8
they saw Jesus *w*............John 6:19
And *w* in the fear of....... Acts 9:31
of your children *w*...........2 Jn 4

WALKS
is the man Who *w*...........Ps 1:1
He who *w* uprightly.........Ps 15:2
Who *w* in darkness and....Is 50:10
do good to him who *w*.....Mic 2:7
If anyone *w* in the day.....John 11:9
he who *w* in darkness...... John 12:35
adversary the devil *w*.......1 Pe 5:8

WALL
If she is a *w*.................Song 8:9
you, you whitewashed *w*.. Acts 23:3
down the middle *w*..........Eph 2:14
Now the *w* of the city......Rev 21:14

WALLS
you shall call your *w*....... Is 60:18
By faith the *w* of........... Heb 11:30

WANDER
ones cry to God, and *w*... Job 38:41
Oh, let me not *w*............ Ps 119:10
they have loved to *w*....... Jer 14:10

WANDERED
w blind in the streets....... Lam 4:14
"My sheep *w* through...... Ezek 34:6
They *w* in deserts and......Heb 11:38

WANDERING
learn to be idle, *w*......... 1 Ti 5:13
w stars for whom is.........Jude 13

WANT
I shall not *w*.................. Ps 23:1
he began to be in *w*........ Luke 15:14

WAR
There is a noise of *w*.......Ex 32:17
my hands to make *w*....... 2 Sa 22:35
day of battle and *w*.......... Job 38:23
speak, they are for *w*........Ps 120:7
by wise counsel wage *w*... Prov 20:18
will wage your own *w*...... Prov 24:6
shall they learn *w*............Is 2:4
we shall see no *w*............Jer 42:14
Who ever goes to *w*........ 1 Co 9:7
You fight and *w*............. Jas 4:2
fleshly lusts which *w*........ 1 Pe 2:11
w broke out in heaven..... Rev 12:7
He judges and makes *w*... Rev 19:11

WARFARE
to her, that her *w*........... Is 40:2
may wage the good *w*...... 1 Ti 1:18
w entangles.................... 2 Ti 2:4

WARN
w the wicked from his..... Ezek 3:18
w everyone night........... Acts 20:31
w those who are unruly....1 Th 5:14

WARNED
them Your servant is *w*....Ps 19:11
Who has *w* you to flee.....Matt 3:7
Noah, being divinely *w*.... Heb 11:7

WARPED
such a person is *w*..........Tit 3:11

WARRIOR
He runs at me like a *w*....Job 16:14

WARS
He makes *w* cease to.......Ps 46:9
And you will hear of *w*....Matt 24:6
Where do *w* and fights.....Jas 4:1

WASH
w myself with snow.........Job 9:30
W me thoroughly............Ps 51:2
O Jerusalem, *w* your....... Jer 4:14
head and *w* your face...... Matt 6:17
not eat unless they *w*.......Mark 7:3
w His feet with her......... Luke 7:38
w the disciples' feet........ John 13:5
w away your sins............ Acts 22:16

WASHED
w his hands before the.....Matt 27:24
My feet, but she has *w*.... Luke 7:44
So when He had *w*...........John 13:12
w their stripes............... Acts 16:33
But you were *w*............... 1 Co 6:11
Him who loved us and *w* Rev 1:5
w their robes and made... Rev 7:14

WASHING
cleanse it with the *w*........Eph 5:26
us, through the *w*............Tit 3:5

WASTED
The field is *w*.................Joel 1:10
this fragrant oil *w*........... Mark 14:4
w his possessions.............Luke 15:13

WATCH
of them we set a *w*......... Neh 4:9
my steps, but do not *w*.... Job 14:16
is past, And like a *w*....... Ps 90:4
Keep *w* over the door......Ps 141:3
and all who *w* for........... Is 29:20
"*W* therefore..................Matt 24:42
What, could you not *w*.... Matt 26:40
"*W* and pray...................Matt 26:41
W, stand fast in the.........1 Co 16:13
submissive, for they *w*..... Heb 13:17

WATCHED
in the days when God *w*.. Job 29:2
come, he would have *w*... Matt 24:43

WATCHES
w the righteous..............Ps 37:32
She *w* over the ways of....Prov 31:27
Blessed is he who *w*........ Rev 16:15

WATCHFUL
But you be *w* in all......... 2 Ti 4:5
be serious and *w*.............1 Pe 4:7

WATCHING
who listens to me, *w*....... Prov 8:34
the flock, who were *w*..... Zech 11:11
he comes, will find *w*.......Luke 12:37

WATCHMAN
W, what of the night....... Is 21:11
I have made you a *w*.......Ezek 3:17

WATCHMEN
w who go about the........ Song 3:3
I have set *w* on your....... Is 62:6
Also, I set *w* over you..... Jer 6:17
strong, set up the *w*........ Jer 51:12

WATER
Eden to *w* the garden...... Gen 2:10
drinks iniquity like *w*........Job 15:16
I am poured out like *w*.... Ps 22:14
Drink *w* from your own... Prov 5:15
"Stolen *w* is sweet...........Prov 9:17
For I will pour *w*............ Is 44:3
eye overflows with *w*....... Lam 1:16
will be as weak as *w*........Ezek 7:17
you gave Me no *w*........... Luke 7:44
given you living *w*...........John 4:10
rivers of living *w*............John 7:38
blood and *w* came out...... John 19:34
with the washing of *w*...... Eph 5:26
were saved through *w*...... 1 Pe 3:20
the Spirit, the *w*............ 1 Jn 5:8
are clouds without *w*....... Jude 12
let him take the *w*...........Rev 22:17

WATERED
w the whole face.............Gen 2:6
I planted, Apollos *w*........1 Co 3:6

WATERS
and struck the *w*.............Ex 7:20
me beside the still *w*........Ps 23:2
Though its *w* roar and..... Ps 46:3
w have come up to my..... Ps 69:1
your bread upon the *w*.... Eccl 11:1
a well of living *w*............ Song 4:15
w cannot quench love...... Song 8:7
because I give *w*............. Is 43:20
thirsts, come to the *w*...... Is 55:1
fountain of living *w*......... Jer 2:13
the sound of many *w*....... Ezek 43:2
w encompassed me...........Jon 2:5
living fountains of *w*........ Rev 7:17
w became wormwood...... Rev 8:11

WAVES
and here your proud *w*.... Job 38:11
All Your *w* and billows.... Ps 42:7
The noise of their *w*........ Ps 65:7
the multitude of its *w*...... Jer 51:42
was covered with the *w*....Matt 8:24
sea, tossed by the *w*........ Matt 14:24
raging *w* of the sea..........Jude 13

WAX
My heart is like *w*............Ps 22:14
mountains melt like *w*......Ps 97:5

WAY
As for God, His *w*...........2 Sa 22:31
But He knows the *w*........ Job 23:10
the LORD knows the *w*.... Ps 1:6
you perish in the *w*......... Ps 2:12
Teach me Your *w*........... Ps 27:11
I have chosen the *w*........ Ps 119:30
I hate every false *w*......... Ps 119:104
in the *w* everlasting......... Ps 139:24
w which seems right......... Prov 14:12
The *w* of the just is.........Is 26:7
"This is the *w*................ Is 30:21
LORD, who makes a *w*..... Is 43:16
O LORD, I know the *w*.... Jer 10:23
one heart and one *w*....... Jer 32:39
and broad is the *w*.......... Matt 7:13
and difficult is the *w*........Matt 7:14
will prepare Your w......... Matt 11:10
to him, "I am the *w*........ John 14:6
proclaim to us the *w*........Acts 16:17
explained to him the *w*.... Acts 18:26
you a more excellent *w*.... 1 Co 12:31
forsaken the right *w*........ 2 Pe 2:15

- to have known the *w*........ 2 Pe 2:21
- have gone in the *w*........ Jude 11

WAYS
- for all His *w* are........ Deut 32:4
- Show me Your *w*........ Ps 25:4
- transgressors Your *w*........ Ps 51:13
- I thought about my *w*........ Ps 119:59
- For the *w* of man are........ Prov 5:21
- *w* please the LORD........ Prov 16:7
- he will teach us His *w*........ Is 2:3
- "Amend your *w*........ Jer 7:3
- *w* are everlasting........ Hab 3:6
- *misery are in their w*........ Rom 3:16
- judgments and His *w*........ Rom 11:33
- unstable in all his *w*........ Jas 1:8
- their destructive *w*........ 2 Pe 2:2
- and true are Your *w*........ Rev 15:3

WEAK
- then I shall become *w*........ Judg 16:7
- me, O LORD, for I am *w* Ps 6:2
- gives power to the *w*........ Is 40:29
- knee will be as *w*........ Ezek 7:17
- not your hands be *w*........ Zeph 3:16
- but the flesh is *w*........ Matt 26:41
- And not being *w*........ Rom 4:19
- Receive one who is *w*........ Rom 14:1
- God has chosen the *w*........ 1 Co 1:27
- We are *w*........ 1 Co 4:10
- *w* I became as *w*........ 1 Co 9:22
- this reason many are *w*........ 1 Co 11:30
- For when I am *w*........ 2 Co 12:10

WEAKNESS
- I was with you in *w*........ 1 Co 2:3
- It is sown in *w*........ 1 Co 15:43
- is also beset by *w*........ Heb 5:2
- *w* were made strong........ Heb 11:34

WEAKNESSES
- also helps in our *w*........ Rom 8:26
- sympathize with our *w*........ Heb 4:15

WEALTH
- who trust in their *w*........ Ps 49:6
- *w* is his strong city........ Prov 10:15
- *W* makes many friends........ Prov 19:4

WEALTHY
- am rich, have become *w*.. Rev 3:17

WEANED
- *w* child shall put his........ Is 11:8
- Those just *w* from milk........ Is 28:9

WEAPONS
- is better than *w*........ Eccl 9:18
- the LORD and His *w*........ Is 13:5
- For the *w* of our........ 2 Co 10:4

WEARIED
- you have *w* Me with........ Is 43:24
- You have *w* the LORD........ Mal 2:17
- therefore, being *w*........ John 4:6

WEARY
- to Isaac, "I am *w*........ Gen 27:46
- lest he become *w*........ Prov 25:17
- As cold water to a *w*........ Prov 25:25
- No one will be *w*........ Is 5:27
- you may cause the *w*........ Is 28:12
- shall run and not be *w*........ Is 40:31
- to him who is *w*........ Is 50:4
- I am *w* of holding it........ Jer 6:11
- *w* themselves to commit... Jer 9:5
- I was *w* of holding it........ Jer 20:9
- continual coming she *w*........ Luke 18:5
- And let us not grow *w*........ Gal 6:9
- do not grow *w* in........ 2 Th 3:13
- lest you become *w*........ Heb 12:3

WEATHER
- a garment in cold *w*........ Prov 25:20
- 'It will be fair *w*........ Matt 16:2

WEDDING
- were invited to the *w*........ Matt 22:3
- day there was a *w*........ John 2:1

WEEK
- with many for one *w*........ Dan 9:27
- the first day of the *w*........ Matt 28:1
- the first day of the *w*........ Acts 20:7
- the first day of the *w*........ 1 Co 16:2

WEEP
- a time to *w*........ Eccl 3:4
- you shall *w* no more........ Is 30:19
- Blessed are you who *w*........ Luke 6:21
- to her, "Do not *w*........ Luke 7:13
- and you did not *w*........ Luke 7:32
- of Jerusalem, do not *w*........ Luke 23:28
- *w* with those who *w*........ Rom 12:15
- those who *w* as though........ 1 Co 7:30

WEEPING
- *w* as they went up........ 2 Sa 15:30
- face is flushed from *w*........ Job 16:16
- the voice of my *w*........ Ps 6:8
- *w* shall no longer........ Is 65:19
- They shall come with *w*... Jer 31:9
- There will be *w*........ Matt 8:12
- Woman, why are you *w*... John 20:13
- What do you mean by *w*.. Acts 21:13

WEIGHED
- *W* the mountains........ Is 40:12
- You have been *w*........ Dan 5:27
- lest your hearts be *w*........ Luke 21:34

WEIGHT
- a perfect and just *w*........ Deut 25:15
- and eternal *w* of glory........ 2 Co 4:17
- us lay aside every *w*........ Heb 12:1

WELL
- that it may go *w*........ Deut 4:40
- wheel broken at the *w*........ Eccl 12:6
- "Those who are *w*........ Matt 9:12
- said to him, '*W* done........ Matt 25:21
- faith has made you *w*........ Mark 5:34

WELLS
- draw water from the *w*........ Is 12:3
- These are *w* without........ 2 Pe 2:17

WENT
- They *w* out from us........ 1 Jn 2:19

WEPT
- for the people *w*........ Ezra 10:1
- that I sat down and *w*........ Neh 1:4
- down, yea, we *w*........ Ps 137:1
- out and *w* bitterly........ Matt 26:75
- He saw the city and *w*........ Luke 19:41
- Jesus *w*........ John 11:35
- So I *w* much........ Rev 5:4

WHEAT
- but gather the *w*........ Matt 13:30
- *w* falls into the........ John 12:24

WHEEL
- the fountain, or the *w*........ Eccl 12:6
- in the middle of a *w*........ Ezek 1:16

WHEELS
- off their chariot *w*........ Ex 14:25
- the rumbling of his *w*........ Jer 47:3
- appearance of the *w*........ Ezek 1:16
- noise of rattling *w*........ Nah 3:2

WHIRLWIND
- Elijah went up by a *w*........ 2 Ki 2:11
- Job out of the *w*........ Job 38:1
- them away as with a *w*........ Ps 58:9
- *w* will take them away........ Is 40:24
- has His way in the *w*........ Nah 1:3

WHISPERINGS
- backbitings, *w*........ 2 Co 12:20

WHITE
- My beloved is *w*........ Song 5:10
- be purified, made *w*........ Dan 12:10
- for they are already *w*........ John 4:35
- walk with Me in *w*........ Rev 3:4
- behold, a *w* horse........ Rev 6:2
- and made them *w*........ Rev 7:14
- Then I saw a great *w*........ Rev 20:11

WICKED
- *w* shall be silent........ 1 Sa 2:9
- Should you help the *w*........ 2 Ch 19:2
- Why do the *w* live and........ Job 21:7
- *w* are reserved for the........ Job 21:30
- to nobles, 'You are *w*........ Job 34:18
- *w* shall be turned........ Ps 9:17
- do the *w* renounce God... Ps 10:13
- *w* bend their bow........ Ps 11:2
- Evil shall slay the *w*........ Ps 34:21
- *w* shall be no more........ Ps 37:10
- how long will the *w*........ Ps 94:3
- if there is any *w*........ Ps 139:24
- *w* will fall by his own........ Prov 11:5
- LORD is far from the *w*........ Prov 15:29
- *w* flee when no one........ Prov 28:1
- Do not be overly *w*........ Eccl 7:17
- *w* forsake his way........ Is 55:7
- But the *w* are like the........ Is 57:20
- and desperately *w*........ Jer 17:9

WICKEDLY
- God will never do *w*........ Job 34:12
- "Those who do *w*........ Dan 11:32
- yes, all who do *w*........ Mal 4:1

WICKEDNESS
- LORD saw that the *w*........ Gen 6:5
- can I do this great *w*........ Gen 39:9
- *W* proceeds from the........ 1 Sa 24:13
- Is not your *w* great........ Job 22:5
- Oh, let the *w* of the........ Ps 7:9
- alive into hell, For *w*........ Ps 55:15
- I will not know *w*........ Ps 101:4
- *w* is an abomination........ Prov 8:7
- *w* burns as the........ Is 9:18
- have trusted in your *w*........ Is 47:10
- wells up with her *w*........ Jer 6:7
- man repented of his *w*........ Jer 8:6
- not turn from his *w*........ Ezek 3:19
- and cannot look on *w*........ Hab 1:13
- is full of greed and *w*........ Luke 11:39
- sexual immorality, *w*........ Rom 1:29
- spiritual hosts of *w*........ Eph 6:12
- and overflow of *w*........ Jas 1:21

WIDOW
- the fatherless and *w*........ Ps 146:9
- plead for the *w*........ Is 1:17
- Then one poor *w*........ Mark 12:42
- *w* has children or........ 1 Ti 5:4
- Do not let a *w* under........ 1 Ti 5:9

WIDOWS
- and let your *w* trust........ Jer 49:11
- *w* were neglected........ Acts 6:1
- that the younger *w*........ 1 Ti 5:14
- to visit orphans and *w*........ Jas 1:27

WIFE
- an excellent *w* is the........ Prov 12:4
- *w* finds a good thing........ Prov 18:22
- but a prudent *w*........ Prov 19:14
- with the *w* of his........ Mal 2:15
- Whoever divorces his *w*... Mark 10:11
- 'I have married a *w*........ Luke 14:20
- "Remember Lot's *w*........ Luke 17:32
- all seven had her as *w*........ Luke 20:33
- so love his own *w*........ Eph 5:33
- the husband of one *w*........ Tit 1:6
- giving honor to the *w*........ 1 Pe 3:7
- bride, the Lamb's *w*........ Rev 21:9

WILD
- locusts and *w* honey........ Matt 3:4
- olive tree which is *w*........ Rom 11:24

and scribes saw the *w*...... Matt 21:15
our own tongues the *w*.... Acts 2:11

WONDERFULLY

fearfully and *w* made....... Ps 139:14

WONDERS

are the God who does *w*.. Ps 77:14
who alone does great *w*... Ps 136:4
He works signs and *w*...... Dan 6:27
And I will show *w*.......... Joel 2:30
and done many *w*........... Matt 7:22
signs, and lying *w*........... 2 Th 2:9
both with signs and *w*...... Heb 2:4

WOOL

they shall be as *w*........... Is 1:18
head was like pure *w*....... Dan 7:9
hair were white like *w*..... Rev 1:14

WORD

w that proceeds............. Deut 8:3
w is very near you......... Deut 30:14
w I have hidden............. Ps 119:11
w has given me life.......... Ps 119:50
w is a lamp to my feet..... Ps 119:105
w makes it glad............. Prov 12:25
w spoken in due season... Prov 15:23
w fitly spoken is............ Prov 25:11
Every *w* of God is pure... Prov 30:5
The LORD sent a *w*........... Is 9:8
the *w* of our God............ Is 40:8
w be that goes forth........ Is 55:11
But His *w* was in my....... Jer 20:9
But only speak a *w*......... Matt 8:8
for every idle *w*.............. Matt 12:36
The seed is the *w*........... Luke 8:11
mighty in deed and *w*...... Luke 24:19
beginning was the *W*........ John 1:1
W became flesh and......... John 1:14
if anyone keeps My *w*...... John 8:51
w which you hear is........ John 14:24
Your *w* is truth.............. John 17:17
and glorified the *w*......... Acts 13:48
of water by the *w*........... Eph 5:26
holding fast the *w*........... Phil 2:16
Let the *w* of Christ......... Col 3:16
come to you in *w* only..... 1 Th 1:5
in every good *w*............. 2 Th 2:17
all things by the *w*.......... Heb 1:3
For the *w* of God is........ Heb 4:12
the implanted *w*............. Jas 1:21
does not stumble in *w*...... Jas 3:2
through the *w* of God...... 1 Pe 1:23
that by the *w* of God....... 2 Pe 3:5
whoever keeps His *w*....... 1 Jn 2:5
let us not love in *w*......... 1 Jn 3:18
the Father, the *W*........... 1 Jn 5:7
name is called The *W*...... Rev 19:13

WORDS

Let the *w* of my mouth.... Ps 19:14
How sweet are Your *w*.... Ps 119:103
The *w* of the wise are...... Eccl 12:11
pass away, but My *w*....... Matt 24:35
at the gracious *w*........... Luke 4:22
w that I speak to you...... John 6:63
You have the *w* of.......... John 6:68
And remember the *w*...... Acts 20:35
those who hear the *w*...... Rev 1:3
is he who keeps the *w*..... Rev 22:7

WORK

day God ended His *w*...... Gen 2:2
people had a mind to *w*... Neh 4:6
the *w* of Your fingers...... Ps 8:3
the heavens are the *w*...... Ps 102:25
Man goes out to his *w*..... Ps 104:23
w is honorable and.......... Ps 111:3
God will bring every *w*.... Eccl 12:14
and said, 'Son, go, *w*....... Matt 21:28
could do no mighty *w*...... Mark 6:5
This is the *w* of God....... John 6:29
"I must *w* the works........ John 9:4
w which You have given.. John 17:4
know that all things *w*..... Rom 8:28
He will finish the w......... Rom 9:28
w is no longer *w*........... Rom 11:6
Do not destroy the *w*...... Rom 14:20
w will become manifest.... 1 Co 3:13
Are you not my *w*.......... 1 Co 9:1
abounding in the *w*......... 1 Co 15:58
without ceasing your *w*.... 1 Th 1:3
every good word and *w*.... 2 Th 2:17
If anyone will not *w*........ 2 Th 3:10
but a doer of the *w*......... Jas 1:25

WORKER

w is worthy of his........... Matt 10:10
Timothy, my fellow *w*...... Rom 16:21
w who does not need....... 2 Ti 2:15

WORKERS

You hate all *w* of........... Ps 5:5
we are God's fellow *w*..... 1 Co 3:9
dogs, beware of evil *w*..... Phil 3:2

WORKING

everywhere, the Lord *w*... Mark 16:20
My Father has been *w*..... John 5:17
according to the *w*.......... Eph 1:19
through faith in the *w*...... Col 2:12
manner, not *w* at all........ 2 Th 3:11

WORKMANSHIP

For we are His *w*............ Eph 2:10

WORKS

the wondrous *w* of God... Job 37:14
are Your wonderful *w*...... Ps 40:5
manifold are Your *w*....... Ps 104:24
The *w* of the LORD are.... Ps 111:2
w shall praise You.......... Ps 145:10
and let her own *w*........... Prov 31:31
show Him greater *w*........ John 5:20
w that I do in My........... John 10:25
w that I do he will do...... John 14:12
might stand, not of *w*...... Rom 9:11
let us cast off the *w*........ Rom 13:12
not justified by the *w*...... Gal 2:16
the spirit who now *w*....... Eph 2:2
not of *w*, lest anyone....... Eph 2:9
with the unfruitful *w*........ Eph 5:11
for it is God who *w*......... Phil 2:13
w they deny Him............ Tit 1:16
zealous for good *w*.......... Tit 2:14
repentance from dead *w*... Heb 6:1
but does not have *w*........ Jas 2:14
He might destroy the *w*... 1 Jn 3:8
"I know your *w*.............. Rev 2:2
their *w* follow them......... Rev 14:13
according to their *w*........ Rev 20:12

WORLD

He shall judge the *w*....... Ps 9:8
For the *w* is Mine........... Ps 50:12
"The field is the *w*.......... Matt 13:38
He was in the *w*............. John 1:10
For God so loved the *w*... John 3:16
the Savior of the *w*......... John 4:42
w cannot hate you........... John 7:7
You are of this *w*............ John 8:23
w will see Me no more.... John 14:19
"If the *w* hates you......... John 15:18
I have overcome the *w*.... John 16:33
do not pray for the *w*...... John 17:9
w has not known You...... John 17:25
w may become guilty....... Rom 3:19
be conformed to this *w*.... Rom 12:2
w is foolishness.............. 1 Co 3:19
w has been crucified........ Gal 6:14
without God in the *w*...... Eph 2:12
loved this present *w*........ 2 Ti 4:10
unspotted from the *w*...... Jas 1:27
w is enmity with God...... Jas 4:4
Do not love the *w*........... 1 Jn 2:15
w is passing away........... 1 Jn 2:17
w does not know us........ 1 Jn 3:1
They are of the *w*.......... 1 Jn 4:5
And all the *w* marveled... Rev 13:3

WORLDS

also He made the *w*........ Heb 1:2

WORM

But I am a *w*............... Ps 22:6
w does not die and the.... Mark 9:44

WORMS

you, and *w* cover you...... Is 14:11
And he was eaten by *w*... Acts 12:23

WORMWOOD

end she is bitter as *w*....... Prov 5:4
of the star is *W*............. Rev 8:11

WORRY

to you, do not *w*............ Matt 6:25
Therefore do not *w*......... Matt 6:31

WORSHIP

I will go yonder and *w*..... Gen 22:5
He is your Lord, *w*......... Ps 45:11
Oh come, let us *w*......... Ps 95:6
and have come to *w* Him Matt 2:2
will fall down and *w*........ Matt 4:9
And in vain they w......... Matt 15:9
w what you do not know.. John 4:22
the One whom you *w*...... Acts 17:23
w the God of my........... Acts 24:14
false humility and *w*........ Col 2:18
the angels of God w........ Heb 1:6
make them come and *w*... Rev 3:9
w Him who lives............ Rev 4:10
w Him who made.......... Rev 14:7

WORSHIPED

"Our fathers *w*............... John 4:20
w Him who lives............ Rev 5:14
on their faces and *w*........ Rev 11:16
w God who sat on the..... Rev 19:4

WORTHLESS

looking at *w* things.......... Ps 119:37
A *w* person.................... Prov 6:12
Indeed they are all *w*....... Is 41:29

WORTHLESSNESS

long will you love *w*....... Ps 4:2

WORTHY

"I am not *w* of the.......... Gen 32:10
sandals I am not *w*.......... Matt 3:11
inquire who in it is *w*...... Matt 10:11
invited were not *w*.......... Matt 22:8
should do this was *w*....... Luke 7:4
and I am no longer *w*...... Luke 15:19
present time are not *w*..... Rom 8:18
apostles, who am not *w*... 1 Co 15:9
to have a walk *w*............ Eph 4:1
"*The laborer is w*............ 1 Ti 5:18
the world was not *w*........ Heb 11:38
white, for they are *w*....... Rev 3:4
"You are *w*.................... Rev 4:11
W is the Lamb who......... Rev 5:12

WOUND

I *w* and I heal............... Deut 32:39
My *w* is incurable........... Job 34:6
But God will *w* the......... Ps 68:21
and my *w* incurable......... Jer 15:18
and *w* their weak........... 1 Co 8:12
and his deadly *w*............ Rev 13:3

WOUNDS

And binds up their *w*...... Ps 147:3
Faithful are the *w*........... Prov 27:6
and bandaged his *w*......... Luke 10:34

WRATH

speak to them in His *w*.... Ps 2:5
Your fierce *w* has gone.... Ps 88:16
The king's *w* is like......... Prov 19:12
in My *w* I struck you....... Is 60:10
I will pour out my *w*....... Hos 5:10

— Y —

— Z —

Index to Maps

The following index is divided into two parts, one for Map 5, Jerusalem, and the other for all the other maps. Place names are usually given as shown on the maps; sometimes they are followed by alternate names and spellings, which are set in parentheses. If a place name is not given as shown on the map, it is followed, in parentheses, by the alternate name or spelling that does appear on the map (example: *Melita* (*Malta* on map)). Where a place name refers to a large area, the index gives the location of the name. Where a name refers to a river, the index gives the source and mouth of the river.

In the index to Maps 1 through 4 and 6 through 9, major political divisions, such as countries and regions, are shown in capital letters (examples: EGYPT, PALESTINE). Cities are shown in upper and lower case as usual (example: Hebron). Geographical features are shown in italics (example: *Jordan River*).

INDEX TO MAPS

Map 1. The Nations of Genesis 10
Map 2. The Exodus from Egypt
Map 3. The Conquest of Canaan
Map 4. The Kingdom Years
Map 6. Palestine in Christ's Time
Map 7. Paul's First and Second Journeys
Map 8. Paul's Third and Fourth Journeys
Map 9. The Holy Land in Modern Times

Map 5. Jerusalem—From David to Christ

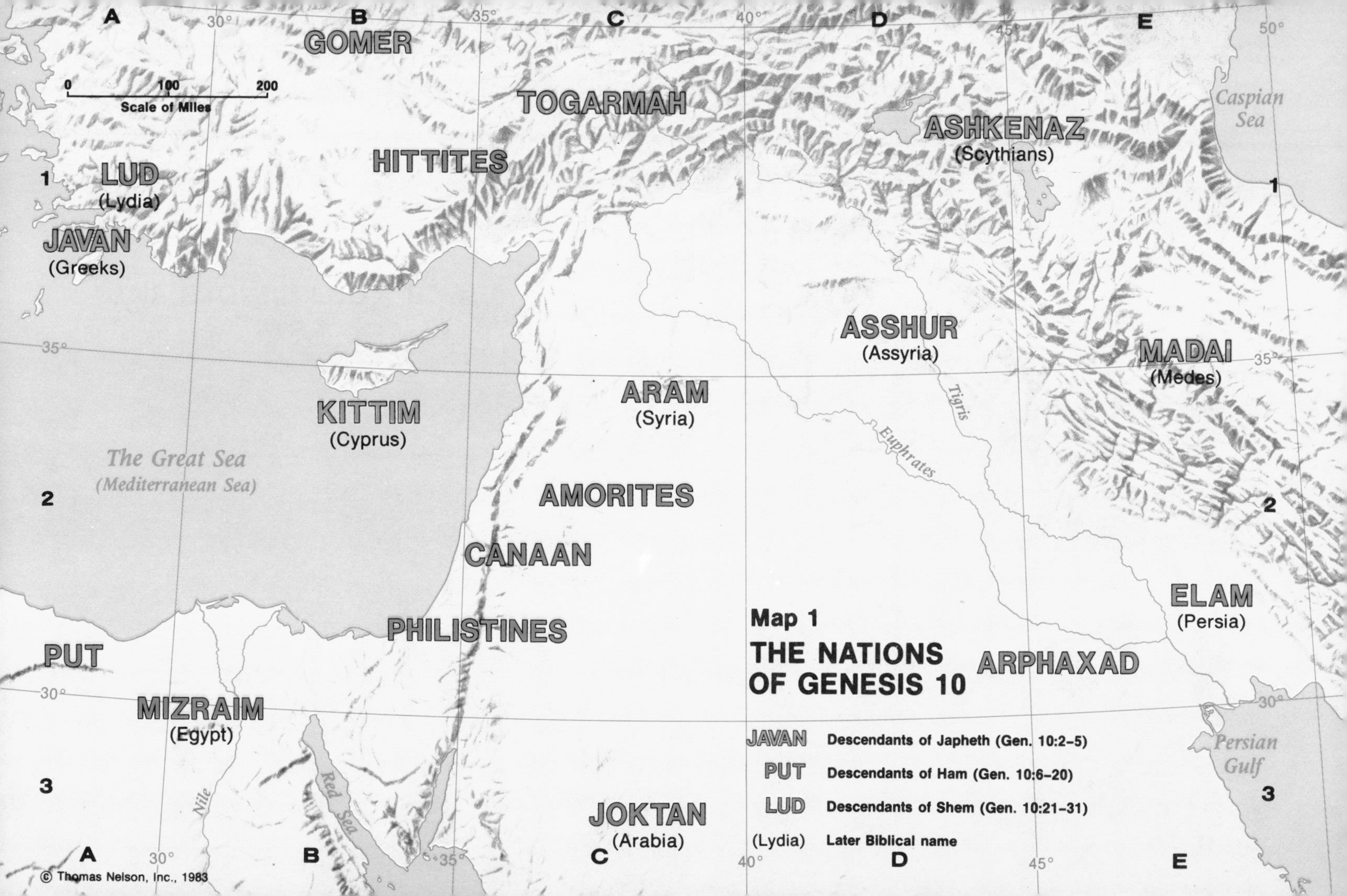
Map 1
THE NATIONS OF GENESIS 10
GOMER
TOGARMAH
ASHKENAZ
(Scythians)
HITTITES
LUD
(Lydia)
JAVAN
(Greeks)
Caspian Sea
ASSHUR
(Assyria)
MADAI
(Medes)
KITTIM
(Cyprus)
ARAM
(Syria)
The Great Sea
(Mediterranean Sea)
AMORITES
CANAAN
PHILISTINES
ELAM
(Persia)
ARPHAXAD
PUT
MIZRAIM
(Egypt)
JOKTAN
(Arabia)
Tigris
Euphrates
Nile
Red Sea
Persian Gulf
0 100 200
Scale of Miles
JAVAN Descendants of Japheth (Gen. 10:2–5)
PUT Descendants of Ham (Gen. 10:6–20)
LUD Descendants of Shem (Gen. 10:21–31)
(Lydia) Later Biblical name
A B C D E
1 2 3
30° 35° 40° 45° 50°

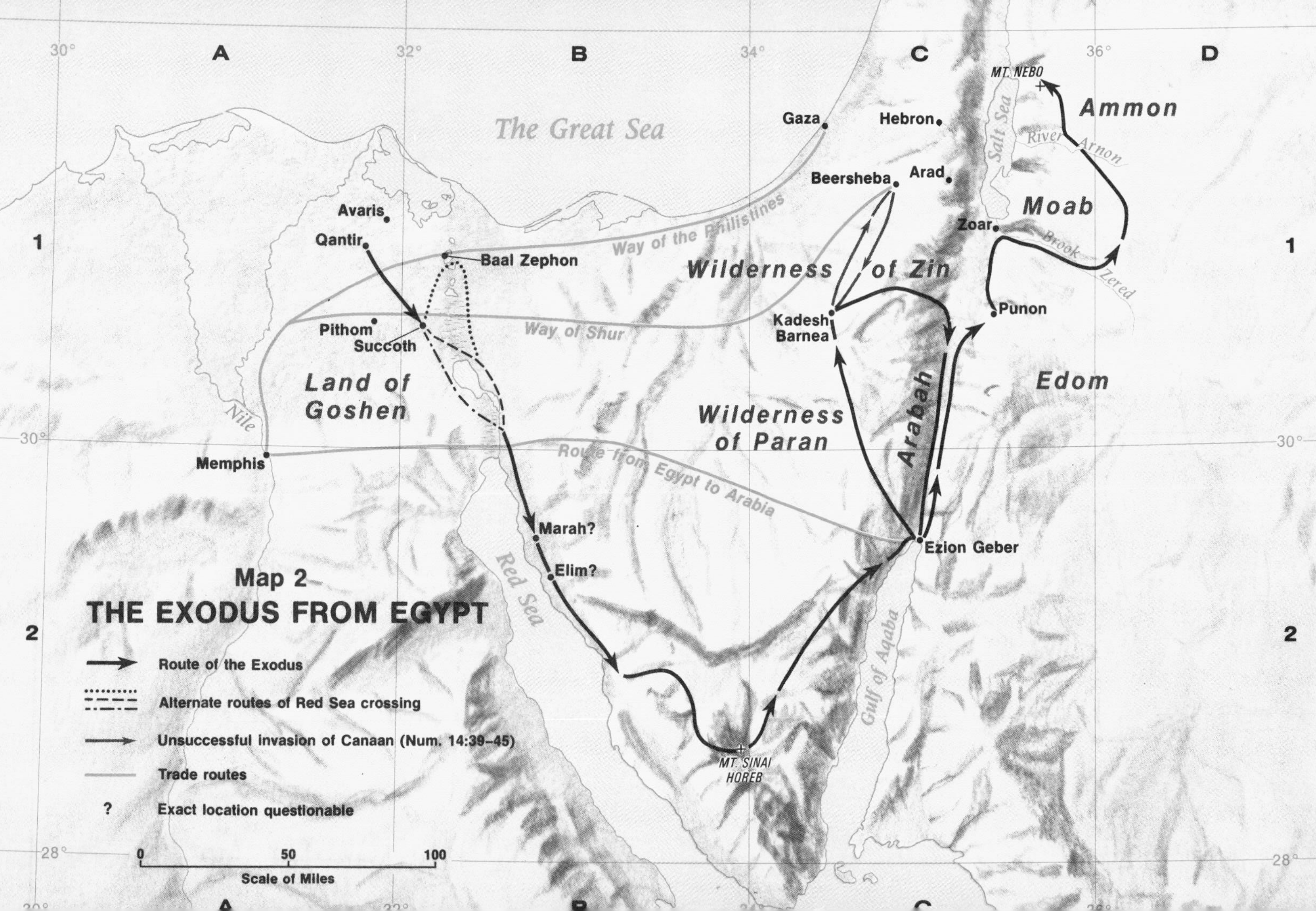

Map 2
THE EXODUS FROM EGYPT
Route of the Exodus
Alternate routes of Red Sea crossing
Unsuccessful invasion of Canaan (Num. 14:39–45)
Trade routes
? Exact location questionable
0 50 100
Scale of Miles
The Great Sea
Gaza
Hebron
Beersheba
Arad
Salt Sea
MT. NEBO
Ammon
River Arnon
Moab
Zoar
Brook Zered
Avaris
Qantir
Baal Zephon
Way of the Philistines
Wilderness of Zin
Kadesh Barnea
Punon
Pithom
Succoth
Way of Shur
Land of Goshen
Edom
Arabah
Wilderness of Paran
Nile
Memphis
Route from Egypt to Arabia
Marah?
Elim?
Ezion Geber
Red Sea
Gulf of Aqaba
MT. SINAI HOREB
A
B
C
D
1
2
30°
32°
34°
36°
28°

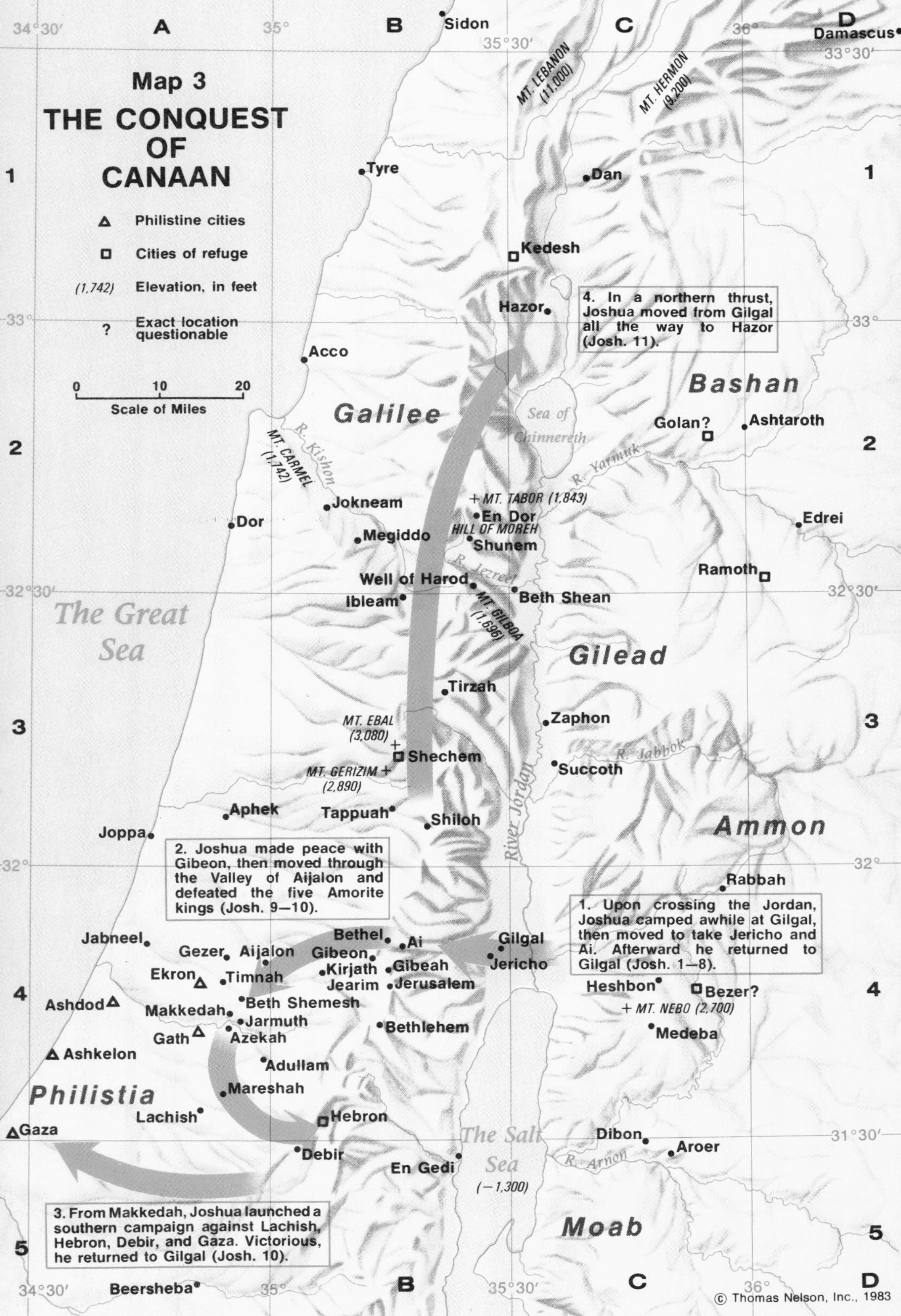

Map 3
THE CONQUEST OF CANAAN
Philistine cities
Cities of refuge
(1,742) Elevation, in feet
? Exact location questionable
0 10 20
Scale of Miles
A
B
C
D
1
2
3
4
5
34°30′
35°
35°30′
36°
33°30′
33°
32°30′
32°
31°30′
Sidon
Damascus
MT. LEBANON (11,000)
MT. HERMON (9,200)
Tyre
Dan
Kedesh
Hazor
4. In a northern thrust, Joshua moved from Gilgal all the way to Hazor (Josh. 11).
Acco
Bashan
Galilee
Sea of Chinnereth
Golan?
Ashtaroth
R. Kishon
MT. CARMEL (1,742)
R. Yarmuk
+ MT. TABOR (1,843)
Jokneam
En Dor
HILL OF MOREH
Shunem
Dor
Megiddo
Edrei
R. Jezreel
Well of Harod
Ramoth
MT. GILBOA (1,696)
Ibleam
Beth Shean
The Great Sea
Gilead
Tirzah
MT. EBAL (3,080)
Zaphon
Shechem
R. Jabbok
MT. GERIZIM (2,890)
Succoth
River Jordan
Aphek
Tappuah
Shiloh
Ammon
Joppa
2. Joshua made peace with Gibeon, then moved through the Valley of Aijalon and defeated the five Amorite kings (Josh. 9—10).
Rabbah
1. Upon crossing the Jordan, Joshua camped awhile at Gilgal, then moved to take Jericho and Ai. Afterward he returned to Gilgal (Josh. 1—8).
Jabneel
Bethel
Ai
Gilgal
Gezer
Aijalon
Gibeon
Jericho
Ekron
Timnah
Kirjath Jearim
Gibeah
Jerusalem
Heshbon
Bezer?
Ashdod
Makkedah
Beth Shemesh
+ MT. NEBO (2,700)
Gath
Jarmuth
Azekah
Bethlehem
Medeba
Ashkelon
Adullam
Philistia
Mareshah
Lachish
Hebron
Gaza
The Salt Sea
(−1,300)
Dibon
Aroer
Debir
En Gedi
R. Arnon
3. From Makkedah, Joshua launched a southern campaign against Lachish, Hebron, Debir, and Gaza. Victorious, he returned to Gilgal (Josh. 10).
Moab
Beersheba

Map 4
THE KINGDOM YEARS
Probable extent of Israelite control during the Kingdom of Solomon, c. 950 B.C.
The Kingdoms of Israel and Judah, c. 860 B.C.
Boundary between Israel and Judah
? Exact location questionable
0 25 50
Scale of Miles
A
B
C
1
2
3
4
5
6
34°
35°
36°
37°
33°
32°
31°
30°
Riblah
Zobah
Byblos
Phoenicia
MT. LEBANON
MT. HERMON
Sidon
Zarephath
Damascus
Tyre
Dan
Syria
Kedesh
Hazor
Acco
Sea of Chinnereth
Ashtaroth
The Great Sea
MT. CARMEL
R. Yarmuk
Golan?
Jokneam
Dor
Megiddo
Jezreel
Ramoth Gilead
Taanach
MT. GILBOA
Jabesh Gilead
Dothan
Tirzah
Jordan R.
Zaphon
Samaria
Succoth
Shechem
R. Jabbok
Aphek
Shiloh
Ammon
Joppa
ISRAEL
Rabbah
Mizpah
Bethel
Jabneh
Gezer
Ramah
Philistia
Heshbon
Jerusalem
Beth Shemesh
Bethlehem
Medeba
Ashkelon
Tekoa
Adullam
Eglon?
Dibon
Gaza
Hebron
The Salt Sea
Aroer
Debir
R. Arnon
Ziklag?
Arad
Moab
Beersheba
Kir Hareseth
Zoar
R. Zered
JUDAH
Bozrah
Kadesh Barnea
Brook of Egypt
Edom
Teman
Note: Other place names significant during the time of the Kingdoms are found on Map 3.
Ezion Geber
Elath
© Thomas Nelson, Inc., 1983

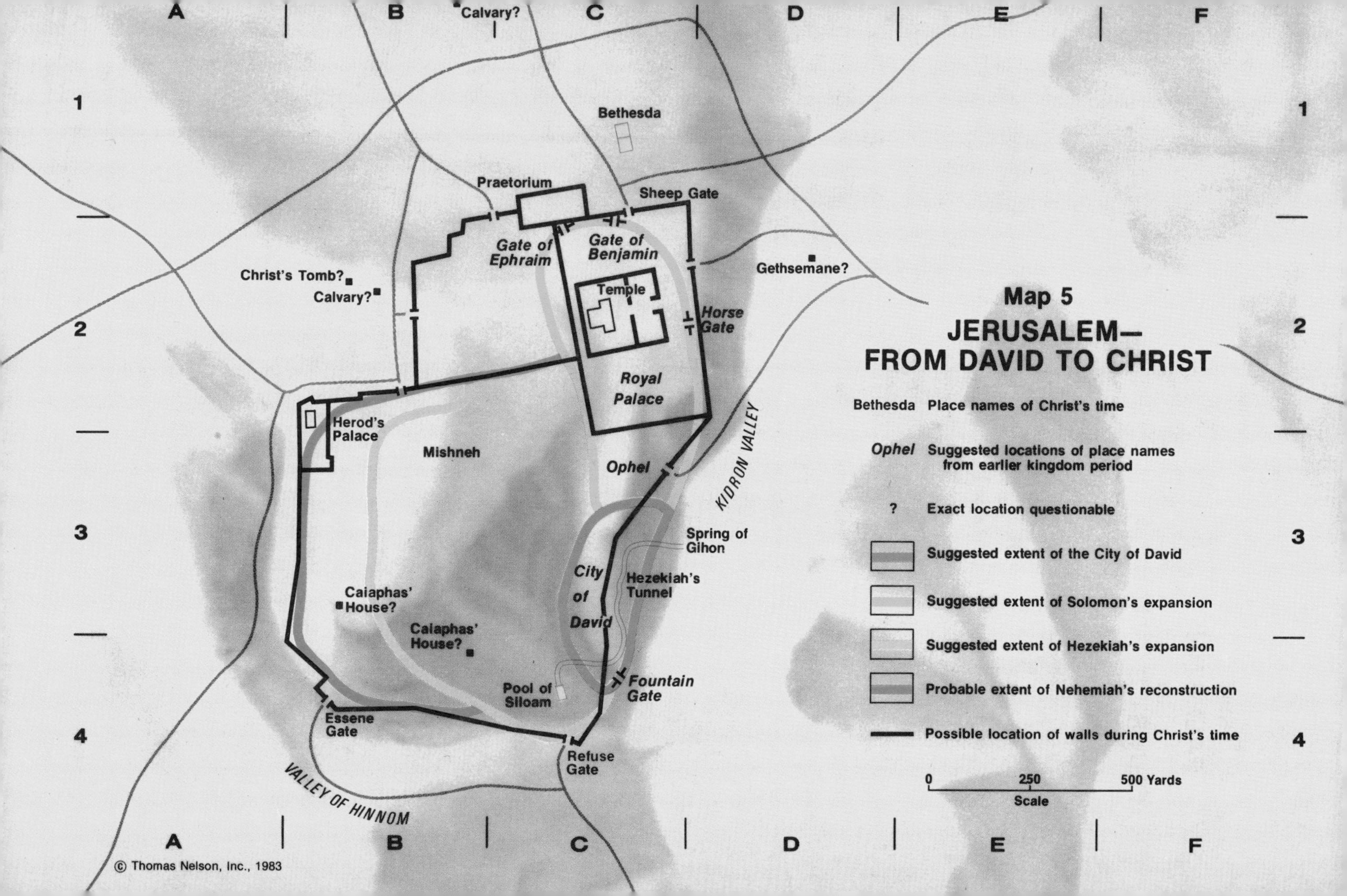
Map 5
JERUSALEM—
FROM DAVID TO CHRIST
Bethesda Place names of Christ's time
Ophel Suggested locations of place names from earlier kingdom period
? Exact location questionable
Suggested extent of the City of David
Suggested extent of Solomon's expansion
Suggested extent of Hezekiah's expansion
Probable extent of Nehemiah's reconstruction
Possible location of walls during Christ's time
0
250
500 Yards
Scale
Calvary?
Bethesda
Praetorium
Sheep Gate
Gate of Ephraim
Gate of Benjamin
Gethsemane?
Christ's Tomb?
Calvary?
Temple
Horse Gate
Royal Palace
Herod's Palace
Mishneh
Ophel
KIDRON VALLEY
Spring of Gihon
City of David
Hezekiah's Tunnel
Caiaphas' House?
Caiaphas' House?
Pool of Siloam
Fountain Gate
Essene Gate
Refuse Gate
VALLEY OF HINNOM
A
B
C
D
E
F
1
2
3
4

Map 6
PALESTINE IN CHRIST'S TIME
(1,742) Elevation, in feet
? Exact location questionable
0 10 20
Scale of Miles
34°30′
A
35°
B
35°30′
C
36°
D
Damasc
33°30′
33°
32°30′
32°
31°30′
1
2
3
4
5
Sidon
Zarephath
MT. LEBANON (11,000)
MT. HERMON (9,200)
Phoenicia
Iturea
Tyre
Panias
(Caesarea Philippi)
Trachonitis
Galilee
Ptolemais
Chorazin
Capernaum
Bethsaida?
Sea of Galilee
Magdala
Gergesa
Cana
Tiberias
R. Kishon
MT. CARMEL (1,742)
R. Yarmuk
Nazareth
+ MT. TABOR (1,843)
Gadara?
Nain
Esdraelon
Caesarea
Scythopolis
MT. GILBOA (1,696)
The Great Sea
Decapolis
Samaria
Samaria
Gerasa
Sychar
R. Jabbok
MT. GERIZIM + (2,890)
River Jordan
Antipatris
Joppa
Perea
Arimathea
Gadara?
Ephraim
Lydda
Philadelphia
Emmaus
Jericho
Kirjath Jearim
Bethabara
Jerusalem
Bethany
Azotus
Beth Haccerem
Qumran
Bethlehem
Medeba
Ashkelon
Herodium
Judea
Machaerus
Hebron
Gaza
The Salt Sea
R. Arnon
(−1,300)
Masada
Idumea
Beersheba

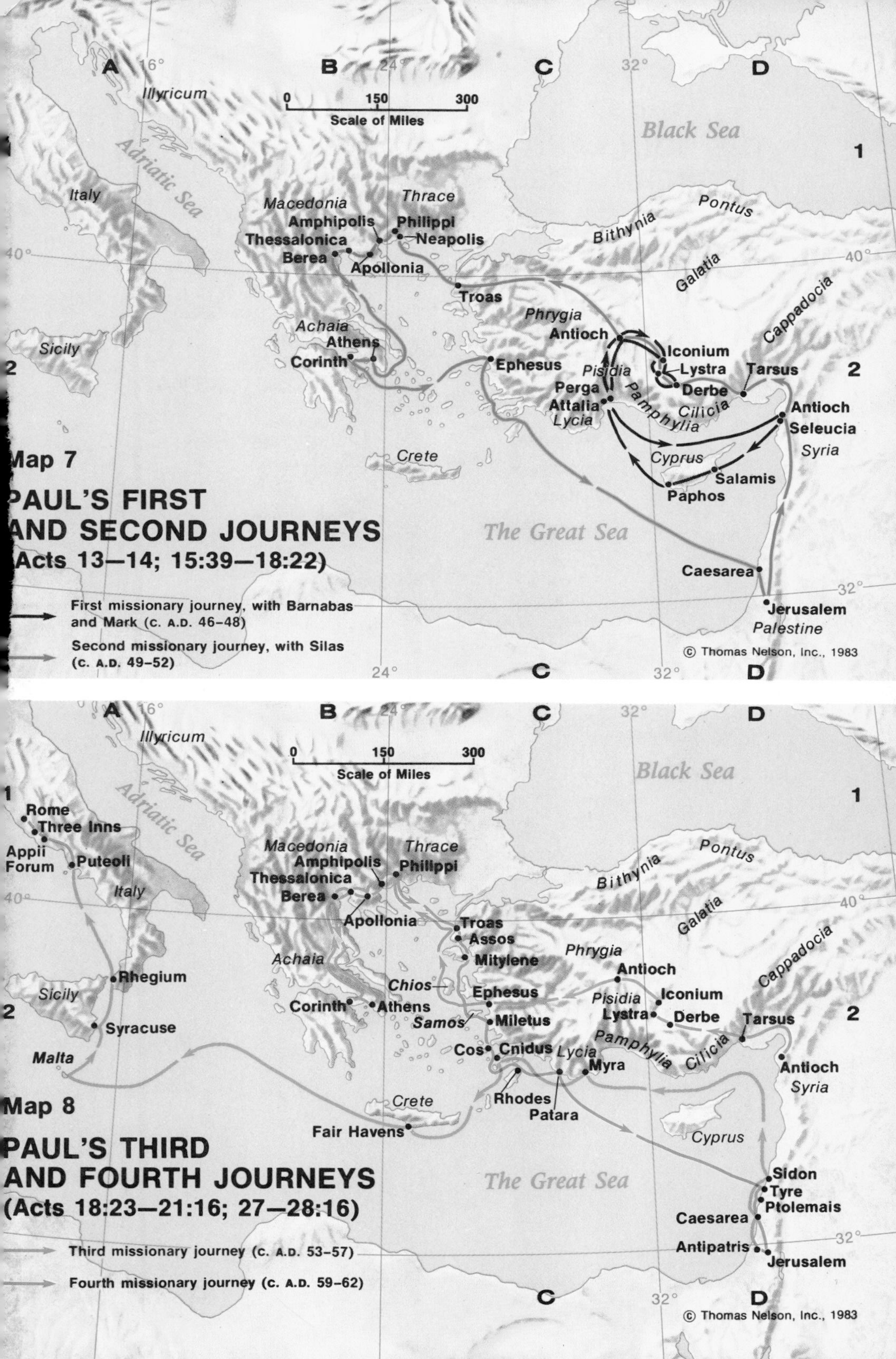
Map 7
PAUL'S FIRST AND SECOND JOURNEYS
(Acts 13–14; 15:39–18:22)
First missionary journey, with Barnabas and Mark (c. A.D. 46–48)
Second missionary journey, with Silas (c. A.D. 49–52)
© Thomas Nelson, Inc., 1983
A
B
C
D
1
2
16°
24°
32°
40°
0
150
300
Scale of Miles
Illyricum
Adriatic Sea
Italy
Sicily
Macedonia
Thrace
Amphipolis
Philippi
Neapolis
Thessalonica
Berea
Apollonia
Troas
Achaia
Athens
Corinth
Ephesus
Crete
Black Sea
Pontus
Bithynia
Galatia
Cappadocia
Phrygia
Antioch
Iconium
Lystra
Derbe
Pisidia
Perga
Attalia
Lycia
Pamphylia
Cilicia
Tarsus
Antioch
Seleucia
Syria
Cyprus
Salamis
Paphos
The Great Sea
Caesarea
Jerusalem
Palestine
Map 8
PAUL'S THIRD AND FOURTH JOURNEYS
(Acts 18:23–21:16; 27–28:16)
Third missionary journey (c. A.D. 53–57)
Fourth missionary journey (c. A.D. 59–62)
© Thomas Nelson, Inc., 1983
Rome
Three Inns
Appii Forum
Puteoli
Italy
Rhegium
Sicily
Syracuse
Malta
Illyricum
Adriatic Sea
Macedonia
Thrace
Amphipolis
Philippi
Thessalonica
Berea
Apollonia
Troas
Assos
Mitylene
Achaia
Chios
Ephesus
Corinth
Athens
Samos
Miletus
Cos
Cnidus
Rhodes
Patara
Crete
Fair Havens
Black Sea
Pontus
Bithynia
Galatia
Cappadocia
Phrygia
Antioch
Pisidia
Iconium
Lystra
Derbe
Lycia
Myra
Pamphylia
Cilicia
Tarsus
Antioch
Syria
Cyprus
The Great Sea
Sidon
Tyre
Ptolemais
Caesarea
Antipatris
Jerusalem

Map 9
THE HOLY LAND
IN MODERN TIMES
Area occupied by Israel since June, 1967
0
25
50
Scale of Miles
A
B
C
D
E
1
2
3
4
5
6
34°
35°
36°
37°
33°
32°
31°
30°
Tripoli
LEBANON
BEKAA VALLEY
Beirut
LEBANON MTS.
ANTI-LEBANON MTS.
Sidon
Damascus
Tyre
Dan
U.N. Buffer Zone
1973 Line
SYRIA
Qiryat Shemona
Quneitra
Nahariyya
1967 Cease-Fire Line
Safad
Golan Heights
Akko
Sea of Galilee
Haifa
Tiberias
Dera
Nazareth
Mediterranean Sea
Afula
Ramtha
Beth Shean
Hadera
Netanya
Tulkarm
Jordan River
Jarash
Nablus
Herzliyya
West Bank
Tel Aviv
Petah Tiqwa
Yafo
Rishon le Zion
Lod
Ramalah
Amman
Ramla
Ashdod
Jericho
Jerusalem
Bethlehem
Madaba
Ashqelon
Qiryat Gat
Hebron
Dead Sea
Gaza
En Gedi
Dhiban
Beersheba
Al-Arish
Karak
JORDAN
ISRAEL
EGYPT
Negev
Arabah
Sinai
Elat
Aqaba